BLOOMSBURY
ENGLISH
DICTIONARY

BLOOMSBURY
ENGLISH
DICTIONARY

BLOOMSBURY

A BLOOMSBURY REFERENCE BOOK
Created from the Bloomsbury Dictionary Database
www.wordquery.com

© Bloomsbury Publishing Plc 1999, 2004

First edition published 1999
Second edition published 2004

Published by Bloomsbury Publishing Plc,
38 Soho Square, London W1D 3HB

This Dictionary includes words on the basis of their usage in the English
language today. Words that are known to have current trademark or
proprietary registrations are identified as such. The inclusion of any
such word or identification in this Dictionary is not, however, to be
regarded as an expression of the Publisher's opinion as to whether or
not it is subject to proprietary rights. Neither the presence nor absence
of any such word or identification in the Dictionary is to be regarded as
affecting in any way whatever the validity or status of any trademark or
other proprietary rights throughout the world.

Microsoft® and Encarta® are either registered trademarks or trademarks
of Microsoft Corp. in the United States and/or other countries. Other
product and company names herein may be trademarks of their
respective owners.

British Library Cataloguing in Publication Data is available on request

ISBN 0-7475-6243-1

All papers used by Bloomsbury Publishing are natural, recyclable
products made from wood grown in well-managed forests.
The manufacturing processes conform to the environmental regulations
of the country of origin.

Typeset by Selwood Systems, Midsomer Norton, United Kingdom
Printed in the United States of America

Contents

Editor-in-Chief
Dr Kathy Rooney

Publisher
Nigel Newton

Dictionaries Publisher
Faye Carney

Executive Editor
Susan Jellis

US General Editor
Anne H. Soukhanov

Database Manager
Edmund Wright

Senior Lexicographer
Lesley Brown

Project Manager
Katy McAdam

Project Coordinator
Joel Adams

Chief Etymologist
John Ayto

Chief Phonetician
Dinah Jackson

Production Director
Penny Edwards

Production Editor
Nicky Thompson

EDITORIAL CONTRIBUTORS TO THE SECOND EDITION

Lexicographers
David Barnett
Carol Braham
Robert Clevenger
Dewayne Crawford
Steve Curtis
Rosalind Fergusson
Scott Forbes
Jennifer Goss Duby
David Hallworth
Ruth Hein
Georgia Hole
Ann-Marie Imbornoni
Barbara Kelly
Imogen Kerr

Duncan Marshall
Michael Munro
Julie Plier
Jane Rogoyska
Howard Sargeant
Karen Stern
Fraser Sutherland
Megan Thomson
Donald Watt
Pamela White

Science and Technical Editors
Rich Cutler
Pam England

Robert Hine
Alan D. Levy
James E. Shea
Tom Shields

Etymologies
Lesley Brown
Martha Mayou
Dr Susan Sigalas
Dr David M. Weeks

Usage and Language Heritage Notes
John Ayto
Lesley Brown

Rosalind Fergusson
Anne H. Soukhanov

Proofreaders
Sandra Anderson
Pat Bulhosen
Christina Gleeson
Isabel Griffiths
Ruth Hillmore
Irene Lakhani
Jill Leatherbarrow
Clea McEnery
Mark Miller
Vanessa Mitchell
Susan Turner

vi

ADDITIONAL CONTRIBUTORS

**Editorial,
Keyboarding,
and Administrative
Assistance**
Sara Al-Bader
Simon Arnold
Heather Bateman
Emma Harris
Sarah Lusznat
Rebecca McKee
Simone Potter
Charlotte Regan
Darren Treend

Illustrations
Wendy Bramwell
Chris Lyon
Annabel Milne
Sylvie Rabbe
Beatriz Waller
David Wood

Tables
Nigel Partridge
Jeffrey Petts
Ruth Bateson
Anthony Duke

Annotations
Andrew Clarke

Maps
Digital Wisdom Publishing Ltd

Design
William Webb
Fiona Knowles
Mercer Design

Jacket Design
William Webb
Yeti McCaldin

ADVISERS AND CONSULTANTS TO THE BLOOMSBURY DICTIONARY DATABASE

Clark Adams
Professor, Department of Wildlife and
Fisheries Sciences, Texas A&M University
(Hunting)

Michael Allaby
Writer and science consultant
(Life Sciences)

Robert Allen
Editor and lexicographer
(English Language)

Christopher Arnison
Professor, Royal Agricultural College
(Agriculture)

Michele Aina Barale
Professor of English and of Women's and
Gender Studies, Amherst College,
Massachusetts (English Language)

Dr Tallis Barker
(Music)

Alan Barnard
Professor, University of Edinburgh
(Anthropology)

LynnDianne Beene
Professor, Department of English,
University of New Mexico
(English Language)

Stephen C. Behrendt
George Holmes Distinguished Professor of
English, University of Nebraska
(English Language)

Philip D. Beidler
Professor, University of Alabama
(English Language)

Joseph J. BelBruno
Professor, Dartmouth College, Hanover,
New Hampshire (Chemistry)

Erin Belieu
Assistant Professor, Department of English,
Ohio State University (English Language)

Dr Bethan Benwell
Department of English Studies, University
of Stirling (English Language)

Teresa Bevin
Author and Professor, Montgomery
College (Hispanic English)

David F. Bjorklund
Professor, Department of Psychology,
Florida Atlantic University (Psychology)

Donald Black
Professor, College of Food and Natural
Resources, University of Massachusetts
(Agriculture)

David Blair
Senior Research Fellow, Department of
English, Macquarie University
(Australian English)

Sheila S. Blair
Norma Jean Calderwood University
Professor of Islamic and Asian Art, Boston
College (Arabic Words and Places)

Clive Bloom
Professor, Middlesex University (Media)

Joseph Donald Blount
Professor, Department of English,
University of South Carolina Aiken
(English Language)

Suzanne Bordelon
Assistant Professor, Department of
Rhetoric and Writing Studies, San Diego
State University (English Language)

Robert H. Brinkmeyer Jr
Professor and Chair, Department of
English, University of Arkansas
(English Language)

Allan Brooks
Editor and writer; member, US
Government Technical committees, Sr. VP
Electro-Lite Corp. (Engineering)

Charles Butcher
Specialist writer and editor
(Chemical Engineering)

Col. John A. Calabro
US Army, Retired. Adjunct Professor of
English, US Military Academy, West Point
(Military)

Colin Callander
Freelance journalist and former editor of
Golf Monthly (Golf)

Paul A. Carling
Professor, University of Lancaster
(Geography)

Teena A. M. Carnegie
Assistant Professor, Department of English,
University of Iowa (English Language)

Ronald Carter
Professor of Modern English Language,
University of Nottingham
(English Language)

Dr Christopher Chippindale
Reader in Archaeology & curator for
British archaeology collections,
Cambridge University Museum of
Archaeology & Anthropology
(Archaeology)

William Leon Coburn
Associate Professor, Department of
English, University of Nevada, Las Vegas
(English Language)

N. J. Collar
Leventis Fellow in Conservation Biology,
BirdLife International and Cambridge
University (Ornithology)

Timothy Collings
Motor racing correspondent, Reuters and
Daily Telegraph (Motor Sports)

Peter Colvin
Faculty Librarian for Languages and
Cultures, School of Oriental and African
Studies (Islamic Culture)

Nikolas Coupland
Professor, Centre for Applied English
Language Studies, University of Wales
(English in Wales)

Helen Cowie
Professor, Director of UK Observatory for
the Promotion of Nonviolence, University
of Surrey, Guildford (Psychology)

Michael Crane
Director, British Isles Backgammon
Association (Backgammon)

Dr Andrew Dalby
Honorary Fellow, Institute of Linguists,
author of *Dictionary of Languages* and
Language in Danger (Languages)

Robert Day
Chairman, Suffolk Advanced
Motorcyclists Club (DIY, Motorcycles)

Dr Scott Delancey
Department of Linguistics, University of
Oregon (Native American English)

Col. Michael Dewar
Formerly Deputy Director, Institute of
Strategic Studies (Military)

Robert Ditton
Professor, Department of Wildlife and
Fisheries Sciences, Texas A&M University
(Ecology, Recreational Fishing)

Paul B. Diehl
Associate Professor, Department of
English, University of Iowa
(English Language)

Kenneth L. Donelson
Professor, Department of English, Arizona
State University (English Language)

Bethany K. Dumas
Professor, Department of English,
University of Tennessee (Law)

Stephen Dundas
Teacher of English, St Bede's School,
Redhill, Surrey (English Language)

Dr Catherine Emmott
Senior Lecturer, Department of English
Language, University of Glasgow
(English Language)

Dr Roy Evans
Formerly Faculty of Education,
Roehampton Institute, London
(Education)

Dr Alan Ewart
University of Northern British Columbia
(Mountaineering / Climbing)

Margery Fee
Professor, Department of English,
University of British Columbia; co-author,
Oxford Guide to Canadian Usage
(Canadian English)

Joshua Fishman
Professor, City University of New York
(Yiddish)

Nancy Flynn
Cornell University (Botany)

Tom Gallagher
Writer (Baseball)

Bruce Ganem
Professor, Department of Chemistry and
Chemical Biology, Cornell University
(Chemistry)

Shirley Nelson Garner
Professor and Associate Dean of the
Graduate School, University of Minnesota
(English Language)

Andrew Goldsbrough
St John's Innovation Centre, Cambridge,
UK (Biotechnology)

Lynne Goldstein
Professor and Chair, Department of
Anthropology, Michigan State University
(Anthropology / Archaeology)

David Graddol
The English Company (UK) Ltd
(World English)

James Gramann
Professor, Department of Recreation, Park
and Tourism Sciences, Texas A&M
University (Leisure)

Jeremy Gray
Open University (Mathematics)

Dr A. C. Grayling
Reader in Philosophy, Birkbeck College,
London (Philosophy)

Eugene Green
Professor, Department of English, Boston
University (English Language)

Jonathon Green
Writer, broadcaster, author of a history of
lexicography *Chasing the Sun: Dictionary
Makers and the Dictionaries They Made*,
and leading slang lexicographer; author,
Cassell Dictionary of Slang

Fayal Greene
Gardening writer and editor (Gardening)

Steven Griffiths
UK civil servant (Transport / Environment)

Trevor Griffiths
Professor and Programme Director,
Department of Humanities, Arts and
Languages, London Metropolitan
University (Theatre)

Dr Anthea Fraser Gupta
School of English, University of Leeds
(English Language)

Dr Eva Hertel
English Language and Linguistics,
TU Chemnitz (East Africa)

David Hoover
Associate Professor of English, New York
University (English Language)

Andrew Howard
Middlesex University (Politics)

Alastair Hudson
Reader in Equity and Law, Queen Mary,
University of London (Law)

Philip Johansson
Managing Editor, Earthwatch Institute
(Zoology)

Bridget Jones
Cookery editor and writer, member of the
Guild of Food Writers (Food)

Darlene Juschka
Professor, University of Toronto
(World Religions)

Kathryn Kavanagh
Formerly Executive Director, Dictionary
Unit for South African English, Rhodes
University (South African English)

David Kemp
VP and Euro Director, London, ABN-
AMRO Bank N. V. (Currencies)

Alison Kervin
Editor, *Rugby World* (Rugby)

Kate Kiefer
Professor, Colorado State University
(English Language)

Betty Kirkpatrick
Editor, author, and lexicographer
(English Language)

Ira Konigsberg
Professor, University of Michigan, Ann
Arbor; author, *Complete Film Dictionary*
(Cinema)

Tracy Lake
Head of English, Skegness Grammar
School, Skegness (English Language)

Dr Jacqueline Lam
Language Centre, Hong Kong University
of Science & Technology
(Hong Kong English)

Dr John Laurence
Boyce Thomson Institute, Cornell
University (Botany)

Bryan Lawson
Professor and Dean, Faculty of
Architectural Studies, University of
Sheffield (Architecture)

Andrew Leclair
Professor, Newman Laboratory, Cornell
University (Physics)

Dr Becky Lee
Associate Professor,
Division of Humanities and School of
Women's Studies, York University,
Toronto (Christianity and
The Bible)

Naomi C. Losch
Assistant Professor in Hawaiian,
Department of Hawaiian and Indo-Pacific
Languages, University of Hawaii at Manoa
(Hawaiian English)

Dr Caroline Macafee
University of Aberdeen
(Scottish, Northern Irish)

Carolyn Marcus
Gardening writer and editor, ESOL lecturer
(Gardening)

Donald G. Marshall
Professor and Fletcher Jones Chair of Great
Books, Humanities and Teacher Education
Division, Pepperdine University
(English Language)

Aya Matsuda
Assistant Professor, Department of English,
University of New Hampshire
(English Language)

Dr Tom McArthur
Editor, *English Today: The International
Review of the English Language* (1985-)
and *The Oxford Companion to the English
Language* (1992-); author, *The Oxford
Guide to World English* (2002)

Dr Joy McEntee
Lecturer, Discipline of English, University
of Adelaide, Australia (English Language)

Alastair McIver
Editor, *Tennis World* (Tennis)

Jeffrey McQuain
Writer and researcher, *New York Times*;
word columnist and researcher for William
Safire; author, *Power Language* (Politics)

Anthony Middleton
Formerly editor, RAF in-house
publications service; formerly Technical
Publications Editor, GEC-Marconi
(Engineering)

Mark Miller
Editor (Literature)

Dr Frank Molloy
Senior Lecturer, Department of English,
School of Humanities, Charles Sturt
University, New South Wales, Australia
(English Language)

Martyn Moore
Editor, *Practical Photography*
(Photography)

Philip D. Morehead
Lyric Opera of Chicago (Music)

David Morton
Professor, School of Biomedical Science
and Ethics, University of Birmingham
(Veterinary Science)

Bruce Murphy
Professor, Faculty of Veterinary Medicine,
University of Montreal (Biology)

Adrian Napper
Formerly Department of Architecture,
Edinburgh College of Art
(Building and Construction)

Dr Mark Newbrook
Honorary Research Associate in
Linguistics, Monash University; Honorary
Research Associate in Linguistics,
University of Sheffield
(English in Malaysia and Singapore)

Ronald B. Newman
Associate Professor of English, University
of Miami (English Language)

Susan North
Textiles and Fashion, Victoria and Albert
Museum (Fashion)

Kathleen O'Grady
Trinity College, University of Cambridge
(Religion and Mythology)

Thomas S. Oliver Jr
Former Chair, Department of English,
University of the District of Columbia
(English Language)

Alex Orenstein
Professor, City University of New York
(Philosophy)

Lee Pederson
Charles Howard Professor of English
Language, Emory University, Atlanta GA
(US regionalisms, History of US English)

Anthony Pellegrini
PhD and Professor, Department of
Educational Psychology, University of
Minnesota (Education)

Sandra Poulton
Teacher of English Language, Weald of
Kent Grammar School, Tonbridge, Kent
(English Language)

Dr Terry K. Pratt
Professor Emeritus, Department of English
Language and Literature, University of
Prince Edward Island (English Language)

Verbie Lovorn Prevost
Katharine Pryor Professor of English,
University of Tennessee at Chattanooga
(English Language)

Michael Quinion
Lexicographer and editor (New Words)

Lilita Rodman
Assistant Professor Emerita, University of
British Columbia (Canadian English)

John Ross
Writer and editor (Computing)

Dr Edward Ruddell
Department of Parks, Recreation and
Tourism, University of Utah (Martial Arts)

M. Elizabeth (Betsy) Sargent
Associate Professor, Department of
English, University of Alberta
(English Language)

Mary Scott MA
Former Head of English, Hills Road Sixth
Form College, Cambridge
(English Language)

Dr Mark Sebba
Department of Linguistics, Lancaster
University (British Black English)

Dr Robert N. Smead
Associate Professor of Spanish Linguistics,
Brigham Young University
(Hispanic English)

Geneva Smitherman
University Distinguished Professor;
Director, African American Language and
Literacy Program; Director, 'My Brother's
Keeper' Program, Department of English,
Michigan State University
(African American English)

Richard Soffe
University of Plymouth Business School
(Agriculture and Countryside)

Ian M. Spackman
Editor (Computer Games)

Tony Spybey
Professor, Department of Sociology,
Staffordshire University (Sociology)

Kamal Keskar Sridhar
Associate Professor, India Studies and
Linguistics and Director, Center for India
Studies, State University of New York
(South Asian English)

Peter N. Stearns
Professor and Dean, College of Humanities
and Social Sciences, Carnegie Mellon
University; author, *Encyclopedia of World
History* (History)

James M. Steele
Professor, School of Architecture,
University of Southern California
(Architecture and Building)

Sol Steinmetz
Formerly Editorial Director, Random
House Dictionaries (English Language)

Rebecca Stott
Professor and director of the Speak-Write
Project, Department of English, Anglia
Polytechnic University, Cambridge
(English Language)

Robert Strong
Professor of Finance, Maine Business School, University of Maine (Finance)

Bruce Thom
Professor Emeritus, Visiting Professor, University of New South Wales (Geography)

Dr Peter Timmer
Bisant Interactive Ltd (Computing)

Loreto Todd
Professor, Academy for Irish Cultural Heritages, University of Ulster (Irish English, UK regional English, World English)

Diane Tolomeo
Associate Professor, Department of English, University of Victoria, British Columbia (English Language)

Roger Trigg CChem FRSC
Formerly Principal Pharmaceutical Officer, British Pharmacopoeia Commission (Pharmacy)

Dr Amos Turk
Professor Emeritus, Department of Chemistry, City College of New York (Chemical Engineering)

Dr Heather Valencia
University of Stirling (Judaism)

Robert Veltman MA
Lecturer in Applied Linguistics, Department of English Language and Linguistics, University of Kent at Canterbury, Kent (English Language)

Gregory A. Waller
Professor and Chair, Department of English, University of Kentucky (English Language)

Barbara Wallraff
Usage columnist, *The Atlantic*, author, *Word Court* (2000) and *Your Own Words* (2004)

Michael J. Walsh
Editor of *The Heythrop Journal* and archivist, Heythrop College, University of London (The Bible)

John Wells
Professor of Phonetics, University College, London (Phonetics)

Rosemary Wilkinson
Crafts publisher (Crafts and Design)

Gillian Williams
Editor, *Ski and Board Magazine* (Skiing)

John Williams
Sir Norman Chester Centre for Football Research, University of Leicester (Soccer)

Deborah Wills
Associate Professor, Department of English, Mount Allison University, New Brunswick (English Language)

Dr Lise Winer
Faculty of Education, McGill University (Caribbean English)

Ellen Wohl
Professor, Colorado State University (Geography)

Susan J. Wolfe
Professor, Department of English, University of South Dakota (English Language)

Jill Wolvaardt
Director, Dictionary Unit for South African English, Rhodes University (South African English)

Shawn H. Wong
Professor and Director of the University Honors Program at the University of Washington (English Language)

Dr Alison Wray
Reader, Centre for Language and Communication Research, Cardiff University (English Language)

Philip C. Wright
Professor, University of New Brunswick (Business and Management)

Ben Yagoda
Professor, Department of English, University of Delaware (English Language)

Dr Robert Youngson MB, ChB
Author, *Royal Society of Medicine Encyclopedia of Family Health* and *Collins Medical Dictionary*, formerly consultant advisor on ophthalmology to British Army (Medicine and Pharmacology)

Foreword

The *Bloomsbury English Dictionary* is the second edition of the *Encarta® World English Dictionary* which was published in 1999. This new edition continues to define the English language from a global perspective. The need for such a dictionary became apparent to me after 16 years of living as an American in Britain and travelling around the world. It was clear in this period towards the end of the twentieth century that the English language was gaining a level of adoption by non-native speakers which could never have been dreamed even a few decades earlier. English has become the preferred language of communication in the same way that so many propositions that have been around for a long time suddenly achieve widespread acceptance, as, for example, the idea that the Earth orbits the Sun, rather than the Sun orbiting the Earth, gained currency during the seventeenth century.

This Dictionary was the first to use the world as its cultural perspective, to move beyond the hitherto national frontiers which confined dictionaries and their writers. The English language today can no longer be said to be the British language originally defined by James Murray in the first *Oxford English Dictionary* or the language of America that Noah Webster set out to define. Today English is the language of the world. What does this mean? It is interesting to note that in the current edition of a leading English dictionary the term 'imperial' is defined as 'of or relating to an empire: *Britain's imperial era*'. The *Bloomsbury English Dictionary* defines the same term as 'concerning or involving an empire or its ruler'. The point is that a dictionary of the world's *lingua franca* in the third millennium should reflect a neutral cultural perspective rather than the history of nations that once held power over others.

Our goal was to create a dictionary of the world's language that would become the most widely used around the world. In order to realize that vision, we assembled a global partnership of publishers. We have been fortunate in the great strength this partnership has given the project. Our team of over 320 lexicographers, editors, and special consultants created, edited, and updated the text of the Dictionary. As they live in many countries around the world, they brought to the text a global perspective that distinguishes this Dictionary from its rivals.

We also live in a multimedia age. This Dictionary was the first to be planned and created with the specific aim of being published in both book and electronic form. There are many people who will find the electronic edition of this Dictionary, published by Microsoft, to be the most useful one. The market for the print form of the Dictionary, however, is still a large one. It has been observed that a book is a superior piece of mid-technology, like the bicycle, which has continued to flourish in the age of the car. Indeed, unless one's computer is already switched on, a dictionary in book form is probably the fastest random-access device available.

When the world wants to communicate, especially if it wants to communicate or do business beyond a country's own borders, English tends to be the chosen means of communication. One century ago that language might have been French, and several centuries earlier it would have been Latin. Landmarks in the spread of English range from the decision by air-traffic controllers in the 1950s to adopt English as their world language on the one hand, through the worldwide popularity of Hollywood movies and American TV shows, to the fact that almost 70 per cent of Internet webpages are in English.

In the *Bloomsbury English Dictionary*, we are not asserting the primacy of one form of English over another. We are celebrating the richness and diversity of the many varieties of English encountered in daily life. In today's global village, the influences on English from all over the world are intense. We read Canadian novels, some watch Australian soap operas on television, while American language and style dominate software programs. The *Bloomsbury English Dictionary* takes a new view of today's world language and will in years to come continue to reflect the changes and developments in the language in which most of the world chooses to communicate.

Nigel Newton,
Chairman,
Bloomsbury Publishing Plc,
London,
25 May 2004

Introduction

English can be called the world's favourite language. Approximately 375 million people speak English as their first language. Over 375 million people speak English as their second language. Unlike Chinese, Arabic, Spanish, and other major world languages, English is the language in which speakers of other languages choose to communicate with one another. English is the main international language of science and technology, business, pop music, sport, advertising, academic conferences, travel, airports, air-traffic control, diplomacy, and the military. English is the main language of the Internet as about 70 per cent of the information stored on the Web is in English. It is estimated that by the year 2050 over 50 per cent of the world's population will have some competence in English, an increase of almost 20 per cent in 50 years.

The *Bloomsbury English Dictionary*, the second, totally revised edition of the *Encarta® World English Dictionary*, reflects this worldwide status of English, having been compiled in the two main spelling forms of the language (British English and American English), while also covering the other main varieties of our language, from Canada, Australia, New Zealand, Africa, Asia, the Caribbean, and the Pacific Rim, as well as regional variations within both the UK and US. This gives the Dictionary a truly world perspective that accurately reflects the worldwide presence of the English language today.

This Dictionary is first and foremost a dictionary of the English language of today. The audience for this dictionary is diverse, worldwide, encompassing a wide range of ages and backgrounds. It is also a multimedia audience, for the Dictionary appears in both print and electronic forms. For this reason we have made the language of the definitions as natural as possible, avoiding jargon where feasible. We have tried to create clear, informative, and readable definitions that readers will understand without difficulty. Our definitions identify and focus clearly on the characteristics that distinguish and differentiate a word from related terms

and include features that are picked up in extended usage.

Where some other dictionaries might be described as literary, based on historical principles, or scientific, the *Bloomsbury English Dictionary* should be described as modern, for it focuses on the language needs of general dictionary users today. These needs encompass definitions of both the newest scientific and slang terms, and of literary or historical language that users of the Dictionary may encounter especially in their reading. Our guiding principle has been to define the language that our readers are likely to encounter in their everyday lives. Part of the role of our dictionary editors is to monitor where specialized terms move over into everyday usage, where technical jargon becomes part of the mainstream. This can happen, for example, through television shows that bring medical or law-enforcement vocabulary into the homes of millions.

Traditionally, dictionaries have provided definitions of terms, information on how to pronounce words, explanations of where words have come from and, in some instances, information on how to use words. The *Bloomsbury English Dictionary* is no exception to these conventions. We include over 100,000 headwords (the words you look up), and almost four million words of text.

But what else should readers reasonably expect from a dictionary aimed at the language needs of the twenty-first century? The stance of this Dictionary is both to define today's English and to offer clear advice and guidance on how to use our language well. Research with our advisors and readers has shown that this is what readers want from their dictionaries. Problems with spelling and how to use English correctly are perceived as increasing problems for many. Bloomsbury's dictionaries pay particular attention to these issues. This Dictionary includes over 900 frequently misspelt words together with their correct spellings. In our highly computerized era people increasingly find it difficult to distinguish between words that sound or look alike and that a

computer spellchecker will not detect as potential errors. Examples include *hoard/horde* or *principal/principle*. To help our readers avoid errors of this type we have included in this Dictionary several hundred Spellcheck notes that explain the difference between such terms. We give further advice on frequent grammatical and language problems in our Usage essays, while our Synonym essays help readers distinguish between words of similar meaning.

Dictionary editors require hard data to make sure that the definitions they write are based on good linguistic evidence. For earlier dictionary writers such evidence was garnered and stored on cards or slips of paper. In recent years the advent of the computer has meant that such cumbersome and time-consuming methods have been replaced by computerized corpora. A corpus is like a huge filing cabinet, filled with millions of words of real language (taken from fiction, nonfiction, and journalism, for example). Software developed specifically for this project has enabled our editors to call up examples of the use of any term at the touch of a computer key. The Internet is also a huge repository of information about language and how it is used today – but one that our editors must analyse with great care as the material available is not always reliable.

People use dictionaries to find out what words mean, and often these words are scientific or technical. However, many dictionaries define such terms in ways that can seem just as technical as the term itself. In writing this Dictionary we have tried to bring the same criteria of clarity, concision, and transparency to our scientific and technical definitions that have characterized our approach to other definitions. We have applied these criteria across all our specialized entries. In doing so, we combined the skills of our technical definers with contributions from our many subject advisers who checked the accuracy of our definitions and patiently answered thousands of queries. Thus, the Dictionary tries to paint a word picture that the reader can understand by keeping use of specialist terminology to a minimum.

Our research has also indicated that today's dictionary users want to find the information they are seeking quickly. In response to that need, we developed the 'quick definition' feature that is unique to this Dictionary. Quick definitions appear in small capital letters at all entries with more than two senses. They provide a brief gloss of the headword for the user who does not want, or need, the full picture, providing a thumbnail sketch rather than a full analysis of the meaning. The quick definitions are also important in helping readers to navigate through the many senses of a long entry.

When deciding on the order of sense categories, our general principle has been 'most frequent first, least frequent last' as judged by current usage and evidence from our Corpus and language research. This is to make certain that the most common senses occur early in the entry, to enable readers to find what they want quickly. We have, however, in some instances overridden this principle where more frequent senses clearly develop out of a less frequent (probably more technical) sense. Senses within the same part of speech are grouped together in an entry. Informal and slang senses usually come before dated or archaic senses but after stylistically neutral senses.

In sense division, we have tried to strike a balance midway between broad and narrow categorization of senses. The primary consideration has always been ease of use by the reader. We have applied a similar priority when deciding which words and senses should be expanded by example phrases and sentences. We have tried to include these wherever they will help the reader grasp the meaning more easily.

The pronunciation system has been specially developed for this Dictionary to provide a system that speakers of English will find easy to decode. Rather than using the International Phonetic Alphabet (IPA), an excellent system for learners of our language, we felt that we should provide a more up-to-date system that our users, mainly speakers of the English language, would find easier to understand.

Language is a powerful tool, one that can hurt and offend. We have endeavoured to write definitions that convey the meaning of the word in an appropriately clear but sensitive way. Since the Dictionary is a snapshot of the language today, we include some terms that some users may find offensive or even highly offensive. It has been our policy throughout to indicate clearly when such terms are likely to cause offence. A number of lexical entries labelled *offensive* or *taboo* must be defined as entries in any adult dictionary that attempts to cover the whole range of the language. However, in writing the Dictionary, we have tried to avoid sexist, ethnic, ethnocentric, ethnophobic, ageist, racist, and physiologically or otherwise offensively stereotypical language in the Dictionary text. This thoroughly modern editorial policy reflects the standards of changing times during which a great many people deplore what they deem a 'coarsening of the language' by some users, especially ones who, having seen a questionable word in a dictionary, justify their use of the word by dint of the mere fact that it is neither labelled nor stigmatized.

Since the English language has a multifaceted history,

we have paid particular attention to tracing the histories of words (etymologies). These are written in clear language, using as few symbols and abbreviations as possible. We have also included hundreds of extended word history essays. In addition to extended paragraphs on word histories, we have included similar brief essays on World English, regional English, Cultural Notes, and key quotations from leading figures that appear at our biographical entries. The essays form a stepping stone from the dictionary text into the wider world of cultural reference. Language Heritage essays, a new feature for this edition, trace the words that have been absorbed into English from the world's other main language traditions, such as Arabic, German, Italian, and Yiddish.

This Dictionary and its first edition were compiled by a team of over 320 dictionary editors (lexicographers), word history experts (etymologists), pronunciation specialists (phoneticians), and over 120 special subject and World English consultants. Our team was drawn from around the world and included, for example, a Canadian poet and an English lecturer in Hong Kong. I would like to thank sincerely everyone who has contributed to this Dictionary and our Dictionary Database.

It is estimated that there are in the region of one million words in the English language ranging from the most frequently used everyday vocabulary to the most highly specialized technical jargon, the most informal slang, and the most arcane regional terminology. This total continues to grow, especially in science, technology, business, media, sport, and food.

Since it absorbed thousands of French words after the Norman Conquest of 1066, English has always welcomed the new. The 9,600 new words and senses added to this Dictionary since our first edition only five years ago bear witness to this.

The most exciting challenge for dictionary editors today is to keep up with the changes in our language as new words come in and linguistic norms and conventions change and develop in response to technological and cultural innovation. The work of the lexicographer has never been more exciting – defining an ever-evolving language and providing clear advice to readers on how to use English.

Kathy Rooney
May 2004

How to Use the Dictionary

INTRODUCTION

Structurally, a dictionary is a complex mosaic of different elements relating to what you want from such a reference book – spelling, pronunciation, meanings, examples of use, advice on grammar or usage, and an explanation of the origins of words. This section outlines the different elements in the text, so that you can find what you want in the *Bloomsbury English Dictionary* quickly and easily.

How the dictionary page is laid out

Guide words

Each page has two **guide words** that show, on the left, the first **boldface** dictionary entry on that page, and, on the right, the last, so that you can quickly find the word you are looking for.

Layout of the text

The text is designed in three columns for maximum coverage and legibility. Important elements of the text appear in **boldface** type. Quick definitions appear in SMALL CAPITALS. Full

definitions appear in roman type and examples and citations in *italic* type. Quotations by key figures appear after the entries for those people, in roman type and within quotation marks.

Graphic illustrations and tables

Illustrations appear as close as possible to the entries to which they refer. An explicit cross-reference is given if an illustration or table falls on a different page from its entry.

guide word – first entry ——————

guide word – last entry

illustration

pronunciation key ——————

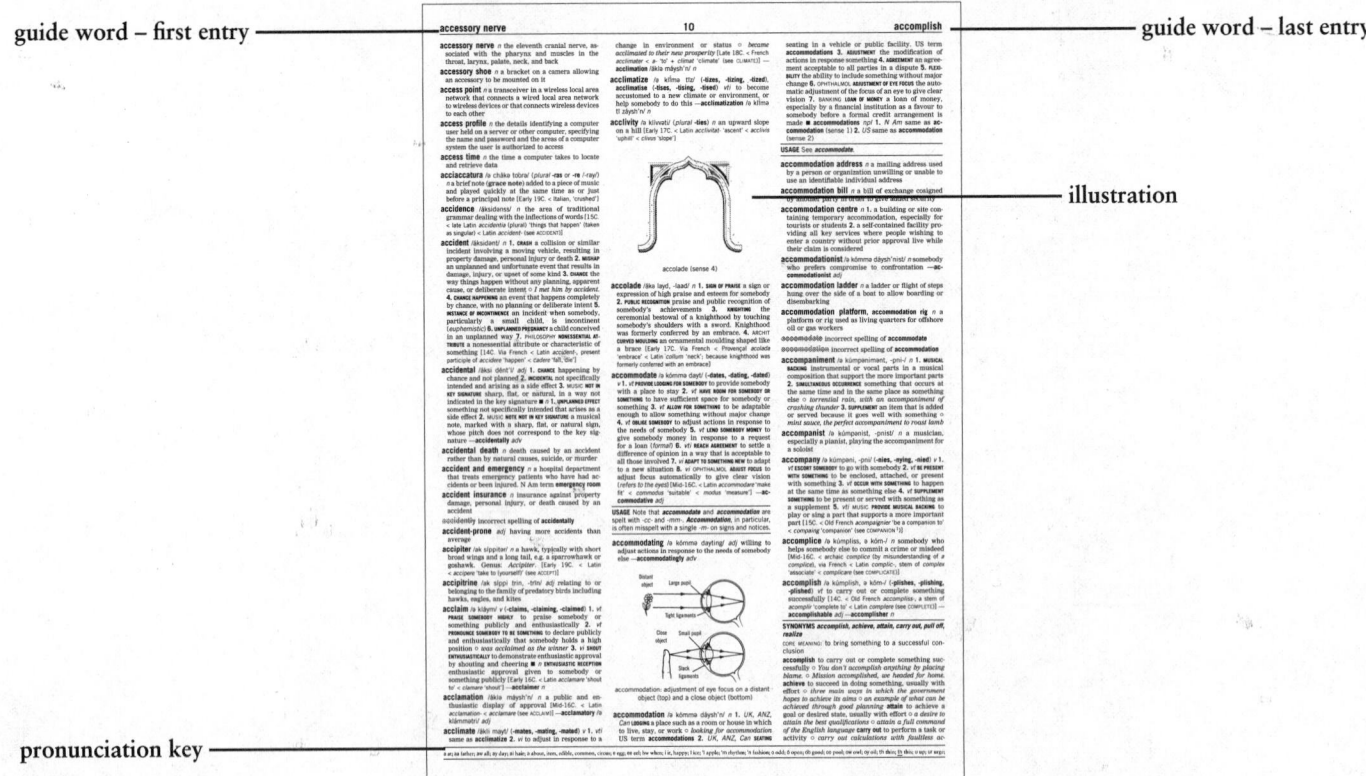

Finding the word you are looking for

This Dictionary contains over 400,000 individual elements that you might want to look up. Here is a guide to finding the different types of information quickly.

Headwords

The *Bloomsbury English Dictionary* contains over 100,000 **headwords** (the words you look up), including approximately 10,000 entries about people and places – the biographical and geographical entries (see page xxi for a discussion of these 'nonlexical' biographical and geographical entries). There are also over 3,700 'list words' – words beginning with a common prefix such as *anti-* or *non-* that are entered without definitions because their meanings are self-explanatory.

Headwords are listed in strict alphabetical order, ignoring internal or end punctuation and other characters:

brandied /brándid/ *adj* cooked or preserved in brandy

branding /bránding/ *n* the use of advertising, distinctive design, and other means to make consumers associate a specific product with a specific manufacturer

branding iron *n* an iron tool that is heated and pressed onto a surface, especially an animal's hide, in order to leave a permanent identifying mark

brandish /brándish/ (**-dishes, -dishing, -dished**) *vt* to wave something about, especially a weapon, in a menacing, theatrical, or triumphant way [14C. < French *brandiss-*, stem of *brandir* < *brand* 'sword'] —**brandisher** *n*

brand leader *n* the best-selling product in a particular category

brandling /brándling/ *n* a small reddish-brown earthworm that is often used as bait by anglers. Latin name: *Eisenia foetida*. [Mid-17C. Because of its colouring, like a burning brand]

brand loyalty *n* the tendency to buy a particular brand of a product

brand name *n* a trade name for a product or service produced by a particular company. It may or may not be a registered trademark. ○ *A computer with a brand name can cost 10 per cent more.* —**brand-named** *adj*

brand-new *adj* completely new and unused [As if newly made in a furnace]

Words with the same spelling

Words with the same spelling (**homographs**) but with different pronunciations or origins (**etymologies**) are listed with superscript, or raised, numbers to differentiate them. The order of these numbers broadly reflects usage and frequency of occurrence:

baste[1] /bayst/ (**bastes, basting, basted**) *vt* to moisten meat or fish at intervals during cooking with a liquid such as melted fat or cooking juices [15C. Origin ?]

baste[2] /bayst/ (**bastes, basting, basted**) *vt* to beat somebody severely (*dated informal*) [Mid-16C. Origin ?]

baste[3] /bayst/ (**bastes, basting, basted**) *vt N Am* HANDICRAFT same as **tack**[1] *v* (sense 6) [14C. Via Old French *bastir* < Germanic, 'join together with bast']

Alternative spellings of headwords

The Dictionary recognizes instances when a word has more than one possible spelling (**variant**). Such entries appear in **boldface** type following their headwords:

falafel /fə laáf'l/, **felafel** *n* a deep-fried ball of ground chickpeas seasoned with onions and spices, originating in Southwest Asia [Mid-20C. Via Egyptian Arabic *falāfil* < Arabic *fulful* 'pepper']

At the entry for the alternative spelling, a cross-reference directs you back to the entry where the word is defined:

felafel *n* FOOD another spelling of **falafel**

Inflections

Inflections are grammatical forms of headwords that include the principal tenses of verbs, the comparative and superlative forms of adjectives and adverbs, and irregular plurals of nouns. These forms are shown after the pronunciation where the inflection applies to the whole headword, or at a specific sense or group of senses where appropriate:

adieu /ə dyoó/ *interj*, *n* (*plural* **adieux** /ə dyoóz/ or **adieus** /ə dyoóz/) used to say goodbye (*literary*) ○'...*the more gentle adieus of her sisters were uttered without being heard*' (Jane Austen, *Pride And Prejudice*; 1813) [14C. < French, '(I commend you) to God']

shoo /shoo/ *interj* used to tell a child or animal to go away ■ *vti* (**shoos, shooing, shooed**) to say shoo and gesture to a child or animal to go away ○ *shooed the pigeons away* [15C. Natural exclamation]

cagey /káyji/ (**-gier, -giest**) **cagy** *adj* secretive and refusing to be open, frank, or direct (*informal*) [Late 19C. Origin ?] —**cagily** *adv* —**caginess** *n*

When a headword has a plural form with the same spelling, this is indicated by the label *plural same*:

aircraft /aír kraaft/ (*plural same*) *n* any vehicle capable of flight

Important irregular inflections also appear as headwords in their own right, cross-referred back to their main entries:

calyces BOT plural of **calyx**

fled past participle, past tense of **flee**

Abbreviations and acronyms

Abbreviations and acronyms are included in the alphabetical headword list, grouped together according to their punctuation and their status as either an abbreviation or symbol. Our Corpus of World English has shown that punctuation within abbreviations varies considerably. This Dictionary gives the most common form; important alternative forms are also shown. Meanings are ordered alphabetically:

C1 (*plural* **C1s**) *n* in the market research system that classifies people according to their occupation, somebody in a clerical or junior management position

C2 (*plural* **C2s**) *n* in the market research system that classifies people according to their occupation, somebody in a skilled manual job

C2B *abbr* E-COMMERCE consumer-to-business

ca *abbr* Canada (*used in Internet addresses*) See table at **domain name**

Ca *symbol* CHEM ELEM calcium

CA *abbr* **1.** MAIL California **2.** GEOG Central America **3.** GEOG Central American **4.** ONLINE certificate authority (*used in e-mails*) **5.** ACCT chartered accountant **6.** ACCT chief accountant **7.** chronological age **8.** INTERNAT REL consular agent **9.** COMM Consumers' Association

ca. *abbr* HIST circa (*used before dates*)

C/A *abbr* **1.** FIN capital account **2.** FIN credit account **3.** *also* **c/a** BANKING current account

CAA *abbr* AVIAT Civil Aviation Authority

CAAT *abbr* E-COMMERCE certificate authority administration tool

When an abbreviation is more frequently used than its full form, we give the definition at the abbreviation:

BSE *n* a disease that affects the nervous system of cattle, believed to be caused by a transmissible protein particle (**prion**) and related to Creutzfeldt-Jakob disease in humans. Full form **bovine spongiform encephalopathy**

Foreign words and phrases

Based on information in our Corpus of World English, foreign words and phrases are included in the A-Z list as entries if they have established English pronunciations and are used, without being explained, in contemporary literature, journalism, general writing, or general conversation:

du jour /doo zhoór/ *adj* **1.** offered or served today ○ *the soup du jour* **2.** being the latest in a series, sequence, or trend [< French, 'of the day']

Two- and three-word verbs (phrasal verbs)

Phrasal verbs are two- or three-word verbs, each consisting of a common verb plus an adverb or preposition such as *out* or *up*, whose meaning is not self-explanatory, for example *do up*, *put up with*. These are listed after the entries for their root verbs:

keel /keel/ *n* **1.** NAUT SHIP'S STRUCTURAL ELEMENT the main structural element of a ship, stretching along the centre line of its bottom from the bow to the stern. It sometimes extends farther downwards into the water to provide extra stability. **2.** AVIAT AIRCRAFT'S STRUCTURAL ELEMENT a structure that looks or acts like a ship's keel, e.g. the main structural element of an aircraft's fuselage **3.** BIRDS PART OF BIRD'S BREASTBONE a ridge-shaped part in the breastbone of a bird to which the flight muscles are anchored. Technical name **carina 4.** BIOL PART LIKE RIDGE any ridge-shaped part of an organism **5.** same as **ship** (*literary*) ■ *vti* (**keeled, keeling, keels**) NAUT CAPSIZE to capsize a vessel, or capsize [14C. < Old Norse *kjölr*] ◇ **on an even keel** in a stable steady condition
keel over *v* **1.** *vi* to collapse or fall over, often through exhaustion or illness (*informal*) **2.** *vti* NAUT same as **keel**

Idiomatic phrases

Idiomatic phrases such as *on the run* and *let the cat out of the bag* are shown at the ends of many entries, introduced by the symbol ◇:

fun /fun/ *n* **1.** AMUSEMENT a time or feeling of enjoyment or amusement ○ *Just for fun, we wore silly hats.* ... [Late 17C. < obsolete *fon* 'fool', origin ?] ◇ **fun and games** difficulty or trouble (*informal; used ironically*) ○ *A broken sprinkler in the stockroom overnight gave us some fun and games in the morning.* ◇ **like fun** (*informal*) **1.** with great speed or effort ○ *We'll have to work like fun to finish this order on time.* **2.** US certainly not ○ *Like fun I am!* ◇ **make fun of somebody** *or* **something** to make somebody or something appear ridiculous ◇ **poke fun at somebody** *or* **something** to mock or ridicule somebody or something

Incorrect spellings

This Dictionary includes in its A-Z text over 900 frequently misspelt words, which are entered at their own alphabetical places where users are most likely to look them up. This list of misspellings was compiled using the help of our advisers on English usage and the evidence in our own Corpus of World English and Internet research. In order to avoid reinforcing an erroneous idea of the spelling of a word, we have shown the incorrect form with a line through it:

~~Carribean~~ incorrect spelling of **Caribbean**

See also the section titled 'Spellchecks', on page xx.

Cross-references

Cross-references in this Dictionary serve various purposes. They take the place of definitions, and indicate that the information you need is given at other entries with the same meanings as the words you have looked up:

abele /ə beél/ *n* TREES same as **white poplar** (sense 1) [13C. Directly or via Dutch *abeel* < Old French *a(u)bel* < Latin *albus* 'white']

bannister *n* ARCHIT another spelling of **banister**

armor *n* US spelling of **armour**

Cross-references in the form of *plural of, past tense of,* and so on, refer from inflected forms to their root words:

children plural of **child**

Full form of refers from the expanded form of an abbreviation or acronym to its abbreviation, where a definition is given:

disc jockey *n* MUSIC, MEDIA full form of **DJ**[1] (sense 1)

DJ[1] *n* **1.** somebody who plays records or other recorded music, e.g. at a live dance or on the radio. Full form **disc jockey 2.** somebody who composes rap or techno music using samples of recorded music [Abbreviation of DISC JOCKEY] —**DJ** *vi*

The boldface symbol ♦ directs you to another nonlexical, i.e. geographical or biographical entry, where you will find a definition:

Bonaparte /bóne paart/ ♦ **Napoleon I**

Dakota[2] /də kótə/ ♦ **North Dakota, South Dakota** — **Dakotan** *n, adj*

A lightface arrow ◊ after a definition directs you to a related lexical entry where you will find additional relevant information:

Celsius /sélssi əss/ *adj* using or measured on an international metric temperature scale on which water freezes at 0° and boils at 100° under normal atmospheric conditions. The term 'Celsius' is usually preferred to 'centigrade', especially in technical contexts. ◊ **Fahrenheit** [Mid-19C. After Anders *Celsius* (1701–44), Swedish astronomer]

coldboot /kóld boot/ (**-boots, -booting, -booted**) *vt* to restart a computer by turning it off and on. ◊ **warmboot**

Derivative words

At the ends of many entries there are additional boldface words with no definitions (**undefined runons**). These consist of the headwords plus common suffixes such as *–able, –ly,* or *–ness,* or the headwords shown in other parts of speech. They do not require definitions because they correlate predictably in usage and meaning with their headwords. Where appropriate, these derivative words have been given pronunciations, for example, when their stress patterns differ significantly from those of their headwords:

changeable /cháynjəb'l/ *adj* capable of changing, or liable to change or vary —**changeability** /cháynjə bílləti/ *n* —**changeableness** *n* —**changeably** *adv*

Words beginning with common prefixes

The Dictionary includes several lists of self-explanatory words (**list words**) made up of a word defined elsewhere in the text and a common prefix, such as *anti-, non-,* or *un-.* These words do not need definitions, as their meanings can be easily deduced from their elements. Here we show the first and last pairs of words of the list at *ultra*:

ultra- *prefix* **1.** more than normal, excessively, completely ○ *ultrasophisticated* **2.** outside the range of ○ *ultrasound* [< Latin *ultra* 'beyond' < Indo-European]

ultracareful *adj*
ultracasual *adj*
[etc.]
ultrathin *adj*
ultraviolent *adj*

ultrabasic /últrə báyssik/ *adj* describes igneous rock that is high in iron and magnesium and contains no free quartz ■ *n* a rock of ultrabasic composition

Similar lists of self-explanatory words can be found at the following prefixes: *anti-, co-, cyber-, e-, hyper-, ill-, inter-, mis-, multi-, neo-, non-, out-, over-, post-, pre-, pro-, pseudo, quasi-, re-, self-, semi-, sub-, super-, ultra-, un-, under-* and *well-.*

Finding the meaning you are looking for

Entries with more than one meaning

Many words have more than one meaning, or definition. The different meanings are indicated by numbers that appear in **boldface** type. Meanings are ordered according to usage and frequency, with the most frequent sense given first:

> **puerile** /pyoŏr īl/ *adj* **1.** regarded as childishly silly or immature **2.** relating to or characteristic of childhood (*formal*) [Late 16C. Directly or via French < Latin *puerilis* < *puer* 'child, boy'] —**puerilely** *adv* —**puerility** /pyoor rílləti/ *n*

Parts of speech

Part-of-speech labels, in *italic type*, indicate whether the headword functions as a noun, adjective, verb, and so on. If an entry contains meanings that have different parts of speech, they are grouped together (all noun meanings together, all verb meanings, and so on). A change of part of speech within an entry is introduced by the symbol ■:

> **bodycheck** /bóddi chek/ *n* in some sports, especially ice hockey or soccer, an illegal act of using the body to obstruct an opposing player ■ *vt* (**-checks, -checking, -checked**) in some sports, especially ice hockey or soccer, to use the body to obstruct an opposing player illegally

The part-of-speech labels used in the Dictionary are:

abbr	abbreviation
adj	adjective
adv	adverb
aux v	auxiliary verb
conj	conjunction
contr	contraction
det	determiner
interj	interjection
modal v	modal verb
n	noun
npl	plural noun
prefix	prefix
prep	preposition
pron	pronoun
symbol	symbol
suffix	suffix
vt	verb
vi	intransitive verb
vr	reflexive verb
vt	transitive verb
vti	transitive / intransitive verb

The label *tdmk* indicates trademarks.

Quick definitions

The **Quick Definitions** are a unique feature of this Dictionary and are designed to guide you through longer entries. They appear in SMALL CAPITALS and act as brief summaries of the full definitions, so that you can easily find your way to the appropriate sense:

> **extremity** /ik strémməti/ *n* (*plural* **-ties**) **1.** HAND OR FOOT a limb of a person or animal, or the part of a limb that is farthest from the body, especially somebody's hand or foot (*often used in the plural*) **2.** FARTHEST POINT a point that is the farthest out, especially from the centre ○ *the southernmost extremity of the continent* **3.** HIGHEST DEGREE the highest degree or greatest intensity of something ○ *in the extremity of her grief* **4.** DANGER a situation or state of great danger or distress ○ *They prayed for help in their extremity.* ■ **extremities** *npl* DRASTIC MEASURES drastic or unreasonable measures (*formal*)

Specialist meanings

The Dictionary includes the main specialized meanings you are likely to encounter in general publications and consumer magazines. **Subject labels** such as COMP (computing) and FIN (finance) signal meanings belonging to specialist subject areas and help you identify them readily in an entry (a full list of the subject labels used in the Dictionary is given on p. xxii):

> **export** *v* /ik spáwrt, éks pawrt/ (**-ports, -porting, -ported**) **1.** *vti* COMM SEND GOODS ABROAD to send goods for sale or exchange to other countries **2.** *vt* SOC SCI SPREAD ONE SOCIETY'S CULTURE TO ANOTHER to cause the spread of ideas, values, or a way of life from one society, culture, or nation to another **3.** *vt* COMPUT ALTER FORMAT OF COMPUTER DATA to convert data from a computer program into a form suitable for a different program or environment ■ *n* /éks pawrt/ **1.** COMM SELLING OF GOODS ABROAD the selling of goods to other countries **2.** COMM PRODUCT SOLD ABROAD a product sold and transported to another country **3.** BEVERAGES TYPE OF SCOTTISH BEER a strong brown beer brewed in Scotland [15C. < Latin *exportare* 'carry away' < *portare* 'carry'] —**exportability** /ik spáwrtə bílləti, éks pawrtə-/ *n* —**exportable** *adj* —**exportation** /éks pawr táysh'n/ *n* —**exporter** *n*

Some information that occurs routinely in scientific and technical definitions, for example the sources of minerals or the uses to which chemicals are put, is shown in a concise form for greater accessibility and consistency:

> **beta-blocker** *n* a drug that regulates the activity of the heart. Use: treatment of high blood pressure.

> **calcium carbonate** *n* a white crystalline solid that is one of the most common natural substances. Source: chalk, limestone, marble, animal shells, bones. Use: antacids, paint, cement, toothpaste. Formula: $CaCO_3$.

> **gardenia** /gaar deéni ə/ *n* an evergreen tree or bush with shiny leaves. Flowers: white, fragrant. Native to: Africa, Asia. Genus: *Gardenia*. [Mid-18C. < modern Latin, after Alexander *Garden* (1730–91), Scottish-American naturalist]

Information on how a word is used

Illustrative examples

The Dictionary has thousands of illustrative examples that clarify the definitions and place them in context. These are drawn from our 200-million-word Corpus of World English. The symbol ○ introduces examples:

> **believe** /bi leév/ (**-lieves, -lieving, -lieved**) *v* **1.** *vt* ACCEPT SOMETHING AS TRUE to accept that something is true or real ○ *I don't know which story to believe.* **2.** *vt* ACCEPT SOMEBODY AS TRUTHFUL to accept that somebody is telling the truth ○ *Nobody will believe you!* ○ *I don't believe him.* **3.** *vt* CREDIT SOMEBODY WITH SOMETHING to accept that somebody or something has a particular quality or ability ○ *No one believed her capable of such a malicious remark.* **4.** *vi* THINK THAT SOMETHING EXISTS to be of the opinion that something exists or is a reality, especially when there is no absolute proof of its existence or reality ○ *believe in reincarnation* **5.** *vi* HAVE TRUST to be confident that somebody or something is worthwhile or effective ○ *We all believe in you.* **6.** *vi* THINK SOMETHING IS GOOD to be of the opinion that something is right or beneficial and, usually, to act in accordance with that belief ○ *believed strongly in freedom of expression* **7.** *vi* HAVE RELIGIOUS FAITH to have a belief in God or in a religion's gods [Old English *belyfan* < Germanic, 'to love, trust'] —**believer** *n* ◇ **make believe** to pretend, especially in play

Quoted citations

The Dictionary also includes many quotations taken from written sources (**citations**) such as fiction, nonfiction, and journalism. These citations are also drawn from our Corpus of World English:

> **excepted** /ik séptid/ *adj* with the exception of a particular person or thing ○ *present company excepted* ○ '*Hazel eyes excepted, two years more might make her all that he wished.*' (Jane Austen, *Emma*; 1816)

mingy /mínji/ (**-gier, -giest**) *adj* **1.** STINGY ungenerous or stingy (*informal*) **2.** INSUFFICIENT excessively or unacceptably small in quantity or amount (*informal*) ○ *a mingy helping* **3.** SHODDY IN QUALITY creating a negative impression on others because of being shoddy (*informal*) ○*'Finally, they will have to change the mingy, defensive, consultant-driven style of recent campaigns.'* (Joe Klein *Newsweek*; 19 May 2003) [Early 20C. Origin ?]

Style levels, registers of usage, and currency

The Dictionary uses *italic* labels to give information on the style, register, and currency of a word or meaning. If a label applies to all meanings of a word, it appears before the first numbered meaning; if it applies to a specific meaning, it appears after that meaning:

back-seat driver *n* (*informal*) **1.** a passenger in a vehicle who continually pesters the driver with unwanted advice or criticism **2.** somebody who gives unwanted advice or criticism while somebody else does something

gat[2] /gat/ *n* same as **handgun** (*dated slang*) [Early 20C. Shortening of GATLING GUN]

The following labels are used in the Dictionary to indicate stylistic level or degree of currency:

Currency

archaic	not used since before World War II
dated	used at some stage between 1945 and 1990 but no longer part of the current idiom

Register

literary	used in literature and poetry and for special effect, but not used in everyday contexts
formal	used in formal situations and formal writing, but inappropriate in everyday contexts
technical	marks specialist terms that have an everyday equivalent
informal	used in relaxed conversation or writing but avoided in more formal contexts
humorous	pompous or formal or dated terms typically used self-consciously for humorous effect
disapproving	marks a derogatory attitude on the part of the speaker
slang	highly informal language, completely inappropriate in formal contexts, and often with a crude edge
babytalk	used by adults when talking to young children and babies
nonstandard	not considered part of correct or educated usage, though current in spoken usage

Offensiveness

insult	a pejorative term that would be likely to insult or upset somebody if said directly to the person
offensive	likely to be offensive to many people, for example because of being racist or sexual
taboo	marks classic taboo words referring to sex and bodily functions

Some lexical entries commonly regarded as offensive or taboo require inclusion in a dictionary of this size and scope. However, the editors have attempted to ensure that these and other offensive or potentially offensive lexical items and areas of reference are not used in the defining language and other elements of the text.

Words not universally regarded as offensive but likely to give offense in varying degrees are qualified accordingly: *often considered offensive*, *sometimes considered offensive*, and *offensive in some contexts*.

Offensive terms have been defined by glosses rather than substitutable definitions.

Regional varieties of English: global and domestic

In the Dictionary, we give a global and domestically regional view of the English language. Globally, we have included information on the two main spelling forms of English – British and American – and have differentiated the main varieties of World English when alternative terms are preferred. American usage is explicitly labelled only where it differs from other varieties of World English:

boohai /boʻo hī/, **booai** /boʻo ī/, **booay** *n NZ* a remote rural area (*informal*) [Mid-20C. Origin ?]

nukkad /nu kúd/ *n S Asia* a street corner or other place where people gather to chat [Late 20C. < Hindi]

spaza /spaʻaza/ *n S Africa* a small informal shop, often run from a home in a township [Late 20C. Origin?]

supply teacher *n UK* a teacher who takes the place of another temporarily. ANZ term **relief teacher**. N Am term **substitute teacher**

The Dictionary uses the following *italic* labels to indicate the geographical area where a word is used:

ANZ	Australian and New Zealand English
Aus	Australian English
Can	Canadian English
Carib	Caribbean English
Cockney	Cockney
E Africa	East African English
Hawaii	Hawaiian English
Hong Kong	Hong Kong English
Ireland	Irish English
Isle of Man	Isle of Man
Malaysia	Malaysian English
Midwest	Midwestern United States
N Am	North American English (US and Canada)
N England	Northern England
NZ	New Zealand English
New England	New England
Northeast US	Northeastern United States
Northwest US	Northwestern United States
Philippines	Philippines English
S Africa	South African English
S Asia	South Asian English
S England	Southern England
Scot	Scottish English
Singapore	Singapore
Southern US	Southern United States
Southwest England	Southwestern England
Southwest US	Southwestern United States
UK	British English
US	American English
W Africa	West African English
Wales	Welsh English
Western US	Western United States

The label *regional* indicates that a word or meaning has widespread use in English dialects. The labels *UK regional* and *US regional* indicate dialectal use in British English and American English, respectively. See also the section titled 'World English and regional essays' on page xx.

Other restrictions on usage

Other restrictions on the usage of words are shown by italic comments in brackets. These Usage notes spell out useful syntactic information beyond the basic part of speech, for example *takes a singular verb*; they give information on the typical users of a word or phrase, for example *used mainly by children*; and they give information on the speaker's attitude or tone of voice, for example *often used ironically*:

city slicker *n* a worldly resident of a city (*informal disapproving*)

fine[1] /fīn/ *adj* (**finer, finest**) **1.** QUITE WELL OR SATISFACTORY in a good, acceptable, or comfortable condition (*informal*) ○ *Everything's fine, thank you.* ... **9.** UNPLEASANT extremely unsuitable or undesirable (*informal; used ironically*) ○ *This is a fine mess!*

hardening of the arteries *n* MED same as **atherosclerosis** (*not in technical use*)

Trademarks, trade names, and proprietary terms

The Dictionary includes words on the basis of their usage in the English language today. Words that are known to have current trademark or proprietary registrations have been given the label *tdmk*. They are defined with glosses, not substitutable definitions.

Graphic illustrations and tables

The Dictionary illustrates over 4,000 items with photographs, drawings, and maps. Their main function is to help you by adding to and complementing the text, providing additional contexts for the definitions, and placing the definitions in their context. The Dictionary contains 24 tables. Cross-references to illustrations and tables are shown after their definitions:

caesium /seézi əm/ *n* a rare ductile silver-white element of the alkali metals group that is the most reactive of the elements. Use: photoelectric cells. Symbol **Cs**. See table at **element** [Mid-19C. < modern Latin < Latin *caesius* 'bluish-grey'; from its blue spectral lines]

Special features of the dictionary entry

In addition to definitions, the Dictionary includes information on the pronunciation of headwords and the origin and development of headwords. It also contains additional features that give information on a specific aspect of a word, going beyond the scope of the standard dictionary entry. These features include extended notes on spelling, grammar, and usage; regionalisms; varieties of World English; notes on contributions by other languages to British English; sets of synonyms; cultural notes incorporating cultural references; and quotations at key biographical entries.

Pronunciation

Our pronunciation system has been developed specifically for the *Bloomsbury English Dictionary*. It relies on familiar combinations of letters of the alphabet, so that you can use it without constant reference to a table of explanations and symbols. An abbreviated pronunciation key appears at the bottom of each page, and the entire pronunciation system is explained in full on pp. xxiv–xxv.

Word origins

The principal aim of the word origins (**etymologies**) in the Dictionary is to present the etymologies of the entries with as much accuracy as present-day knowledge permits, in a way that is accessible and interesting to general readers. As far as possible, etymologies have been written in plain English, with few abbreviations or technical terms. Whenever possible, etymologies include the century when the headword was first recorded, an account of the word's origin, and other relevant information likely to be of interest to you. The symbol < , meaning 'from', indicates the various stages in a word's development. A question mark [?] is used after the word 'Origin' when the ultimate origin of a word is not definitely known:

capeesh /ka peésh/ *interj* do you understand? [Mid-20C. < Italian *capisce* 'he or she understands', form of *capire* 'understand']

gravlax /gráv laks/ **gravadlax** /grávvəd-/ *n* a Scandinavian dish consisting of thin slices of dried salmon marinated in sugar, salt, pepper, and herbs, especially dill, and usually served as an appetizer [Mid-20C. < Swedish or Norwegian *gravlaks* 'buried salmon' (because originally marinated in a hole in the ground)]

hanker /hángkər/ (**-kers, -kering, -kered**) *vi* to want something very badly and persistently ○ *hankers after something she can't have* [Early 17C. Origin ?]

At some entries we explain why a word is used with a particular meaning. This may be because of a development of a meaning in English or in a source language, or an association with a person or place, or a visual image or stereotype:

Ruritania /roÓori táyni ə/ *n* a place of romance, adventure, and intrigue [Late 19C. After a fictional central European kingdom in novels by Anthony Hope (1863–1933)] —**Ruritanian** *adj, n*

In addition, over 200 short word history essays, entitled **ORIGIN**, give additional information of etymological interest that applies to more than one headword, for example at *ocular*:

ocular /ókyoŏlər/ *adj* relating to, perceived by, or performed by the eye ■ *n* an eyepiece in an optical instrument [Late 16C. Via French *oculaire* < late Latin *ocularis* < Latin *oculus* 'eye']

ORIGIN The Indo-European word from which *ocular* is derived is also the ancestor of English *atrocious*, *eye*, *ferocious*, *inoculate*, *optic*, and *window*.

Finally, a unique series of 28 extended essays, entitled **LANGUAGE HERITAGE** trace the influence of languages such as Arabic, Dutch, Spanish, and Hebrew on English vocabulary over the centuries:

Tupi-Guarani *n* a Native South American language family whose principal members are Tupi and Guarani. It is itself a branch of the Andean-Equatorial family of languages. —**Tupi-Guarani** *adj*

LANGUAGE HERITAGE *Tupi-Guarani* Much of English is made up of words from other languages, and the *Tupi-Guarani* group of South American languages is a small but significant contributor in this respect. Names of unfamiliar animals and birds reached English relatively soon after Europeans discovered the New World (usually via Portuguese, Spanish, or sometimes French): the *agouti* and the *toucan* in the mid-16th century, the *capybara*, *eyra*, *jaguar*, and *tanager* in the early 17th, followed later by, for example, *cougar*, *jabiru*, *piranha*, and *tapir*. Foodstuffs were adopted: *manioc* (mid-16th century), *cashew* (late 16th), *cayenne pepper*, and *tapioca*, for example. Valuable products and their sources became known and used, for instance *ipecac* (a plant from whose roots an emetic is made, early 17th century), *jacaranda* (a tree with a valuable wood), and *jaborandi* (a bush whose dried leaves yield the drug pilocarpine). Tupi also gave us (via Portuguese) the sound of the *maraca* (early 17th century).

Usage essays

The Usage essays complement the Usage notes by providing more extended information on particularly thorny usage problems. Meanings that may be challenged as to the legitimacy of their usage are signalled by a lightface triangle △. Usage essays appear after the heading **USAGE**:

nonplussed /nón plúst/ *adj* **1.** surprised, confused, and uncertain what to do or say **2.** △ calm and unperturbed (*informal*)

USAGE The adjective *nonplussed* means 'surprised, confused, and uncertain what to do or say'. It is increasingly used in the almost opposite sense of 'untroubled', especially in US English (*Nonplussed by the criticism, she continued to direct her films in the very same offbeat manner for which she was famed.*). This new meaning is not yet accepted as standard, and it may cause ambiguity in sentences such as *He seemed nonplussed by the news.* It possibly derives from a misunderstanding of the *non-* element, perhaps also influenced by *nonchalant* which does mean 'calm and unconcerned'. But *nonplussed* goes back to Latin *non plus* 'no more', and does not have a positive or affirmative form *plussed*.

Spellchecks

A common spelling problem today is confusion over homophones, or words with similar sounds but different meanings or spellings such as *ware, wear, were,* and *where.* Although this confusion has always existed, it is our belief that increasing reliance on automatic spellcheckers, which do not, of course, distinguish homophones as errors, has exacerbated the problem in recent years. For this reason the Dictionary features pairs or sets of common homophones that are routinely confused in written texts, after the heading **SPELLCHECK**. The Spellcheck notes are entered at the first word of the pair or set, regardless of relative frequency, with cross-references from the other homophones to the entries with the Spellchecks. Unlike incorrect spellings, Spellcheck terms are all valid forms:

ware[1] /wair/ *n* **1.** SIMILAR THINGS similar things, or things that are made of the same material (*usually used in combination*) ○ *glassware* **2.** CERAMICS ceramic articles of a particular kind or made by a particular manufacturer (*often used in combination*) ○ *delftware* ■ **wares** *npl* **1.** THINGS FOR SALE articles offered for sale **2.** MARKETABLE SKILLS skills or talents offered as a service or a commodity [Old English *waru*]

SPELLCHECK ware, wear, were, or **where?** Do not confuse the spelling of *ware, wear, were,* and *where,* which sound similar. *Ware* (referring to similar things, or things made of the same material), is most likely to be confused with *wear* (referring to clothing) in compound words such as *software, tableware, footwear,* and *knitwear.* *Were* is the past tense of *are* (as in *We were all young once*), and *where* is used to ask about or indicate the place that somebody or something is in, at, going to, or coming from: *Where were you last night? They still live in the town where they were born.*

Synonym essays

Synonym essays distinguish between sets of words that are close in meaning. Examples help to clarify nuances of meaning, and cross-references from individual synonyms direct you from them to the Synonym essays at which they appear:

annoy /ə nóy/ (-noys, -noying, -noyed) *v* **1.** *vt* IRRITATE SOMEBODY to make somebody feel impatient or mildly angry **2.** *vt* HARASS SOMEBODY to harass somebody repeatedly **3.** *vi* BE IRRITATING to be a source of irritation ○ *Barking dogs are bound to annoy.* [13C. Via Old French *anoier* < late Latin *inodiare* 'make loathsome' < Latin *in odio* 'in hatred']

SYNONYMS *annoy, irritate, exasperate, vex, irk*

CORE MEANING: to cause a mild degree of anger in somebody
annoy to make somebody feel impatient or mildly angry ○ *His constant complaining annoys everyone.* ○ *We're annoyed that no-one told us how long the alterations would take.* **irritate** to annoy somebody slightly ○ *The loud humming quickly started to irritate her.* ○ *We were irritated to find that everyone had left early.* **exasperate** to make somebody angry or frustrated, often by repeatedly doing something annoying ○ *The frequent breakdowns and delays exasperated even loyal customers.* ○ *We soon became exasperated with his laziness and excuses.* **vex** to make somebody slightly annoyed or upset, especially over a relatively unimportant matter ○ *The mistake vexed him but did not worry him unduly.* ○ *It vexed her that she had almost wanted to laugh at his remark.* **irk** to annoy somebody slightly by being tiresome or tedious ○ *What irked her more than anything else was that Jo was probably right.* ○ *He also irked his colleagues with frequent TV appearances and public pronouncements.*

irk /urk/ (irks, irking, irked) *vt* to annoy somebody slightly, especially by being tedious [14C. Perhaps < Old Norse *yrkja* 'to work'; originally N English, 'grow weary or vexed']

SYNONYMS See *annoy* and *bother.*

World English and regional essays

The World English coverage in the Dictionary is underpinned by a number of essays on specific varieties of English, both domestically regional and global:

earwig /eér wig/ *n* SLENDER INSECT WITH PINCERS a common insect with a slender shiny body, small forewings, antennae, and pincers at the end of its abdomen. Order: Dermaptera. ■ *v* (-wigs, -wigging, -wigged) **1.** *vti* EAVESDROP to eavesdrop, or eavesdrop on something (*humorous*) **2.** *vt* TRY TO INFLUENCE SOMEBODY to try to influence somebody, e.g. a judge, privately or clandestinely [Old English *ēarwicga* < *ēare* 'ear' + *wicga* 'insect']

REGIONAL NOTE From the proliferation of existing forms, *earwigs* must have been very familiar in all parts of the British Isles. Among the synonyms are *battle-twigs, cat-o'-two-tails, earlywigs, earywigs, harry-wiggles, skutchy-bells,* and *urrins.* Many of these names, like the insect, are no longer common.

Malaysian English *n* a variety of English spoken in Malaysia

WORLD ENGLISH *Malaysian English* is the variety of English used in Malaysia since the formation of the nation-state in 1963. Prior to independence from Britain the term *Anglo-Malay* was used, indicating the influence of the Malay language. From the earlier period come such general English words of Malay origin as *amok, durian, kampong, mango, orang-utan, sago,* and *sarong.* Malaysian English pronounces *r* in such words as *art, door,* and *worker.* There is a tendency towards full vowels in all syllables (e.g. *seven* pronounced 'seh-ven', not 'sevn'), and a reduction in consonant clusters at the ends of words ('muss' for *must,* 'bes' for *best,* 'liv' *lived,* 'relac' *relax*). In grammar, reflexive pronouns are used for emphasis, often without the verb *to be,* as in 'Himself sick', and certain general-purpose particles are used, such as *lah,* indicating informality and intimacy, as in 'Can do it lah?' ('Can you do it?'). There is considerable hybridization between Malay and English, as in: 'She wanted to beli some barang-barang' ('She wanted to buy some things').

Cultural notes

Cultural Notes form stepping stones from particular senses of words to their wider cultural contexts. Cultural Notes typically refer to titles of books, films, plays, works of art, and musical pieces, especially those that have passed into the language:

catch-22 /-twenti too/ *n* a situation or predicament from which it is impossible to extricate yourself because of built-in illogical rules and regulations [After the novel *Catch-22* by Joseph Heller]

CULTURAL NOTE *Catch-22,* a novel (1961) by US writer Joseph Heller. The title of this dark satire relates to the skewed military logic that entraps the protagonist, Yossarian, a pilot serving in Italy during World War II. He tries to get himself grounded by being pronounced insane, but is told that only an insane person would want to fly, and his desire not to fly proves that he is, in fact, sane, and so must continue to fly. The term *Catch-22* eventually came to have a more general meaning of a situation in which somebody is trapped by illogical conditions and restrictions.

enigma /i nígmə/ *n* somebody or something that is not easily explained or understood [Mid-16C. Via Latin < Greek *ainigma* < *ainos* 'fable']

CULTURAL NOTE *The Enigma Variations,* an orchestral work (1899) by British composer Edward Elgar. Elgar's most popular and widely performed work, it was originally entitled *Variations on an Original Theme.* Each of the variations is a musical portrait of a friend of Elgar, identified in the score only by his or her initials or nickname. The title of Elgar's piece influenced the Berlin engineer who built the now-famed German military cipher machine known as *Enigma,* a typewriter-like device capable of producing an infinite number of ciphers.

'Nonlexical' entries for people and places

The Dictionary contains thousands of entries for people (biographical entries) and places (geographical entries) in the A–Z list. Though the Dictionary does not presume to be an exhaustive source of such items because its primary mission is recording British and World English words, it nevertheless includes a representative, broad sampling of some of the more important people and places you might have occasion to look up as a very first step in a reference search.

Entries for people and places

Biographical entries for people and geographical entries for placenames are listed alphabetically. Whenever one biographical surname appears in more than one entry, the entries appear in alphabetical order following the comma, with a pronunciation at the first occurrence of the name:

Sutherland /súthərlənd/ former county of northern Scotland. Since 1975 it has been part of Highland council area.

Sutherland, Graham (1903–80) British painter. He is noted for his semiabstract works, portraits, and the design for the tapestry *Christ in Majesty* (1952–58) for Coventry Cathedral. Full name **Sutherland, Graham Vivian**

Sutherland, Dame Joan (*b.* 1926) Australian operatic soprano. In a career stretching from 1947 to 1990, she became an opera singer of international renown, noted especially for her coloratura roles in Italian opera.

Sutherland Falls waterfall on the South Island, New Zealand. It is one of the highest in the world. Height: 580 m/1,904 ft.

Biographical Quotations

At some biographical entries, quotations by or about the people have been included when it is felt that their words characterize them or serve to validate their historical or cultural significance:

Thatcher /tháchər/, **Margaret, Baroness Thatcher of Kesteven** (*b.* 1925) British prime minister (1979–90). The leader of the Conservative Party from 1975, and the first woman prime minister of Great Britain, she pursued policies of privatization and economic deregulation. Born **Roberts, Margaret Hilda**. See table at **prime minister**

'We must find ways to starve the terrorist and the hijacker of the oxygen of publicity on which they depend.'
[Margaret Thatcher, *Speech to the American Bar Association, London*; 15 July 1985]

'Remember, George: this is no time to go wobbly.'
[Margaret Thatcher, *to President George H.W. Bush during the Persian Gulf War*, 8 March 1991. Quoted in *The New Yorker*; 7 December 1992]

Subject Labels for Specialist Areas

ACCT	Accounting	COMMUNICATION	Communication	HOCKEY	Hockey
ACOUSTICS	Acoustics	COMPASS	Compass points	HORSERACING	Horseracing
AEROSP	Aerospace	COMPUT	Computing	HOUSEHOLD	Household items
AGRIC	Agriculture	COMPUT GAMES	Computer games	HR	Human resources
AIR FORCE	Air force	CONSTR	Construction	HUNTING	Hunting
ALPHA	Alphabet	COOK	Cookery	ICE SKATING	Ice skating
ALTERN MED	Alternative medicine	COSMETICS	Cosmetics	IMMUNOL	Immunology
AMERICAN FOOTBALL	American football	COVERINGS	Coverings	INDUST	Industry
AMPHIB	Amphibians	CRICKET	Cricket	INFO SCI	Information science
ANAT	Anatomy	CRIME	Crime	INSECTS	Insects
ANCIENT HIST	Ancient history	CRYSTALS	Crystals	INSUR	Insurance
ANTHROP	Anthropology	CUE GAMES	Cue games	INTERNAT REL	International relations
ARCHAEOL	Archaeology	CULTL ANTHROP	Cultural anthropology	ISLAM	Islam
ARCHERY	Archery	CYCLING	Cycling	JEWELLERY	Jewellery
ARCHIT	Architecture	DANCE	Dance	JUDAISM	Judaism
ARMS	Arms and weapons	DENT	Dentistry	JUD-CHR	Judaeo-Christian religion
ARMY	Armed forces	DESIGN	Design	LANG	World languages
ART	Art	DRUGS	Drugs	LANGUAGE	Language
ARTS	Arts	ECOL	Ecology	LAW	Law
ASTROL	Astrology	E-COMMERCE	E-commerce	LEISURE	Leisure
ASTRON	Astronomy	ECON	Economics	LIBRARIES	Libraries
ATHLETICS	Athletics	EDUC	Education	LING	Linguistics
AUTOMOT	Automotive	ELEC	Electricity	LITERAT	Literature
AVIAT	Aviation	ELEC ENG	Electrical engineering	LOGIC	Logic
BALLET	Ballet	ELECTRONICS	Electronics	MAIL	Mail
BANKING	Banking	EMERGENCIES	Emergencies	MANAGEMT	Management
BASEBALL	Baseball	ENG	Engineering	MANUF	Manufacturing
BASKETBALL	Basketball	ENVIRON	Environment	MAPS	Maps
BEVERAGES	Beverages	ETHICS	Ethics	MARINE BIOL	Marine biology
BIBLE	Biblical terms	EXTREME SPORTS	Extreme sports	MARKETING	Marketing
BIOCHEM	Biochemistry	FASHION	Fashion	MARTIAL ARTS	Martial arts
BIOL	Biology	FENCING	Fencing	MATHS	Mathematics
BIOTECH	Biotechnology	FIN	Finance	MEASURE	Measurements
BIRDS	Birds	FISH	Fish	MECH ENG	Mechanical engineering
BOARD GAMES	Board games	FISHERIES	Fisheries	MED	Medicine
BOATING	Boating	FISHING	Fishing	MEDIA	Media
BOT	Botany	FITNESS	Fitness	METALL	Metallurgy
BOWLING	Bowling	FOOD	Food	METEOROL	Meteorology
BOWLS	Bowls	FOOD INDUST	Food industries	MICROBIOL	Microbiology
BOXING	Boxing	FOOTBALL	Football	MIL	Military
BREED	Breed of animal	FORESTRY	Forestry	MIN EXTRACT	Mineral extraction
BROADCAST	Broadcasting	FREIGHT	Freight	MINERALS	Minerals and mineralogy
BUDDHISM	Buddhism	FUNGI	Fungi	MONEY	Currencies
BUILDINGS	Buildings	FURNITURE	Furniture	MOTOR SPORTS	Motor sports
BUSINESS	Business	GAMBLING	Gambling	MOTORCYCLES	Motorcycles
CALENDAR	Calendar terms	GARDENING	Gardening	MUSIC	Music
CAMPING	Camping	GENETICS	Genetics	MYTHOL	Mythology
CANOEING	Canoeing	GEOG	Geography	NAUT	Nautical
CARDS	Card games	GEOL	Geology	NAVIG	Navigation
CARS	Cars	GLASS	Glassware	NAVY	Navy
CERAMICS	Ceramics and pottery	GOLF	Golf	OCCUPATIONS	Occupations
CHEM	Chemistry	GOV	Government	OCEANOG	Oceanography
CHEM ELEM	Chemical elements	GRAM	Grammar	ONLINE	Online
CHESS	Chess	GYM	Gym	OPHTHALMOL	Ophthalmology
CHR	Christianity	GYMNASTICS	Gymnastics	OPTICS	Optics
CINEMA	Films	HAIR	Hairdressing	PALAEONT	Palaeontology
CIV ENG	Civil engineering	HANDICRAFT	Handicraft	PAPER	Papermaking
CLIMBING	Climbing	HEALTH	Health	PARANORMAL	Paranormal
CLOTHING	Clothing and costume	HEALTH SERVICES	Health services	PARAPSYCHOL	Parapsychology
COINS	Coins and coin collecting	HERALDRY	Heraldry	PEOPLES	Peoples
COLLECTING	Collecting	HINDUISM	Hinduism	PHARM	Pharmacology
COLOURS	Colours	HIST	History	PHILOSOPHY	Philosophy
COMM	Commerce	HOBBIES	Hobbies	PHON	Phonetics

PHOTOGRAPHY	Photography	ROADS	Roads	SWIMMING	Swimming
PHYS	Physics	ROLLER SKATING	Roller skating	TECH	Technology
PHYSIOL	Physiology	ROWING	Rowing	TELECOM	Telecommunications
PLANES	Planes	RUGBY	Rugby	TENNIS	Tennis
PLANTS	Plants	SAFETY	Safety	TEXTILES	Textiles
POL	Politics	SAILING	Sailing	THEATRE	Theatre
POLICE	Police	SCI	Science	TIME	Time
PREHIST	Prehistory	SCULPTURE	Sculpture	TOWN PLAN	Town Planning
PRINTING	Printing	SEISMOL	Seismology	TRANSP	Transport
PSYCHIAT	Psychiatry	SHIPPING	Shipping	TRAVEL	Travel
PSYCHOANAL	Psychoanalysis	SHOW JUMPING	Show jumping	TREES	Trees
PSYCHOL	Psychology	SKIING	Skiing	UTIL	Public utilities
PUBL	Publishing	SOC SCI	Social sciences	VEHICLES	Vehicles
PUBLIC ADMIN	Public administration	SOC WELFARE	Social welfare	VERTEB	Vertebrates
QUANTUM PHYS	Quantum physics	SOCCER	Soccer	VET	Veterinary medicine
RACKET GAMES	Racket games	SOCIOL	Sociology	WATER SKIING	Waterskiing
RAIL	Railways	SOFTBALL	Softball	WINE	Wine and winemaking
RECORDING	Recording	SPORTS	Sport in general	WOODWORK	Woodwork
RELIG	Religions	STAMPS	Stamps	WRESTLING	Wrestling
REPT	Reptiles	STATS	Statistics	YOUTH ORG	Youth organizations
RIDING	Riding	SURFING	Surfing	ZODIAC	Astrology
RIFLERY	Riflery	SURG	Surgery	ZOOL	Zoology

Abbreviations and Symbols

C	century (in etymologies)	kmph	kilometres per hour	■	precedes new part of speech
cgs	centimetre-gram-second	l	litre(s)	○	precedes illustrative example
cl	centilitre(s)	lb	pound(s)	◇	precedes idiomatic phrase
cm	centimetre(s)	m	metre(s)	⇗	precedes cross-reference to related entry
cu.	cubic	mi.	mile(s)		
e.g.	for example	ml	millilitre(s)		
fl	flourished (in dates)	mm	millimetre(s)	◆	precedes cross-reference to geographical or biographical entry where meaning is given
fl.	fluid	mph	miles per hour		
ft	foot/feet	oz	ounce(s)		
gal.	gallon(s)	sq.	square		
in.	inch(es)	pt	pint(s)	⚠	marks a contraindicated usage
kg	kilogram(s)	yd	yard(s)		
km	kilometre(s)				

Pronunciation Guide

Pronunciations in the *Bloomsbury English Dictionary* are given in a pronunciation system specially developed for the Dictionary. It relies on familiar combinations of letters of the alphabet so that it can be interpreted without constant reference to a table of explanations. The only symbol taken from outside the ordinary alphabet is the *schwa* /ə/, which stands for the sound represented by **a** in **approve** and **megabyte**. In the Dictionary the pronunciations follow the headword or sense number and appear between forward slashes / /.

PRONUNCIATION KEY

a	at
aa	father
ai	hair
aw	all
ay	day
b, bb	but, ribbon
ch	chin
d, dd	do, ladder
ə	about, edible, item, common, circus
e	egg
ee	eel
f, ff	fond, differ
g, gg	go, giggle
h	hot
hw	when
i	it, happy, medium
ī	ice
j, jj	juice, pigeon
k	key, thick
l, ll	let, silly
m, mm	mother, hammer
n, nn	not, funny
ng	song
o	odd
ō	open
oŏ	good
oo	school
ow	owl
oy	oil
p, pp	pen, happy
r, rr	road, carry, hard
s, ss	say, lesson
sh	sheep
th	thin
<u>th</u>	this
t, tt	tell, butter
u	up
ur	urge
v, vv	very, savvy
w	wet
y	yes
z, zz	zoo, blizzard
<u>zh</u>	vision

´ over a vowel indicates the syllable with the strongest (primary) stress, e.g. **depend** /di pénd/.

` over a vowel also indicates the syllable with medium (secondary) stress, e.g. **antiseptic** /ánti séptik/.

' before /l/, /m/, or /n/ shows that the consonant is syllabic (takes the function of a vowel), e.g. **bottle** /bótt'l/.

I. Consonants

The following are used to describe the sound they usually stand for in ordinary spelling:

/b d f g h j k l m n p r s t v w y z/

befriend	/bi frénd/
hug	/hug/
strap	/strap/
milk	/milk/
jazz	/jaz/
yes	/yess/

The following two-consonant combinations also denote the sound they stand for in ordinary spelling:

/ch ng th/

church	/church/
thing	/thing/
shop	/shop/

For the sound in 'this' (**voiced dental fricative**) we have used /<u>th</u>/:

mother	/mú<u>th</u>ər/
that	/<u>th</u>at/

For the central sound in 'vision' (**voiced palatoalveolar fricative**) we have used /<u>zh</u>/:

vision	/ví<u>zh</u>'n/
pleasure	/plé<u>zh</u>ər/

Double consonants

This Dictionary uses double consonants to show many sounds in the middle of words because English spelling normally doubles letters in these positions. Consonants are doubled when they are preceded by the stressed vowels /á, é, í, ó, ú, oŏ/ and followed by either a vowel or a syllabic consonant, or by /l, r, y, or w/:

rubber	/rúbbər/
metric	/méttrik/
travel	/trávv'l/
inward	/ínnwərd/
deputy	/déppyəti/
supposition	/súppə zísh'n/

In order to show clearly that /s/ is required, not /z/, we double the /s/ additionally at the end of a syllable and with voiced consonants:

face	/fayss/
miscue	/míss kyoŏ/
mincer	/mínssər/

But not with voiceless consonants:

wasp	/wosp/
first	/furst/
tax	/taks/

The consonant /k/ is not doubled:

flicker	/flíkər/
tackle	/ták'l/

There is no doubling of the two-consonant combinations /ch, sh, th, ng, <u>th</u>, <u>zh</u>/:

touching	/túching/
passion	/pásh'n/
rhythm	/rí<u>th</u>'m/
measure	/mé<u>zh</u>ər/
hanger	/hángər/

II. Vowels

The traditional short vowels /a, e, i, o, u/ denote the sounds they usually stand for in ordinary spelling:

cat	/kat/
head	/hed/
myth	/mith/
swan	/swon/
double	/dúbb'l/

For the short vowel as in 'put' we use /oŏ/:

good	/goŏd/
could	/koŏd/
full	/foŏl/

For the weak vowel as in the first syllable of 'along' and the second syllable of 'butter' we use the symbol /ə/ (schwa):

along	/ə lóng/
butter	/búttər/
flattering	/fláttəring/

For the vowel in 'goose' and 'soup' we use /oo/:

food	/food/
move	/moov/
rude	/rood/

When this is preceded by a y-sound we use /yoo/:

music	/myoóozik/
acute	/ə kyoót/
sinuous	/sínnyoo əss/

In words such as 'sure' and 'pure' we have used /oor/ and /yoor/ respectively:

cure	/kyoor, kyawr/
during	/dyoóring/

For the diphthongs in 'gray', 'flee', and 'boy', the respellings /ay/, /ee/, and /oy/ are used:

great	/grayt/
niece	/neess/
voice	/voyss/

For the diphthongs in 'high', 'low', and 'cow' we use /ī/, /ō/, and /ow/ respectively:

write	/rīt/
goat	/gōt/
micro	/mīkrō/
loud	/lowd/
frown	/frown/

For the vowel of 'nurse' we use /ur/:

turn	/turn/
stern	/sturn/
first	/furst/

For the stressed vowel of 'father' we use /aa/:

father	/faáathər/
bravado	/brə vaádō/

For the vowel of 'start' in words where there is an 'r' in the spelling we have used /aar/:

farm	/faarm/
starry	/staári/

We have used /aw/ for the vowel of 'thought':

thought	/thawt/
tall	/tawl/

For the vowel of 'north' in words where there is an 'r' in the spelling we have used /awr/:

short	/shawrt/
war	/wawr/
sport	/spawrt/
story	/stáwri/

For the vowels in 'near' and 'square' we have used /eer/ and /air/ respectively:

beer	/beer/
beard	/beerd/
weary	/weéri/
declare	/di kláir/

scarce	/skáirss/
vary	/váiri/

For the vowels in 'fire' and 'sour' we have used /īr/ and /owr/:

inspire	/in spír/
virus	/vírəss/
hour	/owr/
dowry	/dówri/

Consonants that take the place of a vowel in a syllable (**syllabic consonants**) are preceded by /'/:

apple	/ápp'l/
garden	/gaárd'n/
station	/stáysh'n/
dental	/dént'l/

In the vowel at the end of words such as 'happy' we have used /i/. The same applies to vowels such as the central one in 'various':

happy	/háppi/
coffee	/kóffi/
various	/váiri əss/
radiate	/ráydi ayt/

III. Stress

Single syllable words (**monosyllables**) have no stress marks. In words with more than one syllable (**polysyllables**) we have indicated the primary (main) stress with an acute accent /´/:

another	/ə núthər/
collide	/kə líd/
cosmetic	/koz méttik/

There are two types of secondary stress. We have used an acute accent /´/ to show those that occur **after** the main stress (**posttonic stresses**):

academic	/ákə démmik/
seventeen	/sévv'n teén/

IV. When are pronunciations given?

The *Bloomsbury English Dictionary* shows pronunciations at headwords except where the headword is made up of separate or hyphenated words that are given pronunciations elsewhere in the Dictionary. Thus we include pronunciations for all entries that are different headwords with the same spelling (**homographs**) such as *bank* or *bow*. Capitalized forms of common names are not given a pronunciation unless they are geographical or biographical entries. In geographical and biographical entries where the names are repeated, the first occurrence only is given a pronunciation. Important variants in pronunciation are covered in the Dictionary, as are changes in pronunciation or stress in undefined entries (**runons**) and pronunciations of plural or other forms where the pronunciation or stress changes from that of the headword.

V. Spacing

As it is easier to work out the pronunciation of a word if longer respellings are broken up into easily processed pieces, we have inserted spaces within the respelling of a word in the following cases:
(i) before a stressed syllable or other syllable containing a strong vowel (for this purpose, any vowel other than /ə i ō oo yoo oŏ/):

allow	/ə lów/
detect	/di tékt/
unknown	/ún nōn/
celebrate	/séllə brayt/
cucumber	/kyoó kumbər/

(ii) between the elements of a compound in which each element retains its usual pronunciation:

bedtime	/béd tīm/
teakettle	/teé ket'l/

(iii) between any two successive vowel or diphthong symbols:

payee	/pay eé/
chaos	/káy oss/
radiate	/ráydi ayt/

(iv) between /ng/ and a following /g/:

anger	/áng gər/

VI. Foreign pronunciations

In occasional cases – particularly proper names – we have used the following to indicate non-English sounds:
/hl/ as in Welsh Llangollen
/kh/ as in Scottish loch, German Bach, Spanish Gijón
/N/ to show nasalization of the preceding vowel as in the French pronunciation of **un bon vin blanc** /öN boN vaN blaaN/
/ö/ as in French b**oeuf**, German sch**ön**
/ü/ as in French r**ue**, German gem**ü**tlich

English: the Word Web
John Ayto

English is a member of the Indo-European family of languages, which is over 7,000 years old. We do not know for certain where this language family originated, but good evidence suggests that it had its beginnings in the general area to the north of the Black Sea. Over the millennia the people of those lands migrated northwestwards and southeastwards, into Europe and the northern part of India.

As the people spread more and more widely, their language became differentiated into distinct groups, which form the basis of the languages spoken today in the areas where they settled. Immediately to the south and southeast are the Iranian languages, including Farsi (Modern Persian), Pashto (spoken in Afghanistan), and Kurdish. In India, ancient Sanskrit evolved into a multiplicity of modern languages, including Bangla (Bengali), Gujarati, Hindi, Punjabi, Sinhalese, Urdu, and also Romany. Also among these easterly branches are Armenian and the now extinct Hittite and Tocharian.

To the west and north, fragmentation produced the Slavic languages (Russian, Polish, Czech, Slovak, Bulgarian, Serbo-Croat, etc.) in eastern Europe; the Baltic languages (Latvian and Lithuanian, which of all these modern languages most closely resembles its Indo-European ancestor); Greek in Greece; Albanian in Albania; the Romance languages (French, Provençal, Italian, Spanish, Catalan, Portuguese, Romanian, Rhaeto-Romance – descendants of Latin) further west; and the Celtic languages (Welsh, Irish and Scottish Gaelic, Breton, Cornish, Manx) at the very western edge of Europe.

One particular group of migrants had settled in northern Europe, in the area around the River Elbe, about 3,000 years ago. Around the second century BC the language they spoke, known as Common Germanic, began to split up into three different dialects, one of which was East Germanic. (The only written evidence we have of this is in the now extinct Gothic language.) The second was North Germanic, which has evolved into modern Swedish, Danish, Norwegian, Icelandic, and Faroese. And lastly there was West Germanic, the ancestor of modern German, Dutch (and Afrikaans), Flemish, Frisian, Yiddish – and English.

The ancestor of modern English crossed the English Channel, in the form of a set of mutually intelligible Germanic dialects, in the fifth and sixth centuries AD, brought by peoples from the northeastern corner of the European mainland, around Jutland and modern Denmark – the Angles, Saxons, and Jutes. The story of its subsequent development is told in **A Brief History of the English Language** (see p. xxviii)

English has never abandoned its roots, but it has changed almost beyond recognition over the past millennium and a half. The lexicon of English is now probably larger and more eclectic than that of any other language; as the Language Heritage notes in this dictionary show, there is not a major language in the world that has not over the past 500 years made some contribution to English. There was a huge influx of French vocabulary after the Norman Conquest and of Latin and Greek words during and after the Renaissance; the spread of English speakers round the world later sucked in thousands of words from sources as diverse as Nahuatl (*tomato*), Tibetan (*lama*), Maori (*kiwi*), Finnish (*sauna*), Swahili (*safari*), Inuit (*kayak*), Czech (*pistol*), and Hawaiian (*ukulele*); and new words continue to pour into the language at the rate of over a thousand a year.

All down these centuries of development and assimilation runs a complicated web of descent – often muddled, interrupted, cancelling itself out, or losing itself in dead ends. Many of the word history essays in this dictionary show how one ancestor can be responsible for a surprising number of English words: for example the Latin *gradus* 'step' is the source of *grade, gradation, gradient, gradual,* and *graduate,* but also of *aggression, congress, degrade, degree, digress, ingredient, progress, regress, retrograde,* and *transgress.*

Often, too, the unseen web of interconnections conceals patterns that link the unlikeliest of English partners. It seems scarcely plausible, for instance, that *symphony* and *fate* should be related, or *acrobat* and *oxygen*, but they are, as the diagrams opposite prove. Both *symphony* and *fate* go back to the same Indo-European root *bha-*, meaning 'speak', *symphony* being derived from the Greek *phōnē* 'voice, sound', and *fate* from Latin *fatum*, 'destiny' – more literally, 'that which is spoken (by the gods)'. The family of *acrobat* and *oxygen* is linked by the idea of 'pointed' or 'sharp': an *acrobat* is literally someone who walks on tiptoe, on the 'points' of the feet, while *oxygen* literally means 'acid-producer'.

The Dictionary, and the word history essays in it, uncover more of the unexpected connections between English words, revealing the links in the word web that centuries of language change have obscured.

Routes into English

The diagrams below take two related groups of English words and trace them back to their Indo-European sources, namely *ak-* meaning 'sharp' and *bha-* meaning 'speak'. The complex web of links shows how these two roots evolved into seemingly unconnected English words, and traces the stages of their development via languages such as French and Latin.

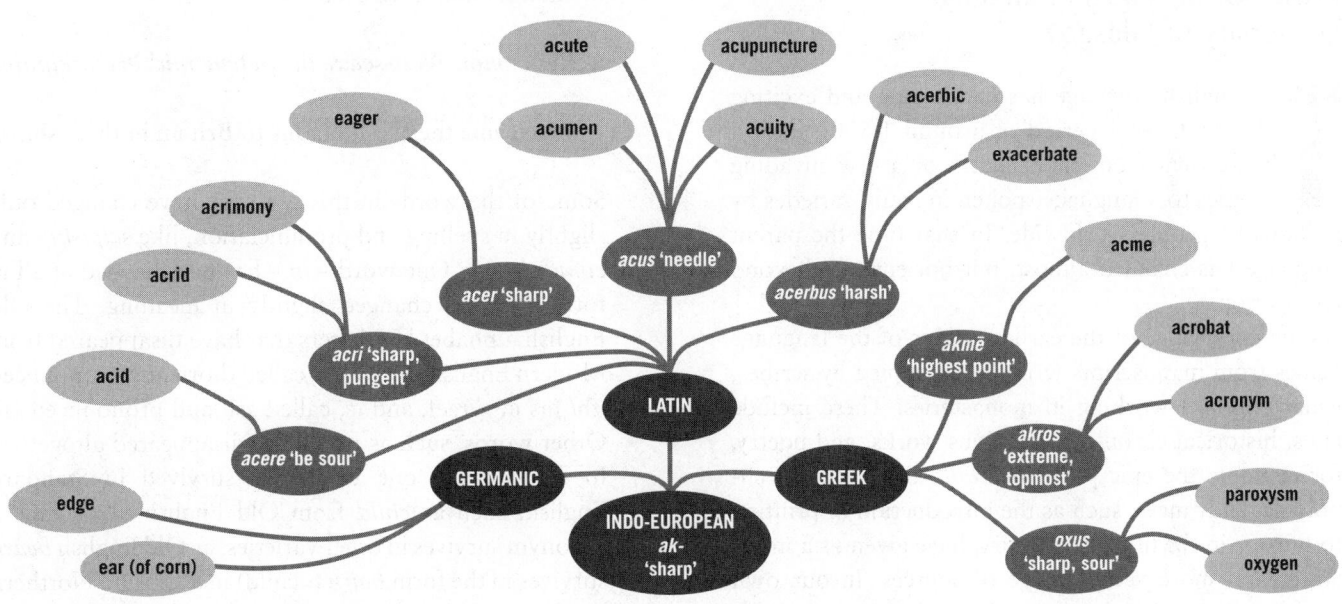

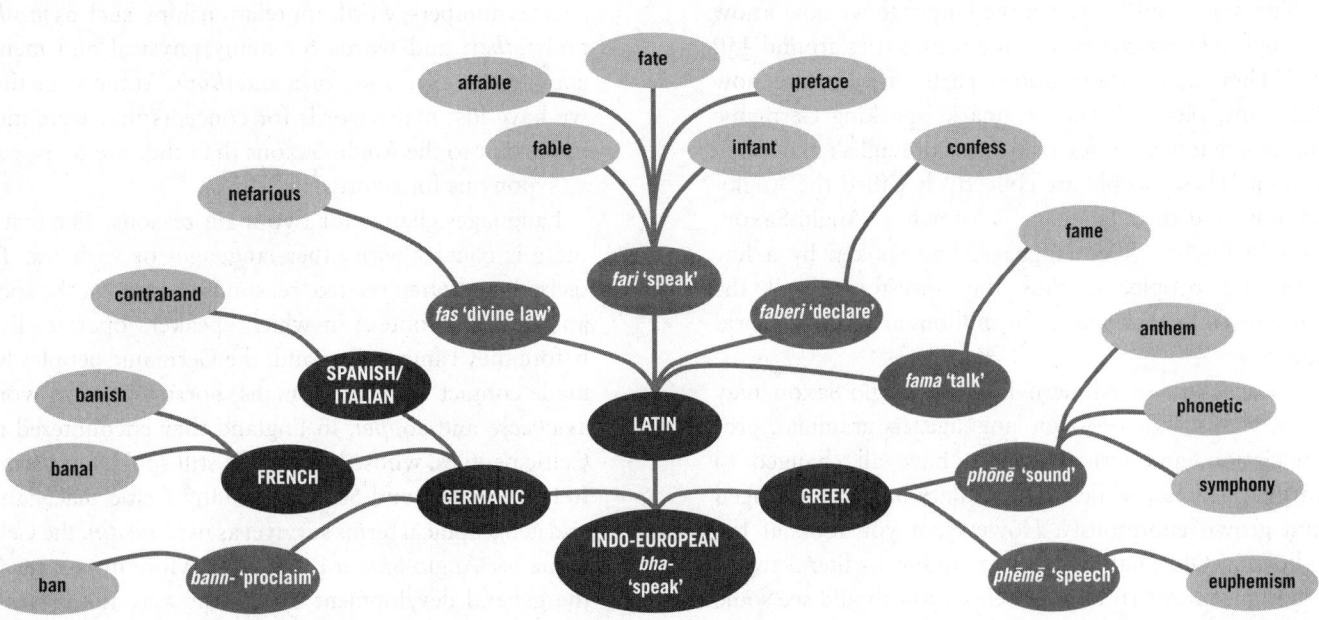

A Brief History of the English Language

Professor Christian J. Kay
Professor of English Language
University of Glasgow

The English language has had a long and exciting history. Over a period of around 1,500 years, it has grown from the dialects of a few invading peoples to a language spoken in many varieties by millions of people worldwide. In that time the parent language has changed almost, but not entirely, beyond recognition.

Our knowledge of the earliest stages of the language comes from manuscripts written and copied by scribes, usually monks working in monasteries. These include laws, historical chronicles, religious works, and poetry, for example the epic poem *Beowulf*. Since then, technological advances, such as the introduction of printing to Europe in the fifteenth century, have given us a much larger and more varied range of sources. In our own age, the ability to record speech, and to compile huge electronic text databases, means that we can monitor the language as never before.

The first people to speak the language we now know as English began to arrive in the British Isles around 450 AD. They came from various parts of what are now Germany, Holland, and Denmark, speaking Germanic dialects that were to form the basis of English dialects in Britain. These people are collectively called the Anglo-Saxons, and their language is known as Anglo-Saxon, or Old English. This language, first spoken by a few thousand people, is thus the ancestor of all the varieties of English spoken by millions around the world today.

To speakers of Modern English, Anglo-Saxon may seem almost like a foreign language. Its grammar, pronunciation, and writing system have all changed to varying degrees, while its vocabulary has both changed and grown enormously. However, if you look at the following Old English sentence, and at its literal translation into Modern English below, you should see some of the connections between the two as well as the kinds of changes that have occurred.

Her comon West-seaxe in Bretene mid Prim scipum.

Here came the West-Saxons to Britain in three ships.

Some of the words in this sentence have changed only slightly in spelling and pronunciation, like *scip/ship* and *comon/came*. One word – *in* – has not changed at all in form, but has changed slightly in meaning. The Old English alphabet had letters that have disappeared from Modern English, such as þ, called thorn and pronounced /th/ (as in *three*), and æ, called ash and pronounced /a/. Other words, such as *mid*, have disappeared altogether. In some cases, one word has survived in Standard English, such as *child* from Old English *cild,* while a synonym survives in other varieties, as Old English *bearn* survives in the form *bairn* (=child) in Scots and Northern English. Many of our most basic words come from Old English: words for things in the world around us, such as *earth, sun, moon,* and *stars*; words for measurements such as numbers; words for relationships, such as *mother* and *father*; and words for many physical and mental activities, such as *run, love,* and *think*. At the same time, we have lost many words for concepts that were more important to the Anglo-Saxons than they are to us, such as synonyms for swords and ships.

Languages change for two main reasons. The first of these is contact with other languages or varieties. The second, and often related, reason is changes in the social and cultural context in which speakers operate. Even before they came to England, the Germanic peoples had made contact with the Romans, borrowing such words as *cheese* and *copper*. In England they encountered the Celtic peoples, whose language is still spoken in parts of Ireland, Wales, and Scotland. Many Celtic placenames and geographical terms survive, as in *Dunedin*, the Celtic name for Anglo-Saxon Edinburgh. More important for the general development of English were the waves of

invasions by Scandinavian Vikings that started in the late eighth century. Some came simply to plunder, but others settled down. Unlike the Celts, their language was quite similar to that of the Anglo-Saxons, making communication between the two groups possible. They added many everyday words to English, such as *sky*, *egg*, and *law*, the verb *to take*, and the pronoun *they*. Grammatical changes, such as the *-s* ending in such forms as *she walks*, spread into English from Scandinavian areas.

By far the most important contact, however, was the Norman Conquest of 1066, when the Norman-French Duke William defeated the Anglo-Saxon King Harold at the Battle of Hastings and became King William I of England. The Anglo-Saxon aristocracy was destroyed and their lands given to William's nobles, who built many of the castles that still dominate the British landscape. French became the language of government, although the bulk of the population continued to work on the land and speak English. Communication between French and English speakers became increasingly necessary, and, as in any bilingual situation, the languages influenced each other. French words were used in English and its grammar was simplified. By the end of this period, generally known as Middle English, English was much more recognizably the language we know today. Thus in the late fourteenth century, the poet Geoffrey Chaucer wrote of one of his characters:

He was a verray parfit gentil knyght.

He was a very perfect gentle knight.

The words *he*, *was*, *a*, and *knyght* are Old English in origin, but *verray*, *parfit*, and *gentil* were borrowed into English from French and from there can be traced back to Latin. *Knyght* has changed in meaning since Old English, where it meant 'boy' or 'servant', while the use of *gentle* to mean 'noble' or 'courteous' differs somewhat from its modern meaning. Such changes in the meanings of words are typical of the way languages develop. These Middle English borrowings from French show the beginnings of one of the most characteristic features of modern English – its large and varied vocabulary. French words come from many vocabulary areas, such as government, law, religion, cooking, the arts, and courtly life. Sometimes words from both sources survive side by side, as with *kingly* (Old English) and *royal* (French). Sometimes their meanings are differentiated, as in *calf* (Old English) and *veal* (French), originally the animal, but developing to mean only the meat.

Detail from an early illuminated manuscript of Chaucer's *The Canterbury Tales*, showing Chaucer as a pilgrim on horseback.

Because French and Latin were the official languages during the early Middle English period, English was slow to develop a standard form in speech or writing. There was considerable diversity in the dialects people spoke, as there still is in their modern descendants in Britain or elsewhere. When English began to be written again, the scribes tended to write the words as they were pronounced, which is helpful to modern scholars interested in reconstructing the language of the past.

From the point of view of Modern English, continuing changes in grammar are also significant. In Old English grammatical relationships between words were expressed mainly by changing their endings, as were distinctions such as past/present or singular/plural. The majority of the world's languages have this kind of grammar. This system began to break down through contact with Scandinavian speakers, whose language had a similar system but different endings, and the process was accelerated by the contact with French. In the course of this process English began to move towards its present system of expressing grammatical relationships largely through word order and the use of prepositions. It also lost its system of grammatical gender and began to develop the complex system of verb forms that we know today.

By the end of the Middle English period, generally put at around 1500, a more uniform written language was emerging, based on the dialect of London. This development was promoted both by the greater physical and social mobility of the population and by the rapid

spread of printed books. The printers were less tolerant of spelling variation than the medieval scribes had been, and a standardized system began to emerge. Unfortunately for modern users of English, this system predated various changes in the pronunciation of vowels, especially a series known as the Great Vowel Shift. This situation led to apparently illogical spelling variations such as *made/maid*, *flood/food*, or *great/dream*; in the first pair, the vowels used to be pronounced differently, whereas in the others they were once the same. However illogical English spelling seems, there is usually a reason for it!

Early Modern English saw major grammatical patterns being established. Shakespeare and his contemporaries in the late sixteenth century could use either older forms such as 'Why go you?' or 'He speaks not', or newer ones such as 'Why do you go?' and 'He does not speak'. They could choose between the older 'Thou goest, he goeth' or the more modern 'You go, he goes'. They could express wishes through the old subjunctive form, 'Long live the Queen', or the newer 'May the Queen live long'. In all these cases the older forms were in decline and died out as modern English progressed. At the same time, the verbal group developed, producing forms unavailable to Shakespeare, such as 'When are you going?' or 'He would have been surprised'. An indicator of social change was the fact that speakers gradually ceased to use the singular and plural pronouns *thou* and *you* to distinguish between those of lower and higher rank.

Vocabulary has also continued to grow throughout Modern English. Partly as a result of the renaissance of learning in Europe, the Early Modern period saw an upsurge in Latin borrowings in order to develop terminologies for new approaches to subjects such as science, philosophy, and medicine. National pride increasingly demanded that English, not Latin, should be used in all kinds of writing. Formal prose styles developed, often favouring Latinate words above native ones: *fraternal* might be considered more elegant than the native *brotherly*, or *illuminate* preferred to *light up*. English thus acquired a multilayered vocabulary, able to express a concept at different stylistic levels. This process of borrowing, changing, or inventing words to accommodate new intellectual developments continues to this day, as can be seen from the vocabulary of industrialization in the nineteenth century or of computers or space travel in the twentieth into the twenty-first century.

During the Early Modern period English-speaking traders and adventurers were also setting out to explore the world, reaching the Americas, Africa, India, the Far East, and later Australia and New Zealand. Exotic objects were collected or described, and words such as *chocolate*, *wigwam*, *banana*, *gorilla*, *tea*, and *outback*

were added to the language. Like their ancestors before them, some of the invaders settled down, thus laying the foundations of English as a world language and contributing to its continual development.

The same patterns of a heritage gained from a country's first settlers, borrowings from local languages and peoples, and continuing development and change in response to geographical, cultural, social, and other factors characterize the continuing changes to the English language in its many manifestations today. Australian and New Zealand Englishes have been enriched by words from Aboriginal and Maori traditions; the English of South Asia bears testament to the many local languages and varied cultural heritage of that vast subcontinent. South Africa's Anglo-Dutch heritage yields a multiplicity of words from that dual background as well as from local languages. In the many territories of the Pacific Rim the same process has given rise to a continuing enrichment of English with new words and senses.

In the early years of this new millennium English can reasonably be regarded as the first worldwide *lingua franca* since Latin. This Dictionary has been written to reflect this phenomenon. It will fall to our dictionary editors to monitor the continuing development of the English language in its manifold forms around the world.

Title page of the original Bodleian copy of the First Folio edition of Shakespeare (1623).

The Formation of New Words in English

John Ayto

The vocabulary of English is in a state of continuous, accelerating expansion. On average, nearly a thousand new items found a place for themselves in our lexicon each year in the twentieth century, and there is no reason to suppose that the language will stop growing at a comparable rate in the foreseeable future. What drives it on?

For one thing, many more people are using English as each decade passes. There are now almost 375 million native speakers of English in the world, approximately three times as many as there were a hundred years ago, and the numbers of second-language English users are growing even faster. It would be surprising if more speakers did not produce more words.

The effect is multiplied by the fragmentation of the language into a number of regional, ethnic, and national varieties (for example Singapore English, East African English), each of which increasingly feels sanctioned to revitalize its own vocabulary.

And then, of course, with every passing year, new things in the world need names – from the *hot dog* in 1900 to the *webcam* in 1995 to *SARS* in 2002. (Indeed, human beings' ability to conceptualize something that does not yet exist means that not a few words predate the objects they name – the term *atomic bomb*, for instance, is first recorded in 1914.) Nor is the phenomenon limited to 'things': a growing perception in the mid-twentieth century that English lacked a title common to married and unmarried women led to the emergence of the use of *Ms* for both.

Language also has a key role in cementing and defining social groups, and the need to maintain its exclusionary power is a considerable spur to the introduction of new vocabulary – hence the rapid turnover of words in many areas of slang, baffling to outsiders.

These are all the forces of the external world operating on the language. The changes they cause can be termed 'socially triggered'. But alterations within the language can produce new vocabulary, too. Change in meaning, a major contributor to lexical evolution, is very often attributable to gradual, unconscious shifts in the application of a word. For example, in the thirteenth century *nice* meant 'ignorant, stupid, or foolish'. By the fourteenth century it had taken on yet another pejorative meaning, 'wanton or lascivious'. Over centuries of various changes, *nice* has lost its original meanings, now coming to mean, among other things, 'pleasing and agreeable'. The obverse can happen to a meaning of a word: *silly*, which once meant 'blessed, innocent, helpless', has lost that meaning and has taken on the pejorative one we are all familiar with. And what might originally have been described (and condemned) as a wrong interpretation of a word's inner structure can easily survive to become an accepted form: *umpire*, for instance, was once *numpire* but evolved into the spelling we use today by the process of *false division*.

The vocabulary of English takes in new words by any of five basic methods: combining existing words or word parts; shortening existing words; using existing words with new meanings; taking words from other languages; and coining entirely new words.

Combination. By far the most common way of forming words in present-day English is to take words or word parts that already exist and join them together. Combination accounts for at least three quarters of the new vocabulary that comes into the language. It usually involves either adding one word to another (a process called *compounding*), so that *sail* + *board* becomes *sailboard*; or adding a prefix or suffix to a word (a process called *affixation* or *derivation*), so that *bio-* + *terrorism* becomes *bioterrorism*. One particular type of compound that became especially popular in the twentieth century is the *blend*. It involves merging the beginning of the first word into the end of the second, so that the two form a

new whole: thus *camera* + *recorder* becomes *camcorder*. Sometimes more than one developmental process is involved: *blog*, formed from *(we)b* + *log*, involves combining two words and then shortening the result. Such is the inventiveness of word formation.

Shortening or **abbreviation**. The most straightforward way of shortening a word is to remove its final or first element or elements: so *discotheque* becomes *disco*, and *magazine* becomes *zine*. More specifically, a word containing a suffix can have its suffix removed, usually resulting in a change in its word class; thus the noun *destruction* gives rise to the verb *destruct* in a process linguists call *back-formation*. More radically, all the latter part of a word can be removed, leaving only the first letter. Sequences of such letters are known as *initialisms*: *DVT* for *deep vein thrombosis*, *CEO* for *chief executive officer*. When the letters are pronounced as an ordinary word, the sequence is called an *acronym*: *OFSTED* for *Office for Standards in Education*, *NIMBY* for *not in my back yard*, and *SARS*, mentioned above, for *severe acute respiratory syndrome*.

Change in meaning. Words are constantly being redeployed to new uses. So, for example, an *anorak* becomes 'an obsessive enthusiast', *plastic* becomes 'credit card', and *mail* becomes 'an e-mail, or e-mail generally'. Included in this category is the use of trademarks and surnames, altered or not, in such a way that they take on their own distinct meanings; thus, the all-too-familiar *Teflon* presidency, *Churchillian* oratory, and *Bushism*.

A particular type of verbal reassignment is *functional shift*, also known as *conversion* or *zero derivation*. A word is taken from its existing word class (say, a noun) and is put into a new one. In essence, the word changes its grammatical function; hence, the technical descriptor *functional shift*. When this happens, for example, *access* becomes a verb, meaning 'to retrieve data or a computer file' and *embed* becomes a noun, meaning 'a journalist who travels with troops in a combat zone and files reports on operations'.

Borrowing. From its earliest days, English has enriched itself by taking words from other languages, and in the centuries after the Norman Conquest, its entire nature was changed by the huge number of French words it took in. The 'borrowing' frenzy has never reached quite that height again, but English now gets a healthy five percent of its new vocabulary from foreign sources. The borrowing tends to be concentrated on areas of cultural contact (for example, assimilation of foreign cuisines has provided English with terms as diverse as *focaccia*, *taco*, and *sushi*) and on areas in which another language is dominant (for instance, France's lead in aviation technology at the beginning of the twentieth century means that many English aeronautical terms are French in origin: *aileron*, *fuselage*, *hangar*, and so on).

Coinage. It is comparatively rare that new words are simply dreamed up out of nothing, unconnected to any existing English word, with the exception of many proprietary product names. Such coinages account for less than one per cent of twentieth-century neologisms. The practice is not uncommon, though, as can be seen in these genuine scientific and technical coinages: *byte*, *dongle*, *googol*. Writers of science fiction and fantasy are fond of inventing words, too (*Dalek*, *hobbit*, *Muggle*).

This unceasing surge of words presents a problem to dictionary makers. Clearly, not all new words can be included in 'the dictionary': the existing vocabulary would be swamped. Some sort of selection process must be followed. How does it work?

For one thing, some items exclude themselves: for example, highly technical terms of very limited circulation would be wasted in a dictionary for the general user; and, where space is at a premium, terms whose meaning can be easily deduced (such as *leg brace*) are unlikely to gain entry. But the main flood of new words and meanings must be passed through a series of filters, designed to trap only those that the dictionary editor thinks are suitable for entry. The raw material – the lexical evidence – nowadays comes mainly in the form of a database of texts that can be read and analysed by a computer. All sorts of information useful in the description and definition of words – for example, which prepositions are most typically used with a particular verb – can be extracted from these databases by increasingly sophisticated computer programs. Decisions on what to include and exclude, however, rest mainly on three simpler calculations.

First, and most basic, how common is this word or meaning? Are there large numbers of examples of it in our database, or a thin trickle? Then, what is its chronological profile? Has it only just appeared, or have we got evidence for it going back over several years? And how consistent is that evidence – is its timeline fairly level, or was there a brief explosion of popularity to begin with, followed by years in the doldrums? Third, how even is the word's distribution? Has it been in reasonably general use, or, when we examine the evidence more closely, does it turn out that it is the preferred usage of only a small group, or even of a single individual, and that it has never spread widely throughout the language community?

There is no single right answer to these three questions, no magic number of citations collected or years passed that will guarantee a word's admission to the dictionary – not least because different types and sizes of dictionary will dictate different criteria. It is the overall profile presented by the various statistics that determines the lexicographer's decision: in or out.

There is evidently an assumption underlying these calculations, and it is this: the more clearly it can be demonstrated that a given usage has established a long-term place for itself in the language, the more likely it is to be included in the dictionary. This has always been an assumption lexicographers have followed, and it underpins the whole notion of dictionaries as normative, standard-setting texts. But it is a slightly slippery one. After all, if the question is asked, 'How can we tell if a word is "established" in the language?', many people's reply is likely to be 'It's established if it's in the dictionary' – closing a perilous logical circle.

Such caution made commercial sense in the days of hot-metal printing, when a new edition of a large dictionary represented a major capital investment and each new entry had to prove its stamina, chiefly by maintaining its staying power over a period of roughly 10 to 12 years in a broad group of publications. But nowadays, with computerized typesetting, new entries can be put in and with ease taken out again next time round, and the advent of the online dictionary offers at least the prospect of a constantly updated flow of new entries (that could, if desired, be unfiltered). This situation would mirror quite accurately the lexical mobility of English, but it would put a severe strain on the dictionary's traditional role as a repository of 'standard' usage.

Modern data-gathering techniques mean that dictionaries can be based on a far wider range of evidence than in the past. Until the late twentieth century their standard evidence base was printed books, newspapers, and journals: language carefully considered and revised. Now we can access far more spontaneous language – spoken English, for example, and the English of the Internet. This too will challenge the traditional standard-setting role of 'the dictionary'.

The general perception of what is a 'dictionary word', a word or expression fit to be entered in the lexicon, will probably broaden out over the coming century, but as long as we have dictionaries in book form (as we assuredly will) there will be several thousand hopefuls that fail the audition each time around. So, in this edition of the *Bloomsbury English Dictionary* we might have had, for example, *Bladerunneresque* 'reminiscent of the bleak futuristic vision of the science-fiction film *Blade Runner*', but it missed the cut.

A Brief History of Dictionaries and Dictionary-Makers

Jonathon Green

The first dictionary, a very distant ancestor of today's CD-ROMs, online dictionaries, and spellcheckers, was a list of words committed to a clay tablet around 2000 BC. The conquest of Sumeria (roughly in the region of today's Iraq) by the neighbouring territory Akkad required, as such things do, that the conquerors absorb the language of the conquered. In this case the Akkadians were particularly anxious to take on board the sophistication of the Sumerian legal system. So the tablets were filled with glossaries of legal, and soon other, words offering the Sumerian term followed by the Akkadian term.

Such early compilations, however, remained isolated. It was only in the fourth century BC that the Greeks took up dictionary-making. They feared that the language of Homer was becoming 'dead', even to scholars, and began to compile glossaries of his more obscure vocabulary. This same process was repeated later by the Romans, who also were seeking to preserve the language of their 'dead' authorities and authors.

From then through the scholars of Byzantium, of the Middle Ages, and of the Renaissance, the flow of dictionaries was maintained, mainly as bilingual glossaries that translated words from one language into another. One of the most ambitious was the *Calepine*, first created by the monk Ambrosio Calepino in 1502. Edition followed edition, and at its peak its massive folio pages encompassed words in no fewer than 11 discrete languages for every single entry.

Precursors to today's English dictionaries first appeared in the eighth century. Four glossaries (the *Corpus*, the *Leiden*, the *Epinal*, and the *Erfurt* (named for the libraries that now hold them) are each dedicated to translating the vocabulary of a single text and were written to give scholars access to what were seen as the harder words of specific, usually ecclesiastical texts, by translating the original Latin into Anglo-Saxon English.

ALPHABETICAL ORDER

Early glossaries were usually based only on 'A-order'. This meant that all the words starting with the same letter were listed together, but with no attempt to refine the order further. It would take several centuries before full alphabetization was finally in place.

Over subsequent centuries the production of such text-specific lists began to be amalgamated, offering scholars translations of more than one work in the same list. Such lists, it should be noted, were rudimentary. All these dictionaries – some 20 major works between 1440 and 1600 – were bilingual, the usual mix being Latin-English, although some involved European languages. One of these, John Florio's *A World of Words* (1598), introduced so many new English words in his translations that it provided a huge step in English dictionary-making in itself.

WORDS FOR WORD BOOKS

Among the titles given to word books have been an *abecedarium* (an alphabetical order), an *alveary* (beehive), a *catholicon* (cure-all), an *ortus* (garden), a *medulla* (marrow or pith), a *glossary*, a *manipulus* (a handful), a *sylva* (wood), a *promptuarium*, a *vocabulary*, and a *vulgar* (common thing).

By 1700 *dictionary*, from the medieval Latin *dictionarius*, a repertory of words, had won out, and ever since it has been the predominant term.

In 1604 the first dictionary that defined rather than translated words appeared. Robert Cawdrey's *Table Alphabeticall, Contayning and Teaching the True Writing and Understanding of Hard Usuall English Words* was the first true English–English dictionary. It contained barely 3,000 entries, and its goal was to explain the meanings of difficult words.

Cawdrey had many successors who formed major way stations in the development of lexicography in English. Among the 'hard words' lexicographers were John Bullokar (in 1616), Henry Cockeram (1623), Thomas Blount (1656), Edward Philips (1658), and Elisha Coles, whose dictionary, appearing in 1676, would be the first mainstream English work to include slang (the dedicated collection of which had begun in Copland's *Hye Way to the Spittel House* in 1531). These were in response to the emergence in the seventeenth century of a middle class and thus a surge in literacy.

If the seventeenth century had reflected the expansion of literacy beyond the universities and churches, then the eighteenth reflected that of England itself beyond its own territorial borders. The century that saw the expansion and consolidation of the British colonies demanded new efforts to establish English as a major language, specifically as a rival to French. The creation in 1635 of the *Académie Française* and the publication in 1694 of its authoritative *Dictionnaire* promoted much comment across the English Channel. Such literary figures as John Dryden, Robert Hooke, Daniel Defoe, and Jonathan Swift variously called for some form of English Academy and suggested that its primary task would be to produce a purified version of truly standard English.

These ruminations led in 1746 to the commissioning by a group of booksellers (who, as was the custom, were also publishers) of one Samuel Johnson, then best known as an essayist and parliamentary writer for the *Gentleman's Magazine*, to prepare a *Dictionary of the English Language*. That dictionary, which appeared in 1755, represents a great turning point in English-language dictionary-making.

Lexicography is an ever developing craft, for the language does not reform and reappear mint-new in time for every successive lexicon. Johnson used his predecessors, especially Nathaniel Bailey, whose own major work, the *Universal Etymological English Dictionary* (published in 1730), provided massive assistance in compiling the basic word lists. Nor did Johnson invent any of the processes seen to such advantage in his work, namely etymology, illustrative citations, and basic guides to pronunciation. All of these had been attempted before, but Johnson brought them together and did so more skilfully than had ever been done before.

Johnson did not, however, fix the language, as he and his publishers had once felt was feasible. Instead, recognizing reality, he would declare that such fantasies were 'the dreams of a poet doomed at last to wake a lexicographer' and that thus to pursue perfection was

Samuel Johnson

reminiscent of ancient tribes who would 'chace the sun, which, when they had reached the hill where he seemed to rest, was still beheld at the same distance from them'. Language changes and lexicographers, now as much as then, must reflect such changes in their work. Johnson's decision to accept such a reality has influenced the growth of English ever since.

In a nice twist of coincidence, the very first US dictionary, *The School Dictionary* (1798), was written by one Samuel Johnson, a teacher. And others would follow, among them titles from this Johnson and his coeditor the Reverend John Elliott (1800), from another preacher Caleb Alexander (1800), from Richard Coxe (1813) and, in 1807, from Sarah Rowson, a British actor who had quit London and gained a new reputation as a best-selling US novelist.

The first major US dictionary, Noah Webster's two-volume *American Dictionary of the English Language*, appeared in 1828. Webster was a New England school-teacher whose *American Spelling Book*, popularly dubbed the 'Blue-Backed Speller' (1783), sold over 70 million copies within a century of its publication, an astounding feat. He was a great pioneer of US English, as opposed to British English. For him the establishment of a national language, based upon but independent of its source, was as politically important as the American Revolution itself. In *Dissertations on the English Language* (1789), Webster wrote: 'Several circumstances render a future separation of the American tongue from the English necessary and unavoidable'. The respelling of terms such as *theater* for 'theatre' and *color* for 'colour' is Webster's legacy, as is his inclusion of meanings of words

Noah Webster

that applied specifically, and only, to life in North America, for example, *plantation* and *senate*.

The *Oxford English Dictionary* (*OED*) is arguably still the world's greatest dictionary on historical principles (offering the usage history and development of a word as well as definition and highly detailed etymology). Conceived in 1857, it would override a false start (in 1865) to begin once more in 1878 with the appointment of James Murray, a self-educated school-teacher and philologist, as its editor. The first 352-page section, offering words from *A* to *Ant*, appeared in 1884 and the dictionary was eventually completed in 1928 after Murray's death.

With the exception of Webster, lexicography has never really been a solo craft. Even Johnson had his assistants, the eight 'harmless drudges' who did the basic work of compilation, while the *OED* lists dozens of individuals, from Murray's coeditors through to the ranks of sub-editors and readers, all enlisted on the great work. Today's dictionaries, the products of publishers (whether academic or popular), are rarely associated with a single individual. Modern lexicography is in every sense a corporate endeavour – the large number of lexicographers and consultants enlisted for this project are typical. Such a finely tuned exercise may have sacrificed a degree of idiosyncrasy (after all, is not the decision by one individual to compile a dictionary, 'chasing the panting syllable' as one poet had it, somewhat eccentric in itself?), but has gained an infinity of expertise. It may be less romantic, but today's user wants accuracy and information first.

And not only have dictionaries become available on computer, but computers are central to every stage of the production. The great dictionaries of the past depended on armies of amateur readers, scanning texts for examples of usage. Today's compilers have the great corpora, literally 'bodies' of real language, available for consultation. Such a corpus was compiled for this dictionary, ensuring that every nuance of a word's existence can be laid down, and backed up with illustrative quotations. Not only that, but the keyboarding of a great dictionary into a permanent, if evolving, database, renders the great consumers of the lexicographer's time – inserting new and updating old entries and inserting and verifying cross-references – infinitely simpler than the most sophisticated of pre-electronic systems could ever manage.

Perhaps the most important aspect of lexicographic change, and never more so than as illustrated here, is the change in the word list itself. All these earlier dictionaries tried to be language-specific; not so today. World English is the name of the modern game. This dictionary, like its predecessor, is aimed at a worldwide audience. Incorporating multinational expertise in its compilation and in the entries that have been produced, it is proof in itself of the extent to which English has long since burst through its territorial confines.

The Internet, the globally encompassing electronic forum, presents a special challenge for lexicography and its potential enhancement. While the old identity of the 'information superhighway' seems to have vanished with the dotcom boom that spawned it, the Internet remains an unrivalled source of language. At its worst it is no more than a vast library still lacking a proper index, but at its best it is a superb repository of infinitely wide-ranging (and continually expanding) source material. And it is undeniable, and telling, that its primary language is English. Setting aside its role as a marketplace, the Net has speeded up the proliferation of language, rendered the formerly arcane massively accessible, and in every way, and quite literally, 'spread the word'.

For dictionary-makers this proliferation is undoubtedly challenging. To assess the state of a globally reaching language is hard enough with no more than the printed word and the visual media to analyse. With the countless 'documents' of whatever sort on offer via the Net – be they century-old newspapers or yesterday's hip-hop lyrics – that task is rendered even harder. Yet simultaneously it is hugely empowering. Indeed, some lexicographers suggest that this generation will be the last to go searching among terrestrial libraries for usage examples, with the inevitable pursuit of 'first use'. In a few decades, with everything digitized, one will need to do no more than perform a search, and every example

will be there, first to most recent, online. How feasible this is – it will require both dedication and, equally important, extensive funding – remains to be seen. But for anyone working on language, and especially language reference, the potential is hugely exciting. The lexicographer is not and never has been, in Johnson's ironic, now hackneyed phrase, a 'harmless drudge'. Lexicographers hold a strange position, employed in an unglamorous task, yet occupying a position of power and influence by virtue of defining what the words in our language mean. That those words, once confined to a small elite of scholars, are now the property of many differing millions and available in myriad variations is both a challenge and a reward to the dictionary-maker.

ENGLISH AROUND THE WORLD

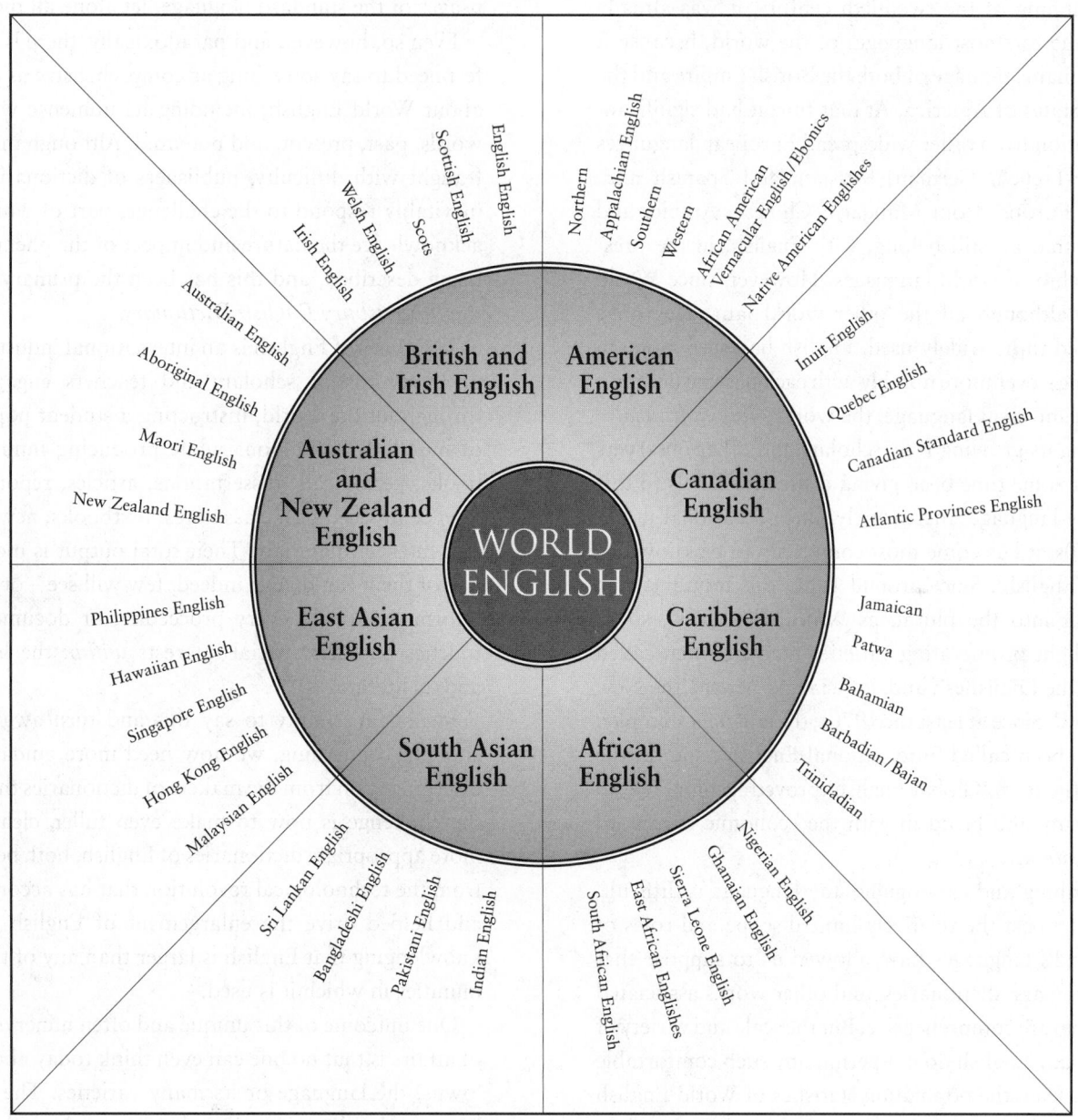

There are many varieties of World English; some of the main ones are included in this diagram.

World English

Tom McArthur

In the early years of a new century and a new millennium, English is the most used – and studied – language in the history of the human race. At the beginning of the twentieth century, it was already one of the foremost languages of the world, because it was the main language of both the British Empire and the United States of America. At that time it had significant competition from other widespread European languages such as French, German, Russian, and Spanish and, beyond Europe, from Mandarin Chinese, Arabic, and Swahili that all still belong, with English, in the prestigious club of world languages. However, since World War II, although all the other world languages have continued to be widely used, English has been alone in becoming – ever more notably with each passing decade – the sole universal language, the world's *lingua franca*.

Noting its growing role, scholars and other observers have for some time been giving distinctive labels to this runaway language. Increasingly, since occasional use in the 1930s, it has come most commonly to be known as 'World English'. Since around 1980, this term has also been put into the plural, as 'World Englishes', so as to highlight proliferating varieties that are often called simply 'the Englishes', and, in Asia and Africa, 'the New Englishes'. Since at least the 1970s, the language complex has also been called 'International English', and, in the 1990s, the term 'Global English' proved fashionable, to accompany and blend in with the economic buzzword *globalization*.

Describing and cataloguing any language is difficult, but in the past the relatively limited scope and roles of the world's languages have allowed us to suppose that the grammars, dictionaries, and other works associated with them are comprehensive. But the scale and variety of present-day English do not permit any such comfortable illusion. Even the population statistics of World English are uncertain, ranging hazily from over three hundred million people who are assumed to be native speakers to over a billion users of English of all kinds, from the most informed and fluent to the most casual and halting. The unnumbered varieties and uses of this language (whether thought, spoken, written, typed, printed, broadcast, taped, telephoned, faxed, e-mailed, texted, or disseminated on the World Wide Web) are so complex that no individual, group, or system can catch them all. Even the most extensive and flexible computer corpus currently imaginable cannot encompass all the registers and usages of the standard language, let alone all the rest.

Even so, however, and paradoxically, there is a manifest need to say something as comprehensive as possible about World English, including its immense wealth of words, past, present, and potential. Although the task is fraught with difficulty, publishers of dictionaries must inevitably respond to the challenge, part of which is to acknowledge the nature and impact of the phenomenon being described, and this has been the primary goal of the *Bloomsbury English Dictionary*.

The *study* of English is an international industry. Tens of thousands of scholars and teachers engage in it throughout the world, instructing a student population of hundreds of millions while producing innumerable books, periodicals, dissertations, articles, reports, conference proceedings, class notes, textbooks, newsletters, and Internet materials. Their total output is more than any of them can digest; indeed, few will see – or even be informed about – every proceeding or document that touches on their special interests *within* the language and its literatures.

But again, simply to say this and turn away is not enough. If anything, we now need more guidance and discrimination from the makers of dictionaries than ever: the challenge is now to make even fuller, clearer, and more appropriate dictionaries of English, both benefiting from the technological revolution that has accompanied and helped drive the enlargement of English and acknowledging that English is larger than any of the communities in which it is used.

One outcome of this unique and often unnerving state of affairs is that no one can even think today about who 'owns' the language or its many varieties. The English language has become a global resource. As such, it does not owe its existence – or its future – to any nation, group, or individual. Inasmuch as a language belongs to any individual or community, English is the possession of every individual and community that wishes to use it, wherever they are in the world. It is in effect as democratic and universal an institution as humankind has ever possessed.

The Future of English
David Graddol

The history of English is traditionally divided into three major periods – Old English, Middle English, and Modern English. We may now, however, be witnessing the transition to a fourth era – that of World English.

There is wide agreement that English has become a (some would say 'the') global language but despite the fact that this phenomenon, about which we know a great deal, occurred relatively recently, exactly *how* and *why* it happened remains tantalizingly obscure. Here are a few of the theories that have been put forward in recent years:

- English was intrinsically suited to becoming a *lingua franca*. This argument points to how English already contains a vast number of words borrowed from many sources. Often described as a language that is easy for learners to speak badly, though difficult to speak well, it has relatively little complexity in the way it inflects, for example, and is potentially more open than most languages to rapid change.
- World English arose from the process of British colonization that over several centuries brought English first to America, and then to Asia and Africa.
- It arose from a postcolonial process, in which the social elites of former colonies encouraged the use of English for their own benefit.
- Its roots lie in the Industrial Revolution and the creation of new kinds of capitalism and world trade in the nineteenth century, dominated first by Britain and then America.
- It arose as a result of the massive globalizing impact of two world wars and their aftermath, in which much of the world came into contact with English-speaking military forces.
- It arose from a conspiracy between the United States and Britain in the 1940s and 1950s, nations that secretly agreed to promote English in Asia and Middle East to counter Communist propaganda during the Cold War. And so, the reasoning goes, the world today still reflects this 'carve-up' into US English and British English territories.
- It arose because economic globalization, communication technologies such as the Internet, and cheap world travel have made the world a global village in which speakers need a world language to communicate.

The explanation for the emergence of World English probably lies in all these, since each provides a partial explanation at different points in history. The origins of World English are multiple and complex and its emergence as a global *lingua franca* has depended on a centuries-long chain of events and processes. At various moments in history, its future might have been redirected. What if the industrial revolution had started in China, not Britain? What if there had been no World War II? We can expect the future of English as a World Language to be as complex as its history, and as dependent on the lack of major disruption in its next phase.

The demographic future of English

The development of languages depends much on their external context: economic, social, technological, and political. But a counter-trend has quietly been subverting the position of English in the world. During the last few decades, the proportion of the world's population who speak English as a native language has actually been declining. The world's population rose rapidly during the twentieth century, but the major increase took place in less developed countries. This trend, decade upon decade, is transforming the ranking of languages in the global league table, as based on native-speaker numbers. Table 1a (see next page) shows the 'top ten' languages at the end of the twentieth century. Table 1b shows the likely impact of global population increase by 2050.

Estimating speaker numbers for the larger – and otherwise best documented – languages such as English is surprisingly difficult. Perhaps the best-established international database is the Ethnologue, provided by SIL International (the Summer Institute of Linguistics, a service organization that studies and documents the world's lesser-known languages). But the Ethnologue data for English includes such a diverse mix of sources, some dating from the 1960s, that it provides an unreliable snapshot of the present-day situation. The numbers provided here in Table 1 are based on UN population projections and estimates of the linguistic demography of each country – a technique that is still approximate but that allows principled estimates for future language usage to be made.

TOP TEN WORLD LANGUAGES

	Table 1a (1995)		Table 1b (2050)
1	Chinese	1	Chinese
2	English	2	Hindi/Urdu
3	Hindi/Urdu	3	Arabic
4	Spanish	4	English
5	Arabic	5	Spanish
6	Portuguese	6	Portuguese
7	Russian	7	Bangla (Bengali)
8	Bangla (Bengali)	8	Russian
9	Japanese	9	Japanese
10	German	10	Malay
11	French	11	German
12	Italian	12	French

Table 1a: The rank ordering of languages in the world in 1995, according to native-speaker numbers.

Table 1b: The expected rank ordering of languages in the world in 2050, according to estimated numbers of native speakers aged 15-24.

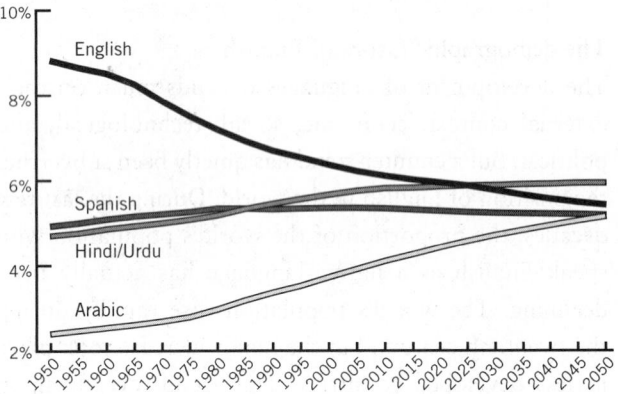

Figure 1

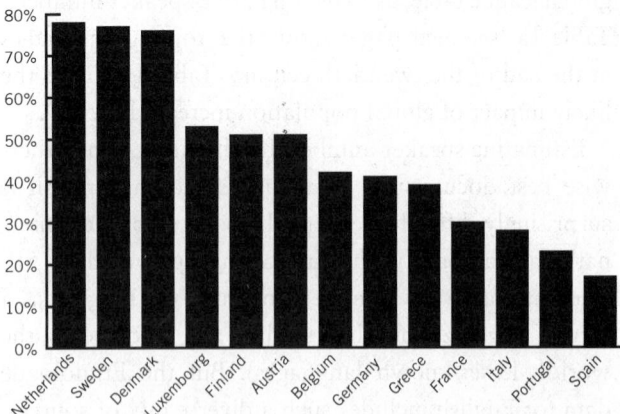

Figure 2

The decline of native speakers is shown in Figure 1, which indicates a one-hundred-year period: the left side of the graph represents history; the right hand, a projection for the future. In the mid-twentieth century, nearly 10 per cent of the global population grew up speaking English as their first language, but that proportion is declining – towards nearer 5 per cent by 2050. In absolute terms, the number of native English speakers is rising, but not as fast as the populations speaking other languages.

Chinese (whether one counts only Mandarin or all the Chinese dialects sharing a common writing system) is already well established as the world's largest language in terms of native speakers and its position will remain unchallenged. Significant change is affecting the next four major languages (English, Spanish, Hindi/Urdu, and Arabic), which are gradually converging and are likely to be equally ranked by 2050, with Arabic rising as English declines.

The rise of English as a second language

Figures for native speakers of English tell only part of the story of World English. Since the nineteenth century, speakers using English as their second language have been regarded as a relatively marginal group – an anomaly brought about by the British Empire, on the one hand, and large-scale immigration, especially to the United States, on the other. This situation created two different, but equally marginal, groups of speaker: those who would be assimilated as native speakers after a generation, and those who formed a bilingual social elite in their countries. Today, however, people speaking English as their second language cannot be regarded as marginal. In number they overtook native speakers early in the twenty-first century. In future, they will form the dominant community of English speakers.

A multilingual future

Another feature of World English is the spread of English into formerly monolingual communities where the populaces speak only one language, transforming them into bilingual ones, where the populaces now speak two. Bilingualism is indeed a global trend. In Europe a wave of English has been spreading from North to South. In Sweden, Denmark, and the Netherlands, around 80 per cent of the population now claim fluency in the language (see Figure 2); France is a state of transition; in Italy, Spain, Greece, and Portugal learning English is now big business. The spread of English and other major languages beyond their traditional territories has eroded the idea that 'one country one language' is the norm. In the new world order most people will speak more than one language and expect to switch between languages to perform different functions in their daily lives. In future people who can only speak English may find themselves

unable to operate fully in a multilingual society. What all this means is that we will have to think differently about what it means to speak English, or to learn and teach it. The very notion of 'native speaker' is under challenge, as is the idea that any language naturally 'belongs' to certain territories, and the expectation that someone should aspire to perfect competence in a foreign language.

Future trends in English

In the past, English has been subject to two contradictory tendencies: on the one hand, it has been diversifying, fragmenting into an increasing number of local forms, and in the process raising anxiety that English is turning into a new family of mutually unintelligible languages. This trend has been counterbalanced, however, by a centralizing, standardizing one in which institutions such as publishing and schools encourage a standard usage.

The development of English has, for some centuries now, resolved this contradiction by allowing local forms of language to develop alongside a more standard form. In other words, native speakers have been increasingly required to use two dialects of the same language. But the dynamic that will shape the future of English may be rather different for several reasons:

- The major national varieties of English are themselves gradually moving away from a single standard, becoming more tolerant of variety and eroding the clear distinction between written and spoken forms of language. The reasons for this process lie in a complex mix of culture, technology, and economics.

- There are more standards now to choose from. Many of the New Englishes have been undergoing a process of standardization themselves, so that we now have concepts of standard Indian English, standard Singapore English, and so on.

- The domains in which English is used as a global language are largely specialist ones developing within global but restricted communities. European bureaucratic English, for example, arises from particular institutions and practices that may not be understood by outsiders. English is the language of scholarly research papers – an estimated 80 to 90 per cent of papers in scientific journals in some fields are now written in English – but it may not be understood across disciplines.

These trends suggest that the emergence of a single, unified standard World English is unlikely.

The decline of idiomatic English

English learners across the world are apparently trained in such curious English idioms as *it is raining cats and dogs*, despite the fact that corpus linguistics (the study of language using large collections of machine-readable texts) has shown that the expression is rarely used by native speakers. However, corpus linguists have also helped us to understand much better what gives native-speaker English its special character. Each word in the language has its own preferred patterns of collocation. Much of the grammar of the language can be explained by examining the linguistic life of individual words.

This use of corpora provides a powerful tool for exploring World English, since it transpires that patterns of collocation (groups of words that tend to occur together) vary widely from one variety of English to another. As an example, Indian English is distinctive not just because of its vocabulary but also in the way words collocate. Where in British English a cup of tea may be 'weak', in Indian English it might be 'light'. In the future we can expect to learn more about the way even shared vocabulary might be used differently in different varieties.

A potentially more significant trend, however, may be the emergence of *lingua franca* forms of English. Strong patterns of collocation arise from large vocabularies and communities of speakers who have a shared experience of language usage. Speakers of *lingua franca* English, who have more experience of communicating with each other than with native speakers, may not show the same kind of patterning in vocabulary.

The Future of English texts

Certainly, there is much work ahead for corpus linguists, as texts change their nature almost faster than they can be analysed. As texts become shorter and more fragmentary, using pictures, colour, sound, and kinetics as well as words, so will strategies of interpretation and ways of reading adapt. A degree of tension is now arising between the author and reader, the producer and consumer of texts. On the one hand, multimedia texts are becoming more and more common and need more attention by designers and editors to marshal the disparate forms of information into a coherent whole. But against them there is a movement demanding free access to 'content', arguing that publishers, editors, and designers are part of a capitalist conspiracy to add cost and block free access to knowledge. Readers may be left to make sense of competing and chaotic streams of information, and in some domains we may lose the linguistic ability to create and interpret longer, unified texts. Hence the future of World English may be subject to contradictory driving forces just as in earlier periods of its history. But the nature of the dynamic may be different.

a¹ /ay/ (*plural* **a's**), **A** (*plural* **A's** or **As**) *n* **1.** the first letter of the English alphabet, representing a vowel sound **2.** a written representation of the letter 'a'

a² *symbol* **1.** PHYS acceleration **2.** used to refer to the first vertical row of squares from the left on a chessboard

a³ *abbr* **1.** MEASURE are² **2.** TRANSP arrives

a⁴ *stressed* /ay/; *unstressed* /ə/ CORE MEANING: a determiner, used before a singular countable noun to refer to one person or thing not previously known or specified, in contrast with 'the', referring to somebody or something known to the listener ○ *I need a new car.*

det **1.** INDICATES TYPE used before a noun to indicate that somebody or something has some of the same qualities as the person or thing mentioned ○ *a Hercules* ○ *He's a genius.* **2.** ONE used instead of 'one' with words of measurement ○ *a teaspoonful of salt* **3.** PER in each or in every ○ *twice a day* **4.** INDICATES SOMEBODY NOT KNOWN PERSONALLY used to indicate somebody not personally known, but known of ○ *There's a Mr O'Flynn here to see you.* **5.** ANY used in negative structures to emphasize a complete absence of something ○ *He doesn't have a hope!* [Old English, shortening of *ān* (see ONE)]

USAGE a or an? *A* is the form of the indefinite article used before words that are pronounced with an initial consonant sound (even if the spelling does not begin with a consonant): *a banana; a hunk; a ewe. An* is used before words that begin with a vowel sound (even if an unpronounced consonant comes first): *an elephant; an heir.* The same rule regarding sound rather than spelling applies to abbreviations: *a CD* but *an LP.* The practice of using **an** before words beginning with *h* and an unstressed syllable (for example *an hotel, an historic occasion*) is falling out of use, and it is much more usual now to hear *a hotel* and *a historic occasion*, with the *h* sounded in each word.

A¹ *symbol* **1.** CHEM activity **2.** BIOCHEM adenine **3.** MEASURE ampere **4.** *also* **Å** MEASURE angstrom **5.** ROADS used to indicate a main road other than a motorway **6.** PHYS mass number **7.** COMPUT 10 (*used in hexadecimal notation*)

A² /ay/ (*plural* **A's** or **As**) *n* **1.** 'A'-SHAPED OBJECT something shaped like a letter 'A' **2.** MUSIC 6TH NOTE IN C MAJOR the sixth note of a scale in C major. The A above middle C is often used to tune instruments and is standardized at a frequency of 440 hertz. **3.** MUSIC SOMETHING THAT PRODUCES A a string, key, or pipe tuned to produce the note A **4.** MUSIC SCALE BEGINNING ON A a scale or key that starts on the note A **5.** MUSIC WRITTEN SYMBOL OF A a graphic representation of the tone of A **6.** EDUC HIGHEST GRADE the highest grade in a series, e.g. a top grade for academic work ○ *straight As in her exams.* **7.** MED HUMAN BLOOD TYPE a human blood type of the ABO system, containing the A antigen. Somebody with this type of blood can donate to people of the same group or of the AB group, and can receive blood from people with this type or with type O. **8.** SOC SCI SENIOR MANAGER OR PROFESSIONAL in the market research system that classifies people according to their occupation, somebody in a senior management, professional, or administrative position ◇ **from A to B** from one place to another ◇ **from A to Z 1.** extremely thoroughly **2.** all the way from the beginning to the end

a-¹ *prefix* in a particular place, condition, or manner ○ *abed* ○ *adrift* ○ *aloud* [Old English, < *an*, alternative for *on* (see ON)]

a-² *prefix* without, not ○ *agnostic* ○ *amoral* [< Greek]

A1, A-1, A-one *adj* **1.** in excellent or first-rate condition (*informal*) **2.** describes a boat as being well equipped and in excellent condition [Mid-19C. < Lloyd's Register, an annual British shipping list; *A* indicated a hull in first-class condition, *1* that the ship was well-provisioned and well-equipped]

A2 *n* in England, Wales, and Northern Ireland, the second year of a full A-level course, or the examination taken at the end of that year

aa /aá aa/ *n* solidified lava with a rough jagged surface and sharp angular features [Mid-19C. < Hawaiian *a-'a*]

AA¹ *abbr* Alcoholics Anonymous

AA² *n* a UK company that provides breakdown and other services to motorists and travellers. Full form **Automobile Association**

AAA *abbr* **1.** /three áyz/ *UK* Amateur Athletic Association **2.** /tripp'l áy/ *N Am* American Automobile Association **3.** /tripp'l áy/ antiaircraft artillery **4.** *Aus* Australian Automobile Association

a.a.e. *abbr* according to age and experience

aah *interj, vi, n* another spelling of **ah**

aajaa *n Carib* another spelling of **aja**

aajee *n Carib* another spelling of **aji**

Aalto /aáltō/, **Alvar** (1898–1976) Finnish architect. He designed the Helsinki Hall of Culture (1958) and was noted for his use of organic materials and forms. Full name **Aalto, Hugo Alvar Henrik**

AAM *abbr* ARMS air-to-air missile

A & E *abbr* HEALTH SERVICES accident and emergency

A & M *abbr* (Hymns) Ancient and Modern

A & R *abbr* MUSIC, RECORDING artists and repertoire

aapa /aápə/ *n S Asia* somebody's elder sister (*used by Muslims*) [< Urdu *ápa*]

aardvark

aardvark /aárd vaark/ *n* a burrowing mammal with a long snout, powerful claws, long tongue, and heavy tail. Native to: southern Africa. Latin name: *Orycteropus afer.* [Late 18C. < Afrikaans, 'earth pig']

aardwolf /aárd woolf/ (*plural* **-wolves** /-woolvz/) *n* a striped nocturnal mammal, related to the hyena, that feeds mainly on termites. Native to: southern Africa. Latin name: *Proteles cristatus.* [Mid-19C. < Afrikaans, 'earth wolf']

aargh /aá/ *interj* used to express annoyance or disgust at something or somebody (*informal; often used humorously*) [Late 18C. Lengthened form of AH]

Aarhus another spelling of **Århus**

Aaron /áirən/ *n* in the Bible, the first Jewish high priest and elder brother of Moses. With Moses, he led the Israelites out of Egypt but died before reaching the Promised Land.

Aaron's beard *n* PLANTS same as **rose of Sharon** (sense 1) [After AARON, who had a long beard (Psalms 133:2), because of the flower's prominent hairy stamens]

Aaron's rod *n* a tall smooth-stemmed plant. Flowers: yellow. Native to: Asia, Europe, North America. [After the rod belonging to AARON, said to have flowered (Numbers 17:8)]

aarti *n, v* HINDUISM another spelling of **arti**

A'asia *abbr* Australasia

AAVE *abbr* African American Vernacular English

Ab /ab/, **Av** /av/ *n* in the Jewish calendar, the fifth month of the religious year, lasting 30 days and falling about the same time as July to August. See table at **calendar** [Late 18C. < Hebrew *āb*]

AB¹ *abbr* **1.** able-bodied seaman **2.** Alberta

AB² *n* a human blood type of the ABO system, containing the A and B antigens. Somebody with this type of blood can donate to people of the same group and receive blood from people with this type or with type O, A, or B.

A.B. *abbr* **1.** able-bodied seaman **2.** *US* EDUC Bachelor of Arts

ab- *prefix* away from, off ○ *aboral* ○ *abaxial* [< Latin < Indo-European, 'off, away']

aba /ábbə/ *n* **1.** a cloth made in Syria using hair from goats or camels **2.** a loose sleeveless outer garment worn by boys and men in North Africa and Southwest Asia [Early 19C. < Arabic *'abā*]

ABA *abbr* **1.** Amateur Boxing Association **2.** *also* **A.B.A.** American Bar Association

abaca /ábbəkə/ *n* **1.** TEXTILES same as **Manila hemp 2.** a large plant from whose leaves Manila hemp is produced. It is related to bananas. Latin name: *Musa textilis.* [Mid-18C. Via Spanish < Tagalog *abaká*]

abaci MATHS, ARCHIT plural of **abacus**

aback /ə bák/ *adv* **1.** SAILING WITH WIND BLOWING TOWARDS BOW with the wind blowing against the forward part of a sail or sails, so that a vessel cannot move ahead **2.** BACKWARDS backwards or towards the back (*archaic*) **3.** *Carib* FORMERLY in the past [Old English *on bæc* 'towards the back, backwards'] ◇ **aback of** *Carib* at the back of or behind something ◇ **take somebody aback** to surprise somebody and make him or her unsure how to react

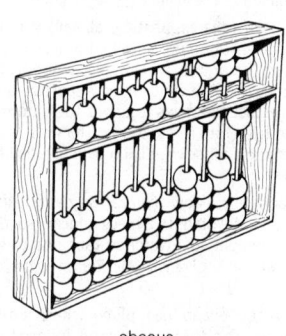

abacus

abacus /ábbəkəss/ (*plural* **-cuses** or **-ci** /-sī/) *n* **1.** a mechanical device for making calculations consisting of a frame mounted with rods along which beads or balls are moved. See illustration on previous page **2.** a flat slab at the top of an architectural column [14C. Via Latin < Greek *abakos* 'board strewn with dust on which to draw or write' (later 'slab, table')]

Abadan /ábbə daan/, **Ābādān** city in southwestern Iran. It is a major petroleum-refining and shipping centre. Population: 296,081 (1996).

abaft /ə baáft/ *adv* towards the rear of a boat ■ *prep* to the rear of an area on a boat [14C. < Old English *an* + *be* (see BY[1]) + *æften* 'behind']

Abakan /ábbə kaan/ capital of the autonomous republic of Khakassia in eastern Russia. Population: 168,047 (1999).

abalone /ábbə lṓ ni/ *n* an edible invertebrate sea animal that breathes through holes in its ear-shaped shell. The pearly interior of the shell is used for making jewellery. Genus: *Haliotis*. [Mid-19C. Via American Spanish *abulón* < Shoshonean *aulun*]

abampere /ab ám pair/ *n* the centimetre-gram-second unit of electromagnetic current equal to ten amperes

abandon /ə bándən/ *v* (**-dons, -doning, -doned**) **1.** *vt* LEAVE SOMEBODY BEHIND to leave somebody or something behind for others to look after, especially somebody or something meant to be a personal responsibility ○ *pets abandoned by their owners* **2.** *vt* LEAVE PLACE BECAUSE OF DANGER to leave a place or vehicle, especially for reasons of safety and without intending to return soon ○ *had to abandon their vehicles in the snow* **3.** *vt* RENOUNCE SOMETHING to renounce or reject something previously done or used ○ *The practice was abandoned long ago.* **4.** *vt* GIVE UP CONTROL OF SOMETHING to surrender control of something completely to somebody else ○ *As troops closed in the town was abandoned to its fate.* **5.** *vt* HALT SOMETHING IN PROGRESS to stop doing something before it is completed, usually because of difficulty or danger ○ *abandoning the rescue attempt* **6.** *vt* GIVE UP TO INSURER to surrender part of an insured property to the insurer in order to make a claim for total loss **7. abandon yourself** *vr* GIVE IN TO EMOTION to give yourself over to a powerful emotion ○ *He abandoned himself to his grief.* ■ *n* LACK OF RESTRAINT complete lack of inhibition or self-restraint [14C. < Old French *abandoner* < *a bandon* 'under control' < Latin *bannum* 'proclamation'] —**abandonment** *n*

abandoned /ə bándənd/ *adj* **1.** EMPTY left empty because of not being used or lived in any more **2.** ALONE left alone without being cared for or supported **3.** UNRESTRAINED without restraint or self-control

abandonment option *n* in a contract, a clause relating to the possibility of abandoning a project and terminating the contract earlier than originally planned

abandonment value *n* the value that can be realized by terminating a business project or disposing of a business before its anticipated maturity

abase /ə báyss/ (**abases, abasing, abased**) *v* **1.** *vt* to make somebody feel belittled or degraded **2. abase yourself** *vr* to behave in a way that lowers your sense of dignity or self-esteem [14C. < Old French *abaissier* < *baissier* 'to lower' < Latin *bassus* 'short of stature'] —**abasement** *n*

abash /ə básh/ (**abashes, abashing, abashed**) *vt* to make somebody feel ashamed, embarrassed, or uncomfortable [14C. < Anglo-Norman *abaïss-* < Old French *baïr* 'astound'] —**abashment** *n*

abate /ə báyt/ (**abates, abating, abated**) *v* **1.** *vti* BECOME LESS to lessen or make something lessen gradually (*formal or literary*) **2.** *vti* LAW END to suppress or end a nuisance, act, or writ, or be suppressed or ended **3.** *vt* FIN REDUCE SOMETHING to lower the amount or rate of something such as a tax (*formal*) [13C. < Old French *abatre* 'beat down' < Latin *batt(u)ere* 'fight, beat'] —**abatement** *n*

abatis /ábbətiss, -tee/ (*plural same* or **-tises**) *n* a rampart made of felled trees placed so that their bent or sharpened branches face out towards the enemy [Mid-18C. < French < Old French *abatre* 'beat down, fell' (see ABATE)]

abattoir /ábbə twaar/ *n* a place where animals are slaughtered for their meat and by-products [Early 19C. < French < *abattre* 'fell' < Old French *abatre* (see ABATE)]

abaxial /ab áksee əl/ *adj* used to describe the underside of a leaf or other surface that faces away from the stem

Abba /ábbə/ *n* **1.** in the Bible, a name used to address God **2.** in the Syrian Orthodox and Coptic Churches, a title given to bishops and patriarchs [14C. Via ecclesiastical Latin and New Testament Greek < Aramaic *'abbā* 'father']

abbacy /ábbəssi/ (*plural* **-cies**) *n* the rank, jurisdiction, or term of office of an abbot or abbess [15C. < ecclesiastical Latin *abbacia* < *abbat-* (see ABBOT)]

AKG London

Claudio Abbado

Abbado /ə baádō/, **Claudio** (*b.* 1933) Italian conductor. He began his career with the La Scala Opera, Milan, Italy, and became artistic director of the Berlin Philharmonic Orchestra, Germany (1989–2002).

Abbas /ábbəss/ (566?–653) Arabian merchant. He was instrumental in spreading the tenets of Islam. The prophet Muhammad was his nephew. Full name **Al-Abbas ibn al-Muttalib**

Abbas I (1571–1629) shah of Persia member of the Safavid dynasty. He ruled from 1588 until his death. Known as **Abbas the Great**

Abbasid /ə bássid, ábbə sid/ *n* a member of a dynasty that ruled an Islamic empire from Baghdad from 750 to 1258. Descended from Muhammad's uncle, Abbas, the Abbasids often wielded little political power but were great patrons of Islamic art and culture. —**Abbasid** *adj*

abbatial /ə báysh'l/ *adj* relating to an abbey, abbot, or abbess [Late 17C. < French, or < medieval Latin *abbatialis*, both < ecclesiastical Latin *abbat-* (see ABBOT)]

~~**abbatoir**~~ incorrect spelling of **abattoir**

abbé /ábbay/ *n* an abbot or member of a religious order in a French-speaking area [Mid-16C. Via French < ecclesiastical Latin *abbat-* (see ABBOT)]

abbess /ábbess/ *n* the nun in charge of a convent [13C. < Old French *abbesse* < ecclesiastical Latin *abbat-* (see ABBOT)]

Abbevillean /ab vílli ən/ *adj* relating to or typical of early Lower Palaeolithic culture in Europe [Mid-20C. < French *Abbevillien*, after the town of *Abbeville* in N France]

abbey /ábbi/ (*plural* **-beys**) *n* **1.** a building or buildings occupied by monks under an abbot, or nuns under an abbess, especially the church building **2.** a church that is or was used by a community of monks or nuns [13C. < Old French *ab(b)eïe* < ecclesiastical Latin *abbat-* (see ABBOT)]

abbot /ábbət/ *n* the monk in charge of a monastery [Pre-12C. Via ecclesiastical Latin *abbat-*, stem of *abbas* < Aramaic *'abbā* 'father'] —**abbotship** *n*

abbr, **abbr.**, **abbrev.** *abbr* abbreviation

abbreviate /ə breé vi ayt/ (**-ates, -ating, -ated**) *vt* **1.** to shorten a word by leaving out some of its letters or sounds **2.** to shorten a piece of text by cutting sections or paraphrasing it [15C. < Latin *abbreviat-*, past participle of *abbreviare* 'shorten' < *brevis* 'short'] —**abbreviator** *n*

abbreviation /ə breévi áysh'n/ *n* **1.** a shortened form of a word or phrase **2.** the shortening of a word or phrase to be used to represent the full form

USAGE Types of **abbreviation**: There are four main kinds of abbreviation: shortenings, contractions, initialisms, and acronyms. **1 Shortenings** of words usually consist of the first few letters of the full form and are usually spelt with a final full stop when they are still regarded as abbreviations, for example *cont.* = continued, *etc.* = et cetera. In the cases where they form words in their own right, the full stop is omitted, for example *hippo* = hippopotamus. Such shortenings are often but not always informal. Some become the standard forms, and the full forms are then regarded as formal or technical, for example *bus* = omnibus, *pub* = public house, *zoo* = zoological garden. **2 Contractions** are abbreviated forms in which letters from the middle of the full form have been omitted, for example *Dr* = doctor, *St* = saint or street. Practice varies with regard to adding a full stop, but in modern usage it is increasingly usual to omit it. Another kind of contraction is the type with an apostrophe marking the omission of letters: *can't* = cannot, *didn't* = did not, *you've* = you have. **3 Initialisms** are made up of the initial letters of words and are pronounced as separate letters: *CIA* (or *C.I.A.*), *pm* (or *p.m.*), *US* (or *U.S.*). Practice again varies with regard to full stops, with current usage increasingly in favour of omitting them, especially when the initialism consists entirely of capital letters. **4 Acronyms** are initialisms that have become words in their own right, or similar words formed from parts of several words. They are pronounced as words rather than as a series of letters, for example *Aids, laser, scuba, UNESCO*, and do not have full stops. In many cases the acronym becomes the standard term and the full form is only used in explanatory contexts.

ABC[1] *n* **1.** the alphabet, especially in referring to basic reading and writing **2.** the basic facts or essential details of a subject ○ *the ABC of building your own home* ▶ N Am term **ABCs** ◇ **as easy as ABC** extremely easy

ABC[2] *abbr* American Broadcasting Company

ABC[3] *n* in Australia, the government-funded organization that provides radio and television services. Full form **Australian Broadcasting Corporation**

abcoulomb /ab kóo lom/ *n* the centimetre-gram-second unit of electrical charge equal to ten coulombs

ABCs *npl N Am* same as **ABC**[1] ○ *learned her ABCs* ○ *the ABCs of carpentry*

Abd al-Hamid /ab daal hámmid/ ♦ **Abdulhamid II**

abdicate /ábdi kayt/ (**-cates, -cating, -cated**) *v* **1.** *vti* to give up a high office formally or officially, especially the throne **2.** *vt* to fail to fulfil a duty or responsibility ○ *The company seems to have abdicated all responsibility for the damage.* [Mid-16C. < Latin *abdicat-*, past participle of *abdicare* 'renounce' < *dicare* 'proclaim'] —**abdication** /ábdi káysh'n/ *n* —**abdicator** *n*

abdomen /ábdəmən/ *n* **1.** BODY SECTION CONTAINING STOMACH the part of the body of a vertebrate that contains the stomach, intestines, and other organs. In mammals it is situated between the pelvis and the thorax. **2.** BELLY the surface of the body of a vertebrate around the stomach **3.** INSECTS REAR PART OF INSECT the elongated portion of the body of an arthropod, located behind the thorax. It is usually segmented. [Mid-16C. < Latin] —**abdominal** /ab dómmin'l/ *adj*

abducens nerve /ab dyóoss'nz-/, **abducent nerve** /ab dyóoss'nt-/ *n* a nerve conveying impulses from the brain to the muscle that moves the eye laterally in its socket, one of a pair of cranial nerves [*Abducens* < modern Latin, present participle of *abducere* (see ABDUCT)]

abduct /əb dúkt/ (**-ducts, -ducting, -ducted**) *vt* **1.** to take somebody away by force or deception **2.** to pull something, e.g. a muscle, away from the midpoint or midline of the body or of a limb [Early 17C. < Latin *abduct-*, past participle of *abducere* 'lead out' < *ducere* 'lead'] —**abduction** *n*

abductor /ab dúktər/ *n* **1.** somebody who takes somebody else away by force or deception **2.** a muscle that pulls the body or a limb away from a midpoint or midline

Abdulhamid II /ab dóol hámmid/ (1842–1918) Ottoman sultan. He suspended the constitution (1877) and fought Western influences. He was deposed by the Young Turks' revolt (1909).

Abdullah /ab dúllə/ (*b.* 1939) prime minister of Malaysia. A member of the United Malays National Organization party, he entered parliament in 1978, became deputy prime minister in 1999, and prime

minister in 2003. Full name **Datuk Seri Abdullah Ahmad Badawi**

Abdullah II (b. 1962) king of Jordan. He was commander of the Jordanian army's Special Forces and succeeded his father Hussein in 1999. Full name **Abdullah bin Hussein**

Abdullah et Taaisha /-et tī eésha/ (1846–99) Sudanese nationalist resistance leader who led the uprising against the Egyptian administration of Sudan and was defeated by Lord Horatio Kitchener (1898)

Abdullah ibn Husein /-ib'n hŏŏ sáyn/ (1882–1951) king of Jordan. He was emir of Transjordan (1921–46) and the first king of the modern state of Jordan (1946–51).

Abdul Rahman /ab dŏŏl raˊamən/, **Tunku** (1903–90) Malayan politician. He was the first prime minister of the Federation of Malaya (1957–63) and of Malaysia (1963–70).

abeam /ə beˊem/ adv to or at the side of a boat or aircraft, especially at right angles to its length

abecedarian /áy bee see dáiri ən/ n somebody learning the basics of literacy or a subject [Early 17C. < medieval Latin abecedarium 'book containing the alphabet' < the names of the first four letters of the alphabet]

abed /ə béd/ adv in or confined to bed (archaic)

Abednego /ə bédni gō/ n in the Bible, one of Daniel's companions thrown into the furnace of Nebuchadnezzar II (Daniel 3:12–20)

abeer n HINDUISM another spelling of **abir**

Abel /áyb'l/ n in the Bible, a shepherd and the second son of Adam and Eve, who was killed by his brother Cain (Genesis 4)

Abelard /ábbə laard/, **Peter** (1079–1142) French philosopher and theologian whose correspondence with his pupil and lover Héloïse became a literary classic

> 'We call the intention good which is right in itself, but the action is good, not because it contains within it some good, but because it issued from a good intention.'
> [Peter Abelard, *Abailard's Ethics*; 1935 (tr. J. McCallum)]

abele /ə beˊel/ n TREES same as **white poplar** (sense 1) [13C. Directly or via Dutch *abeel* < Old French *a(u)bel* < Latin *albus* 'white']

Abeles /áyb'lz/, **Sir Peter** (1924–99) Hungarian-born Australian business executive. He was a director of several major national freight and airline corporations in Sydney, Australia. Full name **Abeles, Sir Emil Herbert Peter**

abelia /ə beˊeli ə/ n a widespread ornamental bush. Flowers: white to purple, tubular. Native to: East Asia. Genus: *Abelia*. [Mid-19C. < modern Latin, after Clarke Abel (1780–1826), English botanist]

Abelian group /ə beˊeli ən-/ n an algebraic group in which the result of the operation is independent of the sequence of the operands, e.g. ab = ba or a+b = b+a [Mid-19C. After Niels Abel (1802–29), Norwegian mathematician]

Abenaki /ab naˊaki, -náki/ (plural same or **-kis**), **Abnaki** n a member of a Native North American people who once lived throughout New England and southeastern Canada, but who now live in Maine and southern Quebec [Early 18C. Via French *Abénaqui* < Montagnais *ouabanākionek* 'people of the eastern country'] — **Abenaki** adj

ABEND /áb end/ n 1. also **abend** a sudden failure of a computer program. Full form **abnormal end** 2. used in the subject line of e-mails to warn correspondents of an imminent loss of Internet access. Full form **absent by enforced Net deprivation**

Abeokuta /áybi ō kŏŏtə/ city and port in southwestern Nigeria. It is the capital of Ogun state. Population: 416,800 (1995).

Aberdeen /ábbər deˊen/ 1. city, port, and industrial centre in northeastern Scotland, located at the mouth of the rivers Dee and Don. It is known as the Granite City as many of its buildings are constructed of granite. Population: 212,125 (2001). 2. council area in northeastern Scotland. Population: 218,220 (1993). Area: 186 sq. km/72 sq. mi. Official name **City of Aberdeen** —**Aberdonian** /ábbər dōni ən/ n, adj

Aberdeen Angus (plural same or **Aberdeen Anguses**) n UK, Can a cow belonging to a short-haired, black, hornless breed of beef cattle. US term **Angus**[1] [Mid-19C. After ABERDEENSHIRE and ANGUS[2]]

Aberdeenshire /ábbər deˊenshər/ Scottish administrative county since 1998, formerly in Grampian Region. The county headquarters are in Aberdeen. Area: 5,103 sq. km/1,971 sq. mi.

Aberfan /ábbər ván/ coalmining village in southern Wales, where in 1966 a landslide killed 144 people

abernethy /ábbər néthi/ (plural **-thies**) n a crisp semisweet biscuit flavoured with caraway [Mid-19C. Probably after John Abernethy (1764–1831), English physician]

aberrant /ə bérrənt/ adj deviating from what is normal or desirable [Mid-19C. < Latin *aberrant-*, present participle of *aberrare* (see ABERRATION)] —**aberrance** n —**aberrantly** adv

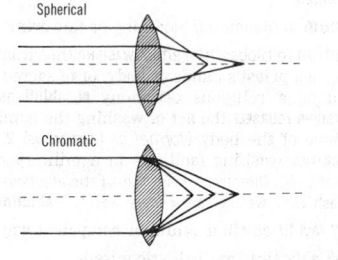

aberration: lenses with defects causing a distorted image (top) and an image with coloured edges (bottom)

aberration /ábbə ráysh'n/ n 1. DEVIATION a departure from what is normal or desirable ○ *in a moment of aberration* 2. LAPSE a temporary departure from somebody's normal mental state 3. OPTICS OPTICAL DEFECT a defect in a lens or mirror, causing a distorted image or one with coloured edges 4. ASTRON APPARENT DISPLACEMENT IN STAR'S POSITION a small periodic change in the apparent position of a star or other astronomical object, caused by the motion of the Earth around the Sun [Late 16C. < Latin *aberration-* < *aberrare* 'go astray' < *errare* 'wander, err'] —**aberrational** adj

Aberystwyth /ábbər rístwith, -rústwith/ seaside resort and university city in Ceredigion, Wales. Population: 11,154 (1991).

abet /ə bét/ (**abets, abetting, abetted**) vt to assist somebody to do something, especially something illegal [14C. < Old French *abeter* 'urge, stimulate' < *beter* 'hound, drive on'] —**abettor** n

abeyance /ə báy ənss/ n 1. temporary inactivity or nonoperation ○ *a law that has been in abeyance for some time* 2. a condition in which legal ownership of an estate has not been established [Late 16C. < Old French *abeance* 'expectation, desire' < *abaer* 'desire' < *baer* 'gape' < medieval Latin *batare*] —**abeyant** adj

abfarad /ab fárrad, -fárrəd/ n the centimetre-gram-second unit of electrical capacitance equal to 10^9 farads

abhenry /ab hénri/ (plural **-ries**) n the centimetre-gram-second unit of electrical conductance equal to 10^{-9} of a henry

abhor /əb háwr/ (**-hors, -horring, -horred**) vt to disapprove of or reject something very strongly [15C. < Latin *abhorrere* 'shrink back in horror' < *horrere* 'shudder, bristle'] —**abhorrer** n

abhorrence /əb hórrənss/ n 1. a feeling of intense disapproval of something 2. somebody or something that is strongly disapproved of ○ *The mere idea was an abhorrence to her.*

SYNONYMS See *dislike*.

abhorrent /əb hórrənt/ adj 1. arousing strong feelings of repugnance or disapproval ○ *a practice abhorrent to all animal lovers* 2. incompatible or conflicting with something (literary) —**abhorrently** adv

abide /ə bíd/ (**abides, abiding, abode** /ə bód/ or **abided**) v 1. vt TOLERATE SOMETHING to find somebody or something

acceptable or bearable ○ *couldn't abide his superior attitude* 2. vi DWELL to live or reside in a place (archaic) 3. vt AWAIT SOMETHING to wait for somebody or something (archaic) 4. vt WITHSTAND SOMETHING to endure or withstand something (archaic) [Old English *ābīdan* 'wait for, expect' < *bīdan* 'wait' (see BIDE)] —**abidance** n —**abider** n

abide by vt to comply with or act in accordance with something such as a decision or rule ○ *Applicants must agree to abide by the rules.*

abiding /ə bíding/ adj permanent or long-lasting ○ *my abiding memory of her* —**abidingly** adv

Abidjan /ábbi jáan/ cultural and commercial capital of the Côte d'Ivoire, in the southeastern part of the country. Population: 1,929,079 (1988).

abietic acid /ábbi éttik-/ n a naturally occurring yellowish powder. Source: rosin. Use: varnishes, lacquers, soaps. Formula: $C_{20}H_{30}O_2$. [< Latin *abiet-* 'fir', from which rosin is obtained]

Abigail /ábbi gayl/ n in the Bible, a woman who averted an attack by David and his followers by taking provisions to them. She later married David (1 Samuel 25).

Abilene /ábbə leen/ city in central Texas. It is a centre for agriculture and the oil industry. Population: 115,225 (2002 estimate).

ability /ə bílləti/ (plural **-ties**) n 1. BEING ABLE a natural tendency to do something successfully or well ○ *The vehicle has the ability to perform well on really rough terrain.* 2. INTELLIGENCE OR COMPETENCE a high degree of intelligence or competence ○ *We need people of your ability.* 3. NATURAL GIFT FOR SOMETHING a particular gift for doing something well ○ *a student with impressive musical abilities* [14C. Via Old French *ablete* < Latin *habilitas* 'suitability, aptness' < *habilis* (see ABLE)]

SYNONYMS *ability, skill, competence, aptitude, talent, capacity, capability*

CORE MEANING: the necessary skill, knowledge, or experience to do something

ability a natural tendency to do something successfully or well ○ *an event open to people of all ages and abilities* ○ *Honeybees show a remarkable ability to respond collectively to external stimuli.* **skill** the ability to do something well gained through training or experience ○ *She made all the arrangements with consummate skill and professionalism.* ○ *good communication skills* **competence** the ability to do something well, measured against a standard, especially ability acquired through experience or training ○ *the professional competence built up over the preceding 20 years* ○ *has reached a high level of competence in arithmetic* **aptitude** a natural tendency to do something well, especially one that can be further developed ○ *These students show a natural aptitude for mechanical construction.* **talent** an unusual natural ability to do something well, especially in artistic areas that can be developed by training ○ *had considerable talent as a teacher, as well as in music* ○ *a talent for modelling with clay* **capacity** mental or physical ability for something or to do something ○ *his youthful energy and capacity for hard work* ○ *a limited capacity to sustain interest in politics* **capability** the power or practical ability necessary for doing something ○ *It is beyond our official capability to influence these things.* ○ *the relationship between a company's size and its technological capabilities*

ab initio /áb i níshi ō/ adv 1. from the beginning (formal) 2. without any previous knowledge of a subject being studied ○ *study Spanish ab initio* [Early 17C. < Latin]

abiogenesis /áy bī ō jénnəssiss/ n the hypothesis that life can come into being from nonliving materials [Late 19C. < Greek *abios* 'without life' < *bios* 'life'] — **abiogenetic** /áy bī ō jə néttik/ adj —**abiogenetical** adj —**abiogenist** /áy bī ójjənist/ n

abiotic /áy bī óttik/ adj 1. describes the physical and chemical aspects of an organism's environment 2. not containing or supporting life —**abiosis** /-óssiss/ n —**abiotically** adv

abir /a beˊer/, **abeer** n the red-purple dye thrown on people during the Hindu Holi festival [Late 20C. Via Hindi < Arabic, 'mica powder']

abject /áb jekt/ adj 1. MISERABLE allowing no hope of improvement or relief ○ *abject poverty* 2. HUMBLE extremely or excessively humble, e.g. in making an

apology or request ○ *an abject apology* **3.** DESPICABLE utterly despicable or contemptible ○ *abject cruelty* [15C. < Latin *abjectus*, past participle of *abjicere* 'throw away, reject' < *jacere* 'throw'] —**abjection** /ab jéksh'n/ *n* —**abjectly** *adv* —**abjectness** *n*

abjure /əb jóor/ (**-jures, -juring, -jured**) *vt* **1.** to give up a previously held belief, especially formally or solemnly **2.** to abstain from, reject, or avoid something (*literary*) [15C. < Latin *abjurare* 'deny on oath' < *jurare* 'swear'] —**abjuration** /áb joor ráysh'n/ *n* —**abjurer** *n*

Abkhaz /ab kaáz/ *n* **1.** somebody who comes from between the eastern shores of the Black Sea and the Great Caucasus mountain range in the Republic of Georgia **2.** an Abkhaz-Adyghean language spoken in northwestern Georgia. Native speakers: 80,000–100,000. [Mid-19C. After a territory in the Caucasus] —**Abkhaz** *adj*

Abkhaz-Adyghean /-aadi gáy ən/ *n* a group of Caucasian languages spoken in Georgia and southern Russia —**Abkhaz-Adyghean** *adj*

Abkhazia /ab kaázi ə/ autonomous republic in northwestern Georgia, bordered to the north by Russia and to the southwest by the Black Sea. Area: 8,600 sq. km/3,300 sq. mi. Population: 537,500 (1990).

ablate /ə bláyt/ (**-lates, -lating, -lated**) *vt* **1.** to remove diseased or unwanted tissue from the body by surgical or other means **2.** to remove or reduce snow and ice from a glacier by melting and evaporation [15C. < Latin *ablat-* (see ABLATIVE)]

ablation /ə bláysh'n/ *n* **1.** MED REMOVAL OF TISSUE the removal of diseased or unwanted tissue from the body by surgical or other means **2.** AEROSP MELTING OF SPACECRAFT'S OUTER SURFACE the melting or erosion of the protective outer surface of a spacecraft during re-entry through the Earth's atmosphere **3.** GEOL MELTING OF SNOW AND ICE the removal of snow and ice by melting and sublimation from a glacier or iceberg

ablative /ább lətiv/ *n* **1.** a grammatical form (**case**) that identifies the source, agent, or instrument of action of the verb in some inflected languages and affects nouns, pronouns, and adjectives **2.** a word or phrase in the ablative [15C. Directly or via French *ablatif* < Latin *ablativus* < *ablat-*, past participle of *auferre* 'carry away'] —**ablative** *adj*

ablator /ə bláytər/ *n* a heat shield on a spacecraft

ablaut /áb lowt/ *n* in Indo-European languages, a regular change of vowels in a related series of words or forms, e.g. 'sing', 'sang', 'sung' [Mid-19C. < German < *ab* 'off' + *Laut* 'sound']

ablaze /ə bláyz/ *adj* **1.** ON FIRE burning strongly **2.** BRIGHTLY LIT very brightly lit **3.** SHOWING STRONG EMOTION displaying great emotion or excitement, especially on the face

able /áyb'l/ *adj* (**abler, ablest**) **1.** IN POSITION TO DO SOMETHING physically or mentally equipped to do something, especially because of circumstances and timing ○ *Were you able to reach her before she left?* **2.** CAPABLE OR TALENTED having the necessary resources or talent to do something ○ *a very able administrator* **3.** EDUC GOOD AT LEARNING quick to learn in an educational environment ○ *schoolwork to extend able children* ■ *vt* (**ables, abling, abled**) *Carib* **1.** BE ABLE TO DO SOMETHING to be able or have the ability to do something **2.** TOLERATE SOMETHING to put up with something [14C. Via Old French *(h)able* < Latin *habilis* 'easy to hold or handle' < *habere* 'have, hold']

SYNONYMS See *intelligent*.

-able *suffix* **1.** capable of or fit for ○ *readable* **2.** tending to ○ *changeable* [< Latin *-abilis*] —**-ability** *suffix*

able-bodied /áyb'l bóddid/ *adj* **1.** not physically or mentally disabled **2.** healthy and physically strong

able-bodied seaman *n* a member of a ship's crew, especially the crew of a merchant ship, who possesses basic skills and qualifications

abled /áyb'ld/ *adj* **1.** having particular abilities **2.** *US* having all physical or mental functions

ableism /áyb'lizəm/ *n* discrimination in favour of those who are not physically or mentally disabled —**ableist** *adj, n*

able rate, able rating *n* a non-commissioned sailor in the Royal Navy who possesses basic skills and qualifications

LANGUAGE HERITAGE ***Aboriginal*** Much of English is made up of words from other languages, and when English-speaking settlers arrived in Australia in the 1780s it was inevitable that they would adopt names for flora, fauna, and cultural objects from the Aboriginal peoples who already inhabited the land. There were about 200 different Aboriginal languages to encounter, including Dharuk, Dhurga, Dieri, Nyungar, Kamilaroi, Pitjantjatjara, Wiradhuri (now extinct), Yagara, and Yuwaalaraay. By the end of the 18th century the word ***boomerang*** was already in use in English, as well as the names ***dingo***, ***kangaroo***, ***koala***, ***potoroo***, and ***wombat*** for various, largely unfamiliar, animals. The word ***corroboree***, later to be extended in Australian English to any noisy gathering or party, also became the English word for a gathering of Aboriginal people in the late 18th century, and ***koradji*** 'traditional healer' and ***waratah***, the bush that is the emblem of New South Wales, are also recorded before the turn of the century.

During the 19th century and into the early 20th names that migrated into English include: for animals, ***bilby***, ***euro***, ***joey***, ***perentie***, ***quokka***, ***tammar***, ***wallaby***, and ***wallaroo***; for birds, ***budgerigar***, ***currawong***, ***galah***, and ***kookaburra***; for fish ***yabby***; for trees and plants, ***bindi-eye***, ***bunya***, ***coolibah***, ***gidgee***, ***jarrah***, ***mallee***, ***mulga***, and ***quandong***; for cultural objects, ***didgeridoo*** and ***kylie***. Names for geographical features were less frequently adopted, though ***billabong*** was (mid-19th century), and is known outside Australia through the song 'Waltzing Matilda'.

able seaman *n* **1.** a sailor in the Canadian navy of a rank above ordinary seaman **2.** same as **able-bodied seaman**

abloom /ə blóom/ *adj* blooming or flowering

ablution /ə blóosh'n/ *n* RITUAL WASHING the ritual cleansing of a priest's hands or body, or of sacred vessels, during a religious ceremony ■ **ablutions** *npl* **1.** WASHING YOURSELF the act of washing the hands or the whole of the body (*formal or humorous*) **2.** WASHING FACILITIES washing facilities in a military camp or base [14C. Directly or via French < Latin *ablution-* < *abluere* 'wash away, wash clean' < *luere* 'wash'] —**ablutionary** *adj*

ably /áybli/ *adv* in a skilful or competent way

ABM *abbr* ARMS antiballistic missile

abn *abbr* airborne

ABN *n Aus* a numerical code assigned to a business so that it can be identified by the Australian Taxation Office and other government departments. Full form **Australian Business Number**

Abnaki *n, adj* PEOPLES another spelling of **Abenaki**

abnegate /ábni gayt/ (**-gates, -gating, -gated**) *vt* to give up or renounce something (*formal*) [Early 17C. < Latin *abnegat-*, past participle of *abnegare* 'refuse, reject' < *negare* 'deny'] —**abnegation** /ábni gáysh'n/ *n* —**abnegator** *n*

abnormal /ab náwrm'l/ *adj* unusual or unexpected, especially in a way that causes alarm or anxiety ○ *X-rays of the lung showed nothing abnormal.* [Mid-19C. < French *anormal* < Latin *abnormis* 'deviating from a rule'] —**abnormally** *adv*

abnormality /áb nawr mállәti/ (*plural* **-ties**) *n* **1.** a variation from the usual structure or function of the mind or body ○ *The blood test detected no abnormalities.* **2.** any condition that is not the usual or expected one

Abo /ábbō/ (*plural* **Abos**), **abo** (*plural* **abos**) *n Aus* a highly offensive term for an Aboriginal (*taboo*) [Early 20C. Shortening]

USAGE See *insult*.

aboard /ə báwrd/ *adv, prep* **1.** on, onto, in, or into a ship, aeroplane, train, or other vehicle **2.** in or into an organization or group (*informal*)

abode[1] /ə bṓd/ *n* (*literary*) **1.** the house or other place where somebody lives **2.** a period of living somewhere [13C. < ABIDE] ◇ **of no fixed abode** having no permanent place in which to live (*formal*)

abode[2] past participle, past tense of **abide**

abohm /ab ṓm/ *n* the centimetre-gram-second unit of electrical resistance equal to 10^{-9} ohms

abolish /ə bóllish/ (**-ishes, -ishing, -ished**) *vt* to put an end to something such as a law ○ *'Critics of advertising usually forget that if it were eliminated or abolished, other methods would necessarily be substituted for it.'* (Daniel Starch, *Principles of Advertising*; 1923) [15C. < French *aboliss-*, stem of *abolir* < Latin *abolere* 'destroy'] —**abolishable** *adj* —**abolisher** *n* —**abolishment** *n*

abolition /ábbə lísh'n/ *n* **1.** the act of officially ending a law, regulation, or practice **2.** *also* **Abolition** the official ending of the practice of slavery. In British territories the slave trade was abolished in 1807 and slavery in 1833. [Early 16C. Directly or via French < Latin *abolition-* < *abolere* 'destroy'] —**abolitionary** *adj*

abolitionist /abə lísh'nist/ *n* **1.** *also* **Abolitionist** an antislavery campaigner in the 18th and 19th centuries **2.** a supporter of the abolition of something, e.g. capital punishment —**abolitionism** *n*

abomasum /ábbō máyssəm/ (*plural* **-sa** /-sə/) *n* the fourth and final chamber of the digestive system of cattle and other ruminants, where enzymatic or true digestion takes place

A-bomb *n* ARMS same as **atom bomb** [Mid-20C. Contraction]

abominable /ə bómminəb'l/ *adj* **1.** extremely repugnant or offensive **2.** of very bad quality, or very unpleasant to experience [14C. Via Old French < Latin *abominabilis* < *abominari* 'shun something as being a bad omen' < *omen* 'omen'] —**abominably** *adv*

ORIGIN Between the 14th and the 17th centuries ***abominable*** was often spelt *abhominable* because of a widely held belief that it was derived from Latin *ab hominem*, literally 'away from humankind', hence 'unnatural, beastly'. Shakespeare puns on this sense when Hamlet speaks of incompetent actors who 'imitate humanity abominably'.

Abominable Snowman *n* same as **yeti**

abominate /ə bómmi nayt/ (**-nates, -nating, -nated**) *vt* to dislike and disapprove of somebody or something intensely (*formal*) [Mid-17C. < Latin *abominat-*, past participle of *abominari* (see ABOMINABLE)] —**abominator** *n*

abomination /ə bómmi náysh'n/ *n* **1.** SOMETHING HORRIBLE an object of intense disapproval or dislike **2.** SOMETHING SHAMEFUL something that is immoral, disgusting, or shameful **3.** INTENSE DISLIKE a feeling of intense dislike or disapproval towards somebody or something (*literary*)

aboral /ab áwrəl/ *adj* situated away from or opposite the mouth ○ *the aboral surface of a starfish*

aboriginal /ábbə ríjjinəl/ *adj* existing in a place from the earliest known times ■ *n* a member of a people who has lived in an area from the earliest known times [Mid-17C. < Latin *aborigines* (see ABORIGINE)] —**aboriginality** /ábbə rijji nállәti/ *n* —**aboriginally** *adv*

SYNONYMS See *native*.

Aboriginal *n* a descendant of any of the indigenous peoples who inhabited Australia before the arrival of European settlers —**Aboriginal** *adj*

aborigine /ábbə ríjjini/ *n* **1.** a member of a people who has lived in an area from the earliest known times (*often offensive*) **2.** an animal or plant that has existed in a place since earliest times [16C. Back-formation < Latin *aborigines*, the pre-Roman inhabitants of Latium < *ab origine* 'from the beginning']

Aborigine *n* a member of any of the indigenous peoples who inhabited Australia before the arrival of European settlers

aborning /ə báwrning/ *adv N Am* while being born, created, or realized

abort /ə báwrt/ (**aborts, aborting, aborted**) *v* **1.** *vt* REMOVE FOETUS to remove an embryo or foetus from the womb in order to end a pregnancy **2.** *vi* HAVE MISCARRIAGE to give birth to an embryo or foetus before its independent survival is possible. Survival is usually possible at about 24 weeks for human foetuses. (*technical*) **3.** *vti* END SOMETHING PREMATURELY to bring something to an end or come to an end at an early stage **4.** *vti* ABANDON MISSION to end a space flight or similar mission before it is completed **5.** *vti* COMPUT QUIT COMPUTER PROGRAM to abandon a computer program, command, or operation before it has fin-

ished [Mid-16C. < Latin *abort-*, past participle of *aboriri* 'miscarry' < *oriri* 'come into being']

abortifacient /ə báwrti fáysh'nt/ *adj* describes a drug or device that causes abortion —**abortifacient** *n*

abortion /ə báwrsh'n/ *n* **1.** **OPERATION TO END PREGNANCY** an operation or other intervention to end a pregnancy by removing an embryo or foetus from the womb **2.** MED same as **miscarriage** (sense 1) (*technical*) **3.** **OFFENSIVE TERM** an offensive term for something so badly done or made that it is a complete failure **4.** AEROSP **CANCELLATION OF MISSION** the ending of a flight or mission before it is completed

abortion doctor *n* a doctor whose job is to perform abortions

abortionist /ə báwrsh'nist/ *n* somebody who performs abortions. The term, used in the past often in contexts reflecting the former illegality of the procedure, is still used disapprovingly by some, but not by all, groups.

abortion pill *n* a drug that induces an abortion at a very early stage of pregnancy

abortion trauma syndrome *n* a set of symptoms associated with the period following an abortion including guilt, anxiety, depression, low self-esteem, eating and sleeping disorders, and suicidal thoughts

abortive /ə báwr tiv/ *adj* **1.** failing to reach completion **2.** describes an organ that has had its development terminated —**abortively** *adv*

ABO system *n* a system that classifies human blood by dividing it into the four groups A, B, AB, and O. Classification is based on the presence or absence of two chemical groups (**antigens**), A and B, on the red blood cells.

Aboukir, Bay of ➧ **Abukir, Bay of**

aboulia *n* PSYCHOL another spelling of **abulia**

abound /ə bównd/ (**abounds, abounding, abounded**) *vi* **1.** to be present in large numbers or quantities **2.** to contain something in large numbers or amounts [14C. Via Old French *abunder* < Latin *abundare* 'overflow' < *undare* 'surge' < *unda* 'wave'] —**abounding** *adj* —**aboundingly** *adv*

about /ə bówt/ CORE MEANING: a grammatical word that refers to different sides or aspects of something from some point of orientation ○ (prep) *a book about a dog* ○ (adv) *There's a lot of laziness about.*

1. *prep* **IN CONNECTION WITH** in connection with or relating to ○ *think about problems* **2.** *prep* **APPROXIMATELY** close to in number, time, or degree ○ *inviting about fifteen people* **3.** *prep* **DOING OR ATTENDING TO** with or in an activity ○ *go about your business* **4.** *prep* **CLOSE BY** situated, moving, or happening in all directions from a central point of reference ○ *frantic activity going on all about us* **5.** *prep, adv* **AT HAND** somewhere in a place or on a person ○ *I don't have any cash about me.* ○ *She must be about. I saw her a minute ago.* **6.** *adv, prep* **IN VARIOUS PLACES** positioned here and there ○ *scattered about the house* **7.** *adv, prep* **IN VARIOUS DIRECTIONS** from place to place in different directions or in no particular direction ○ *children running about everywhere* **8.** *adv* **IN CIRCULATION** available, prevalent, or in circulation ○ *There was never much money about.* **9.** *adv* **ALL AROUND** on every side of or all the way around ○ *'He proceeded to the banks of the Hudson, and looked about among the vessels.'* (Jules Verne, *Around the World in 80 Days*; 1873) **10.** *adv* **INTO REVERSED POSITION** in or to the opposite or a different direction ○ *the wrong way about* **11.** *adv* **ADDS EMPHASIS** used to emphasize a statement, usually when expressing impatience or anger (*informal*) ○ *Well, it's about time you showed up!* **12.** *adv* SAILING **TO OPPOSITE TACK** on or to the opposite tack [Old English *onbūtan* 'on or around the outside of' < *on* (see ON) + *būtan* (see BUT[1])] ◇ **be about** ⚠ to have something as an essential characteristic or be fundamentally equivalent to ○ *Being successful is all about energy, drive, and commitment.* ◇ **be about to** to be on the point of doing something ○ *The game was about to start.* ◇ **be what something** *or* **somebody is (all) about** ⚠ to be what something or somebody involves or has as a purpose (*informal*) ◇ **not about to** ⚠ used to emphasize that somebody is certainly not going to do something (*informal*) ○ *I'm not about to apologize!*

USAGE The use of the preposition ***about*** in *be about* meaning 'be fundamentally the equivalent of' in formal contexts is sometimes criticized. Avoid usages like these: *The main character in the novel is about power. She's about winning and nothing more.* Here, the contested use of ***about*** is an attempt to establish equivalent relationships, however vague they may be, among pairs of entities (i.e. *main character, she*) and the things those entities supposedly illustrate or represent (i.e. *power, winning*). Say instead: *The central interest of the main character in the novel is power. She is obsessed with winning and nothing more.*

USAGE See ***round***[2].

about-face *vi, n US* MIL same as **about-turn**

about-ship *vi* in sailing, to turn to a new tack

about-turn *vi* **TURN AROUND** to turn to face in the opposite direction (*usually used as a command*) ■ *n* **1.** **REVERSAL** a sudden and complete reversal of a previous opinion or policy **2.** **TURN** a turn to face in the opposite direction

above /ə búv/ CORE MEANING: a grammatical word indicating a position directly overhead, on top of, or higher than something ○ (prep) *The bird flew up above the trees.* ○ (adv) *gazing at the sky above*

1. *prep* **OVER** over, higher than, or on top of ○ *hanging over the fireplace* **2.** *prep, adv* **MORE THAN** greater than an amount or level ○ *100 pounds above the ideal body weight* **3.** *prep, adv* **SUPERIOR TO** higher in status or power ○ *You can rise above your station.* **4.** *prep* **TOO GOOD FOR** too good or important to be affected by or involved in something ○ *They felt they were above small town gossip.* **5.** *prep* **BEYOND** not subject to something negative such as criticism or reproach ○ *'He wanted her to know that here too his conduct should be above suspicion.'* (George Eliot, *Middlemarch*; 1872) **6.** *prep* **IN MORE RESPECTED POSITION THAN** in a position that is valued more or considered more important than other people or things ○ *We put the people above everything else.* **7.** *prep* **TOO DIFFICULT FOR** outside or beyond somebody's understanding ○ *The lecture was completely above me.* **8.** *prep* **LOUDER THAN** louder than or over another sound ○ *She couldn't hear him above the roar of the band.* **9.** *prep* **NORTH OF** lying north of a place ○ *a small town just above London* **10.** *prep* **UPSTREAM FROM** lying upstream from a place **11.** *adv, adj* **IN PREVIOUS PLACE IN WRITING** appearing previously in a piece of writing (*often used in hyphenated compounds*) ○ *using the information from the table above* **12.** *adv* RELIG **IN HEAVEN** to or in heaven (*literary*) **13.** *adv* **ON TOP** overhead, in a higher position, or on top [Old English *abufan* < *an* (see ON) + *bufan* 'above' < Indo-European] ◇ **above all** used to indicate the most important thing or the main point of a statement ◇ **get above yourself** to become conceited

aboveboard /ə búv báwrd/ *adj* honest, legal, and without deception ■ *adv also* **above board** honestly, legally, and without deception [Late 16C. Originally a gambling term indicating that the player's hands were above the gaming table and nothing was being concealed]

aboveground /ə búv grównd/ *adj* on or above the surface of the ground ○ *aboveground plant parts* ○ *aboveground tests*

above-mentioned *adj* written or listed above, or referred to previously ■ *n* a person previously referred to in a text

above-the-fold *adj* relating to the portion of a webpage that can be seen without scrolling downwards. Commercially this is the most valuable portion of the page, as it is seen by everybody who calls it up. ◊ **below-the-fold**

above-the-line *adj* **1.** describes the profit after taxation that a company makes on its ordinary activities **2.** describes advertising for which payment is made and for which a commission is paid to an advertising agency

above-the-title *adj* shown in film credits before the title is seen, and therefore in a starring role ○ *an above-the-title mention*

ab ovo /ab ṓvō/ *adv* from the very beginning [Late 16C. < Latin, 'from the egg']

abracadabra /àbbrəkə dábbrə/ *interj* **MAGIC WORD** used to ensure the supposed success of a magic trick (*used by magicians and conjurors*) ■ *n* **1.** **MAGIC SPELL** a supposedly magical charm or spell **2.** **GIBBERISH** deliberately nonsensical language [Mid-16C. Via Latin < Greek]

abrade /ə bráyd/ (**abrades, abrading, abraded**) *vti* to wear something away or be worn away by friction [Late 17C. < Latin *abradere* < *radere* 'scrape']

Abraham /áybrə ham/, **Abram** /áybrəm/ *n* in the Bible, the first patriarch, seen by Jews as the father of the Israelites through his son Isaac, and by Muslims, who call him Ibrahim, as the father of Arab peoples through his son Ishmael

Abraham, Plains of /áybrə ham/ plateau in eastern Canada, in the city of Quebec, on the St Lawrence River. It was the scene of a battle between British and French forces in 1759.

Abrahams /áybrə hamz/, **Harold** (1899–1978) British athlete. His victory in the 100 metres at the 1924 Paris Olympic Games was featured in the film *Chariots of Fire* (1981).

Abram *n* BIBLE another spelling of **Abraham**

abrasion /ə bráyzh'n/ *n* **1.** **WEARING AWAY** the process of wearing away by friction **2.** MED **SCRAPED AREA OF SKIN** an area on the skin, or some other surface of the body, that has been damaged by scraping or rubbing ○ *dental abrasion* **3.** GEOG **WEARING AWAY OF ROCK** the erosion of bedrock by continuous friction caused by rock fragments in water, wind, or ice [Mid-17C. < Latin *abrasion-* < *abras-* (see ABRASIVE)]

abrasive /ə bráyssiv/ *adj* **1.** **USING FRICTION** using friction and roughness of texture to smooth or clean a surface ○ *an abrasive cleaner* **2.** **HARSH IN MANNER** aggressively direct and insensitive ■ *n* **SMOOTHING SUBSTANCE** a substance such as pumice or emery that is used to smooth or polish a surface by grinding or scraping [Mid-19C. < Latin *abras-*, past participle of *abradere* (see ABRADE)]

abreact /àbbri ákt/ (**-acts, -acting, -acted**) *vt* to release unconscious psychological tension by talking about or reliving the events that caused it —**abreaction** *n*

abreast /ə brést/ *adv* side by side and facing the front ■ *adj* up to date with something

~~abreviation~~ incorrect spelling of **abbreviation**

abridge /ə bríj/ (**abridges, abridging, abridged**) *vt* **1.** **SHORTEN SOMETHING** to shorten a text, e.g. by cutting or summarizing it ○ *abridged for television in three episodes* **2.** **CUT SOMETHING SHORT** to reduce something in scope or extent ○ *They abridged the meeting as best they could.* **3.** **RESTRICT SOMEBODY'S RIGHTS** to deprive somebody of rights or privileges (*archaic*) [14C. Via Old French *abreg(i)er* < Latin *abbreviare* 'shorten' < *brevis* 'short'] —**abridgable** *adj* —**abridged** *adj* —**abridger** *n* —**abridgment** *n*

abroad /ə bráwd/ *adv* **1.** **AWAY FROM YOUR OWN COUNTRY** in or to another country or other countries **2.** **IN CIRCULATION** in public or into general circulation **3.** **EVERYWHERE** over a wide area **4.** **OFF TARGET** wide of the mark (*literary*) **5.** *Ireland* **NOT AT HOME** away from your house or home ■ *n* **OTHER COUNTRIES** countries other than a specific one

~~abroard~~ incorrect spelling of **abroad**

abrogate /ábbrə gayt/ (**-gates, -gating, -gated**) *vt* to end an agreement or contract formally and publicly (*formal*) [Early 16C. < Latin *abrogat-*, past participle of *abrogare* 'repeal a law' < *rogare* 'ask, propose a law'] —**abrogation** /àbbrə gáysh'n/ *n*

SYNONYMS See ***nullify***.

abrupt /ə brúpt/ *adj* **1.** **SUDDEN** sudden and unexpected **2.** **BRUSQUE** brief and making no effort to be friendly **3.** **STEEP** with a sudden steep slope **4.** **DISCONNECTED** not passing smoothly from topic to topic [Late 16C. < Latin *abruptus* 'broken off, steep', past participle of *abrumpere* 'break off' < *rumpere* 'break'] —**abruptly** *adv* —**abruptness** *n*

abruption /ə brúpsh'n/ *n* the sudden breaking off of a part from a larger mass (*formal*) [Early 17C. < Latin *abruption-* < *abruptus* (see ABRUPT)]

Abruzzi /ə bróotsi/ agricultural region of central southern Italy consisting of the provinces of L'Aquila, Chieti, Pescara, and Teramo. Area: 10,795 sq. km/4,168 sq. mi. Population: 1,279,016 (2000).

abs /abz/ *npl* the abdominal muscles, or exercises done to firm them (*informal*) [Late 20C. Shortening]

ABS[1] *n* a type of strong plastic **(copolymer)**. Use: moulded casings, pipes, car parts. Full form **acrylonitrile-butadiene-styrene**

ABS[2] *n* a system of electronically controlled brakes that prevents a vehicle's wheels locking if the driver brakes suddenly. Full form **antilock braking system**

Absalom /ábssələm/ *n* in the Bible, the third son of David, King of Israel. He rebelled against his father and was killed by Joab (2 Samuel 13–18).

abscess /áb sess/ *n* a pus-filled cavity resulting from inflammation and usually caused by bacterial infection ■ *vi* **(-scesses, -scessing, -scessed)** to form an abscess, or be the site where one develops [Mid-16C. < Latin *abscessus* < *abscedere* 'go away' (referring to bodily humours going away in the pus) < *cedere* 'go'] —**abscessed** *adj*

abscisic acid /ab síssik-/ *n* a plant hormone that promotes leaf and fruit fall, and dormancy in seeds and buds

abscissa /ab síssə/ (*plural* **-sas** or **-sae** /-see/) *n* in mathematics, the horizontal coordinate or x-coordinate of a point in a two-dimensional system of Cartesian coordinates. It is the distance from the vertical axis or y-axis measured along a line parallel to the horizontal axis or x-axis. [Late 17C. < modern Latin *abscissa linea* 'line cut off']

abscission /ab sísh'n/ *n* **1.** the act of suddenly cutting something off **2.** the natural process by which leaves or other parts are shed from a plant [Early 17C. < Latin *abscission-* < *abscindere* 'cut off' < *scindere* 'cut up, divide']

abscond /əb skónd, ab-/ **(-sconds, -sconding, -sconded)** *vi* **1.** to run away secretly, especially in order to avoid arrest or prosecution **2.** to escape from a place of detention [Mid-16C. < Latin *abscondere* 'hide or put away' < *condere* 'stow'] —**absconder** *n*

abseil /áb sayl/ *vi* **(-seils, -seiling, -seiled)** to descend a steep slope or vertical face using a rope that is secured at the top and passed around the body ■ *n* a descent of a steep slope or vertical face by abseiling ▶ N Am term (all senses) **rappel** [Mid-20C. < German *abseilen* < *ab* 'down' + *Seil* 'rope'] —**abseiler** *n* —**abseiling** *n*

absence /áb'snss/ *n* **1. NOT BEING PRESENT** the fact of somebody's not being in a specific place ○ *took note of certain people's absence* **2. TIME AWAY** a period during which somebody is away ○ *returning after a short absence* **3. NONEXISTENCE** the lack or nonexistence of a quality or feature ○ *in the absence of any fresh information* [14C. Via French < Latin *absentia* < *abesse* (see ABSENT[1])] ◇ **absence makes the heart grow fonder** separation makes love or affection for somebody grow stronger

~~**absense**~~ incorrect spelling of **absence**

absent[1] /ábs'nt/ *adj* **1.** not attending a place or event, especially when expected to ○ *absent from school* **2.** not paying attention ○ *His face took on an absent expression.* [14C. < Latin *absent-*, present participle of *abesse* 'be away' < *esse* 'be']

absent[2] /ab sént/ **(-sents, -senting, -sented)** *vr* **absent yourself** to stay away from or leave something such as an event or occasion ○ *absented themselves from the meeting* [14C. Directly or via French *absenter* < Latin *absentare* 'keep or be away' < *absent-* (see ABSENT[1])]

absentee /áb s'n teé/ *n* somebody who is not present at an event

absentee ballot *n* N Am POL same as **postal vote**

absenteeism /áb s'n teé izəm/ *n* persistent absence from work or some other place without good reason

absentee landlord *n* a landlord who lives away from the accommodation or land rented out, especially one who neglects the needs of tenants

absently /áb s'ntli/ *adv* in an inattentive or absent-minded way

absent-minded *adj* tending to be preoccupied or forgetful —**absent-mindedly** *adv* —**absent-mindedness** *n*

absent without leave *adj* absent from military duties without permission, but not assumed to have deserted

absinthe /ábssinth/, **absinth** *n* **1.** a highly alcoholic liqueur tasting of aniseed and made from wormwood and herbs. Absinthe is now banned in many countries because of its toxicity. **2.** PLANTS same as **wormwood** (sense 1) [Early 17C. Via French < Greek *apsinthion* 'wormwood']

absolute /ábssə loot/ *adj* **1. ADDS EMPHASIS** used to give strong emphasis to what is being said ○ *an absolute disaster* **2. UNBOUNDED** to the very greatest degree possible ○ *absolute confidence in her ability to win* **3. UNEQUIVOCAL** completely unequivocal and not capable of being viewed as partial or relative ○ *absolute proof* **4. INDEPENDENT AND UNMODIFIABLE** not depending on or qualified by anything else ○ *absolute truth* **5. POSSESSING UNLIMITED POWER** having total power and authority ○ *an absolute monarch* **6.** GRAM **INDEPENDENT OF SENTENCE SYNTAX** not syntactically dependent on the main clause of a sentence, e.g. 'It being sunny' in the sentence 'It being sunny, they went to the pool' **7.** GRAM **WITHOUT DIRECT OBJECT** used without an explicit direct object. The usage of 'satisfy' is absolute in the sentence 'We aim to satisfy'. **8.** GRAM **USED AS NOUN** used without an explicit noun. 'The rich and the poor' are absolute adjectival uses. **9.** PHYS **MEASURED RELATIVE TO VACUUM** involving or relating to measurements made relative to the vacuum state **10.** PHYS **ACCORDING TO STANDARDIZED MEASURES** relating to or using basic units of length, time, mass, and charge **11.** PHYS **MEASURED RELATIVE TO ABSOLUTE ZERO** measured on or relating to a scale that has as its lowest temperature absolute zero, the point at which all molecular motion ceases **12.** LAW **FULL AND UNCONDITIONAL** complete and in no way conditional on any future evidence or behaviour ○ *an absolute pardon* **13.** LAW **OWNED OUTRIGHT** having unconditional ownership of a title or property, unrestricted by trusts or entails (*often used after a noun*) **14.** MATHS **ALWAYS TRUE ALGEBRAICALLY** true for all values of a variable in an algebraic expression **15.** MATHS **CONSTANT IN VALUE** not changing in value in varying mathematical expressions **16.** MATHS **WITHOUT VARIABLES** not containing an algebraic variable ■ *n* **1. UNQUESTIONABLE RULE** a principle or value that is held to be always true or valid **2.** *also* **Absolute** PHILOSOPHY **ULTIMATE REALITY** in some schools of philosophy, the one ultimate reality that does not depend on anything, and is not relative to anything else [14C. < Latin *absolutus*, past participle of *absolvere* 'set free' (see ABSOLVE)]

absolute ceiling *n* the maximum height above sea level at which an aircraft can maintain horizontal flight

absolutely /ábssə lootli, -lóotli/ *adv* **1.** ⚠ **ADDS EMPHASIS** used to give strong emphasis to what is being said **2.** ⚠ **THAT'S RIGHT** used in speech or dialogue as an emphatic way of agreeing with the other speaker ○ *Absolutely!* **3. NOT IN RELATIVE WAY** in a way that is independent of circumstances and never variable or modified **4.** GRAM **WITH NO GRAMMATICAL OBJECT** used syntactically with an implied direct object or noun head **5.** LAW **UNCONDITIONALLY** with no conditions or restrictions, especially constitutional or legal ones

USAGE Some people dislike the use of ***absolutely*** to give strong emphasis (*That is absolutely disgraceful.*). Also controversial is its use to express agreement. It retains some meaning in uses such as *'Do you like it?' 'Yes, absolutely'*, but is simply an intensifier when used with answers that are factual rather than expressing an opinion: *'Have you been to Paris?' 'Yes, absolutely'*.

absolute majority *n* the winning total of votes that amounts to more than half of the votes cast

absolute music *n* music whose meaning is derived solely from the music itself and that does not evoke another source, e.g. a visual scene

absolute pitch *n* **1.** the ability to identify the pitch of a single note without reference to any other sound **2.** the exact pitch a tone is expected to have, measured by its number of vibrations per second

absolute temperature *n* temperature derived from the laws of thermodynamics rather than being primarily derived from properties of substances

absolute value *n* **1.** the magnitude of a number, irrespective of whether it is positive or negative, symbolized by placing the number within vertical bars, thus $|7| = |-7| = 7$ **2.** MATHS same as **modulus**

absolute zero *n* the temperature at which hypothetically all molecular motion ceases, equal to 0 degrees K and equivalent to -273.16°C or -459.69°F

absolution /ábssə ló͝osh'n/ *n* **1.** forgiveness for somebody's sins, especially when formally given in a Christian church **2.** a spoken blessing used in a Christian church to grant absolution to somebody [13C. Via French < Latin *absolution-* 'acquittal, perfection' < *absolutus* (see ABSOLUTE)]

absolutism /ábssə lootizəm/ *n* **1. POLITICAL SYSTEM** a political system in which the power of a ruler is unchecked and absolute **2.** PHILOSOPHY **THEORY OF OBJECTIVE VALUES** a philosophical theory in which values such as truth or morality are absolute and not conditional upon human perception **3. SOMETHING ABSOLUTE** a standard, principle, or theory that is absolute **4.** CHR **PREDESTINATION** a strict form of the doctrine of predestination —**absolutist** *n, adj*

absolve /əb zólv/ **(-solves, -solving, -solved)** *vt* **1. PRONOUNCE SOMEBODY BLAMELESS** to state publicly or officially that somebody is not guilty and not to be held responsible **2. RELIEVE SOMEBODY OF OBLIGATION** to release somebody from an obligation or requirement **3. FORGIVE SOMEBODY** to forgive somebody's sins, especially formally in a Christian church service or sacrament [15C. < Latin *absolvere* 'set free' < *solvere* 'loosen'] —**absolvable** *adj* —**absolver** *n*

absorb /əb sáwrb, -záwrb/ **(-sorbs, -sorbing, -sorbed)** *vt* **1. TAKE SOMETHING UP OR IN** to soak up a liquid or take in nutrients or chemicals gradually **2. NOT TRANSMIT SOMETHING** to take up light, noise, or energy and not transmit it at all ○ *built to absorb the shock of a collision* **3. TAKE SOMETHING IN MENTALLY** to see, read, or hear something and understand it fully ○ *He hasn't yet absorbed the news.* **4. ENGROSS SOMEBODY** to hold somebody's attention or occupy somebody's time completely **5. INCORPORATE SOMETHING INTO WHOLE** to incorporate something into a larger entity in such a way that it loses much of its own identity ○ *The islands were later absorbed into the Roman Empire.* **6. ADAPT TO SOMETHING** to adapt to a changing situation without being adversely affected **7. NOT PASS COSTS ON** to accept increased costs without passing them on to somebody else ○ *forced to absorb the cost of tax increases* **8. REQUIRE SOMETHING IN QUANTITY** to require something in considerable quantities, usually without significant results ○ *absorbing a huge amount of money* [15C. Via French *absorber* < Latin *absorbere* 'swallow' < *sorbere* 'suck in'] —**absorbable** *adj* —**absorbed** *adj* —**absorber** *n*

absorbance /əb sáwrbənss, -záwrb-/ *n* the capacity of a substance to absorb radiation. Symbol **A**

absorbent /əb sáwrbənt, -záwrb-/ *adj* **1.** capable of soaking up liquid **2.** capable of absorbing light, noise, or energy instead of reflecting it (*often used in combination*) ○ *shock-absorbent* [Early 18C. < Latin *absorbent-*, present participle of *absorbere* 'swallow' (see ABSORB)] —**absorbency** *n*

absorbent cotton *n* N Am same as **cotton wool** (sense 1)

absorbing /əb sáwrbing, -záwrb-/ *adj* extremely interesting and therefore occupying the attention completely —**absorbingly** *adv*

~~**absorbtion**~~ incorrect spelling of **absorption**

absorptance /əb sáwrptənss, -záwrp-/ *n* a measure of the ability of an object or substance to absorb radiant energy, equal to the ratio of the absorbed energy to the total energy reaching the object or substance. Symbol α [Mid-20C. < Latin *absorptus* (see ABSORPTION)]

absorption /əb sáwrpsh'n, -záwrp-/ *n* **1. PREOCCUPATION** a state in which the whole attention is occupied **2. SOAKING UP** the uptake of liquid into the fibres of a substance **3. INCORPORATION** the incorporation of something into a larger group or entity **4.** PHYSIOL **ASSIMILATION BY BODY** the passage of material through the lining of the intestine into the blood or through a cell membrane into a cell **5.** PHYS **ABILITY OF SUBSTANCE TO ABSORB ENERGY** the ability of a substance to absorb light, noise, or energy, or the fact that it does so **6.** PHYS **REDUCTION IN RADIATED ENERGY** the reduction in intensity of radiated energy within a medium, caused by converting some or all of the energy into another form **7.** IMMUNOL **REMOVAL OF ANTIBODIES** the elimination of antibodies or antigens by the use of a chemical reagent [Late 16C. < Latin *absorption-* < *absorptus*, past participle of *absorbere* 'swallow' (see ABSORB)] —**absorptive** *adj*

absorption spectrum *n* the pattern of dark bands that is seen when electromagnetic radiation passes through an absorbing medium and is observed with a spectroscope. It is the result of unequal absorption of the radiation as it passes through the medium.

absquatulate /ab skwóttyōō layt/ (-lates, -lating, -lated) *vi US* to leave, especially in a hurry or under suspicious circumstances (*archaic or humorous*) [Mid-19C. < Latin *ab* 'away' + SQUAT¹ + -*ulate* (as in CONGRATULATE)]

abstain /əb stáyn/ (-stains, -staining, -stained) *vi* 1. not to vote for or against a proposal when a vote is held 2. to choose not to do something [14C. Via Old French *abstenir* < Latin *abstinere* 'hold yourself away' < *tenere* 'hold'] —**abstainer** *n*

abstemious /əb stéemi əss/ *adj* not indulging in or characterized by excessive eating or drinking [Early 17C. < Latin *abstemius* < *abs-* 'away from' + *temetum* 'intoxicating liquor'] —**abstemiously** *adv* —**abstemiousness** *n*

abstention /əb sténsh'n/ *n* 1. a refusal to vote either for or against a proposal 2. the deliberate choice not to do something [Early 16C. < late Latin *abstention-* < Latin *abstentus*, past participle of *abstinere* (see ABSTAIN)]

abstinence /ábstinənss/ *n* restraint from indulging a desire for something, e.g. alcohol or sexual relations [14C. Via Old French < Latin *abstinentia* < *abstinent-*, present participle of *abstinere* (see ABSTAIN)] —**abstinent** *adj* —**abstinently** *adv*

abstract *adj* /áb strakt/ 1. NOT CONCRETE not relating to concrete objects but expressing something that can only be appreciated intellectually 2. THEORETICAL based on general principles or theories rather than on specific instances ○ *abstract arguments* 3. ARTS NONREPRESENTATIONAL not aiming to depict an object but composed with the focus on internal structure and form 4. MUSIC CONCEPTUAL describes music that is intended to have no programmatic or emotional content 5. IRREGULARLY PATTERNED decorated with irregular areas of colour that do not represent anything concrete 6. IMPERSONAL emotionally detached or distanced from something ■ *n* /áb strakt/ 1. SUMMARY a summary of a longer text, especially of an academic article 2. INTELLECTUAL CONCEPT a concept or term that does not refer to a concrete object but denotes a quality, emotion, or idea 3. ARTS ABSTRACT ARTWORK a work of art, especially a painting, in an abstract style ■ *vt* /əb strákt/ (-stracts, -stracting, -stracted) 1. CONCEPTUALIZE SOMETHING to develop a line of thought from a concrete reality to a general principle or an intellectual idea 2. SUMMARIZE SOMETHING to make a summary of the main points of an argument or text 3. EXTRACT SOMETHING to remove something from a place, usually with some difficulty 4. STEAL SOMETHING to steal something by taking it unobtrusively (*used euphemistically*) 5. ENVIRON PUMP WATER to remove water from a river or other source for industrial use [14C. < Latin *abstractus*, past participle of *abstrahere* 'drag away' < *trahere* 'drag'] —**abstracted** *adj* —**abstractedly** *adv* —**abstracter** /áb straktər/ *n* —**abstractly** *adv* —**abstractness** *n*

abstract expressionism *n* a school of painting, originating in New York in the 1940s, that combined abstract forms with spontaneity of artistic expression

abstraction /əb stráksh'n/ *n* 1. GENERALIZED CONCEPT a generalized idea or theory developed from concrete examples of events 2. GENERALIZING PROCESS the formation of general ideas or concepts from concrete examples 3. PREOCCUPATION a state in which somebody is deep in thought and not concentrating on his or her surroundings 4. PHILOSOPHY CONCEPTUALIZATION the philosophical process by which people develop concepts either from experience or from other concepts 5. ART ABSTRACT ART an abstract painting or sculpture 6. EXTRACTION the removal or theft of something, usually with some difficulty 7. ENVIRON PUMPING OF WATER FROM RIVER the removal of water from a river or other source for industrial use

abstractionism /əb stráksh'nizəm/ *n* the principles and practice of abstract art —**abstractionist** *n*

abstract noun *n* a noun signifying a concept, quality, or other abstract idea

abstract of title *n* a summary of the details of the ownership of a piece of land

abstruse /əb strōóss/ *adj* difficult to understand [Late 16C. Directly or via French < Latin *abstrusus*, past participle of *abstrudere* 'thrust away' < *trudere* 'thrust'] —**abstrusely** *adv* —**abstruseness** *n*

SYNONYMS See *obscure*.

absurd /əb súrd/ *adj* 1. LUDICROUS ridiculous because of being irrational, incongruous, or illogical ○ *an absurd notion* 2. PHILOSOPHY MEANINGLESS lacking any meaning that would give purpose to life ○ *the notion that existence is absurd* ■ *n also* **Absurd** MEANINGLESSNESS the condition of living in a meaningless universe where life has no purpose, especially as a concept in some 20th-century philosophical movements [Mid-16C. Via French < Latin *absurdus* 'inharmonious', literally 'away from the (right) sound'] —**absurdly** *adv* —**absurdness** *n*

absurdism /əb súrdizəm/, **Absurdism** *n* the idea that the universe is without meaning or rational order and that human beings, in attempting to find a sense of order, conflict with it —**absurdist** *n, adj*

absurdity /əb súrdəti/ (*plural* -**ties**) *n* 1. ridiculousness because of being irrational, incongruous, or illogical 2. something that is ridiculous because of being irrational, incongruous, or illogical

ABTA /ábtə/ *abbr* Association of British Travel Agents

Abu Bakr /ə bōō bákər/ (570?–634) Arabian religious leader who was the first caliph of Islam. He was responsible for uniting Arabia and spreading Islam.

Abu Dhabi /ábbōō daábi/ capital of the United Arab Emirates, on the island of Abu Dhabi in the Persian Gulf. Population: 904,000 (1999).

Abuja /ə bōōjə/ official capital of Nigeria since December 1991. It is located in the Federal Capital Territory in central Nigeria. Population: 403,000 (1999).

Abukir, Bay of /ábbōō keer/, **Aboukir**, **Abū Qīr** bay in the Nile Delta that was the site of Lord Nelson's defeat of the French fleet in 1798

abulia /ə byóoli ə, ə bóoli ə/, **aboulia** /ə bóoli ə/ *n* a lack of will or motivation, usually manifested as an inability to make decisions or to set goals [Mid-19C. < Greek < *a-* 'without, not' + *boulē* 'will'] —**abulic** *adj*

abundance /ə búndənss/ *n* 1. LARGE AMOUNT a more than plentiful quantity of something ○ *the abundance of art treasures in Florence* ○ *food and drink in abundance* 2. AFFLUENCE a lifestyle with more than adequate material provisions ○ *living in careless abundance* 3. FULLNESS a fullness of spirit that overflows ○ *the abundance of her soul* 4. CHEM, GEOL RATE OF INCIDENCE the extent to which an element is present in the earth or in a rock 5. PHYS PROPORTION OF ISOTOPE ATOMS the proportion of one isotope of an element, expressed by number of atoms, to the total quantity of the element [14C. Via Old French < Latin *abundantia* < *abundant-* (see ABUNDANT)]

abundant /ə búndənt/ *adj* 1. present in great quantities 2. providing a more than plentiful supply of something ○ *abundant in natural resources* [14C. < Latin *abundant-*, present participle of *abundare* 'overflow' (see ABOUND)] —**abundantly** *adv*

~~**abundent**~~ incorrect spelling of **abundant**

Abū Qīr, Bay of ♦ Abukir, Bay of

abuse *n* /ə byōóss/ 1. MALTREATMENT the physical, psychological, or sexual maltreatment of a person or animal 2. IMPROPER USE the illegal, improper, or harmful use of something ○ *allegations of abuse of government powers* 3. IMPROPER PRACTICE an illegal, improper, or harmful practice ○ *human rights abuses* 4. INSULTS insulting or offensive language 5. DRUG USE the harmful use of drugs or alcohol ■ *v* /ə byōóz/ (**abuses, abusing, abused**) 1. *vt* MALTREAT SOMEBODY to treat a person or animal cruelly, whether physically, psychologically, or sexually, especially on a regular or habitual basis 2. *vt* MISUSE SOMETHING to use something in an improper, illegal, or harmful way 3. *vt* INSULT SOMEBODY to speak insultingly or offensively to somebody 4. **abuse yourself** *vr* MASTURBATE to masturbate (*disapproving*) [15C. Via French *abus* < Latin *abusus*, past participle of *abuti* 'use up, misuse' < *uti* 'use'] —**abuser** /ə byōózər/ *n*

SYNONYMS See *mistreat* and *misuse*.

Abu Simbel: Great Temple of Rameses II

Abu Simbel /ábbōō símb'l/ site of two carved rock temples in southern Egypt, built in the reign of Rameses II in the 13th century BC. They were moved to higher ground in the 1960s to avoid possible damage from the construction of the Aswan High Dam.

abusive /ə byóossiv/ *adj* 1. INSULTING intended to insult or offend somebody ○ *abusive language* 2. HARMFUL involving physical, psychological, or sexual maltreatment ○ *an abusive relationship* 3. WRONGFUL involving illegal, improper, or harmful activities ○ *using abusive methods to secure power* —**abusively** *adv* —**abusiveness** *n*

abut /ə bút/ (**abuts, abutting, abutted**) *vti* to touch or be adjacent to something along one side [15C. Partly < Anglo-Latin *abuttare* < *butta* 'ridge or strip of land'; partly < Old French *aboter* 'aim at' < *boter* 'strike' < Germanic] —**abutter** *n*

abutilon /ə byóotilən/ *n* a tropical plant or bush. Flowers: red, yellow, or white, bell-shaped. Genus: *Abutilon*. [Late 16C. Via modern Latin < Arabic *ubutilun*]

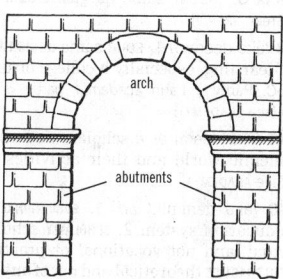
abutment (sense 4)

abutment /ə bútmənt/ *n* 1. ADJACENCY the state of touching or being adjacent to an object or piece of land along one side 2. MEETING POINT the point at which two things abut 3. MAKING THINGS ABUT the positioning of two things so that they abut 4. SUPPORT STRUCTURE a structure that supports or bears the thrust of something

abuttal /ə bútt'l/ *n* same as **abutment** (senses 1–2) ■ **abuttals** *npl* the boundaries of a piece of land in relation to an adjoining piece of land (*standard*)

abuzz /ə búz/ *adj* full of lively conversation or activity

abvolt /áb vōlt/ *n* the centimetre-gram-second unit of electromotive force or potential difference equal to 10^{-8} of a volt [Mid-20C. < *ab-*, abbreviation of ABSOLUTE + VOLT¹]

abwatt /áb wot/ *n* the centimetre-gram-second unit of electrical power, equal to one ten millionth (10^{-7}) of a watt

abysmal /ə bízm'l/ *adj* 1. extremely bad or severe 2. similar in depth to that of an abyss [Mid-17C. < *abysm*, via Old French < medieval Latin *abysmus*, alteration of late Latin *abyssus* (see ABYSS)] —**abysmally** *adv*

abyss /ə bíss/ *n* 1. CHASM a chasm or gorge so deep that its extent is not visible 2. ENDLESS SPACE something that is immeasurably deep or infinite 3. TERRIBLE SITUATION a situation of apparently unending awfulness 4. HELL thought of as a bottomless pit [14C. Via late Latin *abyssus* < Greek *abussos* 'bottomless' < *bussos* 'bottom']

abyssal /ə bíss'l/ adj found in the very deepest areas of the oceans or on the deep ocean floor

abyssal plain n a broad flat area of seafloor at the deepest part of an ocean basin

Abyssinia /ábbə sínni ə/ former name for **Ethiopia** — **Abyssinian** adj, n

Abyssinian cat n a short-haired domestic cat belonging to a breed with dark brown or black markings on its brown coat

abyssopelagic /ə bíssō pə lájjik/ adj relating to or living in the water just above the deep ocean floor [< Greek abussos 'abyss' (see ABYSS) + pelagikos 'of the sea' (see PELAGIC)]

Abzug /áb tsoog/, **Bella** (1920–98) US feminist, lawyer, and politician. She was an outspoken critic of the Vietnam War and an advocate for civil and minority rights and feminism, an agenda she vigorously pursued as a Democratic US Representative (1970–76). Born **Savitsky, Bella**

ac abbr (used in Internet addresses) **1.** academic organization **2.** Ascension Island ▶ see table at **domain name**

Ac symbol CHEM ELEM actinium

AC abbr **1.** ELEC ENG alternating current **2.** ATHLETICS Athletic Club (used in club names) **3.** air conditioning **4.** WINE appellation contrôlée **5.** ante Christum (used before dates)

ac- prefix same as **ad-** (used before c, k, and q)

-ac suffix person affected with a particular condition ○ amnesiac [Via modern Latin -acus < Greek -akos]

a/c abbr **1.** account **2.** account current

A/C abbr **1.** ACCT account **2.** ACCT account current **3.** air conditioning

acacia /ə káyshə/ (plural **-cias** or same) n **1.** a bush or tree that has narrow leaves and dark fruit pods. Flowers: small, yellow. Native to: tropics, subtropics. Genus: Acacia. **2.** a tree or plant similar to the acacia **3.** INDUST same as **gum arabic** [14C. Via Latin < Greek akakia]

academe /ákə deem/ n **1.** EDUC same as **academia 2.** a place of learning, especially a college or university [Late 16C. Partly < Latin academia, partly < Greek Akadēmeia (see ACADEMY)]

academia /ákə deémi ə/ n scholars and students of the academic world and their activities [Mid-20C. < Latin (see ACADEMY)]

academic /ákə démmik/ adj **1.** EDUCATIONAL relating to the education system **2.** SCHOLARLY scholarly and intellectual, and not vocational or practical **3.** IRRELEVANT IN PRACTICE theoretical and not of any practical relevance **4.** NOT LIVELY dry and intellectual in approach, concentrating on structure, form, or historical conventions ■ n **1.** UNIVERSITY TEACHER somebody teaching or conducting research at an institution of higher learning **2.** SCHOLARLY PERSON somebody with a scholarly background or attitudes —**academical** adj —**academically** adv

academic dress n formal garments for students or university staff, usually including a gown and hood

academician /ə káddə mísh'n/ n a member of an academy or society concerned with the arts or sciences

academicism /ákə démməsizəm/, **academism** /ə káddəmizəm/ n a reliance on conventional artistic techniques or an emphasis on the formal aspects of an art form such as painting or poetry

academic year n the annual cycle of teaching and study at an educational institution. It usually starts part of the way through the calendar year and is divided into sessions or terms.

academism n ARTS same as **academicism**

academy /ə káddəmi/ (plural **-mies**) n **1.** SOCIETY a formal society whose purpose is to promote a particular aspect of knowledge or culture **2.** SPECIALIZED SCHOOL an educational institution devoted to a particular subject **3.** SCHOOL NAME a secondary school, often a private one (usually used in school names) [Mid-16C. Via Latin academia < Greek Akadēmeia, the school of philosophy founded by Plato, after the park on the outskirts of Athens where he taught]

Academy n the school Plato founded to teach his philosophy

Academy Award n an award given annually by the Academy of Motion Picture Arts and Sciences in the United States for work in film-making or acting

Acadia /ə káydi ə/ n former French colony in North America that encompassed present-day New Brunswick, Nova Scotia, Prince Edward Island, and parts of Quebec and New England —**Acadian** n, adj

Acadian orogeny n the stage of mountain formation that occurred in the Appalachian Mountains of the United States during the Devonian Period

acalculia /áy kal kyóoli ə/ n an inability, or the loss of the ability, to carry out basic arithmetical calculations [Early 20C. < A-² + Latin calculare (see CALCULATE)]

acanthi PLANTS, ARCHIT plural of **acanthus**

acantho- prefix thorn ○ acanthopterygian [< Greek akanthos 'thorn plant' (see ACANTHUS)]

acanthocephalan /ə kánthō séffələn/ n ZOOL same as **spiny-headed worm** [Mid-19C. < ACANTHO- + Greek kephalē 'head' (see CEPHALO-)] —**acanthocephalan** adj

acanthopterygian /ákən thoptə ríjji ən/ n a fish with toothed scales and spiny rays on the fins, e.g. a mackerel, perch, or bass. Superorder: Acanthopterygii. [Mid-19C. < Greek akantha 'thorn' + pterugion 'fin', literally 'small wing' < pterux 'wing'] —**acanthopterygian** adj

acanthus

acanthus /ə kánthəss/ (plural **-thuses** or **-thi** /-ī/ or same) n **1.** a spiny-leaved bush or perennial plant. Flowers: white, purple. Native to: Mediterranean. Genus: Acanthus. **2.** a design characteristic of the capital of a Corinthian column, representing acanthus leaves [Mid-16C. Via Latin < Greek akanthos < akantha 'thorn']

a cappella /aàkə péllə, ákə-/ adv, adj unaccompanied by musical instruments [Late 19C. < Italian, 'in chapel style', that is, 'in the style of church music']

Acapulco /ákə póolkō/ seaport and resort on the Pacific coast in southern Mexico. Population: 722,499 (2000).

acari ZOOL plural of **acarus**

acariasis /ákə rí əssiss/ n infestation of the skin with mites or ticks

acaricide /ə kárri sīd/ n a substance that kills mites or ticks

acarid /ákərid/ n a mite or tick. Order: Acarina.

acaroid resin /ákəroyd-/, **acaroid gum** n a red resin exuded by some grass trees. Use: varnishes, coatings for paper.

acarology /ákə rólləji/ n the study of mites and ticks — **acarologist** n

acarophobia /ákərə fóbi ə/ n an irrational fear of mites or ticks

acarus /ákərəss/ (plural **-ri** /-rī/) n a mite or tick (technical) [Mid-17C. Via modern Latin < Greek akari 'mite', literally 'too short to cut, tiny' < kar- 'cut']

ACAS /áy kass/, **Acas** n an organization that mediates between employers and employees or trade unions in industrial disputes. Full form **Advisory, Conciliation, and Arbitration Service**

acatalectic /áy kattə léktik/ adj having the full number of syllables in the final foot of a line of verse ■ n a line of verse that has the full number of syllables in the final foot [Late 16C. Via Latin acatalecticus < Greek akatalēktos 'complete' < katalēktos 'incomplete']

acaudal /ay káwd'l/, **acaudate** /-dayt/ adj without a tail (technical)

acaulescent /áy kaw léss'nt, ákaw-/ adj having no stem or one that is very short

acc. abbr **1.** ACCT account **2.** GRAM accusative

acca /ákə/ n Aus somebody who teaches or undertakes research at an institution of higher education (informal) [Shortening of ACADEMIC]

~~accademic~~ incorrect spelling of **academic**

ACCC /áy trípp'l see/ abbr Aus Australian Competition and Consumer Commission

accede /ək seéd/ (**-cedes, -ceding, -ceded**) vi **1.** ASSENT to give consent or agreement to something **2.** COME TO POWER to attain an important and powerful position **3.** SIGN TREATY to become a party to an international agreement or treaty [15C. < Latin accedere 'come to' < cedere 'come'] —**accedence** n — **acceder** n

---

SPELLCHECK accede or exceed? Do not confuse the spelling of **accede** and **exceed**, which sound similar. **Accede** is usually followed by to, as in accede to our requests, accede to the throne. **Exceed** means 'be greater than' or 'go beyond': Income exceeds expenditure. Do not exceed the speed limit.

---

accelerando /ak séllə rándō, ə chéllə-/ adv, adj with gradually increasing speed (used as a musical direction) [Early 19C. < Italian, 'accelerating']

accelerant /ək séllərənt/ n **1.** CHEM same as **accelerator** (sense 3) **2.** a substance that is used to intensify a fire

accelerate /ək séllə rayt/ (**-ates, -ating, -ated**) vti **1.** to move increasingly quickly, or cause something to do this **2.** to happen or develop faster, or cause something to do this [Early 16C. < Latin acceleratus, past participle of accelerare 'quicken' < celer 'quick'] — **accelerated** adj —**accelerative** /-rətiv/ adj

accelerated graphics port n a computer interface that allows the display of three-dimensional graphics

acceleration /ək séllə ráysh'n/ n **1.** INCREASE IN SPEED the rate at which something increases in velocity **2.** INCREASE IN RATE OF PROGRESS an increase in the rate at which something happens or develops **3.** ACT OF ACCELERATING the act of accelerating, or the process of being accelerated **4.** PHYS MEASURE OF INCREASE IN VELOCITY a measure of the rate of increase in the velocity of something per unit of time. Symbol a

acceleration clause n a clause in the terms of a loan or mortgage stipulating that payments must be made earlier in specific circumstances

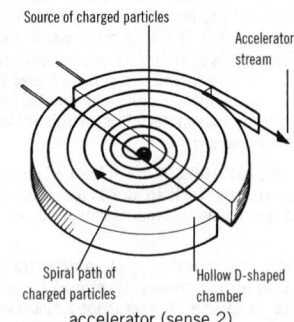

Source of charged particles

Accelerator stream

Spiral path of charged particles

Hollow D-shaped chamber

accelerator (sense 2)

accelerator /ək séllə raytər/ n **1.** SPEED-INCREASING CONTROL a pedal or other control mechanism used to cause a vehicle to increase speed **2.** PHYS DEVICE FOR GIVING PARTICLES HIGH VELOCITIES a machine used to increase the velocity, and hence the kinetic energy, of subatomic particles or nuclei, usually in preparation for collision with a target **3.** CHEM PROMOTER OF CHEMICAL REACTION a substance that speeds up a chemical reaction

accelerator card, **accelerator board** n a circuit board that adds a faster central processing unit to a computer

accelerometer /ək séllə rómmitər/ n an instrument or device for measuring acceleration, especially one in which a sensor converts acceleration into an electrical signal

accent *n* /áks'nt/ **1.** MANNER OF PRONUNCIATION a way of pronouncing words that indicates the place of origin or social background of the speaker **2.** INTONATION a way of using intonation or inflection to convey the speaker's mood or character **3.** STRESS ON SYLLABLE the prominence given to a syllable within a word or to a word within a phrase **4.** MARK ABOVE LETTER a symbol used in print or writing to indicate stress or the pronunciation of a vowel **5.** MAIN EMPHASIS an aspect of a situation or issue that is emphasized ○ *The accent is on safety.* **6.** CONTRASTING DETAIL a contrasting decorative feature used to add interest ○ *a blue room with green accents in the furnishings* **7.** STYLE a distinctive style that is characteristic of a particular person, region, or artistic school **8.** MUSIC STRESS ON NOTES stress placed on specific notes in a piece of music, or the symbol printed above the notes to indicate this stress **9.** MUSIC RHYTHM the rhythm of a piece of music, represented as the stress on the first beat of each bar **10.** MATHS, MEASURE same as **prime**[1] *n* (sense 3) ■ *vt* /ak sént/ (**-cents, -centing, -cented**) **1.** EMPHASIZE SOMETHING to stress or emphasize something, e.g. to pronounce a word or syllable more prominently than those surrounding it or play a musical note or beat with greater volume or attack **2.** MARK SOMETHING WITH ACCENT to mark something such as a letter or word with a written or printed accent [Early 16C. Via French < Latin *accentus* < *ad* 'to' + *cantus* 'singing', literal translation of Greek *prosōidia* 'accompanied song']

REGIONAL NOTE An ***accent*** refers to a method of pronunciation and every speaker has one; a regional accent is often incorrectly referred to as a *dialect*. There is no single standard pronunciation for British English although, for centuries, an educated southeastern English accent has been associated with privilege and prestige. Irish, Scottish, and West Country accents tend to be 'rhotic', that is, they pronounce the 'r' in 'dear' and 'warm'; most English and Welsh accents are not.

accent lighting *n* lighting that highlights an area or feature of a room, e.g. a painting or an alcove

accentor /ək séntər, -tawr/ *n* a songbird distinguished from a house sparrow by its thin, finely pointed beak. Hedge sparrows are one type of accentor. Native to: Europe, Asia, Africa. Family: Prunellidae.

accentual /ək sénchoo əl/ *adj* **1.** involving or associated with accent or stress **2.** employing a structure based on the number of stresses in a poetic line instead of the number of syllables

accentuate /ək sénchoo ayt/ (**-ates, -ating, -ated**) *vt* **1.** to make a feature of something more noticeable **2.** to emphasize a syllable, word, or phrase when saying it [Mid-18C. < medieval Latin *accentuatus*, past participle of *accentuare* 'emphasize' < Latin *accentus* (see ACCENT)] —**accentuation** /ək sénchoo áysh'n/ *n*

accept /ək sépt/ (**-cepts, -cepting, -cepted**) *v* **1.** *vt* TAKE SOMETHING OFFERED to take something that is offered, e.g. a gift or payment **2.** *vti* SAY YES TO INVITATION to reply in the affirmative to an invitation or offer **3.** *vt* COME TO TERMS WITH SOMETHING to acknowledge a fact or truth and come to terms with it **4.** *vt* ENDURE SITUATION to tolerate something without protesting or attempting to change it **5.** *vt* BELIEVE SOMETHING to acknowledge that something is true **6.** *vt* LAW AGREE TO TERMS to indicate formal agreement to the terms and conditions in a contract **7.** *vt* ADMIT to admit the blame or responsibility for something **8.** *vti* TAKE ON DUTY to agree to take on a duty, responsibility, or position **9.** *vt* PROCESS SOMETHING to be able to process something or be operated by something ○ *old machines that won't accept the new cards* **10.** *vt* ALLOW SOMEBODY TO JOIN to allow somebody to join an organization or attend an institution **11.** *vt* BE WELCOMING TO SOMEBODY to treat somebody as a member of a group or social circle **12.** *vt* RECEIVE FOR REVIEW to receive something such as a report for official action or review [14C. Via French *accepter* < Latin *acceptare* < *accipere* 'take to (yourself)' < *capere* 'take'] —**accepted** *adj*

USAGE accept or **except**? Do not confuse these two, even though they have similar pronunciations. ***Accept*** is a verb only; it means variously 'to take something offered', 'to believe something', and 'to agree to something', as in *We cannot accept* [not *except*] *such a lame excuse.* ***Except*** can work as a preposition meaning 'to the exclusion of', 'excluding', as in *All students except* [not *accept*] *the first years are eligible.* It is also a conjunction meaning 'if it were not for the fact that' and 'otherwise than', as in *I would have finished the course except* [not *accept*] *that I became ill at the end of term. The demonstrators did not quieten down except* [not *accept*] *to regroup and create new slogans for use later.* Finally, it is a verb used most often in the passive voice in the meaning 'to leave out or exclude', as in *Only children were excepted* [not *accepted*] *from attendance.*

acceptable /ək séptəb'l/ *adj* **1.** ADEQUATE considered to be satisfactory **2.** APPROVED OF likely to gain somebody's approval **3.** WELCOME likely to please the person who receives it (*usually modified by an adverb such as 'most' or 'quite'*) —**acceptability** /ək séptə bílləti/ *n* —**acceptableness** *n* —**acceptably** *adv*

acceptable daily intake *n* the highest daily intake level of a chemical that, if continued over the whole life of a person, is considered to pose no health risk

acceptance /ək séptənss/ *n* **1.** AGREEMENT TO INVITATION OR OFFER a written or verbal indication that somebody agrees to an invitation or offer **2.** ACT OF WILLINGLY TAKING GIFT the willing receipt of a gift or payment **3.** WILLINGNESS TO BELIEVE willingness to believe that something is true **4.** COMING TO TERMS WITH SOMETHING the realization of a fact or truth and the process of coming to terms with it **5.** TOLERATION the toleration of something without protest **6.** SOCIAL TOLERANCE willingness to treat somebody as a member of a group or social circle **7.** POSITIVE RESPONSE TO APPLICATION an offer to allow somebody to join an organization or attend an institution **8.** LAW AGREEMENT TO TERMS formal written or verbal agreement showing that somebody assents to the terms and conditions in a contract **9.** LAW AGREEMENT TO PAY a formal agreement by a debtor to pay a draft or bill of exchange when it becomes payable

acceptation /áksep táysh'n/ *n* **1.** a generally favourable reception of something **2.** the sense in which a word or phrase is generally understood

accepter *n* LAW another spelling of **acceptor** (sense 1)

accepting /ək sépting/ *adj* able to endure something difficult or unpleasant without complaint or protest ○ *Illness brought many restrictions, but he was very accepting of them.* —**acceptingly** *adv*

accepting house *n* a financial institution that guarantees bills of exchange

acceptor /ək séptər/ *n* **1.** somebody who accepts liability for a bill of exchange **2.** an atom or group of atoms that accepts electrons to form a coordinate bond during the formation of a chemical compound

access /ák sess/ *n* **1.** ENTRY OR APPROACH a means of entering or approaching a place ○ *Thieves gained access to the premises via a side door.* **2.** OPPORTUNITY FOR USE the opportunity or right to experience or make use of something **3.** RIGHT TO MEET SOMEBODY the opportunity to meet somebody **4.** ENTRY TO COMPUTER SYSTEM the right or ability to log on to a computer system or use a computer program ○ *software that allows network access* **5.** OUTBURST a sudden strongly felt burst of emotion (*literary*) ○ *'With a sudden access of tenderness he flung his arm about me.'* (Rider Haggard, *She*; 1887) ■ *adj* FOR UNQUALIFIED STUDENTS designed as a course of study for people without formal educational qualifications, in order to give them entry to higher education ■ *vt* (**-cesses, -cessing, -cessed**) **1.** ENTER PLACE to find a means of entering or approaching a place **2.** ⚠ GET INFORMATION to have the opportunity or right to experience or make use of something (*see usage note below*) **3.** CALL UP DATA to retrieve data or a computer file (*see usage note below*) ○ *The program can be accessed using the correct password.* [14C. Directly or via Old French *acces* < Latin *accessus*, past participle of *accedere* 'come near' (see ACCEDE)]

SPELLCHECK access or **excess**? Do not confuse the spelling of ***access*** and ***excess***, which sound similar. ***Access*** refers to a right or opportunity for approach, entry, contact, or use: *gain access to secret information, to access a computer program.* ***Excess*** refers to something extra or more than enough: *temperatures in excess of 100 degrees, excess baggage.* Note also the literary use of ***access*** to mean 'an outburst of emotion', as in *an access of tenderness*, and do not confuse it with ***excess*** meaning 'a surplus of emotion', as in *an excess of enthusiasm.*

USAGE access as a verb: There is normally no problem with using ***access*** as a verb in computing contexts (although even this is objected to by some people), but there is more resistance to using it in general contexts such as accessing bank accounts or biographical information.

~~**accessable**~~ incorrect spelling of **accessible**

accessary *n, adj* LAW another spelling of **accessory** *n* (sense 3), *adj* (sense 2)

USAGE See *accessory.*

access code *n* a sequence of letters or numbers that have to be keyed in to allow somebody access to a restricted area, e.g. a building or a computerized network

access course *n* a course of study designed for people without formal educational qualifications, so that they can gain entry to higher education

accessible /ək séssəb'l/ *adj* **1.** EASILY REACHED easy to enter or reach physically **2.** EASILY UNDERSTOOD able to be appreciated or understood without specialist knowledge **3.** EASILY AVAILABLE able to be obtained, used, or experienced without difficulty **4.** APPROACHABLE not aloof and not difficult to talk to or meet **5.** SUSCEPTIBLE susceptible to or likely to be influenced by something (*literary*) **6.** EASY FOR DISABLED PEOPLE TO USE suitable or adapted for people with disabilities **7.** LOGIC OBSERVABLE FROM ANOTHER WORLD able to be referred to from another possible world, so that the truth value of statements about it can be given —**accessibility** /ək séssə bílləti/ *n* —**accessibly** *adv*

accession /ək sésh'n/ *n* **1.** TAKING UP OF POSITION the assumption of an important position, usually a position of power **2.** LAW ACCEPTANCE OF TREATY the formal acceptance by a state of an international treaty or convention **3.** ASSENT agreement or consent, usually when given unwillingly **4.** ADDITION TO COLLECTION an item added to a collection **5.** SUDDEN MOOD a sudden and unexpected display of a particular mood or emotion (*literary*) **6.** LAW INCREASE TO PROPERTY addition to property by natural growth or improvement **7.** LAW RIGHT TO INCREASE IN PROPERTY the right of an owner to add to a property by natural growth or improvement ■ *vt* (**-sions, -sioning, -sioned**) CATALOGUE ADDITIONS TO COLLECTION to make a formal record of an addition to a collection —**accessional** *adj*

accession country *n* a country that has been formally accepted as a member of the EU

access number *n* the telephone number used to link to an Internet service provider or other network provider using a dial-up connection

accessorize /ək séssə rīz/ (**-izes, -izing, -ized**), **accessorise** (**-ises, -ising, -ised**) *v* **1.** *vti* to wear or use items such as gloves, hats, and handbags to complete an outfit of clothing **2.** *vt* to fit accessories to something

accessory /ək séssəri/ *n* (*plural* **-ries**) **1.** OPTIONAL PART an optional part that may be fitted to something to perform an additional function or enhance performance **2.** FASHION ARTICLE an item of clothing that is worn or used for fashionable effect with an outfit ○ *'designers who create neckties as fashion accessories'* (*International Herald Tribune*; June 1997) **3.** *also* **accessary** LAW SOMEBODY WHO HELPS CRIMINAL somebody who aids somebody else in committing a crime or avoiding arrest but who does not participate in the crime itself ■ *adj* **1.** ADDITIONAL supplementary or subsidiary to something more important **2.** *also* **accessary** LAW ASSISTING IN CRIME aiding a criminal act although not participating in the crime itself —**accessorial** /ák se sáwri əl/ *adj* —**accessorily** *adv* —**accessoriness** *n*

USAGE ***Accessory*** is the usual spelling. ***Accessary*** is an older form that is still occasionally used, especially in some legal contexts.

accessory after the fact (*plural* **accessories after the fact**) *n* somebody who helps a criminal after a crime

accessory before the fact (*plural* **accessories before the fact**) *n* somebody who incites or helps a criminal before a crime

accessory mineral *n* a mineral in igneous rock that occurs in small quantities

accessory nerve *n* the eleventh cranial nerve, associated with the pharynx and muscles in the throat, larynx, palate, neck, and back

accessory shoe *n* a bracket on a camera allowing an accessory to be mounted on it

access point *n* a transceiver in a wireless local area network that connects a wired local area network to wireless devices or that connects wireless devices to each other

access profile *n* the details identifying a computer user held on a server or other computer, specifying the name and password and the areas of a computer system the user is authorized to access

access time *n* the time a computer takes to locate and retrieve data

acciaccatura /ə cháka toóra/ (*plural* **-ras** or **-re** /-ray/) *n* a brief note (**grace note**) added to a piece of music and played quickly at the same time as or just before a principal note [Early 19C. < Italian, 'crushed']

accidence /áksidənss/ *n* the area of traditional grammar dealing with the inflections of words [15C. < late Latin *accidentia* (plural) 'things that happen' (taken as singular) < Latin *accident-* (see ACCIDENT)]

accident /áksidənt/ *n* **1.** CRASH a collision or similar incident involving a moving vehicle, resulting in property damage, personal injury or death **2.** MISHAP an unplanned and unfortunate event that results in damage, injury, or upset of some kind **3.** CHANCE the way things happen without any planning, apparent cause, or deliberate intent ○ *I met him by accident.* **4.** CHANCE HAPPENING an event that happens completely by chance, with no planning or deliberate intent **5.** INSTANCE OF INCONTINENCE an incident when somebody, particularly a small child, is incontinent (*euphemistic*) **6.** UNPLANNED PREGNANCY a child conceived in an unplanned way **7.** PHILOSOPHY NONESSENTIAL ATTRIBUTE a nonessential attribute or characteristic of something [14C. Via French < Latin *accident-*, present participle of *accidere* 'happen' < *cadere* 'fall, die']

accidental /áksi dént'l/ *adj* **1.** CHANCE happening by chance and not planned **2.** INCIDENTAL not specifically intended and arising as a side effect **3.** MUSIC NOT IN KEY SIGNATURE sharp, flat, or natural, in a way not indicated in the key signature ■ *n* **1.** UNPLANNED EFFECT something not specifically intended that arises as a side effect **2.** MUSIC NOTE NOT IN KEY SIGNATURE a musical note, marked with a sharp, flat, or natural sign, whose pitch does not correspond to the key signature —**accidentally** *adv*

accidental death *n* death caused by an accident rather than by natural causes, suicide, or murder

accident and emergency *n* a hospital department that treats emergency patients who have had accidents or been injured. N Am term **emergency room**

accident insurance *n* insurance against property damage, personal injury, or death caused by an accident

~~**accidently**~~ incorrect spelling of **accidentally**

accident-prone *adj* having more accidents than average

accipiter /ak síppitər/ *n* a hawk, typically with short broad wings and a long tail, e.g. a sparrowhawk or goshawk. Genus: *Accipiter*. [Early 19C. < Latin < *accipere* 'take to (yourself)' (see ACCEPT)]

accipitrine /ak síppi trin, -trīn/ *adj* relating to or belonging to the family of predatory birds including hawks, eagles, and kites

acclaim /ə kláym/ *v* (**-claims, -claiming, -claimed**) **1.** *vt* PRAISE SOMEBODY HIGHLY to praise somebody or something publicly and enthusiastically **2.** *vt* PRONOUNCE SOMEBODY TO BE SOMETHING to declare publicly and enthusiastically that somebody holds a high position ○ *was acclaimed as the winner* **3.** *vi* SHOUT ENTHUSIASTICALLY to demonstrate enthusiastic approval by shouting and cheering ■ *n* ENTHUSIASTIC RECEPTION enthusiastic approval given to somebody or something publicly [Early 16C. < Latin *acclamare* 'shout to' < *clamare* 'shout']—**acclaimer** *n*

acclamation /ákla máysh'n/ *n* a public and enthusiastic display of approval [Mid-16C. < Latin *acclamation-* < *acclamare* (see ACCLAIM)]—**acclamatory** /ə klámmətri/

acclimate /ákli mayt/ (**-mates, -mating, -mated**) *v* **1.** *vti* same as **acclimatize 2.** *vi* to adjust in response to a

change in environment or status ○ *became acclimated to their new prosperity* [Late 18C. < French *acclimater* < *a-* 'to' + *climat* 'climate' (see CLIMATE)]—**acclimation** /ákla máysh'n/ *n*

acclimatize /ə klíma tīz/ (**-tizes, -tizing, -tized**), **acclimatise** (**-tises, -tising, -tised**) *vti* to become accustomed to a new climate or environment, or help somebody to do this —**acclimatization** /ə klīmə tī záysh'n/ *n*

acclivity /ə klívvəti/ (*plural* **-ties**) *n* an upward slope on a hill [Early 17C. < Latin *acclivitat-* 'ascent' < *acclivis* 'uphill' < *clivus* 'slope']

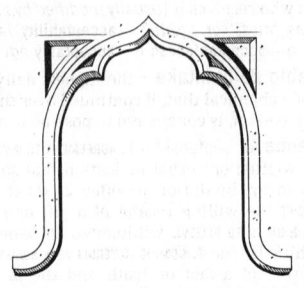

accolade (sense 4)

accolade /ákə layd, -laad/ *n* **1.** SIGN OF PRAISE a sign or expression of high praise and esteem for somebody **2.** PUBLIC RECOGNITION praise and public recognition of somebody's achievements **3.** KNIGHTING the ceremonial bestowal of a knighthood by touching somebody's shoulders with a sword. Knighthood was formerly conferred by an embrace. **4.** ARCHIT CURVED MOULDING an ornamental moulding shaped like a brace [Early 17C. Via French < Provençal *acolada* 'embrace' < Latin *collum* 'neck'; because knighthood was formerly conferred with an embrace]

accommodate /ə kómma dayt/ (**-dates, -dating, -dated**) *v* **1.** *vt* PROVIDE LODGING FOR SOMEBODY to provide somebody with a place to stay **2.** *vt* HAVE ROOM FOR SOMEBODY OR SOMETHING to have sufficient space for somebody or something **3.** *vt* ALLOW FOR SOMETHING to be adaptable enough to allow something without major change **4.** *vt* OBLIGE SOMEBODY to adjust actions in response to the needs of somebody **5.** *vt* LEND SOMEBODY MONEY to give somebody money in response to a request for a loan (*formal*) **6.** *vti* REACH AGREEMENT to settle a difference of opinion in a way that is acceptable to all those involved **7.** *vi* ADAPT TO SOMETHING NEW to adapt to a new situation **8.** *vi* OPHTHALMOL ADJUST FOCUS to adjust focus automatically to give clear vision (*refers to the eyes*) [Mid-16C. < Latin *accommodare* 'make fit' < *commodus* 'suitable' < *modus* 'measure'] —**accommodative** *adj*

USAGE Note that **accommodate** and **accommodation** are spelt with -*cc*- and -*mm*-. **Accommodation**, in particular, is often misspelt with a single -*m*- on signs and notices.

accommodating /ə kómma dayting/ *adj* willing to adjust actions in response to the needs of somebody else —**accommodatingly** *adv*

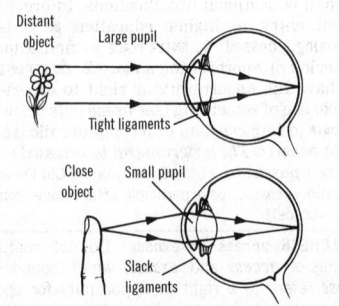

accommodation: adjustment of eye focus on a distant object (top) and a close object (bottom)

accommodation /ə kómma dáysh'n/ *n* **1.** UK, ANZ, Can LODGING a place such as a room or house in which to live, stay, or work ○ *looking for accommodation* US term **accommodations 2.** UK, ANZ, Can SEATING

seating in a vehicle or public facility. US term **accommodations 3.** ADJUSTMENT the modification of actions in response something **4.** AGREEMENT an agreement acceptable to all parties in a dispute **5.** FLEXIBILITY the ability to include something without major change **6.** OPHTHALMOL ADJUSTMENT OF EYE FOCUS the automatic adjustment of the focus of an eye to give clear vision **7.** BANKING LOAN OF MONEY a loan of money, especially by a financial institution as a favour to somebody before a formal credit arrangement is made ■ **accommodations** *npl* **1.** N Am same as **accommodation** (sense 1) **2.** US same as **accommodation** (sense 2)

USAGE See **accommodate**.

accommodation address *n* a mailing address used by a person or organization unwilling or unable to use an identifiable individual address

accommodation bill *n* a bill of exchange cosigned by another party in order to give added security

accommodation centre *n* **1.** a building or site containing temporary accommodation, especially for tourists or students **2.** a self-contained facility providing all key services where people wishing to enter a country without prior approval live while their claim is considered

accommodationist /ə kómma dáysh'nist/ *n* somebody who prefers compromise to confrontation —**accommodationist** *adj*

accommodation ladder *n* a ladder or flight of steps hung over the side of a boat to allow boarding or disembarking

accommodation platform, accommodation rig *n* a platform or rig used as living quarters for offshore oil or gas workers

~~**accomodate**~~ incorrect spelling of **accommodate**

~~**accomodation**~~ incorrect spelling of **accommodation**

accompaniment /ə kúmpənimənt, -pni-/ *n* **1.** MUSICAL BACKING instrumental or vocal parts in a musical composition that support the more important parts **2.** SIMULTANEOUS OCCURRENCE something that occurs at the same time and in the same place as something else ○ *torrential rain, with an accompaniment of crashing thunder* **3.** SUPPLEMENT an item that is added or served because it goes well with something ○ *mint sauce, the perfect accompaniment to roast lamb*

accompanist /ə kúmpənist, -pnist/ *n* a musician, especially a pianist, playing the accompaniment for a soloist

accompany /ə kúmpəni, -pni/ (**-nies, -nying, -nied**) *v* **1.** *vt* ESCORT SOMEBODY to go with somebody **2.** *vt* BE PRESENT WITH SOMETHING to be enclosed, attached, or present with something **3.** *vt* OCCUR WITH SOMETHING to happen at the same time as something else **4.** *vt* SUPPLEMENT SOMETHING to be present or served with something as a supplement **5.** *vti* MUSIC PROVIDE MUSICAL BACKING to play or sing a part that supports a more important part [15C. < Old French *acompaignier* 'be a companion to' < *compaing* 'companion' (see COMPANION¹)]

accomplice /ə kúmpliss, ə kóm-/ *n* somebody who helps somebody else to commit a crime or misdeed [Mid-16C. < archaic *complice* (by misunderstanding of *a complice*), via French < Latin *complic-*, stem of *complex* 'associate' < *complicare* (see COMPLICATE)]

accomplish /ə kúmplish, ə kóm-/ (**-plishes, -plishing, -plished**) *vt* to carry out or complete something successfully [14C. < Old French *accompliss-*, a stem of *acomplir* 'complete to' < Latin *complere* (see COMPLETE)] —**accomplishable** *adj* —**accomplisher** *n*

SYNONYMS *accomplish, achieve, attain, carry out, pull off, realize*

CORE MEANING: to bring something to a successful conclusion

accomplish to carry out or complete something successfully ○ *You don't accomplish anything by placing blame.* ○ *Mission accomplished, we headed for home.* **achieve** to succeed in doing something, usually with effort ○ *three main ways in which the government hopes to achieve its aims* ○ *an example of what can be achieved through good planning* **attain** to achieve a goal or desired state, usually with effort ○ *a desire to attain the best qualifications* ○ *attain a full command of the English language* **carry out** to perform a task or activity ○ *carry out calculations with faultless ac-*

curacy ○ *She found it hard to believe that Julius would actually carry out his threat.* **pull off** (*informal*) to achieve something impressive, particularly through a combination of skill and luck ○ *The goalkeeper pulled off a fine save.* ○ *He pulled off an immediate coup by appointing a well-known entrepreneur as patron.* **realize** to fulfil a specific vision, plan, or potential ○ *realize your potential* ○ *His dream was realized when he signed for Manchester United.*

accomplished /ə kúmplisht, ə kóm-/ *adj* **1. TALENTED** having considerable talent and skill **2. HAVING SOCIAL GRACES** possessing social skills and talents **3. BEYOND DOUBT** fully established ○ *an accomplished fact*

accomplishment /ə kúmplishmənt, ə kóm-/ *n* **1. ACHIEVING OF SOMETHING** the completion or fulfilment of something **2. FEAT** a remarkable or successful achievement **3. TALENT** a skill or talent that has been developed

Acconci /ə kónssi/, **Vito** (*b.* 1940) US artist. He explored the concept of space through film, video, and installations that doubled as meeting places. He has collaborated with architects to design landscaping for public places.

accord /ə káwrd/ *v* (**-cords, -cording, -corded**) **1.** *vt* **RENDER SOMEBODY SOMETHING** to give somebody or something a particular status or treatment ○ *was accorded the same privileges as her predecessor* **2.** *vi* **AGREE** to be in agreement or come to an agreement ○ *accords with my own view* **3.** *vt* **GRANT SOMETHING** to bestow something such as a blessing on somebody ■ *n* **1. AGREEMENT** a treaty or settlement agreed by two or more parties **2. CONSENSUS** general agreement as to what is right **3. HARMONY** a state in which things are in harmony with each other [Pre-12C. < Old French *acorder* < Latin *ad* 'to' + *cord-*, stem of *cor* 'heart'] ◇ **of your own accord** of your own free will ◇ **with one accord** together and with everyone agreeing (*formal*)

accordance /ə káwrd'nss/ *n* **1. CONSENSUS** consensus as to the right course of action **2. ADHERENCE TO CORRECT PROCESS** conformity with specific procedures or actions ○ *in accordance with official guidelines* **3. BESTOWAL** the bestowal of a particular status or treatment on somebody or something

according as /ə káwrding-/ *conj* depending on whether, or corresponding to the extent to which ○ *were deemed approved or unapproved, according as each matched the specification*

accordingly /ə káwrdingli/ *adv* **1.** in a way that is appropriate **2.** in accordance with what has been said or with a principle or practice

according to *prep* **1. ON SOMEBODY'S OR SOMETHING'S AUTHORITY** as stated by somebody or indicated by something ○ *the gospel according to St Luke* **2. RELATED TO** depending on and corresponding in extent to something ○ *salary according to experience* **3. AS DETERMINED BY** on the basis of and in line with a method or principle ○ *arranged according to alphabetical order* **4. AS LAID DOWN BY** in the way that a plan or system stipulates ○ *done exactly according to the instructions*

accordion /ə káwrdi ən/ *n* a musical instrument with a keyboard or buttons on one side, buttons on the other, and a bellows in the middle that forces air through metal reeds [Mid-19C. < German *Akkordion* < *Akkord* 'chord' < Italian *accordare* 'tune (an instrument)']

accordion pleats *npl* sharp pleats in a garment or piece of fabric, like the folds in an accordion's bellows

accost /ə kóst/ (**-costs, -costing, -costed**) *vt* to approach and stop somebody in order to speak to that person, especially in an aggressive, insistent, or suggestive way [Late 16C. Via French < Latin *accostare* 'adjoin' < *costa* 'rib, side'] —**accoster** *n*

account /ə kównt/ *n* **1. REPORT** a written or spoken report of something **2. EXPLANATION** an explanation of something that has happened, especially one given to somebody in authority **3.** BANKING **BANK ARRANGEMENT** an arrangement by which a customer keeps money in a bank or building society and is offered financial services in exchange **4.** BANKING **MONEY IN BANK** the money that a customer keeps in a bank **5.** FIN **FINANCIAL ARRANGEMENT** an arrangement with a shop, company, stockbroker, or other business, by which financial services are provided, e.g. credit **6.** ONLINE **NETWORK ACCESS CONTRACT** a contractual agreement between a user and an Internet or e-mail service provider establishing a directory and other system information and giving the user access to a network, e.g. the Internet, in return for a fee or other consideration **7.** ACCT **RECORD OF FINANCES** a regular printed statement of financial transactions conducted through an account **8.** FIN **PERIOD OF TRANSACTION** the period during which transactions are made, usually lasting two weeks, and at the end of which settlements are made **9.** BUSINESS **CUSTOMER** a customer who has a regular business relationship with a company **10.** BUSINESS **WORK CARRIED OUT FOR CLIENT** an area of business handled by a company on behalf of another, e.g. advertising, design, or publicity ■ **accounts** *npl* ACCT **LIST OF FINANCIAL INFORMATION** a detailed list of everything that a person or company earns or spends, kept primarily for tax purposes ■ *vt* (**-counts, -counting, -counted**) **CONSIDER** to consider somebody or something to have a particular quality (*formal*) ○ *We would account it a privilege to serve you.* [14C. < Old French *aconte* 'a counting up' < *aconter* < Latin *computare* 'sum up'] ◇ **by all accounts** according to what most people say ◇ **call somebody to account** to demand that somebody explains what he or she has done ◇ **give a good account of yourself** to do something in a way that does justice to your abilities or character ◇ **of no account** of no importance ◇ **on account** on credit ◇ **on account of** because of ◇ **on no account** for no reason, whatever the circumstances ◇ **on somebody's account** out of concern for somebody's wellbeing ◇ **take account of somebody or something, take somebody or something into account** to consider somebody or something when making a decision ◇ **turn something to good account** to use or deal with something in a way that puts it to good use

account for *vt* **1. EXPLAIN SOMETHING** to provide an explanation for something ○ *And how do you account for his behaviour?* **2. BE RESPONSIBLE FOR SOMETHING** to be responsible for something or be an important factor in something ○ *Export sales account for at least half of our total business.* **3. KILL OR DESTROY SOMEBODY OR SOMETHING** to be responsible for killing, destroying, or neutralizing somebody or something

accountable /ə kówntəb'l/ *adj* **1.** responsible to somebody or for something **2.** capable of being explained (*formal*) —**accountability** /ə kówntə bílləti/ *n* —**accountably** *adv*

accountancy /ə kówntənssi/ *n* the work or profession of an accountant

accountant /ə kówntənt/ *n* somebody who maintains the business records of a person or organization and prepares reports for tax or other financial purposes

account day *n* the day on which payments and deliveries that have been agreed on during the preceding two-week period are made

account executive *n* an employee, especially in an advertising or public relations company, who handles all of a client's business

accounting /ə kównting/ *n* the activity, practice, or profession of maintaining the business records of a person or organization and preparing reports for tax or other financial purposes

accounting rate of return (*plural* **accounting rates of return**) *n* a calculation of the anticipated net profit from an investment in an asset or project, expressed as a percentage of the money invested

accounts payable *npl* a record that shows how much a firm owes suppliers for the purchase of supplies or services on credit

accounts receivable *npl* a record that shows how much is owed to a company by customers who have purchased supplies or services on credit

~~**accoustic**~~ incorrect spelling of **acoustic**

accouter *vt* MIL US spelling of **accoutre**

accouterment *n* MIL US spelling of **accoutrement**

accoutre /ə kóotər/ (**-tres, -tring, -tred**) *vt* to equip and clothe somebody, especially for military purposes [Mid-16C. < French *accoutrer* 'equip with something, especially clothes' < assumed Latin *consutura* 'sewn together' < *sutura* 'sewn']

accoutrement /ə kóotrəmənt/ *n* **1.** an accessory or piece of equipment associated with a specific object, task, or role **2.** a piece of military equipment carried by soldiers in addition to their standard uniform and weapons

accra *n* another spelling of **akara**

Accra /ə kráa/ capital of Ghana. It is located on the Gulf of Guinea in southeastern Ghana. Population: 1,904,000 (1999).

accredit /ə kréddit/ (**-its, -iting, -ited**) *vt* **1. GIVE OFFICIAL RECOGNITION TO SOMEBODY** to officially recognize a person or organization as having met a standard or criterion (*usually passive*) **2. APPOINT SOMEBODY AS ENVOY** to appoint somebody as an envoy or ambassador to another country **3. GIVE SOMEBODY AUTHORITY** to give somebody the authority to perform a function (*usually passive*) **4. ATTRIBUTE QUALITY TO SOMEBODY** to regard somebody as having a particular quality ○ *accredited them with more intelligence than they have* **5. ASCRIBE SOMETHING TO SOMEBODY** to consider something as belonging to or attributable to somebody ○ *We cannot accredit all the problems to immigration.* **6.** *NZ* **PASS STUDENT ON INTERNAL ASSESSMENT** to award a pass in an external examination on an assessment made within a school [Early 17C. < French *accréditer* 'believe (firmly)' < *crédit* (see CREDIT)] —**accreditation** /ə kréddi táysh'n/ *n*

accrete /ə kréet/ (**-cretes, -creting, -creted**) *vti* to increase in size, or increase the size of something, especially by accumulation or the growing together of separate things [Late 18C. < Latin *accret-*, past participle of *accrescere* < *crescere* 'grow']

accretion /ə kréesh'n/ *n* **1. INCREASE** an increase in size as a result of accumulation or the growing together of separate things **2. SOMETHING ACCUMULATED** something formed by or resulting from accretion **3.** FIN **ADDITION** something added to something such as a fund of money from an external source **4.** ASTRON **ATTRACTION OF MATTER BY GRAVITY** a process in which matter revolving around an astronomical object is gradually pulled in and added to the body's mass **5.** GEOL **INCREASE IN LAND MASS** a process by which a body of rock or a land mass increases in size as a result of material accumulating on or around it **6.** GEOL **INCREASE IN SIZE OF CONTINENTS** a process by which the size of a continent increases as a result of the moving together and deforming of tectonic plates —**accretionary** *adj*

accretion disc *n* a band of matter revolving around and being pulled towards an astronomical object with an intense gravitational field, e.g. a star or black hole

~~**accross**~~ incorrect spelling of **across**

accrual /ə króo əl/ *n* **1.** something that has accrued **2.** the process of accruing or of being accrued

accrual method *n* a method of accounting that counts income or expenses at the time they are earned or incurred, irrespective of when money is received or paid out

accrue /ə króo/ (**-crues, -cruing, -crued**) *v* **1.** *vi* **INCREASE** to increase in amount or value ○ *The money had started to accrue in my account.* **2.** *vt* **ACCUMULATE AMOUNT** to gather together an amount, especially over a period of time ○ *investments accruing interest* **3.** *vi* **COME AS RESULT** to come as a result or consequence of something, especially over a period of time ○ *environmental benefits that will accrue to the area* **4.** *vi* LAW **BECOME ENFORCEABLE** to become legally enforceable (*refers to claims or rights*) [15C. Via Anglo-Norman < Latin *accrescent-*, present participle of *accrescere* (see ACCRETE)] —**accruement** *n*

acct *abbr* ACCT, BANKING, FIN account

acculturate /ə kúlchə rayt/ (**-ates, -ating, -ated**) *v* **1.** *vi* to absorb and assimilate the culture of another group of people or another person **2.** *vt* to change somebody's cultural behaviour and thinking through contact with another culture [Mid-20C. Back-formation < ACCULTURATION] —**acculturative** *adj*

acculturation /ə kúlchə ráysh'n/ *n* **1.** a change in the cultural behaviour and thinking of a person or group of people through contact with another culture **2.** the process by which somebody absorbs the culture of a society from birth onwards [Late 19C. < AC- + CULTURE + -ATION] —**acculturational** *adj*

accumulate /ə kyóomyoo layt/ (**-lates, -lating, -lated**) *vti* to collect or obtain a large amount of something over a period of time ○ *The magazines she had accumulated over 20 years filled the shelves.* ○ *The report suggests that the herbicide accumulates in the*

soil. [15C. < Latin *accumulat-*, past participle of *accumulare* 'heap up in addition' < *cumulus* 'heap'] —**accumulable** /ə kyoōmyoōləb'l/ *adj*

SYNONYMS See *collect*[1].

accumulation /ə kyoōmyoō láysh'n/ *n* **1.** PROCESS OF GATHERING the process of gathering together and increasing in amount over a period of time **2.** COLLECTION OF THINGS a number of things that have collected or been collected over a period of time **3.** FIN GROWTH THROUGH INTEREST the growth of a sum by the addition of earned interest

accumulative /ə kyoōmyoōlətiv/ *adj* **1.** growing by gradual additions **2.** tending to gather or collect things —**accumulatively** *adv* —**accumulativeness** *n*

accumulator /ə kyoōmyoō laytər/ *n* **1.** BET ON SEVERAL RACES a bet made on a chosen number of horse races, with the stake and any winnings from one race being automatically bet on the next **2.** BATTERY a rechargeable battery consisting of one or more cells for producing electrical energy from stored chemical energy. N Am term **storage battery 3.** SHORT-TERM ELECTRONIC MEMORY a section of short-term memory in a computer or calculator

accuracy /ákyoōrəssi/ *n* **1.** the correctness or truthfulness of something **2.** the ability to be precise and avoid errors

accurate /ákyoōrət/ *adj* **1.** CORRECT giving a correct or truthful representation of something ○ *Their account of the incident was not entirely accurate.* **2.** FREE FROM ERRORS precise or free from errors ○ *an accurate typist* **3.** PROVIDING INFORMATION TO ACCEPTED STANDARD capable of providing information in accordance with an accepted standard ○ *an accurate watch* [Late 16C. < Latin *accuratus* 'done with care' < *cura* 'care'] —**accurately** *adv*

accursed /ə kúrssid, ə kúrst/, **accurst** /ə kúrst/ *adj* **1.** horrible or hateful (*dated*) **2.** enduring the effects of a curse (*archaic or literary*) [12C. < *a-* 'on' (< Old English *ar-*) + CURSE] —**accursedly** /ə kúrssidli/ *adv* —**accursedness** /ə kúrssidnəss/ *n*

accusation /ákyoō záysh'n/ *n* **1.** a claim that somebody has done something illegal or wrong **2.** the accusing of somebody, or the state of having been accused of something

accusative /ə kyoōzətiv/ *n* **1.** a grammatical case that identifies the direct object of a verb or other grammatical parts in some inflected languages and that affects nouns, pronouns, and adjectives **2.** a word or phrase in the accusative [15C. < Latin *accusativus* < *accusare* (see ACCUSE)] —**accusative** *adj* —**accusatively** *adv*

accusatorial /ə kyoōzə táwri əl/ *adj* **1.** containing or making an accusation (*formal*) **2.** describes a legal system in which the prosecution is required to provide proof of guilt beyond reasonable doubt, with the evidence being assessed by an impartial judge and jury —**accusatorially** *adv*

accusatory /ə kyoōzətəri, ákyoō záytəri/ *adj* same as **accusatorial** (sense 1) (*formal*)

accuse /ə kyoōz/ (**-cuses, -cusing, -cused**) *v* **1.** *vti* to confront somebody with a charge of having done something illegal, wrong, or undesirable **2.** *vt* to charge somebody formally with having committed a crime [14C. Via French < Latin *accusare* 'call somebody to account' < *ad causa* 'to the (legal) case'] —**accuser** *n*

accused /ə kyoōzd/ *n* somebody being charged with wrongdoing in a criminal case

accusing /ə kyoōzing/ *adj* containing or suggesting a claim that somebody has done something wrong —**accusingly** *adv*

accustom /ə kústəm/ (**-toms, -toming, -tomed**) *vt* to make yourself or somebody else used to something through frequent or prolonged contact or use [15C. < Anglo-Norman *acustomer* < *custome* 'habit' (see CUSTOM)]

accustomed /ə kústəmd/ *adj* habitual or usual ◇ **accustomed to** used to or familiar with something or somebody ○ *I've grown accustomed to life in a small town.*

AC/DC *adj* **1.** able to be powered by battery or by connection to the mains. Full form **alternating current/direct current 2.** an offensive term meaning bisexual (*slang*)

ace /ayss/ *n* **1.** PLAYING CARD a playing card that has a single mark on it, or the single mark itself **2.** SINGLE-SPOTTED SIDE a single-spotted side of a dice or domino, or the single spot itself **3.** TENNIS WINNING SERVE in tennis, a serve that an opponent cannot reach **4.** GOLF HOLE IN ONE the hitting of a golf ball from the tee into a hole in one stroke, or a score resulting from such a stroke **5.** AIR FORCE FIGHTER PILOT a top fighter pilot, especially one who has shot down a number of enemy aircraft **6.** SOMEBODY WITH EXCEPTIONAL SKILL somebody who is outstandingly good at something, e.g. a sport (*informal*) ■ *vt* (**aces, acing, aced**) TENNIS BEAT WITH SERVE in tennis, to beat an opponent by serving an ace ■ *adj* EXCELLENT very good (*informal*) [14C. Via French *as* < Latin, 'unit, unity'] ◇ **have an ace up your sleeve** to have a hidden advantage (*informal*) ◇ **hold all the aces** to have all the advantages (*informal*) ◇ **within an ace of** very close to

ACE[1] /ayss/ *n* an enzyme that increases blood pressure. Full form **angiotensin-converting enzyme**

ACE[2] *abbr* **1.** Advisory Centre for Education **2.** Allied Command Europe

-acean *suffix* same as **-aceous**

acebutolol /ássi byoōtə lol/ *n* a drug that reduces the heart rate and the force of heart muscle contraction. Use: treatment of high blood pressure and irregular heart rhythms. [Mid-20C. < ACETYL + BUTYL]

acedapsone /ássə dápsōn/ *n* a sulphur-containing drug. Use: treatment of malaria and leprosy. [Mid 20C. Blend of *acetylated* + DAPSONE]

ACE inhibitor *n* a drug that blocks an enzyme that raises blood pressure

acentric /ay séntrik/ *adj* **1.** without a centre **2.** describes a chromosome that lacks the structure at which the two arms of a chromosome join (**centromere**)

-aceous, **-acean** *suffix* resembling or related to ○ *herbaceous* [< Latin *-aceus*]

acephalous /ay séffələss/ *adj* describes an animal that has no head [Mid-18C. Via medieval Latin < Greek *akephalos* 'without a head' < *kephalē* 'head']

acepromazine /ássə prómə zeen/ *n* an antipsychotic drug, often used as a tranquillizer in veterinary medicine [< *aceprom-* + *-azine*, INN stem]

acer /áyssər/ *n* a deciduous tree or bush grown for its ornamental foliage. Native to: Europe, Asia, North America. Genus: *Acer*. [Late 19C. < Latin, 'maple']

acerbate /ássər bayt/ (**-bates, -bating, -bated**) *vt* (*formal*) **1.** to annoy or irritate somebody **2.** to make something taste bitter [Mid-18C. < Latin *acerbat-*, past participle of *acerbare* 'make harsh' < *acerbus* (see ACERBIC)]

acerbic /ə súrbik/ *adj* bitter or sharp in tone, taste, or manner ○ *an acerbic remark* [Mid-19C. < Latin *acerbus* 'harsh' < Indo-European] —**acerbically** *adv* —**acerbity** *n*

~~**acessory**~~ incorrect spelling of **accessory**

acet- *prefix* same as **aceto-** (*used before vowels*)

acetabulum /ássi tábbyoōləm/ (*plural* **-la** /-lə/) *n* **1.** the curved cavity on the side of the hipbone where the end of the thighbone fits **2.** a round cup-shaped sucker found on flatworms, leeches, and molluscs such as the octopus [14C. < Latin, 'vinegar cup, cup-shaped cavity' < *acetum* 'vinegar'] —**acetabular** *adj*

acetal /ássi tal/ *n* **1.** a colourless volatile liquid. Use: solvent, perfumes. Formula: $C_6H_{14}O_2$. **2.** an organic compound similar to acetal that contains the chemical group $-CH(OR_1)OR_2$

acetaldehyde /ássi táldi hīd/ *n* a colourless volatile liquid with a pungent smell. Use: manufacture of acetic acid, acetic anhydride, and butanol. Formula: C_2H_4O.

acetamide /ə séttə mīd, ássi tá-/ *n* a white crystalline solid that absorbs water readily. Use: solvent, manufacture of organic chemicals. Formula: CH_3CONH_2.

acetaminophen /ə seétə mínnəfən, ássitə-/ *n N Am* PHARM same as **paracetamol**

acetanilide /ássi tánni līd/ *n* a white crystalline compound. Use: manufacture of chemicals, dyes, and rubber. Formula: C_8H_9NO. [Mid-19C. < ACETYL + ANILINE + -IDE]

acetate /ássi tayt/ *n* **1.** a salt or ester of acetic acid **2.** CHEM same as **cellulose acetate 3.** a product made of or containing acetate

acetic /ə seétik/ *adj* containing, producing, or made from vinegar or acetic acid [Late 18C. < French *acétique* < Latin *acetum* 'vinegar']

acetic acid *n* a colourless acid with a pungent odour that is the main component of vinegar. Use: manufacture of drugs, dyes, plastics, and fibres. Formula: CH_3COOH.

acetic anhydride *n* a colourless liquid with a pungent odour. Use: manufacture of aspirin and plastics. Formula: $C_4H_6O_3$.

acetify /ə sétti fī/ (**-fies, -fying, -fied**) *vti* to turn into, or cause something to turn into, acetic acid or vinegar —**acetification** /ə séttifi káysh'n/ *n* —**acetifier** *n*

aceto- *prefix* acetic acid ○ *acetify* [< Latin *acetum* 'vinegar']

acetohexamide /ə seétō héksə mīd/ *n* a sulphur-containing drug. Use: treatment of diabetes. [< ACETO- + HEXA- + AMIDE]

acetone /ássitōn/ *n* a colourless flammable liquid with a slightly sweet smell. Use: paint and nail polish solvent, manufacture of organic chemicals. Formula: C_3H_6O.

acetone body *n* BIOCHEM same as **ketone body**

acetophenone /ə seétō fénnōn/ *n* a colourless liquid with a sweet pungent smell and taste. Use: perfumes, solvent, flavouring. Formula: C_8H_8O. [Mid-19C. < ACETO- + PHENYL + -ONE]

acetous /ássitəss, ə seé-/ *adj* like, containing, or producing acetic acid or vinegar [14C. < late Latin *acetosus* < Latin *acetum* 'vinegar']

acetyl /ássi tīl, ə seé-/ *adj* relating to or containing the chemical group CH_3CO-

acetylate /ə sétti layt/ (**-lates, -lating, -lated**) *vt* to introduce the acetyl group into a compound —**acetylation** /ə sétti láysh'n/ *n*

acetylcholine /ássi tīl kō leen/ *n* a white crystalline compound released from the ends of nerve fibres and involved in the transmission of nerve impulses. Formula: $C_7H_{17}NO_3$.

acetylcholinesterase /ássi tīl kōlin éstə rayz/ *n* an enzyme, present in blood and some nerve endings, that aids the breakdown of acetylcholine and suppresses its stimulatory effect on nerves

acetyl coenzyme A, **acetyl CoA** *n* a coenzyme produced during metabolism of carbohydrates, fatty acids, and amino acids

acetylene /ə sétti leen/ *n* a colourless gaseous flammable hydrocarbon. Use: welding, manufacture of organic chemicals. Formula: C_2H_2. —**acetylenic** /ə sétti lénnik/ *adj*

acetylide /ə sétti līd/ *n* any acetylene-derived compound containing a metal atom, often very explosive

acetylsalicylic acid /ássi tīl sálli síllik-/ *n* the drug aspirin (*technical*)

acey-deucy /áyssi dyoōssi/ *n* a version of backgammon in which a dice throw of one or two wins an additional turn [< ACE, DEUCE[1]]

ach /aakh/ *interj Scotland* used to express emotion, e.g. annoyance, surprise, or resignation, often as an introduction to saying something [15C. < Celtic]

ACH *n* in e-commerce, a wholesale payment network for interbank clearing and payment settlement, accessible through points of sale or cashpoints. Full form **automated clearing house**

Achaea /ə keé ə/, **Achaia** /ə kī ə, ə káy ə/ **1.** administrative department in the Northern Peloponnese, Greece. Area: 3,209 sq. km/1,239 sq. mi. Population: 300,078 (1991). **2.** in ancient Greece, province in the northern Peloponnese

Achaean /ə keé ən, ə káy ən/, **Achaian** /ə kī ən, ə káy ən/ *n* **1.** a member of an ancient Hellenic people thought to have founded the Mycenaean civilization on the Peloponnese **2.** somebody who comes from the modern Greek department of Achaea —**Achaean** *adj*

Achaia, etc another spelling of **Achaea, etc**

achalasia /ákə láyzi ə/ *n* a failure of smooth muscle

bands such as those in the gullet to relax [Early 20C. < A-² + Greek *khalasis* 'relaxation' < *khalan* 'loosen']

achar /ə chaár, **achaar** n a pungent pickle made of mango, lemon, and ginger, used in South Asian and Caribbean cooking [Late 16C. Via Hindi < Persian *āchār*]

acharya /ə chaári ə/ n S Asia a learned religious teacher and guide

achcha /úchə/ interj S Asia 1. used to express agreement 2. used to express surprise or doubt [< Hindi *acchā*]

ache /ayk/ vi (**aches**, **aching**, **ached**) 1. FEEL PAIN to feel or be the site of a dull constant pain 2. YEARN to yearn for the presence of somebody or something 3. WANT BADLY to want something very much (informal) ○ *aching to tell her the news* ■ n CONSTANT PAIN a feeling of constant dull pain [Old English *æce* (noun), *acan* (verb), origin ? The *ch* spelling arose from a mistaken association with Greek *akhos* 'pain'] —**achingly** adv

Achebe /ə cháybi/, **Chinua** (b. 1930) Nigerian novelist. He is the author of *Things Fall Apart* (1958) and *Anthills of the Savannah* (1987).

'I feel that English will be able to carry the weight of my African experience. But it will have to be a new English, still in communion with its ancestral home but altered to suit its new African surroundings.'
[Chinua Achebe, *Morning Yet on Creation Day*; 1964]

~~acheive~~ incorrect spelling of **achieve**

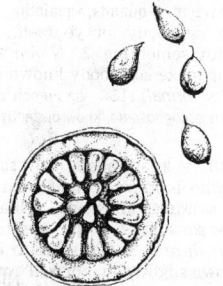

achene: cross-section of the fruit of the dog rose

achene /ə keén/, **akene** n a dry single-seeded fruit that does not open to release its seed. Dandelions and sunflowers have achenes. [Mid-19C. < modern Latin *achaenium* 'not gaping' < Greek *khainein* 'gape']

Acheron /ákərōn/ n in Greek mythology, one of the rivers that ran through Hades

Acheson /áchəss'n/, **Dean** (1893–1971) US secretary of state (1949–52). He played an important role in the development of the Truman Doctrine, the Marshall Plan, and NATO. Full name **Acheson, Dean Gooderham**

'A memorandum is written not to inform the reader but to protect the writer.'
[Dean Acheson. Quoted in *Wall Street Journal*; 8 September 1977]

Acheulian /ə shoōli ən/ n a period of the Palaeolithic era during which people made symmetrical stone hand axes [Early 20C. After the French village of Saint-Acheul near Amiens] —**Acheulian** adj

à cheval /áshə vál/ adv by placing a bet on two adjacent numbers, e.g. in roulette or cards [< French, 'on horseback', used to mean 'with one foot on each side'. Because the risk is shared equally between two cards]

achieve /ə cheév/ (**achieves**, **achieving**, **achieved**) vt to succeed in doing or gaining something, usually with effort [14C. < French *achever* 'bring to an end or head' < *a chief* 'to a head' (see CHIEF)] —**achievability** /ə cheévə billəti/ n —**achievable** adj —**achievably** adv

SYNONYMS See *accomplish*.

achieved /ə cheévd/ adj US showing great skill or accomplishment

achievement /ə cheévmənt/ n 1. SUCCESS something that somebody has succeeded in doing, usually with effort 2. FINISHING WELL the act or process of finishing something successfully 3. HERALDRY FULL COAT OF ARMS

a full coat of arms that includes standing figures such as lions or unicorns (**supporters**), the family symbol (**crest**), and the family motto

achievement age n the age at which a child should be able to perform a specific task successfully

achiever /ə cheévər/ n 1. a successful and motivated person 2. somebody who succeeds in an activity ○ *low achievers*

Achilles /ə kílleez/ n in Greek mythology, the principal hero of the Trojan War, made invulnerable by being dipped in the river Styx as a baby, except for the heel he was held by. He killed the Trojan hero Hector before being fatally wounded in the heel with an arrow fired by Paris.

Achilles heel n a weakness that seems small but makes somebody or something fatally vulnerable

Achilles tendon n the tendon that connects the heel bone to the calf muscles

achiral /ay kírəl/ adj describes a molecule having neither left-handed nor right-handed configuration

achkan /áchkən/ n a man's formal knee-length coat that buttons down the front from a high collar, worn especially in northern South Asia [Early 20C. < Hindi *ackan*]

achlorhydria /áy klaw hídri ə/ n an absence of or reduction in hydrochloric acid in the gastric juice —**achlorhydric** adj

achondrite /ə kón drīt/ n a stony meteorite that does not contain rounded grains (**chondrules**) —**achondritic** /áy kon dríttik/ adj

achondroplasia /ə kondrō pláyzi ə/ n a genetic disorder in which cartilage fails to develop into bone during early stages of development, resulting in dwarfism [Late 19C. < Greek *akhondros* 'without cartilage'] —**achondroplastic** /-plástik/ adj

achoo /ə choó/ interj a representation of the sound of somebody sneezing [Late 19C. An imitation of the sound]

achromat /ákrə mat/ n 1. PHYS same as **achromatic lens** 2. OPHTHALMOL same as **monochromat** [Early 20C. Back-formation < ACHROMATIC]

achromatic /ákrə máttik/ adj 1. WITHOUT COLOUR without colour and therefore white, grey, or black in appearance 2. PHYS WITHOUT SPECTRUM COLOURS able to reflect or refract light without spectral colour separation 3. BIOL NOT EASILY STAINED describes cells of organisms that cannot easily be stained with standard dyes 4. MUSIC WITHOUT SHARPS OR FLATS using a musical scale with no sharps or flats —**achromatically** adv —**achromaticity** /áykrōmə tíssəti/ n —**achromatism** /ə krōmətizəm/ n

achromatic colour n a colour with no hue or chromatic component

achromatic lens n a composite lens in which two or more lenses with different properties are combined to prevent distortion (**chromatic aberration**)

achromatic prism n a composite prism in which two or more prisms deflect, but do not disperse, light

achromatopsia /ə krōmə tópsi ə, ay krōmə tópsi ə/ n MED same as **monochromatism** [Mid-19C. < Greek *akhrōmatos* 'without colour' < *a-* 'without, not' + *khrōmato-* (see CHROMATO-) + *-opsia* (see -OPSY)]

achy /áyki/ (**-ier**, **-iest**) adj feeling or being the site of a constant dull pain —**achiness** n

aciclovir /ay síklə veer/, **acyclovir** n an antiviral drug. Use: treatment of herpes cold sores.

acicula /ə síkyoōlə/ (plural **-lae** /-lee/) n a needle-shaped part, e.g. a spine, bristle, or crystal (technical) [Mid-19C. < late Latin, 'little needle'] —**aciculate** /ə síkyoō layt/ adj —**aciculated** adj

acid /ássid/ n 1. CHEM CORROSIVE SUBSTANCE a sour-tasting compound that releases hydrogen ions to form a solution with a pH of less than 7, reacts with a base to form a salt, and turns blue litmus red 2. CHEM COMPOUND FORMING COVALENT BOND WITH BASE a compound that can donate a proton or accept a pair of electrons to form a covalent bond with a base 3. DRUGS same as LSD (slang) 4. SHARPNESS a sharp, bitter, or sarcastic quality in speech or writing ■ adj 1. HAVING ACIDIC PROPERTIES with the properties of or containing an acid 2. SOUR-TASTING having a sour or sharp taste 3. SARCASTIC sharp, bitter, or sarcastic in tone ○ *acid comments* 4. METEOROL POLLUTED describes rain or snow that contains dilute acid resulting from pol-

lution 5. GEOL HIGH IN SILICA describes igneous rocks that have a high silica content [Late 17C. Directly or via French < Latin *acidus* < *acere* 'be sour'] —**acidity** /ə síddəti/ n —**acidly** adv ◇ **put the acid on somebody** ANZ to put pressure on somebody to obtain a favour (informal)

ORIGIN The Indo-European word from which *acid* is ultimately derived is also the ancestor of English *acme*, *acrid*, *acrobat*, *acute*, *alacrity*, *eager*, *edge*, *oxygen*, and *vinegar*.

acid anhydride n CHEM same as **anhydride**

acid chloride n CHEM same as **acyl chloride**

acid deposition n a deposit of water vapour formed in the atmosphere, e.g. dew, rain, snow, hail, or fog, that is high in acid content because of atmospheric pollution

acid drop n a boiled sweet that has a sharp lemony taste

acid house n electronic dance music of the late 1980s, using pulsating rhythms and associated with the use of the drug ecstasy

acidic /ə síddik/ adj 1. SOUR-TASTING sour or bitter in taste 2. SARCASTIC sour, bitter, or sarcastic in manner or tone 3. CHEM CONTAINING ACID containing or having the properties of an acid 4. CHEM FORMING ACID IN WATER forming an acid in water

acidify /ə síddi fī/ (**-fies**, **-fying**, **-fied**) vti to turn something acid, or become acid —**acidifiable** adj —**acidification** /ə síddifi káysh'n/ n —**acidifier** n

acidimeter /ássi dímmitər/ n an instrument for measuring the amount of acid in a solution —**acidimetric** /ássidi méttrik/ adj —**acidimetry** /ássi dímmətri/ n

acidity /ə síddəti/ n (plural **-ties**) n 1. the concentration of acid in a substance, of which pH is a measure 2. the quality or condition of being acid 3. MED same as **hyperacidity**

acid jazz n a mixture of funk, jazz, and soul music that first appeared in the 1980s

acidophil /ássi dōfil, ə síddōfil/, **acidophile** /ássi dō fīl, ə síddōfīl/ n 1. a microorganism or plant that flourishes in an acid environment 2. a cell that stains readily with acidic dyes

acidophilic /ássidō fíllik/ adj 1. describes cells that are easily stained by an acid dye 2. describes microorganisms or plants that flourish in an acid environment

acidophilus /ássi dóffiləss/ (plural **acidophili** /-lī/) n a bacterium with slender rod-shaped cells, usually in chains, that thrives in acidic conditions and is beneficial to the intestinal tract. Use: yoghurt manufacture. Latin name: *Lactobacillus acidophilus*. [Mid-19C. < modern Latin, 'acid-loving']

acidophilus milk n milk to which acidophilus culture has been added but which has not fully fermented as has yogurt. Use: treatment of digestive disorders.

acidosis /ássi dōssiss/ n a failure of the mechanism that controls the acidity of the blood, other body fluids, or body tissues, commonly caused by untreated diabetes

acid protease n a protein-digesting enzyme activated in stomach acid

acid rain n rain that contains dilute acid derived from burning fossil fuels and that is potentially harmful to the environment

acid reflux n upward ejection of acid from the stomach into the oesophagus, causing pain known as heartburn

acid rock n electric rock music popular in the late 1960s, with instrumental effects and lyrics suggesting or promoting psychedelic experiences

acid test n a decisive test that establishes the worth or credibility of something ○ *'The treatment accorded Russia by her sister nations in the months to come will be the acid test of their good will.'* (Woodrow Wilson, *Speech on the Fourteen Points*; 1918) [< the use of nitric acid to test gold]

acidulate /ə síddyoō layt/ (**-lates**, **-lating**, **-lated**) vti to make something slightly acid, or become slightly acid —**acidulation** /ə síddyoō láysh'n/ n

acidulous /ə síddyoōləss/ adj 1. slightly sour in taste

(*formal*) **2.** cutting and sharp in speech or tone [Mid-18C. < Latin *acidulus* < *acidus* (see ACID)]

aciduria /ássi dyoŏri əl/ *n* a condition in which there is a higher level of acidity of the urine than is usual or desirable

acierate /ássi ə rayt/ (**-ates, -ating, -ated**) *vt* to make iron into steel by combining it with carbon and other elements [Mid-19C. < French *aciérer* < *acier* 'steel']

acinus /ássinəss/ (*plural* **-ni** /-nī/) *n* **1.** ANAT a rounded sac containing secretory cells, found at the ends of the ducts in an exocrine gland **2.** ANAT same as **alveolus** (sense 1) **3.** BOT any of the small globes (**drupelets**) that make up an aggregate fruit such as a blackberry or raspberry [Mid-18C. < Latin, 'berry growing in a cluster, kernel'] —**acinar** *adj* —**acinous** *adj*

ack-ack /ák ak/ *n* (*informal*) **1.** ARMS same as **antiaircraft gun 2.** antiaircraft fire [Representing *AA* 'antiaircraft' in a former system of spelling out messages]

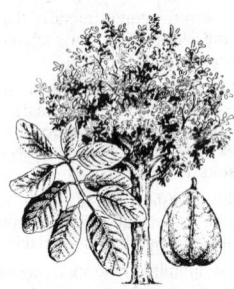

ackee

ackee /ákee/ (*plural* **-ees** or *same*), **akee** *n* **1.** a red pear-shaped fruit with poisonous seeds, edible when ripe but poisonous at other times **2.** an evergreen tree cultivated in the Caribbean and Florida for ackees. Native to: tropical western Africa. Latin name: *Blighia sapida*. [Late 18C. Perhaps < Kru]

REGIONAL NOTE *Ackee*, used especially in the phrase *ackee rice*, has been introduced into British English by the Caribbean community. The flesh of the fruit is often eaten with rice and saltfish.

ack-emma /ák émmə/ *adv* in the morning (*dated informal*) [Representing A.M. in a former system of spelling out messages]

Ackerman steering /ákərmən-/ *n* the steering system used in most motor vehicles, in which the wheels swivel at each end of the axle, instead of the whole axle beam swivelling at its central point

acknowledge /ək nóllij/ (**-edges, -edging, -edged**) *v* **1.** *vti* ADMIT SOMETHING to admit or accept that something exists, is true, or is real **2.** *vti* SHOW AWARENESS OF SOMETHING to respond to something such as a greeting or message to show it has been noticed or received **3.** *vt* SHOW APPRECIATION OF SOMETHING to show appreciation or express thanks for something such as a letter or gift **4.** *vt* RECOGNIZE SOMEBODY OR SOMETHING LEGALLY to recognize or admit the existence, rights, or authority of somebody or something, especially in a legal context **5.** *vt* THANK SOMEBODY OFFICIALLY to officially or publicly recognize somebody's help or work [15C. Probably < KNOWLEDGE after obsolete *aknow* 'recognize, acknowledge' (< KNOW)] —**acknowledgeable** *adj* —**acknowledged** *adj* —**acknowledger** *n*

acknowledgment /ək nóllijmənt/, **acknowledgement** *n* **1.** ACCEPTANCE OF FACTS the act of accepting the truth or existence of something **2.** SIGN OF RECOGNITION a sign showing that somebody has seen or heard somebody else **3.** OFFICIAL RECOGNITION official or public recognition of somebody's help or work **4.** INDICATION OF RECEIPT a letter or message sent to say that something has been received **5.** THANKS an expression of thanks or appreciation for something ■ **acknowledgments** *npl* AUTHOR'S THANKS a section in a book or other piece of writing where an author thanks those who have helped

~~aclaim~~ incorrect spelling of **acclaim**

aclarubicin /áklə roŏbissin/ *n* an antibiotic that is toxic to dividing cells. Use: treatment of leukaemia.

aclinic line /ay klínnik-/ *n* GEOG same as **magnetic equator** [< Greek *aklinēs* 'not leaning' < *klinein* 'to lean']

ACLU *abbr* American Civil Liberties Union

ACM *abbr* **1.** AIR FORCE air chief marshal **2.** COMPUT Association for Computing Machinery

acme /ákmi/ *n* the highest point of perfection or achievement [Late 16C. < Greek *akmē* 'highest point']

acne /ákni/ *n* a disease of the oil-secreting glands of the skin that often affects adolescents, producing eruptions on the face, neck, and shoulders that can leave pitted scars [Mid-19C. < Latin, misreading of Greek *akmē* 'highest point'] —**acned** *adj*

acne rosacea *n* MED same as **rosacea**

acoelomate /ə seélə mayt/ *n* an organism with no cavity (**coelom**) between its digestive tract and outer wall, e.g. a flatworm or jellyfish

acolyte /ákə līt/ *n* **1.** a follower or assistant ○ *the acolytes of this powerful leader* **2.** somebody, especially a young person, who assists a member of the clergy in the performance of rites [14C. Directly or via Old French < ecclesiastical Latin *acolytus* < Greek *akolouthos* 'follower' < *a-* 'together' + *keleuthos* 'path']

~~accommodate~~ incorrect spelling of **accommodate**

~~accommodation~~ incorrect spelling of **accommodation**

~~accompany~~ incorrect spelling of **accompany**

Aconcagua /ákən kágwə/ highest mountain in the Andes and in the western hemisphere, located in western Argentina near the Chilean border. Height: 6,960 m/22,834 ft.

aconite /ákə nīt/ *n* **1.** an extract of the dried poisonous root of some plants of the genus. Latin name: *Aconitum*. Use: homeopathic remedy. **2.** a plant with poisonous roots. Flowers: purplish-blue or white, hooded. Native to: northern temperate regions. Genus: *Aconitum*. **3.** PLANTS same as **winter aconite** [Mid-16C. Directly or via French < Latin *aconitum* < Greek *akoniton*]

~~acording~~ incorrect spelling of **according**

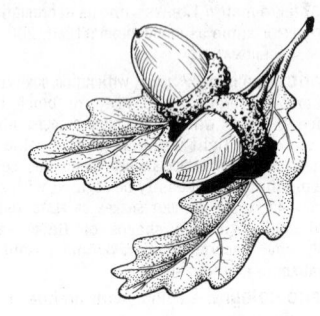

acorn

acorn /áy kawrn/ *n* the hard fruit of an oak tree, consisting of a smooth single-seeded nut that is set in a cup-shaped base and ripens from green to brown [Old English *æcern*, perhaps < *æcer* 'open land'; later interpreted as 'oak-corn']

acorn barnacle *n* an invertebrate sea animal with a conical shell that attaches itself to rocks and catches food using tendrils. Latin name: *Balanus balanoides*.

acorn squash

acorn squash *n N Am* an acorn-shaped winter squash with a ridged dark green rind and yellow or orange flesh

acorn worm *n* a burrowing invertebrate sea animal

resembling a worm with an acorn-shaped snout that it uses to dig for food. Native to: shallow coastal waters. Phylum: Chordata.

acouchi /ə koŏshi/ (*plural* **-chis** or **-chies**), **acouchy** (*plural* **-chies**) *n* an agile rodent similar to an agouti. Native to: South America. Genus: *Myoprocta*. [Late 18C. Via French < Tupi]

acoustic /ə koŏstik/, **acoustical** /-stik'l/ *adj* **1.** OF SOUND relating to sound, hearing, or the study of sound **2.** DESIGNED FOR USE WITH SOUND designed to control, absorb, or carry sound **3.** MUSIC NOT AMPLIFIED describes music or a musical instrument that is not electronically amplified, e.g. a guitar ■ *n* MUSIC same as **acoustics** *npl* [Early 18C. < Greek *akoustikos* < *akouein* 'hear' < Indo-European] —**acoustically** *adv*

acoustic nerve *n* MED same as **auditory nerve**

acoustic neuroma *n* a benign tumour that develops on the auditory nerve causing hearing loss, loss of balance, and headaches

acoustics /ə koŏstiks/ *n* the scientific study of sound (*takes a singular verb*) ■ *npl* the characteristic way in which sound carries or can be heard within an enclosed space such as an auditorium (*takes a plural verb*) —**acoustician** /ákoo stísh'n/ *n*

acoustic tile *n* a ceiling or wall tile designed to stop or diminish the transmission of sound

acoustic trauma *n* physical damage or changes in the body caused by sound waves, e.g. hearing loss, disorientation, motion sickness, and dizziness

acoustoelectric /ə koŏstō i léktrik/ *adj* ACOUSTICS same as **electroacoustic** —**acoustoelectrically** *adv*

acquaint /ə kwáynt/ (**-quaints, -quainting, -quainted**) *vt* **1.** to make somebody, or yourself, aware of or familiar with something **2.** *N Am* to introduce somebody or make somebody known to somebody else (*dated or formal*) [13C. Via French *acointier* 'make known' < Latin *accognoscere* 'know perfectly' < *cognoscere* 'know']

acquaintance /ə kwáyntənss/ *n* **1.** SOMEBODY KNOWN somebody who is known slightly rather than intimately **2.** KNOWLEDGE knowledge, usually slight, of somebody or something ○ *only a basic acquaintance with French theatre* **3.** PEOPLE SLIGHTLY KNOWN people who are known slightly but not well ○ *a wide circle of acquaintance* —**acquaintanceship** *n* ◇ **have a nodding acquaintance with somebody** *or* **something** to know somebody or something slightly ◇ **make somebody's acquaintance** to meet somebody for the first time

acquaintance rape *n US* a rape committed by a perpetrator who is known to the victim

acquainted /ə kwáyntid/ *adj* **1.** having some, often not very much, knowledge of something ○ *not acquainted with this software* **2.** known to somebody or to each other from a previous introduction

acquiesce /ákwi éss/ (**-esces, -escing, -esced**) *vi* to agree or comply with something in a passive or reserved way [Early 17C. < Latin *acquiescere* 'remain resting', hence 'agree tacitly' < *quiescere* 'to rest'] —**acquiescence** *n* —**acquiescent** *adj* —**acquiescently** *adv*

SYNONYMS See *agree*.

acquire /ə kwír/ (**-quires, -quiring, -quired**) *vt* **1.** GET SOMETHING to get or obtain possession of something **2.** DEVELOP SOMETHING to learn or develop something ○ *a habit I acquired in the army* **3.** LOCATE SOMETHING BY RADAR to locate an object such as an aircraft or ship by the use of radar or other detector [15C. Via Old French *acquerre* < Latin *acquirere* 'get something extra' < *quaerere* 'try to get or obtain'] —**acquirable** *adj* —**acquired** *adj*

SYNONYMS See *get*[1].

acquired character, **acquired characteristic** *n* a characteristic that an organism develops in response to its environment and that cannot be passed on to the next generation

acquired immune deficiency syndrome, **acquired immunodeficiency syndrome** *n* MED full form of **Aids**

acquired taste *n* a liking that develops for something that seems unpleasant at first

acquirement /ə kwírmənt/ *n* **1.** the act or process of acquiring something **2.** something learnt or attained, especially a skill

acquirer /ak kwīrər/ *n* **1.** somebody or something that acquires something **2.** a financial institution that processes transactions paid for by credit or debit card, supplying payment to the retailer and notifying the card issuer of the debt incurred by the purchaser

acquis communautaire /a kée kə moonō táir/ *n* the body of legislation governing the EU [< French, literally 'community knowledge']

acquisition /ákwi zísh'n/ *n* **1.** ACQUIRING the act of acquiring something **2.** NEW POSSESSION something that has recently been bought or obtained **3.** SKILL DEVELOPMENT the development of a new skill, practice, or way of doing things ○ *language acquisition* **4.** LOCATING BY RADAR the location of an object such as an aircraft or ship by the use of radar or other detector [14C. < Latin *acquisition-* < *acquisit-*, past participle of *acquirere* (see ACQUIRE)]

acquisitions /ákwi zísh'nz/ *n* the department in a company responsible for taking over other businesses (*takes a singular verb*) ○ *I work in acquisitions and mergers.*

acquisitive /ə kwízzətiv/ *adj* eager to acquire things, especially possessions [Mid-17C. < Latin *acquisit-* (see ACQUISITION), after French *acquisitif*] —**acquisitively** *adv*—**acquisitiveness** *n*

acquit /ə kwít/ (**-quits, -quitting, -quitted**) *v* **1.** *vt* LAW DECLARE SOMEBODY INNOCENT to declare officially that somebody is not guilty of a charge **2. acquit yourself** *vr* BEHAVE to conduct yourself in a particular way ○ *The band acquitted itself well at the performance.* **3.** *vt* FREE SOMEBODY FROM OBLIGATION to free somebody from a duty or obligation (*formal*) **4.** *vt* REPAY SOMETHING to repay something such as a debt (*archaic*) [13C. Via Old French *a(c)quiter* < assumed Latin *acquitare* 'bring to rest', hence 'set free' < *quies* 'quiet'] —**acquitter** *n*

acquittal /ə kwítt'l/ *n* a judgment given by a court of law that somebody is not guilty of a charge

acquittance /ə kwítt'nss/ *n* release from a debt or obligation, or a record of this (*dated*)

acre /áykər/ *n* UNIT OF AREA a unit of area used in some countries, including the United States and the United Kingdom, equal to 4,046.86 sq. m./4,840 sq. yd ■ **acres** *npl* **1.** LAND land, especially a large amount of land **2.** LARGE AMOUNT a large amount or area of something (*informal*) ○ *acres of space in the new headquarters* [Old English *æcer*. Ultimately probably 'area over which ploughing oxen can be driven in a day' < Indo-European, 'drive']

Acre /áykər/ industrial seaport in northern Israel. Population: 44,800 (1999).

acreage /áykərij/ *n* land, or an area of land, measured in acres

acre-foot *n* the volume of water that would cover an area of one acre to a depth of one foot, equal to 1,233.5 cu m/43,560 cu ft

acre-inch *n* the volume of water that would cover an area of one acre to a depth of one inch, equal to one-twelfth of an acre-foot or 102.8 cu m/3,630 cu ft

acrid /ákrid/ *adj* **1.** unpleasantly strong and bitter in smell or taste **2.** sharp or bitter in tone or character [Early 18C. < Latin *acri-* 'sharp, pungent', after ACID] —**acridity** /ə kríddəti/ *n*—**acridly** *adv*—**acridness** *n*

acridine /ákri deen/ *n* a colourless crystalline solid. Source: coal tar. Use: manufacture of dyes and pharmaceuticals. Formula: $C_{13}H_9N$. [Late 19C. < German *Acridin* < Latin *acri-* 'sharp, pungent']

acriflavine /ákri fláy veen/ *n* an orange-brown crystalline solid. Use: as an antiseptic in solution. Formula: $C_{14}H_{14}N_3Cl$.

~~**acrilic**~~ incorrect spelling of **acrylic**

acrimonious /ákri mṓni əss/ *adj* full of or displaying anger and resentment —**acrimoniously** *adv* —**acrimoniousness** *n*

acrimony /ákriməni/ *n* bitterness and resentment, especially in speech, attitude, or tone [Mid-16C. Directly or via French < Latin *acrimonia* < *acri-* 'sharp, pungent']

acrivastine /ə krívvə steen/ *n* a drug that inhibits the production of histamine. Use: treatment of rhinitis, urticaria, and eczema. [Late 20C. < ACRYLIC ACID + *-astine*, INN stem]

acro- *prefix* top, tip, height ○ *acrocentric* ○ *acrophobia* [< Greek *akros* 'extreme, topmost' < Indo-European]

acrobat /ákrə bat/ *n* **1.** a performer of gymnastic feats as entertainment **2.** somebody whose opinions or positions change readily to suit the circumstances [Early 19C. Via French < Greek *akrobatos* 'walking on tiptoe' < *akros* (see ACRO-) + *bainein* 'to walk']

acrobatic /ákrə báttik/ *adj* **1.** relating to or involving acrobatics **2.** showing or demanding agility and energy —**acrobatically** *adv*

acrobatics /ákrə báttiks/ *n* **1.** MOVEMENTS OF ACROBAT the skill or performance routines of an acrobat (*takes a singular or plural verb*) **2.** ACTIVITY REQUIRING AGILITY an activity that requires great skill or agility (*takes a plural verb*) ○ *mental acrobatics* **3.** VIRTUOSO PERFORMANCE performance of something that is marked by skill and artistry (*takes a plural verb*) ○ *verbal acrobatics in her summing-up*

acrocentric /ákrō séntrik/ *adj* describes a chromosome that has arms of unequal length, because the structure at which the two arms join (**centromere**) is located towards one end

acrocephaly /ákrō séffəli/ *n* MED same as **oxycephaly** —**acrocephalic** /ákrō sə fállik/ *adj* —**acrocephalous** *adj*

acrocyanosis /ákrō sī ə nṓssis/ *n* a disorder affecting the fingers and toes causing them to become blue and cold at low temperatures. Acrocyanosis is a feature of raynaud's disease.

acrodont /ákrə dont/ *adj* describes the teeth of some reptiles that have no roots and are joined to the jawbone ■ *n* a reptile with acrodont teeth

acrolect /ákrō lekt/ *n* the language variety among a group of related varieties that is closest to the standard form of the language

acrolein /ə krṓli in/ *n* a colourless poisonous pungent aldehyde. Use: manufacture of chemicals and pharmaceuticals. Formula: CH_2CHCHO. [Mid-19C. < ACRID + Latin *oleum* 'oil']

acrolith /ákrō lith/ *n* a statue, especially in ancient Greece, with a wooden body and hands, feet, and head of stone

acromegaly /ákrō méggəli/ *n* overproduction of growth hormones, resulting in enlarged bones in the hands, feet, jaw, nose, and ribs of adults —**acromegalic** /ákrō mi gállik/ *adj*

acromion /ə krṓmi ən/ (*plural* **acromia** /-mi ə/) *n* a bony projection from the outer end of the spine of the shoulder blade, to which the collarbone is attached [Late 16C. < Greek *akrōmion* < *akros* (see ACRO-) + *ōmos* 'shoulder']

acronym /ákrənim/ *n* a word formed from the initials or other parts of several words, e.g. 'NATO', from the initial letters of 'North Atlantic Treaty Organization' [Mid-20C < ACRO- + *-nym* < Greek *onuma* 'name', after SYNONYM etc] —**acronymic** /ákrə nímmik/ *adj*—**acronymous** /ə krónniməss/ *adj*

USAGE See ***abbreviation.***

acropetal /ə króppit'l/ *adj* describes leaves or flowers that grow in order from the base of a plant or stem towards the apex —**acropetally** *adv*

acrophobia /ákrə fṓbi ə/ *n* an irrational fear of being in high places —**acrophobic** *adj*

acropolis /ə króppəliss/ *n* in ancient Greece, the fortified citadel of a city [Early 17C. < Greek *akropolis*]

Acropolis *n* the ancient citadel of Athens in Greece that was the religious focus of the city. It contains the remains of several classical temples, including the Parthenon.

acrosome /ákrō sōm/ *n* a structure at the end of a sperm cell that releases enzymes to digest the cell membrane of an egg, enabling the sperm to penetrate the egg

across /ə króss/ CORE MEANING: a grammatical word indicating that somebody or something is on the opposite side of something or moves or reaches from one side to the other ○ (prep) *I live across the street from you.* ○ (adv) *a bridge wide enough to walk across*

1. *prep* ON OPPOSITE SIDE at or on the opposite side of something ○ *across the road* **2.** *prep* FROM ONE SIDE TO OTHER from one side of something to the opposite side ○ *ran across the road* ○ *a bridge across the river* **3.** *prep* IN SPITE OF BOUNDARIES in such a way that boundaries or borders are transcended ○ *united across cultures* **4.** *adj, adv* SO AS TO CROSS SOMETHING in such a way as to intersect or form a cross with something ○ *placed one board across the other* **5.** *prep* THROUGHOUT all over something or somewhere ○ *all across America* **6.** *adv* AT OR TO OTHER SIDE at, on, or to the other side of something ○ *Once we were across, we felt safe.* **7.** *adv* MEASURED IN WIDTH as measured from one side of something to the other ○ *about an inch across* **8.** *adv* HORIZONTALLY ON CROSSWORD in a horizontal position in a crossword ○ *couldn't find the solution to 3 across* [13C. < Old French *à croix* or *en croix* 'transversely' < Latin *crux* 'cross']

across-the-board *adj, adv* affecting everyone or everything equally or proportionally ■ *adj US* used to describe an each-way bet —**across the board** *adv*

acrostic /ə króstik/ *n* a number of lines of writing, especially a poem or word puzzle, in which a combination of letters from each line spells a word or phrase [Late 16C. Via French *acrostiche* < Greek *akrostikhis* < *akros* 'outermost' + *stikhos* 'line of verse' (< *steikhein* 'go')] —**acrostically** *adv*

acrylamide /ə kríllə mīd/ *n* **1.** a poisonous colourless crystalline solid. Use: manufacture of polymers. Formula: $C_{17}H_{10}O$. **2.** a polymer made with acrylamide [Late 19C. < ACRYLIC]

acrylate /ə kríllayt/ *n* **1.** a salt or ester of acrylic acid **2.** CHEM same as **acrylate resin** [Mid-19C. < ACRYLIC]

acrylate resin *n* a resin derived from acrylic or other related acids. Use: paints, sizing, adhesives, plastics.

acrylic /ə kríllik/ *n* **1.** SYNTHETIC FIBRE a synthetic textile fibre produced from acrylonitrile **2.** SOMETHING MADE FROM ACRYLIC ACID something containing or made from acrylic acid **3.** PAINT a paint containing acrylate resin, used especially in painting pictures [Mid-19C. < ACROLEIN + -YL] —**acrylic** *adj*

acrylic acid *n* a colourless corrosive acid. Use: manufacture of acrylate resins. Formula: $C_3H_4O_2$.

acrylic resin *n* CHEM same as **acrylate resin**

acrylonitrile /ákrilō nī trīl/ *n* a colourless toxic liquid. Use: manufacture of acrylic fibres and resins, rubbers, and thermoplastics. Formula: C_3H_3N. [Late 19C. < ACRYLIC]

act /akt/ *n* **1.** SOMETHING DONE something that somebody does **2.** DOING SOMETHING the action of carrying something out **3.** PART OF PLAY one of the main sections of a play or other dramatic performance **4.** ONE OF SEVERAL PERFORMANCES a short performance, especially one that is part of a varied programme or show ○ *The next act is a barbershop quartet.* **5.** PERFORMER the performer or performers who take part in an act **6.** PERSONAL BEHAVIOUR somebody's actions or behaviour considered as entertainment or used as an assessment of that person's worth (*informal*) ○ *a class act* **7.** PRETENCE behaviour that is intended to impress or deceive other people ○ *He's just putting on an act.* **8.** POL RECORD REGARDING LAW a record or statement of the decision made by a parliamentary or judicial body **9.** FORMAL RECORD a formal written record of the proceedings of a society, committee, or elected group **10.** PHILOSOPHY SOMETHING DONE INTENTIONALLY something brought about by human will ■ *v* (**acts, acting, acted**) **1.** *vi* DO SOMETHING to do something to change a situation, e.g. to solve a problem or prevent one arising ○ *need to act at once* **2.** *vti* BEHAVE IN PARTICULAR WAY to adopt a particular way of behaving ○ *You've been acting funny all morning.* ○ *Stop acting the fool.* ○ *'I even liked him when he was 'difficult' and official, because I thought I knew why he acted like that.'* (Paul Scott, *The Jewel in the Crown*; 1966) **3.** *vi* PRETEND to behave in a way intended to impress or deceive other people **4.** *vi* FUNCTION AS SOMETHING to serve a particular purpose or perform a particular function ○ *The ozone layer acts as a barrier against harmful radiation.* **5.** *vi* REPLACE SOMEBODY to be a substitute for somebody or something else ○ *Since the director cannot attend, his deputy will act for him.* **6.** *vi* HAVE EFFECT to create, produce, or bring about an effect or result ○ *Once the medicine acts, you'll feel better.* **7.** *vti* PLAY ROLE to play the part of a character in a dramatic performance ○ *a chance to act Othello* **8.** *vi* BE ACTOR to pursue a career in films or drama **9.** *vti* PERFORM SOMETHING, OR BE PERFORMED to stage a dramatic performance, or be capable of being staged ○ *The company will act a different play tomorrow night.* [14C. Directly or via French *acte* < Latin *actus, actum* 'public transaction' < past participle of *agere*

'do'] —**actable** *adj* ◇ **a hard** *or* **tough act to follow** somebody or something that sets a standard difficult to reach by others who come later ◇ **catch somebody in the act** to see or meet somebody just as he or she is doing something, especially something wrong ◇ **clean up your act** to improve your behaviour ◇ **get in on the act** to join in something in order to share in its success or profit (*informal*) ◇ **get your act together** to do something to become more organized (*informal*)

act on, act upon *vt* **1.** to be guided by somebody's advice or suggestion **2.** to have an effect on something

act out *v* **1.** *vt* to perform something or portray it in action **2.** *vti* to express a negative feeling or impulse by behaving in a socially unacceptable way

act up *vi* to cause trouble or pain

ACT *abbr* **1.** advance corporation tax **2.** Australian Capital Territory

Actaeon /ak tée ən/ *n* in Greek mythology, a hunter who was turned into a stag after inadvertently seeing the goddess Artemis bathing

ACTH *n* a pituitary hormone that stimulates the adrenal cortex to produce steroid hormones. Full form **adrenocorticotrophic hormone**

actin /áktin/ *n* a protein present in all cells and in muscle tissue where it plays a role in contraction [Mid-20C. < Latin *actus* (see ACT)]

actin- *prefix* same as **actino-** (*used before vowels*)

actinal /áktənəl/ *adj* **1.** describes the side of an invertebrate sea animal such as a jellyfish or sea anemone from which the arms or tentacles radiate, or on which the mouth area is situated **2.** having rays or tentacles

acting /ákting/ *n* **PERFORMING IN PLAYS** the art, profession, or performance of an actor ■ *adj* **1. TEMPORARY** carrying out particular duties or doing somebody else's job temporarily ○ *the acting manager* **2. WITH DIRECTIONS FOR STAGING** including directions in a play's text to be used in staging a performance ○ *a copy of the acting edition of the play*

actinian /ak tínni ən/ *n* MARINE BIOL same as **sea anemone** (*technical*) [Late 19C. < modern Latin *Actinia* < Greek *aktin-* 'ray']

actinic /ak tínnik/ *adj* relating to radiation such as ultraviolet radiation that produces a chemical effect —**actinically** *adv*

actinide /ákti nīd/ *n* an element in the series of radioactive elements beginning with actinium and ending with lawrencium [Mid-20C. < ACTINIUM, after LANTHANIDE]

actinism /áktinizəm/ *n* the property of radiation that makes photochemical change possible

actinium /ak tínni əm/ *n* a radioactive silvery-white metallic element. Source: pitchblende. Use: source of alpha rays. Symbol **Ac**. See table at **element** [Early 20C. < Greek *aktin-* 'ray']

actino- *prefix* **1.** radial ○ *actinomorphic* **2.** radiation [< Greek *aktin-*, stem of *aktis* 'ray']

actinolite /ak tínnə līt/ *n* a green or greyish green silicate mineral of the amphibole group, containing calcium, magnesium, and iron

actinometer /ákti nómmitər/ *n* a device for measuring the intensity of radiation, especially that from the Sun —**actinometric** /áktinō méttrik/ *adj* —**actinometry** /ákti nómmətri/ *n*

actinomorphic /áktinō máwrfik/, **actinomorphous** /-máwrfəss/ *adj* spreading out symmetrically around a central point and so making identical halves when divided along any vertical axis. Tulips and starfish are actinomorphic. —**actinomorphy** *n*

actinomycete /áktinō mī seet/ *n* a rod-shaped or filamentous bacterium belonging to a large group that includes some that cause diseases and some that are the sources of antibiotics. Order: Actinomycetales. [Early 20C. Back-formation < modern Latin *actinomycetes*, plural of *actinomyces* < ACTINO- + Greek *mukēs* 'fungus'] —**actinomycetous** *adj*

actinomycin /áktinō mīssin/ *n* an antibiotic. Use: treatment of childhood cancers.

actinouranium /áktinō yoo ráyni əm/ *n* the only naturally occurring, naturally fissile, radioactive isotope of uranium. Use: nuclear reactors, weapons.

action /áksh'n/ *n* **1. DOING SOMETHING TOWARDS GOAL** the process of doing something in order to achieve a purpose **2. SOMETHING DONE** something that somebody or something does **3. MOVEMENT** the way somebody or something moves or works, or the movement itself ○ *the action of a piston* **4. VERVE** energetic activity ○ *a woman of action* **5.** LAW **LEGAL PROCEEDINGS** legal proceedings in a court to obtain compensation for something or to enforce a right ○ *decided not to take action* **6. EVENTS** the important events in a narrative composition such as a novel or film **7. FUNCTION OR INFLUENCE** the way in which something functions, or the effect it produces ○ *the action of water on stone* **8. FIGHTING DURING WAR** a small battle, or the fighting that takes place during a war ○ *wounded in action* ○ *a campaign of brief actions* **9. EXCITING OR PROFITABLE ACTIVITY** involvement in something that brings excitement, profit, or pleasure (*informal*) ○ *a piece of the action* **10. OPERATING MECHANISM** the operating parts of a mechanism or instrument, e.g. a watch or piano **11.** MUSIC **SPACE UNDER STRINGS** the space between the fingerboard and strings of a string instrument such as a violin or a guitar **12.** PHYS **FORCE** the force applied to a body **13.** PHYS **PROPERTY OF SYSTEM USED IN DYNAMICS** twice the average kinetic energy of a system in a given time multiplied by the time ■ *interj* CINEMA **START PERFORMING** a command from a film director telling actors to start acting as filming has begun ■ *vt* (**-tions, -tioning, -tioned**) ⚠ **PUT PLAN INTO OPERATION** to take action on something such as a proposal or request [14C. Directly or via Old French < Latin *action-* < *actus* (see ACT)] ◇ **missing in action** absent after combat and not known to be captured, injured, or dead

---

USAGE The use of ***action*** as a verb, as in *Criticism was levelled at the way the operation was actioned*, has crept into ordinary usage from business jargon. It is disliked by people who maintain that simpler words such as *do*, *achieve*, and *complete* are just as effective. The use is particularly unwelcome in cases such as *to action dismissal*, as in *Dismissal will be actioned if any employee violates this rule*, when a simple verb is available (*Any employee who violates this rule will be dismissed*). It is always better to use the more straightforward word when this conveys the meaning just as well.

---

actionable /áksh'nəb'l/ *adj* **1.** giving a basis for somebody to take legal action **2.** able or ready to be acted upon or put into action ○ *A marketing consultancy must provide actionable and effective marketing solutions.*

actioner /áksh'nər/ *n* a film that features a great deal of usually extreme action (*informal*) ○ *a made-for-TV actioner with a little-known cast*

action figure *n* a small usually plastic doll with movable legs and arms, often based on a character from an action adventure

action game *n* a computer game that simulates exciting or violent action, especially shooting

action group *n* a group of people formed to achieve a social or political objective ○ *a pro-merger action group*

action man *n* a man who takes part in many energetic and exciting activities (*informal*)

action-packed *adj* involving or containing a large number of exciting events

action painting *n* a technique used by artists of the Abstract Expressionism movement in which paintings are created by splashing, dripping, spattering, or smearing paint

action potential *n* a temporary change in electrical potential that occurs between the inside and the outside of a nerve or muscle fibre when a nerve impulse is transmitted

action replay *n UK* a reshowing of a brief part of a televised event, often in slow motion. ANZ, N Am term **instant replay**

action stations *UK, Aus, Can npl* **POST FOR COMBAT** the posts assigned to people during or in readiness for combat ■ *interj* **1. GO TO COMBAT POSTS** used as a command ordering people to take up the posts assigned to them during or in readiness for combat **2. GET READY** used to warn people to get ready to carry out their assigned tasks (*informal*) ▶ US term (all senses) **battle stations**

activate /ákti vayt/ (**-vates, -vating, -vated**) *v* **1.** *vti* **MAKE SOMETHING CAPABLE OF ACTION** to make something active or operational, or become active or operational ○ *Any sound in the room will activate the alarm.* ○ *The detonator will activate in 30 seconds.* **2.** *vt* PHYS **MAKE SOMETHING RADIOACTIVE** to make a substance radioactive **3.** *vt* CHEM **MAKE SOMETHING REACTIVE** to increase the rate of a chemical reaction, e.g. by applying heat **4.** *vt* CHEM **INCREASE POWER OF ADSORPTION OF SOMETHING** to treat a substance such as charcoal so as to increase its capacity for adsorption **5.** *vt* PHYSIOL **PREPARE SOMETHING BY STIMULATION OR CONVERSION** to prepare an organ, body part, or body chemical for activity by stimulating it or converting an inactive form into one capable of action **6.** *vt* INDUST **PURIFY SEWAGE WITH AIR** to purify sewage by aerating it —**activation** /ákti váysh'n/ *n* —**activator** *n*

activated alumina /ákti vaytid-/ *n* a highly adsorbent form of aluminium oxide. Use: removing moisture from gases, filtering oil, catalyst.

activated carbon, **activated charcoal** *n* a highly adsorbent powdered or granular form of carbon. Use: liquid and gas purification, chemical extraction, solvent recovery, poison antidote.

activated sludge *n* aerated sewage containing microorganisms, added to untreated sewage to purify it by accelerating its bacterial decomposition

activation energy *n* the energy needed to make molecules of a substance take part in a chemical reaction

active /áktiv/ *adj* **1. MOVING ABOUT** moving about, working, or doing something, and not resting or sleeping **2. BUSY** full of or involved in busy activity ○ *an active life* **3. DOING SOMETHING** carrying out, or able to carry out, an action or process ○ *an active ingredient* **4. SHOWING INVOLVEMENT OR ENERGY** characterized by involvement, energy, or action ○ *played an active part* **5. NEEDING AND USING ENERGY** requiring a lot of energy and movement ○ *active pastimes* **6.** COMPUT **READY FOR INPUT FROM COMPUTER OPERATOR** describes the part of a computer screen or window that is currently in use or ready to accept input from the user ○ *active cell* ○ *active window* **7.** GEOL **NOT EXTINCT** describes a volcano that is not extinct and still erupts occasionally **8.** GRAM **RELATING TO ROLE OF VERB'S SUBJECT** describes a verb whose subject is the person or thing performing the action described by the verb **9.** ASTRON **SHOWING VARIABLE SURFACE FEATURES** describes the Sun when it is displaying large numbers of dark patches (**sunspots**) and bright patches (**faculae**), and high variability in radio-wave emissions **10.** COMM **USED TO PRODUCE PROFIT** producing or being used to produce profits or dividends ○ *an active account* **11.** FIN **TRADING IN LARGE VOLUME** bought and sold in large quantities ○ *the ten most active stocks* **12.** ELECTRONICS **WITH POWER SOURCE** describes electronic networks and components that contain a power source and are capable of operating ■ *n* GRAM **VERB VOICE** the active voice, or a verb in the active voice [14C. Directly or via Old French < Latin *activus* < *actus* (see ACT)] —**actively** *adv* —**activeness** *n*

active cell *n* a spreadsheet cell in which values or formulas may be entered

active duty *n N Am* full-time service in the armed forces with full pay and benefits

active immunity *n* immunity generated by the production of antibodies by the body when it is exposed to antigens

active list *n* a list of officers on or available for full duty

active-matrix display *n* a flat liquid-crystal display with high colour resolution that is particularly suitable for use in laptop and notebook computers

active packaging *n* food packaging that interacts chemically or biologically with its contents to extend shelf-life or modify the product during storage

active server page *n* a page in HyperText Markup Language with scripts that are processed on a server before being sent to a user

active service *n* **1.** *UK* service with the armed forces in an operational area **2.** *N Am* MIL same as **active duty**

active site *n* the part of an enzyme molecule that binds the substance the enzyme acts on (**substrate**)

active transport *n* the movement of substances across cell membranes from low to high concentrations, requiring energy and proteins that act as carriers

active vocabulary *n* the range of words that somebody normally uses in speech or writing, as opposed to words he or she understands when used by others

activism /áktivizəm/ *n* vigorous and sometimes aggressive action in pursuing a political or social end —**activist** *n, adj* —**activistic** /ákti vístik/ *adj*

activity /ak tívvəti/ (*plural* **-ties**) *n* **1.** SOMETHING SOMEBODY DOES something that somebody takes part in or does (*often used in the plural*) ○ *leisure activities* **2.** PHYSICAL EXERCISE energetic physical movement or exercise **3.** STATE OF DOING SOMETHING the state or process of doing something or being active ○ *Activity in the newsroom has reached fever pitch.* **4.** CHEM POTENTIAL FOR CHEMICAL REACTION the ability of a substance to undergo a chemical reaction **5.** BIOL NATURAL PROCESS a process or function that takes place naturally in a living organism ○ *activities such as eating or sleeping* **6.** EDUC LEARNING EXPERIENCE an educational exercise designed to provide direct experience of something ○ *an activity to accompany the geography lesson* **7.** PHYS RADIOACTIVITY the emission of radiation from a radioactive substance (*technical*) Symbol *A*

act of contrition *n* a short prayer of penitence

act of faith *n* an action motivated by belief in something for which there is no concrete evidence

act of God *n* a sudden uncontrollable event produced by natural forces, e.g. an earthquake or a tornado

Act of Union *n* **1.** the 1707 Act of Parliament by which Scotland was united with England to form Great Britain **2.** the 1801 Act of Parliament by which Ireland was united with Great Britain to form the United Kingdom

actomyosin /áktō mí əssin/ *n* a complex of actin and myosin formed in muscle cells during contraction [Mid-20C. < ACTIN]

actor /áktər/ *n* **1.** somebody who acts in plays, films, or television **2.** somebody who pretends to be somebody else or to feel something so as to impress or deceive

actress /áktrəss/ *n* **1.** a woman or girl who acts in plays, films, or television **2.** a woman or girl who pretends to be somebody else or to feel something so as to impress or deceive

USAGE Many actresses now prefer to refer to themselves as actors.

Acts of the Apostles *n* a book of the Bible that describes the early history of the Christian Church (*takes a singular verb*) See table at **Bible**

ACTU *abbr Aus* HR Australian Council of Trade Unions

actual /ákchoo əl, ákchəl/ *adj* **1.** REAL real and existing as fact ○ *Is that her actual title?* **2.** ⚠ USED FOR EMPHASIS used for emphasis, e.g. to stress that somebody or something being referred to is genuinely the person or thing involved ○ *This is the actual place where Wellington stood.* **3.** EXISTING NOW existing or occurring at the moment ○ *actual as opposed to projected income* [14C. Via Old French < late Latin *actualis* < Latin *actus* (see ACT)]

USAGE **Actual** is often overused as a mere emphatic term, without any real meaning: *He wanted to know if any (actual) damage had been done.* In this sentence **actual** could be removed without any significant change to the sense. In the sentence *The actual total was much higher than we had expected,* **actual** is legitimately used to mark a contrast with projected or estimated totals.

actualise *vti* another spelling of **actualize**

actuality /ákchoo álləti/ (*plural* **-ties**) *n* **1.** something that is real, as opposed to what is expected, intended, or feared ○ *Let's deal with actualities.* **2.** everything that does or could exist or happen in real life

actualize /ákchoo ə līz/ (**-izes**, **-izing**, **-ized**), **actualise** (**-ises**, **-ising**, **-ised**) *vt* **1.** to make something actual or real, or make something come about ○ *expectations actualized by deeds* **2.** to portray or represent something realistically —**actualization** /ákchoo ə lī záysh'n/ *n*

actually /ákchoo əli, ákchəli/ *adv* **1.** ⚠ used to emphasize that something really is so or really exists, e.g. when it may be hard to believe or when it contrasts with what has already been said ○ *He's actually over 35, although he looks much younger.* **2.** used to express an opinion, often a contradictory one, or to change the subject ○ *Actually, I'd prefer it if you left right now.* ○ *He's in India – he's always wanted to go there, actually.*

USAGE ***Actually***, like **actual**, is used most effectively when it contrasts with what is theoretical or only apparent: *It sounds difficult, but it's actually quite straightforward.* It is regarded as poor style to use it as a sentence filler with no real meaning, although this practice is common in informal conversation: *Actually, I prefer her to her cousin.*

actuarial /ákchoo áiri əl/ *adj* **1.** relating to the statistical calculation of risk or life expectancy for insurance purposes **2.** relating to actuaries and their work

actuarial science *n* the branch of statistics that deals with the calculation of risk, life expectancy, and insurance premiums

actuary /ákchoo əri/ (*plural* **-ies**) *n* a statistician who calculates insurance premiums, risks, dividends, and annuity rates [Mid-16C. < Latin *actuarius* < *actus* (see ACT)]

actuate /ákchoo ayt/ (**-ates**, **-ating**, **-ated**) *vt* **1.** to make somebody act or behave in a specific way (*often used in the passive*) ○ *was actuated by self-interest* **2.** to make a device move or start working (*formal*) [Late 16C. < medieval Latin *actuatus*, past participle of *actuare* 'cause something to be done' < Latin *actus* (see ACT)] —**actuation** /ákchoo áysh'n/ *n* —**actuator** *n*

ACT-UP /ákt up/ *n* an Aids activist organization in the United States and United Kingdom. Full form **Aids Coalition To Unleash Power**

ACU *abbr* MONEY Asian currency unit

acuity /ə kyoó əti/ *n* keenness of hearing, sight, or intellect [Mid-16C. Directly or via French *acuité* < medieval Latin *acuitas* < Latin *acuere* (see ACUTE)]

aculeate /ə kyoóli ət/ *adj* **1.** describes an insect that has a sting **2.** describes a plant or plant part that has prickles [Mid-17C. < Latin *aculeatus* < *aculeus* 'small needle' < *acus* (see ACUTE)]

acumen /ákyoōmən/ *n* the ability to make quick accurate intelligent judgments about people or situations ○ *political acumen* [Late 16C. < Latin, 'point, sharpness' < *acuere* (see ACUTE)]

acuminate /ə kyoómīnət/ *adj* describes leaves that taper to a sharp point [Late 16C. < late Latin *acuminatus*, past participle of *acuminare* 'sharpen to a point' < Latin *acumen* (see ACUMEN)]

~~acumulate~~ incorrect spelling of **accumulate**

acupressure /ákyoo preshər/ *n* a form of alternative therapy similar to acupuncture that uses manual pressure instead of needles [Mid-19C. *Acu-* < ACUPUNCTURE]

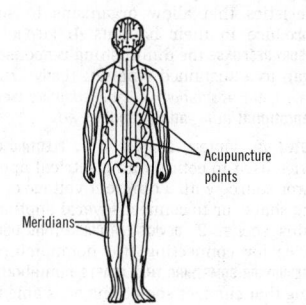

Acupuncture points

Meridians

acupuncture: points and energy flow paths (meridians) in the human body

acupuncture /ákyoō pungkchər/ *n* the treatment of disorders by inserting needles into the skin at points where the flow of energy is thought to be blocked (**meridians**) [Late 17C. < Latin *acus* 'needle'] —**acupuncturist** *n*

~~acurate~~ incorrect spelling of **accurate**

acute /ə kyoót/ *adj* **1.** VERY GREAT OR BAD extremely serious, severe, or painful ○ *an acute financial crisis* **2.** PERCEPTIVE keenly perceptive and intelligent ○ *an acute grasp of foreign affairs* **3.** SENSITIVE very powerful and sensitive to detail ○ *acute eyesight* **4.** MATHS LESS THAN 90° describes an angle that is less than 90° **5.** MATHS WITH ANGLES LESS THAN 90° describes a triangle that has three internal angles each of less than 90° **6.** MED SEVERE AND OF SHORT DURATION describes a disease that is brief, severe, and quickly comes to a crisis **7.** BOT POINTED describes leaves that end in a short narrow point ■ *n also* **acute accent** LANGUAGE ACCENT OVER LETTER in some languages, a mark placed above a letter to show that it is sounded in a specific way, as in *é, ó*. In Spanish, the acute indicates a stressed syllable, as in *cupón*; in French, a specific pronunciation of *e*, as in *blé*; and in classical Greek, a vowel sounded at a higher pitch. See table at **diacritic** [14C. < Latin *acutus*, past participle of *acuere* 'sharpen' < *acus* 'needle'] —**acutely** *adv* —**acuteness** *n*

USAGE See **chronic**.

acute arch *n* ARCHIT same as **lancet arch**

acute dose *n* a fatal amount of radiation received over a short period

acute lymphocytic leukaemia *n* a form of leukaemia affecting mainly children, characterized by anaemia, weight loss, bone pain, and fatigue

acute nonlymphocytic leukaemia *n* a form of leukaemia affecting mainly adults, characterized by anaemia, fatigue, and weight loss

ACVE *abbr* EDUC Advanced Certificate of Vocational Education

ACW *abbr* AIR FORCE aircraftwoman

acyclic /ay síklik, -síklik/ *adj* **1.** having a molecular structure in which the atoms are arranged in a string whose ends do not meet (**open chain**) **2.** describes flowers that have their parts arranged in a spiral, not a whorl

acyclovir *n* PHARM another spelling of **aciclovir**

acyl /áyssīl/ *adj* relating to or containing a chemical group derived from a carboxylic acid by removal of a hydroxyl group [Late 19C. < ACID]

acylation /áyssī láysh'n/ *n* the introduction of an acyl group into a chemical compound

acyl chloride *n* a chemical group containing the compound -COCl

ad[1] /ad/ *n* MARKETING same as **advertisement** (*informal*) [Mid-19C. Shortening]

ad[2] *abbr* TENNIS advantage

ad[3] *abbr* Andorra (*used in Internet addresses*) See table at **domain name**

AD[1], **AD** *adv* used to indicate a date that is a particular number of years after the birth of Jesus Christ. Full form **anno Domini**

USAGE **AD before or after the date?** Because of its literal Latin meaning, 'in the year of the Lord', **AD** is traditionally put before the numeral to which it relates, so that it makes grammatical sense if understood in its expanded form: *AD 1453.* In practice, **AD** is usually put after the numeral, and it is also acceptable to put it after the identification of a century, as in *the fifth century* **AD**. Some writers prefer to use **PE** (Present Era) or **CE** (Common Era) as alternatives in order to avoid the association with Christianity.

AD[2] *abbr* MED Alzheimer's disease

ad- *prefix* **1.** to, towards ○ *adsorb* ○ *advance* **2.** near ○ *adrenal* [< Latin *ad* 'towards, near' < Indo-European]

-ad *suffix* to, towards ○ *cephalad* [< Latin *ad* (see AD-)]

A/D *abbr* analogue to digital

Ada /áydə/ *n* a high-level computer programming language used for military and other complex applications [Late 20C. After Augusta *Ada* Byron, Countess of Lovelace (1815–52), British mathematician]

ADA deficiency *n* a genetic disease resulting from the deficiency of a metabolic enzyme (**adenosine deaminase**), characterized by low numbers of some lymphocytes and increased susceptibility to lymphomas and chronic infections [*ADA* contraction of ADENOSINE DEAMINASE]

adage /áddij/ *n* a traditional saying that expresses something considered to be a general truth ○*'Oysters are said to be best in months containing the letter R, according to an old adage.'* (Barbara Sturm, *Living Page*; 1997) [Mid-16C. Via French < Latin *adagium* < *ad* 'to' + variant of *aio* 'I say']

adagio /ə dáaji ŏ/ *adv* slowly, but faster than lento (*used as a musical direction*) ■ *n* (*plural* **-gios**) a movement or piece of music played or marked adagio [Late 17C. < Italian, 'at ease'] —**adagio** *adj*

Adam /áddəm/ *n* in the Bible, the first man, created by God ◇ **not know somebody from Adam** to have never met or seen somebody before

Adam /a daàm/, **Adolphe** (1803–56) French composer who wrote 60 operas and the ballet *Giselle* (1841). Full name **Adam, Adolphe Charles**

Adam /áddəm/, **Robert** (1728–92) British architect and interior designer who built grand neoclassical country and town houses, including Kenwood House (1768) and Osterley Park (1761–80)

adamant /áddəmənt/ *adj* very determined and not influenced by appeals to reconsider a position or decision ○*'They did their best to persuade her, but Mother was adamant.'* (Gerald Durrell, *Birds, Beasts and Relatives*; 1969) ■ *n* a legendary, extremely hard stone, sometimes identified as diamond or lodestone (*archaic*) [Pre-12C. Via Old French *adamaunt* and Latin *adamant-* 'adamant, steel, diamond' < Greek *adamas* 'unbreakable' < *daman* 'break down'] —**adamantly** *adv*

adamantine /áddə mán tīn/ *adj* (*literary*) **1.** extremely hard or unyielding **2.** like a diamond in hardness and brilliance

Adamawa-Eastern /áddə maáwə-/ *n* one of the major branches of the Niger-Congo family of African languages. Native speakers: 12 million. [Mid-20C. After the *Adamawa* Massif in Cameroon] —**Adamawa-Eastern** *adj*

Adamite /áddə mīt/ *n* **1.** a human being regarded as a descendant of Adam **2.** in North Africa in the second century AD, a member of a Christian religious group whose members preferred not to wear clothes

Adamov /áddə mov/, **Arthur** (1908–70) Russian poet and dramatist. He was one of the chief exponents of the Theatre of the Absurd.

Adams /áddəmz/, **Abigail** (1744–1818) US first lady and early feminist. She married John Adams, 2nd president of the United States. Her letters to him were published by her grandson. Born **Smith, Abigail**

'Whilst you are proclaiming peace and good will to men, emancipating all nations, you insist upon retaining absolute power over your wives. But you must remember that arbitrary power is most like other things which are very hard, very liable to be broken.'
[Abigail Adams, *Letter to John Adams*; 7 May 1776]

Adams, Ansel (1902–84) US photographer, noted for his dramatic photographs of the North American wilderness landscape

Adams, Gerry (*b.* 1948) Northern Irish politician and president of Sinn Fein, the political wing of the Irish Republican Army. He was elected to the British Parliament (1983–92, 1997) but declined to take his seat. Full name **Adams, Gerard**

Adams, John (1735–1826) 2nd president of the United

John Adams

States (1797–1801). He served as the first vice president (1789–97) and succeeded Washington to the presidency in 1797. He was a member of the committee that drafted the Declaration of Independence (1776). See table at **president**

'English is destined to be in the next and succeeding centuries more generally the language of the world than Latin was in the last or French is in the present age.'
[John Adams, *A Letter to the President of Congress*; 1780]

Adams, John Quincy (1767–1848) 6th president of the United States (1825–29). As secretary of state to President James Monroe (1817–25), he helped to formulate the Monroe Doctrine opposing foreign intervention in the American continents. See table at **president**

Adams, Philip Andrew (*b.* 1939) Australian writer, broadcaster, and film producer. He chaired the Australian Film Commission (1983–90). Published collections of his work include *The Unspeakable Adams* (1977).

Adam's apple *n* the hard lump at the front of the neck formed by the thyroid cartilage of the larynx [< the belief that it results from the forbidden apple being stuck in Adam's throat]

Adam-Smith, Patsy (1926–2001) Australian writer and historian. She wrote *The Anzacs* (1978). Full name **Adam-Smith, Patricia Jean**

Adam's needle *n* a yucca with spiny pointed leaves. Flowers: white, in spikes. Native to: North America. Latin name: *Yucca filamentosa*. [In allusion to Adam and Eve sewing fig leaves together to cover themselves (Genesis 3:7)]

Adana /áddənə/ city in southern Turkey and capital of the province of the same name. Population: 1,131,198 (1997).

adapt /ə dápt/ (**adapts, adapting, adapted**) *v* **1.** *vti* CHANGE TO MEET REQUIREMENTS to change something to suit different conditions or a different purpose, or be changed in this way **2.** *vti* ADJUST TO SOMETHING to become, or make somebody or something become, used to a new environment or different conditions **3.** *vt* REWRITE BOOK OR PLAY to rewrite a book or a play in order to make it into a film or television programme [15C. Via French *adapter* < Latin *adaptare* 'fit to' < *aptus* 'attached']

adaptable /ə dáptəb'l/ *adj* **1.** able to adjust easily to a new environment or different conditions **2.** capable of being modified to suit different conditions or a different purpose ○ *adaptable for different voltages* —**adaptability** /ə dáptə bíllɨti/ *n* —**adaptableness** *n* —**adaptably** *adv*

adaptation /áddap táysh'n, -əp-/, **adaption** /ə dápsh'n/ *n* **1.** ADAPTING the process or state of changing to fit a new environment or different conditions, or the resulting change **2.** SOMETHING ADAPTED TO FIT NEED something that has been modified to suit different conditions or a different purpose ○ *a film adaptation of a novel* **3.** BIOL CHANGE TO SUIT ENVIRONMENT the development of physical and behavioural characteristics that allow organisms to survive and reproduce in their habitats **4.** PHYSIOL DIMINISHING SENSORY RESPONSE the diminishing response of a sense organ to a sustained stimulus [Early 17C. Via French < late Latin *adaptation-* < Latin *adaptare* (see ADAPT)] —**adaptational** *adj* —**adaptationally** *adv*

adapter /ə dáptər/, **adaptor** *n* **1.** ELECTRIC CONNECTOR a device used to connect an electrical appliance to a power source with a different voltage or a different plug shape, or to connect several appliances to one mains socket **2.** DEVICE FOR CONNECTING UNLIKE PARTS a device for connecting two nonmatching parts **3.** SOMEBODY OR SOMETHING THAT ADAPTS somebody or something that changes something or is able to adjust to suit different conditions

adaption *n* same as **adaptation**

adaptive /ə dáptiv/ *adj* able to be adjusted for use in different conditions —**adaptively** *adv*

adaptive radiation *n* the evolutionary diversification of a group of organisms from an ancestral form into several different forms that adapt to different environments

adaptive reuse *n* a use of a building that is different

from its original or previous use, often involving conversion work

adaptor *n* ELEC another spelling of **adapter**

Adar /ə daár/ *n* in the Jewish calendar, the 12th month of the religious year, lasting 29 or 30 days and falling about the same time as February to March. ◇ **Adar Rishon**. See table at **calendar** [14C. < Hebrew *ădār*]

Adar Rishon /-ríshon/ *n* in the Jewish calendar, the name given to the month of Adar during a leap year, when an additional month (**Adar Sheni**) follows it [*Rishon* < Hebrew *ri'šōn*, 'first']

Adar Sheni /-sháyni/ *n* in the Jewish calendar, a 13th month, lasting 29 days, added after Adar in leap years and falling around March to April. See table at **calendar** [*Sheni* < Hebrew *šēnî* 'second']

adaxial /ad áksi əl/ *adj* describes the upper side of a leaf or other surface that faces towards the stem

ADC *abbr* ELECTRONICS analogue-to-digital converter

Adcock, Fleur (*b.* 1934) New Zealand poet, author of *The Inner Harbour* (1979). Full name **Adcock, Kareen Fleur**

A-D conversion *n* an electronic process that converts an analogue signal to a multilevel digital signal

ad court *n* the left-hand side of a tennis court, from which alternate odd points are played (*informal*) [< shortening of ADVANTAGE]

add /ad/ (**adds, adding, added**) *v* **1.** *vt* UNITE OR COMBINE THINGS to put something into or join something onto something else ○ *I'll add your name to the list.* **2.** *vti* CALCULATE TOTAL OF SOMETHING to calculate the total of two or more numbers or amounts **3.** *vt* PUT IN INGREDIENT to mix in an ingredient that is part of a recipe ○ *Add six eggs to the flour.* **4.** *vt* INTRODUCE QUALITY to give something a particular quality or more of a particular quality ○ *The flowers add a touch of cheerfulness.* **5.** *vi* INTENSIFY SOMETHING to increase the effect of something ○ *This adds to our problems.* **6.** *vt* SUPPLEMENT SPEECH OR WRITING to say or write something as a further remark ○ *'Don't forget your umbrella,' she added.* [14C. < Latin *addere* < *dare* 'give'] —**addable** *adj*

add up *v* **1.** *vti* MAKE TOTAL to calculate the total of two or more numbers or amounts, or reach a total **2.** *vi* MAKE SENSE to make a sensible or believable story or explanation ○ *His story just doesn't add up.* **3.** *vi* FORM LARGE AMOUNT to make a large total or amount ○ *If everyone gives a little, it soon adds up.*

add up to *vt* to amount to or result in a particular sum or thing

ADD *abbr* MED attention deficit disorder

add. *abbr* **1.** addendum **2.** MATHS addition **3.** address

adda /ə daá/ *n* S Asia **1.** an establishment that sells alcoholic drinks illegally **2.** informal talk among several people [< Hindi, 'perch for birds']

addax

addax /áddaks/ (*plural* **-daxes** or *same*) *n* an antelope that has long spiralling horns. Native to: desert regions of North Africa. Latin name: *Addax nasomaculatus*. [Late 17C. < Latin < an African word]

addend /áddend, ə dénd/ *n* a number that is to be added [Late 17C. Shortening of ADDENDUM]

addendum /ə déndəm/ (*plural* **-da** /-də/) *n* **1.** something that is or has been added **2.** a supplement to a book or magazine [Late 17C. < Latin < *addere* (see ADD)]

adder

adder[1] /áddər/ n somebody or something that adds, especially an electronic device that adds numbers [Late 16C. < ADD]

adder[2] /áddər/ n a small venomous snake that is dark grey with a black zigzag pattern on its back. Native to: Europe. Latin name: *Vipera berus*. [Old English *næd(d)re* 'snake' < Germanic. The initial *n* was lost when 'a nadder' was misanalysed as 'an adder']

adder's tongue

adder's tongue n 1. a fern with a spore-bearing stalk at the base of a pointed frond. Native to: northern hemisphere. Genus: *Ophioglossum*. 2. PLANTS same as **dogtooth violet**

addict /áddikt/ n 1. somebody who is physiologically or psychologically dependent on a potentially harmful drug 2. somebody who is very interested in a particular thing and devotes a lot of time to it ○ *soap opera addicts* [Mid-16C. < Latin *addictus*, past participle of *addicere* 'award, devote' < *dicere* 'say']

addicted /ə díktid/ adj 1. physiologically or psychologically dependent on a potentially harmful drug 2. very interested in a particular thing and devoting a lot of time to it ○ *addicted to football*

addiction /ə díksh'n/ n 1. a state of physiological or psychological dependence on a potentially harmful drug 2. great interest in a particular thing to which a lot of time is devoted ○ *Internet addiction*

addictionology /ə díksh'n ólləji/ n the study and treatment of addictions —**addictionologist** n

addictive /ə díktiv/ adj making or likely to make somebody an addict —**addictively** adv

addictive personality n a personality predisposed towards becoming addicted to something

add-in n COMPUT same as **add-on**

Addington /áddingtən/, **Henry, 1st Viscount Sidmouth** (1757–1844) British prime minister (1801–04). He resigned the premiership after criticism of his conduct of the Napoleonic Wars. He went on to serve as home secretary (1812–22).

Addis Ababa /áddiss ábbəbə/ capital of Ethiopia. Population: 2,424,100 (1999).

Addison /áddiss'n/, **Joseph** (1672–1719) English essayist and politician. An originator of the modern essay, he was cofounder (with Richard Steele) of *The Spectator* (1711).

'Thus I live in the world rather as a Spectator of mankind, than as one of the species, by which means I have made myself a speculative statesman, soldier, merchant, and artisan, without ever meddling with any practical part of life.'

[Joseph Addison, *The Spectator*; 1 March 1711]

Addison, Thomas (1793–1860) British physician who correctly ascribed the symptoms of Addison's disease to adrenal malfunction

Addison's disease n a wasting disease caused by failure of the adrenal glands to function normally and characterized by bronzing of the skin, low blood pressure, and weakness [Mid-19C. After Thomas ADDISON]

addition /ə dísh'n/ n 1. PUTTING IN OR ON the act of adding something onto or into something else 2. ADDED PERSON OR THING somebody or something that is added 3. MATHS CALCULATION the process of calculating the sum of two or more numbers or amounts 4. CHEM CHEMICAL REACTION a chemical reaction in which two or more compounds combine to produce a new compound ○ *an addition-type reaction* [14C. Directly or via French < Latin *addition-* < *additus*, past participle of *addere* (see ADD)] ◇ **in addition** 1. used to introduce an additional point or relevant fact 2. also ◇ **in addition to** as well as

additional /ə dísh'nəl/ adj added on to something else

additionality /ə dísh'ə nálləti/ n a principle of funding in the European Union by which funds for a project are only granted to a member state if the latter also contributes

additionally /ə dísh'nəli/ adv 1. FURTHER further to what has just been said ○ *Additionally, each machine is checked hourly.* 2. TOO also 3. EVEN MORE to an even greater extent (*literary*) ○ *'The atmosphere of the place was heavy and mouldy, being rendered additionally oppressive by the closing of the door which led into the church.'* (Wilkie Collins, *The Woman in White*; 1860)

Additional Member System n a method of voting in which votes are cast separately for parties and candidates, and parties may acquire extra seats according to their share of the total vote

additive /áddətiv/ n something added to something else to alter or improve it in some way, e.g. to change the colour or texture of food ■ adj involving or produced by addition or by the addition of something (*formal*) [Late 17C. < late Latin *additivus* < *additus* (see ADDITION)]

additive identity n a quantity that, when added to another, leaves it unchanged. For ordinary numbers this is zero.

additive inverse n a number or quantity that gives zero when added to another. For example, the additive inverse of 3 is –3.

additive printing n a printing process in which colours are produced by adding proportionate amounts of three primary colours

addle /ádd'l/ (**-dles, -dling, -dled**) vti 1. to confuse or muddle somebody, or become confused or muddled 2. to make something rotten or spoiled, or become rotten or spoiled [Old English *adela* 'filth, liquid manure' < Germanic]

addle-headed adj regional an offensive term that deliberately insults somebody's intelligence [< addle 'empty, idle']

REGIONAL NOTE Many of the terms used in the past would now be considered politically incorrect, among them those for supposed stupidity. We find *addle-headed*, *barmy*, *bull-skulled*, *daft*, *dozy*, *dummel-headed*, and supposedly stupid people may be *noggin-heads*, *noodle-noggins*, *num(b)skulls*, or *staups*. Like many terms of abuse, they could be used affectionately: *You wee pet, you! You dummel-headed wee darling!*

add-on, add-in n a piece of computer equipment added to another to expand its capabilities

address /ə dréss/ n 1. PHYSICAL LOCATION the number, street name, and other information that describes where a building is or where somebody lives 2. WRITTEN FORM OF ADDRESS the address of a person or organization when written on a letter or an item of mail 3. FORMAL TALK a formal speech or report 4. COMPUT NUMBER FOR LOCATION a number that specifies a location in a computer's memory 5. STATEMENT FROM PARLIAMENT a statement of opinions or desires sent to the sovereign by either or both of the Houses of Parliament ■ **addresses** npl COURTSHIP attention paid

to somebody that is intended as courtship (*archaic*) ■ v (**-dresses, -dressing, -dressed**) 1. vt WRITE DIRECTIONS ON MAIL to write or print on an item of mail details of where it is to be delivered 2. vt SPEAK OR MAKE SPEECH TO SOMEBODY to say something to somebody, or make a speech to an audience 3. vt USE CORRECT TITLE FOR SOMEBODY to use the proper name or title in speaking or writing to somebody ○ *You should address him by his last name.* 4. vr BEGIN TASK to set about doing some task ○ *'Through this program of action we address ourselves to putting our own national house in order.'* (Franklin D. Roosevelt, *First Inaugural Address*; 1933) 5. vt DEAL WITH ISSUE to face up to and deal with a problem or issue ○ *failure to address the main issue* 6. vt FACE SOMEBODY OR SOMETHING to stand facing a dance partner or an archery target 7. vt GOLF PREPARE TO HIT GOLF BALL to take up the correct stance beside a golf ball before hitting it [14C. Via Old French *adresser* < assumed Vulgar Latin *addrictiare* 'direct to' < Latin *directus* (see DIRECT)] —**addressable** adj

addressee /áddre seé, ə dréss eé/ n a person or organization to whom an item of mail is to be delivered

address harvester n a computer program that collects e-mail addresses from the Internet

adduce /ə dyóoss/ (**-duces, -ducing, -duced**) vt to offer something as evidence, a reason, or proof (*formal*) [15C. < Latin *adducere* 'bring forward' < *ducere* 'lead'] —**adducible** adj

adduct /ə dúkt, a-/ vt (**-ducts, -ducting, -ducted**) to pull a leg or arm towards the central line of the body or a toe or finger towards the axis of a leg or arm ■ n a chemical compound formed by an addition reaction between two or more different compounds or elements [Mid-19C. Back-formation < adduction, directly or via French < Latin *adduction-* < *adductus*, past participle of *adducere* (see ADDUCE)] —**adduction** n —**adductive** adj

adductor /ə dúktər/ n a muscle that pulls a leg or arm towards the central line of the body or a toe or finger towards the axis of a leg or arm [Early 17C. < modern Latin < Latin *adductus* (see ADDUCT)]

Ade /ayd/, **George** (1866–1944) US writer. He wrote a dozen popular Broadway plays (1900–10), but is best remembered for his satirical fables, written in Midwestern vernacular and published in several collections including *People You Know* (1903).

-ade suffix 1. a sweetened drink ○ *orangeade* 2. an action ○ *cannonade* [Via Old French < Latin *-ata*, feminine of *-atus* (see -ATE)]

Adelaide /ádd'l ayd/ city in southeastern Australia, on the Gulf of St Vincent. It is the state capital and main port of South Australia. Population: 1,088,400 (1998). —**Adelaidian** /ádd'l áydi ən/ n, adj

Aden /áyd'n/ 1. port and second largest city of Yemen, situated on a peninsula that juts into the Gulf of Aden. Population: 400,783 (1993 estimate). 2. former British colony and protectorate that became part of South Yemen in 1967 and is now part of Yemen

aden- prefix same as **adeno-** (*used before vowels*)

Adenauer /áddə now ər/, **Konrad** (1876–1967) chancellor of the Federal Republic of Germany (1949–63). He also served as foreign minister (1951–55) and led West Germany into NATO in 1955.

'We must free ourselves from thinking in terms of nation states.'
[Konrad Adenauer, *Speech*; May 1953]

adenectomy /áddə néktəmi/ (*plural* **-mies**) n the surgical removal of a gland

adenine /áddə neen/ n a purine base found in DNA, RNA, and energy-carrying molecules such as ATP. Symbol **A**

adenitis /áddə nítiss/ n inflammation of a gland or a lymph node

adeno- prefix gland ○ *adenovirus* [< Greek *adēn*]

adenocarcinoma /áddinō kaarssi nṓmə/ (*plural* **-mas** or **-mata** /-mətə/) n 1. a malignant tumour in glandular tissue. Breast cancers are often adenocarcinomas. 2. a malignant tumour with cells arranged in patterns similar to those of a gland —**adenocarcinomatous** adj

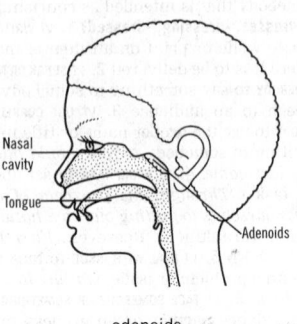

adenoids

adenoid /áddə noyd/ *adj* **1.** RELATING TO GLANDS relating to or similar to a gland **2.** CONCERNING LYMPHOID TISSUE relating to lymphoid tissue **3.** MED same as **adenoidal** (sense 1) ■ **adenoids** *npl* THROAT TISSUE a mass of tissue at the back of the nose and throat that can restrict breathing if enlarged

adenoidal /áddi nóyd'l/ *adj* **1.** displaying symptoms caused by enlarged adenoids, e.g. a nasal voice or breathing difficulties **2.** relating to the adenoids

adenoidectomy /áddi noy déktəmi/ (*plural* **-ies**) *n* the surgical removal of adenoids

adenoma /áddi nṓmə/ (*plural* **-mas** or **-mata** /-mətə/) *n* **1.** a benign tumour in glandular tissue **2.** a benign tumour with cells arranged in patterns similar to those of a gland —**adenomatoid** *adj*

adenoma sebaceum /-sə báyshəm/ *n* a skin condition of the face characterized by raised red vascular bumps, usually beginning in late childhood or early adolescence [< modern Latin, 'sebaceous adenoma']

adenopathy /áddi nóppəthi/ *n* a diseased condition in a gland or lymph node, e.g. inflammation or enlargement

adenosine /ə dénnō seen/ *n* **1.** a compound of adenine and a ribose found in nucleic acids and energy-carrying molecules such as ATP **2.** a drug used to treat irregular heartbeat [Early 20C. Blend of ADENINE + RIBOSE]

adenosine deaminase *n* an enzyme that catalyses the removal of an amino group from adenosine to form inosine during purine metabolism. Lack of adenosine deaminase marks ADA deficiency.

adenosine diphosphate BIOCHEM full form of **ADP**[1]

adenosine monophosphate *n* BIOCHEM full form of **AMP**

adenosine triphosphatase /-trī fósfə tayz/ *n* BIOCHEM full form of **ATPase**

adenosine triphosphate BIOCHEM full form of **ATP**[1]

adenosis /áddi nṓssiss/ *n* **1.** the unusual enlargement or development of a gland **2.** a disease characterized by adenosis

adenovirus /áddinō vírəss/ *n* a virus that causes respiratory infections in humans [< its occurrence in adenoid tissue]

adenylate cyclase /ə dénnə layt-/, **adenyl cyclase** /áddənīl-/ *n* an enzyme involved in the formation of cyclic AMP from ATP

adept *adj* /ə dépt/ highly proficient or expert at something ■ *n* /ádd ept/ somebody who is highly proficient or expert at something [Mid-17C. < Latin *adeptus*, past participle of *adipisci* 'acquire' < *apisci* 'pursue'] —**adeptly** *adv* —**adeptness** *n*

adequate /áddikwət/ *adj* **1.** sufficient in quality or quantity to meet a need or qualify for something **2.** just barely sufficient in quality or quantity to meet a need or qualify for something [16C. < Latin *adaequatus*, past participle of *adaequare* 'make equal, match' < *aequus* 'equal'] —**adequacy** *n* —**adequately** *adv* —**adequateness** *n*

~~adequatly~~ incorrect spelling of **adequately**

Ader /a dáir/, **Clément** (1841–1926) French engineer who constructed a steam-powered aircraft and made the first heavier-than-air powered flight (1890)

à deux /aa dố/ *adv*, *adj* involving only two people and therefore private [Late 19C. < French]

ADH *abbr* BIOCHEM antidiuretic hormone

ADHD *abbr* MED attention deficit hyperactivity disorder

adhere /əd heér/ (**-heres**, **-hering**, **-hered**) *vi* **1.** OBEY to be conscientious in supporting or following somebody or something ○ *adhere to the rules* **2.** SUPPORT to hold firmly to a belief, idea, or opinion ○ *on account of the opinion to which they consistently adhere* **3.** STICK FIRMLY to stick firmly to a surface or an object [15C. Directly or via French *adhérer* < Latin *adhaerere* < *haerere* 'to stick'] —**adherence** *n*

adherent /əd heérənt/ *n* a supporter of a cause or of a leader ■ *adj* able to stick firmly to a surface or an object (*formal*)

adhesion /əd heézh'n/ *n* **1.** STICKING POWER the ability to stick firmly to something **2.** ABSENCE OF SLIPPERINESS the ability to make firm contact with a surface without slipping **3.** SUPPORT loyal support for a cause or for a leader **4.** MED JOINING OF BODY PARTS the joining of normally unconnected body parts by bands of fibrous tissue **5.** PHYS INTERMOLECULAR ATTRACTION intermolecular attraction between substances that are unlike and in surface contact, causing them to cling together [15C. Directly or via French < Latin *adhaesion-* < *adhaes-*, past participle of *adhaerere* (see ADHERE)]

adhesive /əd heéssiv, -ziv/ *n* a substance used to stick things together ■ *adj* able to stick to something or to stick things together [Late 17C. < Latin *adhaes-* (see ADHESION)] —**adhesively** *adv* —**adhesiveness** *n*

ad hoc /ad hók/ *adj* done or set up solely in response to a specific situation or problem, without considering wider or longer-term issues ○ *ad hoc measures* [Mid-17C. < Latin, 'to this'] —**ad hoc** *adv*

ad hocism /ad hókizəm/ *n* the taking of decisions or the implementation of measures solely in response to a specific situation or problem, without considering wider or longer-term issues (*disapproving*)

adhocracy /ad hókrəssi/ (*plural* **-cies**) *n* an organization that does not have a fixed bureaucratic structure and can adapt to changing circumstances [Late 20C. Blend of AD HOC + BUREAUCRACY]

ad hominem /ad hómmi nem/ *adj* **1.** appealing to people's emotions and prejudices instead of their ability to think (*formal*) **2.** S Africa on the basis of personal merit ○ *ad hominem promotion* [Late 16C. < Latin, 'to the person'] —**ad hominem** *adv*

adiabatic /áddi ə báttik/ *adj* describes a thermodynamic process that happens without loss or gain of heat [Late 19C. < Greek *adiabatos* 'impassable' < *a-* 'not' + *diabainein* 'go through'] —**adiabatically** *adv*

adiaphorism /áddi áffərizəm/ *n* especially in Protestant Christianity, the view that things not specifically forbidden by the Scriptures may be treated with indifference [Early 17C. < Greek *adiaphoros* 'indifferent' < *a-* 'not' + *diaphoros* 'different'] —**adiaphoristic** /-afə rístik/ *adj*

~~adict~~ incorrect spelling of **addict**

Adie's pupil /áydiz-/ *n* a condition of the eyes in which one pupil is much larger than the other and less responsive to light [Early 20C. After William John Adie (1886–1935), Australian-born British neurologist]

adieu /ə dyoó/ *interj*, *n* (*plural* **adieux** /ə dyoóz/ or **adieus** /ə dyoóz/) used to say goodbye (*literary*) ○ *'...the more gentle adieus of her sisters were uttered without being heard'* (Jane Austen, *Pride And Prejudice*; 1813) [14C. < French, '(I commend you) to God']

Adi Granth /aadi grúnt/ *n* the principal Sikh scripture, which contains the teachings of the first five gurus and also poems and hymns [< Sanskrit *ādigrantha* 'first book' < *grantha* 'tying, work of literature']

ad infinitum /ád infi nítəm/ *adv* endlessly, or for so long as to seem endless [Early 17C. < Latin, 'to infinity']

ad interim /ad íntərim/ *adv* for the meantime ■ *adj* done or created for the meantime only [< Latin, 'to the meanwhile']

adios /áddi óss/ *interj* used to say goodbye (*informal*) [Mid-19C. < Spanish, '(I commend you) to God']

adipic acid /ə díppik-/ *n* a white crystalline solid. Use: making nylon, production of chemicals. Formula: $C_6H_{10}O_4$. [< Latin *adip-* 'fat' (see ADIPO-), because the acid was originally made by oxidizing fats]

adipo- *prefix* fat, fatty ○ *adipocyte* [< Latin *adip-*, stem of *adeps* 'fat']

adipocyte /áddi pō sīt/ *n* a cell that synthesizes and stores fat [Mid-20C. < modern Latin *adiposus* (see ADIPOSE)]

adipose /áddi pṓss/ *adj* containing fat ■ *n* fat under the skin and surrounding major organs, providing stored energy, insulation, and protection [Mid-18C. < modern Latin *adiposus* 'fatty' < Latin *adip-* (see ADIPO-)] —**adiposity** /áddi póssəti/ *n*

adipose tissue *n* connective tissue in human or animal bodies that contains fat

adipsin /ay dípsin/ *n* a protein that is believed to control appetite. Use: obesity treatment. [Late 20C. < A[2] + Greek *dipsa* 'thirst']

Adirondack Mountains /áddə rón dak-/, **Adirondacks** /-daks/ mountain chain in northeastern New York State, known for spectacular scenery and recreational activities. The highest peak is Mount Marcy 1,629 m/5,344 ft.

adit /áddit/ *n* a nearly horizontal shaft used for giving access to a mine or for drainage [Early 17C. < Latin *aditus* 'approach, entrance' < past participle of *adire* 'go towards' < *ire* 'go']

Adivasi /aadi vaássi/ (*plural same* or **-sis**) *n* **1.** MEMBER OF ANCIENT S ASIAN PEOPLE a member of an aboriginal people of South Asia **2.** DESCENDANT OF ANCIENT ADIVASI a descendant of the ancient Adivasi, living mainly in the Bangla and Bihar regions of India **3.** MEMBER OF S ASIAN ABORIGINAL PEOPLE a member of any of the aboriginal peoples of S Asia [Mid-20C. < Hindi *ādivāsi* 'original inhabitant']

adj, adj. *abbr* **1.** GRAM adjective **2.** MATHS adjoint **3.** LOGIC adjunct **4.** BANKING, INSUR adjustment **5.** MIL adjutant

Adj, Adj. *abbr* adjutant

adjacent /ə jáyss'nt/ *adj* **1.** situated near or close to something or each other, especially without touching **2.** describes either a pair of vertices in a graph that have common edges or a pair of edges in a graph that have a common vertex [15C. < Latin *adjacent-*, present participle of *adjacere* 'lie near' < *jacere* 'to lie'] —**adjacency** *n*

USAGE **adjacent** or **adjoining**? Two houses are said to be **adjoining** when they are next to each other with a common wall. **Adjoining** tables are next to each other, end to end, forming one surface (they are, to use a more technical word, *contiguous*). In other words, **adjoining** items *join*. **Adjacent** houses, on the other hand, can have a space between them or even be on opposite sides of the road, as long as there is nothing significant between them (such as another house) and they are close enough for you to pass easily from one to the other. **Adjacent** tables are next to each other but not necessarily touching. Note also that **adjoining**, being a form of a verb, can govern an object (*the house adjoining ours*), whereas **adjacent** needs the addition of *to* (*the house adjacent to ours*).

adjacent angle *n* either of the two angles that are formed by the intersection of two straight lines and lie on the same side of one line

adjective /ájjiktiv/ *n* GRAM WORD DESCRIBING NOUN a word that describes or qualifies a noun or pronoun ■ *adj* **1.** GRAM ACTING AS ADJECTIVE relating to, forming, or functioning as an adjective **2.** LAW PRACTISED IN COURT relating to court practice and procedure rather than the principles of law [14C. Via French *adjectif* < Latin *adjectivus* < *adjicere* 'throw to' < *jacere* 'to throw'] —**adjectival** /ájjik tív'l/ *adj* —**adjectivally** *adv* —**adjectively** *adv*

USAGE See **adverb**.

adjoin /ə jóyn/ (**-joins**, **-joining**, **-joined**) *v* **1.** *vti* to be next to or share a common border with something, especially an area of land ○ *The two properties adjoin.* **2.** *vt* to attach or add on something (*archaic*) [14C. < Old French *ajoin-*, stem of *ajoindre* < Latin *adjungere* 'join to' < *jungere* 'to join']

adjoining /ə jóyning/ *adj* situated next to and touching something or each other

USAGE See **adjacent**.

adjoint /ájjoynt/ *n* a matrix formed from a given square matrix, each element being derived from its cofactors, the determinants of the given matrix obtained by removing the row and column con-

taining the element [Late 16C. < French, past participle of *ajoindre* (see ADJOIN)]

adjourn /ə júrn/ (**-journs, -journing, -journed**) *v* **1.** *vti* SUSPEND PROCEEDINGS to suspend the business of a court, legislature, or committee temporarily or indefinitely, or become suspended temporarily or indefinitely ○ *The court adjourned at one o'clock.* **2.** *vti* POSTPONE MEETING to postpone a meeting to another time, or become postponed **3.** *vt* DEFER SOMETHING to defer a matter or an action to another time **4.** *vi* MOVE AS GROUP to move together from one place to another ○ *We adjourned to the lounge.* **5.** *vi* STOP DOING SOMETHING to stop the current activity (*informal*) ○ *Time to adjourn for today.* [14C. < Old French *ajourner* < *à jorn* (*nomé*) 'to an (appointed) day'] —**adjournment** *n*

adjournment debate *n* in the House of Commons, a debate on the motion that Parliament be adjourned, used as a formal device for raising other topics

Adjt *abbr* MIL adjutant

adjudge /ə júj/ (**-judges, -judging, -judged**) *vt* **1.** MAKE JUDGMENT ABOUT SOMEBODY OR SOMETHING to judge somebody or something in a particular way ○ *She was adjudged to be an accomplished musician.* **2.** DETERMINE SOMETHING JUDICIALLY to decide something in a judicial proceeding **3.** DECREE SOMETHING LEGALLY to pronounce something by law **4.** GRANT MONEY IN JUDGMENT to make somebody an award of damages or costs in a legal judgment [14C. Via Old French *ajuger* < Latin *adjudicare* (see ADJUDICATE)]

adjudicate /ə joŏdi kayt/ (**-cates, -cating, -cated**) *vti* **1.** to reach a judicial decision on something **2.** to make an official decision about a problem or dispute [Early 18C. < Latin *adjudicat-*, past participle of *adjudicare* 'award in arbitration' < *judic-* 'a judge'] —**adjudication** /ə joŏdi káysh'n/ *n* —**adjudicative** /-kətiv/ *adj* —**adjudicator** *n*

adjunct /ájjungkt/ *n* **1.** SOMETHING ADDED ON AS EXTRA something inessential added to something else **2.** ASSISTANT an assistant or subordinate **3.** INESSENTIAL PART OF SENTENCE a part of a sentence that is not the subject or predicate [Early 16C. < Latin *adjunctus*, past participle of *adjungere* (see ADJOIN)] —**adjunction** /ə júngksh'n/ *n* —**adjunctive** *adj*

adjure /ə joŏr/ (**-jures, -juring, -jured**) *vt* **1.** to order somebody to do something, especially under oath **2.** to make an earnest appeal to somebody [14C. < Latin *adjurare* 'swear by oath' < *jurare* 'swear' (see JURY)] —**adjuration** /ájjoŏ ráysh'n/ *n* —**adjurer** *n*

adjust /ə júst/ (**-justs, -justing, -justed**) *v* **1.** *vt* CHANGE SOMETHING SLIGHTLY to make slight changes in something to make it fit or function better **2.** *vti* ADAPT TO NEW CIRCUMSTANCES to adapt to a new environment or condition **3.** *vt* REARRANGE to put something back in order, especially clothing, so that it is tidy [Early 17C. Via obsolete French *adjuster* < assumed Vulgar Latin *adjuxtare* 'put close to' < Latin *juxta* 'close'] —**adjustable** *adj* —**adjustment** *n*

adjustable-rate mortgage *n* *N Am* FIN same as **variable-rate mortgage**

adjustable spanner *n* *UK* a spanner with a head that can be adjusted by means of a screw to fit different sizes of nuts and bolts. Aus term **shifting spanner**. NZ, N Am term **adjustable wrench**

adjuster /ə jústər/ *n* *N Am* INSUR same as **loss adjuster**

adjutant /ájjoŏtənt/ *n* **1.** a military officer who acts as an administrative assistant to a commanding officer **2.** BIRDS same as **adjutant stork** [Early 17C. < Latin *adjutant-*, present participle of *adjutare* 'keep on helping' < *adjuvare* (see ADJUVANT)]

adjutant general (*plural* **adjutants general**) *n* **1.** an army general responsible for administration and personnel **2.** an executive officer of an army general

adjutant stork

adjutant stork *n* a large, often carrion-eating stork with a naked yellow head and neck, black wings, and white undersides. Native to: Southeast Asia. Latin name: *Leptoptilos dubius* or *Leptoptilos javanicus.* [< the similarity of its walk to that of a military staff officer]

adjuvant /ájjoŏvənt/ *n* **1.** PHARM DRUG-ENHANCING AGENT a drug or agent added to another drug or agent to enhance its medical effectiveness **2.** PHARM ANTIGEN-ENHANCING DRUG a substance injected along with an antigen to enhance the immune response stimulated by the antigen **3.** HELPING AGENT something that helps or assists ■ *adj* ASSISTING helping by supplementing [Late 16C. Directly or via French < Latin *adjuvant-*, present participle of *adjuvare* 'give help to' < *juvare* 'to help']

ADL *npl* MED a scale used by geriatricians and occupational therapists to assess the capacity of older patients or those with disabilities to live independently. Full form **activities of daily living**

Adler /áddlər/, **Alfred** (1870–1937) Austrian psychiatrist who stressed the importance of the inferiority complex. His books include *The Neurotic Constitution* (1912).

ad lib /ád líb/ *adj, adv* **1.** without any advance preparation **2.** MUSIC same as **ad libitum** [Early 19C. Shortening of AD LIBITUM]

ad-lib /ád líb/ *vti* (**ad-libs, ad-libbing, ad-libbed**) IMPROVISE SPEECH OR PERFORMANCE to make up a speech or a musical or dramatic performance on the spot without a fixed text or score ■ *adj* UNPLANNED improvised or made up on the spot ■ *n* IMPROVISED PART OF PERFORMANCE something said by an actor or other performer that is not in the script —**ad-libber** *n*

ad libitum /ád líbbitəm/ *adj, adv* to be performed in the way the performer chooses [Early 17C. < Latin, 'at your pleasure']

ad litem /ád lítem/ *adj* appointed by a court to represent a minor [Mid-18C. < Latin, 'for the purpose of a lawsuit']

Adm. *abbr* **1.** Admiral **2.** Admiralty

adman /ád man/ (*plural* **-men** /-men/) *n* a man who works in advertising (*informal*)

admass /ád mass/ *n* the part of society that can be influenced by advertising or publicity [Mid-20C. Coined by the British writer J. B. Priestley from AD- + MASS]

admeasure /ad mézhər/ (**-ures, -uring, -ured**) *vt* to divide something up to be shared out (*formal*) [14C. Via Old French *amesurer* < medieval Latin *admensurare* 'apply a measure to'] —**admeasurement** *n*

admin /ád min/ *n* (*informal*) **1.** the administrative work involved in running a business or organization **2.** *N Am* an administrative assistant [Mid-20C. Shortening]

administer /əd mínnistər/ (**-ters, -tering, -tered**) *v* **1.** *vt* BE IN CHARGE OF AFFAIRS to manage the affairs of a business, organization, or institution **2.** *vt* DISPENSE SOMETHING to preside over the dispensation of something ○ *He administered justice in the fairest possible manner.* **3.** *vt* GIVE MEDICATION to give somebody a measured amount of a medication, often by physically introducing it into the body **4.** *vt* PERFORM MEDICAL PROCEDURE to apply a medical technique or procedure to somebody **5.** *vt* PERFORM RITUAL to carry out a set ritual or religious ceremony on behalf of a person or group of people **6.** *vi* SUPERVISE TAKING OF OATH to oversee the taking of an oath by somebody **7.** *vi* LOOK AFTER SOMEBODY to look after and tend to the needs of somebody **8.** *vt* LAW ORGANIZE HANDOVER OF PROPERTY to manage the distribution of a deceased person's property in accordance with the law [14C. Via Old French *aministrer* < Latin *administrare* 'serve, manage' < *ministrare* 'serve'] —**administrable** *adj*

administrate /əd mínni strayt/ (**-trates, -trating, -trated**) *vti* to oversee or organize the affairs of something, especially a business, organization, or institution [Mid-16C. < Latin *administrat-*, past participle of *administrare* (see ADMINISTER)]

administration /əd mínni stráysh'n/ *n* **1.** MANAGEMENT OF BUSINESS the management of the affairs of a business, organization, or institution **2.** MANAGEMENT STAFF the staff of a business, organization, or institution whose task is to manage its affairs **3.** MANAGEMENT OF GOVERNMENT the management of public affairs or the affairs of a government **4.** STAFF OF GOVERNMENT a government's staff whose task is to manage its affairs **5.** TERM OF OFFICE the duration of a term of office, usually a political one **6.** GOVERNMENT a government, especially its executive branch **7.** LAW LEGAL DISPOSAL OF ESTATE the legal disposal or management of a deceased person's estate or an estate held in trust **8.** ADMINISTERING OF SOMETHING TO SOMEBODY the act of administering something such as an oath, medicine, or sacrament **9.** SOMETHING ADMINISTERED something that is administered to somebody, especially an oath, medicine, or sacrament

administration order *n* **1.** a court order appointing somebody to run a company in financial trouble, in order to return it to successful trading or to oversee the sale of its assets **2.** a court order appointing somebody to administer the estate of a debtor

administrative /əd mínnistrətiv/ *adj* relating to the administration of a business, organization, or institution —**administratively** *adv*

administrative area *n* a part of a country under the control of a local government administration

administrative assistant *n* an employee whose task is to assist a superior with the day-to-day affairs of running a business or department

administrative law *n* the area of law dealing with the affairs of agencies of the executive branch of a government, and with the judicial review of public bodies generally

administrative officer *n* an employee who carries out administrative tasks in an institution or government body, usually at a fairly junior level

administrator /əd mínni straytər/ *n* **1.** somebody whose job is to manage the affairs of a business, organization, or institution **2.** somebody appointed by a court to manage the estate of a deceased person, especially when there is no competent executor

admirable /ádmərəb'l/ *adj* deserving to be admired [15C. < Latin *admirabilis* < *admirari* (see ADMIRE)] —**admirableness** *n* —**admirably** *adv*

admiral (sense 3)

admiral /ádmərəl/ *n* **1.** NAVAL COMMANDER an officer in the Royal Navy or the US Navy or Coast Guard of a rank above vice-admiral **2.** NAVAL OFFICER a high-ranking naval officer entitled to fly a personal flag **3.** INSECTS BRIGHTLY COLOURED BUTTERFLY a brightly coloured butterfly of temperate regions. Family: Nymphalidae. [13C. Via French *amiral* < Arabic *amir-al* 'commander of' in such phrases as *amir-al-bahr* 'commander of the sea'] —**admiralship** *n*

Admiral of the Fleet *n* an officer in the Royal Navy of the highest rank

Admiral's Cup *n* **1.** an international yacht race held every two years off the southern coast of England between teams of three yachts **2.** the trophy awarded to the winning team in the Admiral's Cup

admiralty /ádmərəlti/ *n* the office or jurisdiction of an admiral

Admiralty *n* a former UK government department that administered the affairs of the Royal Navy

Admiralty Board *n* a committee of the UK Ministry of Defence responsible for the administration of the Royal Navy

Admiralty Islands /ádmərəlti-/ island group in the Bismarck Archipelago, north of New Guinea in the western Pacific Ocean, part of Papua New Guinea. The group's largest island is Manus. Area: 2,072 sq. km/800 sq. mi.

admiration /ádmə ráysh'n/ n 1. warm approval or appreciation of somebody or something ○ was filled with admiration for her courage 2. somebody or something regarded with approval, appreciation, or respect ○ a house that was the admiration of the neighbourhood

SYNONYMS See *regard*.

admire /əd mír/ (-mires, -miring, -mired) vt 1. to regard somebody or something with approval, appreciation, or respect ○ I admire your determination. 2. to look at somebody or something beautiful or attractive with enjoyment ○ admired the view from the summit [Late 16C. Directly or via French admirer < Latin admirari 'wonder at' < mirari 'to wonder']

admirer /əd mírər/ n 1. somebody who admires another person or thing 2. somebody, especially a man, who feels sexually attracted to another person ○ We think Ellen has a secret admirer.

admiring /əd míring/ adj full of admiration for somebody or something —**admiringly** adv

~~admision~~ incorrect spelling of **admission**

~~admissable~~ incorrect spelling of **admissible**

admissible /əd míssəb'l/ adj 1. ALLOWABLE allowed to be done 2. ALLOWED TO COME IN able or deserving to enter 3. ALLOWED TO BE USED IN COURT accepted as evidence in court [Early 17C. Directly or via French < medieval Latin admissibilis < Latin admiss- (see ADMISSION)] —**admissibility** /əd míssə bílləti/ n —**admissibleness** n —**admissibly** adv

admission /əd mísh'n/ n 1. ENTRY the right, ability, or permission to enter a place or an organization or institution ○ Admission is by invitation only. 2. FEE FOR ENTRY a fee paid for entrance to a place or event 3. CONFESSION a confession to having committed a crime or having made a mistake ○ an admission of guilt 4. DECLARATION an acknowledgment that something is true ○ The letter contained a clear admission of the error. ■ **admissions** npl 1. PROCESS OF ACCEPTING STUDENTS the process of accepting students for study at a university or college ○ a new system of admissions ○ an admissions tutor 2. NUMBER OF STUDENTS ACCEPTED the number of students accepted into a university or college ○ a drop in admissions [15C. < Latin admission- < admiss-, past participle of admittere (see ADMIT)]

admissive /əd míssiv/ adj granting or showing admission

admit /əd mít/ (-mits, -mitting, -mitted) v 1. vti CONFESS to confess to having committed a crime or having made a mistake 2. vti ACKNOWLEDGE TRUTH to acknowledge that something is true ○ You must admit it is a tempting offer. 3. vt ALLOW SOMEBODY TO ENTER to allow somebody or something entrance or access ○ 'Admits one' 4. vti OFFER POSSIBILITY to permit the possibility of something ○ Their conduct admits of only one explanation. [14C. < Latin admittere 'let go into' < mittere 'let go']

admittance /əd mítt'nss/ n 1. PERMISSION TO GO IN permission or right to enter a place 2. ENTRANCE TO PLACE physical entry to a place 3. PHYS MEASURE OF FLOW OF CURRENT the reciprocal of impedance, a measure of the ability of an electrical current to flow. Symbol **Y**

admittedly /əd míttidli/ adv as must be acknowledged

admix /əd míks/ (-mixes, -mixing, -mixed) vt to mix something into something else [Early 16C. Probably back-formation < ADMIXTURE]

admixture /əd míkschər/ n 1. PRODUCT OF MIXING something produced by incorporating an item into something else 2. INGREDIENT something added to something else by mixing 3. PROCESS OF MIXING INGREDIENTS the mixing of something into something else [Early 17C. < AD- + MIXTURE]

admonish /əd mónnish/ (-ishes, -ishing, -ished) vt 1. REBUKE SOMEBODY to rebuke somebody mildly but earnestly 2. ADVISE SOMEBODY to advise somebody to do or, more often, not to do something 3. REPRIMAND SOMEBODY OFFICIALLY in the UK police force, to reprimand an employee severely for misconduct [14C. < Old French amonester < assumed Vulgar Latin admonere < Latin monere 'warn'] —**admonisher** n —**admonishment** n

admonition /ádmə nísh'n/ n 1. a mild but earnest rebuke 2. advice for or against doing something —**admonitory** /əd mónnitəri/ adj

ad nauseam /ad náwzi am/ adv to an extreme or annoying extent [Mid-17C. < Latin, 'to sickness']

~~ad nauseum~~ incorrect spelling of **ad nauseam**

adnexa /ad néksə/ npl adjoining structural parts of the body [Late 19C. < Latin < adnectere 'tie together' < nectere 'to tie'] —**adnexal** adj

adnominal /əd nómmin'l/ n a word that modifies a noun [Mid-19C. < Latin adnomen, alteration of agnomen (see AGNOMEN)] —**adnominal** adj

adnoun /ád nown/ n an adjective that is used as a noun, e.g. 'meek' in 'Blessed are the meek' [Mid-18C. < AD- + NOUN, after adverb]

ado /ə doó/ n excited activity or bother [14C. Contraction of N English dialect at do < Old Norse at 'to' + DO¹] —**without further** or **more ado** without wasting any time

CULTURAL NOTE *Much Ado About Nothing*, a play (1598?) by William Shakespeare. A comedy set in the court of the Duke of Messina in Sicily, it tells of the love of a soldier, Claudio, for the Duke's daughter, Hero, and the eventually unsuccessful attempts of Claudio's enemy, Don John, to prevent their marriage.

adobe /ə dóbi/ n 1. EARTHEN BRICK brick made from earth and straw and dried by the sun 2. BUILDING MADE OF ADOBE a structure made with adobe bricks 3. EARTH THAT FORMS ADOBE earth used to make adobe bricks [Mid-18C. Via Spanish < Arabic at-tūb 'the bricks']

adobe flat n in the United States, a gently sloping plain of clay soil deposited by desert floods

adobo /ə dóbō/ (plural -bos) n SE Asia a Philippine dish of marinated meat or fish seasoned with vinegar, garlic, soy sauce, and spices [Mid-20C. < Spanish]

adolescence /áddə léss'nss/ n 1. the period from puberty to adulthood in human beings 2. the stage in the development of something such as a civilization before it reaches maturity

adolescent /áddə léss'nt/ n 1. SOMEBODY IN PERIOD PRECEDING ADULTHOOD somebody who has reached puberty but is not yet an adult ■ adj 1. EXPERIENCING ADOLESCENCE going through the period of adolescence ○ adolescent males 2. HAPPENING DURING ADOLESCENCE typically occurring during the period of adolescence 3. IMMATURE involving, relating to, or meant for somebody who is immature [15C. Via French < Latin adolescent-, present participle of adolescere 'be nourished, grow up' < alere 'nourish']

~~adolesent~~ incorrect spelling of **adolescent**

Adonai /áddo ní/ n a name used in Judaism instead of the unspeakable name of God [14C. < Hebrew 'ăḏōnay]

Adonic /ə dónnik/ adj 1. LITERAT OF CLASSICAL VERSE STYLE describes a line in classical verse consisting of a dactyl followed by either a spondee or trochee 2. MYTHOL RELATING TO ADONIS relating to or like Adonis ■ n LITERAT CLASSICAL LINE OR POEM an Adonic line or poem [Late 16C. Via French < medieval Latin adonicus < Greek Adōnis (see ADONIS)]

Adonis /ə dóniss/ n 1. in Greek mythology, a handsome youth loved by Aphrodite and Persephone. He was killed while hunting boar, but was allowed by Zeus to divide his time between Aphrodite on earth and Persephone in the underworld. 2. also adonis an extremely handsome young man [Late 16C. < Greek Adōnis < Phoenician ædōnī 'my lord']

adopt /ə dópt/ (adopts, adopting, adopted) vt 1. LEGALLY RAISE ANOTHER'S CHILD to raise a child of other biological parents as if it were your own, in accordance with formal legal procedures 2. CHOOSE AND DECIDE TO USE SOMETHING to take up something such as a plan, idea, cause, or practice and use or follow it ○ decided to adopt a wait-and-see policy 3. ASSUME WAY OF ACTING to assume an attitude or way of behaving ○ adopted an air of innocence 4. CHOOSE AS CANDIDATE to choose somebody as a political candidate 5. START USING NEW NAME to take on and use a new name or title ○ plans to adopt a pseudonym 6. POL VOTE IN FAVOUR OF SOMETHING to vote to accept something such as a committee's decision or a parliamentary bill [15C. Directly or via French adopter < Latin adoptare 'choose for yourself'

< optare 'choose'] —**adoptable** adj —**adopted** adj —**adoptee** /a dóp teé/ n —**adopter** n

USAGE **adopted** or **adoptive**? Parents who adopt a child have an **adopted** child, and the child has **adoptive** parents. Any children related to the parents by birth have an **adopted** brother or sister; the **adopted** child has **adoptive** siblings.

adoption /ə dópsh'n/ n 1. a formal legal process to adopt a child 2. an instance of adopting somebody or something such as an idea, name, or attitude [14C. Directly or via French < Latin adoption- < adoptare (see ADOPT)]

adoptive /ə dóptiv/ adj describes a parent who adopts a child, or somebody who is related to somebody else by adoption (see usage note) ○ her adoptive sister

USAGE See **adopt**.

adorable /ə dáwrəb'l/ adj charming, lovable, and usually very attractive —**adorability** /ə dáwrə bílləti/ n —**adorableness** n —**adorably** adv

adore /ə dáwr/ (adores, adoring, adored) vt 1. LOVE SOMEBODY DEEPLY to love somebody intensely 2. LIKE SOMETHING VERY MUCH to like something or somebody very much (informal) 3. WORSHIP GOD to worship God, a god, or a spirit [14C. Via Old French < late Latin adorare 'pray to' < Latin orare 'pray'] —**adoration** /áddə ráysh'n/ n —**adorer** n

adoring /ə dáwring/ adj showing love or admiration for somebody —**adoringly** adv

adorn /ə dáwrn/ (adorns, adorning, adorned) vt 1. to add decoration or ornamentation to something 2. to add to the beauty or glory of something or somebody [14C. Via Old French < Latin adornare 'embellish with ornaments' < ornare 'embellish'] —**adorner** n —**adornment** n

Adorno /a dáwrnō/, **Theodor** (1903–69) German philosopher, sociologist, and musicologist. His works include *Dialectic of Enlightenment* (1947) and *Minima Moralia: Reflections from Damaged Life*. Born **Wiesengrund, Theodor Ludwig**

ADP¹ n a chemical compound (**nucleotide**) involved in energy transfer reactions in living cells. Full form **adenosine diphosphate**

ADP² abbr COMPUT automatic data processing

adperson /ád purss'n/ (plural -persons or -people /-peep'l/) n somebody who works in advertising (informal)

Adrastea /ə drásti ə/ n a small natural satellite of Jupiter, discovered in 1979

ad rem /ad rém/ adv to the point or purpose (formal) [Late 16C. < Latin, 'to the matter or business'] —**ad rem** adj

adren- prefix same as **adreno-** (used before vowels)

adrenal /ə dreén'l/ adj 1. relating to or on the kidneys 2. describes parts or effects of the adrenal glands ■ n ANAT same as **adrenal gland** [Late 19C. < AD- + RENAL, because the adrenal glands are next to the kidneys] —**adrenally** adv

adrenalectomy /ə dreénə léktəmi/ (plural -mies) n the surgical removal of one or both of the adrenal glands

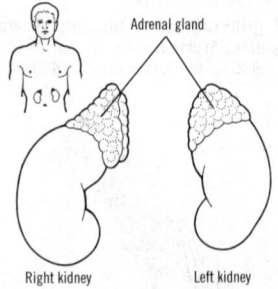

adrenal gland

adrenal gland n an endocrine gland located above each kidney. The inner part (**medulla**) of each gland secretes adrenaline and the outer part (**cortex**) secretes steroids.

adrenaline /ə drénnəlin/, **adrenalin** *n* a hormone secreted by the adrenal glands and by some nerve endings, that increases the speed and force of heart contraction (*often nontechnical*) ○ *get the adrenaline pumping* [Early 20C. < ADRENAL + -IN]

USAGE adrenalin or **adrenaline**? In British English, the spellings ***adrenaline*** or ***adrenalin*** are used. In American usage, ***adrenaline*** is the more usual spelling, and ***Adrenalin*** (with a capital initial letter) is a trademark for a commercial drug. An alternative term, especially in American English, is *epinephrine*.

adrenergic /áddrə núrjik/ *adj* producing or activated by adrenaline or a similar substance [Mid-20C. < ADREN- + Greek *ergon* 'work'] —**adrenergically** *adv*

adreno- *prefix* relating to adrenaline or the adrenal glands ○ *adrenochrome* [< ADRENAL or ADRENALINE]

adrenochrome /ə dreénō krōm/ *n* a naturally occurring mixture of quinones, brick red in colour, produced by the oxidation of adrenaline, that reduces the permeability of small blood vessels. Use: control of bleeding.

adrenocortical /ə dreénō káwrtik'l/ *adj* involving, located in, or produced by the cortex of the adrenal glands

adrenocorticosteroid /ə dreénō kawrtikō steér oyd, -stérr oyd/ *n* **1.** any steroid hormone released from the adrenal cortex **2.** a drug that mimics steroids produced by the adrenal cortex

adrenocorticotrophic /ə dreénō káwrtikō tróffik/, **adrenocorticotropic** /-tróppik/ *adj* describes hormones or drugs that stimulate the adrenal cortex to produce corticosteroids

adrenocorticotrophic hormone *n* BIOCHEM full form of **ACTH**

adrenocorticotrophin /ə dreénō káwrtikō trṓfin/, **adrenocorticotropin** /-trṓpin/ *n* BIOCHEM same as **ACTH**

adrenocorticotropic, etc BIOCHEM another spelling of **adrenocorticotrophic, etc**

adrenoleukodystrophy /ə dreénō lóokə dístrəfi/ *n* a hereditary disorder of the nervous system in boys that affects the adrenal glands

adrenolytic /ə dreénō líttik/ *adj* blocking the action of the adrenergic nerves or inhibiting the response to adrenaline ■ *n* an adrenolytic drug or agent

adrenoreceptor /ə drénnō ri séptər/ *n* a nerve ending that is activated by adrenaline or related substances

~~**adress**~~ incorrect spelling of **address**

Adriatic /áydri áttik/ *adj* relating to the area that borders on the Adriatic Sea, or islands in that sea ■ *n* same as **Adriatic Sea**

Adriatic Sea /áydri áttik-/ arm of the Mediterranean Sea, east of Italy. Area: 132,000 sq. km/51,000 sq. mi.

adrift /ə dríft/ *adj, adv* **1. FLOATING WITHOUT DIRECTION** floating freely without being steered in a specific direction **2. WITHOUT PURPOSE** living life without a goal **3. OFF TARGET** astray, off target, or amiss

adroit /ə dróyt/ *adj* **1.** displaying physical or mental skill **2.** able to react quickly in thought or actions [Mid-17C. < French *à droit* 'by right, properly'] —**adroitly** *adv* —**adroitness** *n*

ADSL *abbr* asymmetrical digital subscriber line

adsorb /ad sáwrb, -záwrb/ (**-sorbs, -sorbing, -sorbed**) *vti* to undergo, or cause something to undergo, adsorption [Late 19C. Back-formation < ADSORPTION] —**adsorbable** *adj*

adsorbate /ad sáwr bayt, -záwr-/ *n* a substance that is adsorbed

adsorbent /ad sáwrbənt, -záwrbənt/ *adj* able to adsorb ■ *n* a substance capable of adsorbing

adsorption /ad sáwrpsh'n, -záwrpsh'n/ *n* the adhesion of a thin layer of molecules of some substance to the surface of a solid or liquid [Late 19C. Blend of AD- + ABSORPTION] —**adsorptive** *adj*

adspeak /ád speek/ *n* the language thought of as typical of advertisements, especially characterized as misleading or exaggerated

adspend /ád spend/ *n* the amount of money spent on advertising for a product or activity

ADT *abbr N Am* TIME Atlantic Daylight Time

aduki bean *n* PLANTS, FOOD same as **adzuki bean**

adularia /áddyoō láiri ə/ *n* a white or transparent precious stone that is a variety of orthoclase. Use: gems. [Late 18C. < French *adulaire* < *Adula*, mountains in the Swiss Alps]

adulate /áddyoō layt/ (**-lates, -lating, -lated**) *vt* to admire or flatter somebody excessively [Mid-18C. Back-formation < ADULATION] —**adulator** *n* —**adulatory** /áddyoō láytəri/ *adj*

adulation /áddyoō láysh'n/ *n* excessive flattery or admiration [14C. Directly or via French < Latin *adulation-* < *adulari* 'flatter']

adult /áddult, ə dúlt/ *n* **1. FULLY GROWN LIFE FORM** a fully mature person, animal, plant, or other form of life **2. SOMEBODY LEGALLY ADULT** somebody who has reached the age of legal majority ■ *adj* **1. COMPLETELY GROWN** fully developed and mature ○ *an adult male* ○ *adult life* **2. FOR SOMEBODY MATURE** involving, relating to, or meant for mature people ○ *adult education* **3. UNSUITABLE FOR CHILDREN** considered unsuitable for young people because of pornography, violence, or sexually explicit language [Mid-16C. < Latin *adultus*, past participle of *adolescere* (see ADOLESCENT)] —**adulthood** *n* —**adultness** *n*

adult child *n* **1.** somebody's grown-up son or daughter ○ *a photo of the bride and groom and their adult children* **2.** an adult who, because of a psychiatric disorder, thinks and behaves like a child

adult education *n* EDUC same as **continuing education** (sense 1)

adulterant /ə dúltərənt/ *n* something that makes something else less pure —**adulterant** *adj*

adulterate /ə dúltə rayt/ *vt* (**-ates, -ating, -ated**) to make something less pure by adding inferior or unsuitable elements or substances to it ■ *adj* **1.** made less pure **2.** same as **adulterous** (*literary*) [Mid-16C. < Latin *adulterat-*, past participle of *adulterare* 'change, corrupt, commit adultery' < *alterare* (see ALTER)] —**adulteration** /ə dúltə ráysh'n/ *n* —**adulterative** /-rətiv/ *adj* —**adulterator** *n*

adulterine /ə dúltərin/ *adj* **1. IMPURE** characterized by adulteration **2. ILLEGAL** not within the law **3. BORN FROM ADULTERY** born from an adulterous relationship (*literary*)

adulterous /ə dúltərəss/ *adj* relating to or involved in adultery [Early 17C. < obsolete *adulter* 'adulterer' < Latin *adulterare* (see ADULTERATE)] —**adulterously** *adv*

adultery /ə dúltəri/ *n* voluntary sexual relations between a married person and somebody other than his or her spouse [15C. Directly and via Old French *avout(e)rie* < Latin *adulterare* (see ADULTERATE)] —**adulterer** *n*

adultescent /áddul téss'nt/ *n* a young person, aged 25–34, who enjoys entertainment such as computer games or books intended for a much younger audience [Early 21C. < ADULT + ADOLESCENT]

adult-onset diabetes *n* a form of diabetes mellitus that develops slowly in some adults as the body becomes unable to use insulin effectively

~~**adultry**~~ incorrect spelling of **adultery**

adumbrate /áddum brayt/ (**-brates, -brating, -brated**) *vt* **1. SKETCHILY INDICATE SOMETHING** to give an incomplete or faint outline or indication of something **2. FORESHADOW SOMETHING** to give a vague indication or warning of something to come **3. CONCEAL SOMETHING** to overshadow and obscure something [Late 16C. < Latin *adumbrat-*, past participle of *adumbrare* 'overshadow' < *umbra* 'shade'] —**adumbration** /áddum bráysh'n/ *n* —**adumbrative** /ə dúmbrətiv/ *adj* —**adumbratively** *adv*

adv, adv. *abbr* **1.** GRAM adverb **2.** adverbial

ad val. *abbr* FIN ad valorem

ad valorem /ád və láw rem/ *adj, adv* in proportion to the value of something [Late 17C. < Latin, 'according to value']

advance /əd vaánss/ *v* (**-vances, -vancing, -vanced**) **1.** *vti* **MOVE AHEAD** to move, or move somebody or something, forward in position **2.** *vt* **SUGGEST SOMETHING** to put something forward as a proposal **3.** *vt* **GIVE SOMETHING AHEAD OF TIME** to supply something or part of something, especially money, before it is due **4.** *vt* **LEND MONEY OR GOODS** to supply money or goods on credit **5.** *vti* **RISE IN STATUS** to rise, or make or help somebody rise, in rank or position **6.** *vt* **BRING SOMETHING FORWARD IN TIME** to make something happen earlier than originally expected **7.** *vti* **PROGRESS** to further the progress or improvement of something such as a cause, or undergo progress or improvement **8.** *vti* **RISE IN AMOUNT** to increase in price, rate, or amount, or increase the price, rate, or amount of something ■ *n* **1. DEVELOPMENT** progress or improvements **2.** FIN **PAYMENT AHEAD OF TIME** a sum of money paid before it is due **3. MOVEMENT AHEAD** a forward movement in position **4. FRIENDLY APPROACH** an approach made to somebody in an attempt to form a relationship or come to an agreement (*often used in the plural*) **5.** COMM **PROVIDING SOMETHING BEFORE BEING PAID** the act of supplying money or goods before payment is received **6.** COMM **SOMETHING RECEIVED BEFORE BEING PAID FOR** a quantity of money or goods supplied before payment is made or repayments begin **7.** FIN **LOAN** a loan of money **8.** FIN **PRICE RISE** an increase in price or rate ■ *adj* **1. AHEAD OF TIME** made, given, or sent ahead of time **2. GOING IN FRONT** going ahead of the main group [13C. Via Old French *avancer* < assumed Vulgar Latin *abantiare* < *abante* '(from) before' < Latin *ante* 'before'] —**advancer** *n* ◇ **in advance** before an event takes place

advance copy (*plural* **advance copies**) *n* a copy of a book made available before the actual publication date

advance corporation tax *n* a tax paid by any company that pays a dividend, calculated by deducting the basic rate of income tax from the grossed-up value of the dividend

advanced /əd vaánst/ *adj* **1. MORE HIGHLY DEVELOPED** at a higher stage of development or progress than other similar people or things ○ *an advanced class* **2. FAR ALONG** at a point late in the progress or development of something **3. FUTURISTIC** considered to be radical or ahead of its time

advanced degree *n N Am* a university degree higher than a bachelor's

Advanced Higher *n* in Scotland, an examination in a single subject, above and in addition to a Higher, usually taken after six years of secondary education

advance guard *n* a body of troops sent ahead of a main force to prepare an area for operations

advancement /əd vaánssmənt/ *n* **1. PROMOTION** a promotion in rank or position **2. ADVANCING** an act or instance of moving ahead **3. IMPROVEMENT** the progress or development of something **4.** LAW **USE OF LEGACY BEFORE DUE** the use of money from a legacy by or on behalf of its beneficiary before that person is strictly entitled to it

advance party (*plural* **advance parties**) *n* **1.** a group of soldiers or units sent ahead of a larger force to prepare an area for operations **2.** a small group sent on ahead of any main party, e.g. on an expedition

advance person *n US* somebody employed by a politician or other public figure to travel ahead on trips to organize schedules, publicity, security, and other arrangements

advance woman *n US* a woman employed by a politician or other public figure to travel ahead on trips to organize schedules, publicity, security, and other arrangements

advantage /əd vaántij/ *n* **1. SUPERIOR POSITION** a superior or favourable position in relation to somebody or something ○ *hoping to gain an advantage in the negotiations* **2. FACTOR FAVOURING SOMEBODY** a circumstance or factor that places somebody in a favourable position in relation to others ○ *have the advantage of a stable home* **3. PROFIT** a benefit or gain ○ *Their mistakes worked to our advantage.* **4.** TENNIS **POINT AFTER DEUCE** in tennis, the point scored after deuce ■ *vt* (**-tages, -taging, -taged**) **BENEFIT SOMEBODY** to put somebody in a superior or favourable position in relation to others [14C. < Old French *avantage* < *avant* 'before' < assumed Vulgar Latin *abante* (see ADVANCE)] ◇ **take advantage of somebody** to use somebody in a selfish way in order to achieve a personal benefit, usually by exploiting a weakness ◇ **take advantage of something 1.** to make use of something that is available for personal benefit **2.** use somebody or something in a selfish way in order to achieve a personal benefit ◇ **to advantage** in a way that emphasizes the positive aspects of somebody or something

advantageous /ádvən táyjəss/ *adj* **1.** giving an advantage **2.** of use or benefit —**advantageously** *adv* —**advantageousness** *n*

advect /əd vékt/ (**-vects, -vecting, -vected**) *vt* to transfer something by advection [Mid-20C. Back-formation < ADVECTION]

advection /əd véksh'n/ *n* the horizontal transfer of a property such as heat, caused by air movement [Early 20C. < Latin *advection-* < *advehere* 'carry to' < *vehere* 'carry']

advent /ád vent/ *n* the arrival of something important or awaited [Mid-18C. < ADVENT]

Advent *n* the four-week period leading up to Christmas, beginning on the fourth Sunday before Christmas Day [Pre-12C. < Latin *adventus* 'arrival' < *advenire* 'come to' < *venire* 'come']

Advent calendar *n* a large decorated card with numbered doors on it, one of which is opened each day from 1 to 24 December, revealing a picture

Adventist /ádvəntist/ *n* a member of a Christian denomination such as the Seventh-Day Adventists who believes that the Second Coming of Jesus Christ is imminent —**Adventism** *n*

adventitia /ád ven tíshi ə/ *n* the outer covering of an organ or body part, especially that of a blood vessel [Late 19C. < medieval Latin < neuter plural of *adventitius* (see ADVENTITIOUS)]

adventitious /ádvən tíshəss/ *adj* **1.** added from an outside and often unexpected source rather than intrinsic **2.** developing in an unusual position, as does a root growing downwards from a branch [Early 17C. < medieval Latin *adventitius* 'coming from outside', alteration of Latin *adventicius* < *adventus* (see ADVENT)] —**adventitiously** *adv*

adventive /əd véntiv/ *adj* describes a plant or animal found in an environment where it is not native and is not fully established ■ *n* an adventive plant or animal —**adventively** *adv*

Advent Sunday *n* the fourth Sunday before Christmas, marking the start of Advent. It is regarded as the beginning of the Christian ecclesiastical year.

adventure /əd vénchər/ *n* **1.** EXCITING EXPERIENCE an exciting or extraordinary event or series of events **2.** BOLD UNDERTAKING an undertaking involving uncertainty and risk **3.** INVOLVEMENT IN BOLD UNDERTAKINGS the participation or willingness to participate in things that involve uncertainty and risk ○ *Where's your sense of adventure?* **4.** FINANCIAL SPECULATION a risky or speculative financial undertaking ■ *v* (**-tures, -turing, -tured**) **1.** *vt* RISK SAYING SOMETHING to risk saying something that other people may disagree with or find offensive **2.** *vt* PUT SOMETHING AT RISK to put something at risk or in danger (*dated*) **3.** *vi* RISK DANGER to dare to go somewhere new or engage in something dangerous (*dated*) [13C. Via French *aventure* < Latin *adventurus* 'about to arrive', future participle of *advenire* (see ADVENT)]

adventure game *n* a puzzle-solving computer game in which players take on the role of characters in the game world but that generally lacks the numerical characteristics of role-play games

adventure playground *n* an outdoor play area for children with slides, climbing frames, ropes, and sometimes materials with which to build things

adventurer /əd vénchərər/ *n* **1.** SOMEBODY IN SEARCH OF ADVENTURE somebody who enjoys exciting or risky activities **2.** SOMEBODY PURSUING MONEY OR POSITION somebody who is unscrupulous in trying to gain wealth or status **3.** SPECULATOR a financial speculator (*archaic*)

adventuresome /əd vénchərsəm/ *adj* willing or eager to participate in exciting or risky activities —**adventuresomely** *adv* —**adventuresomeness** *n*

adventure sport *n* a sport involving strenuous physical activity with an element of risk, e.g. bungee jumping

adventuress /əd vénchərəss/ *n* a woman who uses unscrupulous means in order to gain wealth or social position (*dated*)

adventure travel *n* a type of holidaying involving strenuous and often risky outdoor activities in remote areas

adventurism /əd vénchərizəm/ *n* **1.** involvement in risky financial enterprises **2.** reckless intervention by one government in the affairs of another —**adventurist** *n*

adventurous /əd vénchərəss/ *adj* **1.** willing or eager to participate in risky or exciting activities **2.** involving risk —**adventurously** *adv* —**adventurousness** *n*

adverb /ád vurb/ *n* a word that modifies a verb, an adjective, another adverb, or a sentence, e.g. 'happily', 'very', or 'frankly' [15C. Directly or via French < Latin *adverbium* (after Greek *epirrhēma* 'added word')]

USAGE adjective or **adverb**? Some adjectives are used as adverbs without changing their form: *a fast car. You're driving too fast.* Other adjectives can be used as adverbs, instead of the *-ly* adverb form, in a restricted range of contexts: *Hold on tight* [or *tightly*]. *He spelt my name wrong* [or *wrongly*]. In most cases, however, it is incorrect to use an adjective as an adverb: *I want it badly* [not *bad*]. *She was really* [not *real*] *pleased.*

adverbial /ad vúrbi əl/ *adj* relating to or functioning as an adverb ■ *n* an adverb, or a phrase or clause that functions as an adverb —**adverbially** *adv*

ad verbum /ad vúrbəm/ *adv* word for word (*formal*) [< Latin, 'in accordance with the word']

adversarial /ád vur sáiri əl/ *adj* **1.** relating to conflict or adversaries **2.** describes a legal system or proceeding that involves conflicting parties or interests. N Am term **adversary**

adversary /ádvərsəri/ *n* (*plural* **-ies**) an opponent in a conflict, contest, or debate ■ *adj N Am* same as **adversarial** (sense 2) [14C. Via Old French < Latin *adversarius* 'enemy' < *adversus* (see ADVERSE)]

adversative /əd vúrsətiv/ *adj* expressing opposition or contrast ■ *n* a word, phrase, or clause that expresses opposition or contrast, e.g. 'but' or 'although' [Mid-16C. Directly or via French < late Latin *adversativus* 'opposed' < Latin *adversus* (see ADVERSE)] —**adversatively** *adv*

adverse /ád vurss, ad vúrss/ *adj* **1.** UNFAVOURABLE creating unfavourable, undesirable, or harmful results ○ *adverse conditions* **2.** ANTAGONISTIC acting with or characterized by opposition or antagonism ○ *adverse publicity* **3.** CONTRARY creating momentum in a direction away from that desired **4.** BOT FACING STEM describes a leaf or flower that faces the main stem [14C. Via Old French < Latin *adversus* 'turned against, hostile' < past participle of *advertere* (see ADVERT[1])] —**adversely** *adv* —**adverseness** *n*

USAGE adverse or **averse**? Both words mean 'opposed' in different ways. ***Adverse*** describes something unfavourable or difficult and is normally used before an abstract noun: *adverse circumstances, adverse conditions.* ***Averse*** describes people who are disinclined to do something or have a strong dislike specified by the word that follows *to*: *As an actor he is not averse to publicity.* ***Averse*** is never used before a noun, as ***adverse*** normally is, and is most often accompanied by 'not'.

adverse possession *n* the possession or occupation of land or property without the owner's permission as a method of acquiring legal ownership

adversity /əd vúrssəti/ (*plural* **-ties**) *n* **1.** hardship and suffering **2.** an extremely unfavourable experience or event

advert[1] /əd vúrt/ (**-verts, -verting, -verted**) *vi* to call attention or make reference to something [15C. Via Old French *advertir* 'notice' < Latin *advertere* 'turn towards' < *vertere* 'to turn'] —**advertence** *n*

advert[2] /ád vurt/ *n* MARKETING same as **advertisement** (sense 2) (*informal*) [Mid-19C. Shortening]

advertise /ádvər tīz/ (**-tises, -tising, -tised**) *v* **1.** *vti* PRAISE COMMERCIAL PRODUCT to publicize the qualities of a product, service, business, or event in order to encourage people to buy or use it **2.** *vti* PUBLICLY ANNOUNCE AVAILABILITY OR NEED to publicize something such as a job vacancy or item for sale ○ *advertise for a new flatmate* **3.** *vt* TELL OTHERS ABOUT SOMETHING to make something known to others ○ *She advertised her arrival with a shout.* [15C. < Old French *advertiss-*, stem of *advertir* (see ADVERT[1])] —**advertiser** *n*

advertisement /əd vúrtissmənt/ *n* **1.** a public announcement in a newspaper or on the radio, television, or Internet advertising something such as a product for sale or an event **2.** the act of advertising something

advertising /ádvər tīzing/ *n* **1.** PUBLIC PROMOTION OF SOMETHING the public promotion of something such as a product, service, business, or event in order to attract or increase interest in it **2.** INDUSTRY THAT CREATES ADVERTISEMENTS the business of producing advertisements **3.** ADVERTISEMENTS advertisements considered collectively

~~**advertisment**~~ incorrect spelling of **advertisement**

advertorial /ádvər táwri əl/ *n* an advertisement in a publication that looks like one of its normal articles [Mid-20C. Blend of ADVERTISEMENT + EDITORIAL]

advice /əd víss/ *n* **1.** somebody's opinion about what another person should do ○ *May I give you some advice?* **2.** formal or official information about something, usually received from a distance (*often used in the plural*) [13C. < French *avis* 'opinion' < Latin *ad (meum) visum* 'in (my) view or opinion' (*visum*, past participle of *videre* 'to see')]

USAGE advice or **advise**? ***Advice*** is a noun only, spelt with a *-c-*: *I followed the doctor's advice*; ***advise*** is a verb only, spelt with an *-s-*: *She advised me to seek a doctor's advice.*

advice column *n* a section of a newspaper or magazine in which advice and answers to questions or problems sent in by readers are printed

advice note *n* a formal document from a supplier to a customer containing details of goods that have been sent

~~**advid**~~ incorrect spelling of **avid**

advisable /əd vízəb'l/ *adj* being a sensible or desirable thing to do —**advisability** /əd vízə bílləti/ *n* —**advisably** *adv*

advise /əd víz/ (**-vises, -vising, -vised**) *v* **1.** *vti* OFFER ADVICE to offer a personal opinion to somebody ○ *I won't choose until somebody can advise me.* **2.** *vt* RECOMMEND SOMETHING to give advice to somebody on a subject or course of action ○ *We were advised against staying longer.* ○ *'I have advised him to join a club or get a hobby but he is determined to feel sorry for himself.'* (Sue Townsend, *The Secret Diary of Adrian Mole Aged 13¾*; 1982) **3.** ⚠ *vt* INFORM SOMEBODY to tell somebody about something [14C. < French *aviser* < *avis* 'opinion' (see ADVICE)]

USAGE The use of the verb ***advise*** to mean 'tell somebody about something' is often regarded as jargon and is best avoided in formal usage: *Please advise us of* [better *tell us*] *your new address. I will advise them* [better *inform them*] *of the new time of the meeting.*

SYNONYMS See ***recommend.***

advisedly /əd vízidli/ *adv* after careful consideration

advisee /əd vī zée/ *n* somebody who receives advice

advisement /əd vízmənt/ *n* **1.** careful consideration or deliberation ○ *will take it under advisement* **2.** the act of giving advice [14C. < French *avisement* < *aviser* (see ADVISE)]

adviser /əd vízər/, **advisor** *n* **1.** somebody who gives advice **2.** a teacher who is a specialist in a subject and is appointed by an education authority to advise school heads and teachers on the teaching of that subject

USAGE adviser or **advisor**? Both spellings are used for 'somebody who gives advice'. ***Adviser*** is often regarded as more correct because *-er* is the more usual suffix for words formed directly from other English words. ***Advisor*** is common in American English and is probably influenced by the form of the adjective ***advisory*** or the spelling of Latin *advisor.*

advisory /əd vízəri/ *adj* **1.** GIVING ADVICE providing or of the nature of advice **2.** HAVING FUNCTION OF GIVING ADVICE having the function of giving advice, usually with the implication that the advice given need not be followed ○ *an advisory committee* ■ *n US* WARNING OF SOMETHING TO COME an advance notice of something, e.g. a warning of impending severe weather ○ *a small craft advisory*

advisory teacher *n* EDUC same as **adviser** (sense 2)

advocaat /ádvō kaa, -kaat/ *n* an alcoholic beverage similar to eggnog, containing eggs, sugar, and brandy [Mid-20C. < Dutch, 'advocate', because supposed to help clear the throat]

advocacy /ádvəkəssi/ (*plural* **-cies**) *n* **1.** active verbal support for a cause or position **2.** support for people who are thought likely to be disregarded or to have difficulty in gaining attention, so that their opinion

is listened to [14C. Via Old French *advocacie* < medieval Latin *advocatia* < Latin *advocatus* (see ADVOCATE)]

advocacy group *n* a group of people working together to promote a cause

advocate *vt* /ádvə kayt/ (**-cates, -cating, -cated**) **RECOMMEND OR SUPPORT SOMETHING** to support or speak in favour of something ■ *n* /ádvəkət, -kayt/ **1. SOMEBODY GIVING SUPPORT** somebody who supports or speaks in favour of something ○ *a tireless advocate of social reform* **2. HELPER** somebody who acts or intercedes on behalf of another **3. LAW LEGAL REPRESENTATIVE** somebody such as a lawyer, who pleads another's case in a legal forum **4. LAW SCOTTISH BARRISTER** the equivalent of an English barrister in Scotland [14C. Via Old French *avocat* 'advocate' < Latin *advocatus* < *advocare* 'call to' < *vocare* 'to call'] —**advocator** *n* —**advocatory** /ádvə káytəri, ádvəkətəri/ *adj*

SYNONYMS See *recommend*.

Advocate Depute (*plural* **Advocates Depute**) *n* a law officer in Scotland, appointed to prosecute cases on behalf of the Lord Advocate. The equivalent in the English and US legal systems is a public prosecutor.

advt *abbr* advertisement

adwoman /ád woomən/ (*plural* **-women** /-wimən/) *n* a woman who works in advertising (*informal*)

Adyghe /aádi gay, -gáy/, **Adygei** *n* an Abkhaz-Adyghean language spoken in the northwestern region of the Republic of Georgia. Native speakers: 100,000. — **Adyghe** *adj*

adynamic /áy dī námmik/ *adj* characterized by loss of normal function ○ *adynamic ileus*

adytum /ádditəm/ (*plural* **-ta** /-tə/) *n* the most sacred part in an ancient temple, restricted to priests [Early 17C. < Latin < Greek *adutos* 'not to be entered' < *duein* 'enter']

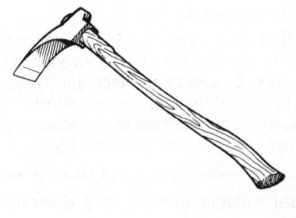

adze

adze /adz/, **adz** *n* a tool similar to an axe, with an arched blade set at right angles to the handle. Use: trimming and shaping wood. [Old English *adesa, eadesa*, origin ?]

adzuki bean /ad zóoki-/, **aduki bean** /ə dóoki-/, **azuki bean** /ə zóoki-/ *n* **1.** a small, slightly sweet, red-brown bean. Use: in vegetarian dishes in Europe and North America, in sweet dishes in East Asian cooking. **2.** a plant that produces adzuki beans. Latin name: *Vigna angularis*. [< Japanese *azuki* 'red bean']

ae /ay/ *det Scotland* a single (*literary*) [Variant of A²]

AEA *abbr* Atomic Energy Authority

aecia FUNGI plural of **aecium**

aecidia FUNGI plural of **aecidium**

aecidiospore /ee síddi ō spawr/ *n* FUNGI same as **aeciospore** [Late 19C. < AECIDIUM]

aecidium /ee síddi əm/ (*plural* **-ia** /-i ə/) *n* FUNGI same as **aecium** [Mid-19C. < modern Latin < Greek *aikia* (see AECIUM)]

aeciospore /éessi ə spawr/ *n* a spore produced in the reproductive organ (**aecium**) of a rust fungus with two genetically distinct nuclei [Early 20C. < AECIUM]

aecium /éessi əm/ (*plural* **-cia** /-si ə/) *n* a cup-shaped reproductive organ (**fruiting body**) produced by some rust fungi in the tissue of their host plant, in which spores (**aeciospores**) are formed [Early 20C. Via modern Latin < Greek *aikia* 'injury'; from the harm caused by the fungi]

aedes /ay ée deez/ (*plural* **same**) *n* a mosquito that can transmit serious diseases such as yellow fever and dengue. Native to: tropics and subtropics. Latin name: *Aedes aegypti*. [Early 20C. < modern Latin < Greek *aēdēs* 'unpleasant'; because it carries diseases]

aedile /ée dīl/ *n* in ancient Rome, a magistrate responsible for public works and buildings, games, markets, and the grain and water supplies [Mid-16C. < Latin *aedilis* < *aedes* 'building']

Aegean Sea /i jée ən-/ arm of the Mediterranean Sea, situated between Greece and Turkey, containing numerous islands divided into three main groups, the Cyclades, Dodecanese, and Sporades. Area: 207,200 sq. km/80,000 sq. mi.

aegis /éejiss/ *n* in Greek mythology, the shield of Zeus or Athena [Early 17C. Via Latin < Greek *aigis* 'goatskin shield of Zeus'] ◇ **under the aegis of somebody** or **something** with the support or protection of somebody or something (*formal*)

aegrotat /ígrō tat, éegrō-, ee grō-/ *n* **1.** a certificate granted to a university student crediting the student with passing an examination missed because of illness **2.** a degree or other qualification granted to a university student by an aegrotat [Late 18C. < Latin, 'he or she is ill']

Aelfric /álfrik/ (955?–1020?) Anglo-Saxon monk and writer. As abbot of Eynsham from 1005 he wrote several works, including *Lives of the Saints* (993– 998) and a Latin grammar.

-aemia, -haemia, -emia, -hemia *suffix* blood ○ *anaemia* [Via modern Latin < Greek *-aimia* < *haima* 'blood']

Aeneas /i née əss/ *n* in Greek and Roman mythology, a Trojan hero who escaped after the fall of Troy and spent seven years travelling before settling near the site of Rome in Italy. His travels are the subject of Virgil's *Aeneid*.

Aeolia ♦ **Aeolis**

aeolian /ee óli ən/ *adj* carried or produced by the wind ○ *aeolian deposits* [Early 20C. < AEOLUS]

Aeolian /ee óli ən/, **Eolian** *n* **1. MEMBER OF HELLENIC PEOPLE** a member of an ancient Hellenic people who lived in Aeolis and Lesbos about 1100 BC **2. LANG** same as **Aeolic** ■ *adj* **1. OF AEOLIS** relating to Aeolis, or its people, language, or culture **2. OF AEOLUS** relating to Aeolus [Late 16C. < Latin *Aeolius*]

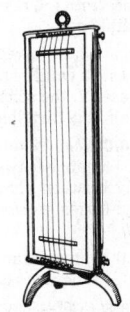

aeolian harp: 18th-century French three-sided aeolian harp

aeolian harp, **Aeolian harp** *n* a box-shaped musical instrument with strings of equal length that are tuned in unison and sounded when the wind blows over them

Aeolian Islands ♦ **Lipari Islands**

Aeolian mode *n* a medieval scale of notes that consists of the eight notes of the diatonic scale rising from A to A, corresponding to the modern minor scale

Aeolic /ee ólik/, **Eolic** *n* a dialect of Ancient Greek spoken mainly in Aeolis, Thessaly, and Boeotia — **Aeolic** *adj*

Aeolis /ée ə liss/, **Aeolia** /ee óli ə/ ancient region on the northwestern coast of Asia Minor, settled by the Aeolian Greeks about 1100 BC

Aeolus /ée ə ləss/ *n* in Greek mythology, the god of wind

aeon /ée ən, -on/, **eon** *n* **1.** a division of geological time comprising two or more eras **2.** a period of time that is boringly or dishearteningly long (*informal*; *usually plural*) ○ *take aeons to finish* [Mid-17C. Via late Latin < Greek *aiōn* 'age, lifetime'] —**aeonian** *adj*

aepyornis /éepi áwrniss/ (*plural* **-nises** or **same**) *n* a giant extinct flightless bird that lived in Madagascar. It reached a height of 2.7 m/9 ft and weighed up to 450 kg/1,000 lb. Genus: *Aepyornis*. [Mid-19C. < modern Latin < Greek *aipus* 'high' + *ornis* (see ORNITHO-)]

aer- *prefix* same as **aero-** (*used before vowels*)

aerate /áir rayt/ (**-ates, -ating, -ated**) *vt* **1.** to allow circulating air to reach or penetrate something **2.** to charge a liquid with a gas, especially when using carbon dioxide to make carbonated drinks **3.** PHYSIOL same as **oxygenate** [Late 18C. < Latin *aer* 'air' < Greek *aēr*] —**aeration** /air ráysh'n/ *n* —**aerator** *n*

aerenchyma /a réngkəmə/ *n* the spongy tissue in some water plants that keeps them afloat and helps in the exchange of gases [Late 19C. < Greek *aēr* 'air' + *egkhuma* 'infusion']

aeri- *prefix* same as **aero-**

aerial /áiri əl/ *n* **1.** BROADCAST **METAL ROD FOR RADIO WAVES** a metallic rod or wire for sending and receiving radio waves or microwaves. An aerial is attached to a radio or TV to improve the reception. N Am term **antenna 2.** HOCKEY **HIGH BALL IN HOCKEY** in hockey, a ball passed by being raised off the ground ■ *adj* **1. RELATING TO AIR** consisting of, typical of, or relating to the air **2. INVOLVING AIRCRAFT** done by or involving aircraft ○ *an aerial bombardment* **3. IN AIR** living, happening, or moving in the air ○ *a plant with aerial roots* **4. LIGHT IN WEIGHT** like the air in being light and insubstantial (*literary*) **5. IMAGINARY** existing only in the imagination (*literary*) [Early 17C. < Latin *aerius* < Greek *aerios* < *aēr* 'air']

aerialist /áiri əlist/ *n* an acrobat who performs on a tightrope or trapeze

aerial ladder *n* N Am same as **turntable ladder**

aerial perspective *n* the use in painting of gradations in colour and definition to suggest distance

aerie *n* BIRDS US spelling of **eyrie**

aeriform /áiri fawrm/ *adj* **1.** existing as air or gas **2.** having no substance or material form

aero¹ /áirō/ *adj* used in aircraft or aeronautics

aero² *abbr* aviation industry (*used in Internet addresses*) See table at **domain name**

aero-, aeri- *prefix* **1.** air, atmosphere, gas ○ *aerodynamic* **2.** aviation ○ *aerospace* [< Greek *aēr* 'air']

aeroballistics /áirō bə lístiks/ *n* the branch of ballistics that deals with projectiles fired or dropped from aircraft (*takes a singular verb*) —**aeroballistic** *adj*

aerobatics /áirō báttiks/ *n* the flying of an aircraft in daring manoeuvres, often as an entertainment (*takes a singular or plural verb*) [Early 20C. < AERO-, after ACROBATICS] —**aerobatic** *adj*

aerobe /áirōb/ *n* a microorganism that requires oxygen for metabolism [Late 19C. < AERO- + Greek *bios* 'life']

aerobic¹ /air róbik/ *adj* **1.** living or taking place only in the presence of oxygen **2.** having or providing oxygen [Late 19C. < French *aérobie*, coined by Louis Pasteur < Greek *aēr* 'air' + *bios* 'life'] —**aerobically** *adv*

aerobic² /air róbik/ *adj* **1.** increasing respiration and heart rates ○ *aerobic exercise* **2.** used in or relating to aerobics [Mid-20C. < AEROBICS]

aerobic respiration *n* the breakdown of foodstuffs to create energy in the presence of oxygen

aerobics /air róbiks/ *n* (*takes a singular or plural verb*) **1.** an active exercise programme done to music, often in a class **2.** exercises such as walking, jogging, cycling, and swimming that increase respiration and heart rates [Mid-20C. < AEROBIC¹, after GYMNASTICS]

aerobiology /áirō bī ólləji/ *n* the study of airborne biological materials and organisms such as allergens and disease-causing microorganisms — **aerobiological** /áirō bī ə lójjik'l/ *adj* —**aerobiologically** *adv*

aerobiosis /áirō bī óssiss/ *n* life in the presence of oxygen [Early 20C. < modern Latin < Greek *aēr* 'air' + *biōsis* (see -BIOSIS)]

aerodrome /áirō drōm/ *n* UK, ANZ, Can a small airfield with limited facilities. US term **airdrome** [Early 20C. < AERO- + -DROME]

aerodynamic /áirō dī námmik/ *adj* **1.** designed to reduce air resistance, especially to increase fuel efficiency or maximum speed **2.** involving or typical of aerodynamics —**aerodynamically** *adv*

aerodynamics /áirō dī námmiks/ *n* the study of moving gases, especially the study of the forces experienced by objects moving through air (*takes a singular verb*) ■ *npl* the aerodynamic properties of an object (*takes a plural verb*) —**aerodynamicist** /-issist/ *n*

aerodyne /áirō dīn/ *n* an aircraft such as an aeroplane or helicopter that is heavier than air and whose lift in flight results from forces caused by its motion through the air [Early 20C. Back-formation < AERODYNAMIC]

aeroembolism /áirō émbəlizəm/ *n* MED same as **air embolism**

aerofoil /áirō foyl/ *n* a part of an aircraft's or other vehicle's surface that acts on the air to provide lift or control, e.g. an aileron, wing, or propeller. N Am term **airfoil**

aerogel /áirō jel/ *n* a highly porous, extremely lightweight solid formed by replacing the particles in a gel with a gas

aerogram /áirə gram/, **aerogramme** *n* a single sheet of lightweight paper for airmail use that, once written on, can be folded and sealed to form its own envelope [Late 19C. After TELEGRAM]

aerography /air róggrəfi/ *n* the study of atmospheric conditions —**aerographer** *n* —**aerographic** /áirə gráffik/ *adj*

aerolite /áirō līt/ *n* a meteorite with a high silicate content —**aerolitic** /áirō líttik/ *adj*

aerolization /áirō līt záysh'n/, **aerolisation** *n* the airborne transmission of a substance in the form of a vapour or fine particles —**aerolize** *vt*

aerology /air rólləji/ *n* the study of the lower layers of the Earth's atmosphere —**aerologic** /áirə lójjik/ *adj* —**aerological** *adj* —**aerologist** *n*

aeromagnetic /áirō mag néttik/ *adj* relating to the study or measurement of the Earth's magnetic field from aircraft —**aeromagnetically** *adv* —**aeromagnetics** *n*

aeromechanics /áirō mi kánniks/ *n* the study of gases in motion and in equilibrium, including the study of the mechanical effects of gases upon objects (*takes a singular verb*) —**aeromechanical** *adj* —**aeromechanically** *adv*

aeromedicine /áirō médss'n/ *n* MED, AVIAT same as **aviation medicine** —**aeromedical** /-méddik'l/ *adj*

aerometeorograph /áirō meéti ərə graaf, -graf/ *n* an instrument on board an aircraft that records temperature, atmospheric pressure, and humidity

aerometer /air rómmitər/ *n* an instrument for measuring the mass or density of air or another gas [Late 18C. < French *aéromètre*]

aeronaut /áirə nawt/ *n* somebody who flies in an airship or balloon [Late 18C. < French *aéronaute* < *aéro-* (< Greek *aēr* 'air') + Greek *nautēs* 'sailor']

aeronautical /áirə náwtik'l/, **aeronautic** /-náwtik/ *adj* relating to aircraft or their flight [Early 19C. < French *aéronautique* < *aéronaute* (see AERONAUT)] —**aeronautically** *adv*

aeronautics /áirə náwtiks/ *n* the science, art, theory, and practice of designing, building, and operating aircraft (*takes a singular verb*)

aeroneurosis /áirō nyoō rōssiss/ *n* anxiety and fatigue in airline pilots brought on by prolonged periods of flying

aeronomy /air ónnəmi/ *n* the study of the upper atmosphere of the Earth above 50 km/31 mi., including its reaction with cosmic and ionizing radiation —**aeronomer** *n* —**aeronomic** /áirə nómmik/ *adj* —**aeronomical** *adj* —**aeronomist** *n*

aeropause /áirə pawz/ *n* the part of the Earth's upper atmosphere above which air is too thin for aircraft to fly

aerophagy /air róffəji/, **aerophagia** /áirə fáyji ə, -fáyjə/ *n* the spasmodic swallowing of air, a common cause of flatulence and belching [Late 19C. After French *aérophagie*]

aerophobia /áirə fóbi ə/ *n* an unusual fear of draughts of air —**aerophobic** *adj*

aerophyte /áirə fīt/ *n* BOT same as **epiphyte**

aeroplane /áirəplayn/ *n* a vehicle with wings and a jet engine or propellers that is heavier than air and is able to fly. N Am term **airplane** [Late 19C. < French *aéroplane* < *aéro-* (< Greek *aēr* 'air') + -*plane*]

aeroponics /áirə pónniks/ *n* the growing of plants without soil, their nutrients being supplied in a water spray (*takes a singular verb*) [Late 20C. After HYDROPONICS]

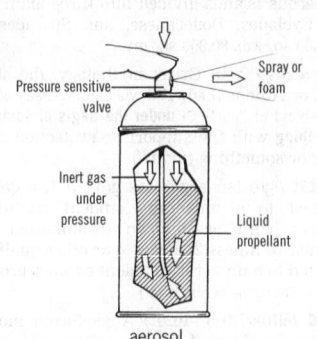

aerosol

aerosol /áirə sol/ *n* **1.** CONTAINER WITH GAS UNDER PRESSURE a small container holding a substance that can be dispensed under pressure by a propellant as a spray **2.** SUBSTANCE SPRAYED a substance held in a small container from which it can be dispensed under pressure by a propellant as a spray **3.** SUSPENSION OF PARTICLES IN GAS a suspension of solid or liquid particles in a gaseous medium

aerosol bomb *n* US same as **aerosol** (sense 1)

aerosolize /áirəssə līz/ (-izes, -izing, -ized), **aerosolise** (-ises, -ising, -ised) *vt* to convert a substance into a fine spray or colloidal suspension

aerospace /áirō spayss/ *n* the Earth's atmosphere and outer space ■ *adj* relating to the design, manufacture, and flight of vehicles or missiles that fly in and beyond the Earth's atmosphere

aerostat /áirə stat/ *n* a hot-air or gas-filled aircraft, e.g. an airship or balloon [Late 18C. < French *aérostat* < *aéro-* (< Greek *aēr* 'air') + Greek *statos* 'standing'] —**aerostatic** /áirə státtik/ *adj*

aerostatics /áirə státtiks/ *n* (*takes a singular verb*) **1.** the study of gases in equilibrium and objects in equilibrium in space **2.** the science of aircraft that are lighter than air, e.g. dirigibles and balloons

aerothermodynamics /áirō thurmō dī námmiks/ *n* the study of the heat exchange between gases and solid objects, especially between air and aircraft flying at high velocity (*takes a singular verb*) —**aerothermodynamic** *adj*

aery /áiri/ (-ier, -iest) *adj* insubstantial and unworldly (*literary*) [Late 16C. < Latin *aerius* (see AERIAL)]

Aeschylus /éeskələss/ (525?–456 BC) Greek dramatist. The earliest of the classical Greek tragic dramatists whose work survives, he is believed to have written 90 plays. Seven survive, including his great trilogy *The Oresteia*, first performed in 458 BC.

Aesculapian /éeskyoō láypi ən/ *adj* relating to medicine and the healing arts [Early 17C. < Latin *Aesculapius*, the Roman god of medicine]

aesculapian snake *n* a long slender brown nonvenomous snake. Native to: forests of Europe and western Asia. Latin name: *Elaphe longissima*. [< the common depiction of Aesculapius (see AESCULAPIAN) in antiquity with such a snake]

Aesop /éessəp/ (620?–560? BC) Greek writer, reputedly a former slave. His fables were popularized by the Roman poet Phaedrus (1st century AD). See Cultural note at **fable**

AEST *abbr* Australian Eastern Standard Time

aesthesia /eess theézi ə/ *n* the ability to feel or experience through the senses [Early 18C. Via modern Latin < Greek *aisthēsis* 'perceiving' < *aisthesthai* 'perceive']

aesthete /éess theet/ *n* somebody who has or affects a highly developed appreciation of beauty, especially in the arts [Late 19C. Back-formation < AESTHETIC, after ATHLETE]

aesthetic /eess théttik, iss-/ *adj* **1.** BEAUTIFUL pleasing in appearance **2.** ARTS APPRECIATING BEAUTY sensitive to or appreciative of art or beauty **3.** PHILOSOPHY RELATING TO AESTHETICS relating to the philosophical principles of aesthetics ■ *n* ARTS SET OF PRINCIPLES a set of principles about art ○ *the modernist aesthetic* [Early 19C. < Greek *aisthētikos* 'perceptual' < *aisthesthai* 'perceive'] —**aesthetically** *adv*

aestheticism /eess théttisizəm, iss-/ *n* **1.** ARTS BELIEF IN IMPORTANCE OF AESTHETICS the belief that the principles of aesthetics are of the highest importance in the arts **2.** PHILOSOPHY DERIVATION OF MORAL PRINCIPLES FROM BEAUTY the philosophical doctrine that all moral principles are derived from beauty **3.** LOVE OF BEAUTY appreciation of and devotion to beauty

aestheticize /eess thétti sīz, iss-/ (-cizes, -cizing, -cized) *vt* to show something in its best or most artistic light

aesthetics /eess théttiks, iss-/ *n* **1.** OUTWARD APPEARANCE the way something looks, especially when considered in terms of how pleasing it is (*takes a singular or plural verb*) **2.** IDEA OF BEAUTY an idea of what is beautiful or artistic (*takes a singular or plural verb*) **3.** ARTS STUDY OF ART the study of the rules and principles of art (*takes a singular verb*) **4.** PHILOSOPHY STUDY OF BEAUTY the branch of philosophy dealing with the study of aesthetic values, e.g. the beautiful and the sublime (*takes a singular verb*) [Early 19C. Via modern Latin *aesthetica* < Greek *aisthētikos* (see AESTHETIC), perhaps after ATHLETICS] —**aesthetician** /éessthə tísh'n, éss-/ *n*

aesthetic surgery *n* SURG same as **cosmetic surgery**

aestival /ee stív'l, éstiv'l/ *adj* relating to or happening during summer (*technical or literary*) [14C. Via French < Latin *aestivalis* < *aestas* 'summer']

aestivate /éesti vayt, ésti-/ (-vates, -vating, -vated) *vi* **1.** to spend the summer in a particular place or activity (*formal*) **2.** to be dormant during the summer or during months of drought (*refers to animals, especially certain amphibians, reptiles, and insects*) [Early 17C. < Latin *aestivat-*, past participle of *aestivare* < *aestas* 'summer']

aestivation /éesti váysh'n, ésti-/ *n* **1.** PARTICULAR SUMMER ACTIVITY the spending of summer in a particular place or activity **2.** SUMMER DORMANCY dormancy in some animals during the summer or months of drought **3.** ARRANGEMENT OF FLOWER BUD PARTS the arrangement of the sepals and petals in a flower bud

aether *n* SCI another spelling of **ether** (senses 3–5)

aethereal *adj* another spelling of **ethereal** (*literary or archaic*)

aetiology /éeti ólləji/, **etiology** *n* **1.** STUDY OF CAUSES the philosophical investigation of causes and origins **2.** STUDY OF CAUSES OF DISEASE the study of the causes and origins of disease **3.** CAUSE OF DISEASE the set of factors that contributes to the occurrence of a disease [Mid-16C. Via Latin *aetiologia* < Greek *aitiologiā* 'statement of the cause' < *aitiā* 'cause'] —**aetiologic** /éeti ə lójjik/ *adj* —**aetiologically** *adv* —**aetiologist** *n*

Aetius /éeti əss/, **Flavius** (AD 390?–454) Roman general who ruled the Western Roman Empire for Valentinian III (AD 425–455) and defeated Attila the Hun (AD 451)

AEU *abbr Aus* EDUC Australian Education Union

af *abbr* Afghanistan (*used in Internet addresses*) See table at **domain name**

AF *abbr* **1.** AIR FORCE air force **2.** Anglo-French **3.** audio frequency **4.** PHOTOGRAPHY autofocus

Af. *abbr* **1.** Africa **2.** African

af- *prefix* same as **ad-** (*used before f*)

AFAIK *abbr* as far as I know (*used in e-mails or text messages*)

afar /ə faár/ *adv* at, to, or from a great distance (*literary*) [14C. < A-[1] + FAR] ◇ **from afar** from a place far away

AFC *abbr* **1.** AEROSP automatic flight control **2.** ELECTRONICS automatic frequency control

afeard /ə feérd/, **afeared** *adj regional* same as **afraid** (*archaic*) [Old English *afæred*, past participle of *afæren* 'frighten' < *færen* 'to fear']

afebrile /a feéb rīl, ay-/ *adj* having no fever, or marked by absence of fever

affable /áffəb'l/ *adj* good-natured, friendly, and easy to talk to [15C. Via French < Latin *affabilis* 'easy to speak

to' < *(af)fari* 'speak (to)'] —**affability** /àffə bíllәti/ *n* —**affably** *adv*

affair /ə fáir/ *n* **1.** BUSINESS MATTER a matter that has been attended to or that requires attention, especially in business **2.** OCCURRENCE an event or occurrence that has been referred to or is known about ○ *that odd affair at work last year* **3.** MATTER OF CONCERN a concern of a particular person or group ○ *What he does with the information is his own affair.* **4.** SOCIAL EVENT a social event or gathering **5.** SOMETHING OF PARTICULAR KIND an object or item of a particular kind ○ *The house is a ramshackle affair.* **6.** SEXUAL RELATIONSHIP a sexual relationship between two people not married to each other **7.** SCANDALOUS INCIDENT an incident that attracts public attention or notoriety ○ *the Profumo affair* ■ **affairs** *npl* **1.** PUBLIC MATTERS OF BUSINESS public, government, or professional business or activities ○ *affairs of state* ○ *consumer affairs* **2.** PERSONAL DUTIES personal responsibilities or business ○ *He must settle his affairs in Paris before returning home.* ○ *the family's financial affairs* [12C. < Anglo-Norman *afere*, Old French *afaire* < *à faire* 'to do']

affaire de coeur /a fáir də kúr/ (*plural* **affaires de coeur** /*pronunc. same*/), **affaire** *n* a love affair or romantic attachment (*literary*) [Early 19C. < French, 'affair of the heart']

affect[1] /ə fékt/ (**-fects, -fecting, -fected**) *vt* **1.** INFLUENCE SOMEBODY OR SOMETHING to act upon or have an effect on somebody or something **2.** STIR SOMEBODY'S EMOTIONS to move somebody emotionally **3.** CAUSE SOMEBODY TO HAVE DISEASE to infect or harm somebody or something with disease [14C. < Latin *affect-*, past participle of *afficere* 'act on' < *facere* 'do']

USAGE affect or **effect**? In general use, ***affect*** is only used as a verb, whereas ***effect*** is commonly used as a noun and only in formal contexts as a verb. What causes confusion is that they have very similar pronunciations and closely related meanings. If one thing ***affects*** [acts upon] another, it has an ***effect*** on it [causes it to change]. Notice also that you can ***affect*** [cause a change in] people as well as things, but you can only ***effect*** [bring about] things such as changes: *The election has affected our entire society, for it has effected major changes in the government. The bad weather has a bad effect* [not *affect*] *on him.*

affect[2] /ə fékt/ (**-fects, -fecting, -fected**) *vt* **1.** PRETEND TO BE SOMETHING to give the appearance or pretence of something **2.** ADOPT SOMETHING to adopt a use, style, or manner of doing something **3.** ACT LIKE SOMEBODY to imitate somebody else's style or character **4.** COME TO BE OR HAVE SOMETHING to assume a particular form or state ○ *affect a liquid state* [15C. Directly or via French *affecter* < Latin *affectare* 'strive for' < *affect-* (see AFFECT[1])] —**affecter** *n*

affect[3] /áffekt, ə fékt/ *n* an emotion or mood associated with an idea or action, or the external expression of such a feeling [Late 19C. < German *Affekt*]

affectation /àffek táysh'n/ *n* **1.** feigned or unnatural behaviour that is often meant to impress others **2.** an appearance or manner assumed as a show or pretence, often to impress others [Mid-16C. Directly or via French < Latin *affectation-* 'influence' < *affectare* < *affect-* (see AFFECT[1])]

affected /ə féktid/ *adj* **1.** INFLUENCED BY SOMETHING acted upon or influenced by somebody or something **2.** MOVED EMOTIONALLY emotionally moved by something **3.** INFECTED OR DAMAGED infected or harmed by disease **4.** TRYING TO IMPRESS behaving in an unnatural way intended to impress others **5.** INTENDED TO IMPRESS done or assumed with the intention of impressing others —**affectedly** *adv* —**affectedness** *n*

affecting /ə fékting/ *adj* able to stir the emotions —**affectingly** *adv*

affection /ə féksh'n/ *n* fond or tender feeling towards somebody or something ■ **affections** *npl* feelings of fondness or tenderness, sometimes as opposed to reason [12C. Via Old French, 'emotion' < Latin *affection-* 'inclination' < *afficere* (see AFFECT[1])] —**affectional** *adj* —**affectionally** *adv*

SYNONYMS See ***love***.

affectionate /ə féksh'nət/ *adj* feeling or showing affection [15C. Directly or via French < Latin *affectionatus* 'devoted' < *affection-* (see AFFECTION)] —**affectionately** *adv* —**affectionateness** *n*

affective /ə féktiv/ *adj* **1.** relating to an external expression of emotion associated with an idea or action **2.** same as **affecting** [15C. Via French < late Latin *affectivus* < Latin *affect-* (see AFFECT[1])] —**affectively** *adv* —**affectivity** /àffek tívvəti/ *n*

affective disorder *n* a psychiatric disorder with a central emotional component, e.g. depression

affectless /ə féktləss/ *adj* feeling or showing no emotion —**affectlessness** *n*

affenpinscher

affenpinscher /áffən pinshər/ *n* a small dog with wiry hair and a tufted muzzle, belonging to a breed developed in Europe [Early 20C. < German, 'ape terrier']

afferent /áffərənt/ *adj* describes nerves that carry impulses from the body towards the brain or spinal cord, or blood vessels that carry blood to an organ [Mid-19C. < Latin *afferent-*, present participle of *afferre* 'bring towards'] —**afferently** *adv*

affettuoso /a féchoo ṓssō/ *adv, adj* played or sung musically with feeling (*used as a musical direction*) [Early 18C. < Italian < Latin *affect-* (see AFFECT[1])]

affiance /ə fī́ ənss/ (**-ances, -ancing, -anced**) *vt* to promise somebody or yourself in marriage to somebody else (*literary; often passive*) [14C. < Old French *afiancer* < *afiance* 'trust' < medieval Latin *affidare* 'to trust']

affidavit /àffi dáyvit/ *n* a written declaration made on oath before somebody authorized to administer oaths, usually setting out the statement of a witness for court proceedings [Late 16C. < medieval Latin, 'he or she has sworn', form of *affidare* 'trust, affirm' < *fidus* 'faithful']

affiliate *vti* /ə fílli ayt/ (**-ates, -ating, -ated**) to come, or bring a person or group, into a close relationship with another, usually larger group ■ *n* /ə fílli ət, -ayt/ a group that is closely connected with a larger group, or a person who joins with others to form a group [Mid-18C. < Latin *affiliat-*, past participle of *affiliare* 'adopt as a son' < *filius* 'son'] —**affiliated** *adj* —**affiliation** /ə fílli áysh'n/ *n*

affiliate marketing *n* the use of a central website to market the products and services of other sites

affiliation order *n* a court order requiring a man adjudged to be the father of an illegitimate child to pay money towards its maintenance

affiliation proceedings *npl* legal proceedings usually initiated by a woman seeking to prove that the man against whom the case is brought is the father of her child, especially in order to claim monetary support from him

affine /áffīn/ *n* **1.** MATHS a geometrical transformation that maps points and parallel lines to points and parallel lines **2.** ANTHROP a relative by marriage [Early 20C. < Latin *affinis* (see AFFINITY)] —**affinal** *adj*

affinity /ə fínnəti/ (*plural* **-ties**) *n* **1.** FEELING OF IDENTIFICATION a natural liking for or identification with somebody or something **2.** CONNECTION a similarity or connection between people or things **3.** SOMEBODY ATTRACTIVE somebody to whom somebody else is attracted **4.** CULTL ANTHROP KINSHIP BY MARRIAGE a relationship by marriage, not by blood **5.** BIOL, LANGUAGE SIMILARITY IN STRUCTURE a similarity in structure, e.g. in species or languages, that may suggest a common origin **6.** CHEM LIKELIHOOD OF CHEMICAL REACTION a measure of the likelihood of a chemical reaction taking place between two substances **7.** IMMUNOL ANTIGEN-ANTIBODY ATTRACTION the attraction between an antigen and an antibody [14C. < Old French *afinité* 'close relationship' < Latin *affinis* 'bordering on something' < *finis* 'border']

affinity card *n* a credit card that benefits a specific charity or specific charities every time it is used

affirm /ə fúrm/ (**-firms, -firming, -firmed**) *v* **1.** *vt* DECLARE SOMETHING TO BE TRUE to declare positively that something is true ○ *affirmed that the rumour is true* **2.** *vt* DECLARE SUPPORT FOR SOMETHING to declare support or admiration for somebody or something ○ *affirmed their commitment to peace* **3.** *vt* LAW CONFIRM SOMETHING to confirm something as binding or valid **4.** *vi* LAW MAKE FORMAL STATEMENT to make a statement formally but not under oath [13C. Via Old French < Latin *affirmare* 'strengthen' < *firmus* 'firm'] —**affirmable** *adj* —**affirmably** *adv* —**affirmant** *n* —**affirmer** *n*

affirmation /àffər máysh'n/ *n* **1.** ACT OF AFFIRMING an assertion of support or agreement **2.** SOMETHING AFFIRMED a positive statement or declaration of the truth or existence of something ○ *an affirmation of his love* **3.** LAW FORMAL LEGAL DECLARATION a formal declaration acceptable in a court, usually made by somebody who has a conscientious objection to taking an oath **4.** PSYCHOL POSITIVE STATEMENT OF ACHIEVEMENT a positive thought or statement affirming that a desired goal has been reached or is within reach [15C. Directly or via French < Latin *affirmation-* < *affirmare* (see AFFIRM)]

affirmative /ə fúrmətiv/ *adj* **1.** TRUE confirming or asserting that something is true **2.** INDICATING AGREEMENT indicating agreement or giving assent **3.** LOGIC RELATING TO TYPE OF PROPOSITION relating to or consisting of a categorical proposition in which the predicate's extension is contained partially or wholly within the subject, as in 'All humans are mammals' ■ *n* **1.** POSITIVE ASSERTION an emphatic statement that something is true **2.** WORD CONVEYING AGREEMENT a word or statement conveying agreement or approval **3.** *N Am* SIDE SUPPORTING PROPOSITION IN DEBATE the side in a debate that supports a proposition ■ *interj* YES a signal code word expressing agreement or compliance —**affirmatively** *adv*

affirmative action *n N Am* same as **positive discrimination**

affix *vt* /ə fíks/ (**-fixes, -fixing, -fixed**) **1.** FASTEN SOMETHING to fasten something to something else **2.** ADD SOMETHING AT END to add something at the end of something, e.g. a signature to a document **3.** ATTRIBUTE SOMETHING to ascribe something such as responsibility or blame, to somebody ■ *n* /áffiks/ **1.** GRAM PART ADDED TO WORD a form added to the beginning, middle, or end of another word that creates a derivative word or inflection **2.** SOMETHING ATTACHED an attachment or addition to something [Mid-16C. Directly or via French *affixer* < medieval Latin *affixare* 'keep on fastening to' < Latin *affigere* 'fasten to' < *figere* 'fasten'] —**affixable** *adj* —**affixer** *n*

affixation /àffik sáysh'n/ *n* the addition of a prefix, suffix, or infix to a word in order to create a new word or an inflected form

afflatus /ə fláytəss/ *n* creative inspiration, usually thought of as divine (*formal*) [Mid-17C. < Latin, 'act of blowing on' < *flare* 'to blow']

afflict /ə flíkt/ (**-flicts, -flicting, -flicted**) *vt* to cause severe physical or mental distress to somebody [14C. < Latin *afflict-*, past participle of *affligere* 'strike down, cause to suffer' < *fligere* 'to strike'] —**afflicter** *n* —**afflictive** *adj* —**afflictively** *adv*

USAGE afflict or **inflict**? The chief difference is in the grammatical construction: you ***inflict*** something unpleasant *on* somebody, whereas you ***afflict*** somebody *with* something unpleasant (or, more usually, somebody is ***afflicted***) *with* or *by* something unpleasant: *They promoted measures to avoid inflicting further harm on the environment. The population was afflicted by a series of natural disasters.*

affliction /ə flíksh'n/ *n* **1.** a condition of great physical or mental distress **2.** something that causes great physical or mental distress [14C. Via Old French < Latin *affliction-* < *afflict-* (see AFFLICT)]

affluent /àffloo ənt/ *adj* having an abundance of material wealth ■ *n* GEOG a stream or river that flows into another [15C. Via Old French < Latin *affluent-*, present participle of *affluere* 'flow towards' < *fluere* 'flow'] —**affluence** *n* —**affluently** *adv*

CULTURAL NOTE *The Affluent Society*, a book (1958) by US economist John Kenneth Galbraith. One of Galbraith's most widely read works, it attacks what he views as the American obsession with production and material

zh vision. In foreign words: kh German Bach; aN French vin; aaN French blanc; ö German schön, French feu; oN French bon; öN French un; ü as in French rue. Stress marks: ´ as in secret /séekrət/, academic /àkə démmik/

goods, and urges greater government expenditure on the country's infrastructure and public services.

afflux /áffluks/ *n* a flow inwards or towards a point, e.g. of blood towards a body organ [Early 17C. < medieval Latin *affluxus* < Latin *affluere* (see AFFLUENT)]

afford /ə fáwrd/ (**-fords, -fording, -forded**) *vt* **1.** BE ABLE TO BUY SOMETHING to be able to meet the cost of something without unacceptable difficulty **2.** BE ABLE TO DO SOMETHING to be able to do or provide something without unacceptable or disadvantageous consequences ○ *We can't afford to be late.* **3.** BE ABLE TO SPARE SOMETHING to be able to spare something without unacceptable or disadvantageous consequences ○ *I'd like to come but I can't afford the time.* **4.** PROVIDE SOMETHING to supply or provide something (*formal*) ○ *The film will afford you much pleasure.* [Old English *geforþian* 'accomplish' < *forþian* 'to further'] —**affordable** *adj*

affordable housing *n* housing for people on lower incomes in which rent or mortgage costs are subsidized

afforest /ə fórrist/ (**-ests, -esting, -ested**) *vt* to convert land not previously forested into forest by planting trees [Early 16C. < medieval Latin *afforestare* < *foresta* 'forest'] —**afforestation** /ə fórri stáysh'n/ *n*

affray /ə fráy/ *n* a fight or noisy disturbance in a public place [14C. Via Anglo-Norman *afrayer* 'disturb' < assumed Vulgar Latin *exfridare* 'take out of peace']

affricate /áffrikət/, **affricative** /ə fríkətiv/ *n* a composite speech sound made up of a stop immediately followed by a fricative [Late 19C. < Latin *affricat-*, past participle of *affricare* 'rub against' < *fricare* 'rub'] —**affricative** *adj*

affright /ə frít/ (*archaic or literary*) *vt* (**-frights, -frighting, -frighted**) to overwhelm somebody with sudden fear ■ *n* sudden overwhelming fear [Late 16C. < obsolete *fright* 'frighten' < Old English *fryhtan* < Germanic] —**affrightment** *n*

affront /ə frúnt/ *n* an open insult or giving of offence to somebody ■ *vt* (**-fronts, -fronting, -fronted**) to insult or offend somebody openly [14C. Via Old French < Vulgar Latin *affrontare* 'strike in the face' < *ad frontem* 'to the face']

afghan /áf gan, áfgən/ *n* **1.** a knitted or crocheted blanket or shawl, often with geometric designs **2.** a large carpet woven in a geometric design **3.** CLOTHING same as **afghan coat** [Mid-19C. < AFGHAN]

Afghan /áf gan, áfgən/ *n* **1.** somebody who comes from Afghanistan **2.** LANG same as **Pashto** (sense 1) **3.** BREED same as **Afghan hound** [Early 18C. < Pashto *afghāni* 'of Afghanistan'] —**Afghan** *adj*

afghan coat *n* a sheepskin coat or jacket, fashionable in the late 1960s and 1970s, usually embroidered and with the fleece left long around the edges as trimming

Afghan hound

Afghan hound *n* a tall dog with a long silky coat, belonging to a breed originally developed in Afghanistan as hunting dogs and sheepdogs

afghani /af gánni, -gaáni/ (*plural* **-is**) *n* the main unit of Afghan currency. See table at **currency** [Early 20C. < Pashto *afghāni*]

Afghanistan

Afghanistan /af gánni staan, -stan/ landlocked country in Southwest Asia, between Iran and Pakistan. Language: Pashto, Dari (Persian). Currency: afghani. Capital: Kabul. Population: 28,717,213 (2003). Area: 652,225 sq. km/251,825 sq. mi. Official name **Islamic State of Afghanistan**

aficionada /ə físhə naádə, ə físsi ə-/ *n* a woman who is enthusiastic and knowledgeable about something

aficionado /ə físhə naádō, ə físsi ə-/ (*plural* **-dos**) *n* **1.** somebody who is enthusiastic and knowledgeable about something **2.** a devotee of bullfighting [Mid-19C. < Spanish, 'somebody who likes something' < Latin *affection-* (see AFFECTION)]

afield /ə feéld/ *adv, adj* **1.** distant from home ○ *wandered far afield* **2.** off the point or subject

afikomen /aáfi kómən/ *n* in Judaism, the unleavened bread that completes the festive meal (**Seder**) on the first night of Passover [Late 19C. Via Hebrew *aphīqōmān* < Greek *epikōmion* 'festival']

afire /ə fír/ *adj, adv* **1.** on fire or blazing **2.** passionately interested in something

AFL *abbr* Australian Football League

aflame /ə fláym/ *adj* **1.** in flames or blazing **2.** highly aroused or impassioned

aflatoxin /áfflə tóksin/ *n* a toxin produced by some moulds in crops, especially peanuts [Mid-20C. < modern Latin *Aspergillus flavus* + TOXIN]

AFL-CIO *abbr* American Federation of Labor and Congress of Industrial Organizations

afloat /ə flót/ *adj, adv* **1.** FLOATING floating on water **2.** ON BOARD SHIP on board a ship or at sea **3.** FLOODED covered with water **4.** WITHOUT PURPOSE lacking purpose or guidance **5.** IN CIRCULATION circulating among the public **6.** FINANCIALLY SOLVENT free of debt or financial problems

AFLP *abbr* BIOTECH amplified fragment length polymorphism

aflutter /ə flúttər/ *adj, adv* **1.** in a state of agitation or excitement **2.** flapping or waving, e.g. as a flag does in the breeze

AFM *abbr* PHYS atomic force microscope

AFNOR /áf nawr/ *n* the French industrial standards authority. Full form **Association française de normalisation**

afoot /ə foót/ *adj, adv* **1.** in the process of happening **2.** on foot or by walking [13C. Partly after Old Norse *á fótum* 'on foot']

afore /ə fáwr/ *adv, prep, conj regional* same as **before** [Old English *onforan* < *foran* 'in front, before']

aforementioned /ə fáwr mensh'nd/ (*formal*) *adj* previously mentioned ■ *n* the previously mentioned person or people

aforesaid /ə fáwr sed/ *adj* previously named or stated (*formal*)

aforethought /ə fáwr thawt/ *adj* thought about or planned beforehand

a fortiori /ay fáwrti áwr ī, aa fáwrti áwree/ *adv* for an even stronger reason [Early 17C. < Latin, 'from the stronger (reason)' < *fortis* 'strong']

afoul /ə fówl/ *adj, adv* **1.** in or into trouble or conflict with somebody or something **2.** entangled or in collision with something

AFP *abbr* **1.** BIOCHEM alpha-foetoprotein **2.** POLICE Australian Federal Police

Afr. *abbr* **1.** Africa **2.** African

afraid /ə fráyd/ *adj* **1.** FRIGHTENED frightened or apprehensive about something **2.** RELUCTANT feeling hesitation or disinclination towards something **3.** REGRETFUL feeling regret about something [14C. Originally past participle of AFFRAY, after Anglo-Norman *affrayé*]

CULTURAL NOTE *Who's Afraid of Virginia Woolf?*, a play (1962) by US dramatist Edward Albee. Albee's first full-length play examines the sour relationship between a middle-aged underachieving academic and his embittered wife. A dinner party with a younger, not dissimilar couple forces them to confront the reality of their past and present.

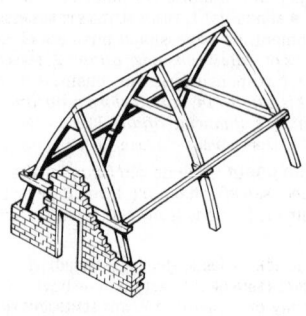

A-frame

A-frame *adj* built in the shape of a capital letter A ■ *n* a building shaped like a capital letter A, with a triangular front and back, and a roof that slopes to the ground to form the sides of the building

afreet /áffreet, ə freét/, **afrit** /ə freét/ *n* in Arabian mythology, an evil spirit or powerful monster [Late 18C. < Arabic *afrīt*]

afresh /ə frésh/ *adv* once again, especially from the beginning

Africa /áffrikə/ the second largest continent, lying south of Europe, with the Atlantic Ocean to the west and the Indian Ocean to the east. Population: 875,027,307 (2004). Area: 30,243,910 sq. km/11,677,239 sq. mi.

African /áffrikən/ *adj* OF AFRICA relating to any part of the African continent, or its peoples, languages, or culture ■ *n* **1.** SOMEBODY FROM AFRICA somebody who comes from Africa **2.** SOMEBODY OF AFRICAN DESCENT somebody descended from a people of Africa [Pre-12C. < Latin *Africanus* < *Afri* 'the ancient inhabitants of N Africa']

African American *n* an American of African descent —**African American** *adj*

African American Vernacular English *n* the variety of English spoken by many African Americans

African buffalo *n* a reddish-brown to black wild buffalo, either the Cape buffalo or the smaller forest or dwarf buffalo. Native to: Africa. Latin name: *Synceros caffer* or *Synceros nanus*.

African Caribbean *n* somebody of African descent who lives in or comes from the Caribbean —**African Caribbean** *adj*

African daisy *n* a plant of the composite family that resembles a daisy. Flowers: colourful, large. Native to: Africa. Genera: *Dimorphotheca* or *Gerbera* or *Lonas*.

Africander *n* BREED same as **Afrikander**

African English *n* the variety of English spoken in Africa. See panel on next page

Africanism /áffrikənizəm/ *n* a cultural feature associated with Africa or Africans, especially a linguistic feature found in a language that is not itself African

Africanist /áffrikənist/ *n* a specialist in African affairs, cultures, or languages

Africanize /áffrikə nīz/ (**-izes, -izing, -ized**), **Africanise** (**-ises, -ising, -ised**) *vt* **1.** to make something African in character **2.** in postcolonial Africa, to replace white employees with Black African staff in a business or political organization

Africanized bee /áffrikə nīzd-/ *n* an aggressive honeybee that was accidentally hybridized in Brazil

from African and European strains and has spread north into Mexico and southern Texas

African lily *n US* same as **agapanthus**

African mahogany *n* **1.** a hard wood similar in appearance to that of tropical American mahogany. Use: furniture-making. **2.** a tree that produces African mahogany. Native to: Africa. Genera: *Khaya* or *Entandrophragma*.

African National Congress *n* a South African political party founded in 1912 that fought against apartheid and formed South Africa's first multiracial, democratically elected government in 1994

African sleeping sickness *n* MED same as **sleeping sickness**

African Union *n* an organization of African states founded in 2002 for mutual cooperation, superseding the Organization of African Unity

African violet

African violet *n* a tropical plant with fleshy leaves, grown as a houseplant. Flowers: violet, white, or pink. Native to: Africa. Genus: *Saintpaulia*.

Afrikaans /áffri ka'anss/ *n* an official language of South Africa, also spoken in Namibia, that is descended from the Dutch spoken by 17th-century settlers. Native speakers: 10 million. ■ *adj* relating to the Afrikaner people, or their language or culture [Early 20C. < Dutch, 'African']

LANGUAGE HERITAGE See *Dutch*.

Afrikander /áffri kándər/, **Africander** *n* **1.** a long-horned hump-backed animal with a reddish colour, belonging to a South African breed of beef cattle **2.** a sheep belonging to an indigenous South African breed [Variant of AFRIKANER]

Afrikaner /áffri ka'anər/ *n* a South African whose first language is Afrikaans, usually descended from 17th-century settlers (**Boers**) [Early 19C. < Afrikaans < *Afrikaan* 'African person', after *Hollander* 'Dutch person'] —**Afrikaner** *adj*

afrit *n* MYTHOL same as **afreet**

Afro /áffrō/ *n* (*plural* **-ros**) a hairstyle with thick tight curls ■ *adj* African in origin or style [Mid-20C. < AFRO-AMERICAN or AFRO-]

Afro- *prefix* Africa, African ○ *Afro-Cuban* [< Latin *Afr-*, stem of *Afer* 'an African']

Afro-American *n* same as **African American** (*dated*) — **Afro-American** *adj*

Afro-American English *n* LANG same as **African American Vernacular English**

Afro-Asian *adj* relating to the continents of Africa and Asia, or to their peoples or shared cultural phenomena

Afro-Asiatic *n* a large family of languages spoken across North Africa and Southwest Asia. Native speakers: 250 million. —**Afro-Asiatic** *adj*

Afro-Caribbean *n* PEOPLES same as **African Caribbean**

Afrocentric /áffrō séntrik/ *adj* centred on or originating in Africa or African culture

Afro-Cuban *adj* relating to Cuban culture as influenced by Africa, especially a style of jazz based on Cuban interpretations of African rhythms

afrormosia /áffrawr mōzi ə/ *n* a hard wood, similar to teak, from tropical African trees [Mid-20C. < modern Latin < *Afro-* 'Africa(n)' + *Ormosia* genus name (< Greek *hormos* 'necklace', probably because the wood was used to make jewellery)]

aft /aaft/ *adv, adj* towards or at the rear of a ship, submarine, or aircraft [Early 17C. Shortening of ABAFT]

after /a'aftər/ *prep* **1.** LATER THAN later in time than **2.** BEHIND behind in order or place **3.** IN PURSUIT OF in pursuit of or looking for **4.** REGARDING about or regarding **5.** FOLLOWING FROM subsequent to and considering **6.** LIKE in imitation or in the manner of ○ *a painting after the style of Cézanne* **7.** AGREEING WITH in agreement with or in conformity to **8.** WITH SAME NAME AS with the name of a particular person or thing given because of family relationships or out of respect ○ *We called her after her grandmother.* **9.** *N Am* PAST HOUR OF later than a particular hour ○ *a quarter after seven* ■ *adv* **1.** LATER later in time or place **2.** NAUT, AVIAT FARTHER BACK farther towards the rear of a ship, submarine, or aircraft ■ *conj* FOLLOWING TIME WHEN following a time when, and sometimes as a result ○ *You'll miss me after I've gone.* ■ *adj* **1.** SUBSEQUENT later in time **2.** NAUT, AVIAT REAR situated farther towards the rear of a ship, submarine, or aircraft [Old English *æfter.* Assumed to be a comparative form, 'farther away' < Indo-European, 'away, off'] ◇ **after all 1.** used to emphasize something that should be taken into consideration in spite of what has happened or been said **2.** used to show that in the end something happened, was done, or was recognized in spite of expectations to the contrary or efforts to prevent it

afterbeat /a'aftər beet/ *n* MUSIC same as **backbeat**

afterbirth /a'aftər burth/ *n* the placenta and foetal membranes expelled from the womb after a birth [Late 16C. Perhaps after German *Aftergeburt*]

afterburner /a'aftər burnər/ *n* **1.** a system for increasing the thrust of an aircraft jet engine by feeding fuel into the hot exhaust gases **2.** a device in the exhaust system of an internal combustion engine for burning or catalytically destroying potentially harmful unburnt or incompletely burnt carbon compounds

aftercare /a'aftər kair/ *n* **1.** HEALTH SERVICES CARE AFTER LEAVING HOSPITAL care or support that somebody receives after leaving a hospital, prison, or other institution, often provided by a community nurse or social worker **2.** HEALTH SERVICES CARE AFTER ILLNESS care given in a hospital to a patient who is recovering from an illness or operation **3.** COMM UPKEEP OF PRODUCT PURCHASED the maintenance in good condition of a product after purchase, or a service provided by a company to its customers to support this **4.** *US* PSYCHOL COUNSELLING OF BEREAVED counselling of bereaved clients by funeral home staff after a death and the funeral **5.** ENVIRON POLLUTION PREVENTION arrangements for preventing pollution from occurring after an environmentally sensitive activity such as landfill of waste has ended

afterdamp /a'aftər damp/ *n* gaseous fumes remaining in a mine after an explosion of firedamp

afterdeck /a'aftər dek/ *n* the part of the main open deck of a boat that extends from the bridge or midships to the stern

aftereffect /a'aftər i fekt/ *n* **1.** DELAYED RESULT an effect, usually unpleasant, that follows its cause after an interval of time (*usually used in the plural*) ○ *The stock markets are still showing the aftereffects of last month's rise in interest rates.* **2.** PHYSIOL SECONDARY REACTION a secondary response that follows the primary response to a physiological stimulus **3.** PSYCHOL DELAYED REACTION a delayed reaction to a psychological stimulus

afterglow /a'aftər glō/ *n* **1.** radiated light that remains visible after a source of light or energy has been removed, e.g. the glow sometimes seen in the sky after sunset **2.** a feeling of pleasure or a favourable impression that remains after a positive experience ○ *basking in the afterglow of victory*

afterimage /a'aftər immij/ *n* a visual image that remains briefly after light stimulation has ended

afterlife /a'aftər līf/ *n* **1.** a form of existence believed to continue after death **2.** the period of somebody's life that follows a specific event or role ○ *Is there an afterlife for retired football players?*

aftermarket /a'aftər maarkit/ *n* subsequent sales opportunities resulting from an original sale, especially the demand for parts and services that follows the purchase of something such as a car

aftermath /a'aftər math, -maath/ *n* **1.** the consequences of an event, especially a disastrous one, or the period of time during which these consequences are felt ○ *in the aftermath of the war* **2.** a second crop or growth of grass in the same season, after the first harvest or mowing [15C. < *math* 'mowing' < Old English *mæþ*]

aftermost /a'aftər mōst/, **aftmost** /a'aft mōst/ *adj* nearest to the stern of a boat

afternoon /a'aftər noón/ *n* **1.** DAYTIME BETWEEN MIDDAY AND EVENING the period of the day between noon or lunchtime and evening **2.** LATTER PART the latter part of something, especially of somebody's life (*literary*) ■ *interj* GREETING a greeting used to say 'good afternoon' (*informal*)

afternoons /a'aftər noónz/ *adv* in any or during every afternoon (*informal*)

afterpains /a'aftər paynz/ *npl* pains experienced by some women just after giving birth, similar to labour pains and caused by contractions of the womb

afterpiece /a'aftər peess/ *n* a short entertainment, usually comic, performed after a play

afters /a'aftərz/ *n* the sweet or dessert course of a meal (*informal; takes a singular or plural verb*) ○ *What's for afters?*

aftersales /a'aftər saylz/ *adj* occurring or provided after the sale of a product

after-school *adj* occurring after school, especially from the end of the school day until the end of the normal working day ○ *an after-school club*

aftersensation /a'aftər sen saysh'n/ *n* a sense impression that remains after the immediate stimulus has been removed

aftershave /a'aftər shayv/ *n* a liquid applied after shaving to soothe and scent the skin of the face

aftershock /a'aftər shok/ *n* **1.** a small earthquake, usually one of several, that follows a larger one **2.** a delayed psychological or physical reaction to a serious event or trauma

aftertaste /a'aftər tayst/ *n* **1.** a taste left in the mouth by food or drink after swallowing **2.** a feeling or sensation, especially an unpleasant one, left behind after an experience

afterthought /a'aftər thawt/ *n* **1.** something not thought of, said, or done originally, but added afterwards **2.** a child born several years after other children in the same family (*humorous*)

afterward /a'aftərwərd/ *adv US* same as **afterwards**

afterwards /a'aftərwərdz/ *adv* at a later time or after an event that has been mentioned previously ○ *Let's have breakfast now and go skiing afterwards.*

USAGE See *towards*.

afterword /a'aftər wurd/ *n* a short concluding section added at the end of a literary work as an epilogue or a commentary of some kind

afterworld /a'aftər wurld/ *n* in some religions, a world

that people are believed to go to and live in after death

aftmost *adj* NAUT same as **aftermost**

AFV *abbr* MIL armoured fighting vehicle

ag *abbr* Antigua and Barbuda (*used in Internet addresses*) See table at **domain name**

Ag *symbol* CHEM ELEM silver [Shortening of Latin *argentum* 'silver']

AG *abbr* **1.** ARMY Adjutant General **2.** LAW Attorney General

ag- *prefix* same as **ad-** (*used before g*)

aga /áagə/, **agha** *n* used as a title for a military commander or important official in Islamic countries, especially during the Ottoman Empire ○ *the Aga Khan* [Mid-16C. < Turkish *aghā* 'chief, master, lord']

Aga /áagə/ *tdmk* a trademark for a large iron stove used for both cooking and heating that includes two or more ovens designed to cook at different temperatures

Agadir /ággə deér/ port and city in Morocco. Population: 550,200 (1994).

again /ə gén, ə gáyn/ *adv* **1.** AT ANOTHER TIME at another time or on another occasion, repeating what has happened or been done before ○ *I hope to come here again some day.* **2.** AS BEFORE to the place, person, or state where somebody or something was earlier ○ *Will I ever be able to walk again?* **3.** IN ADDITION in addition to a previously mentioned quantity ○ *You'll need all that and half as much again.* **4.** MOREOVER similarly and in addition ○ *Again, that is something that the court must take into account.* **5.** *Carib* THESE DAYS nowadays or any longer ○ *He doesn't live here again.* **6.** *Carib* AFTER ALL used to indicate that what has happened or been done represents a change of plan or is contrary to expectations ○ *What happen, you not doing Accounting again?* **7.** *Carib* MORE in addition ○ *How long again do you have to go?* [Old English *ongēan* 'in a direct line with, facing' or 'back to a starting point' < Germanic] ◇ **again and again** repeatedly

against /ə génst, ə gáynst/ CORE MEANING: a preposition indicating opposition to or conflict with somebody or something, either physically or intellectually ○ (*prep*) *a battle against cancer*
prep **1.** IN COMPETITION WITH with somebody or something as an opponent in a competitive situation, especially in sport ○ *It's Australia against Sweden in the finals.* **2.** IN CONTACT WITH BY LEANING in a position so that part or all of something touches another object or surface, by leaning or resting on the side of it ○ *I leaned against a tree.* **3.** INTO SUDDEN CONTACT OR COLLISION WITH so as to briefly touch or suddenly collide with a usually stationary object while in movement ○ *banged his head against the beam* **4.** IN OPPOSITE DIRECTION TO in the opposite direction to the movement, angle, or position of something or somebody ○ *to swim against the current* **5.** SEEN IN CONTRAST WITH seen in contrast with physical surroundings ○ *The dark green pines are lovely against the blue sky.* **6.** IN RELATION TO EVENTS in relation to, or contrasted with, a set of events or circumstances ○ *Government action makes sense against the background of rising tensions.* **7.** AS PROTECTION FROM in order to prevent or avoid something, or to be protected from something ○ *vaccinate against disease* **8.** IN PAYMENT OF in partial or total payment of, or as a charge on ○ *I'd like to put this money against the amount I owe you.* **9.** AS DISADVANTAGE TO to the disadvantage of somebody or something ○ *Will you hold it against me if I don't come to your party?* **10.** COMPARED WITH in comparison with something ○ *weighed the cost of hiring someone against that of promoting existing staff* **11.** CONTRARY TO contrary to, or not approved or allowed by somebody or something ○ *It's against the law.* **12.** IN PREPARATION FOR in preparation for something, usually an expected unpleasant event (*dated*) ○ *to save against hard times* [14C. < AGAIN + adverbial suffix *-es* + *-t*, after such words as AMIDST]

Aga Khan III /áagə káan/ (1877–1957) religious leader, born in Karachi, India, now Pakistan. He was imam of the Ismaili Muslim religious group and president of the League of Nations Assembly (1937).

Aga Khan IV (*b*. 1936) Swiss-born Muslim leader. He became imam of the Ismaili religious group in 1957. Born **Karim al Hussaini Shah**

agama /ággəmə/ *n* **1.** a small, long-tailed, often colourful lizard. Native to: tropical Africa, Asia. Genus: *Agama.* **2.** REPT same as **agamid** [Late 18C. < modern Latin and Spanish, probably < Carib *mami* 'lizard']

Agamemnon /ággə mém non/ *n* in Greek mythology, the commander of the Greek army in the Trojan War. When Agamemnon returned from the war, he was murdered by his wife Clytemnestra and her lover Aegisthus. His death was later avenged by his son Orestes.

agamic /ə gámmik/, **agamous** /ə gámməss/ *adj* describes an organism that multiplies asexually [Mid-19C. < Greek *agamos* 'unmarried' < *gamos* 'marriage'] — **agamically** *adv*

agamid /ággəmid/ *n* a small long-tailed insect-eating lizard. Native to: tropical Africa, Asia. Family: Agamidae. [Late 19C. < modern Latin *Agamidae* < *agama* (see AGAMA)]

agamogenesis /áy gamō jénnəssiss, ággəmō-/ *n* asexual reproduction, e.g. by cell division or budding [Mid-19C. < Greek *agamos* 'unmarried' + -GENESIS]

agamospermy /ággəmō spurmi/ *n* the asexual formation of seeds without fertilization [Mid-20C. < Greek *agamos* 'unmarried' + SPERM[1] + -Y[1]]

agamous *adj* BIOL same as **agamic**

agapanthus /ággə pánthəss/ (*plural same* or **-thuses**) *n* UK, ANZ, Can a plant of the lily family. Flowers: bluish or white, funnel-shaped, in ball-shaped clusters. Native to: southern Africa. Genus: *Agapanthus.* US term **African lily** [Late 18C. < modern Latin < Greek *agapē* 'brotherly love' + *anthos* 'flower']

agape[1] /ə gáyp/ *adv, adj* (*literary*) **1.** with the mouth wide open, usually in surprise or wonder **2.** opened widely ○ *The door to the room was agape.* [Mid-17C. < A-[1]]

agape[2] /ággəpi/ *n* **1.** NONSEXUAL LOVE love that is wholly selfless and spiritual **2.** CHR CHRISTIAN LOVE selfless love felt by Christians for their fellow human beings **3.** CHR CHRISTIAN COMMUNAL MEAL a communal meal held by a Christian community, especially in early Christian times, in commemoration of the Last Supper [Mid-17C. < Greek *agapē* 'brotherly love']

agar /áygər, -gaar/, **agar-agar** *n* **1.** a powdered seaweed extract. Use: setting agent, thickener. **2.** a culture medium based on a seaweed extract. Use: growing microorganisms in laboratories. [Late 19C. < Malay *agar-agar* 'jelly']

agarbatti /úggər buti/ (*plural same* or **-tis**) *n* S Asia same as **joss stick** [< Hindi]

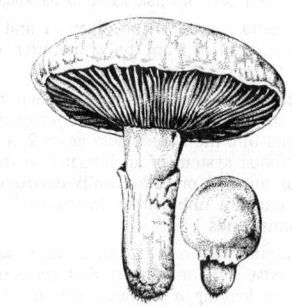

agaric

agaric /ággərik, ə gárrik/ *n* a fungus with a large cap resembling an umbrella with numerous radiating gills on the underside. Some types are edible and some are poisonous. Family: Agaricaceae. [15C. Directly or via French < Latin *agaricum* < Greek *agarikon* 'tree fungus']

agarose /ággə rōss, -rōz/ *n* a complex carbohydrate (**polysaccharide**) obtained from agar. Use: as a medium in chromatography and electrophoresis.

Agartala /úggəta laa/ capital city of Tripura state in northeastern India. Population: 158,000 (1991).

Aga saga *n* a novel about middle-class people, especially those living in the shire counties of England [Because the AGA is thought to symbolize the lifestyle of the main characters]

Agassi /ággəssi/, **Andre** (*b*. 1970) US tennis player. He won Wimbledon in 1992, the US Open in 1994 and

1999, and a gold medal in the Atlanta Olympics in 1996.

agate /ággət/ *n* **1.** a hard fine-grained semiprecious stone with variously coloured bands, markings, and areas of clouding that is a form of chalcedony. Use: gems. **2.** a playing marble made of agate or of glass that looks like agate [Late 16C. Via French < Greek *akhātēs*, perhaps after *Achates*, river in Sicily]

agate line *n* US a measure of page space, e.g. in classified advertising, one column wide and 1.8 mm deep

agateware /ággət wair/ *n* decorative pottery made using a cross-section of layers of clay of contrasting colours

agave

agave /ə gáyvi, ə gaávi, ággayv/ (*plural* **-ves** or *same*) *n* a spiny-leaved plant with a single tall flower stalk. Use: fibre, alcoholic drinks, especially tequila. Native to: America. Genus: *Agave.* [Late 18C. Via Latin < Greek *Agauē*, mother of Pentheus in Greek mythology]

agbiotech /ag bĭ ō tek/, **agbiotechnology** /ag bĭ ō tek nólləji/ *n* agriculture or an agricultural industry using products and processes developed through biotechnology [Late 20C. Shortening of *agbiotechnology* < shortening of AGRICULTURAL or AGRICULTURE]

AGC *abbr* ELECTRONICS automatic gain control

age /ayj/ *n* **1.** LENGTH OF SOMEBODY'S OR SOMETHING'S EXISTENCE the length of time that somebody or something has existed, usually expressed in years **2.** STAGE OF LIFE a stage or phase in the lifetime of somebody or something ○ *at an early age* **3.** LEGAL ADULTHOOD the age at which somebody is legally considered to be an adult **4.** STATE OF HAVING LIVED LONG the condition of having lived many years ○ *the wisdom of age* **5.** *also* **Age** HIST HISTORICAL PERIOD a period in history, especially a long period or one associated with and named after a distinctive characteristic, achievement, or influential person ○ *the space age* **6.** *also* **Age** GEOL GEOLOGICAL PERIOD a relatively short division of recent geological time, shorter than an epoch ○ *the Ice Age* **7.** EDUC LEVEL OF DEVELOPMENT a level of development equivalent to that of an average person of a particular age ○ *a reading age of 7* **8.** GENERATION a generation of people (*literary*) ○ *the greatest writer of her age* ■ **ages** *npl* **1.** LONG TIME a very long time (*informal*) **2.** HISTORY human history ○ *People have warred with one another throughout the ages.* ■ *v* (**ages, ageing** or **aging, aged**) **1.** *vti* GROW OR CAUSE TO GROW OLD to become old, develop the characteristics of being old, or cause somebody or something to become or seem old ○ *Too much sun ages the skin.* **2.** *vti* FOOD IMPROVE OVER TIME to cause a food or wine to mature, develop a desired flavour, or become more tender, or to be improved in this way over time ○ *The wine is aged in oak barrels.* **3.** *vt* ELECTRONICS STABILIZE DEVICE THROUGH USE to stabilize an electronic device by using it [13C. Via Old French *aage* < Latin *aetat-* 'period of life' < Indo-European] ◇ **come of age** to reach the age when people are legally considered to be adults ◇ **of a certain age** no longer young (*humorous*)

-age *suffix* **1.** action or result of an action ○ *breakage* ○ *coinage* **2.** collection of things ○ *signage* ○ *mileage* **3.** housing ○ *orphanage* **4.** condition, office ○ *brigandage* ○ *peerage* **5.** charge ○ *dockage* ○ *postage* [Via French < assumed Vulgar Latin *-aticum* < Latin *-aticus*, suffix forming adjectives]

age bracket *n* the range of ages included between two particular ages ○ *the 30–40 age bracket*

aged *adj* **1.** /áyjid/ OLD very advanced in years **2.** /ayjd/ OF PARTICULAR AGE of a particular age ○ *a person aged 50* **3.** /ayjd/ IMPROVED WITH TIME stored for a period of time in order to mature, develop a desired flavour, or become more tender ○ *well-aged wine* **4.** /ayjd/ GEOL ERODED showing evidence of advanced erosion ■ /áyjid/ *npl* ELDERLY PEOPLE people of advanced years, especially those whose physical or mental health has diminished (*formal*) [15C. Probably after French *âgé*]

age discrimination *n* same as **ageism**

age-diverse employment *n* employment practices that include recruiting, training, and promoting employees without regard to age

age diversity *n* the inclusion of people of all age groups, especially in the workplace

aged worker /ayjd-/ *n Aus* a worker certified as being of a particular age and therefore able to earn less than the statutory minimum wage in his or her trade or profession

Agee /áyji/, **James** (1909–55) US poet, novelist, screenwriter, and film critic. He cowrote *Let Us Now Praise Famous Men* with Walker Evans (1941) and wrote the screenplay for *The African Queen* (1951).

age gap *n* the difference in age between two people

age-grade *n* a group of people in a society who are the same sex and approximately the same age. Age-grades and the relationships between them are an important part of the organization of some cultures.

age group *n* a group of people whose ages are approximately the same or fall within a particular range

ageing /áyjing/, **aging** *n* **1.** PROCESS OF GROWING OLD the process of growing old, especially of acquiring the physical and mental characteristics of old age **2.** MATURING PROCESS the natural or chemically assisted process of bringing foods to maturity or of making materials like wood appear older ■ *adj* BECOMING OLD growing old, especially by acquiring the physical and mental characteristics of old age ■ present participle of **age**

ageism /áyjizəm/, **agism** *n* discrimination or prejudice against people of specific ages, especially in employment —**ageist** *adj*

ageless /áyjləss/ *adj* **1.** never growing or seeming to grow older **2.** not typical of or confined to a specific period of time ○ *the ageless search for the truth* —**agelessly** *adv* —**agelessness** *n*

age limit *n* a restriction limiting participation in an activity to people above or below a particular age

agency /áyjənssi/ (*plural* **-cies**) *n* **1.** BUSINESS, MANAGEMT COMPANY ACTING AS AGENT an organization, especially a company, that acts as the agent, representative, or subcontractor of a person or another company ○ *an employment agency* **2.** GOV GOVERNMENT ORGANIZATION an administrative division of a government or international organization ○ *a United Nations agency* **3.** AGENCY OFFICES the building or offices where an agency is located **4.** SEPARATE PART OF UK CIVIL SERVICE a part of the civil service in the United Kingdom that has some autonomy to deal with an aspect of administration such as issuing passports or benefits ○ *the Child Support Agency* **5.** MEANS the action, medium, or means by which something is accomplished [Mid-17C. < medieval Latin *agentia* < Latin *agent-* (see AGENT)]

agenda /ə jéndə/ *n* **1.** LIST OF THINGS TO DO a formal list of things to be done in a specific order, especially a list of things to be discussed at a meeting **2.** MATTERS NEEDING ATTENTION the various matters that somebody needs to deal with at a specific time ○ *What's your agenda for today?* **3.** PERSONAL MOTIVATION an underlying personal viewpoint or bias ○ *Of course she's in favour, but then she has her own agenda.* ■ plural of **agendum** [Early 17C. < Latin, plural of *agendum* 'thing to be done' < *agere* 'to do'] ◇ **set the agenda** to be the major influence or force affecting something ○ *It is the environmental lobby that is setting the agenda in this round of negotiations.*

USAGE Although ***agenda*** is strictly speaking a plural noun meaning 'things to be done', the singular form *agendum* is formal and no longer used; ***agenda*** is used in the singular as if it were 'a list of things to be done', with a plural form ***agendas***: *The agenda for tomorrow's meeting has been changed. This item has appeared on a number of previous agendas.* The use of ***agenda*** as a verb (*We will agenda that for the next meeting*) is criticized and is better avoided.

Agenda 21 *n* the global environmental programme and statement of principles emphasizing sustainable development agreed at the Earth Summit in Rio de Janeiro in 1992

agendum /ə jéndəm/ (*plural* **-dums** or **-da** /-də/) *n* an item on an agenda (*formal*) [Early 17C. < Latin (see AGENDA)]

USAGE See *agenda*.

agenesis /ay jénnəssiss/ *n* the incomplete development or total absence of a body part ○ *ovarian agenesis*

agent /áyjənt/ *n* **1.** SOMEBODY REPRESENTING ANOTHER somebody who officially represents somebody else in business **2.** SOMEBODY PROVIDING SERVICE somebody who provides a particular service for another ○ *a travel agent* **3.** CAUSATIVE SUBSTANCE something such as a chemical substance, organism, or natural force that causes an effect ○ *a cleansing agent* **4.** MEANS EFFECTING RESULT the means by which an effect or result is produced ○ *As director you will be expected to be the main agent of change.* **5.** COMPUT PROGRAM FOR ROUTINE TASKS a computer program that works automatically on routine tasks such as sorting e-mail or gathering information [15C. < Latin *agent-*, present participle of *agere* 'drive, lead, act, do'] —**agential** /ay jénsh'l/ *adj*

ORIGIN The Latin word *agere* 'to drive, act, do' from which ***agent*** is derived is also the source of English *act, active, actual, agile, agitate, ambiguous, cogent, essay, exact, examine,* and *prodigal.*

agent-general (*plural* **agents-general**) *n* a representative of a Canadian province or Australian state in a foreign country

Agent Orange *n* a toxic herbicide sprayed by the US military during the Vietnam War to defoliate jungle areas and expose enemy forces [< the orange stripe on its storage drums]

agent provocateur /ázhoN prə vokə túr/ (*plural* **agents provocateurs** /*pronunc. same*/) *n* somebody employed to gain the trust of suspects and then tempt them to do something illegal so that they can be arrested and punished [< French, 'provocative agent']

Age of Aquarius *n* an astrological era in which increased spirituality and harmony are said to characterize people's lives

age of consent *n* the age at which somebody is legally old enough to consent to marriage or sexual intercourse

Age of Reason *n* the period from the middle to the end of the 18th century during which there was an emphasis on rationalism in philosophy, religion, and society

age-old *adj* dating from a very long time ago and still in existence

age pension *n Aus* a social security payment made to men over 65 and women over an age between 60 and 65 depending on the date of birth

ageratum /ájjə ráytəm/ (*plural same* or **-tums**) *n* a low-growing garden plant. Flowers: blue, white, or purplish, in thick clusters. Genus: *Ageratum*. [Mid-16C. < modern Latin < Greek *agēratos* 'ageless, everlasting' < *gēras* 'old age']

age-related *adj* relating to or typical of the age that somebody has reached ○ *a normal age-related risk*

age-related macular degeneration *n* an eye condition associated with ageing in which the yellowish spot (**macula**) in the middle of the retina breaks down or becomes damaged as a result of leaking blood vessels. Symptoms include blurry central vision and diminished colour perception.

Aggadah *n* JUDAISM same as **Haggadah**

aggiornamento /ə jáwrnə méntō/ *n* the process of modernizing the ritual and policy of the Roman Catholic Church [Mid-20C. < Italian < *aggiornare* 'bring up to date']

agglomerate *vti* /ə glómmə rayt/ (**-ates, -ating, -ated**) COLLECT IN ROUND MASS to gather something or form into a rounded mass ■ *n* /ə glómmərət/ **1.** JUMBLED COLLECTION a jumbled mass or collection of something (*formal*) **2.** GEOL VOLCANIC ROCK rock produced by a volcanic eruption, consisting of fragments of different rock types, sizes, and shapes set in fine-grained solidified volcanic ash ■ *adj* /ə glómmərət/ IN ROUND MASS gathered into or forming a rounded mass [Mid-17C. < Latin *agglomerat-*, past participle of *agglomerare* 'heap up' < *glomer-* 'ball'] —**agglomeration** /ə glómmə ráysh'n/ *n* —**agglomerative** /ə glómmərətiv, -raytiv/ *adj* —**agglomerator** *n*

agglutinate /ə glóoti nayt/ (**-nates, -nating, -nated**) *vti* **1.** ADHERE OR CAUSE TO ADHERE to be joined or glued together, or cause things to do this **2.** CLUMP OR CAUSE CELLS TO CLUMP to cause cells such as red blood cells or bacteria to form clumps, or gather together in clumps **3.** LING FORM COMPOUND WORD to combine simple words without changing their form to make a new word, or be combined in a new word in this way [Mid-16C. < Latin *agglutinat-*, past participle of *agglutinare* 'fasten with glue' < *gluten* 'glue'] —**agglutinability** /ə glóotinə bíllәti/ *n* —**agglutinable** *adj* —**agglutinant** *n, adj* —**agglutination** /ə glóoti náysh'n/ *n*

agglutinative /ə glóotinətiv/ *adj* **1.** able or likely to agglutinate **2.** LING forming new words by combining simple words without changing their form ○ *an agglutinative language*

agglutinin /ə glóotinin/ *n* a substance that causes cells to clump together, e.g. an antibody or lectin

agglutinogen /ágglōō tínnəjən/ *n* an antigen responsible for the formation of an agglutinin

aggrade /ə gráyd/ (**-grades, -grading, -graded**) *vt* to build up a land surface or stream bed through the natural deposition of material [Early 20C. Back-formation < *aggradation* < AG- + DEGRADATION] —**aggradation** /ággrə dáysh'n/ *n* —**aggradational** *adj*

~~**aggragate**~~ incorrect spelling of **aggregate**

aggrandize /ə grán dīz, ággrən-/ (**-dizes, -dizing, -dized**), **aggrandise** (**-dises, -dising, -dised**) *vt* **1.** to increase or improve the power, wealth, influence, or status of somebody or something, especially by a deliberate plan **2.** to make somebody or something seem bigger or better than is actually the case, especially through exaggerated praise (*formal*) ○ *aggrandizing the value of her accomplishments* [Mid-17C. < French *agrandiss-*, stem of *agrandir* < *grandir* 'increase' < Latin *grandis* 'great'] —**aggrandizement** /ə grán dizmənt, -dīzmənt/ *n* —**aggrandizer** *n*

aggravate /ággrə vayt/ (**-vates, -vating, -vated**) *vt* **1.** ⚠ to irritate or anger somebody, especially with a continuing or trivial annoyance (*informal*) **2.** to make something become even worse or even more severe than before [Mid-16C. Probably via Old French < Latin *aggravat-*, past participle of *aggravare* 'make heavier' < *gravis* 'heavy'] —**aggravating** *adj* —**aggravatingly** *adv* —**aggravator** *n*

USAGE aggravate meaning 'annoy': Many people still dislike the use of ***aggravate*** to mean 'irritate or anger somebody', despite a history of usage dating back to the 17th century: *We were aggravated by the continuous loud noise from the street. Their bad behaviour has been very aggravating.* Except in informal conversation, it is usually better to use an alternative word such as *annoy, exasperate,* or *irritate.*

aggravated /ággrə vaytid/ *adj* having features that make something a worse criminal offence ○ *aggravated assault*

aggravation /ággrə váysh'n/ *n* **1.** IRRITATION a feeling of irritation or anger, especially when caused by a continuing or trivial annoyance **2.** SOURCE OF IRRITATION somebody or something that causes continuing irritation or anger **3.** WORSENING the worsening of an already bad situation, or somebody or something that makes a bad situation even worse ○ *Exercising before you have fully recovered may lead to an aggravation of your condition.* **4.** TROUBLE annoyance or bother, often aggressive in nature (*informal*) ○ *I get a lot of aggravation from dissatisfied customers.*

aggregate *adj* /ággrigət, -gayt/ **1.** FORMING WHOLE collected together from different sources and considered as a whole (*formal*) **2.** GEOL RESEMBLING ROCK describes a mixture of minerals or rock fragments that resembles rock ○ *an aggregate structure* ■ *n* /ággrigət, -gayt/ **1.** SUM TOTAL a total or whole made up of different parts from often disparate sources (*formal*) ○ *Her portfolio consisted of an aggregate of*

shares from different countries. **2.** SPORTS **TOTAL OF SCORES** the overall score gained by a team or player in a series of games in a competition ○ *won 4–2 on aggregate* **3.** CONSTR **INGREDIENTS OF CONCRETE** broken stone, gravel, and sand used in road construction and, when mixed with cement and water, for making concrete **4.** GEOL **MINERAL MIXTURE RESEMBLING ROCK** a mixture of minerals or rock fragments that resembles rock ■ *v* /ággri gayt/ (**-gates, -gating, -gated**) **1.** *vti* **UNITE** to come together, or bring different things together, into a total, mass, or whole ○ *Aggregate the different totals to get the overall cost.* **2.** *vt* MATHS **ADD UP TO NUMBER** to amount or add up to a number ○ *The company's earnings aggregate £175,000.* [15C. < Latin *aggregat-*, past participle of *aggregare* 'add to' < *greg-* 'flock'] —**aggregately** *adv* —**aggregation** /àggri gáysh'n/ *n* —**aggregative** *adj* —**aggregator** *n* ◇ **in the aggregate** considered or taken together as a whole

aggress /ə gréss/ (**-gresses, -gressing, -gressed**) *vi* to attack first, or begin a war, fight, or argument (*formal*) [Late 16C. Via obsolete French *aggresser* < Latin *aggress-*, past participle of *aggredi* 'approach, attack' < *gradi* 'walk']

aggression /ə grésh'n/ *n* **1.** threatening behaviour or actions **2.** hostile action, especially a physical or military attack, directed against another person or country, often without provocation [Early 17C. Directly or via French < Latin *aggression-* < *aggress-* (see AGGRESS)]

aggressive /ə gréssiv/ *adj* **1. LIKELY TO ATTACK** showing a readiness or having a tendency to attack or do harm to others **2. ATTACKING** attacking or taking action without provocation or without waiting for an enemy to make the first move **3.** ⚠ **ASSERTIVE** characterized by or exhibiting determination, energy, and initiative ○ *an aggressive investment policy* **4.** MED **SPREADING QUICKLY** describes a disease or a pathological growth such as a tumour that spreads or grows quickly **5.** EXTREME SPORTS **EMPHASIZING STUNTS** describes a type of in-line skating, skateboarding, or snowboarding that focuses on performing stunts —**aggressively** *adv* —**aggressiveness** *n*

USAGE Note that the correct spelling of ***aggressive*** and ***aggression*** is with *-gg-* and *-ss-*.

USAGE Aggressive or **assertive**? ***Aggressive*** normally implies hostility and even the threat of violence, and is best avoided when the meaning required is 'forceful' or 'assertive': *The sales team is encouraged to be assertive but not to use aggressive methods.*

aggressive growth fund *n* a unit trust that takes risks in the hope of making large long-term gains by investing in companies that are expected to grow fast

aggressor /ə gréssər/ *n* a person or country that attacks or starts a war, fight, or argument, often without being provoked [Mid-17C. < late Latin < Latin *aggress-* (see AGGRESS)]

aggressor force *n* the force that assumes the role of the enemy in military training exercises

aggrieve /ə gréev/ (**-grieves, -grieving, -grieved**) *vt* **1.** to cause somebody pain, trouble, or distress (*formal*) **2.** LAW to inflict an actionable injury on somebody [13C. Via Old French *agrever* 'make heavier' < Latin *aggravare* (see AGGRAVATE)] —**aggrieved** *adj*

aggro /ággrō/ *n* (*slang*) **1.** threatening behaviour, especially troublemaking or fighting ○ *We don't want any aggro.* **2.** trouble or difficulty ○ *He's having a lot of aggro with the garage.* [Mid-20C. Shortening of AGGRAVATION or AGGRESSION]

agha *n* POL another spelling of **aga**

Agha Mohammad Khan /àagə mə hámməd kaán/, **Shah** (1742–97) Iranian ruler who was self-proclaimed Shah (1796–97). He founded the Qajar dynasty, which reigned from 1794 until 1925.

aghast /ə gaást/ *adj* overcome with shock and dismay [13C. < the past participle of obsolete *agast* 'frighten' < Old English *gǣst* 'spirit, ghost']

agile /ájjīl/ *adj* **1.** able to move quickly and with suppleness, skill, and control **2.** able to think quickly and intelligently [Late 16C. Via French < Latin *agilis* 'able to be moved easily, nimble, quick' < *agere* 'move, do'] —**agilely** *adv* —**agileness** *n* —**agility** /ə jílləti/ *n*

agin /ə gín/ *prep regional* same as **against**

aging *n, adj* another spelling of **ageing**

agio /ájji ō/ (*plural* **-os**) *n* FIN **1.** an amount charged as a premium or percentage for changing one country's currency into that of another **2.** an allowance or discount given when paying in a foreign currency to compensate for the costs of exchanging the currency [Late 17C. Via Italian < medieval Greek *allagion* 'exchange' < *allagē* 'change' < *allos* 'other']

agiotage /ájji ə tij/ *n* **1.** the business of exchanging currencies between countries **2.** speculation in stocks, securities, or foreign currencies [Late 18C. < French < Italian *agio* (see AGIO)]

agism *n* SOC SCI another spelling of **ageism**

agitate /ájji tayt/ (**-tates, -tating, -tated**) *v* **1.** *vt* **MAKE SOMEBODY ANXIOUS** to make somebody feel anxious, nervous, or disturbed **2.** *vi* **AROUSE PUBLIC INTEREST** to attempt to arouse public feeling, interest, or support for or against something **3.** *vt* **MOVE SOMETHING VIOLENTLY** to cause something to move vigorously or violently, e.g. by shaking or blowing it ○ *Agitate the mixture until the sediment is thoroughly dispersed.* [Late 16C. < Latin *agitat-*, past participle of *agitare* 'move to and fro' < *agere* 'drive, move'] —**agitated** *adj* —**agitatedly** *adv* —**agitative** /ájjitətiv/ *adj*

agitation /àjji táysh'n/ *n* **1. ANXIETY** nervous anxiety **2. PUBLIC CAMPAIGNING** actions intended to arouse public feeling, interest, or support for or against something **3. SHAKING** vigorous or violent shaking, stirring, or other disturbance of something, especially a liquid ○ *Observe the mixture after agitation.*

agitato /àjji taátō/ *adj, adv* in a restless, tense, or excited manner (*used as a musical direction*) [Early 19C. Via Italian < Latin *agitat-* (see AGITATE)]

agitator /ájji taytər/ *n* **1.** somebody who attempts to arouse feeling about something, especially a political cause **2.** a machine or machine part that causes vigorous movement in a liquid or other substance

agitprop /ájjit prop/ *n* **1.** political propaganda, especially when disseminated through literature, drama, music, or art **2.** artistic work or works serving as a vehicle for political propaganda [Early 20C. < Russian < *agitatsiya* 'agitation' + *propaganda* 'propaganda']

Aglaia /ə glī́ ə, ə gláy ə/ *n* in Greek mythology, one of the three Graces who lived on Mount Olympus and tended the goddess Aphrodite. Aglaia was the daughter of Zeus and Euronyme.

agleam /ə gléem/ *adj* emitting or seeming to emit light (*literary*) ○ *She was laughing, her eyes agleam.*

aglet /ágglət/ *n* **1.** a plain or ornamental metal or plastic sheath covering the end of a shoelace or ribbon **2.** a metallic ornament such as a stud, cord, or badge worn on clothing [15C. < French *aiguillette* (see AIGUILLETTE)]

agley /ə gláy, ə glī́, ə gleé/ *adv, adj N England, Scotland* awry or askew ○ *'The best laid schemes o' mice and men / Gang aft agley'* (Robert Burns, *To a Mouse*; 1785) [Late 18C. < A-[1] + *gley* 'squint', origin ?]

aglimmer /ə glímmər/ *adj* glimmering with light (*literary*)

aglitter /ə glíttər/ *adj* glittering with light (*literary*)

aglow /ə glṓ/ *adj* radiating light, warmth, excitement, or happy emotion

AGM *abbr* annual general meeting

agma /ágmə/ *n* in phonetics, the symbol (ŋ) used to represent a velar nasal consonant, as in the final sound of 'long' [Mid-20C. < Greek, 'fragment']

agnail /ág nayl/ *n* ANAT same as **hangnail** [Old English *angnægl* < *ang-* 'narrow, painful' + *nægl* 'nail']

agnate /ág nayt/ (*formal*) *n* a relative who is descended from a man who is also the ancestor of other relatives, especially through the male line ■ *adj* **1.** ANTHROP same as **patrilineal** **2.** related or similar in any way [15C. < Latin *agnatus* 'born in addition' < Old Latin *gnatus*, past participle of *gnasci* 'be born'] —**agnatic** /ag náttik/ *adj* —**agnatically** *adv* —**agnation** /ag náysh'n/ *n*

Agnes /ágnəss/, **St** (*d.* AD 304?) Roman Christian martyr and saint. As a young woman she rejected marriage because of her devotion to Jesus Christ, and was put to death for her faith.

Agnew /ág nyoo/, **Spiro T.** (1918–96) vice president of the United States (1969–73). He was Richard Nixon's vice president and was forced to resign as a result of charges of illegal financial dealings during his period as governor of Maryland (1966–68). Full name **Agnew, Spiro Theodore**

Agni /úgni/ *n* in Hinduism, the god of fire [< Sanskrit, 'fire, the fire god']

agnolotti /ànnyə lótti/ *npl* small pieces of semicircular pasta stuffed with meat, cheese, or other filling and sealed at the edges [Late 20C. < Italian dialect, alteration of Italian *anellotto* 'little ring']

agnomen /ag nṓm en/ (*plural* **-nomina** /-minə/) *n* **1.** in ancient Rome, a fourth name that was occasionally bestowed on somebody as an honour **2.** a nickname (*literary*) [Mid-17C. < Latin, 'additional name' < *(g)nomen* 'name']

agnosia /ag nṓzi ə/ *n* the total or partial loss of the ability to recognize familiar people or objects, usually caused by brain damage [Early 20C. < Greek, 'lack of knowledge' < *gnōsis* (see GNOSIS)]

agnostic /ag nóstik/ *n* **1.** somebody who believes that it is impossible to know whether or not God exists **2.** somebody who doubts that a question has one correct answer or that something can be completely understood ○ *I'm an agnostic concerning space aliens.* [Mid-19C. < A-[2] + GNOSTIC] —**agnostic** *adj* —**agnostically** *adv*

agnosticism /ag nóstissizəm/ *n* the belief that it is impossible to know whether or not God exists

agnus castus /ágnəss kástəss/ *n* a preparation of the dried fruit of the chaste tree. Use: in alternative medicine, to treat various disorders of the female reproductive system. [14C. < Latin *agnus* < Greek *agnos*, the tree + *castus* 'chaste']

Agnus Dei /ágnooss dáy ee/ *n* **1. LAMB AS SYMBOL OF CHRIST** a lamb, usually depicted with a halo and holding a cross and banner, symbolizing Jesus Christ **2. CHRISTIAN PRAYER** a Christian prayer that begins in Latin with the words 'Agnus Dei', or 'Lamb of God', part of the liturgy of the Mass **3. MUSIC FOR AGNUS DEI PRAYER** a musical setting of the Christian prayer beginning 'Agnus Dei' [15C. < Latin, 'Lamb of God']

ago /ə gṓ/ *adv, adj* before the present time ○ *He only left about five minutes ago.* [14C. < the past participle of Old English *āgān* 'go away, pass by' < *gān* 'go']

USAGE ago and **since**: If ***ago*** is used it should be followed by *that* and not ***since*** in a following clause: *It was several weeks ago that I saw them.* If ***ago*** is left out, then ***since*** is used: *It is several weeks since I last saw them.* Note also that in sentences of this type, ***ago*** is preceded by a verb in the past tense (*was*) and ***since*** by a verb in the present tense (*is*).

agog /ə góg/ *adj* intensely interested, excited, or eager ○ *agog at the new twist to the scandal* [15C. Probably based on Old French *en gogues* 'enjoying yourself', literally 'in enjoyment']

-agog *suffix* another spelling of **-agogue**

à gogo /ə gṓ gō/ *adj* as much as anybody could want (*dated informal*) ○ *caviar à gogo* [Mid-20C. < French, 'joyfully' < *en gogues* (see AGOG) by repeating the *go-*]

-agogue, -agog *suffix* substance promoting the flow of something ○ *galactagogue* [Via French < Greek *agōgos* 'a drawing off' < *agein* 'lead']

agonise, etc another spelling of **agonize, etc**

agonist /ággənist/ *n* **1. COMPETITOR** somebody involved in a struggle, contest, or competition with somebody else (*formal*) **2.** ANAT **MUSCLE ACTING AGAINST ANOTHER** a muscle whose action is balanced by that of another associated muscle **3.** BIOCHEM **DRUG MIMICKING BODILY CHEMICAL** a hormone, neurotransmitter, or drug that triggers a response by binding to specific cell receptors [Early 17C. < Greek *agōnistēs* 'contestant, actor' < *agōn* 'contest']

agonistic /àggə nístik/, **agonistical** /àggə nístik'l/ *adj* **1. TRYING FOR EFFECT** striving to achieve an effect but appearing contrived or exaggerated (*literary*) **2. ARGUMENTATIVE** tending to argue and eager to win an argument (*literary*) **3.** ZOOL **AGGRESSIVE** characteristic of aggressive interaction between individuals, usually of the same species [Mid-17C. Via late Latin < Greek *agōnistikos* < *agōnistēs* (see AGONIST)] —**agonistically** *adv*

agonize /ággə nīz/ (**-nizes, -nizing, -nized**), **agonise** (**-nises, -nising, -nised**) *v* **1.** *vi* SPEND TIME WORRYING to think about something intensely and anxiously, usually in great detail and for a long time, before making a decision ○ *to agonize over the answer to every question* **2.** *vti* SUFFER OR CAUSE SOMEBODY PAIN to suffer, or cause somebody to suffer, extreme pain or mental anguish **3.** *vi* STRUGGLE to make a desperate or strenuous effort (*literary*) [Late 16C. Directly or via French < late Latin *agonizare*, after Greek *agōnizesthai* 'take part in a contest' < *agōn* 'contest']

agonized /ággə nīzd/, **agonised** *adj* expressing or characterized by severe pain or anxiety ○ *an agonized scream* ○ *an agonized search for the missing person*

agonizing /ággə nīzing/, **agonising** *adj* **1.** extremely painful **2.** causing much difficulty or unpleasantness ○ *an agonizing decision* —**agonizingly** *adv*

agony /ággəni/ (*plural* **-nies**) *n* **1.** GREAT PAIN OR ANGUISH intense physical pain or mental anguish **2.** INTENSE EMOTION a consuming emotion ○ *an agony of indecision* **3.** SUFFERING PRECEDING DEATH a period of struggle or suffering immediately preceding death (*literary*) ○ *last agony* [14C. Directly or via French < Latin *agonia* < Greek *agōnia* '(mental) struggle, anguish' < *agōn* 'contest'] —**agonal** *adj* ◇ **prolong the agony** to make a period of misfortune or anxiety last longer than necessary

agony aunt *n* a woman who gives personal advice to readers in a regular column in a newspaper or magazine or to callers on a radio or television programme

agony column *n* **1.** a regular column in a newspaper or magazine in which a columnist gives advice to readers who have written in about their personal problems **2.** a newspaper column of personal advertisements, usually enquiring about missing relatives or friends (*archaic*)

agony uncle *n* a man who gives personal advice to readers in a regular column in a newspaper or magazine or to callers on a radio or television programme

agora[1] /ággərə/ (*plural* **-rae** /-rī/ or **-ras**) *n* in ancient Greece, an open space in a town where people gathered, especially a marketplace [Late 16C. < Greek, 'marketplace, place of assembly' < *ageirein* 'assemble']

agora[2] /ággə ráa/ (*plural* **-rot** /-rṓt/) *n* a subunit of Israeli currency. See table at **currency** [Mid-20C. < Hebrew *agōrāh* 'small coin']

agorae ANCIENT HIST plural of **agora**[1]

agoraphobia /ággərə fṓbi ə/ *n* a condition characterized by an irrational fear of public or open spaces [Late 19C. < Greek *agora* 'open place' (see AGORA[1])] —**agoraphobic** *adj, n*

agorot MONEY plural of **agora**[2]

agouti /ə gṓoti/ (*plural* **-tis** or **-ties**) *n* **1.** a rabbit-sized rodent with short ears and clawed feet. Native to: tropical Central and South America. Genus: *Dasyprocta*. **2.** an irregularly striped pattern in the individual hairs of the fur of an agouti [Mid-16C. Via French or Spanish < Tupi-Guarani *akutí*]

AGP *abbr* COMPUT accelerated graphics port

Agra /aágrə/, **Āgra** city in Uttar Pradesh state, northern India. It is famous as the site of the Taj Mahal. Population: 1,321,410 (2001).

~~agragate~~ incorrect spelling of **aggregate**

Agrahayana /ágrəhī aánə/ *n* HINDUISM, CALENDAR same as **Margasirsa**

agranulocytosis /ə grànnyōolō sī tṓssiss, ay-/ *n* a sometimes fatal acute illness characterized by a decrease in granular white blood cells and by lesions of the throat, gastrointestinal tract, and skin. The condition often occurs as a toxic effect of specific drugs. [Early 20C. < A-[2] + GRANULOCYTE]

agrapha /ággrəfə/ *npl* sayings of Jesus Christ not recorded in the Bible but found in other early Christian writings [Late 19C. < Greek, plural of *agraphon* 'unwritten']

agraphia /ə gráffi ə, ay-/ *n* loss of the ability to write, resulting from neurological damage such as a brain lesion [Mid-19C. < A[3] + Greek *graphia* 'writing'] —**agraphic** *adj*

agrarian /ə gráiri ən/ *adj* **1.** OF LAND relating to land, especially its ownership and cultivation **2.** OF RURAL LIFE dominated by or relating to farming or rural life **3.** PRO-FARMER promoting the interests of farmers, especially in seeking a more equitable basis of land ownership ○ *an agrarian political party* ■ *n* LAND REFORMER somebody, often a member of an agrarian political movement, who believes in the fair distribution of land, especially the redistribution of large amounts of land owned by the rich [Early 17C. < Latin *agrarius* < *agr-* 'field, land'] —**agrarianism** *n*

agrarianism /ə gráiri ənizəm/ *n* a political movement or philosophy that promotes the interests of the farmer, especially the redistribution of land owned by the rich or by government

agree /ə grée/ (**agrees, agreeing, agreed**) *v* **1.** *vi* BE IN ACCORD to have the same opinion about something as somebody else ○ *Scientists don't agree about what causes these reactions.* **2.** *vi* CONSENT to consent to or approve a course of action ○ *They agreed on a postponement.* **3.** *vti* ADMIT AS TRUE to admit that something is true ○ *I had to agree that the room looked better with a coat of paint.* **4.** *vti* DECIDE to come to an understanding or reach a settlement regarding something ○ *Do you think we can agree on a plan?* **5.** *vi* BE CONSISTENT to be consistent with something in content, meaning, or characteristics ○ *The witnesses' stories agree in most details with the accused's.* **6.** *vi* BE SUITABLE to suit or be good for somebody ○ *The climate doesn't agree with me.* **7.** *vt* MAKE SOMETHING CORRESPOND to make something equal or consistent with something else ○ *to agree the incomings with the outgoings* **8.** *vi* GRAM MATCH EACH OTHER GRAMMATICALLY to have the same grammatical number, case, person, or gender, especially in the same sentence [14C. < French *agréer* 'please' < Latin *ad* 'to' + *gratus* 'pleasing'] ◇ **agree to differ** to stop arguing and accept that the opposing viewpoints are irreconcilable

---

SYNONYMS ***agree, concur, acquiesce, consent, assent***

CORE MEANING: to accept an idea, plan, or course of action that has been put forward

agree to have the same opinion about something as somebody else ○ *We agreed on an appointment at nine o'clock the next morning.* ○ *They have agreed in principle to lease the land.* **concur** to have the same opinion as somebody else, or reach agreement independently on a specific point ○ *I'd like to concur with my colleague's comment.* ○ *Do both sides in the negotiations concur that a settlement needs to be achieved very soon?* **acquiesce** to agree or comply with something in a passive or reserved way ○ *Peter refused at first, but later acquiesced.* ○ *The ministers acquiesced in a decision to seek funding for the project.* **consent** to give formal permission for something to happen ○ *consented to the marriage* **assent** to accept something formally ○ *a nation in which everyone assented to a common identity*

---

agreeable /ə grée əb'l/ *adj* **1.** PLEASING pleasing to the senses or to somebody's taste ○ *The climate here is very agreeable.* **2.** FRIENDLY pleasant, friendly, and ready to please others ○ *an agreeable companion* **3.** WILLING TO COMPLY willing to consent to or consider something ○ *If the committee is agreeable, you can start work straight away.* **4.** CONSISTENT consistent or in keeping with something —**agreeableness** *n* —**agreeably** *adv*

agreed /ə gréed/ *adj* **1.** DETERMINED BY CONSENSUS previously decided and assented to by two or more people ○ *the agreed procedure* **2.** SHARING OPINION sharing the same view as somebody else or others ○ *Are we all agreed on the proposal?* ■ *interj* YES used to confirm agreement with somebody else

agreement /ə gréemənt/ *n* **1.** FORMAL CONTRACT a contract or arrangement, either written or verbal and sometimes enforceable by law **2.** SITUATION OR ACT OF CONSENT the state of having come to the same opinion or having made the same decision as somebody else, or an expression of this state ○ *There is general agreement about the need for better transport.* ○ *Do we have your agreement on this issue?* **3.** CONSENSUS OF OPINION a situation in which everyone accepts the same terms or has the same opinion ○ *everyone is in agreement* **4.** GRAM MATCH BETWEEN GRAMMATICAL ELEMENTS correspondence of the number, case, gender, or person of one word with that of another word, especially in the same sentence

~~agression~~ incorrect spelling of **aggression**

~~agressive~~ incorrect spelling of **aggressive**

~~agressor~~ incorrect spelling of **aggressor**

agrestal /ə grést'l/ *adj* describes a plant that grows on cultivated land or among crops [Mid-19C. < Latin *agrestis* 'of fields' < *agr-* 'field, land']

agrestic /ə gréstik/ *adj* (*literary*) **1.** associated with the rural or rustic life **2.** lacking the qualities associated with sophistication [Early 17C. < Latin *agrestis* (see AGRESTAL)]

agri- *prefix* same as **agro-**

agribusiness /ággri biznəss/ *n* the operations and businesses that are associated with large-scale farming

agrichemical *n* AGRIC same as **agrochemical**

Agricola /ə gríkələ/, **Gnaeus Julius** (AD 40–93) Roman colonial administrator and governor of Britain (78–84). He encouraged Romanization, and was recalled to Rome and retirement in 85.

agricultural /ággri kúlchərəl/ *adj* **1.** involving or relating to agriculture ○ *agricultural equipment* ○ *agricultural college* **2.** with farming as the dominant way of life ○ *one of the earliest agricultural communities* —**agriculturalist** *n* —**agriculturally** *adv*

agriculture /ággri kulchər/ *n* the occupation or business of cultivating the land, producing crops, and raising livestock [15C. Directly or via French < Latin *agricultura* < *agri* 'of the land' (< *agr-* 'field, land') + *cultura* 'cultivation'] —**agriculturist** /ággri kúlchərist/ *n*

agri-food /ággri-/ *adj* describes industries involved in the mass production, processing, and inspection of food products made from agricultural commodities

agrimony /ággriməni/ (*plural* *same* or **-nies**) *n* **1.** a perennial plant with compound leaves and spiny fruits. Flowers: small, yellow, in spikes. Genus: *Agrimonia*. **2.** PLANTS same as **hemp agrimony** [Pre-12C. Via Old French < Latin *agrimonia*, misreading of *argemonia* < Greek *argemōnē* 'poppy']

Agrippa /ə gríppə/, **Marcus Vipsanius** (63–12 BC) Roman general and a principal aide of the Emperor Augustus. He won the naval battle of Actium (31 BC).

Agrippina (the Elder) /àggrə péenə/ (13? BC–AD 33) Roman noblewoman. The daughter of Agrippa and the granddaughter of Augustus, she married the general Germanicus, by whom she became the mother of Caligula and Agrippina the Younger. Renowned for her virtue and heroism, she starved herself to death after being banished by Tiberius.

Agrippina (the Younger) (AD 15–59) Roman noblewoman. The daughter of Agrippina the Elder and Germanicus, she was the mother of Nero. She ensured Nero's accession to the throne by poisoning her third husband, the emperor Claudius, and ruled the empire through her son until she was murdered at his order.

agriterrorism /ággri térrə rizəm/, **agroterrorism** /ággrō-/ *n* terrorism against a nation that involves the poisoning of agricultural livestock, meats, grains, and vegetables

agro-, **agri-** *prefix* **1.** soil ○ *agronomy* **2.** agriculture ○ *agroindustrial* [< Latin *agri* (form of *ager*) and Greek *agros* 'field' < Indo-European]

agrobiology /àggrō bī óllәji/ *n* the branch of biology concerned with agricultural production, especially crop growth —**agrobiological** /àggrō bī ə lójjik'l/ *adj* —**agrobiologically** *adv* —**agrobiologist** *n*

agrochemical /àggrō kémmik'l/, **agrichemical** /ággri-/ *n* a chemical used in farming, e.g. a fertilizer or pesticide

agroforestry /àggrō fórristri/ *n* **1.** the method or practice of integrating the raising of trees into farming to provide fuel, fruits, forage, shelter for animals or crops, and other benefits **2.** forestry conducted purely to produce timber, without any regard for sporting or recreational pursuits

agroindustrial /àggrō in dústri əl/ *adj* **1.** relating to the production or provision of materials needed by both agriculture and industry, e.g. water **2.** used in, produced by, or involved in the industrial processing of agricultural products

agroindustry /àggrō indəstri/ *n* **1.** AGRIC same as **agribusiness** **2.** the operations and businesses that are

associated with the industrial processing of agricultural products

agronomic /ággrə nómmik/, **agronomical** /-nómmik'l/ *adj* **1.** relating to the scientific study of soil management, land cultivation, and crop production **2.** describes plant characteristics that are important during growth and development of a crop, e.g. height and stem strength

agronomics /ággrə nómmiks/ *n* the branch of economics that is concerned with the use and productivity of land (*takes a singular verb*) [Mid-19C. < AGRO- + ECONOMICS]

agronomy /ə grónnəmi/ *n* the science of soil management, land cultivation, and crop production [Early 19C. < French *agronomie* < Greek *agronomos* 'overseer of land' < *agros* 'land' + *-nomos* 'dispensing, administering'] —**agronomist** *n*

aground /ə grównd/ *adj, adv* onto or on ground, especially a shore, a reef, rocks, or the bottom of shallow water

aguardiente /ág waardi énti/ *n* rough brandy distilled in Spain, Portugal, or Latin America, sometimes flavoured with anise [Early 19C. < Spanish < *agua* 'water' + *ardiente* 'fiery']

Aguascalientes /ággwəss kal yén tayz/ **1.** state in central Mexico on the Anahuac Plateau. The resort city of Aguascalientes is its capital. Population: 944,285 (2000). Area: 5,197 sq. km/2,007 sq. mi. **2.** capital city of Aguascalientes State and a popular health resort in central Mexico. Population: 643,360 (2000).

ague /áy gyoo/ *n* **1.** a feverish condition involving alternating hot, cold, and sweating stages, especially as a symptom of malaria **2.** a fever or shivering fit (*archaic*) [14C. Via French < medieval Latin *acuta*, short for *febris acuta* 'sharp fever'] —**aguish** *adj* —**aguishly** *adv* —**aguishness** *n*

ah /aa/, **aah** *interj* **1.** EXPRESSING EMOTION used to express emotions ranging from blissful contentment to acute discomfort to disgust, depending on the speaker's tone of voice **2.** EXPRESSING RECOGNITION used to express surprise or recognition and understanding ○ *Ah, I see.* ■ *vi* (**ahs, ahing, ahed; aahs, aahing, aahed**) SAY 'AH' to say 'ah' ■ *n* UTTERANCE OF 'AH' an exclamation of 'ah' expressing any of various emotions [13C. < Old French *a(h)*, natural exclamation]

AH *adv* CALENDAR used to indicate a date that is a particular number of years after the Hegira (AD 622), a key date in the Islamic calendar. Full form **anno Hegirae**

A.h. *abbr* MEASURE ampere-hour

aha /aa haá/ *interj* used when discovering something, especially to express triumphant satisfaction or excitement ○ *Aha, I caught you in the act!* [14C. < AH + HA¹]

AHA *abbr* CHEM alpha-hydroxy acid

Ahab /áy hab/ (*fl* 9th century BC) king of Israel. He ruled Israel from 869 BC to 850 BC.

ahead /ə héd/ *adv, adj* **1.** IN FRONT in front of somebody or something ○ *They are in the white car just ahead.* **2.** FORWARDS onwards or in a forward direction ○ *Keep walking straight ahead and it's on your left.* **3.** TO FUTURE in or into the future ○ *We expect more news in the weeks ahead.* **4.** EARLIER before or in advance of something or somebody ○ *You need to learn to plan ahead!* **5.** BETTER in or into a more advanced or desirable state ○ *Our company is definitely ahead compared to competition.* **6.** IN FIRST PLACE in a winning position in a contest or competition ○ *They were ahead by 6 points to 4.* ◇ **ahead of 1.** in front of **2.** at an earlier time than **3.** in a more advanced or advantageous position than ○ **get ahead** to succeed, do well, or advance financially (*informal*)

ahem /ə hém/ *interj* used in writing to indicate the sound of a quiet cough made to attract attention, express disapproval or doubt, or gain time [Mid-18C. An imitation of the sound]

Ahern /ə húrn/, **Bertie** (*b.* 1951) Irish politician who became leader of the Fianna Fáil political party in 1994 and was elected Taoiseach (prime minister) in 1997

'It is an observable phenomenon in Northern Ireland—and elsewhere—that tension and violence tend to rise when com-

promise is in the air.'
[Attributed to Bertie Ahern]

ahimsa /ə hím saa/ *n* the Hindu, Buddhist, and Jain philosophy of revering all life and refraining from harm to any living thing [Late 19C. < Sanskrit < *a-* 'without' + *himsā* 'injury']

ahistorical /áy hi stórrik'l/, **ahistoric** /áy hi stórrik/ *adj* not concerned with or not taking into account history or historical development, especially when examining a phenomenon that changes over time

ahold /ə hóld/ *n* US a firm grasp on something, usually with the hand (*informal*) ◇ **get ahold of** (*informal*) **1.** N Am get somebody or something or reach somebody by phone or similar means **2.** US to regain emotional control after a shock or state of distress, fear, anxiety, or excitement

aholehole /ə hóli hóli/ (*plural same* or **-les**) *n* a silvery tropical fish with spiny fins that is caught for food in the Pacific and Indian oceans. Family: Kuhlidae. [< Hawaiian]

-aholic *suffix* dependent on or with an extreme fondness for ○ *workaholic* [< ALCOHOLIC]

A-horizon *n* the uppermost layer of soil containing humus, topsoil, and organic debris

ahoy /ə hóy/ *interj* **1.** used by sailors to greet another ship or person or to attract attention ○ *Ahoy there!* **2.** used by sailors to announce that something, usually another ship or land, is in sight ○ *Land ahoy!* [Mid-18C. Probably blend of AHA + *hoy* < Middle Dutch *hoei* 'barge, ship']

Ahriman /áarimən/ *n* the spirit of evil in Zoroastrianism, and the opponent of Ahura Mazda [Via Persian < Avestan *angrō mainiiuš* 'evil spirit']

Ahura Mazda /ə hóorə mázdə/ *n* the creator god in Zoroastrianism, and the opponent of Ahriman [< Avestan *ahurō mazdå* 'wise lord']

ah we, **ahwee** *pron Carib* another spelling of **awe**²

ai *abbr* Anguilla (*used in Internet addresses*) See table at **domain name**

AI *abbr* **1.** artificial insemination **2.** COMPUT artificial intelligence

aid /ayd/ *vti* (**aids, aiding, aided**) GIVE HELP TO SOMEBODY to provide somebody or something with help or with what is needed to achieve something ○ *Better sewage systems aid in the fight against cholera.* ■ *n* **1.** MONEY OR SUPPLIES financial or material assistance, e.g. that provided by a government or international organization, especially in times of crisis **2.** ASSISTANCE anything done or provided that assists somebody or something ○ *I wouldn't have made it without the aid of my friends.* **3.** SOMEBODY OR SOMETHING HELPFUL a person, device, resource, or material that helps or assists with something ○ *visual aids such as maps* ○ *This book is an aid to using the Internet for research.* **4.** ASSISTANT an assistant or aide **5.** CLIMBING AID any device that is used to help a climber ascend a cliff or mountain face **6.** FORMER PAYMENT TO FEUDAL LORD formerly, a monetary payment by a vassal to an English feudal lord **7.** FORMER SUBSIDY FOR ENGLISH KING a special subsidy formerly granted to the English king by parliament. Aids for extraordinary expenses were granted from the time of the Norman Conquest into the 18th century. [15C. Via French < Latin *adjutare* 'to help'] ◇ **aid and abet** to assist somebody in commission of a crime ◇ **in aid of** in order to help, or for a particular reason or purpose (*informal*)

AID *abbr* **1.** MED acute infectious disease **2.** INTERNAT REL Agency for International Development **3.** MED artificial insemination by donor (*dated*)

aida /ī eédə/ *n* a fabric that comes in different sizes of weave. Use: cross-stitch embroidery.

aid agency *n* a usually charitable organization that gives money, food, or other material assistance to a country or area at a time of crisis

Aidan /áyd'n/, **St** (AD 600?–651) Irish monk who became bishop of Northumbria (635) and founded the monastery of Lindisfarne

aid climbing *n* climbing mountains or rocks with the assistance of artificial aids such as pitons

aide /ayd/ *n* **1.** an assistant to somebody in public office or to somebody providing a professional service, who may also offer advice ○ *The letter was*

signed by one of the Prince's aides. **2.** MIL same as **aide-de-camp** [Late 18C. Shortening of AIDE-DE-CAMP]

SYNONYMS See **assistant**.

aide-de-camp /áyd də kaáN/ (*plural* **aides-de-camp** /*pronunc. same*/) *n* a military officer acting as confidential assistant to a general or senior officer [Late 17C. < French, 'camp assistant']

aide-mémoire /áyd mem waár/ (*plural* **aide-mémoires** /*pronunc. same*/ or **aides-mémoire** /*pronunc. same*/) *n* (*formal*) **1.** a brief written summary or outline of the items on which agreement was reached in a meeting **2.** something, e.g. a mnemonic device, book, or document, that is an aid to remembering something else [Mid-19C. < French, 'help-memory']

Aids /aydz/, **AIDS** *n* a disease of the immune system caused by infection with the retrovirus HIV, which destroys some types of white blood cell and is transmitted through blood or bodily secretions such as semen. Patients lose the ability to fight infections, often dying from secondary causes such as pneumonia or kaposi's sarcoma. [Late 20C. Acronym < *Acquired Immune Deficiency Syndrome*]

Aids dementia *n* a dementia caused by HIV infection of the brain and characterized by neurological and psychiatric symptoms, e.g. severe cognitive impairment and degeneration of motor nerves and the spinal cord

Aids-related complex *n* the set of symptoms associated with infection by HIV, including weight loss and fever

aid station *n* US a military medical installation for troops in the field

aid worker *n* somebody who works for an aid agency either as an employee or volunteer

aight /īt/ *interj* same as **all right** *interj* (sense 2) (*slang; used in Black English*) [Representing a pronunciation]

aigrette /áy gret, ay grét/ *n* **1.** a tuft of long upright plumes, especially the tail feathers of an egret, worn on the head or on a hat for decoration **2.** a piece of jewellery that resembles a plume of feathers, usually worn on the head or on a hat [Mid-17C. < French, 'egret, heron']

aiguille: Teton Mountains, Jackson Hole, Wyoming, United States

aiguille /ay gwéel, ággweel/ *n* a mountain peak or large rock that is tall and sharply pointed [Early 19C. < French, 'needle']

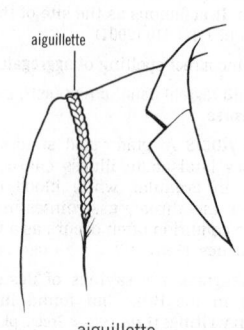
aiguillette

aiguillette /áygwi lét/ *n* a decorative cord with hanging points worn on the shoulder of some military uniforms [Mid-16C. < French, 'little needle' < *aiguille* 'needle']

AIH *abbr* MED artificial insemination by husband

aikido /ī kéedō, íki-/ *n* a martial art originating in Japan that is similar to judo but incorporates blows made with the hands and feet [Mid-20C. < Japanese *aikidō* < *ai* 'mutual' + *ki* 'spirit' (< Middle Chinese *khì*) + *dō* 'art' (< Middle Chinese *daw*)]

ail /ayl/ (**ails, ailing, ailed**) *vt* to cause pain or discomfort to somebody or something (*archaic or literary*) ○'*Oh what can ail thee, knight at arms/Alone and palely loitering*' (John Keats, *La Belle Dame Sans Merci*; 1820) [Old English *eglian* < Indo-European, 'be afraid or distressed']

SPELLCHECK Do not confuse the spelling of *ail* and *ale* ('beer'), which sound similar.

ailanthus /ay lánthəss, ī-/ *n* a tree or bush with long feathery leaves, winged fruit, and dense flower clusters. Native to: Asia. Genus: *Ailanthus*. [Early 19C. Via modern Latin < Ambonese *ai lanto* 'tree of heaven', influenced by plant names ending in *-anthus*]

aileron /áylə ron/ *n* a hinged flap on the trailing edge of an aircraft wing, used to control banking movements [Early 20C. < French, 'small wing' < *aile* 'wing' < Latin *ala*]

Ailey /áyli/, **Alvin** (1931–89) US dancer and choreographer. He founded the Alvin Ailey American Dance Theater (1958). His works, known for their fusion of ballet, jazz, modern dance, and African American dance influences, include *Revelations* (1960).

ailing /áyling/ *adj* **1.** performing below an expected standard ○ *the nation's ailing steel industry* **2.** affected or weakened by an illness

ailment /áylmənt/ *n* a mild illness or injury, especially a persistent one

Ailsa Craig /áylssə kráyg/ rocky islet in the Firth of Clyde, Scotland. Height: 340 m/1,114 ft.

ailurophile /ī lóorə fīl, ī lyóorə-/ *n* somebody who loves cats [Mid-20C. < Greek *ailuros* 'cat']

ailurophobe /ī lóorə fōb, ī lyóorə-/ *n* somebody who hates or fears cats [Early 20C. < Greek *ailuros* 'cat'] —**ailurophobia** /ī lóorə fóbi ə, ī lyóorə-/ *n*

aim /aym/ *v* (**aims, aiming, aimed**) **1.** *vti* POINT OBJECT to point a weapon or object or direct a blow at somebody or something **2.** *vi* PLAN TO DO SOMETHING to intend or plan to do something **3.** *vt* DIRECT MESSAGE to target words, a message, an action, or a product at a person or group ■ *n* **1.** INTENTION a plan to do or achieve something **2.** ACT OF AIMING an act or manner of aiming ○ *Take aim and fire.* **3.** SKILL IN AIMING skill at hitting a target ○ *Her aim was perfect.* **4.** DEGREE OF ACCURACY the level of accuracy of a weapon ○ *A rifle has more precise aim than a shotgun.* [14C. < Old French *esmer* 'estimate', *aesmer* 'aim at' < Latin *aestimare* (see ESTIMATE)] —**aimer** *n*

aimless /áymləss/ *adj* without purpose or direction —**aimlessly** *adv* —**aimlessness** *n*

ain't /aynt/ *contr* ⚠ a contraction of 'am not', 'is not', 'are not', 'have not', or 'has not' (*nonstandard*)

USAGE *Ain't* is one of the most informal verb contractions in English, and its use may be criticized in formal contexts because it is associated with careless speech. It is slightly more acceptable as a contraction of *am not*, and in the form *ain't I?* is more common as a question in informal American English: *Ain't I right?* British English uses the form *aren't I?* or (more formally) *am I not?* Otherwise *ain't* is best avoided, except as a deliberate rhetorical device and in allusive expressions such as *You ain't seen nothing yet.*

Ainu /ī noo/ (*plural same* or **-nus**) *n* **1.** a member of a Japanese people who now live in the north of the Japanese island of Hokkaido, and on the Kurile Islands and the island of Sakhalin **2.** a language spoken by the Ainu on Hokkaido that is considered to be unrelated to any other language [Early 19C. < Ainu, 'person'] —**Ainu** *adj*

aioli /ī óli/ *n* mayonnaise flavoured with garlic, used especially to garnish fish and vegetables [Early 20C. Via French < Provençal < *ai* 'garlic' + *oli* 'oil']

air /air/ *n* **1.** GASES FORMING ATMOSPHERE the mixture of gases, mainly nitrogen and oxygen, that forms the Earth's atmosphere **2.** ATMOSPHERE IN OPEN SPACE the atmosphere of an open space as opposed to that of

an enclosed space ○ *I need to get some air.* ○ *in the open air* **3.** ATMOSPHERE WE BREATHE the atmosphere in a place or enclosed space ○ *The air in here is too stuffy.* **4.** SKY the sky or the empty space above the Earth ○ *It flew through the air and landed at our feet.* **5.** TRAVEL IN AIRCRAFT travel in or transportation by aircraft (*often used before a noun*) ○ *sending the package by air* ○ *an air terminal* **6.** SOMEBODY'S DISTINCTIVE QUALITY a distinctive quality in somebody's appearance or manner ○ *her air of superiority* ○ *an air of sadness about him* **7.** MUSIC MELODY a melody or tune, especially a light or cheerful one **8.** LIGHT WIND a very light wind **9.** AERIAL SKATING OR BOARDING TRICK in skateboarding, in-line skating, and snowboarding, a trick performed with the whole board off the ground ■ *adj* OF ZODIAC SIGNS relating to the Aquarius, Gemini, or Libra signs of the zodiac ■ *v* (**airs, airing, aired**) **1.** *vti* BROADCAST OR BE BROADCAST to broadcast something or be broadcast on radio or television ○ *will be aired in the spring* **2.** *vt* MAKE SOMETHING KNOWN to express something such as an opinion or complaint ○ *air your views* **3.** *vti* EXPOSE TO AIR to be exposed to the air, or expose something to the air in order to dry it, cool it, or ventilate it [13C. Partly via Old French and Latin < Greek *aēr* 'air, atmosphere', partly via French, 'nature, place of origin' < Latin *ager* 'field', *area* 'open space'] ◇ **airs and graces** affected or pretentious behaviour ◇ **clear the air** to remove the tension, uncertainty, or misunderstanding from a situation ◇ **in the air** happening or about to happen ○ *The rumour is that a merger is in the air.* ◇ **off (the) air** not being broadcast on radio or television, e.g. because a person or programme has stopped or finished broadcasting ◇ **on (the) air** being broadcast on radio or television ◇ **punch the air** to thrust your arm upwards or outwards with your fist clenched as a gesture of triumph ◇ **take the air** to go for a walk (*formal*) ◇ **up in the air** undecided or uncertain ◇ **vanish into thin air** to disappear completely ◇ **walk** *or* **tread on air** to be extremely happy

SPELLCHECK *air, ere, err,* and *heir.* Do not confuse the spelling of *air, ere, err,* and *heir,* which sound similar. *Air* is the most common of the four words, as in *the air that we breathe, an air of superiority, to air an opinion. Ere* is a literary word meaning 'before' (as in *ere long*), *err* is a verb meaning 'make a mistake' (as in *to err is human, err on the side of caution*), and *heir* is a noun meaning 'legal inheritor' (as in *the heir to the throne*).

AIR *abbr* S *Asia* All India Radio

air bag *n* **1.** a safety device in a car consisting of a bag that automatically inflates on impact to protect the occupant of the seat **2.** a strong inflatable bag used to bring sunken items to the surface or by rescue workers to lift heavy machinery or debris under which somebody is trapped

air base *n* a place from which military aircraft operate

air bed *n* an inflatable mattress, especially a plastic or rubber one used by sunbathers

air bladder *n* **1.** an air-filled sac above the alimentary canal in most fishes that regulates buoyancy and, in some, aids in respiration **2.** an air-filled sac that aids buoyancy in some types of seaweed

airboat /áir bōt/ *n* same as **swamp boat** [Because it is driven with a propellor and steered with a rudder like an aeroplane's]

airborne /áir bawrn/ *adj* **1.** CARRIED BY AIR carried along by movements of air ○ *airborne infections* **2.** BY AIRCRAFT carried out or transported by aircraft ○ *airborne troops* **3.** IN FLIGHT in flight or in the air ○ *A meal will be served once we are airborne.*

air brake *n* **1.** a brake operated by compressed air, especially in a heavy motor vehicle **2.** a flap or small parachute on an aircraft operated to increase drag and thus slow the aircraft

airbrick /áir brik/ *n* a brick with holes through it, incorporated in structures to increase ventilation

air bridge *n* an air transport link between two places, especially where travel by land is not possible

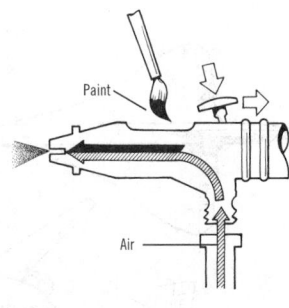

airbrush

airbrush /áir brush/ *n* a device for spraying paint using compressed air ■ *vt* (**-brushes, -brushing, -brushed**) to paint something or alter or improve a picture using an airbrush ○ *The blemish had been airbrushed out.*

airburst /áir burst/ *n* an explosion of a bomb, shell, or missile in the air

Airbus /áir bus/ *tdmk* a trademark for a large passenger jet aircraft manufactured by aerospace companies from different European countries working as a consortium

air chamber *n* **1.** an enclosed space with air in it **2.** a chamber in a hydraulic system in which air expands and compresses to control the flow of a fluid

air chief marshal *n* an officer in the Royal Air Force of a rank above air marshal

air commodore *n* an officer in the Royal Air Force of a rank above group captain

air-condition (**air-conditions, air-conditioning, air-conditioned**) *vt* to cool and control the humidity and purity of the air circulating in a space with an air conditioner —**air conditioned** *adj*

air conditioner *n* a device for cooling and controlling the humidity and purity of the air circulating in a space

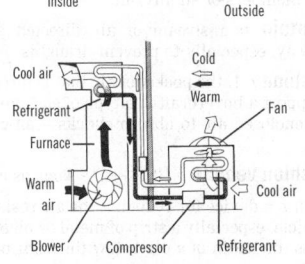

air conditioning

air conditioning *n* a system for cooling and controlling the humidity and purity of the air circulating in a space

air-cool (**air-cools, air-cooling, air-cooled**) *vt* to cool something, especially an engine, by a flow of air rather than a water system —**air-cooled** *adj*

air cooler *n* a device, e.g. a portable air-conditioning unit, for cooling the air inside a building, room, or vehicle

air corridor *n* a defined route that aircraft should take through airspace in which flying is restricted

air cover *n* the provision of an airborne defence for ground forces against an enemy air attack, or the aircraft providing the defence

aircraft /áir kraaft/ (*plural same*) *n* any vehicle capable of flight. See illustration on next page.

aircraft carrier *n* a warship with a long flat deck designed to allow aircraft to take off and land on it

aircraftman /áir kraaftmən/ (*plural* **-men** /-mən/) *n* a serviceman in the Royal Air Force of the lowest rank

aircraftwoman /áir kraaft wŏŏmən/ (*plural* **-women**

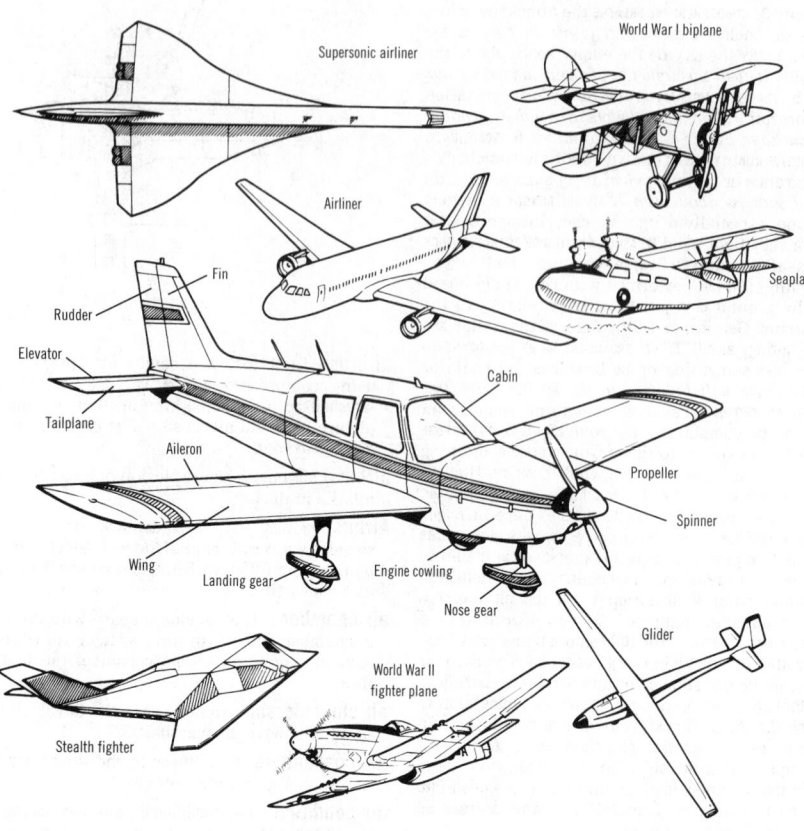

Supersonic airliner

World War I biplane

Airliner

Seaplane

Fin

Rudder

Elevator

Tailplane

Aileron

Cabin

Propeller

Spinner

Wing

Landing gear

Engine cowling

Nose gear

Glider

World War II
fighter plane

Stealth fighter

aircraft

/-wimin/) *n* a servicewoman in the Royal Air Force
of the lowest rank

aircrew /áir kroo/ *n* the pilot, navigator, and other
crew members of an aircraft

air curtain *n* a stream of air directed across a
doorway, especially to prevent draughts

air cushion *n* **1.** the pocket of air that is forced down
to support a hovercraft **2.** a type of suspension that
uses enclosed air to absorb shocks —**air-cushioned**
adj

air cushion vehicle *n US* VEHICLES same as **hovercraft**

air dam *n* a device for reducing the air resistance of
a vehicle, especially a strip of metal or plastic fitted
across the width of a car below the front bumper

airdate /áir dayt/ *n* the date on which a radio or
television programme is scheduled to be broadcast

air door *n* a strong current of air directed upwards
in an entrance to take the place of a door

airdrome /áir drōm/ *n US* same as **aerodrome** [Early
20C. < AIR + -DROME]

airdrop /áir drop/ *n* a landing of troops or supplies by
parachute from an aircraft ■ *vt* (**-drops, -dropping,
-dropped**) to land troops or supplies by parachute
from an aircraft

air-dry *v* (**air-dries, air-drying, air-dried**) to dry something by exposing it to air ■ *adj* dry to the point
where continued exposure to air will remove no
further moisture

Airedale /áir dayl/, **Airedale terrier** *n* a large terrier
belonging to a breed with rough tan-coloured hair
and a black patch on the back [Late 19C. After a district
in W Yorkshire]

air embolism *n* the presence of air in a blood vessel
resulting from injury, from moving too rapidly from
high to lower atmospheric pressure, or from using
a heart-lung machine during cardiopulmonary
bypass

airer /áirər/ *n* a frame on which to hang clothes to
dry indoors

Airedale

air exchanger *n* a device that expels stale air from
a room and brings in fresh air from outside, and
may also heat or cool the incoming air

airfare /áir fair/ *n* the price of a journey in an aircraft

airfield /áir feeld/ *n* an area where aircraft can take
off and land

airflow /áir flō/ *n* a flow of air, especially around a
moving vehicle

airflown /áir flōn/ *adj Malaysia* describes goods that
have been imported by air ○ *We have particularly
good airflown beef.*

airfoil /áir foyl/ *n N Am* same as **aerofoil**

air force *n* a military organization that uses aircraft
in war, especially a branch of a nation's armed
forces

Air Force One *n* the official aeroplane of the President
of the United States

airframe /áir fraym/ *n* the whole body of an aircraft,
apart from its engines

airfreight /áir frayt/ *n* **1.** TRANSPORTATION OF GOODS BY AIR the
transportation of freight by air **2.** CHARGE FOR AIRFREIGHT
the charge made for transporting freight by air ■
vt (**-freights, -freighting, -freighted**) TRANSPORT GOODS BY
AIR to transport goods by air

air gas *n* CHEM same as **producer gas**

airglow /áir glō/ *n* a faint light observed in the night
sky caused by photochemical reactions generated
by solar radiation in the upper atmosphere

air guitar *n* an imaginary guitar held by somebody
pretending to play a real instrument, especially
when miming to rock music (*informal*)

air gun *n* a pistol or rifle that fires a projectile by
releasing compressed air

airhead /áir hed/ *n* **1.** an area in enemy territory
captured and held by airborne forces and used when
flying troops and supplies in or out of the territory
2. somebody regarded as unintelligent and superficial (*slang insult*) [In sense 1 after BEACHHEAD]

air hole *n* **1.** a hole to allow the passage of air **2.** an
unfrozen area in the surface of a frozen body of
water, especially one where water mammals
surface to breathe **3.** METEOROL same as **air pocket**
(sense 1)

air hostess *n* a woman flight attendant on a large
passenger aeroplane (*dated*)

airily /áirili/ *adv* **1.** in a carefree or light-hearted way
as if something was unimportant **2.** in a delicate or
light way

airing /áiring/ *n* **1.** DRYING exposure to air or heat,
especially for drying, removal of dampness, or ventilation **2.** MAKING SOMETHING KNOWN the exposure to
public attention of somebody's opinions or ideas
3. RADIO OR TELEVISION BROADCAST a radio or television
broadcast **4.** WALK OR DRIVE a walk or drive in the open
air

airing cupboard *n* a warm or heated cupboard where
laundry can be aired or kept dry

air intake *n* an opening through which air enters a
duct, a confined space, or a fuel-burning engine

air jacket *n* **1.** an air-filled casing around a machine
to insulate it against heat loss or gain **2.** SAFETY
same as **life jacket**

air-kiss (**air-kisses, air-kissing, air-kissed**) *vt* greet
somebody by making a kissing gesture near to, but
not actually making contact with, his or her cheek
(*informal*) ○ *The guests were welcomed in a flurry of
air-kissing and delighted squeals.* —**air kiss** *n*

air lane *n* a regular route used in air travel

air layering *n* a plant propagation method in which
a growing branch is cut or stripped of bark and the
area wrapped in moist compost to encourage root
formation

airless /áirləss/ *adj* **1.** WITH STALE AIR with stale rather
than fresh air ○ *an airless room* ○ *an airless night*
2. STILL without wind or movement of air **3.** WITHOUT
AIR completely lacking any air —**airlessness** *n*

airlift /áir lift/ *n* the transport of people or things by
air, especially when alternative means cannot be
used ■ *vt* (**-lifts, -lifting, -lifted**) to transport people or
things by air, especially when alternative means
cannot be used

airline /áir līn/ *n* **1.** a system of commercial scheduled
flights transporting people and goods, or a company
that operates such a system **2.** a tube through which
air is passed under pressure

airliner /áir līnər/ *n* a large commercial passenger-
carrying aircraft

airlock /áir lok/ *n* **1.** an airtight chamber between two
areas of differing air pressure in which air pressure
can be altered to match that of either area **2.** an
obstruction to the flow of a liquid in a pipe, caused
by a bubble of air

airmail /áir mayl/ *n* **1.** SENDING OF MAIL BY AIR the system
of transporting letters and parcels in aircraft **2.** MAIL
SENT BY AIR mail transported in aircraft ■ *adj* SENT BY
AIR sent by airmail ■ *vt* (**-mails, -mailing, -mailed**) SEND
BY AIR to send a letter or parcel by airmail

airman /áirmən/ (*plural* **-men** /-mən/) *n* **1.** a pilot,
especially of a military aircraft **2.** an enlisted person
in the US Air Force

air marshal *n* **1.** an officer in the Royal Air Force of
a rank above air vice-marshal **2.** an officer in the
Royal Australian Air Force of the highest rank **3.**
TRAVEL same as **sky marshal**

air mass *n* a large body of air with temperature,
pressure, and moisture uniform throughout its

mass but changed by the environment through which it passes

air mile *n* a unit of distance used in air travel, equal to one international nautical mile

Air Miles *tdmk* a trademark for points worth miles of free or discounted air travel, issued by retailers and other businesses

airmobile /áir mō bīl/ *adj* able to be transported into a combat zone by air, especially by helicopter

air officer *n* an officer in the Royal Air Force of any rank above group captain

airpack /áir pak/ *n* a device consisting of a portable supply of oxygen connected to a face mask that allows somebody to enter an area where the air is unsafe to breathe

airperson /áir purss'n/ (*plural* **-persons** or **-people** /-peep'l/) *n* a member of an aircrew

air pistol *n* a pistol that fires a projectile by releasing compressed air or another gas

airplane /áir playn/ *n N Am* same as **aeroplane**

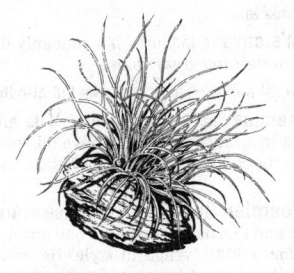

air plant

air plant *n* a plant that obtains nutrients and moisture from the air and rain, especially one grown as a houseplant for the novelty value of its requiring no soil or compost

airplay /áir play/ *n* the playing on radio of a piece of recorded music

air pocket *n* **1.** a small area of lower air density or a downward air current that makes an aircraft abruptly lose height **2.** an air bubble that impedes the flow of liquid or gas in a pipe

airport /áir pawrt/ *n* an area where civil aircraft may take off and land, especially one equipped with surfaced runways and facilities for handling passengers and cargo

airport tax *n* a tax levied on passengers departing on a flight from an airport, sometimes included in the cost of the airline ticket

airpower /áir power/ *n* military capability in terms of combat power delivered from the air

air pressure *n* METEOROL same as **atmospheric pressure**

air pump *n* a device for compressing air or forcing it into or out of something

air quality index *n* a numerical scale that indicates how polluted the air is

air rage *n* disruptive or aggressive behaviour by passengers aboard an aircraft that is liable to endanger the safety of other passengers

air raid *n* an attack by aircraft on something on the ground, especially a nonmilitary target (*hyphenated before nouns*)

air rifle *n* a rifle that fires a projectile by releasing compressed air or another gas

air sac *n* **1.** ANAT same as **alveolus** (sense 1) **2.** BIRDS an air-filled cavity in a bird, formed as an extension of the respiratory system and growing into the bones, that aids respiration and decreases bone mass **3.** INSECTS a thin-walled bulge (**diverticulum**) that aids respiration, located in the tubes that transport air through the bodies of some insects

Air Scout *n* a member of the Scout movement who belongs to a troop that goes flying or gliding

airscrew /áir skroo/ *n* a propeller on an aircraft

air-sea rescue *n* a rescue at sea in which aircraft are used

Barnaby's

airship

airship /áir ship/ *n* an aircraft that is lighter than air, powered, and navigable

airshow /áir shō/ *n* a public exhibition at an airfield of aircraft in flight and on the ground

air shower *n* a device in which jets of air are used to remove dust or particles from the clothes of people who work in a clean environment

airsickness /áir siknəss/ *n* motion sickness caused by air travel —**airsick** *adj*

airside /áir sīd/ *n* the area of an airport where the aircraft take off and land, load, or unload

air sign *n* each of the three signs of the zodiac, Gemini, Libra, and Aquarius, traditionally associated with thought, communication, and social interaction

air sock *n* AVIAT same as **windsock**

airspace /áir spayss/ *n* **1.** the part of the atmosphere directly above an area of land or water, especially a part over which a state claims jurisdiction **2.** the space in the air that a flying aircraft occupies or needs to manoeuvre

air speed *n* the speed of an aircraft in relation to the air through which it moves

air splint *n* a splint consisting of an inflatable cylinder that surrounds an injured limb

air spray *n* same as **aerosol** (senses 1–2)

air station *n* a small airfield with facilities for maintenance of aircraft

airstream /áir streem/ *n* **1.** a wind, especially one blowing at a high altitude **2.** AEROSP same as **airflow**

air strike *n* an attack by aircraft on something on the ground, especially an enemy position or formation —**airstrike** /áir strīk/ *vt*

airstrip /áir strip/ *n* a place for aircraft to take off and land that has no facilities and is often temporary

air stripping *n* a technique for removing pollutants from water by breaking the water into minute particles

airt /airt/ *n Scotland* a direction or quarter, especially one of the cardinal compass points [15C. Via Scottish Gaelic *aird* < Old Irish, 'point of the compass']

air taxi *n* a small commercial aircraft used for brief flights between places that do not have regularly scheduled flights

air terminal *n* a building in a city used by passengers being transported to or from an airport by train or bus

air terrorism *n* the use of skyjacking, aircraft bombing, and other terrorist acts involving aeroplanes in an attempt to achieve a political objective or get international publicity

airtight /áir tīt/ *adj* **1.** IMPERMEABLE BY AIR not allowing air in or out **2.** FLAWLESS without flaws or vulnerable points ○ *an airtight alibi* ■ *n W Africa* METAL BOX a metal box

airtime /áir tīm/ *n* **1.** the amount of time given to a programme or subject in radio or television broadcasting **2.** the time at which an item is scheduled to be broadcast

air-to-air *adj* moving or passing from one aircraft to another while in flight

air-to-surface *adj* moving or passing from a flying aircraft to a point on the ground

air traffic *n* the movement of aircraft in an area

air-traffic control *n* the system or organization responsible for directing the movement of aircraft over an area, operated by ground staff in radio contact with pilots —**air-traffic controller** *n*

air vesicle *n* same as **air bladder**

air vice-marshal *n* **1.** an officer in the Royal Air Force, Royal Australian Air Force and formerly in the Royal Canadian Air Force of a rank above air commodore **2.** the highest-ranking officer in the Royal New Zealand Air Force

air walk *n US* a high-level passageway connecting two buildings, usually made from a transparent material

airwaves /áir wayvz/ *npl* radio waves as used in broadcasting

airway /áir way/ *n* **1.** BREATHING PASSAGE a passage for air from the nose or mouth to the lungs **2.** TUBE TO KEEP AIRWAY OPEN a device for keeping an unconscious person's airway open, incorporating a tube inserted into the throat **3.** VENTILATION PASSAGE a passage for ventilation in a mine or tunnel **4.** AIR ROUTE an air route, especially one used by regular commercial flights (*often used in the plural*)

Airways /áir wayz/ *n* a company that operates a system of commercial flights (*used in company names; takes a singular or plural verb*)

airwoman /áir woomən/ (*plural* **-women** /-wimən/) *n* a woman who is a member of an aircrew

airworthy /áir wurthi/ *adj* in good enough condition to be safe to fly [Early 19C. After SEAWORTHY] —**airworthiness** *n*

airy /áiri/ (**-ier, -iest**) *adj* **1.** ROOMY well ventilated and having plenty of space **2.** LOFTY positioned or performed high in the air **3.** CAREFREE lighthearted and unconcerned ○ *an airy wave of her hand* **4.** ETHEREAL ethereal or insubstantial ○ *airy concepts* **5.** GRACEFUL light and graceful in movement (*literary*) ○ *an airy step* **6.** HIGH IN AIR at a great height in the sky (*literary*) —**airiness** *n*

airy-fairy *adj* fanciful or not grounded in reality (*informal*)

Aisha /aá ee shaa, ai eeshə/, **Ayesha** (AD 614?–678) wife of the prophet Muhammad. She was the daughter of the prophet Muhammad's chief adviser Abu Bakr and was Muhammad's favourite among his nine wives. Her political manoeuvring led to her exile in 656.

aisle /īl/ *n* **1.** PASSAGEWAY BETWEEN SEATS a passageway between areas of seating, especially in a church, theatre, or passenger vehicle **2.** PASSAGEWAY BETWEEN GOODS a passageway between stacks or displays of goods, especially in a supermarket or warehouse **3.** DIVISION IN CHURCH an area of a church separated from the nave or central area by pillars, especially one forming a passage between seats [14C. < Old French *ele* 'wing' < Latin *ala*, influenced by ISLE and, later, French *aile* 'wing'] ◇ **rolling in the aisles** laughing very heartily (*informal*)

SPELLCHECK *aisle* or *isle*? Do not confuse the spelling of *aisle* and *isle*, which sound similar. An *aisle* is a passageway, for example in a church or supermarket: *The bride walked down the aisle*. *Isle* is a literary word for a small island that is also sometimes used in place names: *the Isle of Wight*.

ait /ayt/ *n regional* a small island, especially in a river [Old English *īgeþ* 'small island' < *īeg* 'island']

aitch /aych/ *n* the letter 'h', or its sound [Mid-16C. < French *hache*, via late Latin *ach* < Latin *ah*, alteration of *ha*]

REGIONAL NOTE Pronunciations involving initial *h* have been a source of problems for almost a thousand years. In parts of the English-speaking world, *h* is pronounced *haitch*, not *aitch*, and such a difference is often enough used to distinguish Ulster Catholics from Protestants. In most other parts *haitch* is thought to be an uneducated pronunciation. Dialect speakers have often been described as *aitch-droppers*, and so they 'appily 'and their 'ats to 'arry. The illogicality of such prejudices becomes clear when we realize that it is prestigious to drop the *h* in *heir*, *honest*, and *hour*.

aits /īts/ *interj* used as a greeting, especially among

Rastafarian people (*slang*; *used in Black English*) [Origin ?]

Aix-en-Provence /éks aaN pro vaáNss/ city in the Bouches-du-Rhône Department in the Provence-Alpes-Côte d'Azur Region of southeastern France. It was the first Roman settlement in Gaul. Population: 134,222 (1999).

Aizawl /í jəl/ capital city of Mizoram state in north-eastern India. Population: 155,240 (1991).

aja /ájjə/, **aajaa** *n Carib* the father of somebody's father [Late 20C. < Hindi *daadaa*]

AJA *abbr Aus* Australian Journalists' Association

Ajaccio /ə jáksi ŏ/ main port and capital of Corsica. Population: 52,880 (1999).

ajar /ə jáar/ *adj, adv* neither shut nor wide open ○ *left the door ajar* [Late 17C. < later form of Old English *cierr* 'turn']

Ajax /áy jaks/ *n* in Greek mythology, a powerful warrior who fought in the Trojan War as leader of the Salamis forces. He was stricken by madness by the goddess Athena and killed himself when he was not awarded the armour of the dead Achilles.

AJC *abbr Aus* Australian Jockey Club

aji /ájee/, **aajee** *n Carib* the mother of somebody's father [Late 20C. < Hindi *daadii* 'grandmother']

ajoupa /ə jóopə/, **ajupa** *n Carib* a simple shelter or house with a thatched roof [Mid-20C. < Carib *ajouppa*]

a.k.a., AKA *abbr* also known as

Akan /aá kaan/ (*plural same* or **Akans**) *n* **1.** a member of a people who live in southern Ghana, southeastern Ivory Coast, and parts of Togo **2.** a language spoken in Ghana and Ivory Coast, belonging to the Kwa group of Niger-Congo languages. Native speakers: 8 million. [Late 17C. < Twi *akaŋ*] —**Akan** *adj*

akara /ákərə/, **accra** /ákrə/ *n* in Caribbean countries and western Africa, a fritter made from black-eyed beans or another pulse, or sometimes from fish [Late 19C. < Yoruba *àkàrà* 'bean cake']

akaryote /áy kárri ŏt/ *n* a cell that has no nucleus [< A-[2] + Greek *karuon* 'kernel'] —**akaryotic** /áy kárri óttik/ *adj*

Akbar /ák baar/ (1542–1605) emperor of India. During his reign (1556–1605), he conquered a vast realm in the north of the Indian subcontinent. Regarded as the most important of the Mughal emperors, he established a modern administrative system and promoted religious tolerance, economic development, and the arts. Known as **Akbar the Great**

akee *n* TREES another spelling of **ackee**

Akela /aa káylə/ *n UK, Can* the adult leader of a Cub Scout pack [Early 20C. After a wolf in Kipling's *Jungle Book*]

akene *n* BOT another spelling of **achene**

akhara /ə kaárə/ *n S Asia* same as **gymnasium** [< Hindi]

Akhenaton /aákə naát'n, aàk-/, **Ikhnaton** /ik-/ (*fl.* 14th century BC) Egyptian pharaoh. He ruled from about 1353 to 1337 BC and introduced a monotheistic religion based on the worship of the sun god Aton. He was married to Nefertiti.

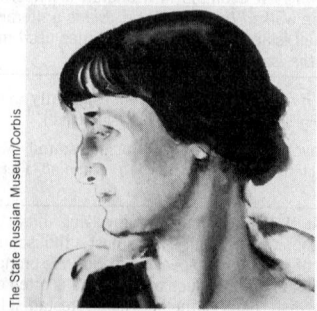

Anna Akhmatova: detail of a portrait (1928) by Nikolai Tyrsa

Akhmatova /ákmə tŏvə/, **Anna** (1889–1966) Russian poet. She was a leading figure in an early 20th-century movement that advocated precision and brevity in poetic language. Pseudonym of **Gorenko, Anna Andreyevna**

'And the stone word fell / Upon my still living breast. / Never mind, I was prepared for this. / Somehow, I shall stand the test.'
[Anna Akhmatova, 'The Sentence'; 22 June 1939]

Akiba ben Joseph /ə keébə ben jŏzəf, -jŏssəf/ (AD 50?–135?) Palestinian Jewish rabbi. He lived near Jaffa and was executed by the Romans for teaching Judaism.

Akihito /áki heétŏ/ (*b.* 1933) emperor of Japan. He succeeded his father, Hirohito, in 1989.

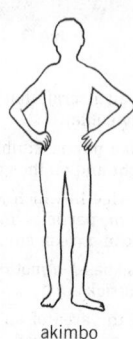

akimbo

akimbo /ə kímbŏ/ *adj, adv* with the hands on the hips and the elbows turned outwards [14C. Origin ?]

akin /ə kín/ *adj* **1.** SIMILAR similar or closely related to something **2.** RELATED related by blood **3.** SHARING COMMON ORIGIN describes languages that share a common origin or ancient forms [Mid-16C. < *a*, reduced form of OF]

akinesia /áy ki neéssi ə, -kī-, á-/ *n* the loss or reduction of the usual power of movement [Mid-19C. < Greek *akinēsia* 'lack of movement' < *kinein* 'to move'] —**akinetic** /áy ki néttik/ *adj*

Akira Yoshimura /ə keérə yóshi moórə/ (*b.* 1927) Japanese writer. His prize-winning novels and non-fiction works include *Journey to the Stars* (1966) and *Von Siebold's Daughter* (1978).

Akita /ə keétə/ capital city of Akita Prefecture on the Sea of Japan (East Sea), northwestern Honshu Island, Japan. Population: 312,926 (2002).

Akkad /á kad/ ancient city and region of the same name situated in central Northern Mesopotamia. It was most influential during the third millennium BC.

Akkadian /ə káydi ən/ *n* **1.** somebody who came from the ancient city or region of Akkad **2.** the extinct Semitic language of Mesopotamia, written in cuneiform [Mid-19C. < *Akkad*, city in ancient Babylonia] —**Akkadian** *adj*

Akmolinsk /ak móllinsk/ former name for **Astana** (1824–1960)

~~acknowledge~~ incorrect spelling of **acknowledge**

akrasia /ə kráyzi ə/ *n* weakness of will, especially a failure to act according to a sense of moral obligation [< Greek, variant of *akrateia* 'powerlessness' < *kratos* 'strength' (see -CRACY)] —**akratic** /ə kráttik/ *adj*

Akubra /ə kúbrə/ *tdmk Aus* a trademark for a traditional Australian wide-brimmed hat, usually made of felt made from rabbit fur and worn in the bush or country, particularly in outback areas

Akutagawa Ryunosuke /aá kootə gaáwə roónə soóki/, **Akutagawa Ryūnosuke** (1892–1927) Japanese author. He is noted for stories set in Japan's feudal era, e.g. *Rashomon* (1915).

akvavit *n* BEVERAGES same as **aquavit**

al *abbr* Albania (*used in Internet addresses*) See table at **domain name**

Al *symbol* aluminium

al. *abbr* **1.** alcohol **2.** alcoholic

-al[1] *suffix* **1.** relating to or characterized by ○ *delusional* **2.** action, process ○ *disposal* [Via French < Latin *-alis, alia*]

-al[2] *suffix* aldehyde ○ *chloral* [< ALDEHYDE]

à la /aá laa, állə/ *prep* in the style of somebody

or something [Late 16C. < French, shortening of *à la mode de* 'in the fashion of']

Alabama /állə bámmə/ state in the southeastern United States, bordered by Georgia, the Gulf of Mexico, Mississippi, and Tennessee. Capital: Montgomery. Population: 4,486,508 (2002 estimate). Area: 135,293 sq. km/52,237 sq. mi. —**Alabaman** *adj, n* — **Alabamian** /-báymi ən/ *adj, n*

alabaster /állə baastər, -bastər/ *n* **1.** TYPE OF GYPSUM a white or transparent form of gypsum. Use: decorative carving. **2.** TYPE OF CALCITE a hard semitranslucent type of calcite, occasionally with banding ■ *adj* **1.** OF ALABASTER made of alabaster ○ *alabaster ornaments* **2.** WHITE white and translucent like alabaster ○ *her alabaster skin* [14C. Via Old French < Greek *alabastros*]

à la carte /aá laa kaárt, állə-/, **a la carte** *adj, adv* with each dish on a menu priced separately [Early 19C. < French, 'by the menu']

alack /ə lák/ *interj* used to express regret (*archaic or literary*) [15C. < LACK, after ALAS]

alacrity /ə lákrəti/ *n* promptness or eager and speedy readiness [Early 16C. < Latin *alacritas* < *alacer* 'lively'] — **alacritous** *adj*

Aladdin's cave /ə láddinz-/ *n* a suddenly discovered place containing great riches

al-Adha /ál aádə/ *n* ISLAM same as **Eid al-Adha**

à la grecque /aá laa grék, állə-/, **a la grecque** *adj* cooked in a sauce made with olive oil, lemon, wine, and herbs, and served cold [< French, 'in the Greek style']

Alain-Fournier /állaN foor nyay/ (1886–1914) French writer and journalist. He wrote one novel, *Le Grand Meaulnes* (1913), lyrical in style. He was killed in World War I. Pseudonym of **Fournier, Henri-Alban**

à la king /aá laa kíng, állə-/, **a la king** *adj* cooked in a cream sauce with green peppers and mushrooms

Alamein, El ♦ El 'Alamein

Alamo /álləmŏ/ chapel in San Antonio, Texas, besieged by Mexican forces in 1836 when all 187 Texan defenders were killed

alamode /álləmŏd/ *n US* a light silk. Use: shawls. [Mid-17C. < French (see À LA MODE)]

à la mode /aá laa mŏd, állə-/, **a la mode** *adj* in the latest fashion (*dated*) [Late 16C. < French, 'in the style']

Alamogordo /álləmə gáwrdŏ/ city in southern New Mexico, northeast of White Sands Missile Range, the site of the first atom bomb explosion, on 16 July 1945. Population: 35,107 (2002 estimate).

alanine /állə neen, -nīn/ *n* an amino acid found in protein foods and also synthesized by the body [Mid-19C. < German *Alanin* < *Aldehyd* 'aldehyde']

alannah /ə lánnə/ *interj Ireland* used to address a child affectionately [Mid-19C. < Irish *a leanbh* 'O child' < Old Irish *lenab* 'child']

alar /áylər/ *adj* describes a part of an animal or plant that is shaped like a wing or is associated with such a part [Mid-19C. < Latin *alaris* < *ala* 'wing']

Alaric /állərik/ (AD 370?–410?) king of the Visigoths (395–410) who sacked Greece (395) and Rome (410)

alarm /ə laárm/ *n* **1.** WARNING DEVICE a device for giving a warning of danger **2.** SECURITY DEVICE a security device fitted to property, especially a house or car, to make a warning sound if a break-in or theft is attempted **3.** SOUND OF WARNING OR SECURITY DEVICE the sound made by a warning or security device **4.** same as **alarm clock 5.** FEAR fear caused by perception of imminent danger **6.** CALL TO ARMS a summons to prepare to fight (*archaic*) **7.** FENCING CHALLENGE MADE BY STAMPING a warning or challenge to a fencer made by stamping the leading foot ■ *vt* (**alarms, alarming, alarmed**) **1.** FRIGHTEN SOMEBODY to make somebody frightened or apprehensive **2.** FIT SOMETHING WITH SECURITY DEVICE to fit property, especially a building or vehicle, with a security device that sounds a warning if a break-in or theft is attempted **3.** WARN SOMEBODY to give somebody warning of danger [Early 16C. < archaic *alarm* adverb, via French < Italian *all' arme* 'to arms!'] —**alarmed** *adj*

alarm clock *n* a clock that can be set to sound a buzzer or bell at a desired time, especially to wake somebody

alarming /ə laárming/ *adj* frightening or disturbing —
alarmingly *adv*

alarmist /ə laármist/ *n* **1.** somebody who spreads unnecessary fear or warnings of danger **2.** somebody
who becomes afraid easily —**alarmism** *n* —**alarmist**
adj

alarm reaction *n* the initial response of a person or
animal to stress, including increased heart rate and
hormonal activity

alarum /ə lárrəm, ə laárəm/ *n* same as **alarm** *n* (sense
6) (*archaic*) [Variant]

alas /ə láss/ *interj* used to express sorrow or pity ■
adv unfortunately or regrettably [13C. Via French
hélas < Latin *lassus* 'weary']

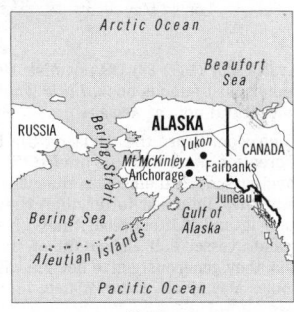

Alaska

Alaska /ə láskə/ US state of northwestern North
America, bordered by Canada and the Pacific and
Arctic Oceans. Capital: Juneau. Population: 643,786
(2002 estimate). Area: 1,593,438 sq. km/615,230 sq.
mi. —**Alaskan** *adj*, *n*

Alaska Highway *n* a road built in 1942 from Dawson
Creek, British Columbia, to Fairbanks, Alaska.
Former name **Alcan Highway**

Alaskan Peninsula peninsula of southern Alaska
separating the Pacific Ocean from the Bering Sea
to the northwest. Length: 644 km/400 mi.

Alaska Range mountain range in southern Alaska,
extending in a 640 km/400 mi. semicircle north of
Anchorage. It includes the highest peak in North
America, Mount McKinley 6,194 m/20,320 ft.

Alaska Standard Time, **Alaska Time** *n* the standard
time in the time zone centred on longitude 135°
W, which includes Alaska, apart from the western
Aleutian Islands. It is nine hours behind Universal
Time.

alastrim /ə lástrim/ *n* a mild form of smallpox, found
especially in South America and West Africa [Early
20C. < Portuguese < *alastrar* 'spread']

alate /áy layt/, **alated** /-laytid/ *adj* describes insects
with wings, or seeds with parts resembling wings
[Mid-17C. < Latin *alatus* < *ala* 'wing']

alb /alb/ *n* a long white robe with long sleeves worn
by priests [Pre-12C. Via ecclesiastical Latin (*vestis*) *alba*
'white (garment)' < Latin *albus* 'white']

Alb. *abbr* **1.** Albania **2.** Albanian

albacore /álbə kawr/ (*plural* same or **-cores**) *n* **1.** a
large tuna with a long pectoral fin. Native to: warm
waters of the Atlantic and Pacific. Latin name:
Thunnus alalunga. **2.** the flesh of an albacore used
as food [Late 16C. < Portuguese *albacor*]

Alban /áwlbən/, **St** (*fl* 3rd century AD) Roman-born
English martyr. A Roman soldier, he was converted
to Christianity by a priest, and beheaded by the
Roman authorities on the site of St Albans Abbey
in Hertfordshire.

Albania

Albania /al báyni ə/ country in southeastern Europe,
bordering the Adriatic Sea. A former Communist
state, it became a parliamentary democracy in 1991.
Language: Albanian. Currency: lek. Capital: Tirana.
Population: 3,582,205 (2003). Area: 28,748 sq.
km/11,100 sq. mi. Official name **Republic of Albania**

Albanian /al báyni ən/ *n* **1.** the official language of
Albania that is also spoken in parts of nearby
countries and is a branch of the Indo-European
languages. Native speakers: 4 million. **2.** somebody
who comes from Albania —**Albanian** *adj*

Albany /álbəni/ **1.** capital of New York State, situated
on the western bank of the Hudson River. Population: 93,779 (2002 estimate). **2.** coastal town in
southwestern Western Australia, an important port
and tourist destination. Population: 20,493 (1996).

albatross

albatross /álbə tross/ (*plural* **-trosses** or *same*) *n* **1. LARGE
SEABIRD** a large long-winged seabird that spends most
of its life in flight. Native to: cool southern oceans.
Family: Diomedeidae. **2. OPPRESSIVE BURDEN** an oppressive burden or hindrance **3. GOLF THREE BELOW PAR**
in golf, a score of three below par for a hole. N Am
term **double eagle** [Late 17C. Alteration (after Latin *albus*
'white') of Spanish and Portuguese *alcatraz* < Arabic *al-
ġaṭṭās* 'the diver'] ◇ **an albatross round somebody's neck**
a burden from which somebody cannot escape

albedo /al beédō/ (*plural* **-dos**) *n* the fraction of light
hitting an object that is reflected by that object,
especially a planet reflecting the Sun's light [Mid-
19C. < ecclesiastical Latin, 'whiteness' < Latin *albus* 'white']

Albee /álbi/, **Edward** (*b.* 1928) US playwright and
author of *Who's Afraid of Virginia Woolf?* (1962).
His play *Three Tall Women* (1991) won him his third
Pulitzer Prize for drama. See Cultural note at **afraid**.
Full name **Albee, Edward Franklin**

> 'Sometimes a person has to go a very long
> distance out of his way to come back a
> short distance correctly.'
> [Edward Albee, *The Zoo Story*; 1960]

albeit /awl beé it/ *conj* used to introduce a statement
that modifies a statement just made ○ *a difficult,
albeit rewarding job* [14C. < ALL + BE[1] + IT[1], 'all though
it may be']

albendazole /al béndə zōl/ *n* a veterinary drug used
to prevent parasitic worms [Mid-20C. < ALBUMEN +
ENDO- + AZOLE]

Alberich /álbərikh/ *n* in medieval Germanic mythology, king of the dwarves and guardian of the
treasures of the Nibelung

Albers /álbərz, áwl-/, **Josef** (1888–1976) German-born
US painter and designer. He taught at the Bauhaus
school of design. After 1933 he worked in the United
States.

albert /álbərt/ *n* a short chain used to attach a pocket
watch to a waistcoat [Mid-19C. After Prince ALBERT, who
wore such a chain]

Albert /álbərt/ (1819–61) German-born prince consort
to Queen Victoria. A supporter of technological
innovation and patron of the arts, he organized the
Great Exhibition (1851). The proceeds financed the
building of several museums and the Royal Albert
Hall (1871).

Albert, Lake lake in east-central Africa, on the border
between Uganda and the Democratic Republic of
the Congo, in the north of the Rift Valley system.
Area: 5,600 sq. km/2,160 sq. mi. Length: 160 km/99
mi.

Alberta /al búrtə/ Canada's westernmost Prairie Province and a leading producer of oil and natural
gas. Capital: Edmonton. Population: 3,113,600 (2002).
Area: 661,848 sq. km/255,541 sq. mi.

Albert Edward Nyanza /-ni ánzə/ former name for
Edward, Lake

Alberti /al báirti/, **Leon Battista** (1404–72) Italian architect and writer. His architectural designs are characterized by a pure classical style. His treatise *On
Painting* (1436) expounded the principles of perspective and was an important source for artists of
his and future generations.

albertite /álbər tīt/ *n* a solid black variety of bitumen
found in oil-bearing rock strata [Mid-19C. After *Albert*
County, New Brunswick, Canada]

Albertus Magnus /al búrtəss mágnəss/, **St** (1200?–80)
German cleric and philosopher. He wrote on logic,
natural and moral sciences, and theology. He taught
St Thomas Aquinas.

albescent /al béss'nt/ *adj* becoming white or whitish
(*technical or literary*) [Early 18C. < Latin *albescent-
< albus* 'white']

Albigenses /álbi jén seez/ *npl* a heretical Christian
religious group in southern France during the 12th
and 13th centuries. They believed that everything
in the material world is evil. [Early 17C. < medieval
Latin < *Albiga* 'Albi', city in S France] —**Albigensian** *adj* —
Albigensianism *n*

albinism /álbinizəm/ *n* congenital lack of pigmentation in the skin and hair of a person or animal
or in the coloration of a plant —**albinistic** /álbi nístik/
adj

albino: dwarf Russian hamsters with albino shown right

albino /al beénō/ (*plural* **-nos**) *n* **1.** a person or animal
whose skin and hair lack pigmentation and whose
irises are pink because of a hereditary condition
(**albinism**) **2.** a plant that lacks pigmentation in
its coloration because of a hereditary condition
(**albinism**) [Early 18C. < Portuguese < Latin *albus* 'white']

Albion /álbi ən/ ancient name for England or the
island of Britain

albite /ál bīt/ *n* a usually white form of feldspar. Use:
glass, ceramics. [Early 19C. < Latin *albus* 'white'] —
albitic /al bíttik/ *adj*

ALBM *abbr* air-launched ballistic missile

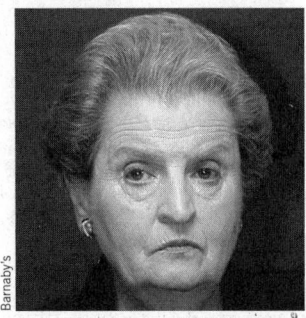

Madeleine Albright

Albright /áwl brīt/, **Madeleine** (*b.* 1937) Czech-born US
secretary of state (1997–2001). A Democrat, she was
appointed US ambassador to the United Nations in
1993 and later became the first woman to hold the
post of US secretary of state. Full name **Albright,
Madeleine Korbel**

'Words are cheap; actions are the coin of the realm.'
[Madeleine Albright. On Iraq's massing of 80,000 troops while accusing the US of harbouring ill will, *Time*; 31 October 1994]

album /álbəm/ *n* **1.** BLANK BOOK a book or binder with blank pages or pockets for keeping collected items such as postage stamps, photographs, mementos, and autographs **2.** MUSIC RECORDING a music recording, sometimes including more than one CD, cassette, or record, issued as a single item **3.** RECORD HOLDER a cardboard holder for gramophone records, similar to a book in shape **4.** COLLECTION a collection in book form of short literary or musical pieces or pictures (*dated*) [Early 17C. < Latin, 'blank tablet' < *albus* 'white']

ORIGIN The Latin word *albus* 'white', from which *album* is derived, is also the source of English *alb*, *albino*, *albumen*, *auburn*, and *daub*.

albumblatt /álbəm blat/ (*plural* **-blatts** or **-blätter** /-blettər/) *n* a short light instrumental piece popular in the 19th century, usually bound together in a set with other similar pieces [< German, 'page from an album']

albumen /álbyooۡmin, al byooۡmin/ *n* **1.** the clear water-soluble protein that surrounds the yolk of an egg and provides nutrition for the embryo (*technical*) **2.** the protein component of egg white, which includes albumin [Late 16C. < Latin < *albus* 'white']

albumin /álbyooۡmin, al byooۡmin/ *n* a common water-soluble protein coagulated by heat, found in egg white, blood plasma, and milk —**albuminous** /al byooۡminəss/ *adj*

albuminoid /al byooۡmi noyd/ *adj* resembling albumin ■ *n* BIOCHEM same as **scleroprotein** —**albuminoidal** /al byooۡmi nóyd'l/ *adj*

albuminuria /al byooۡmi nyoorۡi ə, ál byooۡmi-/ *n* the presence of albumin in urine, usually an indication of kidney disease

Albuquerque /álbə kurki/ city and tourist resort on the Rio Grande and the largest city in New Mexico, United States. Population: 463,874 (2002 estimate).

Albury-Wodonga /áwlbəri wə dóng gə/ urban area in southeastern Australia consisting of the cities of Albury in New South Wales and Wodonga in Victoria. Population: 67,316 (1996).

alc. *abbr US* **1.** BEVERAGES, CHEM alcohol **2.** MED alcoholic

alcahest *n* HIST another spelling of **alkahest**

Alcaic /al káy ik/ *adj* describes lyric poetry written in the metrical form of a stanza of four lines, each containing four feet ■ *n* a lyric poem or line written in the Alcaic form (*often used in the plural*) [Mid-17C. < late Latin *alcaicus* < Greek *Alkaios* 'Alcaeus', lyric poet credited with inventing the form]

alcalde /al káldi, -kaۡaldi/ *n* the mayor or chief magistrate of a town in a Spanish-speaking area [Mid-16C. Via Spanish < Arabic *al-ḳāḍī* 'the judge']

Alcan Highway /ál kan/ *n* former name for **Alaska Highway** [Contraction of *Alaska-Canada*]

Alcatraz /álkə traz/ island in San Francisco Bay, California, site of a federal prison from 1933 to 1963. It has been part of the Golden Gate National Recreation Area since 1972.

alcazar /álkə zaۡar/ *n* in Spain, a fortress or palace, especially one built by the Moors [Early 17C. Via Spanish < Arabic *al-ḳaṣr* 'the castle' < Latin *castrum* 'camp']

Alcestis /al séstiss/ *n* in Greek mythology, the daughter of Pelias and wife of Admetus, King of Pherae. She agreed to die to save her husband's life, but was later rescued from Hades by Heracles.

alchemise *vt* another spelling of **alchemize**

alchemist /álkəmist/ *n* somebody who practises alchemy —**alchemistic** /álkə místik/ *adj*

CULTURAL NOTE *The Alchemist*, a play (1610) by Ben Jonson. An energetic satire set in London, it tells the story of a servant, Face, and his friends Subtle and Doll Common. They pose as alchemists, convincing a series of gullible characters that they can help them attain wealth and happiness.

alchemize /álkə mīz/ (**-mizes**, **-mizing**, **-mized**), **alchemise** (**-mises**, **-mising**, **-mised**) *vt* to transform

something into gold or into a much purer or brighter form by alchemy

alchemy /álkəmi/ *n* **1.** an early, unscientific form of chemistry that sought to change base metals into gold and discover a life-prolonging elixir, a universal cure for disease, and a universal solvent (**alkahest**) **2.** a power supposedly like alchemy, especially of enchantment or transformation [14C. Via Old French *alquemie* and medieval Latin *alchimia* < Arabic *al-kīmiyā* 'the chemistry' < Greek *khēmeia*] —**alchemic** /al kémmik/ *adj* —**alchemical** /al kémmik'l/ *adj*

alcheringa /álchə ríng gə/, **alchera** /álchərə/ *n* MYTHOL same as **Dreaming** [Late 19C. < Aranda *aljerre-nge* 'in the Dreaming']

alchol incorrect spelling of **alcohol**

Alcibiades /álsi bíۡ ə deez/ (450?–404 BC) Athenian general and political leader. His command contributed to the defeat of Athens in the Peloponnesian War.

alclometasone /álkló méttə sōn/ *n* a synthetic steroid drug. Use: treatment of dermatosis. [Late 20C. < *alclo-* + *-metasone*, INN stem]

ALCM *abbr* air-launched cruise missile

Alcmene /alk meéni/ *n* in Greek mythology, wife of Amphitryon and mother of Heracles and Iphicles

Alcock /áwl kok/, **Sir John William** (1892–1919) British aviator. With Arthur Brown, he made the first transatlantic flight, from Newfoundland to Ireland, which took 16 hours 12 minutes.

alcohol /álkə hol/ *n* **1.** LIQUID FOR DRINKS OR SOLVENTS a colourless liquid, produced by the fermentation of sugar or starch, that is the intoxicating agent in fermented drinks. Formula: C_2H_5OH. **2.** DRINKS WITH ALCOHOL intoxicating drinks containing alcohol **3.** ORGANIC COMPOUND an organic compound containing one or more hydroxyl groups bound to carbon atoms [Mid-16C. Via medieval Latin, 'fine powder, distilled essence' < Arabic *al-kuḥl* 'the antimony powder']

alcohol dehydrogenase *n* an enzyme found in the liver and stomach that promotes the conversion of alcohols to aldehydes

alcoholic /álkə hóllik/ *adj* **1.** CONTAINING ALCOHOL relating to or containing alcohol ○ *alcoholic beverages* **2.** CAUSED BY ALCOHOL caused by alcohol consumption ○ *alcoholic dehydration* **3.** ADDICTED TO ALCOHOL addicted to drinking beverages containing alcohol ■ *n* ALCOHOL ADDICT somebody who is addicted to alcohol

alcoholic cardiomyopathy *n* a disease of the heart muscle caused by prolonged exposure to the toxic effects of alcohol or its by-product

alcoholic hepatitis *n* inflammation of the liver caused by prolonged exposure to the toxic effects of alcohol or its by-products, often a precursor to cirrhosis

alcoholicity /álkə ho líssəti/ *n* the amount of alcohol contained in something

Alcoholics Anonymous *n* an organization for alcoholics that offers mutual support to members to help them overcome their dependency

alcoholism /álkə holizəm/ *n* **1.** dependence on alcohol consumption to an extent that adversely affects social and work-related functioning and produces withdrawal symptoms when intake is stopped or greatly reduced **2.** a physical disorder caused by the toxic effects of excessive alcohol consumption

alcopop /álkó pòp/ *n* a drink made of a soft drink, e.g. lemonade, mixed with alcohol. Technical name **flavoured alcoholic beverage** [Late 20C. < ALCOHOL + POP[1]]

Alcoran /ál kaw raۡan/ *n* ISLAM same as **Koran** —**Alcoranic** /-ránnik/ *adj*

Alcott /áwl kət/, **Amos Bronson** (1799–1888) US transcendentalist and writer who founded the Concord Summer School of Philosophy and Literature in 1879

'The true teacher defends his pupils against his own personal influence.'
[Amos Bronson Alcott, 'The Teacher', *Orphic Sayings. From The Dial*; July 1840]

Louisa May Alcott

Alcott, **Louisa May** (1832–88) US novelist. Her novels include her most famous book, *Little Women* (1868–69). See Cultural note at **woman**

'When women are the advisers, the lords of creation don't take the advice till they have persuaded themselves that it is just what they intended to do; then they act upon it, and if it succeeds, they give the weaker vessel half the credit of it; if it fails, they generously give her the whole.'
[Louisa May Alcott, *Little Women*; 1868–69]

alcove /álkōv/ *n* **1.** INTERNAL RECESS a recess in the wall of a room **2.** EXTERNAL RECESS a recess in an exterior wall, usually with a roof or other covering structure **3.** SECLUDED PLACE a shady or secluded place in a garden [Late 16C. Via French *alcôve* and Spanish *alcoba* < Arabic *al-ḳubba* 'the vault, the arch']

alcuronium /álkyoo róni əm/ *n* a drug used as a muscle relaxant [Late 20C. < ALLYL + CURARE]

Aldabra /al dábbrə/ group of four islands in the Seychelles in the Indian Ocean. Area: 154 sq. km/59 sq. mi.

Aldebaran /al débbərən/ *n* the brightest star in the constellation Taurus and one of the brightest stars in the sky

Aldeburgh /áwldbərə/ seaside town in Suffolk, eastern England. An annual music festival is held there. Population: 2,654 (1991).

aldehyde /áldi hīd/ *n* an organic compound containing a carbon atom connected to an oxygen atom by a double bond and to a hydrogen atom ■ *adj* relating to the chemical group composed of a carbon atom connected to an oxygen atom by a double bond and to a hydrogen atom [Mid-19C. Contraction of modern Latin *alcohol dehydrogenatum* 'dehydrogenated alcohol'] —**aldehydic** /áldi híddik/ *adj*

al dente /al dén tay, -dénti/ *adj* cooked just long enough to be still firm, and not too soft [< Italian, 'to the tooth']

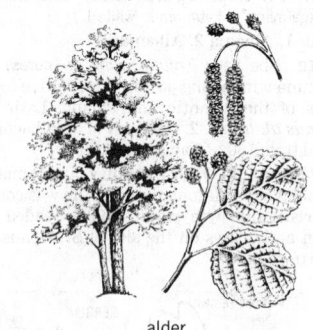

alder

alder /áwldər/ *n* **1.** a deciduous tree or bush with male catkins and cone-shaped fruits, common in wet places. Native to: northern temperate areas. Genus: *Alnus*. **2.** the rot-resistant wood of an alder tree. Use: in underwater structures, carving, furniture making. [Old English *alor* < Indo-European, 'reddish-brown']

alderman /áwldərmən/ (*plural* **-men** /-mən/) *n* **1.** SENIOR COUNCIL MEMBER a man who was a senior member of an English or Welsh local council before the local government reorganization of 1974 **2.** MEMBER OF US TOWN LEGISLATING BODY a man who is a member of the

legislating body of some towns or cities in the United States and Canada **3. LOCAL GOVERNMENT MEMBER IN AUSTRALIA** a member of local government elected by the constituents of a municipality in Australia **4.** HIST another spelling of **ealdorman** [Old English *ealdorman* < *ealdor* 'an elder' + MAN] —**aldermancy** *n* —**aldermanic** /áwldər mánnik/ *adj*

Aldermaston /áwldər maastən/ village in southern England, the site of the Atomic Weapons Research Establishment

Alderney[1] /áwldərni/ third largest and most northerly of the Channel Islands. Population: 2,297 (1991). Area: 17.95 sq. km/3.07 sq. mi.

Alderney[2] /áwldərni/ *n* a cow belonging to a breed of small dairy cattle originally from the Channel Islands

alderperson /áwldər purss'n/ (*plural* -**persons** or -**people** /-peep'l/) *n* a member of the legislating body of some towns or cities in the United States and Canada

Aldershot /áwldər shot/ town and military centre in Hampshire, southern England. Population: 51,356 (1991).

alderwoman /áwldər woomən/ (*plural* -**women** /-wimin/) *n* **1. WOMAN SENIOR COUNCIL MEMBER** a woman who was a senior member of an English or Welsh local council before the local government reorganization of 1974 **2. WOMAN MEMBER OF TOWN LEGISLATING BODY** a woman who is a member of the legislating body of some towns or cities in the United States and Canada **3. WOMAN LOCAL GOVERNMENT MEMBER IN AUSTRALIA** a woman who is a member of local government elected by the constituents of a municipality in Australia

aldesleukin /ál dez lookin/ *n* a genetically engineered drug. Use: treatment of cancer. [Late 20C. < aldes- + -leukin, INN stem]

Aldington /áwldingtən/, **Richard** (1892–1962) British writer. He was a founder member of the imagist movement with Ezra Pound and his first wife, Hilda Doolittle. Much of his writing was influenced by his experiences as a soldier in Europe in World War I.

Aldis lamp /áwldiss-/ *n* a signalling device in the form of a portable lamp used to flash messages in Morse code [Early 20C. After A. C. W. *Aldis* (1878–1953), British inventor]

aldohexose /áldō héksōss, -héksōz/ *n* a sugar containing six carbon atoms and an aldehyde group, e.g. glucose or mannose [Early 20C. Contraction of ALDEHYDE + HEXOSE]

aldol /ál dol/ *n* **1.** a colourless or pale yellow oily liquid. Use: catalyst in the vulcanization of rubber, solvent, perfumes. **2.** an organic compound containing an aldehyde group and an alcohol group on neighbouring carbon atoms

aldolase /áldə layss, -layz/ *n* an enzyme that aids the breakdown of fructose [Mid-20C. < German]

aldose /áldōss, -dōz/ *n* a sugar (**monosaccharide**) that contains an aldehyde group

aldosterone /al dóstərōn/ *n* a steroid hormone, secreted by the adrenal cortex, that controls mineral and water balance

aldosteronism /al dóstərənizəm/ *n* a condition caused by excessive secretion of aldosterone by the adrenal cortex, characterized by weakness, high blood pressure, and large fluid intake and urinary output

Aldrich /áwldrich/, **Thomas Bailey** (1836–1907) US writer. The editor of *The Atlantic Monthly* (1881–90) and the author of stories and poems, he is best remembered for the autobiographical novel *The Story of a Bad Boy* (1870).

> 'We vivisect the nightingale / To probe the secret of his note.'
> [Thomas Bailey Aldrich, 'Realism', *The Poems of Thomas Bailey Aldrich*; 1907]

Aldrin /áwldrin/, **Buzz** (b. 1930) US astronaut. He was the second man to walk on the Moon (1969). Full name **Aldrin, Jr. Edwin Eugene**

> 'Magnificent desolation!'
> [Buzz Aldrin. Message to NASA upon walking with Neil Armstrong on the Moon; 20 July 1969]

ale /ayl/ *n* **1.** a type of beer, brewed from a cereal and originally distinguished from beer by the absence of hops **2.** same as **beer** (sense 1) **3.** N Am an alcoholic drink made from rapidly fermented malt to which hops have been added [Old English *ealu* < Germanic, perhaps 'intoxicating drink']

SPELLCHECK See *ail*.

aleatory /áyli ətəri/ *adj* **1.** depending on chance or contingency **2.** *also* **aleatoric** /áyli ə táwrik/ having the sequence of given notes or passages in a piece of music chosen at random by the performer or left to chance [Late 17C. < Latin *aleatorius* < *alea* 'dice']

Alecto /ə léktō/ *n* in Greek mythology, one of the three Furies

alee /ə leé/ *adv, adj* on or to the leeward side

alef *n* another spelling of **aleph**

alehouse /áyl howss/ *n* **1.** same as **pub** (sense 1) (*dated*) **2.** a place where ale was sold and served (*archaic*)

~~alein~~ incorrect spelling of **alien**

Alemanni /állə mánni, -maáni/ *npl* a group of Germanic peoples who settled in areas around the Rhine, Main, and Danube rivers at the beginning of the 4th century AD [< Latin < Germanic, perhaps 'all the peoples']

Alemannic /állə mánnik/ *n* **1. GERMAN DIALECTS** a group of High German dialects spoken in Alsace, Switzerland, and southwestern Germany **2. ANCIENT GERMANIC LANGUAGE** the language of the Alemanni ■ *adj* **1. OF ALEMANNI** relating to the Alemanni, or their language or culture **2. OF ALEMANNIC** relating to Alemannic

Alembert /a ləm bér, a laaN bér/, **Jean le Rond d'** (1717–83) French philosopher, mathematician, and encyclopedist. He formulated d'Alembert's principle, a landmark in the study of mechanics, in 1743, and collaborated with Denis Diderot on the great *Encyclopédie* (1751–80).

> 'The imagination in a mathematician who creates makes no less difference than in a poet who invents...Of all the great men of antiquity, Archimedes may be the one who most deserves to be placed beside Homer.'
> [Jean le Rond d'Alembert, *Discours préliminaire de l'encyclopédie (Preliminary Discourse to the Encyclopedia)*; 1751]

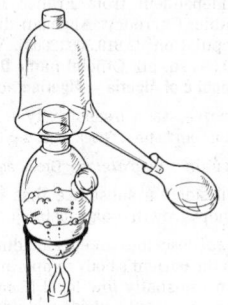

alembic

alembic /ə lémbik/ *n* an apparatus formerly used in distillation [14C. Via Old French and medieval Latin *alembicus* < Arabic *al-'anbīk* 'the still' < Greek *ambix* 'cup']

alendronic acid *n* a drug used as its sodium salt. Use: treatment of osteoporosis and Paget's disease.

aleph /állef, aá lef/, **alef** *n* the first letter of the Hebrew alphabet, transliterated as an apostrophe and pronounced as a glottal stop. See table at **alphabet** [14C. < Hebrew and Phoenician *āleph* 'first letter of the alphabet, ox']

Aleppo /ə léppō/ city in northwestern Syria, northeast of Homs, an important centre on an ancient trade route to the East. Population: 1,582,930 (1994). Former name **Beroea**

Aleppo boil *n* a skin disease caused by infection with a protozoan and characterized by the formation of nodules and sores

alert /ə lúrt/ *adj* **1. WATCHFUL** watchful and ready to deal with whatever happens **2. MENTALLY LIVELY** clear-headed and responsive ■ *n* **1. WARNING OF DANGER** an alarm or warning of danger **2. TIME OF DANGER** a period of time during which an alert remains in force ■ *vt* (**alerts, alerting, alerted**) **WARN SOMEBODY** to make somebody aware of a possible danger or difficulty ○ *Police have alerted the public to the danger.* [Late 16C. Via French *alerte* < Italian *all'erta* 'on the lookout'] —**alertly** *adv* —**alertness** *n* ◇ **on the alert** watchful and ready to deal with whatever happens

à l'espagnole *adj* prepared in a style inspired by Spanish cookery, usually containing tomatoes, sweet peppers, onions, and garlic, and fried in olive oil [< French, 'in the Spanish style']

Alessandri Palma /állə sándri pálmə/, **Arturo** (1868–1950) president of Chile (1920–24, 1925, and 1932–38). Elected president in 1920 on a reform platform, he resigned in 1924 when a military junta seized power. In his second and third terms, he drafted a long-standing constitution and established a central bank.

alethic /ə leéthik/ *adj* relating to the philosophical concepts of truth and possibility and especially to the branch of logic that formalizes them [Late 20C. < Greek *alētheia* 'truth' < *alēthēs* 'true']

aleurone /ə lyoórōn/, **aleuron** /-on/ *n* a protein occurring as granules in some plants, especially in seeds [Mid-19C. Alteration of Greek *aleuron* 'wheat flour'] —**aleuronic** /állyoō rónnik/ *adj*

Aleut /álli oot, ə lyoót/ (*plural same* or **Aleuts**) *n* **1.** a member of an indigenous people who live in the Aleutian Islands and coastal southwestern Alaska **2.** an Eskimo-Aleut language spoken in the Aleutian Islands and coastal parts of Alaska. Native speakers: 500. [Late 18C. < Russian] —**Aleut** *adj* —**Aleutian** /ə loósh'n/ *adj*

Aleutian Islands /ə loósh'n-/ chain of islands stretching westwards for about 1,800 km/1,100 mi. from the tip of the Alaska Peninsula and separating the Pacific Ocean from the Bering Sea to the north

A level *n* **1.** in England, Wales, and Northern Ireland, the advanced level of any subject studied to gain a General Certificate of Education qualification. It is divided into two levels, AS level, taken after the first year of study, and A2, taken after the second year. **2.** a pass in an examination in a subject studied at A level [Shortening of *Advanced level*]

alevin /álləvin/ *n* a young salmon or trout with the yolk sac still attached [Mid-19C. Via French < assumed Vulgar Latin *allevamen* 'something that is raised' < Latin *levare* (see LEVER)]

alewife /áyl wīf/ (*plural* -**wives** /-wīvz/) *n* a herring that migrates up rivers to spawn. It appears off the Atlantic coast of North America in early summer and can be eaten as food. Latin name: *Alosa pseudoharengus.* [14C. < ALE + WIFE 'woman']

alexander /állig zaándər/ *n* a cocktail made from crème de cacao, sweet cream, and gin or brandy [Early 20C. < the name *Alexander*]

Alexander II /állig zándər/ (1818–81) tsar of Russia. He emancipated the serfs in 1861 and sold the Russian lands in North America (now Alaska) to the United States in 1867.

Alexander III (1105?–81) pope. He was pope from 1159 to 1181, during which time he imposed penance on Henry II of England for the murder of St Thomas à Becket. Born **Bandinelli, Rolando**

Alexander, William, Earl of Stirling (1567?–1640) Scots poet. Tutor to Prince Henry of Scotland, he later went to England on the accession of James I. His works include *Four Monarchicke Tragedies* (1604–07).

Alexander technique *n* a method of improving the posture that involves developing awareness of it [Mid-20C. After Frederick *Alexander* (1869–1955), Australian physiotherapist]

Alexander the Great (356–323 BC) king of Macedonia. He conquered most of the ancient world from Asia Minor to Egypt and parts of India.

Alexandra /állig zaándrə/ (1872–1918) empress of Russia. The wife of Tsar Nicholas II, she was executed by the Bolsheviks at Ekaterinberg.

Alexandria /állig zaándri ə/ city and Mediterranean seaport in northern Egypt, on the delta of the River Nile. Founded by Alexander the Great in 332 BC, it was a major cultural centre of the ancient world,

renowned for its library. Population: 3,328,000 (1998). —**Alexandrian** adj

Alexandrina, Lake /állig zan dréenə/ coastal lagoon in southeastern South Australia, situated at the mouth of the Murray River. Area: 680 sq. km/260 sq. mi.

alexandrine /állig zán drīn, -zaán-, -drin/ n **1. ENGLISH VERSE FORM** in English poetry, a line of verse that has six iambic feet and usually a caesura after the third foot **2. FRENCH VERSE FORM** in French poetry, a line of verse that has twelve syllables and usually a caesura after the sixth syllable ■ adj **LIKE OR IN ALEXANDRINES** typical of or written in alexandrines [Late 16C. < French, after the romance *Alexandre* about Alexander the Great, which was written in this metre]

alexandrite /állig zán drīt, -zaán-/ n a precious stone that is a green chrysoberyl. Use: gems. [Mid-19C. < German *Alexandrit*, after *Alexander* II (1818–81), tsar of Russia, because it was discovered on the day of his majority]

alexia /ə léksi ə/ n a loss of the ability to read, caused by a disorder of the central nervous system [Late 19C. < A³ + Greek *lexis* 'speech'; meaning influenced by Latin *legere* 'read']

Alexis Mikhailovich /ə léksiss mi kíləvich/ (1629–76) tsar of Russia (1645–76). Ruling from 1645 to 1676, he legitimized serfdom (1649) and suppressed a peasant revolt (1670–71).

alf /alf/ n *Aus* somebody, especially an Australian, regarded as unsophisticated (*informal insult*)

ALF abbr Animal Liberation Front

alfa n, adj another spelling of **alpha**

~~alfabet~~ incorrect spelling of **alphabet**

alfacalcidol /àlfə kálssə dœl/ n a derivative of vitamin D used by the body in the regulation of calcium and phosphate, and as a drug in the treatment of vitamin D deficiency [Late 20C. < *alfa* + *calcidol*, INN stem]

alfalfa /al fálfə/ n a plant of the pea family. Use: hay, forage crop. Native to: Europe, Asia. Latin name: *Medicago sativa*. [Mid-19C. Via Spanish < Arabic *al-faṣfaṣa* 'the best kind of fodder']

Al Fatah /ál fáttə/ n a Palestinian political group that seeks to establish an independent Palestinian state. Formed in the 1950s, it became part of the Palestine Liberation Organization in 1968. [Late 20C. < Arabic *al* 'the' + acronym < *Ḥ(arakat) T(aḥrīr) F(ilastīn)* 'Movement for the Liberation of Palestine' (resembling *fatah* 'conquer')]

alfentanil hydrochloride /al fént'nil-/ n a drug that is an opium derivative. Use: general anaesthesia. [< *al-* + *-fentanil*, INN stem]

Alfieri /álfi áiri/, **Vittorio, Count** (1749–1803) Italian poet and dramatist. He wrote 28 plays, including *Cleopatra* (1775).

al-Fitr /al fíttər/ n *ISLAM* same as **Eid al-Fitr**

Alfonso XIII /al fónsō/ (1886–1941) king of Spain. His reign (1886–1931) was marked by riots and revolts. He was forced into exile when Spain became a republic.

Alfredo /al fréddō/ adj served with a rich sauce made from cream, butter, and Parmesan cheese [Late 20C. Origin ?]

Alfred the Great /álfrid/ (AD 849–901) king of Wessex. He reigned from 871 until his death, reconquering Danish territories in England. He also translated several Latin works into English.

alfresco /al fréskō/ adv outdoors or in the open air ■ adj taking place or located outdoors [Mid-18C. < Italian, 'in the fresh (air)']

Alfven /al vén/, **Hannes Olof Gosta** (1908–95) Swedish theoretical physicist who worked on the harnessing of nuclear fusion power and was awarded the Nobel Prize in physics (1970)

Alfven wave n a magnetic disturbance that travels along magnetic field lines in a plasma

Alg. abbr **1.** Algeria **2.** Algerian

alga /álgə/ (*plural* **-gae** /-jee, -gee/) n a photosynthetic organism of a group that lives mainly in water and includes the seaweeds. Algae differ from plants in not having true leaves, roots, or stems. [Mid-16C. < Latin, 'seaweed'] —**algal** adj —**algoid** /ál goyd/ adj

---

USAGE alga or **algae**? *Alga* is singular and *algae* is plural; it is generally regarded as incorrect to use *algae* as a singular noun.

---

algal bloom n an excessive growth of algae on or near the surface of water, occurring naturally or as a result of an excess of nutrients from organic pollution

Algarve /al gaárv/ region in southern Portugal. Its coastline is the country's leading holiday area.

algebra /áljibrə/ n **1.** the branch of mathematics in which symbols, usually letters of the alphabet, represent unknown numbers **2.** the study of structures in mathematics such as groups, rings, fields, and categories [Mid-16C. Via Italian and medieval Latin < Arabic *al-jabr* 'the reuniting', in the title of a treatise by the mathematician al-Khwarizmi] —**algebraist** /álji bráyist/ n

algebraic /álji bráyik/, **algebraical** /-bráyik'l/ adj **1.** relating to or involving algebra **2.** relating to or using only finite numbers, expressions, and operations —**algebraically** adv

Algeciras /áljə seérəss/ port and resort near the southern tip of Spain. Population: 106,710 (2002).

Alger /áljər/, **Horatio** (1834–99) US writer and member of the clergy. He wrote many novels, including *Ragged Dick* (1867) and *Tattered Tom* (1871). His works feature boys born into poverty who, through hard work, achieve wealth and success.

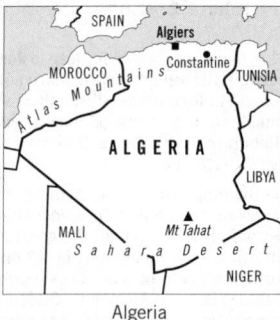
Algeria

Algeria /al jeéri ə/ country in northwestern Africa. It became independent from France in 1962. Language: Arabic. Currency: Algerian dinar. Capital: Algiers. Population: 32,818,500 (2003). Area: 2,381,741 sq. km/919,595 sq. mi. Official name **Democratic and Popular Republic of Algeria** —**Algerian** adj, n

algesia /al jeézi ə, -ssi ə/ n sensitivity to or perception of pain [< modern Latin < Greek *algēsis* < *algos* 'pain']

-algia suffix pain ○ *neuralgia* [< Greek *algos* 'pain']

algicide /álji sīd/ n a substance that kills algae or prevents their growth —**algicidal** /álji síd'l/ adj

algid /áljid/ adj describes an episode during a severe fever when the patient's body temperature suddenly drops to an unusually low level [Early 17C. < Latin *algidus* < *algere* 'be cold'] —**algidity** /al jíddəti/ n

Algiers /al jeérz/ capital, chief port, and largest city of Algeria. Population: 2,561,992 (1998).

algin /áljin/ n a viscous liquid, especially alginic acid or an alginate. Source: seaweed. Use: thickener or emulsifier in plastics or food. [Late 19C. < ALGA + -IN]

alginate /álji nayt/ n a salt or ester of alginic acid. Use: thickener or emulsifier in plastics or food.

alginic acid /al jínnik-/ n an insoluble powdery acid. Source: brown seaweed. Use: thickener in foods; adjuvant in pharmaceuticals; in antacid preparations, cosmetics, textiles. Formula: $(C_6H_8O_6)_n$.

algo- prefix pain ○ *algophobia* [< Greek *algos* 'pain']

ALGOL /ál gol/, **Algol** n a high-level computer programming language that uses algebraic symbols in solving mathematical and scientific problems. Full form **algorithm-oriented language** [Mid-20C. Contraction of *algorithm-oriented language*]

algolagnia /álgō lágni ə/ n sexual pleasure experienced through inflicting or experiencing pain [Early 20C. < Greek *algos* 'pain' + *lagneia* 'lust'] —**algolagnic** adj —**algolagnist** n

---

algology /al gólləji/ n the branch of botany concerned with the scientific study of algae —**algological** /álgə lójjik'l/ adj —**algologist** n

Algonkian n, adj *LANG, PEOPLES* another spelling of **Algonquian**

Algonkin n, adj *LANG, PEOPLES* another spelling of **Algonquin**

Algonquian /al góngki ən, -kwi-/ (*plural same* or **-ans**), **Algonkian** /-ki-/ n **1.** a group of Native North American languages that are, or were, spoken in central and eastern Canada and parts of the central and eastern United States. Algonquian includes the languages of the Arapaho, Blackfoot, Cheyenne, Delaware, Fox, Ojibwa, Sauk, and Shawnee peoples. **2.** a member of an Algonquian-speaking people [Late 19C. < ALGONQUIN] —**Algonquian** adj

LANGUAGE HERITAGE See *Native North American*.

Algonquin /al góngkin, -kwin/ (*plural same* or **-quins**), **Algonkin** /-kin/ (*plural same* or **-kins**) n **1.** a member of a group of Native North American peoples living along the Ottawa and St Lawrence Rivers in eastern Canada. Historically, the Algonquin were allies of the French against the Iroquois people. **2.** a Native North American language spoken in Quebec and Ontario. Native speakers: 3,000. [Early 17C. Via Canadian French < Algonquian] —**Algonquin** adj

algophobia /álgə fóbi ə/ n an unusually intense fear of pain

algorithm /álgə rithəm/ n **1.** a logical step-by-step procedure for solving a mathematical problem in a finite number of steps, often involving repetition of the same basic operation **2.** a logical sequence of steps for solving a problem, often written out as a flow chart, that can be translated into a computer program [Late 17C. Alteration, after Greek *arithmos* 'number', of *algorism*, via Old French and medieval Latin < Arabic *al-Kwārizmī*, name of the 9C mathematician who introduced algorithms to the West] —**algorithmic** /álgə ríthmik/ adj

Algren /áwlgrin/, **Nelson** (1909–81) US writer. His gritty fiction, often set in his native Chicago, includes the novels *The Man with the Golden Arm* (1949) and *A Walk on the Wild Side* (1956), both of which were made into successful films. Born **Abraham, Nelson Ahlgren**

Alhambra /al hámbrə/ n a citadel and palace in Granada, Spain, built for Moorish kings in the 12th and 13th centuries

Alhazen /ál hə zén/ (965–1040) Arab scientist. He made important contributions in optics, astronomy, and mathematics. Arabic name **Abu Ali al-Hasan ibn al-Haytham**

Ali /aa lí/ cousin and son-in-law of Muhammad. He became the fourth caliph. After his assassination in AD 661 following a civil war, Islam divided into two branches, the Sunni and the Shia.

Muhammad Ali

Ali, Muhammad (*b.* 1942) US boxer, three times world heavyweight champion (1964–71, 1974–78, 1978–80). Born **Clay, Cassius Marcellus**

> 'At home I am a nice guy: but I don't want the world to know. Humble people, I've found, don't get very far.'
> [Muhammad Ali, *The Sunday Express*; 13 January 1963]

Alia /áali ə/, **Ramiz** (*b.* 1925) president of Albania (1982–92). He succeeded Enver Hoxha as leader of the

---

communist party in 1985 and paved the way for general elections in 1990. He resigned in 1992 after his party was defeated at the polls.

alias /áyli əss/ *n* **1.** FALSE NAME an assumed name that somebody uses **2.** FILE OR DIRECTORY NAME a name assigned to a computer file or directory, e.g. to make it more convenient to locate or manipulate ■ *adv* ALSO KNOWN AS otherwise or also known as [15C. < Latin, 'otherwise']

alibi /álli bī/ *n* (*plural* **-bis**) **1.** ACCUSED'S CLAIM OF HAVING BEEN ELSEWHERE a form of defence against an accusation in which the accused person claims or proves that he or she was somewhere else at the time that a crime was committed **2.** SOMEBODY OR SOMETHING GIVING ALIBI somebody or something used by an accused person to prove that he or she was somewhere else at the time that a crime was committed **3.** ⚠ EXCUSE an explanation offered to justify something (*informal*) ■ *vt* (**-bis, -biing, -bied**) GIVE ALIBI FOR SOMEBODY to provide an alibi or excuse for somebody [Late 17C. < Latin, 'elsewhere']

USAGE alibi meaning 'excuse': ***Alibi*** should only be used informally in the weakened meaning 'an explanation offered to justify something', because it has a precise legal meaning that is in danger of being compromised. Avoid overuse when *excuse* is the more natural word to use: *He used his illness as an excuse* [not *as an alibi*] *for leaving work early.*

Alicante /álli kánti/ city and port in southeastern Spain. Population: 293,629 (2002).

Alice band /álliss-/ *n* a band of velvet or ribbon worn across the top of the head to hold the hair back off the face [Because Alice is shown wearing one in the original illustrations to *Through the Looking-Glass* by Lewis CARROLL]

Alice-in-Wonderland /állis in wúndər land/ *adj* absurd, fantastic, or completely at odds with reality [Early 20C. < *Alice's Adventures in Wonderland* (1865), fantasy by Lewis CARROLL]

Alice Springs /álliss-/ town in the southern part of Australia's Northern Territory, a centre of tourism. Population: 26,306 (2002 estimate).

alicyclic /álli sīklik, -sík-/ *adj* describes organic compounds that have carbon atoms joined in a string (**open chain**) as well as in rings [Late 19C. Blend of ALIPHATIC + CYCLIC]

alidade /álli dayd/ *n* an instrument consisting of a rule with sights at both ends, used in surveying for measuring angles and directions [14C. Via French and Spanish < Arabic *al-idada* 'the revolving radius']

alien /áyli ən/ *n* **1.** EXTRATERRESTRIAL BEING a being from another planet or another part of the universe, especially in works of science fiction **2.** NONCITIZEN RESIDENT OF COUNTRY a citizen of a country other than the one he or she is currently in **3.** OUTSIDER somebody who does not belong to or does not feel accepted by a group or society ■ *adj* **1.** STRANGE outside somebody's normal or previous experience and seeming strange and sometimes threatening ○ *an alien practice* **2.** INCONSISTENT WITH SOMEBODY OR SOMETHING not in keeping or totally incompatible with the nature of somebody or something ○ *ideas that were alien to her philosophy* **3.** NOT FROM COUNTRY not a citizen of, or not belonging to, the country in question **4.** EXTRATERRESTRIAL from another world or part of the universe, or relating to extraterrestrial beings, especially in works of science fiction ○ *an alien spacecraft* ■ *vt* (**-ens, -ening, -ened**) LAW same as **alienate** (sense 4) [14C. Directly or via Old French < Latin *alienus* < *alius* 'other']

alienable /áyli ənəb'l/ *adj* capable of being transferred by a legal process to another owner —**alienability** /áyli ənə bílləti/ *n*

alienate /áyli ə nayt/ (**-ates, -ating, -ated**) *vt* **1.** MAKE SOMEBODY UNFRIENDLY to cause somebody to change his or her previously friendly or supportive attitude and become unfriendly, unsympathetic, or hostile ○ *His selfishness succeeded in alienating all of his friends.* **2.** MAKE SOMEBODY FEEL DISAFFECTED to make somebody feel that he or she does not belong to or share in something, or is isolated from it (*often passive*) ○ *The long-term unemployed often feel alienated from society.* **3.** TURN SOMETHING AWAY to cause something, especially somebody's affections, to be directed towards somebody or something else **4.** LAW TRANSFER OWNERSHIP TO SOMEBODY to transfer the ownership of property or a right to somebody [15C. < Latin *alienat-*, past participle of *alienare* 'make somebody else's, alienate' < *alienus* (see ALIEN)] —**alienation** /áyli ə náysh'n/ *n* —**alienator** *n*

alienee /áyli ə nee/ *n* somebody to whom property or a right is transferred by a legal process

alienist /áyli ənist/ *n* **1.** *US* an expert witness, usually a psychiatrist, who is accepted by a court of law as qualified to assess the psychological state of somebody appearing in court **2.** same as **psychiatrist** (*archaic*) [Mid-19C. < French *aliéniste* < Latin *alienare* 'estrange, make irrational' (see ALIENATE)]

alienor /áyli ənər/ *n* somebody who transfers property or a right to somebody else by a legal process

aliform /álli fawrm, áyli-/ *adj* shaped like a wing (*technical*) [Early 18C. < Latin *ala* 'wing']

Alighieri /alli gyáiri/ ➧ **Dante**

alight[1] /ə līt/ (**alights, alighting, alighted** or **alit** /ə lít/) *vi* **1.** GET OUT OF VEHICLE to step down or dismount from something onto the ground or a platform ○ *The VIPs alighted from their train.* **2.** LAND to land or settle after a flight ○ *A magpie alighted on a branch.* **3.** FIND BY CHANCE to happen to find, spot, or come to rest on something ○ *alighted on a suitable candidate* [Old English *alīhtan* < *a-* 'away, up, out' + *līhtan* 'make lighter in weight']

alight[2] /ə līt/ *adj* **1.** ON FIRE on fire or burning ○ *set the bonfire alight* **2.** LIT UP lit up or full of light ○ *The sky was alight with fireworks.* **3.** FULL OF ENERGY filled with or radiating energy, excitement, interest, or pleasure ○ *His face was alight with joy.* [Old English *aliht* 'illuminated', past participle of *alihtan* 'light up']

align /ə līn/ (**aligns, aligning, aligned**), **aline** (**alines, alining, alined**) *v* **1.** *vti* BRING SOMETHING INTO LINE to place something in a straight line or in an orderly position in relation to something else, or be placed in this way **2.** *vti* BRING OR COME INTO CORRECT POSITION to bring something such as different parts of a machine or structure, into the correct position with respect to each other or something else, or come into this position **3.** *vti* DECLARE SUPPORT FOR SOMEBODY OR SOMETHING to declare your support, or the support of somebody or something you represent, for a person, group, argument, or point of view ○ *The government aligned itself behind NATO.* **4.** *vi* FORM LINE to become arranged in a line ○ *The marching band aligned behind the drum major.* [15C. < Old French *alignier* < Latin *linea* 'line'] —**aligner** *n*

alignment /ə līnmənt/, **alinement** *n* **1.** LINEAR OR ORDERLY ARRANGEMENT the arrangement of something in a straight line or in an orderly position in relation to something else **2.** POSITIONING OF SOMETHING FOR PROPER PERFORMANCE the correct position or positioning of different components with respect to each other or something else, so that they perform properly ○ *The wheels are out of alignment.* **3.** SUPPORT OR ALLIANCE support for, or a political alliance with, a person, group, argument, or point of view ○ *shifting alignments within the legislature* **4.** GROUND PLAN a ground plan, especially one showing the course of a road or railway line **5.** ORDERING OF TYPE the ordering of lines of type relative to a margin or line ○ *Try changing the alignment from left to right.* ○ *The vertical alignment looks uneven.*

alike /ə līk/ *adj* similar in appearance or character ○ *They're so alike, it's difficult to tell them apart.* ■ *adv* in a similar or the same way ○ *The film will please young and old alike.* [Old English *gelīc* 'alike, similar' < Germanic, 'body, form'] —**alikeness** *n*

aliment /állimənt/ *n* something that feeds, sustains, or supports something else (*formal*) [15C. Via French < Latin *alimentum* < *alere* 'nourish'] —**aliment** *vt* —**alimental** /álli mént'l/ *adj* —**alimentally** *adv*

alimentary /álli méntəri/ *adj* (*formal*) **1.** OF FOOD OR NUTRITION relating to food or nutrition **2.** PROVIDING NOURISHMENT providing food or nourishment **3.** PROVIDING SUPPORT providing support or maintenance

alimentary canal *n* the tubular passage between the mouth and the anus, including the organs through which food passes for digestion and elimination as waste

alimentation /álli men táysh'n/ *n* (*formal*) **1.** the providing of food or nourishment **2.** the providing of support or maintenance —**alimentative** /álli méntətiv/ *adj*

alimony /állimənі/ *n* maintenance paid to a former spouse [Early 17C. < Latin *alimonia* 'subsistence' < *alere* 'nourish']

aline *vti* another spelling of **align**

A-line *adj* resembling the outline of the letter A, especially in a garment by flaring out from the top to the bottom ○ *an A-line dress*

alinement *n* another spelling of **alignment**

aliphatic /álli fáttik/ *adj* describes organic compounds that have carbon atoms joined in a string (**open chain**) [Late 19C. < Greek *aleiphat-* 'fat', because originally applied to fatty acids]

aliquant /állikwənt, -kwont/ *adj* describes a number or quantity that cannot divide another number or quantity without leaving a remainder [Late 17C. < Latin *aliquantum* 'somewhat']

aliquot /álli kwot/ *adj* describes a number or quantity that will divide another number or quantity without leaving a remainder ■ *n* an aliquot part [Late 16C. Via French < Latin, 'a certain number']

A list *n* the people most sought after or most in demand for an activity such as a social function or for recruitment to a team or organization (*informal*; *hyphenated when used before a noun*)

alit past participle, past tense of **alight**[1]

aliterate /ay líttərət/ *n* somebody who, though usually able to read, is completely uninterested in reading or literature —**aliteracy** *n* —**aliterate** *adj*

alive /ə līv/ *adj* **1.** LIVING living, especially still living, and not dead **2.** OF ALL PEOPLE LIVING of all people currently living (*usually used with a superlative*) ○ *the luckiest person alive* **3.** STILL IN EXISTENCE still existing, continuing, or functioning ○ *The movement remained alive by going underground.* **4.** FULL OF LIFE full of energy and vigour, and with a zest for and interest in life ○ *He feels alive only when he is writing his book.* **5.** ANIMATED active or animated, especially full of busy activity or a sense of excitement ○ *The place doesn't come alive till after midnight.* **6.** STILL INTERESTING still interesting, relevant, or vividly imaginable for people in the present day ○ *Her brief was to make the subject come alive for a modern audience.* **7.** SWARMING WITH SOMETHING full of or swarming with people or animals ○ *The floor of the tent was alive with ants.* **8.** AWARE OF SOMETHING sensitive to or aware of things ○ *alive to the danger involved in the operation* [Old English *on līfe* 'in life'] —**aliveness** *n* ◇ **alive and kicking** still active, healthy, or functioning vigorously (*informal*)

aliyah /álli yaá/ *n* **1.** immigration into Israel by Jews **2.** the honour of being nominated to give a reading from the Torah [Mid-20C. < Hebrew, 'ascent']

alizarin /ə lízzərin/ *n* an orange-red or brownish-yellow crystalline compound. Source: coal tar, formerly madder root. Use: dyes. Formula: $C_{14}H_8O_4$. [Mid-19C. < French *alizarine*, probably < Arabic *alizari* 'madder']

Al Jazeera /ál jə zeérə/, **Al Jezera** *n* an independent Arab television station in Qatar [< Arabic *Al-Jazīrah*, literally 'the peninsula']

al-Kadr *n* ISLAM same as **Lailat al-Qadr**

alkahest /álkə hest/, **alcahest** *n* a hypothetical universal solvent sought by alchemists [Mid-17C. Coined by Paracelsus, in imitation of Arabic] —**alkahestic** /álkə héstik/ *adj*

alkalescent /álkə léss'nt/ *adj* slightly alkaline, or becoming alkaline —**alkalescence** *n*

alkali /álkə lī/ (*plural* **-lis** or *same*) *n* **1.** a water-soluble chemical that reacts with acids to form salts, has a pH above 7, and turns red litmus paper blue **2.** a soluble mineral salt found in some dry soils and natural waters at levels harmful to agriculture [14C. Via medieval Latin < Arabic *al-kalī* 'the ashes of saltwort', from which it was first obtained]

alkali metal *n* a metallic element belonging to group 1 of the periodic table, either lithium, sodium, potassium, rubidium, caesium, or francium, characterized by being soft, white, and highly reactive

alkalimeter /álkə límmitər/ *n* an instrument used for measuring the concentration of alkalis in a solution —**alkalimetric** /álkəli méttrik/ *adj* —**alkalimetrically** *adv* —**alkalimetry** *n*

alkaline /álkə līn/ *adj* having the properties of an alkali, or containing an alkali or alkalis

alkaline-earth metal, **alkaline earth** *n* a metallic element belonging to group 2 of the periodic table, either beryllium, magnesium, calcium, strontium, barium, or radium, characterized by having a valency of two

alkaline phosphatase *n* an enzyme that controls hydrolysis. Use: in clinical diagnosis of many illnesses.

alkalinity /álkə línnəti/ *n* the concentration of alkali in a solution, measured in terms of pH

alkalize /álkə līz/ (**-lizes, -lizing, -lized**), **alkalise** (**-lises, -lising, -lised**) *vti* to make something alkaline, or become alkaline

alkaloid /álkə loyd/ *n* a group of nitrogen-containing compounds that are physiologically active as poisons or drugs [Early 19C. < ALKALI, because their chemical properties are similar to it] —**alkaloidal** /álkə lóyd'l/ *adj*

alkalosis /álkə lṓssiss/ *n* an unusually high level of alkalinity in the blood, other body fluids, or body tissues, causing a high blood pH —**alkalotic** /álkə lóttik/ *adj*

alkane /ál kayn/ *n* an open-chain hydrocarbon containing only carbon-to-carbon or carbon-to-hydrogen single bonds and belonging to a series whose members all have the same general chemical formula. Formula: C_nH_{2n+2}.

alkanet /álkə net/ (*plural* **-nets** or *same*) *n* **1.** RED DYE a red dye obtained from the roots of a European plant **2.** EUROPEAN DYE PLANT a plant related to borage with red roots that produce alkanet. Flowers: small, blue. Native to: Europe. Latin name: *Alkanna tinctoria.* **3.** PLANT RELATED TO ALKANET a bristly plant related to alkanet. Flowers: blue. Native to: Europe, Asia, Africa. Genus: *Anchusa.* [14C. Probably via Old Spanish *alcaneta* < Arabic *al-hinnā'* 'the henna']

alkaptonuria /al káptə nyoóri ə/ *n* a rare genetic disease characterized by arthritis and the destruction of connective tissue and bone [Late 19C. < German *Alkapton*, an acid + -URIA]

alkene /ál keen/ *n* an open-chain hydrocarbon containing one carbon-to-carbon double bond and belonging to a series whose members all have the same general chemical formula. Formula: C_nH_{2n}.

alkie *n* SOC SCI another spelling of **alky** (*slang offensive*)

alkoxide /al kóksīd/ *n* a salt formed by replacing the hydroxyl ion of an alcohol with a metal [Late 19C. < ALKALI + OXY- + -IDE]

alky /álki/ (*plural* **-kies**), **alkie** *n* an offensive term for somebody who is an alcoholic or who drinks to excess (*slang*) [Mid-20C. Shortening]

alkyd /ál kid/, **alkyd resin** *n* a sticky resin that is prepared from phthalic acid and glycerol and becomes liquid or plastic when heated. Use: paints, lacquer. [Early 20C. < ALKYL + ACID]

alkyl /ál kil/ *adj* describes a hydrocarbon group derived from an alkane, e.g. the ethyl group [Late 19C. < German < *Alkohol* 'alcohol' + -YL]

alkylation /álki láysh'n/ *n* the addition of an alkyl group to a chemical compound through the replacement of a hydrogen atom

alkyne /ál kīn/ *n* an open-chain hydrocarbon containing one carbon-to-carbon triple bond and belonging to a series whose members all have the same general chemical formula. Formula: C_nH_{2n-2}.

all /awl/ CORE MEANING: a grammatical word used to indicate that the whole of a particular thing, amount, group, or area is involved or affected ○ (det) *all men and all women* ○ (pron) *All of the computers are down.* ○ (pron) *All that glitters is not gold.*

1. *det* WHOLE OF used to indicate that the whole of an amount, area, quantity, or thing is involved or affected ○ *All Europe was in the grip of freezing temperatures.* **2.** *det* EVERY every one of ○ *all employees over 30* **3.** *det* ANY any whatever (*used after a negative word such as 'refuse' or 'deny'*) ○ *Deny all connection with the plot.* **4.** *det* MOST the greatest possible ○ *with all speed* **5.** *det* CHARACTERIZED BY dominated in mood or character by something (*informal*) ○ *He was all smiles.* **6.** *adv* VERY very, completely, or totally (*informal*) ○ *I got all confused.* **7.** *adv* APIECE to or for each one ○ *The score was thirty all.* **8.** *pron* EVERY ONE OR WHOLE the whole number or amount (*takes a plural verb*) ○ *All of us are going to the match.* **9.** *pron* EVERYONE OR EVERYTHING the whole quantity or group ○ *All that glitters is not gold.* **10.** *n* SOMEBODY'S BEST EFFORT the greatest amount of somebody's ability or effort ○ *He gave his all in the performance.* [Old English *eall* < Germanic] ◇ **all along** from the start, or for the whole time that something else was taking place ○ *I knew all along he was lying.* ◇ **all but** almost ○ *I was all but asleep when the phone rang.* ◇ **all how** *Carib* **1.** completely **2.** no matter how ◇ **all now** *Carib* **1.** right away **2.** same as **still**[2] **3.** by this time ◇ **(all) in all** when everything has been taken into account ○ *All in all, it was a good party.* ◇ **all of** no less than (*informal*) ○ *It took us all of three hours to get here.* ◇ **all or nothing** used to indicate that only complete success or obtaining everything counts, and that anything less than that has no value ◇ **all that** very, particularly, or to that extent (*informal; usually used in negative statements or questions*) ○ *I'm not all that worried about it.* ◇ **all the same 1.** none the less ○ *It rained a bit but the children enjoyed their day out all the same.* **2.** used to indicate that it is unimportant to the speaker which of two or more things is done or chosen ○ *I'd rather go by train, if it's all the same to you.* ◇ **all there** fully alert, aware of what is going on, and able to deal with it (*informal*) ◇ **all very well** used to indicate that there is some kind of objection or drawback, despite the fact that somebody else is apparently satisfied with the situation ○ *That's all very well, but it's still my responsibility.* ◇ **be all over somebody** to be extremely or excessively friendly or effusive towards somebody (*informal*) ◇ **in all** in total ○ *That makes 52 votes in all for our candidate.*

SPELLCHECK Do not confuse the spelling of ***all*** and ***awl*** ('a sharp-pointed tool'), which sound similar.

USAGE all or **all of**? You have a choice between ***all*** and ***all of*** when the following noun is qualified by *the, this, that, these, those*, or a possessive determiner such as *my* and *your*: *All my life I've wanted to be a singer. All of my life I've wanted to be a singer. All these things worried them. All of these things worried them.*

alla breve /állə bráyvi/ MUSIC *n* a time signature represented by a C with a slash through it, specifying a beat of two or four minims to the bar ■ *adv* at twice the normal speed (*used as a musical direction*) [< Italian, 'according to the breve'] —**alla breve** *adj*

all-age *adj* intended or suitable for all age groups

all-age personals *npl* advertisements by people of all ages who have an interest in finding romantic partners, usually placed with an online dating agency

Allah /állə/ *n* in Islam, the name of God [Late 16C. < Arabic *'allāh*]

Allahabad /álləhə bad/ city in northern India in Uttar Pradesh State. Located at the confluence of the Yamuna and Ganges rivers, it is an important pilgrimage destination for Hindus. Population: 858,213 (1991). Former name **Prayag**

allamanda /állə mándə/ (*plural* **-das** or *same*) *n* an evergreen bush. Flowers: yellow, purple, trumpet-shaped. Native to: tropical America. Genus: *Allamanda.* [Late 18C. After J. N. S. *Allamand* (1713–87), Swiss scientist]

all-American *adj* **1.** OF OR ABOUT UNITED STATES of or about the United States, its people, or their way of life, or representing them at their best **2.** BEST IN UNITED STATES selected and honoured as the best amateur player or athlete in the United States in a position or event ○ *an all-American linebacker* **3.** MADE OF US COMPONENTS made up entirely of people, materials, or components from the United States **4.** OF ALL AMERICAS including all the countries of North and South America, or representatives from them ○ *an all-American agreement* ■ *n* **1.** BEST US ATHLETE a player or athlete chosen as being the best in the United States in a position or event **2.** TEAM OF BEST US PLAYERS a team made up of the best US players or athletes

allantoin /ə lántō in/ *n* a drug used in the treatment of skin disorders [Mid-19C. < ALLANTOIS, because first found in the allantoic fluid of cows]

allantois /állən tṓ iss/ (*plural* **-ides** /-ideez/) *n* a membranous sac that grows from the lower gut in mammal, bird, and reptile embryos. In mammals, it combines with the chorion to form the umbilical cord and placenta. [Mid-17C. Via modern Latin < Greek *allantoeidēs* 'sausage-like', because of its shape] —**allantoic** *adj*

allargando /állaar gándō/ *adv* at a gradually slower tempo, with a broadening stately sound (*used as a musical direction*) ■ *n* (*plural* **-dos** or **-di** /-gándi/) a section of a piece of music played allargando [Late 19C. < Italian, 'broadening'] —**allargando** *adj*

all-around *adj US* same as **all-round**

allay /ə láy/ (**-lays, -laying, -layed**) *vt* **1.** to calm a strong emotion such as anger, or diminish and set at rest somebody's fears or suspicions **2.** to relieve or reduce the severity of pain or a painful emotion [Old English *ālecgan* 'lay aside' (see LAY[1]). The meaning was influenced by Old French *aleger* 'lighten' and *aleier* 'moderate'] —**allayer** *n*

All Blacks *npl* the New Zealand international Rugby Union team

all-choice *adj US* describes a school system that allows people to choose a school to attend

all clear *n* **1.** SIGNAL THAT DANGER IS OVER a signal that a period of danger is over, especially one sounded on a siren after an air raid **2.** SIGNAL TO PROCEED a signal or notification that something may proceed ○ *We've got the all clear to start building.* **3.** FOOTBALL SIGNAL THAT GOAL KICK IS VALID in Australian Rules football, a signal given by the field umpire to the goal umpire to indicate that there has been no foul play before a kick on goal. The goal umpire then indicates whether a goal or a behind has been scored.

all-comers *npl* everyone who wants to participate in a competition or sport

all-consuming *adj* absorbing somebody's attention, time, or energy to the exclusion of everything else

~~alledged~~ incorrect spelling of **alleged**

allegation /álli gáysh'n/ *n* **1.** an assertion, especially relating to wrongdoing or misconduct on somebody's part, that has yet to be proved or supported by evidence **2.** the alleging of something, especially wrongdoing

allege /ə léj/ (**-leges, -leging, -leged**) *vt* **1.** to state or assert something, especially by accusing somebody of wrongdoing without offering proof of it or with a view to proving it later ○ *The prosecutor alleged that Simmons knew about the planned hold-up.* **2.** to put something forward as a reason or excuse for your actions or conduct (*formal*) ○ *He declined the invitation, alleging a prior appointment.* [14C. Via Anglo-Norman, 'declare before a legal tribunal' < assumed Vulgar Latin *exlitigare* 'clear of charges' < Latin *litigare* (see LITIGATE)] —**allegeable** *adj* —**alleger** *n*

alleged /ə léjd/ *adj* asserted but not yet proven to have taken place, have been committed, or be as described —**allegedly** /ə léjjidli/ *adv*

Alleghenies same as **Allegheny Mountains**

Allegheny /állə gáyni/ river in Pennsylvania and New York, flowing north from its headwaters in Pennsylvania into New York before turning south again to join the Monongahela River at Pittsburgh to create the Ohio River. Length: 523 km/325 mi.

Allegheny Mountains, **Alleghenies** /állə gayniz/ western mountain range of the Appalachian Mountains, in Pennsylvania, Maryland, West Virginia, and Virginia. The range is the divide between those rivers emptying into the Gulf of Mexico and those flowing into the Atlantic Ocean. The highest peak is Spruce Knob 1,482 m/4,861ft.

allegiance /ə leéjənss/ *n* **1.** LOYALTY TO RULER OR STATE a subject's or citizen's loyalty to a ruler or state, or the duty of obedience and loyalty owed by a subject or citizen **2.** DEVOTED SUPPORT loyalty to or support for a person, cause, or group ○ *The match was a treat for all fans, whatever their allegiance.* **3.** FEUDAL OBLIGATION the feudal obligation of a vassal to a liege lord [14C. < Anglo-Norman variant of Old French *ligeance* < *lige* (see LIEGE)] —**allegiant** *adj*

~~allegience~~ incorrect spelling of **allegiance**

allegorical /álli górrik'l/, **allegoric** /-górrik/ *adj* **1.** expressing something through an allegory **2.** relating to or used in allegory —**allegorically** *adv*

allegorize /álligə rīz/ (**-rizes, -rizing, -rized**), **allegorise** (**-rises, -rising, -rised**) *v* **1.** *vti* to express something

in the form of an allegory **2.** *vt* to interpret or treat something as an allegory —**allegorization** /álligə rī záysh'n/ *n* —**allegorizer** *n*

allegory /álligəri/ (*plural* **-ries**) *n* **1. SYMBOLIC WORK** a work in which the characters and events are to be understood as representing other things and symbolically expressing a deeper, often spiritual, moral, or political meaning **2. SYMBOLIC EXPRESSION OF MEANING IN STORY** the symbolic expression of a deeper meaning through a story or scene acted out by human, animal, or mythical characters ○ *the poet's use of allegory* **3. GENRE** allegories considered as a literary or artistic genre **4. SYMBOLIC REPRESENTATION** a symbolic representation of something [14C. < Latin *allegoria* < Greek *allegorein* 'say otherwise' < *allos* 'other' + *agoreuein* 'speak in public'] —**allegorist** *n*

allegretto /álli gréttō/ *adv* at a fairly quick tempo (*used as a musical direction*) ■ *n* (*plural* **-tos**) a piece of music, or a section of a piece, played allegretto [Mid-18C. < Italian, 'less than allegro'] —**allegretto** *adj*

allegro /ə láygrō, ə léggrō/ *adv* at a quick and lively tempo (*used as a musical direction*) ■ *n* (*plural* **-gros**) a piece of music, or a section of a piece, played allegro [Late 17C. < Italian, 'lively'] —**allegro** *adj*

allele /ə leél/ *n* one of two or more alternative forms of a gene, occupying the same position (**locus**) on paired chromosomes and controlling the same inherited characteristic [Mid-20C. < German *Allel*, shortening of *Allelomorph* 'allelomorph'] —**allelic** *adj* —**allelism** *n*

allelo- *prefix* one another ○ *allelopathy* [< Greek *allēlōn* < *allos* 'other' (see ALLO-)]

allelochemical /ə leélə kémmik'l/ *n* a chemical produced by one plant that is toxic to another

allelomorph /ə leélə mawrf, ə léllə-/ *n* GENETICS same as **allele** —**allelomorphic** /ə leélə máwrfik, ə léllə-/ *adj* —**allelomorphism** *n*

allelopathy /álli lóppəthi/ *n* the release into the environment by one plant of a substance that inhibits the germination or growth of other potential competitor plants of the same or another species —**allelopathic** /ə leélə páthik, -léllə-/ *adj*

allelotoxin /ə leélə tóksin/ *n* BOT same as **allelochemical**

alleluia *interj, n* same as **hallelujah**

allemande /álli mand/ *n* **1. MUSICAL MOVEMENT FORMING PART OF SUITE** a stately piece of music in moderate tempo and four-four time, often used as the opening movement of a baroque or classical suite **2. POPULAR 18C DANCE** a stately dance of German origin popular in France in the 18th century **3. DANCE MOVEMENT** a movement used in country dancing that involves partners changing positions, often by interlinking arms [Late 17C. < French, 'German']

all-embracing *adj* including all or everything without discrimination

Allen /állən/ ◗ **Van Allen, James**

Allen, Paul (*b.* 1953) US business executive. He was a cofounder of Microsoft Corporation (1975) and after his retirement in 1983 extended his business interests to multimedia and communications companies and sports teams.

Allen, Peter (1944–92) Australian singer and songwriter. His songs include 'I Go to Rio' (1977). Born **Woolnough, Peter**

Allen, Woody (*b.* 1935) US film director, actor, screenwriter, playwright, and humorous essayist. His films include the Academy Award-winning *Annie Hall* (1977). Born **Konigsberg, Allen Stewart**

> 'I don't want to achieve immortality through my work...I want to achieve it through not dying.'
> [Woody Allen. Quoted in *Woody Allen and His Comedy*, Eric Lax; 1975]

Allenby /állənbi/, **Edmund Henry Hynman, 1st Viscount** (1861–1936) British soldier who commanded the Third Army in France in World War I and also took Jerusalem from the Turks (1917)

all-encompassing *adj* including or affecting everyone or everything

Allende /aa yén day/, **Isabel** (*b.* 1942) Chilean author. She fled to Venezuela in 1973 when her uncle, Salvador Allende, president of Chile, died during a military coup. Her novel *La casa de los espíritus* (1982) (*The House of Spirits* (1985) combines elements of magic, realism, and intensely personal material.

Allende, Salvador (1908–73) president of Chile (1970–73). A founder of the Chilean socialist party, he died during the military coup led by General Pinochet that ended his presidency. Full name **Allende Gossens, Salvador**

allene /álleen/ *n* a colourless unstable gas. Use: manufacture of chemicals. Formula: C_3H_4. [Late 19C. Contraction of *allylene*, a gaseous hydrocarbon]

Allen key *n UK, Aus, Can* a tool in the form of an L-shaped rod, hexagonal in cross section, made in different sizes to turn corresponding sizes of Allen screws. US term **Allen wrench** [See ALLEN SCREW]

Allen screw *n* a screw with a hexagonal recess in its head that allows it to be turned using an Allen key [Mid-20C. After the *Allen* Manufacturing Company of Hartford, Connecticut, US]

Allen wrench *n Aus, N Am* same as **Allen key**

allergen /állər jen, -jən/ *n* any substance that causes an allergic reaction —**allergenic** /állər jénnik/ *adj*

allergic /ə lúrjik/ *adj* **1. HAVING ALLERGY** having an allergy to a substance ○ *allergic to dust mites* **2. CAUSED BY ALLERGY** typical of or caused by an allergy ○ *an allergic reaction* **3. HAVING DISLIKE** having a strong aversion to something or somebody (*informal*) ○ *allergic to loud music*

allergic purpura *n* a form of the skin condition purpura caused by inflammation of blood vessels, found most often in children

allergist /állərjist/ *n* a doctor who specializes in allergies and their treatment

allergy /állərji/ (*plural* **-gies**) *n* **1.** unusual sensitivity to a normally harmless substance that provokes a strong reaction from a person's body. The body is sensitized by the immune system's response to the first exposure to the substance, and the reaction takes place only upon subsequent exposures. **2.** a strong aversion to something (*informal*) ○ *an allergy to washing* [Early 20C. < German *Allergie* < Greek *allos* 'other' (see ALLO-), after *Energie* 'energy']

allethrin /a léthrin/ *n* a clear or amber-coloured viscous liquid. Use: insecticide. Formula: $C_{19}H_{26}O_3$. [Mid-20C. Blend of ALLYL + PYRETHRIN]

alleviate /ə leévi ayt/ (**-ates, -ating, -ated**) *vt* to make something such as pain or hardship more bearable or less severe ○ *Nothing could alleviate her despair.* [Early 16C. < late Latin *alleviat-*, past participle of *alleviare* 'lighten' < Latin *levis* 'light (in weight)'] —**alleviation** /ə leévi áysh'n/ *n* —**alleviative** /-ətiv/ *adj* —**alleviator** *n* —**alleviatory** *adj*

alley[1] /álli/ (*plural* **-leys**) *n* **1. SMALL STREET** a short or narrow street **2. NARROW PASSAGE** a narrow passageway or lane, especially one running between or behind buildings **3. PATH IN GARDEN OR PARK** a path in a garden or park, especially one between trees or bushes **4.** BOWLING same as **bowling alley** (sense 2) **5.** *N Am* TENNIS **PART OF TENNIS COURT** either of the two spaces, one on each side of a court, between the singles and doubles sidelines [14C. < Old French *alee* 'a walk' < Latin *ambulare* (see AMBULATE)] ◇ **right up** *or* **down somebody's alley** *US* completely suited to somebody's interest, expertise, or line of work

alley[2] /álli/ *n* a large playing marble [Early 18C. Shortening of ALABASTER, from which they were originally made]

Alley /álli/, **Rewi** (1897–1987) New Zealand poet and translator, author of *Today and Tomorrow* (1975). He lived in China for 60 years, where he organized workers' cooperatives.

alley cat *n* **1.** a stray cat, usually in bad condition or half wild, that lives on the streets **2.** *US* somebody thought to be disreputable or fierce-tempered, or thought to have loose morals

alley-oop /álli óop/ *interj* **ENCOURAGEMENT ON GETTING UP** used as a word of encouragement to somebody who is getting up, being helped up, or lifting something (*dated*) ■ *n* **1. TYPE OF MOVE IN BASKETBALL** in basketball, a play in which a player jumps up to receive a pass over the basket and immediately puts the ball into the net from above **2. TYPE OF PASS IN BASKETBALL** in basketball, a pass aimed to allow a player to jump up to receive it over the basket **3. SNOWBOARDING AND SURFING MANOEUVRE** in snowboarding and surfing, a rotation of 180° or more made in the air while moving in an uphill or upwards direction (*slang*) **4. SKATEBOARDING MANOEUVRE** in skateboarding, a trick performed in the opposite direction to which the skateboarder is moving (*slang*) [Early 20C. < French *allez* 'come on!' + *houp* 'upsadaisy!']

alleyway /álli way/ *n* an alley or narrow passageway

all-fired *adv US* in an excessive or inordinate way (*informal*) ○ *Don't act so all-fired high and mighty.* [Early 19C. Alteration of *hell-fired*]

All Fools' Day *n* CALENDAR same as **April Fools' Day**

all fours *n* CARDS same as **seven-up** ◇ **on all fours** crawling along or crouched down on the hands and knees

Allhallows /awl hállōz/ (*plural same*), **Allhallowmas** /-hállōməss/ *n* CALENDAR same as **All Saints' Day** (*archaic; takes a singular verb*) [Old English *ealra hālgena* 'of all saints' < *hālga* 'saint' < *hālig* 'holy' (see HOLY)]

Allhallows' Eve *n* CALENDAR same as **Halloween** (*archaic*)

allheal /áwl heel/ (*plural* **-heals** or *same*) *n* a plant traditionally believed to have healing powers, e.g. valerian or selfheal

alliance /ə lī́ ənss/ *n* **1. ASSOCIATION OF GROUPS WITH COMMON AIM** an association of groups, people, or nations who agree to cooperate to achieve a common goal **2. FORMING OF ALLIANCE** the establishment of or participation in an alliance **3. MEMBERS OF ALLIANCE** the nations, people, or groups that make up an alliance ○ *the enemy alliance* **4. CLOSE RELATIONSHIP** a close relationship, based on similar aims or characteristics ○ *the first university to emphasize research in alliance with teaching* **5. MARRIAGE** a marriage uniting family interests ○ *an alliance between the king's daughter and the emperor* [13C. < Old French *aliance* < *alier* 'to ally' (see ALLY)]

Alliance /ə lī́ ənss/ *n* in New Zealand, a left-wing political party formed from a coalition of smaller parties in 1991. It has been in government in coalition with the Labour Party since 1999.

allied /állīd, ə lī́d/ *adj* **1. JOINED WITH OTHERS IN ALLIANCE** joined in an alliance with other nations, people, or groups **2. ASSOCIATED** in a close relationship ○ *allied banks* **3. OF SIMILAR TYPE** of a similar or related type ○ *sociology and allied studies*

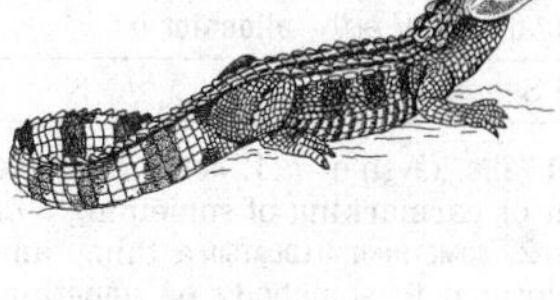

alligator

alligator /álli gaytər/ *n* **1.** (*plural* **alligators** or *same*) **LARGE REPTILE** a large reptile that lives near water, has thick scaly skin, powerful jaws, a long tail, and a shorter and broader snout than a crocodile. Native to: southern United States, China. Genus: *Alligator*. **2. LEATHER** leather made from alligator skin **3. TOOL OR MACHINE WITH MOVABLE JAW** a tool or machine with a strong, movable, often toothed jaw for gripping or crushing [Mid-16C. Alteration of Spanish *el lagarto* 'the lizard' < Latin *lacertus*]

alligator clip *n Aus, N Am* a narrow clasp with a spring and serrated jaws for making temporary electrical connections. UK term **crocodile clip** [Because it resembles an alligator's jaws]

alligator pear *n N Am* FOOD same as **avocado** (sense 1) [Mid-18C. Alteration of American Spanish *aguacate* 'avocado', perhaps because of the rough dark skin of some varieties]

alligator snapping turtle, alligator snapper *n* a large freshwater snapping turtle. Native to: Gulf States of the United States. Latin name: *Macroclemys temmincki*.

all-important *adj* vitally important or necessary

all in *adj* 1. including everything, especially all costs (*hyphenated when used before a noun*) ○ *Is that the all-in price?* 2. extremely tired (*informal*) ○ *We were all in by the time we got back to the hotel.*

all-inclusive *adj* including or encompassing everything that is expected or appropriate

Allingham /állingəm/, **Margery** (1904–66) British writer. She produced a long series of detective novels, including *Tiger in the Smoke* (1952).

all-in-one *adj* 1. performing two or more functions, or made up of two or more things 2. describes a single-piece garment —**all-in-one** *n*

all-in wrestling *n* a style of professional wrestling with relatively few restrictions on the permissible types of hold, blow, or throw

alliterate /ə lítti rayt/ (**-ates, -ating, -ated**) *v* 1. *vi* to begin consecutive or neighbouring words with the same consonant sound, or contain such sound matches 2. *vti* to use alliteration in speaking or writing, or arrange words or construct sentences so as to achieve the effect of alliteration [Late 18C. Back-formation < ALLITERATION] —**alliterative** /ə líttirətiv/ *adj* —**alliteratively** *adv*

alliteration /ə líttə ráysh'n/ *n* a poetic or literary effect achieved by using several words that begin with the same or similar consonants, as in 'Whither wilt thou wander, wayfarer?' [Early 17C. < medieval Latin *alliteration-* < Latin *littera* 'letter of the alphabet']

~~allmost~~ incorrect spelling of **almost**

all-night *adj* lasting, open, or available throughout the night, or throughout a specific night ○ *an all-night rave*

all-nighter /áwl nītər/ *n* a study or work session, entertainment, or other event that lasts throughout an entire night (*informal*)

allo- *prefix* other, different, alternate ○ *allosteric* ○ *allophone* [< Greek *allos* 'other' < Indo-European, 'other of more than two']

Alloa /állō ə/ seaport on the River Forth in Scotland. It is an important engineering centre. Population: 18,842 (1991).

allocate /állə kayt/ (**-cates, -cating, -cated**) *vt* 1. to give something to or set something aside for a person or purpose ○ *Each team member has been allocated a specific task.* 2. to share out or divide up something between a number of different people or projects ○ *Much depends on how we allocate the time available for discussion.* [Mid-17C. < medieval Latin *allocat-*, past participle of *allocare* 'put in place' < Latin *locus* 'place'] —**allocable** /álləkəb'l/ *adj* —**allocator** *n*

SYNONYMS See ***share***[1].

allocation /állə káysh'n/ *n* 1. ACT OF ALLOCATING the assignment or earmarking of something ○ *allocation of duties* 2. SOMETHING ALLOCATED a thing, amount, or share allocated to somebody or something ○ *The department has already used its entire allocation.* 3. ACCT SYSTEM OF DIVIDING INCOME AMONG DEPARTMENTS the system or practice of dividing a company's income and overheads among its various departments

allochthonous /ə lókthənəss/ *adj* 1. describes features of the landscape or elements of its geological structure that have been moved to their current position through tectonic forces 2. describes flora, fauna, or inhabitants that have moved to the region in which they are found from elsewhere [Early 20C. < Greek *allochthon* < *allo-* 'other' + *khthōn* 'soil']

allocution /állə kyóosh'n/ *n* a formal speech or address, especially one that contains an authoritative statement on a subject or an exhortation to somebody [Early 17C. < Latin *allocution-* < *alloqui* 'speak to' < *loqui* 'speak']

allogamy /ə lóggəmi/ *n* the process of cross-fertilization in flowering plants —**allogamous** *adj*

allogeneic /állō jə née ik/, **allogenic** /-jénnik/ *adj* describes tissues that are genetically different and therefore incompatible when transplanted [Mid-20C. < ALLO- + Greek *genea* 'race, generation'] —**allogeneically** *adv*

allograft /állō graaft/ *n* a graft of tissue from one member of a species to a genetically different member of the same species

allograph /állə graaf, -graf/ *n* 1. something, especially a signature, written by one person on another's behalf 2. a letter or combination of letters that is one of a set that can be used to represent the same speech sound (**phoneme**), e.g. 's', 'ss', and 'c' in English

allomerism /ə lómmərizəm/ *n* similarity in the crystal structure of substances that are chemically different —**allomerous** *adj*

allometry /ə lómmətri/ *n* measurement of the rate of growth of a part or parts of an organism relative to the growth of the whole organism. This rate determines the organism's final shape. —**allometric** /állə méttrik/ *adj*

allomone /állə mōn/ *n* a chemical substance produced by a plant in response to attack by other organisms [Late 20C. < ALLO- + PLANT HORMONE]

allomorph /állə mawrf/ *n* 1. a letter or combination of letters that is part of a set used to represent the same basic grammatical element (**morpheme**) of a language. '-ed' and '-t' both form the English past tense and are allomorphs. 2. a different crystal form of the same mineral, chemical compound, or element [Mid-20C. < ALLO- + MORPHEME] —**allomorphic** /állə máwrfik/ *adj* —**allomorphism** *n*

allopathy /ə lóppəthi/ *n* the treatment of a disease by using remedies whose effects differ from those produced by that disease. This is the principle of mainstream medical practice, as opposed to that of homeopathy. —**allopath** /állə path/ *n* —**allopathic** /állə páthik/ *adj* —**allopathically** *adv*

allopatric /állə páttrik/ *adj* describes species or populations that do not interbreed because they are geographically isolated from one another [Mid-20C. < ALLO- + Greek *patra* 'homeland' < *patēr* 'father'] —**allopatrically** *adv* —**allopatry** /ə lóppətri/ *n*

allophane /állə fayn/ *n* an amorphous, variously coloured, hydrated aluminosilicate mineral [Early 19C. < Greek *allophanēs* 'appearing otherwise' (because it changes colour when heated) < *allos* 'other' + *phainesthai* 'appear']

allophone /állə fōn/ *n* one of the slightly differing forms that the same single speech sound (**phoneme**) can take [Mid-20C. < ALLO- + PHONEME] —**allophonic** /állə fónnik/ *adj* —**allophonically** *adv*

allopurinol /állō pyóori nol/ *n* a drug that blocks production of uric acid. Use: gout treatment. [Mid-20C. < ALLO- + PURINE]

All-Ordinaries Index *n* an index of the daily change in share prices on the Australian Stock Market, based on the average price change in the shares of a selection of top Australian companies

All-Ords *n Aus* FIN same as **All-Ordinaries Index** (*informal*)

all-or-none *adj US* functioning or taking effect either completely or not at all

all-or-nothing *adj* 1. bound to result either in complete success or total failure 2. unwilling to accept anything less than all ○ *an all-or-nothing approach to negotiating*

allosaurus /állə sawrəss/ *n* a very large carnivorous theropod dinosaur of the late Upper Jurassic period. Native to: North America. Genus: *Allosaurus.* [Late 19C. < modern Latin < Greek *allos* 'other'+ *sauros* 'lizard']

allosteric /állō stéerik/ *adj* describes a binding site on an enzyme at which interaction induces altered activity at another site —**allosterically** *adv* —**allostery** /ə lóstəri/ *n*

allot /ə lót/ (**-lots, -lotting, -lotted**) *vt* 1. to give something to somebody as a share of what is available or what has to be done ○ *I was allotted the task of sweeping up.* 2. to earmark or reserve something for a purpose ○ *allotting ten shelves to books* [15C. < Old French *aloter* < *lot* 'portion' < Germanic] —**allottee** /ə lot ée/ *n* —**allotter** *n*

USAGE See ***lot***.

SYNONYMS See ***share***[1].

allotment /ə lótmənt/ *n* 1. PLOT OF LAND a small plot of publicly owned land rented to a person for growing vegetables or flowers 2. ALLOTTING OF SOMETHING the assignment or earmarking of something ○ *the allotment of shares* 3. SOMETHING ALLOTTED a thing or amount allotted to somebody or something

allotransplant *vt* /állō transs plaant, -traanss-/ (**-plants, -planting, -planted**) to transplant an organ or body tissue from one member of a species to a genetically different member of the same species ■ *n* /állō tránss plaant, -traanss-/ an organ or piece of body tissue transplanted from one member of a species to a genetically different member of the same species

allotrope /állə trōp/ *n* one of many forms in which a chemical element occurs, each differing in physical properties, e.g. diamonds and coal as forms of carbon —**allotropic** /állə tróppik/ *adj* —**allotropically** *adv*

allotropy /ə lóttrəpi/, **allotropism** /-izəm/ *n* the existence of a chemical element in more than one form (**allotrope**), each having different physical but the same chemical properties

all'ottava /állə taávə/ *adv* to be played an octave higher or lower than written (*used as a musical direction*) [Early 19C. < Italian, 'on the octave'] —**all'ottava** *adj*

allottee /ə lot ée/ *n* somebody to whom something is allotted

all out *adv* with maximum effort, at full power, or at top speed

all-out *adj* 1. involving the maximum possible effort or every available resource ○ *an all-out attempt to break the record* 2. describes a strike involving the whole workforce

all over *adv* (*informal*) 1. same as **everywhere** 2. used to stress that a description or action is characteristic of a particular person or type of person ○ *That's Jack all over: late again!*

all-over *adj* covering the whole surface area of something ○ *an all-over tan*

allow /ə lów/ (**-lows, -lowing, -lowed**) *v* 1. *vt* LET SOMETHING HAPPEN to permit something to happen or somebody to do something ○ *I can't allow you to throw this chance away.* ○ *He's allowed the toast to burn.* 2. *vt* LET SOMEBODY ENTER OR BE PRESENT to let somebody or something enter or be present in a place ○ *Children are not allowed after nine o'clock.* 3. *vt* LET SOMEBODY HAVE SOMETHING to let somebody or yourself have something, often a benefit or pleasure of some kind ○ *Allow yourself a few minutes to catch your breath.* 4. *vti* MAKE PROVISION FOR SOMETHING to take something into consideration or make provision for it when making a plan or decision ○ *We allowed an extra 20 minutes but were still late.* ○ *allow for shrinkage* 5. *vt* ADMIT SOMETHING to admit something or accept it to be true or valid (*formal*) ○ *You must allow that it was rather harsh.* 6. *vi* PRESENT AS POSSIBLE to present something as possible or reasonable (*dated*) ○ *The events allow of only one interpretation.* 7. *vt Southern US* SAY OR THINK to state or suppose ○ *He allowed it was time to go.* [14C. Via Old French *allouer* < Latin *allaudare* 'to praise' and medieval Latin *allocare* 'assign' (see ALLOCATE)] —**allowable** *adj* —**allowably** *adv* —**allowed** *adj*

allowance /ə lów ənss/ *n* 1. BUDGETED AMOUNT an amount of something given out at regular intervals or for a specific purpose ○ *a mileage allowance as well as expenses* 2. PERMITTED AMOUNT the amount of something that is allowed, especially according to regulations ○ *We're going to exceed the baggage allowance when we go home.* 3. FIN INCOME NOT TAXABLE an amount of a person's income that is exempt from taxation and is deducted from the total to be taxed ○ *the married person's allowance* 4. EDUC SALARY SUPPLEMENT GIVEN TO TEACHER a salary supplement paid to a teacher for taking on extra duties or responsibilities 5. *N Am* same as **pocket money** (sense 1) 6. DISCOUNT money deducted from the selling price of something by the seller as a discount or in exchange for something 7. TOLERATION the allowing of something to happen, or the toleration of it 8. MECH ENG AMOUNT OF VARIATION ALLOWED a small amount of variation permitted in the dimensions of closely fitting machine parts 9. *US* HANDICAP a handicap or advantage in some sports ■ *vt* (**-ances, -ancing, -anced**) 1. *US* GIVE SOMEBODY ALLOWANCE to restrict somebody to a fixed regular amount of something ○ *Members of the sales staff are allowanced for monthly expenses.* 2. HAND SOMETHING OUT to supply something, especially an amount of money, in limited amounts (*archaic*) ◇ **make allowance** *or* **allowances (for somebody** *or* **something) 1.**

to take a charitable view of somebody or something and take mitigating circumstances into account **2.** to take something into consideration when making a plan, decision, or judgment

allowedly /ə lówidli/ *adv* admittedly or by general agreement ○ *Allowedly, the salary is modest.*

alloy *n* /álloy/ **1.** METALL **MIXTURE OF METALS** a substance that is a mixture of two or more metals, or of a metal with a nonmetallic material **2.** DEBASING ADDITION something that detracts from the value or quality of the thing it is added to or mixed with ○ *The film is weakened by the alloy of sentimentality.* **3.** BLEND any mixture, amalgam, or compound of different materials ■ *vt* /ə lóy/ (**-loys, -loying, -loyed**) **1.** METALL **MIX METALS** to mix one metal with another, or mix a metal with a nonmetallic material **2.** DEBASE SOMETHING to detract from the quality, purity, or value of something by the addition of something inferior ○ *principles alloyed with cynicism* **3.** COMBINE SOMETHING to mix or combine different things [Mid-17C. Via Old French dialect *allai* (noun), *allayer* (verb) < Latin *alligare* 'bind to' < *ligare* 'bind']

SYNONYMS See *mixture*.

all-party *adj* involving all political parties ○ *all-party talks*

all-pervading *adj* spread or present throughout everything ○ *a sense of all-pervading gloom*

all-points bulletin *n* US a message broadcast to all police in an area, usually containing urgent information or a warning

all-powerful *adj* possessing unlimited authority or power —**all-powerfulness** *n*

all-purpose *adj* suitable for a wide variety of uses

all-purpose flour *n* N Am same as **plain flour**

~~allready~~ incorrect spelling of **already**

all right *adj* **1.** SATISFACTORY generally good, satisfactory, or pleasing (hyphenated when used before a noun) ○ *Everything's going to be all right.* **2.** JUST ADEQUATE just about acceptable or adequate, but not very good ○ *The new job's all right, I guess.* **3.** UNINJURED not injured or unwell **4.** IN GOOD CONDITION in good condition or order, and not defective or damaged ■ *interj* **1.** YES used to express agreement or approval ○ *'Will you come along?' 'All right.'* **2.** GREETING used as a greeting and informal enquiry, meaning hello and how are you (*informal*) ■ *adv* **1.** SATISFACTORILY in a generally good, satisfactory, or pleasing way ○ *My old drill still works all right.* **2.** CERTAINLY without any doubt ○ *He's his father's son all right.* ◇ **it's all right for some** some people are more privileged or have more advantages than others (*used humorously*)

USAGE **all right** or **alright**? Some people think the one-word spelling is justified by the analogy of *already* and *altogether*, and that it is sometimes useful to be able to distinguish between **all right** and **alright** (as with *altogether* and *all together*): *The answers were alright* (= satisfactory). *The answers were all right* (= all correct). But *alright* has never been accepted as good usage.

all round *adv* **1.** in every respect or taking everything into consideration ○ *I think, all round, it was a pretty successful effort, don't you?* **2.** for, from, or involving everyone ○ *There was a sigh of relief all round when he made the announcement.*

all-round *adj* **1.** WITH MANY ABILITIES able to do many things well, or useful in a number of different ways, and not specialized ○ *the best all-round player for both attack and defence* **2.** ALL-INCLUSIVE broad or comprehensive in scope ○ *for all-round news coverage* **3.** IN ALL DIRECTIONS in all directions

all-rounder *n* somebody who is good at many things, especially in sports

All Saints' Day, All Saints *n* the day in the Christian calendar set aside to celebrate the lives of saints. Date: 1 November.

all-season *adj* usable in every season of the year, regardless of weather conditions

all-seater *adj* providing seats for all spectators and having no standing room ○ *an all-seater stadium*

all-seeing *adj* seeing or appearing to see everything

all-singing all-dancing *adj* **1.** extraordinarily versatile or impressive (*informal humorous*) **2.** elaborate

and containing many interesting or useful features (*informal*)

All Souls' Day, All Souls *n* the day set aside in the Roman Catholic Church calendar for prayer for the souls of those who have died and are believed to be in purgatory. Date: 2 November.

allspice

allspice /áwl spīss/ *n* **1.** the ground dried berries of a tropical evergreen tree, used as a spice **2.** (*plural* **allspices** or *same*) an evergreen tree whose aromatic berries make allspice. Native to: tropical America. Latin name: *Pimenta dioica*. [Because it is thought to combine the flavours of cinnamon, cloves, and nutmeg]

all-star *adj* made up of very famous and talented performers or players ■ *n* N Am a member of an all-star team

All-Star game *n* a baseball game between teams composed of the best professional players, played every summer in the United States

Allston /áwlstən/, **Washington** (1779–1843) US artist and writer, author of the Gothic novel *Monaldi* (1841)

all-suite *adj* describes a hotel room that has a sitting-room and kitchenette as well as the standard features of hotel accommodation

all-terrain bike *n* a bicycle or motorcycle designed for use in open country as well as on roads

all-terrain boarding *n* a form of skateboarding using a modified board with larger wheels that enables the rider to travel over all types of terrain, especially down mountain slopes —**all-terrain board** *n*

all-terrain vehicle *n* a motor vehicle designed for use on rough, sandy, or marshy ground, as well as on roads. It usually has only one seat.

~~allthough~~ incorrect spelling of **although**

all-ticket *adj* describes an event to which people are only admitted if they have bought a ticket in advance

all-time *adj* having never yet been bettered, or the best, greatest, or most popular ever (*informal*) ○ *an all-time record for this distance*

all told *adv* when everything or everyone is included or taken into account ○ *A dozen people made it, all told.*

allude /ə loód/ (**-ludes, -luding, -luded**) *vi* to refer to something or somebody indirectly, without giving a precise name or explicit identification ○ *I presume you are alluding to the alleged financial discrepancy.* [Mid-16C. < Latin *alludere* 'play to' < *ludere* < *ludus* 'play']

SPELLCHECK **allude** or **elude**? Do not confuse the spelling of *allude* and *elude*, which sound similar. *Allude* is usually followed by *to*, as in alluding to the *disappearance of her husband*. *Elude* means 'escape from', 'avoid', or 'be beyond': *He eluded his pursuers. Her name eludes me.*

USAGE **allude** or **refer**? The sentence *She alluded to her husband by name* is a self-contradiction, because *allude* means 'to mention indirectly'. When the reference is direct, the word to use is *refer*. So if she mentioned 'the man at home looking after the children', she was *alluding* to her husband, whereas if she mentioned 'George' or 'my husband' directly, she was *referring* to him: *She referred to her husband frequently.*

allure /ə lyoor, ə loor/ *n* an attractive or tempting quality ○ *They couldn't resist the allure of the big city.* ■ *vti* (**-lures, -luring, -lured**) to exert a very powerful and often dangerous attraction on somebody [15C. < Anglo-Norman *alurer*, Old French

aloirrier, aleurier 'bring to the bait' < *leure* 'bait' (see LURE) —**allurement** *n*

alluring /ə lyooring, ə looring/ *adj* extremely attractive, tempting, or glamorous, and able to arouse strong desire in people —**alluringly** *adv*

allusion /ə loozh'n/ *n* **1.** an indirect reference to somebody or something ○ *He made an allusion to marital problems.* **2.** the act of making an indirect reference to somebody or something [Early 17C. Directly or via French < late Latin *allusion-* < Latin *allus-*, past participle of *alludere* (see ALLUDE)]

USAGE **allusion, delusion,** or **illusion**? *Allusion* and *illusion* are the closest in sound but the furthest apart in meaning: an *allusion* is an indirect reference to a person, thing, or event: *The story contained an allusion to her childhood in Africa.* An *illusion* is something that deceives the senses or mind: *The shimmering effect on a hot road is an optical illusion.* By shutting himself in his room for hours he kept up an illusion of studying hard. *Illusion* and *delusion* are similar in meaning, but *delusion* denotes a false or mistaken belief or idea, rather than a wrong impression received: *Visitors often suffer under the delusion that the weather is always hot here.*

allusive /ə loossiv/ *adj* **1.** making or containing an indirect reference to something or somebody **2.** characterized by the use of indirect references or subtle suggestion —**allusively** *adv* —**allusiveness** *n*

SPELLCHECK See *elusive*.

alluvia GEOL plural of **alluvium**

alluvial /ə loovi əl/ *adj* relating to, consisting of, or formed by sediment deposited by flowing water

alluvial fan *n* a fan-shaped deposit of sediment formed at the point where a stream enters a valley or plain or another, larger stream

alluvion /ə loovi ən/ *n* **1.** the flow or wash of the sea or other body of water against a shore **2.** the expansion of a land area through the build-up of alluvial deposits or the receding of a body of water [Mid-16C. Via French < Latin *alluvion-* < *alluvius* (see ALLUVIUM)]

alluvium /ə loovi əm/ (*plural* **-viums** or **-via** /-vi ə/) *n* sediment deposited by flowing water, especially soil formed in river valleys and deltas from material washed down by the river [Mid-17C. < Latin, form of *alluvius* 'washed against' < *lavare* 'to wash']

~~allways~~ incorrect spelling of **always**

all-weather *adj* usable in or able to stand up to all types of weather

ally /ə lī, álī/ *n* (*plural* **-lies**) **1.** MEMBER OF ALLIANCE a person, group, or state that is joined in an association with another or others for a common purpose **2.** BIOL RELATED ORGANISM an organism that is closely related to another ■ *v* (**-lies, -lying, -lied**) **1.** *vti* JOIN IN MUTUALLY SUPPORTIVE ASSOCIATION to join, or enlist somebody, in an association with one or more other states, organizations, or people for a common purpose **2.** *vt* RELATE THINGS to connect something with something else through similarity or common features (*usually passive*) ○ *These plants are allied to lilies.* **3.** *vti* CONNECT PEOPLE, OR BE CONNECTED to connect people or families, or form a connection with another person or family, especially through marriage [14C. Via Old French *al(e)ier* < Latin *alligare* 'bind to' (see ALLOY)]

allyl /álīl, álil/ *adj* describes a compound containing the chemical group C_3H_5- [Mid-19C. < Latin *allium* 'garlic' (because first obtained from garlic)]

allyl alcohol *n* a colourless, strong-smelling liquid. Use: manufacture of resins, plasticizers.

Alma-Ata /al maʼə taʼə/ former name for **Almaty**

Almagest /álmə jest/ *n* **1.** a text on astronomy written by Ptolemy in the 2nd century AD setting out his view of the universe with the Earth at its centre surrounded by spheres **2.** *also* **almagest** an important medieval treatise on a subject, especially on astronomy, astrology, or alchemy [14C. Via Old French < Arabic *al-mijistī* 'the greatest' < Greek *megistē* 'greatest', superlative of *megas* 'great' (see MEGA-)]

alma mater /álmə maʼətər, -máytər/, **Alma Mater** *n* the school, college, or university that somebody

formerly attended [< Latin, 'bounteous mother', title given by the Romans to several goddesses]

almanac /áwlmə nak, álmə-/ n **1.** an annual publication that includes a calendar for the year as well as astronomical information and details of anniversaries and events **2.** an annually published book of information relating to a subject or activity ○ *a sports almanac* [14C. < medieval Latin *almanac(h)*]

almandine /álməndin, -dīn/ n a precious stone coloured deep red by iron that is a variety of garnet. Use: gems. [15C. Via French < Latin *alabandina (gemma)* '(gem) of Alabanda' (city in Asia Minor where the gem was originally cut and polished)]

Alma-Tadema /álmə táddimə/, **Sir Lawrence** (1836–1912) Dutch-born British painter. He specialized in subjects and scenes from classical antiquity such as *Tarquinius Superbus* (1867).

Almaty /al maáti/ city and former capital of Kazakhstan, in the southeastern part of the country, east of Bishkek in Kyrgyzstan. Population: 1,135,000 (2000). Former name **Alma-Ata, Verny**

almighty /awl míti/ adj **1. ALL-POWERFUL** having supreme unquestionable power over everything ○ *almighty God* **2. EXTREME** extreme or excessive of its kind (*informal*) ○ *an almighty quarrel* ■ adv **EXTREMELY** to an extreme or excessive degree (*informal*) ○ *almighty proud* [Old English *ælmeahtig* < *æl* 'completely' (see ALL) + *meahtig* (see MIGHTY)] —**almightiness** n

Almighty n **RELIG** same as **God** ○ *pray to the Almighty*

Al-Minya /al mínyə/ city and trading centre in eastern Egypt, in the Nile valley. Population: 208,000 (1992).

almirah /al mírə/ n S Asia a wardrobe, cabinet, or cupboard

ALMO /álmō/ abbr PUBLIC ADMIN arm's length management organization

Almodóvar /álmə dóvər/, **Pedro** (b. 1951) Spanish film director of comedies such as *Women on the Verge of a Nervous Breakdown* (1988) and *All About My Mother* (1999)

almond

almond /aámənd, aálmənd/ n **1. EDIBLE OVAL NUT** an edible, oval-shaped, brown-skinned nut that is widely used in cooking **2. SMALL TREE PRODUCING ALMONDS** a tree that bears almonds. Native to: western Asia. Latin name: *Prunus dulcis.* **3. ALMOND-SHAPED OBJECT** something oval and pointed in shape like an almond ■ adj **SHAPED LIKE ALMOND** oval and pointed in shape like an almond [14C. Via Old French *alemande, a(l)mande* < Greek *amugdalē*]

almoner /aámənər/ n **1.** formerly, somebody attached to a hospital as a social worker for its patients **2.** in former times, somebody who distributed alms to the needy, especially on behalf of a church, monastery, or wealthy family [15C. Alteration of obsolete *aumener*, via Old French *aumoner* < ecclesiastical Latin *eleemosynarius* 'connected with alms' < *eleemosyna* (see ALMS)]

almost /áwlmōst, awl mṓst/ adv not exactly, not yet, or not in fact, but very close to being or happening as described ○ *I almost wrecked the car.*

alms /aamz/ npl in former times, money or other assistance given to people in need as charity [Pre-12C. Via assumed Vulgar Latin *alimosina* < ecclesiastical Latin *eleemosyna* < Greek *eleēmosynē* 'compassionateness' < *eleos* 'compassion, mercy']

almshouse /aámz howss/ (*plural* **-houses** /-howziz/) n a house formerly built as accommodation for a poor or old person or family and maintained by private

charitable funds. Almshouses are usually small and were built in groups.

alnico /álnikō/ n an alloy of iron, aluminium, and nickel together with one or more of cobalt, copper, and titanium. Use: strong permanent magnets. [Mid-20C. < ALUMINIUM + NICKEL + COBALT]

aloe

aloe /állō/ n **1.** a plant with fleshy toothed leaves. Flowers: red, yellow. Native to: southern Africa. Genus: *Aloe.* **2.** PLANTS same as **aloe vera** (sense 2) [14C. Via Latin < Greek *aloē*, probably of Asian origin]

aloes /állōz/ n (*takes a singular verb*) **1.** a bitter-tasting aloe leaf extract. Use: laxative. **2.** *also* **aloes wood** the fragrant wood of the eaglewood tree from which a resin is obtained. Use: making perfumes.

aloe vera /-veérə/ n **1.** a soothing, moisturizing extract made from the leaves of a species of aloe. Use: drugs, cosmetics. **2.** the Mediterranean species of aloe from which aloe vera is extracted. Latin name: *Aloe barbadensis.* [< modern Latin, 'true aloe']

aloft /ə lóft/ adv **1.** upwards, high up, or in a higher position (*literary*) **2.** in or into the rigging of a sailing ship [13C. < Old Norse *á lopt(i)* 'in the air' < *lopt* 'air, sky' (see LOFT)]

alogical /ay lójjik'l/ adj unable to be dealt with by, or having nothing to do with, logic —**alogically** adv

aloha /ə lṓ ə, aa lṓ haa/ interj Hawaii used as a greeting or farewell [Early 19C. < Hawaiian, 'love, affection']

aloin /állō in/ n a bitter-tasting aloe derivative. Use: manufacture of laxatives. [Mid-19C. < ALOE + -INE]

alone /ə lṓn/ CORE MEANING: a grammatical word meaning without any other person or thing nearby ○ (adj) *I like to be alone sometimes.* ○ (adv) *wandering alone in the wilderness*
1. adv **WITHOUT HELP FROM OTHERS** without help or support from anybody or anything else ○ *I can't do this job alone.* **2.** adv, adj **WITHOUT COMPANY** without any other person or thing nearby or in attendance, for company, or to give assistance ○ *She left with the others but returned alone.* **3.** adj **UNIQUE IN SOME RESPECT** being the only one of a group to do, achieve, or think something ○ *Am I alone in thinking this?* **4.** adj **DONE WITHOUT OTHERS** carried out by somebody or assigned to somebody without the assistance or company of others ○ *an assignment that was too much for one person alone* [13C. < *all one* 'completely by yourself'] —**aloneness** n

along /ə lóng/ CORE MEANING: a preposition indicating that something is situated or moves over all or part of the length of something ○ *came racing along the path*
1. prep **PARALLEL WITH** following a course or line parallel with or beside ○ *freighters sailing along the coastline* **2.** prep **SIMILAR TO** in accordance with or similar to **3.** adv **FORWARDS** forwards, onwards, or in a particular direction ○ *Move along there!* **4.** adv **WITH SOMEBODY** with you, with somebody, or with the rest of the group when going somewhere ○ *I asked if I could come along.* ○ *Next time you come, bring your guitar along.* **5.** adv **AT OR TO PLACE** arriving at or coming or going to a place ○ *There'll be a bus along in a minute.* [14C. < Old English *andlang* 'against the long' < *lang* 'long'] ◇ **along with** together with, or as well as

alongshore /ə lóng sháwr/ adv near to, beside, or along a shore ○ *The water was too shallow to bring the ship alongshore.* ■ adj located on or near a shore or moving along a shore

alongside /ə lóng síd, ə lóng sīd/ prep also **alongside of** close up against, near, or parallel to the side of ○ *pulled the boat alongside the pier* ■ adv in or into a position along or by the side of something ○ *anchored alongside*

Alonso /ə lónzō/, **Alicia** (b. 1921) Cuban ballerina, choreographer, and dance teacher who was instrumental in establishing the National Ballet of Cuba

aloo /aalóo/, **alu** n S Asia cooked potato in South Asian cooking [Via Hindi, Urdu < Sanskrit *ālū*]

aloof /ə lóof/ adj **1.** uninvolved or unwilling to become involved with other people or events ○ *always courteous but aloof* ○ *tried to stay aloof of the infighting and scandals* **2.** physically distant or apart [Mid-16C. Probably < *a luff* 'in a windward direction', hence 'away from the shore', after Dutch *te loef*] —**aloofly** adv —**aloofness** n

alopecia /állə peéshi ə, -peéshə/ n loss or the absence of hair, especially from the human head [14C. Via Latin < Greek *alōpekia* 'baldness, fox mange' < *alōpek-* 'fox'] —**alopecic** adj

alopecia areata /-ari áttə/ n a reversible patchy hair loss of the scalp and beard caused by inflammation [< modern Latin, 'alopecia with patches']

aloud /ə lówd/ adv **1.** using an audible speaking voice ○ *reading aloud* **2.** in a loud voice ○ *cried aloud for mercy*

aloxiprin /ə lóksə prín/ n a compound of aluminium hydroxide and aspirin. Use: analgesic. [Blend of ALUMINIUM + OXY- + ASPIRIN]

alp /alp/ n **1.** a high mountain, especially one capped with snow **2.** a high mountain pasture in Switzerland [15C. Via French *Alpes* 'Alps' < Latin < Greek *Alpeis*]

ALP abbr POL Australian Labor Party

alpaca

alpaca /al pákə/ n **1.** (*plural* **alpacas** or *same*) S AMERICAN MAMMAL a domesticated, long-haired South American animal of the camel family, related to the llama and similar in appearance. Latin name: *Lama pacos.* **2.** WOOL FROM ALPACA wool or cloth made from the long shaggy hair of the alpaca **3.** GLOSSY CLOTH a thin glossy cotton, wool, or rayon fabric made to simulate alpaca cloth [Late 18C. Via Spanish < Aymara *alpako* < *pako* 'reddish-brown', from the colour of its hair]

alpenglow /álpən glṓ/ n a reddish glow on snow-covered mountain peaks at sunset or sunrise, caused by reflected weak sunlight [Late 19C. Partial translation of German *Alpenglühen* 'glowing of the Alps']

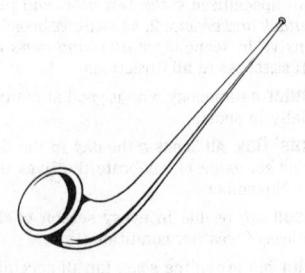

alpenhorn

alpenhorn /álpən hawrn/, **alphorn** /álp-/ n a traditional wooden wind instrument with a long tube that rests

on the ground and curves up at the end [Late 19C. < German, 'horn of the Alps']

alpenstock /álpən stok/ *n* a long staff with an iron spike at one end, formerly used by mountain climbers [Early 19C. < German, 'staff of the Alps']

alpestrine /al péstrin/ *adj* describes a plant that grows at high altitudes [Late 19C. < Latin *alpestris* 'alpine' < *Alpes* (see ALP)]

alpha /álfə/, **alfa** *n* **1.** 1ST LETTER OF GREEK ALPHABET the first letter of the Greek alphabet represented in the English alphabet as 'a'. See table at **alphabet 2.** EDUC **HIGHEST MARK** the highest mark in a system that uses Greek letters to grade examinations or pieces of academic work ■ *adj* **1.** ALPHABETICAL relating to or being in alphabetical order ○ *in alpha order* **2.** COMPUT **OF FIRST TEST VERSION** describes the first working version of a new hardware or software product or upgrade. Some features of the product may not be implemented in the alpha version and the discovery of significant bugs is usually anticipated. **3.** CHEM **RELATING TO NEAREST ATOM** describes the atom nearest to a particular atom or group of atoms in an organic molecule **4.** CHEM **RELATING TO MAJOR FORM OF ELEMENT** describes the major form of a chemical element with more than one physical form (**allotrope**) [13C. Via Latin < Greek, related to Hebrew and Phoenician *āleph* (see ALEPH)]

Alpha *n* **1.** a code word for the letter 'A', used in international radio communications **2.** the brightest or main star in a constellation (*followed by the Latin genitive*) ○ *Alpha Centauri*

alpha and omega *n* **1.** the beginning and end of something **2.** the most important aspect of something [< their being the first and last letters of the Greek alphabet]

alphabet /álfə bet/ *n* **1.** LETTERS USED TO REPRESENT LANGUAGE a set of letters, usually listed in a fixed order, used in writing a language and representing its basic speech sounds ○ *the Cyrillic alphabet*. See table on next page **2.** SYMBOLS FOR COMMUNICATING a set of symbols representing units used in communication, especially speech sounds or words ○ *the alphabet in Braille* **3.** BASIC PRINCIPLES the basic principles of something (*formal*) [Early 16C. Via late Latin *alphabetum* < Greek *alphabētos* < Greek *alpha* and *bēta*, the first and second letters of the alphabet]

alphabetical /álfə béttik'l/, **alphabetic** /-béttik/ *adj* **1.** ordered like the letters of the alphabet **2.** based on, typical of, or relating to an alphabet —**alphabetically** *adv*

alphabetize /álfə bet īz/ (**-izes, -izing, -ized**), **alphabetise** (**-tises, -tising, -tised**) *vt* **1.** to arrange words or items in alphabetical order **2.** to provide a language with an alphabet —**alphabetization** /álfə bet ī záysh'n/ *n* —**alphabetizer** *n*

alphabet soup *n* **1.** soup containing small pieces of pasta formed as letters of the alphabet **2.** a confusing mass of letters, especially with unintelligible abbreviations (*informal*)

alpha-blocker *n* a drug that prevents the constriction of blood vessels. Use: treatment of high blood pressure.

Alpha Centauri /álfə sen táwri, -táwrī/ *n* a multiple star that is the brightest star in the constellation Centaurus. It consists of two bright stars and a red dwarf in orbit around each other.

alpha-chymotrypsin /álfə kīmō trípsin/ *n* a hydrolytic enzyme (**chymotrypsin**), synthesized in the pancreas, that has an unusually reactive serine residue in the active site

alpha decay *n* a radioactive decay process in which an alpha particle is emitted from a nucleus

alpha emission *n* the emission of alpha particles from an atomic nucleus —**alpha emitter** *n*

alpha-foetoprotein *n* **1.** a protein in the liver of a human foetus, the presence of which in very high or low quantities in the amniotic fluid may indicate spina bifida or Down's syndrome **2.** a blood protein produced in the liver, yolk sac, and gastrointestinal tract of a foetus and used as an indicator of cancer and other diseases in adults

alpha helix *n* a helical protein structure consisting of amino acids stabilized by hydrogen bonds

alpha-hydroxy acid *n* an organic acid in which a hydroxyl acid is bonded to a carbon atom. Use: skin care products.

alpha male *n* **1.** a male in a pack of wolves, or a similar pack or troop of animals, that other members submit to and follow and that takes priority in mating with females **2.** a man who controls the activities of a group and to whom others defer (*informal*)

alphanumeric /álfənyoo mérrik/, **alphanumerical** /-mérrik'l/, **alphameric** /álfə mérrik/ *adj* using both letters and numbers ○ *an alphanumeric code* [Mid-20C. Blend of ALPHABET + *numeric*] —**alphanumerically** *adv*

alpha particle *n* a particle consisting of two neutrons and two protons that is identical to the helium nucleus and is emitted during some radioactive transformations

alpha ray *n* a stream of alpha particles

alpha-receptor *n* a protein molecule in the cell membrane that specifically binds adrenaline or noradrenaline, triggering a response in the cell

alpha rhythm *n* the pattern of electrical activity in the brain of somebody awake but relaxed or drowsy, registering on an electroencephalograph at a reading between 8 and 13 hertz

alpha source *n* a radioactive atom that emits alpha particles, e.g. polonium

alpha stock *n* a security that is among the 100–200 most profitable on the Stock Exchange

alpha test *n* a first test by the manufacturer of new or upgraded software or hardware [< the idea of being first in a series] —**alpha-test** *vt*

alphatocopherol /álfə to kóffə rol/ *n* BIOCHEM same as **vitamin E**

Alphege /álfij/, **St** Archbishop of Canterbury (954–1012) English martyr. Captured by the Danes (1011), he was murdered after refusing to save himself at the expense of his tenants.

alphonso /al fónssō/ (*plural* **-sos**) *n* a highly regarded variety of mango originally grown in western India [< Portuguese *Alfonso*, a personal name]

alphorn *n* MUSIC same as **alpenhorn**

alpine /álp īn/ *adj* **1.** TYPICAL OF HIGH MOUNTAINS relating to, typical of, or found in high mountains ○ *an alpine climate* **2.** USED IN MOUNTAINEERING used in or involving mountain climbing **3.** BOT SITUATED OR GROWING ABOVE TREE LINE describes the zone of vegetation on high mountains between the tree line and snow line and any plant that grows in or originates from that zone **4.** SKIING, EXTREME SPORTS another spelling of **Alpine** (senses 2–3) ■ *n* MOUNTAIN PLANT a plant that originates from or can grow in the alpine zone on mountains, above the tree line [15C. < Latin *alpinus* < *Alpes* (see ALP)]

Alpine *adj* **1.** OF ALPS relating to the Alps **2.** SKIING **RELATING TO DOWNHILL SKIING** describes competitive skiing on steep downhill courses, especially downhill and slalom events **3.** **DESCRIBES SNOWBOARD AND SNOWBOARDING STYLE** describes a type of snowboard that is thinner than average and more like a standard ski, or a type of snowboarding that concentrates on fast runs and freecarving

alpine-style *adj* describes a type of mountaineering in which the climbers carry all the necessary equipment with them on a single ascent to a mountain summit —**alpine-style** *adv*

alpinist /álpinist/ *n* a mountain climber, especially one who climbs in the Alps or mountains of similar height [Late 19C. < French *alpiniste* < Latin *alpinus* (see ALPINE)] —**alpinism** *n*

Alport's syndrome /ál pawrts-/, **Alport syndrome** *n* a genetic disease characterized by kidney disease and hearing and sight loss

alprostadil /al próstə dil/ *n* a drug that dilates blood vessels. Use: treatment of impotence, prevention of coagulation, treatment of neonates. [Late 20C. < *al-* + *-prost-*, INN stem + *-a-* + VASODILATOR]

Alps

Alps /alps/ mountain range in southern Europe, extending about 800 km/500 mi. from southeastern France to Austria. The highest peak is Mont Blanc. Height: 4,807 m/15,771 ft.

al-Qaeda /al kī eédə/, **al-Qaida** /al káydə/ *n* an international Islamic fundamentalist organization associated with several terrorist incidents, including the attack on the World Trade Center, New York (2001). Al-Qaeda was established by Osama bin Laden in 1989 and was based in Afghanistan until driven out by US and coalition forces in 2001. [Late-20C. < Arabic 'the base']

al-Quds /al koŏdz/ *n* ISLAM Arabic name for **Jerusalem**

already /awl réddi, áwl redi/ CORE MEANING: an adverb indicating that something has happened before now, happened in the past before a particular time, or will have happened by or before a particular time in the future ○ *I already know what you're going to say.* ○ *She had already left when I arrived.* *adv* **1.** by or at an earlier time than expected ○ *Have you finished already?* **2.** N Am used after a command, exclamation, or other statement to give it emphasis or express exasperation (*informal*) ○ *Enough already!* [14C. < *all ready* 'completely ready']

USAGE already or **all ready**? These words do not mean the same thing, and so they are not interchangeable. *Already*, an adverb, means 'by or at an earlier time than expected', as in *Have they already* [not *all ready*] *left? All ready* means 'all or totally prepared', as in *Is everything all ready* [not *already*] *for tomorrow?*

alright /awl rít, áwl rīt/ (*nonstandard*) *adv* ⚠ in a generally good, satisfactory, or pleasing way ■ *adj* ⚠ generally good, satisfactory, or pleasant

USAGE See **all right**.

ALS *abbr* MED amyotrophic lateral sclerosis

Alsace /al sáss/ region and former province of France, situated west of the River Rhine. Capital: Strasbourg. Population: 1 734 145 (1999). Area: 8,280 sq. km/3,197 sq. mi.

Alsace-Lorraine /-lə ráyn/ area of France on the German border. Now divided into two administrative regions, Alsace and Lorraine. The area was disputed by France and Germany between 1871 and 1945. Population: 3,930,100 (1990). Area: 31,827 sq. km/12,288 sq. mi.

Alsatian /al sáysh'n/ *n* **1.** UK LARGE DOG a large powerful dog belonging to a short-haired breed with erect ears, a face rather like a wolf's, and a brown and black coat. ANZ, N Am term **German shepherd 2.** SOMEBODY FROM ALSACE somebody who comes from Alsace ■ *adj* FROM ALSACE relating to Alsace, or its people, language, or culture [Late 19C. < medieval Latin *Alsatia* 'Alsace']

alsike clover /ál sīk-, álsik-/ *n* a perennial clover widely grown for forage. Flowers: white or pink. Native to: Europe. Latin name: *Trifolium hybridum*. [Mid-19C. After *Alsike*, town in Sweden]

also /áwlsō/ *adv* **1.** IN ADDITION used to indicate that something is true or is the case in addition ○ *got his picture in the paper and also won a prize* **2.** LIKEWISE OR SIMILARLY like or in the same way as somebody or something else ○ *Her niece was also called Jean.* ○ *When they withdraw their forces, we shall also withdraw ours.* **3.** MOREOVER and in addition to that (*used to modify a whole sentence or clause*) ○ *Also, you must complete the task in one hour.* [Old English *ealswā, allswā* (see ALL, SO[1])]

MAJOR ALPHABETS OF THE WORLD

Phoenician 20 letters, no cases			Early Greek 21 letters, no cases			Hebrew 23 letters, no cases			Classical Roman 23 letters, capitals only	Modern Greek 24 letters[1]			Cyrillic 31 letters[2]		Modern Arabic 28 letters[3]		
	sound	name		sound	name		sound	name			sound	name		sound		sound	name
ΚΚ	[']	'aleph	Χ	[a]	alpha	א	[']	aleph	A	Αα	[a]	alpha	Аа	[a]	ا ا	[']	'alif
99	[b]	bĕth	∂∂	[b]	beta	אב	[b,bh]	beth	B	Ββ	[b]	beta	Бб	[b]	ب ب ت ت	[b]	bā
٦	[g]	gaml, gimel	٦	[g]	gamma	ג	[g,gh]	gimel	C	Γγ	[g,n]	gamma	Вв	[v]	ت ت ث ث	[t]	tā
△△	[d]	dag, dāleth	△	[d]	delta	ד	[d,dh]	daleth	D	Δδ	[d]	delta	Гг	[g]	ث ث خ خ	[t]	thā
ꓱ	[ḥ]	hĕ	ꓱ	[ĕ]	e (psilon)	ה	[h]	he	E	Εε	[e]	epsilon	ЕеЁё	[e,ë][5]	ح ح ج ج	[j]	jīm
Ύ	[w]	wāw	ꓵ	[w]	wau, digamma	ו	[w]	vav	F	Ζζ	[z]	zēta	Жж	[zh]	ح ح ح ح	[ḥ]	ḥā
Ⅱ	[z]	zayin	Ⅱ	[z]	zēta	ז	[z]	zayin	G	Ηη	[ē]	ēta	Зз	[z]	خ خ خ خ	[kh]	khā
ꓯ	[h]	hĕth	B	[h,ē]	ēta	ח	[ḥ]	heth	H	Θθ	[th]	thēta	ИиЙй	[i][6]	د د	[d]	dāl
2Z	[y]	yōdh	ꓱ	[i,y]	iŏta	ט	[ṭ]	teth	I	Ιι	[i]	iota	Кк	[k]	ذ ذ	[dh]	dhāl
↓↓	[k]	kaph	ꓘ	[k]	kappa	י	[y]	yod	K	Κκ	[k]	kappa	Лл	[l]	ر ر	[r]	rā
＜∠	[l]	lāmedh	Λ	[l]	lambda	ךכ	[k,kh]	kaph	L	Λλ	[l]	lambda	Мм	[m]	ز ز	[z]	zāy
ξ๗	[m]	mĕm	M	[m]	mu	ל	[l]	lamedh	M	Μμ	[m]	mu	Нн	[n]	س س س س	[s]	sīn
Ƨৈ	[n]	naḥš, nūn	Ν	[n]	nu	םמ	[m]	mem	N	Νν	[n]	nu	Оо	[o]	ش ش ش ش	[sh]	shīn
ꓩ	[s]	samekh	Ξ	[ks]	xi	ןנ	[n]	nun	O	Ξξ	[x]	xi	Пп	[p]	ص ص ص ص	[ṣ]	ṣād
O	[']	'ayin	O	[ŏ]	o (micron)	ס	[s]	samekh	P	Οο	[o]	omicron	Рр	[r]	ض ض ض ض	[ḍ]	ḍād
ꓬ٦	[p]	pĕ	ꓵ	[p]	pi	ע	[']	ayin	Q	Ππ	[p]	pi	Сс	[s]	ط ط ط ط	[ṭ]	ṭā
Φ	[q]	qōph	Φ	[q]	koppa	ףפ	[p,ph]	pe	R	Ρρ	[r,rh]	rhō	Тт	[t]	ظ ظ ظ ظ	[z]	zā
94	[r]	rōsh, rēsh	ꓼ	[r]	rhō	ץצ	[ṣ]	sadhe	S	Σσς	[s]	sigma[4]	Уу	[u]	ع ع ع ع	[']	'ayn
Ｗ	[th,š]	thann, shin	ꓝ≷	[s]	sigma	ק	[q]	qoph	T	Ττ	[t]	tau	Фф	[f]	غ غ غ غ	[ġ]	ghayn
＋Χ	[t]	tāw	Т	[t]	tau	ר	[r]	resh	V	Υυ	[y,u]	upsilon	Хх	[kh]	ف ف ف ف	[f]	fā
			Υ	[ū,w]	u (psilon)	שׁ	[ś]	sin	X	Φφ	[ph]	phi	Цц	[ts]	ق ق ق ق	[q]	qāf
						שׁ	[šh]	shin	Y	Χχ	[kh]	chi/khi	Чч	[ch]	ك ك ك ك	[k]	kāf
						ת	[t,th]	tav	Z	Ψψ	[ps]	psi	Шш	[sh]	ل ل ل ل	[l]	lām
										Ωω	[ō]	ōmega	Щщ	[shch]	م م م م	[m]	mīm
													Ъъ	["]	ن ن ن ن	[n]	nūn
													Ыы	[y]	ه ه ه ه	[h]	hā
													Ьь	[']	و و	[w]	wāw
													Ээ	[e]	ي ي ي ي	[y]	yā
													Юю	[yu]			
													Яя	[ya]			

Notes

1 In the modern Greek alphabet, each letter has an uppercase and lowercase form.

2 In the Cyrillic alphabet, each letter has an uppercase and lowercase form.

3 In the modern Arabic alphabet, each letter has between two and four forms each.

4 The classical and modern Greek letter *sigma* has two lowercase forms.

5 The Cyrillic letter *e* has two forms, each with uppercase and lowercase.

6 The Cyrillic letter *i* has two forms, each with uppercase and lowercase.

also-ran *n* **1.** LOSING RUNNER a horse or other entrant in a race that does not finish in any of the winning places **2.** LOSING COMPETITOR a losing entrant in any contest **3.** SOMEBODY UNIMPORTANT somebody of little or no consequence or significance [Because newspaper racing results formerly listed horses that finished fourth or lower under the heading 'Also Ran']

alstroemeria /álstrə meéri ə/ (*plural* **-as** or *same*) *n* a tuberous plant of the amaryllis family. Flowers: long-lasting, variously coloured. Native to: South America. Genus: *Alstroemeria*. [Late 18C. < modern Latin, after Klas von *Alstroemer* (1736–96), Swedish naturalist]

alt *abbr* **1.** alteration **2.** BOT alternate **3.** ASTRON, MEASURE, MATHS altitude **4.** MUSIC alto

Alt *abbr* COMPUT Alt key

alt- *prefix* same as **alto-** (*used before vowels*)

Alta *abbr* Alberta

Altaic /al táy ik/ *n* a family of languages that consists of Turkic, Mongolic, and Tungusic, sometimes considered as part of a wider Ural-Altaic family [Mid-19C. After the ALTAI MOUNTAINS] —**Altaic** *adj*

Altai Mountains /al tí-/ mountains in Central Asia, on the Kazakhstan-Mongolia border, south of Russia and north of China. The highest peak is Mount Belukha 4,620 m/15,157 ft.

altar: Roman Catholic Church altar

altar /áwltər/ *n* **1.** a raised, typically flat-topped structure or area where religious ceremonies are performed **2.** the table or other raised structure in a Christian church on which the bread and wine of Communion are prepared [Pre-12C. < Latin *altare* < *altaria* 'burnt offerings', probably < *adolere* 'burn up'] ◇ **lead somebody to the altar** to marry somebody (*dated informal*)

SPELLCHECK altar or **alter**? Do not confuse the spelling of **altar** and **alter**, which sound similar. **Altar** is a noun referring to a ceremonial structure where religious ceremonies take place, and **alter** is a verb meaning 'change', as in *I had to alter the wording of the document.*

altar boy *n* a boy who assists the priest during services, especially in the Roman Catholic Church

altarpiece /áwltər peess/ *n* a work of art, usually a painting, placed above and behind an altar

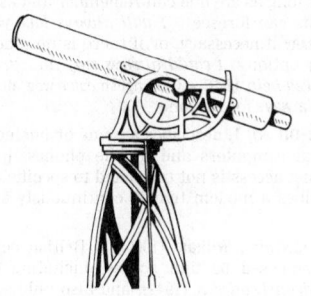

altazimuth

altazimuth /al tázziməth/ *n* **1.** an instrument, incorporating a telescope that can move vertically and horizontally, used to measure the altitude and azimuth of an astronomical object **2.** an instrument similar to a theodolite used in surveying to measure horizontal and vertical angles [Mid-19C. Blend of ALTITUDE + AZIMUTH]

alteplase /áltə playz, -playss/ *n* a tissue plasminogen activator produced by recombinant DNA technology. Use: treatment of heart failure.

alter /áwltər/ (**-ters, -tering, -tered**) *v* **1.** *vti* CHANGE to make changes to something or somebody, or be changed or become different ◇ *We'll have to alter our plans.* **2.** *vt* ADJUST GARMENT FOR BETTER FIT to make adjustments to a piece of clothing so that it fits better ◇ *The trousers are fine, but the jacket will have to be altered.* **3.** *vt* Aus, N Am CASTRATE ANIMAL to castrate or spay an animal (*informal*) [14C. Via French < late Latin *alterare* < Latin *alter* 'other'] —**alterability** /áwltərə bílləti/ *n* —**alterable** *adj*

SPELLCHECK See **altar**.

SYNONYMS See **change**.

alteration /áwltə ráysh'n/ *n* **1.** CHANGE a change, modification, or adjustment made to something **2.** DIFFERENCE a difference in something resulting from change ◇ *I don't see any alteration in the patient's condition.* **3.** PROCESS OF CHANGING the process of changing something or of being changed ◇ *undergoing alteration*

altercation /áwltər káysh'n/ *n* a heated argument, quarrel, or confrontation [14C. Via French < Latin *altercation-* < *altercari* 'to dispute' < *alter* 'other'] —**altercate** /áwltər kayt/ *vi*

alter ego /áwltər eégō/ (*plural* **alter egos**) *n* **1.** a second side to somebody's personality, different from the one that most people know **2.** a very close and trusted friend [< Latin, 'other self']

alternant /awl túrnənt/ *adj* changing from one to the other (*formal*)

alternate *vi* /áwltər nayt/ (**-nates, -nating, -nated**) **1.** FOLLOW IN INTERCHANGING PATTERN to follow each other and take each other's place in a regular pattern ◇ *as night alternates with day* **2.** FLUCTUATE to shift back and forth, especially regularly or constantly, between one state and another ◇ *Her mood alternates between elation and despair.* **3.** BE UNDERSTUDY to act as an understudy for another performer ■ *adj* /áwl túrnət/ **1.** ARRANGED IN ALTERNATING PATTERN arranged or happening in a regular pattern in which the one thing alternates with the other ◇ *alternate spells of sun and showers* **2.** EVERY OTHER every other or second of a series ◇ *They babysit for each other on alternate weekends.* **3.** N Am same as **alternative** *adj* (sense 1) **4.** BOT NOT ALIGNED describes flowers, buds, or leaves that are arranged singly and at different levels on either side of the stem of a plant, as opposed to being in pairs or groups ■ *n* /áwl túrnət/ N Am SOMEBODY WHO FILLS IN somebody who substitutes for somebody else [Early 16C. < Latin *alternat-*, past participle of *alternare* 'do things one after another' < *alternus* 'one after another' < *alter* 'other']

USAGE alternate or **alternative**? The adjective **alternate** is often used instead of **alternative**, especially in US English, to mean 'different from or able to serve as a substitute', as in *The band decided to go with the song's alternate title.* However, **alternate** has a quite distinct meaning, namely 'every other', as in *We meet on alternate Sundays* (= every other Sunday).

alternate angle *n* one of a pair of angles on opposite sides and at opposite ends of a line that cuts two other lines

alternately /awl túrnətli/ *adv* **1.** by following one immediately after the other in a regular repeated pattern or sequence **2.** same as **alternatively**

alternating current *n* an electric current that regularly reverses direction

alternation /áwltər náysh'n/ *n* **1.** a process of change in which one thing follows, or is made to follow, another in a regular repeated pattern **2.** LOGIC a proposition of the form 'p or q', that is, either sentence 'p' is true or sentence 'q' is true

alternation of generations *n* the existence in the life cycle of an organism of two or more alternating forms or reproductive modes, e.g. sexual and asexual cycles

alternative /awl túrnətiv/ *n* **1.** OTHER POSSIBILITY something different from, and able to serve as a substitute for, something else ◇ *You could take the bus as an alternative to driving.* **2.** POSSIBILITY OF CHOOSING the possibility of choosing between two different things or courses of action ◇ *We gave you the alternative; you decided to stay.* **3.** ⚠ OPTION either one of two, or one of several, things or courses of action to choose between ◇ *I can't decide which of the two alternatives is worse.* ■ *adj* **1.** UK, Aus, Can SERVING AS BACKUP different from and serving, or able to serve, as a substitute for something else ◇ *There are alternative courses we can take.* US term **alternate** **2.** MUTUALLY EXCLUSIVE of which only one can be true, or only one can be used or chosen, or take place at any one time ◇ *There are two alternative theories as to why this phenomenon occurs.* **3.** UNCONVENTIONALLY NONTRADITIONAL outside the establishment or mainstream, and often presented as being less institutionalized or conventional, or more natural or economical with resources ◇ *alternative methods of painting* **4.** LOGIC same as **disjunctive** *adj* (sense 3)

USAGE See **alternate**.

USAGE alternative meaning 'two or more': Some people maintain that the noun sense of **alternative** cannot be used in the sense 'an option' if there are more than two choices but this restriction is largely dying out.

alternative comedy *n* any form of comedy characterized by subject matter and a style of presentation deliberately made different from mainstream comedy —**alternative comedian** *n*

alternative curriculum *n* in England and Wales, any available course of study that is not included in the National Curriculum

alternative energy *n* any form of energy obtained from the Sun, wind, waves, or other natural renewable source, in contrast to energy generated from fossil fuels

alternative lifestyle *n* a way of living adopted by people who reject the prevailing lifestyle, often because they consider it to be too materialistic or too dependent on technology

alternatively /awl túrnətivli/ *adv* or instead of that ◇ *Alternatively, you could drive there.*

alternative medicine *n* the treatment of illness using remedies such as homoeopathy or naturopathy that are not considered part of mainstream medicine

alternative vote *n* a system of voting in which electors vote for several candidates in order of preference, their votes being transferred to the second choice if the first choice fails to receive a majority

alternator /áwltər naytər/ *n* a device that generates alternating current

~~**alternitive**~~ incorrect spelling of **alternative**

altho /awl thṓ/ *conj* US another spelling of **although** (*informal*)

althorn

althorn /ált hawrn/ *n* an alto brass wind instrument of either the saxhorn or the flügelhorn family, used mainly in brass or military bands [Mid-19C. < German < *Alt* 'alto' + *Horn* 'horn']

although /awl thṓ/ *conj* granting or in spite of the fact that ◇ *Although the children were sleepy, they kept watching the movie.* [14C. < ALL in the sense 'even' + THOUGH]

USAGE although or **though**? In many uses **although** and **though** are interchangeable, but **though** is a generally more versatile word, capable of occupying different positions in a sentence and having more grammatical flexibility. It is the only choice in the phrases *as though* and *even though*, and in the following types of use: *I don't like them, though. It is true, though, that they have*

been kind to us. The chair, though damaged, could still be used. We enjoyed the day out, cold though it was.

USAGE although or **however**? Do not use the conjunction ***although*** as a substitute for the adverb ***however***. ***However*** is used to add contrasting and surprising information, and, unlike ***although***, is followed by a comma. Compare *We were from different backgrounds. However, we got along really well.* and *We got along very well, although we were from different backgrounds.*

alti- *prefix* same as **alto-**

altimeter /al tímmitər, álti meetər/ *n* an instrument that shows height above sea level, especially one mounted in an aircraft and incorporating an aneroid barometer that senses differences in pressure caused by changes in altitude —**altimetric** /álti méttrik/ *adj* —**altimetry** /al tímmətri/ *n*

altiplano /álti plaánō/ (*plural* **-nos**) *n Southwest US* especially in Mexico or the Andes of South America, a high plateau [Early 20C. < American Spanish, 'high plain']

Altiplano /álti plaánō/ region of the Andes Mountains extending from southwestern Bolivia to southern Peru. Height: about 3,650 m/12,000 ft.

altissimo /al tíssimō/ *adv* [Late 18C. < Italian, 'highest', superlative of *alto* (see ALTO)] ◇ **in altissimo** in the octave beginning on the G one octave above the G at the top of the treble stave

altitude /álti tyood/ *n* **1. HEIGHT ABOVE SEA LEVEL** the height of something above a specific level, especially above sea level or the Earth's surface **2. HIGH PLACE** a place or region situated high above sea level (*often used in the plural*) **3.** MATHS **DISTANCE** in a geometrical figure, the perpendicular distance from the vertex to the base **4.** ASTRON **ANGLE OF ASTRONOMICAL OBJECT ABOVE HORIZON** the angle of an astronomical object above an observer's horizon, measured from the horizon along the circle passing through the object and the point above the observer **5. HIGH RANK OR POSITION** a high rank or high position in a society or group [14C. < Latin *altitudo* < *altus* 'high'] —**altitudinal** /álti tyóodin'l/ *adj*

altitude sickness *n* a condition caused by low levels of oxygen in the air at high altitudes, resulting in nausea and breathlessness

Alt key /áwlt-/ *n* a computer key that is pressed together with another key to change its function

AKG London

Robert Altman

Altman /áwltmən/, **Robert** (*b.* 1925) US film director and screenwriter. His films include *M*A*S*H* (1970) and *The Player* (1992).

> 'What's a cult? It just means not enough people to make a minority.'
> [Robert Altman, *Observer*, 11 April 1981]

alto /áltō/ (*plural* **-tos**) *n* **1.** MUSIC same as **contralto** (sense 1) **2. HIGHEST MAN'S VOICE** the highest singing voice for a man, achieved by using falsetto **3. ALTO SINGER** a singer with an alto or contralto voice **4. INSTRUMENT BETWEEN SOPRANO AND TENOR** in a family of instruments, the instrument whose size and pitch fall between the soprano and tenor instruments [Late 16C. Via Italian, 'high' < Latin *altus*]

alto-, alti- *prefix* high, altitude ○ *altocumulus, altimeter* [< Latin *altus* 'high, deep' < Indo-European, 'grow']

alto clef *n* the C clef indicating that middle C is on the third line of the stave

altocumulus /áltō kyóomyooləss/ (*plural* **-li** /-lī/) *n* white or grey patchy cloud with a rounded outline

altogether /áwltə géthər, -geth-/ *adv* **1. WITH EVERYTHING INCLUDED** when everything is included or taken into account ○ *Altogether, your bill comes to £75.99.* **2. TOTALLY** entirely or utterly ○ *I'm not altogether satisfied.* **3. ON THE WHOLE** considered as a whole ○ *Altogether, it's been a highly successful day.* [12C. < ALL 'the whole group' + TOGETHER] ◇ **in the altogether** naked (*informal*)

USAGE altogether or **all together**? These words mean different things. ***Altogether*** means 'with everything included', 'totally', or 'on the whole' and is an adverb. ***All together*** means 'everyone together', 'all at the same place or time', and functions as an adjectival phrase. Usually the word *all* can be removed without affecting the grammar or the sense: *They arrived (all) together at nine. The plates are (all) together on a separate shelf.*

altoist /áltō ist/ *n* a musician who plays an alto saxophone

alto-relievo /áltō ri leévō/ (*plural* **alto-relievos**), **alto-rilievo** /-rillee áy vō/ (*plural* **alto-rilievos**) *n* SCULPTURE same as **high relief** [Mid-17C. < Italian *alto-rilievo*]

altostratus /áltō straátəss, -stráytəss/ (*plural* **-ti** /-tī/) *n* greyish cloud in thin sheets or layers of uniform appearance, through which the Sun can be seen

altricial /al trísh'l/ *adj* describes birds or mammals that are helpless when young and dependent on their parents for food ■ *n* a bird or mammal that produces young that are unable to move or feed themselves without help [Late 19C. < modern Latin *Altrices* (former division of birds), plural of Latin *altrix* 'female nourisher' < *alere* 'nourish']

alt rock /áwlt-/ *n* rock music played by lesser known performers and considered as alternative to the music promoted by large record companies [< shortening of ALTERNATIVE]

altruism /áltroo izəm/ *n* **1.** an attitude or way of behaving marked by unselfish concern for the welfare of others **2.** the belief that acting for the benefit of others is right and good [Mid-19C. < French *altruisme* < Italian *altrui* 'that which belongs to other people' < Latin *alter* 'other'] —**altruist** *n* —**altruistic** /áltroo ístik/ *adj* —**altruistically** *adv*

alu *n S Asia* FOOD another spelling of **aloo**

ALU *abbr* COMPUT arithmetic logic unit

alula /ályoolə/ (*plural* **-lae** /-lee/) *n* the part of a bird's wing that corresponds to a thumb and contains a few short feathers [Late 18C. < modern Latin, 'little wing' < Latin *ala* 'wing'] —**alular** *adj*

alum /álləm/ *n* **1.** a colourless crystalline solid that turns white in air. Use: astringents, pigments, dyes, water purification, leather dressing. Formula: $KAl(SO_4)_2.12H_2O$. **2.** an inorganic chemical having a structure like alum [14C. Via French < Latin *alumen*]

alumina /ə lóominə/ *n* a white or colourless oxide of aluminium. Source: corundum, bauxite. Use: catalysts, abrasives, manufacture of artificial rubies and sapphires. Formula: Al_2O_3. [Late 18C. < Latin *alumin-* (see ALUMINIUM), after words such as SODA and MAGNESIA]

aluminate /ə lóomi nayt/ *n* any salt of aluminium and a metallic oxide

aluminiferous /ə lóomi nífferəss/ *adj* containing or being a source of alumina or aluminium

aluminise *vt* INDUST another spelling of **aluminize**

aluminium /állə mínni əm/ *n* a silvery-white, light metallic element that is ductile, malleable, and resistant to corrosion. Source: bauxite. Use: lightweight construction, corrosion-resistant materials. Symbol **Al**. See table at **element** [Early 19C. < Latin *alumin-*, stem of *alumen* 'alum']

aluminium chloride *n* a white or yellowish crystalline powder. Use: medicines, cosmetics, pigments, antiperspirants. Formula: $AlCl_3$ or Al_2Cl_6.

aluminium foil *n* aluminium in the form of a very thin sheet. Use: wrapping food to be roasted or baked.

aluminium hydroxide *n* a white solid. Use: antacid, catalyst, drying agent, glass and ceramics manufacturing. Formula: $Al(OH)_3$ or $Al_2O_3.3H_2O$.

aluminium oxide *n* CHEM same as **alumina**

aluminium sulphate *n* a white crystalline solid. Use: paper, textiles, water purification. Formula: $Al_2(SO_4)_3$.

aluminize /ə lóomi nīz/ (**-nizes, -nizing, -nized**), **aluminise** (**-nises, -nising, -nised**) *vt* to treat or coat something with aluminium

aluminosilicate /ə lóominō sílli kayt/ *n* a silicate that contains aluminium. The minerals feldspar and beryl are aluminosilicates.

aluminothermy /ə lóominō thúrmi/ *n* a process for extracting a metal from its oxide that involves burning the oxide together with aluminium powder

aluminous /ə lóominəss/ *adj* **1.** resembling aluminium or alum **2.** CHEM same as **aluminiferous** [15C. < Latin *aluminosus* < *alumin-* (see ALUMINIUM)]

aluminum /ə lóominəm/ *n US* CHEM same as **aluminium**

alumna /ə lúmnə/ (*plural* **-nae** /-nī, -nee/) *n* a female graduate or former student of a school, college, or university [Late 19C. < Latin, feminine form of ALUMNUS]

alumnus /ə lúmnəss/ (*plural* **-ni** /-nī, -nee/) *n* a male graduate or former student of a school, college, or university [Mid-17C. < Latin, 'pupil, foster child' < *alere* 'nourish']

alunite /ályoo nīt/ *n* a white, grey, or reddish mineral composed of hydrated potassium aluminium sulphate. Source: altered volcanic rocks. Use: fertilizers. [Mid-19C. < French < *alun* 'alum' < Latin *alumen* (see ALUMINIUM)]

Alvarez /álvə rez/, **Luis W.** (1911–88) US physicist. He developed the first proton linear accelerator and liquid hydrogen bubble chamber, and won the Nobel Prize in physics (1968) for his work on subatomic particles. Full name **Alvarez, Luis Walter**

alveolar /álvi ólər, al veé ələr/ *adj* **1.** ANAT **RELATING TO AIR SAC IN LUNG** relating to the air sacs in the lungs (**alveoli**) **2.** ANAT **RELATING TO JAWBONE** relating to the part of the upper or lower jaw that contains the roots of the teeth **3.** PHON **WITH TONGUE NEAR UPPER TEETH RIDGE** describes a consonant that is sounded with the tongue touching or close to the ridge behind the teeth of the upper jaw ■ *n* PHON **CONSONANT** an alveolar consonant, e.g. 't', 'd', or 's' in English —**alveolarly** *adv*

alveolar ridge *n* a hard ridge in the mouth immediately behind the roots of the teeth

alveolectomy /álvi ə léktəmi/ (*plural* **-mies**) *n* surgical excision of a portion of the tooth socket or ridge

alveoli ANAT plural of **alveolus**

alveolitis /álvi ə lítiss/ *n* inflammation of the air sacs of the lungs

alveolus /álvi óləss, al veé ələss/ (*plural* **-li** /-lee, -lī/) *n* **1.** a tiny thin-walled air sac found in large numbers in each lung, through which oxygen enters and carbon dioxide leaves the blood **2.** a socket in the jaw bone in which a tooth is rooted [Late 17C. < Latin, 'little cavity' < *alveus* 'cavity' < *alvus* 'belly']

always /áwl wayz, -wiz/ *adv* **1. AT ALL TIMES** used to indicate that something happens or is done continuously, repetitively, or on every occasion ○ *She's always very polite.* **2. THROUGH ALL PAST OR FUTURE TIME** throughout all past time or all future time, or for as long as anyone can remember and as long as anyone can foresee ○ *I will always love you.* **3. IF NECESSARY** if necessary, or if there is no other or no better option ○ *I could always stay an extra day if you need help.* [14C. < Old English *ealne weg* 'all the way'] ◇ **for always** for all time

always-on *adj* **1.** describes a home or business with several computers and mobile phones, in which Internet access is not restricted to specific times **2.** describes a modem that is continuously switched on

Alwyn /áwlwin/, **William** (1905–85) British composer. He composed 60 film scores, including one for *Squadron Leader X* (1942), and also published *The Technique of Film Music* (1957).

Alyawarr /al yáwərə/, **Alyawarra, Alyawarre** *n* an Australian Aboriginal language spoken in the central-eastern Northern Territory. Native speakers: 1,370.

alyssum /állissəm/ *n* **1.** PLANTS same as **sweet alyssum** **2.** *UK, Aus, Can* a perennial plant with oval hairy grey-green leaves. Flowers: bright yellow. Native to: Europe. Latin name: *Aurinia saxatilis*. US term **basket-of-gold** [Mid-16C. Via modern Latin < Greek *alysson*

'madwort' (believed to cure rabies) < *a-* 'without' + *lyssa* 'rabies']

Alzheimer's disease /álts hī́mərz-/, **Alzheimer's** *n* a degenerative disorder that affects the brain and causes dementia, especially late in life [Early 20C. After Alois *Alzheimer* (1864–1915), German neurologist]

am[1] *abbr* **1.** TELECOM amplitude modulation **2.** Armenia (*used in Internet addresses*) See table at **domain name**

am[2] *stressed* /am/; *unstressed* /əm/ 1st person singular present of **be**[1] [Old English *eom* < Indo-European]

Am[1] *abbr* BIBLE Amos

Am[2] *symbol* CHEM ELEM americium

AM *abbr* **1.** MIL Albert Medal **2.** MEDIA amplitude modulation **3.** associate member **4.** US EDUC Master of Arts **5.** Member of the Order of Australia [In sense 4 Latin *Artium Magister*]

Am. *abbr* American

a.m., A.M., am, AM *adj, adv* in the period between midnight and noon. Full form **ante meridiem**

Amadeus, Lake /ə maádi əss/ large salt lake in the southern part of the Northern Territory, Australia. Area: 2,400 sq. km/927 sq. mi.

Amado /ə maádō, ə maádoo/, **Jorge** (1912–2001) Brazilian novelist and Communist politician. His works include *Dona Flor and Her Two Husbands* (1966, English version 1969).

amah /aámə/ *n* in East and South Asia, a woman employed as a children's nurse, domestic servant, office cleaner, or attendant [Mid-19C. Via Portuguese *ama* 'nurse' < medieval Latin *amma* 'mother']

amalgam /ə málgəm/ *n* **1.** MIXTURE a combination of two or more characteristics ○ *an amalgam of liberal and socialist ideas* **2.** FILLING MATERIAL FOR TEETH a substance used as filling for tooth cavities, consisting of a paste of powdered mercury, silver, and tin that quickly hardens **3.** METALL MERCURY ALLOY an alloy of mercury and another metal [15C. Directly or via French < medieval Latin *amalgama*]

SYNONYMS See *mixture*.

amalgamate /ə málgə mayt/ (**-mates, -mating, -mated**) *vti* **1.** to combine two or more organizations or things into one unified whole, or take the form of one unified whole **2.** to alloy a metal with mercury, or be alloyed with mercury —**amalgamator** *n*

amalgamation /ə málgə máysh'n/ *n* **1.** COMBINING THINGS the process of amalgamating things into a unified whole **2.** RESULT OF COMBINING THINGS something that is a combination of different things or results from their amalgamation **3.** BUSINESS MERGER a combination of two or more business concerns so as to form one **4.** METAL EXTRACTION FROM ORE a method of extracting a precious metal from an ore by using mercury to form an amalgam with the metal

Amalthea /ámmal thee ə/ *n* a natural satellite of Jupiter, discovered in 1892

amandine /aámən deen, -deén, ámmən-/ *adj* filled, cooked, or served with almonds ○ *salmon amandine* [Mid-19C. < French < *amande* 'almond']

amantadine /ə mántə deen/ *n* an antiviral drug that is also used to treat Parkinson's disease [Mid-20C. Blend of AMINE + *adamantane*]

amanuensis /ə mánnyoo énssiss/ (*plural* **-enses** /-én seez/) *n* (*literary*) **1.** somebody employed by a person to write from his or her dictation or to copy manuscripts **2.** a writer's assistant with research and secretarial duties [Early 17C. < Latin < *a manu* 'by hand' (in *servus a manu* 'enslaved servant with secretarial duties')]

amaranth /ámmə ranth/ (*plural* **-ranths** or *same*) *n* **1.** PLANT WITH DROOPING FLOWERS a plant grown for ornament and sometimes as a grain crop or leafy vegetable. Flowers: green, red, or purple, in long drooping heads. Genus: *Amaranthus*. **2.** LEGENDARY FLOWER according to legend, a flower that never fades **3.** FOOD DYE a synthetic red food dye [Mid-16C. Via French *amarante* or modern Latin *amaranthus* < Latin *amarantus* < Greek *amarantos* 'not corruptible, not fading']

amaranthine /ámmə rán thīn, -thin/ *adj* **1.** undying or unfading, like the legendary amaranth (*literary*) **2.** of a dark reddish-purple colour

amaretti /ámmə rétti/ *npl* small crisp Italian biscuits flavoured with almonds [< Italian, plural of *amaretto* (see AMARETTO)]

amaretto /ámmə réttō/ *n* an Italian almond-flavoured liqueur [Mid-20C. < Italian, 'little bitter (one)' < *amaro* 'bitter' < Latin *amarus*]

Amarillo /ámmə ríllō/ city in northwestern Texas, near the centre of the Texas Panhandle. Population: 177,010 (2002 estimate).

amaryllis

amaryllis /ámmə rílliss/ (*plural* **-lises** or *same*) *n* **1.** a plant grown from a bulb, usually indoors. Flowers: large, red, pink, or white, trumpet-shaped, at the head of a single stalk. Native to: southern Africa. Latin name: *Amaryllis belladonna.* **2.** a tropical American plant related to the southern African amaryllis. Genus: *Hippeastrum.* [Late 18C. Via modern Latin < Greek *Amarullis*, shepherdess in pastorals]

amass /ə máss/ (**amasses, amassing, amassed**) *vt* to bring a large quantity of things together over time ○ *amassed a fortune in the 1950s* [15C. < French *amasser* < *masser* 'gather into a mass' < Latin *massa* (see MASS)] —**amassable** *adj* —**amasser** *n*

SYNONYMS See *collect*[1].

amateur /ámmətər, -choor/ *n* **1.** SOMEBODY DOING SOMETHING FOR PLEASURE somebody who does something for pleasure rather than payment ○ *a competition open only to amateurs* **2.** UNSKILLED PERSON somebody with limited skill in, or knowledge of, an activity ○ *Whoever handled your rewiring must have been an amateur.* **3.** SOMEBODY WHO LOVES SOMETHING somebody who loves or is greatly interested in something (*literary*) ○ *She is an amateur of classical sculpture.* ■ *adj* **1.** BEING AMATEUR engaging in something as an amateur ○ *a talented amateur golfer* **2.** BY AMATEURS for, by, or consisting of amateurs **3.** NOT DONE WITH SKILL done in an unskilful or unprofessional way [Late 18C. Via French < Latin *amator* 'lover' < *amare* 'to love']

amateurish /ámmətərish, -choor-/ *adj* lacking the skill of a professional, or unskilfully or unprofessionally done —**amateurishly** *adv* —**amateurishness** *n*

amateurism /ámmətərizəm, -choor-/ *n* amateur status, participation by amateurs, or the principle that something should be reserved for amateurs ○ *one of the last bastions of true amateurism in sport*

Amati /ə maáti/ family of Italian violin makers including **Andrea** (*d.* 1578), his son **Girolamo** (1556?–1630?), and grandson **Nicolò** (1596–1684), the most eminent of the Amati family, known for the extreme elegance of his instruments

amatol /ámmə tol/ *n* an explosive made from ammonium nitrate and TNT. Use: bombs. [Early 20C. < AMMONIUM + TOLUENE]

amatory /ámmətəri/, **amatorial** /ámmə táwri əl/ *adj* relating to, involving, expressing, or typical of physical love (*formal*) ○ *amatory adventures* [Late 16C. < Latin *amatorius* < *amator* (see AMATEUR)]

~~amatuer~~ incorrect spelling of **amateur**

amaurosis /ámmaw róssiss/ *n* partial or complete vision impairment, especially when there is no obvious damage to the eye [Mid-17C. < Greek *amaurōsis* < *amauroun* 'darken' < *amauros* 'dark'] —**amaurotic** /-róttik/ *adj*

amaurosis fugax /-fyoó gaks/ *n* a brief episode of partial blindness occurring when there is no obvious damage to the eye [*Fugax* < Latin < *fugere* 'flee']

amautik /ə mówtik/, **amauti** /-ti/ *n Can* among the Inuit, a woman's jacket that has a fur-lined hood for carrying an infant or small child [< Inuktitut]

amaze /ə mayz/ (**amazes, amazing, amazed**) *vt* to fill somebody with wonder or astonishment [Old English *āmasian* 'stupefy, stun', origin ?] —**amazed** *adj*

amazement /ə máyzmənt/ *n* a strong feeling of wonder or surprise at the extraordinariness of something

amazing /ə máyzing/ *adj* **1.** so extraordinary or wonderful as to be barely believable or to cause extreme surprise ○ *an amazing escape* **2.** outstandingly good, skilful, or admirable (*informal*) ○ *an amazing concert* —**amazingly** *adv* —**amazingness** *n*

amazon /ámməz'n/ *n* a medium-sized parrot that typically has green feathers and a short tail. Native to: tropical America. Genus: *Amazona.* [Late 19C. After the AMAZON[2]]

Amazon[1] /ámməz'n/ *n* **1.** in Greek mythology, a member of a group of women warriors who lived in Scythia, an area of present-day Ukraine, or elsewhere at the northern limits of the world. According to one version, they fought in the Trojan war on the side of Troy. **2.** *also* **amazon** a notably tall, physically strong, or strong-willed woman [14C. Via Latin < Greek *Amazōn*] —**Amazonian** /ámmə zóni ən/ *adj*

Amazon

Amazon[2] /ámməz'n/ world's second longest river. It flows east from northern Peru, traversing northern South America and emptying into the Atlantic Ocean in Brazil. Length: 6,400 km/4,000 mi. —**Amazonian** /ámmə zóni ən/ *adj*

Amazonas /ámmə zónəss/ state in Northwestern Brazil. Capital: Manaus. Population: 2,389,279 (1996). Area: 1,577,820 sq. km/609,200 sq. mi.

Amazon dolphin *n* a freshwater dolphin with a long snout. Native to: upper Amazon and Orinoco rivers. Latin name: *Inia geoffrensis.*

amazonite /ámməzə nīt/ *n* a green or bluish-green precious stone that is a variety of microcline. Use: gems. [After the AMAZON[2], where similar green stones were formerly found]

ambassador /am bássədər/ *n* **1.** DIPLOMATIC REPRESENTATIVE a diplomatic official of the highest rank sent by one country as its long-term representative to another **2.** OFFICIAL REPRESENTATIVE an official representative of an organization or movement ○ *visiting this country as an ambassador for an organization dedicated to saving endangered species* **3.** UNOFFICIAL REPRESENTATIVE somebody or something regarded as an unofficial representative or a symbol of something ○ *The swallow is an ambassador of spring.* [14C. Via French *ambassadeur* < Italian *ambasciator* < Latin *ambactus* 'vassal' < Gaulish, 'servant'] —**ambassadorial** /am bássə dáwri əl/ *adj* —**ambassadorship** *n*

CULTURAL NOTE *The Ambassadors*, a novel (1903) by US writer Henry James. Sometimes regarded as James's masterpiece, it tells the story of Lambert Strether, a middle-aged editor sent by his wealthy New England patron and fiancée to Paris to persuade her expatriate son Chad to return home.

ambassador at large (*plural* **ambassadors at large**) *n* N Am an ambassador not assigned to one specific country

amber /ámbər/ *n* **1.** YELLOW FOSSIL RESIN a hard translucent fossil resin varying in colour from yellow to light brown. Use: jewellery, ornaments. **2.** BROWNISH-YELLOW COLOUR a yellow to brown colour **3.** SIGNAL FOR

CAUTION in a system of road traffic lights or railway signalling, the yellow-coloured light that advises caution [14C. Via French *ambre* < Arabic *anbar* 'ambergris', from a perceived similarity between the two] —**amber** *adj*

Amber alert *n US* a system of bulletins issued by police to the media and sometimes on electronic road signs, requesting vital information leading to the rapid rescue of a kidnapped child [Early 21C. After *Amber* Hagerman, a child kidnapped and murdered in Texas in 1996]

amber fluid *n Aus* BEVERAGES same as **beer** (senses 1–2) (*informal*)

amber gambler *n* a driver who takes risks by not stopping at traffic lights when they are at amber (*informal*)

ambergris /ámbər greess, -griss/ *n* a grey waxy substance, consisting mainly of cholesterol, secreted from the intestines of the sperm whale. It is found floating in tropical waters or on beaches. Use: perfume-making. [15C. < French *ambre gris* 'grey amber']

amberjack /ámbər jak/ (*plural* **-jacks** or *same*) *n* **1.** a large sea fish that has golden markings. Native to: warm waters. Genus: *Seriola*. **2.** a fish with a black-blue, yellow-banded body and a mouth that is a brilliant orange colour inside. Native to: the eastern and western coasts of Australia. Latin name: *Seriola purpurascens*.

amber nectar *n Aus* BEVERAGES same as **beer** (senses 1–2) (*informal*)

amberoid /ámbə royd/ *n* a synthetic form of amber made by heating and compressing valueless small pieces of amber with other resins

ambi- *prefix* both ○ *ambiversion* [< Latin *ambi* 'around, on both sides' < Indo-European]

ambiance *n* another spelling of **ambience**

ambidextrous /ámbi dékstrəss/ *adj* **1.** able to use the right and the left hand with equal skill **2.** very skilful and versatile [Mid-17C. < late Latin *ambidexter* 'right-handed on both sides' < Latin *dexter* 'right-handed'] —**ambidexterity** /-dek stérrəti/ *n* —**ambidextrously** *adv*

ambience /ámbi ənss, -onss/, **ambiance** *n* the typical atmosphere or mood of a place ○ *a restaurant with a welcoming ambience* [Mid-20C. < French *ambiance* < *ambiant* < Latin *ambient-* (see AMBIENT)]

ambient /ámbi ənt/ *adj* in the immediately surrounding area ○ *ambient temperature* ■ *n* MUSIC same as **ambient music** [Late 16C. Directly or via French < Latin *ambient-*, present participle of *ambire* 'go round' (see AMBITION)]

ambient music *n* music that is usually instrumental and repetitive and often contains soothing electronic sounds, used to create an atmosphere of calm or relaxation

ambiguity /ámbi gyóo əti/ (*plural* **-ties**) *n* **1.** a situation in which something can be understood in more than one way and it is not clear which meaning is intended **2.** an expression or statement that has more than one meaning

ambiguous /am bíggyoo əss/ *adj* **1.** having more than one possible meaning or interpretation ○ *an ambiguous response* **2.** causing uncertainty or confusion ○ *an ambiguous result* [Early 16C. < Latin *ambiguus* 'undecided' < *ambigere* 'wander about' < *agere* 'to lead'] —**ambiguously** *adv* —**ambiguousness** *n*

USAGE ambiguous or **ambivalent?** Both words describe uncertainty in understanding what is meant. The principal difference is that ***ambivalent*** is used of people and their attitudes, whereas ***ambiguous*** refers to information or context. If people are ***ambivalent*** about disarmament, they are unsure about the advantages and disadvantages and cannot easily decide between the various arguments, whereas if a political leader makes an ***ambiguous*** statement about disarmament, then the statement has more than one possible interpretation.

ambiguous genitalia *n* a congenital condition in which the outer genitals do not have the typical appearance of either sex (*takes a singular verb*) ■ *npl* outer genitals that do not have the typical appearance of either sex (*takes a plural verb*)

ambisexual /ámbi sékshoo əl/ *adj* **1.** describes secondary sexual characteristics that are common to both sexes **2.** sexually responsive or attracted to both sexes —**ambisexuality** /-sékshoo álləti/ *n*

ambisonics /ámbi sónniks/ *n* a recording and reproduction system that uses separate channels and speakers to create the effect of being surrounded by sound (*takes a singular verb*) —**ambisonic** *adj*

ambit /ámbit/ *n* the scope, extent, or limits of something ○ *within the ambit of the court's jurisdiction* [Late 16C. < Latin *ambitus* 'circuit' < *ambire* (see AMBITION)]

ambit claim *n Aus* a claim made to an arbitration authority by workers who expect to negotiate and therefore make extravagant initial demands

ambition /am bísh'n/ *n* **1.** a strong feeling of wanting to be successful in life and achieve great things ○ *She lacks ambition.* **2.** an aim or objective that somebody is trying to achieve [14C. Via French < Latin *ambition-* < *ambire* 'canvass for votes, go round' < *ire* 'go']

ambitious /am bíshəss/ *adj* **1.** HAVING STRONG DESIRE FOR SUCCESS having a strong desire to be successful in life **2.** NEEDING GREAT EFFORT TO SUCCEED sounding impressive but difficult to achieve because very high standards have been set or a great deal of work is required ○ *an ambitious plan to increase market share* **3.** STRONGLY DESIROUS with a strong desire to have or do something ○ *ambitious to be the youngest person ever to win the championship* —**ambitiously** *adv* —**ambitiousness** *n*

ambivalence /am bívvələnss/ *n* **1.** the presence of two opposing ideas, attitudes, or emotions at the same time **2.** a feeling of uncertainty about something due to a mental conflict [Early 20C. < German *Ambivalenz*, after *Äquivalenz* 'equivalence']

ambivalent /am bívvələnt/ *adj* having mixed, uncertain, or conflicting feelings about something

USAGE See ***ambiguous***.

ambiversion /ámbi vúrsh'n/ *n* a personality pattern that has characteristics of both introversion and extroversion —**ambivert** /ámbi vurt/ *n*

amble /ámb'l/ *vi* (**-bles, -bling, -bled**) to walk slowly in a relaxed way ○ *'I took off shoes and socks and ambled along carrying them, enjoying the evening sun.'* (Dick Francis, *The Danger*; 1983) ■ *n* a slow and relaxed walk or style of walking [14C. Via French *ambler* < Latin *ambulare* 'walk'] —**ambler** *n*

amblygonite /am blíggə nīt/ *n* a white or greyish-green mineral. Use: source of lithium. [Early 19C. < Greek *amblugōnios* 'obtuse-angled']

amblyopia /ámbli ṓpi ə/ *n* an impairment of the vision in one eye that does not have a physical cause [Early 18C. Via modern Latin < Greek *ambluōpia* 'dim-sightedness'] —**amblyopic** /-óppik/ *adj*

ambo[1] /ámbō/ (*plural* **-bos** or **-bones** /am bṓ neez/) *n* a lectern or pulpit in early Christian churches [Mid-17C. Via medieval Latin < Greek *ambōn* 'raised edge (of a dish)']

ambo[2] /ámbō/ (*plural* **-bos**) *n Aus* an ambulance driver (*informal*) [Late 20C. Shortening and alteration]

Amboinese *n, adj* PEOPLES, LANG same as **Ambonese**

ambones CHR plural of **ambo**[1]

Ambonese /ámbə neéz/ (*plural same*), **Amboinese** /ám boy-/ *n* **1.** somebody who was born or brought up on the island of Ambon in eastern Indonesia **2.** the form of Malay spoken on the island of Ambon [Mid-19C. < *Ambon*] —**Ambonese** *adj*

Ambrose /ámbrōz/, **St** (AD 340?–397) Roman priest and theologian. As bishop of Milan from 374 he combated Arianism and introduced much Greek theology to the West.

ambrosia /am brṓzi ə/ *n* **1.** FOOD OF CLASSICAL GODS in classical mythology, the food of the deities, which was supposed to make those who ate it immortal **2.** INSECTS same as **beebread** **3.** FRUIT AND COCONUT DISH a dessert or salad made from oranges, bananas, and coconut **4.** SOMETHING DELICIOUS a substance that tastes or smells delicious (*literary*) [Mid-16C. Via Latin < Greek < *ambrotos* 'immortal'] —**ambrosial** *adj*

ambry /ámbri/ (*plural* **-bries**), **aumbry** /áwmbri/ *n* **1.** a small recess near the altar in a church, where sacred vessels are kept **2.** a small cupboard or pantry (*archaic*) [14C. Via French *armarie* < Latin *armarium* (see ARMOIRE)]

ambulacrum /ámbyoo láykrəm/ (*plural* **-ra** /-rə/) *n* in a starfish, sea urchin, or similar animal, each of the five radial areas on the underside of the body along which the blood vessels and nerves run and through which the feet extend [Early 19C. < Latin, 'avenue' < *ambulare* 'to walk'] —**ambulacral** *adj*

ambulance /ámbyooləns/ *n* a vehicle designed and equipped for carrying people to and from hospital [Mid-19C. < French < *hôpital ambulant* 'field hospital', literally 'walking hospital' < Latin *ambulant-*, present participle of *ambulare* 'walk']

ambulance chaser *n* a lawyer who, in order to earn large fees, seeks out accident victims and encourages them to claim heavy damages (*slang disapproving*)

ambulant /ámbyoolənt/ *adj* **1.** moving around from place to place **2.** MED same as **ambulatory** *adj* (sense 3) [Early 17C. Via French < Latin *ambulant-* (see AMBULANCE)]

ambulate /ámbyoo layt/ (**-lates, -lating, -lated**) *vi* to walk or move from one place to another (*formal*) [Early 17C. < Latin *ambulat-*, past participle of *ambulare* 'walk']

ambulatory /ámbyoo láytəri/ *adj* **1.** RELATING TO WALKING relating to or equipped for walking (*formal*) **2.** WALKING OR MOVING walking or moving around, or done while walking or moving (*formal*) ○ *ambulatory activities* **3.** MED NOT CONFINED TO BED describes a patient who is able to walk and does not have to be kept in bed ○ *an ambulatory patient* **4.** LAW REVOCABLE able to be revoked ○ *an ambulatory will* ■ *n* (*plural* **-ries**) WALKWAY IN CHURCH OR CLOISTER an aisle at the end of a choir or chancel in a church, or a covered walkway of a cloister —**ambulatorily** *adv*

ambuscade /ámbə skáyd/ (*literary*) *n* an ambush set for somebody ■ *vt* (**-cades, -cading, -caded**) to ambush somebody [Late 16C. Via French *embuscade* and Italian *imboscata* < assumed Vulgar Latin *imboscare* (see AMBUSH)]

ambush /ámboosh/ *n* **1.** SURPRISE ATTACK an unexpected attack from a concealed position **2.** CONCEALMENT BEFORE ATTACK concealment before a surprise attack ○ *They lay in ambush and waited for their victims.* **3.** SOMEBODY WAITING IN AMBUSH one or more people concealed in order to make a surprise attack ■ *vt* (**-bushes, -bushing, -bushed**) ATTACK SOMEBODY OR SOMETHING to attack somebody or something suddenly from a concealed position [14C. Via Old French *embusche* < assumed Vulgar Latin *imboscare* 'hide in a bush' < assumed *boscus* 'bush'] —**ambusher** *n*

amchoor /um choór/ *n* unripe mangoes sliced, dried, and ground into powder, used in Indian and Middle Eastern cooking to give food a sweet-and-sour flavour or to tenderize meat [< Hindi < *aam* 'mango' + *choor* 'powder']

AMD *abbr* MED age-related macular degeneration

am dram /ám dram/ *n* the performance and production of plays for the theatre by nonprofessionals (*informal*) [Shortening of *amateur dramatics*]

ameba, etc. *n* MICROBIOL US spelling of **amoeba, etc**

amelanchier /ámmə lángki ər/ (*plural* **-ers** or *same*) *n* a small tree or bush of the rose family that produces small, edible, dark blue fruits. A common variety is the serviceberry. Flowers: white, in clusters. Native to: North America. Genus: *Amelanchier*. [Mid-18C. < Savoy dialect *amelancier* 'medlar']

ameliorate /ə meéli ə rayt/ (**-rates, -rating, -rated**) *vti* to make something better, or become better (*formal*) [Mid-18C. Alteration of MELIORATE, after French *améliorer*] —**ameliorable** /-rəb'l/ *adj* —**amelioration** /ə meéli ə ráysh'n/ *n* —**ameliorative** /-rətiv/ *adj* —**ameliorator** *n*

amen /aá mén, áy-/ *interj* **1.** said or sung at the end of a prayer or hymn to affirm its content **2.** used to express strong agreement ○ *amen to that* [Pre-12C. Via late Latin and Greek < Hebrew *'āmēn* 'truly' < *'āman* 'confirm']

amenable /ə meénəb'l/ *adj* **1.** WILLING TO COOPERATE responsive to suggestion and likely to cooperate **2.** ABLE TO BE AFFECTED susceptible to being affected in a particular way ○ *The tumour is not amenable to treatment.* **3.** ACCOUNTABLE required to account for your behaviour to an authority **4.** LIABLE TO BE JUDGED likely or available to be tested or judged [Late 16C. < Anglo-Norman < Old French *amener* 'bring to' < Latin *minari* 'threaten' < *minae* 'threats'] —**amenability** /ə meénə bílləti/ *n* —**amenably** *adv*

amend /ə ménd/ (**amends, amending, amended**) *vt* **1.** to make changes to something, especially a piece of text, in order to improve or correct it **2.** to revise or alter formally a motion, bill, or constitution [13C. Via French *amender* < Latin *emendare* 'to correct' < *menda* 'error'] —**amendable** *adj* —**amendatory** *adj*

USAGE amend or **emend**? The word to use in general contexts involving change for the better or legislative alterations is *amend*. *Emend* is normally restricted to the correction of errors in a printed or written text: *The ambiguous wording at the beginning of the document needs amending* (= changing to something clearer). *By emending two words* (= suggesting alternatives for them because they may have been copied wrongly) *it is possible to make the sentence intelligible.*

amendment /ə méndmənt/ *n* **1. ALTERATION TO SOMETHING** a change, correction, or improvement to something **2. CHANGE TO LEGAL DOCUMENT** an addition or alteration to a motion, bill, or constitution **3. PROCESS OF ALTERING SOMETHING** the process of changing, correcting, or improving something ○ *The bill was passed without amendment.*

amends /ə méndz/ *n* something done or given as compensation for a wrong (*takes a singular or plural verb*) ○ *a desire to make amends after the misunderstanding* ○ *No amends were forthcoming even after we proved that they were in the wrong.* [14C. < Old French *amendes*, plural of *amende* 'reparation' < *amender* (see AMEND)]

Amenhotep III /áä men hó tep/ (*fl* 15th-14th century BC) king of Egypt (1417–1379 BC). His reign was characterized by the building of monuments and other architectural works.

Amenhotep IV ♦ Akhenaton

amenity /ə meénəti/ (*plural* **-ties**) *n* **1.** a useful or attractive feature or a service, e.g. leisure facilities (*often used in the plural*) ○ *the amenities of a luxury hotel* **2.** the experience of a place as pleasant or attractive ○ *thoroughly enjoyed the amenity of the clean mountain air in the summer* [14C. Directly or via French *aménité* < Latin *amoenitas* < *amoenus* 'pleasant']

amenorrhoea /áy menə reé ə/, **amenorrhea** *n* the suppression or unusual absence of menstruation —**amenorrhoeic** *adj*

ament /ə mént/, **amentum** /ə méntəm/ (*plural* **-ta** /tə/) *n* BOT same as **catkin** (*technical*) [Mid-18C. < Latin *amentum* 'strap']

Amer. *abbr* American

Amerasian /ámmə ráyzh'n/ *n* somebody of mixed American and Asian parentage ■ *adj* having mixed American and Asian parentage [Mid-20C. Blend of AMERICAN + ASIAN]

amerce /ə múrss/ (**amerces, amercing, amerced**) *vt* (*archaic*) **1.** to punish somebody with a fine **2.** to punish somebody in an arbitrary way [14C. < Anglo-Norman *amercier* 'place at somebody's mercy (as to the amount of a fine)' < Old French *a merci* 'at (your) mercy'] —**amerceable** *adj* —**amercement** *n*

America /ə mérrikə/ *n* **1.** ⚠ **UNITED STATES** the United States of America **2. N, S, AND CENTRAL AMERICA** a landmass comprising North America, South America, and Central America **3.** ⚠ **N AMERICA** North America (*informal*) [Early 16C. < *Americus*, Latinized form of *Amerigo* Vespucci (1454–1512), Italian navigator]

USAGE The use of *America* to mean the United States may cause offence to people from Canada and Central and South America, and should be avoided. The term *North America* may be used to refer to the United States and Canada together.

American /ə mérrikən/ *n* **SOMEBODY FROM UNITED STATES** somebody who comes from the United States ■ *adj* **1. OF UNITED STATES** relating to the United States, or its people, languages, or cultures **2. OF N, S, OR CENTRAL AMERICA** relating to North, South, or Central America or the landmass comprising them [Mid-16C. < modern Latin *Americanus* < AMERICA] —**Americanness** *n*

Americana /ə mérri ka'ánə/ *n* things from or about the United States, especially items that are valued by collectors (*takes a singular or plural verb*)

American aloe *n* PLANTS same as **century plant**

American Black English *n* LANG same as **African American Vernacular English**

American chameleon *n* REPT same as **anole**

American cheese *n* US a smooth processed cheese with a mild taste similar to cheddar

American dream *n* the idea that everyone in the United States has the chance to achieve success and prosperity

American eagle *n* BIRDS same as **bald eagle**

American English *n* the variety of English spoken in the United States

American football *n* UK, ANZ, Can a game played in the United States by two teams of 11 players who carry, throw, or kick an oval ball. Points are scored by carrying the ball across the opposing team's goal line or by kicking it through open-topped goal posts. US term **football**

American goldfinch *n* a goldfinch with yellow and black markings. Native to: United States and Canada. Latin name: *Carduelis tristis*.

American Gothic (1930) by Grant Wood
Corbis-Bettmann

American gothic, American Gothic *adj* depicting or representing hard work, frugality, and conservative social attitudes associated with rural and small-town United States

American Indian *n, adj* ANTHROP same as **Native American** (*sometimes considered offensive*)

USAGE See *Indian*.

Americanise *vti* another spelling of **Americanize**

Americanism /ə mérrikənizəm/ *n* **1.** a word, phrase, or custom that originated in, or is regarded as characteristic of, the United States **2.** strong affection or support for the United States

Americanist /ə mérrikənist/ *n* **1.** an expert on the life, history, language, or culture of the United States **2.** a student of or specialist in the languages and cultures of Native Americans

Americanize /ə mérrikə nīz/ (**-izes, -izing, -ized**), **Americanise** (**-ises, -ising, -ised**) *vti* to give something the form, style, or qualities associated with or used in the United States, or take on such qualities — **Americanization** /ə mérrikə nī záysh'n/ *n*

American kestrel *n* BIRDS same as **sparrowhawk** (sense 2)

American Legion *n* an organization of veterans of the US armed services, founded in 1919

americano /ə mérri ka'ánō/ (*plural* **-nos**) *n* an espresso coffee diluted with hot water and containing no milk [Late 20C. < Italian, 'American']

American plan *n* N Am same as **full board**

American Revolution *n* N Am same as **American War of Independence**

American saddle horse *n* a high-stepping saddle

horse originally bred in Kentucky and trained to walk, trot, canter, gallop, and pace

American Samoa US territory, consisting of a group of South Pacific islands, in the Samoan island chain. Pago Pago is the seat of government. Population: 67,084 (2001). Area: 195 sq. km/75 sq. mi.

American shorthair *n* a short-haired domestic cat belonging to a US breed with a broad head and thick coat

American Sign Language *n* a system of communication used by people with impaired hearing that uses motions or gestures of the hands

American Spanish *n* the form of Spanish that is spoken in the United States

American Standard Code for Information Interchange *n* COMPUT full form of **ASCII**

American War of Independence *n* the war in which the American colonies won independence from Great Britain (1775–83). N Am term **American Revolution**

Americas /ə mérrikəz/ *npl* same as **America** (sense 2)

americium /ámmə ríssi əm/ *n* a white radioactive metallic element. Source: beta decay of plutonium. Use: alpha particle source for research. Symbol **Am**. See table at **element** [Mid-20C. After AMERICA]

Amerindian /ámmə ríndi ən/ *n* same as **Native American** (*sometimes considered offensive*) [Late 19C. Contraction of AMERICAN INDIAN] —**Amerindian** *adj* —**Amerindic** *adj*

USAGE See *Indian*.

Ameslan /ámmə slan/ *n* LANG same as **American Sign Language** [Late 20C. Acronym]

Ames test /áymz-/ *n* a test used to determine the cancer-causing potential of a chemical or other agent by measuring its effect on bacteria [Late 20C. After Bruce Ames (1928–), US biochemist]

amethocaine /ə méthō kayn/ *n* MED same as **tetracaine** [Mid-20C. Origin ?]

amethyst /ámməthist/ *n* **1.** VIOLET QUARTZ a translucent violet precious stone that is a variety of quartz. Use: gems. **2.** PURPLE SAPPHIRE a purple variety of sapphire. Use: gems. **3.** BLUISH-PURPLE a bluish-purple colour [13C. Via French and Latin < Greek *amethustos* 'not intoxicating' < *methu* 'wine'] —**amethyst** *adj* —**amethystine** /ámmə thís tīn/ *adj*

Amex /ámmeks/, **AMEX** *abbr* FIN American Stock Exchange

Amexica /ə méksikə/ *n* the Mexican presence on the US-Mexican border, in other non-border western states, and in large Midwest urban centres (*informal*) [Late 20C. Blend of AMERICA + MEXICO]

Amexican /ə méksikən/ *n* English as influenced by Latin American, especially Mexican, Spanish and spoken in the southwestern United States and in Latin American communities elsewhere in the country

amfetamine /am féttə meen/ *n* DRUGS same as **amphetamine** (*technical*)

Amharic /am hárrik/ *n* the official language of Ethiopia, belonging to the Semitic branch of Afro-Asiatic languages and written in Ethiopic script. Native speakers: 15 million. [Early 19C. < *Amhara*, province in NW Ethiopia] —**Amharic** *adj*

amiable /áymi əb'l/ *adj* **1.** friendly and pleasant to be with **2.** characterized by friendly feelings [14C. Via French < Late Latin *amicabilis* (see AMICABLE), influenced in meaning by French *aimable* 'lovable'] —**amiability** /áymi ə bílləti/ *n* —**amiableness** *n* —**amiably** *adv*

amianthus /ámmi ánthəss/ *n* a type of asbestos with thin silky fibres [Early 17C. Via Latin < Greek *amiantos* 'undefiled' < *miainein* 'defile']

amicable /ámmikəb'l/ *adj* characterized by or done in friendliness, without anger or bad feelings ○ *an amicable divorce* [15C. < Late Latin *amicabilis* < Latin *amicus* 'friend' < *amare* 'to love'] —**amicability** /ámmikə bílləti/ *n* —**amicableness** *n* —**amicably** *adv*

amice /ámmiss/ *n* a length of white fabric worn by a Christian priest around the neck [13C. Probably via Old French *amit* < Latin *amictus* 'cloak' < *amicire* 'to cover' < *iacere* 'throw']

AMICUS /ámmikəs/ *n* a trade union formed by a

---

merger between the AEEU and MSF in January 2002

amicus curiae /a míkəss kyoóri ee/ (*plural* **amici curiae** /a míssee-/), **amicus** (*plural* **-ci**) *n* somebody whose counsel provides information to a court on legal issues involved in a case [Early 17C. < modern Latin, 'friend of the court']

amid /ə míd/, **amidst** /ə mídst/ *prep* **1.** surrounded by things or people ○ *a small lake amid the hills* **2.** used to indicate the circumstances or events around or accompanying something ○ *I sat down amid roars of laughter.* [12C. < A¹ + MID]

Amida /a meédə/ *n* BUDDHISM same as **Amitabha** [< Sanskrit *amita* 'immeasurable, unlimited']

amide /ámmīd/ *n* **1.** any organic compound derived from ammonia, formed by the replacement of one or more hydrogen atoms with acyl groups **2.** any inorganic compound derived from ammonia and containing the NH_2 ion [Mid-19C. < AMMONIA] —**amidic** /ə míddik/ *adj*

amidol /ámmi dol/ *n* a colourless water-soluble crystalline compound. Use: photographic developer. Formula: $C_6H_3(NH_2)_2OH\cdot HC$. [Late 19C. < German, a trademark]

amidships /ə mídships/ *adv*, *adj* near or in the middle of a boat or ship

amidst *prep* same as **amid**

amigo /ə meégō/ (*plural* **-gos**) *n* a friend, or somebody thought likely to be friendly (*used especially in Spanish-speaking regions*) [Mid-19C. Via Spanish < Latin *amicus* 'friend']

amikacin /ámmi káyssin/ *n* a synthetic antibiotic. Use: treatment of infections caused by aerobic bacteria. [Late 20C. < *ami-* + *-kacin*, INN stem]

Amin /aa meén/, **Idi** (1925–2003) Ugandan president. Under his presidency (1971–79), approximately 70,000 Asians were expelled from Uganda, and perhaps as many as 300,000 Ugandans were killed.

amine /ámmeen/ *n* any organic derivative of ammonia formed by the replacement of hydrogen with one or more alkyl groups [Mid-19C. < AMMONIA]

-amine *suffix* amine ○ *tryptamine* [< AMINE]

amino /ə meénō/ *adj* describes a chemical compound containing the NH_2 group of atoms [Independent use of AMINO-]

amino- *prefix* containing an NH_2 group combined with a nonacid radical ○ *aminophenol* [< AMINE]

amino acid *n* a compound belonging to a class that contains an amino group. Amino acids make up proteins and are important components of cells. Some can be synthesized by the body (**nonessential amino acids**) and others must be obtained through the diet (**essential amino acids**).

aminobenzoic acid /ə meénō ben zō ik-/ *n* a crystalline solid derived from benzoic acid, especially PABA. Use: sunscreen lotions. Formula: $C_7H_7NO_2$.

amino caproic acid /ə meénō kap rō ik-/, **aminocaproic acid** *n* a type of amino acid. Use: treatment of excessive bleeding.

aminoglutethimide /ə meénō gloo téthə mīd/ *n* a drug that acts on the adrenal cortex, affecting the production of steroids. Use: treatment of breast cancer.

aminoglycoside /ə meénō glíkō sīd/ *n* an antibiotic belonging to a group in which amino sugars are linked as glycosides, e.g. streptomycin. Source: species of *Streptomyces* or *Micromonospora*. Use: treatment of aerobic bacterial infections.

aminopeptidase /ə meénō pépti dayz, -dayss/ *n* an enzyme that breaks down dietary peptides into amino acids

aminophenol /ə meénō fee nol/ *n* a white soluble organic compound. Use: dyes, photographic developers. Formula: C_6H_7NO.

aminophylline /ámmi nóffi leen, -nóffilin/ *n* a drug that causes widening of the bronchial tubes. Use: treatment of asthma. [Mid-20C. < AMINO- + THEOPHYLLINE]

aminoquinolone /ə meénō kwínnə lōn/ *n* a drug belonging to a group used in the prevention of malaria

---

aminotransferase /ə meénō tránsfə rayz, -rayss/ *n* BIOCHEM same as **transaminase**

amiodarone /ámmi óddərōn/ *n* a drug that blocks the displacement of calcium ions from active cell membranes. Use: treatment of irregular heartbeat.

amir *n* POL, ISLAM same as **emir**

Amis /áymiss/, **Sir Kingsley** (1922–95) British novelist. He received critical acclaim for his first novel, *Lucky Jim* (1954), and was awarded the Booker Prize in 1986 for *The Old Devils*.

Amish /áamish/ *npl* members of a Protestant group who migrated from Europe to North America in the 18th century. The Amish seek to maintain a lifestyle based on the Bible. [Late 19C. Probably < German *amisch*] —**Amish** *adj*

amiss /ə míss/ *adj* incorrect, inappropriate, or not as it should be ○ *We knew immediately from the disorder in the house that something was amiss.* ■ *adv* incorrectly or inappropriately ○ *Things began to go amiss after she left.* [13C. < Old Norse *á mis* 'so as to miss'] ◇ **not go** *or* **come amiss** to be welcome or useful ◇ **take something amiss** to be upset or offended by something, even though no offence was intended

Amitabha /ámmi taábə/ *n* an incarnation of Buddha as lord of paradise, into which the souls of the pure are reborn [< Sanskrit, 'infinite light']

amitosis /ámmi tőssiss/ *n* cell division by simple division of the nucleus and cytoplasm, without the appearance of chromosomes [Late 19C. < A-² + MITOSIS] —**amitotic** /-tóttik/ *adj*

amitriptyline /ámmi tríptə leen/ *n* a sedative drug. Use: treatment of depression and chronic pain. [Mid-20C. < AMINE + triptyline, INN stem]

amity /ámməti/ *n* friendliness and peaceful relations (*formal*) [15C. Via French *amitié* < medieval Latin *amicitas* < Latin *amicus* 'friend' (see AMICABLE)]

amlodipine /am lóddi peen/ *n* a drug that blocks the displacement of calcium ions from active cell membranes. Use: treatment of hypertension and angina. [Late 20C. < *amlo-* + *-dipine*, INN stem]

amma /úmmə/ *n* S Asia same as **mother**¹ *n* (sense 1) (*informal; often used as a form of address*) [Probably < children's first attempts at speaking, influenced by AMAH]

Amman /ə maán/ capital of the Hashemite Kingdom of Jordan, in the northwestern part of the country, northeast of the Dead Sea. Population: 1,147,447 (2000).

~~ammendment~~ incorrect spelling of **amendment**

ammeter /ámmeetər/ *n* an instrument used for measuring electric current in amperes [Late 19C. < AMPERE + -METER]

ammine /ámmeen/ *n* a compound containing one or more ammonia molecules attached to a salt or similar compound through coordinate bonds [Late 19C. < AMMONIA]

ammo /ámmō/ *n* ARMS same as **ammunition** (*informal*) [Early 20C. Shortening]

ammocoete /ámmə seet/ *n* the filter-feeding larva of the lamprey [Mid-19C. < modern Latin *Ammocoetes* < Greek *ammos* 'sand' + *koitē* 'bed']

ammonate /ámmə nayt/ *n* CHEM same as **ammine**

ammonia /ə mőni ə/ *n* **1.** a colourless pungent gas that is highly soluble in water. Use: refrigerant, manufacture of fertilizers, explosives, and plastics. Formula: NH_3. **2.** a solution of ammonia in water. Use: household cleaner, manufacture of fertilizers and textiles. [Late 18C. < modern Latin < Latin *sal ammoniacus* 'salt of Ammon' < Greek *Ammōn* 'Ammon', Egyptian god near whose temple ammonia and ammoniac were said to be obtained]

ammoniac /ə mőni ak/ *n* a strong-smelling brownish-yellow gum resin. Source: Asian plant of the carrot family. Use: medicine, porcelain, cement. ■ *adj* CHEM same as **ammoniacal** [14C. Via French < Latin *ammoniacus* (see AMMONIA)]

ammoniacal /ə mőni nī ək'l/ *adj* containing or resembling ammonia

ammoniate /ə mőni ayt/ (**-ates, -ating, -ated**) *vt* to treat or combine something with ammonia or an ammonia compound —**ammoniation** /ə mőni áysh'n/ *n*

ammonia water *n* CHEM same as **ammonia** (sense 2)

---

ammonification /ə mónnifi káysh'n/ *n* **1.** treatment with ammonia or an ammonium compound **2.** the formation of ammonia or ammonium compounds through the bacterial decomposition of organic matter

ammonify /ə mónni fī/ (**-fies, -fying, -fied**) *vti* to treat something with ammonia, or to undergo ammonification —**ammonifier** *n*

ammonite /ámmə nīt/ *n* **1.** an extinct invertebrate sea animal with a flat partitioned spiral shell, belonging to the ammonoids **2.** the fossilized shell of an ammonite [Mid-18C. < modern Latin *ammonites* < medieval Latin *cornu Ammonis* 'horn of Ammon'] —**ammonitic** /ámmə níttik/ *adj*

Ammonite /ámmə nīt/ *n* a member of an ancient Semitic people in the Bible who lived between the Syrian desert and the River Jordan between the 13th and 6th centuries BC. They were constant enemies of the Israelites. [Mid-16C. < late Latin < Hebrew *'Ammōn* 'Ammon (son of Lot)']

ammonium /ə móni əm/ *adj* relating to or containing the NH₄+ ion derived from ammonia [Early 19C. < AMMONIA]

ammonium bicarbonate *n* a white crystalline solid. Use: baking powder. Formula: NH_4HCO_3.

ammonium carbonate *n* a white crystalline solid. Use: smelling salts, baking powder. Formula: $(NH_4)_2CO_3$.

ammonium chloride *n* a white crystalline solid. Use: expectorant, soldering flux, dry cell electrolyte. Formula: NH_4Cl.

ammonium hydroxide *n* a solution of ammonia in water

ammonium nitrate *n* a white crystalline solid. Use: fertilizers, herbicides, insecticides, explosives. Formula: NH_4NO_3.

ammonium sulphate *n* a white crystalline solid. Use: fertilizer, water purification. Formula: $(NH_4)_2SO_4$.

ammonoid /ámmə noyd/ *n* an extinct cephalopod mollusc with a partitioned shell [Mid-19C. < modern Latin *Ammonoidea* < *ammonites* (see AMMONITE)]

ammunition /ámmyʊ́ níshʼn/ *n* **1.** BULLETS AND MISSILES bullets, shells, missiles, and other projectiles used as weapons **2.** EXPLOSIVE MATERIAL bombs, grenades, and other explosive devices or substances used as weapons **3.** SUPPORTING FACTS facts and information that can be used to support a point of view in an argument [Late 16C. < French, alteration (due to mistaking *la munition* for *l'amunition*) of *munition* (see MUNITION)]

amnesia /am neé zi ə/ *n* loss of memory as a result of shock, injury, psychological disturbance, or medical disorder [Late 18C. < Greek *amnēsia*, alteration of *amnēstia* 'forgetfulness' < *amnēstos* 'not remembered' < *mnasthai* 'remember'] —**amnesiac** /-ak/ *n, adj* — **amnestic** /-néstik/ *adj*

amnesty /ámnəsti/ *n* (*plural* **-ties**) **1.** PARDON a general pardon, especially for those who have committed political crimes **2.** PROSECUTION-FREE PERIOD a period during which crimes can be admitted or illegal weapons handed in without prosecution ■ *vt* (**-ties, -tying, -tied**) PARDON SOMEBODY to grant an amnesty to somebody [Late 16C. Via French < Greek *amnēstia* (see AMNESIA)]

Amnesty International *n* an international human rights organization concerned with prisoners of conscience under any type of political regime

amnia ANAT plural of **amnion**

amnio /ámni ō/ (*plural* **-os**) *n* MED same as **amniocentesis** (*informal*) [Late 20C. Shortening]

amniocentesis /ámni ō sen teéssiss/ (*plural* **-teses** /-teé seez/) *n* a test performed to determine the health, sex, or genetic constitution of a foetus by taking a sample of amniotic fluid through a needle inserted into the womb of the mother [Mid-20C. < AMNION + Greek *kentēsis* 'pricking' (from *kentein* 'prick')]

amniography /ámni óggrəfi/ *n* an X-ray of the womb, taken after a substance that will be shown up by the X-rays has been injected into the bloodstream [Mid-20C. < AMNION + -GRAPHY]

amnion /ámni ən/ (*plural* **-nions** or **-nia** /-ni ə/) *n* **1.** the inner of the two membranes enclosing the embryo of a bird, reptile, or mammal and its surrounding fluid **2.** the fluid-filled sac within which the embryo

of a bird, reptile, or mammal develops [Mid-17C. < Greek, 'caul' < *amnos* 'lamb'] —**amniotic** /ámni óttik/ *adj*

amniote /ámni ōt/ *n* a vertebrate that develops from an embryo within an amnion, e.g. a bird, reptile, or mammal [Early 20C. < modern Latin *Amniota* < AMNION]

amniotic fluid /ámni óttik-/ *n* the fluid that surrounds a foetus while it is developing. It flows out in the 'breaking of the waters' before a baby is born.

amniotic sac *n* ANAT, MED same as **amnion** (sense 2)

amobarbital /ámmō baárbit'l/ *n* a barbiturate drug. Use: sedative, hypnotic. [Mid-20C. < AMYL + BARBITAL]

amodiaquine /ámmō dí ə kween/ *n* a bitter yellow crystalline solid. Use: prevention of malaria.

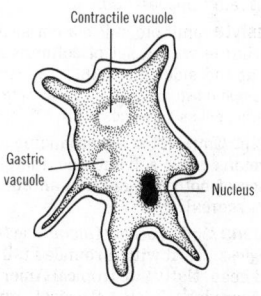

Contractile vacuole

Gastric vacuole

Nucleus

amoeba

amoeba /ə meébə/ (*plural* **-bae** /-bee/ or **-bas**) *n* a single-celled organism found in water and in damp soil on land, and as a parasite of other organisms. Lacking a fixed form and supporting structures, an amoeba consists of a protoplasmic mass in a thin membrane, and forms temporary projections (**pseudopodia**) in order to move. Genus: *Amoeba.* [Mid-19C. Via modern Latin < Greek *amoibē* 'change' < *ameibein* 'to change'] —**amoebic** *adj* —**amoeboid** *adj*

amoebiasis /ámmi bí əssiss/ *n* an infection or disease affecting the bowel, caused by the amoeba *Entamoeba histolytica*

amoebic dysentery *n* an inflammation of the colon causing diarrhoea of varying degrees of severity and resulting from infection by the amoeba *Entamoeba histolytica*

amoebicide /ə meébə sīd/ *n* a chemical agent used to kill amoebae

amoebocyte /ə meébə sīt/ *n* a cell that moves like an amoeba, e.g. a blood cell that can engulf particles

amok /ə mók/, **amuck** /ə múk/ *adj* frenzied and out of control [Early 16C. Directly or via Portuguese *am(o)uco* < Malay *amuk* 'fighting frenziedly'] ◇ **run amok** to be or become out of control, especially in a frenzied way

among /ə múng/, **amongst** /ə múngst/ CORE MEANING: a preposition indicating that something or somebody is surrounded by people, things, ideas, or circumstances ○ *You're among friends here.*
prep **1.** OF GROUP belonging to a particular group or class ○ *Her carvings are among the world's finest.* **2.** IN GROUP in or by a particular group ○ *a widely-held notion among physicists* **3.** BETWEEN GROUP MEMBERS by, between, or to each person or thing in a group ○ *divided among six of us* **4.** IN ADDITION TO in addition to other things or people ○ *The photos showed, among other things, a birthday party.* [Old English *on* (ge)*mong* < *on* 'in' + (ge)*mong* 'crowd' < Indo-European]

USAGE See **between**.

amontillado /ámmonti laádō/ *n* a pale medium-dry sherry from Spain [Early 19C. < Spanish]

amoral /ay mórrəl/ *adj* **1.** not concerned with or amenable to moral judgments **2.** not caring about good behaviour or morals (*disapproving*) —**amoralism** *n* — **amorality** /áymo rálləti/ *n* —**amorally** *adv*

amoretto /ámmə réttō/ (*plural* **-ti** /-ti/) *n* an artistic representation of a small naked boy or winged cherub as a symbol of love [Early 17C. < Italian, 'small cupid' < *amore* 'love' < Latin *amor*]

amorist /ámmərist/ *n* somebody who writes about love or is in love (*literary*) [Late 16C. < French *amour* 'love' or Latin *amor*]

Amorite /ámmə rīt/ *n* a member of an ancient Semitic people who lived in Mesopotamia, Syria, and Palestine between about 2600 and 1200 BC [Mid-16C. < Hebrew *'ĕmōrī* < Akkadian *Amurru(m)*, the land inhabited by the Amorites] —**Amorite** *adj*

amoroso[1] /ámmə róssō/ *adv, adj* to be played or sung in a gentle loving way (*used as a musical direction*) [Late 18C. Via Italian < medieval Latin *amorosus* (see AMOROUS)]

amoroso[2] /ámmə róssō/ *n* a sweet dark sherry [Late 19C. Via Spanish < medieval Latin *amorosus* (see AMOROUS)]

amorous /ámmərəss/ *adj* showing or feeling romantic love or sexual attraction [14C. Via Old French < medieval Latin *amorosus* < Latin *amor* 'love'] —**amorously** *adv* —**amorousness** *n*

amorphous /ə máwrfəss/ *adj* **1.** WITHOUT SHAPE without any clear shape, form, or structure **2.** NOT CLASSIFIABLE not obviously belonging to any category or type **3.** CHEM, GEOL NOT CRYSTALLINE without a crystalline structure [Mid-18C. Via modern Latin < Greek *amorphos* 'without shape' < *morphē* 'shape'] —**amorphously** *adv* — **amorphousness** *n*

amortize /ə máwr tīz/ (**-tizes, -tizing, -tized**), **amortise** (**-tises, -tising, -tised**) *vt* **1.** REDUCE DEBT BY INSTALMENTS to reduce a debt by making payments against the principal balance in instalments or regular transfers **2.** WRITE OFF COST OF ASSET to write off the cost of an asset over a period of time in a statement of accounts **3.** TRANSFER PROPERTY to transfer land or other assets to an ecclesiastical body (*archaic*) [14C. Via French *amortiss*- 'alienate in mortmain' < assumed Vulgar Latin *admortire* 'deaden' < Latin *mort*- 'death'] —**amortizable** *adj* —**amortization** /ə máwr tī záysh'n/ *n*

Amos /áymoss/ *n* **1.** in the Bible, a Hebrew prophet who lived in the 8th century BC and delivered judgments against Judah, Samaria, and Israel **2.** a book of the Bible that contains the prophecies traditionally attributed to Amos. See table at **Bible**

amotivational syndrome /áy mōti váysh'nəl-/ *n* a psychological condition characterized by a loss of the motivation to carry out socially accepted behaviours and tasks, usually associated with the use of marijuana

amount /ə mównt/ *n* a quantity or degree of something, considered as a unit or total [14C. < Old French *amonter* 'rise' < *amont* 'upwards' < Latin *ad montem* 'to the mountain']

USAGE **amount** or **number**? *Amount* is normally used with singular words or words that have no plural, that is so-called uncountable or mass nouns, for example *cheese*, *happiness*, and *warfare*: *a large amount of cheese; any amount of happiness.* In contrast, *number* is used with plural nouns, for example *books, questions, ships,* and *cheeses* (= types of cheese): *a large number of books; an excessive number of questions; a good number of cheeses.* In everyday speech, *amount* is sometimes used when *number* is strictly called for: *a large amount of books.* This should be avoided in more formal speaking and writing.

amount to *vt* **1.** to come to a total when added up **2.** to be equivalent to something ○ *Their statement amounts to nothing more than a slick evasion.*

amour /ə moór/ *n* a love affair, especially one that is clandestine (*dated*) [14C. Via French < Latin *amor* 'love']

amour-propre /ámmoor próprə/ *n* self-respect or estimation of your true worth (*formal*) [Late 18C. < French, 'self-love']

amoxapine /ə móksə peen/ *n* an antidepressant drug taken orally. Use: treatment of neurotic and psychotic depressive disorders. [Late 20C. < amox- + -apine, INN stem]

amoxycillin /ə móksi síllin/ *n* an antibiotic with properties similar to those of ampicillin, used to treat a broad range of conditions [Late 20C. < amoxi- + -cillin, INN stem]

Amoy /ə móy/ *n* the dialect of Chinese spoken on the island of Xiamen and in neighbouring areas in southeastern China [Mid-19C. After Amoy (XIAMEN)] — **Amoy** *adj*

amp /amp/ *n* **1.** same as **ampere 2.** same as **amplifier** (sense 1) (*informal*) [Late 19C. Shortening]

AMP *n* a compound (**nucleotide**) involved in energy transfer reactions in living cells. Full form **adenosine monophosphate**

amped /ampt/, **amped up** adj US feeling or showing great excitement or agitation (slang) [Late 20C. < AMP, literally 'amplified, powered up']

amperage /ámpərij/ n the number of amperes measured in an electric current

ampere /ám pair/ n the basic unit of electric current in the SI system, equal to a current that produces a force of 2x10⁻⁷ newtons per metre between two parallel conductors in a vacuum. Symbol **A** [Late 19C. After André-Marie Ampère (1775–1836), French physicist]

ampere-hour n a measure of quantity of electricity equal to the amount of electricity that passes in one hour through a conductor with a current of one ampere

ampersand /ámpər sand/ n the symbol '&', meaning 'and' [Mid-19C. < and per se and '(the character) "&" by itself (means) and']

amphetamine /am féttə meen/ n a drug formerly used to treat depression and as an appetite suppressant, or any of its derivatives. Technical name **amfetamine** [Mid-20C. Contraction of alpha-methyl-phenethylamine]

amphi- prefix both ○ amphibious [Via Latin < Greek amphi 'on both sides' < Indo-European]

amphibian /am fíbbi ən/ n 1. a cold-blooded vertebrate that spends some time on land but must breed and develop into an adult in water. Frogs, salamanders, and toads are amphibians. Class: Amphibia. 2. an aircraft or vehicle designed to operate on land or water ■ adj ZOOL same as **amphibious** (sense 1) [Mid-19C. < modern Latin Amphibia < Greek amphibion 'amphibious being' < amphibios (see AMPHIBIOUS)]

amphibious /am fíbbi əss/ adj 1. LIVING ON LAND AND IN WATER describes an animal that lives in water during early development and on land as an adult 2. OPERATING ON LAND AND IN WATER taking place or operating both on land and in water ○ made an amphibious assault on the island ○ amphibious vehicles 3. OF MIXED TYPE with two different qualities or features resulting in a mixed type [Mid-17C. < Greek amphibios 'living on both (land and water)' < bios 'life'] —**amphibiously** adv

amphibole /ámfi bōl/ n a hydrous silicate mineral containing varying amounts of aluminium, calcium, iron, magnesium, and sodium [Early 19C. < French < Greek amphibolos 'ambiguous' < ballein 'to throw'; because the mineral is able to appear in a variety of forms] —**amphibolic** /ámfi bóllik/ adj

amphibolite /am fíbbə līt/ n a metamorphic rock consisting mainly of amphibole with some plagioclase

amphibology /ámfi bólləji/ (plural -gies), **amphiboly** /am fíbbəli/ (plural -lies) n a phrase or sentence that can be interpreted in two ways, usually because of the grammatical construction rather than the meanings of the words themselves. The phrase 'the boy on the chair with a broken leg' is an amphibology. [Late 16C. < late Latin amphibologia 'ambiguity' < Latin amphibolia < Greek -logia 'speech'] —**amphibological** /am fíbbə lójjik'l/ adj —**amphibologically** adv —**amphibolous** /am fíbbələss/ adj

amphibrach /ámfi brak/ n a metrical foot of three syllables with the stress on the second syllable, or of one long syllable between two short syllables. The word 'contentment' and the phrase 'a mushroom' are amphibrachs. [Late 16C. Via Latin amphibrachys < Greek amphibrakhus 'short on both sides' < brakhus 'short'] —**amphibrachic** /ámfi brákik/ adj

amphictyony /am fíkti əni/ (plural -nies) n in ancient Greece, a group of neighbouring states or communities that shared responsibility for shrines and temples. The amphictyony maintaining the shrine of Apollo at Delphi is a famous example. [Mid-19C. < Greek amphiktuones, literally 'dwellers around' < ktizein 'to found'] —**amphictyonic** /am fíkti ónnik/ adj

amphigenetic /ámfijə néttik/ adj produced by or involving both sexes ○ amphigenetic reproduction

amphigory /ám figgəri/ (plural -ries), **amphigouri** /ámfí goori/ (plural -ris) n a nonsensical piece of writing, usually in verse [Early 19C. < French amphigouri]

amphimacer /am fímməssər/ n a metrical foot of three syllables with the stress on the first and third syllables, or of one short syllable between two long syllables. The phrase 'happy days' is an am-

phimacer. [Late 16C. Via Latin < Greek amphimakros 'long on both sides' < makros 'long']

amphimixis /ámfi míksiss/ n sexual reproduction involving the fusion of reproductive cells (**gametes**) from two organisms [Late 19C. < modern Latin < Greek amphi- 'on both sides' + mixis 'mingling' < mignunai 'to mix'] —**amphimictic** adj

amphioxus /ámfi óksəss/ (plural -oxi /-óksī/ or -oxuses) n MARINE BIOL same as **lancelet** [Mid-19C. < modern Latin, 'sharp at both sides' < Greek amphi- 'at both sides' + oxus 'sharp']

amphipod /ámfi pod/ n a small fresh or saltwater crustacean with a thin body and without a carapace. Order: Amphipoda. [Mid-19C. < modern Latin Amphipoda < Greek amphi- 'both' + pod-, stem of pous 'foot', because there are two types of feet in this order] —**amphipodous** /am fíppədəss/ adj

amphiprostyle /ámfi prố stīl/ n a classical temple or other building with a set of columns at each end but not at the sides [Early 18C. Via French and Latin < Greek amphiprostulos 'with pillars at both ends' < prostulos 'having pillars' (see PROSTYLE)]

amphiprotic /ámfi prótik/ adj producing and reacting with protons as a solvent and therefore having properties of both an acid and an alkali [Mid-20C. < AMPHI- + PROTON]

amphisbaena /ámfiss bēenə/ (plural -nae /-nee/ or -nas) n 1. a legless lizard with a rounded tail resembling a second head. Native to: tropical America. Family: Amphisbaenidae. 2. in classical mythology, a poisonous snake with a head at each end of its body, allowing it to move in either direction [14C. Via Latin < Greek amphisbaina 'going both ways' < amphis 'both ways' + bainein 'go'] —**amphisbaenic** adj

amphistylar /ámfi stīlər/ adj describes a building, especially a classical temple, that has a set of columns on both ends or sides [19C. < AMPHI- + Greek stulos 'column']

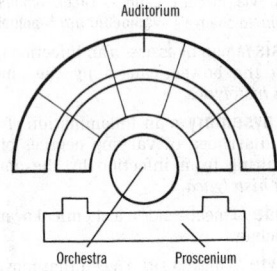

amphitheatre

amphitheatre /ámfi theertər/ n 1. CIRCULAR BUILDING a round or oval building without a roof that has a central open space surrounded by tiers of seats, especially one used by the ancient Romans for public entertainments 2. PLACE FOR SPORTS a large enclosure where sporting activities or public entertainments take place 3. SEATING FOR SPECTATORS a gallery of seats arranged in semicircular tiers for the audience in a theatre or lecture room 4. LECTURE ROOM a lecture hall or operating room where seating is arranged in semicircular tiers [Mid-14C. Via Latin < Greek amphitheatron, 'theatre on both sides' (because the typical classical Greek theatre had seating on one side only) < theatron (see THEATRE)] —**amphitheatric** /ámfithi áttrik/ adj —**amphitheatrically** adv

amphora

amphora /ámfərə/ (plural **-rae** /-ree/ or **-ras**) n in ancient Greece and Rome, a jar, usually made of clay, with a narrow neck and two handles, used for holding oil or wine [15C. Via Latin < Greek amphiphoreus < amphi- 'on both sides' + phoreus 'bearer' < pherein 'to bear'; from its two handles]

amphoteric /ámfə térrik/ adj able to react chemically as either an acid or a base [Mid-19C. < Greek amphoteroi 'both of two', comparative form of amphō 'both']

amphotericin /ámfə térrissin/ n a mixture of two antibiotic drugs used intravenously. Use: treatment of fungal infections.

ampicillin /ámpi síllin/ n a semisynthetic form of penicillin. Use: treatment of respiratory infections. [Mid-20C. < AMINO- + -cillin, INN stem]

ample /ámp'l/ (-pler, -plest) adj 1. as much or as many as required, usually with some left over 2. large, especially in physical size (often used euphemistically) [15C. Via French < Latin amplus 'large, plentiful'] —**ampleness** n

amplexus /am pléksəss/ n the mating posture of a pair of frogs or toads, in which the male clasps the female from behind during egg release and fertilization [Mid-20C. < Latin < past participle of amplecti 'embrace']

amplicon /ámpli kón/ n a nucleic acid fragment that is the product of the artificial large-scale reproduction of genetic material [Late 20C. < AMPLIFICATION]

amplidyne /ámpli dīn/ n a specialized direct-current generator in which small changes in power input produce large changes in output. It is used especially in servo systems. [Mid-20C. Blend of AMPLIFIER + Greek dynamis 'power' (see DYNAMIC)]

amplification /ámpli fi káysh'n/ n 1. PROCESS OF MAKING LOUDER the act or process of making something louder 2. ENLARGEMENT OF SOMETHING the act or process of making something larger, greater, or stronger 3. ADDITION OF DETAIL the act or process of making a spoken or written account fuller or clearer 4. ELECTRONICS INCREASE IN SIGNAL MAGNITUDE the increase in the magnitude of a signal produced by an amplifier 5. DETAIL ADDED a detail, explanation, or illustration added to a spoken or written account to make it fuller or clearer 6. GENETICS GENE REPRODUCTION the production of many copies of a section of DNA, naturally or by technological means

amplified fragment length polymorphism n a rapid method for detecting variations in DNA sequences between individuals, using the polymerase chain reaction technique

amplifier /ámpli fī ər/ n 1. a device that makes sounds louder, especially one increasing the sound level of musical instruments 2. an electronic device that increases the magnitude of a signal, voltage, or current

amplify /ámpli fī/ (-fies, -fying, -fied) vti 1. MAKE LOUDER to become louder, or make a sound become louder, by electronic or other means 2. INCREASE to become, or make something become, greater in scope or stronger 3. ADD DETAIL to make a spoken or written account fuller, clearer, or more detailed 4. ELECTRONICS INCREASE SIGNAL to increase the magnitude of a signal using an amplifier, or undergo such an increase [15C. Via French amplifier < Latin amplificare 'enlarge' < amplus 'large' + fic-, a stem of facere 'make'] —**amplifiable** adj

SYNONYMS See **increase**.

amplitude /ámpli tyood/ n 1. LARGENESS largeness in size, volume, or extent 2. BREADTH breadth of range 3. ABUNDANCE an amount that is more than required 4. PHYS DISTANCE FROM MEAN POINT the farthest distance that a vibrating or oscillating system such as a pendulum travels from a mean or zero point 5. ELECTRONICS MAXIMUM VALUE OF SIGNAL the maximum value of an alternating signal 6. MATHS ANGLE OF VECTOR REPRESENTING COMPLEX NUMBER the angle between a vector representing a complex number and the positive real axis 7. SPORTS HEIGHT REACHED BY SNOWBOARDER in snowboarding, the degree of height a rider can attain above the lip of a pipe [Mid-16C. Via French < Latin amplitudo 'size, greatness, grandeur' < amplus 'large']

amplitude modulation n the modulation of the amp-

litude of a radio wave in such a way as to encode the wave with audio or visual information

amply /ámpli/ *adv* to a more than adequate degree

ampoule /ám pool, -pyool/, **ampule** *n* a small sealed glass container that holds a measured amount of a medicinal substance to be injected [Early 20C. Via French < Latin *ampulla* (see AMPULLA)]

ampulla /am póollə/ (*plural* **-lae** /-lee/) *n* **1.** a small container for a consecrated substance, especially oil, water, or the wine used in the Christian Communion **2.** in ancient Rome, a round two-handled bottle to hold wine, oil, or perfume [Late 14C. < Latin, 'little amphora' < *ampora*, variant of *amphora* (see AMPHORA)]

amputate /ámpyoŏ tayt/ (**-tates, -tating, -tated**) *vti* to cut off a limb or other appendage of the body, especially in a surgical operation [Mid-16C. < Latin *amputat-*, past participle of *amputare* 'cut around' < *ambi-* 'around' + *putare* 'cut'] —**amputation** /ámpyoŏ táysh'n/ *n* —**amputator** *n*

amputee /ámpyoŏ teé/ *n* somebody who has had a limb or part of a limb cut off

amrita /am reétə/, **amreeta** *n* **1.** in Hinduism, a substance prepared by the deities that makes those who drink it immortal **2.** in Hinduism, immortality gained by drinking amrita [Late 18C. < Sanskrit *amṛta* 'without death' < *mṛta* 'death']

Amritsar /əm rítsər/ city in Punjab State in north-western India. It is a holy city for Sikhs. Population: 1,011,327 (2001).

Amsterdam /ámstər dám/ capital and commercial centre in the Netherlands, situated where the River Amstel flows into the IJsselmeer. Population: 735,328 (2002).

amu *abbr* atomic mass unit

amuck *adv, adj* same as **amok**

Amu Darya /aámoo daáryə/ the longest river in Central Asia, flowing from the Pamir plateau towards the Aral Sea. Length: 1,415 km/879 mi.

amulet /ámmyoŏlət/ *n* **1.** a piece of jewellery that supposedly protects its wearer against evil, injury, disease, or bad luck **2.** an ordinary object that is supposed to provide protection against bad luck or negative forces [Late 16C. < Latin *amuletum*]

Amun /aámən/ *n* in Egyptian mythology, the supreme god. Amun was originally a local god of Thebes, but was elevated during the eighteenth dynasty.

Amundsen /ámməndss'n/, **Roald** (1872–1928) Norwegian explorer. He was the first person to reach the South Pole (1911).

Amur /ə moór/ river in east-central Asia that forms the boundary between Manchuria and Siberia before flowing north into the Tatar Strait. Length: 4,345 km/2,700 mi. Chinese name **Heilong Jiang**

amuse /ə myoóz/ (**amuses, amusing, amused**) *vt* **1.** to make somebody smile or laugh or think that something is funny **2.** to keep somebody occupied or entertained by providing entertainment or an interesting task [15C. < French *amuser* 'cause to stare stupidly' < *muser* 'stare stupidly'] —**amused** *adj*

ORIGIN The history of the word *amuse* is very similar to that of *distract* and *divert*: all three have moved from the notion of 'leading the mind astray' in a negative sense to the notion of 'entertainment'.

amusement /ə myoózmənt/ *n* **1.** FEELING SOMETHING IS FUNNY the feeling that something is funny or entertaining **2.** RECREATIONAL ACTIVITY an enjoyable activity such as a game, hobby, or form of entertainment **3.** RIDE OR GAME a ride, game, or other attraction found in an amusement park or arcade **4.** KEEPING SOMEBODY HAPPILY OCCUPIED the act of keeping somebody occupied or entertained

amusement arcade *n* an indoor or covered area containing a variety of coin-operated machines for playing games. They are often found in shopping malls and at holiday resorts. N Am term **arcade**

amusement park *n* an outdoor area with a variety of mechanical rides, games, and other attractions that people pay to use

amusing /ə myoózing/ *adj* causing somebody to smile or laugh or be amused, often in a subdued way — **amusingly** *adv*

SYNONYMS See *funny*.

Amvets /ám vets/, **AMVETS** *n* in the United States, a private organization of ex-servicemen of World War II and the Korean and Vietnam wars

amygdala /ə mígdələ/ (*plural* **-lae** /-lee/) *n* an almond-shaped mass of grey matter, one in each hemisphere of the brain, associated with feelings of fear and aggression and important for visual learning and memory [Pre-12C. Via Latin < Greek *amugdalē* 'almond']

amygdalin /ə mígdəlin/, **amygdaline** /-lin, -leen/ *n* a white crystalline bitter-tasting sugar derivative (**glycoside**). Source: almond, apricot, and peach seeds. Use: expectorant. [Mid-19C. < Latin *amygdala* 'almond' (see AMYGDALA)]

amyl /ámmil, áy mīl/ *adj* CHEM same as **pentyl** [Mid-19C. < Latin *amylum* < Greek *amulon* 'finely ground meal' < *mulē* 'mill']

amyl- *prefix* CHEM same as **amylo-** (*used before vowels*)

amylaceous /ámmi láyshəss/ *adj* having or resembling starch (*technical*)

amyl acetate *n* a colourless volatile liquid that smells like pears. Use: flavouring agent, solvent. Formula: $CH_3CO_2C_5H_{11}$.

amyl alcohol *n* a colourless alcohol or mixture of any of the eight related amyl alcohols. Use: solvent, manufacture of organic chemicals and drugs. Formula: $C_5H_{12}O$.

amylase /ámmi layz, -layss/ *n* an enzyme in saliva and pancreatic juice that breaks down starch into simple sugars

amylmetacresol /ámm'l metə kreé sol/ *n* an antiseptic. Use: treatment of minor infections of the mouth and throat.

amyl nitrite *n* a pale yellow fragrant liquid. Use: inhalant to dilate blood vessels. Formula: $C_5H_{11}NO_2$.

amylo- *prefix* starch ○ *amylopectin* [< Latin *amylum* (see AMYL)]

amylobarbitone /ámmələ baárbə tōn/ *n* PHARM former name for **amobarbital**

amyloid /ámmi loyd/ *n* **1.** WAXY PROTEIN a waxy translucent substance composed of complex protein fibres and polysaccharides that is formed in body tissues in some degenerative diseases, e.g. Alzheimer's disease **2.** STARCHY SUBSTANCE a substance that resembles starch in composition or function ■ *adj* STARCHY resembling a starch (*technical*)

amyloidosis /ámmi loy dóssiss/ *n* a condition marked by the accumulation of a protein-based substance (**amyloid**) in the body's organs and tissues

amylopectin /ámmilō péktin/ *n* a branched polysaccharide that is an insoluble component of starch

amylose /ámmi lōz, -lōss/ *n* an unbranched polysaccharide that is a soluble component of starch

amyotonia /áy mī ə tóni ə/ *n* a medically significant lack of muscle tension [< A-² + MYO- + Greek *tonos* 'tension, tone']

amyotrophic /ámmi ə tróffik/ *adj* characterized by degeneration of the muscles (**amyotrophy**)

amyotrophic lateral sclerosis *n* a fatal degenerative disease of the nervous system marked by progressive muscle weakness and atrophy. It is a form of motor neurone disease.

amyotrophy /ámmi óttrəfi/ *n* a degeneration of the muscles caused by nerve disease [Late 19C. < A-² + MYO- + -TROPHY]

an¹ *stressed* /an/; *unstressed* /ən/ *det* used instead of 'a', the indefinite article, in front of words with an initial vowel sound [Old English, unstressed form of *ān* 'one']

USAGE See *a⁴*.

an² /an, ən/, **an'** *conj* same as **if** (*archaic*) [12C. Reduced form of AND 'if']

an³ *abbr* Netherlands Antilles (*used in Internet addresses*) See table at **domain name**

an- *prefix* same as **a-²** (*used before vowels*) [< Greek]

-an¹ *suffix* **1.** of or relating to ○ *Minoan* ○ *agrarian* **2.** somebody of or resembling a particular kind ○ *librarian* [Via French < Latin *-anus*]

ORIGIN English words in which the original form of the Old French suffix *-an* is preserved include *captain*, *chamberlain*, *chaplain*, and *fountain*. English *sovereign* is descended from a Latin word with the suffix *-anus*.

-an² *suffix* an unsaturated carbon compound ○ *dextran* [Alteration of -ANE]

ana¹ /aánə/ (*plural same* or **-as**) *n* **1.** a collection of things connected with a famous person, place, or period, especially spoken or written information, anecdotes, or sayings **2.** an item in an ana [Mid-18C. < -ANA]

ana² /ánnə/ *adv* of each of the ingredients specified in a medical prescription in equal amounts [< Greek *ana-* (see ANA-)]

ana- *prefix* **1.** up, upward ○ *anamorphic* **2.** back, backward, away ○ *anaphase* **3.** again ○ *anaplastic* [< Greek < *ana* < Indo-European, 'on']

-ana *suffix* a collection of objects or information about a topic, person, or place ○ *Shakespeareana* [Via modern Latin < Latin, neuter plural of *-anus* 'relating to']

anabaptism /ánnə báptizəm/ *n* the advocacy of adult baptism on the grounds that only as adults can people responsibly accept and declare their faith [See ANABAPTISM]

Anabaptism /ánnə báptizəm/ *n* the doctrines or beliefs of the Anabaptists [Mid-16C. Via ecclesiastical Latin *anabaptismus* < Greek *anabaptismos* 'second baptism' < *baptismos* 'baptism']

Anabaptist /ánnə báptist/ *n* a member of a 16th-century Protestant movement promoting the doctrine of adult baptism on the grounds that only adults can accept and declare their faith on their own behalf [Mid-16C. < ecclesiastical Latin *anabaptista* < Greek *ana-* 'again, afresh' + *baptistēs* 'baptizer' < *baptizein* (see BAPTIZE)] —**Anabaptist** *adj*

anabatic /ánnə báttik/ *adj* describes winds that move or blow upwards during the daytime as warm air rises up mountain slopes [Mid-20C. < Greek *anabatikos* 'relating to mounting' < *anabainein* 'go up, mount' < *bainein* 'go']

anabolic /ánnə bóllik/ *adj* promoting tissue growth [Late 19C. Blend of ANA- + METABOLIC]

anabolic steroid *n* **1.** a synthetic steroid hormone. Use: to increase muscle mass and strength. **2.** a naturally occurring hormone that promotes tissue growth

anabolism /ə nábbəlizəm/ *n* a metabolic process in which energy is used to make compounds and tissues from simple molecules [Late 19C. Blend of ANA- + METABOLISM]

anabolite /ə nábbə līt/ *n* a substance resulting from anabolism

anabranch /ánnə braánch/ *n* a stream that separates from a river and follows its own course before re-entering the same river farther downstream [Mid-19C. Blend of *anastomosing* (< ANASTOMOSE) + BRANCH]

anachronism /ə nákrənizəm/ *n* **1.** CHRONOLOGICAL MISTAKE something from a different period of time, e.g. a modern idea or invention wrongly placed in a historical setting in fiction or drama **2.** SOMETHING FROM DIFFERENT HISTORICAL PERIOD a person, thing, idea, or custom that seems to belong to a different time in history **3.** MAKING OF CHRONOLOGICAL MISTAKE the representation of somebody or something out of chronological order or in the wrong historical setting [Mid-17C. < French *anachronisme* < late Greek *anakhronizesthai* 'be timed backwards' < *khronos* 'time'] —**anachronous** *adj* —**anachronously** *adv*

anachronistic /ə nákrə nístik/ *adj* **1.** belonging to a time other than the one being represented, especially in fiction or drama **2.** out-of-date or inappropriate at the time in question —**anachronistically** *adv*

anaclitic /ánnə klíttik/ *adj* characterized by strong emotional dependence on a mother or other nurturing person, especially to the extent of exhibiting or causing serious developmental and psychological disturbances [Early 20C. < Greek *anaklitos* 'for reclining' < *anaklinein* 'lean upon' < *klinein* 'lean'] —**anaclisis** /-klíssiss/ *n*

anacoluthon /ánnəkə loŏ thon, -th'n/ (*plural* **-tha** /-thə/) *n* an instance of abandoning a grammatical construction in speech or writing before it is

complete and continuing with another. The sentence 'The subject of the lecture was – I didn't really understand it' contains an anacoluthon. [Early 18C. Via late Latin < Greek *anakolouthon* 'illogicality, inconsistency' < *anakolouthos* 'not following' < *akolouthos* 'following'] —**anacoluthic** *adj*

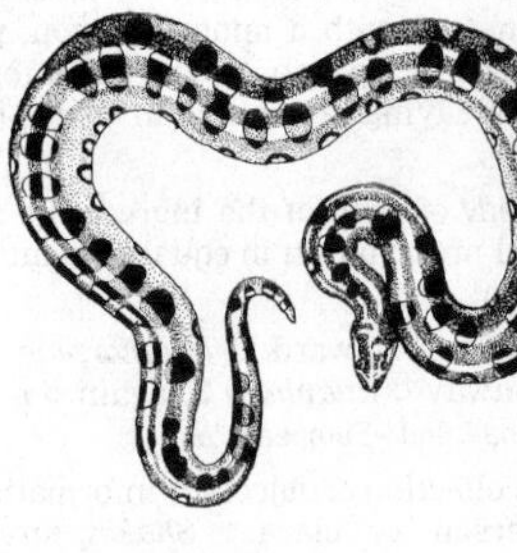

anaconda

anaconda /ánnə kóndə/ *n* a nonvenomous snake that lives in or near water and in trees. It is the largest snake in the boa family. Native to: South America. Latin name: *Eunectes murinus*. [Mid-18C. Origin ?]

Anacreon /ə nákri on/ (570?–478 BC) Greek lyric poet. He is well known for celebrating love and wine in his verse.

Anacreontic /ə nákri óntik/, **anacreontic** *adj* written in the style or treating the subjects of the Greek poet Anacreon ■ *n* an Anacreontic poem [Early 17C. < Latin *Anacreonticus* < Greek *Anakreont-*, stem of *Anakreōn* 'Anacreon']

anacrusis /ánnə kroossiss/ (*plural* **-cruses** /-kroo seez/) *n* **1.** one or more unstressed syllables at the beginning of a line of verse that are not considered part of the metrical pattern of the line **2.** one or more unaccented notes immediately before the first downbeat of a bar of music [Mid-19C. < modern Latin < Greek *anakrouein* 'strike up (a tune)' < *krouein* 'strike'] —**anacrustic** /ánnə krústik/ *adj*

anadiplosis /ánnə di plṓssiss/ (*plural* **-ploses** /-plṓ seez/) *n* the rhetorical repetition of the last word or words of one phrase or sentence at the beginning of the next. The sentence 'He was tormented by fears – fears that were soon to be realized' uses anadiplosis. [Late 16C. < Latin < Greek *anadiploein* 'double back' < *diploein* 'to double']

anadromous /ə náddrəməss/ *adj* describes fish such as salmon and shad that return from the sea to the rivers where they were born in order to breed [Mid-18C. < Greek *anadromos* 'running up (a river from the sea)' < *dromos* 'a running']

anaemia /ə neémi ə/, **anemia** *n* **1.** a blood condition in which there are too few red blood cells or the red blood cells are deficient in haemoglobin, resulting in poor health. Common causes include a lack of dietary iron, heavy blood loss, or the production of too few red blood cells due to disorders such as leukaemia. **2.** lack of vitality or courage [Early 19C. Via modern Latin < Greek *anaimia* 'being without blood' < *haima* 'blood']

anaemic /ə neémik/, **anemic** *adj* **1.** MED **HAVING ANAEMIA** having some form of anaemia **2. SICK-LOOKING** pale and not looking well **3. WEAK** lacking vitality, strength, or courage —**anaemically** *adv*

anaerobe /ánnə rōb/ *n* a microorganism that does not require oxygen for metabolism [Late 19C. Back-formation < French *anaérobie* 'living without air' < Greek *an-* 'not' + French *aéro-* 'air' + Greek *bios* 'life']

anaerobic /ánnə rṓbik, án air-/ *adj* **1.** living or taking place in the absence of oxygen, especially not requiring oxygen for metabolism **2.** having or providing no oxygen —**anaerobically** *adv*

anaerobic process *n* a chemical or biological process such as decay or decomposition that does not require oxygen. Such processes are often used to dispose of wastes while generating useful gases.

anaerobic respiration *n* the production of energy without the presence of oxygen. Anaerobic respiration occurs in some yeasts and bacteria, and in muscle tissue during strenuous exercise when there is insufficient oxygen.

anaerobiosis /ánnərō bī ṓssiss, án airō-/ *n* life in the absence of free or atmospheric oxygen [Late 19C. < ANAEROBIC + -BIOSIS] —**anaerobiotic** /ánnərō bī óttik, án airō-/ *adj*

anaesthesia /ánnəss theézi ə/, **anesthesia** *n* **1. MEDICALLY INDUCED INSENSITIVITY TO PAIN** induced loss of sensitivity to pain in all or a part of the body for medical reasons. Methods include drugs, acupuncture, and hypnosis. The procedure may render the patient unconscious (**general anaesthesia**) or merely numb a body part (**local anaesthesia**). **2. LOSS OF SENSATION** the loss of sensation caused by damage to a nerve **3. APATHY** a state of apathy or mindlessness [Early 18C. Via modern Latin < Greek *anaisthēsia* 'lack of sensation' < *aisthēsis* 'feeling, sensation' (see AESTHESIA)]

anaesthesiologist /ánnəss theezi óllәjist/ *n* US HEALTH SERVICES same as **anaesthetist** (sense 1)

anaesthesiology /ánnəss theezi ólləji/ *n* US MED same as **anaesthetics**

anaesthetic /ánnəss théttik/, **anesthetic** *n* a substance that reduces sensitivity to pain and may cause unconsciousness, especially a drug used in medicine [Mid-19C. < Greek *anaisthētos* 'without feeling' < *aisthētos* 'capable of feeling' < *aisthesthai* 'perceive'] —**anaesthetic** *adj* —**anaesthetically** *adv*

anaesthetics /ánnəss théttiks/ *n* UK, Aus, Can the medical study and application of anaesthetic substances (*takes a singular verb*) US term **anesthesiology**

anaesthetise *vt* SURG another spelling of **anaesthetize**

anaesthetist /ə neésthətist/, **anesthetist** *n* **1.** UK, ANZ, Can a senior doctor who specializes in administering anaesthetics. US term **anesthesiologist** **2.** somebody qualified to administer anaesthetics, especially a nurse or technician

anaesthetize /ə neésthə tīz/ (**-tizes, -tizing, -tized**), **anesthetize, anaesthetise** /ə neésthətīz/ (**-tises, -tising, -tised**) *vt* to administer an anaesthetic to somebody —**anaesthetization** /ə neésthə tī záysh'n/ *n*

anaglyph /ánnə glif/ *n* **1.** a decoration carved in low relief, so that the shape of the design projects only slightly from the background **2.** a three-dimensional visual effect created by dyeing each of two images a different colour, usually red and green, and then viewing them through complementary-coloured filters, one over each eye [Late 16C. < Greek *anagluphē* 'low-relief sculpture' < *gluphein* 'carve'] —**anaglyphic** /-glíffik/ *adj* —**anaglyptic** /-glíptik/ *adj*

Anaglypta /ánnə glíptə/ *tdmk* a trademark for a thick embossed wallpaper, designed to be painted

anagoge /ánnə gōji/, **anagogy** /ánnə gōji, -gogi/ (*plural* **-gies**) *n* **1.** a spiritual or mystical interpretation of a word or passage, especially in a sacred text, in contrast to a literal or moral interpretation **2.** an allegorical interpretation of a passage in the Bible as an allusion to or foreshadowing of people or events in the New Testament [Mid-16C. Via Latin < Greek *anagōgē* 'reference' < *anagein* 'take back' < *agein* 'take'] —**anagogic** /ánnə gójjik/ *adj* —**anagogical** *adj* —**anagogically** *adv*

anagram /ánnə gram/ *n* a word or phrase that contains all the letters of another word or phrase in a different order. 'Astronomers' is an anagram of 'no more stars'. [Late 16C. Directly or via French *anagramme* < modern Latin *anagramma*, probably < Greek *anagrammatismos* 'transposition of letters' < *anagrammatizein* (see ANAGRAMMATIZE)] —**anagrammatic** /ánnəgrə máttik/ *adj*

anagrammatize /ánnə grámmə tīz/ (**-tizes, -tizing, -tized**), **anagrammatise** (**-tises, -tising, -tised**) *vt* to rearrange the letters of a word or phrase to form a different word or phrase [Late 16C. Perhaps < Greek *anagrammatizein* 'rearrange the letters of a word' < *gramma* 'letter']

Anaheim /ánnə hīm/ city in southwestern California. It is home to the Disneyland™ amusement park. Population: 332,642 (2002 estimate).

anal /áyn'l/ *adj* **1.** ANAT **RELATING TO ANUS** relating to or situated near the anus **2.** PSYCHOANAL **RELATING TO CHILDHOOD INTEREST IN DEFECATION** in Freudian theory, relating to a stage of childhood psychosexual development during which the focus is on the anal region and functions **3.** PSYCHOANAL **OBSESSIVELY SELF-CONTROLLED** in Freudian theory, relating to adult personality traits that are considered to have originated during or be characteristic of the anal stage of development, e.g. obsessive neatness, stubbornness, and meanness [Mid-18C. < modern Latin *analis* < *anus* (see ANUS)] —**anally** *adv*

anal. *abbr* **1.** analogous **2.** analogy **3.** analysis **4.** analytic

analcime /ə nál seem/, **analcite** /ə nál sīt/ *n* a white or light-coloured form of the mineral zeolite composed of hydrated sodium aluminium silicate. Source: igneous rocks. [Early 19C. < French < Greek *analkimos* 'not strong' (in reference to the mineral's weak electric current) < *alkimos* 'strong' < *alkē* 'strength'] —**analcimic** /ánn'l símmik/ *adj*

analects /ánnə lekts/, **analecta** /ánnə léktə/ *npl* passages selected from one or more literary or philosophical works, especially when published as a collection [Early 17C. Via Latin < Greek *analekta* 'collected, or selected, things' < *analegein* 'gather up' < *legein* 'gather'] —**analectic** /ánnə léktik/ *adj*

analemma /ánnə lémmə/ (*plural* **-mas** or **-mata** /-mətə/) *n* a scale, found on some sundials and globes, that is shaped like a figure eight and marked to indicate the declination of the Sun and to allow the calculation of apparent solar time [Mid-17C. Via Latin, 'sundial, pedestal of a sundial' < Greek *analēmma* 'pedestal, support' < *analambanein* 'take up, support' < *lambanein* 'take']

analeptic /ánnə léptik/ *adj* describes a type of medication that is restorative or invigorating, especially after an illness ■ *n* a drug that stimulates the central nervous system [Mid-17C. Via Latin < Greek *analēptikos* 'restorative' < *analambanein* (see ANALEMMA)]

anal fin *n* a single fin on the underside of some fish, behind the anus

analgesia /ánn'l jeézi ə/ *n* **1.** the lack of sensibility to pain while somebody is conscious **2.** treatment to control pain [Early 18C. Via modern Latin < Greek *analgēsia* 'lack of feeling, insensibility' < *algeein* 'feel pain' < *algos* 'pain'] —**analgetic** /ánn'l jéttik/ *adj*

analgesic /ánn'l jeézik/ *adj* describes a type of medication that alleviates pain without loss of consciousness —**analgesic** *n*

anal intercourse *n* a form of sexual intercourse in which a man puts his penis into the anus of a man or woman

analog /ánnə log/ *adj* COMPUT same as **analogue** ■ *n* US CHEM same as **analogue** *n* (sense 3) [Mid-20C. Variant]

analogical /ánnə lójjik'l/ *adj* relating to or working by means of analogy [Late 16C. Directly or via French *analogique* < Latin *analogicus* < Greek *analogikos* < *analogos* (see ANALOGOUS)] —**analogically** *adv*

analogize /ə nállə jīz/ (**-gizes, -gizing, -gized**), **analogise** (**-gises, -gising, -gised**) *v* **1.** *vt* to compare two things that are similar in some respects, especially in order to explain something or to support an argument **2.** *vi* to make use of an analogy

analogous /ə nálləgəss/ *adj* **1.** similar in some respects, allowing an analogy to be drawn **2.** describes body parts and organs that have equivalent functions but that have evolved independently of one another in different plants or animals. The wings of birds, bats, and insects are analogous. [Mid-17C. < French *analogue* or Latin *analogus* < Greek *analogos* < *analogon* 'in due ratio' < *ana* 'according to' + *logos* 'ratio'] —**analogously** *adv* —**analogousness** *n*

USAGE ***Analogous***, correctly used, should include a notion of *analogy*, that is of similarity in some particular respects: *The Commission has set up guidelines for broadcasters that are analogous to those for journalists.* It is better to avoid ***analogous*** when the comparison is only general and when more straightforward words such as *similar, equivalent, comparable*, or *corresponding* serve just as well, as in *The new system is comparable* [not *analogous*] *to that used in the electronics industry.*

analogue /ánnə log/ *n* **1. CORRESPONDING THING** a thing, idea, or institution that is similar to or has the same function as another ○ *'They had no exact analogue for our word "home", any more than they had for our Roman-based "family".'* (Charlotte Perkins Gilman, *Herland*; 1915) **2.** BIOL **EQUIVALENT BUT INDEPENDENT ORGAN** a body part or organ that has an equivalent function to one in a different plant or animal but that evolved independently. The wings of birds, bats, and insects are analogues. **3.** UK, ANZ, Can CHEM **SIMILAR CHEMICAL** a chemical with a

similar structure to another but differing slightly in composition. US term **analog** **4.** FOOD **FOOD SUBSTITUTE** a food or dish made to resemble another by the substitution of inferior ingredients ■ *adj UK* **USING PHYSICAL REPRESENTATION** relating to a system or device that represents data variation by a measurable physical entity. ANZ, N Am term **analog** [Early 19C. Via French < Greek *analogon* (see ANALOGOUS)]

analogue clock *n* a clock that shows the time by means of hands on a dial

analogue computer *n* a computer that uses a variable physical quantity such as voltage to represent data

analogue watch *n* a watch that shows the time by means of hands on a dial

analogy /ə nálləji/ (*plural* **-gies**) *n* **1.** **COMPARISON** a comparison between two things that are similar in some way, often used to help explain something or make it easier to understand **2.** **SIMILARITY** a similarity in some respects **3.** BIOL **EQUIVALENCE BETWEEN INDEPENDENT PARTS** equivalence in biological function between body parts or organs that have appeared independently in different plants and animals **4.** LOGIC **FORM OF REASONING** a form of logical inference, reasoning that if two things are taken to be alike in one way, they are alike in other ways **5.** LING **STANDARDIZATION OF LINGUISTIC FORMS** the development or production of linguistic forms and patterns that resemble those already predominating in a language [15C. Via French *analogie* or Latin *analogia* < Greek *analogia* 'proportion' < *analogos* (see ANALOGOUS)]

analphabetic /án alfə béttik, an álfə-/ *adj* **1.** **NOT ALPHABETICAL** not in alphabetical order (*formal*) **2.** **ILLITERATE** not knowing how to read or write (*formal*) **3.** **NOT OF ALPHABET** not belonging to or concerning an alphabet ■ *n* **1.** **PRINTING CHARACTER** a typographical character used with the alphabet but not part of its order, e.g. a punctuation mark **2.** **ILLITERATE PERSON** somebody who cannot read or write (*formal*) [Late 19C. < Greek *analphabētos* 'not knowing the alphabet' < *alphabētos* 'alphabet']

anal-retentive *adj* PSYCHOANAL same as **anal** (sense 3) —**anal retention** *n* —**anal-retentive** *n* —**anal-retentiveness** *n*

anal sex *n* same as **anal intercourse**

analysand /ə nálli sand/ *n* somebody who is undergoing psychoanalysis [Mid-20C. < ANALYSE, after *operand*]

analyse /ánnə līz/ (**-lyses, -lysing, -lysed**), **analyze** (**-lyzes, -lyzing, -lyzed**) *vt* **1.** **STUDY SOMETHING CLOSELY** to examine something in great detail in order to understand it better or discover more about it **2.** **BREAK SOMETHING DOWN INTO COMPONENTS** to find out what something is made up of by identifying its constituent parts **3.** **EXAMINE STRUCTURE** to study the structure of something or how its constituent parts are put together **4.** GRAM **EXPRESS SOMETHING USING FUNCTION WORDS** to express grammatical relationships by using function words or word order rather than inflectional endings **5.** PSYCHIAT same as **psychoanalyse** [Early 17C. Perhaps back-formation < ANALYSIS, or < French *analyse* 'analysis' used as a verb; reinforced by French *analyser* 'analyse'] —**analysable** *adj* —**analyser** *n*

analysis /ə nállississ/ (*plural* **-yses** /-i seez/) *n* **1.** **CLOSE EXAMINATION** the examination of something in detail in order to understand it better or draw conclusions from it **2.** **SEPARATION INTO COMPONENTS** the separation of something into its constituents in order to find out what it contains, to examine individual parts, or to study the structure of the whole **3.** **ASSESSMENT** an assessment, description, or explanation of something, usually based on careful consideration or investigation **4.** **LIST OF PARTS** a statement giving details of all the constituent parts of something and how they relate to each other **5.** MATHS **BRANCH OF MATHEMATICS** the branch of mathematics dealing with differential calculus, functions, and limits **6.** LING **WAY OF EXPRESSING GRAMMATICAL RELATIONSHIPS** the use of function words or word order, rather than inflectional forms, to express grammatical relationships in a language **7.** PSYCHIAT same as **psychoanalysis** (sense 2) [Late 16C. Via medieval Latin < Greek *analusis* 'a breaking up into elements' < *analuein* 'unloose, dissolve into elements' < *luein* 'loosen'] ◇ **in the final** *or* **last analysis** used to introduce or indicate a summary conclusion to a complex subject

analysis of variance *n* in statistics, the analysis of the difference in outcomes of an experiment to determine the factors contributing to the variations

analyst /ánnəlist/ *n* **1.** somebody with specialist knowledge or skill who studies or examines something by separating it into its constituent parts and gives an assessment, description, or explanation of it **2.** somebody who practises psychoanalysis [Mid-17C. < French *analyste* < *analyse* 'analysis' (see ANALYSE)]

~~**analysys**~~ incorrect spelling of **analysis**

analyte /ánnə līt/ *n* the substance being identified and measured in a chemical analysis [Late 20C. Irregularly < ANALYSIS]

analytic /ánnə líttik/ *adj* **1.** same as **analytical** (senses 1–2) **2.** LOGIC **TRUE BY MEANING ALONE** true by definition or by virtue of the meaning of the words used **3.** MATHS **DIFFERENTIABLE AT ALL POINTS IN DOMAIN** describes a function of a complex variable that is differentiable at all points in its domain **4.** GRAM **USING FUNCTION WORDS** expressing grammatical relationships by means of function words or word order rather than inflections [Late 16C. Via late Latin < Greek *analutikos* < *analuein* (see ANALYSIS)]

analytical /ánnə lítik'l/ *adj* **1.** connected with or involving analysis **2.** able or inclined to separate things into their constituent elements in order to study or examine them, draw conclusions, or solve problems **3.** MATHS same as **analytic** (sense 3) —**analytically** *adv*

analytical balance *n* an accurate scale used in laboratories for weighing minute objects or quantities

analytical engine *n* a programmable calculating machine, the forerunner of the modern computer, invented by Charles Babbage in 1833

analytical geometry *n* a branch of mathematics dealing with geometric properties using algebraic operations and notation to locate points within a coordinate system. US term **analytic geometry**

analytical philosophy *n* a 20th-century philosophy primarily concerned with resolving philosophical problems through the analysis and clarification of language

analytical psychology *n* a system of psychoanalysis based on the psychological theories of Carl Jung. US term **analytic psychology**

analytical reagent *n* a chemical almost free of impurities

analytics /ánnə líttiks/ *n* the branch of logic involved with the analysis of propositions (*takes a singular verb*)

analyze *vt* another spelling of **analyse**

anamnesis /án am néessiss/ (*plural* **-neses** /-née seez/) *n* **1.** a recollection of events, especially from a supposed past existence (*technical*) **2.** the medical history of a patient, especially in the patient's own words [Late 16C. < Greek, 'remembrance' < *anamimnēskein* 'call back to mind' < *mimnēskein* 'call to mind']

anamnestic /án am néstik/ *adj* showing a secondary immunological response to an antigen at some time after initial immunization [Early 18C. < Greek *anamnēstikos* < *anamimnēskein* (see ANAMNESIS)] —**anamnestically** *adv*

anamorphic /ánnə máwrfik/ *adj* relating to or producing image distortion caused by unequal magnification along different perpendicular axes

anamorphosis /ánnə mawr fóssiss, -máwrfəssiss/ (*plural* **-phoses** /-fó seez/) *n* **1.** a distorted image or drawing of a distorted image that appears normal when viewed with or reflected from a special device **2.** the process of making distorted images by means of special mirrors or other devices [Mid-18C. < Greek, 'transformation' < *anamorphoein* 'change shape again' < *morphoein* 'change shape' < *morphē* 'shape']

ananda /ə núndə/ *n* in Hinduism, a state of bliss that is considered the highest state of being and results from a release from all sense of the body and its demands [Mid-19C. < Sanskrit *ānanda* 'joy']

Ananke /ə nángki/ *n* a small natural satellite of Jupiter, discovered in 1951

Anansi /ə nánssi/ *n* in West African folk tales, a popular spider god who is both devious and very wise [< Twi *ananse* 'spider']

anapaest /ánnə peest, -pest/, **anapest** *n* a metrical foot of three syllables with the stress on the third syllable, or of two short syllables followed by a long syllable. The word 'unconcerned' and the phrase 'up the hill' are anapaests. [Late 16C. Via Latin < Greek *anapaistos* 'struck backwards' (from its being a reversed dactyl), past participle of *anapaiein* < *paiein* 'strike'] —**anapaestic** /ánnə péestik, -péstik/ *adj*

anaphase /ánnə fayz/ *n* a late stage of cell division during which chromosomes move to the poles of the spindle

anaphora /ə náffərə/ *n* **1.** **REFERRING BACK** reference to a word or phrase used earlier, especially to avoid repeating the word or phrase by replacing it with something else such as a pronoun. In the sentence 'I told Paul to close the door and he did so', the clause 'he did so' makes use of anaphora. **2.** **REPETITION FOR EFFECT** the use of the same word or phrase at the beginning of several successive clauses, sentences, lines, or verses, usually for emphasis or rhetorical effect. 'She didn't speak. She didn't stand. She didn't even look up when we came in' is an example of anaphora. (*formal*) **3.** CHR **PART OF COMMUNION** the offering of the bread and wine in the Christian Communion [Late 16C. Via Latin < Greek, 'reference, repetition' < *anapherein* 'carry back' < *pherein* 'carry'] —**anaphoric** /ánnə fórrik/ *adj* —**anaphorically** *adv*

anaphoresis /ánnə fə réessiss/ *n* the movement towards the anode of suspended particles in solution

anaphrodisia /án affrə dízzi ə/ *n* absence or reduction of sexual desire [20C. < Greek, 'inability to inspire love' < *aphrodisia* (see APHRODISIAC)]

anaphrodisiac /án affrə dízzi ak/ *adj* tending to reduce sexual desire —**anaphrodisiac** *n*

anaphylactic /ánnəfi láktik/ *adj* relating to or caused or characterized by extreme sensitivity to a substance (**anaphylaxis**) —**anaphylactically** *adv*

anaphylactic shock *n* a sudden severe and potentially fatal allergic reaction in somebody sensitive to a substance, marked by a drop in blood pressure, difficulty in breathing, itching, and swelling

anaphylaxis /ánnəfi láksiss/ *n* **1.** extreme sensitivity to a substance such as a protein or drug **2.** MED same as **anaphylactic shock** [Early 20C. < modern Latin < Greek *ana-* 'again' (because a substance is reintroduced) + *-phylaxis* 'guarding, watching'] —**anaphylactoid** *adj*

anaplasia /ánnə pláyzi ə/ *n* the reversion of cells, usually within a tumour, to a simpler or less differentiated form

anaplastic /ánnə plástik/ *adj* relating to or characterized by the loss of distinctive cell features (**anaplasia**)

anaptyxis /ánnap tíksiss/ *n* the insertion of a weak vowel sound between two consonants in order to make a word or phrase easier to pronounce. Saying 'go thataway' rather than 'go that way' is an example of anaptyxis. [Late 19C. Via modern Latin < Greek *anaptuxis* 'an unfolding' < *anaptussein* 'unfold' < *ptussein* 'fold']

anarchic /an aárkik, ən-/, **anarchical** /-kik'l/ *adj* **1.** **LAWLESS** showing no respect for established laws, rules, institutions, or authority **2.** **CHAOTIC** characterized by a lack of organization or control **3.** **ENCOURAGING ANARCHY** likely to cause the overthrow of a formal system of government or a breakdown of law and order —**anarchically** *adv*

anarchism /ánnər kizəm/ *n* **1.** **DOCTRINE REJECTING GOVERNMENT** an ideology that rejects the need for a system of government in society and proposes its abolition **2.** **ACTIONS OF ANARCHISTS** behaviour intended to overthrow or weaken a society's formal system of government **3.** **RESISTANCE TO CONTROL** resistance to all forms of authority or control

anarchist /ánnərkist/ *n* **1.** somebody who believes that governments should be abolished as unnecessary **2.** somebody who tries to overthrow a government or behaves in a lawless way —**anarchistic** /ánnər kístik/ *adj*

anarchy /ánnərki/ *n* **1.** a situation in which there is a

total lack of organization or control **2.** the absence of any formal system of government in a society [Mid-16C. Via medieval Latin < Greek *anarkhia* < *anarkhos* 'without a ruler' < *arkhos* 'ruler']

anarthria /an áarthri ə/ *n* the loss of the ability to articulate words [Late 19C. Via modern Latin < Greek < *anarthros* (see ANARTHROUS)] —**anarthric** *adj*

anarthrous /an áarthrəss/ *adj* used or occurring without a definite or indefinite article [Early 19C. < Greek *anarthros* 'not joined or articulated, inarticulate' < *arthron* 'article, joint']

anasarca /ánnə saárkə/ *n* the accumulation of watery fluid in connective tissue and cavities, resulting in swelling **(oedema)** [14C. Via medieval Latin < Greek *anasarx*, describing oedema, < *ana sarka* 'throughout the flesh'] —**anasarcous** *adj*

Anastasia /ánnə stáyzi ə, -staázi ə/ (1901–18) Russian grand duchess. Daughter of Tsar Nicholas II, she died when the Bolsheviks executed the Romanovs (July 1918), but the obscurity of her death led to many women claiming to be her. Born **Romanova, Anastasia Nikolaevna**

anastigmat /an ástig mat, ánnə stíg mat/ *n* a lens or combination of lenses free from astigmatism [Late 19C. < German, back-formation < *anastigmatisch* 'anastigmatic' < Greek *stigmat-* 'point']

anastigmatic /ánnə stig máttik/ *adj* describes a lens that is corrected for or free from astigmatism

anastomose /ə nástə mōz, -stə mōss/ (**-moses, -mosing, -mosed**) *vt* to join blood vessels or other tubular parts in a surgical operation **(anastomosis)** [Late 17C. Probably back-formation < ANASTOMOSIS]

anastomosis /ə nástə mṓssiss/ (*plural* **-moses** /-mō seez/) *n* **1. NATURAL JOINT** the connection or place of connection of two or more parts of a natural branching system, e.g. of blood vessels, leaf veins, stems of woody plants, or rivers **2.** SURG **SURGICAL UNION OF TUBULAR PARTS** the surgical union of two hollow organs, e.g. blood vessels or parts of the intestine, to ensure continuity of the passageway **3.** FUNGI **FUSING OF FUNGAL FILAMENTS** a fusion between fungal filaments **(hyphae)** to form a network [Early 17C. Via modern Latin < Greek, 'outlet, opening, interconnection of openings' < *anastomoein* 'supply with a mouth or opening' < *stoma* 'mouth'] —**anastomotic** /ə nástə móttik/ *adj*

anastrophe /ə nástrəfi/ *n* an alteration of the normal order of words or phrases in a grammatical construction, usually for rhetorical effect. Coleridge's 'The helmsman steered; the ship moved on; yet never a breeze up blew' ends with an anastrophe. [Mid-16C. < Greek, 'a turning back, inversion' < *stroph-*, stem of *strephein* 'to turn']

anat. *abbr* MED **1.** anatomical **2.** anatomy

anatase /ánnə tayz/ *n* a blue or yellowish-brown mineral consisting of titanium dioxide. Source: igneous rocks. [Early 19C. Via French < Greek *anatasis* 'extension' (from the elongated crystals) < *teinein* 'to stretch']

anathema /ə náthəmə/ *n* **1. OBJECT OF LOATHING** somebody or something that is greatly disliked or detested and is therefore shunned **2.** RELIG **SOMEBODY OR SOMETHING FORMALLY DENOUNCED** somebody or something cursed, denounced, or excommunicated by a religious authority **3. GENERAL CURSE** a forceful curse or denunciation **4.** RELIG **ECCLESIASTICAL CURSE** a curse from a religious authority that denounces something or excommunicates somebody [Early 16C. Via ecclesiastical Latin < Greek, 'something devoted to evil' < *anatithenai* 'set up']

anathematize /ə náthəmə tīz/ (**-tizes, -tizing, -tized**), **anathematise** (**-tises, -tising, -tised**) *vti* to formally curse, denounce, or excommunicate somebody or something [Mid-16C. Via ecclesiastical Latin *anathematizare* 'ban, curse' < Greek *anathematizein* 'dedicate to evil' < *anathemat-*, stem of *anathema* (see ANATHEMA)] —**anathematization** /ə náthəmə tī záysh'n/ *n*

Anatolia /ánnə tṓli ə/ Asian part of Turkey, forming the westernmost peninsula of Asia

Anatolian /ánnə tṓli ən/ *n* **1.** somebody who comes from Anatolia **2.** a group of extinct Indo-European languages spoken more than 3,000 years ago in central and western Turkey —**Anatolian** *adj*

Anatolian Plateau /ánnə tṓli ən-/ mountainous region extending across much of Turkey. The highest peak is Mount Erciyes 3,916 m/12,848 ft.

anatomical /ánnə tómmik'l/, **anatomic** /-tómmik/ *adj* relating to or showing the physical structure of animals or plants —**anatomically** *adv*

anatomically correct *adj* describes a doll, model, or other representation of the human body that has an accurate representation of the genitals and other bodily details

anatomical position *n* the standard position of the body in the study of anatomy from which all directions and positions are derived. In it the body is assumed to be standing, the feet together, the arms to the side, and the head, eyes, and palms facing forward.

anatomize /ə náttə mīz/ (**-mizes, -mizing, -mized**), **anatomise** (**-mises, -mising, -mised**) *vt* **1.** BIOL same as **dissect** (sense 1) **2.** to analyse or examine something in great detail, thus revealing features that are not obvious —**anatomization** /ə náttə mī záysh'n/ *n*

anatomy /ə náttəmi/ (*plural* **-mies**) *n* **1. STUDY OF STRUCTURE OF BODY** the branch of science that studies the physical structure of animals, plants, and other organisms **2. PHYSICAL STRUCTURE OF ORGANISM** the physical structure, especially the internal structure, of an animal, plant, or other organism, or of any of its parts **3. BOOK ABOUT ANATOMY** a book or other written work about the physical structure of animals, plants, or other organisms **4. BODY** the human body (*informal*) **5. ANALYSIS** a detailed analysis of something [14C. Via French *anatomie* and late Latin *anatomia* < Greek *anatomē* 'cutting up' < *temnein* 'to cut'] —**anatomist** *n*

ORIGIN From the 16th century to the early 19th century ***anatomy*** was used to mean 'skeleton', and in this sense it was often misinterpreted as *an atomy*, as if the initial *an-* were the indefinite article: 'My bones…will be taken up smooth, and white, and bare as an atomy', Tobias Smollett (1755).

Anaxagoras /án ak sággərəss/ (500?–428 BC) Greek philosopher. He stated that matter was infinitely divisible and was the first person to explain solar eclipses.

Anaximander /ə náksi mándər/ (611?–547? BC) Greek philosopher. He put forward an evolutionary theory of the origins of life, claiming that human beings evolved from more primitive species.

Anaximenes /á nak símmə neez/ (570?–500? BC) Greek philosopher. He believed that the universe consisted of air or vapour in various stages of condensation, and that the movement of air changed the structure of physical objects.

ANC *abbr* POL African National Congress

-ance *suffix* **1.** action ○ *utterance* **2.** *also* **-ancy** state or condition ○ *elegance*

ancestor /án sestər, ánsəstər/ *n* **1. DISTANT RELATION SOMEBODY IS DESCENDED FROM** somebody from whom somebody else is directly descended, especially somebody more distant than a grandparent **2. FORERUNNER** a predecessor of somebody, e.g. in the development of an art form **3.** BIOL **EARLIER SPECIES** an animal or plant from which a species has evolved **4. EARLIER MODEL** a device that was an earlier form of a modern invention or was used as a basis for developing it [14C. Via Old French *ancestre* < Latin *antecessor* 'somebody who goes before' < *cess-*, past participle of *cedere* 'give way']

ancestral /an séstrəl/ *adj* relating to something belonging to former generations of somebody's family [15C. < Old French *ancestrel* < *ancestre* (see ANCESTOR)] —**ancestrally** *adv*

ancestry /án sestri, ánsəs-/ *n* the former generations of somebody's family ○ *was rumoured to have a buccaneer in his ancestry* [14C. Alteration of Old French *ancesserie* < *ancessour* < Latin *antecessor* (see ANCESTOR)]

anchar /an chaár/ *n* FOOD same as **achar** [Late 20C. Alteration of ACHAR after Hindi *aam* 'mango']

Anchises /an kī́ seez/ *n* in Greek and Roman mythology, a Trojan prince and the father of Aeneas by the goddess Aphrodite. In later life, Anchises was saved during the Greek sack of Troy when Aeneas carried him from the burning city on his back.

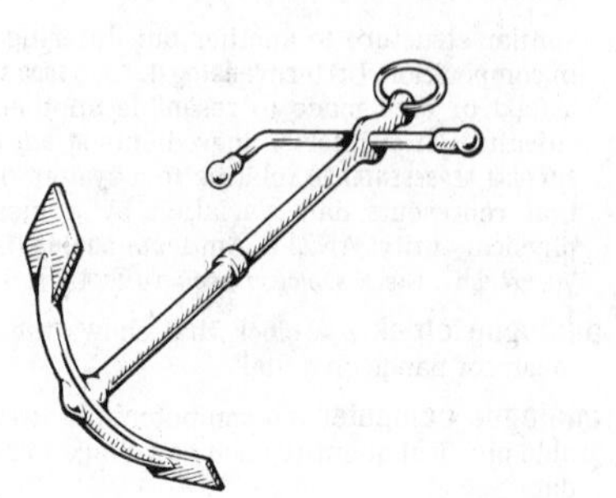

anchor

anchor /ángkər/ *n* **1. DEVICE TO HOLD SHIP IN PLACE** a heavy, traditionally double-hooked, device for keeping a ship or floating object in place **2. DEVICE KEEPING OBJECT IN PLACE** any device that keeps an object in place **3. SOMETHING DEPENDABLE** somebody who or something that provides stability ○ *She was my anchor during the crisis.* **4.** BROADCAST **PRESENTER OF NEWS PROGRAMME** a presenter on a news programme, providing links between the studio and reporters based outside **5.** ATHLETICS **SOMEBODY POSITIONED LAST** the team member who is responsible for the last leg in a relay race or who is at the back in a tug of war **6.** CLIMBING **CLIMBER'S ROPE ATTACHMENT** a point to which a climber's rope is fixed, e.g. on a rock face or in ice ■ *adj* **ATTACHING** used for securing or connecting something ■ *v* (**-chors, -choring, -chored**) **1.** *vt* **HOLD SOMETHING IN PLACE** to hold something securely in place **2.** *vti* NAUT **PUT DOWN ANCHOR** to moor a ship by lowering its anchor so that it remains stationary in a place ○ *anchored off the Nigerian coast* **3.** *vt* BROADCAST **PRESENT NEWS PROGRAMME** to be the presenter on a news programme [Pre-12C. Via Latin *ancora* < Greek *agkura*] ◇ **at anchor** held on the water by an anchor

anchorage /ángkərij/ *n* **1. PLACE TO HOLD BOATS SECURE** a place in or near a harbour where boats are moored **2. CHARGE FOR ANCHORING BOAT** a charge for anchoring a boat in a harbour **3. SOMETHING HOLDING OBJECT IN PLACE** a device used to hold an object in place **4. ANCHORING** the securing of a ship with an anchor **5. SECURITY** a source of stability, or a stable condition

Anchorage /ánkərij/ city and port in southern Alaska, at the eastern end of Cook Inlet. Population: 268,983 (2002 estimate).

anchorite /ángkə rīt/ *n* somebody who lives a reclusive life of prayer [15C. Via medieval Latin *anc(h)orita* < ecclesiastical Greek *anakhōrētēs* < Greek *anakhōrein* 'withdraw' < *ana-* 'away' + *khōrein* 'move']

anchorman /ángkər man/ (*plural* **-men** /-men/) *n* **1.** a man who is an anchor for a news programme **2.** a man or boy who is the anchor in a relay race or for a tug-of-war team

anchorperson /ángkər purss'n/ (*plural* **-persons** or **-people**) *n* BROADCAST, ATHLETICS same as **anchor** *n* (senses 4–5)

anchorwoman /ángkər wŏŏmən/ (*plural* **-women** /-wimin/) *n* **1.** a woman who is an anchor for a news programme **2.** a woman or girl who is the anchor in a relay race or for a tug-of-war team

anchovy /ánchəvi, an chṓvi/ (*plural* **-vies** or *same*) *n* **1.** a small silvery sea fish that travels in large schools. Family: Engraulidae. **2.** the flesh of an anchovy as food, often sold salted and canned in oil [Late 16C. < Spanish *anchova*]

ancien régime /aaN syaN ray zhéem/ (*plural* **anciens régimes** /*pronunc. same*/) *n* **1.** the political and social system of France before the revolution of 1789 **2.** an outmoded system, method, or way of life [Late 18C. < French, 'old regime']

ancient /áynshənt/ *adj* **1. OLD** very old **2. OF DISTANT PAST** belonging to the distant past, especially to the time before the collapse of the Western Roman Empire in AD 476 ■ *n* **1. SOMEBODY FROM PAST CIVILIZATION** a member of a civilization of the distant past **2. SOMEBODY OF ADVANCED YEARS** a very mature or venerable person ■ **ancients** *npl* **1. PEOPLE OF ANCIENT WESTERN CIVILIZATIONS** the people who lived in one of the ancient civilizations, especially Greece and Rome **2. ANCIENT GREEK AND ROMAN AUTHORS** the authors of ancient Greece and Rome, whose writings form the basis of the classics as a

subject of study [14C. Via French *ancien* < assumed Vulgar Latin *anteanus* < Latin *ante* 'before'] —**anciently** *adv* —**ancientness** *n*

Ancient Greek *n* the forms of the Greek language spoken from about 1500 BC to about AD 500

ancient history *n* 1. the study of the cultures of the distant past, especially those of Greece and Rome 2. things that happened a long time ago (*informal*)

ancient lights *n* the legal right to receive daylight through windows (*takes a singular verb*)

Ancient Mariner *n* somebody who tends to talk at length (*informal humorous*) [< the title of a poem by Samuel Taylor Coleridge]

ancient monument *n* a building or part of a building, usually dating from at least medieval times, that is preserved and protected by law

Ancient of Days *n* a name for God, used by the prophet Daniel (Daniel 7:9) [Translation of Latin *antiquus dierum*]

ancillary /an sílləri/ *adj* 1. PROVIDING SUPPORT providing support for somebody or something, e.g. non-technical assistance to people who work in an industry or profession 2. SUBORDINATE in a position of lesser importance ■ *n* (*plural* **-ries**) 1. SUBORDINATE PART a subordinate part or element, e.g. a branch of an organization 2. EMPLOYEE PROVIDING NONTECHNICAL SUPPORT a worker who provides nontechnical assistance or support to the core workers in an industry or profession [Mid-17C. < Latin *ancillaris* < *ancilla* 'handmaid', feminine of *anculus* 'manservant']

ancthea /ángk thi ə/ *n* in African cuisine, a plant whose leaves are boiled then cooked with meat and ground seeds

ancylostomiasis /ángki lōstə mī́ əssiss, ánssi-/, **ankylostomiasis** /ángki-/ *n* a tropical disease caused by infestation of the small intestine by hookworms, with symptoms of anaemia and tiredness [Late 19C. < modern Latin *Ancylostoma*, genus of hookworms < Greek *agkulos* 'hooked' + *stoma* 'mouth']

and *stressed* /and/; *unstressed* /ənd, ən/ CORE MEANING: a conjunction used to indicate an additional thing, situation, or fact. 'And' in this case links words and phrases of the same grammatical value. ○ *a sister and two brothers* ○ *We need to clean the house and pack our suitcases.* ○ *switching back and forth between different systems*
conj 1. THEN used to link two verbs or statements about events to indicate that the second follows the first ○ *Just add water and stir.* 2. AS RESULT used to introduce a situation or event that is a consequence of something just mentioned ○ *Their work was excellent and won several awards.* 3. USED TO STRESS REPETITION OR CONTINUITY used to link identical words or phrases in order to emphasize repetition or continuity ○ *It gets better and better.* 4. PLUS used to link two numbers or quantities to indicate that they are to be added together ○ *One and one are two.* 5. BUT used to introduce a contrasting statement ○ *My dentist says to eat fruit and avoid refined sugar.* 6. MOREOVER used to introduce a statement that continues or adds weight to a statement just made ○ *The kids needed clothes, and I hadn't been paid in weeks.* 7. USED TO CONNECT IDEAS used to connect clauses or sentences, especially in spoken conversation ○ *I like the head waiter, but the work's hard. And the hours are very long.* 8. INDICATES INFINITIVE VERB used instead of 'to' before an infinitive verb, usually with verbs such as 'try', 'go', and 'come' (*informal*) ○ *I usually try and visit her once a week.* 9. IF used to introduce a conditional clause (*archaic*) ○ *and it please you* [Old English *and, ond* < Germanic] ◇ **and (all)** **that** and everything else that is similar or included (*informal*) ○ *I've painted the doors and window frames and all that.* ◇ **and how** used to show strong agreement with or to emphasize something that has just been said (*informal*)

USAGE The notion that **and** should not be used at the beginning of a sentence arose from too literal an understanding of the 'joining' function of conjunctions. The same objection is also raised with regard to *but*. If initial **and** is overdone, the effect is of poor style, but it is not a matter of grammatical correctness. Using **and** at the beginning of a sentence can often be an effective way of drawing attention to what follows: *'You can't get away with this,' he threatened. And we knew he meant it.*

AND /and/ *n* 1. a binary operator in Boolean algebra whose result is true only if both its operands are true 2. a logic circuit, used especially in computers, that gives a high-voltage output if its input carries a low voltage and a low-voltage output otherwise [Mid-20C. < AND]

Andalusia /ándə loóssi ə/ autonomous region of southern Spain bordered by the Mediterranean Sea and the Atlantic Ocean. It contains the historic cities of Seville, Granada, and Cadiz and many examples of Moorish architecture. Population: 7,357,558 (2001). Area: 87,599 sq. km/33,822 sq. mi. Spanish name **Andalucía** —**Andalusian** *adj*

andalusite /ándə loó sīt/ *n* a variously coloured precious stone that is composed of aluminium silicate. Use: gems. [Early 19C. After ANDALUSIA]

Andaman and Nicobar Islands /ándəmən ənd níkə baar-/ union territory of eastern India, comprising two island groups in the Bay of Bengal between India and Myanmar. Capital: Port Blair. Population: 356,265 (2001). Area: 8,249 sq. km/3,185 sq. mi. —**Andamanese** *n*

Andaman Islands northern part of the Indian union territory of the Andaman and Nicobar Islands, situated between the Bay of Bengal and the Andaman Sea. The Andaman Islands consist of five large islands and over 200 islets. Population: 240,089 (1991). Area: 6,500 sq. km/2,500 sq. mi.

andante /an dánti, -tay/ *adj, adv* at a moderate musical tempo but slower than moderato (*used as a musical direction*) ■ *n* a title given to musical pieces or movements that are to be played andante [Early 18C. < Italian, 'walking', present participle of *andare* 'go, walk']

andantino /án dan teé nō/ *adj, adv* at a moderate musical tempo slightly faster than andante (*used as a musical direction*) ■ *n* (*plural* **-nos**) a title given to musical pieces or movements that are to be played andantino [Early 19C. < Italian, 'little andante']

AND circuit *n* ELECTRONICS same as **AND** (sense 2)

Andean /ándi ən/ *adj* relating to the Andes ■ *n* somebody who lives in the Andes

Andean-Equatorial *n* a family of Native South American languages, one of whose main branches is Tupi-Guarani —**Andean-Equatorial** *adj*

Andean margin *n* an area of tectonic plate convergence along the Andes Mountain Range, characterized by thicker than normal crust and high mountains

Andersen /ándərss'n/, **Hans Christian** (1805–75) Danish writer. His fairy tales include 'The Ugly Duckling' (1843) and 'The Snow Queen' (1844).

'It doesn't matter about being born in a duckyard, as long as you're hatched from a swan's egg.'
[Hans Christian Andersen, 'The Ugly Duckling', *Fairy Tales*; 1843]

Anderson /ándərss'n/, **Elizabeth Garrett** (1836–1917) British doctor. Refused entry to medical school, she studied privately and gained her licence to practise in 1865, the first British woman to do so.

'Because I prefer to earn a thousand rather than twenty pounds a year.'
[Elizabeth Garrett Anderson. Reply when asked why she did not train to be a nurse. Quoted in *Dr Elizabeth Garrett Anderson*, Louisa Garrett Anderson; 1939]

Anderson, John (1893–1962) Scottish-born Australian philosopher. He was professor of philosophy at the University of Sydney (1927–58), where his espousal of independent critical thinking influenced many local intellectuals.

Anderson, Laurie (*b.* 1947) US composer and performance artist. She combines speech, song and other vocal techniques, dance, film and projection, and unusual instruments in works such as *United States* (1984).

'I think a Benedictine convent is very close to the art world in a lot of ways. The nuns are isolated, but these are people who think and feel and have a relationship to—to a kind of ideal, a spiritual or intellectual ideal.'
[Laurie Anderson. Quoted in 'Laurie An-

derson', *View*, Robin White (interviewer); January 1990]

Library of Congress
Marian Anderson

Anderson, Marian (1897–1993) US contralto. She was the first African American singer to appear at the Metropolitan Opera in New York (1955).

'Where there is money, there is fighting.'
[Marian Anderson, *Marian Anderson, A Portrait*, Kosti Verhanen; 1941]

Anderson, Philip W. (*b.* 1923) US physicist. He shared the Nobel Prize in physics (1977). Full name **Anderson, Philip Warren**

'You never understand everything. When one understands everything, one has gone crazy.'
[Attributed to Philip W. Anderson]

Anderson shelter *n* a small arch of corrugated metal designed to act as a shelter during air raids in World War II [Mid-20C. After its designer, David A. *Anderson*, but popularly associated with British Home Secretary Sir John Anderson]

Anderssen /ándərss'n/, **Adolf** (1818–79) German chess master. He won the first modern international tournament (1851). He used combination plays to force opponents into making immediate decisions.

Andes

Andes /án deez/ huge South American mountain system that extends north to south along the west coast from Panama to Tierra del Fuego. It consists of several ranges and has its highest peak at Aconcagua 6,960 m/22,835 ft.

andesine /ándi zeen, -zin/ *n* a hard colourless mineral of the feldspar group. Source: andesite. [Because found in the ANDES]

andesite /ándi zīt/ *n* a fine-grained greyish volcanic rock characterized by feldspar minerals [Because found in the ANDES] —**andesitic** /ándi zíttik/ *adj*

Andhra Pradesh /ándrə prə désh/ Indian state in the southeast of the country on the Bay of Bengal. Capital: Hyderabad. Population: 75,727,541 (2001). Area: 275,045 sq. km/106,195 sq. mi.

andiron /ánd ī ərn/ *n* either of a pair of metal stands used to hold logs in a fireplace. See illustration on next page [14C. Alteration (influenced by IRON) of Old French *andier* < Celtic]

andolan /aán dōlən/ *n S Asia* an angry protest or other act of opposition by a group of people [< Hindi]

and/or /ánd áwr/ *conj* a short way of saying that either or both of two options may be valid ○ *Bring mosquito netting and/or insect repellent.*

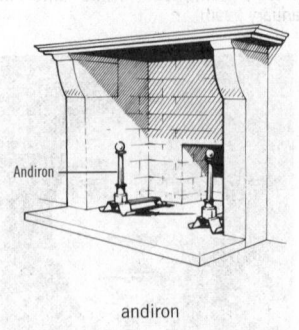

andiron

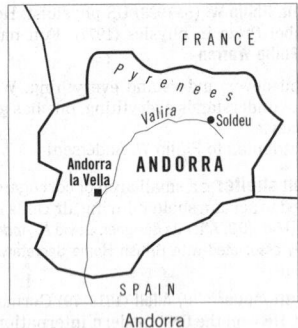

Andorra

Andorra /an dáwrə/ principality in the Pyrenees Mountains between France and Spain. Language: Catalan. Currency: Euro. Capital: Andorra la Vella. Population: 69,150 (2003). Area: 468 sq. km/181 sq. mi. Official name **Principality of Andorra** —**Andorran** *adj*, *n*

Andorra la Vella /-lə véllə/ capital of the Principality of Andorra. Population: 25,000 (1999).

andr- *prefix* same as **andro-** (used before vowels)

andradite /ándrə dīt/ *n* a variously coloured precious stone that is a variety of garnet and is composed of calcium iron silicate. Use: gems. [Mid-19C. After José Bonifácio de *Andrada* e Silva (1763?–1838), Brazilian geologist and independence leader]

Andre /áan dray/, **Carl** (*b.* 1935) US sculptor. He is known for abstract minimalist sculptures made of mass-produced objects such as bricks and metal plates.

Andrea del Sarto /an dráy ə del saártō/ (1486–1530) Italian High Renaissance painter based in Florence. He is best known for his series of frescoes depicting the life of John the Baptist.

Andreessen /an dráyss'n/, **Marc** (*b.* 1971) US computer scientist. He developed and commercialized Internet browser software.

Andreotti /án dray ótti/, **Giulio** (*b.* 1919) Italian prime minister (1972–73, 1976–79, and 1989–92). A Christian Democrat, he held several ministerial posts in coalition governments before becoming prime minister for the first time in 1972.

Andrew /ándroo/ (*b.* 1960) **Prince, Duke of York** Second son of Queen Elizabeth II and Prince Philip, Duke of Edinburgh, he married Sarah Ferguson in 1986. They separated in 1992 and divorced in 1996. Full name **Andrew Albert Christian Edward**

Andrew, St (*d.* AD 60) one of the 12 apostles of Jesus Christ. He preached the Gospel in Scythia and was crucified in Achaea. He is the patron saint of Russia, Greece, and Scotland.

Andrewes /ándrooz/, **Lancelot** (1555–1626) English Anglican bishop and writer. He became bishop of Winchester in 1619 and helped to translate the Authorized Version of the Bible.

Andrews /ándrooz/, **Julie** (*b.* 1935) British-born US actor and singer. She made her Broadway debut in the musical *My Fair Lady* (1956) and starred in the popular films *Mary Poppins* (1964) and *The Sound of Music* (1965). Born **Wells, Julia Elizabeth**

andro- *prefix* male, masculine ○ *androgen* [< Greek < *andr-*, stem of *anēr* 'man']

Androcles /ándrə kleez/ *n* in Roman legend, a slave who was forced to fight a lion, which spared his life after recognizing Androcles as the man who had once removed a thorn from its paw

androecium /an dreéssi əm/ (*plural* **-cia** /-si ə/) *n* the set of stamens in a single flower [Mid-19C. < modern Latin < Greek *andro-* 'man, male' + *oikion* 'house'] —**androecial** *adj*

androgen /ándrəjən/ *n* a natural or artificial male sex hormone responsible for the development of male sexual characteristics. Testosterone and androsterone are androgens. —**androgenic** /ándrə jénnik/ *adj*

androgenize /an drójjə nīz/ (**-nizes**, **-nizing**, **-nized**), **androgenise** (**-nises**, **-nising**, **-nised**) *vt* to cause a female to acquire some male sexual characteristics —**androgenization** /an drójjə nī záysh'n/ *n*

androgyne /ándrə jīn/ *n* **1.** somebody who seems to have both male and female sexual characteristics **2.** BIOL same as **hermaphrodite** (sense 1) [Mid-16C. Via French and Latin < Greek *androgunos* < *andro-* 'man' + *gunē* 'woman']

androgynous /an drójjənəss/ *adj* **1.** BLENDING MASCULINE AND FEMININE neither male nor female in appearance but having both conventional masculine and feminine traits and giving an impression of ambiguous sexual identity ○ *androgynous looks* **2.** PHYSIOL HERMAPHRODITE having both male and female physical characteristics **3.** BOT WITH BOTH MALE AND FEMALE FLOWERS describes a plant species in which both male and female flowers occur in the same flower head [Early 17C. < Latin *androgynus* 'hermaphrodite' (see ANDROGYNE)] —**androgynously** *adv* —**androgyny** *n*

android /án droyd/ *n* in science fiction, a robot that looks and behaves like a human being [Early 18C. < modern Latin *androides* < Greek *andro-* 'man']

Andromache /an drómməki/ *n* in Greek mythology, a princess of Troy and the wife of Hector, who led the Trojan women throughout the Trojan War

andromeda /an drómmidə/ (*plural* **same** or **-das**) *n* an evergreen bush of the heath family. Flowers: pink, drooping in clusters. Genera: *Andromeda* or *Pieris*. [Mid-18C. < modern Latin, after ANDROMEDA (sense 1)]

Andromeda Galaxy: photographed from the Palomar Observatory, California Institute of Technology

Andromeda /an drómmidə/ *n* **1.** in Greek mythology, the daughter of Cassiopeia, who was saved from a sea monster by her future husband, Perseus **2.** a constellation of the northern hemisphere containing a spiral galaxy (**Andromeda Galaxy**) that can be seen with the naked eye. See illustration at **constellation**

andropause /ándrō pawz/ *n* PSYCHOL same as **male menopause** [Late 20C. After MENOPAUSE] —**andropausal** /ándrō páwz'l/ *adj*

Andropov /an dróppov/, **Yuri** (1914–84) president of the former Soviet Union (1983–84). He was chairman of the KGB (1967–82), general secretary of the Communist Party from 1982, and succeeded Brezhnev as president in 1983. Full name **Andropov, Yuri Vladimirovich**

androstenedione /ándrō steén dīōn/ *n* a dietary supplement that increases testosterone production, energy, strength, and muscle development. Unwanted side effects include disruption of hormonal balance, leading to aggressive behaviour and mood swings, and hair loss. [Mid-20C. < ANDROSTERONE + -ENE + DI-[1] + -ONE]

androsterone /an dróstə rōn/ *n* a weak male sex hormone produced by males and females [Mid-20C. < ANDRO- + STEROL + -ONE]

-andry *suffix* **1.** the condition of having a particular number of males or husbands ○ *polyandry* **2.** the condition of having a particular number of stamens ○ *monandry* [< Greek *-andria* < *andr-*, stem of *anēr* 'man'] —**-androus** *suffix*

-ane *suffix* a saturated hydrocarbon ○ *methane* [After -ENE, -ONE]

anecdotal /ánnik dót'l/ *adj* **1.** consisting of or based on second-hand accounts rather than firsthand knowledge or experience or scientific investigation ○ *anecdotal evidence* **2.** relating to anecdotes or in the form of anecdotes —**anecdotally** *adv*

anecdote /ánnik dōt/ *n* a short personal account of an incident or event [Early 18C. Directly or via French < modern Latin *anecdota* < Greek *anekdota* 'things unpublished' < *an-* 'not' + *ekdidonai* 'publish']

anecdotic /ánnik dóttik/ *adj* same as **anecdotal**

anechoic /ánni kó ik/ *adj* producing or characterized by few or no echoes (*technical*)

Aneirin /ə nírin/ (*fl* early 6th century AD) Scottish-born Welsh court poet. He celebrated Britons fallen in battle against the Saxons in his principal work *Y Gododdin*.

anemia, etc. MED another spelling of **anaemia, etc.**

anemo- *prefix* wind ○ *anemography* [< Greek *anemos* 'wind' < Indo-European, 'breathe']

anemochore /ə neémō kawr/ *n* a plant that depends on the wind to disperse its seeds or fruits

anemography /ánni móggrəfi/ *n* the process of measuring wind speed

anemometer /ánni mómmitər/ *n* an instrument that measures the force and direction of the wind

anemometry /ánni mómmətri/ *n* the process of measuring the force and direction of the wind —**anemometrical** /-mə méttrik'l/ *adj*

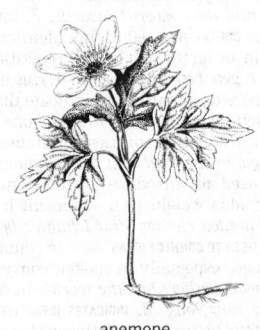

anemone

anemone /ə némməni/ (*plural* **-nes** or **same**) *n* **1.** a perennial flowering plant of the buttercup family with wild and cultivated types. Genus: *Anemone*. **2.** MARINE BIOL same as **sea anemone** [Mid-16C. Via Latin < Greek *anemōnē*]

anemone fish *n* a small colourful damselfish with stinging cells, found in close association with sea anemones. Native to: tropical coral reefs. Genus: *Amphiprion*.

anemophilous /ánni móffələss/ *adj* describes a plant species that is pollinated by the wind —**anemophily** *n*

anencephaly /án en séffəli/ *n* the absence of all or a part of the brain and part of the skull at birth —**anencephalic** /án ensə fállik/ *adj*

~~anenome~~ incorrect spelling of **anemone**

anergy /ánnərji/ *n* decreased immunity or lack of immunity to an antigen [Late 19C. < modern Latin *anergia* < Greek *an-* 'without' + *ergon* 'work'] —**anergic** /a núrjik/ *adj*

aneroid /ánnə royd/ *adj* not containing or using liquid [Mid-19C. < French *anéroïde* < Greek *a-* 'without' + *nēron* 'water, liquid']

aneroid barometer *n* an instrument for indicating atmospheric pressure on a circular dial

anesthesia MED another spelling of **anaesthesia**

anesthesiologist /ánnəss theezi ólləjist/, **anaesthesiologist** *n US* same as **anaesthetist** (sense 1)

anesthesiology /ánnəss theezi ólləji/, **anaesthesiology** *n US* same as **anaesthetics**

anesthetic, etc. MED another spelling of **anaesthetic, etc.**

anestrous, etc. ZOOL US spelling of **anoestrous, etc.**

aneuploid /ánnyoo ployd/ *adj* describes a cell or organism with fewer or more chromosomes than usual —**aneuploid** *n* —**aneuploidy** *n*

aneurysm /ánnyoorizəm/, **aneurism** *n* a fluid-filled sac in the wall of an artery that can weaken the wall [15C. < Greek *aneurusma* 'dilation, swelling' < *aneurunein* 'widen out' < *ana-* 'through' + *eurus* 'wide'] —**aneurysmal** /ánnyoo rízm'l/ *adj*

anew /ə nyoo/ *adv* 1. once more 2. in a new way or form that is unlike the previous one [14C. < *a-* (reduced form of *of*) + NEW; probably after Old French *de neuf, de nouveau*]

anfractuosity /án frakchoo óssəti/ (*plural* -**ties**) *n* (*literary*) 1. a twist or turn, e.g. in a road or in the plot of a novel 2. the twisting turning nature of something [Late 16C. < French *anfractuosité* < late Latin *anfractuosus* < Latin *anfractus* 'bending'] —**anfractuous** /an frákchoo əss/ *adj*

Angas /áng gəss/, **George Fife** (1789–1879) British-born Australian philanthropist. He encouraged the settlement of South Australia and raised money to found its capital, Adelaide.

angel /áynjəl/ *n* 1. HEAVENLY BEING in some religions, a divine being who acts as a messenger of God 2. PICTURE OF HEAVENLY BEING a depiction of an angel as a human figure with wings 3. KIND PERSON somebody who is kind or beautiful (*informal*) 4. GUARDIAN AND GUIDE a spirit that protects and offers guidance 5. FINANCIAL BACKER somebody who provides financial support for an enterprise, e.g. a theatrical venture (*informal*) 6. MEMBER OF LOWEST ANGELIC ORDER an angel of the first of the nine orders of angels in the traditional Christian hierarchy. The nine orders are, in ascending order, angels, archangels, principalities, powers, virtues, dominations, thrones, cherubim, and seraphim. 7. OLD ENGLISH COIN a gold coin that was a unit of currency in England between the 15th and early 17th centuries [13C. Via Old French and ecclesiastical Latin < Greek *aggelos* 'messenger']

CULTURAL NOTE *An Angel at My Table* (1984), the second volume of a three-part autobiography by New Zealand writer Janet Frame. It describes the author's commitment to a mental institution where she was erroneously diagnosed as schizophrenic. She narrowly avoided a leucotomy when a surgeon discovered she had published a collection of stories. The book was made into a film by Jane Campion in 1990.

SYNONYMS See *backer*.

angel cake *n* a whitish light-textured cake with a delicate flavour, made with egg whites. Aus, N Am term **angel food cake**

angel dust *n* the illegal hallucinogenic drug phencyclidine (*slang*)

Angeleno /anjə leéno/ (*plural* -**nos**) *n* somebody who comes from Los Angeles, California [Late 19C. < American Spanish *angeleño*]

Angel Falls /áynjəl fáwlz/ the world's highest waterfall, located in southeastern Venezuela in the Guiana Highlands. Height: 979 m/3,212 ft.

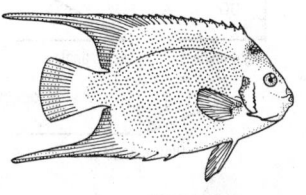
angelfish

angelfish /áynjəl fish/ (*plural* same or -**fishes**) *n* 1. a freshwater fish with a broad striped body and large fins that is often kept in aquariums. Native to: the tropical rivers of South America. Latin name: *Pterophyllum scalare*. 2. a brightly coloured sea fish that has a broad flat body. Native to: tropics. Family: Chaetodontidae or Pomacanthidae. 3. FISH same as **angel shark**

angel food cake *n US* same as **angel cake**

angel hair *n* pasta in the form of long, very fine strands

angelic /an jéllik/, **angelical** /-jéllik'l/ *adj* 1. KIND OR BEAUTIFUL very kind or beautiful 2. WELL-BEHAVED not disturbing or annoying other people 3. OF ANGELS relating to angels —**angelically** *adv*

angelica /an jéllikə/ (*plural* -**cas** or same) *n* 1. bright green, candied plant stems. Use: decorating cakes and biscuits. 2. a tall hollow-stemmed plant of the carrot family that is the source of angelica. Native to: Europe, Asia. Genus: *Angelica*. [Early 16C. < medieval Latin, short for *herba angelica* 'angelic plant']

angelical *adj* same as **angelic**

Angelico /an jéllikō/, **Fra** (1400?–55) Italian religious painter. He became a Dominican monk. He is noted for his frescoes in Florence, including the *Annunciation* and the *Coronation of the Virgin*. Born **Guido di Pietro**

angel of mercy *n* somebody who brings welcome assistance

Angel of the North *n* a large metal sculpture by Antony Gormley of an angel, erected on a hill outside Gateshead, northeastern England, in 1997. It has a wingspan of 54 m/177 ft and has been described as a symbol of renewal in a region undergoing social and economic change.

Maya Angelou

Barnaby's

Angelou /ánjəloo/, **Maya** (*b.* 1928) US writer. Her novels and poetry are notable for their depiction of assertive African American women.

'History, despite the wrenching pain, / Cannot be unlived, but if faced / With courage, need not be lived again.'
[Maya Angelou, poem read at President Bill Clinton's Inauguration; 20 January 1993]

angel shark *n* a small shark with a flat body, broad head, and enlarged pectoral fins, giving it the appearance of a ray. Genus: *Squatina*. [< its wing-like pectoral fins]

Angelus /ánjiləss/, **angelus** *n* 1. in the Roman Catholic Church, a set of prayers to commemorate the Annunciation and the Incarnation 2. a bell rung to announce the time for the Angelus [Mid-17C. < Latin *Angelus domini* 'the angel of the Lord', the first words of the prayers]

anger /áng gər/ *n* a strong feeling of grievance and displeasure ■ *vti* (-**gers**, -**gering**, -**gered**) to become or make somebody extremely annoyed [13C. < Old Norse *angr* 'trouble, sorrow']

CULTURAL NOTE *Look Back in Anger*, a play (1956) by John Osborne. Seen at the time of its first performances as a landmark play that reflected the disaffection of many young people, this domestic drama focuses on Jimmy Porter, a working-class graduate who feels stifled by the middle-class family into which he has married and trapped by social conventions.

SYNONYMS *anger, annoyance, irritation, resentment, indignation, fury, rage, ire, wrath*

CORE MEANING: a feeling of strong displeasure in response to an assumed injury

anger a strong feeling of grievance and displeasure ○ *His face turned white with anger.* ○ *She could feel the anger bubbling up inside her.* **annoyance** mild anger and impatience ○ *Her untidiness was a source of annoyance to him.* ○ *I couldn't find my credit card, much to the annoyance of people queuing behind me.* **irritation** a feeling of impatience or exasperation ○ *replied with ill-concealed irritation* ○ *a sign of his intense irritation with his distant superiors* **resentment** aggrieved feelings caused by a sense of having been badly treated ○ *The policy provoked bitter resentment throughout the police force.* ○ *Try to overcome your feelings of resentment at being denied this experience.* **indignation** anger because something seems unfair or unreasonable ○ *The woman protested in righteous indignation at the idea.* **fury** violent anger ○ *Their eyes were fixed on each other in cold fury.* ○ *Fury at the rejection welled up in him.* **rage** sudden and extreme anger ○ *jealous rage* ○ *Toby flew into a rage.* **ire** (*literary*) strong anger ○ *a change that raised the ire of union members* ○ *This decision drew the ire of rights activists.* **wrath** strong anger, often with a desire for revenge ○ *the wrath of God* ○ *I don't want to incur the wrath of my manager by changing the plan.*

Angers /aáN zhay/ capital of Maine-et-Loire Department in the Pays de la Loire Region in western France. Population: 151,279 (1999).

Angevin /ánjəvin/ *n* SOMEBODY FROM ANJOU somebody who comes from the Anjou region in southwestern France ■ *adj* 1. OF ANJOU relating to the Anjou region in France 2. OF ANJOU AND PLANTAGENET DYNASTIES relating to the House of Anjou, especially the branch that includes the Plantagenet kings of England [Mid-17C. Via French < medieval Latin *Andegavinus* < *Andegavia* 'Anjou']

angina /an jínə/, **angina pectoris** /-péktəriss/ *n* a medical condition in which lack of blood to the heart causes severe chest pains [Mid-16C. < Latin, 'quinsy', alteration (after *angere* 'to squeeze') of Greek *agkhonē* 'strangling' < *agkhein* 'to squeeze, strangle']

angio- *prefix* 1. blood or lymph vessel ○ *angiogram* 2. pericarp ○ *angiosperm* [< modern Latin < Greek *aggeion* 'blood vessel' < *aggos* 'vessel']

angiocardiography /ánji ō kaardi óggrəfi/ *n* X-ray examination of the heart and related blood vessels after a substance that will show up when X-rayed has been injected into the bloodstream — **angiocardiographic** /-ə gráffik/ *adj*

angiogenesis /ánji ō jénnisiss/ *n* the formation of new blood vessels, e.g. in an embryo or as a result of a tumour

angiogram /ánji ō gram/ *n* an X-ray photograph of a blood vessel

angiography /ánji óggrəfi/ *n* X-ray examination of blood vessels after a substance that will show up when X-rayed has been injected into the bloodstream —**angiographic** /ánji ə gráffik/ *adj*

angiology /ánji ólləji/ *n* the branch of medicine that deals with blood vessels and the lymphatic system

angioma /ánji ōmə/ (*plural* -**mas** or -**mata** /-mətə/) *n* a benign tumour made up of blood or lymph vessels — **angiomatous** *adj*

angiopathy /ánji óppəthi/ (*plural* -**thies**) *n* a disease of the blood vessels or lymph vessels

angioplasty /ánji ō plasti/ (*plural* **-ties**) *n* a surgical operation to clear a narrowed or blocked artery

angiosarcoma /ánji ō saar kṓmə/ (*plural* **-mas** or **-mata** /-mətə/) *n* a malignant tumour consisting of vascular cells, often in the liver

angioscope /ánji ə skōp/ *n* a long fine surgical viewing instrument threaded into a patient's blood vessels to allow surgeons to observe and perform operations without large incisions —**angioscopy** /ánji óskəpi/ *n*

angiospasm /ánji ō spazəm/ *n* a spasmodic contraction of a blood vessel

angiosperm /ánji ō spurm/ *n* a plant in which the sex organs are within flowers and the seeds are in a fruit [Early 19C. < ANGIO- + Greek *sperma* 'seed'] —**angiospermous** /ánji ō spúrməss/ *adj* —**angiospermy** *n*

angiostatin /ánji ə statin/ *n* a naturally occurring protein in the body that plays a role in inhibiting the formation of new blood vessels

angiotensin /ánji ō ténssin/ *n* a hormone that causes blood pressure to rise, formed in the blood by a series of processes that can be influenced by drugs [Mid-20C. < ANGIO- + HYPERTENSION + -IN]

angiotensin-converting enzyme inhibitor *n* PHARM full form of **ACE inhibitor**

Angkor

Angkor /áng kawr/, **Ângkôr** ancient capital city of early Khmer civilization, now deserted but noted for its temples and monuments, built AD 850–900. It is in present-day northwestern Cambodia. Area: 13 sq. km/5 sq. mi.

angle[1] /áng g'l/ *n* **1.** SPACE BETWEEN DIVERGING LINES the space between two diverging lines or planes, or a measure of the space **2.** FIGURE FORMED BY DIVERGING LINES a figure formed by two lines diverging from a common point or two planes diverging from a common line **3.** MATHS same as **solid angle 4.** PART THAT STICKS OUT a projecting part of something **5.** POSITION FOR VIEWING SOMETHING a position from which somebody can look at something ○ *a sculpture seen from three angles* **6.** WAY OF CONSIDERING SOMETHING a way of looking at a situation ○ *Consider the matter from this angle.* ■ *v* (**-gles**, **-gling**, **-gled**) **1.** *vti* PLACE SOMETHING, OR BE PLACED, OBLIQUELY to direct or place something obliquely, or move or be placed obliquely **2.** *vt* PRESENT SOMETHING WITH BIAS to present something with a particular audience in mind or in order to express a particular point of view **3.** *vi* CHANGE DIRECTION SHARPLY to turn in a sharply different direction [14C. Directly or via French < Latin *angulus* 'corner']

angle[2] /áng g'l/ (**-gles**, **-gling**, **-gled**) *vi* **1.** to fish with a hook, line, and rod **2.** to attempt to obtain a compliment or an advantage (*informal*) [Old English *angul* 'fishhook' < Indo-European, 'to bend, hook']

Angle /áng g'l/ *n* a member of a Germanic people who invaded and settled eastern and northern England in the 5th and 6th centuries AD [Pre-12C. < Latin *Angli* 'people from Angul' (in N Germany)] —**Anglian** /áng gli ən/ *adj, n*

angle bar *n* CONSTR same as **angle iron**

angle bracket *n* either of a pair of marks (< or >) used to enclose text

angle iron *n* an iron or steel bar that is L-shaped in cross section

angle of attack *n* the acute angle between the direction of airflow and the line linking the leading and trailing edges of an aircraft wing

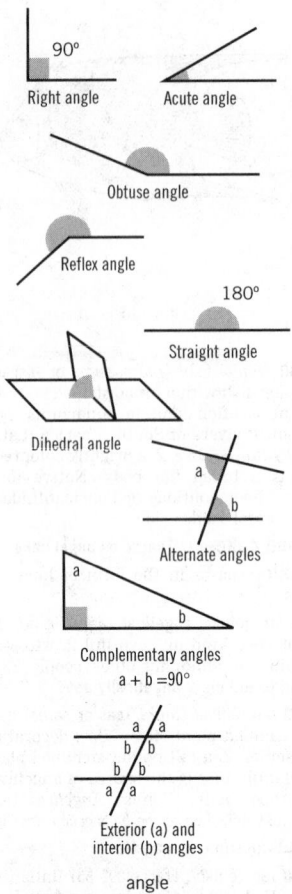

Right angle   Acute angle

Obtuse angle

Reflex angle

Straight angle   180°

Dihedral angle

Alternate angles

Complementary angles
a + b =90°

Exterior (a) and interior (b) angles

angle

angle of incidence *n* the angle between an incoming ray of light and the line perpendicular to the surface at the point of arrival

angle of reflection *n* the angle between a reflected ray of light and the line perpendicular to the surface at the point of reflection

angle of refraction *n* the angle between a refracted ray of light and the line perpendicular to the surface at the point of refraction

angle of repose *n* the maximum slope or angle at which unconsolidated material such as sand can be made into a mound before it begins to slide

angle plate *n* an L-shaped metal plate used to support a framework

Anglepoise /áng g'l poyz/ *tdmk* a trademark for a desk lamp that allows the angle of the light to be adjusted without moving the base

angler /áng glər/ *n* **1.** somebody who fishes with a hook, line, and rod **2.** FISH same as **anglerfish**

CULTURAL NOTE *The Compleat Angler*, a handbook (1653) by Izaak Walton. Although presented as a discourse on fishing in the form of a dialogue between a fisherman, a hunter, and a fowler, the work's affectionate portrait of country life and its references to social issues transform it into a work of great literary and historical value.

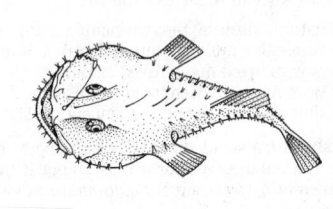
anglerfish

anglerfish /áng glər fish/ (*plural same* or **-fishes**) *n* a sea fish that uses a long dorsal fin extending over its mouth to attract prey. Order: Lophiiformes.

Anglesey /áng g'lssi/ island off the coast of northwestern Wales, the largest island in England and Wales. Population: 66,829 (2001). Area: 676 sq. km/261 sq. mi.

anglesite /áng g'l sīt/ *n* a colourless, white, or lightly tinted lead sulphate mineral [Mid-19C. < ANGLESEY]

Anglican /áng glikən/ *adj* relating to the Anglican Church ■ *n* a member of an Anglican Church [Early 17C. < medieval Latin *Anglicanus* 'English' < Latin *Angli* 'the Angles'; from its originally denoting the Church of England]

Anglican Church *n* a group of Christian churches including the Churches of England, Ireland, and Wales, and the Episcopal Church of Scotland

Anglican Communion *n* a worldwide association of churches related to the Church of England, with the Archbishop of Canterbury at its head

Anglicanism /áng glikənizəm/ *n* the doctrines of the Church of England and other Anglican churches

anglicise *vti* another spelling of **anglicize**

Anglicism /áng gli sizəm/, **anglicism** *n* **1.** a term that is peculiar to British English as opposed to other varieties of English **2.** an English word or phrase used in a foreign language [Mid-17C. < medieval Latin *Anglicus* 'English' < Latin *Angli* 'the Angles']

anglicize /áng gli sīz/ (**-cizes**, **-cizing**, **-cized**), **Anglicize**, **anglicise** (**-cises**, **-cising**, **-cised**), **Anglicise** *vti* to become or make somebody or something more English [Early 18C. < medieval Latin *Anglicus* (see ANGLICISM)] —**anglicization** /áng gli sī záysh'n/ *n*

angling /áng gling/ *n* the sport of catching fish with a hook, line, and rod

Anglo /áng glō/ (*plural* **-glos**), **anglo** *n* (*informal*) **1.** Aus AUSTRALIAN FROM BRITISH ISLES OR N AMERICA an Australian citizen of British, Irish, or North American origin **2.** *N Am* NON-HISPANIC WHITE PERSON an English-speaking white person in the United States who is not of Hispanic origin **3.** *Can* ENGLISH-SPEAKING CANADIAN an English-speaking person in Canada, especially in Quebec [Early 19C. < ANGLO-]

Anglo- *prefix* England, the English, British ○ *Anglophile* ○ *Anglo-Irish* [< Latin *Angli* 'the Angles']

Anglo-American *n N Am* a citizen of the United States or Canada whose ancestors were originally from Great Britain and whose language and culture derive from Great Britain

Anglo-Asian *n* somebody from the United Kingdom whose family originally came from South Asia

Anglo-French *adj* relating to the links that exist between France and the United Kingdom

Anglo-Indian *adj* FROM SOUTH ASIAN LANGUAGE introduced into English from a South Asian language ■ *n* **1.** SOMEBODY WITH BRITISH AND INDIAN ANCESTRY somebody of both British and South Asian descent **2.** BRITISH PERSON RESIDENT IN INDIA a British person who lived or has lived a long time in South Asia, especially during the time of former British India, from 1765 to 1947

Anglo-Irish *npl* IRISH PEOPLE WITH ENGLISH ANCESTRY people of English descent who were born or who live in Ireland ■ *adj* **1.** ENGLISH AND IRISH relating to the United Kingdom and Ireland or the Republic of Ireland **2.** OF THE ANGLO-IRISH of English descent but from or living in Ireland

Anglo-Latin *n* a form of Latin used in medieval England, having some English loanwords and forms

Anglo-Norman *adj* ENGLISH AND NORMAN relating to the 11th-century Norman conquerors of England ■ *n* **1.** HIST NORMAN IN ENGLAND a Norman inhabitant of England after 1066 **2.** LANG FRENCH SPOKEN IN MEDIEVAL ENGLAND the variety of Norman French spoken in medieval England

Anglophile /áng glō fīl/ *n* an admirer of England or English people —**Anglophilia** /áng glō fílli ə/ *n* —**Anglophilic** /ánglō fíllik/ *adj*

Anglophobe /áng glō fōb/ *n* somebody who hates England or English people —**Anglophobia** /áng glō fṓbi ə/ *n* —**Anglophobic** /ánglō fṓbik/ *adj*

anglophone /áng glə fōn/ *n* somebody who speaks English, especially as a first language ■ *adj* de-

scribes countries or regions where English is spoken by most people as their first language

Anglo-Saxon n 1. PEOPLES MEMBER OF GERMANIC PEOPLE a member of a West Germanic people who settled in Britain from the 5th century AD and were dominant until 1066. They included the Angles, Saxons, and Jutes. 2. LANG same as **Old English** (sense 1) 3. ENGLISH NATIVE SPEAKER a white speaker of English as a first language ■ adj 1. LANG FROM OLD ENGLISH describes a word in Modern English that comes from Old English 2. OF ENGLISH SPEAKERS relating to white English speakers

ang mo /áng mő/ (plural **ang mos**) n Malaysia, Singapore an inhabitant of the West, especially western Europe or North America (informal) [< Hokkien, 'red hair']

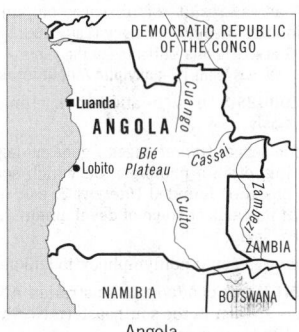

Angola

Angola /ang gőla/ country in west-central Africa that gained its independence from Portugal in 1975. Language: Portuguese. Currency: kwanza. Capital: Luanda. Population: 10,766,471 (2003 estimate). Area: 1,246,700 sq. km/481,530 sq. mi. Official name **Republic of Angola** —**Angolan** adj, n

angora /ang gáwrə/ n 1. wool made from the hair of an angora goat or rabbit (often used before a noun) 2. a rabbit, goat, or cat belonging to a breed with long silky fur [Early 19C. < ANGORA]

Angora /ang gáwrə/ former name for **Ankara** (until 1930)

angostura /áng gə styoórə/, **angostura bark** n the bitter aromatic bark of either of two South American citrus trees. Use: flavouring in bitters and formerly to relieve fever. [After Angostura (now Ciudad Bolívar), Venezuela]

Angostura bitters /-bíttərz/ tdmk a trademark for a bitter-tasting flavouring for alcoholic drinks, made from herbs and spices

Angoulême /aaN goo lem/, **Charles, Duc d'** (1573–1650) French soldier and the illegitimate son of Charles IX. He commanded the siege of La Rochelle (1627).

angrez /ung ráyz/ (plural **-grezi** /-ráyzi/ or **-grezlog** /-ráyz lőg/) n S Asia somebody who was born or brought up in England (informal) [< Hindi, 'Englishman'] — **angrez** adj

angrily /áng grəli/ adv 1. in a way that conveys extreme annoyance or displeasure 2. in a stormy threatening way

angry /áng gri/ (-**grier**, -**griest**) adj 1. FEELING VERY ANNOYED feeling extremely annoyed, often about an insult or a wrong 2. EXPRESSING ANNOYANCE expressing extreme annoyance ○ Low growls and angry snarls assailed our ears on every side...' (Edgar Rice Burroughs, The Gods of Mars; 1913) 3. STORMY stormy-looking 4. INFLAMED inflamed and painful-looking ○ an angry bruise [14C. < ANGER]

angry young man n 1. also **Angry Young Man** a member of a group of British men writing in the 1950s who were hostile to authority. The setting for their works is typically working-class, and the central character typically a lone man. (often used in the plural) 2. a young man who is hostile to authority

angst /angst/ n 1. in existentialist philosophy, a feeling of dread arising from an awareness of free choice 2. any feeling of dread or anxiety [Early 20C. < German]

SYNONYMS See **worry**.

angst-ridden adj dominated by a feeling of dread or anxiety

angstrom /ángstrəm, -strom/ n 1. also **angstrom unit** a unit of length equal to one ten-billionth of a metre (10^{-10} m), used to measure the wavelengths of electromagnetic radiations. Symbol **Å** 2. the letter 'a' with a mark (°) placed above it, used in some Scandinavian languages to indicate a change in pronunciation from 'a' to 'aw'. See table at **diacritic** [Late 19C. After Anders Jonas Ångström (1814–74), Swedish physicist]

Anguilla /ang gwíllə/ one of the Leeward Islands, in the eastern Caribbean, east of Puerto Rico. Area: 91 sq. km/35 sq. mi. Population: 12,446 (2002 estimate)

anguish /áng gwish/ n extreme anxiety or emotional torment ■ vti (-**guishes**, -**guishing**, -**guished**) to feel or cause somebody to feel anguish [12C. < Old French anguis < Latin angustus 'narrow, tight']

anguished /áng gwisht/ adj feeling or producing extreme anxiety or torment

angular /áng gyoõlər/ adj 1. SHARPLY DEFINED describes an object with a lot of angles 2. THIN thin and bony 3. AWKWARD AND UNGAINLY stiff, awkward, and ungainly 4. MATHS MEASURED BY ANGLES measured by an angle or rate of change of an angle [14C. < Latin angularis < angulus 'corner'] —**angularly** adv

angular acceleration n the rate at which the rotation of a rotating body changes. Symbol α

angular displacement n the angle through which something has been rotated about an axis, usually measured in radians

angular frequency n the frequency of a repeating rotation expressed in radians per second and multiplied by 2π. Symbol ω

angularity /áng gyoõ lárrəti/ (plural -**ties**) n 1. the thin and bony appearance of somebody's body 2. a sharp corner or angle (often used in the plural)

angular momentum n the momentum that a body has due to its rotation about an axis, calculated as the product of its mass and its angular velocity. Symbol L

angular stomatitis n a condition of the lips, mouth, and cheeks characterized by cracks and fissures and caused by a bacterial infection

angular velocity n the rate of rotation of a body around an axis. Symbol ω

Angus[1] /áng gəss/ (plural same or -**guses**) n US BREED same as **Aberdeen Angus**

Angus[2] /áng gəss/ historic Scottish county

anhinga /an híng gə/ (plural -**gas** or same) n US same as **darter** (sense 2) [Mid-18C. Via Portuguese < Tupi áyinga]

Anhui /án hwáy/, **Anhwei** province in east-central China bordered by the provinces of Jiangsu, Zhejiang, Jiangxi, Hubei, and Henan. Capital: Hefei. Population: 60,700,000 (1997). Area: 139,899 sq. km/54,015 sq. mi.

anhydride /an hí drīd, -drid/ n a compound formed from another by the removal of water [Mid-19C. < ANHYDROUS]

anhydrite /an hí drīt/ n a colourless or lightly tinted anhydrous calcium sulphate mineral. Use: cement, fertilizers. [Early 19C. < ANHYDROUS]

anhydrous /an hídrəss/ adj describes compounds that contain no water, or crystals that lack chemically bound water (**water of crystallization**) [Early 19C. < Greek anudros 'waterless' < hudōr 'water']

ani /aáni/ (plural **anis** or same) n a glossy black long-tailed bird that has a heavy arched beak and lays eggs in a communal nest. Native to: tropical America. Genus: Crotophaga. [Early 19C. Via Spanish or Portuguese < Tupi anú]

Aniakchak National Monument and Preserve /ánni ák chak-/ national park in southwestern Alaska. One of its outstanding natural features is the Aniakchak Crater, a volcanic crater 610 m/2,000 ft deep.

anicca /ánnikə/ n in Buddhism, the cycle of birth, life, and death [Via Pali < Sanskrit anitya- 'not eternal' < nitya- 'constant, perpetual']

aniconic /án ī kónnik/ adj describes images of deities that are not human or animal in form

~~anihilation~~ incorrect spelling of **annihilation**

anil /ánnil/ (plural -**ils** or same) n a bush that is the source of indigo dye. Native to: Caribbean. Latin name: Indigofera suffruticosa. [Late 16C. Via French and Portuguese < Arabic an-nīl 'the indigo' < Arabic and Persian nīl < Sanskrit nīla- 'dark blue']

anile /ánnīl, áy-/ adj resembling a woman of advanced years (literary) [Mid-17C. < Latin anilis < anus 'venerable woman']

aniline /ánnilin, -leen/ n a colourless poisonous oily liquid. Use: manufacture of dyes, resins, pharmaceuticals, explosives. Formula: $C_6H_5NH_2$. [Mid-19C. < ANIL, because first obtained by distilling indigo with alkali]

aniline dye n a synthetic dye derived from aniline

anilingus /áyni líng gəss/ n the act of sexually stimulating the anus with the tongue or mouth [Mid-20C. < modern Latin < Latin anus 'anus', after CUNNILINGUS]

anima /ánnimə/ n 1. in Jungian psychology, the true inner self as opposed to the outer persona 2. in Jungian psychology, the feminine aspect of a man's personality [Early 20C. < Latin, 'breath, soul, spirit']

animadversion /ánni mad vúrsh'n/ n a critical comment or comments, especially those reproaching somebody (formal)

animadvert /ánni mad vúrt, -məd-/ (-**verts**, -**verting**, -**verted**) vi to comment critically or unfavourably (formal) [Mid-17C. < Latin animadvertere 'turn the mind towards' < animus 'mind' + advertere (see ADVERT[1])]

animal /ánnim'l/ n 1. LIVING ORGANISM WITH INDEPENDENT MOVEMENT a living organism that is distinguished from plants by independent movement and responsive sense organs 2. MAMMAL a land mammal other than a human being 3. BRUTISH PERSON somebody regarded as vulgar or brutish (informal) 4. INSTINCT-DRIVEN INNER SELF the instinctive inner self as opposed to the one subject to self-restraint 5. TYPE OF PERSON OR THING somebody or something of a particular type (informal) ○ The laser printer is a completely different animal. ■ adj 1. FROM ANIMALS derived from animals ○ animal fats 2. INSTINCTIVE belonging to the realm of instincts and urges ○ animal urges [14C. < Latin animal(e) < animalis 'living, breathing' < anima 'breath, life, soul']

animalcule /ánni mál kyool/, **animalculum** /ánni málkyoõləm/ (plural -**la** /-kyoõlə/) n a microscopic organism such as an amoeba that moves about, eats other microbes, or resembles an animal in some other way (archaic) [Late 16C. < modern Latin animalculum 'little animal' < Latin animal(e) (see ANIMAL)] —**animalcular** adj

animal husbandry n the branch of agriculture concerned with breeding and rearing farm animals

animalise vt another spelling of **animalize**

animalism /ánniməlizəm/ n 1. THEORY OF HUMANS' NON-SPIRITUAL NATURE the theory that human beings are driven by physical appetites rather than spiritual needs 2. PREOCCUPATION WITH PHYSICAL SIDE OF LIFE preoccupation with physical rather than spiritual needs 3. TYPICAL ANIMAL BEHAVIOUR behaviour that is typical of animals —**animalistic** /ánnimə lístik/ adj

animalist /ánnim'list/ n 1. SOMEBODY PREOCCUPIED WITH PHYSICAL NEEDS somebody who is preoccupied with physical rather than spiritual needs 2. SOMEBODY DENYING HUMANS' SPIRITUAL NATURE somebody who holds that humans are driven by physical rather than spiritual needs 3. ANIMAL RIGHTS SUPPORTER a supporter of animal rights, especially a militant one (informal)

animality /ánni málləti/ n 1. the characteristics of animals, as opposed to those of plants 2. the physical needs of human beings, as opposed to the spiritual needs

animalize /ánnimə līz/ (-**izes**, -**izing**, -**ized**), **animalise** (-**ises**, -**ising**, -**ised**) vt to bring out somebody's brutal or instinctive nature —**animalization** /ánnimə lī záysh'n/ n

animal liberation n the movement to free animals from what is held to be human exploitation (often used before a noun)

animal magnetism n somebody's strong physical attractiveness (informal humorous)

animal rights npl basic rights for animals, e.g. the right to live free from suffering inflicted by human beings ○ an animal rights activist

animal spirits *npl* natural energy and high spirits

animal welfarist *n* a supporter of animal rights

animate *vt* /ánni mayt/ (**-mates, -mating, -mated**) **1. MAKE SOMEBODY OR SOMETHING LIVELY** to make a person, subject, or event lively **2. INSPIRE SOMEBODY** to rouse or inspire somebody to take action or to have strong feelings **3.** CINEMA **PRESENT SOMETHING USING ANIMATION TECHNIQUES** to present or record something in the form of a sequence of moving still images **4. MAKE SOMEBODY ACTIVE** to arouse somebody or something into activity or motion ○ *leaves animated by a stiff breeze* **5. CAUSE TO LIVE** to bring somebody or something to life ■ *adj* /ánnimət/ **1. PHYSICALLY ALIVE** in a physically live state, as opposed to being dead or inert **2. LIVELY** full of liveliness or energy [14C. < Latin *animat-*, past participle of *animare* 'give life to' < *anima* 'breath, soul, spirit'] —**animated** *adj*

animation /ánni máysh'n/ *n* **1.** CINEMA **PRODUCTION OF ANIMATED FILMS** the making of films by photographing a sequence of slightly varying drawings or models so that they appear to move and change when the sequence is shown **2.** CINEMA **ANIMATED FILMS** a film or films consisting of a series of drawn, painted, or modelled scenes **3.** COMPUT **COMPUTER-GENERATED GRAPHICS** the production of moving images by computer techniques, or the image produced ○ *smooth and realistic animations* **4. LIVELINESS** liveliness in the way somebody speaks or behaves

animato /ánni maátō/ *adj, adv* to be played in a lively animated manner (*used as a musical direction*) [Early 18C. < Italian < Latin *animare* (see ANIMATE)]

animator /ánnimaytər/ *n* **1.** a maker of animated films **2.** somebody who or something that makes things lively, exciting, or interesting

animatronics /ánnimə trónniks/ *n* the use of computer technology and a form of radio control to animate puppets or other models, e.g. for a film (*takes a singular verb*) [Late 20C. Blend of ANIMATE + ELECTRONICS] —**animatronic** *adj*

anime /ánni may, ánnimə/ *n* a Japanese style of animated cartoon, often with violent or sexually explicit content [Late 20C. < Japanese < English ANIMATION]

animé /ánni may/ *n* resin obtained from various tropical American trees. Use: varnishes, perfumes. [Late 16C. Via French < Tupi *wana'ni*]

animism /ánnimizəm/ *n* **1. BELIEF THAT NATURE HAS SOUL** the belief that things in nature, e.g. trees, mountains, and the sky, have souls or consciousness **2. BELIEF IN ORGANIZING FORCE IN UNIVERSE** the belief that a supernatural force animates and organizes the universe **3. BELIEF IN EXISTENCE OF SEPARATE SPIRIT** the belief that people have spirits that do or can exist separately from their bodies [Mid-19C. < Latin *anima* 'soul'] —**animist** *adj, n* —**animistic** /ánni místik/ *adj*

animosity /ánni móssəti/ (*plural* **-ties**) *n* a feeling or spirit of hostility and resentment [15C. Directly or via French *animosité* < late Latin *animositas* 'spiritedness' < *animosus* 'spirited' < *animus* 'mind, spirit']

SYNONYMS See ***dislike***.

---

animus /ánniməss/ *n* **1. HOSTILITY** a feeling or display of animosity **2. MOTIVATION** an attitude or feeling that motivates somebody's actions **3.** PSYCHOL **WOMAN'S MASCULINE SIDE** in Jungian psychology, the masculine aspect of a woman's personality [Early 19C. < Latin, 'mind, spirit']

Anindilyakwa /ə níndəl yakwə/ *n* an Australian Aboriginal language spoken on Groote Eylandt in the Northern Territory. Native speakers: 1,310.

anion /án ī ən/ *n* a negatively charged ion, especially one that is attracted to an anode, either during electrolysis or within a vacuum tube [Mid-19C. Blend of ANODE + ION] —**anionic** /án ī ónnik/ *adj* —**anionically** *adv*

anion-exchange resin *n* a solid resin in which the functional group is positive and thus attracts negative ions. Use: chemical and radioactive waste cleanup, chemical separation.

anise /ánniss/ *n* **1.** FOOD same as **aniseed 2.** an aromatic plant with liquorice-flavoured seeds (**aniseed**). Use: medicines, flavouring for food and drink. Native to: Mediterranean. Latin name: *Pimpinella anisum*. [13C. Via French *anis* and Latin *anisum* < Greek *anison*]

aniseed /ánni seed/ *n* the liquorice-flavoured seeds of anise, used whole or in ground spice mixtures as a flavouring in foods and drinks

aniseikonia /án ī sī kōni ə/ *n* a condition in the lens of one eye that results in its seeing an image that differs in size and shape from the image seen by the other eye [Mid-20C. < ANISO- + Greek *eikōn* 'image']

anisette /ánni zét, -sét/ *n* a sweet liqueur flavoured with aniseed [Mid-19C. < French, 'little anise' < *anis* (see ANISE)]

aniso- *prefix* differing, not equal ○ *anisogamy* [< Greek *anisos* < *an-* 'not' + *isos* 'equal']

anisogamete /án ī sō gámmeet, -gə meét/ *n* BIOL same as **heterogamete** (sense 1)

anisogamy /án ī sóggəmi/ *n* BIOL same as **heterogamy** (sense 1) —**anisogamic** /án īssə gámmik/ *adj* —**anisogamous** *adj*

anisole /ánni sōl/ *n* a colourless liquid with a pleasant smell. Use: solvent, perfume, flavouring. Formula: $C_6H_5OCH_3$. [Mid-19C. < ANISE + -OLE]

anisomeric /án īssō mérrik/ *adj* describes a compound that does not form structurally different molecules (**isomers**)

anisometric /á n īssō méttrik/ *adj* **1.** not isometric or symmetrical ○ *an anisometric particle* **2.** describes a crystal that does not have three perpendicular axes of equal length and is therefore not regular

anisometropia /án īssōmə trṓpi ə/ *n* lack of balance between each eye's ability to refract light [Late 19C. < ANISO- + Greek *metron* 'measure' + -OPIA] —**anisometropic** /án īssōmə tróppik/ *adj*

anisotropic /án īssō tróppik/ *adj* describes something with physical properties that are different in different directions, e.g. crystals that measure differently along each of two or more axes —**anisotropically** *adv* —**anisotropism** /án ī sóttrəpizəm/ *n* —**anisotropy** /án ī sóttrəpi/ *n*

anistreplase /a nístrə playz, -playss/ *n* a drug that breaks down fibrous tissue. Use: to dissolve blood clots blocking arteries. [Late 20C. < *anistre-* + *-plase*, INN suffix]

Anjou[1] /aán zhoó, óN-/, **Anjou pear** *n* a variety of pear with green skin and firm flesh [After ANJOU[2]]

Anjou[2] /oN zhoó/ former province in western France in the lower Loire valley. Once part of the Plantagenet domain, it was claimed for France in 1481.

Ankara /ángkərə/ capital of Turkey, in the north-central part of the country, on the River Ankara, northwest of Adana and southeast of Bursa. Population: 3,023,000 (2000). Former name **Angora**

ankerite /ángkə rīt/ *n* a white, grey, brown, or reddish carbonate mineral containing calcium, magnesium, iron, and sometimes manganese [Mid-19C. < German *Ankerit*, after M. J. *Anker* (1772–1843), Austrian mineralogist]

ankh /angk/ *n* a symbol consisting of a cross with a loop for the top extension and a short crossbar, used in ancient Egypt to signify life [Late 19C. < Egyptian, 'life']

ankle /ángk'l/ *n* **1.** the joint that connects the leg bones with the highest bone in the foot **2.** the slender part of the leg immediately above the ankle [14C. < assumed Old Norse *ankula*, which replaced related Old English *ancleōw*, < Indo-European]

ankle-biter *n Aus, US* a young child (*informal humorous*)

anklebone /ángk'l bōn/ *n* ANAT same as **talus**[2]

ankle boot *n* a boot that extends up to the ankle but not much beyond

ankle-length *adj* reaching up to or down to the ankles

ankle sock *n UK, ANZ, Can* a sock that extends up to the ankle but not much past it. US term **anklet**

anklet /ángklət/ *n* **1.** a piece of jewellery or some other ornament worn round the ankle **2.** *US* same as **ankle sock**

anklewarmer /ángk'l wawrmər/ *n* a knitted tube that covers the ankles and sometimes also the calves and top of the foot

ankus /ángkəss/ (*plural same* or **-kuses**) *n S Asia* a stick used to goad an elephant [Late 19C. < Hindi]

ankylosaur /ángkələ sawr/ *n* a plant-eating dinosaur with short legs, a heavy thickset body, and bony dorsal plates. It lived during the Cretaceous period. [Late 20C. < modern Latin *Ankylosaurus* < Greek *agkulōsis* (see ANKYLOSIS) + *sauros* 'lizard']

ankylose /ángkilōz, -lōss/ (**-loses, -losing, -losed**) *vti* to cause bones to fuse and a joint to become stiff as a result of injury or disease, or intentionally through surgery, or to fuse and become stiff [Late 18C. Back-formation < ANKYLOSIS]

ankylosing spondylitis /ángkilōssing-, -lōzing-/ *n* a disease of the spine that causes the vertebrae to form a solid inflexible column

ankylosis /ángki lṓssiss/ (*plural* **-loses** /-lṓ seez/) *n* **1.** the fusion of bones of a joint, often as a result of disease or injury, or intentionally through surgery **2.** stiffness or immobility in a joint caused by bones fusing as a result of disease or injury, or intentionally through surgery [Early 18C. Via modern Latin < Greek *agkulōsis* 'stiffening of the joints' < *agkuloun* 'bend' < *agkulos* 'bent'] —**ankylotic** /ángki lóttik/ *adj*

ankylostomiasis *n* MED another spelling of **ancylostomiasis**

anlage /án laagə/ (*plural* **-lagen** /-gən/ or **-lages**) *n* **1.** something, often a principle, on which something else is based or founded (*literary*) **2.** BIOL a part or organ in its earliest stage of development [Late 19C. < German, 'layout']

ANLL *abbr* MED acute nonlymphocytic leukaemia

Anmatyerr /ánmə chérrə/ *n* an Australian Aboriginal language spoken in the southeastern Northern Territory. Native speakers: 860.

ANN *abbr* COMPUT artificial neural network

ann. *abbr* **1.** annals **2.** annual **3.** FIN annuity

anna /ánnə/ *n* a copper coin formerly used in South Asia, worth one-sixteenth of a rupee [Early 17C. < Hindi *ānā*]

Anna Ivanovna /ánnə i vaánəvnə/ (1693–1740) empress of Russia. She was the niece of Peter the Great. While she was empress (1730–40), her German advisers administered the country.

annalist /ánn'list/ *n* somebody who compiles annals

annals /ánn'lz/ *npl* **1. ANNUAL RECORDS** a record of events arranged chronologically by year **2. RECORDED HISTORY** history in general, as it is recorded in books and other documents ○ *Her achievements have secured her place in the annals of our nation.* **3. LEARNED JOURNAL** a periodical that records events and reports in a field of research [Mid-16C. Directly or via French < Latin *annales* < *annalis* (see ANNUAL)]

~~**annalysis**~~ incorrect spelling of **analysis**

Annam /a nám/ region in Vietnam forming a narrow strip along the South China Sea. It became a protectorate of France in 1883, gaining autonomy after World War II until Vietnam was partitioned in 1954. —**Annamese** /ánnə meéz/ *adj, n*

Annan /a nán, ánnən/, **Kofi** (*b.* 1938) Ghanaian Secretary General of the United Nations. As the United Nations special envoy to the former Yugoslavia, he oversaw the Dayton Accords in 1995 that ended the Bosnian-Croatian-Serbian war. He was appointed Secretary General of the United Nations in 1996 and awarded the Nobel Peace Prize in 2001.

'The best way of using force is to show it in order not to have to use it.'
[Attributed to Kofi Annan]

Annapolis /ə náppəliss/ capital of Maryland, situated near the Chesapeake Bay. The US Naval Academy is here. Population: 36,196 (2002 estimate).

Annapurna /ánnə púrnə/ mountain in the Himalaya range in north-central Nepal, one of the world's highest peaks. Height: 8,091 m/26,545 ft.

Ann Arbor /an aárbər/ city in southeastern Michigan, home to the main campus of the University of Michigan. Population: 115,213 (2002 estimate).

annatto /ə náttō/ (*plural* **-tos**) *n* **1.** a yellowish-red dye made from the pulp around the seeds of a tropical tree. Use: food colouring, fabric dye. **2.** the tree from whose seeds annatto dye is made. Native to: tropical America. Latin name: *Bixa orellana*. [Early 17C. < Carib]

Anne /an/ (1665–1714) queen of Great Britain and Ireland. The daughter of James II, she inherited the

throne from William III. She ruled from 1702 to 1714 and provided for the Hanoverian succession after her death.

Anne, the Princess Royal (*b.* 1950) The daughter of Queen Elizabeth II and Prince Philip, Duke of Edinburgh, she became president of the Save the Children Fund in 1970. Full name **Anne Elizabeth Alice Louise**

Anne (of Austria) (1601–66) queen of France. She was the wife of Louis XIII of France and became queen regent for her son Louis XIV in 1643.

Anne (of Cleves) /-kleevz/ (1515–57) German-born queen of England. She married Henry VIII in a match made for political expediency (1540). He divorced her the same year.

Anne (of Denmark) (1574–1619) queen of England, Scotland, and Ireland. She married James VI of Scotland (later James I of England) in 1589 and was the mother of Prince Henry and Charles I.

anneal /ə néel/ *v* **1.** *vt* **MAKE SOMETHING MORE RESOLUTE** to make something, especially an opinion, a feeling, or an intention, stronger, firmer, or more resolute (*literary*) **2.** *vti* METALL, GLASS **MAKE SOMETHING STRONGER THROUGH HEATING** to subject an alloy, metal, or glass to a process of heating and slow cooling to make it tougher and less brittle **3.** *vti* BIOL **SEPARATE STRANDS OF NUCLEIC ACID** to subject nucleic acid to a process of heating and cooling in order to separate its strands [Old English *onælan* < *ælan* 'burn' < Germanic]

annelid /ánnəlid/ *n* an invertebrate organism with a flat body that is divided into segments. Earthworms and leeches are annelids. Phylum: Annelida. [Mid-19C. < modern Latin *Annelida* < French *annelés* 'ringed' < Latin *an(n)ulus* (see ANNULUS)]

annex /ə néks/ *vt* (**-nexes, -nexing, -nexed**) **1. TAKE OVER TERRITORY** to take over territory and incorporate it into another political entity, e.g. a country or state **2. ADD SOMETHING TO SOMETHING** to attach something subsidiary to a larger thing (*usually passive*) ○ *The new pool will be annexed to the gymnasium.* **3. ATTACH QUALITY TO SOMETHING** to add something such as a consequence, quality, or condition (*usually passive*) ○ *Annexed to his feeling of guilt was a sense of having let everybody down.* **4. STEAL SOMETHING** to take something without permission (*informal*) ○ *He returned to find that his assistant had annexed his chair.* ■ *n* **1.** *N Am* BUILDINGS same as **annexe** (sense 1) **2.** *Aus, US* INFO SCI same as **annexe** (sense 2) [14C. Via French *annexer* < Latin *annectere* 'tie together' < *nectere* 'to tie'] —**annexation** /ánnek sáysh'n/ *n*

annexe /ánneks/ *n* **1.** a building added onto another building or serving as an auxiliary building to a larger one **2.** *UK, Can* an appendix, epilogue, or other additional material attached to a larger document. Aus term **annex** ▶ US term **annex**

Annigoni /ánni gṓni/, **Pietro** (1910–88) Italian painter who used traditional oil techniques to paint portraits, including those of President Kennedy (1961) and Queen Elizabeth II (1955 and 1970)

annihilate /ə nī ə layt/ (**-lates, -lating, -lated**) *v* **1.** *vt* **DESTROY SOMETHING** to destroy something completely, especially so that it ceases to exist **2.** *vt* **DEFEAT SOMEBODY** to defeat somebody easily and decisively (*informal*) **3.** *vi* PHYS **BE DESTROYED IN PARTICLE COLLISION** to be mutually destroyed when a particle collides with a corresponding antiparticle [Early 16C. < late Latin *annihilat-*, past participle of *annihilare* 'reduce to nothing' < Latin *nihil* 'nothing'] —**annihilator** *n*

annihilation /ə nī ə láysh'n/ *n* **1. DESTRUCTION** the complete destruction of something **2. DEFEAT OF OPPONENT** the decisive defeat of an opponent (*informal*) **3.** PHYS **DESTRUCTIVE COLLISION OF PARTICLE AND ANTIPARTICLE** the process in which a particle combines with its antiparticle, destroying both and releasing their energy in the form of radiation or other particles ○ *annihilation radiation*

Anning /ánning/, **Mary** (1799–1847) British pioneer of fossil-collecting. She discovered the first complete plesiosaur skeleton (1810) and the first Early Jurassic pterosaur (1828).

anniversary /ánni vúrssəri/ (*plural* **-ries**) *n* **1.** a date that is observed on an annual basis because it is the same date as a noteworthy event in a past year **2.** a celebration or other commemorative ritual marking the date of a noteworthy event [13C. Directly or via French *anniversaire* < medieval Latin *anniversarium* < Latin *anniversarius* 'returning yearly' < *annus* 'year' + *versus*, past participle of *vertere* 'turn']

anno Domini /ánnō dómmi nī/ *adv* CALENDAR full form of **AD**[1] [Mid-16C. < Latin, 'in the year of the Lord']

anno Hegirae /ánnō hə jīri/ *adv* CALENDAR, ISLAM full form of **AH** [Late 19C. < Latin, 'in the year of the Hegira']

~~**annoint**~~ incorrect spelling of **anoint**

~~**annonymous**~~ incorrect spelling of **anonymous**

annotate /ánnə tayt/ (**-tates, -tating, -tated**) *vt* to add critical or explanatory notes to a text (*usually passive*) [Mid-18C. < Latin *annotat-*, past participle of *annotare* 'note down' < *nota* 'mark'] —**annotative** *adj* —**annotator** *n*

annotation /ánnə táysh'n/ *n* **1.** the addition of explanatory or critical comments to a text **2.** an explanatory or critical comment that has been added to a text

announce /ə nówns/ (**-nounces, -nouncing, -nounced**) *v* **1.** *vt* **TELL SOMETHING PUBLICLY** to declare or report something publicly **2.** *vt* **SAY SOMETHING** to say something in a formal, forceful, or aggressive way ○ *the day they announced to the children they were selling the house* **3.** *vt* **DECLARE ARRIVAL OF SOMEBODY OR SOMETHING** to tell others formally that somebody or something has arrived **4.** *vt* **SIGNIFY OR FORETELL SOMETHING** to be a sign that something has arrived or is imminent **5.** *vti US* **SERVE AS PRESENTER OF SOMETHING** to act as a presenter of something, e.g. a television or radio show [15C. Directly or via French *annoncer* < Latin *annuntiare* < *nuntius* 'messenger']

announcement /ə nównssmənt/ *n* **1.** a public statement giving people information or news, or the making of the statement **2.** a formal written notice, often a card or newspaper item, giving the news of a birth, wedding, or other event

announcer /ə nównssər/ *n* **1.** somebody who makes announcements, e.g. on a public address system at an airport **2.** a television or radio commentator who gives news bulletins or programme information

annoy /ə nóy/ (**-noys, -noying, -noyed**) *v* **1.** *vt* **IRRITATE SOMEBODY** to make somebody feel impatient or mildly angry **2.** *vt* **HARASS SOMEBODY** to harass somebody repeatedly **3.** *vi* **BE IRRITATING** to be a source of irritation ○ *Barking dogs are bound to annoy.* [13C. Via Old French *anoier* < late Latin *inodiare* 'make loathsome' < Latin *in odio* 'in hatred']

SYNONYMS ***annoy, irritate, exasperate, vex, irk***

CORE MEANING: to cause a mild degree of anger in somebody

annoy to make somebody feel impatient or mildly angry ○ *His constant complaining annoys everyone.* ○ *We're annoyed that no-one told us how long the alterations would take.* **irritate** to annoy somebody slightly ○ *The loud humming quickly started to irritate her.* ○ *We were irritated to find that everyone had left early.* **exasperate** to make somebody angry or frustrated, often by repeatedly doing something annoying ○ *The frequent breakdowns and delays exasperated even loyal customers.* ○ *We soon became exasperated with his laziness and excuses.* **vex** to make somebody slightly annoyed or upset, especially over a relatively unimportant matter ○ *The mistake vexed him but did not worry him unduly.* ○ *It vexed her that she had almost wanted to laugh at his remark.* **irk** to annoy somebody slightly by being tiresome or tedious ○ *What irked her more than anything else was that Jo was probably right.* ○ *He also irked his colleagues with frequent TV appearances and public pronouncements.*

annoyance /ə nóy ənss/ *n* **1.** feelings of mild anger and impatience **2.** something that causes somebody to be mildly angry or impatient ○ *Living in this neighbourhood is not without its annoyances.*

SYNONYMS See *anger.*

annoying /ə nóy ing/ *adj* causing mild anger or impatience —**annoyingly** *adv*

annual /ánnyoo əl/ *adj* **1. ONCE A YEAR** happening once a year **2. FOR PERIOD OF ONE YEAR** based on or accumulating over one year **3.** BOT **DYING AFTER ONE SEASON** describes a plant that flowers, produces seed, and dies in one growing season ■ *n* **1.** BOT **PLANT THAT DIES AFTER ONE SEASON** a plant that flowers, produces seed, and dies in one growing season **2.** PUBL **YEARLY BOOK OR MAGAZINE** a book or magazine published once a year, especially one for children [14C. Directly or via French *annuel* < late Latin *annualis*, blend of Latin *annuus* + *annalis* 'yearly' < *annus* 'year']

annual general meeting *n UK, ANZ, Can* a yearly gathering of members of an organization, at which officers are elected and the year's activities, including financial dealings, are discussed. US term **annual meeting**

annualize /ánnyoo ə līz/ (**-izes, -izing, -ized**), **annualise** (**-ises, -ising, -ised**) *vt* **1.** to calculate or adjust figures so that they reflect a period of a year **2.** to put something on, or change something to, a once-a-year schedule ○ *Let's annualize the newsletter.*

annually /ánnyoo əli/ *adv* every year or once a year

annual meeting *n US* same as **annual general meeting**

annual report *n* a document that outlines and analyses the activities, especially the financial dealings, of a company or other organization over the past year

annual ring *n* TREES same as **growth ring**

annuitant /ə nyóo itənt/ *n* somebody who receives an annuity

annuity /ə nyóo əti/ (*plural* **-ties**) *n* **1. MONEY PAID AT REGULAR INTERVALS** an amount of money paid to somebody yearly or at some other regular interval **2. INVESTMENT PAYING ANNUAL SUM** an investment that earns the investor a fixed amount of money each year for a number of years, often the investor's lifetime **3. CONTRACT FOR ANNUAL PAYMENT** the right to receive or the obligation to pay an annuity [15C. Via French *annuité* < medieval Latin *annuitas* < Latin *annuus* (see ANNUAL)]

annul /ə núl/ (**-nuls, -nulling, -nulled**) *vt* **1. MAKE SOMETHING INVALID** to declare a legal document or agreement invalid **2. DECLARE MARRIAGE INVALID** to declare that a marriage was never a proper marriage in the eyes of a church, e.g. because one of the parties was not completely committed to it **3. DESTROY SOMETHING** to wipe out or destroy the effect or existence of something ○ *not able to annul my fears* [14C. Via Old French *anuller* < late Latin *annullare* 'make into nothing' < Latin *nullus* 'nothing'] —**annulment** *n*

SYNONYMS See *nullify.*

annular /ánnyóolər/ *adj* shaped like or forming a ring (*technical*) [Late 16C. Directly or via French *annulaire* < Latin *an(n)ularis* < *an(n)ulus* (see ANNULUS)]

annular eclipse *n* a solar eclipse in which all but the outermost rim of the Sun is blocked by the Moon, leaving a ring of sunlight visible round the Moon

annular ligament *n* a ring-shaped ligament that surrounds an ankle joint or a wrist joint and holds other ligaments in place

annulate /ányóo layt/, **annulated** /ányoolaytid/ *adj* with ring-shaped parts, or consisting of rings [Early 19C. < Latin *an(n)ulatus* < *an(n)ulus* (see ANNULUS)]

annulation /ánnyóo láysh'n/ *n* **1.** the formation of rings or ring-shaped parts **2.** any part that is shaped like a ring

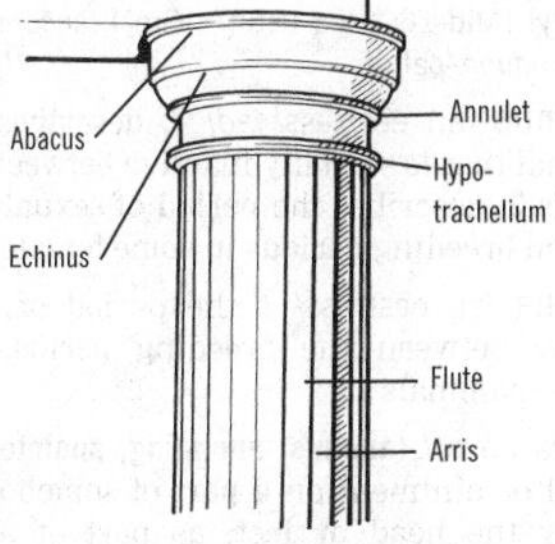
Abacus
Annulet
Hypo-
trachelium
Echinus
Flute
Arris
annulet

annulet /ánnyóolət/ *n* **1.** in architecture, a ring-shaped moulding round a column **2.** a ring-shaped object on a heraldic shield [Late 16C. < Latin *an(n)ulus* (see ANNULUS)]

annulus /ánnyóoləss/ (*plural* **-li** /-lī/ or **-luses**) *n* **1.** BIOL a ring-shaped part or arrangement of parts in a plant or animal, e.g. a growth ring on fish scales **2.**

MATHS the area bounded by two concentric circles [Mid-16C. < Latin *an(n)ulus* 'small ring' < *anus* 'ring']

annunciate /ə núnssi ayt/ (**-ates, -ating, -ated**) *vt* to announce or proclaim something (*archaic*) [14C. < Latin *annuntiat-*, past participle of *annuntiare* (see ANNOUNCE)]

annunciation /ə núnssi áysh'n/ *n* the announcing of something, or an announcement (*archaic*) [14C. Via Old French < late Latin *annuntiation-* < Latin *annuntiare* (see ANNOUNCE)]

Annunciation (1513?) by Lucas Cranach the Elder

Annunciation *n* **1.** in the Bible, the archangel Gabriel's visit to the Virgin Mary to announce that she had been chosen to be the mother of Jesus Christ (Luke 1:26–38) **2.** the Christian festival known as the feast of the Annunciation. Date: 25 March.

annunciator /ə núnssi aytər/ *n* an electronic signalling device, e.g. a switchboard device that indicates the source of incoming telephone calls

annus horribilis /ánnəss hə ríbbiliss/ (*plural* **anni horribiles** /ánni̅ hə ríbbi layz/) *n* a year of great unhappiness or misfortune [Late 20C. < Latin, 'horrible year']

annus mirabilis /ánnəss mi ráabiliss/ (*plural* **anni mirabiles** /ánni̅ mi ráabi layz/) *n* a year that is remarkable for its great events [Mid-17C. < Latin, 'wonderful year']

anode /ánnōd/ *n* **1.** the negative terminal of a battery **2.** the positive electrode in an electrolytic cell [Mid-19C. < Greek *anodos* 'way up' < *hodos* 'way']

anodize /ánnō di̅z/ (**-dizes, -dizing, -dized**), **anodise** (**-dises, -dising, -dised**) *vt* to coat a metal, e.g. aluminium, with a protective or decorative oxide by making the metal the anode of an electrolytic cell —**anodization** /ánnō di̅ záysh'n/ *n*

anodontia /ánnə dónshə, -dónshi ə/ *n* the absence of some or all teeth, because the teeth have never developed

anodyne /ánnō di̅n/ *adj* **1.** BLAND harmless, inoffensive, or uncontroversial to the point of being dull ○ *a rather anodyne speech, given the nature of the crisis* **2.** SOOTHING serving to soothe, relax, or comfort (*literary*) ○ *the anodyne effects of a weekend in the mountains* **3.** PHARM PAINKILLING bringing relief from pain or discomfort ■ *n* **1.** PHARM PAINKILLER a drug that relieves pain, e.g. aspirin or codeine **2.** COMFORTING THING something that soothes, comforts, or relaxes (*literary*) [Mid-16C. Via Latin < Greek *anōdunos* 'without pain' < *odunē* 'pain']

anoestrous /an ée̅strəss/ *adj* **1.** describes a female mammal that is sexually inactive between breeding periods **2.** describes the period of sexual inactivity between breeding periods in some female mammals

anoestrus /an ée̅strəss/ *n* the period of sexual inactivity between the breeding periods of some female mammals

anoint /ə nóynt/ (**anoints, anointing, anointed**) *vt* **1.** to rub oil or ointment on a part of somebody's body, usually the head or feet, as part of a religious ceremony, e.g. in a Christian baptism **2.** to install somebody officially or ceremonially in a position or office [14C. < Old French *enoint*, past participle of *enoindre* < Latin *inungere* < *ungere* 'to smear'] —**anointment** *n*

anointing of the sick *n* in the Roman Catholic Church, the sacrament of anointing people who are very ill, praying for their recovery, and offering confession and absolution of sins

anole /ə nṓ li/ *n* a tree-climbing lizard that can change colour. Genus: *Anolis*. [Early 18C. Via modern Latin *Anolis* < Carib *anolí*]

anomalistic month /ə nómmə lístik-/ *n* the average time taken by the Moon to orbit the Earth once, starting from the point in its orbit at which it is nearest the Earth, measured as 27.554 days

anomalistic year *n* the time taken by the Earth to orbit the Sun once, starting from the point in its orbit at which the Earth is nearest the Sun, measured as 365.26 days

anomalous /ə nómmələss/ *adj* **1.** deviating from the norm or from what people expect ○ *We're getting anomalous readings on the heart monitor.* **2.** strange and difficult to identify or classify ○'*Individuals would occasionally give rise to new species having anomalous habits.*' (Charles Darwin, *On the Origin of Species*; 1859) [Mid-17C. < late Latin *anomalus* < Greek *anōmalos* 'uneven' < *homalos* 'even']

anomaly /ə nómməli/ (*plural* **-lies**) *n* **1.** IRREGULARITY something that deviates from the norm or from expectations ○ *looking for anomalies in the blood tests* **2.** PECULIARITY something strange and difficult to identify or classify ○ *The space probe has encountered an anomaly.* **3.** ASTRON ANGLE IN PLANET'S ORBIT the angle between a planet's position, the Sun, and the point in the planet's orbit when it is closest to the Sun

anomic /ə nómmik/ *adj* **1.** SOCIOL UNSTABLE BECAUSE OF MORAL BREAKDOWN unstable because moral and social codes have been eroded or abandoned ○ *an anomic society* **2.** PSYCHOL AFFECTED BY ALIENATION feeling alienated from society and disorientated by the perceived absence of a social or moral framework ■ *n* PSYCHOL SOMEBODY AFFECTED BY ALIENATION somebody who feels alienated and disorientated because of the lack of a social and moral framework

anomie /ánnōmi/, **anomy** *n* **1.** instability in society caused by the erosion or abandonment of moral and social codes **2.** a feeling of disorientation and alienation from society caused by the perceived absence of a supporting social or moral framework [Late 16C. Via French < Greek *anomia* 'lawlessness' < *anomos* 'lawless' < *nomos* 'law']

anon /ə nón/ *adv* (*archaic or literary*) **1.** at an unspecified future time ○ *I'll see you anon.* **2.** in a short while ○ *more of these grotesque escapades anon* [Old English *on ān* 'in one']

anon. /ə nón/ *abbr* anonymous

anonym /ánnənim/ *n* **1.** UNNAMED AUTHOR an author whose name is not known or not given **2.** PSEUDONYM a name used by somebody to hide his or her identity **3.** PUBLICATION WITH UNNAMED AUTHOR a publication whose author is unnamed or unknown [Early 19C. < French *anonyme* < Greek *anōnumos* (see ANONYMOUS)]

anonymity /ánnə nímməti/ (*plural* **-ties**) *n* **1.** FREEDOM FROM IDENTIFICATION the state of not being known or identified by name, e.g. as the author or donor of something ○ *preserve the anonymity of your informant* **2.** LACK OF DISTINCTIVENESS a lack of distinctive features that makes things seem bland or interchangeable ○ *detested the anonymity of the city-centre hotels* **3.** UNNAMED PERSON an unnamed or unacknowledged person **4.** STATE OF BEING UNNOTICED the state of blending into a crowd and going unnoticed ○ *I always preferred the anonymity of the big city.*

anonymizer /ə nónnə mi̅zər/ *n* a website through which a person browsing can visit the World Wide Web without leaving any identity traces

anonymous /ə nónnimass/ *adj* **1.** UNNAMED whose name is not known or not given ○ *the anonymous author* **2.** WITH NAME WITHHELD with the performer's, maker's, or creator's identity withheld ○ *an anonymous letter* **3.** INDISTINCTIVE lacking individuality or distinctiveness ○ *a quirkiness unsuited to an anonymous shopping mall* [Early 17C. < late Latin *anonymus* < Greek *anōnumos* 'unnamed' < *onuma* 'name']

anonymous FTP *n* a type of Internet file transfer in which no password is needed, used by some organizations to make their file archives publicly accessible

anonymously /ə nónnimassli/ *adv* without being named or acknowledged

anopheles /ə nóffəleez/ (*plural* **same**) *n* a mosquito belonging to a genus that includes some that can carry and transmit malaria to humans. Genus: *Anopheles*. [Late 19C. Via modern Latin < Greek *anōphelēs* 'useless']

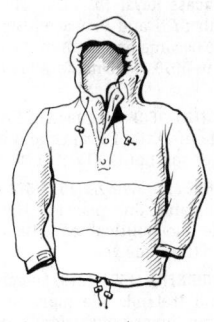

anorak

anorak /ánnə rak/ *n* **1.** a warm thick waterproof hip-length jacket with a hood **2.** a boring, unfashionable, or studious person, especially somebody who is excessively devoted to a hobby or interest (*humorous*) ○ *You can be into something without becoming a total anorak about it.* [Early 20C. < (Greenlandic) Inuit *annoraaq*] —**anoraky** *adj*

anorectic /ánnə réktik/ *adj* relating to pathological loss of appetite ■ *n* a medicine that suppresses the appetite [Late 19C. < Greek *anorektos* 'without appetite' < *orexein* 'to desire']

anorexia /ánnə réksi ə/ *n* **1.** PSYCHIAT same as **anorexia nervosa 2.** persistent loss of appetite [Late 16C. Via modern Latin < Greek, 'lack of appetite' < *orexis* 'appetite' < *orexein* 'to desire']

anorexia nervosa /-nur vṓssə/ *n* an eating disorder, marked by an extreme fear of becoming overweight, that leads to excessive dieting to the point of serious ill-health and sometimes death [< modern Latin, 'nervous anorexia']

anorexic /ánnə réksik/ *adj* **1.** OF ANOREXIA NERVOSA relating to or affected by anorexia nervosa **2.** VERY THIN extremely thin, especially unhealthily or unattractively so (*informal*) ■ *n* SOMEBODY WITH ANOREXIA NERVOSA somebody who is affected by anorexia nervosa

anorthite /a náwr thi̅t/ *n* a rare white, grey, or reddish-grey feldspar mineral. Source: mainly in igneous rocks. Use: glass, ceramics. —**anorthitic** /ánnawr thíttik/ *adj*

anorthosite /a náwrthə si̅t/ *n* a coarse-grained igneous rock composed of at least 90% feldspar [Mid-19C. < French *anorthose*, type of feldspar < Greek *anorthos* 'not straight'; from its crystals] —**anorthositic** /a náwrthə síttik/ *adj*

anosmia /a nózmi ə/ *n* absence or loss of the sense of smell [Early 19C. < AN- + Greek *osmē* 'smell'] —**anosmic** *adj*

another /ə núthər/ *det, pron* **1.** ONE MORE an additional ○ *need another person to help* ○ *May I have another?* **2.** ONE THAT IS DIFFERENT somebody or something that is separate or different ○ *We need another accountant because ours is moving.* ○ *This one is too dark; I would prefer another.* **3.** SOME OTHER some other one, or any other one ○ *at one time or another*

A. N. Other /áy en úthər/ *n* somebody who has not as yet been named, e.g. in an incomplete list of participants or contributors

another place *n* used by the House of Lords to refer to the House of Commons, and vice versa

Anouilh /ánnoo ee/, **Jean** (1910–87) French dramatist. His plays include *Antigone* (1942), *Ring Round the Moon* (1947), and *Becket* (1959).

> 'There will always be a lost dog somewhere that will prevent me from being happy.'
> [Jean Anouilh, *La Sauvage (The Restless Heart)*; 1938]

anovulant /a nóvvyŏŏlənt/ *n* a drug that prevents ovulation, e.g. a birth-control pill [Mid-20C. < AN- + OVULATE] —**anovulant** *adj*

anovulation /án ovvyŏŏ láysh'n/ *n* the state of not ovulating because of a medical condition, suppression by drugs, or menopause —**anovulatory** /án ovvyŏŏ láytəri/ *adj, n*

anoxaemia /ánnok seémi ə/ *n* a deficiency of oxygen in the blood flowing through the arteries —**anoxaemic** *adj*

anoxemia *n* MED US spelling of **anoxaemia**

anoxia /a nóksi ə/ *n* MED same as **hypoxia** —**anoxic** *adj*

ansate /án sayt/ *adj* with a handle or a part shaped like a handle [Late 19C. < Latin *ansatus* < *ansa* 'handle']

ansate cross *n* same as **ankh**

Anselm /án selm/, **St** (1033?–1109) Italian theologian and philosopher. His most famous work is his ontological proof of God's existence, completed in 1078. His tenure as Archbishop of Canterbury (1093–1109) was marked by conflict with England's kings.

> 'I do not seek to understand so that I may believe, but I believe so that I may understand.'
> [St Anselm, *Proslogion*; 1078]

Ansermet /aáNssər may/, **Ernest** (1883–1969) Swiss conductor. He conducted Sergei Diaghilev's Ballets Russes (1915–23), and interpreted Igor Stravinsky and other 20th-century composers.

Ansett /ánssət/, **Sir Reginald Myles** (1909–81) Australian aviator and business executive. He was founder (1936) of Ansett Airways Ltd.

ANSI /ánssi/ *abbr* American National Standards Institute

answer /aánssər/ *n* **1.** RESPONSE TO QUESTION the information requested by a spoken or written question **2.** WAY OF SOLVING SOMETHING the solution to a problem ○ *trying to find an answer to our ecological problems* **3.** RESPONSE TO ACTION a reaction intended to deal with something that somebody says or does ○ *She had no answer to her opponent's lethal backhand.* **4.** RESPONSE TO CALL a response to a summons, e.g. a ringing telephone, a doorbell, or somebody calling your name ○ *I tried phoning him, but there was no answer.* **5.** CORRESPONDING THING something designed to match or correspond to something else ○ *The Space Needle is Seattle's answer to the Eiffel Tower.* **6.** LAW PLEA IN COURT a defendant's plea in response to a charge, lawsuit, or summons ■ *v* (**-swers, -swering, -swered**) **1.** *vti* REPLY TO SOMETHING to reply to something written or spoken ○ *answered with a stinging rebuttal* **2.** DO SOMETHING IN REACTION to do something as a reaction to something that somebody says or does **3.** *vti* RESPOND TO CALL to respond to a summons such as a ringing telephone, a doorbell, or somebody calling your name **4.** *vti* CORRESPOND TO SOMETHING to match or correspond to something ○ *nobody who answers to that description* **5.** *vti* MEET NEED to fulfil a need or wish ○ *Her arrival answered our need for an experienced radiologist.* **6.** *vi* SERVE PURPOSE to be adequate in serving a purpose (*formal*) ○ *an upturned box that answers for a seat* **7.** *vt* LAW RESPOND TO CHARGE IN COURT to offer a plea in response to a charge, lawsuit, or summons ○ *The defendant will now answer the charges.* [Old English *andswaru* < Germanic, 'swear against'] —**answerer** *n* ◇ **be the answer to a maiden's prayer** to be exactly what is desired or sought after (*humorous*) ◇ **know** *or* **have all the answers 1.** to be admirably knowledgeable about a subject **2.** to be irritatingly eager to demonstrate or claim superior knowledge

SYNONYMS *answer, reply, response, retort, riposte, rejoinder*
CORE MEANING: something said, written, or done in acknowledgment of a question or remark, or in reaction to a situation
answer the information requested by a spoken or written question ○ *He wasn't sure he had given the right answer to Question 3a.* ○ *She searched for a suitable answer to Cyril's question about job prospects.* **reply** a reaction, usually written or spoken, to a question, letter, or situation ○ *a written reply to our letter* ○ *'How do you know that?' she asked, but her friend only giggled in reply.* **response** a spoken or written answer, or a reaction to a situation ○ *Could I have your response by Wednesday?* ○ *His comments sparked an angry response in the press.* ○ *a steady improvement in ambulance response times* **retort** a sharp spoken reply, often to criticism ○ *Polly managed to bite back a cutting retort.* **riposte** a quick or witty reply, usually spoken ○ *You can never manage to deliver a witty riposte at the time, but always think of one later.* ○ *a less than diplomatic riposte to their approach* **rejoinder**

(*formal*) a sharp, critical, angry, or clever reply, usually spoken ○ *'Of course the school is to blame', came the parents' angry rejoinder.*

answer back *vti* to reply to somebody impudently or disrespectfully

answer for *vt* **1.** to be accountable or responsible for something ○ *You'll have to answer for this broken window.* **2.** to give an assurance about the good character of somebody ○ *She can be trusted, but I can't answer for the rest of the team.*

answer to *vt* to be accountable to somebody for something

answerable /aánssərəb'l/ *adj* **1.** responsible or accountable to somebody for something ○ *You're answerable to your boss for any losses you incur.* **2.** having a possible solution or a correct response —**answerability** /aánssərə bílləti/ *n*

answerback /aánssər bak/ *n* a response in a two-way radio transmission

answering machine *n* a recording device that is connected to or part of a telephone and can be activated to play a message to callers and record messages from them

answering service *n* a business that receives telephone calls on behalf of other people or organizations and takes messages for them

answer machine *n* TELECOM same as **answering machine**

ant

ant /ant/ *n* **1.** an insect that lives in complex well-organized colonies and is noted for its ability to carry objects heavier than itself. Male ants have wings, as do fertile females (**queens**) after mating. Family: Formicidae. **2.** a smuggler who makes repeated trips across a border carrying such things as cigarettes, liquor, or weapons (*slang*) [Old English *æmette* < Germanic, 'cut off'] ◇ **have ants in your pants** to be excited or impatient about something (*informal*)

REGIONAL NOTE British dialects abound in words for *ants*, suggesting perhaps that they once played a bigger role in people's lives, and in those of country people in particular. Among the best-known synonyms are *emmets*, *muryans*, *nants*, *pismires*, *piss-annats*, and *pissy-beds*, a name they share with dandelions.

ant. *abbr* **1.** antiquarian **2.** antiquity **3.** LING antonym

Ant. *abbr* Antarctica

ant- *prefix* same as **anti-** (*used before vowels*)

-ant *suffix* **1.** performing a particular action ○ *coolant* **2.** being in a particular condition ○ *hesitant* [< Latin *-ant-*, stem of *-ans*, a present participle ending]

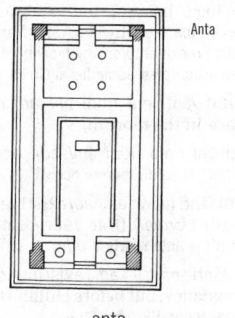

anta

anta /ántə/ (*plural* **-tae** /-ti/) *n* a thicker end of the side wall of a Greek temple that forms one side of a porch [Mid-18C. Back-formation < Latin *antae* 'square pilasters']

antacid /an tássid/ *n* a drug that reduces or neutralizes stomach acid ■ *adj* preventing, counteracting, or neutralizing acidity, especially in the stomach

antae plural of **anta**

antagonise *vt* another spelling of **antagonize**

antagonism /an tággənizəm/ *n* **1.** HOSTILITY hostility or hatred causing opposition and ill will **2.** OPPOSITION opposition between forces or principles ○ *the antagonism between good and evil* **3.** BIOCHEM NEUTRALIZING INTERACTION BETWEEN CHEMICALS the interaction between two or more chemical substances in the body that diminishes the effect that each of them has individually **4.** PHYSIOL OPPOSITION BETWEEN MUSCLES the opposing force that usually exists between pairs of muscles

antagonist /an tággənist/ *n* **1.** OPPONENT somebody or something opposing or in conflict with another ○ *several antagonists locked in a power struggle* **2.** CHARACTER IN CONFLICT WITH HERO a major character in a book, play, or film whose values or behaviour are in conflict with those of the protagonist or hero **3.** PHARM NEUTRALIZING AGENT a drug that neutralizes the effect of a substance on the body **4.** PHYSIOL OPPOSING MUSCLE a muscle that acts with and limits the action of another muscle

antagonistic /an tággə nístik/ *adj* showing or expressing hostility or opposition —**antagonistically** *adv*

antagonize /an tággə nīz/ (**-nizes, -nizing, -nized**), **antagonise** (**-nises, -nising, -nised**) *vt* to cause a person or animal to become hostile [Mid-17C. < Greek *antagōnizesthai* 'struggle against' < *agōnizesthai* 'struggle' < *agōn* 'contest']

Antakya /an taákyə/ city in southern Turkey on the River Orontes. Founded in 301 BC, it was the capital of the eastern Roman Empire from 64 BC to AD 260. Population: 123,871 (1990). Former name **Antioch**

Antalya /an taályə/ city in southwestern Turkey, situated on the Gulf of Antalya. Population: 564,914 (1997).

Antananarivo /ántə nánnə reé vō/ capital of Madagascar, located in the central part of the island. Population: 1,689,000 (2001). Former name **Tananarive** (until 1977)

Antarctic /an taárktik/ region lying south of the Antarctic Circle —**Antarctic** *adj*

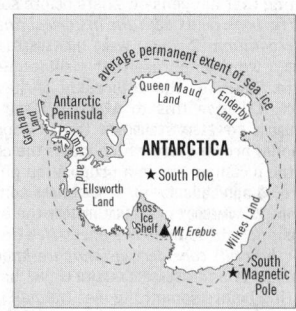

Antarctica

Antarctica /an taárktikə/ uninhabited continent surrounding the South Pole, consisting of an ice-covered plateau and high mountain peaks. Area: 14,000,000 sq. km/5,400,000 sq. mi.

Antarctic Circle *n* parallel of latitude at 66°30'S, encircling Antarctica and its surrounding seas, marking the Northern limit of the area in which the sun does not set during the summer solstice and does not rise during the winter solstice

Antarctic Current ocean current circling Antarctica. Moving eastwards, it circulates water from one ocean to another.

Antarctic Ocean the waters that surround the South Pole and Antarctica, consisting of the waters of the southern Atlantic, Indian, and Pacific oceans. Depths exceed 6,000 m/20,000 ft.

~~Antartic~~ incorrect spelling of **Antarctic**

antazoline /an tázzə leen/ *n* a white odourless compound. Use: control of allergic reactions. [Late 20C. < ant- + -azoline, INN stem]

ant bear *n* ZOOL same as **aardvark**

antbird /ánt burd/ *n* a bird that follows army ants and feeds on insects, frogs, and lizards disturbed by the ants. Native to: South America. Family: Formicariidae.

ante /ánti/ *n* the amount a card player puts into the gambling pot before cards are dealt ■ *vti* (**-tes, -teing, -ted** or **-teed**) to place betting stakes before cards are dealt [Early 19C. < Latin (see ANTE-)] ◇ **up the ante** (*informal*) **1.** to increase the amount of money required to do something **2.** to demand more in a situation, especially in an extortionate way **ante up** *vti N Am* to pay money that is owed (*informal*) ○ *We know you've got the cash, so ante up now!*

ante- *prefix* before, in front ○ *antechamber* [< Latin *ante* 'before' < Indo-European, 'front']

anteater

anteater /ánt eetər/ *n* **1.** a long-snouted toothless mammal that has long claws and a sticky tongue for catching prey, usually ants and termites. Native to: Central and South America. Family: Myrmecophagidae. **2.** ZOOL same as **pangolin 3.** ZOOL same as **aardvark**

antebellum /ánti bélləm/ *adj* **1.** preceding a war, or characteristic of the time preceding a war **2.** *US* belonging or relating to the time before the American Civil War [Mid-19C. < Latin *ante bellum* 'before the war']

antecede /ánti seéd/ *vt* (**-cedes, -ceding, -ceded**) to precede something in time or order (*formal*) [Early 17C. < Latin *antecedere* 'go before' < *cedere* 'give way']

antecedent /ánti seéd'nt/ *n* **1.** SOMETHING COMING BEFORE something that happens or exists before something else ○ *The book deals with the historical antecedents of the revolution.* **2.** GRAM WORD THAT SUBSEQUENT WORD REFERS TO a word or phrase that a subsequent word refers to. 'Mary' is the antecedent of 'her' in the sentence 'I'll give this to Mary if I see her'. **3.** LOGIC CLAUSE EXPRESSING CONDITION the first part of a conditional proposition, which states the condition and is the p component in a proposition phrased 'if p then q' ■ **antecedents** *npl* **1.** ANCESTORS somebody's ancestors **2.** SOMEBODY'S PERSONAL HISTORY the events or circumstances in somebody's past ○ *He's done pretty well for himself, considering what we know of his antecedents.* ■ *adj* OCCURRING EARLIER IN TIME happening or existing before something else (*formal*) [14C. Directly or via French < Latin *antecedent-*, present participle of *antecedere* (see ANTECEDE)] —**antecedence** *n* —**antecedently** *adv*

USAGE Antecedents Relative clauses need something such as nouns to refer to, and the relationship ought to be clear. Avoid constructions like these where the antecedents (words or phrases that subsequent material refers to) are either absent or unclear: *I'd sign up for advanced calculus if I were smart, which I'm not.* The clause *which I'm not* has no antecedent; also, *if I were smart* already tells the reader that I am not smart. Don't try to make an entire clause an antecedent for a relative clause, as in *I need to purchase an entirely new computer system, which upsets me.* Say instead *I need to purchase an entirely new computer system, and this* [or *that*] *upsets me.* Similarly, avoid relative clause constructions with vague antecedents: *She crashed the ultralight aircraft into the cliff, which was her own fault.* Since the cliff was definitely not her own fault but the

crash indeed was, reword the sentence: *Crashing the ultralight aircraft into the cliff was her own fault* or *She crashed the ultralight aircraft into the cliff in an accident that was her own fault.*

antechamber /ánti chaymbər/ *n* a small room leading into a larger room and often used as a waiting area [Mid-17C. < French *antichambre*, translation of Italian *anticamera* 'room in front']

antechoir /ánti kwír/ *n* an area at the entrance to the choir in a church, reserved for clergy and choir members

antedate /ánti dáyt/ *vt* (**-dates, -dating, -dated**) **1.** OCCUR EARLIER THAN SOMETHING to exist or happen at an earlier date than something else ○ *These tapestries antedate the development of synthetic dyes.* **2.** PUT EARLIER DATE ON SOMETHING to assign something a date that is earlier than its true or original date ○ *This vase was mistakenly antedated to the Ming dynasty.* ■ *n* EARLIER DATE a date assigned to something that is earlier than its true or original date

antediluvian /ánti di loóvi ən/ *adj* **1.** extremely old-fashioned or outdated (*humorous*) **2.** in or from the time before the biblical Flood [Mid-17C. < ANTE- + Latin *diluvium* 'flood']

SYNONYMS See **old-fashioned**.

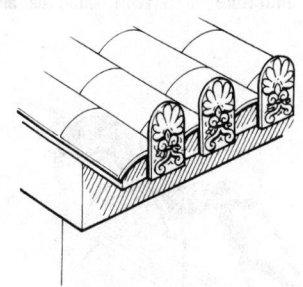
antefix

antefix /ánti fiks/ (*plural* **-fixes** or **-fixa** /-fiksə/) *n* an ornamental edging on the eaves of an ancient building with a tiled roof that hides the joints of the roof tiles [Mid-19C. < Latin *antefixum* < *antefigere* 'fasten before' < *figere* 'fasten'] —**antefixal** /ánti fíks'l/ *adj*

antegrade amnesia /ántə grayd-/ *n* a form of amnesia in which the memory loss relates to events occurring after a traumatic event [After RETROGRADE]

antelope

antelope /ántəlōp/ (*plural* **-lopes** or same) *n* a cud-chewing mammal with a smooth brown or grey coat, two-toed hooves, and unbranched horns. Native to: Africa, Southwest Asia. Family: Bovidae. [15C. Via Old French *antelop* 'mythical horned creature said to live by the Euphrates' < medieval Greek *antholops*]

antemeridian /ánti mə ríddi ən/ *adj* relating to or taking place in the morning

ante meridiem /-mə ríddi əm/ *adj, adv* full form of **a.m.** [Mid-16C. < Latin, 'before noon']

antemortem /ánti máwrtəm/ *adj* existing or happening before death (*formal*) [Late 19C. < Latin *ante mortem* 'before death'] —**ante mortem** *adv*

antenatal /ánti náyt'l/ *adj* existing or happening during pregnancy, but before childbirth. N Am term **prenatal** —**antenatally** *adv*

antenna /an ténnə/ (*plural* **-nae** /-nee/ or **-nas**) *n* **1.** a thin movable sensory organ found in pairs on the heads of some organisms, including insects and crustaceans **2.** somebody's inquisitive or enquiring sense (*informal; often used in the plural*) **3.** *N Am* BROADCAST same as **aerial** *n* (sense 2) [Mid-17C. < Latin, 'pole supporting a sail'] —**antennal** *adj*

antenuptial /ánti núpsh'l/ *adj S Africa* same as **prenuptial**

antenuptial contract /ánti núpsh'l-/ *n S Africa* LAW same as **prenuptial agreement**

antepartum /ánti paártəm/ *adj* relating to the period before birth, especially the period of labour before a baby is delivered [Late 19C. < Latin *ante partum* 'before birth']

antependium /ánti péndi əm/ (*plural* **-dia** /-di ə/) *n* a decorative cloth that hangs on the front of an altar or lectern [Late 16C. < medieval Latin < Latin *ante* 'before' + *pendere* 'hang']

antepenult /ánti pi núlt/ *n* the third from last syllable in a word ○ *The antepenult is stressed in the word 'superfluous'.*

antepenultimate /ánti pi núltimət/ *adj* third from last in a series ○ *the antepenultimate word in the paragraph* ■ *n* GRAM same as **antepenult**

ante-post *adj* describes odds offered or bets placed before the starting places of the competitors are known, especially in horseracing

anterior /an teéri ər/ *adj* **1.** IN FRONT at, near, or from the front of something (*formal*) ○ *an anterior view of the building* **2.** EARLIER existing or happening before something else (*formal*) **3.** ANAT NEAR FRONT OF BODY situated at or near the front of the body or of a body part **4.** BOT SITUATED AWAY FROM STEM describes a leaf or flower part that is situated farthest away or facing away from the stem of a plant [Mid-16C. Directly or via French < Latin, 'earlier' < *ante* 'before'] —**anteriority** /an teéri órrəti/ *n*

anteroom /ánti room, -rŏom/ *n* a subsidiary room that opens into a larger room, often used as a waiting area

antetype /ánti tīp/ *n* an earlier form of something

anteversion /ánti vúrsh'n/ *n* an unusual tilting forward of an organ, especially the uterus

anthelion /an theéli ən/ (*plural* **-lia** /-li ə/) *n* a luminous spot appearing occasionally in the sky opposite the Sun [Late 17C. < Greek, 'opposite the Sun' < *hēlios* 'Sun']

anthelix /ant heéliks, an theé-/ (*plural* **-lixes** or **-lices** /-li seez/), **antihelix** /ánti heéliks/ *n* a ridge of cartilage located behind the folded lobe (**helix**) of the outer ear and running more or less parallel to it

anthelmintic /ánthəl míntik/, **anthelminthic** /anthel mínthik/ *adj* describes a natural or pharmaceutical substance that destroys or expels intestinal parasitic worms ■ *n* a natural or pharmaceutical substance that kills or expels intestinal parasitic worms [Late 17C. < Greek *anti* 'against' + *helminth-* 'worm']

anthem /ánthəm/ *n* **1.** SONG OF ALLEGIANCE a song praising and declaring loyalty to something, e.g. a country, cause, or organization ○ *a national anthem* **2.** ROUSING POPULAR SONG a stirring, often commercially popular, song that has become associated with a group, period, or cause and celebrates a sense of solidarity with it ○ *rock anthems* **3.** SHORT HYMN FOR CHOIR a short hymn with words from the Bible, sung by a choir as part of a Christian church service **4.** RELIGIOUS SONG WITH PARTS a religious song with parts for different singers or groups, especially a hymn sung in a Christian church with parts sung by different members of the congregation [Pre-12C. < late Latin *antiphona* 'antiphon' < Greek *antiphōnos* 'responsive' < *phonē* 'sound']

anthemion /an theémi ən/ (*plural* **-mia** /-mi ə/) *n* a motif of radiating leaves found in classical Greek art and design. See illustration on next page [Mid-19C. < Greek, 'small flower' < *anthos* 'flower']

anther /ánthər/ *n* a male flower part forming the top part of a stamen and bearing the pollen in sacs [Early 18C. Via Latin, 'medicine made from (the pollen-bearing part of) flowers' < Greek *anthēra* 'flowery' < *anthos* 'flower']

antheridium /ánthə ríddi əm/ (*plural* **-dia** /-di ə/) *n* the

anthemion

male reproductive organ in algae, ferns, fungi, and mosses

anthesis /an theéssiss/ *n* **1.** the opening of a flower bud **2.** the period of time between the opening of a flower and the formation of the fruit [Mid-19C. Via modern Latin < Greek *anthēsis* 'bloom' < *anthein* 'to flower' < *anthos* 'flower']

anthill /ánt hil/ *n* a mound of earth formed by ants during the construction of their nest

antho- *prefix* flower ○ *anthozoan* [< Greek *anthos*]

anthocyanin /ántho sí ənin/ *n* a water-soluble pigment that produces blue, violet, and red colours in plants [Mid-19C. < ANTHO- + CYANINE]

anthologize /an thóllə jīz/ (**-gizes, -gizing, -gized**), **anthologise** (**-gises, -gising, -gised**) *v* **1.** *vt* to gather works from different writers, musicians, or artists, into a collection ○ *O. Henry's stories are often anthologized.* ○ *a much anthologized writer* **2.** *vi* to compile or publish an anthology —**anthologist** *n*

anthology /an thólləji/ (*plural* **-gies**) *n* **1.** COLLECTION OF DIFFERENT WRITERS' WORKS a book that consists of essays, stories, or poems by different writers **2.** COLLECTION OF MUSICAL OR ARTISTIC WORKS a collection of works from different musicians or artists **3.** COLLECTION OF THINGS a collection of various things or ideas ○ *an anthology of complaints* [Mid-17C. Via medieval Latin < medieval Greek *anthologia* 'collection of flowers' < Greek *anthos* 'flower']

Anthony (of Padua), St /ántəni/ (1195–1231) Italian friar. He joined the Franciscan order in 1227. A renowned preacher, he taught theology in Italy and France. Born **Fernando**

Susan B. Anthony

Anthony, Susan B. (1820–1906) US social reformer. She helped to found the National Woman Suffrage Association (1869). Full name **Anthony, Susan Brownell**

'The true republic: men their rights and nothing more; women their rights and nothing less.'
[Susan B. Anthony. Motto on the front of her newspaper, *The Revolution*; 1868–70]

anthophilous /an thóffiləss/ *adj* describes an insect that feeds on or lives among flowers

anthozoan /ánthə zṓ ən/ *n* an invertebrate sea animal with a roundish hollow body, e.g. a coral or sea anemone. Class: Anthozoa. [Late 19C. < modern Latin *Anthozoa* < ANTHO- + Greek *zōia* 'animals'] —**anthozoic** *adj*

anthracene /ánthrə seen/ *n* an aromatic crystalline solid with a faint blue glow. Source: coal tar. Use: manufacture of dyes, organic chemicals. Formula: $C_{14}H_{10}$. [Mid-19C. < Greek *anthrax* 'coal']

anthraces plural of **anthrax**

anthracite /ánthrə sīt/ *n* a hard shiny black coal that is clean-burning, high in carbon content, and low in volatile matter [Early 19C. Via Latin < Greek *anthrakitēs* < *anthrax* 'coal'] —**anthracitic** /ánthrə síttik/ *adj*

anthracnose /an thráknōss/ *n* a fungal disease of beans and vines that produces dark sunken spots on fruit, stems, and leaves [Late 19C. < French < Greek *anthrax* 'coal' + *nosos* 'disease']

anthracosis /ánthrə kṓssiss/ *n* a disease of the lungs caused by long-term inhalation of coal dust [Mid-19C. < Greek *anthrax* 'coal']

anthraquinone /ánthrə kwínnōn/ *n* a yellow crystalline chemical. Use: manufacture of dyes. Formula: $C_{14}H_8O_2$. [Late 19C. Blend of ANTHRACENE + QUINONE]

anthrax /án thraks/ (*plural* **-traces** /-thrə seez/) *n* **1.** a highly infectious, often fatal, bacterial disease of mammals, especially cattle and sheep, that is transmissible to humans and causes skin ulcers (**cutaneous anthrax**) or a form of pneumonia when inhaled (**pulmonary anthrax**) **2.** an open sore on the skin that results from infection with anthrax [14C. Via Latin, 'carbuncle' < Greek, 'coal, carbuncle']

anthrobotics /ánthrə bóttiks/ *n* the study and development of robots that are intended to behave like or resemble human beings (*takes a singular verb*) [Late 20C. Blend of ANTHROPO- + ROBOTICS]

anthrop. *abbr* **1.** anthropological **2.** anthropology

anthropic principle /an thróppik-/ *n* **1.** the principle that the observed values of all physical and cosmological quantities require that humankind, as the observer, must evolve **2.** the principle that the universe has properties that make the evolution of intelligent life inevitable [< Greek *anthrōpikos* < *anthrōpos* 'human being']

anthropo- *prefix* human being ○ *anthropology* [< Greek *anthrōpos*]

anthropocentric /ánthrəpō séntrik/ *adj* **1.** regarding humans as the universe's most important entity **2.** seeing things in human terms, especially judging things according to human perceptions, values, and experiences ○ *anthropocentric responses to the condition of animals* —**anthropocentrically** *adv* —**anthropocentrism** *n*

anthropogenesis /ánthrəpō jénnəssiss/, **anthropogeny** /ánthrō pójjəni/ *n* the scientific study of the origin of humankind and how it has developed

anthropogenic /ánthrəpō jénnik/, **anthropogenetic** /ánthrəpōjə néttik/ *adj* **1.** relating to or resulting from the influence that humans have on the natural world **2.** relating to the origin and development of human beings —**anthropogenically** *adv*

anthropogeny *n* ANTHROP same as **anthropogenesis**

anthropoid /ánthrə poyd/ *adj* **1.** OF APES AND MONKEYS relating to the group of animals that includes monkeys, gibbons, great apes, and humans **2.** LIKE HUMANS physically resembling human beings or human parts **3.** CLUMSY OR UNINTELLIGENT rough-mannered, clumsy, ugly, or unintelligent, as apes are sometimes characterized (*informal*) ■ *n* **1.** PRIMATE an animal belonging to the group that includes monkeys, gibbons, great apes, and humans. Suborder: Anthropoidea. **2.** ZOOL same as **anthropoid ape** —**anthropoidal** /ánthrə póyd'l/ *adj*

anthropoid ape *n* a tailless animal with long arms and a highly developed brain that belongs to the family that includes the gorillas, chimpanzees, orang-utans, and gibbons

anthropological /ánthrəpə lójjik'l/ *adj* relating to the study of humankind, especially the study of cultures —**anthropologically** *adv*

anthropological linguistics *n* a branch of linguistic research that investigates the relationship between language and culture (*takes a singular verb*)

anthropology /ánthrə pólləji/ *n* **1.** the study of humankind in all its aspects, especially human culture or human development. It differs from sociology in taking a more historical and comparative approach. **2.** the parts of Christian doctrine that are concerned with the nature, origin, and destiny of humankind —**anthropologist** *n*

anthropometry /ánthrə pómmətri/ *n* the study of

human body measurements. The uses of anthropometry include the creation of ergonomic furniture designs and the examination and comparison of populations. —**anthropometric** /ánthrəpə méttrik/ *adj* —**anthropometrically** *adv* —**anthropometrist** *n*

anthropomorphise *vt* another spelling of **anthropomorphize**

anthropomorphism /ánthrəpō máwrfizəm/ *n* the attribution of a human form, human characteristics, or human behaviour to nonhuman things, e.g. deities in mythology and animals in children's stories —**anthropomorphic** *adj* —**anthropomorphically** *adv*

anthropomorphize /ánthrəpə máwr fīz/ (**-phizes, -phizing, -phized**), **anthropomorphise** (**-phises, -phising, -phised**) *vt* to give a nonhuman thing a human form, human characteristics, or human behaviour ○ *our tendency to anthropomorphize wild animals* —**anthropomorphization** /ánthrəpə máwr fī záysh'n/ *n*

anthropomorphous /ánthrəpə máwrfəss/ *adj* having the shape of the human body or a human body part

anthropopathism /ánthrə póppəthizəm/, **anthropopathy** /ánthrə póppəthi/ *n* the attribution of human emotions to a nonhuman thing, e.g. a deity or an object of worship [Mid-19C. < ANTHROPO- + -PATHY]

anthropophagus /ánthrə póffəgəss/ (*plural* **-gi** /-jī/) *n* somebody who eats human flesh (*technical*) [Mid-16C. < Latin < Greek *anthrōpophagos* 'eating humans' < *anthrōpos* 'human being'] —**anthropophagic** /ánthrəpə fájjik/ *adj* —**anthropophagous** *adj* —**anthropophagy** /-póffəji/ *n*

anthroposophy /ánthrə póssəfi/ *n* a religious philosophy developed by Rudolf Steiner from theosophy, holding that spiritual development should be humankind's foremost concern —**anthroposophical** /ánthrəpə sóffik'l/ *adj* —**anthroposophist** *n*

anthurium /an thyoóri əm/ *n* a tropical evergreen plant with showy foliage. Flowers: glossy, heart-shaped, red or white, enclosing a spike of yellow florets. Native to: America. Genus: *Anthurium*. [Mid-19C. < modern Latin < Greek *anthos* 'flower' + *oura* 'tail']

anti /ánti/ (*informal*) *adj* expressing or holding an opposing view, especially with regard to a political issue or moral principle ■ *n* (*plural* **-tis**) somebody with an opposing view, particularly on a political issue or moral principle ○ *Are you a pro or an anti?* [Late 18C. < ANTI-]

anti- *prefix* **1.** against or preventing ○ *anticlerical* ○ *anticoagulant* **2.** opposite ○ *anticlimax* ○ *antiparticle* [Via Latin < Greek *anti* 'opposite, against']

antiabortion *adj*	**antichurch** *adj*
antiabortionist *n*	**anticlassical** *adj*
antiacademic *adj*	**anticlergy** *adj*
antiacne *adj*	**anticling** *adj*
antiageing *adj*	**anticlogging** *adj*
antiaggression *adj*	**anticlotting** *adj*
antialcohol *adj*	**anticolonial** *adj*
antiallergic *adj*	**anticolonialism** *n*
anti-American *adj*	**anticommercial** *adj*
anti-Americanism *n*	**anticommercialism** *n*
antiapartheid *adj*	**anticommunism** *n*
antiasthma *adj*	**anti-Communism** *n*
antiauthoritarian *adj*	**anticommunist** *adj, n*
antiauthoritarianism *n*	**anti-Communist** *adj, n*
antiauthority *adj*	**anticonstitutional** *adj*
antibacterial *adj, n*	**anticonsumer** *adj, n*
anti-Black *adj*	**anticorrosion** *adj*
antibleeding *adj*	**anticorrosive** *adj*
anti-Bolshevik *adj, n*	**anticorruption** *n*
antibourgeois *adj*	**anticrime** *adj*
anti-British *adj*	**anticruelty** *adj*
antibureaucratic *adj*	**anticult** *adj*
antiburglar *adj*	**antidandruff** *adj*
anticaking *adj*	**anti-Darwinian** *adj*
anticancer *adj*	**anti-Darwinism** *n*
anticapitalism *n*	**antidemocratic** *adj*
anticapitalist *adj, n*	**antidiarrhoeal** *adj, n*
anticarcinogen *n*	**antidiscrimination** *adj*
anticarcinogenic *adj*	**antiegalitarian** *adj*
anticaries *adj*	**antielite** *adj*
anti-Catholic *adj, n*	**anti-English** *adj*
anti-Catholicism *n*	**antiestablishment** *adj*
anticellulite *adj*	**anti-European** *adj*
anticensorship *adj*	**anti-Europeanism** *n*
anti-Christian *adj*	**antifascism** *n*

antifascist *adj, n*
antifederal *adj*
antifeminism *n*
antifeminist *n, adj*
antifog *adj*
antifogging *adj*
antifraud *adj*
antifriction *adj*
antifungal *adj, n*
antifur *adj*
antigambling *adj*
antigay *adj*
antigovernment *adj*
antigrowth *adj*
antihomosexual *adj*
antihunting *adj*
anti-immigration *adj*
anti-imperialism *n*
anti-imperialist *n, adj*
anti-inflammatory *adj, n*
anti-inflationary *adj*
anti-intellectual *adj*
anti-intellectualism *n*
anti-isolationism *n*
anti-isolationist *n*
antilabour *adj*
antiliberal *adj, n*
antiliberalism *n*
antimalarial *adj, n*
antimarket *adj*
antimicrobial *adj, n*
antimilitarism *n*
antimilitarist *n, adj*
antimilitary *adj*
antimodernism *n*
antimodernist *n, adj*
antimonarchist *n, adj*
antimonopolistic *adj*
antimonopoly *adj*
antinarcotic *adj, n*
antinationalism *n*
antinationalist *n*
anti-Nazi *adj, n*
anti-Nazism *n*
antipacifism *n*
antipacifist *n*
antiparasitic *adj, n*
antiplaque *adj*
antipole *n*
antipolitical *adj*

antipollution *adj*
antipollutionist *n*
antipoverty *n*
anti-Protestant *adj, n*
anti-Protestantism *n*
antiracism *n*
antiracist *adj, n*
antiradar *adj*
antiradical *adj, n*
antireligious *adj*
antirepublican *adj, n*
antirepublicanism *n*
antirevolutionary *adj, n*
antiriot *adj*
antiroyalist *n, adj*
antirust *adj*
antisatellite *adj*
antiscientific *adj*
antisexism *n*
antisexist *adj*
antishoplifting *adj*
antiskid *adj*
antislavery *adj*
antislip *adj*
antismog *adj*
antismoking *adj*
antisocialist *adj, n*
anti-Soviet *adj*
antispam *adj*
antistate *adj*
antistatic *adj*
antistress *adj*
antisubmarine *adj*
antitakeover *adj*
antitank *adj*
antitheft *adj*
antitobacco *adj*
antitrespassing *adj*
antitumour *adj*
antitumoural *adj*
antiunion *adj*
antiviral *adj*
antivirus *adj*
antivivisection *adj*
antivivisectionism *n*
antivivisectionist *adj, n*
antiwar *adj*
antiwrinkle *adj*
anti-Zionism *n*
anti-Zionist *adj, n*

antiadrenergic /ánti áddrə núrjik/ *adj* counteracting the physiological effects of adrenaline ■ *n* a drug that counteracts the physiological effects of adrenaline

antiaircraft /ánti áir kraaft/ *adj* designed and used to destroy enemy aircraft

antiaircraft gun *n* a piece of artillery designed and used to destroy enemy aircraft

antialiasing /ánti áyli əssing/ *n* the technique of smoothing the jagged edges of diagonal lines in computer graphics by varying the colour at the edges

antiangina /ánti an jínə/ *adj* controlling or preventing the symptoms of angina

antiarrhythmic /ánti ay ríthmik/ *adj* counteracting irregular heart action ■ *n* a drug that counteracts irregular heart action

antiart /ánti aart/ *n* the art of the Dada movement, begun during World War I, that rejected conventional artistic practices and tastes ■ *adj* rejecting conventional artistic practices and tastes

antiatom /ánti áttəm/ *n* an atom made up of antiparticles

antiballistic missile /ánti bə lístik-/ *n* a missile used to prevent a ballistic missile from reaching its target by destroying it in flight

Antibes /on teéb/ port and resort southwest of Nice in the Alpes-Maritimes Department in the Provence-Alpes-Côte d'Azur Region of France. Population: 72,412 (1999).

antibiosis /ánti bī óssiss/ *n* a relationship between organisms that is harmful to one of them, e.g. the production by one microorganism of chemicals that harm another [Late 19C. < ANTI-, after *symbiosis*]

antibiotic /ánti bī óttik/ *n* a naturally produced substance that kills or inactivates bacteria, but has

no effect against viruses, used as a medication —
antibiotic *adj* —**antibiotically** *adv*

antibody /ánti bodi/ (*plural* **-ies**) *n* a protein produced by B cells in the body in response to the presence of an antigen, e.g. a bacterium or virus. Antibodies are a primary form of immune response in resistance to disease and act by attaching themselves to a foreign antigen and weakening or destroying it. [Early 20C. Translation of German *Antikörper*, contraction of *anti-toxischer Körper* 'antitoxic body' or a similar phrase]

antic /ántik/ *n* CLOWN an actor or performer playing a comic role requiring ludicrously eccentric behaviour (*archaic*) ■ **antics** *npl* SILLY PRANKS amusing, frivolous, or eccentric behaviour ■ *adj* STRANGE ludicrously eccentric (*archaic*) [Early 16C. Via Italian *antico* 'old, old-fashioned' < Latin *anticus, antiquus*]

anticatalyst /ánti káttəlist/ *n* 1. CHEM same as **inhibitor** (sense 1) 2. a substance that inhibits or prevents the action of a catalyst

anticathode /ánti káthōd/ *n* the anode in a vacuum tube, e.g. an X-ray tube, towards which electrons flow

antichoice /ánti chóyss/ *adj* opposed to the principle or practice of legal abortion

anticholinergic /ántikōli núrjik/ *adj* blocking nerve impulses that are part of the stress response ■ *n* a drug of a group used to control stress

anticholinesterase /ántikōli néstə rayz, -rayss/ *n* a substance that blocks the activity of the enzyme cholinesterase, increasing the concentration of acetylcholine in the body

Antichrist /ánti kríst/ *n* 1. an antagonist of Jesus Christ, expected by the early Christians to spread evil throughout the world, but then to be overcome by the second coming of Christ 2. *also* **antichrist** a person or power opposed to Jesus Christ [Pre-12C. Via ecclesiastical Latin < Greek *antikhristos*]

anticipate /an tíssi payt/ (*-pates, -pating, -pated*) *vt* 1. EXPECT SOMETHING to think or be fairly sure that something will happen ○ *We anticipate a few problems in the early stages.* 2. LOOK FORWARD TO SOMETHING to feel excited, hopeful, or eager about something that is going to happen ○ *anticipating Saturday's concert* 3. ACT BEFOREHAND TO ADDRESS SOMETHING IMMINENT to imagine or consider something before it happens and make any necessary preparations or changes ○ *anticipate flooding next week* 4. PREVENT SOMETHING to succeed in preventing or avoiding something by acting in advance 5. START SOMETHING AHEAD OF OTHERS to say or do something before it becomes common or fashionable (*formal*) 6. ACT IN HOPE OF SOMETHING HAPPENING to act on the promise or expectation of something, before it has been given or confirmed (*formal*) ○ *frequently anticipated his salary* [Mid-16C. < Latin *anticipat-*, past participle of *anticipare* 'catch beforehand' < *capere* 'seize, take'] —**anticipative** /-tíssipətiv/ *adj* —**anticipator** *n*

USAGE Anticipating trouble: If you *anticipate* trouble, it often just means that you are expecting or foreseeing trouble; the word's more traditional meaning is that you are taking steps to prevent trouble, that is forestalling rather than expecting it.

anticipation /an tíssi páysh'n/ *n* 1. EXPECTANT WAITING the feeling of looking forward, usually excitedly or eagerly, to something that is going to happen 2. FIN PREMATURE USE OF FUNDS the seizure or use of funds before they are legally available, especially from a trust fund 3. MUSIC NOTE PLAYED BEFORE CHORD a note related to a chord that is played just before the chord itself

anticipatory /an tíssipətəri/ *adj* experienced or done in the expectation of a future event

anticlerical /ánti klérrik'l/ *adj* opposed to the involvement of the church or clergy in politics or public affairs —**anticlericalism** *n*

anticlimax /ánti klí maks/ *n* 1. an ordinary or unsatisfying event that follows an increasingly exciting, dramatic, or unusual series of events or a period of increasing anticipation and excitement 2. an unexpected change in tone or subject matter from the high-minded, serious, or compelling to the trivial, comic, or dull —**anticlimactic** /ánti klí máktik/ *adj* —**anticlimactically** *adv*

anticline /ánti klín/ *n* an arch-shaped formation of layers of sedimentary rock folded upwards by movements in the Earth's crust [Mid-19C. < ANTI- + Greek *klinein* 'to lean', after INCLINE] —**anticlinal** /ánti klín'l/ *adj*

anticlockwise /ánti klók wīz/ *adj, adv* in the opposite direction to the way the hands of a clock move. N Am term **counterclockwise**

anticoagulant /ánti kō ággyōōlənt/ *n* a natural or synthetic agent that prevents blood clots from forming ■ *adj* preventing blood from clotting

anticodon /ánti kó don/ *n* a set of three nucleotides in transfer RNA involved in the formation of a protein

anticoincidence /ánti kō ínssidənss/ *adj* describes an electronic circuit that produces an output pulse if one, but not both, of its input terminals receives a pulse within a specific time frame

anticompetitive /ántikəm péttətiv/ *adj* likely or certain to discourage competition

anticonvulsant /ántikən vúlssənt/ *adj* preventing or reducing seizures ■ *n* a drug that prevents or reduces seizures. Use: epilepsy control. —**anticonvulsive** *n, adj*

Anticosti Island /ánti kósti-/ island in the Gulf of St Lawrence, Quebec, Canada. Its abundant forests shelter diverse wildlife. Area: 7,941 sq. km/3,066 sq. mi.

anticyclone /ánti síklōn/ *n* a large system of atmospheric high pressure marked by circulating winds moving clockwise from the centre in the northern hemisphere and anticlockwise in the southern hemisphere, bringing generally settled weather —**anticyclonic** /ánti sī klónnik/ *adj*

antidepressant /ánti di préss'nt/ *n* a drug used to prevent or reduce depression ■ *adj* acting to prevent or reduce depression —**antidepressive** *adj*

antidiabetic /ánti dī ə béttik/ *adj* reducing the effects of diabetes

antidiuretic /ánti dīyoō réttik/ *adj* preventing the excessive output of urine ○ *an antidiuretic hormone* ○ *antidiuretic drugs* ■ *n* a drug for preventing the excessive output of urine

antidiuretic hormone *n* BIOCHEM same as **vasopressin**

antidote /ántidōt/ *n* 1. a substance that counteracts the effects of a toxin 2. something that will take away or reduce the bad effects of something unpleasant or undesirable ○ *an antidote to boredom* [15C. Via Latin < Greek *antidoton* < *antididonai* 'give against' < *didonai* 'give'] —**antidotal** /ánti dōt'l/ *adj*

antiemetic /ánti i méttik/ *adj* preventing vomiting ■ *n* a drug that prevents vomiting

Antietam /an teétəm/ village in northwestern Maryland, southeast of Sharpsburg. On 17 September 1862, Robert E. Lee's army crossed nearby Antietam Creek and was repelled by George McClellan's forces in one of the bloodiest battles of the American Civil War. In the southern US, the engagement is usually called the Battle of Sharpsburg.

antifebrile /ánti feéb rīl/ *adj, n* MED same as **antipyretic**

antifederalist /ánti féddərəlist/ *n* 1. SOMEBODY OPPOSED TO FEDERALISM an opponent of the division of power between a central government and regional governments 2. *also* **Antifederalist** HISTORICAL OPPONENT OF US CONSTITUTION somebody who opposed the US Constitution when it was being drawn up ■ *adj* AGAINST FEDERALISM opposed to the idea or practice of federalism —**antifederalism** *n*

antiferromagnetic /ánti férrō mag néttik/ *adj* describes substances that behave like paramagnetic substances with respect to their permeability but behave like ferromagnetic substances when their temperature is changed —**antiferromagnet** /ánti férrō mágnit/ *n* —**antiferromagnetism** /-mágnitizəm/ *n*

antifouling paint /ánti fówling-/ *n* a poisonous paint used to prevent barnacles and other organisms from growing on the bottom of a boat or ship

antifreeze /ánti freez/ *n* a substance added to a liquid to lower its freezing point. An antifreeze such as ethylene glycol is added to or substituted for the water in a vehicle's radiator to stop it from freezing in winter.

antigen /ántijən/ *n* a substance, usually a protein, on the surface of a cell or bacterium that stimulates

the production of an antibody [Early 20C. Via German < French *antigène* < *anti-* 'anti-' + Greek *-genēs* (see -GEN)] —**antigenic** /ánti jénnik/ *adj*

antigen feeding *n* the oral administration of a protein antigen to encourage immune-system tolerance to it

antigenic drift *n* changes of a minor nature in the antigenic structure of a virus strain. Antigenic drift is the result of natural selection after mixing with a partially immune population.

Antigone /an tíggəni/ *n* in Greek mythology, the daughter of Oedipus and his mother and wife Jocasta. Sentenced to death for defying an order that her brother should not be buried, she committed suicide.

Antigonus I /an tíggənəss/ (382?–301 BC) Greek general and king of Macedonia (306–301 BC). He secured a large part of Asia Minor after the empire of Alexander the Great broke up in 323 BC.

antigravity /ánti grávvəti/ *n* a hypothetical force that would counteract the effects of gravity or of high acceleration ■ *adj* counteracting the effects of gravity or of high acceleration

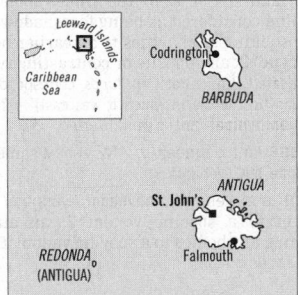

Antigua and Barbuda

Antigua and Barbuda /an teˈegə ənd baar boˈodə/ island nation in the Leeward Islands, east of Puerto Rico and north of Venezuela in the Caribbean Sea. It became a member of the Commonwealth in 1981. Language: English. Currency: East Caribbean dollar. Capital: St John's. Population: 67,897 (2001). Area: 442 sq. km/171 sq. mi. —**Antiguan** *adj, n*

antihelix *n* ANAT same as **anthelix**

antihero /ánti heerô/ (*plural* -roes) *n* the central character in a story who is not a traditionally brave or good hero —**antiheroic** /ánti hə rô ik/ *adj* — **antiheroism** /ánti hérrô izəm/ *n*

antihistamine /ánti hístə meen/ *n* a drug that blocks the action of histamine. Use: to control allergies. (*often used before a noun*) —**antihistaminic** /ánti hístə mínnik/ *adj*

antihypertensive /ánti hípər ténssiv/ *adj* controlling high blood pressure ■ *n* an agent or means to control high blood pressure

antiknock /ánti nók/ *n* a substance added to petrol. Use: to reduce or stop faulty fuel combustion associated with a knocking sound.

Anti-Lebanon Mountains /ánti lébbənən-/ mountain range in southwestern Syria and eastern Lebanon, parallel to the Mediterranean coast. Highest peak: Mount Hermon 2,814 m/9,232 ft.

antilepton /ánti lépton/ *n* the antiparticle of a lepton

antilife /ánti lìf/ *adj* regarded as preventing or opposed to living life fully in tune with the natural world (*informal*) ○ *antilife legislation* ○ *It is absurd and antilife to have to sit in an office all day.*

Antilles ♦ **Greater Antilles, Lesser Antilles**

antilock /ánti lók/ *adj* describes an electronically controlled braking system or brakes that prevent the vehicle's wheels from locking if the driver brakes very suddenly

antilogarithm /ánti lóggərithəm/, **antilog** /ánti log/ *n* a number for which the logarithm is a given number, so for logarithm $_a b = c$, then antilogarithm $_a c = b$

antilogy /an tílləji/ (*plural* -ogies) *n* a phrase that contradicts itself or negates its meaning [Early 17C. Via French < Greek *antilogia* 'speaking against' < *-logia* (see -LOGY)]

antimacassar /ánti mə kássər/ *n* a piece of fabric placed over the back of an armchair to keep it clean [Mid-19C. < ANTI- + *Macassar*, brand of hair oil]

antimagnetic /ánti mag néttik/ *adj* describes a material that does not become permanently magnetized in a magnetic field

antimasque /ánti maask/, **antimask** /an interlude in or prelude to a 17th-century masque that contrasts with the main performance and often involves grotesque costume and dancing

antimatter /ánti matər/ *n* a hypothetical form of matter composed of subatomic particles (**antiparticles**) that correspond to and can annihilate other elementary particles

antimere /ánti meer/ *n* a part of a radially symmetrical animal that is the opposite of a corresponding part of the animal —**antimeric** /ánti mérrik/ *adj*

antimetabolite /ánti mə tábbə lìt/ *n* a synthetic substance similar to one needed for normal cell growth that disrupts cell development by replacing the natural metabolite. Antimetabolites may be used in cancer therapy.

antimissile missile /ánti míssìl-/ *n* a missile used to prevent another missile from reaching its target by destroying it in flight

antimitotic /ánti mī tóttik/ *adj* preventing cell division (**mitosis**) —**antimitotic** *n*

antimony /ántiməni, an tímməni/ *n* a toxic crystalline element that occurs in metallic and nonmetallic forms. Source: ores, e.g. stibnite. Use: alloys, electronics. Symbol **Sb**. See table at **element** [15C. < medieval Latin *antimonium*]

antimycotic /ánti mī kóttik/ *adj* **1.** preventing, killing, or reducing the growth of fungi **2.** a drug for preventing, killing, or reducing the growth of fungi [< ANTI- + Greek *mukētes* 'fungi']

antineoplastic /ánti nee ō plástik/ *adj* preventing or inhibiting the growth of cancers —**antineoplastic** *n*

antineutrino /ánti nyoo treˈenô/ (*plural* -nos) *n* the antiparticle of a neutrino. When a neutrino and an antineutrino are brought together, mutual annihilation occurs.

antineutron /ánti nyóo tron/ *n* the antiparticle of a neutron. When a neutron and an antineutron are brought together, mutual annihilation occurs.

anting /ánting/ *n* a behavioural practice in which birds pick up ants in their beaks and rub them on their feathers to spread fluids repellent to parasites

antinociception /ántinō si sépsh'n/ *n* a reduction in pain sensitivity produced within neurons when an endorphin or similar opium-containing substance (**opioid**) combines with a receptor —**antinociceptive** *adj*

antinode /ántinōd/ *n* a point of maximum amplitude of a wave characteristic in a system in which the wave form is stationary in time

antinoise /anti nóyz/ *n* sound generated to mask unwanted noise by cancelling the interference pattern of the unwanted noise

antinomian /ánti nômi ən/ *n* CHRISTIAN BELIEVING SALVATION DEPENDS ON FAITH a Christian who believes that faith and divine grace bring about salvation and that it is therefore not necessary to accept established moral laws ■ *adj* **1.** HAVING ANTINOMIAN BELIEFS holding antinomian Christian beliefs **2.** REJECTING FIXED MORAL LAWS refusing to accept established moral laws that apply to everybody [Mid-17C. < medieval Latin *Antinomi* 'antinomians' < Latin *antinomia* (see ANTINOMY)]

antinomianism /ánti nômi ənizəm/ *n* **1.** in Christian doctrine, the belief that Christians are not bound by established moral laws, but should rely on faith and divine grace for salvation **2.** the belief that it is impossible to apply a universal moral code because it will have a different meaning for different people

antinomy /an tínnəmi/ (*plural* -mies) *n* **1.** PHILOSOPHY a contradictory and illogical conclusion produced by two apparently correct and reasonable statements or facts **2.** LAW a contradiction between two laws, principles, or authorities [Late 16C. Via Latin *antinomia* < Greek, literally 'against law' < *nomos* 'law, rule'] —**antinomic** /ánti nómmik/ *adj*

antinovel /ánti nov'l/ *n* a work of fiction that lacks the

features traditionally used in a novel, e.g. consistent characters, a coherent plot, and a constant authorial perspective —**antinovelist** /ánti nóvvəlist/ *n*

antinuclear /ánti nyoˈokli ər/ *adj* **1.** opposed to nuclear weapons or power **2.** reactive with or destructive to cell nuclei

antinucleon /ánti nyóokli on/ *n* an antiproton or antineutron. When a nucleon and an antinucleon are brought together, mutual annihilation occurs.

Antioch /ánti ok/ former name for **Antakya**

antioncogene /ánti óngkə jeen/ *n* a recessive gene that is thought to suppress cancers by limiting cell multiplication

antioxidant /ánti óksidənt/ *n* a substance that inhibits the destructive effects of oxidation, e.g. in the body or in foodstuffs or plastics

antiparallel /ánti párrə lel/ *adj* parallel but opposite in linear or rotational direction

antiparticle /ánti paartik'l/ *n* an elementary particle with the same mass as its corresponding particle but with opposite values for other properties such as charge. When an antiparticle and its particle interact, mutual annihilation occurs.

antipasto /ánti pastô/ (*plural* -ti /-ti/ or -tos) *n* a food served at the beginning of an Italian meal or as a snack [Early 17C. < Italian, 'before food']

antipathetic /ántipə théttik/ *adj* **1.** feeling or expressing anger, hostility, strong opposition, or disgust towards somebody or something **2.** causing anger, hostility, strong opposition, or disgust [Early 17C. < ANTIPATHY, after PATHETIC] —**antipathetically** *adv*

antipathy /an típpəthi/ (*plural* -thies) *n* **1.** strong hostility or opposition towards somebody or something **2.** somebody or something that causes anger, hostility, strong opposition, or disgust [Late 16C. Via French *antipathie* < Greek *antipathēs* 'feeling the opposite' < *pathos* 'feeling']

SYNONYMS See *dislike*.

antiperiodic /ánti peeri óddik/ *adj* preventing the periodic recurrence of symptoms or of a disease such as malaria —**antiperiodic** *n*

antiperistalsis /ánti perri stálsiss/ (*plural* -stalses /-stál seez/) *n* contractions of the intestine in the reverse direction to what is usual, tending to cause vomiting —**antiperistaltic** *adj*

antipersonnel /ánti purssə nél/ *adj* intended to injure and kill enemy personnel rather than to destroy buildings, structures, arsenals, or missiles

antiperspirant /ánti púrspərənt/ *n* an astringent preparation applied especially under the arms to reduce or prevent perspiration. Antiperspirants are produced in many forms, including aerosols, roll-ons, and sticks. ■ *adj* used to reduce or prevent perspiration

antiphase /ánti fáyz/ *adj* relating to a boundary, e.g. in an alloy, where an ordered pattern of atoms meets a random pattern

antiphon /ántifən/ *n* **1.** MUSIC SUNG IN ALTERNATING PARTS a hymn or psalm performed by two groups of singers chanting alternate sections **2.** SECTION OF FORMAL CHURCH SERVICE a short piece of biblical or devotional text that is chanted or sung before or after a psalm verse in a Roman Catholic or Anglican church service **3.** RESPONSE a response or reply (*literary*) [15C. < ecclesiastical Latin *antiphona* < Greek *antiphōnos* 'sounding in response' < *phōnē* 'sound']

antiphonary /an tíffənə ri/ (*plural* -ies) *n* a book, often large and richly decorated, containing antiphons or anthems to be sung or chanted responsively

antiphony /an tíffəni/ (*plural* -nies) *n* **1.** CHR same as antiphon (sense 1) **2.** responsive chanting, recitation, or singing, e.g. of liturgical antiphons **3.** a musical response or answering phrase —**antiphonal** *adj*

antiphrasis /an tíffrəssiss/ *n* the use of a word or phrase to mean the opposite of its usual or literal sense, e.g. saying on a rainy day, 'What a lovely day for a picnic!' [Mid-16C. < late Latin < Greek *antiphrazein* 'express oppositely' < *phrazein* 'declare']

antipode /ántipōd/ *n* an exact or diametric opposite [Early 17C. Back-formation < ANTIPODES]

antipodean /an típpə deˈe ən/, **Antipodean** *adj* coming from or relating to Australia or New Zealand

antipodes /an típpə deez/ *npl* **1.** places at opposite sides of the world to each other, or the areas at the side of the world opposite to a given place **2.** two points, places, or things that are diametrically opposite each other [14C. Via French or late Latin < Greek *antipodes* 'those who have their feet opposite' < *pod-*, stem of *pous* 'foot'] —**antipodal** *adj*

Antipodes *npl* Australia and New Zealand, from the perspective of the United Kingdom or Europe (*informal*)

antipope /ántipōp/ *n* an alternative pope elected in opposition to a standing pope [15C. Via French *antipape* < medieval Latin *antipapa* < *papa* 'pope', after *antichristus* 'Antichrist']

antiprostaglandin /ánti próstə glándin/ *n* a drug or agent used to limit the release of prostaglandins

antiproton /ántiprō ton/ *n* the antiparticle of a proton. When a proton and an antiproton are brought together, mutual annihilation occurs.

antipruritic /ánti proor ríttik/ *adj* alleviating the symptoms of itching ■ *n* a drug or other agent that controls itching

antipsoriasis /ánti sə rī əssiss/ *adj* alleviating the symptoms of psoriasis —**antipsoriatic** /ánti sáwri áttik/ *adj*

antipsychiatry /ántī sī kī ətri/ *n* a way of treating people with psychiatric disorders that is derived from psychoanalysis and is opposed to conventional medication

antipsychotic /ánti sī kóttik/ *adj* relieving the symptoms of psychosis ■ *n* a drug that relieves the symptoms of a psychiatric disorder

antipyretic /ánti pī réttik/ *adj* reducing fever ■ *n* a drug or other agent that reduces fever —**antipyresis** /ánti pī réessiss/ *n*

antiq. *abbr* **1.** antiquarian **2.** antiquity

antiquarian /ánti kwáiri ən/ *adj* relating to or dealing with antiques or antiquities, especially rare and old books ■ *n* same as **antiquary** —**antiquarianism** *n*

antiquark /ánti kwaark/ *n* the antiparticle of a quark. When a quark and an antiquark are brought together, mutual annihilation occurs.

antiquary /ántikwəri/ (*plural* -**ies**) *n* a collector, scholar, or seller of antiques or antiquities [Mid-16C. < Latin *antiquarius* < *antiquus* 'old']

antiquate /ánti kwayt/ (-**quates, -quating, -quated**) *vt* **1.** to cause something to become out of date or old **2.** HANDICRAFT same as **antique** [Late 16C. < ecclesiastical Latin *antiquat-*, past participle of *antiquare* 'make old' < Latin *antiquus* 'old']

antiquated /ánti kwaytid/ *adj* out of date, old-fashioned, or in need of updating or replacing —**antiquatedness** *n*

SYNONYMS See *old-fashioned*.

antique /an teék/ *n* (*plural* -**tiques**) **1.** COLLECTABLE OLD ITEM a collectable decorative or household object that is valued because of its age **2.** CLASSICAL ART the style, traditions, and qualities of ancient times, especially the art and sculpture of ancient Greece and Rome (*formal*) ■ *adj* **1.** DEALING IN ANTIQUES dealing in antiques **2.** MADE LONG AGO old and often valuable, of interest to collectors, and characteristic of a period and style of manufacture **3.** FROM CLASSICAL TIMES derived from a period of ancient history, especially ancient Greece and Rome, or stylistically typical of such a period (*formal*) **4.** ANCIENT very old or old-fashioned (*informal*) ■ *vt* (-**tiquing, -tiqued**) HANDICRAFT MAKE SOMETHING APPEAR OLD to treat something, especially a new object, so that it looks antique or worn with time [15C. Via French < Latin *antiquus* 'old']

antiquity /an tíkwəti/ (*plural* -**ties**) *n* **1.** ANCIENT HISTORY ancient history, especially the period of time during which the ancient Greek and Roman civilizations flourished **2.** PEOPLE OF ANCIENT TIMES the people of ancient civilizations, especially those of ancient Greece and Rome **3.** OLDNESS the state of being very old or ancient ○ *a sculpture of great antiquity* **4.** OLD OBJECT an object, especially a collectable, decorative, valuable, or interesting, that dates from a previous era

antirejection /ánti ri jéksh'n/ *adj* designed to prevent the immune system from rejecting a newly grafted organ or tissue

antiretroviral /ánti réttrō vírəl/ *adj* effective against retroviruses —**antiretroviral** *n*

antirheumatoid /ánti roomə toyd/ *adj* preventing or relieving the symptoms of rheumatism

antiroll bar /ánti rṓl baar/ *n* a cross-mounted metal bar incorporated in the suspension system of a motor vehicle, designed to prevent the vehicle from swinging dangerously or overturning

antirrhinum /ánti rínəm/ *n* PLANTS same as **snapdragon** [Mid-16C. Via Latin < Greek *antirrhinon*, literally 'counterfeiting a nose' < *rhin-* 'nose'; from the flower's shape]

anti-Semitic *adj* hating or discriminating against Jews

anti-Semitism *n* policies, views, or actions that harm or discriminate against Jews —**anti-Semite** *n*

antisense /ánti sénss/ *adj* relating to or having a strand of DNA complementary to other genetic material, so that the expression of a trait can be regulated

antisepsis /ánti sépsiss/ *n* **1.** the reduction or prevention of infection, especially by the elimination or reduction of the growth of microorganisms that cause disease or decay **2.** the condition of being free from microorganisms

antiseptic /ánti séptik/ *adj* **1.** CONTROLLING INFECTION reducing or preventing infection, especially by the elimination or reduction of the growth of microorganisms that cause disease or decay **2.** DULL unexciting and unimaginative **3.** UNCONTENTIOUS not contentious, controversial, or offensive in any way ■ *n* AGENT FOR CONTROLLING INFECTION an agent that reduces or prevents infection, especially by eliminating or reducing the growth of microorganisms that cause disease or decay —**antiseptically** *adv*

antiserum /ánti seerəm/ (*plural* -**rums** or -**ra** /-rə/) *n* an animal or human blood serum containing one or more ready-made antibodies that can provide immunity against a disease or counteract a venom

antisocial /ánti sṓsh'l/ *adj* **1.** hostile or indifferent to the comfort or needs of other members of a community or society as a whole **2.** preferring not to spend time with other people —**antisociality** /ánti sṓshi álləti/ *n* —**antisocially** *adv*

USAGE See *unsociable*.

antispasmodic /ánti spaz móddik/ *adj* controlling spasms ■ *n* a drug or other agent that controls muscle spasms

Antisthenes /an tísthə neez/ (444?–371? BC) Greek philosopher. He believed that happiness depends on moral virtue and founded the Cynic school of philosophy.

antistrophe /an tístrəfi/ *n* **1.** SECOND PART OF GREEK CHORAL ODE in a classical Greek drama, the second section of an ode sung by the chorus after the first section (**strophe**) **2.** RETURN MOVEMENT IN ANCIENT GREEK DRAMA in a classical Greek drama, the second of two movements made by the chorus, back in the opposite direction to that of the first movement (**strophe**) **3.** LITERAT SECOND METRICAL FORM IN POEM the second type of metrical form in a poem that alternates two contrasting metrical forms [Mid-16C. Via late Latin < Greek *antistrophē* < *antistrephein* 'turn back' < *strophē* (see STROPHE)]

antiterrorism /ánti térrərizəm/ *n* the combating of terrorists in their attempts to carry out violent and illegal activities against society or property (*often used before a noun*)

antiterrorist /ánti térrərist/ *adj* designed or put in place to make it difficult for terrorists to carry out violent and illegal activities against society or property

antithesis /an títhəssiss/ (*plural* -**eses** /-ə seez/) *n* **1.** DIRECT OPPOSITE the complete or exact opposite of something **2.** FIGURE OF SPEECH a use of words or phrases that contrast with each other to create a balanced effect **3.** PHILOSOPHY CONTRASTING PROPOSITION a proposition that is the opposite of another already proposed (**thesis**) [Early 16C. < late Latin < Greek *antithenai* 'set against' < *tithenai* 'set']

antithetical /ánti théttik'l/, **antithetic** /ánti théttik/ *adj* **1.** expressing or constituting the complete or exact opposite (*formal*) ○ *policies that are antithetical to the prevailing mood of the country* **2.** relating to or consisting of a proposition that is the opposite of

another already proposed [Late 16C. < Greek *antithetikos* < *antitithenai* (see ANTITHESIS)] —**antithetically** *adv*

antithyroid /ánti thī royd/ *adj* counteracting thyroid overactivity, especially in the production of thyroid hormone

antitoxic /ánti tóksik/ *adj* acting to counteract toxins

antitoxin /ánti tóksin/ *n* **1.** an antibody produced in response to a specific toxin **2.** PHARM same as **antiserum**

antitrade /ánti trayd/ *n* a wind in the planetary wind system that is above the trade winds and blows in the opposite direction from them

antitragus /an títtrəgəss/ (*plural* -**gi** /-jī/) *n* a bump of cartilage just below the opening of the external ear

antitrust /ánti trúst/ *adj* N Am intended to oppose trusts and cartels, e.g. by preventing them from using monopolistic business practices to make unfair profits

antituberculosis /ánti tyoō búrkyoō lṓssiss/ *adj* effective against tuberculosis

antitussive /ánti tússiv/ *adj* controlling coughing ■ *n* a drug that controls coughing

antitype /ánti tīp/ *n* **1.** in the Bible, somebody or something considered as being foreshadowed by or having striking similarities to an earlier person or thing (**type**) **2.** an opposite or contrasting type [Early 17C. Via late Latin < Greek *antitupos* 'corresponding as an impression (to the die in which it was cast)' < *tupos* (see TYPE)] —**antitypical** /ánti típpik'l/ *adj*

antivenene /ánti vénneen/ *n* ANZ PHARM same as **antivenin** [Late 19C. Variant]

antivenin /ánti vénnin/, **antivenom** /-vénnəm/ *n* **1.** an antitoxin to a specific venom **2.** an antiserum containing antibodies to a specific venom [Early 20C. < ANTI- + VENOM + -IN]

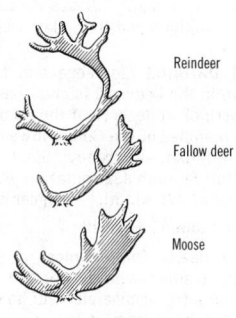

Reindeer

Fallow deer

Moose

antler

antler /ántlər/ *n* a solid bony branched horn found in pairs on the head of an animal, especially a male, of the deer family, including caribou and elk. Antlers are shed each year. [14C. < Anglo-Norman variant of Old French *antoillier*] —**antlered** *adj*

Antlia /ántli ə/ *n* a faint constellation of the southern hemisphere near Centaurus and Hydra

ant lion *n* a nocturnal insect that resembles a damselfly when adult. The larvae lie buried under sand at the bottom of a cone-shaped pit and trap insects such as ants. Family: Myrmeleontidae. [Translation of Greek *murmēkoleōn*; from its usual prey and its fierce-looking jaws]

Antofagasta /ántōfə gástə/ city in northern Chile, on the fringes of the Atacama Desert. Population: 251,429 (1998).

Antonello da Messina /ántə néllō daa mə seénə/ (1430?–79) Sicilian painter who was influenced by Flemish realism

Antonescu /ántə nés kyoo, -nés koo/, **Ion** (1882–1946) Romanian general and politician who became prime minister of a pro-German Romanian government in 1940. He was executed for war crimes.

Antoninus Pius /ántə nínəss pī əss/ (AD 86–161) Roman emperor. He succeeded Hadrian and enjoyed a peaceful and prosperous reign (AD 138–161). Full name **Titus Aurelius Fulvus Boionius Arrius Antoninus**

Antonioni /án tōni óni/, **Michelangelo** (*b.* 1912) Italian film director whose films include *L'Avventura* (1960) and *Zabriskie Point* (1970)

'I don't work from a written script. My work begins when I look through the viewfinder of the camera—that for me is the moment of creation.'
[Michelangelo Antonioni, *Interview, Times*; 29 November, 1960]

antonomasia /ántənə máyzi ə/ *n* **1.** the use of a title or formal description such as 'Your Highness' or 'His Excellency' in place of somebody's proper name **2.** the use of a proper name as a common noun to refer to somebody or something with associated characteristics, e.g. when a strong young man is called 'a Hercules' [Mid-16C. < Latin < Greek *antonomazein* 'name instead' < *anti-* 'against, instead' + *onoma* 'name']

Antony /ántəni/, **Mark** (83?–30 BC) Roman politician and general. He fought in Republican Rome's last civil war in alliance with Cleopatra and was defeated by Octavian. Latin name **Marcus Antonius**

antonym /ántənim/ *n* a word that means the opposite of another word. For example 'hot' is the antonym of 'cold'. [Mid-19C. < French *antonyme* < Greek *anti-* 'against, opposite' + *onuma* 'name'] —**antonymous** /an tónnəməss/ *adj*

antra plural of **antrum**

Antrim /ántrim/ **1.** historic town in County Antrim, Northern Ireland. Population: 20,878 (1991). **2.** historic county in Ulster Province, Northern Ireland

Antrim Coast and Glens /-glénz/ Area of Outstanding Natural Beauty in Northern Ireland. Area: 706 sq. km/273 sq. mi.

antrostomy /an tróstəmi/ (*plural* **-mies**) *n* the surgical creation of an opening into an antrum, usually for drainage purposes [< ANTRUM]

antrum /ántrəm/ (*plural* **-tra** /-trə/) *n* a cavity within a bone, especially a sinus cavity [Early 19C. Via Latin, 'cave' < Greek *antron*]

antsy /ántsi/ (**-sier, -siest**) *adj* N Am (*informal*) **1.** feeling nervous, apprehensive, or tense **2.** moving or squirming about in a restless, bored, or impatient way [Mid-20C. Probably < *have ants in your pants*]

Antwerp /án twurp/ leading port of Belgium, situated on the Schelde river estuary 88 km/55 mi. from the sea. Population: 447,632 (1999).

ANU *abbr* Australian National University

~~annual~~ incorrect spelling of **annual**

Anubis /ə nyóobiss/ *n* in Egyptian mythology, a god represented with the head of a jackal, who leads the dead to judgment

anuran /ə nyóorən/ *n* an amphibian such as a frog or toad that does not have a tail as an adult and has long powerful hind legs. Order: Anura. [Late 19C. < modern Latin *Anura* < Greek *an-* 'without' + *oura* 'tail']

anuria /a nyóori ə, ə-/ *n* inability of the kidneys to form urine, so that toxic waste builds up in the blood —**anuric** *adj*

anurous /ánnyŏorəss/ *adj* without a tail

anus /áynəss/ *n* the opening at the lower end of the alimentary canal through which faeces are released [15C. < Latin, 'ring']

Anuszkiewicz /ánnə skáyvich/, **Richard** (*b.* 1930) US artist. A former student of Josef Albers, he is considered one of the major figures of the Op Art movement. His works often feature geometric designs and bold colour blocks in two or, in *Spiral* (1967), three dimensions.

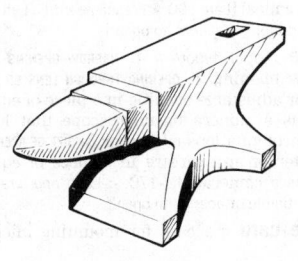

anvil

anvil /ánvil/ *n* **1.** a sturdy piece of iron onto which heated metal is placed to be beaten into the required shape, especially by a blacksmith **2.** ANAT same as **incus** [Old English *anfilte, anfealt* < Indo-European, 'to beat']

anvil technique *n* a prehistoric method of making chipped stone tools that involves striking a stone repeatedly against a static boulder used as an anvil

anxiety /ang zí əti/ (*plural* **-ties**) *n* **1.** FEELING OF WORRY nervousness or agitation, often about something that is going to happen **2.** SOMETHING THAT WORRIES SOMEBODY a subject or concern that causes worry **3.** STRONG WISH TO DO SOMETHING the strong wish to do something, especially if the wish is unnecessarily or unhealthily strong ○ *his anxiety to please* **4.** PSYCHIAT EXTREME APPREHENSION a medical condition marked by intense apprehension or fear of real or imagined danger [Early 16C. < French *anxiété* < Latin *anxius* (see ANXIOUS)]

SYNONYMS See *worry*.

anxiety disorder *n* a psychiatric disorder causing feelings of persistent anxiety, e.g. panic disorder or post-traumatic stress disorder

anxiety neurosis *n* a persistent panic disorder characterized by emotional distress, constant worry, and a strong tendency to avoid specific situations

anxiolytic /ángzi ə líttik/ *adj* relieving anxiety ■ *n* a drug that relieves anxiety [Mid-20C. < ANXIETY + -*lytic*]

anxious /ángkshəss/ *adj* **1.** FEELING NERVOUS worried or afraid, especially about something that is going to happen or might happen **2.** EAGER wanting to do something very much, or in a tense or uneasy way **3.** PRODUCING ANXIETY producing feelings of nervousness or agitation ○ *a few anxious moments* [Early 17C. < Latin *anxius* < *anx-*, past participle of *angere* 'torment', literally 'strangle'] —**anxiously** *adv* —**anxiousness** *n*

any /énni/ CORE MEANING: a grammatical word used to indicate one, some, or several, when the quality, type, or number is not important. It is also used as an intensifier with comparative adjectives and adverbs and a few other words. ○ (det) *Do you have any books on gardening?* ○ (pron) *for any who wish to enter* ○ (adv) *I'm not getting any younger.*
1. *det, pron* EVEN ONE OR LITTLE even one or even the least amount (*used in negative statements*) ○ *I don't want any dessert.* ○ *I didn't see any.* ○ *This isn't any of your business.* **2.** *det, pron* EVERY every person or thing of a particular category or description, no matter who or what ○ *Any financial adviser would agree.* **3.** *det* WITHOUT LIMIT an unlimited or indefinite amount or number of ○ *any number of foods including soups, stews, and salads* **4.** *adv* IN SOME DEGREE to even the smallest extent or degree (*before adjectives and adverbs*) ○ *Is it getting any louder?* ○ *You don't look any different.* **5.** △ *adv* US AT ALL used after a verb to add emphasis (*informal*) ○ *I still don't like him any.* ○ *Her manners haven't improved any.* [Old English *ænig* < Indo-European, 'one of a kind']

USAGE Singular or plural? *Any* used as a pronoun is followed by a singular or plural verb depending on the intended meaning: *Any of these suggestions is acceptable. Are any of the children coming?* [implies more than one of several children] *Is any of the children coming?* [implies that one is expected, with uncertainty as to which].

USAGE Do not use *any old* as an emphatic form of *any* in formal writing: *You can use any* [not *any old*] *glue, provided that it is not soluble in water. Old* should only be added where *old* is meant, as in *Any old rag from the attic will do.*

USAGE American **any**. The use of *any* as an adverb meaning 'at all' is a distinctly American idiom that is not used in British English: *Her manners haven't improved any.*

anybody /énni bodi, -bədi/ *pron* same as **anyone**

USAGE See *anyone*.

anycast /énni kaast/ *n* an act of sending data across a computer network from a single user to the nearest receiver

anyhow /énni how/ *adv* **1.** IN ANY CASE no matter what the situation is or no matter what may be true ○ *What does it matter, anyhow?* **2.** IN CARELESS WAY in a haphazard, careless, or untidy way ○ *ideas produced*

anyhow **3.** NEVERTHELESS in spite of something ○ *I asked him to wait, but he left anyhow.*

any more /énni máwr/ *adv* (*used in negative statements and questions*) **1.** at present and continuing from a point in the past ○ *They don't make them like this any more!* **2.** from the present and ongoing ○ *I'm not tolerating this any more.*

USAGE any more or anymore? In British English, *any more* used as an adverbial phrase after a negative or a question is normally written as two words: *She doesn't live here any more.* In North American English and in some other varieties such as Australian and South African English it is also, though not exclusively, written as one word, **anymore**. There are signs that this is occurring in British contexts too, although it is not standard.

anyone /énni wun/ CORE MEANING: an indefinite pronoun used to mean one or more people, when exactly which person or which people is not known or not important ○ *Can I get anyone more coffee?* ○ *Did anyone show up?* ○ *There isn't anyone at home.*
pron **1.** EVERY PERSON any or every person who could be named or thought of ○ *more qualified than anyone in the business* **2.** EVEN ONE PERSON used to emphasize the unlikelihood of finding even one person to match a description or criteria ○ *Why would anyone want to hurt me?* **3.** UNIMPORTANT PERSON an unimportant and unknown person ○ *It's not just anyone, it's your sister!*

USAGE anyone or any one? *Anyone* is rather more common than *anybody* (which has the same meaning), and is used only of people and after a negative or a question: *Has anyone seen my pen?* The words *any* and *one* are written separately when they mean any one particular person or thing: *Any one of them could have started the fire. The tables are all free, so you can sit at any one you like.*

anyplace /énni playss/ *adv* N Am at, in, or to any place (*informal*)

USAGE American **anyplace** and **anytime**: In British English, **any place** and **any time** are not yet regarded as a unit and are usually spelt as two words in each case, whereas in North American English they are more often spelt as single words and are entered that way in dictionaries: *I don't recall seeing him anyplace. You can come anytime you like.*

anyroad /énni rōd/, **anyroads** /énni rōdz/ *adv* N England anyway

anything /énni thing/ *pron* any object, event, action, situation, or fact ○ *Is there anything I need to know?* ■ *adv* in any way (*used in negative statements and questions*) ○ *He isn't anything like his brother.* ◇ **anything but** used as an emphatic way of contradicting or negating a statement

anytime /énni tīm/ *adv* N Am at some undecided time, or whenever seems convenient or appropriate (*informal*)

USAGE See *anyplace*.

anyway /énni way/ CORE MEANING: an adverb meaning no matter what the situation is ○ *Anyway, we have to pay whether it was accidental or not.* ○ *Recycling, according to some anyway, is the best way of teaching respect for the environment.*
adv **1.** IN ANY CASE no matter what ○ *Don't worry about the damage; I was going to buy a new one anyway.* **2.** REGARDLESS OF SOMETHING in spite of the situation ○ *I knew it would be a sad film but I went anyway.* **3.** IN CARELESS WAY in a careless, haphazard, or lazy way ○ *According to my mother, packing is a skilled operation, not throwing your clothes into a case just anyway.* **4.** *also* **any way** BY ANY MEANS in any manner or way (*informal*) ○ *We have to teach our children moral values anyway we can.*

anyways /énni wayz/ *adv* N Am same as **anyway** (*nonstandard or regional*)

anywear /énni wair/ *n* clothing that can be worn for both casual and more formal occasions (*informal*)

anywhere /énni wair/ CORE MEANING: an indefinite pronoun and adverb referring to one or many places unknown or unspecified ○ (pron-indef) *Is there anywhere you prefer?* ○ (pron-indef) *Anywhere we live now will seem warm.* ○ (adv) *She can sleep anywhere.*
1. *pron* SOME UNIDENTIFIED PLACE one or many places

unknown or unspecified **2.** *adv* **TO ANY PLACE** to one or many places unknown or unspecified ○ *I'll follow you anywhere!* **3.** *adv* **AT OR IN ANY PLACE** in, at, or to any place ○ *We couldn't find her anywhere.* ○ *will live anywhere with a beach* ◇ **anywhere from...to...** used to indicate an approximate measurement of something by giving the smallest and largest possible measurements ○ *weighing anywhere from six to ten pounds*

anywise /énni wīz/ *adv Can, US regional* in any way or in any case (*archaic; usually used in negative statements*)

Anzac /án zak/ *n* **1.** *ANZ* **WORLD WAR I SOLDIER** a soldier who served in the Australian and New Zealand Army Corps in World War I **2.** *Aus* **SOLDIER** any Australian soldier **3.** *Aus* **TYPICAL AUSTRALIAN MAN** a typical Australian man seen as having the courage and spirit shown by the soldiers at Gallipoli in World War I [Early 20C. Acronym]

Anzac biscuit, **anzac biscuit** *n Aus* a biscuit made from wheat flour, oats, coconut, and syrup [< its use by Anzac soldiers in World War I]

Anzac Day *n* in Australia and New Zealand, a public holiday marking the anniversary of the landing of the Australian and New Zealand Army Corps at Gallipoli in 1915 and commemorating all those who have fought in recent times. Date: 25 April.

Anzio /ánzi ō/ port and resort on the western coast of Italy 60 km/37 mi. south of Rome. Heavy fighting occurred there during World War II when Allied forces secured a beachhead in January 1944. Population: 36,952 (2001).

ANZUS /ánzəss/ *n* a defence treaty agreed between Australia, New Zealand, and the United States in 1951. Full form **Australia, New Zealand, & United States**

ao *abbr* Angola (*used in Internet addresses*) See table at **domain name**

AO *abbr* Officer of the Order of Australia

a/o, A/O *abbr* ACCT account of

AOAI *abbr UK* Area of Archaeological Importance

AOB *abbr* any other business

AOC *abbr* appellation d'origine contrôlée

ao dai /ów dī/ *n* a long tunic worn over trousers by Vietnamese women that has a high neck and is slit at both sides below the waist [Mid-20C. < Vietnamese *ào dái* 'long blouse']

A-OK /áy ō káy/, **A-okay** *adj* in excellent condition or working order (*informal*) [Mid-20C. < *all (systems) OK*]

AONB *n* an area of countryside officially designated for the purposes of town and country planning as being special and deserving of protection. Full form **Area of Outstanding Natural Beauty**

AOR *abbr* MUSIC adult-oriented rock

aorist /áy ərist, áirist/ *n* a verb tense used to express a past action in an unqualified way, without specifying whether that action was repeated, continuing, or completed or how long it lasted, found especially in classical Greek [Late 16C. < Greek *aoristos* 'indefinite' < *a-* 'not' + *horistos* 'delimited' < *horizein* 'delimit' (see HORIZON)] —**aoristic** /áy ə rístik, air-/ *adj* —**aoristically** *adv*

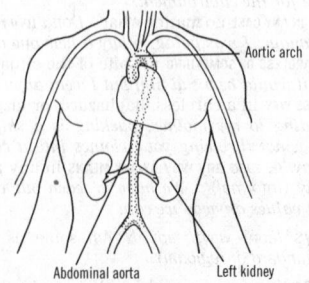

Aortic arch

Abdominal aorta   Left kidney

aorta

aorta /ay áwrtə/ (*plural* **-tas** or **-tae** /-tee/) *n* the main artery in mammals that carries blood from the left ventricle of the heart to all the branch arteries in the body except those in the lungs [Mid-16C. Via modern Latin < Greek *aortē* < *aeirein* 'raise'; perhaps from

the notion that the heart was held up by the aorta] —**aortal** *adj* —**aortic** *adj*

aortic arch *n* **1.** the section of the largest artery (**aorta**) in the body that forms the curve between the ascending and descending parts. As it leaves the heart, the aorta goes upwards and then bends back on itself to form the arch. **2.** a set of paired curved arteries, one of several in the vertebrate embryo that begin in the aorta, rise through the pharynx, and join with the dorsal arterial system

aortic valve *n* the valve in the largest artery (**aorta**) in the body at the point where it leaves the heart. It allows the blood to flow out but not back into the heart.

aortography /áy awr tóggrəfi/ *n* X-ray examination of the largest artery (**aorta**) in the body —**aortographic** /áy awrtə gráffik/ *adj*

Aotearoa /áa ō tee ə rố ə/ *n NZ* Maori name for **New Zealand** (*often used in combination*) ○ *Aotearoa-New Zealand* [< Maori, 'land of the long white cloud', < *ao* 'cloud' + *tea* 'white' + *roa* 'long, tall']

aoudad /ów dad, áa oo dad/ *n* a wild sheep that has long curved horns and a long fringe of hair on the neck and forelegs. Native to: North Africa. Latin name: *Ammotragus lervia*. [Early 19C. Via French < Berber *udád*]

Aouita /ow éetə/, **Said** (*b.* 1960) Moroccan runner who set many world records, including 1,500 and 5,000 metres (1985), 2,000 and 5,000 metres (1987), and 3,000 metres (1989)

AP *abbr* **1.** MIL Air Police **2.** MIL antipersonnel **3.** PUBL Associated Press

a.p. *abbr* **1.** FIN additional premium **2.** PUBL author's proof **3.** PHARM before a meal (*used in prescriptions*)

ap-[1] *prefix* same as **ad-** (*used before p*)

ap-[2] *prefix* same as **apo-** (*used before vowels and h*)

apace /ə páyss/ *adv* **1.** at a good or fast pace **2.** *N Am* at a sufficient rate to keep up with or be alongside somebody or something [14C. < Old French *a pas* 'on step']

Apache /ə páchi/ (*plural same* or **-es**) *n* **1.** a member of a Native North American people who formerly lived throughout the present-day southwestern United States and northern Mexico, but now live in Arizona, New Mexico, and Oklahoma **2.** an Athabaskan language spoken in parts of Arizona, New Mexico, and Oklahoma. Native speakers: 50,000. [Mid-18C. < American Spanish] —**Apache** *adj* —**Apachean** *adj*

~~apalling~~ incorrect spelling of **appalling**

apanage *n* HIST another spelling of **appanage**

~~aparatus~~ incorrect spelling of **apparatus**

~~aparent~~ incorrect spelling of **apparent**

~~aparently~~ incorrect spelling of **apparently**

apart /ə páart/ CORE MEANING: a grammatical word meaning separated in space or time ○ (adv) *scheduled appointments a month apart* ○ (adv) *living apart* ○ (adj) *hard to be apart* ○ (adj) *sitting with legs apart*
1. *adv* **NOT TOGETHER** separated in space or time ○ *She placed the chairs some distance apart.* **2.** *adv* **INTO PIECES** into separate parts or sections ○ *take the machine apart* ○ *pulled the two scuffling children apart* **3.** *adv* **MOVING AWAY AFTER BEING TOGETHER** away from somebody or something after previously being together ○ *We've drifted apart over the years.* **4.** *adv* **REMOVED FROM CONSIDERATION** set aside or excluded from consideration, or taken as an exception ○ *The orange-flowered tie apart, it was a rather smart outfit.* **5.** *adv* **INTO DIFFICULTY** into a bad or difficult condition ○ *ripped the peace process apart* **6.** *adv* **OF SEPARATE KIND** different and consequently separate from others ○ *a world apart* **7.** *adj* **SEPARATED** away from each other in position or location ○ *I think of her all the time we're apart.* [14C. < Old French *a part* 'to the side'] —**apartness** *n* ◇ **apart from 1.** with the exception of somebody or something **2.** in addition to something, or besides something

apartheid /ə páart hayt, -hīt/ *n* a political system in South Africa from 1948 to the early 1990s that separated the different peoples living there and gave privileges to those of European origin [Mid-20C. < Afrikaans, 'separateness' < Dutch *apart* 'separate' < French]

apartment /ə páartmənt/ *n* **1.** *N Am* same as **flat**[2] *n* (sense 1) **2.** a single room in a residential building (*formal*) ■ **apartments** *npl* a suite of adjoining rooms, e.g. an office, entertainment suite, or place to live (*formal*) [Mid-17C. < French *appartement* < Italian *a parte* 'apart', literally 'to the side']

apartment building, **apartment block** *n* a block of flats

apartment complex *n US* a group of several apartment buildings

apathetic /áppə théttik/ *adj* not taking any interest in anything, or not bothering to do anything [Mid-18C. < APATHY, after *pathetic*] —**apathetically** *adv*

SYNONYMS See *impassive*.

apathy /áppəthi/ *n* **1.** lack of interest in anything, or the absence of any wish to do anything **2.** inability to feel normal or passionate human feelings or to respond emotionally [Early 17C. < French *apathie* < Greek *apathēs* 'without feeling' < *pathos* 'feeling']

apatite /áppə tīt/ *n* a glassy, variously coloured calcium phosphate mineral. Use: fertilizers, source of phosphorus. [Early 19C. < Greek *apatē* 'deceit'; from its diversity of form and colour]

apatosaurus /ə páttə sáwrəss/, **apatosaur** /ə páttə sawr/ *n* a large plant-eating dinosaur that lived in North America during the Jurassic period and had a small head, short front legs, and a long neck and tail. Genus: *Apatosaurus.* Former name **brontosaurus** [Late 19C. < modern Latin < Greek *apatē* 'deceit' + *sauros* 'lizard']

APB *abbr* all-points bulletin

ape /ayp/ *n* **1.** **TAILLESS PRIMATE** a tailless primate such as a chimpanzee, gorilla, or orang-utan. Family: Pongidae. **2.** **PRIMATE** a primate of any type (*informal*) **3.** **IMITATOR** an imitator or mimic of somebody or something **4.** *N Am* **CLUMSY PERSON** somebody regarded as clumsy or unintelligent (*informal insult*) ■ *vt* (**apes, aping, aped**) **MIMIC SOMEBODY OR SOMETHING** to act like somebody else in an absurd or grotesque way [Old English *apa* < Germanic] ◇ **go ape** to lose self-control, because of either anger or excitement (*slang*)

SYNONYMS See *imitate*.

apeak /ə peek/ *adj, adv* in a vertical position or direction [Late 16C. < French *à pic* 'at the peak']

~~apear~~ incorrect spelling of **appear**

APEC /áy pek/ *abbr* Asia-Pacific Economic Co-operation

apeman /áyp man/ (*plural* **-men** /-men/) *n* any extinct primate believed to be an ancestor of modern humans (*informal; not in technical use*)

Apennines /áppə nīnz/ mountain range that forms the backbone of peninsular Italy. It extends about 1,290 km/800 mi. from the area north of Genoa to the toe of Italy. The highest peak is Monte Corno 2,912 m/9,554 ft.

aperçu /áppər syoó/ *n* (*formal*) **1.** a revealing glimpse or insight **2.** a concise outline or summary [Early 19C. < French, 'something perceived']

aperient /ə peéri ənt/ *n* a mild laxative [Early 17C. < Latin *aperient-*, present participle of *aperire* 'to open'] —**aperient** *adj*

aperiodic /áy peeri óddik/ *adj* **1.** happening at irregular intervals ○ *aperiodic floods* **2.** describes a mechanical or electrical system that does not exhibit resonance when a periodic disturbance is applied —**aperiodically** *adv* —**aperiodicity** /-ə díssəti/ *n*

aperitif /ə pérrə teéf/ *n* an alcoholic beverage drunk before a meal [Late 19C. < French *apéritif* < Latin *apertus*, past participle of *aperire* 'to open']

aperture /áppər tyoór/ *n* **1.** **NARROW OPENING** a small narrow opening **2.** **OPENING THROUGH LENS OR MIRROR** a fixed or adjustable opening in a piece of equipment such as a camera or microscope that lets light pass through a lens or mirror **3.** **SIZE OF APERTURE** the diameter of an aperture in a piece of equipment such as a camera [Mid-17C. < Latin *apertura* < *apert-*, past participle of *aperire* 'to open']

aperture card *n* a card for mounting microfilmed pages

aperture priority *n* the system in a semiautomatic camera in which the user sets the lens aperture

and the camera then selects the appropriate shutter speed automatically

aperture stop n PHOTOGRAPHY same as **f-stop**

apeshit /áyp shit/ adj an offensive term meaning unreasonably angry or excited (taboo slang)

~~apetite~~ incorrect spelling of **appetite**

apex /áy peks/ (plural **apexes** or **apices** /áypi seez, ápp-/) n 1. HIGHEST POINT the highest point of something 2. MOST SUCCESSFUL POINT the most successful part of something, especially somebody's career or life ○ at the apex of his career 3. TIP OF SOMETHING the tip or top of something, especially something that is pointed, e.g. a triangle [Early 17C. < Latin]

Apex /áy peks/, **APEX** n a system whereby air or rail tickets are available at a reduced price when bought a specific period of time in advance [Acronym < advance-purchase excursion]

Apgar score /áp gaar-/ n a score that is given after assessing the condition of a newborn baby in the five areas of heart rate, breathing, skin colour, muscle tone, and reflex response. Each area has a maximum of two points. [After Virginia Apgar (1909–74), US physician]

aphaeresis /a féerəssiss, ə-/ n the loss of a syllable from the beginning of a word, e.g. in 'coon' for 'raccoon' [Mid-16C. Via late Latin < Greek aphairesis < aphairein 'take away' < hairein 'take'] —**aphaeretic** /áffə réttik/ adj

aphagia /ə fáyji ə/ n the inability or refusal to swallow

aphakia /ə fáyki ə/ n a medical condition in which the internal crystalline lens of the eye is absent [Mid-19C. < A³ + Greek phakos 'lentil', because of the lens's shape]

aphanite /áffə nīt/ n an igneous rock with mineral components that are too fine to be seen by the naked eye [Early 19C. < Greek aphanēs 'unseen' < phan-, stem of phainein (see PHENOMENON)] —**aphanitic** /áffə níttik/ adj

aphasia /ə fáyzi ə, -zhə/ n the partial or total inability to produce and understand speech as a result of brain damage caused by injury or disease [Mid-19C. < Greek < aphatos 'speechless' < phanai 'speak'] —**aphasic** /ə fáyzik/ adj

aphelandra /áffə lándrə/ n an evergreen bush with shiny leaves and brightly coloured flowers, often grown as a houseplant. Native to: tropical America. Genus: Aphelandra.

aphelion /a féeli ən, ap héeli ən/ (plural **-a** /-li ə/) n the point in the orbit of a planet, comet, or other astronomical object that is farthest from the Sun [Mid-17C. < modern Latin aphelium < Greek apo- 'away' + hēlios 'sun'] —**aphelian** adj

apheresis /áffə réessiss/ n 1. the retransfusion of a donor's or patient's own blood from which some constituents have been removed 2. LING same as **aphaeresis** [Variant of APHAERESIS]

aphesis /áffississ/ n the loss of an unstressed vowel at the beginning of a word, e.g. in 'squire' for 'esquire' [Late 19C. < Greek, 'letting go' < aphienai 'send away' < hienai 'send'] —**aphetic** /ə féttik/ adj —**aphetically** adv

aphid /áy fid/ n an insect that has specially adapted mouthparts for piercing and sucking the sap from plants. Many aphids transfer viruses from plant to plant as they feed. Family: Aphididae. [Late 19C. < modern Latin aphid-, stem of Aphis, genus name] —**aphidian** /ə fíddi ən/ adj —**aphidious** /ə fíddi əss/ adj

aphonia /ay fóni ə/ n loss of the power of speech. This may be as a result of injury or disease of the larynx or mouth or may arise from various psychological conditions. [Late 17C. < Greek aphōnos 'having no voice' < phōnē 'sound'] —**aphonic** /áy fónnik/ adj

aphorise vi LANGUAGE another spelling of **aphorize**

aphorism /áffərizəm/ n a succinct statement expressing an opinion or a general truth [Early 16C. < French aphorisme < Greek aphorizein 'define' < horizein 'delimit' (see HORIZON)] —**aphorist** n —**aphoristic** /áffə rístik/ adj —**aphoristically** adv

aphorize /áffə rīz/ (**-rizes, -rizing, -rized**), **aphorise** (**-rises, -rising, -rised**) vi to speak or write using aphorisms

aphotic /ə fóttik/ adj describes those parts of the ocean that are not reached by sunlight, or plants that grow there without photosynthesizing

aphrodisiac /áffrə dízzi ak/ n something that arouses or intensifies sexual desire [Early 18C. < Greek aphrodisiakos 'arousing sexual desire' < aphrodisia 'sexual pleasures' < Aphroditē 'Aphrodite'] —**aphrodisiac** adj —**aphrodisiacal** /áffrədi zī ək'l/ adj

Aphrodite /áffrə dīti/ n in Greek mythology, the goddess of love and beauty. She was the daughter of Zeus. Roman equivalent **Venus**

aphtha /áfthə/ (plural **-thae** /-thee/) n a small white ulcer that appears in groups in the mouth and on the tongue as a result of the fungal condition thrush (technical; usually used in the plural) [Mid-17C. Via Latin < Greek] —**aphthous** adj

Apia /ə pée ə/ capital of Samoa, on northern Upolu Island in the South Pacific Ocean, northeast of Nuku'alofa in Tonga. Population: 35,000 (2000 estimate).

apian /áypi ən/ adj relating to or resembling bees [Early 19C. < Latin apianus < apis 'bee']

apiarist /áypi ərist/ n somebody who keeps bees, often for commercial purposes

apiary /áypi əri/ (plural **-ies**) n a place where beehives are kept and bees are raised for their honey [Mid-17C. < Latin apiarium 'beehive' < apis 'bee'] —**apiarian** /áypi áiri ən/ adj

apical /áppik'l, áy-/ adj 1. situated at the top or tip of something 2. describes a consonant that is pronounced with the tip of the tongue, e.g. 't' or 'd' [Early 19C. < Latin apic-, stem of apex 'apex'] —**apically** adv

apical dominance n the inhibition exerted on the growth of lateral buds by the terminal bud of a growing plant shoot

apical meristem n the zone of actively dividing tissue at the tip of a shoot or root that produces new tissue, mainly to increase length

apices plural of **apex**

apiculate /ə píkyŏŏlət, -layt/ adj describes a leaf that has a short broad tip [Early 19C. < modern Latin apiculus 'little apex' < apic- 'apex']

apiculture /áypi kulchər/ n the keeping of bees, especially for commercial purposes [Mid-19C. < Latin apis 'bee'] —**apicultural** /áypi kúlchərəl/ adj —**apiculturist** /áypi kúlchərist/ n

apiece /ə péess/ adv to or for each one ○ gold watches, from £150 to £550 apiece [Mid-16C. < A⁴ + PIECE]

apish /áypish/ adj 1. silly, ridiculous, or boorish 2. imitating somebody else or somebody's style —**apishly** adv —**apishness** n

aplacental /áyplə sént'l/ adj used to describe mammals such as marsupials that do not develop a placenta

aplanatic /ápplə náttik/ adj describes a lens that does not have, or is corrected for, spherical aberration and so produces a clear undistorted image [Late 18C. < Greek aplanētos 'without error' < planasthai 'wander']

aplasia /ə pláyzi ə/ n the absence or partial development of an organ, part of an organ, or tissue

aplastic /ay plástik/ adj unable to develop new cells or tissue

aplastic anaemia n severe anaemia in which the capacity of bone marrow cells to generate red blood cells is diminished. The condition can be congenital or it can be caused by exposure to radiation, toxic chemicals, or drugs.

aplenty /ə plénti/ adj in large or excessive amounts ○ There are apples aplenty for all of you.

aplite /ápp līt/ n a light-coloured fine-grained igneous rock [Late 19C. < German Aplit < Greek haplous 'single'] —**aplitic** /ə plíttik/ adj

aplomb /ə plóm/ n confidence, skill, and poise, especially in difficult or challenging circumstances [Early 19C. < French à plomb 'perpendicular']

apnea n MED US spelling of **apnoea**

apneusis /ap nyóossiss/ n a form of breathing, caused by brain damage, in which each full inhalation is held for a prolonged period —**apneustic** adj

apnoea /ápni ə, apní ə/ n a temporary suspension or absence of breathing [Early 18C. Via modern Latin < Greek apnoia 'not breathing' < pnein 'breathe']

apo- prefix away from, detached ○ apolune ○ apocarpous [< Greek apo 'off, away' < Indo-European]

Apoc. abbr BIBLE 1. Apocalypse 2. Apocrypha

apocalypse /ə pókə lips/ n 1. the destruction or devastation of something, or an instance of this 2. a revelation concerning the future [13C. Via late Latin < Greek apokalupsis 'revelation' < apokaluptein 'uncover' < kaluptein 'to cover']

CULTURAL NOTE Apocalypse Now, a film (1979) by US director Francis Ford Coppola. This surreal, hallucinatory account of the Vietnam War is based loosely on Joseph Conrad's Heart of Darkness. It follows a US captain on his mission to assassinate a rebel officer, played by Marlon Brando, conducting his own independent war in the heart of the jungle.

Apocalypse n BIBLE same as **Revelation**

apocalyptic /ə pókə líptik/ adj 1. PREDICTING DISASTER warning about a disastrous future or outcome ○ an apocalyptic scenario of global warming 2. INVOLVING DESTRUCTION involving widespread destruction and devastation 3. BIBLE RELATING TO APOCALYPSE relating to the events in the Book of Revelation in the Bible —**apocalyptically** adv

apocarpous /áppə ka'árpəss/ adj describes a flower that has separate carpels [Mid-19C. < APO- + Greek karpos 'fruit'] —**apocarpy** /áppə kaarpi/ n

apochromat /áppə krōmat/ n a lens that is corrected for chromatic aberration by incorporating different types of glass

apochromatic /áppəkrō máttik/ adj describes a lens that has been corrected for chromatic aberration —**apochromatism** /áppə krōmətizəm/ n

apocope /ə pókəpi/ n the loss or omission of one or more sounds from the end of a word, e.g. the shortening of 'margarine' to 'marge' [Mid-16C. Via late Latin < Greek apokopē 'cutting off' < koptein 'to cut'] —**apocopate** vt

apocrine /áppə krīn, -krin/ adj describes glands that secrete part of their secreting cells with the secretory products [Early 20C. < APO- + Greek krinein 'to separate']

apocrypha /ə pókrifə/ n writings or reports that are not regarded as authentic [14C. Via ecclesiastical Latin, < Greek apokruphos 'hidden away' < kruptein 'to hide']

Apocrypha n 1. books of the Bible that are included in the Vulgate and Septuagint versions of the Christian Bible, but not in the Protestant Bible or the Hebrew canon (takes a singular or plural verb) See table at **Bible** 2. a group of Christian writings dating from the early centuries AD that are not included in the Bible

apocryphal /ə pókrif'l/ adj 1. probably not true, but widely believed to be true 2. also **Apocryphal** relating to the Apocrypha —**apocryphally** adv

apodal /ápped'l/, **apodous** /áppədəss/ adj without limbs, feet, or pelvic fins. Eels and snakes are apodal organisms. [Mid-18C. < Greek apod- 'footless' < pous 'foot']

apodictic /áppə díktik/, **apodeictic** /-dík-/ adj demonstrably or indisputably true [Mid-17C. < Latin apodicticus < Greek apodeiknunai 'demonstrate' < deiknunai 'to show' (see DEICTIC)] —**apodictically** adv

apodosis /ə póddəssiss/ (plural **-oses** /-əseez/) n the main clause explaining the consequence in a conditional statement, e.g. 'we can watch the film' in 'If you come early, we can watch the film.' In logic, the apodosis is the 'q' component of propositions of the form 'if p then q'. [Early 17C. < late Latin, < Greek apodidonai 'give back' < didonai (see DOSE)]

apodous adj ZOOL same as **apodal**

apoenzyme /áppō én zīm/ n the inactive protein component of an enzyme that has no physiological effect without attachment of a specific molecule (**coenzyme**)

apogamy /ə póggəmi/ n the development of an embryo without prior fertilization. Apogamy occurs in some ferns, algae, and fungi. —**apogamic** /áppə gámmik/ adj

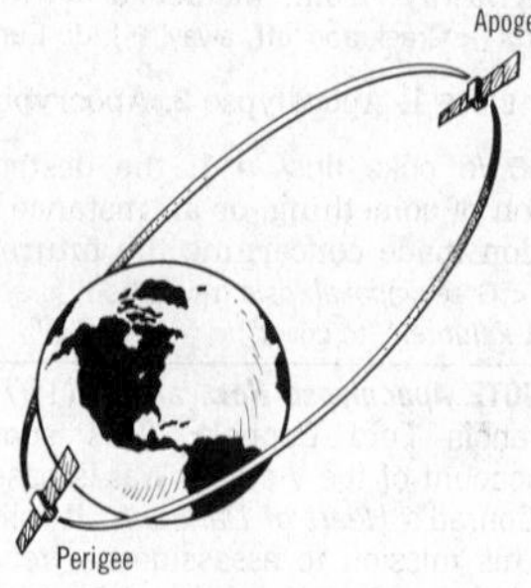

apogee (sense 2)

apogee /áppə jee/ *n* **1.** the best or greatest point **2.** the point at which a satellite orbiting an astronomical object is farthest from the centre of the object being orbited [Late 16C. < French < Greek *apogaios* 'away from the Earth' < *gaia* 'Earth'] —**apogean** /áppə jée ən/ *adj*

apolipoprotein /áppō lípō prō teen/ *n* a protein that combines with a lipid to form a constituent of lipoproteins

apolitical /áypə líttik'l/ *adj* having no interest in politics, or not concerned with politics —**apolitically** *adv*

Apollinaire /ə pólli náir/, **Guillaume** (1880–1918) Italian-born French poet. His verse includes *Les Alcools* (1913) and *Calligrammes* (1918). His play *Les Mamelles de Tirésias* (1917) coined the word 'surrealist'.

> 'A structure becomes architecture and not sculpture when its elements no longer have their justification in nature.' [Guillaume Apollinaire. Quoted in *The Cubist Painters*, L. Abel (tr.); 1944]

Apollo /ə póllō/ *n* **1.** in Greek and Roman mythology, the god of prophecy, sunlight, music, and healing. He was the son of Zeus and Leto, and Artemis was his twin sister. **2. Apollo** (*plural* **-los**), **apollo** a very handsome young man (*literary*) [Via Latin < Greek *Apollōn*] —**Apollonian** /áppə lṓni ən/ *adj*

apologetic /ə póllə jéttik/ *adj* **1.** expressing apology or contrition for something **2.** defending something in speech or writing [Mid-17C. Via French and Latin < Greek *apologētikos* < *apologeisthai* 'speak in your own defence' < *apologia* (see APOLOGY)] —**apologetically** *adv*

apologetics /ə póllə jéttiks/ *n* a branch of theology that is concerned with proving the truth of Christianity (*takes a singular verb*)

apologia /áppə lṓji ə/ *n* a formal, usually written, defence or justification of a belief, theory, or policy (*formal*) [Late 18C. < Latin (see APOLOGY)]

apologise *vi* another spelling of **apologize**

apologist /ə póllәjist/ *n* somebody who defends a doctrine or ideology

apologize /ə póllə jīz/ (**-gizes, -gizing, -gized**), **apologise** (**-gises, -gising, -gised**) *vi* **1. EXPRESS REMORSE FOR SOMETHING** to say that you are sorry for something that has upset or inconvenienced somebody else **2. ACKNOWLEDGE THAT SOMETHING IS NOT IDEAL** to acknowledge that something is not as it should be, especially when you feel embarrassed or guilty about it **3. DEFEND SOMETHING FORMALLY** to defend something formally in writing or speech [Late 16C. < Greek *apologizesthai* < *apologia* (see APOLOGY)] —**apologizer** *n*

apologue /áppə log/ *n* a fable that is intended to teach a moral lesson, especially one that has animals as characters [Mid-16C. Via French or late Latin < Greek *apologos* 'story' < *logos* 'speech' (see LOGOS)]

apology /ə pólləji/ (*plural* **-gies**) *n* **1. STATEMENT EXPRESSING REMORSE** a written or spoken statement expressing remorse for something **2. NOTIFICATION OF NONATTENDANCE AT MEETING** a notification that somebody cannot attend a meeting (*formal*) **3. INFERIOR EXAMPLE** an inferior or bad example of something (*humorous*) ○ *I can't work in this apology for an office!* **4. FORMAL JUSTIFICATION** a formal defence or justification of something [Mid-16C. Via French *apologie* and Latin *apologia* < Greek, 'speech in defence' < *logos* 'speech' (see LOGOS)]

apolune /áppə loon/ *n* the point at which a spacecraft orbiting the moon is farthest from the Moon's centre [Mid-20C. < APO- + Latin *luna* 'moon' (see LUNAR), after APOGEE]

apomictic /áppə míktik/ *adj* describes an organism that reproduces asexually —**apomict** /áppə mikt/ *n* —**apomictically** *adv*

apomixis /áppə míksiss/ *n* asexual reproduction in organisms that are also able to reproduce sexually, in which embryos are formed without fertilization or the creation of specialized reproductive cells [Early 20C. < APO- + Greek *mixis* 'mingling' (see AMPHIMIXIS)]

aponeurosis /áppō nyoo rōssiss/ (*plural* **-roses** /-rō seez/) *n* a broad sheet of fibrous tissue or expanded tendon that joins muscles together or connects muscle to bone [Late 17C. < modern Latin < Greek *aponeurousthai* 'become like a tendon' < *neuron* 'sinew'] —**aponeurotic** /áppō nyoo róttik/ *adj*

apophasis /ə póffəsiss/ *n* the rhetorical device of alluding to something by denying that it will be mentioned, as in 'I shall not bring up the question of age now that you are forty' [Mid-17C. < late Latin < Greek *apophanai* 'deny' < *phanai* 'say' (see -PHASIA)]

apophthegm /áppə them/, **apothegm** *n* a terse saying that embodies an important truth, e.g. 'Haste makes waste' [Mid-16C. < Greek *apophthegma* < *apophtheggesthai* 'speak plainly' < *phtheggesthai* 'speak'] —**apophthegmatic** /áppə theg máttik/ *adj*

apophyge /ə póffəji/ *n* the outward curve at the top of an architectural column where it joins the capital, or at the bottom where it joins the base [Mid-16C. < Greek *apophugē* 'fleeing away' < *pheugein* 'flee']

apophyllite /áppə fíllīt, ə póffi līt/ *n* a white, pale pink, or pale green hydrated silicate mineral containing potassium, calcium, and fluorine [Early 19C. < APO- + Greek *phullon* 'leaf', because it peels when heated]

apophysis /ə póffəsiss/ (*plural* **-yses** /-ə seez/) *n* **1.** a natural swelling or outgrowth on an animal or plant, e.g. a bony protuberance on a vertebra **2.** a small offshoot or network of veins from a large mass of igneous rock such as granite [Late 16C. Via modern Latin < Greek < *apophuein* 'grow out' < *phuein* 'grow'] —**apophysate** *adj* —**apophysial** /ə póffə sée əl/ *adj*

apoplectic /áppə pléktik/ *adj* **1.** overcome with anger **2.** having the symptoms of a stroke (*archaic*) [Early 17C. Via French or late Latin < Greek *apoplēktikos* < *apoplēxia* (see APOPLEXY)] —**apoplectically** *adv*

apoplexy /áppə pleksi/ *n* **1.** a fit of anger **2.** a cerebral stroke, usually caused by a haemorrhage in the brain (*archaic*) [14C. Via French and Latin < Greek *apoplēxia* < *apoplēssein* 'strike completely' < *plēssein* 'to strike']

apoprotein /áppō prō teen/ *n* the protein part of a protein molecule that also contains a nonprotein component

aporia /ə páwri ə/ *n* a confusion in establishing the truth of a proposition [Mid-16C. Via late Latin < Greek < *aporos* 'without passage' < *poros* 'passage' (see PORE[1])] —**aporetic** /áppə réttik/ *adj*

aport /ə páwrt/ *adv, adj* on or towards the left side of a boat as somebody faces forward

aposematic /áppə se máttik/ *adj* describes natural colours and bright markings on an animal that warn predators that it is poisonous ○ *aposematic coloration*

aposiopesis /áppə sī ə péessiss/ (*plural* **-peses** /-pée seez/) *n* a sudden break in speaking, giving the impression that the speaker does not want to or cannot continue, e.g. in the sentence 'On Tuesday morning I came in just as I always do, and I saw – I can't go on' [Late 16C. Via Latin < Greek *aposiōpēsis* < *aposiopan* 'stop speaking' < *siopē* 'silence'] —**aposiopetic** /áppə sī ə péttik/ *adj*

apospory /áppə spawri, ə póspəri/ *n* the process of asexual reproduction in some ferns and mosses without the occurrence of cell division (**meiosis**) or spore formation [Late 19C. < APO- + SPORE + -Y[2]]

apostasy /ə póstəssi/ *n* the renunciation of a religious or political belief or allegiance [14C. Via French < Greek *apostasis* 'standing away' < *histasthai* 'to stand']

apostate /ə pó stayt/ *n* somebody who renounces a belief or allegiance [14C. Via French and Latin < Greek *apostatēs* 'somebody caused to stand away' < *stat-*, related to *histanai* 'cause to stand']

apostatize /ə póstə tīz/ (**-tizes, -tizing, -tized**), **apostatise** (**-tises, -tising, -tised**) *vi* to renounce a religious faith, a political party, a set of principles, or a moral allegiance (*formal*)

a posteriori /áy pos terri áw rī, àa-, -teeri-/ *adj, adv* reasoning from observed facts or events back to their causes [< Latin, 'from what comes later']

apostle /ə póss'l/ *n* **1. PROMOTER OF IDEA OR CAUSE** somebody who tries to persuade others to share an idea or cause ○ *an apostle of free trade* **2. PROMINENT CHRISTIAN MISSIONARY** a prominent Christian missionary, especially one who is responsible for first converting a people **3. MORMON OFFICIAL** a member of the 12-person administrative council of the Church of Jesus Christ of Latter-Day Saints [Pre-12C. Via ecclesiastical Latin *apostolus* < Greek *apostolos* 'somebody sent out' < *stellein* 'send'] —**apostleship** *n*

Apostle *n* any of the 12 followers of Jesus Christ chosen by him to preach the news about Christianity

apostlebird /ə póss'l burd/ *n* a medium-sized grey bird, usually found in small flocks. Native to: Australia. Latin name: *Struthidea cinerea.* [Because they congregate in small flocks]

Apostles' Creed *n* a statement of Christian belief ascribed to the Apostles and dating from around AD 500. It is frequently used in services in Eastern Orthodox, Anglican, and Lutheran churches.

apostle spoon *n* a silver spoon with the figure of an Apostle on the handle. Apostle spoons were traditionally given as presents at baptisms.

apostolate /ə póstə layt/ *n* **1.** the duties or mission of an apostle **2.** a group involved in converting new followers to a religion or doctrine [Mid-17C. < ecclesiastical Latin *apostolatus* < *apostolus* (see APOSTLE)]

apostolic /áppə stóllik/ *adj* **1.** relating to, given by, or on behalf of the pope **2.** relating to the Apostles or their teachings [Mid-16C. Via French and ecclesiastical Latin < Greek *apostolos* (see APOSTLE)] —**apostolical** *adj* —**apostolically** *adv*

apostolic delegate *n* a representative of the pope who is sent to a country that has no formal diplomatic relations with the Vatican

Apostolic Father *n* a Christian church leader of the first or second century AD who was contemporary with or lived shortly after the Apostles

Apostolic See *n* the area of jurisdiction (**see**) of the pope

apostolic succession *n* the doctrine of some Christian denominations that the ordination of bishops follows in an unbroken line of succession from the Apostles, providing the basis of their spiritual authority

apostrophe[1] /ə póstrəfi/ *n* the punctuation mark (') used to show where letters are omitted from a word, to mark the possessive, and sometimes to form the plural of numbers, letters, and symbols [Mid-16C. < French < Greek *apostrophos* 'turned away' < *apostrephein* 'turn away' < *strephein* 'to turn']

USAGE The ***apostrophe*** is used in contractions such as *we've, it's, hadn't, 'em* and some literary words such as *e'en* and *ne'er* to show that a letter or letters have been omitted. Do not confuse the contraction *it's*, meaning *it is* or *it has*, with the possessive *its*, which does not have an apostrophe: *It's* [= it has] *lost all its hair.* When used to mark the possessive form of nouns, the apostrophe is followed by *s* unless the noun is plural and already ends in *s*: *the cat's tail; London's theatres; my children's computer; the companies' accounts; the boys' behaviour.* For singular nouns ending in *s* it is often acceptable to use either *'* or *'s*: *Dickens' best-loved novel* or *Dickens's best-loved novel.* Note that the possessives *its, hers, yours,* and *theirs* do not have an apostrophe. An apostrophe may also be used to indicate relationships of description (*a summer's day*) or measurement (*ten days' absence*). The use of an apostrophe in forming the plural of numbers and letters is optional: *the word has two Ts/T's; in the 1990s/1990's.* However, *'s* is preferable where confusion may arise, especially in showing plural forms of lowercase letters: *dot the i's and cross the t's.*

apostrophe[2] /ə póstrəfi/ *n* a rhetorical passage in which an absent or imaginary person or an abstract or inanimate entity is addressed directly [Mid-16C. Via Latin < Greek *apostrophē* < *apostrephein* (see APOSTROPHE[1])] —**apostrophic** /áppə stróffik/ *adj*

apostrophize /ə póstrə fīz/ (**-phizes, -phizing, -phized**), **apostrophise** (**-phises, -phising, -phised**) *vti* to address

an absent or imaginary person or a personified abstraction

apothecaries' measure *n* a system of liquid measures formerly used in pharmacy

apothecaries' weight *n* a system of weights formerly used in pharmacy and based on a troy ounce equal to 480 grains and a pound equal to 12 ounces

apothecary /ə póthəkəri/ (*plural* **-ies**) *n* (*archaic*) **1.** OCCUPATIONS same as **pharmacist 2.** COMM same as **pharmacy** (sense 2) [14C. Via French < late Latin *apothecarius* 'storekeeper' < Greek *apothēkē* 'storehouse' < *apotithenai* 'put away' < *tithenai* 'put']

apothecium /àppə théessi əm/ (*plural* **-cia** /-si ə/) *n* a disc-shaped or cup-shaped spore-bearing structure found in some fungi, including the fungal component of most lichens [Early 19C. < modern Latin < Greek *apothēkē* (see APOTHECARY)] —**apothecial** *adj*

apothegm *n* LANGUAGE same as **apophthegm**

apotheosis /ə póthi óssiss/ (*plural* **-oses** /-ō seez/) *n* **1.** HIGHEST LEVEL OF GLORY OR POWER the highest point of glory, power, or importance **2.** BEST EXAMPLE OF SOMETHING the best or most glorious example of something ○ *the apotheosis of Romantic music* **3.** TRANSFORMATION INTO DEITY the supposed transformation of a human being into a deity [Late 16C. Via late Latin < Greek *apotheōsis* < *apotheoun* 'make into a god completely' < *theos* 'god']

apotheosize /ə póthi ə sīz/ (**-sizes, -sizing, -sized**), **apotheosise** (**-sises, -sising, -sised**) *vt* **1.** to glorify or exalt somebody or something **2.** to elevate somebody to the status of a deity

apotropaic /àppətrə páy ik/ *adj* intended to ward off evil or bad luck [Late 19C. < Greek *apotropaios* < *apotrepein* 'turn away' < *trepein* 'to turn'] —**apotropaically** *adv* —**apotropaism** *n*

app /ap/ *n* a computer application (*informal*)

app. *abbr* **1.** apparatus **2.** PUBL appendix **3.** applied **4.** appointed **5.** apprentice **6.** approved **7.** approximate

appal /ə páwl/ (**-pals, -palling, -palled**) *vt* to make somebody feel shock, horror, or disgust [Mid-16C. < Old French *apallir* 'grow pale or faint' < *pale* (see PALE [1])]

USAGE Note the spelling with *-pp-* and a single *-l* in the root form, although in American English the usual spelling is **appall**. The verb has the inflected forms **appalled** and **appalling**, with *-ll-*.

Appalachia /àppə láychi ə/ part of the United States that includes the southern Appalachian Mountains, extending roughly from southwestern Pennsylvania through West Virginia and parts of Kentucky and Tennessee to Northwestern Georgia

Appalachian /àppə láychi ən/ *adj* **1.** OF APPALACHIAN MOUNTAINS relating to the Appalachian Mountains **2.** OF APPALACHIA relating to Appalachia, or its people or culture ■ *n* SOMEBODY FROM APPALACHIA somebody who comes from Appalachia in the United States [Late 17C. < *Apalachee*, Native North American people]

Appalachian Mountains /àppə láychi ən-/, **Appalachians** North American mountain system, stretching from southeastern Canada to central Alabama. Major ranges include the White, Green, Catskill, Allegheny, Blue Ridge, Great Smoky, and Cumberland mountains. The highest peak is Mount Mitchell 2,037 m/6,684 ft.

Appalachian Trail *n* a long-distance footpath in the eastern United States, extending about 3,298 km/2,050 mi. from Mount Katahdin in central Maine to Springer Mountain in northern Georgia. It is one of the longest continuous mountain trails in the world.

appall *vt* US spelling of **appal**

appalled /ə páwld/ *adj* feeling or appearing to be shocked by something dreadful or awful ○ *an appalled look*

appalling /ə páwling/ *adj* **1.** causing shock or horror **2.** causing dismay —**appallingly** *adv*

Appaloosa /àppə lóossə/, **appaloosa** *n* a saddle horse with white hair and dark patches, belonging to a breed originating in northwestern North America and formerly much used by Native Americans [Mid-19C. Origin ?]

appanage /áppənij/, **apanage** *n* **1.** a source of revenue set aside for children, especially land given by a sovereign for the maintenance of a younger member of the royal family **2.** something that naturally or usually accompanies something else [Early 17C. < French < medieval Latin *appanare* 'provide with subsistence' < *panis* 'bread']

~~apparantly~~ incorrect spelling of **apparently**

apparat /àppə ráat/ *n* the administrative organization or staff of the Communist Party in the former Soviet Union and other Communist states [Mid-20C. Via Russian < German, 'apparatus']

apparatchik /àppə rátchik, -ráat-/ *n* **1.** a subordinate who is unquestioningly loyal to a powerful political leader or organization **2.** a member of the administrative organization or staff (**apparat**) of the Communist Party in the former Soviet Union and other Communist states [Mid-20C. < Russian]

apparatus /àppə ráytəss, -ráa-, -ráttəss/ (*plural* **-tuses** or *same*) *n* **1.** EQUIPMENT a piece of machinery, a tool, or a device used for a specific purpose ○ *breathing apparatus* **2.** SYSTEM ALLOWING SOMETHING TO FUNCTION the system or structure in which a process occurs or an organization functions ○ *a complex bureaucratic apparatus* **3.** ANAT SYSTEM OF ORGANS a group or system of organs that work together to perform a specific function [Early 17C. < Latin, past participle of *apparare* 'prepare' < *parare* 'prepare']

apparel /ə párrəl/ *n* **1.** CLOTHING clothing, especially outer or decorative clothing (*formal*) ○ *sports apparel* **2.** NAUT SHIP'S EQUIPMENT a ship's gear and equipment ■ *vt* (**-els, -elling, -elled**) CLOTHE SOMEBODY to dress somebody, especially in formal clothes (*archaic*) [13C. < Old French *apareil* 'preparation' < Latin *apparare* (see APPARATUS)]

apparent /ə párrənt/ *adj* **1.** CLEAR clearly seen or understood ○ *From the type of clay used, it's apparent that pottery in Miletus was made locally.* **2.** SEEMING appearing to be shown as a quality, feeling, or attribute but perhaps not genuine ○ *her apparent indifference* **3.** PHYS DIRECTLY OBSERVED BUT NEGLECTING MODIFYING FACTORS directly observed or measured but not taking into account factors or effects that should be allowed for, e.g. distortion caused by the measuring instruments themselves [14C. < Old French *aparant*, present participle of *aparoir* (see APPEAR)]

apparent horizon *n* GEOG same as **horizon** (sense 1)

apparently /ə párrəntli/ *adv* according to what seems to be the case but may not actually be so

apparent magnitude *n* ASTRON same as **magnitude** (sense 6)

apparent wind /-wínd/ *n* a combination of the actual wind and the wind created by a ship's motion

apparition /àppə rísh'n/ *n* **1.** an appearance of a supposed ghost or something ghostly **2.** an appearance of something or somebody unexpected or strange [15C. Directly or via French < Latin *apparition-*, < *apparere* (see APPEAR)] —**apparitional** *adj*

~~appartment~~ incorrect spelling of **apartment**

appassionato /ə pàssyə náa tō/ *adj, adv* to be performed in an impassioned way (*used as a musical direction*) [< Italian, 'impassioned']

appeal /ə péel/ *n* **1.** EARNEST OR URGENT REQUEST an earnest or urgent request to somebody for something ○ *an emotional appeal for forgiveness* **2.** CAMPAIGN TO RAISE MONEY a campaign to raise money or resources ○ *The hospital has launched an appeal for funds.* **3.** ATTRACTION the quality that makes somebody or something pleasant or desirable ○ *The film's appeal lies in its humour and charm.* **4.** FORMAL REQUEST a formal request to a higher authority requesting a change in or confirmation of a decision ○ *An appeal to the boss might solve the matter.* **5.** LAW HEARING OF CASE BEFORE SUPERIOR COURT the hearing by a superior court of part or the whole of a previously tried case, a request for such a hearing, or the right to have such a hearing **6.** CRICKET REQUEST FOR UMPIRE TO DISMISS BATSMAN a verbal request to the umpire to declare a batsman out ■ *v* (**-peals, -pealing, -pealed**) **1.** *vi* EARNESTLY REQUEST SOMETHING to make an earnest or urgent request for something ○ *We are appealing to the public to let us know if they see anything suspicious.* **2.** *vi* REQUEST MONEY to ask for or campaign to raise money or resources ○ *The charity is appealing for books and toys.* **3.** *vi* MAKE FORMAL REQUEST TO SUPERIOR to make a formal request to a higher authority for a change in or confirmation of a decision ○ *You will have to appeal to a senior officer.* **4.** *vi* ATTRACT OR FASCINATE SOMEBODY to be interesting or desirable ○ *Starting up my own business really appeals to me.* **5.** *vti* LAW APPLY TO SUPERIOR COURT FOR HEARING to apply to a superior court for a hearing of the whole or part of a case previously tried in a lower court **6.** *vi* CRICKET ASK UMPIRE TO DISMISS BATSMAN to make a verbal request to the umpire to declare a batsman out **7.** *vi* CHALLENGE UMPIRE'S DECISION to challenge the decision of an umpire or referee [14C. Via Old French *apeler* < Latin *appellare* 'address, entreat', related to *pellere* 'push'] —**appealable** *adj* —**appealer** *n*
◇ **on appeal** at the stage of a court case that involves reconsideration of the decision made at a previous trial

ORIGIN The Latin word *pellere* 'to push', from which ***appeal*** is derived, is also the source of English *compel, dispel, expel, impel, propel, pulse*[1], *push, repeal*, and *repel*.

Appeal Court *n* LAW same as **Court of Appeal**

appealing /ə péeling/ *adj* **1.** having pleasing or attractive qualities **2.** appearing to request help or sympathy ○ *a timid appealing glance* —**appealingly** *adv*

appear /ə péer/ (**-pears, -pearing, -peared**) *v* **1.** *vi* COME INTO VIEW to come into view, or become visible ○ *The main menu will appear whenever you turn on the computer.* **2.** *vi* BEGIN TO EXIST to come into existence ○ *When did this rash appear?* **3.** *vi* BECOME AVAILABLE to become available, especially as a product for sale ○ *Cheaper and better printers have appeared on the market.* **4.** *vti* SEEM LIKELY to seem likely or true ○ *The three men appear to have left the city.* **5.** *vi* BE SEEN IN PUBLIC to come before the public, especially to perform a duty or to act ○ *His dream was to appear on Broadway.* **6.** *vi* LAW BE IN LAW COURT OFFICIALLY to be present in a court of law as a defendant, plaintiff, witness, or legal adviser ○ *due to appear in court next week* **7.** *vi* FORMALLY PRESENT YOURSELF TO SOMEBODY to present yourself formally to somebody after receiving an official request ○ *He was ordered to appear in the district superintendent's office.* [13C. Via Old French *aparoir* < Latin *apparere* 'show, become visible to' < *parere* 'show']

appearance /ə péeranss/ *n* **1.** COMING INTO EXISTENCE the act of emerging, arriving, or coming into existence ○ *the appearance of the first spring flowers* **2.** WAY SOMEBODY OR SOMETHING LOOKS the way somebody or something looks or seems to other people ○ *a youthful appearance* **3.** OUTWARD ASPECT an outward aspect of somebody or something that creates a particular impression (*often used in the plural*) ○ *The place gives the appearance of prosperity.* ○ *Don't be fooled by appearances.* **4.** PERFORMANCE OR EXHIBITION IN PUBLIC a performance or exhibition before a public audience ○ *It was the band's first British appearance.* **5.** ATTENDANCE IN COURT attendance in court as a defendant, plaintiff, witness, or legal adviser ○ *The prospect of an appearance in court was daunting.* ◇ **keep up appearances** to maintain an appearance of wellbeing despite difficulties ◇ **put in an appearance (at something)** to attend something, often only for a short time or to fulfil an obligation

~~appearence~~ incorrect spelling of **appearance**

appease /ə péez/ (**-peases, -peasing, -peased**) *vt* **1.** to say or do something in order to make somebody less angry or aggressive, especially by giving in to demands that have been made **2.** to satisfy a need for something, especially a physical appetite ○ *appeased their thirst with a long cool drink* [14C. < Old French *apaisier* < *pais* 'peace'] —**appeaser** *n*

appeasement /ə péezmənt/ *n* **1.** the political strategy of pacifying a potentially hostile nation in the hope of avoiding war, often by granting concessions **2.** an attempt to stop complaints or reduce difficulties by making concessions

appel /ə pél/ *n* **1.** a stamp of the foot that signals a fencer's intention to start attacking **2.** in fencing, a sharp blow with the blade made to procure an opening [< French, 'call']

appellant /ə péllənt/ *n* a person or group of people in a legal action who bring an appeal [Late 16C. < Old French *apelant*, present participle of *apeler* (see APPEAL)]

appellate /ə péllət/ *adj* having the jurisdiction to hear appeals and review the decisions of lower courts [Mid-18C. < Latin *appellatus*, past participle of *appellare* (see APPEAL)]

appellate court *n* a court with the power to review and reverse the decisions of lower courts

appellate jurisdiction *n* the power vested in an appellate court authorizing it to review the decisions of lower courts

appellation /àppə láysh'n/ *n* the name or title by which something or somebody is known (*formal*) [15C. Via French 'naming' < Latin *appellation-* < *appellare* (see APPEAL)]

appellation contrôlée /àppə lássyoN koN trṓ lay/ (*plural* **appellations contrôlées** /*pronunc. same*/), **appellation d'origine contrôlée** /-dórrijeen-/ (*plural* **appellations d'origine contrôlées**) *n* a certification for French wine that guarantees its origin and verifies that it meets production regulations [< French, 'controlled name (of origin)']

appellative /ə péllətiv/ *n* **1.** same as **appellation** (*formal*) **2.** GRAM same as **common noun** ■ *adj* **1.** connected with a name or title **2.** used as a common noun to describe a class of things —**appellatively** *adv*

append /ə pénd/ (**-pends, -pending, -pended**) *vt* **1.** ADD EXTRA INFORMATION to add extra information to something, especially to a document **2.** ADD AUTHORIZED SIGNATURE to add an authorized signature to a bill or an official agreement as a final part of the ratification or agreement process (*formal*) ○ *All principals to the sale must append their signatures.* **3.** ATTACH SOMETHING to attach or fasten something to something else [Mid-17C. < Latin *appendere* 'hang upon' < *pendere* 'hang']

appendage /ə péndij/ *n* **1.** a body part or organ that projects from the main part of the body, e.g. a tail, wing, or fin **2.** something fastened to something else as a small or secondary attachment ○ *feeling like an appendage of a large company*

appendant /ə péndənt/ *n* **1.** ATTACHMENT something that is attached or added to something larger or more important **2.** LAW SOMETHING ADDED TO LEGAL DOCUMENT a secondary document that is attached to the main body of a legal document, e.g. a codicil altering the terms of a will ■ *adj* ATTACHED attached or added to something larger or more important [Early 16C. < Old French *apendant*, present participle of *apendre* < Latin *appendere* (see APPEND)]

appendectomy /àppən déktəmi/ (*plural* **-mies**), **appendicectomy** /əppəndi séktəmi/ *n* a surgical operation to remove the appendix [Late 19C. < Latin *appendic-*, stem of *appendix* (see APPENDIX)]

appendices ANAT, PUBL plural of **appendix**

appendicitis /ə péndi sītiss/ *n* inflammation of the appendix, causing severe pain

appendicular /àppən díkyŏŏlər/ *adj* **1.** describes body parts that are associated with the limbs ○ *appendicular muscles* **2.** describes the appendix [Mid-17C. < Latin *appendicula* 'small appendix' < *appendix* (see APPENDIX)]

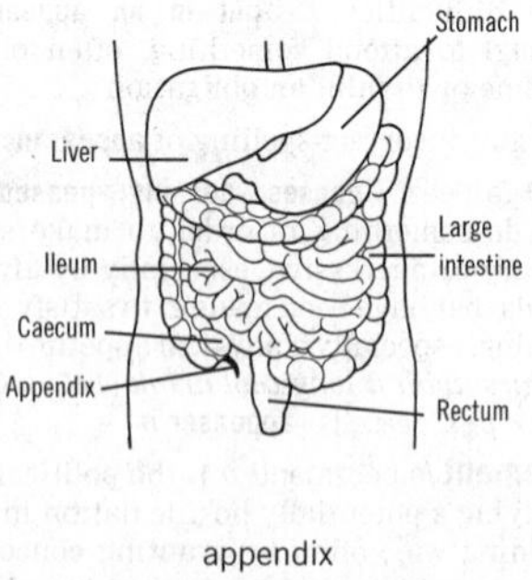

appendix

appendix /ə péndiks/ (*plural* **-dixes** or **-dices** /-di seez/) *n* **1.** SMALL OUTGROWTH FROM LARGE INTESTINE a blind-ended tube leading from the large intestine (**caecum**), near its junction with the small intestine. In humans it is small, occurs in the lower right-hand part of the abdomen, and contains cells of the immune system. **2.** ADDITIONAL INFORMATION a collection of separate material at the end of a book or document **3.** PROJECTING PART a part that projects from something larger [Mid-16C. < Latin < *appendere* (see APPEND)]

apperceive /àppər seév/ (**-ceives, -ceiving, -ceived**) *vt* to comprehend or assimilate something such as a new idea in terms of previous experiences or perceptions [Late 19C. < APPERCEPTION]

apperception /àppər sépsh'n/ *n* the comprehension or assimilation of something such as a new idea, in terms of previous experiences or perceptions [Mid-18C. < modern Latin *apperception-* < Latin *perception-* (see PERCEPTION)] —**apperceptive** *adj*

appertain /àppər táyn/ (**-tains, -taining, -tained**) *vi* to belong or relate to something (*formal*) ○ *another issue that appertains to the policy under discussion* [14C. Via Old French *apartenir* < late Latin *appertinere* 'belong completely to' < *pertinere* 'belong to' (see PERTAIN)]

appestat /áppə stat/ *n* the region of the brain that controls appetite and eating [< APPETITE + -STAT]

appetence /áppətənss/, **appetency** /-tənssi/ (*plural* **-cies**) *n* a desire or longing for something (*technical or literary*) [Early 17C. Via French < Latin *appetentia* < *appetent-*, present participle of *appetere* (see APPETITE)]

appetiser, etc another spelling of **appetizer, etc**

appetite /áppi tīt/ *n* **1.** a natural desire for food **2.** a strong desire or craving for something [14C. Via French < Latin *appetitus* 'desire' < *appetere* 'seek after' < *petere* 'seek' (see PETITION)] —**appetitive** /ə péttitiv/ *adj*

appetizer /áppi tīzər/, **appetiser** *n* **1.** a small dish of food served at the beginning of a meal to stimulate the appetite **2.** a sample of something that is meant to stimulate an interest [Mid-19C. Back-formation < APPETIZING]

appetizing /áppi tīzing/, **appetising** *adj* appealing to or stimulating the appetite [Mid-17C. Anglicization of French *appétissant* < *appétit* (see APPETITE)] —**appetizingly** *adv*

applanation tonometry /àpplə náysh'n tə nómmetri/ *n* a technique for measuring the force per unit area required to flatten the cornea, used in diagnosing glaucoma [< modern Latin *applanare* 'flatten, level' < Latin *planus* 'flat']

applaud /ə pláwd/ (**-plauds, -plauding, -plauded**) *v* **1.** *vti* to clap hands as a sign of welcome, enjoyment, appreciation, or approval **2.** *vt* to praise somebody or something ○ *applauded the students' achievement* [15C. Directly or via French < Latin *applaudere* 'clap at' < *plaudere* 'clap'] —**applaudable** *adj* —**applauder** *n*

applause /ə pláwz/ *n* the clapping of hands as a sign of welcome, enjoyment, appreciation, or approval [Late 16C. < Latin *applausus* < *applaus-*, past participle of *applaudere* (see APPLAUD)]

apple /ápp'l/ *n* **1.** a firm round fruit with a central core, red, green, or yellow skin, and white or yellow flesh **2.** a tree that bears apples. Latin name: *Malus pumila.* [Old English *æppel* < Indo-European] ◇ **she's apples, she'll be apples** *Aus* everything is, or will be, fine ◇ **the apple of somebody's eye** somebody or something very much loved and favoured by another person

apple butter *n* a smooth spread made of stewed apples flavoured with spices

applecart /ápp'l kaart/ *n* in former times, a street vendor's cart or barrow from which apples were sold ◇ **upset the applecart** to spoil a plan or arrangement

apple green *n* a bright yellowish-green colour —**apple-green** *adj*

Apple Isle /ápp'l-/ *n Aus* Tasmania (*informal*) —**Apple Islander** *n*

applejack /ápp'l jak/ *n* **1.** a type of brandy distilled from cider **2.** an alcoholic beverage made from the liquid remaining after cider has been frozen

apple pear *n Can* FOOD, TREES same as **Asian pear**

apple pie *n* a dessert made by cooking sliced apples in a pastry case or in a dish with a pastry top

apple-pie *adj* characteristic of or embodying the virtues that Americans believe to be characteristic of US culture, e.g. neighbourliness, civic pride, and honesty (*informal*) ○ *apple-pie generosity* ◇ **in apple-pie order** neat and tidy

apple-pie bed *n* a way of making a bed with the sheet folded up on itself so that it is impossible to lie full length in the bed [Probably alteration of French *nappe pliée* 'folded sheet']

apples and pears *npl Cockney* stairs (*informal*) [Rhyming slang]

apple sauce *n* a sauce of sweetened stewed apples, traditionally served with roast pork

applet /ápplit/ *n* **1.** a simple computer program that performs a single task, run from within a larger application **2.** a small piece of computer code, often embedded in a webpage, that is transferred over the Internet and executed by the recipient's computer [Late 20C. < APPLICATION + -LET]

Appleton /ápp'ltən/, **Edward Victor** (1892–1965) British physicist. He discovered the F region of ionized gas in the upper atmosphere.

Appleton layer *n* METEOROL same as **F region**

appliance /ə plī́ ənss/ *n* **1.** an electrical device or machine that is used for a specific purpose in the home, e.g. a vacuum cleaner or washing machine **2.** EMERGENCIES same as **fire engine** **3.** the act of putting something into effect

applicable /ə plíkəb'l, ápplikəb'l/ *adj* affecting, connected with, or relevant to a person, group of people, or situation [Mid-16C. < French < Latin *applicare* (see APPLY)] —**applicability** /ə plíkə bílləti, àpplikə-/ *n* —**applicably** /ápplikəbli/ *adv*

applicant /ápplikənt/ *n* somebody who has formally applied for something such as a job, a grant of money, or a place at a university [Early 19C. < Latin *applicant-*, present participle of *applicare* (see APPLY)]

SYNONYMS See *candidate*.

application /àppli káysh'n/ *n* **1.** FORMAL REQUEST FOR SOMETHING a formal and usually written request for something such as a job, a grant of money, or a place at a university **2.** USE OF SOMETHING the use something is put to or the process of putting it to use **3.** RELEVANCE the relevance or value that something has, especially when it is applied to a specific field or area ○ *the industrial applications of biochemical research* **4.** SPREADING LIQUID ON SURFACE the act of spreading a liquid such as paint or medicine on a surface **5.** HARD WORK concentration and hard work **6.** COMPUTER SOFTWARE a computer program or piece of software designed to perform a specific task [15C. Via French < Latin *application-* < *applicare* (see APPLY)]

application service provider *n* a company that provides one or more program functions such as accounting on behalf of an enterprise, freeing it to concentrate on its primary business

applicative /ə plíkətiv/ *adj* capable of being applied [Mid-17C. < Latin *applicat-* (see APPLICATOR)] —**applicatively** *adv*

applicator /áppli kaytər/ *n* a device used to apply a liquid or powder to a surface [Mid-17C. < Latin *applicat-*, past participle of *applicare* (see APPLY)]

applicatory /ə plíkətəri/ *adj* easily or suitably applied [Mid-17C. < Latin *applicat-* (see APPLICATOR)]

applied /ə plī́d/ *adj* able to be put to practical use, especially as a branch of a subject that has both practical and theoretical aspects

appliqué /ə pleé kay/ *n* shaped pieces of fabric sewn on a foundation fabric to form a design or pattern [Mid-18C. < French, 'applied'] —**appliqué** *vt*

apply /ə plī́/ (**-plies, -plying, -plied**) *v* **1.** *vi* FORMALLY REQUEST SOMETHING to make a formal, usually written, request for something ○ *How do I apply for the job?* **2.** *vt* USE SOMETHING to make use of something to achieve a result ○ *applied his first-aid skills to help the accident victims* **3.** *vi* BE RELEVANT to be relevant to somebody or something ○ *The requirement applies only if you are over 65.* **4.** *vt* SPREAD SOMETHING to spread a liquid or other material over a surface ○ *Apply a thin layer of cream to the face and neck.* **5. apply yourself** *vr* WORK HARD to work hard or spend a significant amount of time on something ○ *I could have done better if I'd applied myself a bit more.* [14C. Via Old French *aplier* < Latin *applicare* 'fold towards' < *plicare* 'to fold' (see PLY²)] —**applier** *n*

appoggiatura /ə pójjə tóorə/ (*plural* **-ras** or **-re** /-ray/) *n* in music, an ornamental dissonant note resolving, usually downwards by a step, into a principal note [Mid-18C. < Italian, 'something supported by another']

appoint /ə póynt/ (**-points, -pointing, -pointed**) *vt* **1.** SELECT SOMEBODY FOR POSITION OR JOB to select a person or a group of people for an official position or to do a job ○ *She's been appointed director.* **2.** AGREE ON TIME OR PLACE to fix or agree on a time or place for something to happen (*formal*) **3.** LAW EMPOWER TRUSTEE to authorize a trustee to transfer trust property to beneficiaries [14C. < Old French *apointier* 'arrange, settle' < *a point* 'to a point'] —**appointee** /ə póyn teé/ *n* —**appointer** *n*

appointed /ə póyntid/ *adj* **1.** previously agreed on ○ *met at the appointed time* **2.** decorated, furnished, or equipped (*usually used in combination*) ○ *a well-appointed flat*

appointive /ə póyntiv/ *adj* **1.** describes trust property that is managed by a trustee with the power to transfer it to beneficiaries ○ *legally sufficient to dispose of the appointive property* **2.** *N Am* describes a position to which somebody is appointed rather than elected ○ *an appointive board*

appointment /ə póyntmənt/ *n* **1. ARRANGEMENT TO MEET SOMEBODY** an arrangement to have a meeting or be somewhere at a specific time **2. CHOICE OF SOMEBODY FOR JOB** the selection of somebody for a position, office, or job **3. POSITION OR JOB** a position, office, or job to which somebody is appointed **4. SOMEBODY APPOINTED TO JOB** somebody who has been appointed to a position, office or job **5.** LAW **SELECTION OF TRUSTEE** the selection of a trustee to whom power is given to transfer trust property to beneficiaries ■ **appointments** *npl* **FURNITURE AND FITTINGS** the furniture, fittings, and equipment belonging to a place

appointment book *n US* same as **diary** (sense 3)

appointor /ə póyntər/ *n* somebody responsible for selecting a trustee to supervise and transfer trust property

~~**appologize**~~ incorrect spelling of **apologize**

~~**appology**~~ incorrect spelling of **apology**

apport /ə páwrt/ *n* **1.** the production of objects at a spiritualist's seance, supposedly by paranormal means **2.** an object produced at a spiritualist's seance, supposedly by paranormal means [15C. < French *aport* 'bringing to' < *aporter* 'carry to' < *porter* 'carry']

apportion /ə páwrsh'n/ (**-tions, -tioning, -tioned**) *vt* to divide and allocate something among different people or groups [Late 16C. Directly or via French < medieval Latin *apportionare* < Latin *portion-* (see PORTION)]

apportionment /ə páwrsh'nmənt/ *n* **1.** the division and allocation of something among different people or groups **2.** *US* the distribution of seats in the US House of Representatives or a state legislature, based proportionally on the population of states or electoral districts

appose /ə pṓz/ (**-poses, -posing, -posed**) *vt* to be placed near something, or place or move something next to something else (*formal*) [Late 16C. < Latin *apponere* (see APPOSITE), after COMPOSE and EXPOSE]

apposite /áppəzit/ *adj* especially well suited to the circumstances [Early 17C. < Latin *appositus*, past participle of *apponere* 'add to, put near' < *ponere* 'put' (see POSITION)] —**appositely** *adv* —**appositeness** *n*

apposition /áppə zísh'n/ *n* **1. JUXTAPOSITION** the relative position of two things that are next to each other **2.** GRAM **RELATIONSHIP BETWEEN NOUN PHRASES** the relationship between two usually consecutive nouns or noun phrases that refer to the same person or thing and have the same relationship to other sentence elements. In the sentence 'My son, an actor, lives with me', the phrase 'My son, an actor' is an example of apposition. **3.** PHYSIOL **CELL GROWTH IN LAYERS** cell growth in which layers of material are deposited on existing ones —**appositional** *adj* —**appositionally** *adv*

appositive /ə pózzətiv/ *adj* describes words or phrases that refer to the same person or thing and have the same relationship to other sentence elements —**appositive** *n* —**appositively** *adv*

appraisal /ə práyz'l/ *n* **1.** a judgment or opinion on something or somebody, especially one that assesses effectiveness or usefulness **2.** an estimate of how much money something is worth, especially one given by an expert

appraise /ə práyz/ (**-praises, -praising, -praised**) *vt* **1. VALUE SOMETHING** to make or give an estimate of how much money something is worth **2. ASSESS MERITS OR QUALITY** to form or give an opinion of somebody's merits or something's quality **3.** HR **ASSESS FORMALLY** to make a formal assessment of an employee's performance following an agreed set of criteria [15C. Alteration of APPRIZE, after PRAISE] —**appraisable** *adj* —**appraisement** *n* —**appraiser** *n*

USAGE appraise or **apprise**? ***Appraise***, meaning 'to evaluate', is used with reference to people or (more usually) the things they do or achieve: *She appraised their work at the end of each week.* ***Apprise***, meaning 'to inform', is a more formal word, and is used with reference to people: *He apprised them of the decisions.*

appreciable /ə préeshəb'l/ *adj* large or important enough to be noticed ○ *There is no appreciable difference between them.* —**appreciably** *adv*

appreciate /ə préeshi ayt/ (**-ates, -ating, -ated**) *v* **1.** *vt* **FEEL GRATITUDE** to feel grateful for something ○ *I'd appreciate it if you didn't repeat this to anyone.* **2.** *vt* **VALUE SOMEBODY OR SOMETHING HIGHLY** to recognize and like the qualities in somebody or something ○ *I don't feel appreciated.* **3.** *vt* **UNDERSTAND SOMETHING** to understand fully the meaning or significance of a situation ○ *I hadn't appreciated how upset he felt.* **4.** *vt* **ACKNOWLEDGE SOMETHING** to accept something as valid ○ *We appreciate that these people have rights as well.* **5.** *vi* **GAIN IN VALUE** to increase in value, especially over time [Mid-17C. < late Latin *appretiare* 'value, estimate, rate, appraise' < *pretium* 'money spent, worth, value']

USAGE Opinions on ***appreciate*** vary widely. Some people, explaining that the word's history has to do with accurate valuation, consider that it should be used only in neutral contexts (*I appreciate your position*). Others, pointing out that ***appreciation*** is admiration or gratitude, say that it should be used only in favourable contexts (*I appreciate your frankness*). Still others argue that the object of this verb should always be a noun (*I appreciate your annoyance*), not a clause (*I appreciate how angry you must feel*). Certainly it is worth remembering the verb's continuing ties to the ideas of valuation and gratitude, and worth remembering, too, that no one objects to *recognize*, *realize*, or *understand* in negative contexts or before clauses.

appreciation /ə préeshi áysh'n/ *n* **1. GRATEFULNESS** a feeling or expression of gratitude ○ *a token of my appreciation* **2. POSITIVE OPINION** a favourable opinion of something ○ *clapped and cheered their appreciation* **3. VALUING SOMETHING HIGHLY** recognition and liking of something's qualities ○ *a course in music appreciation* **4. STATEMENT OF PRAISE** a written or spoken statement of somebody's qualities **5. FULL UNDERSTANDING** a full understanding of the meaning and importance of something ○ *an appreciation of our funding problems* **6. GROWTH IN VALUE** an increase in value, especially over time ○ *the rapid appreciation of property*

appreciative /ə préeshi ətiv, -shətiv/ *adj* expressing or feeling gratitude or approval —**appreciatively** *adv* —**appreciativeness** *n*

apprehend /áppri hénd/ (**-hends, -hending, -hended**) *vt* **1. ARREST SOMEBODY** to take somebody suspected of wrongdoing into legal custody **2. UNDERSTAND SOMETHING** to grasp the importance, significance, or meaning of something **3. BECOME AWARE OF SOMETHING** to become aware of something by use of the senses (*formal*) **4. BE FEARFUL OF SOMETHING** to await an impending disaster or other calamity with fear or dread (*formal*) [14C. Directly or via French < Latin *apprehendere* 'take hold of' < *prehendere* 'seize']

apprehensible /áppri hénssəb'l/ *adj* capable of being understood

apprehension /áppri hénsh'n/ *n* **1. DREAD** a feeling of anxiety or fear that something bad or unpleasant will happen **2. IDEA** an idea formed by observation or experience **3. ARREST** the taking of a criminal suspect into custody (*formal*) **4. ABILITY TO UNDERSTAND** the power or ability to grasp the importance, significance, or meaning of something (*formal*) [14C. Directly or via French < late Latin *apprehension-* < Latin *apprehens-*, past participle of *apprehendere* (see APPREHEND)]

apprehensive /áppri hénssiv/ *adj* **1.** worried that something bad will happen **2.** aware or cognizant of something nonphysical such as implications or results (*formal*) —**apprehensively** *adv* —**apprehensiveness** *n*

apprentice /ə préntiss/ *n* **1. TRAINEE** somebody being trained by a skilled professional in an art, craft, or trade **2. INEXPERIENCED PERSON** a novice or amateur ■ *vt* (**-tices, -ticing, -ticed**) **TAKE ON SOMEBODY AS TRAINEE** to give somebody work as an apprentice to a skilled professional ○ *apprenticed to an electrician* [14C. < Old French *aprentis* < *aprendre* 'learn' < Latin *apprehendere* (see APPREHEND)] —**apprenticeship** *n*

SYNONYMS See ***beginner***.

appressed /ə prést/ *adj* describes a part of a plant that is pressed closely against another part without being joined to it ○ *appressed leaves* [Late 18C. < Latin *appressus*, past participle of *apprimere* 'press to' < *premere* 'press']

apprise /ə prīz/ (**-prises, -prising, -prised**) *vt* to inform or give notice to somebody about something (*formal*) [Late 17C. < French *appris*, past participle of *apprendre* 'make learn, teach' (see APPRENTICE)]

USAGE See ***appraise***.

apprize /ə prīz/ (**-prizes, -prizing, -prized**) *vt* to value something very highly, e.g. because of its monetary worth (*archaic*) [15C. Via Old French *aprisier* < Latin *appretiare* (see APPRECIATE)]

appro /áprō/ *n* (*informal*) [Late 19C. Shortening] ◇ **on appro** on approval

approach /ə prṓch/ *v* (**-proaches, -proaching, -proached**) **1.** *vti* **MOVE CLOSER** to move closer to somebody or something ○ *He motioned to us to approach.* **2.** *vt* **ASK SOMEBODY** to speak to somebody with a view to asking for something ○ *approached me about volunteering* **3.** *vt* **TREAT SOMETHING IN PARTICULAR WAY** to deal with something in a particular way ○ *Try approaching the article from a fresh angle.* **4.** *vt* **COME CLOSE TO BEING SOMETHING** to be almost at a particular level or state ○ *statements approaching libel* **5.** *vti* **COME CLOSER IN TIME** to come nearer in time to something ○ *As spring approaches I notice people smiling more.* **6.** *vi* GOLF **HIT BALL TOWARDS GREEN** in golf, to make a shot from the fairway towards a green ■ *n* **1. COMING NEARER** a coming nearer in space or time **2. METHOD** a way of doing or solving something ○ *an incremental approach to reform* **3. REQUEST OR PROPOSAL** an informal request, offer, suggestion, or proposal made to somebody (*often used in the plural*) ○ *had several approaches from Hollywood agents* **4. APPROXIMATION** one thing that is very similar in its nature or qualities to another ○ *an approach to an apology* **5. ACCESS** a way of reaching or gaining access to a building or place **6.** AVIAT **COURSE OF LANDING AIRCRAFT** the path that an aircraft follows as it prepares to land **7.** GOLF **SHOT TOWARDS GREEN** in golf, a shot made from the fairway towards a green **8.** BOWLING **MOVEMENT TO RELEASE BALL** in bowling, the steps a bowler takes before releasing the ball, or the part of the bowling lane used for doing this [14C. Via Old French *aproch(i)er* < late Latin *appropiare* 'go nearer to' < *prope* 'near']

approachable /ə prṓchəb'l/ *adj* **1. INVITINGLY FRIENDLY** friendly and easy to talk to **2. EASILY ACCESSIBLE** able to be reached with ease, especially in terms of transportation **3. USER-FRIENDLY** easy for nonspecialists to understand —**approachability** /ə prṓchə bílləti/ *n* —**approachableness** *n* —**approachably** *adv*

approaching /ə prṓching/ *adj* coming near in space or time

approach shot *n* **1.** in tennis, a shot hit deep into the opponent's court, designed to give the player time to approach the net for the next shot **2.** GOLF same as **approach** *n* (sense 7)

approbation /áppra báysh'n/ *n* **1.** a favourable opinion about something or somebody **2.** the official approving, authorizing, or sanctioning of something —**approbative** /áppra baytiv/ *adj* —**approbatory** *adj*

~~**approch**~~ incorrect spelling of **approach**

appropriacy /ə prṓpri əssi/ *n* the precise suitability of a word to its context

appropriate *adj* /ə prṓpri ət/ **FITTING** suitable for the occasion or circumstances ■ *vt* /ə prṓpri ayt/ (**-ates, -ating, -ated**) **1. TAKE SOMETHING FOR OWN USE** to take something that belongs to or is associated with somebody else for yourself, especially without permission ○ *She soon appropriated the role of chief confidante.* **2. USE MONEY FOR PURPOSE** to set aside an amount of money for a particular use [15C. < Latin *appropriatus*, past participle of *appropriare* 'make your own' < *propius* 'own'] —**appropriable** *adj* —**appropriately** *adv* —**appropriateness** *n* —**appropriator** *n*

appropriation /ə prṓpri áysh'n/ *n* **1.** the taking of something that belongs to or is associated with somebody else, especially without permission **2.** a sum of money that has been set aside from a budget,

especially a government budget, for a specific purpose (*often used in the plural*)

approval /ə pro͞ov'l/ *n* **1.** a favourable opinion or feeling about something **2.** formal or official agreement or permission ◇ **on approval** with the opportunity to try something before deciding whether you really want to buy it

approve /ə pro͞ov/ (**-proves, -proving, -proved**) *v* **1.** *vi* to have a favourable opinion of somebody or something **2.** *vt* to give formal confirmation that something is satisfactory [14C. Via Old French < Latin *approbare* 'assent to as good' < *probus* 'good'] —**approvable** *adj* —**approved** *adj* —**approving** *adj* —**approvingly** *adv*

approved school *n* a reform school or detention centre for young offenders (*dated*)

approx. *abbr* **1.** approximate **2.** approximately

approximal /ə próksim'l/ *adj* used to describe teeth that are side by side or set close together

approximate *adj* /ə próksimət/ **1.** NEARLY EXACT not quite exact, but only slightly more or less in number or quantity ○ *giving an approximate value* **2.** SIMILAR similar in nature, appearance, or characteristics to something else ○ *gives you an approximate idea* ■ *v* /ə próksi mayt/ (**-mates, -mating, -mated**) **1.** *vti* BE SIMILAR to be or become similar to something in nature, size, or extent ○ *There was nothing in the terms of the treaty that even approximated to the negotiators' original thinking.* **2.** *vt* ESTIMATE SOMETHING to make or provide an estimate, usually a rough estimate, of something **3.** *vti* COME OR BRING CLOSE to come or bring something close to something else [15C. < late Latin *approximatus*, past participle of *approximare* 'draw near to' < Latin *proximus* 'near'] —**approximateness** *n* —**approximation** /ə próksi máysh'n/ *n* —**approximative** *adj*

approximately /ə próksimətli/ *adv* not exactly, but nearly or roughly

~~**approximatly**~~ incorrect spelling of **approximately**

appt *abbr* appointment

appulse /ə púlss/ *n* a near approach of two astronomical objects that does not result in a partial concealment or an eclipse [Early 17C. < Latin *appulsus*, past participle of *appellere* 'drive to, force towards' < *pellere* 'drive']

appurtenance /ə púrtinənss/ *n* **1.** ACCESSORY an accompanying part or feature of something (*formal*; *often used in the plural*) ○ *an athletic club with all the usual appurtenances* **2.** LAW PROPERTY RIGHT a legal right or privilege attached to a property and inherited with it ■ **appurtenances** *npl* EQUIPMENT the equipment needed for an activity (*formal*) [14C. < Anglo-Norman < late Latin *appertinere* (see APPERTAIN)] —**appurtenant** *adj*

APR *abbr* FIN **1.** annual percentage rate **2.** annual purchase rate (*used to show repayment rates in hire-purchase schemes*)

Apr. *abbr* April

apraxia /ay práksi ə, ə-/ *n* the inability to perform complex movements, often as a result of brain damage, e.g. following a stroke [Late 19C. Via German < Greek, 'inaction'] —**apraxic** *adj*

~~**apreciate**~~ incorrect spelling of **appreciate**

après /ápppray/ *prep* after an activity [Mid-20C. < French, 'after']

après-ski /ápray skee/ *n* social activities taking place after skiing ■ *adj* taking place during or appropriate to the period of time after skiing [Mid-20C. < French, 'after skiing']

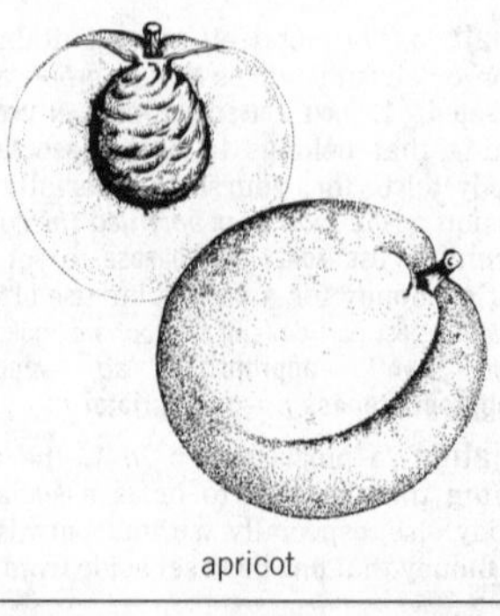

apricot

apricot /áypri kot/ *n* **1.** FRUIT a small round fruit with a soft furry yellowish-orange skin and a single stone **2.** FRUIT TREE a fruit tree that produces apricots. Latin name: *Prunus armeniaca*. **3.** YELLOWISH-ORANGE COLOUR a pale yellowish-orange colour [Mid-16C. Via obsolete Catalan *abrecoc* < Arabic *al-barqūq* 'the apricot'] —**apricot** *adj*

ORIGIN The ***apricot*** got its name because the Romans regarded it as a type of early ripening peach. They therefore applied to it the epithet *praecocus* (a variant of *praecox*, from which English gets *precocious*). This passed via Byzantine Greek *berikokkia* into Arabic where, with the definite article *al*, it became *al-birqūq* or *al-barqūq*. Catalan adopted this as *abrecoc*, which is how English acquired the word (the earliest recorded English spelling is *abrecock*). The final *-t* came soon after, from French.

April /áyprəl/ *n* in the Gregorian calendar, the fourth month of the year, lasting 30 days. See table at **calendar** [14C. < Latin *Aprilis* < Etruscan *apru* < Greek *Aphrō*, shortening of *Aphroditē* 'Aphrodite']

April fool *n* **1.** JOKE a practical joke played on somebody on April Fools' Day **2.** TARGET OF JOKE the target of a practical joke on April Fools' Day ■ *interj* REVEALING JOKE used to tell somebody that he or she has been the target of an April Fools' Day joke

April Fools' Day *n* a day on which practical jokes are played on people. Date: 1 April.

a priori /áy prī áwrī, àa pri áwri/ *adj* **1.** working from something that is already known or self-evident to arrive at a conclusion **2.** known or assumed without reference to experience [Mid-17C. < Latin, 'from the previous (one, cause, hypothesis)'] —**a priori** *adv* —**apriority** /-órrəti/ *n*

apron /áyprən/ *n* **1.** PROTECTIVE GARMENT TIED OVER CLOTHES a garment worn over the front of clothes to keep them clean during working, especially cooking **2.** AVIAT PARKING AREA FOR PLANES the surfaced area immediately in front of airport buildings, on which aircraft are loaded and unloaded **3.** PROTECTIVE PART a shield or plate fitted to a machine that protects the user from flying debris **4.** PROJECTING EDGE the projecting edge of a platform such as a theatre stage, dock, or loading bay **5.** GOLF BORDER AROUND GREEN in golf, the outer edge of a putting green **6.** BOXING AREA OUTSIDE BOXING RING in boxing, the part of the floor of a boxing ring that is outside the ropes **7.** GEOG LOW-ANGLED SURFACE a gently sloping surface of sand, gravel, or bare rock, usually in front of a mountain range **8.** MANUF CURVING CONVEYOR BELT a conveyor belt made of slats loosely attached to each other in a way that allows the belt to go around curves **9.** ENG same as **skirt** *n* (sense 4) [14C. < Old French *naperon* 'small cloth' < *nape* 'tablecloth' < Latin *mappa* 'napkin'; by interpreting 'a napron' as 'an apron']

apron strings *npl* the strings that secure an apron ◇ **be tied to somebody's apron strings** to be dependent on and controlled by a woman, especially a wife or mother

apropos /áprə pṓ/ (*formal*) *prep* WITH REGARD TO on the subject of ○ *We've had further correspondence from them apropos our application for funds.* ■ *adj* JUST RIGHT appropriate in a specific situation ■ *adv* INCIDENTALLY by the way ○ *Apropos, do you think we should delay the announcement?* [Mid-17C. < French *à propos* 'to the purpose']

~~**apropriate**~~ incorrect spelling of **appropriate**

aprotic /ay prṓtik/ *adj* describes a solvent that is unable to donate protons [Mid-20C. < A-^{2} + PROTON]

aprotinin /ay prṓtinin/ *n* a polypeptide obtained from animal organs. Use: treatment of pancreatitis.

~~**aproximately**~~ incorrect spelling of **approximately**

apse /aps/ *n* **1.** a semicircular projecting part of a building, especially the east end of a church, which contains the altar **2.** ASTRON same as **apsis** (sense 1) [Early 19C. < Latin *apsis* (see APSIS)]

apsidal /ap sīd'l, ápsid'l/ *adj* **1.** relating to the apse of a building **2.** relating to an apsis or the apsides of an orbit [Mid-19C. < Latin *apsid-*, stem of *apsis* (see APSIS)]

apsis /ápsiss/ (*plural* **-sides** /-si deez/) *n* **1.** either of the two points in an orbit that are nearest to and farthest from the centre of gravitational attraction **2.** BUILDINGS same as **apse** (sense 1) [Late 16C. Via Latin < Greek *(h)apsis* 'rim of a wheel, wheel, arch, vault']

apt /apt/ *adj* **1.** VERY APPROPRIATE especially suited to the circumstances ○ *an apt comment* **2.** LIKELY often doing something and likely to do it again ○ *apt to get angry* **3.** QUICK TO LEARN enthusiastic and quick to learn new things ○ *an apt pupil* [14C. Directly or via Old French < Latin *aptus*, past participle of *apere* 'fit, fasten, join'] —**aptly** *adv* —**aptness** *n*

ORIGIN The Latin word *apere* 'to fit, fasten', from which ***apt*** is derived, is also the source of English *adapt*, *attitude*, and *inept*. Its Indo-European ancestor is in turn the source of English *copulate* and *couple*.

APT *abbr* advanced passenger train

apt. *abbr* apartment

apteral /áptərəl/ *adj* **1.** describes a classical temple that has no columns along its sides **2.** describes a church that has no aisles [Mid-19C. < Greek *apteros* 'wingless' < *pteron* 'wing, feather']

apterous /áptərəss/ *adj* describes an insect that has no wings [Late 18C. < Greek *apteros* (see APTERAL)]

aptitude /ápti tyood/ *n* **1.** a natural tendency to do something well, especially one that can be further developed ○ *a natural aptitude for teaching* **2.** quickness and ease in learning

SYNONYMS See ***ability*** and ***talent***.

aptitude test *n* a test to determine whether somebody is likely to be able to develop the skills required for a specific kind of work

Apuleius /áppyoo lée əss/, **Lucius** (AD 125?–200?) Numidian-born Roman philosopher and writer. His most famous work, the satirical *Metamorphoses* or *The Golden Ass*, influenced many later writers including Boccaccio and Henry Fielding.

Apus /áypəss/ *n* a faint constellation near the south celestial pole. See illustration at **constellation**

apyrase /áppə rayz, -rayss/ *n* an enzyme that aids the breakdown of ATP, producing energy [Mid-20C. Contraction of *adenypyrophosphatase*]

apyrexia /áypī réksi ə, áppī-/ *n* absence of fever, or a period during which a patient experiences no fever [Mid-17C. Via modern Latin < Greek *apurexia* < *purexis* (see PYREXIA)] —**apyretic** *adj* —**apyrexial** *adj*

aq *abbr* Antarctica (*used in Internet addresses*) See table at **domain name**

AQ *abbr* EDUC achievement quotient

aq. *abbr* **1.** PHARM aqua **2.** GEOL, CHEM aqueous

Aqaba, Gulf of /ákəbə/ northeastern arm of the Red Sea, bordered by Egypt's Sinai Peninsula on the east, Israel on the north, and Saudi Arabia on the west. It is of great strategic importance, as it provides Israel with its only access to the Red Sea. Length: 160 km/99 mi.

Aqmola /aak mṓlə/ former name for **Astana** (1991–98)

aqua /ákwə/ *n* **1.** COLOURS same as **aquamarine** (sense 2) **2.** water, especially when used in the pharmaceutical industry as a solvent (*technical*) [14C. < Latin, 'water'] —**aqua** *adj*

aqua- *prefix* water ○ *aquanaut* [< Latin *aqua*]

aquacrop /ákwə krop/ *n* a crop produced by cultivating organisms that live in the sea or fresh water, e.g. fish produced by fish-farming [Late 20C. < AQUACULTURE + CROP]

aquaculture /ákwə kulchər/, **aquiculture** /ákwi-/ *n* **1.** the farming of sea and freshwater plants and animals for human consumption **2.** BOT same as **hydroponics** [Mid-19C. After AGRICULTURE] —**aquacultural** /ákwə kúlchərəl/ *adj* —**aquaculturist** *n*

~~**aquaduct**~~ incorrect spelling of **aqueduct**

aquadynamic /ákwə dī námmik/ *adj* having a smooth or streamlined surface in order to reduce drag when passing through water [Late 20C. After AERODYNAMIC]

aquaerobics *n* FITNESS same as **aquarobics**

~~**aquaint**~~ incorrect spelling of **acquaint**

~~**aquaintance**~~ incorrect spelling of **acquaintance**

aqualung /ákwə lung/ *n* an underwater breathing apparatus used by divers

aquamarine /ákwə mə réen/ *n* **1.** a precious stone that is a greenish-blue variety of beryl. Use: gems. **2.** a greenish-blue colour [Late 16C. < Latin *aqua marina* 'sea water'] —**aquamarine** *adj*

aquanaut /ákwə nawt/ *n* somebody with training and equipment to spend long periods working or swimming underwater [Late 19C. < AQUA- + Greek *nautēs* 'sailor', after ARGONAUT]

aquaphobia /ákwə fṓbi ə/ *n* an irrational fear of water

aquaplane /ákwə playn/ *n* WATER-SKIING BOARD a water-skiing board on which somebody stands while being towed by a motorboat ■ *vi* (**-planes, -planing, -planed**) **1.** RIDE ON AQUAPLANE to be towed by a motorboat on an aquaplane **2.** LOSE CONTROL IN WET CONDITIONS to skid out of control at high speed on a surface that is so wet that it causes the vehicle's tyres to lose contact with the road. N Am term **hydroplane**

aqua regia /-reêji ə/ *n* a fuming, highly corrosive mixture of nitric and hydrochloric acids. Use: dissolving gold and other metals. [Early 17C. < Latin, 'royal water'; because it can dissolve 'noble' metals]

aquarelle /ákwə rél/ *n* **1.** a painting technique that uses transparent washes of watercolour **2.** a painting produced using the aquarelle technique [Mid-19C. Via French < obsolete Italian *acquarella* 'watercolour' < *acqua* 'water'] —**aquarellist** *n*

aquaria plural of **aquarium**

aquarist /ákwərist/ *n* somebody who looks after an aquarium as a hobby or a profession

aquarium /ə kwáiri ə/ *n* (*plural* **-iums** or **-ia** /-ri ə/) *n* **1.** a water-filled transparent container, often box-shaped, in which fish and other water animals and plants are kept **2.** a building in which fish and other water animals are kept and shown to the public [Mid-19C. < Latin *aquarius* (see AQUARIUS) after VIVARIUM]

Aquarius /ə kwáiri əss/ *n* **1.** CONSTELLATION IN SOUTHERN HEMISPHERE a zodiacal constellation of the southern hemisphere between Pisces and Capricornus. See illustration at **constellation 2.** 11TH SIGN OF ZODIAC the 11th sign of the zodiac, represented by a man pouring water, and lasting from approximately 20 January to 18 February. Aquarius is classified as an air sign and its ruling planets are Saturn and Uranus. **3.** SOMEBODY BORN UNDER AQUARIUS somebody whose birthday falls between 20 January and 18 February [14C. < Latin, 'water carrier' < *aquarius* 'of water' < *aqua* 'water'] —**Aquarian** *n* —**Aquarius** *adj*

aquarobics /ákwə rṓbiks/, **aquaerobics** /ákwair-/ *n* aerobic exercises done to music in a swimming pool (*takes a singular or plural verb*) [Late 20C. Blend of AQUA- + AEROBICS]

aquatic /ə kwáttik/ *adj* **1.** OF WATER connected with, consisting of, or dependent on water **2.** LIVING IN WATER living or growing in water **3.** DONE IN WATER played or performed in or on water ○ *aquatic sports* ■ *n* WATER PLANT OR ANIMAL a plant or animal that lives or grows in water —**aquatically** *adv*

aquatics /ə kwáttiks/ *n* sports played in or on water (*takes a singular or plural verb*)

aquatint /ákwə tint/ *n* **1.** a method of etching a copper plate in which the prints produced from it resemble watercolours in the shading of different areas **2.** an etching produced by the aquatint process [Late 18C. Via French *aquatinte* < Italian *acquatinta* 'tinted water'] —**aquatinter** *n* —**aquatintist** *n*

aquavit /ákwəvit/, **akvavit** /ákvəvit/ *n* a potato- or grain-based spirit flavoured with caraway seeds, produced in Scandinavia [Late 19C. Via Danish, Norwegian, Swedish *akvavit* < Latin *aqua vitae* 'water of life']

aqua vitae /ákwə ví tee, -veé tī/ *n* a strong spirit, especially brandy [14C. < Latin, 'water of life']

aqueduct: ancient Roman aqueduct in Tarragona, Spain

Barnaby's

aqueduct /ákwi dukt/ *n* **1.** STRUCTURE CARRYING CANAL a structure in the form of a bridge that carries a canal across a valley or river **2.** CHANNEL FOR WATER a pipe or channel for moving water to a lower level, often across a great distance **3.** ANAT CHANNEL CARRYING FLUID IN BODY a channel in an organ or body part through which fluid passes [Mid-16C. Via medieval Latin *aqueductus* < Latin *aquae ductus* 'water conveyance']

aqueous /áykwi əss, ákwi-/ *adj* **1.** containing, dissolved in, or consisting mostly of water **2.** describes rocks or deposits that are formed from material carried by water [Mid-17C. < medieval Latin *aqueus* < Latin *aqua* 'water']

aqueous humour *n* the transparent fluid that circulates in the eye chamber between the back of the cornea and the front of the iris and pupil and permeates the vitreous humour behind the lens

aqui- *prefix* water ○ *aquifer* [< Latin *aqua*]

aquiclude /ákwi klood/ *n* a layer of rock, sediment, or soil through which ground water cannot flow [Late 20C. < AQUI- + EXCLUDE]

aquiculture *n* AGRIC same as **aquaculture**

aquifer /ákwifər/ *n* a layer of permeable rock, sand, or gravel through which ground water flows, containing enough water to supply wells and springs

Aquila /ákwilə, ə kwíllə/ *n* a constellation near the celestial equator containing the bright star Altair. See illustration at **constellation**

aquilegia /ákwi leéji ə/ *n* (*plural* **-as** or *same*) *n* a perennial plant with leaves that have five rounded lobes. Flowers: drooping, purple, pink, blue, or red, on tall stalks. Genus: *Aquilegia*. N Am term **columbine** [Late 16C. < medieval Latin]

aquiline /ákwi līn/ *adj* **1.** thin, curved, and pointed like an eagle's beak ○ *an aquiline nose* **2.** resembling or connected with eagles [Mid-17C. < Latin *aquilinus* < *aquila* 'eagle'] —**aquilinity** /ákwi línnəti/ *n*

Aquinas /ə kwínəss/, **Thomas, St** (1225–74) Italian philosopher and theologian. He sought to reconcile the philosophy of Aristotle with the theology of St Augustine.

> 'Whatever is in motion must be moved by something else. Moreover, this something else...must itself be moved by something else, and that in turn by yet another thing...So we reach a first mover which is not moved by anything. And this all men think of as God.'
> [Thomas Aquinas, *Summa Theologica*; 1266–73]

Aquino /ə keénō/, **Corazón** (*b.* 1933) Filipino politician. She was president of the Philippines (1986–92) after the uprising against Ferdinand Marcos. Born **Maria Corazón Cojuangco**

> 'One must be frank to be relevant.'
> [Corazón Aquino, chiding the UN for its non-support of the opposition to the Ferdinand Marcos regime; 22 September 1986]

~~**aquire**~~ incorrect spelling of **acquire**

~~**aquit**~~ incorrect spelling of **acquit**

Aquitaine /ákwi tayn/ region of southwestern France. It includes the departments of Dordogne, Gironde, Landes, Lot-et-Garonne, and Pyrénées-Atlantiques. It corresponds roughly to the Roman administrative region of Aquitania. Capital: Bordeaux. Population: 2,908,359 (1999). Area: 41,309 sq. km/15,949 sq. mi.

~~**aquittal**~~ incorrect spelling of **acquittal**

aquiver /ə kwívvər/ *adj* quivering, especially from excitement or agitation

Ar *symbol* CHEM ELEM argon

AR *abbr also* **A/R** account receivable

ar. *abbr* **1.** arrival **2.** arrive

Ar. *abbr* **1.** Arabia **2.** Arabian **3.** Arabic

-ar *suffix* of, relating to, or resembling ○ *nebular* [Via Old French *-ar* < Latin *-aris*, alternative for *-alis*]

Ara /áarə/ *n* a faint constellation of the southern hemisphere lying in the Milky Way near Scorpius. See illustration at **constellation**

ARA *abbr* Associate of the Royal Academy

ara-A /árrə áyl/ *n* PHARM same as **vidarabine** [Late 20C. < contraction of *arabinoside* (< ARABINOSE) + A[1] (sense 2)]

Arab /árrəb/ *n* a member of a Semitic Arabic-speaking people who live throughout North Africa and Southwest Asia ■ *adj* PEOPLES same as **Arabian** [14C. Via French and Latin < Greek *Arab-* < Arabic *arab*]

USAGE Arab, Arabic, or **Arabian?** *Arab* denotes a person, and is also used before nouns as a modifier (*the Arab world*; *Arab customs*). *Arabian* is an adjective referring to *Arabia* in geographical terms (*the Arabian Peninsula*). *Arabic* is a noun and an adjective meaning the language of the *Arab* people (*She speaks Arabic and knows Arabic literature*). *Arabic* is written with a capital initial letter in *Arabic numerals* (1, 2, 3, etc.), and with a small initial letter in the term *gum arabic*, a substance obtained from African acacia trees.

Arab. *abbr* **1.** Arabia **2.** Arabian **3.** Arabic

arabesque /árrə bésk/ *n* **1.** ORNATE DESIGN an intricate and often symmetrical design incorporating curves, geometric patterns, leaves, flowers, and animal shapes **2.** BALLET FORMAL POSE OF BALLET DANCER a ballet position in which the dancer stands on one leg with the other extended back and both arms stretched out, usually one forwards and the other backwards **3.** MUSIC CLASSICAL MUSIC WITH ORNATE MELODY a piece of classical music characterized by decorative melodies, especially one written for solo piano [Early 17C. Via French < Italian *arabesco* 'in the Arabian style']

Arabia /ə ráybi ə/, **Arabian Peninsula** peninsula of Southwest Asia, bordering the Persian Gulf, the Arabian Sea, and the Red Sea. It includes the nations of Saudi Arabia, Yemen, Oman, the United Arab Emirates, Qatar, Kuwait, and the island state of Bahrain. Area: 3,000,000 sq. km/1,158,306 sq. mi.

Arabian /ə ráybi ən/ *adj* relating to Arabia, or its peoples or cultures ■ *n* **1.** somebody who comes from a country of the Arabian Peninsula **2.** BREED same as **Arabian horse**

USAGE See *Arab*.

Arabian camel *n* ZOOL same as **dromedary**

Arabian Desert /ə ráybi ən-/ mountainous dry region of eastern Egypt, between the Nile and the Red Sea. Area: 225,000 sq. km/86,870 sq. mi.

Arabian Gulf same as **Persian Gulf**

Arabian horse *n* a horse belonging to a breed known for its intelligence, graceful build, and speed. Native to: Arabia.

Arabian Peninsula ♦ Arabia

Arabian Sea part of the Indian Ocean, extending from the Arabian Peninsula to South Asia

Arabic /árrəbik/ *n* SEMITIC LANGUAGE a Semitic language that is the official language of several countries of North Africa and Southwest Asia. Native speakers: 150 million. Other speakers: 175 million. See panel on next page ■ *adj* **1.** OF ARABIA relating to Arabia, or its peoples, language, or cultures **2.** OF ARABIC relating or belonging to the language Arabic

USAGE See *Arab*.

arabica /ə rábbikə/ *n* **1.** a widely grown species of coffee bush producing high-quality coffee. Latin name: *Coffea arabica*. **2.** coffee made with arabica coffee beans [Early 20C. < modern Latin, 'Arabic']

Arabicize /ə rábbi sīz/ (**-cizes, -cizing, -cized**), **Arabicise** (**-cises, -cising, -cised**) *v* **1.** *vt* to adapt a word or other language feature for use in Arabic **2.** *vti* same as **Arabize** —**Arabicization** /ə rábbi sī záysh'n/ *n*

Arabic numeral *n* a symbol of the type 0, 1, 2, 3, 4, 5, 6, 7, 8, and 9 that is used to represent a number

arabinose /ə rábbinōz, -nōss/ *n* a sugar (**aldose**) derived from various plant gums. Use: biological culture medium. Formula: $C_5H_{10}O_5$. [Late 19C. < GUM ARABIC + -IN + -OSE[1]]

Arabise *vti* another spelling of **Arabize**

Arabism /árrəbism/ *n* **1.** ARAB IDENTITY Arab cultural identity **2.** ARAB NATIONALISM support for Arab causes or political positions **3.** ARABIC EXPRESSION an Arabic word or phrase

Arabist /árrəbist/ *n* **1.** a student of or expert on the Arabs, their language, or their culture **2.** somebody who favours Arab causes or political positions

Arabize /árrə bīz/ (**-izes, -izing, -ized**), **Arabise** (**-ises, -ising, -ised**) *vti* to conform, or make something

LANGUAGE HERITAGE ***Arabic*** Much of English is made up of words from other languages, and Arabic is an important contributor in this respect. Arabic is an intermediate, direct, or ultimate ancestor of many English words opening with *al-*, where the definite article in Arabic becomes a formative element in English and in other languages, for example Spanish, Portuguese, Latin, French, and Italian, through which many Arabic words transited into English. Among these borrowings are, for example, ***albatross*** (ultimately from Arabic *al-ġaṭṭās* 'the diver'), ***alcaide*** ('the commander'), ***alcazar*** ('the castle'), ***alchemy***, ***alcohol***, ***alcove***, ***alembic***, ***alfalfa*** ('the best kind of fodder'), ***algebra***, and ***alkali***.

Arabic is also the direct or ultimate source of some very common English words, for example ***ghoul***, ***sash*** (from Arabic *šāš* 'muslin'), ***candy*** (via French), ***cotton*** (via French), ***lemon*** (via French), ***lime*** (via French and Spanish), ***giraffe*** (via French or Italian, both words from Arabic *zarāfa*), ***magazine*** (via French and Italian), and ***zero*** (via French and Italian, ultimately from Arabic *ṣifr* 'emptiness', the source of English ***cipher***).

Another émigré with an interesting history is ***mohair***. Going back in English to the late 16th century, it was respelt from *mocayre* because English speakers, unfamiliar with *-ayre*, likened it to *hair*, a familiar English form, which they substituted for *-ayre*, in a process called 'folk etymology'. *Mocayre* is ultimately from Arabic *mukayyar* 'cloth of goat's hair', literally 'select, choice', the past participle of the Arabic verb *kayyara* 'prefer'.

Arabic has also been an intermediate transport medium in migrations of words from other languages into English. For instance, ***sugar***, first recorded in English in the 13th century, came into English via an early form of French *sucre*, which itself came via medieval Latin from Arabic *sukkar*, and finally from Sanskrit *śarkarā* 'grit, ground sugar'. ***Elixir*** entered English in the 14th century via medieval Latin from Arabic *al-iksir*, from Greek *xērion* 'dry powder for treating wounds', from *xēros* 'dry'.

Arabic occasionally combines with English to yield compound words, for example ***seif dune***, first recorded in English in the early 20th century, denoting an enormous desert dune formed in parallel ridges, *seif* coming from Arabic *sayf* 'sword'. Some Arabic borrowings have taken on English affixes: ***jihadist***, ***Islamism***, and ***Islamize*** are examples.

English also contains a number of direct borrowings from Arabic: for example ***hashish*** (16th century, from *ḥašīš* 'dry herb, powdered hemp', also the source of English ***assassin***), ***fatwa*** (early 17th), ***shrub***, a fruit-and-alcohol drink (early 18th), ***loofah*** (late 19th), and ***intifada*** (late 20th, from *intifāḍa* 'a shaking off').

Apart from other direct borrowings readily recognizable as Arabic émigrés, for example ***falafel***, ***kebab***, ***imam***, ***madrasa***, and ***wadi***, a few derive from placenames. For example, ***saluki***, the name of a breed of dog, going back in English to the early 19th century, comes from Arabic *salūķī*, from *Salūk*, a town in Yemen. And ***tabby***, the fabric and striped pattern of cat's fur, first recorded in the late 16th century, came into English via French *tabis* from Arabic *'attābī*. It was named after *al-'Attābiyya*, a quarter of Baghdad, Iraq, where the fabric, originally with stripes, was made.

conform, to Arab customs or culture —**Arabization** /àrrə bī záysh'n/ *n*

arable /árrəb'l/ *adj* **1. SUITABLE FOR GROWING CROPS** describes land that can be cultivated for growing crops **2. RELATING TO LARGE-SCALE CULTIVATION** relating to, involving, or produced by the large-scale cultivation of field crops such as cereals and potatoes ■ *n* **LAND SUITABLE FOR CULTIVATION** land that is fit for planting crops [15C. Via French < Latin *arabilis* < *arare* 'to plough'] —**arability** /àrrə bíllәti/ *n*

Arab League *n* a political and economic association of Arab states, formed in 1945

Araby /árrəbi/ *n* Arabia (*archaic or literary*) [12C. < Old French *ar(r)abi* 'Arabian', probably < Arabic *arab* 'Arab']

aracari /àrrə saári, àrrə kaári/ (*plural* **-ris** or *same*) *n* a toucan that has a long, slim, gently curved beak with serrated edges. Native to: South America. Genus: *Pteroglossus*.

arachidonic acid /àrrəkə dónnik-/ *n* an essential fatty acid found in most animal fats that is a precursor of prostaglandins [< modern Latin *arachid-* 'peanut' (< Greek *arakhos* 'type of leguminous plant') + -ONE]

arachis oil /árrəkiss-/ *n* FOOD same as **peanut oil**

arachnid /ə ráknid/ *n* an animal with four pairs of legs and a body with two segments, belonging to a large class that includes spiders, scorpions, and mites. Class: Arachnida. [Mid-19C. < modern Latin *Arachnida* < Greek *arakhnē* 'spider, spider's web'] —**arachnidan** *adj*

arachnodactyly /ə ráknō dáktəli/ *n* a condition characterized by unusually long fingers and toes

arachnoid /ə rák noyd/ *n* **1.** ANAT the middle of the three membranes that envelop the brain and spinal cord **2.** ZOOL same as **arachnid** ■ *adj* ZOOL resembling or related to an arachnid [Mid-18C. Via modern Latin < Greek *arakhnoeidēs* 'like a spider's web' < *arakhnē* 'spider's web']

arachnology /àrrak nólləji/ *n* the branch of zoology concerned with the study of spiders and other arachnids [Mid-19C. < Greek *arakhnē* 'spider'] —**arachnologist** *n*

arachnophobia /ə ráknə fóbi ə/ *n* an unusually strong fear of spiders [Early 20C. < Greek *arakhnē* 'spider'] —**arachnophobe** /ə ráknəfōb/ *n* —**arachnophobic** *adj*

Arafat /árrə fat/, **Yasir** (*b.* 1929) president of the Palestinian National Authority (1996–). He became chairman of the Palestine Liberation Organization (1968) and shared the Nobel Peace Prize with Itzhak Rabin and Shimon Peres (1994).

Arafura Sea /àrrə fóorə-/ area of the Pacific Ocean between the northern coast of Australia, New Guinea, and eastern Indonesia

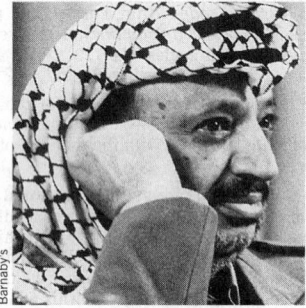

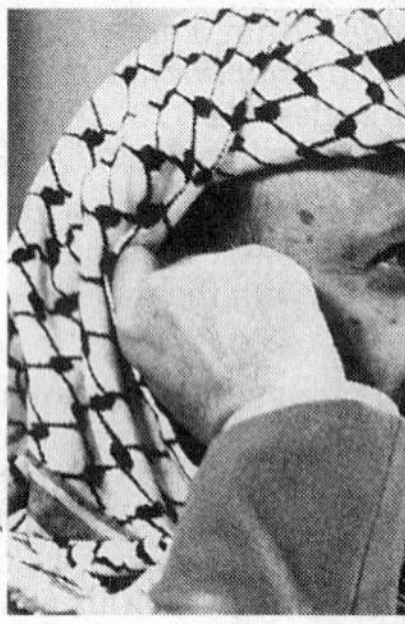
Barnaby's

Yasir Arafat

Aragon /árrə gon/, **Louis** (1897–1982) French writer who wrote surrealist texts and cofounded the magazine *Littérature* with André Breton. He also wrote social realistic novels (1933–51).

> 'The function of genius is to furnish cretins with ideas twenty years later.'
> [Louis Aragon, 'La Porte-plume (The Pen)', *Traité du style (Treatise on Style)*; 1928]

Aragón /árrə gon, ara gón/ autonomous region and former kingdom in northeastern Spain. It contains the provinces of Huesca, Zaragoza, and Teruel. Capital: Zaragoza. Population: 1,188,817 (1991). Area: 47,669 sq. km/18,405 sq. mi.

aragonite /ə rággə nīt/ *n* a colourless, blue to violet, or yellow mineral consisting of calcium carbonate [Late 18C. After *Aragón*]

aralia /ə ráyli ə/ (*plural* **-as** or *same*) *n* a plant widely grown as a houseplant for its ornamental leaves. Genera: *Aralia* or *Polyscias*. [Mid-18C. < modern Latin]

Aral Sea /árrəl-/ inland sea straddling the Kazakhstan-Uzbekistan border in Central Asia, east of the Caspian Sea. Area: 31,220 sq. km/12,050 sq. mi.

Aram /áirəm/, **Eugene** (1704–59) English scholar who explored possible links between Celtic and Indo-European languages. He was hanged for murder.

Aramaic /àrrə máy ik/ *n* a Semitic language of the ancient Near East, dating from about 300 BC and still spoken in the region. Native speakers: 50,000–100,000. [Mid-19C. < Greek *Aramaios* 'of Aram' (ancient Syria)] —**Aramaic** *adj*

Aran /árrən/ *adj* describes a traditional style of heavy knitted garments made from thick unbleached wool with complex cable patterns [Mid-20C. After the ARAN ISLANDS]

Aranda *n, adj* PEOPLES, LANG same as **Arrernte**

Aran Islands /árrən-/ group of three islands, Inishmoor, Inishmaan, and Inisheer, situated at the mouth of Galway Bay in western Ireland. Population: 1280 (2002). Area: 47 sq. km/18 sq. mi.

Arapaho /ə ráppəhō/ (*plural same* or **-hos**) *n* **1.** a member of a Native North American people who formerly lived on the Great Plains, and now live in Colorado, Wyoming, and Montana **2.** an Algonquian language of western North America. Native speakers: 1,500. [Early 19C. < Crow *alappahó* 'many tattoo marks'] —**Arapaho** *adj*

Ararat, Mount /árrə rat/ mountain in eastern Turkey, which rises in two peaks, Great Ararat 5,137 m/16,854 ft and Little Ararat 3,914 m/12,840 ft. According to the Bible, it was the landing place of Noah's Ark.

Araucanian /àrraw káyni ən/ *n* **1.** a member of a Native South American people who live in central Chile and western Argentina **2.** a South American language spoken in parts of Chile and western Argentina. Native speakers: 300,000. [Early 19C. < Spanish *Araucanía*, region of Chile] —**Araucanian** *adj*

araucaria /àrraw káiri ə/ (*plural* **-as** or *same*) *n* an evergreen coniferous tree with stiff sharp leaves. Monkey puzzle is a species of araucaria. Native to: southern hemisphere. Genus: *Araucaria*. [Mid-19C. < modern Latin < *Arauco*, province in Chile]

Arawak /árrə wak/ (*plural same* or **-waks**) *n* **1.** a member of a Native South American people who live in Guyana, Suriname, and French Guiana **2.** a South American language of the Arawakan family, spoken in Guyana and neighbouring countries [Mid-18C. < Carib *aruac*] —**Arawak** *adj*

Arawakan /àrrə wákən/ *n* a family of Native South American languages, spoken by widely scattered peoples in South America. Native speakers: 300,000. —**Arawakan** *adj*

arb /aarb/ *n* FIN same as **arbitrageur** (*slang*) [Late 20C. Shortening]

arbalest /aárbəlist, -lest/, **arbalist** /-list/ *n* a large medieval crossbow used to propel stones, arrows, and other missiles [Pre-12C. Via Old French *arbaleste* < late Latin *arcuballista* < *arcus* 'bow' + *ballista* (see BALLISTA)] —**arbalester** /-lestər/ *n*

arbiter /aárbitər/ *n* **1. SOMEBODY MAKING JUDGMENT** somebody who can settle a dispute or decide an issue **2. INFLUENTIAL PERSON** somebody with great influence over what people say, think, or do **3.** LAW **SCOTTISH JUDGE OF DISPUTE** in the Scottish legal system, somebody designated to hear both sides of a dispute and make a judgment [14C. Directly or via French < Latin, 'judge, umpire'] —**arbitral** *adj*

arbitrage /aárbitrij, -traazh/ *n* the simultaneous buying and selling of the same negotiable financial instruments or commodities in different markets in order to make an immediate profit without risk ■ *vi* (**-trages, -traging, -traged**) to engage in arbitrage [Mid-19C. < French < *arbitrer* 'to judge' < Latin *arbitrari* (see ARBITRATE)]

arbitrageur /aárbi traa zhúr/ *n* somebody who engages in arbitrage [Mid-19C. < French < *arbitrage* (see ARBITRAGE)]

arbitrary /aárbitrəri/ *adj* **1. BASED ON WHIM** based solely on personal wishes, feelings, or perceptions, rather than on objective facts, reasons, or principles ○ *an arbitrary decision* **2. RANDOM** chosen or determined at random ○ *the arbitrary order of the entries* **3. AUTHORITARIAN** with unlimited power ○ *arbitrary government* **4.** LAW **NOT ACCORDING TO RULE** based on the decision of a judge or court rather than in accordance with any rule or law ○ *arbitrary arrest* **5.** MATHS **ASSIGNED NO SPECIFIC VALUE** describes a mathematical constant that is not assigned a specific value [15C. < Latin *arbitrarius* 'uncertain, depending on the judgment of an arbiter' < *arbiter* 'judge'] —**arbitrarily** /aárbitrərəli, aàrbi tráirəli/ *adv* —**arbitrariness** *n*

arbitrate /aárbi trayt/ (**-trates, -trating, -trated**) *v* **1.** *vti* to act as a judge in a dispute between others **2.** *vt* to submit a dispute to be decided by a third party [Late 16C. < Latin *arbitrat-*, past participle of *arbitrari* 'judge, decide' < *arbiter* 'judge'] —**arbitrable** *adj*

arbitration /aárbi tráysh'n/ *n* the process of resolving disputes between people or groups by referring them to a third party, either agreed by them or provided by law, who makes a judgment —**arbitrational** *adj*

arbitrator /aárbi traytər/ *n* somebody designated to hear both sides of a dispute and make a judgment

arbor[1] /aárbər/ *n* **1.** AXLE ON MACHINE OR POWER TOOL a shaft, axle, or spindle on a machine or a power tool **2.** SUPPORTING PIECE a machine part that holds an object being worked on **3.** REINFORCING PART OF MOULD a part that reinforces the core of a mould used to cast metal [Mid-17C. Via French < Latin, 'tree, mast, lever, shaft']

arbor[2] *n* US spelling of **arbour**

Arbor Day *n* in the United States, a day set aside for the planting and appreciation of trees. Date: typically the last Friday in April, but varying from state to state.

arboreal /aar báwri əl/ *adj* **1.** describes a species that lives in trees **2.** relating to, resembling, or consisting of trees —**arboreally** *adv*

arboreous /aar báwri əss/ *adj* covered with trees (*formal*)

arborescent /aárbə réss'nt/ *adj* resembling a tree, especially in developing branches or similar parts [Mid-17C. < Latin *arborescent-*, present participle of *arborescere* 'grow into a tree' < *arbor* 'tree'] —**arborescence** *n*

arboretum /aárbə reétəm/ (*plural* -**tums** or -**ta** /-tə/) *n* an area planted with many types of tree for study, display, and preservation [Mid-19C. < Latin, 'place grown with trees, plantation of trees' < *arbor* 'tree']

arboriculture /aárbəri kulchər, aar báwri-/ *n* the cultivation of trees and bushes for study, ornament, or profit [Mid-19C. Blend of Latin *arbor* 'tree' + AGRICULTURE] —**arboricultural** *adj* —**arboriculturist** *n*

arborio /aar báwri ṓ/, **arborio rice** *n* a short-grained rice used to make risotto and other Italian dishes [Late 20C. < Italian]

arborise *vi* another spelling of **arborize**

arborist /aárbərist/ *n* an expert in the cultivation and care of trees

arborize /aárbə rīz/ (-**rizes**, -**rizing**, -**rized**), **arborise** (-**rises**, -**rising**, -**rised**) *vi* to develop many branching parts or formations —**arborization** /aárbə rī záysh'n/ *n*

arbor vitae /aárbər vītee, -veétī/, **arborvitae** *n* an ornamental coniferous tree with flat leaves that fit closely like scales. Native to: Asia, North America. Genus: *Thuja*. [Mid-17C. < Latin, 'tree of life']

arbour /aárbər/ *n* **1.** a shaded place formed by the leaves and branches of trees and plants that interweave naturally or are trained to grow around a trellis **2.** a trellis or other structure used to support plants that form an arbour [14C. Via Old French (h)erb(i)er < late Latin *herbarium* (see HERBARIUM)]

arbovirus /aárbə vīrəss/ *n* a virus transmitted by bloodsucking arthropods such as ticks and fleas. Arboviruses contain RNA, exist in over 500 species, and include the viruses that cause encephalitis, yellow fever, and dengue. [Mid-20C. Contraction of *arthropod-borne virus*] —**arboviral** /aárbə vīrəl/ *adj*

Arbus /aárbəss/, **Diane** (1923–71) US photographer, known for her unconventional and occasionally morbid portraits of unusual characters

'There are things nobody would see if I didn't photograph them.'
[Diane Arbus. Quoted in *Diane Arbus*; 1972]

arbutus /aar byoótəss/ (*plural* -**tuses** or *same*) *n* **1.** a bush or tree that bears reddish fruits. Flowers: white, pink. Native to: southern Europe. Genus: *Arbutus*. **2.** PLANTS same as **trailing arbutus** [Mid-16C. < Latin, 'wild strawberry']

arc /aark/ *n* **1.** CURVE a curved or semicircular line, direction of movement, or arrangement of items ○ *The ball curved in a high arc.* **2.** MATHS SECTION OF CIRCLE a section of a circle, ellipse, or other curved figure **3.** ASTRON VISIBLE PART OF ASTRONOMICAL OBJECT'S PATH a section of the path that a planet or other astronomical object appears to follow, especially that seen above the horizon **4.** ELEC ENG ELECTRIC DISCHARGE a luminous discharge caused by an electric current flowing across a gap in an electrical circuit **5.** GEOL same as **island arc** ■ *vi* (**arcs, arcing** or **arcking, arced** or **arcked**) **1.** FORM OR MOVE IN ARC to form a curve or move along a curved path **2.** ELEC ENG SPARK ACROSS GAP to produce a luminous discharge across a gap in an electrical circuit [14C. Via French < Latin *arcus* 'bow, curve']

ARC *abbr* MED Aids-related complex

arcade /aar káyd/ *n* **1.** PASSAGEWAY WITH ARCHES a passageway or building with a series of arches and supporting columns **2.** AVENUE OF SHOPS a covered passage with shops on both sides **3.** *N Am* LEISURE same as **amusement arcade 4.** SERIES OF ARCHES a series of arches and the columns supporting them **5.** COMPUT GAMES same as **video arcade** ■ *adj* COMPUT GAMES OF VIDEO GAMES relating to or typical of video arcade games [Mid-18C. Via French < Italian *arcata* < Latin *arcus* 'bow, curve, arch'] —**arcaded** *adj*

arcade game *n* a coin-operated game played in amusement arcades, e.g. a one-armed bandit, pinball machine, or video game

Arcadia[1] /aar káydi ə/ *n* **1.** *also* **arcadia** a place in which people are imagined or believed to enjoy a perfect life of rustic simplicity **2.** the imagined rural paradise used as the setting for much Greek and Roman poetry and some Renaissance literature [Late 19C. Via Latin < Greek *Arkadia*, mountainous district in the Peloponnese]

Arcadia[2] /aar káydi ə/ mountainous region of the central Peloponnese, southwestern Greece

Arcadian /aar káydi ən/ *adj* **1.** *also* **arcadian** relating to the imagined rural paradise or perfect life of rustic simplicity of Arcadia **2.** relating to the region of Arcadia in southwestern Greece —**Arcadian** *n*

arcana /aar káynə/ *n* either of two divisions of a pack of tarot cards ■ *plural* of **arcanum**

arcane /aar káyn/ *adj* **1.** difficult or impossible to understand **2.** requiring secret knowledge to be understood [Early 16C. < Latin *arcanus* 'closed, secret' < *arca* 'box'] —**arcanely** *adv* —**arcaneness** *n*

SYNONYMS See *obscure*.

arcanum /aar káynəm/ (*plural* -**na** /-nə/) *n* (*usually used in the plural*) **1.** a secret known only to the members of a small select group **2.** a secret of nature, of the kind that was formerly sought by alchemists [Late 16C. < Latin, form of *arcanus* (see ARCANE)]

AKG London
Arc de Triomphe, Paris, France

Arc de Triomphe /aárk də treé omf/ *n* a triumphal arch at the end of the Avenue des Champs Elysées in Paris, completed in 1835. It was commissioned by Napoleon to commemorate military victories, and is now used as a war memorial.

arc furnace *n* a furnace in which an electric arc supplies the heat

arch[1] /aarch/ *n* **1.** CURVED STRUCTURE a curved structure that forms the upper edge of an open space such as a window, a doorway, or the space between a bridge's supports **2.** PASSAGE UNDER ARCH an entrance or passageway under an arch **3.** ARCH SHAPE the shape of an arch, resembling an inverted 'U', or an object with such a shape ○ *the arch of his eyebrows* **4.** ANAT CURVED BODY PART a body part with the shape of an arch, especially the bony structure in the foot **5.** GEOL CURVED ROCK FORMATION a naturally occurring arch-shaped span of rock found in dry, especially desert, regions ■ *v* (**arches, arching, arched**) **1.** *vt* FORM CURVED SHAPE to form something into the shape of an arch **2.** *vi* MOVE IN CURVING LINE to follow a trajectory in the shape of an arch **3.** *vt* SPAN to extend across something **4.** *vt* BUILD ARCH to build something in the shape of an arch or with arch-shaped supports [13C. Via Old French *arche* < Latin *arcus* 'bow, curve, arch'] —**arched** *adj*

arch[2] /aarch/ *adj* **1.** greatest, especially most hostile **2.** expressing playfulness, mischief, or shared humour in a knowing way [Mid-16C. < ARCH-] —**archly** *adv* —**archness** *n*

arch. *abbr* **1.** archaic **2.** archaism **3.** archery **4.** GEOG archipelago **5.** architect **6.** architecture

Arch. *abbr* GEOG Archipelago

arch- *prefix* **1.** chief, most important ○ *archrival* **2.** extreme ○ *archconservative* [Via Old French and Latin *arche* < Greek *arkhi-* 'first, chief' (see ARCHI-)]

-arch *suffix* leader, ruler ○ *matriarch* [Via French and late Latin < Greek *arkhos* < *arkhein* 'to rule'] —**-archic** *suffix* —**-archy** *suffix*

archae- *prefix* same as **archaeo-** (*used before vowels*)

archaea /aárkeé ə/ *npl* members of one of two distinct groups of the most primitive living single-celled organisms, similar in size to bacteria but different in molecular organization [Late 20C. Shortening of ARCHAEBACTERIA]

Archaean /aar keé ən/, **Archean** *n* the earliest aeon of geological time, dating from about four billion years ago. See table at **geological time** [Late 19C. < Greek *arkhaios* 'old, ancient' + AN[2]] —**Archaean** *adj*

archaebacteria /aárki bak teéri ə/ *npl* MICROBIOL same as **archaea** [Late 20C. Because believed to be of ancient origin] —**archaebacterial** *adj*

archaeo-, archeo- *prefix* ancient ○ *archaeobotany* [Via modern Latin < Greek *arkhaios*]

archaeoastronomy /aárki ṓ ə strónnəmi/, **archeoastronomy** *n* the study of the astronomical beliefs, practices, and discoveries of prehistoric and ancient cultures —**archaeoastronomer** *n* —**archaeoastronomical** /aárki ṓ astrə nómmik'l/ *adj*

archaeobotany /aárki ṓ bóttəni/, **archeobotany** *n* the scientific study of excavated plant remains from ancient times —**archaeobotanist** *n*

archaeological /aárki ə lójjik'l/, **archeological**, **archaeologic** /-lójjik/, **archeologic** *adj* relating to archaeology, or carried out for the purposes of archaeology —**archaeologically** *adv*

archaeological dating *n* the use of the decay rates of biological specimens to determine the age of an archaeological site, effective back to about 50,000 years

archaeology /aárki ólləji/, **archeology** *n* the scientific study of ancient cultures through the examination of their material remains such as buildings, graves, tools, and other artefacts usually dug up from the ground —**archaeologist** *n*

archaeomagnetism /aárki ṓ mágnətizəm/, **archeomagnetism** *n* a method of dating excavated artefacts by measuring the degree of their magnetization

archaeometry /aárki ómmətri/, **archeometry** *n* the systematic dating of archaeological objects —**archaeometrical** /aárki ə méttrik'l/ *adj* —**archaeometrically** *adv* —**archaeometrist** *n*

archaeopteryx

archaeopteryx /aárki óptəriks/ *n* an extinct bird of the Jurassic period that had the feathers of modern birds but the jaw and sharp teeth of reptiles. It is considered to be a link between reptiles and birds. Latin name: *Archaeopteryx lithographica*. [Mid-19C. < ARCHAEO- + Greek *pteryx* 'wing']

archaic /aar káyik/ *adj* **1.** ANCIENT belonging or relating to a much earlier period **2.** NO LONGER IN ORDINARY LANGUAGE describes a word or phrase that is no longer in general use but is still encountered in older literature and still sometimes used for special effect **3.** OUTMODED no longer useful or efficient [Mid-19C. Via French < Greek *arkhaikos* < *arkhaios* 'old, ancient' < *arkhē* 'beginning'] —**archaically** *adv*

SYNONYMS See ***old-fashioned.***

archaise *vt* another spelling of **archaize**

archaism /aar kay izəm, -ki-/ *n* **1.** a word, expression, practice, or method from an earlier time that is no longer used **2.** the use of expressions, techniques, and fashions from an earlier period [Mid-17C. Via modern Latin < Greek *arkhaismos* < *arkhaizein* 'copy the ancients, give an archaic air to' < *arkhaios* (see ARCHAIC)] —**archaist** *n* —**archaistic** /àar kay ístik, -ki-/ *adj*

REGIONAL NOTE Dialects often retain archaisms, that is, pronunciations, words, and structures that have been discarded by users of the standard language. The forms *emmet* 'ant' and *musheroon* 'mushroom' were the accepted forms 500 years ago; *tay* 'tea' was the refined pronunciation in the 17th century; and the North of England speakers who continue to use *thou* and *thee* can trace such pronouns back to the earliest recorded writings in the language.

archaize /áark ay īz/ (**-izes, -izing, -ized**), **archaise** (**-ises, -ising, -ised**) *vt* to make something seem much older than it is by using old forms or styles —**archaizer** *n*

archangel /áark aynjəl/ *n* **1.** a chief or principal angel **2.** an angel of the second of the nine orders of angels in the traditional Christian hierarchy **3.** PLANTS same as **angelica** (sense 2) [Pre-12C. Via Anglo-Norman < ecclesiastical Greek *arkhaggelos* < Greek *arkhi-* 'chief' (see ARCHI-) + *aggelos* 'messenger'] —**archangelic** /àark an jéllik/ *adj*

Archangel /áark aynjəl/ English name for **Arkhangelsk**

archbishop /aarch bíshəp/ *n* a bishop of the highest rank, who heads an archdiocese or an ecclesiastical province

archbishopric /aarch bíshəprik/ *n* **1.** the area of an archbishop's jurisdiction **2.** the status or term of office of an archbishop [Pre-12C. < ARCHBISHOP + Old English *rice* 'realm']

arch bridge *n* a bridge whose span curves in the shape of an arch

archconservative /áarch kən súrvətiv/ *n* somebody with strong conservative views

archd. *abbr* **1.** CHR archdeacon **2.** archduke

archdeacon /aarch déekən/ *n* a member of the clergy who ranks just below a bishop and assists the bishop with ceremonial and administrative duties —**archdeaconate** *n* —**archdeaconship** *n*

archdeaconry /aarch déekənri/ (*plural* **-ries**) *n* **1.** the status or term of office of an archdeacon **2.** the residence of an archdeacon

archdiocese /aarch dī əssiss/ *n* the area for which an archbishop has ecclesiastical responsibility —**archdiocesan** /áarch dī óssəss'n/ *adj*

archducal /aarch dyóok'l/ *adj* relating or belonging to archdukes, archduchesses, or archduchies

archduchess /aarch dúchiss/ *n* **1.** an archduke's wife or widow **2.** a princess of the former Austrian imperial family

archduchy /aarch dúchi/ (*plural* **-ies**) *n* the land ruled by an archduke or archduchess

archduke /áarch dyóok/ *n* a senior duke in some countries, especially Austria [Early 16C. Via Old French *archeduc* < late Latin *archidux* < *archi-* 'chief, first' + *dux* 'leader']

Archean *n, adj* GEOL another spelling of **Archaean**

archegonia BOT plural of **archegonium**

archegoniate /àarki gṓni ət/ *adj* bearing archegonia ■ *n* a plant that bears archegonia

archegonium /àarki gṓni əm/ (*plural* **-nia** /-ni ə/) *n* the female reproductive organ of mosses, ferns, liverworts, and most gymnosperms. It contains a single egg cell. [Mid-19C. < modern Latin < Greek *arkhegonos* < *arkhe-* 'chief, first' + *gonos* 'people'] —**archegonial** *adj*

archenemy /áarch énnəmi/ (*plural* **-mies**) *n* **1.** somebody's main or worst enemy **2.** *also* **Archenemy** the devil

archenteron /aar kéntə ron, -tərən/ *n* a digestive cavity in animal embryos that develops into the gut [Late 19C. < Greek *arkhē* 'beginning'+ *enteron* 'intestine'] —**archenteric** *adj*

archeo-, etc another spelling of **archaeo-, etc**

archer /áarchər/ *n* somebody who uses a bow and arrow [13C. < Anglo-Norman *archer*, Old French *archier* < Latin *arcus* 'bow, curve']

Archer *n* ZODIAC same as **Sagittarius** (sense 2)

Archer /áarchər/, **Frederick Scott** (1813–57) British photographer. He invented the collodion or wet-plate process for reproducing photographs (1851).

Archer, Robyn (*b.* 1948) Australian singer and actor noted for her performances of the works of Bertolt Brecht and her one-woman show *A Star is Torn* (1982)

Archer, William (1856–1924) British drama critic who translated the plays of Henrik Ibsen and encouraged George Bernard Shaw early in his career

archerfish /áarchər fish/ (*plural same* or **-fishes**) *n* a freshwater fish that hunts insects by spitting water at them. Native to: Australia, Southeast Asia. Family: Toxotidae.

archery /áarchəri/ *n* **1.** USE OF BOW AND ARROW the activity of shooting with a bow and arrow **2.** TROOP OF ARCHERS a troop of soldiers armed with bows and arrows **3.** ARCHERS' WEAPONS the bows and arrows used by archers

archesporium /àarki spáwri əm/ (*plural* **-ria** /-ri ə/), **archespore** /áarki spawr/ *n* the tissue that gives rise to spore-producing cells in a sporangium in fungi [Late 19C. < *arche-*, alteration of ARCHI- + SPORE + -IUM]

archetype /áarki tīp/ *n* **1.** TYPICAL SPECIMEN a typical, ideal, or classic example of something ○ *It was described as an archetype of the interior design of the period.* **2.** ORIGINAL MODEL something that serves as the model or pattern for other things of the same type ○ *The film was one of the archetypes of the American Western.* **3.** PSYCHOANAL IMAGE FROM COLLECTIVE UNCONSCIOUS in Jungian psychology, an inherited memory represented in the mind by a universal symbol and observed in dreams and myths **4.** ARTS RECURRING SYMBOL an image or symbol that is used repeatedly in art or literature [Mid-16C. Via Latin *archetypum* < Greek *arkhetupon* 'first moulded as a model' < *arkhe-* 'first, chief' + *tupon* 'mould, model'] —**archetypal** /áarki tīp'l, -tīp'l/ *adj* —**archetypic** /àarki típpik/ *adj* —**archetypical** *adj* —**archetypically** *adv*

archfiend /áarch féend/ *n* **1.** a supremely wicked person or being **2.** *also* **Archfiend** the devil

archi- *prefix* **1.** chief, most important ○ *archimandrite* **2.** primitive, primary ○ *archenteron* [Via French < Greek *arkhi-* < *arkhein* 'be first, rule']

Archibald /áarchi bawld/, **Jules François** (1856–1919) Australian journalist. He was cofounder of the journal *The Bulletin* (1880), and the Archibald Prize for portrait painting took its name from him. Born **Archibald, John Feltham**

Archibald Prize *n* an annual prize awarded for portrait painting in Australia. It was first awarded in 1921.

archidiaconal /àarki dī ákənəl/ *adj* relating to the work or position of an archdeacon [15C. < Latin *archidiaconus* < *diaconus* (see DEACON)]

archidiaconate /àarki dī ákənət/ *n* an archdeacon's position, area of jurisdiction, or term of office [Mid-18C. < Latin *archidiaconus* (see ARCHIDIACONAL)]

Archie /áarchi/ *n* an Internet database used to search for files and programs that can be downloaded using FTP. The master server is at McGill University in Montreal. [Late 20C. < ARCHIVE + -IE, after the name *Archie*]

archiepiscopal /àarki ə pískəp'l/ *adj* relating to an archbishop or an archdiocese [Early 17C. < ecclesiastical Latin *archiepiscopus* 'archbishop' < ecclesiastical Greek *arkhiepiskopos* < *episkopos* (see BISHOP)] —**archiepiscopally** *adv* —**archiepiscopate** *n*

archimandrite /àarki mán drīt/ *n* in the Eastern Orthodox Church, a senior priest who heads a monastery or group of monasteries [Mid-17C. Directly or via French < ecclesiastical Latin *archimandrita* < ecclesiastical Greek *arkhimandritēs* < *arkhi-* 'first, chief' + *mandra* 'enclosure, monastery']

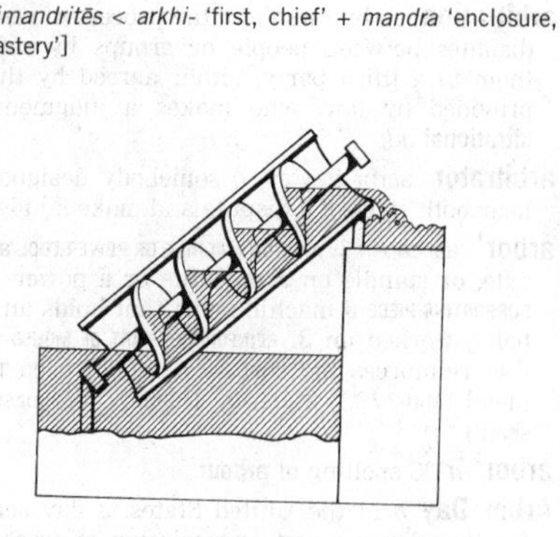

Archimedean screw

Archimedean screw /àarkə mée dee ən-/ *n* an ancient method of raising water, using either a large screw inside a sloping tube or a spiral tube curling around a sloping axis, that causes water to flow upwards when the screw or tube is turned [After ARCHIMEDES]

Archimedes /àarki mée deez/ (287–212 BC) Greek mathematician. He wrote on geometry, arithmetic, and mechanics.

Archimedes' principle *n* the principle that an object immersed in a liquid experiences an upward thrust equal to the weight of liquid it displaces, so that light objects float and heavy objects sink

Archimedes' screw *n* ENG same as **Archimedean screw**

archine /aar shéen/ *n* a unit of length equal to about 71 cm/28 in, used formerly in Russia and Turkey [Mid-18C. < Russian]

archipelago /àarki péllə gō/ (*plural* **-gos** or **-goes**) *n* **1.** a group or chain of islands (*often used in placenames*) **2.** an area of sea with many islands [Early 16C. < Italian *arcipelago* < Greek *arkhi-* 'chief, main' + *pelagos* 'sea'] —**archipelagic** /àarkipə lájjik/ *adj*

archit. *abbr* architecture

architect /áarki tekt/ *n* **1.** BUILDING DESIGNER somebody whose job is to design buildings and advise on their construction **2.** CREATOR somebody who creates or invents something ○ *the architect of her own fortune* **3.** COMPUTER SYSTEM DESIGNER the developer of the structure of a computer system or program [Mid-16C. Directly or via French and Italian < Latin *architectus* < Greek *arkhitektōn* 'chief builder' < *tektōn* 'builder']

architectonic /àarki tek tónnik/ *adj* **1.** relating to architecture or the qualities such as design and structure that architecture requires **2.** relating to the classification of knowledge used in metaphysics [Mid-17C. Via Latin < Greek *arkhitektonikos* < *arkhitektōn* (see ARCHITECT)] —**architectonically** *adv*

architectonics /àarki tek tónniks/ *n* **1.** SCIENCE OF ARCHITECTURE the science of architecture (*takes a singular verb*) **2.** STRUCTURAL DESIGN OF COMPLEX THING the way in which the parts of a complex object or system fit together (*takes a plural verb*) ○ *the architectonics of a good novel* **3.** PHILOSOPHY CLASSIFICATION OF KNOWLEDGE in metaphysics, the classification of knowledge (*takes a singular verb*)

architecture /áarki tekchər/ *n* **1.** BUILDING DESIGN the art and science of designing and constructing buildings **2.** BUILDING STYLE a style or fashion of building, especially one that is typical of a period of history or of a particular place **3.** STRUCTURE OF COMPUTER SYSTEM the design, structure, and behaviour of a computer system, microprocessor, or system program, including the characteristics of individual components and how they interact ○ *network architecture* —**architectural** /àarki tékchərəl/ *adj* —**architecturally** *adv*

architrave /áarki trayv/ *n* **1.** in classical architecture, the lowest section of an entablature, which comes into contact with the top of the columns. See illustration on next page **2.** a decorative strip of wood or plaster forming a frame around a door or window [Mid-16C. Via French < Italian, 'main beam' < *trave* 'beam' < Latin *trab-*]

archive /áar kīv/ *n* **1.** COLLECTION OF DOCUMENTS a collection of documents such as letters, official papers, photographs, or recorded material, kept for their historical interest (*often used in the plural*) ○ *We'll have to check the archives.* **2.** PLACE WHERE ARCHIVES ARE HELD a

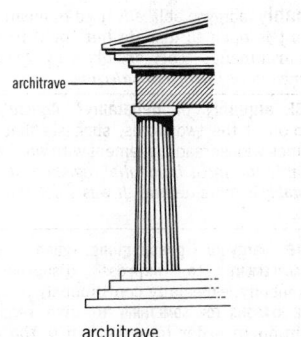
architrave

building or room that houses archives **3.** COMPUT **BACKUP OF COMPUTER FILES** a copy of computer files stored, often in compressed form, on tape or disk **4.** COMPUT **FILE OF COMPRESSED COMPUTER FILES** a computer file containing other compressed files **5.** ONLINE **INTERNET DIRECTORY** a directory of files that Internet users can access using anonymous File Transfer Protocol ■ *vt* (**-chives, -chiving, -chived**) **1.** PUT DOCUMENT IN ARCHIVE to store a document in an archive **2.** COMPUT **STORE DATA EXTERNALLY** to transfer data from a computer's hard disk to a disk or, formerly, a tape for storage. Optical disks are used to archive files as they are more reliable than floppy disks for long-term storage. **3.** COMPUT **COMBINE COMPUTER FILES** to store compressed copies of computer files in a single file [Early 17C. Via French < Latin *archiva, archia* < Greek *arkheia* 'things kept at the public office', plural of *arkheion* 'ruler's house, public office' < *arkhē* 'beginning, government'] —**archival** /aar kīv'l/ *adj*

archivist /aarkivist/ *n* somebody employed to collect, catalogue, and look after the items in an archive

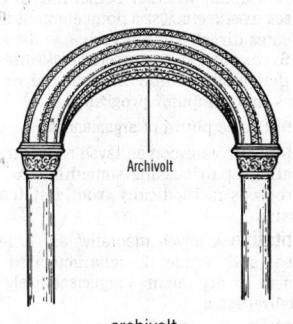
archivolt

archivolt /aarki vōlt/ *n* **1.** a decorative moulding or band on the face of an arch **2.** the underside of an arch [Mid-17C. Directly or via French *archivolte* < Italian *archivolto* < Latin *arcus* 'arch' + *volta* 'vault']

archon /aarkən, -kon/ *n* in ancient Greece, one of the nine chief Athenian magistrates [Late 16C. < Greek *arkhōn* < *arkhein* 'to rule'] —**archonship** *n*

archpriest /aarch preest/ *n* **1.** HIGH-RANKING EASTERN ORTHODOX PRIEST in the Eastern Orthodox Church, a married priest of the highest rank **2.** ROMAN CATHOLIC PRIEST WITH SPECIFIC DUTY in the Roman Catholic Church, a title given to a priest who has a specific important duty or function **3.** ROMAN CATHOLIC BISHOP'S SENIOR ASSISTANT formerly, a title given to the senior Roman Catholic priest in a cathedral chapter, who acted as the bishop's principal assistant [14C. Via Old French *archeprestre* < late Latin *archipresbyter* 'chief priest']

archrival /aarch rīv'l/ *n* somebody's main or most dangerous rival

archway /aarch way/ *n* an entrance or passage under one or more arches, or an arch that forms an entrance

Archytas /aar kītəss/ (*fl* early 4th century BC) Greek mathematician. He calculated the mathematical relationships of musical notes and scales.

Arcimboldo /aarchim bōldō/, **Giuseppe** (1530?–93) Italian painter and designer. He produced pictures of fantastic heads composed of items such as vegetables and animals.

arc lamp, **arc light** *n* an intensely bright electric light with numerous uses, e.g. in floodlights and spotlights on film sets. The light is generated by passing electric current through ionized gas.

arco /aarkō/ *adv* played using the bow of a stringed instrument, usually after a passage played by plucking the strings (**pizzicato**) (*used as a musical direction*) [Mid-18C. < Italian, 'bow'] —**arco** *adj*

arctic /aarktik/ *adj* extremely cold (*informal*) ■ *n* US a high waterproof overshoe with a warm lining [14C. Via Old French *artique* < Greek *arktikos* < *arktos* 'bear', also 'the constellation Ursa Major (the Great Bear)']

Arctic /aarktik/ region that lies around the North Pole, inside the Arctic Circle —**Arctic** *adj*

arctic char *n* a fish of the salmon family, similar to a trout. Native to: northern hemisphere. Latin name: *Salvelinus alpinus*.

Arctic Circle

Arctic Circle *n* the line of latitude at 66°30'N that marks the boundary of the Arctic. North of this latitude there are periods of continuous night in the winter and continuous day in the summer.

arctic fox *n* a small fox with thick fur that is brownish-grey in summer and white or blue in winter. Native to: Arctic. Latin name: *Alopex lagopus*.

arctic hare *n* **1.** a large hare with white fur that in southern regions turns brown in the summer. Native to: Arctic North America, Greenland. Latin name: *Lepus arcticus*. **2.** ZOOL same as **mountain hare**

Arctic Ocean the world's smallest ocean, mostly ice-covered, situated north of the Arctic Circle and surrounding the North Pole. Area: 14,056,000 sq. km/5,427,100 sq. mi. Depth: 5,500 m/17,880 ft.

arctic tern *n* a black-headed seabird that breeds in Arctic regions and migrates to southern Africa, South America, and the Antarctic. Latin name: *Sterna paradisaea*.

arctiid /aarkti id/ (*plural* **-ids** or *same*) *n* a small-to medium-sized moth. There are 8,000 species of arctiid, including the tiger moth. Family: Arctiidae. [< modern Latin *arctiidae* < Greek *arktos* 'bear']

arctophile /aarktō fīl/ *n* a collector of teddy bears [Late 20C. < Greek *arktos* 'bear']

Arcturus /aark tyoŏrəss/ *n* the brightest star in the constellation Boötes and the fourth brightest star in the sky

arcuate /aarkyoo ət/ *adj* in the shape of an arc or a bow [15C. < Latin *arcuatus* < *arcus* 'bow, arch'] —**arcuately** *adv*

arcus senilis /aarkōŏss se neéliss/ *n* an opaque circle around the cornea of the eye that can develop late in life [< Latin, 'bow of advanced age']

arc welding *n* the joining of metal components by fusing them with heat from an electric arc struck between two electrodes

ARD *abbr* acute respiratory disease

-ard, -art *suffix* somebody characterized by a given quality ○ *sluggard* [< Old French < Germanic]

Arden /aard'n/, **John** (*b.* 1930) British playwright. He used experimental techniques and forms in plays such as *Serjeant Musgrave's Dance* (1959) and *The Ballygombeen Bequest* (1972).

Ardennes /aar den/ forested and thinly populated plateau in southeastern Belgium, extending into Luxembourg and northeastern France. The Battle of the Bulge took place in the Ardennes in 1944. The highest peak is Botrange, near Belgium's border with Germany, with a height of 694 m/2,277 ft.

ardent /aard'nt/ *adj* **1.** PASSIONATE feeling great passion, or felt very passionately **2.** ENTHUSIASTIC feeling or showing great enthusiasm or eagerness ○ *one of his most ardent supporters* **3.** GLOWING shining or glowing brightly, with a fiery quality (*literary*) ○ *ardent embers* [14C. Via Old French *ardant* < Latin *ardent-*, present participle of *ardere* 'to burn'] —**ardently** *adv*

ardent spirits *npl* distilled alcoholic beverages such as whisky and rum

ardor *n* US spelling of **ardour**

ardour /aardər/ *n* great passion, enthusiasm, or eagerness ○ *repeated attempts to dampen their revolutionary ardour* [14C. Via French < Latin *ardor* < *ardere* 'to burn']

Ards /aardz/ local government region in Northern Ireland, covering the Ards Peninsula. The administrative headquarters are in Newtownards. Population: 73,244 (2001). Area: 381 sq. km/147 sq. mi.

arduous /aardyoo əss/ *adj* **1.** requiring hard work or continuous physical effort **2.** very difficult to traverse, endure, or overcome [Mid-16C. < Latin *arduus* 'steep, difficult'] —**arduously** *adv* —**arduousness** *n*

SYNONYMS See *hard*.

are[1] *stressed* /aar/; *unstressed* /ər/ *v* 1st person plural present of **be**[1]. 2nd person singular present of **be**[1]. 2nd person plural present of **be**[1]. 3rd person plural present of **be**[1] [Old English *eoron* < Germanic]

are[2] /aar/ *n* a metric unit of area, equal to 100 sq. m. There are 100 ares in a hectare. [Late 18C. Via French < Latin *area* (see AREA)]

area /áiri ə/ *n* **1.** MEASUREMENT OF SURFACE the extent of part of a surface enclosed within a boundary, or the extent of the surface of all or part of a solid. The area of a square or rectangle can be calculated by multiplying together the lengths of two adjacent sides. **2.** PART OF SURFACE a distinct part of the surface of something, especially a piece of land ○ *The storms resulted in flooding over a large area.* **3.** SPACE OR PART WITH SPECIFIC FUNCTION a space, part, or surface of something, especially when intended for a specific use ○ *an area of the brain used for memory* **4.** REGION OR DISTRICT a region or district, either a distinct political or administrative division or a place that has specific qualities or features **5.** SUBJECT a subject of study, field of knowledge, or sphere of activity ○ *in the area of genetic research* **6.** SOCCER same as **penalty area** [Mid-16C. < Latin, 'flat piece of unoccupied land']

area code *n* digits indicating a specific area of a country that are dialled before the local number in calls from outside that area

Area of Archaeological Importance *n* an area of land, usually an urban one, designated and protected by law because it is known to contain archaeological remains. Notice has to be given of any operations that might disturb the ground, so that archaeologists have time to investigate the site before the operation proceeds.

Area of Outstanding Natural Beauty *n* ENVIRON full form of **AONB**

areca /ə reèkə, árri-/ *n* a tall palm tree with white flowers. Native to: Southeast Asia. Genus: *Areca*. [Late 16C. Via Portuguese < Malayalam *aṭekka*]

Arecibo /aárə seébō/ port, commercial and industrial centre in northern Puerto Rico. Population: 93,385 (1990).

areg GEOG plural of **erg**[2]

ARELS /árrəlz/ *abbr* EDUC Association of Recognized English Language Schools

arena /ə reénə/ *n* **1.** STADIUM an indoor or outdoor area surrounded by seating for spectators, where shows or sports events take place **2.** SCENE OF ACTIVITY a place or situation where there is conflict or intense activity ○ *A new contestant has entered the political arena.* **3.** CENTRE OF ROMAN AMPHITHEATRE the open area inside a Roman amphitheatre, in which gladiatorial contests and other entertainments were staged [Early 17C. < Latin, 'sand, sand-strewn place']

arenaceous /árri náyshəss/ *adj* **1.** describes rocks or deposits that are composed of sand grains or have a sandy texture **2.** describes plants that grow best in sandy soil [Mid-17C. < Latin *arenaceus* 'of sand' < *arena* 'sand']

arena theatre n THEATRE same as **theatre-in-the-round**

Arendt /aarənt/, **Hannah** (1906–75) German-born US philosopher and political theorist. Her major works include *Origins of Totalitarianism* (1951) and *Eichmann in Jerusalem* (1963).

> 'It was as though in those last minutes he [Eichmann] was summing up the lessons that this long course in human wickedness had taught us–the lesson of the fearsome, word-and-thought-defying *banality of evil*.'
> [Hannah Arendt, *Eichmann in Jerusalem: A Report on the Banality of Evil*; 1963]

arene /árreen/ n an aromatic hydrocarbon [Mid-20C. < AROMATIC]

arenicolous /árri níkələss/ adj living, burrowing, or thriving in sand [Mid-18C. < Latin *arena* 'sand' + -*cola* 'inhabiting']

aren't /aarnt/ contr (informal) **1.** am not (only used in questions) ○ *I'm allowed to go too, aren't I?* **2.** are not ○ *They aren't coming.*

USAGE Use of **aren't**: English does not have a convenient contracted form of *am I not?* (The logically expected form *amn't I* is used in some parts of Scotland and Ireland but has never been part of standard English.) The usual form used is *aren't I*, borrowing *are* from other parts of the verb *be*, whereas in American English *ain't I* is used, though only informally. There is no contraction for *I am not* that corresponds to *I don't* and *I haven't* (as distinct from *I'm not*, which places greater emphasis on the *not*), and this is why the nonstandard form *ain't* tends to be used for want of anything better, although it is extremely informal.

areola /ə reé ələ/ (plural -**lae** /-lee/ or -**las**) n **1.** the small circular dark area around the nipple in humans **2.** a small circular reddened area such as an inflamed ring around a spot [Mid-17C. < Latin, 'little area'] — **areolar** /ə reé ələt/ adj —**areolate** /ə reé ələt/ adj —**areolation** /ə reé ə láysh'n/ n

areole /árri ōl/ n **1.** a small clearly defined area, e.g. that between veins on a leaf **2.** a depression on the surface of a cactus that the spines, hairs, or flowers grow from [Mid-19C. Via French < Latin *areola* 'little area']

Arequipa /árri keépə/ city in southern Peru in the Andes. It is an important commercial centre. Population: 710,103 (1998).

Ares /aá reez/ n in Greek mythology, the god of war and the son of Zeus and Hera. Roman equivalent **Mars**

arête /ə ráyt, -rét/ n a narrow ridge of bare rock situated between two or more deep smooth-sided semicircular areas (**cirques**), found in a mountainous area that has been glaciated [Early 19C. Via French < Latin *arista* 'ear of grain, fish bone, spine', from its shape]

Aretino /árrə teénō/, **Pietro** (1492–1556) Italian poet. He served under various nobles including Giovanni de Medici, who became Pope Leo X and withdrew his sponsorship after Aretino wrote his *Lewd Sonnets* (1524).

argal n CHEM same as **argol**

argali /aárgəli/ (plural same) n a large wild mountain sheep. Native to: central and northern Asia. Latin name: *Ovis ammon*. [Late 18C. < Mongolian]

argent /aárjənt/ n **1.** the metal or the colour silver (archaic or literary) **2.** the colour white or silver on a coat of arms [14C. Via French < Latin *argentum* 'silver'] — **argent** adj

argentic /aar jéntik/ adj containing silver with a valency of 2

argentiferous /aárjən tíffərəss/ adj describes rocks or deposits containing silver

Argentina /aárjən teénə/, **Argentine, the** /aárjən teen, -tīn/ country that occupies most of the southern tip of South America. It was settled by the Spanish in the 16th century and became independent in 1816. Language: Spanish. Currency: peso argentino. Capital: Buenos Aires. Population: 38,740,807 (2003). Area: 2,780,400 sq. km/1,073,518 sq. mi. Official name **Argentine Republic** —**Argentinian** /aárjən tínni ən/ adj, n

Argentina, La ♦ **La Argentina**

argentine /aárjən tīn/ adj silvery in colour (archaic or

Argentina

literary) ■ n the metal silver, or a material that looks like silver

Argentine[1] /aárjən teen, -tīn/ n somebody who was born or brought up in, or who is a citizen of, Argentina ■ adj relating to Argentina, or its people, language, or culture

Argentine[2] ♦ **Argentina**

argentite /aárjən tīt/ n a grey to black silver sulphide mineral, forming cubic crystals [Mid-19C. < Latin *argentum* 'silver']

argie-bargie n another spelling of **argy-bargy** (informal)

argil /aárjil/ n clay, especially potter's clay [14C. Via Old French *argille* < Greek *argillos* 'clay']

argillaceous /aárji láyshəss/ adj describes sedimentary rock that is made up of clay or silt particles

argillite /aárji līt/ n rock that is made up of clay or silt particles, especially a hardened mudstone

arginase /aárji nayz, -nayss/ n a liver enzyme involved in the production of urea

arginine /aárji neen, -nīn/ n an essential amino acid, one of the constituents of protein. Source: guanidine in plant and animal tissue. Formula: $C_6H_{14}N_4O_2$. [Late 19C. < German]

Argive /aár gīv, -jīv/ adj GREEK relating to ancient Greece, especially the city of Argos ■ n **1.** ANCIENT GREEK somebody from ancient Greece (literary) **2.** CITIZEN OF ARGOS somebody from the city of Argos [Mid-16C. < Latin *Argivus* 'of Argos']

Argo /aárgō/ n a large constellation in the southern hemisphere, now usually regarded as consisting of the smaller constellations of Puppis, Vela, Carina, and Pyxis

argol /aár gol/, **argal** /aárg'l/ n potassium hydrogen tartrate, formed in wine casks [14C. < Anglo-Norman *argoile*]

argon /aár gon/ n an inert gaseous element that makes up about one per cent of the Earth's atmosphere. Use: electric lights, gas shield in welding. Symbol **Ar**. See table at **element** [Late 19C. < Greek *argos* 'inactive, idle' < *a*- 'without' + *ergon* 'work']

argonaut /aárgə nawt/ n ZOOL same as **paper nautilus** [Mid-19C. < modern Latin *Argonauta* (see ARGONAUT)]

Argonaut /aárgə nawt/ n **1.** in Greek mythology, one of the heroes who sailed with Jason in his ship, the Argo, to find the Golden Fleece **2.** also **argonaut** an adventurer, especially somebody who took part in the Californian gold rush of 1849 [Late 16C. Via Latin *argonauta* < Greek *argonautēs* 'sailor in the ship Argo']

Argonne /aar gón, aár gon/ wooded highland region in northeastern France, forming a natural barrier between Champagne and Lorraine

argosy /aárgəssi/ (plural -**sies**) n a large richly laden merchant ship, or a fleet of such ships (literary) [Late 16C. Probably < Italian *Ragusea* '(ship from the port of) Ragusa']

argot /aárgō, -gət/ n the special language used by a particular group of people [Mid-19C. < French] — **argotic** /aar góttik/ adj

SYNONYMS See *jargon*[1].

arguable /aárgyoo əb'l/ adj **1.** able to be supported or proved with evidence or arguments ○ *an arguable case for global warming* **2.** not obviously true or accurate, and therefore likely to be questioned or argued about ○ *It's arguable whether he really is the world's best guitarist.*

arguably /aárgyoo əbli/ adv used to mean that a statement is open to dispute but could be defended in an argument ○ *They are arguably the best team to come out of Europe this decade.*

USAGE arguably or **debatably**? *Arguably*, the more common of the two words, suggests that the speaker assumes widespread agreement with what is being said: *arguably the most influential legislator in the country.* **Debatably** is more neutral: *It was a debatably rude thing to do.*

argue /aárgyoo/ (-**gues**, -**guing**, -**gued**) v **1.** vi EXPRESS DISAGREEMENT to express disagreement with somebody, especially continuously or angrily **2.** vti GIVE REASONS FOR SOMETHING to give reasons for an opinion in order to support it ○ *You could argue that this calls for greater freedom, not less.* **3.** vt PERSUADE SOMEBODY to persuade somebody to do something by giving reasons ○ *argued her out of leaving* **4.** vti PROVIDE EVIDENCE FOR SOMETHING to be evidence or a sign of something ○ *The increase in crime argued for tougher jail sentences, said some.* [14C. Via French *arguer* < Latin *argutari* 'assert repeatedly' < *arguere* 'make clear, assert'] —**arguer** n

SYNONYMS See *disagree*.

~~**argueing**~~ incorrect spelling of **arguing**

~~**arguement**~~ incorrect spelling of **argument**

argufy /aárgyoo fī/ (-**fies**, -**fying**, -**fied**) vi Southern US to argue about something that is unimportant (informal)

argument /aárgyoomənt/ n **1.** DISAGREEMENT a disagreement in which different views are expressed, often angrily **2.** REASON a reason put forward in support of or in opposition to a point of view ○ *the arguments for and against the planned development* **3.** STATED POINT OF VIEW the main point of view expressed in a book, report, or speech **4.** DISCUSSION debate or discussion about whether something is correct **5.** GRAM NOUN ELEMENT IN CLAUSE a noun element in a clause that relates directly to the verb, e.g. the subject or object **6.** COMPUT FEATURE CONTROLLING COMPUTER PROGRAM a value that modifies how a command or function operates in a computer program

argumenta LOGIC plural of **argumentum**

argumentation /aárgyoomən táysh'n/ n **1.** the process of debating or discussing something **2.** reasoning that proceeds methodically from a statement to a conclusion

argumentative /aárgyoo méntətiv/ adj **1.** tending to disagree and argue **2.** characterized by disagreement or argument —**argumentatively** adv —**argumentativeness** n

argumentum /aárgyoo méntəm/ (plural -**ta** /-tə/) n a series of statements or a demonstration that leads to a logical conclusion (formal) [Mid-17C. < Latin, 'argument, rationale' < *arguere* 'make clear, assert']

Argus /aárgəss/ n **1.** in Greek mythology, a giant with 100 eyes. He was sent by the jealous Hera to watch over her husband Zeus's lover, Io, but was later lulled to sleep and killed by Hermes. **2.** an alert watchful person (literary)

argus pheasant n a large brownish pheasant, the male of which has a very long tail like a peacock's. Native to: Southeast Asia, Indonesia. Latin name: *Argusianus argus*. [From its tail-spots, reminiscent of Argus's eyes]

argy-bargy /aárji baárji/ (plural **argy-bargies**), **argie-bargie** (plural **argie-bargies**) n an animated or heated quarrel, or animated or heated quarrelling (informal) [Late 19C. Playful development of ARGUMENT]

argyle

argyle /aar gī́l/ *adj* knitted with a pattern of coloured diamond shapes ■ *n* a sock or sweater made in an argyle design [Mid-20C. < being based on the tartan of Campbells from Argyll in Scotland]

Argyle, Lake /aár gīl/ large reservoir in northwestern Australia, created in 1972 by damming the River Ord. Area: 740 sq. km/290 sq. mi.

Argyll and Bute /aar gīl ənd byoót/ administrative area in Scotland created in 1996, formerly part of Strathclyde Region. It includes the historic county of Argyllshire. The administrative headquarters are in Lochgilphead.

arhat /aárhət/ *n* a Buddhist who has reached the highest state of peace and enlightenment [Late 19C. Via Pali < Sanskrit, 'deserving, meritorious'] —**arhatship** *n*

Århus /áwr hooss, aár-/, **Aarhus** city, port, and seat of Århus County on the Jutland Peninsula and Århus Bay in eastern Jutland, Denmark. Population: 216,564 (1999).

aria /aári ə/ *n* a melody sung solo or as a duet in an opera, oratorio, or cantata [Early 18C. Via Italian < Latin *aer* 'air' (see AIR)]

Ariadne /árri ádni/ *n* in Greek mythology, the daughter of King Minos of Crete. She gave Theseus the ball of thread that he used to find his way out of the labyrinth after killing the Minotaur.

Arian[1] /áiri ən/ *n* ZODIAC same as **Aries** (sense 3) —**Arian** *adj*

Arian[2] /áiri ən/ *n* a follower of the ancient Greek Christian theologian Arius, who argued that Jesus Christ was the highest created being, but was not divine. This doctrine was pronounced heretical in the 4th century AD. —**Arianism** *n*

Arias Sánchez /aári aass sán chez/, **Oscar** (*b.* 1941) president of Costa Rica (1986–90). He was awarded the Nobel Peace Prize (1987) for his contribution to the restoration of peace in Central America.

ariboflavinosis /ay rībō flayvi nṓssiss/ *n* a condition caused by a dietary deficiency of vitamin B_2 (**riboflavin**). The symptoms are mouth lesions and excessive oiliness of the skin and hair. [Mid-20C. < A-[2] + RIBOFLAVIN]

arid /árrid/ *adj* **1.** describes a region in which annual rainfall is less than 25 cm/10 in. **2.** completely lacking in interest or excitement [Mid-17C. Directly or via French < Latin *aridus* < *arere* 'be dry'] —**aridity** /ə ríddəti/ *n* —**aridly** *adv* —**aridness** *n*

SYNONYMS See *dry*.

arid zone *n* either of two zones of latitude that are between 15° and 30° north and south of the equator, consisting mostly of desert or semidesert

Ariel /áiri əl/ *n* a natural satellite of Uranus with a radius of 580 km, discovered in 1851

Aries /áireez/ *n* **1.** ASTRON **CONSTELLATION IN NORTHERN HEMISPHERE** a zodiacal constellation of the northern hemisphere lying between Pisces and Taurus. See illustration at **constellation 2.** ZODIAC **FIRST SIGN OF ZODIAC** the first sign of the zodiac, represented by a ram and lasting from approximately 21 March to 19 April. Aries is classified as a fire sign and its ruling planet is Mars. **3.** ZODIAC **SOMEBODY BORN UNDER ARIES** somebody whose birthday falls between 21 March and 19 April [Pre-12C. < Latin *aries* 'ram'] —**Aries** *adj*

arietta /árri éttə/ *n* a short simple aria in an opera, oratorio, or cantata [Early 18C. < Italian, 'little aria']

aright /ə rī́t/ *adv* in the correct or proper way (*archaic*)

aril /árril/ *n* a fleshy, often brightly coloured seed covering in some plants. Its function is to draw attention to the seed to aid its dispersal by birds. [Mid-18C. Via modern Latin *arillus* < medieval Latin *arilli* 'dried grape pips'] —**ariled** *adj* —**arillate** /árri layt/ *adj*

arioso /aári ṓzō, árri ṓssō/ *adj, adv* with intense lyricism or feeling (*used as a musical direction*) ■ *n* (*plural* **-sos**) a short lyrical aria or instrumental work [Early 18C. < Italian, 'like an aria']

Ariosto /árri óstō/, **Ludovico** (1474–1533) Italian poet. His best-known work is the epic poem *Orlando Furioso* (1532).

> 'Nature made him, and then broke the mould.'
> [Ludovico Ariosto, *Orlando Furioso*; 1532]

arise /ə rī́z/ (**arises, arising, arose** /ə rṓz/, **arisen** /ə rízz'n/) *vi* **1.** **OCCUR** to appear or come into existence ○ *When did the problem arise?* **2.** **BE CAUSED BY SOMETHING** to happen or exist as a result of something ○ *a shortage of qualified staff arising from a lack of investment in training* **3.** **BECOME ACTIVE OR VOCAL** to rise from a quiet, inactive, or subjugated state to become active, vocal, or rebellious (*literary*) **4.** **STAND UP** to stand up from a sitting, lying, or kneeling position (*literary*) [Old English *arisan* 'rise up' < Germanic]

arista /ə rístə/ (*plural* **-tae** /-tay, -tee/) *n* **1.** BOT same as **awn 2.** a bristly part of the antennae of some flies [Late 17C. < Latin, 'ear of grain']

Aristarchus of Samos /árri staárkəss-/ (310?–250? BC) Greek astronomer. He proposed that the Earth rotates on its axis and orbits the Sun.

Aristides the Just /árri stī́ deez-/ (530–468 BC) Athenian general. He took part in the battles of Marathon (490 BC), Salamis (480 BC), and Plataea (479 BC) against the Persians.

Aristippus /árri stíppəss/ (435?–360? BC) Greek philosopher. A student of Socrates, he founded the Cyrenaic school of hedonism, believing that pleasure is the highest good.

aristo /ə rístō/ (*plural* **-tos**) *n* same as **aristocrat** (sense 1) (*informal*) [Mid-19C. < French, abbreviation of *aristocrate* 'aristocrat']

aristocracy /árri stókrəssi/ (*plural* **-cies**) *n* **1.** **PEOPLE OF HIGHEST SOCIAL CLASS** people of noble families or the highest social class **2.** **SUPERIOR GROUP** a group believed to be superior to all others of the same kind **3.** **GOVERNMENT BY ELITE** government of a country by a small group of people, especially a hereditary nobility **4.** **STATE RUN BY ELITE** a state governed by an aristocracy [15C. Via French *aristocratie* < Greek *aristokratia* 'rule by the best' < *aristos* 'best' + *kratos* 'power, rule' (see -CRACY)]

aristocrat /árristə krat/ *n* **1.** **MEMBER OF HIGHEST SOCIAL CLASS** a member of the nobility or the highest social class in a country **2.** **SUPPORTER OF ARISTOCRATIC RULE** a member of a governing aristocracy, or somebody who supports government by an aristocracy **3.** **SUPERIOR PERSON** a person, thing, or group believed to be superior to all others of the same kind

aristocratic /árristə kráttik/ *adj* **1.** relating or belonging to the highest social class, especially the nobility **2.** characteristic of noble families, e.g. in having a grand lifestyle or elegant manners —**aristocratically** *adv*

Aristophanes /árri stóffə neez/ (448?–385 BC) Greek dramatist. He satirized social and intellectual pretensions in comedies such as *The Birds* (414 BC) and *The Clouds* (423 BC).

Aristotelian /árristə teéli ən/ *adj* expressing or based on the ideas of the Greek philosopher Aristotle ■ *n* a follower of Aristotle's philosophy

Aristotelian logic *n* the system of logic developed by Aristotle, based on the kind of reasoning (**syllogism**) that reaches a conclusion from two independent statements with a common factor

Aristotle /árri stott'l/ (384–322 BC) Greek philosopher and scientist. He was one of the most influential philosophers in Western history.

arithmetic *n* /ə ríthmətik/ **1.** **BASIC MATHS** the branch of mathematics that deals with addition, subtraction, multiplication, and division **2.** **CALCULATION** one or more calculations using basic mathematics **3.** **USE OF NUMBERS** the use of numbers in calculation, or educational exercises involving this **4.** **ABILITY TO DO ARITHMETIC** somebody's ability to add, subtract, multiply, and divide (*informal*) ■ *adj* /árrith méttik/ **RELATING TO ARITHMETIC** relating to, using, or based on arithmetic [13C. Via Old French *arismetique* < Greek *arithmētikē (tekhnē)* 'counting (art)' < *arithmein* 'reckon' < *arithmos* 'number'] —**arithmetical** /árrith méttik'l/ *adj* —**arithmetically** *adv* —**arithmetician** /-tísh'n/ *n*

arithmetic logic unit *n* the circuit in a computer's central processing unit that makes decisions based on the results of calculations

arithmetic mean *n* the average of a set of numbers, calculated by adding them together and then dividing their sum by the number of terms

arithmetic progression *n* a sequence of numbers in which a constant figure (**common difference**) is added to each term to give the next. For example, 3, 8, 13, 18 is an arithmetic progression in which the common difference is 5.

-arium *suffix* a place or device for or relating to something ○ *herbarium* [< Latin]

Arizona /árri zṓnə/ state in the southwestern United States, bordered by New Mexico, Mexico, California, Nevada, and Utah. Capital: Phoenix. Population: 5,456,453 (2002 estimate). Area: 295,274 sq. km/114,006 sq. mi. —**Arizonan** *adj, n* —**Arizonian** *adj, n*

Arjuna /aárjoŏnə/ *n* a major character in the *Mahabharata*. Krishna, serving as his charioteer, explains Hindu doctrine to him.

ark /aark/ *n* **1.** BIBLE in the Bible, the ship that Noah was instructed to build by God to save his family and the animals from the Flood **2.** *also* **Ark** JUD-CHR same as **Ark of the Covenant 3.** *also* **Ark** JUDAISM in a synagogue, a cupboard in a synagogue in which the scrolls of the Torah are kept [Old English *ærc*, via Germanic < Latin *arca* 'chest, box'] ◇ **out of the ark** extremely old or old-fashioned (*informal*)

CULTURAL NOTE ***Schindler's Ark***, a novel (1982) by Thomas Keneally. It tells the true story of a German industrialist, Oskar Schindler, who helped thousands of Jews avoid the Nazi death camps by employing them in his factories. It was made into a film called *Schindler's List* by Steven Spielberg in 1993.

Arkan /aárkan/ ➧ **Raznatovic, Zeljko**

Arkansas /aárkən saw/ **1.** state in the southern United States, bordered by Missouri, Tennessee, Mississippi, Louisiana, Texas, and Oklahoma. Capital: Little Rock. Population: 2,710,079 (2002 estimate). Area: 137,741 sq. km/53,182 sq. mi. **2.** major river of the central United States, rising in central Colorado and flowing south and eastwards to join the Mississippi River in southeastern Arkansas. The main cities along its course are Tulsa, Oklahoma, and Little Rock, Arkansas. Length: 2,350 km/1,460 mi. —**Arkansan** /aar kánz'n/ *n, adj*

Arkhangelsk /aar kán gelsk/, **Archangel** /aárk aynjəl/ city in northwestern Russia, capital of Arkhangelsk Oblast, on the Northern Dvina (Severnaya Dvina) River, near its mouth on the White Sea. It was Russia's chief seaport in the 17th century. Population: 367,200 (1999).

Ark of the Covenant, Ark of the Testimony *n* in the Bible, the chest in which Moses placed the two stone tablets containing the Ten Commandments. The Hebrews treasured it as the most sacred sign of God's presence among them.

arkose /aárkōss, -ōz/ *n* a coarse-grained sedimentary rock rich in feldspar and quartz [Mid-19C. < French, probably < Greek *arkhaios* 'ancient']

Arkwright /aárk rīt/, **Sir Richard** (1732–92) British industrialist. He invented the cotton spinning frame (1768) and introduced steam power into his works in Nottingham (1790).

ARL *abbr Aus* Australian Rugby League

Arles /aarl/ city in the Bouches-du-Rhône Department in the Provence-Alpes-Côte-d'Azur region in France, situated northwest of Marseilles. It was a major Roman city and, after the 10th century, was the capital of a kingdom of the same name. Population: 50,513 (1999).

Arlington /aárlingtən/ **1.** city in northeastern Virginia, near Washington, DC It is home to Arlington National Cemetery and the Pentagon. Population: 189,927 (2002 estimate). **2.** city situated between Fort Worth and Dallas in northeastern Texas. Population: 349,944 (2002 estimate).

arm[1] /aarm/ *n* **1.** **UPPER HUMAN LIMB** a limb attached to the shoulder of the human body **2.** **PART OF GARMENT** the part of a piece of clothing that covers the arm **3.** **PART OF SEAT** a side piece of a chair or sofa, designed to support the arms of somebody sitting in it **4.** **ANIMAL'S LIMB** a part of an animal's body that is similar to the human arm **5.** **INVERTEBRATE'S LIMB** a flexible limb in an invertebrate such as an octopus **6.** **PROJECTING PART** a long thin part projecting from something larger ○ *an arm of the sea* **7.** **DIVISION OF LARGER GROUP** a branch of an organization, especially a section of the armed forces ○ *infantry as a combat arm* [Old English *arm, earm* < Indo-European, 'fit, join'] —**armful** *n* ◇ **arm in arm** holding each other affectionately by linking arms ◇ **at arm's length** in a position or

situation that avoids involvement or familiarity ◇ **chance your arm** to attempt something despite unfavourable odds (*informal*) ◇ **put the arm on somebody** *US* **1.** to try to force somebody to do something (*slang*) **2.** to borrow money from somebody (*informal*) ◇ **the long arm of the law** the far-reaching power of the police (*humorous*) ◇ **twist somebody's arm** to try to persuade somebody to do something against his or her will (*informal*) ◇ **with open arms** in a friendly and welcoming way ◇ **would give your right arm for something** would be willing to do or give almost anything to get something that you want (*informal*)

arm[2] /aarm/ *v* (**arms, arming, armed**) **1.** *vti* MIL **EQUIP SOMEBODY WITH WEAPONS** to equip a person or a country with weapons **2.** *vt* MIL **MAKE WEAPON READY FOR USE** to prepare a weapon so that it is ready to use **3.** *vt* **PROVIDE SOMEBODY WITH INFORMATION OR TOOLS** to provide somebody with the information or equipment needed to do something ○ *armed myself with statistics before the meeting* ■ *n* MIL **WEAPON** a weapon, especially one used in warfare (*often used in the plural*) ■ **arms** *npl* **1.** MIL **WARFARE** fighting or military activity **2.** HERALDRY **HERALDIC BADGE** the coat of arms of a family, university, or town [12C. Via Old French *armer* < Latin *armare* < *arma* (plural) 'weapons'] ◇ **be up in arms** to protest or complain angrily ◇ **lay down your arms** to stop fighting ◇ **take up arms** to enter, or prepare to enter, a battle

armada /aar maáda/ *n* a large fleet of ships [Mid-16C. Via Spanish < medieval Latin *armata* (see ARMY)]

armadillo

armadillo /aárma díllō/ (*plural* **-los** *or* **same**) *n* a burrowing mammal whose body is covered in hard plates, related to the anteater and sloth. Native to: temperate and tropical Americas. Family: Dasypodidae. [Late 16C. < Spanish, 'little armed man' < Latin *armare* (see ARM[2])]

armageddon /aárma gédd'n/ *n* a final and decisive war or conflict, e.g. a worldwide nuclear war [Early 19C. < ARMAGEDDON]

Armageddon /aárma gédd'n/ *n* in the Bible, the battle between the forces of good and evil that is predicted to mark the end of the world and precede the Day of Judgment. (Revelation 16:16). [Via late Latin < Hebrew *har megiddōn* 'hill of Megiddo']

Armagh /aar maá/ **1.** town in the province of Ulster, southern Northern Ireland. Population: 14,640 (1991). **2.** historic county of Northern Ireland, in the province of Ulster. Area: 667 sq. km/258 sq. mi.

Armagnac /aárma nyak/ *n* a brandy made in southwestern France [Mid-19C. After a historical region]

armament /aármamant/ *n* **1.** the guns and other weapons on a military aircraft, vehicle, or ship (*often used in the plural*) **2.** the provision of weapons and equipment in preparation for war [Late 17C. < Latin *armamentum* < *armare* (see ARM[2])]

armamentarium /aárma men táiri am/ (*plural* **-iums** *or* **-ia** /-i ə/) *n* the complete range of equipment, medicines and techniques that a medical practitioner has at his or her disposal [Late 19C. < Latin, 'arsenal, armoury' < *armare* (see ARM[2])]

Armani /aar maáni/, **Giorgio** (*b.* 1934) Italian fashion designer. He founded the Giorgio Armani fashion design company in 1975.

> 'I realized that fashion was moving in a very brutal, nostalgic and sometimes vulgar direction, and I refused it.'
> [Giorgio Armani, *The Fashion Conspiracy*; 1989]

armature /aármachar/ *n* **1.** **KEEPER FOR MAGNET** a bar of soft iron or steel placed across the poles of a magnet to maintain its strength **2.** ELEC ENG **MOVING PART IN ELECTROMAGNETIC DEVICE** the moving part in an electromagnetic device, wound with coils that carry a current. In a dynamo, an electric current is induced in the coils when they revolve through a magnetic field. **3.** BIOL **PROTECTIVE PART** a protective outer covering or structure, e.g. quills on a porcupine or spines on a plant **4.** SCULPTURE **FRAMEWORK FOR MODEL** a framework that supports a sculpture while it is being modelled [15C. Via French < Latin *armatura* < *armat-*, past participle of *armare* (see ARM[2])]

armband /aárm band/ *n* a band of fabric worn around the upper arm

arm candy *n* somebody good-looking whom a person takes to a public event in order to impress others and enhance his or her status (*slang offensive*)

armchair /aárm chair/ *n* a chair with arms, especially a comfortable upholstered chair ■ *adj* having no direct experience, only second-hand or theoretical knowledge ○ *an armchair tourist*

armed /aarmd/ *adj* **1.** **EQUIPPED WITH WEAPON** equipped with one or more weapons ○ *armed robbers* **2.** **INVOLVING WEAPONS** involving the use of weapons ○ *armed conflict* **3.** **WITH EXPLODING MECHANISM ACTIVE** prepared and ready for use as a weapon, especially with a fuse or detonator activated **4.** **PROVIDED WITH NECESSARY INFORMATION OR TOOLS** equipped with the information or tools needed to achieve something ○ *armed with the latest statistics*

armed forces *npl* the combined bodies of troops of a country, who fight on land, at sea, or in the air

Armenia

Armenia /aar meéni ə/ country in western Asia between the Black Sea and the Caspian Sea, bordered by Azerbaijan, Azerbaijan-Nakeivan enclave, Iran, Turkey, and Georgia. Language: Armenian. Currency: dram. Capital: Yerevan. Population: 3,326,448 (2003). Area: 29,800 sq. km/11,500 sq. mi. Official name **Republic of Armenia**

Armenian /aar meéni ən/ *n* **1.** somebody who comes from Armenia **2.** the national language of Armenia, also spoken in Turkey and in other parts of the world, that forms a branch of Indo-European. Native speakers: 4 million. —**Armenian** *adj*

armhole /aárm hōl/ *n* either of the holes at the top of a garment for the wearer's arms to go through

Armidale /aármi dayl/ town in eastern New South Wales, Australia, home to the University of New England. Population: 21,330 (1996).

armiger /aármijər/ *n* somebody entitled to have a coat of arms (*archaic*) [Mid-16C. < Latin, 'bearing weapons' < *arma* 'weapons']

armillary sphere

armillary sphere /aar mílləri-, aármiləri-/ *n* a spherical model of the universe, first used by early Greek astronomers, in which the relative positions of the Earth and other astronomical objects are represented by intersecting metal rings [< modern Latin *armillaris* < Latin *armilla* 'arm bracelet' < *armus* 'shoulder']

Arminian /aar mínni ən/ *adj* relating to or following the Protestant theologian Arminius or his doctrines, which rejected the Calvinist view of absolute predestination ■ *n* a follower of Arminius or his doctrines [Early 17C. < *Arminius*, Latinized surname of Jakob Hermandszoon (1560–1609)] —**Arminianism** *n*

armistice /aármistiss/ *n* a truce in a war to discuss terms for peace [Early 18C. Directly or via French < modern Latin *armistitium* 'stoppage of weapons' < Latin *arma* 'weapons']

Armistice Day *n* the former annual celebration of the armistice that ended World War I on 11 November 1918, now incorporated into the observance of Remembrance Sunday

armlet /aármlət/ *n* **1.** a band worn on the upper arm **2.** a short narrow arm of a lake or the sea

armlock /aárm lok/ *n* a tight immobilizing grip around one or both of somebody's upper arms, e.g. in wrestling or judo

armoire /aar mwaár/ *n* a tall cupboard or wardrobe, often ornately decorated. Originally, an armoire was used for storing weapons. [Late 16C. Via French < Latin *armarium* 'chest' < *arma* 'weapons']

armor *n* US spelling of **armour**

armorial /aar máwri əl/ *adj* relating to or decorated with a coat of arms ○ *armorial bearings* [Late 16C. < obsolete *armory* 'heraldry' < Old French *armoi(e)rie* < *armoier* 'to blazon' < *armes* 'weapons' < Latin *arma*]

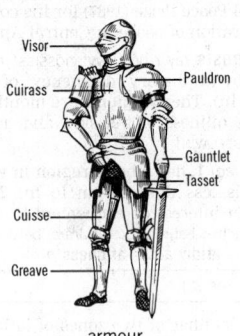

armour

armour /aármər/ *n* **1.** MIL, HIST **PROTECTION FOR SOLDIERS** protective clothing of metal or leather worn in battle by soldiers in former times **2.** MIL **PROTECTION FOR MILITARY VEHICLES** the protective layer of metal covering military vehicles, ships, and aircraft **3.** BIOL **COVERING ON PLANTS OR ANIMALS** a protective layer covering a plant or animal **4.** **PROTECTION** something that gives protection or acts as a safeguard **5.** GEOG **GRAVEL ON RIVER BED** a surface layer of gravel on a river bed preventing erosion of the material below **6.** HERALDRY **COATS OF ARMS** coats of arms, or the symbols and designs used on them [13C. < French *armure* < Latin *armatura* (see ARMATURE)]

armoured /aármərd/ *adj* **1.** MIL **HAVING PROTECTIVE METAL COVERING** equipped with a protective metal covering against bullets or missiles **2.** MIL **USING ARMOURED VEHICLES** equipped with and using armoured vehicles **3.** BIOL **HAVING NATURAL PROTECTIVE COVERING** having a natural protective covering such as a shell

armoured car *n* **1.** a lightly armoured military vehicle used mainly for reconnaissance **2.** a vehicle such as a security van with an extra layer of thick metal to protect the occupants from bullets or other weapons

armourer /aármərər/ *n* **1.** **MAKER OF ARMS** somebody who makes armour and weapons **2.** **SOMEBODY MAINTAINING SMALL ARMS** somebody who repairs and maintains small arms **3.** **SOMEBODY LOADING WEAPONS FOR TRANSPORTATION** a soldier, sailor, or airman who loads weapons onto vehicles, aircraft, or missiles

armour plate *n* MIL same as **armour** (sense 2) —**armour-plated** *adj*

armoury /aárməri/ (*plural* **-ies**) *n* **1.** **STORE FOR WEAPONS** a

building in which weapons are stored **2. COLLECTION OF WEAPONS** a store or collection of weapons **3. US BUILDING FOR MILITARY TRAINING** a building used for drilling and training US National Guard units **4. RESOURCES AVAILABLE FOR DEALING WITH OPPONENT** a range of equipment and skills available to somebody, used especially in dealing with opponents [14C. < Old French *armoi(e)rie* 'weaponry' (see ARMORIAL)]

armpit /aárm pit/ *n* **1.** the hollow area under the arm where it joins the body **2.** a place that is the worst of its kind (*slang*)

armrest /aárm rest/ *n* a projecting part on a seat, designed to support the arm of somebody sitting down

arms control *n* reduction or limitation in the number or type of weapons held by some countries, especially as a result of mutual agreement

arm's-length *adj* without close contact or an intimate relationship ○ *the companies' arm's-length trading arrangement*

arm's-length management organization *n* a private management company set up to operate a public service such as local authority housing

arms race *n* a competition between countries for superiority in the number and power of weapons held

Armstrong /aárm strong/, **Gillian** (*b.* 1950) Australian filmmaker. She directed *My Brilliant Career* (1979) and *Oscar and Lucinda* (1997). Full name **Armstrong, Gillian May**

Louis Armstrong

Armstrong, Louis (1901–71) US jazz musician. He was known for his trumpet playing and gravelly singing voice. Full name **Armstrong, Daniel Louis**. Known as **Satchmo**

'Folk music? Why, daddy, I don't know no other kind of music *but* folk music. I ain't never heard a horse sing a song.'
[Louis Armstrong. Quoted in *The Jazz Book*, Joachim E. Berendt; 1983]

Neil Armstrong

Armstrong, Neil (*b.* 1930) US astronaut. He was the first person to set foot on the Moon (1969).

'That's one small step for man, one giant leap for mankind.'
[Neil Armstrong. Message to NASA; 20 July 1969]

Armstrong, William (1810–1900) British engineer and industrialist. He became a major figure in the arms and shipbuilding industries and helped found the Vickers Armstrong company.

arm-twisting *n* heavy-handed or unfair pressure on somebody to do something (*informal*)

arm wrestling *n* a contest of strength between two people in which they sit opposite each other with one elbow each on a table, clasp hands, and try to force the other's hand onto the table

army /aármi/ (*plural* **-mies**) *n* **1. BRANCH OF ARMED FORCES** the branch of a country's armed forces trained to fight on land **2. LARGE ARMED GROUP** a trained or armed fighting force **3. LARGE ORGANIZED GROUP** a large group of people, especially one that has been organized to do a specific thing ○ *an army of volunteers cleared the wasteland* **4. LARGE GROUP OF THINGS** a very large number of similar things [14C. Via French *armée* < medieval Latin *armata* < past participle of Latin *armare* (see ARM[2])]

army ant *n* a nomadic tropical ant that forages in large groups

army brat *n* somebody who is born into, or grows up in, the family of a member of the army (*informal*) ○ *As an army brat, she's lived all over the world.*

Army List *n* an official list of all serving commissioned officers and reserve officers in the army

armyworm /aármi wurm/ *n* the larva of an insect that travels in large migratory groups destroying vegetation and crops

Arne /aarn/, **Thomas** (1710–78) British composer. He wrote operas, composed songs for the theatre, and wrote *Rule Britannia* (1740). Full name **Arne, Thomas Augustine**

Arnhem /aárnəm/ city in the eastern Netherlands. It was the scene of a major battle in World War II, when Allied airborne troops fought unsuccessfully to secure Rhine bridges in September 1944. Population: 138,020 (2000).

Arnhem Land region in Northern Australia, situated between the Roper and South Alligator rivers in the Northern Territory, and the site of one of Australia's largest Aboriginal reserves

arnica /aárnikə/ (*plural* **-cas** or same) *n* **1.** a liquid preparation made from the dried flower heads of a perennial herb. Use: treating bruises and sprains in alternative medicine. **2.** a perennial plant from which arnica is prepared. Flowers: yellow, resembling daisies. Native to: northern Europe. Genus: *Arnica*. [Mid-18C. < modern Latin]

Arno /aárnō/ chief river of the Tuscany region in central Italy. It rises in the Tuscan Apennines and flows through Florence and Pisa. Length: 240 km/150 mi.

Arnold /aárn'ld/, **Benedict** (1741–1801) American officer who later betrayed the American cause by planning to surrender West Point to the British (1780) during the American War of Independence (1775–83)

Arnold, Sir Malcolm (*b.* 1921) British composer. He wrote symphonies, concertos, operas, ballets, and film scores, including that for *The Bridge on the River Kwai* (1957).

Arnold, Matthew (1822–88) British poet and critic. He was professor of poetry at Oxford (1857), and in addition to poetry wrote critical and religious works.

'And we are here as on a darkling plain / Swept with confused alarms of struggle and flight, / Where ignorant armies clash by night.'
[Matthew Arnold, 'Dover Beach'; 1867]

Arnold, Thomas (1795–1842) British educator. He was the father of Matthew Arnold and the influential reforming headmaster of Rugby school (1828–42).

'What we must look for here is, first, religious and moral principles; secondly, gentlemanly conduct; thirdly, intellectual ability.'
[Thomas Arnold. Address to the scholars of Rugby. Quoted in *The Life and Correspondence of Thomas Arnold*, Penrhyn Stanley; 1844]

Arnside and Silverdale /aárn sīd ənd sílvər dayl/ Area of Outstanding Natural Beauty on the coast of Cumbria, northwestern England. Area: 75 sq. km/29 sq. mi.

A-road *n* a primary route other than a motorway, given the prefix 'A' in the national road numbering and classification system

aroha /aárōhə/ *n* NZ **1.** love **2.** sympathy and understanding [< Maori]

aroid /árroyd/ *adj* relating to or belonging to the arum family of perennial plants [Late 19C. < ARUM]

aroma /ə rómə/ *n* **1.** a smell, especially a pleasant one **2.** a subtle impression or quality ○ *an aroma of scandal* [12C. Via Latin < Greek *arōma* 'spice']

SYNONYMS See *smell*.

aromatase /ə rómə tàyz/ *n* an enzyme that converts androgens to oestrogens

aromatase inhibitor *n* a chemical belonging to a group that block the action of the substance that converts androgens into oestrogens. Use: control of breast cancer.

aromatherapy /ə rómə thérrəpi/ *n* the use of oils extracted from plants to alleviate physical and psychological disorders, usually through massage or inhalation [Mid-20C. < French *aromathérapie*] —**aromatherapist** *n*

aromatic /árrə máttik/ *adj* **1. HAVING FRAGRANT SMELL** giving off a distinctive and pleasant smell **2. CHEM OF CLASS OF ORGANIC COMPOUNDS** describes organic compounds that contain one or more rings of carbon atoms and undergo chemical reactions that are characteristic of benzene. About half of all organic compounds are aromatic. ■ *n* **FRAGRANT SUBSTANCE OR PLANT** a substance or plant that has a distinctive pleasant smell [14C. Via French < Greek *arōmatikos* < *arōma* 'spice'] —**aromatically** *adv*

aromatize /ə rómə tīz/ (**-tizes, -tizing, -tized**), **aromatise** (**-tises, -tising, -tised**) *vt* **1.** to make something fragrant, or release the fragrance of something **2.** to convert a nonaromatic (**aliphatic**) chemical compound to an aromatic compound —**aromatization** /ə rómə tī záysh'n/ *n*

arose past tense of **arise**

around /ə równd/ CORE MEANING: a grammatical word used to indicate that something surrounds a place or object or is situated on or moves from place to place on all sides of it ○ (prep) *She came in and looked at the mess all around her.* ○ (prep) *A crumbling wall still stood around the old town.* ○ (adv) *From this spot you could see the countryside for miles around.*
1. *prep* **TO OTHER SIDE OF** moving or looking to the other side of ○ *There is a chemist's around the corner.* **2.** *prep* **SURROUNDING** so as to surround or be on all sides of ○ *a belt around his waist* ○ *A crowd gathered around them.* **3.** *prep, adv* **TURNING ON AXIS** revolving round a centre or axis ○ (prep) *satellites moving around the planet* **4.** *prep, adv* **IN ALL DIRECTIONS** situated, moving, or happening in all directions from a central point of reference ○ (adv) *The area was built up for several kilometres around.* **5.** *prep* **REGARDING** with regard to ○ *There is a lot of anxiety around the issue of change.* **6.** *prep* **SO AS TO AVOID** so as to sidestep or otherwise avoid something unpleasant or difficult ○ *finally found a way around the problem* **7.** *prep, adv* **TO EVERYONE** to all members in a group, from person to person ○ (adv) *passed the plate of sandwiches around* **8.** *prep* US **NEAR** in the near vicinity of ○ *She lives around the Boston area.* **9.** *adv* **TO REVERSED POSITION** in or to a different or the opposite direction ○ *wheeled around and jogged off* **10.** *adv* **PRESENT** in existence ○ *since computers have been around* **11.** *adv, prep* **IN VARIOUS PLACES** positioned here and there ○ *There were vases of flowers around the room.* **12.** *adv, prep* **AT HAND** in the vicinity, sometimes with no definite purpose or intent ○ *lounged around in the hotel lobby* ○ *Is the boss around?* **13.** *adv, prep* **IN VARIOUS DIRECTIONS** from place to place in different directions or in no particular direction ○ *rushing around* **14.** *adv* **IN CIRCULATION** available, prevalent, or in circulation ○ *There's lots of illness around at the moment.* **15.** *adv, prep* **APPROXIMATELY** close to in number, time, or degree ○ *around £600 a month* **16.** *adv, adj* **ALIVE OR EXISTING** present, alive, or in existence (*informal*) ○ *What's amazing is that nearly everyone from that era is still around.* [13C. < A-[1] 'on' + ROUND[1], probably after Old French *à la reond* 'in the round, roundabout'] ◇ **have been around** to have had enough experience of life and the ways of the world not to be easily deceived (*informal*)

USAGE See *round*[2].

around-the-clock *adj* happening constantly, with no breaks, for 24 hours a day

arouse /ə rówz/ (**arouses, arousing, aroused**) *v* **1.** *vt* STIMULATE SOMETHING to evoke a feeling, response, or desire ○ *aroused their interest* **2.** *vt* STIMULATE SEXUAL DESIRE IN SOMEBODY to cause feelings of sexual desire in somebody **3.** *vt* ANNOY SOMEBODY to make somebody angry **4.** *vti* WAKE UP to wake up, or wake somebody up, from sleep or unconsciousness (*formal*) [Late 16C. < ROUSE] —**arousal** *n*

AKG London

Jean Arp

Arp /aarp/, **Jean** (1887–1966) French sculptor. A co-founder of the Dada movement (1916), he produced organic abstract sculptures based on natural forms.

> 'I love nature but not its substitutes. Naturalistic, illusionistic art is a substitute.' [Jean Arp. Quoted in *On My Way, Poetry and Essays. 1912...1947*, Ralph Manheim (tr.); 1948]

ARP /aarp/ *abbr* air-raid precautions

ARPAnet /áarpə net/ *n* a wide area computer network of the late 1960s linking US government, academic, business, and military sites

arpeggio /aar péjji ō/ (*plural* **-os**) *n* a sounding of the notes of a chord one after the other in rapid succession, instead of simultaneously [Early 18C. < Italian < *arpeggiare* 'play on the harp' < *arpa* 'harp']

arquebus *n* ARMS same as **harquebus**

arr. *abbr* **1.** MUSIC arranged **2.** TRAVEL arrival **3.** TRAVEL arrived **4.** TRAVEL arrives

Arrabal /árrə bál/, **Fernando** (*b.* 1932) Moroccan-born Spanish dramatist and novelist. His plays, including *And They Put Handcuffs on the Flowers* (1971), were banned in France and Sweden for their deliberately shocking imagery.

arraign /ə ráyn/ (**-raigns, -raigning, -raigned**) *vt* **1.** to bring somebody to court to answer a charge (*usually passive*) **2.** to call somebody to account for a fault or mistake (*formal*) [14C. Via Anglo-Norman *arainer* < assumed Vulgar Latin *adrationare* 'call to account' < Latin *ratio* 'reason'] —**arraigner** *n* —**arraignment** *n*

Arran /árrən/ island in the Firth of Clyde in western Scotland. It is noted for its mountain scenery. Area: 433 sq. km/167 sq. mi.

arrange /ə ráynj/ (**-ranges, -ranging, -ranged**) *v* **1.** *vt* PUT SOMEBODY OR SOMETHING IN ORDER to put people or things in a position or order ○ *All the CDs were arranged alphabetically.* **2.** *vt* PREPARE FOR SOMETHING to do what is necessary to make something happen in the future ○ *arrange a meeting* **3.** *vti* MAKE AGREEMENT FOR SOMETHING TO HAPPEN to make an agreement so that something can happen or somebody can have something ○ *She's arranged for the painters to start next week.* **4.** *vti* MUSIC ADAPT MUSIC to adapt a piece of music for playing or singing in a different manner (*often passive*) [Mid-18C. < Old French *arangier* 'put in a line to' < *rangier* (see RANGE)] —**arrangeable** *adj* —**arranged** *adj* —**arranger** *n*

arranged marriage *n* a marriage in which the parents choose a bride or bridegroom for their son or daughter

arrangement /ə ráynjmənt/ *n* **1.** PREPARATION something that has to be done so that something else can happen in the future, or the making of such preparations (*often used in the plural*) **2.** AGREEMENT an agreement made with somebody to do something, or the making of such an agreement **3.** PLEASING DISPLAY a group of things organized in a way that is meant to be pleasing to look at, or the arranging of such a group **4.** ORGANIZATION the way in which something is organized **5.** MUSIC MUSICAL ADAPTATION a version of a piece of music adapted for playing or singing in a different manner, or the scoring of such a version

arrant /árrənt/ *adj* used to emphasize that somebody or something is an extreme example of something disapproved of ○ *an air of arrant self-importance* [Mid-16C. Alteration of ERRANT 'wandering'] —**arrantly** *adv*

arras /árrəss/ *n* a tapestry used as a wall-hanging or hanging screen [15C. < Anglo-Norman *draps d'Arras* 'cloth of Arras' (French town famous for its woollens and tapestry)]

array /ə ráy/ *n* **1.** COLLECTION a large number or wide range of people or things ○ *a dazzling array of talent* **2.** STRIKING ARRANGEMENT a group of things arranged in an impressive or structured way ○ *an array of Greek sculptures* **3.** CLOTHING FINE CLOTHES fine, expensive, or impressive clothes (*literary*) **4.** MATHS ORDERED SET OF NUMBERS a set of numbers or symbols, e.g. experimental data, usually arranged in a specific order **5.** TELECOM GROUP OF AERIALS a group of aerials arranged to increase their effectiveness **6.** COMPUT DATA STRUCTURE an arrangement of items of computerized data in tabular form for easy reference. A computer program references an item by naming the array and the position of the item in it. **7.** LAW JURORS a panel of jurors, or the group of people from whom a jury is selected ■ *vt* (**-rays, -raying, -rayed**) **1.** ARRANGE SOMETHING to arrange something for display or in readiness for use (*formal; usually passive*) **2.** MIL DEPLOY TROOPS to arrange troops for battle (*literary; usually passive*) **3.** CLOTHING CLOTHE SOMEBODY to clothe somebody in particular attire (*literary; often passive*) ○ *was arrayed in ermine and diamonds* [14C. Via Anglo-Norman < Old French *arei* < *areer* 'to array' < assumed Vulgar Latin *arredare* 'arrange' < Latin *ad* 'to' + a Germanic word, 'prepare']

arré /úrray/ *interj S Asia* used to attract another person's attention, or to express emotions such as interest, surprise, or irritation [Via Hindi < Sanskrit *are*, used to summon somebody of inferior rank]

arrearage /ə réerij/ *n* **1.** the debt that remains after part of an overdue debt has been paid **2.** the state of being overdue in the payment of a debt

arrears /ə réerz/ *npl* unpaid debts, especially debts accumulating as a result of the debtor's failure to make regular payments [15C. < obsolete *arrear* 'to the rear, overdue', via Old French < medieval Latin *adretro* < Latin *ad* 'to' + *retro* 'backwards, behind'] ◇ **in arrears 1.** behind in making regular payments of money owed **2.** paid only after some work has been done or a period of time has elapsed

arrector pili /ə rék tawr péeli/ *n* a small muscle connecting a hair follicle to the dermis that contracts to make the hair stand erect in response to cold or fear [< modern Latin, 'raiser of hair']

Arrernte /árrəndə/, **Aranda** *n* **1.** a member of an Aboriginal people who live in southern central Australia **2.** a Pama-Nyungan language spoken in parts of Australia's Northern Territory. Native speakers: 2,000. [Late 19C. < Arrernte] —**Arrernte** *adj*

arrest /ə rést/ *vt* (**-rests, -resting, -rested**) **1.** LAW TAKE SOMEBODY INTO CUSTODY to take somebody into custody on suspicion of having committed a crime **2.** STOP SOMETHING to stop or slow something (*formal*) ○ *a mechanism that arrests the motion of the flywheel* **3.** TAKE HOLD OF SOMETHING to suddenly capture and hold something, especially somebody's attention (*formal*) ○ *an astonishing sight that arrested our attention* **4.** SEIZE SOMETHING LEGALLY to seize or detain something by legal authority (*formal*) ■ *n* **1.** LAW TAKING OF SOMEBODY INTO CUSTODY the taking of somebody into custody on suspicion of having committed a crime ○ *a case of wrongful arrest* **2.** LAW CUSTODY the state of being held in custody on suspicion of having committed a crime ○ *You're under arrest!* **3.** STOPPING OF SOMETHING the stopping or slowing of something **4.** LAW LEGAL SEIZURE OF SOMETHING the legal seizure or detention of something (*formal*) ○ *the arrest of the suspect merchant ship by customs officers* [14C. Via Old French < assumed Vulgar Latin *arrestare* 'cause to stop' < Latin *restare* 'stay behind' (see REST²)] —**arrestee** /ə réss tée/ *n* —**arrestment** *n*

arrester /ə réstər/, **arrestor** /ə réstər, -awr/ *n* **1.** NAVY same as **arresting cable 2.** somebody who takes a suspect into legal custody on suspicion of having committed a crime

arresting /ə résting/ *adj* so good-looking or so unusual that people's attention is immediately caught —**arrestingly** *adv*

arresting cable *n* one of a set of cables strung across the deck of an aircraft carrier to catch the tail hook of a landing aircraft and bring it to a halt (*usually used in the plural*)

arrest of judgment *n* a delay in acting on the verdict of a court on the grounds of possible error

arrestor *n* same as **arrester**

Arrhenius /ə réenee əss/, **Svante August** (1859–1927) Swedish chemist. His theory of ions carrying electrical charges became one of the cornerstones of modern physical chemistry and electrochemistry.

Arrhenius equation *n* an equation in physical chemistry that relates the increase in the rate of a chemical reaction to a rise in temperature

arrhythmia /ə ríthmi ə, ay-/ *n* an irregularity in a rhythmic action such as a heartbeat or breathing [Late 19C. < Greek < *arruthmos* 'without measure' < *rhuthmos* (see RHYTHM)]

arrhythmic /ə ríthmik, ay-/ *adj* **1.** describes an irregular rhythmic action of a heartbeat or breathing **2.** without a regular or recognizable rhythm ○ *an arrhythmic tapping on the glass* —**arrhythmically** *adv*

arrière-pensée /árri air póN say/ (*plural* **arrière-pensées** /*pronunc. same*/) *n* (*formal*) **1.** a mental reservation **2.** an unspoken intention [Early 19C. < French, literally 'behind-thought']

arris /árriss/ (*plural same* or **-rises**) *n* a sharp edge or ridge made by the meeting of two surfaces on an architectural column or moulding [Late 17C. Via French *areste* 'sharp edge' < Latin *arista* (see ARÊTE)]

arrival /ə rív'l/ *n* **1.** ARRIVING the reaching of a place after coming from another place ○ *Her arrival caused a buzz of comment.* **2.** NEWCOMER somebody or something recently arriving at a place or joining a group ○ *a late arrival* **3.** PASSENGER VEHICLE ARRIVING SOMEWHERE an aircraft, train, or bus arriving at an airport or station **4.** BEGINNING the moment when something begins or becomes important ○ *The arrival of television changed the world.* **5.** BIRTH the birth of a baby **6.** REACHING OF SOMETHING the achieving or reaching of something after much work or effort ○ *Their arrival at a decision seems unlikely.*

arrive /ə rív/ (**-rives, -riving, -rived**) *vi* **1.** GET TO PLACE to reach a place after coming from another place **2.** BE DELIVERED to be delivered or brought to somebody or something **3.** BECOME AVAILABLE to become available or common **4.** BEGIN to begin or happen after a period of time or waiting ○ *We've got to finish the work before summer arrives.* **5.** WORK OUT SOLUTION to reach a decision after thinking about or discussing a problem ○ *How did you arrive at the idea of using strings?* **6.** ENTER LIFE to be born **7.** SUCCEED to become successful or famous (*informal*) ○ *You haven't arrived until you've eaten in this restaurant.* [12C. Via French < assumed Vulgar Latin *arripare* 'come to shore' < Latin *ripa* 'shore'] —**arriver** *n*

arrivederci /ə reevə dúrchi/ *interj* goodbye for now [Late 20C. < Italian *a rivederci* 'until we see each other again' < *rivedere* 'see again']

arriviste /árri véest/ *n* somebody who has recently become influential or socially prominent and is regarded as an upstart [Early 20C. < French, 'somebody who arrives']

arrogant /árrəgənt/ *adj* feeling or showing self-importance and contempt for others [14C. Via French < Latin *arrogant-*, present participle of *arrogare* 'claim for yourself' < *rogare* 'ask'] —**arrogance** *n* —**arrogantly** *adv*

SYNONYMS See ***proud***.

arrogate /árrə gayt/ (**-gates, -gating, -gated**) *vt* (*formal*) **1.** to take or claim something for yourself without the right to do so **2.** to assign or attribute something to another in a way that is not warranted [Mid-16C. < Latin *arrogat-*, past participle of *arrogare* (see ARROGANT)] —**arrogation** /árrə gáysh'n/ *n* —**arrogator** *n*

arrondissement /a róN deess móN/ (*plural* **-ments** /*pronunc. same*/) *n* **1.** an administrative area in France that is the largest subdivision of a department **2.** an administrative area in some large

cities in France, including Paris [Early 19C. < French < *arrondiss-*, stem of *arrondir* 'make round']

arrow /árrō/ *n* **1. MISSILE SHOT FROM BOW** a long thin missile pointed at one end and usually with feathers at the other, fired from a bow **2. DIRECTION SIGN** a direction sign consisting of a horizontal stroke finishing in the middle of a V shape **3.** *Carib* **FLOWER ON STALK** a sugar cane flower and its stalk ■ *v* (**-rows, -rowing, -rowed**) **1.** *vi* **DART** to move quickly like an arrow shot from a bow **2.** *vt Malaysia* **SELECT SOMEBODY** to choose somebody to do something unpleasant (*informal*) ○ *The teacher arrowed me because I was dreaming in class.* **3.** *vi Carib* **PRODUCE BLOOMS** to come into flower (*refers to sugar cane*) [Old English *arwe* < Old Norse *örv-* < Indo-European]

arrowhead /árrō hed/ *n* **1.** a sharp pointed tip fixed to an arrow **2.** a water plant with arrow-shaped leaves. Flowers: white, in clusters. Native to: Asia, North America. Genus: *Sagittaria*.

arrow key *n* one of four computer keys marked with an up, down, left, or right arrow, used to move the cursor

arrow-poison frog *n* a brightly coloured frog whose skin glands produce poison that is used by local peoples for smearing on arrow tips. Native to: South America. Family: Dendrobatidae.

arrowroot /árrō root/ (*plural same* or **-roots**) *n* **1. STARCH** edible starch obtained from the rhizomes of a tropical plant. Use: thickener for clear sauces. **2. CENTRAL AMERICAN PLANT** a plant with rhizomes that yield arrowroot. Native to: tropical Central America. Latin name: *Maranta arundinacea*. **3. EDIBLE RHIZOME** the edible rhizome of the arrowroot plant [Late 17C. By folk etymology < Arawak *aru-aru* 'meal of meals'; from its use to absorb poison from arrow wounds]

arrow worm *n* an invertebrate sea animal that has an arrow-shaped body and spines on its head for catching prey. Phylum: Chaetognatha. [< the spines on its head]

arroyo /ə róy ō/ (*plural* **-os**) *n Southwest US* **1.** a steep-sided dry gully in a desert area that is wet only after heavy rain **2.** a small stream of running water [Mid-19C. Via Spanish < Latin *arrugia* 'mineshaft']

Arroyo /a róy ō/, **Gloria** (*b.* 1947) president of the Philippines (2001–). Elected to the senate in 1992 and 1995 and as vice president in 1998, she was sworn in as president when her predecessor was forced to resign following allegations of corruption. Full name **Arroyo, Maria Gloria Macapagal**

arse /aarss/ *n* (*taboo*) **1.** a highly offensive term for the buttocks or anus. N Am term **ass**[2] **2.** a highly offensive term that deliberately insults somebody's intelligence or value [Old English *ærs, ears* < Indo-European] ◇ **move** *or* **shift your arse** a highly offensive phrase meaning to hurry up (*taboo*) ◇ **not know your arse from your elbow** a highly offensive phrase meaning to know very little (*taboo*)

arse about, arse around *vi* a highly offensive term meaning to waste time behaving in a silly irritating way (*taboo*)

arsehole /áarss hōl/ *n* **1.** a highly offensive term that deliberately insult's somebody's value or importance (*taboo insult*) **2.** a highly offensive term for the anus (*taboo*)

arse licker *n* a highly offensive term for somebody who flatters or obediently carries out the orders of a superior in order to gain favour (*taboo*) N Am term **ass kisser** —**arse-licking** *n*

arsenal /áarss'nəl/ *n* **1. STORE FOR WEAPONS** a building where weapons and military equipment are stored **2. ARMAMENTS** a stockpile of weapons and military equipment **3. RESOURCES** a supply of methods or resources ○ *an arsenal of teaching strategies* [Early 16C. Directly or via French < Italian *arzanale* < Venetian Italian *arzanà* < Arabic *dār-(aṣ-)ṣinā'a* 'workshop, factory']

ORIGIN ***Arsenal*** is derived from an Arabic word *dār-(aṣ-)ṣinā'a*, meaning 'workshop' or 'factory'. When the original Arabic word was borrowed into Venetian Italian, the initial *d* was lost, possibly because it was misinterpreted as the Italian preposition *di* 'of'. The word came to mean 'dock possessing naval stores', and in Venice, the leading naval power in the Mediterranean in the 15th century, the dockyard is known to this day as the *Arzenale*. The Romance languages retain this meaning in words from the same ancestor that still show the Arabic *d*, in Italian *darsena* 'dock', for example; in English too, 'dockyard' was the original sense, giving way from the late 16th century to 'military storehouse'.

arsenate /áarssə nayt, -nit/ *n* any salt of arsenic acid [Early 19C. < ARSENIC]

arsenic /áarssnik/ *n* **1.** a steel-grey poisonous solid element that is a brittle crystalline metalloid. Source: realgar, arsenopyrite. Use: in glass manufacture to remove impurities of colour, in alloys to harden lead. Symbol **As**. See table at **element 2.** CHEM same as **arsenic trioxide** ■ *adj* relating to or containing arsenic, especially with a valency of 5 [14C. Via French < Greek *arsenikon* 'yellow orpiment' < Arabic *az-zarnīk* 'the orpiment' < Persian *zar* 'gold']

ORIGIN The term ***arsenic*** was originally applied to a lemon-yellow mineral that is a compound of arsenic, hence its origin in *zar*, the Persian word for gold. The Arabic derivative of this word was misinterpreted by foreign listeners as including the definite article *al*, and in Greek the supposed beneficial effects on virility led the term to be associated by folk etymology with the similar-sounding words *arsenikos*, 'masculine', and *arsēn*, 'manly'. In English the word still referred to the mineral at first (for which *orpiment* was the other current name), and it was not until the early 17th century that it was applied to white arsenic or arsenic trioxide. The element arsenic itself was isolated and so named at the start of the 19th century.

arsenic acid /aar sénnik-/ *n* a white poisonous crystalline solid containing arsenic. Use: manufacture of pigments and insecticides. Formula: H_3AsO_4.

arsenical /aar sénnik'l/ *adj* relating to or containing arsenic ■ *n* a substance that contains arsenic, e.g. a drug or insecticide

arsenic trioxide /áarssnik trī óksīd, aar sénnik-/ *n* a white poisonous solid that contains arsenic. Use: insecticide, rodenticide, herbicide, manufacture of glass and pigments. Formula: As_2O_3.

arsenide /áarssə nīd/ *n* a chemical compound of arsenic and a metal [Mid-19C. < ARSENIC]

arsenious /aar seéni əss/ *adj* relating to or containing arsenic, especially with a valency of 3 [Early 19C. < ARSENIC]

arsenopyrite /áarssinō pír īt, aar sénnə-/ *n* a grey to white metallic mineral consisting of a sulphide of iron and arsenic [Mid-19C. < ARSENIC]

arsenotherapy /áarsənō thérrəpi/ *n* the treatment of disease with arsenic or one of its derivatives or preparations [< ARSENIC]

arses LITERAT plural of **arsis**

arsine /áar seen/ *n* a colourless, very poisonous gas with an odour like garlic. Use: manufacture of organic chemicals, transistors, chemical weapons. Formula: AsH_3. [Late 19C. < ARSENIC]

arsis /áarssiss/ (*plural* **arses** /áar seez/) *n* **1.** in classical Greek and Roman verse, the short syllable or syllables in a metrical foot **2.** in modern verse, the accented syllable in a metrical foot [14C. Via late Latin, 'raising of the voice to greater force, accented part of the metrical foot' < Greek, 'raising (of the foot in beating time)']

arson /áarss'n/ *n* the burning of a building or other property for a criminal or malicious reason [Late 17C. < legal Anglo-Norman *arsoun* < Latin *arsus*, past participle of *ardere* 'to burn'] —**arsonist** *n*

arsy-versy /áarssi vúrssi/ *adv* backwards or upside down (*dated informal; sometimes considered offensive*) [Mid-16C. < ARSE + Latin *versus* 'turned', perhaps after VICE VERSA]

art[1] /aart/ *n* **1. CREATION OF BEAUTIFUL THINGS** the creation of beautiful or thought-provoking works, e.g. in painting, music, or writing **2. BEAUTIFUL OBJECTS** beautiful or thought-provoking works produced through creative activity **3. BRANCH OF ART** a branch or category of art, especially one of the visual arts **4. ARTISTIC SKILL** the skill and technique involved in producing visual representations **5. STUDY OF ART** the study of a branch of the visual arts **6. CREATION BY HUMANS** creation by human endeavour rather than by nature **7. TECHNIQUES OR CRAFT** the set of techniques used by somebody in a particular field, or the use of those techniques ○ *the art of the typographer* **8. ABILITY** the skill or ability to do something well ○ *the art of conversation* **9. CUNNING** the ability to achieve things by deceitful or cunning methods (*literary*) ■ **arts** *npl* **1. FORMS OF CREATIVE BEAUTY** activities enjoyed for the beauty they create or the way they present ideas, e.g. painting, music, and literature **2. NONSCIENTIFIC SUBJECTS** nonscientific and nontechnical subjects at school or university [13C. Via French < Latin *art-* 'skill'] ◇ **have something down to a fine art** to be able to do something very skilfully

ORIGIN The Latin stem *art-* 'skill', from which ***art*** is derived, is also the source of English *artificial*, *artisan*, and *inert*.

art[2] /aart/ 2nd person singular present of **be**[1] (*archaic or literary*)

ART *abbr* MED assisted reproductive technology

art. *abbr* **1.** article **2.** artificial **3.** MIL artillery **4.** artist

-art *suffix* same as **-ard**

artal MEASURE plural of **rotl**

art deco: Chrysler Building, New York City (1930), designed by William van Alen

art deco /-dékō/, **Art Deco** *n* a style of architecture, interior design, and jewellery most popular in the 1930s that used geometric designs and bold colours and outlines [Mid-20C. < French, shortening of *arts decoratifs* 'decorative arts']

art director *n* the person in charge of the sets and costumes when something is being filmed or photographed

artee *n, v* HINDUISM another spelling of **arti**

artefact /áarti fakt/, **artifact** *n* **1.** an object made by a human being, especially one that has archaeological or cultural interest **2.** something in a biological specimen that is not present naturally but has been introduced or produced during a procedure [Early 19C. < Latin *arte* 'by skill' + *factum* 'thing made' (see FACT)]

artel /aar tél/ *n* a workers' or producers' cooperative in pre-Revolutionary Russia or the Soviet Union [Late 19C. < Russian]

Artemis /áartəmiss/ *n* in Greek mythology, the goddess of hunting and the Moon, and of childbirth. She was the daughter of Zeus and the sister of Apollo. Roman equivalent **Diana**

artemisia /áarti meézi ə, -mízzi ə/ (*plural* **-as** or *same*) *n* an aromatic plant with greyish-green leaves. Flowers: profuse, small. Native to: northern hemisphere. Genus: *Artemisia*. [14C. Via Latin < Greek, 'wormwood' < *Artemis* 'Artemis', to whom it was sacred]

arterial /aar teéri əl/ *adj* **1. OF ARTERIES** relating to, affecting, or used in arteries **2. OXYGENATED** describes the bright red blood in the arteries that has absorbed oxygen **3. MAIN** constituting a main route in a road, rail, or river system —**arterially** *adv*

arterialize /aar teéri ə līz/ (**-izes, -izing, -ized**), **arterialise** (**-ises, -ising, -ised**) *vt* to convert venous blood into arterial blood by replenishing its oxygen —**arterialization** /aar teéri ə lī záysh'n/ *n*

arterio- *prefix* artery, arterial ○ *arteriovenous* [< Greek *artēria* 'artery']

arteriogram /aar teéri ə gram/ *n* an X-ray of the arteries made after a substance that shows up on an X-ray has been injected into the bloodstream

arteriography /aar teéri óggrəfi/ *n* X-ray examination of the arteries —**arteriographic** /aar teéri ə gráffik/ *adj*

arteriole /aar teéri ōl/ *n* a blood vessel that branches off from an artery [Mid-19C. < French *artériole* 'little artery' < *artère* 'artery' < Latin *arteria* (see ARTERY)] —**arteriolar** /aar teéri ōlər/ *adj*

arteriosclerosis /aar teˈeri ō skləˈróssiss/ *n* MED same as **atherosclerosis** —**arteriosclerotic** /-sklə róttik/ *adj*

arteriovenous /aar teˈeri ō véenəss/ *adj* involving both a vein and an artery

arteritis /aˈartə rítiss/ *n* inflammation of the walls of an artery

artery /aˈartəri/ (*plural* **-ies**) *n* **1.** a blood vessel that is part of the system carrying blood under pressure from the heart to the rest of the body **2.** a main route in a road, rail, or river system [14C. Via Latin < Greek *artēria*]

artesian aquifer /aar teˈezi ən-/ *n* an aquifer that has an impermeable bed both above and below it and is under enough pressure for water to be forced upwards [See ARTESIAN WELL]

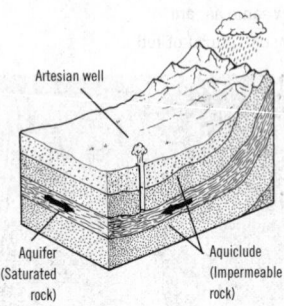

artesian well

artesian well /aar teˈezi ən-/ *n* a well drilled through impermeable rocks into strata where water is under enough pressure to force it to the surface without pumping [Mid-19C. < French *artésien* 'of Artois' (*Arteis* in Old French), region in NE France where such wells were first drilled]

art film *n* a film that is made as a work of art rather than for mass entertainment

art form *n* **1.** a creative activity or type of artistic expression that is intended to be beautiful or thought-provoking **2.** something that is done in such a sophisticated or skilful way that it can be seen as artistic

artful /aˈartf'l/ *adj* **1.** using clever, subtle, and sometimes dishonest means to achieve things **2.** done skilfully or with taste ○ *an artful arrangement of blue and green ceramics* —**artfully** *adv* —**artfulness** *n*

artful dodger *n* somebody skilled at avoiding difficult situations and having to answer questions [After a young pickpocket in *Oliver Twist* by Charles Dickens]

art gallery *n* **1.** a building where works of art are displayed **2.** an establishment that displays and sells works of art

art house *n* a cinema where art films are shown

arthr- *prefix* same as **arthro-** (*used before vowels*)

arthralgia /aar thráljə/ *n* pain in a joint —**arthralgic** *adj*

arthrectomy /aar thréktəmi/ (*plural* **-mies**) *n* a surgical operation to remove a joint

arthritis /aar thrítiss/ *n* a medical condition affecting a joint or joints, causing pain, swelling, and stiffness [Mid-16C. Via Latin < Greek, 'joint disease' < *arthron* 'joint' (see ARTHRO-)] —**arthritic** /aar thríttik/ *adj*, *n*

arthro- *prefix* joint of the body ○ *arthroscopic* [< Greek *arthron* < Indo-European, 'fit together']

arthrogram /aˈarthrə gram/ *n* an X-ray of the inside of a damaged joint made after a substance that shows up on an X-ray has been injected into the joint

arthrography /aar thróggrəfi/ *n* X-ray examination of the inside of a damaged joint

arthropathy /aar thróppəthi/ *n* a disease or medically noteworthy condition of a joint

arthroplasty /aˈarthrə plasti/ (*plural* **-ties**) *n* surgical repair of a joint, or replacement of a joint or part of one by metal or plastic parts

arthropod /aˈarthrə pod/ *n* an invertebrate animal that has jointed limbs, a segmented body, and an exoskeleton made of chitin, e.g. an insect, arachnid, centipede, or crustacean. Phylum: Arthropoda. [Late 19C. < modern Latin *Arthropoda* < Greek *arthron* 'joint'

(see ARTHRO-) + *pod-* 'foot' (see -POD)] —**arthropod** *adj* —**arthropodal** /aar thróppəd'l/ *adj*

arthroscopy /aar thróskəpi/ (*plural* **-pies**) *n* inspection of the inside of a joint of the body using an endoscope —**arthroscope** /aˈarthrəskōp/ *n* —**arthroscopic** /aˈarthrə skóppik/ *adj*

arthrosis /aar thróssiss/ (*plural* **-throses** /-thrō seez/) *n* **1.** a degenerative disease of a joint **2.** a joint between two bones (*technical*) [Mid-17C. Via Latin < Greek *arthrōsis* < *arthroun* 'to articulate' < *arthron* 'joint' (see ARTHRO-)]

arthrotomy /aar thróttəmi/ (*plural* **-mies**) *n* a surgical operation that involves cutting into a joint of the body

Arthur[1] /aˈarthər/ *n* in medieval legend, a king of the Britons whose court was based at Camelot. He was the leader of the Knights of the Round Table. —**Arthurian** /aar thyoóri ən/ *adj*

Arthur[2] ◇ **not know whether you are Arthur or Martha** *Aus* to be very confused (*informal*)

Arthur /aˈarthər/, **Chester A.** (1829–86) 21st president of the United States. A Republican president (1881–85), he enacted sweeping civil service reforms (1883) that lost him the support of his party. Full name **Arthur, Chester Alan.** See table at **president**

Arthur, Owen (*b.* 1949) prime minister of Barbados (1994–). A member of the Barbados Labour Party, he became leader of the opposition in 1993 and won general election victories in 1994 and 1999. Full name **Arthur, Owen Seymour**

> 'A rising tide can also overturn small boats.'
> [Owen Arthur, *New York Times*; 12 December 1994]

Arthurs Pass National Park /aˈarthərz-/ national park in the South Island of New Zealand. It was established in 1929. Area: 980 sq. km/378 sq. mi.

arti /aˈarti/, **aarti**, **artee** *n* a Hindu ritual in which a small fire in a flat container or lamp is moved in a circular motion in front of a god or person during a puja ■ *vt* (**-ties**, **-tiing**, **-tied**; **-tees**, **-teeing**, **-teed**) *Carib* to give a blessing to somebody, or receive a blessing from somebody [Late 20C. Via Hindi < Sanskrit *aartrika*]

artic[1] /aar tík/ *n* VEHICLES same as **articulated lorry** (*informal*) [Mid-20C. Shortening]

~~**artic**[2]~~ incorrect spelling of **arctic**

~~**artical**~~ incorrect spelling of **article**

artichoke

artichoke /aˈartichōk/ (*plural* **-chokes** or *same*) *n* **1.** a large flower bud with parts that can be eaten after cooking **2.** a plant that produces artichokes. Native to: Europe, Asia. Latin name: *Cynara scolymus*. **3.** FOOD same as **Jerusalem artichoke** (sense 1) [Mid-16C. < N Italian *articiocco*, *arciciocco* < Italian *arciciòffo*, via Spanish *alcarchofa* < Arabic *al-karšūf(a)*]

article /aˈartik'l/ *n* **1.** NEWSPAPER OR REFERENCE PIECE a piece of nonfiction writing in a newspaper, magazine, or reference book ○ *an article on ecology* **2.** ITEM an object or item, especially one that is part of a group ○ *articles of clothing* **3.** GRAM WORD BEFORE NOUN a word used with a noun that specifies whether the noun is definite or indefinite. In English the indefinite articles are 'a' and 'an', and the definite article is 'the'. **4.** ONLINE NEWSGROUP MESSAGE a message or posting to a newsgroup **5.** LAW LEGAL PARAGRAPH a section of a legal document that deals with a specific point ■ *vt* (**-cles**, **-cling**, **-cled**) LAW BIND SOMEBODY BY CONTRACT to bind somebody by the articles of a

contract, especially somebody training in the legal profession [12C. Via French < Latin *articulus* 'joint, section' < *artus* 'joint, limb']

articled clerk /aˈartikəld-/ *n* in the United Kingdom, a former title of a person being trained as a solicitor while working in a solicitor's office

article of faith *n* **1.** any one of the items that must be believed as part of a creed or statement of faith **2.** something that somebody believes completely

articles of association *npl* the regulations and constitution that a registered company is legally required to have by the British Companies Acts

articles of incorporation *npl* in the United States, a document that, once approved by an appropriate state authority, creates a corporation

articular /aar tíkyoólər/ *adj* relating to or involving a joint of the body [15C. < Latin *articularis* < *articulus* 'joint' (see ARTICLE)] —**articularly** *adv*

articular facet *n* a small surface of a bone such as a vertebra that articulates with another bone such as a rib

articulate *v* /aar tíkyoó layt/ (**-lates**, **-lating**, **-lated**) **1.** *vt* COMMUNICATE SOMETHING to express thoughts, ideas, or feelings coherently ○ *unable to articulate his grief* **2.** *vti* SPEAK DISTINCTLY to pronounce something or speak clearly **3.** *vti* JOIN TO ALLOW MOVEMENT to form the kind of joint or connection that allows movement **4.** *vi* SPEAK INTELLIGIBLY to utter intelligible speech ■ *adj* /aar tíkyoólət/ **1.** ELOQUENT able to express thoughts, ideas, or feelings coherently **2.** COHERENT spoken or expressed clearly **3.** ABLE TO SPEAK possessing the power of speech **4.** JOINTED with joints or jointed segments, as in the bodies of higher vertebrates and arthropods (*technical*) [Mid-16C. < Latin *articulatus*, past participle of *articulare* 'divide into joints, speak distinctly' < *articulus* 'joint' (see ARTICLE)] —**articulable** *adj* —**articulacy** *n* —**articulately** *adv* —**articulateness** *n*

articulated /aar tíkyoó laytid/ *adj* made up of two or more sections connected by a joint that can pivot

articulated lorry *n* a lorry made up of two parts, tractor and trailer, connected by a joint that can pivot. Aus term **semitrailer**. N Am term **tractor-trailer**

articulation /aar tíkyoó láysh'n/ *n* **1.** COMMUNICATION coherent expression of thoughts, ideas, or feelings **2.** SPEECH the pronouncing of words, or the manner in which they are pronounced **3.** JOINTING the connection of the different parts of something by joints, or the way the parts fit together **4.** ANIMAL'S JOINT a joint in an animal (*technical*) **5.** PLANT NODE a node of a plant, or the space on a stem between two nodes (*technical*) —**articulative** /aar tíkyoólətiv/ *adj* —**articulatory** /-tíkyoólətəri, -láytəri/ *adj*

articulator /aar tíkyoó laytər/ *n* **1.** somebody who communicates clearly **2.** a part of the vocal organs that helps form speech sounds. Active articulators include the pharynx, soft palate, lips, and tongue, while the passive articulators include the upper teeth, the alveolar ridge, and the hard palate.

artifact *n* another spelling of **artefact**

artifice /aˈartifiss/ *n* (*formal*) **1.** CLEVER TRICK a clever trick or stratagem **2.** CLEVERNESS the use of clever stratagems or tricks **3.** INSINCERE BEHAVIOUR the deception of people using cleverness or subtlety [Early 17C. Via French < Latin *artificium* 'craft, art, cunning' < *artific-* 'artisan, contriver' < *art-* 'skill' + *facere* 'make']

artificer /aar tíffissər/ *n* (*dated*) **1.** somebody whose work requires manual skill **2.** same as **inventor** [14C. < Anglo-Norman, probably < Old French *artificien* < Latin *artificium* 'craft, cunning' (see ARTIFICE)]

artificial /aˈarti físh'l/ *adj* **1.** MADE BY HUMANS made by human beings rather than occurring naturally **2.** SYNTHETIC made in imitation of something natural **3.** INSINCERE without sincerity or spontaneity ○ *an artificial smile* **4.** CREATED BY CULTURE produced as a result of political or cultural forces ○ *artificial barriers to promotion* [14C. Directly or via French < Latin *artificialis* < *artificium* 'craft, cunning' (see ARTIFICE)] —**artificiality** /aˈartifishi álləti/ *n* —**artificially** *adv*

artificial climbing *n* climbing on indoor or other human-made environments such as walls specifically designed and built for this activity

artificial feeding *n* the feeding of somebody by means that do not occur naturally, e.g. feeding

a patient on life support intravenously or bottle-feeding a baby

artificial horizon *n* an instrument that displays, usually pictorially, the amount of pitch or bank of an aircraft relative to the horizon

artificial insemination *n* a method of inducing pregnancy in a woman or other female mammal by injecting sperm into the womb

artificial intelligence *n* **1.** a branch of computer science that develops programs to allow machines to perform functions normally requiring human intelligence **2.** the ability of computers to perform functions that normally require human intelligence

artificialize /aárti fishə līz/ (**-izes, -izing, -ized**), **artificialise** (**-ises, -ising, -ised**) *vt* to give something an artificial appearance or quality —**artificialization** /aárti físhə lī záysh'n/ *n*

artificial language *n* a language that has been invented for international communication or for use with computers. The best-known artificial language is Esperanto.

artificial life *n* the use of computer systems to embody and simulate aspects of natural human behaviour such as learning and reproduction

artificial neural network *n* an information processing system with interconnected components analogous to neurons, based on mathematical models that mimic some features of biological nervous systems and the ability to learn through experience

artificial respiration *n* any method of forcing air into the lungs of somebody who has stopped breathing, especially the method that involves blowing air into the mouth

artificial selection *n* selection by humans of animals and plants with desirable characteristics for use in breeding over several generations

artificial sweetener *n* a synthetic sugar substitute

artillery /aar tílləri/ *n* **1.** heavy-calibre firearms, e.g. cannons, howitzers, missile-launchers, and mortars **2.** soldiers who specialize in operating large powerful firearms, regarded as a group or unit [14C. < French *artillerie* < *artiller*, variant of *atillier* 'equip, arm', influenced by *art* 'skill']

artilleryman /aar tíllərimən/ (*plural* **-men** /-mən/) *n* a soldier in an artillery unit

artillery plant *n* a plant with fleshy leaves and stamens that discharge their pollen by exploding. Native to: tropical America. Latin name: *Pilea microphylla.*

artiodactyl /aárti ō dáktil/ *n* a herbivorous hoofed mammal with an even number of toes on each foot, e.g. a cow or deer. Order: Artiodactyla. [Mid-19C. < modern Latin *artiodactyla* < Greek *artios* 'even, fitting' + *dactylos* 'finger, toe'] —**artiodactyl** *adj*

artisan /aárti zan, -zán/ *n* somebody who is skilled at a craft [Mid-16C. Via French < Italian *artigiano* < Latin *artit-*, past participle of *artire* 'instruct in the arts' < *art-* 'skill'] —**artisanship** /aártiz'n ship/ *n*

artist /aártist/ *n* **1.** CREATOR OF ART somebody who creates art, especially paintings or sculptures **2.** PERFORMER a professional entertainer **3.** SKILLED PERSON somebody who does something skilfully and creatively **4.** PERSON GOOD AT SOMETHING somebody who is very good at a particular thing (*slang*) ○ *a rip-off artist* [Late 16C. Via French *artiste* < Italian *artista* < *arte* 'art']

artiste /aar teést/ *n* **1.** a professional entertainer, especially a singer or dancer **2.** somebody who aspires to being artistic (*humorous*) [Early 19C. < French (see ARTIST)]

artistic /aar tístik/ *adj* **1.** GOOD AT ART good at a form of creative expression **2.** OF ART involving or relating to art or artists **3.** TASTEFUL showing taste, skill, and imagination **4.** APPRECIATIVE OF ART able to appreciate the beauty and worth of art —**artistically** *adv*

artistic director *n* somebody responsible for the artistic content of an enterprise in one of the arts

artistry /aártistri/ *n* **1.** the creative ability and skill of an artist, or the expression of this **2.** great ability and skill in doing something

artless /aártləss/ *adj* **1.** WITHOUT DECEPTION without guile or deception **2.** TOTALLY NATURAL completely natural and unforced **3.** INELEGANT lacking skill, knowledge, or elegance —**artlessly** *adv* —**artlessness** *n*

art nouveau /aárt noo vṓ, aár-/, **Art Nouveau** *n* a style of art, architecture, and decoration popular in the 1890s that used stylized natural forms and flowing lines [Early 20C. < French, 'new art']

art paper *n* a high-quality paper coated with china clay or something similar to give it a smooth shiny surface

arts and crafts *n* the art of decorative design applied to everyday objects (*takes a singular or plural verb*)

Arts and Crafts *n* a movement in the late 19th and early 20th centuries in Britain and the United States that stressed the value of artisanship

art song *n* a lyric song composed in the classical tradition

artsy /aártsi/ *adj US* same as **arty**[1] (*informal*)

artsy-craftsy /aártsi kraáftsi/ *adj N Am* same as **arty-crafty** (*informal*) [Early 20C. < ARTS AND CRAFTS]

artsy-fartsy /aártsi faártsi/ *adj N Am* same as **arty-farty** (*informal*)

art therapy *n* a form of psychotherapy that encourages the expression of emotions in artistic media such as paint or sculpture

artwork /aárt wurk/ *n* **1.** a work or works of art **2.** the illustrations that are to be printed in a publication

arty[1] /aárti/ (**-ier, -iest**) *adj* self-consciously and pretentiously artistic (*informal*)

arty[2] *abbr* MIL artillery

arty-crafty /aárti kraáfti/ *adj* (*informal*) **1.** relating to handicrafts or objects decorated by hand **2.** decorated in a pretentiously artistic way ▶ N Am term **artsy-craftsy** [Early 20C. < ARTS AND CRAFTS]

arty-farty /aárti faárti/ *adj* representing an elitist or self-indulgent side of the arts (*informal*) N Am term **artsy-fartsy**

Aruba /ə roóbə/ island off the Venezuelan coast, formerly a Dutch dependency and since 1986 a self-governing part of the Netherlands. Language: Dutch, Papamiento. Capital: Orangestad. Population: 70,007 (2001). Area: 193 sq. km/75 sq. mi.

arugula /ə roógyoōlə/ (*plural* **-las** or *same*) *n N Am* PLANTS same as **rocket**[2] (sense 1) [Mid-20C. Probably related to dialectal Italian (Lombard) *arigola* and Venetian Italian *rucola*]

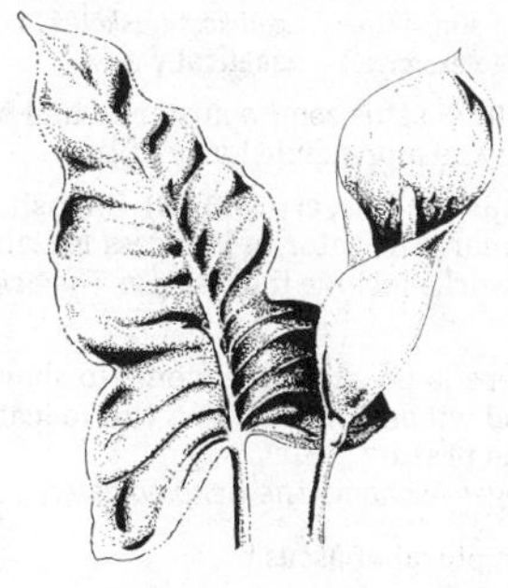

arum

arum /áirəm/ (*plural* **-ums** or *same*) *n* a perennial plant that grows from tubers and has arrow-shaped leaves. Native to: Europe. Genus: *Arum.* [14C. Via Latin < Greek *aron*]

arum lily *n* an ornamental lily with a white funnel-shaped cone around a long yellow spike bearing the actual flowers. Native to: southern Africa. Latin name: *Zantedeschia aethiopica.* N Am term **calla lily**

Arunachal Pradesh /aárə naák'l prə désh/, **Arunāchal Pradesh** union state of India. Situated in north-eastern India, it has borders with China and Myanmar. A portion of this state's territory is claimed by China. Capital: Itanagar. Population: 1,091,117 (2001). Area: 83,743 sq. km/32,333 sq. mi.

arundo /ə rúndō/ *n* a giant reed that grows in warm climates and is considered invasive in some areas. Use: for reeds in woodwind instruments, ornament. Native to: Mediterranean. Latin name: *Arundo donax.* [< Latin *(h)arundo* 'reed']

Arup /áwrəp/, **Sir Ove** (1895–1988) Danish-born British civil engineer who was involved in the rebuilding of Coventry Cathedral (1956–62)

aruspex *n* ANCIENT HIST same as **haruspex**

arvo /aárvō/ (*plural* **-vos**) *n Aus* TIME same as **afternoon** *n* (sense 1) (*informal*) [Mid-20C. < *arv-* (representing an Australian pronunciation of first syllable of AFTERNOON) + -O]

-ary *suffix* of or relating to ○ *functionary* [Via Old French *-arie* < Latin *-arius*]

Aryan /áiri ən, árri-/ *n* **1.** NAZI IDEAL in Nazi ideology, a person of non-Semitic descent regarded as racially superior **2.** LANG INDO-EUROPEAN LANGUAGE the hypothetical parent language of the Indo-European languages (*dated*) **3.** PEOPLES INDO-EUROPEAN ANCESTOR somebody who spoke the hypothetical parent language of Indo-European languages (*dated*) [Mid-19C. < Sanskrit *ārya* 'noble, of good family'] —**Aryan** *adj*

aryl /árril/ *adj* describes a chemical group derived from an aromatic hydrocarbon

arytenoid /árri teén oyd/, **arytenoidal** /árriti nóyd'l/ *adj* **1.** describes either of the two small cartilages of the larynx to which the vocal cords are attached **2.** describes any of the small muscles of the larynx [Early 18C. Via modern Latin < Greek *arutainoeidēs* 'ladle-shaped' < *arutaina* 'ladle, funnel' < *aruein* 'draw water'] —**arytenoid** *n*

as[1] *stressed* /az/; *unstressed* /əz/ CORE MEANING: a grammatical word indicating simultaneity, causality, comparison, or the identity or function of somebody or something ○ (conj) *Once again, as I started my interview, the telephone rang.* ○ (conj) *I'll drop the book off, as I'll be passing your house anyway.* ○ (conj) *Here, take this pencil as it's sharper than yours.* ○ (prep) *Data is stored on the disk as magnetic patterns.* ○ (conj) *It is stored much as music is stored on an audiotape or cassette.*

1. *conj* AT TIME THAT used to indicate that something happens at the same time as something else ○ *A woman stands near the water's edge as two large golden retrievers frolic in the river.* **2.** *conj* WHAT that which ○ *Do as you like!* **3.** *conj* BECAUSE seeing that ○ *I'm not sure where we are in maths, as I've been absent for the last week.* **4.** *conj* USED FOR COMPARISON used to compare things, people, or situations ○ *He is almost as tall as she.* ○ *I'm working as hard as before but getting less done.* **5.** *conj* EMPHASIZES AMOUNTS used to indicate that an amount is small or large **6.** *conj* INTRODUCES CLAUSE used to introduce a short clause referring to a previous or subsequent statement ○ *As you know, I have been in this job for a long time.* **7.** *conj* IN WAY THAT used to indicate the way that something happens or exists ○ *Did everything go as planned?* **8.** *conj* IN SAME WAY THAT used to indicate that something happens or exists in the same way as something else ○ *Her attitude to life was very practical, as her mother's had been.* **9.** *conj* THOUGH in spite of the fact that ○ *Hard-working as she is, she can't compete with the others.* **10.** *prep* AT TIME WHEN used to indicate a stage in somebody's life ○ *As a teenager I was quite shy.* **11.** *prep* IN CAPACITY OF used to indicate the capacity in which somebody or something exists or acts ○ *uses it as a short cut* [12C. Contraction of earlier form of ALSO] ◇ **as against** used to indicate comparison or contrast between two facts or amounts ◇ **as ever** used to indicate that a situation is the same as usual ◇ **as far as** to the extent to which a situation holds or is relevant ◇ **as for** used to refer back to a topic and introduce further information about it or comment on it ◇ **as from** same as **as of** ◇ **as how 1.** used to mean 'that' in the phrases 'seeing as how' and 'allowed as how' (*informal*) ○ *Seeing as how they were almost finished, I waited.* ○ *She allowed as how I had helped her more than anybody.* **2.** *Carib* because **3.** *Carib* seeing that **4.** *Carib* in the same way as ◇ **as if 1.** in a way that suggests something ○ *He looked as if he'd been crying.* **2.** used to indicate that the speaker is saying something ridiculous ○ *As if I'd say a thing like that!* ◇ **as is** in the present condition, with whatever faults there may be ◇ **as it were** used to indicate qualification, uncertainty, or lack of definiteness in a statement ◇ **as long as 1.** provided that ○ *You can go, as long as you're home by midnight.* **2.** because or seeing that ○ *As long as we're here we may as well look round.* ◇ **as much again** twice as much ◇ **as of** on and after a particular date or time ◇ **as per** in accordance with ◇ **as such 1.** used to indicate that a word or phrase does not apply exactly to a situation (*often used with a negative*) ○ *I have no qualifications as such, but I feel I could do the job.* **2.** used to indicate that something is being considered separately ○ *After the earthquake, the village as such*

virtually ceased to exist. ◇ **as though** same as **as if** ◇ **as to** same as **as for** ◇ **as yet** used to indicate that a situation has lasted up to the present time ○ *She has never once mentioned the terrible accusation nor has she, as yet, said that she is sorry.* ◇ **as you were** a military command to return to the same position as before

USAGE As meaning 'in the capacity of': In this use, the preposition ***as*** shows the capacity in which somebody or something exists or acts: *She has a job as a copywriter. As a doctor I understand these problems.* Avoid making false links with the ***as*** clause when they result in ambiguity or apparent absurdity: *As a journalist, you know I do not like being asked such questions* (which one is the journalist?).

USAGE See ***because***.

as² *abbr* American Samoa (*used in Internet addresses*) See table at **domain name**

As *symbol* CHEM ELEM arsenic

AS¹ *abbr* **1.** BANKING after sight **2.** *also* **A.S.** LANG, PEOPLES Anglo-Saxon **3.** ARMS antisubmarine

AS² *n* same as **AS level**

As. *abbr* **1.** Asia **2.** Asian

ASA¹ *adj* used to indicate the speed of photographic film [Abbreviation of *American Standards Association*]

ASA² *abbr* Advertising Standards Authority

Asadha /áasədə/ *n* in the Hindu calendar, the fourth month of the year, lasting 31 days and falling about the same time as June to July. See table at **calendar**

asafoetida /ássə féttidə, -fée-/, **asafetida** *n* **1.** a bitter brownish acrid-smelling plant resin. Use: South Asian cooking. **2.** a plant of the parsley family that produces asafoetida. Latin name: *Ferula assafoetida.* [14C. < medieval Latin < *asa* (< Persian *āzā* 'mastic') + *fetida* 'fetid', form of *fetidus* (see FETID)]

asana /áassənə/ *n* a posture used in yoga [Mid-20C. < Sanskrit *āsana* 'manner of sitting' < *āste* 'he sits']

a.s.a.p. *abbr* as soon as possible

ASAT, **Asat** *abbr* MIL antisatellite

asbestos /ass béss toss, əz béstəss/ *n* a fibrous carcinogenic silicate mineral. Use: formerly, heat-resistant materials. [Early 17C. < Greek, 'unslaked lime' < *sbestos* 'extinguished' < *sbennunai* 'extinguish'] —**asbestine** /ass béss teen, -béstin/ *adj*

asbestosis /áss bess tṓssiss, áz-/ *n* inflammation of the lungs caused by prolonged inhalation of asbestos fibres [Early 20C. < ASBESTOS + -OSIS]

ASCAP *abbr* ARTS American Society of Composers, Authors, and Publishers

ascariasis /áskə rī́ əssiss/ *n* infestation of the intestines by common roundworms or related nematode worms (**ascarids**) [Late 19C. < ASCARID + -IASIS]

ascarid /áskərid/ *n* a parasitic nematode worm, e.g. a common roundworm. Family: Ascaridae. [Late 17C. Back-formation < modern Latin *ascarides*, plural of *ascaris* < Greek *askaris* 'intestinal worm' < *askarizein* 'to jump']

ascend /ə sénd/ (**-cends, -cending, -cended**) *v* **1.** *vi* MOVE UPWARDS to go upwards, usually vertically or into the air **2.** *vti* CLIMB SOMETHING to climb up something such as a hill or staircase **3.** *vi* LEAD UPWARDS to rise or lead to a higher level **4.** *vti* RISE TO HIGHER CAREER POSITION to rise through the ranks to a higher status **5.** *vt* TAKE UP POSITION to succeed to an important position, especially as a monarch (*formal*) ○ *ascend the throne* [14C. < Latin *ascendere* 'climb to' < *scandere* 'to climb'] —**ascendable** *adj*

ascendance /ə séndənss/, **ascendence** *n* **1.** succeeding or rising to a powerful position **2.** same as **ascendancy**

ascendancy /ə séndənssi/, **ascendency** *n* a position of power or domination over others

ascendant /ə séndənt/, **ascendent** *adj* **1.** MOVING UPWARDS moving into a higher position (*literary*) **2.** DOMINANT having a position of power or domination over others (*formal*) **3.** BOT same as **ascending** (sense 2) ■ *n* POINT ON ECLIPTIC in astrology, the point on the ecliptic or the sign of the zodiac that is rising in the east at a specific time

ascendence, etc another spelling of **ascendance, etc**

ascender /ə séndər/ *n* **1.** SOMEBODY OR SOMETHING THAT GOES UP somebody or something that moves upwards **2.** LETTER PART EXTENDING UPWARDS the part of a lowercase letter such as h, d, or b that projects above the body of the letter **3.** LETTER WITH ASCENDER a lowercase letter with an ascender

ascendeur /ássoN dúr/ *n* a metal grip on a rope that can be loosened, moved up, and tightened to help a climber ascend the rope [Late 20C. < French, 'ascender']

ascending /ə sénding/ *adj* **1.** moving upwards, especially on a scale **2.** describes a plant part that grows upwards

ascension /ə sénsh'n/ *n* an act of ascending something (*formal*) [14C. Via French < Latin *ascension-* < *ascens-*, present participle of *ascendere* (see ASCEND)] —**ascensional** *adj*

Ascension *n* in Christian belief, the rising of Jesus Christ from earth to heaven after the Resurrection

Ascension Day *n* the day when Christians celebrate the rising of Jesus Christ from earth to heaven after the Resurrection. Date: Thursday, forty days after Easter Day.

Ascension Island /ə sénsh'n-/ island in the South Atlantic Ocean to the northwest of Saint Helena, by which it is administered as a British dependency. Population: 1,007 (1988). Area: 88 sq. km/34 sq. mi.

ascent /ə sént/ *n* **1.** CLIMB an act of climbing a mountain or hill ○ *the ascent of Everest* **2.** UPWARD MOVEMENT an upward vertical movement **3.** UPWARD SLOPE a slope in an upward direction **4.** WAY UP MOUNTAIN a climbers' route up a mountain or hill **5.** RISE TO IMPORTANCE the process by which somebody becomes more important, successful, or powerful [Late 16C. < ASCEND, after DESCEND, DESCENT]

SPELLCHECK ascent or **assent**? Do not confuse the spelling of ***ascent*** and ***assent***, which sound similar. ***Ascent*** is only used as a noun, denoting an upward movement or slope, as in *the lift's rapid ascent.* ***Assent*** can be used as a noun or verb, referring to agreement or acceptance: *She nodded in assent. He assented to our request.*

ascertain /ássər táyn/ (**-tains, -taining, -tained**) *vti* to find out something with certainty (*formal*) [Late 16C. < Old French *acertain-*, stem of *acertener* < *certain* (see CERTAIN)] —**ascertainable** *adj* —**ascertainably** *adv* —**ascertainment** *n*

ascetic /ə séttik/ *adj* choosing or reflecting austerity and self-denial as personal or religious discipline ■ *n* somebody who is self-denying and lives with minimal material comforts [Mid-17C. Directly or via medieval Latin < Greek *askētikos* < *askētēs* 'monk, hermit' < *askein* 'to exercise'] —**ascetically** *adv*

asceticism /ə séttisizəm/ *n* austerity and self-denial, especially as a principled way of life

Ascham /áskəm/, **Roger** (1515–68) English humanist and scholar. The tutor to Princess Elizabeth (1548–50), his works include the treatise *The Scholemaster* (1570).

> 'There is no such whetstone, to sharpen a good wit and encourage a will to learning, as is praise.'
> [Roger Ascham, *The Scholemaster*, 1570]

asci FUNGI plural of **ascus**

ascidia BOT plural of **ascidium**

ascidian /ə síddi ən/ (*plural* **-ans** *or* *same*) *n* MARINE BIOL same as **sea squirt** (*technical*) [Mid-19C. < modern Latin *Ascidia* < Greek *askidion* 'little wineskin' < *askos* 'wineskin, leather bag']

ascidium /ə síddi əm/ (*plural* **-ia** /-i ə/) *n* a part of a plant or fungus shaped like a pitcher [Mid-18C. Via modern Latin < Greek *askidion* (see ASCIDIAN)]

ASCII /áski/ *n* a standard that identifies letters, numbers, and various symbols by code numbers for exchanging data between different computer systems. Full form **American Standard Code for Information Interchange**

ASCII art *n* illustrations using only ASCII characters, often used in e-mails

ASCII file *n* a computer file that contains only ASCII characters

ascites /ə sī́t eez/ *n* an accumulation of fluid (**serous fluid**) in the peritoneal cavity, causing abdominal swelling [14C. Via late Latin < Greek *askitēs* 'oedema' < *askos* 'wineskin, leather bag'] —**ascitic** /ə síttik/ *adj*

asco- *prefix* ascus ○ *ascocarp* [Via modern Latin < Greek *askos* 'wineskin, leather bag']

ascocarp /áskə kaarp/ *n* a fleshy structure in specific fungi (**ascomycetes**) containing sexually produced spores (**ascospores**) in a membranous spore case (**ascus**)

ascogonium /áskə gṓni əm/ (*plural* **-nia** /-ni ə/) *n* a female reproductive part in specific fungi (**ascomycetes**)

ascoma /a skṓmə/ (*plural* **-mata** /-mətə/) *n* FUNGI same as **ascocarp**

ascomycete /áskə mī séet/ *n* a fungus that produces spores sexually inside a membranous spore case (**ascus**), e.g. a yeast or truffle. Class: Ascomycetes. —**ascomycetous** *adj*

ascorbate /ə skáwr bayt, -bət/ *n* any salt of ascorbic acid

ascorbic acid /ə skáwrbik-/ *n* BIOCHEM same as **vitamin C** [< A-² + SCORBUTIC]

ascospore /áskə spawr/ *n* a fungal spore produced sexually inside a membranous spore case (**ascus**) —**ascosporic** /áskə spáwrik/ *adj* —**ascosporous** /áskə spáwrəss/ *adj*

ascot /áskət/ *n* a broad cravat with square ends, often held in place with an ornamental stud [Early 20C. After ASCOT]

Ascot /áskət/ town in southern England where horse races are held. Population: 13,500.

ascribe /ə skrī́b/ (**-cribes, -cribing, -cribed**) *vt* (*formal*) **1.** GIVE SOMETHING AS CAUSE to believe or say that something was caused by a particular thing ○ *His rivals could only ascribe his success to sheer good luck.* **2.** GIVE SOMEBODY AS AUTHOR to believe or say that something was originally written or said by a particular person ○ *The researcher was confident enough to ascribe the newly discovered poems to Burns.* **3.** GIVE SOMETHING AS CHARACTERISTIC to believe that something belongs to or characterizes a person or group ○ *to ascribe contentment to the unambitious* [15C. < Latin *ascribere* 'add to in writing' < *scribere* 'write'] —**ascribable** *adj* —**ascription** /ə skrípsh'n/ *n*

ascribed status /ə skrī́bd-/ *n* the status that somebody possesses by reason of age, sex, ethnic background, family background, or another factor outside personal control

ascription /ə skrípsh'n/ *n* **1.** ATTRIBUTION the attributing of a relationship between something and somebody or something else (*formal*) **2.** STATEMENT OF ATTRIBUTION a statement that assigns or attributes something to somebody or something else (*formal*) **3.** SOCIAL STATUS BY BIRTH the social status derived from the circumstances into which somebody is born [Late 16C. < Latin *ascription-* < *ascript-*, past participle of *ascribere* (see ASCRIBE)]

ascus /áskəss/ (*plural* **-ci** /-sī, -kī/) *n* a membranous spore case formed by specific fungi (**ascomycetes**) that contains eight sexually produced spores (**ascospores**) [Mid-19C. Via modern Latin < Greek *askos* 'wineskin, leather bag']

asdic /ázdik/ *n* an early version of sonar [Early 20C. Acronym < *Anti-Submarine Detection Investigation Committee*]

-ase *suffix* enzyme ○ *polymerase* [< DIASTASE]

ASEAN /ássi an/ *abbr* Association of Southeast Asian Nations

aseismic /ay sī́zmik/ *adj* **1.** not subject to earthquakes **2.** built to withstand earthquakes

aseismic creep *n* movement of tectonic plates below the Earth's crust that is not caused by earthquakes or other seismic disturbance

aseismic ridge *n* a long linear mountainous ridge in an ocean basin, usually the result of volcanic activity generated as an ocean plate travels over a hot spot in the Earth's mantle

asepsis /ay sépsiss/ *n* **1.** a condition in which no living disease-causing microorganisms are present **2.** the process or methods of bringing about a condition in which no disease-causing microorganisms are present

aseptic /ay séptik/ *adj* **1.** free of disease-causing microorganisms **2.** designed to prevent infection from pathogenic microorganisms ○ *aseptic techniques* —**aseptically** *adv* —**asepticism** /-sizəm/ *n*

asexual /ay sékshoo əl/ *adj* **1.** SEXUALLY INACTIVE without sexual desire or activity **2.** WITHOUT SEX-LINKED FEATURES lacking any apparent sex or sex organs **3.** WITHOUT

SEXUAL FUSION describes reproduction in which there is no fusion of male and female sex cells (**gametes**), e.g. vegetative reproduction or budding —**asexuality** /áy sekshoo álləti/ n —**asexually** adv

Asgard /áss gaard/ n in Norse mythology, the home of the deities and of heroes killed in battle

ash[1] /ash/ n 1. **REMAINS OF FIRE** the powdery substance that is left when something has been burnt (often used in the plural) 2. **VOLCANIC DUST** fine-grained lava that erupts or flows from a volcano before settling on the ground ■ **ashes** npl **BURNT REMAINS OF BODY** the remains of somebody's body after it has been cremated ■ adj **SILVERY GREY** of a silvery grey colour [Old English æsce < Indo-European, 'burn, be dry'] ◇ **rise (like a phoenix) from the ashes** to come into existence or popularity again, seemingly from a state of ruin or destruction

ash

ash[2] /ash/ n 1. (plural **ashes** or same) **DECIDUOUS TREE** a deciduous tree that has compound leaves with paired leaflets and winged fruits. Native to: temperate regions. Genus: *Fraxinus*. 2. **WOOD OF ASH** the hard durable wood of an ash tree. Use: furniture, tool handles. 3. **SYMBOL FOR VOWEL SOUND** the character 'æ', representing the vowel sound of the modern English word 'pad', used in Old English and the International Phonetic Alphabet [Old English æsc < Germanic]

ashamed /ə sháymd/ adj 1. feeling full of shame 2. embarrassed or regretful ○ *I'm ashamed to say I didn't acknowledge their invitation.* [Old English āscamod < sceamu 'shame'] —**ashamedly** /-mədli/ adv

Ashanti[1] /ə shánti/ (plural same or -**tis**), **Ashante** (plural same or -**tes**) n 1. somebody who comes from Ashanti in central Ghana 2. a language spoken in central Ghana, often regarded as a form of Akan [Early 18C. < Twi *Asante*] —**Ashanti** adj

Ashanti[2] /ə shánti/ former kingdom and present-day administrative area in central Ghana

A share n a share in a company that does not entitle the holder to voting rights and that may carry other restrictions

ash blonde, **ash blond** adj light or whitish blonde in colour (hyphenated when used before a noun) ■ n somebody with ash blonde hair

Ashburton /ásh burt'n/ river in northwestern Western Australia. Length: 650 km/404 mi.

Dame Peggy Ashcroft

Ashcroft /ásh kroft/, **Dame Peggy** (1907–91) British actor who played leading theatrical roles from the 1930s to the 1950s. Her films include *A Passage to India* (1984). Born **Ashcroft, Edith Margaret Emily**

Ashdown /ásh down/, **Paddy** (b. 1941) British pol-

itician. A former Royal Marine, he became an MP (1983) and leader of the Liberal Democrat Party (1988–99). He was knighted in 2000 and became a Life Peer in 2001. Full name **Ashdown, Jeremy John Durham**

Ashe /ash/, **Arthur** (1943–93) US tennis player who was the first African American to become men's tennis champion. Full name **Ashe, Jr., Arthur Robert**

> 'The ideal attitude is to be physically loose and mentally tight.'
> [Arthur Ashe, *New York Times*; 8 February 1993]

ashen[1] /ásh'n/ adj 1. extremely pale in appearance 2. resembling or consisting of ashes [15C. < ASH[1]]

ashen[2] /ásh'n/ adj relating to the ash tree or its wood (archaic) [12C. < ASH[2]]

Ashes /áshiz/ n in cricket, the trophy awarded to the winner of a series of test matches between England and Australia [Late 19C. < a mock obituary for English cricket after a defeat, and the subsequent presentation to the English of an urn containing ashes, which became the trophy]

ashet /áshit/ n N England, Scotland, NZ a large plate or shallow dish, usually oval in shape, used for serving food [Mid-19C. < French *assiette* 'place at table, plate' < *asseoir* 'to seat' (see ASSIZE)]

ash flow n 1. an avalanche of hot volcanic ash and debris down the sides of a volcano 2. a deposit of volcanic ash and debris resulting from an ash flow

Ashgabat /áshgə bat/ capital of Turkmenistan, located in the southern part of the country near the Turkmenistan-Iran border and the Kara Kum desert. Population: 605,000 (1999). Former name **Ashkhabad**

Ashkenazi /áshkə náazi/ (plural -**nazim** /-im/) n a member of a Jewish people originating in Germany and northern Europe [Mid-19C. < modern Hebrew < medieval Hebrew *Ashkenaz* 'Germany' < Hebrew *Ashkēnāz*, a grandson of Noah] —**Ashkenazi** adj —**Ashkenazic** adj

Ashkhabad /áshkə bad/ former name for **Ashgabat**

ashlar /áshlər/, **ashler** n 1. a thin slab of squared stone, used for facing walls or in building 2. masonry using thin slabs of squared stone as facing material [14C. Via Old French *aisselier* 'plank' < medieval Latin *axicellus* < Latin *axis* 'plank, axletree']

ashlaring /áshləring/ n the construction of a building using ashlars

ashler n CONSTR another spelling of **ashlar**

Ashley /áshli/, **Laura** (1925–85) British fashion designer who created a chain of shops selling clothes, fabrics, and wallpapers based on 19th-century designs. Born **Mountney, Laura**

Ashmore and Cartier Islands /ásh mawr ənd kaárti ay-/ external territory lying 500 km/323 mi. off the northwestern coast of Australia. It comprises Ashmore Reef and the Cartier Islands. Area: 5 sq. km/2 sq. mi.

Ashora /ə sháwrə/, **Ashura** /ə shóorə/ n an Islamic festival associated by Shia Muslims with the death of Muhammad's grandson Husain. Date: tenth day of Muharram. [Mid-19C. < Arabic *'āshūrā* 'tenth']

ashore /ə sháwr/ adv to the land from the water, or on land as opposed to on a ship or boat ○ *All but the captain went ashore.*

~~**ashphalt**~~ incorrect spelling of **asphalt**

ashram /áshrəm, áash-/ n 1. a retreat for the practice of yoga or other Hindu disciplines 2. a commune or communal house whose members share spiritual goals and practices [Early 20C. < Sanskrit *āśramaḥ* 'hermitage']

Ashton /áshtən/, **Sir Frederick** (1904–88) British dancer and choreographer. He helped found the Ballet Rambert and Sadlers Wells, which became the Royal Ballet, London. Full name **Ashton, Sir Frederick William Mallandaine**

Ashton-under-Lyne /-līn/ engineering town in Greater Manchester, northwestern England. Population: 43,906 (1991).

Ashton-Warner /-wáwrnər/, **Sylvia** (1905–84) New Zealand novelist and teacher. She was the author of *Spinster* (1958).

Ashtoreth /áshtə reth/ n MYTHOL ▶ **Ishtar**

ashtray /ásh tray/ n an open receptacle for the ash from a cigarette, cigar, or pipe and for cigarette ends

Ashura n CALENDAR, ISLAM same as **Ashora**

Ashurbanipal /áshoor bánni pal/ (fl 7th century BC) king of Assyria. He ruled the Assyrian empire from 669 to 627 BC and founded the first library in Southwest Asia in his capital at Nineveh.

Ash Wednesday n a Christian holy day marking the first day of Lent [Because of the Roman Catholic custom of marking the heads of penitents with ashes on this day]

ashy /áshi/ (-**ier**, -**iest**) adj 1. extremely pale or greyish in appearance (literary) 2. resembling or covered in ash

Asia /áyzhə, áyshə/ the world's largest continent, bordered by the Ural and Caucasus mountains and the Arctic, Pacific, and Indian oceans. Population: estimated 3,460,000,000 (2001 estimate). Area: 44,391,000 sq. km/17,139,400 sq. mi.

Asiadollar /áyzhə dollər, áyshə-/ n a US dollar used in Asian banks and currency markets

Asia Minor historic region in the extreme west of Asia, roughly corresponding to Asian Turkey

Asian /áyzh'n, áysh'n/ adj OF ASIA relating to Asia, or its peoples, languages, or cultures ■ n 1. SOMEBODY FROM ASIA somebody who comes from Asia, or is of Asian descent 2. SOMEBODY FROM SOUTH ASIA somebody who comes from South Asia, or is of South Asian descent [15C. Via Latin < Greek *Asianos* < *Asia* 'Asia']

USAGE *Asian* has largely replaced *Asiatic*, both as a noun and as an adjective. When the reference is to people, *Asiatic* is now regarded as derogatory and should be strictly avoided. In British English, *Asian* is also used to refer to people from South Asia (the Indian subcontinent), or their descendants now living in Britain. In North American English, *Asian* usually refers to people of East Asian origin or ancestry, for example from China, Japan, or Korea.

Asian-American n an American of Asian descent — **Asian-American** adj

Asian flu, **Asian influenza** n influenza that occurs in sporadic worldwide epidemics, caused by a strain of virus thought to have originated in China in the mid-1950s and related strains

Asian pear n 1. a fruit resembling a brownish-yellow apple with crisp juicy flesh 2. a tree that produces Asian pears. Genus: *Pyrus*. ▶ ANZ term **nashi**

Asia-Pacific n a commercial region encompassing some of the countries of East and Southeast Asia and the Pacific Rim

Asiatic /áyshi áttik, áyzi-/ adj describes things relating to Asia or of Asian origin such as flora, fauna, or climatic conditions ○ *Asiatic plants and animals* ○ *parts of the Asiatic steppes* [Early 17C. Via Latin < Greek *Asiatikos* < *Asia* 'Asia']

USAGE See **Asian**.

Asiatic cholera n MED same as **cholera**

aside /ə sīd/ adv 1. AWAY OR TO ONE SIDE to one side of somebody or something ○ *Stand aside and let the people through.* 2. OUT OF WAY out of the way, or away from the area of main concern ○ *brush aside all criticism* 3. IGNORED ignored for the sake of argument ○ *Budget constraints aside, is the deadline feasible?* 4. FOR FUTURE USE for special or future use ○ *put aside some money each week* ■ n 1. ACTOR'S COMMENT a remark made by an actor, usually to the audience, that the other characters on stage supposedly cannot hear 2. CONFIDENTIAL COMMENT IN UNDERTONE a spoken remark not directed to all listeners and usually made in a quiet voice 3. DIGRESSION a digression from a main point ◇ **aside from** N Am same as **apart from** (sense 1) ○ *Aside from his medical practice he is also a lawyer.*

A-side n the side of a pop, rock, or jazz single that contains the more important recording, usually the title track (dated)

Asimov /ázzi mof/, **Isaac** (1920–92) Russian-born US scientist and writer, author of around 500 books, including textbooks and science fiction

> 'The good earth is dying; so in the name of humanity let us move. Let us make our hard but necessary decisions. Let us do it quickly. Let us do it now.'

[Isaac Asimov, *The Roving Mind: A Panoramic View of Fringe Science, Technology, and the Society of the Future*; 1987]

asinine /ássi nīn/ *adj* **1.** utterly ridiculous or lacking sense **2.** relating to or resembling an ass [15C. < Latin *asininus < asinus* 'ass'] —**asininely** *adv* —**asininity** /ássi nínnəti/ *n*

ASIO /áyzi ō/ *abbr* Australian Security Intelligence Organization

as is *adj* used to imply that goods may not be in perfect condition ○ *all merchandise sold as is*

ASIS /ássiss/ *abbr* Australian Secret Intelligence Service

asity /ássiti/ *n* a small round-bodied bird with a short tail and rounded wings that feeds on fruit. Native to: Madagascar. Family: Philepittidae.

ask /aask/ (**asks**, **asking**, **asked**) *v* **1.** *vti* QUESTION SOMEBODY to communicate with somebody in order to get information ○ *Ask them how long it will take.* **2.** *vti* MAKE REQUEST to make a request for something ○ *They asked me for my opinion.* **3.** *vt* INVITE SOMEBODY to invite somebody to a social event ○ *Only close friends were asked to dine.* **4.** *vt* REQUIRE SOMETHING to require somebody to give or contribute something ○ *The job asks a lot more of me than I expected.* **5.** *vt* NAME PRICE to name an amount as an acceptable price ○ *They're asking £100,000 for the house.* [Old English *āscian* < Indo-European, 'to wish'] —**asker** *n* ◇ **a big ask** a request or expectation that is difficult to meet (*informal*) ○ *It's a big ask to beat a team as good as the French.* ◇ **for the asking** available at no cost

ask after *vt* to enquire about somebody's welfare ○ *She asks after the children whenever we meet.*

ask for *v* **1.** *vti* REQUEST SOMETHING to request that something be provided ○ *I asked for a cup of coffee.* **2.** *vt* REQUEST SOMEBODY'S APPEARANCE to request somebody's appearance, especially to speak to **3.** *vt* REQUEST TELEPHONE CONVERSATION WITH SOMEBODY to request that somebody be called to the telephone ○ *A man on the phone is asking for the manager.* **4.** *vt* INVITE SOMETHING UNPLEASANT to behave in a way that deserves something unpleasant ○ *You're asking for a lot of problems if you do that.* ○ *just asking for it*

ask out *vt* to invite somebody to go on a date

askance /ə skánss, ə skáanss/ *adv* with doubt or suspicion ○ *'They surveyed each other askance, feeling that they were rivals, and mentally calculating each other's chances.'* (Horatio Alger, Jr., *Ragged Dick*; 1868) [15C. Origin ?]

askari /a skáari/, **askar** /áss kaar/ *n* a soldier or police officer in various Islamic countries of eastern Africa [Late 19C. < Arabic *askarī* 'soldier']

askew /ə skyoo/ *adj, adv* at an angle ○ *with his hat askew*

asking price *n* the price set by a seller before any negotiation

ASL *abbr* N Am LANG American Sign Language

aslant /ə slaant/ *adv* at an angle ○ *books all aslant on the shelves*

asleep /ə sleep/ *adj* **1.** NOT AWAKE in or into a state of sleep ○ *After tossing and turning for some hours I eventually fell asleep.* **2.** NOT ALERT not alert enough to function or operate properly ○ *asleep on the job* **3.** NUMB describes part of the body that has become numb ○ *My arm's gone asleep.*

ASLEF /ázz lef/, **Aslef** *abbr* Associated Society of Locomotive Engineers and Firemen

AS level *n* in England, Wales, and Northern Ireland, a school examination taken at an advanced level in a subject. It is the first year of a full A-level course. (*hyphenated when used before a noun*) ○ *AS-level biology* Full form **Advanced Supplementary level**

aslope /ə slōp/ *adj, adv* at a sloping angle (*archaic or literary*)

ASM *abbr* MIL air-to-surface missile

Asmara /ass máarə/ capital and largest city of Eritrea. It is also the name of one of the ten provinces within Eritrea. Population: 514,000 (1999).

asocial /ay sṓsh'l/ *adj* **1.** UNWILLING TO MIX SOCIALLY averse to human social interaction **2.** UNSUITED TO SOCIETY not conforming to normal social standards, or showing a lack of consideration for others ○ *asocial behaviour* **3.** NOT INTERACTING SOCIALLY describes animals that do not interact socially

association incorrect spelling of **association**

Asoka /ə sṓkə/ (291?–232 BC) king of Maghada. After conquering most of the Indian subcontinent, he renounced violence and converted to Buddhism, actively propagating that faith in his own kingdom and abroad. His reign (273?–232 BC) was marked by religious tolerance and public and charitable works.

asp /asp/ *n* **1.** a small poisonous snake that caused the death of Cleopatra, thought to have been a member of the cobra family. Native to: Africa, Asia, Europe. Latin name: *Naja haje.* **2.** a snake of the viper family, resembling a small adder. Native to: southern Europe. **3.** REPT same as **horned viper** [14C. Directly or via Old French < Latin *aspis* < Greek]

ASP *abbr* COMPUT **1.** active server page **2.** application service provider

asparaginase /ə spárrəji nayz, -nayss/ *n* an enzyme that catalyses the breakdown of asparagine

asparagine /ə spárrə jeen, -jin/ *n* an amino acid found in many plant seeds that can also be produced by humans and other animals. Formula: $C_4H_8N_2O_3$. [Early 19C. < ASPARAGUS, from which it was first obtained]

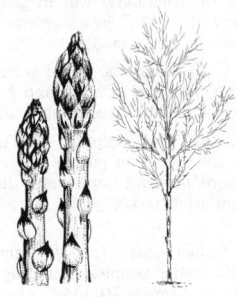

asparagus

asparagus /ə spárrəgəss/ *n* **1.** spear-shaped young plant shoots, eaten cooked as a vegetable **2.** a perennial plant that produces asparagus. Latin name: *Asparagus officinalis.* [Pre-12C. Via Latin < Greek *asparagos*]

asparagus fern *n* a plant with feathery leaves and purplish-black berries grown as a houseplant. Flowers: small, white. Use: foliage for bouquets. Native to: South Africa. Latin name: *Asparagus setaceus.*

aspartame /ə spaar taym/ *n* a protein produced from aspartic acid. Use: synthetic sweetener. [Late 20C. < ASPARTIC ACID]

aspartate /ə spaar tayt/ *n* a salt or ester of aspartic acid

aspartic acid /ə spaártik-/ *n* an amino acid occurring in many plant proteins that can also be produced by humans and other animals. Formula: $C_4H_7NO_4$. [Mid-19C. < French *aspartique* < Latin *asparagus* (see ASPARAGUS)]

aspect /áss pekt/ *n* **1.** ONE SIDE OR PART a facet, phase, or part of a whole ○ *consider the various aspects of the problem* **2.** APPEARANCE the appearance of something to the mind or eye ○ *The stone has a greenish aspect in this light.* **3.** VIEWPOINT a view or point of view ○ *the aspect of the mountain from the river* ○ *seeing life from a new aspect* **4.** EXPOSURE exposure to a particular direction, weather, or other influence ○ *This plant requires a sunny aspect.* **5.** ASTRON ANGLE BETWEEN ASTRONOMICAL OBJECTS the apparent angular separation of two astronomical objects, especially as observed from Earth **6.** ASTROL POSITIONS OF PLANETS in astrology, the relative positions of the stars and planets, believed to influence human affairs **7.** GRAM CATEGORY OF VERBS a grammatical category of verbs that considers qualities of action independent of tense, e.g. the progressive or continuous and perfect aspects in English [14C. < Latin *aspectus*, past participle of *aspicere* < *specere* 'look at']

aspect ratio *n* **1.** in television and the cinema, the ratio of the width of the picture on the screen to its height. This ratio was 4:3 until the 1950s, when it increased in the cinema to 1.85:1 in the United States and 5:3 in Europe. **2.** the ratio of the length of an aircraft's wing to the mean distance between the front and back edge of the wing. Aircraft op-

erating at low speeds, e.g. gliders, need a high aspect ratio and have long narrow wings while for supersonic flight a low aspect ratio is created by swinging the wings back.

aspectual /a spéktyoo əl/ *adj* relating to the aspects of a verb

aspen /áspən/ (*plural* **-pens** or *same*) *n* a poplar with leaves that rustle and flutter in the breeze. Native to: Europe, northern United States. Latin name: *Populus tremens* or *Populus tremuloides.* [14C. < *asp* 'aspen' < Germanic]

Aspen /áspən/ city in the Rocky Mountains, at an altitude of 2,410 m/7,900 ft, in west-central Colorado. It is a popular ski resort. Population: 5,902 (2002 estimate).

Asperger's syndrome /áspurjərz-/, **Asperger syndrome** /áspurjər-/ *n* a severe developmental disorder, similar to autism, characterized by difficulties with social relations, strange behaviour patterns, concentration on details of objects, and often a heightened ability to memorize [After Hans *Asperger* (1906–80), Austrian paediatrician]

asperges /a spúr jeez/ *n* a religious ceremony of the Roman Catholic Church in which holy water is sprinkled over the altar, clergy, and congregation before High Mass [Late 16C. < Latin, 'you will sprinkle', the first word of the rite]

aspergill *n* CHR same as **aspergillum**

aspergilla CHR *plural* of **aspergillum**

aspergillosis /ə spúrji lṓssiss/ *n* a disease affecting mucous membranes, lungs, and sometimes bones that is caused by infection with the fungus *Aspergillus*

aspergillum

aspergillum /áspər jílləm/ (*plural* **-la** /-ə/ or **-lums**), **aspergill** /áspər jíl/ *n* a brush or perforated container for sprinkling holy water [Mid-17C. < modern Latin, 'little sprinkler' < Latin *aspergere* 'to sprinkle']

asperity /a spérrəti/ (*plural* **-ties**) *n* **1.** HARSHNESS OR SEVERITY harshness or severity of manner or tone (*formal*) **2.** HARDSHIP something that is hard to bear because of its harshness or severity (*formal*) **3.** ROUGHNESS the roughness of a surface (*literary*) **4.** PHYS AREA WHERE SURFACES TOUCH a region of contact between two load-bearing flat surfaces [13C. Via French *aspérité* < Latin *asperitas* < *asper* 'rough']

aspermia /ə spúrmi ə/ *n* a medical condition in which no spermatozoa are present in the seminal fluid [Mid-19C. < A³ + Greek *sperma* 'seed'] —**aspermic** *adj*

aspersion /ə spúrsh'n/ *n* **1.** a statement that attacks somebody's character or reputation (*often used in the plural*) ○ *cast aspersions on his integrity* **2.** the making of defamatory remarks

aspersorium /áspər sáwri əm/ (*plural* **-ria** /-ri ə/) *n* same as **aspergillum** [Mid-19C. < medieval Latin < Latin *aspers-*, past participle of *aspergere* 'to sprinkle']

asphalt /áss falt, -fawlt/ *n* **1.** SEMISOLID BITUMINOUS SUBSTANCE a brownish-black solid or semisolid substance. Source: oil-bearing rocks, by-product of petroleum distillation. Use: surfacing roads and paths, waterproofing, fungicides. **2.** MATERIAL USED FOR SURFACING ROADS surfacing material composed mainly of asphalt and gravel that hardens on cooling and is used for making roads and paths ■ *vt* (**-phalts, -phalting, -phalted**) COVER SOMETHING WITH ASPHALT to surface a roadway, pavement, or other area with asphalt [14C. Via late Latin < Greek *asphaltos*] —**asphaltic** /ass fáltik/ *adj*

asphaltite /ass fál tīt, áss fal tīt/ n a solid organic compound resembling asphalt and belonging to a group that occurs naturally in veins and beds below ground

asphalt jungle n a big city or urban area with little natural landscape

aspheric /ay sférrik/, **aspherical** /ay sférrik'l/ adj not perfectly spherical

asphodel /ásfə del/ (plural -dels or same) n 1. FLOWERING PLANT a perennial plant of the lily family. Flowers: white, pink, yellow, in clusters. Native to: southern Europe. Genera: Asphodelus or Asphodeline. 2. PLANT RESEMBLING ASPHODEL a plant similar to the true asphodel, e.g. bog asphodel 3. MYTHOL FLOWER OF HADES in Greek mythology, the flower of Hades that was sacred to Persephone [15C. Via Latin < Greek asphodelos]

asphyxia /ass fíksi ə, əss-/ n suffocation as a result of physical blockage of the airway or inhalation of toxic gases, causing a lack of oxygen and unconsciousness [Early 18C. Via modern Latin < Greek asphuxia 'lack of pulse' < sphuxis 'heartbeat' < sphuzein 'to throb'] —**asphyxiant** adj, n

asphyxiate /ass fíksi ayt, əss-/ (-ates, -ating, -ated) vti to deprive a person or animal of oxygen, or be deprived of oxygen, usually leading to unconsciousness or death —**asphyxiation** /ass fíksi áysh'n, əss-/ n —**asphyxiator** n

aspic /áspik/ n a jelly often used to form a mould of fish, meat, eggs, or vegetables [Late 18C. < French, 'asp', alteration of Old French aspe (see ASP)]

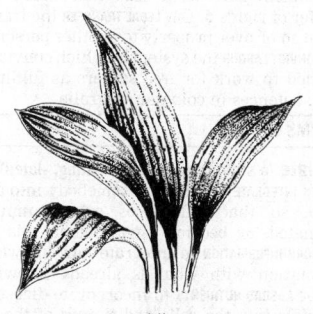
aspidistra

aspidistra /áspi dístrə/ n a common houseplant of the lily family with large glossy leaves. Flowers: small, brownish. Native to: Asia. Genus: Aspidistra. [Early 19C. < modern Latin < Greek aspid-, stem of aspis 'shield'; from the shape of the leaves]

CULTURAL NOTE Keep the Aspidistra Flying, a novel (1936) by George Orwell. The story of a young writer struggling to cope with poverty, it celebrates traditional English values of stoicism and community, symbolized by the hardy aspidistra plant.

aspirant /áspirənt, ə spírənt/ n somebody who is hoping to achieve distinction or advancement ○ an aspirant to the presidency ■ adj seeking or hoping to attain something

SYNONYMS See candidate.

aspirate vt /áspi rayt/ (-rates, -rating, -rated) 1. PRONOUNCE WHILE BREATHING OUT to pronounce a sound or word while breathing out, e.g. the letter 'h' at the beginning of words such as 'house' and 'hat' in standard English 2. INHALE SOMETHING to inhale something, especially a liquid, into the lungs 3. REMOVE LIQUID to remove liquid or gas by suction, especially from a body cavity (technical) ○ using a syringe to aspirate the fluid from the cyst ■ n /áspərət/ BREATHY LETTER a sound pronounced while breathing out, e.g. the sound of the letter 'h' at the beginning of many English words ■ adj /áspərət/ PRONOUNCED WITH BREATH pronounced while breathing out [Late 17C. < Latin aspirat-, past participle of aspirare 'breathe towards' < spirare 'breathe']

aspiration /áspi ráysh'n/ n 1. AMBITION a desire or ambition to achieve something 2. BREATHY PRONUNCIATION pronunciation accompanied by breathing out 3. SUCTION the withdrawal by suction of fluids or gases from the body or a body cavity 4. INHALATION drawing matter into the lungs along with the breath —**aspiratory** /ə spírətəri, áspirətəri/ adj

aspirational /áspi ráysh'nəl/ adj showing a desire or ambition to achieve something, especially self-improvement or material success ○ the aspirational working class

aspirational voter n Aus a traditionally working class but now upwardly mobile voter whose vote can be won by offering policies that will increase his or her wealth

aspiration pneumonia n pneumonia caused by foreign matter such as food entering the lungs

aspirator /áspi raytər/ n an apparatus for drawing out fluids or gases from the body or a body cavity by suction

aspire /ə spír/ (-pires, -piring, -pired) vi 1. to seek to attain a goal ○ aspire to public office 2. to soar to a great height (literary) [14C. < Latin aspirare 'breathe towards' (see ASPIRATE)] —**aspirer** n —**aspiring** adj

aspirin /ásprin/ (plural -rins or same) n 1. a drug that relieves pain and inflammation, lowers fever, and reduces blood clotting 2. a tablet containing aspirin [Late 19C. < German < contraction of acetylierte Spirsäure 'acetylated spiraeic acid' (former name of salicylic acid)]

Aspiring, Mount /ə spíring/ mountain in the southwest of the South Island, New Zealand. Height: 3,036 m/9,961 ft.

~~asprin~~ incorrect spelling of aspirin

asquint /ə skwínt/ adv from the corner of the eye, as if suspiciously

Asquith /áskwith/, Herbert Henry (1852–1928) British prime minister (1908–16). His government introduced retirement pensions and national insurance, and passed the Parliament Act (1911) that removed the power of veto from the House of Lords. See table at prime minister

'We shall never sheath the sword which we have not lightly drawn until Belgium recovers in full measure all and more than she has sacrificed, until France is adequately secured against the menace of aggression, until the rights of the smaller nationalities of Europe are placed upon an unassailable foundation, and until the military dominance of Prussia is wholly and finally destroyed.'
[Herbert Henry Asquith, Speech, Guildhall, London; 9 November 1914]

ass

ass¹ /ass/ n 1. an animal resembling a small horse with long ears, sometimes used as a beast of burden. The donkey is a domesticated descendant of the wild ass. Genus: Equus. 2. an offensive term that deliberately insults somebody's intelligence, consideration for others, or general value (slang insult) [Old English assa, via Celtic < Latin asinus]

ass² /ass/ n N Am 1. same as arse (sense 1) (offensive) 2. a highly offensive term for sexual intercourse (taboo) [Mid-19C. Euphemistic alteration of ARSE] ◇ cover your ass N Am a highly offensive phrase meaning to behave in a way that ensures you will not be blamed for something later (taboo) ◇ haul ass N Am a highly offensive phrase meaning to move or start to move quickly (taboo) ◇ have somebody's ass in a sling or bind US a highly offensive phrase meaning to get somebody into trouble (taboo) ◇ kick (some) ass N Am a highly offensive phrase meaning to behave aggressively or ruthlessly in order to achieve a goal (taboo) ◇ kiss ass N Am a highly offensive phrase meaning to flatter or obediently carry out the orders of a superior in order to gain favour (taboo)

Assad /ə sád/, Bashar al- (b. 1965) president of Syria (2000–). The second son of Hafez al-Assad, he studied ophthalmology in Damascus and London (1988–94) before reaching the rank of colonel at a military academy in 1999.

Assad, Hafez al- (1928–2000) Syrian politician. He served as minister of defence (1966–70) before being elected president of Syria (1971–2000).

assagai n ARMS another spelling of assegai

assail /ə sáyl/ (-sails, -sailing, -sailed) vt 1. to attack somebody vigorously with words or actions ○ assailed by furious criticism 2. to overwhelm the mind or senses of somebody ○ 'Low growls and angry snarls assailed our ears on every side.' [Edgar Rice Burroughs, The Gods of Mars; 1913] [13C. Via Old French asaill-, stem of asalir < assumed Vulgar Latin assalire 'leap at' < Latin salire 'leap'] —**assailable** adj —**assailer** n —**assailment** n

assailant /ə sáylənt/ n somebody who violently attacks somebody else, usually causing physical injury

Assam /ə sám/ state in northeastern India. Capital: Dispur. Population: 26,638,407 (2001). Area: 78,438 sq. km/30,285 sq. mi. Language: Assamese.

Assamese /ássə meéz/ (plural same) n 1. somebody who comes from Assam, India 2. an Indic language spoken in Assam and in Bangladesh that shares a script with Bangla. Native speakers: 11 million. —**Assamese** adj

~~assasin~~ incorrect spelling of assassin

assassin /ə sássin/ n a killer, especially of a political leader or other public figure [Mid-16C. Via French < Arabic ḥašāšīn 'hashish users']

assassinate /ə sássi nayt/ (-nates, -nating, -nated) vt 1. to kill somebody, especially a political leader or other public figure, by a sudden violent attack 2. to harm or destroy something such as somebody's reputation maliciously or treacherously —**assassinator** n

SYNONYMS See kill.

assassination /ə sássi náysh'n/ n 1. the killing of somebody, especially a political leader or other public figure, by a sudden violent attack ○ an unsuccessful assassination attempt 2. the destruction of something such as somebody's reputation by malicious or treacherous means

assassin bug n a large long-legged insect with powerful mouthparts that kills and sucks the blood of other animals. Family: Reduviidae.

assault /ə sáwlt/ n 1. PHYSICAL OR VERBAL ATTACK a violent physical or verbal attack 2. THREAT OF BODILY HARM an unlawful threat or attempt to do violence or harm to somebody else 3. LAW same as sexual assault 4. ATTEMPT TO DESTROY SOMETHING a campaign or series of actions that aims to challenge or destroy something ○ The proposals are under assault by various special interest groups. ■ vt (-saults, -saulting, -saulted) 1. ATTACK SOMEBODY to attack somebody physically or verbally in a violent way 2. MAKE MILITARY ATTACK to attack a place with a military force [13C. Via Old French assaut < assumed Vulgar Latin assaltus, past participle of assalire (see ASSAIL)] —**assaulter** n

assault and battery n the crime of doing bodily harm to somebody

assault course n UK an area of land on which there are various obstacles to be climbed over, crawled under, and run through, used by soldiers for training and keeping fit. Aus, N Am term obstacle course

assaultive /ə sáwltiv/ adj extremely aggressive or disposed to attack

assault weapon n a weapon designed for use in warfare, especially when used in noncombat situations such as terrorism

assay /ə sáy, ássay/ n 1. ANALYSIS OF SOMETHING an examination and analysis of something 2. CHEM CHEMICAL ANALYSIS OF SUBSTANCE chemical testing carried out to determine the composition of a substance or the concentration of its components 3. SAMPLE OF MATERIAL a sample of material for analysis 4. ATTEMPT AT SOMETHING an attempt to do something (archaic) ■ vt (-says, -saying, -sayed) 1. EXAMINE SOMETHING to examine or test something with a view to evaluating it 2. ATTEMPT SOMETHING to make an attempt to do something

(*formal*) **3.** CHEM **ANALYSE SUBSTANCE** to analyse a substance such as an ore in order to discover its components and their concentration [14C. < Old French *assai* 'test' and its source *assaier* 'to test', variant of *essaier* (see ESSAY)] —**assayable** /ə sáy əb'l/ *adj* —**assayer** /ə sáy ər/ *n*

assegai /ássə gī/, **assagai** *n* a slender hardwood spear with an iron tip, used especially by the Zulu peoples of southern Africa [Early 17C. Via obsolete French *azagaie* < Berber *zaġāya* 'spear']

assemblage /ə sémblij/ *n* **1.** a gathering of things or people at one point ○ *an assemblage of world-famous actors* **2.** a work of art made from a collection of different objects

assemble /ə sémb'l/ (**-bles, -bling, -bled**) *v* **1.** *vt* to fit the parts of something together to make a finished whole ○ *assembled a model* **2.** *vti* to bring people or things together, or gather together in one place ○ *A crowd began to assemble.* [13C. Via French *assembler* < assumed Vulgar Latin *assimulare* 'put together' < Latin *simul* 'together'] —**assembled** *adj*

SYNONYMS See ***collect***[1].

assembler /ə sémblər/ *n* **1.** a person, machine, or company that puts together the parts of a machine or piece of equipment when it is being built **2.** a computer program that converts assembly language into machine language **3.** COMPUT same as **assembly language**

assembly /ə sémbli/ (*plural* **-blies**) *n* **1. FITTING COMPONENTS TOGETHER** the putting together of parts to make a finished product **2. COMPONENTS** a set of components before they are put together to make a finished product **3. SCHOOL MEETING** a regular formal gathering of all the students in a school **4.** *also* **Assembly LEGISLATIVE MEETING** a group of people meeting as a deliberative or law-making body **5. GATHERING** the coming together of people for a common purpose ○ *freedom of assembly* **6. MILITARY GATHERING** the gathering together of a military unit prior to an event or operation **7. MILITARY SIGNAL** a signal for soldiers or other personnel to gather **8. TRANSLATION OF COMPUTER LANGUAGE** the translation of assembly language into machine language [14C. < French *assemblée*, feminine past participle of *assembler* (see ASSEMBLE)]

assembly language *n* a low-level computer language consisting of mnemonic codes and symbolic addresses corresponding to machine-language instructions

assembly line *n* a series of workstations at which individual steps in the assembly of a product are carried out by workers or machines as the product is moved along

assemblyman /ə sémblimən/ (*plural* **-men** /-mən/) *n* a man who is a member of a legislative assembly

assemblyperson /ə sémbli purss'n/ (*plural* **-persons** or **-people** /-peep'l/) *n* a member of a legislative assembly

assemblywoman /ə sémbli wòomən/ (*plural* **-women** /-wimin/) *n* a woman who is a member of a legislative assembly

assent /ə sént/ *n* a formal expression of agreement or acceptance ■ *vi* (**-sents, -senting, -sented**) to accept a concept or course of action formally ○ *She will never assent to their marriage.* [13C. Via French < Latin *assentire* 'feel towards' < *sentire* 'feel'] —**assenter** *n* —**assentingly** *adv*

SPELLCHECK See ***ascent***.

SYNONYMS See ***agree***.

assentient /ə sénshi ənt/ (*formal*) *adj* agreeing or accepting ■ *n* a person or party that agrees [Mid-19C. < Latin *assentient-*, present participle of *assentire* (see ASSENT)]

assert /ə súrt/ (**-serts, -serting, -serted**) *v* **1.** *vt* **STATE SOMETHING** to state something as being true ○ *She asserted that she had never seen the man before.* **2.** *vt* **INSIST ON RIGHTS** to insist on or exercise your rights ○ *He asserted his right to remain silent and refused to testify.* **3. assert yourself** *vr* **BEHAVE FORCEFULLY** to exercise your power, influence, and prerogatives in an obvious way ○ *The new management quickly began to assert itself after the takeover.* **4.** *vr* **BECOME KNOWN OR EFFECTIVE** to start to have an effect or become noticeable ○ *The relationship went well until their age difference began to assert itself.* [Early 17C. < Latin *assert-*, past participle of *asserere* 'join to' < *serere* 'join, connect'] —**assertable** *adj* —**asserter** *n*

assertion /ə súrsh'n/ *n* **1.** a strong statement that something is true **2.** the act of stating emphatically that something is true ○ *the assertion of their rights*

assertive /ə súrtiv/ *adj* confident in stating a position or claim ○ *Modern education encourages the assertive student.* —**assertively** *adv* —**assertiveness** *n*

USAGE See ***aggressive***.

assertiveness training *n* teaching people how to overcome shyness and assert themselves

assess /ə séss/ (**-sesses, -sessing, -sessed**) *vt* **1. JUDGE SOMETHING** to examine something in order to judge or evaluate it ○ *not enough information to assess whether the event occurred* **2. DETERMINE AMOUNT** to calculate a value based on various factors ○ *Loss adjusters are assessing the damage.* **3.** FIN **CALCULATE VALUE FOR TAX** to calculate the value of something in order to establish how much tax must be paid ○ *property assessed at £300,000* [15C. < Old French *assesser* < Latin *assess-*, past participle of *assidere* 'sit beside' < *sedere* 'sit'] —**assessable** *adj*

assessment /ə séssmənt/ *n* **1. EVALUATION** a judgment about something based on an understanding of the situation ○ *a fair assessment of the project* **2. PROPERTY VALUATION** a calculation of the value of something, made especially for tax or insurance purposes **3. AMOUNT CALCULATED** an amount assessed, e.g. on a property **4. EDUCATIONAL EVALUATION** a method of evaluating student performance and attainment

assessor /ə séssər/ *n* **1. SOMEBODY WHO CALCULATES** somebody who calculates amounts to be paid or assessed, especially for tax or insurance purposes **2. SOMEBODY WHO EVALUATES** somebody who evaluates the work of somebody else **3. JUDGE'S ADVISER** a specialist in a subject who advises a judge or committee of enquiry

asset /ásset/ *n* **1. SOMEBODY OR SOMETHING USEFUL** somebody or something that is useful and contributes to the success of something ○ *Good health is a great asset.* **2. VALUABLE THING** a property to which a value can be assigned ■ **assets** *npl* **1. OWNED ITEMS** the property that is owned by a person or organization **2.** LAW **SEIZABLE PROPERTY** the property of a person that can be taken by law for the settlement of debts or that forms part of a dead person's estate **3.** ACCT **BALANCE SHEET ITEMS** the items on a balance sheet that constitute the total value of an organization [Mid-16C. Via Anglo-Norman *assetz* 'sufficient goods' (to settle an estate) < Latin *ad satis* 'sufficiency']

asset demand *n* the desire of a person or organization to acquire money, property, or other assets

asset-stripping *n* the practice of buying a company cheaply and making a profit by selling all its assets individually —**asset-stripper** *n*

asseverate /ə sévvə rayt/ (**-ates, -ating, -ated**) *vt* to state something earnestly or solemnly (*formal*) [Mid-16C. < Latin *asseverat-*, past participle of *asseverare* < *severus* 'serious'] —**asseveration** /ə sévvə ráysh'n/ *n*

asshole /áss hōl/ *n US* same as **arsehole** (*taboo offensive*)

assibilate /ə síbbi layt/ (**-lates, -lating, -lated**) *v* **1.** *vt* to utter something with a hissing sound like that of the letter 's' or 'z' **2.** *vi* to be transformed into a hissing sound (**sibilant**) [Mid-19C. < Latin *assibilat-*, past participle of *assibilare* 'hiss at' < *sibilare* (see SIBILANT)] —**assibilation** /ə síbbi láysh'n/ *n*

assiduity /ássi dyòo əti/ *n* great care and attention in doing something ■ **assiduities** *npl* constant attentiveness shown towards somebody

assiduous /ə síddyoo əss/ *adj* showing persistent and hard-working effort in doing something [Mid-16C. < Latin *assiduus* < *assidere* (see ASSESS), in a late sense 'apply yourself'] —**assiduously** *adv* —**assiduousness** *n*

SYNONYMS See ***careful***.

assign /ə sín/ *vt* (**-signs, -signing, -signed**) **1. GIVE SOMEBODY TASK OR DUTY** to give somebody a job to do ○ *assign extra duties to the latecomers* **2. SEND SOMEBODY TO DO SOMETHING** to send somebody to work in a particular place or with a particular group of people ○ *I assigned him to the post room.* **3. DETERMINE QUALITY OF SOMETHING** to determine that somebody or something has a particular quality, name, use, or category ○ *The words are assigned a rating based on frequency.* **4. SET SOMETHING ASIDE FOR SOMETHING** to designate something for a particular use ○ *The new radio station has been assigned a frequency by the authorities.* **5.** MIL **ORDER SOLDIER** to put a soldier or military unit under a particular command **6.** LAW **TRANSFER PROPERTY** to transfer property or rights to another person by an official act **7.** COMPUT **PLACE VALUE** to designate a value for a computer memory location corresponding to a named variable ■ *n* LAW same as **assignee** (senses 1–2) [14C. Via French < Latin *assignare* < *signare* 'mark out, designate' < *signum* 'mark'] —**assignability** /ə sínə bílləti/ *n* —**assignable** *adj* —**assignably** *adv* —**assigner** *n* —**assignor** *n*

assignation /ássig náysh'n/ *n* **1.** an appointment to meet a lover, especially secretly **2.** the act of giving somebody a specific job or designating something for a specific use **3.** LAW same as **assignment** (sense 5) [14C. Via French < Latin *assignation-* < *assignare* (see ASSIGN)]

assignee /ássī nee/ *n* **1. SOMEBODY RECEIVING RIGHT OVER PROPERTY** somebody to whom a right over property is given or transferred **2. PROXY** somebody who is appointed to act for another **3. INHERITOR** a person or a generation that inherits something, e.g., a set of values, a culture, or a group of problems

assignment /ə sínmənt/ *n* **1. TASK** a task that is assigned or undertaken ○ *All team members have received their assignments.* **2. APPOINTMENT** a position, duty, or job for which somebody is chosen ○ *an assignment in Japan* **3. PROCESS OF ASSIGNING** the process of giving a value, use, task, or position to somebody or something **4.** LAW **LEGAL TRANSFER DOCUMENT** a document such as a deed that effects a legal transfer of rights **5.** LAW **LEGAL TRANSFER** the transfer of a right in or over property to another person **6.** *Aus* HIST **CONVICT LABOUR** the system by which convicts were assigned to work for free settlers as fulfilment of their sentences in colonial Australia

SYNONYMS See ***job***.

assimilate /ə símmi layt/ (**-lates, -lating, -lated**) *v* **1.** *vti* SOC SCI **INTEGRATE** to integrate somebody into a larger group, so that differences are minimized or eliminated, or become integrated in this way **2.** *vt* **ABSORB INFORMATION** to integrate new knowledge or information with what is already known **3.** *vt* PHYSIOL **ABSORB NUTRIENTS** to incorporate digested food materials into the cells and tissues of the body ○ *assimilate protein* **4.** *vti* PHON **MAKE SPEECH SOUND LIKE ADJACENT SOUND** to make a speech sound similar to an adjacent sound, or to become similar to an adjacent sound [15C. < Latin *assimilat-*, past participle of *assimilare* 'make the same' < *similis* 'like'] —**assimilable** /-ləb'l/ *adj* —**assimilator** *n* —**assimilatory** /-lətəri, -láytəri/ *adj*

assimilation /ə símmi láysh'n/ *n* **1. ACT OF BECOMING PART OF SOMETHING** the process of becoming part of or more like something greater **2. INTEGRATION INTO GROUP** the process in which one group takes on the cultural and other traits of a larger group **3. LEARNING PROCESS** the integration of new knowledge or information with what is already known **4.** PHYSIOL **NUTRIENT CONVERSION** the incorporation of nutrients into the cells and tissues of plants and animals involving digestion, photosynthesis, and root absorption **5.** PHON **SPEECH SOUND CHANGE** the changing of a speech sound under the influence of an adjacent sound

assimilationism /ə símmi láysh'nizəm/ *n* a policy of assimilating differing ethnic or cultural groups —**assimilationist** *n, adj*

Assiniboin /ə sínnə boyn/ (*plural same* or **-boins**), **Assiniboine** (*plural same* or **-boines**) *n* **1.** a member of a Native North American people who once lived in the northern Great Plains, and who now live mainly in Saskatchewan, Alberta, and Montana **2.** a Siouan language spoken in southern and western Canada and in Montana by the Assiniboin [Late 17C. Via Canadian French < Ojibwa *assini:-pwa:n* 'stone Sioux'] —**Assiniboin** *adj*

Assisi /ə sees si/ town in central Italy, famous as the birthplace of St Francis in 1182. The Basilica of St Francis suffered considerable earthquake damage in 1997. Population: 25,304 (2001).

Assisi embroidery *n* embroidery in which designs are outlined, some design areas are left open, and the background is filled in with cross-stitch

assist /ə síst/ *vti* (**-sists, -sisting, -sisted**) **HELP SOMEBODY** to help somebody to do or accomplish something ○

a programme to assist new parents ■ *n* **1. HELP BY TEAM PLAYER** an act by a player in a sport that enables another member of the team to score or achieve a successful defensive move **2.** *N Am* **ACT OF HELPING** an act or series of actions helping another person [15C. Via French < Latin *assistere* 'stand beside' < *sistere* < *stare* 'to stand'] —**assister** *n*

assistance /ə sístənss/ *n* help given or made available to another ○ *technical assistance*

assistant /ə sístənt/ *n* **1. HELPER** somebody who works to somebody else's instructions, often in a paid capacity **2. SHOP EMPLOYEE** somebody who serves in a shop ■ *adj* **1. HELPING** subordinate to or helping another person ○ *an assistant teacher* **2. HELPFUL** serving to help or be useful

SYNONYMS ***assistant, helper, deputy, aide***

CORE MEANING: somebody who helps another person in carrying out a task

assistant somebody who works to somebody else's instructions, often in a paid capacity ○ *Each supervisor usually works with an assistant.* ○ *She was appointed assistant to the Director of Education.* **helper** somebody who helps with something, often in an informal or voluntary capacity ○ *volunteer helpers* ○ *He had a helper in the shape of his daughter, Celestine.* **deputy** an assistant who is authorized to act in a superior's place ○ *decided to appoint a deputy to take over some tasks* ○ *a committee headed by a chairperson with three deputies with different responsibilities* **aide** an assistant to somebody in public office or to somebody providing a professional service, who may also offer advice ○ *a close aide to the President*

assistant professor *n N Am* a member of a college or university faculty ranking typically above an instructor and below an associate professor

assistantship /ə sístəntship/ *n US* an academic position that provides financial support in exchange for teaching or research services, typically for a postgraduate student

assisted conception /ə sístid-/ *n* MED same as **assisted reproduction**

assisted living *n* the provision of independent residential care in a home environment for older people needing some medical care and help with their daily living

assisted place *n* a place at a fee-paying school or university for which funding is granted by an official body

assisted reproduction, **assisted conception** *n* the use of a technique such as in vitro fertilization to aid human reproduction in cases where this is problematic

assisted suicide *n* the suicide of a patient, usually somebody who is terminally ill, that is aided by a carer or especially a doctor, by the express wish and consent of the patient

assize /ə síz/ *n US* a judicial inquest, or the verdict of the jurors involved ■ **assizes** *npl* periodic judicial proceedings held until 1971 in the counties of England and Wales and presided over by itinerant judges. They were replaced by the Crown Courts. [14C. < Old French *assise*, past participle of *asseoir* 'settle' < Latin *assidere* (see ASSESS)]

ass kisser *n N Am* same as **arse licker** (*taboo offensive*) —**ass-kissing** *n*

associate *v* /ə sṓshi ayt, ə sṓssi-/ (**-ates, -ating, -ated**) **1.** *vt* **CONNECT THINGS IN MIND** to connect one thing with another in the mind **2.** *vi* **PASS TIME WITH SOMEBODY** to spend time together with somebody ○ *Before the race she associated only with other skiers.* **3.** *vi* **MIX SOCIALLY OR PROFESSIONALLY** to be involved with somebody or something in a personal or professional capacity ○ *associates with members of the legal profession* **4. associate yourself** *vr* **BE CONNECTED WITH SOMEBODY OR SOMETHING** to allow yourself to be connected with somebody or something, or voluntarily connect yourself with somebody or something ○ *refused to associate herself with the petition* ■ *n* /ə sṓshi ət, -ayt, ə sṓssi-/ **1. PARTNER** a partner in a business or other undertaking ○ *my associates in the firm* **2. CONNECTED PERSON** somebody who is known to spend time with another person ○ *I couldn't identify any of his associates.* **3. MEMBER** a member of an organization such as a club or a law firm, especially a newly licensed attorney, who does not have full status, rights, or privileges ■ *adj* /ə sṓshi ət, -ayt, ə sṓssi-/ **1. ALLIED** joined with others on an equal or nearly equal basis **2. SECONDARY** with subordinate status or less than full membership in an organization ○ *an associate member* ■ *v* /ə sṓshi ayt, ə sṓssi-/ (**-ates, -ating, -ated**) *vi* **FORM ASSOCIATION** to become involved with somebody regarded as unsuitable ○ *refused to associate with former inmates* [14C. < Latin *associat-*, past participle of *associare* < *socius* 'ally, companion'] —**associable** /ə sṓshi əb'l, ə sṓshəb'l, ə sṓssi-/ *adj* —**associateship** *n* —**associator** *n* ◇ **be associated with somebody** *or* **something 1.** to be involved with somebody or something considered undesirable **2.** to join a person or people in a professional relationship, or belong to an organization in a professional capacity **3.** to connect with or result from something else ○ *The swelling is associated with inflammation of the joint.*

associate degree *n* in the United States, a degree earned on completion of a two-year course at a community college, junior college, technical school, or other institution of higher education

associated statehood /ə sṓshi aytid-/ *n* the status of several former British colonies, mostly in the Caribbean, after dissolution of direct rule from Britain but before full independence

associate professor *n N Am* a member of a college or university faculty ranking typically above an assistant professor and below a professor

association /ə sṓssi áysh'n, ə sṓshi-/ *n* **1. GROUP** a group of people or organizations joined together for a purpose ○ *form an association to represent dairy farmers* **2. CONNECTION** a linking or joining of people or things ○ *She hasn't profited from her association with him.* **3. COMING TOGETHER** coming together and social interaction between people ○ *freedom of association* **4.** PSYCHOL **PSYCHOLOGICAL CONNECTION** a connection of ideas, memories, or feelings with each other, or with events **5. LINKED IDEA** a thought, idea, or feeling that is linked with an event **6.** CHEM **GROUPING OF MOLECULES** the formation of groups of loosely bound molecules **7.** ECOL **GROUPING OF ORGANISMS** a major ecological community dominated by one or more species, e.g. oak in a deciduous forest —**associational** *adj*

association football *n* same as **football** (sense 1) (*formal*)

associationism /ə sṓssi áysh'nizəm, ə sṓshi-/ *n* a psychological theory that explains complex thoughts and feelings in terms of associations with simpler elements —**associationist** *n* —**associationistic** /ə sṓssi ayshə nístik, ə sṓshi-/ *adj*

associative /ə sṓshi ətiv, ə sṓssi-/ *adj* **1.** relating to the association of ideas, events, or experiences **2.** MATHS, LOGIC giving the same result irrespective of the order taken, thus since a + (b + c) = (a + b) + c, addition is associative. Multiplication is also associative but subtraction and division are not. —**associatively** *adv*

associative learning *n* a learning process in which separate ideas and beliefs are linked in order to increase learning effectiveness

associative memory *n* computer memory organization in which stored information is accessed by content rather than memory address

assonance /ássənənss/ *n* the similarity of two or more vowel sounds or the repetition of two or more consonant sounds, especially in words that are close together in a poem [Early 18C. < French < Latin *assonare* 'respond to' < *sonare* 'to sound'] —**assonant** *adj*

assort /ə sáwrt/ (**-sorts, -sorting, -sorted**) *v* **1.** *vt* to sort things by type or category **2.** *vi* to fit into a group [15C. < Old French *assorter* < *sorte* 'a sort' (see SORT)] —**assorter** *n*

assorted /ə sáwrtid/ *adj* **1.** consisting of various kinds ○ *arrived with assorted excuses* **2.** arranged in groups

assortment /ə sáwrtmənt/ *n* a collection of various kinds ○ *an assortment of drawings*

ASSR *abbr* POL Autonomous Soviet Socialist Republic

asst *abbr* assistant

asstd *abbr* **1.** assisted **2.** assorted

assuage /ə swáyj/ (**-suages, -suaging, -suaged**) *vt* to provide relief from something distressing or painful (*formal*) ○ *Constant reassurance could not assuage their fears.* [13C. Via Old French *assuagier* < assumed Vulgar Latin *assuaviare* 'sweeten' < Latin *suavis* 'sweet'] —**assuagement** *n* —**assuager** *n* —**assuasive** /ə swáyssiv, -ziv/ *adj*

assume /ə syoóm/ (**-sumes, -suming, -sumed**) *vt* **1. SUPPOSE SOMETHING** to accept that something is true without checking or confirming it ○ *Don't assume that all has been revealed.* **2. TAKE RESPONSIBILITY FOR SOMETHING** to start being responsible for something ○ *She assumed all of her brother's debts when he died.* **3. ADOPT SOMETHING** to adopt or take on a quality ○ *The task facing them assumed Herculean proportions.* **4. UNDERTAKE ROLE** to undertake a role or function ○ *assume a new role as sales director* **5. PRETEND SOMETHING** to put on a pretence of something, usually in order to hide true feelings ○ *He assumed an air of indifference.* [15C. < Latin *assumere* 'take up' < *sumere* (see SUMPTUARY)] —**assumable** *adj* —**assumed** *adj*

SYNONYMS See ***deduce***.

assumed name /ə syoomd-/ *n* a false name, especially one used by somebody doing something illegal

assuming /ə syoóming/ *adj* expecting too much of other people ■ *conj* if it is assumed that —**assumingly** *adv*

assumpsit /ə súmpsit/ *n* LAW **1.** an oral or written agreement, contract, or promise that exists without being on the record or under seal **2.** an attempt to recover damages from a breached assumpsit [Late 16C. < Latin, 'he or she has undertaken']

assumption /ə súmpsh'n/ *n* **1. SOMETHING TAKEN FOR GRANTED** something that is believed to be true without proof ○ *Make no assumptions before looking at the evidence.* ○ *'Cruelty will be slyly advocated by the assumption that its only opposite is sentimentality.'* (C. S. Lewis, *Reflections on the Psalms*; 1961) **2. BELIEF WITHOUT PROOF** the belief that something is true without having any proof **3. ACT OF UNDERTAKING SOMETHING** the act of taking something upon yourself ○ *With the assumption of power comes responsibility.* **4. ACCEPTANCE OF RESPONSIBILITY FOR SOMETHING** the act of taking over responsibility for something **5. INCLINATION TO HIGH EXPECTATIONS** the tendency to expect too much **6.** LOGIC **UNPROVED STARTING POINT** something taken as a starting point of a logical proof rather than given as a premise [13C. < Latin *assumption-* < *assumpt-*, past participle of *assumere* (see ASSUME)]

AKG London

Assumption (1649–50) by Nicolas Poussin

Assumption, **Assumption of the Virgin Mary** *n* **1.** the ascent of the Virgin Mary to heaven at her death, as believed by some Christians **2.** a Christian feast that celebrates the Assumption. Date: 15 August.

assumptive /ə súmptiv/ *adj* based on an assumption or a set of assumptions

assurance /ə sháwrənss, ə shoórənss/ *n* **1. PLEDGE OR PROMISE** a declaration that inspires or is intended to inspire confidence ○ *They gave us every assurance it would arrive on time.* **2. CONFIDENCE** confidence in personal ability or status ○ *He steered the ungainly machine with smooth assurance.* **3. CERTAINTY** freedom from uncertainty ○ *took heart in the assurance that the problem was solved* **4. MAKING SOMETHING CERTAIN** making something certain or overcoming doubt **5. INSURANCE AGAINST CERTAINTY** insurance against something that is certain to happen such as death, rather than something that might happen such as loss of or damage to property ○ *life assurance*

USAGE assurance or **insurance**? An ***insurance*** policy provides financial protection against undesirable events that may or may not happen, for example loss, damage, theft, fire, or illness. An ***assurance*** policy guarantees that a fixed sum will be paid at some time, usually after

somebody's death or at the end of a specified period. This technical distinction applies only to British English and is now rarely observed outside the financial services industry, the term *life insurance* being more frequent than *life assurance* in general use.

assure /ə sháwr, ə shóor/ (**-sures, -suring, -sured**) *vt* **1. MAKE SOMEBODY CONFIDENT** to overcome somebody's doubt or disbelief about something ○ *I can assure you that every word is true.* **2. CONVINCE SOMEBODY** to convince somebody of something ○ *assured us of her sincerity* **3. MAKE SOMETHING CERTAIN** to make something certain to happen ○ *Proper planning assures that the job will be done right.* **4. INSURE AGAINST CERTAINTY** to insure somebody against something that is certain to happen, e.g. death, rather than something that might happen, e.g. loss of or damage to property [14C. Via French *assurer* < assumed Vulgar Latin *assecurare* 'make secure' < Latin *securus* (see SECURE)] —**assurable** *adj* —**assurer** *n*

USAGE assure, ensure, or **insure?** You use *assure* when the meaning is to make somebody sure about something, and *ensure* about something that you want to be sure of: *I assure you it doesn't hurt. She wanted to ensure that it wouldn't hurt.* *Insure* is used generally in connection with insurance (that is, financial protection), and is also an alternative spelling of *ensure* in North American English.

assured /ə sháwrd, ə shóord/ *adj* **1. GUARANTEED** certain to happen ○ *an assured victory* **2. SELF-CONFIDENT** confident about personal abilities or other qualities ○ *the most assured conductor the orchestra had ever seen* **3. INSUR WITH LIFE ASSURANCE** covered by a life assurance policy ■ *n* INSUR **SOMEBODY WITH LIFE ASSURANCE** the person named as the beneficiary in somebody else's life assurance policy —**assuredly** /ə sháwridli, ə shóor-/ *adv*

assured shorthold tenancy *n* in England and Wales, a lease on a residential property under the Housing Act 1988 that runs for a maximum of six months and gives limited security of tenure

assured tenancy *n* in England and Wales, a lease under the Housing Act 1988 that gives limited security of tenure to a tenant and specific means of terminating the lease to the landlord

Assyria /ə sírri ə/ ancient Mesopotamian kingdom with a large empire extending southwards and eastwards, at its height from the ninth to the seventh centuries BC

Assyrian /ə sírri ən/ *n* **1.** the Akkadian language, especially as recorded in cuneiform tablets from Assyria **2.** somebody who lived in Assyria —**Assyrian** *adj*

AST /ast/ *abbr* TIME Atlantic Standard Time

astable /ay stáyb'l/ *adj* **1.** lacking stability **2.** ELEC oscillating between two unstable states

Fred Astaire

Astaire /ə stáir/, **Fred** (1899–1987) US dancer and actor who was known for his performances in Broadway musicals and films. He famously partnered Ginger Rogers. Born **Austerlitz, Frederick**

'At the risk of disillusionment, I must admit that I don't like to wear top hats, white ties, and tails.'
[Fred Astaire. Quoted in *Starring Fred Astaire*, Stanley Green and Burt Goldblatt; 1973]

Astana /ə stáanə/ capital of Kazakhstan. It is situated in the northern part of the country, on the River Ishim. Population: 312,965 (1999). Former name **Aqmola** (1991–98), **Tselinograd** (1960–91), **Akmolinsk** (1824–1960)

Astarte /ə staárti/ *n* MYTHOL ♦ **Ishtar**

astatic /ay státtik/ *adj* unsteady because of poor muscle coordination [Early 19C. < Greek *astatos* 'unstable' < *statos* 'standing'] —**astatically** *adv* —**astaticism** /ay státtissizəm/ *n*

astatic galvanometer *n* an instrument for measuring electric current that is not significantly affected by the Earth's magnetic field

astatine /ássta teen/ *n* an unstable radioactive element, the heaviest in the halogen series. Source: bombardment of bismuth with alpha particles. Use: in medicine as a tracer element. Symbol **At**. See table at **element** [Mid-20C. < Greek *astatos* (see ASTATIC)]

aster /ástər/ *n* **1.** PLANTS an annual plant of the daisy family. Flowers: white, pink, violet. **2.** a star-shaped structure seen during cell division (**mitosis**) [Early 18C. Via Latin < Greek *astēr* 'star']

-aster *suffix* one that is inferior ○ *poetaster* [< Latin]

asteriated /a steéri aytid/ *adj* describes a crystal that reflects light in a star shape [Early 19C. < Greek *asterios* 'starry' < *astēr* 'star']

~~asterick~~ incorrect spelling of **asterisk**

asterisk /ástərisk/ *n* **1.** STAR-SHAPED SYMBOL a star-shaped symbol (*) used in printing **2.** ASTERISK AS LINGUISTIC SYMBOL in linguistics, an asterisk used to mark a sound, form, or structure that is believed to have existed but is unrecorded, or that is wrong or ungrammatical ■ *vt* (**-isks, -isking, -isked**) MARK SOMETHING WITH ASTERISK to mark a printed or written item with an asterisk, especially to draw attention to it [14C. Via late Latin < Greek *asteriskos* 'little star' < *astēr* 'star']

asterism /ástərizəm/ *n* **1.** PRINTING **PRINTER'S MARK OF THREE ASTERISKS** a triangle formed by three asterisks that calls the reader's attention to a following passage **2.** ASTRON **STAR CLUSTER** a cluster of stars smaller than a constellation **3.** CRYSTALS **STAR-SHAPED REFLECTION IN CRYSTALS** an optical effect appearing as a star in the light reflected from some crystals [Late 16C. < Greek *asterismos* 'constellation' < *astēr* 'star']

astern /ə stúrn/ *adv* **1.** IN OR TO STERN in, on, to, or towards the stern of a ship or boat ○ *The deck hand walked astern.* **2.** WITH STERN FOREMOST into a position with the stern pointing in the direction of motion ○ *Bring the captain's gig astern.* ■ *adj* BEHIND BOAT positioned behind a boat ○ *The astern line has been cut.*

asteroid /ástə royd/ *n* **1.** an irregularly shaped rock that orbits the Sun, mostly occurring in a band (**asteroid belt**) between the orbits of Mars and Jupiter. Asteroids range in size from the largest, Ceres, with a diameter of 930 km/580 mi., down to dust particles. **2.** ZOOL same as **starfish** (*technical*) [Early 19C. < Greek *asteroeidēs* 'starlike' < *astēr* 'star'] —**asteroidal** /ástə róyd'l/ *adj*

asteroid belt *n* a region of space where the density of asteroids is high, located between the orbits of Mars and Jupiter

asthenia /ass theéni ə/ *n* a condition marked by loss of strength in the body [Late 18C. < modern Latin < Greek *asthenēs* (see ASTHENIC)]

asthenic /ass thénnik/ *adj* **1.** showing marked physical weakness **2.** having a slender and lightly muscled build [Late 18C. < Greek *asthenikos* < *asthenēs* 'without strength' < *sthenos* 'strength']

asthenosphere /ass thénnə sfeer/ *n* a weak zone in the upper part of the Earth's mantle where rock can be deformed in response to stress, resulting in movement of the overlying crust [Early 20C. < Greek *asthenēs* (see ASTHENIC)]

asthma /ásmə/ *n* a disease of the respiratory system, sometimes caused by allergies, with symptoms including coughing, sudden difficulty in breathing, and a tight feeling in the chest [14C. Via medieval Latin < Greek < *azein* 'breathe hard']

asthmatic /ass máttik/ *adj* **1.** WITH ASTHMA affected with or prone to attacks of asthma **2.** OF ASTHMA relating to the respiratory difficulties associated with asthma ■ *n* SOMEBODY WITH ASTHMA somebody who is affected by asthma [Early 16C. Via Latin < Greek *asthmatikos* < *asthma* (see ASTHMA)] —**asthmatically** *adv*

Asti /ásti/ *n* WINE same as **Asti Spumante** [Mid-19C. After a province in NW Italy]

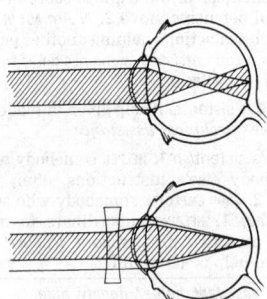

astigmatism: eye condition causing blurred vision (top) and corrected with a concave lens (bottom)

astigmatism /ə stígmətizəm/ *n* **1.** an unequal curving of one or more of the refractive surfaces of the eye, usually the cornea. It prevents light rays lying in specific planes from coming to a focus on the retina, thus producing blurred vision. **2.** a defect in a lens or mirror that prevents light rays from meeting at a single point, producing an imperfect image [Mid-19C. < A^3 + Greek *stigmat-* 'point'] —**astigmatic** /ástig máttik/ *adj*

astilbe /ə stílbi/ (*plural* **-bes** or *same*) *n* a perennial plant widely cultivated in shady damp gardens. Flowers: plume-shaped. Native to: East Asia. Genus: *Astilbe*. [Mid-19C. < modern Latin, 'not glittering' < Greek *a-* 'not' + *stilbos* 'glittering']

astir /ə stúr/ *adj* **1.** awake and moving around, especially out of bed ○ *The children were astir early as usual.* **2.** moving around ○ *leaves astir in the breeze*

Asti Spumante /ásti spyoo mánti/ *n* sparkling white wine from northwestern Italy [< Italian, 'sparkling Asti']

Astley /ástli/, **Thea** (b. 1925) Australian novelist. She wrote *The Slow Natives* (1965). Full name **Astley, Thea Beatrice May**

astonish /ə stónnish/ (**-ishes, -ishing, -ished**) *vt* to amaze somebody to a great degree [Early 16C. < *astone* (see ASTOUND)] —**astonishing** *adj* —**astonishingly** *adv*

astonishment /ə stónnishmənt/ *n* great amazement, often eliciting shock ○ *He was on time, to my astonishment.*

Astor /ástər/, **John Jacob** (1763–1848) German-born US fur trader and property millionaire. Founder of the Astor family and fortune, he endowed the Astor Library, now part of the New York Public Library.

Astor, Nancy, Viscountess (1879–1964) US-born British politician. She was the first woman member of Parliament (elected 1919). Born **Langhorne, Nancy Witcher**

'Superiority we've always had; all we ask is equality.'
[Nancy Astor, on becoming the first woman to sit in the House of Commons, recalled upon her death, press reports; 2 May 1964]

Astoria /ə stóri ə/ city and port in northwestern Oregon. The Lewis and Clark expedition ended here in 1806. Population: 9,730 (2002 estimate).

astound /ə stównd/ (**astounds, astounding, astounded**) *vt* to overwhelm and stun somebody with sudden surprise ○ *was astounded by the viciousness of the attacks* [14C. Alteration of *astoned*, past participle of *astone* 'stun', via Old French *estoner* < assumed Vulgar Latin *extonare* 'thunder out'] —**astounding** *adj* —**astoundingly** *adv*

astr- *prefix* same as **astro-** (*used before vowels*)

astraddle /ə strádd'l/ *prep, adv* with one leg or part on each side of something

astragal /ástrəg'l/ *n* **1.** a narrow convex moulding, often taking the form of beads **2.** *Scotland* a bar that is part of the frame of each pane that makes up a window [Mid-17C. Via French < Latin *astragalus* (see ASTRAGALUS)]

astragalus /ə strággələss/ (*plural* **-li** /-lee/) *n* ANAT same as **talus**[2] [Mid-16C. Via Latin < Greek *astragalos*]

astrakhan /ástrə kán, -kaán/ *n* **1.** fur fabric made from the curly dark fleece of lambs from Astrakhan, southern Russia, or an acrylic imitation. Use: hats, trims on coats. **2.** a brimless hat rising to a ridge, made of astrakhan or similar material

astral /ástrəl/ *adj* **1.** relating to, characteristic of, or consisting of stars **2.** in theosophical belief, belonging to the ethereal region that is believed to exist throughout and at a higher level than the material world, in which personal auras are said to be perceived [Early 17C. < late Latin *astralis* < Greek *astron* (see ASTRO-)] —**astrally** *adv*

astral body *n* in theosophical belief, a second body, not directly perceivable by the human senses, believed to coexist with and survive the death of the physical body

astral plane *n* in theosophical belief, a level of existence where the counterpart of the human body (**astral body**) goes between death and entry into the spirit world

astral projection *n* in theosophical belief, the ability to send the astral body outside the physical body, while both remain connected

astray /ə stráy/ *adv* **1.** OFF RIGHT PATH away from the right path ○ *went astray and ended up lost* **2.** INTO ERROR OR SIN in or into an evil or undesirable course of life ○ *led astray by unsuitable companions* ■ *adj* Ireland UPSET deeply upset and disturbed [13C. < Old French *estraie*, past participle of *estraier* 'to stray'] ◇ **go astray** to be mislaid or missing

astride /ə stríd/ *prep* **1.** WITH LEGS AROUND on top of and with a leg on each side of something ○ *astride a horse* **2.** EXTENDING ACROSS extending across in terms of influence or power ○ *a military colossus astride the world* ■ *adv* WITH LEGS APART with legs spread wide apart ○ *He stood with arms folded and legs astride.*

astringent /ə strínjənt/ *n* a substance that draws tissue together ■ *adj* speaking or writing in a manner that is critical and hurtful in tone and content [Mid-16C. < Latin *astringent-*, present participle of *astringere* 'bind to' < *stringere* 'bind'] —**astringency** *n* —**astringently** *adv*

astro- *prefix* **1.** star, the stars, outer space ○ *astrobiology* **2.** aster of a cell ○ *astrocyte* [< Greek < *astron* 'star' < *astēr* (see ASTER-)]

astrobiology /ástrō bī ólləji/ *n* same as **exobiology** —**astrobiological** /ástrō bī əl lójjik'l/ *adj* —**astrobiologist** *n*

astrobleme /ástrə bleem/ *n* a depression, usually circular, on the surface of the Earth that is caused by the impact of a meteorite [Mid-20C. < ASTRO- + Greek *blēma* 'wound from a missile']

astrochemistry /ástrō kémmistri/ *n* the chemistry of astronomical objects and interstellar space —**astrochemist** *n*

astrocompass /ástrō kumpəss/ *n* a nonmagnetic navigational instrument used to determine the position of true north relative to an astronomical object

astrocyte /ástrə sīt/ *n* a star-shaped cell in the central nervous system's supportive tissue (**glia**)

astrocytoma /ástrə sī tṓmə/ (*plural* **-mas** or **-mata** /-mətə/) *n* a commonly occurring malignant brain tumour made up of star-shaped cells (**astrocytes**)

astrodome /ástrədōm/ *n* a transparent dome on an aircraft or spacecraft through which astronomical observations are made in order to navigate

astrodynamics /ástrō dī námmiks/ *n* the study of the effects of gravitational and other forces on the motion of natural and artificial bodies in outer space (*takes a singular verb*) —**astrodynamic** *adj*

astrogeology /ástrō ji ólləji/ *n* the study of the origin, history, and structure of cosmic bodies other than Earth —**astrogeologist** *n*

astrol. *abbr* ASTROL **1.** astrologer **2.** astrological **3.** astrology

astrolabe /ástrə layb/ *n* an early instrument used to observe the position and determine the altitude of the Sun or other astronomical object. The astrolabe was used for navigation from the Middle Ages until the 18th century when it was replaced by the

sextant. [14C. Via Old French and medieval Latin < Greek *astrolabon*, literally 'take a star']

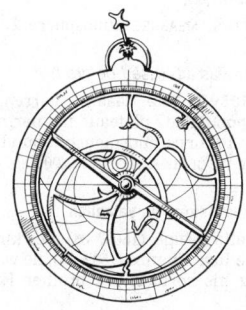
astrolabe

astrology /ə strólləji/ *n* the study of the positions of the Moon, Sun, and other planets in the belief that their motions affect human beings [14C. Via French < Greek *astrologia* 'account of the stars' < *astron* (see ASTRO-) + *-logia* (see -LOGY)] —**astrologer** *n* —**astrological** /ástrə lójjik'l/ *adj* —**astrologically** *adv* —**astrologist** *n*

astrometry /ə strómmətri/ *n* the measurement of the real and apparent motions and the positions of astronomical objects —**astrometrical** /ástrə méttrik'l/ *adj*

astron. *abbr* ASTRON **1.** astronomer **2.** astronomical **3.** astronomy

astronaut /ástrə nawt/ *n* **1.** somebody trained to travel and perform tasks in space **2.** *N Am* an East or Southeast Asian immigrant whose family is settled in Canada, the United States, Australia, or New Zealand but who frequently travels to Asia to work (*informal*) [Early 20C. < ASTRO-, after *aeronaut*]

astronautics /ástrə náwtiks/ *n* **1.** the science and technology of designing and building spacecraft (*takes a singular verb*) **2.** the skills and activities associated with the operation of a spacecraft (*takes a plural verb*) [Early 20C. < ASTRO-, after *aeronautics*] —**astronautic** *adj* —**astronautically** *adv*

astronavigation /ástrō navi gáysh'n/ *n* **1.** the navigation of a spacecraft among astronomical objects, especially stars **2.** ASTRON same as **celestial navigation** —**astronavigate** /ástrō návvi gayt/ *vti* —**astronavigator** /ástrō návvi gaytər/ *n*

astronomical /ástrə nómmik'l/, **astronomic** /-nómmik/ *adj* **1.** relating to astronomy **2.** immeasurably numerous, high, or great (*informal*) ○ *reached astronomical proportions* —**astronomically** *adv*

astronomical clock *n* a clock that shows astronomical information such as the phases of the Moon

astronomical telescope *n* a telescope used to view astronomical objects

astronomical twilight *n* the period of time during which the Sun is at 18° below the horizon

astronomical unit *n* a unit of astronomical distances, especially within the solar system, equal to the mean distance between the Earth and the Sun, about 150 million km/93 million mi.

astronomical year *n* ASTRON same as **solar year**

astronomy /ə strónnəmi/ *n* the scientific study of the universe, especially of the motions, positions, sizes, composition, and behaviour of astronomical objects. These objects are studied and interpreted from the radiation they emit and from data gathered by interplanetary probes. [13C. Via Old French and Latin < Greek *astronomia* 'star-arranging' < *astron* (see ASTRO-) + *-nomia* (see -NOMY)] —**astronomer** *n*

astrophotography /ástrō fə tóggrəfi/ *n* the art of photographing astronomical objects and events for astronomical studies

astrophysics /ástrō fízziks/ *n* the study of the physical properties, origin, and development of astronomical objects and events (*takes a singular verb*) —**astrophysical** *adj* —**astrophysically** *adv* —**astrophysicist** *n*

AstroTurf /ástrō turf/ *tdmk* a trademark for synthetic turf resembling grass

Asturias /a stóori əss/, **Miguel Ángel** (1899–1974) Guatemalan writer, author of anti-imperialist novels rooted in Native American tradition. He won the Nobel Prize (1967).

astute /ə styóot/ *adj* shrewd and discerning, especially where personal benefit is to be derived ○ *an astute investor* [Early 17C. < Latin *astutus* < *astus* 'cleverness, skill'] —**astutely** *adv* —**astuteness** *n*

astylar /ay stílər/ *adj* describes a classical building that has no columns [Mid-19C. < Greek *astulos* 'without pillars' < *stulos* 'pillar']

ASU *abbr* Australian Services Union

Asunción /a sŏónssi ón/ capital of Paraguay and of the Asunción and Central departments and the largest city in Paraguay, located on the River Paraguay. Population: 1,262,000 (2002).

asunder /ə súndər/ *adv* into separate parts, pieces, or places (*literary*) [Old English *onsundran* 'into parts' < *on* 'into' + *sundran* 'parts' < Germanic]

asura /ússoorə/ *n* in Hindu mythology, a member of a class of nonhuman beings who are enemies of heavenly beings [< Sanskrit, 'demon']

Asvina /áshvinə/ *n* in the Hindu calendar, the seventh month of the year, lasting 30 days and falling about the same time as September to October. See table at **calendar**

Aswan /a swaán/ city on the River Nile in southern Egypt. The Aswan High Dam, south of the city, holds back Lake Nasser. Population: 220,000 (1992).

aswarm /ə swáwrm/ *adj* full of moving living things

aswirl /ə swúrl/ *adj* moving with a swirling or twirling motion

aswoon /ə swŏón/ *adj* experiencing a swoon or faint (*literary*)

ASX *abbr* Australian Stock Exchange

asyllabic /áy si lábbik/ *adj* describes a speech sound that does not constitute a syllable

asylum /ə síləm/ *n* **1.** PROTECTION FROM EXTRADITION protection and immunity from extradition granted by a government to somebody who has fled another country, e.g. because of political oppression **2.** SHELTER AND PROTECTION protection from danger or imminent harm provided by a sheltered place **3.** OFFENSIVE TERM an offensive term for an institution for people with psychiatric disorders (*dated*) **4.** HIST PLACE OF SANCTUARY a place that once offered shelter to criminals and debtors, especially a church [15C. Via Latin < Greek *asulon* 'refuge' < *asulos* 'without right of seizure' < *sulon* 'right of seizure']

asylum seeker *n* somebody who applies for asylum as a refugee

asymmetrical /ássi méttrik'l/, **asymmetric** /-méttrik/ *adj* **1.** NOT SYMMETRICAL not balanced or regularly arranged on opposite sides of a line or around a central point ○ *an asymmetrical flower arrangement* **2.** NOT EQUAL lacking equality, balance, or harmony ○ *two countries wholly asymmetrical in their relations* **3.** CHEM WITH ALTERNATIVE ATOMIC ARRANGEMENTS describes a carbon atom bonded to four different atoms or radicals whose arrangement in space may occur in two different configurations (**stereoisomerism**) **4.** ELEC ENG WITH VARYING CONDUCTIVITY describes a substance or a device that exhibits varying or different conductivities for currents flowing through it in different directions **5.** AEROSP WITH UNEQUAL THRUST describes an aircraft that is unbalanced because of unequal thrust from two or more sources, e.g. when one engine of a pair is not functioning properly **6.** LOGIC, MATHS NOT INTERCHANGEABLE describes a relation between two things in which the first has a relation to the second, but the second cannot have the same relation to the first —**asymmetrically** *adv*

asymmetrical digital subscriber line *n* a high-speed telephone line that can transmit voice and video data over copper wires

asymmetrical warfare *n* highly decentralized unconventional warfare carried out against nation-states and civilians by paramilitaries, guerrillas, and terrorists

asymmetry /ay símmətri, ay-/ *n* **1.** the condition of being asymmetrical in arrangement ○ *some asymmetry in the design* **2.** LOGIC, MATHS a relation between two things in which the first has a relation to the second, but the second cannot have the same relation to the first. Asymmetry is illustrated in the statement 'A is the father of B', since B cannot be the father of A.

asymptomatic /áyssimptə máttik/ *adj* not showing or producing indications of a disease or other medical condition ○ *The operation was successful, and she has remained asymptomatic ever since.* —**asymptomatically** *adv*

asymptote /ássimptōt/ *n* a line that draws increasingly nearer to a curve without ever meeting it [Mid-17C. Via modern Latin < Greek *asumptōtos* 'not adapted to fall together' < *sun-* 'together' + *ptōtos* 'adapted to fall'] —**asymptotic** /ássimp tóttik/ *adj* —**asymptotically** *adv*

asynapsis /áy si nápsiss/ *n* the failure of chromosomes that are alike (**homologous**) to pair during cell division (**meiosis**)

asynchronism /ay síngkrənizəm/ *n* in computing and electronics, the occurrence of two or more processes at different times

asynchronous /ay síngkrənəss/ *adj* relating to or using an electronic communication method that sends data in one direction, one character at a time —**asynchronously** *adv*

asynchrony /ay síngkrəni/ *n* TECH same as **asynchronism**

asyndeton /a sínditən, ə-/ (*plural* **-ta** /-tə/) *n* the omission of conjunctions in sentence constructions in which they would usually be used [Mid-16C. < late Latin < Greek *asundetos* 'not bound together' < *sundein* 'bind together'] —**asyndetic** /ássin déttik/ *adj* —**asyndetically** *adv*

asynergy /ay sínnərji/, **asynergia** /áy si núrji ə/ *n* a failure of coordination between different muscle groups so that delicate, skilled, or rapid movements become impossible [Mid-19C. < A-[2] + Greek *sunergia* (see SYNERGY)] —**asynergic** /áy si núrjik/ *adj*

asystole /ay sístəli/ *n* the absence of any heartbeat —**asystolic** /áy si stóllik/ *adj*

at[1] *stressed* /at/; *unstressed* /ət/ CORE MEANING: a preposition used to indicate general position or location. In order to be more precise about exact physical location, other prepositions such as 'on', 'over', 'under', and 'by' are used instead. ○ *a conference at the school* ○ *Someone's at the door.* ○ *I work at home.* *prep* **1.** ATTENDING attending regularly ○ *not at school yet* **2.** FROM INTERVAL OF used to describe the position of something by indicating its distance or angle ○ *She followed them at a distance.* **3.** INDICATES WHEN SOMETHING HAPPENS used to indicate the time or age when something happens ○ *Lunch is at noon.* **4.** DURING EVENT while present during an event ○ *had a good time at the carnival* **5.** INDICATES RATE OR FREQUENCY used to indicate the rate, frequency, level, or price of something ○ *driving at 65 miles per hour* **6.** TOWARDS to or in the direction of somebody or something ○ *He glanced at her.* **7.** AS REACTION TO used to indicate what somebody is reacting to ○ *amazed at what had happened* **8.** IN STATED ACTIVITY used to indicate an activity or subject that a judgment about somebody relates to ○ *an expert at windsurfing* **9.** IN CONDITION OR STATE indicating the condition or state that somebody or something is in ○ *at risk of infection* **10.** DOING engaged or occupied in ○ *hard at work* **11.** IN MANNER OF used to indicate how something is done ○ *set off at a run* **12.** INDICATES REPEATED ACTIONS used to indicate the object of a repeated action ○ *She just picks at her food.* **13.** ACCORDING TO SOMEBODY'S WISHES in response to or based on somebody's wish or decision ○ *Spend this money at your discretion.* **14.** *Carib* AT OR TO THE HOUSE OF used to indicate location at somebody's house ○ *I'm living at my aunt.* ○ *I'm going at Eugene.* [Old English *æt* < Indo-European] ◇ **at all** in any way, to any extent, or under any conditions ○ *don't like it at all* ◇ **at that 1.** in addition ○ *It was a coincidence, and a happy one at that.* **2.** nevertheless, or in spite of something else ○ *It just might work at that.* **3.** at a specific point or place ○ *I think we'll leave it at that for today.* ◇ **where it's** *or* **something is at** where all the action and excitement is happening (*slang*)

USAGE The symbol @ means 'at', and until the 1990s it was mainly used in commercial or technical contexts: *25 kg @ £3.50 per kg; 150 miles @ 30 mph.* Its most familiar use today, however, is in e-mail addresses, where it usually comes between the user's personal screen name and the domain name of his or her organization or Internet service provider: *rtjackson @scotrack.com.*

at[2] *abbr* Austria (*used in Internet addresses*) See table at **domain name**

At *symbol* CHEM ELEM astatine

AT *abbr* **1.** MIL antitank **2.** TIME Atlantic Time **3.** EDUC attainment target

at. *abbr* **1.** PHYS, MEASURE atmosphere **2.** PHYS, ARMS atomic

at- *prefix* same as **ad-** (*used before t*)

Atacama Desert /áttə káámə-/ barren, dry, and sparsely populated plateau in northern Chile known for its once enormously abundant nitrate and copper resources. Area: 363,000 sq. km/140,000 sq. mi.

ataghan *n* ARMS same as **yataghan**

Atahualpa /áttə wáalpə/ (1500?–33) Inca king. The last ruler of the Inca Empire (1532–33), he was executed for having his coruler, his brother Huascar, assassinated.

ataman /áttəmən, -man/ *n* a Cossack chieftain [Mid-19C. Via Russian < Turkic, 'great father']

Atanasoff /ə tánnə sof/, **John V.** (1903–95) US mathematical physicist

atar *n* PHARM another spelling of **attar**

ataractic /áttə ráktik/, **ataraxic** /-ráksik/ *adj* describes a drug or other agent that tranquillizes ■ *n* a tranquillizer (*technical*) [Mid-20C. < Greek *ataraktos* 'not disturbed' < *tarassein* 'disturb']

ataraxia /áttə ráksi ə/ *n* freedom from worry or any other preoccupation [Mid-19C. < Greek < *ataraktos* (see ATARACTIC)]

ataraxic *adj, n* MED same as **ataractic**

Mustafa Kemal Atatürk

Atatürk /áttə turk/, **Mustafa Kemal** (1881–1938) Turkish politician. He was the founder and the first president of the republic of Turkey (1923–38). Born **Pasha, Mustafa Kemal**

> 'If a society consisting of men and women is content to apply progress and education to one half of itself, such a society is weakened by half.'
> [Mustafa Kemal Atatürk, *Speech*; 1926]

atavism /áttəvizəm/ *n* **1.** the recurrence of a genetically controlled feature in an organism after it has been absent for several generations, usually because of an accidental recombination of genes **2.** *also* **atavist** /áttəvist/ an organism showing atavism [Mid-19C. < French *atavisme* < Latin *atavus* 'beyond a grandfather' < *avus* 'grandfather']

atavistic /áttə vístik/ *adj* **1.** relating to or displaying the recurrence of a genetic feature that has been absent for several generations **2.** relating to or displaying the kind of behaviour that seems to be a product of impulses long since suppressed by society's rules —**atavistically** *adv*

ataxia /ə táksi ə/, **ataxy** /ə táksi/ *n* the inability to coordinate the movements of muscles [Late 19C. Via modern Latin < Greek, 'without order' < *taxis* (see TAXIS)] —**ataxic** *adj*

ATB *abbr* **1.** VEHICLES all-terrain bike **2.** EXTREME SPORTS all-terrain boarding

ATC *abbr* **1.** air-traffic control **2.** AIR FORCE Air Training Corps

ate past tense of **eat**

-ate *suffix* **1.** having, characterized by ○ *lobate* **2.** office, rank ○ *archdeaconate* **3.** to act on in a particular way ○ *fluoridate* **4.** a chemical compound derived from a particular element or compound ○ *borate* [< Latin *-atus*, past participle ending of verbs in *-are*]

A-team *n* a group of people who are the very best of their type (*informal*)

atelectasis /áttə léktəssiss/ *n* **1.** a partial or total collapse of a lung **2.** a condition in which the lungs fail to expand completely at birth [Mid-19C. < Greek *atelēs* 'incomplete' + *ektasis* 'extension']

atelier /ə télli ay/ *n* a studio or workshop where an artist works [Late 17C. < French, 'carpenter's workshop' < late Latin *astella* 'board']

a tempo /aa témpō/ *adv, adj* in or back into a previous musical tempo (*used as a musical direction*) [< Italian, 'in time']

atemporal /ay témpərəl/ *adj* independent of or unaffected by time

atempt incorrect spelling of **attempt**

atenolol /ə ténnə lol/ *n* a drug. Use: blood pressure and angina management. [Late 20C. < *anten-* + *-olol*, INN stem]

Athabasca /áthə báskə/ river flowing northeast from the Rocky Mountains in Alberta, Canada, into Lake Athabasca. Length: 1,231 km/765 mi.

Athabasca, Lake fourth largest lake in Canada, bridging the border of Alberta and Saskatchewan. Area: 7,935 sq. km/3,064 sq. mi.

Athabaskan /áthə báskən/, **Athapaskan** /-páskən/ *n* **1.** a group of Na-Dene languages spoken in northwestern Canada and parts of Alaska, Oregon, and California. Native speakers: 180,000. **2.** a member of an Athabaskan-speaking people [Mid-19C. After Lake ATHABASCA] —**Athabaskan** *adj*

Athanasian Creed /áthə náyzh'n-, -náysh'n-/ *n* a 5th-century Christian statement of belief of unknown authorship, formerly attributed to St Athanasius, Greek patriarch of Alexandria

Athanasius /áthə náyshəss/, **St** (AD 293?–373?) Greek theologian. He was patriarch of Alexandria and Primate of Egypt and wrote on the threefold nature of God.

Athapaskan *n, adj* LANG, PEOPLES same as **Athabaskan**

atheism /áythi izəm/ *n* disbelief in the existence of God or deities [Late 16C. < French *athéisme* < Greek *atheos* 'godless' < *theos* 'god']

atheist /áythi ist/ *n* somebody who does not believe in God or deities

atheistic /áythi ístik/, **atheistical** /-ístik'l/ *adj* relating to or characteristic of atheists or atheism —**atheistically** *adv*

athelete incorrect spelling of **athlete**

atheling /átheling/ *n* an Anglo-Saxon nobleman or prince, usually the heir to a throne [Old English *æpeling* < Germanic, 'noble']

Athelstan /áthelstən/ (AD 895?–939) king of Wessex and Mercia. The grandson of Alfred the Great, he was the first monarch to claim the title 'King of all Britain' (926?). He defeated an alliance of Scots, Welsh, and Vikings at the battle of Brunanburh (937).

athematic /áthi máttik, áy thee-/ *adj* describes music that is not based on themes or tunes

Athena /ə theenə/, **Athene** /ə theeni/ *n* in Greek mythology, the goddess of wisdom and warfare, and the patron goddess of Athens. She was born from Zeus's head. Roman equivalent **Minerva**

athenaeum /áthi neé əm/ *n* **1.** an institution that encourages learning, e.g. an academy of science **2.** an institution where reading materials are made available to the public, e.g. a library [Mid-18C. Via Latin < Greek *Athēnaion*, the temple of Athena in Athens, used for teaching]

Athenagoras I /ə theenə gáwrəss/ (1886–1972) Greek religious leader. He was patriarch of the Eastern Orthodox Church (1948–72).

Athene *n* MYTHOL same as **Athena**

atheneum *n* EDUC US spelling of **athenaeum**

Athens /áthənz/ capital and largest city of Greece, situated in the southeastern part of the country. Population: 571,702 (2001). —**Athenian** /ə theeni ən/ *adj, n*

atheoretical /áytheer réttik'l/ *adj* without a theoretical basis

atherogenesis /áthərō jénnəssiss/ *n* the origination and formation of fatty deposits (**atheromas**) in ar-

teries [Mid-20C. < ATHEROMA] —**atherogenic** *adj* —**ather-ogenicity** /áthərōjə níssəti/ *n*

atheroma /áthə rṓmə/ (*plural* **-mas** or **-mata** /-mətə/) *n* an accumulation in the inner lining of an artery of a plaque of cholesterol and other constituents (**atheromatous plaque**) [Late 16C. Via Latin < Greek *athērōma* < *athērē* 'porridge', from its texture] —**atheromatosis** /-rōmə tṓssiss/ *n* —**atheromatous** /-rómmətəss, -rṓmətəss/ *adj*

atherosclerosis /áthərōsklə róssiss/ *n* a common arterial disease in which raised areas of degeneration and cholesterol deposits (**plaques**) form on the inner surfaces of the arteries obstructing blood flow [Early 20C. < ATHEROMA] —**atherosclerotic** /-sklə róttik/ *adj* —**atherosclerotically** *adv*

Atherton /áthərtən/, **Mike** (*b.* 1968) British cricketer and captain of the England cricket team (1993–98). Full name **Atherton, Michael Andrew**

athetosis /áthə tṓssiss/ *n* a condition characterized by involuntary slow movements of the fingers, toes, hands, and feet and usually caused by a brain lesion [Late 19C. < Greek *athetos* 'without a place' < *tithenai* 'to place']

~~**athiest**~~ incorrect spelling of **atheist**

athirst /ə thúrst/ *adj* **1.** eager or longing for something (*literary*) **2.** same as **thirsty** (*archaic*) [Old English *ofpyrst* < past participle of *ofpyrstan* 'thirst greatly' < *þurst* (see THIRST)]

athlete /áth leet/ *n* **1.** somebody with the abilities to participate in physical exercise, especially in competitive games and races **2.** a competitor in track or field events [15C. Via Latin < Greek *athlētēs* < *athlein* 'contend for a prize']

athlete's foot *n* a contagious fungal infection affecting the feet

athletic /ath léttik/ *adj* **1.** relating to athletes, athletics, or other sports activities ○ *athletic uniforms* **2.** possessing a large skeletal structure and strong muscles ○ *an athletic build* [Early 17C. Via French and Latin < Greek *athlētikos* < *athlētēs* (see ATHLETE)] —**athletically** *adv* —**athleticism** /-léttissizəm/ *n*

athletics /ath léttiks/ *n* **1.** TRACK-AND-FIELD EVENTS sports activities carried out on a field, e.g. discus, high jump, and long jump, or on a track, e.g. running (*takes a singular or plural verb*) N Am term **track and field 2.** *N Am* SPORTS ACTIVITIES activities such as sports and exercises that require physical skill and strength (*takes a singular or plural verb*) **3.** METHODS OF ATHLETIC TRAINING the methods, systems, or principles of training and practice for athletic activities (*takes a plural verb*)

athletic shoe *n N Am* same as **trainer** (sense 3)

athletic support *n* CLOTHING same as **jockstrap**

athodyd /áthədid/ *n* a simple tubular jet engine [Mid-20C. Contraction of *aero-thermodynamic duct*]

at-home *n* an informal social gathering in somebody's own home

-athon *suffix* activity or event lasting a long time, especially one done for charity ○ *talkathon* [< MARATHON]

athwart /ə thwáwrt/ *prep* **1.** so as to be across or positioned crosswise over something **2.** so as to oppose or obstruct something

athwartships /ə thwáwrtships/ *adv* from one side of a boat to the other

atilt /ə tílt/ *adv, adj* in or into a slanting position ○ *Her hat was atilt on her head.*

atingle /ə tíng g'l/ *adj* feeling a tingling sensation, often associated with excitement ○ *atingle with anticipation*

-ation *suffix* an action or process, or the result of it ○ *alienation* ○ *presentation* [Via French < Latin *-ation-*, forming nouns from verbs in *-are*]

~~**atitude**~~ incorrect spelling of **attitude**

-ative *suffix* having a particular characteristic ○ *argumentative* [Via French < Latin *-ativus* < *-atus* (see -ATE)]

Atkins diet /átkinz-/ *n* a weight-loss programme that advocates a high-protein, high-fat, low-carbohydrate diet [After Robert C. *Atkins* (1930–2003), US physician]

Atkinson /átkinss'n/, **Sir Harry** (1831–92) British-born premier of New Zealand (1876–77, 1883–84, 1887–

91). As New Zealand's treasurer, he introduced a national insurance scheme in 1882. Full name **Atkinson, Sir Harold Albert**

Atlanta /at lántə/ capital of Georgia, United States, and its largest city. It was an important Civil War battle site. Population: 424,868 (2002 estimate).

atlantes ARCHIT plural of **atlas** (sense 3)

Atlantic /ət lántik/ *adj* relating to or situated in or near the Atlantic Ocean ■ *n* **1.** same as **Atlantic Ocean 2.** a group of West African languages, often considered to belong to the Niger-Congo language family [15C. Via Latin < Greek *Atlantikos* < *Atlas*, the Titan Atlas]

Atlantic City city in southeastern New Jersey, on the Atlantic Ocean, noted for its beaches and casinos. Population: 40,172 (2002 estimate).

Atlantic Conveyor Belt *n* GEOG same as **North Atlantic Conveyor**

Atlantic Intracoastal Waterway /-intrə kṓst'l-/ system of protected inland waterways along the US Atlantic Ocean coast, stretching from Cape Cod, Massachusetts, to southern Florida. It is mostly used by pleasure boats.

Atlanticism /ət lántissizəm/ *n* a doctrine assuming that both western Europe and the United States can benefit politically and economically from cooperation, especially in military matters —**Atlanticist** *n*

Atlantic Ocean the world's second largest ocean, which separates Europe and Africa from North and South America. Area: 82,400,000 sq. km/31,800,000 sq. mi.

Atlantic Provinces Canadian provinces of New Brunswick, Nova Scotia, Prince Edward Island, and Newfoundland

Atlantic Rim *n* the countries that border the Atlantic Ocean, especially the northern Atlantic

Atlantic salmon *n* **1.** a species of salmon that lives in northern Atlantic waters and swims up rivers in northern America and Europe to spawn. Latin name: *Salmo salar.* **2.** the flesh of an Atlantic salmon as food

Atlantic Standard Time, **Atlantic Time** *n* the standard time in the time zone centred on longitude 60° W, which includes Puerto Rico and the Canadian Maritime Provinces. It is four hours behind Universal Time.

Atlantis /at lántiss, ət-/ *n* in Greek mythology, an idyllic island that sank below the sea in an earthquake

atlas /átləss/ *n* **1.** MAP BOOK a book containing maps and vital statistics relating to geographical regions **2.** ANAT TOP BONE IN NECK the vertebra that is at the top of the spinal column and supports the skull. The atlas locks with the skull on rotation and turns with the head. **3.** (*plural* **atlantes** /at lán teez/) ARCHIT FIGURE OF MAN USED AS SUPPORT a figure of a man, either standing or kneeling, used as a support for the upper part of a classical building [Late 16C. Via Latin < Greek]

Atlas /átləss/ *n* **1.** in Greek mythology, a Titan who was forced by Zeus to support the heavens on his shoulders as a punishment **2.** a small natural satellite of Saturn, discovered in 1980

atlas moth *n* a large moth with a wingspan of 25 cm/10 in. or more and strongly hooked and boldly patterned wings. Native to: tropical Asia and Australia. Latin name: *Attacus atlas.*

Atlas Mountains /átləss-/ system of mountain ranges that extends through Morocco, Algeria, and Tunisia. The highest peak is Jebel Toubkal in Morocco. Height: 4,165 m/13,665 ft.

~~**atlass**~~ incorrect spelling of **atlas**

atlatl /át latt'l/ *n* a spear-throwing device, usually a stick fitted with a thong or socket, used to steady the butt of the spear during the throwing motion [Late 19C. < Nahuatl *ahtlatl*]

ATM *n ANZ, N Am* an electronic machine that enables customers to withdraw paper money or carry out other banking transactions on insertion of an encoded plastic card. UK term **cashpoint** [Acronym < *automated teller machine*]

atm. *abbr* METEOROL, PHYS **1.** atmosphere **2.** atmospheric

atlatl

atman /áatmən/ *n* in Hinduism, a person's essence or real self [Late 18C. < Sanskrit *ātman* 'breath, spirit']

Atman *n* in Hinduism, Brahman regarded as the Universal Soul

atmo- *prefix* gas, vapour [< Greek *atmos* 'breath, vapour' < Indo-European, 'to blow']

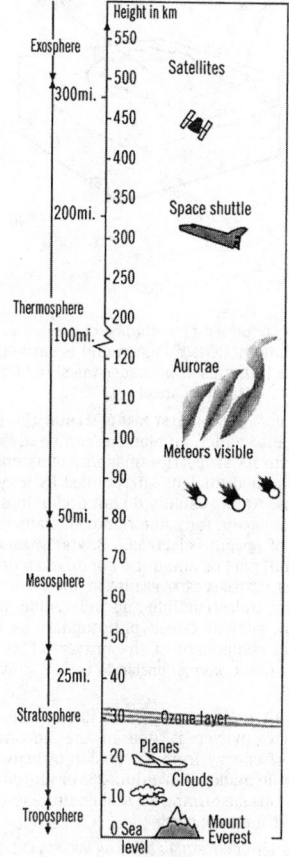

atmosphere: divisions of the Earth's atmosphere

atmosphere /átməss feer/ *n* **1.** GAS AROUND ASTRONOMICAL OBJECT the mixture of gases that surrounds an astronomical object such as Earth **2.** AIR OR CLIMATE the air or climate in a given place **3.** MOOD OR TONE a prevailing emotional tone or attitude, especially one associated with a specific place or time ○ *'The atmosphere of the place was heavy and mouldy, being rendered additionally oppressive by the closing of the door which led into the church.'* (Wilkie Collins, *The Woman in White*; 1860) **4.** MOOD OR TONE OF ARTWORK the prevailing tone or mood of a work of art **5.** INTERESTING MOOD OF PLACE an interesting or exciting mood characteristic of a place ○ *a jazz club with lots of atmosphere* **6.** PHYS UNIT OF PRESSURE a unit of pressure defined as the pressure that will support a 760 mm column of mercury at 0°C at sea level, equal to 1.01325×10^5 newtons per square metre [Mid-17C. < modern Latin *atmosphaera* 'sphere of vapour' < Greek *atmos* (see ATMO-) + Latin *sphaera* (see SPHERE)]

atmospheric /átməss férrik/, **atmospherical** /-férrik'l/

adj **1.** relating to the atmosphere of an astronomical object such as Earth ○ *atmospheric pollution* **2.** evoking or producing an emotional tone or aesthetic quality ○ *a mural with a misty atmospheric effect* —**atmospherically** *adv*

atmospheric pressure *n* the downward pressure exerted by the weight of the overlying atmosphere. It has a mean value of one atmosphere at sea level but decreases as elevation increases.

atmospherics /átməss férriks/ *n* **1.** STUDY OF ATMOSPHERIC INTERFERENCE the study of electromagnetic radiation emanating from natural sources in the atmosphere (*takes a singular or plural verb*) **2.** ATMOSPHERIC INTERFERENCE WITH ELECTRONIC SIGNALS static on a radio or flickering white spots (**snow**) on a television screen caused by electromagnetic radiation from natural sources in the atmosphere (*takes a singular or plural verb*) **3.** PREVAILING MOOD the mood or atmosphere suffusing a situation, group, or place (*takes a plural verb*)

at. no. *abbr* CHEM atomic number

ATO *abbr* Australian Taxation Office

ATOL *abbr* Air Travel Organizers' Licence

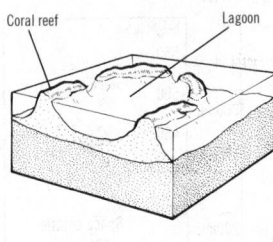

Coral reef   Lagoon

atoll

atoll /áttol, ə tól/ *n* a ring-shaped coral reef and small island that encloses a lagoon and is surrounded by open sea (*often used in placenames*) ○ *Bikini Atoll* [Early 17C. < Maldivian *atolu*]

atom /áttəm/ *n* **1.** SMALLEST PART OF ELEMENT the smallest portion into which an element can be divided and still retain its properties, made up of a dense, positively charged nucleus surrounded by a system of electrons. Atoms usually do not divide in chemical reactions except for some removal, transfer, or exchange of specific electrons. **2.** VERY SMALL AMOUNT a very small part or amount ○ *not an atom of truth* **3.** PARTICLE OF MATTER IN GREEK PHILOSOPHY the basic particle of matter, indestructible and indivisible, first proposed by ancient Greek philosophers as the fundamental component of the universe [16C. < Latin *atomus* < Greek *atomos* 'unable to be cut' < *temnein* 'to cut']

atom bomb *n UK* an explosive device whose great destructive power is due to the uncontrollable release of energy from the fission of heavy nuclei such as the nuclei of uranium-235 or plutonium-239, by neutrons sustaining a rapid chain reaction. Aus, N Am term **atomic bomb**

atomic /ə tómmik/ *adj* **1.** BASED ON NUCLEAR ENERGY based on or using nuclear energy **2.** RELATING TO ATOM relating to an atom or atoms ○ *atomic theory* **3.** TINY extremely small **4.** LOGIC UNANALYSABLE describes a proposition, sentence, or formula that cannot be analysed into a coherent structure —**atomically** *adv*

Atomic Age *n* the present era, starting with 1945 and the first use of atomic weaponry, considered in terms of the discovery, uses, and social implications of nuclear energy

atomic bomb *n Aus, N Am* an explosive device whose destructive power is due to the uncontrollable release of energy from the fission of heavy nuclei, usually uranium-235 or plutonium-239, by neutrons sustaining a rapid chain reaction. UK term **atom bomb**

atomic clock *n* an extremely accurate timekeeping device regulated by the natural regular oscillations of an atom or molecule. An atomic clock powered by a hydrogen atom (**maser**) is accurate to 1 part in 2 quadrillion.

atomic cocktail *n* a radioactive substance in liquid form, used to diagnose or treat cancer (*informal*)

atomic energy *n* PHYS same as **nuclear energy**

atomic force microscope *n* a microscope that measures forces at the atomic level using a very sensitive crystal-tipped cantilever to probe a sample surface —**atomic force microscopy** *n*

atomic heat *n* a value obtained by multiplying the specific heat of an element by its relative atomic mass

atomicity /átta míssəti/ *n* **1.** the number of atoms in a molecule of a chemical element **2.** the state of being composed of atoms **3.** CHEM same as **valency** (sense 1)

atomic mass *n* PHYS same as **relative atomic mass**

atomic mass unit *n* a unit used to express the masses of atoms and molecules, equal to one-twelfth of the mass of a carbon-12 atom or about 1.660×10^{-27} kg. Symbol **u**

atomic number *n* the number of protons in the nucleus of an atom of an element and its isotopes, used to determine that element's position in the periodic table ○ *The atomic number of carbon is 6.* Symbol **Z**

atomic particle *n* a particle that is a part of an atom, e.g. a proton, electron, or neutron

atomic physics *n* the physics of elementary particles and their interactions and processes (*takes a singular verb*)

atomic radius *n* a length equal to half the distance between the nuclei of two covalently bonded atoms

atomic theory *n* any theory proposing that matter is composed of atoms

atomic weight *n* MEASURE same as **relative atomic mass**

atomise, etc another spelling of **atomize, etc**

atomism /áttəmizəm/ *n* **1.** the theory that all matter in the universe is made up of small, individual, finite, and indivisible particles **2.** a theory of psychological states that attempts to reduce them to simple elements —**atomist** *n* —**atomistic** /átta místik/ *adj* —**atomistically** *adv*

atomize /átta mīz/ (**-izes, -izing, -ized**), **atomise** (**-ises, -ising, -ised**) *v* **1.** *vt* SEPARATE SOMETHING INTO ATOMS to reduce something to atoms or separate something into free atoms **2.** *vti* MAKE INTO SPRAY to convert a liquid into fine particles, or to spray particles converted in this way **3.** *vt* DESTROY SOMETHING to destroy something with atomic weapons —**atomization** /átta mī záysh'n/ *n*

atomizer /átta mīzər/, **atomiser** *n* a device that converts a liquid into fine particles

atom smasher *n* a device that speeds up subatomic particles (*informal*)

atomy /áttəmi/ (*plural* **-mies**) *n* a skeleton (*archaic*) [Late 16C. < ANATOMY, understood as *an atomy*, in phrases such as *study anatomy*]

atonal /ay tón'l/ *adj* describes music in which the notes are not related by any mode or key —**atonally** *adv*

atonalism /ay tón'lizəm/ *n* the process of composing music in an atonal style or using atonality —**atonalist** *n*, *adj*

atonality /áy tō nálləti/ *n* in music, the fact of consisting of notes that are not related by any mode or key

atone /ə tón/ (**atones, atoning, atoned**) *vi* to make reparation for a sin or a mistake (*formal*) ○ *atoned for his misdeeds* [Mid-16C. < *at one* 'in agreement', as in (*set*) *at one* 'reconcile'] —**atonable** *adj* —**atoner** *n*

atonement /ə tónmənt/ *n* **1.** the making of reparation for a sin or a mistake **2.** *also* **Atonement** in Christian belief, the reconciliation between God and people brought about by the death of Jesus Christ

atonic /ay tónnik/ *adj* **1.** describes a syllable or sound that is not accented or stressed **2.** relating to, caused by, or showing a lack of muscle tone [Mid-18C. < ATONY, after TONIC] —**atonicity** /áyta níssəti/ *n*

atony /átt'ni/ *n* **1.** lack of stress or accent **2.** lack of normal muscle tone [Late 17C. Via French or late Latin *atonia* 'weakness' < Greek < *atonos* 'lacking tone' < *tonos* (see TONE)]

atop /ə tóp/ *prep*, *adv* on or at the top of something

atopic /ay tóppik, ə-/ *adj* describes a medical condition that is caused by a hereditary tendency to react

to specific allergens, as in hay fever, some skin irritations, and asthma [Early 20C. < Greek *atopia* 'unusualness' < *atopos* 'out of place' < *topos* 'place'] —**atopy** /áttəpi/ *n*

-ator *suffix* something or somebody that acts in a given way ○ *demonstrator* —**-atory** *suffix*

atorvastatin /ə táwrvə státtin/ *n* a drug that blocks the biosynthesis of cholesterol, reducing the level present in the blood, and is effective in reducing heart attacks and strokes

A to Z *n* **1.** a book containing maps and alphabetical lists of street names and map references for a town or city **2.** an alphabetically arranged reference work ○ *an A to Z of cooking terms*

ATP[1] *n* a chemical compound (**nucleotide**) in living organisms that releases energy for cellular reactions when it converts to ADP. Full form **adenosine triphosphate**

ATP[2] *abbr* Association of Tennis Professionals

ATPase /áy tee peé ayz, -ayss/ *n* an enzyme that aids the breakdown of ATP into ADP with a release of energy. Full form **adenosine triphosphatase**

atrabilious /áttrə bílli əss/ *adj* (*literary*) **1.** tending to feel very sad **2.** inclined to peevishness and irritability [Mid-17C. < Latin *atra bilis* 'black bile' (translation of Greek *melankholia*), the bodily fluid formerly thought to cause sadness and irritability] —**atrabiliousness** *n*

atracurium besilate /áttrə kyoori əm béssilət/, **atracurium besylate** *n* a drug administered intravenously that acts as a neuromuscular blocking agent. Use: anaesthesia. [< *atra-* + *-curium*, INN stem for substances resembling curare]

atrazine /áttrə zeen/ *n* a white compound. Use: agricultural herbicide. Formula: $C_8H_{14}N_5Cl$. [Mid-20C. < Latin *atr-* 'black' (because it prevents photosynthesis) + TRIAZINE]

atremble /ə trémb'l/ *adj* shaking or trembling from a strong emotion such as fear or excitement (*literary*)

atresia /ə treézi ə, -zhə/ *n* the often hereditary absence of a usual body opening such as the anus or ear canal [Early 19C. < A[3] + Greek *trēsis* 'perforation']

Atreus /áytri əss/ *n* in Greek mythology, king of Mycenae and father of Agamemnon and Menelaus

atria BUILDINGS, ANAT plural of **atrium**

atrial fibrillation /áytri əl-/ *n* an irregularity in heartbeat (**arrhythmia**) caused by involuntary contractions of small areas of heart-wall muscle

atrioventricular /áytri ō ven tríkyoŏlər/ *adj* relating to the atria and ventricles of the heart or to their interconnection [Mid-19C. < ATRIUM]

atrip /ə tríp/ *adj* describes an anchor that has just been raised clear of the sea bottom

at-risk *adj* exposed to danger or harm of some kind

atrium /áytri əm/ (*plural* **atriums** or **atria** /áytri ə/) *n* **1.** CENTRAL HALL WITH SKYLIGHT a central hall usually with a glass roof or skylight and extending the full height or several storeys of a building **2.** ROMAN COURTYARD the open central courtyard of an ancient Roman house. See illustration on next page **3.** ANAT BODY CAVITY a cavity of the body, especially one of the upper chambers of the heart that takes blood from the veins and pumps it into a ventricle [Late 16C. < Latin]

atrocious /ə tróshəss/ *adj* **1.** appallingly bad ○ *atrocious manners* **2.** extremely evil or cruel ○ *atrocious crimes* [Mid-17C. < Latin *atroc-* 'fierce, cruel' < *ater* 'dark'] —**atrociously** *adv* —**atrociousness** *n*

atrocity /ə tróssəti/ (*plural* **-ties**) *n* **1.** SHOCKINGLY CRUEL ACT a shockingly cruel act, especially an act of wanton violence against an enemy in wartime ○ *to deplore the atrocities of war* **2.** EXTREME CRUELTY extreme evil or cruelty ○ *an act of atrocity* **3.** SOMETHING VERY BAD something repellent or extremely bad of its kind ○ *That design is an atrocity!* [Mid-16C. Directly or via French < Latin *atrocitas* < *atroc-* (see ATROCIOUS)]

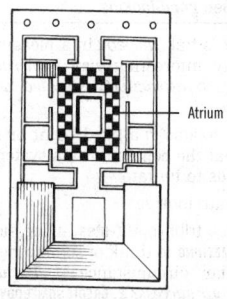

atrium (sense 2)

atrophic /a tróffik/ *adj* relating to or affected by atrophy

atrophic gastritis *n* inflammation of the stomach caused by the inability to secrete sufficient acid to kill bacteria

atrophic vaginitis *n* inflammation of the vagina caused by oestrogen deficiency and characterized by thinning and shrinking of the tissues of the vagina

atrophy /áttrəfi/ *n* **1.** WASTING AWAY the shrinking in size of some part or organ of the body, usually caused by injury, disease, or lack of use ○ *muscle atrophy* **2.** LESSENING OF ABILITY weakening or lessening of some ability ■ *vi* (**-phies, -phying, -phied**) WEAKEN to weaken or waste away through disuse or the effects of disease [Early 17C. Via late Latin *atrophia* < Greek, 'lack of food' < *trophē* 'food']

atropine /áttrə peen, -pin/, **atropin** /-pin/ *n* a poisonous alkaloid obtained from the deadly nightshade plant. Use: muscle relaxant. [Mid-19C. < modern Latin *Atropa*, genus name of belladonna]

Atropos /áttrə poss/ *n* in Greek mythology, one of the three Fates who influenced human destiny. Atropos was known as the Inexorable, and carried the shears that cut the thread of life.

ATS *abbr* Applications Technology Satellite

ATSIC *n* in Australia, a federal authority representing the interests of Australia's indigenous peoples. Full form **Aboriginal and Torres Strait Islander Commission**

att. *abbr* **1.** attached **2.** attention **3.** LAW attorney

attaboy /áttə boy/ *interj* N Am used to express enthusiastic encouragement or approval to a man or boy (*slang*) [Early 20C. Alteration of *That's the boy!*]

attach /ə tách/ (**-taches, -taching, -tached**) *v* **1.** *vt* SECURE SOMETHING TO SOMETHING ELSE to secure one thing to another ○ *attached the door to the frame* **2.** *vt* ADD SOMETHING TO SOMETHING ELSE to append or fasten one thing to another ○ *attached copies of the contracts* **3.** *vt* ASCRIBE SOMETHING to assign a character or quality to something under consideration ○ *I attach no importance whatsoever to their claims.* **4.** *vi* BE ASSOCIATED WITH SOMETHING to have a close inherent relationship to something ○ *little prestige attached to this post* **5.** *vr* JOIN IN WITH SOMEBODY OR SOMETHING to join and go along with somebody or something, often without an invitation ○ *attached himself to our group* **6.** *vt* BIND SOMEBODY EMOTIONALLY to bind somebody emotionally to somebody else or to something (*usually passive*) **7.** *vt* MIL PLACE SOMEBODY ON TEMPORARY DUTY to assign military personnel to a military group on a temporary basis **8.** *vt* LAW SEIZE SOMETHING LEGALLY to seize people or property by legal writ ○ *They've attached her salary for nonpayment of taxes.* [14C. < Old French *atachier*, alteration of *estachier* 'fasten with a stake' < Germanic] —**attachable** *adj*

attaché /ə tásh ay/ *n* somebody on the staff of a diplomatic mission who has specific responsibilities ○ *a military attaché* [Early 19C. < French, past participle of *attacher* 'attach']

attaché case *n* a hard flat rectangular briefcase used for carrying business documents

attached /ə tácht/ *adj* **1.** ENCLOSED fastened to or enclosed with something else ○ *Please see the attached documents and call if you have any questions.* **2.** COMMITTED EMOTIONALLY TO SOMEBODY committed to an emotional relationship with somebody else (*informal*) **3.** DEVOTED devoted to or fond of somebody or something **4.** *Malaysia, Singapore* EMPLOYED having a permanent job with a person or organization ○ *My brother is*

attached to the Ministry. **5.** TOUCHING ANOTHER STRUCTURE sharing a wall with another building, and thus not standing alone

attachement incorrect spelling of **attachment**

attachment /ə táchmənt/ *n* **1.** PART ATTACHED an accessory attached or designed to be attached to a machine **2.** MEANS OF ATTACHING SOMETHING a means by which something is attached to something else **3.** EMOTIONAL BOND an emotional bond or tie to somebody or something **4.** ONLINE ATTACHED TEXT a document or file attached to another or to an e-mail message **5.** ACT OF ATTACHING the action of attaching one thing to another **6.** LAW LEGAL SEIZURE the legal seizure of people or property, especially to acquire jurisdiction over them or it

attachment of earnings *n* a court order directing a third party, usually an employer, to withhold somebody's wages in order to satisfy unpaid debts or to pay maintenance to the person's former spouse

attack /ə ták/ *v* (**-tacks, -tacking, -tacked**) **1.** *vti* HARM USING VIOLENCE to use violence to try to harm somebody or to defeat an enemy or capture an enemy position **2.** *vt* CRITICIZE SOMEBODY OR SOMETHING to subject somebody or something to strong or vehement criticism ○ *The press has repeatedly attacked his plan.* **3.** *vti* INFECT SOMEBODY OR DAMAGE SOMETHING to cause an infection, illness, or damage in somebody or something ○ *The disease can attack at any age.* **4.** *vt* MAKE VIGOROUS START ON SOMETHING to begin something such as work with enthusiasm or determination and deal vigorously with it **5.** *vti* TRY TO WIN to attempt to defeat, or score against, an opponent in a competition or team sport ○ *The chess game began sluggishly, with both sides slow to attack.* ■ *n* **1.** ACTION OF ATTACKING the process or an instance of attacking ○ *The proposals have come under attack.* **2.** BOUT OF ILLNESS an occurrence of something such as a medical disorder that is temporarily debilitating ○ *an attack of asthma* **3.** ATTACKING MEMBERS OF TEAM the attacking members of a team, especially the forwards in a football team (*takes a singular or plural verb*) **4.** MUSIC ENERGETIC WAY OF PLAYING the decisive or energetic way in which a musician begins to play a piece or passage [Early 17C. Via French *attaquer* < Italian *attacare battaglia* 'join battle'] —**attacker** *n*

attack dog *n* **1.** a powerful dog of a breed that is naturally fierce and aggressive, or is trained to be so **2.** an aggressive proponent, mouthpiece, or supporter of a politician or political party (*slang*)

attagirl /áttə gurl/ *interj* US used to express enthusiastic encouragement or approval to a woman or girl (*slang*) [Early 20C. Alteration of *That's the girl!*]

attain /ə táyn/ (**-tains, -taining, -tained**) *vt* **1.** to achieve a goal or desired state, usually with effort **2.** to reach an age, speed, or size [13C. Via Old French *ataindre* < Latin *attingere* 'reach to' < *tangere* 'to touch'] —**attainability** /ə táynə billəti/ *n* —**attainable** *adj* —**attainableness** *n*

SYNONYMS See **accomplish**.

attainder /ə táyndər/ *n* formerly, the loss of civil rights or property as a result of being outlawed or sentenced to death for having committed a serious crime, often treason [15C. < Anglo-Norman, variant of Old French *ataindre* 'affect, dishonour' (see ATTAIN)]

attainment /ə táynmənt/ *n* **1.** the achievement of the goals that somebody has set **2.** a skill, accomplishment, or distinction, especially one achieved through effort (*often used in the plural*)

attainment target *n* the required level of ability that schoolchildren should demonstrate in a subject at a key stage in the National Curriculum

attaint /ə táynt/ (**-taints, -tainting, -tainted**) *vt* formerly, to take away the civil rights of somebody outlawed or sentenced to death for having committed a serious crime, often treason (*archaic; often passive*) [14C. < Old French *atainte*, feminine past participle of *ataindre* 'affect, dishonour' (see ATTAIN)]

attapulgite /áttə púlgīt/ *n* a hydrated silicate of aluminium and magnesium. Use: in filters, an absorbent in medicine.

attar /áttər, á taar/, **atar** *n* essential oil extracted from flowers, especially rose petals ○ *attar of roses* [Mid-17C. < Arabic dialect *aṭar*]

attempt /ə témpt/ *vti* (**-tempts, -tempting, -tempted**) TRY TO DO SOMETHING to try to do something, especially

without much expectation of success ■ *n* **1.** EFFORT TO DO SOMETHING an act of trying to do something ○ *a successful attempt at cooking* **2.** ATTACK an attack or assault ○ *an attempt on her life* [14C. Via Old French < Latin *attemptare* 'try for' < *temptare* 'to try, test'] —**attemptable** *adj* —**attempter** *n*

SYNONYMS See **try**.

Attenborough /átt'nbərə/, **Sir David** (*b.* 1926) British naturalist and broadcaster. He created documentary series such as *Life on Earth* (1979) and *The Living Planet* (1984). Full name **Attenborough, Sir David Frederick**

Attenborough, **Sir Richard, Baron Attenborough of Richmond-upon-Thames** (*b.* 1923) British actor and director. He acted in films such as *Brighton Rock* (1947) and went on to produce and direct films including *Gandhi* (1982). Full name **Attenborough, Sir Richard Samuel**

attend /ə ténd/ (**-tends, -tending, -tended**) *v* **1.** *vti* GO TO EVENT to go to or be present at an event ○ *Hundreds attended the wedding.* **2.** *vti* REGULARLY GO TO PARTICULAR ESTABLISHMENT to go regularly to an institution such as a school, church, or hospital for instruction, worship, or treatment **3.** *vi* LISTEN OR WATCH CAREFULLY to listen or pay close attention to somebody or something (*formal*) **4.** *vt* OCCUR ALONG WITH SOMETHING to accompany something or be associated with it (*formal; usually passive*) **5.** *vt* BE SOMEBODY'S ATTENDANT to escort somebody or act as an attendant to somebody (*formal; usually passive*) **6.** *vi* RESULT FROM SOMETHING to be the consequence of something (*literary*) [14C. Via Old French *atendre* < Latin *attendere* 'reach towards' < *tendere* 'to stretch'] —**attender** *n*

attend to *vt* to deal with or look after somebody or something ○ *patients to attend to* ○ *attend to business*

attendance /ə téndənss/ *n* **1.** an instance of being at an event, or the practice of regularly going to a school, church, or other institution **2.** the number of people who are present at an event or institution ◇ **dance attendance on somebody** to be ready to carry out all somebody's wishes

attendance allowance *n* a tax-free state benefit paid to disabled people to cover the cost of constant care or supervision

attendance centre *n* a centre to which young offenders are required to report regularly by the court, as an alternative to a custodial sentence

attendant /ə téndənt/ *n* **1.** SOMEBODY SERVING IN PUBLIC PLACE somebody employed to serve or help members of the public in a public institution or place ○ *a museum attendant* **2.** ESCORT somebody who escorts or serves another person ■ *adj* OCCURRING ALONG WITH SOMETHING associated with something, or resulting or following from it ○ *parenthood and its attendant anxieties*

attendee /ə tén deé, á ten-/ *n* somebody attending something, especially a conference, course, or seminar

attendence incorrect spelling of **attendance**

attention /ə ténsh'n/ *n* **1.** CONCENTRATION mental focus, serious consideration, or concentration ○ *pay attention* **2.** INTEREST notice or interest ○ *media attention* ○ *a letter for the attention of Mr Brown* **3.** APPROPRIATE TREATMENT care, tending, or appropriate treatment **4.** AFFECTIONATE ACT a polite, considerate, or affectionate act (*formal; often used in the plural*) **5.** FORMAL MILITARY POSTURE a formal standing attitude assumed by members of the armed forces in drill and often when receiving orders, with feet together, eyes forward, and arms at the sides ■ *interj* MILITARY ORDER a shouted military order to assume a posture of attention [14C. < Latin *attention-* < stem of *attendere* (see ATTEND)]

attention deficit disorder, **attention deficit hyperactivity disorder** *n* a condition, occurring mainly in children, characterized by hyperactivity, inability to concentrate, and impulsive or inappropriate behaviour

attention economy *n* a view of the economy in the late 20th century that suggests that people's attention to websites is a valuable and tradable commodity

attention-grabbing *adj* attracting notice or interest, especially by being sensational or lurid ○ *attention-grabbing headlines*

attention line *n* a line in a formally addressed letter indicating for whom the letter is intended

attention-seeker *n* somebody who tries to attract attention, especially from somebody whose notice is craved —**attention-seeking** *n*

attention span *n* the length of time that somebody can concentrate effectively on a task or activity

attentive /ə téntiv/ *adj* **1.** listening or watching carefully and with concentration **2.** behaving towards somebody in a way that shows special regard or affection [14C. < French *attentif* < *atendre* (see ATTEND)] —**attentively** *adv* —**attentiveness** *n*

attenuate /ə ténnyoo ayt/ (**-ates, -ating, -ated**) *v* **1.** *vti* to reduce the size, strength, or density of something, or become thinner, weaker, or less dense **2.** *vt* to reduce the virulence of a bacterium or virus, e.g. by exposing it to heat or producing a culture of it in a special medium. Attenuated bacteria or viruses are used in some vaccines. [Mid-16C. < Latin *attenuat-*, past participle of *attenuare* 'make thin' < *tenuis* 'thin'] —**attenuation** /ə ténnyoo áysh'n/ *n*

attenuated /ə ténnyoo aytid/ *adj* long, narrow, and sometimes tapering

attenuator /ə ténnyoo aytər/ *n* a device for reducing the strength of a wave, especially an electrical signal

attest /ə tést/ (**-tests, -testing, -tested**) *vti* **1.** to show that something exists or is true or valid **2.** to state that something is true, especially in a formal written statement [15C. Via French < Latin *attestari* 'to witness to' < *testis* 'witness'] —**attestant** *n* —**attestation** /átte stáysh'n/ *n* —**attestor** *n*

Att. Gen. *abbr* LAW Attorney General

attic /áttik/ *n* a room or the area that occupies the space under a pitched roof [Late 17C. Via French *attique* 'Attic' < Latin *Atticus* (see ATTIC)]

Attic /áttik/ *adj* **1.** OF ATTICA relating to the ancient Greek territory of Attica or to the modern Greek department of Attica **2.** ELEGANTLY WITTY elegantly succinct or drily witty ■ *n* ANCIENT GREEK DIALECT a dialect of ancient Greek that was spoken in Attica [Late 16C. Via Latin < Greek *Attikos* < *Attikē* 'Attica']

Attica /áttikə/ **1.** department of east-central Greece. Capital: Athens. Area: 14,257 sq. km/5,466 sq. mi. **2.** peninsula region of ancient Greece that was divided into 12 states

Atticism /áttissizəm/ *n* a witty or elegantly simple and concise turn of phrase [Late 16C. < Greek *Attikismos* < *Attikos* (see ATTIC)]

Attila /ə tíllə/ (AD 406?–453?) Hunnish warrior king who led an army of Mongolian nomads and subdued lands from the Rhine to the frontiers of China

attire /ə tír/ (*formal*) *n* clothing worn on a specific occasion ■ *vt* (**-tires, -tiring, -tired**) to dress yourself or somebody else, especially in clothes of a particular type [13C. < Old French *atirier* 'to array' < *tire* 'order' (see TIER)]

attitude /átti tyood/ *n* **1.** PERSONAL VIEW OF SOMETHING an opinion or general feeling about something ○ *a positive attitude to change* **2.** BODILY POSTURE a physical posture, either conscious or unconscious, especially while interacting with others **3.** CHALLENGING MANNER an arrogant or assertive manner or stance assumed as a challenge or for effect (*informal*) ○ *a streetwise teenager with attitude* **4.** AVIAT ORIENTATION OF AIRCRAFT'S AXES the angle of an aircraft in relation to the direction of the airflow or to the horizontal plane **5.** AEROSP ORIENTATION OF SPACECRAFT the angle of a spacecraft in relation to its direction of movement [Late 17C. Via French < late Latin *aptitudo* 'disposition' < Latin *aptus* (see APT)]

attitudinal /átti tyoódinəl/ *adj* **1.** relating to or involving personal attitudes towards specific issues or things in general ○ *attitudinal and behavioural changes* **2.** *US* insisting strongly on your rights —**attitudinally** *adv*

attitudinize /átti tyoodi nīz/ (**-nizes, -nizing, -nized**), **attitudinise** (**-nises, -nising, -nised**) *vi* to strike exaggerated or unspontaneous poses, or adopt extreme opinions, for effect

Clement Attlee

Attlee /áttli/, **Clement, 1st Earl Attlee** (1883–1967) British prime minister (1945–51). He served as deputy prime minister in Churchill's wartime coalition government. His postwar government, the first majority Labour government, introduced the welfare state and granted independence to India (1947). See table at **prime minister**

'We believe in a League system in which the whole world should be ranged against an aggressor.'
[Clement Attlee, *Speech to Parliament, Hansard*; 11 March 1935]

attn *abbr* attention

atto- *prefix* one quintillionth (10^{-18}) [< Danish or Norwegian *atten* 'eighteen']

attorney /ə túrni/ (*plural* **-neys**) *n* **1.** somebody legally empowered by a document (**power of attorney**) to make decisions and act on behalf of somebody else **2.** *US* a qualified lawyer, especially one who represents clients in court proceedings [14C. < Old French *atorne*, past participle of *atorner* 'appoint' < *torner* < Latin *tornare* (see TURN)] —**attorneyship** *n*

attorney at law (*plural* **attorneys at law**) *n* LAW same as **solicitor** (*archaic*)

attorney general (*plural* **attorney generals** or **attorneys general**) *n* **1.** COUNTRY'S CHIEF LEGAL OFFICER a country's chief legal officer, and its government's chief legal adviser. In the United Kingdom, the attorney general is a government minister giving advice on English law. **2.** CHIEF LEGAL OFFICER OF US STATE in the United States, the chief law officer of a state, and its government's chief legal adviser **3.** CHIEF LAW OFFICER OF AUSTRALIA the chief law officer of the Australian Commonwealth or one of its states or territories

~~attornies~~ incorrect spelling of **attorneys**

attract /ə trákt/ (**-tracts, -tracting, -tracted**) *v* **1.** *vt* ENTICE SOMEBODY to be appealing enough to make people visit a place or spend their money **2.** *vt* GET RESPONSE to win or elicit a response from people, especially support or encouragement **3.** *vt* DRAW SOMEBODY'S ATTENTION to draw or secure somebody's attention, or become the focus of somebody's attention ○ '*It takes a big idea to attract the attention of consumers and get them to buy your product.*' (David Ogilvy, *Ogilvy on Advertising*; 1985) **4.** *vt* APPEAL TO PEOPLE to appeal to people or awaken a response in them **5.** *vti* BE OBJECT OF SEXUAL FEELINGS to be the focus or object of sexual interest **6.** *vt* DRAW SOMETHING CLOSER to draw objects nearer, e.g. as a magnet draws iron objects towards it [15C. < Latin *attract-*, past participle of *attrahere* 'draw towards' < *trahere* 'to draw, pull'] —**attractable** *adj* —**attracter** *n*

attractant /ə tráktənt/ *n* a substance or other agent that attracts something, especially one that attracts animals to food or members of the opposite sex

attraction /ə tráksh'n/ *n* **1.** POWER OF ATTRACTING the power of attracting or the feeling of being attracted ○ '*Our mutual attraction was immediate, and we enjoyed one another's company.*' (Peter Ustinov, *Dear Me*; 1977) **2.** APPEALING QUALITY OR FEATURE a quality or feature that attracts somebody ○ *The idea has its attractions.* **3.** THING OR PLACE THAT DRAWS TOURISTS something such as a historical site or building that people, especially tourists, like to see or visit

attractive /ə tráktiv/ *adj* **1.** GOOD-LOOKING good-looking or sexually desirable **2.** AGREEABLE pleasing in appearance or manner **3.** INTERESTING interesting or appealing because of the probable advantages ○ *an attractive proposition* —**attractiveness** *n*

SYNONYMS See *good-looking*.

attractively /ə tráktivli/ *adv* in a pleasing, appealing, or sexually interesting way ○ *attractively priced furnishings* ○ *attractively situated a few minutes from the beach*

attractor /ə tráktər/ *n* a fixed point or state of equilibrium that the behaviour of a system is attracted to and tends to imitate

attrib. *abbr* attributive

attribute *vt* /ə tríbbyoot/ (**-utes, -uting, -uted**) **1.** ASCRIBE CAUSE TO SOMETHING to think of something as caused by a particular circumstance ○ *To what do you attribute your success?* **2.** CREDIT SOMEBODY WITH SOMETHING to give credit for something such as a work of art or a saying to a particular person, often wrongly ○ *It's a bon mot that is often wrongly attributed to Saki.* **3.** ASSIGN QUALITIES TO SOMEBODY OR SOMETHING to regard somebody or something as having particular qualities ○ *the wisdom that she attributes to her favourite writers* ■ *n* /áttri byoot/ QUALITY OR PROPERTY a quality, property, or characteristic of somebody or something [14C. Directly or via French < Latin *attribut-*, past participle of *attribuere* 'allot to' < *tribuere* (see TRIBUTE)] —**attributable** *adj* —**attributer** *n*

attribution /áttri byoosh'n/ *n* the ascribing of something to somebody or something, e.g. a work of art to a specific artist or circumstances to a specific cause

attributive /ə tríbbyootiv/ *adj* forming part of a noun phrase and typically preceding the noun. For example, the adjective 'tiny' in the noun phrase 'one tiny problem' is in the attributive position. —**attributively** *adv*

attrit /ə trít/ (**-trits, -tritting, -tritted**) *vt* *US* to wear something down little by little, especially enemy forces by persistent attacks (*informal*) [Mid-20C. Back-formation < ATTRITION]

attrition /ə trísh'n/ *n* **1.** WEARING AWAY OF SURFACE the wearing away of a surface, typically by friction or abrasion **2.** WEAKENING BY PERSISTENT ATTACK the gradual wearing away of morale and the powers of resistance by persistent attacks **3.** LOSS OF STAFF the gradual reduction of the size of a workforce that occurs when staff lost through retirement or resignation are not replaced **4.** SORROW FOR SIN remorse for sin engendered by the fear of damnation [15C. < French < Latin *attrit-*, past participle of *atterere* 'rub away' < *terere* 'rub']

attune /ə tyoon/ (**-tunes, -tuning, -tuned**) *vt* to adjust or accustom something to be receptive or responsive to something else

Atty. Gen. *abbr* LAW, GOV Attorney General

ATV *abbr* VEHICLES all-terrain vehicle

Margaret Atwood

Atwood /át wood/, **Margaret** (*b.* 1939) Canadian writer. Her works include poems and novels such as *The Handmaid's Tale* (1986) and *The Blind Assassin*, which won the Booker Prize in 2000.

'Everyone thinks writers must know more about the inside of the human head, but that is wrong. They know less, that's why they write. Trying to find out what everyone else takes for granted.'
[Margaret Atwood, 'Lives of the Poets', *Dancing Girls*; 1977]

at. wt. *abbr* CHEM atomic weight

atypical /ay típpik'l/ *adj* not conforming to the usual type or expected pattern

au *abbr* Australia (*used in Internet addresses*) See table at **domain name**

Au *symbol* gold [< Latin *aurum*]

AU *abbr* **1.** angstrom unit **2.** astronomical unit

a.u. *abbr* **1.** PHYS angstrom unit **2.** ASTRON astronomical unit

aubade /ō baʹad/ *n* a song, poem, or piece of instrumental music celebrating or greeting the dawn [Late 17C. Via French < Provençal *albada* < *alba* 'dawn' < Latin *albus* 'white']

aubergine /óbər zheen/ *n* **1.** UK VEGETABLE a large fruit with shiny purple skin, eaten cooked as a vegetable. ANZ, N Am term **eggplant 2.** UK AUBERGINE PLANT a bushy perennial plant of the potato family that bears aubergines. Latin name: *Solanum melongena.* ANZ, N Am term **eggplant 3.** DARK PURPLE a dark reddish-purple colour [Late 18C. Via French, Catalan, and Arabic < Persian *bādingān*]

Aubrey /áwbri/, **John** (1626–97) English antiquary whose biographical anecdotes were collected as *Brief Lives* (1813)

auburn /áwbən, áw burn/ *adj* dark coppery red or reddish-brown ○ *auburn hair* [15C. < Old French (influenced in sense by the similarity of the variant spelling *abrun* to *brun* 'brown') < medieval Latin *alburnus* 'whitish' < Latin *albus* 'white'] —**auburn** *n*

AUC *abbr* **1.** ab urbe condita (*used by Roman classical writers to specify the dates of events in terms of the number of years since Rome's foundation in 753* BC) **2.** Australian Universities Commission

Auckland /áwklənd/ **1.** administrative region of New Zealand, located in the northwest of the North Island and including the city of Auckland. Population: 1,158,891 (2001). Area: 16,282 sq. km/6,287 sq. mi. **2.** largest city in New Zealand, located in the northwest of the North Island. Founded in 1840, it is a commercial and industrial centre and port. Population: 367,737 (2001).

Auckland Islands group of uninhabited islands in the southern Pacific Ocean, 467 km/290 mi. south of New Zealand. The islands are part of New Zealand. Area: 606 sq. km/234 sq. mi.

au contraire /ó kon tráir/ *adv* used to suggest that the opposite is really the case (*literary or humorous*) [< French, 'to the contrary']

au courant /ó kōō ráaN/ *adj* abreast of the latest developments [< French, 'in the current']

auction /áwksh'n/ *n* **1.** SALE BY BIDDING a sale of goods or property at which intending buyers bid against one another for individual items, each of which is sold to the bidder offering the highest price ○ *an Internet auction* **2.** CARDS BIDDING in a game of bridge, the bidding phase during which players contract to win a specific number of tricks if a specific suit is trumps ■ *vti* (**-tions, -tioning, -tioned**) SELL THINGS BY AUCTION to sell goods to the highest bidder [Late 16C. < Latin *auction-* 'increase' < *augere* 'to increase'] —**auctionable** *adj*

auction bridge *n* a form of bridge in which all tricks won count towards the score, as distinct from contract bridge, in which only those tricks contracted to win count

auctioneer /áwkshə neér/ *n* somebody who is in charge of an auction —**auctioneering** *n*

AUD *abbr* MONEY Australian dollar

aud. *abbr* **1.** ACCT audit **2.** ACCT, OCCUPATIONS auditor

audacious /aw dáyshəss/ *adj* bold, daring, or fearless, especially in challenging assumptions or conventions [Mid-16C. < Latin *audac-*, stem of *audax* 'bold' < *audere* 'to dare' < *avidus* (see AVIDITY)] —**audaciously** *adv* —**audaciousness** *n*

audacity /aw dássəti/ *n* **1.** daring or willingness to challenge assumptions or conventions or tackle something difficult or dangerous **2.** lack of respect in somebody's behaviour towards another person

W. H. Auden

Auden /áwd'n/, **W. H.** (1907–73) British-born US poet and dramatist. One of the most influential poets of his generation, he wrote numerous works including 'September 1939' and 'Lullaby', and won the Pulitzer Prize for *The Age of Anxiety* (1947). Full name **Auden, Wystan Hugh**

'Some books are undeservedly forgotten; none are undeservedly remembered.'
[W. H. Auden, 'Reading', *The Dyer's Hand*; 1963]

audi- *prefix* same as **audio-**

audial /áwdi əl/ *adj* relating to hearing or sounds [Mid-20C. < AUDIO]

~~audiance~~ incorrect spelling of **audience**

audible /áwdəb'l/ *adj* loud or clear enough to be heard ○ *an audible gasp from the crowd* [15C. < late Latin *audibilis* < Latin *audire* 'hear'] —**audibility** /áwdə bílləti/ *n* —**audibleness** *n* —**audibly** *adv*

audience /áwdi ənss/ *n* **1.** PEOPLE WATCHING PERFORMANCE a group of people assembled to watch and listen to a show, concert, film, or speech **2.** PEOPLE WATCHING OR LISTENING TO BROADCAST the viewers of a film or a television programme, or the listeners to a radio programme **3.** AUTHOR'S READERSHIP the people who read a writer's books **4.** FORMAL INTERVIEW a formal, usually prearranged, interview with somebody important [14C. Via French < Latin *audientia* 'a hearing' < *audire* 'hear']

audile /áw dīl/ *adj* PHYSIOL same as **auditory** [Late 19C. < Latin *audire* 'hear']

audio /áwdi ō/ *n* the recording and reproduction of sound [Early 20C. < AUDIO-]

audio- *prefix* sound, hearing ○ *audiogram* [< Latin *audire* 'hear']

audio book *n* a commercial recording, usually on a cassette tape, of somebody reading the text of a popular book

audiocassette /áwdi ō kə sét/ *n* a cassette containing an audiotape, for use in a tape recorder

audio clip *n* an extract from a longer sound recording, e.g. from a film soundtrack, that can be listened to on a personal computer

audioconferencing /áwdi ō konfərənssing/ *n* the holding of a conference, meeting, or discussion in which the participants are linked by telephone

audio console *n* a cabinet for vertically stacked pieces of audio equipment, typically a radio, record player, cassette recorder, and compact disc player

audio frequency *n* a frequency that is audible to the human ear, between 20 and 20,000 hertz in people with normal hearing

audiogram /áwdi ō gram/ *n* a tracing produced by an audiometer, recording the sharpness of somebody's hearing

audiology /áwdi ólləji/ *n* the scientific study of hearing, especially for diagnosing and treating hearing loss —**audiological** /áwdi ə lójjik'l/ *adj* —**audiologist** *n*

audiometer /áwdi ómmitər/ *n* an instrument for testing the ability of a human ear to detect sounds over a range of frequencies and intensities —**audiometric** /áwdi ō méttrik/ *adj* —**audiometry** *n*

audiophile /áwdi ō fīl/ *n* somebody who has an enthusiasm for sound reproduction, especially high-fidelity music recordings

audiotape /áwdi ō tayp/ *n* **1.** magnetic tape for recording sound, or a length of this, typically in a cassette **2.** a sound recording on magnetic tape, especially for use in a tape recorder

audiotyping /áwdi ō típing/ *n* the skill or activity of typing up recorded dictation while listening to it —**audiotypist** *n*

audiovisual /áwdi ō vízhoo əl/ *adj* **1.** relating to sound and vision, especially when combined, e.g. in a presentation using both film and sound recordings **2.** relating to the faculties of hearing and seeing ■ *n* N Am same as **audiovisual aid** (*often used in the plural*)

audiovisual aid *n* a teaching or lecture aid that combines sound and vision, e.g. in the form of video equipment, software programs, or slides accompanied by sound recordings (*often used in the plural*) US term **audiovisual**

audit /áwdit/ *n* **1.** CHECK OF FINANCIAL ACCOUNTS a formal examination, correction, and official endorsing of financial accounts, especially those of a business, undertaken annually by an accountant **2.** EFFICIENCY CHECK a systematic check or assessment, especially of the efficiency or effectiveness of an organization or a process, typically carried out by an independent assessor ■ *vt* (**-dits, -diting, -dited**) **1.** CHECK FINANCIAL ACCOUNTS to carry out an audit of the financial accounts of a firm, department, or organization to establish accuracy or efficiency **2.** N Am SIT IN ON CLASS to attend a class without asking for or receiving graduation credit for it, usually attending all the sessions but not doing the assignments [15C. < Latin *auditus* 'hearing' < *audit-*, past participle of *audire* 'hear'] —**auditable** *adj*

auditee /áwdi teé/ *n* a person or organization that is being audited

audition /aw dísh'n/ *n* **1.** TEST PERFORMANCE BY CANDIDATE a test in the form of a short performance, e.g. by an actor applying for a role in a film or play **2.** HEARING the sense, faculty, or process of hearing ■ *vti* (**-tions, -tioning, -tioned**) GIVE AUDITION to do an audition, or give somebody an audition for a role [Late 16C. < Latin *audition-* 'hearing' < *audire* 'hear']

auditive /áwditiv/ *adj* PHYSIOL same as **auditory** [Early 17C. < French < Latin *audire* 'hear']

auditor /áwditər/ *n* **1.** SOMEBODY CHECKING ACCOUNTS OR SYSTEMS somebody who checks accounts or conducts an audit of an organization **2.** HEARER a hearer or listener, e.g. a member of an audience or somebody listening to somebody who is talking (*formal*) **3.** N Am STUDENT SITTING IN ON CLASS a student who attends a class without asking for or receiving graduation credit for it [14C. Via Anglo-Norman < Latin, 'hearer' < *audire* 'hear']

auditor-general (*plural* **auditor-generals** or **auditors-general**) *n* an officer of the Australian government who monitors government expenditure and ensures that it is authorized by Act or regulation

auditorium /áwdi táwri əm/ (*plural* **-riums** or **-ria** /-ri ə/) *n* **1.** the area of a theatre or concert hall where the audience sits **2.** a lecture theatre or a hall that is used for lectures, concerts, and other events [Early 17C. < Latin, 'place for hearing' < *audire* 'hear']

auditory /áwditəri/ *adj* relating to the organs of hearing or the process of hearing [Late 16C. < late Latin *auditorius* < Latin *audire* 'hear']

auditory nerve *n* a nerve that conveys impulses relating to hearing and balance from the inner ear to the brain

audit trail *n* **1.** a sequential record of financial transactions, calculations, and other evidence examined by an auditor **2.** a record showing what operations a computer or computer user has performed in a specific period of time

Audubon /áwdəbən/, **John James** (1785–1851) Haitian-born US ornithologist, naturalist, and artist. An outstanding wildlife artist, he is best known for *The Birds of America* (1827–38), which contains life-size, hand-coloured illustrations of more than 1,000 American birds.

Auerbach /ówər bak/, **Frank** (*b.* 1931) German-born British painter. He is noted for landscapes and portraits characterized by thickly applied oil paint.

au fait /ō fáy/ *adj* familiar with the latest de-

velopments in or facts about something [< French, 'to the fact']

Aufbau principle /ówf bow-/ *n* a principle that each successive chemical element in a sequence can be created by adding a proton to the nucleus and an electron to an orbital of the preceding element [< German, 'construction']

auf Wiedersehen /ówf veédər zayn, zay ən/ *interj* goodbye till the next time we see each other [< German, 'until seeing again', translation of French *au revoir*]

Aug. *abbr* CALENDAR August

Augean /aw jeé ən/ *adj* **1.** disgustingly dirty, like the Augean stables **2.** extremely difficult and unpleasant

Augean stables *npl* in Greek mythology, the stables owned by King Augeas that had not been cleaned in 30 years. One of Heracles' tasks was to clean them in one day, which he achieved by diverting two rivers through them.

auger /áwgər/ *n* a hand tool with a corkscrew-shaped bit for boring holes, or a larger tool, using the same principle, for boring holes in the ground [Old English *nafogār* < NAVE[2] + *gār* 'spear' (see GORE[1]); *n* lost in 16C by false division of *a nauger* as *an auger*]

SPELLCHECK **auger** or **augur**? Do not confuse the spelling of *auger* and *augur*, which sound similar. *Auger* is only used as a noun, denoting a tool for boring holes. *Augur* can be used as a noun, denoting a foreteller of the future, or as a verb, meaning 'indicate what will happen in the future': *This does not augur well for the company's expansion plans.*

Auger effect /ṓ zhay-/, **Auger process** *n* the emission of an electron from an excited positive ion resulting in a doubly charged ion [Mid-20C. After Pierre *Auger* (1899–1993), French physicist]

aught /awt/ *pron* anything whatever (*literary or archaic*) [Old English *āwiht* 'ever a thing' < Germanic]

augite /áw gīt/ *n* a dark green mineral of the pyroxene group, containing aluminium, calcium, iron, and magnesium. Source: igneous rocks. [Early 19C. Via Latin *augites*, a precious stone (possibly turquoise) < Greek *augitēs* < *augē* 'lustre']

augment /awg mént/ *v* (-ments, -menting, -mented) **1.** *vti* INCREASE to add to something in order to make it larger or more substantial, or to grow in this way (*formal*) **2.** *vt* MUSIC INCREASE MUSICAL INTERVAL to enlarge a perfect or major musical interval by a semitone ■ *n* GRAM PREFIXED VOWEL in Greek or Sanskrit grammar, a vowel prefixed to a verb, or added to its initial vowel so as to lengthen it into a diphthong, to form a past tense [14C. < French *augmenter* < Latin *augere* 'to increase' < Indo-European] —**augmented** *adj* —**augmenter** *n*

SYNONYMS See *increase*.

augmentation /áwg men táysh'n, -mən-/ *n* **1.** the increasing, or growth, of something in number, amount, size, strength, or intensity, or the amount by which something grows or is added to ○ *augmentation in costs* **2.** in music, the technique of varying a theme by increasing its note values proportionally

augmentation mammoplasty *n* surgical enlargement of the breasts

augmentative /awg méntətiv/ *adj* **1.** CAUSING INCREASE tending to add to or increase something or to enable something to grow or increase (*formal*) **2.** GRAM DENOTING GREAT SIZE OR IMPORTANCE describes an affix that signifies great size or importance, or a word to which an affix of this kind has been added. Spanish '-ote' and Italian '-one' are augmentative affixes. ■ *n* GRAM AUGMENTATIVE AFFIX OR WORD an affix signifying great size or importance, or a word to which an affix of this kind has been added

au gratin /ṓ gráttaN/ *adj* sprinkled with breadcrumbs, sometimes mixed with grated cheese, and browned before serving [< French, 'with a gratin crust']

Augsburg /ówgz burg/ city in Bavaria in southern Germany, situated northwest of Munich. Population: 262,110 (1997).

augur /áwgər/ *n* **1.** INTERPRETER OF MESSAGES FROM ROMAN DEITIES in ancient Rome, a religious official who interpreted natural phenomena as signs that the deities favoured or disapproved of actions proposed by the city **2.** SOOTHSAYER OR PROPHET any soothsayer, prophet, or diviner ■ *vti* (-gurs, -guring, -gured) INDICATE WHAT WILL HAPPEN to suggest or indicate what will happen in the future or how well or badly things will turn out ○ *Recent events do not augur well for world peace.* ○ *Every circumstance augured success.* [14C. < Latin] —**augural** /áwgyoőrəl/ *adj*

SPELLCHECK See *auger.*

augury /áwgyoŏri/ *n* (*plural* -ries) *n* **1.** the art, activity, prophecies, or pronouncements of an augur, soothsayer, or diviner **2.** an indication of what will happen in the future

august /aw gúst/ *adj* full of solemn splendour and dignity (*formal*) [Mid-17C. Directly or via French < Latin *augustus*] —**augustly** *adv*

August /áwgəst/ *n* in the Gregorian calendar, the eighth month of the year, lasting 31 days. See table at **calendar** [Pre-12C. < Latin *augustus*, after the Roman emperor AUGUSTUS]

Augusta /ə gústə/ **1.** city on the western bank of the Savannah River, in east-central Georgia, United States. It was previously known as Fort Cornwallis. Population: 197,842 (2002 estimate). **2.** capital city of Maine and holiday resort, in the southwest of the state, on the Kennebec River. Population: 18,551 (2002 estimate).

Augustan /aw gústən/ *adj* **1.** OF AUGUSTUS OR HIS TIME relating to the Roman emperor Augustus, to his reign, or to the classical writers, including Virgil, Ovid, and Horace, who flourished during this period **2.** CHARACTERIZED BY CLASSICAL WRITING relating or belonging to a period during which writing in the classical style flourished, especially the 17th century in France or the 18th century in England ■ *n* AUGUSTAN WRITER OR STUDENT a writer from an Augustan period, or somebody who studies Augustan literature

Augustine /aw gústin/, St (AD 354–430) Roman priest and theologian. His masterpiece, *The City of God*, greatly influenced the development of Christianity. He was bishop of Hippo, North Africa, from 395 until his death. Known as **St Augustine of Hippo**

Augustine, St (d. AD 604) Roman priest. Sent by Pope Gregory I to convert the Anglo-Saxons, he became the first Archbishop of Canterbury (597–604). Known as **St Augustine of Canterbury**

Augustinian /áwgə stínni ən/ *adj* relating to St Augustine of Hippo, his teachings, or any of the Christian religious orders living according to his rule or system of monastic life ■ *n* a follower of St Augustine of Hippo, especially a member of one of the religious orders living according to his rule

Augustus /aw gústəss/ (63 BC–AD 14) Roman emperor. The founder of the Roman Empire, he was the adopted son of Julius Caesar. He succeeded his adoptive father as absolute ruler in 27 BC after a period of civil war.

au jus /ṓ zhoŏ/ *adj* describes meat that is served in its own cooking juices ○ *roast beef au jus* [< French, 'with the juice']

auk

auk /awk/ *n* a small black-and-white heavy-bodied seabird. Native to: cool northern seas. Family: Alcidae. [Late 17C. Via Norwegian *alk* < Old Norse *álka*]

auklet /áwklət/ *n* a small auk that nests in burrows or rock slides. Native to: northern Pacific. Family: Alcidae.

auld lang syne /áwld lang zín/ *n Scotland* old times,

or times long gone (*archaic*) [Literally 'old long since', 'old long ago']

Aum *n* RELIG, BUDDHISM another spelling of **Om**

aumbry *n* CHR same as **ambry**

au naturel /ṓ náttyoŏ rél/ *adv, adj* **1.** served simply and plainly, e.g. uncooked or without seasoning or salt **2.** wearing no clothes (*humorous*) [< French, 'in the natural state']

Aung San /áwng sán/, **U** (1914?–47) Burmese nationalist leader. He became prime minister of British Burma (1945–47) and successfully negotiated Burmese independence, but was assassinated before independence was achieved.

Aung San Suu Kyi

Aung San Suu Kyi /áwng san soo keé/, **Daw** (b. 1945) Burmese human rights activist. She established Myanmar's National League for Democracy (NLD) party, and won the Nobel Peace Prize (1991).

'Development requires democracy, the genuine empowerment of the people.' [Daw Aung San Suu Kyi, *Times*; 22 November 1994]

aunt /aant/ *n* the sister of somebody's mother or father, or the wife of somebody's uncle [13C. Via Anglo-Norman < Latin *amita* 'father's sister'] —**aunthood** *n*

Aunt /aant/ *n* used, before a name or alone, as a form of address or reference to an aunt (*formal*)

auntie /áanti/, **aunty** (*plural* -ies) *n* an aunt, or a close woman friend of a child's parents (*informal*)

Auntie /áanti/, **Aunty** *n* (*informal*) **1.** FORM OF ADDRESS TO PARENTS' FRIEND used, before a name or alone, as a form of address or reference to an aunt or a close woman friend of a child's parents **2.** BBC a nickname for the BBC, or British Broadcasting Corporation, in reference to its image as a kindly and well-intentioned, if old-fashioned, guardian of standards **3.** *Aus* ABC a nickname for the Australian Broadcasting Corporation **4.** *Malaysia, S Asia, Singapore* FORM OF ADDRESS TO WOMAN used as a form of address or reference to an unfamiliar woman of middle age or beyond ○ *Auntie, do you want to buy some?*

Aunt Sally /-sálli/ (*plural* **Aunt Sallies**) *n* **1.** FAIRGROUND GAME a traditional throwing game played at fairgrounds and pubs, in which players throw sticks or balls at a target **2.** FAIRGROUND TARGET a target used in Aunt Sally, traditionally shaped like the head of a woman, typically with a clay pipe in her mouth **3.** BUTT OF CRITICISM a person or organization that is the constant target of criticism and abusive comment **4.** ARGUMENT TO BE DEMOLISHED in formal discussion, an argument put forward so that it can be demolished and dismissed

aunty *n* another spelling of **auntie**

au pair /ṓ páir/ *n* a young person from abroad living with a family to learn the language, and helping with childcare and domestic work in return for board and accommodation [< French, 'on equal terms']

aura /áwrə/ (*plural* -ras or -rae /-ree/) *n* **1.** DISTINCTIVE QUALITY a characteristic or distinctive impression created by somebody or something ○ *an aura of mystery* **2.** PARANORMAL FORCE EMANATING FROM SOMEBODY OR SOMETHING a force that is said to surround all people and objects, discernible, often as a bright glow, only to people of unusual psychic sensitivity **3.** MED WARNING SENSATION BEFORE EPILEPTIC EPISODE a distinctive sensation or visual disturbance that may signal the beginning of an epileptic episode or a migraine [Mid-18C. Via Latin, 'gentle breeze' < Greek]

aural /áwrəl/ *adj* relating to the ear or hearing, or to receptiveness and response to speech or other sounds ○ *the extent to which our visual and aural perceptions of painting and music depend on our prior knowledge of the pieces* [Mid-19C. < Latin *auris* 'ear'] —**aurally** *adv*

USAGE aural or **oral**? These two words are often confused because they are pronounced in a similar way and have meanings that are close. Essentially, *aural* is to do with hearing, whereas *oral* is to do with speaking or the mouth. An *aural test* is an examination testing comprehension by listening, whereas in an *oral test* the answers are spoken rather than written.

auranofin /aw ránnəfin/ *n* a pharmaceutical compound containing gold, taken orally. Use: treatment of arthritis.

aurar MONEY plural of **eyrir**

aurate /áw rayt/ *n* a salt containing an anionic grouping of gold and another element

aureate /áwri ayt, -ət/ *adj* **1.** made of, containing, covered with, or coloured like gold **2.** expressed or written in a highly or excessively ornamented, florid, or elaborate style [15C. < Latin *aureatus* < *aureus* 'golden' < *aurum* 'gold']

aurei MONEY plural of **aureus**

Aurelian /aw reeli ən/ (AD 215?–275) Roman emperor. Elected Roman emperor by the army (270–75), he recovered Gaul and made the Danube the empire's frontier.

Aurelius /aw reeli əss/, **Marcus** (AD 121–180) Roman emperor and philosopher. Much of his time as emperor (161–180) was spent fighting on the empire's northern and eastern fronts. While on campaign he wrote *Meditations* (170–180), a 12-volume work that shows his interest in Stoic philosophy. Full name **Aurelius Antoninus, Marcus Aelius**

> 'Time is like a river made up of the events which happen, and its current is strong; no sooner does anything appear than it is swept away, and another comes in its place, and will be swept away too.'
> [Marcus Aurelius, *Meditations*; 170–180]

aureole /áw ri ŏl/, **aureola** /aw ree ələ, áw ri ŏlə/ *n* **1.** a painted or carved representation of a circle of light around the head of a divine being or a saint **2.** METEOROL same as **corona** (sense 2) [Mid-19C. Via French < late Latin *corona aureola* 'golden crown']

aureus /áwri əss/ (*plural* **-rei** /-ī/) *n* a gold coin that was a unit of currency in the Roman Empire between 30 BC and AD 310 [Early 17C. < Latin, noun use of *aureus* 'golden' (see AUREATE)]

au revoir /ō rə vwaár/ *interj* goodbye till we see each other again [< French, 'until seeing again']

auri-[1] *prefix* ear, hearing ○ *auriform* [< Latin *auris* 'ear']

auri-[2] *prefix* gold ○ *auriferous* [< Latin *aurum*]

auric /áwrik/ *adj* containing gold with a valency of three ○ *auric oxide* [Early 19C. < Latin *aurum* 'gold']

Auric /aw reek/, **Georges** (1899–1983) French composer who produced orchestral works, ballets, and film scores. He was a member of the Paris-based group of composers known as 'Les Six', and was director of the Paris Opera and the Opéra Comique in Paris (1962–68).

auricle /áwrik'l/ *n* **1.** the part of the external ear that projects outwards from the head **2.** an ear-shaped muscular part that sticks out from the surface of each upper chamber (**atrium**) of the heart **3.** ANAT same as **atrium** (*dated*) [Mid-17C. < Latin *auricula* 'little ear' < *auris* 'ear'] —**auricled** *adj*

auricula /aw ríkyoolə/ (*plural* **-las** or **-lae** /-lee/) *n* an alpine primrose with leaves shaped like a bear's ear. Flowers: yellow. Latin name: *Primula auricula*. [Mid-17C. < Latin (see AURICLE)]

auricular /aw ríkyoolər/ *adj* **1.** EAR-SHAPED shaped like an ear **2.** OF ORGANS OF HEARING relating to the ear or the sense of hearing **3.** OF HEART CHAMBERS relating to the ear-shaped muscular part (**auricle**) on the surface of each upper chamber (**atrium**) of the heart

auriculate /aw ríkyoo layt/ *adj* **1.** describes leaves that

have an attachment at the base that is shaped like an ear **2.** describes an animal that has ears, auricles, or extensions that resemble earlobes

auriferous /aw ríffərəss/ *adj* describes rock or minerals that contain gold

Auriga /aw rígə/ *n* a prominent constellation of the northern hemisphere containing the bright star Capella. See illustration at **constellation**

Aurignacian /áwrig náysh'n/ *adj* belonging to a prehistoric culture associated with Cro-Magnon people in Europe around the period 30,000 to 22,000 BC [Early 20C. After *Aurignac*, France]

Auriol /áwri ol/, **Vincent** (1884–1966) first president of the French Fourth Republic (1947–54). He served as finance minister (1936–37) and minister of justice (1937–38) before World War II. He was imprisoned (1940–43) for his opposition to the Vichy government and joined the Free French cabinet in 1945.

Aurobindo /áwrō bíndō/ ♦ **Ghose, Aurobindo**

aurochs /áwroks/ (*plural same*) *n* a long-horned wild ox, now extinct but thought to be an ancestor of modern domestic cattle. Native to: North Africa, Europe, Southwest Asia. [Late 18C. < German, variant of *Auerochs* 'original ox']

aurora /ə ráwrə/ (*plural* **-ras** or **-rae** /-ree/) *n* **1.** a phenomenon occurring in the night sky around the polar regions, caused by atmospheric gases interacting with solar particles to create streamers, folds, or arches of coloured light **2.** the dawn, usually personified (*literary*) [15C. < Latin, 'dawn'] —**auroral** *adj*

Aurora[1] /ə ráwrə/ *n* in Roman mythology, the goddess of the dawn. Greek equivalent **Eos**

Aurora[2] /ə ráwrə/ city in northeastern Colorado, near Denver. Population: 286,028 (2002 estimate).

aurora australis /-o stráyliss/ *n* the coloured lights seen in the skies around the South Pole [< modern Latin, 'southern aurora']

aurora borealis /-bawri áyliss/ *n* the coloured lights seen in the skies around the North Pole [< modern Latin, 'northern aurora']

AUS *abbr* Australian Union of Students

Aus. *abbr* **1.** Australia **2.** Australian **3.** Austria **4.** Austrian

Auschwitz /ów shvits/ site of the largest Nazi concentration camp, where between 1.5 and 4 million people were murdered between 1941 and 1945. Situated in southern Poland, it is now a museum and archive.

auscultation /áwsk'l táysh'n/ *n* the act of listening to the sounds made by a patient's internal organs, especially the heart, lungs, and abdominal organs, usually with a stethoscope, in order to make a diagnosis [Mid-17C. < Latin *auscultation-* < *auscultare* 'listen to'] —**auscultate** /áwsk'l tayt/ *vt*

Auslese /ówss layzə/ *n* the grade of high-quality German table wine above Spätlese, made from selected late-picked grapes and typically medium sweet to sweet [Mid-19C. < German, 'selection']

auspice /áwspiss/ *n* a sign or token for the future, especially a happy or promising one [Mid-17C. Via French < Latin *auspicium* 'taking omens' < *auspex* 'soothsayer', originally 'somebody who foretells the future by studying the flight pattern of birds' < *avis* 'bird' + *specere* 'to look'] ◇ **under the auspices of somebody or something** with the help or support of a person or organization

auspicious /aw spíshəss/ *adj* marked by lucky signs or good omens, and therefore by the promise of success or happiness —**auspiciously** *adv* —**auspiciousness** *n*

Aussie /ózzi/ *n* PEOPLES same as **Australian** *n* (sense 1) (*informal*) [Early 20C. Shortening] —**Aussie** *adj*

Aust. *abbr* **1.** Australia **2.** Australian **3.** Austria **4.** Austrian

AUSTEL /ós tel, óz-/ *abbr* Australian Telecommunications Authority

Jane Austen

Austen /óstin/, **Jane** (1775–1817) British novelist, writer of elegant, satirical fiction, including *Pride and Prejudice* (1813). See Cultural note at **park, pride, sense**

> 'For what do we live, but to make sport for our neighbours, and laugh at them in our turn?'
> [Jane Austen, *Pride and Prejudice*; 1813]

> 'A woman, especially if she have the misfortune of knowing anything, should conceal it as well as she can.'
> [Jane Austen, *Northanger Abbey*; 1818]

austenite /áwstə nīt, óstə-/ *n* a solid solution of carbon in iron that occurs as a component of steel at a specific stage of manufacture [Early 20C. After Sir William Roberts-*Austen* (1843–1902), British metallurgist] —**austenitic** /áwstə níttik, óstə-/ *adj*

austere /aw steer, o-/ *adj* **1.** SUGGESTING PHYSICAL HARDSHIP imposing or suggesting physical hardship **2.** UNSMILING grimly unsmiling, humourless, or suggesting strict self-denial **3.** PLAIN AND WITHOUT LUXURY plain and simple, without luxury or self-indulgence ○ *lived an austere life on the frontier* **4.** PLAIN IN STYLE OR DESIGN severely plain in design or lines, without distractions or decoration [14C. Via French and Latin < Greek *austēros*] —**austerely** *adv*

austerity /aw stérrəti, o-/ (*plural* **-ties**) *n* **1.** SEVERITY OR PLAINNESS severity of discipline, regime, expression, or design **2.** ECONOMY MEASURE a saving, economy, or act of self-denial, especially in respect of something regarded as a luxury **3.** ECON ENFORCED THRIFT thrift imposed as government policy, with restricted access to or availability of consumer goods

Austerlitz /áwsterlits, ów-/ site of a major battle in 1805 in what is now the eastern Czech Republic, at which Napoleon defeated Russian and Austrian forces

Austin /áwstin/ capital of Texas and university city in the south of the state, on the Colorado River. Population: 671,873 (2002 estimate).

austral /áwstrəl/ *adj* relating to, belonging to, or coming from the south [15C. < Latin *australis* < *auster* 'south']

Austral. *abbr* **1.** Australasia **2.** Australia **3.** Australian

Australasia /áwstrə láyzhə/ region consisting of Australia, New Zealand, New Guinea, and neighbouring islands of the South Pacific —**Australasian** *adj*, *n*

Australia /o stráyli ə/ **1.** the world's smallest continent, situated between the Pacific and Indian oceans. Population: 20,000,000 (2003). Area: 7,614,500 sq. km/2,939,974 sq. mi. **2.** country encompassing the continent of Australia and the island of Tasmania. It is the sixth largest country in the world. It became an independent member of the Commonwealth in 1931. Language: English. Currency: Australian dollar. Capital: Canberra. Population: 19,881,500 (2003). Area: 7,682,300 sq. km/2,966,200 sq. mi. Official name **Commonwealth of Australia**

Australia Day *n* an Australian public holiday marking the landing of the British First Fleet at Port Jackson, now Sydney Harbour, in 1788. Date: first Monday after 26 January.

Australian /o stráyli ən/ *adj* **1.** OF AUSTRALIA relating to Australia, or its people, languages, or cultures **2.** OF ABORIGINAL LANGUAGES OF AUSTRALIA relating to the family of languages spoken in Australia before European settlement. Most Australian languages are now

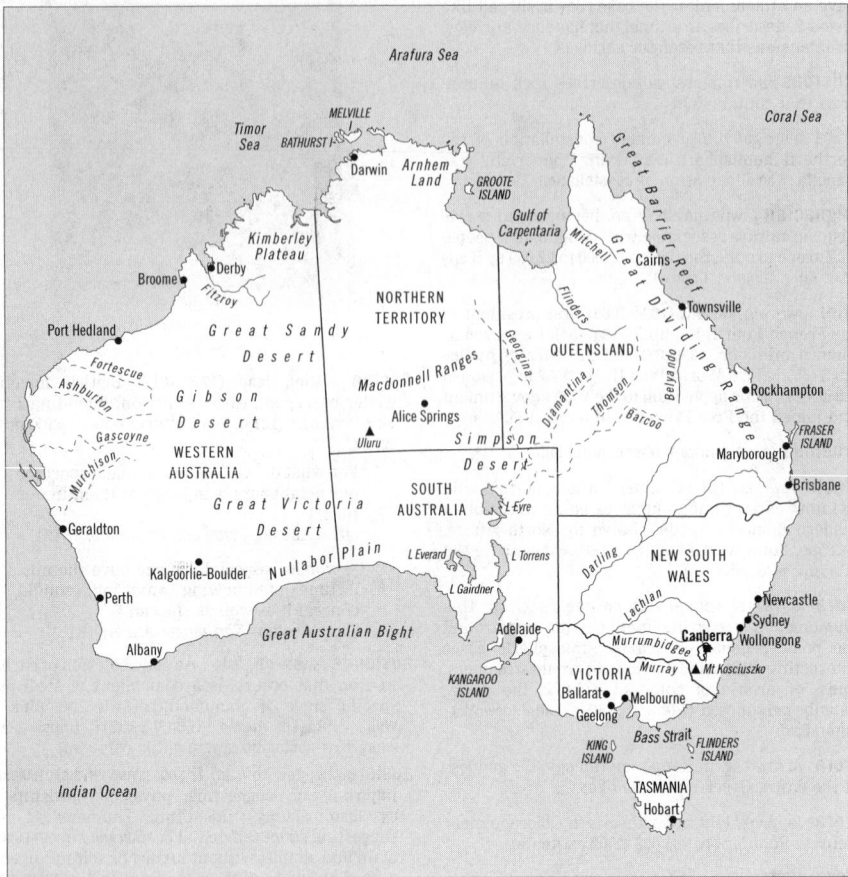

Australia

Austria

WORLD ENGLISH *Australian English* is the English language as used in the Commonwealth of Australia, population over 19 million, which is, with Canada, third in size and distinctness among the primary English-speaking countries. English has been used in Australia for about 200 years.

Australian English is markedly homogeneous, with three kinds of accent: (1) *Cultivated Australian*, similar to Received Pronunciation in the United Kingdom, and formerly highly regarded; (2) *Broad Australian*, often compared with Cockney; and (3) *General Australian*, the majority variety, occupying the social middle ground. Australian English does not pronounce *r* in words such as *art*, *door*, and *worker*. The vowel in *can't dance* is closer to that in 'kent dense' than in 'cahnt dahnce' or 'kaynt daynce', and the Broad version of *I'm going there today* sounds to some ears like 'I'm going there to die'.

Australian English and British English spelling are generally identical (with some ambivalence in the *-or/our* endings, most notably in US-style *Labor*, the name of a political party). Grammar is comparable to general usage in both Britain and the United States, but Australian English has a large and distinctive home-grown vocabulary that includes: (1) adoptions from Aboriginal languages, with a penchant for spelling with double letters (as in *corroboree* and *kookaburra*) and mainly relating to animals, plants, objects, and localities (as, for example, *billabong*, *boomerang*, *didgeridoo*, *dingo*, *koala*, *Murrumbidgee*, *Woomera*), a process similar to American English's adoption from Native American languages; (2) extensions in meaning of everyday words, for example *to feel crook* 'to feel ill', *to farewell somebody* 'to give somebody a farewell party', *mob* 'a flock or group (of sheep, kangaroos, etc.)', *station* 'a ranch', as in *sheep station*; (3) extensions or shifts in the meaning of British dialect words, for example *cobber* 'a friend, mate', *dinkum* 'reliable, genuine', *dunny* 'a lavatory', *wowser* 'somebody regarded as a spoilsport or prude'; (4) distinctive informal word endings, for example *-o* in abbreviations such as *arvo* 'afternoon' and *journo* 'journalist', and *-ie* in names for workers such as *truckie* 'truck-driver' and *wharfie* 'stevedore'. See **New Zealand English**.

extinct or approaching extinction. ■ *n* **1.** SOMEBODY FROM AUSTRALIA somebody who comes from Australia **2.** AUSTRALIAN ENGLISH the variety of English spoken in Australia

Australian Alps /o stráyli ən-/ mountain range in southeastern Australia, straddling the border between New South Wales and Victoria and forming part of the Great Dividing Range. It includes Australia's highest peak, Mount Kosciuszko, 2,228 m/7,310 ft.

Australian Antarctic Territory uninhabited region incorporating part of the continent of Antarctica and a number of adjacent islands. Area: 6,100,000 sq. km/2,355,223 sq. mi.

Australian ballot *n* US POL same as **secret ballot**

Australian Broadcasting Corporation *n* full form of **ABC**

Australian Business Number *n* BUSINESS full form of **ABN**

Australian Capital Territory internal federal territory in southeastern Australia, which incorporates Canberra, the national capital. Capital: Canberra. Population: 322,900 (2003). Area: 2,400 sq. km/930 sq. mi.

Australian Democrats *n* in Australia, a political party that has held the balance of power in the Australian upper house for most of the time since its formation in 1977

Australian English *n* the form of English spoken in Australia as distinct from other forms of English

Australianism /o stráyli ənizəm/ *n* a word or expression that originated in, or is used mainly in, Australia

Australian Labor Party *n* in Australia, the principal political party of the left and one of the two main political parties. Founded in 1891, it is Australia's oldest political party.

Australian Museum *n* a museum in Sydney that contains the Australian national collections of natural history and anthropology. It was founded in 1836.

Australian National Gallery *n* former name for **National Gallery of Australia**

Australian Rules *n* an Australian game resembling rugby, played on an oval pitch with 18 to a team and a large oval ball that can be punched, kicked, or carried (*takes a singular verb*)

Australian terrier *n* a short stocky terrier with erect ears and a straight wiry coat that is normally blue- or silver-grey with brown patches on the muzzle and feet

Australoid /óstrə loyd/ *adj* relating to Australian Aboriginals and some other Southeast Asian and Pacific peoples —**Australoid** *n*

australopithecine /óstrəlō píthə seen/ *adj* describes or relating to a prehistoric primate of southern and eastern Africa whose fossilized remains resemble those of humans [Mid-20C. < modern Latin *Australopithecus* < Latin *australis* 'southern' + Greek *pithēkos* 'ape'] —**australopithecine** *n*

Austrasia /aw stráyzhə/ eastern part of the medieval kingdom of the Franks, consisting of what are now parts of France, Germany, and the Netherlands

Austria /óstri ə/ country in central Europe. Language: German. Currency: euro. Capital: Vienna. Population: 8,188,207 (2003). Area: 83,858 sq. km/32,378 sq. mi. Official name **Republic of Austria** —**Austrian** *adj, n*

Austrian blind *n* a fabric window blind with panels that can be gathered up vertically into loose folds

Austro- *prefix* southern ○ *Austro-Asiatic* [< Latin *auster*]

Austro-Asiatic /óstrō-/ *n* a large family of languages spoken in Southeast Asia and eastern India. Native speakers: 70 million. —**Austro-Asiatic** *adj*

Austronesia /óstrō néezhə, -néeshə/ region consisting of Indonesia, Melanesia, Micronesia, Polynesia, and neighbouring islands in the Pacific Ocean

Austronesian /óstrō néezh'n, -néesh'n/ *adj* relating to Austronesia, or its peoples, languages, or cultures ■ *n* a family of languages spoken in Taiwan, parts of Southeast Asia, the Pacific Islands, New Zealand, and Madagascar. Native speakers: 250 million.

AUT *abbr* Association of University Teachers

aut- *prefix* same as **auto-** (*used before vowels*)

autarchy /áw taarki/ (*plural* **-chies**) *n* **1.** UNLIMITED POLITICAL POWER absolute power, especially such power wielded by a despotic ruler **2.** SELF-GOVERNMENT self-government of a country by representatives drawn from among its own citizens **3.** COUNTRY WITH DESPOTIC RULER a country governed by a ruler who has absolute power **4.** SELF-GOVERNING COUNTRY an independent country with its own government, as distinct from a colony or dependency [Mid-17C. < Greek *autarkhos* 'self-governing' < *arkhein* 'rule'] —**autarchic** /aw taárkik/ *adj* —**autarchical** *adj* —**autarchist** *n*

autarky /áw taarki/ (*plural* **-kies**) *n* **1.** an economic policy or situation in which a nation is independent of international trade and not reliant upon imported goods **2.** a nation that is economically self-sufficient [Early 17C. < Greek *autarkeia* 'self-sufficiency' < *autarkēs* 'self-sufficient' < *arkein* 'be sufficient'] —**autarkic** /aw taárkik/ *adj* —**autarkical** *adj*

autecology /áwti kólləji/ *n* the study of individuals or populations of a single species and their relationship to their environment —**autecological** /áwtikə lójjik'l/ *adj*

auteur /aw túr/ *n* a film director whose films are so distinctive that he or she is perceived as a film's creator [Mid-20C. < French, 'author']

auteurism /aw túriz əm/ *n* belief in or practice of auteur theory —**auteurist** *adj*

auteur theory *n* film criticism that considers the director of a film to be its primary creator

auth. *abbr* **1.** authentic **2.** author **3.** authority **4.** authorized

authentic /aw théntik/ *adj* **1.** NOT FALSE OR COPIED genuine and original, as opposed to being a fake or reproduction **2.** TRUSTWORTHY shown to be true and trustworthy **3.** LAW VALID legally valid because all necessary procedures have been followed correctly **4.** MUSIC IN STYLE OF ORIGINAL PERIOD performed in the musical style current at the time of composition, and on instruments similar to those of the time **5.** MUSIC, CHR WITH UPWARD RANGE FROM MAIN NOTE describes church music such as Gregorian chant that has an upward range from the keynote of the scale [14C. Via French < Greek *authentikos* 'genuine' < *authentes* 'master, doer' < *autos* 'self'] —**authentically** *adv*

authenticate /aw thénti kayt/ (**-cates, -cating, -cated**) *vt* **1.** to establish that something is genuine or that an account is true **2.** to establish something such as a deed or document as legally valid —**authenticator** *n*

authentication /aw thénti káysh'n/ *n* **1.** the act of proving something to be genuine or valid, or the evidence used in so doing **2.** a security measure using data encryption that identifies the user and verifies that the message was not tampered with (*used in e-commerce*)

authenticity /áw then tíssəti, áwthən-/ *n* **1.** the genuineness or truth of something **2.** the legal validity or correctness of a legal document

author /áwthər/ *n* **1.** WRITER somebody who writes a book or other text such as a literary work or a report **2.** PROFESSIONAL WRITER somebody who writes books as a profession **3.** CREATOR OR SOURCE the creator or cause of something ■ *vt* (**-thors, -thoring, -thored**) **1.** WRITE SOMETHING to write or be responsible for the final form of a book, report, or other text **2.** WRITE COMPUTER PROGRAM to create a computer application such as a multimedia document, usually using special software ○ *authoring systems* **3.** CAUSE SOMETHING to be the cause, creator, or originator of something [14C. Via French < Latin *auctor* 'creator, originator' < *augere* 'originate, increase'] —**authorial** /aw tháwri əl/ *adj* —**authorship** *n*

USAGE Although the verb ***author*** has been around for over 400 years, many people dislike it in contexts such as *She has authored several books*, because it does not simply imply 'to write', but 'to be responsible for the content of a printed or published document'. However, there is no problem with the use of the verb ***author*** in computing contexts, where it refers specifically to the creation of databases, multimedia products, and other applications.

authoress /áwthərəss, -réss/ *n* a woman who writes books (*dated*)

authoring /áwthəring/ *n* the creation of computer applications such as multimedia documents, usually done by nonprogrammers using special software (*often used before a noun*) ○ *authoring systems*

authoring language *n* a software development system that lets users develop applications without using formal programming language

authorise, etc another spelling of **authorize, etc**

authoritarian /aw thórri táiri ən/ *adj* **1.** favouring strict rules and established authority **2.** belonging to or believing in a political system in which obedience to the ruling person or group is strongly enforced —**authoritarian** *n* —**authoritarianism** *n*

authoritative /aw thórritətiv/ *adj* **1.** RELIABLE convincing, reliable, backed by evidence, and showing deep knowledge **2.** BACKED BY AUTHORITY backed by an established and accepted authority **3.** SHOWING AUTHORITY showing confidence in or the expectation of being obeyed —**authoritatively** *adv* —**authoritativeness** *n*

authority /aw thórrəti/ (*plural* **-ties**) *n* **1.** RIGHT TO COMMAND the right or power to enforce rules or give orders **2.** HOLDER OF POWER somebody or something with official power **3.** POWER GIVEN TO SOMEBODY power to act on behalf of somebody else, or official permission to do something **4.** SOURCE OF RELIABLE INFORMATION a source of reliable information on a subject **5.** ADMINISTRATIVE BODY an official body that is set up by a government to administer an area of activity (*often used in the plural*) ○ *the local port authority* **6.** JUSTIFICATION a statement that makes somebody believe something is true **7.** QUALITY THAT IS RESPECTED the ability to gain the respect of other people and to influence or control what they do **8.** OBVIOUS KNOWLEDGE AND EXPERIENCE knowledge, skill, or experience worthy of respect **9.** LAW SOURCE OF PRECEDENT OR PRINCIPLE a law or legal decision that is cited as establishing a precedent or a principle **10.** LEGITIMATE POWER a form of rule that is seen as legitimate [13C. Via French < Latin *auctoritas* < *auctor* (see AUTHOR)]

authority figure *n* somebody who is, or appears to be, strong and powerful and able to command and influence others

authorization /áwthə rī záysh'n/, **authorisation** *n* **1.** PERMISSION official power or permission to do something **2.** DOCUMENT GIVING PERMISSION a letter or document that confirms that somebody has permission to do something or be somewhere **3.** E-COMMERCE TRANSACTION RISK ASSESSMENT the process of assessing the degree of risk involved in an e-commerce transaction in terms of a customer's debt limits and available credit

authorize /áwthə rīz/ (**-rizes, -rizing, -rized**), **authorise** (**-rises, -rising, -rised**) *vt* to give somebody or something power, permission, or authorization to do something or be somewhere [14C. Via French < medieval Latin *auctorizare* < Latin *auctor* (see AUTHOR)] —**authorized** *adj* —**authorizer** *n*

Authorized Version /áwthə rīzd-/ *n* a version of the Bible published in England in 1611 and authorized by James I for use in the Church of England. N Am term **King James Bible**

autism /áwtizəm/ *n* a disturbance in psychological development in which use of language, reaction to stimuli, interpretation of the world, and the formation of relationships are not fully established and follow unusual patterns [Early 20C. < Greek *autos* 'self']

autistic /aw tístik/ *adj* showing evidence of autism, e.g. failure to use language and perceive surroundings in the expected way —**autistically** *adv*

autistic savant *n* somebody who has a learning disability or psychiatric disorder but who is exceptionally gifted in one specific area, e.g. rapid mathematical calculation or music

auto /áwtō/ (*plural* **-tos**) *n N Am* CARS same as **car** (sense 1) (*informal*) [Late 19C. Shortening of AUTOMOBILE]

auto. *abbr* **1.** automatic **2.** MECH ENG automotive

auto- *prefix* **1.** self ○ *autograft* **2.** automatic ○ *autopilot* [< Greek *autos* 'self']

autoantibody /áwtō ánti bodi/ (*plural* **-ies**) *n* an antibody that reacts against normal substances present in the organism producing it and is present in autoimmune diseases

autobahn /áwtō baan, ówtō-/ *n* a motorway in a German-speaking country or region [Mid-20C. < German, 'automobile track']

autobiography /áwtō bī óggrəfi/ (*plural* **-phies**) *n* an account of somebody's life written by that person —**autobiographer** *n* —**autobiographical** /-bī ə gráffik'l/ *adj*

autobus /áwtō buss/ *n US* same as **bus**

autocatalysis /áwtō kə tállissis/ *n* the speeding up of a chemical reaction by a catalyst that is a product of the reaction —**autocatalytic** /áwtō káttə líttik/ *adj* —**autocatalytically** *adv*

autocephalous /áwtō séffələss/, **autocephalic** /áwtō si fállik/ *adj* describes an Eastern Orthodox church that is governed by its own elected bishop or patriarch [Mid-19C. < AUTO- + Greek *kephalē* 'head']

autochthon /aw tókthən, -thon/ (*plural* **-thons** or **-thones** /-thə neez/) *n* **1.** BIOL NATIVE PLANT OR ANIMAL a plant or animal that originated in the country where it is found **2.** ABORIGINAL PERSON a descendant of the earliest inhabitants of a region **3.** GEOL GEOLOGICAL DEPOSIT ORIGINATING WHERE FOUND a rock formation, mineral deposit, or geological feature that was formed in the area where it is now found [Early 19C. < Greek *autokhthōn* 'indigenous' < *khthōn* 'earth, soil'] —**autochthonism** *n* —**autochthony** *n*

autochthonous /aw tókthənəss/ *adj* **1.** BIOL PRESENT FROM EARLIEST TIMES descended from the original flora, fauna, or inhabitants of the region in which it is found **2.** GEOL FORMED WHERE FOUND describes a rock, mineral deposit, or geological feature that was formed in the area where it is found **3.** PHYSIOL PRODUCED WHERE SITUATED describes a physical function or disorder that originates in the part of the body where it is found —**autochthonously** *adv*

SYNONYMS See ***native***.

autocidal /áwtō sī́d'l/ *adj* describes a method of pest control in which sterile or genetically altered insects are released to reduce the breeding success of the local insect population

autoclave /áwtō klayv, áwtə-/ *n* **1.** STERILIZATION EQUIPMENT a strong steel vessel that can be pressurized. Use: steam sterilization of objects, pressurized chemical reactions at high temperature. **2.** STEAMER FOR CONCRETE an apparatus with which newly cast concrete is cured by steam under pressure ■ *vt* (**-claves, -claving, -claved**) PLACE SOMETHING IN AUTOCLAVE to use an autoclave to steam something [Late 19C. < French < Greek *autos* 'self' + Latin *clavus* 'nail' or *clavis* 'key'; because self-fastening]

autocorrelation /áwtō kórri láysh'n/ *n* in statistics, a property displayed by some sequences of adjacent items not being independent of each other

autocracy /aw tókrəssi/ (*plural* **-cies**) *n* **1.** RULE BY ONE PERSON a government in which somebody holds unlimited power **2.** RULER'S ABSOLUTE POWER the unlimited political power of a single ruler **3.** PLACE RULED BY ONE PERSON a country governed by a single ruler who has unlimited power [Mid-17C. < Greek *autokrateia* < *autokratēs* (see AUTOCRAT)]

autocrat /áwtə krat/ *n* **1.** a ruler who holds unlimited power and is answerable to no other person **2.** somebody who dominates others [Early 19C. Via French *autocrate* < Greek *autokratēs* 'independent authority' < *kratos* 'power'] —**autocratic** /áwtə kráttik/ *adj* —**autocratically** *adv*

autocross /áwtō kross/ *n* timed motor racing across rough ground [Mid-20C. Contraction of AUTOMOBILE + CROSS-COUNTRY]

Autocue /áwtō kyoo/ *tdmk* a trademark for a device that displays an enlarged line-by-line text on a television screen to a speaker while remaining unseen to the audience

auto-da-fé /áwtō də fáy/ (*plural* **autos-da-fé** /*pronunc. same*/) *n* a sentence of death pronounced on a heretic by a court of the Spanish Inquisition and carried out by the civil authorities. The condemned person was burned at the stake. [Early 18C. < Portuguese, 'act of the faith']

autodeconstruction /áwtō deékən strúksh'n/ *n* critical analysis of artistic works that is done by the artists themselves rather than critics

autodestruct /áwtō di strúkt/ *vi* (**-structs, -structing, -structed**) to undergo self-destruction ○ *The missile auto-destructed after a failed launch.* ■ *adj* allowing or causing something to destroy itself

autodial /áwtō dī əl/ *n* a device that automatically dials a prerecorded number in response to an input signal such as pressing a button —**autodialler** *n*

autodidact /áwtō dī dakt/ *n* somebody whose knowledge is self-taught [Mid-18C. < Greek *autodidaktos* < *didaskein* 'teach'] —**autodidactic** /áwtō dī dáktik, -di-/ *adj*

autodyne /áwtō dīn/ *adj* describes a radio device containing an element such as a transistor that acts simultaneously as a detector and oscillator [Early 20C. < AUTO- + Greek *dunamis* 'force, power'] —**autodyne** *n*

autoecious /aw teéshəss/ *adj* living as a pest or parasite on a single host species [Late 19C. < AUTO- + Greek *oikia* 'house'] —**autoecism** *n*

autoeroticism /áwtō i róttisizəm/, **autoerotism** /áwtō érrətizəm/ *n* sexual arousal and gratification from self-stimulation —**autoerotic** *adj*

autofocus /áwtō fōkəss/ *n* a device that automatically adjusts the focus of a camera

autogamy /aw tóggəmi/ *n* **1.** the process by which some flowering plants fertilize themselves **2.** the division and subsequent reunification of a single cell in the reproductive processes of some simple

one-celled animals and algae —**autogamic** /áwtə gámmik/ *adj* —**autogamous** /aw tóggəməss/ *adj*

autogenesis /áwtō jénnississ/ *n* BIOL same as **abiogenesis** —**autogenetic** /áwtō ji néttik/ *adj* —**autogenetically** *adv*

autogenic /áwtō jénnik/ *adj* BIOL same as **autogenous** —**autogenically** *adv*

autogenics /áwtō jénniks/ *n* PSYCHOL same as **autogenic training** (*takes a singular verb*)

autogenic training *n* a method of relieving stress by using meditation and other mental exercises to produce physical relaxation

autogenocide /áwtō jénnə sīd/ *n* the extermination of people by members of their own society

autogenous /aw tójjənəss/ *adj* **1. PRODUCED INSIDE SOMETHING** produced or created within something itself, without external help or influence **2.** MED **PRODUCED FROM SOMETHING FROM RECIPIENT'S BODY** produced in, or with tissue from, the body of the person to whom it will be given ○ *an autogenous vaccine* **3.** INSECTS **NOT NEEDING BLOOD** describes insects that do not require a meal of blood in order to produce viable eggs [Mid-19C. < Greek *autogenēs* < *gignesthai* 'be born'] —**autogenously** *adv*

autogiro /áwtō jīrō/ (*plural* **-ros**) *n* an aircraft that uses a propeller for forward motion and an unpowered horizontal rotor for lift and stability [Early 20C. < Spanish, 'self-turning' < *giro* 'gyration']

autograft /áwtə graaft/ *n* **1.** a graft of skin or other tissue obtained from a patient's own body **2.** SURG same as **autotransplant**

autograph /áwtə graaf, -graf/ *n* **1. SOMEBODY'S SIGNATURE** a signature, especially the signature of a famous person **2. HANDWRITTEN TEXT** a copy of a document or text handwritten by its creator (*technical*) ■ *vt* (**-graphs, -graphing, -graphed**) **WRITE SIGNATURE ON SOMETHING** to write your signature on something such as a book or photograph ○ *autographing pictures of the band* [Early 17C. Via French or late Latin < Greek *autographon* 'written with your own hand' < *graphein* 'write']

autograph hunter *n* somebody who collects the signatures of famous people (*informal*)

autoharp /áwtō haarp/ *n* a musical instrument with many strings on which chords are played by strumming and the strings that are not to be sounded are held down by a button-controlled damper

autohypnosis /áwtō hip nṓssiss/ *n* a process by which somebody hypnotizes himself or herself —**autohypnotic** /áwtō hip nóttik/ *adj*

autoimmune /áwtō i myóon/ *adj* caused by the reaction of an antibody to substances that occur naturally in the body —**autoimmunity** *n* —**autoimmunization** /áwtō ímmyōō nī záysh'n/ *n*

autoimmune disease *n* a disease caused by the reaction of antibodies to substances occurring naturally in the body. Three common autoimmune diseases are lupus erythematosus, Addison's disease, and rheumatoid arthritis.

autoimmune haemolytic anaemia *n* a form of anaemia involving autoantibodies of red cell antigens

autoinfection /áwtō in féksh'n/ *n* infection caused by an organism already present in another part of the body or by the larval reproduction of a parasite already present in the body

autoinoculation /áwtō i nokyōō láysh'n/ *n* a disease that occurs when an infection spreads from one part of the body to another —**autoinoculable** /-nókyōōləb'l/ *adj*

autointoxication /áwtō in tòksi káysh'n/ *n* poisoning by a substance that has been produced within the body of the person who is poisoned

autojumble /áwtō jumb'l/ *n* components and spares for obsolete vehicles, often found on sale at classic car and commercial vehicle rallies, country shows, or car boot sales (*informal*)

autoload /áwtō lōd/ *adj US* ARMS same as **semiautomatic** *adj* (sense 1) —**autoloader** *n*

autologous /aw tólləgəss/ *adj* derived from a patient's own body [Early 20C. < AUTO- + *-logous* < -LOGY]

autolysate /aw tóllə sayt, -zayt/ *n* a product of the process (**autolysis**) by which cells are broken down by enzymes produced in the cells themselves

autolysin /aw tóllissin, áwtə líssin/ *n* an enzyme that causes autolysis

autolysis /aw tóllississ/ *n* the digestion of cells by their own enzymes —**autolytic** /áwtə líttik/ *adj*

automaker /áwtō maykər/ *n N Am* a manufacturer of motor vehicles

automata ENG plural of **automaton**

automate /áwtə mayt/ (**-mates, -mating, -mated**) *vti* to convert a process or workplace to automation, or utilize the techniques of automation [Mid-20C. Back-formation < AUTOMATION]

automated clearing house /áwtə maytid-/ *n* BANKING full form of **ACH**

automated teller machine *n* BANKING full form of **ATM**

automatic /áwtə máttik/ *adj* **1. STARTING OR FUNCTIONING BY ITSELF** started, operated, or regulated by a process or mechanism without human intervention **2. DONE BY PRIOR ARRANGEMENT** beginning when specific conditions are fulfilled, without the need for a decision or action **3. DONE WITHOUT THOUGHT** done without conscious thought as the result of habit or custom ○ *gave an automatic answer to the child* **4. INDEPENDENT OF SOMEBODY'S WILL** done without intention, especially as the result of a physical reflex ○ *automatic blinking of the eyes* ■ *n* **1. MACHINE OPERATING WITHOUT HUMAN INTERVENTION** a machine that controls its own operating process, e.g. a washing machine **2. MOTOR VEHICLE NOT REQUIRING MANUAL GEAR** a motor vehicle that has a built-in mechanism (**automatic transmission**) for changing gears without requiring the driver to do it **3. GUN THAT FIRES CONTINUOUSLY** a gun that continues to fire and eject used cartridges for as long as the trigger is pressed [18C. < Greek *automatos* 'acting by itself'] —**automatically** *adv*

automatic exposure *n* a control system in a camera that sets the lens aperture and shutter speed according to the amount of light that is present

automatic frequency control *n* a control system in a radio or television receiver that keeps it tuned to a signal in spite of minor variations in the signal's frequency

automatic gain control *n* a radio receiver control system by which the amplifier is adjusted to compensate for variations in the volume of the signal, so that the volume of the output is constant

automaticity /àwtəmə tíssiti/ *n* the processing of information in response to stimuli by an organism in a way that is automatic and involuntary, occurring without conscious control

automatic pilot *n* **1. AUTOMATIC STEERING SYSTEM** a control in the steering system of a ship, aircraft, or spacecraft that can be set to put or keep it on a steady course **2. PRESET OR INSTINCTIVE BEHAVIOUR** a condition in which somebody is not fully aware of what he or she is doing but is acting in a habitual and unthinking way, e.g. because of stress **3. OPERATION WITHOUT GUIDANCE OR CONTROL** a state in which something is operating without guidance or control ○ *The company has been on automatic pilot since she resigned.*

automatic transmission *n* a transmission system for motor vehicles in which changes of gear are made automatically in response to the speed of the vehicle

automatic writing *n* the production of writing while in a trance or similar state as an attempt to make contact with the writer's unconscious or telepathically with a supposed spirit

automation /áwtə máysh'n/ *n* **1.** a system in which a workplace or process has been converted to one that replaces or minimizes human labour with mechanical or electronic equipment **2.** the act of automating something, or the state of being automated [Mid-20C. < AUTOMATIC]

automatise *vt* INDUST another spelling of **automatize**

automatism /aw tómmətizəm/ *n* **1.** PHYSIOL **INVOLUNTARY ORGANIC FUNCTION** a physical reflex or involuntary activity of the body **2.** PHILOSOPHY, LAW **THEORY THAT ACTIONS ARE PERFORMED AUTOMATICALLY** the philosophical theory that all bodily actions have involuntary physical or physiological causes, or the legal defence that an action had such a cause **3.** PSYCHOL **ACTIVITY NOT CONSCIOUSLY CAUSED** behaviour that is not consciously motivated, e.g. sleepwalking or involuntary repetitive actions **4.** ARTS **ARTISTIC METHOD** an artistic approach, associated with the surrealists, in which the painter or writer empties the mind and allows the unconscious to direct the work —**automatist** *n*

automatize /aw tómmə tīz/ (**-tizes, -tizing, -tized**), **automatise** (**-tises, -tising, -tised**) *vti* **1.** INDUST same as **automate 2.** to make or become automatic —**automatization** /aw tómmə tī záysh'n/ *n*

automaton /aw tómmətən, -ton/ (*plural* **-tons** or **-ta** /-tə/) *n* **1.** a machine that contains its own power source and can perform a complicated series of actions, including responses to external stimuli, without human intervention **2.** somebody who behaves like a machine in emotionlessly obeying instructions and performing repetitive actions [Early 17C. Via Latin < Greek, neuter of *automatos* 'acting by itself'] —**automatous** *adj*

automobile /áwtə mə beel/ *n* a road vehicle, usually with four wheels and powered by an internal-combustion engine, designed to carry a small number of passengers [Late 19C. < French, 'self-mobile']

Automobile Association *n* AUTOMOT full form of **AA**[2]

automobilia /áwtə mə beeli ə/ *npl* things to do with cars or motoring that appeal to collectors and enthusiasts [Late 20C. < AUTOMOBILE, after MEMORABILIA]

automotive /áwtə mṓtiv/ *adj* **1.** relating to or involving motor vehicles **2.** propelled by its own motor or engine

autonomic /áwtə nómmik/ *adj* **1. CONTROLLED BY AUTOMATIC RESPONSES** describes functions of the nervous system not under voluntary control, e.g. the regulation of heartbeat or gland secretions **2. WITHOUT THOUGHT** describes an action or response that occurs without conscious control **3. FROM INTERNAL STIMULI** produced or caused by internal stimuli —**autonomically** *adv*

autonomic nervous system *n* the part of the nervous system in humans and other vertebrates that controls involuntary activity such as the action of the heart and glands, breathing, digestive processes, and reflex actions

autonomous /aw tónnəməss/ *adj* **1. SELF-GOVERNING** politically independent and self-governing **2. ABLE TO CHOOSE** able to make decisions and act on them as a free and independent moral agent **3. SELF-SUFFICIENT** existing, reacting, or developing as an independent, self-regulating organism —**autonomously** *adv*

autonomous republic *n* a division of the Russian Federation that has more rights than the other administrative regions. The 21 autonomous republics have their own constitutions and state languages.

autonomy /aw tónnəmi/ *n* **1.** POL **SELF-GOVERNMENT** political independence and self-government **2.** PHILOSOPHY **EXISTENCE AS INDEPENDENT MORAL AGENT** personal independence and the capacity to make moral decisions and act on them **3.** LITERAT **INDEPENDENCE OF TEXT** the status of a text as an aesthetic object not to be judged or commented on in the light of external knowledge such as the biography of the author [Early 17C. < Greek *autonomia* < *autonomos* 'having its own laws' < *nomos* 'law'] —**autonomist** *n*

autopilot /áwtō pīlət/ *n* NAVIG, PHYSIOL, PSYCHOL same as **automatic pilot**

autopista /áwtō peestə/ *n* in a Spanish-speaking country or region, a motorway [Mid-20C. < Spanish, 'automobile track']

autoplasty /áwtə plasti/ (*plural* **-ties**) *n* the repair of a patient's body using tissue, e.g. skin, taken from another part of the patient's body —**autoplastic** /áwtə plástik/ *adj* —**autoplastically** *adv*

autopoiesis /áwtō poy éessiss/ *n* a process whereby a system, organization, or organism produces and replaces its own components and distinguishes itself from its environment —**autopoietic** /-poy éttik/ *adj*

autopsy /áwt opsi/ *n* (*plural* **-sies**) **1. EXAMINATION TO FIND CAUSE OF DEATH** the medical examination of a dead body in order to establish the cause and circumstances of death **2. EXHAUSTIVE EXAMINATION** an exhaustive critical examination of something ■ *vt* (**-sies, -sying, -sied**) **PERFORM AUTOPSY ON BODY** to perform an autopsy on a person or organ [Mid-17C. Via French or modern Latin < Greek *autopsia* 'seeing with your own eyes' < *autoptēs* 'eyewitness']

auto racing *n US* MOTOR SPORTS same as **motor racing**

autoradiograph /áwtō ráydi ə graaf, -graf/, **autoradiogram** /-gram/ *n* a photograph that reveals how radioactivity is distributed in a specimen or sample, made by exposing a photographic plate to the radiation —**autoradiographic** /-raydi ə gráffik/ *adj* —**autoradiography** /-raydi óggrəfi/ *n*

autoresponder /áwtō ri spóndər/ *n* an e-mail software application that enables Internet users to indicate automatically that they are unavailable to respond to incoming e-mail

autorickshaw /áwtō rík shaw/ *n* a vehicle with three wheels, like a covered motor scooter with a back seat for passengers, that is used as a taxi in South Asia

autorotation /áwtō rō táysh'n/ *n* the continuous rotation of an object such as a propeller caused by aerodynamic forces only

autoroute /áwtō root/ *n* in a French-speaking country or region, a motorway [Mid-20C. < French, 'automobile route']

autosave /áwtō sayv/ *n* a computer program feature in which data is saved automatically at predetermined intervals to minimize data loss in the event of a crash

autosome /áwtə sōm/ *n* a chromosome other than one that determines sex —**autosomal** /áwtə sṓm'l/ *adj* —**autosomally** *adv*

autostrada /áwtō straadə/ *n* a motorway in an Italian-speaking country or region [Early 20C. < Italian, 'automobile road']

autosuggestion /áwtō sə jéschən/ *n* the process by which somebody's perceptions, behaviour, or physical condition may be altered by means of his or her power of suggestion —**autosuggest** *vt* —**autosuggestibility** /-jestə bílləti/ *n* —**autosuggestible** *adj* —**autosuggestive** *adj*

autotelic /áwtō téllik, -teélik/ *adj* **1.** done for its own sake rather than to gain a material reward or avoid a punishment **2.** PHILOSOPHY used to describe an entity or event that has within itself the purpose of its existence or occurrence [Early 20C. < Greek *autotelēs* < *autos* 'self' + *telos* 'end'] —**autotelism** *n*

autotimer /áwtō tīmər/ *n* an automatic timing device, e.g. on a cooker

autotomy /aw tóttəmi/ *n* the casting off of part of the body by an animal when it is caught or attacked by a predator. Lizards, snakes, worms, and crustaceans, e.g., can escape by autotomy. —**autotomic** /áwtə tómmik/ *adj*

autotoxaemia /áwtō tok seémi ə/ *n* MED same as **autointoxication**

autotoxin /áwtə tóksin/ *n* a substance that poisons the system within which it is formed

autotransformer /áwtō transs fáwrmər/ *n* a transformer in which the primary and secondary coils share all or some windings

autotransfusion /áwtō transs fyoózh'n/ *n* a blood transfusion using the patient's own blood

autotransplant /áwtə transs plaant/ *n* a surgical procedure in which tissue from one area of a living organism is removed and grafted to another site

autotrophic /áwtə tróffik/ *adj* describes organisms, especially green plants, that are capable of making nutrients from inorganic materials [Late 19C. < Greek *autos* 'self' + -TROPHIC[1]] —**autotroph** /áwtə trōf/ *n* —**autotrophically** *adv* —**autotrophy** /aw tóttrəfi/ *n*

autowinder /áwtō wīndər/ *n* a device that automatically winds the film in a camera forward after a photograph is taken

autoxidation /aw tóksi dáysh'n/ *n* **1.** oxidation at normal temperatures due to contact with air **2.** oxidation that occurs only in the presence of another substance undergoing oxidation

~~**autum**~~ incorrect spelling of **autumn**

autumn /áwtəm/ *n* **1.** *UK, ANZ, Can* the season occurring between summer and winter. Autumn traditionally lasts from 22 September to 21 December in the northern hemisphere, and from 21 March to 21 June in the southern hemisphere. US term **fall 2.** a time in the development of something that follows its most vigorous and successful phase, before its decline ○ *in the autumn of his career as a cellist* [14C. < Latin *autumnus*] —**autumnal** /aw túmn'l/ *adj*

autumnal equinox *n* **1.** the first day of autumn, when the Sun crosses the plane of the Earth's equator and makes day and night approximately of equal length. It occurs about 22 September in the northern hemisphere and 21 March in the southern hemisphere. **2.** the position of the Sun during the autumnal equinox

autumn crocus *n* an autumn-flowering plant. Flowers: crocus-shaped, purple or pink, growing directly from the ground after the leaves have died down. Latin name: *Colchicum autumnale.*

autunite /áwtə nīt/ *n* a yellow radioactive fluorescent mineral consisting of hydrated calcium uranium phosphate [Mid-19C. After *Autun*, France]

aux. *abbr* auxiliary

auxesis /awg zeéssiss, -seéssiss/ *n* growth in animals or plants caused by an increase in the size of cells, not by cellular division [Mid-19C. Via late Latin < Greek] —**auxetic** /awk séttik/ *adj* —**auxetically** *adv*

auxiliary /awg zíllyəri, -zílləri/ *adj* **1.** GIVING SUPPORT acting to support or supplement a group of people **2.** HELD IN RESERVE available as backup for a system, process, or piece of equipment **3.** SECONDARY secondary to something larger **4.** NAUT WITH MOTOR AND SAILS describes a boat with an engine to supplement or replace the sails ■ *n* (*plural* **-ries**) **1.** SUPPORTING PERSON OR THING somebody who or something that has a supporting or supplementary role **2.** GRAM same as **auxiliary verb 3.** MIL MEMBER OF SUPPORTING TROOPS a member of a separate troop, often from another country, that fights with an army as allies or mercenaries and has its own command structure (*often used in the pl*) **4.** NAUT BOAT WITH SAILS AND ENGINE a boat with an engine to supplement or replace the sails **5.** NAVY NAVAL SUPPORT VESSEL a naval vessel such as a tug or transport ship that does not engage in combat [Early 17C. < Latin *auxiliarius* < *auxilium* 'help, assistance']

auxiliary device *n* a peripheral piece of computer hardware, e.g. a printer or scanner

auxiliary language *n* a language that is used by speakers of other languages in order to communicate

auxiliary note *n* in music, a note that falls between two adjacent notes of the same pitch and is not an overtone

auxiliary rotor *n* the tail rotor of a helicopter

auxiliary verb *n* a verb that is used with another verb to indicate person, number, mood, tense, or aspect

~~**auxillary**~~ incorrect spelling of **auxiliary**

auxin /áwksin/ *n* a natural plant hormone or synthetic substance that affects the growth and development of all plant parts [Mid-20C. < Greek *auxein* 'to increase'] —**auxinic** /awk sínnik/ *adj* —**auxinically** *adv*

auxotonic /áwksə tónnik/ *adj* occurring against increasing force as part of a muscle contraction [< Greek *auxein* 'to increase' + TONIC]

auxotroph /áwksə trōf/ *n* a mutant strain of an organism, e.g. a bacterium, that has lost the ability to synthesize a specific nutrient **(growth factor)** and must obtain it from its environment to survive [Mid-20C. < Greek *auxein* 'to increase'] —**auxotrophic** /áwksə trṓfik/ *adj*

Av *n* CALENDAR, JUDAISM same as **Ab**

AV *abbr* **1.** MEDIA audiovisual **2.** BIBLE Authorized Version

av. *abbr* **1.** avenue **2.** average **3.** MEASURE avoirdupois

Av. *abbr* avenue

a.v., a/v, A/V *abbr* FIN ad valorem

avadavat /ávvədə vát/ *n* a songbird of the waxbill family often kept as a cagebird. The male of one species is green and the male of the other species is red. Native to: South Asia. Genus: *Amandava.* [Late 17C. Alteration of *Ahmadabad*, city in W India where these birds were sold]

avail /ə váyl/ *v* (**avails, availing, availed**) **1. avail yourself** *vr* USE SOMETHING to make use of something useful or helpful while you have the opportunity ○ *avail yourself of the facilities* **2.** *vti* HELP to help somebody or something succeed, or be helpful or useful (*formal*) ○ *Negotiation could not avail the deadlocked diplomats.* ■ *n* HELP OR ADVANTAGE help, advantage, or success in achieving something (*used in negative statements*) ○ *His defence was of no avail: a conviction was secured.* [14C. < Old French *vail-*, stem of *valoir* 'be worth' < Latin *valere* 'be strong']

available /ə váyləb'l/ *adj* **1.** ABLE TO BE GOT able to be used, obtained, or relied on ○ *The government intends to make more land available for development.* **2.** UNATTACHED not currently involved in a romantic or sexual relationship but free to engage in one (*informal*) **3.** *US* POL ELIGIBLE FOR OFFICE eligible and willing to undertake a public office or stand for election —**availability** /ə váylə bílləti/ *n* —**availably** *adv*

~~**availible**~~ incorrect spelling of **available**

avalanche /ávvə laanch/ *n* **1.** DOWNHILL FALL OF SNOW a rapid downhill flow of a large mass of something dislodged from a mountainside or the top of a precipice, especially snow or ice **2.** OVERWHELMING QUANTITY a sudden overwhelming quantity of something **3.** PHYS INCREASE IN NUMBER OF IONS an increase in the number of ions or electrons, usually within a medium exposed to an applied electromagnetic field, caused by collisions of the ions or electrons with the medium ■ *v* (**-lanches, -lanching, -lanched**) **1.** *vti* FLOW DOWN IN LARGE QUANTITY to descend in a large mass on somebody or something **2.** *vt* INUNDATE SOMEBODY OR SOMETHING to overwhelm somebody or something by arriving in large numbers or quantities [Late 18C. Via French < Romansh *avalantze*]

Avalon /ávvə lon/ *n* in Celtic mythology, an island paradise in the west. King Arthur is said to have been taken to Avalon after being apparently mortally wounded.

avant-garde /ávong gaárd/ *n* ARTISTS WITH NEW IDEAS AND METHODS writers, artists, filmmakers, or musicians whose work is innovative, experimental, or unconventional, considered as a group (*takes a singular or plural verb*) ■ *adj* **1.** ARTISTICALLY NEW artistically innovative, experimental, or unconventional **2.** OF AVANT-GARDE ARTISTS belonging to the group of writers, artists, filmmakers, or musicians whose work is innovative, experimental, or unconventional [Early 20C. < French, 'before the guard'] —**avant-gardism** *n* —**avant-gardist** *n*

Avar /aá vaar, áv-/ *n* a North Caucasian language spoken in Dagestan. Native speakers: 601,000. [Late 18C. < Avar] —**Avar** *adj*

avarice /ávvəriss/ *n* an unreasonably strong desire to obtain and keep money [13C. Via French < Latin *avaritia* < *avarus* 'greedy' < *avere* 'to desire']

avaricious /ávvə ríshəss/ *adj* showing an unreasonably strong desire to obtain and keep money —**avariciously** *adv* —**avariciousness** *n*

avascular /ə váskyoōlər/ *adj* lacking blood vessels in body tissue —**avascularity** /ə váskyoō lárrəti/ *n*

avascular necrosis *n* the death of cells in tissue or organs as a result of deficient blood supply

avast /ə vaást/ *interj* used by sailors as a command to stop doing something or to ignore a previous order [Early 17C. Alteration of Dutch *hou'vast*, shortening of *houd vast* 'hold fast']

avatar /ávvə taar/ *n* **1.** INCARNATION OF HINDU DEITY an incarnation of a Hindu deity in human or animal form, especially one of the incarnations of Vishnu such as Rama and Krishna **2.** EMBODIMENT OF SOMETHING somebody who embodies an idea or concept **3.** ONLINE IMAGE OF SOMEBODY IN VIRTUAL REALITY a movable three-dimensional image used to represent somebody in cyberspace **4.** COMPUT GAMES COMPUTER GAME PERSONA in computer games, a character or persona of a player with a graphical representation [Late 18C. < Sanskrit *avatāra* 'descent' (of a god to earth)]

AVC *abbr* FIN additional voluntary contribution

avdp. *abbr* MEASURE avoirdupois

ave /aá vay, áavi/, **Ave** *n* **1.** CHR same as **Hail Mary 2.** TIME FOR PRAYER the time when the Hail Mary is to be said, marked by the ringing of a bell **3.** ROSARY BEAD a small bead on a rosary, used for keeping track of how many times the Hail Mary has been said ■ *interj* GREETING OR FAREWELL used as a greeting or farewell (*archaic*) [13C. < Latin, imperative of *avere* 'be or fare well']

Ave., ave. *abbr* avenue (sense 1)

Avebury /áyvbəri/ village in Wiltshire, southwestern England, the site of the largest ancient stone circle in the country

Avedon /ávvə don/, **Richard** (b. 1923) US photographer. He is best known for his pictures of political and literary figures and celebrities.

'Beauty can be as isolating as genius, or deformity. I have always been aware of a relationship between madness and beauty.'
[Richard Avedon. Quoted in *Model: The Ugly Business of Beautiful Women*, Michael Gross; 1995]

Ave Maria /áav ay mə reé ə, aávi-/ n CHR same as **Hail Mary** [13C. < Latin]

avenge /ə vénj/ (**avenges, avenging, avenged**) vt 1. to inflict punishment because of a wrong done ○ *swore to avenge his death* 2. to retaliate on behalf of yourself or somebody else for a wrong done ○ *determined to avenge his brother* [14C. < Old French *avengier* < *vengier* < Latin *vindicare* (see VINDICATE)] —**avenger** n

USAGE **avenge** or **revenge**? Both words are about repaying a wrong. The differences between them have to do with grammar and shades of meaning, though there is considerable overlap in meaning, dictated by usage over time. Grammatically speaking, **avenge** is a verb only; **revenge** is a verb and more usually a noun. **Avenge** traditionally relates not only to repaying a wrong but to getting justice on somebody else's behalf as a remedy for that wrong (*They sought to avenge their sister's murder* [or *their murdered sister*]). **Revenge**, often connoting malice, traditionally relates to getting even with an adversary by inflicting punishment or harm (*In an act of revenge for the bombing of the ship, the navy shelled the terrorists' training camps*). Though both **avenge** and **revenge** can be used as transitive verbs with reflexive pronouns, **avenge** is commoner in this use: *The dictatorship avenged itself on the partisans' radio station by burning it to the ground*.

avens /ávvinz, áyvənz/ (*plural same*) n PLANTS same as **mountain avens** [12C. < Old French *avence*]

aventurine /ə véntyōorin, -reen/, **aventurin** /-rin/ n 1. dark brown or green glass that contains sparkling mineral particles 2. a variety of quartz or feldspar containing minute particles of mica or haematite. Use: gems. [Early 18C. Via French < Italian *avventurino* 'chance' (because discovered accidentally)]

avenue /ávvə nyoo/ n 1. WIDE STREET a wide street or road in a town 2. TREE-LINED ROAD a road lined with trees, especially a tree-lined path leading through grounds to a country residence 3. MEANS OF APPROACH a course of action to be taken in order to approach, attain, or gain access to somebody or something ○ *need to explore all avenues* [Early 17C. < French, 'approach', feminine past participle of *avenir* 'arrive' < Latin *advenire* (see ADVENT)]

aver /ə vúr/ (**avers, averring, averred**) vt (*formal*) 1. to assert something confidently 2. to state or allege that something is true [14C. < French *avérer* < Latin *verus* 'true'] —**averment** n —**averrable** adj

average /ávvərij/ n 1. TYPICAL AMOUNT the level, amount, or degree of something that is typical of a group or class of people or things 2. MATHS NUMBER CONSIDERED TYPICAL OF NUMBER GROUP a number regarded as typical of a group of numbers, obtained by adding each member of the group and dividing the total by the number of members 3. SPORTS MEASURE OF PLAYING PERFORMANCE a measure of a player's or team's achievement, reached by dividing the number of opportunities for successful performances by how many times a successful performance was achieved 4. FIN INTERMEDIATE PRICE a measure of stock exchange performance based on the total of prices for a group or class of securities divided by the number of securities 5. LAW LOSS AT SEA in maritime law, the loss or damage of a ship and its cargo, or the division of the costs of this loss or damage among the owner or partners involved ■ adj 1. TYPICAL lacking any extraordinary, untypical, or exceptional characteristic ○ *just an average person* 2. NOT VERY GOOD not bad, but not very good either ○ *The performance was no better than average.* 3. MATHS CALCULATED AS TOTAL DIVIDED BY MEMBERS obtained by adding the numerical value for each member of a group and dividing the total by the number of members ■ vt (**-ages, -aging,**

-aged) 1. MATHS CALCULATE NUMERICAL AVERAGE OF SOMETHING to calculate the average of a group of numbers by adding each member of the group and dividing the total by the number of members 2. HAVE SOMETHING AS AVERAGE to have or show a particular number or amount as an average 3. DO SOMETHING AS AVERAGE to do, produce, or receive a particular number or amount of something as an average ○ *She averages one trip to Asia each year.* [15C. Alteration, after DAMAGE, of French *avarie* < Arabic *'awār* 'damage to goods'] —**averagely** adv —**averageness** n

average down vi to purchase more shares of a security when its price is falling, in the hope of reducing costs and increasing profits

average out v 1. vi to result in a particular average number or amount ○ *My earnings average out at 400 pounds a week.* 2. vt to calculate the numerical average of something

average up vi to purchase more shares of a security when its price is rising, in the hope of increasing profits

average deviation n STATS same as **mean deviation**

averse /ə vúrss/ adj 1. strongly opposed to or disliking something (*formal*) ○ *The board is not averse to the idea of further talks.* ○ *risk-averse* 2. describes a leaf or flower that is turned away from the main stem or axis [Late 16C. < Latin *aversus* 'turned away', past participle of *avertere* (see AVERT)] —**aversely** adv —**averseness** n

USAGE See **adverse**.

SYNONYMS See **unwilling**.

aversion /ə vúrsh'n/ n 1. a strong feeling of dislike of somebody or something 2. somebody or something strongly disliked

SYNONYMS See **dislike**.

aversion therapy n 1. a method of therapy that attempts to eliminate undesired behaviour by associating it repeatedly with painful or unpleasant effects 2. therapy aimed at eliminating an irrational fear or dislike by making somebody experience the thing feared or disliked in remote or indirect ways that gradually become closer and more direct

aversive /ə vúrssiv/ adj inducing dislike of something —**aversively** adv —**aversiveness** n

avert /ə vúrt/ (**averts, averting, averted**) vt 1. to prevent something from occurring, especially something harmful 2. to turn your eyes away from something [14C. Via French < Latin *avertere* 'turn away' < *vertere* 'turn'] —**avertible** adj

Avery /áyvəri/, **Oswald** (1877–1955) Canadian-born US bacteriologist and geneticist. He discovered that genetic information was transferred through DNA and not through proteins. Full name **Avery, Oswald Theodore**

Avesta /ə véstə/ n the sacred book of the Zoroastrian religion [Early 16C. < Middle Persian *Avastāk* 'original text']

Avestan /ə véstən/, **Avestic** /ə véstik/ n an ancient Iranian language that was spoken in various parts of Southwest Asia. The sacred writings of the Zoroastrians are written in Avestan. —**Avestan** adj

avg. abbr average

avi abbr a file extension for a multimedia video format file. Full form **audio/video interleaved**

avian /áyvi ən/ adj relating to, belonging to, or characteristic of birds [Late 19C. < Latin *avis* 'bird']

avian flu n a type of influenza that affects birds including domestic chickens and is capable of infecting humans

aviary /áyvi əri/ (*plural* **-ies**) n an enclosure or large cage for birds [Late 16C. < Latin *aviarium* < *avis* 'bird']

aviate /áyvi ayt/ (**-ates, -ating, -ated**) vi to pilot or fly in an aircraft (*formal*) [Late 19C. Back-formation < AVIATION]

aviation /áyvi áysh'n/ n the design, manufacture, use, or operation of aircraft [Mid-19C. < French < Latin *avis* 'bird']

aviation medicine n the branch of medicine concerned with the physical and psychological effects of flying in aircraft

aviator /áyvi aytər/ n the pilot of an aircraft

aviator glasses npl spectacles with oval tinted lenses and a metal frame

aviatrix /áyvi áytriks/ (*plural* **-trices** /-trisiz/) n a female pilot of an aircraft (*dated*) [Early 20C. Feminine of AVIATOR]

aviculture /áyvi kulchər, ávvi-/ n the care and rearing of birds in cages, aviaries, or enclosures [Late 19C. < Latin *avis* 'bird'] —**aviculturist** n

avid /ávvid/ adj eager for or enthusiastic about something [Mid-18C. Back-formation < AVIDITY] —**avidly** adv —**avidness** n

avidin /ávvidin/ n a protein found in egg white that inactivates the vitamin biotin [Mid-20C. < AVID, because of its 'avidity' for BIOTIN]

avidity /ə víddəti/ n 1. great eagerness or enthusiasm for something 2. CHEM same as **affinity** (sense 6) 3. IMMUNOL a measure of the strength with which an antibody binds to an antigen [15C. Directly or via French < Latin *aviditas* < *avidus* < *avere* 'to desire']

Aviemore /ávvi mawr/ village in northeastern Scotland. It is a holiday resort and winter skiing centre. Population: 2,214 (1991).

avifauna /áyvi fáwnə, ávvi-/ (*plural* **-nas** or **-nae** /-neeʹ/) n all the birds present in a region, environment, or period of time [Late 19C. < Latin *avis* 'bird'] —**avifaunal** adj

Avignon /ávvee nyoN/ capital of the Vaucluse Department in the Provence-Alpes-Côte d'Azur Region in southeastern France. Population: 85,935 (1999).

avionics /áyvi ónniks/ n the development and use of electric and electronic equipment for aircraft and spacecraft (*takes a singular verb*) ■ npl the electrical and electronic equipment of an aircraft or spacecraft (*takes a plural verb*) [Mid-20C. Blend of AVIATION + ELECTRONICS] —**avionic** adj

avirulent /ay vírrŏolənt, -ryŏo-/ adj describes microorganisms that are not likely to cause disease in another organism —**avirulence** n

avitaminosis /áy vitəmin óssiss/ (*plural* **-oses** /-ō seez/) n a disease caused by deficiency of a specific vitamin —**avitaminotic** /-óttik/ adj

Aviv /ə veév/ n JUDAISM same as **Nisan**

AVM abbr AIR FORCE Air Vice-Marshal

avo /ávvoo/ (*plural* **avos**) n a subunit of currency in Macau. See table at **currency** [Early 20C. < Portuguese, shortened < *oitavo* 'eighth' < Latin *octavus* < *octo* 'eight']

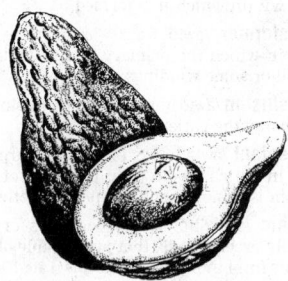
avocado

avocado /ávvə kaádō/ (*plural* **-dos**) n 1. also **avocado pear** GREEN-FLESHED EDIBLE FRUIT a fruit with a leathery dark green or blackish skin, a large stony seed, and soft smooth-tasting pale green flesh, eaten raw in salads or dips 2. TREE ON WHICH AVOCADOS GROW a tropical tree that bears avocados. Latin name: *Persea americana*. 3. CREAMY GREEN a creamy green colour, like that of the flesh of an avocado [Mid-17C. < Spanish, alteration of *aguacate* < Nahuatl *ahuacatl* 'testicle' (because of the shape of the fruit)] —**avocado** adj

avocation /ávvə káysh'n/ n (*formal*) 1. a calling or occupation 2. a hobby or pastime [Early 17C. < Latin *avocation-* 'distraction' < *vocare* 'to call'] —**avocational** adj —**avocationally** adv

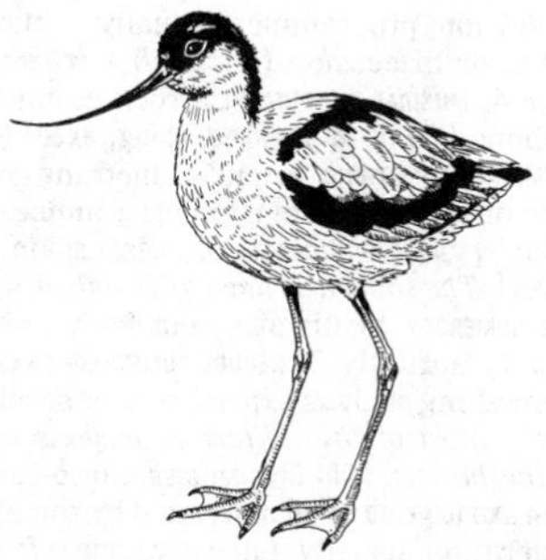
avocet

avocet /ávvə set/ *n* a shorebird with black and white feathers and a long slender upward-curving beak. Genus: *Recurvirostra*. [Late 17C. Via French *avocette* < Italian *avosetta*]

Avogadro /ávvə gaádrō/, **Amedeo, Conte di Quaregna e Ceretto** (1776–1856) Italian physicist and chemist who formulated Avogadro's law. Full name **Avogadro, Lorenzo Romano Amedeo Carlo**

Avogadro's constant *n* PHYS, CHEM same as **Avogadro's number**

Avogadro's law *n* a principle in physics stating that equal volumes of different gases at the same temperature and pressure contain the same number of molecules [Late 19C. After Amedeo AVOGADRO]

Avogadro's number, Avogadro's constant *n* the number of atoms or molecules, 6.022×10^{23} mole$_{-1}$, contained in one mole of a substance. Symbol N_A [Late 19C. After Amedeo AVOGADRO]

avoid /ə vóyd/ (**avoids, avoiding, avoided**) *v* **1.** *vt* NOT GO NEAR SOMEBODY OR SOMETHING to keep away from somebody or something ○ *a place to be avoided* **2.** *vti* NOT DO SOMETHING OR PREVENT SOMETHING to manage not to do something, or manage to stop something happening ○ *I narrowly avoided colliding with it.* **3.** *vt* LAW STATE SOMETHING IS NOT VALID to say that something is void or invalid [14C. < Anglo-Norman < Old French *vuide, voide* 'empty' (see VOID)] —**avoidable** *adj* —**avoidably** *adv* —**avoider** *n*

USAGE avoid, evade, or **elude**? All three words involve keeping away from somebody or something or keeping somebody or something away from you. The main difference between ***avoid*** and ***evade*** is that ***avoid*** is neutral in tone, whereas ***evade*** implies dishonesty or deception, or at least some sort of ulterior motive. If you ***avoid*** a responsibility, you take measures to prevent it from being necessary, whereas if you ***evade*** a responsibility you get out of it in an underhand or deceitful way. ***Avoid*** can be followed by a verbal noun in *-ing*, whereas ***evade*** must be followed by an ordinary noun: *We avoided having to pay. We evaded payment.* ***Elude*** implies clever or ingenious avoidance. It also has the extended meaning 'be beyond understanding or recall', as in *Her name eludes me.*

avoidance /ə vóydənss/ *n* **1.** ACT OF NOT GOING NEAR the act of keeping away from somebody or something **2.** ACT OF NOT DOING SOMETHING the act of refraining from doing something or preventing something from happening **3.** LAW ACT OF MAKING SOMETHING INVALID the act of making something void or invalid

USAGE avoidance or **evasion**? The difference between these two nouns corresponds to the difference between *avoid* and *evade*. In particular, *tax avoidance* means a legal method of reducing a liability to pay tax, whereas *tax evasion* means an illegal method.

avoirdupois /ávv waar dyoo pwaá, ávvərdə poyz/ *n* **1.** MEASURE same as **avoirdupois weight 2.** the amount that somebody weighs (*humorous*) [14C. < Old French *aveir de peis* 'goods of weight']

avoirdupois weight *n* a system for measuring weights based on the pound

Avon /áyvən/ **1.** river in central England, rising in Northamptonshire and flowing through Stratford to join the River Severn. Length: 154 km/96 mi. **2.** river in southwestern England, rising in Gloucestershire and flowing through Bristol to the Bristol Channel. Length: 120 km/75 mi. **3.** river in southern England, rising in Wiltshire and flowing through Salisbury to the English Channel. Length: 96 km/60 mi. **4.** former county (1974–98) in the west of England

avow /ə vów/ (**avows, avowing, avowed**) *vt* to state or affirm that something is true (*formal*) [13C. Via Old French *avouer* 'acknowledge' < Latin *advocare* 'summon' (see ADVOCATE)] —**avowable** *adj* —**avowably** *adv* —**avowedly** /-idli/ *adv*

avowal /ə vów əl/ *n* a frank statement or admission (*formal*)

avulsion /ə vúlsh'n/ *n* **1.** MED the tearing away or separation of part of the body, resulting from an accident or performed during surgery **2.** LAW the sudden separation of part of one person's land and its attachment to another's, especially as a result of a flood [Early 17C. Directly or via French < Latin *avulsion-* < *vellere* 'pull']

avuncular /ə vúngkyŏŏlər/ *adj* **1.** resembling an uncle, especially one who is friendly, helpful, or good-humoured **2.** relating to or deriving from an uncle (*formal or humorous*) [Mid-19C. < Latin *avunculus* 'maternal uncle'] —**avuncularity** /ə vúngkyŏŏ lárrəti/ *n* —**avuncularly** *adv*

avunculate /ə vúngkyŏŏlət/ *n* in some patrilineal societies, a special relationship similar to that of father and son that exists between a man and his sister's sons —**avunculate** *adj*

aw /aw/ *interj Scotland, N Am* used to express surprise, disappointment, or pity (*informal*) [Mid-19C. Natural exclamation]

A/W *abbr* MEASURE actual weight

AWACS /áy waks/ *n* a radar and computer system carried in an aircraft to track large numbers of low-flying aircraft. Full form **Airborne Warning and Control System**

await /ə wáyt/ (**awaits, awaiting, awaited**) *v* **1.** *vti* to wait for, expect, or look for somebody or something **2.** *vt* to be going to happen to or be given to somebody ○ *'Where we find a difficulty we may always expect that a discovery awaits us.'* (C. S. Lewis, *Reflections on the Psalms*; 1961) [13C. < Anglo-Norman *awaitier* < Old French *guaitier* < Germanic]

USAGE await, await for, wait, or **wait for**? You ***await*** or ***wait for*** test results or the arrival of a professor, and you travel to exotic lands where great adventures ***wait*** or ***await***. You do not *await for* anybody: *Let's take a break as we wait for* [not *await for*] *the judge to arrive in the courtroom* or *...while we await the judge's arrival.*

Awakabal /a wákə bal/ (*plural same* or **-bals**) *n* **1.** a member of an Australian Aboriginal people of New South Wales **2.** the language of the Awakabal people, now extinct [Early 19C. < an Aboriginal language] —**Awakabal** *adj*

awake /ə wáyk/ *adj* **1.** NOT ASLEEP fully conscious and not asleep **2.** ALERT alert and vigilant about what is going on all around you ○ *'The colour had come back to his face, and his eyes were clear, and fully awake and aware.'* (J. R. R. Tolkien, *The Fellowship of the Ring*; 1954) **3.** AWARE OF SOMETHING fully aware of something ○ *awake to all the possibilities* ■ *vti* (**awakes, awaking, awoke** /ə wṓk/ or **awaked, awoken** /ə wṓkən/ or **awaked**) **1.** EMERGE FROM SLEEP to rouse somebody, or be roused, from sleep **2.** BECOME OR MAKE AWARE to become, or make somebody become, aware of something **3.** AROUSE FROM DAZE OR DREAM to arouse somebody, or be aroused, from a dazed or dreaming state **4.** AROUSE FEELINGS to arouse feelings or memories, or be aroused [Old English *āwæcnan* < *wacian* 'be awake' and assumed *wacen* 'wake up' < Germanic]

USAGE awake, awaken, wake, or **waken**? Although all four verbs are interchangeable in both the transitive (with an object) and the intransitive (without an object) uses, in practice ***awake*** and ***awaken*** are preferred in figurative meanings: *At last we awoke to the dangers that faced us.* When used in literal meanings ***awake*** and ***awaken*** are normally used intransitively or in the passive: *He awoke at four in the morning. I was awoken by shouts in the street. Will you wake us at four?* ***Wake*** is the only one of these verbs that can be followed by *up*: *I woke up at six this morning.*

awaken /ə wáykən/ (**-ens, -ening, -ened**) *vti* to wake up from sleep or a similar state [Old English *āwæcnian* < *wæcnan* 'waken' < Germanic] —**awakener** *n*

USAGE See ***awake***.

awakening /ə wáykəning/ *adj* JUST BEGINNING just beginning or growing ■ *n* **1.** AROUSAL FROM SLEEP the act or process of waking from sleep **2.** RENEWED ATTENTION TO SOMETHING a revival or renewal of interest in something, especially religion **3.** SUDDEN AWARENESS a sudden recognition or realization of something

award /ə wáwrd/ *n* **1.** SOMETHING GIVEN FOR ACHIEVEMENT something such as a prize that is given in recognition of somebody's merit or an achievement **2.** LAW SOMETHING GRANTED BY LAW COURT something bestowed, granted, or assigned to somebody by a court of law or by arbitration **3.** *ANZ* HR LEGAL DECISION ON WAGES a court decision on wages or conditions of work, or the legal agreement which ratifies this ■ *vt* (**awards, awarding, awarded**) **1.** GIVE SOMETHING FOR MERIT to give somebody something in recognition of merit or an achievement ○ *awarded the prize to the whole class* **2.** LAW BESTOW AS RESULT OF COURT'S DECISION to bestow, grant, or assign something to somebody by a judicial decision or by arbitration [14C. Via Anglo-Norman, 'decide a legal case' < Old French *warder* 'judge' < Germanic] —**awardable** *adj* —**awardee** /ə wáwr deé/ *n* —**awarder** *n*

award rate *n ANZ* same as **award wage**

award wage *n ANZ* a statutory minimum rate of pay set by an industrial court for a specific type of work

aware /ə wáir/ *adj* **1.** KNOWING SOMETHING having knowledge of something from having observed it or been told about it ○ *We are already aware of the problem, and we are dealing with it.* **2.** NOTICING OR REALIZING SOMETHING knowing that something exists because you notice it or realize that it is happening ○ *He became aware of a pain in his left side.* **3.** KNOWLEDGEABLE well-informed about what is going on in the world or about the latest developments in a sphere of activity ○ *More financially aware investors were starting to sell their stock.* [Old English *gewær* 'very watchful' < *wær* 'watchful' < Indo-European, 'perceive, watch out for'] —**awareness** *n*

SYNONYMS ***aware, conscious, mindful, cognizant, sensible***

CORE MEANING: having knowledge of the existence of something

aware having knowledge of something from having observed it or been told about it ○ *I wasn't aware of any problem.* ○ *The leadership has been made well aware of the current position.* **conscious** fully appreciating the importance of something ○ *conscious of the need to make progress* ○ *He was conscious that his predecessor had not lasted long in the job.* **mindful** actively attentive, or deliberately keeping something in mind ○ *mindful of the need to proceed cautiously* ○ *mindful that the current licence expires in early May* **cognizant** (*formal*) having knowledge about something ○ *making people cognizant of the fact that their decision will be final* **sensible** (*formal*) very aware of something ○ *We are sensible of the liberality of your offer.*

awash /ə wósh/ *adj* **1.** COVERED IN WATER covered in water or another liquid **2.** OVERSUPPLIED having more of something than is desirable or manageable ○ *an office awash with letters of complaint* **3.** NAUT WITH WATER RUNNING OVER SIDES describes a boat that has sunk so low that water is able to come in over the sides

away /ə wáy/ CORE MEANING: a grammatical word used to indicate that somebody or something moves so as to leave a particular place ○ *I really need to spend some time away for a while.* ○ *The truck drove away leaving us stranded.* ○ *The cat scampered away.* ○ *We have an away game next week.*

1. *adv* UNINVOLVED separated or far from somebody or something ○ *I try to stay away from trouble.* **2.** *adv* IN DIFFERENT DIRECTION in a different direction from the one somebody was originally facing or looking in ○ *He turned his face away.* **3.** *adv* INTO DISTANCE towards the distance ○ *olive groves stretching away towards the sea* **4.** *adv* IN FUTURE at a particular time in the future (*follows a span of time*) ○ *Christmas is only a week away.* **5.** *adv* INTO STORAGE OR SAFEKEEPING into the place where something is normally stored or kept safe ○ *We filed the valuable papers away.* **6.** *adv* OFF SOMETHING so as to remove or separate something, or so as to be removed or separated (*follows a verb*) ○ *a tool to chip away the old paint* **7.** *adv* TO OR FROM SOMEBODY into or out of the possession of somebody or something (*follows the verb or object of the verb*) ○ *stopped them from stealing away our clients* **8.** *adv* UNTIL SOMETHING IS USED UP so as to make something disappear or be expended (*follows a verb and pre-*

cedes the object) ○ *frittered away his inheritance* **9.** *adv* **GRADUALLY** gradually until something ceases or is no longer noticed ○ *The music gradually died away.* **10.** *adv* **SO AS TO SHOW CHANGE** so that a perceptible change from one thing to another occurs ○ *a shift away from heavier taxation* **11.** *adv* **WITHOUT STOPPING** continuously and usually energetically over a period of time ○ *hammering away in the garage* **12.** *adv, adj* **IN ANOTHER PLACE** not in a specific place or the place where somebody usually is, especially at home or at work ○ *I'll be away until Thursday.* ○ *She works away from the office.* **13.** *adv, adj* **IN DISTANCE OR TIME** as measured in distance or time from here (*follows a measure or indication of distance or time*) ○ *He works about 10 minutes away.* ○ *The mountains are not far away.* **14.** *adv, adj* **ON OPPOSING TEAM'S GROUND** played on an opponent's ground ○ *Their next three games will be played away.* ○ *Their away record has been very bad this season.* **15.** *adj* GOLF **FARTHEST FROM HOLE** in golf, placed farthest from the hole [Old English *aweg* < *on weg* 'on (your) way']

awe[1] /aw/ *n* **1. MIXTURE OF WONDER AND DREAD** a feeling of amazement and respect mixed with fear that is often coupled with a feeling of personal insignificance or powerlessness ○ *Filled with awe, they gazed at the ruins of the massive temple.* ○ *I was completely in awe of her.* **2. ABILITY TO INSPIRE DREAD** the ability to inspire dread or reverence (*archaic*) ■ *vt* (**awes, awing, awed**) **CAUSE AWE IN SOMEBODY** to make somebody feel awe (*usually passive*) ○ *The visiting ambassadors were awed by this display of military might.* [13C. < Old Norse *agi*]

awe[2] /áwi/, **a-wee, ahwee, ah we** *pron Carib* **1.** same as **we 2.** same as **us**[1] *pron* (sense 1) **3.** same as **our** [Mid-20C. Contraction of ALL + WE]

aweary /ə wéeri/ *adj* feeling very tired (*archaic or literary*) ○*'By my troth, Nerissa, my little body is aweary of this great world!'* (Shakespeare, *The Merchant of Venice*; 1596)

aweather /ə wéthər/ *adv* towards the windward side

~~**aweful**~~ incorrect spelling of **awful**

aweigh /ə wáy/ *adj* hanging clear of the bottom of a body of water ○ *Anchors aweigh!*

awe-inspiring *adj* so impressive as to make a person feel humble or slightly afraid

awesome /áwsəm/ *adj* **1.** so impressive or overwhelming as to inspire a strong feeling of admiration or fear ○ *the awesome destructive power of a tornado* **2.** used as a general term of enthusiastic approval (*slang*) ○ *The second track on this CD is totally awesome.* —**awesomely** *adv* —**awesomeness** *n*

awestruck /áw struk/, **awestricken** /-strikən/ *adj* filled with a feeling of awe

awful /áwf'l/ *adj* **1. EXTREMELY BAD** very bad or unpleasant ○ *an awful smell* **2. CAUSING SHOCK OR SADNESS** extremely shocking, saddening, or unpleasant ○ *an awful accident* **3. ILL** in poor health ○ *I feel awful this morning.* **4. VERY GREAT** enormous in size, amount, number, or extent (*informal*) ○ *We spent an awful lot of money on furniture.* **5. AWE-INSPIRING** so impressive as to inspire awe (*literary*) ■ *adv* **EXTREMELY** to an extreme degree or extent (*informal*) ○ *It's awful hot this morning.* [13C. < AWE[1]] —**awfulness** *n*

USAGE The most common use of ***awful*** in current English has nothing to do with inspiring awe, but has the generalized meaning 'very bad or unpleasant', as in the example *The weather has been awful*, and in certain common phrases, for example *an awful shame* and *an awful cheat*, in which ***awful*** intensifies the meaning of the word it accompanies (here, *shame* and *cheat*). This use of ***awful*** is deep-rooted in idiomatic English and is normally unexceptionable, but it is better to avoid it in more formal contexts.

awfully /áwfli, -fəli/ *adv* **1.** to an extremely great degree ○ *I'm awfully grateful to you for helping me out.* **2.** in a very bad or unpleasant way ○ *treated them awfully*

awhile /ə wíl/ *adv* for a short time

USAGE awhile or **a while**? Both expressions are derived from the word *while*, but they have a different role in the sentence. ***Awhile*** is an adverb: *Let us wait awhile* [not *for awhile*]. **A while** – written as two words – is a noun phrase and is normally preceded by *for*: *I'm going to be away for a while.* Sometimes, however, the word *for* is left out, making **a while** look more like an adverbial phrase, although it is still strictly a noun phrase: *We had to wait quite a while.* This use is fairly easy to identify because *while* is qualified in some way, for example *quite a while* or *a long while.*

awhirl /ə wúrl/ *adj* **1.** in a dizzy state of excitement or confusion ○ *Her mind was awhirl with new ideas.* **2.** moving round and round (*literary*) ○ *red and golden leaves awhirl in the autumn breeze*

awkward /áwkwərd/ *adj* **1. EMBARRASSING** embarrassing and requiring great tact or skill to resolve ○ *I find myself in an awkward situation.* **2. DIFFICULT OR UNCOMFORTABLE TO USE** difficult to use because requiring the body to be moved into an uncomfortable position ○ *I find the gear lever very awkward to use when I move the seat forward.* **3. PERFORMED GRACELESSLY** performed in a way that lacks grace and looks uncomfortable ○ *walked with an awkward gait* **4. WITHOUT GRACEFUL COORDINATION** lacking physical coordination and grace ○ *an awkward, gangling adolescent* **5. SHYLY UNCOMFORTABLE** shy, uncomfortable, and embarrassed ○ *He was always awkward around kids.* **6. UNCOOPERATIVE** showing no willingness to cooperate or be reasonable ○ *I think she's being deliberately awkward.* [Mid-16C. < obsolete *awk* 'turned the wrong way' (< Old Norse *afugr* 'turned backwards') + -WARD] —**awkwardly** *adv* —**awkwardness** *n*

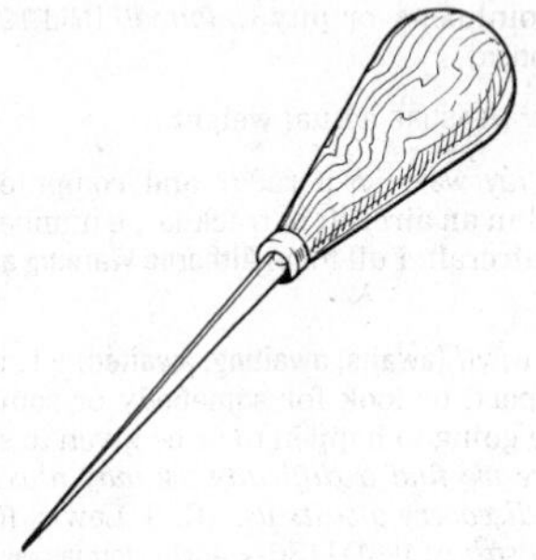

awl

awl /awl/ *n* a tool consisting of a handle and a slim metal shaft with a sharp point, used for boring small holes in leather or wood [Old English *æl*, origin ?]

SPELLCHECK See ***all.***

awn /awn/ *n* a stiff bristle projecting from the tip of a plant organ such as the sheath surrounding a cereal or grass seed [12C. < Old Norse *agn-* 'chaff'] —**awned** *adj*

awning /áwning/ *n* a plastic, canvas, or metal roof supported by a frame and often foldable, placed over a shop front, doorway, window, or the side of a caravan [Early 17C. Origin ?]

awoke past tense of **awake**

awoken past participle of **awake**

AWOL /áy wol/ *adj* absent from a post, especially a military post, without official permission [< *a(bsent) w(ith)o(ut) l(eave)*]

Awolowo /ə wóllәwə/, **Obafemi** (1909–87) Nigerian Yoruba chief and political leader. He became leader of the opposition in the Nigerian federal parliament (1960–62) and was imprisoned until the coup of 1966.

> 'In honest hands, literacy is the surest and the most effective means to true education. In dishonest hands, it may be a most dangerous, in fact a suicidal, acquisition.'
> [Obafemi Awolowo, *Voice of Reason: Selected Speeches of Chief Obafemi Awolowo* (1981), vol. 2]

awry /ə rí/ *adj* **1.** not in the proper position, but turned or twisted to one side ○ *The cushions were awry and there was mud on the carpet.* **2.** not in keeping with plans or expectations ○ *Our plans have gone awry.* [14C. < *on wry* 'in a twist']

ax *n, vt* US spelling of **axe**

axe /aks/ *n* **1. TOOL FOR CUTTING** a tool consisting of a flat heavy metal head with a sharpened edge attached to a long handle, used to chop wood or fell trees **2. JOB LOSS** an abrupt dismissal from a job (*informal*) ○ *Her secretary got the axe yesterday.* **3. TERMINATION** the termination of something such as a service or series of television programmes, usually without prior warning or discussion (*informal*) ○ *schemes facing the axe* **4. MUSICAL INSTRUMENT** a rock guitar or a jazz saxophone (*slang*) ■ *vt* (**axes, axing, axed**) (*informal*) **1. TERMINATE SOMETHING** to end something such as a service or series of television programmes, usually without prior warning or discussion (*usually passive*) ○ *The show was axed after only five episodes.* **2. FIRE SOMEBODY** to dismiss somebody from a job, especially abruptly **3. REDUCE SOMETHING DRASTICALLY** to cut something such as expenditure or services drastically ○ *Most of the welfare provisions were axed from the budget.* [Old English *æcs* < Indo-European] ◇ **have an axe to grind** to be motivated by some personal consideration, usually a negative one ○ *It was clear from their hostile questioning that certain reporters had an axe to grind on this issue.*

axel /áks'l/ *n* a figure-skating jump in which the skater takes off from the forward outside edge of one skate, turns in midair, and lands on the rear outside edge of the other skate [Mid-20C. After *Axel* Rudolph Paulser (1885–1938), Norwegian skater]

axeman /áksmən, -man/ (*plural* **-men** /-mən, -men/) *n* **1.** a man who carries or uses an axe either as a tool or a weapon **2.** a rock guitarist or jazz saxophone player (*slang*)

axenic /ay zéenik/ *adj* describes a culture of an organism that is free from contamination by other living organisms [Mid-20C. < Greek *a-* 'not' + *xenikos* 'alien, strange']

axes SCI, POL plural of **axis**[1]

axial /áksi əl/ *adj* **1.** MATHS **OF AXIS** relating to or forming an axis **2.** CRYSTALS **LOCATED ALONG PLANE OF AXIS** located on or in the plane of an axis of a crystal **3.** ANAT **OF AXIS OF ORGANISM** relating to or located in the axis of an organism —**axially** *adv*

axial plane *n* a plane that intersects the crest or trough of a geological fold in such a way that the sides of the fold are symmetrical about the plane

axial skeleton *n* the bones that make up the vertebral column and skull

axil /áksil/ *n* the space between a leaf or branch and the stem to which it is attached [Late 18C. < Latin *axilla* (see AXILLA)]

axilla /ak síllə/ (*plural* **-lae** /-lee/) *n* **1.** a person's armpit (*technical*) **2.** the hollow underneath the wing of a bird [Early 17C. < Latin, 'little wing' < *ala* 'wing, upper arm']

axillar /ak síllər/ *n* a feather growing from the hollow (**axilla**) under a bird's wing

axillary /ak síllәri/ *adj* **1.** ANAT relating to or near the armpit **2.** BOT relating to or growing in the space (**axil**) between a leaf or branch and the stem ■ *n* (*plural* **-ies**) BIRDS same as **axillar**

axinite /áksi nīt/ *n* a brilliant brown borosilicate mineral containing calcium and aluminium, occurring in wedge-shaped crystals [Early 19C. < Greek *axinē* 'axe']

axiology /áksi ólləji/ *n* the study of the nature, types, and governing criteria of values and value judgments [Early 20C. < French *axiologie* < Greek *axia* 'value'] —**axiological** /áksi ə lójjik'l/ *adj* —**axiologically** *adv* —**axiologist** *n*

axiom /áksi əm/ *n* **1.** a statement or idea that people accept as self-evidently true **2.** MATHS, LOGIC a basic proposition of a system that, although unproven, is used to prove the other propositions in the system [15C. Directly or via French < Latin *axioma* < Greek *axiōma* 'something worthy' < *axios* 'weighty, worthy']

axiomatic /áksi ə máttik/ *adj* **1.** self-evidently true, or universally accepted as being true **2.** MATHS, LOGIC consisting of or based on axioms [Late 18C. < Greek *axiōmatikos* < stem of *axiōma* (see AXIOM)] —**axiomatically** *adv*

axis[1] /áksiss/ (*plural* **axes** /ák seez/) *n* **1.** MATHS **LINE AROUND WHICH OBJECT ROTATES** an imaginary straight line around which an object such as Earth rotates **2.** MATHS **LINE AROUND WHICH SHAPE IS SYMMETRICAL** a straight line around which a geometric figure or three-dimensional object is symmetrical **3.** MATHS **LINE FOR MEASURING COORDINATES** one of two or more lines on which coordinates are measured. Often on a graph two axes form its left and lower margins. **4. ALLIANCE** an alliance or association between two or more people, organizations, or countries that is thought

of as forming a centre of power or influence ○ *the Paris-Bonn axis* **5.** AVIAT LINE DEFINING DIRECTION OF AIRCRAFT one of the three mutually perpendicular lines in an aircraft that define its orientation **6.** ANAT SECOND VERTEBRA IN NECK the second vertebra in the neck, which acts as the pivot on which the head and first vertebra turn **7.** BOT CENTRAL PART OF PLANT the main part of a plant, usually the stem and the root, from which all subsidiary parts develop **8.** OPTICS LINE PERPENDICULAR TO LENS OR MIRROR the axis of symmetry of an optical system, especially a line perpendicular to the surface of a lens or mirror **9.** GEOL LINE AT MAXIMUM CURVATURE an imaginary line along the crest of an anticline or the trough of a syncline at the point of maximum curvature **10.** CRYSTALS LINE PASSING THROUGH CRYSTAL an imaginary line, one of three or four that pass through the centre of a crystal and are used to define its symmetry and the arrangement of its atoms [14C. < Latin, 'axle, pivot']

axis[2] /áksiss/ *n* ZOOL same as **axis deer** [Early 17C. < Latin, an unidentified wild animal in S Asia]

Axis /áksiss/ *n* the military and political alliance of Germany, Italy, and, later, Japan that fought the Allies in World War II [Mid-20C. < Mussolini's idea of 'an axis round which nations could assemble']

axis deer *n* a deer with a reddish-brown, white-spotted coat. Native to: South Asia. Latin name: *Axis axis*.

axis of rotation *n* MATHS same as **axis**[1] (sense 1)

axis of symmetry *n* MATHS same as **axis**[1] (sense 2)

axisymmetric /áksi si méttrik/, **axisymmetrical** /-mét-trik'l/ *adj* symmetrical with respect to an axis —**axisymmetrically** *adv*

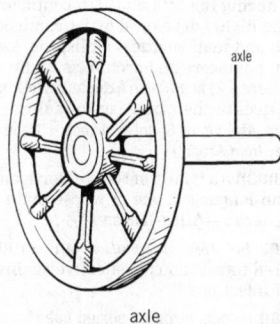

axle

axle /áks'l/ *n* **1.** a shaft on which a wheel or set of wheels revolves, especially a shaft under the body of a vehicle that connects a pair of wheels **2.** the spindle on which one or more wheels revolve [Late 16C. Shortening of AXLETREE]

axletree /áks'l tree/ *n* a shaft that runs underneath the body of a vehicle such as a cart or carriage and connects a pair of wheels [13C. < Old Norse öxultré < öxull 'axle' + tré 'tree, beam']

Axminster /áksminstər/ *n* a high-quality carpet with a cut pile that is usually woven into a colourful pattern [Early 19C. After *Axminster*, SW England]

axolemma /áksə lémmə/ *n* the membranous sheath that encloses the long thin extension of a nerve cell (**axon**) [Late 19C. < Greek *axōn* 'axis' + *lemma* 'skin, husk']

axolotl

axolotl /áksə lott'l/ (*plural* **-lotls** *or* same) *n* a sala-mander that lives in water and often retains its external gills as an adult. Native to: Mexico, western

United States. Genus: *Ambystoma*. [Late 18C. < Nahuatl < *atl* 'water' + *xolotl* 'servant']

axon /ák son/, **axone** /áksōn/ *n* an extension of a nerve cell, similar in shape to a thread, that transmits impulses outwards from the cell body [Late 19C. < Greek *axōn* 'axis']

axoneme /áksə neem/ *n* a bundle of fibrils that form the central core of a cilium or flagellum. It consists of nine pairs of microtubules surrounding a central pair. [Early 20C. < Greek *axōn* 'axis' + *nēma* 'thread']

axonometric /áksənō méttrik/ *adj* describes a method of drawing a three-dimensional object so that the vertical and horizontal axes are drawn to scale but the curves and diagonals appear distorted

axoplasm /áksə plazəm/ *n* the cytoplasm of a nerve cell extension (**axon**) —**axoplasmic** /áksə plázmik/ *adj*

ay[1] *n*, *adv*, *interj* POL another spelling of **aye**[1]

ay[2] *adv* another spelling of **aye**[2] (*archaic or regional*)

Ayacucho /ī ə kōochō/ city in southern Peru. It is an important centre for agriculture and manu-facturing. Population: 118,960 (1998).

ayah /ī yə/ *n* S Asia in South Asia, a maid whose duties include the care of children [Late 18C. Via Portuguese *aia* 'woman tutor' < Latin *avia* 'grandmother']

ayatollah /ī ə tóllə/ *n* a Shiite religious leader, often one who takes an important political as well as religious role [Mid-20C. Via Persian < Arabic *'āyatu-llāh* 'miraculous sign of God' < *'āya* 'sign, miracle' + *allāh* 'God']

Ayckbourn /áyk bawrn/, **Alan** (*b.* 1939) British drama-tist. His plays include *Relatively Speaking* (1967), *Absurd Person Singular* (1973), and *The Norman Conquests* (1974).

'Few women care to be laughed at and men not at all, except for large sums of money.'
[Alan Ayckbourn, *The Norman Conquests*; 1974]

aye[1] /ī/, **ay** /ay/ *adv*, *interj* used to say yes (*archaic or regional*) ■ *n* a vote in favour of a motion, or some-body who casts a vote in favour [Late 16C. Origin ?]

aye[2] /ī/, **ay** *adv* always or forever (*archaic or regional*) [13C. < Old Norse *ei, ey*]

aye-aye

aye-aye /ī ī/ *n* a small nocturnal primate that lives in trees and has a long bushy tail, long bony fingers, and teeth resembling those of a rodent. Native to: Madagascar. Latin name: *Daubentonia mada-gascariensis*. [Late 18C. Via French < Malagasy *aiay*; prob-ably an imitation of its cry]

Ayer /air/, **A. J.** (1910–89) British philosopher. He was a logical positivist whose works include *Language, Truth, and Logic* (1936). Full name **Ayer, Sir Alfred Jules**

'In nature one thing just happens after another. Cause and effect have their place only in our imaginative arrangements and extensions of these primary facts.'
[A. J. Ayer, *The Central Questions of Phil-osophy*; 1973]

Ayers Rock /áirz-/ former name for **Uluru**

Ayesha another spelling of **Aisha**

ayin /áa yin/ *n* the 16th letter of the Hebrew alphabet, transliterated as a reversed apostrophe and pro-nounced approximately like an 'o'. See table at **alphabet** [Early 19C. < Hebrew *'ayin* 'eye']

Aylesbury /áylzbəri/ historic town in Buck-inghamshire, southern England. Population: 58,058 (1991).

Aylesbury Vale local government district in Buck-inghamshire, southern England. Population: 165,748 (2001).

Aymara /īmə ráa/ (*plural same* or **-ras**) *n* **1.** a member of a Native South American people who live around Lake Titicaca in Bolivia and Peru. The great ruins at Tiahuanaco are believed to have been built by the Aymara around AD 500. **2.** a language of Bolivia and Peru, related to Quechua. Native speakers: 2 million. [Mid-19C. < Bolivian Spanish] —**Aymara** *adj* —**Aymaran** *adj*

Aymé /e máy/, **Marcel** (1902–67) French writer. His novels, stories, and plays satirize contemporary corruption.

'When Paris has a sniffle, the whole of France blows her nose.'
[Marcel Aymé, *Silhouette du scandale (The Silhouette of Scandal)*; 1938]

ayo /áyō/ *Carib adj* describes a kite when the string is cut and it flies away quickly ■ *vti* (**ayoes, ayoing, ayoed**) to leave or finish something, especially quickly [Late 20C. Via French Creole, 'goodbye' < French *adieu*]

Ayr /air/ historic town in South Ayrshire, Scotland. Population: 47,962 (1991).

Ayrshire[1] /áirshər/ former county of southwestern Scotland, now divided into North Ayrshire, East Ayrshire, and South Ayrshire

Ayrshire[2] /áirshər/ *n* a cow belonging to a largely white breed of dairy cattle

aysh *interj* S Africa another spelling of **eish** (*informal*)

Ayub Khan /íyoōb kaán/, **Muhammad** (1907–74) Paki-stani soldier and head of state. He became president of Pakistan (1958–69), but resigned after an un-successful war with India and charges of cor-ruption.

Ayurveda /áa yoor vaydə, -veedə/ *n* ALTERN MED same as **Ayurvedic medicine** [Early 20C. < Sanskrit *āyur-veda* 'medicine' < *āyur-* 'life, vital power' + *veda* 'knowledge'] —**Ayurvedic** *adj*

Ayurvedic medicine /áa yoor váydik-, -veédik-/ *n* a traditional Hindu system of healing that assesses somebody's constitution and lifestyle, and recom-mends treatment based on herbal prep-arations, diet, yoga, and purification

az *abbr* Azerbaijan (*used in Internet addresses*) See table at **domain name**

az. *abbr* **1.** ASTRON azimuth **2.** HERALDRY azure

Azad Kashmir /áa zad-/ section of western Kashmir that is under the control of Pakistan. Area: 1,680 sq. km/650 sq. mi.

azalea

azalea /ə záyli əl/ (*plural* **-eas** *or* same) *n* a flowering bush related to the rhododendron. Some azaleas are deciduous and some are evergreen, and they range in size from very low-growing plants to small trees. Flowers: pink, purple, white, yellow, or orange, sometimes fragrant. Genus: *Rhododendron*. [Mid-18C. Via modern Latin < Greek *azaleos* 'dry']

azan /aa zaán/ *n* the Islamic call to prayer that a muezzin repeats five times a day from the minaret of a mosque [Mid-19C. < Arabic *aḏān* 'announcement']

Azania /ə záyni əl/ *n* S Africa a name for South Africa used by resistance movements in the apartheid era

Azapo /ə záppō/ *n* a Socialist political movement in South Africa [Late 20C. Acronym < *Azanian People's Organization*]

azapropazone /ázzə próppə zōn/ *n* a ketone derivative of pyrazole with analgesic and anti-inflammatory properties. Use: treatment of rheumatoid arthritis.

azatadine /ə záttə deen, ay-/ *n* an antihistamine taken orally. Use: treatment of allergic rhinitis, urticaria.

azathioprine /ázzə thī́ ō preen/ *n* a drug that suppresses the immune response. Use: after transplant surgery to prevent rejection. [Mid-20C. < *aza-* + THI- + PURINE]

azelaic acid /ázzə láy ik-/ *n* a dicarboxylic acid that is a yellowish to white powder. Use: treatment of skin cancer and other skin disorders. [< AZO- + Greek *elaion* 'oil']

azelastine /ázzə lásteen/ *n* an antihistamine drug inhaled through the nose [Late 20C. < *azel* + *-astine*, INN stem]

azeotrope /ə zeé ə trōp/ *n* a mixture of liquids that has a different boiling point from any of its components and retains its composition as a vapour [Early 20C. < A[3] + Greek *zeo*, form of *zein* 'to boil' + *-tropos* 'turning, changing'] —**azeotropic** /áyzi ə tróppik/ *adj* —**azeotropy** /áyzi óttrəpi/ *n*

Azerbaijan

Azerbaijan /ázzər bī́ jaán/ country of Southwest Asia bisected by Armenia. It is also surrounded by the Caspian Sea, Russia, Georgia, and Iran. Language: Azeri. Currency: manat. Capital: Baku. Population: 7,830,764 (2003). Area: 86,600 sq. km/33,400 sq. mi. Official name **Azerbaijani Republic** —**Azerbaijani** *n*, *adj*

Azeri /ə záiri/ *n*, *adj* the Turkic official language of the country of Azerbaijan, also spoken in the province of Azerbaijan in northwestern Iran, belonging to the Altaic family of languages. Native speakers: 14 million.

azerty /ə zúrti/, **AZERTY** *adj* describes a computer or typewriter keyboard layout in continental Europe, where the top row of letters, beginning from the left, runs A, Z, E, R, T, Y

azide /áy zīd/ *n* a chemical compound containing a group of three adjacent nitrogen atoms. Formula: N_3. [Early 20C. < AZO- + -IDE]

azidothymidine /ə zíddō thī́mə deen/ *n* PHARM full form of **AZT**

Azikiwe /áˈa zee keˈe way/, **Nnamdi** (1904–96) president of Nigeria. He became Nigeria's first president in 1963, but was overthrown by a military coup in 1966.

'Tell a man whose house is on fire to give a moderate alarm; tell a man moderately to rescue his wife from the arms of a ravisher; tell a mother to extricate gradually her babe from the fire into which it has fallen; but do not ask me to use moderation in a cause like the present.'
[Nnamdi Azikiwe. Quoted in *Zik: A Selection from the Speeches of Nnamdi Azikiwe*; 1961]

Azilian /ə zílli ən/ *n* a prehistoric culture that existed in Spain and southwestern France from around 10,000 to 8,000 BC. The distinctive artefacts produced by this culture include flat bone harpoons and painted pebbles. [Late 19C. After Mas d' *Azil* in the French Pyrenees]

azimuth /ázziməth/ *n* **1.** the angle measured from north, eastwards along the horizon, to the point where a vertical circle through an astronomical object intersects the horizon **2.** the angular distance along the horizon between a point of reference, usually the observer's bearing, and another object [Early 17C. Via French *azimut* < Arabic *as-samūt*, plural of *as-samt* 'the way' < *samt* 'way, direction'] —**azimuthal** /ázzi múth'l/ *adj* —**azimuthally** *adv*

azimuthal equidistant projection *n* a method of map projection in which a straight line from the centre to any given point represents the shortest distance to that point and can be measured to scale

azine /áyzin/ *n* an organic chemical compound with a six-sided ring structure containing one or more atoms of nitrogen [Late 19C. < AZO- + -INE]

azithromycin /ázzithrō míssin/ *n* an antibiotic taken in combination with other drugs. Use: treatment of toxoplasmosis, heart disease, Aids.

Aznar /ath naár, ass naár/, **José María** (*b.* 1953) prime minister of Spain (1996–2004). Elected president of the newly formed centre-right Popular Party in 1990, he won two election victories in 1996 and 2000, standing down after two terms in office.

azo /áyzō, ázzō/ *adj* relating to or containing two adjacent nitrogen atoms. Formula: –N=N–. [Late 19C. < AZO-]

azo- *prefix* containing a nitrogen group ○ *azole* [< French *azote* 'nitrogen' < Greek *a-* 'not' + *zōē* 'life'; because living creatures cannot breathe it]

azobenzene /áyzō bén zeen/ *n* a yellow or orange crystalline solid. Use: making dyes. Formula: $C_6H_5N=NC_6H_5$.

azo compound *n* a compound containing two adjacent nitrogen atoms attached to aromatic groups

azo dye *n* an artificial dye, usually orange, yellow, or brown, containing an azo group. Source: amines.

azoic /ə zṓ ik/ *adj* **1.** relating to or belonging to a geological period before the appearance of living organisms on Earth **2.** exhibiting no trace of life or organic remains [Mid-19C. < Greek *azōos* 'without life' < *zōē* 'life']

azole /áyzōl, ə zṓl/ *n* an organic chemical compound with a ring of five linked atoms, of which at least one is nitrogen [Late 19C. < AZO- + -OLE]

azonal /ay zṓn'l/ *adj* **1.** not divided into zones **2.** *also* **azonic** /-ik/ not restricted to a specific zone or geographical area

azoospermia /ay zṓ ə spúrmi ə/ *n* MED same as **aspermia**

Azores /ə záwrz/ archipelago in the North Atlantic Ocean, west of Portugal, of which it is an autonomous region. There are nine main islands. Capital: Ponta Delgada. Population: 237,800 (1993). Area: 2,247 sq. km/868 sq. mi.

Azorín /ázzə reˈen/ (1873–1967) Spanish writer. A member of a group of writers that rejected traditional literary forms, he wrote the novel *Don Juan* (1922). Born **Ruiz, José Martínez**

azotaemia /ázzə teˈemi ə/ *n* MED same as **uraemia** [Early 20C. < obsolete *azote* 'nitrogen' (see AZO-) + -AEMIA] —**azotaemic** *adj*

azotic /ay zóttik/ *adj* relating to or containing nitrogen [Late 18C. < obsolete *azote* < French (see AZO-)]

azotobacter /ə zṓtō baktər/ *n* a rod-shaped or spherical bacterium found in soil and water that converts atmospheric nitrogen to a stable or biologically available form. Family: Azotobacter. [Early 20C. < modern Latin < French *azote* 'nitrogen' (see AZO-) + *bacterium*]

Azov, Sea of /ázzov, áy zov/ shallow inland sea in southern Russia, linked with the Black Sea by the Kerchenskiy Strait. Area: 37,555 sq. km/14,500 sq. mi.

AZT *n* an antiviral drug used in the treatment of Aids. It works by inhibiting the enzyme reverse transcriptase, which the Aids virus requires to reproduce. Full form **azidothymidine**

Aztec /áz tek/ *n* **1.** a member of a Native Middle American people whose empire dominated central Mexico during the 14th and 15th centuries. As well as having highly developed artistic, musical, astronomical, and mathematical skills, the Aztecs were excellent engineers and architects. **2.** LANG same as **Nahuatl** (sense 2) ■ *adj also* **Aztecan** /az ték'n/ relating to the Aztecs or their language or culture [Late 18C. Via French *Aztèque* or Spanish *Azteca* < Nahuatl *aztecatl* 'somebody from Aztlan']

Aztec-Tanoan *n* a family of Native North and Central American languages, one of whose main branches is Uto-Aztecan —**Aztec-Tanoan** *adj*

aztreonam /az treˈe ə nam/ *n* an antibiotic administered intravenously, effective against a broad range of infections

azuki bean *n* FOOD same as **adzuki bean**

azure /ázhər, áy-/ *adj* **1.** DEEP BLUE deep blue, like the colour of a clear sky on a sunny day (*literary*) ○ *the azure depths of the ocean* **2.** HERALDRY BLUE coloured blue on a coat of arms ■ *n* (*literary*) **1.** BLUE SKY a clear blue sky **2.** DEEP BLUE HUE a deep blue colour, like that of a clear sky on a sunny day ○ *the azure of her eyes* [13C. Via Old French *azur* < medieval Latin *azzurum* < Arabic *al-lāzaw ard* 'the lapis lazuli' < Persian *lāžward* 'lapis lazuli']

azurite /ázhoͦo rīt/ *n* a deep blue semiprecious stone that is composed of hydrated copper carbonate. Use: source of copper, gems.

azygous /ázzigəss/ *adj* occurring as a single muscle or vein, and not as a pair [Mid-17C. < Greek *azugos* 'without yoke' < *zugon* 'yoke']

b¹ /bee/ (*plural* **b's**), **B** (*plural* **B's** or **Bs**) *n* **1.** the second letter of the English alphabet, representing a consonant sound **2.** a written representation of the letter 'b'

b² *symbol* used to refer to the second vertical row of squares from the left on a chessboard

b³ *abbr* **1.** PHYS barn **2.** MUSIC bass¹ **3.** MUSIC basso **4.** ACOUSTICS bel **5.** billion **6.** book **7.** born **8.** CRICKET bowled **9.** breadth **10.** CRICKET bye¹

B¹ /bee/ (*plural* **B's** or **Bs**) *n* **1.** 'B'-SHAPED OBJECT something shaped like a letter 'B' **2.** MUSIC 7TH NOTE IN C MAJOR the seventh note of a scale in C major **3.** MUSIC SOMETHING THAT PRODUCES B NOTE a string, key, or pipe tuned to produce the note B **4.** MUSIC SCALE BEGINNING ON B a scale or key that starts on the note B **5.** MUSIC WRITTEN SYMBOL OF B a graphic representation of the tone of B **6.** EDUC 2ND HIGHEST GRADE the second highest grade in a series, e.g. an above-average grade for academic work **7.** MED HUMAN BLOOD TYPE a human blood type of the ABO system, containing the B antigen. Somebody with this type of blood can donate to people of the same group or of the AB group, and can receive blood from people with this type or with type O. **8.** SOC SCI MIDDLE MANAGER OR INTERMEDIATE PROFESSIONAL in the market research system that classifies people according to their occupation, somebody in a middle-management or intermediate professional or administrative position

B² *symbol* **1.** black (*used on pencils to indicate that the lead is soft*) **2.** CHEM ELEM boron **3.** COMPUT eleven (*used in hexadecimal notation*) **4.** PHYS magnetic flux density **5.** ROADS a secondary road

B³ *abbr* **1.** EDUC bachelor (*used in degree titles*) **2.** MUSIC bass¹ **3.** MUSIC basso **4.** PHYS Baumé scale **5.** GEOG Bay (*used on maps*) **6.** ACOUSTICS bel **7.** billion **8.** CHESS bishop **9.** book **10.** breadth

B2B *abbr* E-COMMERCE business-to-business (*used in e-mails or text messages*)

B2C *abbr* E-COMMERCE business-to-consumer (*used in e-mails or text messages*)

B4 *abbr* before (*used in e-mails or text messages*)

B4N *abbr* bye for now (*used in e-mails or text messages*)

Ba *symbol* CHEM ELEM barium

BA *abbr* **1.** EDUC Bachelor of Arts **2.** British Academy **3.** British Airways **4.** British Association (for the Advancement of Science)

baa /baa/ *vi* (**baas, baaing, baaed**) BLEAT LIKE SHEEP to make the long wavering cry characteristic of a sheep or lamb ■ *n* (*plural* **baas**) **1.** CRY OF SHEEP the long wavering cry characteristic of a sheep or lamb **2.** *Ireland, N England* CHILD a child, especially a youngest child (*informal*) ○ *Where's the baa? Is he sleeping?* [Early 16C. An imitation of the sound]

Baal /baal, báyəl/ (*plural* **-alim** /baálim, báyəlim/ or **-als**) *n* **1.** a fertility or nature god worshipped by the Canaanites and the Phoenicians, and considered a false god by the ancient Hebrews **2.** *also* **baal** (*plural* **-alim** or **-als**) an idol or false god

Baalbek /baál bek/ city in eastern Lebanon between the Litani and Asi rivers. It is the site of the ancient ruins of Heliopolis. Population: 50,000 (1981).

baal teshuvah /baál tə shoovə, -choovə, báyəl-/ (*plural* **baalei teshuvah** /baál lay-, báy ə lay-/), **baal tshuva** (*plural* **baalei tshuva**) *n* somebody who returns to Orthodox Jewish practice after abandoning it [< Hebrew, 'master of return']

baap /baap/ *n S Asia* same as **father** *n* (sense 1) [< Hindi]

baas /baass/ *n S Africa* a form of address used mainly during the apartheid era by non-whites to show respect when addressing a white man or boy, especially an employer [Late 18C. Via Afrikaans < Dutch, 'master']

baaskap /baáss kap/ *n S Africa* the domination of other peoples by white people in South Africa under Nationalist rule until the elections of 1994, or the system that ensured it [Mid-20C. Via Afrikaans, 'domination, mastership' < Dutch *baasschap* < *baas* 'master']

Baath /baath/, **Ba'ath** /baa aáth/ *n* a Socialist party in several Arab countries, including Iraq and Syria, founded in 1943 [Mid-20C. < Arabic *ba'ṯ* 'resurrection']

Baathism /baáth izəm/ *n* the ideology of the Baath Party that combines pan-Arabism, state control, anti-Semitism, and the cult of a single authoritarian ruler. Baathism was predominant in Iraq until the overthrow of Saddam Hussein in 2003, but it remains predominant in Syria. —**Baathist** *n, adj*

Bab /baab/ *n* the title of the Persian religious leader, Mirza Ali Muhammad (1819–50), who founded Babism as a reform of Shiite Islam in Persia in the 19th century [Mid-19C. Via Persian < Arabic *bāb* 'gate, intermediary']

baba¹ /baá baa, -bə/ (*plural* **-bas**) *n* a dessert made of leavened dough soaked in a rum-flavoured syrup and baked in a tin [Early 19C. Via French < Polish, 'married (peasant) woman']

baba² /baá baa/ *n S Asia* **1.** RESPECTFUL ADDRESS FOR OLDER MAN a respectful form of address for an older man (*informal*) **2.** TITLE FOR HOLY MAN a title and form of address for a holy man **3.** same as **father** *n* (sense 1) (*informal; often a form of address*) **4.** CHILD a child, especially a boy (*informal; often an endearment or form of address*) [< Hindi *bābā*]

Baba /baábbə/ *n Malaysia* a man of Chinese origin who was born in Melaka and speaks Malay as a first language [Mid-19C. < Malay]

babalaas /baábbə laass/ *n S Africa* a hangover [Late 20C. < Zulu *ibabalazi*]

Babangida /bə báng geedə/, **Ibrahim** (*b.* 1941) Nigerian soldier and politician. He was president of Nigeria from 1985 to 1993.

babassu /baábbə soó/ (*plural* **-sus** or *same*) *n* a tall palm tree that produces oil. Use: manufacture of soap, margarine, cosmetics, cooking oil. Genus: *Orbignya*. [Early 20C. < Brazilian Portuguese *babaçú* < Tupi *ybá* 'fruit' + *guasu* 'large']

Babbage /baábbij/, **Charles** (1791–1871) British mathematician and inventor. He designed and attempted to build mechanical calculating machines that were forerunners of the computer.

babbitt /baábbit/ *n* a bearing made of babbitt metal ■ *vt* (**-bitts, -bitting, -bitted**) to cover or line a surface with babbitt metal or a similar alloy [Late 19C. See BABBITT METAL]

Babbitt /baábbit/ *n N Am* a self-satisfied narrow-minded man who cannot see beyond his own business and social interests ○ *'His name was…Babbitt, and…he was nimble in the calling of selling houses for more than people could afford to pay.'* (Sinclair Lewis, *Babbitt*; 1922) [Early 20C. After the main character in the novel *Babbitt* (1922) by Sinclair Lewis] —**Babbittry** *n*

Babbitt /baábbit/, **Milton** (*b.* 1916) US composer. He was a leader in the development of serialism and electronic music. Full name **Babbitt, Milton Byron**

babbitt metal *n* a soft alloy originally consisting of tin, copper, and antimony, but now often containing lead. Use: in manufacture of antifriction bearings. [Late 19C. After Isaac *Babbitt* (1799–1862), US inventor]

babble /baább'l/ *v* (**-bles, -bling, -bled**) **1.** *vti* SAY OR SPEAK INCOHERENTLY to say something rapidly and incoherently without pausing, usually because of excitement or fear ○ *She babbled something I didn't catch and then dashed out.* **2.** *vi* SPEAK IRRELEVANTLY to talk rapidly or at length about things that seem irrelevant or foolish ○ *He babbled on about the importance of some new gadget.* **3.** *vi* MURMUR CONTINUOUSLY to make a continuous low murmuring or bubbling sound ○ *a brook babbling through the pasture* **4.** *vti* BLURT SOMETHING OUT to reveal something thoughtlessly or impulsively that is supposed to be secret or confidential ○ *immediately babbled the whole story to the neighbours* ■ *n* **1.** SOUND OF LOUD UNINTELLIGIBLE VOICES the sound of voices speaking too excitedly and rapidly to be heard properly ○ *the babble of guests in the hallway* **2.** FOOLISH TALK irrelevant or foolish chatter **3.** SOUND OF RUNNING WATER the low continuous murmuring or bubbling sound made by water as it flows along **4.** TELECOM BACKGROUND INTERFERENCE ON PHONE LINES background noise on a telephone line caused by interference from other conversations [13C. Probably < Middle Low German or Middle Dutch *babbelen*, an imitation of the sound, or a similar formation in English] —**babblement** *n*

babbler /baábblər/ *n* **1.** somebody who babbles, especially giving away secrets **2.** a small bird of the family that includes the laughing thrush, often kept as a cagebird. Native to: forests and bush of the Middle East, Asia, and Africa. Family: Timaliidae.

babe /bayb/ *n* **1.** LOVER used as an affectionate term of address to a lover or somebody loved (*slang*) **2.** YOUNG WOMAN CONSIDERED GOOD-LOOKING a young woman who is considered good-looking (*slang; sometimes considered offensive*) **3.** *N Am* HANDSOME YOUTH an attractive young man (*slang*) **4.** BABY a baby or small child (*literary or archaic*) [14C. Probably < obsolete *baban* 'baby', an imitation of childish utterances] ◇ **a babe in the woods** a naive excessively trusting person

babe in arms (*plural* **babes in arms**) *n* **1.** a baby too young to walk who needs to be carried **2.** a very inexperienced or naive person who may be incapable of handling a difficult situation or easily duped ○ *We were simply babes in arms when it came to dealing with a real professional.*

babel /báyb'l/ *n* (*literary*) **1.** a confused noise, especially the noise of loud unintelligible voices all talking at once **2.** a scene or place of noisy confusion [Early 16C. < the TOWER OF BABEL]

Babel /báyb'l/ BIBLE ♦ **Tower of Babel**

babe magnet *n* a man or possession considered irresistible to good-looking young women (*slang*)

babesiosis /bə beézi óssiss/, **babesiasis** /baábbi zí əssiss/ *n* a disease of humans and animals caused by protozoan infection of red blood cells and transmitted by a tick bite [Early 20C. < modern Latin *Babesia*, after Victor *Babès* (1854–1926), Romanian bacteriologist]

Babi /baábbi/ (*plural* **-bis**) *n* a follower of the Bab or of Babism [Mid-19C. Via Persian < Arabic < *bāb* (see BAB)]

Babington /baábbingtən/, **Antony** (1561–86) English conspirator. He planned to murder Elizabeth I and

release Mary, Queen of Scots. He and his fellow conspirators were captured and executed.

Babinski reflex /bə bínski-/, **Babinski's reflex** *n* a curling upwards of the big toe when the sole of the foot is stroked. It is a normal reflex in children up to two years old but an indicator of disease of the brain or spinal cord in older people. [Early 20C. After J. F. F. *Babinski* (1857–1932), French neurologist]

babirusa /baàabi roòssə/ (*plural* **-sas** or *same*), **babirussa**, **babirousa** *n* a wild pig that has almost hairless skin and very large curved tusks. Native to: Indonesia, Malaysia. Latin name: *Babyrousa babyrussa*. [Late 17C. < Malay < *babi* 'pig' + *rusa* 'deer']

Babism /baàabizəm/ *n* a religion founded by the Bab as a reform of Shiite Islam in Persia in the 19th century

baboo *n* another spelling of **babu**

baboon

baboon /bə boòn/ *n* **1.** a large ground-dwelling monkey with a prominent snout resembling a dog's muzzle, large teeth, and bare pink patches on the buttocks. Native to: Africa, Asia. Genus: *Papio*. **2.** somebody regarded as rude or oafishly clumsy (*insult*) [15C. < French *babuin* 'gaping figure, baboon' or medieval Latin *babewynus*]

babu /baà boo/, **baboo** *n S Asia* **1.** HINDI COURTESY TITLE a courtesy title or form of address in Hindi equivalent to 'Mr' **2.** OFFENSIVE TERM an offensive term for a bureaucrat (*insult*) **3.** OFFENSIVE TERM in former British India, an offensive term for an Indian, especially a clerk or official, with limited knowledge of the English language and culture (*offensive*) [Late 18C. < Hindi *bābū* 'father']

babul /baa boòl, baà bool/ (*plural* **-buls** or *same*) *n* a tree that produces gum arabic, tannin, and hardwood. Native to: North Africa, South Asia. Latin name: *Acacia nilotica*. [Early 19C. Via Hindi *babūl*, Bangla *bābul* < Sanskrit *babbūla*]

babushka /bə boòshkə/ *n* **1.** a headscarf folded and tied under the chin in the style of Russian peasant women **2.** a traditional Russian grandmother figure [Mid-20C. < Russian, 'grandmother']

Babuyan Islands /baà boo yaàn-/ island group in the northern Philippines. Area: 595 sq. km/230 sq. mi. Population: 24,500

baby /báybi/ *n* (*plural* **-bies**) **1.** VERY YOUNG CHILD a very young child who is not yet able to walk or talk **2.** UNBORN CHILD a child who is still in the womb **3.** CHILDISH PERSON somebody regarded as childish or overly dependent ○ *told him not to be such a baby* **4.** YOUNGEST MEMBER the youngest member of a family or group ○ *the baby of the team* **5.** IMMATURE ANIMAL a very young animal **6.** TERM OF ENDEARMENT an affectionate term of endearment, especially for a woman (*slang; sometimes considered offensive*) ■ *adj* SMALLER AND YOUNGER describes vegetables that are smaller and younger than usual ○ *baby carrots* ■ *vt* (**-bies, -bying, -bied**) TREAT SOMEBODY WITH GREAT CARE to show a great or inordinate amount of care to something or somebody [14C. Pet form of BABE] —**babyhood** *n* ◇ **be left holding the baby** to be left in a situation of being solely responsible for something because other people have abdicated their own responsibility ◇ **throw out the baby with the bathwater** to reject something in its entirety without discriminating between good and bad parts

ORIGIN In Old English, the term for what we would now call a *baby* was *child*, and it seems only to have been from about the 11th century that *child* began to extend its range to the slightly more mature age that it now

covers. Then when the word *baby* came into the language in the 14th century, it was also used in this developed sense of 'child', and only gradually came to refer to infants not yet capable of speech or walking.

baby blue *n* a pale blue colour —**baby-blue** *adj*

baby-blue-eyes *n* a spreading annual plant with serrated grey-green leaves. Flowers: small, bowl-shaped, blue with white centres. Latin name: *Nemophila menziesii*. [< the fancied resemblance of its flowers to eyes]

baby blues *n* PSYCHIAT same as **postnatal depression** (*informal; takes a singular or plural verb*)

baby bond *n* **1.** same as **Child Trust Fund** (*informal*) **2.** *US* a bond issued for an amount lower than $1,000, usually between $25 and $500

baby book *n* a book in which to keep photographs of somebody as a baby and record notable first actions such as smiling and walking

baby boom *n* a sudden large increase in the birthrate over a specific period, especially the 15 years after World War II

baby boomer *n* somebody born during a baby boom, especially the one following the end of World War II

baby boomlet *n* an increase in the birthrate smaller than a baby boom

baby bouncer *n* a harness with elastic straps that allows a baby to be seated within it and suspended from a doorway, letting the infant bounce up and down

baby buggy *n* same as **buggy**[1] (sense 1)

baby carriage *n N Am* same as **pram**[1]

babycino /báybi cheènō/ *n Aus* a small cup of warm, frothy milk topped with powdered chocolate, prepared for toddlers and children

Baby Doc ♦ **Duvalier, Jean-Claude**

baby-dolls *npl* women's nightwear consisting of a short loose top and loose shorts [Because worn in the film *Baby Doll* (1956)]

baby face *n* **1.** a smooth round face that gives somebody a childlike innocent look **2.** somebody with a baby face

baby fat *n N Am* same as **puppy fat**

baby food *n* food that has been prepared or manufactured in such a way that it can be fed to a baby

baby grand *n* a small grand piano about 1.5 m/5 ft long

Babygro /báybi grō/ *tdmk* a trademark for a baby's all-in-one suit made from stretch fabric

babyish /báybi ish/ *adj* **1.** like a baby in appearance, sound, or behaviour ○ *She has a really babyish voice.* **2.** suitable for a baby or for a younger child ○ *Clothes like these are too babyish for a child his age.* —**babyishly** *adv* —**babyishness** *n*

Babylon[1] /bábbilən/, -lon/ capital of ancient Babylonia, sited on the Euphrates in modern Iraq. It was known for its opulence, and the Hanging Gardens there were one of the Seven Wonders of the World.

Babylon[2] *n* **1.** PLACE OF IMMORALITY a place of great luxury or immorality **2.** PLACE OF EXILE a place of exile or captivity **3.** OFFENSIVE TERM an offensive term for the police (*slang; used in Black English*) **4.** OFFENSIVE TERM an offensive term for the Establishment, regarded as dominated by white people (*slang; used in Black English*) **5.** RELIG same as **hell** *n* (sense 1) (*slang; used in Black English*)

Babylonia /bábbi lóni ə/ empire in Mesopotamia that flourished from the first half of the second millennium BC until its conquest by Persia in 539 BC

Babylonian /bábbi lóni ən/ *n* **1.** somebody who lived in ancient Babylon or Babylonia **2.** the Akkadian language, especially as recorded in cuneiform texts from Babylonia —**Babylonian** *adj*

Babylonian captivity *n* the period of time that the Jews spent in exile in Babylonia in the 6th century BC

baby milk *n* a preparation that imitates the composition of human breast milk and that may be used for feeding babies. It can be a liquid, or a powder to be mixed with water.

baby minder *n* somebody whose job is to look after other people's babies or very young children, especially while their parents are at work

baby oil *n* a gentle oil used to moisturize the skin, especially that of a baby

baby's breath (*plural same* or **baby's breaths**) *n* **1.** a plant with a mass of delicate branched stems, often used in bouquets and floral arrangements. Flowers: small, fragrant, white or pink. Latin name: *Gypsophila paniculata*. **2.** a perennial plant with a mass of tiny flowers, especially a plant of the madder family [< the delicate scent]

baby shower *n ANZ, N Am* a party given by the female friends of somebody who is pregnant, at which she is given presents for the baby

babysit /báybisit/ (**-sits, -sitting, -sat** /-sat/) *v* **1.** *vti* to look after a child or children in the child's home while the parents are out **2.** *vt* to look after somebody or something unable to be left unsupervised or needing constant attention (*informal*) ○ *Would you babysit my plants next week?* —**babysitter** *n*

babysitting /báybisiting/ *n* the activity of looking after children in their own home while their parents are out

babysitting circle *n* a child-care arrangement by which a group of parents agree to look after one another's children in the children's own homes for points instead of money, with the accrued points being used for others in the group to take care of the sitters' children. N Am term **babysitting co-op**

baby snatcher *n* **1.** same as **cradle snatcher** (*informal humorous*) **2.** somebody who steals a baby (*slang*)

baby talk, **babytalk** /baybi tawk/ *n* the simplified or specially modified language and exaggerated intonation that adults use when talking to very small children

baby tooth *n* DENT same as **milk tooth**

baby walker *n* a frame mounted on wheels that helps keep babies upright when they are learning to walk. N Am term **walker**

babyware /báybi wair/ *n* clothes and equipment for babies

babywear /báybi wair/ *n* clothing designed to be worn by babies

BAC *abbr* BIOTECH bacterial artificial chromosome

Bacall /bə káwl/, **Lauren** (*b.* 1924) US actor. She starred in musicals and films including *To Have and Have Not* (1944) and *The Big Sleep* (1946). Her first husband was Humphrey Bogart. Born **Perske, Betty Joan**

> 'I think your whole life shows in your face and you should be proud of that.'
> [Lauren Bacall, *Remark*; 1988]

Bacău /bə ków/ city in eastern Romania. It is the capital of Bacău County, and a major rail junction. Population: 209,689 (1997).

baccalaureate /bákə láwri ət/ *n* **1.** an examination taken at the conclusion of a student's secondary school studies, especially in France, that enables successful candidates to enter university **2.** a bachelor's degree (*formal*) [Mid-17C. Directly or via French < medieval Latin *baccalaureatus* < *baccalaureus* 'bachelor']

baccarat /bákə raa, -raà/ *n* a gambling card game in which the winning hand is the one that totals nine points or is closest to nine points without exceeding it [Mid-19C. < French *baccara*]

baccate /bák ayt/ *adj* resembling a berry in shape [Early 19C. < Latin *baccatus* < *bacca* 'berry']

Bacchae /bákee/ *npl* in ancient Greek and Roman religion, the priestesses and women who participated in the orgiastic rites of Bacchus [Early 20C. Via Latin < Greek *Bakkhai*, plural of *Bakkhē* 'priest of Bacchus' < *Bakkhos* 'Bacchus']

bacchanal /bákə náll/ *n* **1.** PARTICIPANT IN ORGIASTIC RITES a participant in the orgiastic rites of Bacchanalia **2.** LOUD DRUNK a riotous drunken reveller (*literary*) **3.** DRUNKEN PARTY a noisy drunken celebration or spree (*literary*) **4.** *Carib* LIVELY PARTY an enjoyably riotous party or occasion, especially with vigorous dancing, drinking, and activities **5.** *Carib* OUT-OF-CONTROL EVENT an event or an occasion that has become uncontrolled and argumentative **6.** *Carib* PUBLIC OUTCRY

scandal or uproar over immoral behaviour ■ *adj* OF BACCHUS relating to Bacchus or the worship of Bacchus [Mid-16C. < Latin *bacchanalis* 'of Bacchus' < *Bacchus* 'Bacchus']

bacchanalia /bákə náyli ə/ *npl* riotous drunken revels [Late 16C. < Latin, plural of *bacchanalis* (see BACCHANAL)] —**bacchanalian** *adj*

Bacchanalia *n* in ancient Rome, festivities in honour of Bacchus that involved orgiastic rites (*takes a singular or plural verb*) —**Bacchanalian** *adj*

bacchant /bákənt/ *n* in ancient Greece or Rome, a priest or other devotee of Bacchus [Late 16C. Via French *bacchante* < Latin *bacchant-*, present participle of *bacchari* 'celebrate the feast of Bacchus' < *Bacchus* 'Bacchus']

bacchante /bə kánti/ *n* in ancient Greece or Rome, a priestess or woman devotee of Bacchus [Late 18C. < French *bacchante* (see BACCHANT)]

bacchantic /bə kántik/ *adj* relating to the worship of Bacchus and the orgiastic rites associated with it

bacchic /bákik/ *adj* characterized by riotous drunkenness (*literary*)

Bacchic /bákik/ *adj* relating to Bacchus

bacchius /ba kī́ əss/ (*plural* **-i** /-ī/) *n* a metrical foot of one short syllable followed by two long ones [Late 16C. Via Latin < Greek *bakkheios (pous)* 'Bacchic (foot)' < *Bakkhos* 'Bacchus']

Bacchus /bákəss/ *n* in Greek and Roman mythology, the god of wine, identified with the Greek god Dionysus and the Roman god Liber. He was worshipped with orgiastic and ecstatic rites. [Via Latin < Greek *Bakkhos*]

Bacchus Marsh /bákəss-/ town in Victoria, southeastern Australia. Population: 9,689 (1991).

bacciferous /bak síffərəss/ *adj* describes plants that produce berries [Mid-17C. < Latin *baccifer* 'bearing berries' < *bacca* 'berry']

baccy /báki/ *n regional* same as **tobacco** [Early 19C. Shortening and alteration]

bach[1] /bach/, **batch** (*informal*) *vi* (**baches, baching, bached; batches, batching, batched**) *ANZ, US* to live alone as a single man and keep house for yourself ■ *n NZ* a cottage or holiday home [Mid-19C. Shortening of BACHELOR]

bach[2] /baakh, baak/ *n Wales* used as an affectionate form of address to a man or boy, alone or after somebody's name ○ *Alan bach, how are you?* [Late 19C. < Welsh, 'small']

REGIONAL NOTE Terms of endearment are often carried over into English by speakers of other mother tongues. We see it with Welsh *bach* and *fach*, literally 'small' and implying 'loved one', and with Irish *alannah*, literally 'child' but suggesting 'darling'. ***Bach*** is often replaced by *boy*, as in *There's nice for you, boy.*

Bach /baak, baakh/, **C. P. E.** (1714–88) German composer. The son of Johann Sebastian Bach, he composed numerous concertos and sonatas as well as chamber and church music. He also wrote *The True Art of Clavier Playing* (1753). Full name **Bach, Carl Philipp Emanuel**. Known as **Berlin Bach, Hamburg Bach**

Bach, J. C. (1735–82) German composer. The youngest son of Johann Sebastian Bach and a composer of church music and operas, he settled in London (1762) and was musician to Queen Charlotte. Full name **Bach, Johann Christian**. Known as **London Bach, English Bach**

AKG London

Johann Sebastian Bach

Bach, Johann Sebastian (1685–1750) German composer and organist. Known as a supreme master of counterpoint, he wrote many organ works, chamber and keyboard works, and oratorios, and over 295 cantatas. His works include the *Brandenburg Concertos* (1720–21) and *St Matthew Passion* (1727).

Bach, W. F. (1710–84) German composer. He led a dissolute life despite being a gifted organist and composer. He was the eldest son of Johann Sebastian Bach. Full name **Bach, Wilhelm Friedemann**. Known as **Halle Bach**

bachcha /búchə/ *n S Asia* **1.** a child or young adult **2.** a naive or immature person [< Hindi *baccā* 'child']

bachelor /báchələr/ *n* **1.** UNMARRIED MAN a man who is not or has never been married **2.** HIST YOUNG KNIGHT a young knight in feudal times who served under the banner of another knight or a great lord **3.** MARINE BIOL YOUNG MALE SEAL a young male seal, especially a fur seal, that older male seals keep from having access to breeding grounds [13C. Via Old French *bacheler* 'young man aspiring to knighthood' < assumed Vulgar Latin *baccalaris*] —**bachelordom** *n* —**bachelorhood** *n* —**bachelorship** *n*

bachelorette /báchələ rét/ *n US* a young woman who has never been married

bachelorette party *n N Am* same as **hen party**

bachelor girl *n* a young unmarried woman, usually one who is self-supporting (*dated*)

Bachelor of Arts *n* a college or university degree awarded to somebody who has successfully completed an undergraduate course in an aspect of the arts or humanities

Bachelor of Letters *n* a university degree awarded to somebody who has successfully completed a postgraduate course in an aspect of the arts or humanities [Translation of Latin *Baccalaureus Litterarum*]

Bachelor of Literature *n* **1.** EDUC same as **Bachelor of Letters 2.** especially in South Asia, a college or university degree awarded to somebody who has successfully completed an undergraduate course in literary studies

Bachelor of Science *n* a college or university degree awarded to somebody who has successfully completed an undergraduate course in an aspect of the sciences or technology

Bachelor of Surgery *n* a university degree awarded to somebody who has successfully completed an undergraduate course in medicine [Translation of Latin *Chirurgiae Baccalaureus*]

bachelor pad *n* a flat where an unmarried man lives alone. N Am term **bachelor apartment**

bachelor party *n NZ, N Am* a party that is given for a man on the night before his wedding and that is usually attended only by men. UK term **stag night**. Aus term **buck's party**

bachelor's degree *n* a degree awarded on the successful completion of an undergraduate course at a college or university and, at some universities, on completion of a usually short postgraduate course

Bach flower remedies /bách-/ *npl* a healing method using extracts of 38 flowers, each treating a different emotional disorder, to promote physical health [Late 20C. After Edward *Bach* (1886–1936), British physician]

Bach trumpet /baak-, baakh-/ *n* a modern valve trumpet, smaller than an ordinary trumpet, specially designed for playing the high-pitched trumpet parts in baroque music [After J. S. BACH]

bacillary /bə sílləri/ *adj* **1.** relating to or caused by rod-shaped bacteria (**bacilli**) **2.** shaped like a small rod, or consisting of small rod-shaped parts

bacillus /bə sílləss/ (*plural* **-li** /-síl ī/) *n* an aerobic, rod-shaped, spore-producing bacterium. Bacilli occur mainly in chains and include many saprophytes, some parasites, and the bacterium that causes anthrax. Genus: *Bacillus*. [Late 19C. < late Latin, 'little rod' < *baculus* 'rod, stick']

bacitracin /bássi tráyssin/ *n* an antibiotic produced by a strain of bacterium. Use: topically, in the treatment of skin infections. [Mid-20C. < BACILLUS + Margaret *Tracy*, in whom the substance was discovered in a wound]

back /bak/ *n* **1.** ANAT REAR PART OF BODY the rear part of the human body between the neck and the pelvis ○ *carrying a baby on her back* ○ *back pain* **2.** ANAT SPINE the spinal column **3.** ANAT AREA OF VERTEBRATE'S BODY the area of a vertebrate animal's body on each side of the backbone **4.** PART AT REAR the part that is at the rear of something or is furthest from the front ○ *Someone at the back of the crowd called out.* **5.** SIDE NOT USUALLY SEEN the side of something such as a sheet of paper or a photograph that carries less information or is away from the viewer **6.** PART OF GARMENT the part of a garment designed to cover the wearer's back **7.** PART OF PIECE OF FURNITURE the part of a seat designed to support somebody's spine **8.** PART TO WHICH PAGES ARE FIXED the part of a book where the pages are glued or stitched to the binding **9.** SPORTS DEFENSIVE PLAYER a player in sports such as soccer or hockey whose role is mainly to prevent the other team from scoring ■ *adv* **1.** IN REVERSE DIRECTION in the opposite direction to the one in which somebody or something was previously facing or travelling ○ *She looked back over her shoulder.* **2.** AT DISTANCE at a distance from where something is situated or taking place ○ *Stay back, the dog might bite.* **3.** IN RESERVE as a reserve or supply kept for future use ○ *I kept back part of the proceeds.* **4.** SO AS TO UNCOVER SOMETHING away from something so as to leave something else uncovered or revealed ○ *roll back the carpet* **5.** SO AS TO RECLINE in or into a reclining position ○ *Sit back and relax.* **6.** IN OR INTO PAST used to indicate a time in the past ○ *Back then, people grew their own food.* ○ *It happened about three weeks back.* **7.** TO MORE DISTANT TIME used to indicate movement in time away from the present ○ *will put the clocks back* ○ *postponed the wedding and moved it back to next year* **8.** TO ORIGINAL OWNER to or into the keeping of the original or former owner or possessor ○ *You can have it back now, because I've finished with it.* **9.** IN RETURN as a reaction or response to something ○ *She called me while I was out, so I called her back.* **10.** INDICATES DIRECTION AND DISTANCE in the distance behind something, especially somebody's present position ○ *We passed it about two miles back.* **11.** RETURNED TO CONDITION OR TOPIC used to indicate a return to a state, situation, or subject of discussion ○ *to get back to your point* **12.** INTO POPULARITY AGAIN into fashion or popularity again ○ *The 1960s are back, and short skirts are back with them.* ■ *adj* **1.** LOCATED AT REAR located at the rear of something, or at the part furthest from the front ○ *Use the back entrance.* ○ *a back room* **2.** ISSUED EARLIER published or issued at an earlier date ○ *a back issue* **3.** REMAINING FROM EARLIER TIME due at or owed from an earlier date ○ *paid the back taxes in full* **4.** LOCATED AWAY FROM MAIN ROADS located away from the main roads or the centre of a town ○ *a quiet back street* **5.** REMOTE situated away from the main centres of population or activity ○ *explored the back areas of the valley* **6.** REVERSE moving in an opposite direction to the usual one **7.** PHON FORMED AT REAR OF MOUTH formed at or towards the rear of the mouth, as the vowel in 'ball' is ○ *a back vowel* ■ *v* (**backs, backing, backed**) **1.** *vti* MOVE BACKWARDS to move backwards, or make somebody or something move backwards ○ *The vehicle in front backed into me.* **2.** *vt* SUPPORT PERSON OR CAUSE to give a person or cause financial, political, or moral support **3.** *vt* BET ON OUTCOME OF RACE to bet money on the person, team, or animal thought likely to win a race or competition **4.** *vt* PROVIDE PROOF TO SUPPORT SOMETHING to provide evidence or proof in support of a statement ○ *But can they back their allegations?* **5.** *vt* REINFORCE SOMETHING to reinforce something by adding a support or backing (*often passive*) ○ *coloured paper backed with cardboard* **6.** *vt* BE BEHIND SOMETHING to be situated behind something (*usually passive*) ○ *a lake backed by a range of mountains* **7.** *vt* MUSIC PROVIDE MUSICAL ACCOMPANIMENT FOR SOMEBODY to provide an instrumental or vocal accompaniment for the main performer of a piece of popular music or jazz **8.** *vi* METEOROL CHANGE DIRECTION to change direction, moving in an anticlockwise direction (*refers to winds*) [Old English *bæc* < Germanic] ◇ **back and fill 1.** to adjust the sails of a vessel to allow the wind to move in and out of them in an alternating manner while manoeuvring in a narrow channel **2.** to dither or vacillate in actions or decision-making ◇ **back of** *N Am* at the back of or behind something ◇ **behind somebody's back** when somebody is not present ◇ **be** *or* **get on somebody's back** to criticize or pressurize somebody (*slang*) ◇ **get off somebody's back** (*slang*) **1.** to stop criticizing or pressurizing somebody **2.** to make somebody feel annoyed or defensive ◇ **get your back up** to become annoyed or angry (*informal*) ◇ **have your back to the wall** to be in a very difficult situation,

with little chance of getting out of it ◇ **in back (of something)** *N Am* at the back of or behind something (*informal*) ◇ **know something like the back of your hand** to know something extremely well ○ *He knew the city like the back of his hand, having lived there for nearly 50 years.* ◇ **put somebody's back up** to annoy or antagonize somebody (*informal*) ◇ **put your back into something** to put effort, especially physical strength, into doing something ◇ **stab somebody in the back** to do or say something harmful to somebody after pretending to be a friend ○ *After promising not to tell anyone, he stabbed me in the back and went to the press.* ◇ **the back of beyond** a remote inaccessible place that has few amenities ○ *They bought a small cottage in the back of beyond, just to get away from it all.* ◇ **turn your back on somebody** or **something** to ignore or reject somebody or something ◇ **you scratch my back, I'll scratch yours** if you help me, I will help you in return (*often refers to unofficial or dishonest business dealings*)

USAGE Movement in time: *Back* as it applies to the past refers to a change to an earlier time. *They have moved its estimated date of origin back a hundred years* would mean a change from, say, AD 1000 to AD 900. As the word applies to the future, however, it usually signifies a change to a later time: *The forecast is for rain, so let's move the picnic back a week.* What the two uses have in common is movement in time away from the present. *Forward* in future contexts is used less consistently than *back*; it is best avoided. All these words become particularly confusing when the subject is, for example, a decision, now in the past, about what was at the time the future: *Last month she told me she wanted to move my appointment back.* In a context like this, *make earlier* or *make later* is clearer.

---

back away *vi* **1.** to walk backwards away from somebody or something, usually because of fear **2.** to withdraw from a situation or previous position ○ *We think they'll back away from any direct confrontation over sanctions.*

back down *vi* to abandon a claim, opinion, or commitment because of the degree of opposition it arouses

back off *vi* **1.** to move away backwards **2.** to stop putting pressure on somebody to do something

back out *v* **1.** *vi* to withdraw from a previous commitment ○ *The buyer backed out before the papers were signed.* **2.** *vti* to move out backwards, or cause something to move out backwards

back up *v* **1.** *vt* SUPPORT SOMEBODY to provide support for a person or idea ○ *I'm sure you'll back me up on this.* **2.** *vt* PROVE STATEMENT to supply proof that a statement is true ○ *Evidence of growth is backed up by recent economic statistics.* **3.** *vt* COMPUT COPY COMPUTER FILES to make a copy of computer data to keep in case anything goes wrong with the original **4.** *vti* GO BACKWARDS to go or move something backwards **5.** *vti* ACCUMULATE to build up, or cause something to build up, especially because normal flow is obstructed ○ *Traffic was backed up three miles from the accident.* **6.** *vt* PRINTING PRINT OTHER SIDE OF SHEET to print the other side of a sheet that has already been printed on one side **7.** *vi* CRICKET START TO RUN EARLY to begin moving down the wicket towards the receiving batsman in anticipation of a run before the ball is bowled

backache /bák ayk/ *n* an ache or pain affecting the back, most commonly the lower back

back-alley *adj* performed illegally or secretly by an unskilled or untrained person

back-and-forth *n N Am* the repeated exchange of ideas, opinions, or information

back bacon *n* a cut of bacon that provides very lean rashers, from the back of the pig in front of the rear haunches

backbeat /bák beet/ *n* a loud rhythmic beat occurring on the off beats of a bar of music, used especially in rock

backbench /bák bench/ *n UK, ANZ, Can* **1.** AREA FOR MPS NOT IN GOVERNMENT a rear bench in a legislative assembly reserved for backbenchers (*usually used in the plural*) **2.** GROUP OF MPS the group of backbenchers in a legislative assembly (*often used in the plural*) ■ *adj* OF BACKBENCHERS relating to backbenchers

backbencher /bák bénchər/ *n UK, ANZ, Can* a member of the lower house of a legislative assembly who is not a government minister or an official Opposition spokesperson

backbend /bák bend/ *n* an exercise in gymnastics in which somebody bends over backwards from a standing position until the hands touch the floor

backbite /bák bīt/ (**-bites, -biting, -bit** /-bit/, **-bitten** /-bitt'n/ or **-bit**) *vti* to make spiteful or slanderous comments about somebody who is not present — **backbiter** *n*

backblocks /bák bloks/, **back blocks** *npl ANZ* a remote area far from the main population centres [Late 19C. Originally a block of land farther than others from water or grass]

backboard /bák bawrd/ *n* **1.** a board that forms the back of something such as a cart or boat **2.** in basketball, the vertical board situated behind the basket that serves to rebound the ball into the basket or onto the court

back boiler *n* a water tank or set of pipes placed behind a fireplace so that a domestic fire will also heat water

backbone /bák bōn/ *n* **1.** ANAT same as **spinal column** **2.** SOMETHING SIMILAR TO SPINAL COLUMN something that is similar in shape or position to a spinal column ○ *the Pennine Hills, the backbone of England* **3.** CENTRAL SUPPORTING PART the part of an organization or system that is its strongest unifying factor and main support ○ *the working people who are the backbone of the nation* **4.** FORTITUDE strength of character and determination ○ *He doesn't have the backbone to stand up to his critics.* **5.** ONLINE HIGH-SPEED RELAY a high-speed relay that feeds smaller channels in corporate computer networks and the Internet **6.** COMPUT CORE OF ELECTRONIC NETWORK the core of an electronic network, e.g. a physical cable connection or a routing protocol

back boundary line *n* on a badminton court, either of two lines parallel to the net that mark the rear limit of the playing area

backbreaker /bák braykər/ *n* **1.** in wrestling, a hold in which somebody's back is bent backwards over the opponent's knee or shoulder **2.** an exhausting or physically demanding task (*informal*)

backbreaking /bák brayking/ *adj* involving enormous physical effort

backburn /bák burn/ (**-burns, -burning, -burnt** /-burnt/ or **-burned**) *vt ANZ* **1.** to prevent a bushfire from spreading by lighting another fire in its path **2.** to clear an area of bush or grassland by setting fire to it into or against the wind

back burner ◇ **put something on the back burner** to assign something a lower priority or give something less prominence ○ *The project has been put on the back burner.*

back catalog *n* US spelling of **back catalogue**

back catalogue *n* the complete collection of recordings, films, or books made by an artist or a company to date

back channel *n* a covert way of exchanging sensitive information in politics or diplomacy that circumvents the usual procedures

backchat /bák chat/ *n* rude or impertinent answers or comments ○ *I don't want any backchat if he asks you whether you like school.* N Am term **back talk**

backcheck /bák chek/ (**-checks, -checking, -checked**) *vti* in ice hockey, to skate back towards your own goal while trying to block an opponent with your body or stick, or block an opponent while doing this —**backchecker** *n*

backcloth /bák kloth/ *n* THEATRE same as **backdrop** (sense 2)

backcomb /bák kōm/ (**-combs, -combing, -combed**) *vt UK* to comb hair with quick short movements towards the roots so that it stands up away from the head and can be brushed into a bouffant hairstyle. ANZ, N Am term **tease**

back copy *n* same as **back number**

back country *n ANZ, N Am* a remote, sparsely populated rural area, often used for various forms of outdoor recreation, including backpacking and camping

backcountry snowboarding *n* snowboard riding that, like off-piste skiing, is done away from resorts or marked terrain

backcourt /bák kawrt/ *n* **1.** REAR OF COURT in tennis, the area between the baseline and the service line of a

court, or in similar games, the area of a court nearest the back boundary line or back wall **2.** DEFENDED HALF OF BASKETBALL COURT in basketball, the half of a court where the basket being defended is located **3.** DEFENSIVE PLAYERS in basketball, the players who defend the backcourt

back crawl *n* SWIMMING same as **backstroke** (sense 1)

backcross /bák kross/ *vt* (**-crosses, -crossing, -crossed**) CROSS HYBRID WITH PARENT to cross an organism, especially a hybrid, with one of its parents or an individual genetically identical to that parent ■ *n* **1.** HYBRID OBTAINED BY BACKCROSSING a hybrid obtained by backcrossing organisms **2.** ACT OF BACKCROSSING the act or the process of backcrossing organisms

backdam /bák dam/ *n Carib* **1.** a dam marking the rear boundary of a plantation **2.** an area beyond the plantation fields used by labourers to grow crops

backdate /bák dayt/ (**-dates, -dating, -dated**) *vt* **1.** to put a date on a document that is earlier than the actual date of its writing or signing **2.** to make an agreement or document valid from an earlier date than the present date

back dive *n* a dive made when the diver's back is facing the water

back door *n* **1.** REAR DOOR a door or entrance at the rear of a building **2.** DISHONEST ADVANTAGE underhand or indirect access that gives somebody an unfair advantage **3.** COMPUT DELIBERATE GAP IN SECURITY SYSTEM an opening deliberately left in a security system to allow access for technicians

backdoor /bák dawr/ *adj* carried out in secrecy or in a surreptitious way ○ *There's been a lot of backdoor pressure on her to step down.* ■ *n* another spelling of **back door** (sense 2)

backdown /bák down/ *n* the abandonment of a course of action or an opinion in the face of opposition from other people

backdrop /bák drop/ *n* **1.** a setting or context ○ *The ski-jumping took place against the backdrop of jagged mountain peaks.* **2.** a large painted cloth hung at the back of a stage that usually depicts the setting in which the action of a scene takes place

backed /bakt/ *adj* having a back, backing, or support (*often used in combination*) ○ *a UN-backed conference on biodiversity*

back EMF *n* an electromagnetic force that opposes any change of current in an inductive circuit

back emission *n* the production of electrons from the anode of a vacuum tube

back end *n* **1.** a main processing computer, often with a smaller interactive computer **2.** a software program that controls operations not specified by the user **3.** *regional* same as **fall** *n* (sense 6), autumn

back end load *n* a unit trust sales charge paid when shares are sold

backer /bákər/ *n* **1.** somebody who gives moral or financial support to somebody or something **2.** somebody who bets on somebody or something

---

SYNONYMS *backer, angel, guarantor, patron, sponsor*

CORE MEANING: somebody who provides financial support

backer a person who gives moral or financial support ○ *The project's main backer has withdrawn his support.* **angel** a person who provides financial support for an enterprise such as a theatrical venture ○ *Business angels pump money into private companies in return for shares.* **guarantor** a person who gives a legal undertaking to be responsible for somebody else's debts or obligations ○ *My father acted as guarantor for the loan.* **patron** a person who gives financial or moral support to a person, institution, or charity, especially in the arts ○ *kings who were great patrons of the arts* ○ *a 21-year-old architect who apparently spent all his patron's money* **sponsor** a person or organization that contributes money to help fund an event, usually in return for publicity, or gives money to a person taking part in a fundraising activity ○ *looking for sponsors for her next project* ○ *We would like to thank our sponsors for donating the prizes.*

---

backfield /bák feeld/ *n* **1.** AREA OF FIELD in American football, the area of the playing field behind the line of scrimmage **2.** PLAYERS the players who line up behind the line of scrimmage **3.** POSITIONS the pos-

---

itions of the players who line up behind the line of scrimmage

backfile /bák fīl/ *n* an archive consisting of previous issues of a newspaper or magazine

backfill /bákfil/ *vt* (-fills, -filling, -filled) to refill a trench or other excavation with the soil dug out of it ■ *n* the soil used to refill a trench

backfire /bák fīr/ *vi* (-fires, -firing, -fired) **1.** HAVE OPPOSITE EFFECT to have an effect opposite to the one intended ○ *The policy of mandatory testing may well backfire and do more harm than good.* **2.** AUTOMOT MAKE EXPLOSION IN EXHAUST PIPE to produce an explosion of prematurely ignited fuel in an internal-combustion engine, or of unburnt exhaust gases in the exhaust pipe **3.** FORESTRY START FIRE TO CREATE FIREBREAK to start a fire in the path of an advancing fire in a forest in order to halt its advance ■ *n* **1.** AUTOMOT EXPLOSION IN CAR EXHAUST an explosion of prematurely ignited fuel in an internal-combustion engine or of unburnt exhaust gases in the exhaust pipe **2.** FORESTRY FIRE STARTED TO CREATE FIREBREAK a fire deliberately started in a forest in order to clear the ground in front of an advancing fire to halt its advance

backflip /bák flip/ *n* a backward midair somersault with the arms and legs extended, performed in gymnastics, diving, and board sports such as skateboarding and snowboarding

backflow /bák flō/ *n* the flowing back of something towards the source

back-formation *n* **1.** a process of word formation in which a new word is coined by removing a real or imagined affix from an existing word **2.** a word formed by back-formation, e.g. 'greed' from 'greedy', or 'televise' from 'television'

back four *n* in football, a defensive formation that consists of two wing backs and two centre backs deployed in a straight line across the field

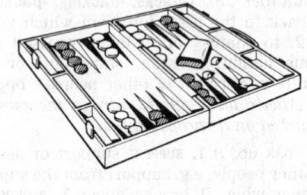

backgammon

backgammon /bák gamən/ *n* **1.** a board game for two players who move pieces according to throws of a pair of dice, the object being to remove all one player's counters from the board **2.** the most complete form of victory in backgammon. It occurs when a player removes all 15 pieces while the other still has a piece furthest from the point at which he or she can remove pieces from the board. [Mid-17C. < BACK + *gamen*, early form of GAME¹; probably from the pieces sometimes being put 'back' on the table]

background /bák grownd/ *n* **1.** PERSONAL CIRCUMSTANCES AND EXPERIENCES the personal circumstances and experiences that shape somebody's life, e.g. ethnic and social origins, upbringing, education, and work experience ○ *a group of people from very different backgrounds* **2.** CAUSES OF EVENT the circumstances leading up to an event that explain its cause ○ *The meeting takes place against a background of rising tension.* **3.** AREA BEHIND SOMETHING the area that is behind something, forming the setting for it ○ *A silvery lake shone against a background of tall dark firs.* **4.** PART OF PICTURE the part of a picture or pattern that appears to be in the distance or behind the most important part **5.** INFORMATION information that helps to explain what somebody or something is like or why something is happening **6.** INCONSPICUOUS POSITION a position of relative inconspicuousness or unimportance ○ *working tirelessly in the background* **7.** COMPUT LOW-PRIORITY COMPUTER ENVIRONMENT the low-priority environment in computers that can perform multiple tasks **8.** PHYS same as **background radiation 9.** ELECTRONICS, ACOUSTICS SIGNAL CAUSING DISTORTION OR INTERFERENCE an extraneous signal, often in

the form of electronic or acoustic noise, that can cause distortion or affect an instrument reading (*often used before a noun*) ○ *background interference* ■ *adj* **1.** AS PART OF BACKGROUND situated or depicted in, or forming part of, the background to something **2.** ACCOMPANYING functioning or suitable as an accompaniment to something else

background music *n* music used as an accompaniment to action or dialogue in a film, or to create a pleasant atmosphere for an activity or a public place

background noise *n* noise that is sufficiently loud to be heard but not so loud as to obscure what is actually being listened to

background processing *n* execution of computer tasks that continues while the user is working with another application. Once started, background tasks such as printing or copying data take place without user input.

background radiation *n* low-level radiation occurring naturally as a result of radioactivity present in the air, soil, and buildings and other structures

backhand /bák hand/ *n* **1.** RACKET GAMES BACKHANDED STROKE in tennis and other racket games, a stroke made with the back of the hand turned towards the ball or shuttlecock as the arm moves outwards from a position across the body **2.** RACKET GAMES SIDE FOR BACKHANDS the side of a tennis or other racket court, or of the body, on which a player would naturally play a backhand. It is the left-hand side for a right-handed player. **3.** HANDWRITING SLOPING LEFTWARDS a style of handwriting in which the letters slope to the left ■ *adj* **1.** RACKET GAMES WITH BACK OF HAND TOWARDS BALL in tennis and other racket games, used to describe a stroke carried out with the back of the hand towards the ball or shuttlecock, usually with the arm across the body **2.** DONE WITH BACKHANDED MOVEMENT carried out with the back of the hand turned towards the direction of any movement ■ *adv* WITH BACKHAND STROKE with the back of the hand facing in the direction in which a stroke, movement, or blow is made ■ *vt* (-hands, -handing, -handed) **1.** SPORTS CONTACT BALL WITH BACKHAND to strike a ball with a backhand stroke ○ *She backhanded the ball just over the net.* **2.** HIT SOMEBODY WITH BACK OF HAND to hit somebody or something with the back of the hand ○ *accidentally backhanded an opponent*

backhanded /bák hándid/ *adj* **1.** WITH BACK OF HAND carried out with the back of the hand, or with the back of the hand facing in the direction in which the stroke, movement, or blow is made ○ *a backhanded return* **2.** WITH DOUBLE MEANING with a doubtful or double meaning, especially one that can be understood equally as a compliment or as an insult ○ *a backhanded compliment* **3.** WRITTEN WITH LETTERS SLOPING LEFTWARDS written in a style of handwriting in which the letters slope to the left ■ *adv* WITH BACKHANDED STROKE with the back of the hand, or with the back of the hand facing in the direction in which a stroke, movement, or blow is made

backhander /bák handər/ *n* **1.** BACKHANDED BLOW a blow struck with the back of the hand ○ *caught the opposing team member with a terrific backhander across the face during hard play* **2.** RACKET GAMES same as **backhand** *n* (sense 1) **3.** BRIBE an illicit payment made as a bribe (*informal*) **4.** BACKHANDED COMPLIMENT a backhanded compliment or veiled verbal attack on somebody (*informal*)

backhoe /bák hō/ *n* a digging machine or attachment consisting of a hinged scoop attached to a jointed mechanical arm that drags the scoop back towards the tractor from which it is operated

backing /báking/ *n* **1.** SUPPORT OR HELP active approval, support, or help, often in financial form, given to a person, organization, or cause **2.** SUPPORTERS the people or organizations giving support to a person or cause **3.** REAR SURFACE material forming or covering the back of something, especially to strengthen, stiffen, or protect it **4.** MUSICAL ACCOMPANIMENT the music or singing that accompanies the playing or singing of the main performer of a piece of popular music or jazz

backing track *n* a recorded musical accompaniment for use by a solo performer

back issue *n* NZ, N Am a previous issue of a magazine or newspaper. UK, Aus term **back number**

back kitchen *n* a pantry or other small room off a kitchen (*informal*)

backlash /bák lash/ *n* **1.** STRONG REACTION a strong adverse reaction among a group of people to an event, development, or trend, especially one that benefits another group **2.** VIOLENT BACKWARD MOVEMENT a sudden violent backward jerking movement, e.g. when a cable breaks under strain **3.** MECH ENG RECOIL BETWEEN MACHINE PARTS a jarring recoil that sometimes occurs when worn or badly fitting parts of a mechanism come together **4.** MECH ENG PLAY BETWEEN MACHINE PARTS excessive play between adjacent parts in a mechanism such as a set of gears, usually as a result of the parts being worn or badly fitted **5.** FISHING TWISTED FISHING LINE a tangle in a fishing line wound on a reel

backless /bákləss/ *adj* with the back cut very low ○ *a backless dress*

backlight /bák līt/ *n* light that illuminates the subject of a photograph or painting from behind ■ *vt* (-lights, -lighting, -lighted or -lit /-lit/) to illuminate a subject from behind —**backlighting** *n*

backlist /bák list/ *n* the range of books already published by a publisher that are still in print ○ *The departing editor had built up a highly respectable backlist.*

backlit past participle, past tense of **backlight**

backlog /bák log/ *n* **1.** a quantity of unfinished business or work that has built up over a period of time and must be dealt with before progress can be made ○ *She faced a backlog of unanswered letters when she came back.* **2.** a large log placed at the back of an open fire

back matter *n* the parts of a book that appear after the main text, e.g. the index or an appendix

backmost /bák mōst/ *adj* farthest back from a specific point ○ *Spectators in the backmost seats couldn't hear a thing.*

back mutation *n* the reversion of a mutated gene to its original form

back number *n* **1.** a previous issue of a magazine or newspaper. NZ, N Am term **back issue 2.** a person or thing considered to be out of date (*informal*)

back o' Bourke /bák ə búrk/, **back of Bourke** *adv* Aus in an extremely remote or undeveloped place [*Bourke*, the most remote town in W New South Wales]

back office *n* **1.** BUSINESS OPERATIONS OTHER THAN POLICYMAKING the business operations performed by people who do not make policy, or the place where they work **2.** SECURE AREA OF SOFTWARE a secure area of e-commerce software where details of store properties, tax tables, and products are held ■ *adj* RELATING TO INTERNAL MATTERS relating to or concerned with the administration and internal workings of a business organization rather than its contacts with the public

backpack

backpack /bák pak/ *n* **1.** HIKERS' KNAPSACK a large canvas bag, often on a metal frame, worn on the back and used by walkers **2.** STUDENTS' BOOK BAG a knapsack used to carry schoolbooks, school supplies, or personal items **3.** EQUIPMENT CARRIED ON BACK a carrier for a piece of equipment such as an astronaut's personal life-support system that is designed to be strapped on the user's back ■ *v* (-packs, -packing, -packed) **1.** *vi* HIKE WITH BACKPACK to travel, especially hike, carrying belongings or supplies in a backpack ○ *She spent a month backpacking in the outback.* **2.** *vt* CARRY SOMETHING ON BACK to transport something, usually equipment or supplies, in a pack on the back ○

astronauts backpacking oxygen during a spacewalk —**backpacker** *n*

back pain *n* persistent pain in part of the back

back pass *n* in football, a pass from an outfield player back to the goalkeeper. Goalkeepers are forbidden to handle back passes with their hands.

back passage *n* the anal canal (*informal*)

back pay *n* pay that is owed to an employee for work done before the current payment period and is either overdue or results from a backdated pay increase

backpedal /bák ped'l/ (**-als, -alling, -alled**) *v* **1.** *vti* **PEDAL BACKWARDS** to turn the pedals of a bicycle backwards in order to operate a brake **2.** *vi* **MOVE BACKWARDS** in sports, to move quickly backwards in order to get away from an opponent or to catch a ball **3.** *vi* **RETRACT STATEMENT** to try to escape the consequences of a statement or action by retracting it, modifying it, or toning it down

backplate /bák playt/ *n* a piece of armour protecting the back

back pocket *n* in Australian Rules football, either of two defenders playing in the back line of defence on each side of the fullback

back pressure *n* **1.** **RESISTANT PRESSURE** resistant pressure exerted by a solid, liquid, or gas to the forward motion of a system, especially the pressure opposing the exhaust stroke of a piston in an internal-combustion engine **2.** INDUST **OIL OR GAS PRESSURE** the pressure exerted by fluids in the bore of an oil well on the oil and gas in the reservoir. Careful control of this pressure ensures an even supply of oil. **3.** MED **PRESSURE DUE TO OBSTRUCTION** pressure within a blood vessel or the urinary system that builds up when there is an obstruction to the flow of fluid

back projection *n* the cinematic technique of projecting a film onto a translucent screen from behind, usually to provide a moving background against which other action can be filmed

backrest /bák rest/ *n* a part of a seat designed to support the user's back

backroom /bák room, -ro͝om/ *n also* **back room** a place away from the centre of activities where important and usually secret research or planning is supposed to be carried out ■ *adj also* **back-room** taking place unobtrusively, but usually important or influential nonetheless

back row *n* in rugby union, the players forming the third row of a scrum, traditionally the two wing forwards and the number eight

backsaw /bák saw/ *n* a small saw stiffened and strengthened by a strip of metal on its noncutting edge

backscatter /bák skatər/ *n* **1.** the deflection of radiation or particles through angles of greater than 90 degrees measured with respect to the original direction of travel through a medium **2.** radiation or particles deflected more than 90 degrees while passing through a medium

backscratcher /bák skrachər/ *n* **1.** a long-handled implement, often ending in a claw or hand shape, for scratching your own back **2.** somebody who does favours for others in order to receive similar favours from them (*informal*)

backscratching /bák skraching/ *n* the doing of favours for other people in return for similar favours from them (*informal*) —**backscratch** *vi*

back seat *n* **1.** a seat at the back of a vehicle **2.** a less important or active role ◇ **take a back seat (to somebody)** to allow somebody else to direct or control something while taking on a relatively less important role yourself

back-seat driver *n* (*informal*) **1.** a passenger in a vehicle who continually pesters the driver with unwanted advice or criticism **2.** somebody who gives unwanted advice or criticism while somebody else does something

backset /bák set/ *n* an eddy or a current flowing against the direction of the main current in a body of water

back shift *n UK* **1.** a period of work beginning in the afternoon and ending at night and overlapping with the day shift and the night shift **2.** a group of employees working on a back shift ▶ ANZ, N Am term **swing shift**

backshore /bák shawr/ *n* the area of a shore that is above the high-water mark except in very severe weather

backside /bák sīd, bák sīd/ *n* **1.** **BUTTOCKS** a person's buttocks (*informal*) **2.** *S Asia* **BACK** a person's back **3.** *Malaysia* **REAR OF SOMETHING** the rear part of a vehicle or building

backsight /bák sīt/ *n* **1.** an aiming device on the part of a firearm nearest to the aimer's eye **2.** a reading taken by a surveyor back towards a position from which a previous reading has been made

back slang *n* slang in which words are disguised by being pronounced as if spelt backwards

backslap /bák slap/ (**-slaps, -slapping, -slapped**) *vti* to treat somebody, or treat each other, in a hearty, jovial, and enthusiastically complimentary way, with or without physical slaps on the back ○ *a political candidate who backslapped his way around the country* —**backslapper** *n*

backslash /bák slash/ *n* a keyboard character (\) with various uses in computing and computer programming

USAGE See *slash.*

backslide /bák slīd/ (**-slides, -sliding, -slid** /-slid/, **-slid** /-slid/ or **-slidden** /-slidd'n/) *vi* to fall back into wrongdoing or a bad habit after an attempt to act in a better way —**backslider** *n*

backspace /bák spayss/ (**-spaces, -spacing, -spaced**) *vi* to move the cursor of a computer or the carriage of a typewriter back one or more spaces using the key designed for this purpose

backspin /bák spin/ *n* spin that makes a ball rotate in the opposite direction to its line of movement so that when it lands or strikes something its forward momentum will be reduced

backsplash /bák splash/ *n N Am* same as **splashback**

backstab /bák stab/ (**-stabs, -stabbing, -stabbed**) *vt* to do or say something harmful to somebody after pretending to be a friend [Early 20C. < *stab somebody in the back*] —**backstabber** *n* —**backstabbing** *n*

backstage /bák stáyj/ *adv* **1.** behind the area of a theatre stage that is visible to an audience, e.g. in the areas where stage technicians work or in the dressing rooms ○ *Journalists were allowed backstage to interview the star.* **2.** in private, or out of the view of the general public —**backstage** *adj*

backstairs /bák stairz/ *npl* a set of stairs in a private part of a house, often originally for the use of servants ■ *adj* carried on secretly or furtively

backstay /bák stay/ *n* **1.** something that supports or strengthens the back of something else, e.g. a piece of leather covering the back seam of a shoe **2.** a rope leading backwards from the top of a ship's mast to the side or stern and giving support to the mast

backstitch /bák stich/ *n* a method of stitching in which each new stitch starts from the middle of the previous stitch —**backstitch** *vti*

backstop /bák stop/ *n* **1.** **ADDITIONAL SUPPORT** somebody or something providing additional support or protection in case somebody or something else fails **2.** **SCREEN TO STOP BALL** a screen or barrier to stop a ball travelling out of the playing area **3.** BASEBALL same as **catcher** (sense 2) **4.** MECH ENG **CATCH STOPPING BACKWARD MOVEMENT** a catch on a mechanism often designed as a safeguard to prevent it from moving back too far

back-story *n* **1.** the events that are supposed to have taken place before the action of a film, television programme, or novel begins (*informal*) **2.** MEDIA same as **prequel**

back straight *n* the straight section of a racing circuit opposite the home straight. N Am term **back stretch**

backstreet /bák street/ *n also* **back street** **MINOR STREET** a small street off the main roads in a city or town ■ *adj also* **back-street** **1.** **IN BACKSTREET** situated or taking place in a backstreet **2.** **ILLICIT** carried out furtively or illicitly in a place where it is unlikely to attract public attention

back stretch *n N Am* SPORTS same as **back straight**

backstroke /bák strōk/ *n* **1.** SWIMMING a method of swimming on the back in which the swimmer makes circular backward movements with each arm alternately while kicking the legs rhythmically up and down **2.** MECH ENG a stroke or movement in the opposite direction to that of the original or forward one **3.** *N Am* RACKET GAMES same as **backhand** *n* (sense 1) —**backstroke** *vi* —**backstroker** *n*

backswept /bák swept/ *adj* angled, slanting, or brushed backwards ○ *a backswept hairstyle*

backswing /bák swing/ *n* the backward movement of a player's club, bat, or racket away from the eventual point of contact with the ball in preparation for playing the actual stroke

backsword /bák sawrd/ *n* **1.** a sword with a cutting edge on one side of the blade only **2.** a stick with a basket-shaped hilt used in fencing practice

back talk *n N Am* same as **backchat**

back tax *n* tax due at or owed from an earlier date

back-to-back *adj* **1.** **WITH BACKS TO EACH OTHER** standing or sitting with backs turned to, and sometimes touching, one another **2.** **BUILT CLOSE TOGETHER** describes houses that are built so that their backs join or are only narrowly separated ○ *street after street of back-to-back houses* **3.** **CONSECUTIVE** following immediately one after the other ○ *We had back-to-back meetings prior to the new-product launch.* ■ *n* **HOUSE BUILT BACK TO BACK** a house built with its back touching the back of another house or only narrowly separated from it —**back to back** *adv*

back-to-back loan *n* a loan in which two companies in separate countries borrow each other's currency for a particular period, and repay each other's currency at an agreed rate upon maturity

back to front *adv* with the back part at the front, or in reverse order ○ *I hadn't noticed I'd put my sweater on back to front.*

back-to-nature *adj* relating to or adopting a simple self-sufficient way of life using little modern technology

backtrack /bák trak/ (**-tracks, -tracking, -tracked**) *vi* **1.** to go back in the direction from which you have come **2.** to change, or distance yourself from, a previous action, opinion, statement, or policy, especially as a result of other people's opposition to it ○ *After a lot of public outrage, the government backtracked on its proposed ban.*

backup /bák up/ *n* **1.** **SUPPORT** support or assistance from other people, e.g. support from the supplier of a product when it breaks down **2.** **REINFORCEMENTS** reinforcements to help personnel already committed, especially police officers ○ *The officers at the scene are calling for backup from another force.* **3.** **SUBSTITUTE OR RESERVE** a substitute or reserve that can be used if the thing normally used fails **4.** **SECURITY COPY** a copy of computer data that is stored, e.g. a copy stored on a floppy disk **5.** **COPYING** the procedure for copying computer data with which somebody is working ○ *The backup is done automatically every morning.* **6.** **BUILDUP OF SOMETHING** an excess quantity of something that builds up when normal flow is obstructed ○ *a backup of traffic* —**backup** *adj*

backup light *n N Am* same as **reversing light**

backward /bákwərd/ *adj* **1.** **TOWARDS REAR** facing or turned in the opposite direction to somebody or something **2.** **REVERSED** positioned the opposite way round, arranged in the opposite order, or proceeding in the opposite direction to the normal one **3.** **NOT ACHIEVING USUAL OR EXPECTED STANDARD** lagging behind the progress and development of others of comparable status (*sometimes considered offensive*) ○ *a backward economy* **4.** **RETROGRADE** causing or representing a return to a previous or less advanced, and usually less satisfactory, state ○ *a backward step developmentally* **5.** **TOWARDS PAST** directed towards the past ○ *a backward look over the city's progress during the last century* **6.** **SHY** shy or lacking in self-confidence ■ *adv* same as **backwards** —**backwardly** *adv* —**backwardness** *n* ◇ **not be backward in coming forward** to be quick and eager to present yourself for something, especially to claim something that could benefit you (*informal*)

USAGE **backward** or **backwards**? ***Backward*** is the only form available for the adjective: *a backward glance.* In British, Canadian, Australian, and New Zealand English,

backwards is used more often than **backward** for the adverb: *The vehicle moved slowly backwards/backward.* In American English **backward** is more common for the adverb.

backwardation /bákwər dáysh'n/ *n* **1.** the amount by which the price of goods for immediate delivery differs from the price of goods for delivery at a future time **2.** on the London Stock Exchange, the right to delay delivery of securities purchased by somebody until the next settlement period, or the percentage paid by the seller for this right (*dated*)

backward-looking *adj* more concerned with or relevant to a past state of affairs than the present

backwards /bákwərdz/ *adv* **1.** BACK FIRST with your back or the back of an object facing in the direction in which you move or the object moves ○ *She walked backwards out of the room.* **2.** TOWARDS REAR behind you, or in a direction away from the front of something **3.** WRONG WAY ROUND the opposite way round, or in the reverse order or direction to the usual ○ *The kids are trying to say the alphabet backwards.* **4.** TOWARDS PAST towards or into the past ○ *Critics accused the report of going backwards in time.* **5.** INTO WORSE CONDITION into a state that is worse or less advanced than the previous or original one ○ *Everything's gone backwards since the new committee took over.* ◇ **bend** *or* **fall** *or* **lean over backwards** TRY HARD TO DO SOMETHING to make an exceptional effort to do something, especially to help or please somebody ◇ **know something backwards** to know something very well

backwards compatible *adj* describes a computer hardware or software product that is compatible with its predecessors to the extent that it can use interfaces and data from earlier versions

backwash /bák wosh/ *n* **1.** RETREATING WAVE the movement of water back down a beach after a wave has broken **2.** WATER PUSHED BACKWARDS a backward movement or flow in water produced by a ship's propeller or by oars **3.** AIR PUSHED BACKWARDS a backward rush of air produced by an aircraft propeller or jet engine **4.** CONSEQUENCES the consequential effects of an event or action, especially unpleasant or unsettling ones

backwater /bák wawtər/ *n* **1.** SMALL STAGNANT BRANCH OF RIVER a still body of water connected to a river but not affected by its current **2.** STILL WATER a still body of water held back by a dam, obstruction, or prevailing countercurrent **3.** DULL PLACE a place or situation regarded as cut off from the mainstream of activity and consequently regarded as quiet or unimportant

backwind /bák wind/ (**-winds, -winding, -winded**) *vt* to divert wind from one sail into the back of another

backwoods /bák woŏdz/ *npl* **1.** a sparsely inhabited forested area distant from the main centres of population **2.** an area regarded as remote, rustic, and culturally unsophisticated —**backwoods** *adj*

backwoodsman /bák woŏdzmən/ (*plural* **-men** /-mən/) *n* **1.** somebody who lives in the backwoods **2.** a member of the House of Lords who does not often attend, especially before reforms reduced the number of hereditary peers eligible to sit (*informal*)

backword /bák wurd/ (**-words, -wording, -worded**) *vti regional* to break a promise or commitment to somebody —**backword** *n*

back yard *n* **1.** YARD BEHIND HOUSE a yard behind a house **2.** SOMEBODY'S NEIGHBOURHOOD somebody's immediate neighbourhood, or the area considered as somebody's home ground ○ *The gangs know better than to cause trouble in each other's back yards.* **3.** *N Am* GARDEN a back garden ◇ **not in my back yard** used to object to something unpleasant or dangerous taking place or being located in your neighbourhood

baclava *n* FOOD another spelling of **baklava**

bacon /báykən/ *n* meat from the back and sides of a pig that has been salted, dried, and often smoked [14C. < Old French < Germanic, 'back meat'] ◇ **bring home the bacon** to earn the money on which a family lives (*informal*) ◇ **save somebody's bacon** to save somebody from serious trouble, punishment, injury, or danger (*informal*)

Bacon, /báykən/, **Sir Francis, 1st Baron Verulam and Viscount St Albans** (1561–1626) English philosopher, lawyer, and politician. A pioneer of modern scientific thought, he wrote *The Advancement of Learning* (1605) and *Essayes* (1597–1625). He was Lord Chancellor (1618–21), but was dismissed for bribery.

'Knowledge itself is power.'
[Sir Francis Bacon, 'De Haeresibus (Of Heresies)', *Meditationes Sacrae (Religious Meditations)*; 1597]

'He that will not apply new remedies must expect new evils: for time is the greatest innovator.'
[Sir Francis Bacon, 'Of Innovations', *Essays*; 1597–1625]

Bacon, **Francis** (1909–92) Irish-born British painter. A major late-20th-century artist, he often used gory and shocking imagery, as in *Head Surrounded by Sides of Beef (Study After Velázquez)* (1954).

'How can I take an interest in my work when I don't like it?'
[Attributed to Francis Bacon]

Bacon, **Roger** (1214?–94) English philosopher and scientist. A Franciscan monk, he published works on mathematics, philosophy, and logic, including his *Great Work* (1266–67). He was imprisoned by the Franciscans for his 'novelties'. Known as **Doctor Mirabilis ('Wonderful Doctor')**

'Reasoning draws a conclusion and makes us grant the conclusion, but does not make the conclusion certain, nor does it remove doubt.'
[Roger Bacon, *Opus Maius (Great Work)*; 1266–67]

bacon-and-eggs *n* PLANTS same as **bird's-foot trefoil** [< its yellow flowers streaked with red]

baconer /báykənər/ *n* a pig reared to produce bacon

Baconian /bay kóni ən/ *adj* OF WORKS OF SIR FRANCIS BACON relating to or based on the philosophy of Sir Francis Bacon, particularly his method of inductive reasoning in which the emphasis is placed on collecting instances rather than testing theories ■ *n* **1.** PHILOSOPHY FOLLOWER OF SIR FRANCIS BACON a student or follower of the philosophy of Sir Francis Bacon **2.** LITERAT BELIEVER IN BACON AS AUTHOR OF SHAKESPEARE'S PLAYS somebody who believes that Shakespeare's plays were actually written by Sir Francis Bacon

BACS /baks/ *abbr* Bankers' Automated Clearing Services

bact. *abbr* **1.** bacteria **2.** bacteriology

bacteraemia /báktə réemi ə/ *n* the presence of bacteria in the blood —**bacteraemic** *adj* —**bacteraemically** *adv*

bacteremia *n* MED US spelling of **bacteraemia**

bacteri- *prefix* same as **bacterio-** (*used before vowels*)

bacteria MICROBIOL plural of **bacterium**

bacterial /bak téeri əl/ *adj* consisting of, caused by, or connected with bacteria —**bacterially** *adv*

bacterial artificial chromosome *n* a sequence of DNA taken from another organism and expressed in a bacterium to reveal its function

bactericide /bak téeri sīd/ *n* a substance or agent that destroys bacteria —**bactericidal** *adj*

bacterio- *prefix* bacteria, bacterial ○ *bacteriostat* [< BACTERIUM]

bacteriol. *abbr* bacteriology

bacteriology /bak téeri ólləji/ *n* the scientific study of bacteria, especially in relation to medicine and agriculture —**bacteriological** /bak téeri ə lójjik'l/ *adj* —**bacteriologically** *adv* —**bacteriologist** *n*

bacteriolysis /bak téeri óllississ/ *n* the dissolution or destruction of a bacterial cell, e.g. as a result of the use of a bactericidal agent during disinfection —**bacteriolytic** /bak téeri ə líttik/ *adj*

bacteriophage /bak téeri ə fayj/ *n* a virus that infects bacteria and may integrate into the genetic material of its host cell. Bacteriophages are used as vectors in gene cloning and have other biotechnological uses. —**bacteriophagic** /bak téeri ə fájjik/ *adj* —**bacteriophagous** /bak téeri óffəgəss/ *adj* —**bacteriophagy** /bak téeri óffəji/ *n*

bacterioplankton /bak téeri ō plángktən/ *n* the component of plankton consisting of bacteria —**bacterioplanktonic** /-plangk tónnik/ *adj*

bacteriostasis /bak téeri ō stáyssiss/ *n* inhibition of bacterial growth and multiplication by a chemical agent

bacteriostat /bak téeri ə stat/ *n* a substance that restricts the growth and activity of bacteria without killing them —**bacteriostatic** /bak téeri ə státtik/ *adj* —**bacteriostatically** *adv*

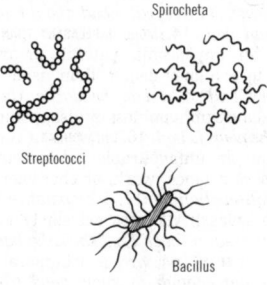

Spirocheta

Streptococci

Bacillus

bacterium

bacterium /bak téeri əm/ (*plural* **-ria** /-ri ə/) *n* a single-celled, often parasitic microorganism without distinct nuclei or organized cell structures. Various species are responsible for decay, fermentation, nitrogen fixation, and many plant and animal diseases. Kingdom: *Eubacteria*. [Mid-19C. < Greek *baktērion* 'little rod' (because the first ones discovered were rod-shaped) < *baktron* 'rod'] —**bacteroid** /báktə royd/ *adj*

USAGE **bacterium** or **bacteria**? *Bacterium* is singular and *bacteria* is plural. The word is more commonly found in the plural, which can lead to its being wrongly treated as a singular noun taking a singular verb.

bacteriuria /bak téeri yoŏri ə/ *n* the presence of bacteria in urine

Bactria /báktriə/ ancient country in Central Asia, in what is now part of Afghanistan, Uzbekistan, and Tajikistan. It was an eastern province of the Persian Empire before its conquest by Alexander the Great in 328 BC. After his death it became a state ruled by his successors, the Seleucids.

Bactrian camel

Bactrian camel /báktri ən-/ *n* a two-humped camel. Native to: Gobi Desert. Latin name: *Camelus bactrianus*. [Early 17C. < Latin *Bactrianus* < *Bactria*, ancient country in central Asia]

baculiform /bə kyoŏli fawrm/ *adj* shaped like a rod [< Latin *baculum* 'rod']

bad /bad/ *adj* (**worse** /wurss/, **worst** /wurst/) **1.** OF POOR QUALITY below an acceptable standard in quality or performance ○ *bad driving* **2.** UNSKILFUL lacking the skill or competence to perform a task adequately ○ *I've always been bad at remembering dates.* **3.** NOT FUNCTIONING PROPERLY not functioning properly because of a fault ○ *bad TV reception* **4.** INCORRECT incorrect according to the normal rules, especially those governing the use of language ○ *used bad grammar in the essay* **5.** WICKED morally evil, blameworthy, or unacceptable ○ *It's how you tell the good guys from the bad guys.* **6.** MISBEHAVING AND DISOBEDIENT troublesome or annoying, usually through rudeness, disobedience, or mischievousness ○ *Bad dog!* **7.** ANGRY AND UNPLEASANT characterized by anger and unpleasantness towards other people ○ *in a bad mood* **8.** OFFENSIVE likely to cause offence to other people because it deals with a taboo subject or expresses violent feelings ○ *swearing and other bad language* **9.** HARMFUL liable to damage health or cause injury ○

Reading in a dim light is bad for the eyes. **10. ROTTEN** deteriorated in quality to the point of being unfit to eat or drink ○ *This milk is bad.* **11. INJURED OR DISEASED** affected by an injury or disease, or not functioning properly, and often causing pain ○ *She's got a bad tooth.* **12. UNWELL** unwell or in pain ○ *I've been feeling bad for a couple of days.* **13. UNEASY** uneasy or regretful about something, or causing somebody to feel this way ○ *I feel really bad about having had to reprimand you.* **14. MORE UNPLEASANT THAN USUAL** possessing an unpleasant, painful, or troublesome quality to a higher degree than usual ○ *Was the pain very bad?* ○ *a bad headache* **15. DISTRESSING** likely to cause unhappiness or disappointment ○ *I'm afraid the news is bad.* **16. UNFAVOURABLE** containing or indicating an unfavourable assessment of somebody's performance, work, or character ○ *received a bad job evaluation* **17.** (*comparative* **badder,** *superlative* **baddest**) **VERY GOOD** extremely good (*slang*; *originally used in Black English*) ○ *the baddest outfit at the party* ■ *n* **1. EVIL** wrong or immoral behaviour ○ *You're old enough to know good from bad.* **2. UNSATISFACTORY OR UNPLEASANT THINGS** things or events that are unsatisfactory or unpleasant ○ *You've got to take the good with the bad.* ■ *adv* (*informal*) **1. BADLY** in an unsatisfactory manner ○ *We didn't do too bad.* **2. VERY MUCH** to an intense or extreme degree ○ *He's got it bad!* [13C. Perhaps < Old English *bæddel* 'effeminate man'] —**baddish** *adj* —**badness** *n* ◇ **go bad** to become rotten or unfit to eat ◇ **go from bad to worse** to become even more unpleasant, unsatisfactory, or morally unacceptable than before ◇ **go to the bad** to adopt or fall into a way of life that other people consider morally or socially debased and unacceptable (*dated*) ◇ **my bad** *US* used to acknowledge that something is your own fault or error (*slang*) ◇ **not bad** fairly good or of a standard that is admitted to be satisfactory, sometimes grudgingly or cautiously, but often in a positive or definitely approving way ○ *That's not bad for a first attempt.*

USAGE See *badly.*

REGIONAL NOTE In many Caribbean pidgins and creoles (forms of language that develop when speakers of different languages have to communicate with each other) *bad* means 'very much, very good', as in: *A laikam bad.* 'I like it very much indeed'. This usage has been popularized in Britain by young people of Afro-Caribbean ancestry: *It's bad, man.* means 'It's really good'. This *bad* is distinguished from traditional *bad* by intonation and often by a lengthening of the vowel. Other words that have undergone a similar transformation are *wicked* and *crucial.*

badam /bə dám/ (*plural same*) *n S Asia* an almond, or almonds processed for use in cooking [< Hindi *badām*]

bad apple *n* somebody thought to be a bad influence on others (*informal*) [< the idea that one bad apple can spoil a whole batch]

badass /bád ass/ *N Am n* a highly offensive term for somebody who is regarded as bad-tempered or aggressive (*taboo insult*) ■ *adj* a highly offensive term meaning tough, intimidating, or powerful (*slang*)

Badawi /bə dáawi/ ♦ **Abdullah**

bad blood *n* an intense and usually long-lasting feeling of hatred, anger, or resentment

bad breath *n* unpleasant-smelling breath

bad cheque *n* a cheque that is invalid because there are insufficient funds in the account to cover it

bad debt *n* a sum of money owed that is unlikely to be repaid

baddie /báddi/, **baddy** (*plural* **-dies**) *n* somebody, especially a character in a film or a novel, who does evil or criminal things (*informal*)

bade past tense of **bid**

Baden-Baden /báad'n báad'n/ resort and spa town in the Black Forest in Baden-Württemberg State, southwestern Germany. Population: 52,570 (1997).

Baden-Powell /báyd'n pów əl, -pố əl/, **Agnes** (1858–1945) British founder of the Girl Guides Association. Together with her brother Robert, she set up the Girl Guides (1910) as the companion organization to the Boy Scouts.

Baden-Powell /báyd'n pówəl, -pố əl/, **Robert, 1st Baron Baden-Powell of Gilwell** (1857–1941) British soldier and founder of the Scout movement. He is famed

for defending Mafeking during the Boer War (1899–1900). Full name **Baden-Powell, Robert Stephenson Smyth**

'Be Prepared...the meaning of the motto is that a scout must prepare himself by previous thinking out and practising how to act on any accident or emergency so that he is never taken by surprise; he knows exactly what to do when anything unexpected happens.'
[Robert Baden-Powell, *Scouting for Boys*; 1908]

Baden-Württemberg /báad'n vúrtəm burg/ state in southwestern Germany. It is bordered to the west by France and to the south by Switzerland. Capital: Stuttgart. Population: 10,426,040 (1998). Area: 35,752 sq. km/13,804 sq. mi.

Bader /báadər/, **Sir Douglas** (1910–82) British fighter pilot. He lost both legs in a flying accident (1931), and later commanded an RAF squadron in World War II. He was knighted (1976) for his work with people with disabilities. Full name **Bader, Sir Douglas Robert Stuart**

'Don't listen to anyone who tells you that you can't do this or that. That's nonsense. Make up your mind you'll never use crutches or a stick, then have a go at everything...never, never let them persuade you that things are too difficult or impossible.'
[Sir Douglas Bader. Quoted in *Flying Colours*, Laddie Lucas; 1980]

bad faith *n* insincerity, especially as evidenced by actions that do not accord with somebody's stated intentions

bad feeling *n* same as **ill feeling**

badge /baj/ *n* **1. EMBLEM** A small distinctive piece of fabric, metal, or plastic worn on clothing to show rank, membership, or personal enthusiasm and support for something **2. IDENTIFYING FEATURE** a characteristic or identifying mark of a particular brand, quality, or type of person ■ *vt* (**badges, badging, badged**) **1. PUT IDENTIFYING MARK ON SOMETHING** to put a badge or a distinctive identifying mark on something **2. PUT BRAND NAME ON SOMETHING** to market a product under different badges or brand names [14C. < Old French *bage*]

badger

badger /bájjər/ *n* a medium-sized burrowing animal that is related to the weasel and has short legs, strong claws, and a thick coat. It usually has black and white stripes on the sides of its head. Subfamily: Melinae. ■ *vt* (**-ers, -ering, -ered**) to pester or annoy somebody continually ○ *kept badgering me to go shopping* [Early 16C. Perhaps < BADGE, because of the markings on its head]

bad guy *n US* same as **baddie** (*informal*)

bad hair *n Carib* hair that is regarded as too tightly curly

bad hair day *n* a day during which somebody experiences a series of difficulties or annoyances (*slang*)

badinage /báddi naazh, -naaj, báddi naazh/ *n* the exchange of playful or joking remarks between people in conversation [Mid-17C. < French < *badin* 'fool, joker' < assumed Vulgar Latin *badare* 'yawn, gape']

badlands /bád landz/ *npl* a barren area of gullies and bare mountain peaks or mesas formed by erosion

bad lot *n* somebody whose character and behaviour

is strongly disapproved of and who is considered to be immoral or pernicious (*dated insult*)

bad luck *n* an unpleasant experience, disappointment, or failure that seems to happen to somebody by chance or undeservedly ■ *interj* used to show sympathy for somebody when something has gone wrong and to suggest that what happened was probably beyond his or her control

badly /báddli/ *adv* (**worse, worst**) **1. POORLY** in an unsatisfactory, incompetent, or incorrect way ○ *The paintwork had been badly finished.* **2. UNHAPPILY** in such a way as to cause suffering, sorrow, or disappointment to the people involved ○ *felt badly about the mistake* **3. SEVERELY** to a degree that causes serious concern for the person or thing involved ○ *Two of the survivors were very badly burned.* **4. VERY MUCH** to a great extent ○ *We're badly in need of new ideas.* **5. WICKEDLY** in a way that is immoral, or that causes trouble, offence, or annoyance to other people ○ *had been behaving badly* **6. REMORSEFULLY** full of remorse or regret ○ *feel badly about it* ■ *adj N England* **ILL** unwell or ill ○ *She's still badly after that accident.*

USAGE badly or **bad**? *Bad* is an adjective; it is also a highly informal adverb meaning 'badly', a usage that has never gained acceptance in formal writing. Avoid sentences like this: *The southeast needs rain bad. My back ached so bad that I thought I would die.* Substitute *badly* for *bad* in all these sentences. Another problem is this: do I use *bad* or *badly* after the verb *feel?* After this verb, use the adjective *bad*, not the adverb *badly* if you mean that you are experiencing, or feeling, physical distress: *After chemotherapy, I felt bad.* On the other hand, if you are experiencing or feeling emotional – not physical – distress, use the adverb *badly*, not the adjective *bad*: *I feel badly about the accident because it was entirely my fault.* In the last example, *badly* works just like some other *-ly* adverbs, for example *strongly* or *emphatically*, in conveying the idea of emotions, as in *The president feels strongly* [not *strong*] *about the need for both sides of the armed conflict to return to the negotiating table. The leaders feel emphatically* [not *emphatic*] *that each side must prove good faith before they will resume their talks.* See also *good* and *well*[2].

badly off (**worse off, worst off**) *adj* **1.** short of money or having a lower than average income (*hyphenated when used before a noun*) ○ *badly-off families* **2.** poorly or inadequately supplied with something ○ *We're badly off for good singers at the moment.*

badmash /búd maash/ *n S Asia* **1.** somebody considered to be aggressive, violent, or evil **2.** used as a term of mock reproof, especially when scolding children ○ *What badmash could have made all this mess?* [Mid-19C. < Urdu < Persian *bad* 'evil' + Arabic *ma'āš* 'means of livelihood']

badminton /bádmintən/ *n* **1.** a game similar to tennis, played usually on an indoor court, using rackets to strike a shuttlecock back and forth across a high net **2.** a long drink based on claret, with sugar and soda water added [Mid-19C. After BADMINTON]

Badminton /bádmintən/ village in southwestern England, known for the country house of the Duke of Beaufort, Badminton House, where horse trials are held annually

badmouth /bád mowth, -mowth/ (**-mouths, -mouthing, -mouthed**) *vt* to make disparaging remarks about somebody (*slang*)

bad news *n* somebody or something that is likely to cause trouble and should be avoided (*slang*) ○ *Something tells me this guy's bad news.*

bad off *adj US* having a low income or very little money (*hyphenated before a noun*)

bad-pay *vt Carib* to fail to pay a debt or fulfil a financial obligation

bad-tempered *adj* characterized by anger and unpleasantness towards other people —**bad-temperedly** *adv* —**bad-temperedness** *n*

Baeda /béedə/ ♦ **Bede**

Baedeker /báydikər/, **baedeker** *n* a guidebook for travellers [Mid-19C. After Karl BAEDEKER]

Baedeker /báydikər/, **Karl** (1801–59) German publisher. His *Rhine Handbook* (1839) was the first of the famous guidebooks that still bear his name.

'The traveller need have no scruple in limiting his donations to the smallest pos-

sible sums, as liberality frequently becomes a source of annoyance and embarrassment.'
[Karl Baedeker, 'Gratuities', *Northern Italy*; 1895]

Baekeland /báykələnd/, **Leo** (1863–1944) Belgian-born US chemist. A pioneer of the modern plastics industry, he invented Bakelite™, a plastic resin, and founded the General Bakelite Corporation (1909). Full name **Baekeland, Leo Hendrik**

bael /báy əl/ *n* a pear-shaped thick-shelled fruit similar to a quince. Use: in South Asia, food, medicine for dysentery. [Early 17C. Via Hindi *bel* < Tamil *viḷavu*]

Baeyer /bí ər/, **Johann** (1835–1917) German chemist. He explained the mechanism of photosynthesis and synthesized indigo dye. He received the Nobel Prize in chemistry (1905). Full name **Baeyer, Johann Friedrich Wilhelm Adolf von**

Baez /bí ez, bī éz, bīz/, **Joan** (b. 1941) US folk singer and activist. From the 1960s, she was widely known for her folk and protest songs and for her human rights campaigning.

> 'You don't get to choose how you're going to die. Or when. You can only decide how you're going to live. Now.'
> [Joan Baez, *Daybreak*; 1970]

Baffin /báffin/, **William** (1584–1622) English navigator. While trying to find the Northwest Passage (1612–16), he explored the Hudson Strait and Baffin Island.

Baffin Bay large bay separating Greenland and Canada. It is bordered by the Atlantic Ocean to the south and the Arctic Ocean to the north and west, and is covered by ice most of the year.

Baffin Island Canada's largest island, located in the northeast of the country, forming part of Nunavut. Area: 507,451 sq. km/195,928 sq. mi.

baffle /báff'l/ *vt* (**-fles, -fling, -fled**) **1.** PUZZLE SOMEBODY to prove too difficult or complicated for somebody to understand, solve, or deal with, causing a feeling of confusion or helplessness **2.** FRUSTRATE SOMETHING to hinder or thwart an action or intention (*formal*) **3.** TECH CONTROL SOMETHING to impede or control the movement of a fluid or gas or the emission of sound or light waves ■ *n* **1.** TECH RESTRAINING DEVICE a device used to control or impede the flow or emission of something, e.g. a flap behind a zip that retains heat or a silencing device in a vehicle's exhaust system **2.** ACOUSTICS PARTITION IN LOUDSPEAKER a partition in a loudspeaker or microphone intended to prevent sound waves of different frequencies from interfering with one another [Mid-16C. Perhaps blend of French *bafouer* 'ridicule' + Scots *bauchle* 'revile'] —**bafflement** *n*

bafflegab /báff'l gab/ *n* N Am pretentious and obscure talk full of technical terminology or circumlocutions (*slang*)

baffling /báffling/ *adj* impossible for the mind to understand, and causing a feeling of confusion or helplessness —**bafflingly** *adv*

Bafta /báftə/ *n* an award given for films and television programmes in Britain ○ *The film won two Baftas.*

BAFTA /báftə/ *abbr* British Academy of Film and Television Arts

bag /bag/ *n* **1.** FLEXIBLE CONTAINER a flexible container that opens at one end and is used for carrying things **2.** AMOUNT IN FLEXIBLE CONTAINER the amount that can be contained in a bag, often used as a measure ○ *eating a bag of crisps* **3.** PORTABLE CONTAINER FOR EQUIPMENT OR BELONGINGS a portable container made of strong flexible material for carrying somebody's belongings or equipment ○ *I threw everything into a bag and rushed out.* **4.** ITEM OF BAGGAGE an item of traveller's baggage that can be carried by hand, e.g. a suitcase (*often used in the plural*) ○ *Our bags went missing at the airport.* **5.** HANDBAG a handbag **6.** FIELD SPORTS NUMBER OF ANIMALS SHOT the number of animals shot or captured by a hunter or hunting party **7.** OFFENSIVE TERM an offensive term deliberately insulting a woman's age and appearance (*slang insult*) **8.** SOMEBODY'S SPECIALITY something that somebody is particularly interested in or good at (*slang*) **9.** BASEBALL same as **base**[1] *n* (sense 7) **10.** DRUGS SMALL QUANTITY OF ILLEGAL DRUG a small quantity of an illegal drug in a piece of folded paper, a plastic bag, or a similar

container (*slang*) ■ **bags** *npl* **1.** LOOSE SKIN UNDER EYES prominent folds of skin beneath the eyes, often caused by fatigue **2.** TROUSERS a pair of trousers (*dated informal*) ■ *v* (**bags, bagging, bagged**) **1.** *vt* PUT SOMETHING IN BAG to put something into a bag **2.** *vti* BULGE to bulge or become baggy, or cause something to do this **3.** *vt* FIELD SPORTS SHOOT OR CAPTURE ANIMAL to shoot or capture a game animal or bird ○ *He bagged a six-point buck.* **4.** *vt* OBTAIN SOMETHING to take, catch, seize, or steal something, usually in an opportunistic way (*informal*) ○ *They've got hold of our address list and are using it to try and bag some of our customers.* **5.** *vt* CLAIM SOMETHING FOR YOURSELF to claim or get possession of something for yourself before anyone else can claim it (*informal*) ○ *She quickly bagged the window seat.* **6.** *vt* SPOT SOMETHING to do, acquire, or see something that is of particular interest or value to you and counts as an achievement in terms of one of your regular hobbies or pursuits (*informal*) **7.** *vt* Aus CRITICIZE SOMETHING to make disapproving comments about something (*slang*) ■ *interj* **bags I WANT** used to indicate that the speaker wants to claim the right to have or do something, or demands that a particular thing should happen (*informal*; usually used by children*) ○ *Bags I go first!* [13C. < Old Norse *baggi*] —**bagful** *n* —**bagger** *n* ◇ **bag and baggage** with all your belongings ◇ **bag of tricks 1.** everything, especially all the equipment necessary to do something (*informal*) ○ *They picked up the whole bag of tricks and slung it onto the back of a truck.* **2.** a magician's collection of equipment and props ◇ **bags of** a huge amount or number of something (*informal*) ◇ **in the bag** certain to be achieved or obtained (*informal*) ◇ **rough as bags** ANZ uneducated, uncouth, or common

Baganda /bə gándə/ *npl* a people living in East Africa, mainly in Uganda [Late 19C. < Bantu]

bagasse /bə gáss/ *n* **1.** the pulp or dry refuse left after the juice has been extracted from sugar cane. Use: fuel, cattle feed, making paper. **2.** paper made from bagasse [Early 19C. Via French < Spanish *bagazo* 'dregs' < Latin *baca* 'berry']

bagatelle /bággə tél/ *n* **1.** SOMETHING UNIMPORTANT a thing of little importance (*formal*) ○ *a mere bagatelle* **2.** BOARD GAME a game played on a board or table, in which balls have to be propelled by a cue or spring-loaded launcher past obstacles and into numbered holes **3.** MUSIC SHORT PLAYFUL PIECE OF MUSIC a short piece of classical music, usually for piano, written in a playful style [Mid-17C. Via French < Italian *bagatella*]

Bagdad ♦ **Baghdad**

Bagehot /bájjət/, **Walter** (1826–77) British economist and journalist. The editor of *The Economist* from 1860 until his death, he also wrote *The English Constitution* (1867), still a standard text.

> 'Poverty is an anomaly to rich people. It is very difficult to make out why people who want dinner do not ring the bell.'
> [Walter Bagehot. Quoted in *Literary Studies*, Hartley Coleridge; 1879]

bagel /báyg'l/ *n* a glazed ring-shaped bread roll with a slightly chewy texture [Early 20C. < Yiddish *beygl* < Old High German *boug* 'ring']

baggage /bággij/ *n* **1.** PACKED SUITCASES AND BAGS suitcases and other containers holding the belongings of people who are travelling **2.** PRECONCEIVED IDEAS ideas, beliefs, or practices retained from somebody's previous life experiences, especially insofar as they affect a new situation in which they may be no longer relevant or appropriate (*informal*) ○ *emotional baggage* **3.** MIL PORTABLE EQUIPMENT the equipment and supplies that a military force carries with it on campaign (*dated*) **4.** IMPUDENT GIRL OR WOMAN a girl or woman who is thought of as impudent or obstinate (*often considered offensive*) **5.** PROSTITUTE an immoral woman, especially a prostitute [15C. < French *bagage* < Old French *bague* 'bundle']

baggage car *n* N Am same as **luggage van**

baggage claim *n* ANZ, N Am the area in an airport where arriving passengers collect their luggage. UK term **baggage reclaim**

baggage handler *n* somebody whose job it is to load and unload baggage onto and off aeroplanes

baggage reclaim *n* UK the area in an airport where arriving passengers collect their luggage. ANZ, N Am term **baggage claim**

baggage room *n* US same as **left-luggage office**

baggage storage *n* ANZ TRANSP same as **left-luggage office**

baggies /bággiz/ *npl* (*informal*) **1.** very baggy men's trousers cut low at the crotch and worn hanging loosely from the hips **2.** US clothing that is cut extra large for the size of the wearer and hangs loosely on the body

bagging /bágging/ *n* **1.** coarse material used for making bags **2.** Aus a verbal attack or critically hostile response or reception

baggy /bággi/ (**-gier, -giest**) *adj* hanging loosely, puffed out, or bulging, either as a deliberate style or as a result of being too big for the wearer or having stretched while being worn —**baggily** *adv* —**bagginess** *n*

baggy green *n* Aus the green cap worn by Australian Test cricketers ◇ **wear the baggy green** Aus to play cricket for Australia

bagh /baag/ *n* S Asia same as **garden** *n* (senses 1–2) [Via Hindi < Persian *bāg*]

Baghdad /bág dad/, **Bagdad, Baghdād** capital of Iraq in the eastern part of the country, on the River Tigris, northwest of Basra. Population: 4,797,000 (2000).

bag lady *n* a homeless woman who carries her possessions in shopping bags (*informal*)

bagman /bágmən/ (*plural* **-men** /-mən/) *n* **1.** COMM same as **travelling salesman** (*dated informal*) **2.** Aus a homeless person or vagrant worker (*informal*)

bagna cauda /bánnyə kówdə/ *n* a warm sauce of olive oil, garlic, and anchovies, served as a dip for raw vegetables [< Italian dialect, literally 'hot bath']

bagnio /bánnyō, baán-/ (*plural* **-gnios**) *n* **1.** same as **brothel** (*literary*) **2.** a prison, especially in Asian Turkey (*archaic*) [Late 16C. Via Italian *bagno* 'bath' < Latin *balneus*]

Bagnold /bág nōld/, **Enid** (1889–1981) British author and playwright. She is best known as the author of *National Velvet* (1935).

bag person *n* a homeless person who carries his or her possessions in shopping bags (*informal*)

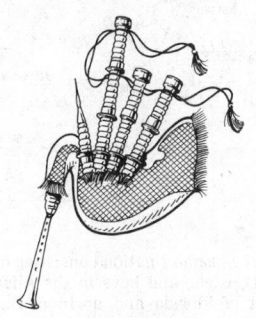

bagpipe

bagpipe /bág pīp/ *n* a wind instrument consisting of an inflatable bag with an inlet pipe and one or more outlet pipes that produce either one fixed note or several notes. The player squeezes the inflated bag under his or her arm, forcing the air out through the speaking pipes and using finger holes to control the pitch of the note. (*usually used in the plural*) —**bagpiper** *n*

bag-snatcher *n* a thief who specializes in taking women's handbags from them in public places and running away (*informal*) —**bag-snatch** *n* —**bag-snatching** *n*

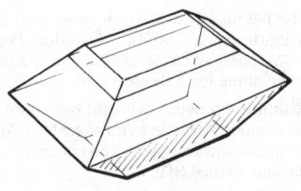

baguette (sense 2)

baguette /ba gét/ n **1.** FOOD STICK-SHAPED LOAF a long thin loaf of French bread **2.** RECTANGULAR GEM a gem cut into a long rectangular shape. See illustration on previous page **3.** RECTANGULAR SHAPE the shape of a baguette gem **4.** ARCHIT CONVEX MOULDING a small narrow rounded convex moulding on a wall or column [Early 18C. < French < Latin *baculum* 'rod']

baguette bag n a handbag that is relatively long from side to side and small from top to bottom

Baguio /bággi ō/ city on Luzon Island, the Philippines. It is the country's summer capital. Population: 268,772 (1999).

bagwash /bág wosh/ (plural **-washes**) n (archaic) **1.** the process or business of washing clothes but not drying or pressing them, or an amount of washing to be dealt with in this way **2.** a laundry where clothes are washed but not dried or pressed [Because finished when the clothes are in the bag]

bagwig /bág wig/ n an 18th-century wig with the back hair gathered in a decorative bag

bagwoman /bág wŏomən/ (plural **-women** /-wimən/), **bag woman** n same as **bag lady** (informal)

bah /baa/ interj expresses scornful irritation, disgust, or contempt

bahadur /baáhə door, bə haádər/ n S Asia **1.** in former British India, a title of respect used before a South Asian surname, originally applied to officers **2.** a Nepalese surname [Late 18C. Via Urdu and Persian *bahādur* < Mongolian, 'brave man']

Baha'i /bə hī, baa-, bə haá i, -hī i/ (plural **-ha'is**) n **1.** a religion founded in Iran in 1863 that maintains that the teachings of all religions are of value and humankind is spiritually one, and advocates world peace **2.** somebody whose religion is Baha'i [Late 19C. Via Persian *bahā'ī* < Arabic *bahā'* 'splendour'] —**Baha'i** adj —**Baha'ism** n —**Baha'ist** n

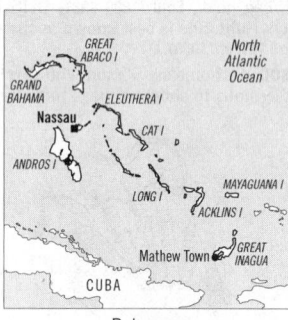

Bahamas

Bahamas /bə haáməz/ nation consisting of hundreds of islands, islets, and keys in the Atlantic Ocean southeast of Florida and north of Cuba. It was settled by the British in the 17th century and became an independent member of the Commonwealth in 1973. Language: English. Currency: Bahamian dollar. Capital: Nassau. Population: 297,852 (2001). Area: 13,939 sq. km/5,382 sq. mi. Official name **Commonwealth of the Bahamas** —**Bahamian** /bə háymi ən/ n, adj

Bahasa Indonesia /baa haássə-/ n the form of Malay that is the official language of Indonesia [< Malay, 'language of Indonesia']

Bahasa Malaysia /bə haássə-/ n the form of Malay that is the official language of Malaysia [< Malay, 'language of Malaysia']

Bahawalpur /bə haáwəl poor, báhə wólpər/ city, district, and division of Punjab Province, Pakistan, situated on the River Sutlej. Population: 180,263 (1981).

Bahia /bə hee ə, -eé ə/ **1.** state in eastern Brazil on the Atlantic coast. Capital: Salvador. Population: 12,541,675 (1996). Area: 567,295 sq. km/219,034 sq. mi. **2.** former name for **Salvador**

Bahía Blanca /bə hee ə blángkə, baa eé ə-/ city and port in Buenos Aires Province, eastern Argentina. It is an important transport and commercial centre. Population: 260,096 (1991).

Bahia grass /bə hee ə-/ n a perennial American grass, grown in the southern United States. Native to: Central and South America. Use: lawns, forage. Latin name: *Paspalum notatum*.

bahookie /bə hoŏki/ n Scotland the buttocks (humorous)

Bahrain

Bahrain /baa ráyn/, **Bahrein** independent island state on the Persian Gulf off the coast of Saudi Arabia, northwest of Qatar. Language: Arabic, English, Farsi, Urdu. Currency: Bahraini dinar. Capital: Manama. Population: 667,238 (2003). Area: 707 sq. km/273 sq. mi. Official name **State of Bahrain** —**Bahraini** n, adj

baht /baat/ (plural **bahts** or same) n the main unit of Thai currency. See table at **currency** [Early 19C. < Thai *bāt*]

bahuvrihi /baá hoo vreé hee/ (plural **-his**) n a compound word in which the first part describes the second or governs it grammatically, and the second element cannot be substituted for the whole, e.g. 'yellowhammer' or 'afternoon' [Mid-19C. < Sanskrit *bahuvrīhi* 'possessing much rice', a typical example of this class]

bai /bī/ S Asia n **1.** FORM OF ADDRESS FOR WOMAN a polite form of address for a woman **2.** CALL GIRL in Bihar and Uttar Pradesh, a prostitute ■ suffix **-bai** INDICATING RESPECT in Maharashtra and parts of Karnataka, a respectful form of address added after a woman's name [< Marathi, 'lady']

baigan n Carib FOOD another spelling of **bhaigan**

Baikal, Lake /bī kaál/ lake in southern Siberia, Russia. It is the world's deepest lake and the largest freshwater lake in Europe and Asia. Area: 31,500 sq. km/12,200 sq. mi. Depth: 1,637 m/5,371 ft.

bail[1] /bayl/ n **1.** SECURITY FOR APPEARANCE IN COURT a sum of money deposited to secure an accused person's temporary release from custody and to guarantee that person's appearance in court at a later date. If the person fails to appear in court on the date set, the money is forfeited. **2.** RELEASE UNDER SECURITY temporary release from custody after bail has been paid ○ Her brother was out on bail. **3.** SOMEBODY WHO PAYS BAIL somebody who pays bail ■ v (**bails, bailing, bailed**) **1.** vt FREE SOMEBODY BY PAYING BAIL to release an accused person from custody after bail has been paid (usually passive) ○ He has been bailed to appear before the magistrates again on 11th October. **2.** vi CRASH in snowboarding, to crash or fall (slang) [14C. < Old French, 'temporary custody' < baillier 'take charge of' < Latin bajulus 'somebody who carries (responsibility)'] —**bailable** adj ◇ **jump** or **skip bail** to fail to appear in court as promised at the end of a bail period (informal)

bail out vt to secure somebody's release from legal custody by paying bail

bail[2] /bayl/ (**bails, bailing, bailed**), **bale** (**bales, baling, baled**) vti to empty water out of a boat, using a bucket or similar container ○ We bailed the sinking boat for an hour. [Early 17C. < obsolete bail 'bucket', via French < assumed Vulgar Latin bajula 'water carrier'] —**bailer** n

bail out, bale out v **1.** vti EMPTY WATER OUT OF BOAT to empty water out of a boat, using a bucket or similar container ○ bailing water out as the boat slowly sank **2.** vi PARACHUTE FROM PLANE to escape from a plane that is in danger of crashing by making a parachute jump **3.** vi ESCAPE FROM DIFFICULT SITUATION to abandon hurriedly and unceremoniously a situation that is dangerous or difficult (informal) ○ When the company hit the skids, she was the first to bail out. **4.** vt HELP SOMEBODY OUT OF TROUBLE to help somebody out of a difficult situation (informal)

bail[3] /bayl/ n **1.** in cricket, either of the two short pieces of wood laid on top of the stumps to make

the wicket **2.** a pole or framework used to separate horses in a barn or stable [Mid-18C. Probably via Old French < Latin *baculum* 'rod']

bail up vt Aus to stop a person in order to speak to him or her, often in a situation where that person does not want to be stopped or spoken to (informal) ○ I was hoping I wouldn't have to speak to him, but he bailed me up as I was leaving. [< BAIL[3]]

bail[4] /bayl/, **bale** n **1.** HINGED BAR a hinged bar on a typewriter or printer that holds the paper against the platen **2.** SEMICIRCULAR HANDLE a semicircular handle, e.g. a bucket handle **3.** SEMICIRCULAR SUPPORT a semicircular support, e.g. one that holds up the canopy on a covered wagon [15C. Probably < Old Norse]

Bail /bayl/, **Murray** (b. 1941) Australian writer. He is best known for his novels *Homesickness* (1980) and *Eucalyptus* (1998).

bail bandit n an accused person released on bail who commits a crime while awaiting trial for the original offence, or who fails to appear in court on the date set (informal)

bail bar n PRINTING same as **bail**[4] (sense 1)

bail bond n a document in which the prisoner released on bail and the person who pays the bail money promise that the prisoner will appear in court at a set time

bail bondsman n N Am a man engaged in the business of providing bail money, or acting as surety, for an accused person

bail bondsperson n N Am somebody engaged in the business of providing bail money, or acting as surety, for an accused person

bail bondswoman n N Am a woman engaged in the business of providing bail money, or acting as surety, for an accused person

bailee /báy leé/ n somebody to whom goods are temporarily entrusted by bailment

bailey /báyli/ (plural **-leys**) n **1.** the outermost wall surrounding a castle **2.** a courtyard inside the walls, especially the outermost walls, of a castle [13C. Probably alteration of BAIL[3], influenced by medieval Latin *ballium*]

Bailey /báyli/, **David** (b. 1938) British photographer. He is best known for his fashion and portrait photography of the 1960s and 1970s. Full name **Bailey, David Royston**

> 'The only reason I ever did fashion was because of the girls. It was the gates of heaven. But I only wanted to photograph girls I liked.'
> [David Bailey, *Sunday Times*; March 1989]

Bailey bridge n a temporary steel bridge made of prefabricated parts and designed for quick construction [Mid-20C. After Sir D. Coleman *Bailey* (1901–85), British engineer]

bailie /báyli/ n Scotland an honorary title sometimes given to senior members of a local council in Scotland. Formerly, the title was reserved for municipal magistrates. [13C. Variant of BAILIFF]

bailiff /báylif/ n **1.** LAW SHERIFF'S OFFICER a legal officer who serves under a sheriff and is empowered to take possession of a debtor's property, forcibly if necessary, to serve writs, and to make arrests **2.** STEWARD a steward or agent of a landowner or landlord **3.** HIST SENIOR OFFICIAL a senior officer with judicial powers representing the sovereign in a district, e.g. a mayor or sheriff, especially the chief officer of a hundred. The word is still retained as an honorary title in some districts. [13C. Via Old French *baillif* 'overseer' < assumed medieval Latin *bajulivus* < Latin *bajulus* 'somebody who carries (responsibility)']

bailiwick /báyli wik/ n **1.** an area of activity in which somebody has specific responsibility, knowledge, or ability ○ Export permits are her bailiwick. **2.** the area over which a bailiff has jurisdiction [15C. < BAILIFF + obsolete *wick* 'town' (via Germanic < Latin *vicus* 'village, homestead')]

Baillie /báyli/, **Dame Isobel** (1895–1983) British soprano. She regularly performed with Sir Thomas Beecham and Arturo Toscanini, and gave over 1,000 performances of George Frederick Handel's *Messiah*.

bailment /báylmənt/ n **1.** the temporary entrusting, subject to a contract, of goods to somebody for a

particular purpose **2.** the granting of bail to somebody in custody

bailor /báy láwr, báylər/ n somebody who entrusts goods to another person by bailment

bailout /báyl owt/ n an intervention by a person or company to help another person or company out of financial difficulties

bailsman /báylzmən/ (plural **-men** /-mən/) n N Am LAW same as **bail bondsman**

Baily's beads /báyliz-/ npl bright points of sunlight that briefly appear around the Moon immediately before and after a total eclipse of the Sun. They are caused by sunlight shining through valleys on the Moon. [Mid-19C. After Francis Baily (1774–1844), British astronomer]

báinín /báa neen/, **bawneen** /báw-/ n Ireland **1.** a collarless jacket for men, made of white wool **2.** white wool prepared with some of the natural oil retained. Use: jackets, skirts. [Early 20C. < Irish bán 'white']

bain-marie

bain-marie /báN mə reé/ (plural **bain-maries**) n a cooking utensil containing hot water into which another container is placed to keep food warm or cook it gently [Early 19C. < French, via medieval Latin translation < Greek kaminos Marias 'alchemist's apparatus', literally 'furnace of Maria' (alchemist and sister of Moses)]

Bairam /bī ráam/ n either of two Islamic festivals, the **Lesser Bairam** marking the end of Ramadan or the **Greater Bairam** seventy days later, marking the end of the Islamic year [Late 16C. Via Turkish bayram < Persian bazrām]

Baird /baird/, **John Logie** (1888–1946) British inventor. He demonstrated an electromechanical television system in 1926. He also researched into radar and fibre optics.

Bairiki /bī reéki/ administrative centre of Kiribati, situated on Tarawa atoll in the western Pacific Ocean. Population: 25,000 (1990).

bairn /bairn/ n N England, Scotland a young child [Old English bearn < Indo-European, 'carry, bear children']

Bairnsdale /báirnz dayl/ town in southeastern Victoria, Australia, situated on the Mitchell River near Lake King. Population: 10,770 (1991).

Baisakhi /bī sáki/ n a Sikh festival commemorating the founding of the Khalsa order by Gobind Singh in 1699 and marking the New Year. Date: 13 April.

bait[1] /bayt/ n **1.** FOOD FOR ATTRACTING ANIMALS a piece of food used as a lure in fishing or trapping ○ fishing with live bait **2.** ENTICEMENT something used to lure a person or animal into being caught ■ vt (**baits, baiting, baited**) **1.** PUT FOOD ON HOOK to put a food attractant on a hook or in a trap ○ This line's baited with a minnow. **2.** HARASS SOMEBODY to persecute, tease, or harass somebody ○ Stop baiting the dog, please. **3.** ATTACK ANIMAL WITH DOGS to set dogs onto a tethered animal, usually a bear or bull, for sport [13C. < Old Norse beit 'food', beita 'hunt with dogs'] —**baiter** n ◇ **rise to the bait** to react to something, especially to temptation or provocation, in precisely the way that somebody wants you to, e.g. by getting angry when somebody teases you

bait[2] vi another spelling of **bate**[1]

bait and switch, **bait advertising** n a tactic used in sales in which buyers are tempted by an advertised bargain but are then persuaded to buy a more expensive item instead

bait casting, **bait cast** n a fishing rod with a line to which live or dead bait is attached

baiza /bīzə/ (plural **-zas** or same) n a subunit of Omani currency. See table at **currency** [Late 20C. Via Arabic < Hindi paisā]

baize /bayz/ n a green woollen cloth, similar to felt. Use: tops of billiard, snooker, and card tables. [Late 16C. < French baies, plural of bai 'bay-coloured' (see BAY[4]), probably because of its original colour]

Baja California /báa haa-/ **1.** peninsula in Northwestern Mexico between the Gulf of California and the Pacific Ocean, divided into the states of Baja California and Baja California Sur. Length: 1,200 km/760 mi. **2.** state in northwestern Mexico in the northern part of the Baja California peninsula. Capital: Mexicali. Population: 2,486,367 (2000). Area: 71,576 sq. km/27,636 sq. mi.

Baja California Sur /-súr/ state in western Mexico in the southern part of the Baja California peninsula. Capital: La Paz. Population: 424,041 (2000). Area: 71,428 sq. km/27,579 sq. mi.

bajada /bə háadə/ n a broad plain formed at the base of a mountain or mountain range resulting from the coalescing of sedimentary deposits from a number of streams [Mid-19C. < Spanish, 'slope, descent']

Bajan /báyjən/ n Carib a Barbadian (informal) [Mid-20C. Shortening and alteration of Barbadian] —**Bajan** adj

Bajazet same as **Bayazid I**

bajee n FOOD another spelling of **bhaji**

bajra /báaj raal/, **bajri** /-ri/, **bajree** n S Asia grain such as pearl millet [Early 19C. < Hindi bājrā, bājrī]

bak abbr a file extension for a backup file

bake /bayk/ v (**bakes, baking, baked**) **1.** vti COOK FOOD IN OVEN to cook food in an oven by dry heat, or be cooked in this way **2.** vti HARDEN BY HEAT to become hardened, or harden something, by exposing it to dry heat **3.** vi BE VERY HOT to be or feel very hot (informal) ○ You must be baking in that heavy coat. ■ n **1.** AMOUNT BAKED a number of things baked at the same time **2.** OVEN-COOKED DISH a dish of food that is cooked in the oven ○ a cheese and vegetable bake **3.** Scotland TYPE OF BISCUIT a type of biscuit **4.** N Am PARTY WITH BAKED FOOD a party at which baked food is served (informal; often used in combination) ○ an oyster bake on the shore [Old English bacan < Indo-European, 'to warm'] ◇ **bake blind** to cook the pastry case for a pie, tart, or flan, usually lined with weighted paper to prevent it from rising, before the filling is added

baked Alaska n a dessert of cake that is topped with ice cream, covered with meringue, and then quickly browned in a very hot oven

baked beans npl baked haricot beans in a tomato sauce, usually bought in tins

baked potato n a potato that has been baked in its skin, served plain or with a topping

bakehouse /báyk howss/ n COMM same as **bakery** (sense 1)

Bakelite /báykə līt/ tdmk a trademark for any of various synthetic resins used in many manufacturing applications

baker /báykər/ n **1.** somebody who makes baked foods, especially bread and cakes **2.** a portable oven

Baker /báykər/, **Dame Janet** (b. 1933) British mezzo-soprano. After performing as a soloist for Sir John Barbirolli in the 1960s, she moved on to opera, and is especially associated with English music. Born **Abbott, Janet**

AKG London

Josephine Baker

Baker, Josephine (1906–75) US-born French dancer and entertainer. She performed as a singer and dancer in New York before settling in Paris in 1925. Highly popular in Europe, she campaigned for racial equality in the United States in the 1950s and 1960s. Born **McDonald, Freda Josephine**

'A violinist had his violin, a painter his palette. All I had was myself. I was the instrument that I must care for.'
[Josephine Baker, Josephine; 1976]

Baker, **Sir Samuel** (1821–93) British explorer. He searched for the sources of the Nile and reached present-day Lake Mobutu Sese Seko, which he called Lake Albert (1864). Full name **Baker, Sir Samuel White**

baker's dozen n a set of thirteen items [Because retailers of bread formerly received an extra loaf with each dozen from the baker, which they were entitled to keep as profit]

Bakersfield /báykərz feeld/ city in south-central California in the valley of the San Joaquin River. Population: 260,969 (2002 estimate).

bakery /báykəri/ (plural **-ies**) n **1.** a building or part of a building where items of food, especially bread and cakes, are baked **2.** a shop or part of a store where items of baked food, especially bread and cakes, are sold

Bakewell /báyk wel/, **Robert** (1725–95) British agriculturalist. He used selective breeding to improve farm livestock and established the Leicester breed of sheep.

Bakewell tart n a tart with a pastry base covered with jam and topped with almond-flavoured sponge [After the town of Bakewell in Derbyshire]

Bakhtaran /báktə ráan/, **Bākhtarān** city in western Iran and capital of Bakhtaran Province, situated on the Hamadan-Baghdad trading route. Population: 692,986 (1996).

baking /báyking/ n **1.** COOKING OF BREAD AND CAKES the cooking of bread, cakes, and other foods by dry heat in an oven ○ did the baking early in the morning **2.** AMOUNT BAKED AT ONE TIME a quantity of items baked at one time ○ a baking of 46 rolls ■ adj VERY HOT very hot and dry ○ a baking sun

baking powder n a mixture containing sodium bicarbonate, or sometimes ammonium bicarbonate or ammonium carbonate, starch, and acids. Use: leavening agent, especially for cakes.

baking sheet n N Am HOUSEHOLD same as **baking tray**

baking soda n sodium bicarbonate, especially when used as a raising agent, for cleaning, or in toothpaste

baking tray n a flat metal tray used for baking food in an oven

Bakke decision /báki-/ n a US Supreme Court ruling that made it unlawful for universities to reserve a specific number of places for students from minority groups, and so prevent applicants who are not minority groups from competing for those places [After Allan Bakke, who was denied a place at medical school in spite of having higher qualifications than others admitted]

bakkie /báki/ n S Africa a pick-up truck with an open back

baklava /báaklə vaa, bákləvə/, **baclava** n a dessert of filo pastry layered with nuts, with syrup or honey poured over it after baking. It originated in southwestern Asia. [Mid-17C. < Turkish]

bakra /bákrə/ n Carib a white person, especially one from the British Isles [Mid-18C. < Ibibio and Efik (m)bakara 'European, master']

baksheesh /bák sheesh, bák sheesh/ n money given as a tip or bribe, or as charity, especially in North Africa and southwestern Asia [Mid-18C. Ultimately < Persian bakšīš]

Baku /baa koó/ capital of Azerbaijan, on the shores of the Caspian Sea, in the centre of an oil-producing region in the eastern part of the country. Population: 1,708,000 (1999).

Bakunin /bə koónin/, **Mikhail** (1814–76) Russian anarchist. Born an aristocrat, he was sent into exile in Siberia in 1857, but escaped to England in 1861 to spread his anarchistic views throughout Europe. Full name **Bakunin, Mikhail Aleksandrovich**

'The urge for destruction is also a creative urge!'
[Mikhail Bakunin, *Die Reaktion in Deutschland (The Reaction in Germany)*; 1842]

BAL *n* MED same as **dimercaprol** [Acronym < *British anti-lewisite*]

Bala, Lake /bállə/ lake in north Wales, the chief source of the River Dee. Area: 10 sq. km/4 sq. mi.

Balaam /báyləm, báy lam/ *n* in the Bible, a Mesopotamian seer who, when called on to curse the Israelites, instead praised them after being reproached by his ass (Numbers 22–24)

balachan /bállə chán/ *n* in Southeast Asian cookery, a paste or powder made from fermented shrimp or other small fish and used to flavour soups and curries [Early 20C. < Malay]

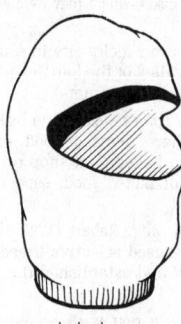

balaclava

balaclava /bállə kláàvə/, **balaclava helmet** *n* a close-fitting knitted covering for the head and neck that leaves only the face or eyes exposed [Late 19C. After the village of *Balaklava* in the Crimea, probably because worn by infantry in the campaign there]

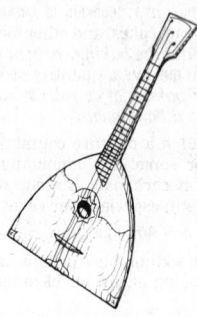

balalaika

balalaika /bállə líkə/ *n* a Russian musical instrument with a triangular soundbox and three strings that are plucked or strummed [Late 18C. Via Russian < Turkic]

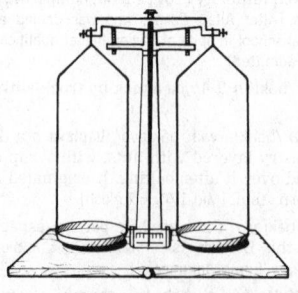

balance (sense 5)

balance /bálləns/ *n* **1.** STEADY STATE ON NARROW BASE a state in which a body or object remains reasonably steady in a particular position while resting on a base that is narrow or small relative to its other dimensions. For human beings, this most commonly involves remaining upright and steady on the feet. ○ *He lost his balance and fell from the beam.* **2.** OPPOSITION OF EQUAL FORCES a state in which two opposing forces or factors are of equal strength or importance so that they effectively cancel each other out and stability is maintained **3.** HARMONY a

state in which various parts form a satisfying and harmonious whole and nothing is out of proportion or unduly emphasized at the expense of the rest **4.** EMOTIONAL STABILITY a state of emotional and mental stability in which somebody is calm and able to make rational decisions and judgments **5.** WEIGHING MACHINE a simple mechanical device for weighing objects, often consisting of a pivoted horizontal beam with a pan suspended from each end. Material to be weighed is put in one pan and weights of a fixed value are gradually added to the other until the beam returns to the horizontal. **6.** COUNTERWEIGHT something that offsets or counters the weight or influence of another element ○ *a system of checks and balances* **7.** GREATER PART a significant or influential amount of something ○ *The balance of evidence was in her favour.* **8.** REMAINDER a remaining or outstanding amount, e.g. the amount remaining in a bank account after a withdrawal or the amount still to be paid to settle a bill **9.** ACCT EQUAL DEBIT AND CREDIT a position where the amounts on the debit and credit sides of an account are equal and cancel each other out **10.** ACCT DIFFERENCE BETWEEN DEBIT AND CREDIT the amount by which the debit and credit sides of an account differ **11.** MATHS, CHEM EQUALITY OF ELEMENTS IN EQUATION a state in which the elements of a mathematical or chemical equation are equal on both sides ■ *v* (**-ances, -ancing, -anced**) **1.** *vti* REMAIN IN OR GIVE SOMETHING EQUILIBRIUM to achieve or maintain, or cause somebody or something to achieve or maintain, a position of steadiness while resting on a narrow base ○ *balanced precariously on a branch* **2.** *vti* PLACE IN PRECARIOUS POSITION to place an object in a position where it is or seems to be in imminent danger of falling, or to be in such a position (*often passive*) **3.** *vt* ASSESS SOMETHING to compare the relative importance of different factors or alternatives before making a choice or decision ○ *balanced the pros and cons of the plan before moving ahead with it* **4.** *vt* WEIGH SOMETHING IN BALANCE to weigh something in a balance or by an action or method that resembles the working of a balance **5.** *vti* EQUAL OR CANCEL OUT to be equal to something in force, weight, or importance, or cancel it out **6.** *vt* ARTS BRING ELEMENTS INTO HARMONY to arrange the different parts of something so that they form a harmonious and well-proportioned whole **7.** *vt* MATHS, CHEM BRING EQUATION INTO EQUALITY to bring the elements of a chemical or mathematical equation into a state of equality **8.** *vt* ACCT ASSESS ACCOUNT to assess the relative positions of the debit and credit sides of an account **9.** *vt* ACCT EQUALIZE ACCOUNT to make the debit and credit sides of an account equal [13C. Via Old French *(libra) bilanx* '(scales) with two pans' < *lanx* 'plate, pan'] —**balanceable** *adj* —**balancer** *n* ◇ **hang in the balance** to be in a critical situation in which two diametrically opposed outcomes are possible and the possibility of an unfavourable one is real and greatly feared ◇ **hold the balance 1.** to have the power to decide in which way a situation will develop or which of two opposing sides will prevail **2.** to control the key to maintaining an existing state of equilibrium between two opposing forces ◇ **on balance** having taken all the relevant factors into consideration and assessed their relative significance ○ *The situation, on balance, is relatively hopeful.* ◇ **redress the balance** to make the situation more fair or equal, usually by giving something to or assisting somebody who was previously at a disadvantage ◇ **strike a balance** to reach a compromise between two extremes ◇ **throw somebody off balance** to surprise or confuse somebody

USAGE **Balance** meaning 'remainder': *Balance* has been used informally to mean 'the remaining amount' in general contexts, as in *The balance of the work must be finished tomorrow*, but this is thought to be in poor style where simpler and more suitable words are available. *The rest of the work must be finished tomorrow* is preferable.

balance out *v* **1.** *vti* to act as an equal and opposing weight, force, or value to something and either neutralize or complement its effect ○ *This gain balances out last month's losses.* **2.** *vi* to arrive at a state of equality or harmony, usually over a period of time ○ *These things tend to balance out in the end.*

Balance *n* ZODIAC same as **Libra** (sense 2)

balance beam *n* N Am same as **beam** *n* (sense 9)

balanced /bállənst/ *adj* **1.** EVEN-HANDED taking account of all sides on their merits without prejudice or

favouritism ○ *a balanced assessment* **2.** HEALTHY containing different parts in suitable quantities or suitably arranged to produce a satisfying and effective whole ○ *a balanced diet* **3.** MENTALLY STABLE in a state of mental and emotional stability and able to make rational judgments

balance of payments *n* the difference between the amount paid by a national government to other countries and the amount it receives from them

balance of power *n* **1.** the distribution of power among two or more states, where the pattern of force and dominance among them is balanced in such a way that no single state has dominance over the others **2.** the power of a single country, group, or person to affect a situation decisively by supporting either of two opposing sides whose powers are equally balanced

balance of trade *n* the difference between the value of the total imports and total exports of a country as assessed over a fixed period

balance sheet *n* a statement showing the assets and liabilities of a company or institution at a particular time

balance weight *n* a weight used to counterbalance a moving part in a machine

balance wheel *n* a wheel in a machine, especially in a clock, that regulates the rate of movement of the main mechanism

Balanchine /bállən cheen, bállən cheèn/, **George** (1904–83) Russian-born US dancer and choreographer. Cofounder of the New York City Ballet (1948), he revolutionized classical ballet with his innovative choreography. Born **Balanchivadze, Georgy Melitonovich**

'Dance has to look like the music. If you see music simply as an accompaniment, then you don't hear it. I occupy myself with how not to interfere with the music.'
[George Balanchine. Quoted in *Portrait of Mr B.*, Lincoln Kirstein; 1984]

balancing act *n* **1.** a skilful or precarious attempt to deal with opposing groups or opinions or with a large variety of tasks (*informal*) **2.** an entertainment in which the performer balances or keeps objects balanced in precarious positions

balanitis /bállə nítiss/ *n* inflammation of the head of the penis, usually caused by an infection [Mid-19C. < Greek *balanos* 'acorn, glans penis']

balas /bálləss, báyləss/, **balas ruby** *n* a ruby that is a red spinel. Use: gems. [15C. Via Old French *balais*, Spanish *balax* < Arabic *balakš* < Persian *Badakšān*, region of Afghanistan]

balata /bállətə/ *n* **1.** a gum made from tree sap and resembling rubber. Use: gaskets, chewing gum, gutta-percha substitute. **2.** *UK, NZ, Can* a tropical tree that yields the sap from which balata is made. Latin name: *Manilkara bidentata*. Aus, US term **bully tree** [Early 17C. < Carib *balatá*]

Balaton, Lake /bállə ton/ largest lake in central Europe and resort centre in west-central Hungary. Area: 601 sq. km/232 sq. mi.

balboa /bal bó ə/ *n* the main unit of Panamanian currency. See table at **currency** [Early 20C. After Vasco Núñez de BALBOA]

Balboa /bal bó ə/ town and port in Panama where the Panama Canal flows into the Gulf of Panama. Population: 1,214 (1990).

Balboa, Vasco Núñez de (1475?–1519) Spanish explorer. He was the first European to reach the Pacific Ocean (1513).

balbriggan /bal bríggən/ *n* a knitted unbleached cotton fabric. Use: making underwear. [Late 19C. After the town of *Balbriggan*, Ireland]

balchan *n* FOOD same as **balachan**

Balcon /báwlkən/, **Sir Michael** (1896–1977) British film producer. He was in charge of production at Ealing Studios (1938–57). His films include *Whisky Galore* (1949) and *The Lavender Hill Mob* (1951). Full name **Balcon, Sir Michael Elias**

balcony /bálkəni/ (*plural* **-nies**) *n* **1.** a platform projecting from the interior or exterior wall of a building, usually enclosed by a rail or parapet **2.** an area of seating raised entirely above the floor level in a theatre, cinema, or concert hall [Early 17C.

Via Italian *balcone* < Old Italian, 'scaffold' < Germanic] — **balconied** *adj*

bald /bawld/ *adj* **1.** WITH HAIRLESS HEAD having little or no hair on the head **2.** WITHOUT NATURAL COVERING having little or no hair, fur, grass, or other natural covering ○ *a bald patch on the grass* **3.** WORN describes tyres with a very worn-down tread **4.** PLAIN plain and direct, with no attempt to elaborate or explain ○ *a bald statement of the facts* **5.** UNORNAMENTED plain, bare, and without ornamentation, often to the point of seeming dull or prosaic **6.** ZOOL WITH WHITE MARKINGS describes birds and mammals that have white markings on the face or head [14C. Perhaps < obsolete *bal* 'white spot or streak, especially on a horse's face'] — **baldness** *n*

baldachin /báwldəkin/ *n* **1.** CANOPY a canopy made of cloth or stone erected over an altar, shrine, or throne in a Christian church **2.** PORTABLE CANOPY a canopy carried above a priest or venerated object during a religious procession **3.** TEXTILES BROCADE a rich silk and gold brocade [Late 16C. < Italian *baldacchino* < *Baldacco* 'Baghdad']

bald cypress *n* a deciduous coniferous tree, often found in swamps or near water, that yields a hard timber. Native to: North America. Latin name: *Taxodium distichum*. [*Bald* because the tree sheds its needles, unlike most members of its family]

bald eagle

bald eagle *n* a large eagle, the adult of which has a white head and tail. Native to: lakes and rivers of North America. Latin name: *Haliaeetus leucocephalus*.

Balder /báwldər/ *n* in Norse mythology, one of Odin's sons, who was god of the summer sun. He was vulnerable only to mistletoe, by which he was killed.

balderdash /báwldər dash/ *n* senseless or pointless talk or writing [Late 16C. Origin ?]

bald-faced *adj N Am* same as **barefaced** (sense 1)

baldhead /báwld hed/ *n* **1.** an offensive term for somebody with a bald head (*informal insult*) **2.** an offensive term for somebody who is not a Rastafarian (*slang; used in Black English*) **3.** an offensive term for a Black person who is regarded as having abandoned his or her Black heritage (*slang; used in Black English*) [Senses 2 and 3 < the association of long hair with Rastafarianism]

baldheaded /báwld héddid/ *adj* with a bald head ■ *adv* impetuously or without restraint (*informal*)

baldie *n* another spelling of **baldy**

balding /báwlding/ *adj* in the process of losing the hair on the head

baldly /báwldli/ *adv* in a simple and blunt way ○ *To put it baldly, she did a lousy job.*

baldpate /báwld payt/ *n* BIRDS same as **wigeon** (sense 2)

baldric /báwldrik/ *n* a sash or belt worn from one shoulder to the opposite hip, used to support a sword [13C. Directly and via Old French *baudre* < Middle High German *balderich*]

Baldwin /báwldwin/, **James** (1924–87) US writer. His novels and essays addressed racism in the United States, and include *Go Tell It on the Mountain* (1953) and *Notes of a Native Son* (1955). Full name **Baldwin, James Arthur**

'There is never a time in the future in which we will work out our salvation. The challenge is in the moment, the time is

James Baldwin

always now.'
[James Baldwin, 'Faulkner and De-segregation', *Nobody Knows My Name*; 1961]

Baldwin, Stanley, 1st Earl Baldwin of Bewdley (1867–1947) British Conservative party leader and prime minister (1923–24, 1924–29, 1935–37). He retired from politics in 1937 amid criticism that he had ignored Germany's preparations for World War II. See table at **prime minister**

'I would rather be an opportunist and float than go to the bottom with my principles round my neck.'
[Attributed to Stanley Baldwin]

baldy /báwldi/ (*plural* **-ies**), **baldie** *n* an offensive term for somebody who is bald or balding (*informal insult*)

bale[1] /bayl/ *n* a large bundle or package of hay or a raw material such as cotton, tightly bound with string or wire to keep it in shape during transportation or storage ■ *vti* (**bales, baling, baled**) to gather and fasten material or goods into bales ○ *baling hay* [14C. < Old French < Germanic]

bale[2] /bayl/ *n* evil or suffering (*archaic or literary*) [Old English *bealu* < Germanic]

bale[3] /bayl/ *vti* another spelling of **bail**[2]

Balearic /bálli árrik/ *adj* belonging to the Balearic Islands

Balearic Islands

Balearic Islands /bálli árrik-/ island group in the western Mediterranean that includes Majorca, Menorca, and Ibiza. It is a province and autonomous region of Spain. Population: 736,865 (1991). Area: 5,014 sq. km/1,936 sq. mi.

baleen /bə leén/ *n* a horny substance that grows as fringed plates from the upper jaws of some whales, acting to strain food, especially small crustaceans, from the water [14C. Via Old French *balaine* < Latin *balaena* 'whale' < Greek *phalaina*]

baleen whale *n* a large whale that has two blowholes and a set of horny fringed plates instead of teeth. Blue, grey, and right whales are baleen whales. Suborder: Mysticeti.

baleful /báylf'l/ *adj* threatening, or seeming to threaten, harm or misfortune ○ *a baleful stare* — **balefully** *adv* — **balefulness** *n*

USAGE **baleful** or **baneful**? *Baleful*, meaning 'causing harm', is a much more common term than *baneful*, meaning 'causing destruction', which is largely confined to literary use.

~~balence~~ incorrect spelling of **balance**

Balfour /bálfər, -fawr/, **Arthur James, 1st Earl of Balfour** (1848–1930) British Conservative prime minister (1902–05) and author of the Balfour Declaration (1917), supporting a Jewish homeland in Palestine. See table at **prime minister**

'History does not repeat itself. Historians repeat each other.'
[Attributed to Arthur James Balfour]

Bali /baáli/ mountainous island east of Java, Indonesia, that is a popular holiday destination. Capital: Denpasar. Population: 3,102,400 (2001). Area: 5,623 sq. km/2,171 sq. mi.

balibuntal /bálli búnt'l/ *n* **1.** fine straw woven into material. Use: hat making. **2.** a hat made from balibuntal [Early 20C. < *Baliuag* in the Philippines + Tagalog *buntal* 'straw from the talipot palm tree']

Balikpapan /baálik paá paan/ city and port in Indonesia, situated on the island of Borneo, on the Makassar Strait. Population: 433,494 (1997).

Balinese /baáli neéz/ *n* **1.** somebody who comes from Bali **2.** an Austronesian language spoken on Bali. Native speakers: 2–3 million. [Early 19C. < Dutch *Balinees* < *Bali* 'Bali'] — **Balinese** *adj*

Baliol /báyli əl/, **Balliol, John de** (1250?–1314) king of Scots. He rebelled against English rule, but was defeated by Edward I at Dunbar (1296) and deposed.

balk *v*, *n* another spelling of **baulk**

Balkan /báwlkən, bólk-/ *adj* relating to the states of the Balkan Peninsula, or their peoples, languages, or cultures [Mid-19C. < Turkish, a mountain chain]

Balkanization /báwlkə nī záysh'n, bólkə-/, **balkanization, Balkanisation** *n* division of an area, region, or group into smaller and often mutually hostile units [Early 20C. < the political fragmentation of the Balkan States between the Treaty of Berlin (1878) and the Balkan Wars (1912–13)] — **Balkanize** *vt*

Balkan Mountains /báwlkən-/ mountain range running across eastern Yugoslavia and central Bulgaria. The highest point is Botev Peak 2,376 m/7,795 ft.

Balkan Peninsula mountainous peninsula in southeastern Europe between the Adriatic and Ionian seas in the west and the Aegean and Black seas in the east

Balkan States, Balkans /báwlkənz/ the countries in the Balkan Peninsula, including Albania, Bosnia-Herzegovina, Bulgaria, Croatia, Greece, Macedonia, the European part of Turkey, and the Federal Republic of Yugoslavia

balky /báwki, báwlki/ (**-ier, -iest**), **baulky** *adj N Am* difficult and uncooperative ○ *a balky mule that stopped dead in its tracks* — **balkily** *adv* — **balkiness** *n*

ball[1] /bawl/ *n* **1.** ROUND OBJECT PLAYED WITH an object, usually round in shape and often hollow and flexible, used in many games and sports in which it is thrown, struck, or kicked **2.** ROUNDED THING something spherical or almost spherical, especially a spherical mass or arrangement of material ○ *a ball of wool* **3.** GAME WITH BALL a game, especially one played by children, in which a ball may be thrown from one player to another in various ways ○ *Who's coming out to play ball?* **4.** BALL PLAYED IN PARTICULAR WAY a particular use, movement, or way of transferring the ball to another player in the course of a game ○ *a long ball into the penalty area* **5.** CRICKET DELIVERY BY BOWLER a single instance of a bowler bowling the ball to a batsman in cricket ○ *the last ball of the over* **6.** BASEBALL PITCH THAT IS NOT STRIKE in baseball, any pitch that does not pass through the strike zone and at which the batter does not swing **7.** RUGBY POSSESSION AFTER SET PIECE useful possession, usually with an opportunity to develop an attacking movement, arising from skilful delivery of the ball by another player **8.** ARMS SOLID PROJECTILE a solid nonexplosive and usually round projectile shot from an old-fashioned pistol, musket, or cannon **9.** ARMS SOLID PROJECTILES COLLECTIVELY a collective term for the solid projectiles fired from old-fashioned guns ○ *The gunners were ordered to change from ball to case-shot.* **10.** ROUNDED BODY PART a rounded part of the body, e.g. at the base of the thumb or just behind the toes ○ *the ball of the foot* **11.** TABOO TERM a highly offensive term for a testicle (*taboo*) ■ *vti* (**balls, balling, balled**) **1.** MAKE INTO OR FORM BALL to mould, gather, or wind something into a ball, or become a ball-shaped mass ○ *She balled her fists.* **2.** TABOO TERM a highly offensive

term meaning to have sexual intercourse (*taboo*) [13C. < Old Norse *böllr* or assumed Old English *beall* < Germanic] ◇ **get** *or* **set** *or* **start the ball rolling** to start something off, especially a conversation or project ◇ **keep the ball rolling** to ensure that an activity continues ◇ **on the ball** aware of what is going on and quick to respond and take action (*informal*) ◇ **play ball (with somebody)** to cooperate together or with somebody (*informal*) ◇ **the ball is in somebody's court** used to say that it is somebody's turn to take action

ball up *vt N Am* to make a complete mess of something by mistake or through lack of skill (*slang*) ■ *n* in Australian Rules football, the bouncing of the ball by the field umpire to restart the game after the ball has failed to emerge from a scrimmage

ball[2] /bawl/ *n* a large-scale formal social event at which the main activity is dancing [Early 17C. < French *bal* < late Latin *ballare* < Greek *ballizein*] ◇ **have a ball** to enjoy yourself very much (*informal*) ○ *It was a great party; we really had a ball!*

Ball /bawl/, **Hugo** (1886–1927) German poet and musician. An important figure in the Dadaist movement, he moved to Switzerland at the start of World War I and founded the Cabaret Voltaire in Zurich in 1916.

Ball, John (1338?–81) English rebel. An excommunicated priest, he was one of the leaders, with Wat Tyler, of the Peasants' Revolt (1381). He was executed for his part in the rebellion.

> 'When Adam delved and Eve span, / Who was then the gentleman?'
> [John Ball, *Sermon on the day before the Peasants' Revolt*; 12 June 1381]

Ball, Lucille (1911–89) US actor. A gifted comedian, she appeared with her husband Desi Arnaz in the television comedy *I Love Lucy* (1951–57), the first of several popular series. She was also a successful television producer. Full name **Ball, Lucille Désirée**

> 'I think knowing what you *cannot* do is more important than knowing what you can do. In fact, that's good taste.'
> [Lucille Ball. Quoted in *The Real Story of Lucille Ball*, Eleanor Harris; 1954]

Ball, Murray Hone (*b.* 1939) New Zealand cartoonist. He created cartoon strips, including *Footrot Flats*.

Balla /bálla/, **Giacomo** (1871–1958) Italian painter, known for using cubist techniques to suggest motion

ballad /bállad/ *n* **1.** a song or poem, especially a traditional one or one in a traditional style, telling a story in a number of short regular stanzas, often with a refrain ○ *The Ballad of Bonnie and Clyde* **2.** a slow romantic popular song ○ *two up-tempo numbers followed by a ballad* [15C. < French *ballade* < late Latin *ballare* (see BALL[2])] —**balladic** /bə láddik/ *adj* —**balladist** *n* —**balladry** *n*

ballade /ba laád, bə-/ *n* **1.** a poem consisting of three stanzas of eight or ten lines and a short concluding explanatory stanza (**envoy**), all of which end with the same refrain **2.** an instrumental piece of music, usually for piano, intended to suggest the telling of a story as in a ballad. The best-known ballades in the classical repertoire are by Chopin and Brahms. [14C. Variant of BALLAD]

balladeer /bálla déer/ *n* a ballad singer

ballad opera *n* a form of opera with spoken dialogue and popular tunes made into songs. The most famous example is John Gay's *The Beggar's Opera*.

Ballance /bállanss/, **John** (1839–93) British-born premier of New Zealand (1891–93). He led the Liberal party (1887–93) and was noted for his progressive legislation.

ball and chain *n* **1.** IRON BALL ON CHAIN a type of restraint formerly used for prisoners consisting of an iron ball on a chain that is attached at its other end to the prisoner's ankle **2.** GREAT HINDRANCE something considered to be a great hindrance or restraint ○ *Censorship can be a ball and chain fettering artistic freedom of expression.* **3.** OFFENSIVE TERM an offensive term deliberately insulting a man's wife (*dated slang*)

ball-and-claw *adj* having a foot or another part modelled in the shape of an animal's claw holding a ball ○ *a ball-and-claw bathtub*

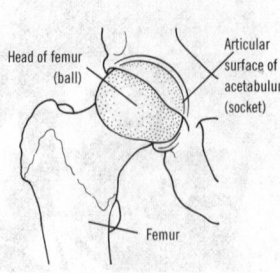
ball and socket joint

ball and socket joint, ball joint *n* **1.** a joint such as the hip joint in which a bone with a rounded end fits into a concave area of the adjoining bone, allowing a wide range of movement **2.** a junction between two moving parts of a mechanism in which the rounded end of one part fits into a cup-shaped socket on the other

Ballarat /bálla rat/ city in southern Victoria, Australia. It was a major gold-mining town in the mid-19th century and is now an industrial centre. Population: 84,846 (2002 estimate).

ballast /bállast/ *n* **1.** STABILIZING HEAVY WEIGHTS heavy material carried in the hold of a ship, especially one that has no cargo, in the keel of a sailing boat, or in the gondola of a balloon, to give the craft increased stability **2.** SOMETHING THAT GIVES BULK OR STABILITY anything that serves no particular purpose except to give bulk or weight to something or that provides additional stability **3.** FOUNDATION MATERIAL stones or gravel when used as a foundation for a road or railway track **4.** INDUST GRAVEL USED IN MAKING CONCRETE gravel used in making concrete and in earthworks **5.** ELEC ENG CIRCUIT LIMITING CURRENT FLOW a circuit that limits the current flow in a fluorescent lamp ■ *vt* (**-lasts, -lasting, -lasted**) **1.** PUT BALLAST ON SOMETHING to load ballast onto something **2.** STABILIZE SOMETHING to give stability to something [Mid-16C. Probably < Old Danish, 'mere weight' < *bar* 'bare, mere' + *last* 'load']

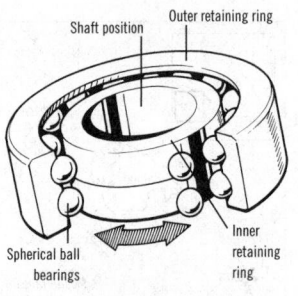
ball bearing

ball bearing *n* **1.** a metal ball used to reduce friction between moving parts **2.** a bearing containing a number of metal balls that rotate freely to reduce friction between moving parts

ball boy *n* **1.** a boy who retrieves balls that go out of play during a tennis match and delivers them to the server when required **2.** a boy who takes care of the balls that are out of play during a baseball game or practice

ballbreaker /báwl braykər/ *n N Am* a highly offensive term that deliberately insults a woman who is regarded as aggressive towards men (*taboo*)

ballbuster /báwl bustər/ *n* **1.** *US* an offensive term for a difficult and unpleasant job (*taboo*) **2.** *N Am* same as **ballbreaker** (*taboo offensive*)

ball clay *n* a sedimentary clay containing kaolin, mica, other minerals, and organic matter. Use: ceramics. [< an obsolete mining process in which clay was handled as rounded cubes ('balls')]

ballcock /báwl kok/ *n* a floating ball on the end of an arm that is connected to a valve controlling the water level in a tank. The valve opens as the ball falls and closes as it rises.

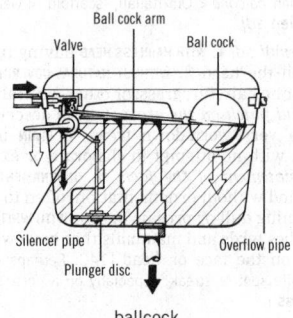
ballcock

ballerina /bálla reéna/ *n* **1.** a woman ballet dancer **2.** *N Am* a woman dancer in a ballet company who is regularly given principal parts [Late 18C. < Italian, 'woman dancing teacher' < *ballare* 'to dance' < Greek *ballizein*]

Ballesteros /bálla steér oss/, **Severiano** (*b.* 1957) Spanish golfer. He won the British Open three times (1979, 1984, and 1988) and in 1980 became the youngest player ever to win the US Masters Tournament.

> 'I look into their eyes, shake their hand, pat their back and wish them luck, but I am thinking, I am going to bury you.'
> [Severiano Ballesteros, *The Guardian*; 14 October 1989]

ballet: Darcy Bussell performing in the ballet *Laurencia* (1990)

ballet /bállay/ *n* **1.** FORM OF DANCE a form of dance characterized by conventional steps, poses, and graceful movements including leaps and spins **2.** STORY PERFORMED BY DANCERS a choreographed presentation of a story or theme performed to music by ballet dancers, or the musical score written for this **3.** GROUP OF DANCERS a company of ballet dancers who perform together [Mid-17C. Via French < Italian *balletto* < *ballo* 'ball (with dancing)']

balletic /ba léttik/ *adj* with the grace of somebody dancing in a ballet

balletomane /bálletō mayn/ *n* a lover of ballet —**balletomania** /-máyni a/ *n*

ballet shoe *n* **1.** a flat light flexible slipper made of silk or leather, worn by ballet dancers for performing and practice **2.** same as **pointe shoe 3.** a light flat hard-soled shoe resembling one worn by a ballet dancer

ball game *n* **1.** any game played with a ball **2.** *N Am* a game of baseball ◇ **a whole new ball game** a completely new or different set of circumstances (*informal*)

ball girl *n* a girl who retrieves balls that go out of play during a tennis match and delivers them to the server when required

ballgown /báwl gown/ *n* a full-length formal dress suitable for wearing to a ball

Ballina /bállina/ coastal town in northeastern New South Wales, Australia, situated at the mouth of the Richmond River. Population: 38,889 (2002 estimate).

Balliol another spelling of **Baliol**

ballista /bə lísta/ (*plural* **-tae** /-tee/) *n* a piece of military equipment that was used in ancient times to hurl stones and other missiles over a distance [Early 16C. < Latin < Greek *ballein* 'throw']

a at; aa father; aw all; ay day; ai hair; ə about, item, edible, common, circus; e egg; ee eel; hw when; i it, happy; ī ice; 'l apple; 'm rhythm; 'n fashion; o odd; ō open; oo good; oo pool; ow owl; oy oil; th thin; th this; u up; ur urge;

ballistic /bə lístik/ *adj* relating to the movements of objects propelled through the air [Mid-18C. < BALLISTA] —**ballistically** *adv* ◇ **go ballistic** to become extremely angry (*informal*)

ballistic missile *n* a missile that maintains a course determined by its initial orientation and engine thrust, rather than one calculated by guidance systems during flight

ballistics /bə lístiks/ *n* **1. STUDY OF PROJECTILES** the study of the movements and forces involved in the propulsion of objects through the air (*takes a singular verb*) **2. STUDY OF FIREARMS** the study of firearms and ammunition (*takes a singular verb*) **3. FIRING CHARACTERISTICS OF WEAPON** the characteristics of a firearm that affect the way missiles are fired (*takes a plural verb*)

ball joint *n* ANAT, MECH ENG same as **ball and socket joint**

ball lightning *n* a rare form of lightning that takes the shape of a moving glowing ball, typically disappearing without explosion

ballocks *npl, interj, vt* another spelling of **bollocks** (*taboo offensive*) [Old English *bealluc* < Germanic, 'little (round) ball']

ball of fire *n* an extremely energetic and dynamic person (*informal*)

ballon d'essai /ba láwn de sáy/ (*plural* **ballons d'essai**) *n* same as **trial balloon** [< French]

balloon /bə lóon/ *n* **1.** LEISURE **GAS-FILLED BAG USED AS TOY** a small coloured bag made of thin rubber or plastic that is inflated with air or helium and used as a toy or decoration **2. GAS-FILLED BAG USED IN AIR TRANSPORT** an extremely large bag filled with a lighter-than-air gas and used as a form of air transport, carrying passengers or equipment in a suspended basket or gondola **3. SPEECH CIRCLE IN CARTOON** a rounded outline with a point directed towards a character in a cartoon that encloses the text of the character's speech or thought **4. BRANDY GLASS** a glass with a large rounded bowl, used for drinking brandy ■ *vi* (**-loons, -looning, -looned**) **1. SWELL** to form a large round swollen shape **2. INCREASE IN AMOUNT** to increase in amount suddenly and rapidly [Late 16C. < French *ballon* or Italian *ballone* 'large (round) ball'] ◇ **go over** *or* **down like a lead balloon** to be completely unsuccessful (*informal*) ◇ **if** *or* **when the balloon goes up** if *or* when the expected or likely trouble or excitement starts (*informal*)

balloon angioplasty *n* the use of a balloon catheter to widen a narrowed artery

balloon catheter *n* a tube that can be inserted into a blood vessel or other body part and inflated while inside, e.g. to widen a narrowed artery

ballooning /bə lóoning/ *n* the sport of riding in or piloting a balloon

balloonist /bə lóonist/ *n* the pilot of a balloon

balloon loan *n* a loan that is repaid with a series of regular payments and one much larger payment at the end

balloon mortgage *n* a mortgage that is paid off in a series of regular payments with one much larger payment at the end

balloon payment *n* a final payment on a loan, especially a mortgage, that is significantly larger than the usual payment and pays off the debt

balloon tyre *n* a pneumatic tyre with a wide tread inflated to a low pressure, used to drive on soft surfaces such as deep sand

balloon vine *n* a vine with ornamental pods shaped like balloons. Native to: tropics. Latin name: *Cardiospermum halicacabum*.

balloon whisk *n* a hand-held whisk made of stiff wires that form a loop at one end and are gathered into a covered handle at the other

ballot /bállət/ *n* **1. VOTING SYSTEM** a system in which eligible people vote, usually in secret, to determine the outcome of an election or make some other collective decision **2. SECRET VOTE** a secret vote held to determine the outcome of an election or some other decision **3.** *N Am* same as **ballot paper 4. TOTAL VOTES** the total number of votes that have been cast in an election ■ *v* (**-lots, -loting, -loted**) **1.** *vt* **ASK PEOPLE TO VOTE** to carry out a ballot on members of an organization or an electorate **2.** *vi* **VOTE** to vote in a ballot [Mid-16C. < Italian *ballotta* 'little ball' < *balla* '(round) ball'] —**balloter** *n*

ballot box *n* **1.** a box in which voters put their ballot papers after marking them **2.** the system in which leaders are elected or decisions are made using a ballot ○ *The people will decide at the ballot box.*

ballot paper, **ballot** *n* a piece of paper or card on which somebody can record a vote. N Am term **ballot**

ballot rigging *n* the use of dishonest or illegal methods of voting to ensure victory for a particular candidate or party in an election

ballpark /báwl paark/ *N Am n* **1. PARK FOR PLAYING BALL GAMES** a stadium or area of land for playing ball games, especially baseball **2.** AEROSP **TOUCHDOWN AREA FOR SPACECRAFT** the approximate area within which a spacecraft is intended to touch down ■ *adj* **APPROXIMATE** rough or approximate (*informal*) ○ *a ballpark figure* ◇ **in the (right) ballpark** within the right general range or scope (*slang*)

ballpeen hammer /báwl peen-/ *n* a hammer that has one end of its head rounded for beating metal

ball-pen *n Malaysia* same as **ballpoint**

ballplayer /báwl playər/ *n* **1.** a football player who has excellent ball control **2.** *N Am* somebody who plays baseball, softball, American football, or basketball

ballpoint /báwl poynt/, **ballpoint pen** *n* a pen with a small rotating ball at its tip that transfers the ink from an inner tube onto the writing surface

ballroom /báwl room, -ròom/ *n* a very large room with a smooth floor and a high ceiling, used for formal dances

ballroom dancing *n* formal dancing with a partner in dances such as the foxtrot, quickstep, and waltz that use a set pattern of steps

balls /bawlz/ *n* (*taboo*) (*takes a singular verb*) **1.** a highly offensive term meaning courage and determination **2.** a highly offensive term meaning nonsense ■ *npl* a highly offensive term for the testicles (*takes a plural verb*)

balls up *vt* a highly offensive term meaning to make a complete mess of something by mistake or through lack of skill (*slang*)

balls-up *n* a highly offensive term for a complete mistake or totally unsuccessful attempt at something (*slang*)

ballsy /báwlzi/ (**-ier, -iest**) *adj N Am* a highly offensive term meaning unusually tough, courageous, or determined (*slang taboo*) [Mid-20C. < BALL[1]]

ball tearer *n Aus* an offensive term for something or somebody regarded as either exceptionally good or exceptionally bad (*taboo*)

ball valve *n* a valve in which a ball moves in and out of a spherical socket in response to changes in fluid or mechanical pressure

bally /bálli/ *adj, adv* used to express anger, frustration, or additional emphasis (*dated informal*) [Late 19C. Alteration of BLOODY, perhaps influenced by the written form *bl-y*]

ballyhoo /bálli hóo/ *n* **1. UPROAR** a noisy argument or disturbance **2. SENSATIONAL ADVERTISING** sensational, loud, or sustained advertising ■ *vt* (**-hoos, -hooing, -hooed**) **ADVERTISE SOMETHING LOUDLY** to advertise or publicize something loudly and insistently [Mid-19C. Origin ?]

Ballymena /bálli méenə/ town in County Antrim, Northern Ireland, the administrative headquarters of the district of Ballymena. Population: 28,717 (1991).

Ballymoney /bálli múnni/ district in County Antrim, Northern Ireland. The administrative headquarters are in Ballymoney town. Population: 26,894 (2001). Area: 417 sq. km/161 sq. mi.

ballyrag *vt* same as **bullyrag**

balm /baam/ *n* **1. SOOTHING OIL** a fragrant oily substance obtained as a resin from various trees. Use: soothing ointments. **2. SOMETHING THAT SOOTHES** something that has the effect of calming, soothing, or comforting ○ *balm to his wounded ego* **3. PLEASANT SCENT** a pleasant scent (*literary*) **4.** PLANTS same as **lemon balm** [13C. Via French *bame* < Latin *balsamum* (see BALSAM)]

Balmain /bál maN/, **Pierre** (1914–82) French couturier, known for his simple and elegant designs. Full name **Balmain, Pierre Alexandre Claudius**

> 'The trick of wearing mink is to look as though you are wearing a cloth coat. The trick of wearing a cloth coat is to look as though you are wearing mink.'
> [Pierre Balmain, *Observer*, 24 December 1955]

Balmain bug /bál mayn-/ *n Aus* a shellfish with a flat wide body, eaten as a delicacy. Native to: Australia. Latin name: *Ibacus peronii*.

Balmer series /bálmər-/ *n* a series of lines in the visible part of the atomic spectrum of hydrogen [Early 20C. After J. J. *Balmer* (1825–98), Swiss physicist]

balm of Gilead /-gílli ad/ *n* **1.** TREES same as **balsam fir 2.** a hybrid poplar tree that has heart-shaped leaves and resinous buds. Genus: *Populus*. **3.** a fragrant resin produced by various trees

Balmoral /bal mórrəl/, **balmoral** *n* **1.** a strong walking shoe that is fastened with laces **2.** a traditional Scottish flat woollen cap [Mid-19C. After the royal estate of *Balmoral* in Scotland]

balmy /baámi/ (**-ier, -iest**) *adj* **1.** pleasantly warm and mild in climate ○ *a balmy summer's evening* **2.** same as **barmy** (*informal*) —**balmily** *adv* —**balminess** *n*

balneology /bálni óllǝji/ *n* a branch of medicine concerned with therapeutic bathing, especially in natural mineral spring water [Mid-19C. < Latin *balneum* 'bath'] —**balneological** /-ə lójjik'l/ *adj* —**balneologist** *n*

balneotherapy /bálni ə thérrəpi/ *n* the medical practice of treatment by immersion in baths, especially those in spas containing water with a high mineral content [Late 19C. < Latin *balneum* 'bath']

Balochi *n, adj* PEOPLES, LANG another spelling of **Baluchi**

baloney /bə lóni/ (*plural* **-neys**) *n* (*informal*) **1.** *N Am* FOOD same as **bologna 2.** silly or stupid talk ○ *Don't talk baloney.* [Early 20C. Origin ?]

~~**baloon**~~ incorrect spelling of **balloon**

Balqash, Lake /bal kásh/ shallow lake in southeastern Kazakhstan into which the River Ili flows. Area: 18,200 sq. km/7,030 sq. mi.

balsa /báwlssə/ (*plural* **-sas** or *same*) *n* **1.** *also* **balsa wood** a lightweight softwood. Use: rafts, toy models, insulation. **2.** a tree that yields balsa. Native to: South America. Genus: *Ochroma*. [Early 17C. < Spanish, 'raft']

balsam /báwlssəm/ *n* **1. OILY PLANT SUBSTANCE** an oily resinous substance (**oleoresin**) obtained from plants, especially one containing benzoic acid or cinnamic acid. Use: perfumes, medicines. **2. PREPARATION CONTAINING BALSAM** a preparation containing or resembling balsam **3. TREE YIELDING RESIN** a tree that yields a fragrant resinous substance, especially a balsam fir **4. FLOWERING PLANT** a plant of the family that includes Busy Lizzie. Family: Balsaminaceae. [Pre-12C. Via Latin < Greek *balsamon*] —**balsamic** /bawl sámmik/ *adj*

balsam fir *n* a pyramid-shaped tree that is the source of canada balsam. Native to: North America. Latin name: *Abies balsamea*.

balsamic vinegar *n* vinegar made from the juice of white grapes matured in wood for 10 to 50 years, giving it a characteristic dark colour and rich sweet-sour taste

balsam of Peru *n* **1.** an aromatic resin obtained from trees. Use: perfumes, skin lotions. **2.** a tree that produces high-quality timber and yields balsam of Peru. Native to: South America. Latin name: *Myroxylon balsamum* var. pareirae.

Balt /bawlt/ *n* **1.** somebody who comes from Lithuania, Latvia, or Estonia **2.** somebody whose native language is Lithuanian, Latvian, or Estonian [Late 19C. < late Latin *balthae*] —**Balt** *adj*

Balthazar[1] /bal tházzə, báltha zaar/ *n* a bottle that contains 12 litres of wine, the equivalent of 16 bottles [Mid-20C. After *Balshazzar*, king of Babylon, who, according to the book of Daniel in the Bible, 'made a great feast...and drank wine before the thousand']

Balthazar[2] /bal tházzə, báltha zaar/, **Balthasar** *n* traditionally one of the three magi who the Bible says brought gifts to Bethlehem to honour the birth of Jesus Christ (Matthew 2:1–12)

balti /báwlti, bál-/ *n* a spicy dish originally from Pakistan that is traditionally served in the bowl-shaped pan it is cooked in (**karahi**) [< Urdu *bāltī*, literally 'pull']

Balti /báwlti, bál-/ *n* a Tibetan language spoken in northern Kashmir [Early 20C. < Ladakhi dialect] —**Balti** *adj*

Baltic[1] /báwltik/ *n* a group of Indo-European languages in northeastern Europe, closely related to the Slavonic group. Native speakers: 5 million. [Late 16C. < late Latin *Balticus*]

Baltic[2] /báwltik/ **1.** ♦ Baltic Sea **2.** ♦ Baltic States

Baltic Exchange *n* a commodity market in the City of London that deals in international trade, especially international bulk shipping

Baltic Sea /báwltik-/ sea in northern Europe. Nearly landlocked, it borders Sweden, Finland, Russia, Estonia, Latvia, Lithuania, Poland, Germany, and Denmark. Area: 422,000 sq. km/163,000 sq. mi.

Baltic States Estonia, Latvia, and Lithuania, considered as a group

Baltimore /báwltə mawr/ port and the largest city in Maryland, near the Chesapeake Bay. It is home to the Johns Hopkins University. Population: 638,614 (2002 estimate).

Baltimore oriole *n* a songbird, the male of which has a black head and upper body with an orange underside and tail. Native to: North America. Latin name: *Icterus galbula*. [Late 17C. After George Calvert, Lord *Baltimore* (1580?–1632), English proprietor of Maryland]

Balto-Slavonic /báwl tō-/, **Balto-Slavic** *n* the Baltic and Slavonic branches of the Indo-European language family, sometimes considered to form a unified grouping —**Balto-Slavonic** *adj*

Baluchi /bə loóchi/ (*plural* **-chis** or *same*), **Balochi** /-lōchi/ *n* **1.** somebody who comes from Baluchistan **2.** an Eastern Iranian language spoken in Baluchistan. Native speakers: 5 million. [Early 17C. < Persian *Balučī*] —**Baluchi** *adj*

Baluchistan /bə loóchi staán/ dry mountainous region in southwestern Pakistan and southeastern Iran

balun /bállən/ *n* a transformer used to couple balanced and unbalanced transmission lines [Contraction of BALANCED + UNBALANCED]

baluster /bálləstər/ *n* **1.** an upright post supporting a handrail, e.g. in the banister of a staircase **2.** a support that is shaped like a long narrow vase, e.g. a chair leg or the stem of a glass [Early 17C. Via French *balustre* < Italian *balaustro* < Greek *balaustion* 'blossom of the wild pomegranate', because early balusters resembled its shape]

balustrade

balustrade /bállə stráyd/ *n* a decorative railing together with its supporting balusters, often used at the front of a parapet or gallery [Mid-17C. Via French < Spanish *balastrada* or Italian *balaustrata* < *balaustro* (see BALUSTER)]

Balzac /bál zak/, **Honoré de** (1799–1850) French novelist. He wrote 90 novels that provide a panoramic social history of France between about 1790 and 1830, and arranged them under the collective title *The Human Comedy*. See Cultural note at **human**. Born **Balssa, Honoré** —**Balzacian** /bal záki ən/ *adj*

'Equality may perhaps be a right, but no power on earth can ever turn it into a fact.'
[Honoré de Balzac, *La Duchesse de Langeais* (*The Duchess of Langeais*); 1834]

bam /bam/ *vti* (**bams, bamming, bammed**) *US* MAKE LOUD NOISE to make a loud hammering or thudding noise ○ *bammed on the door* ■ *n* LOUD NOISE a loud thudding or hammering noise ○ *fell to the floor with a bam* ■ *interj* USED TO INDICATE SUDDEN IMPACT used to indicate sudden impact, the result of such impact, or the sudden occurrence of an event of great significance (*informal*) ○ *All of a sudden, bam! I was 30!* [Early 20C. An imitation of the sound]

Bamako /bámməkō/ capital and largest city of Mali, situated on the River Niger. Population: 1,016,167 (1998).

Bambara /bám baárə, baám-/ (*plural same* or **-ras**) *n* **1.** a member of an African people living mainly in Mali, western Africa **2.** a Niger-Congo language spoken in Mali, Senegal, Burkina Faso, and Côte d'Ivoire. Native speakers: 1–2 million. [Late 19C. < *Bambara*] —**Bambara** *adj*

Bamberg /bám burg/ city and river port north of Nuremberg in Bavaria, Germany. Population: 70,216 (1997).

bambino /bam beénō/ (*plural* **-nos** or **-ni** /-ni/) *n* **1.** a baby or young child (*informal*) **2.** a representation of Jesus Christ as a baby [Early 18C. < Italian, 'baby' < *bambo* 'silly']

bamboo /bam boó/ *n* **1.** the strong hollow stems of a tropical plant. Use: building, furniture, canes, fishing rods. **2.** a plant with long woody, often hollow, stems that grows in dense clumps and produces bamboo. Native to: tropical and semitropical areas. Family: Bambusaceae. [Late 16C. Via Dutch *bamboes*, modern Latin *bambusa* < Malay *mambu*]

bamboo curtain *n* the political, military, and ideological barrier that effectively isolated China from Western countries from the Communist revolution of 1949 until China's relaxation of trade barriers in 1979 [After IRON CURTAIN]

bamboo shoot *n* an edible young shoot of the bamboo plant that is eaten sliced and cooked, particularly in East Asian dishes

bamboozle /bam boóz'l/ (**-zles, -zling, -zled**) *vt* (*informal*) **1.** to trick or deceive somebody through misleading statements or falsehoods **2.** to make somebody confused [Early 18C. Origin ?] —**bamboozler** *n*

ban[1] /ban/ *vt* (**bans, banning, banned**) **1.** FORBID SOMETHING to forbid something officially or legally so that it cannot be done, used, seen, or read **2.** STOP SOMEBODY DOING SOMETHING to forbid somebody to do something or go somewhere **3.** HIST RESTRICT RIGHTS IN SOUTH AFRICA during the apartheid era in South Africa, to punish somebody suspected of breaking the apartheid laws by preventing the person from moving around freely and having contact with other people ■ *n* **1.** ORDER FORBIDDING SOMETHING an order officially or legally forbidding something so that it cannot be done, used, seen, or read **2.** PUBLIC REVILEMENT public condemnation of somebody or something (*archaic*) **3.** CURSE a powerful curse on somebody (*archaic*) [Old English *bannan* 'summon, proclaim' < Germanic; noun via Old French *ban* 'summons for military duty, proclamation' < same Germanic word]

ban[2] /ban/ (*plural* **bani** /baánni/) *n* a subunit of currency in Romania and Moldova. See table at **currency** [Late 19C. Via Romanian < Serbo-Croatian *bān* 'lord' < Turkic *bayan* 'very rich person' < *bay* 'rich gentleman']

Banaba /bə naábə/ one of the 33 islands of Kiribati in the western Pacific Ocean. Population: 284 (1990). Area: 6 sq. km/2 sq. mi. Former name **Ocean Island**

banal /bə naál/ *adj* boringly ordinary and lacking in originality [Mid-19C. < French < *ban* (see BAN[1])] —**banally** *adv*

banality /bə nálləti/ (*plural* **-ties**) *n* **1.** conventional or dull ordinariness **2.** an ordinary remark or feature that lacks originality

banana /bə naánə/ (*plural* **-as** or *same*) *n* **1.** a long and slightly curved fruit with creamy coloured soft flesh and a skin that turns from green to yellow when ripe **2.** a large-leaved tropical plant that bears bananas. Genus: *Musa*. [Late 16C. Via Spanish and Portuguese < Mande] ◇ **go bananas** to become uncontrollably or unreasonably angry or excited (*informal*)

banana bender *n* *Aus* an offensive term for somebody who comes from or lives in Queensland

banana

bananalander /bə naánə landə/ *n* *Aus* same as **banana bender**

banana plug *n* a single conductor plug with a spring metal tip shaped like a banana

bananaquit /bə naánə kwit/ *n* a small brown and yellow songbird common in gardens. Native to: Central and South America, Caribbean. Latin name: *Coereba flaveola*.

banana republic *n* a small country with an unstable government and an economy dependent on the export of a single product or on outside financial help (*disapproving*)

banana skin *n* something that could easily result in an embarrassing mistake or failure

banana split *n* a dessert of peeled banana cut in half lengthways, filled with ice cream, sweet sauce, whipped cream, and chopped nuts

banausic /bə náwzik/ *adj* **1.** with no art, creativity, or imagination **2.** practical or materialistic rather than uplifting or inspiring [Mid-19C. < Greek *banausikos* 'of or for artisans']

Banbridge /bán brij/ district council in County Down, Northern Ireland. The administrative headquarters are in Banbridge town. Population: 41,392 (2001).

banco /bángkō/ *interj* used in baccarat and chemin de fer to declare that a player wishes to place a bet equivalent to the total worth of the bank ■ *n* in baccarat and chemin de fer, a bet placed equivalent to the total worth of the bank [Late 18C. Via French < Italian, variant of *banca* (see BANK[1])]

~~bancrupcy~~ incorrect spelling of **bankruptcy**

band[1] /band/ *n* **1.** MUSICIANS PLAYING TOGETHER a group of musicians who play together, particularly a group playing popular or rock music **2.** GROUP WITH SAME BELIEFS OR PURPOSE a group of people who have the same ideas or beliefs or who are pursuing the same activity together ○ *a growing band of supporters* **3.** CULTL ANTHROP SMALL GROUP WITH SIMPLE SOCIAL STRUCTURE a subdivision of a people that has a relatively simple social structure [15C. < French *bande*] ◇ **to beat the band** to a very great extent or degree (*dated*)

band together *vi* to form a group in order to achieve a goal

band[2] /band/ *n* **1.** STRIP OR LOOP OF MATERIAL a strip of fabric, metal, or elastic placed around something to strengthen it or around several things to hold them together **2.** CONTRASTING STRIPE a long narrow area that is different in material, colour, or texture from the adjacent parts **3.** STRIP OR CIRCLE OF MATERIAL a strip or circle of fabric or elastic used for decoration, identification, or absorbing sweat on the forehead or hands **4.** RING a plain ring worn on a finger ○ *a wedding band* **5.** MOVING BELT a moving belt in a piece of machinery **6.** RANGE OF VALUES WITHIN LARGER RANGE a range of values such as age or amount of tax liability that relate only to some people within a larger group ○ *the highest tax band* **7.** RANGE OF RADIO FREQUENCIES a range of frequencies or wavelengths assigned to a radio station or radio broadcaster **8.** GROUP OF PUPILS TAUGHT TOGETHER a group of pupils from the same school year, taught together because they are at a similar level of ability **9.** PHYS RANGE OF ENERGIES the range of energies possessed by electrons in a solid **10.** GEOL ORE OR MINERAL LAYER a layer of rock with a different composition or texture from the adjacent layers ■ *vt* (**bands, banding, banded**) **1.** PUT BAND ON OR ROUND SOMETHING to put a strip on or round something to decorate or identify it or to hold a number of things together **2.** CATEGORIZE THINGS to

divide things into ranges of value **3.** EDUC **DIVIDE PUPILS INTO GROUPS** to divide pupils from one school year into groups to be taught together because they are at a similar ability level [13C. < Old Norse < Germanic; reinforced by French *bande* < the same Germanic word]

banda /bándə/ *n* a military band used on occasion in operas as an ensemble on or off stage or to provide a contrast to the main orchestra [< Italian, 'band, group']

Banda /bándə/, **Hastings** (1906?–97) Malawian politician. He was prime minister (1964–66), then president (1966–94), of Malawi. Full name **Banda, Hastings Kamazu**

'I wish I could bring Stonehenge to Nyasaland to show there was a time when Britain had a savage culture.'
[Hastings Banda, *Observer*; 10 March 1963]

bandage /bándij/ *n* a long strip of thin or elasticated fabric that is wrapped around a wound or injured part of the body to protect or support it [Late 16C. < French < *bande* (see BAND²)] —**bandage** *vt* —**bandager** *n*

bandanna /ban dánnə/, **bandana** *n* a large square of brightly coloured cotton or silk cloth worn over the hair or around the neck [Mid-18C. Probably via Portuguese < Hindi *bāndhnū*, method of tie-dyeing < *bāndhnā* 'to tie']

Bandaranaike /bándərə nī́ əkə/, **Sirimavo** (1916–2000) Sri Lankan politician. She succeeded her husband S. W. R. D. Bandaranaike to become the world's first woman prime minister (1960–65, 1970–77, 1994–2000). She nationalized schools and foreign-owned plantations in Sri Lanka. Born **Ratwatte Dias, Sirimavo**

Bandaranaike, S. W. R. D. (1899–1959) prime minister of Sri Lanka (1956–59). He was assassinated by a Buddhist monk. Full name **Bandaranaike, Solomon West Ridgeway Dias**

Bandar Seri Begawan /bán daar sérri bə gáawən/ capital of Brunei, in the northern part of the country, on Brunei Bay. Population: 49,902 (1997 estimate).

Banda Sea /bándə-/ sea in the Pacific Ocean in eastern Indonesia, north of the island of Timor and southeast of Sulawesi. Area: 738,147 sq. km/285,000 sq. mi.

B & B *abbr* bed and breakfast (*informal*)

bandbox /bánd boks/ *n* a round lightweight box for carrying accessories such as hats [Mid-17C. Because originally used to carry neckbands]

bandeau /bándō/ (*plural* **-deaux** /-dōz/) *n* **1.** a piece of material worn round the chest to cover the breasts **2.** *N Am* a ribbon or band of material worn around the head to keep the hair in place [Early 18C. < French < Old French *bandel* 'little band' < *bande* (see BAND²)]

banded /bándid/ *adj* marked with bands of different or contrasting colours ○ *banded agate*

banded-iron formation *n* a thin, extremely old, iron-rich layer of sedimentary material of unknown origin, deposited on all continents and containing haematite, magnetite, goethite, and limonite

banderilla /bándə reé ə, -reéyə/ *n* in a bullfight, a long decorated barbed dart that is thrust into the neck or shoulder of a bull by a bullfighter's assistant [Late 18C. < Spanish, 'little banner' < *bandera* 'banner']

banderillero /bándə ree áirrō, -lyáirō/ (*plural* **-ros**) *n* a bullfighter's assistant who sticks a banderilla into the bull during a bullfight [Late 18C. < Spanish < *banderilla* (see BANDERILLA)]

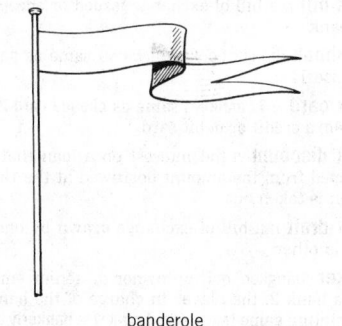

banderole

banderole /bándə rōl/, **banderol**, **bannerol** /bánnə-/ *n* **1.** FLAG ON MASTHEAD a long narrow flag with a divided end that is flown on a ship's masthead **2.** FLAG AT FUNERAL a flag that is carried at a funeral or used to cover a tomb **3.** INSCRIBED BAND a sculpted scroll or band bearing an inscription **4.** HIST RIBBON ON KNIGHT'S LANCE a ribbon or streamer hanging from a knight's lance [Mid-16C. Via French < Italian *banderuola* 'small banner' < *bandiera* 'banner']

bandh /bund/, **bundh** *n S Asia* a short general strike called in a city or district [< Hindi, 'a tying up']

bandicoot

bandicoot /bándi koot/ *n* a marsupial that has a long nose, strong hind legs, and a long tail and eats mainly insects and plants. Native to: Australia, Tasmania, New Guinea. Family: Peramelidae. [Late 18C. < Telugu *pandikokku* 'pig-rat']

bandicoot rat *n* a large rodent that is a serious pest to farmers. Native to: South Asia. Latin name: *Bandicota indica*.

banding /bánding/ *n* EDUC same as **streaming**

bandit /bándit/ (*plural* **-dits** or **-ditti** /-dítti/) *n* **1.** ARMED ROBBER an armed robber who steals from travellers and other people, usually at gunpoint **2.** GANGSTER a member of a gang of violent criminals **3.** *US* EXPLOITATIVE PERSON a swindler or cheat **4.** AIR FORCE ENEMY AIRCRAFT an enemy aircraft sighted by a crew while flying (*informal*) ○ *Bandits at twelve o'clock high!* [Late 16C. < Italian *bandito* < *bandire* 'to ban'] ◇ **make out like a bandit** *or* **bandits** *US* to be extremely successful, especially by making a lot of money in a short period of time (*informal*)

banditry /bánditri/ *n* the occurrence or prevalence of armed robbery and violent crime

banditti CRIME plural of **bandit**

Bandjarmasin ♦ **Banjarmasin**

bandleader /bánd leedər/ *n* the conductor of a band, especially of a dance band

Bandler /bándlər/, **Faith** (*b.* 1918) Australian writer and activist. She was cofounder of the Aboriginal Australian Fellowship (1956). Full name **Bandler, Ida Lessing Faith**

bandmaster /bánd maastər/ *n* the conductor of a band, especially of a brass band or a military band

bandobust /bún dō bust/, **bundobust** *n S Asia* arrangements or preparations made to organize an event, especially security arrangements ○ *police bandobust* [Late 18C. Via Urdu < Persian *band-o-bast* 'tying and binding']

bandog /bán dog/ *n* an aggressive dog produced by cross-breeding a pit bull terrier with a mastiff, Rottweiler, or Rhodesian ridgeback [15C. Blend of BAND² + DOG; originally a dog that was chained up or bound]

bandoleer /bándə leér/, **bandolier** *n* a soldier's belt with loops or small pockets for storing cartridges, worn over the shoulder and across the chest [Late 16C. < French, probably either < Spanish *bandolera* < *banda* 'sash', or < Catalan *bandolera* < *bandoler* 'bandit']

bandoneon /ban dóni ən/ *n* a square concertina, used especially in Argentina [Early 20C. Via Spanish *bandoneón* < German *Bandonion*, after its German inventor Heinrich Band (1821–60)] —**bandoneonist** *n*

bandore /ban dáwr, bán dawr/ *n* a musical instrument of the 16th and 17th centuries, similar to a large guitar or lute [Mid-16C. Origin ?]

band-pass filter *n* **1.** an electronic filter that passes only those frequencies within a specific range **2.** a device transmitting electromagnetic radiation,

especially visible light, within a restricted wavelength range

band saw *n* a stationary power saw with a continuous vertically mounted blade

B and S Ball *n* a social event held in the Australian outback for young people, typically a weekend of music, dancing, and drinking. Guests normally wear formal evening attire, but sleep in tents or in their vehicles. [Shortening of *Bachelor and Spinsters Ball*]

band shell *n* a bandstand with a curved wall at the back that is designed to reflect the sound towards the audience

bandsman /bándzmən/ (*plural* **-men** /-mən/) *n* a man who plays in a brass band or military band

bandsperson /bándz purss'n/ (*plural* **-persons** or **-people** /-peep'l/) *n* somebody who plays in a brass band or military band

bandspreading /bánd spreding/ *n* a function of some radios that allows the user to select a narrow band of frequencies and space them further apart, to make tuning into a specific frequency easier

bandstand /bánd stand/ *n* a platform for a band or small orchestra to perform on, especially outdoors

bandswoman /bándz woomən/ (*plural* **-women** /-wimin/) *n* a woman who plays in a brass band or military band

band theory *n* a theory that explains the electrical conductivity of solids in terms of energy bands containing electrons

Bandung /bán dŏong/ city in southern Indonesia, on western Java Island, southeast of Jakarta. Population: 3,557,665 (1997).

B & W, b & w *abbr* PHOTOGRAPHY black-and-white

bandwagon /bánd wagən/ *n* **1.** a cause or movement that is gaining popularity and support **2.** *N Am* an ornately decorated wagon that musicians perform on during a parade ◇ **jump** *or* **climb on the bandwagon** to join in something only because it is fashionable or likely to be profitable

bandwidth /bánd width/ *n* **1.** TELECOM **RANGE OF RADIO FREQUENCIES** a range of radio frequencies used in radio or telecommunications transmission and reception **2.** ONLINE **COMMUNICATION CAPACITY** the capacity, often measured in bits per second, of a communication channel, e.g. a connection to the Internet **3.** AVAILABLE TIME the time somebody has available to accomplish assigned tasks (*informal*) ○ *Do you have sufficient bandwidth to handle another job?*

bandy /bándi/ *vt* (**-dies, -dying, -died**) to toss words back and forth casually, often without caring whether they are true or what effect they may have ○ *I've heard the name being bandied about.* ■ *adj* (**-dier, -diest**) describes legs that curve outward so that the knees cannot meet [Late 16C. Perhaps < French *bander* 'take sides at tennis']

bandy-bandy (*plural* **bandy-bandies**) *n* a small, mildly venomous snake marked with black-and-white bands. Native to: Australia. Latin name: *Vermicella annulata*. [Early 20C. < an Aboriginal language]

bandy-legged *adj* having legs that curve outward, so that the knees do not touch

bane /bayn/ *n* **1.** SOMETHING THAT CAUSES MISERY something that continually causes problems or misery ○ *It's the bane of my life.* **2.** SOMETHING THAT CAUSES RUIN something that causes death, destruction, or ruin (*literary or archaic*) **3.** DEADLY POISON a fatal poison (*often used in combination in the names of poisonous plants*) [Old English *bana* < Germanic] ◇ **the bane of somebody's life** somebody or something that is a constant source of trouble or annoyance

baneberry /báyn berri/ (*plural* **-ries**) *n* **1.** a poisonous fleshy red or white berry of a baneberry plant **2.** a plant that bears baneberries. Native to: North America, Europe, Asia. Genus: *Rubus fruticosus*.

baneful /báynf'l/ *adj* causing ruin or destruction (*literary*) —**banefully** *adv*

USAGE See *baleful*.

Banff /bamf/ market town and seaport in Aberdeenshire, Scotland. Population: 4,110 (1991).

Banff National Park national park in the Rocky Mountains, southwestern Alberta, Canada. Area: 6,641 sq. km/2,564 sq. mi.

Banffshire /bámfshər/ former county in northeastern Scotland, now part of Aberdeenshire

bang[1] /bang/ n **1.** SUDDEN LOUD NOISE a sudden loud noise, e.g. the sound of a gun firing or a door slamming shut **2.** SHARP HIT a sharp blow or hit ○ *a nasty bang on the head* **3.** ENERGY BURST a burst of energy or activity (*informal*) ○ *start with a bang* **4.** OFFENSIVE TERM an offensive term for the act of having sexual intercourse (*slang*) **5.** INJECTION OF DRUG an injection of an illegal drug such as heroin (*slang*) **6.** *US* PRINTING EXCLAMATION MARK in typesetting, the character ! ■ **bangs** *npl* N Am same as **fringe** n (sense 1) ■ v (**bangs, banging, banged**) **1.** vti HIT to hit something hard, or slam something against a surface ○ *He banged his fist on the table.* **2.** vti HIT SOMETHING ACCIDENTALLY to hit something unintentionally ○ *bang into the furniture* **3.** vti CLOSE HARD AND NOISILY to close suddenly and loudly, or make something close with a sudden loud noise ○ *The door banged shut.* **4.** vi MAKE LOUD NOISE to make a sudden loud noise ○ *children banging on pots and pans* **5.** vi MOVE AROUND NOISILY to move around making a lot of noise ○ *I could hear her banging about in the kitchen.* **6.** vti OFFENSIVE TERM an offensive term meaning to have sexual intercourse with somebody (*slang*) **7.** vti FIN MAKE SHARE PRICES FALL to cause share prices to fall **8.** vi DRUGS INJECT DRUG to inject an illegal drug such as heroin (*slang*) ■ adv **1.** PRECISELY exactly or precisely ○ *Our hotel is bang in the centre of the town.* **2.** SUDDENLY suddenly and unexpectedly ○ *I turned round and bang, there he was!* ■ interj IMITATING EXPLOSIVE SOUND used especially by children to imitate the sound of a gun firing (*informal*) ○ *Bang! You're dead!* [Mid-16C. An imitation of the sound] ◇ **bang for your buck** Aus, N Am value for money spent or effort expended (*slang*) ◇ **bang goes something!** used as a rueful acknowledgment that something is no longer available or likely to happen (*informal*) ◇ **bang on** UK, Can exactly right (*informal*) ◇ **go (off) with a bang** to be very successful ◇ **go out with a bang** to end or finish something in a dramatic way (*informal*)

bang away vi to keep doing something persistently and determinedly

bang on vi to keep on talking about the same topic (*informal*)

bang out vt (*informal*) **1.** to play a tune on a musical instrument, especially a piano, loudly and coarsely **2.** to produce something speedily ○ *bang out an essay overnight*

bang up vt to lock a prisoner in a cell (*informal*)

bang[2] n DRUGS another spelling of **bhang**

Bangalore /báng gə láwr/ capital of Karnataka State in southern India. Population: 5,686,844 (2001).

bangalore torpedo n an explosive device in a metal tube, used to blow holes in barbed-wire fences or to detonate land mines [Early 20C. After BANGALORE]

bangalow /báng gəlō/ n an Australian palm tree. Native to: New South Wales, Queensland. Latin name: *Archontophoenix cunninghamiana*. [Early 19C. < an Aboriginal name]

banger /bángər/ n **1.** SAUSAGE a fried or grilled sausage (*informal*) **2.** OLD CAR an old car that is not in very good condition (*informal*) **3.** LOUD FIREWORK a firework that explodes very noisily

Banghāzī ⟩ Benghazi

Bangka /bángkə/, **Banka** island in western Indonesia forming part of the Malay Archipelago. Pangkalpinang is the largest town. Area: 11,940 sq. km/4,609 sq. mi.

Bangkok /báng kók, báng kok/ capital city and port on the River Chao Phraya, just north of the Gulf of Thailand, southern Thailand. Population: 7,358,300 (1998).

Bangla[1] /báng glə/ n S Asia the Indic national language of Bangladesh and state language of Bangla, India, also spoken in other parts of the world. Native speakers: 170 million. [< Bengali *bānglā*] —**Bangla** adj

Bangla[2] /báng glə/ state in Northeastern India. It consists of the western part of the former Indian state of Bengal. Capital: Kolkata. Population: 80,221,171 (2001). Area: 87,853 sq. km/33,920 sq. mi. Former name **West Bengal**

Bangladesh

Bangladesh /báng glə désh/ country in south-central Asia, formerly part of India and then, from 1947 to 1971, Pakistan. It became a separate nation following a civil war in 1971 and became an independent member of the Commonwealth in 1972. Language: Bangla. Currency: taka. Capital: Dhaka. Population: 138,448,210 (2003). Area: 147,570 sq. km/56,977 sq. mi. Official name **People's Republic of Bangladesh** —**Bangladeshi** n, adj

bangle /báng g'l/ n **1.** a stiff metal, plastic, or wooden bracelet that is worn around the arm, wrist, or ankle **2.** a decorative disc, charm, or other ornament that hangs from a bracelet [Late 18C. < Hindi *bangli* 'coloured glass bracelet']

Bangor /báng gər/ **1.** coastal resort and fishing port in County Down, Northern Ireland. Population: 52,437 (1991). **2.** university city in northern Wales, on the Menai Strait. Population: 12,330 (1991).

Bang's disease /bángz-/ n brucellosis in animals, especially in cattle [Early 20C. After Bernhard L. F. Bang (d. 1932), Danish veterinary surgeon]

bangtail /báng tayl/ n US an envelope with a detachable section that can be used as an order form or to provide marketing information

Bangui /baang gée/ capital city and major port on the River Ubangi, southern Central African Republic. Population: 524,000 (1996).

bani MONEY plural of **ban**[2]

bania /búnnyə/ n S Asia **1.** a merchant or trader **2.** a member of the merchant (**Vaisya**) caste [Late 18C. < Hindi]

banian CLOTHING another spelling of **banyan**

banish /bánnish/ (**-ishes, -ishing, -ished**) vt **1.** to exile somebody from a place **2.** to put something out of your mind ○ *Let us banish from our minds all dark thoughts.* [14C. < French *baniss-*, stem of *banir* 'proclaim' < assumed Vulgar Latin *bannire* < Germanic] —**banisher** n —**banishment** n

banister /bánnistər/, **bannister** n a handrail supported by posts running up the outside edge of a staircase (*often used in the pl*) [Mid-17C. Alteration of BALUSTER]

Banja Luka /bánnyə lóŏkə/ city in northern Bosnia and Herzegovina, on the River Vrbas. Population: 142,644 (1991).

Banjarmasin /bánjə máasin/, **Bandjarmasin** city in southeastern Borneo, Indonesia. It is the capital of South Kalimantan Province. Population: 546,466 (1997).

banjax /bán jaks/ (**-jaxes, -jaxing, -jaxed**) vt Ireland to damage or ruin something (*informal*) [Mid-20C. Origin ?]

banjo /bánjō/ (*plural* **-jos** or **-joes**) n a musical instrument that has a round sound box covered with parchment, a long neck, and five strings that are plucked or strummed [Mid-18C. Probably < an African language]

Banjul /ban jóöl/ capital and largest city of the Gambia. It is situated at the mouth of the River Gambia. Population: 418,000 (2001).

bank[1] /bangk/ n **1.** BUSINESS OFFERING FINANCIAL SERVICES a business that keeps money for individual people or companies, exchanges currencies, makes loans, and offers other financial services **2.** BANK'S LOCAL OFFICE a local office of a bank **3.** FUND OF MONEY OR TOKENS the fund of money, tokens, chips, or other pieces that players can draw out in some gambling games, or the player who holds the fund **4.** SOMETHING STORED a supply of something stored, ready for immediate use, e.g. data, food, or blood **5.** CONTAINER FOR RECYCLING a large container for waste items that can be recycled ○ *a bottle bank* ■ v (**banks, banking, banked**) **1.** vt DEPOSIT MONEY IN BANK to pay money into a bank ○ *banked the cheque immediately* **2.** vi HAVE ACCOUNT WITH FINANCIAL INSTITUTION to have an account with or use a particular bank ○ *bank with a local institution* [15C. Directly or via French *banque* < Italian *banca* 'bank, bench, table' < Germanic] ◇ **break the bank 1.** GAMBLING to win more money than is available **2.** to leave somebody very short of or without money (*informal*)

bank on vt to count on something happening ○ *We're banking on your support.*

bank[2] /bangk/ n **1.** SIDE OF WATERWAY the steep side of a river, stream, lake, or canal **2.** RAISED AREA OF LAND BELOW WATER a ridge of sand or other sedimentary deposit in a river or coastal sea that decreases the depth of the water above it and may become visible at low tide **3.** EARTH OR SNOW WITH SLOPING SIDE a pile of earth, snow, or sand, or a raised area of ground with a sloping side **4.** METEOROL MASS OF CLOUD a large dense area of cloud or fog **5.** SLOPE AT BEND IN RACETRACK an upward slope at a bend in a road or racetrack, designed to reduce the likelihood of drivers going off the road or track when travelling around the bend at speed **6.** AVIAT TURNING ANGLE OF AIRCRAFT the tilt of one wing higher than the other by an aeroplane as it turns **7.** RAIL LONG TRACK GRADIENT a long gradient or slope on a railway **8.** CUE GAMES CUSHION OF BILLIARD TABLE the cushion of a billiard or pool table **9.** MIN EXTRACT MOUTH OF MINE SHAFT the area around the mouth of a mine shaft ■ v **1.** vti FORM INTO PILE to make something into a pile or a large heap or form a pile or heap ○ *snow banked against the fence* **2.** vt MAKE RAISED SLOPE to make a raised slope as an edge or border to something ○ *bank earth along the river* **3.** vt COVER FIRE to cover a fire with ashes or fuel so that it will continue to burn slowly for a long time **4.** vti AVIAT TILT WHILE TURNING PLANE to tilt an aeroplane with one wing higher than the other while turning **5.** vti TILT WHILE DRIVING to tilt a vehicle, especially a motorcycle, while travelling around a bend at speed, or travel around a bend like this **6.** vt BUILD SLOPE INTO ROAD OR RACETRACK to build a slope into a road or racetrack at a bend **7.** vt CUE GAMES HIT BALL INTO CUSHION in billiards or pool, to hit a ball into the cushion [12C. < assumed Old Norse *banki* 'ridge, bank' < Germanic]

bank[3] /bangk/ n **1.** ROW OF SIMILAR THINGS a row or several rows of things of one type ○ *a bank of switches* **2.** NAUT GALLEY ROWERS' BENCH a bench for rowers in a galley **3.** NAUT GALLEY OARS a row of oars in a galley ■ vt (**banks, banking, banked**) PUT THINGS INTO ROWS to arrange things in rows or tiers [13C. < French *banc* 'bench' < Germanic]

Banka another spelling of **Bangka**

bankable /bángkəb'l/ adj **1.** likely to become financially profitable ○ *a bankable movie star* **2.** readily and legally acceptable to a bank —**bankability** /bángkə bílləti/ n

bank account n an arrangement according to which a bank accepts deposits of money and keeps that money available for withdrawal by the named account holder or holders

bank annuities npl FIN same as **consols**

bank balance n the amount of money in a bank account at any given time

bank barn n a two-storey barn built into a hillside that has an entrance to the first storey at the front and an entrance to the second storey at the back

bank bill n a bill of exchange issued or accepted by a bank

bankbook /bángk bŏok/ n BANKING same as **passbook** (sense 1)

bank card n **1.** BANKING same as **cheque card 2.** ANZ, N Am a credit or debit card

bank discount n the interest on a loan that is deducted from the amount borrowed at the time the loan is taken out

bank draft n a bill of exchange drawn by one bank on another

banker /bángkər/ n **1.** an owner or senior employee of a bank **2.** the player in charge of the bank in a gambling game [Mid-16C. < BANK[1]] —**bankerly** adj

banker's draft *n* same as bank draft

banker's order *n* BANKING same as **standing order** (sense 1)

banket /bángkit/ *n* rock containing gold, found in South Africa [Late 19C. < Afrikaans, literally 'almond toffee']

Bankhead /bángk hed/, **Tallulah** (1903–68) US actor. She was famous for her husky voice and extravagant acting style on stage in such plays as Lillian Hellman's *The Little Foxes* (1939) and in films including *Lifeboat* (1944). Born **Brockman, Tallulah**

'In the theater only one man can count on steady work-the night watchman.'
[Tallulah Bankhead, on a revival of Maeterlinck's *Aglavaine and Selysette*, recalled on her death in press reports; 12 December 1968]

bank holiday *n* a weekday public holiday on which banks, government offices, shops, and many businesses are closed

banking /bángking/ *n* the work carried out by banks or bankers

bank Internet payment system *n US* a number that uniquely identifies a financial institution for the purposes of Internet transactions

bank manager *n* somebody in charge of a branch of a bank

banknote /bángk nōt/ *n* a piece of paper money issued by a bank that may be freely exchanged for goods or services

Bank of England *n* the central bank of England and Wales

bank rate *n N Am* same as **base rate**

bankroll /bángk rōl/ *n* **1.** FUND OF MONEY a fund of money used to finance a project **2.** *N Am* ROLL OF PAPER MONEY a roll of banknotes ■ *vt* (-rolls, -rolling, -rolled) FINANCE SOMETHING to provide the money needed to finance a project on a continuing basis (*informal*) —**bankroller** *n*

bankrupt /bángk rupt/ *adj* **1.** UNABLE TO PAY DEBTS judged legally to be unable to pay off personal debts **2.** WITHOUT QUALITIES completely lacking in a particular quality, especially in good or ethical qualities ○ *morally bankrupt* ■ *n* **1.** SOMEBODY WHO CANNOT PAY DEBTS somebody who is unable to pay his or her debts **2.** SOMEBODY WITHOUT QUALITY somebody who completely lacks a particular quality ■ *vt* (-rupts, -rupting, -rupted) DEPLETE SOMEBODY'S FUNDS to cost so much that a person or business will have hardly any money left or will be declared bankrupt [Mid-16C. < Italian *banca rotta* 'broken table' < *banca* (see BANK¹) + *rotto* < Latin *ruptus* 'broken']

bankruptcy /bángk ruptsi/ *n* **1.** the state of having been legally declared bankrupt **2.** the complete lack of a particular quality, especially good or ethical qualities ○ *moral bankruptcy*

Banks /bangks/, **Sir Joseph** (1743–1820) British naturalist. A member of Captain Cook's expedition round the world (1768–71), he helped to establish botany as a science and was instrumental in developing Kew Gardens in London.

banksia /bángksi ə/ (*plural* **-as** *or* same) *n* a small evergreen bush or tree with leathery narrow leaves and cylindrical flowers. Native to: Australia. Family: Proteaceae. [Early 19C. < modern Latin, after Sir Joseph BANKS]

Banks Island island in the Inuvik Region, Northwest Territories, Canada. It has a predominantly Inuit population. Area: 70,028 sq. km/27,038 sq. mi.

Banks Peninsula peninsula on the eastern coast of the South Island of New Zealand, near Christchurch. Length: 48 km/30 mi.

bank statement *n* a document showing all the transactions in a bank account over a specific period of time

banner /bánnər/ *n* **1.** CLOTH SUSPENDED BETWEEN TWO POLES a long piece of cloth, often bearing a symbol or slogan, and attached at each end to a pole or hanging from the top of a pole **2.** GUIDING PRINCIPLE a guiding principle, cause, or philosophy ○ *under the banner of the trade union movement* **3.** NATION'S OR ARMY'S FLAG the flag of a country or army **4.** HIST FLAG OF KING, EMPEROR, OR KNIGHT a flag used by a king, emperor, or knight when going into battle **5.** MEDIA same as

banner headline 6. ONLINE WEBSITE ADVERT a rectangular graphic across a webpage, used as an advertisement, heading, or link ■ *adj N Am* ESPECIALLY GOOD especially good or successful ○ *a banner year for sales* [13C. < Anglo-Norman *banere*, Old French *banière* < medieval Latin *bandum* 'standard']

CULTURAL NOTE *The Star-Spangled Banner*, a patriotic song (1814) with lyrics by US writer Francis Scott Key set to music by English composer John Stafford Smith. Penned by Key after he had witnessed the successful defence of the city of Baltimore by US troops against a British attack in 1814, it soon became a popular patriotic song. It was adopted as the national anthem of the United States on 3 March 1931.

banner ad *n* an advertisement displayed full-width at the top or bottom of a printed page or a screen on a webpage

banneret /bánnərət, -ret/ *n* **1.** formerly, a knight of high rank who was entitled to lead his own men into battle **2.** formerly, a title given by a king or queen for bravery in battle [13C. < Old French *baneret* 'bannered' < *banière* (see BANNER)]

banner headline *n* a headline in large letters that runs across an entire page of a newspaper

bannerol *n* NAUT, HIST same as **banderole**

bannister *n* ARCHIT another spelling of **banister**

Bannister /bánnistər/, **Sir Roger** (b. 1929) British athlete. He was the first person to run the mile in under four minutes (1954). Full name **Bannister, Sir Roger Gilbert**

bannock /bánnək/ *n* a traditional Scottish bread in the shape of a round flat savoury cake cooked on a griddle [Old English *bannuc* < Celtic]

Bannockburn /bánnək burn/ town in central Scotland, where the Scots, led by Robert the Bruce, defeated Edward II of England in 1314. Population: 5,799 (1991).

banns /banz/ *npl* an announcement of a forthcoming marriage, proclaimed in the parish churches of the engaged couple on three successive Sundays [14C. < BAN¹]

banoffee /bə nóffi/, **banoffi** *n* a creamy filling made from bananas and soft toffee, eaten in a pastry or biscuit base ○ *banoffee pie* [Late 20C. Blend of BANANA + TOFFEE]

banquet /bángkwit/ *n* **1.** an elaborate formal meal attended by many guests, often held in honour of a particular person or occasion and followed by speeches **2.** an elaborate or lavish meal of many courses [15C. < French, 'little bank' < *banc* (see BANK³)] — **banquet** *vi* —**banqueter** *n*

banqueting hall *n* a room large enough to accommodate a banquet, usually in a palace, castle, or stately home

banqueting room *n* a room large enough to accommodate a banquet in a hotel or restaurant

banquette /bang két/ *n* **1.** an upholstered bench along a wall, especially in a restaurant **2.** a raised step in a trench or behind a parapet on which a soldier may stand to fire or a gun may be mounted [Early 17C. Via French < Italian *banchetta* 'little bench' < *banca* (see BANK¹)]

banshee /bán shee/ *n* **1.** in Gaelic folklore, a spirit of a woman who appears, wailing, to signal that somebody in the household is going to die **2.** *Ireland* in Gaelic folklore, a female fairy [Late 17C. < Irish *bean sidhe* < Old Irish *ben* 'woman' + *side* 'of the fairy world']

REGIONAL NOTE Old Irish *ben side* meant 'fairy woman'. The term is used of a supernatural being in both Ireland and the Scottish Highlands. The *banshee* wails near a house as a warning that a member of the household is about to die. Not every family has the dubious privilege of a forewarning from a *banshee*. Some clans are visited by a bird, while others are warned by breaking mirrors, falling pictures, and fires that refuse to burn properly.

bantam /bántəm/ *n* **1.** a bird belonging to a breed of small domestic fowl **2.** BOXING same as **bantamweight** (sense 1) ■ *adj N Am* overconfident and slightly aggressive [Mid-18C. After the town of *Bantam* in Java]

bantamweight /bántəm wayt/ *n* **1.** WEIGHT CATEGORY IN PROFESSIONAL BOXING in professional boxing, a weight category for competitors who weigh between 51 and

53.5 kg/112 and 118 lb **2.** WEIGHT CATEGORY IN AMATEUR BOXING in amateur boxing, a weight category for competitors who weigh between 51 and 54 kg/112 and 119 lb **3.** BOXER COMPETING AT BANTAMWEIGHT a professional or amateur boxer who competes at bantamweight **4.** WEIGHT CATEGORY IN WRESTLING in wrestling, a weight category for competitors who weigh between 52 and 57 kg/115 and 126 lb **5.** WRESTLER COMPETING AT BANTAMWEIGHT a wrestler who competes at bantamweight

banter /bántər/ *n* lighthearted teasing or amusing remarks that are exchanged between people ■ *vi* (-ters, -tering, -tered) to exchange lighthearted teasing remarks [Late 17C. Origin ?] —**banterer** *n*

Banting /bánting/, **Sir Frederick Grant** (1891–1941) Canadian physician. He co-discovered insulin with Charles Best (1922), for which he shared the Nobel Prize in physiology or medicine (1923).

Bantu /bán tóo/ (*plural* same *or* **-tus**) *n* **1.** a large group of Niger-Congo languages, spoken in central, eastern, and southern Africa. Native speakers: 150 million. **2.** ⚠ a member of a large group of peoples living in equatorial and southern Africa (*sometimes considered offensive*) [Mid-19C. In some Bantu languages the plural of -*ntu* 'person'] —**Bantu** *adj*

USAGE In South Africa after the apartheid era, *Bantu* is considered highly offensive when used with reference to Black people, especially in the singular to refer to one person, and *Black* or *African* are the normally accepted terms. In technical contexts outside South Africa, for example academic discussions of anthropology and language, *Bantu* continues in use.

bantustan /bán too staan, bán too staán/, **Bantustan** *n* in South Africa during the apartheid era, an area where Black people lived with limited self-government [Mid-20C. < BANTU, after such names as HINDUSTAN]

Banville /ba-áN veel/, **Théodore de** (1823–91) French poet and playwright. He was famed for his facility with difficult verse forms. Full name **Banville, Étienne Claude Jean Baptiste Théodore Faullain de**

'Poetic licence. There's no such thing.'
[Théodore de Banville, *Petit traité de poésie française (Short Treatise on French Poetry)*; 1872]

banyan

banyan /bánnyən, -yan/ *n* **1.** a tree with roots that grow down from the branches into the ground to form new secondary trunks. Native to: South Asia. Latin name: *Ficus benghalensis*. **2.** *also* **banian** /bánni ən, bánnyən, bán yan/ *or* **baniyaan** in parts of South Asia, a cotton shirt worn by men as an undershirt, or in summer as the only shirt [Late 16C. Via Portuguese < Gujarati *vāṇiyo* 'man of the trading class' < Sanskrit *nāṇija* 'merchant']

banzai /ban zí, baan-/ *interj* in Japan, used as a patriotic battle cry or shout of enthusiasm ■ *adj* reckless and utterly ferocious in a military attack [Late 19C. < Japanese,'(may you live) ten thousand years' < *ban* 'ten thousand' (< Middle Chinese *muanh*) + *zai* 'year' (< Middle Chinese *swiajh*)]

baobab /báy ō bab/ *n* a tree with a thick short trunk and edible fruit. Native to: southern Africa and northwestern Australia. Latin name: *Adansonia digitata*. [Mid-17C. Origin ?]

Bao Dai /bów dí/ (1913–97) emperor of Annam. The last emperor (1926–45) of the Nguyen dynasty in Indochina, he renounced his title and headed Vietnam under French rule (1949–55) before being

deposed and forced into exile. Born **Nguyen Vinh Thuy**

Baotou /bów tô/ *city* in Inner Mongolia, northern China, on the Huang He west of Hohhot. Population: 1,340,000 (1995).

bap /bap/ *n* a large soft flattish bread roll [Late 16C. Origin ?]

baptise *vt* CHR another spelling of **baptize**

baptism /báptizəm/ *n* **1.** a religious ceremony in which somebody is sprinkled with or immersed in water to symbolize purification. In some Christian baptisms, the person is named as well as being accepted into the Christian faith. **2.** a ceremony that serves as an initiation or naming ritual —**baptismal** /bap tízm'l/ *adj* —**baptismally** *adv*

baptism of fire *n* **1.** a difficult or dangerous first experience in a new situation **2.** a soldier's first experience of battle

Baptist /báptist/ *n* a member of a Protestant denomination that baptizes people by total immersion when they are old enough to understand and declare their faith —**Baptist** *adj*

baptistery /báptistri/ (*plural* **-ies**), **baptistry** (*plural* **-tries**) *n* **1.** a part of a Christian church used for baptisms **2.** a tank or pool in a Baptist church used for baptisms by total immersion

baptize /bap tíz/ (**-tizes, -tizing, -tized**), **baptise** (**-tises, -tising, -tised**) *v* **1.** *vti* PERFORM CEREMONY OF BAPTISM to sprinkle somebody or immerse somebody in water as a sign that the person has been accepted into the Christian faith **2.** *vt* NAME SOMEBODY IN BAPTISM to give a personal name to somebody during the Christian ceremony of baptism **3.** *vt* INITIATE SOMEBODY to initiate somebody into a new experience or situation [13C. Via French *baptiser* and ecclesiastical Latin *baptisare* < Greek *baptizein* 'baptize' < *baptein* 'dip'] —**baptizer** *n*

bar[1] /baar/ *n* **1.** LENGTH OF SOLID MATERIAL a length of metal, wood, or other solid material used as a barrier, or as part of a structure **2.** SMALL BLOCK a small, solid, usually rectangular, block of some substance ○ *a bar of soap* **3.** BARRIER something that blocks or hinders progress ○ *Aloofness is a bar to making friends easily.* **4.** PLACE FOR DRINKING a place where alcoholic drinks can be bought and drunk **5.** DRINKS COUNTER a counter at which alcoholic drinks and sometimes food are served **6.** PLACE PROVIDING PRODUCT OR SERVICE a commercial establishment, or a counter inside one, where a product or service is provided ○ *a heel bar* **7.** NARROW BAND a narrow stripe or band of colour or light **8.** SOMETHING USED AS STANDARD something referred to as an authority or standard ○ *We need to raise the bar of academic courses for all our students.* **9.** LAW PART OF LAW COURT the railing in a law court that separates the judge, jury, and Queen's Counsel from solicitors, junior barristers, and the public **10.** LAW PLACE FOR DEFENDANT IN COURT the place in a law court where somebody on trial stands or sits **11.** LAW TRIBUNAL a tribunal or court of law **12.** LAW DEFEAT OF LEGAL ACTION the defeat, prevention, or nullification of an action or claim, or the process by which this is achieved **13.** PLACE IN BRITISH PARLIAMENT the place in the House of Commons or House of Lords where nonmembers must stand to address either House **14.** MUSIC UNIT OF TIME IN MUSIC in music, a fundamental unit of time into which a musical work is divided, according to the number of beats **15.** *Aus, N Am* MUSIC VERTICAL LINE SEPARATING MUSICAL UNITS in music, any one of the vertical lines on a score that separates each unit of musical time. UK, NZ, Can term **bar line 16.** MIL INSIGNIA an insignia added to a decoration to show that an award has been won twice **17.** same as **crossbar** (sense 1) **18.** GYMNASTICS same as **horizontal bar** (sense 1) **19.** BALLET another spelling of **barre 20.** HERALDRY LINE ACROSS SHIELD a horizontal line on a shield, usually one of two or three parallel lines **21.** GEOG RIDGE OF SAND a low ridge of sand or shingle in the shallow part of the bed of a body of water **22.** GEOG RIVER'S CRESCENT-SHAPED SAND DEPOSIT a crescent-shaped area of alluvium deposited on the convex bend of a river bed **23.** BOARD GAMES STRIP ON BACKGAMMON BOARD the central dividing strip on a backgammon board ■ *vt* (**bars, barring, barred**) **1.** FIX SOMETHING WITH BAR to fasten something with a bar ○ *barred the door* **2.** BLOCK SOMETHING to block something by means of bars or barriers **3.** NOT ALLOW SOMEBODY ENTRY to refuse somebody entry to a place ○ *He was barred from the club.* **4.** MARK SOMETHING WITH BARS to mark something with stripes

or bands of colour (*usually passive*) **5.** LAW HALT COURT CASE to prevent a court case from going ahead by making a legal objection to it ■ *prep* EXCLUDING except for ○ *our team's finest hour, bar none.* [12C. Via Old French *barre* < Vulgar Latin *barra*] ◇ **behind bars** in prison ○ *spent 20 years behind bars* ◇ **not have a bar of somebody** *or* **something** ANZ to not tolerate somebody or something (*informal*)

bar[2] /baar/ *n* a centimetre-gram-second unit of pressure that can be used in combination with SI units and prefixes, equal to 10^5 newtons per square metre [Early 20C. < Greek *baros* 'weight']

Bar *n* **1.** barristers considered collectively, or the profession of a barrister **2.** in the United States, lawyers considered collectively, or the profession of a lawyer ○ *the federal and state Bars*

bar. *abbr* **1.** METEOROL barometer **2.** METEOROL barometric **3.** MEASURE barrel

Bar. *abbr* **1.** LAW barrister **2.** BIBLE Baruch

Bara /bárrə/, **Theda** (1890?–1955) US actor. She was one of the first women to become a film star, and is best remembered for the line 'Kiss me, my fool!'. Born **Goodman, Theodosia.** Known as **the Vamp**

Barabbas /bə rábbəss/ *n* in the Bible, a condemned thief who was freed by Pilate at Passover instead of Jesus Christ (Matthew 27)

bara brith /bárrə bríth/ *n Wales* a type of traditional cake made with dried fruit soaked in tea before baking

Barak /baá rak/, **Ehud** (*b.* 1942) Israeli soldier and prime minister (1999–2001). He served as chief of general staff (1991–95), minister of the interior (1995–96), and foreign minister (1996–97) before becoming chairman of the Labour Party in 1997. As prime minister he implemented the 1998 Wye Accord and held talks with Syria.

Baranof Island /bárrənəf-/ *island* off southeastern Alaska, part of the Alexander Archipelago. It is named after the first governor of the Russian colony of Alaska, Aleksandr Baranov (1746–1819). Population: 9,000. Area: 4,162 sq. km/1,607 sq. mi.

Barassi /bə rássi/, **Ron** (*b.* 1936) Australian Rules football player and coach. He coached Carlton (1968, 1970) and North Melbourne (1975, 1977) to Australian Rules Grand Final championships. Full name **Barassi, Ronald Dale**

barathea /bárrə theè ə/ *n* a fabric made from a combination of silk, cotton, wool, or synthetic material. Use: coats. [Mid-19C. Origin ?]

baraza /bə raázə/ *n* in East Africa, a public meeting or a place where meetings are held [Late 19C. < Kiswahili]

barb

barb[1] /baarb/ *n* **1.** POINTED TIP a sharp point facing away from the head of an arrow, fishhook, or harpoon, designed to make it difficult to remove **2.** HURTFUL COMMENT a wounding remark **3.** ZOOL PART OF FEATHER a stiff spine that forms the framework of a feather. The barbs stick out on each side of the main shaft. **4.** ZOOL WHISKER ON ANIMAL'S HEAD a growth on an animal's head like a beard or whisker **5.** BOT BRISTLE OF PLANT a hooked projection on some plants and fruits **6.** (*plural* **barbs** *or* same) FISH AQUARIUM FISH a small fish often kept in aquariums. Genera: *Barbus* or *Puntius.* **7.** CLOTHING MEDIEVAL HEADDRESS a white cloth headdress covering the chin and throat, worn by women in the Middle Ages ■ *vt* (**barbs, barbing, barbed**) FIT SOMETHING WITH BARB to provide something with a barb or barbs [14C. Via Old French *barbe* 'beard, appendage like a beard' < Latin *barba* 'beard']

barb[2] /baarb/ (*plural* **barbs** *or* same) *n* a horse noted for speed and stamina, belonging to a breed originally from North Africa [Mid-17C. Via French *barbe* < Italian *barbero* 'of Barbary']

barb[3] /baarb/ *n* PHARM same as **barbiturate** (*slang*) [Mid-20C. Shortening]

BARB /baarb/ *abbr* Broadcasters' Audience Research Board

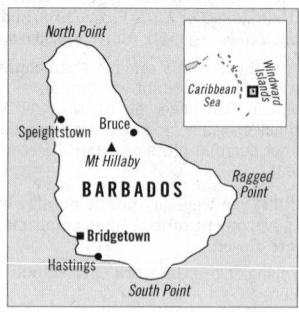

Barbados

Barbados /baar báy doss/ *island nation* of the Windward Islands in the eastern Caribbean off northeastern South America. Settled by the English in the 17th century, it has been an independent state within the Commonwealth since 1966. Language: English. Currency: Barbados dollar. Capital: Bridgetown. Population: 277,264 (2003). Area: 430 sq. km/166 sq. mi. —**Barbadian** *n, adj*

barbarian /baar báiri ən/ *n* **1.** UNCIVILIZED PERSON especially in ancient times, a member of a people whose culture and behaviour was considered uncivilized (*sometimes considered offensive*) **2.** UNCULTURED PERSON somebody with no interest in culture **3.** AGGRESSIVE PERSON an extremely aggressive or violent person [14C. < Old French *barbarien* or Latin *barbarianus* < *barbarus* (see BARBAROUS)] —**barbarianism** *n*

barbaric /baar bárrik/ *adj* **1.** cruel or extremely brutal **2.** uncivilized or unsophisticated when compared to highly developed civilizations (*sometimes considered offensive*) [14C. Directly or via French < Latin *barbaricus* < Greek *barbarikos* < *barbaros* (see BARBAROUS)] —**barbarically** *adv*

barbarise *vti* another spelling of **barbarize**

barbarism /baárbərizəm/ *n* **1.** CRUEL ACT a cruel or brutal act **2.** UNCIVILIZED QUALITY the uncivilized nature of a culture or civilization (*sometimes considered offensive*) **3.** UNCONVENTIONAL OR UNACCEPTABLE THING something that breaks rules of convention or good taste **4.** UNGRAMMATICAL WORD a word or expression considered to be grammatically incorrect [15C. Via French < Latin *barbarismus* < Greek *barbarismos* < *barbarizein* (see BARBARIZE)]

barbarity /baar bárrəti/ (*plural* **-ties**) *n* **1.** a cruel act **2.** an uncivilized condition [Mid-16C. < Latin *barbarus* (see BARBAROUS)]

barbarize /baárbə ríz/ (**-rizes, -rizing, -rized**), **barbarise** (**-rises, -rising, -rised**) *vti* **1.** to become, or make somebody, cruel or brutal **2.** to become less civilized or less cultured, or reduce something to this state [15C. Via late Latin < Greek *barbarizein* 'act or speak like a foreigner, speak gibberish' < *barbaros* (see BARBAROUS)] —**barbarization** /baárbə rí záysh'n/ *n*

Barbarossa /baárbə róssə/ (1483?–1546) Greek-born Ottoman admiral and pirate. Admiral of the Ottoman fleet after 1533, he was feared as a pirate on the Barbary coast. He defeated Holy Roman Emperor Charles V (1538) and sacked Gibraltar (1540). Born **Khair ad-Din**

barbarous /baárbərəss/ *adj* **1.** EXTREMELY CRUEL showing extreme cruelty **2.** UNCIVILIZED characterized by an uncivilized culture (*sometimes considered offensive*) **3.** NOT SOPHISTICATED lacking sophistication or refinement **4.** UNGRAMMATICAL using ungrammatical language [15C. Via Latin *barbarus* < Greek *barbaros* 'non-Greek, foreign, ignorant, uncivilized'] —**barbarously** *adv* —**barbarousness** *n*

Barbary /baárbəri/ *former region* of North Africa stretching from the Atlantic coast to western Egypt. It included the Barbary States of Morocco, Algeria, Tripolitania, Tunisia, and Moorish Spain.

Barbary ape *n* a tailless monkey with greenish-brown hair. Native to: northwestern Africa, introduced to Gibraltar. Latin name: *Macaca sylvana*.

Barbary Coast formerly, the Mediterranean coast of North Africa. It was an important base for pirates between the 16th and 19th centuries.

Barbary sheep *n* ZOOL same as **aoudad**

barbastelle /baárbə stél/ *n* an insect-eating bat with large ears and a wrinkly face. Native to: Europe, Asia. Latin name: *Barbastella barbastellus*. [Late 18C. Via French < Italian *barbastello* < Latin *vespertilio* 'bat']

barbecue /baárbi kyoo/, **barbeque** *n* **1.** an apparatus, including a grill and fuel, used for cooking food outdoors **2.** an outdoor party where people eat food cooked on a barbecue [Mid-17C. < American Spanish *barbacoa*, probably < Arawak *barbakoa* 'frame of sticks'] — **barbecue** *vt*

barbecue sauce *n* a sweet-sour and spicy sauce, sometimes with chilli, used to marinate meat or served as an accompaniment to meat

barbecue stopper *n Aus* an issue that is regarded as vitally important by most people, to the extent that it gets everyone talking and can therefore bring a social event, such as a barbecue, to a halt

barbed /baarbd/ *adj* **1.** with one or more backward-facing points **2.** critical or biting ○ *a barbed comment*

barbed wire *n* strong wire with pointed projections along its length. Use: fences and barriers.

barbel /baárb'l/ *n* **1.** a slender feeler resembling a whisker on the lips or jaws of some fishes **2.** a toothless European fish with barbels that resembles the carp. Genus: *Barbus*. [14C. < Latin *barba* 'beard']

barbell /baár bel/ *n* a metal bar with removable weights at each end, used in weightlifting [Late 19C. Blend of BAR[1] + DUMBBELL] — **barbeller** *n*

barbeque *n* another spelling of **barbecue**

barber /baárbər/ *n* SOMEBODY WHO CUTS HAIR somebody whose profession it is to cut men's hair and shave their beards ■ *v* (**-bers, -bering, -bered**) **1.** *vt* CUT SOMEBODY'S HAIR to cut or shave somebody's hair, especially a man's **2.** *vi* BE BARBER to work as a barber [13C. < Anglo-Norman *barbour* < French *barbe* (see BARB[1])]

CULTURAL NOTE *The Barber of Seville*, an opera (1816) by Italian composer Gioacchino Antonio Rossini. A comedy based on a play (1775) by Beaumarchais, it tells of the attempts of Count Almaviva, disguised as a poor student called Lindoro, to woo Rosina, ward of Doctor Bartolo. Almaviva is assisted in his eventful courtship by the wily local barber, Figaro.

Barber /baárbər/, **Samuel** (1910–81) US composer. His neo-Romantic works, which include *Adagio for Strings* (1936), won two Pulitzer Prizes.

'I have always believed that I need a circumference of silence. As to what happens when I compose, I really haven't the faintest idea.'
[Samuel Barber. Quoted in *American Composers*, David Ewen; 1982]

barberry /baárbəri/ *n* (*plural* **-ries**) *n* a thorny flowering bush widely grown as a garden or hedge plant, especially a yellow-flowered variety that has orange or red berries. Native to: Asia. Genus: *Berberis*. [14C. < Old French *berberis* < medieval Latin *barbaris*, influenced by BERRY]

barbershop /baárbər shop/ *n* a style of popular music for unaccompanied single-sex voices in close harmony, originally for four male voices. There are now many female barbershop groups and larger barbershop choirs.

barber's itch *n* a rash or skin eruption on the face and neck, especially around the beard, caused by a fungal infection

barber's pole *n* a short pole with red and white stripes found outside a barber's shop

barber's rash *n* MED same as **barber's itch**

barbet /baárbit/ *n* a small brightly coloured forest bird with a large head and a thick beak with bristles at its base. Native to: tropics. Family: Capitonidae. [Late 16C. < French, 'small beard' < *barbe* (see BARB[1])]

barbette /baar bét/ *n* **1.** a metal cylinder giving ar-

moured protection to a gun turret on a warship **2.** a mound of earth inside a fortress used as a platform for cannons [Late 18C. < French, 'small beard' (perhaps from the idea of cannon sticking over the parapet like a line of bristles) < *barbe* (see BARB[1])]

barbican

barbican /baárbikən/ *n* a strong defensive tower at the entrance to a town or fortress [13C. Via Old French *barbacane* < Persian *barbarkhana* 'guard house']

Barbican *n* a major arts centre in the City of London, completed in 1982

barbicel /baárbi sel/ *n* a tiny projection linking the filaments (**barbules**) of feathers [Mid-19C. < Italian or modern Latin *barbicella* 'small beard' < Latin *barba* 'beard']

barbie /baárbi/ *n* a barbecue (*informal*) [Late 20C. Shortening]

Barbie /baárbi/, **Klaus** (1913–91) German SS officer. In occupied France during World War II, he deported thousands of Jews to Auschwitz and killed French Resistance workers. He was tried in France after extradition from Bolivia (1983) and imprisoned for life. Known as **The Butcher of Lyons**

bar billiards *n* a billiards-style game, once popular in British pubs, played on a small table with holes instead of pockets and peg-shaped obstacles

Barbirolli /baárbə rólli/, **Sir John** (1899–1970) British conductor. He was long associated with the Hallé Orchestra in Manchester (1943–68). Born **Barbirolli, Giovanni Battista**

barbital /baárbit'l/ *n N Am* same as **barbitone** [Early 20C. < BARBITURIC ACID]

barbitone /baárbitōn/ *n* a barbiturate with a long-lasting sedative or hypnotic effect, formerly prescribed as a white soluble powder. US term **barbital** [Early 20C. < BARBITURIC ACID]

barbiturate /baar bíchoorət/ *n* a drug with sedative and hypnotic properties belonging to a group of derivatives of barbituric acid [Late 19C. < BARBITURIC ACID]

barbituric acid /baárbi tyoórik-/ *n* a white crystalline solid. Use: manufacture of barbiturates. Formula: $C_4H_4N_2O$. [< French *acide barbiturique*, translating German *Barbitursäure* < the name *Barbara*]

Barbizon School /baárbizon-/ *n* a group of mid-19th-century French painters, which included Corot, Millet, Daubigny, and Rousseau, noted for their realistic depictions of landscapes [Late 19C. After the village of *Barbizon* in France]

Barbour /baárbər/ *tdmk* a trademark for a waxed waterproof jacket

Barbuda /baar boódə/ coral island forming part of the independent state of Antigua and Barbuda, in the Caribbean Sea. Population: 1,280 (1995). Area: 417 sq. km/161 sq. mi. ◊ **Antigua and Barbuda** —**Barbudan** *n*, *adj*

barbule /baárbyool/ *n* a slender filament attached to the thicker spines (**barbs**) on a feather's central shaft and interlocking with others [Mid-19C. < Latin *barbula* 'little beard' < *barba* 'beard']

barbwire /baárb wīr/ *n N Am* CONSTR same as **barbed wire**

barcarole /baárkə rōl/, **barcarolle** *n* **1.** a song traditionally sung by Venetian gondoliers **2.** a piece of instrumental music that imitates a barcarole, made popular especially by Chopin and Mendelssohn [Early 17C. Via French < Venetian Italian *barcaruola* < *barcarolo* 'gondolier' < late Latin *barca* 'barque']

Barcelona /baárssə lónə/ second largest city in Spain and a major seaport on the northern Mediterranean coast. It is the capital of Barcelona Province and the autonomous region of Catalonia. Population: 1,527,190 (2002).

BArch *abbr* Bachelor of Architecture

barchan /baár kaan/ *n* a crescent-shaped sand dune in which the tips of the crescent point in the direction of dune movement [Late 19C. < Turkic *barkhan*]

bar chart *n* STATS same as **bar graph**

bar code *n* a sequence of numbers and vertical lines identifying an item and often its price when interpreted by an optical scanner

Barcoo /baar koó/ river in central Queensland, Australia. It rises in the Warrego Ranges and joins the Thomson River upstream of Cooper Creek. Length: 480 km/298 mi.

bard[1] /baard/ *n* **1.** ANCIENT CELTIC POET in ancient Celtic culture, a poet who composed and recited epic poems describing important events **2.** POET WINNING EISTEDDFOD PRIZE a poet who has won a prize at a modern Welsh eisteddfod **3.** POET a poet, especially one of national importance (*literary or humorous*) [15C. < Gaelic *bàrd* < Celtic] —**bardic** *adj*

bard[2] /baard/ *n* ARMOUR FOR HORSE a piece of armour for a horse ■ *vt* (**bards, barding, barded**) **1.** PUT BARD ON HORSE to put a bard on a horse **2.** COOK COVER MEAT WITH FAT to cover meat with fat before roasting it to prevent it from drying out [15C. Via French *barde* < Arabic *barda'a* 'saddle cloth, padded saddle']

Bard, **Bard of Avon** *n* William Shakespeare

Bardeen /baar deén/, **John** (1908–91) US physicist. He shared two Nobel Prizes in physics, for developing the transistor (1956) and for his research in superconductivity (1972).

bar diagram *n* STATS same as **bar graph**

Bard of Avon *n* same as **Bard**

bardolatry /baar dóllətri/ *n* the idolizing of a poet, especially Shakespeare, who is sometimes referred to as the Bard of Avon (*disapproving*)

Bardot /baar dó/, **Brigitte** (*b.* 1934) French actor and activist. She became an international sex symbol in films such as *And God Created Woman* (1956). She retired from films in 1973 to devote herself to campaigning for animal welfare. Born **Javal, Camille**

'I gave my beauty and my youth to men. I am going to give my wisdom and experience to animals.'
[Brigitte Bardot, *Guardian*; 1987]

bare /bair/ *adj* (**barer, barest**) **1.** LACKING CLOTHING not covered by clothing ○ *bare legs* **2.** UNDECORATED lacking the usual furnishings or decorations ○ *The room was bare except for an iron bedstead.* **3.** LACKING PLANTS having no vegetation ○ *a bare hillside* **4.** BASIC simple or essential ○ *the bare facts* **5.** EMPHASIZING SMALLNESS used to emphasize how small something is ○ *the bare minimum of supplies* **6.** MINIMUM only just sufficient ○ *the bare essentials* ■ *vt* (**bares, baring, bared**) **1.** UNCOVER SOMETHING to remove a covering from something ○ *The dog bared its teeth.* **2.** EXPOSE SOMETHING to reveal or expose something secret or concealed ○ *an investigative report that bared the details of the conspiracy* [Old English *bær* < Germanic] —**bareness** *n* ◊ **lay something bare** to expose something that has been concealed or hidden ○ *finally laid bare the whole sorry tale of mismanagement*

SPELLCHECK **bare** or **bear**? Do not confuse the spelling of *bare* and *bear*, which sound similar. *Bare* is an adjective meaning 'not covered or decorated' (as in *bare walls*) or 'minimum' (as in *the bare essentials*). *Bear* is a noun denoting an animal (as in *polar bear, teddy bear*) or a verb meaning 'carry' or 'endure': *I can't bear this oppressive heat*.

SYNONYMS See *naked*.

bareback /báir bak/, **barebacked** /-bakt/ *adv*, *adj* on the back of a horse that has no saddle

bare bones *npl* the essential structure of something, without any elaboration (*informal*)

barebones /báir bōnz/ *adj* containing only the basic components (*informal*) ○ *the cost of a barebones computing system*

barefaced /báir fáyst/ *adj* **1.** shamelessly undisguised ○ *a barefaced lie* **2.** with an uncovered or clean-

shaven face —**barefacedly** /báir fáystli, -fáysidli/ *adv* —**barefacedness** /-fáystnəss, -fáysidnəss/ *n*

barefoot /báir foot/, **barefooted** /-footid/ *adj, adv* wearing nothing on the feet

barefoot doctor *n* an auxiliary health-care worker, especially in rural areas of China

barefooted *adj, adv* same as **barefoot**

barehanded /báir hándid/ *adj, adv* 1. without weapons 2. with hands not protected by gloves —**barehandedness** *n*

bareheaded /báir héddid/ *adj, adv* wearing nothing on the head —**bareheadedness** *n*

Bareilly /bə ráyli/ city in the state of Uttar Pradesh, northern India. Population: 729,800 (2001).

bareknuckle /báir nukl/, **bareknuckled** /-nuk'ld/ *adv* WITHOUT BOXING GLOVES not wearing boxing gloves ■ *adj* 1. USING BARE HANDS using hands not protected by boxing gloves ○ *He was a great bareknuckle champion in his time.* 2. AGGRESSIVE OR COMPETITIVE characterized by open aggression or competitiveness ○ *a bareknuckle exchange in the House*

barelegged /báir légd, -léggid/ *adj, adv* with nothing covering the legs —**bareleggedness** /-léggidnəss/ *n*

barely /báirli/ *adv* 1. scarcely or almost not ○ *They had barely enough money to pay the rent.* ○ *She had barely sat down when the phone rang.* 2. sparsely or simply, with no adornments ○ *a barely furnished office*

USAGE See **hardly**.

Barenboim /bárrən boym/, **Daniel** (*b.* 1942) Argentine-born Israeli pianist and conductor. A noted performer of the classical repertoire, he has regularly conducted major international orchestras, and in 1991 became music director of the Chicago Symphony Orchestra.

Barents /bárrənts/, **Barentz, Willem** (1550?–97) Dutch explorer. In his search for a Northeast Passage to Asia, he discovered Spitsbergen. Barents Sea is named after him.

Barents Sea shallow part of the Arctic Ocean, north of Norway, Finland, and Russia and south of Franz Josef Land. Area: 1,370,350 sq. km/529,096 sq. mi.

Barentz another spelling of **Barents**

barf /baarf/ (*informal*) *vti* (**barfs, barfing, barfed**) VOMIT to vomit the contents of the stomach ■ *n* 1. VOMITING OF FOOD an act of vomiting the contents of the stomach 2. SOMETHING VOMITED vomited food [Mid-20C. Probably an imitation of the sound] —**barfy** *adj*

barfi *n* FOOD another spelling of **burfi**

barfly /baar flī/ (*plural* **-flies**) *n* N Am a frequent drinker in bars (*slang*) [Early 20C. Because regarded as a pest]

bargain /báargin/ *n* 1. CHEAP PURCHASE something offered or bought at less than the usual price 2. PACT an agreement between two people or groups in which each promises to carry out an obligation 3. PRICE AGREEMENT a commercial agreement between two parties that fixes the price of something 4. THINGS RECEIVED BY AGREEMENT goods or services obtained by a commercial agreement ■ *v* (**-gains, -gaining, -gained**) 1. *vi* NEGOTIATE WITH SOMEBODY to negotiate the terms of an agreement with somebody 2. *vt* EXCHANGE SOMETHING to exchange one thing for another [14C. < Old French *bargaignier* 'trade, negotiate, dispute', probably < Germanic] —**bargainer** *n* ◇ **into the bargain** as well ○ *hard-working and very intelligent into the bargain*

bargain away *vt* to lose something by giving it away as part of an agreement that is ultimately disadvantageous

bargain for *vt* to expect or believe something to be of a particular nature, and prepare for it accordingly ○ *The bill was a lot more than we'd bargained for.*

bargain on *vt* to expect or believe that something will happen, and prepare for it accordingly ○ *We hadn't bargained on the train arriving early.*

bargain basement *n* an area of a shop, often in the basement, selling goods cheaply

bargain-basement *adj* lower than usual in quality or price ○ *at bargain-basement prices*

bargain hunter *n* somebody who enjoys finding bargains —**bargain hunting** *n*

bargaining chip, **bargaining counter** *n* something that can be used as leverage in negotiations

bargaining position *n* the ability of somebody to achieve a desired end in a negotiation, as determined by his or her relative strengths or weaknesses ○ *was in a strong bargaining position*

barge /baarj/ *n* 1. FREIGHT BOAT a long narrow flat-bottomed boat used for transporting freight on rivers or canals 2. OPEN BOAT USED CEREMONIALLY a large open boat used in ceremonies 3. SMALL NAVAL BOAT a motor launch used by a high-ranking naval officer for ceremonial occasions ○ *an admiral's barge* ■ *v* (**barges, barging, barged**) 1. *vti* MOVE ROUGHLY to move roughly, colliding with other people ○ *barged his way through the crowd* 2. *vti* PUSH to push somebody or something roughly ○ *He barged the goalkeeper off the ball.* 3. *vt* MOVE SOMETHING IN BARGE to transport freight by barge [13C. < Old French *barge* or medieval Latin *bargia*]

barge in *vt* to enter or intrude suddenly or rudely ○ *Don't just barge in without knocking.*

barge in on *vt* to interrupt somebody in a clumsy or rude manner ○ *Don't barge in on them: they are having a private meeting.*

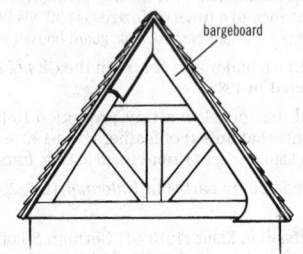

bargeboard

bargeboard

bargeboard /báarj bawrd/ *n* an ornamental board along the gable end of a roof [Mid-19C. < medieval Latin *bargus*, a kind of gallows]

bargee /baar jee/ *n* a crew member or captain of a barge. N Am term **bargeman**

bargello /baar jéllō/ (*plural* **-los**) *n* a straight needlepoint stitch that is worked in zigzags to create chevron or scallop patterns [Mid-20C. After the *Bargello* Palace in Florence]

bargeman /báarjmən/ (*plural* **-men** /-mən/) *n* N Am same as **bargee**

bargepole /báarj pōl/ *n* a long pole used to propel barges ◇ **not touch somebody** or **something with a bargepole** to be unwilling to have any involvement with somebody or something

~~**bargin**~~ incorrect spelling of **bargain**

bar graph *n* a graph consisting of a series of vertical or horizontal bars representing statistical data

barhop /baar hop/ (**-hops, -hopping, -hopped**) *vi* N Am to visit a number of different bars during an evening (*informal*)

Bari /báari/ city and port on the southeastern coast of Italy. It is the capital of Apulia region. Population: 316,532 (2001).

bariatrics /bárri áttriks/ *n* the branch of medicine concerned with the treatment of obesity (*takes a singular verb*) [Mid-20C. < BARO- + -IATRICS] —**bariatric** *adj*

baric /báirik/ *adj* 1. relating to or containing barium 2. relating to barometric pressure

barilla /bə ríllə/ *n* 1. a sodium carbonate and sodium sulphate alkali ash derived from burning various Mediterranean plants and formerly used in the manufacture of soap and glass 2. a plant belonging to various species formerly burned to produce an alkali ash. Native to: Mediterranean, some now naturalized in North America and Australia. Latin name: *Salsola spp.* or *Suaeda spp.* or *Halogeton sativus*. [Early 17C. < Spanish, 'small bar' < *barra* 'bar']

barista /bə rístə/ *n* somebody employed to operate an espresso machine in a coffee bar [Late 20C < Italian, 'worker in or owner of a bar']

barite /báir īt/ *n* N Am same as **barytes** [Mid-19C. < BARIUM]

baritone /bárritōn/ *n* 1. a man's singing voice with a range lower than a tenor and higher than a bass,

or a singer with this voice 2. a wind instrument with the second lowest range in its family [Early 17C. Via Italian *baritono* < Greek *barutonos* 'deep-sounding, baritone']

barium /báiri əm/ *n* a soft silver-white toxic chemical element. Use: alloys. Symbol Ba. See table at **element** [Early 19C. < BARYTA + -IUM]

barium enema *n* the introduction of a barium salt suspension into the rectum and colon before an X-ray is taken

barium meal *n* a barium salt suspension, given by mouth before X-raying the oesophagus, stomach, and upper intestine

barium sulphate *n* a white or yellowish odourless powder. Use: pigment, contrast medium for X-ray photography. Formula: $BaSO_4$.

bark[1] /baark/ *n* 1. DOG'S SOUND the characteristic loud abrupt sound made by a dog or fox 2. ABRUPT SOUND a loud abrupt sound ○ *the bark of guns in the distance* ■ *v* (**barks, barking, barked**) 1. MAKE DOG'S SOUND to make the loud abrupt sound characteristic of a dog or fox 2. *vi* MAKE ABRUPT SOUND to make a loud abrupt sound 3. *vti* UTTER SOMETHING ABRUPTLY to say something in a loud abrupt manner ○ *He barked out an order.* [Old English (ge)beorc (noun), beorcan (verb) < Germanic]

bark[2] /baark/ *n* TREES OUTER LAYER OF TREE the rough outer covering of the woody stems of trees or bushes ■ *vt* (**barks, barking, barked**) 1. GRAZE SKIN to have the skin rubbed off a part of the body through abrasive contact with another object ○ *I barked my shins climbing the fence.* 2. REMOVE OUTER LAYER FROM TREE to remove the bark from a tree or log 3. TAN LEATHER USING BARK to tan leather using tannins derived from bark [13C. < Old Norse *börkr*] —**barky** *adj*

bark[3] *n* another spelling of **barque**

bark beetle *n* a beetle that burrows under the bark of trees. Family: Scolytidae.

barkeeper /baar keepər/ *n* N Am 1. somebody who runs a bar 2. COMM same as **bartender**

barker[1] /báarkər/ *n* 1. somebody who stands outside a fair or carnival and shouts out its attractions 2. a dog that barks a lot

barker[2] /báarkər/ *n* a person or machine that strips bark off trees and logs or prepares bark for tanning

barking /báarking/ *adj* extremely irrational (*informal*)

barking deer *n* ZOOL same as **muntjac**

Barkly Tableland /báarkli táyb'l land/ plateau region situated on the Northern Territory-Queensland border in Australia. Area: 130,000 sq. km/50,200 sq. mi.

Barlee, Lake /báarli/ lake in southwestern Western Australia, between lakes Moore and Ballard. Area: 1944 sq. km/750 sq. mi.

barley /báarli/ *n* 1. the grain from a cereal plant. Use: food, malt production, livestock feed. 2. a cereal plant with a long head of whiskered grains. Latin name: *Hordeum vulgare*. [Old English *bærlic* 'barley-like' < *bære, bere* 'barley' < Indo-European]

barleycorn /báarli kawrn/ *n* 1. a single grain of barley (*archaic*) 2. barley grain, especially used for malt

barley sugar *n* a clear hard orange-yellow sweet made from boiled-down sugar

barley water *n* a sweet cordial made from water, barley extract, and sugar

barley wine *n* very strong, slightly sweet beer

bar line *n* UK, NZ, Can a vertical line on a sheet of music that separates each unit of musical time. Aus, US term **bar**[1]

Barlow knife /báarlō-/ *n* a penknife with one blade for cutting and another for poking or gouging [Late 18C. After a family of cutlers in Sheffield]

barm /baarm/ *n* the foam that rises to the surface during the fermentation of malt liquor [Old English *beorma* < Germanic]

barmaid /baar mayd/ *n* a woman who serves in a pub or bar (*dated*; *sometimes offensive*)

barman /báarmən/ (*plural* **-men** /-mən/) *n* a man who serves in a pub or bar

barmbrack /báarm brak/, **barnbrack** /báarn brak/ *n* Ireland a rich sweet bread with currants in it [Mid-19C. < Irish *bairin breac* 'speckled cake']

Barmecidal /báarmi síd'l/, **Barmecide** /-síd/ *adj* abundant or lavish only in appearance and not in reality (*literary*) [Mid-18C. < *Barmecide*, prince in *The Arabian Nights' Entertainments* who served a series of empty dishes to a hungry beggar to test his sense of humour]

bar mitzvah /baar mítsvə/ *n* **1.** the ritual ceremony that marks the 13th birthday of a Jewish boy, after which he takes full responsibility for his moral and spiritual conduct **2.** a Jewish boy who has reached the age of 13, the age of religious responsibility [Early 19C. < Hebrew *bar miṣwāh* 'son of the commandment']

barmy /báarmi/ (**-ier**, **-iest**) *adj* (*informal*) **1.** unconventional or slightly irrational in behaviour **2.** completely lacking in good sense or reason ○ *That's a barmy idea and you know it.*

REGIONAL NOTE See *addle-headed*.

barn[1] /baarn/ *n* **1.** a large outbuilding on a farm used to store grain or shelter livestock **2.** a large building or room, especially one that is plain and functional ○ *walked into a great barn of a living room* [Old English *ber(e)n* 'barley house' < *bere* 'barley' + *ærn* 'house, place']

barn[2] /baarn/ *n* a unit of area equal to 10^{-28} square metres, used in nuclear physics [Mid-20C. < *as big as a barn door*]

Barnabas /báarnəbəss/, **St** (*fl* 1st century AD) Cypriot missionary. He was a companion of St Paul during Paul's early ministry, and is traditionally thought to have founded the Cypriot church.

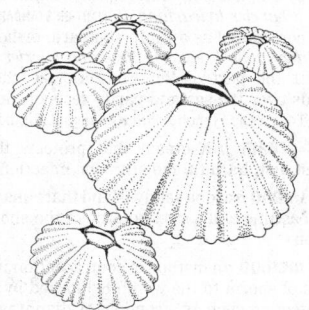
barnacle

barnacle /báarnək'l/ *n* **1.** MARINE BIOL a small invertebrate animal with a shell that clings to rocks and ships and draws food to itself by using slender hairs (**cirri**). Subclass: Cirripedia. **2.** BIRDS same as **barnacle goose 3.** a clinging or dependent person or thing [12C. < medieval Latin *berneca*]

barnacle goose *n* a wild goose with grey wings and a black-and-white head and body. Native to: northern Europe, Greenland. Latin name: *Branta leucopsis.*

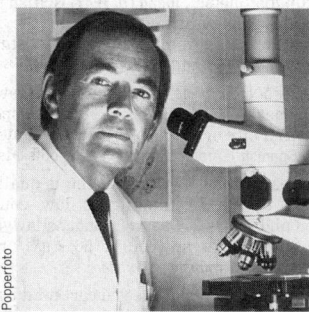
Christiaan Barnard

Barnard /baár naard/, **Christiaan** (1922–2001) South African surgeon. He performed the world's first successful human heart transplant operation in 1967. Full name **Barnard, Christiaan Neethling**

'The prime goal is to alleviate suffering, and not to prolong life. And if your treatment does not alleviate suffering, but only prolongs life, that treatment should be stopped.'
[Attributed to Christiaan Barnard]

Barnardo /bər naárdō/, **Thomas** (1845–1905) Irish-born British doctor and philanthropist. He founded the East End Mission for destitute children in London (1867). His establishments came to be known as Doctor Barnardo's Homes. Full name **Barnardo, Thomas John**

Barnard's star /báarnərdz-, baár naardz-/ *n* a red dwarf star in the constellation Ophiuchus [Early 20C. After Edward Emerson *Barnard* (1857–1923), US astronomer]

Barnaul /baárnə oòl/ capital city of Attay Territory, southwestern Siberia, Russia. Population: 616,299 (1995).

barnbrack *n* FOOD same as **barmbrack**

barn dance *n* **1.** a party, originally held in a barn, with country dancing **2.** a country dance

barn door *n* **1.** either of the huge doors that close the entrance to a traditional wooden barn **2.** an adjustable flap of a set of four on the front of a large industrial light used especially on film sets and in the theatre

barney /báarni/ (*plural* **-neys**) *n* a noisy argument (*informal*) [Mid-19C. Origin ?]

barn owl *n* an owl with white and pale brown feathers that often nests in barns. Latin name: *Tyto alba.*

Barnsley /báarnzli/ industrial town in South Yorkshire, northern England. Population: 218,063 (2001).

barnstorm /baárn stawrm/ (**-storms**, **-storming**, **-stormed**) *v* **1.** *vti* to travel from place to place giving performances **2.** *vi* to perform exhibitions of aerial acrobatics at shows and fairs —**barnstormer** *n* — **barnstorming** *n*

barnstorming /báarn stawrming/ *adj* performing or done in a strikingly enthusiastic and effective way

Barnum /baárnəm/, **P. T.** (1810–91) US showman, known for his spectacular circuses, including 'The Greatest Show on Earth' (1871). With James Bailey (1847–1906) he originated the Barnum and Bailey Circus (1881). Full name **Barnum, Phineas Taylor**

'There's a sucker born every minute.'
[Attributed to P. T. Barnum]

barnyard /baárn yaard/ *n* the area around a barn, where small farm animals roam ■ *adj* crude or vulgar (*informal*) ○ *barnyard humour*

barnyard grass *n* a coarse weedy grass with spiky clusters of flowers, sometimes grown as forage. Latin name: *Echinochloa crusgalli.*

baro- *prefix* pressure, weight ○ *barometer* [< Greek *baros* 'weight']

baroceptor /bárrə septər/ PHYSIOL same as **baroreceptor**

Baroda /bə ró̄də/ former name for **Vadodara** (until 1976)

barogram /bárrə gram/ *n* a record of atmospheric pressure produced by a barograph or other meteorological instrument

barograph /bárrə graaf, -graf/ *n* a barometer that gives a continuous printed record of variations in atmospheric pressure —**barographic** /bárrə gráffik/ *adj*

Barolo /bə róllō/ *n* a full-bodied red wine from northwestern Italy [Late 19C. After a region in NW Italy]

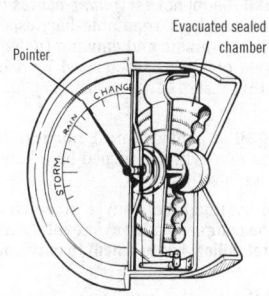
barometer

barometer /bə rómmitər/ *n* **1.** an instrument measuring changes in atmospheric pressure, used in weather forecasting **2.** something that indicates an atmosphere or mood ○ *the barometer of public opinion* —**barometric** /bárrə méttrik/ *adj* —**barometrical** *adj* —**barometrically** *adv* —**barometry** *n*

barometric pressure *n* atmospheric pressure as recorded by a barometer

baron /bárrən/ *n* **1.** NOBLEMAN a nobleman who belongs to the lowest rank of British or Japanese nobility, or to various ranks in some European countries **2.** SOMEBODY POWERFUL somebody with power or influence ○ *an oil baron* **3.** MEDIEVAL NOBLEMAN in the Middle Ages, a nobleman who was given land in return for loyal service [12C. Via Anglo-Norman *barun*, Old French *baron* < medieval Latin *baron-* 'man']

SPELLCHECK baron or **barren**? Do not confuse the spelling of **baron** and **barren**, which sound similar. **Baron** is a noun denoting a nobleman or a powerful person, as in *an oil baron.* **Barren** is an adjective meaning 'not productive', as in *barren land.*

baronage /bárrənij/ *n* **1.** barons considered collectively **2.** a baron's rank or position

baroness /bárrənəss/ *n* **1.** a noblewoman who belongs to the lowest rank of British or Japanese nobility, or to various ranks in some European countries **2.** a baron's wife or widow

baronet /bárrənət/ *n* a British nobleman who holds the lowest hereditary rank

baronetage /bárrənitəj/ *n* **1.** baronets collectively **2.** same as **baronetcy**

baronetcy /bárrənətsi/ *n* a baronet's rank or position

barong /ba róng/ *n* a large knife with a broad blade, used by the Moro people of the Philippines [Late 19C. < Austronesian]

baronial /bə ró̄ni əl/ *adj* **1.** RELATING TO BARON relating to or associated with a baron **2.** LARGE AND IMPRESSIVE large, imposing, or sumptuous ○ *a baronial fireplace* **3.** *Scot* LARGE AND TURRETED describes a large solid-looking country house with turrets

baron of beef *n* a cut of beef consisting of a double sirloin joined at the backbone [After a popular etymology for SIRLOIN]

barony /bárrəni/ (*plural* **-nies**) *n* **1.** a baron's rank or position, or the land held by a baron **2.** a powerful businessperson's area of influence ○ *a newspaper tycoon zealously guarding his barony*

barophilic /bárrə fíllik/ *adj* describes an organism that can tolerate high atmospheric pressure —**barophile** /bárrə fīl/ *n*

baroque /bə rók/ *adj* **1.** relating to or in a highly ornamental style of European architecture and art that lasted from the mid-16th to the early 18th centuries **2.** extravagantly or excessively ornamented or complicated [Mid-18C. Via French, applied to ornate architecture < Italian *barocco*, Portuguese *barroco* 'irregularly shaped pearl'] —**baroquely** *adv*

Baroque *n* **1.** the baroque style of architecture and art, or its period in European history **2.** highly ornamented music of the 17th century written by composers such as Bach, Handel, Vivaldi, and Telemann

baroreceptor /bárrō ri septər/ *n* a nerve ending that is sensitive to blood pressure changes

Barossa Valley /bə róssə-/ major grape-growing region north of Adelaide in South Australia

barothermograph /bárrə thúrmə graaf, -graf/ *n* an instrument that records atmospheric pressure and temperature simultaneously

barotitis /bárrə títiss/ *n* pain in the ear caused by pressure differences, e.g. during air travel

barotrauma /bárrō trawmə/ *n* pain and possible damage caused to an organ by changes in atmospheric pressure

barouche /bə rooʻsh/ *n* a four-wheeled horse-drawn carriage with two facing double seats, a retractable hood, and a box seat at the front for the driver [Early 19C. Via German dialect *Barutsche* < Italian *baroccio* 'two-wheeled' < Latin *birotus* < *rota* 'wheel']

barperson /báar purss'n/ (*plural* **-persons** or **-people** /-peep'l/) *n* somebody who serves in a pub or bar

bar point *n* the seventh point on a large backgammon board, near the bar

barque /baark/, **bark** *n* **1.** a small sailing ship with masts whose sails are fixed breadthways (**square**) except for the last mast, which has its sail running lengthways (**fore-and-aft**) **2.** a small sailing ship [15C. Via French < late Latin *barca*]

Barquisimeto /baar kissi méttō/ city in northwestern Venezuela and the capital of Lara State, on the River Turbio. Population: 602,622 (1991).

Barra /bárrə/ island at the southern end of the Outer Hebrides, western Scotland. Population: 1,200. Area: 90 sq. km/35 sq. mi.

barrack[1] /bárrək/ n MIL same as **barracks** (sense 1) ■ vt (-racks, -racking, -racked) 1. to house soldiers in a barracks 2. to house a group of people in temporary accommodation (often passive) [Late 17C. < BARRACKS] **barrack for** vti Aus to shout support for somebody, especially a player or team (informal) ○ The team ran onto the field with their fans barracking for them all the way.

barrack[2] /bárrək/ (-racks, -racking, -racked) vti to shout at somebody in criticism or protest (informal) [Late 19C. Probably < N Irish dialect barrack 'brag'] —**barracker** n

barrack-room lawyer n somebody who gives unwanted advice or opinions

barracks /bárrəks/ n (takes a singular or plural verb) 1. a building used to accommodate military personnel 2. temporary accommodation for nonmilitary personnel such as people working away from home [Late 17C. Via French baraque < Italian baracca or Spanish barraca 'soldier's tent, barracks']

barracoon /bárrə kóon/ n formerly, a large building used to confine convicts or African slaves temporarily [Mid-19C. < Spanish barracón 'large barracks' < barraca 'barracks']

barracouta /bárrə kóotə/ (plural -tas or same) n 1. a large predatory sea fish with strong teeth and a projecting lower jaw. Native to: Pacific Ocean. Family: Gempylidae. 2. NZ a long thin loaf of bread with a raised crust [Late 17C. Alteration of BARRACUDA]

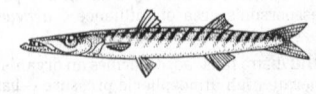

barracuda

barracuda /bárrə kóodə/ (plural -das or same) n a predatory sea fish with a long body and protruding jaws and teeth. Native to: tropics. Genus: Sphyraena. [Late 17C. Via American Spanish < Spanish dialect barraco 'overlapping tooth']

barrage /bárraazh, -j/ n 1. ARMS GUNFIRE BURSTS a long, continuous burst of gunfire 2. ATTACKING FLOW OF SOMETHING a rapid attacking outpouring of something ○ a barrage of criticism 3. CIV ENG RIVER BARRIER an artificial barrier built across a river or canal to provide water or prevent flooding ■ vt (-rages, -raging, -raged) 1. MIL FIRE CONTINUOUSLY ON ENEMY to attack an enemy with rapid and continuous gunfire 2. ATTACK SOMEBODY CONTINUOUSLY to subject somebody to a relentless onslaught ○ Those two have been barraging me with questions all morning. [Mid-19C. < French, 'barrier' < barrer 'to block' < barre (see BAR[1])]

barrage balloon n a large balloon anchored to the ground in wartime to deter enemy aircraft

barramundi /bárrə múndi/ (plural -dis or same), **barramunda** /-múndə/ (plural -das or same) n 1. an edible fish of the perch family. Native to: Australia. Latin name: Lates calcarifer. 2. a freshwater fish with a long robust body and a single dorsal fin near the rounded tail fin, belonging to a group of six species. Native to: tropics. Family: Osteoglossidae. [Late 19C. Probably < a Queensland Aboriginal word]

Barranquilla /bárran kée yə/ river port and capital of Atlántico Department, northern Colombia. It is situated on the Magdalena River, about 13 km/8 mi. inland from the Caribbean Sea. Population: 1,226,000 (1999).

barratry /bárrətri/, **barretry** n 1. BRINGING OF UNREASONABLE LAWSUITS the action of persistently bringing lawsuits for little or no reason, formerly an offence in British law 2. ILLEGAL SHIPPING PRACTICE an illegal practice such as fraud committed by a ship's master or crew that harms its owner or charterer 3. BUYING OF CHURCH OR GOVERNMENT POSITION the sale or purchase of a position in government or the church [15C. < French baraterie 'combat, deceit' < barater 'fight, cheat' < Greek prattein 'do'] —**barrator** n —**barratrous** adj —**barratrously** adv

Barrault /ba rṓ/, **Jean-Louis** (1910–94) French actor and producer. He directed the Théâtre de France in Paris (1959–68). His films include Les enfants du paradis (1945).

> 'Theatre is the first serum to be invented by mankind against that malady, anguish.'
> [Jean-Louis Barrault, 'Comment le théâtre naît en nous (How the Theatre is Born in us)', Nouvelles réflexions sur le théâtre (Reflections on the Theatre); 1961]

Barr body /baar-/ n an inactive X chromosome present in the cells of women and female animals, used in a test to determine sex [Mid-20C. After Murray L. Barr (1908–95), Canadian anatomist]

barre /baar/ n a rail fixed to a wall at about hip height, used by ballet dancers when exercising [Mid-20C. < French (see BAR[1])]

barré /bárray/ n 1. the placing of the index finger over all the strings of a guitar or similar string instrument to raise the pitch of each string simultaneously 2. a chord played on a guitar or similar string instrument in a barré fashion [Late 19C. < French, past participle of barrer (see BARRAGE)]

barred /baard/ adj 1. having strips of colour 2. fitted with or made of bars

barred spiral galaxy n a galaxy in which the stars form a spiral with a bright bar across the centre

barrel /bárrəl/ n 1. LARGE CASK a cylindrical container with a flat top and bottom, used to store liquids 2. QUANTITY IN BARREL the amount held by a barrel 3. MEASURE UNIT OF VOLUME IN OIL INDUSTRY a unit of liquid volume used in the oil industry, usually taken to be 35 imperial gallons or 42 US gallons (approximately 159 litres) 4. MEASURE UNIT OF VOLUME IN BREWING INDUSTRY a unit of liquid volume used in the brewing industry, equal to 36 imperial gallons or 43 US gallons (approximately 164 litres) 5. ARMS TUBE-SHAPED PART OF GUN the tube-shaped part of a gun through which bullets are fired 6. MECH ENG CYLINDRICAL PART a hollow cylindrical device that forms part of a mechanism, e.g. in clocks ■ vi (-rels, -relling, -relled) N Am TRAVEL FAST to move somewhere at high speed (informal) [13C. Via Old French baril < medieval Latin barriclus 'small cask'] —**barrelful** n ◇ **not be a barrel of laughs** to be far from being interesting or amusing ◇ **over a barrel** in a situation of powerlessness ◇ **scrape the (bottom of the) barrel** to use the least desirable person or thing because no one or nothing else is available

barrel chair n US an upholstered chair with a high curved solid back that looks like part of a barrel

barrel-chested adj having a large rounded chest

barrelhead /bárrəl hed/ n the flat circular top of a barrel

barrelhouse /bárrəl howss/ (plural -houses /-howziz/) n 1. N Am a cheap disreputable bar, especially one where there is music and dancing (dated) 2. a loud rough style of jazz characterized by a heavy two-beat rhythm [Late 19C. < the barrels of liquor along the walls]

barrel organ n a mechanical musical instrument consisting of a cylinder turned by a handle to pass air through a set of pipes

barrel roll n a flight manoeuvre in which an aircraft makes one complete sideways revolution ■ vi (barrel rolls, barrel rolling, barrel rolled) to carry out a barrel roll

barrel vault n a ceiling in the shape of a half cylinder

barren /bárrən/ adj 1. BARE OF VEGETATION having no trees or other growing plants 2. NOT FRUITING producing no fruit or seed 3. UNABLE TO HAVE CHILDREN not able to bear children (archaic or literary) 4. WITH NO USEFUL RESULT producing no valuable results or interesting effects ○ It was a barren period in his career. 5. LACKING IN SOMETHING completely lacking in a particular thing (literary) ○ Our writers seem somewhat barren of new ideas. [12C. < Old French baraigne] —**barrenly** adv —**barrenness** n

SPELLCHECK See baron.

barret /bárrət/ n a flat cap similar in shape to a biretta, worn in the Middle Ages by members of the clergy and soldiers [Early 19C. Via French barrette < Italian berretta (see BIRETTA)]

barretry n LAW another spelling of **barratry**

barrette /bə rét/ n a metal or plastic clasp used by women and girls to keep their hair in place [Early 20C. < French, 'small bar' < barre (see BAR[1])]

barricade /bárri káyd, -kayd/ n a barrier that protects defenders or blocks a route ■ vt (-cades, -cading, -caded) to obstruct or protect something, or protect yourself, using a barricade [Late 16C. < French < barrique 'barrel']

Barrie /bárri/, **Sir J. M.** (1860–1937) British author. He wrote Peter Pan (1904) and numerous other plays including The Admirable Crichton (1902). Full name **Barrie, Sir James Matthew**

> 'God gave us our memories so that we might have roses in December.'
> [Sir J. M. Barrie, Rectorial address, St. Andrews University; 3 May 1922]

barrier /bárri ər/ n 1. STRUCTURE BLOCKING ACCESS a structure such as a fence that is intended to stop access or keep one place separate from another 2. SOMETHING THAT OBSTRUCTS something that obstructs or separates, often by emphasizing differences ○ Impatience can act as a barrier to learning. 3. LIMIT OR STANDARD something considered as a limit, standard, or boundary ○ sprinters who break the 10-second barrier 4. GEOG ICE SHELF the part of the Antarctic ice shelf that extends over the sea and partly rests on the ocean floor [14C. < Old French barriere < Vulgar Latin barra 'bar']

barrier cream n a cream that protects the skin against dirt, harmful moisture, or infection

barrier island n a long sandy island that runs parallel to a coastline and serves to protect the shore from erosion

barrier method n a method of contraception in which access of sperm to the womb is blocked by the use of protection such as a condom or diaphragm

barrier nursing n the nursing of patients with infectious diseases in isolation to prevent the spread of infection —**barrier-nurse** vt

barrier reef n a narrow ridge of coral lying parallel and close to a coastline and separated from it by a wide deep lagoon

barrier tape n coloured tape with a repeated warning printed on it, used to cordon off e.g. a crime scene or construction area

barring /baaring/ prep excepting or except for something ○ Barring delays, we'll arrive this afternoon.

Barrington /bárringtən/, **Jonah** (b. 1941) British squash player. He popularized the sport in the United Kingdom, winning the open championships six times between 1967 and 1973.

barrio /bárri ō/ (plural -os) n 1. an area of a town in a Spanish-speaking country 2. US a Spanish-speaking quarter in a city or town in the United States [Mid-19C. Via Spanish < Arabic barr 'open area, outskirts']

barrister /bárristər/ n 1. a lawyer who is qualified to represent clients in the higher law courts in England and Wales 2. Can in Canada, a lawyer who represents clients in any court [15C. < BAR[1], probably after words such as minister, chorister]

barrow[1] /bárrō/ n 1. a two-wheeled cart used by street vendors to sell their wares. N Am term **pushcart** 2. GARDENING, CONSTR same as **wheelbarrow** [Old English bearwe 'stretcher, bier' < Germanic, 'to bear']

barrow[2] /bárrō/ n a large mound of earth above a prehistoric tomb [Old English beorg 'hill, tumulus' < Germanic, 'hide, protect']

barrow[3] /bárrō/ n a pig that has been castrated before sexual maturity [Old English b(e)arg < Germanic]

Barrow /bárrō/, **Clyde** (1909–34) US outlaw. He and Bonnie Parker robbed banks and killed 12 people (1932–34) before being killed by Louisiana police.

barrow boy n a man who sells wares from a barrow

Barrow-in-Furness /-fúrniss/ industrial town on the

Furness Peninsula, Cumbria, northwestern England. Population: 71,979 (2001).

Barrow Island island off the northwestern coast of Western Australia. It is a nature reserve and the site of an important oil field. Population: 100. Area: 200 sq. km/78 sq. mi.

Barry /bárri/ industrial city, seaport, and coastal resort in the Vale of Glamorgan on the Bristol Channel, Wales. Population: 49,887 (1991).

Barry, Sir Charles (1795–1860) British architect. Influenced by the Italian Renaissance, he helped to design the Houses of Parliament in London (1840–70). His other buildings include the Travellers' Club, London (1829–32).

Barrymore /bárri mawr/, **Ethel** (1879–1959) US actor. The sister of John and Lionel Barrymore, she had a long stage career and won an Academy Award for *None but the Lonely Heart* (1944).

> 'For an actress to be a success she must have the face of Venus, the brains of Minerva, the grace of Terpsichore, the memory of Macaulay, the figure of Juno, and the hide of a rhinoceros.'
> [Ethel Barrymore, *The Theater in the Fifties*, George Jean Nathan; 1953]

Barrymore, John (1882–1942) US actor. A handsome leading man, he made numerous films, but was most famous for his performance of Hamlet. He was the brother of Ethel and Lionel Barrymore.

> 'Audiences? No, the plural is impossible. Whether it be in Butte, Montana, or Broadway, it's an audience. The same great hulking monster with four thousand eyes and forty thousand teeth.'
> [John Barrymore, *Letter to playwright Ashton Stevens*; April 1906]

Barrymore, Lionel (1878–1954) US actor. The brother of Ethel and John Barrymore, he won an Academy Award for *Free Soul* (1931) and appeared in the original *Dr Kildare* films.

> 'Half the people in Hollywood are dying to be discovered and the other half are afraid they will be.'
> [Lionel Barrymore. Quoted in *Hollywood, Babble On*, Bose Hadleigh; 1994]

Barsac /báar sak/ *n* a sweet white wine from western France [Early 18C. After a district in W France]

bar sinister (*plural* **bars sinister**) *n* **1.** HERALDRY same as **bend sinister 2.** evidence suggesting that somebody is of illegitimate birth

Bart. *abbr* baronet

bar tack *n* a straight stitch that crosses a piece of cloth at a right angle to a slit, e.g. at the end of a buttonhole

bartender /báar tendər/ *n N Am* somebody who serves in a pub or bar

barter /báartər/ *v* (**-ters, -tering, -tered**) **1.** *vti* EXCHANGE GOODS OR SERVICES to exchange goods or services in return for other goods or services **2.** *vi* NEGOTIATE TERMS OF AGREEMENT to negotiate or argue over the terms of a transaction ■ *n* **1.** EXCHANGE OF GOODS OR SERVICES the practice or system of exchanging goods and services **2.** THINGS BARTERED goods or services that are exchanged [15C. Probably < Old French *barater* (see BARRATRY)] —**barterer** *n*

Barth, John (*b.* 1930) US writer. He is known for his experimentation in literary form in fictional works such as *Giles Goat-Boy* (1966) and *Tidewater Tales* (1987). Full name **Barth, John Simmons**

Barth /baarth, baart/, **Karl** (1886–1968) Swiss theologian. He was a leading theorist of Reformed theology. His numerous writings include *The Epistle to the Romans* (1919) and the monumental *Church Dogmatics* (1932–62).

> 'Men have never been good, they are not good, they never will be good.'
> [Karl Barth, *Time*; 12 April 1954]

Barthes /baart/, **Roland** (1915–80) French philosopher and writer. He was a leading proponent of structuralism and author of the seminal critical work *Writing Degree Zero* (1953). He formulated the literary theory that the 'meaning' of a text lies not in its author's intentions but in its underlying structure. Full name **Barthes, Roland Gérard**

Bartholdi /baar tóldi, -thóldi/, **Frédéric-Auguste** (1834–1904) French sculptor. His best-known work is the *Statue of Liberty* (1886).

Bartholin's gland /báarthəlinz-/ *n* a small gland found on each side of the lower vagina that secretes a lubricating mucus during sexual stimulation [Early 20C. After Kaspar *Bartholin* (1655–1738), Danish anatomist]

Bartholomew /baar thólləmyoo/, **St** (*fl* 1st century AD) one of the 12 apostles of Jesus Christ. He is traditionally believed to have been martyred by being flayed alive.

bartizan

bartizan /báartiz'n, baárti zán/ *n* a small turret that projects from a tower or wall of a fortress or castle, used as a lookout or a defensive position [Mid-16C. Scots variant of *bratticing* 'timberwork' < BRATTICE] —**bartizaned** *adj*

Bartle Frere /báart'l freer/ mountain near the city of Cairns in northeastern Queensland, Australia. It is the highest mountain in Queensland. Height: 1,612 m/5,287 ft.

Bartlett /báartlət/, **Bartlett pear** *n Aus, N Am* FOOD same as **Williams** [Mid-19C. After Enoch *Bartlett* (1779–1860), US merchant]

Bartók /báar tok/, **Béla** (1881–1945) Hungarian composer. Influenced by Hungarian folk music, he wrote piano concertos, string quartets, and the opera *Bluebeard's Castle* (1911).

Barton /báart'n/, **Sir Edmund** (1849–1920) first prime minister of Australia (1901–03). An enthusiastic supporter of federalism, he campaigned for the implementation of the Constitution Bill (1900) that led to the creation of the Commonwealth of Australia. See table at **prime minister**

Baruch /bə róok/ *n* a book of the Roman Catholic Bible and the Protestant Apocrypha traditionally attributed to Baruch, a disciple of the prophet Jeremiah. See table at **Bible**

Barwick /bárrik/, **Sir Garfield** (1903–97) Australian judge and politician. He was federal attorney general (1958–64) and chief justice of the High Court of Australia (1964–81). Full name **Barwick, Sir Garfield Edward John**

barycentre /bárri sentər/ *n* the centre of the mass of a system, especially a system of astronomical objects [Late 19C. < Greek *barus* 'heavy'] —**barycentric** /bárri séntrik/ *adj*

baryon /bárri on/ *n* a subatomic particle belonging to a group that undergoes strong interactions, has a mass greater than or equal to that of the proton, and consists of three quarks [Mid-20C. < Greek *barus* 'heavy' + -ON [1]] —**baryonic** /bárri ónnik/ *adj*

Mikhail Baryshnikov

Baryshnikov /bə ríshnikof/, **Mikhail** (*b.* 1948) Russian-born US dancer and choreographer. He defected from the Soviet Union (1974) and danced for and directed (1980–89) the American Ballet Theatre. Full name **Baryshnikov, Mikhail Nikolayevich**

baryta /bə rítə/ *n* barium oxide or hydroxide [Early 19C. < BARYTES, after SODA] —**barytic** /bə ríttik/ *adj*

barytes /bə rí teez/ *n* a yellow, white, or colourless mineral consisting of barium sulphate. Use: source of barium. N Am term **barite** [Late 18C. < Greek *barutēs* 'weight']

bas /buss/ *interj S Asia* used to tell somebody to stop doing something [Via Hindi < Persian]

BAS[1] *n* a form used by Australian businesses to report the amount of GST and other taxes paid and collected. Full form **business activity statement**

BAS[2] *abbr* **1.** Bachelor of Agricultural Science **2.** Bachelor of Applied Science

basal /báyss'l/ *adj* **1.** at or forming the bottom of something **2.** basic or fundamental —**basally** *adv*

basal body *n* a structure found near the base of cells that have projecting threads (**cilia**)

basal cell *n* a cell forming the deepest layer of the skin

basal cell carcinoma *n* a slow-growing malignant tumour that typically affects the facial skin of people in later life. It rarely spreads to other parts, and is generally curable by surgery or radiotherapy.

basal ganglion *n* a mass of grey matter that lies in the white matter near the base of each cerebral hemisphere of the brain. The basal ganglia help to regulate the body's voluntary movements.

basal metabolic rate *n* the rate at which an organism consumes oxygen while awake but at rest, measured in calories per square metre of body surface per hour

basal metabolism *n* the amount of energy consumed by a resting organism simply in maintaining its basic functions

basalt /bássawlt/ *n* **1.** a hard, black, often glassy, volcanic rock. It was produced by the partial melting of the Earth's mantle. **2.** a hard black unglazed pottery [Early 17C. Via Latin *basaltes*, variant of *basanites* < Greek *basanitēs* 'very hard stone, touchstone' < Egyptian *bakhan* 'slate'] —**basaltic** /bə sáwltik/ *adj*

basalt plateau *n* an extensive continental deposit of basaltic volcanic rock

basaltware /bássawlt wair/ *n* a hard black stoneware pottery made in England and parts of continental Europe in the 18th century

basanite /bássə nīt/ *n* a volcanic basaltic rock containing olivine and additional alkaline minerals [Mid-18C. < Latin *basanites* (see BASALT)]

BASc *abbr* **1.** Bachelor of Agricultural Science **2.** Bachelor of Applied Science

bascule /báss kyool/ *n* **1.** a counterbalanced device that pivots on a central axis so that the unweighted end rises as the weighted end is allowed to fall **2.** *also* **bascule bridge** a bridge with a roadway that can be raised to allow tall boats and ships to pass through [Late 17C. < French, 'seesaw' < *battre* 'to batter' + *cul* 'buttocks']

base[1] /bayss/ *n* **1.** LOWEST PART the lowest, bottom, or supporting part or layer of something **2.** MAIN SUPPORTING ELEMENT the main source of an important component in an economy or sphere of influence ○ *improve our customer base* **3.** FUNDAMENTAL PRINCIPLE the main principle or starting point of a system or theory **4.** CENTRE FROM WHICH ACTIVITIES START a centre from which activities start or are coordinated **5.** MILITARY CENTRE a coordinating or supply centre for military operations **6.** MAIN INGREDIENT a main ingredient to which others are added **7.** BASEBALL FIELD MARKER in baseball, one of the four corners of the diamond-shaped infield that a batter must touch in order to score a run **8.** ARCHIT LOWER PART OF BUILT STRUCTURE the lower part of a built structure such as a wall, pillar, or column **9.** ANAT ATTACHMENT AREA OF BODY ORGAN the part of an organ or body part by which it is attached to a more central structure of an organism **10.** HERALDRY LOWER PART OF HERALDIC SHIELD the lower part of a heraldic shield **11.** MATHS REFERENCE NUMBER the number that is the basis for a system of

Popperfoto

calculation, represented by the total countable digits in the system. The base 10 system contains the ten digits 0–9. **12.** MATHS LOGARITHM REFERENCE a number raised to a power denoted by a superscript. In the equation $10^2 = 100$, 10 is the base. Natural logarithms have a base e (= 2.718). **13.** MATHS LOWER SIDE OF FIGURE the lower side or face of a geometric figure **14.** MEASURE same as **baseline** (sense 1) **15.** SOLVENT a medium in which ingredients or constituents may be dissolved or carried **16.** FIN LOWEST STOCK PRICE the lowest recorded price level of a tradable commodity or security **17.** CHEM CHEMICAL COMPOUND a compound that releases hydroxyl ions to form a solution with a pH greater than 7, reacts with acids to form salts, and turns red litmus paper blue **18.** CHEM CHEMICAL COMPOUND FORMING COVALENT BOND a compound that can accept a proton or donate a pair of electrons to form a covalent bond with an acid **19.** PHOTOGRAPHY FILM FOUNDATION an inert medium supporting the photographic emulsion of films **20.** ELEC ENG MIDDLE REGION OF TRANSISTOR the middle region of a transistor between the emitter and the collector ■ vt (**bases, basing, based**) **1.** MAKE BASE FOR SOMETHING to create or provide a base for something ○ *The board of directors decided to base the new company in Sydney.* **2.** ASSIGN SOMEBODY TO BASE to station, post, or assign somebody to a base ○ *The battalion was based in Aldershot.* **3.** USE SOMETHING AS BASIS to use something as a base or basis for something else ○ *His report is based on the research he carried out in Peru.* [14C. Directly or via French < Latin *basis* < Greek *basis* (see BASIS)] ◇ **have all bases covered** to have made preparations to ensure that every eventuality is provided for ◇ **off base** wrong or inexact (*informal*) ○ *Your calculations are all off base.* ◇ **touch base (with somebody)** to communicate briefly with somebody, e.g. to carry a project forward or exchange current information

---

SPELLCHECK *base* or *bass*? Do not confuse the spelling of *base* and *bass*, which sound similar. Both words refer to something low, but *bass* is used only of sound, as in *a bass voice* or *a bass guitar*. *Base* has a much wider range of meanings and uses, as in *the base of the statue*, *a base unit, base metals, tried to curb his base instincts*, etc.

---

base[2] /bayss/ (**baser, basest**) *adj* **1.** LACKING MORALS lacking proper social values or moral principles **2.** OF POOR QUALITY inferior in value or quality **3.** COUNTERFEIT describes a coin that contains a higher proportion of common inexpensive metals than usual **4.** OFFENSIVE TERM an offensive term meaning of humble or illegitimate birth (*archaic*) **5.** HIST RELATING TO PEASANT relating to a peasant (**villein**) renting land from a feudal lord (*archaic*) [14C. Via French *bas* < medieval Latin *bassus* 'short, low'] —**basely** *adv* —**baseness** *n*

SPELLCHECK See *base*[1]

SYNONYMS See *mean*[2].

Popperfoto
baseball: a batter swings at the ball

baseball /bayss bawl/ *n* **1.** a game played with a bat and ball by two teams of nine players on a field with four bases marking the course the batters must take to score runs. Each team fields and bats alternately, and the aim is to score the most runs. **2.** a hard leather-covered ball about 23 cm/9 in in circumference, used in the game of baseball

baseball cap *n* a close-fitting cap with a long peak, originally worn by baseball players

baseband /bayss band/ *n* the frequency band of a transmitted message

baseboard /bayss bawrd/ *n* **1.** a board that serves as the base of something **2.** *N Am* same as **skirting board**

baseborn /bayss bawrn/ *adj* (*archaic*) **1.** OFFENSIVE TERM an offensive term meaning born of poor parents or of parents regarded as having been disgraced **2.** OFFENSIVE TERM an offensive term meaning born of unmarried parents **3.** CONSIDERED AS IGNOBLE regarded as dishonourable or unworthy

base camp *n* a place used as a temporary store for supplies and from which an activity, especially a mountaineering expedition, starts

base coin *n* a counterfeit coin made of cheap metal

base currency *n* a currency in which a business maintains its accounts and that it uses for buying and selling

Basedow's disease /bázzidōz-/ *n* MED same as **Graves' disease** [Late 19C. After Karl Adolph von *Basedow* (1799–1854), German physician]

base hit *n* in baseball, a hit that enables the batter to reach a base safely

base hospital *n* *Aus* a central hospital that serves an extensive rural area

base jumping *n* the extreme sport of parachuting from the tops of very tall natural objects or constructions such as cliffs, towers, or buildings [Acronym < *building, antenna tower, span, earth*, because jumpers use high buildings, bridges, and cliffs] —**base-jump** *vi*

Basel /baáz'l/, **Basle** /baal/ city in northwestern Switzerland, situated on the highest navigation point of the Rhine. Population: 168,735 (1998).

baseless /bayssləss/ *adj* **1.** without grounds or a factual basis **2.** lacking a base or foundation —**baselessly** *adv* —**baselessness** *n*

base level *n* the lowest level to which moving water can erode a land surface such as the bed of a stream, lake, or sea

baseline /bayss līn/ *n* **1.** MEASURE MEASURING LINE a line used as a basis for measurement, calculation, or location, e.g. in surveying or navigation **2.** STANDARD OF VALUE a standard of value to which other similar things are compared **3.** REFERENCE DATA the data used as a reference with which to compare future observations or results **4.** BOUNDARY LINE AT END OF COURT a boundary line at each end of a court that marks the limit of play in tennis, badminton, or basketball

baseliner /baysslīnər/ *n* a tennis player who prefers to play on or near the baseline and only occasionally moves to the net

base load *n* the average demand placed on an electrical power supply system

baseman /bayssmən/ (*plural* -**men** /-mən/) *n* in baseball, a fielder positioned near first, second, or third base

basement /bayssmənt/ *n* **1.** ARCHIT UNDERGROUND STOREY OF BUILDING a storey of a building that is wholly or partly below ground level **2.** BUILDINGS LOWEST PART OF WALL OR BUILDING the foundation, substructure, or lowest part of a wall or building **3.** GEOL PART OF EARTH'S CRUST the highly folded igneous or metamorphic layer of rocks that lies beneath more recent, softer sedimentary rocks [Mid-18C. Probably via Dutch < Italian *basamento* 'base of a column' < *basare* 'to base']

base metal *n* a common inexpensive metal

basenji /bə sénji/ *n* a small dog belonging to a curly-tailed African breed that rarely barks and has a short smooth coat varying from black to chestnut [Mid-20C. < Bantu]

base on balls *n* in baseball, an advance to first base awarded to a batter who receives four pitches outside the strike zone at which the batter does not swing

base pair *n* a chemical unit linking complementary strands of DNA or RNA. It consists of a purine linked to a pyrimidine by hydrogen bonds.

base pairing *n* the hydrogen bonding between complementary bases that holds together the two strands of the double helix of DNA and RNA

base rate *n* the rate of interest used by UK clearing banks as a basis for calculating their lending rates. N Am term **bank rate**

base runner *n* in baseball, a player on the team

batting who is on a base or is trying to get to one safely

bases plural of **basis**

base unit *n* a fundamental unit within a system of measurement from which other units in the system are derived

bash /bash/ *v* (**bashes, bashing, bashed**) **1.** vt STRIKE SOMEBODY OR SOMETHING HEAVILY to strike somebody or something with a heavy blow (*informal*) **2.** vt SMASH SOMETHING to smash or strike something violently or damagingly (*informal*) **3.** vt DENT SOMETHING to make a dent in something (*informal*) **4.** vi COLLIDE WITH SOMETHING to crash into or collide with something (*informal*) **5.** vt CRITICIZE SOMEBODY OR SOMETHING HARSHLY to criticize somebody or something harshly and usually publicly (*informal*) **6.** vt BATTER SOMEBODY to beat somebody severely (*dated informal*) ■ *n* (*informal*) **1.** HEAVY BLOW a heavy blow dealt to somebody or something **2.** DENT a dent made in something **3.** CELEBRATION a party or celebration [Mid-17C. Probably an imitation of the sound of hitting] ◇ **have a bash (at something)** to make an attempt to do something (*informal*)

bash out *vt* to produce something quickly or in large quantities, but without much care or attention (*informal*)

bash up *vt* to attack and injure somebody (*informal*)

bashful /bashf'l/ *adj* behaving in a shy, self-conscious, or modest way [15C. < shortened form of ABASH] —**bashfully** *adv* —**bashfulness** *n*

bashibazouk /báshibə zoók/ *n* a 19th-century Turkish irregular mercenary soldier, notorious for brutality [Mid-19C. < Turkish *başi bozuk* 'wrong-headed' < *başi* 'head' + *bozuk* 'out of order']

bashing /báshing/ *n* (*slang; usually used in combination*) **1.** PHYSICAL ASSAULT mugging or violence, especially when directed at a particular group of people **2.** CRITICISM hostile comment directed at a specific person or group **3.** EXCESSIVE USE the exposure of something to repetitive or prolonged use

Bashir /bə sheer/, **Omar Hassan al-** (*b.* 1944?) president of Sudan (1989–). He came to power in a military coup and was elected president (1993) and twice re-elected (1996 and 2000) by the Revolutionary Command Council. He presides over a government dominated by members of the National Islamic Front.

Bashkir /bash keer/ (*plural* -**kirs** *or same*) *n* **1.** a member of a Turkic-speaking Muslim people from central Russia **2.** a Turkic language spoken in an area west of the Ural Mountains in central Russia. Native speakers: 1 million. [Early 19C. Via Russian < Turkic *Başkurt*] —**Bashkir** *adj*

Bashkortostan /bash káwrtə staan/ autonomous republic in central Russia, west of the Ural Mountains, bordering the republic of Tatarstan to the Northwest and the republic of Udmurtia to the North. Capital: Ufa. Population: 4,134,000 (1997). Area: 143,600 sq. km/55,440 sq. mi. Former name **Bashkiria** (until 1992)

bashment /báshmənt/ *n* a party, especially a public event, with music provided by a sound system or systems (*slang; used in Black English*)

basho /báshō/ (*plural* -**os**) *n* a sumo wrestling tournament [Late 20C. < Japanese]

Basho /báshō/, **Bashō** (1644–94) Japanese poet, considered an expert in the haiku form. His work was strongly influenced by Zen Buddhism. Pseudonym of **Matsuo Munefusa**

basi- *prefix* same as **baso-**

basic /báyssik/ *adj* **1.** MOST IMPORTANT most important or essential ○ *a few basic guidelines* **2.** ELEMENTARY serving as a starting point or minimum **3.** WITHOUT EXTRA without or before the addition of anything extra ○ *a basic salary* **4.** PLAIN plain and utilitarian rather than luxurious or fancy (*informal*) **5.** CHEM RELATING TO CHEMICAL BASE containing, relating to, or being a chemical base **6.** CHEM ALKALINE having an alkaline reaction **7.** CHEM CONTAINING HYDROXIDE OR OXIDE GROUPS describes a salt that contains hydroxide or oxide anions **8.** GEOL LOW IN SILICA describes rock that contains 45–53 per cent total silica by weight, e.g. basalt **9.** METALL USING BASE IN MAKING STEEL describes a process of making steel in which the furnace is lined with a base that combines with acidic impurities in the ore to produce basic slag ■ **basics** *npl* MOST

IMPORTANT THINGS the most important or fundamental parts of something —**basicity** /bay síssiti/ *n* ◇ **go or get back to basics** to return to the fundamental parts or principles of something, especially when problems are encountered at a more advanced or complex stage ○ *a movement to get back to basics in education*

BASIC /báyssik/, **Basic** *n* a high-level computer programming language that uses common English terms and algebra. Full form **Beginners All-purpose Symbolic Instruction Code**

basically /báyssikli/ *adv* **1.** ⚠ used to emphasize the most important aspect of something, or to give a simplified account of something more complicated ○ *Basically, I'm not interested.* **2.** in a simple way, using only essentials

USAGE **basically** as a sentence adverb: This use, in which **basically** is reduced to adding emphasis (*Basically it's a waste of time*), is common in informal conversation but should be avoided otherwise. So too should the meaning 'essentially', as in *His role is basically to oversee operations.*

Basic Curriculum *n* in schools in England and Wales, the National Curriculum plus religious education

basic education *n* **1.** *N Am* the formal education deemed necessary for somebody to function properly in society **2.** in India, education in which all teaching is linked with learning a craft

Basic English *n* a simplified form of English intended as an introductory version of the language for non-native speakers and for use as an auxiliary international language. It consists of a vocabulary of 850 words for general needs, plus additional international and scientific words.

basic input-output system *n* COMPUT full form of **BIOS**

~~basicly~~ incorrect spelling of **basically**

basic rate *n* **1.** the standard cost or rate of pay excluding any discounts or additions **2.** the standard rate of income tax

basic slag *n* the phosphate-rich slag from making steel using a basic process. Use: fertilizer.

basic training *n* the initial training of a military recruit

basidiomycete /bə síddi ō mī seét/ *n* FUNGI former name for **basidiomycote** [Late 19C. < modern Latin *Basidiomycetes* < *basidium* (see BASIDIUM) + Greek *mukētes* 'fungi'] —**basidiomycetous** *adj*

basidiomycote /bə síddi ō míkōt/ *n* a fungus that produces its spores in a characteristic club-shaped cell (**basidium**). Mushrooms, puffballs, rusts, shelf fungi, and smuts are basidiomycotes. Division: *Basidiomycota*. —**basidiomycote** *adj*

basidiospore /bə síddi ō spawr/ *n* a spore produced by a basidiomycote fungus such as a mushroom, puffball, smut, or rust —**basidiosporous** /bə síddi ō spáwrəss/ *adj*

basidium /bə síddi əm/ *n* (*plural* -**ia** /-i ə/) *n* a club-shaped cell found in some fungi from which external sexual spores are produced [Mid-19C. < modern Latin, 'small base' < Greek *basis* 'step, base'] —**basidial** *adj*

Basie /báyzi/, **Count** (1904–84) US composer and bandleader. He was one of the most enduring popular American musicians as the leader of his own bigband swing ensembles for over four decades, and composed numbers including 'One O'Clock Jump'. Born **Basie, William**

> 'I don't think that a band can really swing on just a kick-off, you know; I think you've got to set the tempo first. If you can do it the other way, that's something else… Anyway we do it our way.'
> [Count Basie. Quoted in *Count Basie*, Alun Morgan; 1984]

basify /báyssifī/ (-**fies, -fying, -fied**) *vt* **1.** to change a chemical into a base **2.** to make something alkaline —**basification** /báyssifi káysh'n/ *n*

basil /bázz'l/ *n* a herb with aromatic leaves. Use: seasoning. Latin name: *Ocimum basilicum*. [15C. Via Old French *basile* < Latin *basilicum* < Greek *basilikon* (*phuton*) 'royal (herb)']

Basil /bázz'l/, **St** (329?–379) Greek prelate and scholar. He studied at Byzantium and Athens, became Bishop of Caesarea (370), and defended Christian philosophy against heresies such as Arianism. Known as **Basil the Great**

basilar /bássilər/ *adj* relating to or situated at the base of a body part such as the skull [Mid-16C. < modern Latin *basilaris* < Latin *basis* (see BASIS)]

Basildon /bázz'ldən/ town in Essex, southeastern England. It was designated a new town in 1949. Population: 165,661 (2001).

basilica /bə zíllikə, -síllikə/ *n* **1.** PRIVILEGED ROMAN CATHOLIC CHURCH a Roman Catholic church or cathedral given ceremonial privileges by the Pope **2.** ANCIENT ROMAN BUILDING in ancient Rome, a building with a central nave, a columned aisle on each side, and typically a terminal semicircular apse. It was used as a court of justice, an assembly hall, or an exchange. **3.** LARGE CHRISTIAN CHURCH a Christian church building formed from a Roman basilica or built to a similar design [Mid-16C. Via Latin, 'royal palace' < Greek *basilikē* < *basilikos* 'royal' < *basileus* 'king'] —**basilican** *adj*

basilisk (sense 2)

basilisk /bázzə lisk/ *n* **1.** a legendary reptile, said to have been hatched by a serpent from a cock's egg, whose look or breath was supposed to be fatal **2.** a lizard, related to the iguana, that is able to run upright on its long hind legs. Native to: Central and South America. Genus: *Basiliscus*. [14C. Via Latin < Greek *basiliskos* 'minor king, kind of serpent' < *basileus* 'king']

basin /báyss'n/ *n* **1.** OPEN CONTAINER FOR WASHING an open metal, ceramic, or plastic container with sloping sides, typically used for holding water or washing **2.** BOWL FOR PREPARING FOOD a deep bowl, especially a round one, used for storing, mixing, or cooking food **3.** BASIN CONTENTS the contents of or amount contained in a basin **4.** DOCK NEAR SEA a dock built in a harbour or river that opens to the sea **5.** GEOG DEPRESSION IN LAND FILLED WITH WATER a depression in the Earth's surface that contains water **6.** GEOG LAND DRAINING INTO RIVER OR LAKE a broad area of land drained by a single river and its tributaries, or draining into a lake **7.** GEOL BOWL-SHAPED DEPRESSION a bowl-shaped depression on land or on the ocean floor into which sediments may be deposited **8.** GEOL CIRCULAR FORMATION OF SLOPING ROCK STRATA a large circular outcrop of rock in which strata dip inwards towards the centre [13C. Via Old French < medieval Latin *ba(s)cinus* < *bacca* 'water container'] —**basinful** *n*

basinet /bássinət/ *n* a lightweight steel helmet, sometimes with a visor, worn in medieval times [14C. < Old French *bacinet* 'little basin', from its shape]

Basingstoke /báyzing stōk/ town in Hampshire, southern England. Population: 77,837 (1991).

Basingstoke and Deane /-deén/ local government district in Hampshire, southern England. Population: 152,573 (2001).

basipetal /bay síppit'l/ *adj* developing from the top of a stem towards the base so that the oldest leaves or flowers are at the top —**basipetally** *adv*

basis /báyssiss/ (*plural* **bases** /báy seez/) *n* **1.** FOUNDATION something that acts as a support or foundation, especially of an idea or argument ○ *Are you sure there is no basis to this rumour?* **2.** STARTING POINT the point from which something starts or is developed ○ *find the basis on which to begin negotiations* **3.** WAY OF PROCEEDING the basic method or system according to which something is done or organized ○ *work on a part-time basis* **4.** MAIN COMPONENT the main component or ingredient of something **5.** MATHS SET OF VECTORS in a vector space, the minimal set of vectors necessary to define all other vectors in the space [Late 16C. Via Latin < Greek, 'step, base' < *bainein* 'go']

USAGE **Basis** does a number of jobs that other words can do better or that need not be done at all. Expressions such as *on a continuing basis, on a daily basis,* and *on a regular basis* are sometimes only wordier ways of saying *continually, daily,* and *regularly.* By the same token, *providing expert resources on a global basis* means providing them everywhere. Careful writers should avoid the unnecessary use of **basis**.

bask /baask/ (**basks, basking, basked**) *vi* **1.** to lie in or expose yourself to enjoyable warmth, especially from the sun **2.** to derive great satisfaction or pleasure from something [14C. Probably < Old Norse *bathask* 'bathe yourself' < Germanic]

Baskerville /báskər vil/ *n* a typeface characterized by serifs [Early 19C. After John BASKERVILLE]

Baskerville /báskər vil/, **John** (1706–75) British printer. The printer to Cambridge University, he designed several typefaces, including the one that now bears his name.

basket /báaskit/ *n* **1.** WOVEN CONTAINER a container made of woven strips of material or wire, often with a handle or handles **2.** BASKET CONTENTS the contents of or amount contained in a basket **3.** CONTAINER a container resembling a basket, e.g. the open gondola attached to a hot-air balloon **4.** GROUP OF RELATED ITEMS a group or collection of similar or related things or ideas **5.** BASKETBALL NET FOR SCORING GOALS in basketball, a mounted horizontal metal hoop with a hanging open net, through which a player must throw the ball in order to score **6.** BASKETBALL GOAL in basketball, a goal scored by throwing the ball through the basket. It is worth 1, 2, or 3 points depending on circumstances. [14C. Origin ?] —**basketful** *n*

basketball: two players attempt to block a pass

basketball /báaskit bawl/ *n* **1.** a game played by two teams of five players, who score points by throwing a ball through a basket mounted at the opponent's end of a rectangular court **2.** a ball of the type used in the game of basketball

basket case *n* **1.** an offensive term for somebody who is affected by severe nervous strain (*insult*) **2.** a nation or organization with serious financial problems (*informal*) ○ *transformed from an economic basket case into a prosperous state*

basket chair *n* a deep chair made of wickerwork or cane

basket hilt *n* a sword hilt with a guard made of interwoven strips —**basket-hilted** *adj*

basket of currencies *n* a group of currencies of which the average value is used as a basis for comparison with another currency

basketry /báaskitri/ *n* **1.** the art or craft of making baskets **2.** baskets collectively

basket weave *n* a textile weave like the chequered pattern of a woven basket

basketwork /báaskit wurk/ *n* HANDICRAFT same as **basketry**

basking shark *n* a large plankton-eating shark measuring up to 13 m/43 ft that often floats on the surface of the sea. Native to: temperate waters. Genus: *Cetorhinus*.

Basle ♦ Basel

basmati /baz máati/ *n* a long-grained aromatic rice [Mid-19C. < Hindi *bāsamatī* 'fragrant']

bas mitzvah *n* JUDAISM same as **bat mitzvah**

baso-, basi- *prefix* **1.** bottom, base ○ *basipetal* **2.** chemical base ○ *basophil* [< Latin *basis* (see BASIS)]

basophil /báyssə fil/ *n* a white blood cell with granules that are readily stained by basic dyes, occurring in some blood diseases

basophilia /báyssə fílli ə/ *n* **1.** the property of some microorganisms and white blood cells of being readily stained with basic dyes **2.** an increase in the blood of the type of cells that stain with basic dyes, occurring in some blood diseases

basophilic /báyssə fíllik/, **basophilous** /bə sóffələss/ *adj* describes cells or cell components that are readily stained by basic dyes

Basotho /bə soó too/ *npl* a Sotho people who live in Lesotho in southern Africa [Mid-19C. < Sesotho]

basque /bask, baask/ *n* **1.** a woman's tight-fitting corset that covers the area from the breasts to the top of the thighs **2.** a part of the bodice of a woman's jacket that extends below the waist [Mid-19C. Origin ?]

Basque /bask, baask/ *n* **1.** a member of a people of unknown origin living in the western Pyrenees, in northwestern Spain and southwestern France **2.** the language spoken by the Basques, having no known relationship with another language. Native speakers: 700,000. [Early 19C. Via French < Latin *Vasco*] — **Basque** *adj*

Basque Country /básk-/ autonomous region of Northern Spain, consisting of the provinces of Álava, Guipúzcoa, and Vizcaya. The regional capital is Vitoria. Population: 2,082,587 (2001). Area: 7,234 sq. km/2,793 sq. mi. Basque name **Euskadi**. Spanish name **País Vasco**

Basra /bázzrə/ city and port in southeastern Iraq, at the northern end of the Shatt al Arab waterway. Population: 406,296 (1987).

bas-relief /baá-/ *n* **1.** sculpture in which the design projects slightly from a flat background, but without any part being totally detached from the background **2.** an example or piece of bas-relief sculpture [Early 17C. < BASSO-RELIEVO, altered after French]

bass[1] /bayss/ *n* **1.** LOWEST SINGING VOICE a singing voice of the lowest range, or somebody with that voice **2.** LOWEST PITCHES the lower half of all the pitches produced by a voice or a musical instrument **3.** LOWEST MUSICAL PART the lowest part in instrumental or vocal part music **4.** LOWEST INSTRUMENT IN FAMILY the instrument with the lowest range in a family of musical instruments **5.** LOW FREQUENCY IN AUDIO REPRODUCTION the low-frequency sound output from an electric amplifier **6.** BASS CONTROL a knob on a piece of audio equipment that controls low-frequency sound output ■ *adj* **1.** DEEP IN TONE deep or grave in tone **2.** LOW IN PITCH low in pitch **3.** OF BASS relating to a bass [15C. Via French *bas* < medieval Latin *bassus*, influenced by Italian *basso* (see BASSO)]

SPELLCHECK See **base[1]**.

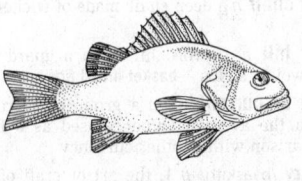

bass

bass[2] /bass/ (*plural same* or **basses**) *n* **1.** a spiny-finned fish found in rivers, lakes, and seas that is caught for food. Families: Centrarchidae or Percichthyidae or Serranidae. **2.** bass as food [15C. Alteration of Old English *bærs, bears* < Germanic]

bass[3] /bass/ *n* **1.** TEXTILES same as **bast** (sense 2) **2.** TREES same as **basswood** [Late 17C. Alteration of BAST]

bass-baritone /bayss-/ *n* a singing voice between baritone and bass, or somebody with that voice

bass clef /bayss-/ *n* a symbol on a musical staff indicating that a note on the fourth line from the bottom represents the F a fifth below middle C

bass drum /bayss-/ *n* a large drum that has a cylindrical body, two drumheads, and a low indefinite pitch

Bassein /ba sáyn/ city in southern Myanmar, about 137 km/85 mi. west of the capital, Yangon (Rangoon). Population: 144,096 (1983).

basset /bássit/ *n* BREED same as **basset hound** [Early 17C. < French < *bas* 'low', from its short legs]

Basseterre /bass táir/ capital of St Kitts and Nevis, in the Leeward Islands. It is situated on the southwestern coast of St Kitts island. Population: 12,220 (1994).

basset horn /bássit-/ *n* an alto clarinet in F, used in classical music [Mid-19C. < German, translating French *cor de basset* < Italian *corno di bassetto*, literally 'cello-horn']

basset hound /bássit/ *n* a dog with short legs, long ears, and a short-haired, white, black, and tan coat, belonging to a breed originally developed for hunting

bass guitar /bayss-/ *n* a four-string guitar, usually electric, that has the same pitch and tuning as a double bass

bassinet /bássi nét/ *n* a baby's bed or pram in the shape of a basket, often with a hood over one end and commonly made of wood or wickerwork [Mid-19C. < French, 'little basin']

bassist /báyssist/ *n* somebody who plays a bass guitar or a double bass

basso /bássō/ (*plural* **-sos** or **-si** /-see/) *n* a bass singer, especially of opera [Early 18C. Via Italian < medieval Latin *bassus* 'low']

basso continuo *n* MUSIC same as **continuo**

bassoon /bə soón/ *n* a low-pitched double-reed instrument of the oboe family. Its wooden body is a long U-shaped tube, attached to the mouthpiece by means of a thin metal pipe. [Early 18C. Via French < Italian *bassone* 'large bass' < *basso* (see BASSO)] — **bassoonist** *n*

basso profundo /-prō fúndō/ (*plural* **basso profundos**) *n* a bass singer with an exceptionally low range [Mid-19C. < Italian, 'deep bass']

basso-relievo /bássō ri leévō/, **basso-rilievo** /-rillee áy vō/ *n* SCULPTURE same as **bas-relief** (sense 1) [Mid-17C. < Italian *basso-rilievo* 'low relief']

Bass Rock /báss-/ steep-sided islet with a lighthouse in the Firth of Forth, Scotland

Bass Strait area of ocean situated between mainland Australia and Tasmania. It is approximately 225 km/140 mi. wide.

bass viol /bayss/ *n* MUSIC **1.** same as **viola da gamba 2.** *N Am* same as **double bass**

basswood /básswood/ *n* the soft light-coloured wood of a lime tree. Use: boxes, carving. [< BASS[3]]

bast /bast/ *n* **1.** BOT same as **phloem 2.** *UK, ANZ, Can* a strong woody fibrous material obtained chiefly from the phloem of plants such as flax, hemp, and jute. Use: ropes, mats, textiles. US term **bast fiber** [Old English *bæst*, origin ?]

bastard /baástərd/ *n* **1.** OFFENSIVE TERM an offensive term for somebody regarded as obnoxious and disagreeable (*slang insult*) **2.** OFFENSIVE TERM an offensive term for somebody born to unmarried parents (*archaic or offensive*) **3.** OFFENSIVE TERM an offensive term for something that is extremely difficult, trying, or unpleasant (*slang*) **4.** INFERIOR THING something that is inferior, debased, or of questionable or mixed origin (*sometimes considered offensive*) **5.** PERSON used to refer to somebody affectionately or humorously (*informal; sometimes considered offensive*) ■ *adj* **1.** NOT GENUINE not the real thing ○ *bastard quartz* **2.** MIXED of mixed origin or in a mixture of styles (*sometimes considered offensive*) **3.** UNUSUAL unusual or irregular in shape, size, or appearance (*sometimes considered offensive*) **4.** ZOOL, BOT SIMILAR AND USUALLY INFERIOR describes plants and animals that are similar but not identical to, and usually slightly inferior to, a particular kind or species ○ *bastard trout* ○ *bastard pine* [14C. Via Old French *bastart* < medieval Latin *bastardus*, probably < *bastum* 'pack saddle', the idea probably being of a child produced from a relationship with a traveller] — **bastardly** *adj*

bastardize /baástər dīz/ (**-izes, -izing, -ized**), **bastardise** (**-ises, -ising, -ised**) *vt* **1.** to lower the value or quality of something **2.** to prove or declare somebody to be illegitimate (*archaic*) — **bastardization** /baástər dī záysh'n/ *n*

bastardry /baástərdri/ *n Aus* behaviour considered to be mean-spirited, treacherous, or obnoxious (*informal*)

bastard title *n* PUBL same as **half title**

bastard wing *n* BIRDS same as **alula**

bastardy /baástərdi/ *n* the state of being a child with unmarried parents (*archaic; sometimes considered offensive*)

baste[1] /bayst/ (**bastes, basting, basted**) *vt* to moisten meat or fish at intervals during cooking with a liquid such as melted fat or cooking juices [15C. Origin ?]

baste[2] /bayst/ (**bastes, basting, basted**) *vt* to beat somebody severely (*dated informal*) [Mid-16C. Origin ?]

baste[3] /bayst/ (**bastes, basting, basted**) *vt N Am* HANDICRAFT same as **tack[1]** *v* (sense 6) [14C. Via Old French *bastir* < Germanic, 'join together with bast']

bast fiber *n US* same as **bast** (sense 2)

basti /bústi/, **bustee** *n S Asia* same as **slum** [Late 19C. < Hindi *bastī*]

Bastia /ba steé ə/ city and capital of Haute-Corse Department on the northeastern coast of the French island of Corsica. Population: 37,884 (1999).

Bastille /ba steél/ *n* a prison in Paris that was stormed and destroyed by a mob on 14 July 1789 at the beginning of the French Revolution

Bastille Day *n* a French national holiday marking the storming of the Bastille in 1789 at the start of the French Revolution. Date: 14 July.

bastinado /básti náydō/ *n* (*plural* **-does**) **1.** PUNISHMENT BY BEATING FEET a punishment or torture in which the soles of the victim's feet are beaten with a stick **2.** THRASHING a beating or a blow with a club **3.** CLUB a stick or club ■ *vt* (**-does, -doing, -doed**) BEAT WITH STICK to beat somebody with a stick, especially on the soles of the feet [Late 16C. < Spanish *bastonada* < *bastón* 'cudgel']

basting /báysting/ *n* loose or temporary stitches, often used to align seams in preparation for final sewing

bastion /básti ən/ *n* **1.** STRONG SUPPORTER somebody or something regarded as providing strong defence or support, especially for a belief or cause **2.** FORTIFICATION a fortified place **3.** PROJECTING PART a projecting part of a wall, rampart, or other fortification [Mid-16C. Via French < Italian *bastione* < *bastire* 'build']

bastnaesite /bástnə sīt/, **bastnasite** *n* a rare yellow to reddish-brown mineral containing lanthanum and cerium. Use: source of rare-earth elements. [Late 19C. After *Bastnäs* in Sweden]

BASW *abbr* British Association of Social Workers

bat[1] /bat/ *n* **1.** CLUB USED IN SPORTS in sports such as cricket, table tennis, and baseball, a club used to strike the ball, usually wooden but sometimes made of metal or plastic **2.** HEAVY STICK OR CLUB a heavy stick or wooden club **3.** BLOW FROM STICK a blow from a heavy stick or club **4.** PACE rate, pace, or speed (*informal*) **5.** AVIAT DEVICE FOR GUIDING AIRCRAFT either of a pair of hand-held devices that look like table-tennis bats and are used by somebody on the ground to guide taxiing or landing aircraft **6.** CRICKET CRICKET BATSMAN OR BATSWOMAN in cricket, a player who strikes the ball ■ *v* (**bats, batting, batted**) **1.** *vt* STRIKE WITH BAT to strike somebody or something with a bat **2.** *vi* SPORTS HAVE TURN AT BATTING in sports such as cricket and baseball, to take a turn at batting [Old English *batt*, origin ?] ◇ **off your own bat** on your own initiative and without instructions or help from anyone (*informal*)

bat[2] /bat/ *abbr* a file extension for a batch file. Full form **batch**

bat

bat[3] /bat/ *n* a small nocturnal flying mammal with leathery wings stretching from the forelimbs to the rear legs and tail. Bats eat fruit or insects, usually hang upside down when resting, and often use echolocation to detect prey and to navigate. Order: Chiroptera. [Late 16C. Alteration of *backe* < N Germanic] ◇ **have bats in the belfry** to be slightly but harmlessly eccentric (*informal*) ◇ **like a bat out of hell** extremely fast (*informal*)

REGIONAL NOTE Changes to farming methods have caused *bats* to become quite rare in Britain. Once, they were found in the eaves of thousands of barns and had different names in different regions. The commonest of these were *batmouse*, *batty-mouse*, *billy-bat*, *blind bat*, *ekkymowl*, *flitterbat*, *flittermouse*, *hairy bat*, *inkmouse*, *leather bat*, and *mouse bat*.

bat[4] /bat/ (**bats**, **batting**, **batted**) *vt* to wink or flutter something, especially the eyes or eyelids [Early 19C. Variant of BATE[1]]

bat. *abbr* **1.** COMPUT batch **2.** MIL battalion

Bataan /bə tán, -taán/ peninsula of Luzon Island in the Philippines, the scene of intense Japanese-American World War II combat. Area: 1,400 sq. km/530 sq. mi.

Batak /báttək/ *n* a group of Austronesian languages spoken in Sumatra, Indonesia. Native speakers: 3 million. [Early 19C. < Batak] —**Batak** *adj*

~~batallion~~ incorrect spelling of **battalion**

Batangas /bə táng gass/ city and port on Luzon Island in the Philippines. It is the capital of Batangas Province. Population: 227,099 (1999).

Batan Islands /bə taán-/ most Northerly island group in the Philippines. Area: 197 sq. km/76 sq. mi. Population: 15,000.

Batavia /bə táyvi ə/ former name for **Jakarta**

batboy /bát boy/ *n* in baseball, a boy employed to look after the team's equipment, especially the bats

batch[1] /bach/ *n* **1.** QUANTITY REGARDED AS GROUP a quantity of people or things treated or regarded as a group, especially when subdivided from a larger group **2.** AMOUNT FOR ONE OPERATION the amount of material prepared or needed for, or produced in, one operation **3.** COOK AMOUNT BAKED the amount of something baked at one time or produced at one baking **4.** COMPUT PROGRAMS PROCESSED TOGETHER a set of programs or jobs processed on a computer at one time ■ *vt* (**batches**, **batching**, **batched**) PROCESS ITEMS AS BATCH to process or assemble items as a batch or in batches [15C. < assumed Old English *bæcce* 'something baked' < *bacan* (see BAKE)]

batch[2] *vi* ANZ, US another spelling of **bach**[1]

bat chayil /baat khaʾayil/, **bat hayill** *n* JUDAISM same as **bat mitzvah** (sense 2) [Late 20C. < Hebrew, 'daughter of valour']

~~batchelor~~ incorrect spelling of **bachelor**

batch file *n* a computer file containing a series of commands to be processed by a computer as if they were entered from the keyboard consecutively. Most personal computers execute a batch file at the start of each operating session to prepare the system for use.

batch-mate *n* S Asia a classmate, or a contemporary at an educational institution

batch processing *n* a mode of computer operation in which programs are executed without the user

being able to influence processing while it is in progress

bate[1] /bayt/ (**bates**, **bating**, **bated**), **bait** (**baits**, **baiting**, **baited**) *vi* to beat the wings wildly or impatiently in an attempt to fly off a perch or a falconer's fist when still attached by a leash (*refers to falcons or other hunting birds*) [13C. < Old French *batre* (see BATTER[1])]

bate[2] /bayt/ *n* a fit of anger (*dated informal*) [Mid-19C. < variant of BAIT[1] (verb)]

bat-eared fox *n* a yellowish-grey fox with large ears. Native to: eastern and southern Africa. Latin name: *Otocyon megalotis*.

bated /báytid/ ◇ **with bated breath** in anxious or excited anticipation

Batei Din *n* JUDAISM plural of **Beth Din**

bateleur /bátta lur/, **bateleur eagle** *n* a black eagle that has a red beak, red legs, almost no tail and often eats carrion. Native to: Africa. Latin name: *Terathopius ecaudatus*. [Mid-19C. < French, 'juggler, rogue']

Bates /bayts/, **Daisy May** (1863–1951) Irish-born Australian journalist and anthropologist. She was the author of *The Passing of the Aborigine* (1938), an account of the many years she spent among the Aboriginals of central Australia. Born O'Dwyer, Daisy May

Bates, H. E. (1905–74) British writer. He wrote plays, short stories, and essays, and is most famous for his novels, including *The Darling Buds of May* (1958). Full name **Bates, Herbert Ernest**

Bates, H. W. (1825–92) British naturalist. He explored Amazonia (1848–59), returning with 14,700 specimens, including 8,000 unknown insect species. Full name **Bates, Henry Walter**

Batesian mimicry /báytsi ən-/ *n* mimicry in which a harmless species is protected from predators by its resemblance to a species that is harmful or unpalatable to them [Late 19C. After H. W. BATES]

batfish /bátfish/ (*plural* same or **-fishes**) *n* an anglerfish that has a flattened head and body and waddles on the sea bottom using pectoral and pelvic fins. Family: Ogcocephalidae.

bath /baath/ *n* (*plural* **baths** /baathz/) **1.** UK LARGE CONTAINER FOR WASHING BODY IN a large container, usually oblong in shape and made of plastic or enamelled metal, that you sit in to wash your body. ANZ, N Am term **bathtub 2.** IMMERSION OF BODY the act of immersing all or part of the body in a bath in order to wash it **3.** BODY TREATMENT the act of immersing all or part of the body in mud or other substance, usually for therapeutic reasons **4.** WATER IN BATH water used for washing in a bath **5.** CHEM LIQUID a liquid, or a liquid and its container, in which something is immersed ■ **baths** *npl* **1.** SWIMMING POOL a swimming pool for public use **2.** BUILDINGS same as **bathhouse 3.** WATER SPA a spa where patrons avail themselves of the water from natural mineral springs (*often in placenames*) ■ *vti* (**baths**, **bathing**, **bathed**) UK, ANZ, Can WASH IN BATH to wash yourself or somebody else in a bath. N Am term **bathe** [Old English *bæp* < Germanic] ◇ **take a bath** to suffer a severe financial setback (*slang*)

USAGE bath or **bathe**? In many varieties of English, both words can be used as noun or verb, with ***bath*** referring to washing and ***bathe*** to swimming. However in US English **bath** is normally used only as a noun (*The bath was deep.*) and **bathe** is used only to mean 'to swim' (*She bathed daily.*). In most varieties of English, **bathe** is also used of immersing things in water to clean or moisten them: *The nurse bathed the wound.*

Bath /baath/ city on the River Avon in Somerset, England. It is the site of the only natural hot springs in England and has been a spa since Roman times. Population: 84,100 (1994).

bat hayill *n* JUDAISM another spelling of **bat chayil**

Bath bun *n* a sweet sticky spiced bun containing dried fruit

bath chair *n* an old-fashioned type of wheelchair, often with a hood [After BATH]

bath cube *n* a cube of soluble material used to perfume and soften bathwater

bathe /bayth/ *v* (**bathes**, **bathing**, **bathed**) **1.** *vi* SWIM OR PADDLE IN OPEN WATER to swim or paddle for pleasure, especially in an area of open water such as the sea

or a river **2.** *vt* CLEANSE WOUND to apply water or another liquid to a wound or part of the body in order to cleanse, heal, or soothe it **3.** *vt* DIP SOMETHING IN LIQUID to immerse something in liquid **4.** *vt* COVER SOMETHING to cover or surround something with light, colour, or a substance ○ *bathed in a golden glow* **5.** *vt* FLOW ALONG EDGE OF SOMETHING to flow along the edge of something **6.** *vti* N Am same as **bath** ■ *n* ACT OF SWIMMING OR BATHING an act of swimming or bathing, especially in an area of open water (*dated*) [Old English *bapian* < Germanic]

USAGE See **bath**.

bather /báythər/ *n* somebody who is swimming

bathers /báythərz/ *npl* Aus a swimming costume (*informal*)

bathetic /bə théttik/ *adj* **1.** showing or characterized by bathos **2.** trite, commonplace, or absurdly sentimental [Late 18C. < BATHOS, after *pathos*, *pathetic*] — **bathetically** *adv*

bathhouse /báath howss/ (*plural* **-houses** /-howziz/) *n* a building equipped with baths, especially for public use

bathing /báything/ *n* the activity of swimming in the sea, a river, or a lake

bathing costume *n* SWIMMING, CLOTHING same as **swimsuit** (*dated*)

bathing machine *n* in the 18th and 19th centuries, a small hut on wheels that bathers changed in. It was pulled to the sea's edge, allowing them to slip into the water modestly.

bathing suit /báything-/ *n* N Am CLOTHING same as **swimsuit**

bathing waters *npl* bodies of seawater or fresh water that are used for public bathing and to which particular water quality standards apply under EU and UK law

bathmat /báath mat/ *n* **1.** a mat that is placed beside a bath or shower for somebody to step out onto **2.** a mat, often made of rubber, that is placed in a bath or shower to prevent somebody from slipping

bath mitzvah *n* JUDAISM another spelling of **bat mitzvah**

batho- *prefix* deep, depth ○ *bathometer* [< Greek *bathos* 'depth']

bathochromic /báthə krṓmik/ *adj* describes a shift towards the red end in a chemical compound's absorption spectrum

batholith /báthəlith/, **batholite** /-līt/ *n* a large mass of igneous rock, composed of granite or gabbro, formed deep in the Earth's crust and intruded in a molten state —**batholithic** /báthə líthik/ *adj*

Bath Oliver *n* a thin dry unsweetened biscuit, usually eaten with cheese [After its creator, Dr William *Oliver* (1695–1764) of BATH]

bathometer /bə thómmitər/ *n* an instrument for measuring the depth of a body of water —**bathometric** /báthə méttrik/ *adj* —**bathometry** *n*

bathophilous /bə thóffiləss/ *adj* describes organisms that are adapted to living in very deep water

bathos /báy thoss/ *n* **1.** in writing or speech, a sudden descent in style or manner from the elevated to the commonplace, producing a ludicrous effect **2.** insincere and excessively sentimental pathos [Early 18C. < Greek, 'depth' < *bathus* 'deep']

bathrobe /báath rōb/ *n* **1.** a loose-fitting garment with a belt, usually made of towelling, worn before or after having a bath or shower **2.** US same as **dressing gown**

bathroom /báath room, -ro̅om/ *n* **1.** a room containing a bath or shower and, usually, a washbasin and a toilet **2.** a room with a toilet

bathroom scales *npl* a step-on device for people to weigh themselves on at home, usually kept in a bathroom

bath salts *npl* soluble mineral salts used to perfume and soften bathwater

Bathsheba /bath sheébə, báthshibə/ *n* in the Bible, the wife of Uriah and later of David, by whom she became the mother of Solomon (II Samuel 11–12)

Bath stone *n* a white limestone used for building, quarried near Bath

bathtub /báath tub/ *n* ANZ, N Am a large container,

often oblong in shape and usually made of enamelled metal or plastic, in which somebody sits to bathe. UK term **bath**

Bathurst /báth urst/ **1.** city and summer holiday resort in northeastern New Brunswick, Canada. Population: 16,427 (1996). **2.** city in central New South Wales, Australia. Founded in 1815, it is Australia's oldest inland town and was the site of the first Australian gold rush. Population: 30,930 (2002 estimate). **3.** former name for **Banjul**

Bathurst Island island in the Timor Sea off the northern coast of the Northern Territory, Australia. Population: 1,000. Area: 2,070 sq. km/799 sq. mi.

bathwater /baáth wawtər/ n the water used for a bath

bathy- prefix deep, depth ○ bathysphere [< Greek bathus 'deep']

bathyal /báthi əl/ adj relating to or living in ocean depths between 200 and 2,000 m/650 and 6,550 ft

bathymetry /bə thímmətri/ n **1.** the measurement of the depth of lakes, oceans, and seas **2.** the data obtained by the use of bathymetry —**bathymetric** /báthi méttrik/ adj —**bathymetrically** adv

bathypelagic /báthipə lájjik/ adj relating to or living in the depths of the ocean, especially between 600 and 3,600 m/2,000 and 12,000 ft

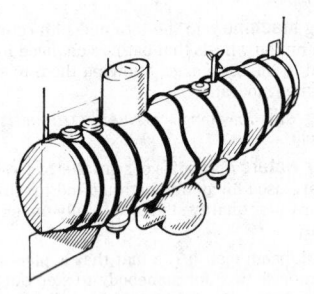

bathyscaphe

bathyscaphe /báthi skayf/, **bathyscaph** n a deep-sea research vessel that has a large flotation hull and an observation cabin attached to its underside, and can dive to depths over 10,000 m/6.2 mi [Mid-20C. < BATHY- + Greek skaphos 'ship']

bathysphere /báthi sfeer/ n a strong steel diving sphere that can be lowered by cable to depths of 900 m/3,000 ft

batik /báttik, bə teék/, **battik** /báttik/ n **1.** FABRIC PRINTING TECHNIQUE a method of hand-printing a fabric by covering with removable wax the parts that will not be dyed **2.** HAND-DYED FABRIC fabric that has been hand-dyed by the batik method **3.** DESIGN IN BATIK a design produced by batik [Late 19C. < Javanese, 'painted']

Batista y Zaldívar /ba teéstə ee zal deé vaar/, **Fulgencio** (1901–73) Cuban soldier and head of state. His presidency of Cuba (1940–44, 1952–59) was ended by Fidel Castro's revolution (1959).

batiste /ba teést/ n a fine soft plain-woven cotton or linen fabric. Use: clothing. [Early 19C. < French]

Batley /báttli/ town in West Yorkshire, northern England. Population: 48,030 (1991).

Batlle y Ordóñez /bátyay ee awr thón yess/, **José** (1856–1929) Uruguayan president (1903–07, 1911–15). He helped to modernize Uruguay's society, economy, and government.

batman /bátmən/ (plural -men /-mən/) n a British military officer's personal servant [Mid-18C. Via Old French < medieval Latin bastum 'pack saddle']

Batman /bát man/, **John** (1801–39) Australian pioneer. He was the first European to explore and recognize the potential of the site of present-day Melbourne.

bat mitzvah /baat mítsvə/, **bath mitzvah**, **bas mitzvah** /baass-/ n **1.** the ritual that marks the 13th birthday of a Jewish girl, after which she takes full responsibility for her moral and spiritual conduct **2.** a Jewish girl who has reached the age of 13, the age of religious responsibility [Mid-20C < Hebrew bat miṣwāh 'daughter of the commandment']

batmouse /bát mowss/ (plural **-mice** /bát/ míss/) n regional ZOOL same as **bat**[3]

REGIONAL NOTE See bat[3].

BATNEEC /bát neek/ n a principle applied to the control of emissions into the air, land, and water from polluting processes, minimizing pollution without requiring technology or methods that are not yet available or unreasonably expensive. Full form **best available technology not entailing excessive cost**

baton /bátton, bátt'n/ n **1.** MUSIC STICK FOR CONDUCTING MUSIC a short thin stick used by a conductor to direct musical performers **2.** POLICE HEAVY STICK USED BY POLICE a short thick stick used as a weapon, especially by police ○ a side-handled baton **3.** SPORTS STICK PASSED BY RELAY TEAM a short stick or hollow cylinder passed by each runner in a relay team to the next runner **4.** SYMBOL OF OFFICE a staff carried by an official such as a field marshal as a symbol of rank or office **5.** DRUM MAJOR'S STICK a long stick with a knob at one or each end, carried and twirled by a drum major or majorette **6.** HERALDRY DIAGONAL LINE ON COAT OF ARMS a shortened narrow diagonal line on a coat of arms, especially one signifying bastardy [Early 16C. Via French < late Latin bastum 'stick']

baton charge n a charge made by people armed with batons, especially police officers

Baton Rouge /bátt'n roózh/ capital of Louisiana, situated on the Mississippi River in the southeastern part of the state. Population: 225,702 (2002 estimate).

baton round n a plastic or rubber bullet used in riot control

batrachian /bə tráyki ən/ n a tailless amphibian, e.g. a frog or toad [Mid-19C. < modern Latin Batrachia < Greek batrakhos 'frog'] —**batrachian** adj

bats /bats/ adj harmlessly eccentric (informal) [Early 20C. < have bats in the belfry]

batsman /bátsmən/ (plural **-men** /-mən/) n **1.** PLAYER WHO BATS OR IS BATTING a cricket or baseball player who bats or is batting **2.** PLAYER WHO SPECIALIZES IN BATTING a cricket player who specializes in batting, rather than bowling or fielding **3.** GROUND OFFICIAL WHO GUIDES AIRCRAFT a ground official who uses a pair of bats to guide landing and taxiing aircraft

batswoman /báts woomən/ (plural **-women** /-wimin/) n a woman cricketer who bats or is batting

batt /bat/ n TEXTILES same as **batting** (sense 2) [Late 19C. Shortening]

battalion /bə tályən/ n **1.** LARGE BODY OF SOLDIERS a large body of soldiers organized to act together **2.** MILITARY UNIT a military unit typically consisting of a headquarters and three or more companies, batteries, or other subunits of similar size **3.** LARGE NUMBER a large group or number (often used in the plural) [Late 16C. Via French < Italian bataglione 'great battle' < late Latin bat(t)uere 'to beat']

~~battallion~~ incorrect spelling of **battalion**

battels /bátt'lz/ npl at Oxford University, the bill or account of a member of a college for accommodation, food, and other expenses [Late 16C. Origin ?]

battement /bát maaN/ n a ballet movement in which one leg is extended, either once or repeatedly, to the front, side, or back, and then beaten against the supporting foot [Mid-19C. < French, 'beating']

batten /bátt'n/ n **1.** BUILDING SUPPORT a thin strip of wood used in building, e.g. to seal or reinforce a joint or to support laths, slates, or tiles **2.** BUILDINGS NARROW PIECE OF WOOD a long narrow piece of wood used for flooring **3.** SAILING STRIP FOR KEEPING SAILS IN SHAPE a thin flexible strip of wood or plastic inserted in pockets in a sail to keep it in shape or support the edge **4.** NAUT SLAT FOR FASTENING DOWN TARPAULIN a narrow metal or wooden slat used to fasten down the edges of a tarpaulin covering a boat's raised hatch in poor weather **5.** THEATRE LIGHTS IN THEATRE a row of lights in a theatre, or the strip or bar that holds it ■ vt (**-tens, -tening, -tened**) PROVIDE WITH BATTENS to provide, strengthen, or secure something with battens [Late 16C. < Old Norse batna 'improve, get better' < Germanic]

Batten /bátt'n/, **Jean** (1909–82) New Zealand aviator. She broke Amy Johnson's record for a solo flight from England to Australia and became the first woman to complete the return trip (1934–35). She wrote Alone in the Sky (1939). Full name **Batten, Jean Gardner**

Battenberg /bátt'n burg/ n an oblong cake coated with marzipan and made of squares of yellow and pink sponge, so that a slice of it has two yellow and two pink squares [Early 20C. After Prince Louis of Battenberg (1820–93)]

batter[1] /báttər/ vt (**-ters, -tering, -tered**) **1.** HIT REPEATEDLY to hit or beat something repeatedly using heavy blows in order to break, bruise, or damage it **2.** SUBJECT TO ATTACK to subject somebody to persistent attack or violence **3.** DAMAGE BY HEAVY BLOWS OR WEAR to damage or injure something by hard blows or heavy wear (often passive) ■ n PRINTING **1.** DAMAGED TYPE a damaged or worn printing type or plate **2.** FAULTY IMPRESSION a defective impression produced by a faulty printing plate [14C. Via Old French batre < late Latin bat(t)uere 'to beat'] —**battered** adj —**batterer** n

batter[2] /báttər/ n a liquid mixture of flour, milk, and eggs used in making cakes, pancakes, and puddings, and for coating foods before frying ■ vt (**-ters, -tering, -tered**) to cover food with batter before frying [14C. < Old French bateüre 'act of beating' < batre (see BATTER[1]); from the idea of beating the mixture]

batter[3] /báttər/ vt (**-ters, -tering, -tered**) to build a wall or similar structure in a way that forms an upwardly receding slope ■ n a receding upward slope of the outer face of a wall, hedge, or similar structure [Mid-16C. Origin ?]

batter[4] /báttər/ n especially in baseball, a player who bats [Late 18C. < BAT[1]]

batterie /báttəri, ba treé/ n a ballet movement in which the dancer beats the feet or calves together during a leap [Early 18C. < French, 'battery']

batterie de cuisine /ba treé də kwi zeén/ (plural **batteries de cuisine** /pronunc. same/) n a set of cooking utensils, pots, and pans [Late 18C. < French, 'set (of implements) for cooking']

battering ram n **1.** a large heavy beam used in ancient times to break down the walls and doors of a fortification under siege **2.** a heavy metal bar used by police officers and firefighters to break down doors

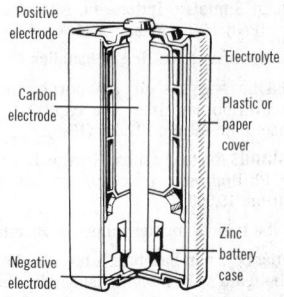

battery: cutaway view of a simple battery

battery /báttəri/ (plural **-ies**) n **1.** POWER SOURCE a number of connected electric cells that produce a direct current through the conversion of chemical energy into electrical energy **2.** GROUPING OF SIMILAR THINGS an array or grouping of similar things intended to be used or considered together **3.** ACT OF BATTERING the act of battering, beating, or pounding something **4.** LAW UNLAWFUL USE OF FORCE ON SOMEBODY the unlawful use of any physical force on another person, including beating or offensive touching without the person's consent **5.** MIL ARTILLERY GROUPING a group of artillery pieces such as guns or missile launchers that function as a single tactical unit **6.** MIL ARMY ARTILLERY UNIT an army artillery unit corresponding to a company in an infantry regiment **7.** MIL GUN EMPLACEMENT a prepared position for artillery **8.** AGRIC SYSTEM OF CAGES FOR REARING ANIMALS a series of cages used for the intensive rearing of livestock, especially poultry **9.** MUSIC PERCUSSION SECTION the percussion section of an orchestra [Mid-16C. < Old French baterie < batre (see BATTER[1])] ◇ recharge your batteries to restore your level of energy and strength (informal)

battery charger n a device for restoring power to electrical batteries

battery pack n a rechargeable high-capacity battery used for powering portable electrical equipment such as laptop computers and video cameras

battik *n* HANDICRAFT, TEXTILES another spelling of **batik**

batting /bátting/ *n* **1.** especially in cricket or baseball, the action or ability of a player or team that hits with a bat **2.** bulky material made from fabric or other fibres. Use: padding, stuffing. [Early 17C. < BAT[1]; in sense 2 from the beating out of impurities from cotton]

batting average *n* **1.** in cricket, a measure of a batsman's performance, calculated by dividing the total number of runs scored in a given period by the number of innings or matches played **2.** *N Am* in baseball, a measure of a batter's performance, calculated by dividing the total of base hits gained in a given period by the number of times at bat

batting crease *n* CRICKET same as **popping crease**

battle /bátt'l/ *n* **1.** ARMED FIGHT a large-scale fight between armed forces involving combat between armies, warships, or aircraft **2.** STRUGGLE a drawn-out conflict between adversaries, or against powerful forces ○ *the battle against malaria* ■ *v* (**-tles, -tling, -tled**) **1.** *vti* FIGHT to fight in a battle **2.** *vi* STRIVE to strive or contend in order to overcome or achieve something ○ *continues to battle to save her career* **3.** *vt* STRUGGLE AGAINST SOMEBODY OR SOMETHING to fight or contend with somebody or something, in or as if in a battle ○ *determined to battle terrorism* [13C. Via French *bataille* < late Latin *battualia* 'military or gladiatorial exercises' < *bat(t)uere* 'to beat'] ◇ **be half the battle** to be an important first part of a difficult task ○ *Shipping the books on time is only half the battle; we have to sell them too.* ◇ **do battle (with somebody** *or* **something)** to fight or struggle against somebody or something ◇ **fight a losing battle** to try hard with no prospect of success

USAGE The use of ***battle*** with a direct object, as in *The people of South Carolina have been battling a hurricane*, instead of with a preposition, as in *battle against* or *battle with something*, is a feature of North American usage that has begun to enter other varieties of English also. This is partly a revival of an older use that died out in the 19th century.

ORIGIN The Latin word *bat(t)uere* 'to beat', from which ***battle*** is derived, is also the source of English *abate, battalion, battery, batter*[1], *combat*, and *rebate*[1].

SYNONYMS See ***fight***.

Battle /bátt'l/ town in East Sussex, southeastern England, the site of the Battle of Hastings in 1066. Population: 5,235 (1991).

Battle, Kathleen (*b.* 1948) US soprano. An internationally renowned concert and opera singer, she sang with the Metropolitan Opera Company in New York City (1977–94).

battleaxe /bátt'l aks/ *n* **1.** a large heavy broad-headed axe used as a weapon **2.** an offensive term for a woman who is considered domineering and fearsome (*insult*)

battle-axe block *n ANZ* a block of land set back from the street behind other blocks and reached via a lane or driveway

battle cruiser *n* a heavily armed warship with lighter armour, fewer guns, greater manoeuvrability, and a faster speed than a battleship

battle cry *n* **1.** a rallying or encouraging shout that soldiers make when going into battle **2.** a slogan used by supporters of a cause to rally fellow supporters

battledore /bátt'l dawr/ *n* **1.** EARLY RACKET GAME an early racket game played by two people with flat wooden rackets and a shuttlecock **2.** RACKET USED IN BATTLEDORE a light racket, smaller than a tennis racket, used for hitting the shuttlecock in battledore **3.** WOODEN BAT a wooden bat formerly used to beat clothes when washing them [15C. Probably < Provençal *batedor* 'beater' < *battre* 'to beat' < late Latin *bat(t)uere*]

battledress /bátt'l dress/ *n* the ordinary uniform worn by a soldier

battle fatigue *n UK, ANZ, Can* a psychological disorder resulting from the stress of being involved in a battle and characterized by acute anxiety, depression, and loss of motivation. US term **combat fatigue**

battlefield /bátt'l feeld/ *n* **1.** the place where a battle is fought **2.** an area of conflict or contention

battlefield detainee *n US* a captured and imprisoned unlawful combatant in a war or other conflict

battlefront /bátt'l frunt/ *n* an area or sector in which combat between armed forces takes place

battleground /bátt'l grownd/ *n* MIL same as **battlefield** (sense 1)

battle line *n* a position along which a battle takes place (*usually plural*) ◇ **draw (up) the battle lines** to prepare for a fight, quarrel, or contest

battlement /bátt'l mənt/ *n* a defensive or decorative parapet with indentations [14C. < French *bateiller* 'fortify'] —**battlemented** *adj*

battlements /bátt'lmənts/ *npl* a series of indentations forming a defensive or decorative parapet

Battle of Britain *n* an aerial battle fought in World War II in 1940 between the German Luftwaffe, which carried out extensive bombing in Britain, and the Royal Air Force, which offered successful resistance

Battle of the Atlantic *n* the struggle during World War II for control of the routes used to bring supplies to Britain across the Atlantic

battle plan *n* **1.** a strategy for fighting a battle **2.** a strategy for any operation or contest

battler /bátt'lər/ *n* **1.** DETERMINED FIGHTER somebody who is courageous or indomitable in a battle or conflict **2.** *Aus* SOMEBODY WHO TRIES HARD somebody who puts a great deal of effort into achieving something **3.** *ANZ* LOW EARNER somebody who works hard for a low wage

battle royal (*plural* **battles royal** or **battle royals**) *n* **1.** a battle involving many combatants, especially a fight to the finish **2.** a passionate conflict, especially one that unfolds in public

battleship /bátt'l ship/ *n* the largest type of warship, which carries the heaviest armour

battleship grey *adj* of a medium grey colour tinged with blue, like the colour in which battleships are commonly painted —**battleship grey** *n*

battle stations *US npl* MIL same as **action stations** ■ *interj* **1.** MIL same as **action stations** *interj* (sense 1) **2.** same as **action stations** *interj* (sense 2) (*informal*)

battle-twig *n regional* INSECTS same as **earwig** [Because its pincers look like weapons]

REGIONAL NOTE See ***earwig***.

battue /ba tóo/ *n* **1.** DRIVING OF GAME IN HUNT the beating of woodland or cover in order to drive game towards hunters **2.** HUNT USING BATTUE a hunt in which battue is used **3.** SLAUGHTER a wholesale massacre or indiscriminate slaughter [Early 19C. < French, past participle of *battre* (see BATTER[1])]

batty[1] /bátti/ (**-tier, -tiest**) *adj* slightly eccentric (*informal*) [Early 20C. < *have bats in the belfry*] —**battiness** *n*

batty[2] /bátti/ (*plural same*) *n Carib* the buttocks (*slang; also used in Black English*) [Mid-20C. Alteration of BOTTY]

batty-bwai /bátti bwī/ (*plural* **batty-bwais**), **batty-boy, batty-man** (*plural* **batty-men**) *n* an offensive term for a gay man (*slang; used in Black English*) [< *batty*, form of *botty*, child's word for BOTTOM + *bwai*, form of BOY]

batty-mouse /bátti mowss/ (*plural* **batty-mice**) *n regional* ZOOL same as **bat**[3] [< BAT[3]]

REGIONAL NOTE See ***bat***[3].

batty-rider *n* a pair of very brief shorts for women (*slang; used in Black English*)

Batumi /baa tóomi/, **Batum** /-tóom/ city and port in southwestern Georgia on the Black Sea, and the capital of Ajaria autonomous region. Population: 137,000 (1990).

batwing sleeve /bátwing-/ *n* a sleeve that is wide at the armhole and tight at the wrist

bauble /báwb'l/ *n* **1.** TRINKET something that is small and decorative but of little real value **2.** CHRISTMAS DECORATION a shiny spherical decoration, often brightly coloured, hung on a Christmas tree **3.** MOCK SCEPTRE a mock sceptre of office carried by a court jester (*archaic*) [14C. < Old French, 'plaything']

baud /bawd/ *n* a unit of data transmission speed, equal to one unit element per second [Mid-20C. After J. M. E. *Baudot* (1845–1903), French engineer]

Baudelaire /bōd lair/, **Charles** (1821–67) French critic and poet. His symbolist verse, notably *Les fleurs du mal* (1857), explored his sense of melancholy, isolation, and the attractions of evil and vice. Full name **Baudelaire, Charles Pierre**

> 'The poet is like the prince of the clouds, / Who rides out the tempest and laughs at the archer. / But when he is exiled on the ground, amidst the clamour, / His giant's wings prevent him from walking.'
> [Charles Baudelaire, 'L'Albatross (The Albatross)', *Les Fleurs du mal (The Flowers of Evil)*; 1857]

Baudouin I /bō dwaN/ (1930–93) king of the Belgians. He spent five years in voluntary exile in Switzerland before ascending the throne on the abdication of his father, Leopold III, in 1951. Full name **Baudouin Albert Charles Leopold Axel Marie Gustave**

> 'It takes twenty years or more of peace to make a man, it takes only twenty seconds of war to destroy him.'
> [Baudouin I, *Address to US Congress*; 12 May 1959]

Bauhaus /bów howss/ *n* an influential German school of architecture and design, founded in 1919 by Walter Gropius. It attempted to synthesize technology, craftsmanship, design, and art, and was noted for a style of functional architecture. [Early 20C. < German < *Bau* 'building' + *Haus* 'house']

baulk /bawk, bawlk/, **balk** *v* (**baulks, baulking, baulked; balks, balking, balked**) **1.** *vi* BE RELUCTANT OR TURN AWAY to hesitate over something or be unwilling to do something, usually because of moral scruples or a natural aversion ○ *I baulked at getting down on my hands and knees to wipe the floor.* ○ *They baulked at the asking price.* **2.** *vti* REFUSE TO TACKLE SOMETHING to refuse to tackle something that presents a difficulty **3.** *vi* STOP SHORT to stop suddenly and refuse to go on, especially when faced with an obstacle ○ *The horse baulked and refused the jump.* **4.** *vt* FOIL SOMEBODY to prevent somebody from carrying out a plan or intention (*often passive*) ○ *acted like a lion baulked of its prey* **5.** *vi* BASEBALL MAKE ILLEGAL PITCHING MOTION in baseball, to make an illegal motion by pretending to pitch but not actually throwing the ball ■ *n* **1.** OBSTACLE something that hinders or frustrates ○ *a baulk to further progress in the peace negotiations* **2.** CONSTR LARGE PIECE OF WOOD a large squared wooden beam **3.** ARCHIT WOODEN BEAM IN HOUSE ROOF a wooden tie beam in the roof of a house **4.** AGRIC UNPLOUGHED RIDGE a ridge of land left unploughed to serve as a boundary or to counter erosion **5.** BASEBALL ILLEGAL PITCHING MOVE in baseball, an illegal motion in which the pitcher pretends to throw the ball towards the plate or to a base but does not release it **6.** *N Am* CUE GAMES AREA BEHIND BAULK LINE the area between the baulk line and the bottom cushion on a billiard table, or in baulk-line billiards between any baulk line and the cushion **7.** CUE GAMES BILLIARDS SHOT a shot from behind the baulk line on a billiards table [< Old English *balca* 'ridge' and Old Norse *bálkr* 'beam, bar' < Indo-European, 'beam'] —**baulker** *n*

baulk line *n* **1.** a straight line parallel to the end of a billiard table, from behind which opening shots with the cue ball are made **2.** one of four lines parallel to the edges of a billiard table that divide it into the central area and eight smaller compartments that are used in a particular variety of billiards —**baulk-line** *adj*

baulk-line billiards *n* the variety of billiards in which baulk lines are used to divide up the table

baulky /báwki, báwlki/ *adj* another spelling of **balky**

Baumé scale /bō máy-, bō may-/ *n* a scale for calibrating hydrometers that are used to ascertain the relative density of liquids [Mid-19C. After Antoine *Baumé* (1728–1804), French chemist]

Baur /bów ər/, **Ferdinand Christian** (1792–1860) German theologian. He studied early Christianity using stringent historical research methods.

Bausch /bowsh/, **Pina** (*b.* 1940) German dancer and choreographer. One of the foremost modern dance choreographers, she created expressionist works, and founded the Wuppertal Dance Theatre in Wuppertal, Germany (1973). Full name **Bausch, Philippine**

bauxite /báwk sīt/ *n* a rock containing aluminium hydroxides that is the principal ore of aluminium [Mid-19C. After the S French village of Les *Baux*]

Bavaria /bə váiri ə/ the largest state of Germany. It is situated in the southeast and has borders with

Baden-Württemberg, Hesse, Thüringen and Saxony states, and the Czech Republic and Austria. Capital: Munich. Population: 12,086,548 (1998). Area: 70,548 sq. km/27,239 sq. mi. —**Bavarian** *n, adj*

bavarois /bávvər wáa/ *n* a dessert of rich flavoured set custard, eaten cold [Mid-19C. < French, 'Bavarian']

bawbee /baw beé, báw beé/ *Scotland n* a former Scottish silver coin worth three Scottish pennies ∎ **bawbees** *npl* money, especially scarce or hard-earned money (*informal*) [Mid-16C. < *Sillebawby*, an estate whose owner, Alexander Orok, was Scottish mintmaster]

bawd /bawd/ *n* a woman who runs a brothel (*archaic*) [14C. Probably < Old French *baude* 'bold, lively' < Germanic]

bawdry /báwdri/ *n* vulgar and lewd language (*literary or archaic*)

bawdy /báwdi/ (**-ier, -iest**) *adj* ribald in a frank, humorous, and often crude way —**bawdily** *adv* — **bawdiness** *n*

bawdyhouse /báwdi howss/ (*plural* **-houses** /-howziz/) *n* same as **brothel** (*archaic*)

bawl /bawl/ *vti* (**bawls, bawling, bawled**) **1.** SHOUT to shout something in a loud and usually aggressive voice **2.** CRY NOISILY to cry very loudly and energetically (*informal*) ∎ *n* LOUD SHOUT a loud cry or shout [15C. Origin ?] —**bawler** *n*

bawl out *vt* to tell somebody off loudly and angrily (*informal*)

bawneen *n Ireland* CLOTHING same as **báinín**

Baxter /bákstər/, **James K.** (1926–72) New Zealand poet. Author of several verse collections, including *Autumn Testament* (1972), he founded a religious community on the Wanganui River, New Zealand (1969). Full name **Baxter, James Keir**

bay[1] /bay/ *n* **1.** an area of sea enclosed by a wide inward-curving stretch of coastline **2.** a lowland area with curving hills partly surrounding it [14C. Via French *baie* < Spanish *bahia*]

bay[2] /bay/ *n* **1.** SPECIAL AREA OR COMPARTMENT an area that is divided off and used for a particular purpose, e.g. in a building, bus station, or aircraft **2.** SPACE BETWEEN TWO PILLARS a section of a wall or building between two vertical structures such as pillars or buttresses **3.** RECESS a recess or alcove in a wall **4.** same as **bay window** [14C. < French *baie* 'opening' < *bayer* 'gape, stand open' < assumed Vulgar Latin *batare* 'yawn, gape']

bay[3] /bay/ *n* **1.** a small evergreen tree of the laurel family with stiff dark green aromatic leaves. Use: flavouring in cooking. Native to: Mediterranean. Latin name: *Laurus nobilis*. **2.** PLANTS same as **laurel** (sense 2) ∎ **bays** *npl* a wreath woven out of laurel leaves, presented to poets and victors in classical antiquity, or the honour conferred by this (*literary*) [14C. Via Old French *baie* < Latin *baca* 'berry']

bay[4] /bay/ *n* **1.** an animal with a reddish-brown coat, especially a horse **2.** a reddish-brown colour [14C. Via Old French *bai* < Latin *badius* 'chestnut-coloured'] —**bay** *adj*

bay[5] /bay/ *v* (**bays, baying, bayed**) **1.** *vi* HOWL to make the howling sound of a hunting dog on the trail of an animal **2.** *vi* MAKE LOUD OUTCRY FOR SOMETHING to call noisily and aggressively for something bad to happen to somebody ○ *an outraged public baying for blood* **3.** *vt* CORNER HUNTED ANIMAL to corner or exhaust a hunted animal so that it must turn and face its hunters ○ *hounds baying a fox* ∎ *n* POSITION OF NO ESCAPE the position in which a hunted animal or a person being pursued has to face the hunters or pursuers [13C. Via Old French *(a)baier* < assumed Vulgar Latin *abbaiare*; an imitation of the sound] ◇ **keep somebody** or **something at bay** to keep somebody or something unpleasant at a distance to avoid difficulty or harm

bayadere /bī ə deér/ *n* a fabric with horizontal stripes of bold contrasting colours [Mid-19C. Via French < Portuguese *bailladeira* 'woman dancer' < *bailar* 'to dance']

Bayamón /bī ə món/ *n* city in northeastern Puerto Rico, west of the River Bayamón, and west of San Juan. Population: 220,262 (1990).

Bayazid I /bī əzid/, **Bayezit I** /-əzit/, **Bajazet I** //bī ə zet/ (1360?–1403?) sultan of the Ottoman Empire. During his reign (1389–1402) he conquered much of the Balkans and Asia Minor, but was eventually defeated by the Tatar Timur. Known as **Yilderim** ('Lightning')

Bayazid II, **Bayezit II**, **Bajazet II** (1448–1512) sultan of the Ottoman Empire. During his reign (1481–1512) he constructed the mosque of Bayazid in Constantinople (1505).

Baybars I /bī baárss/ (1233?–77) sultan of Egypt and Syria. During his reign (1260–77) he extended his control into Armenia, Asia Minor, Nubia, and Arabia.

bayberry /báybəri/ (*plural* **-ries**) *n* **1.** a fruit covered with a waxy substance, borne by a North American bush. Use: making candles. **2.** a bush that bears bayberries. Native to: coast of eastern North America. Genus: *Myrica*. **3.** same as **bay rum tree**

Bayes' theorem /báyz-/ *n* a theorem of conditional probability that allows estimates of probability to be continually revised on the basis of observations of occurrences of events [Mid-19C. After Thomas *Bayes* (1702–61), British mathematician]

Bayeux /bī yúr/ town in Calvados Department, northern France. Population: 14,961 (1999).

Bayeux tapestry *n* a linen embroidery from the 11th century that hangs in Bayeux, France, and depicts the Norman conquest of England in 1066

Bayezit another spelling of **Bayazid I**

bay laurel *n* TREES same as **bay**[3] (sense 1)

Bayle /bayl, bel/, **Pierre** (1647–1706) French philosopher. His *Dictionary* (1697) and his controversial proposition that morality is independent of religion were major influences on the 18th-century European Enlightenment.

> 'If an historian were to relate truthfully all the crimes, weaknesses, and disorders of mankind, his readers would take his work for satire rather than for history.'
> [Pierre Bayle, *Historical and Critical Dictionary*; 1697]

bay leaf *n* the aromatic leaf of the Mediterranean bay tree. Use: flavouring in cooking.

Bay of Pigs /báy-/ bay on the southwestern coast of Cuba that was the site of an abortive attempt by US-backed Cuban exiles to overthrow the government of Fidel Castro in 1961

Bay of Plenty ♦ **Plenty, Bay of**

bayonet

bayonet /báyənit/ *n* **1.** BLADE FITTED TO RIFLE a blade that can be attached to the end of a rifle and used for stabbing **2.** FITTING WITH PROJECTING PINS a fitting with projecting pins that are pushed into a socket and then twisted into slots, as used on electric light bulbs ∎ *vt* (**-nets, -neting, -neted**) USE BAYONET ON SOMEBODY to stab or kill somebody with a bayonet [Early 17C. < French *baïonnette*, after BAYONNE]

Bayonne /bī ón/ city in the Pyrénées-Atlantiques Department of the Aquitaine Region, southwestern France. Population: 61,051 (1998 estimate).

bayou /bī yoo/ (*plural* **-ous**) *n* in the southern United States, an area of slow-moving water, often overgrown with reeds, leading from a river or lake [Mid-18C. Via Louisiana French < Choctaw *bayuk* 'small river forming part of a delta']

bay platform *n* a railway platform at which a line ends in a station where other lines continue, often where a branch line ends in a mainline station

Bayreuth /bī róyt/ city in Bavaria, southern Germany, northeast of Nuremberg. It is the site of an annual Wagner opera festival. Population: 72,840 (1997).

bay rum *n* a liquid made by dissolving the oil of the leaves of the bay rum tree and other fragrant oils in alcohol and water. Use: men's cosmetics. [Because originally made by distilling the oil with rum]

bay rum tree *n* a tree whose leaves produce fragrant oil. Use: bay rum, soaps. Native to: Central and South America. Latin name: *Pimenta racemosa*.

Bay Street *n* **1.** the street in Toronto on which Canada's largest stock exchange is located **2.** the controlling financial interests of Toronto, Canada

bay window *n* a rounded or three-sided window that sticks out from an outside wall and forms a recess on the inside

baywood /báy wŏod/ *n* a light variety of mahogany from southern Mexico and Central America [After the *Bay* of Campeche, Mexico]

bazaar /bə zaár/ *n* **1.** CHARITY SALE a sale of goods to raise money for charity **2.** SHOP SELLING MISCELLANEOUS ITEMS a retail store that sells a wide variety of items (*dated*) **3.** STREET MARKET a street market in North Africa or southwestern Asia [Late 16C. Via Italian and Turkish < Persian *bāzār* 'market']

~~**bazar**~~ incorrect spelling of **bazaar**

bazodee /bə zó dee/ *adj Carib* unable to think clearly, either because of psychological turmoil or because of some physical condition or effect (*slang*) [Mid 20C. Via French Creole < French *abasourdi* 'stunned, bewildered']

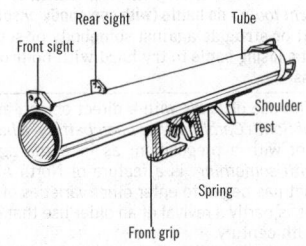

bazooka

bazooka /bə zóokə/ *n* a tube-shaped weapon, fired from the shoulder, that launches a missile that can disable a tank [Mid-20C. Origin ?]

bb[1] *abbr* Barbados (*used in Internet addresses*) See table at **domain name**

bb[2] *symbol* double black (*used to describe pencils with very soft leads*)

BB[1] *n N Am* a pellet fired from a shotgun or air gun [Late 19C. < the official designation of shot that is 0.18 in]

BB[2] *abbr* **1.** Boys' Brigade **2.** bye-bye (*used in e-mails or text messages*)

BBA *abbr* Bachelor of Business Administration

BBC *n* in the United Kingdom, the publicly funded organization that provides radio and television services. Full form **British Broadcasting Corporation**

BBC English *n* a form of English used by newsreaders and announcers on BBC television and radio

BBFC *abbr* British Board of Film Classification

bbl, bbl. *abbr* MEASURE barrel

BBQ *abbr* FOOD barbecue

BBS *abbr* ONLINE bulletin board system

BC[1] *adv* used to indicate a date that is a particular number of years before the traditional date of the birth of Jesus Christ (*used after dates*) Full form **before Christ**

BC[2] *abbr* **1.** because (*used in e-mails or text messages*) **2.** British Columbia

BCD *abbr* COMPUT binary coded decimal

BCE[1] *abbr* **1.** *US* Bachelor of Chemical Engineering **2.** *N Am* Bachelor of Civil Engineering

BCE[2], **B.C.E.** *adv* used after a date as the non-Christian equivalent of BC. Full form **before the Common Era**

B-cell *n* a white blood cell (**lymphocyte**), formed in bone marrow in mammals and present in blood and lymph, that creates antibodies in response to a specific antigen

BCG *n* an antituberculosis vaccine made from a weakened strain of the tubercle bacillus. Full form **bacillus Calmette-Guérin (vaccine)**

BCh *abbr* Bachelor of Surgery [Latin *Baccalaureus Chirurgiae*]

bck *abbr* a file extension for a backup file

BCL *abbr* Bachelor of Civil Law

BCNU *abbr* be seeing you (*used in e-mails or text messages*)

BCNZ *abbr NZ* Broadcasting Corporation of New Zealand

B complex *n* BIOCHEM same as **vitamin B complex**

BC soil *n* soil made up of two distinct layers

bd *abbr* **1.** Bangladesh (*used in Internet addresses*) See table at **domain name 2.** NAUT board **3.** FIN bond **4.** PUBL bound

BD *abbr* **1.** EDUC Bachelor of Divinity **2.** Borna disease

B/D, b/d *abbr* **1.** BANKING bank draft **2.** BANKING bills discounted **3.** ACCT brought down

BDA *abbr* DENT British Dental Association

bdellium /délli əm/ *n* **1.** a transparent yellowish resin. Use: perfumes. **2.** a tree that produces bdellium resin. Native to: Africa, western Asia. Genus: *Commiphora*. [14C. Via Latin < Greek < Semitic]

bd ft *abbr* MEASURE board foot

Bdr *abbr* MIL Bombardier

bds *abbr* **1.** PUBL bound in boards **2.** bundles

BDS *abbr* Bachelor of Dental Surgery

be[1] *stressed* /bee/; *unstressed* /bi/ (*1st person present singular* **am** *stressed* /am/; *unstressed* /əm/, *2nd person present singular* **are** *stressed* /aar/; *unstressed* /ər/, *3rd person present singular* **is** /iz/, *1st person present plural* **are**, *2nd person present plural* **are**, *3rd person present plural* **are**, *present subjunctive* **be**, *1st person singular past indicative* **was** *stressed* /woz/; *unstressed* /wəz/, *2nd person singular past indicative* **were** *stressed* /wur/; *unstressed* /wər/, *3rd person singular past indicative* **was**, *1st person plural past indicative* **were**, *2nd person plural past indicative* **were**, *3rd person plural past indicative* **were**, *past subjunctive* **were**, *past participle* **been** *stressed* /been/; *unstressed* /bin/) CORE MEANING: a verb used most commonly to link the subject of a clause to a complement in order to give more information about the subject, e.g. its identity, nature, attributes, position, or value ○ *This is my colleague.* ○ *He's a very sweet person.* ○ *Her new car is blue.* ○ *The supermarket is on the left.* ○ *The clock was worth £3,000.*

1. *vi* **GIVING DESCRIPTION** used after 'it' as the subject of the clause, to give a description or judgment of something ○ *It is a good thing that we left early.* **2.** *vi* **EXIST OR BE TRUE** used after 'there' to indicate that something exists or is true ○ *There are many problems with her essay.* **3.** *vi* **EXIST** to exist, have presence, or live ○ *I think, therefore I am.* **4.** *vi* **HAPPEN** to happen or take place ○ *The meeting was at four o'clock.* **5.** *vi* **STAY** to stay or visit ○ *I was in Italy during the summer.* **6.** *vi* **HAVE PARTICULAR QUALITY** to have a particular quality or attribute ○ *This sentence is concise.* **7.** *vi* **REMAIN** used to indicate that a particular situation remains ○ *The facts are these: it is cold and unhealthy here.* **8.** *aux v* **EXPRESSING CONTINUATION** used with the present participle of verbs to express continuation ○ *My legs are getting tired.* ○ *I am leaving on the next train.* **9.** *aux v* **FORMING PASSIVE** used with the past participle of transitive verbs to form the passive voice ○ *She was sent on the mission.* **10.** *aux v* **EXPRESSING FUTURE** used to indicate that something is planned, expected, intended, or supposed to happen in the future (*used with an infinitive*) ○ *The meeting is to take place tomorrow.* ○ *What am I to do?* **11.** *aux v* **EXPRESSING UNPLANNED ACTION IN PAST** used when reporting past events to indicate that something happened later than the time reported and was unplanned or uncertain at the time (*used with an infinitive*) ○ *It was to be the last time he ever saw her.* **12.** *aux v* **FORMING PERFECT TENSE** used with the past participle of some intransitive verbs to form a perfect tense (*archaic*) ○ *She is come back.* **13.** *vi* **INTRODUCING SENTENCE** used to introduce a full, often quoted sentence (*informal*) ○ *They were, "The tickets are way too expensive".* [Old English *bēon*, via Germanic, 'exist, dwell' < Indo-European, 'exist, grow'] ◇ **been there, done that (bought the T-shirt)** used to indicate a blasé attitude to a situation (*informal humorous*) ◇ **be off** to leave somewhere ○ *It's already seven o'clock; I'm off.*

ORIGIN The prehistoric Germanic word from which ***be*** is derived, is also the ancestor of English *boor, booth, build, husband*, and *neighbour*, and perhaps also of *bylaw*.

be[2] *abbr* Belgium (*used in Internet addresses*) See table at **domain name**

Be *symbol* CHEM ELEM beryllium

BE *abbr* **1.** Bachelor of Education **2.** Bachelor of Engineering **3.** bill of exchange

be- *prefix* **1.** thoroughly, excessively ○ *bedazzle* ○ *bespatter* **2.** on, over, about ○ *bewail* **3.** to surround or cover with ○ *befog* ○ *bedew* **4.** to supply with ○ *befriend* **5.** to make ○ *belittle* [Old English *be-, bi-* < Indo-European, 'around']

beach /beech/ *n* **COASTAL SAND** a strip of sand or pebbles at the point where land meets the sea or a lake ■ *vti* **(beaches, beaching, beached) 1. HAUL BOAT ASHORE** to pull or run a boat onto a beach, or be pulled onto a beach **2. STRAND OR BECOME STRANDED** to strand or become stranded on shore (*usually passive*) ○ *a whale that had been beached during a storm* [Mid-16C. Origin ?]

SPELLCHECK beach or **beech**? Do not confuse the spelling of ***beach*** and ***beech***, which sound similar. The word ***beach*** can be used as a noun, meaning 'sandy shore' (as in *sunbathing on the beach*), or as a verb, meaning 'haul ashore or be stranded ashore' (as in *to beach a boat, a beached whale*). The word ***beech*** is only used as a noun denoting a tree or its wood.

beach ball *n* a large light easily inflated ball, often brightly coloured, for playing with on a beach

beach buggy *n* a motorized beach vehicle, usually without a top and with oversized tyres to prevent it from getting stuck in sand. N Am term **dune buggy**

beach bum *n* somebody with no regular occupation who spends time idly on beaches (*informal*)

beach chair *n N Am* same as **deck chair**

beachcomber /beéch kōmər/ *n* **1.** somebody who looks for useful or valuable things on beaches **2.** *UK, ANZ, Can* a long high wave that crashes onto a beach. US term **comber**

beach drift *n* debris and sediment transported by waves breaking on the shore at an angle and returning to the sea in a direction determined by the slope of a beach

beached /beecht/ *adj* stranded on a beach or out of the water

beach flea *n* MARINE BIOL same as **sand hopper**

beachfront /beéch frunt/ *n N Am* a strip of land that adjoins a beach

beachhead /beéch hed/ *n* a part of an enemy shoreline that troops have captured and are using as a base for launching an attack [After BRIDGEHEAD]

Beach-la-Mar /beéch lə maár/ *n* a pidgin based on English that developed in Vanuatu, Fiji, and other nearby islands as a trading lingua franca. The modern form that is the national language of Vanuatu is known as Bislama. [Early 19C. < Portuguese *bicho do mar* 'sea cucumber', by association with BEACH] —**Beach-la-Mar** *adj*

beachmobile /beéch mə beel/ *n* a vehicle used to transport surfing equipment onto the beach

beach plum *n* **1.** a dark purple edible plum **2.** a small bushy plum tree with large white flowers that bears beach plums. Native to: coast of northeastern North America. Latin name: *Prunus maritima*.

beach volleyball *n* volleyball played on a beach or sandy surface with only two players on each side

beachwear /beéch wair/ *n* casual clothing designed to be worn on a beach

Beachy Head /beéchi-/ chalk headland on the English Channel near Eastbourne, East Sussex, southern England. Height: 171 m/570 ft.

beacon /beékən/ *n* **1.** NAUT **FLASHING LIGHT FOR SHIPS** a lighthouse or signalling buoy that produces a flashing light to warn or guide ships **2.** NAVIG **RADIO TRANSMITTER PRODUCING NAVIGATION SIGNAL** a radio transmitter that continuously broadcasts a signal that aircraft use for guidance **3. SIGNALLING FIRE ON HILL** a fire lit on a hilltop or tower as part of a national celebration or, formerly, as a signal or warning **4. HILL SUITABLE FOR SIGNALLING FIRES** a prominent hill on which fires were formerly lit as a signal (*often used in placenames*) **5.** ROADS same as **Belisha beacon 6. SOURCE OF INSPIRATION** somebody or something that inspires or guides others (*literary*) [Old English *bēacen* 'signal, sign' < Germanic]

bead /beed/ *n* **1. BALL FOR NECKLACE** a small gemstone or glass, plastic, or wooden ball, pierced for stringing on a cord or sewing onto fabric **2. DROP OF MOISTURE** a drop of moisture, especially of sweat **3.** ARCHIT, FURNITURE **BUILDING OR FURNITURE TRIM** an edge or rim that sticks out on a building or a piece of furniture, traditionally with a pattern of rounded knobs **4.** ARMS **GUN SIGHT** a knob sticking up on the end of the barrel of a gun, forming the front part of the gun's sight **5.** AUTOMOT **SEAL ON TYRE** a projecting lip on the tyre of a motor vehicle that forms a seal to the wheel rim **6.** METALL **DEPOSIT OF METAL** a deposit of metal used in welding ■ **beads** *npl* **1. NECKLACE** a necklace made of beads **2.** RELIG same as **rosary** (senses 2–3) ■ *v* **(beads, beading, beaded) 1.** *vt* **DECORATE SOMETHING WITH BEADS** to trim or ornament something with beads **2.** *vi* **FORM INTO BEADS** to form drops of moisture [Old English *gebed* 'prayer' < Germanic] —**beaded** *adj* ◇ **draw a bead on somebody** *or* **something** to take careful aim at somebody or something ◇ **tell** *or* **say** *or* **count your beads** to say prayers recited in sequence and counted using a rosary

beading /beéding/ *n* an edge or rim that sticks out on a building or a piece of furniture, traditionally with a pattern of rounded knobs

beadle /beéd'l/ *n* **1.** a minor parish official formerly employed in the Church of England to usher and keep order **2.** an official who acts as caretaker of a synagogue and oversees the running of the service [13C. < Old French *bedel* 'proclaimer, messenger' < Germanic]

beadwork /beéd wurk/ *n* **1.** decoration using beads to form a design, e.g. on furniture or knitwear **2.** *US* decorative wooden edging, e.g. on a door or window frame

beady /beédi/ **(-ier, -iest)** *adj* **1. RESEMBLING BEAD** small, round, and shiny like a bead **2. COVERED WITH BEADS** covered or ornamented with beads **3. WATCHFUL** carefully attentive (*informal*) ○ *a beady eye* —**beadily** *adv* —**beadiness** *n*

beagle /beég'l/ *n* a small smooth-haired dog, belonging to a breed with a white, tan, and black coat and long drooping ears, often used for hunting [15C. Origin ?]

Beagle Channel /beég'l-/ strait in the Tierra del Fuego archipelago, at the southernmost tip of South America. Length: 240 km/150 mi.

beagling /beégling/ *n* hunting, especially for rabbits or hares, using beagles —**beagler** *n*

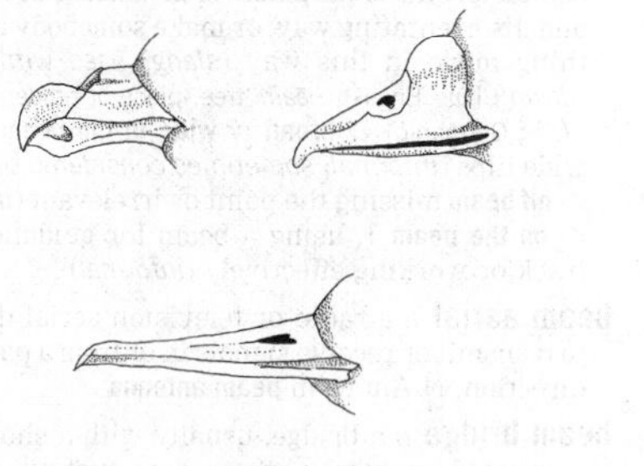

beak

beak /beek/ *n* **1. BIRD'S MOUTH PARTS** the feeding apparatus of a bird, consisting of two pointed jaws protected by a horny covering. Beaks take many different shapes according to the eating habits of individual bird species. **2. PROJECTING PART** a part that sticks out, e.g. the lip of a container **3. SOMEBODY'S NOSE** somebody's nose, especially when it is long or hooked (*informal*) **4. MAGISTRATE** a judge or a magistrate in a court of law (*dated informal*) **5. TEACHER** a headmaster or schoolmaster (*dated informal*) **6.** ZOOL **PROTRUDING PART OF ANIMAL'S MOUTH** a projecting part of the mouth or jaw of animals other than birds, e.g. the sucking mouthpart of an insect or the bony jaw projection of a fish **7.** ZOOL **PART OF INVERTEBRATE ANIMAL SHELL** the oldest part of the shell of an invertebrate animal with a hinged shell, found nearest the hinge

8. ARCHIT **CURVED CORNICE OR MOULDING** a cornice or moulding with a downward-curving edge [13C. Via Old French *bec* < Latin *beccus*] —**beaked** *adj* —**beakless** *adj*

beaked whale *n* a widely found, medium-sized, toothed whale with a long snout. Family: Ziphiidae.

beaker /beékər/ *n* **1.** a wide-mouthed cup, especially a plastic one without a handle **2.** a flat-bottomed glass container used in laboratories [14C. Via Old Norse *bikarr* < assumed Vulgar Latin *bicarium*, perhaps < Greek *bikos* 'wine jar, earthen vessel']

Beaker folk /beékər-/ *npl* a prehistoric people who lived throughout central Europe during the period 2000 to 1000 BC. The remains of pottery beakers are often found in areas where they lived.

beaky /beéki/ (**-ier, -iest**) *adj* having a large, long, or hooked nose (*informal*)

Beale /beel/, **Dorothea** (1831–1906) British educator and suffragette. She founded the first women's teacher training college (1885) and sponsored St Hilda's Hall, Oxford, for women teachers (1893).

be-all ◇ **the be-all and end-all** the thing that is most important

beam /beem/ *n* **1. HORIZONTAL STRUCTURAL SUPPORT** a horizontal structural member, e.g. a long piece of timber, metal, or concrete that spans a gap and supports a floor, roof, or other structure above **2. LINE OF LIGHT** a narrow line of light, e.g. from a flashlight **3. BROAD SMILE** a broad smile of happiness or satisfaction **4.** NAUT **STRUCTURAL CROSSPIECE IN SHIP** a structural member of a ship or boat that joins the sides and supports the deck **5.** NAUT **SHIP'S BREADTH** the full breadth of a ship **6.** NAUT **SIDE OF SHIP** either of the sides of a ship **7.** PHYS **FLOW OF RADIATION** a narrow stream of radiation or particles flowing in one direction **8.** NAVIG **GUIDING SIGNAL** a radio or radar signal intended to guide a ship or aircraft, or the direction indicated by this signal **9.** GYMNASTICS **GYMNASTS' BALANCING BAR** a narrow horizontal wooden bar on legs that women gymnasts stand on to perform balancing exercises, or the event involving this. N Am term **balance beam** **10. HORIZONTAL PART OF BALANCE** the pivoted horizontal bar of a balance on which the two scales hang **11. MAIN SUPPORTING SHAFT** a main bar or shaft, e.g. either of the main stems of a deer's antlers or the central shaft of a plough **12.** MECH ENG **CONNECTING LEVER IN ENGINE** a lever connecting the piston rod and crankshaft in an engine **13.** MANUF **ROLLER IN LOOM** a cylinder in a loom on which either the warp or the cloth is wound ■ *v* (**beams, beaming, beamed**) **1.** *vti* **SMILE BROADLY** to smile broadly with happiness or satisfaction, or express feelings by smiling broadly **2.** *vt* BROADCAST **SEND RADIO OR TV SIGNAL** to send or transmit a programme to a distant place in the form of a radio or television signal **3.** *vti* **SHINE** to shine, or shine something, in a particular direction **4.** *vti* **CHANGE CIRCUMSTANCES SUDDENLY** to move between completely different places or situations in a sudden and disorientating way, or make somebody or something move in this way (*slang; used with 'up' or 'down'*) [Old English *bēam* 'tree, piece of timber, column, ray' < Germanic] ◇ **broad** *or* **wide in the beam** having wide hips (*informal; sometimes considered offensive*) ◇ **off beam** missing the point or irrelevant (*informal*) ◇ **on the beam 1.** using a beam for guidance **2.** on track or working effectively (*informal*)

beam aerial *n* a radio or television aerial designed to transmit or receive signals in or from a particular direction. N Am term **beam antenna**

beam bridge *n* a bridge, usually with a short span, supported on beams whose ends rest on piers or abutments

beam compass *n* a tool for drawing very large circles or arcs, consisting of a horizontal bar with sliding legs

beam-ends *npl* the ends of the beams supporting the deck of a vessel ◇ **on her** *or* **its beam-ends** used to describe a ship leaning so far to one side that its deck is vertical ◇ **on your beam-ends** having very little money to live on (*informal*)

beam engine *n* an early type of steam engine with a piston that pushes a pivoted horizontal beam up and down in a see-saw motion

beamer /beémər/ *n* in cricket, a fast ball that reaches the batsman at head height without bouncing. Beamers usually result from the ball slipping out of the bowler's hand, and to bowl one deliberately is generally considered dangerous and unsporting. [Mid-19C. Origin ?]

Beamer /beémər/, **Beemer** *n* CARS a BMW™ motor car (*informal*) [Late 20C. Alteration]

beamlet /beémlət/ *n* a small amount of low-level radiation, used in noninvasive radiation treatments of cancer

Beamon /beémən/, **Bob** (*b.* 1946) US athlete. He set a world long jump record of 8.9 m/29 ft 2.5 in at the 1968 Olympic Games in Mexico City that stood for 23 years. Full name **Beamon, Robert**

beam splitter *n* a device used in holography to divide a laser light into two beams by means of a prism and mirror to produce a three-dimensional image

beamy /beémi/ (**-ier, -iest**) *adj* **1.** describes a ship with a broad beam **2.** sending out beams of light (*literary*)

bean /been/ *n* **1. EDIBLE GREEN POD** a long thin usually green seed pod eaten cooked whole as a vegetable **2. SMALL ROUND VEGETABLE** a small round or kidney-shaped seed of various colours that is eaten as a vegetable and can be dried to preserve it **3. PLANT WITH EDIBLE PODS AND SEEDS** a tall climbing or small bushy plant that produces beans. Genus: *Phaseolus.* **4. SEED USED IN FOOD OR DRINK** a coffee, cocoa, or carob seed that is processed and used in food or drink ■ **beans** *npl* *N Am* **NOTHING** nothing at all (*informal*) ■ *vt* (**beans, beaning, beaned**) *N Am* **HIT SOMEBODY ON HEAD** to hit somebody on the head (*slang*) [Old English *bēan* < Germanic] ◇ **full of beans** bright and energetic (*informal*) ◇ **not have a bean** to have no money (*informal*) ◇ **not know beans about something** *N Am* to have no knowledge or understanding of something (*informal*) ◇ **spill the beans** to reveal secret information (*informal*)

Bean /been/, **Charles Edwin Woodrow** (1879–1968) Australian writer. He was the general editor and author of six volumes of the *Official History of Australia in the War of 1914–18* (1921–42).

beanbag /beén bag/ *n* **1.** a small cloth bag filled with dried beans or something similar, thrown or otherwise used in children's games **2.** an oversized cushion filled with tiny polystyrene balls, laid on the floor and used for sitting on

bean beetle *n* INSECTS same as **Mexican bean beetle**

bean counter *n* an accountant (*informal insult*)

bean curd *n* tofu, especially as used in Chinese cookery

beanery /beénəri/ (*plural* **-ies**) *n N Am* a cheap restaurant (*informal*)

beanfeast /beén feest/ *n* (*dated informal*) **1.** a party or social gathering **2.** an annual dinner given for employees

beanie /beéni/ *n* a round tight-fitting hat like a skullcap

beano /beénō/ *n* a noisy or enjoyable party or celebration (*dated informal*)

beanpole /beén pōl/ *n* **1.** a stick or pole for supporting a climbing bean plant **2.** somebody tall and thin (*informal insult*)

bean sprouts *npl* long pale shoots of sprouted bean seeds, particularly of mung beans, harvested while crisp and eaten raw or very lightly cooked

beanstalk /beén stawk/ *n* the stem of a bean plant

Beantown /beén town/ *n US* a nickname for Boston (*informal*)

bear[1] /bair/ *n* **1. LARGE FURRY ANIMAL** a large strong omnivorous four-legged animal that has thick shaggy fur and sharp claws, and walks on the flat of its paws. Family: Ursidae. **2. MEDIUM-SIZED FURRY ANIMAL** an animal that resembles but is unrelated to the true bear, e.g. the koala **3.** LEISURE same as **teddy bear** **4. SOMEBODY EASILY ANNOYED** somebody regarded as ill-tempered (*informal*) **5.** FIN **SOMEBODY WHO ANTICIPATES FALLING PRICES** somebody who sells stocks or commodities in anticipation of falling prices [Old English *bera* < Germanic, 'the brown one']

SPELLCHECK See *bare.*

bear[2] /bair/ (**bears, bearing, bore** /bawr/, **borne** /bawrn/) *v* **1.** *vti* **TOLERATE** to be able to endure something without great distress or annoyance (*used in questions and negative statements*) ○ *I can't bear this heat.* **2.** *vt* **SUPPORT SOMETHING** to hold or support a weight or something heavy **3.** *vti* **BE FIT FOR SOMETHING** to withstand being subjected to a particular action ○ *Will her theories bear scrutiny?* **4.** *vt* **MERIT SOMETHING** to be worthy of an action ○ *bear further investigation* **5.** *vt* **ACCEPT SOMETHING AS RESPONSIBILITY** to accept something as a duty or responsibility ○ *bear the expense* **6.** *vt* **BE CHARACTERIZED BY SOMETHING** to have something as a quality, characteristic, or permanent attribute ○ *bears no relation to reality* **7.** *vt* **BE MARKED BY SOMETHING** to show physical signs of something ○ *bears a likeness to his uncle* **8.** *vt* **CARRY SOMETHING** to hold or support and transport somebody or something ○ *The spores are borne on the wind.* **9.** *vt* **PRODUCE SOMETHING** to yield something by a natural process, or produce something desirable or valuable ○ *the tree that bore fruit* **10.** *vt* **GIVE BIRTH TO CHILD** to give birth to a child or young **11.** *vt* **THINK SOMETHING** to hold a particular thought, feeling, or idea in the mind ○ *I bore him no ill will.* **12.** *vi* **HEAD IN PARTICULAR DIRECTION** to move or turn in a particular direction ○ *Bear right when the road divides.* **13.** *vt* **BEHAVE IN PARTICULAR WAY** to conduct or carry yourself in a particular way ○ *bore himself well* **14.** *vt* **TRANSMIT SOMETHING** to hold something in mind and communicate it to others (*formal*) ○ *I will bear your message.* [Old English *beran* < Indo-European] ◇ **bring something to bear (on something)** to use something to force a desired outcome

ORIGIN The prehistoric Germanic word from which ***bear*** is derived is also the ancestor of English *barrow*[1], *berth*, *bier*, *birth*, and *burden*[1]. Its Indo-European ancestor is in turn the source of English *amphora*, *fertile*, and *suffer*.

bear down *vi* to push with the vaginal muscles during childbirth

bear down on *vt* **1.** to move quickly and menacingly towards somebody or something **2.** to exert downward pressure on somebody or something

bear on, bear upon *vt* **1.** to relate to or affect something **2.** to be a problem for or a burden to somebody or something

bear out *vt* to prove something or somebody to be true or justified ○ *This bears out my theory.*

bear up *vi* **1.** to remain cheerful and determined in spite of problems **2.** to remain true or undamaged after being examined or criticized

bear upon *vt* same as **bear on**

bear with *vt* to be patient with somebody who is trying to do something

bearable /báirəb'l/ *adj* not too unpleasant to put up with or accept —**bearably** *adv*

bearbaiting /báir bayting/ *n* the setting of fierce dogs onto a chained bear, once a popular form of public entertainment

bearberry /báirbəri/ (*plural* **-ries**) *n* a trailing evergreen bush with red berries. Native to: Europe, Asia, North America. Latin name: *Arctostaphylos uva-ursi.* [Early 17C. < BEAR[1]]

bearcat /báir kat/ *n* ZOOL same as **red panda**

beard /beerd/ *n* **1. HAIR GROWING ON MAN'S CHIN** the hair on a man's chin and, often, his neck and cheeks **2.** ZOOL **TUFTS GROWING ON ANIMAL OR PLANT** a growth of longer hair on an animal, e.g. on a goat's chin, or a long slender growth on plants, e.g. on barley and wheat heads ■ *vt* (**beards, bearding, bearded**) **OPPOSE SOMEBODY OR SOMETHING** to oppose or confront somebody or something confidently or disrespectfully [Old English, < Indo-European] —**bearded** *adj* —**beardless** *adj*

bearded collie /beérdid-/ *n* a medium-sized grey or brown-and-white dog with a long coat, drooping ears, and a tuft of hair on its chin, belonging to a breed used for herding animals

bearded dragon, bearded lizard *n* a large lizard with a pouch under its chin that inflates to ward off attackers. Native to: Australia. Latin name: *Amphibolus barbatus.*

bearded iris *n* an iris that has large flowers, with numerous hairs, often coloured, along the centre of each drooping lower petal

bearded lizard *n* REPT same as **bearded dragon**

bearded tit *n* a small brownish-orange songbird with a long tail, the male of which has a black patch extending down from the eye. Native to: reed beds in Europe and Asia. Latin name: *Panurus biarmicus.*

bearded vulture *n* BIRDS same as **lammergeier**

Beardsley /beérdzli/, **Aubrey** (1872–98) British artist and illustrator. One of the 'Decadents' in the 1890s, he produced art nouveau illustrations in a dis-

tinctive black-and-white style, including series for *Morte d'Arthur* (1893–4) and *Salomé* (1894). Full name **Beardsley, Aubrey Vincent**

'Really I believe I'm so affected, even my lungs are affected.'
[Attributed to Aubrey Beardsley]

bearer /báirər/ *n* **1.** BRINGER somebody who brings or carries something **2.** FIN HOLDER OF REDEEMABLE NOTE somebody possessing a document redeemable for payment **3.** same as **pallbearer 4.** PORTER a local person employed to carry equipment on an expedition

bearer bond *n* a bond payable only to the person who presents it

bearer instrument *n* a negotiable instrument that may be converted to cash by whoever holds it

bear garden *n* **1.** a noisy or unruly place or occasion **2.** in former times, a place where live bears were on public display and where bearbaiting took place

bear hug *n* **1.** TIGHT EMBRACE an enthusiastic or energetic embrace **2.** TIGHT WRESTLING HOLD in wrestling, a tight, squeezing hold around an opponent's chest and arms **3.** WARNING OF INTENDED CORPORATE TAKEOVER a warning given by one company to another of its intention to assume control of the other

bearing /báiring/ *n* **1.** WAY OF MOVING OR STANDING somebody's way of moving, standing, or behaving generally ○ *her dignified bearing* **2.** MECH ENG HOUSING FOR MOVING MACHINE PART the part of a machine that supports a sliding or rotating part **3.** NAVIG CALCULATION OF DIRECTION OR GEOGRAPHICAL POSITION the location or direction of movement of somebody or something, calculated using a map or compass **4.** RELEVANCE a relation to something ○ *This has no bearing on the matter under discussion.* **5.** ARCHIT SUPPORT FOR BEAM a support for a beam or girder **6.** HERALDRY HERALDIC DEVICE a heraldic device or charge ◇ **find** *or* **get your bearings 1.** to learn exactly where you are and in which direction you should proceed **2.** to become familiar with a new environment ◇ **lose your bearings 1.** to become uncertain about where you are and in which direction you should proceed **2.** to become unable to react in a normal manner

bearing rein *n UK, ANZ, Can* a short rein joining a horse's bit to a hook on the saddle, used to keep the horse's head up. US term **checkrein**

bearish /báirish/ *adj* **1.** BAD-TEMPERED surly or ill-tempered towards people **2.** CLUMSY moving or behaving roughly or clumsily **3.** FIN ANTICIPATING FALLING PRICES conducive to or characterized by selling rather than buying stocks or commodities in anticipation of falling prices

bear market *n* a situation in a stock or commodity market in which shareholders are selling in anticipation of falling prices

béarnaise sauce /báy ər nayz-/ *n* a savoury sauce for meat, thickened with egg yolk and flavoured with tarragon [Late 19C. < French < *Béarn*, district in SW France]

bear raid *n* an attempt to lower a stock or commodity price by selling large numbers of shares, usually in order to buy them back at a lowered price

bear's breech, **bear's breeches** *n* a large garden plant with spiky leaves. Flowers: whitish, purple-streaked. Latin name: *Acanthus mollis.*

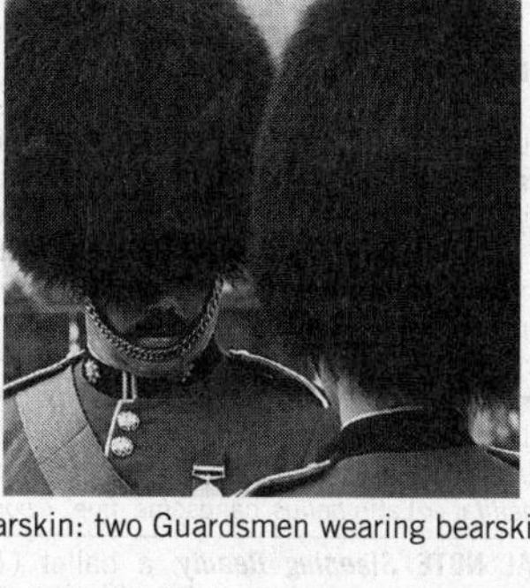

bearskin: two Guardsmen wearing bearskins

bearskin /báir skin/ *n* **1.** BEAR'S PELT a bear's skin with the fur still attached, stripped from the animal **2.** SOLDIER'S TALL FUR HAT a tall fur hat worn as part of the ceremonial uniform of soldiers in the Guards regiments **3.** SHAGGY WOOLLEN CLOTH coarse woollen fabric. Use: overcoats.

beast /beest/ *n* **1.** LARGE ANIMAL an animal, especially a large four-footed mammal **2.** IRRATIONAL SIDE OF SOMEBODY'S PERSONALITY the instinctive, irrational, or aggressive part of somebody's personality **3.** SOMEBODY BRUTAL somebody cruel or aggressive **4.** SOMETHING UNPLEASANT something that is difficult or unpleasant (*informal*) ○ *This is truly a beast of a job!* **5.** SOMETHING WITH PARTICULAR QUALITY something that has a particular quality (*informal*) ○ *The basic beginner's windsurfing board is a hardy beast.* [12C. Via Old French *beste* < Latin *bestia*] —**beastlike** *adj*

beastbwai /beést bwī/ *n* an offensive term for the police (*slang; used in Black English*) [< *bwai*, form of BOY]

beastie /beésti/ *n Scotland, N Am* a small animal, especially an insect or small crawling animal (*informal or humorous*)

beastly /beéstli/ (*dated informal*) *adj* thoroughly unpleasant or objectionable ■ *adv* exceedingly —**beastliness** *n*

beast of burden *n* an animal used to carry or pull things or do other heavy work, e.g. a donkey or an ox

beast of prey *n* an animal that hunts other animals for food

beat /beet/ *v* (**beats, beating, beat, beaten** /beét'n/) **1.** *vt* DEFEAT SOMEBODY IN CONTEST to defeat somebody in a contest, race, or competition ○ *She was beaten in the semifinal.* **2.** *vt* HIT SOMEBODY OR SOMETHING REPEATEDLY to hit somebody or something with repeated heavy blows **3.** *vi* KNOCK AGAINST SOMETHING REPEATEDLY to knock or strike against something repeatedly ○ *waves beating against the rocks* **4.** *vt* FLOG SOMEBODY to inflict physical punishment or injury on somebody using an instrument such as a whip, stick, or belt **5.** *vi* PULSATE to make natural short rhythmic movements (*refers to the heart or pulse*) **6.** *vti* MUSIC HIT DRUM to hit a drum repeatedly to produce a musical rhythm or a signal **7.** *vt* MUSIC SET MUSICAL RHYTHM to show or establish a musical rhythm, e.g. with a conductor's baton or by clapping hands ○ *beating time with her hand* **8.** *vt* COOK STIR INGREDIENTS VIGOROUSLY to mix moist ingredients vigorously to combine them, make them smooth, or incorporate air into them ○ *Now, beat the eggs.* **9.** *vt* OVERCOME OBSTACLES IN SOMETHING to overcome the difficulties or obstacles created by something ○ *You can't beat the system.* **10.** *vt* ARRIVE AHEAD OF SOMEBODY to arrive or finish something sooner than somebody else or before a time limit ○ *She beat me to the office.* **11.** *vt* AVOID LATER DELAYS to take early action to avoid being prevented or delayed by something ○ *Order now and beat the rush!* **12.** *vt* SURPASS SOMETHING to surpass a previous best performance ○ *beat the long jump record* **13.** *vti* BE BETTER THAN SOMETHING to be or do better than a particular thing, activity, or quality (*informal*) ○ *Sitting by the pool certainly beats working.* **14.** *vt* MAKE SOMETHING BY HITTING to shape or make something by pounding or trampling ○ *beat silver into jewellery* **15.** *vti* BIRDS FLAP WINGS to move the wings up and down in flight, or be moved in this way ○ *The vulture beat its wings.* **16.** *vt* FORCE SOMEBODY TO WITHDRAW to force somebody to retreat or accept a weaker position ○ *They beat back the enemy.* **17.** *vti* FIELD SPORTS DRIVE GAME FROM BRUSH to move through or disturb bushes and undergrowth in order to frighten animals and birds for hunting **18.** *vi* SAILING SAIL INTO WIND to sail a boat or ship as nearly as possible in the direction from which the wind is blowing ■ *n* **1.** STEADY THROBBING a rhythmic sound or movement made by something throbbing or pulsating (*often used in combination*) ○ *could hear the beat of his heart* **2.** STROKE an act of striking one thing against another, especially repeatedly and rhythmically, or the sound of one thing striking against another in this way ○ *a drum beat* **3.** MUSIC SET RHYTHM a single element of measured time in a musical piece or poem. Beats occur at regular intervals and are the rhythmic and metrical foundations of music. **4.** MUSIC CONDUCTOR'S SIGNAL a movement made by a conductor's baton or hand to indicate a musical rhythm **5.** MUSIC DOMINANT RHYTHM the dominant rhythm in a piece of music, especially a strong rhythm in rock music **6.** USUAL ROUTE a regular route followed or area covered while working, e.g. a police officer's route ○ *covering her regular beat* **7.** AREA SOMEBODY USUALLY GOES TO the places somebody usually frequents, especially somebody's usual hunting or fishing area ■ *adj* **1.** TIRED OUT completely exhausted (*informal*) **2.** PUZZLED unable to understand or think how to proceed (*informal*) ○ *It has me beat.* **3.** *also* **Beat** OF BEAT GENERATION relating to or produced by members of the Beat Generation [Old English *bēatan*, via Germanic < Indo-European, 'to strike'] ◇ **beat it!** used to tell somebody to go away (*informal*) ◇ **beat somebody to something** to succeed in doing something before somebody else can do it (*informal*) ◇ **it beats me** used to indicate that you do not understand something (*informal*) ◇ **not miss a beat** to show no sign of surprise or upset ◇ **take some beating** to be so good as to be difficult to improve on ○ *Her track record will take some beating.*

SPELLCHECK beat or **beet**? Do not confuse the spelling of ***beat*** and ***beet***, which sound similar. The word ***beat*** can be used as a verb, meaning 'defeat', 'surpass', 'hit repeatedly', or 'pulsate' (as in *beat the world record, beat a drum, his heart was beating*), or as a noun, meaning 'rhythm' or 'usual route' (as in *music with a steady beat, a police officer's beat*). The word ***beet*** is only used as a noun denoting a root vegetable.

SYNONYMS See ***defeat.***

beat down *v* **1.** *vi* to shine intensely or fall heavily from the sky (*refers to sun or rain*) **2.** *vt* to persuade somebody to charge less than the intended selling price (*informal*)

beat off *v* **1.** *vt* to stop an attack or challenge by vigorous action **2.** *vi* a highly offensive term meaning to masturbate (*slang taboo*)

beat up *vt* to injure somebody badly by repeated punches or kicks (*informal*)

beat up on *vt N Am* same as **beat up** (*informal*)

beatbox /beét bòks/ *n N Am* an electronic drum used mainly in hip-hop and rap music to provide accompanying rhythm and sounds (*informal*)

beat-'em-up *n* a video or computer game involving a large amount of simulated hand-to-hand fighting (*informal*)

beaten past participle of **beat**

beaten-up *adj* damaged or in bad condition after long use

beater /beétər/ *n* **1.** TOOL FOR BEATING a tool for beating something, e.g. a shaped stick for beating the dust out of carpets, or an electric food mixer attachment for beating eggs (*often used in combination*) **2.** FIELD SPORTS HUNTER'S ASSISTANT FOR DRIVING BIRDS OUT somebody who flushes out game for hunters to shoot, usually by hitting bushes **3.** SOMEBODY WHO BEATS METAL somebody who hammers metal

Beat Generation *n* **1.** young people in the 1950s who rejected the traditional values, customs, and dress of Western society and experimented with Eastern philosophies, communal living, and illegal drugs **2.** a group of writers associated with the attitudes of the Beat Generation, including Jack Kerouac and Allen Ginsberg

beatific /beé ə tíffik/ *adj* (*literary*) **1.** expressing or radiating great happiness and serenity **2.** bringing or expressing the perfect happiness and inner peace supposed to be enjoyed by the soul in heaven [Mid-17C. Directly or via French *béatifique* < Latin *beatificus* < *beatus* 'blessed'] —**beatifically** *adv*

~~**beatiful**~~ incorrect spelling of **beautiful**

beatify /bi átti fī/ (**-fies, -fying, -fied**) *vt* **1.** in the Roman Catholic Church, to state officially that a dead person lived a holy life, usually as the first step towards making the person a saint **2.** to make somebody extremely happy (*literary*) [Mid-16C. Directly or via French *béatifer* < ecclesiastical Latin *beatificare* < Latin *beatificus* (see BEATIFIC)] —**beatification** /bi áttifi káysh'n/ *n*

beating /beéting/ *n* **1.** an attack or punishment in which somebody is repeatedly hit **2.** a severe defeat or setback, e.g. in a competition or in business

beating reed *n* a reed in woodwind instruments that vibrates as air passes over it

beatitude /bi átti tyood/ *n* (*literary*) **1.** the perfect happiness and inner peace supposed to be enjoyed by the soul in heaven **2.** extreme happiness and serenity [15C. Directly or via French < Latin *beatitud-* < *beatus* 'blessed']

Beatitude *n* **1.** in the Bible, one of the sayings of Jesus Christ in the Sermon on the Mount about the eight groups of people who will receive blessing in heaven (Matthew 5:3–11) **2.** a title given to a senior bishop in non-Orthodox Christian churches of the eastern Mediterranean

The Beatles

Beatles /beet'lz/ (1959–70) British pop music group. This group of musicians from Liverpool, Paul McCartney, John Lennon, George Harrison, and Ringo Starr, revolutionized popular music in the 1960s.

beatnik /beet'nik/ *n* a member of the Beat Generation of the 1950s

Beaton /beet'n/, **Sir Cecil** (1904–80) British photographer and designer. He was a fashion and high-society photographer. He also designed scenery and costumes for *My Fair Lady*, *Gigi*, and other productions. Full name **Beaton, Sir Cecil Walter Hardy**

'Be daring, be different, impractical, anything that will assert integrity of purpose and imaginative vision against the play-it-safers.'
[Sir Cecil Beaton, *Theatre Arts*; 1957]

Beatrix /bee atriks/ (*b.* 1938) queen of the Netherlands. She acceded to the throne on the abdication of her mother, Queen Juliana, in 1980. Full name **Beatrix Wilhelmina Armgard**

Beatty /beeti/, **David, 1st Earl** (1871–1936) British admiral. He was appointed commander of the grand fleet after serving at the Battle of Jutland in 1916. He was First Sea Lord of the Admiralty (1919–27).

beat-up *adj* in bad condition because of overuse (*informal*) ■ *n Aus* a media report that has been sensationalized and made to seem more significant than it really is

beau /bō/ (*plural* **beaus** or **beaux** /bō, bōz/) *n* **1.** a boyfriend or male admirer (*dated*) **2.** a man who is always smartly dressed in the most fashionable clothes (*archaic*) [Late 17C. < French < *beau* 'beautiful' < Latin *bellus* (see BEAUTY)]

beaucoup /bō koo/ *adj US* very many or very much (*slang*) ○ *His new suit cost beaucoup dollars.* [Early 20C. < French]

Beaufort /bṓfərt/, **Henry, Cardinal** (1377?–1447) English prelate and diplomat. He became a cardinal in 1426 and in the 1430s was the real power behind the government of the young King Henry VI.

Beaufort scale /bṓfərt-/ *n* an international scale of wind speeds indicated by numbers ranging from 0 for calm to 12 for hurricane. Each force is recognized by its effects on things such as flags and trees and on the surface of the sea. [Mid-19C. After Sir Francis *Beaufort* (1774–1857), Irish admiral and hydrographer]

Beaufort Sea section of the Arctic Ocean northwest of Canada and north of Alaska. Area: 450,000 sq. km/170,000 sq. mi. Depth: 4,682 m/15,360 ft.

beau geste /bō zhest/ (*plural* **beaux gestes** /*pronunc. same*/) *n* a kind or magnanimous act [Early 20C. < French, 'fine gesture']

Beauharnais /bō aar nay/, **Alexandre, Vicomte de** (1760–94) French soldier and politician. He embraced the French Revolution and became president of the Constituent Assembly (1791), but was later guillotined.

Beauharnais, Joséphine de ♦ **Joséphine**

beau ideal /bṓ ee day aal/ (*plural* **beaux ideals** /bṓz ee

day aal/) *n* **1.** somebody's idea of perfection or beauty **2.** somebody or something considered to be a perfect example of its kind [Early 19C. < French, 'ideal beauty' (but usually taken as meaning 'beautiful ideal')]

Beaujolais /bṓzhə lay/ *n* a light usually red wine from central France [Mid-19C. After a district in central France]

Beaujolais Nouveau /-noo vṓ/ *n* Beaujolais sold in the November and December of the year of its production

Beaulieu /byoo'li/ village in Hampshire, southern England, the site of the Montagu Motor Museum and the ruins of Beaulieu Abbey. Population: 1,200 (1991).

Beaumarchais /bṓ maar shay/, **Pierre Augustin Caron de** (1732–99) French dramatist. He wrote the comedies *The Barber of Seville* (1775) and *The Marriage of Figaro* (1784). These were made into operas by Gioacchino Rossini and Wolfgang Amadeus Mozart respectively. Born **Caron, Pierre Augustin**

beau monde /bṓ mónd/ *n* the part of society made up of the richest and most fashionable people [Late 17C. < French, 'beautiful world']

Beaumont /bṓ mont/, **Francis** (1584–1616) English dramatist. He cowrote plays with John Fletcher, including *Philaster* (1610?) and *A King and No King* (1611).

'All your better deeds / Shall be in water writ, but this in marble.'
[Francis Beaumont, *The Nice Valour*; 1616?]

Beaumont, William (1785–1853) US physician. His principal work was a study of the digestive system (1833).

'Of all the lessons which a young man entering upon the profession of medicine needs to learn, this is perhaps the first—that he should resist the fascination of doctrines and hypotheses till he has won the privilege of such studies by honest labor and faithful pursuit of real and useful knowledge.'
[William Beaumont, *Notebook*; 1833?]

Beaune /bōn/ town on the Bouzaise river at the heart of the Burgundy wine-producing region in east-central France. Population: 22,171 (1990).

~~**beaurocracy**~~ incorrect spelling of **bureaucracy**

beaut /byoot/ (*informal*) *n* a fine or impressive thing ■ *adj, interj ANZ* outstanding or first-rate [Mid-19C. Shortening of BEAUTY or BEAUTIFUL]

beauteous /byooti əss/ *adj* beautiful to look at (*literary*) —**beauteously** *adv* —**beauteousness** *n*

beautician /byoo tish'n/ *n* somebody trained to give beauty treatments such as manicures or facials

beautiful /byoo'təf'l/ *adj* **1.** very pleasing and impressive to look at, listen to, touch, smell, or taste **2.** very good or enjoyable —**beautifully** *adv* —**beautifulness** *n*

SYNONYMS See *good-looking*.

beautiful people *npl* **1.** HIGH SOCIETY rich fashionable people **2.** PEOPLE PARADING THEIR GOOD LOOKS people who like to show off their good looks **3.** HIPPIES in the 1960s, hippies collectively

beautify /byoo'ti fī/ (**-fies, -fying, -fied**) *vt* to make something pleasing and impressive to look at —**beautification** /byoo'tifi káysh'n/ *n* —**beautifier** *n*

beauty /byoo'ti/ (*plural* **-ties**) *n* **1.** PLEASING AND IMPRESSIVE QUALITIES OF SOMETHING the combination of qualities that make something pleasing and impressive to look at, listen to, touch, smell, or taste **2.** PLEASING PERSONAL APPEARANCE personal physical attractiveness, especially with regard to the use of cosmetics and other methods of enhancing it **3.** BEAUTIFUL WOMAN a beautiful woman or girl ○ *her reputation as a great beauty* **4.** FINE EXAMPLE something very good, attractive, or impressive of its kind ○ *Your new car is a real beauty.* **5.** EXCELLENT ASPECT an attractive, useful, or satisfying feature ○ *one of the beauties of working from home* [13C. Via Old French *bealte* < Vulgar Latin *bellitat-*< Latin *bellus* 'handsome, fine' < *bonus* 'good']

CULTURAL NOTE *Sleeping Beauty*, a ballet (1889) by Russian composer Peter Ilich Tchaikovsky. Based on Charles Perrault's fairy tale *La belle au bois dormant*, it tells the story of Princess Aurora, who is condemned to death by the wicked fairy Carabosse. Her sentence is

---

BEAUFORT SCALE

The Beaufort scale was devised in 1805 by Sir Francis Beaufort, a captain (later admiral) in the British Royal Navy, to measure the observable effects of wind force at sea. It was later adapted to include effects on land, and wind speed equivalents were officially incorporated in 1926.

Sailors and forecasters use the Beaufort scale as a standardized way to rate wind speed. Warnings of potentially dangerous conditions for people in small boats are usually issued at a rating of six on the scale. The Beaufort number is also referred to as a 'Force' number, for example, 'Force 10 Gale'.

Beaufort number	Wind speed km/h	Wind speed mph	Description
0	below 1	below 1	Calm
1	1 – 6	1 – 3	Light air
2	7 – 12	4 – 7	Light breeze
3	13 – 19	8 – 12	Gentle breeze
4	20 – 30	13 – 18	Moderate breeze
5	31 – 39	19 – 24	Fresh breeze
6	40 – 50	25 – 31	Strong breeze
7	51 – 62	32 – 38	Moderate gale
8	63 – 74	39 – 46	Fresh gale
9	75 – 87	47 – 54	Strong gale
10	88 – 102	55 – 63	Whole gale
11	103 – 117	64 – 72	Storm
12	above 118	above 73	Hurricane

---

commuted to a hundred years' sleep, from which she is eventually awakened by the handsome Prince Florimund.

beautybush /byóoti bòosh/ *n* a bush grown for its pink flowers and fruit with hairy knobbly skin. Native to: China. Latin name: *Kolkwitzia amabilis*.

beauty contest *n* 1. a competition for women in which a panel of judges decides who is the most beautiful of all the candidates. US term **beauty pageant** 2. same as **beauty parade** 3. *US* in the United States, a primary election in which the votes serve simply to indicate to the political parties which candidate is the most popular (*informal*)

beauty mark *n* N Am same as **beauty spot** (sense 2)

beauty pageant *n* same as **beauty contest**

beauty parade *n* a situation in which several organizations in turn compete in order to persuade another organization to use their services (*informal*)

beauty parlour *n* US same as **beauty salon**

beauty quark *n* QUANTUM PHYS same as **bottom quark**

beauty queen *n* a woman judged to be the most beautiful of all the candidates in a competition

beauty salon, beauty shop *n* UK, ANZ, Can a business establishment where beauty treatments are provided. US term **beauty parlor**

beauty sleep *n* deep restful sleep, especially before midnight, supposed to preserve youthful good looks (*informal*)

beauty spot *n* 1. POPULAR SCENIC PLACE a place that people often visit because of its pleasing scenery 2. SMALL NATURAL MARK ON FACE a mole or other small round mark on somebody's face 3. DOT WORN ON FACE a small black or brown dot of silk or makeup on somebody's face used to emphasize the skin's paleness or hide a blemish. Beauty spots were especially popular among aristocratic women in 18th-century Europe.

Simone de Beauvoir

Beauvoir /bo vwaar/, **Simone de** (1908–86) French writer. She wrote the feminist classic *The Second Sex* (1949) and the novel *The Mandarins* (1954). She was the lifelong companion of Jean-Paul Sartre.

'Man is defined as a human being and woman as a female—whenever she behaves as a human being she is said to imitate the male.'
[Simone de Beauvoir, *The Second Sex*; 1949]

beaux plural of **beau**

beaver

beaver[1] /beévər/ *n* 1. (*plural* **beavers** or *same*) FURRY FLAT-TAILED WATER ANIMAL a water rodent with a broad flat tail and webbed hind feet. Beavers fell trees to build dams and partially submerged dens called lodges. Native to: North America, Europe, Asia. Genus: *Castor*. 2. FUR FROM BEAVER the valuable fur of the beaver 3. MAN'S FUR HAT a man's hat made of beaver fur, felt, or a fabric imitating beaver fur 4. THICK FABRIC a thick woollen or cotton fabric 5. TABOO TERM a highly offensive term for a woman's outer sex organs and pubic hair (*taboo*) ■ *vi* (**-vers, -vering, -vered**) WORK HARD AND CONTINUOUSLY to work hard with unflagging energy and attention (*informal*) [Old English *beofor* < Indo-European, 'brown animal']

beaver[2] /beévər/ *n* the guard for the lower part of the face on a medieval helmet [15C. < French *baviere*, originally 'child's bib' < *baver* 'to slaver']

Beaver, Beaver Scout *n* a member of the most junior branch of the Scout Association, for boys and girls aged between six and eight

beaverboard /beévər bawrd/ *n* N Am a thick board made of compressed wood fibres. Use: ceilings, inner walls.

Beaverbrook /beévər brook/, **Max Aitken, 1st Baron** (1879–1964) Canadian-born British newspaper owner and politician. His news empire included the *Daily Express*, the *Sunday Express*, and the *Evening Standard*. Full name **William Maxwell Aitken**

Beaver Scout *n* YOUTH ORG same as **Beaver**

Bebel /báyb'l/, **August** (1840–1913) German politician. He helped to found the German social democratic movement (1869) and wrote on socialism and the status of women. Full name **Bebel, Ferdinand August**

'The nature of business is swindling.'
[Attributed to August Bebel]

bebop /bee bop/ *n* fast jazz music with complex harmonies and melodies. Charlie Parker was the most famous exponent of the style. [Mid-20C. An imitation of either the two-beat phrase of such music or the nonsense syllables of scat singing] —**bebopper** *n*

becalm /bi kaám/ (**-calms, -calming, -calmed**) *vt* 1. to cause a sailing ship to stop moving because of lack of wind (*usually passive*) 2. to bring peace and quiet to somebody

became past tense of **become**

because /bi kóz, -kəz/ *conj* 1. for the reason that follows ○ *I like her because she's always so friendly.* 2. on the basis of or taking into account what follows ○ *It must have been raining, because the path is wet.* [14C. < *by cause* 'for the reason (that)', after Old French *par chance*] ◇ **because of** indicating the reason or cause of something

USAGE because, as, for, or since? The conjunctions *since, because*, and *as* may be used at the beginning of a sentence, especially when the reason is already well known or when the reason is considered not as important as the main statement: *As you're only staying a little while, we'd better eat now. Because* puts a greater emphasis on the cause: *Because she was witty and lively, she was often invited to be the keynote speaker. Because* and *for* are both used to introduce reasons that justify a statement as distinct from giving a reason for it, though *for* is more literary in style: *You must have forgotten to invite them, because they didn't turn up. He blushed, for he knew he had been caught out. For* as a conjunction is never used at the beginning of a sentence. *As* can also be understood to mean 'at the time that' as well as 'because': *As Louise went back to work, Tony stayed behind to look after the baby.* In this case, it is better to avoid ambiguity and use either *because* or *while* as appropriate. Avoid using *being as* in place of *because* in formal writing: *They left late for the match, because* [not *being as*] *the car would not start.*

USAGE See *due* and *reason*.

béchamel sauce /báyshə mel-/ *n* a rich sauce made from milk thickened with butter and flour and served hot [Late 18C. After Louis, Marquis de *Béchamel* (1630–1703), steward to Louis XIV of France]

bêche-de-mer /bésh də máir/ (*plural* **bêches-de-mer** /*pronunc. same*/ or *same*) *n* MARINE BIOL same as **trepang** [Early 19C. < pseudo-French form of Portuguese *bicho do mar* 'sea cucumber']

Bechuanaland /béchoo aánə land/ former name for **Botswana**

beck[1] /bek/ *n* N England a stream, especially a mountain stream [13C. < Old Norse *bekkr* < Germanic]

beck[2] /bek/ *n* a nod, wave, or similar gesture to attract attention (*literary*) [14C. Shortening of BECKON] ◇ **at somebody's beck and call** always available and ready to carry out somebody's wishes

Beckenbauer /békən bow ər/, **Franz** (*b*. 1945) German footballer. An outstanding midfielder, he captained the West German World Cup championship team in 1974, and coached the national team to another World Cup win in 1990.

Becker /békər/, **Boris** (*b*. 1967) German tennis player. The youngest ever men's singles champion at Wimbledon (1985), he won again in 1986 and 1989.

'It's all about self-belief and a sense of proportion. I say to myself that the worst thing that I can do is lose a tennis match.'
[Boris Becker, *Daily Telegraph*; 4 November 1989]

becket /békit/ *n* a rope with a knot at one end and a small loop or hook at the other. Use: tying down loose equipment on a ship or boat. [Mid-18C. Origin ?]

Becket /békit/, **Thomas à, St** (1118?–70) English saint and martyr. He became Archbishop of Canterbury in 1162 and was assassinated by knights of Henry II. In 1155 he became the first Englishman to hold the office of Chancellor since the Norman Conquest. His strong views on religious prerogative brought him into conflict with Henry II.

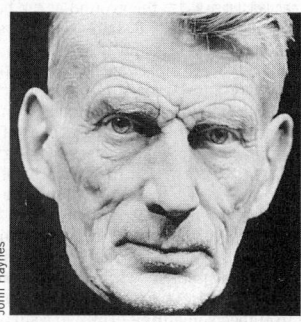

Samuel Beckett

Beckett /békit/, **Samuel** (1906–89) Irish-born writer. His bleak dramas of the absurd include *Waiting for Godot* (1952) and *Not I* (1973). He won a Nobel Prize in literature (1969). Beckett settled in Paris in 1937, and produced novels, plays, and poems in both English and French. Full name **Beckett, Samuel Barclay**

'We are all born mad. Some remain so.'
[Samuel Beckett, *Waiting for Godot*, Act I; 1952]

Beckford /békfərd/, **William** (1760–1844) British writer and art collector. Best known for his Gothic novel, *Vathek: An Arabian Tale* (1782; English version, 1786), he built a celebrated Gothic mansion at Fonthill Abbey (1816) in Wiltshire.

'He did not think...that it was necessary to make a hell of this world to enjoy paradise in the next.'
[William Beckford, *Vathek*; 1782]

Beckham /békəm/, **David** (*b*. 1975) British footballer. An outstanding midfielder and crosser of the ball, he played for Manchester United before moving to Real Madrid in 2003. He became captain of the English national team in 2000.

Beckmann /békmən/, **Max** (1884–1950) German painter. His expressionistic works captured the emotional climate of Germany after 1918.

beckon /békən/ (**-ons, -oning, -oned**) *vti* 1. to signal to somebody to approach with a movement of the hand or head 2. to be an attraction or temptation to somebody (*literary*) [Old English *bēcnan* < Germanic]

becloud /bi klówd/ (**-clouds, -clouding, -clouded**) *vt* (*literary*) 1. to cover or conceal something with cloud or mist 2. to make something confused or difficult to understand

become /bi kúm/ (**-comes, -coming, -came** /-káym/, **-come**) *v* 1. *vi* COME TO BE SOMETHING to change or develop into something ○ *The caterpillar will soon become a moth.* 2. *vt* SUIT SOMEBODY to suit the appearance or

personality of somebody ○ *That colour really becomes you.* **3.** *vt* **BE APPROPRIATE FOR SOMEBODY** to be an appropriate or socially acceptable thing for somebody to do or say (*formal*) [Old English *becuman* < Germanic]

becoming /bi kúmming/ *adj* **1.** attractively suitable for somebody's appearance **2.** appropriate or fitting for somebody —**becomingly** *adv* —**becomingness** *n*

~~**becouse**~~ incorrect spelling of **because**

becquerel /békə rel/ *n* the SI unit for measuring radioactivity, equal to the activity resulting from the decay of one nucleus of radioactive matter in one second. Symbol **Bq** [Late 19C. After Antoine Henri *Becquerel* (1852–1908), French physicist]

BECTU /bék too/ *abbr* Broadcasting, Entertainment, and Cinematograph Technicians Union

bed /bed/ *n* **1.** **FURNITURE ON WHICH TO SLEEP** a piece of furniture on which to sleep, usually consisting of a rectangular frame with a mattress on top **2.** **MATTRESS** a mattress, especially with its coverings **3.** **SLEEP** sleep or rest in bed, or the time for this ○ *time for bed* **4.** **PLACE FOR SLEEPING** a place in which to sleep, or an object on which to sleep ○ *looking for a bed for the night* **5.** **ACCOMMODATION FOR GUEST OR PATIENT** a place for one person to stay or sleep as a guest in a hotel or a patient in a hospital **6.** **PATCH OF SOIL** an area of soil prepared for plants, especially flowers, or an area where particular plants are growing ○ *a rose bed* **7.** **GROUND UNDER WATER** the ground at the bottom of the sea, a river, or a lake **8.** **STATE OF INTIMACY** the state of sexual intimacy associated with being in bed with somebody ○ *the marriage bed* **9.** CONSTR **SURFACE ON WHICH TO BUILD** a prepared surface on which something is built or laid, e.g. the foundation of a road or a railway **10.** COOK **LAYER OF FOOD** a layer of food on which another item of food is placed for serving **11.** FISHERIES **AREA OF WATER WITH SHELLFISH** an area of the sea, a river, or a lake, where a particular kind of shellfish is found or cultivated ○ *oyster beds* **12.** GEOL **LAYER OF ROCK** a layer of rock, normally sedimentary, that is generally homogeneous and was deposited more or less continuously without erosion ■ *v* (**beds, bedding, bedded**) **1.** *vt* **FIX SOMETHING INTO SURROUNDING SURFACE** to embed something firmly in a surrounding mass of a substance such as rock or concrete **2.** *vti* **FORM LAYER** to arrange something, or be arranged, in a layer or stratum **3.** *vt* **HAVE SEXUAL INTERCOURSE WITH SOMEBODY** to have sexual intercourse with somebody (*informal*) [Old English *bedd* < Germanic] ◇ **a bed of nails** an extremely difficult situation or existence ◇ **a bed of roses** an easy, comfortable situation or existence ◇ **get out of bed on the wrong side** to be in an irritable or angry mood right from the start of the day ◇ **go to bed with somebody** to have sexual intercourse with somebody ◇ **put something to bed** to finish work on a newspaper or magazine so it is ready to go to press

ORIGIN ***Bed*** meant both 'sleeping place' and 'garden plot' in Old English, and if the latter is the original sense, it could mean that the word comes ultimately from a prehistoric Germanic ancestor meaning 'dig' (which is also the ancestor of English *fossil*), and that the underlying notion of a ***bed*** was originally of a sleeping place dug or scraped in the ground, like an animal's lair.

bed down *v* **1.** *vi* **GO TO BED** to settle down somewhere, not usually in a proper bed, ready for sleep ○ *I'll bed down on the sofa.* **2.** *vt* **PUT SOMEBODY TO BED** to put a person to bed or an animal in a place with bedding for the night **3.** *vi* **SETTLE INTO POSITION** to sink and settle into position, or become flatter and denser

bed in *vti* to fit something firmly into place, or fit firmly into place

bed out *vt* to put young plants raised indoors into their final growing position outside

BEd /beé ed/ *abbr* EDUC Bachelor of Education

bed and board *n* accommodation and meals provided for somebody

bed and breakfast *n* **1.** **ROOM AND BREAKFAST** overnight accommodation and breakfast provided for paying guests **2.** **GUESTHOUSE** a small hotel or, more often, a private home that offers overnight accommodation and breakfast for paying guests ■ *adj* **INVOLVING SELLING THEN QUICK REACQUISITION** describes transactions involving selling shares late one day and buying them back for less the next morning, to create an apparent financial loss for tax purposes (*informal*)

bedaub /bi dáwb/ (**-daubs, -daubing, -daubed**) *vt* to smear a surface thickly or carelessly with something that spoils it or makes it dirty (*literary*)

bedazzle /bi dázz'l/ (**-zles, -zling, -zled**) *vt* (*literary*) **1.** to astonish somebody by being immediately impressive (*usually passive*) **2.** to make somebody temporarily unable to see by shining a bright light

bed bath *n UK* an all-over wash for somebody confined to bed. ANZ, N Am term **sponge bath**

bed-blocker *n* an elderly hospital patient who need not be treated in hospital but cannot return home to live independently —**bed-blocking** *n*

bedbug /béd bug/ *n* a small wingless bloodsucking insect that infests the bedding and furnishings of houses and the nests of animals. Family: Cimicidae.

bedchamber /béd chaymbər/ *n* same as **bedroom** (*archaic*)

bedclothes /béd klō<u>th</u>z, -klōz/ *npl* the sheets, blankets, duvet, and any other similar coverings on a bed

bedcover /béd kuvər/ *n* any of the coverings for a bed, e.g. a sheet or blanket

beddable /béddəb'l/ *adj* considered desirable enough to make a good sexual partner (*informal*)

bedder /béddər/ *n* **1.** GARDENING same as **bedding plant** **2.** at Cambridge University, somebody who cleans students' rooms

bedding /bédding/ *n* **1.** **BED COVERINGS** the mattress, pillows and coverings such as sheets, quilts, and blankets used to prepare a bed **2.** **SOMETHING USED AS BED** something used to make a bed **3.** **BED FOR ANIMALS** material such as straw put down for animals to lie on **4.** CONSTR **UNDER LAYER** a layer of material put down under something else, especially to serve as a foundation **5.** GEOL **ARRANGEMENT OF ROCK STRATA** the arrangement of a group of rock strata (**beds**) in an area or outcrop

bedding plant *n* a plant suitable for planting in a flower bed for one season's display

Bede /beed/, **St** (673?–735) English theologian and historian. He wrote many grammatical and historical works, including his *Ecclesiastical History of the English People* (completed in 731). Known as **the Venerable Bede**

> 'No reptile is found there [Ireland] nor could a serpent survive; for although serpents have often been brought from Britain, as soon as the ship approaches land they are affected by the scent of the air and quickly perish.'
> [Bede, *Ecclesiastical History*, 731]

bedeck /bi dék/ (**-decks, -decking, -decked**) *vt* to make something look pretty or festive, especially by decorating it with colourful ornaments ○ *trees bedecked with coloured lights*

bedevil /bi dévv'l/ (**-ils, -illing, -illed**) *vt* to be a continual source of problems or irritation to something or somebody —**bedevilment** *n*

bedew /bi dyoō/ (**-dews, -dewing, -dewed**) *vt* to wet or cover something with dew or drops of liquid (*literary*)

bedfellow /béd felō/ *n* **1.** somebody or something paired or allied with another person or thing **2.** somebody who shares a bed with somebody else (*archaic*)

Bedford /bédfərd/ market town on the River Ouse in Bedfordshire, south-central England. Population: 137,451 (1996 estimate).

Bedford cord *n* a heavy ribbed fabric like corduroy

Bedfordshire /bédfərdshər/ county in central England. Population: 381,572 (2001). Area: 1,235 sq. km/477 sq. mi.

bedhead /béd hed/ *n* the upper end of a bed, often with a headboard or rail

bed-hopping *n* casual sex with successive partners (*informal*)

bedim /bi dím/ (**-dims, -dimming, -dimmed**) *vt* (*literary*) **1.** to make the eyes or mind less able to perceive things clearly **2.** to make something appear less bright or distinct

bedizen /bi dīz'n, -dízz'n/ (**-zens, -zening, -zened**) *vt* to dress or decorate somebody or something in a way that seems exaggeratedly or vulgarly showy (*literary*) [Mid-17C. < BE- + *dizen* 'put flax onto a rod'] —**bedizenment** *n*

bed jacket *n* a woman's short light jacket worn over a nightdress when sitting up in bed

bedlam /bédləm/ *n* **1.** a place or situation full of noise, frenzied activity, and confusion **2.** same as **psychiatric hospital** (*archaic*; *sometimes offensive*) [15C. Alteration of BETHLEHEM]

bed linen *n* the sheets, pillowcases, and other fabric coverings that go on a bed

Bedlington terrier /bédlingtən-/, **Bedlington** *n* a dog belonging to a breed of English terriers that have a tapering head and fleecy coat that makes them look similar to lambs [Mid-19C. After a town in N England]

bed load *n* the loose sand and gravel carried by a stream at or just above its bed

Bedloe's Island /bédlōz-/ former name for **Liberty Island**

bed moulding *n* in classical architecture, the lowest section of a cornice, protruding less than the topmost part

Bedouin /béddoo in/ (*plural* **-ins** or *same*), **Beduin** *n* a nomadic Arab of the desert regions of Arabia and North Africa [15C. Via Old French *beduin* < Arabic *badw* 'desert, nomadic desert people'] —**Bedouin** *adj*

bedpan /béd pan/ *n* a shallow container into which a sick or frail person can urinate or defecate while lying in bed

bedplate /béd playt/ *n* a heavy metal base or platform to which the frame of an engine or machine is attached

bedpost /béd pōst/ *n* one of the posts at the corners of a bed, especially a four-poster bed

bedraggled /bi drágg'ld/ *adj* wet, dirty, and unkempt, or with hair or clothes in this state

bedrail /béd rayl/ *n* a rail at the head, foot, or side of a bed

bed rest *n* a period of time spent in bed in order to rest and recover when not well

bedridden /béd rid'n/ *adj* forced to remain in bed because of illness, weakness, or injury [14C. < Old English *bedrida* 'bed-rider']

bedrock /béd rok/ *n* **1.** the facts or principles on which something is based **2.** the solid rock beneath a layer of soil, rock fragments, or gravel

bedroll /béd rōl/ *n* a roll of bedding carried by somebody who is hiking or camping

bedroom /béd room, -rŏom/ *n* a room that has a bed in it and is used mainly for sleeping ■ *adj* involving, depicting, or suggesting sexual activity ○ *a bedroom comedy*

bedroom community *n N Am* same as **dormitory town**

bedroom eyes *npl* a look that seems to indicate a desire to have sex (*informal*)

beds *abbr* bedrooms (*used in advertisements*)

Beds. *abbr* Bedfordshire

bedside /béd sīd/ *n* the side of a bed, or the space next to a bed —**bedside** *adj*

bedside manner *n* a doctor's way of talking to and dealing with patients

bedsit /béd sit, béd sít/ *n* same as **bedsitter** (*informal*) [Mid-20C. Shortening]

bedsitter /béd sitər, -síttər/ *n* a combined bedroom and living room, especially one that is rented and serves as somebody's residence [*sitter* < SITTING ROOM]

bedsitting room *n* same as **bedsitter**

bedsock /béd sok/ *n* either of a pair of socks worn to keep the feet warm in bed

bedsore /béd sawr/ *n* an ulcer on the skin caused by pressure and friction from bedding when somebody is confined to bed for a long time

bedspread /béd spred/ *n* a decorative covering placed on top of bedclothes

bedstead /béd sted/ *n* the structural framework of a bed, excluding the mattress and coverings [Originally the place where a bed stood]

bed tea *n S Asia* morning tea served to a guest in bed

bedtime /béd tīm/ *n* the time when somebody normally goes to bed, or should go to bed

Beduin *n, adj* PEOPLES another spelling of **Bedouin**

bedwarmer /béd wawrmər/ *n* a covered metal container for hot coals, formerly used to warm a bed

bed-wetting *n* urination in bed during sleep, especially by a child —**bed-wetter** *n*

bee

bee /bee/ *n* **1.** a flying insect with a furry body that makes a buzzing sound as it flies. Some species of bees have stings, and some live in hives and produce honey. Superfamily: Apoidea. **2.** *N Am* a gathering at which people combine work or a friendly competition with socializing ○ *a sewing bee* [Old English *bēo* < Germanic] ◇ **have a bee in your bonnet about something** to be so interested in or concerned about something that you rarely stop thinking or talking about it

Beeb /beeb/ *n* the British Broadcasting Corporation (*informal humorous*) [Mid-20C. Shortening of the pronunciation of BBC]

bee balm *n* US same as **bergamot** (sense 4)

beebread /bee bred/ *n* a yellow-brown pollen stored by bees and mixed with honey as food for their larvae

beech /beech/ *n* **1.** a tall tree with smooth grey bark and glossy deciduous leaves. Native to: temperate regions. Genus: *Fagus*. **2.** the wood of the beech tree. Use: furniture. [Old English *bēce* < Germanic]

SPELLCHECK See *beach*.

Beecham /beechəm/, **Sir Thomas** (1879–1961) British conductor and impresario. He founded the London Philharmonic Orchestra (1932) and the Royal Philharmonic Orchestra (1946), and was musical director of Covent Garden (1932–39), London.

'The English may not like music—but they absolutely love the noise it makes.'
[Sir Thomas Beecham. Quoted in *The Wit of Music*, L. Ayre; 1966]

Beeching /beeching/, **Baron Richard** (1913–85) British engineer and administrator. As chairman of the British Railways Board (1963–65) he was responsible for the 'Beeching plan', which substantially reduced the rail network in the United Kingdom.

beech marten *n* ZOOL same as **stone marten** (sense 1)

beech mast *n* the hard fruit of a beech tree enclosed in a prickly case, especially when the fallen fruits form a covering on the ground

beechnut /beech nut/ *n* the small triangular hard edible fruit of a beech tree

beeda /beedə/ *n* a combination of betel leaf and betel nuts, eaten in some Asian countries after a meal to aid digestion [Mid-20C. < Hindi]

beedi *n* another spelling of **bidi**

bee-eater *n* a brightly coloured bird that eats flying insects, especially bees and wasps. Native to: Europe, Asia. Family: Meropidae.

beef /beef/ *n* **1.** MEAT FROM CATTLE meat from a cow, heifer, bull, or bullock **2.** (*plural* **beeves**) ANIMAL USED FOR BEEF a cow, heifer, bull, or bullock being reared for meat **3.** STRENGTH muscular strength or effort (*informal*) **4.** same as **complaint** (senses 1–2) (*slang*) ■ *vi* (**beefs, beefing, beefed**) same as **complain** (sense 1) (*slang*) [12C. Via Anglo-Norman *boef* < stem of Latin *bos* 'ox']

beef up *vt* to make something stronger or more effective (*informal*) ○ *beef up the article with some statistics* —**beefed-up** *adj*

beefalo /beefə lō/ (*plural* same or **-loes**) *n* a cross between the North American bison and domestic cattle that has high resistance to disease. Kept for: lean meat. [Late 20C. Blend of BEEF + BUFFALO]

beefburger /beef burgər/ *n* FOOD same as **hamburger** (senses 1, 3)

beefcake /beef kayk/ *n* a muscular man, considered from the point of view of physical appearance, or pictures of such men (*informal*) [After CHEESECAKE]

beefeater: a Yeoman of the Guard at the Tower of London, with Tower Bridge in the background

beefeater /beef eetər/ *n* one of the Yeomen of the Guard, a group who act as warders of the Tower of London wearing a uniform of Tudor dress

bee fly *n* a fly that resembles a bee, eats pollen and nectar, and whose larvae develop as parasites on insect larvae. Family: Bombyliidae.

beefsteak /beef stayk/ *n* a slice of lean beef that can be grilled or fried

beefsteak fungus, **beefsteak mushroom** *n* an edible bracket fungus with a large reddish cap that grows especially on oak and ash trees. Latin name: *Fistulina hepatica*.

beefsteak tomato *n* ANZ, *N Am* a large, firm-fleshed tomato. UK term **beef tomato**

beef stroganoff /beef strógga nof/ *n* a dish consisting of thin strips of sautéed beef cooked with onions and mushrooms in a sour cream sauce [After Count Paul Stroganoff, 19C Russian diplomat]

beef tea *n* a drink made by boiling beef to extract the juices, formerly given to invalids as a digestible form of nourishment

beef tomato *n* UK a large firm-fleshed tomato. ANZ, N Am term **beefsteak tomato**

beef Wellington *n* a dish consisting of a fillet of beef covered in pâté de foie gras, wrapped in pastry, and baked

beefwood /beef wŏod/ *n* **1.** the hard red wood of an Australian tree. Use: construction, cabinetmaking. **2.** an evergreen hardwood tree that is the source of beefwood. Native to: Australia. Genus: *Casuarina*.

beefy /beefi/ (**-ier, -iest**) *adj* **1.** MUSCULAR strong and muscular **2.** LIKE BEEF containing, produced by, or resembling beef **3.** POWERFUL having strength, power, or substance (*informal*) ○ *a novel with a really beefy plot* —**beefily** *adv* —**beefiness** *n*

beehive /bee hīv/ *n* **1.** HIVE FOR BEES a structure housing a colony of bees **2.** TALL HAIRSTYLE a hairstyle for women, popular around 1960, in which the hair is arranged in a high rounded shape on top of the head ■ *adj* BEEHIVE-SHAPED shaped like a beehive, with a round base rising in a cone to a domed top

Beehive *n* NZ the dome-shaped Parliament building in Wellington, New Zealand

beehive house *n* a round prehistoric house with a domed roof

beekeeper /bee keepər/ *n* somebody who keeps bees for honey or to pollinate crops —**beekeeping** *n*

beeline /bee līn/ *n* a very direct line, path, or other course from one point to another ○ *The kids made a beeline for the swimming pool as soon as we reached the motel.* [< the belief that bees return to their hives in a straight line]

Beelzebub /bi élzi bub/ *n* the devil, or one of the chief devils in hell [Pre-12C. Via Latin < Hebrew *ba'al zĕbūb* 'Lord of Flies', a Philistine god]

Beemer *n* CARS another spelling of **Beamer**

been past participle of **be**[1]

Beenleigh /beenli/ town in southeastern Queensland, Australia, south of Brisbane. Population: 16,387 (1991).

beento /been too, bíntoŏ/ (*plural* **-tos**) *n* W Africa somebody who has spent time in Europe or the United States

bee orchid *n* a European orchid. Flowers: resembling a bee on a flower. Latin name: *Ophrys apifera*.

beep /beep/ *n* SHORT HIGH NOISE a short high-pitched noise emitted as a signal by a piece of electronic equipment or the horn of a vehicle ■ *v* (**beeps, beeping, beeped**) **1.** *vti* MAKE BEEP to make a beep, or cause a vehicle horn or other device to make a beep **2.** *vt* SIGNAL WITH CAR HORN to signal to somebody by using the horn of a vehicle **3.** *vt* N Am PAGE SOMEBODY to try to contact somebody on his or her pager [Early 20C. An imitation of the sound]

beeper /beepər/ *n* COMMUNICATION same as **pager** (*informal*)

bee plant *n* any plant that is particularly attractive to bees

beer /beer/ *n* **1.** DRINK BREWED FROM MALT an alcoholic drink brewed by fermenting malt with sugar and yeast and flavouring it with hops **2.** QUANTITY OF BEER a drink or glass of beer **3.** HERBAL DRINK a fizzy or slightly fermented drink made from or flavoured with the roots, leaves, or seeds of a plant ○ *ginger beer* [Old English *bēor* < late Latin *biber* 'drink' < *bibere* 'to drink']

SPELLCHECK beer or bier? Do not confuse the spelling of *beer* and *bier*, which sound similar. *Beer* is a drink (as in *a glass of beer, ginger beer*), whereas a *bier* is a stand for a coffin.

beer and skittles *n* pleasure and amusement (*informal*)

beer belly *n* an extended stomach often associated with regularly drinking too much beer (*informal*)

Beerbohm /beer bōm/, **Sir Max** (1872–1956) British writer and caricaturist. He wrote *Zuleika Dobson* (1911), a satire on Oxford undergraduate life, and much drama criticism. He also drew witty caricatures of leading literary and political figures. Full name **Beerbohm, Sir Henry Maximilian**. Known as **the Incomparable Max**

'Great men are but life-sized. Most of them, indeed, are rather short.'
[Sir Max Beerbohm, *And Even Now*; 1921]

beer garden *n* an open space or garden, often attached to a pub or similar establishment, where beer and other alcoholic drinks can be purchased and drunk in the open air

beer gut *n* same as **beer belly** (*slang*)

beermat /beer mat/ *n* a small cardboard mat, often displaying brewery advertising, to be placed under a glass to protect a surface in a pub or restaurant

Beersheba /beer sheeba/ city on the edge of the Negev Desert, southwest of Jerusalem, Israel. In biblical times it was in the extreme southern part of Palestine. Population: 163,700 (1999).

beery /beeri/ (**-ier, -iest**) *adj* **1.** characteristic of somebody who is slightly inebriated from having drunk too much beer **2.** smelling or tasting of beer —**beerily** *adv* —**beeriness** *n*

beestings /beestingz/ *n* the first milk secreted by a mammal, especially a cow or goat, after it has given birth [Old English *bŷsting* < Germanic]

bee-stung *adj* full and rounded, as if stung by a bee (*informal*) ○ *bee-stung lips*

beeswax /beez waks/ *n* **1.** WAX MADE BY BEES the dark yellow substance secreted by honeybees and used for building honeycombs **2.** COMMERCIALLY PROCESSED BEESWAX wax produced by bees that has been commercially processed for use in furniture polishes, candles, and crayons ■ *vt* (**-waxes, -waxing, -waxed**) WAX SOMETHING to polish something with beeswax

beeswing /beez wing/ *n* a thin shiny sediment that forms in port and some other wines when they are kept for a long time after bottling

beet

beet /beet/ *n* **1.** a plant with a large swollen root. Use: as a vegetable, as animal feed, for sugar production. Genus: *Beta.* **2.** *N Am* PLANTS, FOOD same as **beetroot** [Old English *bēte* < Latin *beta*]

SPELLCHECK See *beat.*

Ludwig van Beethoven

AKG London

Beethoven /báyt hōvən/, **Ludwig van** (1770–1827) German composer. His symphonies and chamber pieces reached new levels of expressiveness, inspiring the Romantics. He composed 9 symphonies, 32 piano sonatas, and 16 string quartets, among many other works.

'I used to be able to make all my other circumstances subservient to my art. I admit, however, that by so doing I became a bit crazy.'
[Ludwig van Beethoven, *Letter*; February 1818]

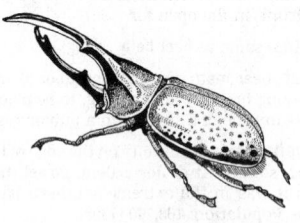

beetle

beetle[1] /beet'l/ *n* **1.** HARD-BACKED INSECT an insect belonging to a large order characterized by a modified outer pair of wings that form a hard covering for the inner pair. Order: Coleoptera. **2.** DICE GAME a game in which players attempt to draw or assemble a complete beetle-shape by throwing a dice and drawing in or collecting the part corresponding to the number thrown ■ *vi* (-tles, -tling, -tled) GO QUICKLY to go somewhere quickly (*informal*) [Old English *bitula, bitela* < *bītan* 'to bite']

beetle[2] /beet'l/ *n* **1.** LARGE MALLET a large tool with a long handle and a heavy wooden head. Use: driving in stakes, ramming, pounding. **2.** TEXTILE-FINISHING MACHINE a machine that beats cloth to give it a smooth finish ■ *vt* (-tles, -tling, -tled) FINISH CLOTH to give a finishing treatment to cloth with a beetle [Old English *bētel, bīetel* < Germanic]

beetle[3] /beet'l/ (*literary*) *vi* (-tles, -tling, -tled) to overhang or jut out ■ *adj* jutting out and bushy ○ *beetle brows* [14C. Origin ?] —**beetling** *adj*

beetle-browed *adj* having thick, bushy, or jutting eyebrows

beetle-crushers *npl* heavy thick-soled boots or shoes (*informal*)

beetle drive *n* a social gathering to play the game of beetle

Beeton /beet'n/, **Isabella Mary** (1836–65) British cookery writer. Her *Book of Household Management* (1861) is one of the most influential cookery books ever written. Born **Mayson, Isabella Mary.** Known as **Mrs Beeton**

beetroot /beet root/ *n* **1.** the dark red root of a beet plant, cooked and usually eaten cold as a salad vegetable or pickled **2.** a beet plant that produces beetroots. Latin name: *Beta vulgaris.* ▶ N Am term **beet**

beet sugar *n* sugar that has been extracted from sugar beet

beeves plural of **beef** *n* (sense 2)

BEF *n* the British Army that served overseas during World War I and World War II. Full form **British Expeditionary Force**

befall /bi fáwl/ (-falls, -falling, -fell /-fél/, -fallen /-fáwlən/) *vti* to happen, or happen to somebody, especially through the unexpected workings of chance or fate (*literary*)

befit /bi fít/ (-fits, -fitting, -fitted) *vt* to be suitable or appropriate for somebody or something —**befitting** *adj* —**befittingly** *adv*

befog /bi fóg/ (-fogs, -fogging, -fogged) *vt* (*literary*) **1.** to make somebody or something vague or confused **2.** to cover or hide something from view with fog

before /bi fáwr/ CORE MEANING: a grammatical word indicating that a point in time, event, or situation precedes another in a sequence ○ (prep) *We try all of the products before deciding to stock them.* ○ (conj) *We lost a lot of manufacturing jobs in the 12 years before I became president.* ○ (conj) *She died at the hospital before her parents could reach her side.* ○ (adv) *He has had this nightmare before.* **1.** *prep, conj, adv* EARLIER earlier than a date, time, or event **2.** *prep, conj* INDICATES SEQUENCE used to indicate a sequence of actions, one preceding the other and closely connected with it **3.** *prep* IN PRESENCE OF in the presence of a person or body of people ○ *spoke before a huge crowd* **4.** *prep* WITH MORE IMPORTANCE THAN indicating that one thing is preferable to or more important than another ○ *Their needs come before yours.* **5.** *prep* INDICATES LOCATION located close to something but just ahead of it **6.** *prep* AHEAD OF stretching ahead of somebody **7.** *adv* PREVIOUSLY on a previous occasion **8.** *conj* RATHER THAN used to indicate that somebody would prefer to do one thing rather than what he or she considers to be a worse thing ○ *I'll die before I'll tell you anything about it.* [Old English *beforan* < Germanic]

beforehand /bi fáwr hand/ *adv* used to indicate that a situation, action, or event happens ahead of time or in advance of something [13C. After Old French *avant main*]

befoul /bi fówl/ (-fouls, -fouling, -fouled) *vt* to make something dirty or impure, or diminish somebody or something's moral purity or reputation (*archaic or literary*) —**befoulment** *n*

befriend /bi frénd/ (-friends, -friending, -friended) *vt* to be friendly to somebody, especially to somebody who has no friends and needs help —**befriender** *n*

befuddle /bi fúdd'l/ (-dles, -dling, -dled) *vt* to make somebody confused or perplexed —**befuddled** *adj* —**befuddlement** *n*

beg /beg/ (begs, begging, begged) *v* **1.** *vti* ASK WITH EMOTION to ask somebody for something such as a favour in a heartfelt, humble, or even humiliating way ○ *begged them for forgiveness* ○ *I beg of you to stop.* **2.** *vti* ASK FOR CHARITY to ask people for gifts of money or food, especially in the street **3.** *vi* SIT UP AND ASK FOR FOOD to ask for food by sitting up and holding out the front legs (*refers to dogs*) **4.** *vt* EVADE MATTER to avoid answering or dealing with a point ○ *beg the question* [Probably < Old English *bedecian* < Germanic]

beg off *vi* to ask to be excused from doing something

begad /bi gád/ *interj* used to add emphasis to something that is said (*archaic*) [Late 16C. Alteration of *by God*]

began past tense of **begin**

beget /bi gét/ (-gets, -getting, -got /-gót/ or -gat /-gát/, -gotten /-gótt'n/ or -got) *vt* **1.** to be the cause of something **2.** to be the father of a child (*archaic*) [Old English *begietan* 'get' < Germanic] —**begetter** *n*

beggar /béggər/ *n* **1.** SOMEBODY WHO BEGS somebody who begs for money or food from strangers **2.** POOR PERSON a very poor person **3.** PERSON a person, often one regarded in a particular light (*informal*) ○ *You lucky beggar!* ■ *vt* (-gars, -garing, -gared) **1.** IMPOVERISH SOMEBODY to make somebody very poor (*literary*) **2.** BE BEYOND BELIEF to be so extraordinary as to be beyond description or belief ○ *a catastrophe that beggars description*

CULTURAL NOTE *The Beggar's Opera*, a ballad opera (1728) by John Gay with music selected and arranged by John Christopher Pepus. Set to traditional melodies, it tells of the relationship between highwayman Macheath and Polly Peachum, daughter of a gang leader. The work is at once a vivid depiction of London lowlife, a satire on political corruption, and a parody of fashionable Italian operas.

beggarly /béggərli/ *adj* insufficient and showing meanness —**beggarliness** *n*

beggar-my-neighbour *n* a simple card game for two players in which cards are won and lost until one person holds them all ■ *adj* involving a ruthless attitude towards another person, organization, or country, especially as regards taking over resources

beggar's lice (*plural same*), **beggar ticks** *n* **1.** PLANTS same as **bur marigold 2.** the burs of a beggar's lice plant

beggary /béggəri/ *n* a state of extreme poverty

~~begger~~ incorrect spelling of **beggar**

begging bowl *n* a bowl carried by somebody who begs for gifts of food or money

begging letter *n* a letter asking for money or help written to somebody who is rich or famous

begin /bi gín/ (-gins, -ginning, -gan /-gán/, -gun /-gún/) *v* **1.** *vti* START to do something that was not being done before ○ *People began to leave.* **2.** *vti* HAVE AS ITS STARTING POINT to have as its starting point, first action, or first part, or be the starting point or first part of something ○ *The story begins with a birthday party.* **3.** *vti* COME OR BRING INTO BEING to come into existence, or cause something to come into existence or take place ○ *The business began as a two-person operation.* **4.** *vt* UNDERTAKE SOMETHING FOR FIRST TIME to undertake, use, or give attention to something for the first time **5.** *vti* START TO SPEAK to start to say something, or start by saying something **6.** *vt* BE CAPABLE OF SOMETHING to be able to succeed in accomplishing a task (*used in negative statements*) ○ *The salary doesn't even begin to meet her expectations.* ○ *I couldn't begin to explain how awful it was.* [Old English *beginnan* < Germanic]

Begin /báygin/, **Menachem** (1913–92) Russian-born prime minister of Israel (1977–83). He shared the Nobel Peace Prize with Egyptian president Anwar al-Sadat (1978) and signed the first-ever Israeli treaty with an Arab state (1979). Full name **Begin, Menachem Wolfovitch**

'The life of every man who fights a just cause is a paradox...We fight, therefore we are.'
[Menachem Begin, *The Revolt*; 1948 and 1977]

~~begining~~ incorrect spelling of **beginning**

beginner /bi gínnər/ *n* somebody who has just started to learn or do something

SYNONYMS *beginner, apprentice, greenhorn, novice, tyro*

CORE MEANING: a person who has not acquired the necessary experience or skills to do something

beginner somebody who has just started to learn or do something ○ *classes for both beginners and advanced students* ○ *a course that teaches even complete beginners to skipper their own yachts* **apprentice** somebody who

is being taught the skills of a trade over an agreed period of time by somebody fully trained ○ *became an apprentice joiner* ○ *Local firms wouldn't take him on as an apprentice.* **greenhorn** somebody who lacks experience and may be naive or gullible ○ *You greenhorns don't understand the situation here at all.* **novice** somebody with no previous experience or skill in the activity undertaken ○ *a political novice with no diplomatic experience* ○ *special events for novice riders* **tyro** somebody who has just started to learn or do something ○ *sensible guidelines for the desktop publishing tyro*

beginner's luck *n* early success that seems inconsistent with somebody's lack of experience

beginning /bi gínning/ *n* **1.** FIRST PART the first part or early stages of something **2.** START the point in time or space at which something starts, comes into existence, or is first encountered ■ **beginnings** *npl* EARLY CONDITIONS the conditions in which something or somebody starts ■ *adj* NEW new to a job or activity ○ *beginning teachers*

begone /bi gón/ *interj* used to tell somebody to go away (*archaic*)

begonia /bi gṓni ə/ *n* a widely grown houseplant and garden plant with ragged-edged leaves. Flowers: round or drooping, brightly coloured. Genus: *Begonia*. [Mid-18C. < modern Latin, after Michel *Bégon*, (1638–1710), governor of French Canada]

begorra /bi górrə/ *interj Ireland* used as an exclamation or a mild oath (*dated*) [Mid-19C. Alteration of *by God*]

begot past participle, past tense of **beget**

begotten past participle of **beget**

begrime /bi grī́m/ (**-grimes, -griming, -grimed**) *vt* to cover something with grime

begrudge /bi grúj/ (**-grudges, -grudging, -grudged**) *vt* **1.** to resent the fact that somebody has something ○ *He's always begrudged me my success.* **2.** to be unwilling to give or pay something

begrudging /bi grújjing/ *adj* showing unwillingness to give somebody something or to let somebody be admired or praised —**begrudgingly** *adv*

beguile /bi gī́l/ (**-guiles, -guiling, -guiled**) *vt* **1.** CHARM SOMEBODY to win and hold somebody's attention, interest, or devotion **2.** DECEIVE SOMEBODY to mislead or deceive somebody (*literary*) **3.** CHEAT SOMEBODY to rob somebody of something, or cheat somebody out of something (*literary*) **4.** PASS TIME to pass time in a pleasant way (*literary*) —**beguilement** *n* —**beguiler** *n*

beguiling /bi gī́ling/ *adj* having the power to gain people's interest or devotion —**beguilingly** *adv*

beguine /bi geén/ *n* a ballroom dance similar to the rumba, originating in the Caribbean [Early 20C. < French *béguine* < *béguin* 'flirtation']

begum /báygəm, beé-/ *n* **1.** a title of respect for a woman in some Muslim communities **2.** a woman of high rank in some Muslim communities [Mid-17C. Via Urdu < East Turkic, 'my mistress']

begun past participle of **begin**

behalf /bi haáf/ [14C. Blend of *on his half* + *by half him*, both meaning 'on his side'] ◇ **on behalf of** *or* **on somebody's behalf 1.** as somebody's representative ○ *We chose James to speak on our behalf.* **2.** for somebody's benefit or support, or in somebody's best interests ○ *I thanked everyone on Jane's behalf.*

USAGE on somebody's behalf or **on somebody's part**: It is important to distinguish ***on somebody's behalf*** from ***on somebody's part*** (= as far as somebody is concerned): *This is a serious error on the part of [not: on behalf of] the minister.* Two participants are required for an action to be ***on somebody's behalf.*** In the United States, *in somebody's behalf* is also used, a use that is found in Shakespeare (*Be thou assured, good Cassio, I will do all my abilities in thy behalf*, *Othello* Act 3, scene 3), but this variant has virtually died out in British English.

Behan /beé ən/, **Brendan** (1923–64) Irish playwright and author. He wrote *The Quare Fellow* (1954), *The Hostage* (1958), and the autobiographical novel *Borstal Boy* (1958). Full name **Behan, Brendan Francis**

> 'When I came back to Dublin, I was court-martialled in my absence and sentenced to death in my absence, so I said they could shoot me in my absence.'
> [Brendan Behan, *The Hostage*; 1958]

behave /bi háyv/ (**-haves, -having, -haved**) *vi* **1.** ACT to act in a particular way that expresses general character, state of mind, or response to a situation or other people ○ *He's been behaving oddly.* **2.** BEHAVE WELL to act in an acceptable way, especially by being polite, good-tempered, and self-controlled ○ *children who won't behave* **3.** PERFORM to perform in or react to particular conditions or circumstances [15C. < BE- + HAVE in the obsolete sense 'conduct yourself']

behavior *n* US spelling of **behaviour**

behaviour /bi háyvyər/ *n* **1.** WAY SOMEBODY BEHAVES the way in which somebody behaves **2.** PSYCHOL RESPONSE the way in which a person, organism, or group responds to a specific set of conditions **3.** WHAT SOMETHING DOES the way that a machine operates or a substance reacts under a specific set of conditions [15C. < BEHAVE, after *haviour* 'possession' < Old French *aveir* 'have'] —**behavioural** *adj* —**behaviourally** *adv*

behavioural contagion *n* the spread of a type of behaviour first exhibited by a few people in a group to the group as a whole

behavioural medicine *n* the interdisciplinary study of behavioural, psychosocial, and biomedical knowledge relevant to the understanding of health and illness

behavioural psychology *n* a branch of psychology based on the observation and modification of the way that people behave

behavioural science *n* **1.** a science such as sociology, psychology, or anthropology that is concerned with the ways in which people or animals behave **2.** the use of scientific methods to study the behaviour of people or animals —**behavioural scientist** *n*

behaviourism /bi háyvyərizəm/ *n* **1.** an approach to the study of psychology that concentrates exclusively on observing, measuring, and modifying behaviour **2.** the theory that statements about the mind and mental states are really about actual or potential behaviour —**behaviourist** *adj, n* —**behaviouristic** /bi háyvyə rístik/ *adj*

behaviour modification *n* psychological treatment that attempts to change somebody's behaviour by rewarding new and desirable responses and making accustomed undesirable ones less attractive

behaviour therapy *n* a form of psychotherapy with the goal of observable changes in problem behaviour rather than changes in mental state

behead /bi héd/ (**-heads, -heading, -headed**) *vt* to cut the head off somebody or something, especially as a form of execution

beheld past participle, past tense of **behold**

behemoth /bi heé moth, bíhi məth/ *n* **1.** something that is enormously big or powerful **2.** *also* **Behemoth** in the Bible, a huge beast usually thought to be a hippopotamus (Job 40:15) [14C. < Hebrew *bĕhēmōt* < *bĕhēmāh* 'beast']

behest /bi hést/ *n* an order or request (*literary*) ○ *arrived at the conference only at her behest* [Alteration of Old English *behǣs* < Germanic, 'to bid, call']

behind /bi hī́nd/ CORE MEANING: a grammatical word indicating that somebody or something is in or is going towards a position at the back or rear of something ○ (prep) *From behind the door we heard country music.* ○ (prep) *She was behind the wheel, and I was in the back.* ○ (adv) *Their car was hit from behind.* ○ (adv) *She had to go back because she'd left her money behind.*

1. *prep, adv* AT BACK OF in or towards a position farther back or at the rear of something **2.** *prep, adv* FOLLOWING following somebody or something **3.** *adv* IN DEBT in debt, or in arrears on a payment ○ *months behind on the payments* **4.** *adv* REMAINING used to indicate that somebody or something is left after another's departure ○ *was left behind* **5.** *prep* IN PAST indicates that an achievement or experience happened in the past ○ *My best days are behind me.* **6.** *prep* LATER THAN indicates that something is not as far advanced as it should be ○ *seven weeks behind schedule* **7.** *prep* CAUSING SOMETHING causing or being responsible for something ○ *the reason behind it* **8.** *prep* SUPPORTING SOMEBODY backing or supporting somebody ○ *I'm behind you all the way on this issue.* **9.** *prep* UNDERNEATH underneath the external appearance of somebody or something ○ *Behind his calm exterior, he was very confused.* **10.** *n* BUTTOCKS somebody's buttocks (*informal*) **11.** *n* ONE POINT SCORED in Australian Rules, a single point scored as a result of the ball being kicked between the goal post and the behind post, hit against a goal post, or punched or handled over the goal line [Old English *behindan* < *hindan* 'from behind' < Germanic] ◇ **get behind somebody** *or* **something** to give somebody or something strong support ○ *The whole community needs to get behind this airport protest.* ◇ **put something behind you** to ensure that something unpleasant can no longer affect you detrimentally

behindhand /bi hī́nd hand/ *adj* **1.** BEHIND SCHEDULE not as well advanced as planned or expected **2.** LAGGING BEHIND behind in development or achievement compared to others **3.** FIN IN ARREARS in arrears for payment of a debt [Mid-16C. After BEFOREHAND]

behind line *n* in Australian Rules football, the line between the goal and the behind posts

behind post *n* in Australian Rules football, either of two posts situated on either side of the taller goal posts

behind-the-scenes *adj* carried out privately or secretly ○ *a lot of frantic behind-the-scenes negotiation*

Behn /ben/, **Aphra** (1640–89) English writer. The first professional woman writer in England, she wrote poems, plays, and the early novel *Oroonoko* (1688?). Born **Amis, Aphra**

> 'Who is't that to women's beauty would submit, / And yet refuse the fetters of their wit?'
> [Aphra Behn, *The Forced Marriage*; 1670]

behold /bi hṓld/ (**-holds, -holding, -held** /-héld/) *vt* to see or observe something or somebody (*archaic or literary; often used in commands*) ○ *'Behold her, single in the field, Yon solitary Highland lass!'* (William Wordsworth, *The Solitary Reaper*) [Old English *bihaldan* < Germanic, 'watch, guard'] —**beholder** *n*

beholden /bi hṓld'n/ *adj* under an obligation to somebody because of something helpful that person has done [14C. Originally past participle of BEHOLD, in the obsolete sense 'hold under obligation']

behoove /bi hóov/ (**-hooves, -hooving, -hooved**) *vt US* same as **behove**

behove /bi hṓv/ (**-hoves, -hoving, -hoved**) *vt* to be right and proper or appropriate for somebody (*formal*) ○ *It ill behoves him to complain.* [Old English *behōfian* 'to need']

Behrens /báirənz/, **Peter** (1868–1940) German architect and designer. He applied the principles of industrial design to all aspects of his work, and influenced Le Corbusier and Walter Gropius.

Behring /báiring/, **Emil von** (1854–1917) German bacteriologist. He developed serum therapy against tetanus and diphtheria (1890) and won the first Nobel Prize in physiology or medicine (1901). Full name **Behring, Emil Adolph von**

Beiderbecke /bī́dər bek/, **Bix** (1903–31) US jazz cornetist, pianist, and composer. He was one of the major jazz musicians of his generation. Born **Beiderbecke, Leon Bismarck**

beige /bayzh/ *adj* VERY PALE BROWN of a very pale brown colour with a tinge of yellow or pink ■ *n* **1.** BEIGE COLOUR a very pale brown colour with a tinge of yellow or pink **2.** TEXTILES UNDYED WOOLLEN CLOTH cloth made of undyed or unbleached wool [Mid-19C. < French, perhaps < late Latin *bombax* 'cotton']

Beijing /báy jíng/ national capital of China as well as a cultural, administrative, and educational centre. It is situated in the northeastern part of the country, northwest of the Bo Hai Gulf. Population: 11,300,000 (1995). Former name **Peking**

being /beé ing/ present participle of **be**[1] ■ *n* **1.** PERSON a human individual **2.** EXISTENCE the state of existing ○ *the turbulent years during which the new nation came into being* **3.** ESSENTIAL NATURE somebody's essential nature or character ○ *loved the child with all her being* **4.** LIVING THING a living thing, especially one conceived of as supernatural or not living on Earth

Beira /bī́rə/ port and capital of Sofala Province, eastern Mozambique, on the Mozambique Channel. Population: 299,300 (1990).

Beirut /bay róot/ capital, port, and largest city in

Lebanon, situated on the Mediterranean Sea. Population: 1,500,000 (1998 estimate).

bejabers /bi jáybərz/ *interj, n Ireland* same as **bejasus** [Early 19C. Alteration of *by Jesus*]

Béjart /báy zhaar/, **Maurice** (*b.* 1927) French dancer and choreographer known for his expressionist fusion of modern dance, ballet, and acrobatics. Born **Berger, Maurice Jean de**

bejasus /bi jáyzəss/, **bejesus** /-jéezəss, -jáyzəss/ *Ireland interj* used as an exclamation or a mild oath ■ *n* used to emphasize a statement or question [Early 20C. Alteration of *by Jesus*]

bejewel /bi jóo əl/ (**-els**, **-elling**, **-elled**) *vt* to decorate something lavishly with jewels or colourful decorative objects —**bejewelled** *adj*

Bekaa Valley /bi kaá/, **Bekáa Valley** valley in Lebanon, east of Beirut, running down the centre of the country between the Lebanon and Anti-Lebanon mountains. Length: 160 km/99 mi.

bel /bel/ *n* a logarithmic unit for comparing the loudness or strength of signals, equal to 10 decibels [Early 20C. After Alexander Graham BELL]

belabor *vt US* spelling of **belabour**

belabour /bi láybər/ (**-bours**, **-bouring**, **-boured**) *vt* **1.** HARP ON SOMETHING to repeat or discuss something unnecessarily or at too great a length **2.** CRITICIZE SOMEBODY to subject somebody to a sustained verbal or literary attack (*literary*) **3.** BEAT SOMEBODY to hit somebody hard and repeatedly with something (*literary or humorous*)

Belarus

Belarus /bélla róoss, byéllə-/ country in eastern Europe. It became an independent nation after the dissolution of the former Soviet Union in 1991. Language: Belarusian, Russian. Currency: Belarusian rouble. Capital: Minsk. Population: 10,322,151 (2003). Area: 207,595 sq. km/80,153 sq. mi. Official name **Republic of Belarus**

Belarusian /bélla rúsh'n/ *n* **1.** somebody who comes from Belarus **2.** the official language of the Republic of Belarus, belonging to the East Slavonic group of Indo-European languages. Native speakers: 11 million. —**Belarusian** *adj*

belated /bi láytid/ *adj* occurring after the appropriate or expected time, especially too late to be effective or useful [Early 17C. < *belate* 'make late, delay'] —**belatedly** *adv* —**belatedness** *n*

Belau ♦ Palau

belay /bi láy/ *vti* (**-lays**, **-laying**, **-layed**) **1.** NAUT FASTEN LINE ON SHIP to fasten a rope or line to a securing point on a ship or boat **2.** CLIMBING SECURE ROPE to fasten or control the rope to which a climber is attached by wrapping it round a metal device or another person **3.** NAUT STOP to stop doing something, or not follow an earlier instruction (*used as a command*) ■ *n* CLIMBING **1.** SECURING OF CLIMBER'S ROPE the fastening or controlling of a climber's rope by wrapping it around a metal device or another person, or the method by which this is done **2.** FASTENING POINT the point to which a climber's rope is fastened [Old English *belecgan* 'surround' < Germanic]

belaying pin /bi láying-/ *n* a large wooden or metal pin that fits into a hole in a rail on a ship or boat and to which a rope can be fastened

bel canto /bel kántō/ *n* **1.** a style of operatic singing that concentrates on producing a pure and even tone. It was developed in Italy in the 17th and 18th centuries. **2.** a style of expressive melodic instrumental playing that uses the principles of bel canto singing [Late 19C. < Italian, 'fine song']

belch /belch/ (**belches**, **belching**, **belched**) *vti* **1.** to let gas from the stomach out through the mouth, making a loud noise in the throat **2.** to send out large amounts of steam, smoke, or gas, or come out of something in a thick cloud ○ *chimneys belching smoke* [Old English *bealcettan*, *bælcan*, perhaps < Germanic] —**belch** *n*

beleaguer /bi léegər/ (**-guers**, **-guering**, **-guered**) *vt* (*usually passive*) **1.** to make somebody feel harassed, hemmed in, or under severe pressure **2.** to surround somebody or something with an army [Late 16C. < Dutch *belegeren* 'camp around, besiege'] —**beleaguerment** *n*

~~beleif~~ incorrect spelling of **belief**

~~beleive~~ incorrect spelling of **believe**

Belém /bə lém/ port and capital of Pará State on the Pará River in northern Brazil. Population: 1,144,312 (1996).

belemnite /bélləm nīt/ *n* a fossilized cylinder-shaped internal shell of an extinct order of cephalopods common in the Mesozoic era [Early 17C. < modern Latin < Greek *belemnon* 'a dart'; from its shape]

bel esprit /bél ess preé/ (*plural* **beaux esprits** /bōz es preé/) *n* a witty, intelligent, and cultured person (*archaic*) [Mid-17C. < French, 'fine mind']

Belfast /bél faast, bel faást/ port and capital of Northern Ireland, located at the head of Belfast Lough on the Lagan River. Population: 277,391 (2001).

Belfast roof *n* a wooden bow-string girder that is made of short lengths of timber but is able to span a length of up to 30 m/100 ft

belfry

belfry /bélfri/ (*plural* **-fries**) *n* **1.** the part of a church steeple or a tower in which bells are hung **2.** a tower on a building, in which a bell or bells are hung [13C. < Old French *berfrei* 'movable siege tower', by association with BELL[1]] —**belfried** *adj*

Belgae /bél zhi, bél gī/ *npl* an ancient Celtic people who lived in northern Gaul and parts of southern England [Early 17C. < Latin]

Belgaum /bel gówm/ city in northern Karnataka State, southwestern India. Population: 506,235 (2001).

Belgian /béljən/ *n* SOMEBODY FROM BELGIUM somebody who comes from Belgium ■ *adj* **1.** OF BELGIUM relating to Belgium, or its people, languages, or cultures **2.** OF FLEMISH OR WALLOON relating to the Flemish or Walloon languages

Belgian Congo former name for **Congo, Democratic Republic of the**

Belgian hare *n* a domestic rabbit belonging to a breed with reddish-brown fur and long legs and ears

Belgium

Belgium /béljəm/ country in northwestern Europe, bordering the North Sea. It became independent in 1830. Language: Flemish, French, German. Currency: Euro. Capital: Brussels. Population: 10,289,088 (2003). Area: 30,528 sq. km/11,787 sq. mi. Official name **Kingdom of Belgium**

Belgrade /bél grayd/ capital of Yugoslavia and the Republic of Serbia that forms part of Yugoslavia. It is situated at the junction of the Danube and Sava rivers. Population: 1,594,483 (1998).

Belgrano /bel graáno/, **Manuel** (1770–1820) Argentine general and diplomat. He led Argentine troops in revolt against Spanish rule, winning major battles (1812 and 1813).

beli /bə leé/ (**-lies**, **-liing**, **-lied**) *vti Malaysia* same as **buy** *v* (sense 1) (*informal; usually used without inflections*) [< Malay]

Belial /beéli əl/ *n* in the Bible, a personification of wickedness or worthlessness, often thought of as a devil or demon [13C. < Hebrew *beliyya'al* 'worthlessness']

belie /bi lí/ (**-lies**, **-lying**, **-lied**) *vt* **1.** to disguise the true nature of something **2.** to show that something is not true or real ○ *The evidence belies the testimony of the witness.* [Old English *belēogan* < Germanic]

belief /bi leéf/ *n* **1.** ACCEPTANCE OF TRUTH OF SOMETHING acceptance by the mind that something is true or real, often underpinned by an emotional or spiritual sense of certainty ○ *belief in an afterlife* **2.** TRUST confidence that somebody or something is good or will be effective ○ *belief in democracy* **3.** SOMETHING THAT SOMEBODY BELIEVES IN a statement, principle, or doctrine that a person or group accepts as true **4.** OPINION an opinion, especially a firm and considered one **5.** RELIGIOUS FAITH faith in God or in a religion's gods [12C. Alteration of Old English *gelēafa* after BELIEVE]

belief system *n* **1.** a set of beliefs, especially religious or political beliefs, that form a unified system **2.** a collection and organization of beliefs prevalent in a community or society

believable /bi leévəb'l/ *adj* seeming to be true or authentic, and capable of being believed or believed in —**believability** /bi leévə bílləti/ *n* —**believably** *adv*

believe /bi leév/ (**-lieves**, **-lieving**, **-lieved**) *v* **1.** *vt* ACCEPT SOMETHING AS TRUE to accept that something is true or real ○ *I don't know which story to believe.* **2.** *vt* ACCEPT SOMEBODY AS TRUTHFUL to accept that somebody is telling the truth ○ *Nobody will believe you!* ○ *I don't believe him.* **3.** *vt* CREDIT SOMEBODY WITH SOMETHING to accept that somebody or something has a particular quality or ability ○ *No one believed her capable of such a malicious remark.* **4.** *vi* THINK THAT SOMETHING EXISTS to be of the opinion that something exists or is a reality, especially when there is no absolute proof of its existence or reality ○ *believe in reincarnation* **5.** *vi* HAVE TRUST to be confident that somebody or something is worthwhile or effective ○ *We all believe in you.* **6.** *vi* THINK SOMETHING IS GOOD to be of the opinion that something is right or beneficial and, usually, to act in accordance with that belief ○ *believed strongly in freedom of expression* **7.** *vi* HAVE RELIGIOUS FAITH to have a belief in God or in a religion's gods [Old English *belyfan*, alteration of *gelēfan* < Germanic, 'to love, trust'] —**believer** *n* ◇ **make believe** to pretend, especially in play

~~beligerent~~ incorrect spelling of **belligerent**

Belinda /bə líndə/ *n* a small natural satellite of Uranus, discovered in 1986 by the Voyager 2 planetary probe

Belisha beacon /bə leéshə-/ *n* a sign at each end of a zebra crossing consisting of an amber ball with a flashing light inside it on top of a black-and-white-striped pole [Mid-20C. After Leslie Hore-*Belisha* (1895–1957), British Minister of Transport]

belittle /bi lítt'l/ (**-tles**, **-tling**, **-tled**) *vt* to reduce or dismiss the importance or quality of somebody or something ○ *I don't want to belittle her achievement.* —**belittlement** *n* —**belittler** *n* —**belittlingly** *adv*

Belize /be leéz, bə-/ country in Central America on the Caribbean Sea, bordered to the west by Mexico and Guatemala. It became a British crown colony in 1862 and an independent member of the Commonwealth in 1981. Language: English, Spanish. Currency: Belizean dollar. Capital: Belmopan. Population: 266,440 (2003). Area: 22,965 sq. km/8,867 sq. mi. See map on next page. Former name **British Honduras** (until 1973) —**Belizean** /be leézh'n, bə-/ *n, adj*

Belize

Belize City city and the main port of Belize on the Caribbean Sea. It was the capital of British Honduras between 1884 and 1972. Population: 53,915 (1997).

Belkic /bélkich/, **Beriz** (b. 1946) Bosniac representative of the presidency of Bosnia and Herzegovina (2001–02) which rotates between a Serb, a Bosnian Muslim, and a Croat

bell[1] /bel/ n **1. OBJECT WITH RINGING SOUND** a hollow open-ended metal instrument with a rounded top that produces a ringing sound when struck. Bells are traditionally used as summonses and signals. **2. ELECTRICAL DEVICE PRODUCING SOUND** a device activated by electricity that produces a ringing or buzzing signal **3. SOMETHING BELL-SHAPED** something with the curved and open-ended shape of a bell, especially a flower **4. MUSIC FLARED END OF WIND INSTRUMENT** the flared end of a wind instrument, from which the sound emerges **5. NAUT DURATION OF SHIP'S WATCH** the time during a watch on a ship, indicated by rings on a bell, one ring for each half hour that has passed ■ **bells** npl MUSIC PERCUSSION INSTRUMENT a percussion instrument consisting of metal tubes or bars hung from a frame that give out a ringing sound when struck ■ vti (**bells, belling, belled**) BECOME OR MAKE WIDER to open out, or open something out, into a curved or flared shape similar to that of a bell [Old English belle < Germanic] ◇ **give somebody a bell** to call somebody on the telephone (informal) ◇ **ring a bell** to evoke a vague memory of something or somebody (informal) ○ Her name doesn't ring a bell. ○ That name doesn't ring a bell with me.

CULTURAL NOTE For Whom the Bell Tolls, a novel (1940) by US writer Ernest Hemingway. Widely viewed as Hemingway's most ambitious work, it is set during the Spanish Civil War and tells the story of Robert Jordan, a US volunteer fighting for the Republicans, who falls in love with a fellow volunteer called Maria. It was made into a film by Sam Woods in 1943.

CULTURAL NOTE Five Bells, a long poem (1939) by Australian poet Kenneth Slessor. This meditation on time and the fragility of human existence is cast as an elegy for Joe Lynch, a friend of the author who drowned in Sydney Harbour.

bell[2] /bel/ n a bellowing sound made by a rutting stag or by a hunting dog during the chase ■ vi (**bells, belling, belled**) to make a bellowing sound [Old English bellan < Germanic]

Bell /bel/, **Alexander Graham** (1847–1922) Scottish-born US inventor and educator. He made the first intelligible telephonic transmission (1876), patented the telephone (1876), and founded the Bell Telephone Company (1877). Among his numerous other inventions were wax cylinder recordings (1886) and the hydrofoil (1917).

Bell, **Sir Francis Henry Dillon** (1851–1936) New Zealand lawyer and politician. He was a Reform Party politician and was briefly prime minister of New Zealand (1925). See table at **prime minister**

Bell, **Gertrude** (1868–1926) British archaeologist and traveller. She travelled extensively in Southwest Asia and left money to found the British Institute of Archaeology in Iraq. Full name **Bell, Gertrude Margaret Lowthian**

Bell, **Vanessa** (1879–1961) British painter and designer. One of the leading British artists to experiment with postimpressionism, she was also a prominent member of the Bloomsbury Group. and the sister of Virginia Woolf. Born **Stephen, Vanessa**

Bella ♦ Ben Bella, Ahmed

belladonna /béllə dónnə/ n **1.** a drug made from deadly nightshade, e.g. atropine **2.** ANZ, N Am an extremely poisonous plant with small black berries, from which belladonna is obtained. Native to: Europe, Asia. Latin name: Atropa belladonna. UK term **deadly nightshade** [Mid-18C. Via modern Latin < Italian, 'beautiful lady'; from the use of belladonna to dilate the pupils]

belladonna lily n PLANTS same as **amaryllis** (sense 1)

bellarmine /béll aar meen/ n a large earthenware or stoneware jug decorated with a bearded face [Mid-17C. After St Robert Bellarmin (1542–1621), Jesuit cardinal]

Bell Bay bay on the northern coast of Tasmania, Australia, beside George Town

bellbird /bél burd/ n a bird with a call that sounds like a bell. Native to: tropical America, Australasia. Genera: Procnias or Oreoica or Anthornis.

bell-bottom trousers, **bell-bottoms** npl trousers that widen below the knees into a bell shape

bellboy /bél boy/ n a man working in a hotel as a porter or page. N Am term **bellhop**

bell buoy n a floating buoy with a bell on top that is rung by the movement of the waves and gives a warning or positional signal to shipping

bell crank n a lever with two arms that share a fulcrum at the point where they join

belle /bel/ n **1.** a beautiful woman **2.** a woman considered to be the most conspicuously good-looking of all those living in a place or attending a social event [Early 17C. < French, 'beautiful']

Belleek ware /bə leék-/, **Belleek** n very thin, typically cream-coloured porcelain with a lustrous glaze [Mid-19C. After a town in N Ireland]

belle époque /bél ay pók/ n an era of cultural refinement, social elegance, and general prosperity and security, especially the last decades of the 19th century and the early years of the 20th prior to World War I [Mid-20C. < French, 'fine period']

Bellerophon /bə lérrəfən/ n in Greek mythology, a hero who tamed the winged horse Pegasus and slew the fire-breathing monster Chimera

belles-lettres /bél léttrə/ n writings that are valued for their elegance and aesthetic qualities rather than for any human interest or moral or instructive content (takes a singular or plural verb) [Mid-17C. < French, 'fine letters'] —**belletrism** /-léttrizəm/ n —**belletrist** /-léttrist/ n

bellflower /bél flowər/ n PLANTS same as **campanula**

bellfoundry /bél fowndri/ (plural -ries) n a foundry that specializes in making bells

bell glass n CHEM same as **bell jar** (sense 2)

bell heather n a heather with deep reddish-purple, bell-shaped flowers. Native to: Europe. Latin name: Erica cineria.

bellhop /bél hop/ n N Am same as **bellboy**

bellicose /béllikōss/ adj ready or inclined to quarrel, fight, or go to war [15C. < Latin bellicosus < bellum 'war'] —**bellicosity** /bélli kóssəti/ n

belligerence /bə líjjərənss/ n the quality of being hostile, ready to start a fight, or ready to go to war

belligerency /bə líjjərənssi/ n **1.** same as **belligerence** **2.** the state of being at war

belligerent /bə líjjərənt/ adj **1. HOSTILE OR AGGRESSIVE** hostile, ready to start a fight, or ready to go to war **2. ENGAGED IN WAR** taking part in warfare, especially in a war recognized by the law of nations **3. OF BELLIGERENT NATION** relating to or characteristic of a participant in war or a fight ■ n **PARTICIPANT IN WAR** a participant in war or a fight, especially a nation engaged in a war recognized by the law of nations [Late 16C. < Latin belligerant-, present participle of belligerare 'wage war' < belliger 'carrying on war' < bellum 'war' + gerere 'carry on'] —**belligerently** adv

Bellingshausen /béllingz howz'n/, **Fabian Gottlieb von** (1778–1852) Russian explorer. He explored an area of the Antarctic Sea (1819–21) that was later named after him.

Bellingshausen Sea predominantly ice-covered sea constituting part of the southern Pacific Ocean, off the coast of Antarctica

Bellini /be leéni/, **Gentile** (1429?–1507) Italian painter. The son of Jacopo Bellini and brother of Giovanni Bellini, he is best known for his portraits and for his large-scale narrative paintings.

Bellini, **Giovanni** (1430?–1516) Italian painter. The son of Jacopo Bellini, he produced calm yet sensuous religious pictures, combining figures and landscape in naturalistic light.

Bellini, **Jacopo** (1400?–70?) Italian painter. He produced stylized paintings and drawings with strong architectural elements.

Bellini, **Vincenzo** (1801–35) Italian composer. His best-known works are the operas La Sonnambula (1831) and Norma (1831).

bell jar n **1.** a glass cover, shaped like a bell, used to protect and display delicate items **2.** a bell-shaped glass cover used to enclose equipment in experiments and prevent gases from escaping or entering

bell-magpie n BIRDS same as **currawong** [< its call]

bellman /bélmən/ (plural **-men** /-mən, -men/) n a man who rings a bell, especially a town crier

bell metal n an alloy of copper with 20 to 25 per cent tin. Use: to cast bells and plain bearings.

Belloc /béllok/, **Hilaire** (1870–1953) French-born British writer. He wrote Cautionary Tales for Children (1907) and biographies of historical figures including Napoleon (1932). He was a leading Roman Catholic and Liberal Member of Parliament (1906–10). Full name **Belloc, Joseph Hilaire Pierre**

> 'Lord Finchley tried to mend the Electric Light / Himself. It struck him dead: And serve him right! / It is the business of the wealthy man / To give employment to the artisan.'
> [Hilaire Belloc, 'Lord Finchley', More Peers; 1911]

bellow /béllō/ (**-lows, -lowing, -lowed**) v **1.** vti to shout something in a loud deep voice **2.** vi to give a bull's loud deep roar or a roar like that of a bull [14C. Origin ?] —**bellow** n —**bellower** n

Bellow /béllō/, **Saul** (b. 1915) Canadian-born US writer. His novel Humboldt's Gift (1975) won the Pulitzer Prize. He won the Nobel Prize in literature (1976).

> 'Socially, psychologically, politically, the very essence of human institutions was an extract of what we assumed about death.'
> [Saul Bellow, Humboldt's Gift; 1975]

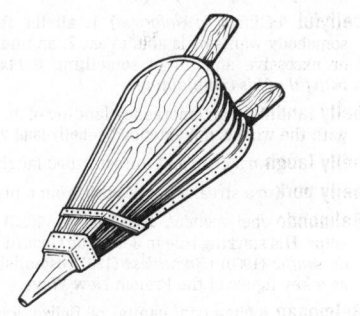

bellows

bellows /béllōz/ (plural same) n **1.** a device or piece of equipment with a chamber that can be expanded to draw air in and compressed to force the air out **2.** something constructed of a pleated material and able to be expanded and contracted, e.g. the part enclosing the lenses on some cameras or photographic enlargers [12C. Probably < Old English belga, shortening of blǣstbelig 'blowing bag']

bell pepper n N Am FOOD same as **sweet pepper** [< its shape]

bell pull n a handle or cord that when pulled makes a bell ring

bell push n a button that when pressed causes an electric bell to ring

bell-ringer n **1.** somebody who rings church bells as an ecclesiastical function or a hobby **2.** a musician who plays handbells —**bell-ringing** n

bells and whistles *npl* special features that are not necessary but are incorporated in a product to make it appear more desirable or useful (*informal*)

Bell's palsy /bélz-/ *n* the inability to move the muscles on one side of the face, so that the expression of the face is distorted. It results from injury to the facial nerve and is usually temporary. [Mid-19C. After Sir Charles *Bell* (1774–1842), Scottish anatomist]

bell tent *n* a tent shaped like a bell or a cone, held up by a central pole

bell tower *n* a tower with a bell or bells housed in it

bellwether /bél wethər/ *n* 1. SHEEP LEADING FLOCK a sheep that leads the rest of the flock, usually wearing a bell around its neck 2. LEADER somebody who leads others 3. INDICATOR OF FUTURE DEVELOPMENTS an indicator of future developments or trends

belly /bélli/ *n* (*plural* **-lies**) 1. MIDDLE PART OF BODY the part of the body of a vertebrate that contains the stomach, intestines, and other organs 2. FRONT OF BODY AROUND STOMACH the surface of the body of a vertebrate around the stomach 3. STOMACH the stomach (*informal*) 4. APPETITE the desire or need for food and drink 5. COURAGE OR DESIRE the courage or desire to have or do something ○ *They have no belly for a fight.* 6. BULGING PART a part of something that bulges out, e.g. a sail 7. INTERIOR CAVITY the interior cavity of a structure, especially a ship 8. MUSIC UPPER SURFACE OF STRINGED INSTRUMENT the top or front surface of the body of a stringed instrument, over which the strings are stretched ■ *vti* (**-lies**, **-lying**, **-lied**) BULGE to bulge or make something bulge ○ *The wind bellied out the sail.* [Old English *belig* 'bag' < Indo-European, 'to swell'] ◇ **go** *or* **turn belly up** to go bankrupt, fail, or fall through

bellyache /bélli ayk/ (*informal*) *n* a painful or upset stomach ■ *vi* (**-aches**, **-aching**, **-ached**) to complain in an annoying manner —**bellyacher** *n*

bellyband /bélli band/ *n* a strap passed around the belly of a draught animal and attached to the shafts of the vehicle it is pulling

bellybutton /béli butt'n/ *n* the human navel (*informal*)

belly chain *n* a chain designed to be worn around the waist or waist area, especially as an ornament

belly dance *n* a dance of North Africa and southwestern Asia, in which the hips and abdomen are moved rapidly —**belly dancer** *n* —**belly dancing** *n*

belly flop *n* 1. a shallow dive in which the front of the diver's body hits the water first 2. AVIAT same as **belly landing** —**belly-flop** *vi*

bellyful /béllifŏol/ *n* (*informal*) 1. all the food that somebody wants or is able to eat 2. an undesirable or excessive amount of something ○ *I've had a bellyful of his complaining.*

belly landing *n* an emergency landing of an aircraft with the wheels not extended —**belly-land** *vti*

belly laugh *n* a deep and unrestrained laugh

belly pork *n* a streaky cut of pork from a pig's belly

Belmondo /bel móndō/, **Jean-Paul** (*b.* 1933) French actor. His starring role in Jean-Luc Godard's *À bout de souffle* (1960) (*Breathless* (1961) established him as a key figure of the French New Wave.

Belmopan /bélmə pán/ capital of Belize, located on the Belize River in the central part of the country. Population: 6,785 (1997).

Belo Horizonte /béllō hori zón tay/ city and capital of Minas Gerais State in eastern Brazil. Population: 2,091,448 (1996).

belong /bi lóng/ (**-longs**, **-longing**, **-longed**) *vi* 1. BE PROPERTY OF SOMEBODY OR SOMETHING to be the property of a person or organization ○ *Who does this coat belong to?* 2. BE LINKED TO SOMEBODY OR SOMETHING to be linked to a particular person, group, place, or time by a relationship such as birth, affection, or membership ○ *belongs to a bridge club* 3. BE CLASSIFIED AS PART OF SOMETHING to be part of a class or group ○ *Tulips belong to the lily family.* 4. BE PART OF to be a part or component of something else ○ *belonging to the assembly mechanism* 5. BE IN RIGHT PLACE to be in an appropriate or usual place ○ *Where does this chair belong?* 6. BE ACCEPTED SOMEWHERE to be accepted or made welcome in a place or group ○ *feeling that I didn't belong* [14C. < BE- + obsolete *long* 'relate to']

Belonger /bi lóngər/ *n Carib* somebody of African descent who was born and lives on a Caribbean island

belonging /bi lónging/ *n* the state of being accepted and comfortable in a place or group ■ **belongings** *npl* the things somebody owns or has with him or her

Belorussia /béllō rúshə/ ◆ **Belarus**

beloved /bi lúvvid/; *predicative adj* /-lúvd/ *adj* very much loved ■ *n* /bi lúvvid/ somebody who is very much loved ○ *a letter from his beloved*

> **CULTURAL NOTE** *Beloved*, a novel (1987) by US writer Toni Morrison. It explores the emotional legacy of slavery among Black people in the United States. Set in the years before, during, and after the American Civil War, it centres on three generations of Black women, Baby Suggs, a woman freed from slavery, her daughter-in-law Sethe, who escapes to the North from vicious slave owners in Kentucky, and Sethe's daughter Denver, raised in freedom but scarred by her inheritance. They are haunted by the ghost of Beloved, another daughter whom Sethe murdered to save her from being raised in slavery. The novel weaves their memories as they come to terms with their personal and collective past.

below /bi lṓ/ CORE MEANING: a grammatical word indicating a position beneath or lower than something ○ (*prep*) *a river below the town* ○ (*adv*) *on the shelf below* 1. *prep, adv* IN LOWER GRADE at or to a level, standard, or grade that is lower than that specified or understood ○ *animals ranked below humans* ○ *below average* ○ *30 degrees below* 2. *adv* FURTHER DOWN lower down or later on in a text, especially on the same page ○ *see below* ○ *on page 29 below* 3. *adv* NAUT LOWER THAN DECK on or to a level of a ship or boat that is lower than the deck [14C. < earlier form of BY[1] + LOW[1]]

belowground /bi lṓ grownd, -grównd/ *adj* situated under the ground ■ *adv* into or under the ground

below-the-fold *adj* relating to the portion of a webpage that is seen only by scrolling down to the middle or bottom of the page and is therefore less commercially valuable. ◊ **above-the-fold**

Belsen /bélss'n/ village in northwestern Germany, about 16 km/10 mi. north of Celle. It is the site of the Bergen-Belsen Nazi concentration camp (1943–45).

Belshazzar /bel sházzər/ *n* in the Bible, a king of Babylon in the sixth century BC whose death is foretold in an inscription that mysteriously appears on the wall of his palace during a feast (Daniel 5)

belt /belt/ *n* 1. STRIP OF MATERIAL ROUND WAIST a strip of material worn round the waist, used to hold up clothing for the lower body, as decoration, or to carry tools or weapons 2. AUTOMOT same as **seat belt** 3. MECH ENG BAND AS PART OF MACHINE a band of strong flexible material used in machinery to transmit motion or power or to move articles ○ *a fan belt* 4. STRIP OF SOMETHING DIFFERENT a band or stripe of a different colour, texture, or substance from what it encircles or crosses 5. PARTICULAR AREA an area or region where a particular item or quality is characteristic ○ *the wheat belt* ○ *the stockbroker belt* 6. SPORTS BELT GIVEN FOR ACHIEVEMENT a belt awarded to a sports competitor, especially in boxing or the martial arts, as a trophy or a sign of having attained a particular grade 7. SPORTS SOMEBODY WITH BELT FOR ACHIEVEMENT somebody awarded a particular belt for an achievement, usually in boxing or one of the martial arts 8. BELT AS SIGN OF RANK a belt worn as a sign of a particular aristocratic rank such as knight or earl 9. BLOW a hard blow (*informal*) 10. EDUC, HIST STRAP USED TO PUNISH a leather strap, usually split into several thongs at one end, formerly used in schools for corporal punishment 11. *N Am* DRINK a drink of spirits (*slang*) ■ *v* (**belts**, **belting**, **belted**) 1. *vt* FIX SOMETHING WITH BELT to fasten or attach something with a belt 2. *vt* HIT SOMEBODY WITH BELT to strike somebody with a belt 3. *vt* HIT SOMEBODY OR SOMETHING HARD to strike somebody or something with a hard blow (*informal*) 4. *vi* MOVE FAST to move or travel very quickly (*informal*) ○ *belted home as soon as we could* [Old English, < Latin *balteus* 'girdle'] ◇ **below the belt** unfair and often hurtful ◇ **have something under your belt** to have done or acquired something that will be of benefit to you in the future ○ *has 12 computer science courses under her belt* ◇ **tighten your belt** to reduce your expenditure

belt down *vt US* to drink a number of alcoholic drinks in very quick succession (*informal*)

belt out *vt* to sing or play something loudly and enthusiastically (*informal*)

belt up *v* 1. *vi* to be quiet or stop talking (*slang*; usually used as a command) 2. *vti* to fasten a safety belt, or secure somebody with a safety belt

Beltane /bél tayn/ *n* an ancient Celtic festival marked by the lighting of bonfires. Date: beginning of May. [15C. Via Gaelic *bealltainn* < Old Irish]

belt bomber *n* a suicide bomber who conceals explosives around the waist, using a specially designed belt to hold them —**belt bomb** *n*

belt drive *n* a system for transmitting power from one shaft to another by means of an endless flexible belt looped over pulleys mounted on the shafts

belted Galloway *n* a cow with a white belt round a black body, belonging to a breed of hornless beef cattle originating in Galloway in southwestern Scotland

belter /béltər/ *n* (*informal*) 1. somebody or something considered remarkable or outstanding 2. a popular song that lends itself to a loud and rousing performance

belting /bélting/ *n* 1. material used for making belts 2. belts considered collectively

belt sander *n* a sander that uses a continuous belt coated with an abrasive

belt-tightening *n* a reduction in spending that results in the loss of something previously enjoyed

beltway /bélt way/ *n N Am* same as **ring road** ◇ **inside** *or* **outside the Beltway** *US* inside or outside the politically and socially insular community of Washington DC

beluga /bə lōogə/ (*plural* **-gas** *or* same) *n* 1. a large white sturgeon. Native to: Black Sea, Caspian Sea. Latin name: *Huso huso* *or* *Acipenser huso*. 2. also **beluga caviar** caviar made from the eggs of the beluga sturgeon 3. MARINE BIOL same as **white whale** [Late 16C. < Russian, 'large white' < *belyǐ* 'white']

belvedere /bélvə deer/ *n* a building or part of a building positioned to offer a fine view of the surrounding area [Late 16C. < Italian, 'beautiful to see']

bema /béemə/ *n* 1. *also* **bima** *or* **bimah** in a synagogue, the raised platform where the scriptures are read 2. in a Christian Orthodox church, the raised area where the altar is located [Late 17C. < Greek *bēma* 'step, platform']

Bemba /bémbə/ (*plural* same *or* **-bas**) *n* 1. a member of an African people who live chiefly in Zambia 2. a Bantu language spoken in east-central Africa and belonging to the Benue-Congo group of languages. Native speakers: 2 million. [Mid-20C. < Bantu] —**Bemba** *adj*

bemire /bi mīr/ (**-mires**, **-miring**, **-mired**) *vt* 1. to soil somebody or something with mud or dirt (*archaic*) 2. to cause somebody or something to become stuck in mud (*archaic or literary*; *usually passive*)

bemoan /bi mṓn/ (**-moans**, **-moaning**, **-moaned**) *vt* to express grief or disappointment about something

bemuse /bi myōoz/ (**-muses**, **-musing**, **-mused**) *vt* to cause somebody to be confused or puzzled —**bemused** *adj* —**bemusedly** /-idli/ *adv* —**bemusement** *n*

ben[1] /ben/ *n Ireland, Scotland* GEOG same as **mountain** (sense 1) (*often used in placenames*) ○ *Ben Nevis* [Late 18C. < Scottish Gaelic and Irish *beann*]

ben[2] /ben/ *n Scotland* the inner room of a house, especially of an old-fashioned rural cottage with two rooms [14C. < Old English *binnan* 'within']

Ben Ali /ben áali/, **Zine al-Abidine** (*b.* 1936) Tunisian politician. As prime minister, he forced the retirement of President Habid Bourgiba and began reforms as the new president (1987–).

Benares /bi náariz/ former name for **Varanasi**

Benaud /bénnō/, **Richie** (*b.* 1930) Australian cricketer and broadcaster. He was the first Australian, and only the second cricketer, to score 2,000 runs and take 200 wickets in international matches. Full name **Benaud, Richard**.

Ben Bella /bén béllə/, **Ahmed** (*b.* 1918?) Algerian politician. A leading figure in Algeria's war of independence from French rule, he was the country's first prime minister (1962–63) and president (1963–

65). Imprisoned from 1965 to 1980, he was exiled in 1980 and returned to Algeria in 1990. Full name **Ben Bella, Mohammed Ahmed**

Benbow /bénbō/, **John** (1653–1702) English naval commander. He commanded the English fleet in the Caribbean, where he died from his wounds after a sea battle against a French force.

bench /bench/ *n* **1.** LONG BACKLESS SEAT a long seat for two or more people, usually made without a back or arms **2.** WORK TABLE a long strong work table **3.** JUDGE'S SEAT the seat where a judge sits in a court **4.** JUDGE the judge or magistrate presiding over a court **5.** JUDGES the judges of a court system **6.** POST OF JUDGE the office or position of a judge **7.** NAUT SEAT IN BOAT a seat for a rower in a boat **8.** SPORTS SEATS FOR NONPLAYING ATHLETES in team sports, the seats for officials and for players not taking part on the field or court **9.** NONPLAYING ATHLETES the officials and players who are not taking part on the field or court **10.** GEOL LEDGE OF LAND a narrow flat ledge of land, often the remnant of a former shoreline **11.** MIN EXTRACT LEDGE IN MINE a ledge formed by excavation in a mine **12.** PLATFORM FOR SHOWING ANIMALS a platform used for displaying dogs, cats, or other animals at a show ■ *vt* (**benches, benching, benched**) **1.** PROVIDE SOMETHING WITH BENCHES to provide a place with benches **2.** DISPLAY ANIMAL AT SHOW to display a dog, cat, or other animal on a bench at a show **3.** EXCLUDE PLAYER in team sports, to exclude or remove a member of a sports team from play [Old English *benc* < Germanic]

bencher /bénchər/ *n* a member of the governing body of an Inn of Court

bench mark *n* a mark made by a surveyor on a permanent object that shows an established position and elevation and is used as a reference point

benchmark /bénch maark/ *n* **1.** STANDARD a standard against which something can be measured or assessed **2.** TEST OF COMPUTER PERFORMANCE a standard test to measure the performance of computer hardware or software ■ *adj* USED AS STANDARD used as a standard for measuring or assessing something ■ *vt* (**-marks, -marking, -marked**) **1.** PROVIDE STANDARD FOR SOMETHING to provide a standard against which something can be measured or assessed **2.** TEST COMPUTER PERFORMANCE to test the performance of computer hardware or software for comparison with similar products

bench press *n* in weightlifting, a lift where somebody lies on a bench with the feet on the floor and raises a weight from chest level to arm's length —**bench-press** *vti*

bench seat *n* a seat that extends across the full width of a motor vehicle

bench test *n* a trial of a machine or part in the laboratory or workshop to confirm that it works properly before it is installed —**bench-test** *vti*

bend[1] /bend/ *v* (**bends, bending, bent** /bent/) **1.** *vti* BECOME OR MAKE CURVED to take on a curved or angled shape, or cause something to do this ○ *The wooden struts bent under pressure.* **2.** *vti* STOOP to make a stooping or inclined movement, or cause somebody to do this ○ *I bent to pick up the ball.* **3.** *vti* CHANGE OR CAUSE TO CHANGE DIRECTION to change direction or course, or cause something to do this ○ *The path bends to the right.* **4.** *vti* YIELD OR FORCE TO YIELD to yield in response to a strong will or force, or force somebody or something to do this **5.** *vt* DISTORT FOR SOMEBODY'S BENEFIT to adapt or interpret something in a way that was not originally intended, especially for personal benefit or to help somebody else ○ *bend the rules* **6.** *vti* CONCENTRATE ON DOING SOMETHING to concentrate the mind on an activity ○ *bent her mind to the task in hand* **7.** *vt* NAUT ATTACH to attach or fasten something, especially a rope ■ *n* **1.** CURVE a curved part of something, especially a curve in a road **2.** ACT OF BENDING an act of bending **3.** NAUT KNOT JOINING TWO ROPES a knot that joins one line to another [Old English *bendan* 'tie, curve' < Germanic] —**bendability** /béndə bílləti/ *n* —**bendable** /béndəb'l/ *adj* —**bendily** *adv* —**bendiness** *n* —**bendy** *adj* ◇ **round the bend** wild, distracted, or irrational (*informal*)

ORIGIN The prehistoric Germanic word from which ***bend*** is derived is also the ancestor of English *band*[2], *bind*, and *bond*, and possibly also of *bundle*.

bend[2] /bend/ *n* a band that crosses a heraldic shield diagonally from top right to bottom left [Old English, < Germanic; later < Old French *bende*]

benday /bén dáy/, **Ben Day** *adj* describes a printing process of adding tone to an image by overlaying a transparent sheet patterned with dots before the image is reproduced to make a plate [Early 20C. After *Benjamin Day*, Jr (1838–1916), US printer]

bended /béndid/ *adj* in a position so as to be curved or bent (*literary*) ○ *on bended knee*

bender /béndər/ *n* **1.** DRINKING SPREE a prolonged bout of alcoholic drinking (*slang*) **2.** TEMPORARY SHELTER a usually dome-shaped temporary shelter made by bending and interweaving branches and covering them with plastic sheeting or tarpaulin (*informal*) **3.** OFFENSIVE TERM an offensive term for a gay man (*slang*)

Bendigo /béndigō/ former gold-mining town in central Victoria, Australia, now an important industrial, commercial, and agricultural centre. Population: 75,900 (1998).

bendrofluazide /béndrō flóo ə zīd/ *n* PHARM former name for **bendroflumethiazide**

bendroflumethiazide /béndrō flóo methī ə zīd/ *n* a diuretic drug that promotes the excretion of salt and water by the kidneys. Use: treatment of oedema and hypertension.

bends /bendz/ *n* decompression sickness, especially in divers (*informal; takes a singular or plural verb*)

bend sinister (*plural* **bends sinister**) *n* a band that crosses a heraldic shield diagonally from top left to bottom right, used to indicate a line of descent from a birth outside marriage

beneath /bi néeth/ CORE MEANING: a grammatical word indicating a position underneath or lower than something

1. *prep, adv* UNDERNEATH in, at, or to a lower position or less superficial level than that specified or understood (*formal*) ○ *beneath the bed* ○ *Beneath his veneer of politeness lay hostility.* **2.** *prep, adv* LOWER in, at, or to a lower level, grade, or standard than that specified or understood (*formal*) ○ *beneath the usual standard* **3.** *prep* TOO LOW FOR too low in status or character for ○ *beneath contempt* ○ *Gossiping is beneath you.* [Old English *binithan, bineothan* 'by or from below' < Germanic]

benedicite /bénnə díssəti/ *n* a blessing or grace used in some Christian religious communities [13C. < Latin, imperative of *benedicere* 'bless']

Benedicite *n* a Latin hymn beginning 'Benedicite omnia opera Domini Domino', traditionally translated as 'O all ye works of the Lord, bless ye the Lord'

Benedict XIV /bénnidikt/, **Pope** (1675–1758) As pope (1740–58) he encouraged the development of education and science. Born **Lambertini, Prospero**

Benedict XV, Pope (1854–1922) As pope (1914–22) he was active in organizing war relief during World War I. Born **della Chiesa, Giacomo**

Benedictine /bénni díktin/ *n* a member of a Christian order of monks and nuns founded by St Benedict of Nursia ■ *adj* relating to or characteristic of St Benedict, his rule, or the Christian order that he founded

benediction /bénni díksh'n/ *n* **1.** EXPRESSION OF APPROVAL an expression of approval or good wishes **2.** PRAYER ASKING FOR GOD'S BLESSING a prayer asking for God's blessing, usually at the end of a Christian service **3.** BLESSEDNESS in Christianity, the state of being blessed **4.** CHR another spelling of **Benediction** [15C. Directly or via French < Latin *benediction-* < *benedicere* 'say well to' < *bene* 'well' + *dicere* 'say'] —**benedictive** *adj* —**benedictory** *adj*

Benediction *n* in the Roman Catholic Church, a devotional service during which the congregation is blessed with the Host

Benedict of Nursia /-núrssi ə, -núrshə/, **St** (480–547) Italian monk. He established a Christian monastery at Monte Cassino and is considered the founder of Western monasticism.

Benedict's solution /bénnidikts-/, **Benedict's reagent** *n* a chemical solution that turns red in the presence of sugars like glucose that are reducing agents. Use: urine tests for diabetes. [Early 20C. After Stanley Rossiter *Benedict* (1884–1936), US chemist]

Benedictus /bénni díktəss/ *n* **1.** a Latin hymn from the Bible beginning 'Benedictus qui venit in nomine Domini' ('Blessed is he who comes in the name of the Lord' Luke 1:68–79) **2.** a Latin hymn from the Bible beginning 'Benedictus Dominus Deus Israel' ('Blessed be the Lord God of Israel' Matthew 21:9) [Mid-16C. < Latin, past participle of *benedicere* (see BENEDICTION)]

benefaction /bénni fáksh'n/ *n* **1.** DOING SOMETHING GOOD the act of doing good **2.** GOOD DEED a good deed, especially an act of charity **3.** DONATION a donation given to a charity [Mid-17C. < late Latin *benefaction-* < Latin *bene* 'well' + *fact-*, past participle of *facere* 'do']

benefactor /bénni faktər/ *n* somebody who aids a cause, institution, or person, especially with a gift of money

benefactress /bénni faktrəss/ *n* a woman who aids a cause, institution, or person, especially with a gift of money

benefice /bénnifiss/ *n* **1.** CHR ENDOWED CHURCH LIVING a church office that provides a living for its holder through an endowment attached to it **2.** CHR REVENUE FOR CHURCH LIVING the revenue or property that provides the living of the holder of a church benefice **3.** HIST FORM OF FEUDAL TENURE a form of feudal tenure in which a vassal held land from a superior, especially in return for military service ■ *vt* (**-fices, -ficing, -ficed**) CHR PROVIDE SOMEBODY WITH BENEFICE to provide a member of the clergy with a church office that will yield a living [14C. Via French < Latin *beneficium* 'doing well' < *bene* 'well' + *fic-*, variant of stem of *facere* 'do']

beneficent /bə néffissənt/ *adj* **1.** doing good or charitable acts **2.** producing benefits or advantages [Early 17C. < Latin *beneficent-*, stem of *beneficentior* 'more beneficent' < *beneficus* < *bene* 'well' + *fic-*, variant of stem of *facere* 'do'] —**beneficence** *n* —**beneficently** *adv*

beneficial /bénni físh'l/ *adj* **1.** producing a good or advantageous effect ○ *The exercise should prove beneficial to his health.* **2.** entitling somebody to or entitled to profits or property [15C. Directly or via French < late Latin *beneficialis* < Latin *beneficium* (see BENEFICE)] —**beneficially** *adv*

beneficiary /bénni físhəri/ *n* (*plural* **-ies**) **1.** SOMEBODY BENEFITING somebody who receives a benefit from something **2.** LEGAL RECIPIENT OF MONEY somebody entitled to money or property under a will, trust, or insurance policy **3.** HOLDER OF BENEFICE a member of the clergy who holds an office that provides a living (**benefice**) **4.** *NZ* SOMEBODY RECEIVING GOVERNMENT ASSISTANCE somebody who receives a state welfare benefit such as unemployment benefit or sickness benefit ■ *adj* RELATING TO BENEFICE relating to a church office that provides a living (**benefice**) or to the member of the clergy who holds it [Early 17C. < Latin *beneficiarius* < *beneficium* (see BENEFICE)]

beneficiary bank *n* a bank that receives money, especially from another bank

benefit /bénnifit/ *n* **1.** ADVANTAGE something that has a good effect or promotes wellbeing ○ *They eventually reaped the benefits of all their hard work.* **2.** GOVERNMENT PAYMENT TO SOMEBODY NEEDING ASSISTANCE a regular payment made by the government under the national insurance scheme or social security to somebody qualified to receive it or in need of financial assistance (*often used in the plural*) **3.** MONEY PAID TO CLAIMANT a payment or form of nonmonetary compensation made to a claimant or entitled person by an employer, insurance company, or other institution **4.** BUSINESS EXTRA EMPLOYEE COMPENSATION compensation over and above salary given to some employees or partially paid for by the employing company, e.g., health insurance, retirement pay, or share options **5.** PERFORMANCE FOR CHARITY a performance by entertainers, athletes, or others to raise money for somebody or something, especially a charity ■ *vti* (**-fits, -fiting** or **-fitting, -fited** or **-fitted**) GIVE OR RECEIVE BENEFIT to give somebody or receive help, an advantage, or another benefit ○ *The research would benefit from an injection of new ideas.* [14C. Via Anglo-Norman *benfet*, Old French *bienfait* < Latin *benefactum* 'good deed' < *bene* 'well' + *facere* 'do'] ◇ **give somebody the benefit of the doubt** to assume that somebody is telling the truth about something or is innocent of something because there is not enough evidence that the person is lying or guilty

benefit of clergy *n* **1.** the official approval or ministration of a Christian church ○ *married without benefit of clergy* **2.** the privilege held by the Christian clergy in the Middle Ages that entitled them

to trial by an ecclesiastical court and exemption from trial by secular authorities

benefit tourism *n* the practice of migrating from a poorer country to a richer country in order to become eligible for its health and social benefits — **benefit tourist** *n*

Benelux /bénni luks/ *n* Belgium, the Netherlands, and Luxembourg The three countries formed a customs union in 1948 that was replaced by the Benelux Economic Union in 1960 [Mid-20C. Acronym < *Belgium, Netherlands, Luxembourg*]

Beneš /bénnesh/, **Eduard** (1884–1948) president of Czechoslovakia (1935–38, 1946–48). He led the Czech government-in-exile during World War II. He resigned after the Communist takeover of his country in 1948.

Benét /bə náy/, **Stephen Vincent** (1898–1943) US author and poet. He wrote the long narrative poem *John Brown's Body* (1928), which won a Pulitzer Prize.

> 'I have fallen in love with American names, / The sharp names that never get fat, / The snakeskin-titles of mining-claims, / The plumed war-bonnet of Medicine Hat, / Tucson and Deadwood and Lost Mule Flat.'
> [Stephen Vincent Benét, *American Names*; 1927]

Benét, **William Rose** (1886–1950) US poet, critic, and editor. The brother of Stephen Vincent Benét, he cofounded the US magazine *The Saturday Review of Literature* in 1924.

benevolent /bə névvələnt/ *adj* **1.** showing kindness or goodwill **2.** performing good or charitable acts and not seeking to make a profit [15C. Via French < Latin *benevolent-*, present participle of *bene velle* 'wish well'] — **benevolence** *n* — **benevolently** *adv*

Bengal /ben gáwl, beng-/ former province of northeastern India. In 1947 it was divided into the Indian state of West Bengal, now Bangla, and East Pakistan, now Bangladesh. — **Bengalese** /ben gáw leéz, béng-/ *n*

Bengal, **Bay of** northeastern section of the Indian Ocean bordered by India, Bangladesh, and Myanmar. Area: 2,172,000 sq. km/839,000 sq. mi.

Bengali /ben gáwli, beng gáwli/ *n* **1.** somebody who comes from Bangladesh or the state of Bangla in India **2.** same as **Bangla**[1] [Late 18C. < Hindi *bangālī*] — **Bengali** *adj*

bengaline /béngəlin, -ə leén/ *n* a heavyweight corded cotton and silk or wool fabric [Late 19C. < French, because of its similarity to cloth made in Bengal]

Benghazi /ben gaázi, beng-/, **Bengasi**, **Banghāzī** city and port in northeastern Libya on the gulf of Sidra. It is near the site of the ancient Greek colony of Euhesperides. Population: 804,000 (1995).

Benguela /ben gwéllə/ city and capital of Benguela District, on the Atlantic coast of western Angola. Population: 155,000 (1983).

David Ben-Gurion

AKG London

Ben-Gurion /ben goóri ən/, **David** (1886–1973) Polish-born prime minister of Israel (1948–53, 1955–63). He was an activist and leader of the movement to establish a Jewish homeland in Palestine, and became Israel's first prime minister. Born **Gruen, David**

~~beneficial~~ incorrect spelling of **beneficial**

~~benifit~~ incorrect spelling of **benefit**

benighted /bi nítid/ *adj* **1.** unenlightened intellectually, socially, or morally (*formal*) **2.** overtaken by night or the dark (*archaic*) — **benightedness** *n*

benign /bi nín/ *adj* **1.** KINDLY having a kind and gentle disposition or appearance **2.** MED NOT LIFE-THREATENING not a threat to life or long-term health, especially by being noncancerous ○ *a benign tumour* **3.** HARMLESS neutral or harmless in its effect or influence **4.** FAVOURABLE mild or favourable in effect ○ *a benign climate* [14C. Via French < Latin *benignus*] — **benignly** *adv*

benignant /bə nígnənt/ *adj* kind and gracious in behaviour or appearance — **benignancy** *n*

benignity /bə nígnəti/ (*plural* **-ties**) *n* **1.** kindness and gentleness of disposition or appearance **2.** a kind or gracious act

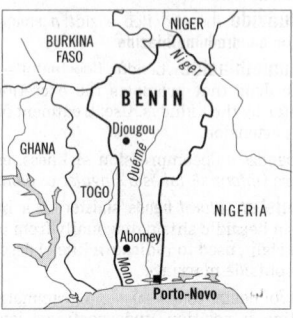

Benin

Benin /bə neén/ country in West Africa between Togo and Nigeria, with a short coastline on the Bight of Benin. It became independent from France in 1960. Language: French. Currency: CFA franc. Capital: Porto-Novo. Population: 7,041,490 (2003). Area: 112,622 sq. km/43,484 sq. mi. Official name **Republic of Benin**. Former name **Dahomey** (until 1975) — **Beninese** /bénni neéz/ *adj, n*

Benin, **Bight of** wide bay in West Africa, the western section of the Gulf of Guinea. It stretches from the mouth of the River Volta to the mouth of the River Niger, with Lagos as one of its principal ports. Length: 720 km/450 mi.

Benin City capital of Edo State in southern Nigeria. It was the capital of the Kingdom of Benin that flourished in the 15th and 16th centuries, producing magnificent brass, bronze, and ivory sculptures. Population: 223,900 (1995 estimate).

benison /bénnizən, -ssən/ *n* a blessing or benediction (*literary*) [12C. Via Old French *benisson* < Latin *benediction-* (see BENEDICTION)]

benjamin /bénjəmin/ *n* CHEM same as **benzoin** [Mid-16C. Alteration of earlier form of BENZOIN after the name *Benjamin*]

Benjamin /bénjəmin/ *n* in the Bible, the youngest son of Jacob and Rachel and father of the smallest tribe of Israel

Benjamin /bénjəmin/, **Walter** (1892–1940) German literary critic. He became a Marxist in the 1920s after meeting Bertolt Brecht. His essays include *The Work of Art in the Age of Mechanical Reproduction* (1936).

> 'Every passion borders on the chaotic, but the collector's passion borders on the chaos of memories.'
> [Walter Benjamin, 'Caution: Steps', *One-Way Street*; 1928]

Ben Lomond /ben lómənd/ mountain in western Scotland, on the eastern side of Loch Lomond. Height: 973 m/3,192 ft.

Benn /ben/, **Tony** (*b.* 1925) British politician. He was first elected as a Labour MP in 1950, and first became a government minister in 1966. The son of Lord Stansgate, he inherited the title but later renounced it in 1963 to stay in the House of Commons. Full name **Benn, Anthony Neil Wedgwood**

> 'The Marxist analysis has got nothing to do with what happened in Stalin's Russia; it's like blaming Jesus Christ for the Inquisition in Spain.'
> [Tony Benn, *Observer*; 27 April 1980]

Bennelong /bénnə long/ (1764?–1813) Australian Aboriginal who was abducted by Governor Arthur Phillip in 1789 and taken to England. On his return he was shunned by both the Aboriginal and European communities.

Bennett /bénnit/, **Alan** (*b.* 1934) British playwright and actor. His many stage and television dramas include *An Englishman Abroad* (1983) and *The Madness of George III* (1991).

> 'I'm not good at precise, coherent argument. But plays are suited to incoherent argument, put into the mouths of fallible people.'
> [Alan Bennett, *Sunday Times*; 24 November 1991]

Bennett, **Arnold** (1867–1931) British novelist. He wrote *The Old Wives' Tale* (1908) and the *Clayhanger* series. Full name **Bennett, Enoch Arnold**

> 'Journalists say a thing that they know isn't true, in the hope that if they keep on saying it long enough it will be true.'
> [Arnold Bennett, *The Title*; 1918]

Bennett, **James Gordon** (1841–1918) US newspaper owner and editor. As editor of the *New York Herald*, he financed H. M. Stanley's African expeditions.

Bennett, **Richard Bedford, 1st Viscount** (1870–1947) Canadian politician and business executive. He was Conservative prime minister of Canada (1930–35). Known as **Iron Heel Bennett**. See table at **prime minister**

Bennett, **Richard Rodney** (*b.* 1936) British composer. His work incorporates the 12-tone scale and jazz influences, and includes the score for the film *Murder on the Orient Express* (1974).

Ben Nevis /-névviss/ highest mountain in the British Isles. It is located in western Scotland, in the Grampian Mountains, overlooking the Great Glen. Height: 1,343 m/4,406 ft.

benny /bénni/ (*plural* **-nies**) *n* an amphetamine tablet, especially Benzedrine™ (*slang*) [Mid-20C. Shortening of BENZEDRINE]

Benny /bénni/, **Jack** (1894–1974) US comedian. He is known for his miserly self-caricature in the *Jack Benny Show* on US radio and television (1932–65). Born **Kubelsky, Benjamin**

bensh /bench/ (**benshes, benshing, benshed**), **bentsh** (**bentshes, bentshing, bentshed**) *vi* to say a Jewish benediction after eating a meal [Via Yiddish *bentshen* < Latin *benedicere* 'bless']

bent[1] /bent/ past participle, past tense of **bend**[1] ■ *adj* **1.** CURVED having a curved, twisted, or angled shape **2.** DETERMINED having a fixed desire to do something ○ *bent on making a name for herself* **3.** OFFENSIVE TERM an offensive term meaning gay (*slang*) **4.** CORRUPT dishonest or corrupt in behaviour (*slang*) ○ *a bent cop* **5.** STOLEN dishonestly acquired or made (*slang*) **6.** SUFFERING FROM BENDS suffering from decompression sickness (*informal*) ■ *n* **1.** NATURAL INCLINATION a strong natural inclination or liking for something **2.** CIV ENG CROSSWISE SUPPORT a crosswise framework or member used to strengthen a structure

SYNONYMS See *talent*.

bent[2] /bent/ *n* **1.** GRASS OF TEMPERATE REGIONS a perennial grass. Use: hay, lawns, putting greens. Native to: temperate regions. Genus: *Agrostis*. **2.** REEDY GRASS a stiff reedy grass (*archaic*) **3.** GRASS STALK a flower stalk of a stiff grass (*archaic*) **4.** HEATH an area of open moor or grassland (*archaic*) [Old English *beonet* < Germanic]

Bentham /bénthəm/, **Jeremy** (1748–1832) British philosopher, jurist, and social reformer. The chief proponent of utilitarianism, he wrote *An Introduction to the Principles of Morals and Legislation* (1789). He helped found University College London.

> 'Every law is an evil, for every law is an infraction of liberty.'
> [Jeremy Bentham, *An Introduction to the Principles of Morals and Legislation*; 1789]

Benthamism /bénthəmizəm/ *n* the utilitarian philosophy of Jeremy Bentham, which argues that the highest good is the happiness of the greatest number — **Benthamite** *n, adj*

benthic /bénthik/, **benthonic** /ben thónnik/ *adj* relating to or characteristic of the bottom of a sea, lake, or

deep river, or the animals and plants that live there [< BENTHOS]

benthos /bénthoss/ *n* the animals and plants that live on or in the sediment at the bottom of a sea, lake, or deep river [Late 19C. < Greek, 'depth of the sea']

Bentley /béntli/, **E. C.** (1875–1956) British writer. He invented the witty four-line verse form known as the 'clerihew'. His writings include the detective novel *Trent's Last Case* (1913). Full name **Bentley, Edmund Clerihew**

bento *n* FOOD same as **obento**

bentonite /bénta nīt/ *n* a light-coloured clay that expands in water. Use: oil drilling, paper, pharmaceutical industries. [Late 19C. After Fort *Benton*, Montana, USA] —**bentonitic** /bénta níttik/ *adj*

bentsh *vi* JUDAISM another spelling of **bensh**

bent-wing moth *n* a large ghost moth whose larvae, up to 15 cm/6 in long, bore into and are harmful to eucalyptus trees. Native to: Australian. Latin name: *Leto staceyi*.

bentwood /bént wŏŏd/ *n* wood that has been bent into a curved shape by being steamed and then put into a mould. Use: furniture.

Benue /bénnoo ay/ the longest tributary of the River Niger in Africa. It rises in northern Cameroon and flows northwards and then westwards across central Nigeria. Length: 1,400 km/870 mi.

Benue-Congo *n* a large group of Niger-Congo languages spoken across central and southern Africa, of which Bantu languages form the largest subgroup —**Benue-Congo** *adj*

benumb /bi núm/ (**-numbs, -numbing, -numbed**) *vt* **1.** to remove the sense of feeling from a faculty or part of the body, especially by exposure to extreme cold **2.** to make somebody incapable of activity or thought (*usually passive*)

Benz /benz/, **Karl** (1844–1929) German engineer and car manufacturer. He built one of the first petrol-driven cars. His company merged with Daimler (1926) to form Daimler-Benz and Company. Full name **Benz, Karl Friedrich**

benz- /benz, bents/ *prefix* same as **benzo-** (*used before vowels*)

benzaldehyde /ben záldi hīd/ *n* a colourless volatile liquid found naturally in and smelling of almonds. Use: manufacture of dyes, flavourings, and perfumes. Formula: C_6H_5CHO.

benzalkonium chloride /ben zal kṓni əm/ *n* a colourless or pale yellow toxic liquid mixture. Use: biocide in the food industry, preservative in pharmaceutical products. [< *benzylalkylammonium*]

Benzedrine /bénzə dreen/ *tdmk* a trademark for an amphetamine preparation

benzene /bén zeen/ *n* a colourless volatile toxic liquid with a distinctive odour. Source: petroleum. Use: manufacture of dyes, polymers, and industrial chemicals. Formula: C_6H_6. Former name **benzol** [Mid-19C. < *benzoic*]

benzene ring *n* a molecular structure common to benzene and its derivatives in which six carbon atoms are bonded in a hexagon by alternating single and double bonds

benzine /bén zeen/, **benzin** /-zin/ *n* a mixture of liquid hydrocarbons with a carefully selected boiling point range. Source: crude oil. Use: industrial solvent. [Mid-19C. < *benzoic*]

benzo- *prefix* benzene, benzoic acid ○ *benzopyrene* [< BENZOIN]

benzoate /bénzō ayt, bénzōit/ *n* a salt or ester of benzoic acid. Benzoates contain the group C_6H_5COO- or the ion $C_6H_5COO^-$.

benzocaine /bénzō kayn/ *n* an anaesthetizing drug. Use: in some throat lozenges and skin creams.

benzodiazepine /bénzō dī áyzə meen/ *n* a drug belonging to a group of minor tranquillizers. Use: short-term treatment for sleeping difficulties.

benzoic acid /ben zṓik-/ *n* a colourless crystalline solid found in some natural resins. Use: food preservative, manufacture of pharmaceuticals and cosmetics. Formula: C_6H_5COOH.

benzoin /bénzō in/ *n* a toxic white crystalline solid occurring in natural resins or manufactured synthetically. Use: medications, perfumes, incense.

Formula: $C_{14}H_{12}O_2$. [Mid-16C. Via French *benjoin* < Arabic *lubānjāwī* 'incense from Sumatra']

benzol /bén zol, /bén/ zōl/, **benzole** *n* CHEM former name for **benzene** [Mid-19C. < *benzoic*]

benzonitrile /bénzō nítrəl, -trīl/ *n* a colourless almond-scented oil with a pungent taste. Use: synthesis of chemicals and resins, solvent.

benzophenone /bénzō feénōn/ *n* a sweet-smelling colourless crystalline solid. Use: manufacture of perfumes, organic compounds. Formula: $(C_6H_5)_2CO$. [Late 19C. < BENZO- + PHENO- + -ONE]

benzopyrene /bénzō pī reen, -zol-/, **benzpyrene** /benz pī reen/ *n* a yellow crystalline solid that is highly carcinogenic. Source: tobacco smoke, coal tar. Formula: $C_{20}H_{12}$.

benzoquinone /bénzō kweénōn/ *n* a yellow crystalline solid with an unpleasant odour. Use: photographic developer, dyes, antioxidants. Formula: $C_6H_4O_2$.

benzoyl /bénzō il, bénzō īl/ *adj* relating to or containing the group C_6H_5CO– [Mid-19C. < German *Benzoesäure* 'benzoic acid' + Greek *hylē* 'wood, matter']

benzpyrene *n* CHEM same as **benzopyrene**

Ben-Zvi /ben zveé/, **Itzhak** (1884–1963) Russian-born president of Israel (1952–63). A leading Zionist, he moved to Palestine in 1907.

benzyl /bénzil/ *adj* relating to or containing the group $C_6H_5CH_2$–

benzyl alcohol *n* a colourless alcohol with a sharp burning taste. Use: synthesis of chemicals, in perfumes and flavourings, solvent.

benzylamine /bénzil áymeen/ *n* an amber toxic liquid that is strongly alkaline. Use: synthesis of chemicals and drugs.

Beowulf /báyō wŏŏlf/ *n* an anonymous Old English epic poem of the eighth century AD describing the exploits of the hero Beowulf, in particular his slaying of the monster Grendel and Grendel's mother

bequeath /bi kweéth, -kweéth/ (**-queaths, -queathing, -queathed**) *vt* **1.** to leave personal or other property to somebody after death by means of a will **2.** to hand down something such as knowledge or a practice to future generations [Old English *becweðan* 'speak about' < *cweðan* 'speak'] —**bequeathal** /bi kweéth'l/ *n* —**bequeather** *n*

bequest /bi kwést/ *n* **1.** ACT OF BEQUEATHING an act of bequeathing something to somebody **2.** SOMETHING LEFT IN WILL something left to somebody in a will **3.** SOMETHING PASSED DOWN TO POSTERITY something such as knowledge or a practice handed down to future generations [14C. < BEQUEATH]

Béranger /báy raaN zhay/, **Pierre Jean de** (1780–1857) French poet. His witty political poems were very popular, though they earned him several spells in jail.

berate /bi ráyt/ (**-rates, -rating, -rated**) *vt* to scold somebody vigorously and at length [Mid-16C. < BE- + *rate* 'berate', origin ?]

Berber /búrbər/ (*plural* **-bers** or *same*) *n* **1.** a member of a people living in North Africa **2.** a group of Afro-Asiatic languages spoken across North Africa, especially in Algeria and Morocco, sometimes regarded as a single language with divergent dialects. Native speakers: 12 million. [Mid-18C. < Arabic *barbar*] —**Berber** *adj*

Berbera /búrbərə/ port on the Gulf of Aden in northwestern Somalia. Population: 65,000 (1987).

berberis /búrbəriss/ *n* TREES same as **barberry** [Late 16C. Via modern Latin or Old French < medieval Latin *barbaris*]

berceuse /bair súrz/ *n* **1.** a lullaby or cradlesong **2.** an instrumental piece of music, usually in 6/8 time, meant to sound like a lullaby [Late 19C. < French < *bercer* 'to rock']

Berchtesgaden /báirktəss gaad'n, báirkhtəss-/ town in southeastern Bavaria, Germany, a popular ski resort. Adolf Hitler's fortified retreat, the Berghof, was nearby. Population: 7,966 (1997).

bereave /bi reév/ (**-reaves, -reaving, -reaved**) *vt* to deprive somebody of a beloved person or a treasured thing, especially through death (*often passive*) [Old English *bereafian* 'deprive, rob' < Germanic] —**bereavement** *n* —**bereaver** *n*

bereaved /bi reévd/ *adj* having lost a loved one

through death ■ *n* (*plural same*) somebody who has suffered the death of a loved one

bereft /bi réft/ *adj* **1.** DEPRIVED deprived of somebody or something loved or valued **2.** LACKING lacking in something desirable or necessary ○ *bereft of new ideas* **3.** FEELING SENSE OF LOSS filled with a sense of loss [Late 16C. Old past participle of BEREAVE]

Berenice's Hair /bérrə níssiz-/ *n* ASTRON same as **Coma Berenices**

Berenson /bérrənss'n/, **Bernard** (1865–1959) Lithuanian-born US art critic and collector. He wrote extensively about Renaissance painting and was an influential art collector and dealer. Born **Valvrojenski, Bernhard**

> 'Between truth and the search for truth, I opt for the second.'
> [Bernard Berenson, *Essays in Appreciation*; 1958]

Beresford /bérrisfərd/, **Bruce** (*b.* 1940) Australian film director. He directed *Breaker Morant* (1980) and the Academy Award-winning *Driving Miss Daisy* (1989).

beret /bérray/ *n* a flat round soft hat, usually woollen, with a tight-fitting headband [Early 19C. Via French < late Latin *birrus* 'hooded cloak']

beretta *n* CHR another spelling of **biretta**

berg[1] /burg/ *n* GEOG same as **iceberg** (sense 1) [Early 19C. Shortening]

berg[2] /burg/ *n* S Africa GEOG same as **mountain** (sense 1) [Early 19C. Via Afrikaans < Dutch *bergh* 'mountain']

Berg /burg/ S Africa same as **Drakensberg** (*informal*)

Berg /bairg/, **Alban** (1885–1935) Austrian composer. He mixed modern and traditional styles in his works, which include the opera *Wozzeck* (1917–22).

Berg /burg/, **Paul** (*b.* 1926) US molecular biologist. He is best known for identifying transfer RNA in 1956, and was awarded the Nobel Prize in chemistry (1980).

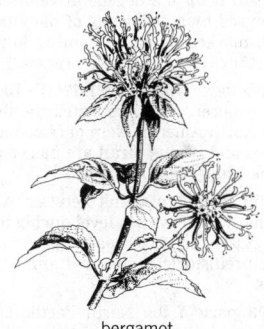

bergamot

bergamot /búrgə mot/ (*plural* **-mots** or *same*) *n* **1.** *also* **bergamot oil** OIL FROM CITRUS FRUIT a fragrant yellow-green essential oil. Source: bergamot fruit rinds. Use: perfumes, flavouring in Earl Grey tea. **2.** *also* **bergamot orange** SPINY ASIAN CITRUS TREE a spiny citrus tree with sour pear-shaped fruit. Native to: Asia. Latin name: *Citrus bergamia*. **3.** MEDITERRANEAN MINT PLANT a mint plant producing a fragrant oil similar to bergamot oil. Native to: Mediterranean. Latin name: *Mentha citrata*. **4.** UK, ANZ, Can N AMERICAN MINT PLANT a wild or garden mint plant. Flowers: scarlet in the wild, white to purple in garden varieties. Native to: North America. Latin name: *Monarda didyma*. US term **bee balm** [Late 17C. After *Bergamo* in N Italy]

Bergen /búrgən/ city and port in southwestern Norway and the administrative capital of Hordaland County. Population: 230,734 (2001).

Bergen-Belsen ♦ **Belsen**

bergenia /bə geéni ə/ (*plural* **-ias** or *same*) *n* a low-growing perennial plant with large leathery leaves. Flowers: early, usually red, purple, or pink on long stalks. Genus: *Bergenia*. [Mid-19C. After Karl August von *Bergen* (1704–60), German botanist and physician]

bergère /bər zháir/ (*plural* **-gères**) *n* a chair or sofa with sides and back made of woven cane [Mid-18C. < French, 'shepherdess']

Bergman /búrgmən/, **Ingmar** (*b.* 1918) Swedish film director. His many films include dark brooding

classics such as *The Seventh Seal* (1957) and *Persona* (1966). Full name **Bergman, Ernst Ingmar**

'Eight hours of hard work each day to get three minutes of film. And during those eight hours there are maybe only 10 or 12 minutes if you're lucky, of real creation…Everything and everyone on a movie set must be attuned to finding those minutes of creativity.'
[Ingmar Bergman, *Interview, Playboy*; June 1964]

Bergman, Ingrid (1915–82) Swedish-born US film actor. Best known for her role in the film *Casablanca* (1942), she acted in numerous US and European films and won three Academy Awards.

'A kiss is a lovely trick designed by nature to stop speech when words become superfluous.'
[Ingrid Bergman, *Viva*; 1977]

bergschrund /búrk shroŏnt/ (*plural* **-schrunds** or **-schrunde** /-shroŏndə/) *n* a crevasse formed at the head of a glacier [Mid-19C. < German, 'mountain cleft']

Bergson /búrgss'n/, **Henri** (1859–1941) French philosopher. One of his most influential ideas was that creative energy plays a central role in human development. He won the Nobel Prize in literature (1927). Full name **Bergson, Henri Louis** —**Bergsonian** /burg sóni ən/ *n, adj*

'The present contains nothing more than the past, and what is found in the effect was already in the cause.'
[Henri Bergson, *Creative Evolution*; 1907]

Bergsonism /búrgss'nizəm/ *n* the philosophy of Henri Bergson, which posits the existence of a universal life-giving force (**élan vital**)

berg wind *n* a hot dry wind that blows from the South African interior to the coast [< BERG², because it comes from the mountains]

beriberi /bérri bérri/ *n* a degenerative disease of the nerves caused by a deficiency of the vitamin thiamine and marked by pain, inability to move, and swelling [Early 18C. < Sinhalese, 'weakness']

Bering /báiring/, **Vitus** (1681–1741) Danish-born Russian explorer. He investigated the theory that Asia and North America were once connected. The Bering Sea and Bering Strait are named after him. Full name **Bering, Vitus Jonassen**

Bering land bridge *n* a link between Alaska and Siberia that was above sea level during the Ice Age between 13,000 and 10,000 years ago and provided a route for prehistoric people and animals into the Americas

Bering Sea part of the North Pacific Ocean surrounded by the Aleutian Islands, Siberia, and Alaska. Area: 2,269,000 sq. km/876,100 sq. mi. Depth: 4,773 m/15,659 ft.

Bering Strait narrow stretch of sea connecting the Bering Sea to the Arctic Ocean, and separating Russia from Alaska. At its narrowest point it is 82 km/51 mi. wide.

Berio /bérri ō/, **Luciano** (1925–2003) Italian composer. His experimental compositions combined prerecorded and electronic sounds, and spoken words.

Berisha /bə reĕshə/, **Sali** (*b*. 1944) president of Albania (1992–97). One of the leaders of post-Communist reform in Albania, he was elected as the country's first non-Communist president since World War II.

berk /burk/, **burk** *n* somebody regarded as stupid or foolish (*slang insult*) [Mid-20C. < rhyming slang *Berkeley Hunt* 'cunt']

Berkeleianism /baˈarkli ə nizzəm/ *n* the philosophy of George Berkeley, particularly his view that the material world is an idea in God's mind and that an object's existence consists in its being perceived [Early 19C. After George BERKELEY] —**Berkeleian** *adj, n*

Berkeley /búrkli/ city in western California on San Francisco Bay, home to the University of California. Population: 103,640 (2002 estimate).

Berkeley /búrkli/, **Busby** (1895–1976) US film director and choreographer. He is famous for his work in Broadway and Hollywood musicals including *42nd Street* (1933). Born **Enos, William Berkeley**

Berkeley /baˈarkli/, **George** (1685–1753) Irish Anglican

bishop and philosopher. He propounded idealist philosophy in *A Treatise Concerning the Principles of Human Knowledge* (1710) and other works.

'We have first raised a dust and then complain we cannot see.'
[George Berkeley, *A Treatise Concerning the Principles of Human Knowledge*; 1710]

Berkeley /baˈarkli, búrk-/, **Sir William** (1606–77) English-born colonial governor. His policies as governor of Virginia (1641–51, 1660–77) resulted in Bacon's Rebellion (1676).

berkelium /bur keĕli əm/ *n* a synthetic radioactive element. Source: bombardment of americium-241 with helium ions. Symbol **Bk**. See table at **element** [Mid-20C. After BERKELEY, California]

Berkoff /búrk of/, **Steven** (*b*. 1937) British actor, director, and dramatist. He founded the London Theatre Group and became known for his controversial adaptations of classical drama.

Berks. /baarks/ *abbr* Berkshire

Berkshire /baˈarkshər/ former county in south-central England. Population: 783,200 (1995). Area: 1,259 sq. km/486 sq. mi.

berley /búrli/, **burley** *Aus n* **1.** FISHING BAIT SCATTERED TO ATTRACT FISH bait scattered into the water to attract fish **2.** NONSENSE thinking or talk considered to be nonsensical (*slang*) ■ *vt* (**-leys, -leying, -leyed**) **1.** FISHING SCATTER BAIT OVER WATER to scatter bait over water to attract fish **2.** HURRY SOMEBODY UP to cause somebody to hurry [Late 19C. Origin ?]

berlin /bur lín/, **berline** /bur leĕn/ *n* a large and luxurious car with a glass partition between the driver and the passengers [Late 17C. After the city of BERLIN; originally a horse-drawn carriage]

Berlin /bur lín/ capital and the largest city of Germany. At the end of World War II (1945), the city was divided into East and West Berlin. It was reunified and became the national capital again following the reunification of East and West Germany in 1990. Population: 3,382,200 (2001). —**Berliner** *n*

Express Newspapers
Irving Berlin

Berlin, Irving (1888–1989) Russian-born US songwriter. One of the all-time great writers of American popular songs, including *God Bless America* (1938) and *White Christmas* (1954), he also wrote numerous musicals, including *Annie Get Your Gun* (1946). Born **Baline, Israel**

'There may be trouble ahead, / But while there's moonlight and music / and love and romance, / Let's face the music / and dance.'
[Irving Berlin, 'Let's Face the Music and Dance', *Follow the Fleet*; 1936]

Berlin, Sir Isaiah (1909–97) Latvian-born British philosopher and historian. He espoused liberal humanism in works such as *Two Concepts of Liberty* (1959), *Vico and Herder* (1976), and *The Crooked Timber of Humanity* (1990).

'The goal of philosophy is always the same, to assist men to understand themselves and thus operate in the open, and not wildly, in the dark.'
[Sir Isaiah Berlin, *Concepts and Categories*; 1978]

Berlin Wall fortified wall surrounding West Berlin, built in 1961 to prevent East German citizens trav-

elling to the West. Its demolition in 1989 marked the end of the Cold War.

Berlin wool *n* a fine wool yarn. Use: clothes, tapestry.

Berlin woolwork *n* needlepoint embroidery stitched with Berlin wools on charts painted by hand, popular especially in the second half of the 19th century

Berlioz /báirli ōz/, **Hector** (1803–69) French composer. He was a seminal figure in 19th-century romanticism. Major works among his symphonies, operas, and masses include the *Symphonie Fantastique* (1831) and the opera *The Trojans* (1856–59). Full name **Berlioz, Louis Hector**

'Time is a great teacher, but unfortunately it kills all its pupils.'
[Attributed to Hector Berlioz]

Berlusconi /báirloo skóni/, **Silvio** (*b*. 1936) prime minister of Italy (1994, 2001–). His coalition government of 1994 collapsed within a year of election. Despite corruption scandals related to his business empire, he led his centre-right party to victory in the 2001 elections.

berm /burm/, **berme** *n* **1.** NARROW PATH a ledge or narrow path along the top or bottom of a slope, at the edge of a road, or along a canal **2.** RIDGE ABOVE HIGH-TIDE MARK a natural ridge or flat platform formed at the rear of a beach, above the high-tide mark **3.** MIL RIDGE OF SAND FOR ANTITANK DEFENCE a ridge of sand or soil erected as a defence against tanks, which in crossing it expose their vulnerable undersides to attack **4.** MIL LEDGE BETWEEN MOAT AND RAMPART a ledge or narrow path between a moat or ditch and a rampart **5.** MIN EXTRACT ROADWAY IN OPEN-CAST MINE a narrow roadway cut in the slope of an open-cast mine **6.** NZ GRASS VERGE OF IN TOWN STREET the grass verge of a suburban street, usually kept mown [Early 18C. Via French < Dutch]

Bermuda /bər myoŏdə/ self-governing British dependency in the western North Atlantic Ocean. It contains more than 150 islands, 20 of which are inhabited. Language: English. Currency: Bermuda dollar. Capital: Hamilton. Population: 64,482 (2001). Area: 53 sq. km/20 sq. mi. —**Bermudan** *n, adj*

Bermuda bag *n* an oval-shaped handbag with wooden handles and removable covers

Bermuda grass *n* a creeping grass with wiry roots. Use: lawns, pastures, stabilizing sand dunes. Native to: southern Europe. Latin name: *Cynodon dactylon*.

Bermuda rig, **Bermudan rig**, **Bermudian rig** /bər myoŏdiən-/ *n* a fore-and-aft arrangement of a boat's mast and sails consisting of a tall pointed mainsail on a sharply raked mast

Bermuda shorts, **Bermudas** /bər myoŏdəz/ *npl* tailored shorts whose legs extend almost to the knee

Bermuda Triangle *n* an area in the western Atlantic Ocean, between Bermuda, Florida, and Puerto Rico, where many ships and aircraft are believed to have disappeared in mysterious circumstances

Bermudian rig *n* SAILING same as **Bermuda rig**

Bern /burn/, **Berne** capital of Switzerland since 1848. Situated on the Aar River in western Switzerland, it is also capital of Bern Canton. Population: 122,500 (2001). —**Bernese** *adj*

Bernadette of Lourdes /búrnə dét-/, **St** (1844–79) French nun and visionary. She said in 1858 that she had received apparitions of the Virgin Mary near her birthplace, Lourdes, which subsequently became a popular place of Roman Catholic pilgrimage. Born **Soubirous, Marie Bernarde**

Bernadotte /búrnə dot/, **Folke, Count** (1895–1948) Swedish diplomat. He was assassinated by Jewish terrorists while serving as a UN mediator in Palestine prior to the creation of Israel.

Bernanos /báirnə noss/, **Georges** (1888–1948) French novelist. He wrote *Diary of a Country Priest* (1936).

'Hell, madame, is to love no more.'
[Georges Bernanos, *Journal d'un curé de campagne (Diary of a Country Priest)*; 1936]

Bernard /bair naˈar, búrnərd/, **Claude** (1813–78) French physiologist. He made important discoveries on the role of the pancreas and liver.

'Man can learn nothing except by going from the known to the unknown.'

[Claude Bernard, *An Introduction to the Study of Experimental Medicine*; 1865]

Bernardine /búrnədin/ *n* **1. CISTERCIAN MONK** a Cistercian monk belonging to the branch of the Roman Catholic order reformed by st bernard of clairvaux **2. NUN** a nun belonging to a non-Cistercian Roman Catholic order that follows a rule based on the original Cistercian rule ■ *adj* **1. OF BERNARDINE** relating to or characteristic of a Bernardine **2. OF ST BERNARD** relating to or characteristic of St bernard of clairvaux or his monastic reforms

Bernard of Clairvaux /búrnərd əv klair vố/, **St** (1090–1153) French theologian. He became the Cistercian abbot of the influential monastery at Clairvaux (1113) and preached the Second Crusade (1146).

Berne ♦ Bern

Berners-Lee /búrnərz leé/, **Tim** (*b.* 1955) British computer scientist and inventor. He designed and introduced the World Wide Web in 1989 and in 1999 became director of the consortium that manages the World Wide Web. Full name **Berners-Lee, Sir Timothy John**

Bernese Alps /búr neez-/ mountain range in southwestern Switzerland, south of Bern. The highest peaks are the Finsteraarhorn, 4,274 m/14,022 ft, and the Jungfrau, 4,158 m/13,642 ft. The region is a major tourist area with many mountain resorts.

Sarah Bernhardt

Bernhardt /búrn haart/, **Sarah** (1844–1923) French actor. Known for her passionate performances in tragedy, she founded her own theatre company in 1899. Among her most famous roles were Marguerite in *La Dame aux Camélias* by Alexandre Dumas fils and the title role in *Phèdre* by Racine. Born **Bernard, Sarah-Marie-Henriette Rosine**

'For the theatre one needs long arms; it is better to have them too long than too short. An *artiste* with short arms can never, never make a fine gesture.'
[Sarah Bernhardt, *Memories of My Life*; 1907]

Bernini /bur neéni/, **Gianlorenzo** (1598–1680) Italian sculptor and architect. The foremost Italian artist of the Baroque period, he produced bronze and marble sculptures and designed many of the most impressive features of St Peter's Cathedral in Rome. Full name **Bernini, Giovanni Lorenzo**

Bernoulli /bur noóli/, **Daniel** (1700–82) Dutch-born Swiss mathematician and physicist. The son of Johann Bernoulli, he formulated the Bernoulli effect governing the conservation of energy in fluid dynamics.

'It would be better for the true physics if there were no mathematicians on earth.'
[Daniel Bernoulli. Quoted in *The Mathematical Intelligencer*; 1991]

Bernoulli, Jacques (1654–1705) Swiss mathematician. The brother of Johann Bernoulli, he wrote *Ars conjectandi* (*The Art of Conjecturing*) (1713) on the theory of probability and made theoretical advances in geometry and calculus.

Bernoulli, Johann or **Jean** (1667–1748) Swiss mathematician. He helped write the first textbook on differential calculus. He was the brother of Jacques Bernoulli and the father of Daniel Bernoulli.

Bernoulli distribution *n* STATS same as **binomial distribution** [After Jacques BERNOULLI]

Bernoulli effect *n* the acceleration of the flow of a fluid as its pressure is reduced, as happens when fluid passes through a pipe of changing diameter [After Daniel BERNOULLI]

Bernoulli's theorem, **Bernoulli's law**, **Bernoulli's principle** *n* **1.** a law in physics whereby the sum of the pressure and the product of one half of the density times the velocity squared is constant along a streamline for steady flow in an incompressible nonviscous fluid at constant height **2.** STATS same as **law of large numbers** [After Jacques BERNOULLI]

Leonard Bernstein

Bernstein /búrn stīn/, **Leonard** (1918–90) US conductor, composer, and pianist. He composed symphonic and choral works and the musicals *Candide* (1956) and *West Side Story* (1957).

'Einstein said that "the most beautiful experience we can have is the mysterious". Then why do so many of us try to explain the beauty of music, thus apparently depriving it of its mystery?'
[Leonard Bernstein, *The Unanswered Question*; 1976]

Berri /bérri/ town in southeastern South Australia, on the Murray River. Population: 3,731 (1991).

berry /bérri/ *n* (*plural* **-ries**) **1. SMALL JUICY FRUIT** a small juicy or fleshy fruit. Berries are usually round and may be edible or inedible. **2. BOT FLESHY SEED-CONTAINING FRUIT** a soft fleshy fruit that contains many seeds. Tomatoes, grapes, and bananas are berries. (*technical*) **3. BOT KERNEL** a seed or kernel, e.g. a coffee bean **4.** MARINE BIOL LOBSTER EGG an egg of a lobster or other egg-carrying crustacean ■ *vi* (**-ries, -rying, -ried**) **1. SEARCH FOR EDIBLE BERRIES** to gather or hunt for berries to eat **2. BEAR BERRIES** to produce berries (*refers to bushes*) [Old English *beri(g)e* < Germanic] —**berried** *adj*

SPELLCHECK **berry** or **bury**? Do not confuse the spelling of **berry** and **bury**, which sound similar. A **berry** is a small soft fruit, and the word with this spelling is only occasionally used as a verb, meaning 'bear or gather berries'. The word **bury** is always used as a verb, meaning 'put in a hole' or 'hide by covering': *The dog buried its bone in the garden.*

Berry /bérri/, **Chuck** (*b.* 1926) US singer, songwriter, and guitarist. He was one of the originators of rock and roll, bringing the influence of rhythm and blues to mainstream popular music and recording such classics of the genre as 'Roll Over Beethoven' (1956) and 'Johnny B. Goode' (1958). Born **Berry, Charles Edward Anderson**

Berry, Halle (*b.* 1968) US actor. She was the first African American woman to win an Academy Award for best actress for her role in *Monster's Ball* (2001).

Berryman /bérrimən/, **John** (1914–72) US poet, writer, and critic. He revealed his own emotional struggles in collections such as *77 Dream Songs* (1964), which won a Pulitzer Prize. Full name **Berryman, John McAlpin**. Born **Smith, John**

'It takes me so long to read the 'paper / said to me one day a novelist hot as a firecracker, / because I have to identify myself with everyone in it, / including the corpses, pal.'
[John Berryman, *77 Dream Songs*; 1964]

berseem /bər seém/ *n* a clover grown especially in the southern United States and the Nile Valley. Use: forage, soil improver. Native to: Mediterranean.

Latin name: *Trifolium alexandrinum*. [Early 20C. Via Arabic *birsīm* < Coptic *bersīm*]

berserk /bər zúrk/ *adj* **1. VERY ANGRY** behaving in an uncontrolled way as a result of anger or irrational feeling ○ *go berserk* **2. VERY EXCITED** extremely excited or enthusiastic about something (*informal*) ○ *The audience went berserk when she finally appeared.* ■ *n* **1. SOMEBODY VERY ANGRY** somebody who behaves in an uncontrolled way as a result of anger or irrational feeling **2.** MIL, HIST same as **berserker** [Early 19C. < Old Norse *berserk* 'wild warrior', probably < the stem of *bjorn* 'bear' + *serkr* 'shirt'] —**berserkly** *adv*

berserker /bər zúrkər/ *n* a member of a group of ancient Norse warriors who fought with wild unrestrained aggression

berth /burth/ *n* **1. BED ON SHIP OR TRAIN** a bed, usually built-in, on a ship or a train **2.** NAUT DOCK FOR SHIP a place, usually alongside a quay or dock, where a boat ties up or anchors **3.** NAUT ROOM TO MANOEUVRE AT SEA sufficient room between a boat and the shore, another boat, or an object to allow safe manoeuvring **4. PARKING PLACE** a place for a motor vehicle to park or be loaded or unloaded **5.** NAUT JOB ON SHIP a post as part of a ship's crew **6.** JOB a job or position of employment (*informal*) ■ *v* (**berths, berthing, berthed**) **1.** *vti* NAUT DOCK SHIP to dock or moor a vessel, or be docked or moored **2.** *vt* NAUT ASSIGN MOORING TO VESSEL to assign a vessel a place to dock or moor **3.** *vt* ALLOCATE BERTH TO SOMEBODY to assign somebody a berth on a ship or train [Early 17C. < BEAR[2] 'carry'] ◇ **give somebody** *or* **something a wide berth** to keep well away from somebody or something considered unpleasant or dangerous

bertha /búrthə/ *n* a wide long collar around the shoulders of a woman's low-necked dress [Mid-19C. < French *berthe*, after *Bertha* (d. AD 783), Carolingian queen]

Bertillon system /búrtilən-/ *n* a former method of identifying people, especially criminals, on the basis of detailed records of their physical measurements and characteristics [Late 19C. After Alphonse *Bertillon* (1853–1914), French criminologist]

Berwickshire /bérrikshər/ former county in southeastern Scotland, now part of the Scottish Borders council area

Berwick-upon-Tweed /bérrik ə pon tweéd/ walled town in Northumberland, northern England. Situated on the mouth of the River Tweed, it was ceded to England by Scotland in 1482. Population: 25,949 (2001).

beryl /bérrəl/ *n* a hard, crystalline mineral, composed of beryllium aluminium silicate, that occurs in white, yellow, pink, green, or blue forms. Use: gems. [12C. Via French and Latin *beryllus* < Greek *bērullos*] —**berylline** *adj*

beryllium /bə rílli əm/ *n* a grey-white metallic element that is light, hard, brittle, and resists corrosion. Source: beryl. Use: alloys, lightweight construction material, windows in X-ray tubes. Symbol **Be**. See table at **element**

Berzelius /bər zeéli əss/, **Jöns Jakob, Baron** (1779–1848) Swedish chemist. He drew up the table of atomic weights and discovered the elements selenium, thorium, and cerium.

besan /báy san/ *n* FOOD same as **gram flour** [< Hindi]

Besançon /bə zóN soN/ city and capital of Doubs Department, in the Franche-Comté Region, eastern France. Population: 117,733 (1999).

Besant /bézz'nt/, **Annie** (1847–1933) British theosophist and politician. She was the first woman elected president of the Indian National Congress (1917). Born **Wood, Annie**

Besant /bə zánt/, **Sir Walter** (1836–1901) British social reformer and novelist. His novels advocated social reform and included *The Children of Gideon* (1886).

beseech /bi seéch/ (**-seeches, -seeching, -sought** /-sáwt/ *or* **-seeched**) *vt* (*literary*) **1.** to ask earnestly or beg somebody to do something ○ *I beseech you to think again.* **2.** to ask urgently for something ○ *beseeching their aid* [12C. < BE- + early form of SEEK] —**beseecher** *n* —**beseeching** *adj* —**beseechingly** *adv*

~~beserk~~ incorrect spelling of **berserk**

beset /bi sét/ (**-sets, -setting, -set**) *vt* (*usually passive*) **1. HARASS SOMEBODY OR SOMETHING** to harass or trouble somebody or something continually (*formal*) **2. SURROUND SOMEBODY OR SOMETHING** to attack somebody or

something from all sides (*formal*) **3.** **SET SOMETHING WITH JEWELS** to surround or set something with jewels or other ornaments (*literary*) —**besetment** *n* —**besetter** *n*

besetting /bi sétting/ *adj* harassing or troubling somebody continually

beside /bi sīd/ *prep* **1.** **AT SIDE OF** in a position next to or alongside ○ *Sit beside me.* ○ *beside the seaside* **2.** **COMPARED WITH** in comparison with ○ *handsome beside his brother* **3.** **AS WELL AS** in addition to ○ *in another dictionary beside this one* [Old English *be sīdan* 'by the side of'] ◇ **beside yourself** in a very excited or agitated state

USAGE beside or **besides**? ***Beside*** is a preposition referring to physical position: *Come and sit beside me.* It is also used to mean 'in addition to', although this can lead to confusion with the meaning 'at the side of'. ***Besides*** is an adverb meaning 'what is more': *It's late and besides, the weather's too cold.* It is also a preposition meaning 'in addition to': *They've already paid a lot for the house besides what they'll need for improvements.* Note that ***besides*** is inclusive, whereas *except* is exclusive, so that *Besides Larry, we'll invite John, Jake, and Renée* means that Larry is also invited, whereas *They are all invited except Larry* means that Larry is not invited.

besides /bi sīdz/ *adv* **1.** **MOREOVER** what is more ○ *He's my cousin. Besides, he's good company.* **2.** **TOO** as well or in addition ○ *I've paid for his education and plenty more besides!* ■ *prep* **AS WELL** in addition to somebody or something specified or understood ○ *Besides fruit, we will also need cheese and crackers.*

USAGE See ***beside***.

besiege /bi séej/ (**-sieges, -sieging, -sieged**) *vt* **1.** **SURROUND PLACE WITH ARMY** to surround a city or stronghold with armed forces in order to bring about its surrender or capture **2.** **CROWD AROUND SOMEBODY** to crowd around somebody in an oppressive way (*usually passive*) ○ *besieged by reporters outside their hotel* **3.** **HARASS SOMEBODY OR SOMETHING** to harass a person or organization with insistent demands or complaints (*usually passive*) ○ *The box office was besieged by fans wanting tickets.* [13C. < BE- + obsolete *assiege* < Old French *asegier* < Latin *sedere* 'sit'] —**besieger** *n*

besmear /bi smeér/ (**-smears, -smearing, -smeared**) *vt* **1.** to spread mud, dirt, or a greasy or sticky substance on somebody or something **2.** to bring shame or disgrace on somebody or something

besmirch /bi smúrch/ (**-smirches, -smirching, -smirched**) *vt* **1.** to bring shame or disgrace on somebody's reputation **2.** to make something dirty (*literary*) —**besmircher** *n*

besom /béezəm/ *n* **1.** **BROOM MADE FROM TWIGS** a broom, especially one made with a bundle of twigs **2.** **CURLING BROOM** in curling, a broom used to sweep the ice in front of a moving stone in order to help it slide **3.** *regional* **WOMAN OR GIRL** used as a mildly derogatory term for a woman or girl (*insult*) [Old English *bes(e)ma* < Germanic] —**besom** *vt*

besotted /bi sóttid/ *adj* **1.** made confused through affection for or attraction to somebody **2.** in a confused mental state, especially through having drunk too much alcohol (*archaic*) [Late 16C. < BE- + obsolete *sot* 'stupefy' < Old French, 'fool']

besought past participle, past tense of **beseech**

bespangle /bi spáng g'l/ (**-gles, -gling, -gled**) *vt* to ornament something with small bright decorations, especially spangles (*literary*)

bespatter /bi spáttər/ (**-ters, -tering, -tered**) *vt* to splash something with mud, paint, or another liquid

bespeak /bi spéek/ (**-speaks, -speaking, -spoke** /-spṓk/, **-spoken** /-spṓkən/) *vt* **1.** **SIGNIFY SOMETHING** to be a sign or indication of something ○ *actions that bespeak complicity* **2.** **ORDER SOMETHING IN ADVANCE** to reserve or order something in advance **3.** **ASK FOR SOMETHING POLITELY** to ask politely for something such as a favour (*formal*) **4.** **ADDRESS SOMEBODY** to speak to somebody (*literary*)

bespectacled /bi spéktək'ld/ *adj* wearing spectacles

bespoke past tense of **bespeak** ■ *adj* made to a customer's specifications ○ *a bespoke suit*

bespoken past participle of **bespeak**

besprinkle /bi spríngk'l/ (**-kles, -kling, -kled**) *vt* to sprinkle small quantities of liquid or something light over the surface of something (*literary; often passive*)

Bessarabia /béssə ráybi ə/ historic region in southeastern Europe, between the Prut and Dniester rivers, corresponding roughly to present-day Moldova and part of Ukraine. A much-contested area, it was a province of Romania between 1918 and 1940.

Bessel /béss'l/, **Friedrich Wilhelm** (1784–1846) German mathematician and astronomer. He identified and determined the distance of the nearest stars, and predicted the existence of a planet beyond Uranus.

Bessemer /béssəmər/, **Sir Henry** (1813–98) British metallurgist. He invented the bessemer process for transforming molten pig iron into steel.

Bessemer process *n* a largely obsolete method of making steel from impure iron by forcing air through the molten metal in a specialized furnace (**Bessemer converter**) [Late 19C. After Sir Henry BESSEMER]

best /best/ CORE MEANING: better than anybody or anything else

1. *adj* **BETTER THAN ALL OTHERS** of the highest quality or standard or the most excellent type ○ *the best days of your life* ○ *wearing her best dress* ○ *the best sprinter this decade* **2.** *adj* **MOST LIKELY TO SUCCEED** most likely to have or come near to the desired outcome ○ *the best thing to do in the circumstances* **3.** *adj* **MOST INTIMATE** liked, trusted, and confided in more than anybody else ○ *my best friend* **4.** *adv* **MORE THAN ALL OTHERS** in the highest degree or to the greatest extent ○ *likes me best* **5.** *adv* **MOST SUCCESSFULLY** in a way that is most likely to have or come near to the desired outcome ○ *It works best if you warm it up first.* **6.** *adv* **TO HIGHEST STANDARD** to a higher standard than anybody or anything else ○ *the best trained horse in the competition* **7.** *n* **WHAT IS BEST** the best possible things or circumstances ○ *want the best for their family* ○ *will only buy the best* **8.** *n* **SOMEBODY OR SOMETHING BETTER THAN OTHERS** somebody or something of the highest quality or standard ○ *is the best at hockey* **9.** *n* **TOP QUALITY** the highest quality or standard that somebody or something is capable of ○ *do your best* ○ *past its best* **10.** *n* **TOP ACHIEVEMENT** the best time or score that somebody has achieved in a sport or game ○ *trying to beat her personal best in the marathon* **11.** *n* **ENDORSEMENT** used as an enthusiastic endorsement of something (*slang*) ○ *How is your hotel? – It's the best!* [Old English *betest*, superlative of GOOD and WELL², < Germanic] ◇ **at best** according to the most favourable interpretation ◇ **at somebody's** *or* **its best** performing at the peak of ability or effectiveness ◇ **at the best of times** even when circumstances are at their most favourable ◇ **do your level best** to make every effort to do something ○ *She did her level best to dissuade us.* ◇ **for the best** likely to have a more favourable outcome ○ *I don't know what to do for the best.* ◇ **make the best of something** to extract what benefit you can from an unsatisfactory or disadvantageous situation

Best /best/, **Charles H.** (1899–1978) US-born Canadian physiologist. With Frederick Banting, he codiscovered insulin (1922). Full name **Best, Charles Herbert**

Best, Elsdon (1856–1931) New Zealand ethnologist. Author of pioneering studies of the Tuhoe people of the Urewera Region of New Zealand, he wrote works that include *The Maori As He Was* (1924).

Best, George (*b.* 1946) Northern Irish footballer. He scored 134 goals for Manchester United (1963–73) and played 37 times for Northern Ireland.

best-ball *adj* in golf, using a scoring method in which a golfer competes against a team of two or three other golfers, with the team recording only the best individual score for each hole

best boy *n* the chief assistant to the electrician in charge of lighting on a film or television set

best-efforts sale *n* in a securities issue, the sale by an underwriter of as many securities as possible with no obligation to buy those not sold to investors

best end *n* meat cut from the end of the neck nearest to the shoulder of a butchered animal

bestial /bésti əl/ *adj* **1.** **INHUMAN** lacking human feelings of pity or remorse ○ *bestial cruelty* **2.** **SEXUALLY DEPRAVED** sexual in a depraved or purely physical manner **3.** **BRUTISH** lacking intellect, reason, or culture **4.** **RELATING TO BEAST** relating to or characteristic of a beast [14C. Via French < late Latin *bestialis* < Latin *bestia* 'beast'] —**bestially** *adv*

bestialise *vt* another spelling of **bestialize**

bestiality /bésti álləti/ *n* **1.** sexual activity between a human being and an animal **2.** an act, behaviour, or condition more appropriate for an animal than a human being

bestialize /bésti ə līz/ (**-izes, -izing, -ized**), **bestialise** (**-ises, -ising, -ised**) *vt* **1.** to make somebody behave or live like an animal **2.** to make somebody inhuman or savage

bestiary /bésti əri/ (*plural* **-ies**) *n* a medieval book containing pictures and moralizing stories about real and imaginary animals [Mid-19C. < medieval Latin *bestiarium* < Latin *bestia* 'beast']

bestir /bi stúr/ (**-stirs, -stirring, -stirred**) *vr* **bestir yourself** to begin to do something after a period of inactivity (*formal*) ○ *After a long afternoon nap, they finally bestirred themselves to start the supper preparations.*

best maid *n Scotland* the chief bridesmaid at a wedding, the counterpart of the best man

best man *n* a man attending a bridegroom and carrying out important duties during the wedding celebrations

best-of-breed *adj* **1.** describes the highest-ranking category of prize-winning animal of a specific breed in competitions and shows **2.** in marketing, sales, and competitive analysis, describes a computer product that is the best available software, hardware, or system in its class

best-off superlative of **well-off**

bestow /bi stṓw/ (**-stows, -stowing, -stowed**) *vt* **1.** to present something, especially something valuable or undeserved, to somebody (*formal*) **2.** to put something somewhere (*archaic*) ○ *'Alonso hence, and bestow your luggage where you found it.'* (William Shakespeare, *The Tempest*; 1611) —**bestowal** *n*

SYNONYMS See ***give***.

best practice *n* the most effective or efficient method of achieving an objective or completing a task

bestrew /bi stróo/ (**-strews, -strewing, -strewed, -strewn** /-stróon/ or **-strewed**) *vt* (*literary*) **1.** to scatter things over something ○ *a church aisle bestrewn with flowers* **2.** to be scattered over something ○ *the confetti that bestrewed the church steps after the wedding*

bestride /bi strīd/ (**-strides, -striding, -strode** /-strṓd/ or **-strid** /-stríd/, **-stridden** /-strídd'n/ or **-strid** *archaic*) *vt* to sit or stand with one foot on or towards each side of something ○ *He bestrode the hearthrug, holding forth on the merits of the case.*

bestseller /bést séllər/ *n* **1.** something, especially a book, that is commercially very successful **2.** an author who writes bestsellers

bestselling /bést sélling/ *adj* **1.** far more popular and successful than other products on sale at the same time ○ *his bestselling account of life in Provence* **2.** writing books that are commercially very successful ○ *a bestselling novelist*

bet /bet/ *vti* (**bets, betting, bet** or **betted**) **1.** **RISK SOMETHING OF VALUE** to agree with somebody that something, usually money, will be forfeited by the person who incorrectly predicts the outcome of a future event to the other or fails in some other prearranged challenge ○ *I bet you £10 you can't lift that rock.* **2.** **THINK SOMETHING IS TRUE** to express certainty that something will happen, has happened, or is true (*informal*) ○ *I bet he's forgotten to bring the keys.* ■ *n* **1.** **ACT OF BETTING** an agreement that the person who incorrectly predicts the outcome of a future event will forfeit something, usually money, to another **2.** **AMOUNT WAGERED** the amount of money that somebody agrees to pay as a bet ○ *She lost her £10 bet.* **3.** **WHAT SOMEBODY EXPECTS OR THINKS** what somebody expects to happen or thinks is true ○ *My bet is they'll decide to overlook the whole thing.* **4.** **SOMEBODY OR SOMETHING LIKELY TO WIN** somebody or something likely to be successful [Late 16C. Origin ?] ◇ **you bet!** used to show emphatic agreement (*informal*) ◇ **your best** *or* **safest bet** the course of action most likely to be productive

beta /beétə/ *n* **1.** **2ND LETTER OF GREEK ALPHABET** the second letter of the Greek alphabet, represented in English as 'b'. See table at **alphabet** **2.** EDUC **ACADEMIC GRADE** a letter such as 'B' used as a grade for good, but not excellent, academic work **3.** FIN **MEASURE OF PRICE SENSITIVITY** a measure of how volatile the price of a security is, compared to the overall market ■ *adj* **1.** COMPUT **READY FOR TESTING BY CUSTOMERS** describes software ready for beta tests ○ *beta version* **2.** PHYS **PRODUCED BY RADIOACTIVITY** describes electrons formed by the splitting of a neutron into a proton and an electron ○ *beta particles* ○ *beta rays* **3.** CHEM **SECOND NEAREST TO DESIGNATED ATOM** describes the second nearest atom to a particular atom or group of atoms in an organic molecule **4.** **BEING MINOR FORM** describes a minor form of a chemical element with more than one form (**allotrope**) **5.** CHEM **BEING ONE FORM AMONG OTHERS** describes a structural form of a chemical compound having more than one form (**isomer**) [14C. Via Latin and Greek < Canaanite *bet* 'house']

Beta *n* the second brightest star in a constellation (*followed by the Latin genitive*) ○ *Beta Centauri*

beta amyloid *n* a protein that accumulates in clumps in the brain as a result of a gene variation, leading to the memory loss and dementia that are features of Alzheimer's syndrome

beta-blocker *n* a drug that regulates the activity of the heart. Use: treatment of high blood pressure.

beta-carotene *n* BIOCHEM same as **carotene**

beta decay *n* the radioactive transformation of an atomic nucleus during which an electron or positron is produced, although the mass number remains unchanged

beta emission *n* the emission of an electron by a radionuclide —**beta emitter** *n*

betaine /beétə een, -in, bi táy-/ *n* a sweet-tasting organic compound. Source: sugar beet. Use: treatment of muscular degeneration. Formula: $C_5H_{11}NO_2$. [Mid-19C. < Latin *beta* 'beet']

betake /bi táyk/ (**-takes, -taking, -took** /-to͝ok/, **-taken** /-táykən/) *vr* **betake yourself** to go somewhere (*archaic or literary*)

betamethasone /beétə méthəzōn/ *n* a steroid drug. Use: treatment of inflammation, asthma, allergies, and rheumatoid arthritis. [Mid-20C. < BETA + METHYL + HYDROCORTISONE]

Betancourt /béttən koor/, **Rómulo** (1908–81) president of Venezuela (1959–64). He helped to found the Democratic Action party (1941) and spent periods in exile. As president he instituted reforms that paved the way for democracy.

beta-oxidation *n* the breakdown of fatty acids during cellular metabolism to produce acetyl coenzyme A

beta particle *n* a high-speed electron emitted from the nucleus of an atom during radioactive decay and created by the splitting of a neutron into a proton and an electron

beta process *n* PHYS same as **beta decay**

beta ray *n* a stream of beta particles

beta-receptor *n* a site on cells in the autonomic nervous system that responds to hormones such as adrenaline and operates to control blood pressure, regulate the heartbeat, and contract muscles

beta rhythm *n* a pattern of electrical waves in the brain of somebody who is awake and active, registering on an electroencephalograph at a reading between 18 and 30 hertz

beta sheet *n* a flat flexible protein structure consisting of parallel polypeptide chains cross-linked by intermolecular hydrogen bonds

beta test *n* a test of a product, especially computer software, by giving it to a few customers to try out, before the final version is put on sale —**beta-test** *vt*

beta transformation *n* PHYS same as **beta decay**

betatron /beétə tron/ *n* a device that accelerates electrons in a circular orbit by means of a rapidly alternating magnetic field. In this way, electrons can reach energies of 340 MeV and may be used to strike a metal target to produce a continuous stream of gamma rays.

betaware /beétə wair/ *n* a version of computer software that is given to a few customers before the final version is put on sale

beta wave *n* a high-frequency electrical wave produced in the human brain and associated with normal wakefulness

betcha /béchə/ *contr* a form of 'bet you' used mainly in conversation (*nonstandard*) ○ *Betcha he asks me out before the weekend.*

betel /beét'l/ (*plural* **-tels** or *same*) *n* an evergreen climbing plant with broad leaves chewed as a mild stimulant and digestive aid. Native to: Asia. Latin name: *Piper betle.* [Mid-16C. Via Portuguese < Malayalam *verrila* < Tamil *vrrilai*]

Betelgeuse /beét'l jurz, /beét'l /jooz/ *n* a bright red variable supergiant star that is the second brightest star in the constellation Orion and the twelfth brightest in the night sky

betel nut *n* the dark red seed of the betel palm that is wrapped in betel leaves with lime and chewed as a mild stimulant in some Asian countries

betel palm *n* a palm tree that has orange fruit and dark red seeds. Native to: Asia. Latin name: *Areca catechu.*

bete noire /bét nwaár/ (*plural* **betes noires** /*pronunc. same*/) *n* somebody or something that is particularly disliked [Mid-19C. < French, 'black beast']

beth /beth/ *n* the second letter of the Hebrew alphabet, represented in the English alphabet as 'b'. See table at **alphabet** [Early 19C. < Hebrew *bēṯ* 'house']

Bethany /béthəni/ village at the foot of the Mount of Olives near Jerusalem in ancient Palestine. According to the Bible, it was the home of Martha, Mary, and their brother Lazarus who was restored to life by Jesus Christ.

Beth Din /bét dín, béth-/ (*plural* **Batei Din** /baá tay-/) *n* a Jewish religious court regulating matters of Jewish law such as dietary laws, divorce, and conversion [Late 18C. < Hebrew *bēṯ dīn* 'house of judgment']

Bethe /báytə/, **Hans** (*b.* 1906) German-born US physicist. He helped develop the atomic bomb (1943–46). His work on stellar nuclear energy won him the Nobel Prize in physics (1967). Full name **Bethe, Hans Albrecht**

bethink /bi thíngk/ (**-thinks, -thinking, -thought** /-tháwt/) *vr* **bethink yourself** to think of or remember something (*archaic*)

Bethlehem /béthli hem/ town in the West Bank near Jerusalem. Part of Israel since 1967, it has been administered by the Palestinian Authority since 1995. Thought to be the birthplace of King David and Jesus Christ, it is regarded as a holy city by Christians. Population: 21,947 (1997).

bethought past participle, past tense of **bethink**

Bethune /be thyo͞on/, **Mary McLeod** (1875–1955) US educator and activist. She founded and was president of what became Bethune-Cookman College, Daytona Beach, Florida. She promoted education for African Americans and founded the National Council of Negro Women (1935).

> 'I don't mind being different. I don't want to be Jim-Crowed to a back seat because I'm black and I don't want to be ushered to a front seat because I'm not white so they can "palaver" over me.'
> [Mary McLeod Bethune. Quoted in *Mary McLeod Bethune*, Emma Gelders Steine; 1957]

beti /bétti/ *n Carib* a daughter, or a young girl [Hindi]

betide /bi tīd/ (**-tides**) *vti* to happen, or happen to somebody (*literary; usually used in the subjunctive*) ○ *Whether good or ill betide you, trust in yourself.*

betimes /bi tīmz/ *adv* (*archaic*) **1.** early or in good time **2.** in a short time [13C. < form of BY[1]]

Betjeman /béchəmən/, **Sir John** (1906–84) British poet. He was poet laureate (1972–84). His books, largely poetic celebrations of rural England, include *A Few Late Chrysanthemums* (1954).

> 'Too many people in the modern world view poetry as a luxury, not a necessity like petrol. But to me it's the oil of life.'
> [Sir John Betjeman, *Observer*; 1974]

betoken /bi tṓkən/ (**-kens, -kening, -kened**) *vt* to be a sign that something exists or will happen (*literary*)

betony /béttəni/ (*plural* **-nies**) *n* **1.** a plant of the mint family. Flowers: purplish. Use: flavourings in herbal teas; herbal medicine. Native to: Europe, Asia. Latin name: *Stachys officinalis.* **2.** a plant resembling true betony [14C. < Latin *betonica*]

betook past tense of **betake**

betray /bi tráy/ (**-trays, -traying, -trayed**) *vt* **1.** **HELP ENEMY** to harm or be disloyal to a country or another person by helping an enemy or giving information that is confidential **2.** **SURRENDER SOMEBODY OR SOMETHING TREACHEROUSLY** to deliver somebody or something to an enemy ○ *He betrayed his own brother to the secret police.* **3.** **GO AGAINST PROMISE** to act in a way that is contrary to a promise made ○ *'If an intelligent person is betrayed repeatedly, and humiliated publicly, yet chooses to remain in that situation, one must ask: what are the rewards?'* (Gail Sheehy, *Vanity Fair*; February 1999) **4.** **REVEAL SOMETHING** to show something, often unintentionally ○ *She said nothing, but her bright eyes betrayed her excitement.* [13C. < BE[1] + Old French *trair* < Latin *tradere* 'hand over'] —**betrayal** *n* —**betrayer** *n*

betroth /bi trṓth/ (**-troths, -trothing, -trothed**) *vt* to promise to marry somebody, or promise that somebody will marry somebody (*archaic*) [14C. < BE- + TRUTH]

betrothal /bi trṓthəl/ *n* the act of becoming engaged to marry somebody, or the state of being engaged to somebody (*formal*)

betrothed /bi trṓthd/ (*plural* **-trotheds** or *same*) *n* the person to whom somebody is engaged to be married (*formal*) —**betrothed** *adj*

Bettelheim /bétt'l hīm/, **Bruno** (1903–90) Austrian-born US psychologist. A member of the University of Chicago faculty, he was best known for his treatment of autistic children and for his study of the meaning of fairy tales, *The Uses of Enchantment* (1976).

> 'No longer can we be satisfied with a life where the heart has its reasons which reason cannot know. Our hearts must know the world of reason, and reason must be guided by an informed heart.'
> [Bruno Bettelheim, *Guardian*; 15 March 1990]

better[1] /béttər/ (**-ters, -tering, -tered**) CORE MEANING: indicating that somebody, something, or an action is superior in some way to something or somebody else or is an improvement upon a situation ○ (adj) *Concentrated laundry detergent is better because it requires a smaller box or bottle.* ○ (adj) *She is gradually getting better, albeit slowly.* ○ (adj) *That's hardly going to make things any better.* ○ (adv) *Treatment programmes may get the job done better.*

1. *adj* **MORE ACCEPTABLE** more pleasing or acceptable than something else ○ *That hairstyle is far better than the one you had before.* **2.** *adj* **OF GREATER QUALITY** of greater quality, usefulness, or suitability than something else ○ *Economic security helps ensure a better future for our children.* ○ *It is better to light a candle than to curse the darkness.* **3.** *adj* **IMPROVED IN HEALTH** in an improved state of health, after not being well ○ *I'm feeling much better today, thank you.* **4.** *adv* **TO HIGHER STANDARD** in a more acceptable, appropriate, or effective way ○ *He plays tennis much better than I do.* ○ *I liked her much better after I got to know her.* **5.** *adv* **PREFERABLY** in a way that is preferable or more advantageous ○ *Such things are better left unsaid.* **6.** *vt* **SURPASS SOMETHING** to improve on something ○ *She hopes to better the record that she set at the Commonwealth Games.* ○ *He summed the whole thing up in a way that I couldn't possibly better.* **7.** *vt* **IMPROVE SELF OR THING** to improve yourself or something (*formal*) ○ *They tried to better themselves by attaining a good education.* ○ *attempts to better the lot of the refugees* **8.** *n* **SUPERIOR PERSON** a person who is superior to another in some way (*often used in the plural*) ○ *They think themselves our betters.* [Old English *bettra* < comparative of Germanic, 'advantageous'] ◇ **better safe than sorry** it is better to be overcautious than to take unnecessary risks ○ *I think I locked the door, but I'll just go back and check – better safe than sorry!* ◇ **for better or worse** whatever the outcome may be ◇ **get the better of somebody 1.** to defeat or be too strong for somebody **2.** to be too strong for somebody to control ◇ **go one better** to do something that has been done before but in a superior or preferable way ◇ **had better do something** ought to or must do something ○ *You'd better tell them soon.*

better[2] /béttər/ *n* somebody who bets. N Am term **bettor** [Early 17C. < BET]

better half *n* somebody's wife or husband (*informal humorous*)

betterment /béttərmənt/ *n* **1.** a change that improves something, especially somebody's financial or social condition (*formal*) **2.** improvement of a building or land that increases its value

better-off comparative of **well-off**

Betti /bétti/, **Ugo** (1892–1953) Italian dramatist and poet. His books include *Corruption in the Palace of Justice* (1944) and the verse collection *The Thoughtful King* (1922).

> 'We cannot bear to regard ourselves simply as playthings of blind chance; we cannot admit to feeling ourselves abandoned.'
> [Ugo Betti, *Struggle Till Dawn*; 1949]

betting /bétting/ *n* the activity of placing bets

betting shop *n* a shop or office that is licensed to take bets on the results of races and other sporting activities

bettong /be tóng/ *n* a small nocturnal member of the kangaroo family, with small rounded ears and a bushy tail. Native to: Australia. Genus: *Bettongia*. [Early 19C. < an Aboriginal language]

between /bi twéen/ CORE MEANING: a grammatical word indicating an intermediate point between two places, people, or times ○ (prep) *I was standing between two other women.* ○ (prep) *I intend to pay off my mortgage between now and 2010.* ○ (adv) *He worked two shifts, with an hour off between.*
prep **1.** TO AND FROM from one place to another ○ *She travels between Oxford and Birmingham most days.* **2.** TOGETHER together or in combination with ○ *Between us we should have enough money to pay for the trip.* **3.** INDICATES COMPARISON indicates a comparison, discussion, or relationship involving two people or groups ○ *Reconciliation was hampered by personality conflicts between company executives.* **4.** INDICATES CHOICES indicates two or more possible courses of action ○ *The court offers them a choice between a fine or community service.* [Old English *betwēonum* 'by two each' < *twēonum* 'two each' < Germanic] ◇ **(just) between you and me, (just) between ourselves, (just) between you, me, and the gatepost** *or* **bedpost** used to indicate that you are about to reveal something confidential

USAGE between or **among**? Although some people insist on using ***among*** and not ***between*** when more than two items or recipients are involved, it is established usage to use ***between*** in this meaning as well, especially when ***among*** might sound too formal: *They shared out the money equally between their five children.* ***Among*** is never used when only two items are involved.

betweenbrain /bi twéen brayn/ *n* ANAT same as **diencephalon**

betweentimes /bi twéen tīmz/ *adv* in the intervals between doing other things

betwixt /bi twíkst/ *adv, prep* same as **between** (*literary*) [Old English *betwēohs* < *tweohs* 'for two' < Germanic] ◇ **betwixt and between** between two groups or categories, without belonging to one or the other

~~**beutiful**~~ incorrect spelling of **beautiful**

Beuys /boyz, boyss/, **Joseph** (1921–86) German artist. His avant-garde artworks included assemblages and happenings. He helped to found Germany's Green Party.

Bevan /bévv'n/, **Nye** (1897–1960) British politician. As health minister for the postwar Labour government (1945–51) he introduced the National Health Service (1948). He edited the left-wing journal *Tribune* (1940–45). Full name **Bevan, Aneurin**

> 'This island is almost made of coal and surrounded by fish. Only an organizing genius could produce a shortage of coal and fish in Great Britain at the same time.'
> [Nye Bevan, *Speech at the Labour Party Conference, Blackpool*; 18 May 1945]

bevel /bévv'l/ *n* **1.** SLANTING EDGE a surface that joins another surface at an angle that is not a right angle **2.** ANGLE the angle at which one surface joins another, when this is not a right angle **3.** TOOL a tool with two legs that can be adjusted to make various angles. Use: measuring or marking angles on something. ■ *vt* (**-els, -elling, -elled**) MAKE SLANTING EDGE to shape the edge of something so that it forms an angle other than a right angle with the main surface ○ *a mirror with edges that had been bevelled* [Late 17C. < assumed Old French]

bevel gear *n* either of a pair of gear wheels, one conical and the other flat or conical, connecting and transmitting power between shafts that are not parallel

bevel square *n* WOODWORK same as **bevel** *n* (sense 3)

beverage /bévvərij/ *n* a drink other than water (*used mainly in commercial contexts*) [14C. < Old French *bevrage* < *bevre*, variant of *boire* < Latin *bibere* 'to drink']

Beveridge /bévvərij/, **William, 1st Baron Beveridge of Tuggal** (1879–1963) Indian-born British economist. His report on social insurance (the so-called 'Beveridge Report', 1942) provided the basis for the creation of the British welfare state. Full name **Beveridge, William Henry**

Beverley /bévvərli/ market town in the East Riding of Yorkshire, northeastern England. It is noted for its ancient minster. Population: 23,632 (1991).

Beverly Hills /bévverli hílz// wealthy residential and commercial city in southwestern California, Los Angeles. Population: 34,857 (2002 estimate).

Bevin /bévvin/, **Ernest** (1881–1951) British trade union leader and politician. The organizer and secretary of the Transport and General Workers' Union (1921–40), he was later minister of labour and foreign secretary.

> 'There never has been a war yet which, if the facts had been put calmly before the ordinary folk, could not have been prevented...The common man, I think, is the great protection against war.'
> [Ernest Bevin, *Speech to Parliament*; 23 November 1945]

bevvy /bévvi/ (*slang*) *n* (*plural* **-vies**) an alcoholic drink ○ *We went out for a few bevvies.* ■ *vi* (**-vies, -vying, -vied**) to drink alcohol [Late 19C. Shortening of BEVERAGE] ◇ **on the bevvy** spending time drinking alcohol (*slang*)

bevy /bévvi/ (*plural* **-ies**) *n* **1.** a group of people **2.** a group of animals or birds, especially quail, larks, or roe deer [15C. Origin ?]

bewail /bi wáyl/ (**-wails, -wailing, -wailed**) *vt* to express great sadness about something (*formal*)

beware /bi wáir/ *vti* to be on guard against somebody or something (*used only as a command and in the infinitive*) [13C. < *be ware* 'be careful' < Old English *wær* 'watchful' < Germanic]

bewdy /byóodi/ *interj Aus* used to show approval (*informal*) [Representing a pronunciation of BEAUTY]

bewhiskered /bi wískərd/ *adj* having whiskers ○ *bewhiskered gentlemen in old photographs*

Bewick /byóo ik/, **Thomas** (1753–1828) British wood engraver. He illustrated the *History of Quadrupeds* (1790) and *Fables of Aesop* (1818).

bewigged /bi wígd/ *adj* wearing a wig

bewilder /bi wíldər/ (**-ders, -dering, -dered**) *vt* to confuse or puzzle somebody completely [Late 17C. < BE[1] + archaic *wilder*, origin ?] —**bewildered** *adj* —**bewilderment** *n*

bewildering /bi wíldəring/ *adj* extremely confusing —**bewilderingly** *adv*

bewitch /bi wích/ (**-witches, -witching, -witched**) *vt* **1.** to fascinate or be very desirable to somebody (*often passive*) ○ *was bewitched by his charm* **2.** to affect somebody or something using a supposed magic spell [13C. < BE- + *witch* 'enchant' < WITCH] —**bewitcher** *n* —**bewitchment** *n*

bewitching /bi wíching/ *adj* fascinating, charming, or very desirable —**bewitchingly** *adv*

bey /bay/ (*plural* **beys**) *n* **1.** a title used for various high-ranking officials in the Ottoman Empire, especially governors of a province **2.** a respectful form of address for men used in Turkey and Egypt [Late 16C. Via Turkish < Old Turkish *beg* 'prince']

beyond /bi yónd/ CORE MEANING: a grammatical word indicating that something is on the other side of something else, either physically or in the abstract ○ (prep) *They are expanding environmental protection programmes beyond the border area.* ○ (prep) *The gift of laughter is beyond price.*
1. *prep, adv* AFTER STATED TIME indicates that something continues after a particular time ○ *will remain the world's leading economy in the next decade and beyond* **2.** *prep* PAST past a stage or situation ○ *Don't attempt to live beyond your income.* **3.** *prep* FURTHER THAN further than a particular state of mind or emotion ○ *The site has proved to be popular beyond anyone's wildest dreams.* **4.** *prep* EXCEPT indicates an exception ○ *He was incapable of any emotion beyond a certain rueful irony.* **5.** *prep* IMPOSSIBLE FOR indicates that something is impossible for somebody to do ○ *I find it quite beyond me to speak about what happened.* **6.** *n* THE HEREAFTER the form of existence that some people believe the spirit reaches after death ○ *He feels that his late parents watch over him from the beyond.* **7.** *n* WHAT IS OUT THERE an area that lies outside what is known ○ *Humanity stands at the edge of the solar system, contemplating the beyond.* [Old English *begeondan* < *be* form of BY[1] + *geondan* (see YOND)]

bezel /bézz'l/ *n* **1.** the face of a cutting tool, especially a chisel, that slopes towards the cutting edge **2.** the groove that holds the glass of a watch, light, or instrument dial in position [Late 16C. < Old French]

Béziers /bézzi ay/ city in Hérault Department in the Languedoc-Roussillon Region of southern France. It is situated in an important wine-producing region. Population: 69,153 (1999).

bezique /bi zéek/ *n* **1.** a card game like whist, played with the highest 64 cards from two packs **2.** the combination of the queen of spades and the jack of diamonds, which gains a high score in the game of bezique [Mid-19C. < French *besigue*]

bezoar /bée zawr/ *n* a hard mass of material such as fruit or hair found in the intestines of a ruminant animal, formerly believed to be an antidote to poison [15C. Via French *bezourd* < Arabic *badhizahr* < Persian *padzahr* < *pad* 'protection (against)' + *zahr* 'poison']

Bezos /báyzōss/, **Jeff** (*b.* 1964) US Internet entrepreneur. A graduate in electrical engineering and computer science, he worked in finance and information technology before setting up a retail site on the Internet in 1995.

bf, b.f., B/F, b/f *abbr* **1.** bloody fool (*dated informal*) **2.** PRINTING boldface **3.** ACCT brought forward

BF *abbr* Belgian franc

BFI *abbr* British Film Institute

BFPO *abbr* British Forces Post Office

bg *abbr* Bulgaria (*used in Internet addresses*) See table at **domain name**

BG *abbr* Brigadier General

B-girl *n* a young woman who is a devotee of hip-hop and rap music culture (*slang*) [Abbreviation of *break* (see BREAKDANCING)]

bh *abbr* Bahrain (*used in Internet addresses*) See table at **domain name**

Bh *symbol* bohrium

Bhadrapada /báadrə paadə/, **Bhadra** /báadrə/ *n* in the Hindu calendar, the sixth month of the year, lasting 31 days and falling about the same time as August to September. See table at **calendar**

Bhagavadgita /búggəvəd géetə/, **Bhagavad-Gita** *n* a Hindu religious text in which the god Krishna teaches the importance of detachment from personal aims, the fulfilment of religious duties, and devotion to God [Late 18C. < Sanskrit *Bhagavadgītā* 'song of the blessed one' (Krishna) < *bhagavant-* 'blessed' + *gītā* 'song']

Bhagwan /bug wáan/ *n S Asia* **1.** RELIG same as **God 2.** a teacher, especially somebody who is revered [Via Hindi *bhagwān* < Sanskrit *bhagavān* < *bhaj* 'adore']

bhai /bī/ *n S Asia* **1.** same as **brother** *n* (sense 1) **2.** used as a friendly form of address for a man [< Hindi *bhāī*, related to Sanskrit *bhrātr* 'brother']

Bhai /bī/ *n* a title of respect that is used after a Sikh man's name to indicate distinction

bhaigan /bī gan/, **baigan** *n Carib* same as **aubergine** (senses 1–2) [< Hindi]

bhajan /bújjən/ *n S Asia* a Sikh or Hindu hymn [Early 20C. < Sanskrit *bhajana*]

a at; aa father; aw all; ay day; ai hair; ə about, item, edible, common, circus; e egg; ee eel; hw when; i it, happy; ī ice; 'l apple; 'm rhythm; 'n fashion; o odd; ō open; ŏŏ good; oo pool; ow owl; oy oil; th thin; th this; u up; ur urge;

bhaji /baáji/ (*plural* **-jis**), **bhajee, bajee, bhajia** /baáji ə/ (*plural same* or **-as**) *n* in South Asian cooking, a spicy deep-fried vegetable fritter, or a dish of these fritters [< Hindi *bhāji* 'fried vegetables']

bhakti /baákti/ *n* in Hinduism, the practice of loving devotion to God as the means of salvation [Mid-19C. < Sanskrit, 'devotion']

bhang /bang/, **bang** *n* a drug made from the Indian hemp or cannabis plant [Late 16C. Via Portuguese < Persian and Urdu *bang*, Hindi *bhan* < Sanskrit *bhanga*]

bhangra /báng grə/ *n* **1.** a style of popular music that mixes Punjabi folk music with western pop music. It originated in South Asia and was popularized by the South Asian community in Britain. **2.** *S Asia* an energetic form of folk dance from the Punjab [Mid-20C. < Punjabi]

bharal /búrrəl/ *n* a wild sheep with a bluish grey coat and horns that curve backwards. Native to: Himalayan region. Latin name: *Pseudois nayaur*. [Mid-19C. < Hindi]

Bharat /búrrət/ *n S Asia* the Hindi name for India [< Sanskrit *Bharata*]

Bharatiya /búrrə tee yə/ *adj S Asia* relating to or originating from India [< Hindi *Bharat* 'India']

Bharatiya Janata Party *n* an Indian political party, founded in 1980, that advocates Hindu nationalism

Bharat Natyam /búrrət naátyəm/ *n* an ancient classical dance from southern India, usually performed by one dancer and based on Hindu mythology, in which the movements of the hands and arms have an elaborate and stylized symbolic meaning [< Sanskrit *bharatanātya* 'dance of Bharata' (reputed author of a famous manual of drama and dance)]

bharta /baártə/ *n* in South Asian cooking, a spicy vegetable dish made with grilled vegetables, especially aubergines, and yogurt

Bhatpara /baat paárə/, **Bhātpāra** city in the state of Bangla, north of Kolkata, India. It was an ancient seat of Sanskrit learning. Population: 304,952 (1991).

bhavan /búvv'n/ *n* in South Asia, a large important house or official building (*often used as part of the name of a building*) ○ *Rasthrapati Bhavan* [< Hindi]

Bhavnagar /baávnəgər/, **Bhāvnagar** city on the Gulf of Khambhat in Gujarat State, western India. Founded in 1723, it is a major industrial and commercial centre. Population: 517,578 (2001).

bhelpuri /báyl poori/ *n* in South Asian cooking, a spicy snack made with puffed rice and onions [< Hindi *bhel* 'mixture' + *pūrī* 'fried unleavened bread' (see PURI)]

bhindi /bíndi/ *n S Asia* FOOD, PLANTS same as **okra** (sense 1) [< Hindi *bhiṇḍī*]

Bhindranwale /bíndrən waali/, **Sant Jarnail Singh** (1947–84) Indian Sikh leader. He led an armed campaign for a separate Sikh state in the early 1980s and was killed by Indian security forces at the Golden Temple at Amritsar, India.

Bhopal /bō paál/, **Bhōpal** city and capital of Madhya Pradesh State, central India. It was the site of the world's worst industrial accident when a gas leak at a chemical plant killed more than 3,300 people in 1984. Population: 1,454,830 (2001).

B horizon *n* an intermediate layer of soil beneath the A horizon, containing some organic matter and clay

bhp *abbr* MECH ENG brake horsepower

BHT *n* a crystalline solid used as an antioxidant for fats and oils, especially in processed foods. Full form **butylated hydroxytoluene**

Bhubaneshwar /boóbə náyshwə/, **Bhubaneswar** capital city of Orissa state in eastern India. Population: 412,000 (1991).

Bhumibol Adulyadej /poómi pōn aa doòn lə dayt/ ◆ **Rama IX**

bhuna /boónə/ *n* a type of roasted vegetable curry originating in southern India

Bhutan

Bhutan /boo taán/ landlocked country in the eastern part of the Himalaya range between India and the Tibet region of China. Language: Dzongkha. Currency: ngultrum. Capital: Thimphu. Population: 2,139,549 (2003). Area: 47,000 sq. km/18,100 sq. mi. Official name **Kingdom of Bhutan** —**Bhutanese** /boótə néez/ *n, adj*

Benazir Bhutto

Bhutto /boótō/, **Benazir** (*b.* 1953) prime minister of Pakistan (1988–90, 1993–96). The daughter of Prime Minister Zulfikar Ali Bhutto (1928–79), she led the Pakistan People's Party.

'You cannot be fuelled by bitterness. It can eat you up but it cannot drive you.'
[Attributed to Benazir Bhutto]

bi[1] /bī/ *adj* same as **bisexual** (sense 1) (*slang*) [Mid-20C. Shortening]

bi[2] *abbr* Burundi (*used in Internet addresses*) See table at **domain name**

Bi *symbol* CHEM ELEM bismuth

bi- *prefix* two, twice, both ○ *biaxial* ○ *bimonthly* [< Latin, stem of *bis* 'twice', *bini* 'two by two' < Indo-European, 'two']

SPELLCHECK bi-, buy, by, or **bye?** Do not confuse the spelling of *bi-, buy, by,* or *bye*, which sound similar. *Bi-* is a prefix meaning 'two' or 'both' (as in *biannual, bilateral*), whereas the prefix *by-* means 'secondary' or 'past' (as in *by-product, bygone*). Note that the noun *by-election* can also be spelt **bye-election**. *Buy* is chiefly used as a verb, meaning 'acquire by payment' (as in *buy a house*), and occasionally as a noun: *These boots were a good buy*. *By* is an adverb or preposition meaning 'beside', 'past', 'through', etc. (as in *stand by the window, as the years flew by*). *Bye* is used as a noun, denoting an automatic advance in a competition, or as a short form of *goodbye*.

Biafra /bi áffrə/ region of eastern Nigeria that was declared a secessionist state by the majority Ibo people between 1967 and 1970. Official name **Republic of Biafra** —**Biafran** *n, adj*

Białystok /bi áwi stok/, **Bialystok** /bi álli-/ capital of Bialystok Province in northeastern Poland. It is an industrial city in a predominantly agricultural region. Population: 282,500 (1997).

Bianca /bi ángkə/ *n* a small natural satellite of Uranus, discovered in 1986 by the Voyager 2 planetary probe

biannual /bī ánnyoo əl/ *adj* happening twice in a year

USAGE biannual or **biennial?** *Biannual* means 'twice a year' whereas *biennial* means 'every two years'. Because many people are unsure about which is which, it is often advisable to use the more straightforward expressions *twice-yearly* and *two-yearly: Interest is paid twice-yearly* (or, less formally, *Interest is paid twice a year*). *They met at a series of two-yearly conferences on the environment.*

Biarritz /beer ríts/ tourist resort on the Bay of Biscay in the Pyrénées-Atlantiques Department, southwestern France. Population: 30,055 (1999).

bias /bī əss/ *n* (*plural* **-ases** or **-asses**) **1.** PREFERENCE an unfair preference for or dislike of something ○ *a bias in favour of internal candidates* **2.** TEXTILES DIAGONAL LINE a line that runs diagonally across the weave of a fabric ○ *a dress cut on the bias* **3.** ELECTRONICS **VOLTAGE APPLIED** the voltage applied across an electronic device, especially a transistor or valve, to determine the conditions under which it operates **4.** BOWLS **UNBALANCED WEIGHT IN BOWLING** a bulge or internal weight in one side of a bowl used in bowling that makes it run in a curved path **5.** BOWLS **CURVED PATH IN BOWLING** the curved path in which a bowl containing a bulge or internal weight runs **6.** STATS **DISTORTION OF RESULTS** the distortion of a set of statistical results by a variable not considered in the calculation, or the variable itself ■ *vt* (**-ases** or **-asses**, **-asing** or **-assing**, **-ased** or **-assed**) INFLUENCE SOMEBODY to influence somebody or something unfairly ■ *adj* DIAGONAL running diagonally across the weave of a fabric ○ *a bias seam* ■ *adv* DIAGONALLY diagonally across the weave of a fabric ○ *The sleeves are cut bias.* [Mid-16C. Via French < Old Provençal *biais* 'slant' < Greek *epikarsios* 'oblique'] —**biased** *adj*

bias binding *n* a long narrow strip of material cut on the bias and used to form the edge of a hem or to bind the edges of a garment. N Am term **bias tape**

bias-cut *adj* cut diagonally across the weave of a fabric ○ *a bias-cut skirt*

bias-ply *adj N Am* same as **cross-ply**

bias tape *n N Am* same as **bias binding**

bias voltage *n* ELEC ENG same as **bias** *n* (sense 3)

biathlon /bī áth lón/ *n* a competition that combines cross-country skiing with rifle shooting at targets along the course [Mid-20C. < BI- + Greek *athlon* 'prize from a contest'] —**biathlete** *n*

biaxial /bī áksi əl/ *adj* having two axes —**biaxially** *adv*

bib /bib/ *n* **1.** PROTECTIVE CLOTHING a small piece of material fastened under a child's chin to protect the clothing while eating **2.** PART OF GARMENT the front part of a pinafore, apron, or pair of dungarees that covers the chest **3.** FISH OF COD FAMILY a sea fish of the cod family. Native to: European coastal waters. Latin name: *Trisopterus luscus*. [Late 16C. Probably < *bib* 'drink frequently' < Latin *bibere* 'to drink'] ◇ **somebody's best bib and tucker** somebody's finest clothes (*informal*) ◇ **keep your bib out** *Aus* to refrain from interfering in something (*informal*) ◇ **stick your bib in** *Aus* to interfere in something (*informal*)

Bib. *abbr* CHR **1.** Bible **2.** biblical

bibb /bib/ *n* a part attached to the mast of a sailing ship to support the trestletrees [Late 18C. Variant of BIB]

bibbed /bibd/ *adj* having a bib ○ *a bibbed apron*

bibber /bíbbər/ *n* somebody who regularly drinks alcohol (*archaic*) [Mid-16C. < *bib* 'drink frequently' (see BIB)]

bibcock /bíb kok/ *n* a tap with a nozzle that is bent downwards [Late 18C. Origin ?]

bibelot /bíbblō/ *n* a small and attractive ornament or piece of jewellery [Late 19C. < French, doubling of *bel* 'beautiful']

bibi /beé bee/ *n S Asia* a non-European woman with whom somebody has a sexual or romantic relationship [Early 19C. < Hindi, Urdu]

bibl. *abbr* LITERAT bibliography

Bible /bíb'l/ *n* **1.** CHRISTIAN HOLY BOOK the sacred book of the Christian religion **2.** JEWISH HOLY BOOK the Hebrew scriptures, the sacred book of the Jewish religion **3.** *also* **bible** HOLY BOOK the holy book of any religion **4.** *also* **bible** COPY OF BIBLE a copy or edition of the Bible **5.** *also* **bible** ESSENTIAL BOOK a book that is considered an authority on a particular subject ○ *a bible for beginning gardeners* [14C. < Latin *biblia*

BOOKS OF THE BIBLE

There is no straightforward explanation of the origin of either the Jewish or the Christian canon of scripture. The Jewish scriptures listed represent the Hebrew Bible as it came to be fixed probably at some time in the 2nd century A D. There existed, however, an alternative version in Greek, known as the Septuagint, which contained seven books that are now found in the Roman Catholic and Eastern Orthodox canons. These are usually known collectively as the Apocrypha, though modern biblical scholars prefer the term deuterocanonical books.

The Old Testament canon was formally fixed for western Christians in the 16th century, when Protestant denominations for the most part adopted the shorter Jewish canon. Roman Catholicism formally embraced the Septuagint as the basis for its Bible at the Council of Trent in 1546. The Orthodox churches accepted effectively the same canon as the Roman Catholic one in 1672 at the Synod of Jerusalem, though the Russian Orthodox Church remained ambivalent, and at least down to the mid-20th century tended to omit the deuterocanonical books from its canon.

*indicates deuterocanonical books

Jewish Scriptures	Old Testament — Roman Catholic and Eastern Orthodox	Protestant
The Law Genesis	Genesis	Genesis
Exodus	Exodus	Exodus
Leviticus	Leviticus	Leviticus
Numbers	Numbers	Numbers
Deuteronomy	Deuteronomy	Deuteronomy
The Prophets Joshua	Joshua	Joshua
Judges	Judges	Judges
	Ruth	Ruth
1 Samuel	1 Samuel	1 Samuel
2 Samuel	2 Samuel	2 Samuel
1 Kings	1 Kings	1 Kings
2 Kings	2 Kings	2 Kings
	1 Chronicles	1 Chronicles
	2 Chronicles	2 Chronicles
	Ezra	Ezra
	Nehemiah	Nehemiah
	Tobit*	
	Judith*	
	Esther	Esther
	1 Maccabees*	
	2 Maccabees*	
	Job	Job
	Psalms	Psalms
	Proverbs	Proverbs
	Ecclesiastes	Ecclesiastes
	Wisdom of Solomon*	
	Ecclesiasticus*	
	Song of Songs	Song of Solomon
Isaiah	Isaiah	Isaiah
Jeremiah	Jeremiah	Jeremiah

Jewish Scriptures	Old Testament — Roman Catholic and Eastern Orthodox	Protestant	New Testament
Prophets (continued)	Lamentations	Lamentations	Matthew
	Baruch*		Mark
Ezekiel	Ezekiel	Ezekiel	Luke
	Daniel	Daniel	John
Hosea	Hosea	Hosea	Acts of the Apostles
Joel	Joel	Joel	Romans
Amos	Amos	Amos	1 Corinthians
Obadiah	Obadiah	Obadiah	2 Corinthians
Jonah	Jonah	Jonah	Galatians
Micah	Micah	Micah	Ephesians
Nahum	Nahum	Nahum	Philippians
Habakkuk	Habakkuk	Habakkuk	Colossians
Zephaniah	Zephaniah	Zephaniah	1 Thessalonians
Haggai	Haggai	Haggai	2 Thessalonians
Zechariah	Zechariah	Zechariah	1 Timothy
Malachi	Malachi	Malachi	2 Timothy
The Writings Psalms			Titus
Proverbs			Philemon
Job			Hebrews
Song of Songs			James
Ruth			1 Peter
Lamentations			2 Peter
Ecclesiastes			1 John
Esther			2 John
Daniel			3 John
Ezra			Jude
Nehemiah			Revelation
1 Chronicles			
2 Chronicles			

(sacra) '(sacred) books' < Greek, plural of biblion (see BIBLIO-)]

Bible-basher n an offensive term for a committed Christian whose outspoken evangelizing is regarded by some as extreme (slang; offensive) N Am term **Bible-thumper** —**Bible-bashing** n

Bible Belt n the areas of the South and Midwest in the United States that are characterized by strong Protestant beliefs and strict interpretation of the Bible

Bible-thumper n N Am same as **Bible-basher** (slang; offensive) —**Bible-thumping** n

biblical /bíbblik'l/, **Biblical** adj 1. relating to the Bible, or written about in the Bible 2. like the Bible, especially in style of language —**biblically** adv

Biblicist /bíbblissist/, **biblicist** n 1. a scholar who studies the Bible 2. somebody who interprets the Bible strictly or literally —**Biblicism** n

biblio- prefix book ○ bibliomania ○ bibliography [< Greek biblion 'small book' < biblos 'papyrus, scroll' < Bublos, Phoenician city from which papyrus was imported]

bibliography /bíbbli óggrəfi/ (plural -phies) n 1. BOOK SOURCES a list of books and articles consulted, appearing at the end of a book or other text 2. BOOKS ON SUBJECT a list of books and articles on a subject 3. LIST OF PUBLICATIONS a list of the books and articles written by a specific author or issued by a specific publisher 4. BOOK HISTORY the history of books and other publications, and the work of classifying and describing them [Late 17C. Directly or via French < modern Latin bibliographia < Greek biblion (see BIBLIO-) + Latin graphia (see -GRAPHY)] —**bibliographer** n —**bibliographic** /bíbbli ə gráffik/ adj —**bibliographical** adj —**bibliographically** adv

bibliomancy /bíbbli ə manssi/ n an attempt to foretell the future or answer a question by picking a passage at random from a book, especially the Bible

bibliomania /bíbbli ə máyni ə/ n an extreme fondness for books, especially the collecting of them —**bibliomaniac** n

bibliophile /bíbbli ə fīl/ n a collector of books

bibulous /bíbbyŏoləss/ adj tending to drink too much alcohol (formal) [Late 17C. < Latin bibulus < bibere 'to drink'] —**bibulously** adv —**bibulousness** n

ORIGIN The Latin word bibere 'to drink', from which **bibulous** is derived, is also the source of English beer, beverage, and imbibe.

bicameral /bī kámmərəl/ adj having two separate and distinct law-making assemblies, e.g. the House of Commons and the House of Lords in Britain [Mid-19C. < BI- + Latin camera 'chamber, vault' (see CAMERA)] —**bicameralism** n —**bicameralist** n

bicarb /bī kaárb/ n FOOD same as **bicarbonate of soda** (informal) [Early 20C. Shortening]

bicarbonate /bī kaárbənət, -nayt/ n CHEM same as **hydrogen carbonate**

bicarbonate of soda n sodium bicarbonate, especially when used as an antacid or a raising agent

bice /bīss/ n a dull blue colour or pigment [14C. < French bis 'dark grey'] —**bice** adj

bice blue n a deep sky-blue colour —**bice blue** adj

a at; aa father; aw all; ay day; ai hair; ə about, item, edible, common, circus; e egg; ee eel; hw when; i it, happy; ī ice; 'l apple; 'm rhythm; 'n fashion; o odd; ō open; ŏŏ good; oo pool; ow owl; oy oil; th thin; th this; u up; ur urge;

bice green *n* a bright leaf-green colour —**bice green** *adj*

bicentenary /bī sen teénəri, -ténn-/ *n* (*plural* **-ries**) an anniversary on which something is 200 years old ■ *adj* marking or celebrating a 200th anniversary ○ *bicentenary celebrations* ▶ N Am term (all senses) **bicentennial**

bicentennial /bī sen ténni əl/ *N Am n* same as **bicentenary** ■ *adj* same as **bicentenary** —**bicentennially** *adv*

bicephalous /bī séffələss/ *adj* having two heads, or two parts resembling heads [Early 19C. < BI- + Greek *kephalē* 'head']

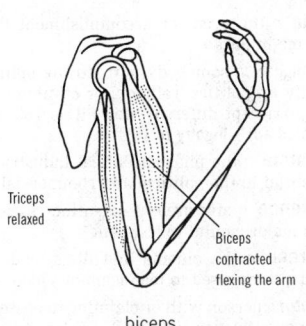

Triceps relaxed

Biceps contracted flexing the arm

biceps

biceps /bī seps/ (*plural same*) *n* a muscle that has two points of attachment at one end, especially one (**biceps brachii**) in the upper arm and one (**biceps femoris**) in the back of the thigh [Mid-17C. Via French < Latin, 'two-headed' < *caput* 'head'] —**bicipital** /bī síppit'l/ *adj*

biche /beesh/ ◇ **break biche** *Carib* to miss attendance at school, deliberately and without legitimate excuse

bicker /bíkər/ (**-ers, -ering, -ered**) *vi* to argue in a bad-tempered way about something unimportant [13C. < Middle Dutch *bicken* 'stab, attack' + English -*er* 'repeatedly']

bickie /bíki/ *n* same as **biscuit** (sense 1) (*informal*) [Early 20C. Alteration and diminutive of BISCUIT]

bicolour /bī kúllər/, **bicoloured** /bī kúllərd/ *adj* having two colours

biconcave /bī kóng kayv/ *adj* describes a lens with two faces that are concave

biconditional /bī kən dísh'nəl/ *n* a proposition in logic involving two statements, one of which is true if, and only if, the other is true

biconvex /bī kón veks/ *adj* describes a lens with two faces that are convex

bicultural /bī kúlchərəl/ *adj* relating to or containing two cultures ○ *a bicultural society* —**biculturalism** *n*

bicuspid /bī kúspid/ *adj* with two cusps or points ○ *a bicuspid tooth* ■ *n* a tooth with two points, especially one of the eight teeth (**premolars**) that come between the canines and the molars in adult humans [Mid-19C. < BI- + Latin *cuspid-*, stem of *cuspis* 'point, spear']

bicuspid valve *n* ANAT same as **mitral valve**

bicycle

bicycle /bī ssik'l/ *n* a vehicle with two wheels and a seat that is moved by pushing pedals with the feet, and steered by handlebars at the front wheel ■ *vi* (**-cles, -cling, -cled**) to travel by bicycle —**bicycler** *n*

bicycle clip *n* either of a pair of circular clips used to prevent the ends of a cyclist's trousers getting in the way of the bicycle chain

bicycle motocross *n* full form of **BMX**

bicyclic /bī síklik, -sík-/ *adj* **1.** consisting of or arranged in two circles, rings, or cycles **2.** describes a molecule containing atoms arranged in two rings

bid /bid/ *v* (**bids, bidding, bade** /bad, bayd/ or **bid** or **bad** *archaic*, **bidden** /bídd'n/ or **bid**) **1.** (*past and past participle* **bid**) *vti* OFFER MONEY AT AUCTION to offer an amount of money for something at an auction **2.** (*past and past participle* **bid**) *vi* OFFER PRICE FOR WORK to offer to do a piece of work for a specific price ○ *bidding for the contract* **3.** (*past and past participle* **bid**) *vti* CARDS STATE NUMBER OF TRICKS to declare the number of card tricks expected to be taken **4.** (*past and past participle* **bid**) *vi* TRY TO ACHIEVE SOMETHING to make an attempt to achieve a goal ○ *He hasn't decided whether or not he'll bid for the presidency.* **5.** *vt* ORDER SOMEBODY to tell somebody to do something (*archaic*) ○ *We were bidden to sit quietly, and so we did.* **6.** *vt* INVITE SOMEBODY to invite somebody somewhere (*archaic*) ■ *n* **1.** OFFER MADE TO PAY an offer of money for something at an auction **2.** OFFER an offer to do a piece of work for a specific price ○ *bids were invited for the contract* **3.** ATTEMPT an attempt to do something or get something ○ *in a desperate bid to save the situation* **4.** CARDS STATEMENT OF TRICKS a statement of the number of tricks that a player expects to take in a card game [Old English *biddan* 'to request', *beodan* 'to offer', both < Germanic] —**bidder** *n*

bid in *vt* to bid at an auction for something already owned, in order to increase its final selling price

bid up *vt* to make bids that are intended to increase the price of something, not to obtain it

b.i.d. *adv* twice a day (*used in prescriptions*) [Latin *bis in die*]

Bidault /bee dṓ/, **Georges** (1899–1983) prime minister of France (1949–50). He was a Resistance leader during World War II, and held several ministerial posts after the Allied liberation of France. Full name **Bidault, Georges Augustin**

> 'The weak have one weapon: the errors of those who think they are strong.'
> [Georges Bidault, *Observer*; 15 July 1962]

biddable /bíddəb'l/ *adj* likely to do as asked or ordered —**biddability** /bíddə bílləti/ *n*

bidden past participle of **bid**

bidding /bídding/ *n* **1.** the making of bids at an auction or in a card game **2.** somebody's orders or instructions ○ *lots of paperwork to do at the boss's bidding*

Biddle /bídd'l/, **Nicholas** (1786–1844) US financier. A lawyer and editor, he was president of the Second Bank of the United States (1823–36).

biddy /bíddi/ (*plural* **-dies**) *n* **1.** an offensive term for a woman whose behaviour is regarded as fussing or interfering (*slang insult*) **2.** same as **chicken** *n* (sense 1) (*regional*) [Early 17C. Origin ?]

biddy-biddy /bíddi bíddi/ (*plural* **biddy-biddies**), **bidi-bidi** (*plural* **bidi-bidis**) *n* a low-growing plant with a clinging seed case. Native to: New Zealand. Latin name: *Acaena novae-zelandiae*. [Mid-19C. Alteration of Maori *piripiri*]

bide /bīd/ (**bides, biding, bided** or **bode** /bōd/, **bided**) *vi* **1.** to stay, remain, or wait (*archaic*) ○ *Bide here with us a while.* **2.** *Scotland* to remain, stay, or reside in a place or situation [Old English *biden* < Indo-European]

bidet /beé day/ *n* a low bathroom plumbing fixture resembling a toilet and equipped with a spray or jet of water, used for washing the genital and anal areas [Mid-17C. < French, literally 'pony' < *bider* 'to trot']

bidi /beédi/, **beedi, biri** /beéri/ *n* S Asia a cheap cigarette made with coarse tobacco [< Hindi *bīdi* 'betel plug, cigar']

bidi-bidi *n* PLANTS another spelling of **biddy-biddy**

bid price *n* the price that a dealer on the stock exchange will pay for a security

Biedermeier /beédər mī ər/ *adj* belonging to or typical of a highly conventional neoclassical style of home decoration and furnishing that was popular among the middle class in 19th-century Germany [Early 20C. < the surname of a fictional poet created by Ludwig Eichrodt (1827–92)]

Bielefeld /beélə felt/ city in North Rhine-Westphalia State, western Germany, situated at the northern edge of the Teutoberg Forest. Population: 324,067 (1997).

Bien Hoa /byén hố ə/ city in southern Vietnam east of Ho Chi Minh City, on the River Dong Nai. Population: 273,953 (1989).

biennial /bī énni əl/ *adj* **1.** happening every two years **2.** describes a plant that lives for two years and produces flowers and fruit in the second year [Early 17C. < Latin *biennis* 'two-yearly' or *biennium* 'two year period'] —**biennial** *n* —**biennially** *adv*

USAGE See *biannual*.

bier /beer/ *n* **1.** a table on which a coffin or a corpse is placed **2.** a wooden frame on which a coffin is carried to where it will be buried (*literary*) [Old English *bǣr* < Germanic]

SPELLCHECK See *beer*.

Bierce /beerss/, **Ambrose** (1842–1914?) US writer. Known for his satirical political articles and short stories, he wrote *The Devil's Dictionary* (1911), first published as *The Cynic's Word Book* (1906). He disappeared in Mexico in 1913. Full name **Bierce, Ambrose Gwinett**

> 'ACCIDENT, n. An inevitable occurrence due to the action of immutable natural laws.'
> [Ambrose Bierce, *The Devil's Dictionary*; 1911]

biethnic /bī éthnik/ *adj* belonging or relating to two different ethnic groups

bifacial /bī fáysh'l/ *adj* **1.** describes leaves with upper and lower surfaces that are different from each other **2.** having two sides or surfaces

bifarious /bī fáiri əss/ *adj* describes plant parts that are arranged in two rows, one on each side of an axis [Mid-17C. < Latin *bifarius* 'doing twice' < -*farius* 'doing'] —**bifariously** *adv*

biff /bif/ (**biffs, biffing, biffed**) *vt* to hit somebody with the fist (*informal*) [Mid-19C. An imitation of the sound caused] —**biff** *n*

bifid /bífid/ *adj* divided at one end into two equal parts [Mid-17C. < Latin *bifidus* 'twice divided' < *findere* 'to divide'] —**bifidity** /bī fíddəti/ *n* —**bifidly** *adv*

bifilar /bī fílər/ *adj* describes a part suspended on two parallel wires or threads, especially the moving part of an electrical measuring instrument [Mid-19C. < BI- + Latin *filum* 'thread']

biflagellate /bī flájjilət, -layt/ *adj* describes a cell that has two slender appendages (**flagella**)

bifocal /bī fók'l/ *adj* describes lenses with sections that have different focal lengths, especially in glasses for near and distant vision ■ **bifocals** *npl* a pair of glasses with bifocal lenses

bifurcate *vti* /bī fur kayt/ (**-cates, -cating, -cated**) to be split or branched off into two parts, or split something into two parts ■ *adj* /-kayt, -kət/ separating or branching off into two parts [Early 17C. < Latin *bifurcat-*, past participle of *bifurcare* 'fork twice' < *furca* 'fork' (see FORK)] —**bifurcation** /bī fur káysh'n/ *n*

big /big/ *adj* (**bigger, biggest**) **1.** OF GREAT SIZE of great size, number, or amount ○ *a big crowd* **2.** OF GREAT POWER of great power or volume ○ *A big cheer went up.* **3.** SIGNIFICANT significant or important to somebody ○ *your big moment* **4.** SIGNIFICANTLY GREAT significantly or surprisingly great ○ *You're making a big mistake.* **5.** IMPORTANT important and powerful ○ *one of the big fashion houses* **6.** MAGNANIMOUS generous or noble ○ *She's a woman with a big heart.* **7.** AMBITIOUS full of boastful or unrealistic ambition ○ *She's not likely to fall for his big talk.* **8.** OLDER older or grown-up (*usually used by or to children*) ○ *When I'm big, I'll be rich and famous.* **9.** ENTHUSIASTIC enthusiastic about something or somebody (*informal*) ○ *I'm a big baseball fan.* **10.** GREAT used to make a word convey greater dislike or disapproval (*informal*) ○ *It's all a big con, really.* **11.** FILLED filled with or swollen by something (*literary*) ○ *eyes big with tears* **12.** PREGNANT in an obvious state of pregnancy (*archaic*) ○ *She was big with child.* **13.** WINE FULL-BODIED full-bodied and full of flavour ○ *The best accompaniment to this dish would be a big Chianti.* ■ *adv* **1.** AMBITIOUSLY in a way that is ambitious, and often boastful or unrealistic ○ *You have to think big if you want to get anywhere.*

2. SUCCESSFULLY in a highly successful way (*informal*) ○ *This approach should go over big at the convention.* [14C. Origin ?] —**bigness** *n* ◇ **big on** enthusiastic about or recognizing the importance of something (*informal*) ◇ **make it big** to be extremely successful (*informal*)

big up (*originally used in Black English*) *vt* (**bigs up, bigging up, bigged up**) (*slang*) **1.** PRAISE SOMEBODY OR SOMETHING to praise or welcome somebody or something enthusiastically **2.** RESPECT SOMEBODY OR SOMETHING to have or show respect for somebody or something ■ *n* THANK YOU an expression of gratitude and thanks ○ *I'd like to say a big up to my parents for their support.*

bigamous /bíggəməss/ *adj* involved in or constituting an illegal marriage made when an existing marriage is still valid [Late 19C. < Latin *bigamus* (see BIGAMY)] —**bigamously** *adv*

bigamy /bíggəmi/ *n* the crime of marrying somebody while being legally married to somebody else [13C. < Latin *bigamus* 'marriage twice' < Greek *gamos* 'marriage']

Big Apple *n* New York City (*informal*) [< APPLE in jazz musicians' sense 'job, engagement']

big band *n* a large jazz or dance band, especially one that was popular in the 1930s and 1940s

big bang *n* the explosion of a single extremely dense mass of matter that started the universe according to a popular theory (**big bang theory**)

big beast *n* (*informal*) **1.** somebody who is regarded as successful or influential in a particular field or activity **2.** a powerful piece of equipment that uses the latest technology

Big Ben /-bén/ *n* **1.** the large clock above the Houses of Parliament in London, or the tower in which it stands **2.** the large bell that chimes the hours in the clock tower of the Houses of Parliament in London [After Sir *Benjamin* Hall, Chief Commissioner of Works]

Big Board *n US* the New York Stock Exchange (*informal*)

big box store *n* a retail superstore that sells a very wide range of merchandise, from large household appliances to items such as groceries and pharmaceuticals [Perhaps because of the sizes of the cardboard boxes in which some of the merchandise is delivered]

big boys *npl* important or influential people in a particular field or activity (*informal*)

Big Brother *n* a person or group who exerts dictatorial control and maintains a constant watch over others, often while presenting a caring image [Used in George Orwell's novel *Nineteen Eighty-Four* (1949)] —**Big Brotherism** *n*

big bucks *npl* a large amount of money (*slang*)

big bud *n* a disease of blackcurrant plants that causes the leaf buds to swell and stop developing, for which the only control is destruction of the plants. It is caused by a gall mite that may also transmit a virus.

big business *n* the activity of large commercial organizations, or these organizations considered as a group

big cat *n* any large carnivorous wild mammal related to the domestic cat. Lions, tigers, leopards, lynxes, and mountain lions are types of big cat. Family: Felidae.

big cheese *n* an important person (*informal*)

big city *n* the largest city in an area ○ *the lure of the big city*

big-city *adj* typical of life in a large metropolitan area ○ *the fast-paced big-city lifestyle*

big crunch *n* the cosmic implosion that one theory of the universe holds will ultimately result if there is enough mass in the universe for gravity to slow, halt, and eventually reverse the current expansion

big daddy *n* (*slang*) **1.** somebody or something that is respected, powerful, or well known ○ *the big daddy of the blues guitar* **2.** the head of an organization, especially one who exerts paternalistic control

big deal (*informal*) *interj* used to counter that something is less impressive or important than somebody thinks it is ○ *So he's head of department. Big deal.* ■ *n* something that is very important ○ *Let's not make a big deal out of a minor misunderstanding.*

big dipper *n* same as **roller coaster** (sense 1)

Big Dipper *n N Am* same as **Plough**

Big Easy *n US* New Orleans, Louisiana (*informal*) [< *The Big Easy* (1970), novel by James Conaway]

big end *n* the larger end of the connecting rod in an internal-combustion engine

bigeneric /bī jə nérrik/ *adj* describes a hybrid produced from two different genera

~~**biger**~~ incorrect spelling of **bigger**

bigeye /bíg ī/ (*plural* **-eyes** or *same*) *n* a small sea fish with rough reddish or silvery scales and very large eyes. Native to: tropical and subtropical waters. Family: Priacanthidae.

big-eye *adj Carib* greedy or covetous

Bigfoot /bíg fo͝ot/ *n* **1.** LEGENDARY HUMANOID OF NW AMERICA a large hairy humanoid said to live in the wilderness areas of northwestern North America, and described as standing 2–3 m/7–10 ft tall **2.** *also* **bigfoot** ESTABLISHED EXPERT a well-known and highly respected expert in a field **3.** *also* **bigfoot** *US* POWERFUL JOURNALIST a powerful journalist employed by a large newspaper, network, or news syndicate (*slang*) [Mid-20C. < the size of the footprints it is said to leave]

big game *n* large wild animals hunted for sport, especially the larger African mammals

biggie /bíggi/ *n* (*informal*) **1.** something that is big **2.** somebody or something that is very significant, important, powerful, or successful ◇ **no biggie** not particularly important or serious (*informal*)

big girl's blouse *n* a man who is thought to behave in ways traditionally attributed to women (*slang insult*)

biggish /bíggish/ *adj* fairly large, although not extremely large ○ *The house is quite nice, and it's got a biggish garden.*

big government *n* government perceived as being excessively high-spending and attempting to control too many aspects of people's lives

Biggs /bigz/, **Ronnie** (*b.* 1929) British train robber. One of the perpetrators of the Great Train Robbery (1963), he escaped from prison (1965) and fled to Brazil. Born **Biggs, Ronald**

big gun *n* a powerful or influential person (*informal*)

big hair *n* hair that is rather long with a lot of body, often backcombed or sprayed so that it stands away from the head (*informal*)

bighead /bíg hed/ *n* somebody regarded as too proud of his or her abilities, achievements, or appearance (*informal insult*)

bigheaded /big héddid/ *adj* too proud of personal abilities, achievements, or appearance (*informal*)

big-hearted *adj* showing kindness and willingness to help and support others —**big-heartedly** *adv* —**big-heartedness** *n*

big hitter *n* a very successful company or product, or a successful or influential person in a particular field (*informal*)

bighorn /bíg hawrn/ (*plural* **-horns** or *same*) *n* a large wild mountain sheep that has a long coarse brown coat and very large curving horns. Native to: western North America. Genus: *Ovis*.

big house *n* **1.** the biggest house in a locality, especially that owned by a family of high social rank **2.** a large prison (*slang*)

bight /bīt/ *n* **1.** a wide curving indent in a shoreline, forming a bay **2.** a loop or slack curve in a rope [Old English *byht* < Indo-European, 'to bend']

big league *n* the highest level of achievement in a field, or the people who occupy the top positions in it (*informal*)

big-league *adj* **1.** among the most successful or influential in a field (*informal*) **2.** of a wholehearted and unrestrained kind (*slang*) ○ *They're into big-league partying.*

Big Man *n* in some cultures, a male leader whose leadership is based on influence, not official or formally recognized authority

big money *n* large sums of money (*informal*)

bigmouth /bígg mowth/ *n* (*informal*) **1.** somebody who cannot keep a secret **2.** somebody regarded as noisy, vulgar, or boastful

bigmouthed /bíg mowthd/ *adj* (*informal*) **1.** unable to keep a secret **2.** loud and boastful

big name *n* a well-known and successful person, organization, or product (*informal*) —**big-name** *adj*

big noise *n* an important or influential person (*informal*)

bignonia /big nṓni ə/ *n* an evergreen woody climbing bush. Flowers: trumpet-shaped, red, orange, or yellow. Native to: tropical America. Genus: *Bignonia.* [Late 18C. < modern Latin, after Abbé J. P. *Bignon* (1662–1743), French librarian]

big-note *vt Aus* to attempt to appear more important or successful by overstating achievements (*informal*)

Big One *n* the event or accomplishment that is of supreme import

bigot /bíggət/ *n* somebody with strong opinions, especially on politics, religion, or ethnicity, who refuses to accept different views [Late 16C. < French] —**bigoted** *adj* —**bigotry** *n*

big pharma *n* the pharmaceutical industry seen as influential in the political and commercial spheres

big science *n* any area of scientific research that needs major capital investment

big screen *n* the cinema and films made for the cinema, as opposed to television or video

big shot *n* a person with or claiming to possess much power or influence (*informal*)

Big Smoke *n* a nickname for a large city, especially a capital city (*informal*)

big stick *n* a threat of force or severe penalties

big tent *n* a group or political party whose members represent a diverse range of opinions and backgrounds ○ *big-tent politics* —**big-tent** *adj*

big-ticket *adj* costing a lot of money (*informal*)

big time (*slang*) *n* the highest level of achievement and success in a profession or other activity ■ *adv* on a grand scale, or to a significant degree ○ *He had messed up his life big time.* —**big timer** *n*

big toe *n* the largest and innermost digit of the foot

big top *n* **1.** a large round tent, especially the main tent, used for circus performances **2.** the performing of circus entertainments

big wheel *n* same as **Ferris wheel**

big white chief *n* the most important person in an organization, often somebody who makes his or her power and influence very obvious (*informal*) ○ *The big white chief says that we all have to work overtime.*

bigwig /bíg wig/ *n* an important person with considerable power or influence (*informal*) [Early 18C. Because important people once wore full-length wigs, whereas ordinary people wore short ones]

Bihac /bi haák/ town in northwestern Bosnia and Herzegovina, devastated by fighting during the Bosnian-Croatian-Serbian War. Population: 50,000 (1999).

Bihar /bi haár/, **Bihār** state in northeastern India that is crossed by the River Ganges and shares a border with Nepal. Capital: Patna. Population: 82,878,796 (2001). Area: 99,199 sq. km/38,301 sq. mi.

Bihari /bi haári/ (*plural same* or **-ris**) *n* a member of a people who live mostly in the Indian state of Bihar, and also in Bangladesh and Pakistan [Late 19C. < Hindi *bihārī*] —**Bihari** *adj*

Bijapur /bi jaá poor/, **Bijāpur** city in northern Karnataka State, southern India. It is known for its medieval Islamic architecture. Population: 253,307 (2001).

bijection /bī jéksh'n/ *n* a mathematical mapping between two spaces in which every element in each space corresponds to only one element of the other space for mapping in either direction [Mid-20C. < BI- + INJECTION] —**bijective** *adj*

bijou /beé zhoo, beé zho͞o/ *adj* small but fashionable and elegant (*humorous*) ○ *a bijou apartment* ■ *n* (*plural* **-jous** /-zhooz/ or **-joux** /-zhoo/) a small delicate jewel or ornamental object [Mid-17C. Via French, 'trinket' < Breton *bizoù* 'jewelled ring' < *biz* 'finger']

Bikaner /beékə neer/, **Bīkāner** walled city in Rajasthan State, northwestern India. It was founded in 1488 and was formerly capital of the princely state of Bikaner. Population: 416,289 (1991).

bike[1] /bīk/ *n* **1.** VEHICLES same as **bicycle** (*informal*) **2.** VEHICLES same as **motorcycle** (*informal*) **3.** an offensive term for a woman who has many sexual relationships (*insult*) ■ *vi* (**bikes, biking, biked**) to ride somewhere on a bicycle or motorcycle (*informal*) [Late 19C. Shortening of BICYCLE] ◇ **on your bike** used as a mildly rude way of telling somebody to go away or of dismissing somebody's suggestion (*informal*)

bike[2] /bīk/, **byke** *Scotland n* a nest of wasps or wild bees ■ *vi* (**bikes, biking, biked; bykes, byking, byked**) same as **swarm**[1] *v* (sense 1) (*refers to bees and wasps*) [13C. Origin ?]

biker /bíkər/ *n* somebody who rides a motorcycle, especially somebody who belongs to a gang of riders

biker jacket *n* a short zip-up leather jacket, originally worn by motorcyclists and popular especially during the 1990s

bikeway /bík way/ *n ANZ, N Am* a route or traffic lane for bicycles. UK term **cycle path**

bikie /bíki/ *n ANZ* same as **biker** (*informal*)

Bikila /bi kéelə/, **Abebe** (1932–73) Ethiopian athlete. The first Black African Olympic gold medallist, he set a world record running barefoot in the marathon in the Rome Olympics in 1960.

bikini /bi kéeni/ *n* a woman's or girl's two-piece swimming costume consisting of a bra-style top and panties-style bottoms ■ **bikinis** *npl* very scanty briefs for women [Mid-20C. After BIKINI] —**bikinied** *adj*

Bikini /bi kéeni/ atoll consisting of 36 islets in the Marshall Islands, in the western Pacific Ocean. It was used as a nuclear testing site by the United States between 1946 and 1958. Area: 5 sq. km/2 sq. mi.

bikini line *n* the area where the top of a woman's thighs meets the lower edge of her bikini or underwear

Biko /béekō/, **Steve** (1946–77) South African political activist. A founder member and the first president of the Black Consciousness Movement, he was arrested several times in the early 1970s and died after being beaten in police custody in 1977. Full name **Biko, Stephen Bantu**

> 'We have set out on a quest for true humanity, and somewhere on the distant horizon we can see the glittering prize...In time we shall be in a position to bestow upon South Africa the greatest gift possible—a more human face.'
> [Steve Biko, 'Black Consciousness and the Quest for a True Humanity', *Steve Biko: I Write What I Like*; 1978]

bilabial /bī láybi əl/ *adj* describes a consonant pronounced by bringing both lips into contact with each other or by rounding them. In English, the bilabial consonants are 'b', 'p', 'm', and 'w'. —**bilabial** *n* —**bilabially** *adv*

bilateral /bī láttərəl/ *adj* **1.** involving or carried out by two groups, especially the political representatives of two countries ○ *bilateral talks* **2.** relating to or affecting both of two sides ○ *bilateral kidney failure* —**bilateralism** *n* —**bilaterally** *adv*

bilateral symmetry *n* symmetry in which an imaginary plane divides an object into right and left halves, each side being a mirror image of the other. Most animals exhibit this symmetry.

bilayer /bí layər/ *n* a membrane that consists of two layers of molecules

Bilbao /bil báa ō/ industrial city and Spain's leading port in the Basque Country, northern Spain. It is the site of the Guggenheim Museum, opened in 1997. Population: 353,950 (2002).

bilberry /bílbəri/ (*plural* **-ries**) *n* **1.** an edible blue-black berry **2.** a wild bush that produces bilberries. Native to: northern Europe. Genus: *Vaccinium.* [Late 16C. Origin ?]

bilby /bílbi/ (*plural* **-bies**) *n* a carnivorous marsupial similar in size to a rat. It has large ears, a pointed nose, a long furry tail and lives in a burrow. Native to: Australasia. Genus: *Macrotis.* [Late 19C. < Yuwaalaraay *bilbi*]

bildungsroman /bíll dòongz rō maan/ *n* a novel about the early years of somebody's life, exploring the development of his or her character and personality [Early 20C. < German, 'education-novel']

bile /bīl/ *n* **1.** PHYSIOL **DIGESTIVE FLUID** a yellowish-green fluid produced in the liver, stored in the gallbladder, and passed through ducts to the small intestine, where it plays an essential role in emulsifying fats **2. BITTERNESS** feelings of bitterness and irritability (*literary*) **3.** HIST **BODILY HUMOUR** according to medieval medicine, one of the four basic fluids of the body (**humours**), an excess of which was thought to make somebody prone to anger [Mid-16C. Via French < Latin *bilis*]

bilection /bəléksh'n/ *n* ARCHIT another spelling of **bolection**

bile duct *n* a tube that carries bile from the liver or gallbladder to the small intestine. The hepatic and cystic ducts merge to form the common bile duct.

bi-level *adj* **1. TWO-LEVEL** having or comprising two levels ○ *a bi-level commuter rail car* ○ *a bi-level approach to process analysis* **2.** *N Am* **HAVING TWO GROUND-FLOOR LEVELS** having two ground-floor levels divided by a vertical partition ■ *n N Am* **BI-LEVEL HOUSE** a bi-level house

bilge /bilj/ *n* **1. LOWER PART OF BOAT** the part of a boat below the water where the sides curve inwards to the keel **2. INSIDE OF LOWER PART OF BOAT** the area inside the bottom of a boat, beneath the lowest floorboards **3. DIRTY WATER IN BOAT BOTTOM** dirty water that collects inside the bottom of a boat **4. BARREL'S WIDEST PART** the widest part of a barrel or cask **5. NONSENSE** ridiculous talk or ideas (*informal*) ○ *a load of bilge* ■ *vti* (**bilges, bilging, bilged**) **SPRING LEAK** to be, or cause a boat to be, damaged in the lower part of the hull and start leaking [15C. Probably alteration of BULGE]

bilge keel *n* either of two fin-shaped underwater projections on each side of a boat's hull, designed to control rolling

bilge water *n* NAUT same as **bilge** *n* (sense 3)

bilharzia /bil háar zi ə/ *n* **1.** ZOOL same as **schistosome** **2.** MED same as **schistosomiasis** [Mid-19C. < modern Latin, after Theodor *Bilharz* (1825–62), German physician]

bilharziasis /bíl haar zí əssiss/ *n* MED same as **schistosomiasis**

biliary /bíllyəri/ *adj* **1.** relating to bile or the transporting of bile **2.** affecting a bile duct or the system of ducts in the liver ○ *biliary cirrhosis* [Mid-18C. < Latin *bilis* 'bile']

bilinear /bī línni ər/ *adj* relating to or representing a mathematical expression with two variables, e.g. x + y, neither of which is squared, cubed, or raised to another power or exponent

bilingual /bī líng gwəl/ *adj* **1. SPEAKING TWO LANGUAGES** able to speak two languages easily and naturally **2. IN TWO LANGUAGES** written, expressed, or conducted in two languages ○ *a bilingual dictionary* ■ *n* **BILINGUAL SPEAKER** somebody who speaks two languages easily and naturally [Mid-19C. < Latin *bilinguis* < *bi-* 'two' + *lingua* 'tongue, speech'] —**bilingually** *adv*

bilingualism /bī líng gwə lizəm/ *n* **1.** the ability to speak two languages easily and naturally **2.** the regular use of two languages in everyday communication

bilious /bílli əss/ *adj* **1. FEELING NAUSEATED** feeling as if about to vomit **2. NAUSEATINGLY UNPLEASANT** extremely unpleasant to look at ○ *The walls were painted a bilious green.* **3. DISAGREEABLE** bad-tempered and irritable (*literary*) ○ *a bilious stare* [Mid-16C. < Latin *biliosus* < *bilis* 'bile'] —**biliously** *adv* —**biliousness** *n*

bilirubin /bílli ròobin, bíli-/ *n* a reddish-yellow bile pigment that is an intermediate product of the breakdown of haemoglobin in the liver. Too much bilirubin in the blood causes jaundice. [Late 19C. < German < Latin *bilis* 'bile' + *ruber* 'red']

biliverdin /bílli vúrdin/ *n* a greenish bile pigment that is an intermediate product of the breakdown of haemoglobin in the liver and in turn breaks down to produce bilirubin [Mid-19C. < German < Latin *bilis* 'bile' + French *vert* 'green']

bilk /bilk/ (**bilks, bilking, bilked**) *vt* **1. CHEAT SOMEBODY** to cheat somebody, especially by swindling him or her out of money (*informal*) **2. AVOID PAYING SOMEBODY OR SOMETHING** to avoid paying a debt or a person to whom money is owed (*informal*) **3. AVOID OR EVADE SOMEBODY** to escape from or elude somebody [Mid-17C. Origin ?] —**bilker** *n*

bill[1] /bil/ *n* **1. STATEMENT OF MONEY OWED** a written statement of how much money is owed for items purchased or services provided ○ *I'll send you the bill.* **2. AMOUNT OWED** the amount of money owed for items or services provided, as shown on a statement ○ *The bill for the meal came to £80!* **3. AMOUNT PAID** the amount that a person, company, or organization has to pay in taxes, salaries, or other charges **4.** POL **LAW PROPOSAL** a written proposal for a new law, discussed and voted upon by the members of a legislative assembly **5. ADVERTISING NOTICE** a notice, poster, or leaflet advertising something **6. LIST OF ITEMS** a list, especially of entertainment features or acts in a show, or the programme of entertainment itself ○ *We've got a brilliant new comedian on the bill tonight.* **7.** *N Am* MONEY same as **banknote** ■ *vt* (**bills, billing, billed**) **1. SEND REQUEST FOR PAYMENT TO SOMEBODY** to send somebody a statement of how much money is owed for items bought or services provided ○ *Bill me for the cost of dry-cleaning.* **2. ADVERTISE SOMETHING** to advertise an event or performance, especially using posters ○ *It's billed as the biggest ice show in Britain.* **3. DESCRIBE SOMETHING AS SOMETHING** to describe something that is going to happen or be produced as having a particular quality ○ *billed as the technological advance of the decade* [14C. Via Anglo-Norman *bille* < medieval Latin *bulla* 'seal on a document'] —**biller** *n* ◇ **fill** *or* **fit the bill** to be suitable for a particular purpose

bill[2] /bil/ *n* **1.** BIRDS, ZOOL same as **beak** (senses 1, 6) **2.** GEOG a narrow strip of land that juts out into the sea (*often used in placenames*) **3.** NAUT the point at the very end of one of the arms of an anchor [Old English *bile*, origin ?] ◇ **bill and coo** to kiss and whisper intimately, as young lovers do, in a way thought to be reminiscent of the affectionate behaviour of doves

bill[3] /bil/, **Bill** *npl* the police (*informal*) ○ *Are the bill still after him for that jewellery job?* [Mid-20C. Probably shortening of OLD BILL]

billabong /bíllə bong/ *n Aus* a pool or water hole formed by a side-channel of a river during the wet season [Mid-19C. < Wiradhuri < *bila* 'river' + *bang* 'watercourse that only runs after rain']

billboard[1] /bíll bawrd/ *n* a very large board erected by the roadside or attached to a building, used for displaying advertisements

billboard[2] /bíll bawrd/ *n* a ledge on the front of a boat or ship to which the anchor is secured

billet[1] /bíllət/ MIL *n* **1. ACCOMMODATION FOR SERVICE PEOPLE** a private home or a guest house providing temporary accommodation for people in the armed forces **2. ORDER TO PROVIDE ACCOMMODATION** an official order to a householder to provide temporary accommodation for a member of the armed forces ■ *v* (**-lets, -leting, -leted**) **1.** *vti* **ASSIGN SOLDIER TO TEMPORARY ACCOMMODATION** to arrange for a member of the armed forces to have temporary accommodation in a particular house, or to have such temporary accommodation **2.** *vt* **PROVIDE TEMPORARY ACCOMMODATION FOR SOLDIER** to provide temporary accommodation for a member of the armed forces [15C. < Anglo-Norman *bilette* 'written orders' < variant of Old French *bulle* (see BULL[2])]

billet[2] /bíllət/ *n* **1. CHUNK OF WOOD** a short thick piece of wood, especially firewood **2.** METALL **METAL BAR IN SEMIFINISHED STATE** a metal bar or block with a simple shape that requires further working **3.** ARCHIT **PART OF DECORATIVE MOULDING** one of a series of short, evenly spaced blocks or cylinders forming part of a decorative moulding [15C. < Old French *billette* 'small log' < *bille* 'log']

billet-doux /bílli dóo/ (*plural* **billets-doux** /bílli dóoz/) *n* a letter expressing affectionate and romantic thoughts [Late 17C. < French, 'sweet note']

billfish /bíll fish/ (*plural same or* **-fishes**) *n* a large fish with jaws resembling spears that lives near the surface and is hunted for sport. Marlin, sailfish, and swordfish are billfish. Native to: tropical and semitropical waters. Family: Xiphiidae. [< BILL[2]]

billfold /bíll fōld/ *n N Am* a pocket-sized folding container for paper money, credit cards, stamps, and photographs, sometimes with a compartment for loose change [< BILL[1]]

billhook /bíll hòok/ *n* a tool with a wooden handle and a large broad curved blade. Use: cutting branches off trees. [< obsolete *bill* 'bladed or pointed weapon']

billiard /bíllyərd/ *adj* relating to or used in billiards ○ *a billiard table*

billiards /bíllyərdz/ *n* an indoor game in which a felt-tipped stick (**cue**) is used to hit three balls across a cloth-covered table into pockets (*takes a singular verb*) [Late 16C. < French *billard* < *bille* 'log']

billing /bílling/ *n* **1. POSITION IN TERMS OF ADVERTISING** the particular importance or prominence given to a performer or event in advertisements ○ *an exciting young band currently getting top billing* **2.** COMM **SENDING OUT OF CUSTOMERS' BILLS** the preparing and sending out of bills to customers ○ *quarterly billing* **3.** *N Am* **ADVERTISING** the advertising or promoting of a performance, event, or product [< BILL[1]]

Billingsgate /bíllingz gayt/ the largest wholesale fish market in London, established on the north bank of the River Thames in the 16th century and, since 1982, located in the Isle of Dogs in the East End of London

billion /bíllyən/ (*plural* **-lions** or *same*) *n* **1. ONE THOUSAND MILLION** one thousand million, written as 1 followed by nine zeros **2. ONE MILLION MILLION** one million million, written as 1 followed by 12 zeros (*dated*) **3. LARGE NUMBER** an extremely large but unspecified number of people or things (*informal*; *often pl*) [Late 17C. < French, 'million million' < *bis* 'twice' + *million* (see MILLION)] —**billionth** *n, adj*

USAGE A **thousand million** or a **million million?** In current use, a ***billion*** means a thousand million. In earlier use it often meant a million million, but a number as large as this is needed far less often. In its informal use, ***billions*** (like *hundreds, thousands*, etc.) has no precise numerical meaning: *I've called his office billions of times. That must have cost billions.* The word now used to mean a million million is *trillion*.

billionaire /bíllyə náir/ *n* **1.** somebody who has money and property worth more than a billion pounds **2.** somebody who is extremely wealthy [Late 19C. After MILLIONAIRE]

bill of entry *n* a list of goods to be imported or exported presented to officials at a customs house

bill of exchange *n* a document setting out an instruction to pay a particular person a fixed sum of money on a particular date or when the person requests payment

bill of fare *n* **1.** a menu of food available in a restaurant or served at a special function **2.** a list of items, especially events in a programme of entertainment (*informal*)

bill of health *n* a certificate stating that the crew of a ship are healthy and are not affected by infectious diseases ◇ **a clean bill of health 1.** a good report on somebody's state of health **2.** a good report about the state of something such as the efficiency or profitability of an organization

bill of indictment *n* a document setting out the criminal charges against somebody, formerly presented to a grand jury

bill of lading *n* a list of goods being transported, especially by ship, together with the conditions that apply to their transportation

bill of rights *n* a list of basic human rights as guaranteed by the laws of a country

Bill of Rights *n* **1.** an English act of law, passed in 1689, guaranteeing people, especially landowners and parliamentarians, freedom and basic rights **2.** the first ten amendments to the US Constitution, which protect people's basic human rights

bill of sale *n* a document stating that something has been sold or transferred to the ownership of another party

billon /bíllən/ *n* **1.** an alloy consisting of a small amount of silver or gold mixed with a base metal such as copper, used especially for making coins **2.** an alloy of silver with copper in high proportion, used especially for making medals [Early 18C. < French, 'ingot, bronze money' < *bille* 'log']

billow /bíllō/ *v* (**-lows, -lowing, -lowed**) **1.** *vti* **SWELL WITH AIR** to fill with air, or cause something made of fabric to fill with air, and swell outwards ○ *the wind billowing their dresses* **2.** *vi* **MOVE IN CURLING MASS** to move upwards or along in a curling or rolling mass ○ *smoke that billowed from the room* ■ *n* **MOVING CURLING MASS** a curling or rolling mass of something such as waves or clouds of smoke that moves upwards or along [Mid-16C. < Old Norse *bylgja* 'wave' < Indo-European, 'to swell'] —**billowy** *adj*

billposter /bíll pōstər/, **billsticker** /-stikər/ *n* somebody who puts up advertising notices in public places ○ *Billposters will be prosecuted.* [< BILL[1]] —**billposting** *n*

billy[1] /bílli/ (*plural* **-lies**) *n N Am* ARMS, POLICE same as **billy club** [Mid-19C. Origin ?]

billy[2] /bílli/ *n* (*plural* **-lies**) a light metal cooking pot with a lid and a semicircular wire handle, used for boiling water or cooking food on a campfire ■ *adj ANZ* cooked or prepared in a pot over a campfire [Mid-19C. Origin ?]

billy[3] /bílli/ (*plural* **-lies**) *n* same as **billy goat**

billy-bat *n regional* ZOOL same as **bat**[3] [Probably < *Billy* pet form of *William*]

REGIONAL NOTE See ***bat***[3].

billycan /bílli kan/ *n* same as **billy**[2] [< BILLY[2]]

billycart /bílli kaart/ *n Aus* a home-made go-cart used by children, usually consisting of a wooden box mounted on a plank attached to wheels [*Billy* in English dialect sense, 'machine']

billy club *n N Am* a short stick or club used as a weapon by a police officer [< BILLY[1]]

billy goat *n* a male goat [< *Billy* pet form of *William*]

Billy the Kid /bílli-/ (1859–81) US outlaw. A notorious robber and cattle rustler on the US Western frontier, he claimed to have killed at least 21 people. He used numerous aliases, and the facts of his life are not clearly known. Born **McCarty, Henry**. Known as **Bonney, William H.**

bilobate /bī lṓ bayt/, **bilobed** /bī lōbd/ *adj* having or consisting of two lobes ○ *a bilobate leaf*

biltong /bíll tong/ *n S Africa* strips of lean meat cured by salting and drying [Early 19C. < Afrikaans < Dutch *bil* 'buttock, rump' + *tong* 'tongue']

Bim /bim/ *n* somebody who comes from Barbados (*informal*) [Mid-19C. Origin ?]

BIM *abbr* British Institute of Management

bima, **bimah** *n* JUDAISM another spelling of **bema** (sense 1)

bimanual /bī mánn yoo əl/ *adj* done with or needing the use of two hands —**bimanually** *adv*

Bimberi Peak /bímbəri-/ mountain in the Australian Capital Territory, southeastern Australia. Height: 1,910 m/6,266 ft.

bimbo /bímbō/ (*plural* **-bos** or **-boes**) *n* (*slang*) **1.** an offensive term for an attractive woman who is regarded as unintelligent and shallow **2.** *N Am* an offensive term for a man or woman who is regarded as unintelligent or superficial [Early 20C. Probably < Italian, 'baby, small child']

bimetallic /bī me tállik/ *adj* containing or consisting of two metals

bimetallic strip *n* a strip composed of two metals fixed together, each with a different coefficient of expansion and, therefore, bending at different rates when heated. Bimetallic strips are used in thermostats, thermal switches, and some thermometers.

bimillenary /bī mi lénnəri/ *adj* relating to or celebrating a 2,000th anniversary ■ *n* (*plural* **-ies**) the 2,000th anniversary of something

bimodal /bī mṓd'l/ *adj* relating to or consisting of a series of observations with two peaks, representing two statistical values that occur with equal frequency and more often than any other value ○ *bimodal distribution* —**bimodality** /bīmō dálləti/ *n*

bimolecular /bī mə lékyŏŏlər/ *adj* relating to, consisting of, or formed from two molecules

bimonthly /bī múnthli/ *adj, adv* **1. OCCURRING EVERY TWO MONTHS** produced or held every two months **2. OCCURRING TWICE MONTHLY** produced or held twice a month ■ *n* (*plural* **-lies**) **BIMONTHLY PUBLICATION** a publication such as a magazine or journal that appears every two months or twice a month

USAGE See ***biweekly***.

bimorphemic /bī mawr féemik/ *adj* consisting of two of the smallest units of meaning in language (**morphemes**). The word 'fallen' is bimorphemic, comprising the free morpheme 'fall' and the bound past participle morpheme '-en'.

bin /bin/ *n* **1. RUBBISH CONTAINER** a container for rubbish or waste paper (*often used in combination*) ○ *a waste-paper bin* **2. LARGE STORAGE CONTAINER** a large storage container, e.g. an industrial container for grain or coal, or an open container holding goods in a shop **3. STORAGE SHELVES FOR WINE** a set of shelves with compartments for storing bottles of wine in a cellar ■ *vt* (**bins, binning, binned**) **1. DISPOSE OF SOMETHING** to throw something away ○ *I bin all the junk mail without even looking at it.* **2. STORE SOMETHING IN BIN** to put something in a storage bin [Old English *binn* < Celtic]

binary /bīnəri/ *adj* **1. IN TWO PARTS** consisting of two parts **2.** MATHS **OF NUMBER SYSTEM BASED ON TWO** using or belonging to a number system that has 2, not 10, as its base ○ *binary notation* **3.** CHEM **HAVING ONLY TWO CHEMICAL ELEMENTS** consisting of two different chemical elements only **4.** CHEM **HAVING TWO CHEMICALS MIXING TOXICALLY** consisting of or using two harmless components that combine to form an extremely toxic product **5.** MUSIC same as **duple** ■ *n* (*plural* **-ries**) **1.** MATHS **BINARY NUMBER SYSTEM** a number system that has 2, not 10, as its base ○ *written in binary* **2.** MATHS **BINARY DIGIT** a binary number or digit **3.** COMPUT **DATA ENCODING PROTOCOL** a protocol for encoding data in a file other than in a sequence of printable characters or human-readable text, or a file encoded in this manner **4.** ASTRON same as **binary star 5.** ARMS same as **binary weapon** [15C. < late Latin *binarius* < Latin *bini* 'two together']

binary code *n* a computer code that uses the binary number system. Numbers and letters are translated into signals that a computer reads as sequences of ones and zeros called binary digits (**bits**).

binary coded decimal *n* a numbering system in which each digit of a decimal is converted into a binary number

binary digit *n* either of the digits 0 and 1, used in the binary system

binary file *n* a computer file that contains data in a raw or nontext state made up of characters that only a computer can read. Executable programs are stored and transmitted in binary files, as are most numerical data files.

binary fission *n* the reproduction of a cell or a one-celled organism by division into two nearly equal parts

binary form *n* a musical form that has two complementary parts, both usually repeated

binary notation *n* COMPUT same as **binary system**

binary star *n* a pair of stars that revolve around their common centre of mass under mutual gravitational attraction

binary system *n* a number system with 2 as its base, numbers being expressed as sequences of the digits 0 and 1. For example, the number 5 is written as 101, representing one 1, no 2s, and one 4, read from right to left.

binary weapon *n* a bomb or artillery shell that contains two chemicals that are harmless in isolation but combine to form a toxic compound before reaching the target

binational /bī násh'nəl/ *adj* relating to or involving two nations

binaural /bī náwrəl, bi-/ *adj* **1.** relating to both ears or the perception of sound by both ears **2.** recorded onto two separate channels using two microphones, so as to sound realistic when heard through headphones [Mid-19C. < Latin *bini* 'two together']

bind /bīnd/ *v* (**binds, binding, bound** /bownd/, **bound**) **1.** *vt* **TIE SOMETHING FIRMLY TO SOMETHING** to tie something firmly to something else by winding a cord tightly and repeatedly round both things **2.** *vt* **TIE SOMEBODY'S HANDS OR FEET TOGETHER** to tie somebody's hands or feet together to make it difficult to escape (*often passive*) ○ *had bound him hand and foot* **3.** *vt* **WRAP SOMETHING TIGHTLY** to wind a cord, tape, or bandage firmly round something to protect it or hold it together ○ *You have to bind the wound firmly.* **4.** *vt* HANDICRAFT **PROTECT EDGE OF FABRIC** to protect or decorate the edge of a piece of material by stitching over it or fixing a strip of fabric to it **5.** *vt* PUBL **PUT BOOK TOGETHER** to fix pages together and put them in a cover to form a book, leaflet, or other publication **6.** *vti* **LINK PEOPLE EMOTIONALLY** to form a link or relationship between people based on loyalty, affection, or a shared experience ○ *the instinct that binds mother and child* **7.** *vti* **STICK TOGETHER** to stick together, or cause things to stick together, so as to form a solid mass ○

The water, sand, and cement bind to form workable mortar. **8.** *vti* CHEM **FORM CHEMICAL BOND** to form a chemical bond with a substance **9.** *vt* MED **MAKE SOMEBODY CONSTIPATED** to make somebody's faeces firmer and more solid (*refers to food or medicine*) **10.** *vi* ENG **BECOME STIFF OR STUCK** to become stiff, stuck, or unable to move freely (*refers to mechanical parts*) ○ *The brakes are binding.* **11.** *vt* **FORCE SOMEBODY TO DO SOMETHING** to oblige or compel somebody to do something, e.g. by invoking a law, contract or promise (*often passive*) ○ *bound by her oath of office* **12.** *vt* **EMPLOY SOMEBODY AS APPRENTICE** formerly, to employ somebody as an apprentice under the terms of an agreement that obliged the apprentice to work for a fixed period, often several years ■ *n* **1. NUISANCE** something that is annoying or causes inconvenience ○ *I have to go to the hospital every two weeks: it's a real bind.* **2.** FENCING **MOVEMENT PUSHING FENCER'S BLADE AWAY** in fencing, a movement that pushes an opponent's blade out of line **3.** CHESS **DOMINANT POSITION IN CHESS** in chess, a position of dominance in the centre of the board that restricts an opponent's moves **4.** MUSIC same as **tie** *n* (sense 8) [Old English *bindan* < Indo-European] ◇ **bound up with somebody** *or* **something** closely involved with or connected to somebody or something ◇ **in a bind** in a difficult or unpleasant situation, especially a situation in which every option leads to difficulties

bind off *vti US* HANDICRAFT same as **cast off** (sense 3)

bind over *vt* to place a legal order on somebody, stating that he or she must behave in a particular way for a particular period of time (*often passive*) ○ *He was fined £200 and bound over to keep the peace for twelve months.*

binder /bíndər/ *n* **1. HARD COVER FOR PAPERS** a stiff cover with clips inside for holding loose sheets of paper or magazines **2. MACHINE FOR BINDING BOOKS OR PAPERS** a machine for fixing sheets of paper together to form a book or booklet **3. BOOKBINDER** somebody whose job is to make books by assembling the pages and putting on the cover **4. CORD OR TIE** a length of cord, string, or tape that is used to tie things together **5. SOMETHING THAT STICKS THINGS** a substance added to form dry ingredients into a solid mass or to maintain an even consistency throughout a liquid or semiliquid substance **6.** AGRIC **DEVICE OR MACHINE FOR MAKING SHEAVES** an attachment on a reaping machine for bundling cut grain into sheaves, or a reaping machine with this attachment

bindery /bíndəri/ (*plural* **-ies**) *n* a place where books are made by assembling the pages and putting on the cover

bindi /bíndi/ (*plural* **-dis**) *n* a small usually red decorative mark worn in the middle of the forehead by women. Traditionally it was worn only by Hindu married women and unmarried girls, but not by widows. [< Hindi *bindī*]

bindi-eye /bíndi-/ (*plural* **bindi-eyes** or *same*) *n* a small plant of the daisy family with fruits that are covered in small hooks or prickles. Native to: Australia. Genus: *Calotis.* [Early 20C. Alteration of Kamilaroi, Yuwaalaraay *bindayaa*]

binding /bínding/ *adj* **OBLIGING SOMEBODY TO DO SOMETHING** creating a legal or moral obligation to do something, with no possibility of withdrawal or avoidance ○ *a binding agreement* ■ *n* **1.** PUBL **BOOK COVERING** the cover of a book, or the material used to cover books **2.** PUBL **SOMETHING HOLDING BOOK'S PAGES TOGETHER** the glue, strip of plastic, or other material that holds the pages of a book or booklet together **3. CORD USED FOR TYING** something that is used to tie or protect things, especially a cord or tape that is wound repeatedly round something **4.** HANDICRAFT **FABRIC EDGING** a strip of fabric or tape attached to the edge of a piece of material to prevent it from fraying **5.** SKIING **SKI FASTENING** one of the fastenings on a ski or snowboard that hold the ski to the boot

binding energy *n* **1.** the energy required to remove a particle from a system, e.g. an electron from an atom **2.** the energy required to separate a system into its individual particles or components

binding site *n* a cavity on the surface of a protein that contains a pattern of amino acids arranged so that they can form a chemical bond only with a specific molecule

bindweed /bínd weed/ *n* a plant with long twining stems, especially a wild plant with large white funnel-shaped flowers, generally regarded as a weed. Genera: *Convolvulus* or *Calystegia.*

bin end *n* one of the last bottles remaining from a single production of wine, often sold at a reduced price

bing /bing/ *n Scotland* a heap or pile of something, especially a slag heap [Early 16C. < Old Norse *bingr* 'heap, bolster']

binge /binj/ *n* **1. HEAVY DRINKING OR EATING SESSION** a short period when somebody drinks or eats too much, especially a period of uncontrolled drinking or eating caused by a disorder such as alcoholism or bulimia **2. SPREE** a short period of time when something is done in an unrestrained way ○ *a shopping binge* ■ *vi* (**binges, bingeing** or **binging, binged**) **1. EAT TOO MUCH** to eat far too much food very quickly, sometimes as a symptom of an eating disorder such as bulimia **2. BE SELF-INDULGENT WITH SOMETHING** to do or consume something in an unrestrained self-indulgent way ○ *stay in all day and binge on old movies* [Early 19C. Origin ?] —**binger** *n*

binge drinking *n* the consumption of an excessive amount of alcohol in a short period of time, usually in order to get drunk

bingle /bíng g'l/ *n Aus* a minor traffic accident (*informal*) [Mid-20C. < dialect *bing* 'thump']

bingo /bíng gō/ *n* **LOTTERY GAME WITH NUMBERED CARDS** a game played with numbered cards in which numbers are selected at random and the first person to cover all or specific numbered slots on his or her card wins ■ *interj* **1. CALL IN BINGO** a shout of success, called by a player who has won a game of bingo **2. EXCLAMATION OF SUCCESS** used to express satisfaction at sudden success or achievement [Early 20C. Origin ?]

Bin Laden /bin láadən/, **Osama** (*b.* 1957) Saudi-born leader of al-Qaeda, a militant Islamic organization associated with several terrorist incidents, including the four attacks on the United States on 11 September 2001

bin liner *n* a plastic bag designed to be put inside a waste bin to make removal of the waste a clean and simple process

binman /bín man/ (*plural* **-men** /-men/) *n* a dustman (*informal*)

binnacle /bínnək'l/ *n* a support or mounting for a ship's compass [15C. Alteration of Spanish *bitácula* < Latin *habitaculum* 'housing' < *habitare* 'inhabit']

binocular /bī nókyōōlər, bi-/ *adj* involving or using both eyes, or relating to vision using both eyes [Mid-18C. < Latin *bini* 'two together' + *oculus* 'eye'] —**binocularity** /bī nókyōō lárrəti, bi-/ *n*

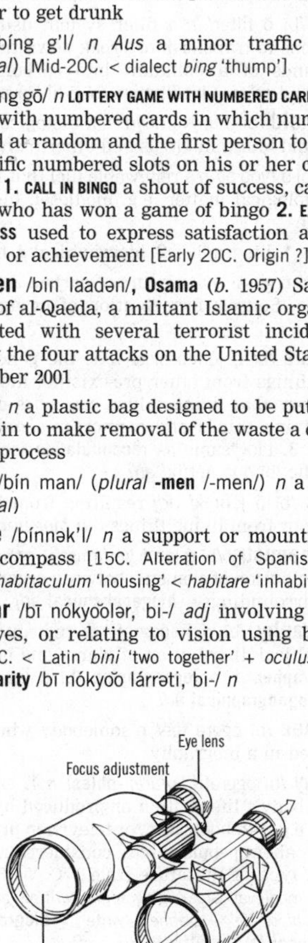
Eye lens
Focus adjustment
Object lens
Reversing prisms

binoculars

binoculars /bī nókyōōlərz, bi-/ *npl* a device for looking at distant objects that magnifies what is seen using a lens for each eye

binomial /bī nṓmi əl/ *n* **1.** MATHS **EXPRESSION WITH TWO TERMS** a mathematical expression made up of two terms linked by a plus or minus sign **2.** BIOL **TWO-PART NAME OF ORGANISM** a pair of Latin or Latinized words forming a scientific name in the classification of plants, animals, and microorganisms. The first word represents the genus and the second the species. ■ *adj* **1.** BIOL **HAVING TWO NAMES** relating to or consisting of the two Latin or Latinized parts of a scientific name in the classification of plants, animals, and microorganisms **2.** MATHS **HAVING TWO MATHEMATICAL TERMS** relating to or consisting of the two terms of a mathematical expression linked by a plus or minus sign [Mid-16C. < modern Latin *binomius* < Latin *bi-* 'two' + Greek *nomos* 'part'] —**binomially** *adv*

binomial coefficient *n* a number that multiplies the variables in a two-part mathematical expression, e.g. the numbers 3 and 4 in the expression 3x-4y

binomial distribution *n* a formula that indicates the probability of achieving a given number of successful outcomes in a predetermined number of statistical trials when the probability of success is the same for each trial

binomial nomenclature *n* the system of assigning two-part Latin or Latinized scientific names to plants, animals, and microorganisms, with the first word denoting the genus and the second the species

binomial theorem *n* a mathematical formula used to calculate the value of a two-part mathematical expression that is squared, cubed, or raised to another power or exponent, e.g. $(x+y)^n$, without explicitly multiplying the parts themselves

bint /bint/ *n* an offensive term for a girl or woman (*slang*) [Mid-19C. < Arabic, 'girl, daughter']

binturong /bíntyōō rong, bin tyóor ong/ *n* a mammal resembling a cat, with a thick black coat, a long tail, and tufts on its ears. The largest of the civet family, it lives in dense forests, uses its tail for grasping branches when climbing, and can swim to catch fish. Native to: Southeast Asia. Latin name: *Arctictis binturong.* [Early 19C. < Malay]

binucleate /bī nyóokli ət/, **binucleated** /-kli aytid/, **binuclear** /-kli ər/ *adj* having two distinct cell nuclei

Binyon /bínnyən/, **Laurence** (1869–1943) British poet. He wrote the World War I poem 'For the Fallen' and translated Dante's *Divine Comedy* (1933–43). Born **Binyon, Robert Laurence**

> 'They shall grow not old, as we that are left grow old: / Age shall not weary them, nor the years condemn. / At the going down of the sun and in the morning / We will remember them.'
>
> [Laurence Binyon, 'For the Fallen', *Poems for the Fallen*; 1914]

bio /bī ō/ (*plural* **-os**) *n* a biographical work (*informal*) ○ *reads mostly fiction and celebrity bios* [Mid-20C. Shortening of BIOGRAPHY]

bio- *prefix* **1.** BIOL life, biology ○ *bioengineering* ○ *biography* ○ *biochemistry* **2.** biological warfare ○ *bioweapon* **3.** involving the use of biological or chemical weapons ○ *bioterrorism* [< Greek *bios* 'life, way of living' < Indo-European, 'to live']

bioaccumulation /bī ō ə kyoomyōō láysh'n/ *n* the accumulation of a harmful substance such as a radioactive element, a heavy metal, or an organochlorine in an organism, especially an organism that forms part of the food chain —**bioaccumulate** /-kyóomyōō layt/ *vi* —**bioaccumulative** /-kyóomyōō lətiv/ *adj*

bioactive /bī ō áktiv/ *adj* producing an effect in living tissue or in a living organism

bioactivity /bī ō ak tívvəti/ *n* the effect that a substance or agent has on an organism or living tissue

bioassay /bī ō ə sáy, -ássay/ *n* a technique for determining the concentration or potency of a substance such as a drug by measuring its effect on an organism —**bioassay** *vt*

bioastronomy /bī ō ə strónnəmi/ *n* the study of the possibility of life in the universe other than on Earth

bioaugmentation /bī ō awg men táysh'n/ *n* the addition of microorganisms to human or industrial waste in order to reinforce the natural biological processes that produce nonpolluting products —**bioaugment** /-awg mént/ *vt*

bioavailability /bī ō ə váylə bílləti/ *n* the extent and rate to which a drug is taken up by the body in a physiologically active form

biocatalysis /bī ō kə tálləssiss/ *n* the stimulation of a chemical reaction by a biochemical agent such as an enzyme —**biocatalyse** /bī ō káttə līz/ *vt* —**biocatalyst** /-káttəlist/ *n* —**biocatalytic** /-káttə líttik/ *adj*

biocenosis *n* ECOL another spelling of **biocoenosis**

biochemical /bī ō kémmik'l/ *adj* relating to the chemical substances present in living organisms and the reactions and methods used to identify or characterize them —**biochemically** *adv*

biochemical oxygen demand *n* a measure of the

pollution present in water, obtained by measuring the amount of oxygen absorbed from the water by the microorganisms present in it

biochemistry /bī ō kémmistri/ *n* **1.** the scientific study of the chemical substances, processes, and reactions that occur in living organisms **2.** the chemistry or composition of a particular organism or system —**biochemist** *n*

biochip /bī ō chip/ *n* a semiconductor chip that uses organic molecules to store and process information

biocide /bī ō sīd/ *n* a chemical designed to kill organisms, especially microorganisms —**biocidal** /bī ō sīd'l/ *adj*

bioclastic rock /bī ō klastik-/ *n* rock formed from organic remains

bioclimatic /bī ō klī máttik/ *adj* relating to the relationship between climate and living organisms, or to the study of bioclimatology

bioclimatology /bī ō klīmə tólləji/ *n* the study of how climate affects living organisms —**bioclimatologist** *n*

biocoenosis /bī ō sə nṓssiss/ (*plural* -**ses** /-seez/), **biocenosis** (*plural* -**ses**) *n* a diverse group of species or organisms with its own distinct habitat, interacting to form an ecological community [Late 19C. < modern Latin < Greek *bios* 'life' + *koinōsis* 'sharing' < *koinos* 'common']

biocompatibility /bī ō kəm pátta bílləti/ *n* the compatibility of a donated organ or an artificial limb with the living tissue into which it is implanted or with which it is brought into contact. Incompatibility leads to toxic reactions or immunological rejection. —**biocompatible** /bī ō kəm páttəb'l/ *adj*

biocomputer /bī ō kəm pyoótər/ *n* a very fast computer whose calculations are performed using biological processes instead of semiconductor technology

biocontrol /bī ō kən tról/ *n* ECOL same as **biological control**

bioconversion /bī ō kən vúrsh'n/ *n* the conversion of one organic substance into another or into energy by biological processes or organisms

biodata /bī ō daytə, -daatə/ *n* **1.** S Asia same as **CV**[2] (*takes a singular or plural noun*) **2.** information relating to a particular person and his or her financial, professional, or educational history, stored in a database and used, e.g. in banking, job recruiting, and marketing (*takes a singular or plural verb*)

biodegradable /bī ō di gráydəb'l/ *adj* made of substances that will decay relatively quickly as a result of the action of bacteria and break down into elements such as carbon that are recycled naturally —**biodegradability** /bī ō di gráydə bílləti/ *n*

biodegrade /bī ō di gráyd/ (**-grades**, **-grading**, **-graded**) *vi* to decay naturally as the result of the action of bacteria —**biodegradation** /bī ō déggrə dáysh'n/ *n*

biodiesel /bī ō deez'l/ *n* a substitute for diesel fuel made wholly or partly from organic products, especially processed vegetable oils such as soya bean oil and groundnut oil

biodiversity /bī ō dī vúrssəti/ *n* the range of organisms present in a particular ecological community or system. It can be measured by the numbers and types of different species, or the genetic variations within and between species.

biodynamics /bī ō dī námmiks/ *n* the study of how energy, motion, and other forces affect living organisms (*takes a singular verb*) —**biodynamic** *adj*

bioelectricity /bī ō ilek tríssəti/ *n* electric current generated by living tissue —**bioelectric** /bī ō iléktrik/ *adj*

bioenergetics /bī ō énnər jéttiks/ *n* (*takes a singular verb*) **1.** the study of the conversion of energy in organisms and biological systems, e.g. in photosynthesis **2.** a therapy, devised by Wilhelm Reich in the 1940s, that uses an analysis of somebody's physical posture and movements to enhance emotional wellbeing —**bioenergetic** *adj*

bioengineering /bī ō énji neéring/ *n* the use of engineering principles and techniques to solve medical problems, e.g. in the design of artificial limbs or in organ replacement —**bioengineer** *n* —**bioengineered** *adj*

bioethanol /bī ō éthə nol/ *n* a fuel for internal-combustion engines that is made by adding alcohol obtained from biological material to petrol so that it produces fewer pollutants

bioethics /bī ō éthiks/ *n* the study of the moral and ethical choices faced in medical research and in the treatment of patients, especially when the application of advanced technology is involved (*takes a singular verb*) —**bioethical** *adj* —**bioethicist** *n*

biofabric /bī ō fabrik/ *n* a fabric impregnated with genetically engineered bacteria that eat odours, absorb sweat, and continually regenerate dirt and dust repellents

biofeedback /bī ō feéd bak/ *n* the use of monitoring devices that display information about the operation of a bodily function that is not normally consciously controlled, e.g. heart rate or blood pressure. This helps a patient to learn to control the function consciously.

biofilm /bī ō film/ *n* a thin layer of cells of a microorganism such as a bacterium or fungus, held to a surface by the material the microorganisms produce. The plaque that forms on teeth is a biofilm.

biofilter /bī ō filtər/ *n* a filter system using microorganisms to transform or break down the organic compounds of a pollutant into carbon dioxide, water, and salts —**biofiltration** /bī ō fil tráysh'n/ *n*

bioflavonoid /bī ō fláyvə noyd/ *n* a biologically active compound found in citrus and other fruits

biofuel /bī ō fyoo əl/ *n* a renewable fuel that is derived from biological matter, e.g. biodiesel, biogas, and methane

biog. *abbr* **1.** biographer **2.** biographical **3.** biography

biogas /bī ō gass/ *n* a mixture of carbon dioxide and methane. Source: fermentation of organic waste. Use: fuel.

biogenesis /bī ō jénnəssiss/ *n* **1.** the generation of living things from other pre-existing life forms **2.** the theory that living things can arise only from other living things and cannot be spontaneously created **3.** BIOL same as **recapitulation** (sense 2) —**biogenetic** /bī ō jə néttik/ *adj*

biogenic /bī ō jénnik/ *adj* resulting from biological activity or from living things ○ *a biogenic amine*

biogeochemistry /bī ō jee ō kémmistri/ *n* the study of the distribution of elements between organisms and their surroundings —**biogeochemical** *adj*

biogeography /bī ō ji óggrəfi/ *n* the study of the geographical distribution of plants and animals —**biogeographer** *n* —**biogeographic** /bī ō jee ə gráffik/ *adj* —**biogeographical** *adj*

biographee /bī óggrə feé/ *n* somebody whose life is described in a biography

biography /bī óggrəfi/ (*plural* -**phies**) *n* **1.** an account of somebody's life written or produced by another person, e.g. as a book, film, or television programme **2.** books about people's lives, considered as a whole or as a type of literature [Late 17C. Via French and Latin < medieval Greek *biographia* 'writing about lives' < Greek *bios* 'life' + *graphein* 'write'] —**biographer** *n* —**biographical** /bī ə gráffik'l/ *adj*

biohazard /bī ō hazərd/ *n* a risk to human beings or their environment, especially one presented by a toxic or infectious agent —**biohazardous** /bī ō házzərdəss/ *adj*

bioinformatics /bī ō infər máttiks/ *n* the use of computers to extract and analyse biological data, especially in studying the nucleotide sequences of DNA and other nucleic acids (*takes a singular verb*) —**bioinformatic** *adj* —**bioinformatician** /bī ō infərmə tísh'n/ *n*

bioinstrumentation /bī ō instroomən táysh'n/ *n* instruments used to record and display information about the body's functions, or the use of such instruments

Bioko /bi ōkō/ island in the Gulf of Guinea that forms part of Equatorial Guinea. It contains the national capital, Malabo. Population: 57,190 (1983). Area: 2,020 sq. km/779 sq. mi. Former name **Fernando Póo** (until 1973), **Macías Nguema** (1973–79)

biol. *abbr* **1.** biological **2.** biology

biolistics /bī ō lístiks/ *n* a method of genetic modification involving the shooting of small particles of gold coated with DNA or messenger RNA directly

into cells or tissues at high velocity (*takes a singular verb*) [Late 20C. Blend of BIOLOGICAL + BALLISTICS] —**biolistic** *adj* —**biolistically** *adv*

biological /bī ə lójik'l/ *adj* **1.** OF LIVING THINGS relating to living organisms ○ *biological diversity* **2.** OF BIOLOGY relating to the science of biology **3.** CONTAINING ENZYMES containing enzymes that are intended to digest stains caused by natural substances ○ *biological detergent* **4.** GENETICALLY RELATED related by birth, not by adoption ○ *my biological mother* ■ *n* MEDICATION OR VACCINE FROM LIVING ORGANISMS a drug or other compound produced by living organisms. It is often a commercially important product of genetic modification. —**biologically** *adv*

biological clock *n* the set of mechanisms within living organisms that link physiological processes with daily, monthly, or seasonal cycles or with stages of development and ageing

biological control *n* a method of reducing or eliminating plant pests by introducing predators or microorganisms that attack the targeted pests but spare other species in the area

biological oxygen demand *n* ENVIRON same as **biochemical oxygen demand**

biological shield *n* a massive structure, usually made of concrete and steel, built around the core of a nuclear reactor to protect operating staff from radiation

biological warfare *n* the use of microorganisms to cause disease or death to humans, animals, or plants

biological weapon *n* a missile, bomb, or other device that delivers harmful biological agents

biology /bī ólləji/ *n* **1.** SCIENCE OF LIFE the science that deals with all forms of life, including their classification, physiology, chemistry, and interactions **2.** LIFE IN ONE PLACE the forms of life in a particular environment and their behaviour, development, and history ○ *the biology of desert regions* **3.** PARTICULAR ORGANISM'S MAKEUP the structure and functioning of a particular organism ○ *the biology of the fruit fly* [Early 19C. Via French < German *Biologie* < Greek *bios* 'life'] —**biologist** *n*

bioluminescence /bī ō loomi néss'nss/ *n* the generation and emission of light by organisms such as fireflies, some bacteria and fungi, and many animals that live in the sea —**bioluminescent** *adj*

biomagnetics /bī ō mag néttiks/ *n* the use of magnets and magnetic fields in the treatment of medical conditions, or the study of this subject (*takes a singular verb*)

biomagnification /bī ō mágnfi káysh'n/ *n* BIOL same as **bioaccumulation**

biomass /bī ō mass/ *n* **1.** MASS OF ORGANISMS IN ECOSYSTEM the mass of living organisms within a particular environment, measured in terms of weight per unit of area **2.** PLANT AND ANIMAL WASTE AS FUEL plant and animal material, especially agricultural waste products, used as a source of fuel **3.** ORGANISM'S DRY WEIGHT the mass of material in a living organism or in a community of organisms, usually measured in terms of dry weight

biomaterial /bī ō mə teeri əl/ *n* **1.** any material that performs, aids, or replaces a natural function, e.g. one used as a medical implant **2.** a biodegradable material of plant origin used for packaging, clothing, and bedding

biomathematics /bī ō mathə máttiks/ *n* the application of mathematical methods and formulas to medical or biological phenomena (*takes a singular verb*) —**biomathematical** *adj* —**biomathematician** /bī ō mathəmə tísh'n/ *n*

biome /bī ōm/ *n* a division of the world's vegetation that corresponds to a defined climate and is characterized by specific types of plants and animals, e.g. tropical rain forest or desert. The world's lakes and oceans may also be considered biomes, although they are less susceptible to climatic influences than terrestrial biomes.

biomechanics /bī ō mi kánniks/ *n* the study of body movements and of the forces acting on the musculoskeletal system (*takes a singular verb*) ■ *npl* the mechanical forces at work in a particular body or organ (*takes a plural verb*) —**biomechanical** *adj* —**biomechanically** *adv*

---

a at; aa father; aw all; ay day; ai hair; ə about, item, edible, common, circus; e egg; ee eel; hw when; i it, happy; ī ice; 'l apple; 'm rhythm; 'n fashion; o odd; ō open; oo good; oo pool; ow owl; oy oil; th thin; th this; u up; ur urge;

biomedical engineering *n* MED same as **bioengineering**

biomedicine /bī ō médss'n/ *n* **1.** the employing of the principles of biology, biochemistry, physiology, and other basic sciences to solve problems in clinical medicine **2.** the study of the body's ability to withstand the stresses of unusual or extreme environments —**biomedical** /bī ō méddik'l/ *adj*

biometrics /bī ō méttriks/ *n* (*takes a singular verb*) **1.** the application of statistical techniques to biological data **2.** the use of measurable, biological characteristics such as fingerprints or iris patterns to identify a person to an electronic system —**biometric** *adj* —**biometrical** *adj* —**biometrically** *adv*

biometry /bī ómmətri/ *n* same as **biometrics** —**biometrist** *n*

biomimetic /bī ō mi méttik/ *n* a complex biochemical molecule such as a peptide protein that is synthesized to resemble a substance occurring naturally in the body

biomineralization /bī ō minərə lī záysh'n/, **biomineralisation** *n* a process in which organisms transform organic matter into mineral matter, e.g. in the formation of bone —**biomineral** /bīō mínnərəl/ *n* —**biomineralized** *adj*

biomolecule /bī ō mólli kyool/ *n* **1.** one of the molecules from which living organisms are made **2.** a molecule of a compound produced by or important to a biological organism —**biomolecular** /bī ō mə lékyōolər/ *adj*

biomonitoring /bī ō mónnitəring/ *n* the measurement and tracking of a chemical substance in a living organism or biological material such as blood or urine, usually for the purpose of monitoring environmental pollution or chemical exposure

biomorphic /bī ō máwrfik/ *adj* relating to a form, pattern, or mechanical system that resembles a living organism in shape, appearance, function, or motion ○ *a biomorphic drug that mimics phosphate* —**biomorph** /bī ō mawf/ *n* —**biomorphism** /bī ō máwrfizəm/ *n* —**biomorphosis** /bī ō mawr fōssiss/ *n*

bionic /bī ónnik/ *adj* **1. HAVING ELECTRONICALLY POWERED ORGANS** in science fiction, used to describe a human being who has had some human organs or functions replaced or enhanced by electronically powered parts that give superhuman capabilities **2. HAVING SUPERHUMAN QUALITIES** having superhuman strength, speed, or intensity (*informal*) ○ *a bionic appetite* **3.** BIOL **INVOLVING BIONICS** relating to or involving bionics [Early 20C. < BIO- + ELECTRONIC]

bionic ear *n Aus* MED same as **cochlear implant** (*informal*)

bionics /bī ónniks/ *n* (*takes a singular verb*) **1.** the study of biological function and mechanics, and their application to machine design **2.** the use of electronic devices to replace damaged limbs and organs

bionomics /bī ō nómmiks/ *n* a theory suggesting that economics can usefully be thought of as similar to an evolving ecosystem (*takes a singular verb*) [Late 19C. < BIO-, after ECONOMICS]

-biont *suffix* an organism that lives under particular conditions ○ *halobiont* [< SYMBIONT]

bioorganic /bī ō awr gánnik/ *adj* describes a carbon-based (**organic**) compound produced by an organism or having biological importance

biopharmaceutical /bī ō faarmə syōotik'l/ *n* a drug produced by biotechnological methods

biophysics /bī ō fízziks/ *n* the science that applies the laws and methods of physics to the study of biological processes (*takes a singular verb*) —**biophysical** *adj* —**biophysically** *adv* —**biophysicist** /-ssist/ *n*

biopic /bī ō pik/ *n* a film about the life of a well-known or interesting person (*informal*) [Mid-20C. Contraction of *biographical picture*]

biopiracy /bī ō pīrəssi/ *n* the commercial development of genetic resources such as plants with medicinal properties or genes for resistance to disease without compensating the inhabitants or government of the area where the substances or materials were originally discovered —**biopirate** *n*

biopolymer /bī ō póllimər/ *n* a polymer produced in living organisms

bioprocess /bī ō prō sess/ *n* a method for producing commercially useful biological material

bioprospecting /bī ō prə spékting, -prós pekting/ *n* the process of searching for and extracting potential pharmaceutical compounds from plants —**bioprospect** *vi* —**bioprospector** *n*

biopsy /bī opsi/ (*plural* **-sies**) *n* the removal of a sample of tissue from a living person for laboratory examination [Late 19C. < BIO- + Greek *opsis* 'a viewing' < *ōps* 'eye'] —**biopsic** /bī ópsik/ *adj* —**bioptic** *adj*

biopsychology /bī ō sī kólləji/ *n* BIOL, PSYCHOL same as **psychobiology**

bioreactor /bī ō ri áktər/ *n* **1.** a microorganism that, through its biochemical reactions, can produce medically or commercially useful materials, e.g., yeast producing beer by fermentation or genetically modified bacteria producing insulin **2.** a large tank for growing microorganisms used in industrial production

bioremediation /bī ō ri meedi áysh'n/ *n* the use of biological methods to restore contaminated land, especially the addition of bacteria and other organisms that consume or neutralize contaminants in the soil

biorhythm /bī ō rithəm/ *n* a cyclic change that takes place within living organisms, e.g. sleeping, waking, or the reproductive cycle. Some people believe that biorhythms affect behaviour, mood, and sense of well-being. (*often used in the plural*) —**biorhythmic** /bī ō ríthmik/ *adj* —**biorhythmically** *adv*

biorhythmics /bī ō ríthmiks/ *n* the branch of science dealing with biorhythms (*takes a singular verb*)

BIOS /bī oss/ *n* a small unerasable computer program that contains the instructions needed to begin operation and controls the data flow between the operating system and application programs and the hardware devices. Full form **basic input-output system**

biosatellite /bī ō satt'l īt/ *n* a satellite designed for living beings, including humans, to live in

bioscience /bī ō sī ənss/ *n* a science that studies structures, functions, interactions, or other aspects of living organisms, e.g. biology, ecology, physiology, or molecular biology

bioscientist /bī ō sī əntist/ *n* a specialist in any of the life sciences such as biology, ecology, physiology, or molecular biology

bioscope /bī ə skōp/ *n S Africa* (*archaic*) **1.** a cinema **2.** a film made for cinema

biosecurity /bī ō si kyōorəti/ *n* the protection of the economy, environment, and health of living things from diseases, pests, and bioterrorism

biosensor /bī ō senssər/ *n* an apparatus that uses a biological agent such as an enzyme or organelle to detect, measure, or analyse chemicals. Biosensors are increasingly used in tests to diagnose medical conditions such as blood pressure.

bioseparation /bī ō seppə ráysh'n/ *n* the use of biological agents such as plants, enzymes, or biological membranes to separate components, e.g. in the purification of proteins or water or in the manufacture of food and pharmaceuticals

biosignature /bī ō sígnəchər/ *n* a substance such as an element, isotope, or molecule present in something such as a meteorite that is characteristic of life and is used as evidence of past or present life

-biosis *suffix* a particular mode of life ○ *necrobiosis* [< Greek *biōsis* 'way of living' < *bioun* 'to live' < *bios* 'life'] —**-biotic** *suffix*

biosphere /bī ə sfeer/ *n* the whole area of Earth's surface, atmosphere, and sea that is inhabited by living things —**biospheric** /bī ə sférrik/ *adj*

biosphere reserve *n* a nationally or internationally protected area managed primarily to preserve natural ecological processes. Biosphere reserves are often open to tourists.

biospheric cycles *npl* the natural recycling processes essential to life on Earth, involving the principal elements that make up the biosphere. They include the oxygen cycle, carbon cycle, nitrogen cycle, and water cycle.

biostatics /bī ō státtiks/ *n* the branch of science dealing with the relationship between the structure and the function of an organism (*takes a singular verb*) —**biostatic** *adj* —**biostatically** *adv*

biostatistics /bī ō stə tístiks/ *n* the application of statistics to biological systems and organisms (*takes a singular verb*)

biostimulation /bī ō stimyōo láysh'n/ *n* the addition of nutrients to a polluted site in order to encourage the growth of naturally occurring chemical-degrading microorganisms

biostratigraphy /bī ō strə tíggrəfi/ *n* the branch of science that uses animal and plant fossils to date and correlate sequences of sedimentary rocks

biostrome /bī ə strōm/ *n* a thin layer in a rock formation that consists of organic material such as fossils deposited at the site where they lived [Early 20C. < modern Latin *biostroma* < Greek *bios* 'life' + *strōma* 'bed, covering']

biosurface /bī ō surfiss/ *n* the region on the surface of a protein, enzyme, or receptor that acts as a binding site for molecules

biosurgery /bī ō surjəri/ *n* the use of living organisms in surgery and post-surgical treatment, especially the use of maggots or leeches to clean wounds

biosynthesis /bī ō sínthəssiss/ *n* the synthesis of chemical substances as the result of biological activity —**biosynthetic** /bī ō sin théttik/ *adj* —**biosynthetically** *adv*

biosystematics /bī ō sistə máttiks/ *n* the study of the relationships among groups of species using criteria such as morphology, biochemistry, and DNA comparisons, especially to determine the history of a species (*takes a singular verb*) —**biosystematic** *adj*

biota /bī ōtə/ *n* the total complement of animals and plants in a particular area ○ *The biotas of tropical forests are the richest of all.* [Early 20C. Via modern Latin < Greek *biotē* 'life' < *bios* 'life']

biotech /bī ō tek/ *n* BIOCHEM, INDUST same as **biotechnology** (sense 1) (*informal*) [Late 20C. Shortening]

biotechnical /bī ō téknik'l/ *adj* relating to or involving biotechnology

biotechnology /bī ō tek nólləji/ *n* **1.** the use of biological processes in industrial production. Early examples of biotechnology include the making of cheese, wine, and beer, while later developments include vaccine and insulin production. **2.** BIOL same as **molecular biology** —**biotechnological** /bī ō teknə lójjik'l/ *adj* —**biotechnologically** *adv* —**biotechnologist** *n*

biotelemetry /bī ō tə lémmətri/ *n* the remote monitoring of vital processes, e.g. by attaching a signalling device to an animal. The information is transmitted to a central processor, where it is analysed electronically.

bioterrorism /bī ō térrərizəm/, **bioterror** /bī ō terrər/ *n* terrorist acts involving the use of biological or chemical weapons —**bioterrorist** *adj, n*

biotherapy /bī ō thérrəpi/ *n* the treatment of disease with substances produced through the activity of living organisms such as sera, vaccines, or antibiotics

biothreat /bī ō thret/ *n* a real or perceived threat of the use of biological or chemical weapons

biotic /bī óttik/ *adj* relating to life and living organisms, or caused by living organisms [Early 17C. Via late Latin < Greek *biōtikos* 'of life, lively' < *bios* 'life']

biotic potential *n* the optimal ability of an organism or species to survive and reproduce successfully

biotin /bī ətin/ *n* a B complex vitamin found in egg yolk and liver, used in fat metabolism. Deficiency can lead to dermatitis, loss of appetite, hair loss, and anaemia. Formula: $C_{10}H_{16}N_2O_3S$. [Mid-20C. < Greek *biotos* 'life, sustenance' < *bios* 'life']

biotite /bī ə tīt/ *n* a black, dark brown, or green silicate mineral of the mica group. Source: igneous and metamorphic rocks. [Mid-19C. After J.-B. *Biot* (1774–1862), French physicist]

biotope /bī ətōp/ *n* a small area with a distinct set of environmental conditions that supports a particular ecological community of plants and animals [Early 20C. < German *Biotop* < Greek *topos* 'place']

biotron /bī ə tron/ *n* a place in a laboratory in which temperature and other environmental conditions can be controlled

biotroph /bí ətröf/ *n* a parasite that feeds on the living tissue of its host

biotype /bí ə tīp/ *n* a naturally occurring group of individuals with the same genetic make-up (genotype) —**biotypic** /bí ə típpik/ *adj*

biowarfare /bí ō wáwr fair/ *n* warfare involving the use of biological weapons

bioweapon /bí ō wepən/ *n* a biological or chemical weapon —**bioweaponry** /bí ō wépənri/ *n*

biparental /bí pə rént'l/ *adj* descended from two parents, male and female, as opposed to being the product of asexual reproduction

biparietal /bí pə rí ət'l/ *adj* relating to or involving both parietal bones of the skull, particularly with respect to the measurement of the distance between their rounded projections

biparous /bíppərəss/ *adj* giving birth to two offspring at one time

bipartisan /bí paarti zán, bī páarti zan/ *adj* relating to, undertaken by, or including two political parties ○ *bipartisan support* —**bipartisanism** *n* —**bipartisanship** *n*

bipartite /bī paár tīt/ *adj* **1.** made or shared by two groups of people ○ *a bipartite agreement* **2.** describes leaves that are almost completely divided into two parts —**bipartitely** *adv* —**bipartition** /bí paar tísh'n/ *n*

biped /bí ped/ *n* an animal with only two legs for locomotion, e.g. a human being [Mid-17C. Directly or via French *bipède* < Latin *biped*- 'two-footed' < *ped*- 'foot']

bipedal /bī peéd'l, -pédd'l/ *adj* describes an animal that has two legs or feet [15C. < Latin *bipedalis* < *biped*- (see BIPED)]

bipedalism /bī peéd'l izəm, -pédd'l-/ *n* the practice of walking upright on two feet, as opposed to moving on all four limbs

biphasic /bī fáyzik/ *adj* having two phases

biphenyl /bī fénn'l, -feén'l/ *n* a white crystalline substance. Use: fungicide, heat transfer agent, synthesis of organic compounds. Formula: $C_{12}H_{10}$.

bipinnate /bī pínnayt/ *adj* describes leaves divided into leaflets that are themselves subdivided —**bipinnately** *adv*

biplane /bí playn/ *n* an aeroplane with two sets of wings, one above the other, of a type built and flown mainly in the early part of the 20th century

bipod /bí pod/ *n* a stand or support that has two legs

bipolar /bī pólər/ *adj* **1.** WITH TWO POLES having two physical poles or extremities **2.** HAVING TWO DIFFERENT IDEAS having two completely different opinions, attitudes, or natures **3.** GEOG RELATING TO EARTH'S POLES relating to, involving, or found at both the North and South Poles **4.** PSYCHIAT HAVING MANIC AND DEPRESSED PERIODS characterized by shifts between episodes of mania and depression **5.** ELECTRONICS USING NEGATIVE AND POSITIVE CHARGE CARRIERS describes electronic devices, especially transistors, in which both negative and positive charge carriers are utilized —**bipolarity** /bī pō lárrəti/ *n*

bipolar disorder *n* a psychiatric disorder characterized by extreme mood swings, ranging between episodes of acute euphoria (**mania**) and severe depression

bipotentiality /bípə ténshi álləti/ *n* the potential in early embryological development for a cell or organ to differentiate in one of two ways, especially for a gonad to become either an ovary or a testis

biprism /bí prizəm/ *n* a glass prism that produces a double image of a single object

bipropellant /bí prə péllənt/ *n* a substance made up of two elements, usually a fuel and an oxidizer, that is used to propel a rocket

BIPS /bips/ *abbr* E-COMMERCE bank Internet payment system

biquadratic /bí kwo dráttik/ *adj* relating to the fourth power of a number ○ *a biquadratic equation* ■ *n* an equation that involves the fourth power of a number

biracial /bī ráysh'l/ *adj* relating to, made up of, or involving people of two different races —**biracialism** *n* —**biracially** *adv*

biradial /bī ráydi əl/ *adj* with both bilateral and radial symmetry, as found in some primitive animals that live in the sea

biramous /bírrəməss, bī ráy-/ *adj* divided into or forming two branches ○ *a biramous appendage*

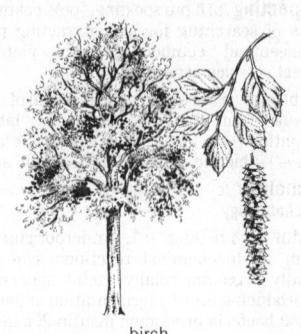
birch

birch /burch/ *n* **1.** TALL TREE WITH PEELING BARK a tall slender tree with papery, peeling bark. Native to: northern hemisphere. Genus: *Betula*. **2.** WOOD OF BIRCH the pale wood of the birch tree **3.** ROD FOR FLOGGING SOMEBODY a birch rod or bundle of twigs, formerly used to beat people as a punishment **4.** PUNISHMENT BY BEATING the action of beating somebody with a birch rod as a punishment ■ *vt* (**birches, birching, birched**) PUNISH SOMEBODY BY BEATING to beat somebody with a birch rod as a punishment [Old English *birce* < Indo-European]

Bircher /búrchər/ *n* a member of the John Birch Society, a right-wing political organization in the United States whose main purpose is fighting Communism [Mid-20C. After John *Birch*, US Baptist missionary]

bird /burd/ *n* **1.** TWO-LEGGED WINGED ANIMAL a two-legged, warm-blooded animal with wings, a beak, and a body covered with feathers. Birds lay eggs from which their young hatch, and most species can fly. Class: Aves. **2.** BIRD EATEN AS FOOD a bird such as a turkey, chicken, duck, or goose cooked and eaten as food **3.** TYPE OF PERSON somebody of a particular type (*informal*) ○ *He's a wise old bird.* **4.** OFFENSIVE TERM an offensive term for a girl or woman (*dated informal*) **5.** US AEROPLANE OR SPACECRAFT an aircraft, satellite, or rocket (*slang*) **6.** SPORTS same as **clay pigeon** (sense 1) [Old English *brid* 'young bird', origin ?] —**birdlike** *adj* ◇ **a bird in the hand is worth two in the bush** it is better to keep something that you can be certain of than risk losing it in an attempt to get something better ◇ **birds of a feather (flock together)** people of similar character, tastes, interests, or opinions (tend to associate with one another) ◇ **do bird** to spend a period in prison (*slang*) ◇ **get the bird** to be received badly, often with booing (*informal*) ◇ **kill two birds with one stone** to achieve two aims with one action ◇ **(strictly) for the birds** worthless or unacceptable (*informal*) ◇ **the birds and the bees** the facts about sexual reproduction in humans (*informal humorous*)

birdbath /búrd baath/ (*plural* **-baths** /-baathz/) *n* a small shallow basin containing water that is placed outside a house for birds to bathe in

birdbrain /búrd brayn/ *n* an offensive term for somebody who is regarded as silly or mildly unintelligent (*informal insult*) —**birdbrained** *adj*

birdcage /búrd kayj/ *n* a cage made of thin bars used to keep birds in captivity

birdcall /búrd kawl/ *n* **1.** the sound or cry of a bird, especially a warning cry **2.** a device that imitates a bird's call, used especially in trying to hunt or catch birds

bird colonel *n* US a full colonel in the US Army, Air Force, or Marine Corps (*informal*) [< the insignia of an eagle worn by a US colonel]

bird dog *n* N Am a dog used to bring back game birds after they have been shot

bird-dog (**bird-dogs, bird-dogging, bird-dogged**) *vti* N Am to watch somebody or something carefully and persistently (*informal*)

birder /búrdər/ *n* ANZ, N Am HOBBIES same as **bird-watcher**

bird flu *n* MED same as **avian flu**

birdhouse /búrd howss/ (*plural* **-houses** /-howziz/) *n* **1.** BIRDS same as **aviary 2.** N Am a small box or shelter built for birds to nest in

birdie /búrdi/ *n* **1.** in golf, a score in which the ball is hit into the hole using one stroke fewer than the accepted standard number of strokes (**par**) for that hole **2.** same as **bird** (sense 1) (*baby talk*) ■ *vt* (**-ies, -ieing, -ied**) to score a birdie in playing a hole in golf

birding /búrding/ *n* ANZ, N Am the hobby of bird-watching

birdlife /búrd līf/ *n* **1.** all the birds that live in an area or region ○ *South African birdlife* **2.** birds in large numbers ○ *The islands are home to a wide variety of birdlife.*

birdlime /búrd līm/ *n* a sticky substance made from plants that is spread on trees to catch birds ■ *vt* (**-limes, -liming, -limed**) to spread a sticky substance on trees in order to catch birds

bird louse *n* a wingless insect with a flattened body that is not truly parasitic but lives on the feathers and skin debris of birds, often causing skin irritation. Suborder: Mallophaga.

bird of paradise *n* **1.** a bird, the male of which often has unusual feathers used in spectacular mating displays. Native to: New Guinea and adjacent islands, eastern Australia. Family: Paradisaeidae. **2.** an ornamental plant. Flowers: orange-and-blue petals resembling a bird's head and crest. Native to: southern Africa, South America. Genus: *Strelitzia*.

bird of passage *n* **1.** a bird that migrates from one region or country to another according to the season **2.** somebody who rarely stays in the same place for long

bird of peace *n* a white dove as a symbol of peace

bird of prey *n* a bird that kills for food and has sharp talons and a sharp curved beak. Owls, eagles, and hawks are birds of prey.

bird pepper *n* **1.** a small pod-shaped hot-tasting fruit eaten cooked or raw as a vegetable **2.** a tropical plant that produces bird peppers. The bird pepper is thought to be the ancestor of the sweet pepper and many hot peppers. Latin name: *Capsicum frutescens*.

birdseed /búrd seed/ *n* seed, or a mixture of seeds, usually used for feeding caged or wild birds

Birdseye /búrdz ī/, **Clarence** (1886–1956) US inventor and business executive. He pioneered the retailing of quick-frozen and dehydrated foods.

bird's-eye *n* **1.** a pattern for fabric composed of diamond shapes with a dot in the middle of each **2.** fabric with a bird's-eye pattern

bird's-eye maple *n* wood from the sugar maple that has a curled pattern in the grain reminiscent of a bird's eye

bird's-eye view *n* **1.** a view that is seen from somewhere very high up **2.** an overall impression or summary of something, without details

bird's-foot trefoil *n* a creeping wild plant with seed pods in the shape of a bird's foot. Flowers: yellow with red tips. Latin name: *Lotus corniculatus*.

birdshot /búrd shot/ *n* small lead shot designed to be fired from a shotgun

bird's nest *n* a food delicacy, usually used in soups, that is obtained from high cliffs in Southeast Asia and is thought to be a swift's nest built with the bird's saliva. It is believed by the Chinese to be good for the skin and lungs. (*hyphenated when used before a noun*) ○ *bird's-nest soup*

bird's-nest fern *n* a fern with long green fronds shaped like a bird's nest that grows on the ground or on trees. Native to: South Asia, parts of Australia, the South Pacific islands. Latin name: *Asplenium nidus*.

birdsong /búrd song/ *n* the sounds made by a bird to attract a mate or defend territory

bird spider *n* a large hairy spider from tropical America that eats birds. Family: Aviculariidae.

bird strike *n* a collision between a bird and an aircraft in flight

Birdsville /búrdz vil/ town in a remote part of southwestern Queensland, Australia. It is the home of the annual Birdsville horse races. Population: 102 (1996).

bird table *n* a small table or platform in a garden on which food is laid out for birds to eat

birdwatcher /búrd wochər/ n somebody who observes birds in their natural habitats as a hobby —**bird-watching** n

birefringence /bí ri frínjənss/ n the splitting of one ray of light into two in an anisotropic medium —**birefringent** adj

bireme /bí reem/ n an ancient warship with two ranks of oars on each side [Late 16C. < Latin biremis 'two-oared' < remus 'oar']

Birendra Bir Bikram Shah Dev /bi réndrə beer bík ram shaa dév/ (1945–2001) king of Nepal. He acceded to the Nepalese throne in 1972 and ruled as an absolute monarch before instituting democratic reforms in 1990. In 2001 he was shot by his son, Crown Prince Dipendra, in a massacre that killed most of the royal family.

biretta /bə réttə/, **beretta** n a stiff hat worn by Roman Catholic clerics that has three upright sections meeting at the centre on top. Priests wear black birettas, bishops purple ones, and cardinals red ones. [Late 16C. < Italian berretta or Spanish birreta < late Latin birrus, birrum 'hooded cape or cloak']

biri /beéri/ n HEALTH same as **bidi**

biriani n FOOD another spelling of **biryani**

Birinus /bi rínəss/, St (d. 650?) Roman-born English missionary. He went to Britain on the orders of Pope Honorius I and converted the king of the West Saxons to Christianity.

Birkenhead /búrkən hed/ town and port in Merseyside, England, opposite Liverpool on the Wirral Peninsula. Population: 93,087 (1991).

Birkenhead, Frederick Edwin Smith, 1st Earl of (1872–1930) British lawyer and politician. He was attorney general (1915–19), and as lord chancellor (1919–22) was an architect of the Anglo-Irish Treaty settlement (1921) and the Law of Property Act (1922).

Birkenstock /búrkən stok/ tdmk a trademark for footwear including sandals and clogs

birl /burl/ (**birls, birling, birled**) v 1. vi Scotland to spin round 2. vt N Am to cause a floating log to spin round in water [Early 18C. Probably an imitation of the sound of something rotating rapidly]

Birmingham /búrmingəm/ 1. second largest city in England and a major industrial centre. Located in the West Midlands, it has three universities, two cathedrals, and the National Exhibition Centre, built in 1976. Population: 977,087 (2001). 2. city in northern Alabama. Just south of the Appalachian Mountains, it is the largest city in the state. Population: 239,416 (2002 estimate).

Biro /bírō/ tdmk a trademark for a pen with a small metal ball at the tip that transfers the ink contained in the pen to the paper

Biro /bírō/, Lazio José (1899–1985) Hungarian inventor. He invented the ballpoint pen in 1944. Born Biro, Laszlo Josef

birr[1] /bur/ Scotland, US vti (**birrs, birring, birred**) MAKE WHIR to make a whirring sound, or cause something to make a whirring sound ■ n 1. WHIR a whirring sound 2. FORCE a forward-moving driving force [14C. < Old Norse byrr 'favourable wind']

birr[2] /bur/ n the main unit of Ethiopian currency. See table at **currency** [Late 20C. < Amharic]

birth /burth/ n 1. EVENT OF BEING BORN the emergence of the young of a human or animal from the mother's womb into the outside world ○ The father was present at the birth. ○ articles give birth and death dates 2. PROCESS OF HAVING BABY the process of having a baby or young emerge from the womb ○ the growing number of home births 3. CIRCUMSTANCES OF BIRTH the time or place at which a baby or other offspring is born 4. SOMEBODY'S HERITAGE somebody's social or national origins ○ a man of noble birth ○ Italian by birth 5. ORIGIN the origin, beginning, or formation of something ○ the birth of jazz ■ adj BIOLOGICALLY RELATED AS PARENT biologically related to somebody, especially as a parent, rather than related by adoption ○ her birth mother ■ vt Can, Southern US HAVE OR DELIVER BABY to have a child emerge from the womb, or deliver a woman's child [13C. < Old Norse byrð < Indo-European] ◇ **give birth 1.** to produce a child or young from the womb **2.** to originate or be responsible for creating something ○ a revolution that gave birth to a free nation

birth canal n the passageway including the cervix and vagina through which a foetus emerges from the womb into the outside world

birth certificate n an official document that states when and where somebody was born and the parents' names

birth control n the deliberate limiting, usually by contraceptive means, of the number of children born

birthday /búrth day, -di/ n 1. the day in each year that is the anniversary of the day somebody was born (often used before a noun) 2. the day on which somebody is born

CULTURAL NOTE *The Birthday Party*, a play (1958) by Harold Pinter. It tells of a young man called Stanley whose comfortable life in a seaside boarding house is disrupted by the arrival of two mysterious and intimidating strangers, Goldberg and McCann. Noted for its sinisterly formal dialogue, the play creates a disturbing atmosphere of paranoia and fear.

Birthday Honours npl honorary titles given by the British sovereign on his or her official birthday to people who have in some way distinguished themselves

birthday suit n a state of nakedness (slang humorous)

birth defect n MED same as **congenital anomaly** (dated informal)

birth family n the family that an adopted child was originally born into ○ Do you have any idea of the whereabouts of the birth family?

birth father (plural **birth fathers** or **birthfathers**) n a person's biological father, especially in the case of an adopted child

birthing /búrthing/ n the process of giving birth, especially when using natural childbirth methods ■ adj designed to facilitate childbirth ○ a birthing pool

birthing chair n a chair designed to support a woman and ease the process of childbirth by enabling gravity to act on the foetus as it moves through the birth canal

birthing room n an area set up for childbirth in a hospital or other building and intended to provide congenial surroundings that do not suggest a clinical context

birthmark /búrth maark/ n a reddish or brown marking seen on the skin of some newborn babies that typically remains visible for life

birth mother (plural **birth mothers** or **birthmothers**) n a person's biological mother, especially in the case of an adopted child

birth pangs npl a difficult or troubled period at the start of something ○ the birth pangs of a new nation-state

birth parent n somebody's biological mother or father, especially in the case of an adopted child

birthplace /búrth playss/ n a place where a particular person was born or where something first started ○ Shakespeare's birthplace ○ the birthplace of classical philosophy

birthrate /búrth rayt/ n the number of live births per 1,000 members of the population in a year ○ a declining birthrate

birthright /búrth rīt/ n 1. a basic right that somebody has or is thought to be entitled to from birth ○ Freedom of speech is our birthright. 2. property or money that somebody feels entitled to because it belongs in the family, especially if the person is the eldest son of the family

birth sign n ZODIAC same as **star sign**

birthstone /búrth stōn/ n a precious or semiprecious stone that is popularly associated with the month in which somebody was born. A birthstone is believed by some people to bring luck.

birthwort /búrth wurt/ n a climbing plant with heart-shaped leaves. Native to: Europe. Latin name: *Aristolochia clematitis*. [Because formerly used to help ease pain during childbirth]

Birtwistle /búrt wiss'l/, Sir Harrison (b. 1934) British composer. He helped form the New Manchester Group for the performance of modern music. His works include *Earth Dances* (1986).

biryani /bírri aáni/, **biriani** n in South Asian cooking, a dish containing spicy coloured rice mixed with meat, fish, or vegetables ○ chicken biryani [Mid-20C. Via Hindi < Persian biriyān 'fried, grilled']

bis /biss/ adv to be played or sung again (used as a musical direction) ■ interj used by members of an audience to call for an encore [Early 17C. Via French and Italian < Latin, 'twice' < Indo-European, 'two']

Biscay, Bay of /bíss kay/ arm of the North Atlantic Ocean between western France and northern Spain. Area: 223,000 sq. km/86,101 sq. mi.

biscotto /bi skóttō/ (plural **-ti** /-ti/) n a hard oblong biscuit, often containing nuts [< Italian, 'biscuit']

biscuit /bískit/ n 1. SMALL FLAT CAKE a small flat dry cake that is usually sweet and crisp and can additionally contain fruit, nuts, or chocolate. Biscuits are often eaten with tea or coffee as a snack. N Am term **cookie** 2. N Am SMALL ROUND PIECE OF BREAD a small round plain piece of bread that rises with baking powder or soda and is then baked in an oven 3. COLOURS LIGHT BROWN HUE a light brown colour 4. CERAMICS UNGLAZED POTTERY pottery that has been fired but not glazed [14C. < Old French bescuit 'twice-cooked' < Latin bis 'twice' + coctus, past participle of coquere 'cook'] —**biscuit** adj ◇ **take the biscuit** to be the worst in a series of bad or annoying things that have already happened (informal)

biscuit firing n the first firing of something made of clay, at a relatively low temperature

biscuit ware n pots or pottery that have been through a first firing at a relatively low temperature

bise /beez/ n a sharp dry northerly wind that blows in Switzerland and neighbouring parts of Italy and France [14C. < French]

bisect /bī sékt/ (**-sects, -secting, -sected**) vt 1. to split something into two parts ○ The river bisects the town. 2. to divide something into two exactly equal parts [Mid-17C. < BI- + Latin sect-, past participle of secare 'cut'] —**bisection** n —**bisectional** adj —**bisectionally** adv

bisector /bī séktər/ n a straight line or plane that divides an angle or another line into two exactly equal parts

bisexual /bī sékshoo əl/ adj 1. ATTRACTED TO BOTH SEXES sexually attracted to both men and women, or engaging in both heterosexual and homosexual activity 2. BOTH MALE AND FEMALE IN CHARACTER having both male and female characteristics 3. HAVING MALE AND FEMALE REPRODUCTIVE ORGANS describes something such as a flower that has both male and female reproductive organs —**bisexual** n —**bisexuality** /bī sékshoo álləti/ n —**bisexually** adv

Bishkek /bish kék/ capital of Kyrgyzstan, in the northern part of the country, on the River Chu, just south of the border with Kazakhstan. Population: 585,800 (1996).

Bisho /beéshō/ capital of Eastern Cape Province in South Africa. Population: 8,000 (1987).

bishop /bíshəp/ n 1. SENIOR CHRISTIAN CLERIC a senior Christian cleric, especially in the Roman Catholic, Anglican, and Orthodox churches, who is in charge of the spiritual life and administration of a particular region (**diocese**) 2. CHESS PIECE a chess piece that can be moved diagonally across the board over any number of squares of the same colour 3. BIRDS AFRICAN WEAVERBIRD a small bird of the weaver family, the males of which have black feathers with red or yellow markings. Native to: Africa. Genus: *Euplectes*. [Old English biscop, via Germanic < variant of Latin episcopus 'bishop, overseer' < Greek episkopos 'overseer' < skopos 'watcher']

Bishop /bíshəp/, Elizabeth (1911–79) US poet. Known for her personal, reflective poetry, she won the Pulitzer Prize for her collection *North and South: A Cold Spring* (1955).

'Is it lack of imagination that makes us come / to imagined places, not just stay at home?'
[Elizabeth Bishop, 'Questions of Travel', *Questions of Travel*; 1965]

bishopric /bíshəprik/ n 1. BISHOP'S DIOCESE an area that a bishop is in charge of 2. BISHOP'S SEE a place where a bishop's cathedral is situated 3. RANK OF BISHOP the rank or office of a bishop [Pre-12C. < BISHOP + Old English rīce 'realm, power']

bishop sleeve n a wide sleeve that is gathered at the wrist

Biskra /biss kraá/ city and oasis on the edge of the Sahara Desert in Biskra Province, northeastern Algeria. Population: 128,280 (1987).

Bislama /bíshlə maá/ *n* the national language of Vanuatu in the Pacific, a modern form of Beach-la-Mar. Native speakers: 128,000. [Late 20C. Representing the local pronunciation of BEACH-LA-MAR] —**Bislama** *adj*

Bismarck /bíz maark/ capital of North Dakota, on the eastern bank of the Missouri River. Population: 56,234 (2002 estimate).

Bismarck, Otto Edward Leopold von, Prince (1815–98) German politician. As Prussian prime minister after 1862, he embarked on the European wars that unified the German states. He was the most powerful politician in Europe as chancellor of the new German Empire from 1871 to 1890. Known as **the Iron Chancellor**

> 'The great questions of our day cannot be solved by speeches and majority votes...but by iron and blood.'
> [Otto Edward Leopold von Bismarck, *Speech given in Prussian Parliament*; 30 September 1862]

Bismarck Archipelago group of over 200 islands, forming part of Papua New Guinea, in the western Pacific Ocean, off New Guinea. Area: 49,658 sq. km/19,173 sq. mi.

Bismarck Sea arm of the southwestern Pacific Ocean northeast of New Guinea and north of New Britain

bismillah /biss míllə/ *interj* an invocation of the name of Allah, often said by Muslims before beginning to do something [Late 18C. < Arabic *bi-smi-llāh(i)*, first word in the Koran]

bismuth /bízməth/ *n* a heavy, brittle, reddish-white, crystalline metallic element. Source: ores of lead, silver, copper, and gold. Use: alloys, medicines. Symbol **Bi**. See table at **element** [Mid-17C. < obsolete German *Bismut*, modern Latin *bisemutum* < Middle High German *wise* 'meadow' + *muth* 'claim to a mine']

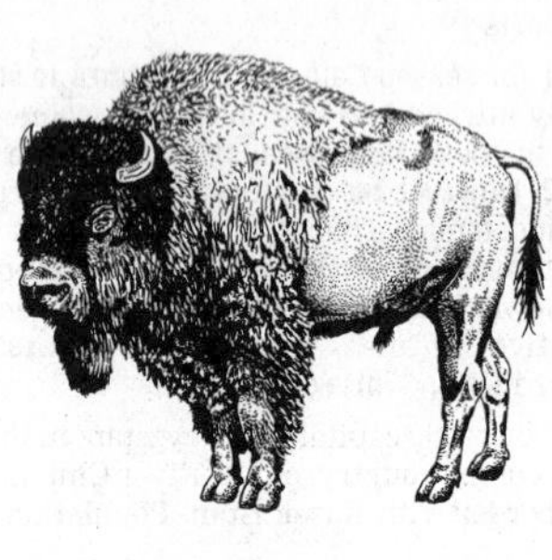

bison

bison /bīss'n/ (*plural same*) *n* a large hairy animal resembling an ox but with a massive head and shoulders and a humped back. Native to: North America, Europe. Genus: *Bison*. [Early 17C. Directly or via French < Latin < Germanic]

bisque[1] /bisk/ *n* a rich soup made from shellfish ○ *lobster bisque* [Mid-17C. < French]

bisque[2] /bisk/ *n* **1.** CERAMICS same as **biscuit** (sense 4) **2.** a pinkish-brown colour [Mid-17C. Alteration of BISCUIT, perhaps after French] —**bisque** *adj*

bisque[3] /bisk/ *n* in a game of tennis, golf, or croquet, an extra turn, stroke, or point that is given as an advantage to a weaker player [Mid-17C. < French]

Bissau /bi sów/ city on the northern shore of the Geba River estuary and capital of Guinea-Bissau since 1941. Population: 233,000 (1995).

bissextile /bi séks tīl/ *adj* having the extra day in a year that makes it a leap year ○ *bissextile month* ■ *n* same as **leap year** [Late 16C. < late Latin *bis(s)extilus* < Latin *bi(s)sextus (dies)* 'twice-sixth (day)', 24 February, the sixth day before 1 March, counted twice in a leap year in the ancient Roman calendar]

bistort /bís tawrt/ *n* a plant with an S-shaped underground stem (**rhizome**). Flowers: bright pink, in spikes. Use: formerly, in medicine. Native to: Europe, Asia. Latin name: *Polygonum bistorta*. [Early 16C. Directly or via French < assumed medieval Latin *bistorta* < Latin *bis* 'twice' + *torta*, feminine past participle of *torquere* 'twist']

bistoury /bístəri/ (*plural* **-ries**) *n* a thin surgical knife designed to cut from the inside outwards, formerly used to cut open abscesses or enlarge fistulas [Mid-18C. < French]

bistro /beéstrō/ (*plural* **-tros**) *n* a small restaurant or bar [Early 20C. < French]

bisulphate /bī súl fayt/ *n* CHEM same as **hydrogen sulphate**

bisulphide /bī súl fīd/ *n* CHEM same as **disulphide**

bisulphite /bī súl fīt/ *n* CHEM same as **hydrogen sulphite**

bit[1] /bit/ *n* **1.** PIECE a small piece of something ○ *There were bits of paper everywhere.* **2.** SMALL AMOUNT a small part or amount of something ○ *a bit of housework* **3.** SHORT AMOUNT OF TIME a very short period of time or distance ○ *I'll do it in a bit.* **4.** EVERYTHING ABOUT ROLE all the aspects of a particular role in life (*informal*) ○ *did the whole two-career marriage bit* **5.** SMALL COIN a small coin of a particular value (*dated informal*) ○ *a threepenny bit* **6.** *N Am* TWELVE-AND-ONE-HALF CENTS an eighth of a dollar (*dated slang; used in the plural*) ○ *two bits* **7.** SHORT PERFORMANCE a short routine, joke, or skit in a performance **8.** SMALL ACTING PART a small part in a film or play (*often used before a noun*) ○ *I was a bit player in one of her films.* [Old English *bita* < *bītan* 'to bite' (see BITE)] ◇ **a bit** somewhat (*informal*) ○ *feels a bit tired* ◇ **a bit much** excessive or unacceptable (*informal*) ◇ **a bit of all right** very good-looking (*informal; sometimes considered offensive*) ◇ **a bit of fluff** an offensive term for a young woman who is regarded as very good-looking but unintelligent, often somebody's girlfriend or lover (*informal*) ◇ **a bit of rough** an offensive term for a person, usually a man, whose physicality and lack of refinement are found sexually attractive by somebody from a higher social class (*informal*) ◇ **a bit of stuff** an offensive term for a woman or girl considered from the point of view of her sexual attractiveness (*dated informal*) ◇ **bit by bit** gradually ◇ **bits and pieces, bits and bobs** (*informal*) **1.** personal belongings **2.** miscellaneous small objects ○ *I collected up my bits and pieces and left.* ◇ **do your bit** to contribute your share to work that needs to be done ◇ **every bit** in every way ○ *She is every bit as skilled as he is.* ◇ **fall to bits 1.** to become broken into small pieces **2.** to become unable to cope ◇ **to bits** very much, or to the greatest degree possible (*informal*) ○ *I just love the kids to bits!*

bit[2] /bit/ *n* **1.** MOUTHPIECE OF BRIDLE a part of a bridle consisting of a metal mouthpiece held in a horse's mouth by the reins and used to control the horse **2.** MECH ENG DETACHABLE PART OF DRILL a small metal tool that is inserted into a drill or brace and used for boring or drilling **3.** WOODWORK TOOL BLADE the part of a plane that is used for cutting **4.** MECH ENG PART OF PINCERS the gripping part of a pair of pincers **5.** METALL TIP OF SOLDERING IRON the tip of a soldering iron that is made from copper ■ *vt* (**bits, bitting, bitted**) PUT BIT ON HORSE to put a bit into the mouth of a horse [Old English *bite* < Indo-European] ◇ **champ** *or* **chafe at the bit** to be impatient for something to happen or because no action is possible ◇ **get** *or* **take** *or* **have the bit between your teeth** to start something and refuse stubbornly to stop

bit[3] /bit/ *n* **1.** in binary notation, either of the digits 0 or 1 used to represent one of only two outcomes, e.g. on or off **2.** the smallest unit of information storable in a computer or peripheral device, expressed as 0 or 1. Eight bits make a byte, the common measure of memory or storage capacity. [Mid-20C. Blend of BINARY + DIGIT]

bit[4] /bit/ past tense of **bite**

bit bucket *n* an imaginary electronic waste bin in cyberspace into which all lost e-mail and news messages disappear (*humorous*)

bitch /bich/ *n* **1.** FEMALE DOG a female dog, or the female of another related animal such as a fox, or of another carnivore such as a ferret **2.** SPITEFUL CONVERSATION a conversation that involves complaining or saying unpleasant things about somebody who is not present (*informal; often offensive*) **3.** OFFENSIVE TERM an offensive term for a woman that deliberately insults her temperament (*slang insult*) **4.** SOMETHING DIFFICULT a difficult thing or situation (*slang; often offensive*) ○ *That lock's a real bitch to open.* **5.** *N Am* COMPLAINT a querulous nagging complaint (*slang; often offensive*) ■ *vi* (**bitches, bitching, bitched**) (*often offensive*) **1.** BE NASTY ABOUT SOMEBODY to talk about somebody who is not present in an unpleasant or malicious way (*slang*) **2.** *N Am* COMPLAIN CONTINUALLY to complain or grumble about something continually [Old English *bicce*, perhaps < Old Norse]

bitchery /bíchəri/ *n* malicious or unpleasant talk about somebody (*informal; often offensive*) ○ *What I couldn't stand was all the bitchery.*

bitch slap *n US* a physical slap as given by a dominant person to a subservient person who cannot hit back (*slang; often offensive*) —**bitch-slap** *vt*

bitchy /bíchi/ (**-ier, -iest**) *adj* malicious or unpleasant in speaking to, talking about, or behaving towards somebody (*slang; often offensive*) —**bitchily** *adv* —**bitchiness** *n*

bite *v* (**bites, biting, bit** /bit/, **bitten** /bítt'n/) **1.** *vti* GRIP WITH TEETH to hold something tightly, tear something off, or cut through something using the teeth ○ *I bit into the fruit.* **2.** *vt* PIERCE SKIN to puncture or tear the skin of a person or animal using fangs, teeth, mouthparts, or a stinger ○ *got bitten by a spider* **3.** *vti* GRIP SOMETHING FIRMLY to make firm or secure contact with something ○ *The wheel's not biting.* **4.** *vi* CORRODE SOMETHING to eat into something with a corrosive action ○ *The acid had bitten into the metal surface.* **5.** *vti* PENETRATE SOMETHING WITH SHARP EDGE to cut into something with a sharpened tool or other sharp-edged object ○ *The saw blade bit the wood.* **6.** *vti* CAUSE DISCOMFORT to cause a cold sharp sensation that is quite painful ○ *an icy wind that bites to the bone* **7.** *vi* TAKE BAIT to attempt to take the bait that has been placed on the end of a fishing line (*refers to fish*) ○ *no fish biting today* **8.** *vi* RISE TO SOMEBODY ELSE'S BAIT to respond when somebody else tries to get you involved in a scheme or an argument (*informal*) ○ *Even though baited by the Opposition, she refused to bite.* **9.** *vt* ANNOY OR UPSET SOMEBODY to annoy or preoccupy somebody, or put somebody in a bad mood ○ *What's biting you today?* **10.** *vi* BE EFFECTIVE to have an effect or influence ○ *The trade sanctions are at last beginning to bite.* **11.** *vt Aus* SCROUNGE FROM SOMEBODY to ask for money or goods from somebody else rather than earning or paying for something personally (*informal*) ○ *Can I bite you for ten bucks?* ■ *n* **1.** SEIZURE OF SOMETHING WITH TEETH the action of taking something between the teeth and tearing it off **2.** MOUTHFUL a piece of food torn off with the teeth **3.** INJURY FROM TEETH OR INSECT an injury that has been caused by an animal or insect puncturing or tearing the skin with teeth, fangs, mouthparts, or a stinger ○ *a mosquito bite* **4.** ATTEMPT BY FISH TO TAKE BAIT an attempt by a fish to eat the bait that has been put on the end of a fishing line **5.** PIQUANCY a pleasantly sharp taste **6.** WIT AND INTELLIGENCE a penetrating and intelligent quality **7.** COLDNESS a cold sharp sensation that is quite painful ○ *There's a bit of a bite in the air today.* **8.** MECH ENG DEPTH OF MACHINE TOOL'S BLADE the depth to which a machine tool can cut **9.** MECH ENG GRIP the grip that something such as a tool has on something else **10.** DENT FIT OF TEETH the way the upper and lower teeth meet and fit together when the jaw is closed **11.** CHEM CORROSIVE EFFECT the corrosive effect of acid on a surface **12.** FISHING PERIOD WHEN FISH EAT a time when fish usually feed and so are more easily caught ○ *The catfish bite is usually the heaviest and best in the evening.* [Old English *bītan* < Indo-European] —**bitable** *adj* —**biter** *n* ◇ **bite off more than you can chew** to take on more than you can deal with (*informal*) ◇ **have two bites at the cherry** to have more than one attempt at doing something (*informal*)

bite back *v* **1.** *vt* to hold back from saying something or openly crying ○ *I bit back my tears.* **2.** *vti* to make a sharp retort

biteplate /bīt playt/ *n* a removable acrylic dental device that sticks to the roof of the mouth and is worn to encourage the back teeth to come through or to correct an overbite

bite-sized, bite-size *adj* small enough to be eaten as a single mouthful ○ *cut the meat into bite-sized pieces*

bit flip *n* the switching of a digital bit from 0 to 1 or from 1 to 0

Bithynia /bi thínni ə/ ancient country of northwestern Asia Minor, on the Black Sea in present-day Turkey

biting /bīting/ *adj* **1.** cold enough to cause discomfort or pain ○ *a biting north wind* **2.** sarcastic and clever —**bitingly** *adv*

biting midge *n UK, ANZ, Can* a fly, almost invisible

to the naked eye, that sucks the blood of animals and other insects, leaving painful itching welts. Family: Ceratopogonidae. US term **punkie**

bit map *n* a representation of a graphics image in computer memory consisting of rows and columns of dots, each corresponding to a pixel. For monochrome images one bit of data is sufficient to represent each dot, while colours and shades of grey require more than one bit per dot.

bit-map (**bit-maps, bit-mapping, bit-mapped**) *vt* to represent a graphics image in computer memory as a matrix of dots, or recreate the image on a computer screen from such a bit map

bitmapped font /bít mapt-/ *n* a screen or printer font with characters formed as a pattern of pixels or dots

BITNET /bít net/ *abbr* COMPUT Because It's Time Network

bitok /bíttok/ *n* fried mince patties served with a sour cream sauce [Via Russian < French *bifteck (haché)* '(minced) beef' < English BEEFSTEAK]

bit part *n* a small role in a film or play

bitser /bítsər/, **bitzer** *n Aus* a dog of mixed breed [Mid-20C. < *bits (and pieces)*]

bit stream *n* a simple unstructured sequence of bits transmitting data in the form of binary digits

bitt /bit/ *n* either of a pair of posts on a ship's deck for fastening cables (*often used in the plural*) ■ *vt* (**bitts, bitting, bitted**) to fasten something round a bitt [15C. Origin ?]

bitten past participle of **bite**

bitter /bíttər/ *adj* **1.** STRONG AND SHARP IN TASTE having a sharp strong unpleasant taste such as the taste of orange peel **2.** RESENTFUL angry and resentful ○ *a bitter smile* **3.** DIFFICULT TO ACCEPT mentally painful, or very hard to accept ○ *a bitter blow* **4.** HOSTILE expressing intense hostility ○ *bitter fighting* **5.** VERY COLD penetratingly and unpleasantly cold ○ *a bitter wind* ■ *n UK* BEVERAGES BEER beer that is made with a lot of hops and has a slightly sharp taste ○ *a pint of bitter* [Old English *biter* < Indo-European] —**bitterly** *adv* —**bitterness** *n*

bitter almond *n* **1.** an almond containing hydrogen cyanide. Use: food flavouring. **2.** a tree that produces bitter almonds

bitter aloes *n* PHARM same as **aloes** (sense 1)

bitter cress *n* a plant belonging to the mustard family that often grows in damp places. Flowers: white, in clusters. Genus: *Cardamine*.

bitter end *n* the very end of something, however unpleasant it is ○ *They held out to the bitter end.* [Originally 'end of a cable or mooring rope secured on board ship', *bitter* perhaps < BITT, but now interpreted as 'painful']

bitter-ender *n US, S Africa* a highly obstinate and inflexible person who takes a stand, refusing to budge until he or she is forced by adverse circumstances to do so

bitterleaf /bíttər leef/ *n W Africa* COOK, BOT same as **ndole**

bitter lemon *n* a fizzy nonalcoholic drink that is flavoured with lemon and is a greyish-green colour

bitterling /bíttərling/ *n* a small brightly-coloured freshwater fish that is often kept in aquariums. Native to: central Europe. Latin name: *Rhodeus sericeus*. [Late 19C. < German, 'small bitter (fish)']

bittern[1] /bíttərn/ *n* a bird of the heron family with mottled brownish feathers and a booming call. It lives among reeds in marshes. Family: Ardeidae. [Early 16C. Alteration of *bitore*, probably < Anglo-Latin *butorius* or Old French *butor* < Latin *butio* 'bittern' + *taurus* 'bull']

bittern[2] /bíttərn/ *n* the bitter liquid that is left after common salt has crystallized from sea water. Use: source of bromides, magnesium. [Late 17C. < BITTER + *-n*, origin ?]

bitternut /bíttər nut/ *n* **1.** a thin-shelled nut with a bitter kernel **2.** a tree that produces bitternuts. Native to: eastern North America. Latin name: *Carya cordiformis*.

bitter orange *n N Am* same as **Seville orange**

bitter pill *n* something unpleasant that nonetheless must be accepted ○ *Not getting the job was a bitter pill for him to swallow.*

bitters /bíttərz/ *n* a slightly alcoholic liquid flavoured with plant extracts. Use: mixer in some cocktails. (*takes a singular verb*) ■ *npl* a bitter-tasting liquid used as a digestive tonic (*takes a plural verb*)

bittersweet /bíttər sweet/ *adj* **1.** BOTH BITTER AND SWEET smelling or tasting both bitter and sweet at the same time **2.** BOTH HAPPY AND SAD causing feelings of happiness and sadness at the same time ■ *n* (*plural* **-sweets** or *same*) **1.** PLANT WITH BRIGHT CAPSULES AND SEEDS a poisonous climbing plant that has orange capsules containing bright red seeds. Native to: North America. Genus: *Celastus*. **2.** *US* PLANTS same as **woody nightshade**

bitty /bítti/ (**-tier, -tiest**) *adj* made up of lots of different parts that do not seem to fit together ○ *a very bitty film* —**bittiness** *n*

bitumen /bíttyoomən/ *n* **1.** a sticky mixture of hydrocarbons found in substances such as asphalt and tar. Source: petroleum. **2.** *Aus* a tarred road or sealed road or system of roads, as opposed to a dirt road [15C. < Latin, 'asphalt'] —**bituminous** /bi tyóominəss/ *adj*

bituminize /bi tyóomi nīz/ (**-nizes, -nizing, -nized**), **bituminise** (**-nises, -nising, -nised**) *vt* to cover or treat something with bitumen, or convert something into bitumen —**bituminization** /bi tyóomi nī záysh'n/ *n*

bituminous coal *n* soft coal that burns with a smoky flame

bitzer /bítsər/ *n Aus* BREED another spelling of **bitser** (*informal*) [Early 20C. < *bits and pieces*]

~~**biulding**~~ incorrect spelling of **building**

bivalence /bī váylənss/, **bivalency** /-lənssi/ *n* in classical systems of logic, the property that a proposition has of being either true or false

bivalent /bī váylənt/ *adj* **1.** GENETICS describes structurally identical (**homologous**) chromosomes that come together during cell division (**meiosis**) **2.** CHEM same as **divalent** ■ *n* GENETICS a pair of bivalent chromosomes

bivalve /bí valv/ *n* a saltwater or freshwater invertebrate animal that has its body contained within two shells joined by a hinge. Oysters, mussels, and cockles are bivalves. —**bivalved** *adj* —**bivalvular** /bī válvyoolər/ *adj*

bivariate /bī váiri ət, -ayt/ *adj* relating to or involving two variables

bivouac /bívvoo ak/ *n* **1.** MILITARY OR MOUNTAINEERING CAMP a very simple temporary camp that is set up and used by soldiers or mountaineers **2.** BRIEF OVERNIGHT STAY a short stay, usually overnight, often with minimum equipment ■ *vi* (**-acs, -acking, -acked**) MAKE CAMP to set up and stay in a very simple temporary camp [Early 18C. < French, probably < Low German *bīwake* < *bi-* 'by' + *wake* 'watch, vigil']

bivvy /bívvi/ (*plural* **-vies**) *n* a very simple shelter or tent (*slang*) [Early 20C. < BIVOUAC]

biweekly /bī weékli/ *adj* **1.** COMING OUT EVERY TWO WEEKS produced or appearing every two weeks **2.** COMING OUT TWICE PER WEEK produced or appearing twice a week ■ *adv* **1.** ONCE EVERY TWO WEEKS at two-week intervals **2.** TWICE PER WEEK twice during a one-week period ■ *n* (*plural* **-lies**) BI-WEEKLY PUBLICATION a publication that appears every two weeks

USAGE How many times is **biweekly**? Confusion is caused by the fact that ***biweekly***, *bimonthly*, and *biyearly* can mean either 'once every two weeks (or months or years)' or 'twice a week (or month or year)'. If you want to avoid doubt, it is better to reword the sentence: *The talks are held twice a week at the local school. The talks are held every two weeks at the local school.*

biyearly /bī yeérli/ *adj* **1.** COMING OUT EVERY TWO YEARS produced or appearing every two years **2.** COMING OUT TWICE PER YEAR produced or appearing twice a year ■ *adv* **1.** ONCE EVERY TWO YEARS at two-year intervals **2.** TWICE PER YEAR twice during a one-year period

USAGE See ***biweekly***.

biz[1] /biz/ *n* (*slang*) **1.** something that is really excellent **2.** a business of a particular type, typically involving fashion, entertainment, or the media [Mid-19C. Shortened < BUSINESS]

biz[2] *abbr* ONLINE business (*used in Internet addresses*) See table at **domain name**

~~**bizare**~~ incorrect spelling of **bizarre**

bizarre /bi záar/ *adj* amusingly or grotesquely strange or unusual [Mid-17C. Via French, 'odd', formerly 'brave, handsome' < Spanish *bizarro* 'brave' < Italian *bizzarro* 'angry'] —**bizarrely** *adv* —**bizarreness** *n*

bizarrerie /bi záarəri/ *n* amusing or grotesque strangeness or oddity [Mid-18C. < French < *bizarre* (see BIZARRE)]

Bizet /beé zay/, **Georges** (1838–75) French composer. He completed the opera *Carmen* just before his death. Born **Bizet, Alexandre César Léopold**

bizonal /bī zón'l/ *adj* made up of two zones

bizzy /bízzi/ (*plural* **-zies**) *n* a police or security officer (*slang*; *usually used in the plural*) [Late 20C. Probably variant of BUSY 'detective']

Bjelke-Petersen /byélki peétərss'n/, **Sir Johannes** (*b.* 1911) New Zealand-born Australian politician. A member of the National Party, he was premier of Queensland, Australia (1968–87).

> 'It is better to tax 25 per cent of something rather than 60 per cent of nothing.'
> [Sir Johannes Bjelke-Petersen, *Sydney Morning Herald*; 6 July 1985]

Bjørnson /byúrnss'n/, **Bjørnstjerne** (1832–1910) Norwegian writer and politician. The national poet of Norway, his work includes the Norwegian national anthem and the novel *The Fisher Girl* (1868). He won the Nobel Prize in literature (1903). Full name **Bjørnson, Bjørnstjerne Martinius**

BJP *abbr* POL Bharatiya Janata Party

bk *abbr* **1.** BANKING bank[1] **2.** book

Bk *symbol* CHEM ELEM berkelium

bks *abbr* **1.** MIL barracks **2.** books

BL *abbr* **1.** Bachelor of Law **2.** Bachelor of Letters **3.** *US* Barrister-at-Law **4.** *also* **B/L** bill of lading **5.** British Library

bl. *abbr* barrel

blab /blab/ *vi* (**blabs, blabbing, blabbed**) (*informal*) **1.** to talk indiscreetly about something that is supposed to be secret **2.** to chatter in a mildly incoherent way ■ *n* same as **blabbermouth** [13C. Probably ultimately < Germanic, an imitation of the sound of vacuous talking]

blabber /blábbər/ (*informal*) *vi* (**-bers, -bering, -bered**) to chatter in a mildly incoherent way ■ *n* **1.** same as **blabbermouth 2.** the sound made by people talking loudly and incoherently [14C. Probably < BLAB]

blabbermouth /blábbər mowth/ (*plural* **-mouths** /-mowthz/) *n* somebody who is regarded as talking too much and revealing secrets (*informal*)

black /blak/ *adj* **1.** OF DARKEST COLOUR being the colour of coal or carbon **2.** DEVOID OF LIGHT completely dark, with no light **3.** PEOPLES another spelling of **Black 4.** BEVERAGES CONTAINING NO MILK served without adding milk or cream ○ *black coffee* **5.** FUNNY AND MACABRE dealing with very serious things in a humorous and often macabre way ○ *black humour* **6.** FULL OF ANGER filled with anger or hostility ○ *in a black mood* **7.** HOPELESS so depressing as to end all hope ○ *The future is looking black.* **8.** DIRTY covered with mud, soil, or any other dark substance **9.** BOYCOTTED boycotted by trade unions, especially in support of industrial action that is being taken by other unions **10.** SERIOUSLY BAD OR UNFORTUNATE causing or associated with severely bad conditions or misfortune ○ *a black day for the industry* **11.** DISHONOURABLE extremely dishonourable and deserving the most serious criticism **12.** EVIL relating to evil ■ *n* **1.** DARKEST COLOUR a colour value that has no hue as a result of the absorption of nearly all light from all visible wavelengths **2.** COAL-COLOURED DYE OR PIGMENT a pigment or dye that is the colour of carbon or coal **3.** PEOPLES another spelling of **Black 4.** TEXTILES, CLOTHING VERY DARK-COLOURED MATERIAL OR CLOTHES fabric or clothing that is black in colour **5.** TOTAL DARKNESS complete darkness **6.** BOARD GAMES BLACK PIECE a black piece in a game such as chess or draughts **7.** CUE GAMES BLACK BALL a black ball in snooker, which is the last ball to be potted ■ *vt* (**blacks, blacking, blacked**) **1.** COLOUR SOMETHING BLACK to make something black or cover something in black **2.** USE BLACK POLISH ON SOMETHING to cover something, especially shoes or boots, with black polish **3.** BRUISE EYE to hit somebody's eye so that it becomes very bruised and turns a purplish-black colour **4.** BOYCOTT to organize a boycott of goods

or of an activity, especially in support of industrial action being carried out by other trade unions [Old English *blæc*, origin ?] —**blackish** *adj* —**blackness** *n* ◇ **in the black** not in debt or overdrawn

USAGE See *Black*.

black out *v* **1.** *vi* MED **LOSE CONSCIOUSNESS** to lose consciousness, sight, or memory temporarily **2.** *vt* ELEC **REMOVE ELECTRICITY SUPPLY FROM PLACE** to cause a place to undergo a failure of its electricity supply **3.** *vt* MIL **EXTINGUISH OR HIDE LIGHTS** to ensure that all lights in an inhabited area are turned off or covered up at night to prevent it being seen from enemy aircraft **4.** *vt* BROADCAST **WITHDRAW PROGRAMMES** to refuse to broadcast radio or television programmes, usually because of a strike **5.** *vt* **ERASE SOMETHING FROM MEMORY** to refuse to remember an upsetting fact, event, or experience **6.** *vt* COMMUNICATION **WITHHOLD INFORMATION** to withhold news or information about a subject **7.** *vi* COMMUNICATION **LOSE RADIO COMMUNICATION** to lose radio communication between an aircraft or ship and headquarters **8.** *vt* **MAKE SOMETHING UNREADABLE** to cover a piece of writing with black colour so that it cannot be read

Black /blak/ *adj* ⚠ belonging to an African people or to another ethnic group with dark skin, e.g. Australian Aboriginals ■ *n* ⚠ a member of an African ethnic group or another ethnic group with dark skin, e.g. Australian Aboriginals

USAGE Terms considered appropriate for different ethnic groups change from place to place and from time to time. The word *Black* is standard in current usage for a dark-skinned person of African or African-Caribbean origin or descent. It is the term that African-Caribbean people in the United Kingdom prefer and is also used by Australian Aboriginals. However, many Americans of African descent prefer the more formal term *African American*, used both as noun and adjective. The term *Black* is sometimes extended to include other peoples who are not white, but this use is generally regarded as unacceptable, the preferable use being specific names such as *Indian* or *Malay*.

Black /blak/, **Hugo** (1886–1971) associate justice of the US Supreme Court (1937–71). He was known for upholding a literal interpretation of the First Amendment of the Constitution. Full name **Black, Hugo LaFayette**

'No higher duty, or more solemn responsibility rests upon this Court than that of translating into living law and maintaining this constitutional shield... for the benefit of every human being subject to our Constitution—of whatever race, creed, or persuasion.'
[Hugo Black, *Speech in a lawsuit*; 1940]

Black, **Sir James Whyte** (*b.* 1924) British pharmacologist. He discovered the first beta-blocking drug, leading to new treatments for heart disease. He shared the Nobel Prize in physiology or medicine (1988).

Shirley Temple

Black, **Shirley Temple** (*b.* 1928) US actor and diplomat. An actor from age 3, she made 25 films, including *The Little Colonel* (1935), that made her Hollywood's biggest box-office draw. Her later diplomatic service included the US ambassadorship to the United Nations (1969–70).

'I stopped believing in Santa Claus at an early age. Mother took me to see him in a department store and he asked me for my autograph.'
[Attributed to Shirley Temple Black]

blackamoor /blákə moor, -mawr/ *n* an offensive term for a Black person or somebody with very dark skin (*archaic*) [Early 16C. Alteration of *black Moor*]

black-and-blue *adj* covered with bruises, or feeling very bruised (*not hyphenated when used after a verb*)

Black and Tan *n* a member of the armed force that was sent by the British to Ireland in 1920–21 to fight Sinn Féin. Their uniform was khaki, with a black beret and armband.

black-and-tan *n* a drink consisting of ale mixed with stout or porter

black-and-tan terrier *n* BREED same as **Manchester terrier**

black and white *n* **1.** material either handwritten or printed **2.** a visual medium without colours, and in hues of black, white, and shades of grey

black-and-white *adj* **1.** **NOT IN COLOUR** representing an image in which colours have been converted to black, white, and shades of grey ○ *a black-and-white photograph* **2.** **REPRODUCING IMAGES NOT IN COLOUR** reproducing images in which colours have been converted to black, white, and shades of grey (*not hyphenated when used after a verb*) ○ *a black-and-white television* **3.** **CLEAR-CUT** clear-cut and straightforward, allowing no room for compromise or doubt (*not hyphenated when used after a verb*) ○ *Everything is black and white as far as she's concerned.*

black arts *npl* forms of magic attempted for evil purposes, calling upon evil spirits or the devil

blackball /blák bawl/ *vt* (**-balls, -balling, -balled**) **1.** **PREVENT SOMEBODY FROM JOINING** to prevent somebody from becoming a member of a club by voting against the person **2.** **EXCLUDE SOMEBODY FROM GROUP** to exclude somebody from a group or profession ■ *n* **1.** **NEGATIVE VOTE** a vote against somebody, especially somebody wanting to join a group **2.** **VOTING TOKEN** a black ball used to show a negative vote (*archaic*)

black bass *n* a large freshwater fish that is popular as a game fish. Native to: North America. Genus: *Micropterus*.

black bean *n* **1.** **DRIED BEAN** a small black seed dried and used in cooking **2.** **FERMENTED SOYA BEAN** a black-seeded soya bean used fermented in East Asian cookery ○ *black bean sauce* **3.** **BEAN PLANT** a soya bean or French bean plant that produces black beans **4.** **TROPICAL TREE** a tree with smooth bark, dark green leaves, and wood that is used in furniture-making. Native to: rainforests of eastern Australia. Latin name: *Castanospermum australe*.

black bear *n* **1.** a bear that lives in forests and ranges from brownish-yellow to black in colour. Native to: North America. Latin name: *Euarctos americanus*. **2.** a bear that has a black coat with a whitish V-shaped mark on its chest. Native to: Central and eastern Asia. Latin name: *Selenarctos thibetanus*.

black belt *n* **1.** **BELT SHOWING SKILL IN MARTIAL ARTS** a belt worn by somebody who has reached the highest level of skill in a martial art such as judo or karate **2.** **SOMEBODY WITH BLACK BELT** somebody at the highest level of skill in a martial art, entitled to wear a belt that is black **3.** *also* **Black Belt** **FERTILE AGRICULTURAL REGION** a region in the southern United States, stretching from Georgia across Alabama and Mississippi, with extremely fertile dark soil

blackberry

blackberry /blákbəri/ *n* (*plural* **-ries**) **1.** **PURPLE FRUIT** a small sweet dark purple fruit composed of a cluster of small round fruitlets **2.** **THORNY BUSH** a large bush with arching, often thorny, stems that produces blackberries. Native to: Europe. Latin name: *Rubus fruticosus*. ■ *vi* **PICK BLACKBERRIES** to look for and pick blackberries

black bile *n* one of the four humours that were once believed to be the base of somebody's character. Black bile was associated with a melancholy temperament.

blackbird

blackbird /blák burd/ *n* **1.** **COMMON BIRD WITH BLACK FEATHERS** a common songbird of the thrush family, the male of which has black feathers and a yellow beak and the female, brown feathers. Native to: Europe. Latin name: *Turdus merula*. **2.** **AMERICAN BIRD WITH BLACK FEATHERS** a bird with black feathers showing a metallic sheen or bold patterns of yellow, orange, or red. Native to: North America. Family: Icteridae. **3.** *Aus* HIST **CAPTIVE WORKER** a Pacific islander taken, often forcibly, to work as a labourer in northeastern Australia, between the 1860s and the early 1900s

blackbirding /blák burding/ *n* Aus HIST the practice, which occurred mainly between the 1860s and the early 1900s, of recruiting Pacific islanders, often forcibly, to work as labourers in northeastern Australia

blackboard /blák bawrd/ *n* a board of either a dark colour or white that is written on with contrasting chalk or erasable markers, used especially in classrooms

black body *n* an ideal object that would absorb all of the radiation incident on it without reflecting any radiation

black-body radiation *n* the thermal radiation that would be emitted by a black body. The distribution of energy in such radiation depends solely on the temperature of the source.

black book *n* **1.** a book in which the names of people who are to be punished or blacklisted are kept **2.** a book in which somebody keeps the names and telephone numbers of private friends, especially boyfriends or girlfriends (*informal*)

black box *n* **1.** AVIAT same as **flight recorder** **2.** an electronic component whose constituents or circuitry are unknown or irrelevant, but whose function is understood

black boy *n* same as **grass tree**

black bread *n* a very dark rye bread that is particularly popular in Germany and Slavic countries

blackbuck /blák buk/ (*plural* **-bucks** or *same*) *n* a rare, small antelope, the male of which has a black back, white underbelly, and spiral horns. Native to: South Asia. Latin name: *Antilope cervicapra*.

black bun *n* Scotland a dark rich fruit cake in a pastry case, traditionally eaten at Hogmanay

Blackburn /blák burn/ industrial town in Lancashire, northwestern England. Population: 139,491 (1996).

blackbutt /blák but/ *n* a eucalyptus tree with sickle-shaped leaves and a tall straight trunk. Use: timber. Native to: eastern Australia. Latin name: *Eucalyptus pilularis*.

blackcap /blák kap/ *n* **1.** a small brown-grey warbler, the male of which has a black-topped head. Native to: Europe, Asia, Africa. Latin name: *Sylvia atricapilla*. **2.** a black cap formerly worn by a judge when passing a death sentence on somebody

black cherry *n* **1.** a large wild cherry tree that has dark bark and white flowers and produces black

cherries. Native to: North America. Latin name: *Prunus serotina*. **2.** a dark-skinned cherry

blackcock /blák kok/ (*plural* **-cocks** or *same*) *n* the male of the black grouse

black cohosh *n* a plant whose roots are used medicinally in the treatment of many gynaecological problems, including menopausal symptoms and painful menstruation. Native to: North America. Latin name: *Cimicifuga racemosa*.

black comedy *n* comedy containing bitter jokes about unpleasant aspects of life

Black Country /blák kuntri/ region of the West Midlands, England, so named because of its former concentration of heavy industries

blackcurrant /blák kúrrənt/ *n* **1.** a small black berry that grows in bunches **2.** a fruit bush that produces blackcurrants. Latin name: *Ribes nigrum*.

blackdamp /blák damp/ *n* atmospheric conditions in a mine that prevent normal breathing because insufficient oxygen remains after an explosion

Black Death *n* the bubonic plague epidemic that killed over 50 million people throughout Asia and Europe in the 14th century [Probably < the colour of the buboes]

black diamond *n* **1.** MINERALS same as **carbonado 2.** the black variety of haematite. Use: source of iron. ■ **black diamonds** *npl* lumps of coal (*informal*)

Blackdown Hills /blák down-/ Area of Outstanding Natural Beauty in Devon and Somerset, southwestern England

black dwarf *n* a white dwarf star that has cooled over a long period of time and no longer emits significant radiation

black economy *n* the part of an economy that consists of unofficial or illegal, and therefore untaxed, earnings

blacken /blákən/ (**-ens, -ening, -ened**) *v* **1.** *vti* to become darker or black, or cause something to become darker or black **2.** *vt* to harm or damage somebody's reputation

Black English *n* **1.** a variety of English that has developed in a Black community **2.** same as **African American Vernacular English**

Blacket /blákit/, **Edmund Thomas** (1817–83) British-born Australian architect. He designed many Gothic-style public buildings in Sydney, including St Andrew's Cathedral and the University of Sydney.

Blackett /blákit/, **Patrick, Baron** (1897–1974) British physicist. He discovered the positron (1932) and received the Nobel Prize in physics (1948) for his work on cosmic radiation. Full name **Blackett, Patrick Maynard Stuart**

black eye *n* an area of bruising round somebody's eye

black-eyed bean *n* **1.** a small beige bean with a black spot **2.** a legume widely cultivated in the southern United States for forage and for its beans. Latin name: *Vigna unguiculata*. ▶ N Am term **black-eyed pea**

black-eyed pea *n N Am* same as **black-eyed bean**

black-eyed Susan /-sóoz'n/ *n* **1.** a plant of the daisy family. Flowers: yellowish-orange with a dark conical centre. Native to: North America. Latin name: *Rudbeckia hirta*. **2.** a climbing plant. Flowers: yellow with purple centres. Native to: tropical Africa. Latin name: *Thunbergia alata*.

blackface /blák fayss/ *n N Am* makeup to blacken the face and other exposed areas of skin, used by a non-Black singer or other performer, especially formerly in minstrel shows

blackfella /blák fellə/, **blackfellow** /-fellō/ *n* a highly offensive term for an Aboriginal (*informal insult*)

blackfish /blák fish/ (*plural same* or **-fishes**) *n* **1.** a small freshwater fish that is very abundant. Native to: Arctic North America and Siberia. Latin name: *Dallia pectoralis*. **2.** a female salmon that has spawned **3.** same as **pilot whale**

black flag *n* same as **Jolly Roger**

black-flag (**black-flags, black-flagging, black-flagged**) *vt* to signal to a racing driver to pull into the pits by waving a black flag

black fly (*plural* **black flies** or *same*) *n* a small dark biting gnat that causes painful itchy welts in people and animals. Family: Simuliidae.

blackfly /blák flī/ (*plural* **-flies** or *same*) *n* a black aphid that infests many plants. Genus: *Aphis*.

Blackfoot /blák fòot/ (*plural* **-feet** /-feet/ or *same*) *n* **1.** a member of a group of Native North American peoples living in Alberta, Saskatchewan, and Montana **2.** an Algonquian language spoken in Alberta and Montana. Native speakers: 8,000. [Late 18C. Translation of Blackfoot *Siksika*, perhaps from walking across burnt prairies] —**Blackfoot** *adj*

Black Forest wooded highland region in Baden-Württemberg State, southwestern Germany that contains the sources of the Danube and Neckar rivers. Area: 5,180 sq. km/2,000 sq. mi.

Black Forest gateau *n UK* a rich chocolate cake that is topped and filled with cherries and whipped cream. Aus, N Am term **Black Forest cake**

Black Friar *n* a member of the Dominican order of friars

black gold *n* petroleum, viewed as a source of wealth (*informal*)

black grouse *n* a large grouse with a lyre-shaped tail, the male of which is black with white patches on its wings. Native to: Europe, western Asia. Latin name: *Lyrurus tetrix*.

blackguard /blággərd, blággaard/ *n* somebody regarded as dishonest or as having few, if any, principles (*dated*) ■ *vt* (**-guards, -guarding, -guarded**) to attack or criticize somebody using abusive language (*archaic*) —**blackguardism** *n* —**blackguardly** *adj*

blackhead /blák hed/ *n* **1.** a small plug of dark fatty matter blocking a follicle on the skin, especially on the face **2.** an infectious disease of turkeys and related fowl resulting in darkened head skin. It is caused by a protozoan.

Blackheath /blak héeth/ village and area of open ground in Greenwich, a borough of London, where golf was introduced to England

Black Hills mountainous region in western South Dakota and northeastern Wyoming, a mining area famous for the granite sculptures of Mount Rushmore National Memorial. The highest point is Harney Peak. Height: 2,207 m/7,242 ft. Area: 15,000 sq. km/6,000 sq. mi.

Black Hills spruce *n* a slow-growing evergreen tree of the pine family with cylindrical cones. Native to: northern part of North America. Latin name: *Picea glauca* var. densata.

black hole *n* **1.** an area in space with such a strong gravitational pull that no matter or energy can escape from it. Black holes are believed to form when stars collapse in on themselves. **2.** a place or thing into which objects disappear and are not expected to be seen again (*humorous*)

Black Hole of Calcutta *n* **1.** a dungeon in Kolkata (formerly Calcutta) in which, in 1756, 123 out of 146 prisoners were said to have died of suffocation **2.** an uncomfortably overcrowded place (*informal*)

black ice *n* a thin, almost invisible, layer of ice formed when rain falls on a surface that is below freezing

blacking /bláking/ *n* polish formerly used to make shoes and stoves black

Black Isle peninsula between the Cromarty and Moray firths, northeastern Scotland

blackjack /blák jak/ *n* **1.** *N Am* CARDS same as **pontoon**[2] **2.** MINERALS **BLACK MINERAL** a black variety of the mineral sphalerite or zinc blende **3.** *N Am* ARMS same as **life preserver** (sense 1) **4.** *S Africa* PLANTS **WEED WITH CLINGING SEEDS** a weed with barbed seeds that cling to clothing and animals. Latin name: *Bidens pilosa*. Same as **bur marigold** ■ *interj N Am* CARDS same as **pontoon**[1] (sense 3) ■ *vt* (**-jacks, -jacking, -jacked**) *N Am* **1. HIT SOMEBODY WITH CLUB** to hit somebody with a short club **2. FORCE** to force somebody to do something (*slang*) [Early 20C. < JACK[1] 'playing card']

black knight *n* a company that makes an unwelcome attempt to take over another company

black lead *n* a commercial form of graphite

blackleg /blák leg/ *n* **1. SOMEBODY WHO WORKS DURING STRIKE** a worker who is criticized and despised by striking colleagues for working during a strike (*disapproving*) **2.** VET **DISEASE OF FARM ANIMALS** an infectious bacterial disease of farm animals that causes swellings on the legs **3.** BOT **POTATO DISEASE** a disease of potato plants caused by the bacterium *Erwinia carotovora* that makes the lower stems rot **4.** GAMBLING **GAMBLER WHO CHEATS** a cheat at cards or horseracing (*informal*) ■ *vi* (**-legs, -legging, -legged**) **WORK DURING STRIKE** to continue to work while colleagues are on strike (*informal*)

black letter *n* PRINTING same as **gothic** *n* (sense 3)

black light *n* **1.** any invisible electromagnetic radiation, e.g. ultraviolet or infrared light **2.** a bulb, tube, or other device that emits black light when stimulated with electrical current

blacklist /blák list/ *n* **1. LIST OF DISAPPROVED PEOPLE** a list of people or groups who are under suspicion or excluded from something ○ *a credit blacklist* **2. LIST OF UNWANTED E-MAILS** a list of e-mail addresses, e.g. of unknown senders, to which somebody does not want to permit access. ◊ **white list** (sense 2) ■ *vt* (**-lists, -listing, -listed**) **1. PUT SOMEBODY ON BLACKLIST** to add somebody's name to a blacklist **2. CONDEMN** to shun or condemn somebody for behaviour that breaks implicit or explicit rules

black lung *n* MED same as **anthracosis**

blackly /blákli/ *adv* **1.** in an angry or threatening way **2.** showing or making use of the colour black

black magic *n* magic attempted for evil purposes, calling upon evil spirits or the devil

blackmail /blák mayl/ *n* **1.** the act of forcing somebody to pay money or do something by threatening to reveal shameful or incriminating facts about him or her **2.** unfair threatening or incriminating of somebody, as a way of achieving a result [Mid-16C. < obsolete *mail* 'tribute, tax' < Old Norse *mál* 'speech, agreement'] —**blackmail** *vt* —**blackmailer** *n*

Blackman /blákmən/, **Charles Raymond** (*b.* 1928) Australian painter. His works include many melancholy paintings of children, in which the figures are often little more than silhouettes.

Black Maria /-mə rī ə/ *n* a police van for transporting prisoners (*dated informal*) [Perhaps < *Maria* Lee, Black Boston woman who brought offenders to jail; partly also from its traditional colour]

black mark *n* a record of something that somebody has done that gives people a bad opinion of him or her ○ *Avoiding the family reunion counted as a black mark against me.*

black market *n* a system of buying and selling officially controlled goods illegally —**black marketeer** *n* —**black marketeering** *n* —**black marketer** *n*

black mass *n* an imitation of a Christian Mass said to be conducted by worshippers of the devil

black money *n* money earned unofficially or illegally

Black Monk *n* a member of the Benedictine order of monks, who wear black cloaks over their white habits

Blackmore /blák mawr/, **R. D.** (1825–1900) British writer. The best known of his novels is *Lorna Doone* (1869). Full name **Blackmore, Richard Doddridge**

> 'Here was I, a yeoman's boy, a yeoman every inch of me, even where I was naked; and there was she, a lady born, and thoroughly aware of it, and dressed by people of rank and taste, who took pride in her beauty, and set it to advantage.'
> [R. D. Blackmore, *Lorna Doone*; 1869]

Black Mountains 1. mountain range in southern Wales, in eastern Carmarthenshire and western Powys. Its highest peak is Carmarthen Van 1,802 m/2,630 ft. **2.** mountain range in southern Wales, in Monmouthshire. Its highest peak is Waunfach, 811 m/2,660 ft.

Black Muslim *n* a member of the Nation of Islam, an almost exclusively African American Islamic denomination based in the United States

Black nationalist *n* a member of a political organization that promotes separate self-governing communities or states for Black people —**Black nationalism** *n*

black nightshade *n* a plant of the nightshade family that has poisonous leaves and black berries. Flowers: white, star-shaped. Latin name: *Solanum nigrum*.

blackout /blák owt/ *n* **1.** MED LOSS OF CONSCIOUSNESS a temporary loss of consciousness, sight, or memory **2.** ELEC LOSS OF ELECTRIC LIGHT a failure of an electricity supply **3.** BROADCAST WITHDRAWAL OF BROADCASTING a refusal to broadcast radio or television programmes, usually because of a strike, **4.** COMMUNICATION WITHHOLDING OF INFORMATION the withholding of news or information about a subject, especially by official sources **5.** COMMUNICATION LOSS OF RADIO COMMUNICATION a loss of radio communication between an aircraft or ship and headquarters **6.** MIL PERIOD OF EXTINGUISHING OR HIDING LIGHTS a period during wartime in which all lights are to be turned off or covered up at night to prevent inhabited areas being seen from enemy aircraft **7.** TRAVEL PERIOD OF FULL-PRICE TRAVEL a period during which promotional offers and benefits, e.g. those given to frequent fliers, cannot by used for air travel

Black Panther *n* a member of a militant African American political organization opposed to white domination that was active in the United States especially in the late 1960s and early 1970s [*Panther* < the emblem used by certain Black Power electoral candidates in Alabama in the mid-1960s]

black pepper *n* dark brown seasoning made by grinding pepper seeds that have not had their black outer covering removed

blackpoll /blák pōl/, **blackpoll warbler** *n* a small songbird with streaky plumage found in conifer forests. Native to: North America. Latin name: *Dendroica striata*.

Blackpool /blák pool/ seaside resort in Lancashire, northwestern England, famous for its tower, built in 1895 and modelled on the Eiffel Tower, Paris. Population: 142,283 (2001).

Black Power *n* a movement formed by Black people to engender social equality and emphasize pride in their racial identity via Black cultural and political institutions and organizations

black pudding *n* a dark sausage made from pig's blood and pork fat. US term **blood sausage**

black rat *n* a common dark-brown rat that is a household pest and a carrier of plague. It was originally from Asia but spread to coastal cities throughout the world. Latin name: *Rattus rattus*.

black rot *n* a plant disease that causes blackening as well as decay

Black Sash *n* originally an organization of white women in South Africa who campaigned against apartheid, now a multiracial organization which promotes civil rights

Black Sea large inland sea linked to the Mediterranean by the Bosporus, the Sea of Marmara, and the Dardanelles. It is bordered by Bulgaria, Romania, Ukraine, Russia, Georgia, and Turkey. Area: 461,000 sq. km/178,000 sq. mi.

black shale *n* a mudstone that contains organic carbon, e.g. an oil-bearing shale

black sheep *n* somebody regarded by the other members of a family or group as not living up to their standards and expectations [Because black wool is less valuable than white]

Blackshirt /blák shurt/ *n* a member of any European fascist movement active before and during World War II, especially a member of the Italian Fascist Party [< the party's uniform]

blacksmith /blák smith/ *n* somebody whose job is making and repairing iron and metal objects such as horseshoes [< *black* applied to iron]

blacksnake /blák snayk/ *n* a dark-coloured poisonous forest-dwelling snake. Native to: eastern Australia. Latin name: *Pseudechis porphyriacus*.

black spot *n* **1.** a place where something bad exists or happens ○ *an unemployment black spot* **2.** a plant disease that causes black patches to form on leaves, particularly on roses

Blackstone /blák stōn, -stən/, **Sir William** (1723–80) British jurist. He wrote the classic *Commentaries on the Laws of England* (1765–69).

> 'It is better that ten guilty persons escape than one innocent suffer.'
> [Sir William Blackstone, *Commentaries on the Laws of England*; 1765–69]

Black Stone *n* the sacred stone in the Kaaba in the great mosque in Mecca, believed to have been given by God. It is reddish-black in colour.

Black Studies *n* an academic subject or curriculum taught mainly in the United States that deals with the history, culture, and literature of Black communities worldwide, often with an emphasis on African American culture (*takes a singular verb*)

black stump *n* *Aus* an imaginary stump marking the farthest edge of civilization (*informal*) ○ *I grew up beyond the black stump and didn't see a city until I was 25.*

black swan *n* a large swan with black plumage and a red beak. Native to: Australia, New Zealand. Latin name: *Cygnus atratus*.

black-tailed deer *n* a mule deer with a tail that is black on top. Native to: western North America. Latin name: *Odocoileus hemionus columbianus*.

black tea *n* **1.** dark-coloured tea leaves that have been fermented before being dried **2.** a tea drink served without milk

blackthorn /blák thawrn/ *n* **1.** a thorny black-stemmed bush with small blue-black berries (**sloes**). Native to: Europe, Asia. Latin name: *Prunus spinosa*. **2.** a walking stick made from the hard wood of the blackthorn

black tie *n* **1.** a black bow tie worn on formal occasions **2.** a formal style in men's dress that includes a black bow tie and a dinner jacket — **black-tie** *adj*

blacktop /blák top/ *N Am n* **1.** ROAD-SURFACING MATERIAL a road-surfacing material bound together with a tarry substance such as asphalt **2.** ROAD MADE WITH BLACKTOP a road or other area with a blacktop surface ■ *vti* (**-tops, -topping, -topped**) COAT SURFACE WITH BLACKTOP to cover a road or other surface with blacktop

black treacle *n* FOOD same as **treacle** (sense 1)

black velvet *n* an alcoholic drink consisting of stout and champagne

Black Vernacular English *n* LANG same as **African American Vernacular English**

black vine weevil *n* INSECTS same as **vine weevil**

black walnut *n* **1.** INDUST N AMERICAN WALNUT WOOD the hard black wood of a North American walnut tree. Use: veneers, cabinets. **2.** EDIBLE NUT the hard-shelled nut of a North American walnut tree **3.** N AMERICAN WALNUT TREE a walnut tree that yields hard black wood and bears black edible walnuts. Native to: North America. Latin name: *Juglans nigra*.

Black Watch *n* the Royal Highland Regiment in the British Army [< its dark tartan]

blackwater fever /blák wawtər-/ *n* a serious condition, developing from malaria, that causes a rapid and massive loss of red blood cells and turns the urine dark red or blackish

black widow

black widow *n* a highly poisonous spider, the female of which has a black body with an hourglass-shaped red marking on the abdomen. Native to: temperate North America and East Asia. Latin name: *Latrodectus mactans*. [< the female's habit of eating her mate]

blackwood /blák wŏŏd/ (*plural* **-woods** or *same*) *n* a large bush or tree with inconspicuous pale yellow flowers and valuable dark brown timber, found in temperate regions of Australia. Latin name: *Acacia melanoxylon*.

bladder /bláddər/ *n* **1.** BODILY SAC FOR LIQUID OR GAS an organ or other body part for storing a liquid or gas, especially the sac that stores urine (**urinary bladder**) or the sac that stores bile (**gallbladder**) **2.** INFLATABLE INNER BAG an inflatable part of something, especially a football, that resembles a bag **3.** BOT SAC IN PLANT a sac found in plants such as bladder wrack that stores air to help the plant to float or, as in bladderwort, traps insects **4.** MED FLUID-FILLED BLISTER a blister or small sac filled with fluid [Old English *blǽdre, blǽddre* < Indo-European] —**bladdery** *adj*

bladder campion *n* a wild plant with a swollen calyx. Flowers: white. Native to: Europe. Latin name: *Silene vulgaris*.

bladdered /bláddərd/ *adj* extremely drunk (*slang*)

bladder fern *n* a small delicate fern that grows in rocks and walls and has a bulbous seed pod. Latin name: *Cystopteris fragilis*.

bladder kelp *n* a brown alga with inflated bladders from which streamers that resemble leaves are suspended

bladdernut /bláddər nut/ *n* **1.** a small tree or bush with clusters of small white flowers and bulbous seed pods. Genus: *Staphylea*. **2.** the seed pod of a bladdernut tree or bush

bladder worm *n* the larva of a tapeworm, shaped like a sac and armed with six hooks. Class: Cestoda.

bladderwort /bláddər wurt/ *n* a water plant with floating leaves bearing small bladders that are used to trap insects. Genus: *Utricularia*.

bladder wrack *n* a brown seaweed that has bulbous air bladders on its fronds that allow them to float. It grows between the high and low water line. Latin name: *Fucus vesiculosus*.

blade /blayd/ *n* **1.** CUTTING PART the flat sharp-edged cutting part of a tool or weapon **2.** LONG THIN FLAT PART a long thin flat part of some tools or machines, e.g. of a propeller **3.** THIN LEAF a long thin leaf, especially of grass **4.** FLAT STRIKING PART the flat striking part of something such as an oar or a golf club **5.** same as **razor blade 6.** PART OF ICE SKATE the metal part of an ice skate that glides on the ice **7.** PHON PART OF TONGUE the flat upper part of the tongue just behind the tip **8.** ARCHAEOL STONE FRAGMENT a parallel-sided stone flake that is at least twice as long as it is wide **9.** ARMS SWORD a sword (*literary*) **10.** DASHING MAN an energetic fun-loving man (*dated informal*) ■ **blades** *npl* **1.** ANZ SHEEP SHEARS hand-operated shears for shearing sheep **2.** *N Am* SKATING IN-LINE ROLLER SKATES in-line roller skates (*informal*) ■ *vi* (**blades, blading, bladed**) *N Am* SKATE ON IN-LINE ROLLER SKATES to skate on in-line roller skates (*informal*) [Old English *blæd* < Germanic] —**bladed** *adj*

blag /blag/ (*slang*) *vt* (**blags, blagging, blagged**) **1.** OBTAIN SOMETHING IN UNDERHAND WAY to obtain something by deceit, scrounging, or cajoling ○ *He blagged his way into the party.* **2.** STEAL SOMETHING FROM SOMEWHERE to steal something, or rob a place, especially using an element of violence, speed, or surprise ■ *n* ROBBERY a theft or robbery, especially one using an element of violence, speed, or surprise ○ *He's done some big bank blags.* [Late 19C. Origin ?] —**blagger** *n* —**blagging** *n*

blah /blaa/ *n* NONSENSE talk or writing that is inane or pretentious (*informal*) ■ **blahs** *npl N Am* MALAISE a condition of feeling bored, restless, and listless ○ *She's got the blahs today.* ■ *vi* (**blahs, blahing, blahed**) TALK NONSENSE to talk or write inane or pretentious nonsense (*informal, often repeated for emphasis*) [Early 20C. An imitation of vacuous talk]

Blainey /bláyni/, **Geoffrey Norman** (*b.* 1930) Australian historian. His works include the popular trilogy *A Vision of Australian History* (1966–80).

Blair /blair/, **Tony** (*b.* 1953) British prime minister. A member of Parliament from 1983, he was elected Labour Party leader in 1994 and became prime minister in 1997. He was re-elected in 2001. Full name **Blair, Anthony Charles Lynton**. See illustration on next page and table at **prime minister**

> 'My vision for the 21st century is of a popular politics reconciling themes which in the past have wrongly been viewed as antagonistic—patriotism and internationalism; rights and responsibilities; the promotion of enterprise and the attack on poverty and discrimination.'
> [Tony Blair, *Lecture to the Fabian Society, London*; 1998]

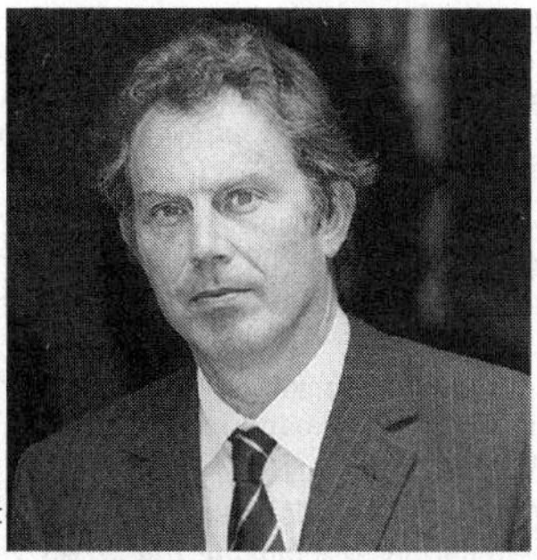
Popperfoto
Tony Blair

Blairism /bláirizəm/ *n* the political policies and style of government of Tony Blair, typified by moderate and gradual social reform, financial prudence, and tight control over policy presentation —**Blairite** /blaírīt/ *n, adj*

Blake /blayk/, **Peter** (*b.* 1932) British painter. An important figure in British Pop Art, he designed the album cover for the Beatles' *Sergeant Pepper's Lonely Hearts Club Band* (1967). His work is often described as deliberately naive and is influenced by folk art and popular culture. Full name **Blake, Peter Thomas**

Blake, Robert (1599–1657) English admiral. He blockaded Lisbon and destroyed Prince Rupert's squadron (1650). In 1657 he destroyed the Spanish treasure fleet off Tenerife.

Blake, William (1757–1827) British poet, painter, and engraver. He wrote *Songs of Innocence* (1789), *The Marriage of Heaven and Hell* (1790–93), and *Jerusalem* (1804–20), illustrating his poetry with highly original engravings and watercolours. He championed mystical wisdom and the unfettered imagination in the face of 18th-century rationalism. See Cultural note at **experience** —**Blakeian** *adj*

> 'O Rose, thou art sick! / The invisible worm / That flies in the night, / In the howling storm, / Has found out thy bed / Of crimson joy: / And his dark secret love / Does thy life destroy.'
> [William Blake, 'The Sick Rose', *Songs of Experience*; 1789–94]

> 'I care not whether a Man is Good or Evil; all that I care / Is whether he is a Wise Man or a Fool. Go! put off Holiness, / And put on Intellect.'
> [William Blake, *Jerusalem*; 1804–20]

Blakey /bláyki/, **Art** (1919–90) US jazz drummer and bandleader. His innovations as a drummer led to the development of bebop and hard bop. His band, the Jazz Messengers (1954), showcased young musicians. Full name **Blakey, Arthur**

blame /blaym/ *vt* (**blames, blaming, blamed**) **1. CONSIDER SOMEBODY RESPONSIBLE** to consider somebody to be responsible for something wrong or unfortunate that has happened ○ *She blames me for the failure of the company.* **2. CRITICIZE SOMEBODY** to find fault with somebody (*used in negative statements and questions*) ○ *I don't blame you for wanting to know what happened.* ■ *n* **RESPONSIBILITY** responsibility for something wrong or unfortunate that has happened ○ *It's still not clear where the blame lies.* ○ *I'm not taking the blame for your mistakes.* [12C. Via Old French *bla(s)mer* < Latin *blastemare*, alteration of *blasphemare* 'revile' (see BLASPHEME)] —**blamable** *adj* —**blameful** *adj* —**blameworthiness** *n* —**blameworthy** *adj* ◇ **be to blame** to be responsible for something wrong or unfortunate that has happened ○ *Who's to blame for the mix-up?*

blame culture *n* a set of attitudes, e.g. within a business organization, characterized by an unwillingness to take risks or accept responsibility for mistakes because of a fear of criticism or prosecution

blameless /bláymləss/ *adj* **1.** not responsible for something wrong or unfortunate that has happened ○ *No one involved is entirely blameless.* **2.** doing nothing bad or wrong ○ *a blameless life* —**blamelessly** *adv* —**blamelessness** *n*

Blamey /bláymi/, **Sir Thomas Albert** (1884–1951) Australian soldier. Commander of the World War II Allied Land Forces in the southwestern Pacific (1942–45), he later became Australia's first field marshal in 1950.

Blanc, Mont ➧ **Mont Blanc**

blanch /blaanch/ (**blanches, blanching, blanched**), **blench** /blench/ (**blenches, blenching, blenched**) *v* **1.** *vi* **TURN PALE** to become pale suddenly ○ *He blanched at the mention of her name.* **2.** *vt* **PUT FOOD BRIEFLY IN BOILING WATER** to put food in boiling water for a few seconds in order to loosen the skin or to kill enzymes **3.** *vt* **WHITEN VEGETABLES BY GROWING IN DARK** to grow vegetables, especially celery and chicory, in dark conditions in order to whiten the stems and improve their flavour **4.** *vti* **LOSE OR REMOVE COLOUR FROM SOMETHING** to lose colour, or cause something to lose colour [14C. < French *blanchir* 'whiten' < *blanche*, feminine of *blanc* 'white'] —**blancher** *n*

blancmange /blə maánj, -maánzh/ *n* a cold dessert similar to jelly made with milk, sugar, flavourings, and cornflour [14C. < Old French *blanc mangier* < *blanc* 'white' + *mangier* 'food' < *mangier* 'eat' (see MANGER)]

bland /bland/ *adj* **1. INSIPID** lacking flavour, character, or interest ○ *a bland diet* **2. FREE OF STRESS** free from anything annoying or upsetting **3. UNEMOTIONAL** without emotion [Mid-17C. < Latin *blandus* 'smooth, flattering'] —**blandly** *adv* —**blandness** *n*

blandish /blándish/ (**-dishes, -dishing, -dished**) *vti* to persuade somebody by flattery (*archaic*) [14C. < Old French *blandiss-* (see BLANDISHMENT)] —**blandisher** *n*

blandishment /blándishmənt/ *n* **1.** a piece of flattery intended to persuade somebody to do something (*formal; often used in the plural*) ○ *impervious to all blandishments* **2.** the use of flattery and enticements to persuade somebody to do something [Late 16C. < archaic *blandish* < Old French *blandiss-*, stem of *blandir* < Latin *blandus* 'smooth, flattering']

blank /blangk/ *adj* **1. NOT MARKED** not written on, drawn on, or printed on ○ *a blank page* **2. UNBROKEN** lacking any features or openings ○ *a sheer, blank rock wall* ○ *a blank corridor* ○ *not a cloud in the blank blue sky* **3. LACKING INTEREST, AWARENESS, OR UNDERSTANDING** having or showing no interest, awareness, or understanding ○ *a blank expression* **4. UNEVENTFUL OR UNPRODUCTIVE** characterized by lack of useful action or result ○ *It was one of those blank periods when nothing particular was happening.* **5. TOTAL** complete or absolute ○ *a blank refusal to cooperate* ■ *n* **1. SPACE IN WHICH TO WRITE** a space left empty in which to write, in a form or document ○ *Fill in the blanks.* **2. DOCUMENT WITH BLANK SPACES** a form or document with spaces for writing in **3. MARK INDICATING MISSING WORD** a mark (–) in writing or print indicating that a word or letter is missing ○ *a word meaning solitary, spelt a l – – e* **4. EMPTINESS OF MIND** a complete absence of awareness or memory ○ *I remember hearing a loud noise; the rest is a blank.* **5. VOID** a period about which nothing is known ○ *There are a lot of blanks in her account of the event.* **6.** *also* **blank cartridge** ARMS = **blank cartridge 7.** MANUF **PIECE FROM WHICH ARTICLE IS MADE** a piece of metal or other material that will be shaped to produce a finished item **8. BULL'S EYE** the bull's eye of a target ■ *v* (**blanks, blanking, blanked**) **1.** *vt* **OBLITERATE SOMETHING** to delete or black something out ○ *The names had been blanked.* **2.** *vi* **FORGET TEMPORARILY** to forget something suddenly and temporarily ○ *I tried to recall their names, but I just blanked.* **3.** *vt N Am* **PREVENT SOMEBODY SCORING** to prevent an opponent from making any score **4.** *vt* **IGNORE SOMEBODY** to ignore or pretend not to see somebody (*informal*) [13C. < French *blanc* 'white'] —**blankly** *adv* —**blankness** *n* ◇ **draw a blank** to be unsuccessful in a search or enquiry ◇ **fire** *or* **shoot blanks** to be unable to impregnate a woman because of a low sperm count (*slang; sometimes considered offensive*) ◇ **go (a) blank** to be unable to think of or remember something ○ *I tried to remember her name but my mind went blank.*

blank out *v* **1.** *vt* **COVER SOMETHING** to cover something completely so that it cannot be seen or read **2.** *vt* **ERASE SOMETHING FROM MIND** to refuse to remember or acknowledge a fact, event, or memory **3.** *vi* **LOSE AWARENESS** to become dazed or unconscious **4.** *vi* **FADE AWAY** to diminish in intensity or loudness

blank cartridge *n* a gun cartridge that contains explosive but no bullet

blank cheque *n* **1.** a signed cheque that has not yet had the amount payable filled in **2.** complete freedom to act or decide (*informal*) ○ *They gave us a blank cheque in our negotiations.*

blank endorsement *n* an endorsement on a bill of exchange that does not name a payee and so may benefit the bearer

blanket /blángkit/ *n* **1. CLOTH BED COVERING** a piece of cloth used especially as a cover for a bed **2. COVERING LAYER** a layer of something covering an area completely **3.** PHYS **LAYER AROUND CORE OF NUCLEAR REACTOR** in a nuclear reactor, a layer of material surrounding the radioactive core used to reflect neutrons or to create more fissile material **4.** PRINTING **SHEET TRANSFERRING IMAGE** a sheet that is wrapped around the cylinder of a printing press which transfers the impression in ink to the surface being printed on ■ *adj* **APPLYING GENERALLY** applying to all areas or situations ○ *We have blanket approval for our proposals.* ■ *vt* (**-kets, -keting, -keted**) **1. COVER SOMETHING WITH LAYER** to cover something with a thick layer ○ *The streets were blanketed with snow.* **2. SUPPRESS SOMETHING** to prevent something from being heard or seen ○ *Background interference keeps blanketing out the recording.* **3.** SAILING **PREVENT WIND REACHING SAILS OF SHIP** to take the wind from the sails of another yacht or ship by sailing to windward of it [14C. < Old N French *blanquet*, Old French *blanchet* < *blanc* 'white']

blanket bath *n UK* HEALTH SERVICES same as **bed bath**

blanket bog *n* a peat bog covering a wide area

blanket bond *n* an insurance contract providing a financial institution with cover against losses resulting from employee dishonesty or theft

blanket finish *n* a situation in which the runners in a race finish very close to one another

blanket stitch *n* looped stitching with wide gaps between stitches, used to reinforce the edge of a piece of fabric

blank verse *n* unrhymed poetry that has a regular rhythm and line length, especially iambic pentameter

blanquette /blong két, blaaN-/ *n* a dish consisting of white meat such as veal cooked in a white sauce ○ *blanquette of veal* [Mid-18C. < French < Old N French *blanquet* (see BLANKET)]

Blantyre-Limbe /blán tīr lím bay/ largest city in Malawi and the administrative headquarters of the Southern Region. Population: 2,000,000 (1998).

blare /blair/ (**blares, blaring, blared**) *v* **1.** *vti* to make a loud harsh noise ○ *speakers blaring out rock music* **2.** *vt* to proclaim something loudly or prominently ○ *'Heiress disappears', the headlines blared.* [14C. Probably an imitation of the sound] —**blare** *n*

blarney /blaárni/ (*informal*) *n* **1. PERSUASIVE FLATTERING TALK** flattering talk intended to persuade somebody **2. NONSENSE** unintelligent or insincere talk ■ *vti* (**-neys, -neying, -neyed**) **WHEEDLE** to persuade somebody with flattery [Late 18C. After the BLARNEY STONE]

Blarney /blaárni/ village in County Cork, southern Republic of Ireland. Population: 2,146 (2002).

Blarney Stone *n* a stone in Blarney Castle, near Cork in Ireland, that is said to give the power of persuasive talk to people who kiss it

blasé /blaá zay, blaa záy/ *adj* not impressed or worried by something, usually because of having experienced it before [Early 19C. < French, 'satiated']

blaspheme /blass feém, blaass-/ (**-phemes, -pheming, -phemed**) *v* **1.** *vi* to swear in a way that insults religion **2.** *vti* to treat God or sacred things disrespectfully through words or action [14C. Via French < ecclesiastical Latin *blasphemare* 'revile' < Greek *blasphēmein* < *blasphēmos* 'evil-speaking'] —**blasphemer** *n*

blasphemous /blássfəməss/ *adj* expressing or involving disrespect for God or sacred things —**blasphemously** *adv*

blasphemy /blássfəmi/ (*plural* **-mies**) *n* **1.** disrespect for God or sacred things **2.** something done or said that shows disrespect for God or sacred things

blast /blaast/ *n* **1. STRONG AIR OR GAS CURRENT** a sudden strong current of air or wind **2. EXPLOSION** an explosion, or a sudden rush of air caused by an explosion ○ *Several homes were destroyed by the*

blast. **3.** LOUD EXPLOSIVE SOUND the sound made by an explosion ○ *We were almost deafened by the blasts.* **4.** INSTRUMENT'S LOUD SOUND a short loud sound made on an instrument, whistle, or car horn **5.** OUTBURST a loud or angry outburst ○ *a blast of criticism* ■ *v* (**blasts, blasting, blasted**) **1.** *vt* BLOW SOMETHING UP WITH EXPLOSIVES to destroy or break open something using explosives ○ *Rescuers blasted a hole in the rock.* **2.** *vti* MAKE LOUD NOISE to come out with great force or volume, or make something do this (*informal*) **3.** *vt* HIT SOMETHING HARD to strike something with great force (*informal*) ○ *She blasted the ball into the net.* **4.** *vt* GIVE SOMEBODY OR SOMETHING STRONG CRITICISM to criticize somebody or something severely (*informal*) ■ *interj* EXPRESSING ANNOYANCE used to express mild annoyance (*informal*) [Old English *blǣst* < Indo-European] —**blaster** *n* ◇ **(at) full blast** at maximum volume or speed

SYNONYMS See *criticize*.

blast away *vi* to fire a gun repeatedly (*informal*)

blast off *vti* to launch a rocket, spacecraft, or astronaut into space, or be launched into space

-blast *suffix* embryonic cell ○ *melanoblast* [< Greek *blastos* 'bud, germ, sprout'] —**-blastic** *suffix*

blasted /blaástid/ *adj, adv* used to express mild annoyance (*informal*) ○ *Then the blasted handle broke.* ■ *adj* affected by a withering disease or a similar destructive force (*literary*) ○ *a blasted heath*

blastema /blas teéma/ (*plural* **-mas** or **-mata** /-mətə/) *n* a group of unspecialized animal cells from which an organ or new tissue develops [Mid-19C. < Greek *blastēma* 'sprout'] —**blastemal** *adj* —**blastematic** /blástə máttik/ *adj* —**blastemic** *adj*

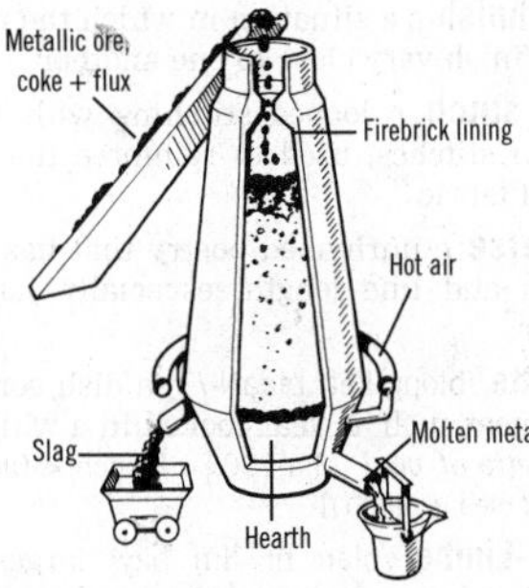
Metallic ore, coke + flux
Firebrick lining
Hot air
Slag
Molten metal
Hearth

blast furnace

blast furnace *n* a vertical shaft furnace for smelting metals. Fuel, ores, and slag-forming rock are loaded from above, and air is blown in from the bottom to raise the temperature. The molten metal is tapped periodically from the base.

blast injection *n* a method of fuel injection that uses air pressure to atomize the fuel as it enters the cylinder of an internal-combustion engine

blasto- *prefix* bud, germ ○ *blastomycosis* [< Greek *blastos* 'bud, germ, sprout']

blastocoel /blástə seel/, **blastocoele** *n* the cavity that forms within the mass of cells (**blastula**) in a developing embryo and fills with fluid [Late 19C. < BLASTO- + Greek *koilos* 'hollow'] —**blastocoelic** /blástə seélik/ *adj*

blastocyst /blástəsist/ *n* a mammalian embryo at the stage when it is implanted in the wall of the womb —**blastocystic** /blástə sístik/ *adj*

blastoderm /blástə durm/ *n* a layer of cells arising from the repeated division of a fertilized mammalian egg that develops into an embryo [Mid-19C. < BLASTO- + Greek *derma* 'skin'] —**blastodermatic** /blástə dur máttik/ *adj* —**blastodermic** /blástə dúrmik/ *adj*

blastodisc /blástō disk/, **blastodisk** *n* the disc-shaped part on the upper surface of the yolk of a fertilized egg where the embryo begins to form, as in reptiles, birds, and some fish

blastoff /blaást of/ *n* the launch of a rocket, spacecraft, or missile

blastogenesis /blástə jénnəssiss/ *n* asexual reproduction by budding —**blastogenetic** /blástə jə néttik/ *adj* —**blastogenic** *adj*

blastomere /blástō meer/ *n* a cell of an animal embryo (**blastula**) formed by the division of a fertilized egg cell

blastomycosis /blástō mī kóssiss/ *n* a fungal infection causing lesions on the lungs, skin, or mucous membranes

blastopore /blástə pawr/ *n* an opening in a young embryo that develops into the anus in some mammals —**blastoporal** /blástə páwrəl/ *adj* —**blastoporic** *adj*

blastosphere /blástə sfeer/ *n* BIOL same as **blastula**

blastospore /blástə spawr/ *n* a fungal spore produced by budding

blastula /blástyoōlə/ (*plural* **-las** or **-lae** /-lee/) *n* an embryo at an early stage of development, consisting of a hollow ball of cells [Late 19C. < modern Latin < Greek *blastos* 'bud, germ, sprout'] —**blastular** *adj* —**blastulation** /blástyoō láysh'n/ *n*

blat[1] /blat/ (**blats, blatting, blatted**) *vi N Am* to make a bleating sound (*informal*) [Mid-19C. An imitation of the sound]

blat[2] /blat/, **blatt** *n US* a tabloid newspaper (*slang*) [Mid-20C. < German *Blatt* 'leaf, sheet (of paper)']

blatant /bláyt'nt/ *adj* **1.** obtrusive and conspicuous in an offensive way, often intentionally ○ *blatant falsehoods* **2.** excessively or offensively noisy (*literary*) [Late 16C. Perhaps alteration of Scottish *blatand* 'bleating', or < Latin *blatire* 'to babble'] —**blatancy** *n* —**blatantly** *adv*

USAGE blatant or **flagrant**? Both words describe openly offensive behaviour, but there is a difference. ***Blatant*** emphasizes the brazen conspicuousness of the offence, as in *a blatant breach of good faith in the negotiations*, whereas ***flagrant*** emphasizes the shocking seriousness or gravity that the offence has: *flagrant racism*. A ***blatant*** lie is one so bare-faced that no one can miss it, whereas ***flagrant*** disregard for human life is unforgivably shameless or outrageous. Avoid using ***blatant*** to mean merely 'obvious': *There seems to be a blatant contradiction...* In sentences like this, substitute *obvious, clear*, or *glaring* for ***blatant***.

blate /blayt/ *adj Scotland* lacking in self-confidence [15C. Origin ?]

blather /bláthər/ (**-ers, -ering, -ered**) (*informal*) *vi* to talk in an unintelligent or inane manner, especially at length ■ *n* foolish and prolonged talk [15C. < Old Norse *blaðra* 'to chatter, babble'] —**blatherer** *n*

blathering /bláthəring/ *n regional* an act of nagging at or scolding somebody

REGIONAL NOTE See *jawing*.

blatherskite /bláthər skīt/, **bletherskite** /bléthər-/ *n* (*dated informal*) **1.** somebody who enjoys silly or unimportant chat **2.** chat about silly or unimportant things [Mid-17C. < Scottish dialect *skate* 'contemptible person']

blatt *n US* MEDIA another spelling of **blat**[2]

Blaxland /bláksland/, **Gregory** (1778–1853) British-born Australian explorer. With William Lawson and William Wentworth, he led the first crossing by Europeans of the Blue Mountains in New South Wales, Australia (1813).

blaxploitation /blák sploy táysh'n/ *n* depiction of Black people in films or other media in a way that appeals to popular and often inaccurate or negative notions of their experiences and qualities (*informal*) [Late 20C. Blend of *Blacks* + EXPLOITATION]

blaze[1] /blayz/ *vi* (**blazes, blazing, blazed**) **1.** BURN BRIGHTLY to burn brightly and fiercely **2.** SHINE to shine or appear to shine brightly **3.** EXPERIENCE STRONG EMOTION to be affected by a strong emotion (*informal*) ○ *blazing with indignation* **4.** FIRE GUN to fire a gun repeatedly ■ *n* **1.** BRIGHT FIRE a brightly or intensely burning fire, or a large fire **2.** CONSPICUOUS DISPLAY a display that attracts attention ○ *a blaze of publicity* ■ **blazes** *npl* ADDING EMPHASIS used to add emphasis (*informal; used euphemistically*) ○ *What the blazes did you do that for?* ○ *run like blazes* [Old English *blæse* 'torch, bright flame' < Germanic]

SYNONYMS See *fire*.

blaze[2] /blayz/ *n* **1.** WHITE MARK ON ANIMAL'S FACE a white streak on the face of a horse or other animal **2.** MARK SHOWING WAY a mark indicating a path, originally a cut made in a tree trunk ■ *vt* (**blazes, blazing, blazed**) **1.** MARK PATH to indicate a new path by making marks **2.** DO SOMETHING NEW to lead the way in doing something new ○ *He blazed the way to the understanding of DNA's structure.* [Mid-17C. Perhaps < Old Norse *blesi*, Middle High German *blasse*, or Middle Low German *bles* 'white mark']

blaze[3] /blayz/ (**blazes, blazing, blazed**) *vt* to spread news or information loudly and clearly ○ *blazed the scandal all over the front page* [14C. < Middle Dutch *blāzen* 'swell' < Indo-European]

blazer /bláyzər/ *n* a jacket, often in the colours of a school or club or bearing its badge [Mid-17C. < the typically bright colour]

blazing /bláyzing/ *adj* **1.** INTENSE feeling or showing intense emotions ○ *a blazing row* **2.** HOT very hot ○ *sitting in the blazing sun* ■ *adv* EXTREMELY extremely or intensely ○ *blazing hot* —**blazingly** *adv*

blazing star *n* **1.** WHITE-FLOWERED PLANT a plant of the lily family. Flowers: white, with long heads. Native to: North America. Latin name: *Chamaelirium luteum*. **2.** WHITE- OR PURPLE-FLOWERED PLANT a plant of the composite family. Flowers: long heads of small white or purplish flowers. Native to: North America. Genus: *Liatris*. **3.** PLANT WITH ROUGH LEAVES a plant with rough leaves that may stick to clothing. Flowers: yellow, orange, or red. Native to: North America. Genus: *Mentzelia*.

blazon /bláyz'n/ *vt* (**-zons, -zoning, -zoned**) **1.** PROCLAIM SOMETHING WIDELY to announce something widely or ostentatiously **2.** HERALDRY DEPICT COAT OF ARMS to create or describe a coat of arms using the traditional symbols ■ *n* HERALDRY COAT OF ARMS a coat of arms, or a technical description of one [13C. < French *blason* 'shield']

blazonry /bláyzənri/ *n* **1.** HERALDRY MAKING OR EXPLAINING COATS OF ARMS the art of creating or explaining coats of arms **2.** HERALDRY COATS OF ARMS coats of arms individually or collectively **3.** BRILLIANT DISPLAY a bright or showy display (*literary*)

bldg *abbr* building

bleach /bleech/ *n* **1.** COLOUR-REMOVING SUBSTANCE a chemical that removes or whitens colour or staining and also cleans and disinfects **2.** APPLICATION OF BLEACH an act of using bleach on something ■ *v* (**bleaches, bleaching, bleached**) **1.** *vt* USE BLEACH ON SOMETHING to clean or whiten something using bleach **2.** *vti* LIGHTEN IN COLOUR to make something whiter or lighter, or become lighter or whiter [Old English *blǣcan* 'make white' < *blǣc* 'pale, shining' < Germanic] —**bleacher** *n*

bleachers /bleéchərz/ *npl N Am* (*sometimes used in the singular*) **1.** seats in an uncovered area of a sports stadium **2.** retractable tiered benches for spectators in an indoor sports arena [Late 19C. < the sun's bleaching of the exposed benches]

bleaching powder *n* a white powder obtained from calcium hydroxide and chlorine. Use: disinfectant, bleaching agent. Formula: CaCl(OCl).

bleak /bleek/ *adj* **1.** DISCOURAGING without hope or expectation of success or improvement ○ *The company's future looks bleak.* **2.** UNWELCOMING providing little comfort or shelter ○ *a cabin on a bleak hilltop* **3.** COLD AND CLOUDY unpleasantly cold, dull, and windy ○ *bleak winter days* [14C. < Old Norse *bleikr* 'pale, white, shining' < Germanic] —**bleakly** *adv* —**bleakness** *n*

CULTURAL NOTE ***Bleak House***, a novel (1852–53) by Charles Dickens. Among the strands of the complex plot are the interminable court case of Jarndyce and Jarndyce; the guilty secret of Lady Dedlock and the tragic consequences of her discovery that her illegitimate daughter, Esther Summerson, is still alive; and Esther's relationship with her kindly and devoted guardian John Jarndyce. The novel combines the excitement of a murder mystery with a bitter satire of the legal system.

blear /bleer/ (**blears, blearing, bleared**) *vt* to make eyes misty or eyesight dim, e.g. with tears (*archaic or literary; usually passive*) [14C. Origin ?]

bleary /bleéri/ (**-ier, -iest**) *adj* **1.** not seeing clearly owing to mistiness or blurring, especially that associated with sleepiness ○ *a bleary gaze* **2.** obscured and not easy to see —**blearily** *adv* —**bleariness** *n*

bleary-eyed *adj* seeing unclearly, especially because of sleepiness or drunkenness

Bleasdale /bléez dayl/, **Alan** (*b.* 1946) British dramatist. His British television dramas include *The Boys from the Blackstuff* (1982).

bleat /bleet/ (**bleats, bleating, bleated**) *vi* **1.** to make the wavering cry of a sheep, goat, or calf **2.** to complain about something in an irritating way (*informal*) [Old English *blǣtan* < Germanic, an imitation of the sound] —**bleat** *n* —**bleater** *n*

bleb /bleb/ *n* **1.** a small blister on the skin **2.** a small bubble, e.g. in glass [Early 17C. Alteration of BLOB] —**blebby** *adj*

bleed /bleed/ *v* (**bleeds, bleeding, bled** /bled/, **bled**) **1.** *vi* LOSE BLOOD to lose blood from the body, through a wound or because of illness ○ *The wound was bleeding heavily.* **2.** *vt* TAKE BLOOD FROM PERSON OR ANIMAL to take blood from a person or animal, especially in order to treat a disease **3.** *vi* FEEL SORROW to feel sadness or pity ○ *My heart bleeds for her in her loss.* **4.** *vi* EXUDE SAP to exude sap from a wound (*refers to plants*) **5.** *vt* TAKE MONEY OR RESOURCES FROM SOMEBODY to use up large amounts of money or resources from a person or organization, especially dishonestly (*informal*) **6.** *vt* DRAW LIQUID OR GAS FROM SOMETHING to draw liquid or gas out of a container or pressurized system ○ *bleed a radiator* **7.** *vi* RELEASE COLOUR to release colour when wet or being washed (*refers to fabrics*) **8.** *vti* PRINTING OVERRUN PAGE to print something, or be printed, so that part of it is cut off by the edge of the page **9.** *vti* PRINTING MAKE COLOURS OF ILLUSTRATION RUN to print something, or be printed, so that colours run into other colours or over the edge of an illustration ■ *n* **1.** INSTANCE OF BLEEDING an instance of losing blood **2.** PRINTING SOMETHING THAT OVERRUNS PRINTED PAGE an illustration or piece of text printed in such a way that part of it is cut off the page [Old English *blēdan* < Germanic]

bleeder /bléedər/ *n* **1.** an offensive term for somebody who is disliked (*slang*) **2.** a blood vessel that bleeds during surgery and requires clamping or other measures to stop it

bleeder resistor *n* a resistor connected across the terminals of a power supply to regulate its output voltage or to discharge capacitors

bleeding /bléeding/ *n* loss of blood from the body as a result of illness or injury ■ *adj, adv* used for emphasis, as a milder form of 'bloody' (*slang*)

bleeding-edge *adj* relating to innovative technology that has yet to be thoroughly tested for feasibility (*informal*) [Suggested by LEADING EDGE and the risk involved in innovation]

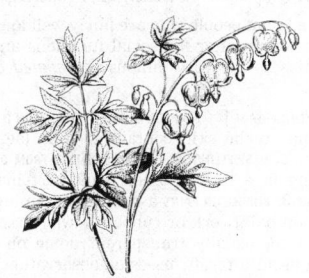

bleeding heart

bleeding heart *n* **1.** a garden plant with arching stems. Flowers: pink, red, white, heart-shaped. Genus: *Dicentra*. **2.** somebody regarded as naively kind or sympathetic, especially towards left-wing or liberal causes

bleed valve *n* a valve that can be opened to let liquid or gas out of a tank or pressurized system, often used for safety purposes to release small amounts of excess fluid or gas

bleep /bleep/ *n* **1.** ELECTRONIC SOUND a short high-pitched electronic noise, intended as a signal and repeated intermittently **2.** COMMUNICATION same as **pager** ■ *v* (**bleeps, bleeping, bleeped**) **1.** *vi* MAKE ELECTRONIC SOUND to make a short high-pitched electronic noise **2.** *vt* CALL SOMEBODY ON BLEEPER to call somebody by sending a signal to a portable electronic receiver **3.** *vt N Am* BROADCAST same as **bleep out** [Mid-20C. An imitation of the sound]
    bleep out *vt* to remove an offensive word from a

broadcast, and replace it with a short high-pitched electronic sound. N Am term **bleep**

bleeper /bléepər/ *n* TELECOM same as **pager**

blemish /blémmish/ *n* **1.** SPOILING MARK OR FLAW a mark or imperfection that spoils the appearance of something ○ *a cream that hides skin blemishes* **2.** SPOILING FAULT something that spoils somebody's reputation or good record ■ *vt* (**-ishes, -ishing, -ished**) MAR to spoil the appearance or reputation of something [14C. < Old French *ble(s)miss-* 'make pale, injure']

SYNONYMS See *flaw*[1].

blench[1] /blench/ (**blenches, blenching, blenched**) *vi* to move back or away in fear [Old English *blencan* 'deceive, cheat', origin ?] —**blencher** *n*

blench[2] /blench/ *vi* COOK, GARDENING same as **blanch**

blend /blend/ *v* (**blends, blending, blended**) **1.** *vti* MIX INGREDIENTS to mix a substance with another substance so that the two do not readily separate ○ *blend the butter and sugar together* **2.** *vt* CREATE PRODUCT BY MIXING DIFFERENT TYPES to create a food or drink by mixing different types of the same substance (*often passive*) ○ *blended tea* **3.** *vti* INTERMINGLE to mix with other people or things without being conspicuous, or mix something in this way ○ *blend fact and fiction* **4.** *vti* MAKE PLEASING COMBINATION to combine things or qualities to create a pleasing effect, or be combined in this way ○ *instruments blending harmoniously* **5.** *vi* SHADE IMPERCEPTIBLY INTO EACH OTHER to shade from one colour to another without obvious transitions or boundaries ■ *n* **1.** MIXTURE something formed by using together two or more things of different types ○ *an interesting blend of traditional styles and modern materials* **2.** FOOD OR DRINK MIXTURE a food or drink created by mixing different types of the same substance ○ *an expensive coffee blend* **3.** WORD MADE BY JOINING TWO WORDS a new word made by joining parts of other words, as in 'telex', formed from 'teleprinter' and 'exchange' [14C. Probably < Old Norse *blend-* 'to mix']

SYNONYMS See *mixture*.

blend in *vi* **1.** to have personal qualities that suit a situation well ○ *He's a likable boy who blends in well.* **2.** to be difficult to see or distinguish from similar things around

blende /blend/ *n* **1.** MINERALS same as **sphalerite 2.** a metallic sulphide ore [Late 17C. < German *blenden* 'deceive']

blender /bléndər/ *n* **1.** an electrical kitchen appliance used to liquidize and blend foods **2.** somebody or something that blends things, especially a person or company that blends foods or drinks

Blenheim[1] /blénnim/ *n* a dog belonging to a breed of spaniel with reddish markings [< *Blenheim* Palace in Oxfordshire]

Blenheim[2] /blénnim/ **1.** site of the Battle of Blenheim in 1704, where an English army, led by the 1st Duke of Marlborough, defeated French and Bavarian troops in the War of the Spanish Succession. It is near the present-day village of Blindheim, southwestern Germany. **2.** wine-producing borough in the Wairau Valley in the South Island of New Zealand. Population: 26,550 (2001).

blenny /blénni/ *n* (*plural* **-nies** *or* **same**) *n* a small scaleless long-bodied fish found in rocky coastal areas and coral reefs. Family: Blenniidae. [Mid-18C. < Latin *blennius* < Greek *blennos* 'slime', from the fish's covering of mucus]

blepharitis /bléffə rítiss/ *n* inflammation of one or both eyelids [Mid-19C. < Greek *blepharon* 'eyelid']

Blériot /blérri ō/, **Louis** (1872–1936) French aviator. He was the first person to fly across the English Channel (1909).

blesbok /bléss bok/ (*plural* **-boks** *or* **same**) *n* a reddish-brown antelope that has a white streak on its nose. Native to: southern Africa. Latin name: *Damaliscus dorcas*. [Early 19C. < Afrikaans < Dutch *bles* 'white facial streak' + *bok* 'buck']

bless /bless/ (**blesses, blessing, blessed, blessed** *or* **blest** /blest/) *vt* **1.** MAKE SOMEBODY OR SOMETHING HOLY to bestow holiness on somebody or something in a religious ceremony ○ *The bishop blessed the new chapel.* **2.** PROTECT SOMEBODY OR SOMETHING to watch over somebody or something protectively ○ *We prayed for God to*

blesbok

bless our marriage. **3.** WISH SOMEBODY OR SOMETHING WELL to declare approval and support for somebody or something ○ *The governor has blessed the new scheme.* **4.** CONFER DESIRABLE QUALITY ON SOMEBODY to give somebody a desirable quality or talent (*usually passive*) ○ *blessed with brains as well as good looks* **5.** THANK SOMEBODY to express heart-felt thanks to somebody (*often expressing a wish*) ○ *Bless you for speaking up for my child!* [Old English *blētsian* < Germanic] —**blesser** *n*

blessed /bléssid/ *adj* **1.** HOLY made holy **2.** BEATIFIED declared holy by the pope, usually as the first stage towards being declared a saint **3.** BESTOWING JOY bringing happiness or good luck ○ *The rain has brought farmers blessed relief from the long drought.* ■ *adj, adv* USED FOR EMPHASIS used to add emphasis in an expression of annoyance (*informal*) ○ *She wouldn't say a blessed thing about it.* —**blessedly** *adv* —**blessedness** *n*

Blessed Sacrament *n* in various Christian churches, the bread and wine that has been blessed for use in Communion

Blessed Virgin Mary, Blessed Virgin *n* a title for Mary, the mother of Jesus Christ, used mainly in Catholic churches

blessing /bléssing/ *n* **1.** GOD'S HELP help believed to come from God or another deity **2.** RELIGIOUS ACT a ceremony in which an ordained person invokes or claims to bestow divine help **3.** PRAYER BEFORE MEAL a prayer of thanks before a meal **4.** APPROVAL approval or good wishes **5.** SOMETHING FORTUNATE something to be glad or relieved about ○ *It's a blessing that you came so quickly.*

blest past participle of **bless**

blether /bléthər/ (*informal*) *vi* UK same as **blather** ■ *n* **1.** *UK* same as **blather 2.** *Scotland* somebody who talks in an unintelligent or inane manner, especially at length

bletherskite *n* same as **blatherskite** (*dated informal*)

blew[1] past tense of **blow**[1]

blew[2] past tense of **blow**[3]

blewits /bloo its/ (*plural same*) *n* an edible fungus with a brown cap and a bluish stem. Genus: *Lepista*. (*takes a singular verb*) [Early 19C. Probably < variant of BLUE, from the colour of its stem]

Bligh /blī/, **William** (1754–1817) British naval officer. Cast adrift in the Pacific by mutineers of the HMS *Bounty* (1789), he navigated nearly 4,000 miles in an open boat to reach Timor. He was promoted to rear admiral in 1811 and vice admiral in 1814.

blight /blīt/ *n* **1.** DESTRUCTIVE FORCE something that spoils or damages things severely **2.** RUINED STATE a severely spoiled or ruined state, especially of an urban area ○ *urban blight* **3.** PLANT DISEASE a plant disease, caused by bacteria, fungi, or viruses, in which symptoms range from brownish blotches on the foliage to withering of the entire plant without rotting **4.** AGRIC same as **potato blight** ■ *vt* (**blights, blighting, blighted**) **1.** RUIN SOMETHING to spoil or damage something severely ○ *a football career blighted by injury* **2.** PLANTS, BOT AFFECT PLANT WITH BLIGHT to cause a plant to wither without rotting [Mid-16C. Origin ?]

blighter /blītər/ *n* **1.** somebody or something considered a source of annoyance (*dated informal insult*) **2.** somebody who is envied or sympathized with (*dated informal*) ○ *poor little blighter* ○ *lucky blighter*

Blighty /blīti/, **blighty** *n* UK England or Great Britain

(*slang dated humorous*) [Early 20C. < Hindi *bilāyatī* 'foreign, European', originally used by British soldiers in India for 'home']

blimey /blīmi/ *interj* used to express amazement or shock (*informal*) ○ *Blimey, that's expensive!* [Late 19C. Alteration of *blind me!* or *blame me!*]

blimp[1] /blimp/ *n* a nonrigid airship, especially one used as a barrage balloon or for observation during World War II [Early 20C. Origin ?]

blimp[2] /blimp/, **Colonel Blimp** *n* somebody, typically a middle-aged military officer, who is pompous and very conservative (*humorous*) [Mid-20C. After a cartoon character invented by David Low (1891–1963)]

blin FOOD plural of **blini**

blind /blīnd/ *adj* **1.** UNABLE TO SEE unable to see, permanently or temporarily **2.** UNABLE TO RECOGNIZE unwilling or unable to understand something ○ *blind to the consequences* **3.** UNCONTROLLABLE so extreme and uncontrollable as to make somebody behave irrationally ○ *blind rage* ○ *blind fear* **4.** UNQUESTIONING not based on fact and usually total and unquestioning ○ *blind prejudice* **5.** UNAWARE lacking awareness ○ *a blind stupor* **6.** NOT GIVING CLEAR VIEW not providing a clear view and possibly dangerous ○ *a blind corner* **7.** HANDICRAFT MADE ON UNDERSIDE OF FABRIC hidden from sight on the underside of a fabric **8.** WITHOUT DOORS OR WINDOWS without doors, windows, or openings ○ *a blind wall* **9.** CLOSED AT ONE END closed off at one end ○ *a blind unused tunnel* **10.** DONE WITHOUT LOOKING done without looking or while unable to see ○ *blind taste tests* **11.** DONE UNPREPARED done without preparation or the relevant information ○ *a blind presentation* **12.** DESIGNED TO BE BIAS-FREE describes scientific experiments or similar evaluations in which information is withheld in order to obtain an unprejudiced result ○ *a blind trial* **13.** BOT WITHOUT GROWING POINT describes a plant in which growth stops because the growing point has been damaged, perhaps by pests, nutrient deficiency, waterlogging of the soil, or drought ■ *adv* **1.** WITHOUT PRIOR EXAMINATION OR PREPARATION without previously thinking about or preparing for something ○ *You shouldn't buy livestock blind.* **2.** AVIAT USING ONLY INSTRUMENTS using information from aircraft instruments, without being able to see ○ *flying blind* **3.** TOTALLY totally or utterly (*informal*) ○ *an unscrupulous lawyer who robbed his clients blind* ■ *vt* (**blinds, blinding, blinded**) **1.** MAKE SOMEBODY PERMANENTLY BLIND to make somebody permanently unable to see **2.** MAKE SOMEBODY TEMPORARILY BLIND to make somebody temporarily unable to see ○ *blinded by the light* **3.** MAKE SOMEBODY UNABLE TO JUDGE PROPERLY to make somebody unable to judge or act rationally ○ *blinded by rage* **4.** CONFUSE SOMEBODY to make it difficult for somebody to understand something ○ *Stop trying to blind us with statistics.* ■ *n* **1.** WINDOW COVERING a device that is pulled down to shut out the light from a window **2.** COVER OR SUBTERFUGE something that is intended to conceal the true nature of somebody's activities **3.** *ANZ, N Am* FIELD SPORTS same as **hide**[1] [Old English, < Indo-European, 'confusion, obscurity'] —**blindly** *adv* —**blindness** *n*

blind alley *n* **1.** a narrow alley or passage that is closed off at one end **2.** something that produces no worthwhile results

blind bat *n regional* a bat [< the popular misconception that bats are blind]

REGIONAL NOTE See ***bat***[3].

blind certificate *n* in e-commerce, a means of tracking visitors to websites anonymously by identifying the user's system but not his or her name

blind date *n* **1.** a date arranged between people who have not seen or met each other before **2.** somebody whom you meet on a blind date

blinder /blīndər/ *n* (*informal*) **1.** something outstanding, especially a performance in a sport **2.** a bout of excessive drinking ■ **blinders** *npl N Am* HORSERACING same as **blinkers** (sense 1; *see* **blinker**)

blindfold /blīnd fōld/ *n* BANDAGE TIED OVER EYES a piece of cloth tied over the eyes to prevent the wearer from seeing ■ *vt* (**-folds, -folding, -folded**) **1.** PUT BANDAGE OVER EYES OF SOMEBODY to prevent somebody from seeing by putting a bandage or other material over the person's eyes **2.** PREVENT SOMEBODY FROM UNDERSTANDING to prevent somebody from understanding clearly ■ *adj* WITH BLINDFOLD wearing a blindfold ■ *adv* **1.** WHILE BLINDFOLDED wearing a blindfold or being unable to see for some other reason **2.** UNPREPARED without consideration or relevant information ○ *had to field their queries blindfold* [Early 16C. By folk etymology (< FOLD[1]) < past tense of obsolete *blindfell* 'make unable to see']

Blind Freddie /-fréddi/, **Blind Freddy** *n Aus* an offensive term for a hypothetical person who represents incompetence and lack of intelligence

blind gut *n* ANAT same as **caecum**

blinding /blīnding/ *adj* **1.** IMPAIRING VISION causing inability to see, especially temporarily, by being bright ○ *a blinding flash of light* **2.** OUTSTANDING outstanding or extraordinary (*informal*) ■ *n* BASE LAYER OF CONCRETE a thin layer of concrete used to seal a surface before more concrete is added —**blindingly** *adv*

blind man's buff *n* a children's game in which one player is blindfolded and has to catch and identify other players by touch [*Buff* shortening of BUFFET[2] 'stroke with the hand']

blind side *n* **1.** the area that is out of your field of vision ○ *The cyclist came up on my blind side.* **2.** in rugby, the side of the field that lies between a scrum and the nearer touchline

blindside /blīnd sīd/ (**-sides, -siding, -sided**) *vt N Am* **1.** to attack somebody suddenly and physically by hitting the person on a side where his or her peripheral vision is obstructed **2.** to take somebody unawares suddenly, with detrimental results to that person

blind snake *n* a small nonvenomous snake with scales over its eyes, adapted for burrowing and eating small soil invertebrates. There are many species. Native to: tropical regions. Families: Typhlopidae or Leptotyphlopidae or Anomalepididae.

blind spot *n* **1.** ANAT same as **optic disc** **2.** AREA OF IGNORANCE a subject that somebody is ignorant about ○ *have a blind spot for maths* **3.** DIRECTION IN WHICH VISION IS OBSCURED an area or direction, especially on a road, in which somebody's vision is obscured **4.** ACOUSTICS ACOUSTICALLY UNSATISFACTORY AREA an area in an auditorium where things cannot be heard clearly **5.** BROADCAST PLACE WITH POOR RADIO RECEPTION an area within the normal range of a radio transmitter where reception is poor

blind trust *n* a legal arrangement in which a trustee manages funds for the benefit of somebody who has no knowledge of the specific management actions taken by the trustee

blindworm /blīnd wurm/ *n* REPT same as **slowworm** [15C. < the animal's small eyes]

bling bling /blíng blíng/, **bling** (*slang*) *adj* RICH having or displaying ostentatious material wealth ■ *n* (*originally used in Black English*) **1.** JEWELLERY OR TRINKETS jewellery or similar expensive shiny objects **2.** OBVIOUS WEALTH ostentatious material wealth [Probably an imitation of the sound of a cash register]

blini /blínni, bleéni/ (*plural* **blinis** or **blin** /blin/ or *same*) *n* a small pancake made with yeast and buckwheat flour, traditional in Russia and other parts of Eastern Europe [Late 20C. < Russian *bliný*, plural (singular *blin*)]

blink /blingk/ *v* (**blinks, blinking, blinked**) **1.** *vti* CLOSE AND REOPEN EYES to close and reopen both eyes rapidly **2.** *vti* LOOK WHILE BLINKING to look at somebody or something while blinking **3.** *vt* REMOVE SOMETHING BY BLINKING to open and shut the eyes rapidly to remove something from them ○ *He blinked away his tears.* **4.** *vi* FLASH to flash on and off, especially as a signal **5.** *vi N Am* WAVER to waver from a course of action ○ *After a ten-week strike, it was the management that finally blinked.* ■ *n* **1.** ACT OF BLINKING EYES a rapid closing and reopening of both eyes **2.** *Scotland* QUICK LOOK a quick look or glance **3.** METEOROL same as **iceblink, snowblink** [13C. Partly variant of BLENCH[1], partly < Middle Dutch *blinken* 'glitter'] ◇ **on the blink** not working properly (*informal*) ○ *The television's on the blink.*

blinker /blíngkər/ *n* FLASHING LIGHT a light that flashes in order to give a message or warning, especially on a motor vehicle. Blinkers were used to send coded messages, especially between ships, to avoid interception of radio signals during World Wars I and II. ■ **blinkers** *npl* **1.** EYE COVERS FOR HORSE a pair of flaps attached to a horse's bridle, one beside each eye, to keep the horse from looking anywhere but straight ahead. N Am term **blinders** (*see* **blinder**) **2.** OBSTRUCTION TO JUDGMENT a mental attitude that prevents somebody from considering a situation rationally ■ *vt* (**-ers, -ering, -ered**) **1.** FIT HORSE WITH BLINKERS to put blinkers on a horse **2.** STOP SOMEBODY FROM JUDGING SITUATION PROPERLY to prevent somebody from considering a situation rationally

blinkered /blíngkərd/ *adj* **1.** unable or unwilling to understand anything outside a very narrow range ○ *took a very blinkered attitude* **2.** wearing blinkers —**blinkeredness** *n*

blinking /blíngking/ *adj* used to add force to an insult or an expression of annoyance (*slang*) ○ *I don't want the blinking thing!* —**blinking** *adv*

blinking green light *n* a tentative affirmative decision on a matter, contingent upon future developments (*slang*) ○ *When I came on board as screenwriter, the project had a blinking green light.*

blintz /blints/, **blintze** /blíntsə/ *n* a pancake folded round a filling and then baked or fried [Early 20C. Via Yiddish *blintse* < Russian *blinets* 'little pancake' < *blin* 'pancake']

blip /blip/ *n* **1.** SPOT ON DISPLAY SCREEN a spot of light, often accompanied by a high-pitched sound, indicating the position of something on a screen ○ *The submarine shows up as a series of faint blips on the screen.* **2.** ELECTRONICS same as **bleep** *n* (sense 1) **3.** SUDDEN DEVIATION a sudden temporary problem in the normal progress of something ■ *vi* (**blips, blipping, blipped**) MAKE BLIP to produce a blip [Late 19C. An imitation of the sound]

bliss /bliss/ *n* **1.** perfect happiness ○ *It was bliss to have a day at home.* **2.** a state of spiritual joy [Old English, alteration of *blīþs* < Germanic, 'gentle, kind']

CULTURAL NOTE ***Bliss***, a novel (1981) by Australian writer Peter Carey. A fable about the battle between good and evil, it tells the story of advertising executive Harry Joy who, after a successful heart bypass operation, becomes convinced that he has woken up in Hell. It was made into a film by Ray Lawrence in 1985.

Bliss /bliss/, **Sir Arthur** (1891–1975) British composer. He was Master of the Queen's Musick (1953–75) and wrote ballets, operas, and chamber music. Full name **Bliss, Sir Arthur Edward Drummond**

blissful /blíssf'l/ *adj* **1.** characterized by perfect happiness ○ *a look of blissful contentment* **2.** serenely happy because of being unaware of something ○ *blissful ignorance* —**blissfully** *adv* —**blissfulness** *n*

B list *n* a list of people who are fairly well known but not as sought after for social functions and other activities as the very famous (*hypenated before a noun*)

blister /blístər/ *n* **1.** MED PAINFUL SWELLING ON SKIN a painful swelling on the skin containing fluid (**serum**) **2.** PLANTS, BOT SWELLING ON PLANT RESULTING FROM DISEASE a swelling in a leaf or other plant part indicating disease **3.** BUBBLE ON PAINT a bubble containing liquid or air on paintwork or rubber **4.** AVIAT AIRCRAFT DOME a rounded, usually transparent dome on the fuselage of an aircraft, used for observation **5.** *ANZ* SHARP COMMUNICATION a strongly worded, usually official, written report (*informal*) **6.** *NZ* COURT SUMMONS a summons to attend court (*informal*) ■ *vti* (**-ters, -tering, -tered**) FORM BLISTERS to be raised in a blister or blisters, or to cause blisters to form on something [14C. Origin ?] —**blistery** *adj*

blister beetle *n* a soft-bodied beetle that secretes for its own defence a substance that raises burning blisters on the skin of vertebrates. Family: Meloidae.

blistering /blístəring/ *adj* **1.** extremely hot **2.** extremely scornful or critical ○ *a blistering attack on the government's failures* —**blisteringly** *adv*

blister pack *n* a packet in which small items such as pills are contained in raised domes of plastic

BLit /beé lít/ *abbr* Bachelor of Literature [Latin *Baccalaureus Litterarum*]

blithe /blīth/ *adj* **1.** happy, cheerful, and carefree **2.** casually indifferent ○ *with a blithe disregard for anyone's feelings* [Old English *blīþe* < Germanic, 'gentle, kind'] —**blithely** *adv* —**blitheness** *n*

blither /blíthər/ *vi* same as **blather** (*informal*) [Mid-19C. Variant]

blithering /blíthəring/ *adj* used to express annoyance with and contempt for somebody or something (*informal*) ○ *It's a blithering nuisance.*

blithe spirit *n* somebody whose characteristic mood is one of carefree happiness (*used approvingly*)

BLitt /bee lít/ *abbr* Bachelor of Literature [Latin *Baccalaureus Litterarum*]

blitz /blits/ *n* **1.** MIL **SUSTAINED AERIAL ATTACK** a heavy air raid intended to obliterate a target **2.** MIL same as **blitzkrieg 3. CONCERTED EFFORT** a concentrated effort to get something done (*informal*) **4.** AMERICAN FOOTBALL **CHARGE ON PASSER** in American football, a direct attack on the passer, by one or more players who usually stay behind the line of scrimmage, to try to prevent a pass ■ *v* (**blitzes, blitzing, blitzed**) **1.** *vt* MIL **DESTROY SOMETHING BY AERIAL BOMBING** to attack or destroy a target by bombardment from the air **2.** *vt* **DEFEAT SOMEBODY COMPREHENSIVELY** to defeat a person or team overwhelmingly in a competition, especially a sports event **3.** *vt* **DEAL WITH SOMETHING ENERGETICALLY** to concentrate a lot of effort on something to get it done (*informal*) **4.** *vt* **TRY TO OVERWHELM SOMEBODY** to subject somebody to an overwhelming amount of something, often in order to force him or her into agreement or submission (*informal*) ○ *blitzed with a stream of facts* **5.** *vti* AMERICAN FOOTBALL **CHARGE PASSER** in American football, to charge the passer in order to prevent a pass [Mid-20C. Shortening of BLITZKRIEG]

Blitz *n* the intensive bombing of British cities by the German Air Force between 1940 and 1941

blitzkrieg /blíts kreeg/ *n* a swift military offensive using ground and air forces [Mid-20C. < German, 'lightning war']

Blixen /blíks'n/, **Karen** ▸ **Dinesen, Isak**

blizzard /blízzərd/ *n* a severe snowstorm with strong winds and poor visibility [Early 19C. Origin ?]

blk *abbr* **1.** block **2.** bulk

BLL *abbr* Bachelor of Laws [Latin *Baccalaureus Legum*]

bloat /blōt/ *vti* (**bloats, bloating, bloated**) **1. SWELL** to become swollen or inflated, or make something do this **2. EXCESSIVELY EXPAND** to increase excessively, or make something do this ■ *n* **1.** *N Am* **EXCESSIVE INCREASE** an excessive amount, or an excessive increase in something ○ *corporate bloat* **2.** VET **CATTLE DISEASE** a disease affecting cattle and sheep, characterized by excessive gas in the main stomach compartment (**rumen**) [Early 17C. Probably < Old Norse *blautr* 'soft, wet']

bloated /blōtid/ *adj* **1. SWOLLEN** swollen with liquid, air, or gas **2. OVERFULL AFTER OVEREATING** overfull and feeling uncomfortable after eating too much **3. TOO LARGE** excessively large ○ *a bloated expense account* —**bloatedness** *n*

bloater /blōtər/ *n* **1.** a large herring that has been soaked in brine and smoked **2.** a common freshwater whitefish. Native to: Great Lakes of North America. Latin name: *Coregonus hoyi.* [Mid-19C. < obsolete *bloat herring*, origin ?]

bloatware /blṓt wair/ *n* a computer program with many, often superfluous features that take up so much memory that the computer's performance is impaired (*informal*) [Late 20C. After SOFTWARE]

blob /blob/ *n* **1. SOFT MASS** a soft lump or drop of something such as paint or glue **2. SMALL SPOT OF COLOUR** a small rounded spot of colour **3. INDISTINCT FORM** an indistinct or shapeless form or object ■ *vt* (**blobs, blobbing, blobbed**) **PUT BLOBS ON SOMETHING** to apply blobs of colour or a soft substance to something [15C. Origin ?]

bloc /blok/ *n* a group of countries or political parties with a shared aim ○ *former Eastern bloc countries* ○ *a 12-nation trading bloc* [Early 20C. < French (see BLOCK)]

SPELLCHECK bloc or **block**? Do not confuse the spelling of ***bloc*** and ***block***, which sound similar. A ***bloc*** is a group of countries or political parties with a common aim. The word ***block*** has a much wider range of meanings and uses: as a noun it may denote a lump, a square object, a large building, or an obstruction (as in *a block of wood, an office block*); as a verb it principally means 'obstruct' (as in *roads blocked by snow*).

Bloch /blok/, **Ernest** (1880–1959) Swiss-born US composer. He incorporated themes from Jewish music in such works as his symphony *Israel* (1912–16).

block /blok/ *n* **1. SOLID LUMP** a large solid piece of a hard substance, usually with flat sides **2.** CONSTR **BUILDING UNIT** a large flat-sided piece of hard material such as stone or wood, used in building **3.** LEISURE same as **brick** *n* (sense 3) **4. CHOPPING BASE** a large piece of wood used for chopping things on **5.** PRINTING **PRINTING DEVICE** a piece of wood, metal, or stone with a design engraved on it, used for printing **6. PLACE FOR BEHEADING PEOPLE** a large piece of wood or stone on which people were beheaded in former times **7. AUCTIONEER'S PLATFORM** a stand on which articles in an auction are displayed **8.** SPORTS same as **starting block 9. PAD OF PAPER** a pad of writing or drawing paper **10. LARGE BUILDING** a building divided into offices or flats **11. SPECIAL-PURPOSE BUILDING** a building or part of a building designed for a particular purpose ○ *the new science block* **12. GROUP OF BUILDINGS** a group of buildings in a town or city bounded on each side by a street ○ *I'm just taking the dog for a walk round the block.* **13.** *N Am* **STREET SECTION** the section of a street between two parallel streets ○ *The post office is in the middle of the next block.* **14.** *US* **DISTANCE** the distance between two parallel streets ○ *They live only three blocks from here.* **15.** *ANZ* **AREA OF RURAL LAND** a large area of rural land, or one offered to somebody by a government **16.** *ANZ* **LAND AREA** an area of land marked for development **17.** *NZ* **AREA OF LAND FOR HUNTING** an area of land over which a hunter is licensed to kill animals **18. UNBROKEN EXPANSE OR AREA** a uniform expanse of something such as colour **19. SET OF SIMILAR ITEMS** a set of similar items sold as a unit ○ *a block of tickets* **20.** STAMPS **GROUP OF POSTAGE STAMPS** a group of four or more postage stamps forming a rectangle **21.** RAIL **LENGTH OF TRACK** a length of railway track on which only one train is permitted at a time **22.** COMPUT **UNIT OF DATA** in computing, a set of contiguous data that performs some action as a unit ○ *a block of text* **23.** POL another spelling of **bloc 24. OBSTRUCTION** something that obstructs or prevents progress **25.** SPORTS **OBSTRUCTION OF PLAY** in some sports, an act of deliberately preventing a ball or another player from moving forward **26.** CRICKET **DEFENSIVE STROKE** in cricket, a defensive stroke made by a batsman, intended only to stop the ball **27.** CRICKET **BATSMAN'S MARK ON CREASE** in cricket, a mark made by a batsman near the popping crease to indicate the position of the bat in relation to the wicket **28.** MED **OBSTRUCTION OF PHYSIOLOGICAL FUNCTION** an interruption of the normal functioning of an organ of the body **29. DISRUPTION OF PSYCHOLOGICAL PROCESSES** an inability to begin or continue a psychological process, often attributed to emotional stress ○ *I forgot – I must have had a mental block.* ■ *v* (**blocks, blocking, blocked**) **1.** *vt* **OBSTRUCT MOVEMENT** to prevent or restrict movement through, into, or out of something ○ *The drains are blocked with leaves.* ○ *He stood in front of me, blocking my way.* **2.** *vt* **HINDER PROGRESS OF SOMETHING** to prevent something from taking place ○ *Her appointment was blocked by the managing director.* **3.** *vt* **OBSTRUCT SIGHT OF SOMETHING** to obstruct somebody's line of sight ○ *blocking my view* **4.** *vti* SPORTS **OBSTRUCT PLAYER OR BALL** in some sports, to prevent a ball or another player from moving forward **5.** *vti* MED **PREVENT NORMAL PHYSIOLOGICAL FUNCTIONING** to prevent the normal functioning of a physiological process ○ *a blocked tear duct* **6.** *vt* **FAIL TO REMEMBER** to fail to remember something, or prevent a memory from being recalled ○ *could not block the memory of the accident* **7.** *vt* **MAKE SOMETHING INTO BLOCK** to shape something into a block **8.** *vt* **SUPPORT SOMETHING WITH BLOCK** to support or strengthen something using a block **9.** *vt* **SHAPE SOMETHING ON BLOCK** to mould something with or on a block **10.** *vt* PRINTING **STAMP SOMETHING USING BLOCK** to stamp a surface with a title or using an engraved block **11.** *vt* THEATRE **REHEARSE BASIC MOVEMENTS FOR SCENE** to plan and rehearse the basic movements and positions for the actors in a scene [14C. Via Old French *bloc* < Middle Dutch *blok* 'tree trunk'] ◇ **knock somebody's block off** to punch somebody in the head (*slang*) ◇ **on the block** *N Am* for sale at an auction

SPELLCHECK See ***bloc.***

SYNONYMS See ***hinder***[1].

block in *vt* **1.** to prevent somebody or something moving from a place by being in the way or by placing something in the way **2.** to fill in the blank spaces on an outline design with colour

block off *vt* **1.** to put up or form a barrier in front of something in order to prevent anybody or anything entering ○ *Police blocked off the street.* **2.** to put up or form a barrier that prevents something from being seen

block out *vt* **1. PUT THOUGHT OUT OF MIND** to prevent a disturbing thought from entering the mind **2. DESCRIBE SOMETHING WITHOUT DETAIL** to describe something in a general fashion, without great detail ○ *block out a proposal* **3.** PHOTOGRAPHY **COVER PART OF NEGATIVE** to cover part of a negative or stencil when printing from it to prevent that part appearing

block up *vti* to prevent movement through something by filling in all the space, or become completely obstructed

blockade /blo káyd/ *n* **1. PREVENTION OF ACCESS** an organized action to prevent people or goods entering or leaving a place **2. FORCES FORMING BLOCKADE** the ships or forces used to maintain a blockade **3. OBSTACLE OR OBSTRUCTION** something that prevents access to a place ■ *vt* (**-ades, -ading, -aded**) **1. SUBJECT PLACE TO BLOCKADE** to impose a blockade on a place **2. BLOCK ACCESS TO PLACE** to obstruct access to a place [Late 17C. Perhaps after AMBUSCADE] —**blockader** *n*

blockage /blókij/ *n* **1.** something that obstructs movement through a pipe or channel ○ *a blockage in an artery* **2.** the act of blocking something

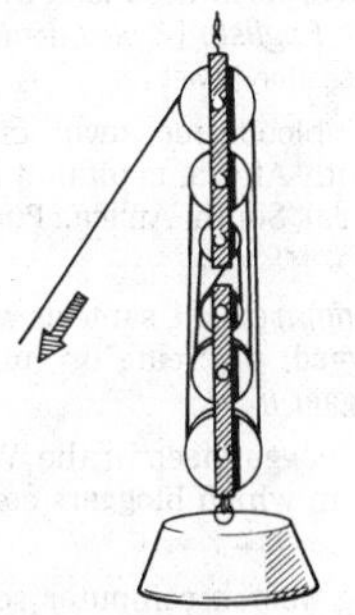

block and tackle

block and tackle (*plural* **blocks and tackles**) *n* a system of two pulley blocks, each with at least one pulley with rope or cable threaded through, used for hoisting or hauling. The greater the number of pulleys, the greater the weight that can be raised by the same force on the rope or cable.

blockboard /blók bawrd/ *n* a plywood composed of soft wood squares or strips between outer layers of veneer. The direction of grain of the wood strips is perpendicular to that of the veneer.

block booking *n* a booking of a large number of tickets for the same event or show

blockbuster /blók bustər/ *n* **1. POPULAR SUCCESS** something such as a book, play, or film that is either very large or achieves enormous commercial success (*informal*) **2.** ARMS **HUGE DESTRUCTIVE BOMB** a large high-explosive bomb designed to demolish buildings over a large area (*dated*) **3.** *US* **PERSON WHO PRACTISES BLOCKBUSTING** somebody who persuades people to sell their houses by instilling fear of declining property values (*informal*)

blockbusting /blók busting/ *adj* sensational and enormously successful commercially ○ *a blockbusting novel* ■ *n US* the practice of persuading homeowners to sell their homes quickly at low prices for fear of declining property values (*informal*)

block capital *n* a plain capital letter that is not joined to other letters ○ *Fill in the form in block capitals.*

block diagram *n* a diagram in which the essential parts of a system or process are represented by labelled rectangles

blocker /blókər/ *n* **1.** a drug that prevents a physiological function **2.** in American football, an offensive player who tries to keep the defence from reaching the ball, kicker, or passer

block grant *n* a grant of money from the government to local authorities to spend on local services

blockhead /blók hed/ *n* somebody who is regarded as very unintelligent (*insult*)

blockhouse /blók howss/ (*plural* **-houses** /-howziz/) *n* **1.** a small military building with apertures to fire through, used as part of a defensive system or an observation post **2.** formerly in North America, a fort constructed from heavy wooden beams

block letter *n* **1.** PRINTING same as **block capital 2.** a compressed sans serif typeface or individual letter

block party *n N Am* a party for all the people who live on the same block or street

block plane *n* a small carpenter's plane with the blade at a low pitch. Use: cutting across the grain of wood.

block printing *n* printing from hand-carved or engraved blocks

block release *n* the release of employees, especially trainees, from work for a continuous period of time to enable them to attend short full-time educational courses at a college

block vote *n* a single vote by a representative, typically of a trade union, on behalf of the members of his or her organization, weighted according to the number of members

blocky /blóki/ (**-ier, -iest**) *adj* three-dimensional, boxy in shape, and seemingly solid

blodclaat /blúd klaat/, **bloodclot** /blúd klot/ *interj* a highly offensive term used as a swearword (*taboo*; *used in Black English*) [< *blod*, form of BLOOD + *claat*, form of CLOTH 'sanitary towel']

Bloemfontein /bloóm fon tayn/ city and judicial capital of South Africa, capital of Free State Province, in central South Africa. Population: 126,867 (1991).

blog /blog/ (*slang*) *n* ONLINE same as **weblog** ■ *vi* (**blogs, blogging, blogged**) to create or run a weblog [Contraction] —**blogger** *n*

blogosphere /blóggə sfeer/ *n* the World Wide Web environment in which bloggers communicate with each other

blogware /blóg wair/ *n* computer software tools for creating a weblog

Blois /blwaa/ capital of Loir-et-Cher Department in central France, on the River Loire, northeast of Tours. It is famous for its magnificent Renaissance chateau. Population: 49,171 (1999).

bloke /blōk/ *n* same as **man** *n* (sense 1) (*informal*) [Mid-19C. < Shelta]

blokeish /blōkish/, **blokish** *adj* relating to the stereotypical character, behaviour, or interests of men, especially when they are in all-male company (*informal*) —**blokeishness** *n*

blonde /blond/, **blond** *adj* **1.** FAIR yellowish or golden in colour **2.** FAIR-HAIRED AND LIGHT-SKINNED with fair hair and a light-coloured skin **3.** LIGHT COLOURED light-coloured, ranging from yellowish-brown to greyish-yellow ○ *blonde wood* ■ *n* FAIR-HAIRED PERSON a person with blonde hair [15C. Via French < medieval Latin *blundus* 'yellow'] —**blondness** *n*

USAGE blonde or **blond**? When describing the colour of somebody's hair, **blond** is normally used of a person of either sex: *Jane has blond hair.* When used as a noun to describe somebody directly, **blonde** is more common, both for a man or boy and a woman or girl: *He is blonde. Jane is blonde/is a blonde.*

Blondin /blóN dáN/, **Charles** (1824–97) French acrobat. He crossed Niagara Falls on a tightrope (1859). Born **Gravelet, Jean François**

blood /blud/ *n* **1.** RED FLUID CIRCULATING IN BODY the red fluid that is pumped from the heart and circulates around the bodies of humans and other vertebrates **2.** BODY FLUID OF INVERTEBRATES a liquid found in invertebrates that has functions similar to those of vertebrate blood **3.** BLOODSHED bloodshed or killing **4.** VITAL LIFE FORCE blood considered as a vital life force **5.** FAMILY OR KINSHIP family background or descent from an ancestor, especially when viewed as determining a person's character or appearance **6.** PURE BREEDING pure breeding in animals, especially horses **7.** MEMBERS OF GROUP people considered for their potential to strengthen and improve an organization (*informal*) ○ *bring in new blood* **8.** YOUNG MAN a fash-

ionable and wealthy young man, especially in the 18th and 19th centuries (*informal humorous*) ■ *vt* (**bloods, blooding, blooded**) **1.** MIL INITIATE TROOPS IN BATTLE to subject troops to their first experience of battle **2.** FIELD SPORTS LET DOG TASTE BLOOD to give a dog its first taste of the blood of a freshly killed animal in order to make it keen to hunt **3.** FIELD SPORTS SMEAR SOMEBODY WITH BLOOD to smear somebody's face with the blood of a hunted animal as an initiation into hunting [Old English *blōd* < Germanic] ◇ **be out for** *or* **after somebody's blood** to be intending to punish somebody ◇ **blood is thicker than water** family ties and loyalties take precedence over other relationships ◇ **have blood on your hands** to be responsible for somebody's death ◇ **in cold blood** deliberately, and in a way that shows a complete lack of emotion ○ *was murdered in cold blood* ◇ **make somebody's blood boil** to make somebody extremely angry ◇ **make somebody's blood run cold** to frighten or horrify somebody ◇ **spill blood** to wound or kill people ◇ **sweat blood** to make a great effort

blood-and-thunder *adj* full of melodramatic adventure and action (*informal*)

blood bank *n* **1.** a place where blood or blood plasma is stored for use in transfusion **2.** the blood or blood plasma stored in a blood bank

bloodbath /blúd baath/ (*plural* **-baths** /-baathz/) *n* a battle or fight characterized by mass killing

blood brother *n* either of two men or boys who have sworn mutual loyalty and friendship

blood clot *n* a thick mass of coagulated blood

blood count *n* **1.** a counting of the number of red and white blood cells and platelets in a given volume of blood **2.** the actual number of cells and platelets found in a blood count

bloodcurdling /blúd kurd'ling/ *adj* arousing extreme fear ○ *bloodcurdling screams*

blood donor *n* somebody who gives blood for use in transfusions

blood doping *n* the practice of reinjecting an athlete with his or her own red blood cells shortly before a competition in order to enhance performance. The practice is illegal in most organized competitions.

blooded /blúddid/ *adj* belonging to a superior breed ○ *blooded mares*

blood feud *n* a long-lasting feud between families or clans involving murder

bloodfin /blúd fin/ *n* a small red-finned freshwater fish, often kept in aquariums. Native to: Argentina. Latin name: *Aphyocharax rubripinnis*.

blood fluke *n* a parasitic flatworm found in human blood that relies on two hosts, humans and some types of snails, to complete its life cycle. Native to: tropical Asia and Africa. Genus: *Schistosoma*.

blood group *n* a class into which human blood is divided for transfusion purposes according to the presence or absence of antigens that determine its immunological compatibility. The ABO system is the most commonly known set of blood groups.

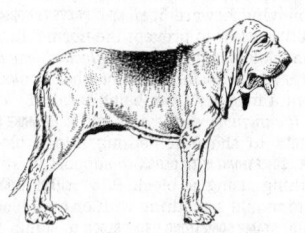

bloodhound

bloodhound /blúd hownd/ *n* **1.** a large powerful dog with drooping ears, sagging jowls, and a keen sense of smell, formerly used for tracking **2.** a detective who is relentless in pursuing people or things (*informal*)

bloodless /blúdləss/ *adj* **1.** WITHOUT KILLING OR VIOLENCE conducted without killing or great violence ○ *a bloodless coup* **2.** PALE AND ANAEMIC pale and anaemic-

looking **3.** LACKING LIVELINESS dull and lacking liveliness ○ *a bloodless performance* **4.** LACKING EMOTION cold and lacking in human emotion ○ *bloodless statistics* **5.** LACKING BLOOD lacking blood or the expected amount of blood —**bloodlessly** *adv* —**bloodlessness** *n*

Bloodless Revolution *n* HIST same as **Glorious Revolution**

bloodletting /blúd leting/ *n* **1.** BITTER QUARRELLING bitter violent fighting between rival groups **2.** MED REMOVAL OF BLOOD FROM BODY the removal of blood, usually by making an incision in a vein, for therapeutic purposes. Although historically common, bloodletting is used only rarely in modern times to treat specific medical conditions. **3.** *N Am* HR EJECTION OF PEOPLE the large-scale laying off of employees in a corporation ○ *corporate bloodletting in which a number of senior managers were let go* —**bloodletter** *n*

bloodline /blúd līn/ *n* a direct line of descent from a specific human or animal ancestor, especially with respect to the common characteristics shared by that ancestor's descendants

blood lust *n* a strong desire to take part in or witness killing or violence

blood meal *n* dried powdered animal blood. Use: to enrich animal feeds, as fertilizer for plants.

blood money *n* **1.** FEE FOR HIRED KILLER the fee paid to a hired killer **2.** REWARD FOR FINDING KILLER a reward paid to somebody for giving information about a criminal, especially a murderer **3.** COMPENSATION PAID FOR KILLING in some cultures, compensation paid to the relatives of somebody who has been killed or murdered

blood orange *n* an orange that has deep red flesh

blood plasma *n* PHYSIOL same as **plasma** (sense 1)

blood poisoning *n* infection of the blood, generally caused either by the presence in the blood of microorganisms (**septicaemia**) or of toxins produced by body cells (**toxaemia**)

blood pressure *n* **1.** the pressure exerted by the blood against the walls of blood vessels. Blood pressure depends on the strength of the heartbeat, thickness and volume of the blood, the elasticity of the artery walls, and general health. **2.** MED same as **hypertension**

blood product *n* a substance such as plasma extracted from donated blood for use in the treatment of various medical conditions

blood pudding *n* FOOD same as **black pudding**

blood red *n* a deep vivid red colour —**blood red** *adj*

blood relation, **blood relative** *n* somebody who is related to another person by birth rather than marriage

bloodroot /blúd root/ (*plural* **-roots** *or* same) *n* a plant that has poisonous deep-red sap in its roots. Native to: eastern North America. Latin name: *Sanguinaria canadensis*.

blood sausage *n N Am* FOOD same as **black pudding**

blood serum *n* MED same as **serum** (sense 1)

bloodshed /blúd shed/ *n* activity resulting in killings or injuries

bloodshot /blúd shot/ *adj* inflamed and red as a result of the widening of small blood vessels in the white of the eye ○ *bloodshot eyes*

blood sport *n* a sport in which animals are killed. Hunting and bullfighting are blood sports.

bloodstain /blúd stayn/ *n* a dark stain left by dried blood —**bloodstained** *adj*

bloodstock /blúd stok/ *n* thoroughbred horses, especially when bred and sold for horseracing

bloodstone /blúd stōn/ *n* a deep green variety of chalcedony with small red spots or streaks of red jasper. Use: gems.

bloodstream /blúd streem/ *n* the flow of blood circulating through the blood vessels of a person or animal

bloodsucker /blúd sukər/ *n* **1.** a parasite that sucks blood from its host, e.g. a leech or mosquito **2.** somebody who exploits somebody else, especially by extortion or blackmail —**bloodsucking** *n, adj*

blood sugar *n* the concentration of glucose in the blood

blood test *n* a scientific analysis of a sample of blood

bloodthirsty /blúd thursti/ (-ier, -iest) *adj* 1. eager to take part in or witness violence and bloodshed 2. full of intentional violence or killing —**bloodthirstily** *adv* —**bloodthirstiness** *n*

blood type *n* MED same as **blood group**

blood vessel *n* an artery, vein, or capillary through which blood flows

bloodwood /blúd wŏŏd/ (*plural* **-woods** or *same*) *n* a eucalyptus tree, found in Australia and parts of Africa, that has reddish timber and yields a dark-red gum. Genus: *Eucalyptus*.

bloodworm /blúd wurm/ *n* 1. the red larva of a freshwater midge. Genus: *Chironomus*. 2. a reddish segmented worm often used as angling bait. Genera: *Tubifex* or *Polycirrus*.

bloody /blúddi/ *adj* (**-ier, -iest**) 1. BLOODSTAINED covered or smeared with blood ○ *Her hands were bloody and shaking.* 2. RELATING TO BLOOD resembling or containing blood 3. INVOLVING MUCH BLOODSHED involving a great deal of killing and bloodshed 4. UNFAIR AND INCONSIDERATE very unfair and inconsiderate (*dated informal*) ■ *adv* SWEARWORD used as a swearword or to add emphasis (*slang; sometimes considered offensive*) ○ *a bloody good job too!* ■ *vt* (**-ies, -ying, -ied**) STAIN SOMETHING WITH BLOOD to stain or smear something with blood —**bloodily** *adv*—**bloodiness** *n* ◇ **bloody well** used to show anger or irritation when contradicting something (*slang; sometimes considered offensive*)

bloody mary (*plural* **bloody marys**), **Bloody Mary** *n* a cocktail consisting of vodka, tomato juice, and spices

bloody-minded *adj* intentionally uncooperative and obstructive (*informal*) —**bloody-mindedly** *adv* —**bloody-mindedness** *n*

bloom[1] /bloom/ *n* 1. FLOWER a flower, especially on a plant cultivated chiefly for its flowers 2. MASS OF FLOWERS the mass of flowers on a single plant 3. FLOWERING the state of being in flower ○ *roses in full bloom* 4. HEALTHY APPEARANCE OR COMPLEXION a fresh, youthful, healthy complexion 5. PRIME the condition of greatest freshness or health (*literary*) ○ *in the bloom of youth* 6. BOT WHITE COATING ON LEAVES OR FRUIT a thin white coating on the leaves of some plants and on fruits 7. WHITE POWDER ON COINS a fine white powder sometimes found on newly minted coins 8. COOK COATING ON CHOCOLATE a mottled white coating on chocolate, usually caused by incorrect temperature during storage 9. ENVIRON same as **algal bloom** ■ *vi* (**blooms, blooming, bloomed**) 1. COME INTO FLOWER to open into flower ○ *The roses bloomed early this year.* 2. PRODUCE PLANTS to produce abundant plant life, especially unexpectedly ○ *make the desert bloom* 3. APPEAR HEALTHY to appear healthy and vigorous (*literary*) 4. PROSPER OR FLOURISH to reach the fullest stage of development or maturity (*literary*) 5. *US* APPEAR SUDDENLY to appear suddenly, usually in a cloud ○ *A cloud of smoke bloomed under the rocket.* 6. ENVIRON BECOME COVERED WITH ALGAE to become discoloured on the surface because of an excessive growth of algae or phytoplankton (*refers to bodies of water*) [13C. < Old Norse *blóm* < Indo-European] —**bloomy** *adj*

bloom[2] /bloom/ *n* a bar of steel or wrought iron hammered or rolled from an ingot ■ *vt* (**blooms, blooming, bloomed**) to convert an ingot of iron or steel into a bloom [Old English *blōma*, origin ?]

bloomer[1] /blóomər/ *n* 1. PLANT THAT FLOWERS a flowering plant, especially considered with respect to the time of its flowering ○ *an early bloomer* 2. DEVELOPER somebody who grows up or reaches a level of competence at a particular stage of development ○ *described herself as a late bloomer* 3. EMBARRASSING MISTAKE a mildly embarrassing mistake (*informal humorous*) [Mid-18C. In sense 3 shortening and alteration of *blooming error*]

bloomer[2] /blóomər/ *n* a large loaf of bread with a rounded top that has diagonal slashes across it [Mid-20C. Origin ?]

Bloomer /blóomər/, **Amelia** (1818–94) US feminist and reformer. She was founding editor of the feminist journal *The Lily* (1849–55), and advocated less constricting clothing for women. Born **Amelia Jenks**

> 'We all felt that the dress was drawing attention from what we thought to be of far greater importance...In the minds of some people the short dress and woman's rights were inseparably connected. With us, the dress was but an incident, and we were not willing to sacrifice greater questions to it.'
> [Amelia Bloomer. Quoted in *The Bloomer Girls*, Charles N. Gattey; 1968]

bloomers /blóomərz/ *npl* (*dated*) 1. BAGGY UNDERWEAR baggy knickers for women or girls, especially garments that reach down to just above the knee 2. WOMEN'S LOOSE SPORTS TROUSERS loose trousers gathered at the knee, worn by women for cycling or swimming in the late 19th century 3. LONG LOOSE WOMEN'S TROUSERS long loose trousers gathered at the ankle and formerly worn by women and girls under a shorter skirt [Mid-19C. After Amelia BLOOMER]

blooming /blóoming, blóoming/ *adj* flourishing and in exceptionally good health or condition ■ *adj, adv* used to add emphasis, as a euphemistic alternative for 'bloody' (*dated informal*) ○ *a blooming nuisance* ○ *not blooming likely*

Bloomsbury Group /blóomzbəri-/ *n* a group of artists and writers who congregated in the Bloomsbury area of London after World War I. They shared political views and an experimental approach to their respective fields.

bloop /bloop/ *vt* (**bloops, blooping, blooped**) in baseball, to hit the ball high and short, so that it lands just beyond the infield ■ *n* BASEBALL same as **blooper** (sense 2) [Early 20C. An imitation of the sound of a missile]

blooper /blóopər/ *n* 1. *N Am* EMBARRASSING MISTAKE a mildly embarrassing mistake (*informal humorous*) 2. BASEBALL HIGH HIT in baseball, a short, high hit that lands just beyond the infield 3. BASEBALL UNDERHAND PITCH in baseball, a lobbed underhand pitch

Bloquiste /blo kéest/ *n Can* a member or supporter of the Bloc Québécois [Late 20C. < Canadian French < *Bloc (Québécois)*]

blossom /blóssəm/ *n* 1. MASS OF FLOWERS ON TREE a mass of flowers appearing on a tree or bush 2. BLOOM a single flower 3. FLOWERING the state of flowering ○ *cherry trees in blossom* ■ *vi* (**-soms, -soming, -somed**) 1. COME INTO FLOWER to open into flower 2. DEVELOP WELL to develop in a pleasing or promising way 3. STOP BEING SHY to stop being shy and reserved [Old English *blōstm* < Indo-European] —**blossomy** *adj*

blossom out *vi* same as **blossom** *v* (senses 2–3)

blot[1] /blot/ *n* 1. STAIN a stain or spot caused by a drop of liquid 2. EYESORE something ugly that spoils the appearance of something ○ *a blot on the landscape* 3. BLEMISH something that spoils somebody or something's good name or reputation ■ *v* (**blots, blotting, blotted**) 1. *vt* DRY SOMETHING WITH ABSORBENT MATERIAL to soak up liquid from the surface of something using absorbent material 2. *vt* BRING DISREPUTE ON SOMEBODY to bring dishonour on somebody's reputation 3. *vti* CREATE BLOT to make a blot on paper [14C. Probably < N Germanic]

blot out *vt* 1. to cover something so that it can no longer be seen 2. to remove something painful from the mind

blot[2] /blot/ *n* in backgammon, a piece placed alone on a point and therefore exposed to capture by the opposing player [Late 16C. Probably < Dutch *bloot* 'exposed, naked']

blotch /bloch/ *n* 1. SPOT OR MARK an irregularly shaped spot or mark 2. BLEMISH ON SKIN a reddish patch on the skin ■ *vti* (**blotches, blotching, blotched**) MARK WITH BLOTCHES to mark something with blotches, or become marked with blotches [Early 17C. Blend of BLOT[1] + BOTCH] —**blotchily** *adv*—**blotchiness** *n* —**blotchy** *adj*

blotter /blóttər/ *n* 1. a sheet of blotting paper that absorbs ink or water 2. *N Am* a book used for recording daily events and transactions ○ *a police blotter*

blotting paper *n* soft paper used for soaking up ink from paper

blotto /blóttō/ *adj* extremely inebriated (*slang*) [Early 20C. < BLOT[1]]

blouse /blowz/ *n* 1. WOMAN'S SHIRT a woman's loose-fitting shirt 2. ETHNIC SMOCK a loose-fitting shirt or smock, often part of traditional costume 3. CADET'S OR SOLDIER'S TUNIC a tunic, sometimes loose and sometimes very snug, that is a part of some military uniforms ■ *vti* (**blouses, blousing, bloused**) HANG IN LOOSE FOLDS to make an item of clothing hang in loose gathers or folds, or hang in this way [Early 19C. < French]

blouson /blóo zon/ *n* 1. a woman's garment resembling a shirt that is gathered at the waist 2. a short jacket that fits closely at the waist and becomes looser over the upper body [Early 20C. < French]

bloviate /blṓ vi ayt/ (**-ates, -ating, -ated**) *vi* to speak at length in a pompous self-aggrandizing way (*slang*) [Mid-19C. Mock Latin alteration of BLOW[1]] —**bloviation** /blṑvi áysh'n/ *n*

blow[1] /blō/ *v* (**blows, blowing, blew** /bloo/, **blown** /blōn/) 1. *vi* BE MOVING AS AIR to be in motion as an air current ○ *It blew all night.* 2. *vt* MOVE WITH AIR CURRENT to move something with an air current, especially air exhaled through the mouth ○ *I blew the dust off the shelf.* 3. *vti* EXHALE to expel a stream of air from the mouth ○ *She blew on her soup.* 4. *vt* FORM SOMETHING BY BLOWING to make bubbles or smoke rings by expelling a stream of air from the mouth 5. *vt* CLEAR NOSE to clear the nose by forcing air through it 6. *vti* SOUND BY BLOWING to make a sound from a musical instrument by blowing air into it, or emit a sound when blown 7. *vt* SEND KISS to send somebody a symbolic kiss by kissing your hand and then blowing across it 8. *vi* EXPEL MOIST AIR to expel moist air from the lungs up through the blowhole (*refers to whales and other sea mammals*) 9. *vi* BREATHE HARD to breathe hard or pant through exertion 10. *vt* EXHAUST HORSE to cause a horse to breathe hard through overexertion 11. *vt* SHAPE HOT GLASS to give shape to molten glass by forcing air into it 12. *vti* DESTROY OR MOVE BY EXPLOSION to destroy or displace something or somebody violently ○ *The blast blew the roof off.* 13. *vt* OPEN SOMETHING BY FORCE to break open something that is firmly shut using explosives 14. *vti* AUTOMOT PUNCTURE to cause a puncture in a tyre, or experience a puncture (*informal*) 15. *vti* ELEC BURN OUT to burn out and break an electrical circuit, or cause a piece of equipment to do this ○ *The toaster blew when I plugged it in.* 16. *vti* BREAK BECAUSE OF PRESSURE to be ruptured, or cause something to rupture, under excess pressure 17. *vt* MISS OPPORTUNITY to fail to take advantage of an opportunity (*slang*) 18. *vt* WASTE MONEY to spend money wastefully (*slang*) ○ *blew a bundle of dough on fast cars* 19. *vt US* ENTERTAIN LAVISHLY to treat or entertain somebody lavishly (*informal*) ○ *The company blew us to a massive dinner.* 20. *vt* EXPOSE SECRET to expose something secret (*slang*) ○ *blew his cover* 21. *vt* DISREGARD SOMETHING to disregard something as trivial (*dated informal; usually used as a command*) ○ *Blow the expense!* 22. (*past participle* **blowed**) *vt* EXPRESSING SURPRISE used to express surprise (*dated informal*) ○ *Blow me down, look who's here!* 23. *vti ANZ, N Am* LEAVE SUDDENLY to leave a place suddenly (*slang*) ○ *When the cops arrived, the thieves blew.* 24. *vi ANZ, US* BOAST to brag (*informal*) 25. *vti* MUSIC PLAY MUSIC INFORMALLY to play music, especially informally or with other musicians (*slang*) 26. *vt US* INHALE DRUG to take a drug by inhalation (*slang*) 27. *vt* OFFENSIVE TERM an offensive term meaning to fellate (*slang*) 28. *vt* BOARD GAMES CAPTURE PIECE IN DRAUGHTS to capture a piece in draughts ■ *interj* EXPRESSING ANNOYANCE used to express annoyance (*informal*) ■ *n* 1. ACT OF BLOWING an act or instance of blowing 2. STRONG WIND a strong wind (*informal*) 3. SHORT WALK a short walk in order to get some fresh air (*informal*) ○ *We went for a blow along the cliffs.* 4. *ANZ, US* BOAST an act of boasting (*informal*) 5. MUSIC same as **jam session** (*slang*) 6. DRUGS same as **cannabis** (sense 1) (*slang*) 7. *N Am* DRUGS same as **cocaine** (*slang*) 8. *ANZ* AGRIC SHEAR STROKE a stroke of the shears in sheep-shearing [Old English *blāwan* < Indo-European] ◇ **blow it** 1. to spoil your chances of success (*slang*) 2. used to express annoyance (*informal*) ◇ **blow something sky-high** to destroy something completely ○ *The results of the survey blew her theory sky-high.*

blow away *vt* (*slang*) 1. KILL SOMEBODY to shoot somebody dead 2. *N Am* DEFEAT SOMEBODY DECISIVELY to subject somebody to an overwhelming defeat 3. *N Am* OVERWHELM SOMEBODY to affect somebody emotionally in an overwhelming way ○ *an epic movie that just blew me away*

blow in *vi* 1. to arrive or enter a place in a casual way (*slang*) ○ *blew in at midnight* 2. to start producing oil (*refers to oil wells*)

blow off *v* **1.** *vti* RELEASE GAS to release a gas or liquid under pressure **2.** *vi* FART to noisily release stomach gases through the anus (*slang*) **3.** *vt N Am* FAIL TO MEET SOMEBODY to disregard an obligation to attend something or meet somebody (*slang*) ○ *Lee blew me off, so I'm free for lunch.* **4.** *vt US* SLIGHT SOMEBODY to treat somebody or something as unimportant (*slang*) ○ *He just blew me off.*

blow out *v* **1.** *vti* EXTINGUISH to extinguish a flame with a blast of air or wind **2.** *vr* DIE DOWN to return to a state of calm after a storm (*refers to storms and winds*) ○ *blow itself out* **3.** *vi* AUTOMOT PUNCTURE to puncture suddenly and at speed (*refers to tyres*) **4.** *vi* INDUST EMIT UNCONTROLLABLY to release oil or gas explosively (*refers to gas or oil wells*) **5.** *vi* OVERINDULGE to overindulge in food or drink (*informal*) **6.** *vt* CANCEL MEETING to cancel a meeting or a performance (*slang*)

blow over *vi* **1.** to become less violent (*refers to storms*) **2.** to no longer excite strong feelings (*informal*) ○ *It was quite a scandal but it all blew over.*

blow up *v* **1.** *vti* DESTROY BY EXPLOSION to destroy something or kill somebody by causing an explosion, or be destroyed in this way **2.** *vti* INFLATE to blow air into something so that it becomes swollen, or swell as a result of being filled with air **3.** *vt* EXAGGERATE SOMETHING to exaggerate the value or importance of something (*informal*) ○ *This affair has been blown up out of all proportion.* **4.** *vt* PHOTOGRAPHY ENLARGE IMAGE to enlarge a photograph **5.** *vi* BECOME ANGRY to become angry suddenly and unexpectedly (*informal*) **6.** *vi* BEGIN TO BLOW to begin to develop or gather force (*refers to winds or storms*) **7.** *vi* ARISE OR COME ABOUT to develop, often unexpectedly, into something more serious

blow² /blō/ *n* **1.** HARD HIT a hard hit with a fist or weapon ○ *a nasty blow on the head* **2.** ACTION HELPING CAUSE an important action that helps a cause or belief ○ *They struck an important blow for civil rights.* **3.** SETBACK a sudden setback ○ *a blow to his confidence* [15C. Origin ?]

blow³ /blō/ (**blows, blowing, blew** /bloo/, **blown** /blōn/) *vti* to blossom, or cause something to blossom (*archaic or literary*) [Old English *blōwan* < Germanic]

Blow /blō/, **John** (1649–1708) English composer. He was organist of Westminster Abbey and a prolific composer of church music.

blowback /blṓ bak/ *n* **1.** MECH ENG REARWARD FLOW OF GASES the reverse flow of gases in a system, e.g. through the carburettor of an internal-combustion engine during the compression cycle **2.** ARMS FIREARM POWDER RESIDUE the powdery residue that is released or ejected upon firing bullets or shells from a weapon **3.** REACTION a reaction or effect resulting from an action or cause, usually a negative reaction (*informal*) ○ *the blowback from the press revelations*

blow-by-blow *adj* describing something in great detail ○ *a blow-by-blow account*

blow-dry *vt* to dry and style hair using a hairdryer ■ *n* a hairstyle produced by blow-drying

blow-dryer *n* **1.** a hand-held hairdryer for blow-drying hair **2.** same as **hairdryer**

blower /blṓ ər/ *n* **1.** a machine that produces a current of air or gas ○ *a leaf blower* **2.** an air compressor that produces air at low pressure **3.** same as **telephone** (*dated informal*)

blowfish /blṓ fish/ (*plural same* or **-fishes**) *n* FISH same as **puffer** (sense 2)

blowfly /blṓ flī/ (*plural* **-flies**) *n* a large fly such as a bluebottle or greenbottle that lays its eggs in rotting meat, in dung, or in open wounds. Family: Calliphoridae. [Early 19C. < BLOW¹ 'deposit eggs']

blowgun /blṓ gun/ *n N Am* ARMS same as **blowpipe** (sense 1)

blowhard /blṓ haard/ *n N Am* somebody who boasts but is considered ineffectual

blowhole /blṓ hōl/ *n* **1.** NOSTRIL OF SEA MAMMAL a nostril in the top of the head of a whale, dolphin, or similar sea mammal that allows the exchange of air from the lungs **2.** BREATHING HOLE IN ICE a hole in ice where water mammals come to the surface to breathe **3.** CIV ENG AIR VENT a vent to permit the escape of air or gas from a tunnel or passage **4.** GEOL HOLE IN CAVE ROOF a hole in the roof of a sea cave through which sea water is forced by waves **5.** *NZ* GEOL VOLCANIC VENT a vent or hole in the ground in a volcanic or thermal area through which gas or steam is forced out

blowie /blṓ i/ *n Aus* INSECTS same as **blowfly** (*informal*) [Mid-20C. Shortening]

blow-in *n Aus* somebody who has just arrived, especially a stranger (*informal*)

blow job *n* an offensive term for an act of fellatio (*slang*)

blowlamp /blṓ lamp/ *n* CONSTR same as **blowtorch**

blown¹ past participle of **blow**¹

blown² past participle of **blow**³

blowoff /blṓ of/, **blow-off** *n* **1.** a discharge of surplus gas or fluid under pressure **2.** a device through which surplus gas or liquid under pressure is released

blowout /blṓ owt/ *n* **1.** TYRE PUNCTURE a sudden puncture of a tyre **2.** FAILURE OF FUSE a sudden burning of a fuse, caused by an electrical overload **3.** GUSH OF OIL OR GAS a sudden rush of oil or gas from an oil well to the surface **4.** same as **flameout** **5.** BIG PARTY a big party with ample food and drink (*slang*)

blowpipe /blṓ pīp/ *n* **1.** TUBE FOR SHOOTING DARTS a long narrow tube through which darts or pellets are shot by blowing. N Am term **blowgun** **2.** CHEM TUBE FOR CONCENTRATING HEAT a small tube that leads a jet of air into a flame to increase its heat **3.** GLASS BLOWER'S TUBE a long narrow iron tube used in glass blowing to shape molten glass

blowsy *adj* another spelling of **blowzy**

blow through *vi Aus* to leave quickly, especially to avoid a duty or potentially awkward encounter (*informal*) ○ *As soon as he heard Jane was coming over, he blew through.*

blowtorch /blṓ tawrch/ *n* a small, usually portable, gas burner that intensifies the heat of its flame by a blast of air or oxygen

blowup /blṓ up/, **blow-up** *n* **1.** PHOTOGRAPHIC ENLARGEMENT an enlargement of a photograph or picture **2.** EXPLOSION an explosion caused by a bomb or similar device **3.** OUTBURST OF TEMPER a sudden outburst of temper (*informal*) ■ *adj* same as **inflatable**

blowy /blṓ i/ (**-ier, -iest**) *adj* windy or breezy (*informal*)

blowzy /blówzi/ (**-zier, -ziest**), **blowsy** (**-sier, -siest**) *adj* **1.** with a reddish face and coarse complexion **2.** slovenly and careless in appearance [Early 17C. < obsolete *blowze* 'wench'] —**blowzily** *adv* —**blowziness** *n*

BLT (*plural* **BLTs** or **BLT's**) *n* a sandwich with a filling of bacon, lettuce, and tomato

blub /blub/ (**blubs, blubbing, blubbed**) *vi* to weep noisily in an uncontrolled way (*informal*) [Early 19C. Shortening of BLUBBER]

blubber /blúbbər/ *v* (**-bers, -bering, -bered**) (*informal*) **1.** *vi* SOB LOUDLY to sob in a loud and unattractive manner **2.** *vt* SAY SOMETHING WHILE SOBBING to say something while sobbing ■ *n* **1.** FAT OF SEA MAMMALS the insulating fat of whales and other large sea mammals. Use: source of oil, food. **2.** UNSIGHTLY FAT unsightly body fat (*informal; sometimes considered offensive*) [14C. Origin ?] —**blubberer** *n* —**blubbery** *adj*

bludge /bluj/ *ANZ* (*informal*) *v* (**bludges, bludging, bludged**) **1.** *vi* LIVE OFF OTHERS to live off somebody else's earnings or on state benefits **2.** *vi* AVOID WORK to avoid work and shirk responsibilities **3.** *vti* CADGE to scrounge something from somebody ■ *n* EASY TASK a task that is easy to perform [Early 20C. Back-formation < *bludger*, contraction of *bludgeoner*] —**bludger** *n*

bludgeon /blújjən/ *n* SHORT HEAVY WEAPON a short heavy club used as a weapon ■ *vt* (**-eons, -eoning, -eoned**) **1.** HIT SOMEBODY WITH HEAVY OBJECT to hit somebody repeatedly with a heavy object ○ *bludgeoned to death* **2.** COERCE OR BULLY SOMEBODY to coerce or bully somebody into doing something [Mid-18C. Origin ?] —**bludgeoner** *n*

blue /bloo/ *adj* (**bluer, bluest**) **1.** OF COLOUR OF SKY having or resembling the colour of the sky on a cloudless day **2.** SLIGHTLY PURPLE IN SKIN COLOUR with the skin appearing slightly purple because of cold, bruising, or exertion **3.** BIOL BLUE-GREY describes animals and plants that are bluish or blue-grey in colour ○ *a blue whale* ○ *a blue spruce* **4.** GLOOMY gloomy or melancholy (*informal*) ○ *feeling blue* ○ *a blue day* **5.** EXPLICIT depicting or referring to sex in an explicit or offensive way (*informal*) ○ *blue jokes* **6.** CONSERVATIVE holding or supporting right-wing views **7.** *N Am* PURITANICAL rigidly conservative in moral and social views (*dated*) **8.** ASTRON HAVING BLUESHIFT describes an astronomical object that exhibits a blueshift ■ *n* **1.** COLOUR OF SKY the colour of the sky on a cloudless day. Blue is one of the three primary colours of light and pigment. **2.** BLUE PIGMENT a blue dye or pigment **3.** DISTANCE the far distance (*informal*) ○ *disappeared off into the blue* **4.** *also* **Blue** OXBRIDGE ATHLETE an athlete who has represented Oxford or Cambridge University in a match between the two universities, winning the right to wear the university's blue colours **5.** ARCHERY BLUE PART OF TARGET the blue ring on the target in archery **6.** CUE GAMES BLUE BALL the blue ball in snooker and similar games **7.** INSECTS BLUE BUTTERFLY a common blue small-winged butterfly. Subfamily: Plebeiinae. **8.** *also* **Blue** *US* MEMBER OF UNION ARMY a member of the Union Army in the American Civil War **9.** *ANZ* FIGHT a fight or quarrel (*slang*) **10.** *ANZ* MISTAKE a mistake or error (*informal*) **11.** *also* **Blue** *ANZ* RED-HAIRED PERSON somebody with red hair (*informal*) ■ *v* (**blues, blueing** or **bluing, blued**) **1.** *vti* MAKE OR BECOME BLUE to make something blue, or become blue **2.** *vt* TREAT SOMETHING WITH BLUING to treat white fabrics or clothing with bluing **3.** *vt* SQUANDER MONEY to spend money wastefully (*dated informal*) [13C. < Old French *bleu* < Indo-European] —**blueness** *n* ◇ **out of the blue** unexpectedly ○ *The offer came out of the blue.*

blue baby *n* a baby born with a bluish skin colour (**cyanosis**) as a result of a congenital heart condition that causes the mixing of venous and arterial blood

bluebeard /blo͝o beerd/, **Bluebeard** *n* a man who marries and then kills successive wives [Early 19C. After *Blue Beard*, translation of French *Barbe Bleue*, character in a story by Charles Perrault (1628–1703)]

bluebell

bluebell /blo͝o bel/ *n* **1.** a woodland plant of the lily family with long thin leaves. Flowers: small, blue, bell-shaped. Native to: Europe. Genus: *Endymion*. **2.** PLANTS same as **harebell** **3.** *N Am* a plant of the borage family. Flowers: blue. Native to: eastern North America. Genus: *Mertenia*.

blue beret *n* a member of a United Nations-controlled military unit

blueberry /blo͝obəri/ (*plural* **-ries**) *n* **1.** a bluish-black edible berry **2.** a cultivated fruit bush that bears blueberries. Native to: North America. Genus: *Vaccinium*.

bluebill /blo͝o bil/ *n* **1.** *US* BIRDS same as **scaup** **2.** a bird of the waxbill family with a heavy metallic-blue bill. Native to: Africa. Genus: *Spermophaga*.

bluebird /blo͝o burd/ *n* a thrush that has bright blue feathers and a bluish or reddish-brown breast. Native to: North America. Genus: *Sialia*.

blue-black *adj* black tinged with blue or with a blue sheen when caught by the light —**blue-black** *n*

blue blood, **blueblood** /blo͝o blud/ *n* **1.** the quality of being royal or aristocratic by birth **2.** somebody of royal or aristocratic birth, or somebody born into a respectable and very wealthy family —**blue-blooded** *adj*

bluebonnet /blo͝o bonit/ *n* **1.** a wide round flat cap of blue wool, formerly worn in Scotland **2.** a low-growing lupin. Flowers: light blue, in spikes. Native to: Texas. Latin name: *Lupinus texensis* or *Lupinus subcarnosus*.

blue book *n* **1.** an official government report bound in a blue cover, especially one published by the British or Canadian government **2.** a book published by a US state government listing its elected officials and employees, and often including a brief history of the state

bluebottle /blo͝o bott'l/ *n* **1.** a large buzzing fly with an iridescent blue body that lays its eggs in decaying plant and animal material. Genus: *Calliphora*. **2.** a blue-flowered plant, especially a cornflower or grape hyacinth **3.** *Aus* MARINE BIOL same as **Portuguese man-of-war** (*informal*)

blue cheese *n* a whitish cheese with veins of blue mould

blue chip *n* **1.** FIN **VALUABLE STOCK IN RELIABLE COMPANY** a stock selling for a high price because it belongs to a company that is considered to be well established, highly successful, and reliable **2.** BUSINESS **VALUABLE ASSET OR COMPANY** an extremely valuable asset, especially a well-established, successful, and reliable company **3.** GAMBLING **POKER CHIP** a blue-coloured gambling chip of high value —**blue-chip** *adj*

blue-chipper *n N Am* **1.** a blue-chip company **2.** a young athlete or sports player that shows great promise (*informal*)

blue cod *n* **1.** a sea fish related to perches that is a popular food fish. Native to: New Zealand. Latin name: *Parapercis colias*. **2.** the flesh of a blue cod used as food

blue-collar *adj* relating to workers who do manual or industrial work that often requires special work clothes or protective clothing —**blue-collar** *n*

blue devil *n US* a capsule containing the narcotic and sedative barbiturate amobarbital (*slang*)

Blue Ensign *n* a blue flag with a Union Jack at the top inner corner, flown by auxiliary vessels of the Royal Navy and by some yacht clubs

blue-eyed boy *n* somebody who is the favourite of another person or group (*informal*) N Am term **fair-haired boy**

blue-eyed soul *n* soul music written and played by white musicians (*informal*)

bluefin /blo͝o fin/, **bluefin tuna** *n* a large tuna that is caught for sport and food. Native to: temperate seas. Latin name: *Thunnus thynnus*.

bluefish /blo͝o fish/ (*plural same* or **-fishes**) *n* **1.** a bluish fish with a silver underside, caught for sport and food. Native to: temperate and tropical regions of the Atlantic and Indian oceans. Latin name: *Pomatomus saltatrix*. **2.** a fish with bluish colouring

blue flag beach *n* a beach with sea water that meets the cleanliness requirements of the European Commission [Because allowed to display an official largely blue flag indicating the award]

blue fox *n* **1.** an arctic fox with a tawny-brown coat that turns pale blue-grey in winter. Latin name: *Alopex lagopus*. **2.** the fur of a blue fox

blue funk *n* a state of great fear (*dated informal*)

bluegill /blo͝o gil/ (*plural* **-gills** or *same*) *n* a freshwater sunfish. Native to: eastern and central North America. Latin name: *Lepomis macrochirus*.

bluegrass /blo͝o graass/ *n* **1.** a style of country music from the southern United States, usually played on fiddle, banjo, guitar, or mandolin and featuring close harmony and instrumental solos (*often used before a noun*) **2.** a blue-green grass. Native to: North America, Europe. Use: fodder, lawns. Genus: *Poa*.

blue-green algae *npl* BIOL same as **cyanobacteria**

blue ground *n* unweathered kimberlite rock lying beneath an oxidized yellow surface layer. Kimberlites occur in volcanic pipes and are the main source of diamonds.

blue gum *n* **1.** a tall eucalyptus tree with aromatic leaves and smooth blue-grey bark. Use: medicinal oil, timber. Native to: Australia. Latin name: *Eucalyptus globulus*. **2.** a eucalyptus tree that has smooth blue-grey bark. Native to: Australia. Genus: *Eucalyptus*.

blue heeler *n Aus* **1.** a dog with a blue-speckled coat, belonging to an Australian breed used for controlling cattle (*informal*) **2.** a police officer (*slang*) [< the dog's practice of urging cattle on by biting their heels]

blueing *n* TEXTILES another spelling of **bluing**

blueish *adj* COLOURS another spelling of **bluish**

blue jay *n* a noisy bird with blue feathers, a crested head, and a white underside. Native to: North America. Latin name: *Cyanocitta cristata*.

blue jeans *npl N Am* a pair of jeans made of blue denim

blue john *n* a blue or purple form of the mineral fluorspar found only in Derbyshire

blue law *n* **1.** in the United States, a law regulating moral conduct, e.g. a law prohibiting the sale of alcohol on Sundays **2.** a law intended to govern moral conduct in colonial New England [*Blue* in the US sense of 'puritanical']

blue line *n* either of two blue lines that divide an ice hockey rink into the defensive, neutral, and offensive zones

Blue Mantle *n* one of the four lowest-ranked heraldic officers of the British College of Arms

blue moon *n* **1.** a long period of time (*informal*) ○ *once in a blue moon* **2.** a second full moon in a calendar month. As there is a full moon every 29.5 days, a blue moon is a comparatively rare event.

Blue Mountains /bloo-/ plateau region about 65 km/47 mi. west of Sydney, Australia, part of the Great Dividing Range. Its highest point is Bird Rock, 1,134 m/3,871 ft. Area: 1,400 sq. km/540 sq. mi.

blue murder *n* a noisy protest (*informal*) ○ *screaming blue murder*

Blue Nile river in northeastern Africa that rises in Ethiopia and supplies about 70 per cent of the water that reaches Khartoum, where it joins the White Nile to form the Nile proper. Length: 1,370 km/850 mi.

bluenose /blo͝o nōz/ *n N Am* somebody excessively concerned with morals (*dated informal*)

blue note *n* a musical note played or sung slightly lower than usual, especially in blues and jazz

blue on blue *adj* describes a friendly-fire attack or casualty occurring during a combat operation on sea or land, or in the air [Late 20C. Perhaps < *blue* 'friendly' in war games and military slang]

blue pages *npl* in the United States and Canada, the section of the telephone book that contains listings of government agencies and departments [Because usually printed on blue paper]

blue-pencil (**blue-pencils, blue-pencilling, blue-pencilled**) *vt* to edit a piece of writing by marking it, in order to shorten, censor, or delete it [< the use of a blue pencil in the editing process]

Blue Peter *n* a blue flag with a white square in the middle, used by ships to signal that they are ready to sail [Because the pattern on the flag represents P in the International Code of Symbols]

blue-plate *adj N Am* describes a main course offered by a restaurant at a lower price than usual ○ *We had the blue-plate special.* [Because cheap fixed-price meals used to be served on blue plates divided into compartments]

blue point *n* a domestic cat, especially a Siamese, that has a bluish-cream coat and dark grey markings on its extremities (**points**)

blueprint /blo͝o print/ *n* **1.** **PRINT OF PLAN** a photographic print of a technical drawing with white lines printed on a blue background, or a similarly produced print with blue lines on a white background, usually of an architectural or engineering design **2.** **PLAN OR GUIDE** a plan of action or a guide to doing something ○ *His administration's policies became a blueprint for those that followed.* ■ *vt* (**-prints, -printing, -printed**) **1.** **MAKE PRINT OF SOMETHING** to make a blueprint of something, especially a technical drawing **2.** **MAKE PLAN FOR SOMETHING** to make or be a plan for something

blue racer *n* a blue-green subspecies of the blacksnake. Native to: central United States. Latin name: *Coluber constrictor flaviventris*.

blue riband *n* the highest distinction or first prize in a particular field. N Am term **blue ribbon** —**blue-riband** *adj*

blue ribbon *n* **1.** an emblem or badge made of blue ribbon and awarded for first prize in a competition **2.** *N Am* same as **blue riband** **3.** a badge made of blue ribbon, worn by members of the Order of the Garter —**blue-ribbon** *adj*

Blue Ridge, Blue Ridge Mountains mountain range in the United States, extending from northern Georgia across western North Carolina and western Virginia into West Virginia. It is the easternmost range of the Appalachian Mountains, with its highest peak at Mount Mitchell 2,037 m/6,684 ft.

blue-rinse *adj* relating to women older than middle age with traditional conservative views (*disapproving*)

blues[1] /blooz/ *n* **1.** **STYLE OF MUSIC** a type of popular music that developed from African American folk songs in the early 20th century, consisting mainly of slow sad songs often performed over a repeating harmonic pattern (*takes a singular or plural verb*) **2.** (*plural same*) MUSIC **PIECE OF MUSIC** a song or instrumental piece of music in the style of the blues ■ *npl* **FEELING OF SADNESS** a feeling of unhappiness or low spirits (*informal*; *takes a plural verb*) [Mid-18C. < dated slang *blue devils* 'depression, low spirits']

blues[2] /blooz/ *n Carib* (*slang*) **1.** a Trinidadian hundred dollar bill, which is blue in colour **2.** an obscene film [< BLUE]

Blues and Royals /blo͞oz ənd róy əlz/ *npl* a regiment of the Household Cavalry [< the *Blues*, the Royal Horse Guards, and the *Royal* Dragoons, amalgamated in 1969]

blues dance *n* a dance, usually held in a private home, for which people pay an admission fee and at which music is provided by a sound system (*slang*; *used in Black English*)

blue shark *n* a shark that has a dark blue back and white underside. Native to: tropical and temperate seas. Latin name: *Prionace glauca*.

blue sheep *n* ZOOL same as **bharal**

blueshift /blo͝o shift/ *n* a displacement in the wavelengths of spectral lines towards the blue end of the visible spectrum, indicating that the radiation source and observer are approaching each other

blue-sky *adj* (*informal*) **1.** purely theoretical and having no concrete goal **2.** idealistic or visionary and without practical application ○ *blue-sky research* ○ *blue-sky thinking* —**blue-sky** *vi*

bluesman /blo͞ozmən/ (*plural* **-men** /-mən/) *n* a man who plays or sings the blues

blue spruce *n* a common evergreen tree with short sharp blue-grey needles. Native to: Rocky Mountains of North America. Latin name: *Picea pungens*.

bluestocking /blo͝o stoking/ *n* an offensive term for a woman who has intellectual, scholarly, or literary interests

ORIGIN At the literary gatherings held at the houses of fashionable mid-18th century hostesses, it became the custom to wear casual rather than formal dress. In the case of gentlemen's stockings, this meant grey worsted (called 'blue' at that time) rather than black silk. This lack of decorum was disapproved of in some quarters, and one Admiral Boscowan dubbed the participants the 'Blue Stocking Society'. Women who attended the gatherings thus became known as 'Blue Stocking Ladies' (even though it was men who had worn the stockings).

bluestone /blo͝o stōn/ *n* **1.** a blue-grey sandstone. Use: building, paving. **2.** the blue mineral form of copper sulphate

blue streak *n* a fast-moving person or thing (*informal humorous*) ◇ **talk a blue streak** *N Am* to talk very quickly and without pausing (*informal*)

blueswoman /blo͞oz wo͝omən/ (*plural* **-women** /-wimin/) *n* a woman who plays or sings the blues

bluesy /blo͞ozi/ (**bluesier, bluesiest**) *adj* composed or performed in or like the style of the blues (*informal*) ○ *a bluesy ballad*

bluet /blo͝o it/ *n* a plant of the madder family. Flowers: small, pale blue to white, four-petalled, with yellow centres. Native to: North America. Genus: *Hedyotis*. [Early 18C. < French *bl(e)uet* 'small blue' < *bleu* 'blue']

bluetit /blo͝o tit/ (*plural* **-tits** or *same*) *n* a small bird that has a blue cap, blue in its wings and tail, and a yellow breast. Native to: Europe. Latin name: *Parus caeruleus*.

bluetongue /blo͝o tung/ (*plural* **-tongues** or *same*), **blue-tongued lizard** *n* a lizard that displays its bright blue tongue when threatened. Native to: Australia. Genus: *Tiliqua*.

Bluetooth /blo͝o tooth/ *tdmk* a trademark for a wireless technology that enables devices such as portable computers, mobile phones, and portable hand-held devices to connect to each other and to the Internet

blue vitriol *n* CHEM same as **copper sulphate** (*archaic*)

blue water *n* the sea far away from the shore

blue whale

blue whale *n* a slate-blue whale, the world's largest living animal, that migrates between polar and equatorial seas. Latin name: *Balaenoptera musculus*.

bluey /bloo i/ (*plural* **-ys**) *n* **1.** *ANZ* somebody with red hair (*informal*) **2.** *Aus* same as **swag** *n* (sense 5)

bluff[1] /bluf/ (**bluffs, bluffing, bluffed**) *v* **1.** *vti* DECEIVE SOMEBODY to deceive, mislead, or instill fear or doubt in somebody by a false show of strength or confidence **2.** *vti* DECEIVE PLAYERS ABOUT CARDS to try to deceive other players in a card game about the true value of the cards you have **3.** *vt Malaysia, Singapore* MISLEAD SOMEBODY to try to mislead somebody about something relatively unimportant (*informal*) [Late 17C. < Dutch *bluffen* 'brag' or *bluf* 'bragging'] —**bluff** *n* —**bluffable** *adj* —**bluffer** *n*

bluff[2] /bluf/ *n* **1.** CLIFF WITH BROAD FACE a high steep bank, cliff, or headland, especially one with a broad face **2.** *Can* GROUP OF TREES ON PRAIRIE a group of trees surrounded by prairie or grassland ■ *adj* BLUNT BUT KIND IN MANNER cheerful and friendly, but outspoken and often insensitive to others' feelings [Early 17C. < Dutch *blaf* 'flat'] —**bluffly** *adv* —**bluffness** *n*

bluing /bloo ing/, **blueing** *n* a substance used in laundering to prevent white materials turning yellow

bluish /bloo ish/, **blueish** *adj* of a colour that is near to blue or contains some blue

Blum /bloom/, **Léon** (1872–1950) French politician. He was France's first socialist prime minister and served three terms (1936–37, 1938, 1946–47).

> 'A French Jew, of a long line of French ancestors, speaking only the language of my country, mainly nourished by its culture, refusing to leave at a moment when I faced the greatest dangers.'
> [Léon Blum. Quoted in *Europe Since 1870*, James Joll; 1970]

Blume /bloom/, **Judy** (*b.* 1938) US writer. Her fiction for young people deals openly with contemporary issues such as divorce and has attracted a large readership.

blunder /blúndər/ *v* (**-ders, -dering, -dered**) **1.** *vi* MAKE SERIOUS MISTAKE to make a serious or embarrassing mistake as a result of carelessness or ignorance **2.** *vi* MOVE CLUMSILY to stumble or move clumsily **3.** *vti* ACT IN CONFUSED WAY to act or speak in a manner that is clumsy, ignorant, or thoughtless ■ *n* SERIOUS MISTAKE a serious or embarrassing mistake resulting from carelessness or ignorance [14C. < N Germanic < Indo-European] —**blunderer** *n* —**blunderingly** *adv*

SYNONYMS See *mistake*.

blunderbuss

blunderbuss /blúndər buss/ *n* **1.** a short wide-muzzled firearm of the 17th century, used to fire shot with a scattering effect at close range **2.** somebody who is clumsy (*informal*) [Mid-17C. Alteration of Dutch *donderbus* < *donder* 'thunder' + *bus* 'gun']

blunge /blunj/ (**blunges, blunging, blunged**) *vt* to mix clay with water and chemicals to create the material for making pottery commercially [Early 19C. Blend of PLUNGE + other *bl-* words such as BLOW[1] and BLEND] —**blunger** *n*

blunt /blunt/ *adj* **1.** NOT SHARP having a cutting edge or point that is not sharp **2.** INSENSITIVELY FRANK OR HONEST very frank or straightforward and showing no delicacy or consideration ■ *v* (**blunts, blunting, blunted**) **1.** *vti* MAKE SOMETHING LESS SHARP to make the cutting edge or point of something less sharp **2.** *vt* LESSEN OR WEAKEN SOMETHING to make something such as a sense or an emotion less effective or less intense [13C. Perhaps < Old Norse *blundr* 'dozing'] —**bluntly** *adv* —**bluntness** *n*

Blunt /blunt/, **Anthony** (1907–83) British art historian and Soviet spy. He was Surveyor of the Queen's Pictures (1945–72), but was stripped of his knighthood and disgraced after the public disclosure (1979) of his role as a Soviet spy in the ring that included Guy Burgess and Donald Maclean. Full name **Blunt, Anthony Frederick**

blur /blur/ *n* **1.** FUZZY OR UNCLEAR IMAGE something that cannot be seen clearly, e.g. because it moves too quickly or because it is not distinctly remembered **2.** SMEAR OR SMEARED AREA a mark on something that makes it unclear, or an area of something that is unclear ■ *vti* (**blurs, blurring, blurred**) **1.** MAKE OR BECOME VAGUE to become less clear or distinct, or make something such as an idea less clear or distinct ○ *blurred the line between right and wrong* **2.** MAKE OR BECOME FUZZY to become fuzzy or unclear, or make something fuzzy or unclear ■ *adj Malaysia, Singapore* CONFUSED confused or uncertain about something (*informal*) ○ *I am very blur about linguistics.* [Mid-16C. Probably variant of BLEAR] —**blurredness** *n* —**blurrily** *adv* —**blurriness** *n* —**blurry** *adj*

blurb /blurb/ *n* a short piece of writing that praises and promotes something, especially a paragraph on the cover of a book [Early 20C. Coined by Gelett Burgess (1866–1951), US humorist] —**blurb** *vt*

blurt /blurt/ (**blurts, blurting, blurted**) *vt* to say something suddenly or impulsively, as if by accident ○ *blurted out an apology* [Late 16C. Probably an imitation of the sound]

blush /blush/ *vi* (**blushes, blushing, blushed**) **1.** BECOME RED IN FACE to turn red in the face because of emotion, especially embarrassment, shame, modesty, or pleasure **2.** BECOME EMBARRASSED to feel embarrassed or ashamed (*formal*) **3.** TURN RED OR PINK to become red or pink (*literary*) ■ *n* **1.** REDDENING OF FACE a reddening of the face caused by emotion, especially embarrassment, shame, modesty, or pleasure **2.** RED OR PINK a red colour or rosy glow **3.** *N Am* COSMETICS same as **blusher** **4.** WINE same as **blush wine** [Old English *blyscan* < Indo-European] —**blushful** *adj* —**blushing** *adj* —**blushingly** *adv*

blusher /blúshər/ *n* a pink or reddish powder or cream applied to the face, especially to accentuate the cheekbones. N Am term **blush**

blush wine *n* wine with a slight pink tinge

bluster /blústər/ *v* (**-ters, -tering, -tered**) **1.** *vti* SPEAK OR SAY LOUDLY OR ARROGANTLY to speak loudly, boisterously, or arrogantly, or say something in this way **2.** *vti* BEHAVE IN BULLYING WAY to behave or do something in a bullying or threatening way **3.** *vi* BLOW LOUDLY IN GUSTS to blow in sudden loud gusts (*refers to winds*) ■ *n* **1.** LOUD ARROGANT SPEECH loud, boisterous, or arrogant speech **2.** BULLYING BEHAVIOUR bullying or threatening behaviour **3.** LOUD GUST a sudden loud gust of wind **4.** LOUD FUSS a loud or angry commotion [Early 15C. < Middle Low German *blustern* 'blow violently'] —**blusterer** *n* —**blusteringly** *adv* —**blustery** *adj*

Blu-tack /bloo tak/ *tdmk* a trademark for a soft malleable substance that is used to stick paper temporarily to walls and other surfaces

Blvd *abbr* ROADS Boulevard

B-lymphocyte *n* IMMUNOL same as **B-cell**

Blyth /blíth/ industrial port in Northumberland, northern England. Population: 35,327 (1991).

Blyth, Chay (*b.* 1940) British yachtsman. He was the first person to sail single-handed around the world travelling east to west (1970–71). Born **Blyth, Charles**

Blyton /blít'n/, **Enid** (1897–1968) British writer. She was the author of over 600 children's books, including such characters as Noddy and the Famous Five. Full name **Blyton, Enid Mary**

bm *abbr* **1.** MEASURE board measure **2.** PHYSIOL bowel movement

BM *abbr* **1.** bench mark **2.** British Museum

BMA *abbr* British Medical Association

BMI *abbr* body mass index

BMJ *abbr* British Medical Journal

B movie *n* a low-budget film that was formerly shown in addition to the main feature —**B-movie** *adj*

bmp *abbr* a file extension for a bit map file. Full form **bit map**

BMus /bee múz/ *abbr* EDUC Bachelor of Music

BMX *n* the riding or racing of bicycles designed for use on rough terrain or open country. Full form **bicycle motocross**

bn[1] *abbr* Brunei (*used in Internet addresses*) See table at **domain name**

bn[2] *abbr* **1.** MIL battalion **2.** billion

Bn *abbr* **1.** baron **2.** MIL battalion

B'nai B'rith /bə náy bə reeth, -bríth/ *n* an international Jewish social service organization founded in New York in 1843 [< Hebrew, 'Sons of the Covenant']

bo *abbr* Bolivia (*used in Internet addresses*) See table at **domain name**

BO[1] *n* an unpleasant smell that comes from somebody because of sweat, lack of hygiene, or a physical disorder (*informal*) Full form **body odour**

BO[2] *abbr* ARTS box office

b.o. *abbr* **1.** BUSINESS branch office **2.** FIN broker's order **3.** FIN buyer's option

B/O *abbr* ACCT brought over

boa /bó ə/ *n* **1.** a nonvenomous, often large snake that kills by winding its body around its prey and suffocating it. Native to: tropical America, Africa, Asia. Family: Boidae. **2.** a long fluffy scarf of feathers or fur worn by women around the neck [14C. < Latin, 'large water snake']

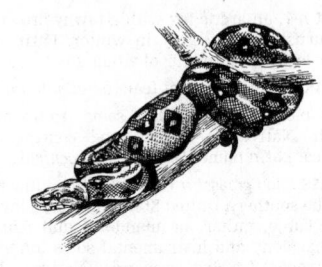

boa constrictor

boa constrictor *n* a large snake of the boa family that kills by winding its body around its prey and crushing it. Native to: tropical Central and South America. Latin name: *Boa constrictor*.

Boadicea ♦ **Boudicca**

boar

boar /bawr/ *n* (*plural* **boars** or *same*) **1.** UNCASTRATED PIG a male pig that has not been castrated **2.** MALE MAMMAL a male mammal, e.g. a male badger, beaver, or raccoon **3.** ZOOL same as **wild boar**. See illustration on previous page ■ *adj Carib* MALE indicating a male animal, e.g. a boar-hog [Old English *bār* < W Germanic]

SPELLCHECK boar or **bore**? Do not confuse the spelling of *boar* and *bore*, which sound similar. The word *boar* is only used as a noun, denoting an animal. The word *bore* is principally used as a verb, meaning 'cause to lose interest' or 'make a hole': *I won't bore you with the details. The insects bore through the bark.* It is also the past tense of the verb *bear: I bore them no ill will.* As a noun, *bore* denotes an uninteresting person or thing, the internal diameter of a pipe or gun barrel, or a large powerful wave.

board /bawrd/ *n* **1.** FLAT PIECE OF WOOD a piece of wood cut into a flat rectangular shape, especially a long narrow piece used for building **2.** FLAT SURFACE FOR PARTICULAR PURPOSE a flat piece of wood, plastic, or other rigid material, used for a particular purpose, e.g. for chopping food **3.** BOARD GAMES FLAT SURFACE FOR GAME a flat surface on which a game is played, especially a piece of wood or cardboard marked with coloured areas for a game such as chess **4.** COMPOSITE MATERIAL PRESSED INTO SHEET a rigid sheet material such as plywood made by compressing layers of other materials **5.** CONTROL PANEL a panel on which the controls of a piece of electrical equipment are mounted **6.** EDUC same as **blackboard 7.** same as **noticeboard 8.** ELECTRONICS same as **circuit board 9.** SWIMMING same as **diving board 10.** SURFING same as **surfboard 11.** same as **scoreboard 12.** SPORTS same as **snowboard 13.** BASKETBALL same as **backboard** (sense 2) **14.** PUBL BOOK COVER either of the pair of pieces of stiff cardboard that together form the front and back covers of a book **15.** NAUT BOAT'S SIDE the side of a boat **16.** GROUP CHOSEN TO MAKE DECISIONS a group of people chosen to make executive or managerial decisions for an organization (*takes a singular or plural verb*) **17.** DAILY MEALS daily meals provided at the place where somebody lives, usually for money or in return for work **18.** TABLE LAID WITH FOOD a table used for meals, especially one with food laid out on it (*archaic*) **19.** SAILING DISTANCE SAILED INTO WIND the distance covered by a sailing vessel in one period of sailing as near as possible into the wind **20.** *ANZ* SHEEP-SHEARING FLOOR the area, sometimes raised like a platform or stage, where sheep are sheared inside a shearing shed ■ **boards** *npl* **1.** THEATRICAL STAGE the stage in a theatre **2.** ICE HOCKEY RINK ENCLOSURE the wooden wall that surrounds an ice hockey rink ■ *v* (**boards, boarding, boarded**) **1.** *vti* GET ONTO VEHICLE AS PASSENGER to get onto a vehicle, especially a train, boat, or plane, as a passenger **2.** *vti* TAKE PASSENGERS ON FOR JOURNEY to take passengers onto a vehicle, especially a train, boat, or plane ○ *This flight is now boarding.* **3.** *vt* NAUT ATTACK OR INSPECT SHIP to come alongside a ship in order for people to go from one ship to another for the purposes of attack or inspection **4.** *also* **board up** *vt* COVER SOMETHING WITH BOARDS to fix boards onto something, especially to cover any openings ○ *The house had been boarded up for the winter.* ○ *The windows were boarded over.* **5.** *vti* BE PROVIDED WITH ROOM AND MEALS to be provided with accommodation and meals in return for money or work, e.g. in a school or guesthouse, or provide somebody with these [Old English *bord* < Germanic, 'board, plank' and 'border, ship's side'] ◇ **go by the board** to be neglected, no longer used, cast aside, or destroyed ◇ **on board 1.** into or on a vehicle, especially a train, boat, or plane **2.** into an existing group or project (*informal*) ○ *As soon as we bring this new analyst on board, the workload should return to normal.* ◇ **take something on board 1.** to understand or realize something fully **2.** to accept or include something such as a suggestion or new idea

SPELLCHECK Do not confuse the spelling of *board* and *bored* ('tired and impatient'), which sound similar.

board bridge *n* BOARD GAMES same as **duplicate bridge**

boarder /báwrdər/ *n* **1.** SOMEBODY PAYING FOR FOOD AND BED somebody who pays to sleep and eat in a private home or boarding house **2.** PUPIL LIVING AT SCHOOL a school pupil who lives at the school during term time **3.** SOMEBODY TRYING TO CAPTURE SHIP somebody who tries to get onto a ship to capture it

board exam *n* **1.** in the United States, an examination taken by somebody in order to qualify for work in a particular field, e.g. medicine or dentistry **2.** in the United States, an examination taken as part of the admission procedure for some colleges and universities

board foot *n* a unit of volume for measuring timber, equal to the volume of a board that is one foot square and one inch thick

board game *n* a game such as chess or backgammon that involves moving pieces around on a board marked with coloured areas

boarding /báwrding/ *n* a number of wooden boards, especially when used for a particular purpose, e.g. to make a floor or a fence

boarding card *n* TRAVEL same as **boarding pass**

boarding house *n* a private home that provides a room and meals to paying guests who are usually long-term residents

boarding pass *n* an additional ticket or document that a passenger must have in order to be allowed onto an aircraft or ship

boarding school *n* a school that provides some or all pupils with accommodation and daily meals

Boardman /báwrdmən/, **Chris** (*b.* 1968) British cyclist. He won a gold medal at the Barcelona Olympics (1992) and broke several world pursuit and endurance records in 1996 and 1997. Full name **Boardman, Christopher Miles**

board measure *n* a system for measuring timber volume based on the board foot

Board of Deputies *n* a representative body that concerns itself with the collective legal and political interests of British Jews

board of trade *n N Am* an organization of businesses and banks that has the goal of promoting commercial interest in a state, city, or other area

Board of Trade *n* a British government department until 1970 that regulated commerce and promoted exports, now part of the Department for Trade and Industry

boardroom /báwrd room, -room/ *n* a room where the members of a board meet

boardsailing /báwrd sayling/ *n* SPORTS same as **windsurfing** —**boardsailor** *n*

board shorts *npl Aus* knee-length swimming shorts often worn by surfers

boardwalk /báwrd wawk/ *n* a raised walkway made of boards, built across marshy ground or sand

Boas /bố az/, **Franz** (1858–1942) German-born US anthropologist. He helped establish anthropology as an academic discipline. He advocated a scientific approach to anthropological investigation and supported the theory of cultural relativism.

> 'Much of what we ascribe to human nature is no more than a reaction to the restraints put upon us by our civilization.'
> [Franz Boas. Quoted in *Coming of Age in Samoa*, Margaret Mead; 1928]

boast[1] /bốst/ *v* (**boasts, boasting, boasted**) **1.** *vti* OVEREMPHASIZE POSSESSIONS OR ACCOMPLISHMENTS to refer immodestly to possessions or achievements **2.** *vt* POSSESS SOMETHING DESIRABLE to possess or contain something, especially something desirable ○ *Our town boasts the world's biggest roller coaster.* ■ *n* **1.** EXCESSIVELY PROUD STATEMENT an immodest reference to possessions or achievements **2.** DESIRABLE POSSESSION something possessed that is desirable [13C. < Anglo-Norman *bost* 'boasting' < N Germanic] —**boaster** *n* —**boastful** *adj* —**boastfully** *adv* —**boastfulness** *n*

boast[2] /bốst/ (**boasts, boasting, boasted**) *vt* to shape stone roughly using a chisel [Early 19C. Origin ?]

boat /bốt/ *n* **1.** SMALL VESSEL FOR TRAVELLING ON WATER a small, often open vessel for travelling on water. See illustration on next page **2.** SHIP OR SUBMARINE a watercraft of any size or type **3.** SOMETHING SHAPED LIKE BOAT an open container shaped like a boat, e.g. one for holding gravy or incense ■ *v* (**boats, boating, boated**) **1.** *vi* TRAVEL BY BOAT to travel by boat, or ride in a boat for pleasure **2.** *vt* CARRY SOMETHING BY BOAT to move or transport something by boat **3.** *vt* FISHING PULL FISH TO BOAT to bring a caught fish to a boat [Old English *bāt* < Germanic] ◇ **in the same boat** in the same situation or having the same problems as somebody else

(*informal*) ◇ **miss the boat** to fail to take advantage of an opportunity (*informal*) ◇ **push the boat out** to spend a lot of money when celebrating something or entertaining somebody (*informal*) ◇ **rock the boat** to cause trouble, especially by questioning an accepted situation (*informal*)

boatbill /bốt bil/ *n* a bird of the heron family with a large, dark, heavy beak. Native to: tropical America. Latin name: *Cochlearius cochlearius*.

boat deck *n* a deck on a ship where the lifeboats are carried

boatel /bō tél/, **botel** *n* **1.** a waterside hotel where people travelling in boats can stay and moor their boats **2.** a ship that functions as a hotel [Mid-20C. Blend of BOAT + HOTEL]

boater /bốtər/ *n* **1.** a circular straw hat with a flat brim, a flat crown, and a hatband **2.** somebody who rides in a boat

boathook /bốt hook/ *n* a long pole with a hook on one end, used for pulling or pushing boats, rafts, or logs, or for picking up items from the water

boathouse /bốt howss/ (*plural* **-houses** /-howziz/) *n* a small building beside water, in which boats are kept

boatie /bốti/ *n ANZ* an enthusiast for boats or sailing (*informal*)

boating /bốting/ *n* the activity of riding in a boat for pleasure

boatload /bốt lōd/ *n* **1.** an amount of something or a number of people that fills a boat **2.** a large amount of something or a large number of people (*informal*)

boatman /bốtmən/ (*plural* **-men** /-mən/) *n* somebody who operates or works on a boat, especially somebody who takes people for rides on a boat or who rents boats out to others —**boatmanship** *n*

boat neck *n* a wide shallow neckline that runs from shoulder to shoulder and is equally deep at the front and back, similar to the neckline of a traditional sailor's blouse

boat people *npl* refugees who leave their country by boat

Boat Race *n* an annual rowing race on the Thames between Oxford and Cambridge Universities, each represented by one boat with a crew of eight

boat-rocker *n* somebody who is unafraid to challenge the status quo or stir up controversy

boatswain /bốss'n/, **bo's'n, bosun** *n* a non-commissioned officer or warrant officer on a ship in charge of the maintenance of the vessel, its boats, and other equipment [Old English *bātswegen* < BOAT + Old Norse *sveinn* 'boy' (see SWAIN)]

boatswain's chair *n* a board supported by ropes, slung over the side of a ship or up in the rigging for somebody to sit on while working

boat train *n* a train that takes people between a dockside and a town, usually timed to coincide with the arrival or departure of a ferry or liner

boatwoman /bốt woomən/ (*plural* **-women** /-wimin/) *n* a woman who operates or works on a boat, especially one who takes people for rides on a boat or who rents boats out to others

boatyard /bốt yaard/ *n* an area where boats are built or maintained

bob[1] /bob/ *vi* (**bobs, bobbing, bobbed**) **1.** BOUNCE to bounce up and down quickly and repeatedly, especially in and out of the water while floating **2.** MAKE CURTSY, BOW, OR NOD to make a quick movement, especially a curtsy, bow, or nod ■ *n* **1.** SMALL HANGING OR BOUNCING OBJECT a small hanging or bouncing object, e.g. a weight on a plumb line or a fishing bobber **2.** CURTSY, BOW, OR NOD a quick movement such as a curtsy, bow, or nod [14C. Probably an imitation of the sound]

bob[2] /bob/ *n* **1.** WOMAN'S SHORT HAIRCUT a woman's short haircut, especially a straight cut at chin length **2.** SOMETHING CUT SHORT something that has been shortened, e.g. a horse's tail when docked, a dog's ears when clipped, or a short line of poetry at the end of a stanza **3.** SPORTS same as **bobsleigh** (*informal*) ■ *vt* (**bobs, bobbing, bobbed**) CUT HAIR SHORT to cut a person's hair or a horse's tail short so that it is all one length [14C. Origin ?]

bob[3] /bob/ (*plural same*) *n* a shilling in the former

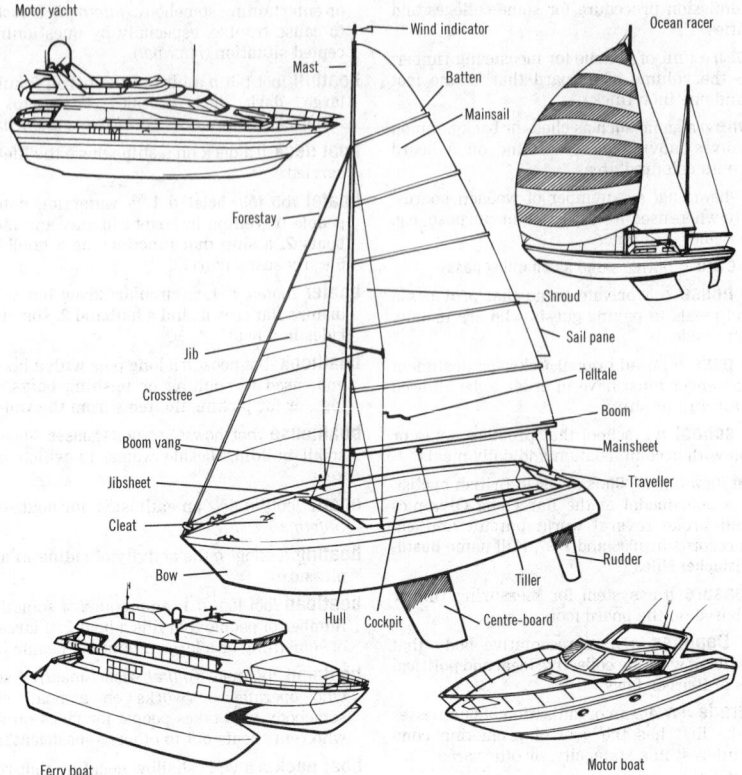

Motor yacht   Wind indicator   Ocean racer

Mast   Batten   Mainsail

Forestay   Shroud   Sail pane   Telltale

Jib   Crosstree   Boom   Mainsheet

Boom vang   Traveller

Jibsheet   Cleat   Rudder

Bow   Tiller   Hull   Cockpit   Centre-board

Ferry boat   Motor boat

boat

British currency system (*informal*) [Late 18C. Origin ?]

bob[4] /bob/ *n* a small polishing wheel of felt or leather ■ *vt* (**bobs, bobbing, bobbed**) to polish something using a bob [Probably < BOB[2]]

Bob /bob/ [Pet form of the name *Robert*] ◇ **Bob's your uncle** used after an explanation of how to do something to say that it will be easy or simple to do (*informal*)

bobber /bóbbər/ *n* a light object attached to a fishing line that floats on the surface of the water to keep the bait at the proper depth

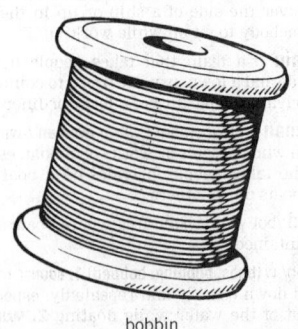

bobbin

bobbin /bóbbin/ *n* **1.** a cylinder wound with thread, yarn, or wire used for sewing, spinning, weaving, knitting, or making lace **2.** a narrow cotton cord, often braided, formerly used for trimming and binding [Mid-16C. < French *bobine* 'sewing instrument' < Old French *balbiner*, probably alteration of *balbier* 'to stutter' < Latin *balbus* 'stuttering']

bobbinet /bóbbi nét/ *n* a machine-made net fabric with a hexagonal mesh

bobbin lace *n* a lace made by winding thread on bobbins around pins stuck into a pillow

bobble /bóbb'l/ *n* **1.** WOOLLEN BALL a woollen ball used as a decoration on clothing, especially on a woollen hat **2.** UP-AND-DOWN MOVEMENT a fast repeated up-and-

down movement ■ *vti* (**-bles, -bling, -bled**) MOVE UP AND DOWN to move, or cause something to move, quickly and repeatedly up and down [Early 19C. Probably < BOB[1]]

bobble hat *n* a woollen hat with a woollen ball on its crown as a decoration

bobby /bóbbi/ (*plural* **-bies**) *n* POLICE same as **policeman** (*informal dated*) [Mid-19C. < pet form of *Robert*, after Sir Robert PEEL, who introduced the 1828 Police Act]

bobby calf *n* a male calf of a dairy cow that is slaughtered before weaning and used for veal [Probably < BOB[2]]

bobby-dazzler *n* an excellent thing or person, especially a good-looking woman (*dated informal*) [*Bobby*, origin ?]

bobby pin *n* ANZ, N Am HAIR a hair clip made of a tightly folded piece of wire that slides into the hair and holds it in place. UK term **hairgrip** [Probably < BOB[2] 'short haircut']

bobby socks /-soks/, **bobby sox** *npl* N Am ankle socks that fold over at the top, popular among teenage girls in the 1940s and 1950s [Probably < BOB[2]]

bobbysoxer /bóbbi soksər/ *n* N Am a teenage girl of the 1940s and 1950s (*informal*)

bobcat /bób kat/ *n* a medium-sized wildcat that is related to the lynx and has reddish-brown fur with black markings, tufted ears, and a short tail. Native to: North America. Latin name: *Lynx rufus*. [Late 19C. < BOB[2], from its short tail]

bobol /bó bol/, **bobbol** *n Carib* corrupt behaviour, usually involving misappropriation of money, the acceptance of bribes, or other fraudulent practices (*slang*)

bobolink /bóbbə lingk/ (*plural* **-links** or *same*) *n* a small bird, white and yellow above and black underneath, that nests in meadowland and has a distinctive bubbly song. Native to: North and South America. Latin name: *Dolichonyx oryzivorus*. [Late 18C. An imitation of the bird's call]

bobotie /bə bóti, bə bóoti/ *n S Africa* a dish of curried minced meat with a baked egg topping [Late 19C. < Afrikaans, probably < Malay]

Bobotov Kuk /bóbbə tof koók/ mountain in Montenegro, Federal Republic of Yugoslavia. It is the highest peak in the Dinaric range. Height: 2,522 m/8,274 ft.

bob skate *n N Am* an ice skate that has two parallel blades, usually used by children [< BOB[2], from its shortness]

bobsled /bób sled/ *n N Am* SPORTS same as **bobsleigh**

bobsleigh /bób slay/ *n* **1.** RACING SLEDGE a long racing sledge with steering, brakes, a seat for two or more people, and two pairs of runners, one in front and one at the back **2.** SLEDGE MADE OF TWO SHORT SLEDGES a long sledge made up of two short sledges attached one behind the other, used for recreation or for carrying things over snow ■ *vi* (**-sleighs, -sleighing, -sleighed**) GO IN BOBSLEIGH to ride or race in a bobsleigh

bobstay /bób stay/ *n* on a sailing boat, a rope used to hold down a bowsprit [*Bob*, origin ?]

bobtail /bób tayl/ *n* **1.** an animal's tail that is naturally short or has been cut short **2.** an animal, especially a horse or dog, that has a short or shortened tail [Mid-16C. < BOB[2], from its shortness] —**bobtailed** *adj*

bobwhite /bób wīt/ (*plural* **-whites** or *same*) *n* a small brown mottled quail with white markings on its head. Native to: central and eastern North America. Latin name: *Colinus virginianus*. [Early 19C. An imitation of the bird's call]

Boccaccio /bo káchi ō/, **Giovanni** (1313–75) Italian writer and humanist. Between 1348 and 1353 he wrote the *Decameron* (published 1353), a collection of 100 tales told by refugees from the Florentine plague of 1348. A classic of world literature, it profoundly influenced English writers such as Shakespeare.

'Although love dwells in gorgeous palaces, and sumptuous apartments, more willingly than in miserable and desolate cottages, it cannot be denied but that he sometimes causes his power to be felt in the gloomy recesses of forests, among the most bleak and rugged mountains, and in the dreary caves of a desert.'
[Giovanni Boccaccio, *Decameron*; 1353]

bocce /bó chee/, **bocci** *n* an Italian game similar to bowling, usually played on a long earth-floored court [Early 20C. Via Italian *bocce*, plural of *boccia* '(round) ball' < Vulgar Latin *bottia* 'boss']

Boccherini /bókə reéni/, **Luigi** (1743–1805) Italian composer and cellist. A prolific writer of chamber music, he composed for the Spanish and Prussian courts. Full name **Boccherini, Luigi Rodolfo**

bocci *n* BOWLS another spelling of **bocce**

Boccioni /bo chóni/, **Umberto** (1882–1916) Italian painter and sculptor. A major theorist of the futurist school, he worked in Paris and Rome.

Boche /bosh/ (*plural* **Boches** or *same*), **boche** (*plural* **boches** or *same*) *n* an offensive term for Germans considered collectively, especially German soldiers of World War I (*dated*) [Early 20C. Shortening of French *alboche*, blend of *allemand* 'German' + *caboche* 'cabbage, blockhead']

Bochum /bókəm, bókhəm/ city in the industrial Ruhr district of North Rhine-Westphalia, Germany. Population: 401,129 (1997).

bod /bod/ *n* (*slang*) **1.** somebody's body or figure **2.** same as **person** (sense 1) [Late 18C. Shortening of BODY]

BOD *abbr* biochemical oxygen demand

bodacious /bō dáyshəss/, **bowdacious** (*informal humorous*) *adj* **1.** *UK, Midwest, Southern US* IMPRESSIVE remarkable or excellent ○ *That's one bodacious boat!* **2.** *Midwest, Southern US* BOLD outrageously arrogant or uninhibited ○ *a bodacious lie* ■ *adv Midwest, Southern US* VERY extremely ○ *I'm bodacious hungry.* [Mid-19C. Perhaps alteration of dialect blend of BOLD + AUDACIOUS] —**bodaciously** *adv*

bode[1] /bōd/ (**bodes, boding, boded**) *vti* to be a particular indication of something that is about to happen ○ *This does not bode well for the future of the organization.* [Old English *bodian* 'announce, foretell' < *boda* 'messenger' < Germanic]

bode[2] past tense of **bide**

bodega /bō dáygə/ *n* in a Spanish-speaking country, a wine shop or a warehouse for the storage of wine [Mid-19C. Via Spanish < Latin *apotheca* 'storehouse']

bodge /boj/ (*informal*) *vti* (**bodges, bodging, bodged**) to make or repair something badly ■ *n* a clumsy piece of work or a badly done repair [Mid-16C. Alteration of BOTCH]

bodgie /bójji/ *adj Aus* FALSE false or fake (*slang*) ■ *n ANZ* **1.** SOMETHING FLAWED something imperfect or without value (*informal*) **2.** JUVENILE DELINQUENT a boy who is a juvenile delinquent (*dated*) [Mid-20C. Probably < BODGE]

Bodhidharma /bóddi daármə/ (*fl* 6th century) Indian monk. He was the founder of the Zen school of Buddhism.

bodhisattva /bóddi sátvə/ *n* in Buddhism, a deity or being who has attained enlightenment worthy of nirvana but who remains in the human world to help others [Early 19C. < Sanskrit *bodhi* 'perfect knowledge' + *sattva* 'being, reality']

bodhrán /bów raan/ *n* a shallow drum used in Irish and sometimes Scottish folk music, covered on one side with goat skin, held in one hand, and played with the other using a stick [Late 20C. < Irish]

bodice /bóddiss/ *n* **1.** the part of a woman's dress or undergarment that covers the upper body **2.** a close-fitting, often laced-up top worn over a blouse in the past or as part of some national costumes [Mid-16C. < plural of BODY]

bodice ripper *n* a popular historical romance in fiction or film that has sexually explicit content and usually involves a melodramatic seduction (*informal*) [< typical scenes where a seducer tears a woman's bodice open]

-bodied *adj, suffix* having a body of a particular kind ○ *a wide-bodied aircraft*

bodiless /bóddiləss/ *adj* having no body or physical substance

bodily /bóddili/ *adj* PHYSICAL relating to, involving, or typical of the body ■ *adv* **1.** PHYSICALLY physically or in the flesh **2.** USING PHYSICAL FORCE by taking hold of somebody or something with the hands and using physical strength ○ *bodily removed him from the building*

bodkin /bódkin/ *n* **1.** LARGE BLUNT NEEDLE a long thick blunt needle with a large eye **2.** HOLE-PUNCHING TOOL a small slender tool with a sharp point used for making holes in cloth or leather **3.** PRINTING TYPE-SETTING TOOL a long sharp typesetting tool [14C. Probably < Celtic, 'small dagger']

Bodleian /bóddli ən/ *n* the library of Oxford University, one of England's copyright deposit libraries [Mid-17C. After Sir Thomas *Bodley*, English diplomat who refounded the library in 1603]

Bodmin /bódmin/ *n* historic town in Cornwall, southwestern England, near Bodmin Moor, an Area of Outstanding Natural Beauty. Population: 12,553 (1991).

bodom /bódəm/ *n* a highly valued Ghanaian bead with a black center made of powdered glass [< Ashanti]

Bodoni /bə dóni/ *n* a font or style of typeface [Late 19C. After Giambattista *Bodoni* (1740–1813), Italian printer]

body /bóddi/ *n* (*plural* **-ies**) **1.** PHYSICAL FORM OF HUMAN OR ANIMAL the complete material structure or physical form of a human being or animal **2.** DEAD HUMAN OR ANIMAL REMAINS the physical remains of a dead person or animal **3.** TORSO the main part of the physical structure of a human being or animal, not including the head, arms, legs, or wings **4.** SOMEBODY'S FIGURE somebody's figure or build, especially with regard to shape and muscle tone ○ *a great body* **5.** GROUP an organized group of people such as lawmakers, students, or soldiers ○ *a legislative body* **6.** COLLECTION a collection or amount of something, considered as a whole ○ *a body of evidence* **7.** MASS an individual mass of something, especially water or land ○ *a large body of water* **8.** MAIN PART OF VEHICLE the main part of a vehicle, e.g. the fuselage of an aircraft or the outer shell of a motor car **9.** MAIN PART OR MAJORITY the main or central part of something, e.g. the majority of a quantity **10.** BUILDINGS NAVE the nave or central part of a church **11.** MUSIC MAIN PART OF MUSICAL INSTRUMENT the largest part of a musical instrument, especially the soundbox of a stringed instrument **12.** MAIN PART OF SOMETHING WRITTEN the main part of a piece of writing ○ *in the body of the text* **13.** FULLNESS OF FLAVOUR IN WINE the extent to which a wine seems full when tasted. Body increases with alcohol content and density. ○ *a French red with plenty of body* **14.** THICKNESS OF LIQUID the thickness or opacity of a liquid such as paint or soup **15.** FULLNESS OF TEXTURE a fullness and bounciness in texture or appearance ○ *designed to give hair more body* **16.** FIRMNESS OF FABRIC the firmness of a type of cloth **17.** *UK* CLOTHING GARMENT FOR TORSO a tight one-piece garment that covers the torso and is fastened at the crotch. ANZ, N Am term **body suit 18.** UPPER PART OF GARMENT the part of a garment that covers the torso **19.** PERSON used to refer to a person or yourself in an impersonal way (*informal*) ○ *This treatment could make a body feel unwelcome!* **20.** CERAMICS MATERIAL FOR MAKING CERAMICS a blend of clay and other raw materials used in making a ceramic piece **21.** PHYS PHYSICAL OBJECT a distinguishable physical object **22.** MATHS OBJECT REPRESENTED MATHEMATICALLY a physical object represented mathematically ■ *vt* (**-ies, -ying, -ied**) GIVE SHAPE TO SOMETHING to give shape or substance to something (*literary*) [Old English *bodig*, origin ?]

body armour *n* a protective covering for the upper part of the torso

body bag *n* a bag designed to hold a dead body, usually made of plastic and fitted with a zip

body blow *n* **1.** something that causes great physical, financial, or emotional damage to somebody or something **2.** a punch that lands between the neck and the waist

body board *n* a short polystyrene surfboard on which a surfer lies rather than stands

body building *n* the practice of developing the muscles of the body through weightlifting and diet (*hyphenated before a noun*) —**body builder** *n*

body cavity *n* **1.** an opening into the body, e.g. the mouth, oesophagus, vagina, rectum, or ear **2.** ZOOL same as **coelom**

body-centred *adj* describes crystals that have an atom in the middle of each unit cell as well as at the corners

bodycheck /bóddi chek/ *n* in some sports, especially ice hockey or soccer, an illegal act of using the body to obstruct an opposing player ■ *vt* (**-checks, -checking, -checked**) in some sports, especially ice hockey or soccer, to use the body to obstruct an opposing player illegally

body clock *n* BIOL same as **biological clock**

body corporate (*plural* **bodies corporate**) *n* **1.** a group of people legally recognized as being able to act as one body **2.** *Aus* a committee that manages common property such as the gardens or entrance hall of a block of flats

body count *n* a count of the number of dead bodies resulting from an incident, especially of soldiers killed after combat

body double *n* somebody whose body is filmed instead of that of an actor, especially in a scene involving nudity

body-flannen //bóddi flanən/ *n regional* a vest [Alteration of FLANNEL]

REGIONAL NOTE See *vest*.

body fluid *n* **1.** a liquid produced by the body, e.g. blood, saliva, semen, vaginal secretions, milk, urine, sweat, or tears **2.** the water content of the body

bodyguard /bóddi gaard/ *n* a person or group of people paid to protect somebody from physical attack

body-hugging *adj* fitting tightly on the body

body image *n* somebody's own impression of how his or her body looks

body language *n* bodily mannerisms, postures, and facial expressions that can be interpreted as unconsciously communicating somebody's feelings or psychological state

bodyline bowling *n* in cricket, fast bowling in which the bowler deliberately aims the ball at the batsman's body

body mass index *n* an index that expresses adult weight in relation to height. It is calculated as weight in kilograms divided by height in metres squared. A body mass index of less than 25 is considered normal, and one of over 30 implies obesity.

body odour *n* HEALTH full form of **BO**

body packer *n* somebody who swallows illegal narcotics in order to smuggle them (*slang*)

body politic *n* the people of a nation or any politically organized state, considered as a group

body popping *n* a type of dancing, popular especially in the 1980s, involving convulsive, sinuous, or robotic movements (*slang*) —**body popper** *n*

body-sark //bóddi saark/ *n regional* a vest [< Old English *serc* 'shirt' < Germanic]

REGIONAL NOTE See *vest*.

body search *n* a thorough physical search of somebody suspected of hiding something such as weapons or narcotics on his or her person

bodyshaper /bóddi shaypər/ *n* a woman's elasticated undergarment reaching from bust to hips, intended to produce a more streamlined body shape

body shield *n UK, ANZ, Can* a small shield attached to the arm for fending off stones and other light projectiles. US term **body bunker**

body shop *n* a workshop where car bodies are repaired (*informal*)

body snatcher *n* in the past, somebody who stole corpses from graves, usually to sell for medical study —**body snatching** *n*

body stocking *n* a close-fitting one-piece garment that covers the body and sometimes the arms and legs

body suit *n ANZ, N Am* a woman's close-fitting, one-piece garment that covers the torso and is fastened at the crotch by snaps. UK term **body**

bodysurf /bóddi surf/ (**-surfs, -surfing, -surfed**) *vi* to surf without a board by lying on a wave and using the body as a surfboard —**bodysurfer** *n* —**bodysurfing** *n*

body wall *n* the part of an animal's body that forms its external surface, encloses the body cavity, and consists of layers of skin and muscle

body warmer *n* a sleeveless quilted jacket, worn outdoors primarily to retain body heat in cold weather

bodywork /bóddi wurk/ *n* **1.** AUTOMOT CAR BODY the outer frame of a car or other motor vehicle **2.** AUTOMOT REPAIR OF MOTOR VEHICLE BODY the work of repairing the outer frame of a car or other motor vehicle **3.** HEALTH MASSAGE OR PHYSICAL MANIPULATION OF BODY physical manipulation of the human body, including all types of massage, to improve general health or posture, or to treat injuries

boehmite /búr mīt/ *n* a light grey to dark red-brown mineral consisting of hydrous aluminium oxide. Source: bauxite. [Early 20C. After Johann *Böhm* (1895–1952), German chemist]

Boeotia /bi óshə/ region of ancient Greece, northwest of Athens. Its city-states formed the Boeotian League under the leadership of Thebes.

Boer /boor, bawr/ *n* **1.** somebody of Dutch descent who lives in South Africa **2.** *S Africa* a police officer (*dated slang*) [Mid-19C. < Dutch *boer* 'farmer'] —**Boer** *adj*

boeremusiek /bóorə myoozik/ *n S Africa* country dance music popular among Afrikaners, usually played by a small band [Mid-20C. < Afrikaans < *boere* 'Afrikaner' + *musiek* 'music']

boerewors /bóorə vawrss/, **boerie** /bóori/ *n S Africa* a large spicy home-made sausage [Mid-20C. < Afrikaans < *boere* 'Afrikaner' + *wors* 'sausage']

Boer War *n* a war fought in South Africa from 1899 to 1902 between the British and the descendants of the Dutch, ending eventually in a British victory

boet /boot, bŏt/ *n S Africa* a friend (*informal*) [19C. < Afrikaans 'brother']

Boethius /bō éethi əss/, **Anicius Manlius Severinus** (480?–524) Roman philosopher. He wrote *The Consolation of Philosophy* (523?), works on logic, and commentaries on Aristotle. His writings influenced scholars in medieval Europe.

'If chance is defined as an event produced by random motion without any causal nexus, I would say there is no such thing as chance.'
[Anicius Manlius Severinus Boethius, *The Consolation of Philosophy*; 523?]

BOF *abbr* COMPUT beginning of file

boff[1] /bof/ n 1. US PUNCH OR SLAP a blow with the fist or open hand (informal) 2. N Am OFFENSIVE TERM an offensive term for sexual intercourse (slang) ■ v (boffs, boffing, boffed) 1. vt US PUNCH OR SLAP SOMEBODY to hit somebody with the fist or open hand (informal) 2. vti N Am OFFENSIVE TERM an offensive term meaning to have sexual intercourse with somebody (slang) [Early 20C. An imitation of the sound of a blow]

boff[2] /bof/ n US (dated informal) 1. a joke that gets a big laugh 2. a big hearty laugh [Mid-20C. Probably contraction of BOX OFFICE, indicating a box-office success]

boffin /bóffin/ n a scientific expert, especially one involved in research, who is regarded as being unconventional or absent-minded (informal) [Mid-20C. Origin ?]

boffo /bóffō/ adj US excellent or extremely successful (dated informal)

Bofors gun /bófarz-/ n a 40 mm antiaircraft gun with one or two barrels, developed in Sweden and used by British and US forces in World War II [After a munitions site in Sweden]

bog /bog/ n 1. an area of wet marshy ground, largely consisting of accumulated decomposing plant material. It supports vegetation such as sedges and moss and may ultimately turn into peat. 2. same as **toilet** (sense 1) (slang) [14C. < Gaelic bognach 'marsh' < bog 'soft'] —**boggy** adj
bog down vt to slow somebody's general progress (informal) ○ got bogged down in unimportant details
bog in vi ANZ to start doing something enthusiastically, especially to begin eating (informal)
bog off vi to go away (slang; usually used as a command)

bogan /bógən/ n Aus an offensive term for somebody regarded as unsophisticated or unfashionable (informal) [From Swahili, 'enclosure']

Humphrey Bogart

Bogart /bó gaart/, **Humphrey** (1899–1957) US film actor. The classic American 'tough-but-tender' leading man, his many films include Casablanca (1942) and The African Queen (1951). Full name **Bogart, Humphrey DeForest**

'The only thing you owe the public is a good performance.'
[Attributed to Humphrey Bogart]

bog asphodel n a plant of the lily family with grassy leaves that is common in boggy areas. Flowers: small, yellow, in clusters. Native to: Europe. Latin name: Narthecium ossifragum.

bogey /bógi/ n (plural **bogeys**) 1. CAUSE OF TROUBLE something that troubles, annoys, or frightens somebody (slang) 2. PIECE OF NASAL MUCUS a lump of mucus in or from somebody's nose (slang) N Am term **booger** 3. POLICE OFFICER a police officer or detective (slang dated) 4. GOLF ONE OVER PAR a golf score of one over par for a particular hole 5. PARANORMAL same as **bogeyman** (sense 1) 6. AIR FORCE UNIDENTIFIED FLYING AIRCRAFT an aircraft in flight that cannot be identified, especially one assumed to be hostile (slang) ■ vt (**bogeys, bogeying, bogeyed**) GOLF SCORE ONE OVER PAR FOR HOLE in golf, to score one over par at a hole [Mid-19C. Alteration of BOGLE]

bogeyman /bógi man/ (plural **-men** /-men/), **bogyman** (plural **-men**) n 1. an imaginary person or monster that causes fear or is invoked to cause fear, especially in children 2. somebody or something regarded as hateful, evil, or frightening ○ The spectre of an election-vote recount is this year's political bogeyman.

boggin /bóggin/ adj regional dirty [< BOG]
REGIONAL NOTE See **manky**.

boggle /bógg'l/ (**-gles, -gling, -gled**) v 1. vi HESITATE WITH SECOND THOUGHTS to hesitate before doing something, usually because of being overwhelmed, afraid, or concerned 2. vti BAFFLE OR BECOME BAFFLED to astonish or confuse somebody or something, or become astonished or confused (informal) ○ The mind boggles! 3. vti US MAKE TRIVIAL MISTAKE to make a trivial mistake, or mismanage something (informal) [Late 16C. Probably related to BOGLE] —**boggler** n

bogie /bógi/ n 1. FRAMEWORK WITH WHEELS a framework mounted on a set of wheels on the undercarriage of a vehicle. Railway vehicles have one at each end and they swivel to allow the vehicle to go round a curve. 2. also **bogy** (plural **-gies**) SMALL RAILWAY TRUCK a small railway truck used for carrying heavy loads 3. S Asia TRAIN COMPARTMENT a compartment of a railway carriage [Mid-19C. Origin ?]

bogle /bóg'l/ n same as **bogeyman** (sense 1) (archaic or regional) [Early 16C. Origin ?]

Bognor Regis /bógnər reéjiss/ seaside resort in West Sussex, southern England. Population: 56,744 (1991).

bogong /bó gong/, **bogong moth, bugong** /boó gong/, **bugong moth** n a large Australian nocturnal moth that is eaten by Aboriginals. Latin name: Agrotis infusa. [< Aboriginal]

Bogong, Mount /bó gong/ the highest mountain in the state of Victoria, Australia and the site of a ski resort. Height: 1,986 m/6,516 ft.

Bogor /bó gawr/ city in Indonesia, near Jakarta, on western Java island. It is known for its botanical gardens. Population: 3,696,848 (1997).

Bogotá /bóggə taá/ capital of Colombia situated on a plateau in the eastern Andes. It is Colombia's largest city and its commercial, cultural, and political centre. Population: 6,422,198 (2000).

bog roll n toilet paper, or a roll of toilet paper (slang)

bog rosemary n a evergreen bush of the heath family. Flowers: pink or white, urn-shaped. Latin name: Andromeda polifolia.

bog spavin n a chronic puffy inflammation of the soft tissue of the hock joint of horses

bog-standard adj basic, ordinary, or lacking any special features (informal) ○ For that price you get your bog-standard production model, without accessories.

bogtrotter /bóg trottər/ n a highly offensive term for an Irish person (slang insult)

bogus /bógəss/ adj 1. false, dishonest, or fraudulently imitating something 2. US not good, pleasant, or acceptable (slang) [Early 19C. < Bogus, a machine for producing counterfeit money, origin ?] —**bogusly** adv —**bogusness** n

ORIGIN The word **bogus** is first recorded in American usage in the 1820s, referring to a machine for producing counterfeit money; its modern uses seem to have developed from there. Its ultimate origins remain unclear, but one suggestion is that it comes from tantrabogus, a word reportedly in use in New England in the early 19th century for 'a sinister-looking object' (which itself may have been based on bogy, meaning 'devil'). Another theory is that it may be related to Hausa boko, meaning 'deceit, fraud', and may have crossed the Atlantic with transported slaves.

bogus caller n somebody who claims to be an official in order to gain entry to a home with the intention of committing theft

bogy n RAIL same as **bogie** (sense 2)

bogyman n same as **bogeyman**

Bo Hai /bó hí/ large inlet of the Yellow Sea on the northeastern coast of China. Former name **Chihli, Gulf of**

bohea /bō heé/ n a low-quality black Chinese tea [Early 18C. < Chinese dialect Bu-yi, variant of Wu-yi, after the Wu-Yi hills in SE China]

bohemia /bō heémi ə/ n 1. a community of artists and other people whose lifestyles are regarded as unconventional 2. the lifestyle considered characteristic of bohemians

Bohemia /bō heémi ə/ historic region in the western Czech Republic. A former kingdom, it was the west-ernmost province of Czechoslovakia from 1918 to 1939 and from 1945 to 1949, but it was then divided into several districts. Area: 52,060 sq. km/20,100 sq. mi.

bohemian /bō heémi ən/ n somebody, often a writer or an artist, who does not live according to the conventions of society —**bohemian** adj —**bohemianism** n

Bohemian /bō heémi ən/ n 1. somebody who comes from Bohemia 2. LANG same as **Czech** (sense 3) (dated) ■ adj belonging to Bohemia, or its people or culture

Bohemian Brethren npl a Protestant Christian society, founded by the Hussites in Bohemia in 1467, that became the Moravian Church in 1722

Böhm /burm/, **Karl** (1894–1981) Austrian conductor. He was especially known for conducting the operas of Wolfgang Amadeus Mozart, and premiered a number of operas of Richard Strauss.

boho /bóhō/ n (plural **-hos**), adj same as **bohemian** (slang)

Bohr /bawr/, **Niels** (1885–1962) Danish physicist. He won the Nobel Prize in physics (1922) for his work on quantum theory. He participated in US atomic bomb development during World War II and later worked for the peaceful application of nuclear technology. Full name **Bohr, Niels Henrik David**

'An expert is a man who has made all the mistakes which can be made in a very narrow field.'
[Attributed to Niels Bohr]

Bohr effect n the effect of carbon dioxide on the binding of oxygen to haemoglobin [Mid-20C. After Christian Bohr (1855–1911), Danish physiologist]

bohrium /báwri əm/ n an unstable radioactive chemical element. Source: produced artificially by nuclear fusion. Symbol **Bh**. See table at **element** [Late 20C. After Niels BOHR]

Bohr theory n a theory of atomic structure postulating that electrons move around a nucleus in distinct orbits and that a jump between orbits is accompanied by the absorption or emission of a photon. It was the earliest important attempt to apply quantum theory to atomic structure. [Mid-20C. After Niels BOHR]

bohunk /bó hungk/ n N Am an offensive term for somebody from central or southeastern Europe (slang insult) [Early 20C. Blend of BOHEMIAN + hunk, shortening of HUNGARIAN]

boil[1] /boyl/ v (**boils, boiling, boiled**) 1. vti HEAT TO OR REACH BOILING POINT to heat a liquid until it forms bubbles and turns to gas, or to reach this state 2. vti CONTAIN OR CAUSE TO CONTAIN BOILING LIQUID to contain liquid that has reached boiling point, or cause the liquid in a container to boil 3. vti COOK IN BOILING LIQUID to cook something by submerging it in boiling liquid for a period of time, or be cooked in this way ○ Boil the spaghetti for about eight minutes. 4. vti PLACE IN BOILING WATER to put something such as clothing into boiling water, e.g. to clean or sterilize it, or be put into boiling water for these purposes 5. vi GET VERY HOT to be or become extremely hot (informal) 6. vi BUBBLE UP ON SURFACE to be stirred up and have bubbles breaking on the surface 7. vi GET VERY ANGRY to be or become very angry ■ n 1. STATE OF BUBBLING AT HIGH TEMPERATURE the point at which a liquid bubbles because it has reached the temperature at which it turns to gas, or the state of bubbling at this temperature 2. Can, Southern US OUTDOOR SEAFOOD PICNIC an outdoor picnic at which shellfish are boiled and eaten (informal) ○ a Low Country crab boil [13C. Via Old French boillir < Latin bullire 'to bubble' < bulla 'a bubble']
boil away vti to turn completely into steam, or turn all of a quantity of liquid into steam by boiling it
boil down v 1. vti to make a liquid mixture thicker and reduce its volume by heating it rapidly until much of the liquid turns to steam, or be made thicker in this way 2. vt to condense or summarize something such as information or text (informal)
boil down to vt to mean or amount to something in essence (informal) ○ It all boils down to the single question: Is he telling the truth?
boil off vti to remove something such as alcohol from a mixture by heating it rapidly until it turns to steam, or be removed in this way
boil over v 1. vti to reach or cause a liquid to reach

boiling point and be so full of bubbles that some of it spills from the container **2.** *vi* to become too intense or out of control ○ *her anger boiled over*

boil² /boyl/ *n* a painful pus-filled abscess on the skin caused by bacterial infection of a hair follicle [Old English *byl* 'inflammation' < W Germanic]

Boileau /bwaálō/, **Nicolas** (1636–1711) French writer. He was the author of *The Art of Poetry* (1674), a statement of the principles of classical verse. Full name **Boileau-Despréaux, Nicolas**

> 'A fool always finds a greater fool to admire him.'
> [Nicolas Boileau, *L'Art poétique (The Art of Poetry)*; 1674]

boiled sweet *n* a hard sweet made by boiling together water, sugar, and flavouring

boiler /bóylər/ *n* **1.** a large tank in which water is heated and stored, either as hot water or as steam, and used for heating or generating power **2.** an old chicken with flesh that is so tough that it must be boiled to make it palatable

boilermaker /bóylər maykər/ *n* **1.** an industrial worker who makes large metal objects, especially boilers **2.** *N Am* a drink of whisky followed by a drink of beer

boilerplate /bóylər playt/ *n* **1.** PLATE USED FOR MAKING BOILERS steel plate used for making boilers **2.** *N Am* CLICHÉD WRITING writing that says nothing new, informative, or interesting **3.** *N Am* FORMULAIC LANGUAGE stock or formulaic language such as that used in legal forms and documents such as powers of attorney and authors' contracts **4.** COMPUT REUSABLE UNIT OF CODE a unit of IT code writing that can be reused

boiler room *n* **1.** an area or room that houses one or more boilers for generating power or hot water **2.** a room from which telemarketers using high-pressure sales tactics, usually by telephone and often illegal, try to sell financial products or property of questionable value (*informal*)

boiler-room *adj US* relating to or being political campaign workers who perform administrative support tasks and make polling phone calls for a candidate

boiler suit *n* a one-piece long-sleeved garment worn over other clothes while doing manual labour or dirty jobs in order to protect them

boiling /bóyling/ *adj* **1.** extremely hot **2.** extremely angry ■ *n Scotland* same as **boiled sweet**

boiling point *n* **1.** the temperature at which a heated liquid turns to gas, e.g. 100°C or 212°F for water at sea level **2.** the point at which people lose their tempers or a situation becomes critical

boing /boyng/ *n* the sound made by something that bounces [Mid-20C. An imitation of the sound]

Bois ♦ Du Bois, W. E. B.

Boise /bóyssi, bóyzi/ capital and largest city of Idaho, on the Boise River. Population: 189,847 (2002 estimate).

boisterous /bóystərəss/ *adj* **1.** full of noisy enthusiasm and energy, and often roughness or wildness **2.** wild, rough, or stormy [13C. Alteration of *boistous*, via Old French *boistos* 'clumsy, rough' < Latin *buxus* 'made from box-tree wood'] —**boisterously** *adv* —**boisterousness** *n*

~~**boistrous**~~ incorrect spelling of **boisterous**

Boito /bō eétō/, **Arrigo** (1842–1918) Italian composer and librettist. He wrote the opera *Mefistofele* (1868) and the texts for Giuseppe Verdi's operas *Otello* (1887) and *Falstaff* (1893). Born **Boito, Enrico Giuseppe Giovanni**

boka /bókkə/ *interj* same as **boo-yah-kah** (*slang; used in Black English*) [Perhaps an imitation of the sound of gunshots]

Bokassa /bə kássə/, **Jean Bédel** (1921–96) Central African national leader and president (1966–77) and emperor (1977–79) of the Central African Republic. He seized power in the Central African Republic (1966) and ruled until his overthrow in 1979, the last two years as self-declared emperor.

bok choy /bók chóy/ *n ANZ, N Am* a Chinese cabbage with long white stalks and narrow green leaves. Latin name: *Brassica chinensis*. UK term **pak choi** [Mid-20C. < Chinese (Guangdang dialect) *baahk-choi* 'white vegetable']

boke /bōk/ *Scotland* (*informal*) *vti* (**bokes, boking, boked**) RETCH OR VOMIT to retch, or vomit something ■ *n* **1.** RETCHING OR VOMITING an act or instance of retching or vomiting **2.** SOMETHING VOMITED something that has been vomited [Mid-16C. Variant of POKE¹]

Bokmål /bók mawl/ *n* an official form of the Norwegian language, which is closer to Danish than Nynorsk [Mid-20C. < Norwegian < *bok* 'book' + *mål* 'language']

Bol. *abbr* **1.** Bolivia **2.** Bolivian

bola /bóllə/, **bolas** /-ləss/ *n* a strong cord with weights attached to the ends, used for catching cows by South American cowhands (**gauchos**) who throw it to entangle the cows' legs [Early 19C. Via Spanish, 'ball' < Latin *bulla* 'bubble']

bola tie *n US* CLOTHING same as **bolo tie**

bold /bōld/ *adj* **1.** FEARLESS AND ADVENTUROUS willing and eager to face danger or adventure with a sense of confidence and fearlessness **2.** REQUIRING OR SHOWING DARING requiring or showing fearlessness, daring, and often originality **3.** IMPUDENT OR PRESUMPTUOUS lacking in modesty or impolitely assertive **4.** CLEAR AND CONSPICUOUS standing out and therefore easily noticed ○ *bold colours* **5.** STEEP rising abruptly and steeply from the surroundings ○ *a bold cliff* **6.** PRINTING DARKER THAN STANDARD having darker thicker lines than standard type, fonts, or lettering ■ *n* PRINTING TYPE DARKER THAN STANDARD type, fonts, or lettering with darker thicker lines than is standard ■ *vt* (**bolds, bolding, bolded**) PRINTING PUT SOMETHING IN BOLD TYPE to set, print, or display text in bold type [Old English *bald* < Indo-European] —**boldly** *adv* —**boldness** *n*

boldface /bóld fayss/ *adj* PRINTING same as **bold** *adj* (sense 6) ■ *n* PRINTING same as **bold** ■ *vt* (**-faces, -facing, -faced**) to make letters darker and thicker for emphasis

boldfaced /bóld fáyst/ *adj* **1.** showing impudence or lack of shame or modesty **2.** PRINTING same as **bold** *adj* (sense 6)

bole¹ /bōl/ *n* the trunk of a tree [14C. < Old Norse *bolr*]

> **SPELLCHECK bole** or **bowl**? Do not confuse the spelling of *bole* and *bowl*, which sound similar. *Bole* is only used as a noun, denoting the trunk of a tree or a reddish-brown clay. The word *bowl* is much more frequent in general usage and can be used as a noun or a verb. As a noun it denotes a round container (as in *a bowl of milk*) or a ball used in bowls or bowling; as a verb it means 'roll or throw a ball' or 'move smoothly and quickly', as in *bowling along the lane*.

bole² /bōl/ *n* a reddish-brown clay used as a pigment [14C. < late Latin *bolus* 'clod of earth' (see BOLUS)]

bolection /bəléksh'n/ *n* a moulding covering an architectural joint and projecting beyond it, usually S-shaped in cross section [Mid-17C. Origin ?]

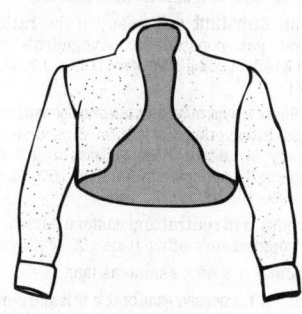

bolero (sense 3)

bolero /bə láirō/ (*plural* **-ros**) *n* **1.** DANCE SPANISH DANCE a Spanish dance in triple time that involves much foot-stamping and dramatic posing **2.** MUSIC SPANISH DANCE MUSIC the music for a bolero. A famous example was written for full orchestra by Ravel. **3.** CLOTHING SHORT OPEN JACKET a short jacket, with or without sleeves, worn open over a blouse or shirt [Late 18C. < Spanish < *bola* 'ball' (see BOLA)]

boletus /bō leétəss/ (*plural* **-tuses** or **-ti** /-tī/) *n* a fungus that has a rounded cap with pores rather than gills on the underside. Cep mushrooms are an edible species of boletus. Genus: *Boletus*. [Early 16C. < Latin]

Boleyn /boo lín/, **Anne** queen of England and Ireland (1507?–36). She was the second wife of Henry VIII

(1533–36) and the mother of Elizabeth I. Henry VIII accused her of adultery and had her beheaded.

> 'The king has been very good to me. He promoted me from a simple maid to be a marchioness. Then he raised me to be a queen. Now he will raise me to be a martyr.'
> [Attributed to Anne Boleyn]

Bolger /bóljər/, **Jim** (*b.* 1935) prime minister of New Zealand (1990–97). A member of the Nationalist Party, he was elected to parliament in 1972 and held his first ministerial post in 1978. His premiership saw an increase in economic growth and closer ties with the United States. Full name **Bolger, James Brendan**. See table at **prime minister**

bolide /bố līd/ *n* a bright meteor that explodes [Early 19C. < French, < Greek *bolis* 'missile']

bolivar /bólli vaar/ (*plural* **-vars** or -vares /bō leevaáress/) *n* the main unit of Venezuelan currency. See table at **currency** [Late 19C. After Simón BOLÍVAR]

Bolívar /bólli vaar, bo leé-/, **Simón** (1783–1830) South American revolutionary. He was the leader of the independence movement that drove the Spanish from Venezuela, Colombia, Ecuador, Peru, and Bolivia (1812–24). Known as **the Liberator**

> 'Do not adopt the best system of government, but the one that is most likely to succeed.'
> [Simón Bolívar, *Letter to Jamaica*; 6 September 1815]

Bolivia

Bolivia /bə lívvi ə/ landlocked country in west-central South America. Part of the Inca empire, it was conquered by the Spanish in 1538 and became independent in 1825. Language: Spanish. Currency: boliviano. Capital: La Paz. Population: 8,586,443 (2003). Area: 1,098,581 sq. km/424,164 sq. mi. Official name **Republic of Bolivia** —**Bolivian** *n, adj*

boliviano /bə lívvi aánō/ (*plural* **-nos**) *n* the main unit of Bolivian currency. See table at **currency** [Late 19C. < Spanish, 'Bolivian']

boll /bōl/ *n* a rounded seed pod or capsule, especially of cotton [15C. < Middle Dutch *bolle* 'round object']

Böll /böl/, **Heinrich** (1917–85) German novelist. His works include *The Lost Honour of Katharina Blum* (1974). He received the Nobel Prize in literature (1972).

> 'Strangely enough I like the kind to which I belong: people.'
> [Heinrich Böll, *The Clown*; 1965]

bollard /bóllaard/ *n* **1.** POST FOR GUIDING TRAFFIC a small post marking the edge of an area that traffic must keep off **2.** NAUT POST FOR MOORING BOATS a strong post on a quay or wharf, or on the deck of a boat, used for securing ropes **3.** CLIMBING ROCK SUITABLE FOR SECURING ROPE in climbing, a spike of rock or a pillar of ice round which a rope can be secured [Mid-19C. Probably < BOLE¹]

bollocking /bólləking/ *n* a highly offensive term for a severe telling-off (*taboo*) [Mid-20C. < BOLLOCKS]

bollocks /bólləks/ *n* a highly offensive term for nonsense (*takes a singular verb*) ■ *npl* a highly offensive term for the testicles (*takes a plural verb*) ■ *interj* a highly offensive term indicating strong disbelief or disagreement ■ *vt* (**-locks, -locking, -locksed**) a highly offensive term meaning to make a mess or muddle of something [Mid-18C. Variant of BALLOCKS]

boll weevil *n* a weevil whose larvae infest and destroy cotton bolls. Native to: southern United States, Mexico. Latin name: *Anthonomus grandis.*

bollworm /bṓl wurm/ *n* a moth larva, especially the corn earworm or pink bollworm, that feeds on and destroys cotton and other crops

Bollywood /bólli wŏŏd/ *n* the extravagantly theatrical Indian film industry [Mid-20C. Blend of BOMBAY + HOLLYWOOD [1]]

bolo /bṓlō/ (*plural* **-los**) *n* in the Philippines, a machete with a single-edged blade [Early 20C. < Philippine Spanish]

bologna /bə lṓnyə/ *n N Am* a large smoked sausage made with a variety of finely minced seasoned meats, usually including beef and pork [Mid-19C. After BOLOGNA, Italy]

Bologna /bə lṓnyə, -lón-/ capital of Bologna Province and Emilia-Romagna Region, in northern Italy. It was an important cultural centre in the Middle Ages and Renaissance. Population: 371,217 (2001).

bolognese /bóllə náyz/, **Bolognese** *adj* **1.** describes an Italian sauce for pasta, made with minced meat and tomato **2.** describes pasta served with bolognese sauce ○ *spaghetti bolognese* [Early 19C. < Italian, '(in the style) of Bologna']

bolometer /bō lómmitər/ *n* an instrument for measuring radiant energy by determining the changes of resistance in an electrical conductor [Late 19C. < Greek *bolē* 'ray'] —**bolometric** /bṓlə méttrik/ *adj* —**bolometry** /bō lómmətri/ *n*

bolo tie /bṓlə-/, **bola tie** *n US* a thin tie made of cord and fastened in front of the neck by a clasp [Alteration of BOLA]

Bolshevik /bólshəvik/ *n* **1.** RUSSIAN COMMUNIST a member of the radical group within the Russian Social Democratic Labour Party that became the Communist Party in 1918 **2.** *also* **bolshevik** COMMUNIST OR COMMUNIST SYMPATHIZER a Communist or somebody who shares the ideals of Communism **3.** *also* **bolshevik** POLITICAL RADICAL a revolutionary or radical socialist (*disapproving*) [Early 20C. < Russian *bol'shevik* < *bol'she* 'more'; because the radicals were in the majority]

Bolshevism /bólshəvizəm/, **bolshevism** *n* **1.** the ideology and policies of the Bolsheviks, especially advocacy of the forcible overthrow of capitalism **2.** Communism or revolutionary socialism (*dated*) —**Bolshevist** *n* —**Bolshevistic** /bólshə vístik/ *adj*

bolshie /bólshi/, **bolshy** *n* (*plural* **-shies**) POL same as **Bolshevik** (*dated informal*) ■ *adj* (*informal*) **1.** tending to be argumentative or uncooperative **2.** politically radical or subversive [Early 20C. < BOLSHEVIK] —**bolshily** *adv* —**bolshiness** *n*

bolster[1] /bṓlstər/ *n* **1.** LONG CYLINDRICAL PILLOW a long firm cylindrical pillow placed under other pillows to support them **2.** MECH ENG PAD PREVENTING FRICTION a pad or cushion fitted to machinery to prevent friction or give support **3.** ARCHIT HORIZONTAL SUPPORTING TIMBER a short horizontal timber positioned between the top of a post and the beam it supports, to spread the load of the post ■ *vt* (**-sters, -stering, -stered**) **1.** ENCOURAGE SOMETHING THROUGH SUPPORT to strengthen something through support or encouragement **2.** KEEP SOMETHING RAISED to prop something up [Old English, 'cushion' < Indo-European, 'to swell'] —**bolsterer** *n*

bolster[2] /bṓlstər/ *n* a chisel with a wide cutting edge, used for cutting stone [Early 20C. Alteration of *boaster* < *boast* 'cut with a chisel', origin ?]

bolt[1] /bōlt/ *n* **1.** BAR FOR FASTENING DOOR a sliding bar that fits into a socket and secures a door or gate **2.** SHORT SCREW a short cylindrical metal bar with a screw thread, used with a nut **3.** METEOROL LIGHTNING FLASH a flash of lightning appearing briefly as a jagged line of light **4.** TEXTILES ROLL OF FABRIC a rolled length of fabric or wallpaper **5.** ARMS ARROW FOR CROSSBOW a short arrow for use with a crossbow **6.** ARMS PART OF GUN in a breech-loading firearm, a sliding rod, bar, or plate that ejects a used cartridge and closes the breech **7.** CLIMBING METAL PIN in climbing, a small metal spike used to provide an anchor in rock faces ■ *v* (**bolts, bolting, bolted**) **1.** *vt* LOCK SOMETHING WITH BOLT to fasten a door or gate by sliding a bolt into a socket **2.** *vi* RUSH AWAY to move suddenly and quickly, especially out of fright **3.** *vt* DEVOUR FOOD HURRIEDLY to swallow food hurriedly without chewing **4.** *vt* FIELD SPORTS EXPEL ANIMAL FROM HIDING-PLACE to flush out a wild animal that is hidden or concealed **5.** *vi* BOT PREMATURELY PRODUCE SEEDS to flower and produce seeds earlier than expected or wanted **6.** *vt* TEXTILES ROLL FABRIC OR PAPER INTO BOLT to roll fabric or wallpaper into a bolt [Old English, 'crossbow bolt', origin ?] ◇ **like a bolt from the blue** very suddenly and unexpectedly ◇ **make a bolt for something** to make a sudden rush towards something ◇ **shoot your bolt** to use all your resources

bolt (sense 2)

bolt[2] /bōlt/ (**bolts, bolting, bolted**), **boult** (**boults, boulting, boulted**) *vt* to filter a substance through a cloth or sieve, especially flour (*archaic*) [12C. < Old French *buleter* < Germanic]

Bolt /bōlt/, **Robert** (1924–95) British playwright. His plays include *A Man for All Seasons* (1960) and *State of Revolution* (1977). Among his screenplays are *Lawrence of Arabia* (1962) and *Dr Zhivago* (1965). Full name **Bolt, Robert Oxton**

> 'Morality's not practical. Morality's a gesture. A complicated gesture learnt from books.'
> [Robert Bolt, *A Man for All Seasons*; 1960]

bolt-action *adj* describes a gun with a sliding bolt that replaces the used cartridge and closes the breech

bolter /bṓltər/ *n* **1.** somebody or something that bolts (*informal*) **2.** *Aus* an escaped convict or a bushranger on the run (*archaic informal*)

bolthole /bṓlt hōl/ *n* a place of escape, especially for an animal fleeing from danger ○ *The rabbit ran down a bolthole.*

Bolton /bṓltən/ industrial town in Lancashire, northwestern England. Population: 261,037 (2001).

bolt-on *adj* **1.** ATTACHABLE WITH BOLT attachable by means of a bolt **2.** ATTACHABLE AS EXTRA attachable as an extra without affecting or requiring change to the rest ■ *n* ADDITIONAL PART something that can be added to a larger structure (*informal*)

boltrope /bṓlt rōp/ *n* a rope sewn along the lower edge or leading edge of a sail to strengthen it

Boltzmann constant /bóltsmən-/ *n* the ratio of the universal gas constant to Avogadro's number. Symbol **k** [After Ludwig *Boltzmann* (1844–1906), Austrian physicist]

bolus /bṓləss/ *n* **1.** INTRAVENOUS INJECTION OF DRUG a rapidly absorbed intravenous injection of a drug **2.** LARGE PILL a very large pill **3.** ROUND MASS a soft rounded ball, especially of chewed food [Mid-16C. Via late Latin < Greek *bōlos* 'clod of earth']

boma[1] /bṓmə/ *n* in central and eastern Africa, a police post or magistrate's office [Late 19C. < Kiswahili]

boma[2] /bṓmə/ *n S Africa* same as **lapa**

bomb /bom/ *n* **1.** EXPLOSIVE PROJECTILE a missile containing explosive or other destructive material **2.** SPECIALIZED EXPLOSIVE DEVICE a device that contains explosive material, especially one designed to explode after some time **3.** *also* **Bomb** ATOM BOMB the atom bomb considered as the absolute weapon of mass destruction (*often used with "the"*) ○ *lived in dread of the Bomb during the Cold War* **4.** MUCH MONEY a great deal of money (*informal*) ○ *It cost a bomb.* **5.** MED DEVICE FOR DIRECTING RADIATION a device that contains radioactive material and is used to beam therapeutic radiation at a patient **6.** GEOL SOLIDIFIED LAVA a solidified rounded or teardrop-shaped mass of lava from a volcano **7.** ARTS ARTISTIC FAILURE a performance that is a commercial or artistic failure (*informal*) **8.** *ANZ* DILAPIDATED VEHICLE a battered or dilapidated vehicle (*informal*) **9.** *US* SOMETHING OR SOMEBODY GOOD something or somebody extremely good or exciting (*slang*) ○ *Their lead singer is the bomb.* ■ *v* (**bombs, bombing, bombed**) **1.** *vti* ATTACK ENEMY TARGETS WITH BOMBS to drop bombs on people or places, or to attack or destroy them with bombs ○ *bombing enemy territory* **2.** *vi* MOVE VERY FAST to move exceptionally fast, especially in a vehicle (*informal*) **3.** *vi* FAIL MISERABLY to fail badly as a performance (*informal*) ○ *The play bombed on Broadway.* **4.** *vi* CRASH SUDDENLY to fail suddenly while in operation (*informal; refers to computers*) [Late 17C. Via French, Italian, and Latin < Greek *bombos* 'booming sound']

bomb out *vt* (*usually passive*) **1.** to destroy a building or structure completely by bombing it **2.** to drive somebody out of a home or workplace by bombing

bombard /bom baárd/ *vt* (**-bards, -barding, -barded**) **1.** ATTACK SOMEBODY OR SOMETHING WITH MISSILES to attack an enemy or enemy territory intensively with sustained artillery fire or bombs **2.** HIT SOMEBODY REPEATEDLY to attack somebody persistently and vigorously **3.** OVERWHELM SOMEBODY to direct towards somebody something such as questions or requests in great quantities **4.** PHYS HIT SOMETHING WITH HIGH-ENERGY PARTICLES to direct high-energy particles against atoms or nuclei ■ *n* HIST, ARMS MEDIEVAL CANNON a cannon used in medieval times to throw large stones [15C. < French *bombarder* < *bombarde* 'cannon' < Latin *bombus* < Greek *bombos* 'booming sound'] —**bombarder** *n* —**bombardment** *n*

bombardier /bómbər deér/ *n* **1.** a member of a military aircraft crew who releases bombs **2.** a non-commissioned officer in the Royal Artillery of a rank below sergeant [Mid-16C. < French < *bombarde* 'cannon' (see BOMBARD)]

bombardier beetle *n* a beetle that squirts volatile acrid liquid when attacked. Latin name: *Brachinus crepitans.*

bombardon /bómbərdən/ *n* **1.** a brass wind instrument of the tuba family **2.** a bass reed stop on an organ [Mid-19C. < Italian *bombardone* < medieval Latin *bombarda* 'bombard' (see BOMBARD)]

bombasine *n* TEXTILES another spelling of **bombazine**

bombast /bóm bast/ *n* language that is full of long or pretentious words, used to impress others [Late 16C. Alteration of Old French *bombace* 'cotton stuffing', via medieval Latin *bombax* 'cotton' < Greek *bombux* 'silk, silkworm'] —**bombastic** /bom bástik/ *adj* —**bombastically** *adv*

Bombay /bom báy/ former name for **Mumbai**

Bombay duck *n* **1.** in South Asian cooking, a fish, especially the bummalo, dried, salted, grilled, and served as a pungent relish **2.** FISH same as **bummalo** [Mid-19C. < Marathi *bombīla* 'bummalo', by association with BOMBAY, from where the fish were exported]

bombay mix *n* a spiced mixture of fried lentils and other dried foods, eaten as a snack or appetizer [After BOMBAY]

bombazine /bómbə zeén, bómbə zeen/, **bombasine** *n* a twilled silk or cotton and worsted material, usually dyed black. Use: formerly, mourning clothes. [Late 16C. Via French *bombasin* < medieval Latin *bombycinus* 'silken' < Latin *bombyx* 'silk, silkworm' < Greek *bombux*]

bomb bay *n* the compartment on board a bomber aircraft in which the bombs are carried

bomb calorimeter *n* a device for measuring calorific values in which substances are burned inside a sealed vessel

bomb disposal *n* the task or process of rendering bombs harmless by defusing them, removing them, or detonating them in a controlled explosion (*hyphenated when used before a noun*) ○ *a bomb-disposal expert*

bombe /bomb/ *n* a dome-shaped frozen or set dessert [Late 19C. < French, 'bomb', from the shape of the mould]

bombé /bom báy/ *adj* describes furniture with a bulging convex shape, typical of French rococo furniture of the 18th century [Early 20C. < French, 'swollen']

bombed /bomd/ *adj* **1.** severely damaged or destroyed by bombing **2.** intoxicated by alcohol or a drug (*slang*)

bombed out *adj* (*hyphenated when used before a noun*) **1.** driven out by bomb damage **2.** made uninhabitable by bombing

bomber /bómmər/ *n* **1.** an aircraft designed for carry-

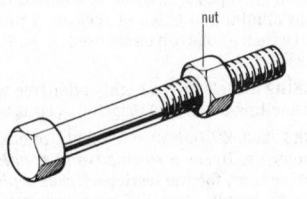

ing and dropping bombs **2.** somebody who plants bombs

bomber jacket *n* a short jacket, usually leather, with an elasticated waist and usually a zip at the front [< the wearing of such jackets by the crew of US bomber aircraft]

bombinate /bómbi nayt/ (**-nates, -nating, -nated**) *vi* to make a humming or buzzing noise (*literary*) [Late 19C. < medieval Latin *bombinat-*, past participle of *bombinare* 'buzz' < Latin *bombus* < Greek *bombos* 'booming sound'] —**bombination** /bómbi náysh'n/ *n*

bombing /bómming/ *n* **1.** the act or process of dropping bombs from aircraft **2.** the act of setting and detonating a bomb with the intent to kill victims

bomblet /bómmlət/ *n* a small bomb or explosive device packed into a larger bomb

bombora /bom báwrə/ *n* Aus **1.** a reef lying just below sea level **2.** a dangerous patch of sea where waves break over a reef [Mid-20C. < an Aboriginal language]

bombproof /bóm proof/ *adj* constructed to withstand the impact of bombs

bomb scare *n* a warning or suspicion of a bomb being in a place, resulting in the evacuation of people from the immediate and surrounding area

bombshell /bóm shel/ *n* **1.** SURPRISING NEWS an unexpected and shocking piece of news (*informal*) **2.** STUNNING WOMAN a very good-looking and glamorous woman (*dated informal*) **3.** ARMS ARTILLERY EXPLOSIVE OR BOMB an artillery shell or a bomb

bomb shelter *n* a building or underground structure designed to protect people from the impact of a bomb

bombsight /bóm sīt/ *n* a device in an aircraft for aiming bombs

bomb site *n* an area devastated by bombs

bombycid /bómbissid/ *adj* belonging to the family of moths that includes the silkworm moths. Family: Bombycidae. [< modern Latin *Bombycidae* < Latin *bombyc-* 'silkworm' < Greek *bombux*] —**bombycid** *n*

Bon, Cape /bon/ peninsula in northeastern Tunisia

Bona, Mount /bónə/ highest peak in the Wrangell Mountains, southern Alaska. Height: 5,005 m/16,421 ft.

bona fide /bónə fīdi/ *adj* **1.** authentic and genuine in nature ○ *a bona fide offer* **2.** without any intention to deceive [< Latin, 'with good faith']

bona fides /-fídeez/ *n* a sincere statement or evidence of good intentions (*takes a singular verb*) ■ *npl* credentials authenticating somebody's true identity, background, intentions, and good faith ○ *a defector whose bona fides could not be established*

Bonaire Island /bo náir-/ island in the Netherlands Antilles off the coast of Venezuela. It is a popular tourist destination. Population: 12,533 (1994). Area: 290 sq. km/112 sq. mi.

bonanza /bə nánzə/ *n* **1.** a source that yields great riches or success **2.** an extremely valuable mineral deposit [Early 19C. Via Spanish < medieval Latin *bonacia* 'calm seas', alteration of *malacia* 'calm seas' after Latin *bonus* 'good']

Bonaparte /bónə paart/ ♦ **Napoleon I**

Bonaparte, Jérôme (1784–1860) French soldier and politician. He was the youngest brother of Napoleon I, who made him king of Westphalia (1807–13).

Bonaparte, Joseph (1768–1844) French soldier and diplomat. He was the older brother of Napoleon I, who made him king of Naples (1806–08) and Spain (1808–13).

Bonaparte, Louis (1778–1846) French soldier and politician. He was a younger brother of Napoleon I, who made him king of Holland (1806–10).

Bonaparte, Lucien (1775–1840) French diplomat and politician. A younger brother of Napoleon I, he opposed Napoleon's despotic reign and spent much of his life in exile.

Bonapartism /bónə paartizəm/ *n* **1.** government by or on the pattern of Napoleon I **2.** support for Napoleon I or Napoleon III or their dynasty —**Bonapartist** *n*, *adj*

bona vacantia /bónə və kánti ə/ *n* in law, property that is unclaimed or that has no known owner (*takes a singular or plural verb*) [< Latin, 'ownerless goods']

Bonaventure /bónnə vénchər/, **Bonaventura** /bónnə ven tyoorə/, **St** (1221?–74) Italian monk and theologian. He was minister general of the Franciscan order (1257) and wrote the official biography of St Francis (1263). Born **Fidanza, Giovanni di**

bonbon /bón bon/ *n* **1.** a sweet confection **2.** something that is sweet and insubstantial [Late 18C. < French, literally 'good-good' < Latin *bonus* 'good']

bonbonnière /bónbə neér, -nyáir/ *n* an ornamental bowl or box for sweets [Early 19C. < French < *bonbon* (see BONBON)]

bonce /bonss/ *n* somebody's head (*informal*) [Mid-19C. Origin ?]

bond /bond/ *n* **1.** SOMETHING THAT BINDS an object such as a rope, band, or chain that binds somebody or something **2.** ADHESION the way in which one surface sticks to another **3.** ADHESIVE SUBSTANCE a substance that makes objects adhere **4.** LINK BETWEEN PEOPLE a link that binds people together in a relationship **5.** RESTRAINT a situation that limits somebody socially, psychologically, or emotionally **6.** LAW SOLEMN PROMISE a solemn agreement promising to do something **7.** LAW DOCUMENT PROMISING TO PAY a document that legally obliges one party to pay money to another **8.** FIN CERTIFICATE PROMISING DEBT REPAYMENT a certificate issued by a government or company promising to pay back borrowed money at a fixed rate of interest on a specified date **9.** Aus SURETY a deposit of money, especially on rented accommodation **10.** CHEM FORCE BINDING ATOMS AND IONS a fundamental attractive force that binds atoms and ions in a molecule. There are different types of bond, e.g. covalent and ionic. **11.** CONSTR TECHNIQUE FOR OVERLAPPING BRICKS an overlapping pattern in which bricks or tiles can be laid **12.** COMM SAFE STORAGE secure storage of goods before payment of duty **13.** INDUST same as **bond paper** ■ *v* (**bonds, bonding, bonded**) **1.** *vti* ADHERE OR MAKE SURFACES ADHERE to stick together, or make two surfaces stick together **2.** *vti* PSYCHOL LINK EMOTIONALLY to link together, or cause people to be linked together, emotionally or psychologically **3.** *vt* COMM STORE GOODS SECURELY to store goods securely until duty is paid **4.** *vti* FIN CONVERT INTO DEBT UNDER BOND to convert something, or be converted, into a debt with a bond as security **5.** *vt* Aus FIN GIVE MONEY DEPOSIT to provide a deposit of money against unforeseen losses **6.** *vi* CHEM HAVE CHEMICAL BOND to be linked with a chemical bond (*refers to atoms or ions*) **7.** *vt* CONSTR OVERLAP BRICKS OR TILES to lay bricks or tiles so that they overlap in a pattern **8.** *vt* HANDICRAFT FUSE FABRICS TOGETHER to fuse two fabrics together [13C. Variant of BAND²] —**bondable** *adj*

Bond, Alan (b. 1938) British-born Australian business executive. He became one of Australia's richest men as chairman of the Bond Corporation (1969–90). It collapsed in 1990, and he was jailed for fraud (1996).

> 'I cannot tolerate strikes. What would my workers say if I go on strike and say I'm not going to sign any more cheques today?'
> [Alan Bond, *Financial Times*; 5 September 1981]

Bond, Edward (b. 1934) British playwright and director. His plays include *Saved* (1965) and *Bingo* (1973).

> 'Imagination creates the real not the illusionary, it exists in the real not in nothingness. Imagination itself – not what it creates – is often illusionary.'
> [Edward Bond, *The Hidden Plot*; 2000]

bondage /bóndij/ *n* **1.** SLAVERY the condition of being enslaved or forced into serfdom **2.** RESTRICTION the condition of being controlled by something that limits freedom **3.** PHYSICAL RESTRAINT DURING SEX the practice of being tied up or restrained physically during sex acts **4.** HIST same as **villeinage** (sense 1) [14C. < Anglo-Norman < Old Norse *bóndi* 'husbandman' < present participle of *búa* 'dwell']

bonded /bóndid/ *adj* **1.** stored securely until duty or tax is paid **2.** chemically attached or fused together in layers

bonded warehouse *n* a warehouse that holds goods awaiting duty or tax to be paid on them

bond energy *n* the amount of energy that has to be supplied to break a chemical bond between two atoms in a molecule

bonder /bóndər/ *n* **1.** somebody who or something that bonds **2.** CONSTR same as **bondstone**

bondholder /bónd hōldər/ *n* an owner of government or company bonds

Bondi Beach /bóndī-/ coastal suburb of Sydney, Australia. It is a popular surfing and tourist centre.

bonding /bónding/ *n* **1.** PROCESS OF BINDING THINGS TOGETHER the process by which something is bonded **2.** PSYCHOL FORMATION OF EMOTIONAL BONDS the formation of a close emotional tie between people, e.g. the establishment of a relationship between a mother and her newly born infant **3.** DENT COATING TOOTH the process of coating a tooth with a durable resinous substance

bondman /bóndmən/ (*plural* **-men** /-mən/) *n* ANZ, US same as **bondsman** (sense 2)

bond paper *n* a strong white paper of high quality

bondservant /bónd survənt/ *n* a serf or enslaved person [15C. < *bond* 'bound in servitude']

bondsman /bóndzmən/ (*plural* **-men** /-mən/) *n* **1.** somebody responsible for a legal bond **2.** UK, Can a man who is enslaved or a serf. ANZ, US term **bondman** [13C. < *bond* 'bound in servitude']

bondsperson /bóndz purss'n/ (*plural* **-persons** or **-people** /-peep'l/) *n* somebody responsible for a legal bond

bondstone /bónd stōn/ *n* building brick or a stone that extends into the interior of a wall in order to strengthen it

bondswoman /bóndz woomən/ (*plural* **-women** /-wimin/) *n* UK, Can a woman who is enslaved or a serf. ANZ, US term **bondwoman**

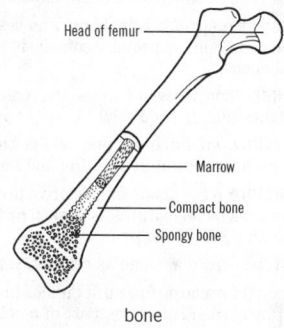

Head of femur
Marrow
Compact bone
Spongy bone

bone

bone /bōn/ *n* **1.** SECTION OF SKELETON one of the hard parts forming the skeleton in vertebrate animals **2.** MATERIAL MAKING UP BONES the main material that forms a vertebrate skeleton, principally collagen fibre and calcium phosphate **3.** SUBSTANCE RESEMBLING BONE something hard that resembles the bone of a vertebrate skeleton, e.g. whalebone or ivory **4.** COLOURS IVORY COLOUR the ivory or off-white colour of bone **5.** CLOTHING STRIP USED AS STIFFENING a flat strip of hard material such as whalebone or plastic used to stiffen a garment ■ **bones** *npl* **1.** DEAD BODY the skeleton or corpse of a dead person or animal **2.** STRUCTURE the structure or framework of something **3.** LIVING BODY somebody's living body (*humorous*) ○ *I must rest my weary bones.* **4.** MUSIC PAIR OF RHYTHMICALLY CLACKING BARS a pair of bars or strips of wood, metal, or bone that are struck together sharply to make musical rhythms **5.** GAMBLING DICE a pair of dice (*slang*) ■ *vt* (**bones, boning, boned**) **1.** COOK REMOVE BONES FROM FOOD to remove the bones from fish, meat, or poultry when preparing it for cooking or eating **2.** CLOTHING STIFFEN GARMENT to add flat strips to stiffen a garment **3.** US OFFENSIVE TERM an offensive term meaning to have sexual intercourse with somebody (*slang*) ■ *adv* VERY extremely or totally ○ *He's bone idle!* ○ *I am bone tired.* [Old English *bān* < Germanic, 'long bone'] ◊ **feel** *or* **know it in your bones** to be sure that something is true without having any proof or being able to explain why ◊ **have a bone to pick with somebody** to have cause for disagreement with somebody ◊ **make no bones about something** to say something openly and frankly ◊ **point the bone** Aus to wish bad luck, or place a jinx on somebody

bone up *vi* to review or study something intensely (*informal*)

bone ash *n* the residue, composed mostly of calcium phosphate, that remains when bones of animals

are burnt to a powder. Use: fertilizer, bone china manufacture.

bone china *n* **1.** a fine white porcelain made from a mixture of clay and bone ash **2.** articles made of bone china

bone dry *adj* containing no moisture at all

bonefire /bón fīr/ *n Ireland* same as **bonfire** [Variant]

bonefish /bón fish/ (*plural same* or **-fishes**) *n* a large game fish found in warm shallow waters. Latin name: *Albula vulpes*.

bonehead /bón hed/ *n* an offensive term for somebody regarded as unintelligent (*insult*) —**boneheaded** /bón héddid/ *adj* —**boneheadedness** *n*

boneless /bónləss/ *adj* having had the bones removed in preparation for cooking or eating

bone marrow *n* a soft reddish substance inside some bones that is involved in the production of blood cells. New white and red blood cells are formed only in the marrow of the flat bones such as the ribs, breastbone, or pelvis in adults.

bone meal *n* ground animal bones, used as a fertilizer or in animal feed [< MEAL²]

bone of contention *n* a subject of constant argument or disagreement between people [< dogs fighting over a bone]

boner /bónər/ *n* **1.** EMBARRASSING MISTAKE an embarrassing mistake (*informal*) **2.** *N Am* ERECTION an erect penis (*slang*) **3.** COOK DEVICE THAT BONES something that is designed for boning something, or somebody who bones something ○ *a fish boner*

boneset /bón set/ (*plural same* or **-sets**) *n* a plant of the daisy family believed to have healing properties. Native to: North America. Genus: *Eupatorium*.

bonesetter /bón setər/ *n* somebody who sets broken or dislocated bones, especially somebody not qualified as a doctor

boneshaker /bón shaykər/ *n* a decrepit or uncomfortable vehicle (*informal*)

bone spavin *n* an inflammation of the bones in a horse's hock, resulting in swelling and lameness

bone structure *n* the shape and relative prominence of somebody's facial features as formed by the bones underneath ○ *good bone structure*

boneyard /bón yaard/ *n* same as **cemetery** (*informal*)

bonfire /bón fīr/ *n* a large fire built outside for burning rubbish or garden refuse, as part of a celebration, or as a signal [14C. < BONE]

CULTURAL NOTE *Bonfire of the Vanities*, a novel (1988) by US writer Tom Wolfe. Using the story of the trial of wealthy New York bond trader Sherman McCoy for the accidental killing of a young African American man, Wolfe satirizes the US media, legal system, and art world. It was made into a film by Brian de Palma in 1990.

Bonfire Night *n* the anniversary of the day on which Guy Fawkes' plot to blow up Parliament (**the Gunpowder Plot**) was discovered in 1605, marked with fireworks and bonfires in the United Kingdom and other Commonwealth countries. Date: 5 November.

bong¹ /bong/ *n, interj* REVERBERATING SOUND a deep resonant sound, especially from a bell ■ *n* CLIMBING METAL PITON a wide piton made out of folded sheet metal ■ *vi* (**bongs, bonging, bonged**) MAKE REVERBERATING SOUND to make a deep resonant sound [Mid-19C. An imitation of the sound]

bong² /bong/ *n* a water pipe for smoking hashish or other drugs (*slang*) [Late 20C. Probably < Thai *baung*]

Bongaree /bóng gə ree/ tourist resort on Bribie Island, off the coast of southeastern Queensland, Australia. Population: 8,425 (1991).

bongo /bóng gō/ (*plural* **-gos** or **-goes** or *same*) *n* a forest-dwelling antelope having a reddish coat with vertical white stripes and distinctive spiralling horns. Native to: central Africa. Latin name: *Boocercus euryceros*. [Mid-19C. < Kikongo]

bongo drums, bongos *npl* a set of two small deep-bodied drums that are held between the knees and beaten with the fingers [< American Spanish *bongó*]

Bonhoeffer /bón höfər/, **Dietrich** (1906–45) German pastor and theologian. He was active in the German Resistance during World War II, and was executed

in 1945 for involvement in a plot to assassinate Adolf Hitler.

'Man has learned to cope with all questions of importance without recourse to God as a working hypothesis.'
[Dietrich Bonhoeffer. Quoted in *Letters and Papers from Prison*, Eberhard Bethge, ed.; 1981]

bonhomie /bónnə mee/ *n* easy good-humoured friendliness [Late 18C. < French *bonhomme* 'good man'] —**bonhomous** /bónnəməss/ *adj*

Boniface /bónni fayss/, **St** (680?–754?) Saxon missionary. Commissioned to preach to the German peoples in 718, he became a bishop in 723. He was killed by non-Christians in Friesia. Born **Wynfrid**. Known as the **Apostle of Germany**

Boniface VIII, Pope (1234?–1303) As pope from 1294 to 1303, he proclaimed the supremacy of the papacy over temporal law. Born **Gaetani, Benedetto**

Bonington /bónningtən/, **Sir Chris** (*b.* 1934) British mountaineer. He led the first British team up the north face of the Eiger (1962) and led numerous other ascents of the world's highest peaks. Full name **Bonington, Sir Christian John Storey**

Bonin Islands /bónin-/ volcanic island group in Japan in the Pacific Ocean. The islands were held under US control from 1945 to 1968. Population: 2,303 (1985). Area: 104 sq. km/40 sq. mi.

bonito /bə neétō/ (*plural* **-tos** or *same*) *n* **1.** FISH OF MACKEREL FAMILY a game fish relating to tuna, with dark stripes on its back. Genus: *Sarda*. **2.** BONITO AS FOOD the flesh of a bonito eaten as food **3.** FISH RESEMBLING BONITO a fish such as the skipjack that resembles or is related to the bonito [Late 16C. Probably < Spanish, 'pretty' < Latin *bonus* 'good']

bonk /bongk/ *v* (**bonks, bonking, bonked**) **1.** *vt* BANG SOMETHING OR SOMEBODY to bang or hit something or somebody (*informal*) **2.** *vti* HIT SOMETHING in snowboarding, to strike or collide with something while riding a snowboard (*slang*) **3.** *vti* OFFENSIVE TERM an offensive term meaning to have sexual intercourse with somebody (*slang*) ■ *n* **1.** SHARP BLOW a sharp blow, typically on the head **2.** OFFENSIVE TERM an offensive term for sexual intercourse (*slang*) [Early 20C. An imitation of the sound of a blow]

bonkers /bóngkərz/ *adj* an offensive term meaning irrational (*slang*) [Mid-20C. Origin ?]

bon mot /bón mó/ (*plural* **bons mots** /*pronunc. same*/) *n* a witty comment [< French, 'good word']

Bonn /bon/ city on the Rhine in North Rhine-Westphalia state, west-central Germany. It was the capital of the former West Germany from 1949 to 1990. Population: 293,072 (1997).

Bonnard /bónnaar, bo naár/, **Pierre** (1867–1947) French painter. In his early career he was a conventional painter of decorative scenes. After 1900 his pictures, often of bathing women, were notable for their use of light and colour.

bonne /bon/ *n* a French woman servant (*dated*) [Late 18C. < French, 'good girl']

bonne bouche /bón boósh/ (*plural* **bonnes bouches** /*pronunc. same*/) *n* a small piece of tasty food [< French, literally 'good mouth']

Bonner /bónnər/, **Neville Thomas** (1922–99) Australian politician. A Liberal Party senator (1971–83), he was the first Aboriginal to be elected to the Australian federal parliament.

bonnet

bonnet /bónnit/ *n* **1.** WOMAN'S HAT a hat framing the face and usually tied under the chin, worn by a woman or girl **2.** COVER OF CAR ENGINE the hinged cover over the engine of a car or other vehicle, usually at the front. N Am term **hood**¹ **3.** *Scotland* SOFT FLAT CAP a soft flat cap, worn by men or boys **4.** NATIVE N AMERICAN HEADDRESS a ceremonial feathered headdress traditionally worn by some Native North Americans **5.** CHIMNEY COWL a wire cover fitted over a chimney pot **6.** MECH ENG PROTECTIVE COVER a protective cap or cover fitting over a machine part **7.** SAILING EXTRA PIECE OF SAIL an extra strip of canvas laced to the base of a foresail, used to extend it when the wind is light [14C. < Old French *bonet* < medieval Latin *abonnis* 'headgear'] —**bonneted** *adj*

bonnethead /bónnət hed/ (*plural* **-heads** or *same*), **bonnethead shark** *n* FISH same as **shovelhead**

Bonneville Salt Flats /bónnəvil-/ barren salt plain in northwestern Utah, the bed of a prehistoric lake. It has been used for setting world land speed records since the 1930s. Area: 260 sq. km/100 sq. mi.

Bonnie Prince Charlie /bónni prinss chaárli/, ◆ **Stuart, Charles Edward**

bonny /bónni/ (**-nier, -niest**), **bonnie** *adj N England, Scotland* **1.** ATTRACTIVE pleasing to look at **2.** SUBSTANTIAL fairly large **3.** EXCELLENT extremely good **4.** HEALTHY plump and healthy [15C. Origin ?] —**bonnily** *adv* —**bonniness** *n*

REGIONAL NOTE The adjective *bonny* is of uncertain origin, although it has often been linked to French *bon(ne)*, meaning 'good'. It is still widely used in the north of England and Scotland to describe a young woman who is attractive both physically and in character.

Bono /bónō/, **Edward de** (*b.* 1933) Maltese-born British psychologist. Director of the Cognitive Research Trust since 1971, he has published widely on thought processes and lateral thinking.

bonobo /bə nōbō, bónnə bō/ (*plural* **-bos**) *n* a rare black arboreal chimpanzee. Native to: West Africa, south of the Congo River. Latin name: *Pan paniscus*. [Mid-20C. < a Central African language]

bonsai

bonsai /bón sī/ (*plural same* or **-sais**) *n* **1.** the art of growing miniaturized forms of trees and bushes by rigorous pruning of roots and branches **2.** a tree or bush miniaturized using bonsai techniques [Early 20C. < Japanese < *bon* 'basin' (< Middle Chinese *bən*) + *sai* 'to plant' (< Middle Chinese *tsəj*)]

bonsella /bon séllə/ *n S Africa* **1.** a tip or gratuity **2.** a small reward, often of sweets, given to a good customer by a trader [Early 20C. < Zulu *bansela* 'express thanks in tangible form, give a small present']

bonspiel /bón speel/ *n* a curling match or tournament [Mid-16C. Probably < Dutch or Low German]

bontebok /bónti buk/ (*plural* **-boks** or *same*) *n* an antelope with a reddish coat, white markings on the face and rump, and white legs. Native to: southern Africa. Latin name: *Damaliscus pygargus*. [Late 18C. < Afrikaans, 'pied buck']

bon ton /bón tón/ *n* (*literary*) **1.** good taste, style, or manners ○ *People thought it bon ton to be seen attending such an occasion.* **2.** fashionable society [< French, 'good tone']

bonus /bónəss/ *n* **1.** UNEXPECTED EXTRA an extra unexpected advantage **2.** FIN EXTRA MONEY an amount of money given in addition to normal pay, especially as a reward **3.** FIN PREMIUM PAID TO SOMEBODY an extra dividend or premium paid to the purchaser, holder,

promoter, or vendor of a stock or insurance policy [Late 18C. < Latin, 'good']

bonus issue *n* an issue of free shares, distributed pro rata by a company to existing shareholders

bon vivant /bóN vee vóN/ (*plural* **bons vivants** /*pronunc. same*/), **bon viveur** /-vee vúr/ (*plural* **bons viveurs** /bóN vee vúr/) *n* somebody who enjoys the luxuries in life, especially good food and wine [*Bon vivant* < French, 'somebody who lives well'; *bon viveur* formed in English after *bon vivant* and French *viveur* 'living person']

bon voyage /bóN vwaa yaázh, bón voy aázh/ *interj* used to wish somebody an enjoyable and safe journey [< French, 'good journey']

bony /bóni/ (**-ier, -iest**) *adj* **1. HAVING PROMINENT BONES** extremely thin and with prominent bones **2.** FOOD **CONTAINING MANY BONES** containing many bones, and often difficult to eat **3.** ANAT **OF OR LIKE BONE** consisting of or resembling bone **4.** FISH **WITH BACKBONE** describes fish that have a skeleton of bone, as distinct from cartilaginous fish such as sharks. The great majority of fish are bony. Class: Osteichthyes. —**boniness** *n*

bonze /bonz/ *n* a Buddhist monk in Southeast Asia, China, or Japan [Late 16C. Via French and Portuguese < Japanese *bonsō* < *bon* 'ordinary' + *sō* 'monk']

bonzer /bónzər/ *adj ANZ* with the best or most pleasing qualities (*dated informal*) [Early 20C. Origin ?]

boo /boo/ *interj* **1. EXPRESSING DISAPPROVAL** used to express dissatisfaction or contempt, especially at a speaker or performer **2. USED TO STARTLE SOMEBODY** used to surprise or startle somebody ■ *n* **SOUND OF DISAPPROVAL OR SURPRISE** an utterance of 'boo!' in order to startle somebody or to show dissatisfaction ■ *vti* (**boos, booing, booed**) **EXPRESS DISAPPROVAL** to shout 'boo!' in order to express dissatisfaction or contempt of somebody, especially a speaker or performer [Early 19C. Originally an imitation of a cow's lowing] ◇ **would not say boo to a goose** to be extremely timid and shy (*informal*)

booai, booay *n NZ* another spelling of **boohai**

boob[1] /boob/, **booby** /boobi/ (*plural* **-bies**) *n* a woman's breast (*slang; often considered offensive; usually plural*) [Mid-20C. < *bubby*, origin ?]

boob[2] /boob/ *n* **1. UNFORTUNATE MISTAKE** an unfortunate and embarrassing mistake (*informal*) **2. UNINTELLIGENT PERSON** somebody who is regarded as unintelligent or ignorant (*slang*) ■ *vi* (**boobs, boobing, boobed**) **MAKE UNFORTUNATE MISTAKE** to make an unfortunate and embarrassing mistake (*informal*) [Early 20C. Shortening of BOOBY[1]]

boobialla /boobi állə/ (*plural* **-las** or *same*) *n* a small tree with a rounded crown, long glossy leaves, and white flowers. Native to: sand dunes and cliffs in Australia. Latin name: *Myoporum insulare.* [Mid-19C. < an Aboriginal language]

boo-boo *n* a mistake or tactless remark (*informal*) [Mid-20C. Probably < BOOB[2]]

boobook /boobook/ (*plural* **-books** or *same*) *n* a small owl with greyish-brown to dark brown feathers and greenish-yellow eyes set in a large facial mask. Native to: Australia, New Zealand. Latin name: *Ninox novaeseelandiae.* [Early 19C. < an Aboriginal language; an imitation of the bird's call]

boob tube[1] *n* a short strapless stretchy top for women (*informal*) [< BOOB[1]]

boob tube[2] *n ANZ, N Am* same as **television** (*informal*) [< BOOB[2]]

booby[1] /boobi/ (*plural* **-bies**) *n* **1. SOMEBODY UNINTELLIGENT** somebody regarded as silly or unintelligent (*dated informal*) **2. POOREST PERFORMER** the poorest performer in a group, or the loser in a game (*informal*) **3. LARGE TROPICAL SEABIRD** a large seabird of the gannet family, with brown, black, and/or white feathers, often with a brightly coloured beak and feet. Native to: tropical regions. Family: Sulidae. [Early 17C. Probably alteration of Spanish *bobo* < Latin *balbus* 'stammering']

booby[2] *n* ANAT same as **boob**[1]

booby hatch *n* **1.** a cover for a small hatchway on a sailing ship **2.** *US* an offensive term for a psychiatric hospital (*slang*) [< BOOBY[1] (sense 3), because a favourite haunt for these birds on a ship]

booby prize *n* a prize given as a joke to the person or team coming last in a competition

booby trap *n* **1.** a bomb that is hidden or disguised and is designed to explode when touched or moved **2.** a trap set as a practical joke

booby-trap (**booby-traps, booby-trapping, booby-trapped**) *vt* to place a booby trap in a place or attach one to something (*often passive*)

boodle /bood'l/ *n* a large amount of money that has been acquired or used in a corrupt way (*slang*) [Early 17C. < Dutch *boedel* 'estate, possessions']

boofhead /boof hed/ *n Aus* an offensive term for somebody who is considered unintelligent or thoughtless (*informal insult*) [Mid-20C. Perhaps < BUFFLEHEAD in the obsolete sense 'simpleton']

boofy /boofi/ *adj Aus* an offensive term for somebody who is considered unintelligent or thoughtless (*informal insult*) [Late 20C. < BOOFHEAD]

booger /booggər/ *n N Am* same as **bogey** *n* (sense 2) (*slang*) [Mid-19C. Probably alteration of BUGGER[1]]

boogie /boogi/ *vi* (**-ies, -ieing, -ied**) to dance to fast rock music (*informal*) ■ *n* MUSIC same as **boogie-woogie** [Mid-20C. Origin ?]

boogie on down *vi* to go off somewhere (*slang*)

boogie board *n* SURFING same as **body board** (*informal*)

boogie-woogie /boogi woogi/ *n* a jazz piano style derived from the blues

boohai /boo hī/, **booai** /boo ī/, **booay** *n NZ* a remote rural area (*informal*) [Mid-20C. Origin ?]

boohoo /boo hoo/ *n, interj* used to represent the sound of noisy weeping ■ *vi* (**-hoos, -hooing, -hooed**) to weep noisily [Mid-19C. An imitation of the sound]

book /book/ *n* **1. BOUND COLLECTION OF PAGES** a collection of printed or manuscript pages sewn or glued together along one side and bound between rigid boards or flexible covers **2. PUBLISHED WORK** a published work of literature, science, or reference, or a work intended for publication **3. BOUND SET OF BLANK SHEETS** a bound set of blank sheets of paper, e.g. for writing in **4. SET OF THINGS BOUND TOGETHER** a set of objects such as matches or fabric samples that are bound together **5. DIVISION OF LITERARY WORK** a major division of a literary work or of the Bible **6. SCRIPT OR LIBRETTO** the script of a play or the libretto of an opera **7. BOOKMAKER'S RECORD** a record kept by a bookmaker of the bets made and of the money paid out **8.** TELECOM same as **telephone directory** (*informal*) **9.** CARDS **NUMBER OF TRICKS NEEDED FOR SCORING** in cards, the number of tricks that need to be won by a player or side before a trick can count as a score **10. MAGAZINE** a magazine or brochure (*informal*) **11. SET OF RULES** the body of rules or procedures relevant to a situation ○ *likes to do things by the book* **12. IMAGINARY RECORD** an imaginary record, archive, or repository of knowledge **13.** THEATRE same as **promptbook 14.** *also* **Book** BIBLE the Christian Bible or Hebrew scripture ■ **books** *npl* **1.** ACCT **FINANCIAL ACCOUNTS** the financial records and accounts of an organization **2. LEARNING** academic study ■ *v* (**books, booking, booked**) **1.** *vti* **RESERVE PLACE** to arrange for somebody to keep a place available at a specified time, e.g. at the theatre or in a restaurant **2.** *vt* **MAKE RESERVATION FOR SOMEBODY** to reserve a place for somebody somewhere, especially on some form of transport **3.** *vt* **ENGAGE SOMEBODY** to engage somebody in advance to do something or be somewhere, especially as a performer (*often passive*) **4.** *vt* LAW **CHARGE SOMEBODY WITH CRIMINAL OFFENCE** to charge somebody with a criminal offence, pending legal proceedings (*often passive*) **5.** *vt* **TAKE NAME OF OFFENDING PLAYER** in sports, to officially record the name of a player who has committed an offence (*often passive*) **6.** *vi US* **DEPART** to leave a place (*slang*) ○ *Yo man, let's book!* [Old English *bōc* 'written document' < Indo-European, 'beech'] —**booker** *n* ◇ **a closed book** somebody or something about which little, if anything, is known or understood ◇ **an open book** somebody or something that is easy to understand or know about because nothing is concealed ◇ **balance the books** to ensure that the debit and credit or income and expenditure sides of an account show the same total, usually by making additional entries ◇ **bring somebody to book** to make somebody account for his or her behaviour ◇ **cook the books** to alter records, especially financial accounts, to conceal irregularities or wrongdoing (*slang*) ◇ **in somebody's book** in somebody's opinion ◇ **in somebody's good** *or* **bad books** in or out of favour with somebody ◇ **throw the book at somebody** to charge somebody with all the offences that he or she may be guilty of, or punish somebody with the maximum penalty

book in *v* **1.** *vti* to reserve accommodation at a hotel or other lodgings **2.** *vi* to sign in at a hotel or other lodgings

book out *vti* to perform the necessary formalities to end a stay at a hotel or other lodgings, or make somebody do this

book up *vi* to reserve accommodation or buy a ticket for something in advance

bookable /bookəb'l/ *adj* **1.** able to be applied for in advance and reserved **2.** describes an offence in sports that is serious enough for the referee to give the guilty player a warning and record his or her name officially

bookbinder /book bīndər/ *n* somebody who binds books, especially as a profession —**bookbindery** *n* —**bookbinding** *n*

bookcase /book kayss/ *n* a set of shelves, either fixed to a wall or free-standing, used for holding books

book club *n* an organization that offers its members books at reduced prices

~~**bookeeping**~~ incorrect spelling of **bookkeeping**

bookend /book end/ *n* either of a pair of supports placed at each end of a row of books ■ *vt* to occur, or make something occur, on both sides or at the beginning and end of something (*informal*) ○ *bookend a speech with anecdotes*

book-entry *adj* relating to the recording of ownership of a security on a financial institution's computer systems instead of using certificates

Booker Prize /bookər-/ *n* a cash prize awarded annually, originally by the company Booker McConnell and now by the Man Group, for a recently published work of fiction by a British, Irish, or Commonwealth writer —**Booker Prizewinner** *n*

bookie /booki/ *n* GAMBLING same as **bookmaker** (sense 1) (*informal*) [Late 19C. < BOOKMAKER]

booking /booking/ *n* **1.** an arrangement by which something such as a theatre seat or hotel room is kept for somebody's use at a specific time **2.** a contract or arrangement for an entertainer to perform somewhere

booking clerk *n* somebody who sells tickets, especially railway tickets

booking office *n* the counter or kiosk in a train or bus station where people buy tickets

bookish /bookish/ *adj* devoted to reading, especially to the exclusion of other things —**bookishly** *adv* —**bookishness** *n*

bookkeeping /book keeping/ *n* the activity or profession of recording the money received and spent by a person, business, or organization —**bookkeeper** *n*

book learning *n* knowledge obtained from books instead of from experience

booklet /booklət/ *n* a small book with a paper cover and few pages, usually containing information about a particular subject

booklore /book lawr/ *n* **1.** same as **book learning 2.** information about books, especially their authors and the circumstances of their publication

booklouse /book lowss/ (*plural* **-lice** /-līss/) *n* a small wingless insect that destroys books by feeding on the paste used in the binding. Order: Psocoptera.

book lung *n* the breathing organ in spiders and other arachnids, with membranous tissue arranged in folds that resemble the leaves of a book

bookmaker /book maykər/ *n* **1.** somebody who takes bets and pays winners **2.** a book designer, printer, or binder —**bookmaking** *n*

bookman /bookmən/ (*plural* **-men** /-mən/) *n* a book enthusiast or collector (*dated*)

bookmark /book maark/ *n* **1. MARKER IN BOOK** a strip of material inserted between the pages of a book to mark a place in it **2.** ONLINE **MARKER IN ELECTRONIC TEXT** an electronic marker in a word-processed document, identifying it for reference or retrieval **3.** ONLINE **ADDRESS OF INTERNET SITE** the address of a favourite Internet site electronically listed ■ *vt* (**-marks, -marking, -marked**) ONLINE **LIST INTERNET ADDRESS** to list the address of an Internet site

bookmobile /book mō beel/ *n N Am* a large motor vehicle equipped as a small lending library, used

for taking books to people, especially in rural areas

Book of Changes *n* PHILOSOPHY same as **I Ching** (sense 2)

Book of Common Prayer *n* the official book giving the order and content of services in the Anglican Church. Since 1980 the Alternative Service Book has also been in use.

book of hours *n* a medieval service book, used especially in monasteries, containing the offices, prayers, and services prescribed for the various canonical hours

Book of Kells /-kéllz/ *n* an illuminated manuscript of the Christian Gospels, produced at Kells in Ireland in the 8th century and now kept in Trinity College, Dublin

Book of Life *n* 1. a comprehensive personal identity document carried by South Africans. It was originally introduced for whites only but went into general use in 1986. 2. CHR same as **Bible**

Book of Mormon *n* a book believed by members of the Church of Jesus Christ of Latter-Day Saints to have been revealed by the prophet Mormon to Joseph Smith. It contains the history of an ancient American people to whom Jesus Christ is believed to have appeared, and is said to have been written originally on golden tablets.

bookplate /bóok playt/ *n* a label for sticking into the front of a book, bearing the name of the owner and sometimes a coat of arms or personal design

bookrest /bóok rest/ *n* a support, often angled, for an open book

bookseller /bóok selər/ *n* somebody who deals in books

bookshelf /bóok shelf/ (*plural* **-shelves** /-shelvz/) *n* a shelf designed for holding books

bookshop /bóok shop/ *n* a shop that specializes in selling books

bookstall /bóok stawl/ *n* 1. a stand in the street or at a railway or bus station where newspapers, magazines, and books are sold 2. a stall where books are sold

bookstand /bóok stand/ *n* 1. same as **bookstall** 2. a support for an open book, often adjustable and made of wood, metal, or plastic

bookstore /bóok stawr/ *n* N Am a shop that sells books

book token *n* a voucher for a specific value that can be exchanged for books and is often given as a present

book value *n* 1. the value of a commodity or asset according to the accounting records of the firm owning it 2. the net value of a business after liabilities have been deducted from assets

bookworm /bóok wurm/ *n* 1. somebody who loves reading (*informal*) 2. an insect whose larvae eat the paper or binding paste in books

Boole /bool/, **George** (1815–64) British mathematician and logician. His system of Boolean algebra, presented in *An Investigation of the Laws of Thought* (1854), applied symbols to logical propositions. Boolean logic is important in designing and programming computers.

Boolean /bóoli ən/ *adj* using a system of symbolic logic that uses combinations of logical operators such as 'AND', 'OR', and 'NOT' (**Boolean operators**) to determine relationships between entities. Boolean operations are extensively used in writing computer programs and in computer searches using keywords. [Mid-19C. After George BOOLE]

Boolean algebra *n* a form of algebra concerned with the logical functions of variables that are restricted to two values, true or false. Boolean algebra is fundamental to circuit design and to the design, function, and operation of computers.

Boolean operator *n* a connecting word or symbol that allows a computer user to include or exclude items in a text search

boom¹ /boom/ *v* (**booms, booming, boomed**) 1. *vi* MAKE LOUD DEEP SOUND to make a loud deep reverberating sound 2. *vt* UTTER SOMETHING LOUDLY to say something in a loud deep voice 3. *vi* ECON EXPERIENCE SIGNIFICANT INCREASE IN TRADE to experience a significant expansion of business and investment, either across an economy or in a specific market ○ *Business is*

booming. ■ *n* 1. LOUD DEEP SOUND a loud deep reverberating sound 2. ZOOL DEEP LOUD BIRD OR ANIMAL NOISE a deep loud cry made by some birds and animals. Bitterns and grouse boom. 3. SIGNIFICANT INCREASE IN AMOUNT a significant increase in the amount of something such as a population level ○ *a population boom* 4. ECON SIGNIFICANT INCREASE IN BUSINESS a significant expansion of business and investment, either across an economy or in a specific market ○ *a boom in sales* [15C. Perhaps < Dutch *bommen* 'to hum, buzz'; an imitation of the sound] —**boomy** *adj*

boom² /boom/ *n* 1. SAILING BEAM HOLDING SAIL AT ANGLE a beam to which the bottom edge of a sail is attached in order to hold the sail at an advantageous angle to the wind 2. CINEMA, MEDIA EXTENDABLE OVERHEAD POLE an extendable pole carrying overhead equipment such as a camera for positioning over a television or film set 3. MIL, INDUST FLOATING BARRIER a floating barrier used to confine or restrict something, e.g. a barrier to protect a harbour from attack or to confine an oil spill 4. FREIGHT POLE USED TO MOVE CARGO a long pole extending from the mast of a derrick to lift or lower cargo 5. AVIAT CONNECTING SPAR FOR AIRCRAFT a spar that connects the tail and the fuselage in some aircraft [Mid-16C. < Dutch, 'beam, pole'] ◇ **lower the boom** N Am to initiate action to prevent something or punish somebody (*informal*)

boom and bust, **boom or bust** *n* the alternation in an economy or market between immoderate growth and collapse and recession

boom box *n* a large radio and cassette or CD player with a built-in speaker at each end, carried by a handle at the top (*informal*)

boomer /bóomər/ *n* 1. N Am same as **baby boomer** (*informal*) 2. Aus a very large male kangaroo (*informal*) 3. NAVY a nuclear-powered submarine armed with ballistic missiles (*slang*)

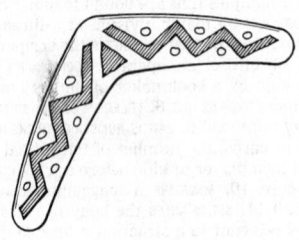

boomerang

boomerang /bóomə rang/ *n* 1. CULTL ANTHROP, ARMS CURVED MISSILE a flat curved piece of wood used as a weapon by Australian Aboriginals that is designed to return to the person who throws it 2. SOMETHING HARMFUL TO INITIATOR something that does inadvertent harm to its initiator ■ *vi* (**-rangs, -ranging, -ranged**) BACKFIRE ON INITIATOR to backfire on the initiator of an action, causing that person harm [Late 18C. < an Aboriginal language]

boomerang kid *n* an adult child who returns home after university, first job, or breakup of a relationship because of financial hardship or lack of employment (*informal humorous*)

booming /bóoming/ *adj* 1. increasingly successful economically ○ *the booming futures market* 2. loud and deep in tone ○ *a booming voice*

boomlet /bóomlət/ *n* a short period of sudden and intense economic growth

boomslang /bóom slang/ (*plural* **-slangs** *or* same) *n* a large greenish tree-dwelling poisonous snake. Native to: southern Africa. Latin name: *Dispholidus typus*. [Late 18C. < Afrikaans, 'tree snake']

boom town *n* a town that significantly increases in size and wealth, often as the result of new and profitable industry

boom vang *n* the pulley that controls the vertical position of the boom

boon /boon/ *n* 1. something that functions as a blessing or benefit to somebody 2. a gift or favour from somebody (*archaic or literary*) [12C. < Old Norse *bón* 'prayer, petition' < Indo-European, 'speak']

boon companion *n* an intimate friend from whom somebody is inseparable [Via French *bon* < Latin *bonus* 'good']

boondocks /bóon doks/ *npl* N Am a place regarded as remote, provincial, and lacking sophistication (*informal*)

boondoggle /bóon dog'l/ *n* N Am an activity or project that is unnecessary and wasteful of time or money, especially one undertaken for personal or political gain (*informal*) [Mid-20C. An invented word: originally a plaited leather cord made by Scouts] —**boondoggle** *vi* — **boondoggler** *n*

Boone /boon/, **Daniel** (1734–1820) American frontiersman. He lived on the frontier from an early age and played a major part in the exploration and settlement of Kentucky.

'I can't say I was ever lost, but I was bewildered once for three days.'
[Attributed to Daniel Boone]

boong /boong/ *n* Aus an offensive term for an Aboriginal (*slang*) [Mid-20C. < an Aboriginal language]

boongary /bóong gari/ (*plural* **-ries** *or* same) *n* a kangaroo that lives in trees. Native to: northern Australia. Latin name: *Dendrolagus lumholtzi*. [Late 19C. < an Aboriginal language]

boonies /bóoniz/ *npl* N Am same as **boondocks**

boor /boor/ *n* somebody who behaves in a crass, insensitive, or ill-mannered way [Mid-16C. < Dutch *boer* 'peasant'] —**boorish** *adj* —**boorishly** *adv* —**boorishness** *n*

Boorman /báwrmən/, **John** (*b.* 1933) British film director. After a successful career making documentaries for the BBC, he directed Hollywood feature films, including *Deliverance* (1972) and *Hope and Glory* (1987).

'Movie-making is the process of turning money into light. All they have at the end of the day is images flickering on a wall.'
[John Boorman. Quoted in *The Oxford Book of Money*, Kevin Jackson, ed.; 1995]

boost /boost/ *vt* (**boosts, boosting, boosted**) 1. IMPROVE SOMETHING to improve, strengthen, or encourage somebody or something 2. INCREASE SOMETHING to cause something to increase ○ *measures to boost productivity* 3. PUSH SOMEBODY OR SOMETHING UP to help somebody or something to get up or over something by giving a push from below 4. ELEC RAISE VOLTAGE to increase the voltage in an electrical circuit 5. COMM PROMOTE SOMETHING to promote or advertise something widely and intensively so that people will buy it 6. N Am STEAL SOMETHING to steal something, especially from a shop (*informal*) ■ *n* 1. IMPROVEMENT something that helps to improve, strengthen, or encourage somebody or something ○ *gave his career a much-needed boost* 2. INCREASE IN SOMETHING an increase or sudden growth in something ○ *a boost in income* 3. PROMOTIONAL CAMPAIGN a campaign promoting or advertising something 4. PUSH FROM BELOW a push from below to help somebody or something to get up or over something [Early 19C. Origin ?]

booster /bóostər/ *n* 1. SOMEBODY OR SOMETHING THAT CAUSES IMPROVEMENT somebody or something that improves, strengthens, or encourages somebody or something (*usually used in combination*) ○ *a morale-booster* 2. ELECTRONICS RADIO-FREQUENCY AMPLIFIER a radio-frequency amplifier that amplifies weak television or radio signals and retransmits them so that they can be received by viewers or listeners 3. AEROSP same as **booster rocket** 4. TECH DEVICE THAT MAKES SOMETHING MORE EFFECTIVE a device used to increase the effectiveness of a piece of equipment 5. IMMUNOL SUPPLEMENTARY DOSE OF VACCINE a repeat dose of a vaccine given some time after the initial course to maintain the level of immunity provided by the previous dose

booster rocket *n* an engine in a space vehicle that is used to give thrust during the launch

booster seat *n* a seat that can be placed over another seat in a motor vehicle or at a table to raise a child into a higher position

boot¹ /boot/ *n* 1. STRONG SHOE EXTENDING UP LOWER LEG a strong item of footwear that covers part of the lower leg (*often used in combination*) ○ *an ankle boot* 2. AUTOMOT LUGGAGE COMPARTMENT IN CAR the compartment of a car used for carrying luggage. N Am term **trunk** 3. HARD KICK the act of kicking somebody or something

with great force **4.** DISMISSAL FROM JOB dismissal from employment or from a personal relationship (*informal*) ○ *was given the boot* **5.** RIDING COVERING FOR HORSE'S LEG a protective covering for the lower part of a horse's leg **6.** HIST INSTRUMENT OF TORTURE an instrument of torture that was used in the past to enclose and crush the victim's foot **7.** MECH ENG PROTECTIVE COVERING a protective covering, e.g. a rubber sheath for protecting a coupling between two shafts **8.** *US* AUTOMOT same as **wheel clamp** ■ *vt* (**boots, booting, booted**) **1.** KICK SOMEBODY OR SOMETHING HARD to kick somebody or something with great force **2.** same as **boot out** (*informal*) **3.** *N Am* AUTOMOT same as **clamp** *v* (sense 3) [14C. < Old French *bote*] ◇ **as tough as old boots** extremely strong and healthy ◇ **boots and all** *ANZ* without holding back in any way ◇ **get too big for your boots** to become overconfident (*informal*) ◇ **lick somebody's boots** to be extremely obsequious to somebody ◇ **put the boot in** to attack or criticize somebody cruelly, often somebody who is vulnerable or already hurt (*informal*)

boot out *vt* to force somebody to leave a place, group of people, or job (*informal*)

boot² /boot/ *n* the process of starting or restarting a computer and loading the operating system ■ *vi* (**boots, booting, booted**) to start or restart a computer and load the operating system, or be started up in this way [Late 20C. Shortening of BOOTSTRAP in *bootstrap loader*, a simple program that enables a computer to start up and load its full operating system]

boot up *vt* to start or restart a computer and load the operating system

boot³ /boot/ [Old English *bōt* 'remedy' < Indo-European, 'good'] ◇ **to boot** in addition or also

Boot /boot/, **Sir Jesse, Baron Trent** (1850–1931) British pharmaceutical manufacturer. He created the largest retail pharmaceutical business in the world, beginning with a single chemist's shop in Nottingham (1877).

bootblack /boot blak/ *n* especially formerly, a person who cleans people's shoes in the street

boot camp *n* (*informal*) **1.** *N Am* CAMP FOR MILITARY RECRUITS a training camp for military recruits **2.** PRISON FOR DELINQUENTS a prison with military-style discipline to which juvenile offenders are sent **3.** TRAINING COURSE a training session or course ○ *a home computing boot camp* [< BOOT¹ 'naval or marine corps recruit']

boot cut *adj* describes trousers with legs that are flared at the end to fit over boots

booted /boot id/ *adj* wearing boots (*archaic or humorous*)

bootee /boo tee/, **bootie** /boot i/ *n* **1.** a soft woollen boot for a baby **2.** an ankle boot for a woman or child

Boötes /bō ō teez/ *n* a constellation of the northern hemisphere, dominated by the bright star Arcturus. See illustration at **constellation** [Mid-16C. Via Latin < Greek *boōtēs* 'ploughman, Boötes' < *bous* 'ox' + *ōthein* 'to push']

booth /booth/ (*plural* **booths** /boothz/) *n* **1.** SMALL TENT OR STALL a tent, stall, or other light structure at a fair or exhibition, offering some form of entertainment or goods for sale **2.** SMALL PARTITIONED ENCLOSURE a partitioned enclosure or small room shaped like a box that offers privacy, e.g. when telephoning, selling tickets, or voting **3.** RESTAURANT COMPARTMENT a small, partly enclosed area in a restaurant with a table and high-backed seats **4.** SMALL ROOM USED IN BROADCASTING a small soundproof room used for recording sound or for broadcasting [12C. < N Germanic]

Booth /booth/, **John Wilkes** (1838–65) US actor and the assassin of Abraham Lincoln. He was the brother of the actor Edwin Booth. A partisan of the Confederacy during the American Civil War, he shot Abraham Lincoln at Ford's Theatre in Washington, DC, on 14 April 1865, and was himself killed soon afterwards.

Booth, William (1829–1912) British religious leader. He founded the Christian Mission (1865), later called the Salvation Army (1878), pursuing social reform and setting up charities in city slums.

Boothia Peninsula /boo thi ə-/ the northernmost tip of mainland North America, in Northwest Territories, Canada, directly west of Baffin Island. Area: 32,300 sq. km/12,500 sq. mi.

Popperfoto

Betty Boothroyd

Boothroyd /boo th royd/, **Betty** (b. 1929) British politician. She was the first woman speaker of the House of Commons (1992–2000) and chancellor of the Open University in 1994, and became a life peer in 2000.

'Good temper and moderation are the characteristics of parliamentary language.'
[Betty Boothroyd, *Independent*; 9 February 1995]

bootie *n* CLOTHING another spelling of **bootee**

bootjack /boot jak/ *n* a device used for gripping the back of a boot when removing it

bootlace /boot layss/ *n* a long shoelace, traditionally a narrow cord or a leather thong, for lacing up boots

bootleg /boot leg/ *vti* (**-legs, -legging, -legged**) DEAL IN ILLEGAL GOODS to make, transport, or sell illegal goods, especially illegally copied or recorded material ■ *n* **1.** SOMETHING ILLEGALLY MADE an illegally made product, especially an illegal recording **2.** ILLEGAL ALCOHOL alcohol or an alcoholic beverage that has been smuggled or illegally distilled ■ *adj* CLOTHING same as **boot cut** [Early 20C. Back-formation < *bootlegger* (late 19C), from alcohol smugglers carrying bottles in their boots] —**bootlegger** *n*

bootless /boot ləss/ *adj* having little or no success [< BOOT³] —**bootlessly** *adv*

bootlick /boot lik/ (**-licks, -licking, -licked**) *vti* to flatter somebody in a position of authority in order to gain an advantage (*informal*) —**bootlicker** *n* —**bootlicking** *n, adj*

boots /boots/ (*plural same*) *n* somebody who polishes boots and shoes, especially at a hotel (*dated*)

boot sale *n* same as **car boot sale**

boots-and-all *adj Aus* characterized by a complete lack of restraint (*informal*) ○ *They had a boots-and-all to-do over the meeting.*

boots and saddles *n US* a bugle call used in the US cavalry to give the signal to mount (*takes a singular verb*) [Alteration of French *boute-selle* 'place saddle']

bootstrap /boot strap/ *n* a leather or fabric loop on the back or side of a boot to help pull it on ◇ **pull yourself up by your (own) bootstraps** to improve your situation in life by your own efforts

bootstrapping /boot straping/ *n* the building of a business from nothing, with minimum outside capital

boot tree *n* **1.** a wooden or metal device shaped like a foot and lower leg, placed inside a boot to preserve its shape **2.** a foot-shaped support for making or repairing boots

booty¹ /boot i/ *n* money or valuables seized or stolen, especially by soldiers in war [15C. Directly or via Old French *butin* < Middle Low German *būte* 'exchange']

booty² /boot i/ *n US* somebody's buttocks (*informal*) [Probably alteration of BODY]

boo-yah-kah /boo yaa kaa/, **booyaka, boo-yah** /boo yaa/ *interj* (*slang; used in Black English*) **1.** used as a greeting, originally among gang members **2.** used to express enjoyment of a performance in a dance hall [Perhaps an imitation of the sound of gunshots]

booze /booz/ (*slang*) *vi* (**boozes, boozing, boozed**) OVER-INDULGE IN ALCOHOL to drink alcohol, especially to excess ■ *n* **1.** ALCOHOL alcoholic drink **2.** SESSION OF HEAVY DRINKING a period of time spent overindulging in alcohol [13C. < Middle Dutch *būsen* 'drink to excess']

booze bus *n NZ* a police patrol unit that stops drivers randomly to test their blood-alcohol levels (*informal*)

boozer /boo zər/ *n* (*slang*) **1.** a public house or bar **2.** a heavy drinker of alcohol

booze-up *n* an occasion when alcohol is drunk to excess (*slang*)

boozy /boo zi/ (**-ier, -iest**) *adj* (*slang*) **1.** WITH EXCESSIVE DRINKING characterized by the drinking of alcohol to excess **2.** CONTAINING ALCOHOL containing or flavoured with alcohol **3.** DRINKING EXCESSIVELY tending to drink alcohol excessively **4.** SHOWING EFFECTS OF EXCESSIVE DRINKING showing the effects of prolonged excessive drinking —**boozily** *adv*

bop¹ /bop/ *vi* (**bops, bopping, bopped**) DANCE to dance to pop music, especially in a disco (*informal*) ■ *n* **1.** PERIOD OF DANCING a session of dancing to pop music (*informal*) ○ *We had one quick bop and left.* **2.** EVENT WITH DANCING a social event organized for the purpose of dancing to pop music (*informal*) **3.** MUSIC same as **bebop** [Mid-20C. Shortening of BEBOP]

bop² /bop/ (*informal*) *vt* (**bops, bopping, bopped**) to hit somebody, especially to punch somebody in the face ■ *n* a blow, especially a punch in the face [Late 19C. An imitation of the sound]

Bophuthatswana /bo poo tət swaa nə/ former homeland in South Africa, now part of North West Province and the Free State

bopper /bop pər/ *n* a jazz musician who plays bebop

~~boquet~~ incorrect spelling of **bouquet**

bora¹ /baw rə/, **Bora** *n* a cold dry strong northeasterly wind that blows down the mountains of central Europe and along the shores of the Adriatic Sea [Mid-19C. < dialect variant of Italian *borea* < Latin *boreas* 'north wind']

bora² /baw rə/ *n* in southeastern Australia, a rite carried out by Aboriginals in which youths pass to manhood. The ceremony takes place within a circle of raised ground. [Mid-19C. < Aboriginal *bor* 'fur belt worn by initiates']

Bora-Bora /baw rə baw rə/ island and tourist resort in the southern Pacific. One of the Leeward Islands of French Polynesia, it was used as a US air base in World War II. Population: 4,225 (1988). Area: 39 sq. km/15 sq. mi.

boracic /bə rass ik/ *adj* **1.** CHEM same as **boric 2.** *Cockney* having no money (*slang*) [Late 18C. < medieval Latin *borac-*, stem of *borax* (see BORAX)]

borage /borr ij/ *n* a hairy plant that has thick leaves that taste of cucumber and produces oil with pharmaceutical uses. Flowers: blue, star-shaped. Native to: Mediterranean. Latin name: *Borago officinalis*. [13C. Via French *bourrache* < Latin *bor(r)ago*]

borane /baw rayn/ *n* a compound containing only boron and hydrogen. Use: rocket and jet engine fuels. [Early 20C. < BORON]

borate /baw rayt/ *n* a boric acid salt or ester [Late 18C. < BORAX]

borax /baw raks/ *n* a white crystalline solid that is an ore of boron. Source: alkaline soils, salt deposits. Use: cleaning agent, water softener, preservative. Formula: $Na_2B_4O_7.10H_2O$. [14C. Via medieval Latin and colloquial Arabic < Pahlavi *būrak*]

borborygmus /baw rbə rigməss/ *n* the rumbling sounds made by the movement of gases in the stomach and intestine (*technical*) [Early 18C. < Greek *borborugmos* < *borborizein* 'have a rumbling in the bowels'] —**borborygmic** *adj*

Bordeaux¹ /bawr dō/ city on the River Garonne and capital of Gironde Department in the Aquitaine Region, southwestern France. It is an important centre for the wine trade. Population: 215,363 (1999).

Bordeaux² /bawr dō/ *n* a red or white wine produced in the region around Bordeaux, southwestern France

Bordeaux mixture *n* a solution of copper sulphate and calcium hydroxide in water. Use: plant fungicide.

bordello /bawr dell ō/ (*plural* **-los**) *n N Am* a house of prostitution [Late 16C. Via Italian < French *bordel* 'cabin, small hut']

Borden /bawrd n/, **Sir Robert** (1854–1937) prime minister of Canada (1911–20). The leader of the Con-

servative Party since 1901, he won a landslide victory after 15 years of Liberal government in 1911. He oversaw his country's participation in World War I and went on to represent Canada on the council of the League of Nations. Full name **Borden, Sir Robert Laird**. See table at **prime minister**

border /báwrdər/ n **1. LINE DIVIDING TWO AREAS** the line that officially separates two countries or regions, or the land on each side of it ○ *across the border* ○ *border country* **2. LAND AT EDGE** the edge of an area of land, or the ground near the edge ○ *a shy animal that rarely comes nearer than the border of the field* **3. STRIP AROUND EDGE** a decorative band that runs along the edge of something such as a printed page or a length of fabric ○ *a handkerchief with a patterned border* **4. GARDENING FLOWERBED** a flowerbed along a wall or at the edge of a lawn or path ■ vti **(-ders, -dering, -dered) 1. FORM FRONTIER WITH PLACE** to form the frontier with another country or the boundary between two regions ○ *Italy borders Austria in the Alps.* **2. RUN ALONG EDGE OF SOMETHING** to form a line along the edge of something ○ *a field bordered by willow trees* [14C. < Old French *bordeūre* < Germanic]

border on vt to be almost the same as something ○ *an admissions policy bordering on the ridiculous*

Border /báwrdər/, **Allan** (b. 1955) Australian cricketer. Captain of the Australian cricket team (1984–94), he retired as the highest scorer of runs in Test cricket with 11,174 runs. Full name **Border, Allan Robert**

Border collie n a dog with a long silky black-and-white coat, belonging to a breed often kept as sheep-dogs [Because originally bred in the border region between England and Scotland]

borderer /báwrdərər/ n somebody who lives in a border area between countries or regions

borderland /báwrdər land/ n **1.** the area near the edge of a country or region, especially a remote area **2.** the indeterminate area between two conditions, categories, or activities that is hard to define because it contains features or qualities of both

borderline /báwrdər līn/ n **SEPARATING LINE** the notional line that separates one state or quality from another very similar one ○ *the borderline between frankness and rudeness* ■ adj **1. AT CATEGORY'S EDGE** not clearly belonging to one or other of two categories ○ *Borderline candidates will take a further oral exam.* **2. PSYCHOL PSYCHOLOGICALLY UNSTABLE** describes a psychological condition characterized by emotional instability and marked by self-destructive, manipulative, and erratic behaviour ○ *a borderline personality* **3. MED ALMOST DEVELOPED** describes a medical condition that a patient is likely to develop unless preventive steps are taken ○ *borderline hypertension*

Border terrier n a small short dog belonging to a breed of terriers with rough coats that are kept as pets [Because originally bred in the border region between England and Scotland]

Bordet /báwr day/, **Jules** (1870–1961) Belgian physiologist and bacteriologist. He discovered the immunity factor in blood serum and the whooping-cough bacterium. Full name **Bordet, Jules Jean Baptiste Vincent**

Borduas /báwrdoo aa/, **Paul Émile** (1905–60) Canadian painter. His exploration of spontaneous painting (**automatism**) led to abstract works such as *L'Étoile noire* (1957).

bordure /báwr dyoor/ n the decorated border round the edge of the shield on a coat of arms, signifying that the bearer is not the chief of the family [14C. Variant of BORDER]

bore[1] /bawr/ vt **(bores, boring, bored)** to make somebody lose interest and so feel tired and annoyed ○ *He bored us stiff with a detailed explanation of his holiday itinerary.* ■ n somebody or something regarded as wholly uninteresting or tiresome ○ *Peeling potatoes is a bore!* [Mid-18C. Origin ?]

SPELLCHECK See *boar*.

bore[2] /bawr/ v **(bores, boring, bored) 1.** vt **MAKE DEEP HOLE IN SOMETHING** to make a deep, neatly formed hole such as one made by a drill, a bullet, or a boring insect **2.** vi **PENETRATE** to penetrate into the inner or hidden parts of somebody or something ○ *questioning that bores deep into their private affairs* ■ n **INTERNAL DIAMETER** the internal diameter of a pipe, gun barrel,

or other hollow cylindrical part [Old English *borian* < Indo-European]

bore[3] /bawr/ n a large powerful wave that the tide causes to move up a river or narrow estuary [Early 17C. Origin ?]

bore[4] past tense of **bear**[2]

boreal /báwri əl/ adj describes a region that has a northern temperate climate, with cold winters and warm summers [15C. Directly or via French < late Latin *borealis* < Latin *Boreas* (see BOREAS)]

Boreas /báwri əss/ n **1.** in Greek mythology, the god who personified the north wind **2.** also **boreas** a wind that blows from the north (*literary*) [14C. Via Latin < Greek]

bored /bawrd/ adj tired of and slightly annoyed by a person or situation that is not interesting, exciting, or entertaining ○ *She grew bored with living in the country.*

SPELLCHECK See *board*.

USAGE The usual preposition to use after the adjective *bored* is *with*, as in *I grew bored with all their squabbling.* However nowadays the preposition *of* is sometimes seen, especially in speech or informal writing, perhaps by analogy with *tired of*. This usage is to be avoided in careful speech or writing.

boredom /báwrdəm/ n the feeling of being bored ○ *I nearly died of boredom.*

borehole /báwr hōl/ n a deep hole drilled into the ground to obtain samples for geological study or to release or extract water or oil

~~**boreing**~~ incorrect spelling of **boring**

borer /báwrər/ n **1.** a machine or hand tool used for boring holes **2.** an organism, especially an insect or a mollusc, that bores into a plant or into wood or rock

Borg /bawrg/, **Björn** (b. 1956) Swedish tennis player. He was the Wimbledon men's singles champion from 1976 to 1980 and won the French singles title six times. Full name **Borg, Björn Rune**

'I want to be known as the best player of all time.'
[Björn Borg, *New York Times*; 8 July 1979]

Borges /báwr hess/, **Jorge Luis** (1899–1986) Argentinian writer. An avant-garde poet and essayist, he is famous for his short stories, of which *Fictions* (1945) and *The Aleph* (1949) are outstanding collections. He was director of Venezuela's National Library from 1955 to 1973.

'To fall in love is to create a religion that has a fallible god.'
[Jorge Luis Borges, 'The Meeting in a Dream', *Other Inquisitions*; 1952]

Borgia /báwrjə/, **Cesare, Duke of the Romagna** (1476?–1507) Italian soldier. The illegitimate son of Pope Alexander VI and the brother of Lucrezia Borgia, he conquered several central Italian city-states in an attempt to found his own kingdom.

Borgia, Lucrezia (1480–1519) Italian art patron. During her third marriage, to the Duke of Este, she attracted Italy's foremost painters and writers to her court in Ferrara. She was the sister of Cesare Borgia.

'My husbands have been very unlucky.'
[Attributed to Lucrezia Borgia]

boric /báwrik/ adj relating to or containing boron [Mid-19C. < BORON]

boric acid n a weak acidic white crystalline solid. Use: fire retardant, antiseptic, manufacture of heat-resistant glass and ceramics. Formula: H_3BO_3.

boring[1] /báwring/ adj stimulating no interest or enthusiasm —**boringly** adv —**boringness** n

boring[2] /báwring/ adj describes animals or tools that make holes in things

Bormann /báwrmən, -man/, **Martin** (1900–45?) German Nazi politician. A close and loyal adviser of Adolf Hitler, he stayed with Hitler to the end of World War II, when he is thought to have been killed by a sniper.

born /bawrn/ adj **1. BROUGHT INTO LIFE** brought into existence as a baby or as young from a mother's womb ○ *a child born in Birmingham* **2. BEGUN** developed

from a particular source or root cause ○ *a realization born of long experience* **3. NATURALLY PREDISPOSED** having a particular natural talent or innate character trait ○ *a born leader* **4. BY BIRTH** given a particular status or condition by or at birth (*often used in combination*) ○ *a Canadian-born singer-songwriter* ◇ **born and bred** coming from a particular place or background and usually having the qualities or character regarded as representative of it

USAGE See *borne*.

Born /bawrn/, **Max** (1882–1970) German-born British physicist. He shared the Nobel Prize (1954) for his work in quantum physics.

'Only two possibilities exist: either one must believe in determinism and regard free will as a subjective illusion, or one must become a mystic, and regard the discovery of natural laws as a meaningless illusion.'
[Max Born, *Bulletin of Atomic Scientists*; 1957]

Borna disease /báwrnə-/ n an often fatal infectious viral disease of horses, sheep, and cattle that can be passed on to human beings, in whom it can cause psychiatric disorders [After *Borna*, city in Saxony, Germany]

born-again adj **1. OF SOMEBODY WITH NEW CHRISTIAN FAITH** relating to somebody with a new and passionately felt and expressed Christian faith **2. EVANGELICALLY CHRISTIAN** relating to evangelical Christianity **3. ENTHUSIASTIC** with all the enthusiasm of somebody who has been recently converted to a cause or an idea ■ n same as **born-again Christian**

born-again Christian n somebody with a new and passionately felt and expressed Christian faith [< John 3:3 'Except a man be born again, he cannot see the kingdom of God' (referring to a spiritual rebirth)]

borne past participle of **bear**[2]

USAGE **borne** or **born**? *Borne* is the past participle of the verb *to bear*: *The following points should be borne in mind. His account is simply not borne out by the facts.* In meanings relating to birth, *borne* is used when the mother is the subject of the verb, or when the verb is passive followed by the preposition 'by': *Maria had already borne six children. The twins were borne by an Italian mother.* But when the subject is the child, *born*, an old past participle of *bear*, is used as an adjective: *I was born on a Tuesday. A child was born to Helga that evening.*

Borneo /báwrni ō/ island of the Malay Archipelago in the Pacific Ocean, divided into Sabah and Sarawak, which are states of Malaysia; Brunei, an independent sultanate; and Kalimantan, part of Indonesia. Population: 10,470,800 (1995). Area: 751,100 sq. km/290,000 sq. mi. —**Bornean** n, adj

Born-Haber cycle /báwrn háybər-/ n a cycle of chemical reactions used for calculating either the energy required to break down a crystalline solid into its constituent ions (**lattice energy**) or the energy required to break a chemical bond into noncrystalline solids (**bond energy**) [Mid-20C. After Max BORN and Fritz *Haber* (1868–1934), German chemist]

Bornholm /báwrn hōlm/ island and tourist area in southeastern Denmark, in the Baltic Sea. Population: 45,067 (1994). Area: 588 sq. km/227 sq. mi.

Bornholm disease n an acute epidemic viral infection whose symptoms include fever and chest pain [Because first identified on BORNHOLM]

bornite /báwr nīt/ n a brown metallic mineral. Use: source of copper. [Early 19C. After Ignatius von *Born* (1742–91), Austrian mineralogist]

boro- prefix boron ○ *borosilicate* [< BORON]

Borodin /bórrədin/, **Aleksander** (1833–87) Russian composer and chemist. A professor of chemistry in St Petersburg, he wrote the opera *Prince Igor* and other orchestral and chamber works. Full name **Borodin, Aleksander Porfiryevich**

Borodino /bórrə deenō/ village in Russia about 110 km/70 mi. west of Moscow. It was the site in 1812 of an important victory by Napoleon.

boron /báw ron/ n a yellow-brown element that is hard and brittle, with properties intermediate between a metal and nonmetal. Source: borax, kernite. Use:

alloys, glass, ceramics, in nuclear reactors to absorb radiation. Symbol **B**. See table at **element** [Early 19C. < BORAX, after CARBON]

boronia /bə róni ə/ *n* an aromatic evergreen bush. Flowers: bowl-shaped, crimson, yellow, or purplish-brown. Native to: Australia. Genus: *Boronia*. [Late 18C. < modern Latin, after Francesco *Borone* (1769–94), Italian botanist]

borosilicate /báwrō síllikət, -kayt/ *n* a salt of boric and silicic acids. Use: manufacture of heat- and chemical-resistant glass.

borough /búrrə/ *n* **1.** an administrative division of a large city, responsible for running local services such as housing and education **2.** in England, a town that once had special privileges granted to it by royal charter [Old English *burg* 'fortress, fortified town' < Germanic, 'protect']

Borromini /bórrə meéni/, **Francesco** (1599–1667) Italian architect. He designed the church of San Carlo alle Quattro Fontane in Rome (1638–41). Born **Castelli, Francesco**

borrow /bórrō/ *v* (-rows, -rowing, -rowed) **1.** *vt* USE SOMEBODY ELSE'S PROPERTY to get temporary possession or use of something belonging to somebody else, usually after asking permission ○ *Dad, can I borrow the car?* **2.** *vti* RECEIVE MONEY AS LOAN to arrange to be given money by somebody or by a bank or other financial institution for a fixed period of time. The money is normally paid back in instalments, with interest. ○ *We've already borrowed heavily this year.* **3.** *vt* TAKE BOOK FROM LIBRARY to take out a book or other item from a library for an agreed period of time **4.** *vti* COPY SOMETHING FROM SOMEBODY'S WORK to copy something from somebody else's work, especially a work of art of some kind ○ *Some shots were clearly borrowed from Hitchcock.* **5.** *vti* LING TAKE SOMETHING FROM ANOTHER LANGUAGE to adopt a word from another language **6.** *vi* GOLF PUTT TO ALLOW FOR SLOPE in golf, to putt to the left or right of a straight line on a green to allow for the effect of the slope **7.** *vi* GOLF VEER LEFT OR RIGHT to veer to the left or right as a result of the slope of a green (*refers to golf balls*) **8.** *vt* LEND to lend something to somebody (*nonstandard*) ■ *n* GOLF EXTENT OF VEERING the degree to which a golf ball veers to the left or right as a result of the slope of a green [Old English *borgian* 'borrow against security' < Germanic, 'protect'] — **borrower** *n*

USAGE borrow, lend, or loan? All these verbs are used in connection with the temporary use or possession of something that belongs to somebody else. When you borrow something from somebody, you get it: *Can I borrow your car for an hour? I borrowed £100 from my brother.* When you **lend** or **loan** something to somebody, you give it: *My brother lent me £100. Will you loan me your car for an hour?* **Lend** can be used figuratively, whereas **loan** cannot: *The old silver lends* [not *loans*] *an air of elegance to an otherwise drab room.* **Borrow** and **lend/loan** are not interchangeable in standard English and should not be confused.

borrow home *vt Malaysia* to borrow something and take it home ○ *Can I borrow this book home?*

Borrow /bórrō/, **George** (1803–81) British writer and traveller. His works include *Lavengro* (1851) and *The Romany Rye* (1857), inspired by his travels with British Roma, and *The Bible in Spain* (1843). Full name **Borrow, George Henry**

borrowing /bórrō ing/ *n* **1.** ACT OF GETTING SOMETHING ON LOAN an act of gaining the temporary possession of something **2.** PROCESS OF BORROWING the process of agreeing to accept money from a bank and pay it back later ○ *an increase in government borrowing* **3.** AMOUNT BORROWED an amount of money borrowed ○ *substantial borrowings in the region of half a million pounds* **4.** LING ADOPTED WORD a word that has been adopted from another language **5.** COPIED IDEA an idea copied from somebody else's work, especially from a work of art of some kind

borrow pit *n* a hole left where stones or other materials have been dug up for use in construction work elsewhere

borscht /bawrsht/ *n* a Russian or Polish soup whose main ingredient is beetroot [Early 19C. < Russian *borshch*]

borstal /báwrst'l/ *n* before 1953 in the United Kingdom, an institution for young offenders that combined features of prison and school. Borstals were re-

placed by detention centres and youth custody centres. ○ *a multimillionaire and former borstal boy* [Early 20C. After the village of *Borstal* in S England]

bort /bawrt/ *n* a diamond of inferior quality that is used industrially on grinding wheels and other abrasive devices [Early 17C. Origin ?]

borzoi /báwr zoy/ (*plural* **-zois**) *n* a tall graceful domestic dog with a long silky coat, belonging to a breed formerly used in Russia to hunt wolves [Late 19C. < Russian < *borzyý* 'swift']

bosberaad /bóssbə raad/ *n S Africa* a meeting of corporate or political management to discuss strategy or planning, usually held away from the normal place of work [Late 20C. < Afrikaans, 'bush summit']

boscage /bóskij/ *n* densely growing trees and bushes [14C. < Old French < Germanic]

Hieronymus Bosch

Bosch /bosh/, **Hieronymus** (1450?–1516) Dutch painter. His allegorical paintings teeming with demons and monsters include *The Seven Deadly Sins* and *The Garden of Earthly Delights*. Born **Aken, Jerome van**

Bose /bōss/, **Sir Jagadis Chandra** (1858–1937) Indian physicist and botanist. He invented a means of measuring minute plant movements and growth and founded the Bose Research Institute, Kolkata, India (1917).

Bose-Einstein condensation *n* a process in which the bosons of a particle system enter the lowest-energy ground state at a specific temperature [After S. N. *Bose* (see BOSON) and Albert EINSTEIN] —**Bose-Einstein condensate** *n*

bosh /bosh/ *interj* used to dismiss as nonsense what has just been said (*dated informal*) [Mid-19C. < Turkish *boş* 'empty, worthless']

bosie /bózi/, **bosey** (*plural* **-seys**) *n Aus* CRICKET same as **googly** [Early 20C. After B. T. *Bosanquet* (1877–1936), English cricketer]

bosky /bóski/ (-ier, -iest) *adj* densely covered with small trees or bushes (*literary*) [Late 16C. < variant of BUSH¹]

Bosman Ruling /bózmən-/ *n* the European Court ruling that made it possible for football players to leave their club at the end of a contract with no transfer fee payable [After Jean-Marc *Bosman*, player who brought the test case to the European Court]

bo's'n *n* NAUT same as **boatswain**

Bosnia /bózni ə/ the northern region of Bosnia and Herzegovina

Bosnia and Herzegovina

Bosnia and Herzegovina /bózni ə ənd húrtsə gō veénə/ country in the former Federal People's Republic of Yugoslavia that declared its independence in 1992. In 1995, following civil war between

Muslims, Serbs, and Croats, it was divided into two self-governing provinces: a Muslim-Croat Federation and a Serb Republic. Language: Serbo-Croatian. Currency: marka. Capital: Sarajevo. Population: 3,989,018 (2003). Area: 51,129 sq. km/ 19,741 sq. mi. Official name **Republic of Bosnia and Herzegovina**

Bosniac /bózni ak/ *n* a Muslim inhabitant of Bosnia and Herzegovina —**Bosniac** *adj*

Bosnian /bózni ən/ *n* **1.** somebody who comes from a region in the north of Bosnia and Herzegovina **2.** somebody who comes from Bosnia and Herzegovina —**Bosnian** *adj*

bosom /bóozzəm/ *n* **1.** SOMEBODY'S CHEST the chest of a man or woman **2.** WOMAN'S BREASTS the breasts of a woman **3.** WOMAN'S BREAST either of the breasts of a woman (*dated*) **4.** CLOTHING COVERING BREASTS the part of a garment that covers a woman's breasts **5.** PROTECTIVE PLACE a familiar source of protection, security, or affection (*literary*) ○ *back in the bosom of her family* **6.** SEAT OF EMOTION the place where emotions are felt (*literary*) ■ *adj* CLOSE IN FRIENDSHIP describes a friend to whom somebody is very close (*informal*) ○ *a bosom buddy* [Old English *bōsm*, origin ?]

bosomy /bóozəmi/ (-ier, -iest) *adj* describes a woman with large breasts

boson /bố zon/ *n* an elementary particle that has zero or integral spin and obeys statistical rules that place no restriction on the number of identical particles that may be in the same state. Photons and alpha particles are bosons. [Mid-20C. After Satyendra Nuath *Bose* (1894–1974), Indian physicist]

Bosporus /bóspərəss/, **Bosphorus** /bósfərəss/ strait linking the Black Sea and the Sea of Marmara. It separates European and Asian Turkey. Length: 31 km/19 mi.

boss¹ /boss/ *n* **1.** SOMEBODY IN CHARGE somebody who is in charge of others, especially in a work environment ○ *asked the boss for some time off* **2.** SOMEBODY DOMINANT the dominant partner in a relationship or the dominant member of a group, who tends to make decisions and give instructions (*informal; often ironic*) **3.** *N Am* POWERFUL POLITICIAN a politician who exerts a controlling influence, e.g. by applying pressure on others to vote in a particular way (*informal*) ■ *vt* (**bosses, bossing, bossed**) *also* **boss around** GIVE SOMEBODY ORDERS to give somebody orders in an authoritarian way that is often resisted or resented ○ *You find the big kids trying to boss the little kids about.* ○ *The big kids try to boss the little ones.* ■ *adj* EXCELLENT so good as to dominate in a group (*dated slang*) ○ *a boss drummer* [Early 19C. < Dutch *baas* 'master'] ◇ **be your own boss 1.** to work under your own authority, e.g. with freelance or self-employed status **2.** to make decisions relating to your own life, instead of having them dictated by others

boss² /boss/ *n* **1.** KNOB a round raised part that sticks out from a surface, e.g. a stud at the centre of a shield **2.** ARCHIT CEILING DECORATION a decorative knob on a vaulted ceiling at points where the ribs meet **3.** COMPUT GAMES HARD-TO-DEFEAT OPPONENT IN COMPUTER GAME in computer games, an opponent who is hard to defeat but must be overcome in order to complete a game level **4.** BIOL SWELLING a round swelling on a plant or on the horn of an animal **5.** MECH ENG SHAFT PART a thicker part of a shaft at a point where another part is attached to it **6.** GEOL VOLCANIC ROCK MASS a mass of volcanic rock with a roughly circular cross section and vertical sides [14C. < Old French *boce*]

BOSS /boss/ *n* a South African intelligence organization during the apartheid era. Full form **Bureau of State Security**

bossa nova /bóssə nővə/ *n* **1.** a lively ballroom dance similar to the samba that originated in Brazil in the early 1960s **2.** the music for a bossa nova [Mid-20C. < Portuguese, 'new trend']

boss battle *n* a battle with a major opponent at the end of a computer game level

boss cocky (*plural* **boss cockies**) *n Aus* a boss who likes giving orders (*informal*) [< COCKY²]

boss-eyed *adj* with one or both eyes out of alignment (*informal*) [Origin ?]

bossy /bóssi/ (-ier, -iest) *adj* fond of or prone to giving

orders ○ *The other children don't like it when you're bossy.* —**bossily** *adv* —**bossiness** *n*

bossyboots /bóssi boots/ (*plural same*) *n* somebody who bosses other people around (*informal*)

boston /bóstən/ *n* a version of whist in which two packs of cards are used and players bid for the right to name trumps [Early 19C. < French, probably after BOSTON, Massachusetts]

Boston /bóstən/ **1.** seaport in Lincolnshire, eastern England. Population: 55,750 (2001). **2.** capital and largest city of Massachusetts. Situated at the mouth of the Charles River on Boston Bay, it is home to Boston College, Boston University, and Northeastern University, among other universities. Population: 589,281 (2002 estimate). —**Bostonian** /bo stṓni ən/ *n, adj*

Boston crab *n* a wrestling hold in which a wrestler is grabbed by the legs, turned face down, and sat on [After BOSTON, Massachusetts]

Boston ivy *n* a cultivated climbing plant with leaves consisting of three black lobes that turn red in autumn. Latin name: *Parthenocissus tricuspidata*. [After BOSTON, Massachusetts]

Boston Tea Party *n* a protest against British taxes made by the citizens of Boston in 1773 that led to the War of American Independence. The protesters boarded three British ships and threw their cargoes of tea overboard.

Boston terrier *n* a stocky dog with a smooth brindled or black coat and white markings, belonging to a breed originating in Boston, Massachusetts that is a cross between a bulldog and a terrier

bosun *n* NAUT same as **boatswain**

Boswell /bóz wel, -wəl/, **James** (1740–95) Scottish lawyer and biographer. He met the writer Samuel Johnson in 1763 and after two decades of close association wrote his *Life of Samuel Johnson* (1791), one of the masterpieces of English biography.

> 'He who praises everybody, praises nobody.'
> [James Boswell, *The Life of Samuel Johnson*; 1791]

Bosworth Field /bózwərth-/ site of a decisive battle in 1485 when Henry Tudor defeated Richard III and claimed the English throne. It is near the town of Market Bosworth, central Leicestershire.

bot[1] /bot/ *n* a larva of a botfly [Early 16C. Probably < Low Dutch]

bot[2] /bot/ *n* a computer program performing routine or time-consuming tasks such as searching websites automatically or semi-independently (*usually used in combination*) [Late 20C. Shortening of ROBOT]

BoT *abbr* Board of Trade

BOT *abbr* **1.** COMPUT beginning of tape **2.** Board of Trade

bot. *abbr* BOT **1.** botanical **2.** botany

botanical /bə tánnik'l/, **botanic** /bə tánnik/ *adj* relating to plants, especially to the scientific study of plants ■ *n* a drug or product made from plants (*often used in the plural*) [Mid-17C. < French *botanique* or late Latin *botanicus* < Greek *botanikos* < *botanē* 'plant'] —**botanically** *adv*

botanical garden, **botanic garden** *n* an area, often open to the public, in which exotic, rare, or scientifically interesting plants are grown and studied (*often used in the plural*)

botanise *vti* another spelling of **botanize**

botanist /bóttənist/ *n* somebody with an expert scientific knowledge of, or a strong interest in, plants [Mid-17C. < French *botaniste* < *botanique* (see BOTANICAL)]

botanize /bótə nīz/ (**-nizes, -nizing, -nized**), **botanise** (**-nises, -nising, -nised**) *vti* to collect or study plants (*informal*) [Mid-18C. Via modern Latin *botanizare* < Greek *botanizein* 'gather plants' < *botanē* 'plant'] —**botanizer** *n*

botany /bóttəni/ (*plural* **-nies**) *n* **1. STUDY OF PLANTS** the scientific study of plants **2. PLANT LIFE OF AREA** the plant life that exists within a particular area **3. BIOLOGICAL CHARACTERISTICS OF PLANT** the biological description of a plant or group of plants [Late 17C. < BOTANICAL]

Botany Bay /bóttəni-/ bay south of Sydney, New South Wales, Australia. It was Captain Cook's first landing site on the continent in 1770.

Botany wool *n* a fine merino wool. Use: yarns, fabrics. [After BOTANY BAY]

botch /boch/ (*informal*) *vt* (**botches, botching, botched**) *also* **botch up** to do something very badly out of clumsiness or lack of care ○ *managed to botch a simple repair job* ■ *n also* **botch-up** a job or task that has been done very badly ○ *made a complete botch of translating the songs* [14C. Origin ?] —**botcher** *n* —**botchily** *adv* —**botchiness** *n* —**botchy** *adj*

botel *n* BOATING, TRAVEL another spelling of **boatel**

botfly /bót flī/ (*plural* **-flies**) *n* a two-winged hairy parasitic fly that lays its eggs under the skin or in the digestive tract, sometimes causing serious illness. Botflies live as parasites on mammals, especially horses, sheep, cattle, and people. Families: Oestridae or Gasterophilidae.

both /bōth/ *det, pron* relating to or consisting of two people or things considered together ○ *For once, I like both candidates.* ○ *There are only two banks in the town, and both are shut on Saturdays.* ■ *conj* used with two facts or alternatives joined by 'and' to indicate that not just one but also the other one is included ○ *Truancy is now treated as both a policing and an educational issue.* [13C. < Old Norse *báðir*]

USAGE ***Both*** has several roles, as a pronoun (*I like both*), determiner (*I like both boys*), or conjunction (*They are both pleasant and cheerful*). Its mobility in a sentence is so great that its meaning can become ambiguous. In the last example, it is not immediately clear whether ***both*** belongs with 'they' or with the complement of the sentence, 'pleasant and cheerful'. In speech, intonation will normally clarify the intention; however when writing, you need to ensure that you are not leaving the reader in doubt. The principal restriction that applies to ***both*** is that it should refer to two people or things and no more; if three or more are meant, it is necessary to use *each*, which behaves grammatically in ways quite similar to ***both***. (However, *each* is regarded as singular while ***both*** is plural, and ***both*** alone allows the construction *I saw them both.*) When pairing ***both*** with *and*, it is important to retain a balance between the two parts of the construction with regard to the position of ***both*** and the types of words linked: *She is both charming and intellectual* [not *She is both charming and an intellectual*] or *He both sings well and likes to paint* [not *He is both a fine singer and likes to paint*]. In terms of possession, *of +* ***both*** is clearer, as in *the parents of both, the responsibility of both*, as opposed to *both their parents* and *both their responsibility* or *both their responsibilities*.

Botha /bóortə, bṓ-/, **P. W.** (*b.* 1916) South African politician. He was prime minister (1978–84) and first executive state president (1984–89) of South Africa. Full name **Botha, Pieter Willem**

> 'South Africa will not allow the double standards and hypocrisy of the Western world, even in the application of legal principles, to stand in the way of our responsibility to protect our country.'
> [P. W. Botha, *Speech*; 1986]

Botham /bṓthəm/, **Ian** (*b.* 1955) British cricketer. One of the world's greatest cricketers, he appeared in 102 Test matches for England. Full name **Botham, Ian Terence**

> 'I'm a bit like an old, battered Escort. You might find one panel that's original. I've had about ten operations—back, shoulder, wrist, knee, cheek.'
> [Ian Botham, *Times*; 30 December 1993]

bother /bóthər/ *v* (**-ers, -ering, -ered**) **1.** *vi* **MAKE EFFORT** to take the time or trouble to do something (*often used in negative statements*) ○ *He didn't even bother to get out of the car.* ○ *I shouldn't bother about a raincoat. It's clearing up.* **2.** *vti* **BE WORRIED OR WORRY SOMEBODY** to feel worried, anxious, or upset, or make somebody feel like this ○ *I never bother about what the neighbours think.* ○ *It bothers me to think of you all on your own.* **3.** *vt* **DISTURB SOMEBODY** to annoy or disturb somebody, e.g. by interrupting or by making unwelcome advances ○ *Is the music bothering you?* **4.** *vt* **CAUSE PHYSICAL PAIN TO SOMEBODY** to make somebody feel physical discomfort or pain ○ *My back is bothering me again.* ■ *n* **1. EFFORT** trouble or effort to do something ○ *Don't go to all that bother for me.* **2. SOURCE OF ANNOYANCE** somebody or something that causes annoyance, e.g. by making noise ○ *I'm sorry to be a bother, but could I use your phone?* ■ *interj* **EXPRESSING MILD ANNOYANCE** used as an expression of mild annoyance ○ *Bother! I've left my glasses in the car.* [Late 17C. Origin ?]

SYNONYMS ***bother, annoy, bug, disturb, trouble, worry***

CORE MEANING: to interfere with somebody's peace or composure

bother to feel worried, anxious, or upset, or make somebody feel like this ○ *Sorry to bother you.* ○ *He is not bothered in the slightest by these hints of change.* **annoy** to harass somebody repeatedly ○ *The wasps buzzing round them as they ate were beginning to annoy them.* **bug** (*informal*) to cause somebody persistent trouble and annoyance ○ *something that's been bugging me* ○ *He's always bugging my son's friends with questions.* **disturb** to interrupt or distract somebody when he or she is doing something ○ *disturbing her while she was reading* **trouble** to put somebody to the inconvenience of doing something ○ *I'm sorry to trouble you, but I need your help.* **worry** to annoy somebody by making insistent demands or complaints ○ *Reporters and photographers kept worrying the family with requests for interviews.*

botheration /bòthə ráysh'n/ *interj* used as an expression of mild annoyance (*dated informal*)

bothersome /bóthərsəm/ *adj* causing annoyance and inconvenience

Bothnia, Gulf of /bóthni ə/ northern part of the Baltic Sea, situated between Finland and Sweden. Area: 117,000 sq. km/45,200 sq. mi.

bothy /bóthi/ (*plural* **-ies**) *n Scotland* a simple house or hut, originally a farmer's or crofter's cottage, now usually a hut providing shelter for hill walkers or climbers [Late 18C. Probably < variant of BOOTH]

Botox /bṓ toks/ *tdmk* a trademark for a preparation of botulinum toxin, a protein that relaxes muscle contractions. It is sometimes injected under the skin to erase facial wrinkles.

bo tree /bṓ-/ *n* a tree of the fig family that is regarded as sacred by Hindus and Buddhists. Native to: South Asia. Latin name: *Ficus religiosa*. [Mid-19C. Partial translation of Sinhalese *bōgaha* < *bō* (< Pali, Sanskrit *bodhi* 'perfect knowledge') + *gaha* 'tree']

botryoidal /bóttri óyd'l/ *adj* describes minerals and plant parts shaped like a bunch of grapes [Late 18C. < Greek *botruoeidēs* < *botrus* 'bunch of grapes']

bots /bots/ *n* an intestinal disease of horses, sheep, and cattle, caused by infection with botfly larvae (*takes a singular or plural verb*)

Botswana

Botswana /bot swáanə/ landlocked country in southern Africa that shares borders with Namibia, Zambia, Zimbabwe, and South Africa. It became an independent member of the British Commonwealth in 1966. Language: English, Setswana. Currency: pula. Capital: Gaborone. Population: 1,573,267 (2003). Area: 581,730 sq. km/224,607 sq. mi. Official name **Republic of Botswana**. Former name **Bechuanaland** (until 1966) —**Botswanan** *n, adj*

botte /bot/ *n* a thrust or hit in fencing [14C. < Old French *bot(te)* 'blow, hit']

Botticelli /bótti chélli/, **Sandro** (1445–1510) Italian painter. He specialized in classical themes, exemplified in paintings such as *The Birth of Venus* and *Primavera*. Born **Filipepi, Alessandro di Mariano**. See illustration on next page

bottle /bótt'l/ *n* **1. CONTAINER FOR LIQUIDS** a container for liquids, usually made of glass or plastic, with a

Sandro Botticelli: *The Birth of Venus* (after 1482)

narrow neck and no handle **2. AMOUNT IN BOTTLE** the amount of liquid contained in a bottle **3. CONTAINER FOR BABY'S MILK** a plastic or glass container with a rubber teat used for feeding a baby, or a feed of milk given from such a container ○ *Has he had his bottle yet?* **4. ALCOHOL** alcoholic beverages, or the habit of drinking alcohol to excess (*informal*) ○ *fond of the bottle* **5. COURAGE** boldness or nerve (*informal*) ○ *didn't have the bottle to say it to her face* ■ *vt* (**-tles, -tling, -tled**) **1. PUT LIQUID IN BOTTLE** to put a liquid that can be consumed in a bottle for storage or sale **2. PRESERVE FOOD IN JARS** to store fruit or vegetables in a preserving liquid in a glass container [14C. Via Old French *boteille* < medieval Latin *butticula* 'little cask' < late Latin *buttis* 'cask, barrel']

bottle out *vi* to lose courage at a crucial moment (*informal*) ○ *He was going to tell her, then he bottled out.*

bottle up *vt* to conceal or repress strong feelings ○ *all the resentment she's been bottling up for years*

bottle bank *n* a large container or group of containers in which members of the public can deposit used glass bottles and jars for recycling

bottlebrush /bótt'l brush/ *n* a bush or small tree that has a mass of spiky flowers with large stamens. Native to: Australia. Genus: *Callistemon* or *Melaleuca*. [< the plant's resemblance to a cylindrical brush for cleaning bottles]

bottled /bótt'ld/ *adj* **1.** stored or sold in bottles **2.** completely inebriated (*slang*)

bottle-feed *vt* to feed a baby or a young animal milk from a bottle, as distinct from breast-feeding or suckling it

bottle gourd *n* a climbing plant that produces bottle-shaped fruits. Use: containers for liquids, when dried. Native to: Europe. Latin name: *Lagenaria siceraria*.

bottle-green *adj* of a dark green colour, like some wine bottles —**bottle green** *n*

bottleneck /bótt'l nek/ *n* **1.** a junction or a narrow section of a road that slows traffic or causes traffic jams **2.** a delay caused when one part of a process or activity is slower than the others and so hinders overall progress

bottle-nosed dolphin, **bottlenose dolphin** /bótt'l nōz-/ *n* a dolphin with a long snout. Native to: warm waters. Latin name: *Tursiops truncatus*.

bottle opener *n* a metal tool used to prise the metal tops off bottles

bottle party *n* a party to which guests bring alcoholic drink

bottler /bótt'lər/ *n* **1.** a company that bottles beverages as part of a manufacturing process **2.** *ANZ* an excellent example of something (*informal*) ○ *a real bottler of a film*

bottle shop *n ANZ, S Africa* a shop where bottles or cans of alcoholic beverages may be bought for consumption elsewhere

bottle store, **bottle shop** *n ANZ* COMM same as **off-licence**

bottle tree *n* a tree with a swollen bottle-shaped trunk and an unpleasant smell. Native to: Australia. Genus: *Brachychiton*.

bottom /bóttəm/ *n* **1. LOWEST PART** the lowest or deepest part of something ○ *From the bottom of the hill it seems a long way up.* **2. UNDERSIDE** the underneath side or surface of something ○ *rust on the bottom of the boat* **3. FARTHEST POINT** the part of something that

is farthest away ○ *ponies grazing at the bottom of the field* **4. LAND UNDER WATER** the ground underneath a sea, lake, or river ○ *Can you dive down and touch the bottom?* **5. END OF LIST** the end of a list or series, especially the lowest level of excellence or achievement ○ *teams at the bottom of the league* **6. ROOT CAUSE** the fundamental, often hidden, cause or origin of something ○ *get to the bottom of the problem* **7. LOWEST RANK** the lowest level in a hierarchy ○ *worked her way up from the bottom* **8. BUTTOCKS** somebody's buttocks, or, particularly when speaking to children, any body part in this general area **9. PART COVERING LOWER BODY** the part of a two-piece garment such as a tracksuit or bikini that covers the lower body (*often used in the plural*) **10. VALLEY** a dry valley or hollow (*often used in placenames*) ○ *Six Mile Bottom* ■ *adj* **1. LOWEST** in the lower or lowest position ○ *Look on the bottom shelf.* **2. LEAST SUCCESSFUL** in the position of least excellence or achievement ○ *determined not to come bottom of the class again* ○ *the bottom five teams* ■ *v* (**-toms, -toming, -tomed**) **1.** *vi* **HIT SEA FLOOR** to scrape the underside against the floor of the sea or a river, because the water is too shallow (*refers to boats*) **2.** *vt* **OVERLOAD TRANSISTOR** to overload a transistor to the point where additional input produces no additional output [Old English *botm* < Indo-European] ◇ **at bottom** in reality, when external appearances are stripped away ◇ **bottoms up** used as a drinking toast (*informal*) ◇ **from the bottom of your heart** with the utmost sincerity ◇ **hit rock bottom** to reach the lowest point in your personal, professional, or emotional life

bottom out *vi* after a decline, to stop falling any lower and stabilize at a low level ○ *After plummeting 200 points, the stock market finally bottomed out.*

bottom dead-centre *n* the position of a piston in an engine or pump when it is at the bottom of its stroke

bottom drawer *n* a collection of household items that a young woman traditionally accumulates in anticipation of marriage. N Am term **hope chest** [Because traditionally kept in the lowest drawer of a chest of drawers]

bottom feeder *n* **1.** a freshwater or saltwater animal, especially a fish that feeds on material drifting to the bottom of a body of water **2.** somebody who profits by taking advantage of other people (*slang insult*)

bottom fishing *n* the purchase of securities, property, or businesses when prices are unusually low as a result of adverse market conditions —**bottom fisher** *n*

bottomless /bóttəmləss/ *adj* **1. VERY DEEP** so deep as to appear to have no bottom **2. PLENTIFUL** with unlimited or seemingly unlimited resources, especially of money ○ *a bottomless fund* **3. UNFATHOMABLE** too well hidden to be discovered or too mysterious to be understood —**bottomlessness** *n*

bottom line *n* **1. UNAVOIDABLE FACTOR** the most important factor that must be accepted, however reluctantly ○ *The bottom line is that the sponsors want a French driver on the team.* **2. PROFIT OR LOSS** the final profit or loss that a company makes at the end of a given period of time **3. LOWEST ACCEPTABLE AMOUNT** the least amount of money regarded as acceptable in a business transaction

bottommost /bóttəm mōst/ *adj* at the very lowest level ○ *the bottommost rung of the ladder*

bottom-of-the-harbour scheme *n Aus* a tax-avoidance strategy that involves setting up a company of assets and then selling it a number of times so that it is hard to trace

bottom quark *n* a quark with an electric charge of $-\frac{1}{3}$, zero charm, zero isotopic spin, and zero strangeness

bottomset bed /bóttəmset-/ *n* a layer of sediment deposited by a river at the base of an accumulating delta

botty /bótti/ *n* (*plural* **-ties**) *n* the buttocks (*baby talk*) [Late 19C. Alteration of BOTTOM]

botulin /bóttyσolin/ *n* a toxin produced by the bacterium *Clostridium botulinum* that causes botulism [Early 20C. < modern Latin *botulinus* (see BOTULINUM)]

botulinum /bóttyσo línəm/, **botulinus** /-línəss/ *n* a bacterium that causes botulism when it is present in food. It is an anaerobic bacterium, requiring the

absence of free oxygen. Latin name: *Clostridium botulinum*. [Early 20C. < modern Latin, neuter of *botulinus* < Latin *botulus* 'sausage'] —**botulinal** *adj*

botulism /bóttyσolizəm/ *n* a serious form of food poisoning caused by eating preserved food that has been contaminated with botulinum organisms. The toxin affects the central nervous system and causes progressive muscular paralysis. [Late 19C. < German *Botulismus* 'sausage-poisoning' < Latin *botulus* 'sausage']

Bouaké /bwaˊa kay/ city and capital of Bouaké Department, central Côte d'Ivoire. Population: 329,850 (1988).

boubou /boˊo boo/ *n* a bird of the shrike family that is black with a white flash on each wing. It is known for singing in pairs. Native to: Africa. Genus: *Laniarius*. [Late 20C. < an African language]

bouchée /boˊo shay, boo shayˊ/ *n* a small bite-sized puff pastry case filled with a savoury mixture [Mid-19C. < French, 'mouthful' < *bouche* 'mouth' < Latin *bucca* 'cheek']

Boucher /boˊo shay/, **François** (1703–70) French painter. He worked at the court of Louis XV, painting mythological and pastoral scenes in the rococo style.

bouclé /boˊo klay/ *n* a yarn with loops or bumps along its length that produces a knobbly effect when knitted or woven (*often used before a noun*) [Late 19C. < French, past participle of *boucler* 'curl' < Latin *buccula* 'cheek strap of a helmet' < *bucca* 'cheek']

Boudicca /boˊodikə/, **Boadicea** /bố ədi seˊə/ (d. AD 62) English tribal queen. The queen of the Iceni, she raised a rebellion against the Romans, who had invaded her kingdom. She sacked London, Colchester, and St Albans, and destroyed the Roman Ninth Legion.

boudin /boˊo daN/ *n* a French black pudding [Mid-19C. < French < Latin *botulus* 'sausage']

boudoir /boˊo dwaar/ *n* a woman's bedroom or private sitting room [Late 18C. < French, 'place to sulk in' < *bouder* 'to pout, sulk']

bouffant /boˊo foN/ *adj* describes a woman's hairstyle in which hair is backcombed or teased to give fullness and height [Early 19C. < French, present participle of *bouffer* 'swell or puff up'] —**bouffant** *n*

bougainvillaea *n* PLANTS another spelling of **bougainvillea**

Bougainville /boˊogənvil/ largest island of the Solomon Islands group in eastern Papua New Guinea, in the southwestern Pacific Ocean. Area: 10,000 sq. km/3,880 sq. mi.

Bougainville /boˊogənvil, boˊo gaN veˊel/, **Louis Antoine, comte de** (1729–1811) French navigator. He made the first French circumnavigation of the world (1766–69).

bougainvillea /boˊogən villi ə/, **bougainvillaea** *n* a climbing woody ornamental plant with attractive red, purple, or pink leaves (**bracts**) around insignificant flowers. Native to: South America. Genus: *Bougainvillea*. [Mid-19C. < modern Latin, after Louis Antoine de BOUGAINVILLE]

bough /bow/ *n* a large main branch of a tree, from which smaller branches grow [Old English *bōg* 'bough, shoulder' < Indo-European, 'arm']

SPELLCHECK bough or bow? Do not confuse the spelling of *bough* and *bow*, which sound similar. *Bough* is only used as a noun, denoting a branch of a tree. The word *bow* (rhyming with 'cow') can be used as a noun, denoting the front part of a boat or ship, or as a verb, meaning 'bend over': *I bowed my head in shame. The branches were bowed down with fruit.*

CULTURAL NOTE The Golden Bough, a book (1890) by the British anthropologist Sir James George Frazer. It is an encyclopedic, rationalist survey of mythology and religion that suggests a strong connection between belief in magic and religious faith. Hugely influential in its time, it notably provided T. S. Eliot with several striking images for his poem *The Waste Land* (1922).

bought /bawt/ past participle, past tense of **buy** ■ *adj* commercially made rather than homemade

bougie /boˊo zhee, boo zheˊe/ *n* a medical instrument in the form of a flexible tube, inserted into a body passage such as the rectum to open it to allow medicines or instruments to be introduced [Mid-18C. < French, after the town of *Bougie* (Arabic *Bijāya*) in Algeria, which traded in wax]

bouillabaisse /bóoyə béss, -báyss/ *n* a rich soup made with fish and originating from the south of France [Mid-19C. Via French < modern Provençal *bouiabaisso*]

bouillon /bóo yoN/ *n* a clear liquid that is traditionally made by boiling meat, bones, and vegetables together. It is sometimes served as a soup, but usually used as a stock for soups and stews. [Mid-17C. < French < *bouillir* (see BOIL[1])]

bouillon cube *n N Am* same as **stock cube**

Boulanger /bóo loN zhay/, **Nadia** (1887–1979) French composer and music teacher. She composed vocal and instrumental music until 1918, then concentrated on teaching composition. Her students included Aaron Copland, Philip Glass, Walter Piston, and Virgil Thomson. Full name **Boulanger, Nadia Juliette**

boulder /bṓldər/ *n* **1.** a large round rock **2.** a large fragment of rock greater than 200 mm/8 in in diameter [15C. Shortening of *boulderstone*, partial translation of a N Germanic word]

Boulder /bṓldər/ resort city in northern Colorado, northwest of Denver, southeast of Rocky Mountain National Park, original home of the University of Colorado, opened in 1877. Population: 94,167 (2002 estimate).

boulder clay *n* GEOL same as **till**[4]

bouldering /bṓldəring/ *n* rock climbing that involves undertaking short and extremely difficult slopes —**boulderer** *n*

boule /bool/ *n* a pear-shaped imitation gemstone made in a furnace from synthetic aluminium oxide (**corundum**) [Early 20C. < French (see BOWL[2])]

boules /bool/ *n* an outdoor game of French origin, similar to bowls. It is traditionally played on open dusty ground in public places with heavy metal balls that are tossed with a backhand action. (*takes a singular verb*) [Early 20C. < French, plural of *boule* (see BOWL[2])]

boulevard /bóol vaar, bóolə vaard/ *n* a wide street, especially one lined with trees (*often used in placenames*) [Mid-18C. Via French, '(promenade on the site of) a rampart' < Middle Low German, Middle Dutch *bolwerk* (see BULWARK)]

boulevardier /bool vaárdi ay, boolə-/ *n* a fashionable sophisticated man who treats life with lighthearted cynicism (*dated*) [Late 19C. < French < *boulevard* (see BOULEVARD)]

Boulez /bóo lez/, **Pierre** (*b.* 1925) French composer and conductor. He has conducted major orchestras in Europe and the United States and championed new music.

boulle /bool/ *n* elaborate inlay work on furniture, using tortoiseshell, ivory, or brass in scroll shapes. It was popular in France in the 17th century. (*often used before a noun*) [Early 19C. < French, after André Charles *Boulle* (1642–1732), French cabinetmaker]

~~**boullion**~~ incorrect spelling of **bouillon**

Boulogne-sur-Mer /boo lóyn syoor máir/, **Boulogne** city and port on the English Channel in Pas-de-Calais Department, northwestern France. Population: 44,859 (1999).

boult *vt* FOOD INDUST another spelling of **bolt**[2]

Boumédienne /boo máydi én/, **Houari** (1932–78) Algerian nationalist and president (1965–78). He commanded the liberation forces during Algeria's war of independence from French rule (1960–62). Born **Boukharouba, Muhammad Brahim**

bounce /bownss/ *v* (**bounces, bouncing, bounced**) **1.** *vti* **SPRING AWAY FROM SURFACE** to move away quickly after hitting a surface, or throw something so that it hits a surface and moves away ○ *bouncing a tennis ball against a wall* ○ *Onlookers saw the car bounce off a tree.* **2.** *vi* **JUMP UP AND DOWN** to jump up and down repeatedly on a soft surface ○ *children bouncing on trampolines* **3.** *vt* **LIFT CHILD ON KNEE** to move a baby or small child gently up and down in your arms or on your knees **4.** *vti* **REFLECT FROM SURFACE** to strike a surface, or cause something to strike a surface, and be reflected back ○ *the use of a fixed orbiting satellite to bounce the transmission signal back to Earth* **5.** *vi* **MOVE UP AND DOWN ON SPOT** to move up and down repeatedly in almost the same location ○ *with her long blonde hair bouncing as she walked* **6.** *vi* **WALK ENERGETICALLY** to walk energetically or cheerfully ○ *She bounced up to the guests and breezily said hello.* **7.** *vti* **REFUSE TO PAY** to refuse payment of a cheque, or be refused by a bank, because there is insufficient money in the account on which it is drawn **8.** *vt* **WRITE BAD CHEQUE** to write a cheque that the bank will not honour **9.** *vt* **COERCE SOMEBODY INTO DOING SOMETHING** to force somebody into doing something by restricting the alternatives (*informal*) ○ *I don't want to get bounced into making unwise investments.* **10.** *vt* **THROW SOMEBODY OUT** to eject somebody from a place or expel somebody from a club or other organization (*slang*) ○ *managed to get themselves bounced out of the restaurant* **11.** *vi* **COME BACK** to be returned undelivered to a sender (*used in e-mails or text messages*) ○ *My last e-mail to you bounced.* ■ *n* **1.** **ACT OF REBOUNDING** a springing away from a surface after hitting it ○ *hit the ball before the second bounce* **2.** **SPRINGINESS** the capacity of a ball or other object to bounce, or of a surface to cause objects hitting it to bounce ○ *not so much bounce in the pitch* **3.** **BOBBING MOVEMENT** a swinging or bobbing movement, or the capacity to swing or bob up and down ○ *a conditioner guaranteed to give your hair added bounce* **4.** **ENERGY** lively energy **5.** FOOTBALL **METHOD OF STARTING AUSTRALIAN RULES MATCH** in Australian Rules football, the bouncing of the ball in the centre circle by the field umpire to start the match [13C. Origin ?] ◇ **bounce something off somebody** to put something, especially an idea or suggestion, to somebody in order to get reactions or opinions (*slang*) ○ *She bounced a couple of theories off the students.*

bounce back *vi* to recover quickly and completely after a bad experience

bouncer /bównssər/ *n* **1.** **GUARD AT NIGHTCLUB** a security guard who usually stands at the door of a nightclub or other place of entertainment and is responsible for preventing undesirable people from entering and for ejecting troublemakers **2.** **BALL BOUNCING HEAD HIGH** in cricket, a ball that is pitched short and bounces at chest or head height to intimidate the batsman **3.** **STRUCK BALL THAT BOUNCES** in baseball, a ball that bounces along the ground after being hit

bouncing /bównssing/ *adj* describes a healthy and active baby ○ *the proud parents of a beautiful bouncing boy*

bouncing Bet /-bét/ *n US* PLANTS same as **soapwort** [Pet form of *Elizabeth*]

bouncy /bównssi/ (**-ier, -iest**) *adj* **1.** **LIVELY** lively and energetic **2.** **BOUNCING WELL** tending to bounce or capable of bouncing well ○ *bouncy material used in making tennis balls* **3.** **SPRINGY** tending to bounce objects hitting it or resting on it —**bouncily** *adv* —**bounciness** *n*

bouncy castle *n* a large inflatable object in the shape of a castle that children can bounce on for fun

bound[1] /bownd/ past participle, past tense of **bind** ■ *adj* **1.** **CERTAIN TO DO SOMETHING** certain to happen or do something because custom, experience, or common sense dictates it ○ *If you play music late at night, people are bound to complain.* **2.** **OBLIGED** obliged to do something or behave in a particular way, e.g. for legal or moral reasons ○ *All the member countries are bound by the provisions of the Treaty of Rome.* **3.** **WITH PERMANENT COVER** describes a book or other written document that has a permanent, usually hard, cover **4.** *US* **DETERMINED** firmly resolved ○ *She was bound to become the best in the business.*

bound[2] /bownd/ (**bounds, bounding, bounded**) *vi* to move quickly and energetically, with large strides or jumps ○ *A puppy came bounding across the lawn.* [Early 16C. Via French *bondir* 'resound, rebound' < Latin *bombire* 'to buzz' < *bombus* < Greek *bombos* 'booming sound'] —**bound** *n*

bound[3] /bownd/ *adj* **1.** travelling towards a particular place (*often used in combination*) ○ *a Spanish trawler bound for the Irish Sea* ○ *homeward bound* **2.** certain to reach or achieve something ○ *young performers bound for international stardom* [Late 16C. Originally *boun* < Old Norse *búinn*, past participle of *búa* 'prepare'; probably influenced by BOUND[1]]

bound[4] /bownd/ *vt* (**bounds, bounding, bounded**) **1.** **SURROUND AREA** to form the boundary to an area or site ○ *grounds bounded on three sides by the river* **2.** **RESTRICT SOMETHING** to impose limits on something ○ *political views not bounded by moral convictions* ■ *n* MATHS **LIMITING NUMBER** a number that represents the upper or lower end of a range of possible values ■ *adj* **1.** LING **NOT CONSTITUTING WORD** describes a unit of meaning (**morpheme**) that cannot be used on its own as a word **2.** GRAM **NOT CONSTITUTING SENTENCE** describes a grammatical element such as a clause that can only be used with another element [14C. < Anglo-Norman *bounde*, Old French *bodne* < medieval Latin *butina*; originally 'boundary marker']

boundary /bówndəri/ (*plural* **-ries**) *n* **1.** **BORDER** the official line that divides one area of land from another ○ *Multinational companies operate across national boundaries.* **2.** **LIMIT** the point at which something ends or beyond which it becomes something else ○ *pushing back the boundaries of human knowledge* **3.** **EDGE OF CRICKET PITCH** the outer limit of the playing area of a cricket pitch **4.** **SHOT CROSSING BOUNDARY** in cricket, a shot that crosses the boundary, scoring either four or six runs [Early 17C. Alteration of *bounder* < BOUND[4]]

Boundary Commission *n* a public body that monitors the boundaries of parliamentary constituencies between elections and recommends changes to them based on shifts in the population

boundary condition *n* the mathematical set of requirements that must be met in order for the solution to a set of differential equations to be found

boundary layer *n* the region of a viscous fluid such as air or water that is closest to the surface of a solid moving relative to the fluid

boundary rider *n Aus* an employee on a sheep or cattle station whose job is to check that boundary fences are in good repair

boundary umpire *n* in Australian Rules football, either of two umpires, positioned on opposite sides of the pitch, who judge whether the ball has gone out of play

bounded /bówndid/ *adj* describes a mathematical set that has an upper and lower limiting number (**bound**)

bounden /bówndən/ past participle of **bind** (*archaic*)

bounder /bówndər/ *n* somebody, especially a man, who behaves in a dishonourable or morally unacceptable way (*dated informal*; *insult*) [Late 19C. < BOUND[2]]

boundless /bówndləss/ *adj* seeming to have no end or limit —**boundlessly** *adv* —**boundlessness** *n*

~~**boundry**~~ incorrect spelling of **boundary**

bounds /bowndz/ *npl* limits, especially restrictions on what can happen or what can be done ○ *a joke that goes beyond the bounds of good taste* ◇ **know no bounds** to be very great, strong, or intense ○ *an ego that knows no bounds* ◇ **out of bounds 1.** outside the area where somebody is allowed to go ○ *The village is out of bounds to the boarding-school boys.* **2.** beyond what is acceptable ○ *Discussion of the candidate's private life is out of bounds.*

bounteous /bównti əss/ *adj* (*literary*) **1.** giving generously **2.** given in generous measure [14C. Alteration (after PLENTEOUS) of Old French *bontif* < *bonté* (see BOUNTY)] —**bounteously** *adv* —**bounteousness** *n*

bountiful /bówntif'l/ *adj* (*literary*) **1.** giving generously, particularly to less fortunate people **2.** in plentiful supply —**bountifully** *adv* —**bountifulness** *n*

SYNONYMS See ***generous***.

---

bounty /bównti/ (*plural* **-ties**) *n* **1.** **REWARD** a reward of money offered for finding a criminal or other wanted person, or for killing a person or a predator **2.** **ABUNDANT SUPPLY** a plentiful or generous supply (*literary*) ○*'As a grand mansion, 'The Broadway Estate' is home to a bounty of rooms, each with a distinct personality.'* (Patti Martinhome, *Living Page*; 1997) **3.** **GENEROSITY** generosity in giving (*literary*) ○*'a trifling additional claim upon your bounty and good nature'* (Sir Walter Scott, *Waverley*; 1814) [14C. Via French *bonté* < Latin *bonitas* 'goodness' < *bonus* 'good']

bounty hunter *n* **1.** somebody who captures criminals for reward money **2.** somebody who hunts animals for reward money

Bounty Islands /bównti-/ group of 13 uninhabited islands in the southwestern Pacific Ocean, 668 km/415 mi. east of New Zealand. The islands are part of New Zealand. Area: 1 sq. km/0.54 sq. mi.

bouquet /boo káy, bō-/ *n* **1.** **BUNCH OF FLOWERS** a bunch of cut flowers that have been specially chosen or arranged **2.** **SCENT OF WINE** the characteristic pleasant smell of a wine **3.** **PRAISE** an expression of

congratulation or praise (*literary*) [Early 18C. < French, 'thicket' < Old French *bois* 'forest' < Germanic]

SYNONYMS See *smell*.

bouquet garni /boo͝o kay gaʹarni/ (*plural* **bouquets garnis** /*pronunc. same*/) *n* a bunch of mixed herbs, or an equivalent dried herb mixture in a sachet, that is used to add flavour to stews, soups, and sauces [Mid-19C. < French, 'garnished bouquet']

bourbon[1] /búrbən/ *n* a type of whisky distilled mainly in the United States from a fermented mixture of hot water and grain (**mash**) containing at least 51% maize [Mid-19C. After *Bourbon* County, Kentucky]

bourbon[2] /boórbən/, **Bourbon** *n* a rectangular chocolate-flavoured biscuit that has two layers sandwiched together with a chocolate cream filling [Mid-18C. After the *Bourbon* dynasty of France]

Bourbon /boórbən/ *adj* relating to a branch of the French royal family who reigned from 1589 to 1793 and again after the French Revolution until the revolution of 1830. The Spanish royal family also belongs to this branch. [Mid-18C. < French, after the town of *Bourbon l'Archambault* in central France] — **Bourbon** *n*

bourdon /boórd'n/ *n* **1.** the bass pipe on a set of bagpipes, or the bass note it produces **2.** the bass stop on an organ, especially on a 16-foot pipe [Mid-19C. < French, 'drone']

Bourdon gauge *n* a pressure gauge with a flattened curved tube that straightens under pressure, allowing the force to be measured [After Eugène *Bourdon* (1808–84), French hydraulic engineer]

bourgeois /boór zhwaa, boor zhwaʹa/ *adj* **1.** associated with affluent middle-class people, who are often characterized as conventional, conservative, or materialistic in outlook **2.** according to Marxist theory, relating to the social class that owns the means of producing wealth and is regarded as exploiting the working class [Mid-16C. < French, 'citizen of a city or borough' < Latin *burgus* 'castle, borough' < Germanic] — **bourgeois** *n*

Bourgeois /boór zhwaa/, **Léon Victor** (1851–1925) French politician. He was one of the founders of the League of Nations, and received the Nobel Peace Prize (1920). Full name **Bourgeois, Léon Victor Auguste**

bourgeoisie /boór zhwaa zeé/ *n* **1.** affluent middle-class people characterized as conventional, conservative, or materialistic in outlook **2.** the social class that, according to Marxist theory, owns the means of producing wealth and is regarded as exploiting the working class [Early 18C. < French < *bourgeois* (see BOURGEOIS)]

bourgeoisify /boór zhwaʹazi fī/ (**-fies, -fying, -fied**) *vt* to impose bourgeois values on somebody or something, or make somebody or something bourgeois in character —**bourgeoisification** /boor zhwaʹazifi káysh'n/ *n*

Bourguiba /boor geébə/, **Habib** (1903–2000) Tunisian politician. He led Tunisia's independence movement against French rule and was the country's first prime minister (1956–57) and president (1957–87). Full name **Bourguiba, Habib ibn Ali**

bourguignonne /boór geen yón/ *adj* cooked in a red wine sauce with mushrooms and small whole onions, in a style that originated in the Burgundy region of France [Early 20C. < French < *Bourgogne* 'Burgundy']

Bourke /burk/ town in northern New South Wales, Australia. It lies on the Darling River. Population: 3,947 (2002 estimate).

Bourke-White /búrk wít/, **Margaret** (1906–71) US photographer and writer. She was a leading photojournalist who was closely identified with *Life*. She was the magazine's staff photographer from 1936 to 1969.

> 'Nothing attracts me like a closed door. I cannot let my camera rest until I have pried it open, and I wanted to be first.'
> [Margaret Bourke-White, *Portrait of Myself*; 1963]

bourn[1] /bawrn, boorn/ *n* (*archaic*) **1.** a boundary between one place or one thing and another ○ *I'll set a bourn how far to be beloved.'* (William Shakespeare, *Antony and Cleopatra*; 1606) **2.** something

that is aimed for or aspired to [Early 16C. Via French *borne* < Old French *bodne* (see BOUND[4])]

bourn[2] /bawrn, boorn/, **bourne** *n* a small stream that flows only in the winter months [14C. S English variant of BURN[2]]

Bournemouth /báwrnməth/ seaside resort on the English Channel in Dorset, southern England. Population: 163,444 (2001).

bourse /boorss/, **Bourse** *n* a European stock exchange, especially the one in Paris [Late 16C. Via French < medieval Latin *bursa* 'bag, purse' < Greek *bursa* 'leather']

boustrophedon /boóstrə feéd'n, bówstrə-/ *n* an ancient method of inscribing and writing in which lines are written alternately from right to left and from left to right [Early 17C. < Greek, 'as the ox turns in ploughing' < *bous* 'ox' + -*strophos* 'turning' < *strephein* 'to turn'] —**boustrophedonic** /boóstrə fee dónnik, bówstrə-/ *adj*

bout /bowt/ *n* **1.** ATTACK OF ILLNESS a temporary or short-lived attack of illness, usually a common and not very serious illness ○ *a recent bout of flu* **2.** SHORT PERIOD OF ACTIVITY a short time spent doing something, often something considered distasteful ○ *periodic bouts of violence* **3.** FIGHT a boxing or wrestling match [Mid-16C. Origin ?]

boutique /boo teék/ *n* **1.** SMALL CLOTHES SHOP a small shop that sells fashionable clothes **2.** SMALL SPECIALIST SHOP a small shop selling specialized, often luxury, goods or services of any kind ■ *adj* SERVING LUXURY MARKET catering for a specialized, often luxury, market ○ *a boutique travel service* [Mid-18C. Via French < Greek *apothēkē* 'storehouse']

boutique brewery *n* US FOOD INDUST same as **microbrewery**

boutique hotel *n* an upmarket, often stylish hotel with an individual character and decor

bouton /boó toN/ *n* the knob or swelling on a nerve-cell extension (**axon**) at the point where it forms a junction (**synapse**) with a neuron [Mid-19C. < French (see BUTTON)]

boutonniere /boó ton yáir, -tonni áir/, **boutonnière** *n* ANZ, N Am same as **buttonhole** *n* (sense 2) [Late 19C. < French < *bouton* (see BUTTON)]

Boutros-Ghali /boó tross gaáli/, **Boutros** (*b.* 1922) Egyptian diplomat. He was the sixth secretary-general of the United Nations (1992–96).

> 'I survived the Egyptian bureaucracy. If you can do that you can run the UN.'
> [Boutros Boutros-Ghali, *New York Times*; 16 October 1993]

bouvier /boóvi ay/ *n* a large powerful dog with a rough fawn or black coat, belonging to a breed originally developed in Belgium to herd cattle [Early 20C. < French, shortened < *bouvier des Flandres* 'cowherd of Flanders']

~~bouy~~ incorrect spelling of **buoy**

~~bouyant~~ incorrect spelling of **buoyant**

bouzouki

bouzouki /boo zoóki/ (*plural* **-kis**) *n* a long-necked stringed musical instrument of Greek origin similar in appearance and sound to a mandolin [Mid-20C. < modern Greek *mpouzouki*]

bovid /bóvid/ *adj* relating or belonging to the family of hollow-horned, hoofed, ruminant animals that includes cattle, sheep, and antelopes. Family: Bovidae. [Late 19C. < Latin *bov-* (see BOVINE)] —**bovid** *n*

bovine /bó vīn/ *adj* **1.** OF CATTLE GENUS relating or belonging to the genus of ruminant animals that in-

cludes cattle, oxen, and buffalo. Genus: *Bos.* **2.** SLOW displaying the slowness regarded as typical of cattle and related animals (*literary*) ■ *n* ANIMAL RELATED TO CATTLE an animal belonging to the same genus as cattle [Early 19C. < late Latin *bovinus* < Latin *bov-*, stem of *bos* 'ox']

bovine somatotrophin, **bovine growth hormone** *n* a hormone in cattle that regulates growth and milk production. It can also be produced artificially by genetic engineering and used to increase milk yields.

bovine spongiform encephalopathy *n* MED, VET full form of **BSE**

bovver /bóvvər/ *n* aggressive behaviour (*slang*) [Mid-20C. Representing a Cockney pronunciation of BOTHER]

bovver boot *n* UK a heavy-duty boot, often with a steel toecap, worn by members of gangs as a fighting weapon and a symbol of toughness. In the 1960s and 1970s, such boots were a standard part of a skinhead's uniform. (*dated informal*)

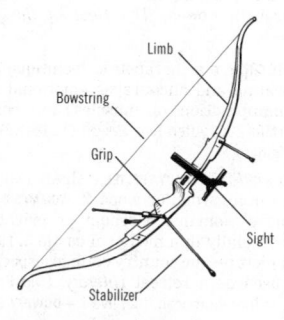

bow (sense 2)

bow[1] /bō/ *n* **1.** LOOPED KNOT a knot in which the loops remain visible, e.g. in tied shoelaces or in ribbons used for decorating gifts or hair **2.** WEAPON FOR FIRING ARROWS a weapon used to fire arrows, consisting of a curved flexible piece of wood and a taut string fastened to the two ends **3.** ROD FOR PLAYING STRINGED INSTRUMENTS a wooden rod with fibres tightly stretched between the two ends, used for playing stringed instruments **4.** CURVED SHAPE OR PART something that has a rounded or semicircular shape, e.g. a part of a building or a loop in a river **5.** ARCHERY, HIST same as **bowman**[1] (*literary*) **6.** METEOROL same as **rainbow** *n* (sense 1) ■ *v* (**bows, bowing, bowed**) **1.** *vti* BEND SOMETHING INTO CURVE to bend, or bend something, into a rounded or bow shape **2.** *vti* USE BOW ON STRINGED INSTRUMENT to draw a bow across the strings of a stringed instrument **3.** *vt* INDICATE BOWING FOR MUSIC to mark a piece of music to indicate which notes are to be played with the bow moving in one direction across the strings and which are to be played with it moving in the opposite direction [Old English *boga* < Germanic, 'to bend']

bow[2] /bow/ *v* (**bows, bowing, bowed**) **1.** *vti* BEND HEAD OR BODY FORWARD to bend the head forward, or to bend forward from the waist, as a signal of respect, greeting, consent, submission, or acknowledgment ○ *bowing her head in shame* **2.** *vti* BEND SOMETHING OR DROOP to bend something over so that it droops, or to be bent in this way ○ *branches bowed down with fruit* **3.** *vi* YIELD to accept something and yield to it, often unwillingly ○ *In the end they had to bow to the inevitable and sell their house.* ■ *n* BENDING FORWARD OF UPPER BODY a bending forward of the upper part of the body to show respect, greeting, consent, submission, or acknowledgment [Old English *būgan* < Germanic, 'to bend'] ◇ **bow and scrape** to be excessively polite or attentive in an attempt to ingratiate yourself with somebody

bow[3] /bow/ *n* **1.** the front section of a boat or ship **2.** the rower closest to the front of a boat [Early 17C. < Low German *boog* or Middle Dutch *boeg*]

SPELLCHECK See *bough*.

Bow /bō/, **Clara** (1905–65) US actor. She enjoyed a brief career in the late 1920s as the most popular female film star in the country, but spent her last three decades in retirement. Known as **the It Girl**

bowdlerize /bówdlə rīz/ (**-izes, -izing, -ized**), **bowdlerise** (**-ises, -ising, -ised**) *vti* to remove parts of a work of literature that are considered indecent [Mid-19C.

< Thomas *Bowdler* (1754–1825), who published an edition of Shakespeare omitting scenes that he considered unsuitable] —**bowdlerism** *n* —**bowdlerization** /bówdlǝ rī záysh'n/ *n* —**bowdlerizer** *n*

bowel /bów ǝl/ *n* **1.** ANAT same as **intestine** (*often used in the plural*) **2.** a section or part of the intestine, especially the part of the intestine that connects to the anus ○ *empty your bowels* ■ **bowels** *npl* the deepest or innermost part of something ○ *the bowels of the ship* [13C. Via Anglo-Norman *buel*, Old French *boël* < Latin *botellus* 'small sausage' < *botulus* 'sausage']

bowel movement *n* **1.** the passing of faeces out of the body through the anus **2.** faeces passed through the anus

Bowen /bố in/, **Elizabeth** (1899–1973) Irish writer. Her fictional depictions of upper-middle-class British life included short stories and the novels *The Death of the Heart* (1938), and *The Heat of the Day* (1949). Full name **Bowen, Elizabeth Dorothea Cole**

'One can live in the shadow of an idea without grasping it.'
[Elizabeth Bowen, *The Heat of the Day*; 1949]

Bowen therapy *n* a therapeutic technique that initiates healing and encourages emotional stability using manipulation of muscles and connective tissues [Mid-20C. After Tom *Bowen* (1916–82), its Australian originator]

bower[1] /bówǝr/ *n* **1.** SHADY SHELTER a shady leafy shelter or recess in a garden or wood **2.** WOMAN'S BEDROOM OR APARTMENTS a woman's bedroom or private apartments, especially in a medieval castle **3.** PICTURESQUE COTTAGE a picturesque country cottage, especially one that is used as a retreat (*literary*) [Old English *būr* 'dwelling' < Indo-European, 'be, live'] —**bowery** *adj*

bower[2] /bówǝr/ *n* the anchor positioned at the bow of a boat [15C. < BOW[3]]

bower[3] /bówǝr/ *n* the jack in euchre and other similar card games [Late 19C. < German *Bauer* 'peasant']

bowerbird

bowerbird /bówǝr burd/ *n* a bird that is noted for the elaborate structures that the male builds for courtship. Native to: New Guinea, Australia. Family: Ptilonorynchidae.

bowfin /bố fin/ (*plural* **-fins** *or* **same**) *n* a freshwater fish with a mottled greenish-brown body and a long dorsal fin. Native to: eastern North America. Latin name: *Amia calva*.

bowfront /bố frunt/ *adj* describes a piece of furniture with a front that curves outwards ○ *a bowfront desk*

bowhead /bố hed/ (*plural* **-heads** *or* **same**) *n* a baleen whale that lives in the Arctic seas and has an arched upper jaw. Latin name: *Balaena mysticetus*.

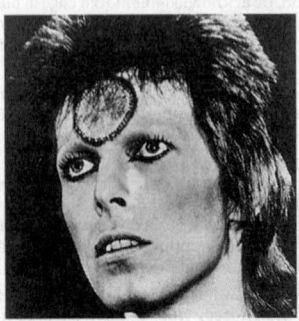

David Bowie

Bowie /bów i/, **David** (*b.* 1947) British pop singer and actor. He pioneered glam rock in the 1970s. His albums include *The Rise and Fall of Ziggy Stardust* and *The Spiders from Mars* (1972). Born **Jones, David Robert**

'The 1970s for me was the beginning of the 21st century—it was the beginning of a true pluralism of social attitudes.'
[Attributed to David Bowie]

Bowie /bố i/, **Jim** (1796?–1836) US pioneer. A colonel in the Texas army, he died at the Battle of the Alamo. Full name **Bowie, James**

bowie knife

bowie knife /bố i-/ *n* a single-edged hunting knife, about 38 cm/15 in long and curved near the point, with a short hilt and a guard for the hand [Mid-19C. After Jim BOWIE, who popularized it]

bowknot /bố not/ *n* a decorative knot in the form of a bow

bowl[1] /bōl/ *n* **1.** ROUND CONTAINER an open container, usually round in shape and wider than it is deep, typically used for holding food and liquids **2.** AMOUNT IN BOWL the contents of a bowl, or the amount a bowl can hold **3.** PART LIKE BOWL a bowl-shaped part of something ○ *a toilet bowl* **4.** DEPRESSION IN GROUND a round depression in the surface of the land **5.** MILDLY ALCOHOLIC DRINK a mildly alcoholic beverage, or the type of cup used for drinking it (*literary*) [Old English *bolla* < Indo-European, 'swell, be round'] —**bowlful** *n*

SPELLCHECK See **bole**[1].

bowl[2] /bōl/ *v* (**bowls**, **bowling**, **bowled**) **1.** *vti* ROLL SMOOTHLY ALONG to roll smoothly, or make something such as a ball roll smoothly, along the ground or some other flat surface ○ *Bowl the ball more gently this time.* **2.** *vti* SEND BALL TO PERSON BATTING in cricket, to send a ball, usually overarm, to a batsman or batswoman **3.** *vt* DISMISS BATSMAN OR BATSWOMAN in cricket, to get a batsman or batswoman out by bowling ○ *He's been bowled!* **4.** *vi* GO BOWLING to take part in a game of bowls or bowling **5.** *vt* SCORE POINTS IN BOWLING in bowling, to score a given number of points ○ *He bowled 250 last night.* **6.** *vi* MOVE QUICKLY to move smoothly and quickly ○ *bowling along down the country lanes* ■ *n* **1.** WOODEN BALL USED IN BOWLS a wooden ball used in the game of bowls, which has slightly flattened sides in order to make it roll in a curve **2.** BOWLING same as **bowling ball 3.** ROLL OF BALL in bowling, one roll of the ball [15C. Via French *boule* < Latin *bulla* 'bubble']

bowl out *vt* CRICKET same as **bowl**[2] *v* (sense 3)

bowl over *vt* **1.** to amaze or delight somebody (*often used in the passive*) ○ *I was completely bowled over by their generous offer.* **2.** to knock something or somebody down, especially accidentally during a headlong rush ○ *The dog bowled three chairs over in its excitement.*

bowlegged /bō léggid, bō légd/ *adj* having legs that curve outwards around or below the knee area [Mid-16C. < BOW[1]]

bow legs *n* a condition in which the legs curve outwards around or below the knee area (*takes a singular verb*) —**bowleg** *n*

bowler[1] /bốlǝr/ *n* **1.** in cricket, the player who bowls the ball **2.** somebody who plays bowls or goes bowling [Early-16C. < BOW[2]]

bowler[2] /bốlǝr/ *n* CLOTHING same as **bowler hat**

bowler hat, **bowler** *n* a hard felt hat, usually black in colour, with a round crown and narrow upturned brim. In the United Kingdom, it was formerly part of the city attire of British businessmen. N Am

term **derby** [Mid-19C. After William *Bowler*, 19C British hatter]

Bowles /bōlz/, **Paul** (1910–99) US writer and composer. He lived in Tangier, Morocco, after 1952. He composed music for films and opera and wrote novels such as *The Sheltering Sky* about US expatriates (1949). Full name **Bowles, Paul Frederick**

bowline /bố lin/ *n* **1.** KNOT FORMING TIGHT LOOP a knot used to form a loop that will not slip at the end of a piece of rope **2.** LINE FOR CONTROLLING SAIL a line for controlling one of the vertical edges of a square sail **3.** KNOT IN END OF CLIMBING ROPE a fixed knot in the end of a climbing rope [14C. < Middle Low German *bōlīne* or Middle Dutch *boechline* 'line from the ship's bow']

bowling /bốling/ *n* **1.** GAME CONSISTING OF ROLLING BALL a game played by rolling a ball so that it either hits pins, as in tenpin bowling, or moves close to another ball, as in bowls **2.** ROLLING OF BALL IN GAME the playing of any form of bowling **3.** THROWING BALL TO PERSON BATTING in cricket, the throwing of the ball, usually overarm, to somebody who is batting

bowling alley *n* **1.** a building for tenpin bowling **2.** the long narrow smooth expanse of floor down which a ball is rolled in tenpin bowling or skittles

bowling ball *n* the heavy ball used in the game of bowling, especially tenpin bowling, that has holes in it for the bowler's thumb and two fingers

bowling crease *n* in cricket, a line that a bowler must not cross before the ball has been bowled

bowling green *n* a piece of natural grass outdoors or a piece of artificial grass indoors for playing the game of bowls

bowls /bōlz/ *n* UK a game in which heavy wooden balls are rolled on a flat surface towards a smaller target ball (*takes a singular verb*) ANZ term **lawn bowls**. N Am term **lawn bowling**

bowman[1] /bốmǝn/ (*plural* **-men** /-mǝn/) *n* somebody who uses a bow and arrows, or a crossbow — **bowmanship** *n*

bowman[2] /bówmǝn/ (*plural* **-men** /-mǝn/) *n* **1.** a man or boy who rows at the bow of a boat **2.** a bowperson on a sailing boat, especially a man

Bowman's capsule /bốmǝnz-/ *n* a cup-shaped part of the kidney that extracts waste and water from the blood and produces urine [Late 19C. After Sir William *Bowman* (1816–92), British surgeon]

bowperson /bốw purss'n/ (*plural* **-persons** *or* **-people** /-peep'l/) *n* **1.** a crew member on a sailing boat who is responsible for the deck and sail work at the bow **2.** somebody who rows at the bow of a boat

Bowral /bówrǝl/ town in the Southern Highlands of east-central New South Wales, Australia. Population: 7,919 (1991).

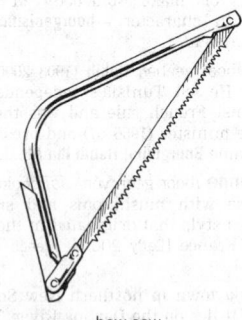

bow saw

bow saw /bố saw/ *n* a saw with a thin blade held in a bow-shaped frame with a narrow handle, used for cutting curves

Bowser /bówzǝr/ *tdmk* **1.** a trademark for a mobile tanker with a pumping apparatus, used to transport fuel for aircraft or military vehicles, or water **2.** ANZ a petrol pump

bow shock /bów shok/ *n* a shock wave, about 21 billion miles from the Sun, caused by solar winds colliding with the Earth's magnetic field [After the crescent-shaped wave made by a ship as it moves through water]

bowshot /bố shot/ *n* the distance that an arrow travels when it has been shot from a bow

bowsprit /bṓ sprit/ *n* a beam that projects forward from the bow of a boat, to which the stays of the foremast are fastened [14C. < Low German *bōgsprēt* or Middle Dutch *boechspriet* 'pole at a ship's bow']

Bow Street Runner /bṓ-/ *n* an officer of Bow Street magistrates' court, London, from 1749 to 1829, whose duty was to pursue and arrest criminals. The Bow Street Runners were the forerunners of the modern British police force.

bowstring /bṓ string/ *n* the taut string on an archer's bow, usually made of strands of hemp

bowstring hemp *n* 1. fibre from the leaves of a tropical perennial plant. Use: bowstrings, mats, nets. 2. a tropical plant with thick leaves grouped in rosettes, from which bowstring hemp is obtained. Native to: Africa, Asia. Genus: *Sansevieria*.

bow tie /bṓ-/ *n* a short tie, knotted in a bow at the neck

bow weight /bṓ-/ *n* the amount of force needed to pull a bowstring back to its fullest extent

bow window /bṓ-/ *n* a bay window that is curved

bow-wow /bów wów, bów wow/ *interj* used to imitate the bark of a dog ■ *n* same as **dog** (*baby talk*) ■ *vi* (**bow-wows, bow-wowing, bow-wowed**) to bark, or imitate the sound of barking [Late 16C. An imitation of the sound]

bowyangs /bṓ yangz/ *npl* ANZ a pair of strings or straps secured round each trouser leg below the knee, worn in Australia and New Zealand by agricultural workers. Their purpose is said to be to prevent insects or small animals crawling up the legs. [Mid-19C. Origin ?]

bowyer /bóyər/ *n* somebody who makes bows for archery [13C. < BOW[1] + -IER]

box[1] /boks/ *n* 1. CONTAINER a container for objects or dry goods, often with a removable or hinged lid, and usually square or rectangular 2. CAPACITY OF BOX the amount of something a box holds or could hold 3. RECTANGULAR SHAPE a square or rectangular shape printed on paper, or on a computer screen, usually containing information or requiring information to be entered in it ○ *Tick the boxes if the following items apply to you.* 4. AREA OR STRUCTURE WITH BEST SEATS an enclosed area in a public building or at a sports venue, especially a theatre, football stadium, or racetrack, that contains the best and most luxurious seats 5. ENCLOSED AREA IN COURTROOM the enclosed area in a courtroom that is reserved for particular participants in a court case ○ *in the witness box* 6. SMALL BUILDING PROVIDING SHELTER a small building that is used as a shelter, especially by military personnel (*usually in combination*) ○ *a sentry box* 7. SMALL BUILDING THAT HOUSES EQUIPMENT a small building that houses equipment and provides shelter for those who use this equipment (*always in combination*) ○ *a police box* 8. EQUIPMENT CONTAINER a container, usually affixed to a wall or on a stand, that houses equipment such as a fire extinguisher, emergency telephone, or first-aid materials 9. ANONYMOUS ADDRESS FOR MAIL an anonymous address for mail to be sent to, used either for administrative purposes or to protect the privacy of the addressee ○ *a PO box* 10. SPORTS PART OF PLAYING AREA in sports such as baseball and football, a marked-off part of the playing area used for a special purpose, or subject to special rules 11. SOCCER PENALTY AREA the penalty area in front of a football goal (*informal*) 12. PROTECTIVE COVERING FOR SPORTSMAN'S GENITALS a protective plastic covering for a sportsman's genitals, worn especially in cricket 13. FIELD SPORTS same as **shooting box** 14. DRIVER'S SEAT IN HORSE-DRAWN COACH a raised seat for the driver in a horse-drawn coach 15. COMPARTMENT FOR LIVESTOCK a compartment for horses or other farm animals, either in a building or in a vehicle 16. TELEVISION the television set (*slang*) ○ *What's on the box tonight, then?* 17. COFFIN a casket for a corpse (*informal*) ○ *The next time he leaves that house it'll be in a box.* 18. NZ MIN EXTRACT WHEELED CONTAINER FOR COAL a high-sided wheeled container used for transporting coal in a mine 19. Aus, N Am OFFENSIVE TERM an offensive term for a woman's vulva and vagina (*taboo slang*) 20. HOLE IN TREE TO COLLECT SAP a hole or hollow cut into the base of a tree in order to collect sap ■ *vt* (**boxes, boxing, boxed**) 1. PACK THINGS IN BOXES to pack individual items into boxes ○ *There are 300 pieces waiting to be boxed before shipping.* 2. OUTLINE SOMETHING WITH BOX to enclose something on a page or on a computer

screen in a box ○ *Box the title to make it stand out more.* 3. CUT HOLE IN TREE FOR SAP to cut a box in the base of a tree to collect the sap 4. ANZ MIX FLOCKS OR HERDS to mix flocks or herds of animals either accidentally or on purpose [Pre-12C. Via late Latin *buxis* < Greek *puxis* 'wooden container' < *puxos* 'boxwood, box tree'] —**boxful** *n* ◇ **out of the box** Aus very good

box in *vt* to surround a person or vehicle with other people or cars, preventing movement

box up *vt* same as **box**[1] *v* (sense 1)

box[2] /boks/ (**boxes, boxing, boxed**) *vti* to fight using the techniques of boxing, or fight somebody in a boxing match ○ *He boxed in exhibition bouts to entertain the crowds.* [14C. Origin ?] ◇ **box clever** to act in a clever and wily manner so as to defeat an opponent

box on *vi* to continue with a boxing match. It is usually a command, given by the referee after a fight has been stopped for a count or other interruption.

box[3] /boks/ (*plural same* or **boxes**) *n* 1. a dense evergreen tree or bush with shiny dark green oval leaves. Use: hedges. Genus: *Buxus*. 2. INDUST same as **boxwood** (sense 2) [Pre-12C. Via Latin *buxus* < Greek *puxos*]

box[4] /boks/ *vti* SAILING same as **boxhaul** [Mid-18C. Origin ?]

Box and Cox /boks ən kóks/ *npl* an arrangement whereby two people can share the use of something in strict rotation (especially accommodation) because they need it at different times [< a farce by British playwright J. M. Morton (1811–91)]

box beam *n* CONSTR same as **box girder**

box bed *n* an old-fashioned bed, enclosed on three sides and the top by a wooden structure resembling a box

boxboard /bóks bawrd/ *n* a tough cardboard made from wood and wastepaper pulp, used for making boxes

box calf *n* black calfskin leather that has been tanned with chromium salts [Early 20C. After Joseph Box, 19C maker of boots in London]

box camera *n* a camera shaped like a box, with a simple lens that has a fixed focus and a single shutter speed

box canyon *n* a canyon with steep walls that can be entered readily only from the downstream direction. Box canyons were formerly often used to pen stock such as cattle and horses.

boxcar /bóks kaar/ *n* N Am in North America, a fully enclosed railway wagon, usually with sliding doors, that is used to transport freight

box coat *n* a coat that hangs loosely from the shoulders

boxed set /bokst-/ *n* COMM same as **box set** (sense 2)

box elder *n* a fast-growing maple tree. Native to: North America. Latin name: *Acer negundo*. [< BOX[3]]

box end spanner *n* UK a wrench with an angled head to allow access to nuts and bolts located in positions not easily reached. ANZ, N Am term **box end wrench**

boxer[1] /bóksər/ *n* a fighter in boxing matches [Late 17C. < BOX[2]]

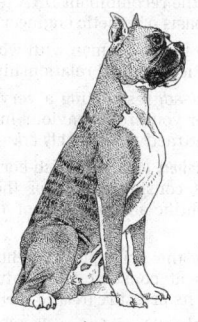

boxer

boxer[2] /bóksər/ *n* a medium-sized dog that has a flat face with a black mask and a short brownish-tan coat, belonging to a breed developed in Germany [Early 20C. Via German < English *boxer*; because of its wide flattened nose]

boxer[3] /bóksər/ *n* a person or machine whose task it is to pack things into boxes

Boxer *n* a member of a secret society in China that launched the Boxer Rebellion [Early 20C. Translation of Chinese *yì hé quán* 'righteous harmonious fists']

Boxer Rebellion *n* an unsuccessful rebellion in China in 1900, the aim of which was to drive out all foreigners, remove all foreign influence, and compel Chinese Christians to give up their religion

boxer shorts *npl* underpants with a gathered waistband and loose-fitting short legs [Because they resemble trunks worn by boxers]

boxfish /bóks fish/ (*plural same* or **-fishes**) *n* FISH same as **trunkfish**

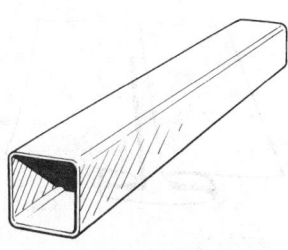

box girder

box girder *n* a hollow girder or beam that is square or rectangular in section

boxhaul /bóks hawl/ (**-hauls, -hauling, -hauled**) *vti* to turn a square-rigged sailing ship onto a new tack by causing the wind to fill the back side of the foresails and steering hard round [Mid-18C. < BOX[4]]

boxing /bóksing/ *n* the sport of fighting with the fists, with the aim of knocking out the opposing boxer, or inflicting enough punishment to cause the other boxer to retire or be judged defeated

Boxing Day *n* a public holiday in England, Wales, and some Commonwealth countries. Date: 26 December. [Because traditionally the day on which Christmas boxes were given to service workers]

boxing glove *n* a thick padded glove tied at the wrist, worn by boxers for fighting

boxing ring *n* a square raised platform with roped-in sides, used as the fighting arena in boxing matches. Each fighter has a designated corner diagonally opposite the other.

box jellyfish (*plural same* or **box jellyfishes**) *n* a highly poisonous jellyfish that has a box-shaped body with venomous tentacles. Native to: tropical Australia. Latin name: *Chironex fleckeri*.

box junction *n* a road junction with yellow crossed lines painted on the road surface, marking an area that traffic is not permitted to block

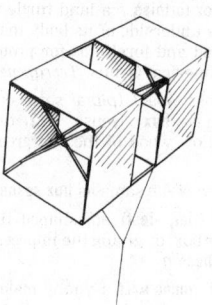

box kite

box kite *n* a square kite without a tail, consisting of two open-ended boxes joined by thin sticks

box lunch *n* N Am same as **packed lunch**

box lyre *n* a plucked stringed instrument, formed from a hollow wooden box with strings running across the soundboard, which are attached to arms jutting out to form a crossbar. Box lyres were known in ancient Sumer in 2800 BC and were widely played in Europe until AD 1000.

box number *n* the number assigned to an anonymous address for mail, either at a post office or as a reference for a reply to a newspaper advertisement

box office *n* **1.** PLACE WHERE TICKETS ARE BOUGHT the place where tickets are bought for entertainments such as films, plays, or concerts **2.** MONEY FROM TICKET SALES ticket sales for a theatrical or cinematic entertainment, or the income from these sales (*informal*; *often used before a noun*) ○ *box office takings* **3.** AUDIENCE POPULARITY drawing power to attract an audience to a theatre (*informal*) ○ *The show makes great box office.* [Originally where a box in the theatre could be reserved]

box-on *n Aus* a fight

box pleat

box pleat *n* a pleat in which fabric is folded under and back again on both sides, and pressed flat

boxroom /bóks room, -rŏŏm/ *n* a small room used either for storage of household items not in regular use or as a bedroom [Early 20C. Because used to store boxes and trunks]

box score *n N Am* a printed summary of a game, especially a baseball game, in table form, listing the players and their positions and performance in the game

box seat *n* **1.** a seat in a box in a theatre or a sports stadium **2.** TRANSP same as **box**¹ *n* (sense 14)

box set *n* **1.** a stage set with a ceiling and three walls **2.** *also* **boxed set** a set of similar items that are packaged together in a box and sold as a single unit, e.g. a set of music recordings ○ *a four-CD box set*

box spanner *n* a spanner in the form of a steel cylinder with a hexagonal end that slips over a nut. N Am term **box wrench**

box spring *n* a base for a mattress consisting of a set of coiled springs in a frame, covered with fabric

box stall *n N Am* same as **loosebox**

box step *n* the basic step in ballroom dancing, in which the feet are moved in a square-shaped pattern

boxthorn /bóks thawrn/ (*plural* **-thorns** or *same*) *n* TREES same as **matrimony vine** [< BOX³]

box turtle, **box tortoise** *n* a land turtle with a hinged shell on the underside of its body that can close up over its head and forelimbs for protection. Native to: North America. Genus: *Terrapene*.

boxwood /bóks wŏŏd/ (*plural same* or **-woods**) *n* **1.** TREES same as **box**³ (sense 1) **2.** the hard close-grained yellow wood of the evergreen box tree or bush

box wrench *n N Am* same as **box spanner**

boxy /bóksi/ (**-ier**, **-iest**) *adj* shaped like a cube or rectangular box, or giving the impression of squareness —**boxiness** *n*

boy /boy/ *n* **1.** YOUNG MALE a young male person ○ *I've had this hobby since I was a boy.* **2.** SON somebody's male child ○ *I'm very proud of that boy of mine.* **3.** YOUNG MAN WITH PARTICULAR JOB a male child or teenager described in terms of his job ○ *a newspaper boy* **4.** MALE FROM PARTICULAR AREA a youth or man who comes from or was brought up in a particular area or has a particular background ○ *He's a local boy.* **5.** WAY OF ADDRESSING MALE ANIMAL a way of addressing a male animal, especially a dog or a horse ○ *Get down, boy!* **6.** *regional* SUITABLE TOOL a tool that will do a particular job (*informal*) ○ *That's just the boy I need to tighten this nut.* ■ **boys** *npl* GROUP OF MALE FRIENDS a group of men of any age who often socialize ○ *I'm off out with the boys.* ■ *interj* EXCLAMATION OF SURPRISE used to express surprise, pleasure, or disgust ○ *Oh boy! Would you just take a look at that!* [13C. Origin ?] —**boyhood** *n* ◇ **boys and their toys** a way of saying that men are fascinated by machines or gadgets, especially in a way that women find hard to understand

SPELLCHECK **boy** or **buoy**? Do not confuse the spelling of **boy** and **buoy**, which sound similar. **Boy** is only used as a noun, denoting a young male, as in *girls and boys*. **Buoy** can be used as a noun, denoting a floating device; as a verb, it means 'mark with a buoy or buoys' or (a separate word) 'keep from falling or sinking', or, with up, 'encourage': *A buoyed channel leads ships safely to the harbour. We were buoyed up by the good news.*

boyakasha /bŏŏ yaa kaáshə/ *interj* same as **boo-yah-kah** (*slang*; *used in Black English*)

boyar /bŏ yaar, bóyər/ *n* between the 12th and early 18th centuries, a member of a class of the higher Russian nobility ranking below a prince. The boyars headed the civil and military administration of the country. [Late 16C. < Russian *boyarin* 'grandee']

boy band *n* a pop group made up of personable young men who sing and dance to synthesized music but do not play instruments

boycott /bóy kot/ (**-cotts, -cotting, -cotted**) *vt* to cease or refuse to deal with something such as an organization, a company, or a process, as a protest against it or as an effort to force it to become more acceptable ○ *Some called for the elections to be boycotted, insisting they were flawed.* [Late 19C. After Captain Charles *Boycott* (1832–97), estate manager in Ireland] —**boycott** *n* —**boycotter** *n*

Boycott /bóy kot/, **Geoff** (*b.* 1940) British cricketer. During a long career he captained Yorkshire (1970–78), played 108 times for England, and scored over 150 centuries. Full name **Boycott, Geoffrey**

Boyd /boyd/, **Arthur Merric** (1862–1940) New Zealand-born Australian painter. Noted for his watercolours, he was the father of Martin à Beckett Boyd and grandfather of Arthur Merric Bloomfield Boyd.

Boyd, **Arthur Merric Bloomfield** (1920–99) Australian artist. His paintings often incorporate biblical and mythological figures. Among his best-known works is *The Australian Scapegoat* (1987).

Boyd, **Benjamin** (1803?–51) British-born Australian pioneer and entrepreneur. He was the founder of whaling ports on Twofold Bay in southeastern New South Wales.

Boyd, **Martin à Beckett** (1893–1972) Swiss-born Australian writer. Author of the novel *Lucinda Brayford* (1946), he was the uncle of Arthur Merric Bloomfield Boyd.

Boyd, **Merric** (1888–1959) Australian potter, the son of Arthur Merric Boyd and father of Arthur Merric Bloomfield Boyd. His works often have religious themes. Full name **Boyd, William Merric**

Boyer /bóy ay/, **Charles** (1897–1978) French actor. He appeared in many romantic roles, including *Mayerling* (1936), and received a special Academy Award in 1943 for his work in promoting Franco-American cultural relations.

Boyer /bóy ər/, **Herbert W.** (*b.* 1936) US biochemist. He codeveloped the recombinant DNA techniques that became the basis of genetic engineering.

boyfriend /bóy frend/ *n* a man with whom somebody has a romantic or sexual relationship

boyish /bóyish/ *adj* resembling a very young man's fresh looks or youthful behaviour in a way that is pleasing or attractive —**boyishly** *adv* —**boyishness** *n*

Boyle /boyl/, **Robert** (1627–91) Irish-born English scientist. He is considered one of the founders of modern scientific method and of the science of chemistry.

Boyle's law *n* the principle that the volume of a confined gas at constant temperature varies inversely with its pressure [Named after Robert BOYLE]

boy-meets-girl *adj* based on a developing romance between a young man and a young woman, and treated in a predictable or hackneyed way in film or print ○ *It's a typical boy-meets-girl story where they live happily ever after.*

Boyne /boyn/ river that rises in the Bog of Allen, County Kildare, Republic of Ireland, and empties into the Irish Sea near Drogheda. The Battle of the Boyne was fought on the banks of the river near Drogheda in 1690, when forces led by William III of England defeated the army of James II.

boy next door *n* a type of man or boy who is unaffected, approachable, and perceived as similar to yourself ○ *an actor who has achieved international stardom without losing his image as the boy next door*

boyo /bóy ŏ/ *n* used as a form of address for a boy or man, or a way of referring, sometimes disparagingly, to a boy or man, particularly one who is Welsh (*informal*; *sometimes disapproving*) ○ *Relax, boyo.*

boy racer *n* a young man who drives very fast to impress people (*informal disapproving*)

Boys' Brigade *n* a Christian organization for boys founded in Britain in 1883 by William Alexander Smith to promote obedience, reverence, discipline, and self-respect

boy scout *n* a man who is considered to be naive or overzealous (*insult*)

Boy Scout *n* **1.** in the United States, a member of the Boy Scouts of America, an organization whose objectives are to develop character, physical fitness, and citizenship, often through community and outdoor activities **2.** another spelling of **boy scout**

boysenberry /bóyz'nbəri/ (*plural* **-ries**) *n* **1.** a large purplish-black fruit with a taste similar to a loganberry **2.** a plant that produces boysenberries, a hybrid of the loganberry, blackberry, and raspberry. Genus: *Rubus*. [Mid-20C. After Rudolph *Boysen* (1895–1950), US botanist]

boys in blue *npl* the police (*informal*)

boy toy *n* **1.** an expensive and high-tech device or other piece of equipment regarded as appealing especially to men **2.** *N Am* a young woman who appears deliberately to try to attract and please men (*informal insult*; *sometimes considered offensive*) **3.** *N Am* same as **toy boy** [Late 20C. Reversal of TOY BOY]

boy wonder *n* a talented and bright young man

bozo /bŏ́zŏ/ *n* an offensive term for somebody who says or does something unwise (*informal insult*) [Early 20C. Origin ?]

bp *abbr* **1.** baptized **2.** CHEM, GENETICS base pair **3.** FIN bills payable **4.** birthplace **5.** CHESS bishop **6.** *also* **b.p.** CHEM boiling point

BP *abbr* **1.** before the present **2.** *also* **B/P** FIN bills payable **3.** MED blood pressure **4.** British Pharmacopoeia (*its use on a product label implies compliance with the specified quality standards*)

BPC *abbr* British Pharmaceutical Codex

BPharm /beé faárm/ *abbr* Bachelor of Pharmacy

BPhil /beé fíl/ *abbr* EDUC Bachelor of Philosophy

bpi *abbr* COMPUT, MEASURE **1.** bits per inch **2.** bytes per inch

bps *n* a measurement of data transfer speed, e.g. in modems and serial ports. Full form **bits per second**

Bq *symbol* MEASURE, PHYS becquerel

b quark *n* PHYS same as **bottom quark**

br¹ *abbr* FIN bills receivable

br² *abbr* Brazil (*used in Internet addresses*) See table at **domain name**

Br *symbol* CHEM bromine

BR *abbr* **1.** bathroom (*used in e-mails or text messages*) **2.** bedroom **3.** RAIL British Rail

br. *abbr* **1.** bills receivable **2.** branch **3.** METALL brass **4.** brief **5.** METALL bronze **6.** brother **7.** brown

Br. *abbr* **1.** Britain **2.** British **3.** Brother

bra /braa/ *n* an undergarment designed to support and shape a woman's breasts [Mid-20C. Shortening of BRASSIERE]

braai /brī/ *n S Africa* COOK same as **barbecue** (senses 1–2) [Mid-20C. Shortening of BRAAIVLEIS]

braaivleis /brī flayss/ (*plural same*) *n S Africa* same as **barbecue** (sense 2) [Mid-20C. < Afrikaans, 'grilled meat']

Brabant /brə bánt/ former duchy from 1190 to 1830 in Western Europe, now divided between the Netherlands and Belgium

Brabham /brábbəm/, **Sir Jack** (*b.* 1926) Australian racing driver. He won the world championship in

1959, 1960, and 1966. Full name **Brabham, Sir John Arthur**

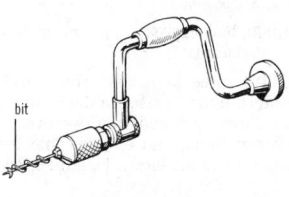

brace

brace[1] /brayss/ n **1.** CLAMP a device that keeps something steady or holds two things together **2.** CONSTR SUPPORT FOR SOMETHING CONSTRUCTED a device used to hold a structure or part steady or upright, e.g. a beam or wooden framework **3.** MED SUPPORT FOR PART OF BODY an orthopaedic appliance that holds or supports part of the body **4.** DENT APPLIANCE FIXED TO TEETH a dental appliance that is fixed to the teeth and can be tightened in order to straighten them (*often used in the plural*) **5.** (*plural same*) PAIR a pair of similar things such as wild birds or animals, hunting dogs, or pistols ○ *two brace of pheasant* **6.** WOODWORK TOOL FOR HOLDING DRILL BIT a tool with an adjustable socket at one end for holding a drill bit, and a handle like a crank at the other for turning the bit **7.** PRINTING, MATHS EITHER OF SYMBOLS { } either of a pair of symbols, { }, used singly in printing or writing to group items together in a table or list or as a pair in mathematical formulae **8.** MATHS SYMBOL OF MATHEMATICAL GROUPING either of a pair of symbols, { }, for additional grouping of mathematical quantities after parentheses and square brackets have been used **9.** MUSIC BRACKET CONNECTING LINES OF MUSIC in music notation, a thick line or bracket connecting a group of staves such as all the choral parts or the accompaniment **10.** MUSIC ADJUSTER FOR DRUM TENSION a sliding loop on the cords of a drum, used to change its tension **11.** ARCHERY, FENCING same as **bracer**[2] ■ **braces** npl UK, ANZ, Can STRAPS FOR HOLDING UP TROUSERS a pair of elasticated shoulder straps attached to the front and back waist of a pair of trousers ■ v (**braces, bracing, braced**) **1.** vt SUPPORT OR STRENGTHEN SOMETHING WITH CLAMP to support or strengthen something, especially part of a building, with a clamping device **2.** vti PREPARE FOR SOMETHING BAD to prepare for something difficult, dangerous, or unpleasant that is about to happen ○ *brace yourself* ○ *The financial markets braced themselves for a rise in interest rates.* **3.** vti ASSUME POSITION PROVIDING SUPPORT FOR BODY to put your body or a part of it into a position intended to provide support or to reduce the effects of an impact or blow ○ *braced her back against the wall* [14C. Via Old French, 'two outstretched arms' < Latin *bracchia*, plural of *brachium* 'arm' (see BRACHIUM)]

brace up vi to be strong and resolute in facing difficulty ○ *Brace up and face the facts.*

brace[2] /brayss/ n on a square-rigged sailing ship, a rope used to control the spar that extends a sail [Early 17C. Perhaps alteration of French *bras de vergue* 'yard arm', after BRACE[1]]

brace and bit n a hand tool for boring holes, consisting of a crank handle at one end and a drill bit at the other

bracelet /bráysslət/ n **1.** JEWELLERY WORN AROUND WRIST OR ARM a piece of jewellery that is worn around the wrist or arm, e.g. a chain or bangle **2.** METAL WRISTWATCH STRAP a metal band attached to a watch that is worn on the wrist ■ **bracelets** npl HANDCUFFS a pair of handcuffs (*slang*) [15C. < French < Latin *bracchiale* 'armlet' < *brachium* 'arm' (see BRACHIUM)]

brace position n a protective position that somebody adopts before impact in a crash, protecting the head with the arms and bringing the legs up underneath the chest

bracer[1] /bráyssər/ n **1.** somebody or something that braces **2.** an invigorating, often alcoholic drink (*informal*) [Mid-16C. < BRACE[1]]

bracer[2] /bráyssər/, **brace** n a leather guard worn by fencers and archers to protect the arm [14C. < Old French *bracière* < *bras* 'arm' < Latin *brachium* (see BRACHIUM)]

brace root n BOT same as **prop root**

brachia ANAT, ZOOL plural of **brachium**

brachial /bráyki əl/ adj relating to or resembling an arm, foreleg, or wing [Late 16C. < Latin *brachialis* < *brachium* (see BRACHIUM)]

brachiate /bráyki ayt/ (**-ates, -ating, -ated**) vi to move along by swinging from one hold to the next with the arms (*refers to tree-dwelling animals*) [Mid-18C. < Latin *brachiatus* < *brachium* (see BRACHIUM)] —**brachiation** /bráyki áysh'n/ n

brachio- prefix arm ○ *brachiocephalic* [< Latin *brachium* (see BRACHIUM)]

brachiocephalic /bráki ō sə fállik, bráyki ō-/ adj relating to or supplying blood to the arms and the head

brachiocephalic artery n ANAT same as **innominate artery**

brachiopod /bráki ə pod, bráyki-/ n an invertebrate sea animal with a hinged shell enclosing tentacles. Phylum: Brachiopoda. [Mid-19C. < modern Latin *Brachiopoda* < Latin *brachium* (see BRACHIUM) + Greek *-pod* (see -POD)] —**brachiopod** adj

brachiosaurus /bráki ə sáwrəss, bráyki-/ (*plural* **-ruses** or **-ri** /-rī/), **brachiosaur** /bráki ə sawr, bráyki-/ n a dinosaur with a massive sloping body up to 30 m/100 ft long. Genus: *Brachiosaurus*. [Early 20C. < modern Latin < Latin *brachium* (see BRACHIUM) (from the unusual length of the animal's humerus bones) + Greek *sauros* 'lizard']

brachium /bráyki əm/ (*plural* **-chia** /-ki ə/) n **1.** an arm, especially the upper arm (*technical*) **2.** a structure that corresponds to an arm, e.g. a wing [Mid-18C. Via Latin < Greek *brakhīōn* 'upper arm', literally 'shorter' < *brakhus* (see BRACHY-)]

brachy- prefix short ○ *brachypterous* [< Greek *brakhus* < Indo-European, 'short']

brachycephalic /bráki sə fállik/, **brachycephalous** /-séffələss/ adj with a short, broad, and almost spherical head —**brachycephalism** /-séffəlizəm/ n —**brachycephaly** /-séffəli/ n

brachydactylic /bráki dak tíllik/, **brachydactylous** /-dáktiləss/ adj with unusually short fingers or toes —**brachydactylia** /-dak tílli ə/ n —**brachydactyly** /-dáktili/ n

brachylogy /bra kílləji/ n **1.** brevity in speech or writing, or an instance of this **2.** a shortened form of an expression, used in informal speech [Mid-16C. Via late Latin < Greek *brakhulogia* 'shortness of speech'] —**brachylogous** /-kílləgəss/ adj

brachypterous /bra kíptərəss/ adj describes insects and some species of diving birds with short or not fully developed wings —**brachypterism** n

bracing /bráyssing/ adj making you feel refreshed or invigorated ○ *a bracing cold shower* ■ n a system of braces that are used to support or strengthen a structure —**bracingly** adv

bracken

bracken /brákən/ (*plural same* or **-ens**) n a large fern with extensive underground stems and large triangular fronds that is poisonous to livestock. Native to: most temperate and tropical regions. Latin name: *Pteridium aquilinum*. [14C. < assumed Old Norse *brakni*]

bracket /brákit/ n **1.** PRINTING UPRIGHT CURVED PUNCTUATION MARK one of a pair of shallow, curved signs, ( ), used to enclose an explanatory word or comment and distinguish it from the sentence in which it occurs (*often used in the plural*) N Am term **parenthesis 2.** N Am PRINTING same as **square bracket 3.** PRINTING PAIRED PUNCTUATION MARK any of the set of signs used in pairs to separate words from surrounding text, including the angle bracket and the brace **4.** GROUP WITHIN SET LIMITS a section of the population that falls within particular defined limits ○ *taxpayers in the £50,000 to £70,000 bracket* **5.** L-SHAPED STRUCTURE ON WALL an L-shaped structure that is fixed to a wall to hold up something such as a shelf or speaker **6.** TYPE OF SHELF a shelf with an integral part that fixes to the wall as its support and can sometimes be swivelled ○ *This TV bracket is too low.* ■ vt (**-ets, -eting, -eted**) **1.** PUT SOMETHING INSIDE BRACKETS to put something, especially text or a mathematical equation, inside brackets **2.** SUPPORT SOMETHING WITH BRACKETS to fix brackets to something, especially a wall, or support something with brackets **3.** GROUP PEOPLE OR THINGS TOGETHER to group or class people or things together, usually because they are similar in some way ○ *The two shows, both about 30-something women, will inevitably be bracketed together.* [Late 16C. Perhaps < French *braguette* 'codpiece' (because of the shape) < Latin *bracae* 'breeches'] —**bracketing** n

USAGE *Brackets* are used around text that adds extra information to what has gone before: *She was suffering from rubella (German measles).* The noun *'dessert'* (with a double 's') is pronounced the same as the verb *'desert'*. *He read an article on GM (genetically modified) crops.* The information within the brackets can usually be omitted without affecting the structure of the sentence. Note that there should be no punctuation directly before the opening bracket in such cases. Brackets are also used around optional or alternative material: *Please write your forename(s) in full*, or to separate something such as a number or symbol from the surrounding text: *I disagree with the proposal, (a) because it is too expensive and (b) because it is unlikely to be effective in the long term.* See also **square bracket**.

bracket clock n a clock that is designed to stand on a shelf or a wall bracket

bracket fungus n a fungus that forms growths that stick out like shelves. The growths generally appear on tree trunks and other wooden structures.

brackish /brákish/ adj rather salty, especially from being a mixture of fresh and salt water [Mid-16C. < Dutch *brak* 'salty water'] —**brackishness** n

Bracknell /brákn'l/ town in central southern England, designated a new town in 1949. Population: 60,895 (1991).

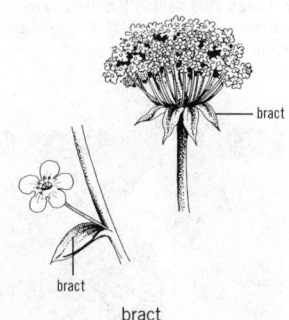

bract

bract /brakt/ n a modified leaf that arises from the stem at the point where the flower or flower cluster develops. Although often green and inconspicuous, bracts may sometimes be large and brightly coloured, as in a poinsettia. [Late 18C. < Latin *bractea* 'thin metal plate, gold leaf'] —**bracteal** /brákti əl/ adj

bracteate /brákti ət/ adj describes a plant that has bracts ■ n a decorated dish or plate made of precious metal [Early 19C. < Latin *bracteatus* < *bractea* 'thin metal plate, gold leaf']

bracteole /brákti ōl/ n an organ resembling a leaf or scale that arises from a branch of a flower cluster where the flowers develop, and where the entire cluster itself develops above a bract [Early 19C. < Latin *bracteola* 'small bract' < *bractea* 'thin metal plate, gold leaf'] —**bracteolate** /brákti ələt, -layt/ adj

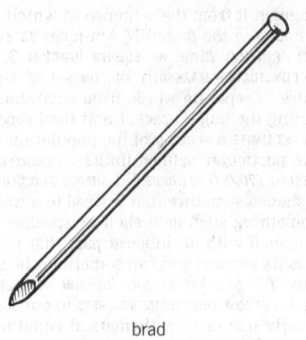

brad

brad /brad/ *n* a thin tapered nail with a head that is small and either circular or flat on one side [13C. < Old Norse *broddr* 'spike']

bradawl /brád awl/ *n* a hand tool with a pointed tip, used for making holes in wood, leather, and other materials, to allow screws and nails to be inserted

Bradbury /brádbəri/, **Malcolm** (1932–2000) British novelist, critic, and scholar. Many of his novels such as *The History Man* (1975) deal with academic life. Full name **Bradbury, Malcolm Stanley**

Bradbury, Ray (*b.* 1920) US writer best known for his science fiction novels and stories, including *The Martian Chronicles* (1950) and *Fahrenheit 451* (1953). Full name **Bradbury, Ray Douglas**

Bradfield /brád feeld/, **John Job Crew** (1867–1943) Australian civil engineer. He created the original plan for and supervised the construction of Sydney Harbour Bridge (opened in 1932).

Bradford /brádfərd/ industrial city in West Yorkshire, northern England. Population: 467,665 (2001).

Bradlaugh /brád law/, **Charles** (1833–91) British social reformer and freethinker. He was elected MP in 1880, but was admitted to the House of Commons only in 1886 because of his insistence on taking an affirmation rather than an oath of allegiance.

Bradley /brádli/, **A. C.** (1851–1935) British literary critic. He held professorships at the universities of Liverpool (1882–89), Glasgow (1890–1900), and Oxford (1901–06). He wrote *Shakespearean Tragedy* (1904). Full name **Bradley, Andrew Cecil**

Bradley, Francis Herbert (1846–1924) British philosopher. A major figure in the idealist movement, his philosophy drew on the work of Hegel. His works include *Principles of Logic* (1883) and *Appearance and Reality* (1893).

Bradley, James (1693–1762) English astronomer. The third astronomer royal (1742–62), he discovered the aberration of light (1729).

Sir Don Bradman

Bradman /brádmən/, **Sir Don** (1908–2001) Australian cricketer. He was Australian Test captain (1936–48), and one of the highest-scoring batsmen of all time, with a Test average of 99.94 runs. Full name **Bradman, Sir Donald George**

Bradstreet /brád street/, **Anne** (1612?–72) English-born American New England poet. An early settler (1630) and the wife of a governor of the Massachusetts Bay Colony, she is regarded as the first English poet in America. Her verse was originally published in England in 1650. Born **Dudley, Ann**

'I am obnoxious to each carping tongue, / Who sayes my hand a needle better fits, /

A Poet's Pen, all scorne, I should thus wrong; / For such despight they cast on female wits: / If what I doe prove well, it won't advance, / They'll say it's stolne, or else, it was by chance.'
[Anne Bradstreet, 'The Prologue', *The Tenth Muse Lately Sprung up in America*; 1650]

Brady /bráydi/, **James** (*b.* 1940) US presidential aide. President Ronald Reagan's press secretary, he was wounded in an assassination attempt on the president in 1981 and with his wife Sarah Brady subsequently became a staunch advocate of gun control legislation. The so-called Brady Bill of 1993 mandating waiting periods and licence fees for firearms takes its name from his efforts.

brady- *prefix* slow ○ *bradycardia* [< Greek *bradus*]

bradycardia /bráddi kaárdi ə/ *n* slowness of the heart rate, usually measured as fewer than 60 beats per minute in an adult human [Late 19C. < BRADY- + Greek *kardia* 'heart'] —**bradycardiac** *adj* —**bradycardic** *adj*

bradykinin /bráddi kínin/ *n* a chemical (**peptide**) produced in the blood when tissues are injured that plays a role in inflammation [Mid-20C. < BRADY- + Greek *kinein* 'to move']

brae /bray/ *n* Scotland a hill or slope (*often used in placenames*) [14C. < Old Norse *brá* 'eyelash']

brag /brag/ *vi* (**brags, bragging, bragged**) TALK WITH TOO MUCH PRIDE to talk with excessive pride about an achievement or possession ○ *The police arrested him after he bragged about the bank robbery to his friends.* ■ *n* **1.** BOASTFUL REMARK a boastful statement or display of arrogant behaviour **2.** CARDS CARD GAME a card game similar to poker [14C. Origin ?] —**bragger** *n* —**bragging** *n*, *adj* —**braggingly** *adv*

Braga /braágə/ city and capital of the mountainous district of Braga, northwestern Portugal. Population: 63,033 (1981).

Brage *n* MYTHOL same as **Bragi**

Bragg /brag/, **Sir Lawrence** (1890–1971) Australian-born British physicist. He collaborated with his father, Sir William Bragg, in developing an X-ray technique for examining crystals. They shared the Nobel Prize in physics (1915). Full name **Bragg, Sir William Lawrence**

Bragg, Sir William Henry (1862–1942) British physicist. With his son, Sir Lawrence Bragg, he developed an X-ray technique for examining crystals. They shared the Nobel Prize in physics (1915).

braggadocio /brággə dóchi ō/ (*plural* **-os**) *n* **1.** empty boasting and swaggering self-aggrandizement **2.** somebody who boasts in a swaggering self-aggrandizing way [Late 16C. Alteration of *Braggadocchio*, personification of boastfulness in Spenser's *Faerie Queene*]

braggart /brággərt/ *n* somebody who talks immodestly or with excessive pride about himself or herself [Late 16C. < French *bragard* < *braguer* 'to brag']

Bragg's law /brágz-/ *n* a law stating the angle at which X-rays reflected from a crystal are most intense [Early 20C. After Sir William Henry BRAGG and Sir Lawrence BRAGG]

Bragi /braági/, **Brage** /braágə/ *n* in Nordic mythology, the god of poetry, eloquence, and music

Brahe /braa, braá ə, braáhi/, **Tycho** (1546–1601) Danish astronomer. He employed extremely precise observations of stars and planets to correct inaccuracies in existing astronomical tables.

Brahma[1] /braámə/ *n* **1.** in Hinduism, the god of knowledge and understanding, regarded as the protector of the world and in later tradition called the creator **2.** HINDUISM same as **Brahman** (sense 1) [< Sanskrit *brāhmaṇa-* < *brahman-* 'priest']

Brahma[2] /braámə/ *n* a large domestic fowl with heavily feathered legs and feet and a small tail and wings, belonging to a breed that originated in Asia [Mid-19C. Shortening of *Brahmaputra fowl*; because first imported from a town on the Brahmaputra river in India]

Brahman /braámən/ *n* **1.** in Hinduism, the ultimate impersonal reality underlying everything in the universe, from which everything comes and to which it returns **2.** HINDUISM same as **Brahma**[1] (sense 1) **3.** *also* **brahman** HINDUISM another spelling of **Brahmin** (senses 1–2) [Late 18C. < Sanskrit *brahman-* 'priest'] —**Brahmanic** /braa mánnik/ *adj* —**Brahmanical** *adj*

Brahmana /braámənə/ *n* a sacred Hindu text belonging to a group of commentaries on the Vedas [< Sanskrit *brāhmaṇam* < *brāhmaṇa-* (see BRAHMIN)]

Brahmani /braáməni/, **brahmani** *n* a woman of the Brahmin caste [Late 18C. < Sanskrit *brāhmaṇī*, feminine of *brāhmaṇa-* (see BRAHMIN)]

Brahmanism, **brahmanism** *n* another spelling of **Brahminism** —**Brahmanist** *n*

Brahmaputra /braámə poótrə/ river in Tibet and northeastern India. It rises in the Himalayan range in Tibet, flows east and southwestwards through northeastern India, and empties into the delta of the Ganges in Bangladesh. Length: 2,900 km/1,800 mi.

Brahmin: a Brahmin priest

Brahmin /braámin/ (*plural* **-mins** or *same*), **brahmin**, **Brahman** (*plural* **-mans** or *same*), **brahman** *n* **1.** the first of the four Hindu castes, the members of which are priests and scholars of Vedic literature **2.** a member of the Brahmin caste [15C. < Sanskrit *brāhmaṇa-* < *brahman-* 'priest'] —**Brahminic** /braa mínnik/ *adj* —**Brahminical** *adj*

Brahminism /braáminizəm/, **brahminism**, **Brahmanism** /braámənizəm/, **brahmanism** *n* the traditional social and religious system of Vedic Hinduism —**Brahminist** *n*

Johannes Brahms

Brahms /braamz/, **Johannes** (1833–97) German composer. His works include four symphonies, two piano concertos, and *A German Requiem* (1868).

Brahui /braa hoó i/ (*plural* **-is** or *same*) *n* **1.** a Dravidian language spoken in southwestern Pakistan. Native speakers: 2 million. **2.** a member of a Brahui-speaking people who live in southwestern Pakistan [Early 19C. < Brahui] —**Brahui** *adj*

braid /brayd/ *n* **1.** TEXTILES DECORATIVE SILKY CORD a decorative and often silky cord or interwoven thread. Use: trimming, binding, decorating uniforms, edging for soft furnishings. **2.** SOMETHING INTERWOVEN something that is made of three or more interwoven strands **3.** HAIR INTERWOVEN STRANDS OF HAIR a length of hair divided into three or more interwoven strands and worn down the back ○ *She wore her hair in braids.* ■ *vt* (**braids, braiding, braided**) **1.** INTERWEAVE STRANDS to interweave three or more strands of something, especially hair **2.** MAKE SOMETHING BY BRAIDING to make something by interweaving strands, strips, or other components ○ *braid a rug* **3.** TRIM SOMETHING WITH DECORATIVE CORD to decorate uniforms or edge furnishings with silky cord [Old English *bregdan* 'weave, lay hold of' < Germanic]

braided /bráydid/ *adj* **1.** INTERWOVEN interwoven from three or more strands **2.** EDGED WITH DECORATIVE CORD decorated or edged with silky cord, especially gold

cord **3.** CONSISTING OF INTERCONNECTED TRACKS OR CHANNELS composed of interconnected tracks or channels that divide and reunite ○ *a braided river*

braiding /bráyding/ *n* **1.** decorative silky cord. Use: trimming uniforms and furnishings. **2.** embroidery worked in decorative silky thread

Bràila /brə éëlə/ city and capital of Bràila County, southeastern Romania. Situated on the Danube, it is Romania's second largest port. Population: 234,648 (1997).

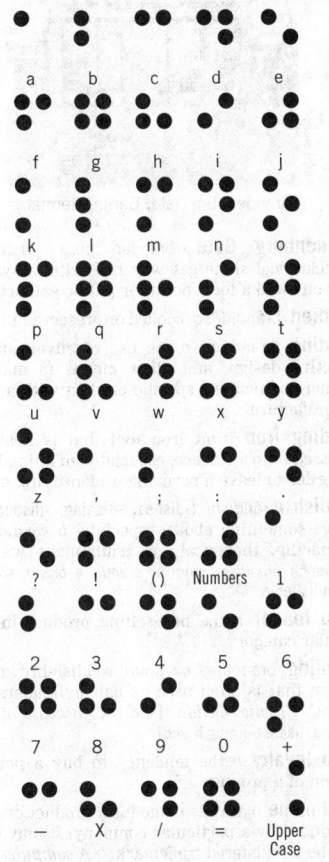

Braille

Braille /brayl/ *n* a writing system for visually impaired people, consisting of patterns of raised dots that are read by touch [Mid-19C. After Louis BRAILLE]

Braille /brayl/, **Louis** (1809–52) French educationist. He was unable to see from early childhood and in 1829 he invented the Braille system of raised dots to enable visually impaired people to read and write.

Brailler /bráylər/, **Braillewriter** /bráyl rītər/ *n* a machine similar to a typewriter that prints Braille

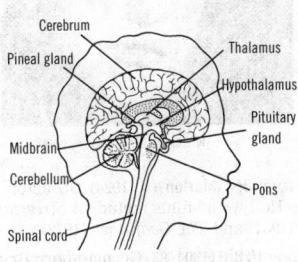

brain: cross-section of human brain

brain /brayn/ *n* **1.** ORGAN OF THOUGHT AND FEELING the controlling centre of the nervous system in vertebrates, connected to the spinal cord and enclosed in the cranium. It consists of a mass of nerve tissue and nerve-supporting and nourishing tissue (**glia**), is the centre of thought and emotions, and regulates bodily activities. **2.** CENTRE OF INVERTEBRATE NERVOUS

SYSTEM a nervous-system centre in some invertebrates that is functionally similar to the brain in vertebrates **3.** MIND somebody's intellectual ability ○ *He's got a good brain.* **4.** INTELLIGENCE somebody's natural intelligence (*usually used in the plural*) ○ *She's got brains as well as beauty.* **5.** SOMEBODY INTELLIGENT somebody very intelligent (*informal*) **6.** MOST INTELLIGENT PERSON IN GROUP the person in a group who is considered the most intelligent and who devises plans or strategies for it (*informal; usually used in the plural*) ○ *Lee's the brains of the family.* ■ **brains** *npl* ANIMAL'S BRAIN AS FOOD the brain of an animal cooked and eaten as food ■ *vt* (**brains, braining, brained**) HIT SOMEBODY ON HEAD to hit somebody violently on the head (*informal*) [Old English *brægen* < W Germanic] ◇ **have something on the brain** to be unable to stop thinking about something (*informal*) ◇ **pick somebody's brains** to ask questions of somebody, in order to learn what he or she knows about something ◇ **rack your brains** to try very hard to solve a problem

brainbox /bráyn boks/ *n* a very clever person (*informal; often used by children*)

brain bucket *n* a protective helmet worn when engaging in sports such as climbing or motorcycling (*slang*)

braincase /bráyn kayss/ *n* the part of the skull enclosing the brain

brain cell *n* one of the millions of cells that make up the brain ◇ **not have a brain cell (between them)** an offensive phrase meaning to be regarded as having very low intellectual ability (*informal*)

brainchild /bráyn chīld/ (*plural* **-children** /-chīldrən/) *n* an original plan or idea attributed to a person or group (*informal*)

brain coral *n* coral that forms rounded colonies resembling the folds of the human brain. Genus: *Meandrina.*

brain damage *n* injury to the brain tissue that can impair its ability to function

brain dead *adj* **1.** lacking functions of the brain and central nervous system as measured by brain wave activity on an electroencephalogram over a specific period of time **2.** an offensive term meaning having extremely low intellectual ability (*slang*)

brain death *n* the end of all functions of the brain and central nervous system as measured by brain wave activity on an electroencephalogram over a specific period of time. There are strict legal criteria for determining brain death, since its occurrence can allow cessation of life support or removal of organs for transplantation.

brain drain *n* the movement of highly skilled people to a country offering better opportunities (*informal*)

brain fever *n* inflammation of the brain or its covering membranes (*archaic*)

brainless /bráynləss/ *adj* lacking or not requiring intelligence (*disapproving*) ○ *a brainless activity* —**brainlessly** *adv* —**brainlessness** *n*

brainpan /bráyn pan/ *n* ANAT same as **braincase**

brainpower /bráyn powər/ *n* somebody's intellectual capability

brain stem *n* the part of the brain between the spinal column and the cerebral hemispheres. It consists of the midbrain, pons, and medulla oblongata.

brainstorm /bráyn stawrm/ *n* **1.** a momentary psychological disturbance **2.** *N Am* same as **brain wave** (sense 2) (*informal*) ■ *vti* (**-storms, -storming, -stormed**) to have an intensive group discussion in order to generate creative ideas and usually to stimulate problem-solving —**brainstormer** *n* —**brainstorming** *n*

brains trust *n* **1.** a group of experts who informally discuss issues of public interest, especially on television or radio **2.** a group of high-level advisers, usually unofficial, to a government or administration. US term **brain trust**

brainteaser /bráyn teezər/ *n* a difficult or complex problem that requires careful thought in order to solve it, often done for amusement (*informal*)

brain trust *n* ANZ, N Am same as **brains trust** (sense 2)

brainwash /bráyn wosh/ (**-washes, -washing, -washed**) *vt* **1.** to impose a set of usually political or religious beliefs on somebody by the use of various coercive methods of indoctrination, including destruction of

the victim's prior beliefs **2.** to induce somebody to believe or do something, e.g. to buy a new product, especially by means of constant repetition or advertising

brainwashing /bráyn woshing/ *n* **1.** the imposition of a set of usually political or religious beliefs on somebody by the use of various coercive methods of indoctrination, including destruction of the victim's prior beliefs **2.** the inducing of somebody to believe or do something, e.g. to buy a new product, especially by means of constant repetition or advertising [Mid-20C. Translation of Chinese *xĭnǎo* < *xĭ* 'to wash' + *nǎo* 'brain']

brain wave *n* **1.** one of the rhythmic waves of voltage arising from electrical activity within brain tissue **2.** a sudden exciting idea (*informal*) N Am term **brainstorm**

brainwork /bráyn wurk/ *n* concentrated intellectual activity, especially that required to do a job

brainy /bráyni/ (**-ier, -iest**) *adj* extremely intelligent (*informal*) —**brainily** *adv* —**braininess** *n*

braise /brayz/ (**braises, braising, braised**) *vt* to cook food, especially meat or vegetables, by browning briefly in hot fat, adding a little liquid, and cooking at a low temperature in a covered pot [Mid-18C. < French *braiser* < *braise* 'live coals']

brake[1] /brayk/ *n* **1.** DEVICE THAT SLOWS OR STOPS MACHINE the part of a machine or vehicle that slows it down or stops it (*often used in the plural*) **2.** RESTRAINT a slowing down or stopping of something such as expenditure or development, or something that causes this ○ *The brake on investment is largely a result of political factors.* **3.** RAIL same as **brake van** ■ *v* (**brakes, braking, braked**) **1.** *vti* SLOW OR STOP MACHINE to slow down or stop, or make something such as a vehicle or a machine slow down or stop ○ *The driver braked hard.* **2.** *vt* SLOW OR HALT DEVELOPMENT to slow down or halt the progress of something or an increase in something [Late 18C. Perhaps < BRAKE[4]]

SPELLCHECK See *break*[1].

brake[2] /brayk/ (*plural same* or **brakes**) *n* PLANTS, BOT same as **bracken** [14C. Perhaps back-formation < BRACKEN]

SPELLCHECK See *break*[1].

brake[3] /brayk/ *n* an area of dense undergrowth, bushes, or brushwood [Old English *bracu*, origin ?]

brake[4] /brayk/ *n* **1.** a tool or machine for crushing and separating flax or hemp fibres **2.** a machine, frequently hydraulically powered, for precision bending and folding of sheet metal [15C. < Middle Low German or Middle Dutch]

brake[5] /brayk/ *n* a lever or handle on a pump or other machine [Early 17C. Origin ?]

brake[6] /brayk/, **break** *n* an open four-wheeled horse-drawn carriage [Mid-19C. Origin ?]

brake block *n* a small rectangular block of rubber that is pressed against the rim of a bicycle wheel when the brake is applied

brake chute *n* AUTOMOT same as **brake parachute**

brake drum *n* the metal cylinder attached to the wheel of a vehicle that slows the rotation of the wheel when pressure is applied by the brake shoe

brake-fade *n* a decrease in the braking efficiency of a motor vehicle, caused by the overheating of the brakes

brake fluid *n* an oily liquid used in hydraulic brakes and clutches to transmit pressure

brake horsepower *n* a measure of the work produced by an engine, calibrated in horsepower and determined by the force exerted on a friction brake

brake light *n* a rear light on a motor vehicle that lights up when the driver brakes

brake lining *n* the renewable thin strip of material attached to a brake shoe

brakeman /bráykmən/ (*plural* **-men** /-mən/) *n* **1.** a member of a train crew or other railway employee who operates, inspects, or repairs brakes, usually a man **2.** somebody who operates the brakes on a bobsleigh, especially in a team of men

brake pad *n* a renewable block of material that presses against the surface of a disc brake

brake parachute *n* a parachute that is attached to the back of a vehicle and acts as a brake

brakeperson /bráyk purss'n/ *n* **1.** a member of a train crew or other railway employee who operates, inspects, or repairs brakes **2.** somebody who operates the brakes on a bobsleigh

brake shoe *n* a curved block that presses a brake lining against a brake drum to slow the turning of a wheel

brakesman /bráyksmən/ (*plural* **-men** /-mən/) *n* somebody who operates the winch at a pithead

brake van *n* formerly, a railway vehicle attached to a goods train from which the guard applied the brakes

brakewoman /bráykwoomən/ (*plural* **-women** /-wimin/) *n* **1.** a female member of a train crew or other railway employee who operates, inspects, or repairs brakes **2.** a woman who operates the brakes on a bobsleigh

braking distance /bráyking-/ *n* the distance that a vehicle needs to come to a complete stop when the brakes have been applied

braless /bráaləss/ *adj, adv* not wearing a bra

Bramante /brə mán tay/, **Donato** (1444–1514) Italian architect and painter. He rebuilt and renovated the Vatican and St Peter's in Rome (1505–06). Born **d'Antonio, Donato di Pascuccio**

bramble /brámb'l/ *n* **1.** BLACKBERRY a blackberry fruit, especially when growing on a wild bush **2.** BLACKBERRY PLANT a wild blackberry plant (*often plural*) **3.** PRICKLY BUSH a prickly bush similar or related to a wild blackberry, e.g. a dog rose ■ *vi* (**-bles, -bling, -bled**) COLLECT BERRIES FROM BRAMBLES to collect berries from brambles in hedgerows [Old English *bræmbel* < Germanic, 'thorny bush']

brambling /brámbling/ *n* a small bird related to the chaffinch, with black and rusty-brown feathers. Native to: northern Europe, Asia. Latin name: *Fringilla montifringilla*. [Mid-16C. Perhaps < BRAMBLE + -LING[1]]

brambly /brámbli/ (**-blier, -bliest**) *adj* covered in or containing prickly bushes, especially blackberries or wild roses ○ *a brambly garden*

Brampton /brámptən/ city and industrial centre in southeastern Ontario, Canada. Population: 325,428 (2001).

bran /bran/ *n* the husks of cereal grain that are removed during milling. Use: supplementary source of dietary fibre. [13C. < French]

Bran /bran/ *n* in Celtic mythology, a giant god who ruled Britain and installed his son, Gwern, as king of Ireland

Branagh /bránnə/, **Kenneth** (*b.* 1960) British actor and director, born in Northern Ireland. His work on stage and in films includes *Henry V* (1989). Full name **Branagh, Kenneth Charles**

> 'I didn't think they gave awards to short ill-tempered megalomaniacs.'
> [Attributed to Kenneth Branagh]

branch /braanch/ *n* **1.** PART OF TREE GROWING FROM TRUNK a woody limb of a tree that grows out from a larger limb or from the trunk **2.** BOT PART OF PLANT STEM OR ROOT a subdivision of the stem, root, or flower cluster of a plant **3.** SOMETHING LIKE TREE BRANCH something that resembles a branch of a tree in structure ○ *the branches of the stag's antlers* **4.** LOCAL UNIT IN ORGANIZATION a shop, bank, or other organization that is part of a larger group and is located in a different part of a geographical area from the parent organization ○ *The account is held at the bank's Oxford branch.* **5.** DISTINCT PART OF LARGE ORGANIZATION a subdivision of a large organization, usually with a specialized mission ○ *The executive branch of government is headed by the president.* **6.** PART OF SUBJECT AREA a part of a large area of study ○ *Ethics is a branch of philosophy.* **7.** FAMILY LINE a line of a family that is descended from a common ancestor ○ *the Peruvian branch of the family* **8.** GEOG TRIBUTARY STREAM a river or stream flowing into another river ○ *a branch of the Colorado River* **9.** COMPUT ALTERNATIVE INSTRUCTION SEQUENCE a sequence of computer program instructions in a set of alternative sequences that are activated according to specific conditions **10.**

MATHS PART OF CURVE a distinctive part of a curve that is separated from the rest of the curve, e.g. by discontinuities or extreme points ■ *v* (**branches, branching, branched**) **1.** *vti* DIVIDE to divide into smaller parts, or cause something to do this ○ *Part of the track branches off towards the river.* **2.** *vi* BOT HAVE BRANCHES to grow branches **3.** *vi* EXPAND ACTIVITIES OR INTERESTS to become involved in something new, especially as a way of extending or expanding personal interests or business activities ○ *The company has branched into multimedia upgrade kits.* **4.** *vi* COMPUT JUMP TO ALTERNATE PROGRAM PATH to execute an alternative sequence of computer program instructions as a result of the detection of a specific condition [13C. Via French *branche* < late Latin *branca* 'paw'] —**branchlet** /braanchlət/ *n*

branch out *vi* to do something different, especially if it involves an element of risk

-branch *suffix* gills ○ *opisthobranch* [< Latin *branchia* (SEE BRANCHIA)]

branchia /brángki ə/ (*plural* **-ae** /-ee/) *n* a gill in water animals or a similar structure found in the embryos of higher animals, including human beings [Late 17C. Via Latin < Greek *bragkhia* 'gills'] —**branchial** *adj* —**branchiate** *adj*

branchial cleft, branchial groove *n* AMPHIB, FISH same as **gill slit** (*technical*)

branchiopod /brángki ə pod/ *n* a small, usually freshwater crustacean with a segmented body and flat gill-bearing appendages. Subclass: Branchiopoda. [Early 19C. < modern Latin *Branchiopoda* < Latin *branchia* 'gills' + Greek *-pod* (see -POD)] —**branchiopod** *adj* —**branchiopodous** /brángki óppədəss/ *adj*

branch line *n* a part of a railway system that connects smaller towns and villages that are not served by a main line

branch officer *n* a warrant officer in the Royal Navy

branch stacking *n* Aus the practice of recruiting new members to a political party for the purpose of achieving a favourable vote in a contest to select new candidates

Brancusi /brang koozi/, **Constantin** (1876–1957) Romanian sculptor. He was a pioneer of 20th-century European sculpture and was particularly concerned with the inner form of his subject.

> 'Architecture is inhabited sculpture.'
> [Constantin Brancusi. Quoted in *Themes and Episodes*, Igor Stravinsky; 1966]

brand /brand/ *n* **1.** COMM PRODUCT OR MANUFACTURER a name, usually a trademark, of a product or manufacturer, or the product identified by this name ○ *What brand of cosmetics does she use?* **2.** RECOGNIZABLE TYPE OF SOMETHING a distinctive type of something ○ *an unusual brand of humour* **3.** AGRIC MARK BURNED ON ANIMAL a mark burned into the hide of an animal to identify it as the property of a particular farm or owner ○ *The Triple S is the brand on all our cattle.* **4.** HIST MARK ON CRIMINAL OR SLAVE formerly, a mark made on the skin of a criminal or a slave, especially to identify the owner **5.** SIGN OR MARK OF DISGRACE a sign or mark of disgrace, infamy, or notoriety ○ *He bore the brand of disloyalty.* **6.** BURNT OR BURNING PIECE OF WOOD a piece of wood that is burnt or smouldering (*archaic*) **7.** TORCH a flaming torch (*literary*) **8.** ARMS same as **sword** (sense 1) (*literary*) **9.** FUNGI FUNGAL DISEASE OF PLANTS a fungal disease that affects garden plants by causing brown spots to appear on leaves ■ *vt* (**brands, branding, branded**) **1.** MARK SKIN OR HIDE OF ANIMAL to mark an animal's skin or hide with a hot iron, especially as a means of identification ○ *All the cattle have been branded.* **2.** DESCRIBE SOMEBODY OR SOMETHING AS BAD to class somebody or something as bad, illegal, or undesirable, often arbitrarily ○ *was branded a cheat* **3.** MAKE INDELIBLE IMPRESSION ON SOMEBODY to make an indelible mark or impression on somebody or something (*literary*) ○ *The traditions of this sport have been branded into my heart.* [Old English, 'burning stick' < Indo-European, 'be hot'] —**brander** *n*

branded /brándid/ *adj* bearing a company name or trademark, usually considered a mark of prestige or quality

Brandeis /brán dīss/, **Louis** (1856–1941) associate justice of the US Supreme Court. He was an important legal theoretician and a liberal member of the Supreme Court (1916–39). Full name **Brandeis, Louis Dembitz**

> 'The federal Constitution is perhaps the greatest of human experiments.'
> [Louis Brandeis. Quoted in *The Words of Justice Brandeis*, Solomon Goldman, ed.; 1953]

AKG London

Brandenburg Gate, Berlin, Germany

Brandenburg Gate /brándən burg-/ *n* a large neoclassical stone gateway in Berlin, a symbol of the city and a focal point for public gatherings

brandied /brándid/ *adj* cooked or preserved in brandy

branding /bránding/ *n* the use of advertising, distinctive design, and other means to make consumers associate a specific product with a specific manufacturer

branding iron *n* an iron tool that is heated and pressed onto a surface, especially an animal's hide, in order to leave a permanent identifying mark

brandish /brándish/ (**-dishes, -dishing, -dished**) *vt* to wave something about, especially a weapon, in a menacing, theatrical, or triumphant way [14C. < French *brandiss-*, stem of *brandir* < *brand* 'sword'] —**brandisher** *n*

brand leader *n* the best-selling product in a particular category

brandling /brándling/ *n* a small reddish-brown earthworm that is often used as bait by anglers. Latin name: *Eisenia foetida*. [Mid-17C. Because of its colouring, like a burning brand]

brand loyalty *n* the tendency to buy a particular brand of a product

brand name *n* a trade name for a product or service produced by a particular company. It may or may not be a registered trademark. ○ *A computer with a brand name can cost 10 per cent more.* —**brand-named** *adj*

brand-new *adj* completely new and unused [As if newly made in a furnace]

Marlon Brando

Brando /brándō/, **Marlon** (*b.* 1924) US actor. His numerous Hollywood films include *A Streetcar Named Desire* (1951) and *The Godfather* (1972).

Brandt /brant/, **Bill** (1904–83) German-born British photographer. The United Kingdom's foremost social documentary photographer, he worked for the *Picture Post* and photographed the London Blitz during World War II. Full name **Brandt, William**

Brandt, Willy (1913–92) German politician. He was mayor of West Berlin (1957–66) and was elected Chancellor of the Federal Republic of Germany in 1969. His pursuit of reconciliation between East and West earned him the Nobel Peace Prize (1971). Born **Frahm, Herbert Ernst Karl**

'A Europe living in peace calls for its members to be willing to listen to the arguments of the others, for the struggle of convictions and interests will continue. Europe needs tolerance. It needs freedom of thought, not moral indifference.'
[Willy Brandt, *Address given on the presentation of a Nobel Peace Prize*; 11 December 1971]

brandy /brándi/ *n* a spirit that is distilled from the fermented juice of grapes or other fruit [Early 17C. Shortening of *brandy-wine* < Dutch *brandewijn* 'burnt (i.e. distilled) wine']

brandy Alexander *n* a cocktail with a base of brandy

brandy butter *n UK* a creamed mixture of butter, sugar, and brandy, traditionally served with Christmas pudding. ANZ, N Am term **hard sauce**

brandy snap *n* a sweet crisp biscuit with a thin lacy texture that is rolled into a cylinder and often filled with cream

brane /brayn/ *n* a spatial dimension in space–time arising out of string theory [Late 20C. Shortening of MEMBRANE]

branks /brangks/ *npl* a device consisting of a metal frame for the head and a bit to restrain the tongue, formerly used to restrain and punish women thought to be quarrelsome or nagging [Mid-16C. Origin ?]

Branson /bránss'n/, **Richard** (b. 1950) British entrepreneur. Under the Virgin corporate umbrella he developed business interests in music retailing, broadcasting, and transportation. Full name **Branson, Richard Charles Nicholas**

'Develop the business around the people; build it, don't buy it; and, then, be the best.'
[Richard Branson, *Speech to the Institute of Directors, London*; May 1993]

brant /brant/ (*plural* **brants** or *same*) *n N Am* BIRDS same as **brent goose** [14C. Variant of BRENT GOOSE]

Brantôme /braaN tŏm/, **Pierre de Bourdeille, Seigneur de** (1540–1614) French writer and courtier. Chamberlain to Charles IX and Henry III of France, he wrote scandalous accounts of the Valois court.

bran tub *n* a tub or barrel containing bran in which small wrapped gifts are hidden at parties or fairs, to be pulled out by people in a game of lucky dip

Braque /braak, brak/, **Georges** (1882–1963) French painter. He was one of the founders, with Pablo Picasso, of the cubist movement.

'There is only one thing in art that has value: that which one cannot explain.'
[Georges Braque. Quoted in 'Late Lyrics: Braque', *Art in America*, Jed Perl; 1983]

brash[1] /brash/ *adj* self-assertive in an aggressive or rude way [Early 19C. Origin ?] —**brashly** *adv* —**brashness** *n*

brash[2] /brash/ *adj* describes wood that is easily cracked or broken (*technical*) [Mid-16C. Origin ?]

brash[3] /brash/ *n* MED same as **heartburn** [Early 19C. Origin ?]

brash[4] /brash/ *n* a pile of loose rubbish, e.g. broken rock or garden refuse [Late 18C. Origin ?]

brashy /bráshi/ (**-ier, -iest**) *adj* **1.** loosely broken or fragmented ○ *soft brashy ice* **2.** easily cracked or broken

Brasília /brə zílyə/ city and capital of Brazil. A relatively new city, laid out on an uninhabited site in 1957, it is in the Federal District, east-central Brazil. Population: 2,051,146 (2000).

Braşov /brásh ov/ city and capital of Braşov County, central Romania. It is situated in a steep-sided valley at the foot of the Transylvanian Alps. Population: 319,908 (1997).

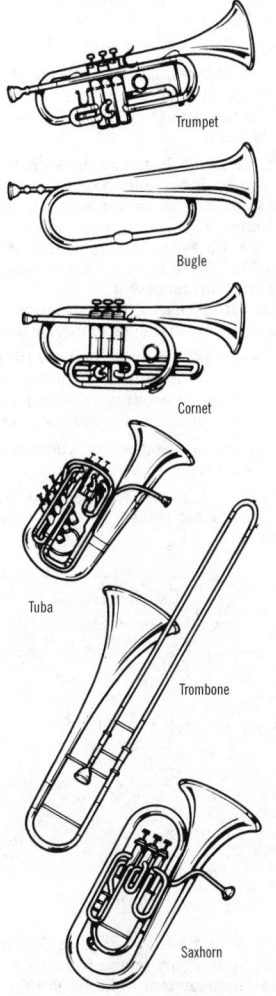

brass: brass musical instruments

(Labels on illustration: Trumpet, Bugle, Cornet, Tuba, Trombone, Saxhorn*)*

brass /braass/ *n* **1.** YELLOW ALLOY a hard yellow shiny metal that is an alloy of zinc and copper, frequently with the addition of other metallic elements to impart specific properties ○ *candlesticks made of brass* **2.** ITEMS MADE OF BRASS a collection of ornaments or items made of brass ○ *clean the brass* **3.** ITEM MADE OF BRASS an ornament or item made of brass (*usually used in the plural*) ○ *horse brasses* **4.** ENGRAVED PLATE OF BRASS an engraved plaque or tablet made of brass, especially one set into the floor or wall of a church **5.** MUSIC BRASS MUSICAL INSTRUMENTS musical instruments made of brass such as trumpets and trombones, considered as a group **6.** MUSIC PLAYERS OF BRASS INSTRUMENTS the players of brass instruments, especially when considered as one of the four main sections of an orchestra **7.** MIL HIGH-RANKING OFFICERS high-ranking officers, especially in the military (*informal*) **8.** MECH ENG RENEWABLE LINER FOR BEARING a renewable brass or bronze liner for a bearing **9.** EXCESSIVE SELF-ASSURANCE extreme and usually excessive self-confidence (*informal*) ○ *He had the brass to lie about every aspect of his background.* **10.** N England MONEY money or cash (*informal*) ○ *Where there's muck, there's brass.* [Old English *bræs*, origin ?]

Brassaï /bra sí/ (1899–1984) Hungarian-born French photographer. His photographs documenting Parisian nightlife in the 1930s were published as *Paris by Night* (1933). Pseudonym of **Halasz, Gyula**

'...there is only one criterion for a good photograph: that it be unforgettable.'
[Brassaï. Quoted in 'Guest Speaker: Brassaï. The Three Faces of Paris', *Architectural Digest*, Avis Berman; July 1984]

brass band *n* a band consisting of brass wind instruments and sometimes percussion instruments

brassbound /braass bownd/ *adj* **1.** trimmed or banded with brass or a similar metal **2.** unreasonably inflexible in manner or character

brassed off /braast-/ *adj* feeling irritated and disappointed (*dated informal*)

brasserie /brásseri/ *n* a restaurant serving a wide range of food and drinks [Mid-19C. < French, 'brewery' < Old French *bracier* 'brew' < Latin *brace* 'malt' < Celtic]

brassica /brássikə/ *n* a plant of the mustard family, e.g. cabbage, kale, broccoli, cauliflower, or mustard. Genus: *Brassica*. [Early 19C. Via modern Latin, genus name < Latin, 'cabbage']

brassie /brássi, braássi/ *n* a golf club, classified as a number two wood, that has a brass-plated sole (*informal*)

brassiere /brássi ər, brázzi ər/ *n* CLOTHING same as **bra** [Early 20C. < French, 'bodice' < *bras* 'arm' < Latin *brachium* (see BRACHIUM)]

brass knuckles *npl* N Am same as **knuckle-duster**

brass-monkey weather, **brass monkeys** *n* extremely cold weather (*informal*) [< *cold enough to freeze the balls off a brass monkey*]

brass neck *n* impudence and a lack of respect (*informal*)

brass rubbing *n* **1.** a copy made by putting paper over an engraved plaque or tablet, especially one in a church, and rubbing it with a soft substance such as chalk or graphite **2.** the process of making a brass rubbing

brass tacks *npl* the most basic or fundamental parts of a situation or issue (*informal*) ○ *Let's get down to brass tacks.*

brassware /braass wair/ *n* items such as plates and ornaments made from brass

brassy /braássi/ (**-ier, -iest**) *adj* **1.** FLASHY AND VULGAR brightly dressed in a cheap and showy way, and behaving too confidently or noisily **2.** SOUNDING LIKE BRASS INSTRUMENTS dominated by or resembling the sounds of brass musical instruments, and therefore typically short, harsh, and high-pitched ○ *a brassy mixture of reggae, funk, calypso, and jazz* **3.** BRAZENLY OVERBEARING brazen or strident in style ○ *a brassy management approach* **4.** OF BRASS made of or containing brass **5.** GOLDEN-YELLOW golden-yellow in colour —**brassily** *adv* —**brassiness** *n*

brat /brat/ *n* somebody, especially a child, who is regarded as tiresomely demanding and selfish in a childish way [Mid-16C. Origin ?] —**brattish** *adj* —**bratty** *adj*

Bratby /brátbi/, **John** (1928–92) British painter. He was an exponent of 'kitchen sink' realism in the 1950s, using thick paint and heavy brushstrokes.

Bratislava /brátti sláavə/ capital and largest city of Slovakia. It lies on the River Danube in the southwest of the country, about 56 km/35 mi. east of Vienna. Population: 449,547 (1999).

brat pack *n* a group of successful or affluent young people, especially actors (*informal*) [After RAT PACK]

Bratsk /braatsk/ town in Siberia, eastern Russia, developed as a home for employees of the Bratsk Dam hydroelectric plant on the Angara River. Population: 301,742 (1995).

Brattain /brátt'n/, **Walter H.** (1902–87) Chinese-born US physicist. He shared a Nobel Prize in physics (1956) for his research on transistors and semiconductors. Full name **Brattain, Walter Houser**

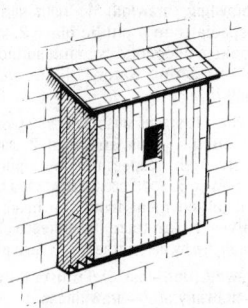

brattice (sense 2)

brattice /bráttiss/ *n* **1.** a partition used to assist ventilation in a mine **2.** in medieval times, a temporary wooden parapet or gallery erected on the battlements of a fortress and used during a siege [13C.

Via Anglo-Norman, Old French *bretesche* < medieval Latin *bretescha (turris)* 'British (tower)']

bratwurst /brát vurst/ *n* a highly seasoned fresh German sausage made of pork or of pork and veal [Early 20C. < German, 'frying-sausage']

Braun ◆ von Braun, Wernher

brava /braa vaa/ *interj, n* a cry of approval for a woman or girl performer by members of a theatre audience [Early 19C. < Italian, 'excellent']

bravado /brə vaadō/ *n* a real or pretended display of courage or boldness ○ *set out to travel the world with more bravado than common sense* [Late 16C. Alteration of Spanish *bravada* < *bravo* (see BRAVE)]

brave /brayv/ *adj* (**braver, bravest**) HAVING OR SHOWING COURAGE having or showing courage, especially when facing danger, difficulty, or pain ■ *n* NATIVE N AMERICAN WARRIOR a Native North American warrior (*dated*) ■ *npl* BRAVE PEOPLE those people who are courageous ■ *vt* (**braves, braving, braved**) 1. FACE ONSLAUGHT OF SOMETHING to face the onslaught of something unpleasant with courage and resolution 2. CHALLENGE SOMETHING to defy something despite there being only a small chance of being victorious [15C. Via French < Italian *bravo* 'bold' or Spanish *bravo* 'brave, savage', < Latin *barbarus* (see BARBAROUS)] —**bravely** *adv* —**braveness** *n*

brave out *vt* to live through something that is difficult or unpleasant

brave new world *n* the world of the future, usually either a technology-based utopia or a sinister totalitarian world devoid of human values (*often ironic*) [Mid-20C. < *Brave New World* (1932), novel by Aldous HUXLEY]

CULTURAL NOTE *Brave New World*, a novel (1932) by Aldous Huxley. Written partly as a response to more utopian writers of the day, it depicts a bleak and sterile future civilization in which feelings are stimulated by drugs, and babies are bred in factories.

bravery /bráyvəri/ *n* courage in the face of danger, difficulty, or pain [Mid-16C. < French *braverie* or Italian *braveria*, both < Italian *bravo* 'bold']

SYNONYMS See *courage*.

bravissimo /braa víssimō/ *interj* used as a cry of great and enthusiastic approval by members of a theatre audience (*formal*) [Mid-18C. < Italian, 'most excellent']

bravo /braávō, braa vṓ/ *interj* AUDIENCE'S SHOUT OF APPROVAL used as a cry of approval by members of a theatre audience ■ *n* (*plural* **-vos**) 1. SHOUT OF 'BRAVO' a cry of 'bravo' to express approval 2. ASSASSIN a hired assassin (*archaic*) [Mid-18C. < Italian, 'excellent']

Bravo *n* a code word for the letter 'B', used in international radio communications

bravura /brə vyoórə/ *n* 1. great skill that is shown when something artistic is done in an exciting or innovative way (*often used before a noun*) ○ *a bravura performance* 2. showy style or behaviour [Mid-18C. < Italian, 'courage, spirit' < *bravo* 'bold']

braw /braw/ *adj Scotland* excellent, attractive, or pleasant [Late 16C. Variant of BRAVE]

brawl /brawl/ *n* 1. NOISY FIGHT a noisy fight, especially in a public place 2. DEEP LOUD SOUND a deep loud roaring sound, especially the sound of rushing water 3. *N Am* LOUD PARTY a noisy boisterous party (*slang*) ■ *vi* (**brawls, brawling, brawled**) 1. FIGHT NOISILY to fight noisily, especially in a public place 2. MAKE DEEP LOUD SOUND to make a deep loud roaring sound, especially the sound of rushing water [14C. Origin ?] —**brawler** *n* —**brawling** *n*

brawn /brawn/ *n* 1. STRONG MUSCLES very strong muscles, especially on the arms and legs 2. BODILY STRENGTH physical strength, especially as opposed to intellectual power 3. FOOD COOKED MEAT FROM ANIMALS' HEADS boiled and jellied meat from the head and feet of pigs or calves. *N Am* term **headcheese** [14C. < Anglo-Norman *braun* 'fleshy part of the leg' < Germanic]

brawny /bráwni/ (**-ier, -iest**) *adj* muscular and strong-looking —**brawnily** *adv* —**brawniness** *n*

bray[1] /bray/ (**brays, braying, brayed**) *v* 1. *vi* to make the sound a donkey makes 2. *vti* to speak, laugh, or say something in a harsh high-pitched rasping voice [13C. < Old French *braire* 'to cry'] —**bray** *n* —**brayer** *n*

bray[2] /bray/ (**brays, braying, brayed**) *vt* 1. to crush something to a fine powder or consistency 2. to spread

ink in a thin layer on a surface [14C. < Anglo-Norman *braier, brei* < Germanic]

Braz. *abbr* 1. Brazil 2. Brazilian

braze /brayz/ (**brazes, brazing, brazed**) *vt* to join two pieces of metal together with a solder that has a high melting point [Mid-16C. < Old French *braser* 'to burn'] —**brazer** *n*

brazen /bráyz'n/ *adj* 1. BOLD AND UNASHAMED showing or expressing boldness and a complete lack of shame 2. HARSH-SOUNDING with an unpleasantly loud and resonant sound 3. OF OR LIKE BRASS made of brass or resembling it, especially in colour or hardness (*literary*) [Old English *bræsen* 'made of brass' < BRASS] —**brazenly** *adv* —**brazenness** *n*

brazen out *vt* to face a difficult situation confidently, without showing shame or embarrassment

brazier[1] /bráyzi ər/ *n* a metal drum with holes in it, used outdoors as a container for burning coal or charcoal, either for cooking or to keep people warm [Late 17C. < French *brasier* < *braise* 'hot coals']

brazier[2] /bráyzi ər/ *n* somebody who works on brass articles [14C. Probably < BRASS, after GLAZIER]

brazil /brə zíl/ *n* 1. INDUST same as **brazilwood** 2. FOOD same as **Brazil nut** (sense 1) [14C. < medieval Latin *brasilium*]

Brazil

Brazil /brə zíl/ largest country in South America. Colonized by the Portuguese from 1500 onwards, it became an independent republic in 1889. Language: Portuguese. Currency: real. Capital: Brasília. Population: 182,032,600 (2003). Area: 8,547,404 sq. km/3,300,171 sq. mi. Official name **Federative Republic of Brazil** —**Brazilian** *n, adj*

Brazil Basin basin of the Atlantic Ocean on the western side of the Mid-Atlantic Ridge. Depth: 5,000 m/16,400 ft.

Brazil nut *n* 1. a long thick edible seed with a hard shell that is nearly triangular in cross section, borne in clusters inside large round capsules 2. an evergreen tree that bears Brazil nuts. Native to: tropical southern America. Latin name: *Bertholletia excelsa*.

brazilwood /brə zíl woŏd/ *n* red wood from various tropical and North American trees, especially a tree native to Brazil. Use: manufacture of red dyes, violin bows.

Brazzaville /brázzə vil/ capital city of the Republic of the Congo and a major port on the Congo River. It was founded in 1880 by the French explorer Pierre Savorgnan de Brazza (1852–1905). Population: 1,187,000 (1999).

BRCS *abbr* British Red Cross Society

BRE *abbr* 1. Bachelor of Religious Education 2. Building Research Establishment

breach /breech/ *n* 1. FAILURE TO MAINTAIN SOMETHING a failure to obey, keep, or preserve something such as a law, trust, or promise ○ *a breach of confidentiality* 2. ESTRANGEMENT a breakdown in friendly relations 3. HOLE a hole in something that is caused by something else forcing its way through 4. GAP a gap that results when somebody or something leaves 5. WHALE'S LEAP a leap out of the water by a whale ■ *v* (**breaches, breaching, breached**) 1. *vt* BREAK LAW OR PROMISE to fail to obey, keep, or preserve something such as a law, trust, or promise 2. *vt* MAKE OPENING THROUGH SOMETHING to break down an obstruction to allow something to pass through it 3. *vt* SURPASS LIMIT to go beyond a target or limit ○ *a proposal to breach the budgetary limit* 4. *vti* LEAP OUT

to leap out of the water (*refers to whales*) [13C. < Old French *breche* < Germanic] —**breachable** *adj*

SPELLCHECK *breach* or *breech*? Do not confuse the spelling of *breach* and *breech*, which sound similar. *Breach* is a noun or verb referring to an opening or the breaking of something, as in *step into the breach*, *a breach of the peace*, *to breach their defences*. *Breech* is a noun denoting the rear part of a gun barrel or of the body, for example, in *a breech birth*.

breach of promise *n* a failure to fulfil a promise, especially formerly the breaking of a promise to marry somebody

breach of the peace *n* the criminal offence of behaving in a noisy and violent way in public

bread /bred/ *n* 1. FOOD MADE FROM FLOUR AND WATER a food typically made by mixing flour, water, and yeast and allowing it to swell before baking it 2. MEANS OF SURVIVAL food, sustenance, or a means of survival or support 3. MONEY money to live on (*dated slang*) [Old English *brēad*, origin ?] ◇ **cast your bread upon the waters** to spend time and effort, especially to help others, without expecting any immediate advantage for yourself (*literary*) ◇ **know which side your bread is buttered (on)** to know what is to your advantage (*informal*)

SPELLCHECK *bread* or *bred*? Do not confuse the spelling of *bread* and *bred* (past tense and past participle of *breed*), which sound similar.

bread and butter *n* 1. a dependable source of income 2. something that is the essential or sustaining part of something else

bread-and-butter *adj* 1. concerned with basic but important things 2. providing the main source of somebody's income or livelihood ○ *a bread-and-butter job*

bread-and-butter letter *n* a letter or note expressing thanks for somebody's hospitality

bread-and-butter pudding *n* FOOD a baked pudding that is made from buttered bread layered in a dish with dried fruit and covered in a mixture of egg, sugar, milk, and spices. N Am term **bread pudding**

bread and circuses *npl* something done or given to keep people happy, especially something provided or encouraged by governments to win popular appeal or avert public unrest [Translation of Latin *panis et circenses*]

breadbasket /bréd baaskit/ *n* 1. an important grower of cereal crops 2. the stomach or abdomen (*dated slang*)

bread bin *n* HOUSEHOLD a container for storing bread. N Am term **breadbox**

breadboard /bréd bawrd/ *n* 1. BOARD FOR CUTTING BREAD ON a board for cutting or kneading bread on 2. ELEC ENG TEST VERSION OF ELECTRICAL CIRCUIT a preliminary version of an electrical or electronic circuit put together for test purposes ■ *vt* (**-boards, -boarding, -boarded**) ELEC ENG MAKE TEST VERSION OF CIRCUIT to make a preliminary version of an electrical or electronic circuit for test purposes

breadbox /bréd boks/ *n N Am* HOUSEHOLD same as **bread bin**

breadcrumb /bréd krum/ *n* a tiny piece of bread, either soft or hard (*often used in the plural*)

breaded /bréddid/ *adj* describes food that is coated in breadcrumbs and fried or baked ○ *breaded chicken fillets*

breadfruit /bréd froot/ *n* (*plural same or* **-fruits**) 1. a large round seedless tropical fruit 2. an evergreen tree that bears breadfruit. Native to: Pacific Islands. Latin name: *Artocarpus altilis*. [Late 17C. Because it has a texture like bread when cooked]

bread knife *n* a knife with a long thin, usually serrated blade, used for cutting bread

breadline /bréd līn/ *n* 1. a very low standard of living, with only just enough food and money to survive ○ *living on the breadline* 2. *N Am* a queue of people waiting for handouts of free food [Originally 'queue of people for unsold bread']

bread mould *n* a fungus that grows on decaying bread and other foods, forming a dense cottony growth. Latin name: *Rhizopus nigricans*.

breadnut /bréd nut/ *n* 1. the large edible seed of a

yellow tropical fruit **2.** a large tree with yellow fruits containing breadnuts. Native to: tropical America. Latin name: *Brosimum alicastrum*.

bread pudding *n* **1.** a rich cake made with ingredients similar to those of bread-and-butter pudding **2.** *N Am* same as **bread-and-butter pudding**

breadroot /bréd root/ *n* **1.** a starchy tuber, formerly used as food by many Native North American peoples **2.** a perennial plant of the pea family that produces breadroot. Native to: North America. Latin name: *Psoralea esculenta*.

bread sauce *n* a milk-based sauce thickened with breadcrumbs and flavoured with onion, traditionally served with poultry

breadth /bredth, bretth/ *n* **1.** DISTANCE FROM SIDE TO SIDE the distance or measurement of something from one side to the other **2.** STANDARD WIDTH OF FABRIC a standardized width that a product, especially fabric, is manufactured in, or a piece of fabric in a standardized width **3.** GREAT EXTENT the extent of something, especially when it is impressively great ○ *the breadth of her knowledge* **4.** BROAD-MINDEDNESS an open and tolerant view of life and the world ○ *breadth of vision* [Early 16C. < obsolete *brede* 'breadth' < Germanic, after LENGTH]

breadthways /brédth wayz/, **breadthwise** /-wīz/ *adv* with the broad side of something facing forwards

breadwinner /bréd winər/ *n* somebody whose earnings are a family's main income

break[1] /brayk/ *v* (**breaks, breaking, broke** /brōk/, **broken** /brōkən/) **1.** *vti* SEPARATE SOMETHING INTO PIECES to become damaged and separate into pieces, or damage something so that it separates into pieces ○ *It broke in two.* **2.** *vti* DAMAGE BODY PART to damage a hard body part such as a bone, or sustain such a break ○ *She broke her leg.* **3.** *vti* DAMAGE PART OF MACHINE to damage a part of a tool or machine so that it stops functioning properly, or become damaged and stop functioning properly ○ *The washing machine is broken.* **4.** *vti* TEAR SURFACE to become torn, or make a tear or hole in a surface or seal, allowing the possibility of a leak or spill ○ *Store the milk in the fridge after breaking open the seal on the bottle.* **5.** *vt* DISOBEY RULE to disobey a rule or law ○ *He's broken the law.* **6.** *vt* GO BACK ON WORD to renege on a promise or agreement ○ *broke her word* **7.** *vt* END BAD SITUATION to end, change, or rectify a difficult or disadvantageous situation ○ *break the deadlock between rival factions* **8.** *vt* END SILENCE to end a period of silence **9.** *vti* FINISH RELATIONSHIP to end an involvement with a person or group **10.** *vt* END SOMETHING to finish something, bring it to an end, or stop somebody doing it ○ *break the coffee-drinking habit* **11.** *vt* INTERRUPT SOMETHING to interrupt something temporarily ○ *The distraction broke her train of thought.* **12.** *vt* RUIN SOMEBODY'S LIFE to destroy somebody's career, resolve, courage, or hope of success ○ *The media can make or break her.* **13.** *vti* ESCAPE to escape from a restraint ○ *break free* **14.** *vi* TAKE PERIOD FOR REST to take a period of leisure ○ *break for lunch* **15.** *vt* STAND BETWEEN PERSON AND SOMETHING to stand in the way of or weaken the force of something such as a fall or blow ○ *He tried to break her fall.* **16.** *vt* BEAT RECORD to beat a previous record **17.** *vt* EXCEED LIMIT to exceed a limit or constraint ○ *break the speed limit* **18.** *vti* REVEAL OR BE REVEALED to reveal something personally, or be revealed, particularly by the media ○ *She broke it to me gently.* ○ *Panic ensued when the news broke.* **19.** *vi* BECOME DEEPER to settle into an adult man's voice register (*refers to a boy's voice*) **20.** *vi* STOP SPEAKING FROM EMOTION to stop speaking and hesitate when overcome with emotion ○ *Her voice broke and tears slid down her face.* **21.** *vi* MUSIC CHANGE TONE WITH REGISTER to change in tone or quality when changing register (*refers to voices or musical instruments*) **22.** *vi* BECOME DAYLIGHT to become light at sunrise **23.** *vi* *US, Carib* MOVE SUDDENLY to move suddenly or quickly towards somebody or something ○ *broke for the nearest shelter from the storm* **24.** *vi* METEOROL CHANGE WEATHER PATTERN to change after a settled period of weather **25.** *vi* METEOROL SUDDENLY START to begin to rain, snow, or hail suddenly **26.** *vi* OCEANOG TURN TO SURF to start collapsing into surf when close to shore or hitting rocks or similar objects (*refers to waves*) **27.** *vt* INTERPRET CODE to understand a code and be able to translate it accurately **28.** *vt* PROVE SOMETHING UNTRUE to prove that something is untrue or wrong ○ *new evidence that broke the defendant's alibi* **29.** *vt* LAW INVALIDATE WILL to use legal means to declare a will invalid **30.** *vt* CRIME BLOW OPEN SAFE to open a safe using explosives **31.** *vt* RIDING TRAIN HORSE TO ACCEPT HARNESS to train a horse to become accustomed to a saddle, bit, and rider **32.** *vt* MONEY SWAP NOTE FOR CHANGE to exchange a note of money for smaller units of money, either coins or smaller notes and coins ○ *break a £20 note* **33.** *vi* MED FLOW OUT IN CHILDBIRTH to flow out when the amniotic sac around an unborn baby breaks during the first stage of labour (*refers to amniotic fluid*) ○ *Her waters have broken.* **34.** *vi* *US* TURN OUT to happen or turn out in a particular way ○ *Things are breaking well.* **35.** *vt* REDUCE TO POVERTY to cause somebody to be extremely poor or bankrupt **36.** *vti* FISH EMERGE OUT OF WATER to emerge or erupt above the surface of a body of water **37.** *vt* MIL DEMOTE SOMEBODY to demote somebody to a lower rank **38.** *vt* ELEC INTERRUPT FLOW OF ELECTRIC CURRENT to interrupt the flow of electricity in an electrical circuit **39.** *vi* FIN FALL SHARPLY to fall in price (*refers to stock exchange quotations*) **40.** *vti* TENNIS WIN GAME OFF OPPONENT'S SERVICE in tennis, to win a game in which the other player is serving **41.** *vi* BOXING, WRESTLING SEPARATE FROM CLINCH to separate after being in a boxing or wrestling clinch **42.** *vi* SPORTS SPEED UP IN RACE to increase speed suddenly in a race **43.** *vi* BASEBALL CHANGE DIRECTION IN AIR to change direction while moving through the air (*refers to a baseball*) **44.** *vi* CRICKET CHANGE DIRECTION ON BOUNCING to change direction after bouncing (*refers to a cricket ball*) **45.** *vt* CRICKET KNOCK OVER WICKET in cricket, to hit and knock over a bail from the wicket **46.** *vi* HORSERACING START OFF IN HORSE RACE in horseracing, to start off at the start of a race **47.** *vi* CUE GAMES TAKE FIRST SHOT in billiards or snooker, to take the opening shot in a game or frame **48.** *vi* PHON BECOME DIPHTHONG to change in pronunciation, becoming a diphthong (*refers to vowels*) **49.** *vt* *Carib* ENTER A PLACE ILLEGALLY to enter a place illegally to steal ○ *They broke two houses last night.* **50.** *vi* *Carib* HAVE ORGASM to have an orgasm (*slang; usually refers to men*) ■ *n* **1.** PERIOD OFF FROM ACTIVITY a period taken away from an activity for a rest, change, or meal ○ *a lunch break* ○ *Let's take a break now.* **2.** BRIEF HOLIDAY a short holiday away from home ○ *a weekend break* ○ *We needed to get away for a short break.* **3.** PERIOD OFF BEFORE CONTINUING a period away from something before continuing it again ○ *a career break* **4.** EDUC TIME OFF IN SCHOOL DAY time off from classes during the school day, when pupils can play or rest. N Am term **recess** **5.** END TO RELATIONSHIP the severance of links with a person or group or an end to a relationship ○ *He wanted to make the break with his partner.* **6.** END an end to something ○ *a break with tradition* **7.** BROADCAST, MARKETING same as **commercial break** **8.** SPORTS INTERVAL IN MATCH an interval in a sports match **9.** PAUSE IN SPEECH a pause when speaking ○ *a break in the conversation* **10.** MED FRACTURE a fracture in a bone **11.** CRACK a crack in something **12.** METEOROL WEATHER CHANGE a change in the weather **13.** LUCKY OPPORTUNITY FOR SUCCESS an unexpected opportunity that allows somebody to achieve something or become successful (*informal*) ○ *He got his first break when he was spotted playing for his college.* **14.** PIECE OF LUCK a piece of good luck or bad luck ○ *a lucky break* ○ *a bad break* **15.** FIN ADVANTAGEOUS FINANCIAL SITUATION an advantageous financial situation in which somebody is repaid or makes a reduced payment ○ *a tax break* **16.** ESCAPE ATTEMPT a sudden attempt to escape ○ *make a break for it* **17.** DISCONTINUITY a discontinuity in something, by which it changes in quality or level **18.** SUNRISE the time when the sun first rises (*literary*) ○ *at the break of day* **19.** TENNIS WINNING OF GAME OFF OPPONENT'S SERVICE in tennis, the winning of a game in which the other player is serving **20.** HORSERACING START OF RACE the start of a horse race **21.** ELEC INTERRUPTION IN FLOW OF ELECTRICITY an interruption in the flow of electricity in an electrical circuit **22.** MUSIC INSTRUMENTAL PART IN SONG an instrumental part in a piece of pop music **23.** MUSIC IMPROVISED JAZZ SOLO an improvised solo part in a piece of jazz music **24.** MUSIC CHANGE IN REGISTER a change in register in a voice or musical instrument **25.** LITERAT same as **caesura** (senses 1–2) **26.** FIN FALL IN PRICES a sudden fall in prices, particularly in a stock market **27.** CUE GAMES SERIES OF SUCCESSFUL SHOTS in billiards or snooker, a sequence of successful shots in one player's turn, or the points scored from them **28.** CUE GAMES FIRST SHOT THAT SCATTERS BALLS in billiards or snooker, an opening shot, which in snooker scatters the balls **29.** BOWLS FAILURE TO KNOCK DOWN ALL PINS a failure to knock down all the pins in ten pin bowling after the second throw **30.** MEDIA ACCESS TO CB RADIO CHANNEL access for a CB radio operator to a radio channel ■ *interj* BOXING, WRESTLING USED TO SEPARATE FIGHTERS used to command boxers or wrestlers to separate from a clinch [Old English *brecan* < Indo-European] ◇ **break even** to make neither a profit nor a loss from a venture ◇ **give somebody a break** to stop nagging or criticizing somebody, or start treating somebody fairly (*informal*) ◇ **if it ain't broke, don't fix it** do not try to improve something that is satisfactory as it is (*informal*) ◇ **make a clean break** to end a relationship or association completely and permanently

---

SPELLCHECK break or brake? Do not confuse the spelling of *break* and *brake*, which sound similar. Both words can be used as nouns or verbs, but *break* has a wider range of meaning and is the more frequent of the two, generally referring to separation, destruction, violation, or interruption, as in *to break a window*, *to break the rules*, *a break for refreshments*. *Brake* means 'a device used to slow or stop a vehicle' or 'apply a brake' and is sometimes used figuratively, as in *put a brake on expenditure*. *Brake* is also another word for bracken or undergrowth.

---

break away *vi* **1.** LEAVE OR GET AWAY to sever relations with or detach from a person or group **2.** DEPART FROM CUSTOM to change or depart from established customs or procedures **3.** PULL AWAY QUICKLY to depart or pull away from somebody or something, usually at high speed **4.** *Carib* BECOME UNCONTROLLABLE to get out of control

break down *v* **1.** *vi* FAIL TO FUNCTION PROPERLY to stop working, or stop working properly, effectively, or usefully **2.** *vt* TEAR DOWN to destroy something, or cause something to fall or collapse **3.** *vti* BECOME OR MAKE EMOTIONAL to become upset emotionally, or cause somebody to become upset emotionally **4.** *vti* EXPERIENCE OR CAUSE HEALTH COLLAPSE to experience, or cause somebody to experience, a physical or psychological collapse **5.** *vti* STOP RESISTING to yield or end any resistance, or cause somebody to yield or somebody's resistance to end **6.** *vti* WEAKEN to become weak and ineffective, or cause somebody or something to become weak and ineffective **7.** *vt* ANALYSE SOMETHING BY DIVIDING INTO PARTS to analyse or examine something by reducing it to its simplest terms or component parts **8.** *vi* BE DIVISIBLE INTO ELEMENTS to divide into separate parts when analysed, or be reducible to separate parts **9.** *vti* DECOMPOSE CHEMICALLY to decompose chemically, or cause something to undergo chemical decomposition **10.** *vi* ELEC ENG EXPERIENCE ELECTRICAL INSULATION FAILURE to experience a sudden failure of an insulating material to halt the current flow

break in *v* **1.** *vi* ENTER FORCIBLY to enter a place or building forcibly and usually illegally **2.** *vi* START TALKING to interrupt a conversation or discussion **3.** *vt* BEGIN USING SOMEBODY OR SOMETHING NEW to begin to employ somebody new, supplying the training needed for good performance, or use something new, providing necessary modifications ○ *breaking the new assistant in gently*

break into *vt* **1.** ENTER BUILDING FORCIBLY to enter a building forcibly and usually illegally **2.** INTERRUPT CONVERSATION to interrupt something that is being said or discussed **3.** DO SOMETHING SUDDENLY to begin an act or activity suddenly ○ *broke into song* ○ *broke into a run* **4.** START WORK IN NEW FIELD to begin working in a profession or field, often after having tried to do so for some time without success ○ *break into television*

break off *v* **1.** *vt* TAKE OFF PIECE OF SOMETHING to separate a piece from a solid mass or the main part of something **2.** *vti* END RELATIONSHIP OR JOINT ACTIVITY to discontinue a relationship or interaction with a person or group **3.** *vi* STOP SPEAKING to stop talking, usually abruptly

break out *v* **1.** *vi* BEGIN ABRUPTLY to happen or begin suddenly and strongly **2.** *vi* HAVE SKIN RASH to develop skin blemishes or a rash, especially suddenly **3.** *vi* BECOME FREE FROM SOMETHING to escape or emerge from something such as a prison that confines, restrains, or traps **4.** *vt* PREPARE SOMETHING FOR USE to open something or get something ready for use or action ○ *broke out the emergency rations* **5.** *vt* CLASSIFY DATA ITEMS to classify, summarize, outline, or separate data items in order to analyse, explain, or identify something

break through *vti* to burst or advance quickly and suddenly through an obstruction or opposition

break up *v* **1.** *vt* DIVIDE OR INTERRUPT SOMETHING to divide

or separate something into pieces, or interrupt its continuity **2.** *vti* END to cause a relationship, interaction, or gathering to end, or come to an end **3.** *vi* DISPERSE to separate and go in different directions, or have members separate **4.** *vti* CAUSE EMOTIONAL RESPONSE to burst into tears or laughter, or cause somebody to burst into tears or laughter **5.** *vi* TELECOM LOSE PHONE COMMUNICATION to start to lose clear communication when using a mobile phone ○ *You're breaking up.*
break with *vt* to separate from somebody or from a tradition, rule, or trend

break² /brayk/ *n* TRANSP another spelling of **brake**⁶

breakable /bráykəb'l/ *adj* likely to be broken if not handled carefully ■ *n* something that is easily broken if not handled carefully (*usually used in the plural*)

breakage /bráykij/ *n* **1.** something that has been broken, usually accidentally (*usually used in the plural*) ○ *All breakages must be paid for.* **2.** the act of breaking something

breakaway /bráykə way/ *n* **1.** SOMETHING BREAKING OFF somebody or something that breaks away or has broken away **2.** SOMETHING MADE TO BREAK OFF something that is designed to break away or break apart from the whole **3.** ACT OF BREAKING AWAY the breaking away of somebody or something **4.** SPORTS QUICK SURGE FORWARD in sports, a sudden attack or movement away from the rest of a group of players or competitors **5.** *Carib* DANCE STYLE a lively style of dancing **6.** *Carib* DANCE MUSIC the music for breakaway dancing, usually calypso ■ *adj* **1.** MADE TO BREAK OFF designed to break away or apart, either as a safety mechanism or to create an illusion **2.** HAVING SEVERED TIES having broken ties or connections to somebody or a group ■ *vi Carib* DANCE WITH INDIVIDUAL STYLE to dance to a section of music that has heavy rhythm and brass, especially with individually improvised movements

breakbeat /bráyk beet/ *n* a drum pattern with a syncopated beat that is electronically looped, used mostly in jungle, drum and bass, and hard-core music

breakbone fever /bráyk bōn-/ *n* MED same as **dengue**

breakdancing /bráyk daanssing/ *n* an acrobatic style of solo dancing to rap music, typically involving spinning of the body on the ground. Breakdancing started in the United States in the 1980s. [Late 20C. Perhaps related to BREAKDOWN 'fast dance'] —**breakdance** *n, vi* —**breakdancer** *n*

breakdown /bráyk down/ *n* **1.** FAILURE TO OPERATE a failure to operate, or an interruption of the operation of a machine or vehicle **2.** DISRUPTION IN COMMUNICATIONS a disruption of the understanding and interaction between people or groups ○ *the breakdown in the talks* **3.** MED PERSONAL HEALTH CRISIS a sudden physical or psychological collapse **4.** DATA SUMMARY OR EXPLANATION a summary, explanation, or analysis of data items collected **5.** TIME WHEN CAR OR MACHINERY FAILS an incident involving a car or piece of machinery stopping working **6.** DECOMPOSITION INTO PARTS a breaking down of something into its essential components or parts **7.** ELEC ENG SUDDEN PASSAGE OF CURRENT THROUGH INSULATOR the sudden passage of electrical current through an insulator **8.** DANCE COUNTRY DANCE a fast US country dance

breakdown lorry, **breakdown truck** *n UK* a lorry that tows a vehicle that has broken down to a garage where it can be repaired. ANZ term **tow truck**. N Am term **wrecker**

breakdown voltage *n* the voltage at which a sudden and large increase in current through an insulator or semiconductor happens

breaker¹ /bráykər/ *n* **1.** LARGE WHITE-CAPPED WAVE a large, usually white-capped, wave that is cresting or breaking, especially onto a shore **2.** ELEC ENG same as **circuit breaker 3.** BREAKDANCER somebody who does breakdancing (*slang*) **4.** BREAKING MACHINE something that is used to crush or break up rocks, fibres, or other substances **5.** HORSE TRAINER somebody who trains horses to be ridden ■ *interj* OPENING MESSAGE OF RADIO TRANSMISSION used by CB radio operators to announce that they are beginning to transmit on a channel [12C. < BREAK¹]

CULTURAL NOTE *Breaker Morant*, a film (1979) by Australian film-maker Bruce Beresford. It is based on the true story of Australian soldier and poet, Breaker Morant, who was court-martialled and executed by the British Army in South Africa, an event that aroused strong anti-British feeling in Australia.

breaker² /bráykər/ *n* a small cask for water, used especially on a lifeboat [Mid-19C. < Spanish *barrica* 'cask']

breakeven /bráyk éev'n/, **breakeven point** *n* the point or level of financial activity at which expenditure equals income or the value of an investment equals its cost, with the result that there is neither a profit nor a loss

breakfast /brékfəst/ *n* the first meal of the day, usually eaten in the morning (*often used before a noun*) [15C. < BREAK¹ + FAST²] —**breakfast** *vi* —**breakfaster** *n* ◇ **eat** *or* **have somebody for breakfast** to defeat or destroy somebody without any difficulty whatsoever (*slang*) ○ *The tabloid media will eat the movie star for breakfast over this revelation.*

breakfast bar *n* **1.** a breakfast served buffet style in a hotel or restaurant with a variety of foods from which to choose **2.** a counter in a kitchen at which informal meals and snacks are served

breakfast shed *n Carib* **1.** a building where schools or charities supply meals at very low cost, usually for children **2.** a restaurant that serves creole and local food, where customers choose which food they want from a number of cooks who share the premises

breakfast television *n* informal, magazine-style television programmes broadcast in the morning

breakfront /bráyk frunt/ *adj* describes a piece of furniture such as a cabinet or bookcase with a central section that juts forward slightly —**breakfront** *n*

break-in *n* an illegal forced entry into a building or enclosed place

breaking /bráyking/ *n* **1.** the changing of a simple vowel into a diphthong when some other speech sounds come before or after it. For example the vowel in 'feet' becomes a diphthong in 'feel'. **2.** DANCE same as **breakdancing** (*slang*)

breaking and entering *n* the crime of forcibly entering property, usually in order to steal from it

breaking point *n* **1.** the point at which somebody loses the ability to deal physically, psychologically, or emotionally with a stressful situation **2.** the point at which a condition or situation reaches a crisis

breakneck /bráyk nek/ *adj* so fast or quick as to be hazardous or reckless ○ *at breakneck speed*

break of day *n* the time when the sun rises in the morning

breakoff /bráyk of/ *n* a discontinuation of something, especially when this is abrupt ○ *the breakoff of negotiations*

breakout /bráyk owt/ *n* a forceful escape or emergence from being confined, restrained, or trapped

break point *n* in tennis, a point that, if won, results in the player who is not serving winning the game

breakpoint /bráyk poynt/ *n* **1.** a point where something stops, pauses, changes, or breaks apart **2.** a pause inserted into a computer program so that the registers and memory locations can be examined to correct a programming logic error

breakthrough /bráyk throo/ *n* **1.** IMPORTANT DISCOVERY an important new discovery, especially in science, medicine, or technology, that has a dramatic and far-reaching effect **2.** REMOVAL OF BARRIER TO PROGRESS an event that causes or marks the breaking down of a barrier to progress **3.** MIL PENETRATION OF ENEMY LINE an attacking army's advance through and beyond an enemy's line of defence ■ *adj* BRINGING PUBLIC RECOGNITION bringing public attention and fame to a performing artist

breakthrough bleeding *n* bleeding from the womb that occurs between menstrual periods

breakup /bráyk up/ *n* **1.** BREAKING APART OR UP the separation of something such as a company or country into separate units ○ *the breakup of the Soviet Union* **2.** END OF RELATIONSHIP the breaking off or discontinuation of a personal relationship **3.** SPRING THAW OF LODGED ICE the melting or breaking apart of

lodged ice in rivers and harbours in the spring **4.** EMOTIONAL BREAKDOWN a loss of control over the emotions

breakup value *n* the amount that a company would be worth if it were liquidated for its assets. It is sometimes expressed as an amount per share.

breakwater /bráyk wawtər/ *n* an offshore barrier that protects a harbour or other coastal area from the full force of the sea

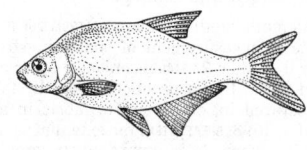

bream

bream¹ /breem/ (*plural same* or **breams**) *n* **1.** THIN-BODIED FRESHWATER FISH a freshwater fish that has a deep thin body and is yellowish in colour. Native to: Europe, Asia. Latin name: *Abramis brama.* **2.** FRESHWATER FISH LIKE BREAM a freshwater fish that resembles the bream. Native to: North America, introduced into Europe and Asia. Genus: *Lepomis.* **3.** FISH same as **sea bream 4.** FOOD the flesh of a bream as food [14C. < Old French *bre(s)me* < Germanic]

bream² /breem/ (**breams**, **breaming**, **breamed**) *vt* to scrape the shells, seaweed, and mud off the bottom of a boat (*archaic*) [Early 17C. Probably < Middle Dutch *bremme* 'broom, furze']

Bream /breem/, **Julian** (b. 1933) British guitarist and lutenist. He studied under Andrés Segovia. Full name **Bream, Julian Alexander**

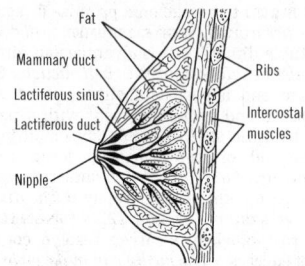

breast: cross-section of female breast

breast /brest/ *n* **1.** ORGAN ON CHEST either of two soft rounded organs on each side of the chest in women and men. In women the organs are more prominent and produce milk after childbirth. **2.** ZOOL MAMMAL'S MILK GLAND a milk-producing gland in mammals that corresponds to the human breast **3.** SOMEBODY'S CHEST the front of the human chest **4.** CLOTHING GARMENT SECTION the part or section of clothing covering the front of the chest **5.** ZOOL ANIMAL'S CHEST the chest of an animal, especially a mammal or bird **6.** FOOD MEAT FROM ANIMAL'S CHEST meat from the chest of an animal, especially from a chicken or other poultry **7.** ROUNDED PART a part that is rounded or projecting, or in some way resembles a breast ○ *the breast of a hill* **8.** SEAT OF EMOTIONS the chest regarded as the place where human emotions reside (*literary*) ○ *with pride filling my breast* **9.** FONT OF NOURISHMENT a source of sustenance or protection (*literary*) ■ *vt* (**breasts**, **breasting**, **breasted**) **1.** PUSH SOMETHING WITH CHEST to touch or push against something with the chest ○ *She breasted the tape just seconds ahead of the next runner.* **2.** REACH HILLTOP to reach the summit of a hill **3.** FACE SOMETHING BOLDLY to confront a difficulty squarely and boldly and deal with it in a determined way [Old English *brēost* < Germanic, perhaps < Indo-European, 'swelling'] ◇ **make a clean breast of something** to confess or admit to something, especially something previously denied or withheld

breastbone /brést bōn/ *n* a long bone running down the front of the chest, flat in many animals but ridged in most birds. In humans, the top seven pairs of ribs are connected to it.

breast-feed *vti* to feed a baby by holding it so that it can suck milk from the breast (*refers to women*)

breastplate /brést playt/ *n* **1.** a piece of armour that covers the chest **2.** a garment worn over the breast by Jewish high priests in ancient times, set with 12 precious stones representing the 12 tribes of Israel

breaststroke /brést strōk/ *n* a swimming stroke in which both arms are extended and pulled back together in a circular motion while both legs are thrust out and pulled back together —**breaststroke** *vi* —**breaststroker** *n*

breastwork /brést wurk/ *n* formerly, an earth wall built at chest height as a temporary barrier for defence

breath /breth/ *n* **1.** AIR BREATHED IN AND OUT the air that a person or animal inhales and exhales **2.** AIR EXHALED the air that somebody exhales, especially with reference to how it feels or smells to somebody nearby **3.** BREATHING OF AIR an inhaling or exhaling of air ○ *take a deep breath* **4.** HINT a faint hint of something ○ *a breath of scandal* **5.** LIFE the vital force or spirit of a living person or animal **6.** SHORT PAUSE a momentary pause or respite **7.** WAFT a fleeting or slight fragrance or movement of air ○ *not a breath of wind* **8.** SOFT SOUND a sound or whispering that is soft and almost inaudible [Old English *bræþ* 'odour, especially of something burning or cooking' < Indo-European, 'heat'] ◇ **a breath of fresh air** somebody or something that is refreshingly new and exciting ◇ **catch your breath 1.** to stop breathing for an instant, especially because of shock or physical pain **2.** to regain a normal breathing rhythm after exertion ◇ **don't hold your breath** used to indicate that it is extremely unlikely that something will happen (*informal*) ◇ **in the same breath** at the same time or shortly afterwards ◇ **out of breath** breathing heavily because of physical exertion ◇ **take somebody's breath away** to astonish or greatly impress somebody ◇ **under your breath** in a whispering or muttering voice ◇ **with bated breath** full of anxious anticipation

USAGE breath or breathe? The noun is **breath** (*not a breath of air moving*), and the verb is **breathe** (*hard to breathe in the sultry air*). Only the verb has the *-e* at the end.

breathable /breéthəb'l/ *adj* **1.** suitable or possible for people to breathe **2.** describes fabric that allows air in and body moisture out in order to keep the wearer cool and dry

breathalyse /bréthə līz/ (**-lyses, -lysing, -lysed**) *vt* to test somebody, especially a driver, for alcohol consumption by making him or her breathe into a Breathalyzer™ [Mid-20C. Back-formation < BREATHA-LYSER]

breathalyser /bréthə līzər/ *n* an apparatus that measures the concentration of alcohol in the breath exhaled by a person, which is related to the level in the bloodstream [Mid-20C. < BREATH + analyser]

Breathalyzer /bréthə līzər/ *tdmk US* a trademark for a breathalyser

breathe /breeth/ (**breathes, breathing, breathed**) *v* **1.** *vti* TAKE IN AIR to repeatedly and alternately take in and blow out air in order to stay alive ○ *breathe in deeply* **2.** *vt* EXPEL SUBSTANCE WITH BREATH to expel fire, smoke, or other gas from the mouth or nose along with the breath, or be exhaled in this way ○ *a dragon breathing fire* **3.** *vt* SMELL SOMETHING to take in the aroma of something **4.** *vti* TAKE IN AIR to take in air, e.g. for combustion or in order to equalize internal and external pressure (*refers to machines*) **5.** *vi* TEXTILES ALLOW AIR THROUGH to allow air and moisture to pass through fabric or clothing **6.** *vt* SAY SOMETHING SECRETIVELY to say something in a soft voice or secretively **7.** *vt* GIVE SOMEBODY OR SOMETHING QUALITY to instil a particular quality in somebody or something ○ *breathed new life into the group* **8.** *vti* EXUDE QUALITY to suggest a quality in abundance, or be suggested or displayed noticeably **9.** *vi* LIVE to be alive **10.** *vi* DEVELOP FLAVOUR THROUGH EXPOSURE TO AIR to be exposed to air in order to develop flavour (*refers to wine*) **11.** *vti* PAUSE TO REST to give a person or an animal such as a horse time to rest and allow a normal breathing rhythm to be restored **12.** *vi* WAFT

GENTLY to blow softly or move gently [13C. < BREATH] ◇ **breathe easy** *or* **easily** to relax and stop worrying about something or things in general

USAGE See breath.

breathed /bretht, breéthd/ *adj* **1.** pronounced without vibrating the vocal cords **2.** with a particular type of breathing (*usually used in combination*)

breather /breéthər/ *n* **1.** PAUSE TO REST a short rest while in the middle of doing something (*informal*) ○ *In extreme heat you have to make sure you take a breather every hour or so.* **2.** VENT a vent in an area or enclosure that is otherwise sealed **3.** BREATHING PERSON somebody who breathes in a particular way (*used in combination*) ○ *a heavy breather*

breathing /breéthing/ *n* **1.** the process of taking air into the lungs and pushing it out again **2.** in ancient Greek, the pronouncing of an initial vowel with an 'h' sound before it (**rough breathing**), or without an 'h' sound (**smooth breathing**), or either of the symbols indicating these pronunciations

breathing space, **breathing room** *n UK, ANZ, Can* the opportunity to relax or sort out problems without pressures, constraints, interruptions, or interference ○ *Going away should give you some breathing space to sort out any relationship problems.*

breathless /bréthləss/ *adj* **1.** UNABLE TO BREATHE PROPERLY experiencing difficulty in breathing, or breathing faster than normal, because of physical exertion or illness **2.** WITH SHALLOW BREATHING breathing very shallowly because of intense emotion such as fear or excitement **3.** EXCITING OR INTENSE capable of causing difficulties in breathing because of intense excitement, emotion, or speed **4.** HOT AND WITHOUT BREEZE lacking any air movement or breeze ○ *a breathless room* **5.** NOT ALIVE dead and no longer breathing (*literary*) —**breathlessly** *adv* —**breathlessness** *n*

breathtaking /bréth tayking/ *adj* evoking strong emotions, especially excitement, awe, or shock —**breathtakingly** *adv*

breath test *n* a test using a device that a person breathes into to determine the level of alcohol in the breath, especially one conducted by police on the driver of a road vehicle

breathy /bréthi/ (**-ier, -iest**) *adj* **1.** with a discernible sound of breathing accompanying spoken words **2.** without proper control of the breath, which creates an uneven or weak vocal or instrumental sound —**breathily** *adv* —**breathiness** *n*

Brébeuf /bráy boŏf/, **Jean de, St** (1593–1649) French-born Canadian missionary. He worked as a Jesuit missionary among the Huron people in Canada after 1625.

breccia /bréchi ə/ *n* coarse-grained sedimentary rock made of sharp fragments of rock and stone cemented together by finer material. Breccia is produced by volcanic activity or erosion, including frost shattering. [Late 18C. < Italian, 'gravel'] —**breccial** *adj* —**brecciate** /-ayt/ *vti* —**brecciation** /bréchi áysh'n/ *n*

Brecht /brekht/, **Bertolt** (1898–1956) German playwright and director. One of the most influential dramatists of the 20th century, he was the author of *The Threepenny Opera* (1928) in collaboration with Kurt Weill, *Mother Courage* (1941), and *The Caucasian Chalk Circle* (1945). After 1948 he worked with the Berliner Ensemble in East Berlin. Full name **Brecht, Eugene Bertolt Friedrich**. See Cultural note at **circle**

'Those who have had no share in the good fortunes of the mighty often have a share in their misfortunes.'
[Bertolt Brecht, *The Caucasian Chalk Circle*; 1945; tr. 1948]

Brecon Beacons National Park /brékən beékənz-/ national park in Powys, Wales, created in 1957. It includes the Black Mountains and is an important tourist area.

bred /bred/ past participle, past tense of **breed** ■ *adj* raised in a particular manner (*used in combination*) ○ *city-bred*

SPELLCHECK See bread.

Breda /breédə/ city in North Brabant Province, the Netherlands, near Rotterdam. Population: 160,398 (2000).

breddah /bréddə/ (*plural* **-ren** /brédrən/) *n* (*slang; used in Black English*) **1.** same as **brother 2.** a form of address for or way of referring to another Black man, especially an Afro-Caribbean or Rastafarian man [Representing a pronunciation]

bred-in-the-bone *adj* **1.** deeply ingrained or firmly established **2.** describes a habit, especially a bad habit, that has become deeply ingrained over time

bredren plural of **breddah** (*slang; used in Black English*)

breech /breech/ *n* **1.** ARMS BACK OF GUN BARREL the rear part of the barrel of a rifle or shotgun, near the stock **2.** MECH ENG PART OF PULLEY the lower part of a pulley block, to which the rope, cable, or chain is fixed **3.** ANAT BUTTOCKS the back lower portion of the trunk of the body [Old English *brēc*, plural of *brōc* 'garment covering the thighs and lower trunk' < Germanic]

SPELLCHECK See breach.

breech birth *n* the delivery of a baby with its buttocks or feet, rather than its head, emerging first

breechblock /breéch blok/ *n* the part of a breech-loading gun that is detached from the barrel to allow cartridges to be loaded into the back of the barrel

breechcloth /breéch kloth/ (*plural* **-cloths**) *n* CLOTHING same as **loincloth**

breech delivery *n* MED same as **breech birth**

breeches /bríchiz/, **britches** *npl* **1.** trousers with legs that come down to the knee **2.** trousers of any kind (*informal*) [13C. Plural of BREECH]

breeches buoy *n* a piece of equipment used for transferring people between moving ships, consisting of a canvas harness suspended from a pulley and line that links the ships

breeching /bríching, breé-/ *n* **1.** RIDING STRAP ON HORSE'S HARNESS the strap of a harness that passes behind the hindquarters of a horse or donkey **2.** ARMS GUN'S BREECH PARTS parts of a gun that form or make up the breech **3.** NAVY ROPE SECURING SHIP'S GUN in former times, ropes used to secure guns to the side of a ship to control the recoil

breechloader /breéch lōdər/ *n* a gun that is loaded by inserting cartridges through the back of the barrel —**breechloading** *adj*

breed /breed/ *n* **1.** BIOL DISTINCT ANIMAL OR PLANT a strain of an animal or plant with identifiable characteristics that distinguish it from other members of its species, especially one whose characteristics are preserved by controlled mating or propagation **2.** SOMEBODY OR SOMETHING OF PARTICULAR TYPE a particular type of thing or person, especially one that can be easily distinguished from other similar things or people ○ *a new breed of manager* ■ *v* (**breeds, breeding, bred** /bred/) **1.** *vti* BIOL MATE AND PRODUCE YOUNG to mate and give birth to offspring **2.** *vt* AGRIC RAISE ANIMALS OR PLANTS to reproduce and raise animals or plants, especially for commercial purposes or for shows and competitions **3.** *vt* GENETICS SELECT ANIMALS OR PLANTS to select animals or plants as part of a process of improving or preserving their special characteristics **4.** *vti* PRODUCE SOMETHING to produce or create something, or be produced or created ○ *Experience breeds confidence.* **5.** *vt* INDUST MAKE NUCLEAR FUEL to make fissionable substances using a breeder reactor [Old English *brēdan* < Indo-European, 'heat']

breeder /breédər/ *n* **1.** SOMEBODY WHO BREEDS ANIMALS OR PLANTS somebody who breeds animals or propagates plants **2.** ANIMAL OR PLANT USED FOR BREEDING an animal or plant kept to produce offspring **3.** CAUSAL FACTOR a cause or a source of something **4.** OFFENSIVE TERM an offensive term for somebody who is heterosexual (*slang insult*) **5.** INDUST same as **breeder reactor**

breeder reactor *n* a nuclear reactor that produces more fuel than it consumes. This kind of reactor is used mainly to produce plutonium.

breeding /breéding/ *n* **1.** UPBRINGING somebody's upbringing, education, and training in manners and other social skills, especially an upbringing that produces the polished manners and self-assurance thought characteristic of the upper classes **2.** ANCESTRY somebody's family or ancestry **3.** REPRODUCTION the mating and producing of young (*often used before a noun*) ○ *prime breeding stock* **4.** GENETICS DEVELOPMENT OF IMPROVED SPECIMENS the development of new types of plant or animal with improved char-

acteristics **5.** INDUST **REACTOR'S FUEL PRODUCTION EXCEEDING CONSUMPTION** production of fissionable material in a breeder reactor in quantities in excess of the fuel it consumes

breeding ground *n* **1.** an area where animals mate and produce young **2.** an environment or situation that is likely to produce or encourage a particular phenomenon ○ *The festival is a breeding ground for new comedy talent.*

breeks /breeks/ *npl N England, Scotland* trousers or breeches (*informal*) [14C. Variant of BREECHES]

breeze /breez/ *n* **1.** METEOROL **LIGHT TO MODERATE WIND** a wind ranging in strength from light to moderate, with a speed of 6 to 50 kph/4 to 31 mph **2.** SOMETHING EASY a task or object that is easily achieved (*informal*) ■ *v* (**breezes, breezing, breezed**) **1.** *vi* GO SOMEWHERE BRISKLY to move quickly and confidently or cheerfully into or out of a place **2.** *vti* ACCOMPLISH SOMETHING EASILY to progress through something easily and with little difficulty or effort ○ *He breezed through his certification test.* [Mid-16C. Probably < Spanish *brisa*, Portuguese *briza* 'northeast wind'] ◇ **shoot the breeze** *N Am* to spend time chatting (*slang*)
breeze through *vti* to do something quickly and easily

breeze block *n* a light rectangular block made from a mixture of cement and the ashes of coal and coke. Use: lightweight or interior walls. N Am term **cinder block** [< French *braise* 'hot coals']

breezeway /bree'z way/ *n N Am* a roofed passageway with open sides that connects two buildings such as a house and a garage

breezily /bree'zili/ *adv* in a lively, cheerful, and relaxed way

breezy /bree'zi/ (**-ier, -iest**) *adj* **1.** with a light to moderate wind **2.** lively, cheerful, and relaxed — **breeziness** *n*

bregma /brég'mə/ (*plural* **-mata** /-mətə/) *n* the place on the skull at the top of the forehead where the frontal bone and the two parietal bones meet, used as a reference point when measuring skulls [Late 16C. < Greek, 'front of the head'] —**bregmatic** /breg máttik/ *adj*

brekky /bréki/ (*plural* **-kies**) *n* FOOD same as **breakfast** (*informal*) [Early 20C. Shortening and alteration]

Brel /brel/, **Jacques** (1929–78) Belgian-born French singer and songwriter. His songs included 'Les bourgeois' and 'Ne me quitte pas', and were widely recorded by other singers, including Frank Sinatra and Ray Charles.

> 'I'm obsessed by those things that are ugly and sordid, that people don't want to talk about.'
> [Jacques Brel. Quoted in *Jacques Brel*, Alan Clayson; 1996]

Bremen /bráymən/ city, major port, and capital of the state of Bremen in northwestern Germany. It is situated on the River Weser, about 69 km/43 mi. from the North Sea. Population: 539,400 (2000).

Bremerhaven /bráymər haávən/ port and city in Bremen State, northwestern Germany, on the River Weser estuary. Population: 130,847 (1997).

bremsstrahlung /brémz shtraaloong/ *n* the electromagnetic radiation that is produced by an electrically charged subatomic particle such as an electron when it is suddenly slowed down by the electric field of an atomic nucleus [Mid-20C. < German < *bremsen* 'brake' + *Strahlung* 'radiation']

Brendan /bréndən/, **St** (486?–578?) Irish saint and traveller. He founded the monastery of Clonfert in County Galway (561). Known as **the Navigator**

Bren gun /brén-/ *n* a light machine gun, used by British and Commonwealth forces in World War II, that is air-cooled and gas-operated and takes .303 calibre ammunition. [Mid-20C. Blend of BRNO, where originally made + Enfield, town in S England where later made under licence]

Brennan /brénnən/, **Christopher** (1870–1932) Australian poet. Noted for his symbolist style, he was the author of *Poems 1913* (1914). Full name **Brennan, Christopher John**

Brennan, William J., Jr. (1906–97) associate justice of the US Supreme Court (1956–90). During his long tenure he was known for his dedication to maintaining freedom of speech. Full name **Brennan, William Joseph, Jr.**

> 'Capital punishment…treats members of the human race…as objects to be toyed with and discarded.'
> [William J. Brennan, Jr., *Address, University of California, Hastings College of Law, Los Angeles Times*; 19 November 1985]

Brenner /brénnər/, **Sydney** (*b.* 1927) South African molecular biologist. He worked on molecular genetics and the DNA code, and shared the 2002 Nobel Prize in Physiology or Medicine with John Sulston and Robert Horvitz.

Brenner Pass Alpine mountain pass linking Innsbruck, Austria, and Bolzano, Italy. With a maximum elevation of 1,371 m/4,497 ft, it has been an important route between Austria and Italy since antiquity.

brent /brent/ *n* BIRDS same as **brent goose**

Brentano /bren taáno/, **Clemens Maria von** (1778–1842) German writer. He produced poems, stories, and plays and compiled a collection of folk poems, *The Boy's Magic Horn* (1805–08), with his brother-in-law, Achim von Arnim.

brent goose /brént-/ *n* BIRDS a small dark-coloured goose with a white mark on its neck. It breeds in the Arctic and Siberia, farther north than any other goose. Native to: coasts of Europe, Pacific coasts of Asia and North America. Latin name: *Branta bernicula*. N Am term **brant** [Origin ?]

Brenton /bréntən/, **Howard** (*b.* 1942) British dramatist. His plays include *Weapons of Happiness* (1976) and *Pravda* (1985, with David Hare).

> 'Shakespeare was something of an Establishment creep…a man who could be trusted to have a safe pair of hands when it came to politics dramatised on the stage.'
> [Howard Brenton, 'Soundbites', *Guardian*; 3 June 1993]

Brentwood /brént wood/ town northeast of London, in Essex, southeastern England. Population: 68,456 (2001).

bresaola /bre sólə, bri zólə/ *n* Italian salt-cured air-dried beef [Late 20C. < Italian < *brasare* 'cook slowly']

Brescia /bréshə/ city and capital of Brescia Province, Lombardy Region, northern Italy. Population: 187,576 (2001).

Bresson /bréssoN/, **Robert** (1907–99) French film director. His films include *Diary of a Country Priest* (1951) and *The Trial of Joan of Arc* (1962).

> 'I never use professional actors nowadays…For in my opinion the moment actors assume certain expressions, the result cannot be true cinema, only filmed theatre.'
> [Robert Bresson, *Interview, Montreal Star*; 16 July 1966]

Brest /brest/ port and largest city in Finistère Department in the Bretagne Region, western France. Population: 149,634 (1999).

brethren /bréthrən/ plural of **brother** *n* (senses 2–3) ■ *npl* **1.** members of the same family, group, class, or community (*literary or humorous*) ○ *the weaker brethren among us* **2.** the members, especially men, of a church or other religious group (*archaic or literary*) [12C. Old plural of BROTHER]

Brethren *npl* a strict Protestant Christian denomination

Breton /bréttən, brétt'n/ *n* **1.** somebody who comes from Brittany **2.** a Celtic language, related to Cornish, that is spoken in mostly rural areas of Brittany. Native speakers: 500,000. —**Breton** *adj*

LANGUAGE HERITAGE See *Celtic*

Breton /bréttoN/, **André** (1896–1966) French poet and essayist. He was a Dadaist and a founder of the surrealist movement.

> 'Subjectivity and objectivity commit a series of assaults on each other during a human life out of which the first one suffers the worse beating.'
> [André Breton, *Nadja*; 1928]

Bretton Woods /brétt'n-/ tourist resort in New Hampshire. In 1944, it hosted the United Nations Bretton Woods Conference where the International

Monetary Fund and the International Bank for Reconstruction and Development were set up. Area: 41 sq. km/16 sq. mi.

Breuer /bróy ər/, **Josef** (1842–1925) Austrian physician. He pioneered the use of hypnosis in the treatment of hysteria and collaborated briefly with Sigmund Freud on the development of catharsis in psychoanalysis.

Breuer, Marcel (1902–81) Hungarian-born US architect. He designed the Whitney Museum of American Art (1966) and other modernist buildings, and is regarded as the designer of the tubular steel-framed chair. Full name **Breuer, Marcel Lajos**

Breughel ♦ **Brueghel, Jan**

breve /breev/ *n* **1.** a mark, ˘, placed over a vowel to show that it has a short sound or used to show a short or unstressed syllable in poetry **2.** a musical note that is equal in length to two semibreves [14C. Variant of BRIEF]

brevet /brévit/ *n* (*plural* **-vets**) a temporary promotion of a military officer without an increase in pay ■ *vt* (**-vets, -vetting** or **-veting, -veted** or **-vetted**) to promote a military officer by brevet [14C. < French, 'little letter' < Old French *brief* 'letter'] —**brevetcy** *n*

breviary /breevi əri, brévvi-/ (*plural* **-ies**) *n* in the Roman Catholic Church, a book that contains the hymns, psalms, and prayers prescribed for each day [15C. < Latin *breviarium* 'summary, abridgment' < *breviare* 'shorten']

brevity /brévvəti/ *n* **1.** shortness in time **2.** the economical use of words in speech or writing [15C. Via French < Latin *brevitas* < *brevis* 'short']

brew /broo/ *vti* (**brews, brewing, brewed**) **1.** MAKE BEER to make beer or similar alcoholic drinks by a process of steeping, boiling, and fermenting grain with hops, sugar, and other ingredients **2.** MAKE TEA OR COFFEE to prepare tea or coffee for drinking by infusing it to develop its flavour, or infuse to develop flavour **3.** DEVELOP THREATENINGLY to form or develop ominously or threateningly, or concoct something ominous or threatening ○ *A scandal was brewing.* ■ *n* **1.** BEER beer, or a type of beer such as lager or ale ○ *What's the local brew?* **2.** BREWED BEVERAGE a drink such as coffee or tea made by infusion, or a serving of such a drink (*informal*) **3.** MIXTURE a combination of ingredients or components of any kind [Old English *breowan* < Germanic] —**brewer** *n* —**brewing** *n*
brew up *vi* to make tea (*informal*)

brewer's yeast *n* the yeast that is used in brewing beer, also used as a dietary source of vitamins, especially vitamin B. Latin name: *Saccharomyces cerevisiae*.

brewery /broo əri/ (*plural* **-ies**) *n* a building where beer or a similar drink is brewed, or a company that brews beer

brewpub /broo pub/ *n* a restaurant or bar where the beer is made on the premises

Brewster /broo stər/, **Sir David** (1781–1868) British physicist. He studied optics and invented the kaleidoscope (1916). Brewster's Law calculates the refraction index of a glass surface.

Brewster's law *n* a law relating a material's index of refraction to the tangent of the material's angle of polarization [After Sir David BREWSTER]

brewup /broo up/ *n* a cup or pot of tea (*informal*)

Brezhnev /brézh nef/, **Leonid Ilyich** (1906–82) Soviet leader. General secretary of the Soviet Communist Party (1964–82) and president of the USSR (1977–82), he exerted strong control over Warsaw Pact countries.

> 'When internal and external forces that are hostile to socialism try to turn the development of some socialist country towards the restoration of a capitalist regime, then socialism in that country and the socialist community as a whole is threatened.'
> [Leonid Ilyich Brezhnev. The 'Brezhnev doctrine', used to justify the Warsaw Pact's invasion of Czechoslovakia (1968), asserted the right of pact states to intervene in each other's internal affairs.]

Brian Bórú /brí ən bə roo/ (941?–1014) king of Ireland. He extended his power across Southern Ireland and was acknowledged as ruler of all Ireland in 1002. He

was killed after defeating the Vikings at Clontarf. Known as **Brian Boroimhe, Boru 'Brian of the Tribute'**

Briand /breˈe aaN/, **Aristide** (1862–1932) French politician. He was elected prime minister of France 11 times between 1909 and 1929. He shared the Nobel Peace Prize (1926) and contributed to the Kellogg-Briand Pact (1928), which outlawed war.

> 'Draw back the rifles, draw back the machine-guns, draw back the cannons— trust in conciliation, in arbitration, in peace!...A country grows in history not only because of the heroism of its troops on the field of battle, it grows also when it turns to justice and to right for the conservation of its interests.'
> [Aristide Briand, *Speech, Geneva, Switzerland*; 10 September 1926]

briar[1] /brī ər/ (*plural* **-ars** or *same*), **brier** (*plural* **-ers** or *same*) *n* **1.** a tobacco pipe made from the wood of a root **2.** a bush of the heather family with hard woody roots from which tobacco pipes are made. Native to: southern Europe. Latin name: *Erica arborea*. [Mid-19C. < French *bruyère* 'wild heather']

ORIGIN English has two words **briar**. Both can also be spelt **brier**, and their meanings are similar, so they tend to get confused. One goes back to Old English, when it was applied to any prickly bush, especially the bramble; in modern usage it is applied to a type of wild rose. The other is much more recent. It refers to a 'wild heather', and it was borrowed from French *bruyère*. At first it was spelt *bruyer* in English, but because of its similarity to **briar** in the 'wild rose' sense, it too came to be spelt **briar**. It is the root of this type of **briar** that is used to make tobacco pipes.

briar[2] /brī ər/, **brier** *n* a thorny wild plant, especially a trailing rose [Old English *brēr*, origin ?] —**briery** *adj*

Briareus /brī áiri əss/ *n* in Greek mythology, a giant with fifty heads who fought alongside Zeus against the Titans

briarroot /brī ər root/ *n* the root of the European briar. Use: source of briarwood. [Mid-19C. < BRIAR[1]]

briarwood /brī ər wŏŏd/ *n* wood from the root of the European briar. Use: making tobacco pipes.

bribe /brīb/ *vti* (**bribes, bribing, bribed**) to give somebody money or some other incentive to do something, especially something illegal or dishonest ■ *n* money or another incentive given to bribe somebody [14C. < Old French *briber, brimber* 'beg' < *bribe* 'morsel of food given to a beggar'] —**bribable** *adj* —**briber** *n*

bribery /brī bəri/ (*plural* **-ies**) *n* the offering of money or other incentives to persuade somebody to do something, especially something dishonest or illegal

bric-a-brac /brī kə brak/ *n* small ornamental objects that are of interest or sentimental value but of little monetary value [Mid-19C. < French < obsolete *à bric et à brac* 'at random']

brick /brik/ *n* **1.** HARD BLOCK USED FOR CONSTRUCTION WORK a rectangular block of clay or a similar material that is baked until it is hard and is used for building houses, walls, and other large permanent structures **2.** BRICKS OR THEIR MATERIAL bricks collectively, or the material they are made of **3.** CHILD'S BUILDING BLOCK a child's wooden or plastic block used with others to make shapes or structures. N Am term **building block 4.** BLOCK a rectangular block of something, e.g. of ice cream **5.** RELIABLE SUPPORTIVE PERSON a helpful or supportive person (*dated informal*) ■ *vt* (**bricks, bricking, bricked**) **1.** MAKE SOMETHING WITH BRICKS to use bricks to build something or as a liner or paving material for something **2.** CLOSE SOMETHING UP WITH BRICKS to close something up or wall something off with bricks and mortar ○ *the window had been bricked up* [15C. < Middle Dutch *bricke*, later reinforced by French *brique*]

brick-and-mortar *adj* E-COMMERCE same as **bricks-and-mortar**

brickbat /brik bat/ *n* **1.** a harshly unfavourable criticism **2.** a broken fragment of something hard that is used as a missile [Mid-16C. < BAT[1] 'piece, lump']

brickie /brik i/ *n* CONSTR same as **bricklayer** (*informal*)

bricklayer /brik lay ər/ *n* somebody trained to construct houses, walls, and other large permanent

structures by cementing bricks together with mortar —**bricklaying** *n*

brick-red *adj* of a warm brownish-red colour similar to that of bricks —**brick red** *n*

bricks-and-mortar, **brick-and-mortar** *adj* having and using actual business or retail premises, as opposed to operating solely or mainly via the Internet

brick veneer *n Aus* an external wall that consists of a timber frame with a decorative facing of bricks

brickwork /brik wurk/ *n* **1.** the brick structure of something such as a wall, building, or walk **2.** the technique or skill of laying bricks

brickworks /brik wurks/ (*plural same*) *n* a factory where bricks are made

brickyard /brik yaard/ *n* a place where bricks are made, stored, or sold

bricolage /breˈe kō laazh, brikō-/ *n* something that is made or put together with whatever materials happen to be available [Mid-20C. < French < *bricoler* 'do odd jobs' < *bricole* (see BRICOLE)]

bricole /brik'l, bri kōl/ *n* **1.** CUE GAMES TYPE OF BILLIARDS SHOT in billiards, a shot where the cue ball touches the cushion after hitting the target ball and before hitting another ball **2.** ARMS ANCIENT MILITARY CATAPULT a catapult that ancient and medieval soldiers used to launch stones **3.** MIL SOLDIER'S HARNESS FOR HAULING GUNS a harness worn by soldiers in the past for hauling guns [Early 16C. Via French < Provençal *bricola* or Italian *briccola*]

bridal /brīd'l/ *adj* for or associated with brides or weddings [Old English *bryd-ealu* 'wedding with much ale' < BRIDE + ALE, altered after -AL[1]]

SPELLCHECK bridal or **bridle**? Do not confuse the spelling of *bridal* and *bridle*, which sound similar. *Bridal* is chiefly used as an adjective, meaning 'of brides or weddings', as in *the bridal party*. The word *bridle* can be used as a noun or verb, referring to part of a horse's harness or, figuratively, a restraint: *He removed the bridle and saddle from his horse. She bridled her rage.* The verb *bridle* can also mean 'show anger or indignation': *He bridled at the criticism.*

bridal party *n* the group of people at a wedding that includes the bride, bridegroom, members of their immediate families, the bridesmaids, and the groomsmen

bridal shower *n ANZ, N Am* a party given by the woman friends of a woman who is about to get married, at which she is given presents

bridal suite *n* a luxurious and expensive room in a hotel, used especially by newlywed couples on their honeymoon

bridal wreath *n* a bush with arching branches. Flowers: small, white. Genus: *Spiraea*.

bride /brīd/ *n* a woman who is about to marry or who has just married [Old English *bryd* < Germanic]

bridegroom /brīd groom, -grŏŏm/ *n* a man who is about to marry or who has just married [Old English *brȳdguma* < BRIDE + *guma* 'man', altered after GROOM]

bride price *n* in some societies, a payment in the form of money or property made by the groom to the bride or her family

bridesmaid /brīdz mayd/ *n* a girl or woman who helps the bride on her wedding day

bride-to-be (*plural* **brides-to-be**) *n* a woman who is about to get married ○ *Greg returns from the States with his bride-to-be next week.*

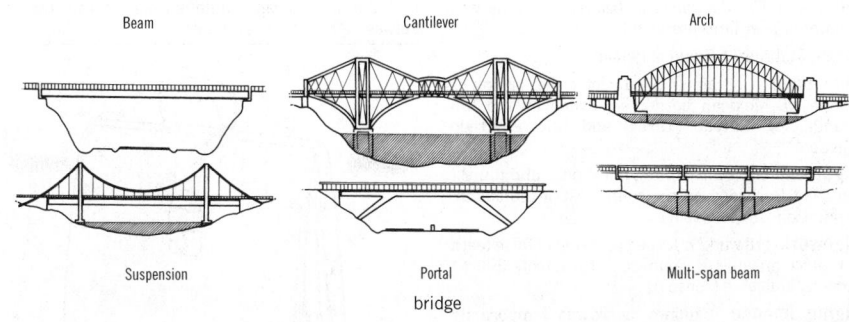

| Beam | Cantilever | Arch |
| Suspension | Portal | Multi-span beam |

bridge

bridge[1] /brij/ *n* **1.** STRUCTURE ALLOWING PASSAGE ACROSS OBSTACLE a structure that is built above and across a river, road, or other obstacle to allow people or vehicles to cross it **2.** LINK OR MEANS OF APPROACH something that provides a link, connection, or means of coming together **3.** NAUT SHIP'S CONTROL ROOM OR PLATFORM the platform or room on a ship or other vessel from which the captain controls its course **4.** DENT PARTIAL FALSE TEETH a set of one or more false teeth that are attached to adjoining teeth. It can be permanently anchored to natural teeth (**fixed bridge**), or set into a metal appliance and temporarily clipped on to natural teeth (**removable bridge**). **5.** ANAT TOP OF NOSE the top bony part of the nose between the eyes **6.** OPHTHALMOL PART OF GLASSES the part of a pair of glasses that connects the two lenses together at the front and rests on the nose **7.** MUSIC PART OF STRINGED INSTRUMENT the part of a stringed instrument that keeps the strings away from its body. It is high and curved on a violin but shallow and straight on a guitar. **8.** MUSIC LINKING PIECE OF MUSIC a transitional or connecting section in a musical work **9.** CUE GAMES CUE REST WITH HIGH END a long-handled support for a player's cue in snooker and billiards, with a high arching end **10.** CUE GAMES HAND USED AS REST the player's hand used as a rest for the cue in billiards and snooker **11.** ELEC ENG PART OF ELECTRICAL CIRCUIT a part of an electrical circuit fitted with a device that measures electrical resistance or capacitance **12.** ONLINE TELECOMMUNICATIONS CONNECTION a telecommunications connection between two local area networks ■ *vt* (**bridges, bridging, bridged**) **1.** CIV ENG BUILD BRIDGE ACROSS SOMETHING to build a bridge across an obstacle to allow people or vehicles to get across it **2.** CREATE UNDERSTANDING BETWEEN PEOPLE to create a means of communication or understanding between people or a means of reconciling their differences [Old English *brycg* < Germanic] —**bridgeable** *adj* ◇ **build bridges** to try to make friends with somebody who has previously been an enemy ◇ **burn your bridges** to do something that makes it difficult or impossible to return to your former position ◇ **cross that bridge when you come to it** to think about or worry about something only when it becomes a reality or a priority

bridge[2] /brij/ *n* a card game derived from whist and played with one deck of cards divided among four players, who play in two pairs. The term is generally used to refer to contract bridge, which is the most popular form of the game. [Late 19C. Origin ?]

bridgehead /brij hed/ *n* **1.** END OF BRIDGE the area immediately surrounding the end of a bridge **2.** MIL DEFENSIVE MILITARY POSITION a fortified position from which troops defend the end of a bridge that is nearest to the enemy **3.** MIL ARMY'S POSITION SEIZED IN ENEMY TERRITORY a forward position seized by advancing troops in enemy territory and serving as a basis for further advances **4.** PIONEERING FOOTHOLD a position from which further advancement can be attained

bridge loan *n N Am* same as **bridging loan**

Bridgend /bri jénd/ county in southern Wales that replaced the southern part of Mid Glamorgan in 1996. Capital: Bridgend. Population: 128,654 (2001). Area: 264 sq. km/102 sq. mi.

Bridge of Sighs *n* a 16th-century canal bridge in Venice, Italy, believed to be named after the sighs of prisoners crossing the bridge to be tried or executed

bridge roll *n* a small torpedo-shaped soft bread roll [Perhaps because eaten at afternoon bridge parties]

Bridges /brij jiz/, **Robert** (1844–1930) British poet. The author of *Eros and Psyche* (1885), *The Spirit of Man*

(1916), and *The Testament of Beauty* (1929), he was appointed poet laureate in 1913.

Bridget, St /bríjjit/ ◆ **Brigid of Ireland**

bridge town *n* either of a pair of cities or towns on the US–Mexican border separated by the Rio Grande, e.g. Laredo (Texas) and Nuevo Laredo (Mexico)

Bridgetown /bríj town/ capital, main port, and tourist centre of Barbados, in the southwest of the island. Population: 136,000 (2001).

bridgework /bríj wurk/ *n* 1. the provision of false teeth to replace missing or removed natural teeth 2. DENT same as **bridge**[1] *n* (sense 4)

bridging finance *n* money borrowed temporarily until a specific event occurs, especially a loan to finance the purchase of a property while another is being sold

bridging finance loan *n* ANZ FIN same as **bridging loan**

bridging loan *n* FIN a sum of money borrowed to finance something until permanent financing can be obtained, especially one to finance the purchase of a new property until an old one is sold. ANZ term **bridging finance loan**. N Am term **bridge loan**

Bridgman /bríjmən/, **P. W.** (1882–1961) US physicist. He won the Nobel Prize in physics (1946) in recognition of his work on thermodynamics. Full name **Bridgman, Percy Williams**

Bridgwater /bríj wawtər/ historic town in Somerset, southwestern England. Population: 34,610 (1991).

bridie /brídi/ *n Scotland* a meat pie made with a circle of puff pasty folded over a meat filling, especially sausagemeat

Bridie /brídi/, **James** (1888–1951) British dramatist. The founder of the Citizens' Theatre in Glasgow, his plays include *The Anatomist* (1930) and *Dr Angelus* (1947). Born **Mavor, Osborne Henry**

bridle /bríd'l/ *n* 1. RIDING HARNESS FOR HORSE'S HEAD a set of leather straps fitted to a horse's head and incorporating the bit and the reins 2. RESTRAINING THING something that acts as a control or restraint ■ *v* (**-dles, -dling, -dled**) 1. *vt* RIDING FIX BRIDLE ON HORSE to provide a horse with a bridle 2. *vi* SHOW ANGER OR INDIGNATION to react with slight anger or indignation, sometimes by rearing the head 3. *vt* EXERCISE CONTROL OR RESTRAINT to show restraint in expressing a feeling or control in curbing something [Old English *brídel* < Germanic]

SPELLCHECK See *bridal*.

bridle path, bridleway /bríd'l way/ *n* a path or trail for horse riding

Brie /bree/ *n* a soft cow's-milk cheese with a whitish rind, originally made in Brie in northeastern France

brief /breef/ *adj* 1. NOT LASTING LONG lasting for only a short time ○ *a brief conversation* 2. CONCISE containing only the necessary information, without any extra details 3. CURT curt and abrupt in conversation ○ *a brief exchange between adversaries* 4. CLOTHING SCANTY describes clothing that leaves much of the wearer's body exposed ■ *n* 1. SYNOPSIS OF DOCUMENTS a synopsis of a larger document or group of documents 2. BRIEFING a briefing, or the information conveyed during one 3. ASSIGNED DUTIES the details of what somebody's job or duties involve 4. LAW SUMMARY OF LEGAL CASE FOR BARRISTER a summary of a client's case prepared for the barrister who will deal with it in court 5. LAW LEGAL REPRESENTATIVE a legal representative, especially a barrister (*informal*) 6. CHR PAPAL LETTER a letter from the Pope, less formal than a papal bull ■ **briefs** *npl* CLOTHING SNUG UNDERWEAR men's or women's close-fitting underwear for the lower body ■ *vt* (**briefs, briefing, briefed**) 1. GIVE INFORMATION TO PREPARE SOMEBODY to give somebody all the necessary information about something in preparation for a discussion or decision 2. SUMMARIZE SOMETHING to make a summary of something, especially in writing [13C. Via Old French < Latin *brevis* 'short'] —**briefer** *n* —**briefly** *adv* —**briefness** *n* ◇ **in brief** used to introduce a summary ○ *In brief, then, you think he should resign.*

CULTURAL NOTE *Brief Encounter*, a film (1945) by the British director David Lean. Noted for its fine central performances by Celia Johnson and Trevor Howard, it tells the story of an unfulfilled extramarital romance between a housewife and a doctor.

briefcase

briefcase /breef kayss/ *n* a small rectangular case with a handle, used for carrying books and papers

briefing /breefing/ *n* 1. a meeting held to provide information about the main facts of an issue or situation 2. the information conveyed at a briefing

brier *n* PLANTS another spelling of **briar**[1]

brig[1] /brig/ *n* 1. SAILING SHIP a two-masted sailing ship with square-rigged sails on both masts 2. *N Am* SHIP'S PRISON a secure area in a ship of the US Navy, which can be used as a prison while the ship is at sea 3. *N Am* MILITARY PRISON a building or part of a building that is used as a prison in a US military installation [Early 18C. Shortening of BRIGANTINE]

brig[2] /brig/ *n N England, Scotland* CONSTR same as **bridge**[1] *n* (sense 1) [13C. Form of BRIDGE[1], influenced by Old Norse *bryggja*]

Brig. *abbr* MIL 1. brigade 2. brigadier

brigade /bri gáyd/ *n* 1. MILITARY UNIT a military unit consisting of two or more combat battalions or regiments and associated support units. It is smaller than a division and is commanded by a brigadier. 2. GROUP WITH COMMON GOAL OR CHARACTERISTIC a group of people organized to achieve a particular goal or characterized by a common trait such as attitude, background, appearance, or activities ■ *vt* (**-gades, -gading, -gaded**) ORGANIZE PEOPLE INTO TASK FORCE to organize a group of people in order to achieve a particular goal [Mid-17C. Via French < Italian *brigata* 'military company' < *brigare* 'contend, brawl' < *briga* 'strife']

CULTURAL NOTE *The Charge of the Light Brigade*, a poem (1845) by Alfred, Lord Tennyson. Based on a contemporary newspaper report, it describes a suicidal attack by the British Light Brigade on the Russian army at Balaclava in the Crimea, on 25 October 1854. While acknowledging that the charge was a military blunder, Tennyson celebrates its heroism.

brigadier /brigga déer/ *n* an officer in the British Army or Royal Marines of a rank above colonel [Late 17C. < French < *brigade* (see BRIGADE)]

brigadier general (*plural* **brigadiers general**), **brigadier** (*plural* **-diers**) *n* an officer in the US or Royal Canadian armies, air forces, or Marines of a rank above colonel

brigalow /brígga lō/ (*plural* **-lows** or *same*) *n* an acacia tree found in dry regions. Native to: Australia. Latin name: *Acacia harpophylla*. [Mid-19C. Origin ?]

brigand /bríggand/ *n* a bandit operating in wild or isolated terrain, usually as a member of a roving band (*literary*) [14C. Via Old French < Italian *brigante* < present participle of *brigare* (see BRIGADE)] —**brigandage** *n* —**brigandism** *n* —**brigandry** *n*

brigandine /bríggən deen/ *n* a coat of chain-mail body armour, worn in medieval times [15C. Directly or via Old French < Italian *brigantina* < *brigante* (see BRIGAND)]

brigantine /bríggən teen, -tīn/ *n* a two-masted sailing ship with square-rigged sails on the foremast and fore-and-aft sails on the mainmast [Early 16C. Directly or via Old French *brigandine* < Italian *brigantino* 'fighting ship' < *brigante* (see BRIGAND)]

Brig. Gen. *abbr* MIL brigadier general

Briggs /brigz/, **Henry** (1561–1630) English mathematician. He was the first Savilian Professor of Geometry at Oxford University and worked with John Napier on logarithms.

Briggs, Robert (1911–83) US embryologist. His research on frog embryos with Thomas J. King at the Institute for Cancer Research in Philadelphia led to the creation of the first amphibian clones in 1951.

bright /brīt/ *adj* 1. SHOWING LIGHT emitting or reflecting strong light ○ *The moon is bright tonight.* 2. ILLUMINATED illuminated with strong natural or artificial light ○ *a bright day* 3. INTENSELY COLOURED intense in colour, or decorated with intense colours ○ *bright blue* 4. INTELLIGENT showing an ability to think, learn, or respond quickly ○ *She was brighter than other children of her age.* 5. CHEERFUL cheerful and lively ○ *He seems much brighter this morning.* 6. LIKELY TO BE SUCCESSFUL likely to be successful ○ *predicted a bright future for the company* 7. ACOUSTICS CLEAR-SOUNDING describes sounds that have a clear crisp quality and little harmonic resonance 8. BEAUTIFUL remarkably beautiful or handsome (*archaic*) ■ *adv* WITH LIGHT with a great deal of light ■ *n* SOMEBODY WITHOUT SUPERNATURAL BELIEFS a person, e.g. an atheist, who has a naturalist, as opposed to a supernaturalist, view of the world, and who therefore considers himself or herself to be more rational than religious believers ■ **brights** *npl N Am* HEADLIGHTS the headlights on a motor vehicle when set to full beam [Old English *beorht* < Indo-European, 'shine'] —**brightish** *adj* —**brightly** *adv*

SYNONYMS See *intelligent*.

Bright /brīt/, **John** (1811–89) British politician. A leading radical, he was associated with the Anti-Corn Law League and the Reform Act of 1867.

'England is the mother of parliaments.'
[John Bright, *Times*; 19 January 1865]

'If our forefathers two hundred years ago …refused to be the bondsmen of a king, shall we be the born thralls of an aristocracy like ours? Shall we, who struck the lion down, shall we pay the wolf homage?'
[John Bright, *Speech, Royal Opera House, Covent Garden, London*; 19 December 1845]

brighten /brīt'n/ (**-ens, -ening, -ened**) *v* 1. *vi* LOOK HAPPY to become enthusiastic, lively, or happy ○ *She brightened visibly at the suggestion.* 2. *vt* ADD INTEREST to add colour or interest to something ○ *Their visit brightened the day for us.* 3. *vi* METEOROL BECOME LESS OVERCAST to become less dull or rainy ○ *It's supposed to brighten this afternoon.* 4. *vti* ILLUMINATE OR GET LIGHTER to increase the amount of light emitted or reflected by something, or be filled with an increasing amount of light 5. *vti* MAKE OR BECOME MORE PROMISING to seem more promising, or make something seem more promising
brighten up *vti* to become brighter, lighter, more colourful, or livelier, or make somebody or something do this

brightener /brīt'nər/, **brightening agent** /brīt'ning-/ *n* a compound added to some washing powders or liquids to make white or light-coloured fabrics look brighter

bright-eyed ◇ **bright-eyed and bushy-tailed** noticeably energetic and lively

bright lights *npl* the entertainment and activities of a big city (*informal*)

bright nebula *n* a cloud of material in space that appears bright because it is illuminated by the stars around it

brightness /brítnəss/ *n* 1. STRENGTH OF LIGHT the intensity of light reflected or emitted by something 2. CLEVERNESS the ability to think, learn, or respond quickly 3. CHEERFULNESS a cheerful and lively manner 4. PROMISE OF SUCCESS the promise of a successful outcome 5. CLARITY OF SOUND a clear crisp sound quality with little harmonic resonance 6. OPTICS LIGHT EMITTED IN PARTICULAR DIRECTION the intensity of light (**luminosity**) emitted by an object in a particular direction, used by an observer to compare the luminosity of other visible objects

Brighton /brít'n/ seaside resort on the English Channel in East Sussex, southern England. Population: 257,817 (2001).

Bright's disease /bríts-/ *n* an inflammatory disease of the kidneys, e.g. glomerulonephritis [Mid-19C. After Richard *Bright* (1789–1858), British physician]

bright spark *n* a clever or ingenious person (*informal; used ironically*) ○ *Some bright spark had the idea of hiding my glasses.*

brightwork /brīt wurk/ *n* fittings or trimmings of polished metal or varnished wood, e.g. on a vehicle or boat

bright young thing *n* **1.** a young clever person thought likely to succeed **2.** a member of a young and fashionable social set in Great Britain in the 1920s and 1930s who regarded themselves as setting new fashions in dress, music, behaviour, and style

Brigid of Ireland /bríjjit-/, **St** (453?–524?) Irish abbess. She founded four religious communities for women in Ireland.

~~**briliant**~~ incorrect spelling of **brilliant**

brill[1] /bril/ (*plural same* or **brills**) *n* an edible flatfish that is closely related to the turbot. Native to: Europe. Latin name: *Scophthalmus rhombus*. [15C. Origin ?]

brill[2] /bril/ *adj, interj* used to express satisfaction with somebody or something (*informal*) [Late 20C. Shortening of BRILLIANT]

Brillat-Savarin /brée yaa sávvə raN/, **Anthelme** (1755–1826) French politician and writer. His *Physiology of Taste* (1825) is a classic of gastronomic literature. Full name **Brillat-Savarin, Jean Anthelme**

> 'Tell me what you eat and I will tell you what you are.'
> [Anthelme Brillat-Savarin, 'Aphorismes, pour servir de prolégomènes (Aphorisms to serve as prolegomena)', *Physiologie du Goût (Physiology of Taste)*; 1825]

brilliance /brillyənss/, **brilliancy** /-yənssi/ *n* **1.** BRIGHTNESS extreme brightness or radiance **2.** GREAT INTELLIGENCE OR TALENT exceptional intelligence, ability, skill, or talent ○ *the technical brilliance of the pianist's performance* **3.** SPLENDOUR imposing splendour or magnificence

brilliant /brillyənt/ *adj* **1.** EXTREMELY BRIGHT OR RADIANT extremely bright or radiant ○ *brilliant sunshine* ○ *a brilliant smile* **2.** VIVID vividly coloured ○ *a brilliant shade of green* **3.** INTELLIGENT OR TALENTED showing exceptional intelligence, ability, skill, or talent ○ *a brilliant mathematician* **4.** EXCELLENT distinguished by excellence **5.** SPLENDID imposingly splendid or magnificent ■ *adj, interj* GREAT used to express great satisfaction with somebody or something (*informal*) [Late 17C. < French *brillant*, present participle of *briller* 'shine' < Italian *brillare*] —**brilliantly** *adv*

brilliant-cut *adj* describes a gemstone that is cut into a multifaceted shape to maximize brilliance. A brilliant-cut gemstone is shaped like two polygonal pyramids joined base to base, with the point of the upper pyramid cut off to form a large flat facet.

brilliantine /brillyən teen/ *n* **1.** an oily hair cream, used by men to keep hair in place and make it look glossy **2.** a shiny lightweight fabric, often made from cotton woven with mohair or worsted [Late 19C. < French *brillantine* < *brillant* (see BRILLIANT)]

brim /brim/ *n* **1.** HAT EDGE the rim around the edge of a hat, shaped to stand out from the head **2.** TOP EDGE the top edge of a container such as a cup or bowl ■ *v* (**brims, brimming, brimmed**) **1.** *vti* BE FULL TO TOP to fill something, or be full, to the top edge ○ *The cup was brimming with hot coffee.* **2.** *vi* BURST to have an unusually plentiful supply of something ○ *He was brimming with ideas.* **3.** *vi* OVERFLOW to be so full as to be overflowing ○ *eyes brimming with tears* [13C. Origin ?] —**brimless** *adj*

brimful /brímfōōl/ *adj* **1.** describes a container that is full to its top edge **2.** having an unusually plentiful supply of something ○ *brimful of energy*

brimstone /brím stōn/ *n* **1.** CHEM same as **sulphur** (sense 1) (*archaic*) **2.** *also* **brimstone butterfly** a medium-sized butterfly, the male of which is bright yellow and the female greenish-white. Native to: gardens and woodlands in Europe and Asia. Latin name: *Gonepteryx rhamni*. [12C. < Old English *byrne* 'burning' < *birnan* (see BURN[1])]

Brindisi /brin déezi/ capital of Brindisi Province, Apulia Region, southern Italy. It is a port and important ferry terminal for ships carrying tourist traffic to or from Greece. Population: 89,081 (2001).

brindle /brínd'l/ *adj* same as **brindled** ■ *n* brindled colouring [Late 17C. Back-formation < BRINDLED]

brindled /brínd'ld/ *adj* tawny brown or grey marked with darker streaks or patches [Late 17C. Alteration of *brinded* (influenced by GRIZZLED or SPECKLED), origin ?]

Brindley /bríndli/, **James** (1716–72) British engineer. He built 584 km/365 mi. of canals in England, including the first, from Worsley to Manchester, opened in 1763.

brine /brīn/ *n* **1.** SALT WATER FOR PRESERVING water containing a significant amount of salt, used for curing, preserving, and developing flavour in food **2.** SEA WATER the salt water of the sea (*literary*) **3.** SALT SOLUTION a strong salt solution ■ *vt* (**brines, brining, brined**) TREAT SOMETHING WITH SALT WATER to preserve, can, pickle, or soak something in salt water [Old English *brīne*, origin ?] —**brinish** *adj*

Brinell hardness /bri nél-/ *n* the hardness of a metal or alloy, determined by pressing a steel ball into its surface under standard pressure and measuring the surface area of the resulting indentation [Early 20C. After Johan *Brinell* (1849–1925), Swedish engineer]

Brinell hardness number, **Brinell number** *n* a number expressing the hardness of a metal or alloy. It is the ratio of the pressure applied to a steel ball forced into the surface of the metal to the surface area of the resulting indentation.

brine shrimp *n* a small crustacean that lives in salt lakes and brine pools and is used as food for aquarium fish. Genus: *Artemia*.

bring /bring/ (**brings, bringing, brought** /brawt/) *v* **1.** *vt* ACCOMPANY OR CARRY SOMEBODY OR SOMETHING to come from one place to another with somebody or something ○ *Please bring me a glass of water.* **2.** *vt* ATTRACT SOMETHING to draw something to yourself or another person ○ *This charm is supposed to bring luck.* **3.** *vt* MAKE SOMETHING HAPPEN to cause something to take place ○ *The heavy rain brought flooding.* **4.** *vt* PUT SOMETHING IN PARTICULAR STATE to force somebody or something to arrive at a particular situation or condition ○ *The chairperson brought the meeting to a close.* **5.** *vt* CAUSE SOMETHING TO ENTER MIND to cause something to enter somebody's mind ○ *Seeing you brings memories of good times.* **6.** *vr* MAKE YOURSELF DO SOMETHING to persuade or force yourself to do something (*usually with negatives or in questions*) ○ *She still can't bring herself to think about the tragedy.* **7.** *vt* SELL FOR PARTICULAR PRICE to be sold for a particular price **8.** *vt* LAW BEGIN ACTION to begin a legal action **9.** *vt* PRESENT EVIDENCE to present evidence before a court **10.** *vt UK regional, Malaysia, Singapore* TAKE SOMEBODY OR SOMETHING to take somebody or something somewhere ○ *I brought my friend to the airport when she left.* [Old English *bringan* < Indo-European] —**bringer** *n*

bring about *vt* to make something happen

bring around *vt* same as **bring round**

bring back *vt* **1.** to evoke memories of something forgotten **2.** to restore something that has been discontinued ○ *widespread support for bringing back on-the-spot fines*

bring down *vt* **1.** TOPPLE SOMEBODY OR SOMETHING to cause the downfall of a person, group, or institution **2.** KILL OR WOUND PERSON OR ANIMAL to make a person or animal fall by wounding or killing it **3.** *ANZ, Can* POL PRESENT BILL to present a bill or other piece of legislation in a parliament

bring forth *vt* **1.** to bear young **2.** to produce fruit or flowers

bring forward *vt* **1.** BRING SOMETHING CLOSER IN TIME to move something such as an appointment or an event to an earlier date or time **2.** SUGGEST SOMETHING FOR CONSIDERATION to offer something for discussion or consideration **3.** ACCT CARRY AMOUNT TO NEXT PAGE to carry a sum from one column or page to the next

bring in *vt* **1.** INTRODUCE SOMETHING to introduce something such as a new policy or law **2.** EARN OR ACQUIRE SOMETHING to acquire money as profits, pay, or interest ○ *She barely brings in enough to live on.* **3.** LAW PRESENT SOMETHING IN COURT to present something in a court of law

bring off *vt* **1.** to succeed in doing something difficult **2.** an offensive term meaning to cause somebody to have an orgasm (*slang*)

bring on *vt* **1.** to be the cause of something happening or appearing ○ *exhaustion brought on by overwork* **2.** to further the development of a quality or of the person who possesses it

bring out *vt* **1.** MAKE SOMETHING KNOWN to cause something to become known **2.** CALL ATTENTION TO SOMETHING to emphasize a quality in somebody or something ○ *That outfit brings out the red in your hair.* **3.** INTRODUCE SOMETHING FOR SALE to produce or issue something for sale to the public ○ *The company has just brought out a new version of the software.* **4.** INTRODUCE SOMEBODY TO SOCIETY to introduce a debutante to society

bring round, **bring around** *vt* **1.** to revive somebody who has lost consciousness **2.** to make somebody change an opinion and agree with you ○ *We eventually brought him round to our view.*

bring to *vt* **1.** to restore somebody to consciousness **2.** to head a ship into the wind in order to slow it down or stop it

bring up *vt* **1.** RAISE SUBJECT to raise a subject for discussion **2.** REAR CHILD to provide care, training, and education for a child until maturity **3.** VOMIT SOMETHING to cough something up, or expel something from the stomach through the mouth **4.** MAKE SOMEBODY OR SOMETHING STOP SUDDENLY to cause somebody or something to come to a standstill

bring-and-buy sale *n* a sale, usually organized to raise funds for a school, church, or charity, where people bring things to sell and buy things others have brought

brinjal /brínjəl/ *n S Africa, S Asia* same as **aubergine** (senses 1–2) [Early 17C. < Portuguese *berinjela* < Arabic *al-bāḏinjān*]

brink /bringk/ *n* **1.** the very edge of something such as a steep drop or river bank **2.** the crucial point in a situation when something disastrous or momentous is about to happen ○ *teetering on the brink of bankruptcy* [13C. < Old Norse *brekka* 'slope']

brinkmanship /bríngkmən ship/ *n* the practice, especially in international relations, of taking a dispute to the verge of conflict in the hope of forcing the opposition to make concessions

brinks /bríngks/ *n* a rich man who gives money and gifts to a partner in a relationship (*slang; used in Black English*) [Origin ?]

briny /brīni/ *adj* (**-ier, -iest**) relating to, containing, or tasting like sea water ■ *n* same as **sea** (sense 1) (*literary*) —**brininess** *n*

brio /brée ō/ *n* lively energy [Mid-18C. < Italian]

brioche /bri ósh/ *n* a sweet French bread roll made from a dough enriched with eggs and butter [Early 19C. < French < Old French *brier* 'knead']

briolette /brée ō lét/ *n* a gem cut in the shape of a teardrop or oval [Mid-19C. < French]

briquette /bri két/, **briquet** *n* a small rectangular block of compressed material such charcoal, sawdust, or coal dust. Use: fuel. ■ *vt* (**-quettes, -quetting, -quetted; -quets, -quetting, -quetted**) to compress a material into small rectangular blocks [Late 19C. < French, 'little brick' < *brique* 'brick']

bris /briss/ (*plural* **brises**) *n* the religious circumcision ceremony for a Jewish boy [Early 20C. < Hebrew *berīṯ (mīlāh)* 'covenant (of circumcision)']

Brisbane /brízbən/ city on the Brisbane River and the capital of Queensland, eastern Australia. Population: 1,574,600 (1998). —**Brisbanite** *n, adj*

brisk /brisk/ *adj* **1.** QUICK done quickly and energetically ○ *a brisk walk* **2.** BRUSQUE speaking or behaving in an abrupt way ○ *a brisk reply* **3.** BUSY showing or experiencing much activity ○ *Business was brisk.* **4.** INVIGORATING refreshingly cool ○ *brisk autumn days* ■ *vti* (**brisks, brisking, brisked**) MAKE OR BECOME LIVELY to become, or make something become, more active or lively ○ *Business brisks up in summer.* [Late 16C. Probably < French *brusque* (see BRUSQUE)] —**briskly** *adv* —**briskness** *n*

brisken /brískən/ (**-ens, -ening, -ened**) *vti* to become, or make something become, faster or livelier ○ *She briskened her pace.*

brisket /brískit/ *n* **1.** a cut of meat, especially of beef, taken from an animal's breast **2.** the breast of a four-legged animal [14C. Origin ?]

brisling /brísslíng, brízz-/ (*plural same* or **-lings**) *n* **1.** a small fish of the herring family. Latin name: *Clupea sprattus*. **2.** the flesh of a brisling used as food [Early 20C. < Norwegian or Danish]

bristle /bríss'l/ *n* **1.** STIFF HAIR a short stiff hair on an animal or plant, or a mass of short stiff hairs growing, especially on a pig's back or a man's face **2.** HAIR ON BRUSH the short stiff natural or synthetic hair on a brush ■ *v* (**-tles, -tling, -tled**) **1.** *vti* HAVE OR SET HAIR ON END to make the hair or fur stand upright in response to fear or anger, or to show such a

response 2. *vi* BECOME OFFENDED to react rather angrily or indignantly to somebody or something ○ *He bristled at the suggestion.* **3.** *vi* ABOUND to have an abundance of something ○ *a mighty battleship bristling with guns* **4.** *vt* GIVE SOMETHING BRISTLES to provide or cover something with bristles [13C. < Old English *byrst* 'bristle']

bristlebird /bríss'l burd/ *n* a small brown and reddish-brown bird that lives in coastal scrub, belonging to three species, two of which are endangered. Native to: Australia. Genus: *Dasyornis.* [Early 19C. < the bristles on its face]

bristlecone pine /bríss'l kōn-/ *n* a small pine tree with bristly cones, the longest-living tree in the world. Native to: California. Genus: *Pinus.*

bristletail /bríss'l tayl/ (*plural* **-tails** or *same*) *n* a wingless insect that has a long segmented abdomen with two or three long bristles at the end. Order: Thysanura.

bristle worm *n* ZOOL same as **polychaete**

bristling /bríssling/ *adj* **1.** thick with stiff hairs **2.** reacting with anger or indignation

bristly /bríss'li/ (**-tlier, -tliest**) *adj* **1.** prickly and rough with bristles **2.** easily provoked to anger or indignation —**bristliness** *n*

Bristol /bríst'l/ university city and seaport on the River Avon in southwestern England. Population: 380,615 (2001).

Bristol board *n* fine smooth lightweight cardboard, used in design and drawing [Early 19C. After BRISTOL]

Bristol Channel arm of the Atlantic Ocean between southern Wales and southwestern England, into which the River Severn flows. Length: 140 km/85 mi.

bristols /bríst'lz/ *npl* an offensive term for a woman's breasts (*slang*) [Mid-20C. Shortening of *Bristol Cities*, rhyming slang for 'titties']

brit /brit/ (*plural* **brits** or *same*) *n* **1.** the young form of some fish including the herring and the sprat **2.** a mass of tiny organisms in the sea, especially crustaceans, that whaleboat whales and some fish feed on [Early 17C. Origin ?]

Brit /brit/ *n* a British person (*informal*) [Early 20C. Shortening]

Brit. *abbr* **1.** Britain **2.** British

Britain /brítt'n/ **1.** island in the Atlantic Ocean off the northwestern coast of Europe, including England, Scotland, and Wales. Area: 229,870 sq. km/88,753 sq. mi. **2.** ♦ **Great Britain**

Britannia[1] /bri tánnyə/ *n* **1.** the personification and symbol of Great Britain, shown as a seated woman wearing a helmet and holding a trident **2.** same as **Britannia coin 3.** *also* **britannia** METALL same as **Britannia metal** [Pre-12C. < Latin *Brit(t)annia*]

Britannia[2] /bri tánnyə/ the Roman name for the southern part of Britain

Britannia coin *n* a British gold coin worth £10, £25, £50, or £100, introduced as an investment coin in 1987 [< the figure depicted on the coin]

Britannia metal, **britannia metal** *n* an alloy of tin, antimony, and copper that is similar to pewter and is used for decorative items and for bearings

Britannic /bri tánnik/ *adj* belonging to Great Britain (*dated formal*) ○ *Her Britannic Majesty*

~~Britanny~~ incorrect spelling of **Brittany**

brith *n* JUDAISM same as **bris**

~~Britian~~ incorrect spelling of **Britain**

Briticism /brítti sizəm/ *n* something such as a word or custom that is characteristic of the British or of Great Britain [Mid-19C. < BRITISH, after SCOTTICISM or GALLICISM]

British /bríttish/ *npl* the people of the United Kingdom of Great Britain and Northern Ireland ■ *n* **1.** LANG same as **British English 2.** the language spoken by the ancient Celtic people who lived in southern Britain [Old English *Brettisc, Brittisc* < *Bret* 'ancient Briton', directly or via Latin *Britto* < Celtic] —**British** *adj*

British Asian *n* somebody of South Asian origin in the United Kingdom

British Black English *n* the variety of English spoken by British-born people of African Caribbean descent in the United Kingdom. It is a form of

---

WORLD ENGLISH *British Black English* is also known in the British context as *Creole* or *Patois*, a form of Jamaican Creole used by British-born Caribbeans. Jamaican Creole was originally brought to Britain by Jamaicans (mainly in the period after 1948) but came to predominate as a heritage language among second-generation Caribbeans, even those without Jamaican ancestry. The likely reasons for this were that Jamaicans were more numerous than other Caribbeans and also that Creole was the language of reggae music and the Rastafarian religious movement, both of which were popular among second-generation Caribbean adolescents.

The British variety of Jamaican Creole was first recognized as a variety distinct from Creole as spoken in Jamaica in the late 1970s. It is influenced in varying degrees by local varieties of English; in London this has given rise to the term *London Jamaican*, referring to a variety of Creole that shows the influence of London English ('Cockney') in certain aspects of grammar and pronunciation. Some Jamaican vocabulary items are little known or unused in Britain (for example words for Caribbean flora and fauna) but new words are coined to refer to objects and activities that are important in the British context. Since virtually all users of Patois are also speakers of English, and in fact most have English as their first language, conversations involving Patois are likely to involve English as well. Thus the term British Black English is sometimes applied to a mode of speaking that involves switching between Patois and a local variety of British English. British Black English is not used for any formal purposes but is used informally between friends and family members, on some local radio programmes, in song lyrics, and in poetry. It is sometimes used in written form, especially in lyrics, poems, and personal letters.

Some typical notable features of British Black English are: 1) The Creole pronoun forms are *me* (also sometimes *I*), *you, him, we, unu, dem.* Because of the influence of Standard English not all speakers distinguish singular and plural second person 'you'. 2) The past tense may be used without 'to' or with 'did', for example *me see him* or *me did see him* 'I saw him'. 3) Verbs may be preceded by *a*, giving a sense similar in many cases to the Standard English progressive, for example *mi a come* 'I am coming'. 4) The verb *to be* is not used before an adjective, for example *dem big* 'they are big'. 5) A separate verb *deh* is used for 'to be in a place', for example *him deh a yaad* 'he's at home'. 6) In questions, an emphasized noun or verb can be placed at the beginning of the sentence, sometimes preceded by a form of the verb *to be* (*is* or *a*), for example *a play we a play* 'we're playing', *is weh de load deh?* 'where's the load?'

WORLD ENGLISH *British English* is the English language as used in the United Kingdom of Great Britain (England, Scotland, and Wales) and Northern Ireland. With a population of over 57 million, the United Kingdom is the second largest primary English-speaking country after the United States, and it continues to have prestige as the place of origin of the English language. The term British English is not, however, precise, being variously used to refer to: all varieties of English in the United Kingdom as a whole; all varieties in Great Britain as a whole; all varieties in England alone; the forms of only the standard language in the United Kingdom as a whole; those forms in Great Britain as a whole; those forms in England alone; and, notably, that variety of the standard language based on upper- and middle-class usage (especially at the turn of the 20th century in southeastern England).

Jamaican Creole, the dialect of English spoken in Jamaica

British Broadcasting Corporation *n* full form of **BBC**

British Columbia /bríttish-/ *n* westernmost province of Canada, situated on the Pacific coast, north of the US border, west of Alberta, and south of Yukon Territory and the Northwest Territories. Capital: Victoria. Population: 3,907,738 (2001). Area: 944,735 sq. km/364,764 sq. mi.

British Commonwealth of Nations *n* POL same as **Commonwealth** (sense 1)

British Council *n* a London-based organization founded by Royal Charter in 1942 to promote the English language and British culture around the world

British Empire *n* a group of colonies, protectorates, and other territories brought under British rule, by the 19th century comprising more than one-quarter of the world's population. Most of Great Britain's former colonies became independent after World War II and, as sovereign states, many joined the Commonwealth.

British English *n* the form of English used by people in the United Kingdom

Britisher /bríttishər/ *n* N Am a British subject or a person from Great Britain (*informal*)

British Guiana former name for **Guyana**

British Honduras former name for **Belize**

British India *n* the part of South Asia under British administration from 1765 to 1947, when the independent states of India and Pakistan were created

British Indian Ocean Territory British overseas territory in the Indian Ocean, consisting of five uninhabited coral islands, the largest of which is Diego Garcia. Area: 60 sq. km/23 sq. mi.

British Isles group of islands in the northeastern Atlantic, separated from mainland Europe by the North Sea and the English Channel. It consists of the large islands of Great Britain and Ireland and almost 5,000 surrounding smaller islands and islets.

British Legion *n* a charitable organization in the United Kingdom that provides help for former members of the armed forces

British Library *n* the United Kingdom's national library in London that contains books, sound recordings, and manuscripts brought together from various national collections such as those of the British Museum. It is one of England's copyright deposit libraries.

British Museum *n* the national museum of the United Kingdom, situated in London. It was founded in the 18th century and contains one of the world's finest collections of antiquities.

British Pharmacopoeia *n* the official compendium of UK quality standards for pharmacologically active substances and drug products. Substances listed put BP after the name on labels.

British Somaliland former British protectorate in East Africa from 1884 until 1960, when it united with Italian Somaliland to form the republic of Somalia

British Standards Institution *n* an organization that issues standards for manufacturing practice and quality control, as well as for measurements and technical terms used in the United Kingdom

British Standard Time *n* the time that was used from 1968 to 1971 in the United Kingdom, one hour ahead of Greenwich Mean Time

British Summer Time *n* the time, one hour ahead of Greenwich Mean Time, used in the United Kingdom from the end of March to the end of October. It is intended to make better use of the hours of daylight in this part of the year.

British thermal unit *n* the amount of heat needed to raise the temperature of one pound of water by one degree Fahrenheit, equal to approximately 1055 joules

British Union of Fascists *n* a fascist organization founded by Sir Oswald Mosley in the 1930s

British Virgin Islands dependent territory of the United Kingdom consisting of 36 islands in the eastern Caribbean Sea, east of Puerto Rico. Capital: Road Town. Population: 20,812 (2001). Area: 153 sq. km/59 sq. mi. See map on next page

British West Indies British dependent territories in the Caribbean, including Anguilla, the British Virgin Islands, the Cayman Islands, Montserrat, and the Turks and Caicos

Briton /brítt'n/ *n* **1.** somebody who comes from Great Britain **2.** a member of an ancient Celtic people

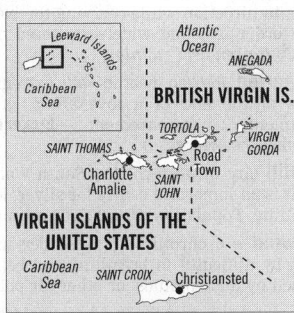

British Virgin Islands and Virgin Islands of the United States

who once lived in southern Britain [13C. Via French *Breton* < Latin *Britton-* < Celtic]

Britpop /brít pop/ *n* a style of pop music originating in the United Kingdom in the 1990s and reminiscent of the rock and roll style of 1960s bands such as the Beatles

britska *n* VEHICLES another spelling of **britzka**

Brittain /brítt'n/, **Vera** (1893–1970) British writer. Her World War I memoir *Testament of Youth* (1933) speaks for a generation of young people whose lives were forever changed by the experience of war. Full name **Brittain, Vera Mary**

'It is probably true to say that the largest scope for change still lies in men's attitude to women, and in women's attitude to themselves.'
[Vera Brittain, *Lady into Woman*; 1953]

Brittany /brítt əni/ peninsular region in northwestern France, between the Bay of Biscay and the English Channel. Its capital is Rennes. Population: 2,906,197 (1999). Area: 27,209 sq. km/10,505 sq. mi.

Britten /brítt'n/, **Benjamin** (1913–76) British composer. Regarded as one of Britain's finest composers, he wrote orchestral works, the operas *Peter Grimes* (1945) and *Billy Budd* (1951), and the *War Requiem* (1961). Full name **Britten, Edward Benjamin, Baron Britten of Aldeburgh**

brittle /brítt'l/ *adj* (**-tler, -tlest**) 1. HARD AND BREAKABLE hard and likely to break or crack ○ *plastic that has become brittle with age* 2. SHARP-SOUNDING describes a voice that has a sharp, unnerving quality 3. NOT FRIENDLY tense, irritable, and lacking personal warmth ○ *a brittle quality to her that I didn't like* ■ *n* TOFFEE-NUT SWEET a crunchy sweet made from caramel and nuts [14C. < Old English *gebryttan* 'shatter'] —**brittlely** *adv* —**brittleness** *n*

brittle-bone disease *n* MED 1. same as **osteoporosis** 2. same as **osteogenesis imperfecta**

brittle star *n* an invertebrate sea animal similar to a starfish but with thinner, longer, and more flexible arms. Class: Ophiuroidea.

Brittonic *adj, n* LANG, PEOPLES same as **Brythonic**

britzka /brítskə/, **britska** *n* a horse-drawn carriage with a rear-facing front seat and a folding top over the back seat [Early 19C. < Polish *bryczka*]

Brix scale /bríks-/ *n* a hydrometer scale used for measuring the sugar content of a solution at a particular temperature [Late 19C. After Adolf *Brix* (1798–1890), German scientist]

Brno /búrnō/ industrial city in the former region of Moravia, southeastern Czech Republic. Population: 384,727 (1999).

bro /brō/ *n* same as **brother** (*informal*)

bro., **Bro.** *abbr* brother

broach /brōch/ *v* (**broaches, broaching, broached**) 1. *vt* BRING UP DIFFICULT SUBJECT to introduce a subject for discussion, usually one that is awkward ○ *He finally broached the question of the loan.* 2. *vt* OPEN CONTAINER to open a container for the first time 3. *vt* PIERCE CASK to make a hole in a cask to draw off liquid 4. *vt* BORE HOLE to make or enlarge a hole in something 5. *vi* NAVY COME THROUGH SURFACE OF WATER to break the surface of water from below without completely emerging (*refers to submarines*) 6. *vi* NAUT TURN SIDEWAYS TO WIND to be turned broadside to the wind, e.g. by heavy seas, with a risk of capsizing (*refers to boats*) ■ *n* 1.

TOOL FOR HOLES a tool for enlarging holes 2. TOOL FOR PIERCING CASKS a tool used for making holes in casks 3. ROASTING SPIT a spit for roasting meat over a fire 4. JEWELLERY same as **brooch** [14C. < Old French *brocher* 'to stitch' < *broche* 'skewer, long needle'] —**broacher** *n*

SPELLCHECK Do not confuse the spelling of **broach** and **brooch** ('a dress ornament'), which sound similar.

broad /brawd/ *adj* 1. WIDE large from one side to the other ○ *a broad forehead* ○ *six inches broad* 2. LARGE AND SPACIOUS extending a great distance in all directions ○ *the broad steppes* 3. MEASURED ACROSS measured from side to side ○ *as broad as it is long* 4. FULL AND CLEAR full and clear to see ○ *a broad grin* ○ *broad daylight* 5. COVERING WIDE RANGE comprehensive in content, knowledge, experience, ability, or application ○ *She has very broad interests.* 6. NOT DETAILED general and lacking detail ○ *I'll give you a broad outline of the project.* 7. WIDESPREAD OR GENERALIZED widespread or generalized throughout a large and diverse group of people ○ *a broad feeling of disillusionment in the party* 8. OBVIOUS meant to be easily understood ○ *dropping broad hints about their plans* 9. UNOBSTRUCTED with nothing blocking the way ○ *in broad view* 10. TOLERANT tending to tolerate or accept the ideas and conduct of other people, even when these are very different from your own ○ *I think I have fairly broad views on the whole.* 11. POTENTIALLY OFFENSIVE potentially offensive to accepted standards of propriety ○ *broad humour* 12. PHON STRONGLY REGIONAL describes a regional accent that is very strong or pronounced 13. PHON SHOWING ONLY MAIN DIFFERENCES describes a phonetic transcription that gives only major differences 14. PHON PRONOUNCED WITH TONGUE DOWN describes a vowel pronounced with the tongue low and flat and the mouth open wide ■ *n* 1. WIDE PART the wide part of something ○ *He slapped Jack across the broad of his back.* 2. GEOG RIVER COVERING LAND a river that expands to cover low-lying land 3. *N Am* OFFENSIVE TERM an offensive term for a woman (*slang*) ■ *adv* COMPLETELY to the fullest extent [Old English *brād* < Germanic] —**broadness** *n*

B-road *n* a road given the prefix 'B' in the national road numbering and classification system because it is less important than an A-road

broadacre /brawd aykər/ *adj Aus* suitable for or used on large farms

broad arrow *n* 1. a mark in the shape of a wide arrowhead identifying government property, formerly used on prison clothing 2. an arrow with a wide barbed head

Broad Australian *n* Australian English spoken with a strong Australian accent

WORLD ENGLISH See *Australian English*.

broadaxe /brawd aks/ *n* a heavy battleaxe with a wide blade

broadband /brawd band/ *adj* 1. using a wide range of electromagnetic frequencies 2. able to transfer large amounts of data at high speed

broad bean *n* 1. a large flat green seed cooked and eaten as a vegetable 2. a plant of the pea family with long pods that produces broad beans. Native to: Europe. Latin name: *Vicia faba*.

broadbill /brawd bil/ (*plural* **-bills** or *same*) *n* a bird with often brightly coloured feathers and a short broad beak. Native to: tropical Africa and Asia. Family: Eurylaimidae.

broad-brush *adj* attempting to cover all situations, conditions, or instances ○ *a broad-brush approach*

broadcast /brawd kaast/ *v* (**-casts, -casting, -cast** or **-casted**) 1. *vti* TRANSMIT RADIO SIGNALS to transmit a programme or information on television or radio 2. *vi* PERFORM ON RADIO OR TV to take part in a radio or television programme 3. *vt* MAKE SOMETHING WIDELY KNOWN to make something known to a large number of people ○ *They broadcast the rumours all over town.* 4. *vt* SCATTER SEED to sow seed by scattering it by hand ■ *n* 1. PROGRAMME a television or radio programme 2. TRANSMISSION a transmission of radio or television signals 3. SCATTERING OF SEED a sowing of seed by scattering it ■ *adv* WIDELY over a wide area —**broadcast** *adj* —**broadcaster** *n*

broadcasting /brawd kaasting/ *n* the making and transmission of television and radio programmes

broad church *n* a group, institution, or political party that has liberal and inclusive attitudes

Broad Church *n* a group within the Church of England that favours a liberal interpretation of doctrine

broadcloth /brawd kloth/ *n* 1. a shiny, closely woven cloth of woollen, cotton, or silk. Use: clothing. 2. a smooth woollen fabric with a plain weave and a dense texture

broaden /brawd'n/ (**-ens, -ening, -ened**) *vti* 1. to make something wider, or become wider 2. to enlarge the range or magnitude of something, or become wider in range or magnitude

broad gauge *n* a railway track that has a distance between the tracks greater than the standard 123.2 cm/48.5 in. Broad gauge allows greater passenger comfort and carrying capacity, but increases the cost of construction.

broad-gauge *adj* 1. relating to or designed for a railway using broad gauge 2. wide in application or range

broad-leaved /-leevd/, **broadleaf** /brawd leef/ *adj* describes deciduous or evergreen trees such as holly or beech that have wide rather than needle-shaped leaves

broadloom /brawd loom/ *adj* describes carpet that is woven on a wide loom so that it can be laid with few or no seams ■ *n* a carpet woven on a wide loom that can be laid with few or no seams

broadly /brawdli/ *adv* 1. GENERALLY in general terms ○ *Broadly speaking, there are two types of tourist.* 2. MOSTLY for the most part ○ *It is broadly based on the German prototype.* 3. WITH ENTHUSIASTIC SMILE with a smile that shows enthusiasm or friendliness ○ *smiling broadly*

broadly-based *adj* involving or covering a wide range of people or things

broad-minded *adj* willing to tolerate a wide range of ideas and behaviour —**broad-mindedly** *adv* —**broad-mindedness** *n*

broad money *n* ECON same as **M2**

Broads /brawdz/ area of over 30 shallow freshwater lakes and lagoons in Norfolk and Suffolk, eastern England. A popular tourist destination, it is managed by the Broads Authority and was made a Special Statutory Authority, with similar status to that of a national park, in 1988.

broadsheet /brawd sheet/ *n* 1. a newspaper that is printed in a large format and is associated with serious journalism as opposed to the smaller-format tabloids 2. *UK, ANZ, Can* PRINTING a large sheet of paper printed on one side. US term **broadside**

broadside /brawd sīd/ *n* 1. NAUT SHIP'S SIDE the side of a ship above the water line from bow to quarter 2. NAUT SHIP'S GUNS all the guns on one side of a ship 3. NAUT FIRING OF SHIP'S GUNS the simultaneous firing of all the guns on one side of a ship 4. STRONG SPOKEN OR WRITTEN ATTACK a strong spoken or written attack on somebody ○ *a vicious broadside on the Prime Minister* 5. LARGE FLAT SURFACE a large flat and usually vertical surface ○ *the broadside of the barn* 6. *US* PRINTING same as **broadsheet** (sense 2) ■ *adv* 1. WITH SIDE with the side facing towards something ○ *The ship hit the rocks broadside on.* 2. WITHOUT OBJECTIVE with no apparent objective ○ *Her proposals were attacked broadside.* ■ *vt* (**-sides, -siding, -sided**) *N Am* HIT SIDE OF SOMETHING to collide with something sideways on ○ *The car was broadsided by the train.*

broad-spectrum *adj* describes antibiotics or other chemicals that destroy a wide range of organisms such as bacteria or agricultural pests

broadsword /brawd sawrd/ *n* a sword with a wide flat blade designed for cutting rather than for thrusting

broadtail /brawd tayl/ *n* 1. the black wavy fur of a prematurely born karakul lamb 2. ZOOL same as **karakul** (sense 2)

broadwalk /brawd wawk/ *n Aus* a wide walkway, especially along a seafront

Broadway /brawd way/ *n* 1. a long avenue in Manhattan, New York City, part of which is the main thoroughfare of the city's theatre district 2. the commercial theatre business in the United States ○ *This is not Broadway material.*

Broadwood /brawd wood/, **John** (1732–1812) British

piano manufacturer. He founded the Broadwood Piano Company (1770) with Burkat Shudi, a Swiss harpsichord-maker.

Brobdingnagian /bróbding nággi ən/ *adj* extraordinarily large (*literary*) [Early 18C. < *Brobdingnag*, fictitious land of giants in Jonathan Swift's *Gulliver's Travels* (1726)]

brocade /brō káyd, brə-/ *n* a heavy silk, cotton, or woollen fabric with a raised design, often in metallic threads ■ *vt* (**-cades**, **-cading**, **-caded**) to weave a fabric with a raised design [Late 16C. Via Spanish or Portuguese *brocado* < Italian *broccato* < *brocco* 'twisted thread, shoot' < Latin *brocchus*] —**brocaded** *adj*

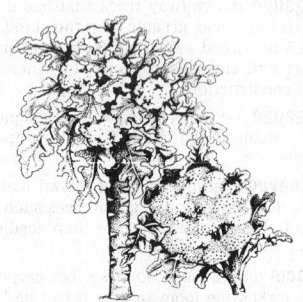
broccoli

broccoli /brókəli/ *n* **1.** heads of tight green, purple, or white flower buds, cooked and eaten as a vegetable **2.** a plant of the cabbage family that produces broccoli. Heading broccoli has green flower heads like cauliflower, and sprouting broccoli has multiple small purple or white flowering shoots. Latin name: *Brassica oleracea* var. *italica*. [Mid-17C. < Italian, plural of *broccolo* 'cabbage sprout' < *brocco* 'shoot' < Latin *brocchus*]

broch /brok, brokh/ *n* a prehistoric fortified dwelling in the shape of a circular stone tower, found especially on the islands and northern mainland of Scotland. They were built by the Picts, a Celtic people. [Mid-17C. Dialect form of BURGH]

brochette /bro shét/ *n* **1.** a small skewer on which chunks of food are grilled or roasted **2.** food, especially meat or fish, that has been cooked on a brochette [15C. < French, 'little skewer' < *broche* 'skewer, long needle']

brochure /bróshər, bro shoór/ *n* a booklet or pamphlet that contains descriptive information or advertising [Mid-18C. < French, 'something stitched together' < *brocher* (see BROACH)]

brochure site *n* a simple, often one-page website advertising a company's products and giving contact details

brock /brok/ (*plural* **brocks** or *same*) *n* ZOOL same as **badger** [Pre-12C. < Celtic]

Brocken /brókən/ the highest point in the Harz Mountains, central Germany. It is associated with folklore and traditional rites, including Walpurgis Night, or the Witches' Sabbath. Height: 1,141 m/3,743 ft.

~~brocoli~~ incorrect spelling of **broccoli**

broderie anglaise /bródəri ong gláyz/ *n* **1.** white cotton or synthetic fabric decorated with an ornamental pattern of small holes with stitched edges. Use: decorative trimming. **2.** embroidery in the form of an ornamental pattern of small holes with stitched edges [Mid-19C. < French, 'English embroidery']

broderie perse /-púrss/ *n* an appliqué technique in which designs are cut from patterned fabric and sewn onto plain fabric [< French, 'chintz embroidery']

Brodsky /bródski/, **Joseph** (1940–96) Soviet-born US poet and essayist. He won the Nobel Prize in literature (1987) and was US poet laureate (1991–92).

'The greatest thing a society can do to a citizen is to leave him alone.'
[Joseph Brodsky. Remarks at Dartmouth College Commencement, *New York Times*; 12 June 1989]

Broederbond /broódər bont/ *n* S Africa formerly, a secret society of Afrikaner nationalists in South Africa, committed to gaining control of vital areas

of government [Mid-20C. Via Afrikaans < Dutch, 'league of brothers']

brog /brog/ *n* Scotland WOODWORK same as **bradawl** [15C. Origin ?]

brogan /brógən/ *n* a heavy ankle-high work boot [Mid-19C. < Irish or Scottish Gaelic *brógan* 'little shoe' < *brog* (see BROGUE[2])]

Broglie /broy/, **Louis Victor, Prince de** (1892–1987) French physicist. He was awarded the Nobel Prize in physics (1929) for his work on electron waves and particles. Full name **Broglie, Louis Victor Pierre Raymond**

brogue[1] /brōg/ *n* a regional accent, especially the accent of Irish people speaking English [Early 18C. Origin ?]

REGIONAL NOTE The Irish word *brog* meaning 'shoe' comes ultimately from an Old Norse word meaning 'leg covering'. The use of the term for 'accent', especially an 'Irish accent', goes back to the early 18th century, but the link between the meanings is tenuous. It is possible that it was applied to the speech of people who called their shoes *brogues*. Certainly, Thomas Sheridan mentioned that the Irish 'brought with them each their several brogues or modes of intonation' in 1775.

brogue[2] /brōg/ *n* **1.** a rugged shoe, usually with a decorative pattern of small holes in the leather across the toe and along the sides. N Am term **wing tip 2.** a simple heavy untanned shoe formerly worn in Ireland and Scotland [Late 16C. Via Irish and Scottish Gaelic *brog* < Old Norse *brók* 'leg covering']

broil[1] /broyl/ (**broils**, **broiling**, **broiled**) *v* **1.** *vti* to make somebody or something extremely hot, or become extremely hot ○ *We had been broiling in the sun all morning.* **2.** *vt* Aus, N Am same as **grill**[1] *v* (sense 2) **3.** *vi* US to be extremely angry [14C. < Old French *bruler*]

broil[2] /broyl/ *n* a brawl (*archaic*) [15C. < Anglo-Norman *broiller* 'mix up, confuse', Old French *bröoillier* < *breu* 'broth'] —**broil** *vi*

broiler /bróylər/ *n* **1.** a young chicken for roasting **2.** Aus, N Am HOUSEHOLD same as **grill**[1] *n* (sense 1)

broiler house *n* a building where broiler chickens are reared

broiler pan *n* Aus, N Am HOUSEHOLD same as **grill pan**

broke[1] past tense of **break**[1]

broke[2] /brōk/ *regional* past participle of **break**[1] (*archaic*) ■ *adj* (*informal*) **1.** without any money to spend **2.** totally bankrupt [Early 18C. Alteration of BROKEN] ◇ **go for broke** to risk everything to achieve a goal (*informal*)

broke[3] /brōk/ *vt* to broker a deal, sale, or contract [Early 20C. Back-formation < BROKER] —**broking** *n*

broken /brókən/ past participle of **break**[1] ■ *adj* **1.** NO LONGER WHOLE in two or more pieces, e.g. after having been dropped or struck with something hard **2.** OUT OF ORDER no longer in working condition ○ *The CD player is broken.* **3.** NOT KEPT not honoured or fulfilled ○ *a broken promise* **4.** NOT CONTINUOUS lacking continuity ○ *a broken line* **5.** UNEVEN having an uneven surface ○ *We travelled over broken terrain.* **6.** WEAKENED physically weakened ○ *His health was broken.* **7.** DESTROYED BY ADVERSITY destroyed or badly hurt by grief or misfortune ○ *a broken man* **8.** SPLIT APART split apart by divorce, separation, or desertion ○ *came from a broken home* **9.** LANGUAGE IMPERFECTLY SPOKEN spoken in an imperfect or halting manner ○ *in broken English* **10.** INCOMPLETE lacking parts necessary to be complete ○ *a broken set of books* **11.** DISORGANIZED lacking order or harmony ○ *escaping in broken ranks* [Old English *brocen*, past participle of BREAK[1]] —**brokenly** *adv* —**brokenness** *n*

Broken Bay /brókən-/ bay on the eastern coast of New South Wales, Australia. It lies at the mouth of the Hawkesbury River, north of Sydney.

broken chord *n* a chord played as a quick succession of notes (**arpeggio**) instead of simultaneously

broken consort *n* a musical ensemble made up of instruments of different types, used especially in music of the Renaissance

broken-down *adj* **1.** damaged or not working ○ *a broken-down old machine* **2.** in very poor condition ○ *a broken-down house*

broken-field *adj* in American football, making quick

changes in direction while carrying the ball downfield in order to avoid widely scattered opposing players ○ *broken-field running*

brokenhearted /brókən haártid/ *adj* extremely sad because of the end of a love affair, great disappointment, or bereavement —**brokenheartedly** *adv* —**brokenheartedness** *n*

Broken Hill city in western New South Wales, Australia. It is an important centre for silver, lead, and zinc mining. Population: 20,908 (2002 estimate).

broken wind *n* a chronic lung disorder in horses marked by difficulty in breathing and believed to be caused by dust, moulds, or other air pollutants

broker /brókər/ *n* **1.** somebody who is paid to act as an agent for others, e.g. in negotiating contracts or buying and selling goods and services **2.** FIN same as **stockbroker 3.** POL same as **power broker** ■ *vt* (**-kers**, **-kering**, **-kered**) to act as an agent in arranging a deal, sale, or contract [14C. < Anglo-Norman *brocour* 'small trader']

brokerage /brókərij/ *n* **1.** PAYMENT TO BROKER a fee paid to somebody who acts as a financial agent for somebody else **2.** BROKER'S BUSINESS the business of being a broker **3.** STOCKBROKING COMPANY a company whose business is buying and selling stocks, shares, and bonds for its clients

broker-dealer *n* in the United Kingdom, somebody employed on the Stock Exchange to buy and sell stocks, shares, goods, or assets on behalf of somebody else

brokered CD *n* a certificate of deposit issued by a bank and sold in bulk to a brokerage for selling on to its customers

brolga /brólgə/ (*plural* **-gas** or *same*) *n* a large grey crane with bare red skin on the sides and back of its neck. Native to: Australia. Latin name: *Grus rubicunda*. [Late 19C. < Kamilaroi *buralga*]

brolly /brólli/ (*plural* **-lies**) *n* same as **umbrella** *n* (sense 1) (*informal*) [Late 19C. Alteration]

brom- *prefix* bromine, bromic ○ *bromate* [< BROMINE, BROMIDE]

bromate /brố mayt/ *n* a salt, ester, or ion of bromic acid ■ *vt* (**-mates**, **-mating**, **-mated**) CHEM same as **brominate**

bromegrass /brốm graass/, **brome** /brōm/ *n* a tall grass with small drooping flower spikes. Some types of bromegrass are cultivated for hay, while others are weeds. Native to: temperate regions. Genus: *Bromus*. [Mid-18C. Via modern Latin *Bromus* < Greek *bromos, brōmos* 'oats']

bromelain /brốmə layn/, **bromelin** /-lin/ *n* an enzyme extracted from pineapples, used in alternative medicine to help the digestion of proteins, reduce blood clotting, counter inflammation, and boost immunity [Late 19C. < modern Latin *Bromelia*, after O. Bromel (see BROMELIAD)]

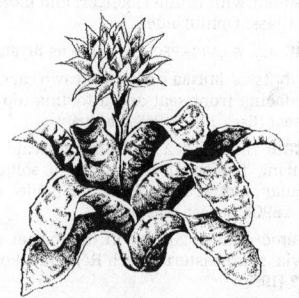
bromeliad

bromeliad /brō meéli ad/ *n* a tropical plant with fleshy leaves forming a funnel that holds water, often growing on another plant for physical support. Native to: Central and southern America. Family: Bromeliaceae. [Mid-19C. After Olaf *Bromel* (1639–1705), Swedish botanist]

bromic /brốmik/ *adj* relating to or containing bromine with a valency of five

bromic acid *n* an unstable colourless acid that is a strong oxidizing agent. Use: manufacture of pharmaceuticals and dyes. Formula: $HBrO_3$.

bromide /brṓ mīd/ *n* **1.** CHEM BROMINE COMPOUND a compound containing bromine and another element or group, e.g. silver bromide **2.** CHEM POTASSIUM BROMIDE potassium bromide, especially when used as a sedative **3.** UNORIGINAL SAYING a saying that lacks originality or significance (*dated*)

bromide paper *n* a light-sensitive photographic paper that is coated with silver bromide emulsion

bromidic /brṓ míddik/ *adj* without originality or interest (*dated*)

brominate /brṓmi nayt/ (**-nates, -nating, -nated**) *vt* to treat or combine a substance with bromine or a bromine compound —**bromination** /brṓmi náysh'n/ *n*

bromine /brṓ meen, -min/ *n* a pungent, dark red, volatile, liquid, nonmetallic element of the halogen series. Use: sedatives, photographic materials. Symbol **Br**. See table at **element** [Early 19C. < French *brome* < Greek *brōmos* 'stench']

Bromley /brómmli/ borough of London, England. Population: 295,532 (2001).

bromobenzene /brṓmō bén zeen/ *n* a heavy colourless liquid with a pungent odour. Use: synthesis of chemicals, solvent.

bromocriptine /brṓmə kríp teen/ *n* a drug that functions like dopamine. Use: treatment of excessive lactation, breast pain, some forms of infertility, growth disorder, and Parkinsonism.

Bromsgrove /brómz grṓv/ town in Worcestershire, west-central England. Population: 26,366 (1991).

bronch- *prefix* ANAT same as **broncho-** (*used before vowels*)

bronchi ANAT plural of **bronchus**

bronchial /bróngki əl/ *adj* relating to or affecting the tubes (**bronchi**) that carry air from the windpipe into the lungs ○ *a bronchial infection* —**bronchially** *adv*

bronchial pneumonia *n* MED same as **bronchopneumonia**

bronchial tube *n* a tubular passage forming part of a network of airways to and within the lungs. Two main tubes (**bronchi**) lead from the windpipe to each lung, dividing into smaller bronchi and subsequently bronchioles.

bronchiectasis /bróngki éktəssiss/ *n* chronic dilation of the airways to and within the lungs, causing coughing and excessive mucus production [Late 19C. < late Latin *bronchia* (see BRONCHIOLE) + Greek *ektasis* 'dilation']

bronchiole /bróngki ōl/ *n* a narrow tube inside the lungs that branches off the main air passages (**bronchi**) [Mid-19C. < modern Latin *bronchiolus* < late Latin *bronchia* < Greek *brogkhos* (see BRONCHUS)] —**bronchiolar** /bróngki ṓlər/ *adj*

bronchitis /brong kítiss/ *n* inflammation of the mucous membrane in the airways (**bronchial tubes**) of the lungs, resulting from infection or irritation and causing breathing problems and severe coughing —**bronchitic** /brong kíttik/ *adj*

broncho- *prefix* bronchus, bronchial ○ *bronchoscope* [Via late Latin < Greek *brogkhos* (see BRONCHUS)]

bronchodilator /bróngkō dī láytər/ *n* a drug that relaxes the main air passages (**bronchi**) and eases breathing. Use: asthma treatment.

bronchopneumonia /bróngkō nyoo mṓni ə/ *n* inflammation of the lungs caused by an infection in the air passages (**bronchioles**)

bronchoscope /bróngkə skōp/ *n* a thin instrument with a light on the end, used for looking inside the air passages (**bronchi**) leading to the lungs — **bronchoscopic** /bróngkə skóppik/ *adj* —**bronchoscopically** *adv* —**bronchoscopist** /brong kóskəpist/ *n* —**bronchoscopy** /-kóskəpi/ *n*

bronchus /bróngkəss/ (*plural* **-chi** /-kī, -kee/) *n* a tube leading from the windpipe to a lung, which provides for the passage of air [Late 17C. Via modern Latin < Greek *brogkhos* 'windpipe' < Indo-European]

bronco /bróng kō/ (*plural* **-cos**) *n* a wild or partly broken horse, used in rodeos [Mid-19C. < Spanish, 'rough, wild']

broncobuster /bróngkō bustər/ *n* N Am a person who breaks in wild horses (*informal*)

Brontë /brónti/, **Anne** (1820–49) British novelist and poet. Sister of Charlotte Brontë and Emily Brontë,

she wrote the novels *Agnes Grey* (published in 1847) and *The Tenant of Wildfell Hall* (published in 1848).

> 'What is it that constitutes virtue, Mrs. Graham? Is it the circumstance of being able and willing to resist temptation; or that of having no temptations to resist.'
> [Anne Brontë, *The Tenant of Wildfell Hall*; 1848]

Charlotte Brontë

Brontë, Charlotte (1816–55) British novelist. Elder sister of Emily Brontë and Anne Brontë, she wrote *Jane Eyre* (1847) and *Villette* (1853).

> 'Conventionality is not morality. Self-righteousness is not religion. To attack the first is not to assail the last. To pluck the mask from the face of the Pharisee, is not to lift an impious hand to the Crown of Thorns.'
> [Charlotte Brontë, *Jane Eyre*; 1847]

Brontë, Emily (1818–48) British poet and novelist. Sister of Charlotte Brontë and Anne Brontë, she wrote *Wuthering Heights* (1847). See Cultural note at **height**

> 'If all else perished, and he remained, I should still continue to be; and if all else remained, and he were annihilated, the universe would turn to a mighty stranger: I should not seem a part of it.'
> [Emily Brontë, *Wuthering Heights*; 1847]

brontosaurus /bróntə sáwrəss/, **brontosaur** /bróntə sawr/ *n* PALAEONT same as **apatosaurus** (*dated*) [Late 19C. < modern Latin *Brontosaurus* < Greek *brontē* 'thunder' + *sauros* 'lizard']

Bronx /brongks/ northernmost of the five boroughs of New York City, located on the mainland with the Harlem and Hudson rivers to the west, Westchester County to the north, Long Island Sound to the east, and the East River to the south. Population: 1,354,068 (2002 estimate).

Bronx cheer *n* N Am same as **raspberry** (sense 3) (*informal*)

bronze /bronz/ *n* **1.** COPPER AND TIN ALLOY a hard yellowish-brown alloy of copper and tin, sometimes containing small amounts of other metals. Bronze is harder than copper and is often cast to make statues. **2.** COPPER-BASED ALLOY an alloy of copper with a substance other than tin, e.g. aluminium or silicon **3.** SCULPTURE BRONZE WORK OF ART an object that is made from bronze, especially a statue or other piece of cast sculpture **4.** SPORTS same as **bronze medal** (*informal*) **5.** COLOURS DEEP YELLOWISH-BROWN COLOUR a deep yellowish-brown colour, like that of bronze ■ *v* (**bronzes, bronzing, bronzed**) **1.** *vt* MAKE SOMETHING LOOK LIKE BRONZE to give something the yellowish-brown sheen or weathered patina of bronze **2.** *vti* TAN SKIN to make somebody's skin suntanned, or become suntanned (*informal*) [Early 18C. Via French < Italian *bronzo*] —**bronze** *adj* —**bronzed** *adj* —**bronzer** *n* —**bronzy** *adj*

Bronze Age *n* a period of cultural history, approximately between 3500 and 1500 BC, that succeeded the Stone Age and was characterized by the use of tools made of bronze

bronze medal *n* a medal that is awarded to a person who is placed third in a competition, especially a sporting event —**bronze medallist** *n*

Bronzino, il /bron dzéeno/ ♦ **il Bronzino**

bronzite /brón zīt/ *n* an iron-containing variety of enstatite with a metallic sheen

brooch /brōch/, **broach** *n* a piece of jewellery that is fastened to a garment by a hinged pin and catch. Brooches are usually worn by women on the upper part of a garment. [13C. < Old French *broche* 'skewer, long needle']

SPELLCHECK See *broach*.

brood /brood/ *v* (**broods, brooding, brooded**) **1.** *vi* WORRY to be preoccupied with a troublesome or unwelcome thought **2.** *vi* THINK UNPLEASANT THOUGHTS to think resentful, dark, or miserable thoughts **3.** *vti* HATCH EGGS to sit on or hatch eggs, or cover nestlings for warmth **4.** *vi* BE HEAVY OR OMINOUS to loom or hang heavily and ominously (*literary*) ○ *dark clouds brooding overhead* ■ *n* **1.** YOUNG OF BIRDS OR ANIMALS the young of an animal, especially young birds, that are born and reared together **2.** FAMILY'S CHILDREN the children of one family (*informal humorous*) **3.** GROUP OF SIMILAR PEOPLE a group whose members share a common origin or background ○ *the latest brood of avant-garde artists* ■ *adj* KEPT FOR BREEDING describes a female farm animal that is kept for the purpose of producing young ○ *a brood mare* [Old English *brōd* < Indo-European, 'heat']

brooder /broodər/ *n* **1.** HEATED PLACE FOR YOUNG ANIMAL a heated area or enclosure for rearing young fowl. It provides an optimum environment in which heat, light, food, and water can be carefully controlled. **2.** FEMALE BIRD SITTING ON EGGS a female bird that sits on eggs to keep them warm before they hatch **3.** PERSON WHO WORRIES somebody who worries a lot about things

brooding /brooding/ *adj* seeming to contain some silent threat or danger (*literary*) ■ *n* somebody's private thoughts about a situation that is a source of anxiety ○ *Her broodings were disturbed by Colette's arrival.* —**broodingly** *adv*

brood mare *n* a mare that is kept specially for breeding

broody /broodi/ (**-ier, -iest**) *adj* **1.** READY TO INCUBATE EGGS describes a hen that is ready to sit on eggs to keep them warm before they hatch, especially a hen that is no longer able to lay eggs **2.** THOUGHTFUL OR SULLEN showing deep thought, anxiety, or resentment ○ *His long broody silences were hard to bear.* **3.** WANTING BABY eager or anxious to have a baby (*informal*) — **broodily** *adv* —**broodiness** *n*

brook[1] /brook/ *n* a small freshwater stream [Old English *brōc* < Germanic]

brook[2] /brook/ (**brooks, brooking, brooked**) *vt* to put up with something (*literary*; *used in negative statements*) ○ *I will brook no interference in this matter.* [Old English *brūcan* < Indo-European]

Brook /brook/, **Peter** (*b.* 1925) British-born director. He was associated with the Royal Shakespeare Company from 1962. Full name **Brook, Peter Stephen Paul**

Brooke /brook/, **Rupert** (1887–1915) British poet. His reputation as a major poet of World War I was secured by the posthumous publication of *1914 and Other Poems* (1915). He died of blood poisoning in the Aegean before seeing action. Full name **Brooke, Rupert Chawner**

> 'These laid the world away; poured out the red / Sweet wine of youth; gave up the years to be / Of work and joy, and that unhoped serene, / That men call age; and those who would have been, / Their sons, they gave, their immortality.'
> [Rupert Brooke, 'The Dead'; 1914]

Brookeborough /brookbərə/, **Basil Stanlake Brooke, 1st Viscount** (1888–1973) British politician. A supporter of Unionist policies, he was prime minister of Northern Ireland from 1943 to 1963.

Brook Farm *n* an experimental cooperative community established by a group of writers and scholars on a farm at West Roxbury, Massachusetts. It lasted from 1841 to 1846.

brookite /brook īt/ *n* a translucent or reddish-brown to black crystalline mineral composed of titanium dioxide [Early 19C. After Henry *Brook* (1771–1857), British mineralogist]

Brooklyn /brooklin/ one of the five boroughs of New York City, located on the western tip of Long Island with Staten Island and Manhattan to the west and Queens to the north and east. Population: 2,465,326 (2000).

Brookner /brŏoknər/, **Anita** (*b.* 1928) British writer. Her novel *Hotel du Lac* (1984) won the Booker Prize.

> 'In real life, of course, it is the hare who wins. Every time. Look around you. And in any case it is my contention that Aesop was writing for the tortoise market...Hares have no time to read. They are too busy winning the game.'
> [Anita Brookner, *Hotel du Lac*; 1984]

Brooks /brŏoks/, **Mel** (*b.* 1926) US film actor and director. His films include *The Producers* (1968) and *Blazing Saddles* (1974). Born **Kaminsky, Melvin**

> 'Tragedy is if I cut my finger. Comedy is if I walk into an open sewer and die.'
> [Mel Brooks, *New Yorker*; 30 October 1978]

brook trout *n* **1.** *N Am* same as **char 2.** the flesh of a brook trout as food

broom /broom, brŏom/ *n* **1.** BRUSH FOR SWEEPING a brush with a head of twigs or bristles attached to a long thin handle, used for sweeping indoors or outdoors **2.** PLANT WITH BRIGHT YELLOW FLOWERS a wild or cultivated bush. Flowers: bright yellow. Native to: Europe, Asia. Latin name: *Cytisus scoparius.* **3.** PLANT LIKE BROOM a bush resembling broom. Flowers: yellow. Native to: Europe, Asia. Genera: *Genista* or *Spartium.* ■ *vt* (**brooms, brooming, broomed**) SWEEP SOMETHING to sweep something with a broom or brush [Old English *brōm* < Germanic]

broomcorn /broom kawrn, brŏom-/ *n* a type of sorghum with long stiff stalks. Use: making brooms. Latin name: *Sorghum bicolor*.

Broome /broom/ town on the northwestern coast of Western Australia, formerly an important pearling centre. Population: 13,673 (2002 estimate).

broomrape /broom rayp, brŏom-/ *n* a plant that lives on the roots of other plants, including crops. Genus: *Orobanche.* [Late 16C. < medieval Latin *rapum* 'tuber']

broomstick /broom stik, brŏom-/ *n* **1.** the long handle of a broom **2.** a long-handled broom with a head of twigs

Broonzy /broonzi/, **Big Bill** (1893–1958) US musician. He incorporated a wide range of influences as a master composer and performer of blues. Born **Conley, William Lee**

bros., **Bros.** *abbr* COMM brothers

brose /brōz/ *n Scotland* a Scottish dish resembling porridge, made from broth, milk, or water stirred into toasted oatmeal. It is sometimes flavoured with vegetables, meat, fish, seafood, or poultry. [Mid-17C. Via Old French *broez* and assumed Vulgar Latin *brodo* < Germanic, 'broth']

broth /broth/ *n* **1.** a nourishing soup of poultry, meat, or vegetables, to which barley or rice is sometimes added **2.** a clear soup made by cooking meat, poultry, fish, seafood, or vegetables in water and then removing them [Old English *broþ* < Indo-European, 'heat, boil']

brothel /bróth'l/ *n* a place where people pay to have sexual intercourse with prostitutes [14C. < Old English *broþen* 'ruined'. Originally 'worthless person, prostitute'; current use a shortening of *brothel-house*]

brothel creepers *npl* men's suede shoes with thick crepe-rubber soles, popular in the 1950s and 1960s

brother /brúthər/ *n* **1.** MALE SIBLING a boy or man who has the same father and mother as another person **2.** (*plural* **brothers** or **brethren** /bréthrən/) FELLOW MEMBER a man who belongs to the same ethnic group, religion, profession, trade, or organization as another man **3.** (*plural* **brothers** or **brethren**) CHR LAY MEMBER a member of a religious order for men **4.** (*plural* **brothers** or **brethren**) CHR DEVOTED RELIGIOUS WORKER a man who devotes himself to the work of a men's religious order without having been professed ■ *interj* EXPRESSING SURPRISE OR ANNOYANCE used to express surprise, annoyance, or disappointment (*informal*) ○ *Oh, brother! What happened here today?* [Old English *brōþor* < Indo-European]

brotherhood /brúthər hŏod/ *n* **1.** GOODWILL a feeling of fellowship and sympathy for other people **2.** GROUP OF MEN an organization of men who are united for a common purpose, e.g. a trade union **3.** ALL MEMBERS all the members of a particular profession or trade **4.** HAVING SAME PARENTS the relationship of brothers

brother-in-law (*plural* **brothers-in-law**) *n* **1.** SISTER'S HUSBAND the husband of somebody's sister **2.** SPOUSE'S BROTHER the brother of somebody's husband or wife **3.** SPOUSE'S SISTER'S HUSBAND the husband of the sister of somebody's husband or wife

brotherly /brúthərli/ *adj* showing feelings that a brother might be expected to have towards his sister or brother —**brotherliness** *n*

brougham /broom, brŏo əm/ *n* a one-horse carriage with an open seat at the front for the driver and a closed compartment at the back for passengers, used in the 19th century [Mid-19C. After Lord *Brougham* (1778–1868)]

brought past participle, past tense of **bring**

broughtupsy /brawt úpsi/ *n Carib* especially in Tobago, good manners indicating that somebody has been brought up well (*informal*) ○ *She eh have no broughtupsy.*

brouhaha /broo haa haa/ *n* **1.** public criticism or protest ○ *all the brouhaha over the drug's side effects* **2.** a noisy commotion or uproar (*informal*) [Late 19C. < French]

brow /brow/ *n* **1.** FOREHEAD the area on somebody's face above the eyes and below the hairline **2.** ANAT same as **eyebrow** (sense 1) **3.** TOP OF HILL the top edge of a hill or the highest part of a slope **4.** MIN EXTRACT TOP OF MINE the top of a mineshaft [Old English *brū* < Indo-European]

browallia /brə wáali ə/ (*plural same* or **-as**) *n* an ornamental plant of the nightshade family. Flowers: blue, white, violet. Native to: America. Genus: *Browallia.* [Late 18C. < modern Latin, after Johann *Browall* (1707–55), Swedish botanist]

browband /brów band/ *n* a strap that is part of a horse's bridle and goes across its forehead

browbeat /brów beet/ (**-beats, -beating, -beat, -beaten** /-beet'n/) *vt* to bully or intimidate somebody sternly ○ *I will not be browbeaten into making a hasty decision.* —**browbeater** *n*

brown /brown/ *n* **1.** COLOUR BETWEEN RED AND YELLOW a colour that varies between red and yellow, similar to the colour of wood or soil **2.** BROWN CLOTHING fabric or clothing that is brown in colour ○ *We had to wear brown for school.* **3.** BROWN PIGMENT OR DYE a pigment or dye that has or is near to the colour of wood or soil **4.** BROWN OBJECT an object that is brown in colour ○ *She decided to take the brown.* ■ *adj* **1.** BROWN IN COLOUR of the colour brown ○ *the fruit was brown and rotten* **2.** SUNTANNED deeply suntanned or sunburnt **3.** UNPROCESSED describes foodstuffs that are partially or wholly unprocessed so that their natural brown colour remains ○ *brown sugar* ■ *vti* (**browns, browning, browned**) MAKE OR BECOME BROWN to make something brown or become brown, e.g. in cooking or sunbathing [Old English *brūn* < Indo-European, 'bright, brown'] —**brownish** *adj* —**brownness** *n*

Brown /brown/, **Sir Arthur Whitten** (1886–1948) British aviator. With John Alcock, he made the first transatlantic flight, from Newfoundland to Ireland, which took 16 hours 12 minutes.

Brown, Bryan (*b.* 1948) Australian actor. He is best known for his work in films such as *Breaker Morant* (1979) and *Gorillas in the Mist* (1988).

Brown, Capability (?1716–83) British landscape gardener. He landscaped the grounds of many English country houses, including Blenheim Palace in Oxfordshire and Chatsworth in Derbyshire, and created a naturalistic style of landscape design. Born **Brown, Lancelot**

Brown, Ford Madox (1821–93) French-born British painter. A Pre-Raphaelite and associate of William Morris, he produced dramatic historical paintings such as *The Last of England* (1855).

Brown, George Mackay (1921–96) British poet and novelist. Influenced by Orkney folklore, his work includes the poetry collection *Loaves and Fishes* (1959) and the novel *Beside the Ocean of Time* (1994).

Brown, James (*b.* 1928) US singer and songwriter. His use of polyrhythmic beats in songs such as 'Papa's Got A Brand New Bag' (1965) and 'Sex Machine' (1970) were highly influential in the development of funk and many subsequent forms of popular dance music. Known as **the Godfather of Soul**

Brown, John (1800–59) US abolitionist leader. Convicted of treason after a failed attempt to launch a slave rebellion, he was hanged in Virginia. The song 'John Brown's Body' commemorates his actions.

> 'I am fully persuaded that I am worth inconceivably more to hang than for any other purpose.'
> [John Brown, *Remark*; 2 November 1859]

brown adipose tissue *n* PHYSIOL same as **brown fat**

brown alga *n* an alga found in the sea that has chlorophyll masked by brown pigment. Kelps and wracks are brown algae. Division: *Phaeophyta.*

brown bear *n* a bear that is mainly brown in colour, e.g. a grizzly bear. Native to: western North America, northern Europe, northern Asia. Latin name: *Ursus arctos.*

Brown Betty /-bétti/ *n N Am* a baked apple pudding made from apples, breadcrumbs, sugar, spices, butter, and sometimes raisins

brown bread *n* bread made using wholemeal flour, or flour that does not contain whole grains but has nevertheless not been bleached or sieved

brown coal *n* a soft brown-black fossil fuel with visible plant remains and a high moisture content

brown dwarf *n* a star that is smaller than a planet and has a mass equivalent to less than one-tenth of the Sun's mass

Browne /brown/, **Sir Thomas** (1605–82) English doctor and essayist. His best-known work, *Religio Medici* (1635?), is a discourse on scientific reasoning and religious faith.

brown earth *n* soil formed in temperate humid regions under deciduous forests and characterized by a dark brown layer rich in organic material

browned-off /brównd-/ *adj* (*dated informal*) **1.** in a state of boredom or low spirits **2.** feeling discouraged or disheartened

browneye[1] /brówn ī/ *n* ◇ **chuck a browneye** *Aus* an offensive term meaning to bend over and expose the naked buttocks and anus to somebody, either as a male joke or as a gesture of defiance (*slang*)

browneye[2] /brówn ī/ (**-eyes, -eyeing** or **-eying, -eyed**) *vt Aus* same as **chuck a browneye** (*informal offensive*)

brown fat *n* a dark-coloured fatty tissue in many mammals, especially hibernating animals and human babies, that produces heat in order to control body temperature

brownfield site /brówn feeld-/ *n UK* an urban development site that has been previously built on but is currently unused. ANZ, N Am term **brownfield** [After GREENFIELD]

brown goods *npl* electrical consumer goods such as televisions and audio equipment that are mainly used for home entertainment, as opposed to conventionally 'white' kitchen appliances such as refrigerators and washing machines

Brownian movement /brówni ən-/, **Brownian motion** *n* the random movement of microscopic particles suspended in a liquid or gas that occurs as a result of collisions with molecules of the surrounding medium [After Robert *Brown* (1773–1858), British botanist]

brownie /brówni/ *n* **1.** in folklore, a small supernatural being believed to do helpful work at night **2.** a piece of flat rich chocolate cake baked in a square or rectangular tin and sometimes containing chopped nuts

Brownie, **Brownie Guide** *n* in the United Kingdom, a member of the junior section of the Guides, aged between seven and ten years [Because of the brown uniform]

Brownie Guider *n* an adult leader of a pack of Brownies, formerly known as 'Brown Owl'

brownie point, **Brownie point** *n* a notional credit earned for doing something helpful, especially in order to please (*informal*) [< the idea that Brownies use a points system for advancement]

brownin /brównin/ *n* a Black person who is light-skinned (*slang; used in Black English*)

browning /brówning/ *n* a substance such as caramelized sugar that is used to give a brown colour to soup or gravy

Browning /brówning/, **Elizabeth Barrett** (1806–61) British poet. Her works include *Sonnets from the Portuguese* (1850), *Aurora Leigh* (1856), and *Poems*

Before Congress (1860). She married Robert Browning in 1846 and lived with him in Italy. Born **Barrett, Elizabeth**

> '"Yes", I answered you last night; / "No", this morning, sir, I say / Colours seen by candle-light / Will not look the same by day.'
> [Elizabeth Barrett Browning, 'The Lady's Yes'; 1844]

Browning, Robert (1812–89) British poet. His works include *Men and Women* (1855), *Dramatis Personae* (1864), and *The Ring and the Book* (1868–69). He married Elizabeth Barrett Browning in 1846.

> 'Ah, but a man's reach should exceed his grasp, / Or what's a heaven for?'
> [Robert Browning, 'Andrea del Sarto', *Men and Women*; 1855]

Browning automatic rifle *n* an air-cooled, gas-operated, magazine-fed rifle with a .30 calibre barrel, capable of firing between 200 and 350 rounds per minute with an effective range of 600 m/2,000 ft [After John M. *Browning* (1855–1926), US arms designer]

Browning machine gun *n* an air- or water-cooled, belt-fed, automatic machine gun with either a .30 or .50 calibre barrel, capable of firing over 500 rounds per minute [See BROWNING AUTOMATIC RIFLE]

brown lacewing *n* an insect with brownish wings that often feeds on agricultural pests. Family: Hemerobiidae.

brownlands /brówn landz/ *npl* land for development that has been previously developed but is currently unused

brown lung disease, brown lung *n* MED same as **byssinosis**

brown mustard *n* 1. the dark reddish-brown, oil-rich seeds of a mustard plant. Use: cooking spice. 2. an annual plant of the mustard family with irregularly lobed leaves that produces brown mustard seeds. Latin name: *Brassica juncea*.

brownnose /brówn nōz/ (**-noses, -nosing, -nosed**) *vti* to be unnaturally subservient or obsequious to somebody in authority (*slang; sometimes offensive*) [Implying willingness to undertake stigmatized intimacy as in the offensive phrase *kiss ass*] —**brownnose** *n* —**brownnoser** *n*

brownout /brówn owt/ *n N Am* 1. **DIMMING OF LIGHTS** a dimming of lights or reduction in the use of electrical appliances in a city or region, especially as an economy measure 2. **POWER REDUCTION** a temporary reduction in electrical power caused by high consumer demand or by a technical malfunction 3. **LAPSE OF CONCENTRATION** a temporary lapse of concentration or focus [Mid-20C. After BLACKOUT]

brown owl *n* BIRDS same as **tawny owl**

Brown Owl *n* formerly, the adult leader of a pack of Brownies. Now called **Brownie Guider**

brown paper *n* thick strong brown-coloured paper used for wrapping parcels

brown patch *n* a soil-borne fungal disease of grass that produces round dead patches

brown rat *n* an extremely destructive rat found in populated areas. Native to: originally Europe and Asia, now worldwide. Latin name: *Rattus norvegicus*.

brown recluse spider *n* a pale brown poisonous spider with a violin-shaped mark on the head area. Native to: United States, South America. Latin name: *Loxosceles reclusa*.

brown rice *n* unpolished rice in which the yellowish-brown outer layer containing the bran remains intact, making it more nutritious than white rice

brown rot *n* a disease of ripe tree fruits such as apples and peaches, caused by fungi. The infected fruit turns brown, and concentric yellow rings appear on the plant. Genus: *Rhizoctonia*.

brown sauce *n* 1. a dark-brown savoury sauce made from fruit, vinegar, sugar, and spices 2. a sauce made from a dark meat stock, thickened with flour that has been browned in fat

brown seaweed *n* MARINE BIOL same as **brown alga**

Brownshirt /brówn shurt/ *n* 1. a member of a Nazi uniformed paramilitary organization that originally formed Adolf Hitler's personal bodyguard and was later used as a militia. Brownshirts assisted Hitler's rise to power, but lost their influence to the SS following the assassination of their leader Erich Röhm in 1934. 2. *N Am* an offensive term for somebody who is regarded as being a violent racist (*insult*) [Translation of German *Braunhemd*, from the brown uniform shirts of the Nazi storm troopers]

brown snake *n Aus* a poisonous brown-coloured snake. Native to: Australia. Genus: *Pseudonaja*.

brownstone /brówn stōn/ *n N Am* 1. a reddish-brown sandstone used as a building material 2. a house or building made from or faced with reddish-brown sandstone, especially a block of flats in New York City

brown sugar *n* 1. **REFINED SUGAR WITH TREACLE** a soft light or dark brown sugar made from refined white sugar combined with a refined treacle and used in cooking 2. **UNREFINED SUGAR** unrefined or partially refined sugar 3. **HEROIN** the drug heroin (*slang*)

brown-tail moth *n* a white and brown moth whose caterpillars destroy the leaves of trees and produce a substance that is toxic to humans. Native to: Europe, eastern United States. Latin name: *Euproctis chrysorrhoea*.

brown trout *n* 1. a common brownish freshwater fish. Native to: Europe, northern America. Latin name: *Salmo trutta*. 2. the flesh of a brown trout as food

browse /browz/ *v* (**browses, browsing, browsed**) 1. *vi* **LOOK THROUGH OR OVER SOMETHING CASUALLY** to look through or over something, especially goods in a shop, in a leisurely manner with the hope of finding something of interest 2. *vti* **READ CASUALLY** to read through something quickly or superficially 3. *vti* COMPUT, ONLINE **SCAN COMPUTER FILES** to scan and view files in a computer database or on the Internet, especially on the World Wide Web 4. *vti* ZOOL **FEED ON LEAVES AND SHOOTS** to feed on tender vegetation such as the shoots, leaves, or twigs above ground level of bushes or trees (*refers to animals such as deer or cattle*) ■ *n* 1. **SESSION OF BROWSING** a superficial read through something such as a newspaper, or a leisurely look over something such as the goods in a shop 2. ZOOL **FEEDING PERIOD** a session during which an animal feeds on tender shoots or twigs of bushes and trees 3. ZOOL **TENDER VEGETATION USED AS FOOD** the tender shoots, leaves, or twigs above ground level of bushes and trees used as food by animals [Early 16C. Via obsolete French *broust* < Old French *brost* < Germanic]

browser /brówzər/ *n* 1. a piece of computer software used to search for information on the World Wide Web 2. somebody who looks at something such as a book or goods for sale, in a leisurely or superficial manner

Broxbourne /bróks bawrn/ town in Hertfordshire, England. Population: 87,054 (2001).

Brubeck /broó bek/, **Dave** (*b.* 1920) US pianist and composer. He is known for his progressive jazz compositions such as *Take Five* (1959). Full name **Brubeck, David William**

> 'Jazz is about the only form of art existing today in which there is freedom of the individual without the loss of group contact.'
> [Dave Brubeck. Quoted in *The Jazz Book*, Joachim Berendt; 1982]

Bruce /brooss/, **Christopher** (*b.* 1945) British dancer and choreographer. He worked for the Ballet Rambert and the English National Ballet in London. His dances include *Ancient Voices of Children* (1975).

Bruce, James (1730–94) British explorer. He traced the upper waters of the Blue Nile in 1770 and wrote *Travels to Discover the Source of the Nile* (1768–73).

Bruce, Stanley Melbourne, 1st Viscount Bruce of Melbourne (1883–1967) prime minister of Australia (1923–29). After his premiership, he served as high commissioner for Australia in London (1933–45), on the council of the League of Nations (1933–35), and in the British war cabinet during World War II. See table at **prime minister**

brucellosis /broóssə lóssiss/ *n* a chronic infectious disease of some domestic animals that can be transmitted to human beings through contaminated milk [Mid-20C. < modern Latin *Brucella*, genus name of causative bacteria, after Sir David *Bruce* (1855–1931), Scottish physician]

Bruch /bro͝okh/, **Max** (1838–1920) German composer. His compositions include a violin concerto and the *Kol Nidrei* variations (1880–81), which draw on Hebrew melodies.

brucine /bro͞o seen/ *n* a poisonous white crystalline alkaloid. Source: nux vomica seeds. Use: denaturation of alcohol. Latin name: *Strychnos nux-vomica*. Formula: $C_{23}H_{26}N_2O_4$. [Early 19C. < modern Latin *Brucea*, genus name of a tree formerly thought to bear the bark that the substance is derived from]

brucite /bro͞oss īt/ *n* a magnesium hydroxide mineral. Source: hydrothermal deposits, metamorphosed limestone. [Early 19C. After Archibald *Bruce* (1777–1818), US mineralogist]

Bruckner /bro͝oknər/, **Anton** (1824–96) Austrian composer. He wrote nine symphonies and four masses. His music was influenced by Wagner and Schubert.

Brueghel /bróyg'l/, **Bruegel, Breughel, Jan** (1568–1625) Flemish painter. The son of Pieter Brueghel, he produced still lifes and landscape paintings.

Brueghel, Bruegel, Breughel, Pieter (1520–69) Flemish painter. He produced religious and moral allegories in contemporary landscapes, depicting peasant life in works such as *Peasant Wedding* (1568). Known as **Pieter Brueghel the Elder**

Bruges /broozh/ capital of West Flanders Province, western Belgium. It is famous for its traditional lace industries. Population: 116,559 (2001).

bruin /bro͞o in/, **Bruin** *n* used as a name for a bear in folklore, fables, and children's stories [15C. < Middle Dutch, 'brown']

bruise /brooz/ *n* 1. **SKIN DISCOLORATION CAUSED BY INJURY** a tender area of skin discoloration caused by blood leaking from blood vessels damaged by pressure or impact 2. **DAMAGE TO PLANT TISSUE** damage to underlying plant or fruit tissue, visible as a soft discoloured area on the unbroken surface and caused by pressure or impact 3. **EMOTIONAL INJURY** an injury that is not physical, e.g. hurt feelings or damaged self-esteem ■ *v* (**bruises, bruising, bruised**) 1. *vti* **INJURE CAUSING SKIN DISCOLORATION** to injure a part of the body, or sustain an injury, resulting in discoloration caused by blood leaking from damaged blood vessels 2. *vti* **DAMAGE PLANT TISSUE** to damage plant tissue by pressure or impact, or sustain such damage, leaving a softened and discoloured surface area 3. *vt* **UPSET SOMEBODY** to injure somebody's feelings or harm somebody's self-esteem ○ *I was bruised by the criticism.* 4. *vt* COOK **CRUSH FOOD** to crush or pound food, especially to extract juice from it or bring out its flavour [Partly < Old English *brȳsan* 'crush', and partly < Anglo-Norman *bruser* 'break' < Germanic]

bruiser /bro͞ozər/ *n* a large strong man or youth, e.g. a boxer, bodyguard, or club bouncer (*informal*)

bruising /bro͞ozing/ *n* bruises or the dark patches left on the surface of bruised skin ■ *adj* causing emotional, psychological, or physical pain

bruit /broot/ *n* 1. **RUMOUR OR REPORT** a story, true or untrue, that is passed about among people (*archaic*) 2. MED **SIGNIFICANT SOUND INSIDE BODY** a medically significant sound heard inside the body, usually with the aid of a stethoscope, and caused by turbulent blood flow within the heart or blood vessels ■ *vt* (**bruits, bruiting, bruited**) **SPREAD STORY** to circulate stories, whether true or untrue [15C. < Old French < past participle of *bruire* 'roar']

Brum /brum/ *n* a nickname for Birmingham (*informal*) [Mid-19C. Shortening of BRUMMAGEM]

brumby /brúmbi/ (*plural* **-bies**) *n ANZ* a wild unbroken horse [Late 19C. Origin ?]

brume /broom/ *n* a weather condition in which fog or mist is present, or the fog or mist itself (*literary*) [Early 18C. Via French, 'fog' < Latin *bruma* 'winter'] —**brumous** *adj*

brummagem /brúmməjəm/, **Brummagem** *n* something, especially imitation jewellery, that is cheap and gaudy ■ *adj* cheap and shoddy [Mid-17C. < BRUMMAGEM, originally referring to counterfeit coins made there]

Brummell /brúmm'l/, **Beau** (1778–1840) British dandy. A courtier and friend of George IV, he was a fashion-setter in Regency England. Born **Brummell, George Bryan**

Brummie /brúmmi/, **Brummy** (*plural* **-mies**) *n* somebody who comes from Birmingham (*informal*) —**Brummie** *adj*

brunch /brunch/ *n* a meal that combines breakfast and lunch, eaten late in the morning [Late 19C. Blend of BREAKFAST + LUNCH]

Brunei

Brunei /broo ní/ country bisected by the Malaysian state of Sarawak in northwestern Borneo, eastern Asia. It became an independent member of the Commonwealth in 1984. Language: Malay. Currency: ringgit or Brunei dollar. Capital: Bandar Seri Begawan. Population: 358,098 (2003). Area: 5,765 sq. km/2,226 sq. mi. Official name **Negara Brunei Darussalam**

Isambard Kingdom Brunel

Brunel /broo nél/, **Isambard Kingdom** (1806–59) British engineer. He designed the Clifton Suspension Bridge and constructed the *Great Western* (1837), the first steamship designed to cross the Atlantic.

Brunelleschi /broónə léski/, **Filippo** (1377–1446) Italian architect and sculptor. One of the greatest Renaissance architects, he designed the dome of the cathedral in Florence (1420–61) and built several churches in Florence. Born **di Ser Brunellesco, Filippo**

brunette /broo nét/ *n* a girl or woman with dark brown hair [Early 17C. < French, feminine form of *brunet*] —**brunette** *adj*

Brunhild /broón híld/, **Brunnhilde** /-híldə/ *n* in medieval Germanic mythology, the queen of Iceland who promises to marry whoever can defeat her in battle. Siegfried does so on behalf of King Gunther.

Bruno /broónō/, **St** (1030?–1101) German monk in the French mountains at Chartreuse. He founded a monastery of hermit monks (1084), which later became the Carthusian contemplative order. Known as **Bruno the Carthusian**

brunt /brunt/ *n* **1.** the main force or effect of something such as a blow or criticism ○ *We always had to bear the brunt of her anger.* **2.** the greater part or the main burden [14C. Origin ?]

bruschetta /broo skéttə, -shéttə/ *n* Italian bread toasted and drizzled with olive oil, usually served with added garlic and chopped tomatoes [< Italian < *bruscare* 'roast over coals']

brush[1] /brush/ *n* **1.** TOOL WITH BRISTLES ATTACHED TO HANDLE an implement consisting of bristles, hair, or wire set into a handle, used for grooming the hair, painting, polishing, scrubbing, or sweeping **2.** USE OF BRUSH the use of a brush, e.g. to groom the hair or to sweep a surface **3.** LIGHT CONTACT a light stroke or momentary contact **4.** SHORT UNPLEASANT ENCOUNTER a brief unpleasant encounter ○ *a brush with evil* **5.** BUSHY TAIL OF FOX a bushy tail, especially the tail of a fox as a hunting trophy **6.** ELECTRICAL CONDUCTOR an electrical conductor that makes sliding contact between a

stationary and a moving part of a generator or motor while completing a circuit and conveying a current **7.** ELEC same as **brush discharge** ■ *v* (**brushes, brushing, brushed**) **1.** *vti* USE BRUSH ON SOMETHING to use a brush to clean, groom, or polish something **2.** *vt* APPLY SOMETHING WITH BRUSH to apply something such as paint or varnish to a surface using a brush **3.** *vt* REMOVE SOMETHING WITH BRUSH to remove something with a brush or a sweeping motion **4.** *vt* REJECT SOMETHING to dismiss, ignore, or rebuff something or somebody in an abrupt or curt manner ○ *They brushed aside the suggestion.* **5.** *vti* GRAZE AGAINST SOMETHING to touch something lightly and briefly in passing [14C. < Old French *broisse*, probably variant of *broce* (see BRUSH[2])] —**brusher** *n* —**brushy** *adj* ◇ **tar somebody with the same brush** to attribute unfairly the faults and failings of somebody to another person

brush off *vt* to dismiss or disregard somebody or something in an abrupt manner

brush up *vt* to refresh or renew knowledge of or skill in something

brush[2] /brush/ *n* **1.** THICK UNDERGROWTH a dense undergrowth of small trees and bushes **2.** LAND COVERED WITH THICK UNDERGROWTH land covered with a dense undergrowth of small trees and bushes **3.** same as **brushwood** (sense 1) **4.** BACKWOODS wild and sparsely populated woodland [14C. < Anglo-Norman *brousse*, variant of Old French *broce* 'broken branches']

brush border *n* a dense layer of tiny protuberances that lines some absorbing cells such as those in the intestine and kidney

brush discharge *n* a luminous electric discharge between two conductors, consisting of a flow of ionized particles with less intensity than a spark [< its appearance]

brushed /brusht/ *adj* **1.** describes a knitted or woven fabric that has a nap produced by brushing it during manufacture **2.** describes a metallic surface with a nonreflective sheen

brush fire *n* **1.** FIRE IN DRY BRUSH a fire in dry brush and scrub that usually spreads quickly **2.** SMALL WAR a localized but often intensely fought war ■ *adj* INVOLVING LOCAL MILITARY involving only small-scale and local military mobilization

brushmark /brúsh maark/ *n* a mark or line left by the bristles of a brush on a painted or varnished surface

brushoff /brúsh of/ *n* an abrupt dismissal, rejection, or snub (*informal*)

brushstroke /brúsh strōk/ *n* a movement of a paintbrush that produces a particular look or mark on a painted surface, or the mark itself

brush turkey *n* a heavy-bodied bird resembling a turkey, with a bare head, black feathers, red head, and yellow wattles. Native to: forests of northeastern Australia. Latin name: *Alectura lathami.*

brushwood /brúsh woŏd/ *n* **1.** cut or broken branches and twigs **2.** same as **brush**[2] (senses 1–2)

brushwork /brúsh wurk/ *n* **1.** the characteristic manner in which an artist applies paint with a brush **2.** the product of an artist's use of a brush in painting

brusque /broŏsk/ *adj* abrupt, blunt, or curt in manner or speech [Early 17C. Via French < late Latin *bruscum* 'coarse, rough'] —**brusquely** *adv* —**brusqueness** *n*

Brussels /brúss'lz/ largest city and capital of Belgium. It is situated in the centre of Belgium and is the headquarters of the European Union and the North Atlantic Treaty Organization (NATO). Population: 954,460 (1999).

Brussels carpet *n* a carpet with a heavy patterned pile of small woollen loops attached to a linen base

Brussels griffon *n* BREED same as **griffon** (sense 1) [Because the breed originated in Belgium]

Brussels lace *n* **1.** a fine lace with a floral design, made with bobbins or with needle and thread, that originated in or near Brussels **2.** a machine-made net lace with an appliqué design

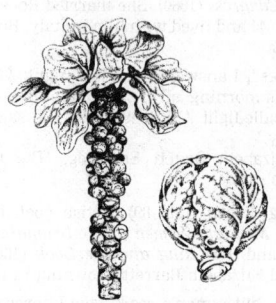

Brussels sprout

Brussels sprout *n* **1.** a small green swollen bud like a tiny cabbage that is eaten as a vegetable **2.** a plant related to cabbage that has a thick stalk lined with Brussels sprouts. Latin name: *Brassica oleracea.* [Because first grown near Brussels]

brut /broot/ *adj* describes wine, especially sparkling white wine, that is extremely dry in taste [Late 19C. < French]

brutal /broot'l/ *adj* **1.** RUTHLESS AND CRUEL extremely ruthless or cruel **2.** HARSH AND SEVERE unrelentingly harsh and severe ○ *a brutal regimen* **3.** DIRECT IN MANNER direct or insensitive in manner or speech ○ *with brutal frankness* [15C. Directly or via French < medieval Latin *brutalis* < Latin *brutus* (see BRUTE)] —**brutally** *adv* —**brutalness** *n*

brutalise *vt* another spelling of **brutalize**

brutalism /broot'lizəm/ *n* a style of modern architecture characterized by massiveness, a lack of exterior decoration, harsh lines, and the exposure of structural materials —**brutalist** *n*, *adj*

brutality /broo tálləti/ *n* (*plural* -**ties**) **1.** cruel, harsh, or ruthless behaviour or treatment **2.** a cruel, harsh, or ruthless act

brutalize /broot'l īz/ (-**izes, -izing, -ized**), **brutalise** (-**ises, -ising, -ised**) *vt* **1.** to make somebody brutal or unfeeling **2.** to treat somebody brutally, cruelly, or harshly —**brutalization** /broot'l ī záysh'n/ *n*

brute /broot/ *n* **1.** SOMEBODY BRUTAL somebody regarded as cruel, ruthless, or insensitive **2.** ANIMAL an animal other than a human being (*literary*) ■ *adj* **1.** PURELY PHYSICAL purely physical or instinctive, rather than intellectual or reasoned **2.** CRUEL OR SAVAGE displaying extreme cruelty and savagery **3.** STARK unremittingly harsh or severe **4.** CRUDE OR BARBARIC describes behaviour, actions, or instincts that are considered crude, especially those prompted by physical desire and hunger **5.** OF BEASTS relating or belonging to lower animals, as opposed to human beings [15C. Via French < Latin *brutus* 'stupid, like an animal' < Indo-European, 'heavy'] —**brutism** *n*

brutish /broótish/ *adj* **1.** SAVAGE cruel, ruthless, or violent in behaviour, actions, or instincts **2.** LACKING INTELLIGENCE coarse or crude in a manner that suggests a lack of intelligence **3.** RELATING TO BEASTS relating to or characteristic of lower animals —**brutishly** *adv* —**brutishness** *n*

Bruton /broot'n/, **John** (*b.* 1947) prime minister of the Republic of Ireland (1994–97)

Brutus /broótəss/, **Lucius Junius** (*fl* late 6th century BC) Roman consul. He drove the Etruscan royal family, the Tarquins, out of Rome and founded the Roman republic. He was elected one of the first two Roman consuls.

Brutus, Marcus Junius (85?–42 BC) Roman general. He sided with Pompey against Caesar during the civil war (49 BC), and was a principal conspirator in Caesar's assassination (44 BC). He was defeated by Mark Antony and Octavian at Philippi (42 BC), and committed suicide.

bruxism /broóksizəm/ *n* the unconscious habit of grinding or gritting the teeth that occurs during sleep or in stressful situations and can lead to excessive wear of the teeth [Mid-20C. < Greek *brukein* 'gnash the teeth']

Brynhild /brínhild/ *n* in Norse mythology, a Valkyrie who is woken from an enchanted sleep by Sigurd and later tricked into marrying his brother-in-law, Gunnar

bryo- *prefix* moss ○ *bryophyte* [< Greek *bruon*]

bryology /brī óllǝji/ *n* the branch of plant science concerned with the study of hornworts, mosses, and liverworts —**bryological** /brī ǝ lójjik'l/ *adj* —**bryologist** *n*

bryonia /brī ṓni ǝ/ *n* a homeopathic remedy prepared from bryony. Use: treatment of flu and other conditions. [Pre-12C. < Latin (see BRYONY)]

bryony /brī́ ǝni/ *n* a climbing plant with large leaves, tendrils, and red or black berries. Native to: Europe, North Africa. Genus: *Bryonia*. [Pre-12C. Via Latin *bryonia* < Greek *bruonia* < *bruein* 'teem']

bryophyte /brī́ ǝ fīt/ *n* a nonflowering plant, often growing in damp places, that has separate gamete-bearing and spore-bearing forms, e.g. moss. Division: *Bryophyta*. —**bryophytic** /brī́ ǝ fíttik/ *adj*

bryozoan /brī́ ǝ zṓ ǝn/ *n* an invertebrate sea animal that reproduces by budding. Bryozoans often form colonies on the sea bottom or attached to seaweed. Phylum: Bryozoa. [Late 19C. < modern Latin *Bryozoa* < Greek *bruon* 'moss' + *zoion* 'animal'] —**bryozoan** *adj*

Brythonic /bri thónnik/, **Brittonic** /-tónnik/ *n* a group of languages that belongs to the Celtic branch of Indo-European languages and includes Breton, Cornish, and Welsh. Native speakers: 1 million. ■ *adj* relating to the Brythons, or their language or culture [Late 19C. < Welsh *Brython* 'Briton']

bs *abbr* Bahamas (*used in Internet addresses*) See table at **domain name**

BS *abbr* **1.** *US* EDUC Bachelor of Surgery **2.** *also* **B/S** LAW bill of sale **3.** British Standard (*as part of the number of a British Standards Institution publication*)

b.s. *abbr* **1.** balance sheet **2.** *also* **b/s** bill of sale

B.S. *abbr N Am* bullshit (*slang taboo*)

BSB *abbr* MEASURE British Standard brass (*used to identify a type of screw thread*)

BSc *abbr* EDUC Bachelor of Science

BSE *n* a disease that affects the nervous system of cattle, believed to be caused by a transmissible protein particle (**prion**) and related to Creutzfeldt-Jakob disease in humans. Full form **bovine spongiform encephalopathy**

BSF *abbr* MEASURE British Standard fine (*used to identify a type of screw thread*)

bsh. *abbr* MEASURE bushel

BSI *abbr* British Standards Institution

B-side *n* the side of a vinyl pop-music or jazz single that does not contain the title track and is considered less important

BSL *abbr* British Sign Language

Bs/L *abbr* bills of lading

BSN *abbr* EDUC Bachelor of Science in Nursing

BSP *abbr* MEASURE British Standard pipe (*used to identify a type of screw thread*)

BSS *abbr* British Standards Specification

BST *abbr* **1.** AGRIC bovine somatotrophin **2.** British Summer Time

BSW *abbr* MEASURE British Standard Whitworth (*used to identify a type of screw thread*)

bt *abbr* Bhutan (*used in Internet addresses*) See table at **domain name**

Bt *abbr* baronet

BT *abbr* British Telecom

BTEC /beé tek/ *abbr* Business and Technology Education Council

BThU *abbr* MEASURE British thermal unit

b-to-b *abbr* business-to-business

btry *abbr* MIL battery

Btu, **btu** *abbr* MEASURE British thermal unit

BTU *n* a unit for measuring electrical energy, equal to 1 kilowatt-hour. Full form **Board of Trade Unit**

BTW, **btw** *abbr* by the way (*used in e-mails or text messages*)

bty *abbr* MIL battery

bu. *abbr* MEASURE bushel

BUAV *abbr* British Union for the Abolition of Vivisection

buaya /bwī́ ǝl/ *n Malaysia, Singapore* a man who tends to flirt (*informal*) [< Malay, 'crocodile']

bub /bub/ *n* **1.** *N Am* used as a term of address to an unnamed male person, especially one encountered and spoken to casually (*slang*) **2.** *Aus* a baby or toddler (*informal*) [Mid-19C. Shortening and alteration of BROTHER]

bubal /byoób'l/ (*plural same* or **-bals**) *n* a large hartebeest. Native to: northern Africa. Latin name: *Alcephalus boselaphus*. [Late 18C. Via French < Latin *bubalus* < Greek *boubalos* 'gazelle']

bubble /búbb'l/ *n* **1.** THIN GLOBE-SHAPED AIR-FILLED FILM a thin spherical or dome-shaped film that is filled with air or a gas **2.** SOMETHING LIKE BUBBLE something spherical or dome-shaped like a bubble **3.** GLOBULE WITHIN LIQUID OR SOLID a globule of air or a gas in a liquid such as a fizzy drink or in a solid such as glass **4.** GURGLING SOUND a gurgling sound made by a boiling or effervescent liquid **5.** SOUND OF MANY BUBBLES BURSTING a sound produced by bubbles forming and bursting **6.** MEDIA same as **balloon** *n* (sense 3) **7.** DOME a dome, usually made of transparent glass or plastic **8.** PROTECTED AREA a protected, isolated, or exempted area **9.** FALSE CONFIDENCE a false feeling of confidence or security ○ *The rocketing housing market is a bubble that will surely burst.* **10.** RISKY SCHEME a risky or unreliable business enterprise or speculative scheme, especially one proving to be fraudulent or unsuccessful ○ *suffered when the dot.com bubble burst* ■ *v* (**-bles, -bling, -bled**) **1.** *vi* EFFERVESCE OR BOIL UP to form or produce spherical or dome-shaped pockets of air or gas in a liquid **2.** *vi* GURGLE to move or flow with a gurgling sound **3.** *vi* EMERGE OR APPEAR to emerge or rise to the surface ○ *the views and attitudes that are now bubbling up* **4.** *vi* BE LIVELY WITH EMOTION to be animated with or display an emotion such as excitement, happiness, or anger ○ *bubbling with mirth* **5.** *vt* EXPRESS SOMETHING ENTHUSIASTICALLY to say something with great animation and friendly enthusiasm **6.** *vt* MAKE SOMETHING BUBBLE to cause something to form bubbles or to move in bubbles through a liquid **7.** *vi Scotland* SOB to blubber or snivel [14C. Probably an imitation of the sound of bubbling water]

bubble and squeak *n* a dish consisting of leftover cooked potatoes and cabbage chopped up and fried together [Because of the sounds during cooking]

bubble bath *n* **1.** a usually perfumed and coloured preparation in liquid or crystal form that is added to bath water in order to make it foam **2.** a bath to which a preparation has been added to make the water foam

bubble car *n* a small two-seater car, usually three-wheeled, with a transparent bubble-shaped dome or a single door in place of a bonnet

bubble chamber *n* a chamber containing a liquid, usually liquid hydrogen just above its boiling point, in which the trail of a particle can be observed as a line of bubbles created by the particle

bubble cut *n* a woman's hairstyle of short full curls

bubblegum /búbb'l gum/ *n* **1.** CHEWING GUM THAT FORMS BUBBLES chewing gum that can be blown from the mouth into large bubbles **2.** POP MUSIC FOR TEENAGERS commercial pop music aimed at the younger teenage market and usually considered to be lacking originality (*informal*) ■ *adj N Am* (*informal*) **1.** APPEALING TO ADOLESCENTS appealing to or characteristic of the style, taste, or behaviour of adolescents, especially when considered immature **2.** BLAND, INSIPID, OR VAPID lacking originality, careful mature thought, or seriousness

bubble-jet printer *n* a printer in which heated ink forms bubbles that burst onto the paper

bubble memory *n* computer memory in which data is stored as binary digits represented by the presence or absence of minute areas of magnetization in a semiconductor

bubble pack *n* MANUF same as **blister pack**

bubble point *n* the temperature at which bubbles first appear when a liquid mixture is heated

bubbler /búbblǝr/ *n* **1.** DEVICE THAT BUBBLES GAS THROUGH LIQUID a device for bubbling gas through a liquid **2.** SOMETHING THAT BUBBLES something that emits bubbles, e.g. a mountain spring **3.** *Aus, US regional* DRINKING FOUNTAIN a drinking fountain, especially one that spouts water from a vertical nozzle

bubble top *n* a transparent glass or plastic dome used in building, e.g. one forming a roof over a swimming pool

bubblewrap /búbb'l rap/ *n* a sheet of plastic material covered with air-filled bubbles, used for wrapping fragile objects in order to protect them in transit

bubbly /búbb'li/ *adj* (**-blier, -bliest**) **1.** CHEERFULLY EXCITED feeling and exhibiting cheerful excitement **2.** FOAMY OR EFFERVESCENT full of or producing bubbles **3.** LIKE BUBBLES resembling a bubble or bubbles in shape or sound ■ *n* CHAMPAGNE sparkling wine, especially champagne (*informal*) —**bubbliness** *n*

Buber /boóbǝr/, **Martin** (1878–1965) Austrian-born Israeli theologian and philosopher. He was an intellectual leader of German Jews before World War II and expounded his influential religious philosophy of dialogue in his best-known work, *I and Thou* (1922).

> 'God does not want to be believed in, to be debated and defended by us, but simply to be realized through us.'
> [Martin Buber. Quoted in *On Judaism*, N. Glazer (ed.), Eva Jose et al. (trs.); 1967]

bubo /byoóbō/ (*plural* **-boes**) *n* swelling and inflammation of a lymph node, especially in the area of the armpit or groin [14C. Via Latin < Greek *boubōn* 'swelling in the groin']

bubonic /byoo bónnik/ *adj* describes a swelling (**bubo**) of the lymph nodes

bubonic plague *n* an infectious fatal epidemic disease, caused by the bacterium *Yersinia pestis* transmitted by fleas that have previously bitten an infected animal or person, and characterized by fever, chills, and the formation of swellings (**buboes**). In the 14th century, an extensive epidemic of it occurred, known as the Black Death. In modern times, infection is limited and sporadic and can be treated successfully with antibiotics. [< Latin *bubon-*, stem of *bubo* (see BUBO)]

bubonocele /byoo bónnǝ seel/ *n* an incomplete hernia of the groin accompanied by swelling [Early 17C. Via modern Latin < Greek *boubōnokēlē* 'groin rupture']

buccal /búk'l/ *adj* **1.** relating to or forming part of the cheek ○ *the buccal surface of a tooth* **2.** relating to the mouth [Early 19C. < Latin *bucca* 'cheek']

buccal smear *n* a gentle scraping of the inside of the cheek with a spatula in order to obtain DNA samples and cells for chromosomal and other studies

buccaneer /búkǝ neér/ *n* **1.** PIRATE a pirate, especially one who preyed on Spanish colonies and shipping in the Caribbean in the 17th century **2.** UNSCRUPULOUS ADVENTURER OR BUSINESSPERSON a ruthless or unscrupulous adventurer, businessperson, or politician ■ *vi* (**-neers, -neering, -neered**) ACT LIKE BUCCANEER to be or behave like a buccaneer [Mid-17C. < French *boucanier* < *boucaner* 'cook over an open fire'] —**buccaneering** *adj, n*

buccinator /búksi naytǝr/ *n* a flat thin muscle that compresses the cheek and is used in blowing and chewing [Late 17C. < Latin < *buccinare* 'blow the trumpet' < *buccina*, a kind of trumpet]

Bucephalus /byoo séffǝlǝss/ *n* the favourite war horse of Alexander the Great, which he tamed when still a boy

Buchan /búkǝn/, **John, 1st Baron Tweedsmuir** (1875–1940) British writer and administrator. Among his many books are *Prester John* (1910) and *The Thirty-Nine Steps* (1915) He was appointed governor general of Canada in 1935.

Buchanan /byoo kánnǝn/, **George** (1506–82) Scottish scholar and humanist. He was a tutor to Mary, Queen of Scots, and tutor to James VI of Scotland (1570–78) and wrote a monumental Latin *History of Scotland* (1582).

Buchanan, James (1791–1868) 15th president of the United States. A Federalist turned Democrat, he was a US Representative (1821–31), Senator (1834–45), and secretary of state (1845–49). During his presidency (1857–61) he was unable to avert the American Civil War (1861–65). See table at **president**

Bucharest /boókǝ rést/ largest city and capital of Romania. It is situated on a plain in the south-eastern part of the country, north of the River Danube. Population: 2,037,005 (1999).

Buchenwald /bo͝okhən vald/ village near Weimar, central Germany, that was the site of a World War II Nazi concentration camp (1937–45)

Buchner /búknər, bo͝okhnər/, **Eduard** (1860–1917) German chemist. He attributed the fermentation of yeast to enzyme reaction and won the Nobel Prize in chemistry (1907) for this discovery.

Büchner /byo͝okhnər/, **Georg** (1813–37) German dramatist. He was an early exponent of expressionist theatre. His plays include *Danton's Death* (1835) and *Woyzeck* (1836). Full name **Büchner, Karl Georg**

> 'Every man's a chasm. It makes you dizzy when you look down it.'
> [Georg Büchner, *Woyzeck*; tr. 1879]

Buchner funnel, Büchner funnel *n* a cylindrical filter funnel with a flat perforated base through which liquids are drawn under reduced pressure [After Eduard BUCHNER]

buchu /bo͞o koo/ (*plural* **-chus** or *same*), **bucku** (*plural* **-ckus** or *same*) *n* a bush with leaves that are used as a mild diuretic and urinary antiseptic. Native to: southern Africa. Genus: *Agathosma.* [Mid-18C. Via Afrikaans < Nama]

Buchwald /búk wawld/, **Art** (*b.* 1925) US journalist. His popular column, first appearing in the *International Herald Tribune* and later widely syndicated in the United States, offered a satirical view of American life and politics. Full name **Buchwald, Arthur**

> 'This is not an easy time for humorists because the government is far funnier than we are.'
> [Art Buchwald, *New York Times*; 28 June 1987]

buck[1] /buk/ *n* **1. MALE ANIMAL** a male animal of some species, including the antelope, deer, goat, kangaroo, and rabbit **2.** (*plural same* or **bucks**) *S Africa* **ANTELOPE OR DEER** an antelope or deer of either sex **3. ARTICLE MADE OF BUCKSKIN** an object made of buckskin, e.g. a shoe **4. VIRILE YOUNG MAN** a man, especially a strong, virile, impetuous, or spirited young man (*dated informal*) **5. DANDY OR FOP** a young man who takes elaborate care to be neat and stylish (*archaic*) [Old English *buc* 'male deer', *bucca* 'male goat' < Germanic]
buck up *v* **1.** *vti* **MAKE OR BECOME MORE CHEERFUL** to become more cheerful, confident, or encouraged, or make somebody do this (*informal*) **2.** *vt* **IMPROVE SOMETHING** to make something better (*informal*) **3.** *vi* **HURRY UP** to hurry or act more quickly (*dated informal*) **4.** *vti* **MEET** to meet somebody by chance, or meet by chance (*slang*; *used in Black English*)

buck[2] /buk/ *v* (**bucks, bucking, bucked**) **1.** *vi* **JUMP UPWARDS** to jump or rear upwards with the back arched and the legs stiff (*refers to horses*) **2.** *vt* **THROW RIDER** to throw a rider by rearing or jumping upwards on the hind legs or forelegs **3.** *vti* **STAND IN OPPOSITION** to oppose or resist something obstinately ○ *buck the trend* **4.** *vt* **GAMBLE AGAINST SOMETHING** to take a risk against something ○ *buck the odds* **5.** *vt* **ENCOURAGE SOMEBODY** to raise somebody's spirits or hopes (*usually passive*) ○ *She was bucked by the good news.* **6.** *vi N Am* **MAKE JOLTING MOTION** to move in a jerky or erratic manner **7.** *vti N Am* **BUTT WITH LOWERED HEAD** to charge against somebody or something with the head lowered ■ *n* **ACT OF BUCKING** the movement or action of bucking [Mid-19C. < BUCK[1]]

buck[3] /buk/ *n ANZ, N Am* (*informal*) **1.** a United States, Canadian, Australian, or New Zealand dollar **2.** a specified or unspecified amount of money [Mid-19C. Shortening of BUCKSKIN, used as a unit of exchange on the American frontier] ◇ **make a fast** *or* **quick buck** to make a profit on a quick and often dishonest transaction

buck[4] /buk/ *n* **1.** a covered block used as a vaulting horse **2.** *N Am* CONSTR same as **sawhorse** [Early 19C. < BUCK[1]]

buck[5] /buk/ *n* a counter or marker formerly used in poker and passed from one player to another to indicate some obligation, especially somebody's turn to deal [Mid-19C. Origin ?] ◇ **pass the buck** to shift responsibility to somebody else (*informal*)

Buck /buk/, **Pearl S.** (1892–1973) US writer. She is best known for novels depicting Chinese life, including *The Good Earth* (1931), which won the Pulitzer Prize. She won the Nobel Prize in literature (1938). Born **Sydenstricker, Pearl**

Buck, Sir Peter (1880–1951) New Zealand anthropologist and politician. A member of New Zealand's parliament (1909–14) and minister for Maori affairs, he later devoted himself to anthropology. He wrote *The Coming of the Maori* (1949). Born **Te Rangi Hiroa.** Full name **Buck, Sir Peter Henry**

buckaroo /búkə ro͞o/ (*plural* **-roos**), **buckeroo** (*plural* **-oos**) *n N Am* a cowhand in the southwestern United States (*informal*) [Early 19C. Alteration of Spanish *vaquero* 'cowboy', after BUCK[2]]

buckbean /búk been/ *n* a marsh plant of the gentian family. Flowers: white, pink, purplish. Native to: northern hemisphere. Latin name: *Menyanthes trifoliata.* [Late 16C. Translation of Flemish *boks boonen* 'goat's beans']

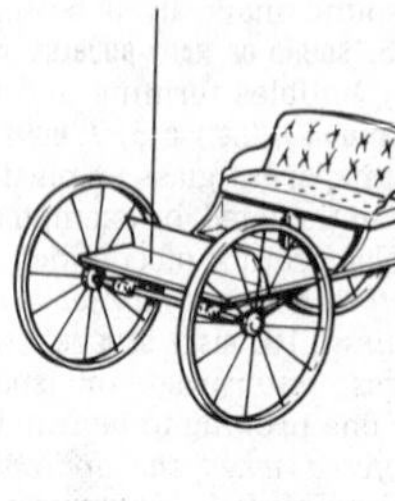

buckboard

buckboard /búk bawrd/ *n N Am* an open four-wheeled horse-drawn carriage with the seat or seats mounted on a flexible board between the front and rear axles [Late 17C. < obsolete *buck* 'belly, body (of a wagon)']

buckeroo *n N Am* AGRIC another spelling of **buckaroo** (*informal*)

bucket /búkit/ *n* **1. CYLINDRICAL CONTAINER** a container, usually cylindrical in shape with an open top and a semicircular handle, used for catching or holding liquids or solids **2. BUCKETFUL** the contents of a bucket, or the amount that a bucket will hold **3. LARGE QUANTITY** a very large quantity or amount of something (*informal*; *often used in the plural*) ○ *buckets of money* **4. SOMETHING LIKE BUCKET** something resembling a bucket in shape or function, e.g. a compartment on the outer edge of a water wheel or the scoop on a mechanical shovel **5.** FOOD INDUST **FOOD CONTAINER** a large plastic or paper container for food, e.g. fried chicken or ice cream **6.** TRANSP same as **bucket seat 7.** BASKETBALL same as **basket** (sense 5) ■ *v* (**-ets, -eting, -eted**) **1.** *vt* **PUT SOMETHING IN BUCKET** to carry, hold, lift, or put something in a bucket **2.** *vi* **POUR WITH RAIN** to rain very heavily (*informal*) **3.** *vi* **MOVE FAST** to move or drive fast, jerkily, haphazardly, or recklessly (*informal*) ○ *We went bucketing down the motorway.* **4.** *vt Aus* **ATTACK SOMEBODY VERBALLY** to criticize somebody severely, or denigrate somebody (*informal*) **5.** *vt* RIDING **RIDE HORSE HARD** to ride a horse hard without consideration for the animal [13C. < Anglo-Norman *buket* < Germanic] ◇ **kick the bucket** to die (*slang*)
bucket down *vi* to rain very heavily (*informal*)

bucket chain *n* a line of people formed to pass buckets of water from hand to hand in order to put out a fire

bucketful /búkitfo͝ol/ *n* **1.** the contents of a bucket or the amount that a bucket will hold **2.** a very large quantity or amount of something (*informal*; *usually used in the plural*)

bucket ladder *n* a continuous chain of buckets used for excavating land or dredging riverbeds (*hyphenated when used before a noun*) ○ *a bucket-ladder dredger*

bucket seat *n* an individual seat with a rounded back in a vehicle or aircraft

bucket shop *n* **1.** a dishonest unregistered stockbroking firm that speculates on stocks and commodities using its clients' capital **2.** any small business that cannot be relied on by customers, especially an unlicensed travel agency that buys airline tickets in bulk and sells them cheaply [Originally a saloon selling liquor from buckets]

buckeye /búk ī/ *n* **1.** a prickly or smooth fruit of a tree or bush of the horse chestnut family, or the large shiny brown poisonous seed it contains **2.** (*plural* **buckeyes** or *same*) the tree or bush that produces buckeyes. Native to: North America. Genus: *Aesculus.* [Mid-18C. Because of the seed's resemblance to a deer's eye]

buck fever *n* (*informal*) **1.** nervous excitement felt by an inexperienced hunter at the sight of game **2.** nervous excitement felt by somebody faced with a new situation, experience, or responsibility

buckhorn /búk hawrn/ *n* **1. MATERIAL FROM BUCK'S HORN** the material from the horn of a male deer or antelope. Use: handles for knives and tools. **2. HORN OF BUCK** the horn of a male deer or antelope **3.** (*plural* **buckhorns** or *same*) **PLANT WITH LEAVES RESEMBLING ANIMAL'S HORN** a plant with leaves shaped like the horns of a deer or antelope. Native to: Europe, Asia. Latin name: *Plantago coronopus.*

buckie /búki/ *n Scotland* **1.** MARINE BIOL **SHELLFISH OR SHELL** a shellfish with a spiral shell, or the shell itself **2. OBSTINATE PERSON** somebody who is obstinate **3. LIVELY PERSON** somebody who is lively [Early 16C. Probably alteration of Latin *buccinum* 'whelk']

Buckingham /búkingəm/, **George Villiers, 2nd Duke of** (1628–87) English courtier. He was a privy councillor to Charles II and one of the most influential political figures of the Restoration. He is remembered for his satirical comedy *The Rehearsal* (1671).

> 'The world is made up for the most part of fools and knaves, both irreconcilable foes to truth.'
> [George Villiers Buckingham, 'To Mr Clifford On His Humane Reason', *Dramatic Works*; 1715]

Buckingham Palace *n* the official London residence of the British monarch, built in 1703

Buckinghamshire /búkingəmshər/ county in southern England, northwest of London. Its administrative centre is Aylesbury. Population: 479,026 (2001). Area: 727sq. km/1,883 sq. mi.

buckjumper /búk jumpər/ *n Aus* an untamed horse that is likely to buck

Buckland /búklənd/, **William** (1784–1856) British geologist and clergyman. An Oxford academic and clergyman, he attempted to reconcile scientific discoveries about the Earth's history with the biblical version of the Creation.

buckle /búk'l/ *n* **1. METAL FASTENER** a clasp, usually consisting of a metal frame with a hinged prong, for fastening two loose ends, especially the ends of a belt, shoe, or strap **2. ORNAMENT LIKE BUCKLE** an ornament that resembles a buckle, e.g. one on a shoe or a hat **3. BULGING OR BENDING PART** a bend or kink in something such as a rope, or a bulge in something such as a piece of wood ■ *v* (**-les, -ling, -led**) **1.** *vti* **FIX SOMETHING WITH BUCKLE** to fasten something such as a shoe or seat belt with a buckle, or be fastened with such a device **2.** *vti* **BEND OR CAUSE SOMETHING TO BEND** to bend out of shape, warp, or crumple, usually because of heat or pressure, or bend something in this way **3.** *vi* **COLLAPSE** to collapse or lose physical strength completely, sometimes as a result of a structural defect or weakness **4.** *vi* **GIVE IN** to succumb or yield to mental or emotional pressure [14C. Via Anglo-Norman *bucle*, Old French *bocle* < Latin *buccula* 'cheek strap of a helmet' < *bucca* 'cheek']
buckle down *vi* to set out to accomplish something with vigour or determination (*informal*)
buckle to *vi* to make a determined or special effort
buckle under *vi* to give in under pressure or stress
buckle up *vti* to fasten the buckle on a belt designed to keep the wearer securely in a seat in a vehicle or an aircraft

buckler /búklər/ *n* a small round shield either worn on the forearm or held by a short handle at arm's length [13C. < Old French *bocler* < *bocle* 'boss of a shield' (see BUCKLE)]

buckler fern *n* a perennial deciduous or semi-evergreen fern that grows to about 1 m/3 ft in height. Native to: Europe. Genus: *Dryopteris.* [Because of the flap of tissue covering the receptacle in which its spores are formed]

Buckley /búkli/, **William F., Jr** (*b.* 1925) US writer and editor. A conservative political commentator, he was founding editor of the *National Review* (1955) and hosted the television program 'Firing Line'

(1966). His books include *The Culture of Liberty* (1993). Full name **Buckley, William Frank, Jr**

Buckley's chance /búkliz-/, **Buckley's hope** *n ANZ* no chance whatsoever of accomplishing something (*informal*) [Late 19C. Origin ?]

buckminsterfullerene /búkminstər fóŏlə reen/ *n* a stable form (**allotrope**) of carbon containing 60 atoms [Late 20C. < the molecule's resemblance to the geodesic dome structure invented by R. Buckminster FULLER]

bucko /búkō/ (*plural* **-os**) *n* 1. a swaggering bully or bossy person (*slang*) 2. *Ireland, N Am* a boy or man (*informal*) [Late 19C. < BUCK[1]]

buck-passing *n* the shifting of blame or responsibility to somebody else (*informal*) [< BUCK[5]]

buckram /búkrəm/ *n* STIFF FABRIC a coarse cotton or linen fabric that has been stiffened with starch, gum, or latex. Use: bookbinding, stiffening clothes. ■ *adj* LIKE BUCKRAM resembling buckram in rigidity ■ *vt* (**-rams, -raming, -ramed**) PUT BUCKRAM ON SOMETHING to stiffen or strengthen something with buckram [14C. < Old French *boquerant* 'cloth from Bukhara']

buck rarebit *n* a Welsh rarebit topped with a poached egg

Bucks. /buks/ *abbr* Buckinghamshire

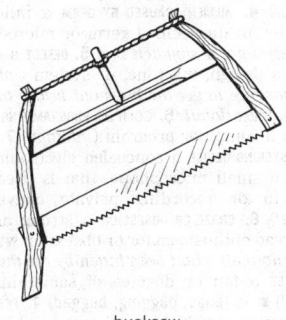

bucksaw

bucksaw /búk saw/ *n* a saw in which the blade is set in an 'H'-shaped frame [Mid-19C. < BUCK[4]]

buck's fizz /búks fízz/, **Buck's fizz** *n* a cocktail made of champagne mixed with orange juice [Mid-20C. After *Buck's Club* in London]

buckshee /búk shee/ (*dated informal*) *adj* 1. FREE given or obtained without charge 2. NOT ASKED FOR given without being asked for ■ *adv* WITHOUT CHARGING free of charge [Early 17C. Alteration of BAKSHEESH]

buckshot /búk shot/ *n* a large size of lead shot used in shotgun shells, especially for hunting game

buckskin /búk skin/ *n* 1. DEERSKIN the skin of a male deer 2. SOFT LEATHER a soft pliable greyish-yellow leather, usually with a suede finish, originally made from deerskin and now usually from sheepskin ■ **buckskins** *npl N Am* BUCKSKIN GARMENTS clothing made from buckskin leather, especially jackets, chaps, hats, and moccasins ■ *adj* GREYISH-YELLOW greyish-yellow in colour

buck's party, **buck's night** *n Aus* same as **stag night**

buckthorn /búk thawrn/ (*plural* **-thorns** or *same*) *n* a thorny bush or small tree with black berries. Genus: *Rhamnus*. [Late 16C. Translation of modern Latin *cervi spina* 'stag's thorn']

bucktooth /búk tóóth/ (*plural* **-teeth** /-teeth/) *n* a protruding upper front tooth (*informal*) —**bucktoothed** *adj*

bucku *n* TREES another spelling of **buchu**

buckwheat /búk weet/ *n* 1. a triangular seed that can be ground into flour. Use: cereal foods, animal fodder. 2. a plant that produces buckwheat. Native to: Asia. Latin name: *Fagopyrum esculentum*. [Mid-16C. Anglicization of Middle Dutch *boecweite* 'beech wheat'; because its grains resemble beech nuts]

buckyball /búki bawl/ *n* a stable ball-shaped molecule of carbon (**fullerene**), especially the molecule containing 60 atoms (**buckminsterfullerene**) (*informal*) [Late 20C. < *Bucky*, nickname of R. Buckminster FULLER]

bucky tube /búki-/ *n* 1. a tube-shaped molecule consisting of carbon atoms, usually 60 (*informal*) 2. CHEM same as **nanotube** [Late 20C. After BUCKYBALL]

buclizine /byoo klı zeen/ *n* an antihistamine drug. Use: control of nausea, vomiting, and some types of migraine.

bucolic /byoo kóllik/ *adj* 1. OF COUNTRYSIDE relating to or characteristic of the countryside or country life ○ *a writer of bucolic poems* 2. OF SHEPHERDS relating to or characteristic of shepherds, herdsmen, or flocks ■ *n* 1. LITERAT PASTORAL POEM a poem about the countryside or country life 2. SOMEBODY FROM COUNTRY a farmer, shepherd, or other person from the country [Early 16C. Via Latin < Greek *boukolikos* < *boukolos* 'cowherd'] —**bucolically** *adv*

bud[1] /bud/ *n* 1. OUTGROWTH ON PLANT STEM an outgrowth on a stem or branch consisting of a shortened stem and immature leaves or flowers, often enclosed by protective scales 2. UNOPENED FLOWER a flower that has not yet opened 3. ZOOL REPRODUCTIVE OUTGROWTH OF SIMPLE ORGANISM an asexually produced outgrowth of a simple organism such as an invertebrate or a yeast that breaks away from the parent and develops into a new individual 4. SOMETHING LIKE PLANT BUD something shaped like a plant bud 5. SOMEBODY OR SOMETHING IMMATURE somebody or something that is small, immature, or not yet fully developed ■ *v* (**buds, budding, budded**) 1. *vi* PRODUCE PLANT BUDS to produce outgrowths that develop into flowers or leaves 2. *vi* START TO GROW to start to develop or grow from a plant bud 3. *vi* BEGIN TO DEVELOP to begin to develop or grow from something small into another, usually larger thing ○ *Seeds of dissent are budding in the heartland.* 4. *vi* ZOOL REPRODUCE ASEXUALLY to reproduce asexually by producing an outgrowth that eventually separates to form a new individual 5. *vt* GARDENING GRAFT BUD INTO ANOTHER PLANT to insert a bud from one plant into the bark of another, usually one of a different variety, in order to propagate a plant from the bud [14C. Origin ?] —**budder** *n* —**budless** *adj* ◇ **in bud** having new buds that have not yet opened ◇ **nip something in the bud** to put an end to something considered undesirable before it can develop (*informal*)

bud[2] /bud/ *n N Am* same as **buddy** *n* (sense 2) (*informal*) [Mid-19C. Shortening]

Budapest /bóŏdə pést/ capital and largest city of Hungary. It is situated on the River Danube in northern Hungary near the Slovak border. Population: 1,811,522 (2001).

buddha: Daibutsu (Great Buddha), Kamakura, Japan

buddha /bóŏddə/, **Buddha** *n* 1. in Buddhism, somebody who has attained perfect enlightenment 2. a statue, picture, or other representation of the Buddha [Late 17C. < Sanskrit, past participle of *budh-* 'wake up, be enlightened']

Buddha /bóŏddə/ (563?–483? BC) Nepalese-born Indian philosopher and founder of Buddhism. About 528, he renounced his life as a prince and began his teaching after having attained enlightenment through meditation. Born **Gautama, Siddharta**. Known as **Sakyamuni**

> 'I do not fight with the world but the world fights with me.'
> [Buddha. Quoted in *Buddhism*, Edward Conze; 1951]

Buddhahood /bóŏddəhóŏd/ *n* the state of spiritual enlightenment attained by the Buddha

Buddhism /bóŏddizəm/ *n* a world religion or philosophy based on the teaching of the Buddha and holding that a state of enlightenment can be attained by suppressing worldly desires

Buddhist /bóŏddist/ *n* somebody who professes Buddhism —**Buddhist** *adj* —**Buddhistic** /bóŏ dístik/ *adj*

buddhu /bóŏ doo/ *n S Asia* an offensive term that deliberately insults somebody's intelligence or capacity to learn (*informal*) [< Hindi]

budding /búdding/ *adj* PROMISING beginning to show a particular talent ○ *a budding actor* ■ *n* 1. BOT DEVELOPMENT OF BUDS the formation and growth of buds on a plant stem 2. GARDENING GRAFTING OF BUD artificial propagation, especially of woody plants, by grafting a bud from one variety onto the stem of another 3. ZOOL ASEXUAL REPRODUCTION a form of asexual reproduction in which an outgrowth of the parent becomes constricted and eventually separates to form a new individual, as occurs in invertebrates and yeasts

buddle /búdd'l/ *n* a sloping trough in which crushed ore is separated from waste by washing with water [Mid-16C. Origin ?]

buddleia /búddli ə/ (*plural* **-ias** or *same*) *n* a deciduous ornamental bush or small tree with flowers that attract butterflies. Flowers: small, scented, purple, in tapering heads. Native to: South America. Latin name: *Buddleja davidii*. [Late 18C. < modern Latin, after Adam *Buddle* (d. 1715), English botanist]

buddy /búddi/ *n* (*plural* **-dies**) 1. *N Am* FRIEND a good friend, colleague, companion, or partner (*informal*) 2. *N Am* TERM OF ADDRESS FOR MALE a form of address to a man or boy (*informal*) ○ *Hey, buddy!* 3. HELPER TO AIDS PATIENT a volunteer who gives help and support to somebody who has Aids ■ *vi* (**-dies, -dying, -died**) HELP SOMEBODY WHO HAS AIDS to act as a helper to somebody with Aids [Mid-19C. Perhaps alteration of BROTHER]

buddy-buddy *adj* appearing to enjoy a close friendship (*informal*)

buddy movie, **buddy film** *n* a film focusing on the adventures and friendship of two central characters of the same gender

buddy system *n* an arrangement by which people are paired for mutual safety, e.g. in mountain climbing

Buderim /búddrəm/ coastal town and resort in southern Queensland, Australia. Population: 7,491 (1991).

budesonide /byoo déssə nīd/ *n* a corticosteroid drug taken by inhalation or in tablets. Use: treatment of hay fever and nasal polyps.

budge[1] /buj/ (**budges, budging, budged**) *vti* 1. to move, or move something, especially with difficulty or effort (*usually used in negative statements*) ○ *I tried moving the machine, but it wouldn't budge.* 2. to change an attitude, decision, or opinion, or make somebody do this ○ *Once she's made up her mind, no amount of persuasion will budge her.* [Late 16C. Via French *bouger* < assumed Vulgar Latin *bullicare* 'keep bubbling up' < Latin *bullire* (see BOIL[1])]

budge[2] /buj/ *n* a fur, usually lambskin, worn with the wool outwards ■ *adj* made from, trimmed with, or lined with budge [14C. Origin ?]

Budge /buj/, **Don** (1915–2000) US tennis player. One of the greatest players of his generation, he was the first tennis player ever to win a grand slam (1938). Full name **Budge, John Donald**

budgerigar /búj jəri gaar/ *n* a small bright green parrot with a yellow head that is often kept as a cagebird. Native to: central Australia. Latin name: *Melopsittacus undulatus*. [Mid-19C. < Yuwaalaraay *gijirigaa*]

budget /búj jit/ *n* 1. PLAN FOR ALLOCATING RESOURCES a plan specifying how resources, especially time or money, will be allocated or spent during a particular period 2. MONEY FOR PARTICULAR PURPOSE the total amount of money allocated or needed for a particular purpose or period of time 3. QUANTITY OR SUPPLY a quantity, stock, or supply of something ■ *adj* CHEAP OR ECONOMICAL suitable for somebody with a limited amount of money to spend ■ *v* (**-ets, -eting, -eted**) 1. *vti* PLAN SPENDING to plan the allocation, expenditure, or use of resources, especially money or time ○ *budget £20 a head* ○ *budget for growth* 2. *vt* PUT SOMETHING IN BUDGET to provide for or enter something in a budget 3. *vi* LIVE WITHIN SPENDING LIMITS to live within a budget ○ *Having budgeted well all their lives, they can afford to retire early.* [15C. < Old French *bougette* 'leather pouch, purse' < *bouge* (see BULGE)] —**budgetary** *adj* —**budgeter** *n*

Budget *n* a statement of the financial position of the United Kingdom for the financial year, with proposals for spending and taxation, presented in a speech by the Chancellor of the Exchequer

budget account *n* an account with a department store or other large organization that enables a customer to pay in regular or monthly instalments for goods or services obtained on credit

budget deficit *n* the amount by which government expenditure exceeds revenue

budgie /bújji/ *n* a budgerigar, especially one kept as a domestic pet (*informal*) [Early 20C. Shortening]

budgie smugglers *npl Aus* close-fitting elasticated briefs worn by men or boys for swimming (*informal*)

bud scale *n* a scaly leaf that is part of a protective sheath around a plant bud and is sometimes hairy or resinous

budworm /búd wurm/ *n* a moth larva that feeds on conifer buds and is one of the most destructive pests in North America. Latin name: *Harmolga fumiferana*.

Buenaventura /bwáynə ven to͝orə, -tyo͝orə/ city and major port on the Pacific Coast of western Colombia. Population: 266,988 (1995).

Buena Vista /bwáynə vístə/ village in Coahuila State, Mexico, the site of a US victory in the Mexican War in 1847

Bueno /bwáynō/, **Maria** (*b.* 1940) Brazilian tennis player. She won singles titles at the US championships (1959, 1963, 1964, 1966) and at Wimbledon (1959, 1960, and 1964). Full name **Bueno, Marie Ester Audion**

Buenos Aires /bwáy noss ī́riz/ capital and largest city of Argentina, situated in the eastern part of the country. It is a port on the Río de la Plata and the nation's commercial and cultural centre. Population: 2,776,138 (2001).

buff[1] /buf/ *n* **1.** COLOURS **PALE YELLOWISH-BEIGE** a dull yellowish-beige colour **2.** INDUST **SOFT LEATHER** a soft thick undyed leather that is made chiefly from the skins of buffalo, elk, or oxen and has a light yellow colour **3.** CLOTHING **LEATHER GARMENT** a garment made of buff leather, e.g. a military uniform coat **4.** TEXTILES **POLISHING CLOTH** a cloth of soft material such as leather or velvet, often mounted on a block and used for polishing **5.** ENG **POLISHING DISC** a revolving disc consisting of layers of cloth impregnated with abrasive powders. Use: polishing metal or other hard bright surfaces. ■ *adj* **1.** COLOURS **PALE YELLOWISH-BEIGE** of a dull yellowish beige colour **2. OF SOFT LEATHER** made of buff leather ■ *vt* (**buffs, buffing, buffed**) **1. POLISH SOMETHING** to clean or polish something with a piece of soft material **2. MAKE SURFACE SOFT** to make the surface of something, especially of leather, soft and velvety like buff by raising a nap [Late 16C. Alteration of French *buffle* 'buffalo' < late Latin *bufalus* (see BUFFALO)] ◇ **in the buff** naked (*informal*)

buff up *vi US* to become or make yourself physically fit and strong through exercise and diet (*informal*)

buff[2] /buf/ *n* somebody who is enthusiastic and knowledgeable about something (*informal*) ○ *a film buff* [Early 19C. < the buff-leather overcoats formerly worn by volunteer firefighters ('fire buffs') in New York City]

buff[3] /buf/ *adj* **1.** *US* physically fit and strong, especially through exercise and a controlled diet (*informal*) **2.** having a handsome or beautiful face and physique (*slang*) [Late 20C. Probably < BUFF[1]]

buffalo /búffəlō/ *n* (*plural* **-loes** or **-los** or *same*) **1. TYPE OF HORNED CATTLE** a type of horned cattle belonging to various species, including the African buffalo and domesticated breeds of the Asian water buffalo. Family: Bovidae. **2.** *N Am* **BISON** a North American bison **3.** FISH same as **buffalo fish** ■ *vt* (**-loes, -loing, -loed**) *N Am* (*informal*) **1. BAFFLE SOMEBODY** to throw somebody into a state of confusion and puzzled bewilderment **2. INTIMIDATE SOMEBODY** to coerce or inhibit somebody aggressively [Mid-16C. Via Portuguese or Italian < late Latin *bufalus* < Greek *boubalos* 'gazelle']

Buffalo /búffəlō/ city and port in western New York State beside Lake Erie and the Niagara River. Population: 287,698 (2002 estimate).

Buffalo, Mount mountain in northern Victoria, Australia, the site of a ski resort. Height: 1,723 m/5,653 ft.

Buffalo Bill /búffəlō bíl/ ➧ **Cody, William Frederick**

buffalo fish *n* a large freshwater fish of the sucker family that resembles the carp and has a humped back. Native to: Mississippi Valley. Genus: *Ictiobus*.

buffalo grass *n* **1.** a short grey-green grass. Use: forage, lawns. Native to: plains of central North America. Latin name: *Buchloë dactyloides*. **2.** *S Africa* a broad-leaved grass. Use: lawns, fodder. Native to: South Africa. Genus: *Panicum*.

buffalo mozzarella *n* a fresh mozzarella cheese made from a combination of water buffalo milk and cow's milk

buffalo wings *npl N Am* fried chicken wings, usually served in barbecue sauce [Because supposedly first served in a restaurant in or named after the city of BUFFALO]

buffer[1] /búffər/ *n* **1. PROTECTOR AGAINST IMPACT** somebody or something that reduces shock or impact or protects against other harm, usually by interception **2.** RAIL **DEVICE ON TRAIN OR TRACK** a spring-loaded or hydraulic pad attached to the end of rolling stock or at the end of a railway track. It stops the train running off the end of the track and may also absorb impact. **3.** COMPUT **MEMORY AREA** a temporary storage area for data being transmitted between two devices that function at different speeds. A buffer enables a faster device such as a computer to complete sending the data and begin another task without waiting for a slower device such as a printer. **4.** CHEM **SUBSTANCE MAINTAINING PH** a substance that minimizes a change in pH of a solution by neutralizing added acids and bases, or a solution containing such a substance ■ *vt* (**-ers, -ering, -ered**) **1. CUSHION SOMETHING AGAINST SHOCK** to protect something against impact, or reduce the shock of an impact **2.** CHEM **ADD BUFFER TO SOLUTION** to add to a solution a substance that will keep its pH constant [Mid-19C. < obsolete *buff* 'hit something softly', perhaps < French *bufe* (see BUFFET[2])]

buffer[2] /búffər/ *n* **1.** an implement or tool for polishing something, especially the fingernails **2.** somebody who polishes something with a buffer **3.** INDUST, TEXTILES same as **buff**[1] *n* (sense 2), *adj* (sense 1) [Mid-19C. < BUFF[1]]

buffer[3] /búffər/ *n* somebody who is regarded as bumbling or indecisive, especially a man (*informal insult*) [Mid-18C. < obsolete *buff* 'stammer', probably an imitation of the sound]

buffer state *n* a small neutral state that lies between two potentially hostile powers and reduces the risk of conflict between them

buffer stock *n* a stock of a basic commodity accumulated by a government when supplies are plentiful and prices low, and held for use when supplies are short to stabilize the price

buffer zone *n* **1.** a neutral area that lies between hostile forces and reduces the risk of conflict between them **2.** an area designed to form a barrier that prevents potential conflict or harmful contact

buffet[1] /bo͝o fay/ *n* **1. SELF-SERVICE MEAL** a meal at which people serve themselves from various dishes set out on a serving counter or table **2. TABLE WITH REFRESHMENTS** a serving counter or table on which meals or refreshments are displayed **3.** RAIL same as **buffet car** **4.** FURNITURE **DINING-ROOM SIDEBOARD** a piece of dining-room furniture with drawers for storing tableware [Early 18C. < French, 'footstool, sideboard']

buffet[2] /búffit/ *n* **1. BLOW STRUCK WITH HAND** a blow struck with the fist or hand **2. REPEATED BLOW** a heavy or repeated blow or stroke **3.** AVIAT same as **buffeting** ■ *v* (**-fets, -feting, -feted**) **1.** *vt* **STRIKE AGAINST SOMETHING REPEATEDLY** to knock or strike against something heavily or repeatedly **2.** *vt* **HIT SOMETHING WITH HAND** to hit somebody or something sharply with the fist or hand **3.** *vi* **STRUGGLE TO PROGRESS** to proceed under difficult conditions [Pre-12C. < Old French, 'small blow' < *bufe* 'blow', an imitation of the sound] —**buffeter** *n*

buffet car *n* a railway carriage where light refreshments and beverages are served

buffeting /búffiting/ *n* an irregular shaking of a part or the whole of an aircraft during flight, usually caused by strong winds

buffi plural of **buffo**

buffing wheel /búffing-/ *n* a wheel covered with a soft material such as lamb's wool, leather, or velvet and used to shine or polish something, especially metal

bufflehead /búff'l hed/ (*plural* **-heads** or *same*) *n* a small diving duck, the male of which has black and white feathers and a large fluffy head, while the female is dark brown. Native to: North America. Latin name: *Bucephala albeola*. [Mid-17C. < obsolete *buffle* 'buffalo' < French (see BUFF[1]); because of its large head]

buffo /bo͝offō/ (*plural* **-fi** /-fee/ or **-fos**) *n* in opera, a male singer of comic roles [Mid-18C. < Italian < *buffare* (see BUFFOON)] —**buffo** *adj*

Buffon /bo͝o foN/, **Georges Louis Leclerc, Comte de** (1707–88) French naturalist. His major work was *Histoire naturelle* (1749–89), the first scientific account of the history of the Earth.

buffoon /bə fo͞on/ *n* **1.** somebody behaving in a silly way **2.** somebody who amuses others by clowning or joking [Mid-16C. Via French < Italian *buffone* < *buffare* 'puff, act the clown', an imitation of the sound]

buffoonery /bə fo͞onəri/ *n* silly behaviour

buff-tip moth *n* a large European moth that resembles a twig when it wraps its cream-tipped wings around its body. Latin name: *Phalera bucephala*.

buff wheel *n* MANUF same as **buffing wheel**

bug /bug/ *n* **1. INSECT WITH PIERCING AND SUCKING MOUTHPARTS** an insect with thickened forewings and mouthparts adapted for piercing and sucking. Order: Hemiptera. **2.** *N Am* **INSECT REGARDED AS PEST** an insect or similar organism, especially one considered to be a pest, e.g. an aphid, bedbug, or cockroach ○ *can't stand having bugs in the house* **3. GERM** an unspecified germ or microorganism that causes mild illness (*informal*) **4. AILMENT CAUSED BY GERM** a mild illness caused by an unspecified germ or microorganism (*informal*) ○ *got a stomach bug* **5. DEFECT** a defect or flaw in a design, machine, or system (*informal*) ○ *We're working to get the bugs out before the system becomes operational.* **6.** COMPUT **PROGRAMMING ERROR** an error in a computer program (*informal*) **7.** TELECOM **HIDDEN LISTENING DEVICE** a concealed electronic device, usually a small microphone, that is used for listening to or recording private conversations (*informal*) **8. CRAZE OR OBSESSION** a strong and often widespread enthusiasm for or obsession with something (*informal*) ○ *had been bitten by the theatre bug* **9. DEVOTEE** a fan or devotee of something (*dated informal*) ■ *vt* (**bugs, bugging, bugged**) **1. PESTER SOMEBODY** to cause somebody persistent trouble and annoyance (*informal*) ○ *Go away and stop bugging me!* **2. HIDE LISTENING DEVICE IN SOMETHING** to conceal an electronic listening device in something ○ *She suspected her office had been bugged.* **3. LISTEN TO SOMETHING SECRETLY** to listen to or eavesdrop on a conversation using an electronic listening device ○ *He thinks someone is bugging his phone conversations.* [14C. Origin ?]

SYNONYMS See ***bother***.

Bug /book, boog/ **1.** river that rises in Ukraine and forms the border between Ukraine and Poland, and between Poland and Belarus before joining the Vistula near Warsaw. Length: 756 km/470 mi. **2.** river in western Ukraine, flowing southeast into the Black Sea. Length: 805 km/500 mi.

bugaboo /búggə boo/ (*plural* **-boos**) *n* something that causes fear, annoyance, or trouble, especially an imagined threat or problem [Mid-18C. Origin ?]

Buganda /bo͞o gándə/ former kingdom in the area north of Lake Victoria, southern Uganda. It became part of Uganda in 1962 and the kingdom was dissolved in 1967.

Bugatti /boo gátti/, **Ettore** (1881–1947) Italian car designer and manufacturer. He is best known for the racing cars he produced in the 1930s. Full name **Bugatti, Ettore Arco Isidoro**

bugbane /búg bayn/ *n* a perennial plant that has large compound leaves. Flowers: small, white, in spike-shaped clusters. Native to: Europe. Latin name: *Cimicifuga foetida*. [Because its flowers are reputed to repel insects]

bugbear /búg bair/ *n* **1. SOURCE OF FEAR** a source of obsessive or groundless fear **2. CONTINUING PROBLEM** a continuing source of annoyance or difficulty **3. GOBLIN** a goblin invented to frighten children, traditionally in the form of a bear that eats those who misbehave [Late 16C. < obsolete *bug* 'hobgoblin' + BEAR[1] (sense 1)]

bug-eyed *adj* (*informal*) **1.** having protruding eyes **2.** wide-eyed with amazement or fear

bugger[1] /búggər/ *n* **1. TABOO TERM** a highly offensive term for somebody who practises anal intercourse (*taboo*) **2. OFFENSIVE TERM** an offensive term for some-

body or something regarded as unpleasant, difficult, or contemptible (*slang*) **3. SOMEBODY OF PARTICULAR TYPE** used to refer to somebody with a particular characteristic or in a particular situation (*slang; often offensive*) ○ *The jammy bugger won the prize.* ■ *v* (**-gers, -gering, -gered**) **1.** *vti* **TABOO TERM** a highly offensive term meaning to practise anal intercourse with somebody (*taboo*) **2.** *vt* **OFFENSIVE TERM** an offensive term meaning to damage, ruin, or spoil something (*slang*) **3.** *vt* **OFFENSIVE TERM** an offensive term meaning to make somebody thoroughly exhausted (*slang*) **4.** *vt* **OFFENSIVE TERM** an offensive term used as a swearword to express annoyance or frustration (*slang; can be in the passive, especially to express an absolute refusal*) ■ *interj* **OFFENSIVE TERM** an offensive term used as a swearword to express annoyance or frustration (*slang*) [Mid-16C. Via French *bougre* 'heretic' < medieval Latin *Bulgarus* 'Bulgarian (belonging to the Orthodox Church)'; from a Western Christian association of heresy with anal intercourse]

bugger about, bugger around *v* (*taboo*) **1.** *vi* a highly offensive term meaning to waste time **2.** *vt* a highly offensive term meaning to cause difficulties for somebody

bugger off *vi* a highly offensive term meaning to go away or get out (*taboo*)

bugger up *vt* a highly offensive term meaning to spoil or ruin something (*taboo*)

bugger[2] /búggər/ *n* somebody who plants listening devices in an object or place [Mid-20C. < BUG]

buggery /búggəri/ *n* **1. TABOO TERM** a highly offensive term for anal intercourse (*taboo*) **2.** LAW **SEXUAL OFFENCE** anal intercourse or bestiality **3. OFFENSIVE TERM** a highly offensive term used as an intensifier (*slang*)

buggy[1] /búggi/ (*plural* **-gies**) *n* **1. WHEELED CHAIR FOR BABY OR TODDLER** a lightweight wheeled chair for pushing a baby or young child around in, especially one that can be folded for easy storage **2. BATTERY-POWERED VEHICLE** a small battery-powered vehicle used for a particular purpose ○ *a golf buggy* **3. HORSE-DRAWN VEHICLE** a lightweight horse-drawn carriage [Mid-18C. Origin ?]

buggy[2] /búggi/ (**-gier, -giest**) *adj* **1.** infested with insects **2.** containing or prone to develop computer bugs (*informal*) [Early 18C. < BUG] —**bugginess** *n*

bugle[1] /byoóg'l/ *n* a brass instrument like a short trumpet without valves, used for military signals [14C. Via Old French < Latin *buculus*, diminutive of *bos* 'ox'] —**bugle** *vi* —**bugler** *n*

bugle[2] /byoóg'l/ *n* a creeping plant related to mint. Flowers: blue, pink, white. Native to: Europe, Asia. Genus: *Ajuga*. N Am term **bugleweed** [13C. Directly or via Old French < late Latin *bugula*]

bugle bead, bugle *n* a tube-shaped bead made of glass or plastic used in embroidery or bead trimmings [Late 16C. Origin ?]

bugleweed /byoóg'l weed/ *n* *N Am* PLANTS same as **bugle**[2]

bugloss /byoó gloss/ *n* a hairy plant related to borage. Flowers: blue, drooping in clusters. Genus: *Lycopsis*. [14C. < Latin *buglossus* < Greek *buglōssus* 'ox-tongued' (from the shape and roughness of the leaves)]

bugong, bugong moth *n* another spelling of **bogong**

buhl /bool/ *n* FURNITURE another spelling of **boulle** [Early 19C. Via German < French *boulle* (see BOULLE)]

buhrstone /búr stōn/, **burstone, burrstone** *n* **1.** a rough hard quartz rock. Use: formerly, millstones, grindstones. **2.** a millstone or grindstone made from buhrstone [Mid-17C. < variant of BURR[1] (because of the stone's roughness)]

build /bild/ *v* (**builds, building, built** /bilt/) **1.** *vt* **MAKE SOMETHING BY JOINING PARTS** to make a structure by fitting the parts of it together ○ *to build a wall* **2.** *vt* **HAVE SOMETHING BUILT** to have a building or other structure made ○ *The emperor built a number of these pavilions.* **3.** *vti* **FORM OR DEVELOP** to form or develop something such as an enterprise or a relationship, or be formed or developed ○ *building a solid business reputation* **4.** *vi* **INCREASE** to increase or mount steadily ○ *Tension is starting to build.* **5.** *vt* **COLLECT SET OF PLAYING CARDS** in card games, to form a set by gathering related cards ■ *n* **1. BODY STRUCTURE** somebody's physical structure, shape, and size ○ *the wrestler's heavy build* **2.** COMPUT **STAGE OF SOFTWARE DEVELOPMENT** a stage in the development of computer software in which two or more independently developed software components are linked so that they can be tested in conjunction with one another ○ *testing the first build of the program* **3. STANDARD OF CONSTRUCTION** the standard of construction of something such as a vehicle [Old English *byldan* 'construct a house' < *bold* 'dwelling' < Germanic, 'dwell']

build in *vt* **1.** to construct a piece of furniture so that it becomes part of the structure of a room, or add an object so that it becomes part of something else ○ *built in bookshelves over the desk* **2.** to add something to a system or organization ○ *The designers will build in options that buyers can choose from.*

build into *vt* to add something as a permanent feature of something else ○ *These safeguards will be built into the system.*

build on *vt* **1.** to use something as a basis for further development or improvement ○ *hoping to build on the success of their first CD* **2.** to add something as an extra part joined to an existing building ○ *The porch was built on about ten years later.*

build up *v* **1.** *vti* **DEVELOP** to increase or develop gradually, or make something do this ○ *Traffic is building up on the motorway.* **2.** *vt* **PRAISE EXCESSIVELY** to emphasize or exaggerate the good qualities of somebody or something ○ *I expected someone more impressive after the way she built him up.* **3.** *vt* **MAKE SOMEBODY STRONGER AND HEALTHIER** to make somebody stronger and healthier, especially by feeding

build up to *vt* to develop towards a point or climax

builder /bíldər/ *n* **1.** a person or company engaged in building or repairing houses or other large structures **2.** a detergent additive that improves cleaning properties

building /bílding/ *n* **1.** a structure with walls and a roof, e.g. a house or factory **2.** the business or task of constructing houses, factories, bridges, and other large structures (*often used before a noun*) ○ *building materials*

building block *n* **1.** *N Am* same as **brick** *n* (sense 3) **2.** an element or component regarded as contributing to the growth of an organization, plan, or system ○ *He acquired companies as building blocks for his financial empire.* **3.** a large block of concrete or similar hard material, used for building houses and other large structures

building line *n* a line on a property beyond which no building is allowed

building paper *n* a damp-proofing and insulating material consisting of a bitumen and fibre mix sandwiched between heavy-duty paper

building sickness *n* MED same as **sick building syndrome**

building site *n* an area where construction, structural alteration, or repair work is being carried out

building society *n* a financial organization that pays interest on savings accounts, lends money for buying and improving houses, and provides other banking services

buildup /bíld up/ *n* **1. ACCUMULATION** a large amount of something or a large number of things gradually accumulated or developed ○ *prevents the buildup of plaque* **2. RUN-UP TO EVENT** a period of time in which preparations are being made for a particular important event **3. IMPRESSIVE DESCRIPTION** a description that emphasizes or exaggerates the good qualities of somebody or something

built past participle, past tense of **build**

built environment *n* buildings and structures made by people, as opposed to natural features

built heritage *n* the part of a country's heritage that consists of buildings and structures, as opposed to natural or aesthetic assets

built-in *adj* **1.** designed or fitted as a fixed or permanent part **2.** forming a natural feature or characteristic

built-in obsolescence *n* INDUST same as **planned obsolescence**

built-up *adj* **1.** containing many buildings **2.** having several layers or added thickness ○ *built-up heels*

~~**buisness**~~ incorrect spelling of **business**

Bujumbura /boójəm boórə/ capital and largest city of Burundi. It is situated in the western part of the country, on Lake Tanganyika. Population: 634,479 (1991 estimate).

Bukavu /boo kaávoo/ capital of Sud-Kivu Region in the eastern Democratic Republic of the Congo. It is situated on Lake Kivu, close to the border with Rwanda. Population: 418,000 (1985).

Bukhara /boŏ khaárə/ city in southern Uzbekistan, in the Amu Darya valley, west of Samarkand. Population: 236,000 (1994).

Bukhari /boŏ khaári/ (810–870) Arabian scholar. He travelled throughout the Muslim world and compiled the oral traditions of the Prophet Muhammad into the Sunni foundation text, *al-Sahih* ('The Genuine'). Full name **Bukhari, Muhammad ibn-Ismail al-**

Bukharin /boo kaárin, -khaárin/, **Nicolay Ivanovich** (1888–1938) Russian revolutionary and political theorist. He was leader of the October Revolution of 1917 and edited the Communist Party newspaper *Pravda* (1917–29). He was arrested in Joseph Stalin's Great Purge (1937) and executed.

Bulawayo /boŏllə wáy ō/ industrial city on the Matsheumlope River, southwestern Zimbabwe. Population: 620,936 (1992).

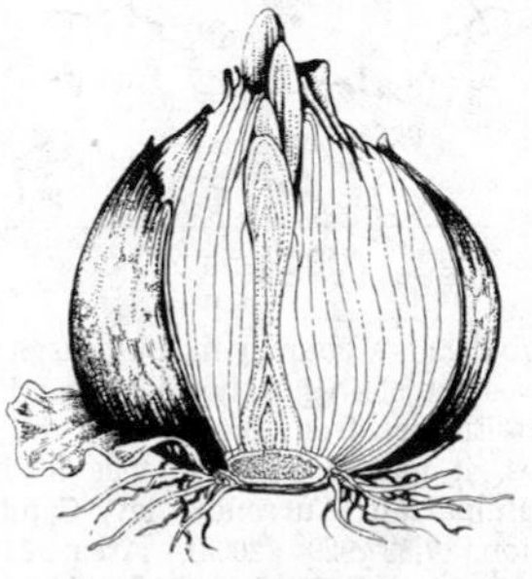

bulb

bulb /bulb/ *n* **1. UNDERGROUND PLANT PART** an underground plant storage organ, e.g. a corm, tuber, or rhizome, from which a new plant grows every year **2. PLANT GROWING FROM BULB** a plant that develops from a bulb or other underground storage organ, e.g. a tulip or crocus **3.** ELEC same as **light bulb** **4. ROUNDED PART** a rounded part of something, e.g. the mercury reservoir of a thermometer or the squeezable rubber ball on a dropper **5.** ANAT **ROUNDED PART OF BODY ORGAN** a rounded or enlarged section of a cylindrical body part [Mid-16C. Via Latin *bulbus* < Greek *bolbos* 'bulbous root, onion']

bulbel *n* BOT another spelling of **bulbil**

bulb fly *n* a fly similar to a wasp, whose larvae live in and eat daffodil bulbs. Family: Syrphidae.

bulbil /búl bil/, **bulbel** /búlb'l/ *n* a new bulb growing like a bud on a plant or leaf stem [Mid-19C. < modern Latin *bulbillus*, diminutive of Latin *bulbus* (see BULB)]

bulbourethral gland /búlbō yoo reéthrəl-/ *n* ANAT same as **Cowper's gland** [< Latin *bulbus* (see BULB)]

bulbous /búlbəss/ *adj* **1.** rounded and swollen-looking **2.** growing from a plant bulb —**bulbously** *adv* —**bulbousness** *n*

bulbul /boŏlboŏl/ *n* **1.** a generally greyish or brownish songbird. Native to: tropical Africa and Asia. Family: Pycnonotidae. **2.** a songbird frequently mentioned in Persian poetry, taken to be a nightingale [Mid-17C. < Persian, an imitation of its song]

Bulfinch /boŏl finch/, **Charles** (1763–1844) US architect. He developed the federal style of American architecture with buildings such as the State House in Boston (completed 1798) and the completion of the US Capitol (1830).

Bulfinch, Thomas (1796–1867) US writer. He wrote a series of books popularizing mythology, including *The Age of Fables* (1855) and *The Age of Chivalry* (1858).

Bulgakov /boŏl gaá kof/, **Mikhail** (1891–1940) Ukrainian writer. Suppressed by the Soviet Communists, his work includes the posthumously-published modern masterpiece *The Master and Margarita* (1966–7). Full name **Bulgakov, Mikhail Afanasyevich**

> 'Love leaped out at us like a murderer jumping out of a dark alley. It shocked us both—the shock of a stroke of lightning, the shock of a flick-knife.'

[Mikhail Bulgakov, *The Master and Margarita*; 1966–7]

Bulganin /bul gánnin/, **Nikolay Aleksandrovich** (1895–1975) premier of the USSR (1955–58). After Joseph Stalin's death, he worked closely with Nikita Khruschev to try to establish détente with the West.

bulgar *n* FOOD another spelling of **bulgur**

Bulgar /búl gaar/ *n* a member of an ancient Slavic people who settled in areas of present-day Bulgaria around the 7th century AD. They abandoned their Finno-Ugric language and adopted the Slavic language and customs of the people they subjugated. [Mid-18C. < medieval Latin *Bulgarus* < Old Church Slavonic *Bulgary* (plural) 'Bulgars']

Bulgaria

Bulgaria /bul gáiri ə/ country in southeastern Europe, on the western shores of the Black Sea. Part of the Ottoman Empire from the 14th to the late 19th centuries, it gained independence in 1908. Language: Bulgarian. Currency: lev. Capital: Sofia. Population: 7,537,929 (2003). Area: 110,994 sq. km/42,855 sq. mi. Official name **Republic of Bulgaria**

Bulgarian /bul gáiri ən/ *n* **1.** somebody who comes from Bulgaria **2.** the official language of Bulgaria, belonging to the South Slavonic group of Indo-European languages. Native speakers: 9 million. — **Bulgarian** *adj*

bulge /bulj/ *vi* (**bulges, bulging, bulged**) **1.** SWELL to expand or swell **2.** BE OVERFILLED to contain so much that the sides expand outwards (*informal*) ○ *The shoppers carried bags bulging with groceries.* ■ *n* **1.** PART THAT EXPANDS OUTWARDS an area or part that curves or has expanded outwards **2.** INCREASE a sudden temporary increase ○ *a bulge in the population figures* **3.** same as **baby boom** (*informal*) [12C. Via Old French *boulge* 'leather sack, bag' < Latin *bulga* < Gaulish] — **bulginess** *n* — **bulging** *adj* — **bulgingly** *adv* — **bulgy** *adj*

bulgur /búlgər/, **bulghur, bulgar, bulgur wheat** *n* wheat that has been parboiled, dried, and cracked into small pieces. It is a common ingredient in southwestern Asian and vegetarian cooking. [Mid-20C. Via Turkish < Persian *bulgūr* 'bruised grain']

bulimia /byoo límmi ə/ *n* a condition in which bouts of overeating are followed by undereating, use of laxatives, or self-induced vomiting. It is associated with depression and anxiety about putting on weight. [14C. Via modern Latin < Greek *boulimia* 'hunger of an ox' < *bous* 'ox' + *limos* 'hunger'] — **bulimic** *adj, n*

bulk /bulk/ *n* **1.** LARGE SIZE large size or mass **2.** MAJORITY the greater part of something ○ *The bulk of the funding will come from the government.* **3.** LARGE BODY a large or overweight person's body ○ *eased his bulk through the narrow passageway* **4.** FIBRE IN FOOD the indigestible fibre that is a constituent of some food **5.** CARGO a ship's cargo **6.** PART OF SHIP FOR CARGO the part of a ship where cargo is stored ■ *adj* IN LARGE QUANTITY in or of a large quantity ■ *vi* (**bulks, bulking, bulked**) GAIN WEIGHT to gain weight, especially by deliberately adding additional muscle mass [15C. Partly < Old Norse *búlki* 'heap' (< Indo-European, 'swell'); partly < Old English *būc* 'belly' (< Germanic)] ◇ **bulk large** to play an important part ◇ **in bulk 1.** in large quantities or amounts **2.** loose, instead of being commercially packaged

bulk up *vti* to increase in size or volume, or make somebody or something do this (*informal*) ○ *We're hoping student numbers will bulk up this year.*

bulkbill /búlk bíl/ (**-bills, -billing, -billed**) *vt Aus* to claim payment for medical care directly from the insurer, Medicare, rather than charging the patient, who must then claim a refund — **bulkbilling** *n*

bulk buy *n* a large amount of something or a number of things bought at one time, usually at a reduced rate — **bulk-buy** *vti* — **bulk buying** *n*

bulk carrier *n* a ship that carries loose unpackaged cargo such as coal or grain

bulkhead /búlk hed/ *n* a partition inside a ship, aircraft, or large vehicle [15C. < Old Norse *bálkr* 'partition']

bulking /búlking/ *n* the increase in the volume of sand, cement, and other building materials when they become damp

bulky /búlki/ (**-ier, -iest**) *adj* **1.** large and awkward to carry or move **2.** heavily built, broad, or muscular — **bulkily** *adv* — **bulkiness** *n*

bull[1] /bool/ *n* **1.** MALE OF CATTLE an uncastrated adult male of any breed of domestic cattle or other bovine animal **2.** MALE MAMMAL a sexually mature male of any of various large mammals, including whales, seals, moose, and elephants **3.** BIG MAN a hefty or aggressive man **4.** FIN BUYER OF RISING SECURITIES an investor who buys securities in anticipation of rising prices, intending to resell them for profit **5.** SPORTS same as **bull's eye 6.** OFFENSIVE TERM an offensive term for a policeman (*slang; used in Black English*) ■ *vt* (**bulls, bulling, bulled**) FIN RAISE PRICES WITH SPECULATIVE BUYING to attempt to raise prices in a particular commodity or market by buying large quantities and thus reducing availability and increasing demand [Pre-12C. < Old Norse *boli*] ◇ **take the bull by the horns** to deal with a difficult situation forcefully and decisively (*informal*)

bull[2] /bool/ *n* a written statement formally issued by the pope and bearing an official seal [13C. Via French < Latin *bulla* 'bubble, seal, sealed document']

bull[3] /bool/ *n Ireland* a glaring mistake in speech, especially a self-contradictory statement [Early 17C. Origin ?]

bull[4] /bool/ *n* an offensive term for talk or writing dismissed as foolish or inaccurate (*slang*) [Early 17C. Origin ? Now often taken as an abbreviation of BULLSHIT] ◇ **shoot the bull** *N Am* to chatter idly (*slang*)

Bull /bool/ *n* ASTRON, ZODIAC same as **Taurus** (sense 2) [Early 16C. Translation of Latin *Taurus*]

Bull /bool/, **John** (1563?–1628) English organist and composer. Organist to James I of England and VI of Scotland, he was the organist of Antwerp Cathedral (1617–28). He was an early exponent of contrapuntal keyboard music.

bulla /boollə/ (*plural* **-lae** /-lee/) *n* **1.** MED same as **blister** *n* (sense 1) (*technical*) **2.** a rounded bony protruding part of the body **3.** the pope's official seal [14C. < Latin, 'bubble, seal, sealed document']

Bullamakanka /boolləmə kángkə/ *n Aus* a remote and backward place (*informal*) [Mid-20C. Origin ?]

bullbaiting /bool bayting/ *n* the former entertainment of setting fierce dogs to attack a bull, popular in medieval times

bull bars *npl* a metal framework mounted on the front of a vehicle to protect it against impact

bulldog

bulldog /bool dog/ *n* **1.** a muscular dog with smooth hair, belonging to a breed developed in England for bullbaiting **2.** an assistant to a proctor at Oxford and Cambridge universities (*informal*)

bulldog ant *n* a large ant with strong jaws and a painful bite. Native to: Australia. Genus: *Myrmecia*.

Bulldog Clip *tdmk* a trademark for a clip with a strong cylindrical spring, used for holding papers together or for fastening them to a board

bulldoze /bool dōz/ (**-dozes, -dozing, -dozed**) *v* **1.** *vt* DEMOLISH SOMETHING WITH BULLDOZER to demolish a building or clear debris using a bulldozer **2.** *vti* FORCE WAY THROUGH SOMETHING to force a way past or through an obstruction (*informal*) **3.** *vt* FORCE SOMEBODY OR SOMETHING to force somebody to do something or something to happen by behaving stubbornly or ruthlessly (*informal*) [Late 19C. Origin ?]

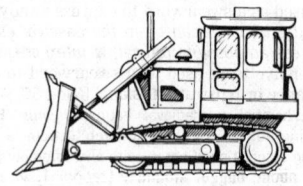

bulldozer

bulldozer /bool dōzər/ *n* a construction vehicle with tracks or large wheels and a wide blade used for moving earth or debris

bull dust *n Aus* **1.** fine dirt or dust on roads **2.** talk or writing dismissed as nonsensical or inaccurate (*informal*)

bull dyke *n* an offensive term for a lesbian whose appearance or behaviour is considered unfeminine (*slang*)

Bullen /boollən/, **Keith** (1906–76) New Zealand geophysicist and mathematician. He collaborated with Sir Harold Jeffreys to create the Jeffreys Bullen Tables (1940), which record the speed of seismic waves as they pass through rocks of different types. Full name **Bullen, Keith Edward**

Buller /boollər/ river in the northwestern part of the South Island, New Zealand. It rises in the Southern Alps near Mount Travers and empties into the Tasman Sea near Westport. Length: 177 km/110 mi.

bullet /boollit/ *n* **1.** AMMUNITION USED IN FIREARM a projectile fired from a handgun, rifle, or other small firearm, usually pointed and cylindrical and made of metal **2.** also **bullet point** DOT a large printed dot used to highlight items in a printed list **3.** FINAL REPAYMENT OF LOAN a final loan payment, representing the initial sum borrowed excluding interest, which was paid during the term of the loan [Early 16C. < French *boulet* 'small ball' < *boule* (see BOWL[2])] ◇ **bite the bullet** to deal with a situation that is unpleasant but unavoidable (*informal*) ◇ **get** *or* **be given the bullet** to be dismissed from a job (*informal*)

bulletin /boollətin/ *n* **1.** NEWS BROADCAST a short broadcast containing a single item of news **2.** ANNOUNCEMENT an official announcement **3.** NEWSLETTER a newsletter issued by an organization or institution [Mid-18C. < Italian *bulletino* 'small papal bull' < *bulla* < Latin (see BULL[2])]

bulletin board *n* **1.** *N Am* same as **noticeboard 2.** also **bulletin board system** an online forum used to exchange e-mails, chat, and access software

bullet loan *n* a loan that is repaid in full in a single payment on a set date

bullet point *n* PRINTING same as **bullet** (sense 2)

bulletproof /boollit proof/ *adj* **1.** able to resist the penetration of bullets ○ *bulletproof glass* **2.** invulnerable to attack or criticism (*informal*) ○ *Nobody's bulletproof in this company.*

~~bullettin~~ incorrect spelling of **bulletin**

bullet train *n* a high-speed passenger train in Japan

bulletwood /boollit wood/ *n* **1.** the tough durable wood of a tropical American tree **2.** a tree grown for its tough durable wood. Native to: tropical America. Latin name: *Manilkara bidentata*.

bull fiddle *n US* same as **double bass** (*informal*)

bullfight /bool fīt/ *n* a traditional public entertainment, especially in Spain and Mexico, in which a bull is baited and killed — **bullfighter** *n* — **bullfighting** *n*

bullfinch /bool finch/ *n* a small bird with a short thick

beak, a black head, and a pink to red breast. Native to: Europe, Asia. Latin name: *Pyrrhula pyrrhula*.

bullfrog /bo͝ol frog/ *n* a large frog with a deep croak. Native to: eastern North America. Genus: *Rana*. [Mid-18C. < its strong croak]

bullhead /bo͝ol hed/ *n* **1.** a large-headed fish such as the freshwater sculpin. Genus: *Cottus*. **2.** a common catfish of rivers and lakes. Native to: North America. Genus: *Ictalurus*.

bullheaded /bo͝ol héddid/ *adj* stubborn and uncooperative (*informal*) —**bullheadedly** *adv* —**bullheadedness** *n*

bullhead rail *n* a railway rail with a narrow base and a bulbous top when viewed in cross-section

bullhorn /bo͝ol hawrn/ *n N Am* COMMUNICATION same as **loudhailer**

bullion /bo͝olli ən/ *n* **1. BARS OF GOLD OR SILVER** gold or silver in the form of bars or ingots **2. MASS OF METAL** metal in the form of an unshaped mass **3.** TEXTILES **GOLD OR SILVER BRAID** gold or silver ornamental braid [15C. < Anglo-Norman, 'mint' < Latin *bullire* 'boil' < *bulla* 'bubble']

bullish /bo͝ollish/ *adj* **1. BRAWNY** broad and strong **2. EXPECTING GOOD STOCK MARKET FIGURES** expecting or producing good results, especially rising stock market prices **3. OPTIMISTIC** confident and optimistic (*informal*) —**bullishly** *adv* —**bullishness** *n*

bull market *n* a stock market in which prices are rising and are expected to continue rising

bull mastiff *n* a large muscular dog with smooth hair, belonging to a breed developed by crossing the bulldog and the mastiff

bullnecked /bo͝ol nékt/ *adj* having a short thick neck

bullnose /bo͝ol nōz/ *n* **1.** a brick with a rounded end **2.** a disease of pigs that causes the snout to swell

bullnosed /bo͝ol nōzd/ *adj* having a rounded protruding front part (*technical*) ○ *a stair tread with a bullnosed edge*

bullock /bo͝ollək/ *n* **1.** a young domestic bull **2.** a castrated domestic bull [Old English *bulluc* < *bula* 'bull']

bullock's heart *n* FOOD same as **custard apple** (sense 1)

bullocky /bo͝ollәki/ (*plural* **-ies**) *n Aus* somebody who drives a team of bullocks (*informal*)

bullpen /bo͝ol pen/ *n* **1.** in baseball, the part of the field where the relief pitchers warm up **2.** *N Am* a cell for prisoners waiting to be brought into court (*informal*)

bullring /bo͝ol ring/ *n* an arena where bullfights are held

bullroarer /bo͝ol rawrər/ *n Aus* a musical instrument used in Aboriginal music and ritual, consisting of a long thin piece of wood that is twirled round on a length of string to create a roaring sound

bullrush /bo͝ol rush/ *n ANZ* PLANTS same as **bulrush**

bull session *n N Am* an informal discussion (*informal*)

bull's eye *n* **1. MIDDLE OF TARGET** the centre of a target, which usually carries the highest score ○ *She hit the bull's eye perfectly.* **2. TOP-SCORING SHOT** a shot that hits the centre of a target **3. HARD SWEET** a hard round peppermint boiled sweet, usually striped **4. ROUND WINDOW** a small round window, especially a disc of thick glass in a ship's deck for letting in light below deck **5. THICK LENS** a small thick lens for intensifying light **6. LAMP** a lamp fitted with a bull's-eye lens **7. PRECISE ACHIEVEMENT** a precise or highly effective achievement (*informal*) ■ *interj* **RECOGNIZING PRECISE ACHIEVEMENT** used to acknowledge and commend a precise or highly effective achievement (*informal*)

bullshit /bo͝ol shit/ (*slang*) *n* an offensive term for talk or writing dismissed as foolish or inaccurate ■ *vti* (**-shits, -shitting, -shitted**) **1.** an offensive term meaning to say things that are completely untrue or very foolish **2.** an offensive term meaning to try to intimidate, deceive, or persuade somebody with deceitful or foolish talk —**bullshitter** *n*

bull-skulled *adj regional* an offensive term that deliberately insults somebody's intelligence (*insult*)

REGIONAL NOTE See ***addle-headed***.

bull snake *n* a large burrowing nonpoisonous snake with yellow and brown markings that feeds mainly on rodents. Native to: North America. Genus: *Pituophis*.

bull terrier *n* a muscular dog with smooth hair, belonging to a breed developed in England by crossing the bulldog with a breed of terrier

bullwhip /bo͝ol wip/ *n* a long heavy whip made of plaited strips of hide, knotted at the end ■ *vt* (**-whips, -whipping, -whipped**) to beat somebody with a bullwhip

bully[1] /bo͝olli/ *n* (*plural* **-lies**) an aggressive person who intimidates or mistreats weaker people ■ *vt* (**-lies, -lying, -lied**) to intimidate or mistreat a weaker person [Mid-16C. Probably < Middle Dutch *boele* 'lover'] —**bullying** *n* ◇ **bully for you!** used to express approval (*dated; used ironically*)

bully[2] /bo͝olli/ *n* FOOD same as **bully beef** (*dated*) [Mid-18C. Anglicization of *bouilli* 'boiled beef' < French, past participle of *bouillir* 'boil' < Latin *bullire*]

bully[3] /bo͝olli/ (*plural* **-lies**) *n* a small river fish. Native to: New Zealand. Genera: *Gobiomorphus* or *Phylinodon*. [Mid-19C. Probably shortened < BULLHEAD]

bully beef *n* tinned corned or pickled beef (*dated*)

bullyboy /bo͝olli boy/ *n* an aggressive bully or thug

bully-off *n* formerly, a way of starting a hockey match, in which two opposing players hit sticks over the ball before each tries to hit it first. ◊ **pushback** [Late 19C. Origin ?]

bully pulpit *n N Am* a position of prominent authority that gives the holder a wide audience, e.g. a political office

bullyrag /bo͝olli rag/ (**-rags, -ragging, -ragged**), **ballyrag** /bálli-/ *vt N Am* to persecute somebody with insults or cruel practical jokes (*informal*) [Late 18C. Origin ?]

bully tree *n Aus, US* a tropical American tree that yields a sap from which a hard rubber substance (**balata**) is made. Latin name: *Manilkara bidentata*. UK, NZ, Can term **balata**

bulrush /bo͝ol rush/ *n* **1.** *UK, ANZ, Can* **TALL MARSH PLANT** a tall marsh plant. Genus: *Typha*. US term **cat's tail** **2. WATERSIDE PLANT** a plant with leaves like grass that grows in wet conditions. Genus: *Scirpus*. **3.** BIBLE **PAPYRUS** in the Bible, a papyrus plant [15C. Probably blend of BULL[1] + RUSH[2]]

bulwark /bo͝olwərk/ *n* **1. DEFENSIVE WALL** a structure such as a wall or fortification built to keep out attackers **2. HARBOUR WALL** a wall built out into the sea to shelter a harbour **3. PROTECTION** somebody or something that gives protection or support ○ *The alliance is regarded as a bulwark of economic stability in the region.* ■ **bulwarks** *npl* **SHIP'S SIDES** the sides of a ship projecting above the deck ■ *vt* (**-warks, -warking, -warked**) **1. PROTECT PLACE WITH WALLS** to fortify or protect a place by building walls round it **2. SAFEGUARD SOMEBODY OR SOMETHING** to defend or support somebody or something strongly [15C. < Middle Dutch, Middle Low German *bolwerk* 'rampart made of tree trunks' < *bole* 'tree trunk' + *werk* 'work']

bum[1] /bum/ *n* the buttocks (*informal*) [14C. Origin ?]

bum out *vt N Am* to annoy or depress somebody (*slang*)

bum[2] /bum/ (*informal*) *n* **1. GOOD-FOR-NOTHING** somebody regarded as irresponsible or worthless **2. DEVOTEE** somebody who is excessively devoted to a particular activity or place ○ *a ski bum* **3.** *N Am* **VAGRANT** a homeless person living on the street (*sometimes considered offensive*) ■ *vt* (**bums, bumming, bummed**) **CADGE** to get something by asking or begging ■ *adj* **USELESS** useless, worthless, or of poor quality ○ *gave me some pretty bum advice* [Mid-19C. Shortening of BUMMER] ◇ **bums on seats** people occupying seats at the theatre, cinema, concerts, or other places of entertainment (*informal*) ◇ **give somebody the bum's rush** *N Am* to order or force somebody abruptly to leave a place (*informal*)

bum bag *n* a pouch for valuables, worn on a belt. N Am term **fanny pack**

bumble[1] /búmb'l/ (**-bles, -bling, -bled**) *v* **1.** *vti* to speak in a hesitant or muddled way **2.** *vt* to move or proceed clumsily [Mid-16C. Origin ?] —**bumbler** *n*

bumble[2] /búmb'l/ (**-bles, -bling, -bled**) *vi* to make a humming sound [14C. An imitation of the sound]

bumblebee /búmb'l bee/ *n* a large hairy bee that nests in burrows and makes a loud droning noise in flight. Native to: North America, Europe, Asia. Genus: *Bombus*.

bumble-puppy *n* **1.** a game that involves hitting a ball attached to a string on a post, so that the string winds round the post. N Am term **tetherball** **2.** bridge or whist played badly (*informal*) [Early 19C. Origin ?]

bumbling /búmbling/ *adj* speaking or behaving in a clumsy or confused way (*informal*)

bumboat /búm bōt/ *n* a small boat that is used for selling goods to ships at anchor [Late 17C. < BUM[2]]

bumbo-claat /búmbō klaat/ (*used in Black English*) *interj* a highly offensive term used as a swearword (*taboo*) ■ *vt* (**bumbo-claats, bumbo-claating, bumbo-claated**) to cheat somebody or behave in a dishonest or dishonourable way towards somebody (*slang*) [< *bumbo* 'vagina, buttocks' + *claat*, form of CLOTH 'sanitary towel']

bumbum /búm bum/ *n Carib* the buttocks

bumf /bumf/, **bumph** *n* unwanted or uninteresting printed material, especially official forms and documents (*informal*) [Late 19C. Shortening of *bum fodder* 'toilet paper']

bumfreezer /búm freezər/ *n* a short jacket for men, especially one that finishes above the waist (*informal*)

bummalo /búmməlō/ (*plural same*) *n* **1.** a small blunt-nosed fish found in brackish water. Native to: South Asia. Latin name: *Harpadon nehereus*. **2.** the flesh of a bummalo used as food [Late 17C. Probably alteration of Marathi *bombīl*]

bummed /bumd/, **bummed out** *adj N Am* unhappy as a result of an unpleasant experience (*slang*)

bummer /búmmər/ *n* (*slang*) **1.** something annoying or unpleasant **2.** a bad reaction to a hallucinogenic drug [Mid-19C. Probably < German *Bummler* 'idler, layabout' < *bummeln* 'stroll or loaf around']

bump /bump/ *v* (**bumps, bumping, bumped**) **1.** *vti* **KNOCK SOMETHING** to hit or knock something, especially accidentally **2.** *vti* **MOVE UNSTEADILY** to jolt or bounce along, or move something in a jolting or bouncing way ○ *We bumped along the dirt track.* **3.** *vt* **TURN AWAY PASSENGER** to turn away an airline passenger with a reserved seat because the flight has been overbooked (*informal*) **4.** *vt* FOOTBALL **NUDGE SOMEBODY OFF BALL** in Australian Rules football, to nudge an opponent off the ball with the hip or shoulder ■ *n* **1. ACCIDENTAL KNOCK** a light blow or impact, especially an accidental one ○ *that bump dented the bodywork* **2. SWELLING ON BODY** a swelling on the body caused by an impact ○ *a bump on the elbow* **3. LUMP ON SURFACE** a raised area on a flat surface ○ *a bump in the road* **4. SOUND OF IMPACT** the dull sound of one thing hitting another **5. RAISED AREA ON SKULL** a raised area at different points on the skull, formerly thought to indicate intelligence or personality type [Mid-16C. An imitation of the sound of a bump] ◇ **bump and grind** to dance erotically, thrusting and rotating the pelvis (*slang*)

bump into *vt* **1.** to knock against or hit somebody or something accidentally **2.** to meet somebody by chance

bump off *vt* to murder somebody (*slang*)

bump up *vt* to increase prices suddenly and sharply (*informal*)

bump up against *vt* **1.** to come into contact with something, usually making a sound **2.** to come into conflict with somebody

bumper /búmpər/ *n* **1. PROTECTING BAR ON VEHICLE** a projecting rim or bar on the front or back of a vehicle, designed to protect it from damage **2.** *US* BROADCAST **DEVICE SEPARATING SECTIONS OF PROGRAMME** a device such as a piece of music that separates the content of a radio or television programme from a commercial break (*slang*) **3.** *ANZ* **CIGARETTE END** a cigarette butt (*informal*) ■ *adj* **LARGE** unusually large or successful ○ *a bumper crop* ○ *a bumper year for apples*

bumper car *n* a small electric car designed to be bumped against other similar cars in a raised enclosure as part of a fairground entertainment

bumper sticker *n* a small adhesive sign, typically mounted on a car bumper or window

bumper-to-bumper *adj, adv* forming a line of close slow-moving vehicles ○ *bumper-to-bumper traffic* ○ *drive bumper-to-bumper*

bumph *n* another spelling of **bumf**

bumpkin[1] /búmpkin/ *n* a country person regarded as unsophisticated (*informal*) [Late 16C. Origin ?]

bumpkin[2] /búmpkin/, **bumkin** /búmkin/ *n* a pole at the back of a boat to which a sail is attached by a rope [Mid-17C. < Dutch *boomken* < *boom* 'tree']

bump-start AUTOMOT *vt, n* same as **push-start**

bumptious /búmpshəss/ *adj* stating opinions aggressively or self-importantly [Early 19C. Blend of BUMP + FRACTIOUS] —**bumptiously** *adv* —**bumptiousness** *n*

bumpy /búmpi/ (**-ier, -iest**) *adj* **1.** having a rough or uneven surface ○ *a bumpy road* **2.** uncomfortably bouncy or rough ○ *a bumpy ride* —**bumpily** *adv* —**bumpiness** *n*

bum rap *n N Am* a false or fraudulent accusation or appraisal (*slang*)

bum steer *n Aus, N Am* a piece of misleading information or bad advice (*slang*)

bun /bun/ *n* **1.** ROUND BREAD ROLL a small round bread roll, sometimes sweetened and with added fruit or spice **2.** SMALL CAKE a small round sweet cake **3.** HAIR COILED AT BACK OF HEAD hair gathered in a tight round coil on the back or top of the head ■ **buns** *npl N Am* BUTTOCKS a person's buttocks (*slang*) [14C. Origin ?] ◇ **have a bun in the oven** to be pregnant (*informal; sometimes considered offensive*)

Bunbury /búnbəri/ coastal town in southwestern Western Australia, a major seaport and administrative centre. Population: 30,6731 (2002 estimate).

bunch /bunch/ *n* **1.** COLLECTION OF THINGS a number of people or things grouped or joined together ○ *people in bunches waiting for the doors to open* ○ *a bunch of parsley* **2.** CLUSTER OF FRUITS a cluster of fruits growing on a stem **3.** GROUP OF PEOPLE a group of people, usually with a common characteristic or interest (*informal*) ○ *a fiercely competitive bunch* **4.** A LOT OF PEOPLE OR THINGS a large number of people or things (*informal*) ○ *Expect a whole bunch of new features in the next version.* ■ **bunches** *npl* HAIR TIED IN TWO CLUMPS hair gathered and tied in two clumps, one at each side of the head ■ *vti* (**bunches, bunching, bunched**) GATHER to gather things or people into a cluster or close group, or gather in this way [14C. Origin ?] —**bunchy** *adj*

Buncho Tani /búnchō taáni/ (1763–1840) Japanese artist. A noted book illustrator, he was responsible for introducing the Western style to Japanese painting.

bunco /búngkō/ (*plural* **-coes**), **bunko** (*plural* **-koes**) *n N Am* a trick or scheme that deceives people into parting with money (*slang*) [Late 19C. Origin ?] —**bunco** *vt*

bund[1] /bund/ *n S Asia* an embankment or dyke that surrounds rice fields or a reservoir and acts as a breakwater to prevent flooding [Early 19C. Via Urdu *band* < Persian]

bund[2] /bŏond/, **Bund** *n* a political organization, especially a socialist Jewish labour movement in tsarist Russia or a German–American group of Nazi sympathizers in the United States in the 1930s and 1940s [Late 19C. < German, 'association']

Bundaberg /búndə burg/ city and port on the Pacific coast of southern Queensland, Australia, an important centre for sugar and timber production. Population: 45,043 (2002 estimate).

bundh *n S Asia* POL another spelling of **bandh**

bundle /búnd'l/ *n* **1.** COLLECTION OF THINGS HELD TOGETHER a number of things tied, wrapped, or held together **2.** A LOT OF MONEY a large sum of money (*slang*) **3.** BIOL BAND OF PARALLEL TISSUES a band of tissue such as muscle or nerve fibres or vascular tissue in plants **4.** COMPUT SET OF COMPUTER EQUIPMENT a package of computer hardware and software supplied at an inclusive price ■ *vt* (**-dles, -dling, -dled**) **1.** TIE THINGS TOGETHER to tie or wrap a number of things together **2.** SHOVE SOMEBODY OR SOMETHING to push somebody or something roughly and hurriedly (*informal*) ○ *bundled the suspect into the police car* **3.** COMPUT SUPPLY COMPUTER EQUIPMENT to package computer hardware and software together at an inclusive price [14C. < Dutch *bundel*] —**bundler** *n* ◇ **drop a bundle** (*slang*) **1.** *N Am* to spend a large amount of money **2.** *ANZ* to give birth ◇ **drop your bundle** *ANZ* to lose your nerve and run away (*informal*) ◇ **go a bundle on something** to be very fond of or enthusiastic about something (*informal*)

bundle off *vt* to send somebody away hurriedly (*informal*) ○ *We bundled the children off to school.*

bundle up *v* **1.** *vt* to gather things into a bundle **2.** *vti* to dress in warm clothes, or dress somebody in warm clothes (*informal*) ○ *Bundle up, it's cold outside.*

bundle sheath cell *n* in some vascular plants, a specialized photosynthetic cell where the initial products of photosynthesis undergo the removal of carbon dioxide

bundobust *n S Asia* another spelling of **bandobust**

bundu /bŏon doo/ *n S Africa* a remote sparsely inhabited area (*slang*) [Mid-20C. Probably < Shona *bundo* 'grasslands']

bundwall /búnd wawl/ *n* a casing of concrete or earth around an oil storage tank [< BUND[1]]

bundy /búndi/ *Aus n* (*plural* **-dies**) a time clock used to record when an employee starts and finishes work or to regulate scheduled services ■ *vi* (**-dies, -dying, -died**) to clock on or off for work [Mid-20C. < trade name of a time clock]

bun fight *n* **1.** a party or large gathering, especially an official dinner (*informal humorous*) **2.** a heated argument (*slang*)

bung /bung/ *n* **1.** STOPPER a stopper or plug, especially one made of cork or rubber **2.** PAYOFF an illicit fee paid to a football player, manager, or agent to facilitate a player transfer (*slang*) ■ *vt* (**bungs, bunging, bunged**) **1.** PLUG HOLE to plug or seal a hole with a bung **2.** PLACE CARELESSLY to put something somewhere roughly or hurriedly (*informal*) ○ *Bung it in the bin when you're finished.* [15C. < Middle Dutch *bonghe*, probably < late Latin *puncta* 'puncture' < Latin *pungere* 'to prick'] ◇ **go bung** *ANZ* to go wrong or cease functioning (*slang*)

bung up *vt* to block or obstruct a hole or passage (*informal*)

bungalow /búng gəlō/ *n* **1.** ONE-STOREY HOUSE a single-storey house **2.** LIGHTWEIGHT TROPICAL HOUSE in Southeast Asia and the South Pacific, a simply built one-storey house with a veranda and a wide, gently sloping roof **3.** *Malaysia, Singapore* DETACHED HOUSE a detached house, usually of two or more storeys [Late 17C. < Hindi *banglā* 'of Bengal']

bungee /búnji/ *n* a cord or rope made from elastic material [Early 20C. Origin ?]

bungee jump *n* a dive from a high place using an elastic cord tied to the ankles as a restraint —**bungee jumping** *n*

bungee running *n* an activity originating in Australia that involves a line of people running from a wall while attached to elastic cords to see how far the line gets before bouncing back (*informal*)

bunger /búngər/ *n Aus* a firework that explodes with a loud noise (*informal*) [Early 20C. Variant of BANGER]

bunghole /búng hōl/ *n* **1.** a hole in a barrel or vat, used for drawing off the contents and closed with a bung **2.** an offensive term for the anus (*slang*)

bungle /búng g'l/ (*informal*) *vt* (**-gles, -gling, -gled**) to cause something to fail through carelessness or incompetence ○ *bungled the job* ■ *n* a careless or clumsy action or mistake [Mid-16C. Probably to suggest the action] —**bungler** *n* —**bungling** *adj* —**bunglingly** *adv*

bunion /búnnyən/ *n* an inflammation of the sac (**bursa**) around the first joint of the big toe, accompanied by swelling and sideways displacement of the joint [Early 18C. Directly or via English dialect *bunny* 'lump, swelling' < Old French *buigne* 'bump on the head']

bunk[1] /bungk/ *n* **1.** SIMPLE BED a simple narrow bed built on a shelf or in a recess **2.** FURNITURE same as **bunk bed** **3.** SLEEPING PLACE any bed or place to sleep (*informal*) ■ *vi* (**bunks, bunking, bunked**) SLEEP SOMEWHERE to sleep in a place away from home (*informal*) ○ *'You may as well bunk at the YMCA and get in on their recreation programs.'* (Garrison Keillor, *We Are Still Married*; 1989) [Mid-18C. Origin ?]

bunk[2] /bungk/ *n* talk or writing dismissed as nonsensical or inaccurate (*slang*) [Early 20C. Shortened < BUNKUM]

bunk[3] /bungk/ (**bunks, bunking, bunked**) *vi* to disappear or depart hurriedly [Late 19C. Origin ?] ◇ **do a bunk** to leave unexpectedly and hurriedly (*informal*)

bunk off *vt* to sneak away or be absent from somewhere without permission, especially from school (*informal*)

bunk bed *n* either of a pair of single beds fitted one on top of the other

bunker /búngkər/ *n* **1.** UNDERGROUND SHELTER an underground shelter, especially one built for troops, with a fortified gun position above ground **2.** GOLF SAND HAZARD a sand-filled hollow on a golf course, built as a hazard **3.** LARGE OUTDOOR CONTAINER a large outdoor bin or chest **4.** SHIPPING FUEL-STORAGE CONTAINER a fuel-storage container on a ship ■ *vt* (**-kers, -kering, -kered**) **1.** GOLF SEND BALL INTO BUNKER to hit a golf ball into a bunker **2.** PUT SOMETHING IN OUTDOOR BIN to put or store something in a large outdoor bin or chest [Mid-16C. Origin ?]

bunker buster *n* a powerful laser-guided bomb designed to penetrate a reinforced target and explode

Bunker Hill /búngkər-/ hill in Boston, Massachusetts, near the site of the first battle of the War of American Independence in 1775. Height: 34 m/110 ft.

bunkhouse /búngk howss/ (*plural* **-houses** /-howziz/) *n N Am* a building providing simple sleeping facilities

bunkum /búngkəm/ *n* talk or writing dismissed as nonsensical or inaccurate (*informal*) [Mid-19C. Alteration of *Buncombe* County, N Carolina, United States, whose congressman defended a dull and irrelevant speech by saying he made it to impress the people of Buncombe]

bunny /búnni/ (*plural* **-nies**) *n* (*informal*) **1.** a child's word for a rabbit **2.** *Aus* a gullible person or scapegoat [Early 17C. < dialect *bun* 'rabbit's tail, rabbit' < Gaelic *bun* 'stump, bottom']

bunny hug *n* a lively ballroom dance popular in the United States in the early 20th century

bunny slopes *npl N Am* SKIING same as **nursery slopes** [Origin ?]

bunodont /byŏonə dont/ *adj* having molar teeth with separate rounded ridges (**cusps**), typical of omnivores [Late 19C. < Greek *bounos* 'mound']

Bunraku /bŏon raá koo/ *n* traditional Japanese puppetry using large wooden puppets, each worked by several puppeteers who are visible to the audience and with a separate narrator offstage [Early 20C. < Japanese, after the *Bunraku-za* theatre]

Bunsen /búnss'n/, **Robert Wilhelm** (1811–99) German chemist and physicist. One of the discoverers of spectrum analysis (1859), he also invented a galvanic battery. He popularized the laboratory gas burner that bears his name.

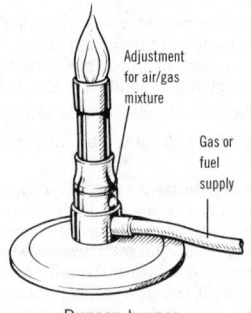

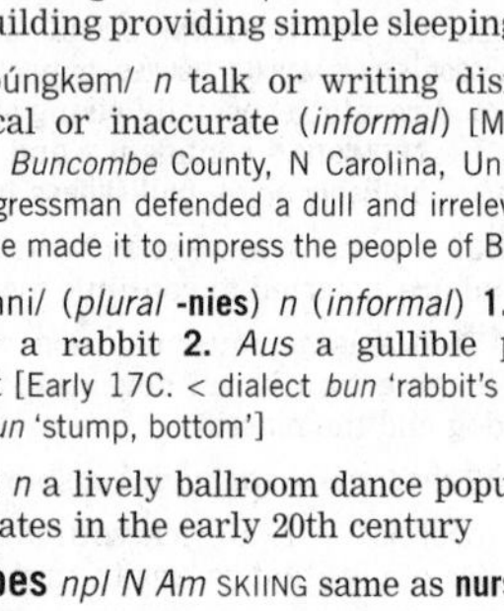
Adjustment
for air/gas
mixture
Gas or
fuel
supply

Bunsen burner

Bunsen burner *n* a portable tube-shaped gas burner with an adjustable hole to control air intake and flame type, used in laboratories [Late 19C. After R. W. BUNSEN]

bunt[1] /bunt/ (**bunts, bunting, bunted**) *vt* **1.** same as **butt**[1] *v* (sense 1) **2.** in baseball, to hit a pitched ball very gently, holding the bat horizontally with both hands [Mid-18C. An imitation of the sound of something being hit] —**bunt** *n* —**bunter** *n*

bunt[2] /bunt/ *n* the baggy middle part of a sail [Late 16C. Origin ?]

buntal /búnt'l/ *n* straw from the large leaves of the talipot palm tree [Early 20C. < Tagalog]

bunting[1] /búnting/ *n* a small seed-eating songbird related to the finch, with a short heavy beak and usually brown or grey feathers. Family: Emberizidae. [13C. Origin ?]

bunting² /búnting/ n strings of cloth or paper decorations for hanging outdoors [Early 18C. Origin ?]

buntline /búnt līn/ n a rope attached to the bottom of a square sail, used to roll up the sail [Early 17C. < BUNT²]

Popperfoto
Luis Buñuel

Buñuel /boon wél/, **Luis** (1900–83) Spanish film director. One of the greatest masters of filmmaking, he incorporated uncompromising social criticisms in works such as *The Discreet Charm of the Bourgeoisie* (1972).

bunya /búnnyə/, **bunya-bunya**, **bunya pine** n a tall tree with cones containing edible seeds. Native to: Australia. Latin name: *Araucaria bidwillii*. [Mid-19C. < Yagara *bunya-bunya*]

Bunyan /búnnyən/, **John** (1628–88) English preacher and writer. A Puritan, he was jailed for 12 years for his religious beliefs. He wrote the autobiographical *Grace Abounding to the Chief of Sinners* (1666) and the great spiritual allegory *The Pilgrim's Progress* (published in two parts 1678, 1684). See Cultural note at **pilgrim**.

'Who would true valour see, / Let him come hither; / One here will constant be, / Come wind, come weather / There's no discouragement / Shall make him once relent / His first avow'd intent / To be a pilgrim.'
[John Bunyan, *The Pilgrim's Progress*; 1684]

bunyip /búnnyip/ n Aus in Aboriginal legend, a monster said to inhabit swamps and water holes of the Australian interior [Mid-19C. < Wemba-Wemba *banib*]

Buonarroti /bwónnə rótti/, **Michelangelo ♦ Michelangelo**

Buoninsegna ♦ Duccio di Buoninsegna

buoy¹ /boy/ n **1.** a large anchored float, often equipped with lights or bells, that serves as a guide or warning to ships **2.** EMERGENCIES same as **life buoy** ■ vt (**buoys, buoying, buoyed**) to use a buoy to mark the location in water of something such as a hazard or a channel [13C. Origin ?]

SPELLCHECK See *boy*.

buoy² /boy/ (**buoys, buoying, buoyed**) vt to keep something from falling or sinking ○ *steps to buoy the country's currency* [Late 16C. < Spanish *boyar* 'to float' < *boya* 'buoy']

buoy up vt **1.** to give support or encouragement to somebody ○ *Buoyed up by a few wise investments, the company went on to prosper the following year.* **2.** to keep somebody cheerful or optimistic in spite of difficulties ○ *The arrival of the children has buoyed us all up.*

buoyancy /bóyənssi/, **buoyance** /-ənss/ n **1.** TENDENCY TO FLOAT the tendency of an object to float **2.** FORCE CAUSING FLOATING the tendency of a liquid or gas to cause less dense objects to float or rise to the surface **3.** POWER TO RECOVER EMOTIONALLY the ability to recover quickly from a disappointment or failure **4.** CHEERFULNESS cheerfulness or optimism

buoyancy tank n a chamber containing air designed to keep a boat afloat if it is swamped or a hovercraft afloat when it is at rest

buoyant /bóy ənt/ adj **1.** ABLE TO FLOAT tending to float or rise to the surface of a liquid or upwards in a gas **2.** PUSHING UPWARDS causing immersed objects to float or rise to the surface of a liquid or upwards in a gas **3.** QUICK TO RECOVER EMOTIONALLY tending to recover quickly from a disappointment or failure **4.** CHEERFUL

cheerful or optimistic [Late 16C. Directly or via French < Spanish *boyante*, present participle of *boyar* (see BUOY²)] —**buoyantly** adv

bupivacaine /byoo pívvə kayn/ n a powerful local anaesthetic. Use: epidural anaesthesia. [Late 20C. < BUTYL + *piperidyl*, chemical compound (< PIPERIDINE) + -*va*- + -*caine*, INN stem]

buprestid /byoo préstid/ n a metallic-coloured beetle that bores into wood during the larval stage. Native to: tropics. Family: Buprestidae. [Mid-19C. < modern Latin *Buprestidae* (plural) < Greek *bouprēstis* 'ox-sweller' < *bous* 'ox']

bur, burr n ENG, BOT another spelling of **burr¹**

Bur. abbr **1.** Burma **2.** Burmese

Burakumin /boō rákoō min/ npl members of the lowest Japanese sector of society [Mid-20C. < Japanese, 'hamlet people']

buran /boo raán/ n a strong wind in central Asia, bringing dust storms in summer and blizzards in winter [Mid-19C. Via Russian < Turkic *boran*]

Buraydah /boō rídə/ city in central Saudi Arabia, north of Unayzah. Population: 248,600 (1992).

burb /burb/, **'burb** n N Am GEOG same as **suburb** (*slang*) [Shortening]

burber /búrbər/ n US soc sci same as **suburbanite** (*slang*)

burble /búrb'l/ v (**-bles, -bling, -bled**) **1.** vi MAKE BUBBLING SOUND to make a gentle bubbling sound, like the sound of running water **2.** vti SPEAK EXCITEDLY to speak or say something in a fast excited way (*informal*) **3.** vi AVIAT HAVE EDDYING MOTION to become turbulent (*refers to the airflow around an aircraft's wing*) ■ n **1.** GENTLE SOUND a gentle bubbling or gurgling sound **2.** STREAM OF TALK a flow of fast excited talking (*informal*) **3.** AVIAT BREAK IN AIRFLOW a break in the flow of air around an aircraft's wing, which causes turbulence [14C. An imitation of the sound] —**burbler** n —**burbly** adv

burbot /búrbət/ (*plural same* or **-bots**) n **1.** a freshwater fish of the cod family. Native to: North America, northern Europe, Asia. Latin name: *Lota lota*. **2.** the flesh of a burbot used as food [14C. < Old French *borbette*]

Burckhardt /búrk haart/, **Jakob** (1818–97) Swiss art historian. Professor of history at Basel University, Switzerland (1843–93), he wrote works on the Italian Renaissance and Greek civilization including the classic *The Civilisation of the Renaissance in Italy* (1860). Full name **Burckhardt, Jakob Christoph**

Burdekin /búrdəkən/ river in Queensland, Australia, that rises in the Seaview Range west of Ingham and empties into the Pacific Ocean near Ayr. Length: 720 km/447 mi.

burden¹ /búrd'n/ n **1.** WORRYING RESPONSIBILITY a difficult or worrying responsibility or duty ○ *the burdens of parenthood* **2.** SOMETHING CARRIED a load being carried ○ *carrying a heavy burden on his back* **3.** SHIPPING SHIP'S CAPACITY the maximum weight of cargo that a ship can carry ■ vt (**-dens, -dening, -dened**) **1.** GIVE RESPONSIBILITY TO SOMEBODY to give somebody a task that is difficult to deal with or something worrying to think about **2.** GIVE SOMEBODY LOAD TO CARRY to cause somebody or something to carry a burden [Old English *byrthen* < Indo-European, 'to bear']

burden² /búrd'n/ n **1.** a chorus in a song **2.** the main or recurring theme in a book, piece of music, speech, or argument (*literary*) [14C. < French *bourdon* 'bass, drone', influenced by BURDEN¹]

SYNONYMS See *subject*.

burden of proof n the responsibility of proving a case or argument, especially in a court of law

burdensome /búrd'nsəm/ adj difficult or worrying to bear or deal with

burdock /búr dok/ n a tall biennial plant with a long taproot. Flowers: small, prickly, purple. Native to: temperate areas. Genus: *Arctium*. [Late 16C. < BURR¹ + DOCK¹]

bureau /byoór rō/ (*plural* **-reaus** or **-reaux** /-rōz/) n **1.** GOVERNMENT DEPARTMENT a government department, or a branch of a government department **2.** ORGANIZATION an organization, or a branch of an organization **3.** WRITING DESK a narrow desk with a writing surface and drawers **4.** N Am CHEST OF DRAWERS a chest of drawers, especially a low one [Late 17C. < French, literally 'baize' (used for desks)]

bureaucracy /byoor rókrəssi/ (*plural* **-cies**) n **1.** FRUSTRATING RULES complex rules and regulations applied rigidly **2.** ADMINISTRATIVE SYSTEM an administrative system, especially in a government, that divides work into specific categories carried out by special departments of nonelected officials **3.** OFFICIALS COLLECTIVELY the nonelected officials of an organization or department **4.** STATE OR ORGANIZATION a state or organization operated by a hierarchy of paid officials [Early 19C. < French *bureaucratie* < *bureau* 'office' + -*cratie* 'rule']

bureaucrat /byoórə krat/ n **1.** an administrative or government official **2.** an official who applies rules rigidly —**bureaucratism** /byoō rókrətizəm/ n

bureaucratic /byoór rə kráttik/ adj **1.** relating to the way administrative systems are organized ○ *the bureaucratic structure* **2.** applying rules rigidly within an administrative system or government —**bureaucratically** adv

bureaucratize /byoō rókrə tīz/ (**-tizes, -tizing, -tized**), **bureaucratise** (**-tises, -tising, -tised**) vt **1.** to change a system into a bureaucracy **2.** to make a system or procedure rigid or complex —**bureaucratization** /byoō rókrə tī záysh'n/ n

bureau de change /byoór rō də shóNzh/ (*plural* **bureaus de change** /byoór rō-/ or **bureaux de change** /byoór rō-/) n an office or part of a bank where foreign currency is exchanged [< French, 'office of exchange']

Buren /byoórən/ ♦ **Van Buren, Martin**

Buren /bü ráN/, **Daniel** (b. 1938) French artist. He is known for his unconventional conceptual and installation works, often characterized by the use of striped material.

'In art, banality soon becomes extraordinary.'
[Daniel Buren. Quoted in 'Beware!', *Conceptual Art*, Ursula Meyer; 1972]

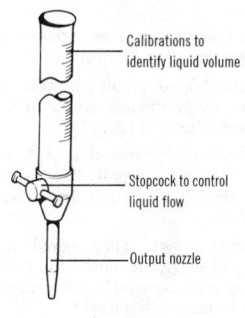
Calibrations to identify liquid volume
Stopcock to control liquid flow
Output nozzle
burette

burette /byoō rét/ n a glass tube with measurements marked on the side and a stopcock at the bottom. Use: in laboratories to release an accurately measured quantity of liquid. [Mid-19C. < French *buire* 'jug']

burfi /búrfi/, **barfi** /búrfi, baárfi/ n in South Asian cooking, a sweet made from milk and sugar, often with nuts or cardamom, and shaped into a square or diamond [Via Hindi < Persian *barfī* 'icy, snowy']

burg¹ /burg/ n an ancient fortress or walled town [Mid-18C. < late Latin *burgus* 'town']

burg² /burg/ n N Am a city or town (*informal*) [Mid-19C. < German *Burg* < Germanic]

Burgas /boor gáss/ Black Sea port and capital of Burgas Province, eastern Bulgaria. Population: 199,470 (1996).

burgee /búr jee/ n an identification flag flown from the top of a mast, e.g. a sailing club pennant [Mid-18C. Origin ?]

burgeon /búrjən/ (**-geons, -geoning, -geoned**) vi (*literary*) **1.** to produce new buds and leaves, or swell and develop into leaves and flowers **2.** to flourish or develop rapidly [14C. < French *bourgeonner* < *bourgeon* 'a shoot or bud' < late Latin *burra* 'wool']

burgeoning /búrjəning/ adj growing or expanding rapidly ○ *burgeoning wealth*

burger /búrgər/ n **1.** FOOD same as **hamburger** (sense 2) **2.** a round flat cake made of chicken, fish, vegetables, or nuts, usually cooked and served in a bun [Mid-20C. Shortened < HAMBURGER]

-burger *suffix* resembling minced beef or a hamburger ○ *veggieburger*

Burgess /búrjiss/, **Anthony** (1917–93) British writer and critic. His books include *A Clockwork Orange* (1962) and *A Dead Man in Deptford* (1993). Born **Wilson, John Anthony Burgess**

'Without class differences, England would cease to be the living theatre it is.'
[Anthony Burgess, *Observer*; 26 May 1985]

Burgess, Guy (1911–63) British Soviet spy. Recruited as a Soviet agent while a student at Cambridge in the 1930s, he worked for MI5 and the Foreign Office. After being charged with serious misconduct, he escaped to the Soviet Union in 1951 with Donald Maclean. Full name **Burgess, Guy Francis de Moncy**

burgh /búrrə/ *n* **1.** in Scotland, a town, especially one incorporated by royal charter **2.** same as **borough** (sense 2) (*archaic*) [Variant of BOROUGH]

Burgh /burg/, **Hubert de, Earl of Kent** (1197–1243?) English politician. He was chief justice of the land and was regent for Henry III from 1219 to 1227.

burgher /búrgər/ *n* **1.** a merchant in a medieval European town **2.** a citizen, especially a prosperous or conservative member of the middle class (*humorous*) [Late 16C. Partly < BURGH, partly < German or Dutch *burger* < *burg* (see BURG¹)]

Burghley /búrli/, **Sir William Cecil, 1st Baron** (1520–98) English politician. He was chief secretary of state to Elizabeth I after 1558, and formulated many of the domestic and foreign policies that made the Elizabethan Age a period of power and prosperity in England.

burglar /búrglər/ *n* somebody who enters a building intending illegally, usually in order to steal something [Mid-16C. < obsolete legal French *burgier*]

burglar alarm *n* an electronic device designed to make a loud noise when somebody enters a building illegally

burglarize /búrglə rīz/ (**-izes, -izing, -ized**) *vt N Am* same as **burgle** (*often passive*)

burglarproof /búrglər proof/ *adj* secured with locks, alarms, or other devices so as to discourage or prevent unauthorized entry

burglary /búrgləri/ (*plural* **-ries**) *n* **1.** the crime of entering a building illegally **2.** an act of entering a building illegally to commit theft —**burglarious** /bur gláiri əss/ *adj*

burgle /búrg'l/ (**-gles, -gling, -gled**) *vt* to enter a building illegally, usually in order to steal something (*often passive*) N Am term **burglarize** [Late 19C. Back-formation < BURGLAR]

~~burgler~~ incorrect spelling of **burglar**

burgomaster /búrgə maastər/ *n* the mayor or chief magistrate in some northern European towns [Late 16C. < Dutch *burgomeester* 'town master']

Burgos /búr goss/ capital of Burgos Province in Castile-Léon, northern Spain. Population: 167,962 (2002).

Burgoyne /bur góyn/, **John** (1722–92) British army general. His attempt to lead a British invasion into New York from Canada was thwarted at Saratoga (1777). He also wrote plays, including *The Heiress* (1786).

'After a fatal procrastination...we took a step as decisive as the passage of the Rubicon, and now find ourselves plunged at once in a most serious war without a single requisition, gunpowder excepted, for carrying it on.'
[John Burgoyne, *Letter from Boston*; April 1775]

Burgundian /bər gúndi ən/ *n* **1.** PEOPLES SOMEBODY FROM BURGUNDY, FRANCE somebody who comes from the Burgundy region of east-central France **2.** HIST MEMBER OF GERMANIC PEOPLE a member of a Germanic people who established a kingdom in Burgundy in the 5th century AD **3.** MUSIC EARLY RENAISSANCE COMPOSER a member of a 15th-century group of European composers noted for their chansons and masses, especially one of those employed by the dukes of Burgundy [Early 17C. < BURGUNDY]

burgundy /búrgəndi/ *n* **1.** burgundy (*plural* **-dies**), Burgundy red or white wine produced in the Burgundy

region of east central France **2.** a deep red colour, like that of red burgundy wine —**burgundy** *adj*

Burgundy /búrgəndi/ region, formerly a kingdom and duchy, located in east-central France. It is an important wine-producing area. French name **Bourgogne**

burial /bérri əl/ *n* the act or ceremony of putting a dead body into the ground or into the sea (*often used before a noun*) ○ *a burial place* [Old English *byrgels* < *byrgan* (see BURY)]

burial chamber *n* a small room or enclosed space where somebody has been buried

burial ground *n* an area of land where dead bodies are buried, especially an ancient site

Buriat *n* PEOPLES, LANG another spelling of **Buryat**

Buridan's ass /byoŏr rid'nz-/ *n* a situation used to demonstrate the impracticality of making choices according to a formal system of reasoning [After Jean Buridan (1300–58), French philosopher]

burin /byoŏr rin/ *n* **1.** an engraver's chisel for making grooves **2.** a prehistoric flint tool resembling a chisel, used for cutting and engraving during the Upper Palaeolithic period [Mid-17C. < French]

burk *n* another spelling of **berk** (*slang*)

burka /búrkə/, **burqa** *n* a garment with veiled eyeholes covering the entire body, worn in public by some Muslim women [Mid-19C. Via Urdu or Persian *burka'* < Arabic *burku'*]

burke /burk/ (**burkes, burking, burked**) *vt* **1.** KEEP SOMETHING QUIET to prevent information from becoming known **2.** KEEP SOMEBODY QUIET to prevent somebody from revealing information **3.** EVADE SOMETHING to evade an issue or question **4.** MURDER SOMEBODY DISCREETLY to murder somebody silently and without leaving marks or wounds, especially by suffocation (*dated*) [Early 19C. After William BURKE]

Burke /burk/, **Edmund** (1729–97) Irish-born British writer, political philosopher, and politician. As a Whig member of Parliament (1765–94), he was one of the greatest orators of the age. He played a leading role in the impeachment of Warren Hastings (1788–95). His *Reflections on the Revolution in France* (1790) condemned the French Revolution and reached a wide European audience.

'If any ask me what a free government is, I answer, that for any practical purpose, it is what the people think so. Liberty, too, must be limited in order to be possessed.'
[Edmund Burke, *Letter to the Sheriffs of Bristol*; 1777]

Burke, Robert O'Hara (1820–61) Irish-born Australian explorer. The leader of an ill-fated expedition across Australia from south to north, he died during the return journey.

Burke, William (1792–1829) Irish murderer. With William Hare he procured corpses to sell to Edinburgh medical schools by murdering people. He was hanged for his crimes.

Burkina Faso

Burkina Faso /bur keénə fássō/ landlocked country in West Africa. A former French territory, it became independent in 1960. Language: French. Currency: CFA franc. Capital: Ouagadougou. Population: 13,228,460 (2003). Area: 274,200 sq. km/105,900 sq. mi. Official name **Democratic Republic of Burkina Faso**. Former name **Upper Volta** (until 1984)

Burkitt's lymphoma /búrkits-/ *n* a rare malignant tumour attacking white blood cells, associated with

a virus spread by insects. It is found mainly in children in Central Africa. [Mid-20C. After Denis Burkitt (1911–93), British surgeon]

burl¹ /burl/ *n* **1.** KNOT ON TREE a knotty growth on a tree trunk **2.** KNOTTY WOOD knotty wood, or a decorative veneer made from a burl of a tree **3.** KNOT IN CLOTH a knot in thread or cloth ■ *vt* (**burls, burling, burled**) REMOVE KNOTS FROM CLOTH to pick knots off newly woven cloth [15C. Via Old French *bourle* 'tuft of wool' < late Latin *burra* 'wool']

burl² /burl/ *n* **1.** *UK regional, Ireland* ACT OF SWINGING an act of swinging or spinning round ○ *How would you like a burl?* **2.** *ANZ* TRY an attempt to do something (*informal*) ■ *vt* (**burls, burling, burled**) *UK regional, Ireland* MAKE SOMEBODY SWING to cause somebody to swing or spin round ○ *He swung me off my feet and burled me through the air.* [Late 19C. Variant of BIRL]

burlap /búr lap/ *n* coarse cloth woven from jute, hemp, or a similar rough thread [Late 17C. Origin ?]

burlesque /bur lésk/ *n* **1.** MOCKERY BY LUDICROUS IMITATION the mocking of a serious matter or style by imitating it in an incongruous way **2.** WORK USING BURLESQUE a literary or dramatic work that uses burlesque **3.** LUDICROUS IMITATION an incongruous imitation of something **4.** *N Am* VARIETY SHOW a variety show of a type that often includes striptease ■ *vt* (**-lesques, -lesquing, -lesqued**) MOCK SOMETHING BY LUDICROUS IMITATION to mock something serious by imitating it in an incongruous way [Mid-17C. Via French < Italian *burlesco* < *burla* 'mockery, fun'] —**burlesquer** *n*

burly /búrli/ (**-lier, -liest**) *adj* strong and with a broad sturdy frame ○ *flanked by two burly bodyguards* [14C. Probably < assumed Old English *borlic* 'excellent' < Indo-European, 'carry'] —**burliness** *n*

Burma /búrmə/ former name for **Myanmar** —**Burman** *adj, n*

bur marigold *n* BOT a wild plant that has barbed seeds that stick to hair, fur, and clothing. Flowers: yellow. Genus: *Bidens*. US term **beggar's lice**

Burmese /búr meéz/ (*plural same*) *n* **1.** somebody who comes from Myanmar, formerly Burma **2.** the official Tibeto-Burman language of Myanmar. Native speakers: 20–27 million. —**Burmese** *adj*

Burmese cat *n* a domestic cat belonging to a breed with a chocolate-coloured or silvery-brown coat and yellow eyes, similar in build to the Siamese cat

burn¹ /burn/ *v* (**burns, burning, burnt** /burnt/ or **burned**) **1.** *vti* BE OR SET ON FIRE to be on fire, or cause something to be on fire **2.** *vti* DESTROY SOMETHING BY FIRE to destroy something by fire, or be destroyed by fire ○ *The house was burnt to the ground.* **3.** *vt* DAMAGE SOMETHING BY FIRE to injure, damage, or affect somebody or something with fire or extreme heat ○ *I burnt my hand on the iron.* **4.** *vti* OVERCOOK SOMETHING to spoil food or a cooking pan by subjecting it to too intense or long a heat, or be spoiled in this way **5.** *vt* USE SOMETHING UP to use up or consume something ○ *You won't burn many calories watching TV.* **6.** *vt* USE SOMETHING AS FUEL to use something for heat or energy ○ *burn gas* **7.** *vti* KILL OR DIE BY FIRE to kill somebody with fire, or die by fire, usually as a form of execution **8.** *vi* SUFFER PAIN to suffer pain through fire **9.** *vi* FEEL FEVERISH to feel or look extremely hot or feverish because of illness or embarrassment ○ *Her cheeks were burning.* **10.** *vti* CAUSE OR FEEL STINGING to feel an intense stinging or smarting sensation, or cause such a sensation in a part of the body ○ *That hot coffee will burn your throat.* **11.** *vi* IMPRESS DEEPLY to create a deep and lasting impression on somebody or something ○ *His words were burning in my brain.* **12.** *vt* MAKE MARK to cause a mark, hole, or other sign of damage to appear in something because of intense heat or fire ○ *I burnt a hole in my shirt with the iron.* **13.** *vti* SUNBURN to become sunburnt, or cause a person or part of the body to become sunburnt ○ *My skin burns easily.* **14.** *vi* EMIT ENERGY to emit heat or light ○ *A light was burning in the front room.* **15.** *vi* CONTAIN FIRE to contain a fire, or operate by means of fire ○ *a fireplace burning brightly* **16.** *vi* FEEL STRONG EMOTION to feel an emotion very intensely ○ *burning with shame* **17.** *vi* YEARN to yearn to do or acquire something ○ *burning to succeed* **18.** *vti* CHEM COMBUST to undergo combustion, or cause something to undergo combustion **19.** *vt* COMPUT COPY DATA TO CD to copy data onto a CD-ROM or DVD-ROM. It can then be used to transport the content or to create

multiple copies. **20.** *vti* CARDS **DISCARD** to exchange or discard unwanted playing cards in the course of a game (*informal*) **21.** *vi* **DRIVE FAST** to drive a motor vehicle at high speed (*informal*) **22.** *vti US* **ELECTROCUTE** to electrocute somebody, or be electrocuted (*informal*) **23.** *vt N Am* **CHEAT SOMEBODY** to cheat or swindle somebody (*informal; usually passive*) ○ *We really got burnt on that deal.* ■ *n* **1.** MED **HEAT INJURY** an injury caused by fire, heat, radiation, chemical action, electricity, or friction, resulting in redness and blistering of the skin and often causing damage to underlying tissues **2. FIRE OR HEAT MARK** a mark or hole left on or in something such as fabric, wood, or plastic as a result of burning **3. STINGING** a stinging sensation or feeling of intense heat ○ *the burn of the iodine on my skin* **4. SKIN BURN** sunburn or windburn **5.** FITNESS **SENSATION OF BURNING** a sensation of burning that occurs during strenuous exercise, and the positive psychological sensation associated with it ○ *You can feel the burn after an hour of aerobics.* **6.** AEROSP **ROCKET ADJUSTMENT** a controlled firing of a rocket's engine for adjusting course and position [Old English *birnan* 'be on fire', *bærnan* 'cause something to burn' < Germanic] —**burnable** *adj*

burn down *vti* to catch fire and burn until almost nothing remains, or burn something such as a building in order to destroy it

burn in *vt* **1.** to expose a specific part of an image on photographic paper while masking other areas so that they are not exposed any further **2.** to operate a semiconductor-based device or piece of software continuously to test for defects

burn off *v* **1.** *vt* **GET RID OF EXCESS FAT** to use up energy or get rid of unwanted fat by exercising ○ *burn off a few extra calories* **2.** *vt* AGRIC **REMOVE VEGETATION** to remove vegetation by fire or with chemicals, either to clear the land or in preparation for harvesting a root crop **3.** *vt* INDUST **GET RID OF EXCESS GAS** to get rid of unwanted gas by burning it, e.g. at an oil-well head **4.** *vti* METEOROL **DISSIPATE** to dissipate fog or clouds by the heat of the sun, or be dissipated in this way

burn out *v* **1.** *vi* **FINISH BURNING** to stop burning when reduced to nothing **2.** *vti* **WEAR OUT THROUGH HEAT** to stop working because of too much heat or friction, or cause something to stop working in this way ○ *The car's clutch has burned out.* **3.** *vti* **BECOME EXHAUSTED** to become exhausted or unwell through too much hard work, stress, or reckless living, or make somebody exhausted or unwell in this way (*informal*) ○ *You'll burn yourself out if you don't slow down.*

burn up *v* **1.** *vti* **DESTROY BY FIRE** to destroy something by intense heat or fire, or be destroyed in this way **2.** *vt* **USE FUEL** to use up fuel by burning **3.** *vi* **BE VERY HOT** to be very hot or overheated ○ *burning up with fever* **4.** *vt* **SPEED OVER ROAD** to drive at high speed on a road or track (*informal*) **5.** *vt* **DRIVE FASTER THAN SOMEBODY** to drive faster than somebody else (*informal*) ○ *Some idiot tried to burn me up on the motorway.*

burn[2] /burn/ *n N England, Scotland* a stream or brook [Old English *burna* < Indo-European, 'to boil']

burned-out *adj* same as **burnt-out**

Burne-Jones /búrn-/, **Sir Edward** (1833–98) British artist and designer. A leading member of the pre-Raphaelite school, he painted classical and mythological subjects in a dreamlike style. His book illustrations and designs for stained glass and tapestries showed the strong influence of medieval art. Born **Jones, Edward Coley**

burner /búrnər/ *n* **1. RING ON COOKER** one of the circular rings or plates on a gas or electric cooker that produces heat or a flame **2. PART OF STOVE OR LAMP** the part of a fuel-burning stove, lamp, or heater that produces a flame when lit **3. FURNACE** an incinerator or furnace that burns fuel, waste products, or rubbish

burnet /búrnit/ (*plural* **-nets** or *same*) *n* a perennial herb of the rose family. Genus: *Sanguisorba*. [14C. < Old French *brunet, brunete* < *brun* 'brown' < Germanic]

Burnet /bər nét, búrnit/, **Sir Macfarlane** (1899–1985) Australian biologist. He was joint winner of the Nobel Prize in physiology or medicine (1960) for his work in immunology. Full name **Burnet, Sir Frank Macfarlane**

Burnett /bər nét/, **Frances Hodgson** (1849–1924) British-born US writer. She wrote children's books, including the classic novel *The Secret Garden* (1911). Born **Hodgson, Frances Eliza**. See Cultural note at **garden**

Burney /búrni/, **Fanny** (1752–1840) British novelist and diarist. Her novels include *Evelina* (1778). Her diaries covering 1768–85, published posthumously, are among the classic documents of late-18th-century British social history. Born **Frances Burney**

> 'Now I am ashamed of confessing that I have nothing to confess.'
> [Fanny Burney, *Evelina*; 1778]

Burnie-Somerset /búrni-/ major port and city on the northern coast of Tasmania, Australia, and the site of a large paper mill. Population: 18,831 (2002 estimate).

burn-in *n* a final test for semiconductor-based devices or software in which they are operated for a prescribed period to find defects

burning /búrning/ *adj* **1. ON FIRE** producing flames, or on fire **2. VERY HOT** extremely hot **3. ARDENT** emotionally intense or strong ○ *He spoke with a burning passion.* **4. IMPORTANT** of immediate or urgent importance ○ *one of the burning issues of the day* ■ *adv* **EXTREMELY** so as to produce intense heat ○ *a burning hot day*

burning bush *n* **1.** a bushy annual plant with narrow light green leaves that turn red in autumn, e.g. kochia **2.** PLANTS same as **gas plant 3.** *N Am* a bush with bright red berries or foliage. Genus: *Euonymus*. [Alluding to Exodus 3]

burning glass *n* a convex lens that can concentrate the sun's rays to produce an intense spot of heat or fire at the focus

burnish /búrnish/ *vt* (**-nishes, -nishing, -nished**) **1. POLISH SOMETHING** to polish metal until it shines **2. MAKE SOMETHING SHINY** to make something such as pottery or fabric shine by rubbing it with a smooth instrument ■ *n* **SHINY SURFACE** a smooth shiny finish ○ *a bowl with a bright burnish* [14C. < Old French *burniss-*, stem of variant of *brunir* 'make bright or brown' < *brun* (see BURNET)] —**burnisher** *n*

burnished /búrnisht/ *adj* **1.** polished until shiny **2.** brown and lustrous or smooth (*literary*) ○ *the burnished coat of the chestnut mare*

Burnley /búrnli/ town in Lancashire, northwestern England, a centre of textile production. Population: 89,542 (2001).

burnoose /bur nóoss/, **burnous, burnouse** *n* a long hooded cloak worn by some Arabs, or a garment resembling this [Late 16C. Via French *burnous* < Arabic *burnus* < Greek *birros* 'hooded cloak']

burnout /búrn owt/ *n* **1. EXHAUSTION** psychological exhaustion and diminished efficiency resulting from overwork or prolonged exposure to stress ○ *reported a high rate of burnout among nurses* **2.** MECH ENG **MACHINE FAILURE THROUGH HEAT** failure of a machine or part of a machine to work because of overuse or excessive heat or friction **3.** AEROSP **ROCKET FAILURE** failure of a rocket or jet engine to work because the fuel supply has been exhausted or cut off **4.** *N Am* **EXTREMELY EXHAUSTED PERSON** somebody affected by psychological exhaustion (*informal*)

burn rate *n* the rate at which a company uses up its cash

Burns /burnz/, **George** (1896–1996) US comedian and actor. He conducted one of the longest-running acts in show business, encompassing vaudeville, radio, movies, and television, and won an Academy Award for *The Sunshine Boys* (1975).

> 'It's nice to be here. When you're 99 years old, it's nice to be anyplace.'
> [George Burns, *USA Today*; 20 June 1995]

Barnaby's

Robert Burns

Burns, Robert (1759–96) Scottish poet. The author of *Poems Chiefly in the Scottish Dialect* (1786) and hundreds of songs, he is regarded as Scotland's national poet. His many works include the songs 'Auld Lang Syne' and 'Scots Wha Hae', and the narrative poem 'Tam O'Shanter'.

> 'Wee, sleekit, cow'rin', tim'rous beastie, /
> O what a panic's in thy breastie!'
> [Robert Burns, 'To a Mouse'; 1786]

burnsides /búrn sīdz/ *npl US* heavy side whiskers and a moustache worn with a clean-shaven chin [Late 19C. After Ambrose *Burnside* (1824–81), US army general]

Burns Night *n Scotland* the anniversary of the birth of Robert Burns, which is traditionally celebrated with a Burns Supper. Date: 25 January.

Burns Supper *n Scotland* a meal celebrating Burns Night, traditionally consisting of haggis, mashed swede, and mashed potato

burnt /burnt/ past participle, past tense of **burn**[1] ■ *adj* describes a pigment or dye that has been darkened through a heating process ○ *burnt umber*

burnt almond *n* a sweet with an almond in the centre and a coating of burnt sugar

burnt offering *n* **1.** in some religions, an animal or other offering that is burnt on an altar as a sacrifice **2.** a dish of burnt or overcooked food that is nevertheless served up (*humorous*)

burnt-out, burned-out *adj* **1.** exhausted physically or emotionally through too much hard work, stress, or reckless living **2.** destroyed on the inside by fire

burnt sienna *n* **1.** a reddish-brown pigment or dye originally obtained by roasting raw sienna **2.** a dark reddish-brown colour —**burnt sienna** *adj*

burnt umber *n* **1.** a dark brown pigment or dye originally obtained by roasting raw umber **2.** a deep brown colour —**burnt umber** *adj*

Burnum /búrnəm/, **Burnum** (1936–97) Australian political activist and writer. The leader of Aboriginal protests during the Australian bicentenary, he was the author of *Aboriginal Australia: A Traveller's Guide* (1988). Born **Penrith, Harry**

burn-up *n* a high-speed drive in a motor vehicle (*slang*)

buroo /bə róo/ *n Ireland, Scotland* (*dated slang*) **1.** an office where unemployed people go to seek work and sign on for state benefit **2.** a state allowance paid to unemployed people seeking work [Mid-20C. Alteration of BUREAU]

burp /burp/ *n* **NOISE MADE THROUGH MOUTH** a noise made through the mouth when air is suddenly forced up through the oesophagus from the stomach ■ *v* (**burps, burping, burped**) **1.** *vi* **BELCH** to make a noise through the mouth when air is suddenly forced up through the oesophagus from the stomach **2.** *vt* **MAKE BABY BRING UP WIND** to make a baby expel air from its stomach through its oesophagus after feeding by rubbing or patting its back [Mid-20C. An imitation of the sound]

burp gun *n US* a lightweight submachine gun (*informal*)

burqa *n* CLOTHING another spelling of **burka**

burr[1] /bur/, **bur** *n* **1. PRICKLY SEED HUSK** a prickly husk covering the seeds of plants such as burdock **2. TREE GROWTH** a lumpy outgrowth of wood on a tree **3.** ENG **ROUGH EDGE** a rough edge on material such as metal after it has been cut or drilled **4.** ENG **TOOL FOR REMOVING BURRS** a tool used for removing the rough edges from metal that has been cut or drilled **5.** SURG **DRILL FOR BONE** an instrument for drilling holes in bone, especially into the skull ■ *vt* (**burrs, burring, burred; burs, burring, burred**) **1. CREATE ROUGH EDGE ON SOMETHING** to create a rough edge on a piece of metal or other piece of work by cutting or drilling **2. REMOVE ROUGH EDGE FROM SOMETHING** to remove a rough edge from a piece of metal or other piece of work [14C. Probably < N Germanic]

burr[2] /bur/ *n* **1.** a whirring or buzzing sound ○ *the steady burr of the machines downstairs* **2.** a rolled or trilled pronunciation of the 'r' sound in some regional accents of English [Mid-18C. Origin ?] —**burr** *vti*

burr[3] /bur/ *n* a washer that fits around the end of a rivet [14C. Shortening of Old English *burg* (see BOROUGH); originally 'circle']

Burr /bur/, **Aaron** (1756–1836) vice president of the United States. He was Thomas Jefferson's first vice president (1801–05). He killed Alexander Hamilton in a duel after a long public feud (1804).

burra /búrrə/ adj S Asia large or important [Early 19C. < Hindi baṛā 'great']

Burra /búrrə/, **Edward** (1905–76) British painter. He produced surreal watercolours of figures set in gritty urban backgrounds or in exotic settings.

Burra Din /-dín/ n S Asia same as **Christmas** [< Hindi din 'day']

burra sahib n **1.** an important or senior man **2.** S Asia an important man or boss

Burrell Collection /búrrəl-/ n an art collection in Glasgow that contains paintings, textiles, glass, ceramics, and many other artefacts that once belonged to the 19th-century Scottish shipping magnate Sir William Burrell (1861–1958)

burrito /bə réetō/ (plural **-tos**) n in Mexican cooking, a flour tortilla wrapped round a filling of meat, beans, or cheese [Mid-20C. < American Spanish, 'small burro' < Spanish burro (see BURRO)]

burro /boörrō/ (plural **-ros**) n N Am a small donkey, especially one that is used as a pack animal [Early 19C. < Spanish, back-formation < borrico 'donkey' < late Latin burricus 'small horse']

Burroughs /búrrōz/, **Edgar Rice** (1875–1950) US writer. He created the character Tarzan in a series of popular novels starting in 1914.

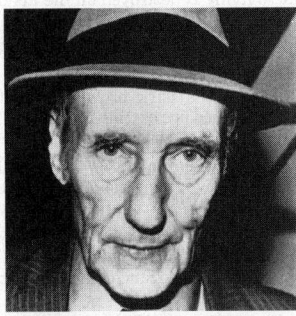

William S. Burroughs

Burroughs, **William S.** (1914–97) US writer. A leading figure of the Beat Generation, he wrote *The Naked Lunch* (1959) and *The Soft Machine* (1961). Full name **Burroughs, William Seward**. See Cultural note at **lunch**

'Writers live the sad truth just like everyone else. The only difference is, they file reports.'
[William S. Burroughs, *The Naked Lunch*; 1959]

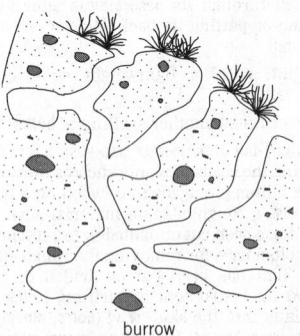

burrow

burrow /búrrō/ n **1.** RABBIT'S HOME a hole or tunnel dug as a living space by a small animal such as a rabbit **2.** SNUG PLACE a small snug place created by digging or hollowing ■ v (**-rows, -rowing, -rowed**) **1.** vti DIG HOLE OR TUNNEL to make a hole or tunnel by digging **2.** vi BE IN BURROW to hide or live in a burrow **3.** vi PENETRATE BY DIGGING to move through something solid by digging or by creating a space ○ He burrowed through the undergrowth. **4.** vi LOOK INTO SOMETHING THOROUGHLY to research or investigate something more thoroughly ○ had spent years burrowing into the history of the era [13C. Variant of BOROUGH] —**burrower** n

burrstone n GEOL another spelling of **buhrstone**

burry[1] /búri/ (**-rier, -riest**) adj **1.** covered in burrs **2.** resembling a burr or burrs [15C. < BURR[1]]

burry[2] /búri/ (**-rier, -riest**) adj characterized by or spoken with a burr [Mid-19C. < BURR[2]]

bursa /búrsə/ (plural **-sas** or **-sae** /-see/) n a fluid-filled body sac that reduces friction around joints or between other parts that rub against one another [Early 19C. Via modern Latin < medieval Latin, 'bag, purse' < Greek, 'wineskin'] —**bursal** adj

Bursa /búrsə/ city in northwestern Turkey, south of the Sea of Marmara, south of Istanbul, and west of Ankara. It was the capital of the Ottoman Empire from 1326 to 1402. Population: 1,095,842 (1997).

bursa of Fabricius /-fə bríshəss/ n an organ in immature birds that produces B lymphocytes. It resembles a sac and is situated in part of the lower pelvic region (**cloaca**). [After Girolamo *Fabrici* (1533–1619), Italian anatomist (Latinized)]

bursar /búrssər/ n **1.** an official who has charge of funds, particularly in a university, college, school, or monastery **2.** a student who holds a bursary [13C. Directly or via French < medieval Latin bursarius < bursa (see BURSA)] —**bursarship** n

bursary /búrssəri/ (plural **-ries**) n **1.** a grant or scholarship offered to a student at a school, college, or university in some countries such as Scotland and Canada **2.** the office or room where a bursar works [Late 17C. < medieval Latin bursaria 'bursar's office' < bursa (see BURSA)] —**bursarial** /bur sáiri əl/ adj

burse /burss/ n in the Roman Catholic Church, a flat case that is used for carrying a special linen cloth (**corporal**) when celebrating Mass [13C. Directly or via French < medieval Latin bursa (see BURSA)]

bursitis /bur sítiss/ n inflammation of a fluid-filled sac (**bursa**) of the body, particularly at the elbow, knee, or shoulder joint

burst /burst/ v (**bursts, bursting, burst**) **1.** vi SPLIT OR BREAK to split or break apart suddenly and violently because of excess internal pressure ○ The suitcase had burst open. **2.** vt MAKE SOMETHING SPLIT to cause something to split open suddenly and disgorge its contents, e.g. by piercing it or applying external pressure **3.** vi BE VERY FULL to be so full as to appear close to splitting open or overflowing ○ Every hotel in town was bursting with tourists. **4.** vt RUPTURE SOMETHING to rupture an internal organ or blood vessel **5.** vt FLOW OVER SOMETHING to overflow the normal limit of containment ○ The river burst its banks. **6.** vi MOVE SUDDENLY to go, come, or move suddenly and with great energy and speed ○ Angry protesters burst in on the meeting. **7.** vi BE OVERWHELMED to feel an emotion so intensely that it is almost overwhelming ○ I thought I would burst with excitement. **8.** vi BECOME SUDDENLY NOTICED to appear suddenly and become noticed and prominent at a particular time and in a particular situation ○ an exciting new product about to burst onto the market **9.** vt DIVIDE PAPER to separate continuous stationery such as computer printout into individual sheets ■ n **1.** EXPLOSION OR RUPTURE a sudden and often noisy splitting or breaking open of something ○ There's a burst in the mains. **2.** SHORT INTENSE PERIOD a short, sudden, and intense period of an activity or phenomenon ○ a burst of publicity **3.** SUSTAINED ACTIVITY a period of sustained activity ○ I read it in two bursts. ○ a burst of speed **4.** GUNFIRE a short, sudden, and noisy volley of gunfire **5.** ONLINE, COMPUT SINGLE AMOUNT OF DATA an amount of data sent or received in one operation [Old English berstan < Germanic] —**burster** n

burst into vt **1.** to start to happen or appear suddenly and often dramatically ○ The truck crashed and burst into flames. ○ Spring saw the landscape burst into life. **2.** to give sudden and full expression to a strong emotion such as laughter or tears ○ burst into tears

burst out v **1.** vi to start expressing something suddenly and fully ○ burst out laughing **2.** vt to say something suddenly, as if a suppressed emotion or opinion had been welling up inside

bursting /búrsting/ adj **1.** OVERFLOWING so full of an emotion or a quality that it is almost impossible to contain it ○ bursting with energy **2.** ABSOLUTELY FULL full to the point of overflowing ○ a city bursting with refugees **3.** EAGER wanting to do something very much (informal) ○ I was bursting to tell her the news. **4.** WITH FULL BLADDER needing desperately to urinate (informal)

bursting disc n a safety device in a vessel used in an industrial process consisting of a thin metal disc that is designed to rupture when subjected to unusually high pressure

burstone n GEOL another spelling of **buhrstone**

bursty /búrsti/ adj moving, transferred, or transmitted in short uneven spurts, as is stellar radiation from a pulsar, traffic at a tollbooth, or data in a computer network

burthen /búrthən/ (archaic) n same as **burden**[1] ■ vt (**-thens, -thening, -thened**) same as **burden**[1] [Variant]

burton /búrt'n/ n a light tackle with double or single blocks used for hoisting [Early 18C. Alteration of obsolete *Breton* (tackle), origin ?] ◇ **go for a burton** to be destroyed, ruined, or dead (dated informal)

Burton /búrt'n/, **Sir Richard** (1821–90) British explorer and linguist. He was one of the first Europeans to enter Mecca and Medina. He also travelled extensively in Africa and translated several books, including *The Arabian Nights* (1885–88) and *The Perfumed Garden* (1886). Full name **Burton, Sir Richard Francis**

Burton, **Richard** (1925–84) Welsh-born British actor. His films include *Look Back in Anger* (1959) and *Cleopatra* (1963).

'An actor is something less than a man while an actress is something more than a woman.'
[Richard Burton. Quoted in *Halliwell's Filmgoer's and Video Viewer's Companion* (8th ed.), Leslie Halliwell; 1990]

Burton, **Robert** (1577–1640) English writer and clergyman. His best-known work is *The Anatomy of Melancholy* (1621).

Burton, **Tim** (b. 1960) US film director. He directed *Batman* (1989) and *Edward Scissorhands* (1990).

Burton-upon-Trent /búrt'n ə pon trént/ town on the River Trent in Staffordshire, central England. It is a historic brewing centre. Population: 60,525 (1991).

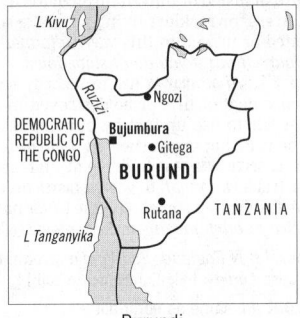

Burundi

Burundi /boŏ roŏndi/ landlocked country in east-central Africa. It is bordered by Rwanda to the north, Tanzania to the east and south, and the Democratic Republic of the Congo to the west. Language: Kirundi, French. Currency: Burundi franc. Capital: Bujumbura. Population: 6,096,156 (2003). Area: 27,834 sq. km/10,747 sq. mi. Official name **Republic of Burundi**. Former name **Ruanda-Urundi** (until 1962) —**Burundian** n, adj

bury /bérri/ (**-ies, -ying, -ied**) v **1.** vt PUT SOMETHING IN HOLE to dig a hole, put something in it, and replace the soil or other material removed ○ a dog burying its bone **2.** vt INTER DEAD BODY to put a dead body in a grave dug in the ground, or sometimes under water, usually as part of a religious ritual ○ He asked to be buried at sea. **3.** vt LOSE SOMEBODY THROUGH DEATH to lose somebody, especially a spouse or a close relative, through death ○ She has buried four husbands. **4.** vt HIDE SOMETHING BY COVERING to hide something by covering it with a lot of things so that it cannot be seen ○ He buried the letter under a pile of books. **5.** vt COVER SOMEBODY OR SOMETHING UP to cover somebody or something completely with something ○ was buried under the rubble **6.** vt OBSCURE SOMETHING to make something difficult to find, notice, or distinguish ○ The announcement was buried at the end of the programme. **7.** vt SINK SOMETHING DEEPLY to sink

something deeply into something else so that it is difficult to see or retrieve ○ *The splinter had buried itself under his nail.* **8.** *vt* HIDE HEAD FROM SIGHT to put the face or head somewhere, usually on or under a soft and yielding surface ○ *She buried her face in her hands.* **9.** *vr* **bury yourself** CONCENTRATE INTENSELY ON SOMETHING to concentrate exclusively and intensely on something ○ *She tended to bury herself in her work.* **10.** *vt* SUPPRESS OR FORGET SOMETHING to suppress or forget something unpleasant or undesirable ○ *their efforts to bury the past* [Old English *byrgan* < Germanic, 'protection, shelter']

SPELLCHECK See *berry*.

Bury /bérri/ town in Lancashire, northwestern England, on the River Irwell. It is part of Greater Manchester and, historically, a weaving centre. Population: 180,608 (2001).

Buryat /boŏri áat/, **Buriat** *n* **1.** a member of a people living in southeastern Russia **2.** an Altaic language spoken by the Buryats, considered to be a dialect of Mongolian. Native speakers: 300,000. [Mid-19C. < Mongolian *Buriyad*] —**Buryat** *adj*

Bury St Edmunds /bérri s'nt édməndz/ market town in Suffolk, eastern England. Its name comes from the Saxon king St Edmund, who is buried there. Population: 31,237 (1991).

bus /buss/ *n* (*plural* **buses** or **busses**) **1.** LARGE PASSENGER VEHICLE a long motor vehicle with many seats, usually divided by a central aisle and often on two decks. Buses transport fare-paying passengers along a specific route. **2.** CAR OR PLANE a vehicle, especially a car or plane (*informal*) ○ *I can't get this old bus to start!* **3.** COMPUT DATA CHANNEL a channel or path for transferring computer data, especially between the central processing unit and a peripheral device **4.** ARMS ROCKET WARHEAD the final stage of a multistage rocket, containing the warhead **5.** AEROSP SPACECRAFT COMPONENT the part of a space exploration vehicle that contains the atmospheric re-entry probes ■ *v* (**buses** or **busses**, **busing** or **bussing**, **bused** or **bussed**) **1.** *vti* GO OR CARRY PASSENGERS BY BUS to travel or transport passengers to a particular destination by bus **2.** *vt* N Am TRANSPORT SCHOOLCHILDREN to transport schoolchildren by bus to a school distant from their homes, especially in an effort to achieve ethnic balance in the school population [Early 19C. Shortening of OMNIBUS] ◇ **miss the bus** to fail to take advantage of an opportunity (*informal*)

bus. *abbr* business

bus bar *n* an electrical conductor or group of electrical conductors used as a connector in a circuit, especially as a bus in a computer system

busboy /búss boy/ *n* N Am somebody employed in a restaurant or café to clear away dishes, set tables, and assist the serving staff

busby /búzbi/ (*plural* **-bies**) *n* a tall fur helmet worn by some soldiers, including some British guards regiments [Mid-18C. Origin ?]

Busby /búzbi/, **James** (1800–71) British government official. He was British Resident in New Zealand (1833–40) and paved the way for the Treaty of Waitangi (1840) by persuading local Maori chiefs to accept government protection.

Busby, Sir Matt (1909–94) British footballer and manager. Injured in the air crash that killed most of the Manchester United team in 1958, he rebuilt the team, which won the European Cup in 1968. Full name **Busby, Sir Matthew**

bus conductor *n* an official on some buses whose job is to sell and check tickets and to signal to the driver when to stop and start

bush[1] /boŏsh/ *n* **1.** WOODY BRANCHED PLANT a woody plant that is smaller than a tree and has many branches growing up from the lower part of the main stem **2.** THICKET a thick clump of bushes **3.** UNCULTIVATED AND UNSETTLED LAND wild, uncultivated, and sparsely populated areas of land covered with natural vegetation, especially in Africa and Australia ○ *living in the bush* **4.** DENSE MASS a dense large mass of something, especially hair or beard ○ *a great bush of black hair* **5.** TABOO TERM a highly offensive term for a woman's pubic hair (*taboo slang*) **6.** BUSHY TAIL a bushy tail, especially of a fox **7.** NZ NEW ZEALAND FOREST AREAS the forests of New Zealand **8.** VINTNER'S SIGN a bunch of ivy hung outside a tavern to show that wine is sold inside (*archaic*) ■ *vi* (**bushes**,

bushing, bushed) BRANCH OUT to branch out, spread, or grow thick like a bush ○ *hair bushing out round her head* [< assumed Old English *bysc* and Old Norse *buski* < Germanic] ◇ **beat about the bush** to discuss a subject without coming to the point ◇ **go bush** Aus to leave urban civilization in order to live a simple, rustic lifestyle in the country

bush[2] /boŏsh/ *n* UK, ANZ, Can a cylindrical metal sleeve used to prevent abrasion, functioning as a bearing or as a guide for tool parts such as valve rods. US term **bushing** [Mid-16C. < Middle Dutch *busse*, via Germanic < Latin *pyxis* 'box, cap' < late Greek *puxis* 'box']

George Bush

(Library of Congress)

Bush /boŏsh/, **George** (b. 1924) 41st president of the United States. A Republican, he was Ronald Reagan's vice president (1981–88) before his election to the presidency. His presidency (1989–93) was notable for the passage of the Americans with Disabilities Act (1990) and, in foreign policy, the Gulf War (1990) against Iraq and the end of the Cold War. Full name **Bush, George Herbert Walker**. See table at **president**

'A line has been drawn in the sand.'
[George Bush, on deploying troops to the Persian Gulf after Iraq's invasion of Kuwait; 8 August 1990]

George W. Bush

(Popperfoto)

Bush, George W. (b. 1946) 43rd president of the United States. The son of former US president George Bush, he was elected Republican governor of Texas in 1994 and 1998 and became president in 2001. Full name **Bush, George Walker**. Known as **Dubya**. See table at **president**

'Terrorist attacks can shake the foundations of our biggest buildings, but they cannot touch the foundation of America. These acts shattered steel, but they cannot dent the steel of American resolve.'
[George W. Bush, *Address to the Nation*; 11 September 2001]

bushbaby /boŏsh baybi/ *n* a small nocturnal primate that lives in trees and has big round eyes, large ears, and a long tail. Native to: Africa. Family: Galagidae.

bush ballad *n* Aus in Australian literature, a poem written in ballad form that takes as its subject some aspect of life in country areas

bushbash /boŏsh bash/ (**-bashes, -bashing, -bashed**) *vi* Aus to hike through bushland by flattening the vegetation to create a path instead of following an existing trail

bush-bath *n* Carib a bath containing herbs, taken

to avert evil influences especially after illness or childbirth or a run of bad fortune

bush bean *n* N Am same as **dwarf bean**

bushbuck /boŏsh buk/ (*plural* **-bucks** or *same*) *n* a small antelope that has a reddish-brown coat, usually with white stripes, and twisted horns. Native to: sub-Saharan Africa. Latin name: *Tragelaphus scriptus*. [Mid-19C. Translation of Afrikaans *bosbok* < Dutch *bosch* 'bush' + *bok* 'buck']

bush clover *n* a plant with three-leaved compound leaves and small flowers. Use: forage, erosion control, and decoration. Genus: *Lespedeza*.

bushcraft /boŏsh kraaft/ *n* ANZ the skills and knowledge that enable somebody to live and function successfully in the bush

bushed /boŏsht/ *adj* (*informal*) **1.** exhausted from overwork or lack of sleep **2.** Aus perplexed and confused [Late 19C. The state typical of somebody wandering in the bush]

Bushehr /boŏ sheér/, **Bushire** /boo shír/ city in southwestern Iran, southwest of Shiraz. It is a major port on the Persian Gulf. Population: 140,615 (1994).

bushel /boŏsh'l/ *n* **1.** FORMER UK UNIT OF VOLUME a unit of dry or liquid measure in the British Imperial system, equal to 8 imperial gallons (36.37 litres), formerly used for measuring items such as wheat, fruit, and liquids **2.** US UNIT OF VOLUME a unit of measure in the US Customary system used for measuring dry goods, equal to 64 US pints (35.24 litres) **3.** CONTAINER a container that has a capacity of one bushel [15C. < Old French *boisell*]

bushfire /boŏsh fîr/ *n* a fire in the bush or in a forest area that spreads quickly and goes out of control easily

bush fly *n* a fly that lays its eggs in animal dung. Native to: Australia. Latin name: *Musca vetustissima*.

bush grass *n* a grass with leaves that grow tall like reeds in damp clay soils. Native to: Europe, Asia. Latin name: *Calamagrostis epigejos*.

bushhammer /boŏsh hamər/ *n* a powered hammer with small pyramidal points cut into the working surface, used to form a rough surface on stonework [Late 19C. Probably translation of German *Boszhammer* < *boszen* 'to beat']

bush house (*plural* **bush houses**) *n* Aus a hut or simple dwelling in the country or in a garden

Bushido /boo sheédō/ *n* the code of honour and behaviour of the Japanese warrior class (**samurai**), emphasizing self-discipline, courage, and loyalty [Late 19C. < Japanese *bushidō* < *bushi* 'warrior' (< Middle Chinese *wushi* + *dō* 'way') (< Middle Chinese *daw*')]

bushie /boŏshi/ *n* ANZ somebody from a remote country area, especially somebody regarded as unsophisticated (*informal insult*)

bushing /boŏshing/ *n* **1.** a layer of electrical insulation that allows a live conductor to pass through an earthed wall **2.** an adaptor or screw-piece for connecting two different sizes of pipe **3.** US ENG same as **bush**[2] [Mid-19C. < BUSH[2]]

Bushire ♦ **Bushehr**

Bushism /boŏshizəm/ *n* a spoken grammatical error or misuse of a word or phrase by US president George W. Bush that changes the intended meaning of a statement or is amusing, or a similar mistake in speech made by somebody else. ○ *'misunderestimate' and other Bushisms* [Late 20C. After George W. BUSH]

bush jacket *n* a lightweight cotton jacket resembling a shirt, with patch pockets and a belt

bushland /boŏsh land, boŏshlənd/ *n* Aus uncultivated and undeveloped land

bush lawyer *n* ANZ **1.** a prickly, trailing plant. Native to: Australia. **2.** somebody who offers legal advice without being qualified (*informal disapproving*)

bush line *n* NZ the height on a mountain or other elevation above which the native forest does not grow

bushman /boŏshmən/ (*plural* **-men** /-mən/) *n* ANZ somebody, usually a man, with experience of living or travelling in remote areas

Bushman /boŏshmən/ (*plural* **-men** /-mən/) *n* an offensive term for a member of the San people

bushman's singlet n NZ a sleeveless black woollen top worn by farmers and other outdoor workers

bushmaster /bŏŏsh maastər/ n a large venomous snake with greyish-brown markings, growing up to 3.6 m/12 ft in length. Native to: Central and South America. Latin name: *Lachesis mutus*.

bush meat n W Africa the flesh of wild animals killed for food

bush medicine n Aus, Carib traditional medical remedies, prepared from plants, especially herbs

bushperson /bŏŏsh purss'n/ (plural **-persons** or **-people** /-peep'l/) n ANZ somebody with experience of living or travelling in remote areas

bush pig n a black or brown wild pig that has small tusks and long tufts of hair on the face and ears. Native to: southern Africa. Latin name: *Potamochoerus porcus*.

bush pilot n a pilot who flies a small plane into and out of areas that are difficult to reach with other means of transportation

bushranger /bŏŏsh raynjər/ n **1.** NZ, N Am SOMEBODY LIVING AWAY FROM HABITATION somebody who lives in or explores the wild parts of the country **2.** ANZ ESCAPED CONVICT formerly, a criminal or escaped convict living on the run in the bush, surviving by robbing passers-by or local people **3.** NZ VOLUNTEER formerly, a member of a settlers' volunteer unit engaged in bush fighting

bush-shrike (plural **bush-shrikes** or same) n a bird of the shrike family, typically olive-backed with a bright yellow or red breast, that chases its prey on foot. Native to: African forests. Genera: *Malaconotus* or *Chlorophoneus*.

bush telegraph n **1.** a method of communicating over distances, e.g. using drumbeats **2.** a method of communicating information or rumours swiftly and unofficially by word of mouth or other means (informal)

bush track n ANZ a rough road in a remote area

bush tucker n Aus (informal) **1.** simple food that can be cooked over a campfire in the bush **2.** food consisting of items collected in the bush, e.g. native plants and fruits

bushwalk /bŏŏsh wawk/ n ANZ a walk through the bush —**bushwalker** n —**bushwalking** n

bushwhack /bŏŏsh wak/ (**-whacks**, **-whacking**, **-whacked**) v **1.** vi Aus, N Am TRAVEL THROUGH WOODS to travel through woods, forest, or the bush **2.** vi Aus, N Am CUT THROUGH WOODS to cut a way through thick woods or forest **3.** vt N Am AMBUSH SOMEBODY to attack somebody suddenly from a concealed position (informal) **4.** vi N Am FIGHT AS GUERRILLA to fight as a guerrilla **5.** vi NZ FORESTRY FELL TIMBER to fell timber for a living

bushwhacker /bŏŏsh wakər/ n **1.** Aus, N Am SOMEBODY TRAVELLING OR LIVING IN BUSH somebody who travels or lives in isolated regions **2.** HIST CONFEDERATE GUERRILLA IN AMERICAN CIVIL WAR a Confederate guerrilla in the American Civil War **3.** US RURAL GUERRILLA a guerrilla who fights in remote or rural areas **4.** NZ CLEARER OF BUSH somebody who clears away bush or undergrowth **5.** NZ FORESTRY WORKER somebody who fells timber for a living **6.** NZ UNSOPHISTICATED RUSTIC an unsophisticated person from the country (slang) **7.** CLEARING TOOL a tool for clearing or cutting a way through bush, trees, or undergrowth

bushy /bŏŏshi/ (**-ier**, **-iest**) adj **1.** THICK very thick and full ○ bushy eyebrows **2.** DENSE AND WOODY with many branches growing up together, producing a rounded shape like a bush **3.** COVERED WITH BUSHES covered or overgrown with bushes —**bushily** adv —**bushiness** n

busily /bízzili/ adv in an active, energetic, and concentrated way ○ busily cleaning the house

~~busines~~ incorrect spelling of **business**

business /bíznəss/ n **1.** LINE OF WORK a particular trade or profession ○ the retail business **2.** COMMERCIAL ORGANIZATION a company or other organization that buys and sells goods, makes products, or provides services ○ take over an ailing business **3.** COMMERCIAL ACTIVITY commercial activity involving the exchange of money for goods or services ○ a good person to do business with **4.** LEVEL OF COMMERCE the amount of commercial activity or custom that exists at a particular time ○ Business is poor right now. **5.** COMMERCIAL PRACTICE commercial practice or procedure ○ It's bad business to neglect smaller clients. **6.** CUSTOM the commercial dealings that a person or organization has with another person or organization ○ If this goes on, I shall take my business elsewhere! **7.** IMPORTANT MATTERS tasks or important things that somebody has to do or deal with ○ We have important business to discuss. **8.** PRIVATE MATTERS personal responsibilities and concerns ○ What business is it of yours? **9.** AFFAIR a situation or event that is characterized by difficulty, fuss, or unpleasantness ○ that business about the tickets **10.** UNSPECIFIED ACTIVITIES activities or things that are not clearly described or defined ○ designing, measuring, and all that kind of business **11.** COMPLICATED TASK an overcomplicated or irritating task or activity ○ It's such a business even getting served in here! **12.** SOMETHING EXCELLENT something very impressive or excellent (informal) ○ He thinks his new car is really the business. **13.** THEATRE ACTOR'S SMALL ACTIONS an action or series of actions performed by an actor for dramatic or comic effect or to fill in a pause when little is happening on stage ■ adj OF COMMERCE relating to, belonging to, or involving commerce and the world of professional workers ○ good business practice ■ vi (**-nesses**, **-nessing**, **-nessed**) BE CONCERNED to care about or be interested in something (slang; used in negative statements in Black English) ○ me no business [Old English bisignis 'anxiety, distress' < bisig 'anxious, busy'] ◇ **do your business** to defecate (informal; euphemistic) ◇ **get down to business** to deal with important matters, leaving extraneous ones behind ◇ **have no business doing something** to have no right to do something ◇ **like nobody's business** very hard or strongly (informal) ◇ **mean business** to be serious and determined about something ◇ **mind your own business** to attend to your own affairs and not interfere in other people's concerns ◇ **not be in the business of doing something** to consider something inappropriate or outside the usual area of responsibility ◇ **out of business** not or no longer trading or operating as a business ○ restaurants that go out of business within a few months of opening

business activity statement n Aus BUSINESS full form of **BAS**

business administration n a course of study at a university, college, or other institution of higher education that teaches the basic principles of business and business practices

business card n a small card printed with somebody's name, job title, business address, and contact numbers

business class n a superior level of service in air travel that is less expensive than first class and caters for business travellers (hyphenated when used before a noun) —**business class** adv

business college n a college of higher education where students learn basic business skills such as accounting and management

business cycle n N Am ECON same as **trade cycle**

business day n a day on which stock exchanges and banks are open for business

business end n the part of a tool or device that performs the intended function, as opposed to the body or handle (informal) ○ the business end of a gun

business hours npl the normal hours that most offices and shops are open, usually between about 9 a.m. and 5.30 p.m.

businesslike /bíznəss līk/ adj **1.** showing qualities or attributes that are useful and desirable in a business context, e.g. efficiency, practicality, and methodicalness ○ a very businesslike operation **2.** practical and unemotional

businessman /bíznəss man/ (plural **-men** /-mən, -men/) n a man who works in business, especially at a senior level

business park n an area designed to accommodate businesses and light industry, with large numbers of companies all grouped together, usually on the outskirts of a town or city

businessperson /bíznəss purss'n/ (plural **-people** /-peep'l/ or **-persons**) n somebody who works in business, especially at a senior level

business plan n a plan that sets out the future strategy and financial development of a business, usually covering a period of several years

business school n US a postgraduate educational establishment that offers MBA courses and related courses of study

business studies n the study of the activities involved in running a business, especially the financial and managerial aspects (takes a singular verb)

business suit n a suit consisting of a jacket and trousers, or a jacket and skirt, appropriate for wearing in the office

business-to-business adj relating to Internet transactions between business organizations, rather than between a business and consumers

businesswoman /bíznəss wŏŏmən/ (plural **-women** /-wimmin/) n a woman who works in business, especially at a senior level

busing /bússing/, **bussing** n N Am the transporting of children by bus to a school distant from their homes in an effort to achieve ethnic balance in the school population

busk[1] /busk/ (**busks**, **busking**, **busked**) vi to entertain in the street or another public place in the hope of receiving money from passers-by ○ two guys busking outside the station [Mid-17C. Via obsolete French busquer 'seek, hunt for' < Italian buscare or Spanish buscar < Germanic] —**busker** n

busk[2] /busk/ n a strip of wood, steel, or whalebone used to stiffen the front of a corset [Late 16C. Via French busc < Italian busco 'splinter' < Germanic]

buskin /búskin/ n **1.** ATHENIAN ACTOR'S BOOT a thick-soled laced boot worn by tragic actors in ancient Greece to give them extra height **2.** GREEK DRAMA tragic drama, particularly in the ancient Greek style (archaic) **3.** MEDIEVAL SANDAL a calf-length laced boot worn in the Middle Ages [Early 16C. Probably via Old French bousequin, variant of brousequin < Middle Dutch broseken]

bus lane n in some cities or towns, a road lane that can only be used by buses during busy hours of the day

busload /bús lōd/ n the number of passengers that a bus carries or can carry ○ demonstrators arriving in busloads

busman's holiday n a holiday or leisure activity that is similar to the work somebody normally engages in (informal) [Probably < drivers of horse-drawn buses being driven around on their own bus]

bus mouse n a mouse attached to a computer bus using a special card or port

bus network n a computer network in which all nodes are connected to a single bus

Buson /bŏŏ son/ (1716–84) Japanese poet and artist. He is noted for his haiku and was regarded as one of the finest painters of his time. Known as **Yosa Buson**

bus pass n a ticket that entitles the holder to multiple rides on buses over a set period of time, either free or at a reduced rate

buss /buss/ n regional a kiss (archaic) [Late 16C. Probably variant of obsolete bass 'to kiss', via French baiser < Latin basiare] —**buss** vti

Buss /buss/, **Frances Mary** (1827–94) British pioneer of women's education. She set up the North London Collegiate School for Ladies, was its head (1850–94), and fought for the entry of women to universities.

Busselton /búss'ltən/ town on the southern coast of Western Australia, a pastoral centre and tourist resort. Population: 24,368 (2002 estimate).

bus shelter n a covered shelter at a bus stop

bussing n US EDUC another spelling of **busing**

bus stop n a designated place along a specific route where a bus stops to pick up or set down passengers

bust[1] /bust/ n **1.** a woman's breasts **2.** a sculpture of somebody's head and shoulders [Mid-17C. Via French buste < Italian busto]

bust[2] /bust/ v (**busts**, **busting**, **busted** or **bust**) **1.** vti MAKE OR BECOME USELESS to stop operating properly, or cause something to stop operating properly (informal) ○ Your brother just busted our telly! **2.** vti BREAK OR GET BROKEN to break or damage something by hitting it or by subjecting it to a powerful impact, or be broken in this way (informal) ○ I busted my leg

skiing. **3.** *vti* BURST to burst something, or undergo bursting **4.** *vt N Am* HIT SOMEBODY to hit somebody hard (*informal*) ○ *He busted the villain over the head.* **5.** *vt US* BREAK UP ORGANIZATION to break up an organization when it has become too powerful (*informal*) **6.** *vt* CRIME RAID PLACE to mount a police raid on a place, especially in connection with illegal drugs (*slang*) **7.** *vt* CRIME CATCH SOMEBODY DOING SOMETHING ILLEGAL to catch and punish somebody for doing something illegal or against the rules (*informal*) ○ *got busted for skipping class* **8.** *vti* FIN MAKE OR BECOME BANKRUPT to make somebody bankrupt, or become bankrupt (*informal*) **9.** *vt N Am* MIL DEMOTE SOMEBODY to demote a member of the armed forces (*informal*) **10.** *vt N Am* RIDING TAME HORSE FOR RIDING to break in a horse (*informal*) **11.** *vi* CARDS GO OVER LIMIT in pontoon, to accumulate cards totalling more than 21 points **12.** *vi* CARDS FAIL TO COMPLETE HAND in poker, to fail to complete a flush or straight ■ *n* **1.** FIN ECONOMIC FAILURE economic or financial failure ○ *periods of boom and bust* **2.** CRIME POLICE RAID a police raid or arrest, especially in connection with illegal drugs (*slang*) **3.** *N Am* FAILURE somebody or something that fails completely (*informal*) ○ *The plan seemed perfect in theory, but it was a bust in reality.* **4.** *N Am* PUNCH a punch or blow (*informal*) **5.** PARTY a disorganized party or celebration (*informal*) ■ *adj* (*informal*) **1.** DAMAGED broken or no longer working **2.** FIN BANKRUPT judged legally to be unable to pay off personal debts ○ *go bust* [Mid-18C. Alteration of BURST] —**busted** *adj*
bust up *v* (*informal*) **1.** *vi* to end a relationship in a violent quarrel **2.** *vt* to disrupt or stop something such as a meeting or gathering

Bustamante /bústə mánti/, **Sir Alexander** (1884–1977) Jamaican politician. He served as independent Jamaica's first prime minister (1962–67). Born **Clarke, William Alexander**

bustard /bústərd/ (*plural* **-tards** or *same*) *n* a bird with long legs, a round body, a long neck, and a fairly short beak. Native to: open grassy land in southern Europe, Asia, Africa, and Australia. Family: Otididae. [15C. Probably < assumed Anglo-Norman *bustarde*, blend of *bistarde* + *oustarde*, both < Latin *avis tarda* 'slow bird']

bustee *n S Asia* ENVIRON another spelling of **basti**

buster /bústər/ *n* **1.** *N Am* used as a jocular or mildly threatening term of address, usually for a man or boy (*informal*) **2.** *N Am* RIDING same as **broncobuster 3.** somebody or something that breaks up or destroys something (*informal; usually in combination*) ○ *a union buster* [Mid-19C. < BUST², or alteration of *burster*]

bustier /bústi ay/ *n* a close-fitting sleeveless and usually strapless bodice worn by women as lingerie or clothing [Late 20C. < French < *buste* (see BUST¹)]

bustle¹ /búss'l/ *vi* (**-tles, -tling, -tled**) to work or behave in an ostentatiously hurried and energetic way ○ *He bustled about in preparation for their arrival.* ■ *n* hurried and energetic activity ○ *a great bustle surrounding the arriving guests* [14C. Origin ?] —**bustler** *n*

bustle² /búss'l/ *n* a pad or frame worn in the 19th century under the top of a woman's long skirt to fill it out at the back [Late 18C. Origin ?]

bustling /búss'ling/ *adj* full of or characterized by hurried and energetic activity —**bustlingly** *adv*

bust-up *n* (*informal*) **1.** the breaking up of something such as a relationship or an organization **2.** a fight or brawl

busty /bústi/ (**-ier, -iest**) *adj* having large breasts (*informal*)

busulfan /byoo súlfən/ *n* a drug used in the treatment of some types of chronic leukaemia [Mid-20C. Blend of BUTANE, BUTYL + SULPHONYL, SULPHONATE]

busulphan *n* PHARM another spelling of **busulfan** (*dated*)

busy /bízzi/ *adj* (**-ier, -iest**) **1.** OCCUPIED fully occupied in a particular activity, especially work ○ *She seemed too busy even to talk to me.* ○ *He was busy writing letters all morning.* **2.** FULL OF BUSTLE full of activity, with a large number of people moving around ○ *the busy city streets* **3.** NOT FREE committed to something that has previously been planned or arranged and so unable to undertake another activity ○ *I'm sorry but I'm busy tomorrow night.* **4.** ACTIVE engaged in or characterized by constant, and usually purposeful, activity ○ *busy people who lead busy lives* **5.** ELABORATE

characterized by overcomplex detail, colours, or patterns ○ *a very busy painting* **6.** *N Am* TELECOM same as **engaged** (sense 3) ■ *v* (**-ies, -ying, -ied**) **1.** *vr* **busy yourself** OCCUPY YOURSELF to start doing something that will keep you occupied and working for a period of time ○ *busied himself with the wedding arrangements* **2.** *vt* OCCUPY SOMEBODY to occupy somebody ○ *The work busied him all afternoon.* [Old English *bisig* 'busy, anxious'] —**busyness** *n*

busy bee *n* somebody who is always very busy and active (*informal*)

busybody /bízzi bodi/ (*plural* **-ies**) *n* somebody who meddles in other people's business (*informal*)

busy Lizzie /-lízzi/ (*plural same* or **busy Lizzies**) *n* BOT a low-growing cultivated species of the balsam family. Flowers: numerous, colourful. Latin name: *Impatiens walleriana*.

busy signal *n N Am* same as **engaged tone**

busywork /bízzi wurk/ *n N Am* activities assigned or undertaken that take up time but do not necessarily yield productive results

but¹ *stressed* /but/; *unstressed* /bət/ CORE MEANING: a grammatical word used in the middle of or at the beginning of a sentence to introduce something that is true in spite of either being or seeming contrary to what has just been said ○ *I thought it was late, but it was only 9 o'clock.* ○ *Not one, but two offers were received.* ○ *Yes, but not now.* ○ *It's true her name is Spanish, but she's actually Greek.* ○ *I'm a blonde, but both my mother and father have dark hair.*
1. *conj* INTRODUCING OPPOSING PROPOSITION used to introduce a statement that disagrees with something just said, or that expresses an emotion such as surprise or disbelief at what was just said ○ *'I don't think you're suitable for the job'. 'But I have all the right qualifications!'* **2.** *conj* INTRODUCING FURTHER INFORMATION used to introduce a clause or a new sentence that adds information such as background or reasoning ○ *Jeff isn't coming with us. But he doesn't like horror movies anyway.* **3.** *conj* EXCEPT THAT used to introduce a dependent clause, e.g. a reason for doing or not doing something ○ *I would have called, but I couldn't find a phone.* **4.** *conj* WITHOUT SOMETHING HAPPENING used to indicate that something does not happen without something else happening or being the case (*formal; usually used after negatives*) ○ *She never leaves home but she forgets her keys.* **5.** *conj* THAT used to introduce a subordinate clause ○ *It's not so difficult but I can't understand it.* **6.** *conj* WHEN than or when (*informal*) ○ *I'd no sooner put the phone down but it rang again.* **7.** *conj, prep* EXCEPT used to indicate the exception to a statement just made ○ *He could do nothing but stand and watch her leave.* ○ *There was nothing but a lump of mouldy bread in the cupboard.* **8.** *adv* ONLY, JUST, OR MERELY used to indicate that something happens or is true just to the extent mentioned and not more (*formal*) ○ *This is but one of the bread-making techniques used.* ○ *He arrived but a minute ago.* ○ *We can but try.* **9.** *adv* UK regional, Aus THOUGH used to introduce a contrastive statement (*used at the end of a sentence*) **10.** *adv* US FOR EMPHASIS used to emphasize a statement (*slang*) ○ *Man, but he's fast!* **11.** *npl* **buts** OBJECTIONS objections to something (*informal*) ○ *Allow time to consider all the ifs and buts from the children.* [Old English *butan* 'outside, without, except, but' < Germanic] ◇ **but for** if not for, or if it had not been for ◇ **but that 1.** except that (*archaic or formal*) ○ *Nothing is important but that I see you again.* **2.** used as a subordinating conjunction equivalent to 'that' following negative words such as 'doubt' and 'deny' (*archaic; follows a negative*)

USAGE Can **but** begin a sentence? Some people object to the use of **but**, like *and*, at the beginning of a sentence, regarding it as a joining word that has to have words on either side of it. However, this is a mistaken notion that has no foundation in English structure and usage. It is, however, advisable to reserve this use for occasions when the special effect that initial position affords is needed; otherwise it can become an awkward affectation.

But is not usually followed by a comma. A comma may precede **but** when an independent clause follows, thus: *I wanted to leave early, but* [not *but,*] *the rest of the group did not.*

Avoid unnecessary redundancy in using **but** and other terms such as *however* together.

When **but** is used to indicate an exception, as in *No*

one but me has (or *No one but I have*) *seen the document*, either wording can be used, according to your interpretation of the function of **but**: is it a preposition, as in the first variation, or is it a conjunction, as in the second variation? Though strong cases have been made for both wordings, the prepositional wording does carry slightly more weight. You can recast the sentence as *No one has seen the document but me*, where its prepositional function is quite clear.

USAGE See **help**.

REGIONAL NOTE But normally functions as a contrastive conjunction. In Ireland, the northeast of England, parts of Scotland, and Australia, it can occur at the end of a sentence as an adverb with no contrastive implications. The following examples taken from spoken English illustrate this usage: *I didn't do it but. It's tasty but.*

but² /but/ *Scotland n* the outer room of a two-roomed cottage in Scotland, usually the living or cooking area ■ *adv* in or towards the outer part of a house, cottage, or other dwelling [Early 18C. < BUT¹]

but- *prefix* containing a group of four carbon atoms ○ *butene* [< BUTYRIC]

butadiene /byoótə dí een/ *n* a colourless flammable gas. Source: petroleum. Use: manufacture of synthetic rubber, nylon, latex paints. Formula: C_4H_6. [Early 20C. < BUTANE]

butanal /byoótənəl/ *n* CHEM same as **butyraldehyde** [Late 20C. < BUTANOL]

but and ben *n Scotland* in parts of Scotland, a two-roomed cottage that consists of a living room and a bedroom

butane /byoo tayn/ *n* a colourless, highly flammable gas that has two different molecular structures (**isomers**). Source: natural gas. Use: lighter fluid, fuel. Formula: C_4H_{10}. [Late 19C. < BUTYL]

butanoic acid /byoótənō ik-/ *n* CHEM same as **butyric acid** [< BUTANE]

butanol /byoótə nol/ *n* a colourless toxic liquid with four different molecular structures (**isomers**). Use: solvents, manufacture of organic compounds. Formula: C_4H_9OH.

butanone /byoótə nōn/ *n* a colourless flammable liquid with an odour similar to acetone. Use: solvent, paint stripper, in resins. [Early 20C. < BUTANE]

butch /booch/ *adj* **1.** MASCULINE AND STRONG describes a man who is extremely masculine and strong **2.** OFFENSIVE TERM an offensive term meaning unfeminine in appearance (*slang*) ■ *n* **1.** OFFENSIVE TERM an offensive term for a woman whose appearance is considered unfeminine (*slang*) **2.** *N Am* HAIR same as **crew cut** [Mid-20C. Probably < the nickname *Butch*]

butcher /boochər/ *n* **1.** MEAT SELLER somebody who sells meat **2.** SLAUGHTERER somebody who slaughters animals for their meat **3.** COMM PREMISES OF BUTCHER a shop that sells prepared raw meat and meat products **4.** BRUTAL KILLER somebody who kills people in a brutal manner **5.** INEXPERT PROPONENT OF SOMETHING somebody who does something badly and produces unattractive results ○ *a butcher of the sonnet form* **6.** *Aus* BEER GLASS in South Australia, a small glass for serving beer, usually containing 170 ml/6 oz ■ *vt* (**-ers, -ering, -ered**) **1.** KILL ANIMAL FOR FOOD to slaughter and prepare the meat of an animal for food **2.** KILL PEOPLE BRUTALLY to kill people in a brutal way **3.** BOTCH SOMETHING to do something badly and produce unattractive results (*informal*) ○ *The original script had been butchered.* [13C. < Anglo-Norman form of Old French *bo(u)chier* 'slaughterer of he-goats' < *boc* 'he-goat'] —**butcherer** *n*

butcherbird /boochər burd/ *n* **1.** a bird of the shrike family that impales its prey on thorns and barbed wire. Genus: *Lanius*. **2.** a songbird, usually with black or black-and-white feathers, that impales insects and other prey on thorns. Native to: Australasia. Genus: *Cracticus*.

butcher knife *n US* HOUSEHOLD same as **butcher's knife**

butcher's /boochərz/ *n* **1.** COMM same as **butcher** *n* (sense 3) **2.** Cockney a look (*informal*) ○ *Let's have a quick butcher's at that.* [Sense 'look' from rhyming slang *butcher's hook*]

butcher's broom *n* an evergreen bush with stiff stems. Use: formerly, making brooms. Native to: Mediterranean. Latin name: *Ruscus aculeatus*.

butcher's knife *n* a large heavy-duty knife for use in the kitchen or for butchering

butchery /boŏcheri/ (*plural* **-ies**) *n* **1.** BRUTAL KILLING brutal, senseless, and cruel slaughter of people, usually in large numbers ○ *an act of appalling butchery* **2.** USE OF KNIVES ON CARCASS the use of knives or other tools to remove meat from an animal's carcass ○ *'The tools are often found in association with broken animal bones, which sometimes show signs of butchery.'* ('Ape at the Brink', *Discover Magazine*; 1994) **3.** BUTCHER'S WORK the work of somebody who sells meat at retail or who slaughters animals for their meat **4.** BOTCHING a terrible botching of a job, performance, or activity (*informal*) ○ *the singer's butchery of the melody* **5.** FOOD INDUST same as **abattoir** (*archaic*) **6.** *S Africa* MEAT SHOP a butcher's shop [14C. < French *boucherie* < Old French *bo(u)chier* (see BUTCHER)]

butch haircut *n N Am* HAIR same as **crew cut**

Bute /byoot/ island off the southwestern coast of Scotland, in the Firth of Clyde. It is separated from the mainland by the Kyles of Bute. Area: 119 sq. km/46 sq. mi.

butene /byoó teen/ *n* a colourless, flammable, easily liquefiable gas with three different molecular structures (**isomers**). Use: manufacture of polymers. Formula: C_4H_8. [Late 19C. < BUTYL]

buteo /byoóti ō/ (*plural* **-os**) *n N Am* same as **buzzard** (sense 1) [Mid-20C. Via modern Latin (genus name) < Latin, '(kind of) hawk or falcon']

Buteshire /byoótsher/ former county in western Scotland, Now part of Argyll and Bute council area. Its main town was Rothesay.

Buthelezi /boóte láyzi/, **Mangosuthu Gatsha** (*b.* 1928) South African politician. He was chief minister of KwaZulu, a Black South African homeland (1976–94), and founded Inkatha, a Zulu nationalist organization. Also known as **Dr Buthelezi**

butler /búttler/ *n* the male head servant in a large or important household, with responsibilities that include overseeing the other staff, taking care of the wine and silverware, and sometimes receiving guests [13C. < Anglo-Norman *buteler*, Old French *boteillier* 'cup-bearer' < *boteille* (see BOTTLE)]

Butler /búttler/, **R. A.** (1902–82) British politician. He served as chancellor of the Exchequer (1951), home secretary (1957), and foreign secretary (1963–4). Full name **Butler, Richard Austen**. Known as **Butler, Rab**

Butler, Reg (1913–81) British sculptor. He used wrought iron and stainless steel constructions in linear forms in his early work. His later work was more realistic in style. Full name **Butler, Reginald Cotterell**

Butler, Samuel (1612–80) English satirist. He wrote *Hudibras*, a poetic satire on the Puritans (published in three parts 1663, 1664, 1678).

> 'Oaths are but words, and words but wind.'
> [Samuel Butler, *Hudibras*; 1664]

butler's pantry, **butlery** /bútleri/ *n* a room situated between a kitchen and dining room, used for serving food and for storage

Butlin /búttlin/, **Sir Billy** (1899–1980) British holiday camp organizer. He opened his first camp at Skegness in 1936 and many more after World War II. Full name **Butlin, Sir William Edmund**

> 'Publicity is something I have always believed in, and I make no apologies for it. There is no point in building a better mousetrap if nobody knows it.'
> [Sir Billy Butlin, *The Billy Butlin Story*; 1982]

Butskellism /bútskillizem/ *n* the perceived consensus politics of the Conservative and Labour parties in the United Kingdom in the 1950s, when R. A. Butler and Hugh Gaitskell were the chancellors of the two parties when in power. [Mid-20C. < blend of *Butler* + *Gaitskell*]

butt[1] /but/ *v* (**butts, butting, butted**) **1.** *vt* RAM SOMEBODY OR SOMETHING to hit or push against somebody or something with the head or horns **2.** *vi* STICK OUT to project or jut out ■ *n* PUSH a push with the head or horns [15C. Via Anglo-Norman *buter*, Old French *bo(u)ter* < Germanic] —**butter** *n*

butt in *vi* to interrupt and attempt to join in a

conversation or activity without being invited ○ *He's always trying to butt in on our conversations.*

butt out *vi* to keep out of other people's business or conversation (*informal*)

butt[2] /but/ *n* **1.** OBJECT OF RIDICULE OR CONTEMPT somebody or something that is an object of ridicule or contempt for other people ○ *He became the butt of their satire.* **2.** HINGE a butt hinge, or either of its two parts **3.** CONSTR same as **butt joint** ■ **butts** *npl* **1.** ARCHERY, RIFLE SHOOTING MOUND BEHIND TARGET in archery and rifle shooting, a mound of earth behind the target, designed to stop any stray bullets or arrows **2.** ARCHERY TARGET RANGE a target range in archery **3.** ARCHERY, RIFLE SHOOTING TARGET a target at a shooting or archery range [14C. < French *but* 'goal']

butt[3] /but/ *n* **1.** THICK END the thicker or larger end of something, e.g. the part of a rifle held against the shoulder **2.** CIGARETTE END the part of a cigarette that remains after the rest has been smoked **3.** *N Am* BUTTOCKS a person's or animal's buttocks (*informal; sometimes considered offensive*) ■ *vti* (**butts, butting, butted**) ABUT to lie with one flat end against the flat end of something else, or place something in such a position ○ *The beam butts against the wall.* [15C. Origin ?]

butt[4] /but/ *n* a large cask for holding wine or ale [15C. Via Anglo-Norman *but*, Old French *bot* < late Latin *buttis*]

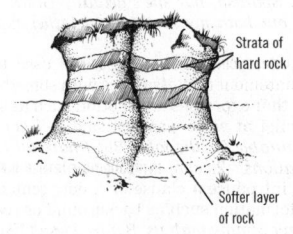

butte

butte /byoot/ *n Can, US regional* a hill that rises abruptly from a flat area of land, with steep sides and a flat top [Mid-19C. < French, 'mound, hillock']

butter /bútter/ *n* **1.** SOFT CREAMY SPREAD a soft, pale yellow, fatty food made by churning cream and used for cooking and spreading on food ○ *bread and butter* **2.** SUBSTANCE LIKE BUTTER a substance that is similar to butter in consistency or appearance ○ *apple butter* ■ *vt* (**-ters, -tering, -tered**) PUT BUTTER ON SOMETHING to spread butter on something, or add butter to something [Old English *butere*, via Germanic < Latin *butyrum* < Greek *bouturon*] ◇ **look as if butter wouldn't melt in your mouth** to look more innocent than you really are

butter up *vt* to flatter somebody in the hope of winning favour or cooperation (*informal*)

butter-and-eggs *n* PLANTS same as **toadflax** (sense 1) (*takes a singular or plural verb*)

butterball /bútter bawl/ *n N Am* **1.** an offensive term for somebody regarded as being overweight (*informal*) **2.** BIRDS same as **bufflehead**

butter bean *n* **1.** a large flat cream-coloured bean, dried before cooking **2.** *Can, US regional* PLANTS, FOOD same as **wax bean**

butterbur /bútter bur/ (*plural* **-burs** or *same*) *n* a waterside plant with large soft leaves. Flowers: purple. Native to: Europe, Asia. Genus: *Petasites*. [Because butter was formerly wrapped in its leaves]

buttercup /bútter kup/ *n* a plant that grows in grassland. Flowers: yellow, cup-shaped. Native to: cold or temperate regions. Genus: *Ranunculus*.

butterfat /bútter fat/ *n* the natural fats found in dairy products

Butterfield /bútter feeld/, **William** (1814–1900) British architect. He designed Keble College, Oxford, and churches in the Gothic Revival style.

butterfingers /bútter fing gerz/ (*plural same*) *n* somebody who tends to drop things accidentally (*informal*) —**butterfingered** *adj*

butterfish /bútter fish/ (*plural same* or **-fishes**) *n* **1.** a small inshore fish, found worldwide, that is a

popular food because of its high lipid content and fine flavour. Family: Stromateidae. **2.** the flesh of a butterfish as food [Late 17C. < its slippery mucous coating]

butterfly

butterfly /bútter flī/ *n* (*plural* **-flies**) **1.** INSECT WITH BIG COLOURFUL WINGS an insect with two pairs of often brightly coloured wings and knobbed antennae. It develops from a caterpillar and lives for only a short time. Order: Lepidoptera. **2.** SWIMMING STROKE a swimming stroke in which both arms are lifted simultaneously above and over the head while both feet are kicked up and down **3.** SWIMMING COMPETITION a race in which swimmers do the butterfly stroke **4.** SOMEBODY LACKING CONCENTRATION somebody who is unable to concentrate for long **5.** PIECE OF METAL FOR FASTENING EARRING a small piece of metal worn on the underside of the lobe of a pierced ear, into which the pin of an earring is fastened **6.** FIN DEAL ON STOCK MARKET the buying and selling of options on the stock market on the same day but at different prices or with different expiry dates ■ **butterflies** *npl* VAGUE NAUSEA a nervous feeling in the stomach ■ *vt* (**-flies, -flying, -flied**) COOK SPLIT FOOD to split a piece of food such as meat or fish along its length, separating it into halves that remain joined [Old English *buttorflēoge*; reference to 'butter' unexplained]

CULTURAL NOTE *Madame Butterfly*, an opera (1904) by Italian composer Giacomo Puccini. Set in Nagasaki, Japan, it tells of the love of a young Japanese woman, Cio-Cio San, for a US naval officer, Lieutenant Pinkerton, who half-heartedly agrees to an arranged marriage with her. When Pinkerton later returns from a three-year sojourn in the United States with another wife, a heartbroken Cio-Cio San commits suicide.

butterfly bush *n* PLANTS same as **buddleia** [Because its flowers attract butterflies]

butterfly chair *n* a chair made from a continuous folded metal rod with four upward-pointing corners on which a fitted canvas seat rests

butterfly diagram *n* a graphic representation of the appearance of sunspots over an 11-year cycle [< its shape]

butterfly effect *n* the supposed influence exerted on a dynamic system by a small change in initial conditions [After a 1979 scientific paper 'Does the flap of a butterfly's wings in Brazil set off a tornado in Texas?' by Edward N. Lorenz]

butterfly fish *n* a small boldly patterned fish with a flattish body and a tapered snout. Native to: tropics. Family: Chaetodontidae.

butterfly nut *n* CONSTR same as **wing nut**

butterfly stroke *n* SWIMMING same as **butterfly** (sense 2)

butterfly valve *n* **1.** a valve consisting of a disc that turns inside a pipe, especially one used as a throttle valve in a carburettor **2.** a valve consisting of two semicircular plates that are hinged around a central spindle, used to allow flow in one direction only [< its shape]

butterfly weed *n* a wild plant whose roots have medicinal properties. Flowers: bright orange, in clusters. Native to: North America. Latin name: *Asclepias tuberosa*. [Because it attracts butterflies]

butterie /bútteri/ *n Scotland* a rich breakfast roll, eaten in the northeast of Scotland

butter knife *n* a small knife with a broad blunt blade, used for spreading butter

In the *butte* illustration: *Strata of hard rock*; *Softer layer of rock*

Buttermere /búttər meer/ lake in the Lake District, in Cumbria, northwestern England. Area: 2 sq. km/0.63 sq. mi. Depth: 28 m/93 ft.

buttermilk /búttər milk/ *n* **1.** the sour-tasting liquid that is left over after milk or cream has been churned to make butter. Use: in baking. **2.** a sour-tasting drink that is made by adding microorganisms to milk

butter muslin *n* a thin, loosely woven cotton fabric. Use: originally, to wrap butter.

butternut /búttər nut/ *n* **1.** a walnut tree that produces edible nuts and yields timber **2.** *ANZ* PLANTS, FOOD same as **butternut squash**

butternut squash *n* a beige-coloured winter squash shaped like a club with a bulbous end and firm yellow-orange flesh. Latin name: *Cucurbita moschata.*

butters /búttərz/ *adj* (*slang*) **1.** lacking appealing physical features, especially facial ones **2.** used as an expression of disgust or strong dismissal

butterscotch /búttər skoch/ *n* **1.** **BRITTLE SUGAR SWEET** a brittle brown-coloured sweet made from butter and brown sugar **2.** **BUTTERSCOTCH FLAVOURING** a flavouring made from the ingredients used in butterscotch **3.** COLOURS **LIGHT BROWN** a light brown colour [Mid-19C. Probably because first made in Scotland] —**butterscotch** *adj*

butterweed /búttər weed/ *n* a wild plant with yellow flowers. Family: Compositae.

butterwort /búttər wurt/ (*plural* **-worts** or *same*) *n* a carnivorous bog plant with a rosette of sticky fleshy leaves that trap and digest insects. Native to: Europe, Asia, North America. Genus: *Pinguicula.*

buttery[1] /búttəri/ (**-ier, -iest**) *adj* resembling, tasting like, or containing butter ○ *a smooth, buttery taste* [14C. < BUTTER] —**butteriness** *n*

buttery[2] /búttəri/ (*plural* **-ies**) *n* **1.** a room in which food or drinks are stored **2.** in some universities, a bar or cafeteria [14C. < Anglo-Norman *boterie*]

butt hinge *n* a hinge consisting of two parts, one of which is attached to a door jamb, the other to the door itself, allowing the door to swing open and shut [< BUTT[2]]

butt joint *n* a joint consisting of two parts of wood or other material that are placed squarely together rather than overlapping or interlocking [< BUTT[2]]

buttock /búttək/ *n* **1.** in humans, either of the two fleshy mounds above the legs and below the hollow of the back (*often used in the plural*) **2.** the rump of an animal [Old English *buttuc* 'end ridge of land' < assumed *butt* 'ridge']

button /bútt'n/ *n* **1.** **DISC FOR HOLDING CLOTHES TOGETHER** a flat and usually round piece of plastic or other material on a piece of clothing that fits into a slit or loop on another part and holds the two parts together **2.** **ELECTRICAL SWITCH** a small disc fitted in an electrical appliance or attached to a surface that activates an electrical connection when pressed **3.** **SMALL ROUND OBJECT** a small round object that resembles a button **4.** *Aus, N Am* **SMALL BADGE WORN ON CLOTHES** a small round flat metal or plastic badge with an image or words printed on it, worn attached to clothes **5.** BIOL **ROUNDED PART** a rounded knob-shaped part or organ, e.g. the head of an unripe mushroom **6.** COMPUT **SMALL ACTIVATING ICON ON COMPUTER SCREEN** a small oblong image in a dialogue box of a computer-screen display, activated to perform a task by clicking with the mouse or pressing the 'Enter' key **7.** COMPUT **ACTIVATING PART OF COMPUTER MOUSE** the part of a computer mouse that, when pressed, performs a function such as inserting the cursor at a specific point **8.** FENCING **PROTECTIVE COVERING ON FOIL** a small rounded plastic or rubber covering placed on the tip of a fencing foil to protect participants from injury **9.** REPT **END OF RATTLESNAKE'S TAIL** the terminal section of a rattlesnake's tail ■ *v* (**-tons, -toning, -toned**) **1.** *vti* **FASTEN WITH BUTTONS** to fasten something with a button or buttons **2.** *vi* **HAVE BUTTONS SOMEWHERE** to have buttons that can be fastened on a particular side of a garment opening or in a particular place on the garment ○ *The dress buttons at the back.* **3.** *vt* **PUT BUTTON IN HOLE** to put a button through a slit or loop designed to receive it ○ *I never button the top button of my shirt.* **4.** *vt* **SHUT MOUTH** to close the mouth or lips and be quiet (*informal*) ○ *Just button it!* [14C. < French *bouton* 'bud, knob' < Germanic] —**buttoner** *n* ◇ **on the button** (*informal*) **1.** exactly right **2.** precisely ○ *She was able to guess the price on the button.* ◇ **press** *or* **push all the right buttons** to do all the right or appropriate things ◇ **push somebody's buttons** to provoke a reaction in somebody deliberately

button up *v* **1.** *vt* **DO UP BUTTONS** to fasten something with buttons **2.** *vt* **CLOSE SOMETHING TIGHTLY** to close or seal something tightly **3.** *vi* **STOP TALKING** to stop talking or refuse to talk (*informal*)

button bar *n* a row of buttons on a computer screen that are clicked on to perform frequently used functions

button day *n Aus* a day on which badges or stickers are sold to raise money for a particular charity

button-down *adj* **1.** describes a collar that has a buttonhole at the end of each flap to fasten it to the front of a shirt **2.** *US* same as **buttoned-down** (*informal*)

buttoned-down /búttənd-/ *adj N Am* having a conservative and traditional manner (*informal*) ○ *stuffy, buttoned-down types*

buttoned-up *adj* unwilling or unable to express feelings (*informal*)

button grass *n* **1.** an annual grass with round flower heads. Native to: Australia. Latin name: *Dactyloctenium radulans.* **2.** a sedge with round flower heads. Native to: Australia. Latin name: *Gymnoschoenus sphaerocephalus.*

buttonhole /búttən hōl/ *n* **1.** **HOLE FOR BUTTON** a slit in a garment through which a button is passed to fasten two pieces of material together **2.** **FLOWER WORN ON LAPEL** a flower or a small spray of flowers worn in or pinned over the buttonhole of a jacket or coat lapel. N Am term **boutonniere** ■ *vt* (**-holes, -holing, -holed**) **1.** **ACCOST SOMEBODY** to compel somebody to listen, allowing no avenue of escape (*informal*) ○ *He buttonholed me outside my office.* **2.** **GIVE SOMETHING BUTTONHOLES** to make buttonholes in something **3.** **SEW WITH BUTTONHOLE STITCH** to sew something with a buttonhole stitch —**buttonholer** *n*

buttonhole stitch *n* a tightly worked looped stitch used for reinforcing buttonholes

buttonhook /bútt'n hŏŏk/ *n* a small hook formerly used for pulling small buttons through buttonholes on tight boots or gloves

buttonmould /bútt'n mōld/ *n* a small piece of plastic, metal, or wood that forms the base of a button covered in fabric or leather

button mushroom *n* an immature unopened mushroom [< its shape]

button nose *n* a small short flattish nose

buttonquail /bútt'n kwayl/ (*plural same* or **-quails**) *n* a small terrestrial bird that has no hind toe and resembles a quail. Native to: southern Europe, Asia, Africa, Australia. Family: Turnicidae.

buttons /bútt'nz/ *n* a pageboy who wears a livery with rows of buttons up the jacket (*archaic informal; takes a singular verb*)

button-through *adj* fastened by a row of buttons from the top to the bottom hem

button tow *n* a ski lift in which the occupant straddles a disc attached to a metal pole suspended from a moving cable

buttonwood /bútt'n wŏŏd/ *n* a mangrove tree that yields button-wood. Native to: American and African tropics. Latin name: *Conocarpus erectus.*

buttress /búttrəss/ *n* **1.** **SUPPORT FOR WALL** a solid structure, usually made of brick or stone, that is built against a wall to support it **2.** **SOMEBODY OR SOMETHING THAT GIVES SUPPORT** somebody or something that acts as a source of support, help, or reinforcement ○ *The constitution is a buttress of our civil rights.* **3.** **PROJECTING ROCK** a large projecting rock mass that appears to support the rock above it **4.** **HOOF PART** the pointed horny rear part of a horse's hoof ■ *vt* (**-tresses, -tressing, -tressed**) **1.** **SUPPORT WALL** to support a wall with a buttress **2.** **SUPPORT OR REINFORCE SOMETHING** to support, help, or reinforce something, especially an argument, analysis, or point of view ○ *He buttressed his views with lengthy quotations from the scriptures.* [14C. < Old French *(ars) bouterez* 'thrusting (arch)' < *bouter* (see BUTT[1])]

butt shaft *n* a blunt-headed arrow used for archery practice [< BUTT[3]]

butt-weld (**butt-welds, butt-welding, butt-welded**) *vt* to weld a joint in which the two pieces are placed end to end rather than overlapped —**butt weld** *n*

butty[1] /bútti, bŏŏtti/ (*plural* **-ties**) *n N England* FOOD same as **sandwich** *n* (sense 1) (*informal*) [Mid-19C. < BUTTER]

butty[2] /bútti/ (*plural* **-ties**) *n regional* a friend, companion, or workmate, especially in a coal mine [Late 18C. Probably < archaic *play booty* 'unite against another player (and share winnings)']

butut /bŏŏt oot/ *n* a subunit of Gambian currency. See table at **currency** [Late 20C. < Wolof]

butyl /byŏŏ tīl/ *n, adj* relating to the group of atoms derived from butane after the loss of a hydrogen atom. Formula: C_4H_9-. [Mid-19C. < BUTYRIC]

butyl acetate *n* CHEM same as **butyl ethanoate**

butyl alcohol *n* CHEM same as **butanol**

butylate /byŏŏti layt/ (**-ates, -ating, -ated**) *vt* to introduce a butyl group or groups into a chemical compound —**butylation** /byŏŏti láysh'n/ *n*

butylated hydroxytoluene /byŏŏti laytəd hī dróksi tóllyoo een/ *n* CHEM full form of **BHT**

butylene /byŏŏti leen/ *n* CHEM same as **butene**

butyl ethanoate /-i thánnō ayt/ *n* a colourless flammable toxic liquid with a fruity odour and three different molecular structures (**isomers**). Use: lacquer solvent. Formula: $C_6H_{12}O_2$.

butyl rubber *n* a synthetic rubber that is extremely resistant to abrasion, tearing, sunlight, and chemical attack. Use: inner tubes, hosepipes, insulation, seals for food jars.

butyraceous /byŏŏtə ráyshəss/ *adj* containing, resembling, or producing butter (*technical*) [Mid-17C. < BUTYRIC]

butyraldehyde /byŏŏtə ráldə hīd/ *n* a colourless flammable liquid. Use: manufacture of solvents, resins, and plasticizers. Formula: C_4H_8O.

butyrate /byŏŏtə rayt/ *n* a salt or ester of butyric acid [Mid-19C. < BUTYRIC]

butyric /byoo tírrik/ *adj* **1.** relating to or containing butanoic acid **2.** relating to or containing butter (*technical*) [Early 19C. < Latin *butyrum* (see BUTTER)]

butyric acid *n* a thick colourless liquid that causes the smell of rancid butter. Use: in flavourings, scents. Formula: C_3H_7COOH.

butyrin /byŏŏtərin/ *n* a colourless liquid ester or oil with three different molecular structures (**isomers**). Source: formed from butanoic acid and glycerol and found in butter. [Early 19C. Blend of BUTYRIC + GLYCERIN]

buxom /búksəm/ *adj* describes a woman with a full figure (*humorous*) [Assumed Old English *(ge)būhsum* 'pliable' < *(ge)būgan* 'to bend' < Germanic] —**buxomly** *adv* —**buxomness** *n*

Buxtehude /bŏŏkstə hŏŏdə/, **Dietrich** (1637?–1707) Danish-born German organist and composer. A prolific composer of sacred music for the organ, he moved to Germany in 1668 and was greatly admired by J. S. Bach and Handel.

Buxton /búkstən/ spa town in the Peak District, Derbyshire, central England, with thermal and chalybeate springs. Population: 19,854 (1991).

buy /bī/ *v* (**buys, buying, bought** /bawt/) **1.** *vti* **ACQUIRE SOMETHING BY PAYMENT** to pay money for something in order to obtain it ○ *They bought me a bike for my birthday.* ○ *People just aren't buying at the moment.* **2.** *vt* **OBTAIN SOMETHING FROM SOMEBODY BY BRIBERY** to obtain information, help, or loyalty from somebody in exchange for money **3.** *vt* **OBTAIN TIME** to obtain more time to reach a desired end by taking strategic action ○ *a manoeuvre that should buy us another week* **4.** *vt* **OBTAIN SOMETHING BY SACRIFICE** to obtain something by sacrificing something else of equivalent value ○ *buy peace with land* **5.** *vi* **BE BUYER FOR COMPANY OR PERSON** to purchase goods on behalf of a company or another person ○ *She buys for a large London store.* **6.** *vt* **BELIEVE SOMETHING** to accept or believe something proposed as true (*informal*) ○ *I don't buy the part about an international conspiracy.* ■ *n* **1.** **SOMETHING BOUGHT** something that you pay money for, considered relative to its worth ○ *a good buy* **2.** **EXCHANGE OF MONEY FOR GOODS** an exchange of money for goods or services [Old English *bycgan* < Germanic] —**buyable** *adj*

SPELLCHECK See *bi-*.

buy back, buy home *vt Malaysia* to buy something and take it home ○ *We bought back pizzas for supper.*
buy in *v* **1.** *vti* PURCHASE SOMETHING IN QUANTITY to purchase something in large quantities, usually in preparation for an expected period of hardship **2.** *vi* PURCHASE SHARES IN COMPANY to purchase shares in a company as the controlling interest **3.** *vi* PAY TO TAKE PART IN SOMETHING to pay in order to take part in or have a share of something **4.** *vt* WITHDRAW ITEM FROM AUCTION to withdraw an item from sale at an auction because it has failed to reach its reserve price
buy into *vt* **1.** PURCHASE SHARES IN COMPANY to purchase an amount of shares in a company **2.** PAY TO PARTICIPATE IN SOMETHING to pay money in order to take part in something ○ *buy into a timeshare* **3.** ACCEPT SOMETHING to accept or believe in a proposition or idea (*informal*) ○ *I don't buy into that 'greed is good' attitude.*
buy off *vt* to bribe somebody in order to prevent something happening or ensure cooperation ○ *They tried to buy off the entire jury.*
buy out *vt* **1.** PAY SOMEBODY TO RELINQUISH INTEREST to pay somebody to relinquish interest in a property or other enterprise ○ *She was bought out by her partners.* **2.** MIL RELEASE SOMEBODY FROM MILITARY SERVICE to pay money to release somebody from military service ○ *He bought himself out of the army and set up a business in London.* **3.** COMM PURCHASE ENTIRE SHARES OF COMPANY to purchase the entire shares of or controlling financial interest in a company or business
buy up *vt* **1.** to purchase all, or all that is available, of a commodity ○ *They've been buying up property in the area.* **2.** to purchase something in great quantity without regard to expense ○ *buying up modern paintings*

buy-back *n* the repurchase of something such as shares, currency, property, or goods, according to a previously made contractual agreement

buydown /bī down/ *n* an advance cash payment on a loan made in order to reduce the interest charge and size of the periodic payment

buyer /bī ər/ *n* **1.** somebody who buys or intends to buy something **2.** somebody whose job is to choose and buy goods for a company or another person

buyer's market *n* a situation in which supply exceeds demand, prices are relatively low, and buyers therefore have an advantage

buy-in *n* commitment to achieving a shared goal ○ *Successful change begins with acquiring employees' buy-in to the change process.*

buyout /bī owt/ *n* **1.** the purchase of a controlling interest in a company ○ *a management buyout* **2.** the purchase of an entire amount or quantity of something

buzz /buz/ *n* **1.** STEADY HUMMING SOUND a steady low humming sound like that of a bee ○ *the low buzz of insects flitting over the flowers* **2.** HUM OF TALK a low murmur of conversation made by a group of people, especially when they are excited or interested in something ○ *a buzz of voices emerging from the living room* **3.** ELECTRONIC HUMMING SOUND the sound made by a buzzer **4.** TELEPHONE CALL a telephone call to somebody (*informal*) **5.** FEELING OF EXCITEMENT a feeling of excitement or satisfaction often linked with a sense of achievement (*informal*) ○ *It gives me a tremendous buzz to hear someone saying the lines that I've written.* **6.** LATEST GOSSIP the latest gossip or information within an industry or a locale (*informal*) ○ *The buzz at the festival was that he'd pick up an award for best director.* **7.** FAD a short-lived interest or enthusiasm (*informal*) **8.** PUBLICITY publicity, or interest generated by publicity (*informal*) ○ *a new book that is generating lots of buzz* **9.** INTOXICATION a feeling of intoxication (*slang*) ■ *v* (**buzzes, buzzing, buzzed**) **1.** *vi* MAKE STEADY HUMMING SOUND to make a steady low humming sound like that of a bee **2.** *vi* BE ANIMATED to be animated by the talk or activity of people ○ *The room was buzzing with excitement.* **3.** *vi* MOVE SPEEDILY to move around speedily and busily ○ *buzzing about in small cars that dodged through traffic* **4.** *vti* WORK BUZZER to activate a buzzer **5.** *vt* LET SOMEBODY INTO BUILDING ELECTRONICALLY to admit somebody to a building by activating an electronic system that controls a door ○ *waiting for them to buzz me in* **6.** *vi* MAKE ELECTRONIC HUMMING SOUND to make an electronic humming noise when activated ○ *When the timer buzzes, turn the oven down.* **7.** *vi* BE EXCITED to be filled with anxious or excited thoughts ○ *My head was buzzing with all the things I'd heard that night.* **8.** *vi* BE RINGING to be filled with a continuous ringing sound, e.g. after being exposed to loud noise ○ *My ears were buzzing after the concert.* **9.** *vt* TELEPHONE SOMEBODY to call somebody on the telephone or on an intercom (*informal*) **10.** *vt* AVIAT FLY LOW OVER PEOPLE OR PLACE to fly an aircraft low over people or buildings, or across the path of other aircraft (*informal*) [14C. An imitation of the sound]
buzz off *vi* to go away (*informal*)

buzzard /búzzərd/ (*plural* **-zards** or *same*) *n* **1.** a large hawk with broad wings and a broad tail. Native to: Europe, Asia, Africa. Genus: *Buteo.* N Am term **buteo** **2.** *N Am* a North American vulture, e.g. the turkey vulture [14C. < Old French *busard*]

buzz bomb *n* MIL same as **V-1**

buzz cut *n N Am* a hairstyle in which the hair is cut very close to the skull with a razor

buzzer /búzzər/ *n* an electronic device that makes a humming or buzzing sound when activated

buzz saw *n N Am* same as **circular saw**

buzzword /búz wurd/ *n* a fashionable word or concept, often associated with a specific group of people and not understood by outsiders (*informal*) ○ *the latest media buzzword*

b.v. *abbr* ACCT book value

B vitamin *n* a water-soluble vitamin belonging to a group that is essential to the working of some enzymes. The B vitamins are B1 thiamine, B2 riboflavin, B6 pyridoxine, B12 cobalamin, B5 pantothenic acid, folic acid, and biotin.

BVM *abbr* Blessed Virgin Mary [Latin *Beata Virgo Maria*]

bw *abbr* **1.** black-and-white **2.** ONLINE Botswana (*used in Internet addresses*) See table at **domain name**

BW *abbr* **1.** bacteriological warfare **2.** biological warfare **3.** *also* **B/W** black-and-white

bwana /bwáanə/ *n E Africa* used as a respectful term of address for a man [Late 19C. < Kiswahili]

BWG *n* a numerical system for specifying the diameter of metal rods. Full form **Birmingham Wire Gauge**

BWI *abbr* **1.** Baltimore-Washington International Airport **2.** British West Indies

BWR *abbr* INDUST boiling-water reactor

BWV *abbr* MUSIC Bach Werke-Verzeichnis (*used before numbers identifying the works of J. S. Bach*)

by[1] /bī/ CORE MEANING: a grammatical word expressing a spatial relationship, indicating that somebody or something is beside or close to somebody or something else ○ (prep) *standing by the window* ○ (adv) *A large crowd of shoppers stood by watching.*
1. *prep, adv* PAST SOMEBODY OR SOMETHING IN SPACE indicates movement past somebody or something, sometimes including a brief stop (*used following a verb expressing movement*) ○ *He drove by his apartment building.* ○ *The waiter strolled by, pouring us some more coffee.* **2.** *prep* ALONG next to or along something **3.** *prep* THROUGH passing through something ○ *entering by the back door* **4.** *prep* BEFORE THAT TIME happening or required at or before a particular time ○ *reservations required by Sunday* **5.** *prep* DURING happening during a particular time period ○ *By day he worked in a canning factory.* **6.** *prep* IN MEASURES OF at a rate based on a particular measure such as time, weight, or volume ○ *sold by weight* **7.** *prep* MATHS INDICATES FACTOR OR DIVISOR used in multiplication and division to indicate a number or quantity being multiplied, or to indicate the number or quantity that divides another ○ *What is 144 divided by 12?* **8.** *prep* MEASURE INDICATES DIMENSIONS used between the measurements of the dimensions of an object, expressing area or volume ○ *2 metres by 3* **9.** *prep* MEASURE DIFFERING IN AMOUNT OF used to indicate an amount, extent, or rate at which something increases, decreases, or differs ○ *Tax rates are to be cut by 0.25%.* **10.** *prep* MEASURE INDICATES DIRECTION used to indicate a direction ○ *north by northwest* **11.** *prep* IN AMOUNTS OF PARTICULAR SIZE in groups or amounts of a particular size ○ *Visitors arrived by the truckload.* **12.** *prep* AFTER SAME THING used to link two identical words to indicate a progression or sequence ○ *One by one we told our stories.* ○ *You can see an improvement day by day.* **13.** *prep* INDICATES CAUSE used to indicate the person or thing performing an action or causing a situation or reaction (*used following a passive verb*) ○ *He was hit by a ball.* **14.** *prep* INDICATES CREATOR, AUTHOR, OR ARTIST used to indicate the person who wrote or created something such as a written piece or work of art ○ *written by A. A. Milne* **15.** *prep* USING METHOD OR MEDIUM used to indicate the particular mode, method, or action through which something occurs or is done ○ *travelling by ocean liner* ○ *She earns a living by playing the harp.* **16.** *prep* INDICATES MEANS used to indicate the action used to achieve something (*followed by a gerund*) ○ *The key to attracting banks to small locales is by attracting more businesses.* **17.** *prep* IN PARTICULAR MANNER with, in, or through a particular manner of doing something ○ *used by permission of the author* **18.** *prep* ACCORDING TO UNCHANGING QUALITY in terms of a particular attribute or function ○ *a teacher by profession and a learner by nature* **19.** *prep* IN COMPLIANCE WITH in order to comply with something, especially the law ○ *By law, patients must have access to their records.* **20.** *prep* AT PARTICULAR PART at a particular part of something, e.g. a hand or corner ○ *held the dancer by the waist* **21.** *adv* IN NAME OF SOMETHING SACRED used to indicate something considered holy when making a solemn oath or promise ○ *By all that is sacred, I ask you to stop.* **22.** *adv* AWAY OR ASIDE into a place for safekeeping for use later ○ *I spent some of the money and put some by for hard times.* **23.** *adv Scotland* PAST over and done with [Old English *bī* < Germanic] ◇ **by and by** after a while (*literary*) ◇ **by the by, by the bye** used to introduce a question or piece of information that is not connected with the subject being discussed

SPELLCHECK See *bi-*.

by[2] *abbr* ONLINE Belarus (*used in Internet addresses*) See table at **domain name**

by-, bye- *prefix* **1.** secondary ○ *byroad* ○ *by-product* **2.** past ○ *bygone* [< BY[1]]

BYAM *abbr* ONLINE between you and me (*used in e-mails or text messages*)

Byatt /bī ət/, **Dame A. S.** (*b.* 1936) British novelist and academic. Her novels include *The Virgin in the Garden* (1978), and the Booker Prize-winning *Possession* (1990). She is the sister of the novelist Margaret Drabble. Full name **Byatt, Dame Antonia Susan.** Born **Drabble, Antonia Susan**

> 'Motherhood meant I have written four fewer books, but I know more about life.'
> [Dame A. S. Byatt, *Sunday Times*; 21 October 1990]

by-bidder *n* somebody who bids at an auction to raise the price —**by-bidding** *n*

Byblos /bíbbləss/ ancient Phoenician city, near modern-day Beirut, Lebanon, on the Mediterranean Sea. It was the principal city of Phoenicia in the second millennium BC, and an important source of papyrus.

by-blow *n* an illegitimate child (*dated*)

by-catch /bī kach/ *n* fish that are caught unintentionally in addition to the required species

~~**bycicle**~~ incorrect spelling of **bicycle**

bye[1] /bī/ *n* **1.** AUTOMATIC ADVANCE TO NEXT ROUND the right to proceed to the next round of a competition without contesting the present round, often through non-appearance of an opponent **2.** INFORMAL MATCH in golf, an informal match contested over remaining holes, once the main competition is over **3.** EXTRA RUN WITHOUT HITTING BALL in cricket, a run scored off a ball that has not been hit by a batsman, awarded to the team as a whole rather than to an individual batsman [Mid-16C. Variant of BY[1]]

bye[2] /bī/ *interj* same as **goodbye** (*informal*) [Early 18C. Shortening]

SPELLCHECK See *bi-*.

bye- *prefix* another spelling of **by-**

SPELLCHECK See *bi-*.

bye-bye[1] *interj* same as **goodbye** (*informal*) [Child's variant]

bye-bye[2] *n N Am* same as **bye-byes**

bye-byes *n* bed or sleep (*baby talk*) N Am term **bye-bye**[2] [< a refrain used in lullabies]

by-election, **bye-election** *n* an election held between official general or local elections to fill a vacant seat, e.g. to replace a member of parliament or a local councillor who has died or resigned

Byelorussia /byéllō rúshə/ *n* former name for **Belarus** —**Byelorussian** *n*, *adj*

by-form *n* a slightly changed form of a word that begins to be used at a later date

bygone /bī́ gon/ *adj* existing or having happened a long time ago ○ *reminders of a bygone age* ▪ *n* something that happened, existed, or was manufactured a long time ago (*often used in the plural*) ◇ **let bygones be bygones** to forgive past offences or resentments

byke *n*, *vi* another spelling of **bike**[2]

BYKT *abbr* ONLINE but you know/knew that (*used in e-mails or text messages*)

bylaw /bī́ law/ *n* **1.** LOCAL LAW a law made by a local authority that applies only in the area that the authority governs **2.** INTERNAL RULE a law or regulation that governs the internal affairs of a company or other organization ○ *company bylaws* **3.** SUBSIDIARY LAW a secondary law [13C. Probably < Old Norse *býlagu* 'town law' < *býr* 'town' + *lagu* 'law']

byline /bī́ līn/ *n* **1.** the name of the author of an article in a newspaper or magazine, printed at the head of the article **2.** SOCCER same as **goal line** ▪ *vt* (**-lines, -lining, -lined**) to write an article that will include a byline

byname /bī́ naym/ *n* same as **nickname**

BYO *n* ANZ a restaurant, party, or event to which guests bring their own alcoholic beverages. Full form **bring your own**

BYOB *abbr* bring your own bottle (*used on party invitations*)

bypass /bī́ paass/ *n* **1.** ROAD ROUND PLACE a road built round a town or city to keep through traffic away from the centre **2.** SURG OPERATION TO REROUTE BLOOD a surgical operation to redirect the blood, usually via a grafted blood vessel, carried out when the existing blood vessel has become blocked ○ *a heart bypass* **3.** MED NEW ROUTE FOR BLOOD a new route for the blood, created by a bypass operation **4.** ELEC ENG same as **shunt** *n* (sense 4) **5.** UTIL EMERGENCY CHANNEL a channel such as a pipe carrying gas or water that is brought into use when the main channel is blocked ▪ *vt* (**-passes, -passing, -passed**) **1.** GO ROUND PLACE to avoid a place by travelling round it **2.** ROADS BUILD ROAD ROUND PLACE to build a bypass round a town or city **3.** AVOID SOMETHING to avoid an obstacle, obstruction, or problem by using an alternative route or method **4.** AVOID STANDARD PROCEDURE to ignore or avoid a standard procedure for doing something, or ignore somebody who is usually consulted

bypath /bī́ paath/ *n* a rarely used path, especially in the country

by-play *n* matters of subsidiary importance or interest that take place while the main action is going on, e.g. in a stage play

by-product *n* **1.** something produced as a secondary result of the manufacture or production of something else, often something useful or commercially valuable **2.** something that happens as an incidental result of something else

Byrd /burd/, **William** (1543–1623) English composer. He was appointed organist for the Chapel Royal in 1572. His work includes three Latin masses (1589–91), madrigals, and instrumental pieces.

byre /bīr/ *n regional* AGRIC same as **cowshed** [Old English *byre*, origin ?]

byroad /bī́ rōd/ *n* a side road carrying a small volume of traffic

Byron, Cape /bī́rən/ cape in northeastern New South Wales, Australia, near the town of Byron Bay. It is the most easterly point on the Australian mainland.

AKG London

Lord Byron

Byron /bī́rən/, **George Gordon Noel, 6th Baron Byron** (1788–1824) British poet. He was an influential figure of the Romantic movement. His major works include *Childe Harold's Pilgrimage* (1812–18) and the long satirical poem *Don Juan* (1819–24). After scandalizing London with his promiscuity, Lord Byron lived abroad, largely in Italy, and died aiding the Greeks in their revolt against the Turks. Known as **Lord Byron**

'Mad, bad, and dangerous to know.'
[Charlotte Lamb, *Journal*; 1812]

Byron Bay tourist resort in northeastern New South Wales, Australia. Population: 5,007 (1991).

Byronic /bī rónnik/ *adj* **1.** relating to or characteristic of Lord Byron or his poetry **2.** describes a brooding and solitary man who seems capable of great passion and suffering

byssi MARINE BIOL, TEXTILES plural of **byssus**

byssinosis /bíssi nṓssiss/ *n* a respiratory disease caused by prolonged inhalation of dust from textile fibres, marked by coughing, wheezing, shortness of breath, and permanent lung damage [Late 19C. < Latin *byssinus* 'of fine linen' < *byssus* (see BYSSUS)]

byssus /bíssəss/ (*plural* **-suses** or **-si** /-sī/) *n* **1.** a mass of strong silky threads that molluscs such as mussels use to attach themselves to rocks and other hard surfaces **2.** fine linen used by the ancient Egyptians to wrap mummies [14C. Via Latin, 'fine linen' < Greek *bussos* < Semitic]

bystander /bī́ standər/ *n* somebody who observes but is not involved in something

bystander effect *n* the reluctance of members of a crowd to intervene in an incident they are witnessing

byte /bīt/ *n* **1.** a group of eight bits of computer information, representing a unit of data such as a number or letter **2.** a unit of computer memory equal to that needed to store a single character [Mid-20C. Probably alteration of BIT[3] after BITE 'morsel', or acronym < *binary digit eight*]

byway /bī́ way/ *n* **1.** a small side road not regularly used by people or traffic **2.** the less important aspects of a particular pursuit or field of knowledge ○ *the byways of numismatics*

byword /bī́ wurd/ *n* **1.** WELL-KNOWN EXAMPLE somebody or something that is well known for a particular quality ○ *The magazine became a byword for cutting-edge style.* **2.** CATCH PHRASE a word or phrase that is in common use at a particular time **3.** PROVERB a proverb in common use at a specific place or time or among a group [Old English *bīwyrde* 'proverb', translation of Latin *proverbium*]

byzantine /bī zán tīn, -teen, bízz'n tīn, -teen/ *adj* **1.** extremely complex or intricate **2.** marked by deviousness or scheming [Mid-20C. < BYZANTINE]

Byzantine /bī zán tīn, -teen, bízz'n tīn, -teen/ *adj* **1.** ANCIENT HIST OF BYZANTIUM relating to the ancient city of Byzantium **2.** HIST OF EASTERN ROMAN EMPIRE relating to the eastern part of the late Roman Empire (**Byzantine Empire**) **3.** ART, ARCHIT OF BYZANTINE ART OR ARCHITECTURE relating to or typical of the colourful religious art or the ornate architecture developed under the Byzantine Empire **4.** CHR OF EASTERN ORTHODOX CHURCH relating to the Eastern Orthodox Church and its traditions ▪ *n* ANCIENT HIST SOMEBODY FROM BYZANTIUM somebody who came from the ancient city of Byzantium or the Byzantine Empire [Late 16C. < Latin *Byzantinus* < *Byzantium* < Greek *Buzantion*]

Byzantine Church *n* CHR same as **Orthodox Church** (sense 1)

Byzantine Empire *n* the eastern part of the late Roman Empire, from AD 330 to 1453, when its capital Constantinople fell to the Ottoman Turks. It was the centre of Orthodox Christianity.

Byzantium /bī zánti əm, bi-, bī zánshi əm, bi-/ ancient Greek city on the site of modern-day Istanbul, conquered by the Romans in AD 196, and rebuilt in AD 330 by Constantine the Great, who renamed it Constantinople. As the capital of the Byzantine Empire (until 1453), it was the largest city in the Christian world.

bz *abbr* ONLINE Belize (*used in Internet addresses*) See table at **domain name**

c¹ /see/ (*plural* **c's**), **C** (*plural* **C's** or **Cs**) *n* **1.** 3RD LETTER OF ENGLISH ALPHABET the third letter of the English alphabet, representing a consonant sound **2.** LETTER 'C' WRITTEN a written representation of the letter 'c' **3.** ROMAN 100 the Roman numeral for 100

c² *symbol* **1.** CHEM concentration **2.** PHYS the speed of light in a vacuum **3.** CHESS used to refer to the third vertical row of squares from the left on a chessboard

c³ *abbr* **1.** cancelled **2.** VERTEB canine **3.** MEASURE carat **4.** BUSINESS carbon (paper) **5.** HOUSEHOLD carton **6.** LAW case **7.** SPORTS catcher **8.** SPORTS caught by **9.** FIN cedi **10.** FIN cent **11.** FIN centavo **12.** MEASURE centi- **13.** FIN centime **14.** MEASURE centimetre **15.** centre **16.** HIST century **17.** PUBL chapter **18.** PHYS charm **19.** CHR church **20.** HIST circa (*used before dates*) **21.** ELEC circuit **22.** MATHS circumference **23.** clockwise **24.** METEOROL cloudy **25.** SCI coefficient **26.** MED cold **27.** ANAT colon **28.** colour **29.** ZOOL colt **30.** MATHS constant **31.** INTERNAT REL consul **32.** MUSIC contralto **33.** COMMUNICATION copy **34.** LAW copyright **35.** MIL corps **36.** FIN cost **37.** MEASURE cubic **38.** PHYS curie

C¹ (*plural* **C's** or **Cs**) *n* **1.** 'C'-SHAPED OBJECT something shaped like a letter 'C' **2.** MUSIC 1ST NOTE IN C MAJOR the first note of a scale in C major **3.** MUSIC SOMETHING THAT PRODUCES C a string, key, or pipe tuned to produce the note C **4.** MUSIC SCALE BEGINNING ON C a scale or key that starts on the note C **5.** MUSIC WRITTEN SYMBOL OF C a graphic representation of the tone of C **6.** EDUC 3RD HIGHEST GRADE the third highest grade in a series, e.g. an average grade for academic work **7.** COMPUT PROGRAMMING LANGUAGE a high-level computer programming language **8.** DRUGS same as **cocaine** (*slang*) ◇ **the big C** cancer (*slang*)

C² *symbol* **1.** ELEC ENG capacitance **2.** CHEM ELEM carbon **3.** BIOCHEM cytosine **4.** PHYS heat capacity

C³ *abbr* **1.** MAPS cape **2.** BUILDINGS castle **3.** CHR Catholic **4.** MEASURE Celsius **5.** MEASURE centigrade **6.** HIST century **7.** POL Chancellor **8.** PHYS charm **9.** MANAGEMT chief **10.** MAPS city **11.** EDUC College **12.** Companion **13.** POL Congress **14.** POL Conservative **15.** MIL corps **16.** ELEC coulomb **17.** SPORTS court **18.** ONLINE see (*used in e-mails or text messages*)

C++ /see pluss plúss/ *n* an object-oriented version of the programming language C, developed in the 1980s

C1 (*plural* **C1s**) *n* in the market research system that classifies people according to their occupation, somebody in a clerical or junior management position

C2 (*plural* **C2s**) *n* in the market research system that classifies people according to their occupation, somebody in a skilled manual job

C2B *abbr* E-COMMERCE consumer-to-business

ca *abbr* Canada (*used in Internet addresses*) See table at **domain name**

Ca *symbol* CHEM ELEM calcium

CA *abbr* **1.** MAIL California **2.** GEOG Central America **3.** GEOG Central American **4.** ONLINE certificate authority (*used in e-mails*) **5.** ACCT chartered accountant **6.** ACCT chief accountant **7.** chronological age **8.** INTERNAT REL consular agent **9.** COMM Consumers' Association

ca. *abbr* HIST circa (*used before dates*)

C/A *abbr* **1.** FIN capital account **2.** FIN credit account **3.** *also* **c/a** BANKING current account

CAA *abbr* AVIAT Civil Aviation Authority

CAAT *abbr* E-COMMERCE certificate authority administration tool

cab /kab/ *n* **1.** CARS same as **taxi** **2.** the part of a large vehicle such as a lorry, a locomotive, or a large crane where the driver or operator sits **3.** a lightweight horse-drawn carriage formerly used for public hire [Early 19C. Shortening of CABRIOLET] ◇ **the first cab off the rank** *Aus* the first to act (*informal*)

CAB *abbr* **1.** Citizens' Advice Bureau **2.** Civil Aeronautics Board

cabal /kə bál/ *n* **1.** GROUP OF PLOTTERS a group of conspirators or plotters, particularly one formed for political purposes **2.** SECRET PLOT a secret plot or conspiracy, especially a political one **3.** CLIQUE an exclusive group of people ■ *vi* (**-bals, -balling, -balled**) CONSPIRE AS GROUP to form a group and plot together against somebody or something [Early 17C. Via French *cabale* < medieval Latin *cab(b)ala* 'secret teaching' (see KABBALAH)]

Cabal /kə bál/ *n* a group of ministers in the court of the English king Charles II, who governed the country between 1667 and 1673. Their surnames were Clifford, Arlington, Buckingham, Ashley, and Lauderdale. [Mid-17C. Acronym < the initials of their names, after CABAL]

Cabala *n* JUDAISM another spelling of **Kabbalah**

cabaletta /kábbə léttə/ *n* **1.** a short simple aria in 19th-century Italian opera, usually found in conjunction with a preceding cavatina **2.** the final section of an aria or duet, typically with a lively rhythm [Mid-19C. < Italian, 'little stanza' < Latin *copula* 'link']

cabalistic /kábbə lístik/, **cabbalistic** *adj* mysterious or esoteric ○ *the cabalistic teachings of the alchemists*

Caballé /kə bál yay, káb ə yáy/, **Montserrat** (*b.* 1933) Spanish soprano, associated especially with the operas of Donizetti and Verdi

caballero /kábbə láirō, kább'l yáirō/ (*plural* **-ros**) *n* **1.** in Spain or Spanish-speaking countries, a knight, cavalier, or gentleman **2.** *Southwest US* a horseman [Mid-19C. Via Spanish < late Latin *caballarius* < Latin *caballus* 'horse']

cabaret /kábbə ray/ *n* **1.** a floor show consisting of singing, dancing, and comic acts, performed in a restaurant, club, or bar **2.** a restaurant, club, or bar offering a cabaret [Mid-17C. Via French < Old French dialect *camberet* 'little room' < Latin *camera* 'room' (see CAMERA)]

cabbage

cabbage /kábbij/ *n* **1.** FOOD LEAVES AS FOOD a roundish head of closely layered green, white, or red leaves, eaten raw or cooked as a vegetable **2.** PLANTS EDIBLE

PLANT WITH CLOSELY LAYERED LEAVES a short-stemmed plant that produces cabbage. Latin name: *Brassica oleracea* var. capitata. **3.** PLANTS PLANT LIKE CABBAGE a plant related to cabbage, e.g. Chinese cabbage **4.** FOOD EDIBLE PALM BUD the bud of a number of species of palm, eaten as a vegetable **5.** OFFENSIVE TERM a highly offensive term for somebody who has no mental awareness or mental activity, usually as a result of brain injury, and who is completely dependent on other people **6.** BORING PERSON a physically and mentally inactive person (*informal insult*) [15C. < Old French *caboche*, variant of *caboce* 'head'] —**cabbagy** *adj*

cabbage butterfly *n* ANZ, N Am a light-colored butterfly whose larvae (**cabbageworms**) feed on the leaves of cabbages and related plants. Family: Pieridae. UK term **cabbage white**

cabbage lettuce *n* a variety of lettuce that has a rounded head like a cabbage

cabbage palm *n* **1.** a palm tree whose leaf buds resemble cabbages and are eaten as a vegetable. Latin name: *Roystonea oleracea*. **2.** a palm or similar plant resembling a cabbage

cabbage palmetto *n* a palm tree with edible leaf buds and fan-shaped leaves that are used in Christian celebrations on Palm Sunday. Native to: southeastern United States, Bahamas. Latin name: *Sabal palmetto*.

cabbage root fly *n* a fly whose larvae feed on cabbages and other plants of the cabbage family such as broccoli, cauliflowers, and Brussels sprouts. Latin name: *Delia radicum*.

cabbage rose *n* a hybrid bush rose grown in gardens. Flowers: fragrant, double-petalled. Latin name: *Rosa centifolia*.

cabbage tree *n* **1.** a small tree with a top that resembles that of a palm tree. Native to: New Zealand. Latin name: *Cordyline australis*. **2.** a large palm tree. Native to: coast of eastern Australia. Latin name: *Livistona australis*.

cabbage white *n* UK a light-coloured butterfly whose larvae feed on the leaves of cabbages and related plants. Family: Pieridae. ANZ, N Am term **cabbage butterfly**

cabbageworm /kábbij wurm/ *n* a larva that feeds on cabbages and related plants, especially the larva of the cabbage white butterfly

Cabbala *n* JUDAISM another spelling of **Kabbalah**

cabbalistic *adj* another spelling of **cabalistic**

cabby /kábbi/ (*plural* **-bies**), **cabbie** *n* a driver of a taxi (*informal*)

caber /káybər/ *n* a long thick wooden pole thrown end over end in an event (**tossing the caber**) in Scottish Highland Games [Early 16C. < Gaelic *cabar* 'pole']

Cabernet Sauvignon /kábbər nay sóvin yon/ *n* **1.** a dry red wine made from a variety of black grape originally grown in southwestern France **2.** a black grape variety. Use: winemaking. [< French]

cabin /kábbin/ *n* **1.** BUILDINGS WOODEN HUT a small simple house, especially one made of wood in forest or mountain areas **2.** TRAVEL SMALL ROOM ON SHIP a small room on a boat or ship, where people live or sleep **3.** NAUT SHELTER ON SMALL BOAT a covered compartment that houses the wheel on a small boat, used for shelter in bad weather and often as a living space **4.** TRANSP same as **cab** (sense 2) **5.** AVIAT AEROPLANE INTERIOR the part of a passenger aeroplane where the

passengers sit, or the part of a cargo aeroplane where the cargo is carried **6.** AEROSP **CREW QUARTERS ON SPACECRAFT** the part of a spacecraft where the crew work, live, or sleep **7.** NAVY **ROOM ON SHIP** the commanding officer's room on a warship **8.** RAIL same as **signal box** ■ *vti* (**-ins**, **-ining**, **-ined**) KEEP SOMEBODY CONFINED to confine somebody in a small enclosed space, or live confined in this way (*literary*; *usually passive*) [14C. Via Old French *cabane* < late Latin *capanna* 'hut']

CULTURAL NOTE *Uncle Tom's Cabin*, a novel (1852) by US writer Harriet Beecher Stowe. Set in the American South, it is the story of an enslaved African American man, Uncle Tom, who is sold by his kindly owners and eventually dies at the hands of a vicious new master named Simon Legree. Such was this abolitionist novel's influence that it was described as one of the causes of the American Civil War.

cabin boy *n* a boy who acted as a servant on board a sailing ship, waiting on officers and passengers (*dated*)

cabin class *n* a class of accommodation on some passenger ships that is lower than first class and higher than tourist class ■ *adj*, *adv* in cabin class on a passenger ship

cabin crew *n* the staff on a passenger aircraft whose job is to attend to passengers

cabin cruiser *n* a large, powerful motor boat with varying amounts of living space

Cabinda /kə beéndə/ Angolan exclave bounded by the Republic of Congo to the north and the Democratic Republic of Congo to the south. Capital: Cabinda. Population: 152,100 (1992). Area: 7,270 sq. km/2,807 sq. mi.

cabinet /kábbinət/ *n* **1.** PIECE OF FURNITURE an upright piece of furniture usually made of wood and consisting of drawers, shelves, and compartments for storing or displaying objects **2.** TV OR RADIO COVERING the outer casing of a television or stereo system, especially the wooden casing of an old-fashioned model **3.** *also* **Cabinet** GOV GROUP OF SENIOR MINISTERS a group of senior government ministers chosen by a prime minister to act as the executive decision-making body of the country (*takes a singular or plural verb*) **4.** PRIVATE ROOM a small private room (*archaic*) ■ *adj* **1.** FOR SMALL ROOM describes furniture and other items intended for a small room or a room in a private home **2.** FOR DISPLAY IN CABINET small or decorative enough to be displayed in a cabinet [Mid-16C. < French, 'small room' < Old Picard *cabine* 'room for gambling']

cabinetmaker /kábbinət maykər/ *n* a skilled worker who specializes in making high-quality furniture —**cabinetmaking** *n*

cabinet minister *n* in Britain, Canada, and some other countries, a senior government minister who is in a cabinet

cabinetwork /kábbinət wurk/, **cabinetry** /kábbinətri/ *n* wooden furniture made to a high standard by a cabinetmaker

cabin fever *n* an emotional condition, marked by irritability, distress, or depression, caused by prolonged isolation or confined living quarters (*informal*)

cable /káyb'l/ *n* **1.** STRONG ROPE OR WIRE a strong thick rope or steel wire, used for lifting, pulling, towing, or securing things **2.** ELEC BUNDLE OF ELECTRICAL WIRES a group of wires for transmitting electrical signals that are bound together and usually have shared or common insulation **3.** NAUT MOORING ROPE OR CHAIN a rope or chain attached to an anchor or used for mooring a ship **4.** TELECOM OVERSEAS TELEGRAM a telegram originally sent by undersea cable, now usually by telephone, radio, or satellite **5.** MEDIA same as **cable television 6.** HANDICRAFT same as **cable stitch** ■ *v* (**-bles**, **-bling**, **-bled**) **1.** *vti* SEND TELEGRAM to send somebody a telegram **2.** *vt* TELECOM SEND SOMETHING VIA TELEGRAM to send something such as money or information to somebody in a distant place by sending a telegram **3.** *vt* FASTEN OR FIT SOMETHING WITH CABLES to fasten something with cables, or fit cables to something **4.** *vt* TELECOM SUPPLY PLACE WITH CABLE TV to connect a building or area to a cable telecommunications network [Pre-12C. Via Anglo-

Norman, Old N French < late Latin *capulum* 'halter' < Latin *capere* 'seize'] —**cabler** *n* —**cabling** *n*

cable-access *adj US* showing programmes that are made locally and often of local interest only, as opposed to commercially produced material ○ *a cable-access channel*

Barnaby's
cable car

cable car *n* **1.** a compartment or cabin suspended from an overhead cable, used to transport passengers up and down steep hills or across valleys **2.** a car on a cable railway

cablecast /káyb'l kaast/ *n* a broadcast over a cable television network [Late 20C. < CABLE + *-cast* < BROAD-CAST] —**cablecaster** *n* —**cablecasting** *n*

cablegram /káyb'l gram/ *n* TELECOM same as **cable** *n* (sense 4)

cable-laid *adj* describes thick ropes made of three thinner ropes, each with three strands, twisted together anticlockwise

cable modem *n* a high-speed modem enabling a computer to connect to the Internet via a cable television network

cable railway *n* a hillside railway consisting of a track along which cars are pulled by a moving cable that is operated by a stationary engine

cable release *n* a cable fitted with a control button and attached to a camera in order to take photographs without shaking the camera, e.g. on long exposures

cable-stayed bridge *n* a suspension bridge with the cables that support the deck connected directly to the bridge's piers rather than to suspenders

cable stitch *n* a knitting stitch that produces a pattern resembling twisted rope

cablet /káyblət/ *n* a cable-laid rope that has a circumference of less than 25 cm/10 in

cable television, **cablevision** /káyb'l vizh'n/, **cable** *n* a television system in which signals are sent to a central antenna and then transmitted by cable to subscribers rather than broadcast

cableway /káyb'l way/ *n* a transportation system consisting of an overhead cable from which are suspended cars or containers

cabochon /kábbə shon/ *n* **1.** a highly polished rounded unfaceted gem **2.** the gem-cutting style that results in a cabochon [Mid-16C. < French, 'little head' < Old French *caboche* 'head'] —**cabochon** *adj*, *adv*

Caboclo /kə bóokloo, -lō/, **caboclo** *n* somebody descended from one or more of the indigenous peoples of Brazil especially a Brazilian [Early 19C. < Brazilian Portuguese]

caboodle /kə boód'l/ [Late 19C. Probably alteration of BOODLE] ◇ **the whole caboodle** all the people or things in question (*slang*)

Caboolture /kə boólchər/ town in southeastern Queensland, Australia, north of Brisbane. It is a fruit-growing and dairy-farming centre. Population: 12,738 (1991).

caboose /kə booss/ *n* **1.** NAUT SHIP'S GALLEY a kitchen on the deck of a boat (*archaic*) **2.** NAUT GALLEY HOUSING the structure on a boat's deck that houses the galley (*archaic*) **3.** *N Am* RAIL GUARD'S VAN the guard's van on a freight train, with eating and sleeping facilities for the train crew. Most freight trains no longer have a caboose. [Mid-18C. < Dutch *cabuyse*]

Cabot /kábbət/, **John** (1450?–99?) Italian explorer. He

made the first recorded contact (1497) with North America after the Vikings. Born Giovanni Caboto

Cabot, **Sebastian** (1476?–1557) Italian-born English navigator and cartographer. He made expeditions to North and South America (1508–09, 1525–28) for Spain and England and published a world map (1544).

cabotage /kábbə taazh, -tij/ *n* **1.** trade, shipping, or navigation that takes place in coastal waters within the boundaries of a single country **2.** the right of a country to operate internal traffic, especially air traffic, using its own carriers and not those of other countries [Mid-19C. < French < *caboter* 'coast along' < Spanish *cabo* 'cape, headland' < Latin *caput* 'head']

caboteur /kábbə túr/ *n Can* a coastal trading ship or boat, especially one plying the Gulf of St Lawrence and the St Lawrence River (*dated*) [< French < *caboter* (see CABOTAGE)]

Cabral /kə braál/, **Pedro Álvares** (1460?–1526?) Portuguese explorer. He was the first European to visit present-day Bahia, Brazil, and declared it a Portuguese territory.

cabriole /kábbri ōl/ *n* **1.** a curving furniture leg tapering into a decorative foot, popular in the early 18th century and used in Chippendale furniture **2.** a ballet movement in which the dancer leaps into the air with one leg outstretched sideways and the other beating against it [Late 18C. < French, 'leap' < *cabrioler*, variant of *caprioler* 'to caper']

cabriolet /kábbri ə lay/ *n* **1.** a two-door convertible car **2.** a two-wheeled, two-seater, horse-drawn carriage with a folding roof [Mid-18C. < French < *cabrioler* 'to caper'; from the bouncing motion of a horse-drawn vehicle]

cabstand /káb stand/ *n US* TRANSP same as **taxi rank**

cac- *prefix* same as **caco-** (*used before vowels*)

cacao /kə káy ō, -kaá ō, -ków/ (*plural* **-os** *or* same) *n* **1.** a dried fatty seed. Use: source of cocoa, chocolate, and other foods and products. **2.** a tropical American evergreen tree with fleshy pods containing cacao seeds. Latin name: *Theobroma cacao*. **3.** INDUST same as **cocoa butter** [Mid-16C. < Spanish < Nahuatl *cacauatl* 'cacao tree']

cacao bean *n* FOOD same as **cocoa bean**

cacao butter *n* INDUST same as **cocoa butter**

cacciatore /kácha táwri/ *adj* cooked with mushrooms, tomatoes, and herbs (*usually used after nouns*) ○ *chicken cacciatore* [Mid-20C. < Italian, 'hunter'; because originally used of a sauce for game]

cachaca /kə shaássə/ *n* a Brazilian rum made from sugar cane

cachalot /káshə lot/ *n* MARINE BIOL same as **sperm whale** [Mid-18C. Via French < Spanish or Portuguese *cachalote*]

cache /kash/ *n* **1.** HIDDEN SUPPLY a hidden store of things, especially weapons or valuables **2.** SECRET PLACE FOR HIDING THINGS a secret place where a store of things is kept hidden **3.** COMPUT MEMORY FOR COMPUTER DATA an area of high-speed computer memory used for temporary storage of frequently used data ■ *vt* (**caches**, **caching**, **cached**) **1.** HIDE SUPPLY OF THINGS to store a hidden supply of things, especially weapons or valuables, in a secret place **2.** COMPUT HOLD DATA IN MEMORY to store data in a cache [Late 18C. < French < *cacher* 'press']

SPELLCHECK cache or **cash**? Do not confuse the spelling of *cache* and *cash*, which sound similar. *Cache* can be used as a noun or verb, referring to a secret hidden supply or to an area of computer memory, as in *an arms cache*, *cached data*. The word *cash*, which is much more frequent in general usage, can also be used as a noun or verb. As a noun it denotes money in the form of coins and banknotes (as in *paid in cash*); as a verb it means 'exchange for cash' (as in *cash a cheque*).

cachectic /kə kéktik, ka-/ *adj* affected by or relating to cachexia [Early 17C. < Greek *kakhektikos*, related to *kakhexia* (see CACHEXIA)]

cache memory *n* COMPUT same as **cache** *n* (sense 3)

cachepot /kásh pō, -pot/ *n* a decorative container for a flowerpot [Late 19C. < French, 'hide pot']

cachet /kásh ay/ *n* **1.** QUALITY THAT ATTRACTS ADMIRATION a quality of distinction and style that people admire and approve of **2.** OFFICIAL MARK an official seal or stamp on a letter or other document **3.** STAMPS COMMEMORATIVE POSTMARK a commemorative mark

stamped on mail to mark an event **4.** STAMPS **COL-LECTOR'S MARK** a small mark made on the back of a postage stamp by a stamp collector **5.** PHARM **EDIBLE MEDICINE SACHET** an edible capsule formerly used for containing unpleasant-tasting medicine [Early 17C. < French, 'stamp' < Old French *cacher* 'press']

cachexia /kə kéksi ə, ka-/ *n* a condition marked by loss of appetite, weight loss, muscle wastage, and general mental and physical debilitation. It is associated with the advanced stage of diseases such as cancer. [Mid-16C. Via French or late Latin < Greek *kakhexia* < *kakos* 'bad' + *hexis* 'habit']

cachinnate /káki nayt/ (**-nates, -nating, -nated**) *vi* to laugh convulsively and loudly (*literary*) [Early 19C. < Latin *cachinnat-*, past participle of *cachinnare*, an imitation of the sound] —**cachinnation** /káki náysh'n/ *n* —**cachinnator** *n*

cachou /ka shoó, káshoo/ *n* **1.** a perfumed pastille that sweetens the breath **2.** CHEM same as **catechu** [Late 16C. Via French < Malayalam *kaccu*]

cachucha /kə choóchə/ *n* **1.** a lively Andalusian dance in 3/4 time for a solo dancer with castanets **2.** the music for a cachucha [Mid-19C. < Spanish]

cacique /kə seék/ *n* **1.** NATIVE AMERICAN CHIEF in South America during colonial times, a Native American chief **2.** POLITICAL LEADER especially in Latin America or Spain, a local political boss **3.** TROPICAL AMERICAN SONGBIRD a boldly coloured blackbird that feeds on fruit and insects, and nests in colonies. Native to: tropical Central and South America. Genus: *Cacicus*. [Mid-16C. Via Spanish or French < Taino]

cack (*slang*) *n* **1.** an offensive term for excrement **2.** an offensive term for dirt **3.** an offensive term for something that is worthless, annoying, or makes no sense **4.** *Aus* an offensive term for somebody or something regarded as amusing ■ *v* (**cacks** /kak/, **cacking, cacked**) **1.** *vi* an offensive term meaning to defecate **2.** *vt* an offensive term meaning to defecate involuntarily, especially in a piece of clothing **3.** **cack yourself** *vr* an offensive term meaning to be very scared or nervous [Pre-12C. Verb via Middle Low German and Middle Dutch < Latin *cacare* 'defecate'; noun (earlier) related]

cack-handed /kák hándid/ *adj* **1.** clumsy (*informal*) **2.** *regional* an offensive term meaning naturally left-handed [Mid-19C. Origin ?] —**cack-handedness** *n*

cackle /kák'l/ *v* (**-les, -ling, -led**) **1.** *vi* LAUGH HARSHLY AND SHRILLY to laugh a harsh high-pitched malicious laugh, often suggesting pleasure at others' misfortune **2.** *vt* SAY SOMETHING WITH HARSH SHRILL LAUGH to say something with a malicious high-pitched laugh **3.** *vi* MAKE SQUAWKING NOISE to squawk shrilly, especially after laying an egg (*refers to hens*) ■ *n* MALICIOUS LAUGH a high-pitched malicious laugh or tone of voice [12C. < Middle Low German or Middle Dutch *kākel(e)n*, an imitation of the sound] —**cackler** *n*

cackling /kák'ling/ *n regional* an act of nagging at or scolding somebody

REGIONAL NOTE See *jawing*.

caco- *prefix* bad ○ *cacology* [< Greek *kakos*]

cacodemon /káka deéman/, **cacodaemon** *n* a supposed evil spirit [Late 16C. < Greek *kakodaimōn*]

cacodyl /káka dil, -dīl/ *n* a poisonous oily flammable liquid that contains arsenic and has an unpleasant garlicky smell. Formula: $C_4H_{12}As_2$. [Mid-19C. < Greek *kakōdēs* 'bad-smelling'] —**cacodylic** /káka díllik/ *adj*

cacography /kə kóggrəfi, ka-/ *n* (*formal*) **1.** poor handwriting **2.** incorrect spelling —**cacographic** /káka gráffik/ *adj* —**cacographical** *adj*

cacomistle /káka miss'l/, **cacomixle** /-miks'l/ *n* a carnivorous mammal resembling a cat with brown fur and a long black-banded tail. Native to: southwestern United States and Mexico. Latin name: *Bassariscus astutus*. [Mid-19C. Via American Spanish *cacomixtle* < Nahuatl *tlacomiztli* 'half mountain lion']

cacophony /kə kóffəni/ (*plural* **-nies**) *n* **1.** an unpleasant combination of loud, often jarring, sounds **2.** the use of harsh unpleasant sounds in language, e.g. for literary effect [Mid-17C. Via French < Greek *kakophōnia* < *kakophōnos* 'bad-sounding'] —**cacophonous** *adj*

cactus

cactus /káktəs/ *n* (*plural* **-ti** /-tī/ or **-tuses** or *same*) a spiny leafless plant with fleshy stems and branches and often with brilliantly coloured flowers. Native to: dry desert regions of the Americas. Family: Cactaceae. ■ *adj Aus* (*slang*) **1.** broken down **2.** same as **drunk** *adj* (sense 1) [Mid-18C. Via Latin, 'cardoon' < Greek *kaktos*] —**cactaceous** /kak táyshəss/ *adj*

cacuminal /kə kyoómin'l, ka-/ *adj* PHON same as **retroflex** (sense 2) [Mid-19C. < Latin *cacuminare* 'make pointed' < *cacumen* 'point']

cad /kad/ *n* **1.** a man whose conduct, especially towards women, is considered unscrupulous or dishonourable (*dated*) **2.** *regional* the smallest or weakest piglet in a litter [Mid-19C. Shortening of CADDIE] —**caddish** *adj* —**caddishly** *adv* —**caddishness** *n*

REGIONAL NOTE See *underling*.

CAD /kad/ *abbr* computer-aided design

cadaster /kə dástər/, **cadastre** *n* an official register containing information on the value, extent, and ownership of land for the purposes of taxation [Late 18C. Via French < Italian *catastico* < Greek *katastikhon* 'list' < *kata stikhon* 'line by line'] —**cadastral** *adj*

cadaver /kə daávər, -dáy-, -dávvər/ *n* a dead body, especially one that is to be dissected [14C. < Latin < *cadere* 'to fall'] —**cadaveric** *adj*

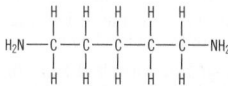

cadaverine

cadaverine /kə dávvə reen/ *n* a thick toxic colourless liquid with an extremely unpleasant smell, produced when flesh rots. Formula: $C_5H_{14}N_2$.

cadaverous /kə dávvərəss/ *adj* **1.** EXTREMELY THIN thin to the point of resembling a skeleton or corpse **2.** PALE deathly pale (*literary*) **3.** OF CORPSES suggesting death or corpses (*formal or literary*)

CADCAM /kád kam/ *abbr* computer-aided design and manufacturing

caddice *n* TEXTILES another spelling of **caddis**

caddice fly *n* INSECTS another spelling of **caddis fly**

caddice worm *n* INSECTS another spelling of **caddis worm**

caddie /káddi/, **caddy** *n* (*plural* **-dies**) a golfer's assistant who carries a bag of clubs and performs other duties ■ *vi* (**-dies, -dying, -died**) to act as a caddie for a golfer [Late 18C. Scots form of CADET]

caddis /káddiss/, **caddice** *n* a coarse woollen fabric, braid, or yarn [Mid-16C. Via French < Provençal]

caddis fly, **caddice fly** *n* an insect with four membranous wings, multijointed antennae, and larvae (**caddis worms**) that live in water. Order: Trichoptera.

caddis worm, **caddice worm** *n* a larva of a caddis fly. Caddis worms live in water inside a protective silken case that is covered with sand and debris.

Caddo /káddō/ (*plural same* or **-dos**) *n* a member of a confederacy of Native North Americans in central Oklahoma who formerly lived in the Red River area of Arkansas, Louisiana, and east Texas [Via American French < Caddoan *kaduhdáĉĉuʔ* in the language of the Caddo people] —**Caddo** *adj*

Caddoan /káddō ən/ *n* a family of Native North American languages spoken by members of the Caddo confederacy, including Pawnee

caddy[1] /káddi/ (*plural* **-dies**) *n* **1.** a small box or tin used for storing something, especially tea **2.** a plastic or metal case for a CD-ROM [Late 18C. Alteration of *catty* < Malay *kati*, a standard measure for tea]

caddy[2] *n, vi* GOLF another spelling of **caddie**

cade[1] /kayd/ *n* a juniper tree whose wood yields a medicinal oil (**cade oil**). Use: treating skin conditions. Native to: southern Europe. Latin name: *Juniperus oxycedrus*. [Late 16C. Via French < medieval Latin *catanus*]

cade[2] /kayd/ *adj* describes animals that have been abandoned by their mother and reared by humans [14C. Origin ?]

Cade /kayd/, **Jack** (?–1450) Irish-born English rebel leader. He led an insurrection against Henry VI and marched on London. Tricked with promises of a pardon, he was killed while fleeing.

-cade *suffix* procession ○ *motorcade* [< CAVALCADE]

cadelle /kə dél/ *n* a small black beetle that feeds on grain and other stored foods. Native to: found worldwide. Latin name: *Tenebroides mauritanicus*. [Mid-19C. Via French < Latin *cadellus* 'little dog']

cadence /káyd'nss/ *n* **1.** RHYTHM the beat or measure of something such as a dance or a march that follows a set rhythm **2.** FALLING TONE a drop in the pitch of the voice, e.g. at the end of a sentence **3.** INTONATION the rise and fall of the voice during speech **4.** RHYTHM IN LANGUAGE the rhythmic flow of poetry or prose **5.** MUSIC MUSICAL SEQUENCE a short sequence of notes that marks the end of a piece or passage of music. In tonal music, a cadence brings about a harmonic resolution. [14C. Via Old French, 'rhythm' < Italian *cadenza* 'falling away' < Latin *cadere* 'to fall'] —**cadenced** *adj*

ORIGIN The Latin word *cadere* 'to fall', from which *cadence* is derived, is also the source of English *accident*, *cadaver*, *cascade*, *case*[1], *chance*, *cheat*, *coincide*, *decay*, *deciduous*, *incident*, *occasion*, and *Occident*.

cadency /káyd'nssi/ (*plural* **-cies**) *n* a genealogical line that descends from a younger member of a family

cadential /kə dénsh'l/ *adj* **1.** relating to rhythm or a rhythmic cadence **2.** relating to cadenzas or a musical cadence

cadenza /kə dénzə/ *n* an elaborate solo passage of virtuoso playing or singing near the end of a section or piece of music, sometimes improvised by the soloist [Mid-18C. < Italian (see CADENCE)]

cade oil /káyd-/ *n* PHARM same as **juniper tar**

cadet /kə dét/ *n* **1.** MILITARY TRAINEE a young man or woman who is training to become a full member of the armed forces or the police force, especially as an officer **2.** YOUNG PERSON IN UNIFORMED ORGANIZATION somebody of school age who is a member of a uniformed organization offering military training **3.** YOUNGER SON a younger son or brother (*dated*) **4.** GENTLEMAN SOLDIER in England in former times, a gentleman, often a younger son, who entered the army without a commission, intending to work his way up to officer rank [Early 17C. < French, originally Gascon dialect *capdet* 'younger son' (because noble Gascon families traditionally sent younger sons into the army) < Latin *caput* 'head'] —**cadetship** *n*

cadge /kaj/ (**cadges, cadging, cadged**) *vti* to scrounge or beg something from somebody (*informal*) [Early 17C. Back-formation < CADGER]

cadger /kájjər/ *n* somebody who habitually borrows things or requests favours (*informal*) [15C. Origin ?]

cadi /kaádi, káydi/, **qadi** *n* in a Muslim community where Islamic law is followed, a minor judge [Late 16C. < Arabic *kāḍī*]

Cadiz /kə díz/, **Cádiz** capital of Cádiz Province and a major port in the autonomous region of Andalusia in southwestern Spain. Population: 136,239 (2002).

cadmium /kádmi əm/ *n* a soft malleable toxic bluish-white metallic element. Source: ores of copper and lead. Use: alloys, electroplating, nuclear reactors, dental amalgams, pigments, electronics. Symbol **Cd**. See table at **element** [Early 19C. < Latin *cadmia* 'zinc ore' < Greek *kadm(e)ia gē* 'earth of Cadmus', because the substance came originally from Thebes]

cadmium sulphide *n* an orange or yellowish-brown poisonous salt. Use: in paints as a pigment, in medicine, in electronic parts. Formula: CdS.

cadmium yellow *n* a bright yellow pigment that contains cadmium sulphide, or a paint prepared with this pigment

Cadmus /kádməss/ *n* in Greek mythology, a prince who slew a dragon and planted its teeth in the ground, from which armed men sprouted and began fighting each other. With the five survivors Cadmus founded Thebes.

cadre /kaadər, káy-/ *n* **1.** MIL MILITARY UNIT a group of experienced professionals at the core of a military organization who are able to train new recruits and expand the operations of the unit **2.** POL CORE OF ACTIVISTS a core group of political activists or revolutionaries **3.** CORE GROUP a controlling or representative group at the centre of an organization **4.** SMALL GROUP OF TEAM-SPIRITED PEOPLE a tightly knit, highly trained group of people **5.** MEMBER OF UNIT a member of a cadre [Mid-19C. Via French, 'frame' < Italian *quadro* 'framework' < Latin *quadrum* 'square']

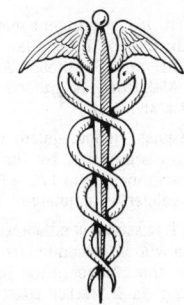

caduceus

caduceus /kə dyoóssi əss, -dyoóshi-/ (*plural* **-i** /-ī/) *n* **1.** in classical mythology, a winged staff entwined with two serpents, the symbol of Hermes or Mercury and associated with the Greek god of healing, Asclepius **2.** a symbol of various medical organizations that is modelled on Hermes' caduceus [Late 16C. Via Latin < Doric Greek *karuk(e)ion* < *kērux* 'herald'] —**caducean** *adj*

caducity /kə dyoóssəti/ *n* (*literary*) **1.** the weakening or loss of physical or mental powers that sometimes occurs in later life **2.** the quality of being perishable or impermanent [Mid-18C. < French *caducité* < *caduc* 'transitory' < Latin *caducus* (see CADUCOUS)]

caducous /kə dyoókəss/ *adj* describes a plant or animal part that drops off or is shed in the early stages of development, as are some leaves or flower parts [Late 18C. < Latin *caducus* 'liable to fall' < *cadere* 'to fall']

CAE *abbr* computer-aided engineering

caeca ANAT plural of **caecum**

caecilian /see sílli ən/ *n* a limbless tropical amphibian that looks like an earthworm, has small or no eyes, and burrows in the soil. Order: Gymnophiona. [Late 19C. < modern Latin *Caecilia* < Latin *caecilia* 'slowworm']

caecum /seékəm/ (*plural* **-ca** /-kə/) *n* the pouch, open at one end, in which the large intestine begins [Early 18C. < Latin *(intestinum) caecum* 'blind (gut)' < *caecus* 'blind'] —**caecal** /seékəl/ —**caecally** *adv*

Caedmon /kádmən/ (650?–680?) English monk and poet. The hymn on the Creation that he composed and that was written down by Bede is the earliest Christian poem in Old English.

Caelum /seéləm/ *n* a constellation of the southern hemisphere [< Latin, 'chisel'; from its shape]

Caen /koN/ capital of the Calvados Department in the Basse-Normandie Region, in northwestern France. It was the scene of heavy fighting in World War II. Population: 113,987 (1999).

caenogenesis /seénō jénnəssiss/, **cainogenesis** /kī́nō-/, **cenogenesis** *n* the development by an embryo, foetus, or larva of organs or body parts that are lost in adult life

Caenozoic *adj, n* GEOL another spelling of **Cenozoic**

Caerleon /kaar lée ən/ town in southeastern Wales. It contains the remains of the Roman fortress of Isca. Population: 8,931 (1991).

Caernarvon /kər naárv'n/ walled town on the Menai Strait, in Ceredigion, Wales. Edward II, the first Prince of Wales, was born in Caernarvon Castle. Population: 9,695 (1991). Welsh name **Caernarfon**

Caernarvonshire /kər naárv'nshər/ former county of Wales, abolished in 1974

caerphilly /kər fílli, kair-/ *n* a pale crumbly cheese made in Wales [Early 20C. After CAERPHILLY.]

Caerphilly /kər fílli, kair-/ town in south Wales, best known for the cheese that bears its name. Population: 28,481 (1991).

caeruloplasmin *n* PHYSIOL another spelling of **ceruloplasmin**

Caesar /seézər/ *n* **1.** the title given to a Roman emperor, especially from the reign of Augustus to that of Hadrian **2.** *also* **caesar** somebody, e.g. a ruler or leader, who acts like a dictator [Old English *casere* < Latin *Caesar*, family name of Julius CAESAR]

Caesar /seézər/, **Julius** (100–44 BC) Roman general who emerged from civil war as dictator of Rome and was assassinated by republican conspirators. Full name **Caesar, Gaius Julius**

> 'I came, I saw, I conquered.'
> [Julius Caesar. Quoted in *The Twelve Caesars*, Suetonius; AD 121?]

Caesarea /seézə rée ə/ ancient seaport on the coast of Samaria, and the Roman capital of Palestine, situated approximately 35 km/22 mi. south of present-day Haifa, Israel

Caesarean /si záiri ən/, **Caesarian** *n* UK, ANZ, Can SURGICAL DELIVERY OF BABY an operation to deliver a baby by cutting through the mother's abdominal wall and womb. US term **cesarean** ■ *adj* **1.** OF OR LIKE CAESAR OR CAESARS relating to or resembling Julius Caesar or the Caesars in general **2.** MED OF CAESAREAN relating to or involving a surgical Caesarean [In the medical sense, from the belief that Julius CAESAR was born this way]

Caesarean section *n* UK, ANZ, Can MED same as **Caesarean**

Caesarian *adj, n* MED, ANCIENT HIST another spelling of **Caesarean**

caesar salad *n* a salad made with lettuce, croutons, Parmesan cheese, and anchovies, with an egg-based dressing [After *Caesar* Gardini, Mexican restaurant proprietor]

caesium /seézi əm/ *n* a rare ductile silver-white element of the alkali metals group that is the most reactive of the elements. Use: photoelectric cells. Symbol **Cs**. See table at **element** [Mid-19C. < modern Latin < Latin *caesius* 'bluish-grey'; from its blue spectral lines]

caesium clock *n* a clock in which caesium atoms are stimulated by an alternating magnetic field and a precise time is determined when the frequencies of the atoms and the field match

caespitose /sésspi tōss/ *adj* describes a plant that grows in tufts or clumps [Late 18C. < Latin *caespit-* 'turf']

caestus *n* BOXING, ANCIENT HIST another spelling of **cestus**²

caesura /si zyoórə/ (*plural* **-ras** or **-rae** /-ree/), **cesura** (*plural* **-ras** or **-rae**) *n* **1.** LITERAT PAUSE IN LINE OF VERSE a pause in a line of poetry, especially to allow its sense to be made clear or to follow the rhythms of natural speech, often near the middle of the line **2.** LITERAT BREAK IN LINE OF VERSE in classical poetry, a break between two words that are part of the same unit of rhythm (**foot**), usually near the middle of the line **3.** MUSIC INTERRUPTION IN MUSIC a brief interruption in a musical phrase **4.** PAUSE a pause or break in speech or conversation (*formal*) [Mid-16C. < Latin, 'cut' < *caedere* 'to cut'] —**caesural** *adj* —**caesuric** *adj*

ORIGIN The Latin word *caedere*, 'to cut', from which *caesura* is derived, is also the source of English *chisel*, *concise*, *decide*, *excise*², *incise*, *precise*, and *scissors*.

CAF *abbr* cost and freight

café /káffay/ *n* **1.** a small informal restaurant serving drinks, snacks, and often light meals **2.** S Africa a small shop near a residential area that stocks food and general household goods and is open long hours [Early 19C. Via French, '(place serving) coffee' < Turkish *kahveh* 'coffee' or Arabic *qahwah* 'coffee, wine']

café au lait /káffay ō láy/ (*plural* **café au laits** /-láyz/ or **cafés au lait** /káffay-/) *n* **1.** coffee with hot milk **2.** a pale brown colour, like that of milky coffee [Mid-18C. < French, 'coffee with milk'] —**café au lait** *adj*

café latte *n* same as **latte**

café noir /káffay nwaár/ (*plural* **cafés noirs** /*pronunc. same*/) *n* coffee without milk or cream [< French, 'black coffee']

café society *n* celebrities and media people who attend fashionable events and visit fashionable restaurants, clubs, and resorts

cafeteria /káffə teéri ə/ *n* a self-service restaurant or coffee bar, especially one in a workplace or department store [Mid-19C. < American Spanish < *café* 'coffee']

cafetière /káffə tyáir, -teér/ *n* a coffee pot fitted with a plunger that is used to push the floating coffee grounds to the bottom of the pot when the coffee is ready to drink. N Am term **French press** [Mid-19C. < French < *café* (see CAFÉ)]

caff /kaf/ *n* a café, especially an old-fashioned British one serving tea and fried breakfasts in unstylish surroundings (*informal*) [Mid-20C. Shortening of CAFÉ]

caffein FOOD INDUST, PHARM another spelling of **caffeine**

caffeinated /káffi naytid/ *adj* containing caffeine

caffeine /káffeen, káffi een/, **caffein** *n* a stimulant found in coffee, tea, and cola nuts. Use: in soft drinks, medicine, and painkillers. [Mid-19C. < French, < *café* 'coffee']

caffeinism /káffee nizəm, káffi een-/ *n* a condition caused by an excessive amount of caffeine in the body, resulting in symptoms of high blood pressure, diarrhoea, palpitations, accelerated breathing, and insomnia

caffe latte, **caffè latte** /káffay láttay/ *n* BEVERAGES same as **latte**

~~caffiene~~ incorrect spelling of **caffeine**

caftan *n* CLOTHING another spelling of **kaftan**

cag /kag/ *n* CLOTHING same as **cagoule** (*informal*) [Late 20C. Shortening]

cage /kayj/ *n* **1.** METAL ENCLOSURE FOR ANIMAL an enclosure, usually made from bars or wire, in which to keep animals or birds **2.** ENCLOSING OR PROTECTING WIRE-MESH STRUCTURE a wire-mesh structure used to protect or enclose something **3.** LIFT PLATFORM the part of a lift that people stand in, particularly a lift in a mine shaft **4.** BASEBALL SCREEN TO STOP BALLS in baseball, a screen behind home plate that stops thrown or fouled balls **5.** BASKETBALL BASKET in basketball, the basket (*informal*) **6.** ICE HOCKEY HOCKEY GOAL the goal in ice hockey (*informal*) **7.** US TEMPORARY PRISON CELL a barred room or strong mesh enclosure for confining prisoners temporarily, e.g. in a police station ■ *vt* (**cages**, **caging**, **caged**) PUT PERSON OR ANIMAL IN CAGE to place or keep a person or animal in a cage [12C. Via Old French < Latin *cavea* 'enclosure, dungeon'] —**caged** *adj* ◇ **rattle somebody's cage** to annoy or upset somebody deliberately ○*We kept after him and kept after him and finally rattled his cage a little bit, he said.' (Cincinnati Post; 1997)

Cage /kayj/, **John** (1912–92) US composer. His avant-garde music includes *4'33"* (1952), in which musicians sit silently with their instruments. Full name **Cage, John Milton, Jr**. See illustration on next page

> 'Composing's one thing, performing's another, listening's a third. What can they have to do with one another?'
> [John Cage, *Silence*; 1961]

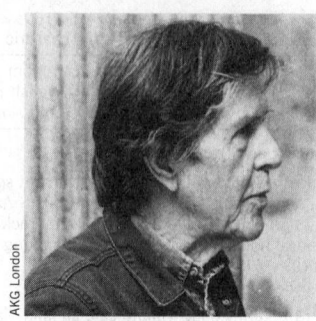

John Cage

Cage, Nicholas (b. 1964) US actor. He frequently plays offbeat film characters, as in his Academy Award-winning performance in *Leaving Las Vegas* (1995).

cagebird /káyj burd/ n a bird that is often kept as a pet in a cage, e.g. a budgerigar or parrot

cageling /káyj ling/ n a bird that is being kept as a pet in a cage (*archaic or literary*)

cagey /káyji/ (**-gier, -giest**), **cagy** adj secretive and refusing to be open, frank, or direct (*informal*) [Late 19C. Origin ?] —**cagily** adv —**caginess** n

SYNONYMS See *cautious*.

cagmag /kág mag/ *regional adj* poorly done, or not properly finished ■ vi (**-mags, -magging, -magged**) to quarrel or nag [Mid-18C. Origin ?]

cagmagging /kág maging/ n regional an act of nagging at or scolding somebody

REGIONAL NOTE See *jawing*.

James Cagney

Cagney /kágni/, **James** (1899–1986) US film actor, known for both comic and tough gangster roles. Full name **Cagney, James Francis**

‘I went into show business strictly from hunger. Starvation helps to turn you into a good actor, I guess.’
[James Cagney. Quoted in *Film-makers Speak*, Jay Leyda (ed.); 1977]

cagoule /kə goól, ka-/ n a lightweight hooded waterproof top that often folds up small and can be carried easily [Mid-20C. Via French, ‘cowl’ < Latin *cucullus* ‘cap, hood’]

cagy adj another spelling of **cagey**

cahier /kaʼa yay/ n (*formal*) 1. a notebook 2. a written report of a meeting, e.g. of a parliamentary group [Late 18C. Via French < Latin *quaternis* ‘set of four’ < *quattuor* ‘four’; because originally a pamphlet made from four folded sheets of paper]

Cahokia Mounds /kə hóki ə-/ group of prehistoric Native American mounds, including the largest prehistoric earthwork in the United States, situated 13 km/8 mi. northeast of East Saint Louis, Illinois

cahoots /kə hoóts/ [Early 19C. Origin ?] ◇ **be in cahoots (with somebody)** to have a secret agreement with somebody, especially to do something dishonest or illegal (*informal*)

Cahuilla /kə weé ə/ (*plural same* or **-las**) n 1. a member of a Native North American people who live in the Sonoran and Mojave desert regions of southern California 2. the language of the Cahuilla, belonging to the Shoshone group of Uto-Aztecan languages,

now spoken by very few people [Mid-19C. < Cahuilla, ‘masters’]

CAI abbr computer-aided instruction

Caiaphas /kíʼ ə fass/ (fl AD 18–37) Jewish high priest. According to the Bible, he presided over the trial of Jesus Christ.

Caicos Islands ▸ **Turks and Caicos Islands**

caiman /káymən/ (*plural* **-mans** or *same*), **cayman** n a reptile related to the alligator but smaller and slimmer and with a proportionally longer tail. Native to: tropical America. Genus: *Caiman*. [Late 16C. Via Spanish < Carib *caymán*]

Cain /kayn/ n in the Bible, the elder son of Adam and Eve, who killed his brother Abel (Genesis 4) ◇ **raise Cain** to cause a noisy disturbance (*informal*)

Caine /kayn/, **Michael** (b. 1933) British actor. His films include *Zulu* (1963) and *Hannah and her Sisters* (1986), for which he won an Academy Award. Born **Micklewhite, Maurice Joseph**

‘Not many people know that.’
[Attributed to Michael Caine. Caine’s catch phrase, which was made the title of his memoirs, is said to have been his comment when habitually offering information garnered from *The Guinness Book of Records*.]

-caine suffix a synthetic alkaloid anaesthetic ○ *phenacaine* [< COCAINE]

cained /kaynd/ adj under the influence of cocaine (*slang*) [< shortening of COCAINE]

cainogenesis n BIOL same as **caenogenesis**

Cainozoic adj, n GEOL same as **Cenozoic**

caipirinha /kíʼ pi reén ya/ n a Brazilian cocktail consisting of cachaca, sugar, crushed lime, and ice

caïque

caïque /kī eék, kaa-/ n 1. a long narrow rowing boat used in the waters around Turkey 2. a small rowing, sailing, or motor boat used in the Greek Islands and the eastern Mediterranean [Early 17C. Via French < Turkish *kayik*]

cairn /kairn/ n 1. a pile of stones set on a hill or mountain to mark a spot for walkers and climbers, or as a memorial to somebody who died there 2. DOGS same as **Cairn** [Mid-16C. < Gaelic *carn* ‘heap of stones’] —**cairned** adj

Cairn /kairn/, **Cairn terrier** n a small terrier with a shaggy coat of rough hair, belonging to a breed originally developed in Scotland

cairngorm /káirn gawrm/, **cairngorm stone** n a smoky yellow, grey, or brown form of quartz, found in Scotland. Use: jewellery. [Late 18C. After the CAIRNGORM MOUNTAINS]

Cairngorm Mountains /káirn gawrm-/, **Cairngorms** /káirn gawrmz/ range of the Grampian Mountains in northeastern Scotland. Its highest peak is Ben Macdhui, 1,309 m/4,296 ft.

Cairngorms National Park national park in northeastern Scotland, established in 2003, and the largest in the United Kingdom. Area: 3,800 sq. km/1400 sq. mi.

Cairngorm stone n MINERALS same as **cairngorm**

Cairns /kairnz/ coastal city in northeastern Queensland, Australia. It is the main gateway to the northern Great Barrier Reef and a major tourist resort. Population: 119,256 (2002 estimate).

Cairn terrier n BREED same as **Cairn**

Cairo /kírō/ capital of Egypt and Africa’s largest city. It is situated on the River Nile, at the southern end of the Nile delta. Population: 6,789,000 (1998).

caisson /káyss'n, kə soón/ n 1. CONSTR **UNDERWATER WORK CHAMBER** a bottomless watertight chamber filled with compressed air, used as a base from which construction work is carried out underwater 2. NAUT **FLOAT TO RAISE SHIPS** a hollow structure attached to a sunken object such as a wrecked ship, then pumped full of air until it acts as a float, raising the object to the surface 3. CIV ENG, NAUT **WATER BLOCK** a floating watertight structure used to keep water from entering a dry dock, canal lock, or basin 4. MIL **HORSE-DRAWN VEHICLE** a two-wheeled horse-drawn vehicle, formerly used to carry ammunition but now often used to carry coffins at state or military funerals 5. ARMS **AMMUNITION BOX** a large container for ammunition 6. **BOX OF EXPLOSIVES USED AS MINE** a box of explosives, formerly used as a land mine 7. ARCHIT same as **coffer** (sense 2) [Late 17C. Via French < Italian *cassone* ‘large box’ < *cassa* ‘box’ < Latin *capsa*]

caisson disease n MED same as **decompression sickness**

Caithness /káyth ness, kayth néss/ former county of northeastern Scotland, abolished in 1973. It is now part of the Highland unitary authority.

caitiff /káytif/ n same as **coward** (*archaic*) [13C. Via Old French *caitif* ‘captive, wretched person’ < Latin *captivus* < *capere* ‘take’] —**caitiff** adj

Caitra /káytrə/ n in the Hindu calendar, the first month of the year, lasting 30 or 31 days and falling about the same time as March to April. See table at **calendar**

cajeput /kájjəpoŏt/ n 1. a pungent medicinal oil 2. a small flowering tree or bush that yields cajeput. Native to: South and Southeast Asia, Australia. Latin name: *Melaleuca leucadendron*. [Late 18C. < Malay *kayuputih* ‘white tree’]

cajole /kə jól/ (**-joles, -joling, -joled**) vti to persuade somebody to do something by flattery or gentle but persistent argument [Mid-17C. < French *cajoler*] —**cajolement** n —**cajoler** n —**cajolery** n

Cajun /káyjən/ n 1. **LOUISIANAN OF FRENCH DESCENT** somebody from Louisiana who is descended from French colonists exiled in the 18th century from Acadia in present-day Canada 2. **FRENCH DIALECT** a dialect of French spoken in Louisiana that developed from the French spoken by 18th-century settlers who were expelled from Acadia, Canada 3. **MUSIC MIXING BLUES AND FOLK** the musical style, consisting of a mixture of blues and folk music, that originated among the Cajuns 4. **SOMEBODY OF MIXED ANCESTRY** a native of southern Alabama or southeastern Mississippi who is of mixed European, African American, or Native American ancestry [Mid-19C. Alteration of *Acadian* ‘(inhabitant) of Acadia’] —**Cajun** adj

cake /kayk/ n 1. **BAKED SWEET FLOUR-BASED FOOD** a baked sweet food usually made from flour, fat, sugar, eggs, and other ingredients 2. **SHAPED PORTION OF SAVOURY FOOD** an individual portion of ground or chopped savoury food, shaped into a flat round piece and cooked, often by frying or grilling ○ *potato cakes* 3. **BLOCK OF SOMETHING** a solid block of something, e.g. soap, ice, or chocolate 4. **THICK LAYER** a thick layer of something that has collected over a period of time 5. **SOMETHING DIVIDED UP** something that is to be shared or divided up, e.g. a fund of money ○ *Everyone wants a slice of the cake.* ■ v (**cakes, caking, caked**) 1. vti **FORM CRUST ON SOMETHING** to form, or cover something with, a thick layer of a substance such as dirt, grease, or grime ○ *My boots were caked with mud after I walked through the field.* 2. vi **FORM INTO CAKE** to form into a solid mass ■ n US **TABOO TERM** a highly offensive term for a woman’s genitals (*taboo*) [12C. < Old Norse *kaka* ‘flat round loaf’] —**cakey** adj ◇ **cakes and ale** an enjoyable activity (*literary*) ◇ **have your cake and eat it (too)** to try to enjoy the advantages of two things, each of which tends to make the other impossible ◇ **take the cake** to be even worse than all the other bad or annoying things that went before (*informal*)

cakehole /káyk hōl/ n somebody’s mouth (*slang*)

cake mix n dried ingredients that can be used to make a cake, sold in a box or packet

cake slice n a kitchen utensil with a flat triangular blade, used for serving slices of cake

cakewalk /káyk wawk/ *n* **1.** SOMETHING VERY EASY something that is very easy to do (*informal*) **2.** COMPETITION BASED ON WALKING an informal contest to music, with a cake as a prize for executing the most elaborate or amusing walking steps, popular among African Americans in the 19th century **3.** DANCE STRUTTING DANCE a popular dance with elaborate or strutting steps **4.** MUSIC MUSIC the music for a cakewalk —**cakewalk** *vi* —**cakewalker** *n*

Cal *abbr* large calorie

CAL[1] *abbr* **1.** CALENDAR calendar **2.** MEASURE calibre

CAL[2] /kal/ *abbr* COMPUT computer-assisted learning

Cal. *abbr* California

Calabar bean /kálla baar-/ *n* the dark-brown poisonous seed of a tropical climbing plant. Use: source of drug physostigmine. Native to: Africa. Latin name: *Physostigma venenosum.* [After *Calabar*, Nigeria]

calabash /kálla bash/ *n* **1.** FRUIT OR GOURD a large ball-shaped fruit of a tropical American tree, or of the bottle gourd or some other gourd **2.** CONTAINER the hollowed-out dried shell of a calabash, bottle gourd, or other gourd **3.** TROPICAL AMERICAN EVERGREEN TREE a tropical evergreen tree that bears calabashes. Flowers: bell-shaped. Native to: tropical America. Latin name: *Crescentia cujete.* **4.** PLANTS same as **bottle gourd** [Mid-17C. Via French *calabasse* < Persian *karbuz* 'melon']

calabrese /kálla bráyzi, -breez/ *n* a variety of green broccoli [Mid-20C. < Italian, 'of Calabria']

Calabria /kə lábbri ə/ region in southern Italy forming the 'toe' of the Italian peninsula. It includes the provinces of Cataranzo, Cosenza, and Reggio di Calabria. Capital: Catanzaro. Population: 2,050,478 (2000). Area: 15,080 sq. km/5,822 sq. mi.

caladium /kə láydi əm/ *n* a tropical plant with white, green, red, or pink variegated leaves, widely grown as a houseplant. Native to: Americas. Genus: *Caladium.* [Mid-19C. < modern Latin, < Malay *keladi*]

Calais /kállay/ seaport on the English Channel in the Pas-de-Calais Department, Nord-Pas-de-Calais Region, in northwestern France. The Calais-Dover route is the shortest crossing between France and the United Kingdom. Population: 77,333 (1999).

calalu /kálləloo/ (*plural* **-lus**), **calaloo** (*plural* **-loos**), **cal-laloo** *n Carib* **1.** CARIBBEAN GREENS the leaves of various plants when used as salad, in soups, or cooked as greens **2.** SOUP a thick soup made of calalu with okra, green peppers, coconut milk, onions, herbs, and crab **3.** MIXTURE a complex mixture or confusion [Mid-18C. < American Spanish *calalú*]

calamanco /kálla máng kō/ *n* a glossy woollen fabric with a checked pattern on one side [Late 16C. Origin ?]

calamander /kálla mandər/ *n* the hard black-and-brown striped wood of a number of Asian trees. Use: furniture-making. [Early 19C < Sinhalese *kalumādirriya*]

calamari /kálla maári/ *npl* squid served as food, especially in Mediterranean cuisine [Late 20C. < Italian, plural of *calamaro* 'squid' < medieval Latin *calamarium* 'pencase' (from the shape of the squid's internal shell) < Latin *calamus* (see CALAMUS)]

calami BIOL plural of **calamus**

calamine /kálla mīn/ *n* a pink zinc oxide and ferric oxide powder. Use: in lotions and creams to soothe irritated skin. [Late 16C. Via Old French < medieval Latin *calamina*, alteration of Latin *cadmia* 'zinc ore' (see CADMIUM)]

calamint /kálləmint/ (*plural* **-mints** or *same*) *n* a plant of the mint family. Flowers: drooping, white, pink, or purple. Genera: *Satureja* or *Calamintha.* [14C. Via Old French *calament* < Greek *kalaminthē*]

calamite /kálla mīt/ *n* a plant that grew in the Palaeozoic era, related to the horsetail. Genus: *Calamites.* [Mid-19C. < modern Latin *calamites* < Latin *calamus* (see CALAMUS)]

calamitous /kə lámmitəss/ *adj* causing great trouble, tragedy, or disaster [Mid-16C. Directly or via French < Latin *calamitosus* < *calamitas* 'disaster'] —**calamitously** *adv*

calamity /kə lámməti/ (*plural* **-ties**) *n* **1.** a disastrous situation or event **2.** misery or distress resulting

from a disastrous event (*archaic*) [14C. Via French < Latin *calamitas* 'disaster']

Library of Congress
Calamity Jane

Calamity Jane /kə lámməti jáyn/ (1852?–1903) US frontierswoman. She worked as a scout in the American West. Born **Canary, Martha Jane**. Real name **Burke** or **Burk, Martha Jane**

calamondin /kálla mundin/ *n* **1.** the small sour orange-yellow fruit of a hybrid citrus tree **2.** a hybrid citrus tree that bears calamondins. Native to: Philippines. Latin name: *Citrofortunella mitis.* [Early 20C. < Tagalog *kalamundíng*]

calamus /kálləməss/ (*plural* **-mi** /-mī/) *n* **1.** ASIAN PALM a tropical Asian palm tree. Use: rattan. Genus: *Calamus.* **2.** ROOT OF SWEET FLAG the aromatic root of the sweet flag plant. Use: source of an oil used in perfumery. **3.** PLANTS same as **sweet flag 4.** FEATHER SHAFT the hollow shaft of a feather [14C. Via Latin < Greek *kalamos* 'reed, pen']

calando /kə lándō/ *adv, adj* played with gradually decreasing volume and slowing tempo (*used as a musical direction*) [Early 19C. < Italian, 'slackening']

calandria /kə lándri ə/ *n* the cylindrical core of a nuclear reactor with vertical holes [Early 20C. < Spanish < Greek *kulindros* 'cylinder']

calathea /kálla thee ə/ *n* a tropical evergreen plant with showy variegated leaves, widely grown as a greenhouse plant and houseplant. Native to: South America. Genus: *Calathea.* [< modern Latin, < Greek *kalathos* 'basket']

calaverite /kə lávvə rīt, kálla váir īt/ *n* a silvery-white or yellowish mineral that contains gold [Mid-19C. After *Calaveras* County, California]

calc- *prefix* same as **calci-**

calcaneus /kal káyni əss/ (*plural* **-i** /-ī/) *n* ANAT same as **heel bone** (*technical*) [Mid-18C. < late Latin, 'heel' < Latin *calc-*] —**calcaneal** *adj*

calcar[1] /kál kaar/ (*plural* **-caria** /-káiri ə/) *n* a spur on a plant or animal part, e.g. on a bird's leg or at the base of a petal [Early 19C. < Latin, 'spur' < *calc-* 'heel']

calcar[2] /kál kaar/ *n* a furnace formerly used in glass-making for burning materials to make frit, the viscous substance from which glass is subsequently made [Mid-17C. < Italian *calcara*]

calcareous /kal káiri əss/ *adj* **1.** containing or characteristic of calcium carbonate **2.** growing on limestone or in earth containing limestone ○ *calcareous algae* [Late 17C. < Latin *calcarius* 'of lime' < *calc-* 'lime'] —**calcareously** *adv*

calcaria BIOL plural of **calcar**[1]

calcariferous /kálkə ríffərəss/ *adj* describes a plant or animal part that has a spur on it [Mid-19C. < Latin *calcar* (see CALCAR[1])]

calceolaria /kálssi ə láiri ə/ *n* a small plant, often grown as a houseplant. Flowers: speckled, slipper-shaped. Native to: tropical America. Genus: *Calceolaria.* [Late 18C. < modern Latin, < Latin *calceolus* 'little shoe']

calces ANAT plural of **calx**

Calchas /kál kass/ *n* in Greek mythology, a soothsayer who accompanied the Greeks during the Trojan War, advising them, among other things, to build the Trojan Horse

calci- *prefix* calcium, calcium salt, lime ○ *calcific* [< Latin *calc-*, stem of *calx* (see CALX)]

calcic /kálssik/ *adj* relating to, containing, or derived from calcium or lime

calciferol /kal síffə rol/ *n* BIOCHEM same as **vitamin D₂** [Mid-20C. < CALCIFEROUS]

calciferous /kal síffərəss/ *adj* producing or containing calcium carbonate or other calcium salts

calcific /kal síffik/ *adj* producing lime salts, or involved in their production

calcifuge /kálssi fyooj/ *n* a plant that is best suited for growth in an acid soil —**calcifugal** /kal síffyoŏg'l, kálssi fyoŏg'l/ *adj* —**calcifugous** /kal síffyoŏgəss, kálssi fyoŏgəss/ *adj*

calcify /kálssi fī/ (**-fies, -fying, -fied**) *vti* **1.** CHEM TURN INTO LIME to convert a substance into lime, or be converted into lime **2.** MED TURN HARD WITH CALCIUM to become, or cause a body part to become, hard or stiff as a result of the deposit of calcium salts **3.** BECOME OR MAKE RIGID AND UNCHANGING to become, or cause something to become, rigid and unchanging (*formal*) —**calcification** /kálssifi káysh'n/ *n*

calcimine /kálssi mīn, -min/ *n* a mixture of zinc oxide, water, and glue, sometimes with a colouring added, brushed onto interior walls as a decorative and sealing finish ■ *vt* (**-mines, -mining, -mined**) to cover a wall with calcimine [Mid-19C. Origin ?]

calcine /kál sīn, -sin/ (**-cines, -cining, -cined**) *vti* to heat a solid to a high temperature, converting it to a powdery residue by drying, decomposing, or oxidizing it, or to undergo this process [14C. < medieval Latin *calcinare* 'burn until like lime' < Latin *calc-* (see CALCIUM)] —**calcination** /kálssi náysh'n/ *n*

calcinosis /kálssi nóssiss/ *n* a medical condition in which nodules of calcium are deposited in soft body tissues

calcite /kál sīt/ *n* a colourless or white crystalline mineral that is a form of calcium carbonate. Source: limestone, marble, chalk. Use: cement, plaster, glass, paints. Formula: $CaCO_3$. —**calcitic** /kal síttik/ *adj*

calcitonin /kálssi tónin/ *n* a hormone, produced by the thyroid and parathyroid glands, that increases the deposition of calcium in bones

calcitriol /kal síttri ol/ *n* a form of Vitamin D. Use: to control or reverse bone loss. [Late 20C. Probably < CALCIUM + TRIOL]

calcium /kálssi əm/ *n* a soft silvery-white element that is an alkaline earth metal constituting about three per cent of the Earth's crust. It is essential to the formation of bones and teeth. Symbol **Ca**. See table at **element** [Early 19C. < Latin *calc-*, stem of *calx* (see CALX)]

calcium acetylide *n* CHEM same as **calcium carbide**

calcium antagonist *n* a drug that dilates the arteries and slows the heart. Use: treatment of angina.

calcium carbide *n* a colourless or greyish-black powdery compound. Use: generation of acetylene gas. Formula: CaC_2.

calcium carbonate *n* a white crystalline solid that is one of the most common natural substances. Source: chalk, limestone, marble, animal shells, bones. Use: antacids, paint, cement, toothpaste. Formula: $CaCO_3$.

calcium chloride *n* a white salt that absorbs moisture easily and quickly. Use: drying gases, de-icing roads, in pulp and paper treatment. Formula: $CaCl_2$.

calcium cyanamide *n* a white or greyish-black crystalline compound that releases ammonia slowly in the presence of water. Use: fertilizers. Formula: $CaCN_2$.

calcium cyanide *n* a white or greyish-black powder that decomposes in humid conditions to produce hydrogen cyanide. Use: formerly, insecticide, rodent poison, in fumigation. Formula: $Ca(CN)_2$.

calcium cyclamate *n* a sweet-tasting salt of cyclamic acid. Use: formerly, sugar substitute. Formula: $Ca(C_6H_{11}NHSO_3)_2.2H_2O$.

calcium fluoride *n* a colourless or white substance occurring naturally as fluorspar. Formula: CaF_2.

calcium gluconate *n* a calcium salt. Use: mineral supplement, treatment of calcium deficiency and osteoporosis. Formula: $CaC_{12}H_{22}O_{14}$.

calcium hydroxide *n* a white alkaline powder. Source: action of water on calcium oxide. Use:

manufacture of cement, plaster, and glass. Formula: $Ca(OH)_2$.

calcium hypochlorite *n* a white crystalline solid, soluble in water, that is a stable chlorine carrier. Use: bleaching agent, disinfectant, bactericide. Formula: $Ca(OCl)_2$.

calcium nitrate *n* a white solid that absorbs moisture very quickly and is a strong oxidizer. Use: fertilizer, explosives. Formula: $Ca(NO_3)_2.4H_2O$.

calcium oxide *n* a white crystalline powder. Use: manufacture of steel and glass, refining of aluminium, copper, and zinc, treatment of sewage. Formula: CaO.

calcium phosphate *n* a phosphate of calcium, existing in different forms. Source: rocks, animal bones. Use: as fertilizer in the form of bone ash.

calcium sulphate *n* a white odourless crystal or powder. Source: anhydrite, gypsum. Use: drying agent, building material. Formula: $CaSO_4$.

calcrete /kál kreet/ *n* an accumulation in the soil of a layer of calcium carbonate and other alkaline minerals just below the surface [Early 20C. Blend of CALC- + CONCRETE]

calcspar /kálk spaar/ *n* MINERALS same as **calcite** [Early 19C. < CALC- + SPAR[3]]

calc-tufa /kálk-/ *n* MINERALS same as **tufa**

calculable /kálkyŏōləb'l/ *adj* **1.** able to be worked out or estimated using mathematics **2.** likely to behave in the way that is expected —**calculability** /kálkyŏōlə bílləti/ *n*

calculate /kálkyŏō layt/ (-lates, -lating, -lated) *v* **1.** *vti* MATHS **WORK SOMETHING OUT MATHEMATICALLY** to work out or estimate a figure using mathematics **2.** *vti* **DECIDE WHAT WILL HAPPEN** to consider a situation carefully and decide what is likely to happen ○ *a speech calculated to reassure investors* **3.** *vt* **INTEND SOMETHING TO HAVE PARTICULAR EFFECT** to intend or design something to have a particular effect or result (*usually used in the passive*) ○ *The attack was calculated to cause maximum loss of life.* **4.** *vi Can, US regional* **INTEND** to be planning or intending to do a particular thing ○ *We were calculating on going home around midnight.* [Late 16C. < late Latin *calculat-*, past participle of *calculare* < Latin *calculus* 'pebble', (see CALCULUS)] —**calculated** *adj* —**calculative** /kálkyŏōlətiv, -laytiv/ *adj*

calculating /kálkyŏō layting/ *adj* **1.** determined to gain the greatest personal advantage **2.** showing that somebody is determined to gain the greatest personal advantage —**calculatingly** *adv*

calculation /kálkyŏō láysh'n/ *n* **1.** MATHS **PROCESS OF CALCULATING SOMETHING** the process of working out the answer to a mathematical problem, or a step in this process **2.** **ESTIMATE** an estimate or answer obtained by calculating **3.** **SCHEMING** consideration of something, especially when thinking of personal advantage —**calculational** *adj*

calculator

calculator /kálkyŏō laytər/ *n* a device used to carry out arithmetical operations, especially a small hand-held electronic device

calculous /kálkyŏōləss/ *adj* relating to hard formations of minerals (**calculi**) in the body

calculus /kálkyŏōləss/ (*plural* **-li** /-lī/ or **-luses**) *n* **1.** MATHS **BRANCH OF MATHEMATICS** a branch of mathematics dealing with the way that relations between some sets (**functions**) are affected by very small changes in one of their variables (**independent variables**) as they approach zero. It is used to find slopes of curves, rates of change, and volumes of curved figures. **2.** MATHS, LOGIC **METHOD OF CALCULATION** a method or system of calculation using symbols or symbolic logic **3.** MED **STONE** a stone or concretion, especially one in the kidney, gall bladder, or urinary bladder (*technical*) **4.** DENT same as **tartar** (sense 1) [Mid-17C. < Latin, 'pebble', diminutive of *calx* (see CALX)]

Calcutta /kal kúttə/ *n* former name for **Kolkata**

caldarium /kal dáiri əm/ (*plural* **-ria** /-ri ə/) *n* the hot room in an ancient Roman bathhouse [Mid-18C. < Latin, < *calere* 'be warm']

Alexander Young Calder

Calder /káwldər, kóld-/, **Alexander** (1898–1976) US painter and sculptor, known for his abstract sculptures, especially mobiles and stabiles

'The sense of motion in painting has long been considered one of the primary elements of composition...Just as one can compose colors, or forms, so I can compose motions.'
[Alexander Calder, 'Alexander Calder: Cosmic Imagery and the use of Scientific Instruments', *October Arts*, Joan M. Marter; 1978]

caldera /kal dáirə, káwldərə/ (*plural* **-ras**) *n* a large crater in a volcano, caused by a major eruption followed by the collapse of the volcanic pipe walls that form the volcano's cone. It may later contain a lake. [Late 17C. Via Spanish < late Latin *caldaria* 'cooking pot' < Latin *caldus* 'warm']

Calderdale /káwldər dayl/ local government unitary authority in northern England, established 1997. Population: 192,396 (2001).

Calderón de la Barca /kálde rón də la baárkə/, **Pedro** (1600–81) Spanish dramatist and poet. He wrote comedies and religious allegories including *Life is a Dream* (1635). Full name **Calderón de la Barca y Henao, Pedro**

'He dreams who thrives and prospers in this life. / He dreams who toils and strives. He dreams who injures, / Offends, and insults. So that in this world / Everyone dreams the thing he is, though no one / Can understand it.'
[Pedro Calderón de la Barca, *Life is a Dream*; 1635]

Caldey Island /káwldi-/ small island off the coast of Pembrokeshire, Wales, and location of a Cistercian monastery. Population: 50. Area: 3 sq. km/1 sq. mi. Welsh name **Ynys Pyr**

caldron *n* HOUSEHOLD another spelling of **cauldron**

Caldwell /káwld wel/, **Erskine** (1903–87) US writer. His novels about rural poverty include *Tobacco Road* (1932). Full name **Caldwell, Erskine Preston**

'Here is hard-core unemployment, widespread and chronic; here is a region of shacks...In this region of steep mountains, a person is exceptionally fortunate if he is able to hack out two or three ten-foot rows of land for potatoes or beans.'
[Erskine Caldwell, *Around About America*; 1964]

Caledonia /kállə dóni ə/ **1.** Roman name for the northern part of Britain **2.** poetic name for Scotland

Caledonian /kálli dóni ən/ *n* **1.** SCOT a Scottish person (*literary*) **2.** GEOLOGICAL ERA the era of geological time in northwestern Europe, 500 million to 395 million years ago, during which many mountains were formed ■ *adj* **1.** OF SCOTLAND relating to Scotland or its people, language, or culture (*literary*) **2.** OF GEOLOGICAL ERA relating to the Caledonian era of geological time

Caledonian Canal /kálli dóni ən-/ major waterway of Scotland. It consists of canals linking Loch Linnhe in the southwest with Loch Lochy, Loch Ness, and the Moray Firth in the northeast. Length: 60 km/97 mi.

calendar /kállindər/ *n* **1.** CHART OF YEAR a chart showing the days and months of the year, especially a particular year **2.** SYSTEM OF CALCULATING YEAR a system of calculating the days and months of the year and when the year begins and ends **3.** TIMETABLE a timetable of events, usually covering a period of a year **4.** LIST an official list of things to be done or considered ■ *vt* (-dars, -daring, -dared) SCHEDULE SOMETHING to enter something in a calendar or diary ► See table on next page [12C. Via Anglo-Norman < Latin *calendarium* 'moneylender's account-book' < *calendae* 'first day of the month']

calendar day *n* the period of 24 hours from midnight to midnight

calendarize /kállindərīz/ *vt* same as **calendar**

calendar month *n* CALENDAR same as **month** (senses 1, 3)

calendar year *n* the period of 365 or 366 days from 1 January to 31 December

calender /kállindər/ *n* a machine with rollers, used to form thin sheets from paper, plastic, or other material, or to impart a desired surface finish [Early 16C. Via French *calendre* < assumed Vulgar Latin *colondra*, alteration (influenced by Latin *columna* 'column') of Latin *cylindrus* 'roller'] —**calender** *vt*

calends /kállendz/, **kalends** *npl* in the ancient Roman calendar, the first day of the month [14C Via French *calendes* < Latin *calendae* 'first day of the month']

calendula /kə léndyŏōlə/ (*plural* **-las** or *same*) *n* PLANTS same as **pot marigold** [Late 16C. < modern Latin < Latin *calendae* 'first day of the month'; from its use in treating menstrual disorders]

calenture /kállən tyoor, -choor/ *n* a fever occurring in tropical regions, formerly believed to be caused by heat [Late 16C. Via French < Spanish *calentura* < Latin *calere* 'be warm']

calf[1] /kaaf/ (*plural* **calves** /kaavz/) *n* **1.** YOUNG COW OR BULL a young cow or bull of a domestic breed of cattle **2.** YOUNG ANIMAL the young of some animals such as elephants, whales, giraffes, and buffalos **3.** INDUST same as **calfskin** (sense 1) **4.** PIECE OF ICEBERG a large piece of ice that has broken away from an iceberg [Old English *cælf* < Germanic] ◇ **kill the fatted calf** to have a great celebration in honour of somebody, usually a family member who has been absent for some time

calf[2] /kaaf/ (*plural* **calves** /kaavz/) *n* the fleshy part at the back of the leg below the knee [14C. < Old Norse *kálfi*]

calf love *n* same as **puppy love** (*literary*)

calfskin /kaaf skin/ *n* **1.** fine leather made from the skin of calves **2.** the skin of a calf

Calgary /kálgəri/ city in southern Alberta, Canada. It is an important centre for transportation, finance, and the petroleum industry. Population: 879,277 (2001).

Cali /kaáli/ capital of Valle de Cauca Department and second largest city in Colombia. It is situated on the Cali River in western Colombia. Population: 2,111,000 (1999).

caliber *n* US spelling of **calibre**

calibrate /kálli brayt/ (-brates, -brating, -brated) *vt* **1.** MEASURE MARK SCALE ON SOMETHING to establish and mark the units on a measuring instrument **2.** MEASURE ENSURE ACCURACY OF SOMETHING to test and adjust the accuracy of a measuring instrument or process **3.** ARMS MEASURE BORE OF SOMETHING to measure the internal diameter of a pipe, cylinder, or the barrel of a firearm —**calibrator** *n*

calibration /kálli bráysh'n/ *n* **1.** the checking of a measuring instrument against an accurate standard to determine any deviation and correct for errors **2.** a mark showing one of the units of measurement on a measuring instrument

CALENDARS AND FESTIVALS

The Gregorian calendar was introduced in 1582 by Pope Gregory XIII, replacing the Julian calendar, and is based on a solar year of 365 days plus an extra day every four years (the leap year) and in centenary years evenly divisible by 400. The other calendars shown are based on lunar months. Each Hindu month is divided in two equal parts: krsna-paksa and sukla-paksa. Both the Hindu and the Jewish calendars are adjusted at intervals to the solar year. The Islamic calendar is not adjusted to the solar year so advances through the solar year on a 32.5 year cycle. The first month of each calendar is marked with a 1. Note, in the Jewish calendar, although Tishri is considered the first month of the civil year, Nisan is the first month of the religious year.

Notes

1 February has 29 days in a leap year.

2 The intercalary month Adar Sheni (29 days) is added every 3 years to adjust the Jewish calendar to the solar year.

3 The month Heshvan has 30 days in some years.

4 The month Kislev has 30 days in some years.

5 Caitra has 31 days in a leap year.

6 The month Dhu al-Hijjah has 30 days in some years.

Gregorian calendar	Jewish calendar	Hindu calendar	Islamic calendar
1 January 31 *days*	Tevet 29 *days*	Pausa 30 *days*	1 Muharram 30 *days*
February 28 *days*[1]	Shevat 30 *days*	Magha 30 *days*	Safar 29 *days*
March 31 *days*	Adar 29 *days*[2]	Phalguna 30 *days*	Rabi I 30 *days*
April 30 *days*	Nisan 30 *days*	1 Caitra 30 *days*[5]	Rabi II 29 *days*
May 31 *days*	Iyar 29 *days*	Vaisakha 31 *days*	Jumada I 30 *days*
June 30 *days*	Sivan 30 *days*	Jyaistha 31 *days*	Jumada II 29 *days*
July 31 *days*	Tammuz 29 *days*	Asadha 31 *days*	Rajab 30 *days*
August 31 *days*	Av 30 *days*	Sravana 31 *days*	Sha'ban 29 *days*
September 30 *days*	Elul 29 *days*	Bhadrapada 31 *days*	Ramadan 30 *days*
October 31 *days*	1 Tishri 30 *days*	Asvina 30 *days*	Shawwal 29 *days*
November 30 *days*	Heshvan 29 *days*[3]	Kartika 30 *days*	Dhu al-Qa'dah 30 *days*
December 31 *days*	Kislev 29 *days*[4]	Margasirsa 30 *days*	Dhu al-Hijjah 30 *days*[6]
	Tevet	Pausa	

Christian festivals	Jewish festivals	Hindu festivals	Islamic festivals
Annunciation *25 March*	**Hanukkah** *25 Kislev for eight days*	**Dussehra** *First half of Asvina*	**Ashora** *10 Muharram*
Ascension *40 days after Easter*	**Passover** *14 Nisan for seven days*	**Diwali** *Second half of Asvina*	**Eid al-Adha** *10 Dhu al-Qa'dah to 1 Dhu al-Hijjah*
Christmas *25 December: Roman Catholic and Protestant churches* *6 January: Eastern Orthodox churches*	**Purim** *14 Adar*	**Ganesh Chaturthi** *Early Bhadrapada*	**Eid al-Fitr** *1 Shawwal*
	Rosh Hashanah *1 and 2 Tishri*	**Holi** *Early Phalguna*	**Lailat al-Miraj** *27 Rajab*
Easter *First Sunday after the full moon of the vernal equinox*	**Shavuoth** *6 Sivan*	**Krishna Jayanti** *Late Sravana*	**Lailat al-Baraah** *15 Sha'ban*
Epiphany *6 January*	**Sukkoth** *15 Tishri for eight or nine days*	**Rakhi Bandham** *Full moon of Sravana*	**Lailat al-Qadr** *27 Ramadan*
Pentecost *Seventh Sunday after Easter*	**Yom Kippur** *10 Tishri*	**Shiva Ratri** *Middle of Magha*	**Mawlid al-Nabi** *12 Rabi I*
Transfiguration *6 August: Roman Catholic and Protestant churches* *19 August: Eastern Orthodox churches*			**Ras al-Am** *1 Muharram*
Trinity *First Sunday after Pentecost*			**Ramadan**

---

calibre /kálliber/ *n* **1. ABILITY** somebody's ability, intelligence, or character ○ *We don't often get candidates of her calibre.* **2. ARMS BORE OF FIREARM** the internal diameter of a pipe, cylinder, or the barrel of a firearm **3. ARMS SIZE OF BULLET** the external diameter of a projectile such as a bullet or a shell [Mid-16C. Via French < Italian *calibro* or Spanish *calibre*, probably < Arabic *kālib* 'mould']

calices RELIG, ANAT plural of **calix**

caliche /ka leechi/ *n* **1.** a layer of clay or sand containing minerals such as sodium nitrate and sodium chloride, found in dry regions of South America **2.** GEOL same as **calcrete** [Mid-19C. < American Spanish]

calicle *n* ZOOL same as **calyculus**

calico /kállikō/ (*plural* **-coes**) *n* **1. WHITE COTTON CLOTH** a white or unbleached cotton cloth **2.** *N Am* **BRIGHT COTTON CLOTH** a coarse cotton cloth with a bright printed pattern **3.** *N Am* **ANIMAL WITH BLOTCHED COAT** an animal with a blotched coat, usually white with black and reddish patches [Mid-16C. Alteration of

Calicut (now KOZHIKODE), India, from which such cloth was exported]

calif *n* ISLAM another spelling of **caliph**

Calif. *abbr* California

califate *n* ISLAM another spelling of **caliphate**

California /kálli fáwrnyə/ the most populous state in the United States, bordered by the Pacific Ocean, Oregon, Nevada, Arizona, and Mexico. Capital: Sacramento. Population: 35,116,033 (2002 estimate). Area: 411,469 sq. km/158,869 sq. mi. —**Californian** *n, adj*

California, Gulf of arm of the Pacific Ocean that extends northwards between mainland Mexico and Baja California. Area: 152,810 sq. km/59,000 sq. mi. Former name **Cortés, Sea of**

California condor *n* a large, dark grey or brown vulture with a wingspan of about 3 m/10 ft and a naked head and neck. It is being rescued from extinction by a captive breeding programme. Native to: southeastern United States. Latin name: *Gymnogyps californianus.*

California Current current in the northern Pacific Ocean. It flows from north to south along the western coast of North America before turning west.

California poppy, Californian poppy *n* an annual plant with bluish divided leaves. Flowers: bright red to yellow. Latin name: *Eschscholzia californica.*

californium /kálli fáwrni əm/ *n* a synthetic radioactive metallic element. Source: bombardment of curium or americium with neutrons. Use: neutron source. Symbol **Cf**. See table at **element** [Mid-20C. Because first synthesized at the University of California]

Caligula /kə líggyoõlə/ (AD 12–41) Roman emperor. A despotic ruler (AD 37–41), he bankrupted the state with his extravagance and was assassinated. Full name **Gaius Julius Caesar Germanicus**

> 'Would that the Roman people had but one neck!'
> [Attributed to Caligula, *Life of Caligula*, Suetonius; 121?]

caliper *n* MED, MEASURE Aus, US spelling of **calliper**

caliph /káylif, kállif/, **calif, kalif, khalif** *n* a title taken by Islamic rulers such as the Turkish sultans that asserts religious authority to rule, derived from that of Muhammad [14C. Via French *caliphe* < Arabic *kalīfa* 'successor, deputy' < *kalafa* 'succeed']

caliphate /kálli fayt, káyli-, -fit/, **califate, kalifate, khalifate** *n* the territory over which a caliph's rule extends, or the time for which it lasts

calix /káyliks, káll-/ (*plural* **-lices** /-li seez/) *n* **1.** a chalice or cup **2.** ANAT same as **calyx** (sense 2) [Early 18C. < Latin (see CHALICE)]

calk[1] /kawk/ *n* a metal spike on a horseshoe to prevent slipping [Late 16C. Origin ?]

calk[2] *vt* CONSTR another spelling of **caulk**

call /kawl/ *v* (**calls, calling, called**) **1.** *vt* NAME SOMEBODY OR SOMETHING to give somebody or something a name ○ *What are you going to call the baby?* **2.** *vt* REFER TO SOMEBODY to use a particular term to address or refer to somebody ○ *He always called his father 'Sir'.* **3.** *vt* DESCRIBE SOMEBODY OR SOMETHING AS SOMETHING to describe or think of somebody or something in a particular way ○ *I'd call him a fool.* **4.** *vti* SAY SOMETHING OR SPEAK LOUDLY to say something or speak in a loud voice ○ *'Supper's ready', he called from the kitchen.* **5.** *vi* CRY to give a characteristic cry (*refers to birds or animals*) **6.** *vt* SUMMON SOMEBODY OR SOMETHING to summon or alert somebody or something by means of a formal request ○ *I'll call a taxi.* **7.** *vti* MAKE REQUEST FOR SOMETHING TO HAPPEN to make an official order or request for something such as a meeting ○ *A council meeting has been called for July 15th.* **8.** *vti* TELEPHONE SOMEBODY to contact somebody by telephone or radio **9.** *vt* READ SOMETHING OUT to read names or numbers from a list **10.** *vi* VISIT SOMEBODY to visit somebody or the place where somebody lives or works ○ *I called to see her yesterday.* **11.** *vi* TRANSP STOP SOMEWHERE to stop at a particular place on a regular bus, coach, or train route ○ *Do you call at George Square?* **12.** *vti* DECLARE CHOICE IN GAME to make a declaration in a game, e.g. to choose heads or tails, or choose trumps in a card game ○ *I'll toss, you call.* **13.** *vt* N Am PREDICT SOMETHING to predict what is going to happen, especially in politics ○ *It's a very hard result to call.* **14.** *vt* SPORTS OFFICIALLY DECIDE SOMETHING IN GAME to make an official decision in a sporting event or a game ○ *called a foul* **15.** *vti* DANCE INSTRUCT DANCERS to direct people who are dancing, e.g. in a square dance **16.** *vt* FIN DEMAND REPAYMENT OF SOMETHING to demand repayment of a loan or bond issue ○ *call a loan* **17.** *vt* ANZ COMMENTATE ON EVENT to commentate on radio or television on a sporting event, especially a horse race ■ *n* **1.** SHOUT a shout or cry **2.** BIRD OR ANIMAL CRY the characteristic sound made by a bird or animal **3.** FIELD SPORTS HUNTER'S DEVICE TO ATTRACT GAME a device that imitates the cry of a bird or other animal, used as a lure in hunting **4.** SIGNAL a signal given by a sound, e.g. on a horn or whistle **5.** TELEPHONE COMMUNICATION a telephone conversation, or an attempt to get in touch with somebody by telephone **6.** REMINDER a reminder, given electronically, by telephone, or in person, that somebody should wake up or that something is about to happen **7.** REQUEST TO COME a request for somebody to come ○ *The emergency services answer thousands of calls a year.* **8.** EXPRESSED WISH a demand or request for something to be done ○ *There have been calls for him to resign.* **9.** FEELING OF DUTY a feeling that a particular job or way of life is a personal duty **10.** VISIT a short visit to somebody at his or her house or place of work ○ *made a few calls on the way home* **11.** DECISION a decision or choice to be made by somebody ○ *It's your call.* **12.** LEISURE DECLARATION IN GAME a declaration made during a game, e.g. the choice of heads or tails when a coin is tossed **13.** STRONG APPEAL OF PLACE OR LIFESTYLE the feeling of strong attraction exerted by a particular place or way of life ○ *the call of the wild* **14.** SPORTS, LEISURE REFEREE'S DECISION a decision made by a referee **15.** DEMAND OR OBLIGATION a demand or obligation that somebody has to fulfil ○ *I'd like to help, but I have a great many calls on my time.* **16.** N Am PREDICTION a prediction of what is about to happen, especially in politics **17.** FIN same as **call option** [12C. < Old Norse *kalla*] ◇ **be on call** to be on duty away from the workplace, available to be summoned ◇ **there's no call for something** *or* **to do something** 1. used to say that a particular remark or action is not welcome or necessary ○ *There's no call to get angry.* **2.** people do not want something, especially a particular commercial product ○ *There's no call for swimsuits at this time of year.*

call back *v* **1.** *vti* TELEPHONE SOMEBODY AGAIN to contact somebody by telephone again ○ *If she's busy, I'll call back later.* **2.** *vti* RETURN TELEPHONE CALL TO SOMEBODY to telephone somebody in order to return that person's telephone call ○ *My money's running out – can you call me back?* **3.** *vi* VISIT SOMEBODY AGAIN to visit somebody again **4.** *vt* ASK TO RETURN to recall somebody, e.g. for a second audition or interview, or to return to a job **5.** *vt* ASK WORKERS BACK TO WORK to contact previously laid-off workers to ask them to return to a job site

call down *vt* **1.** to pray or appeal for good or bad things to happen to somebody **2.** *N Am* to rebuke somebody who has done something wrong ○ *The judge called the lawyers down for their unseemly courtroom antics.*

call for *vt* **1.** MAKE REQUEST FOR SOMETHING TO HAPPEN to make a demand or request for something to be done **2.** NEED to need or require a particular thing or quality **3.** COLLECT to collect somebody

call forth *vt* to inspire an emotion, energy, or courage

call in *v* **1.** *vt* ASK HELP FROM SOMEBODY to ask somebody to come and give advice or help **2.** *vi* PAY QUICK VISIT TO SOMEBODY to make a brief visit to somebody **3.** *vi* TELEPHONE PLACE OF WORK to telephone a place of work in order to collect or leave a message **4.** *vt* ASK FOR SOMETHING TO BE REPAID to ask for a debt or loan to be repaid **5.** *vt* ARRANGE RETURN OF SOMETHING to arrange for or request that something be returned, e.g. outdated currency or defective goods

call off *vt* **1.** to cancel or stop an event **2.** to order a dog or a person to stop attacking somebody

call on *vt* **1.** to ask or tell somebody to do something **2.** to visit somebody, often in a formal manner

call out *vt* **1.** SUMMON SOMEBODY TO HELP to summon a person or an organization to give help **2.** ORDER WORKERS TO STRIKE to tell workers to stop work and go on strike **3.** CHALLENGE SOMEBODY TO FIGHT to challenge somebody to a duel or fight (*archaic*)

call up *vt* **1.** RECRUIT SOMEBODY TO FIGHT to order somebody to join the armed services in time of war. N Am term **draft 2.** SUMMON SOMEBODY OR SOMETHING IN RESERVE to summon somebody or something that is available in reserve **3.** TELEPHONE SOMEBODY to contact somebody by telephone (*informal*) **4.** COMPUT DISPLAY SOMETHING ON COMPUTER SCREEN to instruct a computer to find and display a particular piece of information ○ *call up last month's sales figures* **5.** EVOKE SOMETHING to bring back memories of something

call upon *vt* **1.** to ask somebody in a formal way to do something **2.** to make demands on somebody or on somebody's abilities

calla /kállə/ *n* PLANTS same as **arum lily**

callable /káwləb'l/ *adj* **1.** describes a loan that is repayable on demand **2.** describes a share or bond that is convertible before reaching maturity

Callaghan /kálləhən, -han/, **James, Baron Callaghan of Cardiff** (*b.* 1912) British politician. He was home secretary (1967–70), foreign secretary (1974–76), and Labour prime minister (1976–79). He became a Life Peer in 1987. Full name **Callaghan, Leonard James.** See table at **prime minister**

> 'Britain has lived for too long on borrowed time, borrowed money and even borrowed ideas.'
> [James Callaghan, *Observer*; 3 October 1976]

call alarm *n* a personal alarm used for summoning help in an emergency

calla lily *n N Am* same as **arum lily**

callaloo *n Carib* same as **calalu**

Callao /kə yów/ *city and chief seaport of Peru, situated on Callao Bay 13 km/8 mi. west of Lima. Population: 424,294 (1998).

Maria Callas

Callas /kálləss/, **Maria** (1923–77) US-born operatic soprano. One of the leading opera singers of the mid-20th century, she was known for her incisive portrayals of such characters as Norma and Tosca. Born **Kalogeropoulos, Maria Anna Sofia Cecilia**

callback /káwl bak/ *n* **1.** RETURN CALL a telephone call made to somebody who has recently phoned **2.** RECALLING OF SOMEBODY an act of asking somebody to return, especially for a second audition **3.** *N Am* PRODUCT RECALL the recalling of a faulty product by a manufacturer

call bird *n* a cheap item displayed to attract customers

callboard /káwl bawrd/ *n* a board backstage in a theatre, giving information to actors and other people involved in a production

call box *n* **1.** *UK* TELECOM same as **telephone box 2.** *N Am* a telephone alongside a highway, used for reporting emergencies

callboy /káwl boy/ *n* somebody in a theatre who tells the actors when the time for them to go on stage is approaching

call centre *n* a place that handles high-volume incoming telephone calls on behalf of a large organization

caller /káwlər/ *n* **1.** SOMEBODY PHONING OR VISITING somebody who makes a telephone call or a visit **2.** ANNOUNCER an announcer, e.g. of moves in a square dance or of numbers in a game of bingo **3.** *Aus* SPORTS COMMENTATOR a radio or television commentator for a sporting event, especially a horse race

caller ID *n* an electronic device attached to a telephone that, on a small screen, shows the name and telephone number of somebody who is calling or has called

calleting /kálləting/ *n regional* an act of nagging at or scolding somebody

REGIONAL NOTE See *jawing*.

call girl *n* a prostitute who makes appointments with clients by telephone

calli *vt* DRUGS another spelling of **kali** (*slang; used in Black English*)

calli- *prefix* beautiful ○ *callipygian* [< Greek *kallos* 'beauty']

calligraphy /kə líggrəfi/ *n* **1.** the art or skill of producing beautiful or artistic handwriting **2.** beautiful or artistic handwriting [Early 17C. < Greek *kalligraphia* 'beautiful writing' < *kallos* 'beauty' + *graphein* 'write'] —**calligrapher** *n* —**calligraphic** /kálli gráffik/ *adj* —**calligraphically** *adv* —**calligraphist** *n*

Callil /kə líl/, **Carmen** (*b.* 1938) Australian publisher. She founded the London-based Virago publishing house (1972).

call-in *n N Am* BROADCAST same as **phone-in**

calling /káwling/ *n* **1.** a strong urge to follow a particular career or do a particular type of work **2.** a job or profession

calling card *n* **1.** *N Am* same as **visiting card 2.** TELECOM same as **phonecard 3.** something that serves to identify somebody or something ○ *a drop of blood containing the DNA calling card of an unknown person*

calliope /kə lí əpi/ *n ANZ, N Am* an organ that generates sound by the release of steam or compressed air through pipes, with tunes often played mechanically, as on a player piano. Calliopes are

usually found in fairgrounds or circuses. UK term **steam organ** [Mid-19C. < Latin *Calliope* 'Calliope']

Calliope /kə lī́ əpi/ *n* in Greek mythology, the Muse of epic poetry, one of the nine Muses believed to inspire and nurture the arts [Via Latin < Greek *Kalliopē*, literally 'beautiful-voiced'.]

calliper /kállipər/ *n* **1. MEASURING INSTRUMENT** an instrument used to measure the internal or external dimensions of objects and consisting of two curved hinged legs joined at one end (*usually used in the plural*) **2. LEG BRACE** a leg splint consisting of metal rods and straps that enables the hip bone, rather than the foot, to support weight when walking ■ *vt* **(-pers, -pering, -pered) MEASURE SOMETHING WITH CALLIPER** to measure something using a calliper [Late 16C. Origin ?]

calliper rule *n* a graduated scale with jaws, one fixed and one sliding, set at right angles to it, used to measure the thickness of boards or the diameters of pipes or shafts

callipygian /kálli píjji ən/, **callipygous** /kálli pī́gəss/ *adj* having well-shaped buttocks (*literary*) [Late 18C. < Greek *kallipūgos* 'beautiful buttocks' (applied to a statue of Aphrodite) < *kallos* 'beauty' + *pugē* 'buttocks']

callisthenics /kálliss thénniks/ *npl* vigorous physical exercises for improving fitness and muscle tone, including push-ups, sit-ups, and star jumps (*takes a plural verb*) ■ *n* the practice of performing callisthenics (*takes a singular verb*) [Early 19C. < Greek *kallios* 'beauty' + *sthenos* 'strength'] —**callisthenic** *adj*

Callisto /kə lístō/ *n* **1.** in Greek mythology, a nymph who was changed into a bear by Hera and later became the constellation Ursa Major **2.** a large satellite of Jupiter that was discovered in 1610 [Via Latin < Greek *Kallistō* < *kalos* 'beautiful']

call letters *npl N Am* a group of letters used for identification by a radio transmitting station

call loan *n* a loan that must be repaid on demand

call mark *n* LIBRARIES same as **shelf mark**

call money *n* money that has been borrowed and is repayable on demand

call number *n* LIBRARIES same as **shelf mark**

call of nature *n* a need to urinate or defecate (*humorous*)

call option *n* a financial document that gives somebody the right, but not the obligation, to buy an asset at a particular exercise price on or before a particular date

callose /kállōz/ *n* a polysaccharide found in plant cell walls and formed in flowering plants in response to injury. It consists of chains of linked glucose units. [Mid-19C. < Latin *callosus* (see CALLOUS)]

callosity /kə lóssəti/ (*plural* **-ties**) *n* a local thickening of the outer layer of the skin caused by repeated friction or pressure

Callot /kə lṓ/, **Jacques** (1592–1635) French artist. His realistic and innovatory techniques can be seen in such etchings as *Miseries of War* (1633).

callous /kálləss/ *adj* showing no concern that other people are or might be hurt or upset [14C. Directly or via French < Latin *callosus* 'hardened by friction' < *callus* 'hard skin'] —**callously** *adv* —**callousness** *n*

SPELLCHECK callous or **callus**? Do not confuse the spelling of ***callous*** and ***callus***, which sound similar. ***Callous*** is an adjective meaning 'insensitive or unfeeling', as in *a callous remark*. ***Callus*** is a noun that usually denotes a patch of thickened skin on the hand or foot.

calloused /kálləst/, **callused** *adj* having an area of hard thickened skin

callow /kállō/ *adj* young or immature, and lacking the experience of life that comes with adulthood [Old English *calu* < Germanic] —**callowness** *n*

Calloway /kállə way/, **Cab** (1907–94) US jazz musician, known for his exuberant performances, catch phrase 'hi-de-ho', and scat singing. Full name **Calloway, Cabell**

call sign *n* a signal, often a group of letters and numbers, used for identification by a radio transmitting station or a unit or operator in radio communication with others

call slip *n* a form for requesting a library book that is not kept on the shelves used by the public

call-up *n* MIL an order to join the armed services in time of war. N Am term **draft**

callus /kálləss/ *n* **1. PATCH OF THICKENED SKIN** a hard thickened area of skin, especially on the palm of the hand or the sole of the foot, caused by repeated pressure or friction **2.** MED **MASS FORMED IN HEALING BONE** a mass of fibrous tissue, calcium, cartilage, and bone that forms progressively during the healing of a bone fracture **3.** BOT **PLANT TISSUE** plant tissue that forms at the site of a wound, or that develops during tissue culture of plant parts, giving rise to new plantlets ■ *vti* **(-luses, -lusing, -lused) DEVELOP CALLUS** to develop a callus or calluses, or cause something to do so [Mid-16C. < Latin]

SPELLCHECK See *callous*.

callused *adj* another spelling of **calloused**

call waiting *n* **1.** a facility for taking a telephone call while another is in progress on the same line, usually putting the first on hold **2.** a service offered by a telephone company that allows somebody to answer an additional incoming call without disconnecting from the current call

calm /kaam/ *adj* **1. NOT ANXIOUS** without anxiety or strong emotion **2. NOT STORMY** smooth and without any large waves ○ *smooth sailing on calm seas* **3. NOT WINDY** without wind or storms ○ *forecasting a calm evening after heavy rain* **4. NOT VIOLENT** free from civil disturbance or violence ○ *The city was reported calm after a curfew was imposed.* ■ *n* **1. PEACE AND QUIET** a situation of complete peace and quiet, with no noise, trouble, or anxiety **2. ABSENCE OF WIND** still weather, without wind or waves caused by wind **3.** METEOROL **LOWEST POINT OF BEAUFORT SCALE** a wind of no more than 1.6 km/1 mi. per hour, classified as the lowest force on the Beaufort scale ■ *vt* **(calms, calming, calmed) MAKE SOMEBODY LESS TENSE** to make somebody less anxious or upset [14C. Probably directly or via French *calme* < late Latin *cauma* 'heat of the day' < Greek *kauma*] —**calmly** *adv* —**calmness** *n*

calm down *vti* to become or make somebody become less excited, anxious, or upset

calmative /kaámətiv/ *adj* having a calming or quietening effect

calmodulin /kal móddyoolin/ *n* a calcium-binding protein found in the cells of most living organisms that controls many enzyme processes [Late 20C. Contraction of CALCIUM + MODULATE + -IN]

calomel /kállə mel, -məl/ *n* a mercury compound. Use: fungicide, insecticide, formerly, as a purgative. [Late 17C. < modern Latin]

Calor Gas /kállər-/ *tdmk* a trademark for liquid butane gas sold in cylinders for domestic use

caloric /kə lórrik, kállərik/ *adj* same as **calorific** (sense 1) —**calorically** /kə lórrikli/ *adv*

calorie /kálləri/ *n* **1. UNIT OF ENERGY** a unit of energy equal to 4.1855 joules, originally defined as the quantity of heat required to raise the temperature of 1 g of pure water by 1° C. It has now been superseded by the joule in scientific usage. **2. LARGER UNIT OF ENERGY** a unit of energy equal to the heat required to raise the temperature of 1 kg of pure water by 1° C **3. UNIT OF FOOD ENERGY** a unit of energy-producing potential in food, equal to one large calorie. This energy, if not used, is converted to fat and stored. [Mid-19C. < French < Latin *calor* 'heat' < *calere* 'be warm']

calorific /kállə ríffik/ *adj* **1.** relating to heat or calories, especially the number of calories contained in food **2.** containing many calories, and so likely to be fattening

calorific value *n* the amount of heat released by the combustion of a mass of fuel, typically measured in joules per kilogram

calorimeter /kállə rímmitər/ *n* an apparatus for measuring the amount of heat given out or taken in during a process such as combustion or change of state. The measurements are often made by observing the amount of solid liquefied, or liquid vaporized, under set conditions. —**calorimetric** /kálləri méttrik/ *adj* —**calorimetrically** *adv* —**calorimetry** *n*

calorize /kállə rīz/ **(-rizes, -rizing, -rized)**, **calorise (-rises, -rising, -rised)** *v* to treat the surface of steel or iron with aluminium powder and heat to 800–1,000° C to prevent or reduce rusting [Mid-20C. < Latin *calor* (see CALORIE)]

calotype /kállō tīp/ *n* **1.** a 19th-century photographic process producing a negative on a plate wetted with silver iodide **2.** a photograph produced by the calotype process [Mid-19C. < Greek *kalos* 'beautiful']

Caloundra /kə lówndrə/ city and beach resort in Queensland, Australia, situated north of Brisbane. Population: 78,798 (2002 estimate).

calpac /kál pak/, **calpack, kalpak** *n* a high-peaked felt or sheepskin hat worn by men in Turkey and parts of eastern Central Asia [Late 16C. < Turkish *kalpak*]

calque /kalk/ *n* LANGUAGE same as **loan translation** [Mid-20C. < French, 'copy' < Latin *calcare* (see CAULK)]

caltrop /káltrəp/ *n* **1.** MIL a military device with four spikes arranged so that one will always point upwards, scattered on the ground to lame horses or puncture tyres **2.** (*plural* **caltrops** or *same*) a spiny plant harmful to livestock. Native to: Europe, naturalized in California. Latin name: *Tribulus terrestris.* **3.** PLANTS same as **water chestnut** (sense 3) **4.** PLANTS same as **star thistle** [Pre-12C. Variant of obsolete *calcatrippe* 'thistle' < medieval Latin *calcatrippa*]

calumet /kállyoo met/ *n* a long-stemmed ceremonial pipe used by some Native American peoples [Late 17C. < French, 'pipe', dialect variant of *chalumeau* < Latin *calamus* 'reed']

calumniate /kə lúmni ayt/ **(-ates, -ating, -ated)** *vt* to accuse somebody falsely, or slander somebody (*formal*) [Mid-16C. < Latin *calumniat-*, past participle of *calumniare* < *calumnia* (see CALUMNY)] —**calumniable** *adj* —**calumniation** /kə lúmni áysh'n/ *n* —**calumniator** *n*

calumny /kálləmni/ (*plural* **-nies**) *n* (*formal*) **1.** the making of false statements about somebody with malicious intent **2.** a slanderous statement or false accusation [15C. < Latin *calumnia* 'false accusation' < *calvi* 'deceive'] —**calumnious** /kə lúmni əss/ *adj* —**calumniously** *adv*

calvados /kálvə doss/ *n* apple brandy distilled from cider, made in the Normandy region of France [Early 20C. After *Calvados*, Normandy]

calvarium /kal váiri əm/ (*plural* **-ia** /-i ə/) *n* the upper domed portion of the skull (*technical*) [Late 19C. Alteration of Latin *calvaria* 'skull' < *calvus* 'bald']

calvary /kálvəri/ (*plural* **-ries**) *n* a sculpture representing Jesus Christ's crucifixion [Early 18C. < CALVARY]

Calvary /kálvəri/ *n* a hill just outside the city walls of ancient Jerusalem where the Crucifixion of Jesus Christ took place, according to the Bible [< Latin *calvaria* 'skull', translating Greek *golgotha* (see GOLGOTHA)]

Calvary cross *n* a Christian cross mounted on three symmetrical steps

calve /kaav/ **(calves, calving, calved)** *vti* **1.** to give birth to a calf **2.** to release a mass of ice that breaks away (*refers to a glacier or iceberg*) [Old English *calfian* < *cælf* 'calf']

Calvert /kálvərt, káwl-/, **Cecelius, 2nd Baron Baltimore** (1605–75) English-born American colonial administrator. He inherited Maryland (1632), settled the colony, and implemented the policies written into its charter.

Calvert, Charles, 3rd Baron Baltimore (1637–1715) English-born American colonial administrator. He governed the Maryland colony (1661–89).

Calvert, George, 1st Baron Baltimore (1580?–1632) English-born American absentee colonial administrator. He established the colony of Maryland (1632) and advocated religious tolerance.

Calvert, Leonard (1606–47) English-born American colonial administrator. He was the first governor of Maryland (1633–47).

calves[1] ZOOL plural of **calf**[1]

calves[2] ANAT plural of **calf**[2]

Calvin /kálvin/, **John** (1509–64) French-born Swiss Protestant reformer. He founded a Presbyterian government in Switzerland and developed the doctrine of the Protestant Reformation in *Institutes of the Christian Religion* (1536).

Calvin cycle *n* a series of reactions that take place in photosynthesis by which carbon dioxide is con-

verted to glucose [After Melvin *Calvin* (1911–97), US biochemist]

Calvinism /kálvinizəm/ *n* the religious doctrine of John Calvin, which maintains that salvation comes through faith in God, and also that God has already chosen those who will believe and be saved —**Calvinist** *n*, *adj* —**Calvinistic** /kálvi nístik/ *adj* —**Calvinistically** *adv*

Calvino /kal veénō/, **Italo** (1923–85) Cuban-born Italian novelist. His works, including *If on a Winter's Night a Traveller* (1979), contain a unique blend of realism and fantasy.

> 'I have tried to remove weight, sometimes from people, sometimes from heavenly bodies, sometimes from cities; above all I have tried to remove weight from the structure of stories and from language.'
> [Italo Calvino, *Six Memos for the Next Millennium*; 1988]

calx /kalks/ (*plural* **calxes** or **calces** /kál seez/) *n* **1.** the powdery oxide of a metal that is formed when an ore or a mineral is roasted **2.** the rounded part at the back of the heel [15C. < Latin, 'lime, limestone' < Greek *khalix* 'pebble']

calyces BOT plural of **calyx**

calyculus /kə líkyoŏləss/ (*plural* **-li** /-lī/), **calycle** /kállik'l/, **calicle** *n* a small cup-shaped structure, e.g. the depression at the top of a coral skeleton [Late 19C. < Latin, 'calyx of a flower', diminutive of *calyx* 'husk' (see CALYX)] —**calycular** *adj* —**calyculate** /-layt, -lət/ *adj*

calypso /kə lípsō/ (*plural* **-sos**) *n* **1.** a Caribbean, especially Trinidadian, ballad with a lively dance rhythm, that deals satirically with social and political topics **2.** Caribbean dance music that has syncopated rhythms, is usually improvised, and is often played by a steel band [Early 20C. Origin ?]

Calypso /kə lípsō/ *n* **1.** in Greek mythology, a nymph who kept Odysseus on her island for seven years **2.** a small irregularly-shaped natural satellite of Saturn, discovered in 1980

calyx /káyliks, kálliks/ (*plural* **calyxes** or **calyces** /-li seez/) *n* **1.** the group of sepals, usually green, around the outside of a flower that encloses and protects the flower bud **2.** one of the funnel-shaped hollows in the pelvis of the kidney, through which urine passes to the ureter [Late 17C. Via Latin < Greek *kalux* 'husk, shell' < *kaluptein* 'conceal']

calzone /kal zō nay, -ni/ (*plural* **-nes** /-nis/ or **-ni** /-ni/) *n* a semicircular Italian turnover made from pizza dough with a savoury filling [Late 20C. < Italian, literally 'trouser leg' < Latin *calceus* 'shoe' < *calx* 'heel']

cam /kam/ *n* an irregularly-shaped projection on a rotating shaft that changes rotary motion into a reciprocating up and down motion in another machine part (**cam follower**) that touches it [Late 18C. < Dutch *kam* 'comb']

CAM /kam/ *abbr* COMPUT, MANUF computer-aided manufacturing

Camagüey Archipelago /kámmə gwáy-/ group of coral islands situated off east-central Cuba, including the islands of Romano, Sabinal, and Coco, and extending approximately 241 km/150 mi. from northwest to southeast

camaraderie /kámmə raádəri, -ráddəri/ *n* a feeling of close friendship and trust among a group of people [Mid-19C. < French < *camarade* (see COMRADE)]

Camargue /ka maárg/ delta region of marshes, lagoons, and farmland in the Bouches-du-Rhône administrative region in southern France. The sparsely populated region is known for its wild bulls, white horses, and flamingos.

camarilla /kámmə ríllə/ *n* a group of advisers, especially a secretive group advising an important person [Mid-19C. < Spanish, 'small room' < *camara* 'room']

camas /kámməss/ (*plural* **camasses** or *same*), **camass** (*plural* **camasses** or *same*) *n* a plant with grassy leaves and an edible bulb. Flowers: blue and white, in clusters. Native to: North America. Latin name: *Camassia quamash*. [Early 19C. < Chinook Jargon *qamaš*]

Camb. *abbr* Cambridge

camber /kámbər/ *n* **1.** CONVEX CURVE IN ROAD a slight convex curve in a structure, especially the curve in the surface of a road **2.** SLANT OF VEHICLE'S WHEELS a slant in the steerable wheels on a vehicle that makes them slightly closer together at the bottom than at the top ■ *vti* (**-bers, -bering, -bered**) MAKE CURVED SHAPE to form something with a camber, or be formed in this way [Early 17C. Via French *cambre* 'arched' < Latin *camur* 'curved inwards'] —**cambered** *adj*

Camberley /kámbərli/ town in Surrey, southeastern England, the site of an army staff college. Population: 46,120 (1991).

Camberwell beauty /kámbər wel-/ (*plural* **Camberwell beauties** or *same*) *n UK* a butterfly with purplish-brown wings that are spotted and rimmed with bright yellow. Native to: Europe, North America. Latin name: *Nymphalis antiopa*. ANZ, N Am term **mourning cloak** [Mid-18C. After a district of SE London]

cambist /kámbist/ *n* a dealer in foreign exchange [Early 19C. Via French < Italian *cambista* < medieval Latin *cambium* (see CAMBIUM)]

cambium /kámbi əm/ (*plural* **-biums** or **-bia** /-bi ə/) *n* a cylindrical layer of cells in plant roots and stems that produces the new tissue responsible for increased girth, particularly sap-conducting tissues, xylem and phloem, and bark [Late 17C. < medieval Latin *cambium* 'exchange' < Latin *cambire* 'to exchange'] —**cambial** *adj*

Cambodia

Cambodia /kam bōdi ə/ country in Southeast Asia, in the southern part of Indochina, bordered by Thailand, Laos, Vietnam, and the Gulf of Thailand. Language: Khmer, French. Currency: riel. Capital: Phnom Penh. Population: 13,124,764 (2003). Area: 181,035 sq. km/69,898 sq. mi. Official name **Kingdom of Cambodia**. Former name **Kampuchea** (1976–89), **Khmer Republic** (1970–75)

Cambodian /kam bōdi ən/ *n* **1.** somebody who comes from Cambodia **2.** LANG same as **Khmer**[1] (sense 3) (*dated*) —**Cambodian** *adj*

Camborne-Redruth /kám bawrn réd rooth/ district in Cornwall, southwestern England, southwest of Plymouth. Population: 35,915 (1991).

Cambrai /kám bray, kaáN-/ town in the Nord-Pas-de-Calais region in northern France, south of Lille. Population: 33,738 (1999). Flemish name **Kamerijk**

Cambrian /kámbri ən/ *n* PREHISTORIC PERIOD the period of geological time, 570 million to 500 million years ago, during which invertebrate animal life, including trilobites, appeared, and marine algae developed. See table at **geological time** ■ *adj* **1.** GEOL OF CAMBRIAN relating to the period of geological time known as the Cambrian. See table at **geological time 2.** WELSH relating to or from Wales [Mid-17C. < medieval Latin *Cambria* 'Wales' < Welsh *Cymry*]

Cambrian Mountains /kámbri ən-/ mountain system of Wales, running from north to south and covering about two-thirds of the country. It includes Snowdon, the Brecon Beacons, and the Black Mountains. The highest peak is Aran Fawddwy 905 m/2,970 ft.

cambric /káymbrik/ *n* a thin white linen or cotton fabric [14C. After *Kamerijk* 'Cambrai']

Cambridge /káym brij/ **1.** university city in eastern England. It lies on the River Cam, and is the administrative headquarters of Cambridgeshire and a local government district. Population: 108,863 (2001). **2.** city in Massachusetts. It is home to Harvard University, founded in 1636, Radcliffe College, founded in 1879, and the Massachusetts Institute of Technology, founded in 1865. Population: 101,807 (2002 estimate).

Cambridge blue *n* **1.** LIGHT BLUE COLOUR a light bright blue colour **2.** CAMBRIDGE ATHLETE a representative of Cambridge University in a sports event who has been awarded a blue ■ *adj* COLOURS OF LIGHT BLUE of a light bright blue colour [After CAMBRIDGE, England]

Cambridgeshire /káym brijshər/ county of eastern England. Population: 552,658 (2001). Area: 3,409 sq. km/1,316 sq. mi.

Cambs. *abbr* Cambridgeshire

Cambyses I /kam bí seez/ (*fl* 6th century BC) Persian king. He reigned over a dynasty in present-day Iraq around 600–559 BC. His son, Cyrus the Great, founded the Persian Empire.

Cambyses II (*d.* 522 BC) Persian king. He reigned from 529 BC to 522 BC, and conquered Egypt (525 BC) to expand the Persian Empire.

camcorder

camcorder /kám kawrdər/ *n* a portable video camera and recorder [Late 20C. Blend of CAMERA + RECORDER]

Camden /kámdən/ borough in North London, England. Population: 198,020 (2001).

Camden, William (1551–1623) English antiquary and historian. He compiled a topographical account of the British Isles, *Britannia* (1586).

came past tense of **come**

camel /kámm'l/ *n* **1.** (*plural* **camels** or *same*) a ruminant animal that has either one or two humps on its back and is adapted to a dry climate. Genus: *Camelus*. **2.** COLOURS a light sandy brown colour **3.** NAUT same as **caisson** (sense 2) [Pre-12C. Via Latin < Greek *kamēlos* < Semitic] —**camel** *adj*

cameleer /kámmə leér/ *n* a rider or controller of a camel

camel hair, **camel's hair** *n* **1.** HAIR OF CAMEL hair from the camel. Use: clothing, rugs. **2.** TEXTILES FABRIC soft fabric containing camel hair or a similar fibre. Use: coats. **3.** ART PAINTBRUSH an artist's paintbrush, normally made of squirrel hair and used primarily for watercolours

~~camelia~~ incorrect spelling of **camellia**

camelid /kámm'lid/ *n* a member of the family that includes camels, llamas, and their relatives, all of which have feet with two toes and thick leathery soles. Family: Camelidae.

camellia /kə meéli ə/ (*plural* **-lias** or *same*) *n* **1.** an ornamental bush of the tea family with glossy evergreen leaves and rose-shaped flowers. Latin name: *Camellia japonica*. **2.** a tree or bush of the tea family that resembles a camellia. Genus: *Camellia*. [Mid-18C. < modern Latin < *Camellus*, Latinized name of Joseph *Kamel* (1661–1706), Moravian Jesuit missionary and botanist]

camelopard /kə méllə paard, kámmilə-/ *n* ZOOL same as **giraffe** (*archaic*) [14C. < Latin *camelopardus* < Greek *kamēlopardalis* < *kamēlos* 'camel' + *pardalis* 'pard' (because the animal has a head like a camel and spots like a leopard)]

Camelopardalis /kə méllə paárd'liss/, **Camelopardus** /-dəss/, **Cameloopard** /kə méllə paard, kámmilə-/ *n* a large faint constellation of the northern hemisphere. See illustration at **constellation** [Via Latin < Greek *kamēlopardalis* (see CAMELOPARD)]

Camelot /kámmə lot/ *n* **1.** in Arthurian legend, the city of King Arthur **2.** a place or situation regarded as very enlightened, cultured, beautiful, and peaceful

CULTURAL NOTE *Camelot*, the 1960 musical by Alan Jay Lerner and Frederick Loewe, takes its title from the site of King Arthur's legendary sixth-century English court, and its tragic yet lavishly produced story centres on Arthur, his queen, Guinevere, and Lancelot.

camel's hair *n* INDUST, TEXTILES same as **camel hair**

camel spin *n* in figure skating, a spin in which the skater extends one leg backwards in a raised and horizontal position

Camembert /kámməm bair/ *n* a small round soft French cheese with an edible white rind that becomes more intense in flavour and softer in the centre as it ripens [Late 19C. After a town in Normandy, France]

cameo /kámmi ō/ *n* 1. a semiprecious stone carved to give a raised design in one colour against a background of another, especially a pale head against a darker background 2. a single brief appearance by a famous actor in a film or play [15C. < Italian]

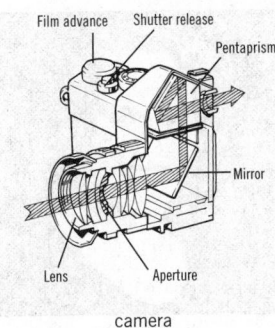

camera

camera /kámmərə/ *n* 1. DEVICE FOR TAKING PHOTOGRAPHS a device for taking photographs by letting light from an image fall briefly onto sensitized film, usually by means of a lens-and-shutter mechanism 2. DEVICE FOR MAKING PICTURES a device that converts images into electrical signals for television transmission, video recording, or digital storage 3. COMPUT GAMES COMPUTER GAME VIEWPOINT in a computer game, an imaginary camera located at the point that would produce the image shown on a computer screen [Early 18C. Via Latin, 'vault, chamber' < Greek *kamara*]

~~cameraderie~~ incorrect spelling of **camaraderie**

camera lucida /-loóssidə/ (*plural* **camera lucidas**) *n* a box or chamber that allows images to be projected onto a surface so they can be traced [Early 18C. < Latin, 'bright chamber']

cameraman /kámmrə man, -mən/ (*plural* **-men** /-men/) *n* a man who operates a film or television camera

camera obscura /-ob skyoórə/ *n* a box or small darkened room into which an image of what is outside is projected using a small hole, and sometimes a simple lens, in one of the sides of the box or room [Early 18C. < Latin, 'dark chamber']

cameraperson /kámmərə purss'n/ *n* an operator of a film or television camera

camera-ready *adj* describes material in its final publishable format, ready to be photographed or electronically scanned for the purpose of preparing printing plates

camera-shy *adj* with a dislike of being photographed or filmed

camerawoman /kámmərə woŏmən/ (*plural* **-women** /-wimin/) *n* a woman who operates a film or television camera

camerawork /kámmərə wurk/ *n* the ways in which cameras are used in films and television, especially their positioning and movement

camerlingo /kámmər líng gō/ (*plural* **-gos**), **camerlengo** /-léng gō/ *n* in the Roman Catholic Church, a cardinal who deals with the Pope's financial and other secular affairs [Early 17C. Via Italian < Frankish]

Cameron /kámmərən/, **Julia Margaret** (1815–79) British photographer. She is known for her sensitive portraits of eminent Victorian figures.

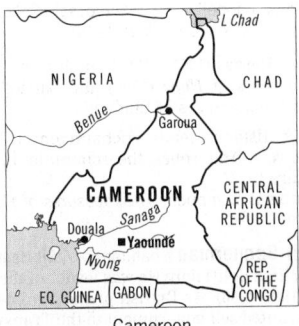

Cameroon

Cameroon /kámmə roŏn/ 1. country in west-central Africa. It became a German protectorate in 1884. After World War I it was divided into French and British Cameroon. French Cameroon became independent in 1960. In 1961, part of British Cameroon joined Nigeria, while the rest joined French Cameroon in a federal republic. Cameroon became a unitary state in 1972 and became an independent member of the Commonwealth in 1995. Language: French, English. Currency: CFA franc. Capital: Yaoundé. Population: 15,746,179 (2003). Area: 475,442 sq. km/183,569 sq. mi. Official name **Republic of Cameroon** 2. active volcano in southwestern Cameroon that had a major eruption in 1982. It is the highest mountain in West Africa. Height: 4,095 m/13,435 ft.

cam follower *n* a machine part that moves up and down in contact with a cam on a rotating shaft

cami /kámmi/ (*plural* **-is**) *n* CLOTHING same as **camisole** (*informal*) [Early 20C. Shortening]

camiknickers /kámmi nikərz/ *npl* 1. a woman's one-piece undergarment that combines a camisole with knickers 2. loose knee-length knickers for women, usually made of silky fabric and decorated with ruffles

camisado /kámmi saádō/ (*plural* **-dos**) *n* a surprise attack at night (*archaic*) [Mid-16C. < Spanish *camisada* 'attack in your shirt' (because attackers wore shirts over their armour in order to recognize each other) < *camisa* 'shirt']

camise /kə meéz/ *n* a style of loose shirt or tunic worn in former times [Early 19C. < Arabic *kamīs*]

camisole /kámmi sōl/ *n* 1. a woman's sleeveless undergarment covering the upper torso 2. a woman's sleeveless top with thin shoulder straps and a straight neckline ○ *a camisole top* [Early 19C. < French < late Latin *camisia* 'linen shirt, nightgown']

Camlan /kámlən/ *n* in Arthurian legend, the battlefield in the southwest of England where King Arthur was mortally wounded by his traitorous nephew Mordred before being carried away to Avalon

camo /kámmō/ *n* camouflage clothes or material used by military personnel (*slang*) [Shortening of CAMOUFLAGE]

Camões /ka móynsh/, **Camoëns** /kámmō ənss/, **Luís (Vaz) de** (1524?–80) Portuguese poet. His best-known work, *Os Lusíades* (*The Lusiads*) (1572), is considered Portugal's national epic.

~~camoflage~~ incorrect spelling of **camouflage**

camogie /kə mógi/ *n* an Irish stick and ball game that is a form of hurling played by women. Camogie was developed in 1900 by women in Dublin and the game has become increasingly popular with more than 400 clubs affiliated to the Camogie League. [Early 20C. < Irish Gaelic *camógaíocht* < *camóg* 'crooked stick']

camomile /kámmə mīl/, **chamomile** *n* 1. the leaves and flowers of an aromatic plant. Use: medicine, herbal teas. 2. an aromatic perennial plant with delicate leaves. Flowers: yellow and white, similar to daisies. Native to: Europe, Asia. Genera: *Anthemis* or *Matricaria*. [14C. Via Old French *camomille* < medieval Latin *chamomilla* < Greek *khamaimēlon* 'earth-apple'; because the flowers smell like apples]

camoodi /kə moŏdi/ (*plural* **-dis**) *n* REPT same as **anaconda** [Early 19C. < Arawak *kamudu*]

Camorra /kə mórrə/ *n* a secret society formed in Italy in the early 1800s that was involved in criminal and terrorist activities. The Camorra allied itself with Garibaldi and helped to eject the ruling Bourbons, then declined in the early 20th century and was suppressed in 1922 by Mussolini's Fascist government. [Mid-19C. < Italian]

camouflage /kámmə flaazh, -flaaj/ *n* 1. CONCEALMENT OF THINGS concealment of things, especially troops and military equipment, by disguising them to look like their surroundings, e.g. by covering them with branches or leaf-clad netting 2. CONCEALING DEVICES devices designed to conceal by imitating the colours of the surrounding environment ○ *a camouflage jacket* 3. PROTECTIVE COLORATION IN ANIMALS the devices that animals use to blend into their environment in order to avoid being seen by predators or prey, especially coloration 4. DISGUISE something that is intended to hide, disguise, or mislead ■ *vt* (**-flages, -flaging, -flaged**) DISGUISE SOMETHING to disguise something in order to mislead somebody, often somebody perceived as a threat ○ *camouflaged his true intentions* [Early 20C. < French < *camoufler* 'to disguise' < Italian *camuffare*] —**camouflager** *n*

camp[1] /kamp/ *n* 1. PLACE WITH REMOVABLE ACCOMMODATION a place where short-term accommodation such as tents or camper vans for holidaymakers has been temporarily erected or sited 2. PLACE FOR TEMPORARY STAY a set of buildings where people are housed temporarily, e.g. as prisoners, refugees, or troops ○ *a prison camp* 3. GROUP a group of people who share the same ideas, beliefs, or aims, or who form one of the sides in a debate ○ *members of the environmentalist camp* ■ *vi* (**camps, camping, camped**) 1. STAY TEMPORARILY to stay in temporary accommodation, especially in a tent ○ *We camped by a stream.* 2. TAKE TEMPORARY POSITION to take up a temporary position somewhere, e.g. as a protester or in alternative accommodation ○ *We'll camp on his doorstep until we get some action.* [Early 16C. Via French < Latin *campus* 'field, site for military exercises']

camp out *vi* 1. to live or sleep outdoors, with or without a tent ○ *camping out under the stars for a few nights.* 2. to take up a temporary position somewhere, e.g. as a protester or in alternative accommodation ○ *Hordes of journalists camped out in the palace grounds.*

camp[2] /kamp/ *adj* 1. AFFECTING CONVENTIONAL FEMININITY exaggeratedly or affectedly feminine, especially in a man 2. AMUSINGLY BRASH deliberately and exaggeratedly brash or vulgar in an amusing, often self-parodying way ■ *n* 1. EXAGGERATED FEMININITY exaggeratedly or affectedly feminine behaviour, especially in men 2. DELIBERATE OUTRAGEOUSNESS deliberate outrageousness for humorous effect ○ *The performance is high camp.* [Early 20C. Origin ?] —**camp** *vi* —**campy** *adj* ◇ **camp it up** (*informal*) 1. to behave in a deliberately outrageous way for humorous effect 2. to behave in an exaggeratedly or affectedly feminine way, especially to emphasize the fact of being gay (*usually refers to men*)

campaign /kam páyn/ *n* 1. PLANNED ACTIONS a planned and organized series of actions intended to achieve a specific goal, especially fighting for or against something or raising people's awareness of something ○ *an advertising campaign* 2. POL VOTE-SEEKING ACTIVITIES a series of events, e.g. rallies and speeches, that are intended to persuade voters to vote for a specific politician or party ○ *ran an expensive nationwide campaign* 3. MIL MILITARY OPERATIONS a series of military or terrorist operations taking place in one area over a period, intended to achieve a specific objective ○ *the Falklands campaign* ■ *vi* (**-paigns, -paigning, -paigned**) WORK TOWARDS GOAL to take part in a campaign to achieve a specific goal ○ *parents campaigning to get the school re-opened* 2. SEEK VOTES to take part in a political campaign ○ *We campaigned particularly strongly in the south.* [Early 17C. < French *campagne* 'open country' < Latin *campus* 'field'] —**campaigner** *n*

~~campain~~ incorrect spelling of **campaign**

Campanella /kámpə néllə/, **Tommaso** (1568–1639) Italian philosopher. He wrote the utopian *City of the Sun* (1623) while imprisoned by the Inquisition. Born **Campanella, Giovanni Domenico**

campanile /kámpə neéli/ (*plural* **-les** or **-li** /-li/) *n* a bell tower, especially a freestanding bell tower of the kind found in Italy. See illustration on next page

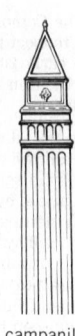

campanile

[Mid-17C. < Italian < *campana* 'bell' < late Latin *campana* (see CAMPANOLOGY)]

campanology /kámpə nólləji/ *n* the study or practice of bell-ringing [Mid-19C. < modern Latin *campanologia* < late Latin *campana* 'bell' < Latin *campanus* 'of Campania' (S Italy), former source of bronze for making bells] —**campanologist** *n*

campanula /kam pánnyoŏlə/ *n* an annual or perennial plant, widely grown as a garden plant. Flowers: bell-shaped, blue, white, or pink. Native to: northern temperate regions. Genus: *Campanula*. [Early 17C. < modern Latin, 'little bell' < late Latin *campana* (see CAMPANOLOGY)]

camp bed *n* a small narrow bed for occasional use that folds for easy storage and carriage, especially one consisting of a canvas sling supported on a sectional framework of metal tubing. N Am term **cot**[1]

Campbell /kámb'l/, **Donald** (1921–67) British motor-racing driver. Son of Sir Malcolm Campbell, he set world land and water speed records and died in an attempt on the latter. Full name **Campbell, Donald Malcolm**

Campbell, Keith (*b.* 1954) British microbiologist. With Ian Wilmut he was responsible for the first successful cloning of a mammal from adult cells.

Kim Campbell

Campbell, Kim (*b.* 1947) Canadian politician. She held several posts in Brian Mulroney's cabinet (1989–93) before becoming Canada's first woman prime minister (1993). Born **Campbell, Avril Phaedra**. See table at **prime minister**

'In a democracy, government isn't something that a small group of people do to everybody else, it's not even something they do for everybody else, it should be something they do with everybody else.'
[Kim Campbell, *Press conference*; 25 March 1993]

Campbell, Sir Malcolm (1885–1948) British motor-racing driver. He was the first man to set the world land speed record above 483 kph/300 mph (1935) in *Bluebird*.

Campbell, Mrs Patrick (1865–1940) British actor. She played Eliza in George Bernard Shaw's *Pygmalion* (1912). Born **Tanner, Beatrice Stella**

Campbell, Roy (1901–57) South African-born British poet, translator, and journalist. Among his works are the satire *The Georgiad* (1931) and the autobiographical *Light on a Dark Horse* (1951).

'South Africa, renowned both far and wide / For politics and little else beside.'

[Roy Campbell, 'The Wayzgoose', *Collected Poems of Roy Campbell*; 1949]

Campbell, Thomas (1777–1844) British poet. He wrote *The Pleasures of Hope* (1799) and patriotic lyrics such as 'Ye Mariners of England'.

''Tis distance lends enchantment to the view, / And robes the mountain in its azure hue.'
[Thomas Campbell, *The Pleasures of Hope*; 1799]

Campbell-Bannerman /-bánnərmən/, **Sir Henry** (1836–1908) British politician. He was leader of the Liberal Party (1899–1908). As British prime minister (1905–08) he granted self-government to the Transvaal and the Orange Free State in South Africa. See table at **prime minister**

Campbell Island uninhabited island in the south-western Pacific Ocean, 644 km/400 mi. south of New Zealand. Area: 166 sq. km/64 sq. mi.

Camp David /-dáyvid/ US presidential retreat in Catoctin Mountain Park, central Maryland, established by President Franklin D. Roosevelt in 1942. President Jimmy Carter hosted talks there in 1978 between Menachem Begin and Anwar al-Sadat, the presidents of Israel and Egypt, that led to the Camp David Accords, offering a framework for peace in the Middle East.

Campeche /kam peéchi, -peécháy/ **1.** state in southeastern Mexico on the Yucatán Peninsula. Capital: Campeche. Population: 690,689 (2000). Area: 56,800 sq. km/21,930 sq. mi. **2.** capital of Campeche State in southeastern Mexico. It is located on the coast in the northwestern part of the state. Population: 229,144 (2000).

camper /kámpər/ *n* **1.** somebody who goes camping ○ *accessories for campers and hikers* **2.** N Am VEHICLES same as **camper van 3.** N Am a trailer equipped as a self-contained travelling home, pulled by a car

camper van *n* a motor vehicle equipped as a self-contained travelling home, smaller than a motor caravan. It has basic facilities for cooking, washing, and sleeping. N Am term **camper**

Campese /kam peézi/, **David Ian** (*b.* 1962) Australian rugby union player, known for his speed and try-scoring ability. He holds the record (64) for tries in international games.

campesino /kámpə seénō/ (*plural* **-nos**) *n* in Latin American countries, a farmer or agricultural worker [Mid-20C. < Spanish < Latin *campus* 'field']

campfire /kámp fī ə/ *n* a wood fire built outside by campers, for cooking on or for warmth

camp follower *n* **1.** a civilian who follows a military unit from place to place in order to earn money by supplying products or services, especially like a prostitute **2.** a supporter of a group or an organization who does not belong to it

campground /kámp grownd/ *n* N Am same as **campsite** (sense 1)

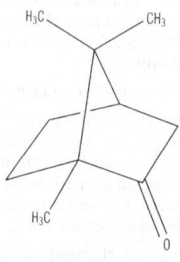

camphor

camphor /kámfər/ *n* a strong-smelling compound. Use: in medicinal creams, manufacture of celluloid, plastics, and explosives. Formula: $C_{10}H_{16}O$. [14C. Directly or via French < medieval Latin *camphora*, via Arabic and Malay < Sanskrit *karpūra*] —**camphoric** /kam fórrik/ *adj*

camphorate /kámfə rayt/ (**-ates, -ating, -ated**) *vt* to treat or impregnate something with camphor

camphor ice *n* an ointment used to relieve minor skin ailments, made of camphor mixed with white wax and castor oil

camphor oil *n* the oil that is distilled from the steamed bark and wood of the camphor tree

camphor tree *n* an evergreen tree, sometimes cultivated as an ornamental, with aromatic wood and bark that are a source of camphor. Native to: East Asia. Latin name: *Cinnamomum camphora*.

campimetry /kam pímmətri/ *n* the measuring of the field of vision or the sensitivity of the retina to colour and space [Early 20C. < Latin *campus* 'field']

Campinas /kam peénəss/ city in eastern São Paulo State, southeastern Brazil, northwest of São Paulo. Population: 908,906 (1996).

camping /kámping/ *n* living outdoors in a tent while on holiday or as a recreational activity ○ *a camping holiday*

campion /kámpi ən/ *n* a flowering plant of the pink family. Flowers: pink, red, white. Native to: northern hemisphere. Genera: *Lychnis* or *Silene*. [Mid-16C. Origin ?]

Jane Campion

Campion /kámpi ən/, **Jane** (*b.* 1954) New Zealand film director. She directed the Academy Award-winning *The Piano* (1993).

Campion, St Edmund (1540–81) English priest. He worked as a Jesuit missionary in England, where he was executed on a false charge of treason.

Campion, Thomas (1567–1620) English poet. In *Observations on the Arte of English Poesie* (1602) he advocated rhymeless verse on a classical model.

'When to her lute Corinna sings, / Her voice revives the leaden strings, / And both in highest notes appear, / As any challenged echo clear. / But when she doth of mourning speak, / Ev'n with her sighs the strings do break.'
[Thomas Campion, *A Book of Airs*; 1601]

campo /kámpō/ (*plural* **-pos**) *n* in South America, a large grassy plain with scattered bushes and small stunted trees [Mid-19C. Via American Spanish or Portuguese, 'field' < Latin *campus*]

Campo Grande /kámpō grándi/ city and capital of Mato Grosso do Sul State, southwestern Brazil. Population: 565,943 (1993).

Campos /kám poss/ city in Rio de Janeiro State, southeastern Brazil, situated on the River Paraíba. Population: 389,547 (1996).

camp oven *n* ANZ a metal pot with three short legs and a lid, used for cooking food over an open fire

camp robin *n* US regional BIRDS same as **grey jay**

campsite /kámp sīt/ *n* **1.** an outdoor area designed for camping, usually providing campers with some facilities such as showers, toilets, and a shop. N Am term **campground 2.** N Am a single unit of land within a campsite, for a camper to pitch a tent on or park a trailer or camper van on

campus /kámpəss/ *n* **1.** an area of land that contains the main buildings and grounds of a university or college ○ *accommodation on campus* **2.** a site on which the buildings of an organization or institution are located ○ *a dormitory for nursing students on the hospital campus* [Late 18C. < Latin, 'field']

campus novel *n* a novel that satirizes university life. The genre appeared in Britain in the late 1970s and early 1980s.

campus university *n* a university whose teaching, administration, and accommodation buildings are located on one main site, usually a rural site, as opposed to being spread around different sites throughout a town

campylobacter /kámpilō báktər/ *n* a rod- or spiral-shaped bacterium that is a common cause of food poisoning in humans and of spontaneous abortion in farm animals [Late 20C. < modern Latin < Greek *kampulos* 'bent' + *baktērion* (see BACTERIUM)]

campylobacter enteritis *n* an intestinal infection by the organism *Campylobacter jejuni* that is usually acquired from contaminated water, milk, or poultry. It is a common cause of travellers' diarrhoea.

CAMRA /kámrə/ *abbr* Campaign for Real Ale

camshaft /kám shaaft/ *n* a shaft that has one or more cams attached, especially one that operates the valves in a vehicle's internal combustion engine

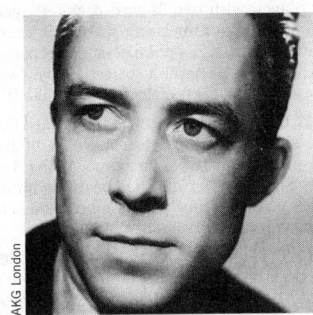

AKG London

Albert Camus

Camus /ka móo/, **Albert** (1913–60) Algerian-born French novelist, essayist, and dramatist. He wrote *The Outsider* (1942) and *The Plague* (1947), and was awarded the Nobel Prize in literature (1957). See Cultural note at **outsider**

> 'I am not made for politics because I am incapable of wishing for, or accepting the death of my adversary.'
> [Albert Camus, *The Rebel*; 1951]

cam wheel *n* a wheel that functions as a cam

camwood /kám wood/ *n* **1.** the hard red wood of a West African tree. Use: formerly, cabinet making, red dye. **2.** a tree that produces camwood. Native to: West Africa. Latin name: *Baphia nitida*. [Late 17C. Probably < Temne *k'am*]

can[1] *stressed* /kan/; *unstressed* /kən/ CORE MEANING: a modal verb used to indicate that it is possible for something to be done or made use of in a particular way ○ *Loans can be made over the phone.*
modal v **1.** BE ABLE TO to have the ability, knowledge, or opportunity to do something ○ *Can you swim?* **2.** BE LIKELY to be likely to be true or to be the case ○ *It can be dangerous.* **3.** BE ALLOWED TO to be allowed to do something, either by legal or moral right or by permission ○ *Can I go?* **4.** BE ACCEPTABLE used to make polite requests, suggestions, or offers ○ *Can I make a suggestion?* **5.** BE POSSIBLE used in questions to emphasize strong feelings about something ○ *What on earth can be the matter?* [Old English *cunnan* < Indo-European]

USAGE **can** or **may**? Many people draw a distinction between **can**, meaning 'be able to', and **may**, meaning 'be allowed to', but the distinction is hard to maintain in practice and the meanings often overlap. In everyday conversation, *Can I go?* is as likely to be used as *May I go?*, and the context, together with intonation, usually makes it clear what is meant. In more formal situations it is wise to maintain the distinction, if only because many people expect it. Note that **may** has ambiguities of its own. *He may go* can mean either 'he is allowed to go' or 'it is possible that he will go'; again, intonation and context clarify the matter. The negative contraction **mayn't** is awkward, and **can't** is usually used instead: *Can't we come too?*

can[2] /kan/ *n* **1.** *N Am* FOOD INDUST same as **tin** *n* (sense 2) **2.** METAL CONTAINER WITH REPLACEABLE LID a metal container with a removable lid or cap, especially one for storing or packaging liquids such as chem-

icals or paint **3.** CONTENTS OF CAN the contents of a metal container ○ *We used up three cans of paint.* **4.** PRESSURIZED CONTAINER a metal container that holds liquid under pressure so that it can be released as a spray ○ *a can of hairspray* **5.** same as **prison** *n* (sense 1) (*slang*) **6.** *N Am* same as **toilet** (senses 1–2) (*slang*) **7.** NAVY same as **ship** *n* (sense 1) (*slang*) **8.** *US* SHIPPING same as **can buoy** ■ *vt* (**cans, canning, canned**) **1.** *N Am* FOOD INDUST same as **tin** *v* (sense 1) **2.** *US* STOP SOMETHING to stop something regarded as inappropriate under the circumstances, e.g. laughter, tears, or jokes (*slang*) ○ *Just can the giggling.* [Old English *canne* < Germanic or late Latin *canna*] —**canful** *n* —**canner** *n* ◇ **carry the can** *UK, Can* to take the blame or responsibility (*informal*) ○ *An unsuspecting junior was left to carry the can.* ◇ **in the can** (*informal*) **1.** in the final edited form ready for broadcasting or distribution ○ *as soon as the film is in the can* **2.** successfully completed or negotiated ○ *At last, after three weeks of tough negotiations, the contract was in the can.*

can[3] *abbr* **1.** cancellation **2.** cancelled **3.** MIL cannon **4.** MUSIC canon[1] (sense 7) **5.** LITERAT canto

Can. *abbr* **1.** Canada **2.** Canadian

Canaan /káynən/ *n* in the Bible, the part of ancient Palestine west of the River Jordan

Canaanite /káynə nīt/ *n* **1.** a member of a Semitic people who lived in Canaan from around 3000 BC until 1000 BC **2.** an extinct Semitic language once spoken in the region between the River Jordan and the Mediterranean Sea —**Canaanite** *adj*

Canada /kánnədə/ federation occupying the northern half of North America and the second largest country in the world. It became an independent member of the Commonwealth in 1931. Language: English, French. Currency: Canadian dollar. Capital: Ottawa. Population: 32,207,113 (2003). Area: 9,970,610 sq. km/3,849,674 sq. mi.

Canada balsam *n* a thick resin secreted from the bark of the balsam fir

Canada goose *n* a large goose with a brownish body, a black head and neck, and a white patch on its

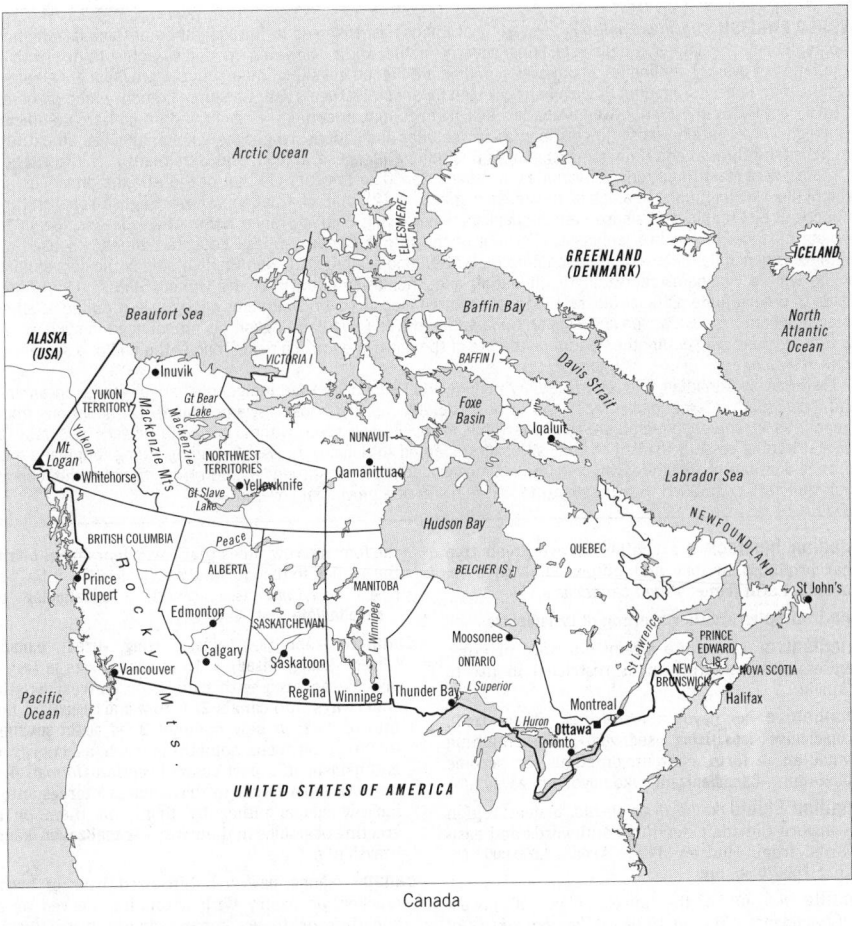

Canada

throat. Native to: North America, introduced into Europe. Latin name: *Branta canadensis*.

Canada jay *n* BIRDS same as **grey jay**

Canada lily

Canada lily *n* a lily with small orange funnel-shaped flowers. Native to: North America. Latin name: *Lilium canadense*.

Canada thistle *n N Am* same as **creeping thistle**

Canadian /kə náydi ən/ *adj* relating to Canada, or its people, languages, or cultures ■ *n* somebody who comes from Canada

Canadian Alliance *n* a Canadian conservative political party dissolved in 2003 when it joined with the Progressive Conservative Party to form the Conservative Party of Canada

Canadian Broadcasting Corporation *n* full form of **CBC**

Canadian English *n* the variety of English spoken in Canada. See panel on next page

Canadian football *n* a form of football that is similar to American football but takes place on a larger field, has 12 players on each team, and uses three rather than four plays to advance at least ten yards or score

Canadian French *n* the variety of French that is spoken in parts of Canada, especially Quebec

WORLD ENGLISH *Canadian English* is the variety of English as it is used in the federation of Canada, which is geographically the largest English-speaking country in the world. However, in demographic terms (with a population of over 31 million, of whom over 7 million are French-speaking, mainly in the province of Quebec), it is the third largest. Canadian English has coexisted for about 230 years with Canadian French, which predates it by a century, as the French were Canada's first main European settlers. English and French are co-official languages in a nation whose linguistic mosaic includes indigenous languages (including Cree, Inuktitut, Iroquois, and Ojibwa) and immigrant languages (including Cantonese, Italian, and Ukrainian).

There are at least three regional varieties of spoken Canadian English: (1) that of the Atlantic provinces, in which the Newfoundland dialect is the most distinctive; (2) that of Quebec, whose English-speakers are influenced by French, and whose French-speakers, when using English, range from native-speaker fluency to varying mixtures of the two languages; (3) that of the rest of Canada, whose educated variety (focused on Ontario) is generally taken as the national norm. Written and printed Canadian English blends the conventions of the United Kingdom (decreasingly influential) and, increasingly, those of the United States. US spelling tends to predominate. Official federal bilingualism often leads to hybrid formulas such as *Jeux Canada Games* (blending French *Jeux Canada* and English *Canada Games*). In Canadian English *r* is pronounced in such words as *art*, *door*, and *worker*. Another feature is the use of the particle *eh* with a rising tone at the end of a sentence, as in *It's nice, eh?*

Distinctively Canadian English vocabulary includes: (1) adoptions from indigenous languages, as in *anorak* and *kayak* (both international), *mackinaw* (a bush jacket), *muskeg* (mossy, swampy land); (2) adoptions from French, as in *anglophone* and *francophone* (both in the French style, without a capital letter), *caboteur* (a coastal trading vessel); (3) British English usages adapted for local purposes, including *riding* (originally one of three divisions of Yorkshire, which in Canada means a political constituency), and *prime minister* (the federal first minister), contrasted with *premier* (the first minister of a provincial government).

Canadian hemlock *n* a coniferous evergreen tree that produces lumber and pulpwood. Native to: Canada. Latin name: *Tsuga canadensis*.

Canadianise *vti* another spelling of **Canadianize**

Canadianism /kə náydi ə nizəm/ *n* a word or other expression originating in or restricted in use to Canada

Canadianize /kə náydi ə nīz/ (-izes, -izing, -ized), **Canadianise** (-ises, -ising, -ised) *vti* to make something Canadian in form, content, or status, or become Canadian —**Canadianization** /kə náydi ə nī záysh'n/ *n*

Canadian Shield /kə náydi ən sheeld/ plateau region of eastern Canada extending southwards and eastwards from Hudson Bay. Area: 4,600,000 sq. km/1,776,070 sq. mi.

canaille /kə nī́/ *n* the lowest class of people (*disapproving*) ○*But to think of her partaking of hospitality; all alone, too; with the canaille of Wynford!'* (L. T. Meade, *A Very Naughty Girl*; 1907) [Late 16C. Via French < Italian *canaglia* 'pack of dogs' < Latin *canis* 'dog']

canal /kə nál/ *n* **1.** TRANSP **WATERWAY** an artificial waterway constructed for use by shipping, for irrigation, or for recreational use. A canal may take in parts of natural rivers along its course. **2.** ANAT **TUBE IN BODY** a tube-shaped passage in the body, carrying air, liquids, or semisolid material **3.** ASTRON **FEATURE ON MARS** an apparent surface marking on Mars, formerly thought to be part of a system of water channels, a view discredited by more recent data [15C. < French, alteration (based on Italian *canale* or Latin *canalis*) of *chanel* < Latin *canalis* 'pipe, canal' < *canna* (see CANE)]

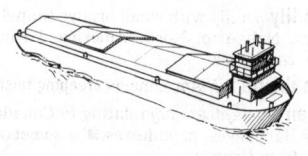

canal boat

canal boat *n* a long boat used on canals to carry freight or for recreational boating

Canal du Midi /kə nál doō meédi/ canal in southern France that links the Bay of Biscay to the Mediterranean Sea

Canaletto /kánnə léttō/, **Antonio** (1697–1768) Italian artist, known especially for his views of Venice and London. Born **Canal, Giovanni Antonio**

canaliculus /kánnə líkyooˈləss/ (*plural* -**li** /-lī/) *n* a minute canal or duct in the body, especially one of the four narrow tubes that carry tears from behind the eyelids to the lacrimal sac [Mid-16C. < Latin, 'little pipe' < *canalis* (see CANAL)] —**canalicular** *adj* —**canaliculate** /-lət, -layt/ *adj*

canalize /kánn'l īz/ (-lizes, -lizing, -lized), **canalise** (-lises, -lising, -lised) *v* **1.** *vt* **BUILD CANALS IN AREA** to provide an area with canals, or convert existing waterways into canals **2.** *vi* **FLOW INTO CHANNEL** to flow into or form a new channel **3.** *vt* **DIRECT SOMETHING** to direct or focus something such as energy or enthusiasm in a particular direction (*formal*) **4.** *vt* MIL **PUSH ENEMY FORCES** to drive enemy forces into a narrow space, either by firing on them or by erecting obstacles in their way —**canalization** /kánn'l ī záysh'n/ *n*

canapé /kánnə pay/ *n* a bite-sized base of bread, cracker, or pastry with a topping, served as an appetizer or to accompany drinks [Late 19C. Via French, literally 'sofa' < medieval Latin *canopeum* (see CANOPY)]

canard /kánnaard, ka naárd/ *n* **1.** HOAX a deliberately false report or rumour, especially something silly intended as a joke (*literary*) **2.** AIRCRAFT PART LIKE WING a small projection like a wing near the nose of an aircraft, fitted to create extra horizontal stability **3.** AIRCRAFT an aircraft fitted with a canard [Mid-19C. < French, literally 'duck', an imitation of the sound]

Canaries /kə náiriz/ ✦ **Canary Islands**

Canaries Current cold current of the North Atlantic Ocean, flowing south from the Canary Islands down the western coast of northern Africa, joining the westward-flowing equatorial current west of Mauritania and Senegal

canary /kə náiri/ (*plural* -**ies**) *n* **1.** BIRDS **YELLOW FINCH** a small yellow songbird of the finch family that has been domesticated as a pet and as a show bird. Native to: Canary Islands and adjacent islands. Latin name: *Serinus canarius*. **2.** WINE **WINE** a sweet wine from the Canary Islands, similar to Madeira **3.** COLOURS same as **canary yellow 4.** DANCE, HIST **DANCE** a lively court dance popular in the 16th century [Late 16C. < French *Canarie*, chief island of the Canary Islands < Latin *Canaria Insula* 'Isle of Dogs', from the large dogs that inhabited it in Roman times] —**canary** *adj*

canary creeper *n* a climbing plant with small yellow flowers. Native to: Peru. Latin name: *Tropaeolum peregrinum*.

canary grass *n* an annual grass plant cultivated for its seeds that are sold as birdseed. Native to: northwestern Africa, Canary Islands. Latin name: *Phalaris canariensis*.

Canary Islands /kə náiri-/, **Canaries** /kə náiriz/ autonomous region of Spain consisting of a group of islands off the northwestern coast of Africa, comprising the provinces of Las Palmas and Santa Cruz de Tenerife. They consist of seven large islands and various islets. The climate is subtropical and tourism is important, especially on the islands of Gran Canaria and Tenerife. Population: 1,631,498 (1995). Area: 7,273 sq. km/2,808 sq. mi. Spanish name **Islas Canarias**

Canary Islands

canary yellow *n* a bright yellow colour —**canary yellow** *adj*

canasta /kə nástə/ *n* **1.** a variant of the card game rummy played with two 52-card packs. Players are dealt 15 cards, the aim being to collect groups of seven similar cards. **2.** a point-scoring set of cards in canasta [Mid-20C. Via Spanish, 'basket' < Latin *canistrum*, because two packs of cards (a 'basketful') are used]

Canaveral, Cape /kə návvərəl/ cape in Brevard County, Florida, situated on the eastern coast of the Canaveral peninsula. It is the home of the John F. Kennedy Space Center and has been the launching site of US crewed space flights since 1961. Former name **Kennedy, Cape** (1963–73)

Canberra /kánbərə/ capital city of Australia, located in the Australian Capital Territory in southeastern Australia. Construction of this new capital began in 1913 and the national parliament moved here from its temporary seat in Melbourne in 1927. Population: 321,819 (2002 estimate). —**Canberran** *n, adj*

can buoy *n* an unlighted marker buoy for shipping, cylindrical or cone-shaped above the water

canc. *abbr* **1.** cancellation **2.** cancelled

cancan /kán kan/ *n* a dance of French origin in which a chorus line of women perform high kicks to reveal their underwear. It originated in the 1840s in the music halls in Paris. [Mid-19C. < French]

cancan skirt *n* a skirt with layers of ruffles and attached knickers that are shown by cancan dancers when the skirt is lifted during the dance

cancel /kánss'l/ *v* (-cels, -celling, -celled) **1.** *vti* **STOP SOMETHING HAPPENING** to stop a previously arranged event from happening ○ *We had to cancel five classes because nobody showed up.* ○ *The guest speaker is ill and has had to cancel.* **2.** *vti* **END CONTRACT** to withdraw officially or legally from a contract ○ *Members are free to cancel at any time.* **3.** *vt* **REVERSE INSTRUCTION** to reverse an instruction to a machine, especially a computer, or bring a machine's operation to an end ○ *Cancel the download from the Internet.* **4.** *vt* **MARK DOCUMENT AS USED** to invalidate a legal or official document to show that it has been used and cannot be reused ○ *machines that cancel postage stamps* **5.** *vt* **DELETE SOMETHING** to mark something for deletion, usually by drawing a line through it **6.** *vti* **NEGATE IDENTICAL FACTOR** to neutralize the effect of another factor or circumstance **7.** *vt* MATHS **REMOVE COMMON FACTOR** to remove a common factor from the numerator and denominator of a fraction or the common terms from the two sides of an equation ○ *The twelves cancel and you end up with 8 by 6 again.*
■ *n* **1.** PRINTING **INSERTED PAGE** a new page or section of a book inserted to replace a missing original or an original that contained errors **2.** PRINTING **PAGE TO BE REPLACED** a faulty page or section of a book replaced by another **3.** same as **cancellation** (sense 3) [14C. Via French < Latin *cancellare* 'cross out' < *cancelli* 'lattice' < *cancer* 'grating, lattice'] —**cancellable** *adj* —**canceller** *n*

cancel out *vt* to combine two opposite or equally powerful things with the result that their strengths, qualities, or effects are neutralized

cancelation *n* US US spelling of **cancellation**

cancelbot /kánss'l bot/ *n* a computer program that cancels unwanted articles sent to an Internet newsgroup by a specific user [Late 20C. < CANCEL + ROBOT]

cancellate /kánssə layt/, **cancellated** /-laytid/ *adj* **1.** ANAT same as **cancellous 2.** forming a mesh or

network [Mid-17C. < Latin *cancellat-* (see CANCELLATION)]

cancellation /kánssə láysh'n/ *n* 1. CANCELLING OF SOMETHING the cancelling of something such as an appointment or order ○ *We had a cancellation, so we can fit you in at two o'clock.* ○ *There is a cancellation charge if you withdraw your order.* 2. THING MADE AVAILABLE something that has become available because the person who reserved it has cancelled, e.g. a seat in a theatre 3. CANCELLING MARK a mark that officially or legally invalidates something, especially a postage stamp [Mid-16C. < Latin *cancellat-*, past participle of *cancellare* (see CANCEL)]

cancellous /kánssələss/ *adj* describes bone that has a mesh of hollows on the inside, as opposed to being compact or dense [Mid-19C. < Latin *cancelli* (see CANCEL)]

cancer /kánssər/ *n* 1. MALIGNANT TUMOUR a malignant tumour or growth caused when cells multiply uncontrollably, destroying healthy tissue. The different forms are sarcomas, carcinomas, leukaemias, and lymphomas. 2. ILLNESS CAUSED BY TUMOUR the illness or condition that is caused by the presence of a malignant tumour 3. FAST-SPREADING BAD PHENOMENON something, usually something negative, that develops or spreads quickly and usually destructively 4. CONSTR GRADUAL DESTRUCTION OF BUILDING MATERIAL gradual erosion or damage occurring in building materials, believed to be caused by inherent manufacturing faults ○ *concrete cancer* [Pre-12C. < Latin, literally 'crab']—**cancerous** *adj*

Cancer /kánssər/ *n* 1. ASTRON CONSTELLATION IN NORTHERN HEMISPHERE a zodiacal constellation of the northern hemisphere between Gemini and Leo. See illustration at **constellation** 2. ZODIAC 4TH SIGN OF ZODIAC the fourth sign of the zodiac, represented by a crab and lasting from approximately 21 June to 22 July. Cancer is classified as a water sign, and its ruling planet is the Moon. 3. ZODIAC SOMEBODY BORN UNDER CANCER SIGN somebody whose birthday falls between 21 June and 22 July [Pre-12C. < Latin (see CANCER); from the constellation's sideways movement across the sky]—**Cancer** *adj*—**Cancerian** /kan séeri ən, -sáiri ən/ *n, adj*

cancerophobia /kánsərō fóbi ə/ *n* an obsessive fear of developing cancer

cancer stick *n* same as **cigarette** (*slang*)

cancroid /káng kroyd/ *adj* like a crab in shape, structure, or movement ■ *n* MED same as **squamous cell carcinoma** [Early 19C. < Latin *cancr-*, stem of *cancer* 'crab, cancer']

Cancún /kan koón/ island resort on the northeastern coast of Quintana Roo state, Mexico. Population: 319,632 (2000).

candela /kan déelə, -déllə/ *n* the basic SI unit of luminous intensity. Symbol **cd** [Mid-20C. < Latin (see CANDLE)]

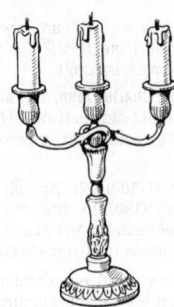

candelabrum

candelabrum /kándə laábrəm/ (*plural* **-bra** /-brə/ or **-brums**) *n* a large decorative candle holder with several arms or branches, or a similarly shaped electric light fitting [Early 19C. < Latin < *candela* (see CANDLE)]

C and F *abbr* FREIGHT cost and freight

C and G *abbr* EDUC City and Guilds

c & i *abbr* FREIGHT cost and insurance

candid /kándid/ *adj* 1. HONEST honest or direct in a way that people find either refreshing or distasteful ○ *a surprisingly candid admission* 2. PHOTOGRAPHED IN-

FORMALLY photographed or filmed without the subject knowing or having the opportunity to prepare or pose ○ *a candid documentary* ■ *n* N Am UNPOSED PHOTOGRAPH an unposed and informal photograph of a person or group [Mid-17C. Directly or via French *candide* 'guileless' < Latin *candidus* 'white, shining' < *candere* 'be white']—**candidly** *adv*—**candidness** *n*

candida /kándidə/ *n* a fungus that can cause yeast infection, especially in the mouth and vagina. Latin name: *Candida albicans*. [Mid-20C. < Latin, feminine of *candidus* 'white' (see CANDID); from its colour]

candidate /kándi dayt, -dət/ *n* 1. APPLICANT FOR OFFICE somebody who is being considered for a political office or an official position ○ *names of candidates for the leadership of the party* 2. APPLICANT FOR JOB an applicant or suitable person for a job ○ *The successful candidate will have had experience with market research.* 3. PERSON SUSCEPTIBLE TO DISEASE OR TREATMENT a patient who seems suitable for a particular treatment, or is likely to be affected by a particular disease ○ *a prime candidate for a heart attack* 4. EXAM TAKER somebody sitting an examination 5. COMPETITOR somebody competing with others for a prize, grant, or award ○ *the candidates for best director* [Early 17C. Directly or via French *candidat* < Latin *candidatus* '(candidate) clothed in white'; from the white togas worn by candidates for election in ancient Rome]—**candidacy** /-dəssi/ *n*—**candidature** /-dəchər/ *n*

SYNONYMS *candidate, contender, contestant, aspirant, applicant, entrant*

CORE MEANING: somebody who is seeking to be chosen for something or to win something

candidate somebody who is being considered for a job, grant, or prize, standing for election, or taking part in an examination ○ *the Liberal Democrat parliamentary candidate* ○ *candidates for the newly created posts* **contender** a competitor, especially somebody who has a good chance of winning ○ *a contender for the best supporting actor award* ○ *He is emerging as a strong contender for the presidency.* **contestant** somebody who takes part in a contest or competitive event ○ *a contestant on a popular TV quiz show* ○ *To win, the contestant must score eleven points.* **aspirant** somebody who is hoping to achieve distinction or advancement ○ *a prime ministerial aspirant* ○ *a challenge from a rival aspirant to the throne* **applicant** somebody who has formally applied to be a candidate for something ○ *the starting salary of the successful applicant* ○ *It's claimed that the company is turning away hundreds of job applicants.* **entrant** somebody who enters a competition or examination ○ *I was the only entrant, so the event was cancelled.*

candid camera *n* the use of hidden cameras to film subjects unawares, often in stage-managed situations intended to elicit amusing responses (*hyphenated when used before a noun*)

candidiasis /kándi dī əssiss/ (*plural* **-diases** /-dī əsseez/) *n* MED same as **yeast infection** (*technical*) [Mid-20C. < CANDIDA]

Candiot /kándi ot/, **Candiote** /-ōt/ *adj* relating to Crete, especially the capital, Heraklion (*literary*) [< *Candy*, old name for Crete]—**Candiot** *n*

candle /kánd'l/ *n* a moulded piece of wax, tallow, or other fatty substance, usually cylindrical in shape, encasing a wick that is burnt to provide light ■ *vt* (**-dles, -dling, -dled**) to test an egg for freshness by looking at it against a bright light [Pre-12C. < Latin *candella*, earlier *candela* < *candere* 'be white, glow'] ◇ **burn the candle at both ends** to get up very early and go to bed very late ◇ **not hold a candle to somebody** to be not nearly as good at something as somebody ○ *As a writer, he doesn't hold a candle to his mother.*

candlefish /kánd'l fish/ (*plural* **-fishes** or *same*) *n* an oily saltwater fish. Native to: northern Pacific Ocean. Latin name: *Thaleichthys pacificus*. [< the former use of the dried fish as a lamp by pushing a piece of bark through it as a wick]

candleholder /kánd'l hōldər/ *n* a holder for a candle, often a decorative one

candlelight /kánd'l līt/ *n* 1. the light that a burning candle provides ○ *reading by candlelight* 2. twilight, the time when candles would have been lit (*literary*)

candlelit /kánd'l lit/ *adj* lit by candles, or done by candlelight ○ *a silent candlelit march through the streets*

Candlemas /kánd'l mass, -məss/ *n* 1. a Christian feast marking the purification of the Virgin Mary and the presentation of the infant Jesus Christ in the Temple. Date: 2 February. 2. in Scotland, one of the four days marking the traditional three-month divisions of the year (**quarter days**). Date: 2 February. [Pre-12C. < CANDLE + MASS]

candlenut /kánd'l nut/ *n* 1. an oil-rich seed of a tropical tree that is sometimes threaded with a wick to serve as a candle in Asia and Polynesia 2. a tropical tree of the spurge family that bears candlenuts. Native to: Asia, Polynesia. Latin name: *Aleurites moluccana*.

candlepin /kánd'l pin/ *n* a slim pin used in the bowling game candlepins [< its shape]

candlepins /kánd'l pinz/ *n* a bowling game using slender pins and a ball smaller than that used in tenpins (*takes a singular verb*)

candlepower /kánd'l powər/ *n* luminous intensity measured in candelas

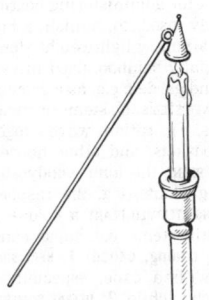

candlesnuffer

candlesnuffer /kánd'l snufər/ *n* a device, usually made of metal, consisting of a small cone on the end of a long thin handle, placed over the flame of a candle to put it out

candlestick /kánd'l stik/ *n* a tall thin holder for a single candle

candlewick /kánd'l wik/ *n* 1. COTTON FABRIC tufted cotton fabric. Use: bedcovers, dressing gowns. 2. EMBROIDERY YARN soft cotton yarn used for embroidery 3. THICK STRING thick string used for candle wicks

candlewood /kánd'l wŏod/ *n* 1. resinous wood burnt for light and fuel 2. a tree or bush that produces candlewood

C and M *abbr* care and maintenance

can-do *adj* keen to take on a job or challenge and confident of success (*informal*) ○ *We're only looking at can-do executives with proven track records.*

Candolle /kan dól/, **Augustin Pyrame de** (1778–1841) Swiss botanist. He was the originator of taxonomy, the science of classification of plants still in general use.

candor *n* US spelling of **candour**

candour /kándər/ *n* honesty or directness, whether refreshing or distasteful ○ *He spoke of their conspicuous candour and bravery.* [14C. < Latin *candor* 'glossy whiteness' < *cand-*, base of *candidus* (see CANDID)]

CANDU reactor /kán doo-/ *n* a form of nuclear reactor designed and built in Canada that uses replaceable fuel bundles and heavy water to moderate fission and cool the reactor core [Acronym < CANADA + DEUTERIUM + URANIUM]

C and W *abbr* MUSIC country and western

candy /kándi/ *n* (*plural* **-dies**) 1. N Am SMALL CONFECTIONS small sweet food items usually eaten for pleasure and not as part of a meal, e.g. chocolate bars, mints, and toffee 2. N Am FOOD same as **sweet** (sense 1) 3. HARD DRUGS heroin, cocaine, or another hard drug (*slang*) ■ *v* (**-dies, -dying, -died**) 1. *vt* STEEP IN SUGAR to dress a food by impregnating it with sugar, in order either to preserve it or to make it more pleasant to eat 2. *vt* COAT WITH SUGAR SYRUP to coat food with sugar or sugar syrup, or be coated with sugar or sugar syrup 3. *vti* TURN SUGAR SOLUTION INTO CRYSTALS to turn a sugar solution into crystals, especially by boiling it, or be converted into sugar crystals [13C. Via Old French *candi* < Arabic *qandī* 'crystallized into sugar' < *qand* 'cane sugar']

candy apple *n N Am* same as **toffee apple**

candy cane *n US* a long slender red-and-white striped hard candy that is bent into a curve at one end

candyfloss /kándi floss/ *n* cooked sugar syrup, coloured and spun from a machine onto a stick in fine strands, eaten traditionally at fairgrounds. Aus term **fairyfloss**. N Am term **cotton candy**

candy man *n US* **1.** a drug trafficker (*slang*) **2.** formerly, an itinerant seller of sweets

candy store *n N Am* same as **sweetshop**

candy-striped *adj* with a pattern of narrow stripes in a single colour on a white background

candytuft /kándi tuft/ *n* a flowering plant with thin leaves. Flowers: white, red, or purple, in clusters. Native to: Europe, Mediterranean. Genus: *Iberis*. [Early 17C. < *Candy*, old name for Crete]

cane /kayn/ *n* **1. WALKING STICK** a stick that people use to help them walk **2. STICK FOR PUNISHMENT BEATINGS** a long flexible stick for administering beatings, especially one formerly used to punish schoolchildren **3. BAMBOO STEM** a hollow lightweight stem of a tropical plant, especially bamboo, used in various ways in the house and garden, e.g. as a growing support for plants **4. WOVEN STEMS** the stems of various palms and grass plants, e.g. rattan, woven together to make furniture, baskets, and other household items **5. STEM OF FRUIT PLANT** the long woody stem of various fruit-bearing plants, e.g. the raspberry or blackberry **6. LONG-STEMMED PLANT** a coarse grass or reed with long stiff stems, e.g. sugar cane or sorghum ■ *vt* (**canes, caning, caned**) **1. BEAT SOMEBODY** to beat somebody with a cane, especially, formerly, to punish a schoolchild **2. DEFEAT SOMEBODY** to subject somebody to a crushing defeat (*slang*) [14C. Via Old French *cane* < Latin *canna* 'reed' < Greek *kanna* < Semitic]

cane beetle *n* a large beetle that lays its eggs in sugar cane. Native to: Australia. Latin name: *Demolepida albohirtum*.

canebrake /káyn brayk/ *n US* an area of land planted or overgrown with cane

cane grass *n* a tall stiff-stemmed grass. Native to: inland wetland areas of Australia. Latin name: *Eragrostis australasica*.

canelle knife /kə nél-/ *n* a small kitchen implement, similar to a vegetable peeler or zester, with a slot and a V-shaped blade for cutting strips from the skins of citrus fruits [< French *canneler* 'to groove, flute' < *cane* (see CANE)]

cane piece *n* in the Caribbean, a field of sugar cane, especially one that is isolated and belongs to a small farmer

caner /káynə/ *n US* a maker or repairer of furniture and other items made of cane

canescent /kə néss'nt/ *adj* **1.** describes plant parts that have a white or whitish-grey covering of fine hairs **2.** becoming white or greyish (*literary*) [Mid-19C. < Latin *canescent-*, present participle of *canescere* 'grow white' < *canus* 'white, hoary'] —**canescence** *n*

cane sugar *n* sucrose obtained from sugar cane or sugar beet

Canes Venatici /káy neez və nátti sī/ *n* a constellation of the northern hemisphere. See illustration at **constellation** [< Latin, 'hunting dogs']

cane toad *n* a large toad introduced into Australia to control pests in sugar cane but now a pest in its own right. Native to: South America. Latin name: *Bufo marinus*.

Canetti /ka nétti/, **Elias** (1905–94) Bulgarian-born British writer. His broad output includes literary criticism, history, memoirs, and his only novel, *Der Blendung* (1936), translated into English (1946) as *Auto-da-Fé*. He won the Nobel Prize in literature (1981).

canfield /kán feeld/ *n* a gambling game developed from the card game patience [Early 20C. After Richard Albert *Canfield* (1855–1914), US gambler]

cangue /kang/, **cang** *n* a heavy wooden yoke worn on the shoulders and enclosing the neck and arms, formerly used in China for punishing petty criminals [Late 17C. Via French < Portuguese *canga* 'yoke' < Vietnamese *gong*]

Canicula /kə níkyōōlə/ *n* ASTRON same as **Sirius** [12C. < Latin (see CANICULAR)]

canicular /kə níkyōōlər/ *adj* relating to the star Sirius [14C. < late Latin *canicularis* < Latin *canicula* 'little dog' < *canis* 'dog']

canid /kánnid, káy-/ *n* a carnivorous mammal of the dog family, which includes foxes, wolves, jackals, dingoes, coyotes, and domestic breeds [Late 19C. < modern Latin *Canidae* < Latin *canis* 'dog']

canine /káy nīn, kánn-/ *adj* relating to dogs ○ *a canine trainer* ○ *members of the canine family* ■ *n* **1.** a pointed tooth between the incisors and the first bicuspids. Most mammals have two in each jaw. **2.** same as **dog** (sense 1) (*often humorous*) [15C. Directly or via French < Latin *caninus* < *canis* 'dog']

canine distemper *n* a viral disease of dogs that causes high fever and is often fatal

canine tooth *n* DENT same as **canine** *n* (sense 1)

caning /káyning/ *n* **1.** a punishment beating with a cane, especially a beating of a kind formerly administered to schoolchildren **2.** a resounding defeat (*informal*)

Canis Major /káyniss-/ *n* a constellation of the southern hemisphere containing the star Sirius. Canis Major and Canis Minor represent dogs following at the heels of Orion the Hunter. See illustration at **constellation** [< Latin, 'greater dog']

Canis Minor /káyniss-/ *n* a constellation near the celestial equator containing the star Procyon. See illustration at **constellation** [< Latin, 'lesser dog']

canister /kánnistər/ *n* **1. PRESSURIZED CONTAINER** a pressurized metal container holding a substance released as a spray **2. SEALED CONTAINER** a strong sealed metal container for hazardous chemicals **3. FOOD CONTAINER** a metal container with a lid, for storing tea, coffee, or other dry foods **4.** ARMS **EXPLOSIVE** a weapon used in former times consisting of a metal shell filled with gas and shot or shrapnel, designed to explode when thrown or fired from a cannon [Late 15C. Via Latin < Greek *kanastron* 'wicker basket' < *kanna* 'reed']

canker /kángkər/ *n* **1.** BOT **PLANT DISEASE** a disease that creates open wounds on the trunks and branches of woody plants. Cankers can be caused by bacteria, fungi, or pests. **2.** VET **ANIMAL DISEASE** a disease of animals, e.g. a disease of horses that makes their hooves spongy, a disease that can cause ulcers in the outer ears of some animals, or a throat infection of some birds **3. EVIL** an evil or corrupting influence that spreads and is difficult to wipe out ○ *'This canker that eats up Love's tender spring'* (William Shakespeare, *Venus and Adonis*; 1593) ■ *vti* (**-kers, -kering, -kered**) **1.** BOT **DEVELOP PLANT DISEASE** to develop canker, or cause the trunks and branches of woody plants to develop canker **2. MAKE OR BECOME CORRUPT** to become a source of spreading corruption or evil, or cause something to decay as a result of spreading corruption or evil [14C. Via Old N French *cancre* < Latin *cancr-* 'crab'] —**cankerous** *adj*

canker sore *n N Am* an ulcer on the lips or inside the mouth

cankerworm /kángkər wurm/ *n* the larva of either of two types of moth that destroys the leaves and fruit of trees in North America. Latin name: *Paleacrita vernata* or *Alsophila pometaria*.

canna /kánnə/ *n* a perennial tropical plant with luxuriant foliage. Flowers: red or yellow, in clusters. Native to: Caribbean, Central America. Genus: *Canna*. [Mid-18C. Via modern Latin *Canna* < Latin *canna* (see CANE)]

cannabidiol /kánnəbə dī ol, kə nábbə-/ *n* one of the chemical constituents of cannabis. Formula: $C_{21}H_{28}(OH)_2$. [Mid-20C. < CANNABIS + DI-[1] + -OL[1]]

cannabinoid /kánnəbi noyd/ *n* an organic chemical substance belonging to a group that comprises the active constituents of cannabis [Mid-20C. < CANNABIS]

cannabis /kánnəbiss/ *n* **1.** a drug produced in various forms from the dried leaves and flowers of the hemp plant, smoked or chewed. Its recreational use is illegal in many countries. **2.** the hemp plant, especially when grown as a source of the drug cannabis. Latin name: *Cannabis sativa*. [Early 18C. Via Latin < Greek *kannabis*]

cannabis resin *n* the drug cannabis in the form of a greenish-black resin

Cannae /kánnee/ battlefield situated near present-day Barletta, southeastern Italy. It was the site of Hannibal's major defeat of the Roman army during the Second Punic War in 216 BC.

canned /kand/ *adj* **1.** *N Am* FOOD INDUST same as **tinned** **2. PRERECORDED** prerecorded in a standardized form for general use, rather than recorded for a specific broadcast or performance ○ *canned laughter* **3. UNVARYING** used repeatedly with little or no variation, and therefore lacking freshness or originality ○ *the familiar canned claim to know about the problem already* **4. DRUNK** extremely drunk (*slang*) **5.** ONLINE **HAVING STANDARD DESIGN** describes a website or its features that are designed according to a standard template rather than to somebody's personal specifications ○ *canned questions* **6.** *S Africa* **OF RESTRICTED HUNTING** relating to hunting conducted in a restricted area with animals that have been raised in captivity, or to the animals that are hunted

cannel /kánn'l/, **cannel coal** *n* a bituminous coal that burns brightly and creates a lot of smoke [Mid-16C. Dialect variant of CANDLE; from its bright flame]

cannelloni /kánnə lōni/ *n* wide tubes or rolls of pasta that are stuffed with a filling, topped with sauce, then baked [Mid-20C. < Italian, plural of *cannellone* 'tubular noodle' < Latin *canna* (see CANE)]

cannelure /kánnəlyoor/ *n* a groove around the cylindrical part of a bullet [Mid-18C. < French < *canneler* 'make a groove in' < *canne* 'reed' < Old French *cane* (see CANE)]

cannery /kánnəri/ (*plural* **-ies**) *n* a factory where food is packaged into tins

Cannes /kan/ resort and seaport on the French Riviera that is the site of an annual international film festival. It is situated in the Alpes-Maritimes Department in the Provence-Alpes-Côtes-d'Azur administrative region of southern France. Population: 67,304 (1999).

cannibal /kánnib'l/ *n* **1.** somebody who eats human flesh **2.** an animal that eats the flesh of other animals of the same species [Mid-16C. < Spanish *Canibales*, variant of *Caribes* < Arawak *carib*, the Carib people] —**cannibalism** *n*

cannibalise *vt* another spelling of **cannibalize**

cannibalistic /kánnibə lístik/ *adj* relating to, involving, or practising cannibalism —**cannibalistically** *adv*

cannibalize /kánnibə līz/ (**-izes, -izing, -ized**), **cannibalise** (**-ises, -ising, -ised**) *vt* **1.** to take parts from something, especially a machine, in order to use them elsewhere ○ *cannibalized the other vehicles for spare parts when their supply line failed* **2.** to eat the flesh of another human being or of an animal of the same species —**cannibalization** /kánnibə lī záysh'n/ *n*

cannikin /kánnikin/ *n* a small can, especially one used for drinking from [Late 16C. < Dutch *kanneken* 'little can' < Middle Dutch *canne* 'can']

Canning /kánning/, **Charles John, 1st Earl Canning** (1812–62) British colonial administrator. He was governor general (1856–58) and first viceroy (1858–62) of British India.

Canning, George (1770–1827) British politician. As foreign secretary (1807–10, 1822–27) he encouraged independence movements in Latin America. He was briefly British prime minister (1827).

> 'Give me the avowed, erect and manly foe; / Firm I can meet, perhaps return the blow; / But of all plagues, good Heaven, thy wrath can send, / Save me, oh, save me, from the candid friend.'
> [George Canning, 'New Morality', *The Anti-Jacobin*; 1821]

Canning Basin arid lowland region in the Great Sandy Desert, Western Australia, extending eastwards from Derby to the Kimberley Plateau and southwards to the River De Grey

Cannizzaro reaction /kánni tsaárō-/ *n* a chemical process in which some aldehydes are broken down into alcohols and acid salts in the presence of a strong alkali [After Stanislao *Cannizzaro* (1826–1910), Italian chemist]

Cannock /kánnək/ former mining town in Staffordshire, central England, situated northwest of Birmingham. Population: 92,126 (2001).

Cannock Chase Area of Outstanding Natural Beauty in Staffordshire, central England. Area: 67 sq. km/26 sq. mi.

cannon /kánnən/ *n* **1.** (*plural* **cannons** or *same*) HISTORICAL WEAPON in former times, a weapon that fired heavy iron balls or other projectiles through a simple iron tube **2.** MODERN WEAPON a modern heavy artillery weapon large enough to need to be mounted for firing, e.g. on a warship or on a tracked vehicle **3.** AIRCRAFT GUN a rapid-firing gun mounted on an aircraft **4.** CUE GAMES BILLIARDS SHOT in cue games, a shot in which the cue ball hits one ball that then hits another ball. N Am term **carom** **5.** BELL LOOP the loop at the top of a bell from which it is suspended ■ *v* (**-nons, -noning, -noned**) **1.** *vi* COLLIDE to collide with something or bounce off it at great speed and with a lot of force ○ *a 35-yard shot that cannoned off the post* **2.** *vt* MIL same as **cannonade** *v* (sense 1) **3.** *vi* CUE GAMES MAKE CANNON SHOT in cue games, to make a shot in which the cue ball hits one ball that then hits another ball. US term **carom** [14C. Via French < Italian *cannone* 'large tube' < Latin *canna* (see CANE)]

SPELLCHECK **cannon** or **canon**? Do not confuse the spelling of ***cannon*** and ***canon***, which sound similar. ***Cannon*** is chiefly used as a noun denoting a weapon, especially one formerly used to fire heavy iron balls. It is also used as a verb, meaning 'collide' or 'rebound': *The car cannoned into the bridge.* The word ***canon*** is a noun with numerous meanings, including 'a rule or decree', 'a list of saints', 'a collection of religious writings or artistic works', and 'a member of the clergy of a cathedral'.

cannonade /kánnə náyd/ *n* **1.** BOMBARDMENT a sustained bombardment with heavy artillery **2.** SOMETHING RESEMBLING BOMBARDMENT something that sounds or feels like an artillery bombardment ○*'The deep cannonade of roaring thunder belched forth its fearsome challenge.'* (Edgar Rice Burroughs, *Tarzan of the Apes*; 1914) ■ *v* (**-ades, -ading, -aded**) **1.** *vti* BOMBARD SOMEBODY OR BE BOMBARDED to subject an enemy to, or be subjected to, a cannonade **2.** *vt* ATTACK SOMEBODY to subject somebody to a sustained attack, e.g. with words of criticism or reproach [Mid-16C. Via French < Italian *cannonata* < *cannone* (see CANNON)]

cannonball /kánnən bawl/ *n* **1.** BALL FIRED FROM CANNON a heavy metal or stone ball fired from a cannon **2.** JUMP INTO WATER a jump into water with the body tucked into a ball, usually with the head down and the knees drawn up to the chest ■ *vi* (**-balls, -balling, -balled**) TRAVEL QUICKLY to travel at great speed (*informal*) ○ *The train cannonballed through the dark tunnel.*

cannon bone *n* a bone in the lower limbs of some hoofed animals, resulting from the fusing of the metatarsals or metacarpals [< its tubular shape]

cannoneer /kánnə néer/ *n* formerly, a soldier who fired a cannon [Mid-16C. Via French < Italian *cannoniere* < *cannone* (see CANNON)]

cannon fodder *n* (*informal*) **1.** members of the lowest ranks of the military, regarded as an expendable resource in wartime **2.** a person or group regarded as a resource to be exploited or sacrificed

cannot /kánnot, -ət, kə nót/ *contr* the usual way of writing 'can not'

USAGE See ***help***.

cannula /kánnyŏŏlə/ (*plural* **-las** or **-lae** /-lī/), **canula** *n* a flexible tube with a sharp-pointed part at one end that is inserted into a duct, vein, or cavity in order to drain away fluid or to administer drugs [Late 17C. < Latin, 'little tube' < *canna* (see CANE)]

cannulate /kánnyŏŏ layt/, **canulate** *vt* (**-lates, -lating, -lated**) to insert a tube (**cannula**) into a duct, vein, or cavity in order to drain away fluid or to administer drugs ■ *adj* having a tubular shape (*technical*) —**cannulation** /kánnyŏŏ láysh'n/ *n*

canny /kánni/ *adj* (**-nier, -niest**) **1.** SHREWDLY KNOWING shrewd enough not to be easily deceived ○ *a canny negotiator* **2.** *N England* GOOD good, pleasant, or excellent (*informal*) **3.** *Scotland* PRUDENT careful and shrewd in money matters **4.** *Scotland* MILD-TEMPERED docile and obedient ■ *adv regional* EXCEEDINGLY used to emphasize the degree or extent of something ○ *We walked a canny long way.* [Late 16C. < CAN[1] 'know'] —**cannily** *adv* —**canniness** *n*

canoe /kə nóo/ *n* a lightweight boat, pointed at each end, that can be paddled by one or two people and can carry passengers. Canoes were originally made from natural materials, but modern canoes are made of aluminium or of moulded plastic and fibreglass. ■ *vi* (**-noes, -noeing, -noed**) to paddle a canoe, often as a sport or hobby [Mid-16C. Via Spanish *canoa* < Carib *canaoua*; modern form influenced by French *canoë*] ◇ **paddle your own canoe** to take control of and responsibility for your own life and affairs (*informal*)

canoeing /kə nóo ing/ *n* the sport, hobby, or activity of paddling a canoe

canoeist /kə nóo ist/ *n* somebody who canoes, especially as a sport or a hobby

can of worms *n* a complicated situation that results from unforeseen problems, especially an issue that seems likely to create conflicts (*informal*)

canola /kə nólə/ *n* **1.** a rape plant that yields oil with high nutritional quality **2.** same as **canola oil** [Late 20C. < CANADA]

canola oil *n* a rapeseed oil that has a high level of monounsaturated fatty acids. Use: cooking oil.

canon[1] /kánnən/ *n* **1.** GENERAL RULE a general rule, principle, or standard ○ *one of the fundamental canons of free-market economics* **2.** RELIG RELIGIOUS DECREE a decree issued by a religious authority, especially one ruling on religious practices **3.** RELIG BODY OF RELIGIOUS WRITINGS a set of religious writings regarded as authentic and definitive and forming a religion's body of scripture **4.** ARTS SET OF ARTISTIC WORKS a set of artistic works established as genuine and complete, e.g. the works of a particular writer, painter, or filmmaker ○ *one of the best-known pictures in the Welles canon* **5.** CHR LIST OF SAINTS in the Roman Catholic Church, the complete list of all the saints **6.** CHR PART OF MASS in the Roman Catholic Mass, the prayer during which the bread and wine are consecrated **7.** MUSIC STAGGERED SINGING OR PLAYING a musical technique in which different instruments or voices enter one after the other, each playing or singing exactly the same sequence of notes, resulting in often complex counterpoint [Pre-12C. Via Latin < Greek *kanōn* 'rule']

SPELLCHECK See ***cannon***.

canon[2] /kánnən/ *n* **1.** a member of the Christian clergy who is on the permanent staff of a cathedral and has specific duties in relation to the running of it **2.** CHR same as **canon regular** [12C. Via Old French *canonie* < ecclesiastical Latin *canonicus* '(somebody living) according to a rule' < Latin *canon* (see CANON[1]); altered after CANON[1]]

cañon *n* GEOG another spelling of **canyon**

canoness /kánnə néss/ *n* in the Roman Catholic Church, a woman who belongs to a religious order in which members live under a rule, not a vow

canonical /kə nónnik'l/, **canonic** /kə nónnik/ *adj* **1.** ARTS OF CANON OF WORKS relating to or belonging to the biblical canon or a canon of artistic works established as genuine and complete **2.** RELIG FOLLOWING CANON LAW conforming to or authorized by canon law **3.** CONFORMING TO GENERAL PRINCIPLES conforming to accepted principles or standard practice **4.** CHR OF CATHEDRAL OR REGULAR CANONS relating to members of the clergy who are canons **5.** MUSIC OF MUSICAL CANON relating to a musical canon, or sung or played in a canon [15C. < medieval Latin *canonicalis* < Latin *canon* (see CANON[1])] —**canonically** *adv*

canonical hour *n* **1.** in the Roman Catholic Church, one of the daily prayer times when specific prayers are said. These times are the matins with lauds, prime, terce, sext, nones, vespers, and compline. **2.** in the Church of England, any time between 8 am and 6 pm when marriages can officially be celebrated

canonicals /kə nónnik'lz/ *npl* ceremonial robes worn by members of the clergy during a religious ceremony

canonicity /kánnə níssəti/ *n* inclusion in a religious or secular canon, or status as an included item

canonize /kánnə nīz/ (**-izes, -izing, -ized**), **canonise** (**-ises, -ising, -ised**) *vt* **1.** DECLARE SOMEBODY AS SAINT in the Roman Catholic Church, to declare a deceased person to be a saint **2.** GIVE RELIGIOUS APPROVAL TO SOMETHING to declare something to be acceptable or valid according to canon law **3.** GLORIFY SOMETHING to idolize somebody or glorify something ○*'And fame in time to come canonize us'* (William Shakespeare, *Troilus and Cressida*; 1601) [14C. < medieval Latin *canonizare* < Latin *canon* (see CANON[1])] —**canonization** /kánnə nī záysh'n/ *n* —**canonizer** *n*

canon law *n* the body of laws that governs the affairs of the Christian church or a particular branch of it

canon regular (*plural* **canons regular**) *n* a member of any of several Roman Catholic orders of monks living in communities that follow Augustinian rules

canonry /kánnənri/ *n* the status or position of a religious canon

canoodle /kə nóod'l/ (**-noodles, -noodling, -noodled**) *vti* to kiss and cuddle somebody in a mildly romantic or sexual way (*informal*) ○ *couples canoodling in the dark* [Mid-19C. Origin ?]

can opener *n N Am* HOUSEHOLD same as **tin-opener**

canopic jar

canopic jar /kə nópik-/, **Canopic jar** *n* a jar used in ancient Egypt to hold the embalmed entrails of a mummy [Late 19C. < Latin *Canopicus* < *Canopus*, port in ancient Egypt]

Canopus /kə nópəss/ *n* the brightest star in the constellation Argo and the second brightest star in the sky after Sirius. Because it is so bright, spacecraft often take Canopus as a reference point for orientation.

canopy /kánnəpi/ (*plural* **-pies**) *n* **1.** COVERING FOR SHELTER a covering fixed above something to provide shelter or for decoration, especially a fabric covering that can be removed or folded away **2.** BOT TREETOPS the uppermost layer of vegetation in a forest, consisting of the tops of trees forming a kind of ceiling **3.** SKY the sky regarded as a covering or ceiling (*literary*) ○ *the vast canopy of stars* **4.** BUILDINGS ROOFED STRUCTURE a roofed structure that covers an area, especially one that shelters a passageway between two buildings **5.** SPORTS PART OF PARACHUTE the part of a parachute that opens and fills with air **6.** AVIAT COCKPIT COVER the transparent cover of an aircraft's cockpit [14C. Via medieval Latin *canopeum* 'canopy above an altar' < Greek *kōnōpeion* 'bed with a mosquito net' < *kōnōps* 'mosquito'] —**canopied** *adj*

~~**canot**~~ incorrect spelling of **cannot**

Canova /kə nóvə/, **Antonio, Marquis of Ischia** (1757–1822) Italian sculptor. His neoclassical works include figures of Napoleon I and George Washington.

Canso /kánssō/ town in Guysborough County, eastern Nova Scotia, Canada, situated on the Atlantic Ocean near Cape Canso. Population: 1,228 (1991).

canst *stressed form* /kanst/; *unstressed form* /kənst/ *v* an archaic form of the verb 'can' used with 'thou'

cant[1] /kant/ *n* **1.** CLICHÉD TALK boring talk filled with clichés and platitudes **2.** HYPOCRITICAL TALK insincere talk, especially regarding morals or religion **3.** JARGON the special language or vocabulary of a particular group, especially a group whom some people look down on ■ *vi* (**cants, canting, canted**) SPEAK CANT to use cant, especially to speak or lecture others hypocritically on matters of religion or morals [Mid-16C. Probably < Latin *cantare* 'sing'] —**canting** *adj* —**cantingly** *adv*

ORIGIN The Latin word *cantare*, 'to sing', from which ***cant*** is probably derived, and the related noun *cantus* 'singing' are also sources of English *accent, cantabile, cantata, canto, chant* and *incantation*.

cant[2] /kant/ *n* **1. SLOPE** slope, degree of slope, or a sloping surface **2. JOLT** a jolt that knocks something out of its straight or level position ■ *vt* **(cants, canting, canted) JOLT SOMETHING** to knock something out of its straight or level position [14C. Via Middle Low German *kante* or Middle Dutch *cant* 'edge' < Latin *cantus* 'tyre']

can't /kaant/ *contr* cannot

Cant. *abbr* 1. Canterbury 2. BIBLE Canticle of Canticles

Cantab /kán tab/ *adj* relating to or belonging to the University of Cambridge (*used after titles of academic awards*) [Shortening of Latin *Cantabrigiensis*]

cantabile /kan taá bi lay/ *adj, adv* in a smooth, flowing, and melodious style (*used as a musical direction*) ■ *n* a cantabile passage or piece of music [Early 18C. < Italian, 'that can be sung']

Cantabrian Mountains /kan táybri ən-/ mountain range extending about 480 km/300 mi. west from the Pyrenees across northern Spain. The highest peak is Torre Cerredo. Height: 2,648 m/8,688 ft.

Cantabrigian /kántə bríji ən/ *n* **1.** a student or graduate of the University of Cambridge, England **2.** somebody who comes from Cambridge, England, or Cambridge, Massachusetts [Mid-16C. < Latin *Cantabrigia* 'Cambridge (England)'] —**Cantabrigian** *adj*

cantaloupe /kántə loop/, **cantaloup** *n* a small round melon with a ridged scaly rind and aromatic orange flesh. Latin name: *Cucumis melo cantalupensis*. [Late 18C. Via French < Italian *Cantaluppi*, papal villa near Rome where the melon was introduced from Armenia]

cantankerous /kan tángkərəss/ *adj* easily angered and difficult to get on with [Mid-18C. Probably alteration of rancorous] —**cantankerously** *adv* —**cantankerousness** *n*

cantata /kan taátə/ *n* a musical composition for voices and instruments, usually on a religious theme, containing arias, choruses, and recitatives [Early 18C. Via Italian < Latin, feminine past participle of *cantare* 'sing' < *canere*]

cant dog *n* FORESTRY same as **cant hook** [< CANT [2] + DOG 'mechanical device']

canteen /kan teén/ *n* **1. CAFETERIA** a place where food is served, especially in a school or workplace **2. SOLDIERS' SHOP** a shop selling food, toiletries, and other items on a military base **3. TEMPORARY FOOD STAND** a mobile or temporary food stand **4. CUTLERY BOX** a box or chest with compartments for storing cutlery **5. PORTABLE DRINKING FLASK** a small container used by campers or soldiers for carrying liquids such as drinking water [Mid-18C. Via French *cantine* < Italian *cantina* 'cellar']

canteen culture *n* sexist and racist behaviour and attitudes prevalent or accepted among a group of colleagues, especially in a traditionally white male occupation, typically the police force ○ *perpetuating an outdated canteen culture*

~~canteloupe~~ incorrect spelling of **cantaloupe**

canter[1] /kántər/ *n* **1. HORSE'S MEDIUM PACE** a smooth easy gait of a horse or donkey, slower than a gallop but faster than a trot **2. HORSE RIDE** a horse ride at a canter ■ *v* **(-ters, -tering, -tered) 1.** *vi* **GO AT CANTER** to move or ride at a canter **2.** *vt* **MAKE HORSE CANTER** to make a horse go at a canter [Early 18C. Shortening of *Canterbury gallop*; from the pace of medieval pilgrims who rode to the shrine of St Thomas à Becket in Canterbury]

canter[2] /kántər/ *n* somebody who talks cant or who uses cant [Early 17C. < CANT [1]]

canterbury /kántərbəri/ (*plural* **-ies**) *n* **1.** a stand with partitions for holding sheet music or magazines **2.** a stand with partitions for holding cutlery and plates [Early 19C. Probably after Charles Manners-Sutton, first Viscount *Canterbury*]

Canterbury /kántərbəri/ **1.** city in Kent, England. Its cathedral is the mother church of the Church of England. Population: 135,278 (2001). **2.** administrative region of New Zealand, in the eastern part of the South Island and including the city of Christchurch. Population: 481,431 (2001). Area: 56,612 sq. km/21,858 sq. mi.

Canterbury bells *n* an ornamental garden plant with blue, bell-shaped flowers. Native to: Europe. Latin name: *Campanula medium*. [Origin ?]

Canterbury Bight wide bay on the eastern coast of the South Island, New Zealand, extending 135 km/84 mi. from the Banks Peninsula to Timaru

Canterbury Plains fertile lowland area in the eastern part of the South Island, New Zealand. It is the largest area of flat land in New Zealand.

cantharis /kánthəriss/ (*plural* **-tharides** /-thárri deez/) *n* INSECTS same as **Spanish fly** (sense 1) [14C. Via Latin < Greek *kantharis*]

canthi ANAT plural of **canthus**

cant hook *n* a wooden pole with a pivoting metal hook at one end, used in forestry for handling logs [< CANT [2]]

canthus /kánthəss/ (*plural* **-thi** /-thī/) *n* the corner or angle at each side of the eye [Mid-17C. Via Latin < Greek *kanthos*]

canticle /kántik'l/ *n* a song or chant, especially a hymn containing words derived from the Bible, used in the Christian liturgy [13C. < Latin *canticulum* 'little song' < *canticum* 'song' < *cantus* (see CANTO)]

Canticle of Canticles *n* BIBLE same as **Song of Solomon**

cantilena /kánti láynə/ *n* a smooth-flowing melodious line in vocal or instrumental music [Mid-18C. Directly or via Italian < Latin, 'song' < *cantus* (see CANTO)]

cantilever /kánti leevər/ *n* **1.** BUILDINGS **PROJECTION SUPPORTED AT ONE END** a projecting structure that is attached or supported at only one end **2.** BUILDINGS **SUPPORTING BRACKET** a bracket that supports a balcony or a cornice **3.** AEROSP **WING WITH NO EXTERNAL BRACE** an aircraft wing constructed without external braces ■ *v* **(-vers, -vering, -vered) 1.** *vt* BUILDINGS **ATTACH SOMETHING AT ONE END** to construct something in such a way that it is attached or supported at only one end **2.** *vi* **EXTEND OUTWARDS** to project outwards with an unsupported end [Mid-17C. Origin ?] —**cantilevered** *adj*

cantilever bridge *n* a bridge consisting of arms projecting outward from supporting piers and joined together by a simple span where the two arms meet

cantillate /kánti layt/ **(-lates, -lating, -lated)** *vti* to chant or intone something, especially passages of the Hebrew scriptures [Mid-19C. < Latin *cantillat-*, past participle of *cantillare* 'sing low' < *cantare* (see CANTATA)] —**cantillation** /kánti láysh'n/ *n*

cantina /kan teénə/ *n Southwest US* a bar or wine shop, especially in a Spanish-speaking country [Late 19C. Via Spanish, 'bar, wine cellar' < Italian, 'cellar']

canting /kánting/ *v regional* an act of nagging at or scolding somebody [Mid-16C. < CANT [1]]

REGIONAL NOTE See *jawing*.

canting arms *npl* a coat of arms that makes a visual reference to the bearer's name [< CANT [1] in the obsolete sense 'say in a particular way']

cantle /kánt'l/ *n* the raised back part of a saddle for a horse [14C. Via Anglo-Norman < medieval Latin *cantellus* 'small corner' < Latin *cant(h)us* (see CANT [2])]

canto /kántō/ (*plural* **-tos**) *n* **1.** a section out of several into which a long poem may be divided **2.** MUSIC same as **cantus** (sense 2) [Late 16C. Via Italian < Latin *cantus* 'song' < *cantare* (see CANTATA)]

canton /kán ton, kan tón/ *n* **1. PART OF COUNTRY** a division of a country, especially one of the states into which Switzerland is divided **2. PART OF FRENCH ARRONDISSEMENT** a division of a French arrondissement **3. PART OF FLAG** a rectangular division in the top corner of a flag, next to the staff **4.** HERALDRY **PART OF SHIELD** a small square or oblong division of a heraldic shield, usually in the top left corner [Early 16C. Via French < Provençal < Latin *cant(h)us* (see CANT [2])] —**cantonal** /kántən'l/ *adj*

Canton /kan tón/ ➧ **Guangzhou**

Cantonese /kántə neéz/ (*plural same*) *n* **1.** the Chinese language of Guangzhou (Canton) and the province of Guangdong, China, also widely spoken elsewhere in the world. Native speakers: 70 million. **2.** somebody who comes from Guangzhou or the surrounding province of Guangdong —**Cantonese** *adj*

cantonment /kan toónmənt/ *n* **1. MILITARY TRAINING CAMP** a large military training camp, especially formerly **2. MILITARY CAMP IN BRITISH INDIA** a permanent military station in India during the time of British imperial rule **3. TEMPORARY TROOP ACCOMMODATION** temporary accommodation for troops, especially the winter quarters of an army **4. ASSIGNMENT OF TROOPS TO QUARTERS** the assignment of troops to temporary quarters **5.** *S Asia* **WESTERNIZED CITY DISTRICT** a Westernized district of a South Asian city [Mid-18C. < French *cantonnement* < *cantonner* 'quarter, billet' < *canton* (see CANTON)]

Canton ware *n* Chinese porcelain and other ceramic ware of types exported from China during the 18th and 19th centuries [Early 20C. Because exported from China by way of CANTON (Guangzhou)]

Cantopop /kántō pop/ *n SE Asia* pop music of Southeast Asia, originally sung in Hong Kong's Cantonese but now also in Mandarin, English, and Japanese. It is characterized by a decorous balladic style sung by musicians who are neatly dressed.

cantor /kán tawr, kántər/ *n* **1.** a Jewish religious official who is the chief singer of the liturgy in a synagogue **2.** somebody who leads the singing in a synagogue or congregation [Mid-16C. < Latin, 'singer' < *cantare* (see CANTATA)]

cantorial /kan táwri əl/ *adj* **1.** JUD-CHR relating to the chief singer of a synagogue or church **2.** CHR describes the part of the choir on the north side of a cathedral or church **3.** CHR, MUSIC same as **cantoris**

cantoris /kan táwriss/ *adj* sung by the part of the choir on the north side of a cathedral or church [Mid-17C. < Latin, 'of the singer', form of *cantor* (see CANTOR)]

cantrip /kántrip/ *Scotland n* **1. WITCH'S SPELL** a witch's spell or trick **2. PRANK** a mischievous trick or prank (*often used in the plural*) ■ *adj* **DONE BY MAGIC** supposedly carried out by means of magic [Late 16C. Origin ?]

cantus /kántəss/ (*plural same*) *n* **1.** MUSIC same as **cantus firmus 2.** the highest vocal part of a harmony in a piece of choral music **3.** a melody or style of singing used in the medieval Christian church [Late 16C. < Latin (see CANTO)]

cantus firmus /-fúrməss/ (*plural* **cantus firmi** /-fúrmī/) *n* a melody, often derived from chant, that forms the basis of a composition to which other melodic lines are added [< Latin, 'firm song']

canty /kánti/ **(-tier, -tiest)** *adj N England, Scotland* cheerful, lively, or sprightly [Early 18C. < Scots and English dialect *cant* 'bold'] —**cantily** *adv* —**cantiness** *n*

Canuck /kə núk/ *n N Am* (*slang*) **1.** somebody from Canada **2.** an offensive term for a French-Canadian person [Mid-19C. Probably < (a Native American pronunciation of) CANADA]

canula MED another spelling of **cannula**

canulate MED another spelling of **cannulate**

Canute /kə nyoót/, **Cnut, Knut** (994?–1035) king of England (1016–35), Denmark (1018–35), and Norway (1028–35). Known for his wise and effective rule, he is said to have ordered the tide to turn back in order to demonstrate his inability to control nature. Popularly, and wrongly, it is thought that he actually expected to turn back the tide.

canvas /kánvəss/ *n* **1.** TEXTILES **HEAVY FABRIC** a strong heavy cotton, hemp, or jute fabric. Use: sails, tents, furnishings. **2.** ART **FABRIC FOR PAINTING ON** a piece of canvas on which a painting is done, especially in oils **3.** ART **PAINTING** a painting that has been done on a canvas **4. BACKGROUND** the background against which events happen **5.** HANDICRAFT **CLOTH FOR NEEDLEWORK** a fabric with a coarse loose weave. Use: embroidery, tapestry. **6.** SAILING **SAIL** a vessel's sail or sails **7.** BOXING, WRESTLING **FLOOR OF BOXING OR WRESTLING RING** the floor of a boxing or wrestling ring when covered with canvas **8.** BOATING, MEASURE **END OF BOAT** the covered section at each end of a racing boat, sometimes used as a unit of length ■ *vt* **(-vases** or **-vasses, -vasing** or **-vassing, -vased** or **-vassed) PUT CANVAS ON SOMETHING** to cover or line something with canvas [14C. Via Old French *canevas* < Latin *cannabis* 'hemp' (from which the cloth was made)] ◇ **under canvas** living in a tent

SPELLCHECK **canvas** or **canvass**? Do not confuse the spelling of ***canvas*** and ***canvass***, which sound similar. The word ***canvas*** is chiefly used as a noun, denoting a heavy fabric, a piece of canvas used for painting, or something made from canvas such as a tent or sail, as

in *spend the night under canvas.* The word ***canvass*** is chiefly used as a verb, meaning 'solicit orders, opinions, or votes', 'debate', or 'inspect'.

canvasback

canvasback /kánvəss bak/ *n* a wild duck, the male of which has a white back and a reddish-brown head and neck. Native to: North America. Latin name: *Aythya valisineria.*

canvass /kánvəss/ *v* (**-vasses, -vassing, -vassed**) **1.** *vti* **VISIT SOMEBODY TO SOLICIT SOMETHING** to travel around an area asking people for something such as sale orders, opinions, or votes **2.** *vt* **DEBATE SOMETHING** to debate or discuss something thoroughly **3.** *vt* **LOOK AT SOMETHING CAREFULLY** to examine something in detail ■ *n* **1. OPINION POLL** a survey of public opinion, especially before an election **2. SALE OFFER TO MEMBERS OF GROUP** an offer of something, especially something for sale, to people in a particular area or group **3. CAREFUL INSPECTION** a detailed examination of something [Early 16C. < CANVAS] —**canvasser** *n*

SPELLCHECK See ***canvas.***

canyon /kánnyən/, **cañon** *n* a deep narrow valley with steep sides, often with a stream running through it [Mid-19C. Via Mexican Spanish *cañón* < Spanish, 'large tube' < *caña* 'pipe' < Latin *canna* (see CANE)]

canyoneering /kányən éering/ *n N Am* same as **canyoning**

canyoning /kánnyəning/, **canyoneering** /kánnyə néering/ *n* the activity of travelling through canyons on foot using skills such as abseiling, climbing, traversing, or swimming. N Am term **canyoneering**

canzona /kan zṓnə/ *n* **1.** MUSIC a song resembling a madrigal but simpler and less serious in form and content **2.** MUSIC an instrumental piece in the style of a canzona **3.** LITERAT same as **canzone** (sense 1) [Late 19C. < Italian < *canzone* 'song' (see CANZONE)]

canzone /kan zṓ nay/ (*plural* **-ni** /-nī/) *n* **1.** a love poem written by a troubadour in medieval Italy or Provence **2.** MUSIC same as **canzona** (senses 1–2) [Late 16C. Via Italian < Latin *cantion-* 'singing' < *cant-*, past participle of *canere* 'sing']

canzonet /kánzə nét/, **canzonetta** /-néttə/ *n* **1.** a short light English song of the 17th or 18th century, originally intended for a group of singers or for a soloist with accompaniment **2.** a Renaissance song with different parts for different singers, similar to the madrigal [Late 16C. < Italian *canzonetta* 'small canzone' < *canzone* (see CANZONE)]

canzoni LITERAT, MUSIC plural of **canzone**

Cao Dai /kow dī/ *n* a religious movement originating in Vietnam that combines features of both eastern and western religions [Mid-20C. < Vietnamese, 'great palace']

cap[1] /kap/ *n* **1. HAT** a covering for the head, usually soft and close-fitting and often with a peak and no brim **2. UNIFORM HAT** a head covering, usually part of a uniform, worn to identify the wearer's occupation or rank **3. PROTECTIVE COVERING FOR HAIR** a head covering worn to protect the hair, usually close-fitting or elasticated around the edge **4. HAT AWARDED TO PLAYER** a hat or beret awarded to a player selected for a special team **5. PLAYER AWARDED HAT** a player who has been selected for a special team such as a national cricket, football, or rugby team **6. HAT WORN AT ACADEMIC CEREMONY** an academic mortarboard, worn with a gown on a ceremonial occasion **7. COVER** a removable cover or lid that closes the end of something when it is not in use ○ *a lens cap* **8. COVERING AT TIP** something that covers the top or tip of something, especially as protection **9.** DENT **COVERING FOR TOOTH** a covering to preserve or replace the crown of a tooth **10.** FUNGI **TOP OF MUSHROOM** the dome-shaped upper part of some fungi such as mushrooms **11.** BOT **SPORE-CAPSULE COVERING** the hood that covers the spore-bearing capsule of mosses and liverworts **12.** BIRDS **PATCH OF COLOUR ON BIRD'S HEAD** a patch of feathers of a distinct colour on the top of a bird's head, extending to the level of the eyes **13. UPPER LIMIT** an upper limit on something, e.g. the amount that may be spent on an item **14. TOP PART** the top part of something such as a hill or mountain **15. EXPLOSIVE FOR TOY GUN** a small quantity of explosive enclosed in paper for use in a toy gun **16.** ARMS same as **percussion cap 17.** ARCHIT **TOP OF COLUMN** the upper part of a column or pedestal **18. CONTRACEPTIVE DEVICE** a contraceptive device that fits over the cervix, e.g. a Dutch cap or a diaphragm (*informal*) **19.** MATHS **SET INTERSECTION SYMBOL** a mathematical symbol (∩) representing the intersection of two sets **20.** GEOL same as **cap rock 21.** BIOL **MOLECULE CLUSTER** an aggregation of molecules at one end of something such as a cell or virus **22.** FIELD SPORTS **COLLECTION AT HUNT** a collection of money taken at a fox hunt **23.** BUILDINGS **WINDMILL ROOF** the roof of a windmill (*technical*) ■ *vt* (**caps, capping, capped**) **1. COVER SOMETHING WITH CAP** to put a cap over something **2. LIE ON TOP OF SOMETHING** to cover the top or tip of something **3. SURPASS SOMETHING** to improve on something that has already happened or been done **4. COMPLETE SOMETHING** to add the finishing touch to something such as an effort or a process **5. IMPOSE LIMIT ON SOMETHING** to put an upper limit on something such as the amount of money to be charged or spent **6.** SPORTS **AWARD PLAYER CAP** to select a player for a special team such as a national side, for which a cap is awarded **7.** *Scotland, NZ* EDUC **GIVE SOMEBODY DEGREE** to award an academic degree to somebody **8.** FIELD SPORTS **ASK FOR MONEY AT HUNT** to take a collection of money at a fox hunt from participants who are not members of the hunt **9.** CHEM **FORM CLUSTER OF MOLECULES** to form a cluster of molecules on something [Pre-12C. < late Latin *cappa* 'hood, hooded cloak'] —**capful** *n* ◇ **cap in hand** with a humble or apologetic attitude ◇ **if the cap fits (wear it)** if you think that a remark could apply to you, then you should take note of it ◇ **set your cap at** *or* **for somebody** to try to attract somebody, especially with a view to marriage (*dated*) ◇ **to cap it all** used to say that something has made a bad situation as bad as it can get

cap[2] *n Aus* same as **cappuccino** [Late 20C. Shortening]

CAP[1] *abbr* POL Common Agricultural Policy

CAP[2] /kap/ *abbr* COMPUT computer-aided production

cap. *abbr* **1.** MEASURE capacity **2.** capital **3.** FIN capitalize **4.** capital letter **5.** ANAT caput

Capa /káppə/, **Robert** (1913–54) Hungarian-born US photographer. He covered combat from the Spanish Civil War to the Vietnam War, where he was killed by a landmine.

capability /káypə bílləti/ (*plural* **-ties**) *n* **1. NATURAL ABILITY** the power or practical ability necessary for doing something ○ *Her capability to increase sales by endorsement is valuable to us.* **2. RANGE OF ABILITY** the potential ability of somebody or something to do something ○ *There is some doubt about the company's technological capabilities.* **3.** COMPUT **FUNCTION** a facility to carry out a particular set of operations ○ *a graphics capability*

SYNONYMS See ***ability.***

capable /káypəb'l/ *adj* **1. DOING SOMETHING WELL** good at a particular task or job or at a number of different things **2. ABLE TO DO PARTICULAR THING** possessing the qualities needed to do a particular thing ○ *not capable of murder* **3. LIABLE TO SOMETHING** permitting or susceptible to something ○ *an action capable of being misinterpreted* **4.** LAW **LEGALLY COMPETENT** considered legally competent to do something [Mid-16C. Via French < late Latin *capabilis* < Latin *capere* 'take']

capably /káypəbli/ *adv* in a competent or efficient way

capacious /kə páyshəss/ *adj* big enough to contain a large quantity [Early 17C. < Latin *capac-* 'able to hold' < *capere* 'take'] —**capaciously** *adv* —**capaciousness** *n*

capacitance /kə pássitənss/ *n* ELEC **1. ABILITY TO STORE ELECTRICAL CHARGE** the ability of a substance to store an electrical charge **2. ABILITY OF COMPONENT TO STORE CHARGE** the ability of an electronic component to store an electrical charge **3. MEASURE OF ELECTRICAL CHARGE STORAGE** a measure of the capacitance of a substance, equal to the surface charge divided by the electrical potential. Symbol **C 4. PART OF ELECTRICAL CIRCUIT** the part of an electrical circuit that has capacitance

capacitate /kə pássi tayt/ (**-tates, -tating, -tated**) *vt* **1. MAKE SOMEBODY CAPABLE** to make somebody able, fit, or qualified to do something (*formal*) **2.** LAW **GIVE SOMEBODY LEGAL POWER** to make somebody legally able to do something **3.** PHYSIOL **CAUSE CHANGE IN SPERM COATING** to cause the coatings on a sperm to be able to interact with proteins on the ovum —**capacitation** /kə pássi táysh'n/ *n*

capacitive /kə pássətiv/ *adj* relating to electrical capacitance —**capacitively** *adv*

capacitor /kə pássitər/ *n* an electrical component, used to store a charge temporarily, consisting of two conducting surfaces separated by a nonconductor (**dielectric**)

capacity /kə pássəti/ (*plural* **-ties**) *n* **1. VOLUME** a measure of the amount that can be held or contained by something **2. MAXIMUM VOLUME** the maximum amount that can be held or taken in **3. MAXIMUM PRODUCTIVITY** the maximum amount of output or productivity **4. MENTAL OR PHYSICAL ABILITY** mental or physical ability for something or to do something **5. OFFICIAL ROLE** an official function or position that somebody has ○ *in my capacity as team captain* **6.** ELEC **MEASURE OF ELECTRICAL OUTPUT** a measure of the electrical output of a battery, generator, or motor **7.** COMPUT **COMPUTER STORAGE SPACE** the amount of data that can be stored by a computer device **8.** LAW **LEGAL COMPETENCE** the legal ability or qualification to do something such as make an arrest or a will [15C. Via French < Latin *capacitas* < *capac-* (see CAPACIOUS)]

SYNONYMS See ***ability.***

caparison /kə párriss'n/ *n* **1. DECORATIVE COVERING FOR HORSE** an ornamental covering for a horse, especially for a warhorse in former times **2. HARNESS OR SADDLE DECORATIONS** a decorative harness for a horse or decorations for its saddle or other fittings **3. ELABORATE CLOTHING** elaborate or rich clothing and ornaments [Early 16C. < obsolete French *caparasson*] —**caparison** *vt*

cape[1] /kayp/ *n* **1. LOOSE OUTER GARMENT** a sleeveless outer garment, shorter than a cloak, that is fastened at the neck and hangs loosely from the shoulders **2. COAT PART LIKE CAPE** a piece of material like a cape that forms part of a coat or other garment **3.** BIRDS **FEATHERS ON BIRD'S SHOULDER** a covering of short feathers on the shoulders of some birds, especially fowl [Mid-16C. Via French < late Latin *cappa* 'hood, hooded cloak']

cape[2] /kayp/ *n* a point of land that juts out into water, especially a headland significant for navigation [14C. Via French *cap* < Latin *caput* 'head']

Cape Breton Island island in northern Nova Scotia, Canada, separated from the mainland by the Strait of Canso. Area: 10,311 sq. km/3,981 sq. mi.

Cape Coast town and capital of Central Region, Ghana. It is situated on the Gulf of Guinea, southwest of Accra. Population: 57,224 (1984).

Cape Coloured *n* in South Africa, somebody of mixed ethnic descent in the Western Cape Province, speaking Afrikaans or English [After the CAPE OF GOOD HOPE]

Cape Dutch *n* **1. 18C ARCHITECTURAL STYLE** a style of architecture characterized by whitewashed houses with high gables that developed in the Cape of Good Hope, South Africa, in the 18th century **2. 18C FURNITURE STYLE** a heavy style of furniture that developed in the Cape of Good Hope, South Africa, in the 18th century **3. DUTCH FORERUNNER OF AFRIKAANS** the form of Dutch that developed into Afrikaans [*Cape* after the CAPE OF GOOD HOPE; *Dutch* refers to the early settlers or the language] —**Cape Dutch** *adj*

capeesh /ka péesh/ *interj* do you understand? [Mid-20C. < Italian *capisce* 'he or she understands', form of *capire* 'understand']

Cape Flats the townships on the outskirts of Cape Town which were built during the apartheid era to house people of mixed race

Cape gooseberry *n ANZ, N Am* a tropical plant of the nightshade family that bears edible yellow berries. Native to: Americas. Latin name: *Physalis*

peruviana. UK term **physalis** [< its cultivation in the CAPE OF GOOD HOPE]

Cape jasmine *n* PLANTS same as **gardenia**

Čapek /cháp ek/, **Karel** (1890–1938) Czech writer. His drama *R.U.R.* (short for 'Rossum's Universal Robots') (1921), satirizes mechanization.

capelin /káyp'lin/, **caplin** /káplin/ *n* a small edible sea fish of the smelt family. Native to: northern and Arctic seas. Latin name: *Mallotus villosus*. [Early 17C. Via French < medieval Latin *cappellanus* 'custodian of St Martin's cloak' < late Latin *cappa* 'hood, hooded cloak']

Capella /kə péllə/ *n* a double star that is the brightest star in the constellation Auriga

capellini /káppə leéni/ *n* long fine noodles, resembling thin spaghetti (*takes a singular or plural verb*) [< Italian, 'little hairs']

Cape Peninsula peninsula that extends south of Cape Town, South Africa, ending in the Cape of Good Hope

Cape pigeon

Cape pigeon *n* a seabird of the petrel family with dappled black-and-white feathers. Native to: southern Atlantic and Antarctic seas. Latin name: *Daption capense*. [After the CAPE OF GOOD HOPE]

Cape primrose *n* BOT same as **streptocarpus** [Probably after the CAPE OF GOOD HOPE or CAPE PROVINCE]

Cape Province former province of South Africa, successor to the British-ruled Cape Colony. In 1994 the region was divided into the three provinces of Eastern Cape, Northern Cape, and Western Cape.

caper[1] /káypər/ *n* **1.** PLAYFUL JUMP a playful leap or dancing step **2.** PLAYFUL ACT OR TRICK a lighthearted adventurous act or prank **3.** QUESTIONABLE ACTIVITY a dangerous or illegal activity, especially one involving robbery (*informal*) ■ *vi* (**-pers, -pering, -pered**) PRANCE HAPPILY to leap or dance about in a happy playful manner [Late 16C. Shortening of CAPRIOLE]

caper

caper[2] /káypər/ *n* **1.** PICKLED FLOWER BUD a flower bud of a bush, eaten pickled or salted as a flavouring (*often used in the plural*) **2.** PLANT WITH EDIBLE BUDS a bush with spiny trailing stems, cultivated for its capers. Native to: Mediterranean. Latin name: *Capparis spinosa*. **3.** PLANT RELATED TO CAPER a plant in the same family as the caper. Family: Capparidaceae. [14C. Directly or via French *câpres* < Latin *capparis* < Greek *kapparis*; modern form from misunderstanding -s as the plural suffix]

capercaillie /káppər káyli/, **capercailzie** /-káyli, -káylzi/ *n* a large woodland bird of the grouse family, with dark grey feathers. Native to: Europe, Asia. Latin name: *Tetrao urogallus*. [Mid-16C. < Gaelic *capull coille* 'horse of the wood']

Capernaum /kə púrni əm/ city of ancient Palestine, situated on the northwestern shore of the Sea of Galilee

caper spurge *n* an annual plant that produces a milky fluid (**latex**) and has seeds with a high oil content, of potential interest as biodiesel. It is reputed to repel moles. Native to: Europe, naturalized in North America. Latin name: *Euphorbia lathyris*. [< CAPER[2]]

capeskin /káyp skin/ *n* a soft light leather made from South African sheepskin [After the CAPE OF GOOD HOPE]

Cape sparrow *n* a common sparrow. Native to: South Africa. Latin name: *Passer melanurus*.

Capetian /kə peésh'n/ *n* a member of the royal dynasty founded by Hugh Capet that ruled France from AD 987 to 1328 ■ *adj* relating to the Capetians or the period of their rule [Mid-19C. < French *Capetien*]

Cape Town legislative capital of South Africa and capital of Western Cape Province. It is situated at the northern end of the Cape Peninsula at the foot of Table Mountain. Population: 2,893,256 (2001). Afrikaans name **Kaapstad**

Cape Verde

Cape Verde /-vúrd/ **1.** island country lying about 644 km/400 mi. off the coast of Senegal in West Africa. A former Portuguese colony, it became independent in 1975. Language: Portuguese. Currency: escudo. Capital: Praia. Population: 412,137 (2003). Area: 4,033 sq. km/1,557 sq. mi. Official name **Republic of Cape Verde**. Portuguese name **Cabo Verde 2.** same as **Cape Vert**

Cape Vert /kap váir/ peninsula in western central Senegal. Its tip is the westernmost point of the African mainland. Length: 32 km/20 mi.

capework /káyp wurk/ *n* the skill of a bullfighter in using a cape to control the movements of a bull [Early 20C. < CAPE[1]]

Cape York Peninsula peninsula in northern Queensland, Australia, the most northerly point on the Australian mainland. Area: 127,200 sq. km/49,100 sq. mi.

cap gun *n* a toy gun that can be loaded with a small quantity of explosive enclosed in paper (**cap**)

Cap-Haitien /káp háysh'n/ seaport in northern Haiti. Population: 92,122 (1995).

capias /káypi as, káppi-/ *n* a warrant authorizing an officer of the law to arrest the person named on the warrant (*dated*) [< Latin, 'you are to seize' < *capere* 'take']

capillaceous /káppi láyshəss/ *adj* **1.** resembling a hair **2.** having many filaments that resemble hair or thread [Early 18C. < Latin *capillaceus* < *capillus* 'hair']

capillarity /káppi lárrəti/ *n* **1.** PHYS same as **capillary action 2.** the state of being capillary [Mid-19C. < French *capillarité* < Latin *capillus* 'hair']

capillary /kə pílləri/ *n* (*plural* **-ies**) **1.** ANAT THIN BLOOD VESSEL an extremely narrow thin-walled blood vessel that connects small arteries (**arterioles**) with small veins (**venules**) to form a network throughout the body **2.** SCI same as **capillary tube** ■ *adj* **1.** PHYS OF CAPILLARY ACTION relating to or involving capillary action ○ *capillary attraction* **2.** ANAT OF BLOOD CAPILLARIES relating to the capillaries of the blood system **3.** RESEMBLING HAIR as fine and slender as a hair **4.** SMALL IN DIAMETER having a very small internal diameter [Mid-17C. < Latin *capillaris* < *capillus* 'hair']

capillary action *n* a phenomenon in which a liquid's surface rises, falls, or becomes distorted in shape

where it is in contact with a solid. It is caused by the difference between the relative attraction of the molecules of the liquid for each other and for those of the solid.

capillary bed *n* the collective mass of capillaries in the body or in a particular part of it

capillary tube *n* a tube with a very small internal diameter, especially a glass tube with a fine bore and thick walls used in thermometers and similar pieces of equipment

capita ANAT plural of **caput**

capital[1] /káppit'l/ *n* **1.** SEAT OF GOVERNMENT a city that is the seat of government of a country, state, or province **2.** CENTRE OF ACTIVITY a city that is the centre of a particular activity **3.** MATERIAL WEALTH material wealth in the form of money or property **4.** CASH FOR INVESTMENT money that can be used to produce further wealth **5.** ADVANTAGE advantage derived from or useful in a particular situation ○ *making political capital out of the dispute* **6.** ECONOMIC RESOURCE a resource or resources that can be used to generate economic wealth ○ *a waste of human capital* **7.** WEALTHY PEOPLE the capitalist class considered as a group ○ *capital's influence on government policy* **8.** NET WORTH the assets of a business that remain after its debts and other liabilities are paid or deducted **9.** LING same as **capital letter** (*often used in the plural*) ■ *adj* **1.** LING UPPERCASE describes the form of letters used at the beginning of sentences and names, e.g. A, B, and C as distinct from a, b, and c ○ *a capital D* **2.** RELATING TO DEATH PENALTY relating to or incurring punishment by death **3.** GRAVE having extremely serious consequences ○ *a capital blunder that sealed their fate* **4.** PRINCIPAL constituting or belonging to the highest category **5.** GEOG, POL GOVERNMENT relating to or functioning as a seat of government ○ *a capital city* **6.** FIN OF FINANCIAL CAPITAL relating to or involving financial capital **7.** same as **excellent** (*dated*) [12C. Via French < Latin *capitalis* 'of the head' < *caput* 'head']

capital[2] /káppit'l/ *n* the upper part of an architectural pillar or column, on top of the shaft and supporting the entablature [13C. Via French < late Latin *capitellum* (see CAPITELLUM)]

capital account *n* a statement of the value of a company's capital at a given time

capital allowance *n* money spent by a company on fixed assets and deducted from its profits before taxes are calculated

capital asset *n* FIN same as **fixed asset**

capital expenditure *n* expenditure on long-term business assets (**fixed assets**) such as buildings

capital gain *n* a profit made from the sale of a financial asset such as shares or a house (*often used in the plural*)

capital gains tax *n* a tax on profit above a fixed level made from the sale of financial assets

capital goods *npl* goods that are used in the production of other goods, as opposed to being sold to consumers

capital-intensive *adj* using or requiring a proportionately large financial expenditure relative to the amount of labour involved

capitalise *vt* another spelling of **capitalize**

capitalism /káppit'lizəm/ *n* an economic system based on the private ownership of the means of production and distribution of goods, characterized by a free competitive market and motivation by profit

capitalist /káppit'list/ *n* **1.** INVESTOR an investor of money in business for profit **2.** BELIEVER IN CAPITALISM a supporter of capitalism, or a participant in a capitalist economy **3.** SOMEBODY RICH somebody who is wealthy, especially somebody made rich by capitalism and considered to be greedy (*informal*) ■ *adj* **1.** OF CAPITALISM relating to or involving capitalism or capitalists **2.** *also* **capitalistic** /káppit'l istik/ FAVOURING CAPITALISM practising or supporting capitalism —**capitalistically** *adv*

capitalize /káppit'l īz/ (**-izes, -izing, -ized**), **capitalise** (**-ises, -ising, -ised**) *v* **1.** *vti* LING USE CAPITAL LETTERS FOR SOMETHING to write or print something with capital letters or an initial capital letter **2.** *vi* BENEFIT FROM SOMETHING to profit by or take advantage of something ○ *to capitalize on an opponent's mistake* **3.** *vt* FINANCE SOMETHING to supply capital for a business enterprise

4. *vt* FIN USE SOMETHING AS CAPITAL to use debt or budgeted expenditure as capital for development **5.** *vt* FIN AUTHORIZE ISSUE OF CAPITAL STOCK to authorize a business enterprise to issue a particular amount of capital stock **6.** *vt* FIN EXCHANGE DEBT FOR STOCK to convert a corporation's debt into shares of stock **7.** *vt* ACCT TREAT EXPENSES AS ASSETS to treat an expenditure as an asset in a business account instead of as an expense **8.** *vt* FIN VALUE FUTURE INCOME to determine the current value of a future cash flow, earnings, or other income —**capitalizable** *adj* —**capitalization** /káppit'l T záysh'n/ *n*

capital letter *n* an alphabetical letter in the larger form used to begin sentences and names, e.g. A, B, and C as distinct from a, b, and c

capital levy *n* a tax on fixed assets or property

capitally /káppit'li/ *adv* in a way that arouses admiration (*dated*)

capital market *n* a financial market involving institutions that deal with securities with a life of more than one year

capital punishment *n* the punishment of death for committing a crime

capital ship *n* a ship that belongs to the largest and most heavily armed class of warships

capital stock *n* **1.** *ANZ, N Am* the amount of money raised by a company through the sale of shares, entitling holders to dividends, some rights of ownership, and other benefits. UK term **stock 2.** the face value of the share capital that a company issues

capital transfer tax *n* in the United Kingdom, a tax levied until 1986 on the total value of gifts and bequests somebody made. It was replaced by inheritance tax.

capitate /káppi tayt/ *adj* **1.** describes a flower head composed of small flowers arranged in a dense cluster **2.** describes a body part that is enlarged and rounded [Mid-17C. < Latin *capitatus* 'having a head' < *caput* 'head']

capitated /káppi taytid/ *adj* numbered or assessed by or for each person ○ *capitated payments* [Late 20C. < CAPITATION]

capitation /káppi táysh'n/ *n* **1.** FIXED TAX PER PERSON a form of taxation in which each person pays the same fixed amount **2.** FIXED FEE PER PERSON a payment or fee charged at an equal amount per person **3.** COUNTING OF HEADS a method of assessing the number of people by counting heads (*formal*) [Early 17C. Directly or via French < late Latin *capitation-* 'poll tax' < Latin *capit-* 'head'] —**capitative** /káppitətiv/ *adj*

capitellum /káppi télləm/ (*plural* **-la** /-lə/) *n* a rounded enlarged part at the end of a bone, especially that of the upper arm bone (**humerus**) that forms the elbow joint with one of the lower bones (**radius**) [Early 18C. < Latin, 'little head' < *caput* 'head']

capitol /káppit'l/ *n* in the United States, a building or group of buildings in which a state legislature meets and where other state government offices may be housed [14C. Via French < Latin *Capitolium*, temple of Jupiter in Rome < *caput* 'head']

Capitol, Washington, DC

Capitol *n* the white marble domed building in Washington, DC where the US Congress meets

Capitol Hill *n* the US Congress (*informal*)

Capitoline Hill /kə pít ō līn-, káppi tō-/ *n* a hill in ancient Rome on which the temple of Jupiter stood, site also of the Tarpeian Rock [Early 17C. < Latin *Capitolinus* < *Capitolium* (see CAPITOL)]

---

capitula BIOL *plural* of **capitulum**

capitular /kə píttyŏŏlər/ *adj* **1.** CHR OF ECCLESIASTICAL CHAPTER relating to or belonging to a cathedral or other ecclesiastical chapter **2.** BOT DENSELY CLUSTERED describes a flower head (**capitulum**) consisting of many small flowers **3.** ANAT ROUNDED describes the rounded end (**capitulum**) of a bone [Early 16C. < late Latin *capitularis* < Latin *capitulum* (see CAPITULUM)] —**capitularly** *adv*

capitulary /kə píttyŏŏləri/ (*plural* **-ies**) *n* **1.** a member of an ecclesiastical chapter **2.** a civil or ecclesiastical decree or set of decrees [Mid-17C. < late Latin *capitularius* < Latin *capitulum* (see CAPITULUM)]

capitulate /kə píttyŏŏ layt/ (**-lates, -lating, -lated**) *vi* **1.** to surrender, especially under agreed conditions **2.** to give in to an argument, request, pressure, or something unavoidable [Late 17C. < French *capituler* 'come to terms' < Latin *capitulare* 'draw up under distinct heads' < *capitulum* (see CAPITULUM)] —**capitulant** *n* —**capitulator** *n* —**capitulatory** /-lətəri/ *adj*

SYNONYMS See *yield*.

capitulation /kə píttyŏŏ láysh'n/ *n* (*formal*) **1.** GIVING UP surrender or a giving up of resistance **2.** TERMS OF SURRENDER a document that sets out the agreed terms of surrender **3.** SUMMARY an outline or summary in document form

capitulum /kə píttyŏŏləm/ (*plural* **-la** /-lə/) *n* **1.** a flower head that looks like a large single flower but consists of numerous tiny flowers clustered together on a disc. Daisies and sunflowers have this type of flower head. **2.** a rounded enlarged body part, e.g. at the end of a bone or at the tips of an insect's antennae [Early 18C. < Latin, 'little head' < *caput* 'head']

capiz /káppiz/ *n* **1.** a small mollusc with a hinged shell. Native to: Philippines. Latin name: *Placuna placenta*. **2.** *also* **capiz shell** the shell of the capiz. Use: jewellery, lampshades, ornaments. [< a language in the Philippines]

caplet /káplət/ *n* a small oval tablet of medicine taken orally

caplin *n* FISH another spelling of **capelin**

cap'n *n* used in writing to represent the pronunciation of 'captain' when addressing or referring to the captain of a ship

capo[1] /káp ō, káy pō/ (*plural* **-pos**) *n* a small movable bar fitted across all the strings of a guitar or similar instrument to raise the pitch [Mid-20C. Shortening of *capo tasto* < Italian, 'head stop']

capo[2] /káp ō/ (*plural* **-pos**) *n* a leader in the Mafia or a similar criminal organization [Mid-20C. Via Italian < Latin *caput* 'head']

capoeira /kápoo áyrə/ *n* a martial art and dance form, originally from Brazil, that is used to promote physical fitness and grace of movement [Late 20C. < Portuguese]

capon /káypən, -pon/ *n* a male chicken castrated to improve its growth and the quality of its flesh for eating [Pre-12C. Via Anglo-Norman < Latin]

caponata /ka'apə naátə/ *n* a dish made from chopped aubergine and other vegetables [Mid-20C. < Italian < Latin *capon-* 'capon']

Al Capone

Capone /kə pón/, **Al** (1899–1947) Italian-born US gangster and racketeer. Active in Chicago during the Prohibition era, he was imprisoned in 1931 for

---

tax evasion. Full name **Capone, Alphonse**. Known as **Scarface**

> 'I've been accused of every death except the casualty list of the World War.'
> [Al Capone, *The Bootleggers*, Kenneth Allsop; 1961]

caporal /káppə raál/ *n* a strong dark coarse tobacco [Mid-19C. < French *tabac du caporal* 'corporal's tobacco' (being superior to *tabac du soldat* 'soldier's tobacco')]

capot /kə pót/ *n* the winning of all the tricks by one player in a game of piquet ■ *vt* (**-pots, -poting, -poted**) to win all the tricks from an opponent in a game of piquet [Mid-17C. < French]

capote /kə pót/ *n* a long coat or cloak, usually with a hood [Early 19C. < French, 'little cape' < *cape* 'cape' < late Latin *cappa* 'hood, hooded cloak']

Truman Capote

Capote /kə pót/, **Truman** (1924–84) US writer. His best-known works are the novel *Breakfast at Tiffany's* (1958) and the widely acclaimed 'nonfiction novel' *In Cold Blood* (1966).

> 'I sat looking at Manhattan and wondering what sort of ruin it would make.'
> [Truman Capote, 'On Brooklyn Heights', *A Capote Reader*; 1987]

Capp /kap/, **Al** (1909–79) US cartoonist, known for his comic strip *L'il Abner* (1934–77). Born **Alfred Gerald Caplin**

cappelletti /káppi létti/ *n* small pieces of pasta shaped like pointed hats, filled with a savoury mixture of cheese or meat (*takes a singular or plural verb*) [Mid-20C. < Italian, 'little hats' < *capella* 'hat' < medieval Latin *capellus* 'little hat' < late Latin *cappa* 'hood, hooded cloak']

capper /káppər/ *n* **1.** a machine that fits caps on bottles **2.** something good or bad that is the last in a string of such events (*informal*)

cap pistol *n* LEISURE, ARMS same as **cap gun**

cappuccino /káppoo cheénō/ (*plural* **-nos**) *n* a drink made with espresso coffee and frothed hot milk, sometimes topped with powdered chocolate or cinnamon [Mid-20C. < Italian, 'Capuchin (friar)' < *cappuccio* 'hood' < late Latin *cappa* 'hood, hooded cloak'; from the colour of the habit]

~~cappucino~~ incorrect spelling of **cappuccino**

Capra /kápprə/, **Frank** (1897–1991) US film director and producer. He is best known for his comic 'little guy' films of the 1930s and 40s. *It Happened One Night* (1934) was the first film to win all five major Academy Awards.

> 'I made mistakes in drama. I thought drama was when actors cried. But drama is when the audience cries.'
> [Frank Capra, *Cinemas No. 12, Antenne 2 (French television)*; February 1983]

Capri /kə preé, káppri/ island resort in Napoli Province, Campania Region, southern Italy. It is situated near the southern entrance to the Bay of Naples. Population: 7,064 (2001). Area: 10 sq. km/4 sq. mi.

capric acid /kápprik-/ *n* a white crystalline acid. Source: animal fats, oils. Use: manufacture of artificial fruit flavours, perfumes, plasticizers, and resins. Formula: $C_{10}H_{20}O_2$. [< Latin *capr-* 'goat'; from its smell]

capriccio /kə preéchi ō, -prích-/ (*plural* **-cios** or **-ci** /-chi/) *n* **1.** LIVELY INSTRUMENTAL WORK a piece of instrumental music with a free form, an

improvisatory style, and usually a lively tempo **2. PRANK** a lighthearted act or prank **3. WHIM** a sudden idea, impulsive decision, or change of mind [Early 17C. < Italian (see CAPRICE)]

capriccioso /kə preéchi ốssō, -prích-/ *adj, adv* in a lively and fanciful manner (*used as a musical direction*) [Mid-18C. < Italian < *capriccio* (see CAPRICE)]

caprice /kə preéss/ *n* **1.** a sudden unexpected action or change of mind **2.** a tendency to sudden impulsive decisions or changes of mind **3.** MUSIC same as **capriccio** (sense 1) [Mid-17C. Via French < Italian *capriccio* 'head with hair standing on end' < *capo* 'head' (< Latin *caput*) + *riccio* 'hedgehog' (< Latin *(h)ericius*)]

capricious /kə príshəss/ *adj* tending to make sudden unexpected changes —**capriciously** *adv* —**capriciousness** *n*

Capricorn /káppri kawrn/ *n* **1.** ZODIAC the tenth sign of the zodiac, represented by a goat with a fish's tail and extending from 22 December to 19 January. Capricorn is classified as an earth sign, and its ruling planet is Saturn. **2.** ZODIAC somebody whose birthday falls between 22 December and 19 January **3.** *N Am* ASTRON same as **Capricornus 4.** GEOG same as **tropic of Capricorn** [Pre-12C. < Latin *capricornus* 'goat's horn' < *caper* 'goat' + *cornu* 'horn'] —**Capricorn** *adj*

Capricornia /káppri káwrni ə/ district in central Queensland, Australia

Capricornian /káppri káwrni ən/, **Capricornean** *n* same as **Capricorn** (sense 2)

Capricornus /káppri káwrnəss/ *n* a zodiacal constellation of the southern hemisphere. N Am term **Capricorn**. See illustration at **constellation**

caprifig /káppri fig/ *n* a fig produced by a wild fig tree [15C. Partial translation of Latin *caprificus*]

caprine /ká prīn/ *adj* relating to or resembling a goat [15C. < Latin *caprinus* < *caper* 'goat']

capriole /kápri ōl/ *n* **1.** in dressage, a vertical leap in which all four of the horse's feet leave the ground and then its hind legs are kicked out **2.** a playful leap or jump performed in ballet [Late 16C. Via French < Latin *capreolus* 'little goat' < *caper* 'goat'] —**capriole** *vi*

capri pants /kə preé-/, **Capri pants**, **capris** /kə preéz/, **Capris** *npl* close-fitting women's trousers that end just below the knee [Mid-20C. After the island of CAPRI]

Caprivi Strip /kə preévi-/ narrow extension of Namibia, running eastwards about 450 km/280 mi. from northeastern Namibia to the River Zambezi. It is bordered by Angola and Zambia to the north and Botswana to the south.

cap rock *n* **1.** a layer of rock that lies above a salt dome and consists of anhydrite, gypsum, or limestone **2.** an impermeable layer of rock that lies above a deposit of gas or oil and prevents it from percolating upwards

caproic acid /kə prố ik-/ *n* a liquid fatty acid. Source: fats, oils, made synthetically. Use: flavourings, medicine. Formula: $C_6H_{12}O_2$. [< Latin *capr-* 'goat'; from its smell]

caprylic acid /kə príllik-/ *n* an oily fatty acid with an unpleasant taste and smell. Source: animal fats. Use: in dyes, perfumes. Formula: $C_8H_{16}O_2$. [< Latin *capr-* 'goat'; from its smell]

caps. *abbr* **1.** capital letters **2.** PHARM capsule

capsaicin /kap sáy issin/ *n* a colourless compound. Source: hot peppers. Use: medicine, flavouring. Formula: $C_{18}H_{27}NO_3$. [Late 19C. Alteration of *capsicine* < CAPSICUM]

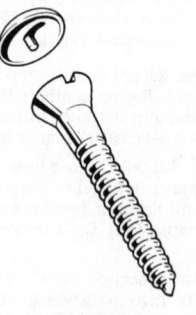
cap screw

cap screw *n* a long-threaded bolt with a head that may be square, hexagonal, slotted, or socketed

Capsian /kápsi ən/ *adj* belonging to a late Palaeolithic culture of northern Africa and southern Europe, characterized by the use of geometrically shaped tools and distinctive art forms such as engraved limestone slabs [Early 20C. < French *capsien* < Latin *Capsa* 'Gafsa', town in Tunisia] —**Capsian** *n*

capsicum /kápsikəm/ *n* **1.** a hot red pepper fruit, eaten raw or cooked as a vegetable, and often dried **2.** FOOD same as **pepper** *n* (sense 4) [Late 16C. < modern Latin]

capsid /kápsid/ *n* the outer coat of protein that surrounds a virus particle [Mid-20C. < Latin *capsa* 'box']

capsize /kap sĩz/ (**-sizes, -sizing, -sized**) *vti* to overturn on the surface of water, or cause a boat to overturn (*refers to boats*) [Late 18C. Origin ?]

cap sleeve

cap sleeve *n* a very short sleeve that hangs over the shoulder but does not extend beyond the armhole on the underside

caps lock *n* a key on a computer keyboard or typewriter that, if pressed once, causes all subsequent letters to be typed as capital letters

capsomere /kápsə meer/ *n* one of the individual protein units that make up the outer coat (**capsid**) of a virus [Mid-20C. < CAPSID]

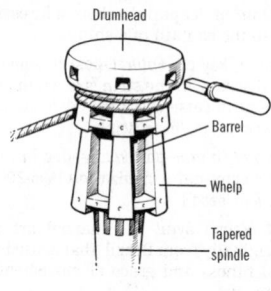
capstan

capstan /kápstən/ *n* **1.** a device consisting of a vertical rotatable drum around which a cable is wound. Use: moving heavy weights, hauling in ropes on a ship. **2.** a rotating shaft in a tape recorder that pulls the magnetic tape past the head [14C. Via Provençal *cabestan* < Latin *capistrum* 'halter' < *capere* 'seize']

capstan bar *n* a long lever used to turn a capstan by hand

capstan lathe *n* a lathe with a head holding several tools that can be rotated so that the tool needed for each operation can be brought in turn into the exact position required. N Am term **turret lathe**

capstone /káp stōn/ *n* **1.** a stone used at the top of a wall or another structure **2.** something considered the highest achievement or most important action in a series of actions

capsular /kápsyŏōlər/ *adj* **1.** relating to or resembling a capsule **2.** enclosed in or in the form of a capsule

capsule /káp syool/ *n* **1.** PHARM PILL OR CASING a small cylindrical soluble container enclosing a dose of medicine, or the container itself **2.** BOT SEED CASE a fruit containing seeds that it releases by splitting open when it is dry and mature **3.** BOT SPORE SAC a sac containing the spores of a moss or a liverwort

4. MICROBIOL GELATINOUS COVERING OF MICROORGANISM a gelatinous covering that surrounds some microorganisms **5.** ANAT MEMBRANE SURROUNDING BODY PART a membrane or sac enclosing an organ or body part **6.** ANAT WHITE MATTER IN BRAIN a layer of white fibres in the forebrain **7.** AEROSP same as **space capsule 8.** AVIAT EJECTABLE COCKPIT a sealed cockpit in an aircraft that can be ejected in an emergency **9.** MANUF SEAL ON BOTTLE a protective seal, e.g. the metal, plastic, or wax covering that protects the cork of a wine bottle **10.** SHORT SUMMARY a very brief summary ■ *adj* **1.** VERY BRIEF expressed in an extremely brief or highly condensed way **2.** COMPACT very small or compact ■ *vt* (**-sules, -suling, -suled**) *N Am* same as **capsulize** [Mid-17C. Via French < Latin *capsula* 'little box' < *capsa* 'box' < *capere* 'take'] —**capsulate** /kápsyŏō layt/ *adj*

capsule collection *n* a set, e.g. of fashion garments and accessories or furniture, comprising all the basic or key items

capsule hotel *n* in Japan, a hotel in which the rooms are lockable cubicles

capsule wardrobe *n* a person's basic collection of coordinating clothes that can be used to form the basis of outfits for all occasions

capsulize /káp syōō līz/ (**-izes, -izing, -ized**), **capsulise** (**-ises, -ising, -ised**) *vt* to put something into a capsule or into the form of a capsule

capsulotomy /kápsyŏō lóttəmi/ (*plural* **-mies**) *n* a surgical procedure involving cutting into the capsule surrounding a body part, e.g. cutting into the lens of the eye during the removal of a cataract

Capt. *abbr* Captain

captain /káptin/ *n* **1.** NAUT SAILOR IN COMMAND the commander of a ship **2.** AEROSP PILOT IN COMMAND the pilot in command of a civil aircraft **3.** NAVY NAVY OFFICER a naval officer of a rank above commander **4.** OFFICER IN BRITISH FORCES an officer in the British Army or Royal Marines of a rank above lieutenant **5.** OFFICER OF OTHER ARMY an officer of corresponding rank in the army of any other country **6.** TEAM LEADER a leader of a team in a sport or game **7.** IMPORTANT PERSON an influential leader in a field or organization ○ *captains of industry* **8.** EDUC HEAD BOY OR GIRL a senior pupil chosen to represent a school and sometimes given supervisory or disciplinary responsibilities ■ *vt* (**-tains, -taining, -tained**) COMMAND SOMETHING to be the captain of something [14C. Via Old French *capitain* < late Latin *capitaneus* 'chief' < Latin *caput* 'head'] —**captaincy** *n*

Captain Cooker /-kŏōkər/ *n NZ* a blue-grey razorbacked wild pig, descended from domestic pigs released by early settlers (*informal*) [Late 19C. After Captain James COOK, whose crew released pigs into the wild in New Zealand]

captain's chair *n* a wooden chair with a saddle seat and a low curved back and arms supported on vertical spindles

captain's mast *n* a disciplinary hearing at which a captain or commanding officer of a navy ship or force hears and acts on cases against enlisted personnel

captan /káp tan/ *n* an agricultural fungicide in the form of a white powder, used on fruits, flowers, and vegetables. Formula: $C_9H_8Cl_3NO_2S$. [Mid-20C. Shortening of MERCAPTAN]

caption /kápsh'n/ *n* **1.** DESCRIPTION OF ILLUSTRATION a short description or title accompanying an illustration in a printed text **2.** CINEMA FILM OR TELEVISION SUBTITLE a printed explanation in a film or on television, especially a translation of dialogue accompanying a scene or an explanation preceding a scene **3.** PRINTING, PUBL HEADING OR SUBHEADING a heading or subheading in a document or article **4.** LAW HEADING OF LEGAL DOCUMENT an attachment to or heading of a legal document that identifies the circumstances of its production and the sources of its authority [14C. < Latin *caption-* 'act of taking' < *capt-* (see CAPTIVE)] —**caption** *vt* —**captionless** *adj*

captious /kápshəss/ *adj* **1.** tending to find fault and make trivial and excessive criticisms **2.** intended to confuse or entrap an opponent in an argument [14C. Directly or via French < Latin *captiosus* < *caption-* (see CAPTION)] —**captiously** *adv* —**captiousness** *n*

captivate /kápti vayt/ (**-vates, -vating, -vated**) *vt* to attract and hold somebody's attention by charm or

other pleasing or irresistible features [Early 16C. < late Latin *captivat-*, past participle of *captivare* 'capture' < Latin *captivus* (see CAPTIVE)] —**captivation** /kápti váysh'n/ *n* —**captivator** *n*

captivating /kápti vayting/ *adj* attracting and holding somebody's attention by charm or other pleasing or irresistible features —**captivatingly** *adv*

captive /káptiv/ *n* **1.** PRISONER a person or animal that is forcibly confined or restrained, especially somebody held prisoner **2.** SOMEBODY DOMINATED BY EMOTION somebody gripped by a strong emotion such as love or anger ■ *adj* **1.** UNABLE TO ESCAPE prevented from escaping **2.** FORCED TO USE OR ACCEPT SOMETHING forced by circumstances to buy, accept, or pay attention to something, usually because there is no other option or no means of escape ○ *a captive audience* **3.** VERY ATTRACTED irresistibly attracted to somebody or something [15C. < Latin *captivus* < *capt-*, past participle of *capere* 'take']

captivity /kap tívvəti/ *n* the state of being a prisoner, or a period of time that somebody is held prisoner

captopril /káptəpril/ *n* a drug that blocks the action of a vasoconstrictor (**angiotensin**). Use: control of high blood pressure. [Late 20C. < MERCAPTAN + -O- + -*pril*, INN stem]

captor /káptər/ *n* a person or animal that takes or holds another person or animal prisoner [Mid-16C. < Latin < *capt-* (see CAPTIVE)]

capture /kápchər/ *vt* (**-tures, -turing, -tured**) **1.** TAKE SOMEBODY PRISONER to catch and then forcibly lock up or restrain a person or animal **2.** SEIZE PLACE to seize or gain control over a place **3.** TAKE SOMETHING IN GAME to win control or gain possession of something in a game or contest **4.** DOMINATE SOMEBODY'S THOUGHTS to enchant or dominate somebody's mind, especially somebody's imagination, or hold somebody's attention ○ *The stories about travel captured their imaginations most.* **5.** REPRESENT SOMETHING ACCURATELY to describe or represent something, especially something fleeting or intangible, in a lasting medium such as painting, writing, film-making, or sculpture ○ *a picture capturing the innocence of childhood* **6.** COMPUT RECORD DATA ON COMPUTER to record and store data in the memory of a computer or as a computer file **7.** PHYS GAIN PARTICLE to gain an additional elementary particle ■ *n* **1.** BEING TAKEN OR TAKING PRISONER the act of being captured or of capturing somebody or something **2.** SOMEBODY OR SOMETHING CAPTURED somebody or something that has been captured and held in captivity **3.** COMPUT RECORDING OF DATA the recording and storage of data in the memory of a computer or as a computer file **4.** PHYS GAIN OF PARTICLE a process in which an atom, ion, molecule, or nucleus gains an additional elementary particle, often followed by an emission of radiation **5.** GEOG DIVERSION OF RIVER OVER TIME the diversion of the headwaters of one river into the channel of another, brought about by erosion over a long period of time [Mid-16C. Via French < Latin *captura* 'seizure' < *capt-* (see CAPTIVE)] —**capturer** *n*

Capua /káppyŏŏ ə/ town in Caserta Province, Campania Region, southern Italy. Population: 19,041 (2001).

~~capuccino~~ incorrect spelling of **cappuccino**

capuche /kə pŏŏsh, -pŏŏch/ *n* a large hood on a cloak, especially the cowl worn by a Capuchin monk [Late 16C. Via French < Italian *cappuccio* (see CAPPUCCINO)]

capuchin

capuchin /kápyŏŏchin, -shin/ *n* **1.** *also* **capuchin monkey** an agile and intelligent long-tailed monkey with a

tuft of hair on its head that resembles a monk's cowl. Native to: forests of Central and South America. Latin name: *Cebus capucinus*. **2.** a hooded cloak formerly worn by women [Mid-18C. < CAPUCHIN]

Capuchin /kápyŏŏchin, -shin/ *n* a member of an independent order of Franciscan friars founded in 1525 in Italy [Late 16C. Via French < Italian *cappuccino* (see CAPPUCCINO)]

capuchin monkey *n* VERTEB same as **capuchin** (sense 1)

caput /káypət, káppət/ (*plural* **-pita** /káppitə/) *n* **1.** the most prominent part of something such as a bodily organ **2.** the head (*technical*) [Mid-17C. < Latin]

capybara

capybara /káppi baárə/ (*plural* **-ras** or *same*) *n* the largest living rodent, resembling a large guinea pig, which can grow to a length of more than 1.2 m/4 ft. Native to: Central and South America. Latin name: *Hydrochoerus hydrochaeris*. [Early 17C. Via Spanish *capibara* or Portuguese *capivara* < Tupi *capiuára* < *capī* 'grass' + *uára* 'eater']

car /kaar/ *n* **1.** CARS PASSENGER-CARRYING ROAD VEHICLE a road vehicle, usually with four wheels and powered by an internal-combustion engine, designed to carry a small number of passengers **2.** RAILWAY PASSENGER VEHICLE a railway vehicle for carrying passengers rather than freight **3.** TRANSP TRAVELLING COMPARTMENT FOR PEOPLE OR THINGS the part of an airship, balloon, or cable car for carrying passengers and cargo **4.** *N Am* RAIL VEHICLE ON RAILS a vehicle designed to run on rails, e.g. a tram or a railway carriage or wagon **5.** VEHICLES same as **chariot** (*archaic or literary*) [14C. Via Anglo-Norman, Old French *carre* < Latin *carrum, carrus* < Celtic] —**carful** *n*

car. *abbr* MEASURE carat

carabid /kárrəbid/ *n* a beetle that lives in the soil. Many species feed on other insects. Family: Carabidae. [Late 19C. < modern Latin *Carabidae* < Latin *carabus* 'sea crab' < Greek *karabos* 'horned beetle']

carabineer /kárribi neér/, **carabinier** *n* a soldier armed with a lightweight short-barrelled rifle (**carbine**) [Mid-17C. < French *carabinier* < *carabine* (see CARBINE)]

carabiner /kárrə beénər/ *n* same as **karabiner**

carabinero /kárrəbi nái rō/ (*plural* **-ros**) *n* **1.** in Spain, a member of the national police force **2.** in the Philippines, a customs officer, coast guard, or revenue officer [Mid-19C. < Spanish < *carabina* 'carbine' < French *carabine* (see CARBINE)]

carabinier *n* MIL another spelling of **carabineer**

carabiniere /kárrə binni áiri/ (*plural* **-ri** /-ri/) *n* in Italy, a member of the national police force [Mid-19C. Via Italian < French *carabinier* (see CARABINEER)]

caracal

caracal /kárrə kal/ (*plural* **-cals** or *same*) *n* **1.** a medium-sized wildcat with long legs, a smooth reddish-brown coat, a short tail, and long tufted ears. Native to: dry savannas of Africa and southern Asia. Latin name: *Lynx caracal*. **2.** the fur of the caracal [Mid-18C. Via French or Spanish < Turkish *karakulak* < *kara* 'black' + *kulak* 'ear']

caracara /kárrə kaárə/ *n* a large long-legged carrion-eating or predatory bird of the falcon family. Native to: Central and South America. Genus: *Polyborus*. [Mid-19C. Via Spanish or Portuguese *caracará* < Tupi-Guarani, an imitation of its cry]

Caracas /kə rákəss/ city and capital of Venezuela, situated at an altitude of approximately 900 m/3,000 ft. Population: 1,975,787 (2000).

carack *n* NAUT another spelling of **carrack**

caracole /kárrəkōl/, **caracol** *n* in dressage, a half turn to the left or right performed by a horse and rider ■ *vti* (**-coles, -coling, -coled; -cols, -coling, -coled**) to perform a caracole, or cause a horse to perform a caracole [Early 17C. < French *caracoler* < *caracol(e)* 'snail's shell, spiral']

Caractacus ♦ **Caratacus**

caracul *n* INDUST another spelling of **karakul**

carafe /kə ráf, -raáf/ *n* **1.** a container with a wide cylindrical base, a narrow neck, and a flared open top, usually made of glass and used to serve liquids, especially wine or water at table **2.** the contents or capacity of a carafe [Late 18C. Via French < Italian *caraffa*]

caramba /kə rámbə/ *interj* used to express surprise, amazement, or dismay (*slang*) [Mid-19C. < Spanish]

carambola /kárrəm bólə/ *n* **1.** a smooth-skinned yellow fruit with lengthways ridges that give it a star-shaped cross section. The thin skin is edible, and the juicy, slightly crisp fruit has a delicate flavour. **2.** a tropical evergreen tree that bears carambolas. Latin name: *Averrhoa carambolas*. [Late 16C. < Portuguese, probably < Marathi *karambal*]

caramel /kárrə mel, -m'l/ *n* **1.** CHEWY SWEET a chewy sweet that can be soft or firm, made with butter, milk, and sugar **2.** BURNT SUGAR sugar melted or dissolved in a small amount of water and heated until it turns golden or dark brown. Use: syrup for ice cream and other desserts. **3.** YELLOWISH-BROWN COLOUR a yellowish-brown colour [Early 18C. Via French < Spanish *caramelo*, alteration of Provençal *canamel* 'sugar cane' < Latin *canna* 'cane' + *mel* 'honey'] —**caramel** *adj*

caramelize /kárrəmə līz/ (**-izes, -izing, -ized**), **caramelise** (**-ises, -ising, -ised**) *vti* to heat sugar or boil dissolved sugar until it turns dark brown, or undergo this process [Mid-19C. < French *caraméliser* < *caramel* (see CARAMEL)] —**caramelization** /kárrəmə lī záysh'n/ *n*

carangid /kə ránjid, -ráng gid/ *n* a spiny-finned sea fish of the family that includes the jack and pompano. Family: Carangidae. [Late 19C. < modern Latin *Carangidae* < *Caranx* < Spanish *caranga* 'shad, horse mackerel']

carapace /kárrə payss/ *n* **1.** a thick hard case or shell made of bone or chitin that covers part of the body, especially the back, of an animal such as a crab or turtle **2.** a method of self-protection, e.g. shy or arrogant behaviour [Mid-19C. Via French < Spanish *carapacho*]

carat /kárrət/ *n* **1.** a standard unit of mass used for precious stones, especially diamonds, equal to 200 milligrams **2.** a unit for expressing the proportion of gold in an alloy on a scale from 1 to 24. For example, an alloy containing 50 per cent pure gold would be classified as 12-carat gold. [15C. Via French < Greek *keration* 'fruit of the carob' < *keras* 'horn'; because carob beans were used as standard weights for small quantities]

SPELLCHECK carat or **carrot**? Do not confuse the spelling of *carat* and *carrot*, which sound similar. The noun denoting a measure of precious stones or gold is spelt *carat*, as in *24-carat gold*. The noun denoting the orange root vegetable, or the plant that produces it, is spelt *carrot*.

Caratacus /kə ráttəkəss/, **Caractacus** /-ráktəkəss/ (*fl* AD 50) British tribal ruler. He was defeated by the Romans.

Caravaggio /kárrə vájji ō/, **Michelangelo Merisi da** (1573–1610) Italian painter. He was an exponent of the baroque style, and his tempestuous life is reflected in his realistic and dramatically lit works.

caravan /kárrə van/ n **1.** TOWED VEHICLE FOR STAYING IN a large vehicle equipped for living in, usually with two wheels and designed to be towed by another vehicle. Caravans are especially used for holidays but are also parked as permanent residences. N Am term **trailer 2.** VEHICLE FOR LIVING IN a large covered vehicle or van used as a travelling home, particularly by Roma people or circus performers **3.** GROUP OF DESERT MERCHANTS WITH CAMELS a group of traders, especially in northern Africa and Asia, crossing the desert together for safety, usually with a train of camels **4.** GROUP OF TRAVELLERS a group of people, vehicles, or supervised animals that are travelling together for security ■ vi (**-vans, -vanning, -vanned**) SPEND TIME IN CARAVAN to holiday or travel about in a caravan [Late 16C. Via French *caravane* < Persian *kārwān* 'group of desert travellers'] **—caravanner** n

caravanning /kárrə vanning/ n travelling or staying in a caravan for pleasure or a holiday

caravan park n same as **caravan site**

caravanserai /kárrə vánssə rī/ (plural **-rais**), **caravansary** (plural **-ries**) n **1.** a large inn with a central courtyard, found in some eastern countries and used by caravans crossing the desert **2.** TRANSP same as **caravan** n (senses 3–4) [Late 16C. < Persian *kārwānsarāī* < *kārwān* 'group of desert travellers' + *sarāī* 'inn']

caravan site n a place where caravans are parked for use as holiday homes or permanent residences, usually providing washing facilities and often shops and entertainment. ANZ term **caravan park**. US term **trailer park**

caravel /kárrə vel/, **carvel** /káarv'l/ n a light sailing ship with two or three masts, used in the Mediterranean from the 14th to the 17th centuries [Early 16C. < French *caravelle*, Portuguese *caravela* 'small ship' < Greek *karabos* 'crayfish']

caraway /kárrə way/ n **1.** a plant with finely divided leaves that bears caraway seeds. Flowers: small, white or pinkish, in clusters. Native to: Europe, Asia. Latin name: *Carum carvi*. **2.** FOOD same as **caraway seed** [13C. Directly or via Old French *carvi* < medieval Latin *carui*]

caraway seed n the aromatic dried ripe fruit of the caraway plant. Use: spice.

carb[1] /kaarb/ n ENG same as **carburettor** (informal) [Mid-20C. Shortening]

carb[2] /kaarb/ n a carbohydrate, or a high-carbohydrate food (slang) [Mid-20C. Shortening of CARBOHYDRATE]

carb- prefix CHEM same as **carbo-** (used before vowels)

carbamate /kaárbə mayt/ n a salt or ester of carbamic acid. Use: pesticides. [Mid-19C. < CARBAMIC ACID]

carbamazepine /kaárbə mázzə peen/ n an analgesic anticonvulsant drug. Use: treatment of epilepsy, pain, bipolar disorder. [Late 20C. Rearrangement of *dibenzazepinecarboxamide*]

carbamic acid /kaar bámmik-/ n an acid that exists only in the form of its salt or ester. Formula: NH₂COOH. [< CARBO- + AMIDE]

carbamide /kaárbə mīd/ n CHEM same as **urea** [Mid-19C. < CARBO- + AMIDE]

carbanion /kaar bánn ī ən/ n an organic ion that has a carbon atom with a negative charge [Mid-20C. < CARBO- + ANION]

carbaryl /kaárbə ril/ n an insecticide used as a substitute for DDT in a broad range of applications [Mid-20C. Blend of CARBAMATE + ARYL]

carbazole /kaárbə zōl/ n a compound derived from coal tar and used in the production of some dyes. Formula: C₁₂H₉N.

carbene /kaár been/ n a highly reactive, short-lived molecule containing a carbon atom with only three bonds

carbenicillin /kaar bénni síllin/ n an antibiotic derived from penicillin [Mid-20C. < carb(oxy)-ben(zyl)pen)i- + -cillin, INN stem]

carbide /kaár bīd/ n **1.** a compound containing carbon and one other element, especially a metal **2.** CHEM same as **calcium carbide** [Mid-19C. < CARBON]

carbimazole /kaar bímmə zōl/ n a drug that inhibits the formation of thyroid hormones. Use: management of hyperthyroidism.

carbine /kaár bīn/ n a lightweight rifle with a short barrel [Early 17C. < French *carabine* < *carabin* 'mounted musketeer']

carbineer /kaárbi neér/ n MIL same as **carabineer**

carbinol /kaárbi nol/ n CHEM same as **methanol** [Mid-19C. < CARBON + -INE]

carbo /kaárbō/ (plural **-bos**) n carbohydrate, or a carbohydrate (slang) ○ *Pasta is a good source of carbo.* [Shortening]

carbo- prefix carbon, carbonic ○ *carbocyclic* [< French < *carbone* (see CARBON)]

carbocyclic /kaárbō síklik/ adj describes a chemical compound containing a closed ring of carbon atoms

carbohydrase /kaárbō hī drayz/ n an enzyme that aids the breakdown of a carbohydrate [Early 20C. < CARBOHYDRATE]

carbohydrate /kaárbō hī drayt/ n **1.** a biological compound containing carbon, hydrogen, and oxygen that is an important source of food and energy **2.** food containing carbohydrates

carbohydrate loading n a controversial practice of first starving the body of carbohydrates, then following a high-carbohydrate diet just before an athletic event in an attempt to increase performance

carbolic acid /kaar bóllik-/ n CHEM same as **phenol** (sense 1) [Mid-19C. < CARBO- + -OL[1]]

carbo-loading n ATHLETICS same as **carbohydrate loading** (slang)

car bomb n an explosive device concealed inside or under a vehicle and detonated by remote control or when the engine is started

car-bomb vt to place a car bomb in or under a vehicle, or use such an explosive-laden vehicle against a target

carbon /kaárbən/ n **1.** CHEM ELEM a nonmetallic element that exists in two main forms, diamond and graphite, and has the ability to form large numbers of organic compounds. Source: coal, petroleum. See table at **element 2.** COMM same as **carbon copy** (sense 1) (informal) **3.** PAPER same as **carbon paper** (informal) **4.** something made of carbon, especially an electrode or a lamp filament [Late 18C. Via French *carbone* < Latin *carbon-* 'coal'] **—carbonous** adj

carbon 12 n an isotope of carbon with relative atomic mass of 12. Use: baseline in determining atomic mass.

carbon 14 n a naturally radioactive isotope of carbon with atomic mass of 14 and a half-life of 5,780 years. Use: as tracer, in carbon dating.

carbon-14 dating, **carbon-14 method** n ARCHAEOL same as **carbon dating**

carbonaceous /kaárbə náyshəss/ adj relating to, containing, or resembling carbon

carbonade n FOOD another spelling of **carbonnade**

carbonado /kaárbə náydō, -naádō/ (plural **-dos** or **-does**) n a dark diamond or cluster of diamonds. Use: drilling, polishing. [Mid-19C. < Portuguese]

carbonara /kaárbə naára/ n a hot pasta dish prepared with eggs, chopped ham or bacon, and cheese ○ *spaghetti carbonara* [Mid-20C. < Italian (*alla*) *carbonara* 'on the charcoal grill' < *carbone* 'charcoal' < Latin *carbon-* 'coal']

carbon arc n an electric discharge between two carbon electrodes or between an electrode and a metal to be welded, characterized by bright light and intense heat

Carbonari /kaárbə naári/ npl in early 19th-century Italy, members of a secret society that sought to establish a unified liberal republican government [Early 19C. < Italian, plural of *carbonaro* 'charcoal burner' < Latin *carbon-* 'coal'; from their use of symbols from the charcoal-burning trade]

carbonate n /kaárbə nayt, -nət/ **1.** CHEM SALT OR ESTER a salt or ester of carbonic acid **2.** MINERALS MINERAL a mineral composed of carbonates ■ vt /kaárbə nayt/

(**-ates, -ating, -ated**) **1.** CHEM CHANGE SUBSTANCE INTO CARBONATE to convert a chemical compound into a carbonate **2.** FOOD INDUST MAKE LIQUID FIZZY to make a liquid fizzy by introducing carbon dioxide into it **3.** CHEM same as **carbonize** (sense 1) **—carbonation** /kaárbə náysh'n/ n **—carbonator** n

carbonate platform n a broad extensive belt-shaped deposit of carbonate materials created in shallow warm oceanic waters during the Cambrian period

carbonatite /kaar bónnə tīt/ n an unusual alkaline igneous rock high in carbonate materials, found in eastern Africa and thought to derive from the Earth's mantle [Early 20C. < CARBONATE]

carbon bisulphide n CHEM same as **carbon disulphide**

carbon black n a form of finely divided carbon. Source: partial combustion of petroleum or natural gas. Use: manufacture of pigment, ink, rubber.

carbon brush n a block of carbon in an engine or generator that conveys current between the moving and the stationary parts

carbon copy n **1.** a duplicate of written or drawn material that is made by using carbon paper **2.** somebody or something that is identical to or very like somebody or something else (informal) ○ *This situation is a carbon copy of last year's crisis.*

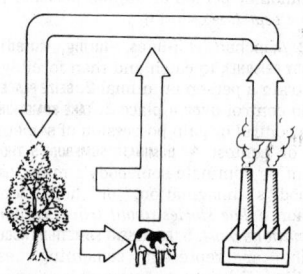

carbon cycle

carbon cycle n **1.** the exchange of carbon between living organisms and the environment. Carbon dioxide is taken from the atmosphere by photo-synthesizing plants and returned by the respiration of plants and animals and by the combustion of fossil fuels. **2.** a chain reaction believed to generate significant energy in some stars, in which carbon is used as a catalyst to fuse four hydrogen nuclei into one helium nucleus

carbon dating n a method of dating organic remains based on their content of carbon 14

carbon dioxide n a heavy colourless odourless atmospheric gas. Source: respiration, combustion. Use: during photosynthesis, in refrigeration, carbonated drinks, fire extinguishers. Formula: CO₂.

carbon disulphide n a colourless poisonous flammable liquid containing impurities that give it a rotten-egg smell. Use: solvents, fumigants, manufacture of cellophane and rayon. Formula: CS₂.

carbon emissions npl carbon dioxide and carbon monoxide produced by motor vehicles and industrial processes and forming pollutants in the atmosphere

carbon fibre n a very strong light carbonized acrylic thread. Use: reinforcing resins, metals, and ceramics, making turbine blades.

carbon fixation n the process by which plants synthesize carbon dioxide into organic compounds

carbonic /kaar bónnik/ adj containing carbon

carbonic acid n a weak acid. Source: dissolving of carbon dioxide in water. Formula: H₂CO₃.

carbonic anhydrase /-an hídrayz, -drayss/ n an enzyme in living tissue such as blood cells, that contains zinc and aids the transfer of carbon dioxide from the tissues to the lungs

carboniferous /kaárbə nífferəss/ adj containing or yielding coal or carbon

Carboniferous /kaárbə nífferəss/ n the period of geological time, 360 million to 290 million years ago, during which true reptiles first appeared and vast swamps create coal-forming sediments. See table at

geological time [Because numerous coal deposits were formed] —**Carboniferous** *adj*

carbonium ion /kaar bṓni əm-/ *n* an organic ion that has a carbon atom bearing a positive charge [Early 20C. < CARBO-, after AMMONIUM]

carbonization /kȧárbən ī záysh'n/, **carbonisation** *n* 1. the burning, fossilization, or chemical treatment of something that turns it into carbon 2. the process of covering or coating something with carbon 3. CHEM same as **destructive distillation**

carbonize /kȧárbə nīz/ (**-izes, -izing, -ized**), **carbonise** (**-ises, -ising, -ised**) *v* 1. *vti* to turn into carbon by partial burning, by fossilization, or through chemical treatment, or turn something into carbon in this way 2. *vt* to cover or coat the surface of something with carbon —**carbonizer** *n*

carbon microphone *n* a microphone containing carbon granules that change resistance according to the vibrating pressure of sound waves, thereby modulating the frequency of the sound waves

carbon monoxide *n* a colourless odourless toxic gas. Source: burning of carbon-containing compounds or fuels with insufficient air. Formula: CO.

carbonnade /kȧárbə náyd, -naad/, **carbonade** *n* a stew made with beef and onions cooked in beer [Mid-17C. < French < *carbone* (see CARBON)]

carbon-neutral *adj* relating to the maintenance of a balance between producing and using carbon, especially balancing carbon-dioxide emissions by activities such as growing plants to use as fuel or planting trees in urban areas to offset vehicle emissions

carbon-nitrogen cycle *n* PHYS, ASTRON, CHEM same as **carbon cycle** (sense 2)

carbon paper *n* paper used for making copies, coated on one side with a waxy pigment that often contains carbon

carbon process, carbon printing *n* a printing process that uses sensitized carbon tissue to produce positive prints

carbon sink *n* a forest or other area of vegetation that absorbs large quantities of carbon dioxide from the atmosphere, especially one planted specifically for this purpose

carbon star *n* a star that has a lower temperature and proportionately more carbon in relation to nitrogen than other stars

carbon steel *n* steel containing carbon with properties that vary according to the carbon content

carbon tax *n* a proposed tax on fossil fuels such as coal, oil, and natural gas that would be proportionately based on their respective carbon content. The purpose of a carbon tax would be to help reduce the emission of greenhouse gases into the atmosphere.

carbon tetrachloride *n* a colourless nonflammable toxic liquid. Use: as a solvent, refrigerant, dry-cleaning agent, in fire extinguishers. Formula: CCl_4.

carbon trading *n* a system of credits that allows a company or country that reduces its carbon-dioxide emissions below a target level to sell the extra reduction as a credit to a company or country that has not met the target level

carbon value *n* a measurement of the extent to which a lubricant forms carbon when in use

carbonyl /kȧárbə nil, -nīl/, **carbonylic** /kȧárbə níllik/ *adj* relating to or containing the group of atoms =C=O found in some organic and inorganic compounds

carbonyl chloride *n* CHEM same as **phosgene**

carbonylic *adj* CHEM same as **carbonyl**

car boot sale *n* a sale of second-hand and new goods from the boots of people's cars, usually taking place on an open-air site hired for the purpose

carborundum /kȧárbə rúndəm/ *n* an abrasive composed of silicon carbide

carboxy- *prefix* carboxyl ○ *carboxypeptidase* [< CARBOXYL]

carboxyhaemoglobin /kaar bóksi heemə glṓbin/ *n* a compound formed when inhaled carbon monoxide binds to haemoglobin

carboxyl /kaar bóksil, -sīl/ *adj* containing the organic acid group of atoms COOH

carboxylase /kaar bóksi layz, -layss/ *n* an enzyme that aids the transfer of carbon dioxide

carboxylate *n* /kaar bóksi layt, -lət/ any salt or ester of a carboxylic acid ■ *vt* /kaar bóksi layt/ (**-lates, -lating, -lated**) to form a carboxylic acid by introducing a carboxyl group or carbon dioxide into a compound —**carboxylation** /kaar bóksi láysh'n/ *n*

carboxylic acid /kȧár bok síllik-/ *n* an organic acid that contains the carboxyl group

carboxymethylcellulose /kaar bóksi mee thīl séllyŏŏ lóss, -méthil-/ *n* a derivative of cellulose. Use: paper production, food processing, medicines.

carboxypeptidase /kaar bóksi pépti dayz, -dayss/ *n* a protein-digesting enzyme secreted from the pancreas

carboy /kȧár boy/ *n* a large container made of plastic or glass, usually protected by a wooden casing and used to hold corrosive liquids such as acids [Mid-18C. Ultimately < Persian *karāba* 'large glass flagon']

carbuncle /kȧár bungk'l/ *n* 1. a multiple-headed boil 2. a red gemstone, especially a garnet, that is smoothly rounded and polished [13C. Via Old French *charbu(n)cle* < Latin *carbunculus* 'small coal' < *carbon-* 'coal'] —**carbuncled** *adj* —**carbuncular** /kaar búng kyŏŏlər/ *adj*

carburation /kȧárbyŏŏ ráysh'n/ *n* the process of mixing the correct proportions of liquid fuel with air to achieve combustion [Late 19C. < CARBURET]

carburet /kȧárbyŏŏ ret, kȧárbyŏŏ rét/ (**-rets, -retting, -retted**) *vt* to mix a gas with hydrocarbons in order to increase fuel energy [Early 19C. < obsolete *carburet* 'carbide' < CARBO- + -*uret*, chemical suffix < modern Latin -*uretum*]

carburetor *n* ENG US spelling of **carburettor**

carburetted /kȧár byŏŏ réttid, kȧárbə-/ *adj* fitted with a carburettor

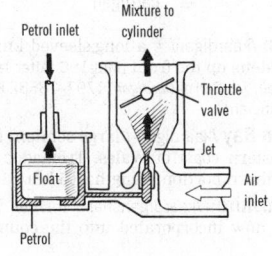

carburettor

carburettor /kȧár byŏŏ réttər, kȧárbə-/, **carburetter** *n* a device in an internal combustion engine that mixes liquid fuel and air in the correct proportions, vaporizes them, and transfers the mixture to the cylinders [Mid-19C. < CARBURET]

carburize /kȧár byŏŏ rīz, -bə-/ (**-rizes, -rizing, -rized**), **carburise** (**-rises, -rising, -rised**) *vt* CHEM same as **carbonize** (sense 2) [Mid-19C. < CARBURET] —**carburization** /kȧár byŏŏ rī záysh'n, -bə-/ *n*

carcass /kȧárkəss/, **carcase** *n* 1. DEAD BODY OF ANIMAL the dead body of an animal, especially one slaughtered and prepared for use as meat 2. PERSON a living person's body (*humorous*) ○ *Move your carcass!* 3. REMAINS OF SOMETHING the remains of something decayed or almost totally destroyed 4. BASIC STRUCTURE the basic structure or framework of something [14C. < Anglo-Norman *carcois*, French *carcasse*]

Carcassonne /kȧárkə són/ city and capital of Aude Department, southern France, situated on the River Aude 92 km/57 mi. southeast of Toulouse. Population: 43,950 (1999).

carcass trade *n* the reconstruction of old worn-out pieces of furniture that are then passed off as valuable antiques (*slang*)

Carchemish /kȧár kə mísh/ ancient city on the River Euphrates, northeast of Aleppo in present-day northern Syria

carcin- *prefix* MED same as **carcino-** (*used before vowels*)

carcino- *prefix* cancer ○ *carcinogenic* [< Greek *karkinos* 'crab, cancer']

carcinogen /kaar sínnəjən, kȧárssinə jen/ *n* a substance or agent that can cause cancer. Radiation and some chemicals and viruses are carcinogens.

carcinogenesis /kȧárssinō jénnəssiss/ *n* the production of cancerous cells

carcinogenic /kȧárssinō jénnik/ *adj* capable of causing cancer —**carcinogenicity** /kȧárssinōjə níssəti/ *n*

carcinoid /kȧárssi noyd/ *n* a small benign or malignant tumour on the walls of the small intestine that sometimes produces physiologically active compounds such as serotonin or prostaglandins that are normally deactivated by the liver [Early 20C. < CARCINOMA]

carcinoid syndrome *n* a condition in which small tumours (**carcinoids**) on the walls of the small intestine release excessive amounts of serotonin or prostaglandins. Symptoms include flushing, headaches, diarrhoea, and asthma.

carcinoma /kȧárssi nṓmə/ *n* a malignant tumour that starts in the surface layer (**epithelium**) of an organ or body part and may spread to other parts of the body [Early 18C. Via Latin < Greek *karkinōma* < *karkinos* 'crab'; from the pattern of the surrounding blood vessels] —**carcinomatoid** *adj* —**carcinomatous** *adj*

carcinomatosis /kȧárssi nṓmə tóssiss/ *n* a condition in which cancer has spread widely throughout the body

carcinosarcoma /kȧárssinō saar kṓmə/ (*plural* **-mas** or **-mata** /-mətə/) *n* a malignant tumour containing features of both a carcinoma and a sarcoma

carcinosis /kȧárssi nóssiss/ *n* MED same as **carcinomatosis**

car coat *n* an overcoat that ends at mid-thigh

Ace

King

Queen

Jack

Joker

Diamond

Spade

Club

Heart

card: playing cards

card[1] /kaard/ *n* 1. PAPER WITH PICTURES AND GREETINGS a folded piece of stiff paper with illustrations, used to send greetings for birthdays, anniversaries, or

other special occasions **2.** CARDS PRINTED STIFF PAPER FOR GAMES a small piece of stiff paper, part of a set, that is printed with symbols or figures and used to play games or tell fortunes **3.** STIFF PAPER SHOWING IDENTITY a small piece of stiff paper or plastic that shows somebody's identity, business position, or membership in a club or organization **4.** PLASTIC CARD STORING INFORMATION a small piece of plastic that holds information in a magnetic strip or microprocessor, used in financial activities such as getting cash from cash machines or making phone calls **5.** COMMUNICATION same as **postcard 6.** SPORTS same as **racecard 7.** INDUST STIFF PAPER stiff paper or thin cardboard **8.** COLLECTING COLLECTABLE STIFF PAPER WITH PICTURE a piece of stiff paper with a picture on one side, collected as part of a set of such items **9.** SOCCER COLOURED CARD SHOWN TO FOOTBALLER in football, a small piece of red or yellow stiff paper that is shown to a player who has violated the rules during a match **10.** AMUSING PERSON an amusing or eccentric person (*dated informal*) **11.** COMPUT same as **punch card 12.** COMPUT CIRCUIT BOARD a printed circuit board **13.** NAVIG same as **compass card 14.** COMPUT same as **expansion card** ■ *vt* (**cards, cárding, carded**) (*informal*) **1.** *N Am* ASK SOMEBODY FOR IDENTIFICATION to ask somebody to show identification, usually to check that the person is of legal age to drink alcohol or be admitted somewhere **2.** GOLF RECORD GOLF SCORE to record a score after playing a hole or round of golf [15C. Via French *carte* < Latin *c(h)árta* 'papyrus leaf' < Greek *khartēs*] ◇ **get** *or* **be given your cards** to be dismissed from your job (*informal*) ◇ **have** *or* **keep a card up your sleeve** to have a secret plan or tactic ready to be used if necessary (*informal*) ◇ **hold all the cards** to be in complete control of a situation (*informal*) ◇ **on the cards** likely to happen (*informal*) ○ *The collapse of the banking giant had been on the cards for some time.* ◇ **play your cards close to your chest** *or* **vest** to be secretive about plans, thoughts, or feelings (*informal*) ◇ **play your cards right** to take the fullest possible advantage of your chances of success (*informal*) ◇ **put** *or* **lay your cards on the table** to reveal openly what your intentions and plans are (*informal*) ◇ **see how the cards stack up** to find out what are the chances of success or otherwise

card[2] /kaard/ *vt* (**cards, carding, carded**) to comb out and clean wool, cotton, or other fibres before spinning ■ *n* a tool or machine with wire teeth used to comb out or clean wool, cotton, or other fibres before spinning [14C. Via French < late Latin *cardus* 'thistle' < Latin *carduus*] —**carder** *n*

Card. *abbr* CHR Cardinal

card- *prefix* MED same as **cardio-**

cardamom /kaárdəməm/, **cardamon** /-mən/, **cardamum** /-məm/ *n* **1.** the aromatic pods and seeds of a tropical plant, used whole or crushed as a spice or flavouring **2.** a perennial tropical plant with large hairy leaves that bears cardamom pods. Flowers: small, white, in clusters. Latin name: *Elettaria cardamomum*. [14C. Directly or via French < Latin *cardamomum* < Greek *kardamōmon* < *kardamon* 'cress' + *amōmon* 'amomum']

cardan joint /kaád'n-/ *n* a universal joint that can rotate when out of alignment [Early 20C. After Gerolamo *Cardano* (1501–76), Italian mathematician]

cardan shaft /kaád'n-/ *n* part of the transmission system in some vehicles [See CARDAN JOINT]

cardboard /kaárd bawrd/ *n* a stiff light material made from wastepaper pulp. Use: especially for making containers or packaging for goods.

cardboard city *n* an area in a city where homeless people gather to sleep, often using large cardboard boxes as shelter (*informal*)

card-carrying *adj* officially listed as belonging to an organization and subscribing to its beliefs (*often disapproving*)

card catalog *n N Am* COMM, LIBRARIES same as **card index**

card file *n* COMM, LIBRARIES same as **card index**

cardholder /kaárd hōldər/ *n* an owner of a card that carries information, especially a credit, debit, bank, or phone card

cardi- *prefix* MED same as **cardio-**

cardia /kaárdi ə/ (*plural* **-ae** /-ee/ *or* **-as**) *n* the opening of the oesophagus into the stomach, or the upper

part of the stomach where it is connected to the oesophagus [Late 18C. < Greek *kardia* 'heart']

cardiac /kaárdi ak/ *adj* **1.** relating to or affecting the heart **2.** relating to the upper part of the stomach, where it is connected to the oesophagus [Early 17C. Via French < Latin *cardiacus* < Greek *kardia* 'heart']

cardiac arrest *n* the sudden stopping of the heartbeat and therefore of the pumping action of the heart. Cardiac arrest requires immediate treatment to prevent brain damage and death.

cardiac compression, **cardiac massage** *n* rhythmic compression of somebody's heart in order to restore or maintain blood circulation after the person has had a heart attack

cardiac output *n* the amount of blood pumped by the heart over a given time period

cardialgia /kaárdi álji ə, -áljə/ *n* **1.** MED same as **heartburn** (*technical*) **2.** pain in or near the heart [Mid-17C. Via modern Latin < Greek *kardialgia* < *kardia* 'heart']

cardie /kaárdi/, **cardy** (*plural* **-ies**) *n* CLOTHING same as **cardigan** (*informal*) [Mid-20C. Shortening]

Cardiff /kaárdif/ capital and largest city of Wales. It is the home of the Welsh Assembly and is an important industrial centre. Population: 305,353 (2001). Welsh name **Caerdydd**

cardigan

cardigan /kaárdigən/ *n* a long-sleeved knitted jacket that fastens up the front [Mid-19C. After James Thomas Brudenell, 7th Earl of *Cardigan* (1797–1868), British soldier and politician]

Cardigan Bay /kaárdigən-/ large semicircular bay on the western coast of Wales. Tremadoc Bay forms its northern portion. Length: 105 km/65 mi.

Cardiganshire /kaárdigənshər/ former county of Wales, now incorporated into the county of Ceredigion

Cardigan Welsh corgi *n* a dog with a long tail belonging to the larger of two breeds of corgi [After CARDIGANSHIRE]

Cardin /kaár daN/, **Pierre** (*b.* 1922) Italian-born French fashion designer. He designed costumes for Jeanne Moreau in the film *La Baie des Anges* (1963).

'The jean! The jean is the destructor...a dictator! It is destroying creativity.'
[Pierre Cardin, *Parade*; June 1976]

cardinal (sense 3)

cardinal /kaárdinəl, -d'nəl/ *n* **1.** CHR ROMAN CATHOLIC DIGNITARY in the Roman Catholic Church, one of the group of clergy, next in rank to the pope, who elect the pope from their own number and act as his advisers **2.** COLOURS DEEP RED a deep strong red colour,

like that of the robes of a cardinal **3.** BIRDS BRIGHT RED N AMERICAN BIRD a crested finch, the male of which has bright red plumage with a black face. Native to: North America. Latin name: *Cardinalis cardinalis*. **4.** MATHS same as **cardinal number 5.** CLOTHING WOMAN'S HOODED CAPE a woman's short cape with a hood, originally scarlet in colour, that was worn in the 17th and 18th centuries ■ *adj* **1.** IMPORTANT fundamentally important **2.** COLOURS BRIGHT RED of a deep strong red colour [12C. Via French < Latin *cardinalis* < *cardin-* 'hinge'] —**cardinally** *adv*

cardinalate /kaárdinəl ayt, -d'nəl-/, **cardinalship** /kaárdinəl ship/ *n* CHR **1.** ALL CARDINALS the cardinals of the Roman Catholic Church regarded collectively **2.** TERM OF OFFICE OF CARDINAL the term of office of a Roman Catholic cardinal **3.** OFFICE OF CARDINAL the rank or office of a Roman Catholic cardinal

cardinal flower *n* a perennial lobelia. Flowers: brilliantly coloured, usually red, in clusters. Native to: central and eastern North America. Latin name: *Lobelia cardinalis*.

cardinal number *n* a number used to denote quantity but not order, e.g. 4 or 42

cardinal point *n* any of the four principal points of the compass, North, South, East, or West

cardinalship *n* CHR same as **cardinalate**

cardinal virtue *n* one of the principal virtues in the classical or Christian traditions. In the classical tradition they are justice, prudence, temperance, and fortitude, and in the Christian tradition they are justice, prudence, temperance, fortitude, faith, hope, and charity.

cardinal vowel *n* a member of a fixed set of vowel sounds, based on the position of the tongue and the shape of the mouth cavity, and spaced at approximately equal acoustic intervals

card index *n* an alphabetical listing of items such as names and addresses or books in a library, with each item on a separate card. N Am term **card catalog**

cardio- *prefix* heart ○ *cardiopulmonary* [< Greek *kardia*]

cardioaccelerator /kaárdi ō ək séllə raytər/ *n* a drug or other agent that increases the heart rate —**cardioacceleration** /kaárdi ō ək séllə ráysh'n/ *n*

cardiogenic /kaárdi ō jénnik/ *adj* resulting from activity or disease of the heart

cardiogram /kaárdi ə gram/ *n* a graphic record made by a cardiograph, especially an electrocardiogram

cardiograph /kaárdi ə graaf, -graf/ *n* an instrument for recording heart activity, used in the diagnosis of heart disorders —**cardiographer** /kaárdi óggrəfər/ *n* —**cardiographic** /kaárdi ə gráffik/ *adj* —**cardiographical** *adj* —**cardiographically** *adv* —**cardiography** /kaárdi óggrəfi/ *n*

cardiology /kaárdi ólləji/ *n* a branch of medicine dealing with the diagnosis and treatment of heart disorders and related conditions —**cardiological** /kaárdi ə lójjik'l/ *adj* —**cardiologist** *n*

cardiomegaly /kaárdi ō méggəli/ *n* pathological enlargement of the heart

cardiomyocyte /kaárdi ōmī ō sīt/ *n* a cell of muscular tissue in the heart —**cardiomyocytic** /kaárdi ōmī ō síttik/ *adj*

cardiomyopathy /kaárdi ō mī óppəthi/ *n* a disease of the heart muscle, usually chronic and with an unknown or obscure cause

cardiopathy /kaárdi óppəthi/ (*plural* **-thies**) *n* a heart disease or disorder

cardiopulmonary /kaárdi ō púlmənəri, -poól-/ *adj* relating to both the heart and the lungs

cardiopulmonary bypass *n* a procedure by which the blood is artificially circulated and oxygenated by a heart-lung machine so that surgery may be carried out on the heart

cardiopulmonary resuscitation *n* an emergency technique to revive somebody whose heart has stopped beating that involves clearing the person's airways and then alternating heart compression with mouth-to-mouth respiration

cardiorespiratory /kaárdi ō rə spírrətəri, -rə spírətəri, -réspərətəri/ *adj* relating to both the heart and the respiratory system

cardiothoracic /kaárdi ō thaw rássik/ *adj* relating to both the heart and the chest

cardiovascular /kaárdi ō váskyŏŏlər/ *adj* relating to both the heart and the blood vessels

carditis /kaar dítiss/ *n* inflammation of the heart [Late 18C. < Greek *kardia* 'heart']

-cardium *suffix* part of the heart ○ *endocardium* [< modern Latin < Greek *kardia* 'heart']

cardoon /kaar dóon/ (*plural same* or **-doons**) *n* a large perennial plant related to the artichoke with spiny leaves and edible roots and leafstalks. Native to: southern Europe. Latin name: *Cynara cardunculus*. [Early 17C. < French *cardon* < Latin *carduus* 'thistle']

cardphone /kaárd fōn/ *n* a payphone operated by a phonecard

cards /kaadz/ *n* a game played using playing cards (*takes a singular verb*)

cardsharp /kaárd shaarp/, **cardsharper** /-shaarpər/ *n* somebody who cheats regularly at cards —**cardsharping** *n*

card table *n* a small table, usually folding and covered with green baize, used for playing card games

cardy *n* CLOTHING another spelling of **cardie**

care /kair/ *v* (**cares, caring, cared**) **1.** *vti* BE CONCERNED to be interested in or concerned about something ○ *I said I couldn't care less if he did leave.* ○ *I don't care whether you come or not.* **2.** *vi* FEEL AFFECTION AND CONCERN to feel affection or love and concern for somebody **3.** *vi* LOOK AFTER SOMEBODY OR SOMETHING to look after or supervise somebody or something **4.** *vi* LIKE OR WANT SOMETHING to like or be in favour of something (*formal*) ○ *Would you care for dessert?* ■ *n* **1.** UPKEEP the process of maintaining something in good condition ○ *a skin care treatment* **2.** CAREFUL ATTENTION careful attention to avoid damage or error **3.** WORRY a worry or cause for anxiety ○ *without a care in the world* **4.** WORRIED STATE OF MIND a troubled state of mind arising from worry or grief (*literary or formal*) **5.** SOC WELFARE ATTENTIVE TREATMENT OF SOMEBODY the providing of whatever is needed for the wellbeing of somebody who is dependent or physically or mentally disabled ○ *responsible for the 20 children in her care* ○ *residential care* **6.** RESPONSIBILITY OF LOCAL AUTHORITY FOR CHILD the custody and maintenance of a child as the legal responsibility of a local authority after a court order ○ *She went to prison and her children were taken into care.* [Old English *caru* 'sorrow' < Indo-European] ◇ **care of** into the temporary possession of an addressee who will ensure that the item will be delivered to the intended recipient ○ *sent the letter to her care of her parents* ◇ **take care 1.** to behave prudently, with regard for your own safety **2.** used as an affectionate farewell to somebody (*informal*) ◇ **take care of somebody** *or* **something 1.** to provide for the needs of somebody or something **2.** to deal with somebody or something effectively

SYNONYMS See *worry*.

CARE /kair/ *abbr* Cooperative for American Relief Everywhere

care and maintenance *n* the condition in which machinery or a site such as a factory or shipyard is kept when it is ready for immediate use at any time

care assistant *n* HEALTH SERVICES same as **care worker**

care attendant *n* somebody employed to look after people in a variety of settings such as retirement or nursing homes

careen /kə réen/ (**-reens, -reening, -reened**) *v* **1.** *vi* SWAY OR SWERVE WHILE MOVING to move forwards at high speed, swaying, lurching, or swerving from one side to the other ○ *a motorcycle careening around sharp curves* **2.** *vi N Am* MOVE RAPIDLY to rush or move carelessly ○ *He seemed to careen from one job to the next.* **3.** *vti* NAUT TURN BOAT ON SIDE to turn a boat over on its side, especially for repairs or cleaning, or turn over onto the side **4.** *vi* SAILING HEEL IN WIND to heel over to one side while sailing [Early 17C. < *careen* 'act of careening a boat', via French *carène* < Latin *carina* 'keel, nutshell'; in senses 1 and 2 influenced by CAREER] —**careener** *n*

career /kə réer/ *n* **1.** LONG-TERM OR LIFELONG JOB a job or occupation regarded as a long-term or lifelong activity **2.** PROFESSIONAL PROGRESS somebody's progress in a chosen profession or during that person's working life **3.** GENERAL PROGRESS the general path or progress taken by somebody or something ○ *a piece of legislation whose career is rich with conflicting amendments* **4.** RAPID FORWARD LURCHING MOTION a rushing onwards while lurching or swaying ■ *adj* PROFESSIONAL FOR LIFE trained for and expecting to work in a particular occupation for an entire working life rather than briefly ○ *a career diplomat* ■ *vi* (**-reers, -reering, -reered**) LURCH RAPIDLY ONWARDS to rush forwards while lurching or swaying [Mid-16C. < French *carrière* < Latin *carrus* (see CAR)]

CULTURAL NOTE ***My Brilliant Career***, a novel (1901) by Australian writer Miles Franklin. It is an account of a young girl's struggle to choose between an independent career and a comfortable life as the wife of a wealthy landowner. It was made into a film directed by Gillian Armstrong in 1979.

career coach *n* somebody who offers another person professional guidance and advice on career change or improvement

career counselor *n N Am* same as **careers officer**

career gapper *n* somebody who takes a prolonged leave from a job to travel or do alternative, especially charitable work, usually abroad

careerism /kə réerizəm/ *n* the behaviour of somebody whose principal motivation is career advancement —**careerist** *n*

careers officer *n* somebody whose job is to advise secondary pupils on possible careers and jobs as they approach school leaving age. N Am term **career counselor**

career woman *n* a woman who has a career or who takes her working life seriously

carefree /káir free/ *adj* having no worries or responsibilities —**carefreeness** *n*

careful /káirf'l/ *adj* **1.** PAINSTAKING showing close attention to accuracy and detail **2.** CAUTIOUS taking reasonable care to avoid risks **3.** WATCHFUL watchful and protective about something **4.** NOT OVERSPENDING OR BEING WASTEFUL ensuring that money or resources are not spent or used wastefully or without thought —**carefully** *adv* —**carefulness** *n*

SYNONYMS ***careful, conscientious, scrupulous, thorough, meticulous, painstaking, assiduous, punctilious, finicky, fussy***

CORE MEANING: exercising care and attention in doing something

careful showing close attention to accuracy and detail ○ *The project was given approval after careful consideration.* ○ *the result of some very careful planning* **conscientious** showing great care, attention, and industriousness in carrying out a task or role ○ *a very conscientious secretary* ○ *Are you always so conscientious about keeping promises?* **scrupulous** having or showing careful regard for what is morally right, or for correct procedure ○ *draw up the contract with scrupulous care* ○ *I shall be absolutely scrupulous in not favouring one candidate.* **thorough** extremely careful to include everything that is needed ○ *a thorough investigation* ○ *a thorough understanding of programming principles* **meticulous** extremely careful and precise ○ *meticulous attention to detail* ○ *pasted the reviews with meticulous care into her cuttings-book* **painstaking** involving or showing great care and attention to detail ○ *years of painstaking research* ○ *a thorough and painstaking investigation* **assiduous** showing persistent and hard-working effort in doing something ○ *paid assiduous attention to the layout of new streets* ○ *He is assiduous in ensuring compliance with the law.* **punctilious** very careful about the conventions of correct behaviour and etiquette ○ *She was usually punctilious about telling her mother if she was going to be late.* ○ *He always has been punctilious in the exercise of his duties.* **finicky** difficult to please, and tending to concentrate on small or unimportant details ○ *Some advocacy groups are finicky about these issues.* ○ *finicky car buyers* **fussy** tending to worry over details or trivial things ○ *She's got every right to be fussy about the seating plan for the wedding.* ○ *This bird isn't all that fussy about its nesting site.*

~~**carefull**~~ incorrect spelling of **careful**

caregiver /káir givər/ *n* **1.** *NZ, N Am* same as **carer** (sense 1) **2.** *N Am* a medical worker or other professional who assists in the management of an illness or disability —**caregiving** *n*

~~**careing**~~ incorrect spelling of **caring**

care in the community *n* a British government policy of reintegrating people with a history of psychiatric disorders into their communities by moving them from long-stay institutions to their families or community centres

care label *n* a label, sewn onto a piece of clothing or other item, that gives cleaning instructions for the item

careless /káirləss/ *adj* **1.** NOT GIVING CAREFUL ATTENTION not giving enough careful attention to the details of something **2.** SHOWING NO CONCERN disregarding or showing no concern about something **3.** NOT CAREFULLY WORKED ON not carefully nurtured or practised, but done or assumed easily and naturally ○ *a careless charm* —**carelessly** *adv*

carelessness /káirləssnəss/ *n* **1.** LACK OF ATTENTION lack of careful attention to the details of something **2.** EXAMPLE OF NEGLIGENCE an example of negligence or of a failure to take enough trouble with something **3.** LACK OF CONCERN lack of concern about something

carer /káirər/ *n* **1.** somebody who has the principal responsibility of caring for a child or an elderly or dependent adult. N Am term **caregiver 2.** somebody employed to visit and help dependent elderly people or people with physical or mental disabilities in their own homes. N Am term **home health aide**

caress /kə réss/ *vt* (**-resses, -ressing, -ressed**) **1.** TOUCH SOMEBODY AFFECTIONATELY to touch or stroke somebody or something affectionately **2.** AFFECT SOMEBODY IN SOOTHING WAY to touch, pass over, or affect somebody in a soothing or pleasant way ■ *n* GENTLE TOUCH a gentle affectionate touch or embrace [Mid-17C. Via French *caresse* < Italian *carezza* < Latin *carus* 'dear'] —**caresser** *n* —**caressive** *adj* —**caressively** *adv*

caressing /kə réssing/ *adj* gentle and soothing —**caressingly** *adv*

caret /kárrət/ *n* a mark (‸) made on printed or manuscript material to show where something such as a letter or word should be inserted [Late 17C. < Latin *caret* 'there is lacking', form of *carere* 'to lack']

caretaker /káir taykər/ *n* **1.** somebody who supervises the care of a property such as an office block or a school **2.** a temporary holder of a post **3.** SOC WELFARE same as **carer** (sense 1)

caretaker government *n* a government that is in power temporarily after the fall of a previous government, e.g. until an election is held

Carew /kə róo, káiroo/, **Thomas** (1595?–1645?) English poet, diplomat and author. He wrote witty lyrics in the Cavalier tradition, as well as the masque *Coelum Britannicum* (1634).

> 'He that loves a rosy cheek, / Or a coral lip admires, / Or, from star-like eyes, doth seek / Fuel to maintain his fires; / As old Time makes these decay, / So his flames must waste away.'
> [Thomas Carew, 'Disdain Returned'; 1640]

careware /káir wair/ *n* COMPUT software that is made available to users in exchange for a donation to charity

care worker *n* somebody employed to help look after people with physical or mental disabilities in residential accommodation

careworn /káir wawrn/ *adj* exhausted or otherwise badly affected by anxiety or worry

Carey /káiri/, **George** (*b.* 1935) British Anglican archbishop. He was bishop of Bath and Wells (1987–91) before being appointed archbishop of Canterbury. He retired in 2002.

> 'My fear will be that in 15 years time, Jerusalem, Bethlehem, once centres of strong Christian presence, might become a kind of Walt Disney Theme Park.'
> [George Carey, *Observer*; 12 January 1992]

Carey, Peter Philip (*b.* 1943) Australian writer. His novels include *Illywhacker* (1985), and he has twice won the Booker Prize, with *Oscar and Lucinda* (1988) and *True History of the Kelly Gang* (2001).

Carey Street /káiri-/ *n* a state of bankruptcy (*dated*)

WORLD ENGLISH *Caribbean English*, also called *West Indian English*, is the variety of English as used in the Caribbean region. Since their European discovery by Columbus in 1492, the islands and coasts of the Caribbean have been claimed, disputed, settled, and governed by the Spanish, Portuguese, French, British, Dutch, Danish, and Americans with obvious long-term varied effects on the languages spoken there. Most of the territories are now independent, but colonization has created a complex inheritance. In such mainland areas as Belize and Guyana, indigenous languages survive; in all territories there is a complex 'continuum' between standard American and British English, Dutch, French, and Spanish on the one hand and their related creoles on the other.
In general terms, the creoles have a majority of European vocabulary items, as well as words from other languages, with varying degrees of African and other structural features. In most Anglo-Caribbean territories, although school-based standard English is the official language, it is a minority form. Apart from Barbados and Guyana, *r* is usually not pronounced in such words as *art, door,* and *worker* in Caribbean English. The most salient differences between the Creole-like varieties of Caribbean English and standard English include the absence of inflected endings in -*ing* and -*ed*, e.g. *name* for *named*; the absence of some past verb forms; the absence of -*s* in third-person singular present verb and plural nouns; the pronunciation of /th/ as /t/ or /d/; and the different usage of parts of speech, e.g. *tired* as both adjective and verb, *hungry* as both adjective and noun.

[After the former location of the Bankruptcy Department of the Supreme Court in London]

carfare /ka'ar fair/ *n N Am* the amount charged for a journey on a bus or tram or in a taxi

carfuffle *n Scotland* another spelling of **kerfuffle** (*informal*)

cargo /ka'argō/ (*plural* -**goes**) *n* **1.** goods carried as freight by sea, road, or air **2.** a load of something [Mid-17C. < Spanish < late Latin *car(ri)care* 'to load' < Latin *carrus* (see CAR)]

cargo cult *n* in some southwestern Pacific islands, a religion whose devotees believe that ancestral spirits will return to the island bringing modern consumer goods and wealth

cargo pants *npl* trousers with cargo pockets, often on the legs

cargo pocket *n* a large pocket with a pleat and a flap, sewn onto the outside of a garment

car guard *n S Africa* somebody, usually a casual worker, paid to watch over parked cars to protect them from theft or vandalism

carhop /ka'ar hop/ *n N Am* somebody who serves food to people in cars at a drive-in restaurant [Mid-20C. < CAR + BELLHOP]

cariad /kárri ad/ *n Wales* used as an affectionate form of address (*informal*) [< Welsh]

~~cariage~~ incorrect spelling of **carriage**

Carib[1] /kárrib/ (*plural* -**ibs** or *same*) *n* **1.** a member of a group of Native American people who live in Central America, northeastern South America, and the Lesser Antilles **2.** a language of the Cariban family spoken in Venezuela and neighbouring countries. Native speakers: 20,000. [Mid-16C. Via Spanish *caribe* < Arawak *carib*] —**Carib** *adj*

Carib[2] *abbr* Caribbean

Cariban /kárriban/ (*plural* -**bans** or *same*) *n* **1.** PEOPLES, LANG same as **Carib**[1] (sense 1) **2.** a group of about 30 languages spoken in northern South America. Native speakers: 40,000. —**Cariban** *adj*

Caribbean[1] /kárri bee ən, kə ríbbi ən/ *adj* **1.** OF CARIBBEAN relating to the Caribbean or its peoples, languages, or cultures **2.** OF CARIBS relating to the Caribs or their language or culture ■ *n* SOMEBODY FROM CARIBBEAN somebody who comes from a Caribbean island

Caribbean[2] /kárri bee ən/ region comprising three main island groups, the Greater Antilles, the Lesser Antilles, and the Bahamas, extending from the southeastern tip of Florida to the coast of Venezuela and separating the Caribbean Sea from the Atlantic Ocean

Caribbean English *n* the variety of English spoken in the Caribbean islands

Caribbean Sea arm of the Atlantic Ocean, surrounded by the Greater and Lesser Antilles, northern South America, and eastern Central America. Area: 2,718,000 sq. km/1,049,000 sq. mi. Depth: Cayman Trench 7,535 m/24,720 ft.

caribou

caribou /kárri boo/ (*plural* -**bous** or *same*) *n* a large deer that lives in large herds and has large branched antlers on both sexes. Native to: northern regions. Genus: *Rangifer*. [Mid-17C. Via Canadian French < Mi'kmaq *ğalipu* 'snow-shoveller'; because it removes snow to find grass]

Caribou Inuit *n* a member of an Inuit people living in the Barren Grounds in northern Canada. They depend upon caribou for survival.

caricature /kárrikə choor/ *n* **1.** COMIC EXAGGERATION a drawing, description, or performance that exaggerates somebody's or something's characteristics for humorous or satirical effect **2.** TRAVESTY a ridiculously inappropriate or unsuccessful version of or attempt at something **3.** ART OF CARICATURES the art of creating caricatures [Mid-18C. < Italian *caricatura* < *caricare* 'exaggerate, load' < late Latin *carricare* (see CARGO)] —**caricatural** *adj* —**caricature** *vt* —**caricaturist** *n*

CARICOM /kárri kom/ *abbr* Caribbean Community and Common Market

caries /kaír eez, kaíri eez/ *n* progressive decay of a tooth or, less commonly, a bone [Late 16C. < Latin] —**carious** *adj*

CARIFTA /ka ríftə/ *abbr* Caribbean Free Trade Association

carillon /kə ríllyən, kárrillyən/ *n* **1.** SET OF STATIONARY BELLS a set of chromatically tuned stationary bells, usually hung in a tower and played from a keyboard **2.** TUNE PLAYED ON SET OF BELLS a tune played on a keyboard connected to a set of stationary bells **3.** ORGAN STOP IMITATING BELLS an organ stop that imitates the sound of a carillon [Late 18C. < French] —**carillon** *vi*

carillonneur /kə ríllyə núr, kárrillyə núr/ *n* somebody who plays a carillon [Late 18C. < French < *carillon* 'carillon']

carina /kə réenə, kə rínə/ *n* **1.** BIRDS same as **keel** *n* (sense 3) (*technical*) **2.** the boat-shaped part of a pea flower, formed by the two fused lower petals **3.** a keel-shaped body part, e.g. the ridge at the base of the windpipe where it divides to form the bronchi [Early 18C. < Latin, 'keel'] —**carinate** /kárri nayt/ *adj*

Carina *n* a constellation of the southern hemisphere containing the star Canopus. See illustration at **constellation**

caring /kaíring/ *adj* **1.** SHOWING CONCERN compassionate or showing concern for others **2.** RELATING TO PROFESSION LOOKING AFTER PEOPLE belonging or relating to a profession that involves looking after people's physical, medical, or general welfare, e.g. nursing or social

work ■ *n* PROVISION OF MEDICAL OR SIMILAR CARE provision of medical or other types of care, either professionally or in general —**caringly** *adv*

carioca /kárri ṓkə/ *n* **1.** a Brazilian dance similar to the samba **2.** the music for a carioca [Mid-20C. < Portuguese < a Tupian language]

Cariocan /kárri ṓkən/, **Carioca** /kárri ṓkə/ *n* somebody who comes from Rio de Janeiro, Brazil —**Cariocan** *adj*

cariogenic /káiri ō jénnik/ *adj* causing tooth decay [Mid-20C. < CARIES]

cariole /kárri ōl/, **carriole** *n* a small open carriage or covered cart, the former drawn by one horse [Mid-18C. Via French < Italian *carriuola* 'little car' < *carro* 'car' < Latin *carrus* (see CAR)]

carjacking /ka'ar jaking/ *n* the crime of holding up a car and either stealing it, robbing the driver, or forcing the driver to drive somewhere for criminal purposes [Late 20C. Blend of CAR + HIJACKING] —**carjack** *vti* —**carjacker** *n*

cark /kaark/ (**carks, carking, carked**) *vi Aus* to fail, break down, or stop working (*slang*) [Late 20C. Origin ?] ■ **cark it** to die (*slang*)

car-lifting *n S Asia* the crime of stealing a motor vehicle

carline /ka'arlin/ (*plural same* or -**lines**) *n* a plant that looks like a thistle, with spiny leaves. Flowers: yellow. Native to: Europe, Asia. Latin name: *Carlina vulgaris*. [Late 16C. Via French < medieval Latin *carlina*]

carling /ka'arling, -lin/ *n* a fore-and-aft wooden beam that supports a boat's deck, especially round an opening in the deck such as a hatchway [14C. < Norse]

Carlisle /kaar líl, ka'ar líl/ town in Cumbria, northwestern England. It is a local government district and the administrative centre of Cumbria. Population: 18,036 (2002).

Carlist /ka'arlist/ *n* a supporter of Don Carlos or his descendants as rightful monarchs of Spain during the 19th century [Mid-19C. < Spanish *carlista* < Don Carlos]

carload /ka'ar lōd/ *n* a full complement of people able to ride in a car

carload rate *n* a reduced rate for shipping freight

Carlos /kar loss/, **Don** (1788–1855) Spanish pretender to the throne. His claim to the Spanish throne (1833), reasserted by his descendants, led to the Carlist Wars (1833–39, 1872–76). Full name **Carlos Maria Isidro**

Carlovingian *n, adj* HIST same as **Carolingian**

Carlow /ka'arlō/ county in Leinster Province, in the southeastern part of the Republic of Ireland. Area: 896 sq. km/346 sq. mi.

Carl XVI Gustaf /ka'arl gṓost af/ (*b.* 1946) king of Sweden. He succeeded his grandfather, Gustaf VI, in 1973.

Carlyle /kaar líl/, **Thomas** (1795–1881) Scottish historian, essayist, and author of *Sartor Resartus* (1833–34), *The French Revolution* (1837), and *Oliver Cromwell's Letters and Speeches, with Elucidations* (1845)

> 'The great law of culture is: Let each become all that he was created capable of becoming.'
> [Thomas Carlyle, 'Jean Paul Friedrich Richter', *Critical and Miscellaneous Essays*; 1838]

> 'A well-written Life is almost as rare as a well-spent one.'
> [Thomas Carlyle, 'Jean Paul Friedrich Richter', *Critical and Miscellaneous Essays*; 1838]

carman /ka'armən/ (*plural* -**men** /-mən/) *n* a man who drives a van or transports goods in other ways (*dated*)

Carmarthen /kər ma'arth'n/ seaport and administrative city of Carmarthenshire. Population: 13,524 (1991). Welsh name **Caerfyrddin**

Carmarthenshire /kər ma'arth'nshər/ county in southern Wales, with its headquarters in Carmarthen.

a at; aa father; aw all; ay day; ai hair; ə about, item, edible, common, circus; e egg; ee eel; hw when; i it, happy; ī ice; 'l apple; 'm rhythm; 'n fashion; o odd; ō open; ōo good; oo pool; ow owl; oy oil; th thin; th this; u up; ur hurry

Population: 172,842 (2001). Area: 2398 sq. km/926 sq. mi.

Carme /káarmi/ *n* a small satellite of Jupiter that was discovered in 1938

Carmel, Mount /káarm'l/ mountain in northern Israel, near the Mediterranean Sea, with many biblical associations. Height: 545 m/1,789 ft.

Carmelite /káarmə līt/ *n* 1. a member of an order of mendicant friars, founded around 1155 and called Our Lady of Mount Carmel 2. a member of the order of nuns of Our Lady of Mount Carmel, founded in 1452 and noted for the strictness of its rule [15C. Directly or via French < medieval Latin *Carmelita*, after CARMEL, MOUNT] —**Carmelite** *adj*

Carmichael /kaar mĭk'l/, **Hoagy** (1899–1981) US singer and songwriter. He wrote the music to the song 'Stardust' (1929). Full name **Carmichael, Hoagland Howard**

carminative /káarminətiv/ *adj* relieving flatulence or colic by expelling gas [15C. < medieval Latin *carminat-*, past participle of *carminare* 'heal by incantation' < Latin *carmin-* 'song'] —**carminative** *n*

carmine /káar mīn, -min/ *n* 1. a deep purplish-red colour 2. a bright red pigment made from cochineal [Early 18C. < French *carmin* < Arabic *ḳirmiz* 'kermes'] —**carmine** *adj*

Carnaby Street /káarnəbi-/ *n* a street in Soho, central London, notable in the 1960s as the heart of the new youth-centred fashion trade

Prehistoric stone monuments at Carnac, France

Carnac /káar nak/ village in Morbihan Department, Bretagne Region, in western France. It is famous for its prehistoric stone monuments, which number more than 3,000.

carnage /káarnij/ *n* 1. widespread and indiscriminate slaughter or massacre, especially of human beings 2. serious injury to a great many people, e.g. in a major accident [Early 17C. Via French < Italian *carnaggio* < medieval Latin *carnaticum* 'flesh (especially as tribute)' < Latin *carn-* 'flesh']

carnal /káarn'l/ *adj* 1. RELATING TO PHYSICAL NEEDS relating to somebody's physical needs or appetites, especially as contrasted with spiritual or intellectual qualities (*formal*) 2. SENSUAL sensual or sexual 3. RELATING TO BODY relating to or consisting of the body (*formal*) [15C. < ecclesiastical Latin *carnalis* < Latin *carn-* 'flesh'] —**carnalist** *n* —**carnality** /kaar nálləti/ *n* —**carnally** *adv*

carnal knowledge *n* same as **sexual intercourse** (*formal*)

carnallite /káarnə līt/ *n* a white or pale hydrous chloride mineral containing magnesium and potassium. Use: source of potassium, fertilizers. [Mid-19C. After Rudolf von *Carnall* (1804–74), German mining engineer]

carnap /káar nap/ (**-naps, -napping, -napped**) *vi* *Philippines* to steal a car (*informal*) —**carnapper** *n*

Carnap /káar nap/, **Rudolf** (1891–1970) German-born US philosopher and logician. He used mathematics and probability statistics to arrive at a system of inductive logic.

'Logic is the last scientific ingredient of Philosophy; its extraction leaves behind only a confusion of nonscientific, pseudo-problems.'
[Rudolf Carnap, *The Unity of Science*; 1934]

carnaptious /kaar nápshəss/ *adj* *Scotland* quar-

relsome and liable to snap at people (*informal*) [Mid-19C]

Carnarvon /kər naárv'n/ town in Western Australia, situated at the mouth of the River Gascoyne. Population: 6,715 (2002 estimate).

Carnarvon Gorge sandstone canyon in southern Queensland, Australia

Carnarvon Range range of mountains in the Little Sandy Desert, Western Australia. Its highest peak is Mount Essendon, 907 m/2,975 ft.

carnassial /kaar nássi əl/ *adj* describes the larger sharp cheek teeth in the upper and lower jaw of a carnivore that are adapted for cutting flesh [Mid-19C. < French *carnassier* 'carnivorous' < Latin *carn-* 'flesh']

Carnatic /kaar náttik/ *adj* GEOG same as **Karnatak** [Early 19C. After *Carnatic*, linguistic region in south-central India between the Eastern Ghats and the Coromandel coast, now part of Madras state < KARNATAKA]

Carnatic music *n* MUSIC same as **Karnatak music**

carnation

carnation /kaar náysh'n/ *n* 1. a perennial plant of the pink family. Flowers: fragrant white, pink, or red with fringed petals, often smelling of cloves. Latin name: *Dianthus caryophyllus*. 2. a pale reddish-pink colour [Mid-16C. Via French < late Latin *carnation-* 'fleshiness' < Latin *carn-* 'flesh'] —**carnation** *adj*

carnauba /kaar nówbə, -náwbə/ (*plural same* or **-bas**) *n* 1. a fan palm with an edible root and leaves that yield carnauba wax. Native to: Brazil. Latin name: *Copernica prunifera*. 2. INDUST same as **carnauba wax** [Mid-19C. Via Portuguese < Tupi]

carnauba wax *n* wax obtained from the young leaves of the carnauba tree. Use: polish, candles.

Carné /káar nay/, **Marcel** (1909–96) French film director. His 'poetic realism' is seen at its height in *Les Enfants du Paradis* (1945) (*Children of Paradise*) (1946).

Carnegie /kaar néggi, -náygi, -neégi, káarnəgi/ usually dry lake situated on the western edge of the Gibson Desert, central Western Australia. Area: 1,338 sq. km/517 sq. mi.

Carnegie, Andrew (1835–1919) Scottish-born US industrialist and philanthropist who made a fortune in the steel industry. His philanthropic gifts endowed numerous public libraries in the United States.

'Concentrate your energy, thought and capital exclusively upon the business in which you are engaged..."Don't put all your eggs in one basket" is all wrong. I tell you "put all your eggs in one basket, and then watch that basket".'
[Andrew Carnegie, *Speech, Curry Commercial College, Pittsburgh*; 23 June 1885]

Carnegie /káarnə gi, kaar néggi/, **Dale** (1888–1955) US writer. His works on public speaking and self-esteem include *How to Win Friends and Influence People* (1936). Born **Carnegey, Dale**

'There is only one way under high heaven to get the best of an argument—and that is to avoid it.'
[Dale Carnegie, *Dale Carnegie's Scrapbook*; 1959]

carnelian /kaar neéli ən/, **cornelian** /kawr-/ *n* a hard reddish translucent semiprecious stone that is a variety of chalcedony. Use: gems. [Late 17C. Alteration

(influenced by Latin *carn-* 'flesh') of *cornelian* < obsolete French *corneline*]

carnet /kaár nay/ *n* 1. a set of travel tickets or coupons costing less than the individual tickets purchased separately 2. a customs document for a car that allows it to be taken across national borders without payment of duty [Early 19C. < French]

carnitine /káarni teen/ *n* an amino acid that transports fatty acids into muscle cells for energy production [Early 20C. < Latin *carn-* 'flesh']

carnival /káarniv'l/ *n* 1. PUBLIC CELEBRATION a public festive occasion or period, often with street processions, costumes, music, and dancing 2. *N Am* same as **fair**[2] (sense 1) 3. PERIOD BEFORE LENT the period just before Lent. It is celebrated in some Roman Catholic areas with a public festival such as Mardi Gras in New Orleans, Louisiana. 4. *Aus* SPORTS MEETING a sports meeting often run like a school sports day [Mid-16C. Via Italian *carnevale* < medieval Latin *carnelevamen* 'cessation of meat-eating' < Latin *carn-* 'flesh']

carnivore /káarni vawr/ *n* 1. FLESH-EATING ANIMAL an animal that eats other animals 2. CARNIVOROUS PLANT a carnivorous plant 3. SOMEBODY WHO EATS MEAT somebody who is not a vegetarian and likes to eat meat (*humorous*) [Mid-19C. Via French < Latin *carnivorus* (see CARNIVOROUS)]

carnivorous /kaar nívvərəss/ *adj* 1. feeding mainly on the flesh of other animals 2. able to catch and digest animals such as insects and small invertebrates ○ *a carnivorous plant* [Late 16C. < Latin *carnivorus* 'meat-eating' < *carn-* 'flesh'] —**carnivorously** *adv* —**carnivorousness** *n*

Carnot cycle /káarnō-/ *n* a theoretical reversible heat-engine cycle that gives maximum efficiency [After Nicholas Léonard Sadi *Carnot* (1796–1832), French physicist]

carnotite /káarnə tīt/ *n* a yellow radioactive mineral. Use: source of radium and uranium. [Late 19C. After Marie Adolphe *Carnot* (1839–1920), French inspector of mines]

Carnot principle /káarnō-/ *n* the principle that the efficiency of a reversible heat engine depends on the maximum and minimum temperatures of the working fluid during the operating cycle [See CARNOT CYCLE]

carny[1] /káarni/ (*plural* **-nies**), **carnie, carney** (*plural* **-neys**) *n N Am* (*informal*) 1. LEISURE same as **fair**[2] (sense 1) 2. a worker in a fairground or carnival [Mid-20C. Shortening of CARNIVAL]

carny[2] /káarni/ (**-nies, -nying, -nied**) *vt* to try to persuade somebody to do something (*informal*) [Early 19C. Origin ?]

Caro /káarō, kárrō/, **Qaro, Joseph ben Ephraim** (1488–1575) Spanish-born Palestinian Talmudic scholar. His *Shulhan Arukh* (1564–65), codifying religious law, is a major text of Orthodox Judaism.

carob /kárrəb/ (*plural* **-obs** or *same*) *n* 1. EDIBLE POWDER LIKE CHOCOLATE an edible powder with a taste similar to that of chocolate, made from the seeds and pods of an evergreen tree 2. EDIBLE POD a long dark-coloured edible pod that contains a sweet-tasting pulp 3. EVERGREEN TREE WITH EDIBLE PODS an evergreen tree with edible pods from which carob powder is made. Flowers: red. Native to: Mediterranean. Latin name: *Ceratonia siliqua*. [Mid-16C. Via obsolete French *car(r)obe* < Arabic *karrūb(a)*]

caroche /kə rósh/ *n* a grand horse-drawn carriage used on ceremonial occasions [Late 16C. Via obsolete French *carroche* < Italian *carraccio* 'large chariot' < Latin *carrum* (see CAR)]

carol /kárrəl/ *n* JOYFUL HYMN a joyful religious song or hymn, especially a Christian song celebrating Christmas ■ *v* (**-ols, -olling, -olled**) 1. *vi* SING CHRISTMAS SONGS to sing hymns that celebrate Christmas, especially as a group going from house to house 2. *vti* SING SOMETHING JOYOUSLY to sing or call out something in a joyful and lively way (*literary*) ○ *The sun shone, and the birds were carolling.* [13C. < Old French *carole*] —**caroller** *n*

CULTURAL NOTE *A Christmas Carol*, a novella (1843) by Charles Dickens. It recounts the story of an avaricious merchant, Ebenezer Scrooge, who is visited by the ghosts of Christmas Past, Christmas Present, and Christ-

mas Yet to Come. Confronted by the effects of his miserly behaviour on others, Scrooge resolves to become a more generous and charitable person. The name *Scrooge* has subsequently come to mean a petty malicious miser.

Carol II /kárrəl/ (1893–1953) king of Romania. He usurped the crown of his son, King Michael, in 1930 but in 1940 was himself dethroned.

Carolean *adj* HIST same as **Caroline**

caroli COINS plural of **carolus**

Carolina /kárr ə lī́nə/ **1.** city in northeastern Puerto Rico, southeast of San Juan. Population: 188,427 (1996). **2.** ◊ **North Carolina, South Carolina**

Carolinas /kárr ə lī́nəz/ *n* the former colonies or present-day US states of North Carolina and South Carolina

Caroline /kárrə līn/, **Carolean** /kárrə lée ən/ *adj* **1.** relating to the English kings Charles I and Charles II or their reigns **2.** relating to any king or emperor called Charles [Early 17C. < medieval Latin *Carolinus* < *Carolus* 'Charles']

Caroline Islands /kárrə līn-, -lin-/ archipelago consisting of more than 600 islands, north of New Guinea in the western Pacific Ocean. Area: 1,165 sq. km/450 sq. mi.

Caroline of Brunswick /kárrə līn-/ (1768–1821) German-born British queen of the United Kingdom. She was the estranged wife of George IV, whose attempt to divorce her (1820) provoked civil disorder.

Carolingian /kárrə línji ən/, **Carlovingian** /kaárlō vínji ən/, **Carolinian** /-línni ən/ *adj* relating to the dynasty of Frankish kings descended from the Emperor Charlemagne that ruled France and Germany from the 8th to the 10th centuries ■ *n* a king of the Frankish dynasty descended from Charlemagne

Carolinian /kárrə línni ən/ *adj* **1.** HIST another spelling of **Carolingian 2.** relating to North or South Carolina, or their people or culture

carolus /kárrələss/ (*plural* **-luses** or **-li** /-lī/) *n* a gold coin named after any king or emperor called Charles, especially Charles I of England [Early 16C. < medieval Latin *Carolus* 'Charles']

carom /kárrəm/ *N Am n* **1.** same as **cannon** *n* (sense 4) **2.** a collision that is followed by one of the objects rebounding off at an angle ■ *v* (**-oms, -oming, -omed**) **1.** *vi* same as **cannon** *v* (sense 3) **2.** *vti* to rebound off another object or series of objects, or cause this to happen [Late 18C. Shortening of *carambole* < Spanish *carambola*, probably < *bola* 'ball']

carotene /kárrə teen/, **carotin** /kárrətin/ *n* an orange or red plant pigment that occurs in several forms (**isomers**), one of which is important in nutrition [Mid-19C. < Latin *carota* (see CARROT)]

carotenoid /kə rótti noyd/, **carotinoid** *n* one of a group of orange or red plant pigments that includes the carotenes —**carotenoid** *adj*

carotid /kə róttid/, **carotid artery** (*plural* **carotid arteries**) *n* a large artery on each side of the neck that supplies blood to the head [Early 17C. Via French *carotide* or modern Latin *carotides* < Greek *karōtides* < *karoun* 'stupefy']

carotid body *n* a cluster of cells and nerve fibres in each carotid that is sensitive to oxygen and acidity levels in the blood and is part of the system that regulates them

carotid sinus *n* a slight bulge in each carotid that contains pressure-sensitive nerve endings and forms part of the system that monitors and controls blood pressure

carotin *n* BIOCHEM another spelling of **carotene**

carotinoid *n* BIOCHEM another spelling of **carotenoid**

carousal /kə rówz'l/ *n* a noisy and boisterous drinking party (*literary*)

carouse /kə rówz/ (**-rouses, -rousing, -roused**) *vi* to drink and become noisy, especially in a group (*literary*) [Mid-16C. < German *gar aus (trinken)* '(drink) right up'] —**carouse** *n* —**carouser** *n*

carousel /kárrə sél, -zél/ *n* **1.** a circular conveyor belt, especially one at an airport displaying luggage for arriving passengers to collect **2.** *N Am* LEISURE same as **merry-go-round** (sense 1) **3.** a circular rotating holder that loads photographic slides into a projector one at a time [Mid-17C. Via French *carrousel* < Italian *carosello* 'tilting match']

carousel retaliation *n US* POL, INTERNAT REL retaliation in a trade dispute, especially one between the United States and the European Union, involving the imposition of punitive import tariffs on a list of imports that is changed at regular intervals to spread the effect more widely

carp[1] /kaarp/ (**carps, carping, carped**) *vi* to keep complaining or finding fault, especially about unimportant things ○ *I wish you'd stop carping, I'm doing my best.* [13C. < Old Norse *karpa* 'brag'] —**carper** *n*

SYNONYMS See ***complain***.

carp[2] /kaarp/ (*plural same* or **carps**) *n* **1.** a large fish with a single fin on its back, found worldwide in lakes and slow-moving rivers. Latin name: *Cyprinus carpio*. **2.** any fish of the carp family, which includes goldfish and koi. Family: Cyprinidae. [14C. Via French < late Latin *carpa*]

-carp *suffix* part of a fruit ○ *pericarp* [< modern Latin *-carpium* < Greek *karpos* (see CARPO-)] —**-carpous** *suffix*

carpaccio /kaar páchi ō, -páchō/ *n* a dish of raw beef sliced thinly, moistened with olive oil and lemon juice, and seasoned [Mid-20C. After Vittore *Carpaccio* (circa 1460–1525), Italian painter who favoured red pigments]

carpal /kaárp'l/ *adj* relating to the bones in the wrist ■ *n* a bone in the wrist [Mid-18C. < CARPUS]

carpal tunnel syndrome *n* a condition of pain and weakness in the hand caused by repetitive compression of a nerve that passes through the wrist into the hand

car park *n* an area in which cars can be parked temporarily. N Am term **parking lot**

Carpathian Mountains /kaar páythi ən-/, **Carpathians** mountain system in eastern Europe, situated along the border between Slovakia and Poland and extending southwards through Ukraine and eastern Romania. Its highest peak is Gerlachovka 2,655 m/8,711 ft.

carpe diem /kaár pay dée em/ *interj* used as an invocation to enjoy the present and not worry about the future [< Latin, 'seize the day']

carpel /kaárp'l/ *n* a female reproductive organ in a flower, enclosing the fertilized ovules that are developing into seeds. It consists of the stigma and usually a style. [Mid-19C. < French *carpelle* or modern Latin *carpellum* 'little fruit' < Greek *karpos* 'fruit'] —**carpellary** *adj* —**carpellate** *adj*

Carpentaria, Gulf of /kaárpən táiri ə/ large gulf on the northern coast of Australia, lying between Arnhem Land in the west and the Cape York Peninsula in the east. Area: 310,000 sq. km/120,000 sq. mi.

carpenter /kaárpintər/ *n* BUILDER OF WOODEN STRUCTURES a builder or repairer of wooden objects or structures ■ *v* (**-ters, -tering, -tered**) **1.** *vi* BUILD WOODEN STRUCTURES to build and repair wooden structures, or the wooden parts of them (*technical*) **2.** *vt* MAKE SOMETHING WOODEN to make something by cutting and joining pieces of wood ○ *He had carpentered a series of perfectly fitting dovetail joints.* **3.** *vt* MAKE SOMETHING IN EFFICIENT WAY to make or devise something efficiently and systematically ○ *They met every day, in the vain attempt to carpenter an agreement that would be acceptable to both sides.* [12C. < Anglo-Norman, Old French *carpentier* < late Latin *carpentarius (artifex)* 'carriage(-maker)' < *carpentum* 'two-wheeled carriage']

carpenter ant *n* a large black or brown ant that bores into wood to make its nest. It usually bores into old or rotten wood, but it can also attack wood in homes and cause much damage. Genus: *Camponotus*.

carpenter bee *n* a bee that bores tunnels into wood to lay its eggs. Families: Xylocopidae or Ceratinidae.

Carpentier /kaar pénti ə/, **Alejo** (1904–80) Cuban writer and musicologist. His novel *Los pasos perdidos* (1953) (*The Lost Steps* (1956) is a fictional diary of a Cuban musician travelling up the Amazon. His blend of realism and surrealism influenced other Central and South American writers.

Carpentier /kaar paaNti ay/, **Georges** (1894–1975) French boxer. Known as 'Gorgeous George', he was world light-heavyweight champion (1920–22).

carpentry /kaárpəntri/ *n* **1.** the work or occupation of building and repairing things made of wood such as houses and boats, or the wooden parts of them ○ *a career in carpentry* **2.** the work or objects produced by a carpenter ○ *fine carpentry for sale*

carpet /kaárpit/ *n* **1.** FLOOR COVERING thick fabric for covering a floor **2.** PIECE OF FLOOR COVERING a piece of thick heavy fabric covering the floor of a room or area **3.** LAYER OR COVERING a layer or covering (*literary*) ○ *a carpet of leaves* ■ *vt* (**-pets, -peting, -peted**) **1.** COVER FLOOR WITH CARPET to cover a floor, or the floor of a room, with a carpet ○ *We could carpet every room in the house with the money she spent on that rug.* **2.** COVER SOMETHING to cover something in a layer (*literary*) ○ *The valley was carpeted with flowers.* **3.** REPRIMAND SOMEBODY to reprimand somebody severely (*informal*) [14C. < Old French *carpite* or medieval Latin *carpita* < Latin *carpere* 'to pluck'] ◇ **roll out the red carpet** to give a special welcome to a distinguished visitor ◇ **sweep something under the carpet** to conceal or ignore something that needs attention

carpetbag /kaárpit bag/ *n* a travelling bag made of a thick fabric such as carpet, commonly used in the 19th century

carpetbagger /kaárpit bagər/ *n* **1.** POST-CIVIL WAR OPPORTUNIST a Northerner who moved to the southern United States after the American Civil War, especially one seeking political or commercial advantage **2.** OUTSIDER SEEKING LOCAL VOTE an outsider whose only interest in coming to a place is to win it as a political seat **3.** OPPORTUNIST MEMBER OF BUILDING SOCIETY a member of a mutual building society or insurance company who campaigns to force it to demutualize, usually for short-term financial gain —**carpetbagging** *adj*

carpetbag steak *n* an Australian dish of a thick beef steak slit horizontally, stuffed with oysters, and grilled

carpet beetle *n* a small beetle whose larvae feed on fabric, furs, or animal remains. Genera: *Anthrenus* or *Attagenus*.

carpet-bomb (**carpet-bombs, carpet-bombing, carpet-bombed**) *vt* **1.** to bomb an area intensively **2.** *US* to conduct an intensive campaign, especially in the media, to sway public opinion or to destroy somebody's reputation —**carpet-bombing** *n*

carpet fitter *n* somebody who cuts and fits wall-to-wall carpet. N Am term **carpetlayer**

carpet grass *n* a coarse grass that forms a tight matted growth and is widely used in warm humid areas for turf and pasture. Genus: *Axonopus*.

carpeting /kaárpiting/ *n* **1.** thick fabric used for covering floors **2.** carpets regarded collectively ○ *How much do you want to spend on carpeting?*

carpet knight *n* somebody considered to be lazy or cowardly, especially a soldier who avoids battle and enjoys social and amorous activity (*archaic*) [< time spent in carpeted chambers instead of on the battlefield]

carpetlayer /kaárpit layər/ *n N Am* same as **carpet fitter**

carpet moth *n* a large moth belonging to a group with mottled wings resembling the pattern of a carpet. Family: Larentidae.

carpet shark *n* a shark with a mottled back resembling the pattern of a carpet. Family: Larentidae.

carpet slipper *n* a slipper with the upper section made of thick fabric

carpet snake *n* a large python with a pattern of scales on its back resembling a traditional carpet. Native to: southern Australia. Latin name: *Morelia variegata*.

carpet sweeper *n* a device for lifting dirt off carpets, with a long handle and revolving brushes in a wheeled casing

carpet tile *n* a square of carpeting laid together with others to cover a floor

carpetweed /kaárpit weed/ *n* a low close-growing weed. Flowers: tiny, greenish-white. Native to: North America. Latin name: *Mollugo verticillata*.

car phone *n* a mobile phone designed for use in a car

carpi ANAT plural of **carpus**

carping /ka'arping/ adj complaining or finding fault, or tending to ○ his usual carping comments —**carpingly** adv

carpo- prefix fruit ○ carpophagous [< Greek karpos < Indo-European, 'gather']

carpology /kaar póllǝji/ n the branch of botany that deals with the study of fruits and seeds —**carpological** /ka'arpǝ lójjik'l/ adj —**carpologist** n

car pool n 1. a group of associated people sharing the use of their cars, each in turn driving the others 2. BUSINESS a number of motor vehicles kept by an organization for use as needed by its personnel. N Am term **motor pool**

car-pool (car-pools, car-pooling, car-pooled) vi to drive or be driven regularly from one place to another as a small group, with each member sharing driving responsibilities

carpool lane n US a lane in an a dual carriageway designated for use only by vehicles with two or more occupants

carpophagous /kaar póffǝgǝss/ adj ZOOL same as **frugivorous**

carpophore /ka'arpō fawr/ n 1. the part of a flower that bears the carpels and stamens 2. the part of some fungi that contains the spores or supports the part that contains them

carport /ka'ar pawrt/ n an open-sided shelter for a parked car, attached to a house or other building

carpospore /ka'arpō spawr/ n a spore that forms in some red algae after fertilization

carpus /ka'arpǝss/ (plural -pi /-pī/) n 1. any bone in the set of eight that form the wrist joint 2. any bone in the set of bones that form the joint between the forelimb of a vertebrate animal and its foot or paw, corresponding to the wrist [Late 17C. Via modern Latin < Greek karpos]

carr /kaar/ n an area of marshy land with clumps of willows or other trees [14C. < Old Norse kjarr 'brushwood']

Carrà /kǝ ra'a/, **Carlo** (1881–1966) Italian painter. A prominent member of the Futurist movement in his early career, he later adopted Giorgio de Chirico's metaphysical style of painting.

Carracci /kǝ ra'achi/ family of Italian painters, including **Annibale** (1560–1609), his brother **Agostino** (1557–1602), and their cousin **Lodovico** (1555–1619), who cofounded an influential academy in Bologna, Italy, in 1585

carrack /kárrǝk/, **carack** n a large trading ship common in the Mediterranean between the 14th and 16th centuries [14C. < French caraque]

carrageen /kárrǝ geen, kárrǝ ge'en/, **carragheen** n 1. PLANTS same as **Irish moss** 2. FOOD INDUST another spelling of **carrageenan** [Early 19C. < Irish carraigín]

carrageenan /kárrǝ geenǝn, kárrǝ ge'enǝn/, **carrageenin** n a complex carbohydrate obtained from edible red seaweeds, especially the seaweed Irish moss. Use: commercial preparation of food and drink. [Late 19C. < CARRAGEEN]

carragheen /kárrǝ geen, kárrǝ ge'en/ n PLANTS, FOOD INDUST another spelling of **carrageen**

~~carraige~~ incorrect spelling of **carriage**

Carrantuohill /kárrǝn toó əl/, **Carrauntuohill, Carrantual** highest mountain in Ireland, in the Macgillicuddy's Reeks range in the southwest of the country. Height: 1,041 m/3,414 ft.

Carrara /kǝ ra'arǝ/ city in Massa-Carrara Province, Tuscany Region, in north-central Italy. It is famous for its quarry, which produces some of the world's finest marble. Population: 65,034 (2001).

Carrauntuohill another spelling of **Carrantuohill**

Carré ♦ Le Carré, John

~~carreer~~ incorrect spelling of **career**

carrel /kárrǝl/, **carrell** n a bay, cubicle, or small room where one person can study in private, e.g. in a library [Late 16C. Alteration of CAROL 'circle']

Carrel /kǝ rél, kárrǝl/, **Alexis** (1873–1944) French biologist and surgeon. He developed the vascular surgical technique that led to organ transplants. He won the Nobel Prize in physiology or medicine (1912).

'Intelligence is almost useless to the person whose only quality it is.'
[Alexis Carrel, Man, the Unknown; 1935]

carrell n LIBRARIES another spelling of **carrel**

Carreras /kǝ ráirǝss/, **José** (b. 1946) Spanish singer. An operatic tenor, he became an international star in the 1970s.

~~carress~~ incorrect spelling of **caress**

carriage /kárrij/ n 1. HORSE-DRAWN VEHICLE a four-wheeled horse-drawn private passenger vehicle, especially one that is large and comfortable 2. RAILWAY COACH a railway passenger coach 3. WHEELED PLATFORM a wheeled platform on which something is carried or supported 4. WAY OF HOLDING BODY the way somebody holds his or her head and body when walking (formal) ○ She was a tall woman with a beautiful upright carriage. 5. TAKING AND DELIVERING GOODS the transporting and delivering of goods 6. CHARGE FOR TAKING AND DELIVERING GOODS a charge made for transporting and delivering goods 7. MOVING PART OF MACHINE a part of a machine that holds and moves another part, e.g. the rotating and sliding paper-holder on a typewriter

carriage bolt n N Am same as **coach bolt**

carriage clock n a small clock set in a case with a handle on top, originally used as a travel clock but now ornamental

carriage dog n VERTEB same as **Dalmatian** (sense 1) [Because the dogs were kept to run in attendance on a carriage]

carriage horse n a horse used to pull carriages

carriage return n the key or lever on a typewriter that sends the paper-holding carriage back and rotates it to move the paper upward, ready to begin a new line

carriage trade n the most wealthy and prestigious of possible customers ○ They carry only the highest quality goods, catering to the carriage trade.

carriageway /kárrij way/ n the part of a main road used for vehicles, especially one side of a major two-way road, carrying traffic in one direction only

~~Carribean~~ incorrect spelling of **Caribbean**

carrick bend /kárrik-/ n an intertwining knot similar to a granny knot, used for tying ropes together [Probably alteration of CARRACK]

carrick bitt n one of the two posts that support a ship's windlass [See CARRICK BEND]

Carrickfergus /kárrik fúrgǝss/ administrative centre of Carrickfergus county, northeastern Northern Ireland, situated on the northern shore of Belfast Lough, northeast of Belfast. Population: 22,885 (1991).

carrier /kárri ǝr/ n 1. TRANSPORTER OF PEOPLE OR GOODS a person or company whose function or business is to transport things or people from one place to another ○ These airlines are among the world's most popular carriers. 2. same as **carrier bag** 3. TRANSMITTER OF DISEASE a person or animal that is infected with a disease without displaying any of the symptoms and can pass it to others 4. SYMPTOMLESS TRANSMITTER OF GENE an individual possessing a gene for a particular genetic trait or disorder without being affected by it, because two copies of the gene, one from each parent, are usually necessary for the characteristic to show itself 5. PART OF MACHINE CONVEYING MOTION a part of a machine that carries and moves something or transmits motion to another part 6. LUGGAGE RACK a metal frame on which luggage can be tied to a road vehicle or bicycle 7. NAVY same as **aircraft carrier** 8. MEANS OF TRANSMITTING ACTIVE SUBSTANCE a neutral substance to which an active ingredient or agent is added as a way of applying or transferring the ingredient or agent ○ Mix the dye and the carrier in equal proportions. 9. BEARER OF ELECTRIC CHARGE something that carries electric current, e.g. an electron or ion 10. RADIO WAVE CARRYING INFORMATION an electromagnetic wave that is modulated to carry a signal in radio or television transmission

carrier air wing n a squadron of aircraft operating from an aircraft carrier

carrier bag n a large plastic or paper shopping bag with handles, especially one supplied by a shop

carrier pigeon n a domestic pigeon trained to deliver messages and return home

carrier wave n TELECOM same as **carrier** (sense 10)

Carrington /kárringtǝn/, **Peter, 6th Baron Carrington** (b. 1919) British politician. He was British foreign secretary (1979–82) and secretary general of NATO (1984–88). Full name **Carrington, Peter Alexander Rupert**

'Detente is like the race in Alice in Wonderland where everyone had to have a prize.'
[Peter Carrington, Speech; March, 1980]

carriole n VEHICLES another spelling of **cariole**

carrion /kárri ǝn/ n 1. the rotting flesh of a dead animal 2. something that is decaying or disgusting (literary) [13C. < Anglo-Norman, Old French caroi(g)ne < Latin caro 'flesh']

carrion crow n a medium-sized crow similar to a rook but with a heavier beak and black face. Native to: Europe. Latin name: Corvus corone.

carrion flower n 1. a climbing plant with small greenish flowers that smell like rotting flesh. Native to: North America. Genus: Smilax. 2. a succulent plant with foul-smelling star-shaped flowers. Native to: tropics. Genus: Stapelia.

Carroll /kárrǝl/, **Lewis** (1832–98) British writer. He wrote the children's classics Alice's Adventures in Wonderland (1865) and Through the Looking-Glass and What Alice Found There (1871). Under his real name, he was also a distinguished geometrician and photographer. Pseudonym of **Dodgson, Charles Lutwidge**. See Cultural note at **wonderland**

'Sentence first–verdict afterwards'
[Lewis Carroll, Alice's Adventures in Wonderland; 1865]

'"The time has come", the Walrus said, / "To talk of many things: / Of shoes –and ships –and sealing wax – / Of cabbages– and kings / And why the sea is boiling hot – / And whether pigs have wings".'
[Lewis Carroll, Through the Looking-Glass and What Alice Found There; 1871]

carronade /kárrǝ nayd/ n a lightweight iron cannon formerly used on ships [Late 18C. After Carron, a district of Falkirk, central Scotland, site of an ironworks]

carrot /kárrǝt/ n 1. THIN ORANGE ROOT VEGETABLE a thin tapering orange-coloured root eaten raw or cooked as a vegetable 2. PLANT WITH EDIBLE ORANGE-COLOURED ROOT a biennial plant that produces carrots. Latin name: Daucus carota. 3. INCENTIVE something tempting, offered in order to persuade somebody to do something ○ They offer you the carrot of a year's free petrol if you buy the car there and then. [15C. Via French < Latin carota < Greek karōton]

SPELLCHECK See **carat**.

carrot-and-stick adj relating to or characterized by the use of persuasion involving a combination of rewards and punishments ○ During the fast-paced negotiations, the diplomats employed a carrot-and-stick strategy.

carrot cake n a cake made with finely grated carrots that give it a moist texture and delicate flavour

carrot fly (plural **carrot flies** or same) n a low-flying insect whose larvae bore into the edible roots of the carrot plant. Latin name: Psila rosae.

carroty /kárrǝti/ adj 1. TASTING LIKE CARROTS like carrots in taste 2. RED describes hair that is red or auburn 3. OF BRIGHT ORANGE COLOUR of a bright reddish-orange colour

carry /kárri/ v (-ries, -rying, -ried) 1. vt HOLD AND TRANSPORT SOMEBODY OR SOMETHING to take somebody or something that you are holding or supporting to another place ○ The case was too heavy for her to carry. 2. vt TAKE SOMEBODY OR SOMETHING TO ANOTHER PLACE to take somebody or something to another place ○ a lorry carrying farm produce 3. vt MOVE SOMEBODY OR SOMETHING BY A FLOW OR IMPETUS to take and move somebody or something by a flow or impetus ○ The current carried them swiftly downstream. ○ She could hear children's voices, carried on the light breeze. 4. vt BE CHANNEL OR ROUTE FOR SOMETHING to be the means by which something passes or is transmitted from one place to another ○ The pipeline will carry oil to the coast. 5. vt TELL

SOMETHING to communicate or convey information, an idea, or a feeling by way of content or in an indirect manner ○ *The article carries wider implications than you may think.* **6.** *vt* **HAVE SOMETHING WITH YOU** to have something with you, e.g. in your pocket or in a handbag ○ *Staff should carry identification at all times.* **7.** *vt* **HAVE TRANSMISSIBLE DISEASE** to be infected with a disease and capable of infecting others ○ *You may be carrying a virus without knowing it.* **8.** *vt* **PUBLISH, BROADCAST, OR DISPLAY SOMETHING** to feature or include an article, picture, item of news, or piece of information ○ *That evening, all the major networks carried the story.* ○ *Every packet carries a government health warning.* **9.** *vt* **KEEP SOMETHING FOR SALE** to keep something as stock in a shop ○ *We don't carry household goods.* **10.** *vi* **BE HEARD AT DISTANCE** to be audible at a distance ○ *Sound carries a long way over water.* **11.** *vt* **SUPPORT WEAKER ELEMENT** to support or compensate for a weaker element or participant ○ *The rest of the department has to carry him.* **12.** *vt* **MAKE SOMEBODY SUCCEED OR ENDURE** to give somebody the incentive, impetus, or encouragement to achieve or deal with something ○ *Their exhilaration at this success may carry them further up the league table.* ○ *The audience cheered, carried along on a wave of enthusiasm.* **13.** *vt* **INCLUDE OR RESULT IN SOMETHING** to have something as a quality, feature, or consequence ○ *Reckless driving carries a heavy penalty.* **14.** *vti* **BE PREGNANT** to be pregnant with a child ○ *She carried the child to term.* **15.** *vt* **DEVELOP IDEA** to develop an idea in discussion or action ○ *If you carry that argument to its logical conclusion, no one should get married at all.* **16.** *vt* **MOVE OR BEHAVE** to move or behave in a particular way, especially with confidence or dignity ○ *He was a handsome man who carried himself with dignity.* ○ *She carried her head high, and looked her accusers in the eye.* **17.** *vt* **BE RESPONSIBLE FOR SOMETHING** to bear the responsibility for something ○ *The Prime Minister carries heavy duties.* **18.** *vti* **ACCEPT OR BE ACCEPTED BY VOTING** to accept a proposal by voting for it, or be so accepted ○ *The nomination was carried, 40–29.* **19.** *vt* **GAIN SOMEBODY'S SUPPORT** to win the support or sympathy of a person or group, especially by making a speech or appeal ○ *It looked for a moment as if he would carry the crowd.* **20.** *vt* **STAY IN TUNE WHEN SINGING** to be able to sing and stay in tune ○ *Can you carry a tune?* **21.** *vt* **TRANSFER ITEM IN ACCOUNT OR CALCULATION** to transfer a figure from one group or column to another in accounts or in a calculation **22.** *vi* **BE HIT PARTICULAR DISTANCE** to reach a particular distance after being struck ○ *Her approach shot didn't carry to the green.* **23.** *vt* **CAPTURE PLACE** to capture a place in battle ○ *Their charge carried the hill.* **24.** *vi* **HAVE FIREPOWER RANGE** to have a particular range of fire ○ *an artillery shell that carried for miles* **25.** *vt* **PALM BALL IN BASKETBALL** in basketball, to keep a hand in illegal contact with the ball **26.** *vt* **PROVIDE FORAGE FOR ANIMALS** to yield enough forage or grazing crops for animals to survive ○ *fields that can carry llamas as well as cattle* **27.** *vt* *N Am* **WIN VOTES OF AREA** to win a majority of the votes in an area or in an election ○ *The incumbent carried all the cities in her district, and won.* **28.** *vt* TRANSP **ACCOMMODATE VEHICULAR TRAFFIC** to be able to withstand a particular degree or amount of vehicular traffic ○ *a motorway that can carry hundreds of thousands of vehicles a day* **29.** *vt* **MOVE WITH BALL IN SPORT** in a sport such as American football, to bring a ball forward a particular distance ○ *Their first rush carried the ball well into the defenders' half.* **30.** *vt* **SUSTAIN EFFECTS OF ALCOHOL** to be able to drink alcohol without showing adverse effects (*informal*) N Am term **hold**[1] ■ *n* (*plural* **-ries**) **1. DISTANCE COVERED** the distance covered by something struck, thrown, launched, or fired, or the reach of something such as a voice **2. ACT OF RUNNING WITH BALL** in American football, a sprint with the ball ○ *a 50-yard carry that won the game* [14C. Directly or via Anglo-Norman < Old French *carier* < *car* (see CAR)]

carry away *vt* to make somebody become less controlled, reasonable, or attentive by arousing his or her emotion or interest (*usually passive*) ○ *I was completely carried away by the beauty of it.*

carry back *vt* to transfer something such as a tax credit so that it is calculated against the previous year's income

carry forward *vt* **1.** to transfer an item to the next section or column in accounts or in a calculation **2.** to transfer something such as a tax credit or liability so that it is calculated against the next year's income

carry off *vt* **1. REMOVE SOMEBODY OR SOMETHING** to take something or somebody away purposefully or by force ○ *carried him off, kicking and screaming, to his crib* **2. WIN SOMETHING** to win a prize (*informal*) ○ *She carried off the award for best newcomer.* **3. DO SOMETHING WELL** to succeed in doing something well or producing a good effect ○ *He was nervous about chairing the meeting, but carried it off in style.* ○ *It's a very sophisticated outfit, but she can't quite carry it off.* **4. CAUSE DEATH OF SOMEBODY** to kill somebody (*usually passive*) ○ *Half the settlers were carried off by smallpox.*

carry on *v* **1.** *vti* **KEEP DOING SOMETHING** to continue to do something ○ *Please just carry on with your work and pretend we're not here.* ○ *She carried on the business after her father retired.* **2.** *vt* **BE INVOLVED IN SOMETHING** to be engaged in something ○ *They were carrying on an intense conversation in a corner of the bar.* **3.** *vi* **BEHAVE FOOLISHLY OR IMPROPERLY** to behave or talk in a way that is socially awkward or improper (*informal*) ○ *I'm ashamed of the way he's been carrying on in public.* **4.** *vi* **HAVE AFFAIR** to have a casual affair with somebody (*informal disapproving*)

carry out *vt* **1.** to complete a task or activity ○ *carry out research* **2.** to do something that has been ordered, planned, or stated as an aim ○ *We shall carry out your instructions to the letter.*

SYNONYMS See ***perform***.

carry over *v* **1.** *vti* **LEAVE SOMETHING TO BE FINISHED LATER** to leave the last part of something to be done at a later date ○ *There were so many candidates that the ceremonies were carried over to the next morning.* **2.** *vt* **TRANSFER ITEM IN ACCOUNT OR CALCULATION** to transfer an item to the next group or column in accounts or in a calculation **3.** *vt* **TRANSFER SOMETHING TO NEXT YEAR** to transfer an allowance or entitlement from one year to the next **4.** *vi* **CONTINUE TO EXIST** to continue to exist or produce an effect in changed circumstances ○ *The dislike he always felt for me has obviously carried over into our relationship at work.* **5.** *vt* FIN **POSTPONE DEAL ON STOCK EXCHANGE** to postpone a payment or settlement on the Stock Exchange until the next account day

carry through *v* **1.** *vt* **DO WHAT WAS PLANNED** to complete or accomplish something planned ○ *We outlined our policy before the election, and we are determined to carry it through.* **2.** *vt* **HELP SOMEBODY SURVIVE** to give somebody the support or strength needed to overcome a difficulty ○ *It was my family's support that carried me through.* ○ *Only his determination not to be humiliated carried him through the next five hours.* **3.** *vi* **SURVIVE** to continue to exist ○ *It is an old tradition that has carried through into the information age.*

carryall /kárri awl/ *n* **1.** *N Am* same as **holdall** **2.** *US* a large passenger vehicle with two facing benches **3.** a covered horse-drawn carriage for four people [Early 18C. Alteration of CARIOLE; partly < CARRY + ALL]

carryback /kárri bak/ *n* an amount of money such as a tax credit that is transferred to the accounts for the previous year

carrycase /kárri kayss/ *n* a small case with a handle, used for carrying a laptop computer, documents, or other things

carrycot /kárri kot/ *n* a lightweight portable bed for a baby, often detachable from a wheeled base

carrying /kárri ing/ *adj* **1.** describes a voice or a sound that can be heard clearly from a distance ○ *speaking in a carrying voice that could be heard in the next office* **2.** *S Asia* expecting a baby ○ *My wife is carrying.*

-carrying /kárri ing/ *suffix* **1.** bearing or transporting a particular thing ○ *passenger-carrying* ○ *disease-carrying* ○ *knife-carrying* **2.** reaching a particular distance ○ *far-carrying*

carrying capacity *n* **1.** the number of animals a region can support **2.** the number of individuals a region can support in terms of its resources

carrying charge *n* **1.** a charge for storing or delivering a customer's goods **2.** the cost to a business of holding or storing assets from which it currently earns no income

carrying-on (*plural* **carryings-on**) *n* behaviour regarded as immature or improper (*informal*) ○ *I won't have that kind of carrying-on in my house.*

carryon /kárri on/ *n* a piece of luggage suitable for taking in the cabin of an aircraft ■ *adj* describes or relating to luggage small enough to be carried and stowed in the cabin of an aircraft

carry-on *n* an annoying incident involving unwise or overexcited behaviour (*informal*) ○ *I've never heard such a carry-on.*

carryout /kárri owt/ *n* **1.** *Scotland, US* **FOOD EATEN OFF PREMISES** an item of ready-to-eat food bought in a shop or restaurant and taken elsewhere to be eaten (*often used before a noun*) ○ *a carryout pizza* **2.** *Scotland* **PLACE SELLING FOOD TO TAKE AWAY** a restaurant or shop that sells cooked food to be taken elsewhere to be eaten **3.** *Scotland* **ALCOHOL BOUGHT IN SHOP** an amount of alcoholic drink bought from a shop and taken elsewhere, especially home, to drink

carryover /kárri ōvər/ *n* **1.** an item transferred to the next group or column in accounts or in a calculation **2.** the postponement of a stock market transaction until the next day, in exchange for a fee

carse /kaarss/ *n Scotland* a stretch of flat land beside a river [14C. Origin ?]

car seat *n* **1.** a small seat for children, fitted or strapped inside a car **2.** a driver's or passenger's seat in a car

car-sharing *n* an urban car rental service whereby customers who sign up as members can reserve a rental car for periods of time as short as one hour, can pick up the car at a designated place in their neighbourhood, and can return the car there

carsick /kaár sik/ *adj* feeling sick from the motion of a vehicle you are travelling in —**carsickness** *n*

Carson /kaárss'n/, **Edward Henry, Baron Carson** (1854–1935) Irish-born British politician and lawyer. A British cabinet minister (1915–18), he later led the Ulster Unionist resistance to Irish home rule.

> 'Ulster is not asking for concessions. Ulster is asking to be let alone.'
> [Edward Henry Carson, *Speech to the Parliament*; 11 February 1914]

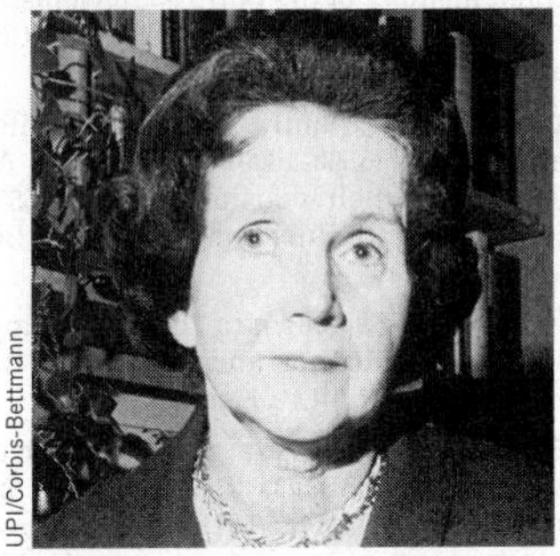
UPI/Corbis-Bettmann

Rachel Carson

Carson, Rachel (1907–64) US ecologist. In *Silent Spring* (1962) she argued that agricultural pesticides damage the food chain.

> 'No witchcraft, no enemy action had silenced the rebirth of new life in this stricken world. The people had done it themselves.'
> [Rachel Carson, *Silent Spring*; 1962]

Carson City capital of Nevada, in the western part of the state, directly east of Lake Tahoe and south of Reno. Population: 54,311 (2002 estimate).

cart /kaart/ *n* **1. HORSE-DRAWN VEHICLE CARRYING GOODS** an open horse-drawn vehicle, especially one with only two wheels, used for carrying goods or as a farm vehicle **2. HORSE-DRAWN CARRIAGE** a light horse-drawn carriage with two wheels **3. VEHICLE PUSHED BY HAND** a light vehicle or barrow pushed by hand **4.** *N Am* **WHEELED CARRIER FOR MERCHANDISE OR BAGGAGE** a container or platform on small wheels on which things are pushed along, e.g. supermarket items or airport baggage **5.** *N Am* **WHEELED TABLE** a small table on wheels, used for taking food and drinks to the table ■ *vt* (**carts, carting, carted**) **1. CARRY SOMEBODY OR SOMETHING ROUGHLY** to take or pull somebody or something roughly or with difficulty (*informal*) ○ *I had to cart*

the Christmas tree home myself. ○ Do you have to cart all those books around? **2. TRANSPORT SOMETHING OR SOMEBODY** to carry or transport something or somebody, especially in a cart ○ carting the produce to market [12C. < Old Norse kartr] —**cartable** adj ◇ **put the cart before the horse** to do or say things in the wrong order

cartage /kaártij/ n the cost of transporting or delivering goods by cart

Cartagena /kaártə jéenə/ **1.** capital of Bolívar Department in northwestern Colombia, a port on the Caribbean Sea's Bay of Cartagena. Population: 877,000 (1999). **2.** city, port, and naval base in the province and autonomous region of Murcia, southeastern Spain. Population: 188,003 (2002).

carte /kaart/ n FENCING same as **quarte**

carte blanche /kaárt blaánsh/ n permission or authority given to somebody to act with freedom or discretion ○ She's been given carte blanche to make whatever changes she thinks necessary. [< French, 'white card']

carte du jour /kaárt də zhoór/ (plural **cartes du jour** /kaárt-/) n a restaurant menu showing what is available on a particular day [< French, 'card of the day']

cartel /kaar tél/ n **1.** an alliance of business companies formed to control production, competition, and prices **2.** a political alliance among parties or groups having common aims [Mid-16C. Via German Kartell < French cartel < Italian cartello 'placard' < Latin c(h)arta (see CARD¹)]

cartelize /kaárti līz/ (-izes, -izing, -ized), **cartelise** (-ises, -ising, -ised) vti to form a cartel of business companies or political groups ○ The market leaders had every incentive to cartelize.

carter /kaártər/ n somebody who uses a cart for transporting goods or for farm work

Carter /kaártər/, **Angela** (1940–92) British writer. Her novels include The Magic Toyshop (1967), Nights at the Circus (1984), and Wise Children (1991).

> 'Myth deals in false universals, to dull the pain of particular circumstances.'
> [Angela Carter, 'Polemical Preface', The Sadeian Woman; 1979]

Carter, Howard (1873–1939) British archaeologist and draughtsman. An Egyptologist, he was largely responsible for discovering the tomb of Tutankhamen in 1922.

The White House

Jimmy Carter

Carter, Jimmy (b. 1924) 39th president of the United States. As Democratic president (1977–81) he negotiated the Panama Canal Treaty (1978) and the Camp David Accords between Israel and Egypt (1978–79). He was awarded the Nobel Peace Price in 2002. Full name **Carter, Jr, James Earl**. See table at **president**

> 'A simple and proper function of government is just to make it easy for us to do good and difficult for us to do wrong.'
> [Jimmy Carter, Acceptance speech, Democratic National Convention, New York City; 15 July 1976]

Cartesian /kaar teézi ən/ adj relating to René Descartes or his writings or theories [Mid-17C. < modern Latin Cartesianus < Cartesius, Latinized form of DESCARTES] —**Cartesian** n

Cartesian coordinate n **1.** one of a pair of coordinates giving the location of a point on a plane, relative to an origin and two perpendicular axes **2.** one of three coordinates giving the location of a point in space, relative to an origin and three mutually perpendicular planes

Cartesianism /kaar teézi ənizəm/ n the philosophy of René Descartes, especially his belief in a distinction between the observing mind and the observed world

Cartesian plane n a plane having all points defined by Cartesian coordinates

Cartesian product n a set of all the pairs of elements from two sets that have their first element from the first set and the second from the second set

Carthage /kaárthij/ site of an ancient city, founded by the Phoenicians on the northern coast of Africa in 814 BC. The site is now in a suburb of Tunis, capital of Tunisia. —**Carthaginian** /kaárthə jínni ən/ n, adj

carthorse /kaárt hawrss/ n a large strong horse bred to pull a cart or for other heavy work

Carthusian /kaar thyoózi ən/ n a member of a contemplative Roman Catholic order of monks and nuns founded in France in the 11th century [Mid-16C. < medieval Latin Carthusianus < Carthusia 'Chartreuse', France, where the order's first monastery was built] —**Carthusian** adj

Cartier /kaárti ay/, **Jacques** (1491–1557) French navigator. He was the first European to explore and chart the St Lawrence River in eastern North America (1534).

Cartier-Bresson /kaárti ay bréss oN/, **Henri** (b. 1908) French photographer. He is known for his black-and-white photographs of French life.

> 'In a portrait, I'm looking for the silence in somebody.'
> [Henri Cartier-Bresson, Observer; 15 May 1994]

Cartier Island /kaárti ay-/ small uninhabited island off the northern coast of Western Australia

cartilage /kaártəlij, kaárt'lij/ n the tough elastic tissue that is found in the nose, throat, and ear and in other parts of the body and forms most of the skeleton in infancy, changing to bone during growth [15C. Via French < Latin cartilago]

cartilaginous /kaártə lájjinəss/ adj **1.** resembling, made of, or relating to cartilage **2.** having a skeleton composed mostly of cartilage

cartilaginous fish n a fish with a skeleton made entirely of cartilage. Shark, rays, and ratfish are cartilaginous fish. Class: Chondrichthyes

Cartland /kaártlənd/, **Dame Barbara** (1901–2000) British novelist. She wrote more than 400 books, mostly popular romances. Born **Hamilton, Mary Barbara**

> 'I'm the only author with 200 virgins in print.'
> [Dame Barbara Cartland, Town & Country; December 1977]

cartload /kaárt lōd/ n **1.** a very large amount (informal) **2.** the amount that a cart can carry

cartogram /kaártə gram/ n a diagrammatic map showing the population and other statistics of a region [Late 19C. < French cartogramme < carte 'map']

cartographic /kaártə gráffik/, **cartographical** /kaártə gráffik'l/ adj **1.** relating to maps ○ cartographic design **2.** in the form of a map ○ cartographic representation —**cartographically** adv

cartography /kaar tóggrəfi/ n the science, skill, or work of making maps [Mid-19C. < French cartographie < carte 'map'] —**cartographer** n

cartomancy /kaártō manssi/ n fortune-telling by using playing cards [Late 19C. < French cartomancie < carte (see CARD¹)]

carton /kaárt'n/ n **1. CARDBOARD BOX** a cardboard box in which something such as goods, movable property, or mail is packaged **2. PLASTIC OR CARD CONTAINER** a container made of plastic or waxed card in which food or drink is sold **3. CONTENTS OF CONTAINER** the contents of a carton ○ drank a whole carton of orange juice **4. RIFLE SHOOTING TARGET CENTRE** the white disc at the centre of a target in competitive shooting ■ vt (-tons, -toning, -toned) **PUT SOMETHING IN CARTON** to put something in a carton ○ Most of our milk is sold

cartoned. [Early 19C. Via French < Italian cartone (see CARTOON)]

cartoon /kaar toón/ n **1. ANIMATED FILM** a film made using animation instead of live actors, especially a humorous film intended primarily for children **2. SEQUENCE OF DRAWINGS** a sequence of drawings that tell a short story, published in a newspaper or magazine **3. SATIRICAL DRAWING** a humorous drawing published in a newspaper or magazine and commenting on a topical event or theme **4. PREPARATORY DRAWING** a drawing done, often in great detail, as a preliminary version of a painting or other work of art [Late 16C. Via Italian cartone 'pasteboard' (on which artists' preparatory drawings were made) < Latin c(h)arta (see CARD¹)] —**cartoonist** n —**cartoony** /kaar toóni/ adj

cartoonish /kaar toónish/, **cartoony** /kaar toóni/ adj resembling a humorous or animated cartoon —**cartoonishly** adv

cartophily /kaar tóffəli/ n the collecting of cigarette cards as a hobby [Mid-20C. < French carte 'card' or Italian carta] —**cartophilist** n

AKG London

cartouche: gold signet ring with cartouche of Tutankhamun (1346–37 BC)

cartouche /kaar toósh/ n **1. CASING FOR GUNPOWDER** the paper casing of a firework or cartridge **2. DECORATIVE PANEL** a decorative panel in the form of a frame or unrolled scroll, sometimes containing writing, forming an artistic or architectural feature **3. FRAME FOR NAME** an oval or oblong shape containing writing, especially one containing a king's name in Egyptian hieroglyphics **4. COOK PAPER KEEPING SOLID INGREDIENTS BELOW SURFACE** a circle or oval of paper placed on top of food that is being cooked in liquid, e.g. in a casserole, to keep the solid ingredients submerged [Early 17C. Via French < Italian cartoccio 'paper cornet' < carta 'paper']

cartridge /kaártrij/ n **1. CASING OF BULLET** a cylindrical case holding an explosive charge and a bullet or shot, which is put into a gun **2. CONTAINER FOR LIQUID OR POWDER** a container for liquid or powder that is loaded into a device, e.g. a removable ink container for a pen or printer ○ toner cartridges **3. CASE FOR LOADING SOMETHING INTO MACHINE** a sealed plastic case containing something such as photographic film, a cassette, or a set of computer disks that can be loaded into an appropriate device **4. PART OF HI-FI TONE ARM** the part of the arm of a record-player that holds the needle [Late 16C. Anglicization of French cartouche (see CARTOUCHE)]

cartridge belt n a belt that holds gun cartridges or cartridge clips

cartridge case n the casing of a gun cartridge

cartridge clip n a container for bullets, loaded directly into an automatic weapon

cartridge paper n thick drawing paper of a good quality with a grained or textured surface

cartridge pen n a pen that holds a replaceable ink cartridge

cart track n a rough track or narrow unsurfaced road used by farm vehicles

cartulary /kaártyoóləri/ (plural -ies) n **1.** a collection of official records, especially those relating to a large estate or a religious community **2.** a room or building where official records are kept [Mid-16C. < medieval Latin c(h)artularium < Latin c(h)artula 'document' < c(h)arta (see CARD¹)]

cartwheel /kaárt weel/ n **1. ACROBATIC MOVEMENT** an acrobatic movement in which the body is turned sideways onto the hands, then over onto the feet again

2. WOODEN WHEEL OF CART a large wooden spoked wheel for a cart ■ *vi* **(-wheels, -wheeling, -wheeled) DO CARTWHEEL** to perform a cartwheel

cartwright /kaárt rīt/ *n* somebody who makes carts

Cartwright /kaárt rīt/, **Edmund** (1743–1823) British inventor and clergyman. He is credited with the invention of the power loom for cotton-spinning (1785).

Cartwright, Dame Silvia (*b.* 1943) New Zealand jurist and politician. She was the first woman to be elected to the New Zealand High Court bench (1993) and became governor-general of New Zealand in 2001.

caruncle /kə rúngk'l/ *n* **1.** a fleshy growth on the head or body, e.g. a cock's comb **2.** a coloured outgrowth of tissue in some types of seed near the point of attachment to the plant [Late 16C. Via obsolete French < Latin *caruncula* 'small piece of flesh' < *caro* 'flesh'] —**caruncular** *adj* —**carunculate** *adj* —**carunculated** *adj* —**carunculous** *adj*

Caruso /kə róossō/, **Enrico** (1873–1921) Italian operatic tenor. A powerful singer and actor, he specialized in the operas of Verdi and Puccini.

carvacrol /kaárvə krol/ *n* an oily liquid with the smell of mint. Source: savory, oregano, thyme. Use: in flavourings, perfumes, as a disinfectant. [Mid-19C. < modern Latin *(Carum) carvi* 'caraway' + Latin *acris* 'sharp']

carve /kaarv/ **(carves, carving, carved)** *v* **1.** *vti* **MAKE SOMETHING BY CUTTING AND SHAPING** to make an object or design by cutting and shaping a hard material such as wood or stone ○ *statues carved from marble* ○ *I remembered carving her name on a tree, years ago.* **2.** *vt* **CUT SUBSTANCE TO MAKE SOMETHING** to cut and shape a material such as wood or stone in order to make an object or design **3.** *vti* **CUT MEAT** to cut cooked meat into slices **4.** *vt* **MAKE SHAPE BY NATURAL FORCE** to make a shape by an eroding action ○ *dunes carved into strange shapes by the wind* [Old English *ceorfan* < Germanic, 'to scratch']

carve out *vt* to make or achieve something through sustained hard work ○ *She carved out a niche for herself in the world of investigative journalism.*

carve up *vt* **1.** to divide something, or ownership of something, into rough or crude parts (*informal*) ○ *Their intention was to invade and carve up the kingdom among themselves.* **2.** to wound somebody with a blade (*slang*)

carvel *n* NAUT same as **caravel**

carvel-built /kaárv'l-/ *adj* describes a boat or ship made of planks of wood with their edges flush, not overlapping

carver /kaárvər/ *n* **1.** COOK same as **carving knife 2. SOMEBODY WHO CARVES** somebody who carves meat **3. DINING CHAIR WITH ARMS** a dining chair with arms, designed to stand at the head of the table ■ **carvers** *npl* **CARVING KNIFE AND FORK** a large knife and fork for carving meat

carvery /kaárvəri/ (*plural* **-ies**) *n* a restaurant or buffet where meat is freshly sliced to order for customers, sometimes offering unlimited servings for a fixed price

carving /kaárving/ *n* **1.** an object or design formed by cutting and shaping a material such as wood or stone ○ *The walls were covered with carvings depicting gods and heroes.* **2.** the work or act of carving something ○ *The carving of the panels was exquisite.*

carving knife *n* a large knife for slicing meat

car wash *n* **1.** a business establishment where motor vehicles are washed automatically by machine or can be washed manually **2.** a shed or structure for washing motor vehicles automatically with revolving brushes and jets of water

Cary /káiri/, **Joyce** (1888–1957) Irish-born British novelist. His bittersweet humour characterizes such works as *The Horse's Mouth* (1944). Full name **Cary, Arthur Joyce Lunel**

> 'It is the misfortune of an old man that though he can put things out of his head he can't put them out of his feelings.'
> [Joyce Cary, *To be a Pilgrim*; 1942]

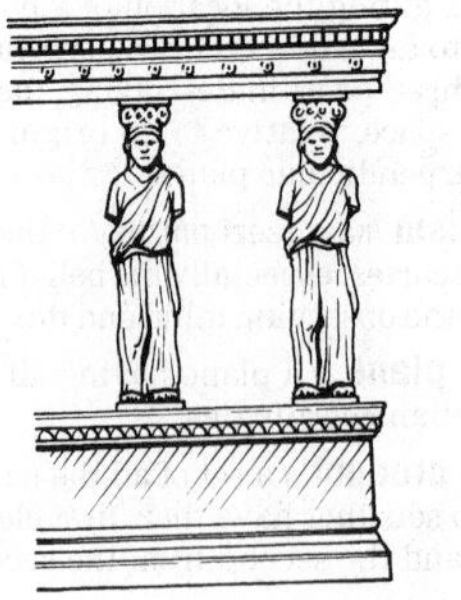

caryatid

caryatid /kárri áttid/ (*plural* **-ids** or **-ides** /-i deez/) *n* a column in the shape of a draped female figure supporting a structure such as the frieze or porch of a classical Greek temple [Mid-16C. Via Latin < Greek *karuatides* 'maidens of Karuai' (Caryae, Greece), priestesses of Artemis]

caryopsis /kárri ópsiss/ (*plural* **-opses** /-ópseez/ or **-opsides** /-si deez/) *n* a dry fruit that looks like a seed, borne by grasses and cereal crops such as wheat [Early 19C. < modern Latin < Greek *karuon* 'nut' + *opsis* 'appearance']

carzey (*plural* **-zeys**) *n* another spelling of **karzy**

casaba /kə saábə/ *n* a winter melon, similar to the honeydew and cantaloupe, with whitish flesh. Latin name: *Cucumis melo* var. inodorus. [Late 19C. After *Kasaba* (now Turgutlu), Turkey]

Casablanca /kássə blángkə, kázzə-/ largest city and chief port in Morocco. It is situated on the Atlantic coast, about 80 km/50 mi. southwest of Rabat. Population: 2,940,623 (1994). Arabic name **Dar el-Beida**

Casals /kə sálz/, **Pablo** (1876–1973) Spanish cellist and composer. He was widely regarded as the greatest cellist of his generation.

> 'The most perfect technique is that which is not noticed at all.'
> [Pablo Casals. Quoted in *The Song of the Birds*, Julian Lloyd Webber (ed.); 1985]

Casanova /kássə nṓvə/ *n* a charming seducer of women who moves quickly from one casual relationship to another or who constantly pesters women in his pursuits [Early 20C. After Giovanni Jacopo CASANOVA]

Casanova /kássə nṓvə/, **Giovanni Giacomo, Chevalier de Seingalt** (1725–98) Italian adventurer and author. He was a soldier, diplomat, and spy whose amorous reputation rests on his posthumously published 12-volume *History of My Life* (1826–38).

> 'This dance is the expression of love from beginning to end, from the sigh of desire to the ecstasy of enjoyment. It seemed to me impossible that after such a dance the girl could refuse anything to her partner.'
> [Giovanni Giacomo Casanova. Describing the *fandango* in Madrid. Quoted in *World History of Dance*, Curt Sachs; 1937]

casbah *n* BUILDINGS another spelling of **kasbah**

cascade /ka skáyd/ *n* **1. WATERFALL** a small waterfall or series of waterfalls **2. DOWNWARD FLOW OF SOMETHING** a fast downward flow of liquid or small objects **3. HANGING MASS** a flowing mass of something that hangs down or lies along a surface ○ *The bride carried a cascade of roses and baby's breath.* **4.** SCI **SUCCESSION** a succession of things such as chemical reactions or components in an electrical circuit, each of which activates, affects, or determines the next ■ *v* **(-cades, -cading, -caded) 1.** *vti* **FLOW** to flow fast and in large amounts, or cause something to flow in this way **2.** *vi* **HANG OR LIE** to hang or lie in a flowing mass ○ *Flowering plants cascaded down the fronts of the buildings.* **3.** *vt* COMPUT **OVERLAP WINDOWS ON COMPUTER SCREEN** to arrange the windows on a computer screen so that they overlap, with the title bar of each visible **4.** *vi* **MOVE ON TO NEXT THING** to move on to others in succession ○ *If it is not claimed, the jackpot will cascade down to the holder of the next numbers drawn.* **5.** *vt* **PASS INFORMATION ON TO OTHERS** to pass on something, especially something that has been learnt, to other people in succession ○ *Trained helpers can then cascade their knowledge to larger groups.* [Mid-17C. Via French < Italian *cascata* < Latin *cadere* 'to fall']

Cascade Range /ka skáyd-/ range of mountains in the western United States, forming the northern continuation of the Sierra Nevada range. Its highest peak is Mount Rainier, 4,392 m/14,410 ft. Length: 1,127 km/700 mi.

cascading menu *n* a menu in a computer program that opens when a choice is selected from another menu

cascara /ka skaárə/ *n* **1.** *also* **cascara buckthorn** a bush or small tree from whose dried bark a strong laxative was formerly made. Native to: northwestern United States. Latin name: *Rhamnus purshiana.* **2.** formerly, a strong laxative made from the dried bark of a North American bush or small tree [Late 19C. Shortening of CASCARA SAGRADA]

cascara sagrada /-sə graádə/ *n* the dried bark of the cascara tree. Use: formerly, as a strong laxative. [< Spanish *cáscara sagrada* 'sacred bark']

case[1] /kayss/ *n* **1. SITUATION** a situation or set of circumstances ○ *I don't think the usual rules apply in this case.* ○ *Sometimes anxiety causes weight loss, but that's not the case here.* **2. INSTANCE** an instance or example of something ○ *This seems to be a case of mistaken identity.* **3. SOMETHING EXAMINED OR INVESTIGATED** a subject of investigation or scrutiny by a professional person such as a doctor or police officer **4. ACTUAL FACT** the reality or truth of a particular situation ○ *The case is that the witness has lied under oath.* **5.** LAW **SOMETHING EXAMINED IN LAW COURT** a matter examined or judged in a court of law ○ *It'll be some weeks before your case comes to trial.* **6.** LAW **ARGUMENTS** a set of arguments and evidence supporting a legal claim in court ○ *He presented his case calmly and with skill.* **7. ARGUMENT FOR OR AGAINST** an argument for or against something ○ *You can make a good case for holding a referendum.* **8.** GRAM **FORM OF WORD SHOWING ROLE IN SENTENCE** a form of a noun, pronoun, or adjective that indicates its syntactic relation to surrounding words **9. TYPE OF PERSON** somebody of a particular type or in a particular condition, especially an unfortunate one (*informal*) ○ *He's a hopeless case.* **10. ODD PERSON** an odd or eccentric person (*informal*) ■ *vt* **(cases, casing, cased) INSPECT PLACE** to assess or survey a place with a view to robbing it (*slang*) [13C. Via Old French *cas* 'event' < Latin *casus* < *cadere* 'to fall'] ◇ **a case in point** a relevant example ○ *A case in point is the steady drop in unit sales.* ◇ **be on somebody's case** (*slang*) **1.** to use influence in order to help somebody **2.** to persist in pestering somebody to do something ◇ **get off somebody's case** (*slang*) **1.** to stop using influence to help somebody **2.** to stop pestering somebody to do something ○ *Get off my case! I'll finish mowing the lawn later.* ◇ **in any case 1.** no matter what may happen ○ *Come over if you want, I'll be home in any case.* **2.** used to support a point that has just been mentioned ○ *Maybe he just got bored. In any case, he left rather early.* ◇ **in case of something** if something happens ○ *In case of fire, leave by the nearest exit.* ◇ **(just) in case 1.** in preparation for an event that may possibly happen ○ *Take your umbrella, just in case.* **2.** used to introduce a piece of information and explain the reason for giving it ○ *In case you're unaware of the fact, this is a nonsmoking area.*

case[2] /kayss/ *n* **1. HOLDER OR OUTER COVERING** something that serves as a container or covering **2. CONTAINER** a container with its contents ○ *bought a case of fizzy drinks* **3. PIECE OF LUGGAGE** an item of luggage, especially a suitcase **4.** PRINTING **KIND OF PRINTED CHARACTER** one of the two kinds of printed character, either a capital or small letter **5.** PRINTING **TRAY HOLDING PRINTING TYPE** in hot-metal printing, a tray with compartments in which individual printing blocks are kept **6. PAIR** a pair, especially of pistols **7.** CIV ENG same as **casing** (sense 3) ■ *vt* **(cases, casing, cased) PUT COVERING ROUND SOMETHING** to enclose something in a covering [13C. Via Old French dialect *casse* < Latin *capsa* 'box' < *capere* 'to hold']

CASE /kayss/ *abbr* COMPUT **1.** computer-aided software engineering **2.** computer-aided systems engineering

casease /káyssi ayss, -ayz/ *n* a bacterial enzyme that aids the breakdown of casein [20C. < CASEIN]

caseate /káyssi ayt/ (**-ates, -ating, -ated**) *vi* to undergo caseation [Late 19C. Back-formation < CASEATION] —**caseous** *adj*

caseation /káyssi áysh'n/ *n* the process by which dead tissue decays into a firm and dry mass, characteristic of tuberculosis [Mid-19C. < medieval Latin *caseation-* < Latin *caseus* 'cheese']

casebook /káyss boˑok/ *n* **1.** a record of legal or medical cases and their conduct **2.** a collection of academic writings on a subject

casebound /káyss bownd/ *adj* PUBL same as **hardback**

cased glass /kayst-/, **case glass** *n* decorative glass consisting of several coloured layers with some areas cut away in different patterns

case grammar *n* a system of grammar that analyses sentences in terms of the semantic relation of the noun or noun phrase and other sentence components to the main verb

case-harden (**case-hardens, case-hardening, case-hardened**) *vt* **1.** to harden the surface of an iron alloy by heating and then cooling in water **2.** to make somebody unsympathetic or unfeeling as a result of extended involvement in dealing with difficult and distressing problems

case history *n* a record of somebody's medical or social history kept by a doctor or social worker

casein /káyssi in, -een/ *n* one of a group of proteins found in milk. Use: in plastics, adhesives, and paints. [Mid-19C. < Latin *caseus* 'cheese']

caseinate /káyssi i nayt, -ee nayt/ *n* a compound of casein and calcium or sodium

caseinogen /kay seˑenəjin, káyssi ínn-/ *n* the main protein in milk, from which casein is formed

case law *n* law established on the basis of previous verdicts according to the doctrine of binding precedent

caseload /káyss lōd/ *n* the number of cases to be dealt with during a specific period by a professional such as a doctor or a lawyer

casemate /káyss mayt/ *n* a fortified compartment on an old sailing ship, or a rampart where a cannon was mounted [Mid-16C. Directly or via French < Italian *casamatta*]

casement

casement /káyssmənt/ *n* a window that opens on hinges located at one side, as distinct from one that slides up and down [15C. Via Anglo-Latin *cassimentum* < Latin *capsa* (see CASE [2])]

Casement /káyssmənt/, **Sir Roger** (1864–1916) Irish-born British consular official and rebel. Knighted for humanitarian work in Africa and South America, he became a militant Irish nationalist and was hanged for treason.

> 'The government of Ireland by England rests on restraint, and not on law; and since it demands no love it can evoke no loyalty.'
> [Sir Roger Casement, *Speech, after being found guilty of treason*; 1916]

caseose /káyssi ōss, -ōz/ *n* a chemical produced in the digestion of cheese [20C. < Latin *caseus* 'cheese']

casern /kə zúrn/, **caserne** *n* a barracks, especially a temporary one [Late 17C. Via French *caserne* < Latin *quaterna* 'hut for four']

case shot *n* formerly, a type of cannon shell containing shrapnel

case stated *n* an outline of the circumstances of a legal case prepared by one court for another court to use in making its decision, e.g. in an appeal hearing or a retrial

case study *n* an analysis of a particular case or situation used as a basis for drawing conclusions in similar situations

case system *n* the teaching of law through the study of important and representative cases rather than by studying theory

casevac /kázzi vak/ *n* also **CASEVAC** the removal, by motor vehicle or aircraft, of wounded or otherwise injured military personnel from a theatre of operations or from a training site, and their transport to a hospital for treatment ■ *vt* (**-vacs, -vacking, -vacked**) MIL, MED to transport wounded or injured military personnel from a theater of operations or a training site to a hospital for treatment [Late 20C. Blend of CASUALTY + EVACUATION]

casework /káyss wurk/ *n* a system in which a social worker is made responsible for particular clients on a long-term basis —**caseworker** *n*

caseworm /káyss wurm/ *n* INSECTS same as **caddis worm** [Early 17C. < the protective case it builds around itself]

cash[1] /kash/ *n* **1.** COINS AND BANKNOTES money in the form of coins or notes as distinct from money orders or credit **2.** CURRENCY OR CHEQUES money used as immediate payment in any form, e.g. currency or cheques (*informal*) ○ *earn some cash* ■ *vt* (**cashes, cashing, cashed**) EXCHANGE SOMETHING FOR READY MONEY to exchange a cheque or money order for coins or banknotes ○ *You can cash your pay cheque at the bank.* [Late 16C. Directly or via obsolete French *casse* < Italian *cassa* 'money box' < Latin *capsa* (see CASE [2])] —**cashable** *adj*

SPELLCHECK See *cache*.

cash in *v* **1.** *vt* to withdraw from a business investment such as an insurance policy and take the money that is due **2.** *vi* to make large amounts of money (*slang*) ○ *When the stock was sold, she really cashed in.*
cash in on *vt* to exploit a situation in order to get personal benefit, especially money ○ *Everyone who knew him wanted to cash in on his rise to fame.*
cash out *v* **1.** *vti* to sell off an asset such as land that has been held for a long time in order to make a profit **2.** *vi* N Am COMM same as **cash up 3.** *vi* US to commit suicide (*slang*)
cash up *vi* to add up the day's takings of a shop or similar business. N Am term **cash out**

cash[2] /kash/ (*plural same*) *n* formerly, a coin of low value in China and some South Asian countries [Late 16C. Via Portuguese *caixa* < Tamil *kācu*]

Cash /kash/, **Martin** (1810–77) Irish-born Australian bushranger. The leader of a gang of outlaws based in Tasmania, Australia, he eventually reformed and was pardoned.

Cash, Pat (*b.* 1965) Australian tennis player. He won the Wimbledon men's singles championship in 1987. Full name **Cash, Patrick Hart**

> 'If the ball is there, hit it.'
> [Pat Cash, *The Sunday Times*; 5 July 1987]

CASH /kash/ *n* US a military field hospital (*informal*) Full form **Combat Support Hospital**

cash and carry *n* (*plural* **cash and carries**) **1.** INEXPENSIVE WHOLESALE STORE a wholesale store selling inexpensive goods that are paid for in cash and taken away by the buyer **2.** POLICY OF SELLING WITHOUT DELIVERY SERVICE a policy of selling items for cash with no delivery service to customers ■ *adj* CASH-ONLY AND WITHOUT DELIVERY sold or operating on a basis of cash-only payments by buyers who take their goods away at the time of purchase

cash bar *n* a bar at a large party or reception at which drinks have to be paid for individually

cashbook /kásh boˑok/ *n* a book for keeping a record of money spent and received

cash box *n* a lockable box for cash, especially one holding the daily takings of a small business

cash card *n* a coded plastic card that a bank customer uses to access an account by means of a cashpoint

cash cow *n* a profitable business or product with

low overheads, often used to fund other businesses or investments (*slang*)

cash crop *n* a crop grown for direct sale, and not for personal consumption

cash desk *n* a counter for payment of goods in a shop

cash dispenser *n* BANKING same as **cashpoint**

cashed up *adj* Aus provided with plenty of money (*informal*) ○ *I just got paid, so I'm cashed up for the weekend.*

cashew /káshoo, ka shoˑo/ *n* **1.** also **cashew nut** a kidney-shaped nut that is edible when roasted **2.** an evergreen tree that produces cashew nuts and oil. Native to: South America. Latin name: *Anacardium occidentale*. [Late 16C. Via Portuguese < Tupi *acajú*]

cashew apple *n* the edible swollen stalk by which a cashew nut is attached to its stem. Use: preserves.

cash flow *n* **1.** the pattern of income and expenses, and its consequences for how much money is available at a given time **2.** the prediction or assessment of a company's income and expenditure over a period of time

cashier[1] /ka sheˑer/ *n* **1.** WORKER TAKING AND PAYING MONEY somebody who works in a bank or shop and handles customers' money transactions **2.** SOMEBODY RESPONSIBLE FOR FINANCIAL TRANSACTIONS an official in an organization who is responsible for receiving and paying out money and keeping financial records ■ *vi* (**-iers, -iering, -iered**) BE CASHIER to work as a cashier, especially in a place of business such as a restaurant or bar [Late 16C. Directly or via Dutch *cassier* < French *caissier* < *casse* (see CASH [1])]

cashier[2] /ka sheˑer/ (**-shiers, -shiering, -shiered**) *vt* to dismiss somebody from the armed forces because of misconduct [Early 16C. Via Dutch *kasseren* 'disband (soldiers)' < French *casser* 'to break' < Latin *quassare* (see QUASH [1])]

cashier's cheque *n* a guaranteed cheque issued by a bank against money taken from a customer's account or against cash provided for this purpose

cash-in-hand *adj, adv* in ready money, instead of by cheque or other traceable means ○ *We were paid cash-in-hand for the job.*

cashless /káshləss/ *adj* using an electronic means of exchanging money instead of dealing in cash

cash machine *n* BANKING same as **cashpoint**

cashmere /kásh meer/ *n* **1.** the soft wool from a Himalayan goat **2.** a woollen fabric made from cashmere [Late 17C. Early spelling of KASHMIR]

cash method *n* a method of accounting that counts income or expenses at the time they are actually received or paid out, irrespective of when they are earned or incurred

cash on delivery *adv* with full payment for ordered goods to be made by the buyer to the person delivering the goods ○ *bought the coat cash on delivery*

cashpoint /kásh poynt/ *n* UK a machine that provides cash and account information on insertion of a machine-readable card. ANZ, N Am term **ATM**

cash-poor *adj* financially sound but having little readily available cash

cash ratio *n* the ratio that a bank must maintain between available cash and total deposits

cash register *n* a machine in a shop that records sales, calculates totals, and has a drawer for takings

cash-starved *adj* having very little money or financial support

cash-strapped *adj* having insufficient money (*informal*)

Casimir III /kázzi meer/ (1309–70) king of Poland. His reign (1333–70) as the 'Peasants' King' saw the introduction of fairer laws and peace through diplomacy. He founded Kraków University (1364). Known as **Casimir the Great**

Casimir force, **Casimir effect** *n* a small electrostatic force between a pair of conductors in a vacuum [After Hendrick *Casimir* (1909–2000), Dutch physicist]

casing /káyssing/ *n* **1.** OUTER COVERING an outer covering, e.g. the sheath of an electrical cable or the skin of a sausage **2.** FRAME FOR DOOR OR WINDOW a frame containing a door, window, or stairway **3.** LINER PIPE IN

WELL a liner pipe or tube in a water, oil, or gas well

casino /kə seénō/ (*plural* **-nos**) *n* **1.** a private club, or a room in a club, hotel, or other establishment, where gambling takes place **2.** *also* **cassino** a point-scoring card game in which players combine cards exposed on the table with cards in their hands, with the 10 of diamonds being the highest-valued card [Mid-18C. < Italian, 'small house' < Latin *casa* 'house']

Casino /kə seénō/ town in northern New South Wales, Australia, a centre of beef and dairy production. Population: 10,152 (1991).

cask /kaask/ *n* **1. BARREL CONTAINING ALCOHOL** a wooden barrel containing alcoholic drink **2. CONTAINER LIKE BARREL** a container resembling a barrel, whether or not of wood **3. CONTENTS OF BARREL** the contents of a barrel or similar container **4.** INDUST same as **flask** (sense 6) [Early 16C. Directly or via French *casque* < Spanish *casco* 'helmet, skull' < Latin *quassare* (see QUASH [1])]

casket /kaáskit/ *n* **1.** a decorative box for valuables **2.** *N Am* same as **coffin** [15C. Origin ?]

Casparian strip /ka spáiri ən-/ *n* a thin impervious band of material in the cell walls of some plants resembling suberin or lignin [After Robert *Caspary*, 19C German botanist]

Caspian Sea /káspi ən-/ large landlocked salt lake lying between south-eastern Europe and Asia. It is the world's largest inland body of water. Area: 371,000 sq. km/143,000 sq. mi.

casque /kask/ *n* **1.** a helmet from a suit of armour **2.** a horny growth on the head of a bird, fish, or reptile, resembling a helmet [Late 17C. < French (see CASK)] —**casqued** *adj*

Cassandra /kə sándrə/ *n* somebody whose warnings of impending disaster are ignored [Early 17C. After *Cassandra*, daughter of Priam, king of Troy, who was granted the gift of prophecy but was condemned never to be believed]

cassata /kə saátə/ *n* **1.** a brightly coloured Italian ice cream containing nuts, candied fruit and layers or streaks of different flavours **2.** a Sicilian sponge cake, layered and coated with sweetened ricotta, flavoured with candied fruit and chopped chocolate, and eaten as a celebration cake or dessert [Early 20C. < Italian]

cassation /ka sáysh'n/ *n* **1.** a court of appeal in countries that follow the Napoleonic code of civil law **2.** an 18th-century instrumental work similar in form to a divertimento [15C. < Latin *cassat-*, past participle of *cassare* 'annul']

Cassatt /kə sát/, **Mary** (1845–1926) US artist. She is known for intimate impressionist portraits of mothers with their children, e.g. *The Bath* (1891).

cassava /kə saávə/ *n* **1.** a large thick-skinned tuber that is poisonous when raw and untreated but like the potato when boiled. Use: as a vegetable in many tropical countries, as a source of tapioca. **2.** a tropical plant that produces cassava. Latin name: *Manihot esculenta*. [Mid-16C. < Taino *casávi*]

Cassegrainian telescope /kássi gráyni ən-/ *n* an astronomical telescope that uses a large concave mirror and a small convex mirror to form an image [Late 19C. After Giovanni *Cassegrain* (1625–1712), French astronomer]

Cassel ♦ **Kassel**

casserole /kássərōl/ *n* **1. COOKED DISH** a stew or other moist food dish, cooked slowly at a low heat in a covered pot or dish **2. COOKING POT** a deep heavy cooking pot suitable for use in an oven **3. LABORATORY CONTAINER** a porcelain container used for heating substances in a laboratory ■ *vt* (**-roles, -roling, -roled**) **COOK FOOD IN LIQUID** to cook food slowly at a low heat with liquid in a covered pot [Early 18C. < French, 'small pan' < *casse* 'pan' < Greek *kuathos* 'cup']

cassette /kə sét/ *n* **1.** a sealed plastic case containing a length of audiotape or videotape wound round spools ready for use **2.** a sealed plastic case containing a supply of something such as ink for insertion into a machine such as a printer [Late 18C. < French, 'small box' < *casse* (see CASH [1])]

cassette deck *n* a tape deck that plays or records audio cassettes

cassette player *n* a machine that plays cassettes, but does not record audio

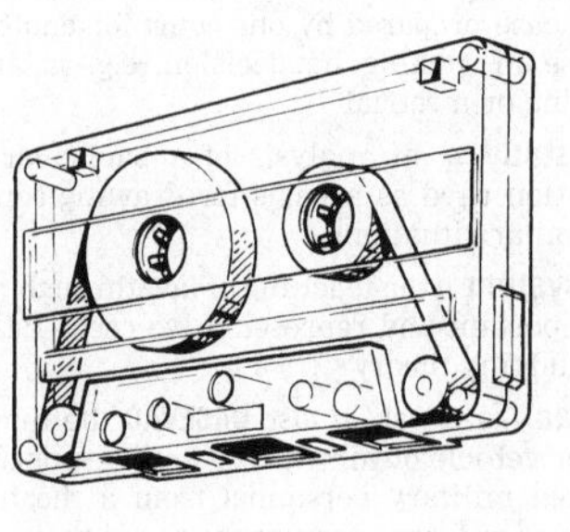

cassette

cassette recorder *n* a machine, especially a portable one, that plays and records audio cassettes

cassia /kássi ə/ *n* an evergreen Asian tree with an aromatic bark. Latin name: *Cinnamomum aromaticum*. [Pre-12C. Via Latin < Hebrew *qĕṣī'āh*]

Cassini division /ka seéni-/, **Cassini's division** *n* the dark area between the two brightest rings, the middle and outermost, of Saturn [Early 20C. After Giovanni Domenico *Cassini* (1625–1712), Italian-born French astronomer]

cassino *n* CARDS another spelling of **casino** (sense 2)

Cassiopeia /kássi ō peé ə/ *n* a constellation of the northern hemisphere. See illustration at **constellation**

cassis /ka seéss/ *n* a syrupy, usually alcoholic, cordial made in France from blackcurrants, often mixed with white wine to make kir [Late 19C. < French, 'blackcurrant', probably < Latin *cassia* (see CASSIA)]

cassiterite /kə síttə rīt/ *n* a dark-coloured mineral consisting of tin oxide. Use: source of tin. [Mid-19C. < Greek *kassiteros* 'tin']

Cassius /kássi əss/ (*fl* 53–42 BC) Roman general and conspirator. A leader in the assassination of Julius Caesar (44 BC), he committed suicide when defeated by Mark Antony. Full name **Gaius Cassius Longinus**

cassock /kássək/ *n* a full-length, usually black robe worn by priests, their assistants, and singers in church choirs [Mid-16C. Via French *casaque* 'long coat' < Italian *casacca* 'riding coat'] —**cassocked** *adj*

Casson /káss'n/, **Sir Hugh** (1910–99) British architect. He was president of the Royal Academy of Arts (1976–84) and author of *Homes by the Million* (1947).

> 'The British love permanence more than they love beauty.'
> [Sir Hugh Casson, *Observer*, 14 June 1964]

cassone /kə sṓni/ *n* a highly decorated Italian chest of the Middle Ages and the Renaissance period [Late 19C. < Italian < *cassa* (see CASH [1])]

cassoulet /kássoo láy, kássoo lay/ *n* a French stew of haricot beans cooked in a casserole with meat [Mid-20C. < French, 'small stew-pan' < Greek *kuathos* 'cup']

cassowary /kássə wairi/ (*plural* **-ies**) *n* a large black flightless bird, with colourful wattles and a large bony head shield, that resembles an ostrich or emu. Native to: northeastern Australia, New Guinea. Genus: *Casuarius*. [Early 17C. < Malay *kesuari*]

cast /kaast/ *v* (**casts, casting, cast**) **1.** *vt* **THROW SOMEBODY OR SOMETHING** to throw somebody or something, especially somebody or something that is light in weight ○ *casting pebbles into a river* **2.** *vt* **CARRY SOMEBODY OR SOMETHING ASHORE** to carry somebody or something to the seashore (*refers to the sea*) ○ *pieces of driftwood cast up by the incoming tide* **3.** *vt* **FLING SOMETHING DOWN OR AWAY** to throw something away from yourself, usually with force ○ *We cast pieces of bread onto the lake to attract fish.* **4.** *vt* FISHING **THROW FISHING LINE INTO WATER** to throw a line, baited hook, or fishing net into the water **5.** *vt* POL **REGISTER VOTE** to register or deposit a vote **6.** *vt* **CAUSE SOMETHING TO APPEAR SOMEWHERE** to make something such as light or shadow appear in a place ○ *The bulb cast an eerie green glow over everything.* **7.** *vt* **HAVE DISPIRITING EFFECT** to produce a dispiriting, sobering, or saddening effect on somebody or something ○ *Her mother's absence cast a shadow over the wedding plans.* **8.** *vt* **CREATE MISTRUST** to generate a sense of uncertainty, distrust, or suspicion about somebody or something ○ *an accident that has cast doubt over the project's future* **9.** *vt* **DIRECT LOOK AT SOMEBODY OR SOMETHING** to direct the eyes or a look towards somebody or something, often in a surreptitious, disapproving, or anxious manner ○ *casting a discreet glance at his watch* **10.** *vt* **DISMISS SOMETHING FROM MIND** to remove or banish something from the mind deliberately, decisively, and often with difficulty (*formal*) **11.** *vt* **PUT SOMEBODY SOMEWHERE ROUGHLY** to put or throw somebody or something somewhere, especially in a rough or brutal way (*formal*) ○ *cast into the dungeon* **12.** *vti* ARTS **SELECT PARTICIPANTS FOR PERFORMANCE** to choose somebody for a particular role in a drama, dance, or other performance, or choose people for all the roles in a production ○ *He was badly cast as Othello.* **13.** *vt* **DESCRIBE SOMEBODY AS SOMETHING** to classify or describe somebody in a particular way ○ *I seem to have been cast as the villain in this affair.* **14.** *vt* MANUF **FORM SOMETHING USING MOULD** to pour something such as molten metal or plaster into a mould and allow it to solidify in order to create an object **15.** *vt* **SHED SOMETHING** to shed something such as the skin ○ *a snake that had cast its skin* **16.** *vt* **DROP SOMETHING** to drop or lose something ○ *a horse that had cast a shoe* **17.** *vt* ACCT **CALCULATE SOMETHING** to add something up or calculate something **18.** *vt* ASTROL **PREDICT SOMEBODY'S FUTURE** to predict somebody's future **19.** *vt Scotland* **USE SOMETHING TO REPROACH SOMEBODY** to use something as a reproach against somebody (*informal*) ■ *n* **1. ACT OF THROWING** the flinging, hurling, or throwing of something, or an instance of this **2. LENGTH OF THROW** the distance that something is thrown ○ *a 20-metre cast of a harpoon* **3.** ARTS **PERFORMERS** the actors or other performers in a drama, dance, or other production (*takes a singular or plural verb*) **4.** MANUF **MOULDED OBJECT** an object that is made by pouring a molten substance, especially metal, into a mould and leaving it to solidify so that it takes on the shape of the mould **5.** MANUF **MOULD** a container of a particular shape into which a molten substance, especially metal, is poured and left to solidify **6.** MED **SUPPORT FOR BROKEN BONE** a stiff plaster of Paris or fibreglass casing that holds a broken bone in place while it is mending ○ *He came back with his leg in a cast.* **7.** MANUF, ARTS **MOLTEN IMPRESSION** an impression formed by pressing soft or molten material over or inside something and letting it harden or dry ○ *a cast of the pianist's hands* **8.** GEOL, PALAEONT **PRESERVED SEDIMENT** preserved sediment that results from an impression such as a footprint being filled in **9. EMOTIONAL OR PSYCHOLOGICAL TYPE** the nature or quality of somebody's character or mind ○ *a sly cast to his face* **10.** OPHTHALMOL same as **squint** **11. OVERSPREADING OF ONE THING ONTO ANOTHER** the overspreading of something, especially an added colour, that results in modification of the hue or general appearance of something else **12. TINGE** a general suggestion of something such as a colour ○ *The mud gave a brown cast to the water.* **13.** FISHING **THROW OF LINE OR NET** a throw of a fishing line or net into the water **14.** FISHING **THROWN LINE OR NET** a fishing line or net that is thrown into the water **15.** GAMBLING, LEISURE **DICE THROW** a throw of dice, or the number that has been thrown **16.** BIOL **SOMETHING SHED BY ORGANISM** a part of an organism that has been shed in a natural recurring process, e.g. an insect casing, a snake skin, or worm faeces [12C. < Old Norse *kasta* 'to throw'] —**castability** /kaástə bílləti/ *n* —**castable** *adj*

SYNONYMS See *throw*.

cast around *or* **about** *vi* to search for something or try to devise a solution to a problem

cast aside *vt* **1.** to reject and abandon somebody or something regarded as no longer interesting or useful ○ *You can't just cast him aside like that!* **2.** to abandon something such as a feeling or belief (*formal*) ○ *You must cast your doubts aside and trust in me.*

cast away *vt* to shipwreck somebody, especially on a desert island

cast off *v* **1.** *vt* **GET RID OF SOMEBODY OR SOMETHING** to reject or abandon somebody or something regarded as no longer useful or attractive ○ *I cast off that old coat years ago.* **2.** *vti* NAUT **UNTIE MOORING LINES** to untie the ropes securing a boat to its mooring so that it can move away **3.** *vti* HANDICRAFT **FINISH KNITTING** to make the last row of stitches in a piece of knitting by looping each stitch over the next and removing it from the needle **4.** *vti* PUBL **FIT TEXT** to calculate the

amount of space a piece of text will take up when it has been typeset

cast on *vti* to make the first row of stitches in a piece of knitting

cast out *v* **1.** *vt* to reject, abandon, or eject somebody or something (*formal*) **2.** *vi* Scotland to have a quarrel with somebody (*informal*)

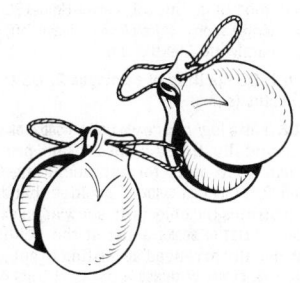

castanets

castanet /kástə nét/ *n* either of a pair of small curved pieces of hard wood or plastic that are joined at the top and used to make a rhythmic clicking sound. They are held in the palm of the hand and tapped together, traditionally by Spanish flamenco dancers and musicians. [Early 17C. < Spanish *castañeta*, literally 'small chestnut' < *castaña* 'chestnut' < Latin *castanea*]

castaway /káːstə way/ *n* the survivor of a shipwreck —**castaway** *adj*

cast down *adj* experiencing feelings of dejection, depression, or sadness

caste /kaast/ *n* **1.** HINDU SOCIAL CLASS one of the four main hereditary classes into which Hindu society is divided, dictating the social position and status of people according to their professions. Though discrimination based on caste has been illegal since 1947, it still occurs in some areas. **2.** HINDU CLASS SYSTEM the Hindu system of organizing society into hereditary classes **3.** SOCIAL CLASS the class and rank or position of somebody in a society, according to birth, occupation, or some other criterion **4.** INSECTS RANK IN INSECT COLONY a group of insects that has a specialized role in a colony or hive of social insects such as ants or bees [Mid-16C. < Spanish, Portuguese *casta* 'pure race' < Latin *castus* 'pure'] —**casteism** *n*

Castel Gandolfo /káss tel gan dólfō/ village in Rome province, Lazio Region, just south of Rome, Italy. It contains a palace that is the summer residence of the pope. Population: 7,930 (2001).

Castella /ka stéllə/, **Robert de** (*b.* 1957) Australian marathon runner. He won gold medals at the Commonwealth Games in 1982 and 1986.

castellan /kástılən/ *n* formerly, the governor or manager of a castle [14C. Via Old N French < medieval Latin *castellanus* < Latin *castellum* (see CASTLE)]

castellated /kástə laytid/ *adj* **1.** ARCHIT HAVING SERRATIONS ALONG TOP having battlements or a serrated top edge like the walls of a castle **2.** INDENTED OR SERRATED having indented or serrated edges ○ *an ornate tablecloth with a castellated edge* **3.** HAVING CASTLE NEARBY having a castle as part of the surroundings or landscape (*literary*) ○ *the castellated French countryside* [Late 17C. < medieval Latin *castellatus* 'having a castle' < Latin *castellum* (see CASTLE)]

caste mark *n* a mark, usually a painted dot on the forehead, that shows a Hindu person's caste

caster /káːstər/ *n* **1.** somebody or something that casts something else **2.** FURNITURE, HOUSEHOLD another spelling of **castor**[1]

caster sugar *n* finely ground white sugar, often used in baking. It is finer than granulated sugar but not as fine as icing sugar.

castigate /kásti gayt/ (**-gates**, **-gating**, **-gated**) *vt* to criticize or rebuke somebody or somebody's behaviour severely (*formal; often passive*) ○ *They were strongly castigated for their refusal to act.* [Early 17C. < Latin *castigat-*, past participle of *castigare* 'chastise' < *castus* 'chaste'] —**castigation** /kásti gáysh'n/ *n* —**castigator** *n* —**castigatory** /kásti gáytəri/ *adj*

SYNONYMS See *criticize*.

Castile /ka steel/ central region of Spain that formed the core of the Kingdom of Castile, under which Spain was united in the 15th and 16th centuries

Castile soap /ka steel-/ *n* hard white unperfumed soap made from olive oil and soda

Castilian /ka stílli ən/, **Castillan** *n* **1.** the standard form of Spanish, based on the dialect spoken in Castile, Spain **2.** somebody who comes from Castile, Spain —**Castilian** *adj*

casting /káːsting/ *n* **1.** MAKING OF OBJECTS USING MOULDS the making of a solid object by pouring molten metal, glass, or plastic into a mould and allowing it to cool **2.** MANUF, ARTS OBJECT MADE WITH MOULD an object made using a mould **3.** FISHING THROW OF FISHING LINE the throwing out of a fishing line or net **4.** SOMETHING THROWN something that is thrown out or thrown off **5.** ARTS SELECTION PROCESS FOR PERFORMERS the choosing of actors or other performers for a drama, dance, or other production, usually by audition, interview, or screen test **6.** ARTS CHOICE OF PERFORMERS the choice of actors or other performers for roles in a drama, dance, or other production, especially as seen as a feature of a particular production ○ *The script was very sharp but the casting was terrible.*

casting couch *n* the granting of usually sexual favours in return for work in a film, television, or other production (*informal*)

casting vote *n* the deciding vote in a ballot or debate, cast by the chairperson or presiding officer when votes for and against something are equally divided

cast iron *n* iron with a high carbon content, so that it is hard but brittle, and must be shaped by casting, rather than by hammering or beating

cast-iron *adj* **1.** METALL OF CAST IRON made from cast iron **2.** VERY STRONG extremely strong or resistant ○ *a politician with a cast-iron will* **3.** ALLOWING NO CHANGE not permitting any alteration of its terms ○ *a cast-iron agreement*

castle /káːss'l/ *n* **1.** FORTRESS a large fortified building or complex of buildings, usually with tall solid walls, battlements, and a permanent garrison, built especially during the Middle Ages **2.** FORTIFIED HOUSE especially in the 18th and 19th centuries, a large magnificent house built to resemble a fortified castle of the past **3.** PRIVATE REFUGE the building, property, or place to which somebody, especially the owner, turns for privacy or refuge **4.** CHESS same as **rook**[2] ■ *vti* (**-tles**, **-tling**, **-tled**) CHESS MOVE KING AND ROOK in chess, to move the king two squares to the left or right and move the nearest rook over the king to the adjacent square on the opposite side [Pre-12C. < Latin *castellum* 'fortified village' < *castrum* 'fortified place'] ◇ **build castles in the air** *or* **in Spain** to have dreams or plans that are extremely unlikely to be realized

Castlebar /káːss'l baːr/ town in County Mayo, western Republic of Ireland. Population: 10,287 (2002).

castled /káːss'ld/ *adj* ARCHIT same as **castellated** (sense 1)

Castlereagh /káːss'l ray/ **1.** district in eastern Northern Ireland. Capital: Belfast. Population: 66,488 (2001). Area: 85 sq. km/33 sq. mi. **2.** river in northern New South Wales, Australia, that rises in the Warrumbungle Range and joins the Macquarie River west of Walgett. Length: 550 km/342 mi.

Castlereagh, **Robert Stewart**, **2nd Marquis of Londonderry** (1769–1822) Irish-born British government official and diplomat. As foreign secretary (1812–22), he secured long-lasting European peace at the Congress of Vienna (1814–15).

cast net *n* a round or cone-shaped net thrown by anglers and withdrawn by means of lines attached to its opening

castoff /káːst of/ *n* **1.** somebody or something that has been rejected or abandoned because no longer considered useful or attractive (*often used in the plural*) ○ *I don't want your old castoffs!* **2.** a calculation of the length of a piece of text made before fitting copy into available space

castor[1] /káːstər/ *n* **1.** SMALL WHEEL UNDER FURNITURE a small wheel on a mount that allows it to turn in all dir-

ections, attached under the corners of heavy furniture and other objects to make them easier to move **2.** SMALL CONDIMENT CONTAINER a small container with a perforated top or open mouth for sprinkling sugar, salt, or other condiments **3.** CONDIMENT STAND a small stand that holds condiment containers [Late 17C. Alteration of CASTER; probably associated with CASTOR[2]]

castor[2] /káːstər/ *n* **1.** BEAVER OIL a brown oily aromatic substance secreted from glands in a beaver's groin. Use: in medicine and perfumes. **2.** BEAVER FUR the fur of a beaver **3.** FUR HAT a hat made of beaver fur or imitation beaver fur [14C. Via French or Latin < Greek *kastōr* 'beaver']

Castor /káːstər/ *n* the second brightest star in the constellation Gemini

Castor and Pollux /-pólləks/ *npl* in Greek and Roman mythology, the twin sons of Leda and the brothers of Helen of Troy and Clytemnestra

castor bean *n* the poisonous seed of the castor-oil plant. Use: source of castor oil.

castor oil *n* a thin yellowish oil obtained from the seeds of the castor-oil plant. Use: laxative, lubricant. [Origin ?]

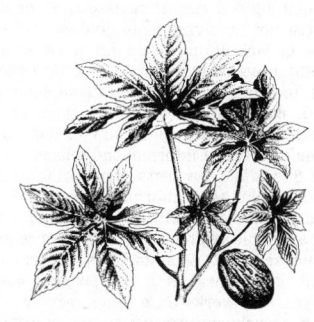

castor-oil plant

castor-oil plant *n* a tall tropical plant with large lobed leaves that is cultivated for ornament and for its seeds, from which castor oil is produced. Native to: Africa. Latin name: *Ricinus communis*.

castor steering *n* a type of steering found in horse-drawn vehicles, steam wagons, traction engines, and trailers, in which the whole front axle swivels around a central point

castrametation /kástrəmə táysh'n/ *n* the creation and laying out of a military encampment [Late 17C. < French *castramétation* < Latin *castra metari* 'measure or mark out a camp']

castrate /ka stráyt/ (**-trates**, **-trating**, **-trated**) *vt* **1.** to remove the testicles of a man or male animal, making reproduction impossible. Animals are sometimes castrated to make them more docile and to prevent disease. **2.** to take away the strength, power, force, or vigour of somebody or something ○ *The department was castrated through heavy budget cuts.* [15C. < Latin *castrat-*, past participle of *castrare* 'cut off'] —**castrater** *n* —**castration** /ka stráysh'n/ *n*

castration complex *n* according to Freudian psychology, a subconscious fear in men of having their genitals removed as a punishment for wanting to have sexual intercourse with their mother

castrato /ka straːtō/ (*plural* **-ti** /-ti/ *or* **-tos**) *n* in the past, a male singer who was castrated before puberty in order to retain a soprano or alto voice [Mid-18C. < Italian, 'castrated one' < Latin *castrat-* (see CASTRATE)]

Castries /ka streess/ capital city of St Lucia. Population: 60,934 (1998).

Castro /kástrō/, **Cipriano** (1858–1924) Venezuelan national leader. He served as president after a coup until he himself was deposed (1899–1908).

Castro, **Fidel** (*b.* 1927) Cuban politician. He led the revolution that overthrew Fulgencio Batista and headed a Communist government as prime minister (1959–76), becoming president in 1976. See illustration on next page

> 'A revolution is not a bed of roses. A revolution is a struggle to the death between the future and the past.'
> [Fidel Castro, *Speech, Havana*; January 1961]

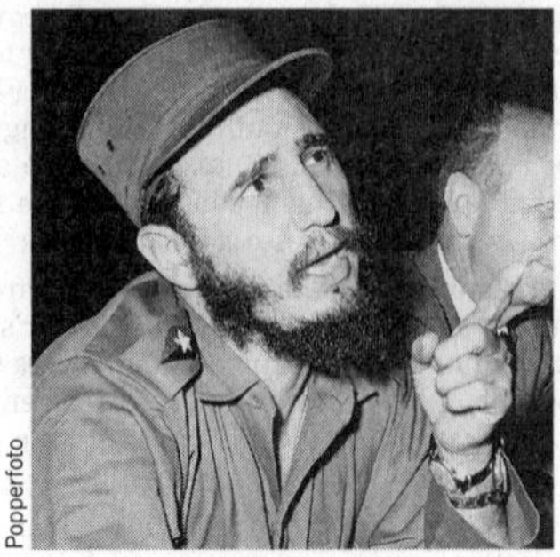

Fidel Castro

Castroism /kástrō izəm/ *n* the Communist political, social, and economic policies of Fidel Castro and his supporters —**Castroist** *n, adj* —**Castroite** *n, adj*

casual /kázhyoo əl/ *adj* **1. CHANCE OR UNPREMEDITATED** happening or done by chance or without prior thought or planning **2. KNOWN ONLY SLIGHTLY** known only slightly or involving only slight knowledge of somebody or something ○ *a casual acquaintance at work* **3. SUPERFICIAL** not involving emotional commitment or loyalty, or lacking in thoroughness or seriousness **4. LENIENT** possessing a permissive or lenient approach to things ○ *very casual about enforcing the rules* **5. INDIFFERENT** showing little interest or enthusiasm **6. NONCHALANT** cool, calm, or nonchalant in manner **7. NOT FORMAL** informal and relaxed ○ *a casual dinner* **8.** CLOTHING **COMFORTABLE** comfortable and suitable for wearing on informal occasions **9.** HR **OCCASIONAL OR TEMPORARY** relating to or taking on work that is available at irregular intervals or seasonally, with no security, benefits, or prospects of permanent employment ■ *n* HR **TEMPORARY WORKER** an employee who works on a temporary or seasonal basis ■ **casuals** *npl* **INFORMAL CLOTHES OR FOOTWEAR** informal comfortable clothes or shoes [14C. Directly or via French < Latin *casualis* < *casus* 'event'] —**casually** *adv* —**casualness** *n*

casualization /kázhyoo ə lī záysh'n/, **casualisation** *n* the changing of working practices so that workers are employed on a freelance and occasional basis instead of being offered full-time contracts ○ *the increasing casualization of labour*

casualty /kázhyoo əlti/ (*plural* **-ties**) *n* **1. ACCIDENT VICTIM** somebody who has a fatal accident or receives a serious injury **2.** MIL **INJURED OR DEAD SOLDIER** a member of the armed forces who is killed or injured during combat **3. VICTIM** somebody or something destroyed or suffering as an indirect result of a particular event or circumstances **4.** *Aus* **HOSPITAL EMERGENCY DEPARTMENT** a hospital's emergency department (*often before nouns*) ○ *rushed to casualty with multiple fractures* N Am term **emergency room** [15C. Alteration of medieval Latin *casualitas* 'chance' < *casualis* (see CASUAL)]

casualwear /kázhyoo əl wair/ *n* comfortable clothes suitable for wearing on informal occasions

casuarina /kázzyoo ə reénə, kázh-, -rínə/ (*plural* **-nas** or *same*) *n* a tree with hard, durable wood and needle-shaped leaves that form whorls at the end of short branches. Native to: Australia, parts of Asia. Genus: *Casuarina.* [Late 18C. < modern Latin < *casuarius* 'cassowary'; from the similarity of its branches to the bird's feathers]

casuist /kázzyoo ist/ *n* **1.** somebody, especially a theologian, who tries to settle questions of ethics or morals by applying general rules and principles to them **2.** a subtle, sophisticated, and sometimes deceptive reasoner, especially on moral issues (*disapproving*) [Early 17C. Via French < modern Latin *casuista* < Latin *casus* 'event'] —**casuistic** /kázzyoo ístik/ *adj* —**casuistical** *adj* —**casuistically** *adv*

casuistry /kázzyoo istri/ *n* **1.** the application of general rules and principles to questions of ethics or morals in order to resolve them **2.** the use of subtle, sophisticated, and sometimes deceptive argument and reasoning, especially on moral issues, in order to justify something or mislead somebody (*disapproving*)

casus belli /káassōoss béll ee/ (*plural same*) *n* a situation or event that causes, or is the pretext for starting, a war or other conflict (*formal*) [< modern Latin, 'occasion of war']

cat /kat/ *n* **1. FURRY ANIMAL THAT PURRS AND MIAOWS** a small domesticated mammal that has soft fur, sharp claws, pointed ears, and, usually, a long furry tail, and makes characteristic purring or miaowing sounds. Cats are widely kept as pets or to catch mice. Latin name: *Felis catus.* **2.** same as **big cat 3. OFFENSIVE TERM** an offensive term for a woman who is regarded as spiteful or malicious (*informal insult*) **4.** *N Am* **MAN** a man (*dated slang*) ○ *He's a real cool cat.* **5.** NAUT **ANCHOR TACKLE OR CATHEAD** a set of heavy tackle used for raising an anchor to the cathead, or the cathead itself **6.** NAVY same as **cat-o'-nine-tails 7.** FISH same as **catfish 8.** same as **catamaran** (*informal*) **9.** same as **catboat** (*informal*) **10.** AUTOMOT same as **catalytic converter** (*informal*) **11.** same as **prostitute** *n* (sense 1) (*archaic*) ■ *v* (**cats, catting, catted**) **1.** *vt* NAUT **RAISE ANCHOR** to raise the anchor to the cathead **2.** *vi* **VOMIT** to vomit (*informal*) ■ *adj regional* **BAD** extremely bad (*slang*) ○ *That game was cat! We lost 5 nil.* [Old English *catt(e)* < Germanic] ◇ **has the cat got your tongue?** used to prompt somebody to speak or to ask the reason for his or her silence ◇ **let the cat out of the bag** to disclose secret or confidential information, usually accidentally ◇ **like a cat on hot bricks** extremely nervous or agitated ◇ **play cat and mouse with somebody** to treat somebody who is in your power in such a way that he or she does not know what you are going to do next ◇ **put** *or* **set the cat among the pigeons** to cause trouble ◇ **rain cats and dogs** to rain very heavily (*informal*) ◇ **when the cat's away the mice will play** when somebody in authority is absent, those he or she is in charge of will misbehave

CAT *abbr* **1.** AVIAT clear-air turbulence **2.** EDUC College of Advanced Technology **3.** FIN computer-aided trading **4.** MED computerized axial tomography

cata- *prefix* **1.** down, apart ○ *catabolism* ○ *catalysis* **2.** against [< Greek *kata*]

catabolism /kə tábbəlizəm/, **katabolism** *n* the production of energy through the conversion of complex molecules into simpler ones [Late 19C. < Greek *katabolē* 'throwing down' < *ballein* 'to throw'] —**catabolic** /káttə bóllik/ *adj* —**catabolically** *adv*

catabolite /kə tábbə līt/ *n* a product of catabolism, especially a waste product

catachresis /káttə kreéssiss/ *n* the incorrect use of words, e.g. by mixing metaphors or applying terminology wrongly [Mid-16C. Via Latin < Greek *katakhrēsis* < *katakhrēsthai* 'to misuse'] —**catachrestic** /-kréstik/ *adj* —**catachrestical** *adj* —**catachrestically** *adv*

cataclysm /káttəklizəm/ *n* **1.** a sudden and violent upheaval or disaster that causes great changes in society **2.** a terrible and devastating natural disaster such as a flood [Early 17C. Via French < Greek *kataklusmos* 'deluge' < *kluzein* 'wash'] —**cataclysmal** /káttə klízm'l/ *adj* —**cataclysmic** *adj* —**cataclysmically** *adv*

catacomb /káttə koom, -kōm/ *n* (*often used in the plural*) **1.** an underground cemetery consisting of passages or tunnels with rooms and recesses used as burial chambers leading off them. In ancient Rome, Christians used catacombs for burial. **2.** an underground network of passages or tunnels [Pre-12C. Via French < late Latin *catacumbas,* subterranean cemetery of St Sebastian in Rome]

catadromous /kə táddrəməss/ *adj* describes fish such as eels that spend most of their lives in fresh water but migrate to salt water to breed [Late 19C. <CATA- after ANADROMOUS]

catafalque /káttə falk/ *n* a raised and decorated platform on which the coffin of a distinguished person lies in state before or during a funeral [Mid-17C. Via French < Italian *catafalco*]

~~**catagory**~~ incorrect spelling of **category**

Catalan /káttə lan/ *n* **1.** the Romance language of Catalonia and the Balearic Islands, Spain, also spoken in Andorra and the French department of Roussillon. Native speakers: 7 million. **2.** somebody who comes from Catalonia —**Catalan** *adj*

catalase /káttə layz, -layss/ *n* an antioxidant enzyme in living cells [Early 20C. < CATALYSIS] —**catalatic** /káttə láttik/ *adj*

catalepsy /káttə lepsi/ *n* actual or apparent unconsciousness during which muscles become rigid and remain in any position in which they are placed. The condition occurs naturally in diseases such as schizophrenia or epilepsy and can be induced by hypnosis or drugs. [14C. Directly or via French < late Latin *catalepsia* < Greek *katalēpsis* 'seizure' < *katalambanein* 'seize upon' < *lambanein* 'seize'] —**cataleptic** /káttə léptik/ *adj* —**cataleptically** *adv*

catalexis /káttə léksiss/ *n* the lack of one syllable in the final foot of a line of verse [Mid-19C. < Greek *katalēxis* 'termination' < *katalēgein* 'leave off' < *lēgein* 'cease'] —**catalectic** /-léktik/ *adj*

catalog *n* **1.** US spelling of **catalogue 2.** *US* EDUC same as **prospectus** (sense 1)

catalogue /káttə log/ *n* **1.** COMM **LIST OF GOODS FOR SALE** a list of priced and illustrated items for sale, presented in book form or in other formats including CD-ROM or video **2. EXHIBITION GUIDE** a booklet that lists and often illustrates the objects on show at an exhibition **3.** LIBRARIES **LIST OF BOOKS** a list of the holdings in a library, usually arranged according to subject, title, or author **4. SERIES OF THINGS** a list of things or events that relate to an issue or person, especially those that are unpleasant or undesirable ○ *a catalogue of disasters* ■ *v* (**-logues, -loguing, -logued**) **1.** *vti* **MAKE CATALOGUE OF ITEMS** to classify and list items to form a catalogue **2.** *vt* **PUT SOMETHING IN CATALOGUE** to enter something in a catalogue ○ *I have catalogued all the new additions to the collection.* **3.** *vt* **LIST SERIES OF THINGS OR EVENTS** to list or describe a series of related events, items, or qualities ○ *a history of the twentieth century that catalogues many examples of human ingenuity* [15C. Via French < Greek *katalogos* 'list' < *katalegein* 'pick out' < *legein* 'choose'] —**cataloguer** *n*

catalogue raisonné /káttə log ráyzə náy/ (*plural* **catalogues raisonnés** /*pronunc. same*/) *n* a detailed list of works by a particular artist, especially one produced to accompany an exhibition or collection [Late 18C. < French, 'reasoned catalogue']

Catalonia /káttə lṓni ə/ autonomous region in northeastern Spain. It contains the provinces of Barcelona, Girona, Lléida, and Tarragona. Capital: Barcelona. Population: 6,343,110 (2002). Area: 32,113 sq. km/12,399 sq. mi. Catalan name **Catalunya**. Spanish name **Cataluña** —**Catalonian** *adj, n*

catalpa /kə tálpə/ *n* a tree with large heart-shaped leaves and long thin pods. Flowers: creamy, bell-shaped, in clusters. Native to: North America, Asia. Genus: *Catalpa.* [Mid-18C. < Creek *katalpa* < *ka* 'head' + *talpa* 'wing', from the shape of the flower]

Catalunya /káttə lo͝onyə/, **Cataluña** ➧ **Catalonia**

catalyse /káttə līz/ (**-lyses, -lysing, -lysed**) *vt* **1.** to increase the rate of a chemical reaction by the action or use of a catalyst **2.** to cause a particular thing to happen, or bring about a particular state of affairs ○ *The hearings have catalysed the passage of financial reforms.* [Late 19C. < CATALYSIS]

catalyser /káttə līzər/ *n* AUTOMOT ➧ **catalytic converter**

catalysis /kə tálləssiss/ (*plural* **-yses** /-ə seez/) *n* an increase in the rate of a chemical reaction as a result of the action or use of a catalyst [Mid-17C. Via modern Latin, 'dissolution' < Greek *katalusis* < *kataluein* 'dissolve' < *luein* 'set free']

catalyst /káttəlist/ *n* **1.** a substance that increases the rate of a chemical reaction without itself undergoing any change **2.** somebody or something that makes a change happen or brings about an event ○ *The quarrel acted as a catalyst for the breakup of their partnership.* [Early 20C. < CATALYSIS]

catalytic /káttə líttik/ *adj* involving or causing an increase in the rate of a chemical reaction by the action or use of a catalyst [Mid-19C. < Greek *katalutikos* 'able to dissolve' < *katalusis* (see CATALYSIS)] —**catalytically** *adv*

catalytic converter *n* in the exhaust system of a motor vehicle, a chamber in which gases mix with air so that pollutants such as carbon monoxide can be oxidized. The chamber contains a platinum-iridium catalyst. See illustration on next page

catalytic cracker *n* an oil-refinery device that breaks down large molecules from crude oil into smaller ones that are useful as fuel, using heat and a catalyst to lower the required temperature

catalyze *vt* CHEM US spelling of **catalyse**

catamaran /káttəmə rán/ *n* **1.** a sailing boat or engine-

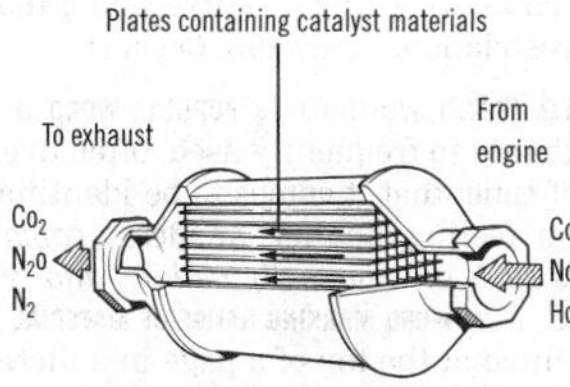

Plates containing catalyst materials
To exhaust
From engine
CO_2
N_2O
N_2
Co
Nox
Hc

catalytic converter

powered boat that has two identical hulls fixed together by a rigid framework **2.** a simple raft made from logs or floats tied together [Early 17C. < Tamil *kaṭṭumaram* 'tied wood']

catamite /káttə mīt/ *n* a boy kept by a man for sexual intercourse (*literary*) [Late 16C. Via Latin *catamitus* < Greek *Ganumēdēs* 'Ganymede']

catamount /káttə mownt/, **catamountain** /-mowntin/ *n* VERTEB same as **puma** [Mid-17C. < *cat of the mountain*]

cat-and-mouse *adj* cruel or sadistic, especially in exploiting, compounding, and enjoying somebody else's suffering or fear

cataphora /kə táffərə/ *n* the use of a word or phrase, usually a pronoun, that refers to something mentioned later, as does 'it' in 'It's easy to make mistakes' [Late 20C. Blend of CATA- + ANAPHORA] —**cataphoric** /káttə fórrik/ *adj*

cataphoresis /káttəfə reéssiss/ (*plural* **-reses** /-reésseez/) *n* SCI same as **electrophoresis** [Late 19C. < CATA- + Greek *phorēsis* 'being carried'] —**cataphoretic** /-fə réttik/ *adj* —**cataphoretically** *adv*

cataplasia /káttə pláyzi ə/ *n* the degeneration of cells or tissue to a more primitive or undeveloped form —**cataplastic** /-plástik/ *adj*

cataplexy /káttə pleksi/ *n* the sudden temporary inability to move, caused by shock, fear, or ecstasy [Late 19C. < Greek *kataplēxis* 'stupefaction' < *kataplēssein* 'strike down' < *plēssein* 'strike'] —**cataplectic** /káttə pléktik/ *adj*

catapult /káttə pult/ *n* **1.** DEVICE FOR FIRING STONES a Y-shaped device of wood, plastic, or metal with a piece of elastic stretched between the two top points of the Y, used for firing stones or pellets. N Am term **slingshot 2.** ARMS PLANE OR MISSILE LAUNCHER a mechanism on an aircraft carrier or warship, used to launch planes or missiles **3.** ARMS, HIST MEDIEVAL WEAPON a large heavy war machine used in medieval times to hurl large stones at an enemy ■ *v* (**-pults, -pulting, -pulted**) **1.** *vti* HURL SOMETHING to throw something with great force from a catapult (*often passive*) ○ *The fighters were catapulted from the carrier at 30-second intervals.* **2.** *vti* FLING OR BE FLUNG to throw somebody or something violently into the air by collision, impact, or a force that has an effect like a catapult, or be thrown in this way ○ *They were catapulted out of their seats by the force of the impact.* **3.** *vt* CHANGE CIRCUMSTANCES FOR SOMEBODY to thrust somebody unexpectedly and suddenly into a particular situation ○ *the hit that catapulted her to fame at the tender age of fifteen* [Late 16C. Directly or via French < Latin *catapulta* < Greek *katapeltēs* < *pallein* 'hurl']

cataract /káttə rakt/ *n* **1.** OPHTHALMOL EYE DISEASE an eye disease in which the lens becomes covered in an opaque film that affects sight, eventually causing total loss of sight. The condition usually affects older people and is generally found in both eyes to varying degrees. It can be treated surgically by replacing the lens with an artificial implant. **2.** OPHTHALMOL FILM OVER EYE LENS the lens of the eye or the membrane surrounding it (**capsule**) that has become opaque as a result of disease **3.** GEOG WATERFALL a series of river rapids and small waterfalls with only moderate vertical drop (*literary*) **4.** FLOOD a heavy downpour of rain or a great flood (*literary*) [15C. < Latin *cataracta* 'portcullis' < Greek *kataraktēs* 'down-dashing' < *katarassein* 'dash down' < *arassein* 'to strike']

catarrh /kə taar/ *n* inflammation of a mucous membrane, especially in the nose or throat, causing an increase in the production of mucus, as happens in the common cold [15C. Via French *catarrhe* < Greek *katarrhous* < *katarrhein* 'flow down' < *rhein* 'flow'] —**catarrhal** *adj* —**catarrhous** *adj*

catarrhine /káttə rīn/ *adj* describes primates that have nostrils set close together and facing downwards ■ *n* an animal with nostrils set close together and facing downwards, e.g. a human or an ape. Suborder: Catarrhini. [Mid-19C. < CATA- + Greek *rhinos* 'nose']

catastrophe /kə tástrəfi/ *n* **1.** DISASTER a terrible disaster or accident, especially one that leads to great loss of life **2.** TOTAL FAILURE an absolute failure, often in humiliating or embarrassing circumstances **3.** THEATRE RESOLUTION OF PLOT the concluding part of the action in a drama, especially a classical tragedy, when the plot is resolved **4.** GEOL VIOLENT SEISMIC CHANGE a sudden and violent change in the Earth's crust caused by an earthquake, flood, or any other natural process **5.** INSUR EVENT CAUSING HUGE INSURANCE CLAIM an event causing losses of insured property above a specific monetary limit and affecting a substantial number of policyholders and insurers [Mid-16C. Via Latin *catastropha* < Greek *katastrophē* 'overturning' < *katastrephein* 'overturn' < *strephein* 'turn']

catastrophic /káttə strόffik/ *adj* **1.** DISASTROUS causing or liable to cause widespread damage or death ○ *The rapid spread of the infection had a catastrophic effect on livestock.* **2.** AWFUL completely unsuccessful or very bad ○ *The party was a catastrophic affair.* **3.** *US* HEALTH SERVICES LIFE-THREATENING AND REQUIRING EXPENSIVE TREATMENT so serious in nature as to require extensive, long-term, and expensive medical treatment ○ *catastrophic illnesses* —**catastrophically** *adv*

catastrophism /kə tástrəfizəm/ *n* **1.** a theory, now discarded, that the geological features of Earth were formed by a series of sudden violent catastrophes rather than a gradual evolutionary process. A more recent version of this theory holds that the evolutionary process of geological development has on occasions been supplemented by such catastrophes. **2.** an outlook or attitude that foresees disaster as the only possible outcome of any action or situation —**catastrophist** *n*

catatonia /káttə tōni ə/ *n* a condition, often associated with schizophrenia, characterized by periods of inertia or apparent stupor and rigidity of the muscles [Late 19C. < CATA- + Greek *tonos* 'tone']

catatonic /káttə tónnik/ *adj* **1.** in a state of inertia or apparent stupor often associated with schizophrenia, characterized by rigidity of the muscles **2.** in a stupefied or unconscious state, especially one caused by drunkenness (*informal*) —**catatonically** *adv*

catawba /kə táwbə/ *n* **1.** a fruity red wine made from a variety of black grape grown in the eastern United States **2.** a reddish-coloured variety of the fox grape. Native to: North America. Use: wine production. [Early 19C. After the *Catawba* River in North and South Carolina]

catbird /kát burd/ *n* a songbird with dark-grey feathers and a black cap whose call sounds like the cry of a cat. Native to: North America. Latin name: *Dumetella carolinensis.*

catbird seat *n N Am* a position or situation that gives somebody power and an edge over others, especially competitors or opponents (*informal*) [Origin ?]

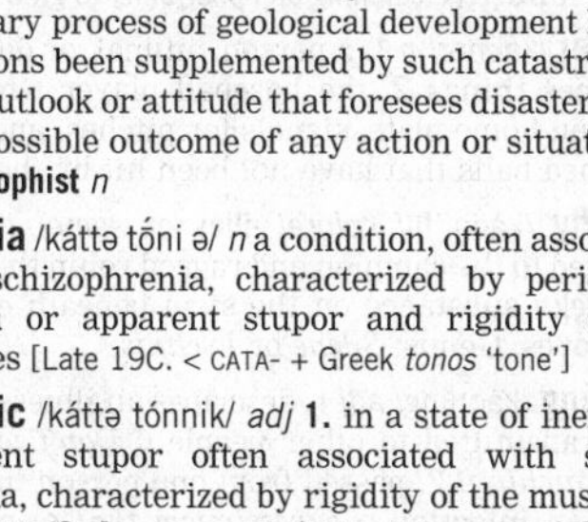

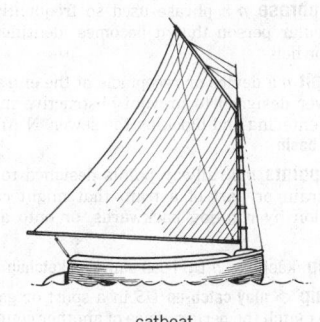

catboat

catboat /kát bōt/ *n* a sailing boat that is broad across the beam and has a single sail on a mast positioned near the front [Late 19C. Origin ?]

cat burglar *n* a burglar who, using stealth and agility, breaks into properties, especially through high windows or small openings [< the burglar's agility, likened to that of a cat]

catcall /kát kawl/ *n* a whistle or shout expressing disapproval or dislike, especially at a live performance [Mid-17C. < the resemblance to cats' nocturnal cries] —**catcall** *vti*

catch /kach/ *v* (**catches, catching, caught** /kawt/) **1.** *vti* STOP SOMETHING WITH HANDS to take hold of or stop something that is travelling through the air **2.** *vt* COLLECT FALLING OBJECTS FROM BELOW to collect from below something such as rain that is falling **3.** *vt* GRASP SOMEBODY OR SOMETHING to take tight hold of somebody or something suddenly ○ *He caught me by the shoulder.* **4.** *vt* CAPTURE ANIMAL to capture or trap an animal **5.** *vt* CAPTURE CRIMINAL to capture somebody, especially a criminal or somebody suspected of wrongdoing, after a search or chase ○ *Have they caught the culprit?* **6.** *vt* REACH SOMEBODY OR SOMETHING to reach or get alongside a person or vehicle moving ahead, usually at speed ○ *trying to catch the car in front* **7.** *vt* GET ON BOARD PUBLIC TRANSPORT to arrive in time to board a bus, train, or other form of public transport ○ *I have a plane to catch.* **8.** *vti* GET DISEASE to become infected with a disease **9.** *vt* SURPRISE SOMEBODY DOING WRONG to surprise or stop somebody who is in the act of doing something illegal or forbidden ○ *He caught her taking money from the till.* ○ *caught me reading her diary* **10.** *vt* SURPRISE SOMEBODY DOING SOMETHING EMBARRASSING to surprise or observe somebody who is doing something considered embarrassing, impolite, or private ○ *I caught him gazing at himself in the mirror.* **11.** *vt* ATTRACT SOMEBODY'S ATTENTION to attract the interest or attention of others ○ *a campaign that had caught the nation's imagination* **12.** *vti* MANAGE TO HEAR SOMETHING to manage to hear what is being said ○ *I'm sorry, I didn't quite catch that.* **13.** *vt* UNDERSTAND SOMETHING to understand the right meaning of something ○ *He didn't seem to catch the drift of what was being said.* **14.** *vt* NOTICE SOMETHING SUBTLE OR FLEETING to notice something subtle in the way somebody is speaking or behaving that tells you how that person really feels ○ *I caught a note of sarcasm in his voice.* **15.** *vt* SEE PERFORMER OR PRODUCTION to see a particular television programme, film, or play, or see a particular person performing in something (*informal*) ○ *If you get the chance, try and catch the new production of 'Hamlet'.* **16.** *vt* MANAGE TO MEET SOMEBODY to manage to meet or talk to somebody, especially somebody who is very busy (*informal*) ○ *I was hoping to catch the doctor before she left.* **17.** *vt* GET SOMETHING YOU NEED to get food, drink, or rest only hurriedly or in small amounts (*informal*) ○ *We can stop and catch a bite to eat.* **18.** *vt* STRIKE SOMEBODY to strike somebody with a blow ○ *a blow that caught him on the side of the head* **19.** *vt* TAKE IMPACT OF SOMETHING to receive the impact or force from something such as a blow or the force of somebody's anger or emotions ○ *He caught the full impact of the blast.* **20.** *vti* ENTANGLE SOMETHING to entangle or hook something such as clothing on something sharp, or become entangled or hooked, sometimes resulting in damage ○ *She caught her blouse on a nail.* **21.** *vti* TRAP SOMETHING to trap something in an opening or door, or become trapped ○ *I caught my fingers in the letter box.* **22.** *vt* DELAY SOMEBODY to delay somebody or hold somebody up (*usually passive*) **23.** *vr* STOP YOURSELF FROM DOING SOMETHING to stop yourself from saying or doing something ○ *He was about to make a sarcastic remark but caught himself just in time.* **24.** *vt* SURPRISE SOMEBODY to take somebody by surprise (*usually passive*) ○ *She got caught in the rain and was absolutely soaked.* **25.** *vt* TRICK SOMEBODY to trick or deceive somebody ○ *a scam that caught most people who had any sense of compassion* **26.** *vt* REPRODUCE ASPECTS OF SOMETHING OR SOMEBODY to reproduce successfully the most typical aspects of somebody or something ○ *a novel that catches the mood of prewar Berlin* **27.** *vt* RECORD SOMETHING ON FILM to record somebody or something on film or tape ○ *the very first time this elusive bird has been caught on film* **28.** *vi* BE CARRIED BY EMOTION to be eager to do something, or reach for something eagerly ○ *She caught at the opportunity of making some extra cash.* **29.** *vi* BEGIN TO BURN to ignite, become alight, or begin to burn ○ *catch fire* **30.** *vi* PLAY BASEBALL AS CATCHER to act as catcher on a baseball team ○ *Clevenger will be catching again in the second game of the season.*

31. *vt* CRICKET **DISMISS BATSMAN** in cricket, to cause the person hitting the ball to be out by catching the ball before it reaches the ground **32.** *vt* **PLACE SOMETHING ON OR AGAINST SOMETHING** to put or rest something on or lean something against something else (*slang; used in Black English*) ■ *n* **1. ACT OF CATCHING SOMETHING** the catching of something such as a ball **2. SOMEBODY WHO CAN CATCH** a skilled catcher of something ○ *He missed the ball again! He's such a lousy catch!* **3. BALL GAME** a game in which people throw a ball to each other and catch it **4. MOVE IN BALL GAMES** a move in ball games such as cricket or rounders in which a player catches a ball hit by another before it touches the ground, forcing that person to retire **5. NUMBER OF THINGS CAUGHT** the amount or number of things caught, e.g. when fishing ○ *Not much of a catch today, I'm afraid.* **6. DEVICE THAT CLOSES OR FASTENS** a device for fastening something such as a door, window, or piece of jewellery **7. SNAG** a hidden or unexpected problem, especially one suspected to exist because everything seems too good to be true (*informal*) ○ *Okay, it sounds great: where's the catch?* **8. BREAK IN VOICE** a brief moment when somebody's voice becomes husky or unclear because of intense emotion ○ *There was a slight catch in his voice as he read out the letter.* **9. IDEAL OR DESIRABLE PERSON** somebody or something regarded as ideal or particularly desirable, especially as a marriage partner (*informal*) ○ *Her friends regarded Tom as quite a catch.* **10. HUMOROUS SONG** a round or canon with humorous, often risqué, words, popular in the 17th and 18th centuries [12C. < Anglo-Norman or Old French *cachier* 'chase' < Latin *captare* 'try to catch' < *capere* 'take'] —**catchable** *adj* ◇ **be caught short** to be taken by surprise and therefore put at a disadvantage ◇ **catch it** to get into trouble (*informal*) ◇ **catch somebody with his** *or* **her pants** *or* **trousers down 1.** to expose somebody in a very embarrassing situation, especially one that suggests hypocrisy or incompetence **2.** to surprise somebody in a state of unpreparedness at a time when alertness is required

catch on *vi* (*informal*) **1.** to become popular or widely used **2.** to understand a new idea, task, or process ○ *pretty slow to catch on*

catch out *vt* **1. DEVISE WAY TO SHOW SOMEBODY'S MISTAKES** to find ways of exposing errors or ignorance in order to embarrass somebody or show superiority (*informal*) ○ *He would try to catch me out by asking awkward questions during safety inspections.* **2. EXPOSE WRONGDOER** to catch somebody doing something wrong or illegal, especially when deliberately setting out to do so (*informal*) **3.** SPORTS **CATCH BALL HIT BY SOMEBODY** in baseball, rounders, or cricket, to catch a ball hit by a player while it is still in the air, forcing the player or the player's team to retire

catch up *v* **1.** *vti* **REACH SOMEBODY OR SOMETHING TRAVELLING AHEAD** to get alongside a person or vehicle that was moving ahead **2.** *vt* **PICK SOMETHING OR SOMEBODY UP** to quickly pick something or somebody up in the hands or arms ○ *He caught up all the papers and strode off.* **3.** *vi* **GET OR BRING UP TO DATE** to make up for lost time by working harder in order to be up to date ○ *I must catch up on my reading.* **4.** *vt* **ENGROSS SOMEBODY** to absorb somebody's attention completely (*usually passive*) ○ *I was so caught up in my work that I didn't have time for lunch.* **5.** *vt* **INVOLVE SOMEBODY UNHAPPILY** to involve somebody in something undesirable (*usually passive*) ○ *They were caught up in the whole messy affair even though they tried to stay out of it.* **6.** *vi Malaysia, Singapore* **STAY EVEN WITH** to progress at the same rate as somebody else **7.** *vi* **HEAR SOMEBODY'S NEWS** to speak to somebody in order to hear what he or she has been doing since the last meeting ○ *We spent an hour catching up with old friends.* ○ *enjoyed catching up on all their news*

catch up on *vt* to have a delayed effect on somebody ○ *Three nights without sleep is beginning to catch up on me.*

catch up with *vt* **1.** to find somebody who has committed a crime or done something wrong, especially after a search or chase ○ *By the time the police caught up with him, he had changed his name and moved to Brazil.* **2.** to finally have an effect on somebody who has, until now, seemed to be free from the usual consequences ○ *All those late nights will catch up with you eventually.*

catch-22 /-twenti tóo/ *n* a situation or predicament from which it is impossible to extricate yourself because of built-in illogical rules and regulations [After the novel *Catch-22* by Joseph Heller]

CULTURAL NOTE ***Catch-22***, a novel (1961) by US writer Joseph Heller. The title of this dark satire relates to the skewed military logic that entraps the protagonist, Yossarian, a pilot serving in Italy during World War II. He tries to get himself grounded by being pronounced insane, but is told that only an insane person would want to fly, and his desire not to fly proves that he is, in fact, sane, and so must continue to fly. The term ***Catch-22*** eventually came to have a more general meaning of a situation in which somebody is trapped by illogical conditions and restrictions.

catchall /kách awl/ *n* something that covers a wide range of possibilities, meanings, ideas, or situations (*often used before a noun*) ○ *one of those catchall phrases that doesn't really mean very much at all*

catch and release *n* a conservation policy adopted by some anglers whereby they release some or all of the fish they catch in order to sustain fish populations

catch-as-catch-can *n* **NO-HOLDS-BARRED WRESTLING** a style of wrestling in which most holds are permitted, including many that are not allowed in other wrestling styles ■ *adj N Am* **MAKING DO** making do with whatever is available ○ *We took a catch-as-catch-can approach to our summer holiday.* ■ *adv N Am* **USING WHAT COMES TO HAND** using whatever happens to be available ○ *The press conference was arranged catch-as-catch-can at very short notice.*

catch basin *n N Am* **1.** CIV ENG same as **catch pit 2.** an area or reservoir for catching drainage water or runoff

catch crop *n* a fast-growing crop grown between the harvest and planting of two main crops, between the rows of a main crop, or as a substitute after a crop failure [< catching an opportunity to grow it]

catcher /káchər/ *n* **1.** a person, animal, or device that catches things **2.** the baseball player who stands behind home plate, signals for pitches, and catches pitched balls that have not been hit by the batter

catchfly /kách flī/ (*plural* **-flies** or *same*) *n* a plant related to the campion and ragged robin that exudes a sticky substance on the stem beneath each pair of leaves. Genus: *Silene* or *Lychnis*.

catching /káching/ *adj* **1.** describes an illness that can be transmitted to other people ○ *Don't worry: it's not catching!* **2.** passed from one person to another like an infection ○ *a pessimism that seemed to be catching*

catchment /káchmənt/ *n* **1. RAINWATER RECEPTACLE** a structure, reservoir, or container for collecting rainwater **2. COLLECTED RAINWATER** the rainwater that collects in a specific container or area **3. COLLECTING OF RAINWATER** the collecting or catching of rainwater especially over an area of land surrounding a river or lake

catchment area *n* **1.** the area from which a particular school, hospital, or doctor will accept pupils or patients **2.** the area of land that drains rainfall into a river or lake

catchpenny /kách penni/ *adj* cheap and made to be sold quickly and easily without much regard for quality (*dated*)

catch phrase *n* a phrase used so frequently by a particular person that it becomes identified with him or her

catch pit *n* a device or receptacle at the entrance of a sewer designed to prevent obstructive material from entering and blocking the sewer. N Am term **catch basin**

catch points *npl* railway points designed to derail any train or part of a train that might cause a collision by running backwards, or onto another track

catchup /kách up/ *n US* FOOD same as **ketchup**

catch-up ◇ **play catch-up** *US* in a sport or game, to try to match the performance of another competitor

catchwater drain /kách wawtər-/ *n* a drain cut along the edge of high ground to catch water from it and divert it so that it does not run onto low-lying ground

catchweight /kách wayt/ *adj* describes a contest in a sport such as wrestling or horseracing that has no weight restrictions [Early 19C. Origin ?]

catchword /kách wurd/ *n* **1. POPULAR WORD** a word or phrase that is so frequently used, often over a short period of time, that it comes to be identified with a particular feeling, quality, or idea ○ *catchwords of the 1980s such as 'upwardly mobile' and 'yuppie'* **2.** *UK, ANZ, Can* **WORD MARKING RANGE OF MATERIAL COVERED** a word printed at the top of a page in a dictionary or other reference book, usually the first or last entry for that page. US term **guide word 3. BINDER'S CUE** the first word of a page of printed text repeated at the bottom right-hand corner of the previous page, originally placed there to draw the binder's attention to it **4.** THEATRE **ACTOR'S CUE** a cue for an actor to come on stage or to speak

catchy /káchi/ (**-ier, -iest**) *adj* **1. MEMORABLE** easy to remember because of having a simple and effective melody or wording **2. ATTRACTING ATTENTION** tending to attract interest or attention because of a notable, unique, or pleasing character or quality ○ *an attempt to come up with a catchy name for a new soft drink* **3. TRICKY** designed to catch people out or trip them up ○ *There were some catchy questions in the English paper.* **4. FITFUL** coming in spasmodic or irregular bursts ○ *light rain with catchy squalls of wind* —**catchiness** *n*

cat cracker *n* INDUST same as **catalytic cracker**

catechesis /kátti kéessiss/ *n* religious instruction given in advance of baptism or confirmation [Early 17C. Via ecclesiastical Latin < Greek *katēkhēsis* 'instruction by word of mouth' < *katēkhein* (see CATECHIZE)] —**catechetical** /kátti kéttik'l/ *adj*

catechin /káttəkin/ *n* a yellow crystalline substance. Use: in tanning and dyeing. Formula: $C_{15}H_{14}O_6$. [Mid-19C. < CATECHU]

catechise *vt* CHR another spelling of **catechize**

catechism /káttəkizəm/ *n* **1. QUESTION-AND-ANSWER TEACHING** instruction in the principles of Christianity using set questions and answers **2. RELIGIOUS QUESTIONS AND ANSWERS** the series of questions and answers that are used to test somebody's religious knowledge in advance of Christian baptism or confirmation **3. QUESTION-AND-ANSWER BOOK** a book containing questions and answers used to test the religious knowledge of somebody preparing for Christian baptism or confirmation **4. BODY OF PRINCIPLES FOLLOWED UNTHINKINGLY** a body of basic beliefs and principles followed unthinkingly **5. INTERROGATION** a close and intense session of questioning on a particular subject, especially forming part of an examination or an interrogation [Early 16C. < ecclesiastical Latin *catechismus* < ecclesiastical Greek *katēkhizein* (see CATECHIZE)] —**catechismal** /káttə kízm'l/ *adj*

catechist /káttəkist/ *n* an instructor in the basic principles of Christianity, especially one who teaches somebody preparing for baptism or confirmation —**catechistic** /káttə kístik/ *adj* —**catechistical** *adj*

catechize /káttə kīz/ (**-chizes, -chizing, -chized**), **catechise** (**-chises, -chising, -chised**) *vt* **1.** to instruct somebody in the basic principles of the Christian religion using questions and answers **2.** to question somebody closely, e.g. in an examination or interrogation [15C. Via ecclesiastical Latin *catechizare* < ecclesiastical Greek *katēkhizein* < *katēkhein* 'sound through' < *ēkhē* 'sound'] —**catechization** /káttə kī záysh'n/ *n* —**catechizer** *n*

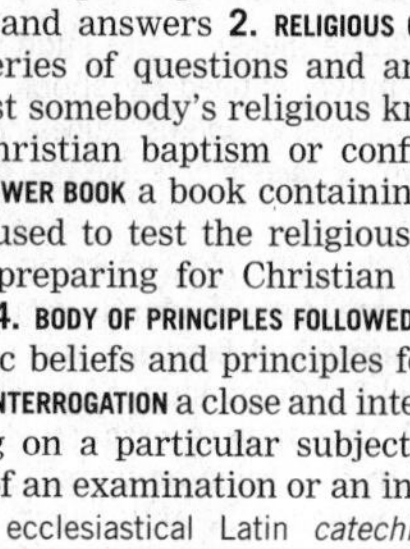

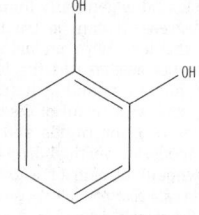

catechol

catechol /kátti kol, -chol/ n a colourless crystalline solid. Use: photographic developer, antioxidant, manufacture of dyes and pharmaceuticals. Formula: $C_6H_6O_2$. See illustration on previous page [Late 19C. < CATECHU]

catecholamine /káttə kólla meen/ n a compound that acts as a neurotransmitter or hormone

catechu /kátta choo, -shoo/ n an astringent water-soluble substance extracted from an Asian acacia tree. Use: in medicine, dyeing. [Late 17C. < modern Latin, alteration of Malay *kacu*]

catechumen /kátta kyoo men, -mən/ n somebody who receives instruction in preparation for Christian baptism or confirmation [14C. Directly or via French < ecclesiastical Latin *catechumenus* < Greek *katēkhoumenos* 'being instructed', form of *katēkhein* (see CATECHIZE)] —**catechumenical** /káttəkyoo ménnik'l/ adj —**catechumenism** n

categorical /kátta górrik'l/, **categoric** /kátta górrik/ adj **1.** leaving no room for doubt, question, or contradiction ○ *The press office has issued a categorical denial of these allegations.* **2.** involving or relating to the use of categories or categorization —**categorically** adv

categorical imperative n according to the moral philosophy of Immanuel Kant, an unconditional moral law applying to all rational beings and independent of all personal desires and motives

categorize /káttigə rīz/ (-**rizes**, -**rizing**, -**rized**), **categorise** (-**rises**, -**rising**, -**rised**) vt to place somebody or something in a particular category and define or judge the person or thing accordingly ○ *It was originally categorized as a cactus, but it's actually a succulent.* —**categorizable** adj —**categorization** /káttigə rī záysh'n/ n

category /káttəgəri/ (plural -**ries**) n a group or set of things, people, or actions that are classified together because of common characteristics ○ *There are choices available in the following categories: leisure, fitness, health.* [15C. Via late Latin < Greek *katēgoria* 'statement' < *katēgorein* 'speak against' < *agora* 'marketplace']

SYNONYMS See *type.*

catena /kə teénə/ (plural -**nae** /-nee/) n a series of connected commentaries on or excerpts of writings, especially comments on the Bible written by early Christian theologians [Mid-17C. < Latin, 'chain']

catenaccio /kátta náchi ō/ n in football, a strongly defensive formation involving one free defender positioned behind his or her team-mates [Late 20C. < Italian, literally 'door bolt' < Latin *catena* 'chain']

catenary /kə teénəri/ (plural -**ies**) n **1.** the curve adopted by a length of heavy cable, rope, or chain of uniform density, hanging between two points, or something with this shape **2.** a suspended overhead power cable that supplies current to trolleybuses, trams, and most electric trains [Mid-18C. < modern Latin *catenaria* < Latin *catena* 'chain'] —**catenary** adj

catenate /kátti nayt/ (-**nates**, -**nating**, -**nated**) vt **1.** to form something into a chain or a series of chains **2.** to form atoms of the same chemical element into a chain held together by chemical bonds [Early 17C. < Latin *catenat-*, past participle of *catenare* 'to chain' < *catena* 'chain']

cater /káytər/ (-**ters**, -**tering**, -**tered**) vti **1.** to provide what is wanted or needed in a particular situation or by a particular group of people ○ *We try to cater for all tastes in our bookshop.* **2.** to provide food and drink for a social or business function ○ *They've been asked to cater the wedding.* [Late 16C. Shortening of obsolete *acater* 'caterer' < Anglo-Norman *acateor* < *ac(h)ater* 'buy' < Latin *capere* 'take'] —**caterer** n

cater-cornered /kátter kawrnərd/, **cater-corner**, **catty-cornered** /kátti-/, **catty-corner** N Am adj DIAGONAL positioned or arranged diagonally ■ adv **1.** DIAGONALLY in a diagonal position or arrangement ○ *They sit cater-cornered in history class.* **2.** OPPOSITE diagonally opposite something or somebody else ○ *Their office is cater-cornered from the bank.* [Cater < dialect, 'diagonally' < French *quatre* 'four']

catering /káytəring/ n the provision of food and drink for the people at a social or business function ○ *a career in catering*

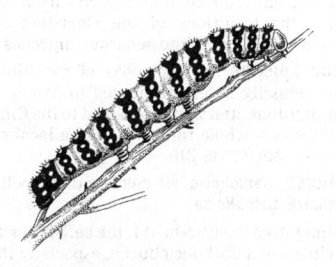
caterpillar

caterpillar /kátter pilər/ n the larva of a butterfly or moth, with a long soft body, many short legs, and often brightly coloured or spiny skin [15C. Alteration of assumed Old French *catepelose* < assumed late Latin *catta pilosa* 'hairy cat']

Caterpillar /kátter pillər/ tdmk a trademark for a continuous metal loop or belt made up of hinged links and fitted instead of wheels on tanks, bulldozers, and similar vehicles

~~caterpiller~~ incorrect spelling of **caterpillar**

caterwaul /kátter wawl/ vi (-**wauls**, -**wauling**, -**wauled**) **1.** YOWL to make a loud howling noise **2.** MAKE LOUD HARSH NOISE to make a loud noise that offends the ears ○ *a street musician caterwauling in the background while we tried to talk* ■ n YOWL a loud howl or cry [14C. Origin ?]

catfight /kát fīt/ n **1.** a fight that takes place among cats **2.** a vicious argument or fight, especially between women (*informal*)

catfish /kát fish/ (plural same or -**fishes**) n a scaleless, usually freshwater fish with long whiskers (**barbels**) around its mouth that are sensitive to touch, taste, and smell. Order: Siluriformes. [< its barbels, likened to a cat's whiskers]

cat flap n a piece of wood or plastic hinged at the top of an opening in a door to enable a pet cat to come and go as it pleases

catgut /kát gut/ n a tough thin cord made from the dried intestines of animals. Use: stringing musical instruments, surgical thread. [Late 16C. Probably < CAT (for unknown reasons)]

cath. abbr ELECTRONICS cathode

Cath. abbr **1.** cathedral **2.** Catholic

Cathar /káthər, -aar/ n a member of a medieval European heretical Christian sect who believed that salvation lay in the adoption of a spiritual way of life [Late 16C. Via medieval Latin *Cathari* 'Cathars' < Greek *katharoi* 'the pure' < *katharos* 'pure'] —**Catharism** n —**Catharist** n —**Catharistic** /káthə rístik/ adj

catharsis /kə thaárssiss/ (plural -**tharses** /-thaár seez/) n **1.** EMOTIONAL RELEASE an experience or feeling of spiritual release and purification brought about by an intense emotional experience **2.** EMOTIONAL PURIFICATION THROUGH GREEK TRAGEDY according to Aristotle, a purifying of the emotions that is brought about in the audience of a tragic drama through the evocation of intense fear and pity **3.** PSYCHOLOGICAL PURGING OF COMPLEXES in psychology, the process of bringing to the surface repressed emotions, complexes, and feelings in an effort to identify and relieve them, or the result of this process **4.** PURGING OF BOWELS cleansing or purging of the bowels [Early 19C. Via modern Latin < Greek *katharsis* < *kathairein* 'to purge' < *katharos* 'pure']

cathartic /kə thaártik/ adj **1.** PURIFYING producing a feeling of being purified emotionally, spiritually, or psychologically as a result of an intense emotional experience or therapeutic technique ○ *a film that had a truly cathartic effect on me* **2.** HAVING PURGATIVE EFFECT ON BOWELS describes a medicine that causes emptying of the bowels ■ n PURGATIVE MEDICINE a medicine that causes emptying of the bowels —**cathartically** adv

Cathay /ka tháy/ medieval name for China

cathead /kát hed/ n a horizontal wooden or iron beam projecting from a ship's bow, where the anchor is carried and hoisted [< CAT 'raise the anchor']

cathect /kə thékt, ka-/ (-**thects**, -**thecting**, -**thected**) vt to concentrate emotional or psychic energy on something such as an object, a person, or an idea [Mid-20C. Back-formation < *cathectic* < CATHEXIS] —**cathectic** adj

cathedra /kə theédrə/ (plural -**dras** or -**drae** /-dree/) n **1.** a bishop's official seat or throne **2.** the official rank, office, or jurisdiction of a bishop [15C. Via Latin < Greek *kathedra* < *kata* 'down' + *hedra* 'seat']

cathedral /kə theédrəl/ n BISHOP'S CHURCH a church that contains a bishop's throne and is the most important church in the bishop's diocese ■ adj **1.** OF BISHOP OR CATHEDRAL relating to, belonging to, or having a bishop or cathedral **2.** LIKE CATHEDRAL resembling or appropriate to a cathedral **3.** MADE BY BISHOP describes an official religious announcement made by a bishop or pope [13C. Via Old French < late Latin *cathedralis* < Latin *cathedra* (see CATHEDRA)]

cathepsin /kə thépsin/ n an enzyme that digests proteins after cell death [Early 20C. < German *Kathepsin* < Greek *kathepsein* 'to digest', literally 'boil down' < *hepsein* 'to boil']

Willa Cather

Cather /káthər/, **Willa** (1873–1947) US writer. Her novels include the Pulitzer Prize-winning *One of Ours* (1922). Full name **Cather, Willa Sibert**

> 'One cannot divine nor forecast the conditions that will make happiness; one only stumbles upon them by chance, in a lucky hour, at the world's end somewhere.'
> [Willa Cather, 'Le Lavandou', *Virago Book of Women Travellers*; 1996]

Catherine I /káthrin/ (1684–1727) empress of Russia (1725–27). An influential adviser to her husband, Peter the Great, she was proclaimed empress after his death. Born **Marta Skavronskaya**

Catherine (of Aragon) /káth'rin əv árrəgən/ (1485–1536) Spanish-born queen of England (1509–33) as the first wife of Henry VIII. The annulment of their marriage in 1533 precipitated the English Reformation.

> 'I came not into this realm as merchandise, nor yet to be married to any merchant.'
> [Catherine (of Aragon), Letter; 1533]

Catherine the Great

Catherine (the Great) (1729–96) German-born empress of Russia (1762–96). After deposing her husband, Tsar Peter III (1762) she extended and consolidated Russian power and culture.

> 'I shall be an autocrat: that's my trade. And the good Lord will forgive me: that's his.'
> [Attributed to Catherine (the Great)]

Catherine de Médicis /-də méddi chee, -me deéchi/, **Catherine de Medici** (1519–89) Italian-born queen of France (1547–59). As the widow of the French king Henry II she was regent of France (1560–63) and may have instigated the St Bartholomew's Day Massacre (1572).

Catherine wheel *n* **1.** a flat spiral-shaped firework that is fastened to a vertical surface with a central pin, on which it spins, shooting out sparks or flames, after being lit. N Am term **pinwheel 2.** in heraldry, a circular window divided by ribs radiating from the centre [Late 16C. After St *Catherine* of Alexandria, executed on a spiked wheel]

catheter /káthitər/ *n* a thin flexible tube that is inserted into a part of the body to inject or drain away fluid or to keep a passage open [Early 17C. Via late Latin < Greek *kathetēr* < *kathienai* 'send down' < *hienai* 'send']

catheterize /káthitə rīz/ (**-izes, -izing, -ized**), **catheterise** (**-ises, -ising, -ised**) *vt* to insert a catheter into a patient or a part of the body — **catheterization** /káthitə rī záysh'n/ *n*

cathexis /ka théksis, kə-/ (*plural* **-thexes** /-thék seez/) *n* the concentration of a great deal of psychological and emotional energy on one particular person, thing, or idea [Early 20C. < Greek *kathexis* 'holding' < *katekhein* 'hold fast' < *ekhein* 'to hold']

cathode /káthōd/ *n* **1.** NEGATIVE ELECTRODE the negative electrode of an electrolytic cell **2.** ELECTRON SOURCE the negatively charged source of electrons in a valve **3.** POSITIVE TERMINAL the positive terminal of a cell that is producing electrical energy by a chemical process that cannot be reversed [Mid-19C. < Greek *kathodos* 'way down' < *hodos* 'way'] —**cathodal** /ka thōd'l/ *adj* —**cathodally** *adv*

cathode ray *n* a stream of electrons that is emitted from a cathode in a vacuum tube

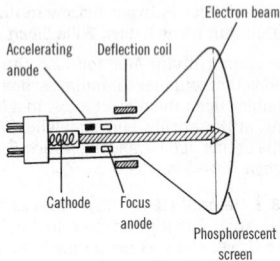

cathode ray tube

cathode ray tube *n* a vacuum tube in which a stream of electrons is produced and directed onto a fluorescent screen, e.g. in a television or visual display unit, creating images and text

cathodic /ka thóddik, ka thódik/ *adj* relating to or involving a cathode —**cathodically** *adv*

cathodic protection *n* the prevention of electrolytic corrosion in something metallic such as an underground pipe or a ship by making it the cathode in an electrolytic cell

cat hole *n* either of two holes at the stern of a ship through which large ropes are passed

catholic /káthlik, káthəlik/ *adj* **1.** ALL-INCLUSIVE including or concerned with all people **2.** USEFUL TO ALL useful or interesting to a wide range of people **3.** ALL-EMBRACING interested in or sympathetic to a wide range of things [14C. Via Latin < Greek *katholikos* 'universal' < *katholou* 'in general' < *kata* 'in regard to' + *holos* 'whole'] —**catholically** /kə thóllikli/ *adv*

Catholic /káthlik, káthəlik/ *adj* **1.** ROMAN CATHOLIC belonging to or characteristic of the Roman Catholic Church **2.** CHRISTIAN belonging to the community of all Christian churches **3.** OF HISTORICAL UNITED CHURCH belonging to the united Christian church that existed before its separation into different churches, or to any church that regards itself as continuing the traditions of that united church ■ *n* CHURCH MEMBER a member of the Roman Catholic Church [14C. Via ecclesiastical Latin < Greek *katholikē* (*ekklēsia*) 'universal (church)' < *katholikos* (see CATHOLIC)]

Catholic Church *n* **1.** CHR same as **Roman Catholic Church 2.** any church that regards itself as continuing the traditions of the Christian church before it was divided into separate churches

Catholic Epistles *npl* the books of the Bible that were originally letters attributed to James, Peter, John, and Jude, and were addressed to the Christian churches as a whole rather than to a local church [< CATHOLIC *adj* (sense 2)]

catholicise, Catholicise *vti* CHR another spelling of **catholicize, Catholicize**

Catholicism /kə thóllisizəm/ *n* **1.** the beliefs, doctrines, and rituals of a Catholic church, especially those of the Roman Catholic Church **2.** membership of a Catholic church, especially of the Roman Catholic Church

catholicity /káthə líssəti/ *n* **1.** wideness of range of tastes or interests **2.** the quality of including or applying to everyone or everything

Catholicity /káthə líssəti/ *n* CHR same as **Catholicism**

catholicize /kə thólli sīz/ (**-cizes, -cizing, -cized**), **catholicise** (**-cises, -cising, -cised**) *vti* to broaden something such as an idea, classification, or range of things, or become broader

Catholicize (**-cizes, -cizing, -cized**), **Catholicise** (**-cises, -cising, -cised**) *vti* to convert somebody to Catholicism, or be converted to Catholicism

cathouse /kát howss/ *n* N Am same as **brothel** (*slang*) [Mid-20C. < CAT 'prostitute']

Catiline /káttə līn/ (108?–62 BC) Roman conspirator. His plan to foment revolution by assassinating Marcus Cicero failed, and he was killed in battle with republican forces. Full name **Lucius Sergius Catilina**

cation /kát ī ən/ *n* an ion that has a positive electrical charge and is attracted towards the cathode in electrolysis [Mid-19C. < Greek *kata* 'down' + ION] —**cationic** /kát ī ónnik/ *adj*

catkin /kátkin/ *n* a long hanging furry cluster of tiny leaves and flowers without petals, produced by trees such as willows, birches, alders, and poplars [Late 16C. < obsolete Dutch *katteken* 'kitten']

Catlins /káttlinz/ scenic area of the southeastern part of the South Island, New Zealand, bounded by the Rata and Beresford ranges

cat litter *n* absorbent material that is used to fill a box in which a cat can urinate and defecate indoors

catmint /kátmint/ *n* a plant of the mint family with greyish leaves and a strong smell that attracts cats. Flowers: blue or white. Genus: *Nepeta*. N Am term **catnip**

catnap /kát nap/ *n* a short light sleep —**catnap** *vi* —**catnapper** *n*

catnip /kátnip/ *n* PLANTS same as **catmint** [Early 18C. < variant of obsolete *nep* 'catmint' < Latin *nepeta*]

cat-o'-nine-tails (*plural same*) *n* a whip with several, usually nine, strands of knotted rope, formerly used for flogging prisoners and as a punishment in the armed forces

catoptric /ka tóptrik/, **catoptrical** /-trik'l/ *adj* relating to or involving a mirror or reflection [Mid-16C. < Greek *katoptrikos* < *katoptron* 'something that looks back' < *op-* 'see']

catoptrics /kə tóptriks/ *n* the branch of optics that deals with mirrors and reflection (*takes a singular verb*)

Cato the Elder /káytō-/, **Marcus Porcius** (234–149 BC) Roman general and politician. As censor he fought against Greek cultural influence and against the luxury and immorality of Rome. Known as **the Censor**

'Carthage must be destroyed.'
[Marcus Porcius Cato the Elder, *Naturalis Historia* (Natural History), Pliny the Elder; 77]

Cato the Younger, **Marcus Porcius** (95–46 BC) Roman politician. Known as a defender of republican Roman values, he opposed the rise of Julius Caesar and committed suicide after his defeat by Caesar in Utica.

cat-o'-two-tails (*plural same*) *n regional* INSECTS same as **earwig** [< its two-tipped tail]

CAT scan *n* ANZ, N Am a diagnostic radiological scan in which cross-sectional images of a part of the body are formed through computerized axial tomography and shown on a computer screen. UK term **CT scan**

CAT scanner *n* ANZ, N Am a diagnostic radiological scanning machine used to make a CAT scan. UK term **CT scanner**

cat's cradle *n* a children's game in which a loop of string is threaded between the fingers of both hands in variable complex patterns [Origin ?]

cat scratch disease, **cat scratch fever** *n* an illness marked by fever and swollen lymph glands, thought to be caused by a bacterium transmitted to humans by the scratch of a cat

cat's eye *n* **1.** a gemstone, especially chrysoberyl or chalcedony, cut so as to reflect a narrow silvery band of light that seems to come from within **2.** a clear glass marble with a core or swirl of colour at the centre

Catseye /káts ī/ *tdmk* a trademark for a small reflecting device that is set into a road surface, kerb, or post to assist drivers at night in staying on the road or within lanes

Catskill Mountains /kátskil-/ group of mountains in the Appalachian system, in southeastern New York State, situated along the western bank of the River Hudson. Its highest peak is Slide Mountain, 1,281 m/4,204 ft.

cat's pajamas, **cat's meow** *n* N Am same as **cat's whiskers**

cat's paw *n* **1.** a victim of trickery who is manipulated into doing something for another person **2.** a hitch with two loops, used for attaching a rope to a hook

cat's tail *n* US same as **bulrush**

catsuit /kát soot, -syoot/ *n* a close-fitting one-piece garment that covers the whole body and has long sleeves and trouser legs [Because it gives a sleek outline]

catsup /kátsəp/ *n* FOOD same as **ketchup**

cat's whiskers *n* an excellent person or thing (*dated slang*) N Am term **cat's pajamas**

cattalo /káttəlō/ (*plural* **-loes** or **-los**) *n* BREED same as **beefalo** [Late 19C. Blend of CATTLE + BUFFALO]

cattery /káttəri/ (*plural* **-ies**) *n* a place where cats are bred or boarded

cattish /káttish/ *adj* same as **catty** —**cattishly** *adv* —**cattishness** *n*

cattle /kátt'l/ *npl* **1.** large domesticated mammals kept for the production of milk, meat, and hides, and also as draught animals. Cows and oxen are common types of cattle. Genus: *Bos*. **2.** people who are regarded as lacking individuality, especially a crowd of people regarded as an undifferentiated mass [13C. Via Anglo-Norman *catel* < Latin *capitale* 'funds']

cattle cake *n* a manufactured food for cattle, concentrated and formed into blocks

cattle dog *n* a dog that has a blue-grey coat, often speckled with black or brown, and black markings on the head, belonging to a breed developed in Australia for herding and guarding cattle

cattle-duffer *n* Aus somebody who steals cattle, usually modifying or removing their brands (*informal*) [Origin ?] —**cattle-duff** *vt*

cattle grid *n* a grid of metal bars over a shallow pit in a road, designed to stop animals but not people or vehicles, leaving an enclosed area. N Am term **cattle guard**

cattle guard *n* N Am same as **cattle grid**

cattleman /kátt'l man, -mən/ (*plural* **-men** /-men/) *n* a man who owns, raises, or works with cattle

cattleperson /kátt'l purss'n/ (*plural* **-persons** or **-people** /-peep'l/) *n* somebody who owns, raises, or works with cattle

cattle plague *n* AGRIC, MED same as **rinderpest**

cattle prod *n* an electrified rod designed for driving and controlling cattle by giving them mild shocks

cattle stop *n* NZ AGRIC same as **cattle grid**

cattle truck *n* a railway wagon for transporting livestock. N Am term **stock car**

cattlewoman /kátt'l woomən/ (*plural* **-men** /-wimmin/) *n* a woman who owns, raises, or works with cattle

cattleya /káttli ə/ (plural **-yas**) n an orchid that is a popular greenhouse plant. Flowers: purple, pink, or white. Native to: tropical America. Genus: *Cattleya*. [Early 19C. < modern Latin, after William *Cattley* (died 1832), British patron of botany]

cat train n N Am a series of linked sledges mounted on runners that is pulled over snow by a tractor with Caterpillar™ treads

catty /kátti/ (**-tier, -tiest**) adj **1.** saying spiteful or malicious things about somebody, especially in a subtle way **2.** resembling a cat, especially in being cautious or secretive —**cattily** adv —**cattiness** n

catty-cornered, **catty-corner** adj N Am same as **cater-cornered**

Catullus /kə túlləss/, **Gaius Valerius** (84?–54? BC) Roman poet. He wrote love poems addressed to 'Lesbia' and satirical attacks on Julius Caesar. —**Catullan** adj

> 'I hate and love.'
> [Gaius Valerius Catullus, *Carmina*; 60? BC]

CATV abbr MEDIA community antenna television

catwalk /kát wawk/ n **1.** a long narrow raised platform along which the models walk in a fashion show **2.** a narrow walkway high above the ground, e.g. along the side of a building or behind the stage in a theatre [Because cats can walk safely on narrow surfaces]

Caucasia /kaw káyzi ə, -zhə/ region of southeastern Europe and southwestern Asia, divided by the Caucasian Mountains and containing Georgia, Armenia, Azerbaijan, and southern Russia. Area: 400,000 sq. km/154,441 sq. mi.

Caucasian /kaw káyzi ən, -zh'n/ adj **1.** WHITE-SKINNED relating to people who are light-skinned or of European origin **2.** OF FORMER ETHNIC GROUP belonging to the light-skinned peoples of Europe, northern Africa, and western and southern Asia, formerly considered a distinct ethnic group (not in technical use) **3.** OF CAUCASIA relating to Caucasia, or its peoples, languages, or cultures **4.** OF LANGUAGES OF CAUCASIA belonging to two unrelated language families spoken in the area around the Caucasus Mountains ■ n **1.** WHITE PERSON somebody light-skinned or of European origin **2.** MEMBER OF FORMER ETHNIC GROUP a member of the people formerly termed Caucasian (not in technical use) **3.** SOMEBODY FROM CAUCASIA somebody who comes from Caucasia **4.** LANGUAGES OF CAUCASIA either of two unrelated language families spoken in the area around the Caucasus Mountains, Kartvelian or South Caucasian, and North Caucasian

Caucasoid /káwkə soyd, -zoyd/ (not in technical use) adj same as **Caucasian** adj (sense 2) ■ n same as **Caucasian** n (sense 2)

Caucasus Mountains /káwkəssəss-/ mountain range that is considered a boundary between Europe and Asia, extending through Georgia, Armenia, Azerbaijan, and southwestern Russia. Its highest peak is El'brus 5,642 m/18,510 ft.

caucus /káwkəss/ n **1.** POLITICAL MEETING a closed meeting of people from one political party, especially a local meeting to select delegates or candidates, or a meeting of party representatives at national level to decide policy **2.** SPECIAL-INTEREST GROUP a group of people, often within a larger group such as a legislative assembly, who unite to promote a particular policy or particular interests ■ vi (**-cuses, -cusing, -cused**) FORM CAUCUS to hold or meet in a caucus [Mid-18C. Origin ?]

caudal /káwd'l/ adj **1.** like or relating to a tail **2.** situated in or extending towards the hind part of the body [Mid-17C. < modern Latin *caudalis* < Latin *cauda* 'tail'] —**caudally** adv

caudal fin n the tail fin of a fish

caudal peduncle n FISH the narrow part of a fish's body just in front of the tail fin

caudate /káw dayt/, **caudated** /-daytid/ adj with a tail or an appendage like a tail [Early 17C. < medieval Latin *caudatus* < Latin *cauda* 'tail'] —**caudation** /kaw dáysh'n/ n

caudex /káw deks/ (plural **-dices** /-diseez/ or **-dexes**) n **1.** a trunk of a tree that bears leaves only at its apex, as in a palm or tree fern **2.** the swollen stem base of some nonwoody perennial plants that survives over the winter and from which new

growth is produced [Late 18C. < Latin, 'tree trunk', variant of *codex* 'block of wood']

caudillo /kow deé yō, -lyō/ (plural **-los**) n in a Spanish-speaking country, a military or political leader, especially a dictator [Mid-19C. Via Spanish, 'leader' < late Latin *capitellum* 'little head' < *caput* 'head']

caught past participle, past tense of **catch**

caul /kawl/ n **1.** the membrane surrounding the amniotic fluid, a part of which sometimes covers a baby's head when it is born **2.** same as **omentum** [14C. Origin ?]

cauldron /káwldrən/, **caldron** n a large metal pot in which liquids are boiled [13C. < Anglo-Norman, Old N French *caudron* < late Latin *caldaria* 'cooking pot' < Latin *calidus* 'hot']

cauliflower

cauliflower /kólli flow ər/ n **1.** a large solid head of tight white or light-green florets, eaten raw or cooked as a vegetable **2.** a plant related to the cabbage that produces cauliflowers. Latin name: *Brassica oleracea* var. botrytis. [Late 16C. Alteration of modern Latin *cauliflora* < Latin *caulis* 'stem' + *flor-* 'flower']

cauliflower cheese n a hot dish of cauliflower coated in cheese sauce

cauliflower ear n an ear that is permanently swollen and misshapen as a result of bleeding into the ear tissues after being repeatedly struck, usually in boxing

caulk /kawk/, **calk** vt (**caulks, caulking, caulked; calks, calking, calked**) **1.** MAKE BOAT WATERTIGHT to make a boat or the seams between its planks watertight by filling the seams with waterproof material such as pitch **2.** STOP SOMETHING UP to stop up the cracks or gaps in something such as a pipe or a window frame using a waterproof material ■ n SOMETHING USED TO FILL GAPS material used to make a boat watertight by filling in its seams, or to stop up the cracks or gaps in something. US term **caulking** [15C. < Old French *cauquer* 'to tread' < Latin *calcare* < *calc-* 'heel'] —**caulker** n

causal /káwz'l/ adj **1.** BEING OR INVOLVING CAUSE involving or being the cause of something else or the relationship of cause and effect **2.** GRAM EXPRESSING CAUSE expressing or indicating a cause or the relationship of cause and effect ■ n GRAM WORD EXPRESSING CAUSE a word or other grammatical element that expresses the reason or cause of something, or a relationship of cause and effect —**causally** adv

causalgia /kaw záljə/ n a persistent burning sensation of the skin, caused usually by injury to a peripheral nerve [Mid-19C. < Greek *kausos* 'burning'] —**causalgic** adj

causality /kaw zálləti/ n **1.** the principle that everything that happens must have a cause **2.** the action that causes an effect, or the ability to cause an effect

causation /kaw záysh'n/ n **1.** the fact that something causes an effect, or the action of causing an effect **2.** the relationship between a cause and its effect

causative /káwzətiv/ adj **1.** INVOLVING CAUSE AND EFFECT involving or being the cause of something or the relationship of cause and effect **2.** EXPRESSING CAUSE describes verbs that express the action of something causing something else ■ n VERB EXPRESSING CAUSE a causative verb, or a form or class of causative verbs —**causatively** adv —**causativeness** n

cause /kawz/ n **1.** WHAT MAKES SOMETHING HAPPEN a person

or thing that makes something happen or exist or is responsible for something that happens ○ *the cause of all the uproar* **2.** REASON a reason or grounds for doing or feeling something ○ *no cause for complaint* **3.** PRINCIPLE a principle or idea that people believe in or work for **4.** INTEREST the interests and aims of a group of people **5.** LEGAL CASE a lawsuit, or the reason that a suit is brought in a court of law **6.** DISCUSSION SUBJECT something under discussion or to be decided (archaic) ■ vt (**causes, causing, caused**) BE REASON FOR SOMETHING to make something happen or exist, or be the reason for somebody doing something or for something happening [13C. Via Old French < Latin *causa* 'reason, motive'] —**causability** /káwzə bílləti/ n —**causable** adj —**causeless** adj —**causer** n

CULTURAL NOTE *Rebel Without a Cause*, a film (1955) by US director Nicholas Ray. The film that made actor James Dean a symbol of an alienated generation, it is the story of Jim, a youth who seems unable to stay out of trouble. His attempts to win the affections of a local girl, Judy, lead to conflict with her boyfriend and, ultimately, tragedy.

'cause /kəz, koz/ conj because (informal) [15C. Shortening]

cause célèbre /kóz sə lébbrə, káwz-/ (plural **causes célèbres** /kóz sə lébbrəz, káwz-/) n a legal case or public controversy that arouses great interest and becomes famous because of the issues or the people involved [< French, 'celebrated case']

causerie /kózəri/ n **1.** a short piece of writing in a light informal style **2.** an informal conversation (literary) [Early 19C. < French < *causer* 'to chat' < Latin *causari* 'discuss' < *causa* 'case, subject']

causeway /káwz way/ n **1.** a raised path or road through a marsh or water or across land that is sometimes covered by water **2.** a road or path with a paved or cobbled surface [15C. < archaic *causey* 'causeway' (via Anglo-Norman *caucie* < medieval Latin *calciata* (via) 'paved (road)' < Latin *calx* 'limestone') + WAY]

Causeway Coast /káwz way-/ region in northeastern Northern Ireland that includes the Giant's Causeway, a World Heritage Site and one of Northern Ireland's top tourist sites

caustic /káwstik/ adj **1.** SARCASTIC very sarcastic and intended to mock, offend, or belittle somebody **2.** CORROSIVE corrosive or burning by chemical action ■ n **1.** SUBSTANCE THAT CORRODES a substance that can corrode or burn away other substances by chemical action, especially a strong alkali **2.** CURVE FORMED BY REFLECTIONS a peaked curve formed on a plane by parallel light rays reflected or refracted from a cylindrical or spherical surface. Caustics can sometimes be seen on the surface of drinks in glazed mugs or cups, or on the base of the mug or cup when empty. [14C. Via Latin < Greek *kaustikos* < *kaustos* 'combustible' < *kaiein* 'to burn'] —**caustical** adj —**caustically** adv —**causticity** /kaw stíssəti/ n

SYNONYMS See *sarcastic*.

caustic potash n CHEM same as **potassium hydroxide**

caustic soda n CHEM same as **sodium hydroxide**

cauterize /káwtə rīz/ (**-izes, -izing, -ized**), **cauterise** (**-ises, -ising, -ised**) vt to seal a wound, or destroy damaged or infected tissue, with a heated instrument, a laser, an electric current, or a caustic substance [14C. < French *cautériser* < Latin *cauterium* (see CAUTERY)] —**cauterization** /káwtə rī záysh'n/ n

cautery /káwtəri/ (plural **-ies**) n **1.** an instrument or substance used to seal a wound or to destroy damaged or infected tissue by burning **2.** the process or action of sealing a wound or destroying damaged or infected tissue by burning [14C. Via Latin *cauterium* < Greek *kauterion* 'branding iron' < *kaiein* 'to burn']

caution /káwsh'n/ n **1.** CAREFULNESS care, thoughtfulness, lack of haste, and close attention that enable somebody to avoid the risks involved in a task or procedure **2.** WARNING a warning to somebody to be careful about something **3.** LAW LEGAL WARNING a formal warning given instead of a penalty to somebody who has done something illegal, advising that punishment will follow if it is repeated **4.** POLICE WARNING ABOUT EVIDENCE a formal warning given by a police officer to somebody who has been arrested that anything he or she says may be used in evi-

dence **5.** UNUSUAL PERSON a surprising or amusing person or thing (*dated*) ■ *vt* (**-tions, -tioning, -tioned**) **1.** WARN SOMEBODY to warn or advise somebody that something is risky or dangerous **2.** LAW GIVE SOMEBODY LEGAL WARNING to give somebody who has done something illegal a formal warning instead of a penalty, advising that punishment will follow if the offence is repeated **3.** LAW GIVE SOMEBODY WARNING ABOUT EVIDENCE to give a formal warning to somebody who has been arrested that anything he or she says may be used in evidence [Late 16C. Via French < Latin *caution-* < *caut-*, past participle of *cavere* 'take heed'] —**cautioner** *n* ◇ **throw caution to the wind(s)** to be reckless

cautionary /káwsh'nəri/ *adj* involving, giving, or being a warning

caution money *n* money deposited as security for good behaviour, e.g. by a student to cover damage to accommodation, furniture, or equipment

cautious /káwshəss/ *adj* having or showing care, thoughtfulness, restraint, and lack of haste [Mid-17C. < CAUTION] —**cautiously** *adv* —**cautiousness** *n*

SYNONYMS ***cautious, careful, chary, circumspect, prudent, vigilant, wary, guarded, cagey***

CORE MEANING: showing care or restraint

cautious having or showing care, thoughtfulness, restraint, and lack of haste ○ *his cautious approach to economic reform* ○ *Years of army training had taught him to be cautious when faced with an unknown situation.* **careful** taking reasonable care to avoid risks ○ *Be very careful when you withdraw money from street cash dispensers.* ○ *I was extra careful not to make any mistakes.* **chary** cautiously reluctant to act ○ *Why had Fenella been so chary of telling the simple truth?* **circumspect** taking into consideration all possible circumstances and consequences before acting ○ *Both men offered only circumspect answers to my question.* ○ *Officials were understandably circumspect about the incident.* **prudent** using good judgment to consider likely consequences and act accordingly ○ *prudent financial planning for foreseeable expenses* ○ *It's certainly prudent to use sunscreen if you are out in the midday sun.* **vigilant** watchful and alert, especially to guard against danger, difficulties, or errors ○ *Doctors are urging the public to be vigilant about the killer virus.* ○ *A vigilant neighbour foiled the attempted burglary.* **wary** showing watchfulness or suspicion ○ *She was always wary of dogs.* ○ *People were becoming more wary about voicing their opinions in public.* **guarded** reluctant to share information with others ○ *Her responses to the questions were heavily guarded.* ○ *His voice was guarded, with a deliberate note of scepticism.* **cagey** (*informal*) secretive and refusing to be open, frank, or direct ○ *She was cagey about why she had rejected the offer.* ○ *Asked about his recent career, he remained cagey.*

Cauvery /káwvəri/, **Kāveri** river in southern India. It rises in the Western Ghats, Karnataka State, and flows through Tamil Nadu to the Bay of Bengal. Length: 760 km/470 mi.

cav., Cav. *abbr* MIL cavalry

cava /kaavə/ *n* a sparkling, typically white wine from northeastern Spain

cavalcade /kávv'l káyd/ *n* **1.** a procession, especially one of people on horses, in carriages, or in cars **2.** a series or procession of things or people, especially a spectacular or dramatic one [Late 16C. Via French < Italian *cavalcata* 'ride on horseback' < medieval Latin *caballicare* < Latin *caballus* 'horse']

cavalier /kávvə léer/ *adj* CARELESS showing an arrogant or jaunty disregard or lack of respect for something or somebody ■ *n* **1.** GENTLEMAN a gallant or chivalrous man, especially one escorting a lady (*formal*) **2.** MOUNTED SOLDIER a knight or soldier in former times who fought on horseback (*archaic*) [Mid-16C. Via French < Italian *cavaliere* 'knight' < medieval Latin *caballarius* 'horseman' < Latin *caballus* 'horse'] —**cavalierly** *adv*

Cavalier *n* a supporter of King Charles I in the English Civil War

cavalier King Charles spaniel *n* BREED same as **King Charles spaniel** (sense 2)

cavalla /kə vállə/ (*plural same* or **-las**) *n* a sea fish with a flat body and forked tail. Native to: tropics. Family: Carangidae. [Early 17C. Via Spanish *caballa* 'horse mackerel' < Latin *caballus* 'horse']

cavalry /kávv'lri/ (*plural* **-ries**) *n* **1.** formerly, the part of an army made up of soldiers trained to fight on horseback **2.** the more mobile part of a modern army, using armoured vehicles and helicopters [Mid-16C. Via French < Italian *cavalleria* 'mounted militia' < *cavallo* 'horse' < Latin *caballus*] —**cavalryman** *n*

cavalryman /kávv'lrimən/ (*plural* **-men** /-mən/) *n* a soldier belonging to a regiment of cavalry

cavalry twill *n* a hard-wearing worsted fabric used for making tailored sporting jackets and trousers [< its use in making riding breeches for soldiers]

Cavan /kávv'n/ county in the Republic of Ireland. It was one of the nine counties that formed the historic province of Ulster. Population: 52,944 (2002). Area: 1,891 sq. km/730 sq. mi.

cavatina /kávvə téenə/ (*plural* **-nas** or **-ne** /-ni/) *n* **1.** a short and simple operatic song, especially a slow aria of Italian opera of the 18th and 19th centuries, usually followed by a livelier cabaletta **2.** a melodious and expressive piece of instrumental music, based loosely on the operatic cavatina [Early 19C. < Italian]

cave /kayv/ *n* a large, naturally hollowed-out place in the ground, or in rock above ground, that can be reached from the surface or from water [13C. < Old French < Latin *cavus* 'hollow']

cave in *v* **1.** *vti* to collapse or cause something to collapse because of pressure or because of being undermined **2.** *vi* to yield to persuasion or threats, after trying to resist

caveat /kávvi at, káy-/ *n* **1.** something said as a warning, caution, or qualification **2.** an official request to a court not to proceed with a case without notice to the person making the request [Mid-16C. < Latin, 'let him or her beware' < *cavere* 'to heed']

caveat emptor /-émp tawr/ *n* the commercial principle that the buyer is responsible for making sure that goods bought are of a reasonable quality, unless the seller is offering a guarantee of their quality [Early 16C. < Latin, 'let the buyer beware']

cavefish /káyv fish/ (*plural same* or **-fishes**) *n* a small fish with underdeveloped eyes that lives in subterranean waters. Native to: North America. Family: Amblyopsidae.

cave-in *n* **1.** COLLAPSE a collapse of something caused by pressure or undermining **2.** FALLEN STRUCTURE a place where a structure such as a roof or floor has collapsed because of pressure or being undermined **3.** YIELDING a giving in to persuasion or threats, after trying to resist

Cavell /kávv'l/, **Edith** (1865–1915) British nurse. She was executed by the Germans during World War I for helping Allied soldiers escape from occupied Belgium.

> 'Standing, as I do, in view of God and eternity, I realize that patriotism is not enough. I must have no hatred or bitterness towards anyone.'
> [Edith Cavell, *Times*; 23 October 1915]

caveman /káyv man/ (*plural* **-men** /-men/) *n* **1.** somebody living in a cave, especially a prehistoric human of the Palaeolithic period **2.** a man who behaves in a brutish or uncivilized way (*informal*)

Cavendish /kávv'ndish/, **Henry** (1731–1810) British chemist and physicist. He identified hydrogen, discovered that water is a compound, and measured the Earth's density.

cave painting *n* a painting made on the wall of a cave by Palaeolithic people

cavern /kávvərn/ *n* LARGE CAVE a large underground cave or a large chamber in a series of caves ■ *vt* (**-erns, -erning, -erned**) **1.** MAKE SOMETHING HOLLOW to make a mountain, cliff, or area of ground hollow **2.** PUT SOMETHING IN CAVE to enclose something in a cave or cavern (*literary*) [14C. Directly or via French < Latin *caverna* < *cavus* 'hollow']

cavernous /kávvərnəss/ *adj* **1.** like or suggestive of a cavern, especially in being large, dark, deep, and hollow **2.** having a hollow, resonating sound —**cavernously** *adv* —**cavernousness** *n*

cavesson /kávvissən/ *n* a stiff noseband used in breaking horses [Late 16C. Via French *caveçon* < medieval Latin *capitium* 'head covering' < Latin *capit-* 'head']

cavetto /kə véttō/ (*plural* **-ti** /-tee/) *n* a concave architectural moulding with a curve that is roughly a quarter circle [Mid-17C. < Italian, diminutive of *cavo* 'hollow' < Latin *cavus*]

cavewoman /káyv wŏŏmən/ (*plural* **-women** /-wimin/) *n* a woman living in a cave, especially a prehistoric woman of the Palaeolithic period

caviar /kávvi aar, -áar/, **caviare** *n* the salted roe of a large fish, particularly the sturgeon, eaten as a delicacy [Mid-16C. Via French < Italian *caviaro* < Turkish *havyar* < Persian dialect *khāvyār*]

cavil /kávv'l, kávvil/ *vi* (**-ils, -illing, -illed**) to make objections about something on small and unimportant points ■ *n* a trivial and unreasonable objection [Mid-16C. Via French *caviller* < Latin *cavillari* < *cavilla* 'mockery'] —**caviller** *n*

caving /káyving/ *n* the activity or sport of exploring and climbing in underground caves and passages —**caver** *n*

cavitand /kávvi tand/ *n* a molecule, especially a synthetic receptor, that is hollow and has one open end [Late 20C. < CAVITY]

cavitate /kávvi tayt/ (**-tates, -tating, -tated**) *vt* to form bubbles or cavities in a substance [Early 20C. Back-formation < CAVITATION]

cavitation /kávvi táysh'n/ *n* **1.** DISTURBANCE OF LIQUID the rapid formation and collapse of bubbles in a liquid, caused by the movement of something in the liquid such as a propeller, or by waves of high-frequency sound **2.** PITTING OF SURFACE the pitting of a solid surface as a result of the forces of repeated cavitation in a surrounding liquid **3.** FORMATION OF CAVITIES IN TISSUE the formation of cavities in body tissue, caused by a disease, e.g. as an effect of tuberculosis on the lungs [Late 19C. < CAVITY]

cavity /kávvəti/ (*plural* **-ties**) *n* **1.** HOLLOW PLACE a hole or hollow space in something **2.** DENT HOLE IN TOOTH a hole in a tooth, caused by decay **3.** ANAT HOLLOW WITHIN BODY a hollow area inside the body [Mid-16C. Via French < late Latin *cavitas* < Latin *cavus* 'hollow']

cavity block *n* a concrete construction block made with cavities inside it

cavity wall *n* an external wall of a building that is made up of two leaves of masonry, bricks, or blocks separated by a cavity. This prevents moisture penetration and improves thermal insulation.

cavo-relievo /kaavō ri léevō, káyvō-/ (*plural* **cavo-relievos** or **cavo-relievi** /-vi/), **cavo-rilievo** (*plural* **cavo-rilievos** or **cavo-rilievi**) *n* a relief sculpture in which even the highest part lies below the level of the original surface, or this style of relief sculpture [Late 19C. < Italian, 'hollow relief']

cavort /kə váwrt/ (**-vorts, -vorting, -vorted**) *vi* to behave in a physically lively and uninhibited way [Late 18C. Origin ?]

Cavour /kə vóor, -váwr/, **Camillo Benso, Conte di** (1810–61) Italian politician. He was prime minister of Piedmont (1852–59, 1860–61) and chief architect of the unification of Italy (1861).

cavy /káyvi/ (*plural* **-vies**) *n* a short-tailed rodent of the family that includes the guinea pig, many of which dig burrows. Native to: South America. Family: Caviidae. [Late 18C. Via modern Latin *Cavia* < Galibi *cabiai*]

caw /kaw/ (**caws, cawing, cawed**) *vi* to make the loud harsh cry of a crow or a related bird, or make a sound like this [Late 16C. An imitation of the sound] —**caw** *n*

Cawdor /káwdər/ parish in the Highland Region, northern Scotland, situated southwest of Nairn

Cawley /káwli/, **Evonne Fay** (*b.* 1951) Australian tennis player. She won the Wimbledon women's singles championship in 1971 and again in 1980, becoming the first Aboriginal tennis player to win a Grand Slam title. Born **Goolagong, Evonne Fay**

Caxton /kákstən/, **William** (1422?–91) English printer. He established the first printing press in England (1476?) and printed over 100 books, including *The Canterbury Tales.*

> 'I, according to my copy, have done set it in imprint, to the intent that noble men

may see and learn the noble acts of chivalry, the gentle and virtuous deeds that some knights used in those days.'
[William Caxton. Quoted in *Le Morte D'Arthur*, Thomas Malory; 1485]

cay /kay, kee/ *n* a small low island or reef in the sea, made of coral or sand, especially in the Caribbean [Late 17C. < Spanish *cayo* 'shoal']

Cayenne /kay én, kī én/ city and capital of French Guiana, situated in the northern coast of Cayenne Island. Population: 41,000 (1990).

cayenne pepper, **cayenne** *n* a very hot-tasting red powder made from the dried and ground fruit and seeds of several kinds of chilli. Use: in cooking. [Early 18C. < Tupi *kyynha*, altered after CAYENNE]

cayman *n* ZOOL another spelling of **caiman**

Cayman Islands /káymən-/ group of three islands, situated in the northwestern Caribbean Sea, approximately 320 km/200 mi. northwest of Jamaica. Capital: George Town. Population: 35,527 (2001). Area: 259 sq. km/100 sq. mi.

Cayuga /kay oógə, kī yoógə/ (*plural same* or **-gas**) *n* a member of an Iroquois people who once lived along Cayuga Lake, and who now live mainly in western New York State, Wisconsin, Ontario, and Oklahoma. The Cayuga were one of the five peoples who formed the Iroquois Confederacy, later known as the Six Nations. [Mid-18C. < Iroquoian, 'the place where locusts were taken out'] —**Cayuga** *adj*

Cayuga Lake /kay oógə-/ one of the Finger Lakes, situated in Cayuga and Seneca counties, central New York State. Area: 170 sq. km/66 sq. mi.

Cazaly /kázz'li/, **Roy** (1893–1963) Australian, Australian Rules footballer. Noted for his ability to take high catches, he spent most of his career with St Kilda.

Cazneaux /káznō/, **Harold Pierce** (1878–1953) New Zealand-born Australian photographer. He was a leading figure in the Australian pictorialist school of photography.

CB *abbr* **1.** ONLINE call back (*used in e-mails or text messages*) **2.** MEDIA Citizens' Band **3.** Companion of the (Order of the) Bath (*used as a title*)

CBC *n* in Canada, the crown corporation that provides radio and television services to the public. Full form **Canadian Broadcasting Corporation**

cbd *abbr* FREIGHT cash before delivery

CBD *abbr* **1.** FREIGHT cash before delivery **2.** BUSINESS central business district

CBE *abbr* Commander of the (Order of the) British Empire (*used as a title*)

CBI *abbr* **1.** computer-based instruction **2.** Confederation of British Industry

CBS *abbr* Columbia Broadcasting System

CBT *abbr* COMPUT, EDUC computer-based training

CBW *abbr* MIL **1.** chemical and biological warfare **2.** chemical and biological weapon

cc *abbr* **1.** Cocos Islands (*used in Internet addresses*) See table at **domain name 2.** cubic centimetre

CC *abbr* **1.** PUBLIC ADMIN City Council **2.** County Council **3.** Cricket Club

cc. *abbr* LITERAT chapters

c.c. *abbr* **1.** BUSINESS (carbon) copy **2.** cubic centimetre ■ *n* **E-MAIL OR PAPER DOCUMENT COPY** a copy of an e-mail or other document sent to a recipient or recipients ○ *sent cc's to all concerned committee members* ■ *v* **SEND COPY TO SOMEBODY** to use the cc line in an e-mail in order to send a copy of the message to another recipient or to others, or to photocopy a document and send it to another recipient or to others

CCA *abbr* **1.** E-COMMERCE cardholder certificate authority **2.** ACCT current-cost accounting

CCD *abbr* COMPUT charge-coupled device

CCF *abbr* MIL Combined Cadet Force

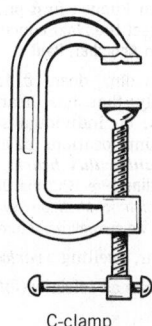
C-clamp

C-clamp *n* a metal clamp shaped like a letter C, with horizontal flat pieces at the ends, that can be adjusted by a screw

C clef *n* a symbol on a musical stave that shows the position of middle C. The alto and tenor clefs are the only commonly used C clefs today, and are found mostly in viola, cello, and bassoon music.

CCTV *abbr* BROADCAST closed-circuit television

CCU *abbr* HEALTH SERVICES coronary care unit

cd[1] *symbol* MEASURE, PHYS candela

cd[2] *abbr* Democratic Republic of the Congo (*used in Internet addresses*)

Cd[1] *symbol* CHEM ELEM cadmium

Cd[2] *abbr* POL command (paper) (*used before a serial number*)

CD *abbr* **1.** BANKING certificate of deposit **2.** MIL Civil Defence **3.** RECORDING, COMPUT compact disc **4.** Corps Diplomatique (*often displayed on the backs of cars that belong to embassies*)

c/d *abbr* **1.** ACCT carried down **2.** FIN cum dividend

CD burner *n* COMPUT same as **CD writer**

CDE *n* a compact disc that can have its contents erased and something else recorded onto it. Full form **compact disc erasable**

cdf *abbr* STATS cumulative distribution function

CDI, **CD-I** *n* an interactive compact disc containing text, video, and audio, and accessed using a self-contained player plugged into a television set. Full form **compact disc interactive**

cDNA *abbr* GENETICS complementary DNA

Cdr *abbr* MIL Commander

CDR[1] *n* a compact disc that can be used to record something but cannot be erased. Full form **compact disc recordable**

CDR[2] *abbr* MIL Commander

Cdre *abbr* NAVY Commodore

CD rewriter *n* a piece of equipment used to record data onto a CD-RW

CD-ROM /see dee róm/ *n* a compact disc containing a large amount of data, including text and images, that can be viewed using a computer but cannot be altered or erased. Full form **compact disc read-only memory**

CD-RW *n* a compact disc that can have its contents erased and something else recorded onto it many times. Full form **compact disc rewritable**

CDT *n* a school subject that combines craft, design, and technology and can be studied to GCSE level. Full form **Craft, Design, and Technology**

CDV *abbr* MEDIA **1.** CD-video **2.** compact video disc

CD-video *n* **1.** a compact disc used to store and play back video images **2.** a player for compact discs that store and play back video images

CD writer *n* a piece of equipment used to record data permanently onto a compact disc

Ce *symbol* CHEM ELEM cerium

CE *abbr* **1.** OCCUPATIONS, CHEM chemical engineer **2.** chief engineer **3.** Church of England **4.** OCCUPATIONS, CIV ENG civil engineer **5.** CALENDAR Common Era **6.** ONLINE creative editing (*used in e-mails*)

USAGE See **AD**[1].

ceanothus /see ə nóthəss/ *n* a bush with small dark green leaves. Flowers: blue, white, or pink, in clusters. Native to: North America. Genus: *Ceanothus*. [Late 18C. Via modern Latin < Greek *keanothos* 'thistle']

~~Ceasar~~ incorrect spelling of **Caesar**

cease /seess/ (**ceases, ceasing, ceased**) *v* **1.** *vt* to put an end or stop to something ○ *The magazine will cease free distribution to nonmembers.* **2.** *vi* to come to an end or stop ○ *The rain ceased as if a tap had been turned off.* [14C. Via French < Latin *cessare* < *cedere* 'give way'] ◇ **without cease** without stopping, or without a break

ceasefire /seéss fīr/ *n* **1.** an agreement between opposing sides in a conflict that they will stop fighting, usually for a limited time during which they will try to reach a more permanent peace agreement **2.** a military order to stop firing

ceaseless /seéssləss/ *adj* without pause or end —**ceaselessly** *adv*

Ceauşescu /chow shéskoo/, **Nicolae** (1918–89) Romanian politician. The Communist president of Romania (1967–89), he was overthrown and executed in a popular revolution.

Cebu /si bóo/ island of the Philippines, in the Pacific Ocean, near the islands of Negros and Mindanao. Population: 2,646,000 (1990). Area: 4,422 sq. km/1,707 sq. mi.

Cecchetti /che kétti/, **Enrico** (1850–1928) Italian ballet dancer, choreographer, and teacher. Dancers trained by his technique included Anna Pavlova, Alicia Markova, and Leonide Massine.

Cecil /séss'l/, **Robert** ♦ Salisbury, Robert Arthur Talbot Gascoyne-Cecil

Cecil, Robert, First Earl of Salisbury (1563–1612) English politician. Chief minister of Queen Elizabeth I and King James I, he prepared the way for the peaceful succession of James to the throne after Elizabeth's death.

Cecil, William ♦ Burghley, Sir William Cecil

Cecilia /sə seéli ə/, **St** (?–230?) Roman Christian martyr. She is regarded as the patron saint of music.

cecropia moth /si krópi ə-/ *n* a large silkworm moth with red, white, and black wings. Native to: North America. Latin name: *Hyalophora cecropia*. [Mid-19C. < modern Latin *Cecropia*, after *Cecrops*, mythological first king of Attica and founder of Athens]

cecum *n* ANAT US spelling of **caecum**

cedar /seédər/ *n* **1. TALL EVERGREEN TREE** a tall evergreen tree with spreading branches, needles, and large rounded upright cones. Native to: Europe, Asia, Africa. Genus: *Cedrus*. **2. TREE LIKE TRUE CEDAR** an evergreen tree that resembles a cedar **3. WOOD FROM CEDAR** the wood of a cedar tree [Pre-12C. Via Old French *cedre* < Greek *kedros*]

cedar of Lebanon

cedar of Lebanon *n* a tall long-lived cedar with horizontally spreading branches. Native to: Lebanon, Turkey. Latin name: *Cedrus libari*.

Cedar Rapids /seédər-/ city in eastern Iowa, on the Cedar River, northwest of Davenport. Population: 122,514 (2002 estimate).

cede /seed/ (**cedes, ceding, ceded**) *vt* to surrender or give up something such as land, rights, or power,

to another country, group, or person [Early 16C. Via French < Latin *cedere* 'give way']

SPELLCHECK cede or **seed**? Do not confuse the spelling of **cede** and **seed**, which sound similar. **Cede**, the less frequent of the two words, is a verb meaning 'surrender or give up', as in *cede territory*. **Seed** is chiefly used as a noun, meaning 'a part or parts of a plant' (as in *grass seed*, *grapes with no seeds*) or 'a graded competitor in some sports' (as in *the number one seed*); it is also used as a verb, meaning 'sow, shed, or remove seeds'.

ORIGIN The Latin word *cedere* 'to give way', from which **cede** is derived, is also the source of English *abscess*, *accede*, *ancestor*, *cease*, *concede*, *decease*, *exceed*, *precede*, *predecessor*, *proceed*, *procession*, *recede*, and *succeed*.

cedi /séedi/ (*plural same*) *n* the main unit of Ghanaian currency. See table at **currency** [Mid-20C. < Fanti *sedi* 'small shell']

cedilla /sə díllə/ (*plural* **-las**) *n* in some languages, a mark placed beneath the letters c (ç) and s (ş) that signals a change in the pronunciation of the letter. In French and Portuguese, it shows that c is pronounced like s, not k. In modern Turkish it shows that c and s are voiceless rather then voiced. See table at **diacritic** [Late 16C. < obsolete Spanish, 'little z' < Latin *zeta*]

Ceefax /sée faks/ *tdmk* a trademark for the teletext service of the BBC

CEGEP /sáy zhép/, **cegep** *n* in Quebec, an institution above secondary level offering two-year programmes leading to university and three-year programmes qualifying students in a variety of professions and trades. Full form **Collège d'Enseignement Général et Professionnel**

ceiba /sáybə/ (*plural* **-bas**) *n UK* a large tropical tree that has seed pods containing a silky fibre. Use: production of kapok. Latin name: *Ceiba pentandra*. ANZ, N Am term **silk-cotton tree** [Early 17C. Via Spanish < Arawak, 'giant tree']

ceil /seel/ (**ceils, ceiling, ceiled**) *vt* **1.** to construct a ceiling for a room **2.** to line a ceiling with a material such as plaster or wood [Early 16C. Origin ?]

ceilidh /káyli/ *n* a party with singing and dancing to Scottish or Irish traditional music and storytelling [Late 19C. Via Irish *céilidhe*, Scottish Gaelic *ceilidh* < Old Irish *célide* 'visit' < *céle* 'companion']

ceiling /séeling/ *n* **1.** INSIDE TOP OF ROOM the overhead surface of a room, or the material used to line this surface **2.** UPPER LIMIT a level above which something such as a price, rent, or wage is not allowed to rise **3.** AVIAT FLYING HEIGHT the maximum height at which an aircraft can fly **4.** METEOROL CLOUD LEVEL the highest point, usually the base of a layer of clouds, from which the surface of Earth can be seen [Mid-16C. < CEIL] —**ceilinged** *adj* ◇ **go through the ceiling** to rise to a very high level ◇ **go through** *or* **hit the ceiling** to become very angry

ceiling rose *n* ARCHIT same as **rose**[1] (sense 8)

ceilometer /see lómmitər/ *n* an instrument for measuring the height of a cloud ceiling [Mid-20C. < CEILING]

Cela /séllə, théllə/, **Camilo José** (1916–2002) Spanish novelist. A starkly realistic writer, he is famous for such works as *La familia de Pascual Duarte* (1942) (*The Family of Pascual Duarte* (1964) and *La colmena* (1951) (*The Hive* (1953). He won the Nobel Prize in literature (1989).

> 'Things are always best seen when they are a trifle mixed-up, a trifle disordered; the chilly administrative neatness of museums and filing cases, of statistics and cemeteries, is an inhuman and antinatural kind of order; it is, in a word, disorder. True order belongs to Nature, which never yet has produced two identical trees or mountains or horses.'
> [Camilo José Cela, *Journey to the Alcarria*; 1948]

celadon /sélladan, -don/ *n* **1.** a pale greyish-green colour **2.** Chinese porcelain with a greyish-green glaze [Mid-18C. < French *céladon*, after a character in D'Urfé's romance *L'Astrée*] —**celadon** *adj*

Celan /sél an/, **Paul** (1920–70) Romanian-born French poet. He wrote in German and his best-known poem,

Todesfuge 'Death Fugue', first published in (1948), takes as its subject the Nazi concentration camp at Auschwitz. Born **Antschel, Paul**

celandine /séllən dīn, -deen/ *n* **1.** a plant of the buttercup family that has heart-shaped leaves. Flowers: yellow, on individual stems. Native to: woodland or damp locations in Europe and Asia. Latin name: *Ranunculus ficaria*. **2.** PLANTS same as **greater celandine** [Pre-12C. Via Old French *celidoine* < Greek *khelidonion* < *khelidōn* 'swallow'; because it flowered in spring, when swallows returned from migration]

-cele *suffix* tumour, swelling ○ *varicocele* [< Greek *kēlē*]

celeb /si léb/ *n* same as **celebrity** (*informal*) [Early 20C. Shortening]

Celebes /séllə beez, se lée beez/ ♦ **Sulawesi**

Celebes Sea part of the Pacific Ocean, surrounded by the Philippines, Borneo, Sulawesi, the Sulu Archipelago, and the Sangihe Islands. Area: 427,348 sq. km/165,000 sq. mi.

celebrant /séllabrant/ *n* **1.** WORSHIPPER a participant in a religious ceremony **2.** OFFICIATING PRIEST a priest officiating at the Christian ceremony of Communion **3.** SOMEBODY CELEBRATING somebody who celebrates something **4.** *ANZ* SOMEBODY OFFICIATING AT CIVIL CEREMONY a secular official who conducts civil ceremonies such as weddings and naming ceremonies [Mid-19C. < Latin *celebrant-*, present participle of *celebrare* (see CELEBRATE)]

celebrate /séllə brayt/ (**-brates, -brating, -brated**) *v* **1.** *vti* SHOW HAPPINESS AT SOMETHING to show happiness that something good or special has happened by doing such things as eating and drinking together or playing music ○ *I told them about my promotion, and we went out to celebrate*. ○ *a noisy crowd of fans celebrating the victory* **2.** *vt* MARK OCCASION to mark a special occasion or day by ceremonies or festivities **3.** *vti* PERFORM RELIGIOUS CEREMONY to perform a religious ceremony according to the prescribed forms **4.** *vt* PRAISE SOMETHING to praise something publicly or make it famous ○ *a popular song celebrating his greatest victory* [Mid-16C. < Latin *celebrat-*, past participle of *celebrare* 'attend a festival' < *celeber* 'frequented, famous'] —**celebration** /séllə bráysh'n/ *n* —**celebrator** *n* —**celebratory** /séllabratəri, séllə bráytəri/ *adj*

celebrated /séllə braytid/ *adj* famous and admired

celebrity /sə lébbrəti/ (*plural* **-ties**) *n* **1.** somebody who is famous during his or her own lifetime **2.** the state of being famous [14C. Directly or via French < Latin *celebritas* < *celeber* 'famous']

celecoxib /sélli kóksib/ *n* an anti-inflammatory drug that is an oxygenase inhibitor. Use: treatment of osteoarthritis and rheumatoid arthritis. [Late 20C. Contraction and alteration of *selective COX-2 inhibitor*]

celeriac /sə lérri ak/ *n* a type of celery that forms a root like an irregularly shaped turnip, eaten cooked or raw as a vegetable. Latin name: *Apium graveolens* var. rapaceum. [Mid-18C. Alteration of CELERY]

celerity /sə lérrəti/ *n* quickness in movement or in doing something (*literary*) [15C. Via French < Latin *celeritas* < *celer* 'swift']

celery

celery /séllǝri/ *n* **1.** LONG-STEMMED VEGETABLE the long crisp flattish leaf stalks of a cultivated plant, eaten raw or cooked as a vegetable **2.** CELERY PLANT the plant that produces celery. Latin name: *Apium graveolens* var. dulce. **3.** SEASONING the seeds of the celery plant. Use: seasoning. [Mid-17C. < French *céleri* < Greek *selinon* 'parsley']

celery pine *n* a tree that has pale shoots resembling celery and yields timber. Native to: New Zealand. Latin name: *Phyllocladus trichomanoides*.

celesta /sə léstə/, **celeste** /sə lést/ *n* a musical instrument with keys that make hammers strike metal plates to create a soft tinkling sound [Late 19C. Alteration of French *céleste* 'celestial' < Latin *caelestis* (see CELESTIAL)]

celestial /sə lésti əl/ *adj* **1.** relating to, suitable for, in, or typical of heaven **2.** relating to, involving, or observed in the sky or outer space [14C. < French < Latin *caelestis* < *caelum* 'sky, heaven'] —**celestially** *adv*

celestial body *n* an object that is permanently present in the sky, e.g. a star or a planet

celestial equator *n* the great circle in which the plane of the Earth's equator intersects the celestial sphere

celestial globe *n* a globe showing the positions of astronomical objects in the sky

celestial horizon *n* ASTRON same as **horizon** (sense 3)

celestial mechanics *n* the branch of astronomy concerned with the motions and positions of astronomical objects in gravitational fields (*takes a singular verb*)

celestial navigation *n* navigation in which the positions of astronomical objects are used to triangulate the position of a ship or aircraft

celestial pole *n* either of the two points where a line in continuation of the Earth's axis intersects the celestial sphere

celestial sphere *n* the imaginary sphere around the Earth on which the Sun, Moon, stars, and planets appear to be placed

celestite /sélla stīt/, **celestine** /séllas teen, -stīn/ *n* a white or coloured mineral consisting of strontium sulphate. Use: source of strontium. [Early 19C. < Latin *caelestis* (see CELESTIAL)]

celiac *adj* ANAT US spelling of **coeliac**

celibate /séllabat/ *adj* **1.** abstaining from sex **2.** unmarried, especially because of a religious vow [Early 19C. < Latin *caelibatus* < *caelebs* 'unmarried'] —**celibacy** *n* —**celibate** *n* —**celibately** *adv*

Céline /se leen, say-/, **Louis-Ferdinand** (1894–1961) French novelist and doctor. Misogyny and anti-Semitism characterize such works as his *Journey to the End of the Night* (1932). Born **Destouches, Louis-Ferdinand**

> 'Truth is a never-ending agony. The truth of this world is death. One must choose— die or lie. I've never been able to kill myself.'
> [Louis-Ferdinand Céline, *Voyage au bout de la nuit (Journey to the End of the Night)*; 1932]

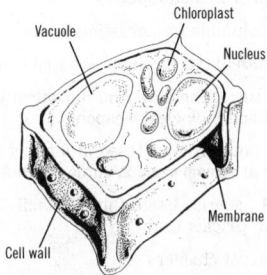
cell: structure of a plant cell

cell /sel/ *n* **1.** BIOL BASIC UNIT OF LIVING THING the smallest independently functioning unit in the structure of an organism, usually consisting of one or more nuclei surrounded by cytoplasm and enclosed by a membrane. Cells also contain organelles such as mitochondria, lysosomes, and ribosomes. **2.** ROOM FOR HOLDING PRISONER a room in a prison, in which one or more prisoners are confined, or a small room in a police station, used to confine somebody who has been arrested **3.** SMALL ROOM a very small and simple room, especially in a monastery or convent **4.** SMALL ENCLOSED STRUCTURE a small contained or hollow unit

in a structure, e.g. a compartment in a honeycomb or the reproductive organs of a plant, or an area on an insect's wing **5.** ELEC, ENG **SOMETHING THAT PRODUCES ELECTRICITY** a device that produces electrical energy by the chemical action of electrodes in an electrolyte **6.** ELEC same as **solar cell 7.** POL **ACTIVIST GROUP** a small group of people who work together and are part of a larger organization, especially members of a political organization who work in secret **8.** TELECOM **RANGE OF MOBILE PHONE TRANSMITTER** the area covered by one of the transmitters in a mobile telephone system that automatically switches a travelling user between short-range radio stations **9.** COMPUT **SPACE IN TABLE** a space for information in a table such as a computer spreadsheet, formed where a row and a column intersect **10.** CHR **DEPENDENT RELIGIOUS COMMUNITY** a small religious house that is dependent on a larger religious community [Pre-12C. Via French < Latin *cella* 'small chamber'] —**celled** *adj* —**-celled** *suffix*

cella /séllə/ (*plural* **-lae** /-lee/) *n* the inner room of a classical Greek or Roman temple, containing the shrine or statue of the god [Late 17C. < Latin, 'small chamber']

cellar /séllər/ *n* **1.** a room wholly or partly underground that is not suitable as living space and is usually used for storage **2.** same as **wine cellar** ■ *vt* (**-lars, -laring, -lared**) to store something, especially wine, in a cellar [13C. Via Anglo-Norman < late Latin *cellarium* 'group of storage chambers' < Latin *cella* 'small chamber']

cellarage /séllərij/ *n* **1.** a fee charged for storing something in a cellar **2.** a cellar or cellars, or the amount of space in a cellar

cellarer /séllərər/ *n* a supervisor of food and drink supplies, especially in a monastery

cellaret /séllə rét/ *n* a cabinet or sideboard for storing bottles of wine and glasses

cellarette *n* FURNITURE US spelling of **cellaret**

cellarman /séllərmən/ (*plural* **-men** /-mən/) *n* a man who is in charge of the cellar in a pub or restaurant and is responsible for maintaining good storage conditions

cellarperson /séllər purss'n/ *n* somebody who is in charge of the cellar in a pub or restaurant and is responsible for maintaining good storage conditions

cellblock /sél blok/ *n* a group of cells forming a unit in a prison

cell body *n* CELL BIOL ➧ **perikaryon**

cell division *n* the process by which a cell divides to form two new cells, either to produce identical cells (**mitosis**) or to produce cells with half the number of chromosomes (**meiosis**)

Cellini /che léeni/, **Benvenuto** (1500–71) Italian sculptor and goldsmith. His autobiography is considered a classic work of Renaissance literature.

cellist /chéllist/ *n* a musician who plays the cello

cellmate /sél mayt/ *n* somebody who shares a cell with another prisoner

cell membrane *n* the membrane that surrounds the cytoplasm, through which substances pass in and out of the cell

cello /chéllō/ (*plural* **-los**) *n* a large stringed instrument of the violin family that is held upright between a seated player's knees and played with a bow. The cello has a full deep sound. [Late 19C. Shortening of VIOLONCELLO]

ORIGIN ***Cello*** is shortened from *violoncello,* an Italian diminutive of *violone* 'double-bass viol'.

cellobiose /séllō bī ōz/ *n* a sugar obtained by the breakdown of cellulose. Formula: $C_{12}H_{22}O_{11}$. [Early 20C. < CELLULOSE + BI- + -OSE[2]]

cellophane /séllə fayn/ *n* a thin transparent waterproof material. Source: wood pulp. Use: wrapping, covering. [Early 20C. < CELLULOSE]

cell phone /sél fōn/ *n* a mobile telephone operated through a cellular radio network [Late 20C. Contraction of *cellular telephone*]

cellular /séllyoōlər/ *adj* **1. CONTAINING SMALL PARTS OR GROUPS** relating to small parts or groups that make up a whole **2.** BIOL **OF LIVING CELLS** relating to or consisting of living cells **3.** TELECOM **ORGANIZED INTO CELLS** organized as a system of cells, especially for radio communication **4.** GEOL, INDUST **POROUS** porous in texture and containing many small cavities **5.** TEXTILES **OPEN-TEXTURED** woven or knitted to produce thick open-textured cloth [Mid-18C. Via French < modern Latin *cellularis* < Latin *cellula* (see CELLULE)] —**cellularity** /séllyoō lárrəti/ *n* —**cellularly** *adv*

cellular phone *n* TELECOM same as **cell phone**

cellular radio *n* a type of radio communication used for mobile phones that consists of a network of transmitters, each covering a small area. The travelling user is automatically switched between radio stations.

cellular telephone *n* TELECOM same as **cell phone**

cellulase /séllyoō layz, -layss/ *n* an enzyme that converts cellulose into sugars [Early 20C. < CELLULOSE]

cellule /séllyool/ *n* a small cell in a living organism [Mid-19C. Via French < Latin *cellula* 'small cell' < *cella* 'small chamber']

cellulite /séllyoō līt/ *n* fatty deposits beneath the skin that give a lumpy or grainy appearance to the skin surface, especially on the thighs or buttocks [Mid-20C. < French < *cellule* (see CELLULE)]

cellulitis /séllyoō lītiss/ *n* infection and inflammation of the tissues beneath the skin

celluloid /séllyoō loyd/ *n* **1. COLOURLESS PLASTIC** a flammable transparent plastic made from nitrocellulose and a plasticizer such as camphor **2.** CINEMA **FILM** the photographic film used for making films **3.** CINEMA **CINEMA AS MEDIUM** the cinema as a medium or art form [Mid-19C. < CELLULOSE] —**celluloid** *adj*

cellulolytic /séllyoōlō líttik/ *adj* describes a process or an organism that can degrade cellulose [Mid-20C. < CELLULOSE]

cellulose /séllyoō lōss, -lōz/ *n* the main constituent of the cell walls of plants and algae. Use: plastics, lacquers, explosives, synthetic fibres. [Mid-19C. < French < Latin *cellula* (see CELLULE)] —**cellulosic** /séllyoō lōssik, -lōzik/ *adj*

cellulose acetate *n* a chemical compound produced by the reaction of acetic or sulphuric acid on cellulose. Use: photographic film, plastics, textile fibres, varnishes.

cellulose nitrate *n* CHEM same as **nitrocellulose**

cell wall *n* the outermost layer of a cell in plants and some fungi, algae, and bacteria, that provides a supporting framework

celosia /sə lōssi ə/ (*plural* **-sias** or *same*) *n* a plant belonging to a genus that includes cockscomb. Flowers: feathery, yellow to purplish-red. Genus: *Celosia.* [Early 19C. < modern Latin < Greek *kēlos* 'burnt']

Celsius /sélssi əss/ *adj* using or measured on an international metric temperature scale on which water freezes at 0° and boils at 100° under normal atmospheric conditions. The term 'Celsius' is usually preferred to 'centigrade', especially in technical contexts. ◊ **Fahrenheit** [Mid-19C. After Anders *Celsius* (1701–44), Swedish astronomer]

celt /selt/ *n* a prehistoric chisel or axe that has a metal or stone head with a bevelled edge [Early 18C. < medieval Latin *celtis* 'chisel']

Celt /kelt, selt/, **Kelt** /kelt/ *n* **1.** somebody who speaks or whose ancestors spoke a Celtic language **2.** a member of an ancient Indo-European people who lived in central and western Europe. They were driven to the western fringes of the continent by the Romans and some Germanic peoples, especially the Angles and Saxons. [Mid-16C. Via Latin *Celtae* 'Celts' < Greek *Keltoi*]

Celtiberian /kélti béeri ən, sélti-/ *n* a member of an ancient Celtic people who lived in the Iberian peninsula [Early 17C. < Latin *Celtiberia*, ancient province of Iberia < *Celtae* (see CELT) + *Iberia*] —**Celtiberian** *adj*

Celtic /kéltik, sélt-/ *adj* **OF CELTS** relating to the Celts, or their languages or cultures ■ *n* **1. INDO-EUROPEAN LANGUAGE GROUP** an Indo-European group of languages that includes Irish, Scottish Gaelic, Welsh, and Breton and has Brythonic and Goidelic subgroups. Native speakers: 1.5 million. **2. ANCESTOR OF MODERN CELTIC LANGUAGES** the reconstructed language that is the ancestor of modern Celtic languages. See panel on next page

Celtic cross *n* a cross that has a broad ring around the intersection of the upright and crossbar

Celtic fringe *n* Scotland, Ireland, and Wales regarded as a collective unit in terms of their culture and history in relation to England

Celticism /kéltissizəm, s-/ *n* **1.** a word or idiom of Celtic origin that has become naturalized in another language. In English, examples include 'plaid' from Scottish Gaelic, 'leprechaun' from Irish Gaelic, and 'eisteddfod' from Welsh. **2.** a custom or belief of Celtic origin

Celtic Sea /kéltik-, sél-/ extension of the Atlantic Ocean between the Republic of Ireland to the north and southwestern England to the south

cembalo /chémbəlō/ (*plural* **-li** /-lee/ or **-los**) *n* MUSIC same as **harpsichord** [Mid-19C. < Italian, contraction of *clavicembalo* < medieval Latin *clavicymbalum* < Latin *clavis* 'key' + *cymbalum* (see CYMBAL)] —**cembalist** *n*

cement /si mént/ *n* **1. POWDER FOR CONCRETE** a fine grey powder of calcined limestone and clay. Use: mixed with water and sand to make mortar, or with water, sand, and aggregate to make concrete. **2. CONCRETE** a building material that sets hard to form concrete, made by mixing cement with water, sand, and aggregate **3. GLUE** a glue or similar bonding substance **4. BOND UNITING PEOPLE** something that unites people or groups **5.** DENT **SUBSTANCE USED IN DENTISTRY** a substance used in dentistry for filling cavities and anchoring bridgework or crowns **6.** ANAT same as **cementum 7.** GEOL **MATERIAL BINDING ROCK** a substance that binds together the particles in sedimentary rocks and fills the spaces ■ *v* (**-ments, -menting, -mented**) **1.** *vti* **FIX OR BECOME FIXED WITH CEMENT** to fix something in place with cement or a similar substance, or become fixed in this way **2.** *vt* **APPLY CEMENT TO SOMETHING** to cover or fill something with cement or a similar substance **3.** *vti* **STRENGTHEN RELATIONSHIP** to make a relationship between people strong or permanent, or become strong or permanent [14C. Via French *ciment* < Latin *caementum* 'quarry stone', (plural) 'stone chips' < *caedere* 'hew'] —**cementer** *n*

cementation /sée men táysh'n/ *n* **1. APPLYING OF CEMENT** the application of cement or a similar substance to something **2.** CIV ENG **CEMENTING OF ROCKS** the injecting of cement into holes or fissures in rocks to make them watertight or strong **3.** METALL **HEATING OF METAL WITH POWDER** the modification of a solid, especially a metal, by heating it with one or more other substances that will diffuse into the surface, e.g. the production of steel by heating it with charcoal **4.** GEOL **SEDIMENTARY ROCK FORMATION** the process in which percolating ground water deposits a cementing material to form a sedimentary rock

cementite /si mén tīt/ *n* a hard brittle compound of iron and carbon that forms in some types of cast iron, in carbon steels, and in alloys of carbon and iron. Formula: Fe_3C.

cement mixer *n* **1.** a transportable machine with a revolving drum in which cement powder, water, sand, and other materials can be mixed to make concrete, mortar, or stucco **2.** a truck with a large revolving drum for mixing, transporting, and pouring concrete

cementum /si méntəm/ *n* the thin layer of bony tissue that covers the dentine of the roots and neck of a tooth [Mid-19C. < Latin *caementum* (see CEMENT)]

~~**cemetary**~~, ~~**cemetry**~~ incorrect spelling of **cemetery**

cemetery /sémmətri/ (*plural* **-ies**) *n* an area of ground in which the dead are buried, especially one that is not in the grounds of a church [14C. Via late Latin *coemeterium* < Greek *koimētērion* 'dormitory' < *koiman* 'put to sleep']

CEN *n* PUBLIC ADMIN same as **CENELEC**

cen. *abbr* **1.** central **2.** TIME century

-cene *suffix* recent ○ *Pliocene* [< Greek *kainos* 'new']

CENELEC /sénnə lek/, **CEN** /sen/ *n* an EU organization that controls the standard of electrical goods. Full form **Commission Européenne de Normalisation Electrique**

ceno- *prefix* another spelling of **coeno-**

cenobite *n* RELIG another spelling of **coenobite**

cenogenesis *n* BIOL another spelling of **caenogenesis**

zh vision. In foreign words: kh German Bach; aN French vin; aaN French blanc; ö German schön, French feu; oN French bon; öN French un; ü as in French rue. Stress marks: ´ as in secret /séekrət/, academic /ákə démmik/

LANGUAGE HERITAGE *Celtic* Much of English is made up of words from other languages, and it might be expected that Celtic, the group of languages spoken by the inhabitants of the British Isles before both the Roman and Anglo-Saxon invasions, would be an important early contributor. In fact the Celtic legacy in Old English is slight: *lough*, the Irish word for a lake that has the same ancestor as Scottish *loch*, is the only significant survivor. The majority of the words of Celtic origin are of later date, and relate primarily to Scottish, Irish, and Welsh culture, history, or landscape. In the cultural sphere Scottish Gaelic has contributed, for example, *caber*, *cairn* (a pile of stones), *claymore* (from Gaelic *claidheamh mor* 'great sword'), and *pibroch* (from Gaelic *piobaireachd* 'art of piping', the first element of which derives from English *pipe*); and especially items of clothing such as *trews* and *plaid*. Some of these migrants have both Scottish and Irish origins, for example *brogue* (via Irish and Scottish Gaelic *brōg* from Old Norse *brók* 'leg covering'), *ceilidh* (via Irish *céilidhe* and Scottish Gaelic *ceilidh* from Old Irish *célide* 'visit'), *clan* (via Gaelic *clan* 'offspring' from Old Irish *cland*, ultimately from Latin *planta* 'sprout'), and *sporran* (via Scottish Gaelic from Middle Irish). Scottish Gaelic has given the world *whisky* (from *usquebea*, *usque beatha* 'water of life'). Irish culture is reflected both in terms of folklore, for example *banshee* and *leprechaun*, and in 20th-century terms relating to the modern Irish state, for example *DáilÉireann* 'Irish assembly', *Garda*, the police force of the Republic of Ireland, and *Taoiseach*, the title of its prime minister. The best-known Welsh cultural migrant is probably *eisteddfod*, 'traditional music and poetry festival'.

The three main Celtic languages are well represented in terms of local geography, geology, and archaeology, but the lesser Breton and Cornish languages also make an appearance in these categories with *menhir* (Breton), 'large single upright prehistoric stone' and *vug* (Cornish), 'small hole in a rock or vein'. Scottish Gaelic and Irish are represented by, for example, *ben* 'mountain', *corrie* 'cirque', *esker* 'long narrow ridge of sand or gravel', *glen* 'long narrow valley', and *inch* 'small island', as well as by *loch* or *lough*; *crag* is also from a Celtic language, probably Welsh *craig* or Gaelic *creagh*. From Welsh come *cist* 'Stone Age coffin', *cromlech* 'circle of prehistoric standing stones' and 'ancient stone burial chamber', and *cwm* 'cirque'. In zoology Cornish makes its contribution with the shark, *porbeagle*, and fish, *wrasse*, Scottish Gaelic with the birds *capercaillie* and *ptarmigan*, and Welsh with the *corgi* dog. In botany the *shamrock*, of course, comes from Ireland.

Less obvious migrants of Celtic origin include *bijou* (immediately from French, but the French word was adopted from Breton *bizoù* 'jewelled ring', from *biz* 'finger'); *bunny*, the child's word for 'rabbit', which goes back to Gaelic *bun* 'stump, bottom'; *galore*, from Irish *go leor* 'sufficiency'; *pillion*, an early migrant to English (15th century), from Gaelic *pillean*, Irish *pillin* 'little couch'; *slew*, an informal North American word for 'large quantity or number', which came in the mid-19th century from Irish *sluagh* 'multitude'; *slogan*, originally the battle cry of a Scottish Highland clan; and *trousers* (from Gaelic *triubhas* 'close-fitting shorts', from which *trews* also derives).

---

cenotaph /sénnə taaf, -taf/ *n* a monument erected as a memorial to a dead person or dead people buried elsewhere, especially people killed fighting a war [Early 17C. < Greek *kenotaphion* 'empty tomb' < *kenos* 'empty' + *taphos* 'tomb'] —**cenotaphic** /sénnə táffik/ *adj*

Cenotaph *n* a monument in London that serves as a memorial to the dead of wars involving British forces since World War I. Designed by Sir Edward Lutyens and erected in Whitehall in 1921, it is the site where heads of state and royalty lay poppy wreaths in a ceremony on Remembrance Sunday.

cenote /si nṓ tay/ *n* a deep natural hole found in limestone, especially in Yucatán, Mexico. Cenotes were holy for the Maya, who used them as places of sacrifice. [Mid-19C. Via Yucatán Spanish < Maya *tzonot*]

Cenozoic /seenō zṓ ik/, **Caenozoic**, **Cainozoic** /kīnə-, káynə-/ *n* the most recent era of geological time, beginning about 65 million years ago, during which modern plants and animals evolved. See table at **geological time** [Mid-19C. < Greek *kainos* 'new'] —**Cenozoic** *adj*

cense /senss/ (**censes**, **censing**, **censed**) *vt* **1.** to perfume a place or worshippers with incense **2.** to burn incense to a deity at an altar or shrine [14C. Shortening of French *encenser* < Latin *incendere* 'set fire to' (see INCENSE[1])]

censer

censer /sénssər/ *n* a container used for burning incense, especially one that is swung in a religious procession or ceremony [13C. < Old French *censier*, shortening of *encensier* < *encens* (see INCENSE[1])]

censor /sénssər/ *n* **1.** OFFICIAL REMOVING OBJECTIONABLE MATERIAL an official who examines plays, films, letters, or publications with a view to removing or banning content considered to be offensive or a threat to

security **2.** SOMEBODY WHO SUPPRESSES SOMETHING somebody or something that suppresses or controls something that may offend or harm others **3.** ANCIENT ROMAN OFFICIAL in ancient Rome, either of two elected magistrates who were responsible for holding censuses, overseeing public morals, and controlling aspects of finance and taxation **4.** PSYCHIAT INHIBITING FORCE IN MIND in psychology, a mechanism believed to be responsible for what can and cannot emerge from the subconscious to the conscious mind. It is thought to prevent harmful memories, ideas, and desires from reaching the conscious level. ■ *vt* (**-sors**, **-soring**, **-sored**) **1.** REMOVE OFFENSIVE PARTS FROM SOMETHING to remove or change any part of a play, film, letter, or publication considered offensive or a threat to security **2.** EXERCISE CONTROL OVER SOMETHING to suppress or control something that may offend or harm others [Mid-16C. < Latin < *censere* 'appraise'] —**censorial** *adj* —**censorial** /sen sáwri əl/ *adj*

USAGE censor or **censure**? Though spelt similarly these two words are pronounced differently and have different meanings. A *censor* is a person who suppresses or removes information (*Military censors have excised some of the photos for security reasons*), while *censure* is severe criticism or condemnation (*The European Parliament is to vote on a motion of censure of the commission*). Both words can be verbs, and as such they preserve their distinct meanings.

censorious /sen sáwri əss/ *adj* **1.** inclined or eager to criticize people or things **2.** expressing strong disapproval or harsh criticism —**censoriously** *adv* —**censoriousness** *n*

censorship /sénssər ship/ *n* **1.** SUPPRESSION OF PUBLISHED OR BROADCAST MATERIAL the suppression of all or part of a play, film, letter, or publication considered offensive or a threat to security **2.** SUPPRESSION OF SOMETHING OBJECTIONABLE the suppression or attempted suppression of something regarded as objectionable **3.** ANCIENT ROMAN OFFICE the office, authority, or term of an ancient Roman censor **4.** PSYCHIAT SUPPRESSION OF MEMORIES the suppression of potentially harmful memories, ideas, or desires from the conscious mind

censure /sénshər/ *n* **1.** DISAPPROVAL severe criticism **2.** OFFICIAL CONDEMNATION official expression of disapproval or condemnation ■ *vt* (**-sures**, **-suring**, **-sured**) **1.** CRITICIZE SOMEBODY OR SOMETHING to make a formal, often public statement of disapproval of somebody or something **2.** CONDEMN SOMEBODY OR SOMETHING OFFICIALLY to express official disapproval or condemnation of somebody or something [14C. < Latin *censura*

'judgment' < *censere* 'appraise'] —**censurable** *adj* —**censurer** *n*

USAGE See **censor**.

SYNONYMS See **criticize** and **disapprove**.

census /sénssəss/ (*plural* **-suses**) *n* **1.** COUNT OF POPULATION an official count of a population carried out at set intervals **2.** SYSTEMATIC COUNT a systematic count or survey **3.** REGISTRATION FOR TAXATION IN ANCIENT ROME in ancient Rome, a registration of the population and their property that was used for assessing taxes [Early 17C. < Latin < *censere* 'appraise']

cent /sent/ *n* a subunit of currency in the United States, Canada, Australia, New Zealand, South Africa, the European Union, and several other countries. See table at **currency** [14C. Directly or via French, 'hundred', or Italian *cento* < Latin *centum*]

cent. *abbr* **1.** MEASURE centigrade **2.** central **3.** TIME century

cent- *prefix* same as **centi-**

cental /sént'l/ *n* a unit of mass equal to 100 lb (45.3 kg). N Am term **hundredweight** [Late 19C. < Latin *centum* 'hundred']

centas /sén tass/ (*plural same*) *n* a subunit of Lithuanian currency. See table at **currency**

centaur

centaur /sén tawr/ *n* in Greek mythology, a creature with the head, arms, and torso of a man joined to the body of a horse at its neck [14C. Via Latin *centaurus* < Greek *kentauros*]

Centaurus /sen táwrəss/ *n* a prominent constellation of the southern hemisphere containing the stars Alpha Centauri and Beta Centauri. See illustration at **constellation**

centavo /sen taávō/ (*plural* **-vos**) *n* a subunit of currency in several Spanish- and Portuguese-speaking countries. See table at **currency** [Late 19C. < Spanish, Portuguese, 'hundredth' < Latin *centum* 'hundred']

Centcom /sént kom/, **CENTCOM** *n* the US military headquarters and its combined service-branch staff responsible for operations in the Arabian Peninsula, Iraq, the northern Red Sea region, the Gulf States, and parts of South and Central Asia and eastern Africa [Late 20C. Acronym of *Central Command*]

centenarian /séntə náiri ən/ *n* 100-YEAR-OLD PERSON somebody who is a hundred years of age or more ■ *adj* **1.** 100 YEARS OLD at least a hundred years of age **2.** OF CENTENARIANS relating to or characteristic of people who are a hundred years of age or more

centenary /sen teénəri, -ténnə-/ *n* (*plural* **-ries**) **1.** 100-YEAR ANNIVERSARY the hundredth anniversary of an event, or a celebration held to mark the anniversary. NZ, N Am term **centennial 2.** CENTURY a period of one hundred years ■ *adj* **1.** MARKING 100 YEARS marking an anniversary of 100 years. NZ, N Am term **centennial 2.** ONCE-A-CENTURY occurring every hundred years **3.** OF CENTURY relating to or involving a period of one hundred years [Early 17C. < Latin *centenarius* 'containing a hundred' < *centeni* 'hundred each' < *centum* 'hundred']

centennial /sen ténni əl/ *adj* **1.** relating to or involving a period of a hundred years **2.** occurring every hundred years **3.** NZ, N Am same as **centenary** *adj* (sense 1) ■ *n* NZ, N Am same as **centenary** *n* (sense 1) [Late 18C. < Latin *centum* 'hundred', after BIENNIAL] —**centennially** *adv*

---

center *n, vti* US spelling of **centre**

~~**centergrade**~~ incorrect spelling of **centigrade**

Centers for Disease Control and Prevention *n* an agency of the US federal government concerned mainly with protecting the health and safety of the people of the United States (*takes a singular verb*)

centesimal /sen téssim'l/ *adj* **1.** IN 100THS divided into hundredths **2.** 1/100TH constituting one one-hundredth of something **3.** USING BASE OF 100 describes a number system that uses a base of 100 ■ *n* 100TH PART one hundredth of something [Late 17C. < Latin *centesimus* 'hundredth' < *centum* 'hundred'] —**centesimally** *adv*

centesimo /sen téssimō/ (*plural* **-mos** or **-mi** /-mi/) *n* a subunit of currency in Uruguay and Panama. See table at **currency** [Mid-19C. < Italian < Latin *centesimus* (see CENTESIMAL)]

centi- *prefix* **1.** hundred ○ *centipede* **2.** hundredth ○ *centipoise* [Via French < Latin *centum* 'hundred']

centigrade /sénti grayd/ *adj* a temperature scale, especially Celsius, based on a range of one hundred

centigram /sénti gram/, **centigramme** *n* a unit of mass equal to one hundredth of a gram. Symbol **cg**

centilitre /sénti leetər/ *n* a unit of volume equal to one hundredth of a litre. Symbol **cl**

centillion /sen tílli ən/ (*plural* **-lions** or *same*) *n* **1.** in the United Kingdom and Germany, the number represented by the figure 1 followed by 600 zeros **2.** *US* in the United States, Canada, and France, the number represented by the figure 1 followed by 303 zeros [Mid-19C. < CENTI-, after MILLION and similar words]

centime /són teem, saán-/ *n* a subunit of currency in some French-speaking countries. See table at **currency** [Early 19C. < French < Latin *centesimus* (see CENTESIMAL)]

centimetre /sénti meetər/ *n* a unit of length equal to one hundredth of a metre. Symbol **cm**

centimetre-gram-second, **centimetre-gramme-second** *adj* relating to or using a measurement system that has the centimetre as the basic unit for length, the gram for mass, and the second for time. In scientific contexts the cgs system has been largely replaced by the SI system.

centimo /séntimō/ (*plural* **-mos**) *n* a subunit of currency in several Spanish-speaking countries. See table at **currency** [Late 19C. Via Spanish < French *centime* (see CENTIME)]

centimorgan /sénti mawrgən/ *n* a unit of measurement used to indicate how closely genes are linked together on the same chromosome [Mid-20C. After Thomas Hunt MORGAN]

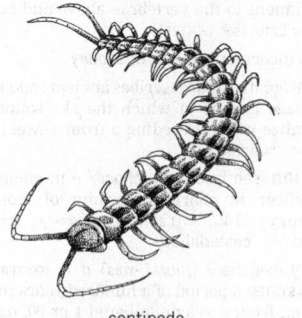
centipede

centipede /sénti peed/ *n* a small fast-moving invertebrate with a long slender body divided into many segments, most of which bear one pair of legs. Class: Chilopoda.

centipoise /sénti poyz/ *n* a unit of measurement for viscosity in the cgs system that is equal to one hundredth of a poise

centner /séntnər/ *n* **1.** BRITISH UNIT OF MASS in the United Kingdom, a unit of mass equal to 45.3 kg/100 lb **2.** EUROPEAN UNIT OF MASS in some European countries, a unit of mass equal to 50 kg/110.23 lb **3.** SOVIET UNIT OF MASS in countries of the former Soviet Union, a unit of mass equal to 100 kg/220.46 lb [Mid-16C. < German *Zentner* < Latin *centenarius* 'of a hundred']

centr- *prefix* same as **centro-** (*used before a vowel*)

centra ANAT plural of **centrum**

central /séntrəl/ *adj* **1.** IN MIDDLE in, near, or forming the middle of something **2.** EQUIDISTANT FROM OTHER POINTS at approximately the same distance from a number of different points or places **3.** IN MAIN PART OF TOWN in the part of a town or city where the main shops, offices, and other facilities are situated **4.** HAVING CONTROL OVER PARTS controlling the activities of connected or subordinate parts ○ *a central authority* **5.** HAVING LINKED COMPONENTS describes a system of linked devices controlled by a single unit or at a single point **6.** CRUCIAL of critical importance or great influence ○ *The notion is central to their thinking on the subject.* **7.** DOMINANT with a major or the principal role **8.** ANAT RELATING TO CENTRUM relating to the centrum of a vertebra **9.** PHON SAID WITH TONGUE IN MIDDLE POSITION describes a vowel articulated with the tongue at or near the middle of the hard palate, as is the final vowel in 'cola' ■ *n* CENTRE OF ACTIVITY a focal point for a particular activity or type of person (*informal*) ○ *Come round, there are lots of people here – it's party central!* [Mid-17C. < Latin *centralis* < *centrum* (see CENTRE)] —**centrally** *adv*

Central /séntrəl/ former administrative region of Scotland from 1975 to 1996

Central African Federation federation from 1953 to 1963 of Nyasaland, Northern Rhodesia, and Southern Rhodesia, equivalent to present-day Malawi, Zambia, and Zimbabwe

Central African Republic

Central African Republic landlocked country in central Africa. Formerly part of French Equatorial Africa, it became independent in 1960. It is bordered by Chad, Sudan, the Democratic Republic of the Congo, the Republic of the Congo, and Cameroon. Language: French. Currency: CFA franc. Capital: Bangui. Population: 3,683,538 (2003). Area: 622,436 sq. km/240,324 sq. mi. Former name **Ubangi-Shari** (until 1958)

Central America the southern part of North America, extending from the southern border of Mexico to northwestern Colombia, South America. It includes the countries of Guatemala, Belize, Honduras, El Salvador, Nicaragua, Costa Rica, and Panama. Population: 31,300,000 (1993). Area: 523,000 sq. km/202,000 sq. mi. —**Central American** *n, adj*

central angle *n* an angle formed in the centre of a circle by the meeting of two radii

Central Asia region comprising the countries of Kazakhstan, Kyrgyzstan, Tajikistan, Turkmenistan, and Uzbekistan

central bank *n* a financial institution whose function is to regulate state fiscal and monetary activities, e.g. the Bank of England. It is responsible for the issue of bank notes and for controlling the flow of currency. —**central banker** *n*

central casting *n N Am* the department in a film production company whose function is to select appropriate actors to audition for parts

Central Committee *n* in a Communist party, the part of the bureaucracy responsible for party policy

Central European Time *n* the standard time adopted by most Western European countries, one hour ahead of Universal Time

central government *n* the area of government that is concerned with national issues such as taxation, defence, international relations, and trade

central heating *n* a system designed to heat a whole building from a single source of heat by pumping hot water or air to room radiators or vents —**centrally heated** *adj*

Central Intelligence Agency *n* full form of **CIA**

centralise *vti* another spelling of **centralize**

centralism /séntrəlizəm/ *n* the concentration of control, especially political control, in a single authority —**centralist** *n, adj* —**centralistic** /séntrə lístik/ *adj*

centrality /sen trálləti/ *n* **1.** CRITICAL ROLE the crucial importance of somebody or something **2.** POSITION IN MIDDLE the location of somebody or something in or near the middle of something **3.** LOCATION IN MAIN PART OF TOWN the location of something in the part of a town or city where the main shops, offices, and other facilities are situated

centralize /séntrə līz/ (**-izes**, **-izing**, **-ized**), **centralise** (**-ises**, **-ising**, **-ised**) *vti* **1.** to remove political or administrative power from local or subordinate levels and concentrate it in a central authority **2.** to concentrate or collect something at a single point —**centralization** /séntrə līzáysh'n/ *n* —**centralizer** *n*

central locking *n* a system in which all the doors and the boot of a motor vehicle are automatically locked or unlocked when somebody locks or unlocks one door

Central Lowlands fertile region of Scotland lying between the Highlands to the north and the Southern Uplands to the south. It contains the valleys of the Clyde, Forth, and Tay rivers.

Central Mount Stuart mountain in central Australia, considered the geographical centre of the continent. Height: 845 m/2,772 ft.

central nervous system *n* the part of the nervous system, consisting of the brain and spinal cord, that controls and coordinates most functions of the body and mind. Impulses from sense organs travel to the central nervous system and impulses to muscles and glands travel from it.

Central Park large park on Manhattan Island in New York City. It was the first urban park to be developed in the United States and served as a model for subsequent city parks.

central processing unit, **central processor** *n* the part of a computer that performs operations and executes software commands

central reservation *n UK* a narrow strip of land that separates lanes of traffic travelling in opposite directions on a dual carriageway or motorway. ANZ, N Am term **median strip**

Central Standard Time, **Central Time** *n* **1.** the standard time in the time zone centred on 90° W longitude, which includes the central states of the United States and the central provinces of Canada. It is six hours behind Universal Time. **2.** the standard time in the time zone centred on longitude 135° E, which includes the central part of Australia. It is nine-and-a-half hours ahead of Universal Time.

central sulcus *n* a deep groove in each of the hemispheres of the brain, separating the frontal and parietal lobes

Central Time *n* TIME same as **Central Standard Time**

centre /séntər/ *n* **1.** MIDDLE POINT OR PART the middle point, area, or part of something that is the same distance from all edges, ends, or opposite sides **2.** MATHS MIDDLE OF CIRCLE OR SPHERE the interior point that is the same distance from all points on the circumference of a circle, the surface of a sphere, or the vertices of a polygon **3.** MATHS MIDDLE OF LINE the point on a line that is the same distance from both ends **4.** FOOD FILLING the filling of a chocolate, doughnut, or other food **5.** MAIN PART OF TOWN the part of a town or city where the main shops, offices, and other facilities are situated **6.** PLACE FOR PARTICULAR ACTIVITY a place where a particular activity is carried on ○ *a sports centre* **7.** FOCUS OF ATTENTION the point that is the focus of attention or interest ○ *the issue at the centre of the controversy* **8.** INFLUENTIAL PLACE OR ORGANIZATION a place, area, or group of people exerting control or influence over somebody or something else ○ *a centre of design innovation* **9.** CLUSTER OR CONCENTRATION a place or part where something is concentrated or focused **10.** also **Centre** POL POLITICAL MODERATES those political parties or the section of a party holding views that are neither left-wing nor right-wing **11.**

PIVOTAL POINT OR AXIS the point or line around which something rotates **12.** PHYS **POINT WHERE FORCE ACTS** in physics, the point at or through which a force is considered to act **13.** SPORTS **ATTACKING PLAYER OR POSITION** in some sports, an attacking player or position in the middle of the field or court **14.** BASEBALL same as **centre field 15.** FOOTBALL **AUSTRALIAN RULES PLAYER IN CENTRE CIRCLE** in Australian Rules football, a player who occupies a position in the centre circle **16.** ANAT **GROUP OF NERVE CELLS REGULATING FUNCTION** a group of nerve cells, especially within the central nervous system, that controls a particular function of the body **17.** MECH ENG **CONICAL PART OF LATHE** the part of a lathe that supports the work to be turned **18.** MECH ENG **MARK TO GUIDE DRILL** a dimple made in metal with a pointed tool (**centre punch**) to mark the centre of a larger hole to be drilled ■ *v* (**-tres, -tring, -tred**) **1.** *vt* **PUT SOMETHING IN MIDDLE** to position something in the middle of something **2.** *vti* **FOCUS ON THEME** to focus on a theme or topic, or cause something to do this ○ *The debate centres on the possible health risks involved.* **3.** *vti* **CONCENTRATE SOMEWHERE** to be concentrated, or cause something to be concentrated, in a particular place **4.** *vt* SPORTS **PASS BALL TOWARDS MIDDLE** in some sports, to pass, hit, or kick a ball or puck from the edge of the playing area towards the middle [14C. Directly or via French < Latin *centrum* < Greek *kentron* 'point' < *kentein* 'to prick']

centre back *n* in various sports, a player or position in the middle of the back line

centre bit *n* a drill attachment or tool for boring or cutting that has a pointed projection in the middle and cutters at the sides

centreboard /séntər bawrd/ *n* a keel in a sailing boat that can be retracted upwards in shallow water

centre bounce *n* FOOTBALL same as **bounce** *n* (sense 5)

centre circle *n* in Australian Rules football, a 3 m/9.75 ft circle marking the centre of the playing field in which the umpire starts and restarts the game by bouncing the ball

centred /séntərd/ *adj* **1.** positioned at the same distance from all edges, ends, or opposite sides **2.** exhibiting confidence, self-awareness, and often a sense of determination —**centredness** *n*

centre field *n* **1.** in baseball, the part of the outfield behind second base **2.** the position of the baseball player who plays centre field —**centre fielder** *n*

centrefold /séntər fōld/ *n* **1.** a single illustration, advertisement, or feature that covers the two facing pages in the middle of a magazine or newspaper, especially a photograph of a naked or nearly naked model **2.** the subject of a centrefold photograph, especially a naked or nearly naked model **3.** MEDIA same as **centre spread** (sense 1)

centre forward *n* in sports such as football and hockey, the player or position in the middle of the forward attacking line

centre half (*plural* **centre halfs**) *n* in football and hockey, the player or position in the middle of the half line

centre half-back *n* in Australian Rules football, a player occupying a position in the middle of the field between the fullbacks and the centreline

centre half-forward *n* in Australian Rules football, a player occupying a position in the middle of the field between the centre line and the full forwards

centreline /séntər līn/ *n* **1.** **LINE DOWN MIDDLE OF ROAD** a solid or dashed line on a road that marks where traffic should flow, either separating lanes going in opposite directions or multiple lanes going in the same direction **2.** **LINE DOWN MIDDLE** a real or imaginary line through or along the middle of something **3.** **THREE PLAYERS ACROSS CENTRE OF FIELD** in Australian Rules football, the three players that form a line across the centre of the playing field, namely the centre and the two wingmen

Centrelink /séntər lingk/ *n* an Australian government agency that offers a range of services to the public such as advice on finding employment and eligibility for social security payments

centre man *n* FOOTBALL same as **centre** *n* (sense 15)

centre of curvature *n* the centre of a circle whose

radius is perpendicular to a line tangent to any point on the concave side of a smooth curve

centre of excellence *n* a place where the highest standards of achievement are aimed for in a particular sphere of activity

centre of gravity *n* **1.** the point through which the sum of gravitational forces on a body can be considered to act **2.** PHYS same as **centre of mass**

centre of mass *n* the point at which the total mass of a body or system is assumed to be centred and upon which the sum of external forces can be considered to act

centrepiece /séntər peess/ *n* **1.** an object placed in the middle of something as decoration or to attract attention **2.** the most important part or feature of something

centre punch *n* in metalworking, a pointed tool used for making a dimple to guide a drill bit prior to drilling a hole

centre spread *n* **1.** the two pages that face each other in the middle of a magazine or newspaper **2.** a magazine or newspaper article featured in the middle to give it prominence

centre square *n* in Australian Rules football, a square measuring 45 sq. m/146.25 sq. ft in the centre of the playing field, containing the centre circle

centre stage *n* **1.** **MIDDLE OF STAGE** the middle area of a theatre stage **2.** **FOCUS OF INTEREST** the centre of people's attention or interest ■ *adv* **1.** **IN MIDDLE OF STAGE** in or to the middle area of a theatre stage **2.** **TO CENTRE OF ATTENTION** at or to the centre of people's attention or interest

centre three-quarter *n* in rugby, either of the two positions in the middle of the three-quarter line, or the players who have those positions

centri- *prefix* same as **centro-**

centric /séntrik/, **centrical** /-trik'l/ *adj* **1.** **AT OR AS MIDDLE** located at or constituting the middle of something **2.** ANAT **OF OR FROM NERVE CENTRE** relating to or issuing from a nerve centre **3.** BOT **WITH CONCENTRIC LAYERS OF TISSUE** describes a plant's vascular bundles in which one type of sap-conducting tissue is surrounded by another **4.** BOT **TAPERING AND CYLINDRICAL** describes leaves that are tapering and cylindrical **5.** MICROBIOL **OF RADICALLY SYMMETRICAL DIATOMS** describes diatoms which are radially symmetrical. Class: Centrales. [Late 16C. < Greek *kentrikos* < *kentron* (see CENTRE)] —**centrically** *adv* —**centricity** /sen tríssəti/ *n*

-centric *suffix* **1.** having a particular number or type of centres ○ *hexcentric* ○ *acentric* **2.** having as its focus of attention, interest, or activity ○ *egocentric* ○ *teen-centric* [< medieval Latin *-centricus* < Latin *centrum* (see CENTRE)]

centrifugal /séntri fyoog'l, sen tríffyoog'l/ *adj* **1.** PHYS **AWAY FROM CENTRE** acting, moving, or pulling away from a centre or axis **2.** TECH **EMPLOYING CENTRIFUGAL FORCE** using or operated by centrifugal force **3.** PHYSIOL same as **efferent 4.** BOT **DEVELOPING OUTWARDS** describes a plant part or tissue that develops from the centre outwards **5.** POL **DECENTRALIZING POWER** tending to disperse political or administrative power away from a central authority ■ *n* TECH **SOMETHING USING CENTRIFUGAL FORCE** an apparatus that uses centrifugal force, or a rotating drum in such an apparatus —**centrifugalism** *n* —**centrifugally** *adv*

centrifugal force *n* an apparent force that seems to pull a rotating or spinning object away from a centre

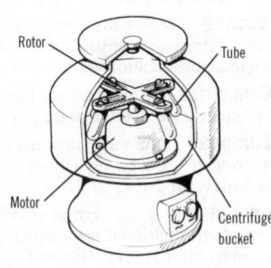

centrifuge

centrifuge /séntri fyooj, -fyoozh/ *n* **1.** a device that rotates rapidly and uses centrifugal force to separate substances of different densities **2.** a rotating apparatus used to simulate the effects of gravity or acceleration on humans or animals [Early 18C. < Latin *centrifugus* 'fleeing the centre' < *fugere* 'flee'] —**centrifugation** /séntri fyoo gáysh'n/ *n* —**centrifuge** *vt*

centriole /séntri ōl/ *n* in an animal cell, a two-part rod-shaped structure with the parts lying at right angles to each other, located in pairs near the nucleus. During cell division, centrioles move to opposite ends of the cell and form the poles of the spindle fibres that pull the chromosomes apart. [Late 19C. < modern Latin *centriolum* 'small centre' < Latin *centrum* (see CENTRE)]

centripetal /sen tríppit'l, séntri peét'l/ *adj* **1.** PHYS **TOWARDS CENTRE** acting, moving, or pulling towards a centre or axis **2.** TECH **EMPLOYING CENTRIPETAL FORCE** using or operated by centripetal force **3.** PHYSIOL same as **afferent 4.** BOT **DEVELOPING INWARDS** describes a plant part or tissue that develops from the perimeter inwards **5.** POL **CENTRALIZING POWER** tending to concentrate political or administrative power in a central authority [Early 18C. < modern Latin *centripetus* 'seeking the centre' < Latin *petere* (see PETITION)] —**centripetally** *adv*

centripetal force *n* a force that pulls a rotating or spinning object towards a centre or axis

centrism /séntrizəm/ *n* the holding or advocating of moderate political or other views —**centrist** *n, adj*

centro- *prefix* centre ○ *centrosome* [< Latin *centrum* (see CENTRE)]

centrobaric /séntrō bárrik/ *adj* relating to a centre of gravity [Early 18C. < Greek *kentrobarikē* 'centre-weight' < *baros* 'weight']

centroid /sén troyd/ *n* PHYS same as **centre of mass** [Late 19C. < CENTRO-]

centrolecithal /séntrō léssithəl/ *adj* used to describe an egg with the yolk in the middle [Late 19C. < CENTRO- + LECITHIN + -AL¹]

centromere /séntrə meer/ *n* the point at which two parts (**chromatids**) of a chromosome join and at which the spindle fibres are attached during cell division (**mitosis**) —**centromeric** /séntrə mérrik, -meérik/ *adj*

centrosome /séntrəsōm/ *n* a small region of cytoplasm near the nucleus of a cell. In animal cells, it contains rod-shaped structures from which the spindle fibres (**centrioles**) develop in cell division. —**centrosomic** /séntrə sómmik/ *adj*

centrum /séntrəm/ (*plural* **-trums** or **-tra** /-trə/) *n* a thick mass of bone in a vertebra that is the point of attachment to the vertebrae above and below [Mid-19C. < Latin (see CENTRE)]

~~centry~~ incorrect spelling of **century**

centum /kéntəm/ *adj* describes ancient Indo-European language groups in which the /k/ sound did not palatalize when preceding a front vowel [Early 20C. < Latin, 'hundred']

centurion /sen tyoóri ən, -choór-/ *n* in ancient Rome, an officer in charge of a unit of foot soldiers (**century**) [14C. < Latin *centurion-* < *centuria* (see CENTURY)] —**centurial** *adj*

century /sénchəri/ (*plural* **-ries**) *n* **1.** **100-YEAR PERIOD IN DATING SYSTEM** a period of a hundred years in a dating system, from a year numbered 1 or 00, e.g. 1901 or 2000, to one ending in 00 or 99, e.g. 2000 or 2099. Centuries are counted forwards or backwards from a significant event, e.g. the birth of Jesus Christ. **2.** **100 YEARS** a period of a hundred years **3.** CRICKET **100 RUNS** in cricket, 100 runs scored by one batsman **4.** **UNIT OF ROMAN SOLDIERS** in ancient Rome, a group of foot soldiers, originally comprising a hundred men but later between sixty and eighty **5.** **GROUP OF ROMAN VOTERS** in ancient Rome, a division of citizens designated for voting purposes **6.** **LONG TIME** a very long time (*informal*; *usually used in the plural*) [14C. < Latin *centuria* 'group of a hundred' < *centum* 'hundred']

USAGE When does a new century begin? Mathematicians will no doubt insist that a new *century* begins on 1 January of a year ending in 01, so that the 22nd century will begin on 1 January 2101. This is because the first century AD began with the year 1 (as

did the first century BC – there was no year 0), and if that century is to have contained its requisite hundred years, the first year of any subsequent century must also end in 1. In most contexts, however, a new century is reckoned from the year ending in 00, since this is psychologically the more significant point. Similarly, a new millennium begins for practical purposes on 1 January of the year ending in 000, not 001.

century plant *n* a plant with greyish-green leaves that takes ten to thirty years to mature and flowers just once before dying. Native to: Mexico, southern United States. Latin name: *Agave americana*. [< the length of its maturation]

CEO *abbr* BUSINESS chief executive officer

ceorl /churl/ *n* in Anglo-Saxon England, a freeman of the lowest class [Old English (see CHURL)]

cep /sep/, **cèpe** /sep, seep/ *n* an edible woodland mushroom with a shiny brown cap and a creamy-coloured underside. It has a rich nutty flavour. Latin name: *Boletus edulis*. [Mid-19C. Via French *cèpe* < Gascon *cep* 'tree trunk, mushroom' < Latin *cippus* 'stake']

cephal- *prefix* same as **cephalo-** (*used before vowels*)

cephalad /séffə lad/ *adv* in or into a position nearer the head or front

cephalic /sə fállik/ *adj* relating to the head, or in the region of the head [15C. Via French and Latin < Greek *kephalikos* < *kephalē* (see CEPHALO-)] —**cephalically** *adv*

-cephalic *suffix* having a particular number of heads or a particular kind of head ○ *monocephalic* ○ *brachycephalic* [< Latin *cephalicus* < Greek *kephalē* (see CEPHALO-)]

cephalic index *n* the ratio of the width to the length of a human skull, measured at the widest and longest points, and multiplied by 100

cephalin /séffəlin/, **kephalin** /kéff-/ *n* one of a group of chemicals found in all tissues, especially the brain

cephalization /séffəlī záysh'n/, **cephalisation** *n* the tendency for sensory, neural, and feeding organs to be concentrated at the front end of the body, leading to the development of a head during both evolution and embryological development

cephalo- *prefix* head, skull ○ *cephalometry* [Via modern Latin < Greek *kephalē* < Indo-European]

cephalometry /séffə lómmətri/ *n* the measurement of human heads, especially using X-rays or ultrasound. It is practised in dentistry to determine if the mouth can accommodate new teeth and in obstetrics to gauge if a foetal head can pass through the birth canal. —**cephalometer** *n* —**cephalometric** /séffəlō méttrik/ *adj*

Cephalonia /séffə lṓni ə, kéffə-/ the largest of the Ionian Islands in western Greece. Population: 39,579 (2001). Area: 750 sq. km/290 sq. mi.

cephalopod /séffələ pod/ *n* an invertebrate sea animal with a large head and tentacles, e.g. an octopus, squid, or cuttlefish. Class: Cephalopoda. —**cephalopod** *adj* —**cephalopodan** /séffə lóppədən/ *adj, n* —**cephalopodic** /séffələ póddik/ *adj* —**cephalopodous** /séffə lóppədəss/ *adj*

cephalosporin /séffəlō spáwrin/ *n* an antibiotic belonging to a group of semisynthetic antibiotics with a broad range of effectiveness [Mid-20C. < modern Latin *Cephalosporium*, genus name of the fungus from which originally isolated < *cephalo-* (see CEPHALO-) + *spora* (see SPORE)]

cephalothorax /séffəlō tháwraks/ (*plural* **-raxes** or **-races** /-rəsseez/) *n* the fused head and thorax typical of spiders and other arachnids and many crustaceans

-cephalous *suffix* having a particular number of heads or a particular kind of head ○ *dicephalous* ○ *autocephalous* [< Greek *-kephalos* < *kephalē* (see CEPHALO-)]

-cephaly *suffix* a particular condition of the head or skull ○ *microcephaly* [< Greek *kephalē* (see CEPHALO-)]

Cepheid /séefi id/, **Cepheid variable** *n* a star that has regular periods of varying brightness, usually lasting from one to fifty days [Early 20C. < CEPHEUS + -ID]

Cepheus /séef yooss, séefi əss/ *n* a constellation of the northern hemisphere. See illustration at **constellation**

ceraceous /si ráyshəss/ *adj* like wax in appearance or texture (*technical*) [Mid-18C. < Latin *cera* 'wax']

ceramal /sə ráym'l/ *n* INDUST same as **cermet** [Mid-20C. Blend of CERAMIC + ALLOY]

ceramic /sə rámmik/ *n* **1.** a hard brittle heat-resistant material made by firing a mixture of clay and chemicals at high temperature **2.** an object made from ceramic [Early 19C. < Greek *keramikos* 'of pottery' < *keramos* 'pottery'] —**ceramic** *adj*

ceramic foam *n* a very light porous solid insulator, made from a ceramic powder and a foaming agent, that can withstand sudden extreme temperature changes

ceramic hob *n* a flat cooking surface of ceramic with heating elements underneath

ceramicist *n* ARTS same as **ceramist**

ceramics /sə rámmiks/ *n* the art, technology, or process of making ceramic objects (*takes a singular verb*)

ceramist /sérrəmist/, **ceramicist** /sə rámməsist/ *n* somebody who makes ceramic objects

Ceram Sea /sə rám-/ sea in the western Pacific Ocean, in central Moluccas, Indonesia, west of New Guinea. Area: 51,800 sq. km/20,000 sq. mi.

cerastes /sə räss teez/ (*plural same*) *n* a poisonous snake that has a projection like a horn above each eye. Native to: North Africa, southwestern Asia. Genus: *Cerastes*. [14C. < Greek *kerastēs* 'horned' < *keras* 'horn']

ceratin *n* BIOCHEM another spelling of **keratin**

ceratoid /sérrə toyd/ *adj* resembling the horn of an animal in appearance or substance

Cerberus /súrbərəss/ *n* in Greek mythology, the fierce dog that guards the entrance to Hades, usually represented as having three heads —**Cerberean** /súrbə rée ən, sə béeri ən/ *adj*

-cercal *suffix* having a particular kind of tail ○ *diphycercal* [< French *-cerque* < Greek *kerkos* 'tail']

cercaria /sur káiri ə/ (*plural* **-ae** /-ee/) *n* the tadpole-shaped larva of various parasitic worms (**flukes**) [Mid-19C. < modern Latin < Greek *kerkos* 'tail'] —**cercarial** *adj*

cercopithecoid /súrkō píthikoyd/ *n* a monkey with cheek pouches, a brightly coloured rump, and downward-pointing nostrils, e.g. a baboon, macaque, or langur. Native to: Africa, Asia. Superfamily: Cercopithecoidea. [Late 19C. < Latin *cercopithecus* < Greek *kerkopithēkos* < *kerkos* 'tail' + *pithēkos* 'ape'] —**cercopithecoid** *adj*

cercus /súrkəss/ (*plural* **-ci** /-see/) *n* either of two sensory appendages at the end of the abdomen of the female mosquito and other insects [Early 19C. Via modern Latin < Greek *kerkos* 'tail'] —**cercal** *adj*

cere /seer/ *n* the thick skin at the base of the upper beak of some birds such as parrots, which contains the bird's nostrils [15C. < Latin *cera* 'wax']

cereal /séeri əl/ *n* **1.** GRAIN OF CROP PLANT the nutritious grain produced by a cultivated plant belonging to the grass family, e.g. oats, barley, rye, wheat, rice, and maize **2.** CROP PLANT a plant that is cultivated for cereal **3.** BREAKFAST FOOD food made from cereal and eaten especially at breakfast, usually with milk [Early 19C. Directly or via French *céréale* < Latin *cerealis* 'of grain cultivation', after CERES]

SPELLCHECK cereal or **serial**? Do not confuse the spelling of ***cereal*** and ***serial***, which sound similar. A ***cereal*** is a type of plant, its grain, or food made from it, as in *cereal crops, breakfast cereal*. The word ***serial*** can be used a noun, denoting a story in episodes, or as an adjective, meaning 'forming a series or doing things in a series', as in *a serial killer*.

cerebellum /sérrə bélləm/ (*plural* **-lums** or **-la** /-lə/) *n* the part of the brain located directly behind the front part (**cerebrum**), typically consisting of two hemispheres connected by a thin central region, and serving to control and coordinate muscular activity and maintain balance. In humans, it lies between the back of the medulla oblongata and the underside of the posterior part of the cerebral hemispheres. [Mid-16C. < Latin, 'small brain' < *cerebrum* 'brain'] —**cerebellar** *adj*

cerebra *n* ANAT plural of **cerebrum**

cerebral /sérrəbrəl, sə rée-/ *adj* **1.** RELATING TO FRONT OF BRAIN relating to or located in the front part of the brain (**cerebrum**) **2.** RELATING TO WHOLE BRAIN relating to or involving the whole brain or any part of it **3.** INTELLECTUAL involving the psychological processes of thinking and reasoning rather than the emotions —**cerebrally** *adv*

cerebral cortex *n* the wrinkled grey outer layer of the front parts of the brain (**cerebral hemispheres**). Its functions include the perception of sensations, learning, reasoning, and memory. Technical name **pallium** (sense 3)

cerebral dominance *n* the normal tendency for one of the two sides of the brain (**cerebral hemispheres**) to have stronger control over some functions of the mind and body. When the left hemisphere is dominant, somebody is likely to be right-handed, and vice versa.

cerebral hemisphere *n* either of the two symmetrical halves of the front part of the brain (**cerebrum**)

cerebral palsy *n* a condition caused by brain damage around the time of birth and marked by lack of muscle control, especially in the limbs —**cerebral-palsied** *adj*

cerebral vascular accident *n* MED same as **cerebrovascular accident**

cerebro- *prefix* brain, cerebrum ○ *cerebrovascular* [< Latin *cerebrum* (see CEREBRUM)]

cerebroside /sérrəbrō sīd, sə rée-/ *n* a fatty chemical (**lipid**) found in the brain and the covering (**myelin sheath**) of some nerves [Late 19C. < CEREBRO- + -OSE [2]]

cerebrospinal /sérrəbrō spīn'l/ *adj* relating to or involving the brain and spinal cord

cerebrospinal fluid *n* the colourless fluid in and around the brain and spinal cord that absorbs shocks and maintains uniform pressure

cerebrospinal meningitis *n* inflammation of the membranes (**meninges**) surrounding the brain and spinal cord, causing high fever and sometimes unconsciousness

cerebrovascular /sérrəbrō váskyōōlər/ *adj* relating to or involving the blood vessels that supply the brain

cerebrovascular accident, **cerebral vascular accident** *n* any physical event, e.g. a cerebral haemorrhage, that may lead to a stroke (*technical*)

cerebrum /sə réebrəm, sérrə-/ (*plural* **-brums** or **-bra** /-brə/) *n* the front part of the brain, divided into two symmetrical halves (**cerebral hemispheres**). In humans, it is where activities including reasoning, learning, sensory perception, and emotional responses take place. [Early 17C. < Latin, 'brain' < Indo-European, 'head']

cerecloth /séer kloth/ *n* fabric coated with melted wax to make it waterproof [Mid-16C. Alteration of *cered cloth* 'waxed cloth', < past participle of *cere* 'to wax' < Latin *cerare* < *cera* 'wax']

Ceredigion /kérrə díggi on/ county and local council in Wales, occupying the area of the historic county of Cardiganshire. Population: 74,941 (2001). Area: 1,793 sq. km/692 sq. mi.

cerement /séermənt, sérrə-/ *n* TEXTILES same as **cerecloth** ■ **cerements** *npl* burial clothes [Early 17C. < *cere* (see CERECLOTH)]

ceremonial /sérrə mṓni əl/ *adj* **1.** RELATING TO FORMAL OCCASIONS used on a formal occasion or at a ceremony **2.** INVOLVING CEREMONY involving or done as part of a ceremony ○ *the ceremonial presentation of the awards* **3.** NOMINAL without real power or authority ○ *a largely ceremonial role* ■ *n* **1.** FORMAL ETIQUETTE the correct way to behave on formal occasions **2.** RITUAL a ceremony or set of ceremonies for an occasion **3.** ORDER OF SERVICE the set order of rites or ceremonies in a Christian church, or a book containing this —**ceremonialism** *n* —**ceremonialist** *n* —**ceremonially** *adv*

USAGE ceremonial or **ceremonious**? ***Ceremonial*** is the more neutral word, describing things that involve ceremony or are a part of it, e.g. *ceremonial occasions*. It is not now used of people. ***Ceremonious*** is used of people or their behaviour: a *ceremonious person*, or a person with a *ceremonious manner*, is somebody who likes and

adheres to formalities, perhaps even excessively. Avoid using ***ceremonious*** where ***ceremonial*** is appropriate.

ceremonious /sérrə mṓni əss/ *adj* **1.** excessively polite or formal, being careful to observe formalities and behave correctly ○ *He replied with ceremonious dignity.* **2.** involving ceremony or consisting of ceremony ○ *ceremonious gestures* —**ceremoniously** *adv* —**ceremoniousness** *n*

USAGE See ***ceremonial.***

ceremony /sérrəməni/ (*plural* **-nies**) *n* **1. RITUAL FOR FORMAL OCCASION** a formal event to celebrate or solemnize something, e.g. a wedding, an official opening, or an anniversary **2. FORMAL ETIQUETTE** the forms of behaviour that are expected or observed on a formal occasion **3. SOCIAL GESTURE** a polite social gesture or ritual performed for the sake of convention [14C. < Latin *caerimonia*] ◇ **stand on ceremony** to behave in a formal manner or insist on formality

Cerenkov effect /chə réngkof-/, **Cherenkov effect** *n* the emission of light by a charged particle as it passes through a transparent medium at a speed greater than that of light in the same medium [Mid-20C. After Pavel A. *Cherenkov* (1904–90), Soviet physicist]

Cerenkov radiation, **Cherenkov radiation** *n* light emitted by a charged particle as it passes through a transparent medium at a speed greater than that of light in the same medium [Mid-20C. See CERENKOV EFFECT]

Ceres /séer eez/ *n* **1.** in Roman mythology, the goddess of agriculture. Greek equivalent **Demeter 2.** the largest asteroid and the first to be discovered, in 1801, orbiting between Mars and Jupiter [< Latin]

cereus /séeri əss/ *n* **1.** a cactus with spiny ribbed stems, especially a Brazilian species that can reach a height of 13 m/40 ft. Genus: *Cereus.* **2.** any cactus related to the true cereus, e.g. the night-blooming cereus [Late 17C. < modern Latin *Cereus* < Latin *cereus* 'candle' < *cera* 'wax']

ceria /séeri ə/ *n* CHEM same as **ceric oxide** [< modern Latin, plural of *cerium* (see CERIUM)]

ceric /séerik/ *adj* relating to or containing cerium with a valency of four [Mid-19C. < CERIUM]

ceric oxide *n* a white crystalline powder. Use: manufacture of ceramics, polishing glass. Formula: CeO_2.

cerise /sə réez, -réess/ *n* a deep vivid pinkish-red colour [Mid-19C. < French, 'cherry' < Greek *kerasos* 'cherry tree'] —**cerise** *adj*

cerium /séeri əm/ *n* a grey malleable metallic element, the most abundant of the rare-earth group. Source: bastnaesite, monazite. Use: metallurgy, glass-making, ceramics, cigarette-lighter flints. Symbol **Ce**. See table at **element** [Early 19C. < modern Latin < CERES; because the asteroid was discovered just before this element]

cermet /súr met, -mit/ *n* a durable substance able to withstand high temperatures, formed by bonding ceramic particles with metal [Mid-20C. Blend of CERAMIC + METAL]

CERN /surn/ *n* an EU organization that carries out research into high-energy particle physics, now called the European Laboratory for Particle Physics. Full form **Conseil Européen pour la Recherche Nucléaire**

cernuous /súrnyoo əss/ *adj* describes flowers and buds that droop naturally [Mid-17C. < Latin *cernuus* 'inclined forward']

cero /séerō, sírrō/ (*plural same* or **-ros**) *n* a large edible sea fish that has silvery sides and large spiny fins. Native to: warm western Atlantic waters. Latin name: *Scomberomorus regalis.* [Late 19C. Alteration of Spanish *sierra* 'saw' < Latin *serra*]

cerotic acid /si róttik-/ *n* a white fatty acid. Source: natural waxes such as beeswax and carnauba wax. Formula: $CH_3(CH_2)_{24}COOH$. [Mid-19C. < Latin *cerotum* 'wax salve' < Greek *kērōton* 'waxed']

cerous /séerəss/ *adj* relating to or containing cerium with a valency of three [Mid-19C. < CERIUM]

cert /surt/ *n* (*informal*) **1.** somebody who is certain to do something **2.** a foregone conclusion or certain outcome [Late 19C. Shortening of CERTAIN or CERTAINTY]

CERT /surt/ *abbr* ONLINE computer emergency response team (*used in e-mails*)

cert. *abbr* **1.** certificate **2.** certification **3.** certified

certain /súrt'n/ *adj* **1. WITHOUT DOUBT** having no doubts about something ○ *I'm certain he's the man I saw.* **2. KNOWN OR SET** definitely known, fixed, or settled **3. INEVITABLE** guaranteed to happen or to do something ○ *It's certain they'll lose.* **4. RELIABLE** able to be relied on **5. NOT DEFINED** undeniable but difficult to define, quantify, or express ○ *a certain hesitation in his voice* **6. NOT NAMED** able to be identified but not named ○ *A certain selfish person has used up all the milk.* **7. UNKNOWN OR UNFAMILIAR** used to indicate that only the name of the person, thing, or place mentioned is known ○ *A certain Mr Esposito was involved.* ■ *det* **SOME** of an imprecise but limited number [13C. Via French < assumed Vulgar Latin *certanus* < Latin *certus* 'determined', past participle of *cernere* 'decide'] ◇ **certain of** some but not all of (*formal*) ◇ **for certain** without any doubt ◇ **make certain 1.** to check that something has been done or is the case **2.** to take action to achieve something

ORIGIN The Latin word *cernere*, 'to separate' or 'to decide', from which ***certain*** is derived, is also the source of English *crime, decree, discern, discreet, discriminate, excrement, excrete, secret,* and *secretary.*

certainly /súrt'nli/ *adv* **1. DEFINITELY** without any doubt or qualification on the part of the speaker ○ *It's certainly a big problem.* **2. USED TO CONCEDE POINT** used to concede a point that has been made ○ *That's certainly an area we could improve upon.* **3. YES** used to indicate unreserved assent ◇ **certainly not** used to indicate emphatic denial or refusal

certainty /súrt'nti/ (*plural* **-ties**) *n* **1. SOMETHING INEVITABLE** a conclusion or outcome that is beyond doubt **2. SOMEBODY OR SOMETHING CERTAIN OF SUCCESS** something that is certain to happen, or somebody assured of a result **3. CONVICTION** complete confidence in the truth of something or an expected outcome ◇ **for a certainty** without any doubt

certifiable /súrti fī əb'l/ *adj* **1. DESERVING CERTIFICATE** authentic or good enough to be given a certificate **2. THAT MUST BE CERTIFIED** requiring to be reported to the appropriate authority (*informal*) ○ *a certifiable disease* **3. REQUIRING PSYCHIATRIC TREATMENT** legally or medically declared to be affected by a psychiatric disorder (*dated*) —**certifiably** *adv*

certificate *n* /sər tíffikət/ **1. DOCUMENT PROVIDING OFFICIAL EVIDENCE** an official document that gives proof and details of something such as personal status, educational achievements, ownership, or authenticity **2. DOCUMENT GIVING STATE OF HEALTH** an official document giving details of somebody's state of health. It may be shown to an employer to confirm that the person is or is not fit for work. **3. ELECTRONIC IDENTIFICATION** an electronic document verifying somebody's relationship, identity, and responsibilities in financial transactions (*used in e-commerce*) ■ *vt* /sər tíffi kayt/ (**-cates, -cating, -cated**) **1. GIVE CERTIFICATE TO SOMEBODY OR SOMETHING** to award a certificate to somebody or something **2. PROVE SOMETHING WITH CERTIFICATE** to authorize or provide evidence of something with a certificate [15C. < medieval Latin *certificatum* < past participle of late Latin *certificare* (see CERTIFY)] —**certification** /súrtifi káysh'n, sər tíffi-/ *n*

certificate authority *n* an organization that issues digital certificates that identify senders of electronic messages

certificate database *n* E-COMMERCE a database storing all certificates issued and used by a certificate authority (*used in e-commerce*)

certificate of origin *n* an official document stating what country a consignment of goods has come from

Certificate of Secondary Education *n* EDUC full form of **CSE**

certificate walker *n* E-COMMERCE a computer software program that reads digital certificates and displays their contents (*used in e-commerce*)

certified accountant *n* an accountant who is a member of the Chartered Association of Certified Accountants and can therefore audit companies' accounts

certified cheque *n* a cheque that the issuing bank guarantees to honour because sufficient funds are present to cover the check

certified mail *n Aus, N Am* a method of postage in which an official record is kept of the sending and delivery of the item concerned. UK, NZ term **recorded delivery**

certified public accountant *n* a public accountant who has met the requirements of a particular US state and is therefore allowed to practise there

certify /súrti fī/ (**-fies, -fying, -fied**) *v* **1.** *vti* **CONFIRM TRUTH OR ACCURACY OF SOMETHING** to state or confirm that something is true or correct **2.** *vt* **PROVE QUALITY OF SOMEBODY OR SOMETHING** to declare that somebody or something has passed a test or achieved an expected standard **3.** *vt* **ISSUE SOMEBODY OR SOMETHING CERTIFICATE** to award a certificate to somebody or something **4.** *vt* **DECLARE SOMEBODY TO HAVE PSYCHIATRIC DISORDER** to declare somebody officially or legally to have a psychiatric disorder and require confinement in a psychiatric hospital (*dated*) **5.** *vt N Am* **GUARANTEE PAYMENT OF CHEQUE** to indicate on a cheque that there are sufficient funds to guarantee payment [14C. Via French *certifier* < late Latin *certificare* 'make certain' < Latin *certus* (see CERTAIN)] —**certifier** *n*

~~**certin**~~ incorrect spelling of **certain**

certiorari /súrti ə ráirī, -raári/ *n* a writ issued by a higher court to obtain records on a case from a lower court so that the case can be reviewed [15C. < late Latin, 'be informed', passive of Latin *certiorare* 'inform' < *certus* (see CERTAIN); because the word occurs in the writ]

certitude /súrti tyood/ *n* **1. FEELING OF CERTAINTY** the feeling of conviction about something, especially an opinion or religious faith **2. DEFINITE TRUTH** the definite truth of something **3. SOMETHING THAT IS CERTAIN** something that is certain to happen or about which somebody can feel sure [15C. < late Latin *certitudo* < Latin *certus* (see CERTAIN)]

cerulean /sə róoli ən/ *adj* of a deep blue colour, like the sky on a clear day (*literary*) [Mid-17C. < Latin *caeruleus* < *caelum* 'sky'] —**cerulean** *n*

ceruloplasmin /sə róolō plazmin/, **caeruloplasmin** *n* a copper-transporting protein present in the blood [Mid-20C. < Latin *caeruleus* (see CERULEAN) + PLASMA]

cerumen /sə róomən/ *n* the waxy secretion of glands lining the canal of the external ear (*technical*) [Late 17C. < modern Latin < Latin *cera* 'wax'] —**ceruminous** *adj*

ceruse /sə róoss/ *n* **1.** a cosmetic used in the past that contained white lead. Lead is now known to damage the skin and is no longer used in cosmetics. **2.** white lead used as a pigment and formerly in cosmetics [14C. Via French < Latin *cerussa*]

cerussite /séerə sīt/, **cerusite** *n* a lead carbonate mineral forming crystals or aggregates of various colours. Use: source of lead. [Mid-19C. < Latin *cerussa* 'ceruse']

Cervantes /sər vánt eez/, **Miguel de** (1547–1616) Spanish novelist and dramatist. His *Don Quixote* (1605–15) greatly influenced the development of the novel. Full name **Cervantes Saavedra, Miguel de**

> **'Too much sanity may be madness. And maddest of all, to see life as it is and not as it should be!'**
> [Miguel de Cervantes, *Don Quixote*; 1605–15]

> **'Every man is as Heaven made him, and sometimes a great deal worse.'**
> [Miguel de Cervantes, *Don Quixote*; 1605–15]

cervelat /súrvəlaa, -lat/ *n* a German cured sausage made from pork and beef, usually smoked, with a mild flavour and a fine texture [Early 17C. Via French < Italian *cervellata* < *cervello* 'brain' < Latin *cerebellum* (see CEREBELLUM); because it was made from brains]

cervical /sər vík'l, súrvik'l/ *adj* **1.** relating or belonging to the cervix of the womb **2.** relating or belonging to the neck, or to any body part that resembles a neck [Mid-19C. < French < Latin *cervic-* 'neck']

cervical cap *n* a small, dome-shaped rubber or plastic contraceptive device for women, placed inside the vagina and fitted tightly over the entrance to the cervix

cervical smear *n* a sample of tissue taken from the cervix of the womb for analysis, to enable early identification of cellular irregularities that could

lead to cervical cancer. Aus, N Am term **Pap smear**

cervices ANAT plural of **cervix**

cervicitis /súrvi sítiss/ *n* inflammation of the cervix of the womb [Late 19C. < Latin *cervic-* 'neck']

cervid /súrvid/ *n* any ruminant mammal characterized by the presence of antlers in the male or sometimes in both sexes, e.g. a deer, elk, or reindeer. Family: Cervidae. [Late 19C. < modern Latin *Cervidae* (plural) < Latin *cervus* 'deer'] —**cervid** *adj*

cervine /súr vīn/ *adj* relating to, resembling, or typical of a deer [Mid-19C. < Latin *cervinus* < *cervus* 'deer']

cervix /súrviks/ (*plural* **-vixes** or **-vices** /-vi seez/) *n* **1.** NECK OF WOMB the neck of the womb, consisting of a narrow passage leading to the vagina. The cervix widens greatly during childbirth to permit delivery of the baby. **2.** NECK the neck (*technical*) **3.** PART RESEMBLING NECK any part of the body that resembles a neck in shape or function [15C. < Latin, 'neck']

cesarean /si záiri ən/ *n* US same as **Caesarean**

cesium *n* CHEM US spelling of **caesium**

České Budějovice /chésk ay bóődə yawvit say/ city in southern Bohemia, Czech Republic. It is situated on the River Vltava, south of Prague. Since the Middle Ages, it has produced Budvar beer. Population: 99,347 (1999).

cespitose *adj* BOT US spelling of **caespitose**

cess[1] /sess/ *n* Ireland, Scotland, S Asia a local tax or levy [Mid-16C. < shortening of ASSESS 'assessment']

cess[2] /sess/ *n* Ireland luck (*informal*) [Mid-19C. Either shortening of SUCCESS, or < CESS[1]]

cessation /se sáysh'n/ *n* a stop, pause, or interruption, especially a permanent discontinuation [15C. < Latin *cessation-* < *cessat-*, past participle of *cessare* 'stop']

cession /sésh'n/ *n* (*formal*) **1.** the ceding or giving up of something, or something ceded in this way, especially land, property, or a right **2.** something ceded or given up, especially land, property, or a right [14C. Directly or via French < Latin *cession-* < *cess-*, past participle of *cedere* 'yield']

Cessnock /séss nok/ town in New South Wales, southeastern Australia. Population: 47,566 (2002 estimate).

cesspit /séss pit/ *n* **1.** a pit for the collection of waste matter and water, especially sewage **2.** UK a foul and putrid place or situation, especially one linked with moral depravity. ANZ, N Am term **cesspool** [Mid-19C. *Cess* < CESSPOOL]

cesspool /séss pool/ *n* **1.** a covered underground tank or well for the collection of waste matter and water, especially sewage **2.** ANZ, N Am same as **cesspit** (sense 2) [Late 17C. Probably alteration of *suspiral* 'drainpipe' < Old French *suspirail* 'breathing hole' < *souspirer* 'breathe']

cesta /séstə/ *n* a curved wicker basket for catching and throwing the ball in the Basque ball sport jai alai [Early 20C. Via Spanish, 'basket' < Latin *cista* (see CHEST)]

cesti ANCIENT HIST, CLOTHING plural of **cestus**[1]

c'est la vie /se laa vée/ *interj* used to express philosophical acceptance of the way things are [Mid-20C. < French, 'that's life']

cestode /séss tōd/ *n* ZOOL same as **tapeworm** (*technical*) [Mid-19C. < modern Latin *Cestoda* (plural) < Latin *cestus* (see CESTUS[1])]

cestus[1] /séstəss/ (*plural* **-ti**), **cestos** (*plural* **-ti** /-tī/) *n* a girdle or belt, especially one worn by women in ancient Greece [Mid-16C. Via Latin < Greek *kestos* 'belt']

cestus[2] /séstəss/ (*plural* **-tuses** or same), **caestus** (*plural* **-tuses** or same) *n* a studded gauntlet made of bull's hide worn by boxers in ancient Rome [Late 17C. < Latin *caestus* < *caedere* 'to hit']

cesura *n* LITERAT another spelling of **caesura**

CET *abbr* **1.** Central European Time **2.** Common External Tariff

cetacean /si táysh'n/ *n* a large sea mammal that has a streamlined body with forelimbs modified as flippers, no hind limbs, and a blowhole on the back, e.g. a whale or a dolphin. Order: Cetacea. [Mid-19C. < modern Latin *Cetacea* (plural) < Latin *cetus* 'whale' < Greek *kētos*] —**cetaceous** /si táyshəss/ *adj*

cetane /sée tayn/ *n* a colourless oily hydrocarbon. Source: petroleum. Use: measuring the ignition quality of diesel fuels, as a solvent. Formula: $C_{16}H_{34}$. [Late 19C. < *cetyl* (see CETYL ALCOHOL)]

cetane number, **cetane rating** *n* the performance rating of a diesel fuel, expressed as the percentage of cetane in a mixture with 1-methylnaphthalene that shows the same ignition properties. The higher the cetane number, the better the performance.

cete /seet/ *n* a group or company of badgers [15C. Origin ?]

ceteris paribus /káytəriss paáribəs, séttəriss párrəbass/ *adv* used to indicate that something would be the case if everything else under consideration remains the same (*formal*) [Early 17C. < modern Latin, 'other things being equal']

cetology /si tólləji/ *n* the branch of zoology concerned with the study of whales, dolphins, and related mammals [Mid-19C. < Latin *cetus* 'whale'] —**cetological** /seétə lójjik'l/ *adj* —**cetologist** *n*

cetrimide /séttrə mīd/ *n* a mixture of ammonium compounds with detergent properties. Use: disinfectant, antiseptic. [Mid-20C. < *ce(tyl)trim-(ethylammonium) (brom)ide*]

Cetus /seétəss/ *n* a constellation of the celestial equator containing the bright star Mira. See illustration at **constellation**

cetyl alcohol /seétīl-, seét'l-/ *n* a white waxy solid. Use: manufacture of cosmetics, pharmaceuticals, detergents. [< Latin *cetus* 'whale'; because originally isolated from spermaceti]

Cévennes /say vén/ mountain range in France extending from the northern Ardèche Department to the southwestern Hérault Department. The highest peak is Mont Mézenc 1,754 m/5,755 ft.

ceviche /se veéchay/, **seviche** *n* a Latin American dish of raw fish or shrimp marinated in lemon or lime juice and served as a type of salad with chopped onions and tomatoes [Mid-20C. < American Spanish *seviche*, probably < Spanish *cebo* 'fish pieces used for bait' < Latin *cibus* 'food']

Ceylon /si lón/ former name for **Sri Lanka** —**Ceylonese** /séllə neéz/ *adj, n*

Ceylon moss *n* a red seaweed that is a source of the gelatinous material agar. Native to: eastern Indian Ocean. Latin name: *Gracilaria lichenoides*.

Ceyx /seé iks/ *n* in Greek mythology, a king of Trachis in Thessaly who died in a shipwreck and whose wife, Alcyone, drowned herself in grief

AKG London

Paul Cézanne: self-portrait

Cézanne /si zán, say-/, **Paul** (1839–1906) French painter. His postimpressionist representation of nature in such paintings as *Rocky Landscape in Aix* (1887?) inspired cubism.

'The day is coming when a single carrot, freshly observed, will set off a revolution.'
[Attributed to Paul Cézanne]

cf *abbr* Central African Republic (*used in Internet addresses*) See table at **domain name**

Cf *symbol* CHEM ELEM californium

CF *abbr* **1.** Chaplain to the Forces **2.** cost and freight **3.** cystic fibrosis

cf. *abbr* compare

c/f *abbr* carried forward

CFA franc *n* a unit of currency used in several francophone African countries. See table at **currency** [Abbreviation of French *Communauté financière africaine* 'African financial community']

CFC *n* a gas containing carbon, hydrogen, chlorine, and fluorine, some forms of which damage the ozone layer in the Earth's atmosphere. Use: refrigerant, aerosol propellant. Full form **chlorofluorocarbon**

CFE *abbr* **1.** College of Further Education **2.** Conventional Forces in Europe

cfi, **CFI** *abbr* SHIPPING cost, freight, and insurance

CFP franc *n* the main unit of currency in several French overseas territories in the South Pacific. See table at **currency** [Abbreviation of French *Communauté Française du Pacifique* 'French Pacific community']

c.f.s. *abbr* cubic feet per second

cg[1] *symbol* MEASURE centigram

cg[2] *abbr* Congo (*used in Internet addresses*) See table at **domain name**

CG *abbr* **1.** captain general **2.** coastguard **3.** Consul General

CGBR *abbr* Central Government Borrowing Requirement

cge *abbr* **1.** FREIGHT carriage **2.** BANKING charge

CGI *abbr* COMPUT **1.** common gateway interface **2.** computer-generated image **3.** computer-generated imagery

cgm *abbr* MEASURE centigram

CGM *abbr* Conspicuous Gallantry Medal

cgs *abbr* MEASURE centimetre-gram-second

CGS *abbr* **1.** MEASURE centimetre-gram-second system **2.** Chief of General Staff

CGT *abbr* capital gains tax

ch *abbr* Switzerland (*used in Internet addresses*) See table at **domain name**

CH *abbr* **1.** clearing house **2.** Companion of Honour **3.** custom house

ch. *abbr* **1.** MEASURE chain **2.** LITERAT chapter **3.** BANKING charge **4.** CHESS check **5.** CHR church

Ch. *abbr* **1.** BROADCAST channel **2.** China

C/H *abbr* central heating

chaat /chaat/, **chat** *n* raw fruits and vegetables in a spicy sauce, eaten as a snack or an accompaniment and originating in northern India [< Hindi]

chabazite /kábbə zīt/ *n* a pink, yellow, white, or colourless aluminosilicate mineral of the zeolite group. Source: cavities in igneous rocks, hot spring deposits. [Early 19C. < French *chabazie* < Greek *khabazie*, misspelling of *khalazie* < *khalaza* 'hail'; from its form and colour]

Chablis /shábbli/, **chablis** *n* a very dry white wine from the Burgundy region of central France

Chabrier /shábbri ay/, **Alexis Emmanuel** (1841–94) French composer. His light operas are rarely performed, but his orchestral rhapsody *España* (1883) remains popular.

Chabrol /sha ból/, **Claude** (*b*. 1930) French film director. He was a leader of the French new wave in the 1950s. His films include *Story of Women* (1988).

'What I like is what people are at the beginning of a scene and what they are at the end of a scene. I'm primarily interested in their relationships, and the plot is just a means to get at the behaviour of the characters.'
[Claude Chabrol, *Interview*, *Times*; 13 May 1972]

cha-cha /chaá chaa/, **cha-cha-cha** /chaá chaa chaá/ *n* **1.** a fast ballroom dance of Latin American origin consisting of three steps and a hip-swaying shuffle **2.** the music for a cha-cha [< American Spanish (Cuban) *cha-cha-cha*, probably an imitation of the musical accompaniment] —**cha-cha** *vi*

chackling /chák'ling/ *n* regional an act of nagging at or scolding somebody [Early 16C. < *chack* 'to chatter, bird's call', an imitation of the sound]

REGIONAL NOTE See *jawing*.

chacma /chákmə/ (*plural* **-mas**) *n* a ground-dwelling baboon with a dark-grey coat and naked face with a long muzzle. Native to: southern Africa. Latin name: *Papio ursinus*. [Mid-19C. < Khoikhoi]

chaconia /chə kóni ə/ (*plural* **-as** or same) *n* a red flower with large, conspicuous sepals that is the

national flower of Trinidad and Tobago. Latin name: *Warszewiczia coccinea*.

chaconne /shə kón/ *n* **1.** an ancient, moderately slow dance, probably of Spanish origin **2.** a musical composition consisting of variations on a fixed bass line continually repeated (**ground bass**) [Late 17C. Via French < Spanish *chacona*, probably < Basque *chucun* 'pretty']

chacun à son goût /shákuN aa soN goó/ used to express the individuality or peculiarity of somebody's taste or choice [< French, 'each to his or her own taste']

chad /chad/ *n* **1.** PIECES PUNCHED OUT the mass of waste paper produced by hole-punching machines, formerly from computer punch cards or tapes **2.** PIECE PUNCHED OUT a small piece of waste paper, card, or tape removed from a sheet by a hole-punching machine or tool **3.** *US* PIECE REMOVED TO REGISTER VOTE a piece removed from a ballot paper by a voter or voting machine in order to register a vote against the name of a candidate [Mid-20C. < ?]

Chad

Chad /chad/ landlocked country in north-central Africa, bordered on the north by Libya, on the east by Sudan, on the south by the Central African Republic, and on the west by Cameroon, Nigeria, and Niger. A former French territory, it became independent in 1960. Language: French. Currency: CFA franc. Capital: Ndjamena. Population: 9,253,493 (2003). Area: 1,284,000 sq. km/495,755 sq. mi. Official name **Republic of Chad** —**Chadian** *adj, n*

Chad, Lake lake in central Africa, situated at the junction of Nigeria, Niger, and Chad. Area: 17,800 sq. km/6,870 sq. mi.

chadar *n* ISLAM another spelling of **chador**

Chadic /cháddik/ *n* a large group of languages, spoken in west-central Africa, that is a branch of the Afro-Asiatic family of languages. Native speakers: 25 million. —**Chadic** *adj*

chador /chúddər/, **chadar**, **chuddar** *n* **1.** a dark traditional garment worn in public by Muslim and sometimes by Hindu women that covers almost all of the head and body **2.** a cloth that is used to cover a Muslim tomb [Early 17C. Directly or via Urdu < Persian *čādar* 'sheet, veil']

chaeta /kéetə/ (*plural* -**tae** /-tee/) *n* a bristle that occurs singly or in clusters in worms such as earthworms and ragworms and helps them to move [Mid-19C. Via modern Latin < Greek *khaitē* 'long hair']

chaetognath /kéetəg nath, kéetə nath/ *n* a torpedo-shaped invertebrate sea animal with an almost transparent body and fins running horizontally down both sides of the trunk and tail. Phylum: Chaetognatha. [Late 19C. < modern Latin *Chaetognatha* < Greek *khaitē* 'long hair' + *gnathos* 'jaw'] —**chaetognathous** /kee tógnəthəss/ *adj*

chafe /chayf/ *v* (**chafes, chafing, chafed**) **1.** *vti* BECOME OR MAKE WORN to become sore or worn by rubbing, or make something sore or worn in this way **2.** *vi* CAUSE FRICTION to rub something, causing friction **3.** *vt* RUB SOMETHING TO WARM IT to warm something, especially the hands or other parts of the body, by rubbing **4.** *vti* BECOME ANNOYED, OR ANNOY SOMEBODY to be or make somebody irritated, annoyed, or impatient ■ *n* **1.** SORENESS OR WEAR soreness or wear caused by rubbing **2.** FEELING OF IRRITATION a feeling of irritation, annoyance, or impatience [13C. Via Old French *chaufer* < Latin *calefacere* 'make warm' < *calere* 'be warm']

chafer[1] /cháyfər/ *n* a large slow-moving scarab beetle, e.g. the cockchafer [Old English *ceafor*, probably < Indo-European, 'jaw, mouth']

chafer[2] /cháyfər/ *n* HOUSEHOLD same as **chafing dish** [15C. Via French *chauffoir* < Latin *calefactorium* < *calefact-*, past participle of *calefacere* (SEE CHAFE)]

chaff[1] /chaaf, chaf/ *n* **1.** SEED COVERINGS REMOVED BY THRESHING the dry coverings (**bracts**) of grains and other grass seeds that are separated by the process of threshing. When cereal crops are harvested mechanically, chaff is removed by the combine harvester and deposited with the straw in the field. **2.** WORTHLESS THING something that is worthless or irrelevant **3.** STRIPS OF METAL TO OBSTRUCT RADAR glass fibres or silvered nylon filaments dispersed into the air as an antiradar measure [Old English *ceaf* < Germanic] —**chaffy** *adj*

chaff[2] /chaaf, chaf/ *v* (**chaffs, chaffing, chaffed**) **1.** *vt* TEASE SOMEBODY LIGHT-HEARTEDLY to tease somebody in fun **2.** *vi* BANTER to exchange light-hearted teasing or joking remarks ■ *n* JOKING light-hearted joking or teasing [Early 19C. Origin ?] —**chaffer** *n*

chaffer /cháffər/ *vi* (-**fers**, -**fering**, -**fered**) **1.** HAGGLE to haggle or bargain about something **2.** BANDY WORDS to chatter idly ■ *n* BARGAINING bargaining or haggling about something [12C. < Old English *ceap* 'bargain' + *faru* 'faring'] —**chafferer** *n*

chaffinch /cháffinch/ *n* a finch with white bars on its wings and a bluish head. Native to: gardens and farmland of Europe and western Asia. Latin name: *Fringilla coelebs*. [Old English *ceaffinc* < *ceaf* 'chaff'; because it pecks among farmyard chaff]

chafing dish /cháyfing-/ *n* a shallow pan with a source of heat beneath it, used for cooking food or keeping food warm at the table

Chagall /sha gál/, **Marc** (1887–1985) Russian-born French painter and designer. His colourful fantasies, anticipating surrealism, stem largely from eastern European Jewish folklore.

'People have reproached me for putting poetry into my pictures. It is true that there are other things to be required of the art of painting. But show me a single great work that does not have its portion of poetry.'
[Marc Chagall. Quoted in *The World of Marc Chagall*, Roy McMullen; 1968]

Chagas' disease /shaágəss-/, **Chagas's disease** /-ssiz-/ *n* an often fatal disease, occurring in South and Central America, that affects the heart and nervous system and is caused by a protozoan parasite transmitted by blood-sucking insects [Early 20C. After Carlos *Chagas* (1879–1934), Brazilian physician]

Chagos Archipelago /chaágəss-/ disputed territory of 52 islands, constituting the British Indian Ocean Territory (a dependency of Great Britain), in the Indian Ocean, south of India. In 1968 the British government forcibly removed the islanders to make way for US military installations but in 2000 a British High Court ruled that this removal was illegal. Area: 60 sq. km/23 sq. mi.

chagrin /shággrin, shə grín/ *n* a feeling of vexation or humiliation due to disappointment about something [Mid-17C. < French] —**chagrin** *vt* —**chagrined** *adj*

~~**chagrinned**~~ incorrect spelling of **chagrined**

chai /chī/ *n* *S Asia* tea or tea leaves [< Hindi or Urdu]

chain /chayn/ *n* **1.** SERIES OF JOINED METAL RINGS a flexible

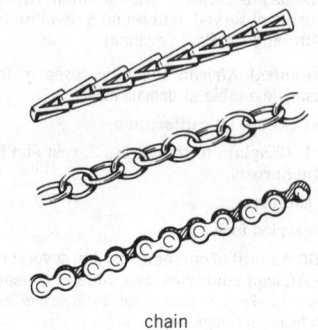

chain

interconnected series of usually metal links that may be used to support, restrain, drive or move something or that may serve as an ornament or decoration **2.** SERIES OF LINKS USED AS ACCESSORY a series of rings, links, or discs used as a necklace, bracelet, or other piece of jewellery **3.** BADGE OF OFFICE a chain worn round the neck as a badge of office **4.** SOMETHING RESEMBLING CHAIN a series of things or people linked or joined together for some purpose ○ *They stood hand in hand to form a human chain round the perimeter.* **5.** COMM BUSINESSES UNDER ONE MANAGEMENT OR OWNERSHIP a number of shops, hotels, restaurants, or other businesses that are owned by the same company and offer similar goods or services but are found in different locations **6.** SEQUENCE OF RELATED EVENTS OR FACTS a sequence of facts or events that happen one after the other and are connected in some way **7.** GEOG SERIES OF GEOGRAPHICAL FORMATIONS a series of associated geographical features or formations such as mountains, lakes, or islands ■ **chains** *npl* RESTRAINING CIRCUMSTANCES feelings or circumstances that restrain or confine somebody (*literary*) ■ *n* **1.** PHYS SERIES OF ATOMS a series of atoms, usually of a single element such as carbon, that are joined in a line or ring within a molecule **2.** MEASURE UNIT OF LENGTH EQUAL TO 66 FT a unit of length that is now rarely used, equal to 20 m/66 ft ■ *vt* (**chains, chaining, chained**) **1.** FASTEN SOMETHING OR SOMEBODY WITH CHAIN to fasten, tie, or restrain something or somebody with a chain or chains **2.** RESTRICT SOMEBODY'S MOBILITY to restrict or confine somebody's freedom of movement or action ○ *She was chained to the computer all day.* [13C. Via Old French *chaeine* < Latin *catena*] —**chained** *adj* —**chainless** *adj*

Chain /chayn/, **Sir Ernst Boris** (1906–79) German-born British biochemist. Together with his colleagues Alexander Fleming and Howard Walter Florey, he developed penicillin. They shared the Nobel Prize in medicine (1945).

chain drive *n* an endless linked chain that meshes with the teeth of two sprocket wheels to transfer energy and motion from one wheel to the other —**chain-driven** *adj*

chaîné /shə náy/ (*plural* -**nés** /-náy/) *n* a series of short, usually fast turns made by a ballet dancer moving in a straight line across a floor or stage [Mid-20C. < French, past participle of *chaîner* 'to chain' < Old French *chaeine* (SEE CHAIN)]

chain ferry (*plural* **chain ferries**) *n* a river ferry that pulls itself along on one or more fixed chains, attached to each bank of the river. Chain ferries are used where there are strong currents and a shallow crossing.

chain gang *n* a group of prisoners who work away from prison and are shackled together, usually with leg irons and a series of chains

chain harrow *n* a farm implement, consisting of a horizontal towing bar attached to heavy chains, that is trailed across soil or pasture to break up clods or disperse manure

chain letter *n* a letter sent to a number of people, each of whom is asked to send copies to the same number of new people, sometimes requesting and promising money

chain lightning *n* *US* same as **forked lightning**

chainlink fence /cháynlingk-/ *n* a fence formed from lengths of strong wire that are interwoven in a diamond pattern —**chainlink fencing** *n*

chain mail *n* interlinked rings of metal forming a flexible piece of armour, worn by knights in medieval times

chain of command *n* a hierarchy of officials in the armed forces or in business, each reporting to and taking orders from the next most senior person

chainplate /cháyn playt/ *n* a metal plate on the hull of a sailing vessel to which the ropes or cables supporting the mast are attached

chain reaction *n* **1.** CONNECTED SEQUENCE OF EVENTS a series of events following on quickly from each other, each of which causes the next one **2.** PHYS SELF-SUSTAINING NUCLEAR FISSION a self-sustaining nuclear reaction in which each fission of an atomic nucleus causes neutrons and energy to be emitted, each collision of neutrons with other nuclei causing a further fission **3.** CHEM SERIES OF CHEMICAL REACTIONS a

series of chemical reactions in which the product from one reaction helps to create the next one — **chain-react** *vi*

chain saw *n* a portable motor-driven saw with cutting teeth made of links that form a continuous chain, used for cutting wood

chain shot *n* two cannonballs or half-balls connected by a chain, formerly used to destroy a ship's rigging

chain-smoke (**chain-smokes, chain-smoking, chain-smoked**) *vti* to smoke cigarettes continuously, often lighting the next from the previous one as it is finished —**chain-smoker** *n*

chain stitch *n* a hand, machine, or crochet stitch in which each stitch forms a loop through the forward end of the previous one to resemble the links of a chain —**chain-stitch** *vti*

chain store *n* one of a series of retail shops, especially department stores or supermarkets, owned by the same company

chair /chair/ *n* **1. SEAT WITH BACK** a seat with a back support, usually for one person. Most chairs have four legs or feet and some have rests for the arms. **2. CHAIRPERSON** somebody presiding over something such as a committee, board, or meeting, or the position of such a person. **3. EDUC PROFESSORSHIP OR PROFESSOR** a university professorship, or the person holding such a position **4. MUSIC RANKED POSITION OF ORCHESTRAL MUSICIAN** the ranked position of a musician in an orchestra **5.** same as **electric chair** (*informal*) **6. RAIL METAL SOCKET ATTACHED TO SLEEPER CAR** a metal socket attached to a railway sleeper car in which a rail is locked into position ■ *vt* (**chairs, chairing, chaired**) **1. PRESIDE OVER SOMETHING** to preside over something such as a committee, board, or meeting **2. CARRY WINNER ON SHOULDERS** to carry a victor or champion on the shoulders in triumph [13C. Via Old French *chaiere* < Latin *cathedra* 'seat']

USAGE *Chair* has been extended to mean 'somebody presiding over a committee or meeting' in order to avoid having to use the gender-specific terms *chairman* or *chairwoman*. An alternative is *chairperson*, though it is disliked by some people.

chairborne /cháir bawrn/ *adj* working at a desk in an office job in the armed forces, rather than having combat or field duties (*informal*)

chair class *n S Asia* a class of travel on railway trains in which passengers are provided with reclinable seats similar to those in aircraft

chair lift

chair lift *n* a series of seats suspended from a moving cable, used to carry passengers up or down a mountain or other slope

chairman /cháirmən/ (*plural* **-men** /-mən/) *n* **1.** the officer who presides over something such as a committee or meeting **2.** *also* **chairman of the board** the chief officer of a business corporation, elected by its board of directors and responsible for corporate policy and supervision of upper management —**chairmanship** *n*

USAGE See *chair.*

chairperson /cháir purs'n/ (*plural* **-sons**) *n* the officer who presides over something such as a committee, board, or meeting

USAGE See *chair.*

chairwoman /cháir woomən/ (*plural* **-women** /-wimmin/)

n a woman who is the presiding officer of something such as a committee, board, or meeting

USAGE See *chair.*

chaise /shayz/ (*plural* **chaises** /pronunc. *same*/) *n* **1.** a light open two-wheeled carriage for one or more people, usually hooded and drawn by one horse **2.** TRANSP same as **post chaise** [Mid-17C. < French]

chaise longue

chaise longue /shayz lóng/ (*plural* **chaise longues** or **chaises longues** /pronunc. *same*/) *n* **1.** a chair with an elongated seat, one armrest, and sometimes an adjustable back, designed for lying on **2.** *N Am* same as **sunlounger** [< French, 'long chair']

~~**chaise lounge**~~ incorrect spelling of **chaise longue**

chakra /chúkrə, chaákrə/ *n* in yoga, any of the centres of spiritual power in the body [Late 18C. < Sanskrit *cakra* 'wheel']

chalaza /kə láyzə, kə lázzə/ (*plural* **-zas** or **-zae** /-zee/) *n* **1.** a spiral chord of albumen that is attached at each end of the yolk to the lining membrane inside a bird's egg, holding it in position **2.** the base of the immature seed of a plant [Early 18C. Via modern Latin < Greek *khalaza* 'hail'] —**chalazal** *adj*

chalazion /kə láyzi ən/ *n* MED same as **meibomian cyst** [Early 18C. < Greek *khalazion* 'small lump' < *khalaza* 'hail']

Chalcedon /kálssidən/ ancient Greek city on the Bosporus near modern-day Istanbul, founded in 685 BC —**Chalcedonian** /kálssi dóni ən/, *adj*, *n*

chalcedony /kal séddəni/ *n* a translucent or greyish semiprecious stone that is a variety of banded quartz. Use: gems, ornaments. [13C. < Latin *c(h)alcedonius* < Greek *khalkēdōn*, mystical stone] —**chalcedonic** /kálssi dónnik/ *adj*

chalcid /kálssid/ *n* a small wasp with bright metallic coloration whose larvae are often parasites of other insects in various stages of life. Superfamily: Chalcidoidea. [Late 19C. < modern Latin *Chalcid-* < Greek *khalkos* 'copper'; from its metallic colour]

chalco- *prefix* copper ○ *chalcopyrite* [< Greek *khalkos*]

chalcocite /kálkə sīt/ *n* a grey to black brittle copper sulphide mineral. Use: source of copper.

chalcography /kal kóggrəfi/ *n* engraving on copper or brass —**chalcographer** *n* —**chalcographic** /kálkə gráffik/ *adj* —**chalcographical** *adj* —**chalcographist** *n*

chalcolithic /kálkə líthik/ *adj* belonging or relating to the transitional period between the Neolithic and Bronze ages, beginning around 400 BC, when the use of copper became more prevalent

chalcopyrite /kálkə pí rīt/ *n* a brassy sulphide mineral containing copper and iron. Use: source of copper.

Chaldaean *n* PEOPLES, LANG another spelling of **Chaldean**

Chaldea /kal dée ə/ ancient region of Mesopotamia, between the Euphrates and the Persian Gulf, in modern-day southern Iraq

Chaldean /kal dée ən/, **Chaldaean** *n* **1.** a member of an ancient Semitic people who lived in Chaldea in southern Babylonia, where they were the dominant ethnic group during the 8th and 7th centuries BC **2.** a dialect of the modern Aramaic language, spoken in Iraq and in the United States [Late 16C. < Latin *Chaldaeus* < Assyrian *kaldū*] —**Chaldaic** /kal dáy ik/ *n*, *adj* —**Chaldean** *adj*

Chaldee /káldee, kal dée/ *n* **1.** the Aramaic language (*dated*) **2.** same as **Chaldean** (sense 1) [14C. Via Old French < Latin *Chaldaeus* (see CHALDEAN)]

~~**chalenge**~~ incorrect spelling of **challenge**

chalet /shállay/ *n* **1.** a house or cottage traditionally made of wood with wide overhanging eaves, in a style originally built in Switzerland **2.** a small house for guests on a holiday camp [Late 18C. < Swiss French]

Chalgrin /shál graN/, **Jean-François-Thérèse** (1739–1811) French architect. He was commissioned by Napoleon in 1806 to design the Arc de Triomphe in Paris, although it was not completed until after his death.

chalice /chálliss/ *n* **1.** a metal drinking cup or goblet (*literary*) **2.** in the Christian church, a gold or silver cup used for serving the wine at Communion [14C. Directly or via French < Latin *calic-* 'cup']

chalicothere /kállikə theer/ *n* an extinct mammal resembling a horse with clawed feet and forelimbs slightly longer than the hind limbs. It lived from about 55 million to about 10,000 years ago. Suborder: Chalicotheriidae. [Early 20C. < modern Latin *Chalicotherium* 'animal found in gravel' < Greek *khalik-* 'pebble' + *thērion* 'small animal' < *thēr* 'animal']

chalk /chawk/ *n* **1. POWDERY WHITE ROCK** a soft white or grey fine-grained sedimentary rock consisting of nearly pure calcium carbonate originally formed under the sea and containing minute fossil fragments of marine organisms **2. SOFT MARKER MADE FROM CHALK** a piece of chalk or a similar substance, sometimes coloured, used for writing or drawing, e.g. on a blackboard **3. PIECE OF CHALK FOR BILLIARD CUE** a small cube of chalk or similar substance used for rubbing the tip of a billiard or snooker cue to increase friction between the cue and the ball ■ *v* (**chalks, chalking, chalked**) **1.** *vti* MAKE CHALK MARK ON SOMETHING to draw, write, or mark something with chalk **2.** *vi* BECOME POWDER to become powdery **3.** *vt* RUB CHALK ON CUE to treat the tip of a billiard or snooker cue with chalk [Old English *cealc* 'lime(stone), chalk', via Germanic < Latin *calc-* 'lime(stone)' < Greek *khalix* 'pebble'] ◊ **as like or different as chalk and cheese** extremely different in important respects (*informal*) ◊ **by a long chalk** by a large margin ◊ **not by a long chalk** not by any means **chalk out** *vt* to outline a plan or proposal

chalk up *vt* **1. SCORE OR KEEP SCORE OF SOMETHING** to score or achieve something, or record a score or victory (*informal*) **2. ATTRIBUTE SOMETHING** to credit or ascribe something to something or somebody (*informal*) **3. CHARGE SOMETHING TO SOMEBODY** to record the cost of something and charge it to somebody or somebody's account [< the custom at pubs or bars of writing up with chalk an account of credit given]

chalk and talk *n* a traditional method of education in which the teacher addresses the students, using a blackboard to provide examples or illustrations

chalkboard /cháwk bawrd/ *n N Am* EDUC same as **blackboard**

chalkface /cháwk fayss/ *n* teaching in a classroom, as distinct from the other duties of a teacher (*informal humorous*) [After COALFACE]

chalkpit /cháwk pit/ *n* a quarry where chalk is excavated

chalkstone /cháwk stōn/ *n* a piece of chalk taken straight from the ground

chalk talk *n N Am* an informal lecture during which illustrations or examples are given on a blackboard

chalky /cháwki/ (**-ier, -iest**) *adj* containing or resembling chalk in colour or texture —**chalkiness** *n*

challah /khaálə, haálə/, **hallah** *n* white bread enriched with eggs, usually in a plaited loaf, traditionally eaten by Jews on Friday evening at the Sabbath meal [Early 20C. < Hebrew *ḥallāh*, probably < *ḥll* 'pierce'; from its original shape]

challenge /chállənj/ *vt* (**-lenges, -lenging, -lenged**) **1. INVITE SOMEBODY TO COMPETE** to invite somebody to participate in a fight, contest, or competition **2. DARE SOMEBODY** to dare somebody to do something **3. CALL SOMETHING INTO QUESTION** to call something into question by demanding an explanation, justification, or proof **4. STIMULATE INTELLECT** to stimulate somebody by making demands on the intellect **5. ORDER SOMEBODY TO PRODUCE IDENTIFICATION** to order somebody to stop and produce identification or a password **6. LAW OBJECT TO INCLUSION OF JUROR** to make a formal objection against the inclusion of a prospective juror on a jury **7. MED TEST WHETHER SOMETHING PRODUCES ALLERGY** to expose a

person or animal to a substance in order to determine whether an allergy or other adverse reaction will occur ■ *n* **1. INVITATION TO TAKE PART IN CONTEST** an invitation to somebody to compete in a fight, contest, or competition **2. STIMULATING TEST OF ABILITIES** a test of somebody's abilities, or a situation that tests somebody's abilities in a stimulating way **3. QUESTIONING OF SOMETHING** a questioning of something by demanding an explanation, justification, or proof **4. DEMAND FOR IDENTIFICATION** an order to somebody to stop and produce identification or a password **5. LAW OBJECTION AGAINST JUROR** an objection against the inclusion of somebody on a jury **6. MED TESTING FOR ALLERGY** exposure of a person or animal to a substance in order to determine whether an allergy or other adverse reaction will occur [13C. Via Old French *c(h)alengier* 'accuse' < Latin *calumniare* 'accuse falsely' < *calumnia* 'false accusation'] —**challengeable** *adj*

challenged /chállənjd/ *adj* **1.** having a particular physical or mental disability ○ *physically challenged* **2.** lacking in a particular quality (*humorous*; *sometimes considered offensive*) ○ *judgmentally challenged*

USAGE In euphemisms for personal disabilities, *challenged* often appears in combinations such as *physically challenged* (= with a disability) and *medically challenged* (= unwell). The intention is to replace a negative-sounding term with a more positive one. But language rarely responds well to such overt manipulation, and in due course a new terminology acquires its own set of context-derived connotations. In British English, *challenged* is usually only used jocularly and the expression is ridiculed in such facetious ad hoc formations as *vertically challenged* (= short).

USAGE See *disabled*.

challenger /chállənjər/ *n* **1.** the issuer of an invitation to a fight, contest, or competition **2.** an opponent of a champion, especially in a boxing match

challenging /chállənjing/ *adj* demanding physical or psychological effort of a stimulating kind —**challengingly** *adv*

challis /shállis, -li/, **challie** /shálli/ *n* a soft lightweight woollen, cotton, or synthetic fabric, often patterned with a small print. Use: clothes. [Mid-19C. Origin ?]

chalone /káy lōn, kállon/ *n* a substance produced by cells that inhibits cell division (**mitosis**). Chalones are usually glycoproteins. [Early 20C. < Greek *khalōn*, present participle of *khalan* 'slacken'] —**chalonic** /ka lónik, kay-/ *adj*

chalta hai /chúltə hī́/ *adj S Asia* tolerant and easy-going (*informal*) [< Hindi]

chalumeau /shállyoŏ mō/ (*plural* **-meaux** /-mō/) *n* **1.** a woodwind instrument of the 17th and 18th centuries that developed into the clarinet **2.** the lowest register of a clarinet, or its warm tone quality [Early 18C. Via French < late Latin *calamellus* 'small reed' < *calamus* 'reed' < Greek *kalamos*]

chalutz /khaa loŏts/ (*plural* **-lutzim** /khaʾa loŏt seém/), **halutz** (*plural* **-lutzim**) *n* a member of a group of Jewish immigrants to Palestine after 1917 who began or worked in agricultural or forestry projects [Early 20C. < Hebrew *ḥaluṣ* 'pioneer']

chalybeate /kə líbbi it/ *adj* **1.** containing iron salts **2.** having a taste like iron [Mid-17C. < modern Latin *chalybeatus* < Latin *chalybs* 'steel' < Greek *khalups*]

chalybite /kálli bīt/ *n* MINERALS same as **siderite** (sense 1) [Mid-19C. < Greek *khalub-* 'steel']

Cham /kam/ (*plural* **Chams** or *same*) *n* **1.** a member of an indigenous people who formed a kingdom in present-day Vietnam between the 2nd and 17th centuries AD and who now live mainly in Cambodia **2.** an Austronesian language spoken in Vietnam and Cambodia. Native speakers: 230,000. —**Cham** *adj*

Chamaeleon /kə meéli ən/, **Chameleon** *n* a faint constellation near the south celestial pole. See illustration at **constellation**

chamaephyte /kámmi fīt/ *n* a perennial plant that produces dormant winter buds on or close to the ground [Early 20C. < Greek *khamai* 'on the ground']

chamber /cháymbər/ *n* **1. OFFICIAL RECEPTION ROOM** a reception room in an official residence or a palace **2. ROOM WITH PARTICULAR FUNCTION** a room used for a particular purpose ○ *in the council chamber* **3. OFFICIAL**

ASSEMBLY a legislative or judicial assembly ○ *The upper chamber is expected to pass the bill.* **4. MEETING PLACE OF LEGISLATURE OR COURT** the place where a legislative or judicial assembly meets ○ *the parliament chamber* **5. ORGANIZED BODY OF PEOPLE** a body of people organized into a group for a specific purpose ○ *the local chamber of commerce* **6. COMPARTMENT OR CAVITY** an enclosed space, compartment, or cavity, e.g. one inside a machine, the body, or a plant ○ *the chambers of the heart* **7. BEDROOM** a bedroom or other room in somebody's home (*archaic or literary*) **8. PLACE IN GUN FOR AMMUNITION** the compartment for a cartridge in a revolver or rifle or for a shell in a cannon **9.** same as **chamber pot** ■ **chambers** *npl* **1. JUDGE'S PRIVATE OFFICE** a judge's private office for discussing cases or legal matters not taken up in open court **2. LAWYERS' OFFICES** a suite of rooms used by lawyers for consulting with clients **3. FLAT OR SUITE OF ROOMS** a flat or suite of private rooms ■ *adj* **OF CHAMBER MUSIC** relating to, written as, or performing chamber music ■ *vt* (**-bers, -bering, -bered**) **1. PROVIDE SOMETHING WITH CHAMBER** to put something in or provide something with a chamber or chambers **2. PUT AMMUNITION IN WEAPON** to insert a round of ammunition in the breech of a weapon [12C. Via French *chambre* < Latin *camera* 'vault, room' < Greek *kamara* 'vault'] —**chambered** *adj*

chambered nautilus *n* MARINE BIOL same as **pearly nautilus**

chamberlain /cháymbərlin/ *n* **1. MANAGER OF ROYAL OR NOBLE HOUSEHOLD** an official who manages the household of a monarch or member of the nobility **2. TREASURER OF MUNICIPALITY** the treasurer of a municipality **3. PRIEST WHO IS PAPAL ATTENDANT** a Roman Catholic priest who is an attendant to the pope, often an honorary position [12C. Via Old French < assumed Frankish *kamarling* 'little room' < Greek *kamara* 'vault']

Chamberlain /cháymbərlin/, **Joseph** (1836–1914) British politician. An MP from 1876, he resigned from the Liberal Party in 1886 over Irish Home Rule and led the Liberal Unionists after 1891.

> 'The day of small nations has long passed away. The day of Empires has come.'
> [Joseph Chamberlain, *Speech, Birmingham*, *Times*; 13 May 1904]

Chamberlain, Neville (1869–1940) British politician. He resigned as prime minister (1937–40) after diplomatic and military failures, most notably his advocacy of appeasement towards Nazi Germany. Full name **Chamberlain, Arthur Neville.** See table at **prime minister**

> 'This is the second time in our history that there has come back from Germany to Downing Street peace with honour. I believe it is peace for our time.'
> [Neville Chamberlain, *Times*; 1 October 1938]

Chamberlain, Owen (b. 1920) US physicist. He shared the Nobel Prize in physics (1959) for his research into atomic nuclei, and discovered the antiproton.

chambermaid /cháymbər mayd/ *n* a woman employed to tidy and clean bedrooms in hotels or guest houses

chamber music *n* classical instrumental music written for a small group such as a quartet or trio and often originally intended for performance in a large room or a small concert hall

chamber of commerce *n* an organization of local business people who work together to promote and protect common interests in trade

chamber of horrors *n* an exhibition depicting macabre or gruesome objects and incidents [< a room in Madame Tussaud's waxwork exhibition in London]

chamber of trade *n* a national organization representing local chambers of commerce

chamber orchestra *n* a small orchestra, usually comprising fewer than 40 players, that performs classical music

chamber pot *n* a large bowl used in a bedroom for urination and defecation

Chambers Pillar /cháymbərz-/ sandstone monolith situated in Chambers Pillar Historical Reserve, south of Alice Springs in central Australia. Height: 50 m/164 ft.

chambray /shám bray/ *n* a fine lightweight cotton or

linen fabric with coloured fibres interlaced with white [Early 19C. Alteration of *Cambrai*, France]

chamcha /chúmchə/ *n S Asia* somebody who agrees enthusiastically with the ideas and views of a superior without offering any criticism [< Hindi *camcā* 'spoon'; from the use of cutlery in imitation of Westerners]

chameleon

chameleon /kə meéli ən/ *n* **1.** a tree-dwelling lizard with long thin legs, a strong curled tail, a long sticky tongue, and the ability to change colour. Native to: Africa, Madagascar. Family: Chamaeleonidae. **2.** somebody who frequently and rapidly changes personality or appearance [14C. Via Latin < Greek *khamaileōn* < *khamai* 'on the ground' + *leōn* 'lion'] —**chameleonic** /kə meéli ónnik/ *adj*

Chameleon *n* ASTRON another spelling of **Chamaeleon**

chameli /chə máyli/ *n S Asia* jasmine [< Hindi *camelī*]

chametz /khaa méts, kháwmits/, **chometz, hametz, hometz** *n* leavened bread or other food that may not be eaten by Jews during Passover [Mid-19C. < Hebrew *ḥāmēṣ*]

chamfer /chámfər/ *n* a shallow cut, edge, or groove made in wood, usually at an angle of 45 degrees to a corner [Mid-16C. Back-formation < *chamfering* 'grooving' < French *chanfrein* 'bevelled edge' < *chanfraindre* 'bevel' < *chant* 'edge' + *fraindre* 'break'] —**chamfer** *vt* —**chamfered** *adj*

chamfron /chámfrən/ *n* a piece of armour used in medieval times to protect a horse's head in battle [15C. < French *chanfrain*]

chamming /chámming/ *n regional* an act of nagging or scolding somebody [15C. < CHAMP [1]]

REGIONAL NOTE See *jawing*.

chamois

chamois /shám waa/ (*plural* **-ois** /-waa/ or **-oix** /-waa/) *n* **1. GOAT ANTELOPE** an agile goat antelope that has slender backward-curving horns and a tawny coat that darkens in winter. Native to: mountains of Europe and southwestern Asia. Latin name: *Rupicapra rupicapra.* **2.** /shámmi/, shám waa/, **chamois leather SOFT PLIABLE LEATHER** soft pliable leather, originally made from the hide of the chamois **3.** /shámmi/ **CLOTH FOR POLISHING** a piece of chamois leather, or a natural or synthetic substitute. Use: cleaning, polishing. **4.** COLOURS **GREYISH-YELLOW** a greyish-yellow colour, like that of chamois leather [Mid-16C. Via French < late Latin *camox*] —**chamois** /shámmi, shám waa/ *adj*

chamomile *n* PLANTS another spelling of **camomile**

Chamorro /chə mórrō/, **Violeta Barrios de** (b. 1929) Nicaraguan politician. The manager of the op-

position newspaper *La Prensa*, she became president of Nicaragua (1990–96).

champ[1] /champ/ *v* (**champs, champing, champed**) **1.** *vti* BITE SOMETHING VIGOROUSLY to bite, chew, or grind something vigorously, noisily, or impatiently **2.** *vt Scotland* MASH FOOD to mash something such as potatoes (*informal*) ■ *n* **1.** BITING, CHEWING, OR GRINDING SOMETHING the process of biting, chewing, or grinding something vigorously, noisily, or impatiently, or the sound that this makes **2.** MASHED POTATOES WITH SPRING ONIONS an Irish dish of mashed potatoes with milk and spring onions eaten with melted butter [Mid-16C. Probably an imitation of the sound] —**champer** *n*

REGIONAL NOTE Occasionally, the food of the poor becomes attractive to the more affluent and, in this way, a dialect word is often retained. In Ireland ***champ*** used to be boiled potatoes mashed with a little milk and butter and flavoured with nettles, leeks, or spring onions. It was the food of people who could rarely afford meat or fish. In later, more affluent times it has featured on menus in Irish restaurants and pubs, with the result that ***champ*** occurs more widely now than it did in the past.

champ[2] /champ/ *n* same as **champion** *n* (sense 1) (*informal*) [Mid-19C. Shortening]

champagne /sham páyn/ *n* **1.** FRENCH WHITE SPARKLING WINE a white sparkling wine from northeastern France, often drunk at special occasions **2.** WHITE WINE LIKE CHAMPAGNE a dry or semisweet white wine resembling champagne and made by a similar process **3.** COLOURS PALE BROWNISH-GOLD a very pale brownish-gold colour ■ *adj* **1.** EXTRAVAGANT involving luxury and indulgence ○ *a champagne lifestyle* **2.** COLOURS PALE BROWNISH-GOLD of the colour champagne

champagne socialist *n* somebody whose luxurious way of life appears to contradict his or her socialist principles (*informal*) —**champagne socialism** *n*

Champaigne /sham páyn/, **Philippe de** (1602–74) Flemish-born French painter. Baroque portraiture, notably of his patron Cardinal Armand Richelieu, gives way to classicism in his later religious subjects.

champak /chúmpuk, chámpak/ (*plural* **-paks** or *same*), **champac** (*plural* **-pacs** or *same*) *n* an evergreen tree sacred to Hindus and Buddhists. Flowers: fragrant, orange-yellow. Native to: Asia. Latin name: *Michelia champaca*. [Late 18C. Via Hindi < Sanskrit *chāmpākā* < Dravidian]

champers /shámpərz/ *n* WINE same as **champagne** *n* (sense 1) (*informal*)

champerty /chámpərti/ (*plural* **-ties**) *n* an illegal agreement between a litigant and somebody who aids or finances litigation in return for a share of the proceeds following a successful outcome [15C. < Anglo-Norman *champartie* < Old French *champart* 'field rent (a portion of produce received by a feudal lord)' < *champ* 'field' + *part* 'portion'] —**champertous** *adj*

champignon /shámpin yoN, cham pínnyən/ *n* a mushroom, especially one cultivated for eating [Late 16C. < French, literally 'little country' < *champagne*, via late Latin *campania* < Latin *Campania*, province in Italy]

champion /chámpi ən/ *n* **1.** SUPREME VICTOR IN CONTEST somebody who competes in and wins a contest, competition, or tournament, either alone or as a member of a team **2.** WINNER OF SHOW something, e.g. an animal or plant, that wins first place in a show **3.** DEFENDER a defender, supporter, or promoter of somebody or something ○ *a champion of human rights* **4.** REMARKABLE PERSON a personal example of excellence or achievement **5.** HERO OR WARRIOR a hero or warrior, especially a knight who fought on behalf of a monarch in former times ■ *vt* (**-ons, -oning, -oned**) DEFEND to defend, support, or promote a cause or person ■ *adj N England* EXCELLENT very good or pleasing ■ *adv N England* VERY WELL in a very good or pleasing way [12C. Via Old French, 'combatant' < late Latin *campion-* 'combatant in the arena' < Latin *campus* 'field']

championship /chámpi ənship/ *n* **1.** CONTEST TO DECIDE CHAMPION a contest, competition, or tournament that is held to decide who will be the overall winner **2.** TITLE OR TIME OF BEING CHAMPION the designation or period of being a champion **3.** DEFENDING OR SUPPORTING SOMEBODY OR SOMETHING the defence, support, or promotion of a person or cause

Champlain, Lake /sham pláyn/ lake situated between Vermont and New York, extending approximately 10 km/6 mi. into Canada. Area: 1,100 sq. km/430 sq. mi. Depth: 122 m/399 ft.

Champlain /sham pláyn/, **Samuel de** (1567?–1635) French explorer. His North American expeditions (1603–08) led to the establishment of New France (Canada). He was later governor of the colony (1633–35).

champlevé /shámplə vay, shaáNlə váy/ *n* enamel work in which coloured enamels are used to fill channels cut into a metal base [Mid-19C. < French < *champ* 'field' + *levé* 'raised'] —**champlevé** *adj*

Champollion /sham pōl yoN/, **Jean François** (1790–1832) French Egyptologist. The founder of the study of ancient Egypt, he became the first person to decode Egyptian hieroglyphics by deciphering the Rosetta stone (1822). Full name **Champollion Le Jeune, Jean François**

Champs Élysées /shaáNz ay lēezay/ *n* a broad avenue in Paris leading from the Place de la Concorde to the Arc de Triomphe

chana /chúnə/, **channa** *n S Asia* **1.** home-made cheese used in South Asian cooking **2.** FOOD another spelling of **channa** (sense 1) [< Hindi]

Chanc. *abbr* **1.** chancellor **2.** chancery

chance /chaanss/ *n* **1.** LIKELIHOOD THAT SOMETHING WILL HAPPEN the degree of probability that something will happen (*often used in the plural*) ○ *There's a strong chance we'll win.* **2.** OPPORTUNITY OR OPPORTUNE TIME an opportunity or a set of circumstances that makes it possible for something to happen ○ *I was given no chance to explain.* **3.** GAMBLE OR RISK a gamble or other act involving uncertainty or risk ○ *You're taking a chance by not wearing a seat belt.* **4.** SUPPOSED FORCE THAT MAKES THINGS HAPPEN the supposed force that makes things happen in a particular way without any apparent cause ○ *It was pure chance that we met.* ○ *a chance encounter* **5.** UNEXPECTED HAPPENING an unexpected event **6.** SOMETHING CAUSED BY LUCK something caused by luck or fortune ■ *v* (**chances, chancing, chanced**) **1.** *vt* DO SOMETHING RISKY to do something knowing that it is risky **2.** *vi* DO SOMETHING UNPLANNED to do something or happen without a cause or plan [13C. Via Anglo-Norman < late Latin *cadentia* 'falling' < present participle of Latin *cadere* 'to fall'] ◇ **by any chance** used to enquire if there is any possibility of something ○ *Is there a copy you could lend me, by any chance?* ◇ **by chance** unexpectedly or without plan ◇ **fat chance** something that is highly unlikely (*informal*) ◇ **given half a chance** if the slightest opportunity should present itself ○ *He did what most of us would do, given half a chance.*

chance on *or* **upon** *vt* to find or encounter somebody or something unexpectedly

chancel /chaánssəl/ *n* an area of a church near the altar for the use of clergy and choir, often separated from the nave by a screen or steps [14C. Via Old French < Latin *cancelli* 'little lattices' < *cancer* 'lattice']

chancellery /chaánssələri, chaánsslәri/ (*plural* **-ies**), **chancellory** *n* **1.** the official residence of a chancellor **2.** the position or rank of a chancellor **3.** *Aus, US* INTERNAT REL same as **chancery** (sense 3) [14C. < French *chancellerie* < *chancelier* (see CHANCELLOR)]

chancellor /chaánssələr, chaánsslər/ *n* **1.** GOV same as **Chancellor of the Exchequer** **2.** POL HEAD OF PARLIAMENTARY GOVERNMENT the chief minister of government in some parliamentary democracies **3.** *UK, Can* EDUC HONORARY HEAD OF UNIVERSITY the honorary head of a university **4.** *N Am* EDUC CHIEF ADMINISTRATIVE OFFICER OF UNIVERSITY the chief administrative officer of some universities **5.** INTERNAT REL EMBASSY SECRETARY the main secretary of an embassy **6.** *US* LAW US PRESIDING JUDGE in some US states, the presiding judge of a court of equity or chancery [Pre-12C. Via Anglo-Norman *c(h)anceler*, Old French *chancelier* < Latin *cancellarius* 'court secretary, attendant at the grating' < *cancelli* (see CHANCEL)] —**chancellorship** *n*

Chancellor of the Duchy of Lancaster *n* an honorary title held by a cabinet minister who legally represents a sovereign in matters concerning the Duchy of Lancaster and who does not have a department

Chancellor of the Exchequer *n* a member of the British government who is the chief minister of finance

chancellory *n* another spelling of **chancellery**

chance-medley *n* **1.** the killing of an assailant in self-defence during an unexpected brawl **2.** a haphazard event or action, or the randomness of chance [15C. < Anglo-Norman *chance medlee* 'mixed chance'; from the idea of being only partly accidental]

chancer /chaánssər/ *n* somebody who takes risks in the interest of personal gain (*informal*)

chancery /chaánssəri/ (*plural* **-ies**) *n* **1.** LAW LORD CHANCELLOR'S COURT in England, the Lord Chancellor's court, one of the five divisions of the High Court of Justice **2.** LAW same as **court of chancery** **3.** *UK, NZ, Can* INTERNAT REL OFFICE ATTACHED TO EMBASSY an office attached to an embassy or consulate, especially the political section. Aus, US term **chancellery** **4.** PUBLIC ARCHIVE a public archive or record office **5.** POL same as **chancellery** (sense 2) [14C. Contraction of CHANCELLERY]

Chancery Division *n* LAW same as **chancery** (sense 1)

chancey *adj* another spelling of **chancy**

chancre /shángkər/ *n* **1.** a small painless highly infectious ulcer or sore that is the first sign of syphilis and some other infectious diseases **2.** a sore or ulcer at the point where a disease-causing organism (**pathogen**) enters the body [Late 16C. Via French < Latin *cancer* 'ulcer'] —**chancrous** *adj*

chancroid /sháng kroyd/ *n* **1.** a sexually transmitted disease that produces a painful ragged ulcer at the site of infection, caused by the bacterium *Haemophilus ducreyi* **2.** a painful ragged ulcer that is characteristic of chancroid —**chancroidal** /shang króyd'l/ *adj*

chancy /chaánssi/ (**-ier, -iest**), **chancey** *adj* **1.** involving risks or danger **2.** occurring in a random or haphazard way —**chancily** *adv* —**chanciness** *n*

chandelier

chandelier /shándə léer/ *n* a decorative hanging light with several branched parts on which are holders for candles or light bulbs [Mid-18C. < French < *chandelle* 'candle' < Latin *candela*] —**chandeliered** *adj*

chandelle /shan dél, shaaN-/ *n* a steep climbing turn in which an aircraft almost stalls as it uses momentum to increase the rate of climb ■ *vi* (**-delles, -delling, -delled**) to climb steeply in an aircraft, turning at the same time and almost stalling [Early 20C. < French (see CHANDELIER)]

Chandigarh /chándi gaár/, **Chandīgarh** city and union territory in northern India, north of Delhi. It is the joint capital of Punjab and Haryana states. Population: 900,914 (2001).

chandler /chaándlər/ *n* **1.** a seller of particular supplies and goods ○ *a ship's chandler* **2.** a seller or maker of candles [14C. < Anglo-Norman *chaundeler*, Old French *chandelier* < *c(h)andelle* (see CHANDELIER)]

Chandler /chaándlər, chánd-/, **Raymond** (1888–1959) US writer. He wrote gritty mystery and crime novels such as *The Big Sleep* (1939) and *The Long Goodbye* (1953). Full name **Chandler, Raymond Thornton**. See illustration on next page

> 'Crime isn't a disease, it's a symptom. Cops are like a doctor who gives you aspirin for a brain tumor, except that the cop would rather cure it with a blackjack.'
> [Raymond Chandler. Quoted in *New York Times*; 1 November 1987]

Raymond Chandler

Coco Chanel

chandlery /cháandləri/ (*plural* **-ies**) *n* **1.** the place where a chandler's goods are sold or stored **2.** the goods that a chandler deals in

Chandrasekhar limit /chaándrə seékə-/ *n* the upper limit for the mass of a white dwarf star beyond which the star collapses to a neutron star or a black hole [After Subrahmanyan *Chandrasekhar* (1910–95), US astrophysicist]

Chanel /shə nél/, **Coco** (1883–1971) French couturier. Her name became synonymous with a distinctively elegant style of women's suit. Full name **Chanel, Gabrielle Bonheur**

'There is nothing more comfortable than a caterpillar and nothing more made for love than a butterfly. We need dresses that crawl and dresses that fly.'
[Coco Chanel. Quoted in *Chanel*, Jean Leymarie; 1987]

Chaney /cháyni/, **Lon** (1883–1930) US silent film actor. He specialized in horror roles, especially in *The Hunchback of Notre Dame* (1923) and *The Phantom of the Opera* (1925). Full name **Chaney, Alonso**

Chang /chang/, **Victor Peter** (1936–91) Chinese-born Australian surgeon. He led the team that performed the first Australian heart-lung transplant (1986).

~~changable~~ incorrect spelling of **changeable**

Changchun /cháng choón/ transportation centre and capital city of Jilin province in northeastern China. Population: 4,150,000 (1995).

change /chaynj/ *v* (**changes, changing, changed**) **1.** *vti* BECOME OR MAKE DIFFERENT to become different, or make something or somebody different ○ *This liquid crystal changes colour when you tilt it.* ○ *The town hasn't changed much since I left.* **2.** *vt* SUBSTITUTE OR REPLACE SOMETHING to exchange, substitute, or replace something ○ *If it doesn't fit, the shop will change it for another size.* **3.** *vti* PASS FROM ONE STATE TO ANOTHER to pass or make something pass from one state or stage to another ○ *Water changes to ice on freezing.* **4.** *vt* FIN CONVERT ONE CURRENCY INTO ANOTHER to replace money of one currency with an equivalent amount in another currency, calculated according to an exchange rate **5.** *vt* FIN EXCHANGE MONEY FOR SMALLER UNITS to exchange a unit of money for an equal amount of money in lower denominations ○ *Can you change me a £10 note for two fives?* **6.** *vti* MOVE FROM ONE VEHICLE TO ANOTHER to get out of one vehicle or means of transportation and continue the journey in another **7.** *vti* REMOVE CLOTHES AND PUT ON OTHERS to remove one or more articles of clothing and replace them with something else ○ *Are you going to change for dinner?*

8. *vt* REMOVE AND REPLACE SOMETHING to remove something dirty or used and replace it with another that is clean or unused ○ *changing the sheets* **9.** *vti* AUTOMOT OPERATE GEARS OF VEHICLE to put a car or other vehicle into a different gear. N Am term **shift** ■ *n* **1.** MAKING OR BECOMING DIFFERENT alteration, variation, or modification, or the result of this ○ *There's been a change of plan.* **2.** EXCHANGE OR REPLACEMENT an exchange, substitution, or replacement of something or somebody **3.** MONEY GIVEN BACK the balance of money given back to a customer who has handed over a larger sum than the cost of the goods or services purchased **4.** COINS coins collectively, especially coins of a small denomination **5.** MONEY EXCHANGED FOR HIGHER DENOMINATION a sum of money given or received for a coin or banknote of a higher denomination **6.** TRANSITION FROM SOMETHING a shift from one state, stage, or phase to another ○ *a change in our thinking* **7.** VARIANCE FROM ROUTINE a variance from a routine or pattern, especially a welcome one ○ *I could do with a change.* **8.** FRESH SET OF SOMETHING a different, clean, or fresh set of something, especially clothes **9.** MUSIC PROCEDURE FOR RINGING BELLS the order in which tuned bells are rung **10.** MED same as **menopause** (*dated informal*) [12C. Via Old French *changer* < late Latin *cambiare* < Latin *cambire* 'exchange'] —**changer** *n* ◇ **ring the changes** to repeat something with variations

SYNONYMS *change, alter, modify, convert, vary, shift, transform, transmute*

CORE MEANING: to make or become different

change to become different, or make something or somebody different ○ *The society we live in is changing rapidly.* ○ *pressure to change public attitudes towards health* **alter** to make changes to something, especially to an aspect of something, or be changed or become different ○ *trying to alter the widely held perception of the north as an industrial area* ○ *From March the situation altered rapidly.* **modify** to make minor changes or alterations, especially in order to improve something ○ *Even extroverts are capable of modifying their behaviour.* ○ *modifying the curriculum so that it is better adapted to the needs of real children* **convert** to change something from one character, form, or function to another, or be changed in character, form, or function ○ *the process by which you take in food and convert it into energy and heat* ○ *Plans are in hand to convert the buildings into luxury dwellings.* **vary** to change within a range of possibilities, or in connection with something else, or make something undergo such a change ○ *Opening times may vary with the season.* ○ *You can vary the menu according to your taste.* **shift** to change from one position or direction to another ○ *The focus of your essay may shift as you write.* ○ *For most of us our native language is alive and constantly shifting.* **transform** to change somebody or something completely, especially improving their appearance or usefulness, or to change in this way ○ *The playground is being transformed into a communal garden.* ○ *A good teacher can still transform the life of a student.* **transmute** to change something from one form, nature, or state to another, or be changed in this way ○ *The Old Norse word 'borg' meaning 'citadel' was later transmuted into 'borough'* ○ *His anger swiftly transmuted into grief.* ○ *The ancient alchemists tried to transmute base metals into gold.*

change down *vi* to change into a lower gear in a car or other vehicle. N Am term **downshift**

change over *vi* **1.** SUBSTITUTE SOMETHING FOR SOMETHING ELSE to replace one system, method, or product with another **2.** EXCHANGE OR REVERSE PLACES OR POSITIONS to exchange or reverse places, positions, or roles **3.** SPORTS EXCHANGE ENDS OF PLAYING FIELD in team sports, to switch to opposite ends of a playing field, usually halfway through a match **4.** SPORTS HAND OVER BATON IN RELAY RACE in a relay race, to pass on the responsibility for participation to another team member by handing over a baton or touching

change round *vti* to reverse or alter places, positions, or roles

change up *vi* to change into a higher gear in a car or other vehicle

changeable /cháynjəb'l/ *adj* capable of changing, or liable to change or vary —**changeability** /cháynjə bílləti/ *n* —**changeableness** *n* —**changeably** *adv*

changeful /cháynjf'l/ *adj* changing frequently

~~changeing~~ incorrect spelling of **changing**

changeless /cháynjləss/ *adj* not liable to change —**changelessly** *adv* —**changelessness** *n*

changeling /cháynjling/ *n* in folklore, a child who is secretly substituted for another one by fairies

change of heart *n* a profound change of attitude or opinion

change of life *n* MED same as **menopause** (*informal*)

change of venue *n* **1.** the removal of a trial to another jurisdiction **2.** a relocation of a public event, especially a play or concert

changeover /cháynj övər/ *n* **1.** COMPLETE CHANGE FROM SOMETHING a conversion, reversal, or complete change from one position, situation, or system to another **2.** EXCHANGE OF ENDS IN PLAYING FIELD in team sports, the switch of teams to opposite ends of a playing field **3.** SPORTS PASSING OF BATON IN RELAY RACE in a relay race, the passing on of responsibility for participation from one team member to another by handing over the baton or touching, or the point at which this is done

change purse *n* N Am same as **purse** *n* (sense 1)

change ringing *n* the ordered ringing of a peal of bells in various combinations so that none of the combinations is repeated and all possible permutations are rung

changeround /cháynj rownd/ *n* a change to a different or opposite position

changing of the guard *n* the action or ceremony in which one shift of guards takes up duty while another leaves, especially outside Buckingham Palace

changing room *n* an area in a sports or leisure centre where clothes can be changed and showers taken

Chang Jiang /cháng ji áng/ ♦ **Yangtze**

Changsha /cháng shaá/ capital of Hunan Province, situated north of Guangzhou, in southeastern China. Population: 1,520,000 (1995).

Changzhou /cháng jö/ city situated in the centre of the River Yangtze Delta, 162 km/100 mi. west of Shanghai. Population: 800,000 (1996).

channa /chúnnə/, **chana** *n* S Asia **1.** chickpeas, often stewed or served roasted or fried as a snack **2.** FOOD another spelling of **chana** (sense 1)

channel[1] /chánn'l/ *n* **1.** TUBULAR PASSAGE FOR LIQUID a long narrow passage or tube along which a liquid can flow ○ *a drainage channel* **2.** GROOVE OR TRENCH a long narrow groove or furrow, e.g. in architecture or sculpture **3.** MEANS OF COMMUNICATION a course or means of communication or expression (*often used in the plural*) ○ *go through the proper channels* ○ *found a channel for his talent in graphic design* **4.** GEOG STRIP OF WATER SEPARATING LAND a wide passage of water between an island and a larger body of land **5.** GEOG ROUTE OF WATERWAY the course of a stream, river, canal, or other waterway **6.** NAUT NAVIGABLE PASSAGE a navigable route through a river or harbour, especially one that has been deepened by dredging **7.** BROADCAST FREQUENCY SPECTRUM USED IN TRANSMISSION the portion of a frequency spectrum that is set aside for a specific purpose such as the broadcasting of a television or radio signal **8.** BROADCAST TV OR RADIO STATION a television or radio station broadcasting on a specific band of the frequency spectrum **9.** ELECTRONICS PATH FOR ELECTRICAL CURRENT a path for an electrical current or signal **10.** COMPUT PATH FOR COMPUTER SIGNALS a path for electronic signals within a computer or between a computer and a peripheral device **11.** ONLINE WEBSITE SENDING UPDATED INFORMATION a preselected website that can automatically send updated information for immediate display or viewing on request **12.** PARAPSYCHOL SUPPOSED SPIRIT MEDIUM in spiritualism, somebody who supposedly acts as a medium for receiving messages from the spirit world ■ *v* (**-nels, -nelling, -nelled**) **1.** *vt* DIRECT SOMETHING ALONG SPECIFIC ROUTE to direct, guide, or convey something through or along a specific route or towards a specific goal ○ *They channelled all their energies into the game.* **2.** *vi* MAKE CHANNEL to make a channel in land or water ○ *channelling through bedrock* **3.** *vt* MAKE GROOVE OR FURROW IN SOMETHING to cut a long narrow groove or furrow in a surface **4.** *vti* PARAPSYCHOL SPEAK FOR SUPPOSED SPIRIT in spiritualism, to act as a medium for a supposed spirit [14C. Via

Old French *chanel* < Latin *canalis* 'groove' (see CANAL)] —**channeller** *n*

channel[2] /chánn'l/ *n* a flat piece of wood or metal projecting horizontally from the side of a ship to increase the spread of the ropes or cables (**shrouds**) supporting the mast [Mid-18C. Alteration of *chainwale* < CHAIN + WALE]

Channel /chánn'l/ GEOG ♦ English Channel

channel deposit *n* a body of sand deposited by a river, often showing an erratic sinuous pattern

channel-hop *vi* UK to use a remote control device to move rapidly through many different television channels, either to see whether there is anything worth watching or without searching for anything in particular (*informal*) ANZ, N Am term **channel-surf** —**channel-hopper** *n*

Channel-hop *vi* to cross the English Channel for a trip to mainland Europe, usually for shopping or sightseeing, and return on the same day —**Channel-hopper** *n*

channeling *n* US spelling of **channelling**

channel iron *n* an iron or steel bar with a U-shaped cross section

channelise *vt* another spelling of **channelize**

Channel Islands group of islands in the English Channel, near the French coast. The islands Jersey, Guernsey, Alderney, and Sark are self-governing Crown dependencies. Language: English; Norman French. Population: 143,534 (1991). Area: 190 sq. km/75 sq. mi.

channelize /chánn'l īz/ (**-izes, -izing, -ized**), **channelise** (**-ises, -ising, -ised**) *vt* 1. to make a channel for something 2. to direct something through a channel —**channelization** /chánn'l ī záysh'n/ *n*

channelling /chánn'ling/ *n* 1. SUPPOSED SPIRITUAL COMMUNICATION THROUGH MEDIUM in spiritualism, the practice of acting as a medium for receiving messages believed to come from the spirit world 2. CREATION OF CHANNEL the making of a channel in or on something 3. TUBING THAT PROTECTS WIRES a protective casing or container that carries one or more cables or wires inside or outside a building

channel-surf *vi* ANZ, N Am same as **channel-hop** (*informal*) —**channel-surfer** *n*

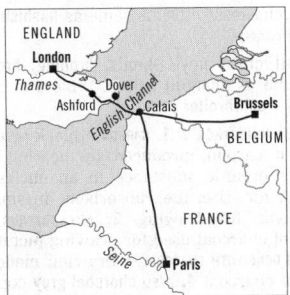

Channel Tunnel: map showing railway routes using the Channel Tunnel

Channel Tunnel *n* a railway tunnel, opened in 1994, that runs underneath the English Channel and links Folkestone in England with Coquelles near Calais in France

chanoyu /chaánaw yoo/ *n* a Japanese ceremony in which tea is ritually prepared, served, and consumed [Late 20C. < Japanese, 'hot water for tea']

chanson /shaaN sóN, shánssən/ *n* a French song, e.g. a satirical cabaret song of the 20th century or a Renaissance song similar to the madrigal [15C. Via French, 'song' < Latin *cantion- < cantare* 'sing']

chanson de geste /shaaN sóN də zhést/ (*plural* **chansons de geste** /*pronunc. same*/) *n* a French epic poem written between the 11th and 14th centuries, usually celebrating legendary events and figures [< French, 'song of heroic deeds']

chant /chaant/ *n* 1. PHRASE SPOKEN REPEATEDLY BY CROWD a phrase or slogan repeated rhythmically and spoken, often with a simple singsong intonation, especially in unison by a crowd or group 2. SOMETHING SPOKEN MONOTONOUSLY OR REPETITIOUSLY a monotonous or repetitive song or intonation of the voice 3. MUSIC

FOR RELIGIOUS TEXT a set of words or syllables sung on the same note, or a single word or syllable sung on a series of notes. Chants are used in psalms, canticles, and other parts of some religious services. 4. HYMN OR PRAYER SUNG AS CHANT a psalm, prayer, or other religious text sung as a chant ■ *vti* (**chants, chanting, chanted**) 1. REPEAT SLOGAN CONTINUALLY to speak a slogan repeatedly and rhythmically with a simple singsong intonation 2. UTTER MONOTONOUSLY to speak or sing something monotonously 3. SING HYMN OR PRAYER AS CHANT to sing or intone a religious text or part of a religious service as a chant [14C. Via French, 'song' < Latin *cantus < past participle of canere* 'sing'] —**chantingly** *adv*

chanter /chaántər/ *n* 1. SOMEBODY CHANTING SLOGAN somebody who chants a slogan 2. SOMEBODY CHANTING PSALM OR HYMN somebody who chants a religious musical passage, e.g. a priest or chorister 3. PIPE WITH FINGER HOLES ON BAGPIPES a pipe with finger holes on which the melody is played 4. PIPE FOR PRACTISING BAGPIPES a pipe used to learn or practise fingering for bagpipes

chanterelle /shaántə rél, chaántə-, shántə-/ *n* an edible mushroom found in temperate woodlands that has a yellow-to-orange trumpet-shaped cap. Latin name: *Cantharellus cibarius*. [Late 18C. Via French < modern Latin *cantharellus* 'little cup' < Latin *cantharus* 'drinking vessel' < Greek *kantharos*]

chanteuse /shaan túrz/ (*plural* **-teuses** /*pronunc. same*/) *n* a female singer, especially in a nightclub or cabaret [Mid-19C. < French]

chantey /chánti, shánti/ (*plural* **-teys**), **chanty** (*plural* **-ties**), **shanty** /shánti/, **shantey** (*plural* **-teys**) *n* US spelling of **shanty**[2] [Mid-19C. Origin ?]

chanticleer /chánti kleer, shánti-/ (*plural* **-ticleers** or **-teclers**) *n* a cock, especially in fairy tales (*literary*) [13C. < Old French *Chantecler < chanter* 'sing' + *cler* 'clear']

Chantilly[1] /shan tílli/ *n* 1. *also* **Chantilly lace** a delicate black or white ornamental lace with an outlined design. Use: bridal and evening gowns. 2. *also* **Chantilly cream** whipped cream, sweetened and often flavoured with vanilla

Chantilly[2] /shan tílli/ a town and resort in Oise Department, Picardie region, northern France. Situated about 42 km/26 mi. north of Paris, it became famous for its lace and porcelain. Population: 10,902 (1999).

chantry /chaántri/ (*plural* **-tries**) *n* 1. an endowment to pay for the saying of masses for the soul of the founder or somebody named by the founder 2. *also* **chantry chapel** a chapel or altar endowed for the performance of chantries [14C. < Anglo-Norman *chaunterie*, Old French *chanterie < chanter* 'sing']

chanty *n* MUSIC another spelling of **shanty**[2]

Chanukah, **Chanukkah** *n* JUDAISM another spelling of **Hanukkah**

chaology /kay ólləji/ *n* the study of chaos theory and chaotic systems —**chaologist** *n*

Chao Phraya /chów prə yaá/ river in west-central Thailand. Length: 365 km/227 mi.

chaos /káy oss/ *n* 1. DISORDER a state of complete disorder and confusion 2. *also* **Chaos** ASTRON EARLIEST CONDITION OF UNIVERSE the unbounded space and formless matter supposed to have existed before the creation of the universe 3. PHYS APPARENT DISORDER the unpredictability inherent in a system such as the weather, in which apparently random changes occur as a result of the system's extreme sensitivity to small differences in initial conditions [15C. Directly or via French < Latin < Greek *khaos* 'void, abyss']

chaos theory *n* a theory that complex natural systems obey rules but are so sensitive that small initial changes can cause unexpected final results, thus giving an impression of randomness

chaotic /kay óttik/ *adj* 1. completely disordered and out of control 2. describes the state of a system according to chaos theory [Early 18C. < CHAOS] —**chaotically** *adv*

chap[1] /chap/ *vti* (**chaps, chapping, chapped**) BECOME SORE AND ROUGHENED to become sore and cracked by exposure to wind or cold, or make skin sore and cracked in this way (*refers to skin*) ■ *n* 1. AREA OF SORE SKIN a sore cracked area of skin, caused by exposure

to wind or cold 2. GEOL CRACK IN GROUND a crack or fissure in dry ground [14C. Origin ?] —**chapped** *adj*

chap[2] /chap/ *n* a man or youth, especially somebody whose name is not known or not relevant (*informal*) [Late 16C. Shortening of *chapman* 'wandering pedlar' < *cēap* (see CHEAP)]

chap[3] /chap/ *n* the lower exterior half of the jaw, especially the cheek [Mid-16C. Origin ?]

chap. *abbr* 1. CHR chaplain 2. LITERAT chapter

chaparral /sháppə rál/ *n* Southwest US a dense thicket of bushes or small trees, especially of evergreen oaks in southern California [Mid-19C. < Spanish < *chaparra* 'dwarf evergreen oak']

chapati /chə paáti, -pátti/ (*plural* **-tis** or **-ties**), **chapatti** *n* a thin round unleavened bread eaten with South Asian dishes [Early 19C. < Hindi *capātī < capānā* 'flatten']

chapbook /cháp book/ *n* a small booklet of poems, ballads, or stories, originally sold by travelling pedlars [Early 19C. Blend of *chapman* (see CHAP[2]) + BOOK]

chape /chayp/ *n* 1. the metal tip of a scabbard 2. the tongue of a buckle [14C. Via French, 'cape, hood' < late Latin *cappa* (see CAP[1])]

chapeau /sha pó/ (*plural* **-peaux** /-pó, -póz/ or **-peaus**) *n* a hat as an item of high fashion or ceremonial dress (*formal*) [15C. Via French < late Latin *cappellum* 'small hooded cloak' < *cappa* (see CAP[1])]

chapel /cháppl/ *n* 1. ROOM FOR CHRISTIAN WORSHIP a place in a hospital, prison, or other institution, or in a large house, consecrated for Christian worship 2. SEPARATE AREA OF CHURCH a separate area in a Christian church, having its own altar and intended for private prayer 3. PROTESTANT CHURCH a place of worship used by a Nonconformist Protestant denomination such as the Methodists or Baptists 4. SERVICE IN CHAPEL a service held in a chapel, especially in a Nonconformist Christian church 5. SMALL ANGLICAN CHURCH a small Anglican church that operates as a branch of a parish church 6. PUBL, MEDIA TRADE UNION BRANCH a branch of a trade union in printing and journalism (+ *sing or pl verb*) 7. PUBL, MEDIA TRADE UNION MEETING a meeting of a printers' or journalists' chapel ■ *adj* BELONGING TO NONCONFORMIST CHURCH belonging to a Nonconformist Christian church (*dated*) [12C. Via Old French *chapele* < medieval Latin *cappella* 'small hooded cloak' < late Latin *cappa* (see CAP[1])]

chapel of ease *n* a Christian church built for people who live a long distance from a parish church

chapel of rest *n* a place at an undertaker's where bodies are kept and may be visited by family and friends

chaperone /sháppərōn/, **chaperon** *n* 1. somebody, especially an older or married woman, who accompanies and supervises a young single woman at social events 2. somebody who accompanies and supervises a group of young people [12C. < French, < late Latin *cappa* (see CAP[1])] —**chaperone** *vti* —**chaperonage** *n*

chaperonin /sháppə rónin/ *n* a protein belonging to a large group of protein families involved in the stabilization, translocation, and unfolding of developing proteins

chaplain /chápplin/ *n* a member of the clergy employed to give religious guidance, e.g. to members of the armed services, schoolchildren, or prisoners [12C. Via Anglo-Norman, Old French *chapelain* < medieval Latin *cappellanus* 'guardian of the cloak of St Martin of Tours' < *cappella* (see CHAPEL)] —**chaplaincy** *n* —**chaplainship** *n*

chaplet /chápplət/ *n* 1. WREATH WORN ON HEAD a decorative circle of beads or flowers worn on the head 2. CHR ROMAN CATHOLIC PRAYER BEADS a string of beads used by Roman Catholics for counting prayers. A chaplet has 55 beads, one third of the number on a rosary. 3. ARCHIT BEADED MOULDING a small moulding resembling a string of beads [14C. < French *chapelet* < late Latin *cappa* (see CAP[1])] —**chapleted** *adj*

Charlie Chaplin

Chaplin /chápplin/, **Charlie** (1889–1977) British-born US film actor, director, and producer who is best known for the tramp character that he played in over 70 films. Full name **Chaplin, Sir Charles Spencer**

> 'Life is a tragedy when seen in close-up, but a comedy in long-shot.'
> [Charlie Chaplin, *Guardian*; 28 December 1977]

chapman /chápmən/ (*plural* **-men** /-mən/) *n* a wandering pedlar (*archaic*) [Old English *cēapman* < *cēap* (see CHEAP)]

Chapman /chápmən/, **George** (1559?–1634) English dramatist and translator who is known for his translations of Homer's *Iliad* and *Odyssey* (1616)

> 'Young men think old men are fools; but old men know young men are fools.'
> [George Chapman, *All Fools*; 1605]

chappal /chúpp'l/ *n S Asia* a leather sandal with a single strap attached at the sides and passing between the first two toes [Late 19C. < Hindi *cappal*]

Chappell /chápp'l/, **Greg** (*b.* 1948) Australian cricketer. He was captain of the Australian Test team (1975–77 and 1979–83) and the country's second-highest scoring Test batsman, with 7,110 runs. Full name **Chappell, Gregory Stephen**

Chappell, Ian (*b.* 1943) Australian cricketer. He was captain of the Australian Test team (1971–75). Full name **Chappell, Ian Michael**

chappie /chάppi/ *n* same as **chap**[2] (*informal*)

chaprasi /chə prússi/ *n S Asia* an office worker who carries out junior tasks, especially carrying messages [Early 19C. < Hindi, literally 'badge wearer']

chaps /chaps/ *npl* protective leather leggings, like a pair of trousers with no seat or crotch, worn on horseback over ordinary trousers by North American ranch workers, rodeo contestants, and cowboys [Late 19C. Shortening of *chaparejos*, alteration of *chaparreras* < *chaparra* (see CHAPARRAL); because worn when riding through chaparral]

chaptalize /chάptə līz/ (**-izes, -izing, -ized**), **chaptalise** (**-ises, -ising, -ised**) *vt* to increase the alcohol content of wine by adding sugar before or during fermentation [Late 19C. After J. A. *Chaptal* (1756–1832), French chemist] —**chaptalization** /chάptə lī záysh'n/ *n*

chapter /cháptər/ *n* **1.** SECTION OF BOOK one of the main sections of a text, usually having a title or number as a heading **2.** PERIOD OF DEVELOPMENT an identifiable period in the history or development of something ○ *Their move to France began a new chapter in their lives.* **3.** SERIES OF EVENTS a series of events having a common characteristic ○ *a turbulent chapter in the history of the country* **4.** BRANCH OF GROUP a branch of a society or organization (*takes a singular or plural verb*) **5.** CHR GROUP OF CANONS the body of canons of a cathedral or collegiate church, or the body of members of an order of knighthood (*takes a singular or plural verb*) **6.** CHR ASSEMBLY OF CHAPTER a meeting of a cathedral or church chapter [12C. Via French *chapitre* < Latin *capitulum* 'small head' < *caput* 'head'] ◇ **give** or **quote chapter and verse** to give exact information and detailed references on a topic

Chapter 11 /-i lévv'n/ *n* a section of the US Federal Bankruptcy Code that allows an insolvent company to be reorganized, sometimes providing for repayment of debts or the creation of a new company

chapter book *n US* a book for young school-age children that is divided into chapters and tells a story in writing rather than through its illustrations

chapter house *n* **1.** a building used for meetings by a religious chapter **2.** a building used by a fraternity or sorority at a North American college

Chapultepec /chə pōōltə pek/ rocky hill in Mexico, fortified by Aztec rulers, situated 5 km/3 mi. southwest of Mexico City

char[1] /chaar/ (**chars, charring, charred**) *v* **1.** *vti* to blacken something or become blackened by burning or scorching **2.** *vt* to turn wood into charcoal by partial burning [Late 17C. Back-formation < CHARCOAL]

char[2] /chaar/ (*plural same* or **chars**), **charr** (*plural same* or **charrs**) *n* a freshwater fish of the salmon family, similar to a trout. Native to: northern hemisphere. Latin name: *Salvelinus fontinalis*. N Am term **brook trout** [Mid-17C. Origin ?]

char[3] /chaar/ *n* same as **charwoman** ■ *vi* (**chars, charring, charred**) to do people's housework, especially cleaning, for pay (*dated informal*) [Old English *cierran* 'to turn' < Germanic]

char[4] /chaar/ *n* BEVERAGES same as **tea** (senses 2–3) (*dated informal*) [Early 20C. < Modern Standard Chinese *chá*]

charabanc /shárrə bang/ *n* a bus or coach, often open-sided, used for pleasure trips or sightseeing [Early 19C. < French *char-à-bancs* 'carriage with benches']

characin /kárrəssin/ (*plural same* or **-cins**), **characid** /-sid/ (*plural same* or **-cids**) *n* a small brightly coloured freshwater fish often kept in aquariums. Native to: Africa, South America. Family: Characidae. [Late 19C. < modern Latin *Characinus* < Greek *kharax* 'pointed stake', also used for a fish]

character /kárrəktər/ *n* **1.** DISTINCTIVE QUALITIES the set of qualities that make somebody or something distinctive, especially somebody's qualities of mind and feeling ○ *It's just not in my character to behave like that.* **2.** POSITIVE QUALITIES qualities that make somebody or something interesting or attractive ○ *an old house full of character* **3.** REPUTATION somebody's public reputation ○ *an attack on his good character that ended in court* **4.** SOMEBODY IN BOOK OR FILM one of the people portrayed in a book, play, or film ○ *None of the central characters is particularly likable.* **5.** UNUSUAL PERSON somebody with an unusual or eccentric personality **6.** INDIVIDUAL somebody considered in terms of personality, behaviour, or appearance ○ *a flamboyant character* **7.** LETTER OR SYMBOL any written or printed letter, number, or other symbol **8.** COMPUT UNIT OF COMPUTER DATA a single letter, number, or symbol that can be displayed on a computer screen or printer and represents one byte of data **9.** GENETICS GENETICALLY CONTROLLED CHARACTERISTIC a genetically controlled characteristic of an organism **10.** HR WRITTEN TESTIMONIAL a written summary of somebody's abilities and personality, written by an employer or other person who knows the person well (*dated*) **11.** CAPACITY OR POSITION a particular role, position, or function that somebody has in society or in an organization (*formal*) ○ *speaking in her character as chairperson* ■ *vt* (**-ters, -tering, -tered**) WRITE to write or carve words carefully and skilfully on paper, stone, or metal (*archaic*) [14C. Via French *caractère* < Greek *kharaktēr* 'tool for marking' < *kharassein* 'engrave' < *kharax* 'pointed stake'] ◇ **in** or **out of character 1.** typical or untypical of the behaviour of a particular person or thing **2.** involved or not involved in the psychological preparations for acting out a particular role in a play, film, or other dramatic work

character actor *n* an actor who specializes in playing the roles of unusual or distinctive characters

character assassination *n* a deliberate and sustained attack on somebody's reputation

character-building, **character-forming** *adj* creating strength of character, usually as a result of testing and difficult experiences

characterful /kárrəktərf'l/ *adj* having many qualities that are interesting or pleasantly unusual

characterise *vt* another spelling of **characterize**

characteristic /kárrəktə rístik/ *n* **1.** DEFINING FEATURE a feature or quality that makes somebody or something recognizable **2.** MATHS WHOLE NUMBER IN LOGARITHM the whole number (**integer**) found to the left of the decimal point in a common logarithm, e.g. the characteristic of 5.4321 is 5 ■ *adj* TYPICAL distinguishing or representative of a particular person or thing —**characteristically** *adv*

characterization /kárrəktər ī záysh'n/, **characterisation** *n* **1.** the way in which the writer portrays the characters in a book, play, or film **2.** a description of the character or nature of somebody or something

characterize /kárrəktə rīz/ (**-izes, -izing, -ized**), **characterise** (**-ises, -ising, -ised**) *vt* **1.** to describe the character or characteristics of somebody or something **2.** to be representative of the way a particular person or thing behaves or looks —**characterizable** /kárrəktə rīzəb'l/ *adj* —**characterizer** *n*

characterless /kárrəktərləss/ *adj* without any interesting or distinctive features ○ *a characterless view* —**characterlessly** *adv* —**characterlessness** *n*

character recognition *n* a magnetic or optical process by which letters, numbers, or symbols are recognized and digitized by a computer

character reference *n* a summary of somebody's abilities and personality, especially with regard to personal integrity or trustworthiness, usually written by a person in authority who knows the subject of the reference well

character set *n* a complete set of letters, numbers, symbols, and control codes that can be used by a computer

character sketch *n* a short description of somebody's character and behaviour

character witness *n* a witness who gives evidence of somebody's good character in a court of law

charade /shə ra̋ad, -ráyd/ *n* **1.** an absurdly false or pointless act or situation **2.** a clue in the game of charades [Late 18C. < French < modern Provençal *charra* 'to chatter']

charades /shə ra̋adz, -ráydz/ *n* a game in which somebody provides a visual or acted clue for a word or phrase, often the title of a book, play, or film, for others to guess (*takes a singular verb*)

charango /chə ráng gō/ (*plural* **-gos**) *n Hispanic* a small guitar from the Andes, traditionally made from the shell of an armadillo [Early 20C. < American Spanish < *charanga* < Spanish, 'light orchestra']

charas /chaárəss/ *n* DRUGS same as **hashish** [Mid-19C. < Hindi *caras*]

charbroil /chaár broyl/ (**-broils, -broiling, -broiled**) *vt N Am* same as **chargrill** [Mid-20C. Blend of CHARCOAL + BROIL[1]] —**charbroiler** *n*

charcoal /chaárkōl/ *n* **1.** CARBON a black or dark grey form of carbon, produced by heating wood or another organic substance in an enclosed space without air. Use: fuel, absorbent, in smelting, in explosives, for drawing. **2.** ART DRAWING IMPLEMENT sticks of charcoal used for drawing pictures **3.** ART DRAWING DONE WITH CHARCOAL a drawing made using a stick of charcoal **4.** *also* **charcoal grey** COLOURS DARK GREY COLOUR a dark grey colour [14C. Origin ?] —**charcoal** *adj*

charcuterie /shaar kóotəri/ *n* **1.** cold cooked, cured, or processed meat and meat products **2.** a shop that specializes in charcuterie [Mid-19C. < French < obsolete *char cuite* 'cooked flesh']

chard /chaard/ *n* PLANTS same as **Swiss chard** [Mid-17C. Via French *carde* < Latin *cardu(u)s* 'thistle']

Chardin /shaar dáN/, **Jean Baptiste Siméon** (1699–1779) French painter. He was a master of lower-middle-class domestic and genre scenes such as *The Benediction* (1740).

Chardonnay /shaárdə nay, shaar dónnay/, **chardonnay** *n* **1.** a dry white wine made from a variety of white grape originally grown in east-central France **2.** a white grape that is used to make Chardonnay [Early 20C. < French]

~~**charecter**~~ incorrect spelling of **character**

charge /chaarj/ *v* (**charges, charging, charged**) **1.** *vti* ASK MONEY FOR SOMETHING to ask somebody for an amount of money as a price or fee ○ *The cafeteria here charges too much for terrible food.* **2.** *vt* HOLD SOMEBODY FINANCIALLY LIABLE to hold a person or organization financially liable for something ○ *That antique shop charges customers for breakage.* **3.** *vti* ARRANGE DEFERRED

PAYMENT to allow, and enter a record of, a deferred payment for something ○ *Charge it to my account.* **4.** *vt* LAW **ACCUSE SOMEBODY OF CRIME** to accuse somebody formally of having committed a crime **5.** *vt* **CRITICIZE SOMEBODY** to criticize somebody for doing something wrong ○ *Her parents unfairly charged her with laziness.* **6.** *vt* **ORDER SOMEBODY TO DO SOMETHING** to order or instruct somebody formally to do something ○ *The judge charged the jury to consider all the facts.* **7.** *vti* **ATTACK IN RUSH** to attack somebody or something by rushing forwards, especially in a battle ○ *Police in riot gear charged the lines of demonstrators.* **8.** *vi* **RUSH** to run somewhere carelessly or clumsily ○ *He came charging in from the garden.* **9.** *vti* ELEC **RESTORE POWER IN BATTERY** to restore the power in a battery by connecting it to a supply of electricity **10.** *vt* **PERVADE SOMETHING** to give an atmosphere of intense interest, excitement, or other strong emotion to a place (*usually passive*) ○ *The concert hall was charged with anticipation.* **11.** *vt* **LOAD OR FILL SOMETHING** to load or fill something, e.g. a gun with explosive, or a glass with drink (*formal*) **12.** *vt* HERALDRY **PUT HERALDIC DEVICE ON SOMETHING** to put a heraldic device on something such as a shield or banner ■ *n* **1. PRICE OR FEE ASKED** the amount of money asked for something that is for sale or available as a result of payment ○ *We had to pay several extra charges before getting the vehicle back.* ○ *an admission charge* **2. RESPONSIBILITY** the responsibility or duty of looking after somebody or something ○ *He took on the children's welfare as an extra charge.* **3. SOMEBODY BEING TAKEN CARE OF** somebody, especially a child or a member of a minister's congregation, for whom somebody else is responsible ○ *The nanny was keeping a close watch on her little charges.* **4.** LAW **ACCUSATION** an accusation of wrongdoing, especially an official statement accusing somebody of committing a crime **5.** MIL **RUSH TO ATTACK** a rush forward to attack, especially in a battle, or the signal for this **6.** ELEC **POWER IN BATTERY** the power stored in a battery **7.** PHYS **ELECTRIC PROPERTY OF MATTER** a fundamental characteristic of matter, responsible for all electric and electromotive forces, expressed in two forms known as positive and negative **8.** PHYS **EXCESS OR LACK OF ELECTRONS** a quantity of electricity caused by an excess or lack of electrons **9.** ARMS **EXPLOSIVE FOR DETONATION** the amount of explosive used to detonate a shell or cartridge **10. ENOUGH TO FILL CONTAINER** the amount required to fill a container or to make a mechanism work **11. INSTRUCTION** a formal order or instruction to do something, e.g. a judge's instructions to a jury **12.** HERALDRY **HERALDIC DESIGN** a design or image used as part of a coat of arms [12C. Via French *charger* 'load, charge' < late Latin *car(ri)care* < Latin *carrus* 'carriage'] ◇ **take charge (of)** to take over control or responsibility for somebody or something

chargeable /chaárjəb'l/ *adj* **1. ABLE TO BE CHARGED** liable or able to be charged to a person, organization, or account **2. LIABLE TO RESULT IN CRIMINAL CHARGE** liable to result in or face a criminal charge **3. SUBJECT TO CHARGE** describes property or land capable of being subject to a charge or tax —**chargeability** /chaárjə bílləti/ *n*

charge account *n ANZ, N Am* an account that allows a customer to buy goods or services and pay at a later date. UK term **credit account**

charge-cap (**charge-caps, charge-capping, charge-capped**) *vt* to put a limit on the amount of flat-rate tax that local authorities in the United Kingdom are allowed to charge people

charge card *n UK, Can* a card issued to customers by a shop or other organization, used to charge purchases to an account for later payment. ANZ, US term **credit card**

charge-coupled device *n* a semiconductor device that converts light patterns into digital signals for a computer, especially in digital cameras and optical scanners

charged /chaarjd/ *adj* tense and causing anxiety, excitement, or anger ○ *a highly charged situation*

chargé d'affaires /shaár zhay da fáir/ (*plural* **chargés d'affaires** /shaár zhay da fáir, shaár zhayz-/) *n* **1.** a diplomat ranking immediately below an ambassador who deputizes in the ambassador's absence **2.** a diplomat who heads a minor diplomatic mission [Mid-18C. < French, 'somebody in charge of affairs']

charge density *n* the amount of electric charge per unit of area or volume. Symbol ρ

charge hand *n* a worker with supervisory responsibilities, ranking below a foreman

charge nurse *n* a nurse in charge of a hospital ward

charger[1] /chaárjər/ *n* **1.** ELEC same as **battery charger** **2.** a large strong cavalry horse **3.** somebody or something that charges [15C. < CHARGE]

charger[2] /chaárjər/ *n* a large flat serving dish of a kind now mainly collected for display [14C. < Anglo-Norman *chargeour* 'something that loads' < Old French *charger* (see CHARGE)]

charge sheet *n* a police document recording criminal charges and court appearances

chargrill /chaár gril/ (**-grills, -grilling, -grilled**) *vt* to grill food over charcoal on a barbecue or on a ridged pan that produces a similar visual effect. N Am term **charbroil** [Blend of CHARCOAL + GRILL [1]]

Chari /shaári/ the main tributary feeding Lake Chad in north-central Africa. It rises in the Central African Republic. Length: 950 km/590 mi.

~~**charicature**~~ incorrect spelling of **caricature**

Chari-Nile *n* a Nilo-Saharan group of languages spoken in northern Chad, Sudan, Uganda, Kenya, and northeastern Republic of Congo

chariot /chárri ət/ *n* **1.** a two-wheeled horse-drawn vehicle without seats, used in ancient times in races, warfare, or processions **2.** a four-wheeled horse-drawn carriage with rear seats only, used especially on ceremonial occasions [14C. < French < Latin *carrus* 'carriage'] —**charioteer** /chárri ə téer/ *n*

charism /kárrizəm/ *n* RELIG same as **charisma** (sense 2) [15C. < ecclesiastical Latin *charisma* (see CHARISMA)]

charisma /kə rízmə/ *n* **1.** the ability to inspire enthusiasm, interest, or affection in others by means of personal charm or influence **2.** (*plural* **charismata** /-mətə/) a gift or power believed to be divinely bestowed [Mid-17C. Via ecclesiastical Latin < Greek *kharisma* < *kharis* 'favour, grace']

USAGE Charisma meaning 'personal charm or influence'. In their generalized meanings, ***charisma*** and ***charismatic*** have moved a long way from their original meanings in theology, where they referred to supernatural gifts of speaking, healing, and so on. The modern meanings have developed from a use in sociology, in which the sense is 'power of leadership or authority', first used in translations of the German sociologist Max Weber (1864–1920).

charismatic /kárriz máttik/ *adj* **1.** possessing great powers of charm or influence **2.** describes Christian groups or worship characterized by a quest for inspired and ecstatic experiences such as healing, prophecy, and speaking in tongues —**charismatic** *n* —**charismatically** *adv*

USAGE See ***charisma***.

charitable /chárritəb'l/ *adj* **1. GENEROUS** generous to people in need **2. SYMPATHETIC** sympathetic, favourable, or tolerant in judging **3. COLLECTIVELY DISPENSING HELP** dispensing assistance to needy people by means of a group or organization —**charitableness** *n* —**charitably** *adv*

charity /chárrəti/ (*plural* **-ties**) *n* **1. ORGANIZATION PROVIDING CHARITY** an organization that collects money and other voluntary contributions of help for people in need **2. PROVISION OF HELP** the voluntary provision of money, materials, or help to people in need **3. MATERIAL HELP** money, materials, or help voluntarily given to people in need **4. TOLERANT ATTITUDE** the willingness to judge people in a tolerant or favourable way **5. IMPARTIAL LOVE** the impartial love of other people, especially as a Christian virtue [12C. Via French *charité* < Latin *caritas* < *carus* 'dear']

Charity Commission *n* in the United Kingdom, an organization that registers and regulates charities —**Charity Commissioner** *n*

charity shop *n* a shop that sells second-hand goods to raise money for a charity

charivari /shaári vaári/ *n* **1.** a noisy mock-serenade with the banging of saucepans, kettles, and similar objects, meant to wish newlyweds well. N Am term **shivaree** **2.** a noise, commotion, or din (*formal*) [Mid-17C. < French]

charkha /chaárk ə/, **charka** *n* a spinning wheel, especially for cotton, used in South Asia [Late 19C. Via Urdu *charkā* < Persian *cark(a)*]

charlady /chaár laydi/ (*plural* **-dies**) *n* same as **charwoman** [Late 19C. < CHARWOMAN]

charlatan /shaárlətən/ *n* somebody who falsely claims to have special skill or expertise [Early 17C. Via French < Italian *ciarlatano* < *ciarlare* 'to babble', an imitation of empty talk] —**charlatanism** *n* —**charlatanry** *n*

Charlemagne /shaárlə mayn/ (742–814) Frankish king and emperor. As emperor of the West (800–814), he inspired the Carolingian Renaissance of European culture.

> 'Our task is, with the aid of divine piety, to defend the Holy Church of Christ with arms...Your task, most holy father, is to lift up your hands to God, like Moses, so as to aid our troops.'
> [Charlemagne, *Letter to Pope Leo III*; 796]

Charleroi /shaárlə roy, -rwaa/ industrial city in Hainault Province, Belgium, south of Brussels. Population: 202,020 (1999).

Charles /chaarlz/, **Prince of Wales** (*b.* 1948) British heir apparent and son of Elizabeth II. He was married to Diana, Princess of Wales, from 1981 to 1996. Full name **Prince Charles Philip Arthur George**

> 'I personally would much rather see my title as Defender of Faith, not the Faith, because it means just one interpretation of the faith, which I think is sometimes something that causes a great deal of a problem.'
> [Charles, 'Charles: The Private Man, the Public Role', *ITV television programme*; 29 June 1994]

Charles I (1600–49) king of England, Scotland, and Ireland (1625–49). He succeeded James I in 1625. His determination to rule without Parliament's authority led to the Civil War (1642–48), which culminated in his execution.

> 'For the people; and truly I desire their liberty and freedom, as much as any body: but I must tell you, that their liberty and freedom consists in having the government of those laws by which their life and their goods may be most their own.'
> [Charles I, *Speech on the scaffold*; 30 January 1649]

Charles II (1630–85) king of England, Scotland, and Ireland (1660–85). He was exiled during Oliver Cromwell's Protectorate (1653–58), but returned to England and formally ascended the throne after the restoration of the monarchy in 1660.

> 'A merry monarch, scandalous and poor.'
> [2nd Earl of Rochester, *A Satire on King Charles II*; 1697]

Charles V (1500–58) Holy Roman Emperor and, as Charles I, king of Spain. During his reign as Holy Roman Emperor (1519–58), he struggled to keep his Roman Catholic empire together and was finally forced to recognize Protestantism.

> 'I speak Spanish to God, Italian to women, French to men, and German to my horse.'
> [Attributed to Charles V]

Charles VII (1403–61) king of France (1422–61). During his reign the Hundred Years' War ended with the English losing most of their possessions in France.

Charles IX (1550–74) king of France (1560–74). His reign was marked by religious wars and dominated by his mother, Catherine de Médicis.

Charles X (1757–1836) king of France (1824–30). He lived in England during the French Revolution. When he returned to France his repressive rule led to the revolution of 1830 and his enforced abdication and exile.

Charles, Bob (*b.* 1936) New Zealand golfer. He won the British Open in 1963 and the World Match Play championship in 1969. Full name **Charles, Robert James**

Charles, Ray (*b.* 1932) US singer and pianist whose rhythm-and-blues style took its roots from country

and western and gospel music. Born **Robinson, Ray Charles**

> 'I believe talent will finally win out in this business. But Jesus could be coming tomorrow, and if no one knew, it wouldn't mean anything. Not even God can afford to ignore promotion.'
> [Ray Charles, 'Back to the Country', *Brother Ray*; 1978]

Charles Martel /-maar tél/ (688?–741) Frankish king (715–741) of Austrasia (in present northeastern France and southwestern Germany). His forces turned back the Moorish invasion of France (732).

Charles's law /chaálziz-/ *n* a law holding that there is a direct relationship between the volume of a gas and its temperature, where its pressure is constant [Late 19C. After J. A. C. *Charles* (1746–1823), French physicist]

Charles's Wain *n* ASTRON same as **Plough** (*archaic*)

Charleston[1] /chaárlstən/ *n* a dance, popular in the 1920s, in which the feet are kicked out sideways with the knees kept together [Early 20C. After CHARLESTON[2], S Carolina]

Charleston[2] /chaárlstən/ **1.** city and port in southeastern South Carolina where the Ashley, Cooper, and Wando rivers meet. Population: 98,795 (2002 estimate). **2.** capital of West Virginia and the largest city in the state. Population: 51,702 (2002 estimate).

Charley *n* MIL another spelling of **Charlie** (sense 2)

charley horse /chaárli-/ *n N Am* a severe muscular cramp, especially of the upper leg (*informal*) [Origin ?]

charlie /chaárli/ *n* **1.** somebody regarded as unintelligent or silly (*informal*) ○ *I felt a proper charlie!* **2.** cocaine used as an illicit drug (*slang*) [Early 19C. Pet form of the name *Charles*. In sense 2 < CHARLIE as abbreviation of the first letter of COCAINE]

Charlie /chaárli/ *n* **1.** a code word for the letter 'C', used in international radio communications **2.** *also* **Charley** *ANZ, US* used to refer to a member of the Viet Cong during the Vietnam War or to the Viet Cong collectively (*dated slang*)

charlock /chaar lok/ (*plural same* or **-locks**) *n* a mustard plant that has hairy stems and leaves and is a common weed. Flowers: yellow. Native to: Europe, Asia. Latin name: *Brassica kaber*. [Old English *cerlic*, origin ?]

charlotte /shaárlət/ *n* a sweet, cold or baked dish prepared in a deep straight-sided container and containing fruit surrounded by sponge cake, biscuits, or bread [Late 18C. < French, probably < the name *Charlotte*]

Charlotte /shaárlət/ city in southern North Carolina, southwest of Winston-Salem and east of the Catawba River. Population: 580,597 (2002 estimate).

Charlotte Amalie /shaárlət ə maályə/ seaport and capital of St Thomas Island and of the US Virgin Islands. Population: 12,000 (1990).

charlotte russe /shaárlət róoss/ (*plural* **charlottes russes** /*pronunc. same*/) *n* a cold set dessert made with cream or custard surrounded by sponge fingers [< French, 'Russian charlotte']

Charlottetown /shaárlət town/ capital city of Prince Edward Island, Canada, situated in the centre of the island, on Hillsborough Bay. Population: 38,114 (2001).

Charlton /chaárltən/, **Bobby** (*b.* 1937) British footballer. He scored 49 goals in 106 appearances for England from 1957 to 1973, and was on the World Cup-winning side in 1966. Born **Charlton, Robert**

Charlton, 'Boy' (1907–75) Australian swimmer and winner of the gold medal in the 1,500 metres at the 1924 Olympic Games. Born **Charlton, Andrew Murray**

Charlton, Jack (*b.* 1935) British footballer and manager. He played for Leeds United (1965–75) and England (1965–70), and managed the Republic of Ireland national team from 1986 to 1996. Born **Charlton, John**

charm /chaarm/ *n* **1. ATTRACTIVENESS** the power to delight or attract people **2. ATTRACTIVE FEATURE** a feature or quality that delights or attracts (*often used in the plural*) **3. SOMETHING SUPPOSED TO BRING LUCK** something carried or worn because it is believed to bring good luck or ward off evil **4. TRINKET** a miniature metal animal, musical instrument, or similar trinket worn on a bracelet or around the neck **5. MAGIC SPELL** a special phrase or rhyme believed to have magical powers **6.** PHYS **CHARACTERISTIC OF ELEMENTARY PARTICLES** a quantum characteristic of elementary particles that accounts for the long lifetime of the J/psi particle, lack of symmetry in hadron interactions, and the failure of some particles to react. Symbol **C** ■ *v* (**charms, charming, charmed**) **1.** *vti* **DELIGHT PEOPLE** to delight or attract people **2.** *vt* **INFLUENCE PEOPLE** to influence somebody or obtain something from somebody by using powers of persuasion and attraction **3.** *vti* **CAST A SPELL** to affect somebody or something by, or as if by, the use of a supposed magic spell [13C. Via French *charme* < Latin *carmen* 'song, incantation' < *canere* 'sing'] —**charmer** *n* —**charmless** *adj*

charm bracelet *n* a chain with charms attached, worn as a bracelet

charmed /chaarmd/ *adj* **1.** so pleasant or lucky as to suggest protection by a magic spell **2.** PHYS describes an elementary particle that has the property of charm

charmed circle *n* a privileged group or elite

charming /chaárming/ *adj* having the power to delight or attract people ○ *a charming village* ○ *a charming young man* ■ *interj* used ironically to express disapproval or distaste at something just done or said (*informal*) —**charmingly** *adv*

charm offensive *n* a campaign to appear more pleasant, attractive, or reasonable in order to gain popularity, e.g. a campaign undertaken by a politician (*informal disapproving*)

charm quark *n* a quark with an electric charge of $+\frac{2}{3}$ and charm of 1

charm school *n* a school for young women that charges tuition and teaches social skills and beauty techniques (*dated*)

charnel /chaárn'l/ *n* BUILDINGS same as **charnel house** ■ *adj* suggestive of death or a tomb [14C. Via Old French < medieval Latin *carnale* < Latin *carn-* 'flesh']

charnel house *n* a building or vault in which bones or dead bodies are placed

Charolais /shárrə lay/ (*plural same*), **Charollais** *n* a large white cow belonging to a breed originating in France. Kept for: beef. [Late 19C. After Monts du *Charollais*, E France]

Charon /káirən/ *n* **1.** in Greek mythology, a ferryman who took the souls of the dead across the River Styx to Hades **2.** the only known satellite of Pluto, discovered in 1978

charoseth, **charoset** *n* JUDAISM another spelling of **haroseth**

Charpentier /shaar paáNti ay/, **Gustave** (1860–1956) French composer. The opera *Louise* (1900) is his best-known work.

Charpentier, Marc-Antoine (1645?–1704) French composer. He composed incidental music for his friend Molière's plays, as well as operas and oratorios. He is best known for his *Te Deum* (1692?).

charpoy /chaár poy/ *n* a light bedstead of webbing stretched across a frame, commonly used in South Asia [Mid-17C. Via Urdu *chārpāī* < Persian]

charr *n* FISH another spelling of **char**[2]

chart /chaart/ *n* **1. DIAGRAM OR TABLE** a diagram or table displaying detailed information **2.** NAVIG **MAP TO NAVIGATE BY** a map for navigation by sea or air **3.** METEOROL **WEATHER MAP** an outline map that shows weather patterns **4.** ASTROL **BASIS FOR HOROSCOPE** a map that shows the relative positions of the planets at the time of somebody's birth, on which his or her horoscope is based **5.** HANDICRAFT **STITCHING PLAN** a squared grid marked with symbols indicating the placement of stitches in embroidery **6.** MUSIC **MUSICAL SCORE** the score of a musical composition (*technical*) ■ **charts** *npl* **LIST OF POPULAR RECORDS** a list of the musical recordings that have sold the most copies during a specific period ■ *v* (**charts, charting, charted**) **1.** *vt* **MAKE CHART OF SOMETHING** to make a map, graph, or diagram of something **2.** *vt* **DESCRIBE PROGRESS** to record or describe how something progresses or develops **3.** *vi* **BE IN MUSIC CHARTS** to appear in the music charts ○ *The band's second album charted the day it was released.* [Late 16C. Via French < Latin *charta* 'paper, papyrus leaf'] —**chartable** *adj*

charter /chaártər/ *n* **1. FORMAL DOCUMENT OF INCORPORATION** a formal document incorporating an organization, company, or educational institution **2. CONSTITUTION** a formal written statement of the aims, principles, and procedures of an organization **3. STATEMENT OF RIGHTS AND RESPONSIBILITIES** a formal written statement describing the rights and responsibilities of a state and its citizens **4. DOCUMENT OF AUTHORIZATION** a document from an organization or society that authorizes the setting up of a new branch **5. SPECIAL PRIVILEGE** a special privilege, immunity, or exemption granted to a particular person or group **6.** TRANSP **HIRE OR LEASE OF TRANSPORT** the hiring or leasing of transport vehicles for personal or special use, or a contract for this purpose **7.** TRANSP **HIRED OR LEASED TRANSPORT** a vehicle chartered for personal or special use **8.** SHIPPING same as **charter party** ■ *vt* (**-ters, -tering, -tered**) **1.** TRANSP **HIRE OR LEASE TRANSPORT** to hire or lease a vehicle for a personal or special purpose **2. GIVE ORGANIZATION A CHARTER** to grant a charter of incorporation to a group or organization [12C. Via French *chartre* < Latin *chartula* < *charta* (see CHART)] —**charterer** *n*

chartered /chaártərd/ *adj* **1.** having been granted a charter **2.** registered with an official body as having satisfied its professional and technical requirements, originally with one granted a royal charter

chartered accountant *n* an accountant who has passed the examinations of a governing professional body that has been granted a royal charter

chartered surveyor *n* a surveyor who is a member of the Royal Institution of Chartered Surveyors

charter flight *n* a flight that has been chartered for a specific journey, especially as part of a holiday package

Charterhouse /chaártər howss/ (*plural* **-houses** /-ziz/) *n* a Carthusian monastery [14C. Alteration of Anglo-Norman *Chartrous* or French *Chartreuse* < medieval Latin *Cart(h)usia* (see CARTHUSIAN)]

Charteris /chaártəriss/, **Leslie** (1907–93) British-born US novelist who created the gentleman-crook, Simon Templar ('The Saint'). Born **Yin, Leslie Charles Bowyer**

charter member *n N Am* a founding or original member of a society or organization

Charter of Rights *n* a section of the Canadian Constitution stating the rights conferred by Canadian citizenship

charter party *n* a contractual arrangement by which the owner of a ship permits another person to use it to carry goods [Via French < medieval Latin *charta partita* 'divided charter']

Charters Towers /chaártərz tów ərz/ town in northern Queensland, Australia. Formerly a gold-mining town, it is now a centre of education and beef production. Population: 8,790 (2002 estimate).

Chartism /chaártizəm/ *n* the principles and practices of a movement advocating political and social reform in England between 1838 and 1848. Among its aims were improvement in the education and living conditions of the working classes, payment for Members of Parliament, adult male suffrage, equal electoral districts, and voting by ballot. [Mid-19C. After the *People's Charter*] —**Chartist** *n, adj*

Chartres /shaártrə/ capital of the Eure-et-Loire Department in northwestern France. It is situated about 80 km/50 mi. southwest of Paris and is famous for its large Gothic cathedral. Population: 40,361 (1999).

chartreuse /shaar trúrz/ *n* a bright yellowish-green colour [Early 19C. < French (see CHARTERHOUSE)] —**chartreuse** *adj*

Chartreuse /shaar trúrz/ *tdmk* a trademark for a yellow or green aromatic liqueur

chart-topping *adj* at the top of the list of musical recordings that have sold the most copies during a specific period —**chart-topper** *n*

charwoman /chaár wŏŏmən/ (*plural* **-women** /-wimmin/) *n* a woman employed to clean a house or office (*dated*) [Late 16C. < Old English *c(i)err* 'turn (of work)']

chary /cháiri/ (**-ier, -iest**) *adj* **1. WARY** cautiously reluctant to do something **2. SPARING** reluctant to

share, give, or use something **3.** **CONCERNED** fussily concerned **4.** **SHY** showing or characterized by shyness or modesty [Old English *cearig* 'sorrowful' < Germanic] —**charily** *adv* —**chariness** *n*

SYNONYMS See *cautious*.

Charybdis /kə ríbdiss/ *n* in Greek mythology, a monster in the form of a dangerous whirlpool at the mouth of the cave of the sea monster Scylla

chase[1] /chayss/ *v* (**chases, chasing, chased**) **1.** *vti* **PURSUE SOMEBODY** to follow somebody quickly in order to catch him or her **2.** *vt* **MAKE SOMEBODY RUN AWAY** to force a person or animal to run away ○ *The kids chased a black cat out of the garden.* **3.** *vi* **RUSH ABOUT** to rush about ○ *I chased about all day.* **4.** *vt* **INVESTIGATE SOMETHING** to follow up or investigate something that has not been done or somebody who has not done something ○ *We need to chase up the plumber to find out when he's going to come.* **5.** *vti* **TRY TO GET SOMETHING** to spend a lot of time and energy trying to acquire something ○ *moving from job to job chasing money* **6.** *vti* **PAY PERSISTENT ATTENTION TO SOMEBODY** to seek the company of somebody for romantic or sexual purposes, especially in an obvious or unsubtle way ■ *n* **1.** **PURSUIT** an act or situation in which something or somebody is being pursued **2.** FIELD SPORTS **SPORT OF HUNTING ANIMALS** the hunting of animals for sport **3.** FIELD SPORTS **LAND MAINTAINED FOR HUNTING** a privately owned area of land where animals are confined or stocked for hunting purposes **4.** FIELD SPORTS **RIGHT TO KEEP GAME OR HUNT** the right to keep game or to hunt on a particular area of land **5.** HORSERACING same as **steeplechase** *n* (sense 1) **6.** **SOMETHING PURSUED** the target of a pursuit, especially an animal **7.** MUSIC **JAZZ DUET** a jazz duet in which the players play alternate phrases and try to outdo each other in virtuosity and invention [13C. Via Old French *chacier* 'seize' < Latin *captare* 'try to seize' < *capere* 'take'] ◇ **cut to the chase** to stop wasting time and get on with what needs to be dealt with (*informal*) ◇ **give chase** to pursue something or somebody forcefully (*formal*)

SYNONYMS See *follow*.

chase[2] /chayss/ *n* **1.** **PART OF GUN BARREL** the external part of a gun barrel just behind the muzzle **2.** **GROOVE** a channel, groove, or trench for something such as a pipe to lie in or fit into ■ *vt* (**chases, chasing, chased**) **1.** **CUT GROOVE IN SOMETHING** to cut or grind a channel, groove, or trench in something **2.** **CUT THREAD IN SCREW** to cut a metal screw thread with a machine tool (**chaser**) [Late 16C. Via French *châsse* < Latin *capsa* 'box']

chase[3] /chayss/ (**chases, chasing, chased**) *vt* to decorate metal or glass by engraving or embossing [15C. Shortening of ENCHASE]

chase[4] /chayss/ *n* a rectangular frame into which metal type or blocks are fitted so that a page or plate can be printed or made [Early 17C. Via French *chas* 'enclosed space' < Latin *capsum* 'thorax, church nave']

chase plane *n* an aeroplane that follows another aircraft either as an escort or to photograph it

chaser[1] /cháyssər/ *n* **1.** **SOMEBODY OR SOMETHING THAT CHASES** somebody or something that forcefully pursues another person or thing **2.** **DIFFERENT DRINK** a second drink, taken with or after one of a different kind, e.g. beer taken after whisky (*informal*) **3.** HORSE-RACING **HORSE FOR STEEPLECHASING** a horse that is ridden in steeplechases **4.** ARMS **NAVAL CANNON** a cannon located at the bow or stern of a vessel and used in pursuing an enemy

chaser[2] /cháyssər/ *n* **1.** an engraver or embosser of metal or glass **2.** a machine tool for cutting screw threads

Chasid *n* JUDAISM another spelling of **Hasid**

chasm /kázzəm/ *n* **1.** **DEEP HOLE IN EARTH** a deep crack or hole in the ground **2.** **WIDE DIFFERENCE** a wide difference in feelings, ideas, or interests **3.** **GAP OR BREAK** a large gap or break in the progress or continuity of something [Late 16C. Via Latin *chasma* < Greek *khasma* 'gulf']

chassé /shá say/ *n* a gliding step, especially in ballet or square dancing [Early 19C. < French, 'chased'] —**chassé** *vi*

Chasseur /sha súr/ *adj* cooked in a rich white-wine and mushroom sauce ■ *n* a soldier in a French special unit equipped and trained for rapid deployment [Mid-18C. < French, 'hunter']

Chassid *n* JUDAISM another spelling of **Hasid**

chassis /shássi/ (*plural* **chassis** /shássiz/) *n* **1.** **MAIN FRAME OF VEHICLE** the frame and wheels that support the engine and body of a motor vehicle, or the frame and wheels of a carriage or wagon **2.** **MOUNTING FOR ELECTRONIC DEVICE** the mounting or supporting structure for the components of an electronic device such as a television **3.** **AIRCRAFT LANDING GEAR** the landing gear of an aircraft **4.** **MOUNTING FOR GUN CARRIAGE** a frame on which a gun carriage can move back and forth [Mid-17C. < French *châssis* < Latin *capsa* 'box']

Chastain /chass táyn/, **Brandi** (*b.* 1968) US soccer player. She played forward on the US women's national soccer team that won a gold medal in the 1996 Olympics and kicked the winning penalty in the World Cup championship in 1999. Full name **Chastain, Brandi Denise**

chaste /chayst/ (**chaster, chastest**) *adj* **1.** **ABSTAINING FROM SEX** abstaining from sex on moral grounds **2.** **SEXUALLY FAITHFUL** not having extramarital sexual relations **3.** **PURE IN THOUGHT AND DEED** behaving in a pure way, with no immoral thoughts **4.** **PLAIN** plain, simple, and unadorned in style [13C. Via French < Latin *castus* 'pure'] —**chastely** *adv* —**chasteness** *n*

chasten /cháyss'n/ (**-tens, -tening, -tened**) *vt* **1.** **MAKE SOMEBODY SUBDUED** to make somebody less self-satisfied or self-assertive and more subdued **2.** **DISCIPLINE SOMEBODY** to subject somebody to discipline **3.** **MODERATE INTENSITY OF SOMETHING** to moderate the intensity of something [Early 16C. < obsolete *chaste* (see CHASTISE)] —**chastened** *adj* —**chastener** *n* —**chastening** *adj*

chaste tree *n* a small tree with aromatic hairy leaves and fragrant clusters of light purplish flowers. Native to: Europe, Asia. Latin name: *Vitex agnus-castus*. [Translation of Latin *agnus castus* < *agnus* 'chaste tree' < Greek *agnos*, confused with *hagnos* 'chaste']

chastise /cha stíz/ (**-tises, -tising, -tised**) *vt* to punish or scold somebody [14C. < obsolete *chaste* 'rebuke', via Old French *chastier* < Latin *castigare* (see CASTIGATE)] —**chastisable** *adj* —**chastisement** *n* —**chastiser** *n*

chastity /chástəti/ *n* **1.** the condition or practice of abstaining from sex on moral grounds **2.** plainness or simplicity of style

chastity belt *n* a locking device passing round the waist and between the legs, used in medieval times to prevent a woman from having sexual intercourse

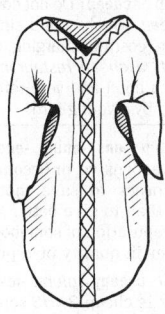

chasuble

chasuble /cházyoŏb'l/ *n* a loose, sometimes sleeveless outer garment worn by a Christian priest when celebrating Mass or Communion [13C. Via French < late Latin *casubla*, alteration of Latin *casula* 'hooded cloak' < *casa* 'house']

chat /chat/ *vi* (**chats, chatting, chatted**) **1.** **TALK INFORMALLY** to talk with somebody in a relaxed informal way **2.** **EXCHANGE MESSAGES BY COMPUTER** to exchange messages in real time with other computer users ■ *n* **1.** **INFORMAL TALK** a relaxed informal conversation with somebody **2.** **EXCHANGE OF MESSAGES BY COMPUTER** an informal exchange of messages in real time with other computer users **3.** **SONGBIRD WITH CHATTERING CRY** a small songbird related to the thrush with a harsh chattering cry. Subfamily: Turdinae. **4.** **AUSTRALIAN CHAT** a bird belonging to any of the five species of Australian chat. Native to: Australia. Genus: *Epthianuridae*. [15C. Shortening of CHATTER]

chat up *vt* to talk to somebody flirtatiously or flatteringly (*informal*)

chateau: Chenonceaux, France

chateau /sháttō/ (*plural* **-teaux** /-tōz, -tō/ or **-teaus** /-tō, -tōz/), **château** (*plural* **-teaux** /-tō, -tōz/) *n* a castle or large house in France, often one that has a vineyard attached and gives its name to wine produced there [Mid-18C. Via French < Latin *castellum* (see CASTLE)]

Chateaubriand /sháttōbri óN/ *n* a thick beefsteak cut from the widest middle part of the fillet [Late 19C. After François René, Vicomte de CHATEAUBRIAND]

Chateaubriand /sháttōbri óN/, **François Auguste René, Vicomte de** (1768–1848) French writer and diplomat. A founder of the Romantic school of French literature, his best-known work is his biography *Mémoires d'outre-tombe* (*Memoir from Beyond the Tomb*) (1849–50).

chatelain /sháttə layn/ *n* formerly, a man who owned or controlled a castle or other large house [15C. Via French *châtelain* < medieval Latin *castellanus* (see CASTELLAN)]

chatelaine /sháttə layn/ *n* **1.** **MISTRESS OF LARGE HOUSE** formerly, a woman who owned or controlled a castle or other large house **2.** **WOMAN'S CHAIN KEY** a chain and clasp formerly worn at the waist by a woman to hold keys and other small items **3.** US **WOMAN WITH LARGE HOUSEHOLD** a woman who is the head of a large fashionable household [Mid-19C. < French *châtelaine*, feminine of *châtelain* (see CHATELAIN)]

chat group *n* a group of people who exchange messages online, especially people who share a common interest

Chatham /cháttəm/ town and former naval dockyard on the estuary of the River Medway in Kent, southeastern England. Population: 71,691 (1991).

Chatham Islands group of islands in the southwestern Pacific Ocean forming part of New Zealand. They are situated 800 km/500 mi. east of the South Island. Population: 717 (2001). Area: 963 sq. km/372 sq. mi.

chatline /chát līn/ *n* a telephone service allowing a number of people to phone the same number and have a conversation

chatoyant /sha tóy ənt/ *adj* having a changeable iridescent lustre ■ *n* a chatoyant gemstone, e.g. a cat's eye [Late 18C. < French, 'shining like a cat's eyes'] —**chatoyancy** *n*

chat room *n* a facility in a computer network where participants exchange messages in real time

chat show *n* UK an informal TV or radio show in which the host interviews celebrities. ANZ, N Am term **talk show**

Chattanooga /cháttə noŏgə/ city and port in southeastern Tennessee, on the Tennessee River, near the Tennessee-Georgia border. Population: 155,404 (2002 estimate).

chattel /chátt'l/ *n* an item of personal property that is not freehold land and is not intangible. Chattels are typically movable property (**chattels personal**), e.g. furniture or cars, but may also be interests in property (**chattels real**), e.g. leases. ■ **chattels** *npl* personal possessions (*formal*) [13C. Via Old French *chatel* 'property' < Latin *capitalis* (see CAPITAL[1])]

chatter /cháttər/ *vi* (**-ters, -tering, -tered**) **1.** **TALK RAPIDLY** to talk or converse rapidly and informally about unimportant things **2.** **MAKE HIGH-PITCHED SOUNDS** to make a rapid series of short high-pitched sounds that seem to resemble speech (*refers to animals or machinery*) **3.** **CLICK TOGETHER** to click together rapidly because of movement of the jaw caused by fear or

cold (*refers to teeth*) **4.** **VIBRATE DURING CUTTING** to vibrate while cutting or being cut by a tool or machine, causing surface flaws (*refers to a saw blade or surface*) ■ *n* **1.** **TRIVIAL CONVERSATION** rapid and informal talk or conversation, especially about unimportant things **2.** **HIGH-PITCHED ANIMAL SOUNDS** rapid short high-pitched sounds made by a bird, animal, or machine that resemble human speech **3.** **SURFACE FLAWS PRODUCED IN MACHINING** imperfections in a surface, caused by vibration while the surface is being cut by a tool or machine [13C An imitation of the sound]

chatterati /cháttə raáti/ *npl S Asia* educated middle-class people who are interested in current affairs and culture and like to make their views known to each other (*disapproving*)

chatterbox /cháttər boks/ *n* somebody who talks a lot, especially about unimportant things (*informal*)

chatterer /cháttərər/ *n* **1.** a talkative person, especially somebody who talks on trivial subjects **2.** BIRDS same as **cotinga**

chattering classes *npl* educated middle-class people with an interest in current affairs and culture who like to make their views known to each other (*disapproving*)

chatter mark *n* **1.** a crack or groove on the surface of rock, caused by the abrasive action of a glacier on bedrock or by the collision of fragments in water **2.** a mark left on something that has been machined, caused by vibration during the machining process

Chatterton /cháttərtən/, **Thomas** (1752–70) British poet and journalist. His pastiches of medieval literature were at first accepted as the work of a 15th-century monk. He committed suicide after they were exposed as frauds. Pseudonym **Rowley, Thomas**

chatty /chátti/ (**-tier, -tiest**) *adj* **1.** talking freely about unimportant things **2.** friendly and informal in tone —**chattily** *adv* —**chattiness** *n*

SYNONYMS See ***talkative***.

chat-up line *n* a prepared phrase or topic that somebody uses when trying to initiate a romantic or sexual relationship (*informal*)

Chatwin /cháttwin/, **Bruce** (1940–89) British writer. His novels, which include *On the Black Hill* (1982), and idiosyncratic travel writings show a distaste for the chaos of modern life.

> 'Being lost in Australia gives you a lovely feeling of security.'
> [Bruce Chatwin, *The Songlines*; 1987]

Chaucer /cháwssər/, **Geoffrey** (1343?–1400) English poet and author of *The Canterbury Tales* (1387–1400), one of the finest early works in English. See Cultural note at **tale** —**Chaucerian** /chaw seéri ən/ *n, adj*

> 'This world nys but a thurghfare ful of wo, / And we ben pilgrymes, passynge to and fro; / Deeth is an ende of every worldly sore.'
> [Geoffrey Chaucer, 'The Knight's Tale', *The Canterbury Tales*; 1390?]

chaudfroid /shō fwaa/ *n* a hot béchamel sauce with aspic that sets when cold and is used to coat cold cooked savoury foods [Late 19C. < French, 'hot-cold']

chaudhuri /chówdəri/ *n S Asia* somebody employed by a government to oversee public works, including the supply of materials and labour [< Hindi]

Chaudhuri /chówdəri/, **Nirad Chandra** (1897–1999) Indian writer and critic of British cultural imperialism in India, notably in *Thy Hand, Great Anarch!* (1987)

chauffeur /shófər/ *n* somebody employed to drive a car ■ *vti* (**-feurs, -feuring, -feured**) to drive somebody from place to place in a car, or be employed to drive a car for somebody [Late 19C. < French, 'stoker (of a steam car)' < *chauffer* 'to heat']

chaulmoogra /chawl moógrə/ *n* a tree with seeds that yield an oil formerly used to treat leprosy. Native to: Southeast Asia. Latin name: *Hydnocarpus kurzii*. [Early 19C. < Bangla *cāul-mugrā*]

Chauvel /shō vel/, **Charles Edward** (1897–1959) Australian film-maker. He was producer and director of films ranging from the silent *Moth of Moonbi* (1926) to *Jedda* (1955), one of the first colour films made in Australia.

chauvinism /shóvənizəm/ *n* **1.** unreasoning, overenthusiastic, or aggressive patriotism **2.** an excessive or prejudiced loyalty to a particular gender, group, or cause [Late 19C. < French *chauvinisme*, after Nicolas *Chauvin*, character in the play *La cocarde tricolore* (1831) by the brothers Cogniard]

chauvinist /shóvənist/ *n* **1.** somebody with an excessive or prejudiced loyalty to a particular gender, group, or cause **2.** an unreasoning, overenthusiastic, and aggressive patriot —**chauvinistic** /shōvə nístik/ *adj* —**chauvinistically** *adv*

chav /chav/, **chavster** /chávstər/ *n* an offensive term stereotyping somebody as lower-class, materialistic, and lacking in culture, fashion sense, and self-restraint (*slang insult*) [Origin ?] —**chav** *adj*

Chávez /cha véz/, **Hugo** (*b.* 1954) president of Venezuela (1999–). He gained considerable popular support for leading a failed coup (1992) and, after serving a two-year prison sentence, launched a new political party, the Fifth Republican Movement, in 1997. Amid a climate of political unrest, he was forced to resign the presidency briefly in April 2002. Full name **Chávez Frías, Hugo Rafael**

chavster *n* same as **chav** (*slang insult*)

chaw /chaw/ (**chaws, chawing, chawed**) *vti regional* to chew [Early 16C. Variant of CHEW]

chayote /chī ōti/ *n* **1.** a pear-shaped, furrowed green or white gourd, cooked and eaten as a vegetable **2.** a climbing plant of the gourd family that bears chayotes. Native to: tropical America. Latin name: *Sechium edule*. [Late 19C. Via Spanish < Nahuatl *chayotli*]

chazan *n* another spelling of **hazzan**

ChB *abbr* Bachelor of Surgery [Latin *Chirurgiae Baccalaureus*]

cheap /cheep/ *adj* **1.** **COSTING LITTLE** low in price or cost, or lower in price than might reasonably be expected **2.** **CHARGING LITTLE** charging low prices but offering good value **3.** **POOR QUALITY** inexpensive and of poor quality **4.** **WORTH LITTLE** worth little or accorded little value ○ *In times of war, life is cheap.* **5.** **UNDESERVING OF RESPECT** not deserving to be respected **6.** **UNFAIR** dishonourable, offensive, or unfair, especially in a way that seems obvious or calculated ○ *a cheap trick* **7.** *N Am* **STINGY** stingy or unwilling to give freely [Old English *cēap* 'trade' < Latin *caupo* 'innkeeper'] —**cheap** *adv* —**cheapish** *adj* —**cheaply** *adv* —**cheapness** *n* ◇ **cheap as chips** costing very little (*informal*) ◇ **on the cheap** at very low cost (*informal*)

SPELLCHECK cheap or **cheep**? Do not confuse the spelling of ***cheap*** and ***cheep***, which sound similar. ***Cheap*** is an adjective meaning 'costing, charging, or worth little', as in *a cheap flight*, *a cheap restaurant*, *a cheap trick*. ***Cheep*** is used as a noun and verb referring to the high shrill sound made by a young bird.

cheapen /cheépən/ (**-ens, -ening, -ened**) *vti* **1.** to make something less expensive, or become less expensive, especially in order to save money or increase profits, rather than to give better value **2.** to lower the quality or reputation of somebody or something, or become lower in quality or reputation

cheapie /cheépi/, **cheapy** (*plural* **-ies**) *n* (*informal*) **1.** something that is cheap **2.** *US* somebody regarded as mean or ungenerous

cheapjack /cheép jak/ *n* a seller of inferior goods ■ *adj* inferior in value or quality [< the name *Jack*]

cheapo /cheépō/ *adj* cheap in price or cost (*informal*)

cheapskate /cheép skayt/ *n* somebody regarded as ungenerous (*informal*) [Late 19C. < US slang *skate* 'worn-out horse, contemptible person' < ?]

cheap thrill *n* something providing only short-lived enjoyment or satisfaction

cheapy *n* another spelling of **cheapie**

cheat /cheet/ *v* (**cheats, cheating, cheated**) **1.** *vt* **DECEIVE SOMEBODY** to deceive or mislead somebody, especially for personal advantage **2.** *vi* **BREAK RULES TO GAIN ADVANTAGE** to break the rules in a game, examination, or contest, in an attempt to gain an unfair advantage **3.** *vi* **BE UNFAITHFUL** to have a sexual relationship with somebody other than a spouse or regular sexual partner **4.** *vt* **ESCAPE SOMETHING** to avoid harm or injury by luck or cunning ■ *n* **1.** **DECEITFUL PERSON** a deceiver who uses trickery to gain an unfair advantage **2.** **DISHONEST TRICK** a dishonest or unfair trick **3.** LAW **DISHONESTLY OBTAINING PROPERTY** the obtaining of somebody else's property by dishonest means **4.** *US* **ANNUAL GRASS** an annual bromegrass. Native to: Europe, naturalized in North America. Latin name: *Bromus secalinus*. [14C. Shortening of ESCHEAT] —**cheater** *n*

cheat code *n* in a computer game, a method of accessing hidden functionality that allows players to cheat, e.g. by becoming invulnerable in a shoot-'em-up or by accessing hidden areas in an adventure game

Chechen /ché chen/ *n* **1.** somebody who comes from Chechnya **2.** the main language in Chechnya, belonging to the Nakh group of North Caucasian languages. Native speakers: 1 million. —**Chechen** *adj*

Chechnya /chéchni ə/ autonomous republic in southwestern Russia that formally separated from Ingushetia in 1992. In 1994, Russia refused to recognize Chechnya's independence, resulting in a conflict that ended formally in 1997. Capital: Grozny. Population: 862,000 (1997). Area: 15,000 sq. km/5,790 sq. mi.

check /chek/ *v* (**checks, checking, checked**) **1.** *vti* **EXAMINE SOMETHING** to examine something in order to establish its state or condition ○ *Check the doors and windows to make sure they're locked.* **2.** *vti* **CONFIRM TRUTH OR ACCURACY OF SOMETHING** to confirm or establish that something is true or accurate ○ *We need to check with the insurance company to find out whether we're covered.* **3.** *vi* **BE CONSISTENT** to be the same as or consistent with something else ○ *What you're telling me now doesn't check with what you told me last week.* **4.** *vt* **HALT OR SLOW SOMETHING** to stop or slow the progress of some unwelcome process ○ *efforts to check inflation* **5.** *vti* **STOP SUDDENLY** to stop or pause suddenly, or make somebody or something stop suddenly ○ *In mid-sentence, he checked himself abruptly, looking terribly embarrassed.* **6.** *vt* **PREVENT SOMETHING BEING EXPRESSED** to prevent or inhibit something from being expressed ○ *Checking the urge to laugh out loud, I buried my head in the newspaper.* **7.** *vt* **REPRIMAND SOMEBODY** to criticize somebody for a fault or bad behaviour **8.** *vt* SPORTS **BLOCK OPPONENT** in sports such as ice hockey, to move directly into the path of an opponent, usually making physical contact, in order to block his or her progress **9.** *vt* FOOTBALL **FOLLOW OPPONENT CLOSELY** in Australian Rules football, to follow an opponent closely, attempting to keep the player clear of the ball by shepherding or bumping **10.** *vt N Am* same as **tick**[1] *v* (sense 3) **11.** *vt N Am* **HAND OVER BAGGAGE** to hand over something, especially baggage, so that it can be transported separately from passengers, usually in the same aircraft or vehicle ○ *You must check your luggage before boarding.* **12.** *vt N Am* **HAND SOMETHING OVER FOR TEMPORARY KEEPING** to hand over something such as a coat in a restaurant or museum, so that it can be looked after until you need it again ○ *Do you want to check your coat?* **13.** *vt* CHESS **PUT OPPONENT'S KING IN JEOPARDY** in chess, to put an opponent's king in a situation in which one of your pieces directly threatens it **14.** *vt* **LOOK AT SOMEBODY OR SOMETHING** to look at or see somebody or something (*informal*) **15.** *vt* **VISIT SOMEBODY** to go and see or find somebody (*slang*; *used in Black English*) ■ *n* **1.** **EXAMINATION** an examination or investigation of something, especially to verify its state or condition ○ *Routine checks should have revealed the cracks in the engine housing.* **2.** **SOMETHING THAT TESTS ACCURACY** something that can be used or referred to in order to test the accuracy, truth, or safety of something else **3.** DESIGN **PATTERN OF SQUARES** a pattern made up entirely of squares in at least two different colours that are arranged alternately **4.** **MEANS OF RESTRAINING SOMEBODY OR SOMETHING** a means of controlling or restraining somebody or something ○ *a check on the dog's aggressive tendencies* **5.** DESIGN **SQUARE IN CHECK PATTERN** a square in a pattern, in which at least two different colours are arranged alternately ○ *Every third check is red.* **6.** CHESS **MOVE ATTACKING KING** in chess, a move by which a piece directly threatens the opposing king, or the position resulting from this move. The king must escape from this position to avoid checkmate. ○ *If you move your king there, you'll be in check.* **7.** SPORTS **BLOCKING MOVE** in sports, a move directly into the path of an attacking opponent **8.** *N Am* **RESTAURANT BILL** the bill in a restaurant or bar **9.** US spelling of **cheque** **10.** *N Am* **NUMBERED TICKET FOR DEPOSITED ITEM** a numbered

ticket or token given out when an item is left at a cloakroom 11. *N Am* same as **tick**[1] *n* (sense 4) ■ *adj* same as **checked** ■ *interj* CHESS **WARNING THAT KING IS IN CHECK** in chess, used to announce that an opponent's king is in check [14C. < Old French *eschec* 'check in chess' < Persian *šāh* 'king' (see SHAH)] —**checkable** *adj* ◇ **checks and balances** features in the way a system operates that prevent any one person or group from having too much power or influence ◇ **in check** restrained and under control ○ *managing to keep her anger in check*

check in *v* 1. *vti* **REGISTER AT HOTEL** to register as a guest, or register a guest, on arrival at a hotel ○ *Has my colleague checked in yet?* 2. *vti* **ARRIVE FOR JOURNEY** to register and go through the necessary formalities before beginning a journey, especially by air ○ *All passengers should check in at least one hour before departure.* 3. *vi* **MAKE CONTACT** to make routine contact with a person or organization to exchange information ○ *The patrols are supposed to check in by radio at half-hourly intervals.*

check into *vt* to investigate something in order to get more information about it or to establish its truth or accuracy ○ *When we checked into his background, we found that he had several convictions for fraud.*

check off *vt N Am* same as **tick off** (sense 1)

check out *v* 1. *vi* **LEAVE HOTEL** to pay the bill and leave a hotel or other place ○ *We'll be checking out later this morning.* 2. *vi N Am* **LEAVE** to leave a particular place or person (*informal*) 3. *vt* **INVESTIGATE SOMETHING** to establish that something is correct or valid (*informal*) ○ *The date is probably 1961. Check it out, will you?* 4. *vt* **TAKE A LOOK AT SOMETHING** to visit a place briefly to get information about it (*informal*) ○ *Let's check out the new pizza place down the High Street.* 5. *vi* **BE PROVED TRUE** to prove after investigation to be correct or valid ○ *If the DNA checks out, he's our man.* 6. *vti US* **PAY IN SUPERMARKET** to pay for something in a supermarket ○ *When I went to check out, I realized I'd left my purse in the car.* 7. *vt US* **TAKE MONEY FOR GOODS AT SUPERMARKET** to calculate and take payment from a customer in a supermarket ○ *This person's in a hurry, so do you mind if I check her out first?*

check over *vt* 1. to examine something to make sure that it is correct or satisfactory ○ *Could you check over my essay to make sure there are no errors, please?* 2. to examine somebody carefully to establish his or her state of health ○ *I've checked her over, and there are no broken bones.*

check through *vt* to examine or review systematically all the parts of something to make sure that it is satisfactory

check up *vi* to make enquiries to establish a point ○ *I checked up: no one of that name lives at that address.*

check up on *vt* to make enquiries or obtain information about somebody or something, often secretly and usually because of suspicion or worry

checkbook *n* BANKING US spelling of **chequebook**

check box *n* a small square on a computer screen that, when clicked on with a mouse, displays a small cross or tick to show that an item has been selected

check dam *n* a dam, usually a small one, that interrupts the flow of a stream and builds up a store of water behind itself

check digit *n* in computing, a digit derived from and added to the other digits in a sequence, used to ensure that the sequence is correct

checked /chekt/ *adj* with a pattern of small squares ○ *a red-and-white checked tablecloth*

checker[1] /chékər/ *n* 1. somebody who checks something 2. *N Am* a cashier in a supermarket or large store

checker[2] US spelling of **chequer** *v*

checkerberry /chékər beri/ (*plural* **-ries**) *n* 1. an edible, red, spicy-flavoured fruit 2. a low-growing evergreen bush that bears checkerberries and has fragrant leathery leaves from which an oil (**oil of wintergreen**) is distilled. Native to: eastern North America. Latin name: *Gaultheria procumbens.*

checkerboard /chékər bawrd/ *n N Am* same as **draughtboard**

checkers /chékərz/ *n N Am* BOARD GAMES same as **draughts**

check-in *n* 1. **REGISTRATION AT HOTEL OR AIRPORT** the process of registering on arrival at a hotel or airport 2. **REGISTRATION DESK** a place where people check in at a hotel or airport 3. *US* **SOMEBODY CHECKING IN** a traveller who checks in at a hotel or airport ○ *Since the flight was overbooked, the five late check-ins had to wait.*

checking account *n US* same as **current account**

checklist /chék list/ *n* a list of names, items, or points for consideration or action

checkmate /chék mayt/ *n* 1. **WINNING CHESS POSITION** in chess, a condition or position in which a player's king cannot escape check and the other player wins the game 2. **CHESS MOVE THAT ENDS GAME** in chess, a move that produces checkmate, or a game that ends in checkmate ○ *The series was declared a draw with three checkmates apiece.* 3. **COMPLETE DEFEAT** a situation of defeat or deadlock ■ *vt* (**-mates, -mating, -mated**) 1. **TRAP KING IN CHESS** in chess, to put an opponent's king in checkmate 2. **THWART SOMEBODY** to make it impossible for somebody to succeed or proceed further ■ *interj* **ANNOUNCEMENT OF CHECKMATE** in chess, used to announce that an opponent's king is in checkmate [15C. Via Old French *eschec mat* < Persian *šāh māt* 'the king is dead']

checkout /chék owt/ *n* 1. **SUPERMARKET TILL** a point in a supermarket at which shoppers pay for their purchases ○ *Only three checkouts were open.* 2. **DEPARTURE FROM HOTEL** the procedure that involves paying a hotel bill and leaving ○ *We'd like to arrange for a later checkout.* 3. *US* **SOMEBODY CHECKING OUT** a traveller checking out at an airport or a hotel ○ *Apart from a couple of late checkouts, everyone seemed to be ready.*

checkpoint /chék poynt/ *n* a place where police or other officials stop and check vehicles

Checkpoint Charlie *n* a border crossing between East and West Berlin during the Cold War. Once situated on the Friedrichstrasse, it has now been demolished.

checkrail /chék rayl/ *n* RAIL same as **guardrail** (sense 2)

checkrein /chék rayn/ *n* 1. *US* same as **bearing rein** 2. a rein used when driving a pair of horses, connecting the driving rein of one horse to the mouthpiece of the other

checkroom /chék room, -ro͝om/ *n N Am* a room in a public building such as a theatre, restaurant, train, or bus station where customers can leave belongings

checksheet /chék sheet/ *n* 1. same as **checklist** 2. a data collection form on which data are entered in categories in order to make analysis easier

checksum /chék sum/ *n* a value transmitted with a data stream, derived from the other elements in the data stream and used to check for transmission errors in the data. If the transmitted checksum differs from the one derived by the receiving computer, a transmission error has probably occurred and the transmission is repeated.

checkup /chék up/, **check-up** *n* a routine examination or inspection, especially one carried out by a doctor or dentist ○ *Regular checkups are required for all pilots.*

check valve *n* a valve designed to allow liquids to flow in one direction only

chedarim EDUC plural of **cheder**

cheddar /chéddər/ *n* a hard pale yellow or orange-red cheese with a flavour that ranges from mild to very strong, depending on its maturity [Mid-17C. After CHEDDAR]

Cheddar /chéddər/ village in the Mendip Hills in Somerset, southwestern England. Population: 4,484 (1991).

Cheddar Gorge deep gorge in the Mendip Hills in Somerset, southwestern England. It is known for its steep limestone cliffs and caves. Height: 137 m/450 ft (cliffs).

cheder /káydər/ (*plural* **-arim** /ke daárim/ or **-ers**) *n* classes in Hebrew language and religious knowledge for younger Jewish children [Late 19C. < Hebrew *ḥeder* 'room']

cheek /cheek/ *n* 1. **SOFT PART OF FACE** the soft side area of the face between the nose and ear 2. **BUTTOCK** either side of the buttocks (*informal*) 3. **BAD MANNERS** impertinent or precocious words or behaviour showing, or appearing to show, disregard for good manners or the feelings of others (*informal*) ○ *He had the cheek to ask me for a lift!* ■ *vt* (**cheeks, cheeking, cheeked**) **SPEAK DISRESPECTFULLY TO SOMEBODY** to speak disrespectfully or rudely to somebody (*informal*) [Old English *cēoce* < W Germanic] —**-cheeked** *suffix* ◇ **cheek by jowl** side by side or very close together ○ *living cheek by jowl in a tiny unheated flat* ◇ **turn the other cheek** to accept injury or insults without resisting or retaliating

cheekbone /cheék bōn/ *n* an arch of bone in the face, below the eyes and above the cheeks

cheekpiece /cheék peess/ *n* either of the two straps on a bridle that lie along the cheeks of a horse and join the bit to the crownpiece

cheek pouch *n* a fold of skin in the mouth of some rodents, mammals, and monkeys that acts as a pouch for storing food

cheek tooth *n* a premolar or molar of a mammal, or any one of the teeth behind the canines

cheeky /cheéki/ (**-ier, -iest**) *adj* 1. insolently or playfully rude or disrespectful 2. amusing or endearing despite offending good manners, especially by being mildly sexually improper (*informal*) ○ *The stories are performed by a raconteur with warmth and a cheeky charm.* —**cheekily** *adv* —**cheekiness** *n*

cheep /cheep/ *n* the high shrill sound made by a young bird ■ *vi* (**cheeps, cheeping, cheeped**) to make a high shrill sound characteristic of young birds [Early 16C. An imitation of the sound]

SPELLCHECK See ***cheap.***

cheer /cheer/ *n* 1. **SHOUT OF APPROVAL** a shout that expresses happiness, excitement, encouragement, or praise ○ *A huge cheer went up as the band walked onto the stage.* 2. **WELL-BEING AND OPTIMISM** a sense of general well-being and optimism ○ *The latest sales figures will bring little cheer.* ■ *v* (**cheers, cheering, cheered**) 1. *vti* **SHOUT ENCOURAGEMENT OR SUPPORT** to shout encouragement, support, or appreciation, especially to people who are performing or competing ○ *The audience clapped and cheered and demanded three encores.* 2. *vt* **MAKE SOMEBODY FEEL CHEERFUL** to make somebody feel more cheerful, confident, or optimistic (*often passive*) ○ *They were cheered by the news.* 3. *vt* **APPROVE OF SOMETHING** to express or feel enthusiasm for something ○ *Business will cheer this decision.* [13C. Via Anglo-Norman *chere* 'face' < Latin *cara* < Greek *kara* 'head'] —**cheerer** *n* —**cheeringly** *adv*

cheer on *vt* to give active or vocal support, especially at a sports event ○ *We went to cheer our team on.*

cheer up *vti* 1. to become, or make somebody feel, less sad ○ *She cheered up a little when I suggested lunch.* 2. to become, or make something, brighter or more attractive and welcoming in appearance ○ *A coat of bright yellow paint will cheer up the dingiest of kitchens.*

cheerful /cheérf'l/ *adj* 1. **HAPPY AND OPTIMISTIC** in a happy and optimistic mood, or happy and optimistic by nature ○ *She remained her usual cheerful self despite recent setbacks.* 2. **BRIGHT AND PLEASANT** causing people to feel cheerful ○ *a cheerful light blue* 3. **WILLING AND UNRESENTFUL** showing willingness or good humour in complying ○ *They set to work cleaning up the mess with cheerful determination.* —**cheerfully** *adv* —**cheerfulness** *n*

cheerio /cheéri ō/ *interj* 1. used to say goodbye (*informal*) 2. a word used to express good wishes when drinking (*dated informal*) [Early 20C. Alteration of CHEER]

cheerleader /cheér leedər/ *n* 1. a member of a group of uniformed performers who encourage the crowd to support a team at sports events in the United States and other places. Cheerleaders direct organized chants and songs, and often perform acrobatic routines. 2. an uncritically enthusiastic supporter (*informal disapproving*)

cheerleading /cheér leeding/ *n* 1. the activity of performing as a cheerleader at a sports event 2. uncritical enthusiastic support for somebody or something (*disapproving*)

cheerless /cheérləss/ adj lacking anything bright, pleasant, or encouraging ○ a gloomy cheerless day —**cheerlessly** adv —**cheerlessness** n

cheers /cheerz/ interj **1.** GOOD HEALTH used to express good wishes just before drinking an alcoholic drink (informal) **2.** THANKS thank you ○ Cheers, you've been a big help! **3.** GOODBYE goodbye or farewell

cheery /cheéri/ (-ier, -iest) adj happy or in good spirits —**cheerily** adv —**cheeriness** n

cheese /cheez/ n **1.** a food made from the pressed curds of the milk of cows, sheep, goats, and some other animals. It can range from hard to semisoft, and from mildly acidic to sharp. Bacteria and acid are added to separate the milk into lumps (**curds**) and a watery liquid (**whey**). The curds are then drained and used to make cheese. **2.** an individual block of cheese [Old English cēse, via Germanic < Latin caseus]

cheeseboard /cheéz bawrd/ n **1.** a piece of wood, plastic, or other material used for serving or cutting cheese **2.** a selection of cheeses offered as an alternative or additional course to the dessert course of a meal

cheeseburger /cheéz burgər/ n a hamburger covered with melted cheese, served in a roll

cheesecake /cheéz kayk/ n **1.** a dessert consisting of a layer of sweetened soft cheese mixed with cream and eggs on a biscuit or pastry base **2.** photographs of women that highlight their physical appearance, especially in a stereotypical way (slang)

cheesecloth /cheéz kloth/ n a light woven cotton material. Use: lightweight clothes, originally, to wrap or strain cheese.

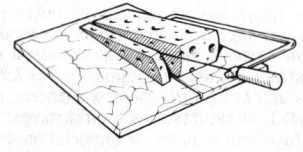

cheese cutter

cheese cutter n a board to which a piece of wire is attached for cutting cheese

cheesed off /cheézd-/ adj feeling annoyed, bored, or frustrated with somebody (informal)

cheesemonger /cheéz mung gər/ n a supplier of cheese and other dairy products

cheeseparing /cheéz pairing/ adj reluctant to spend money [Originally 'a paring of cheese rind', something only the most miserly would save] —**cheeseparing** n

cheese straw n a long thin biscuit of cheese-flavoured pastry, served as a snack

cheesy /cheézi/ (-ier, -iest) adj **1.** having the flavour or smell of cheese **2.** cheap and tawdry (informal) —**cheesiness** n

cheetah

cheetah /cheétə/ (plural **-tahs** or same) n a large member of the cat family with a yellowish-brown, black-spotted coat, small head, slender body, and long legs that is the fastest land mammal. Native to: Africa, southwestern Asia. Latin name: Acinonyx jubatus. [Late 18C. Via Hindi cītā < Sanskrit citraka 'leopard, tiger', literally 'spotted' < citra 'spot']

Cheever /cheévər/, **John** (1912–82) US writer. Many of his novels and short stories are comedies of manners satirizing suburban life.

> 'Fear tastes like a rusty knife and do not let her into your home. Courage tastes of blood. Stand up straight. Admire the world. Relish the love of a gentle woman. Trust in the Lord.'
> [John Cheever, The Wapshot Chronicle; 1957]

chef /shef/ n a professional cook, especially the principal cook in a hotel or restaurant [Early 19C. < French, shortening of chef de cuisine 'head of the kitchen']

chef-d'oeuvre /sháy dúrvrə/ (plural **chefs-d'oeuvre** /pronunc. same/) n a masterpiece, especially one produced by a musician, writer, or artist ○ He regarded that particular speech as his chef-d'oeuvre. [< French, 'chief piece of work']

chef's salad n N Am a tossed green salad with added tomatoes, sliced hard-boiled eggs, and thin strips of meat and cheese

~~cheif~~ incorrect spelling of **chief**

Chekhov /chék of/, **Anton Pavlovich** (1860–1904) Russian writer. His plays and short stories reveal the emotional depth of ordinary lives and include The Seagull (1896) and The Cherry Orchard (1904). See Cultural note at **orchard, seagull, sister** —**Chekhovian** /che kóvi ən/ n, adj

> 'An artist must pass judgment only on what he understands; his range is limited as that of any other specialist.'
> [Anton Pavlovich Chekhov, Letter to A.S. Suvorin; 27 October 1888]

Chekiang /che ki áng/ ♦ **Zhejiang**

chela[1] /keélə/ (plural **-lae** /-lee/) n the end joint that forms a claw on a limb of a lobster, crab, scorpion, or similar animal (**arthropod**) [Mid-17C. Via modern Latin < Greek khēlē 'claw']

chela[2] /cháylə/ n a pupil or disciple of a Hindu religious teacher [Mid-19C. < Hindi celā]

chelate[1] /keé layt/ n COMPOUND OF METAL AND NONMETAL a chemical compound in which metallic and nonmetallic, usually organic, atoms are combined. These compounds are characterized by a ring structure in which a metal ion is attached to two nonmetal ions by covalent bonds. ■ v (-**lates**, -**lating**, -**lated**) **1.** vti COMBINE TO FORM CHELATE to combine, or combine something, with a metal to form a chelate **2.** vt MED TREAT SOMEBODY WITH CHELATING AGENT to treat somebody with a chelating agent in order to remove a heavy metal such as lead from the bloodstream — **chelatable** /ki láytəb'l/ adj —**chelate** adj —**chelation** /ke láysh'n/ n —**chelator** /ki láytər/ n

chelate[2] /keé layt/ adj having chelae, or shaped like a chela

chelated mineral n an essential mineral that has been treated to make it more absorbable by the body when used as a dietary supplement

chelating agent n a chemical that combines with a metal to form a chelate. Use: treatment of metal poisoning.

chelicera /kə líssərə/ (plural **-ae** /-rī/) n either of the first pair of mouthparts of horseshoe crabs and spiders, resembling fangs or pincers and used to grab or poison prey [Mid-19C. < modern Latin < chela (see CHELA[1]) + Greek keras 'horn']

chelicerate /kə líssərət/ n an invertebrate with feeding appendages shaped like pincers, e.g. a spider or crab. Phylum: Chelicerata. [Early 20C. < modern Latin chelicerata < chelicera (see CHELICERA)] —**chelicerate** adj

cheliform /keéli fawrm/ adj used to describe an appendage shaped like a pincer or chela [Late 18C. < modern Latin chela (see CHELA[1])]

Chelmsford /chélmzfərd/ cathedral town in Essex, England. Population: 157,072 (2001).

chelonian /ki lóni ən/ n a reptile, e.g. a turtle or tortoise, that has most of its body enclosed in a hard bony shell. Order: Chelonia. [Early 19C. < modern Latin Chelonia < Greek khelōnē 'tortoise'] —**chelonian** adj

Chelsea /chélssi/ former borough of west-central London, now part of the Royal Borough of Kensington and Chelsea. A popular residential area for artists, writers, and musicians in the 18th century, it is also the site of the Chelsea Royal Hospital.

Chelsea bun n a flat coil-shaped bun, made from yeasted dough, containing currants and sometimes sprinkled with sugar [Early 18C. After Chelsea, London]

Chelsea pensioner n a retired soldier who is a resident of the Chelsea Royal Hospital in London. Chelsea pensioners wear a distinctive uniform with a red tunic.

Cheltenham /chéltnəm, chéltənəm/ spa and residential town in Gloucestershire, west-central England, situated on the western edge of the Cotswold Hills. Population: 110,025 (2001).

Chelyabinsk /chel yaábinsk/ city and capital of Chelyabinsk Oblast, in western Russia, situated 201 km/125 mi. south of Yekaterinburg. Population: 1,393,608 (1995).

chem. abbr **1.** chemical **2.** chemist **3.** chemistry

chem-, chemi- prefix same as **chemo-**

chemical /kémmik'l/ adj **1.** RELATING TO CHEMISTRY produced by or involved in the processes of chemistry **2.** COMPOSED OF CHEMICAL SUBSTANCES composed of or involving the use of substances produced by the process of chemistry ■ n SUBSTANCE USED OR MADE BY CHEMISTRY a substance used in or produced by the processes of chemistry. A chemical has a defined atomic or molecular structure that results from, or takes part in, reactions involving changes in its structure, composition, and properties. [Late 16C. < modern Latin chimicus 'alchemist', shortening of medieval Latin alchimicus < alchimia (see ALCHEMY)] —**chemically** adv

chemical bond n a force resulting from the redistribution of energy contained by orbiting electrons, which tends to bind atoms together to form molecules

chemical dependency n addiction to a chemical substance or drug

chemical element n CHEM same as **element** (sense 6)

chemical energy n the energy released or absorbed in a chemical reaction during the decomposition or formation of compounds

chemical engineering n a branch of engineering that deals with the industrial applications of chemistry and chemical processes —**chemical engineer** n

chemical equation n a representation, using chemical symbols in a form resembling a mathematical equation, of the process involved in a chemical reaction

chemical-free adj US not addicted to drugs or refraining from the use of drugs (informal)

chemical peel n a beauty treatment that uses a chemical solution to remove the outer layers of skin on the face to reveal smooth new skin without lines or wrinkles

chemical reaction n a process that changes the molecular composition of a substance by redistributing atoms or groups of atoms without altering the structure of the nuclei of the atoms

chemical toilet n a portable toilet containing chemicals to neutralize human waste

chemical warfare n military operations involving the use of weapons containing substances such as nerve gas or poison

chemical weapon n a weapon containing a substance such as nerve gas or poison

chemical weathering n the weathering of a rock surface through chemical processes such as oxidation, solution, and hydrolysis

chemiluminescence /kémmi loómi néss'nss/ n emission of light as a result of a chemical reaction, without producing heat —**chemiluminescent** adj

chemin de fer /shə máN də fáir/ n a gambling card game, similar to and derived from baccarat [< French, 'railway'; from the speed at which it is played]

cheminea n COOK another spelling of **chiminea**

chemise /shə meéz/ *n* **1.** a long loose dress, sometimes loosely belted at the waist or hip **2.** a long loose undergarment shaped like a dress [13C. Via Old French < late Latin *camisia* 'shirt']

chemisette /shémmi zét/ *n* a decorative undergarment made of lace or other fine material, worn to fill space left at the neckline of a low-cut dress [Early 19C. < French, 'small chemise' < *chemise* (see CHEMISE)]

chemisorb /kémmi sawrb/ (**-sorbs, -sorbing, -sorbed**), **chemosorb** /keémō-/ *vt* to take up a substance by chemisorption [Mid-20C. Back-formation < CHEMISORPTION]

chemisorption /kémmi sáwrpsh'n/ *n* the process of coating the surface of a substance rather than being absorbed by it, accompanied by chemical bonding between the surface of the material and the adsorbed substance [Mid-20C. Blend of CHEMICAL + ADSORPTION] —**chemisorptive** *adj*

chemist /kémmist/ *n* **1.** a shop where medicines, toiletries, and cosmetics are sold, and where prescriptions are dispensed. N Am term **drugstore 2.** same as **pharmacist 3.** a scientist who works in the field of chemistry [Mid-16C. Via French < modern Latin *chimista*, shortening of medieval Latin *alchimista* 'alchemist' < *alchimia* (see ALCHEMY)]

chemistry /kémmistri/ (*plural* **-tries**) *n* **1.** STUDY OF TRANSFORMATION OF MATTER a branch of science dealing with the structure, composition, properties, and reactive characteristics of substances, especially at the atomic and molecular levels **2.** CHEMICAL PROPERTIES OF SOMETHING the chemical composition, structure, and properties of a substance, or the chemical aspects of an activity ○ *the chemistry of wine-making* **3.** REACTION BETWEEN TWO PEOPLE the spontaneous reaction of two people to each other, especially a mutual sense of attraction or understanding

Chemnitz /kémnits/ city in Saxony, east-central Germany. It is a major industrial city. Population: 274,201 (1997). Former name **Karl-Marx-Stadt** (1953–90)

chemo /keémō/ *n* MED same as **chemotherapy** (*informal*) [Mid-20C. Shortening]

chemo- *prefix* chemical, chemistry ○ *chemoreceptor* [< CHEMICAL]

chemokine /keémō kīn/ *n* a protein secreted by lymph cells (**cytokines**) that activates white blood cells during the development of inflammation [Mid-20C. < CHEMOKINESIS]

chemokinesis /keémō ki neéssiss, -kī-/ *n* increased activity of cells or organisms caused by the presence of a chemical agent

chemolithotroph /keémō líthə trōf, -trof/ *n* a bacterium that obtains its energy from inorganic compounds containing iron, nitrogen, or sulphur, and not from living on decaying organisms —**chemolithotrophic** /keémō líthə trōfik, -tróffik/ *adj*

chemoprophylaxis /keémō profə láksiss/ *n* the use of chemical agents to prevent disease —**chemoprophylactic** *adj*

chemoprotective /keémō prə téktiv/ *adj* protecting the body from the effects of chemicals and diseases such as cancer through the antioxidant or immunity-boosting properties of a specific diet or supplement —**chemoprotection** *n*

chemoreception /keémō ri sépsh'n/ *n* the physiological response of an organism or sense organ to a chemical stimulus —**chemoreceptive** *adj* —**chemoreceptivity** /keémō ree sep tívvəti/ *n*

chemoreceptor /keémō ri séptər/ *n* a sense organ that responds to a chemical stimulus, e.g. a taste bud

chemosensory /keémō sénssəri/ *adj* involved in or relating to the perception of chemical agents, especially in the sense of smell

chemosorb *vt* CHEM another spelling of **chemisorb**

chemosphere /keémō sfeer, kémmō-/ *n* a variable region of the atmosphere, approximately 30 to 190 km/20 to 120 mi. above the Earth's surface, where photochemical reactions take place —**chemospheric** /keémō sférrik, kémmō-/ *adj*

chemostat /keémō stat/ *n* an apparatus designed to permit the growth of bacterial cultures at controlled rates

chemosurgery /keémō surjəri/ *n* surgical removal of dead or diseased tissue by chemical means —**chemosurgical** *adj*

chemosynthesis /keémō sínthəssiss/ *n* the synthesis of organic molecules by microorganisms using energy derived from chemical reactions —**chemosynthetic** /keémōsin théttik/ *adj* —**chemosynthetically** *adv*

chemotaxis /keémō táksiss/ *n* movement or change in the position of a cell or organism in response to the presence of a chemical agent —**chemotactic** /-táktik/ *adj* —**chemotactically** *adv*

chemotaxonomy /keémō tak sónnəmi/ *n* the classification of plants and microorganisms based on their biochemistry —**chemotaxonomic** /keémō taksə nómmik/ *adj* —**chemotaxonomically** *adv* —**chemotaxonomist** *n*

chemotherapy /keémō thérrəpi/ (*plural* **-pies**) *n* the use of chemical agents to treat diseases, infections, or other disorders, especially cancer —**chemotherapeutic** /keémō thérrə pyoótik/ *adj* —**chemotherapeutically** *adv* —**chemotherapist** *n*

chemotropism /kémmō trópizəm/ *n* the movement or growth of an organism or part of an organism in response to a chemical stimulus —**chemotropic** /kémmō tróppik/ *adj* —**chemotropically** *adv*

Chemulpo /chémool pố/ former name for **Inchon**

chemurgy /kémmurji/ *n* US a branch of applied chemistry dealing with the industrial application of organic substances, especially of agricultural origin [Mid-20C. < CHEMICAL] —**chemurgic** /kem úrjik/ *adj* —**chemurgical** *adj*

chemzyme /kém zīm/ *n* a substance that acts like an enzyme to increase the effectiveness of a drug [Late 20C. Blend of CHEMO- + ENZYME]

Chen /chen/ *n* a Chinese dynasty that ruled from AD 557 to 589

Chenab /chi náb/, **Chenāb** river in northwestern India and eastern Pakistan. It flows into the Sutlej, a tributary of the Indus. Length: 960 km/600 mi.

chenette /chénnit/ *n* Carib same as **guinep** (sense 1)

Cheney /cháyni/, **Dick** (*b.* 1941) vice president of the United States. He was a member of the US House of Representatives (1978–89) and US secretary of state (1989–93) before becoming the vice president (2001–). Full name **Cheney, Richard Bruce**

Chengde /chúng dúr/, **Ch'eng-te** city and capital of the former Jehol Province, now Hebei Province, in northeastern China, situated on the River Luan, approximately 177 km/110 mi. northeast of Beijing. Population: 246,799 (1991).

Chengdu /chéng doó/ provincial capital, situated northwest of Chongqing, in Sichuan, China. Population: 4,320,000 (1995).

Ch'eng-te another spelling of **Chengde**

chenille /shə neél/ *n* **1.** a soft thick cotton or silk fabric with a raised pile. Use: furnishings, clothes. **2.** a thick silk, cotton, or worsted cord or yarn. Use: embroidery, fringes, trimmings. [Mid-18C. Via French, 'hairy caterpillar' < Latin *canicula* 'little dog' < *canis* 'dog']

Chenin Blanc /shə naN blaáN/ *n* **1.** a white wine originally from the Loire region of west-central France but now widely made elsewhere **2.** a variety of white grape used to make Chenin Blanc [< French]

Chennai /chə nī/ capital of Tamil Nadu State, on the southeastern coast of India. It is a major port and commercial city. Population: 6,424,624 (2001). Former name **Madras**

Chen Shui-bian /chən shwáy bi án/ (*b.* 1951) president of Taiwan (2000–). A member of the pro-independence Democratic Progressive Party, he served four years as mayor of Taipei (1994–98) before his election to the presidency.

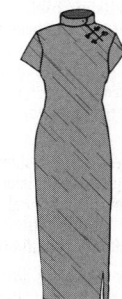

cheongsam

cheongsam /chong sám/ *n* a straight dress with a small stand-up collar and a slit in the skirt, worn by Chinese women [Mid-20C. < Cantonese Chinese, 'long gown']

Cheops /keé ops/ (2549?–2526 BC) Egyptian pharaoh. He commissioned the construction of the Great Pyramid at Giza, near Cairo. Born **Khufu**

Chepstow /chépstō/ town on the River Wye in Monmouthshire, Wales. It is known for its racecourse. Population: 9,461 (1991).

cheque /chek/ *n* a small printed form that, when filled in and signed, instructs a bank to pay a specific sum of money to the person named on it. US spelling **check** [Early 18C. Variant of CHECK]

chequebook /chékboŏk/ *n* a book of detachable cheques

chequebook journalism *n* the payment of large sums of money to secure exclusive rights to a newspaper story

cheque card *n* a small plastic card issued by a bank to a customer that guarantees the customer's cheques up to an agreed limit

cheque guarantee card *n* = **cheque card**

chequer /chékər/ *n* **1.** DESIGN same as **check** *n* (senses 3, 5) **2.** N Am same as **draught** *n* (sense 10) **3.** LEISURE PIECE USED IN CHINESE CHEQUERS a peg, marble, or other piece used in the game of Chinese chequers ■ *vt* (**chequers, chequering, chequered**) **1.** DESIGN MARK SOMETHING WITH CHECKS to mark something with a pattern of checks or with alternating areas of light and shade **2.** DISRUPT CONTINUOUS SUCCESS OF SOMETHING to affect something adversely from time to time ○ *regrettable incidents that chequered his career* ▶ US spelling **checker** [12C. Shortening of EXCHEQUER, which originally denoted the checked chessboard]

chequered /chékərd/ *adj* **1.** DESIGN same as **checked 2.** uneven or inconsistent, and characterized by periods of trouble or controversy as well as periods of success ○ *her chequered past*

chequered flag *n* a flag patterned with black and white squares that is waved as each participant in a motor race crosses the finishing line

Chequers /chékərz/ *n* a country house in Buckinghamshire that is the official country residence of the prime minister

Cher /shair/ (*b.* 1946) US entertainer. She turned to acting after a successful singing career and won an Academy Award for *Moonstruck* (1987). Born **La Piere, Cherilyn Sarkisian**

Cherbourg /sháir boorg/ city and port on the English Channel in the Manche Department of the Basse-Normandie Region, in northwestern France. Population: 25,370 (1999).

Cherenkov effect *n* PHYS another spelling of **Cerenkov effect**

cherimoya /chérri móyə/ (*plural* **-as** or *same*) *n* **1.** an edible heart-shaped fruit with creamy-white scented flesh and green skin that turns purple-black when ripe **2.** the tree that bears cherimoyas. Native to: South America. Latin name: *Annona cherimola*. [Mid-18C. Via Spanish < Quechua *chirimuya* < *chiri* 'cold' + *muya* 'circle']

cherish /chérrish/ (**-ishes, -ishing, -ished**) *vt* **1.** LOVE AND CARE FOR SOMEBODY to feel or show great love or care for somebody ○ *He cherishes that girl.* **2.** VALUE SOMETHING HIGHLY to value something such as a right,

freedom, or privilege highly ○ *I cherish my independence*. **3. RETAIN SOMETHING IN MIND** to retain a memory or wish in the mind as a source of pleasure or as an ambition ○ *his long-cherished dream* [14C. < French *chériss-*, stem of *chérir* 'hold dear' < *cher* 'dear' < Latin *carus*] —**cherishable** *adj* —**cherisher** *n* —**cherishingly** *adv*

Chernenko /chur nyéngkō/, **Konstantin** (1911–85) Soviet politician. A long-time political ally of Leonid Brezhnev, he became general secretary of the Communist Party of the Soviet Union (1984–85). Full name **Chernenko, Konstantin Ustinovich**

> 'Those who try to give us advice on matters of human rights do nothing but provoke an ironic smile among us. We will not permit anyone to interfere in our affairs.'
> [Konstantin Chernenko, *Time*; 2 July 1984]

Chernobyl /chər nôb'l, -nóbb'l/ site of a nuclear power plant near Kiev, in Ukraine, where there was a catastrophic accident in 1986

chernozem /chúrnə zem/ *n* a fertile black or brown topsoil that is rich in humus and can support crops for long periods of time without the addition of fertilizers. It covers a large proportion of the European and Asian steppe, as well as a belt of land stretching from Saskatchewan in Canada through North Dakota into Texas in the United States. [Mid-19C. < Russian, 'black earth'] —**chernozemic** /chúrnə zémmik/ *adj*

Cherokee /chérrə kee/ (*plural same* or **-kees**) *n* **1.** a member of a Native North American people who once lived mainly in the southeastern United States and now live mainly in Oklahoma and North Carolina. The Cherokee were one of the Five Civilized Nations who, under the Removal Act of 1830, were sent to live on reservations in Oklahoma. **2.** the Iroquoian language of the Cherokee. Native speakers: 10,000. [Late 17C. < obsolete Cherokee *tsaraki*] —**Cherokee** *adj*

cheroot /shə róot/ *n* a cigar with two square-cut ends [Late 17C. Via French *cheroute* < Tamil *curuṭṭu* 'roll of tobacco']

cherry

cherry /chérri/ *n* (*plural* **-ries**) **1. FOOD SMALL ROUND FRUIT** a small round fruit that has a single hard stone and varies in colour from bright red or yellow to dark purplish-black **2. TREES FRUIT TREE** a tree that bears cherries. Varieties include the sweet cherry, sour cherry, and morello cherry. Genus: *Prunus*. **3.** INDUST **CHERRY WOOD** the wood of the cherry tree. Use: furniture-making, musical instruments. **4.** COLOURS same as **cherry red 5.** TABOO TERM a highly offensive term for somebody's virginity, or the hymen as a symbol of a woman's virginity (*taboo*) ■ *adj* COLOURS same as **cherry red** [14C. Via Old French *cherise* (taken as plural) < medieval Latin *ceresia* < Greek *kerasos* 'cherry tree']

cherry bomb *n N Am* a powerful round red firecracker that explodes with a loud bang

cherry brandy *n* a sweet cherry-flavoured liqueur usually made by steeping cherries in brandy

cherry laurel *n* an evergreen bush with shiny leaves. Flowers: white. Native to: Europe, Asia. Latin name: *Prunus laurocerasus*.

cherry-pick *vti* **1.** to select only the most lucrative or profitable opportunities, especially in business **2.** to sift through, e.g., evidence or options, selecting only what you like or what supports your strategy, plans, or preconceived notions (*disapproving*)

cherry picker

cherry picker *n* a mobile crane with an enclosed platform that can be raised to allow somebody to work off the ground, e.g. on an overhead street light or cable

cherry plum *n* a plum tree that produces red or yellow fruit resembling cherries. Latin name: *Prunus cerasifera*.

cherry red *adj* of a deep vivid red colour ■ *n* a deep vivid red colour

cherrystone /chérri stōn/ *n* a half-grown quahog clam

cherry tomato *n* a small tomato with a strong sweet flavour. Latin name: *Lycopersicon esculentum*.

cherrywood /chérriwŏod/ *n* INDUST same as **cherry** *n* (sense 3)

chersonese /kúrssə neéss/ *n* GEOG same as **peninsula** (*archaic*) [Early 17C. Via Latin < Greek *khersonēsos* < *khersos* 'dry land' + *nēsos* 'island']

chert /churt/ *n* a brittle microcrystalline quartz. Source: sedimentary rocks. [Late 17C. Origin ?] —**cherty** *adj*

cherub: garden sculptures at Wendens Ambo, Essex, England

cherub /chérrəb/ *n* **1. DEPICTION OF ANGEL** an angel depicted as a chubby-faced child with wings, sometimes simply as a child's head above a pair of wings **2.** (*plural* **cherubim** /chérrəbim/ or **cherubs**) ANGEL OF EIGHTH-HIGHEST ORDER in Christianity, a member of the eighth of the nine orders in the medieval hierarchy of angels **3. WELL-BEHAVED CHILD** a child whose behaviour, disposition, or appearance is attractively innocent and well-behaved [Pre-12C. Via Latin *cherub*, Greek *kheroub* < Hebrew *kĕrūb*, probably < Akkadian; confused with Aramaic *kĕ-rabyā* 'like a child'] —**cherubic** /chə róobik/ *adj* —**cherubically** *adv*

Cherubini /kérroo beéni/, **Luigi** (1760–1842) Italian composer. A prolific composer of operas and sacred music, he was influential as director of the Paris Conservatoire (1821–41). Full name **Cherubini, Maria Luigi Carlo Zenobio Salvatore**

chervil /chúrvil/ *n* **1.** a herb with a mild flavour of aniseed. Use: food seasoning. Latin name: *Anthriscus cerefolium*. **2.** a plant related or similar to the chervil. Genera: *Anthriscus* or *Chaerophyllum*. [Pre-12C. Via Latin *chaerephyllum* < Greek *khairephullon*]

Ches. *abbr* Cheshire[2]

Chesapeake /chéssə peek/ city in Virginia, south of Norfolk and Hampton, and east of the Great Dismal Swamp. Population: 206,665 (2002 estimate).

Chesapeake Bay largest inlet of the Atlantic Ocean on the East Coast of the United States, bounded by

Virginia and Maryland. Area: 8,365 sq. km/3,320 sq. mi.

Cheshire[1] /chéshər/ *n* a mild crumbly cheese that is usually white but sometimes red, originally made in Cheshire

Cheshire[2] /chéshər/ county in northwestern England, between Manchester and the Welsh border. Population: 673,788 (2001). Area: 2,328 sq. km/900 sq. mi.

Cheshire cat *n* a cat in Lewis Carroll's *Alice's Adventures in Wonderland* whose broad grin remained suspended in the air after the cat itself had disappeared

Cheshvan *n* CALENDAR another spelling of **Heshvan**

Chesil Beach /chézz'l-/, **Chesil Bank** narrow shingle ridge on the coast of Dorset, southern England. Length: 27 km/17 mi.

chess

chess[1] /chess/ *n* a game played on a chequered board by two players, each with 16 pieces, whose object is to capture (**checkmate**) the opponent's king. Each player begins with a king, a queen, two bishops, two knights, two rooks or castles, and eight pawns. [12C. Shortening of Old French *esches*, plural of *eschec* (see CHECK)]

chess[2] /chess/ *n* a deck board or floorboard of a pontoon bridge [Early 19C. Origin ?]

chess[3] /chess/ *n US* **1.** PLANTS same as **cheat** *n* (sense 4) **2.** a weedy bromegrass. Genus: *Bromus*. [Mid-18C. Origin ?]

chessboard /chéss bawrd/ *n* a square board divided into 64 alternate light and dark squares, used for playing chess. The eight vertical rows of squares are called files, the eight horizontal rows are called ranks, and the squares that stretch diagonally across the board are called diagonals.

chessel /chéss'l/ *n* a mould or vat used to make cheese [Late 17C. Origin ?]

chessman /chéss man/ (*plural* **-men** /-men/) *n* a piece from a set of 32 used in the game of chess

chess pie *n US* a pie filled with a rich mixture of eggs, butter, and sugar, often with additional flavourings [Origin ?]

chesspiece /chéss peess/ *n* CHESS same as **chessman**

chessylite /chéssi līt/ *n US* MINERALS same as **azurite** [Mid-19C. After *Chessy*, near Lyons in France]

chest /chest/ *n* **1. UPPER BODY** the part of the body between the neck and the stomach, covering the ribs and the organs that the ribs enclose **2. FRONT PART OF BODY** the outside of the chest ○ *a hairy chest* **3. STRONG RECTANGULAR BOX** a strong rectangular box, usually with a lid and sometimes a lock, used for storage or transport **4. CONTENTS OF CHEST** the contents of a strong rectangular box, usually with a lid and sometimes a lock, used for storage or transport [Old English *cest*, via W Germanic < Latin *cista* < Greek *kistē* 'basket'] —**chested** *suffix* ◇ **get something off your chest** to talk openly about something that has been upsetting, annoying, or worrying you, especially in order to reduce or remove those feelings ◇ **keep your cards** *or* **play something close to your chest** to be discreet or secretive about something

Chester /chéstər/ ancient walled cathedral city that is the county town of Cheshire, England. Population: 118,210 (2001).

chesterfield /chéstərfeeld/ *n* **1.** *Can, Northwest US* SOFA a large sofa with upright armrests at the same height as the back, usually upholstered in leather

and with a rolled-over outward curve along the top **2.** *UK, Can* COUCH an upholstered couch or sofa with back and arms of the same height **3.** OVERCOAT an overcoat, usually with concealed buttons and a velvet collar [Mid-19C. After a 19C earl of *Chesterfield*]

Chesterfield /chéstərfeeld/ town in Derbyshire, England, noted for the twisted spire of All Saints' Church. Population: 98,845 (2002).

Chesterfield, Philip Dormer Stanhope, 4th Earl of Chesterfield (1694–1773) British politician and writer. Secretary of state to George III and a literary wit, he wrote *Letters to his Son* (1774).

> 'This man I thought had been a Lord among wits; but, I find, he is only a wit among Lords.'
> [Samuel Johnson. Quoted in *Life of Samuel Johnson*, James Boswell; 1791]

Chester-le-Street /chéstər lə street/ mining town in County Durham, northeastern England. Population: 53,692 (2001).

Chesterton /chéstərtən/, **G. K.** (1874–1936) British writer. His books include the Father Brown detective stories and volumes of literary criticism. Full name **Chesterton, Gilbert Keith**

> 'If a thing is worth doing, it is worth doing badly.'
> [G. K. Chesterton, 'Folly and Female Education', *What's Wrong with the World*; 1910]

> 'A good novel tells us the truth about its hero; but a bad novel tells us the truth about its author.'
> [G. K. Chesterton, *Heretics*; 1905]

chestnut /chéss nut/ *n* **1.** EDIBLE NUT an edible nut that grows inside a prickly case and has a glossy brown skin **2.** (*plural* **chestnuts** or *same*) TREES TREE THAT PRODUCES CHESTNUTS a deciduous tree that has long toothed leaves and produces chestnuts. Native to: Europe, North America, Japan, China. Genus: *Castanea*. ◊ **horse chestnut 3.** INDUST WOOD OF CHESTNUT TREE the coarse-grained durable wood of the chestnut tree **4.** REDDISH-BROWN HORSE a horse with a reddish-brown colour **5.** ANAT CALLUS ON HORSE'S LEG a small hard callus found in several places on the inner surface of a horse's leg and thought to be a vestigial toe **6.** REDDISH-BROWN COLOUR a deep reddish-brown colour **7.** STALE JOKE OR STORY a joke or story that has lost its impact through overuse (*informal*) [Early 16C. < obsolete *chesten*, via Old French *chastaine* < Latin *castanea* < Greek *kastanea*] —**chestnut** *adj*

chestnut blight *n* a disease that kills chestnut trees and is especially destructive to North American chestnuts. It is caused by the fungus *Cryphonectria parasitica* and was probably imported from Asia into the United States in the early 20th century.

chestnut oak *n* a deciduous oak tree with shiny yellow leaves resembling those of a chestnut. Native to: eastern North America. Latin name: *Quercus prinus*.

chest of drawers *n* a piece of furniture consisting of a set of drawers in a wooden frame with a flat top, used for storing clothes

chest voice *n* the lowest register of somebody's speaking or singing voice

chesty /chésti/ (**-ier, -iest**) *adj* **1.** showing the effects of a chest complaint, e.g. by having phlegm in the lungs **2.** having a well-developed chest (*informal*) —**chestiness** *n*

cheth *n* another spelling of **heth**

Chetnik /chétnik/ *n* a Serbian nationalist who was part of a group who fought the Turks before World War I, and was involved in guerrilla warfare in World War I and World War II [Early 20C. < Serbo-Croatian *četnik* < *četa* 'band, troop']

chetrum /chétroóm/ *n* (*plural same* or **-rums**) *n* a subunit of currency in Bhutan. See table at **currency** [Late 20C. < Tibetan]

cheval-de-frise /shə vál də freéz/ (*plural* **chevaux-de-frise** /-vō-/) *n* **1.** an obstacle consisting of barbed wire or spikes attached to a wooden frame, used to block an advancing enemy force **2.** a line of jagged glass, nails, or spikes set into masonry on top of a wall to deter intruders [< French, 'horse of Friesland';

from its use by the Friesians, who lacked cavalry, during the siege of Groningen (1594)]

chevalet /shə vállay, shévvə láy/ *n* the bridge of a stringed musical instrument [Late 19C. < French, 'small horse' < *cheval* 'horse' < Latin *caballus*]

cheval glass /shə vál-/ *n* a long mirror that is mounted in a frame so that it can be tilted [< French *cheval* 'frame', literally 'horse']

chevalier /shə válli ər/ *n* **1.** used as the title of members of the French Legion of Honour and of other orders **2.** a French knight or nobleman of the lowest rank [14C. Via French < medieval Latin *caballarius* < Latin *caballus* 'horse']

chevet /shə váy/ *n* a complex of elaborate architectural structures at the eastern end of a church, especially a French Gothic church, usually consisting of a semicircular or polygonal apse with radiating chapels and many buttresses [Early 19C. < French, 'pillow']

Cheviot /chéevi ət, chévvi ət/ *n* **1.** a hornless sheep belonging to a breed with short thick wool originating in the Cheviot Hills on the border between Scotland and England **2.** *also* **cheviot** a woollen fabric with a coarse twill weave, originally made from the wool of Cheviot sheep

Cheviot Hills /chéevi ət-, chévvi ət-/ range of hills along the border of England and Scotland. The highest peak is the Cheviot, 816 m/2,676 ft.

chèvre /shévrə/ *n* a soft cheese made from goat's milk [Mid-20C. Via French, 'goat' < Latin *capra*, feminine of *caper*]

chevron

chevron /shévrən/ *n* **1.** V-SHAPED SYMBOL a V-shaped symbol, especially one used as a sign of rank on military or police uniforms **2.** HERALDIC ORNAMENT a heraldic ornament in the form of a wide inverted V-shape ■ **chevrons** *npl* ROAD SIGN AT BEND a large rectangular road sign with a pattern of horizontal black and white V-shapes, used to indicate a sharp bend [14C. < French, 'rafter' < Latin *caper* 'goat']

chevrotain /shévrə tayn, -tin/ (*plural* **-tains** or *same*) *n* a small hornless cud-chewing animal similar to a deer, the male of which has projecting canine teeth. Native to: rain forests of west-central Africa and Southeast Asia. Family: Tragulidae. [Late 18C. < French, 'small goat' < *chèvre* (see CHÈVRE)]

chevy *vt* another spelling of **chivvy**

chew /choo/ *v* (**chews, chewing, chewed**) **1.** *vti* GRIND UP FOOD BEFORE SWALLOWING to grind up food or other material with the action of the teeth and jaws **2.** *vti* DAMAGE SOMETHING BY BITING to gnaw at something repeatedly, usually causing damage ○ *chewing her nails* **3.** *vi* *N Am* CHEW TOBACCO to chew a piece of tobacco ■ *n* **1.** ACT OR PERIOD OF CHEWING the act of chewing something, or a period of chewing **2.** SWEET a sweet with a firm texture, which must be chewed before being swallowed ○ *fruit chews* **3.** *N Am* PIECE OF TOBACCO FOR CHEWING a piece of tobacco used for chewing [Old English *cēowan* < Germanic] —**chewable** *adj* —**chewer** *n*

chew out *vt* *N Am* to tell somebody off for doing something wrong (*informal*) ○ *She really chewed me out for being late.*

chew over *vt* to think about or discuss something over a period of time ○ *We chewed the problem over for a couple of days before coming to a decision.*

chew up *vt* **1.** to damage or destroy something, especially something passing through machinery (*informal*) ○ *I'm afraid the machine chewed up your*

tape. **2.** to destroy something by biting or chewing it

Chewa /cháywə/ *n* a language spoken in Malawi, Zambia, and Mozambique, and belonging to the Bantu group of Niger-Congo languages. Native speakers: 8 million. [< Bantu] —**Chewa** *adj*

chewie /choó i/ *n* ANZ FOOD same as **chewing gum** (*informal*) [Early 20C. Shortening]

chewing gum /choó ing-/ *n* a sweet flavoured substance that is chewed but not swallowed. The elastic ingredient in chewing gum used to be chicle from the sapodilla tree, but synthetic equivalents are now commonly used. ○ *a stick of chewing gum*

chew'n'spew *n* *Aus* **1.** cheap takeaway food, such as a hamburger or fish and chips **2.** a café serving cheap takeaway food

chewy /choó i/ (**-ier, -iest**) *adj* having a consistency or texture that requires a good deal of chewing —**chewiness** *n*

Cheyenne[1] /shī án, -én/ (*plural same* or **-ennes**) *n* **1.** a member of a Native North American people who once lived in the western Great Plains. The Cheyenne, along with the Sioux, were instrumental in the defeat of Custer and his forces at the Battle of Little Bighorn. **2.** the Algonquian language of the Cheyenne people. Native speakers: 2,000. [Late 18C. Via Canadian French < Dakota *šahíyena*] —**Cheyenne** *adj*

Cheyenne[2] /shī án, -én/ city, capital of Wyoming, and county seat of Laramie County, situated in southeastern Wyoming 16 km/10 mi. north of the border with Colorado. Population: 53,658 (2002 estimate).

Cheyne-Stokes respiration /cháyn stóks-/ *n* a breathing pattern marked by shallow breathing alternating with periods of rapid heavy breathing found in some medical conditions and also occurring at high altitude [Late 19C. After John *Cheyne* (1777–1836), Scottish physician, and William *Stokes* (1804–78), Irish physician]

chez /shay/ *prep* at somebody's home or business premises, especially a restaurant [Mid-18C. Via French < Latin *casa* 'cottage']

chg. *abbr* **1.** FIN change **2.** BANKING charge

Chhattisgarh /cháttiss gaar/ state in eastern India. Capital: Raipur. Population: 20,795,956 (2001). Area: 135,194 sq. km/52,185 sq. mi.

chi[1] /kī/ (*plural* **chis**), **khi** (*plural* **khis**) *n* the 22nd letter of the Greek alphabet, represented in English as 'ch' or 'kh'. See table at **alphabet** [15C. < Greek *khî*]

chi[2] /chee/, **ch'i, Chi, Ch'i, qi, Qi** *n* in Chinese medicine and philosophy, the energy or life force of the universe, believed to flow round the body and to be present in all living things. The manipulation of chi is the basis of acupuncture and Chinese martial arts. [< Chinese *qì* 'air, breath']

Chiang Ch'ing another spelling of **Jiang Qing**

Chiang Ching-kuo /cháng ching kwó/ (1910–88) Taiwanese politician. He was president of Taiwan (1978–88) and initiated many economic, social, and political reforms.

Chiang Kai-shek

Chiang Kai-shek /cháng kī shék/ (1887–1975) Chinese military leader and politician. He helped to overthrow the imperial government (1912) and developed Taiwan's economy as its president (1949–75).

Chianti /ki ánti/, **chianti** *n* a light red wine from north-

western Italy [Mid-19C. After the *Chianti* Mountains, Tuscany]

Chiapas /chi áppəss/ state in southeastern Mexico. Capital: Tuxtla Gutiérrez. Population: 3,920,892 (2000). Area: 73,724 sq. km/28,465 sq. mi.

chiaroscuro /ki aárə skoórrō/ *n* the use of light and shade in paintings and drawings, or the effect produced by this [Mid-17C. < Italian < *chiaro* 'bright' + *oscuro* 'dark'] —**chiaroscurism** *n* —**chiaroscurist** *n*

chiasma /kī ázmə/ (*plural* **-mas** or **-mata** /-mətə/) *n* **1.** a crossing over of biological tissue, e.g. the intersection of the optic nerves **2.** the point at which two chromatids join during the fusion and exchange of genetic material (**crossing-over**) in cell division [Mid-19C. Via modern Latin < Greek *khiasma* 'crosspiece' < *khiazein* 'mark with an X' < *khi* 'the letter chi'] —**chiasmal** *adj* —**chiasmic** *adj*

chiasmus /kī ázməss/ (*plural* **-mi** /-mī/) *n* a rhetorical construction in which the order of the words in the second of two paired phrases is the reverse of the order in the first. An example is 'grey was the morn, all things were grey'. [Mid-17C. Via modern Latin < Greek *khiasmos* < *khiazein* (see CHIASMA)]

chiastolite /kī ástə līt/ *n* a variety of the mineral andalusite that contains carbon impurities in an X-shape [Early 19C. < Greek *khiastos*, past participle of *khiazein* (see CHIASMA)]

Chiba /cheébə/ capital city of Chiba Prefecture, situated on the eastern shore of Tokyo Bay in Honshu, Japan. Population: 880,164 (2002).

Chibcha /chíbchə/ (*plural same* or **-chas**) *n* **1.** a member of an extinct Native South American people who lived in the Andes Mountains in central Colombia. The Chibcha died out following their defeat by the Spanish conquistador Gonzalo Jeménez de Quesada in the 1530s. **2.** the extinct Chibchan language of the Chibcha people [Early 19C. Via American Spanish < Chibcha *zipa* 'chief']

Chibchan /chíbchən/ (*plural same* or **-chans**) *n* **1.** a group of Native Central American languages spoken in Colombia and Panama. Native speakers: 100,000. **2.** a member of any of the peoples who speak a language belonging to the Chibchan group —**Chibchan** *adj*

Chibemba /chibémbə/ *n* LANG same as **Bemba** (sense 2) [< Bantu] —**Chibemba** *adj*

chic /sheek/ *adj* stylish and elegant ■ *n* fashionable style and elegance [Mid-19C. < French] —**chicness** *n*

Chicago /shi kaágō/ city and port in northeastern Illinois, situated on Lake Michigan. It is the third largest city in the United States, home to the University of Chicago. Population: 2,886,102 (2002 estimate). —**Chicagoan** *n, adj*

Chicago Board of Trade *n* a major commodities exchange in Chicago, in the United States, that deals in grain and metal futures

chicane[1] /shi káyn/ *n* **1.** in motor-racing, a sharp double bend created by placing barriers on the circuit **2.** a bridge or whist hand without trumps or without cards of one suit [Late 19C. < French < *chicaner* 'to quibble']

chicane[2] /shi káyn/ (**-canes, -caning, -caned**) *vi* to practise chicanery [Late 17C. < French *chicaner* 'to quibble'] —**chicaner** *n*

chicanery /shi káynəri/ (*plural* **-ies**) *n* deception or trickery, especially by the clever manipulation of language

Chichester /chíchistər/ cathedral city in West Sussex, southern England, founded by the Romans. Population: 106,450 (2001).

Chichester, Sir Francis (1901–72) British aviator and sailor. His feats included a solo Britain-to-Australia flight in 1929 and a solo round-the-world voyage in 1966–67, in *Gipsy Moth IV*. Full name **Chichester, Sir Francis Charles**

Chichewa /chi cháywə/ *n* LANG same as **Chewa** — **Chichewa** *adj*

chichi /sheé shee/ *adj* trying too hard or too obviously to be chic or modish ○ *All this designer furniture – isn't it just a bit chichi?* ■ *n* affected or self-conscious stylishness [Mid-20C. < French]

Chichimec /cheéchi mek/ (*plural* **-mecs** or *same*) *n* **1.** a member of a group of Native Central American peoples whose ancestors dominated central Mexico from the 11th to the 15th centuries, overthrowing the Toltecs and making way for the Aztecs **2.** the Uto-Aztecan language of the Chichimec peoples. Native speakers: 5,000. [Mid-17C. Via Spanish < Nahuatl *chichimecatl*]

chick[1] /chik/ *n* **1.** BABY BIRD a young bird, especially a young chicken **2.** *N Am* YOUNG WOMAN an attractive girl or young woman (*slang; sometimes considered offensive*) **3.** SMALL CHILD a term of affection used to a baby or small child (*informal*) [14C. Shortening of CHICKEN]

chick[2] /chik/ *n Malaysia, S Asia, Singapore* a hanging screen for a door or a window blind, usually made of split bamboo canes [Late 17C. < Urdu *chik*]

chickabiddy /chíkə biddi/ *n* an affectionate term of address used by adults to children and babies (*archaic*) [Early 19C. < CHICK[1] + BIDDY]

chickadee /chíkə dee/ (*plural* **-dees** or *same*) *n* a small tit that has grey feathers, a darker-coloured top to its head, and a distinctive call. Native to: North America. Genus: *Parus*. [Mid-19C. An imitation of its call]

chickaree /chíkə ree/ (*plural* **-rees** or *same*) *n* a squirrel with red fur that is related to the red squirrel. Native to: western North America. Latin name: *Tamiascurus douglasi*. [Early 19C. An imitation of its cry]

Chickasaw /chíkə saw/ (*plural same* or **-saws**) *n* **1.** a member of a Native North American people who originally lived in northeastern Mississippi and northwestern Alabama, and now live mainly in central and southern Oklahoma. The Chickasaw were one of the Five Civilized Nations who were sent to live on reservations in Oklahoma under the Removal Act of 1830. **2.** the Muskogean language of the Chickasaw. Native speakers: 10,000. [Late 17C. < Chickasaw *čikaša*] —**Chickasaw** *adj*

chicken /chíkin/ *n* **1.** COMMON DOMESTIC FOWL a domestic fowl, usually with brown or black feathers and a fleshy crest on its head. Kept for: meat, eggs. Latin name: *Gallus domesticus*. **2.** MEAT FROM FOWL the meat from a chicken as food **3.** COWARD somebody regarded as cowardly or excessively timid (*informal*) ○ *You'll never do it – you're a chicken!* **4.** DANGEROUS GAME a game or challenge in which two or more people attempt a dangerous or daring feat (*informal*) ■ *adj* COWARDLY showing a lack of courage, or too scared to do a particular thing (*informal; often used by children or young people*) ○ *Are you too chicken to do a high dive?* [Old English *cīcen* < Germanic] ◇ **be running around like a headless chicken** to act in a frantic manner

SYNONYMS See *cowardly*.

chicken out *vi* to fail in or withdraw from something because of a lack of nerve (*slang*) ○ *She chickened out of the climb when she saw how high the cliff was.*

chicken-and-egg situation *n* a situation in which it is impossible to know which of two related circumstances occurred first and caused the other

chicken breast *n* MED same as **pigeon breast** —**chicken-breasted** *adj*

chicken feed *n* an insignificant amount of something, especially money (*informal*)

chicken-fried steak *n US* a cut of beef that has been tenderized, dredged in flour, and then pan-fried

chicken-hearted, **chicken-livered** *adj* easily frightened or lacking sufficient courage, boldness, or confidence —**chicken-heartedness** *n*

chicken louse *n* a biting louse that lives as a parasite on poultry. Latin name: *Menopon pallidum*.

chickenpox /chíkin poks/ *n* a highly infectious viral disease, especially affecting children, characterized by a rash of small itching blisters on the skin and mild fever. Technical name **varicella** [Mid-18C. Origin ?]

chicken salad air *n* in snowboarding, a trick in which the boarder reaches the trailing hand back between the legs and grabs the heel edge of the board, while holding the leading leg rigidly straight

chickenshit /chíkin shit/ *n N Am* (*slang*) **1.** an offensive term for petty or tedious details or tasks **2.** an offensive term for somebody who is regarded as cowardly or timid —**chickenshit** *adj*

chicken soup *n* in skysurfing, a move or jump that does not go as planned (*slang*)

chicken wire *n* lightweight flexible galvanized wire netting, usually made with a hexagonal mesh [< its use as a fence for enclosing chickens]

chick flick *n* a film that is supposedly of interest primarily to women, because of either its content or cast of characters (*slang; sometimes considered offensive*)

chick lit *n* a genre of fiction targeted to, and written by or about, young and sophisticated urban women (*slang*) [Late 20C. Blend of CHICK[1] (sense 2) and LITERATURE]

chickpea /chík pee/ *n* **1.** a pale yellow seed about the size of a large pea, cooked as a vegetable **2.** an annual plant that produces chickpeas. Native to: Asia, Mediterranean. Latin name: *Cicer arietinum*. [Early 18C. Alteration of *chich pease* < *chich* 'chickpea' (< French *chiche* < Latin *cicer*) + *pease* (see PEA)]

chickweed /chík weed/ *n* a common low-growing weed found on cultivated land. Native to: Europe. Latin name: *Stellaria media*. [Because chickens eat the plant]

Chiclayo /chi klī ō/ city in northwestern Peru, situated on the Pacific coast. Population: 375,058 (1998).

chicle /chík'l/ *n* a gummy substance from the latex of the sapodilla tree. Use: main ingredient of chewing gum. [Late 19C. Via American Spanish < Nahuatl *tzictli*] —**chicly** *adj*

chico /cheékō/ *n* PLANTS same as **greasewood** (sense 1) [Shortening of Spanish *chicalote*]

chicory /chíkəri/ *n* **1.** *UK, ANZ, Can* a plant grown for its pale, slightly bitter, succulent leaves. Use: cooked or raw in salads. Latin name: *Cichorium intybus*. US term **endive 2.** a dried, roasted, and ground root. Use: coffee additive or substitute. [15C. Via obsolete French *cicoré* 'endive' < medieval Latin *cichorea* < Greek *kikhorion*]

chide /chīd/ (**chides, chiding, chided** or **chid** /chid/, **chided** or **chid** or **chidden** /chídd'n/) *vti* to reproach somebody gently [Old English *cīdan* < ?] —**chider** *n* — **chiding** *adj* —**chidingly** *adv*

chief /cheef/ *adj* **1.** MOST IMPORTANT most important, basic, or common **2.** HIGHEST IN AUTHORITY highest in authority, position, or rank ■ *n* **1.** LEADER the person with the most authority or highest rank in a group or organization **2.** CULTL ANTHROP same as **chieftain 3.** NAUT SHIP'S PRINCIPAL ENGINEER the principal engineer on a ship **4.** NAUT same as **chief petty officer** (*informal*) **5.** HERALDRY TOP SECTION OF HERALDIC SHIELD the upper third of the surface area of a heraldic shield [13C. Via French *chef* < Latin *caput* 'head'] —**chiefdom** *n* —**chiefship** *n*

chief constable *n* in the United Kingdom, the police officer in overall command of a regional police force

chief education officer *n* in the United Kingdom, the chief administrative officer of a local education authority

chief executive *n* **1.** the highest-ranking member of an executive body, e.g. the head of a government or the governor of a US state **2.** BUSINESS, MANAGEMT same as **chief executive officer 3.** *US* the president of the United States

chief executive officer *n* the highest-ranking executive officer within a company or corporation, who has responsibility for overall management of its day-to-day affairs under the supervision of a board of directors

chief justice *n* **1.** PRESIDING JUDGE a judge who presides over a court that has several judges **2.** PRESIDING JUSTICE OF US SUPREME COURT the presiding justice of the US Supreme Court **3.** SENIOR JUDGE the senior judge in the High Courts of Australia and other Commonwealth countries

chiefly /cheéfli/ *adv* **1.** ABOVE ALL more or more importantly than anyone or anything else ○ *We moved to this area of the city chiefly because it's convenient for getting to work.* **2.** IN MAIN for the most part ○ *The human body consists chiefly of water.* ■ *adj* RELATING TO CHIEF relating to or characteristic of a chief

chief master sergeant *n* a noncommissioned officer

in the US Air Force of a rank above senior master sergeant

chief minister *n* **1.** the leader of a national or provincial government in various countries with a parliamentary system **2.** a ruler's chief executive official

chief of staff *n* **1.** the senior officer serving on a military staff, who has responsibility for managing it and for advising the commander **2.** a general officer in the US Army, Air Force, or Marine Corps who is a member of the Joint Chiefs of Staff

chief operating officer *n* in some US companies, the executive responsible to the board for day-to-day running of the company

chief petty officer *n* a noncommissioned officer in the Royal Navy of a rank above petty officer

chief rabbi *n* the senior religious leader of the Jewish community in the United Kingdom and some other countries

chieftain /chéeftən/ *n* the leader or titular head of a people or similar ethnic group [13C. < Old French *chevetaine*, alteration of late Latin *capitaneus* (see CAPTAIN)] —**chieftaincy** *n* —**chieftainship** *n*

chief technician *n* a noncommissioned officer in the Royal Air Force of a rank below flight sergeant

chief warrant officer *n* **1.** an officer in the US Army, Navy, Marine Corps, or Coast Guard of a rank above warrant officer and below that of second lieutenant or ensign **2.** the highest-ranking noncommissioned officer in the Royal Canadian Army or Air Force

chief whip *n* the most senior of a political party's whips, whose role is to maintain party discipline and ensure that party members attend and vote at debates in the Houses of Parliament

chiel /cheel/, **chield** /cheeld/ *n* Scotland a boy or young man (*regional*) [Variant of CHILD]

chiffchaff /chíf chaf/ *n* a small brownish-yellow bird with a characteristic repetitive song. Native to: Europe, Asia. Latin name: *Phylloscopus collybita*. [Late 18C. An imitation of its song]

chifferobe *n* US FURNITURE another spelling of **chifforobe**

chiffon /shíffon/ *n* LIGHTWEIGHT FABRIC a very light sheer nylon, rayon, or silk fabric ■ *adj* **1.** OF CHIFFON made or consisting of chiffon **2.** LIGHT AND FINE resembling chiffon in lightness and fineness **3.** COOK FLUFFY describes food that has a light fluffy texture, usually created by adding whipped egg whites or gelatin [Mid-18C. < French < *chiffe* 'rag, flimsy stuff']

chiffonade /shíffə naʹad/ *n* vegetables that have been shredded or finely chopped, often used as a garnish for other foods [Late 19C. < French]

chiffonier /shíffə neéer/ *n* **1.** a low cabinet or cupboard with shelves above it **2.** a tall narrow chest of drawers that often has a mirror attached to the back [Mid-18C. < French]

chifforobe /shíffə rōb/, **chifferobe** /shíffrōb/, **chifrobe** /shífrōb/ *n* US a tall piece of furniture with drawers and a space for hanging clothes [Early 20C. Blend of CHIFFONIER + WARDROBE]

Chifley /chíffli/, **Ben** (1885–1951) Australian politician. He was a trade union activist, Labor Party politician, and prime minister of Australia (1945–49). Full name **Chifley, Joseph Benedict**. See table at **prime minister**

chigetai /chíggə tī/ (*plural* same or **-tais**), **dziggetai** /jíg-/ *n* a wild ass related to the onager. Native to: Mongolia. Latin name: *Equus hemionus*. [Late 18C. < Mongolian *chikitei* 'having ears' < *chiki* 'ear']

chigger /chígger/ *n* **1.** INSECTS same as **chigoe** (sense 1) **2.** ANZ, N Am the bright red parasitic larva of a free-living mite that feeds on the skin and other tissues of mammals, including humans, causing irritation and swelling. Some species transmit diseases such as scrub typhus. UK term **harvest mite** [Mid-18C. < CHIGOE]

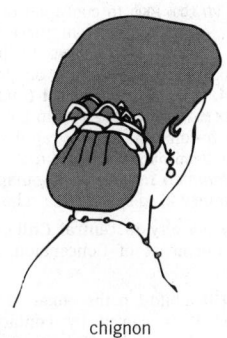
chignon

chignon /shéen yon, -yoN/ *n* a woman's hairstyle consisting of a roll of hair worn at the nape of the neck [Late 18C. < French, 'nape of the neck, chain' < Latin *catena* 'chain']

chigoe /chíggō/ *n* **1.** a small tropical flea, the fertilized female of which burrows under the skin causing painful itching sores that easily become infected. Latin name: *Tunga penetrans*. **2.** INSECTS same as **harvest mite** [Mid-17C. < French *chique* < a W African language]

chihuahua /chi waʹawə/ *n* a very small dog belonging to a breed originally from Mexico that has pointed ears, protruding eyes, and a disproportionately large head [Early 19C. After CHIHUAHUA]

Chihuahua /chi waʹa waa/ **1.** state in northern Mexico. Capital: Chihuahua. Population: 3,0522,907 (2000). Area: 245,945 sq. km/94,960 sq. mi. **2.** city and capital of Chihuahua State, northern Mexico. It is located in the central part of the state. Population: 671,790 (2000).

Chikamatsu /chíkə mátsoo/, **Monzaemon** (1653–1724) Japanese playwright. He is known for his historical romances and domestic tragedies written for the kabuki theatre and Bunraku puppet theatre. Born **Sugimori Nobumori**

chikan /chíkən/ *n* traditional South Asian embroidery with some parts cut out and the edges oversewn or filled, while other parts have crisscross stitches that create a shadowy effect. It is especially associated with Lucknow. [Late 19C. Via Urdu < Persian *čikin*]

chilblain /chíl blayn/ *n* a red itchy swelling on the fingers, toes, or ears caused by exposure to cold and damp (*often used in the plural*) [Mid-16C. < CHILL + *blain* 'inflamed swelling' < Old English *blegen* < W Germanic] —**chilblained** *adj*

child /chīld/ (*plural* **children** /chíldrən/) *n* **1.** YOUNG HUMAN BEING a young human being between birth and puberty **2.** HUMAN OFFSPRING a son or daughter of human parents **3.** SOMEBODY NOT YET OF AGE somebody under a legally specified age who is considered not to be legally responsible for his or her actions **4.** BABY a baby or infant **5.** UNBORN BABY a baby that has not yet been born **6.** IMMATURE ADULT an adult who is regarded as behaving in a childish or inappropriately childlike way **7.** PRODUCT OR RESULT somebody or something considered to be either produced or strongly influenced by a particular environment, period, or historical figure ○ *a child of the 1960s* **8.** DESCENDANT OR MEMBER OF PEOPLE a descendant of somebody, or a member of a people with a common ancestor or geographical origin (*often used in the plural*) ○ *children of Abraham* **9.** regional FEMALE CHILD a female child or infant [Old English *cild*] ◇ **with child** pregnant (*archaic or literary*)

SYNONYMS See *youth*.

Child /chīld/, **Julia** (b. 1912) US cookery expert and author. Since her first television appearance in 1963, she has written several cookery books and hosted a number of popular cookery series. Full name **Child, Julia McWilliams**.

> 'Too many cooks spoil the broth, but it only takes one to burn it.'
> [Julia Child, *Julia Child's Kitchen*; 1975]

child abuse *n* severe mistreatment of a child by a parent, guardian, or other adult responsible for his or her welfare, e.g. physical violence, neglect,

sexual assault, or emotional cruelty —**child abuser** *n*

child-abuse register *n* a register, maintained by a local authority, of people who have been found guilty of child abuse and who are considered likely to offend again

childbearing /chíld bairing/ *n* the process of carrying a child in the womb and giving birth to it (*often used before a noun*) ○ *women of childbearing age*

childbed /chíld bed/ *n* the state of a woman in the process of giving birth to a child (*archaic*)

child benefit *n* in the United Kingdom and New Zealand, a regular payment made by the state to parents towards the maintenance of each child below a specific age

childbirth /chíld burth/ *n* the act or process of giving birth to a child ○ *natural childbirth methods*

childcare /chíld kair/ *n* **1.** the care and supervision of a child by an adult, inside the home or elsewhere and usually for pay, during times when the parents or guardians are at work **2.** the care and supervision by a local authority of children who are homeless or whose home life is severely disrupted

child-centred *adj* adapted to the needs and concerns of children as opposed to those of adults

childe /chīld/ (*plural* **childes**) *n* a young person of noble birth (*archaic*) [Variant of CHILD]

Childe /chīld/, **V. Gordon** (1892–1957) Australian archaeologist. He was a pioneer of the study of prehistory and author of *The Dawn of European Civilisation* (1925). Full name **Childe, Vere Gordon**

Childers /chíldərz/, **Erskine** (1870–1922) British-born Irish nationalist and writer. Author of *The Riddle of the Sands* (1903), he joined the IRA and was executed during the Irish Civil War (1922–23).

child-free /chíld free/ *adj* **1.** not allowing children in a specific place ○ *This restaurant is a child-free environment.* **2.** having decided not to have children ○ *a child-free couple*

child guidance *n* the professional counselling of children who are emotionally disturbed, often also extended to their parents or guardians

childhood /chíld hood/ *n* **1.** the state of being a child, or the period of somebody's life when he or she is a child ○ *a happy childhood* **2.** an early period or stage in the development or existence of something ○ *Interplanetary travel is still in its childhood.*

childish /chíldish/ *adj* **1.** characteristic of or suitable for a child ○ *a childish voice* **2.** regarded as showing a lack of adult qualities such as emotional restraint, seriousness, or good sense ○ *childish behaviour* —**childishly** *adv* —**childishness** *n*

USAGE **childish** or **childlike**? Both words describe people or behaviour that have qualities associated with children. The difference is that *childlike* is complimentary and even affectionate (*childlike innocence*), whereas *childish* is a dismissive and disapproving term: *a childish tantrum.*

child labour *n* the full-time employment of children, especially of those who are legally too young to work

childless /chíldləss/ *adj* not having had children —**childlessness** *n*

child-lifting *n* S Asia the kidnapping of a child

childlike /chíld līk/ *adj* like a child, especially in having a sweet, innocent, unspoiled quality

USAGE See *childish*.

child minder *n* somebody who looks after other people's children in his or her own home, especially when the parents or guardians are working —**child minding** *n*

child prodigy *n* a child who possesses extraordinary abilities or talents, often equal to those of adults

childproof /chíld proof/ *adj* **1.** HARD FOR CHILD TO OPEN designed to be difficult for a child to open, tamper with, or damage ○ *a bottle with a childproof cap* **2.** MADE SAFE FOR CHILDREN made safe for young children to use or be in, e.g. through the removal of potential dangers and the addition of safety devices ○ *a childproof room* ■ *vt* (**-proofs**, **-proofing**, **-proofed**) MAKE SOMETHING SAFE FOR CHILDREN to make something safe for

children to use, or safe against damage or tampering by children

child protective services *npl US* a US government agency charged with the supervision and protection of children at risk from abuse and neglect, or the supervision and protection administered by it

children plural of **child**

Children's Panel *n* in Scotland, a hearing convened by representatives of the appropriate agencies to deal with a child who has committed a crime or is being mistreated by parents or guardians

child restraint *n* a seat belt or detachable seat designed to protect a child travelling in a vehicle or a plane

child seat *n* a detachable seat with a harness, attached to a car seat, used to protect a child too small to wear an adult seat belt

child's play *n* something that is very easy for somebody to do ○ *Skiing these slopes will be child's play for her.*

Child Support Agency *n* a government-sponsored agency whose task is to ensure that absent parents make an adequate financial contribution to their children's maintenance

Child Trust Fund *n* a savings and investment account set up for each child born in the United Kingdom after 1 September 2002, funded initially by a contribution from the government and available to the child at the age of 18

Chile

Chile /chílli/ country in southwestern South America bordered by Peru, Bolivia, Argentina, the Drake Passage, and the Pacific Ocean. Language: Spanish. Currency: peso. Capital: Santiago. Population: 15,665,216 (2003). Area: 756,626 sq. km/292,135 sq. mi. Official name **Republic of Chile** —**Chilean** *n*, *adj*

Chile nitre *n* CHEM same as **Chile saltpetre**

Chile pine *n* TREES same as **monkey puzzle**

Chile saltpetre *n* a form of sodium nitrate that occurs naturally in dry regions, especially in Chile and Peru. Formula: $NaNO_3$.

chili *n* FOOD, PLANTS US spelling of **chilli**

chiliasm /kílli azəm/ *n* CHR same as **millenarianism** (sense 1) [Early 17C. < Greek *khiliasmos* < *khilias* < *khilioi* 'one thousand'] —**chiliast** *n* —**chiliastic** /kílli ástik/ *adj*

chilidog /chílli dog/ *n* N Am a hot dog topped with chilli

chill /chil/ *n* 1. MODERATE COLDNESS a moderate but often unpleasant degree of coldness ○ *a chill in the air* 2. SUDDEN SHORT FEVER a sudden short fever with shivering and a sensation of coldness 3. COLDNESS CAUSED BY FEAR a sudden shuddering feeling of coldness caused by fear, anxiety, or excitement ○ *felt a chill run down my spine* 4. DEPRESSING EFFECT a depressing or dampening effect on people or on an occasion ○ *The news cast a chill over the party.* 5. LACK OF EMOTIONAL WARMTH an emotional coldness or unfriendliness in the atmosphere or in somebody's manner 6. METALL MOULD USED IN CASTING METAL a mould made of a highly conductive material such as iron, used to achieve a rapid even cooling when casting metal. The chill may be water-cooled to accelerate the process. ■ *adj* 1. MODERATELY COLD moderately cold, but usually cold enough to be unpleasant 2. EMOTIONALLY COLD showing no friendliness or emotional warmth ■ *v* (**chills, chilling, chilled**) 1. *vt* MAKE SOMEBODY OR SOMETHING COLD to make somebody or something cold, usually unpleasantly so ○ *a freezing draught that chilled me to*

the bone 2. *vti* COOL FOOD to cool food or drink in a refrigerator, or be left to cool there 3. *vt* BE DISCOURAGING TO SOMEBODY OR SOMETHING to have a discouraging or dampening effect on somebody or something 4. *vi* same as **chill out** (*informal*) 5. *vti* METALL HARDEN METAL, OR BECOME HARD to harden a metal surface, or become hard, by rapid cooling [Old English *ciele* < Germanic] —**chillness** *n*

chill out *vi* (*informal*) 1. to stop being inappropriately anxious or angry 2. to spend time relaxing

Chillán /chi yaán/ city in central Chile, situated 90 km/56 mi. northeast of Concepción. Population: 187,557 (1998).

chilled margin /child-/ *n* the edges of an igneous intrusion as it is cooled by contact with the surrounding colder rocks. The margin is marked by a zone of finer-grained crystals.

chiller /chíllər/ *n* 1. a refrigerated cooling or storage compartment 2. a frightening and suspenseful film or story (*informal*)

chill factor *n* METEOROL same as **wind-chill factor**

chilli /chílli/ (*plural* **-lies**) *n* 1. a narrow red or green hot-tasting pod produced by various types of capsicum pepper plant. Use: flavouring sauces and relishes. 2. FOOD same as **chilli powder** 3. FOOD same as **chilli sauce** 4. FOOD same as **chilli con carne** [Early 17C. Via Spanish *chile* < Nahuatl *chilli*]

SPELLCHECK **chilli** or **chilly**? Do not confuse the spelling of *chilli* and *chilly*, which sound similar. *Chilli* is a noun denoting a hot pepper, as in *chilli con carne*, *chilli powder*. *Chilly* is an adjective meaning 'cold', as in *chilly weather*, *a chilly reception*.

chilli con carne /-kon kaárni/ *n* a highly spiced dish made of chopped or minced meat and beans and usually tomatoes, seasoned with chillies or chilli powder [Mid-19C. < American Spanish, 'chilli with meat']

chilling /chílling/ *adj* causing a feeling of dread or horror ○ *a chilling account of his capture* —**chillingly** *adv*

chilli powder *n* a hot-tasting seasoning consisting of ground chillies blended with other seasonings such as cumin, garlic, and oregano

chilli sauce *n* a highly spiced sauce made with tomatoes, ground dried chillies, and other seasonings

chill-out area *n* an area set aside for quieter or more relaxed or restful activities, e.g. in a public place or club

chill-out zone *n* an area of a dance club where people can relax and where relatively quiet music is played (*informal*)

chillum /chílləm/ *n* a short straight pipe, usually made of clay, for smoking cannabis or tobacco [Late 18C. < Hindi *chilam*]

chilly /chílli/ (**-ier, -iest**) *adj* 1. MODERATELY COLD moderately or noticeably cold, usually enough to cause discomfort ○ *Bring a sweater to the park: it'll be chilly later.* 2. FEELING RATHER COLD feeling cold enough to be uncomfortable 3. SENSITIVE TO COLD prone to feeling cold or sensitive to the cold (*informal*) 4. UNFRIENDLY characterized by a lack of friendliness or by hostility ○ *a chilly reception* —**chillily** *adv* —**chilliness** *n*

SPELLCHECK See *chilli*.

chilly bin *n* NZ a portable insulated container for keeping food and drinks cold (*informal*) Same as **cool bag**

chilopod /kílə pod/ *n* an arthropod of the group that includes the centipedes (*technical*) [Mid-19C. < modern Latin *Chilopoda* < Greek *kheilos* 'lip']

Chiltern Hills /chíltərn-/ range of chalk hills in south-central England, running from Oxfordshire to Bedfordshire. The highest peak is Combe Hill, 260 m/852 ft.

Chiltern Hundreds *n* a nominal office that a Member of Parliament can apply for when wanting to resign from the House of Commons (*takes a singular verb*) [13C. After the CHILTERN HILLS]

Chi-lung /jee loóng/ seaport in northern Taiwan, one of the two ports of Taipei, the major city in Taiwan. Population: 382,118 (1999).

chimaera /kī méerə, ki-/ *n* 1. (*plural* **chimaeras** or *same*) a deep-sea fish with a skeleton of cartilage, a smooth-skinned tapering body, and a tail that resembles a whip. Family: Chimaeridae. 2. GENETICS, BIOCHEM another spelling of **chimera** [Early 19C. < Latin (see CHIMERA)]

Chimaera *n* MYTHOL another spelling of **Chimera**

chimb *n* another spelling of **chime**[2]

Chimborazo /chímbə raázō/ mountain peak in central Ecuador, and the highest point in the Cordillera Real. Height: 6,310 m/20,702 ft.

Chimbote /chim bố tee/ seaport in western Peru, situated at the mouth of the River Santa. Population: 314,700 (1991).

chime[1] /chīm/ *n* 1. SOUND OF BELL the musical ringing sound made by a bell or a set of bells, or a similar sound made by an object such as a doorbell 2. DEVICE FOR STRIKING BELL a device for striking a bell or a set of bells in order to make a musical sound or play a tune (*often used in the plural*) 3. NOTES SOUNDED BY CLOCK a series of musical notes sounded by a clock before striking ■ **chimes** *npl* MUSIC PERCUSSION INSTRUMENT a set of hanging bells, metal bars, or tubes tuned to a scale, used to produce a musical sound when struck ■ *v* (**chimes, chiming, chimed**) 1. *vi* RING MELODIOUSLY to make a melodious ringing sound ○ *Did you hear the bells chiming?* 2. *vt* INDICATE SOMETHING BY CHIMING to indicate something, especially the time, by chiming ○ *The clock chimed three o'clock.* 3. *vt* PRODUCE MUSICAL SOUND to strike a bell or bells so as to produce a musical sound 4. *vi* HARMONIZE to harmonize or be in agreement with something else ○ *Her opinion chimed perfectly with my own.* 5. *vti* SPEAK IN MUSICAL WAY to say something or speak in a rhythmic or musical way [13C. Origin ?] —**chimer** *n*

chime in *vi* 1. to interrupt or join in a conversation between other people, especially in order to voice an opinion 2. to agree or combine harmoniously with something else

chime[2] /chīm/, **chimb** *n* an edge or lip around the rim of a barrel or cask [14C. Probably < assumed Old English *cim*]

chimera /kī méerə, ki-/, **chimaera** *n* 1. SOMETHING TOTALLY UNREALISTIC OR IMPRACTICAL a wildly unrealistic idea or hope or a completely impractical plan 2. GENETICS ORGANISM WITH GENETICALLY DIFFERENT TISSUES an organism, or part of one, with at least two genetically different tissues resulting from mutation, the grafting of plants, or the insertion of foreign cells into an embryo 3. BIOL, BIOTECH ORGANISM WITH DNA FROM DIFFERENT SOURCES an organism that has genetic material from a variety of sources as a result of the insertion of unspecialized cells (**stem cells**) from other species into an embryo [See CHIMERA] —**chimerism** /kī méerizəm, kímərizəm/ *n*

Chimera /kī méerə, ki-/, **Chimaera** *n* 1. in Greek mythology, a female fire-breathing monster, typically represented as a combination of a lion's head, goat's body, and serpent's tail 2. an imaginary monster whose body is a grotesque combination of mismatched animal parts [14C. Via Latin *chimaera* < Greek *khimaira* 'she-goat']

chimeraplast /kī méerə plast/ *n* a hybrid molecule of DNA combined with RNA that is used to repair or modify genes during chimeraplasty

chimeraplasty /kī méerə plasti/ *n* a method of repair or modification of DNA in which a hybrid molecule of DNA combined with RNA is injected into an organism in order to target, bind with, and modify a specific gene —**chimeraplastic** /kī méerə plástik/ *adj*

chimeric /kī mérrik, ki-/ *adj* describes an organism that is composed of genetically different tissues, either naturally or as a result of a laboratory procedure

chimerical /kī mérrik'l, ki-/ *adj* 1. having no existence in reality or no likelihood of existing or happening 2. tending to indulge in unrealistic fantasies (*literary*) —**chimerically** *adv*

chiminea /chímmi náy ə, -née ə/, **chimenea** *n* a large rounded pot with a chimney and an opening in its side, used as a charcoal-burning stove for outdoor heating on patios and at barbecues [< Spanish, 'fireplace']

chimney /chímni/ (*plural* **-neys**) *n* 1. STRUCTURE FOR VENTING GAS OR SMOKE a hollow vertical structure, usually

made of brick or steel, that allows gas, smoke, or steam from a fire or furnace to escape into the atmosphere **2.** PART OF STRUCTURE RISING ABOVE ROOF the part of a chimney that rises above a roof **3.** SMOKE-VENTING PASSAGE INSIDE CHIMNEY a passage or pipe inside a chimney through which smoke or steam escapes **4.** ENG FUNNEL OF STEAM ENGINE a funnel on a railway engine or steamship. N Am term **smokestack 5.** CLIMBING CLEFT IN ROCK FACE a narrow vertical cleft in a rock face that is large enough for a climber to get inside and use as a means of ascending **6.** GLASS TUBE PROTECTING LAMP FLAME a tube, usually made of glass, used to enclose the flame of a lamp in order to promote burning and exclude draughts **7.** *UK, regional* FIREPLACE a large fireplace or hearth, especially one that is very old [13C. Via Old French *cheminée* < late Latin *caminata* < Latin *camera caminata* 'room with a fireplace' < Greek *kaminos* 'oven']

chimney breast *n* a projecting section of an interior wall surrounding a chimney or fireplace

chimney corner *n* a recessed seat, beside or within a large old-fashioned open fireplace

chimneypiece /chímni peess/ *n* BUILDINGS same as **mantelpiece**

chimney pot *n* a short earthenware or metal pipe placed on the top of a chimney in order to increase the draught

chimney stack *n* **1.** same as **chimney** (sense 2) **2.** a tall, often cylindrical, chimney attached to a factory or other large industrial building

chimney sweep *n* somebody whose job is removing soot from chimneys

chimp /chimp/ *n* VERTEB same as **chimpanzee** (*informal*) [Late 19C. Shortening]

chimpanzee

chimpanzee /chím pan zee/ *n* a medium-sized ape with long dark-brown hair covering its body except for its naked face and ears. Native to: equatorial Africa. Latin name: *Pan troglodytes* or *Pan paniscus*. [Mid-18C. Via French < Kikongo]

chin /chin/ *n* PART OF FACE the part of the face below the lips, including the usually protruding front portion of the lower jaw ■ *v* (**chins, chinning, chinned**) **1.** *vti* RAISE CHIN TO HIGH BAR to perform an exercise that involves hanging from a horizontal bar and pulling the body up by the arms until the chin is level with the bar **2.** *vt* PUNCH SOMEBODY ON CHIN to hit somebody on the chin or in the face (*slang*) [Old English *cin* < Germanic] ◇ **keep your chin up** to remain cheerful and hopeful in spite of difficulties or hardships (*informal*) ◇ **take it on the chin** to accept misfortune staunchly, without flinching (*informal*)

Ch'in *n* HIST another spelling of **Qin**

china /chínə/ *n* **1.** PORCELAIN porcelain or a similar high-quality translucent or white ceramic material **2.** THINGS MADE OF CHINA articles made of china, especially plates and decorative objects **3.** *Cockney* MATE a close and trusted friend [Late 16C. < Persian *čīnī* 'porcelain from China'. In sense 3 < *china plate*, rhyming slang for 'mate']

China /chínə/ country in East Asia, the largest in the world by population and the third largest in the world. Language: Modern Standard Chinese. Currency: yuan. Capital: Beijing. Population: 1,286,975,500 (2003). Area: 9,571,300 sq. km/3,695,500 sq. mi. Official name **People's Republic of China**

chinaberry /chínəbəri/ (*plural* -ries) *n* **1.** a deciduous tree of the mahogany family. Flowers: white or purple, in clusters. Use: in the United States, shade tree. Native to: Asia. Latin name: *Melia azedarach*. **2.** TREES same as **soapberry** (sense 2) **3.** a fruit produced by either the chinaberry or soapberry tree

china clay *n* MINERALS same as **kaolin**

Chinaman /chínəmən/ (*plural* -men /-mən/) *n* **1.** an offensive term for a man of Chinese origin (*dated*) **2.** in cricket, a slow off-break bowled by a left-handed bowler to a right-handed batsman

Chinan /chee nán/ ♦ **Jinan**

China

China rose *n* **1.** a rose that is the ancestor of many cultivated varieties. Flowers: fragrant, pink, red, or white. Native to: China. Latin name: *Rosa chinensis*. **2.** a hybrid garden rose derived from the China rose, especially a dwarf rose with crimson flowers. Latin name: *Rosa semperflorens*. **3.** PLANTS same as **hibiscus**

China Sea part of the Pacific Ocean extending from Japan to the southern end of the Malay Peninsula, and divided by Taiwan into the **East China Sea** and the **South China Sea**

china stone *n* finely ground granite stone. Use: porcelain, paper and pharmaceutical industries.

China syndrome *n* a hypothetical accident in which the core of a nuclear reactor melts, allowing the radioactive fuel to burn through the floor of its container and straight down into the ground [< the idea of the molten core sinking through the earth and reaching China]

China tea *n* a tea produced in China that makes a

light-coloured mild brew. China teas are sometimes smoke-cured and flavoured with flower petals.

Chinatown /chína town/ *n* an area of a city inhabited mainly by Chinese people and containing businesses owned by them or selling Chinese products

chinaware /chínə wair/ *n* plates, dishes, and other tableware made of china

Chinawoman /chína woomən/ (*plural* -women /-wimən/) *n* an offensive term for a woman of Chinese origin (*dated*)

chincherinchee /chínchə rínchi/ *n* a plant of the lily family. Flowers: large, fragrant. Native to: southern Africa. Latin name: *Ornithogalum thyrsoides*. [Early 20C. An imitation of the sound created when stalks are rubbed together]

chinchilla

chinchilla /chin chíllə/ (*plural* -las or same) *n* **1.** BUSHY-TAILED RODENT a squirrel-sized rodent with a bushy tail and large round ears. Kept for: fur. Native to: South America. Latin name: *Chinchilla laniger*. **2.** CHINCHILLA FUR the soft silvery-grey fur of a chinchilla **3.** WOOLLEN CLOTH a thick woollen fabric. Use: overcoats. [Early 17C. Via Spanish < Aymara or Quechua]

chin-chin /chín chín/ *interj* used as a greeting, a way of saying goodbye, or as a toast when drinking (*dated informal*) [Late 18C. < Chinese *qing qing*]

Chindit /chíndit/ *n* a soldier of the Allied forces in World War II, who fought behind the Japanese lines in Burma (now Myanmar) [Mid-20C. < Burmese *cinthé*, mythological lion-like creature used by the troops as their badge]

Chindwin /chín dwín/ tributary of the River Irrawaddy, in Myanmar (Burma). Length: 1,200 km/720 mi.

chine[1] /chīn/ n **1.** FOOD JOINT OF MEAT a cut of meat that includes part of the backbone **2.** NAUT BOTTOM CORNER OF BOAT the join between the bottom and sides of some boats, especially those with a flat or V-shaped bottom **3.** regional, S England RAVINE a deep ravine in a cliff wall ■ vt (**chines, chining, chined**) CUT MEAT FROM BACKBONE to cut meat along or across the backbone of a carcass [14C. < Old French eschine < Germanic ancestor of SHIN[1] + Latin spina 'spine']

chine[2] /chīn/ n same as **chime**[2] [15C. Alteration]

Chinese /chī nēez/ (plural same) n **1.** PEOPLES SOMEBODY FROM CHINA somebody who comes from China or whose family came from China **2.** LANG GROUP OF LANGUAGES SPOKEN IN CHINA a group of related Sino-Tibetan languages spoken across most of China and Taiwan, and by large communities elsewhere. Cantonese, Hokkien, and Modern Standard Chinese are the best-known members of the group. **3.** LANG OFFICIAL LANGUAGE OF CHINA the standard language of China and Taiwan and an official language of Singapore, also spoken by large communities elsewhere, that belongs to the Chinese group of Sino-Tibetan languages. Native speakers: 800 million. **4.** RESTAURANT SELLING CHINESE FOOD a restaurant or takeaway run by Chinese people and cooking food in styles from China (informal) **5.** CHINESE MEAL food or a meal from a Chinese restaurant (informal) ▶ See panel on previous page —**Chinese** adj

Chinese anise n PLANTS, FOOD same as **star anise** (sense 2)

Chinese boxes npl a set of matching boxes graduated in size so that each fits inside the next larger one, and as each opens it reveals another waiting to be opened

Chinese burn n a way of inflicting pain that involves grasping somebody's arm and using both hands to twist the skin in opposite directions

Chinese cabbage n **1.** a plant with a long head of overlapping wrinkled leaves and broad stalks, popular as a salad vegetable. Latin name: Brassica pekinensis. **2.** PLANTS same as **pak choi**

Chinese calendar n the traditional calendar used in China that divides the year into 24 fifteen-day periods and is based on both the lunar and solar cycles. It has five months containing 29 days, six months of 30 days, and one month of 20 or 30 days.

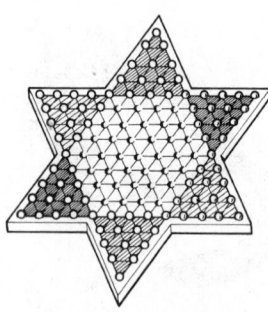

Chinese chequers

Chinese chequers n a game played on a board marked with a six-pointed star studded with small holes. Players move or jump marbles hole by hole towards an opposite point of the star. (takes a singular verb)

Chinese chestnut n a chestnut that is resistant to a blight that affects other chestnuts. Native to: China, Korea. Latin name: Castanea mollissima.

Chinese Empire n China during the rule of the emperors, beginning with the Qin dynasty in the 5th century BC and ending when the republic was established in 1911–12

Chinese gooseberry n PLANTS, FOOD same as **kiwi fruit**

Chinese lantern

Chinese lantern n **1.** a lantern with a collapsible covering made of thin brightly coloured paper supported by thin wires **2.** UK, ANZ, Can a plant with papery orange-red seed cases. Latin name: Physalis alkekengi. US term **winter cherry**

Chinese leaves npl same as **Chinese cabbage** (sense 1)

Chinese New Year n a festival day that falls between January 21 and February 19 and introduces two weeks of celebrations marking the new year

Chinese pheasant n BIRDS same as **ring-necked pheasant**

Chinese puzzle n a puzzle, either in the form of a game or a problem, that is extremely intricate, ingenious, and difficult to solve

Chinese red n a vivid red colour tinged with orange —**Chinese red** adj

Chinese restaurant syndrome n a group of symptoms, including dizziness, headache, palpitations, and sweating, experienced by some people after eating food containing monosodium glutamate, an ingredient often used in preparing Chinese dishes

Chinese wall n **1.** a strong or insurmountable barrier, especially one that obstructs the exchange of information **2.** a set of strict rules intended to prevent the exchange of confidential information that might be used illegally for gain between different departments of a stock-exchange business

Chinese water deer n a small deer without horns, the males of which have small tusks. Native to: China, Korea, naturalized in parts of the United Kingdom and France. Latin name: Hydropotes inermis.

Chinese water torture n a method of psychological torture in which water is persistently dripped onto the victim's forehead

Chinese whispers n a game in which people in a circle pass a message by whispering it into the ear of the person next to them, the message becoming increasingly distorted on the way (takes a singular verb)

Chinese wood block n a hollow slotted wooden block that, when struck, makes a sound similar to that of horses' hooves striking the ground

Chinese wood oil n INDUST same as **tung oil**

Ch'ing n HIST another spelling of **Qing**

chink[1] /chingk/ n NARROW OPENING a small narrow crack or slit ○ Sunlight was coming in through a chink in the curtains. ■ vt (**chinks, chinking, chinked**) **1.** N Am FILL CRACKS IN SOMETHING to fill up cracks or holes in something **2.** US MAKE CRACKS IN SOMETHING to make small cracks in something ○ A flying pebble chinked my car's windshield. [Early 16C. Origin ?] ◇ **a chink in somebody's armour** a slight weakness that makes somebody vulnerable to attack or exploitation, e.g. an aspect of their character or a point in their argument

chink[2] /chingk/ n a short sharp ringing sound, e.g. that of coins or glasses knocking against each other ■ vti (**chinks, chinking, chinked**) to make, or cause glass or metallic objects to make, a short sharp ringing sound ○ We chinked glasses and said a toast. [Late 16C. An imitation of the sound]

Chink /chingk/, **Chinky** /chíngki/ (plural **-ies**) n a highly offensive term for a Chinese person (taboo) [Late 19C. < CHINA]

chinkapin n TREES another spelling of **chinquapin**

chinks /chingks/ vi Carib to be ungenerous ○ Doh chinks wid de rum! [< chink 'small piece']

chinky /chíngki/ adj characterized by small narrow slits or cracks

Chinky n same as **Chink** (taboo)

chinless /chínləss/ adj **1.** having a lower jaw that recedes under the mouth instead of projecting in front of it **2.** lacking strength of character

chinless wonder n somebody, especially an upper-class man, who is considered weak or ineffectual (informal insult)

chin music n **1.** foolish or insignificant talk **2.** in cricket, short-pitched bowling aimed at a batsman's face and intended to intimidate [< the supposed sound of a ball passing close by somebody's face at speed]

chino /chēenō/ n a durable coarse cotton twill fabric, often khaki-coloured. Use: military uniforms, casual trousers. ■ **chinos** npl trousers made of chino [Mid-20C. < American Spanish, 'toasted'; from its original colour]

chinoiserie /shin wáazəri/ n **1.** a style of art and interior design that reflects Chinese influence **2.** an object or decoration in a style reflecting Chinese influence, or such objects and decorations collectively [Late 19C. < French < chinois 'Chinese']

chinook /chi nŏŏk/ n **1.** a moist warm wind that blows from the sea and affects weather along the coast of the northwestern United States **2.** a dry warm wind that blows down the eastern slopes of the Rocky Mountains [Mid-19C. < CHINOOK]

Chinook /chi nŏŏk/ (plural same or **-nooks**) n **1.** a member of a Native North American people who once lived in northwestern Oregon, and who now live in western Washington State **2.** the extinct Penutian language of the Chinook people [Early 19C. < Salish tsinúk] —**Chinook** adj

Chinook Jargon n a pidgin language, once used for trading along the western coast of North America, made up of words borrowed from Chinook, Nootka, various Salishan languages, French, and English

Chinook salmon n **1.** a large salmon found in the northern Pacific Ocean that spawns in the rivers of North America and northern Asia. Latin name: Oncorhyncus tshawytscha. **2.** FOOD the reddish flesh of a chinook salmon used as food

chinquapin /chíngkəpin/, **chinkapin** n **1.** EDIBLE NUT an edible chestnut from a North American tree **2.** SMALL DECIDUOUS TREE a small deciduous tree that produces chinquapins. Native to: eastern United States. Latin name: Castanea pumila. **3.** LARGE EVERGREEN TREE a large evergreen tree that produces chinquapins. Native to: western North America. Latin name: Castanopsis chrysophylla. [Early 17C. < Virginian Algonquian chechinquamin]

chinstrap /chín strap/ n a strap attached to a helmet or hat that passes under the chin and is intended to keep the helmet or hat from falling off

chintz /chints/ n a glazed cotton fabric usually printed with a brightly coloured pattern [Early 17C. Alteration of chints, plural of chint 'calico cloth' < Hindi chīt 'stain' < Sanskrit citra 'variegated']

chintzy /chíntsi/ (**-ier, -iest**) adj **1.** WITH BRIGHTLY COLOURED PATTERN brightly coloured and patterned, in a style associated with chintz fabric ○ chintzy curtains **2.** FUSSY OR QUAINT describes a fussy, quaint, or would-be genteel style of decor (informal) **3.** N Am TRASHY cheap and gaudy ○ Don't buy that chintzy suit; it'll fall apart the first time you have it cleaned. **4.** N Am PENNY-PINCHING unwilling to spend or share money ○ He's so chintzy about money.

chin-up n ANZ, N Am an exercise performed by hanging from a horizontal bar and pulling the body up until the chin has been raised above the bar. UK term **pull-up**

chinwag /chín wag/ n a chat or conversation, especially a long one (informal) —**chinwagger** n —**chinwagging** n

chionodoxa /kī ónnə dóksə/ (plural **-as** or same) n a hardy plant that grows from a bulb and flowers in early spring. Native to: Europe, Asia. Genus: Chionodoxa. [Late 19C. < modern Latin < Greek khíon 'snow' + doxa 'glory']

~~chior~~ incorrect spelling of **choir**

chip /chip/ *n* **1.** SMALL PIECE BROKEN OR CUT OFF a small piece that has been broken, chopped, or cut off something hard or brittle **2.** CRACK a space or crack left in something hard or brittle after a small piece has been broken off or out of it ○ *This cup has a chip in it.* **3.** LONG PIECE OF FRIED POTATO a long finger-shaped wedge of potato traditionally fried in deep fat (*usually used in the plural*) ○ *fish and chips* **4.** PIECE OF THIN CRISP SNACK FOOD a very thin crunchy slice of a starchy food, usually potato or maize, that has been fried until it is crisp ○ *corn chips* **5.** WAFER OF SEMICONDUCTOR MATERIAL a small wafer of semiconductor material, usually silicon, forming the base on which an integrated circuit is laid out, or such a wafer together with its integrated circuit **6.** COUNTER USED AS MONEY a token, often a small round plastic disc, used to represent money in poker and other gambling games **7.** SHORT LOFTED SHOT in various sports, a short hit, kick, or shot that is lofted into the air over an obstacle or another player's head **8.** WOOD CUT AS WEAVING MATERIAL wood, straw, or other material that has been dried and cut for use in weaving **9.** *N Am* DRIED DUNG a piece of dried animal dung, sometimes used for fuel ■ *v* (**chips, chipping, chipped**) **1.** *vt* BREAK SMALL PIECE OFF SOMETHING to break one or more small pieces from something hard or brittle **2.** *vi* LOSE SMALL PIECES to become damaged by having a small piece or small pieces break off ○ *paint that will not chip easily* **3.** *vt* HIT SOMETHING IN HIGH ARC to hit or kick a ball or puck so that it travels a short distance in a high arc **4.** *vi* MAKE CHIP SHOT in golf, to play a chip shot **5.** *vt* CARVE SOMETHING BY REMOVING SMALL PIECES to carve or shape something by cutting small pieces off or out of it **6.** *vt* CHOP SOMETHING INTO CHIPS to cut something up into chips ○ *Will you chip the ice for drinks?* [Pre-12C. < Latin *cippus* 'stake'] ◇ **a chip off the old block** somebody resembling his or her parents (*informal*) ◇ **have a chip on your shoulder** to feel inferior or badly treated and so act in an oversensitive and resentful manner (*informal*) ◇ **have had your chips** to fail, be defeated, or die (*informal*) ◇ **spit chips** *Aus* to be very angry (*slang*) ◇ **when the chips are down** at a time of crisis or when vital matters are at stake (*informal*)

chip away *v* **1.** *vti* to destroy, reduce, or make something weaker by gradually and persistently attacking it ○ *comments designed to chip away at my self-esteem* **2.** *vi* to break small pieces off something solid persistently and over a period of time

chip in *v* **1.** *vti* CONTRIBUTE to contribute something to a common fund or resource (*informal*) **2.** *vi* INTERRUPT to interrupt a conversation in order to make a comment (*informal*) **3.** *vi* PUT MONEY INTO POKER POOL in poker and other games, to put chips or money into the pool in order to play

chip basket *n* a wire basket used to hold food such as chips when frying in deep fat

chipboard /chíp bawrd/ *n* a construction material made from compressed wood chips held together by a synthetic resin and produced in the form of hard flat boards

Chipewyan /chíppə wī ən/ (*plural same* or **-ans**) *n* **1.** a member of a Native North American people who live in northern Saskatchewan, Manitoba, and the Northwest Territories. In the 18th century, they abandoned their nomadic life to settle and become fur traders. **2.** the Athabaskan language of the Chipewyan people. Native speakers: 8,000. [Late 18C. < Cree *cīpwayān* 'parka wearer' literally 'pointed-skin (wearer)'] —**Chipewyan** *adj*

chiphead /chíp hed/ *n* a skilled and enthusiastic user of computers (*slang*)

chip log *n* a wooden chip attached to a line marked off in measured sections that is thrown overboard in order to determine a ship's speed. The speed is calculated from the number of sections of line paid out in a period of 28 seconds.

chipmunk /chíp mungk/ (*plural* **-munks** or *same*) *n* a striped rodent of the squirrel family that lives on the ground, collects nuts and fruit, and stores food in cheek pouches. Native to: North America, Asia. Genera: *Tamias* or *Eutamias*. [Mid-19C. < Ojibwa *aji-damoon⁹* 'squirrel', literally 'one that comes down trees headlong']

chipolata /chíppə laátə/ *n* a small thin sausage, usually made of finely ground pork [Late 19C. Via

chipmunk

French < Italian *cipollata* 'with onions' < *cipolla* 'onion' < Latin *cepa*]

Chipp /chip/, **Don** (*b.* 1925) Australian politician. He was a Liberal government minister who resigned in order to found the centrist political party, the Australian Democrats (1977). Full name **Chipp, Donald Leslie**

chip pan *n* a deep pan, usually enclosing a wire basket, used for frying food, especially chips, in large quantities of oil or fat

Chippendale /chíppən dayl/ *adj* describes furniture in an 18th-century English style characterized by graceful flowing lines, cabriole legs, and elaborate ornamentation [After Thomas CHIPPENDALE] —**Chippendale** *n*

Chippendale /chíppən dayl/, **Thomas** (1718–79) British furniture designer. The influence of his neoclassical, increasingly eclectic style was spread through his book of designs, *The Gentleman and Cabinet Maker's Director* (1754).

chipper[1] /chíppər/ *adj* (*informal*) **1.** cheerful and full of vitality **2.** smartly dressed [Mid-19C. Origin ?]

chipper[2] /chíppər/ *n* a person or thing that chips or cuts [Early 16C. < CHIP]

Chippewa /chíppə waa/ *n* (*plural* **-was** or *same*), *adj* PEOPLES, LANG same as **Ojibwa** [Mid-18C. Alteration]

chippie *n* COMM, CONSTR another spelling of **chippy**[1] (*informal*)

chipping /chípping/ *n* same as **chip** *n* (sense 1) ■ **chippings** *npl* small stones used in surfacing roads

chippy[1] /chíppi/ (*plural* **-pies**), **chippie** (*informal*) **1.** a fish and chip shop **2.** CONSTR same as **carpenter** [Early 20C. < CHIP]

chippy[2] /chíppi/ (**-pier, -piest**) *adj Can* behaving in an aggressive or belligerent way [Late 19C < *have a chip on your shoulder*]

chipset /chíp set/, **chip set** *n* a group of microchips designed to perform one or more related functions as a unit, e.g. to update a computer screen display

chip shop *n* a shop that sells fried fish and chips and various other deep-fried foods

chip shot *n* **1.** in sports, a short-range kick or shot in which the ball or puck rises sharply into the air **2.** in golf, a short approach shot, used to loft the ball onto the green

Chirac /sheér ak/, **Jacques** (*b.* 1932) French politician. He was prime minister (1974–76 and 1986–88) and, after two unsuccessful attempts, was elected president in 1995 and again in 2002. Full name **Chirac, Jacques René**

chiral /kírəl/ *adj* describes a molecule whose arrangement of atoms is such that it cannot be superimposed on its mirror image [Late 19C. < Greek *kheir* 'hand'] —**chirality** /kī rálləti/ *n*

Chi-Rho /kí́ rő/ *n* a monogram and symbol for Jesus Christ, formed by superimposing the Greek letters *chi* (X) and *rho* (P) [< CHI[1] + RHO, the first two letters of Jesus Christ's name in Greek]

Chirico /kírrikō/, **Giorgio de** (1888–1978) Greek-born Italian painter. His metaphysical dreamscapes of 1910 onwards anticipated surrealism.

chiro-, cheiro- *prefix* hand ○ *chiromancy* [Via Latin < Greek *kheir*]

chirography /kī róggrəfi/ *n* ART same as **calligraphy** (sense 1)

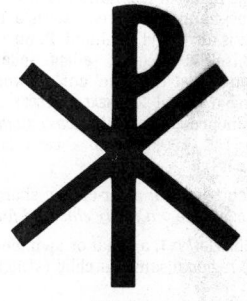

Chi-Rho

chiromancy /kī́rō manssi/ *n* PARANORMAL same as **palmistry** —**chiromancer** *n*

Chiron /kíron/ *n* in Greek mythology, the centaur, known for his great wisdom, who was the tutor of Greek heroes such as Heracles, Achilles, and Jason

chironomid /kī rónnəmid/ *n* a small nonbiting midge that gathers in large breeding swarms, especially near water. Family: Chironomidae. [Late 19C. < modern Latin *Chironomidae* < Greek *kheironomos* 'pantomime dancer']

chiropody /ki róppədi, shi-/ *n* UK, Can the branch of medicine concerned with the care and treatment of the feet. ANZ, US term **podiatry** —**chiropodist** *n*

chiropractic /kírō práktik/ *n* a medical system based on the theory that disease and disorders are caused by a misalignment of the bones, especially in the spine, that obstructs proper nerve functions [Late 19C. < CHIRO- + Greek *praktikos* 'effective'] —**chiropractor** /kírō praktər/ *n*

chiropteran /kī róptərən/, **chiropter** /kī róptər/ *n* a flying mammal with forelimbs that have evolved as membranous wings, e.g. a bat (*technical*) [Mid-19C. < modern Latin *Chiroptera* < CHIRO- + Greek *pteron* 'wing']

chiroptical /kī róptik'l/, **chiroptic** /kī róptik/ *adj* relating to the use of refraction, absorption, and emission of radiation in the study of chiral molecules [Late 20C. < CHIRAL + OPTICAL] —**chiroptically** *adv*

chirp /churp/ *n* SHORT HIGH-PITCHED SOUND a short high-pitched sound, especially as made by a bird ■ *v* (**chirps, chirping, chirped**) **1.** *vi* MAKE CHIRP to make a short high-pitched sound **2.** *vti* SPEAK IN CHEERFUL MANNER to speak, or say something, in a cheerful, lively, or pert voice [15C. An imitation of the sound]

chirpy /chúrpi/ (**-ier, -iest**) *adj* cheerful and lively (*informal*) —**chirpily** *adv* —**chirpiness** *n*

chirr /chur/ *n* a shrill harsh trilled sound made by insects such as grasshoppers ■ *vi* (**chirrs, chirring, chirred**) to make a harsh trilled sound [Early 17C. An imitation of the sound]

chirrup /chírrəp/ *v* (**-rups, -ruping, -ruped**) **1.** *vi* TWITTER to utter a series of chirps **2.** *vti* SPEAK IN HIGH CHEERFUL VOICE to speak or say something in a high-pitched voice, and in a cheerful and lively fashion **3.** *vi* MAKE ENCOURAGING CLUCKING SOUND to make a clucking sound with the lips, e.g. when encouraging a horse to move faster ■ *n* CHIRP a repeated series of chirping or clucking sounds [Late 16C. Alteration of CHIRP] —**chirrupy** *adj*

chisel

chisel /chízz'l/ *n* **1.** TOOL WITH FLAT BEVELLED BLADE a tool for cutting and shaping wood or stone, consisting of a straight flat bevelled blade with a sharp square-cut

bottom edge inserted in a handle. The chisel is often held in one hand and struck with a hammer or mallet, but is also used freehand. **2.** WOODWORK same as **cold chisel** ■ *vti* (**-els, -elling, -elled**) **1.** CARVE SOMETHING WITH CHISEL to carve, cut, or work wood or stone using a chisel **2.** CHEAT SOMEBODY to cheat or swindle somebody (*informal*) ○ *was caught chiselling customers* [14C. < Old French < Latin *caes*-, stem of *caedere* 'to cut']

chiselled /chízz'ld/ *adj* clear-cut or sharply defined in shape or profile ○ *a finely chiselled face*

chiseller /chízzlər/ *n* **1.** a cheat or swindler (*informal*) **2.** *Ireland, regional* same as **child** (*slang*) [Early 20C. Origin ?]

Chisholm /chízzəm/, **Caroline** (1808–77) British philanthropist. She was the creator of employment and welfare programmes for female immigrants to New South Wales, Australia.

Chişinău /kíshi nő/ city and capital of Moldova, situated on a tributary of the River Dniester, 145 km/90 mi. northwest of Odessa, Ukraine. Population: 770,000 (1995). Former name **Kishinev** (1940–91)

chi-square *n* a statistical calculation used to test how well the distribution of a set of observed data matches a theoretical probability distribution. The calculated value is equal to the sum of the squares of the differences divided by the expected values.

chi-square distribution *n* a probability function widely used in testing a statistical hypothesis such as the likelihood that a given statistical distribution of results might be reached in an experiment

chit[1] /chit/ *n* **1.** an official note or document, usually signed by somebody in authority, e.g. a receipt, order, or requisition form **2.** a note, bill, or any small slip of paper with writing on it, especially a statement of money owed for food or drink (*dated*) [Late 18C. Shortening of *chitty*, via Hindi *ciṭṭhī* < Sanskrit *citra* 'spot', referring to the writing]

chit[2] /chit/ *n* a child, girl, or young woman, especially one whose physical slightness seems to be at odds with an impertinent, forceful, or self-confident manner (*dated*) [14C. Origin ?]

chit[3] /chit/ (**chits, chitting, chitted**) *vt* to leave a potato in a light place to cause it to produce shoots before planting it in the ground [Early 17C. < dialect *chit* 'a shoot, sprout', probably < Germanic]

chital /cheet'l/ (*plural same* or **-tals**) *n* ZOOL same as **axis deer** [Late 19C. < Hindi *cittal* < Sanskrit *citrala* 'spotted']

chitchat /chít chat/ *n* casual conversation or small talk, or a casual conversation with somebody (*informal*) [Late 17C. Elaboration of CHAT] **—chitchat** *vi*

chitin /kítin/ *n* a tough semitransparent substance that forms part of the protective outer casing (**cuticle**) of some insects and other arthropods, and the cell walls of some fungi [Mid-19C. Via French *chitine* < Greek *khitōn* 'tunic'] **—chitinoid** *adj* **—chitinous** *adj*

chitlins /chítlins/, **chitlings** /-lings/ *npl Southern US* FOOD same as **chitterlings** [Mid-19C. Contraction]

chiton /kít'n, -ton/ *n* **1.** a small invertebrate sea animal that lives on rocks and has a long body protected by a shell consisting of eight overlapping plates. Class: Polyplacophora. **2.** a loose knee-length woollen tunic worn by women and men in ancient Greece [Early 19C. < Greek *khitōn* 'tunic']

chitosan /kíta san/ *n* a substance derived from the chitin of crab, lobster, and other crustaceans. Use: to stop bleeding and encourage healing; as a moisturizer and dietary supplement. [Late 19C. < CHITIN + -OSE[2] + -AN[2]]

Chittagong /chítta gong/ chief port of Bangladesh and an important industrial city, situated on the southeastern coast of the country. Population: 1,566,070 (1991).

chitter /chíttər/ (**-ters, -tering, -tered**) *vi regional, Scotland* to chatter or shiver with cold [12C. An imitation of the sound of teeth chattering]

chittering /chíttəring/ *n regional* an act of nagging at or scolding somebody

REGIONAL NOTE See *jawing*.

chitterlings /chíttərlingz/ *npl* the small intestines of

pigs, especially when prepared as food [13C. Origin ?]

chivalric /shívv'lrik/ *adj* relating to knights, knighthood, and the knightly code of honour

chivalrous /shívv'lrəss/ *adj* **1.** relating to or reflecting the values of the medieval code of knighthood, especially courtesy, self-sacrifice, and a sense of fair play **2.** describes men, or men's behaviour, characterized by consideration and courtesy, especially towards women **—chivalrously** *adv* **—chivalrousness** *n*

chivalry /shívv'lri/ *n* **1.** QUALITIES OF IDEAL KNIGHT the combination of qualities expected of the ideal medieval knight, especially courage, honour, loyalty, and consideration for others, especially women **2.** CHIVALROUS BEHAVIOUR considerate and courteous behaviour, especially shown by a man towards women **3.** MEDIEVAL KNIGHTHOOD the medieval concept of knighthood, and the customs, practices, social system, and religious and personal ideals associated with knights and their way of life **4.** GROUP OF KNIGHTS knights, noblemen, or armed mounted soldiers, collectively or in a group (*archaic*) [13C. Via Old French *chevalerie* < medieval Latin *caballerius* < Latin *caballus* 'horse']

chive[1] /chīv/ *n* **1.** a long fine hollow leaf with a strong onion flavour. Use: for seasoning food. (*usually used in the plural*) **2.** a plant that produces chives. Flowers: purple, ball-shaped. Latin name: *Allium schoenoprasum*. [14C. Via French < Latin *cepa* 'onion']

chive[2] /chīv/ *n, vt* ARMS same as **shiv** (*slang*)

chivvy /chívvi/ (**-vies, -vying, -vied**), **chivy** (**-ies, -ying, -ied**), **chevy** /chévvi/ *vt* to urge, pester, or harass somebody, usually in order to make him or her do something or do something more quickly [Late 18C. Probably after *Chevy Chase*, site of a battle (1388) in the Anglo-Scottish border wars]

chlamydes CLOTHING plural of **chlamys**

chlamydia /klə míddi ə/ (*plural* **-as** or *same* or **-ae** /-ee/) *n* **1.** a sexually transmitted disease, the most common in developed countries, caused by the bacterium *Chlamydia trachomatis*. Often producing no symptoms, it can cause infertility, chronic pain, or a tubal pregnancy if left untreated. **2.** a spherical bacterium that causes several eye and urogenital diseases in humans and other animals, and psittacosis in pet birds. Genus: *Chlamydia*. [Mid-20C. < modern Latin < Greek *khlamud-* 'mantle']

chlamydial /kləmíddi əl/ *adj* describes infections that are caused by a bacterium of the genus *Chlamydia*, e.g. trachoma and sexually transmitted infections such as urethritis

chlamydospore /klə míddə spawr/ *n* an asexual thick-walled spore produced by some fungi. It is capable of remaining dormant for long periods and surviving adverse conditions. [Late 19C. < Greek *khlamud-*, stem of *khlamus* 'mantle']

chlamys /klámmiss, kláy-/ (*plural* **-yses** or **-ydes** /-i deez/) *n* a short cloak gathered and fastened at the shoulder, worn by men in ancient Greece [Late 17C. < Greek *khlamus* 'mantle']

chloasma /klō ázmə/ *n* dark coloration on the skin of the face caused by hormonal changes related to pregnancy, liver disease, or the use of birth control pills. It is made worse by sunlight. [Mid-19C. < Greek *khloazein* 'become green']

chlor- *prefix* same as **chloro-** (*used before vowels*)

chloracne /klawr ákni/ *n* a skin eruption resembling acne caused by repeated contact with something containing chlorinated hydrocarbons

chloral /kláwrəl/ *n* a colourless oily toxic liquid with a strong odour. Use: manufacture of chloral hydrate and DDT. Formula: CCl_3CHO.

chloral hydrate *n* a colourless crystalline solid that is soluble in water. Use: sedative, hypnotic. Formula: $C_2H_3Cl_3O_2$.

chlorambucil /klawr ámbyəsil/ *n* a drug that is toxic to cells. Use: cancer treatment. [Mid-20C. Shortening of its chemical name *'4-p-di-(2-chloroethyl)amino-phenylbutyric acid'*]

chloramine /kláwrə meen/ *n* an unstable colourless liquid with a pungent odour. Use: manufacture of hydrazine. Formula: NH_2Cl.

chloramphenicol /kláwr am fénni kol/ *n* a powerful antibiotic derived from a soil bacterium. It sometimes has the side effect of causing the failure of blood cell production. [Mid-20C. < CHLOR- + AMIDE + PHEN- + NITRO- + GLYCOL]

chlorate /kláwr ayt/ *n* any salt of chloric acid [Early 19C. < CHLORIC]

chlordane /kláwr dayn/, **chlordan** /-dan/ *n* a thick toxic colourless to amber-coloured liquid that can exist with several different molecular structures (**isomers**). Use: insecticide, fumigant. Formula: $C_{10}H_6Cl_8$. [Mid-20C. < CHLOR- + INDENE + -ANE]

chlordiazepoxide /kláwr dī azzə póksīd/ *n* a yellow crystalline powder. Use: tranquillizer, treatment for alcoholism. Formula: $C_{16}H_{14}ClN_3O$. [Mid-20C. < CHLOR- + DI-[1] + AZO-[1] + EPI- + OXIDE]

chlorella /klə réllə/ *n* a single-celled green alga that is often used in research. Genus: *Chlorella*. [Early 20C. < modern Latin, 'little green (thing)' < Greek *khlōros* 'green']

chlorenchyma /klə réngkimə/ *n* plant tissue that contains chloroplasts, found mainly in leaves [Late 19C. < CHLOROPHYLL]

chloric /kláwrik/ *adj* containing chlorine, especially with a valency of five [Early 19C. < CHLORINE]

chloric acid *n* a toxic unstable acid, known only in solution and as chlorate salts. Formula: $HClO_3$.

chloride /kláwr īd/ *n* a compound containing chlorine and one other element [Early 19C. < CHLORINE] **—chloridic** /klə ríddik/ *adj*

chloride of lime *n* a powder used as a bleach

chloride shift *n* the reversible exchange of bicarbonate and chloride ions from blood serum to red cells during the transport of carbon dioxide

chlorinate /kláwri nayt/ (**-nates, -nating, -nated**) *vt* to combine or treat something with chlorine, especially in order to kill harmful organisms **—chlorinated** *adj* **—chlorination** /kláwri náysh'n/ *n* **—chlorinator** *n*

chlorine /kláwr een/ *n* a gaseous poisonous corrosive greenish-yellow element of the halogen group that is highly reactive and is a product of the electrolysis of sodium chloride. Use: water purification, disinfectant. See table at **element** [Early 19C. < Greek *khlōros* 'green']

chlorite[1] /kláwr īt/ *n* a soft green or black aluminosilicate mineral. Source: metamorphic rocks. [Late 18C. Via Latin < Greek *khlōritis*, green precious stone]

chlorite[2] /kláwr īt/ *n* any salt of chlorous acid [Mid-19C. < CHLORINE]

chloro- *prefix* **1.** green ○ *chlorophyll* **2.** chlorine ○ *chlorobenzene* [< Greek *khlōros* 'green']

chlorobenzene /kláwrō bén zeen/ *n* a combination of chlorine and benzene that produces a colourless flammable liquid smelling of almonds. Use: production of solvents and DDT. Formula: C_6H_5Cl.

chlorofluorocarbon /kláwrō floorō kaárbən, -flawrō-/ *full form of* **CFC**

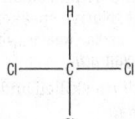

chloroform

chloroform /kláwrə fawrm/ *n* a colourless sweet-smelling toxic liquid that rapidly changes to a vapour and causes unconsciousness if inhaled. It is now known to have damaging effects on the ozone layer. Use: formerly, solvent, cleaning agent, anaesthetic. Formula: $CHCl_3$. ■ *vt* to make a person or animal breathe in chloroform in order to cause unconsciousness [Mid-19C. < CHLORO- + FORMIC]

chloromethane /kláwrō meé thayn/ *n* CHEM same as **methyl chloride**

chlorophyll /klórrəfil/ *n* the pigment in plants that captures the light energy required for photosynthesis. In plants and algae, chlorophyll is contained within numerous minute membranous sacs (**chloroplasts**) within cells of the stems and leaves. —**chlorophyllous** /klórrə fílləss/ *adj*

chloropicrin /kláwrə píkrin/ *n* a colourless toxic liquid that causes tears and vomiting. Use: tear gas, insecticide, disinfectant, in dyes. Formula: CCl_3NO_2. [Mid-19C. < CHLORO- + PICRO-]

chloroplast /kláwrə plast, -plaast/ *n* a membranous sac (**plastid**) that contains chlorophyll and other pigments and is the place where photosynthesis occurs within the cells of plants and algae. While plant cells contain numerous chloroplasts, algal cells often have just one. Each consists of interconnected stacks of disc-shaped membranes in fluid, surrounded by a double membrane. —**chloroplastic** /kláwrə plástik/ *adj*

chloroprene /kláwrə preen/ *n* a colourless liquid. Use: manufacture of neoprene. Formula: C_4H_5Cl. [Mid-20C. < CHLORO- + ISOPRENE]

chloroquine /kláwrə kween/ *n* a bitter-tasting crystalline substance. Use: treatment of malaria and amoebiasis. [Mid-20C. < CHLORO- + QUINOLINE, from which it is derived]

chlorosis /klə rṓssiss/ *n* **1.** a yellowing or whitening of a plant's leaves and stems caused by a lack of chlorophyll **2.** severe iron-deficiency anaemia that produces a greenish tint in the skin —**chlorotic** /-róttik/ *adj* —**chlorotically** *adv*

chlorothiazide /kláwrō thī́ ə zīd/ *n* a drug that relieves fluid retention. Use: treatment of high blood pressure, swelling, and heart failure.

chlorous /kláwrəss/ *adj* relating to or containing chlorine with a valency of three [Mid-19C. < CHLORINE]

chlorpromazine /klawr prṓmə zeen/ *n* a drug. Use: sedative and tranquillizing treatment of psychiatric disorders. [Mid-20C. < CHLOR- + PROMETHAZINE]

chlorpropamide /klawr próppə mīd, -prṓpə-/ *n* a drug that lowers blood sugar. Use: treatment of diabetes. [Mid-20C. < CHLOR- + PROPANE + AMIDE]

chlortetracycline /klawr téttrə sī́klin, -kleen/ *n* an antibiotic drug. Source: soil bacterium. Use: treatment of infections, stimulation of growth in livestock.

ChM *abbr* Master of Surgery

cho /cho/ *interj* used to express disappointment, impatience, scorn, or annoyance (*slang; used in Black English*) [Mid-20C. Natural exclamation]

choc /chok/ *n* a chocolate-covered sweet, especially one from a box of chocolates (*informal*) [Late 19C. Shortening]

chocaholic *n* another spelling of **chocoholic**

chocalate incorrect spelling of **chocolate**

choccy /chóki/ (*plural* **-cies**) *n* chocolate or a chocolate-covered sweet (*informal*) ○ *a box of choccies* [Shortening]

choc ice *n* a small block of ice cream coated in a thin layer of chocolate

chock /chok/ *n* **1.** BLOCK TO STOP SOMETHING MOVING a block of wood or metal used to prevent a wheel from turning, an object from moving, or to support something when it is raised off the ground **2.** SHIP'S FITMENT FOR SECURING CABLES a heavy metal fitment attached to the deck of a ship that has two inward-curving horn-shaped projections around which a cable can be secured **3.** METAL ANCHOR FOR CLIMBING a metal device used to provide anchoring systems for climbing or caving ■ *vt* USE CHOCK FOR BRACE to keep something from turning, moving, or falling by using a chock to block or brace it ○ *chock the plane's wheels* [14C. Probably < Old French *ço(u)che* 'log']

chocka *adj* another spelling of **chocker** (*slang*)

chock-a-block *adj* **1.** so crammed with things or crowded with people as to make it almost impossible to get anything or anybody else in or to move about (*informal*) **2.** having the two blocks in a block and tackle tight up against each other [Mid-19C. Alteration of *chock and block* (nautical) 'with pulleys drawn close together']

chocker /chókər/, **chocka** /chókə/ *adj* **1.** same as **chock-a-block** (sense 1) (*slang*) **2.** completely full up after eating (*slang*) **3.** very fed up or irritated (*dated slang*) ○ *I'm chocker with all this work.* [Mid-20C. Shortening of CHOCK-A-BLOCK]

chockers /chókərz/ *adj* Aus same as **chock-a-block** (sense 1) (*slang*)

chock-full *adj* crammed with something (*informal*)

chocoholic /chókə hóllik/, **chocaholic** *n* a lover of chocolate who is apparently addicted to it (*humorous*) [Late 20C. < CHOCOLATE + -AHOLIC]

chocolate /chóklit/ *n* **1.** SMOOTH SWEET BROWN FOOD a food or flavouring, typically a smooth sweet brown solid, made from roasted and ground cacao seeds usually sweetened and mixed with cocoa butter and dried milk. Chocolate is made into bars or sweets, or used to flavour other foods, especially cakes, desserts, sauces, and biscuits. (*often used before a noun*) ○ *a bar of chocolate* ○ *chocolate cake* **2.** SWEET COVERED IN CHOCOLATE a small sweet coated in chocolate, with a hard or soft centre **3.** CHOCOLATE DRINK a drink, usually served hot or warm, made from sweetened powdered chocolate mixed with water or milk **4.** BROWN COLOUR a deep warm brown colour [Early 17C. Directly or via French < Spanish < Nahuatl *chocolatl* 'bitter water'] —**chocolate** *adj* —**chocolatey** *adj*

chocolate-box *adj* depicting pretty scenes or pretty people in a stereotypical and usually sentimental or romanticized way ○ *chocolate-box portraits*

chocolate chip *n* a small piece of chocolate, used especially in making biscuits and desserts ○ *chocolate chip cookies*

chocolate tree *n* TREES same as **cacao** (sense 2)

chocolatier /chókə látti ər/ *n* a maker or seller of chocolates [Late 19C. < French < *chocolate* (see CHOCOLATE)]

Choctaw /chók taw/ (*plural same* or **-taws**) *n* **1.** a member of a Native North American people who once lived in central and southern Mississippi, and who now live mainly in Oklahoma and southern Mississippi. The Choctaw were one of the Five Civilized Nations who, under the Removal Act of 1830, were sent to live on reservations in Oklahoma. **2.** the Muskogean language of the Choctaw. Native speakers: 10,000. [Early 18C. < Choctaw *čahta*] —**Choctaw** *adj*

choice /choyss/ *n* **1.** ACT OF CHOOSING SOMETHING OR SOMEBODY a decision to choose one thing, person, or course of action in preference to others ○ *Think very carefully before you make a choice.* **2.** POWER TO CHOOSE the chance or ability to choose between different things ○ *They gave us no choice.* **3.** SELECTION OF THINGS a variety of things, people, or possibilities from which to choose ○ *a wide choice of styles and colours* **4.** CHOSEN OBJECT a person, thing, or course of action chosen by somebody from among a range of possibilities ○ *Red would not have been my choice.* **5.** BEST PART the best or most desirable part ■ *adj* (**choicer, choicest**) **1.** HIGH-QUALITY of particularly good quality **2.** RUDE OR EMPHATIC carefully chosen for effectiveness and usually expressing displeasure or dislike in a sufficiently emphatic way (*used euphemistically*) ○ *a few choice words* [13C. < Old French *chois* < *choisir* 'choose' < Germanic] —**choiceness** *n* ◇ **of choice** chosen from among several as being the best or most suitable ○ *the newspaper of choice*

choiceboard /chóyss bawrd/ *n* a program used on the Internet that allows consumers and online companies to communicate in real time

choir /kwīr/ *n* **1.** GROUP OF SINGERS an organized group of singers who perform together, typically combining smaller groups of singers who sing different parts at different pitches (*takes a singular or plural verb*) **2.** AREA FOR CHURCH CHOIR the part of a church where the choir performs **3.** INSTRUMENT GROUP a group of instruments of the same type **4.** MUSIC same as **choir organ** [13C. Via Old French *quer* < Latin *chorus* (see CHORUS)]

choirboy /kwī́r boy/ *n* a boy who sings in a church choir

choirgirl /kwī́r gurl/ *n* a girl who sings in a church choir

choir loft *n* a raised gallery or part of the upper storey in a church where the choir performs during services

choirmaster /kwī́r maastər/ *n* a trainer and conductor of a choir

choir organ *n* a manual organ or section of a large organ with sets of soft-toned pipes suitable for accompanying a choir

choir school *n* a school where the members of a cathedral or church choir are educated and attend ordinary lessons as well as receiving special musical training

choir stalls *npl* enclosed seats or pews in the chancel of a church, reserved for the members of the choir

choke[1] /chōk/ *v* (**chokes, choking, choked**) **1.** *vi* STOP BREATHING THROUGH BLOCKAGE OF THROAT to stop breathing, or breathe with great difficulty, because of a blockage in or restriction of the throat **2.** *vt* CONSTRICT THROAT OF SOMEBODY to prevent somebody from breathing by blocking or squeezing the throat **3.** *vt* BLOCK PASSAGE OR CHANNEL to form an obstruction in a passage, channel, pipe, or roadway and prevent anything from passing along it **4.** *vt* PREVENT PLANTS FROM GROWING to prevent plants from developing by growing over them and depriving them of light and air ○ *The bed was choked with weeds.* **5.** *vti* BECOME TOO MOVED TO SPEAK to be overcome with emotion and unable to speak, or make somebody feel so much emotion that he or she cannot speak (*informal*) **6.** *vi* LOSE NERVE AND FALTER to lose nerve or confidence and falter in the middle of saying or doing something (*informal*) ○ *He gets ahead, two sets to one, and then he chokes!* **7.** *vi* US REFUSE TO COOPERATE to refuse to cooperate when presented with something unacceptable (*informal*) ○ *We choked on their last demand.* ■ *n* **1.** NOISE OF CHOKING a sound or movement made by somebody choking **2.** FUEL MIXTURE REGULATOR FOR ENGINE a device that controls the ratio of air to fuel in the mixture supplied to an internal-combustion engine ○ *pull the choke out* [Old English *āceōcian* < *cēoce* 'cheek'] —**choking** *adj*

choke back *vt* to stop the expression of an emotional response to something by a deliberate effort of self-control ○ *I couldn't choke back my tears any longer.*

choke off *vt* to stop the flow, supply, or development of something, usually abruptly

choke up *vti* same as **choke**[1] *v* (sense 5) ○ *I should have said thank-you, but I choked up completely when I saw everyone there.*

choke[2] /chōk/ *n* the bristly inner inedible part of an artichoke [Shortening]

chokeberry /chṓkbəri/ *n* **1.** (*plural* **chokeberries**) a small bitter red or purplish fruit **2.** (*plural* **chokeberries** or *same*) a bush that bears chokeberries. Flowers: small, white or pink. Native to: North America. Genus: *Aronia*. [Late 18C. < the bitterness of the fruit]

chokebore /chṓk bawr/ *n* **1.** a shotgun bore that tapers towards the muzzle to prevent wide scattering of the shot **2.** a shotgun with a bore that tapers towards the muzzle

choke chain *n* a chain serving as a collar and short lead that fits in a sliding loop around an animal's neck, so that when the animal pulls away the chain gets tighter. Choke chains are used in obedience training for dogs and to restrain powerful animals.

chokecherry /chṓk cheri/ *n* **1.** (*plural* **chokecherries**) a dark red or black bitter fruit of a wild cherry **2.** (*plural* **chokecherries** or *same*) a wild cherry tree that bears chokecherries. Flowers: small, white, in clusters. Native to: North America. Latin name: *Prunus virginiana*.

choke coil *n* an induction coil used to limit or suppress the flow of alternating current without stopping the flow of direct current

choke collar *n* VET same as **choke chain**

choked /chōkt/ *adj* overcome by emotion, usually tenderness, unhappiness, or disappointment (*informal*) US term **choked up**

chokedamp /chṓk damp/ *n* MIN EXTRACT same as **blackdamp**

choked up *adj* N Am same as **choked** (*informal*)

chokehold /chṓk hōld/ *n* a tight hold in which one person restrains another by placing an arm round his or her neck, usually from behind

choke point *n* **1.** AREA OF BLOCKAGE a congested or narrow part where a blockage can occur **2.** NARROW SHALLOW

SEA CORRIDOR a place at sea where geography and water depth combine to create a narrow shallow corridor for submarines and surface ships **3.** *N Am* **STICKING POINT** a point or situation that is an obstacle to an agreement or results in an impasse ○ *amnesty being the choke point in the political settlement*

choker /chṓkər/ *n* **1.** a short length of cloth or ribbon, or a short necklace, that fastens closely around the neck and is worn as an ornament **2.** a high close-fitting collar, e.g. a clerical collar

choke route *n* COMPUT a computer firewall that isolates an internal network from the Internet

chokey *n* CRIME another spelling of **choky**

choko /chṓkō/ (*plural* **-kos**) *n* ANZ a light-green pear-shaped tropical fruit of the chayote plant that tastes like a cucumber and is eaten as a vegetable in Australia, New Zealand, and the Caribbean [Early 20C. Via Spanish < a Native S American language]

chokra /chṓkrə/ *n* S Asia an offensive term for a boy, especially one who works as a servant [Late 19C. < Hindi]

choky /chṓki/, **chokey** *n* CRIME same as **prison** (*dated slang*) ○ *three months in choky* [Early 17C. < Hindi *caukī* 'lock-up', influenced by CHOKE¹]

cholangiography /kō lánji ógrəfi/ *n* X-ray examination of the bile ducts to check for obstructions, carried out after the patient has swallowed a substance that shows up on an X-ray [Mid-20C. < CHOLE-] —**cholangiogram** /kō lánji ə gram/ *n* —**cholangiographic** /-ə gráffik/ *adj*

chole- *prefix* bile, bile ducts, gallbladder ○ *cholelithiasis* [< Greek *kholē* < Indo-European, 'yellow-coloured']

cholecalciferol /kṓlə kal síffərol, kóllə-/ *n* UK, ANZ, Can a form of vitamin D found naturally in fish-liver oils and egg yolks. US term **vitamin D₃**

cholecyst /kṓlə sist, kóllə-/ *n* ANAT same as **gallbladder** (*technical*)

cholecystectomy /kṓlə si stéktəmi, kóllə-/ (*plural* **-mies**) *n* a surgical operation to remove the gall bladder

cholecystitis /kṓlə si stī tiss, kóllə-/ *n* inflammation of the gall bladder, usually caused by a bacterial infection or gallstones

cholecystography /kṓlə si stóggrəfi, kóllə-/ (*plural* **-phies**) *n* X-ray examination of the gall bladder after the patient has swallowed a substance that shows up on an X-ray

cholecystokinin /kṓlə sistə kínin, kóllə-/ *n* a hormone secreted by cells at the top of the small intestine that stimulates the gall bladder, making it contract and release bile [Early 20C. < CHOLECYST + KININ]

cholelithiasis /kṓlə li thī əssiss, kóllə-/ *n* the formation or presence of gallstones in the gall bladder or bile ducts

choler /kóllər/ *n* **1.** anger or bad temper (*literary or archaic*) **2.** one of the four basic fluids (**humours**) of the body according to medieval medicine, thought to make somebody whose body contained too much of it prone to anger and irritability [14C. Via French *colère* < Latin *cholera* 'bile' (see CHOLERA)]

cholera /kóllərə/ *n* an acute and often fatal intestinal disease that produces severe gastrointestinal symptoms and is usually caused by the bacterium *Vibrio cholerae* [14C. Via Latin, 'illness caused by bile' < Greek *kholera* < *kholē* 'bile'] —**choleraic** /kóllə ráy ik/ *adj* —**choleroid** *adj*

choleric /kóllərik/ *adj* showing or tending to show anger or irritation (*literary*) [14C. Directly and via French < Latin *cholericus* 'bilious' < Greek *kholera* (see CHOLERA)] —**cholerically** *adv*

cholestasis /kṓli stáyssiss, -stássiss, kólli-/ *n* a stoppage or slowing of the flow of bile

cholesteatoma /kṓli stee ə tṓmə, kólli-/ *n* a potentially dangerous condition of the middle ear in which a mass of cholesterol and skin scales forms, grows, and invades the local structures, including bone

cholesterol

cholesterol /kə léstə rol/ *n* a steroid alcohol (**sterol**) made by the liver and present in all animal cells. Cholesterol is important to the body as a constituent of cell membranes, and is involved in the formation of bile acid and some hormones. Formula: $C_{27}H_{45}OH$. [Late 19C. < CHOLE- + Greek *stereos* 'stiff']

cholestyramine /kóli steérə meen, kō léstər ámmeen/ *n* a synthetic resin that binds cholesterol with bile acids. Use: to lower blood cholesterol. [Mid-20C. < CHOLE- + STYRENE + -AMINE]

choli /chṓli/ (*plural* **-lis**) *n* S Asia a short fitted top with short sleeves, worn underneath a sari [Early 20C. < Hindi *colī*]

choline /kṓ leen/ *n* a soluble compound (**amine**) found in animal and plant tissue that is involved in fat transportation and the formation of acetylcholine. Formula: $C_5H_{15}NO_2$. [Mid-19C. < CHOLE-]

cholinergic /kóli núrjik/ *adj* **1.** describes nerves that are activated by acetylcholine or that release it **2.** describes drugs that act like acetylcholine [Mid-20C. < CHOLINE + Greek *ergon* 'work'] —**cholinergically** *adv*

cholinesterase /kṓli néstə rayss, -rayz/ *n* BIOCHEM same as **acetylcholinesterase** [Mid-20C. < CHOLINE + ESTERASE]

cholla /chóy ə/ (*plural* **-las** or *same*) *n* a cactus that has cylindrical stem segments and yellow spines. Flowers: vividly coloured in some cultivated types. Native to: southwestern United States, Mexico. Genus: *Opuntia*. [Mid-19C. Via Mexican Spanish < obsolete Spanish, 'top of the head']

Cholula /chə loólə/ town in Puebla State, central Mexico, situated 13 km/8 mi. west of the city of Puebla. Population: 99,794 (2000).

cho-man *interj* same as **cho** (*slang; used in Black English*)

chometz *n* JUDAISM another spelling of **chametz**

chomp /chomp/, **chump** /chump/ (*informal*) *vti* (**chomps, chomping, chomped; chumps, chumping, chumped**) CHEW NOISILY to take big bites of food and chew steadily, noisily, and with obvious satisfaction ■ *n* **1.** NOISY BITE a big noisy bite into something **2.** SOUND OF BITE the sound made by noisy energetic biting or chewing [Mid-17C. Variant of CHAMP¹]

Chomsky /chómski/, **Noam** (*b.* 1928) US linguist. He is known for his transformational-generative grammar, which revolutionized linguistics, and for his political writings. Full name **Chomsky, Avram Noam**

> 'As soon as questions of will or decision or reason or choice of action arise, human science is at a loss.'
> [Noam Chomsky, *Listener*; 30 March 1978]

chon /chon/ (*plural same*) *n* a subunit of currency in North and South Korea. See table at **currency** [Mid-20C. < Korean]

chondr- *prefix* same as **chondro-** (*used before vowels*)

chondral /kóndrəl/ *adj* relating to or consisting of cartilage

chondri- *prefix* same as **chondro-**

chondrify /kóndri fī/ (**-fies, -fying, -fied**) *vti* to change tissue into cartilage, or be changed into cartilage [Late 19C. < Greek *khondros* 'cartilage'] —**chondrification** /kóndrifi káysh'n/ *n*

chondrite /kón drīt/ *n* a stony meteorite that contains spherical masses (**chondrules**) of mainly silicate

minerals [Mid-19C. < Greek *khondros* 'granule'] —**chondritic** /kon dríttik/ *adj*

chondro- *prefix* **1.** cartilage ○ *chondrocranium* **2.** granule ○ *chondrule* [< Greek *khondros*]

chondrocranium /kón drō kráy ni əm/ (*plural* **-niums** or **-nia** /-ni ə/) *n* the part of an embryo's skull that consists of cartilage that later hardens into bone

chondroma /kon drṓmə/ (*plural* **-mas** or **-mata** /-mətə/) *n* a benign growth of cartilage

chondrule /kón drool/ *n* a small spherical mass of mineral matter from outer space, sometimes found in meteorites. Chondrules usually consist of olivine or pyroxene. [Late 19C. < CHONDRITE]

Chong /chong/, **Son** (1676–1759) Korean artist. He was the first Korean to paint in a non-Chinese style, and was noted for his landscapes.

Chongqing /chōong kíng/, **Chungking**, **Ch'ung-ch'ing** city on the Yangtze River in southern Sichuan Province, southwestern China. It was China's capital from 1937 to 1946. Population: 3,470,000 (1995).

Chonju /jún joó/, **Chŏnju** capital of North Cholla Province, South Korea, situated 193 km/120 mi. south of Seoul. Population: 563,406 (1995).

choo-choo /choó choo/, **choo-choo train** *n* a railway train or locomotive (*baby talk*) [Early 20C. An imitation of the sound of a steam train]

choof /choof/ (**choofs, choofing, choofed**) *vi* ○ *Time to choof off now.* [Mid-20C. Variant of chuff 'move with a puffing sound', an imitation of the sound] —**choof off** *vi* Aus to move off or go away (*informal*)

chook /chook, chook/ *n* ANZ **1.** a hen or chicken (*informal*) **2.** an offensive term that deliberately insults a woman's age or appearance (*slang*) [Mid-20C. An imitation of a clucking sound]

choose /chooz/ (**chooses, choosing, chose** /chōz/, **chosen** /chṓz'n/) *vti* **1.** to decide which of a number of different things or people is best or most suitable ○ *chose a partner* **2.** to make a deliberate decision to do something ○ *Jane has chosen to do the midwifery course.* [Old English *cēosan* < Indo-European] —**chooser** *n*

USAGE choose or **chose**? Do not confuse *choose* with *chose*. *Choose*, rhyming with *blues*, is the infinitive and present tense of the verb, whereas *chose*, rhyming with *blows*, is the past tense: *I chose the wrong one last time, so I'll let you choose this time.*

choose up *vti* US to pick the players wanted in a team for a game

choosy /choózi/ (**-ier, -iest**) *adj* very precise or discriminating in preferences (*informal*) —**choosily** *adv* —**choosiness** *n*

Cho Oyu /chṓ ṓ yoo/ mountain in the Himalaya range, one of the world's highest peaks. Height: 8,201 m/26,906 ft.

chop¹ /chop/ *v* (**chops, chopping, chopped**) **1.** *vt* CUT SOMETHING UP WITH SHARP TOOL to cut something into pieces with downward strokes of an axe, knife, or other sharp-bladed tool ○ *chopped a few carrots* **2.** *vt* CUT SOMETHING OFF to use a quick sharp blow or blows to sever or fell something ○ *chopped down the tree* **3.** *vi* MAKE CHOPPING MOVEMENTS to make downward cutting movements with a tool or with the hand **4.** *vt* FORM SOMETHING BY CHOPPING to make something such as a hole or path by chopping with an axe or other tool ○ *He chopped his way through the undergrowth.* **5.** *vt* GET RID OF SOMETHING OR SOMEBODY to get rid of something or somebody, especially jobs or staff, put an end to something, or curtail something drastically (*informal*) ○ *Several junior members of staff have been chopped.* **6.** *vt* HIT BALL WITH SHARP DOWNWARD MOVEMENT to hit a ball with a quick sharp downward movement of a racket or bat, often in order to give the ball backspin **7.** *vt* HIT SHARPLY DOWNWARDS to hit somebody or something with a sharp downward motion ■ *n* **1.** SLICE OF MEAT WITH BONE a small piece of red meat cut from the ribs, loin, or shoulder, usually with the bone still attached ○ *pork chops* **2.** SHARP STROKE DOWNWARDS a sudden strong downward blow with the hand or a cutting tool ○ *a karate chop* **3.** DISMISSAL dismissal from a job (*informal*) ○ *was given the chop* ○ *If the boss finds out, you'll be for the chop.* **4.** CLOSEDOWN the cancellation, closedown, or stoppage of something (*informal*) ○ *Three of our rural offices are to get the chop.* **5.** IRREGULAR WAVE MOTION turbulent

irregular motion in waves or water ○ *a lot of chop on the bay this morning* **6. DISTURBED SEA** a stretch of choppy water, especially on the sea ○ *hit a bad chop at the inlet* [14C. Variant of CHAP ¹]

chop² /chop/ (**chops, chopping, chopped**) *vi* to change direction or have a change of mind, especially suddenly or frequently [15C. Variant of CHAP ³] ◇ **chop and change** to have frequent changes of mind, especially abruptly or in a way that disconcerts or irritates other people

chop³ /chop/ *n* **1.** *Malaysia, Singapore* a wooden, metal, or rubber stamp used to frank documents or seal envelopes **2.** especially in East Asia, a trademark, official stamp, or mark of quality [Early 17C. < Hindi *chāp*] —**chop** *vt*

chop-chop *interj* used to indicate, often in a bossy or arrogant way, that somebody should hurry or do something quickly or right away (*informal*) [Mid-19C. Repetition of pidgin English *chop*, alteration of Cantonese Chinese *gap* 'urgent'] —**chop-chop** *adv*

chophouse /chóp howss/ (*plural* **-houses** /-howziz/) *n* a restaurant serving grilled meat, e.g. chops and steaks, as its speciality, especially formerly

chopin *n* CLOTHING another spelling of **chopine**

Frédéric François Chopin

Chopin /shóp aN, shóp-/, **Frédéric François** (1810–49) Polish composer and pianist. His piano compositions include mazurkas, études, preludes, nocturnes, waltzes, polonaises, sonatas, and two concertos.

Chopin /shóp an/, **Kate** (1850–1904) US novelist, short-story writer, and poet. She wrote *The Awakening* (1899), a pioneering novel of female sexual discovery.

> 'The past was nothing to her; offered no lesson which she was willing to heed. The future was a mystery which she never attempted to penetrate. The present alone was significant.'
> [Kate Chopin, *The Awakening*; 1899]

chopine /cho peén/, **chopin** /chóppin/ *n* a type of high shoe with a very thick sole worn by European women in the 16th and 17th centuries [Late 16C. < Spanish *chapín*]

choplogic /chóp lojik/ *n* the presentation of an argument in a way that is either illogical or pedantic and overcomplicated (*archaic or literary*) [Early 16C. < *chop* 'exchange']

chopper /chóppər/ *n* **1. SMALL AXE** a small axe with a short handle and a relatively large blade **2. CLEAVER** a cutting tool with a handle and a sharp broad blade, used especially for chopping up meat **3.** AVIAT same as **helicopter** (*informal*) **4. BIKE WITH HIGH HANDLEBARS** a motorcycle or bicycle with a lowered seat, raised handlebars, and lengthened forks holding the front wheel **5. INTERRUPTING DEVICE** a device that regularly interrupts an electric current, a beam of light, or some other stream of radiation in order to produce a pulsing flow or beam **6. TABOO TERM** a highly offensive term for a penis (*slang taboo*) ■ **choppers** *npl* TEETH teeth, especially large or false ones (*slang*) ■ *vti* GO BY HELICOPTER to travel or to transport something or somebody by helicopter (*informal*)

chopping block /chópping-/ *n* a heavy block of wood, sometimes mounted on legs, for chopping food or wood on ◇ **somebody's head is on the chopping block** somebody deserves to or is likely to be dismissed from his or her job

chopping board *n* a piece of wood or plastic used for chopping food on. N Am term **cutting board**

choppy /chóppi/ (**-pier, -piest**) *adj* rather rough, with the surface of the water broken up into many small waves made by strong winds —**choppily** *adv* —**choppiness** *n*

chops /chops/ *npl* **1.** the jaws, or the skin covering the jaws (*informal*) **2.** technique or virtuosity in playing an instrument, especially a wind instrument (*slang*)

chop shop *n* N Am a workshop or garage where stolen vehicles are disguised or broken up for spare parts (*slang*)

chopsocky /chóp soki/ *n* the genre of film in which martial arts such as kung fu feature prominently ○ *his latest chopsocky extravaganza* [< CHOP ¹ + SOCK ²]

chopstick /chóp stik/ *n* either of a pair of narrow sticks that are held together in one hand and used when eating or preparing East Asian food [Late 17C. < pidgin English (see CHOP-CHOP)]

chop suey /chop soó i/ *n* a dish of Chinese-American origin made typically of shredded meat and mixed vegetables [Late 19C. < Cantonese Chinese *tsaâp suì* 'mixed bits']

choragus /kaw ráygəss/ (*plural* **-gi** /-jī, -gī/ or **-guses**) *n* the leader of the chorus in ancient Greek drama [Early 17C. Via Latin < Greek *khoragos* 'somebody who leads the chorus'] —**choragic** /-rájjik, -ráyjik/ *adj*

choral /káwrəl/ *adj* **1.** arranged for or performed by a chorus or choir ○ *choral singing* **2.** concerned with choral singing, choruses, or choirs ○ *a choral society* [Late 16C. < medieval Latin *choralis* < Latin *chorus* (see CHORUS)] —**chorally** *adv*

chorale /ko raál/ *n* **1. LUTHERAN HYMN TUNE** a hymn tune, especially a slow and stately one, originally intended for congregational singing in the Lutheran Church **2. PIECE OF MUSIC BASED ON CHORALE** a piece of music, especially a choral work, based on a chorale tune or in a style reminiscent of traditional Lutheran church music **3.** N Am **GROUP OF SINGERS** a group of singers specializing in a particular style of music, especially church music [Mid-19C. < German *Choral(gesang)* 'choral (song)']

chorale prelude *n* an organ prelude based on a chorale tune, used to introduce congregational singing of the chorale on which it is based or performed as a separate piece

chord¹ /kawrd/ *n* two or more musical notes played or sung simultaneously ○ *an F minor chord* [15C. Shortening and alteration of ACCORD after Latin *chorda*] —**chordal** *adj* ◇ **strike** *or* **touch a chord** to produce an emotional, especially a sympathetic, response in somebody, or jog somebody's memory

USAGE chord or **cord**? In musical contexts the spelling is **chord**, and this form is also used in figurative expressions that have to do with feelings: *The speech struck the right chord*. In anatomical contexts (*spinal cord, umbilical cord, vocal cords*), **cord** is more usual. **Cord** is used when referring to a thick, strong string, a belt or cable, and as a measurement of cut wood.

chord² /kawrd/ *n* **1.** MATHS **LINE THROUGH ARC** a straight line connecting two points on an arc or circle **2.** AVIAT **AIRFOIL MEASURE** the shortest distance between the leading and trailing edges of an airfoil **3.** ANAT same as **cord** (sense 4) **4.** CONSTR **HORIZONTAL CONNECTING PART** the horizontal part of a truss designed to absorb tension, e.g. in a roof [Mid-16C. Alteration of CORD, after Latin *chorda*]

chordate /káwr dayt/ *n* an animal that at some stage in its development has a main dorsal nerve cord, a skeletal rod (**notochord**), and gill slits, including all vertebrates and some primitive invertebrate sea animals. Phylum: Chordata. [Late 19C. < modern Latin *chordata* < Latin *chorda* 'cord'] —**chordate** *adj*

chordophone /káwrdə fōn/ *n* MUSIC same as **stringed instrument** (*technical*) [Mid-20C. < CHORD ¹]

chord organ *n* a small electronic organ with special keys to produce chords for accompanying a melody [< CHORD ¹]

chore /chawr/ *n* **1.** a task, especially an ordinary household task, that has to be done regularly (*often used in the plural*) **2.** something that is unpleasant,

difficult, awkward, or boring to do [Mid-18C. < alteration of CHAR ³]

SYNONYMS See *job*.

-chore *suffix* a plant distributed by a particular means ○ *anemochore* [< Greek *khōrein* 'to spread']

chorea /ko reé ə/ *n* jerky spasmodic movements of the limbs, trunk, and facial muscles, common to various diseases of the central nervous system [Late 17C. Via Latin < Greek *khoreia* 'dance'] —**choreal** *adj* —**choreic** *adj*

choreograph /kórri ə graaf/ (**-graphs, -graphing, -graphed**) *v* **1.** *vti* to plan out dance movements to a piece of music **2.** *vt* to plan, coordinate, and supervise an event or activity ○ *His job is to choreograph royal weddings and other state occasions.* [Mid-20C. Back-formation < CHOREOGRAPHY] —**choreographer** /kórri óggrəfər/ *n*

choreography /kórri óggrəfi/ (*plural* **-phies**) *n* **1. COMPOSING DANCES** the planning of movements for dancing **2. DANCE MOVEMENTS FOR PIECE** the steps and movements planned for a dance, or a written record of them **3. PLANNED MOVEMENT** the carefully planned or executed organization of people, things, or an event [Late 18C. < French *chorégraphie* 'dance writing' < Greek *khoreia* 'dance'] —**choreographic** /kórri ə gráffik/ *adj* —**choreographically** *adv*

choriamb /kórri amb, -am/ *n* a poetic foot consisting of two short syllables between two long ones or two unstressed syllables between two stressed ones [Early 17C. Via late Latin < Greek *khoriambos* 'iamb of a chorus'] —**choriambic** /kórri ámbik/ *adj*

choric /kórrik/ *adj* performed by or written for a chorus, especially a chorus in classical Greek theatre [Early 19C. < late Latin *choricus* < Greek *khoros* 'chorus']

chorioallantois /kórri ō ə lán tō iss, -állən tō iss/ *n* a membrane surrounding an embryo. In a bird's or reptile's egg, it lies next to the shell. In mammals, it forms a major part of the placenta. [Mid-20C. < CHORION] —**chorioallantoic** /kórri ō allən tō ik/ *adj*

chorion /káwri ən/ *n* the outer membrane enclosing the embryo of mammals, reptiles, and birds. It has a dense concentration of blood vessels and aids in the formation of the placenta in mammals. [Mid-16C. < Greek *khorion*] —**chorionic** /káwri ónnik/ *adj*

chorionic gonadotrophin *n* a hormone that helps maintain a pregnancy

chorionic villus *n* a tiny outgrowth from the outer membrane (**chorion**) surrounding an embryo that moves into the womb wall with others to form the placenta (*often used in the plural*)

chorionic villus sampling *n* an antenatal screening test carried out by examining cells from the tiny hairy outgrowths (**villi**) of the outer membrane (**chorion**) surrounding an embryo, which have the same DNA as the foetus

chorister /kórristər/ *n* a member of a chorus, choir, or other group of singers [14C. < Anglo-Norman < Old French *cueriste* < Latin *chorus* (see CHORUS)]

chorizo /chə reé zō, -thō/ (*plural* **-zos**) *n* a very spicy Spanish or Mexican pork sausage [Mid-19C. < Spanish]

C-horizon, **C horizon** *n* the lowermost layer of earth immediately above bedrock

chorography /kə róggrəfi/ *n* the preparation of maps in which specific areas or regions are delineated and often highlighted in some way, e.g. by colour-coding [Mid-16C. Directly or via French < Latin *chorographia* < Greek *khōrographia* 'place writing'] —**chorographer** *n* —**chorographic** /kórrə gráffik/ *adj* —**chorographically** *adv*

choroid /káw royd/ *n* also **choroid coat** a brownish membrane between the retina and the white of the eye in vertebrates that contains blood vessels and large pigmented cells ■ *adj* resembling the chorion in being vascular or membranous [Mid-17C. < Greek *khoroeidēs* < *khorion* 'chorion']

choroid plexus *n* a membrane with many small blood vessels in the fluid spaces of the brain that secretes cerebrospinal fluid

chortle /cháwrt'l/ *n* a noisy gleeful laugh [Late 19C. Blend of CHUCKLE + SNORT] —**chortle** *vi* —**chortler** *n*

chorus /káwrəss/ *n* **1. REPEATED PART OF SONG** a set of lines that are sung at least twice in the course of a song, usually being repeated after each verse **2. LARGE GROUP OF SINGERS** a large group of singers who perform choral music or opera together (*takes a singular or plural verb*) **3. GROUP OF PERFORMERS** a group of people who appear, sing, and sometimes dance together as a unit in a performance, usually providing backing for the principal performers (*takes a singular or plural verb*) **4. MUSIC FOR GROUP** a musical composition written for a large group of singers, usually with different parts for the different voice types ○ *the Hallelujah Chorus* **5. MANY VOICES TOGETHER** the words spoken or feelings expressed by a group of people at the same time ○ *a chorus of complaints* **6. GROUP SPEAKING OR MAKING NOISE TOGETHER** a group of people or animals all speaking or making a noise together **7. GROUP OF ACTORS IN GREEK DRAMA** a group of actors in ancient Greek drama who sing or speak in unison, generally commenting on the significance of the events that take place in the play **8. VERSE PASSAGE FOR GREEK DRAMA CHORUS** a verse passage in an ancient Greek drama intended to be sung or spoken by the chorus **9. DRAMA ROLE** a role in some Elizabethan and historical dramas for a solo actor, who speaks the introductory prologue, comments on the action, and delivers the epilogue ■ *vt* (**-ruses, -rusing, -rused**) **SAY SOMETHING TOGETHER** to speak at the same time, saying the same thing or expressing the same feeling or opinion [Mid-16C. Via Latin < Greek *khoros*] ◇ **in chorus** all speaking or making a noise together

chorus boy *n* a man or boy who sings and dances as one of the supporting group of performers in a stage or film production

chorus girl *n* a woman or girl who sings and dances as one of the supporting group of performers in a stage or film production

chorus line *n* the chorus of supporting singers and dancers in a musical or variety show

-chory *suffix* same as **-chore**

chose past tense of **choose**

USAGE See *choose*.

chosen /chōz'n/ past participle of **choose** ■ *adj* picked out from or preferred to the rest ○ *one of the chosen few* ■ *npl* **RELIG** same as **elect** *npl* (sense 2)

chosen people *npl* the Jews, who, according to the Bible and their own belief, were selected by God to play a unique role in world history

chota /chōtə/ *adj S Asia* **1.** small in size **2.** relatively low in importance or rank [Early 19C. < Hindi]

chott /shot/ *n* a basin in the deserts of North Africa that periodically fills with water but dries out and becomes a salt flat when the weather is warmer [Late 19C. < Arabic *satt* 'shore, strand, salt lake']

chouette /shoo ét/ *n* a variation of backgammon in which one player plays against two or more opponents in one game [Late 19C. < French, 'barn owl']

chough /chuf/ *n* a bird of the crow family with glossy black feathers, red legs and feet, and a red or yellow beak. Native to: Europe, Asia. Genus: *Pyrrhocorax*. [12C. Probably an imitation of its call]

Chouteau /shoōtō/, **René Auguste** (1749–1829) American pioneer. He founded St Louis, Missouri (1764), and was an important figure in the local fur trade.

choux pastry /shoō-/ *n* a soft glossy egg-rich pastry that puffs up into a hollow case when baked. It is used in making filled pastries such as cream puffs and éclairs. [< French, literally 'cabbage']

chow[1] /chow/ *n* **1.** same as **food** (sense 2) (*slang*) **2. FOOD** same as **chow-chow** [Late 18C. Shortening of Chinese pidgin English *chow-chow* 'food, mixture']
chow down *vi N Am* to eat food enthusiastically (*informal*)

chow[2] /chow/, **chow chow** *n* a stocky dog with a thick coat, a tail that curls over its back, and a large dark purplish tongue, belonging to a breed originally from China [Late 19C. < pidgin English]

chow-chow *n* **1.** a Chinese mixture of fruit and candied peel in syrup, with stem ginger **2.** a Chinese mixed vegetable pickle in a yellow sauce, similar to piccalilli [see CHOW[1]]

chowder /chówdər/ *n* a thick soup, especially one

made with seafood or fish [Mid-18C. Probably via French *chaudière* 'stew pot' < Latin *calidarium* 'hot bath']

chowderhead /chówdər hed/ *n N Am* an offensive term for somebody regarded as unintelligent or irrational (*informal insult*) [Mid-19C. Alteration of English dialect *jolter-head*] —**chowderheaded** *adj*

chowk /chowk/ *n S Asia* an open area, usually at a road junction, where a market is held [Mid-19C. < Hindi *cauk* 'square']

chowkidar /chówki daar/ *n S Asia* somebody employed to guard an area or building [Early 17C. < Urdu *chaukidar* < Hindi *cauki* 'police station' + Urdu *-dar* 'keeper']

chow mein /chów máyn/ *n* a dish of soft fried noodles, usually cooked with chopped meat and vegetables, originally from China [< Chinese *chǎo miàn* 'fried noodles']

Chr. *abbr* **1.** CHR Christ **2.** CHR Christian **3.** BIBLE Chronicles

chrestomathy /kre stómməthi/ (*plural* **-thies**) *n* a collection of literary passages, especially one assembled for language study [Mid-19C. Directly or via French < Greek *khrēstomatheia* 'useful learning'] —**chrestomathic** /krésta máthik/ *adj*

Jean Chrétien

Chrétien /krétti aN/, **Jean** (*b.* 1934) Canadian prime minister (1993–2003). He became leader of the Liberal Party (1990), leading them to victory in 1993, 1997, and 2000. His premiership was marked by economic restraint and reduced unemployment. Full name **Chrétien, Joseph Jacques Jean**. See table at **prime minister**

'You end up looking like the fish.'
[Jean Chrétien, on why he disliked fishing with US presidents, *New York Times*; 25 February 1995]

Chrétien de Troyes /-də trwaá/ (*fl* 1170) French poet. His epics were the first to incorporate Arthurian legends and the quest for the Holy Grail.

chrism /krízzəm/ *n* **1.** consecrated oil, or a consecrated mixture of balsam and oil, used for anointing people at some ceremonies in the Roman Catholic, Anglican, and Orthodox churches **2.** a ceremonial anointing of somebody with holy oil, especially at confirmation in the Eastern Orthodox churches [Pre-12C. Via medieval Latin *crisma* < Greek *khrisma* 'an anointing' < *khriein* 'anoint'] —**chrismal** *adj*

chrismation /kriz máysh'n/ *n* in the Eastern Orthodox tradition, the act of anointing somebody, or of being anointed, with holy oil in a religious ceremony such as confirmation [Mid-16C. < medieval Latin *chrismation-* < *crisma* (see CHRISM)]

chrisom /krízzəm/ *n* a white robe or shawl worn by an infant for his or her baptism [13C. Alteration of CHRISM]

chrisom child *n* a baby that dies within a month of its baptism (*archaic*)

Chrissie /kríssi/, **Chrissy** *n* same as **Christmas** (*informal*) [Late 20C. Shortening and alteration]

Christ /krīst/ *n* **1.** CHR same as **Jesus Christ** *n* (sense 1) **2.** BIBLE **THE MESSIAH** according to the Bible, a saviour who will come to deliver God's chosen people **3.** CHR **PAINTING OF JESUS CHRIST** an artistic representation of Jesus Christ ■ *interj* **TABOO TERM** a highly offensive term used to express surprise, annoyance, exasperation, or alarm (*taboo*) [Pre-12C. Via Latin *Christus* < Greek *Khristos* 'anointed' < *khriein* 'anoint'] —**Christhood** *n* —**Christly** *adj*

Christadelphian /krístə délfi ən/ *n* a member of a Christian group founded by John Thomas in the United States around 1848. Christadelphians reject the doctrine of the Trinity as not in the Bible and believe in the dead being resurrected with the Second Coming of Jesus Christ. [Mid-19C. < late Greek *Khristadelphos* 'in brotherhood with Christ'] —**Christadelphian** *adj*

Christ child *n* Jesus Christ as an infant, especially as depicted in art

Christchurch /kríst church/ **1.** town and resort in Dorset, southern England, situated at the confluence of the Avon and Stour rivers, 37 km/23 mi. southwest of Southampton. Population: 44,865 (2001). **2.** city situated near the eastern coast of the South Island, New Zealand, 13 km/8 mi. northwest of Lyttelton. Population: 334,107 (2001).

christen /kríss'n/ *vt* **1. BAPTIZE AND NAME SOMEBODY** to make somebody, especially a baby, a member of the Christian Church in a ceremony that includes a form of baptism and, usually, the giving of a Christian name or names **2. GIVE NAME TO SOMETHING OR SOMEBODY** to give a name to something or somebody, with or without an accompanying ceremony ○ *christen a ship* **3. USE SOMETHING FOR FIRST TIME** to use or wear something for the first time (*informal*) ○ *Shall we christen our new coffeepot?* [Pre-12C. < Old English *cristnian* < *cristen* 'Christian' < Latin *christianus*] —**christener** *n*

Christendom /kríss'ndəm/ *n* **1.** all the areas of the world where Christianity is accepted as the main religion **2.** all Christian people considered as a group (*formal*) [Old English *cristendom* 'condition of being Christian' < *cristen* (see CHRISTEN)]

christening /kríss'ning/ *n* a ceremony in a Christian church in which somebody, especially a baby, is baptized and usually given a Christian name or names

Christian /kríschən/ *n* **1. BELIEVER IN JESUS CHRIST AS SAVIOUR** somebody whose religion is Christianity **2.** *Malaysia* CHR same as **Protestant** (sense 1) ■ *adj* **1.** CHR **FROM TEACHINGS OF JESUS CHRIST** based on or relating to a belief in Jesus Christ as the Son of God and the Messiah, and acceptance of his teachings, contained in the Gospels **2. RELATING TO CHRISTIANITY** relating to Christianity, or belonging to or maintained by a Christian organization, especially a church ○ *Christian theology* ○ *a Christian school* **3. KIND AND UNSELFISH** showing qualities such as kindness, helpfulness, and concern for others [13C. < Latin *Christianus* < *Christus* (see CHRIST)] —**Christianly** *adv*

Christian VIII /krísschən, krísti ən/ (1786–1848) king of Denmark. He was first elected to the Norwegian throne in 1814, but was ousted in the same year. During his reign in Denmark (1839–48), his Schleswig-Holstein policy precipitated war with Prussia (1848).

Christian Democratic Party *n* a political party of the moderate right, especially in continental Europe —**Christian Democrat** *n*

Christian Era *n* the period of history dating from the year in which Jesus Christ is believed to have been born. Dates in the early Christian Era are often indicated by AD, and dates before the Christian Era by BC.

Christianise *vt* RELIG another spelling of **Christianize**

Christianity /krísti ánnəti/ *n* **1. RELIGION THAT FOLLOWS JESUS CHRIST'S TEACHINGS** the religion based on the life, teachings, and example of Jesus Christ **2. HOLDING OF CHRISTIAN BELIEFS** the fact of holding Christian beliefs or of being a Christian **3. CHRISTIANS AS GROUP** all Christian people considered as a group

Christianize /krísschə nīz/ (**-izes, -izing, -ized**), **Christianise** (**-ises, -ising, -ised**) *vt* **1.** to change the religious beliefs and practices of a person or group of people from another religion to Christianity **2.** to make somebody or something Christian by imbuing him, her, or it with Christian principles or a Christian spirit —**Christianization** /krísschə nī záysh'n/ *n* —**Christianizer** *n*

Christian name *n* a first name, especially one given at a christening

Christian Science *n* the beliefs and practices of the Church of Christ, Scientist, a religious group founded by Mary Baker Eddy. Its members believe

that illness should be overcome or managed through religious faith and observances alone. —**Christian Scientist** n

Christian Scriptures npl the New Testament of the Bible as distinct from the Hebrew Scriptures

christie /krísti/, **christy** (plural **-ties**) n in skiing, a type of turn used for stopping or rapidly changing direction, in which the skier twists sharply aside while keeping the skis parallel to each other [Early 20C. Shortening of Christiania, former name of Oslo]

Dame Agatha Christie

Christie /krísti/, **Dame Agatha** (1890–1976) British novelist and playwright. She wrote over 70 detective novels featuring the sleuths Hercule Poirot and Miss Marple. Full name **Christie, Dame Agatha Mary Clarissa**

'I don't think necessity is the mother of invention—invention, in my opinion, arises directly from idleness, possibly also from laziness. To save oneself trouble.' [Dame Agatha Christie, An Autobiography; 1977]

Christie, Linford (b. 1960) Jamaican-born British athlete. In 1993, he held the World, Olympic, Commonwealth, and European Cup titles for 100 metres.

'Whoever said losing wasn't important was a loser himself; it's rubbish. Who cares about the people who took part? The only people who are remembered are the winners.' [Linford Christie, Independent on Sunday; 21 August 1994]

Christie, Perry (b. 1943) prime minister of the Bahamas. He was elected leader of the Progressive Liberal Party, then the main opposition party, in 1997, and became prime minister following its electoral victory in 2002. Full name **Christie, Perry Gladstone**

Christina /kri steénə/, **queen of Sweden** (1626–89) In 1644 she negotiated the Peace of Westphalia, bringing to an end the Thirty Years' War

'We grow old more through indolence, than through age.' [Christina, 'Maxims (1660–80)', The Works of Christina of Sweden; 1753]

christingle /krísting g'l/, **Christingle** n a Christmas decoration made by children in some Christian churches, consisting of a candle in an orange symbolizing Jesus Christ as the light of the world [Mid-20C. Probably alteration of German Christkindl 'Christmas present, Christ child', after Kriss Kringle]

Christmas /kríssməss/ n **1. FESTIVAL CELEBRATING BIRTH OF JESUS CHRIST** a Christian festival marking the birth of Jesus Christ. Date: 25 December. **2. CHRISTMAS PERIOD** the period around 25 December, or the Christian church season extending from 24 December to 6 January **3. QUARTER DAY** in England, Wales, and Ireland, one of the four quarter days, falling on 25 December [Old English Cristes mæsse 'mass of Christ']

Christmas beetle n a greenish-gold scarab beetle. Native to: Australia. Genus: Anoplognathus. [Because common around Christmastime]

Christmas box n a gift of money traditionally given at Christmas by a householder or business to workers who have provided a service throughout the year

Christmas bush n any Australian tree whose colourful flowers are used as Christmas decorations

Christmas cactus n a branching cactus cultivated as an ornamental plant. Flowers: red, pink, white, or purplish-red. Native to: Brazil. Latin name: Schlumbergera truncata. [Because it flowers around December]

Christmas cake n a rich dark fruit cake traditionally covered with marzipan and white icing and eaten at Christmastime

Christmas card n an illustrated greetings card sent at Christmas

Christmas carol n a Christian song celebrating Christmas

Christmas club n a savings account in which money is deposited regularly throughout the year in order to buy gifts and additional food and drink for Christmas

Christmas cracker n same as **cracker** (sense 1)

Christmas Day n same as **Christmas** (sense 1)

Christmas disease n a form of haemophilia caused by lack of a protein needed for blood clotting [Mid-20C. After Stephen Christmas, who had the disease]

Christmas Eve n the day or evening of 24 December

Christmas flower n S Africa PLANTS same as **hydrangea** [Because it blooms in December in South Africa]

Christmas Island /kríssməss-/ dependency of Australia in the Indian Ocean, 360 km/224 mi. south of Java. Population: 1,906 (1996). Area: 388 sq. km/150 sq. mi. ■ former name for **Kiritimati** (until 1981)

Christmas pudding n a rich steamed pudding made with dried fruit, spices, and usually candied peel and brandy, prepared and cooked in advance, then reheated for serving at the main Christmas meal

Christmas rose n **1.** an evergreen winter-flowering plant. Flowers: drooping, white. Native to: Europe, Asia. Latin name: Helleborus niger. **2.** S Africa PLANTS same as **hydrangea** [Because it flowers in winter]

Christmas stocking n a stocking or large sock hung up on Christmas Eve by children and supposed to be filled with presents by Father Christmas during the night

Christmassy /kríssməssi/ adj suggesting the Christmas period, or suitable for Christmas (informal) ○ The decorations look really Christmassy.

Christmastime /kríssməss tīm/ n same as **Christmas** (sense 2)

Christmas tree n an evergreen tree, especially a conifer or an artificial version of one, that is decorated with lights and ornaments at Christmas

Christo /krístō/ (b. 1935) Bulgarian-born US artist. He is known for his modern conceptual art, in particular his 'wrapping' of monuments and buildings. Full name **Javacheff, Christo**

Christocentric /krístə séntrik, krístō-/ adj **1.** assuming, implying, or based on Christian values and beliefs **2.** concentrating or based strongly on Jesus Christ and his teachings

Christoff /kríst of/, **Boris** (1914–93) Bulgarian operatic bass. His repertoire spanned around 40 roles in six languages, including acclaimed performances in Modest Mussorgsky's Boris Godunov.

Christology /kri stólləji/ n the branch of theology concerned with the study of the nature, character, and actions of Jesus Christ —**Christological** /krístə lójjik'l/ adj —**Christologist** n

Christopher /krístəfər/, **St** (fl 3rd century) According to legend, he carried Jesus Christ as a child across a river. He is the patron saint of travellers.

Christ's thorn, **Christ thorn** n a thorny Asian bush or tree, especially a jujube, a Jerusalem thorn, or a thorny spurge. Branches of such a plant are popularly believed to have been used for Jesus Christ's crown of thorns

christy n SKIING another spelling of **christie**

chrom- prefix same as **chromo-** (used before vowels)

chroma /krṓmə/ n PHYS same as **saturation** n (sense 8) [Late 19C. < Greek khrōma 'colour']

chromaffin /krṓməfin/ adj describes cells in the adrenal medulla that make noradrenaline [Early 20C. < CHROMO- + Latin affinis 'related']

chromat- prefix same as **chromato-** (used before vowels)

chromate /krṓ mayt/ n any salt or ester of chromic acid [Early 20C. < CHROMIC]

chromatic /krō máttik/ adj **1. USING ALL SEMITONES IN OCTAVE** describes a musical scale that runs through all the semitones in an octave, e.g. using all the keys, black and white, on a keyboard **2. BASED ON CHROMATIC SCALE** describes music that is based on the chromatic scale or that makes frequent use of notes that are outside the key in which it is written **3. RELATING TO COLOUR** relating to colour and phenomena connected with it [15C. Directly or via French < Greek khrōmatikos < khrōma 'colour'] —**chromatically** adv

chromatic aberration n an optical aberration in a lens, caused by a defect, leading to coloured light of different colours being refracted differently

chromaticism /krō máttissizəm/ n the use in music of the chromatic scale or of many notes and harmonies that are foreign to the basic key

chromaticity /krṓmə tíssəti/ n the colour quality of light precisely and uniquely defined in terms of three factors (**chromaticity coordinates**)

chromatics /krō máttiks/ n the science or study of colour (takes a singular verb) —**chromatist** /krṓmətist/

chromatid /krṓmətid/ n either of the two strands into which a chromosome divides in the process of duplicating itself in cell division [Early 20C. < Greek khrōmat- 'colour']

chromatin /krṓmətin/ n the substance that forms chromosomes and contains DNA, RNA, and various proteins [Late 19C. < Greek khrōmat- 'colour'] —**chromatinic** /krṓmə tínnik/ adj

chromato- prefix **1.** colour ○ chromatography **2.** chromatin ○ chromatolysis [< Greek khrōmat- 'colour']

chromatogram /krə mátta gram, krṓmətə gram/ n a pattern formed by substances that have been separated by chromatography

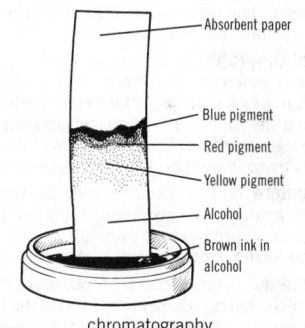
- Absorbent paper
- Blue pigment
- Red pigment
- Yellow pigment
- Alcohol
- Brown ink in alcohol

chromatography

chromatography /krṓmə tóggrəfi/ n a method of finding out which components a gaseous or liquid mixture contains that involves passing it through or over something that absorbs the different components at different rates —**chromatograph** /krə mátta graaf, -graf/ n —**chromatographer** /krṓmətə gráffik/ adj —**chromatographically** adv

chromatolysis /krṓmə tólləssiss/ n the breakdown of the substance that forms chromosomes (**chromatin**) within an injured cell nucleus

chromatophore /krə mátta fawr/ n **1.** a pigment-containing cell in many animals that, when it expands or contracts, causes a change in the animal's skin colouring. Octopus, squid, and some frogs and lizards contain these cells. **2.** BOT same as **chromoplast** —**chromatophoric** /krə mátta fórrik/ adj

chrome /krōm/ n **1. CHROMIUM-PLATED METAL** shiny chromium-plated metal. Use: to trim cars. **2. COMPOUND CONTAINING CHROMIUM** an alloy, dye, or pigment containing chromium **3.** CHEM same as **chromium** ■ vt (**chromes, chroming, chromed**) **1. COAT METAL WITH CHROMIUM** to electroplate a metal with chromium in order to make it shiny and protect it against corrosion **2. TREAT SOMETHING WITH CHROMIUM COMPOUND** to treat a substance with a chromium compound, usually when dyeing or tanning it [Early 19C. Via French < Greek khrōma 'colour'; because compounds containing it are often brightly coloured]

-chrome *suffix* colour, pigment ○ *phytochrome* [< Greek *khrōma* 'colour']

chrome alum *n* a red-violet crystalline solid. Use: fixing agent in dyeing, tanning, and photography. Formula: CrK(SO₄)₂.12H₂O.

chrome green *n* a brilliant green pigment containing chrome yellow and iron blue. Use: fabric dye.

chrome red *n* a bright red-orange pigment containing lead chromate and lead oxide. Use: in paints and dyes.

chrome tape *n* magnetic recording tape that is coated with chromium dioxide

chrome yellow *n* a yellow pigment containing lead chromate and lead sulphate.

chromic /krōmik/ *adj* relating to or containing chromium with a valency of three

chromic acid *n* an unstable oxidizing acid existing only in solution or in the form of a salt. Formula: H_2CrO_4.

chromite /krō mīt/ *n* a brownish-black mineral ore consisting of an oxide of iron and chromium. Use: source of chromium.

chromium /krō mi əm/ *n* a hard bluish-white metallic element. Source: chromite. Use: alloys and electroplating to increase hardness and corrosion resistance. Symbol **Cr**. See table at **element**

chromium dioxide *n* a black crystalline solid. Use: to coat recording tape with magnetic properties. Formula: CrO_2.

chromo /krō mō/ (*plural* **-mos**) *n* PRINTING same as **chromolithograph** [Mid-19C Shortening]

chromo- *prefix* **1.** colour, pigment ○ *chromolithograph* ○ *chromogen* **2.** chromium ○ *chromite* [< Greek *khrōma* 'colour']

chromodynamics /krō mō dī námmiks/ *n* PHYS same as **quantum chromodynamics**

chromogen /krṓməjən/ *n* **1.** any substance that is capable of being converted into a biological pigment or a dye, e.g. through oxidation **2.** any microorganism that produces a pigment —**chromogenic** /krōmə jénnik/ *adj*

chromolithograph /krṓmō líthə graaf, -graf/ *n* a coloured picture produced by making and superimposing multiple lithographs, each of which adds a different colour —**chromolithographer** /krṓməli thóggrəfər/ *n* —**chromolithographic** /krṓmō lithə gráffik/ *adj* —**chromolithography** /krṓmōli thóggrəfi/ *n*

chromomere /krṓmə meer/ *n* a small dense bead-shaped granule of chromatin, found at intervals along a chromosome during cell division —**chromomeric** /krṓmə meérik, -mérrik/ *adj*

chromonema /krṓmə neémə/ (*plural* **-mata** /-mətə/) *n* the coiled central filament that forms the core of a chromosome strand (**chromatid**) [Early 20C. < CHROMO- + Greek *nēma* 'thread'] —**chromonemal** *adj*

chromophore /krṓmə fawr/ *n* a group of atoms in a molecule that produces colour in dyes and other compounds through selective absorption of light, e.g. the azo group —**chromophoric** /krṓmə fórrik/ *adj*

chromoplast /krṓmə plast/ *n* a membrane-surrounded structure (**plastid**) in a plant cell that contains pigment. Red, yellow, or orange chromoplasts contain carotenoid pigments, and green chromoplasts (**chloroplasts**) contain chlorophyll.

chromoprotein /krōmə prṓ teen/ *n* a protein combined with a pigment

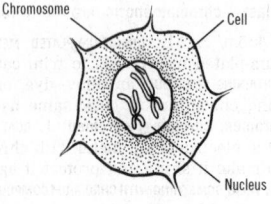

chromosome

chromosome /krṓmə sōm/ *n* a rod-shaped structure, usually found in pairs in a cell nucleus, that carries the genes that determine sex and the characteristics an organism inherits from its parents. A human body cell usually contains 46 chromosomes arranged in 23 pairs. [Late 19C. < German *Chromosom* < Greek *khrōma* 'colour' + *sōma* 'body'; because chromosomes readily take up dye] —**chromosomal** /krōmə sōm'l/ *adj*

chromosome band *n* a pattern produced in a chromosome by using a stain, making the chromosome identifiable from other chromosomes

chromosome map *n* same as **genetic map**

chromosome number *n* the number of chromosomes present in the cell nucleus of a species of plant or animal. A human body usually has a chromosome number of 46.

chromosphere /krṓmə sfeer/ *n* **1.** the lower region of the Sun's atmosphere, between the photosphere and the corona **2.** the lower region of the atmosphere of any star —**chromospheric** /krṓmə sférrik/ *adj*

chromous /krṓməss/ *adj* relating to or containing chromium, especially chromium in its divalent state [Mid-19C. < CHROMIUM]

chron. *abbr* **1.** LITERAT chronicle **2.** TIME chronological **3.** TIME chronology

Chron. *abbr* BIBLE Chronicles

chron- *prefix* TIME same as **chrono-** (*used before vowels*)

chronic /krónnik/ *adj* **1.** LONG-LASTING describes an illness or medical condition that lasts over a long period and sometimes causes a long-term change in the body **2.** WITH LONG-TERM ILLNESS having a particular long-term illness or condition ○ *a chronic asthmatic* **3.** ALWAYS PRESENT always present or recurring **4.** HABITUAL repeatedly doing something or behaving compulsively ○ *a chronic liar* **5.** ⚠ DIRE terrible or appalling (*informal*) [15C. Via French < Greek *khronikos* 'of time' < *khronos* 'time'] —**chronically** *adv* —**chronicity** /krə níssəti/ *n*

USAGE *Chronic*, used both of illness and in figurative contexts (as in *a chronic problem*), essentially denotes continuation over a long period of time, as its origin in the Greek word for 'time' suggests, rather than severity, although this is often also the case. Its opposite is *acute*, which denotes suddenness and intensity. So a *chronic* pain is one that persists, whereas an *acute* pain is one that comes on suddenly and may last only a short time. In its informal meaning 'terrible' or 'appalling', *chronic* has lost all its sense of time, and for this reason and because of its apparent trivialization of a meaning used in serious contexts, many people dislike it: *Drink! My word! Something chronic.* (G. B. Shaw, *Pygmalion*).

chronic daily headaches *npl* a condition in which the patient is affected by a series of extremely painful recurring migraine and tension headaches that are present for 15 or more days a month [Early 21C.]

chronic fatigue syndrome *n* an illness without a known cause that is characterized by long-term exhaustion, muscle weakness, depression, and sleep disturbances. It may be a reaction to a viral infection in somebody already debilitated.

chronicle /krónnik'l/ *n* **1.** HISTORICAL ACCOUNT an account of events presented in chronological order **2.** NARRATIVE a narrative or fictional account ■ *vt* (**-cles, -cling, -cled**) MAKE RECORD OF HAPPENINGS to record an event or series of events in chronological order [14C. < Anglo-Norman *cronicle*, alteration of Old French *cronique* < Greek *khronika* (plural) 'annals' < *khronos* 'time'] —**chronicler** *n*

Chronicles /krónnik'lz/ *n* either of two books of the Bible that tell the story of the Israelites from the creation of Adam to the middle of the 6th century BC (*takes a singular verb*) See table at **Bible**

chronic wasting disease *n* a highly contagious brain disease in deer and elk that has no early overt symptoms but results in the brain deteriorating and taking on a spongy appearance. It is believed to be caused by an abnormal transmissible protein (**prion**) and related to BSE in cattle.

chrono- *prefix* time ○ *chronograph* [< Greek *khronos* 'time']

chronobiology /krónnə bī ólləji, krṓnō-/ *n* the study

of recurring cycles of events in the natural world —**chronobiologic** /krónnə bī ə lójjik, krṓnō-/ *adj* —**chronobiologist** *n*

chronogram /krónnə gram, krṓnə-/ *n* a phrase or inscription containing letters indicating a date. Roman numerals are often used in this way. —**chronogrammatic** /krónnəgrə máttik, krṓnō-/ *adj* —**chronogrammatically** *adv*

chronograph /krónnə graaf, krṓnə-, -graf/ *n* an instrument such as a stopwatch that records time with great accuracy —**chronographic** /krónnə gráffik, krṓnə-/ *adj* —**chronographically** *adv*

chronol. *abbr* TIME **1.** chronological **2.** chronology

chronological /krónnə lójjik'l, krṓnə-/ *adj* **1.** presented or arranged in the order in which events occur or occurred **2.** relating to chronology —**chronologically** *adv*

chronological age *n* somebody's real age, as opposed to the age suggested by his or her mental or physical development

chronology /krə nólləji/ (*plural* **-gies**) *n* **1.** ORDER OF EVENTS the order in which events occur, or their arrangement according to this order **2.** LIST OF EVENTS a list or table of events arranged in order of occurrence **3.** STUDY OF ORDER IN TIME the study of the order in which things occur, or the science of determining this [Late 16C. < modern Latin *chronologia* 'discourse of time' < Greek *khronos* 'time'] —**chronologist** *n*

chronometric /krónnə méttrik, krṓnə-/, **chronometrical** /-méttrik'l/ *adj* relating to or designed for the accurate measurement of time —**chronometrically** *adv*

chronometry /krə nómmətri/ *n* the study of the accurate measurement of time —**chronometer** *n*

chronon /krṓ non/ *n* a unit of time equal to the time that it would take for a photon to cross the diameter of an electron, taken as approximately 10^{-24} seconds [< CHRONO- + -ON¹]

chronoscope /krónnə skōp, krṓnə-/ *n* an electronic instrument that is designed to measure very small intervals of time with extreme precision —**chronoscopic** /krónnə skóppik, krṓnə-/ *adj*

chrysalid /kríssəlid/ *adj* describes the stage between larva and adult in an insect and the protective covering formed at this time ■ *n* (*plural* **chrysalids** or **chrysalides** /kri sálli deez/) INSECTS same as **chrysalis** [Late 18C. < Latin *chrysa(l)lid-*, stem of *chrysa(l)lis* (see CHRYSALIS)]

chrysalis /kríssəliss/ (*plural* **-lises**) *n* **1.** INSECT BETWEEN LARVA AND ADULT an insect at the stage of changing from larva to adult, during which it is inactive and encased in a hard cocoon **2.** INSECT COCOON the hard cocoon that protects a butterfly, moth, or other pupa during its change from larva to adult **3.** THING DEVELOPING anything in an early or intermediate stage of development (*literary*) [Early 17C. Via Latin *chrysal(l)is* < Greek *khrūsalis* < *khrūsos* 'gold'; from the colour or sheen of some pupae]

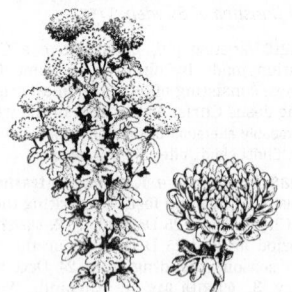

chrysanthemum

chrysanthemum /krə sánthəməm, -zán-/ *n* a perennial garden plant with many cultivated varieties. Flowers: brightly coloured, many varied shapes, small densely clustered petals. Genus: *Chrysanthemum*. [Mid-16C. < Greek *khrūsanthemon* 'gold flower'; from the colour of the corn marigold]

Chryse /kríssi/ lowland plain in the northern equatorial region of Mars where Viking 1 landed in 1976

chryselephantine /kríss eli fántīn/ *adj* describes classical Greek sculptures that are made of or overlaid with gold and ivory [Early 19C. < Greek *khrūselephantinos* < *khrūsos* 'gold' + *elephas* 'elephant, ivory']

chryso- *prefix* gold, golden ○ *chrysotile* [< Greek *khrūsos* 'gold' < Semitic]

chrysoberyl /kríssə berəl/ *n* a green, yellow, or brown variety of beryl. Use: gems. [Mid-17C. < Latin *chrysoberyllus* < Greek *khrūsos* 'gold' + *bērullos* 'beryl']

chrysomelid /kríssə méllid, -meélid/ *n* a small brightly coloured leaf-eating beetle. Colorado beetles are chrysomelids. Family: Chrysomelidae. [Late 19C. < modern Latin *Chrysomelidae* (plural) < *Chrysomela* < Greek *khrūsomēlon* 'golden apple']

chrysoprase /kríssə prayz/ *n* a bright green semiprecious stone that is a variety of chalcedony. Use: gems. [13C. Via French < Greek *khrūsoprasos* 'golden leek']

Chrysostom /kríssəstəm/, **John, St** (349?–407) Syrian theologian and orator. He was bishop of Constantinople and a church father of both the Roman Catholic and the Eastern Orthodox traditions.

chrysotile /kríssə tīl/ *n* a green, grey, or white fibrous variety of the mineral serpentine. Use: formerly in heat-resistant materials. [Mid-19C. < CHRYSO- + Greek *tilos* 'fibre' < *tillein* 'to pluck']

chthonic /thónnik, khthó-/, **chthonian** /thṓni ən, kthṓ-/ *adj* relating to the underworld as described in Greek mythology [Late 19C. < Greek *khthōn* 'earth']

chub /chub/ (*plural* **chubs** or *same*) *n* a fish with a thick rounded body found in fresh water. Family: Cyprinidae. [15C. Origin ?]

chubby /chúbbi/ (**-bier, -biest**) *adj* pleasantly or charmingly plump, especially in the way that healthy babies and toddlers often are —**chubbily** *adv* —**chubbiness** *n*

chuck[1] /chuk/ *vt* (**chucks, chucking, chucked**) **1. THROW SOMETHING CARELESSLY** to throw something, especially in a careless or casual way (*informal*) **2. DISCARD SOMETHING** to get rid of something unwanted (*informal*) **3. EJECT SOMEBODY** to remove somebody from a place or a position (*informal*) **4. ABANDON SOMETHING** to give something up, especially a job (*informal*) **5. BREAK OFF WITH SOMEBODY** to end a relationship with a boyfriend or girlfriend (*informal*) **6. TICKLE SOMEBODY UNDER CHIN** to give somebody an affectionate pat or tickle under the chin ■ *n* **1. CARELESS THROW** a throw, especially a careless or casual one (*informal*) **2. AFFECTIONATE TICKLE UNDER CHIN** an affectionate pat or tickle under somebody's chin [Early 16C. Origin ?]

SYNONYMS See *throw*.

chuck in *v* (*informal*) **1.** *vt* to give something up, especially a job **2.** *vi* to contribute to the cost of something
chuck up *vti* same as **vomit** *v* (sense 1) (*informal*)

chuck[2] /chuk/ *n* **1.** a clamping device with three or four adjustable jaws. Use: to hold a piece of woodwork or metalwork in a lathe or a bit in a drill. **2.** a cut of beef that extends from the neck to the shoulder blade [Late 17C Variant of CHOCK]

chuck[3] /chuk/ *vi* (**chucks, chucking, chucked**), *n* same as **cluck** *v* (sense 1) [14C. An imitation of the sound] —**chuck** *n*

chuck[4] /chuk/ *n N England, regional* used as an affectionate way of addressing a man or a woman [Late 16C. Alteration of CHICK[1]]

chuckhole /chúk hōl/ *n Midwest* ROADS same as **pothole** (sense 1) [Mid-19C. < CHUCK[1]]

chuckie /chúki/ *n regional, Scotland* a small stone [Mid-18C. < CHUCK[1]]

chuckle /chúk'l/ *vti* (**-les, -ling, -led**) to laugh quietly or to yourself, or say something with a quiet laugh ■ *n* a quiet or inward laugh [Late 16C. < CHUCK[3]] —**chuckler** *n*

chuckwalla /chúk wolə/ (*plural* **-las** or *same*) *n* a large lizard with a dark body and a blunt yellow tail. Native to: deserts of southwestern United States and Mexico. Latin name: *Sauromalus obesus*. [Late 19C. Via Mexican Spanish *chachuala* < Cahuilla *tcàxxwal*]

chuck-will's-widow *n* a large bird of the nightjar family with mottled brown markings. Native to: central and southern United States. Latin name: *Caprimulgus carolinensis*. [Late 18C. An imitation of its call]

chuddar *n* ISLAM another spelling of **chador**

chuddies /chúddiz/ *npl* same as **underpants** (*informal; used especially in British Asian English*) [Late 20C. Probably alteration of CHURIDARS] ◇ **kiss my chuddies** used to express contempt or defiance, especially as a playground taunt (*informal*)

chufa /choófə/ *n* a plant of the sedge family with an edible tuber that looks like a nut. Native to: Africa. Latin name: *Cyperus esculentus*. [Mid-19C. < Spanish, 'fluff, nonsense']

chuffed /chuft/ *adj* very pleased or satisfied (*informal*) [Mid-20C. < English dialect *chuff* 'plump, chubby, happy', origin ?]

chug[1] /chug/ *vi* (**chugs, chugging, chugged**) **1. MAKE REPEATED THUDDING SOUND** to make a repetitive thudding sound like that of a small engine **2. MOVE WITH CHUGGING SOUND** to move along slowly with a chugging sound under the power of an engine **3. CONTINUE IN STEADY FASHION** to continue steadily doing the usual things (*informal*) ■ *n* **CHUGGING NOISE** the chugging noise that an engine makes [Mid-19C. An imitation of the sound]

chug[2] /chug/ (**chugs, chugging, chugged**) *vt N Am* to drink something, especially beer, quickly and in one go (*slang*) [Late 20C. An imitation of the sound of gulping]

chugger /chúggər/ *n* somebody who stops passers-by on the street and solicits regular donations for a charitable organization (*slang*) [Late 20C. Blend of CHARITY + MUGGER[1]] —**chugging** *n*

chukar /chu kaár, choŏ kaar/ *n* a greyish-brown partridge with red legs and beak. Native to: South Asia. Latin name: *Alectoris chukar*. [Early 19C. < Hindi *cakor*, probably an imitation of its cry]

Chukchi /chúkchi, choŏk-/ (*plural same* or **-chis**), **Chukchee** /choŏk chee, chúk-/ (*plural same* or **-chees**) *n* **1.** a member of an indigenous people of northeastern Siberia. The Chukchi were the first to breed huskies as working dogs. **2.** a language spoken in northeastern Siberia, belonging to a small isolated language family. Native speakers: 12,000. [Early 18C. < Russian] —**Chukchi** *adj*

Chukchi Sea /chúkchi-, choŏk-/ part of the Arctic Ocean, situated north of the Bering Strait between Asia and North America

chukka /chúkə/ *n* **1.** any of the six periods of continuous play in a polo match, each lasting for approximately 7.5 minutes **2.** *also* **chukka boot** a casual ankle-high lace-up boot, typically made of suede [Late 19C. < Hindi *cak(k)ar* 'circular course' < Indo-European]

chukker /chúkər/, **chukkar** *n* US spelling of **chukka** (sense 1)

Chulalongkorn /choŏlə lóng kawrn/, **Rama V** (1853–1910) Siamese monarch who ruled from 1868 until 1910, and was noted for his modernization programmes

chum[1] /chum/ *n* (*dated informal*) **1. FRIEND** a close friend **2. WAY OF ADDRESSING MAN** used as a term of address for a man ■ *v* (**chums, chumming, chummed**) **1.** *vi* **BE FRIENDS** to be friends with somebody, or behave in a friendly way towards somebody **2.** *vt regional, Scotland* **GO WITH SOMEBODY** to accompany somebody somewhere [Late 17C. Probably shortening of *chamber-fellow*]

chum[2] /chum/ *n* **1.** *N Am* **FISH BAIT** an angler's bait, especially chopped fish, scattered on the water **2. CHEAP TRINKETS** inexpensive trinkets such as cuff links and pins bearing the US presidential seal (*slang*) ■ *vti* (**chums, chumming, chummed**) **USE FISH CHUM** to fish using chum on the water [Mid-19C. Origin ?]

chum[3] /chum/ (*plural* **chums** or *same*) *n* FISH same as **chum salmon** [Early 20C. < Chinook Jargon *tzum (samun)* 'spotted (salmon)']

chummy /chúmmi/ (**-mier, -miest**) *adj* friendly or on close terms (*informal*) [Late 19C. < CHUM[1]] —**chummily** *adv* —**chumminess** *n*

chump[1] /chump/ *n* **1. THICK END OF MEAT** a thick end of a piece of meat, particularly of a leg of lamb or mutton (*often used before a noun*) ○ *a chump chop* **2. UNWISE PERSON** an unwise person, especially somebody whom the person using the term is rather fond of (*dated informal*) **3. HEAD** somebody's head or mind (*dated slang*) **4. THICK PIECE OF WOOD** a short thick piece of wood [Early 18C. Origin ?]

chump[2] /chump/ *vti, n* same as **chomp**

chump change *n US* an insignificant amount of money (*slang*)

chum salmon *n* a salmon with wavy vertical green streaks and blotches. Native to: northern Pacific waters. Latin name: *Oncorhynchus keta*. [< CHUM[3]]

chunder /chúndər/ *vti* (**-ders, -dering, -dered**) same as **vomit** *v* (sense 1) (*slang*) ■ *n* same as **vomit** (*informal*) [Mid-20C. Probably shortening of *chunder loo*, rhyming slang for *spew*, after *Chunder Loo of Akim Foo*, cartoon character in Australian boot-polish advertisements]

Chungking, **Ch'ung-ch'ing** ➧ **Chongqing**

chunk /chungk/ *n* **1.** a thick squarish piece of something, e.g. bread, wood, or meat **2.** a large amount or part of something [Late 17C. Alteration of CHUCK[2]]

chunky /chúngki/ (**-ier, -iest**) *adj* **1. WITH LUMPS** containing lumps or bits **2. SQUARE AND SOLID** solid and squarish ○ *a chunky table* **3. MADE OF THICK MATERIAL** made from thick material, especially wool **4. SHORT AND BROAD** short, broad, and sometimes overweight (*informal*) —**chunkily** *adv* —**chunkiness** *n*

Chunnel /chúnn'l/ *n* same as **Channel Tunnel** (*informal*) [Early 20C. Blend of CHANNEL[1] + TUNNEL]

chunni /choŏnni/ (*plural* **-nis**) *n S Asia* CLOTHING same as **dupatta** [< Punjabi]

chunter /chúntər/ (**-ers, -ering, -ered**) *vi* to say something or complain to yourself in a quiet voice (*informal*) [Late 17C. Probably an imitation of the sound]

chup /chup/ *interj S Asia* used to tell somebody to be quiet [< Hindi *cuprao*]

chuppah /hoŏppə/ (*plural* **chuppahs** or **chuppot** /-pot/ or **chupoth** /-poth/), **huppah** (*plural* **-pahs** or **-pot** or **-poth**) *n* **1.** the canopy under which a Jewish wedding ceremony is performed **2.** the Jewish wedding ceremony [Late 19C. < Hebrew *ḥuppāh* 'canopy']

church /church/ *n* **1. RELIGIOUS BUILDING** a building for public worship, especially in the Christian religion **2.** *also* **Church RELIGION'S FOLLOWERS AS GROUP** all the followers of a religion, especially the Christian religion, considered collectively **3. RELIGIOUS SERVICE** a religious service that takes place in a church ○ *go to church* **4. CLERGY** the clergy as distinct from lay people **5.** *also* **Church RELIGIOUS AUTHORITY** religious authority as opposed to the authority of the state **6.** *also* **Church BRANCH OF CHRISTIAN RELIGION** a denomination or branch of the Christian religion ■ *vt* (**churches, churching, churched**) CHR **GIVE SOMEBODY CHURCH BLESSING** to give a blessing in church to somebody, especially a woman who has recently given birth (*dated; often passive*) [Old English *cir(i)ce*, via Germanic < Greek *kuriakon dōma* 'house of the lord' < *kurios* 'lord']

Church Army *n* a voluntary organization founded by the Church of England in the 19th century to help parish priests evangelize

Church Commissioners *npl* a group of representatives of church and state who are responsible for the administration of the finances and property of the Church of England

church father *n* a Christian writer of the pre-8th century group of scholars who established the doctrines and practices of Christianity in their work (*usually used in the plural*)

churchgoer /chúrch gō ər/ *n* an attender of a church service or church services —**churchgoing** *n, adj*

Churchill /chúrchil/ **1.** seaport in northeastern Manitoba, Canada, situated on Hudson Bay at the mouth of the River Churchill. Population: 1,089 (1996). **2.** river that flows across south-central Labrador, Newfoundland, Canada, from Ashuanipi Lake, emptying into Lake Melville. The river provides hydroelectric power. Length: 335 km/208 mi. **3.** river that flows through numerous lakes from Lac la Loche in Saskatchewan through Manitoba, into Hudson Bay. Length: 1,600 km/1,000 mi.

Churchill, Charles (1731–64) British poet. His satirical verse includes *The Rosciad* (1761).

> 'Fashion—a word which knaves and fools may use, / Their knavery and folly to excuse.'
> [Charles Churchill, *The Rosciad*; 1761]

Churchill, Randolph, Lord (1849–95) British politician. The father of Sir Winston Churchill, he was secretary for India (1885–86).

'I should never be allowed out in private.'
[Randolph Churchill. Quoted in *Randolph: A Study of Churchill's Son*, B. Roberts; 1984]

Sir Winston Churchill

Churchill, **Sir Winston** (1874–1965) British politician and writer. As prime minister (1940–45, 1951–55) he led Britain through World War II. He wrote *The Second World War* (1948–53) and won the Nobel Prize in literature (1953). Full name **Churchill, Sir Winston Leonard Spencer**. See table at **prime minister** —**Churchillian** /chur chílyən/ *adj*

'We shall fight in France, we shall fight on the seas and oceans, we shall fight...in the air, we shall defend our island, whatever the cost may be, we shall fight on the beaches, we shall fight on the landing grounds, we shall fight in the fields and in the streets, we shall fight in the hills; we shall never surrender.'
[Sir Winston Churchill, *Speech to Parliament*; 4 June 1940]

church key *n N Am* a metal tool with a bottle opener at one end and a sharp-pointed triangular head for opening tins at the other end

churchly /chúrchli/ *adj* similar to, suitable for, or typical of a church —**churchliness** *n*

churchman /chúrchmən/ (*plural* -**men** /-mən/) *n* **1.** a man who is a member of the clergy **2.** a man who is a practising member of a church —**churchmanship** *n*

church mode *n* any of a group of eight scales used for church music in the Middle Ages, e.g. the Dorian, Phrygian, or Lydian mode

Church of Christ, Scientist *n* the official name of the Christian Science Church

Church of England *n* the church that is the established church in England, governed by bishops and with the reigning monarch as its titular head

Church of Jesus Christ of Latter-Day Saints *n* a church founded by Joseph Smith in 1830, based on teachings in the Book of Mormon, and centred in Salt Lake City, Utah

Church of Rome *n* CHR same as **Roman Catholic Church**

Church of Scotland *n* the Presbyterian church that is the established church in Scotland

church parade *n* a parade in church of members of the armed forces or other uniformed organizations as part of a special church service

churchperson /chúrch purss'n/ (*plural* -**people** /-peep'l/ or -**persons**) *n* **1.** somebody who is a member of the clergy **2.** somebody who is a practising member of a church

church school *n* a school that provides children with a general education, and was founded or is supported by the Church of England

Church Slavonic *n*, *adj* LANG same as **Old Church Slavonic**

churchwarden /chúrch wáwrd'n/ *n* **1.** a lay person who manages secular matters in an Anglican church **2.** a long-stemmed clay tobacco pipe

churchwoman /chúrch woomən/ (*plural* -**women** /-wimin/) *n* **1.** a woman who is a member of the clergy **2.** a woman who is a practising member of a church

churchy /chúrchi/ (-**ier**, -**iest**) *adj* **1.** zealously, even intolerantly, religious **2.** resembling or suggesting a church

churchyard /chúrch yaard/ *n* an area surrounding a church that is usually used as a graveyard

churidars /choóri daarz/ *npl* long close-fitting trousers worn by both men and women in or from northern parts of South Asia [< Hindi]

churinga /chə ríng gə/ *n Aus* a small carved or painted piece of wood or stone, regarded as sacred by Australian Aboriginals [Late 19C. < Aranda *tjwerrenge*]

churl /churl/ *n* somebody regarded as having bad manners [Old English *ceorl* 'man, freeman of the lowest rank' < Germanic]

churlish /chúrlish/ *adj* **1.** characteristic of somebody with bad manners **2.** surly, sullen, or miserly —**churlishly** *adv* —**churlishness** *n*

churn /churn/ *n* **1.** MILK CAN a large metal container for transporting milk **2.** BUTTER MAKER a container or device in which milk or cream is stirred vigorously to produce butter ■ *v* (**churns, churning, churned**) **1.** *vt* STIR MILK OR CREAM to stir or beat milk or cream vigorously to make butter **2.** *vt* MAKE BUTTER to make butter by beating milk or cream **3.** *vti* SPLASH VIOLENTLY to move about violently, or cause a liquid or soft solid to move about violently **4.** *vi* FEEL UNSETTLED to move unpleasantly, as if in a churn ○ *My stomach was churning.* **5.** *vt* FIN TRADE STOCKS FREQUENTLY FOR COMMISSION to buy and sell stocks and bonds on a frequent basis in order to earn brokerage commissions [Old English *cyrin* < Germanic] —**churner** *n*
churn out *vt* to produce or issue something quickly or regularly and in large quantities

churr /chur/ (**churrs, churring, churred**), **chirr** (**chirrs, chirring, chirred**) *vi* to make the high-pitched vibrating sound typical of some birds such as the nightjar, and some insects such as the cicada [Mid-16C. An imitation of the sound] —**churr** *n*

Churriguera /chúrri gáirə/, **José Benito** (1665–1725) Spanish architect. His high baroque style is characterized by spiral pillars and elaborate ornamentation. —**Churrigueresque** /chúrrigə résk/ *adj*

chute[1] /shoot/ *n* **1.** SLOPE TO DROP THINGS DOWN an inclined channel or passage that something can slide down **2.** LEISURE CHILDREN'S SLIDE a children's slide in a park or swimming pool **3.** SNOW-COVERED SLOPE a snow- or ice-covered slope or channel for sports such as tobogganing or bobsleighing **4.** SLOPE OR DROP ON WATERCOURSE a waterfall, rapids, or steep descent in a river or stream **5.** AGRIC SLOPING PASSAGE FOR ANIMALS a narrow passageway through which animals are driven to be branded, sheared, loaded, dipped, or sprayed [Early 19C. < French, 'fall' < Latin *cadere* 'to fall']

SPELLCHECK chute or **shoot**? Do not confuse the spelling of *chute* and *shoot*, which sound similar. *Chute* is chiefly used as a noun, denoting a slope to slide or drop things down. *Chute* is also a short form of *parachute*. The word *shoot* is a verb or noun with a wide range of meanings and uses. As a verb it can mean 'fire a weapon at somebody or something', 'move fast', 'take a photograph of somebody or something', 'attempt to score a goal', etc., as in *shoot a pheasant, he shot off down the road*. As a noun it can mean 'a new plant growth', 'an occasion for photography', or 'a hunting party'.

chute[2] /shoot/ *n* AVIAT same as **parachute** *n* (sense 1) (*informal*) [Early 20C. Shortening] —**chutist** *n*

chutney /chútni/ (*plural* -**neys**) *n* **1.** a sweet and spicy relish made from fruit, spices, sugar, and vinegar **2.** *Carib* a popular Caribbean form of song with a quick beat, much influenced by calypso in rhythm and choice of subjects [Early 19C. < Hindi *caṭnī*]

chutzpah /hoótspə, kh-/, **hutzpah, chutzpa** *n* (*informal*) **1.** boldness coupled with supreme self-confidence **2.** impudent rudeness or lack of respect [Late 19C. Via Yiddish < Aramaic *ḥuṣpā*]

Chuvash /choo vaásh/ *n* a Turkic language spoken west of the Urals in central Russia. Native speakers: 2 million. [Via Russian < Chuvash *čăvaš*] —**Chuvash** *adj*

chyle /kil/ *n* a milky fluid consisting of lymph and emulsified fat that forms in the small intestine during digestion [15C. Via late Latin < Greek *khūlos* 'animal or plant juice'] —**chylaceous** /kī láyshəss/ *adj* —**chylous** *adj*

chylomicron /kílō míkron/ *n* a microscopic particle, containing fats, cholesterol, phospholipids, and protein, formed in the small intestine and absorbed into the blood during digestion

chyme /kīm/ *n* a thick fluid mass of partially digested food and gastric secretions passed from the stomach to the small intestine [Early 17C. Via late Latin < Greek *khūmos* 'animal or plant juice' < Indo-European] —**chymous** *adj*

chymopapain /kīmōpə páy in, -pī in/ *n* an enzyme found in papayas that helps digest proteins. Use: medicines, meat tenderizer.

chymosin /kíməssin/ *n* BIOCHEM same as **rennin** [< CHYME + -OSE[2]]

chymotrypsin /kīmō trípsin/ *n* a protein-digesting enzyme in pancreatic juice [Mid-20C. < CHYME] —**chymotryptic** *adj*

chymotrypsinogen /kīmō trip sínnəjən/ *n* the inactive form of chymotrypsin that is converted into chymotrypsin by the enzyme trypsin

chypre /sheéprə/ *n* perfume made from sandalwood [Late 19C. < French, 'Cyprus']

ci *abbr* ONLINE Côte d'Ivoire (*used in Internet addresses*) See table at **domain name**

Ci[1] *abbr* METEOROL cirrus

Ci[2] *symbol* MEASURE, PHYS curie

CI *abbr* **1.** Cayman Islands **2.** Channel Islands

CIA *n* a US federal bureau responsible for gathering foreign intelligence and conducting counter-intelligence activities. Full form **Central Intelligence Agency**

ciabatta /chə báttə/ *n* a flat white Italian bread made with olive oil [Late 20C. < Italian, 'slipper'; from the shape of the loaf]

ciao /chow/ *interj* used to say hello or goodbye (*informal*) [Early 20C. < Italian, literally 'I am your slave']

CIB *abbr* **1.** BANKING Chartered Institute of Bankers **2.** POLICE Criminal Investigation Branch

ciborium /si báwri əm/ (*plural* -**ria** /-ri ə/) *n* **1.** a canopy that stands on four pillars over the altar in some Christian churches **2.** a small container with a lid, used to hold the consecrated wafers for Communion [Mid-16C. Via medieval Latin < Greek *kibōrion* 'seed vessel of a water lily']

cicada

cicada /si kaádə/ (*plural* -**das** or -**dae** /-dee/) *n* a large winged insect that lives in trees and tall grass, the male of which makes a shrill sound. Family: Cicadidae. [15C. < Latin]

cicatrice /síkətriss/ *n* MED same as **cicatrix**

cicatrise /síkətrīz/ *vti* MED another spelling of **cicatrize**

cicatrix /síkətriks/ (*plural* **cicatrices** /síkə trī seez/), **cicatrice** /síkətriss/ *n* **1.** MED same as **scar**[1] *n* (sense 1) (*technical*) **2.** a scar left on a stem where a leaf used to be attached [Mid-17C. < Latin, 'scar'] —**cicatricial** /síkə trísh'l/ *adj* —**cicatricose** /si káttrikōss/ *adj*

cicatrize /síkə trīz/ (-**trizes, -trizing, -trized**), **cicatrise** (-**trises, -trising, -trised**) *vti* to heal and form a scar, or cause a wound to heal and form a scar (*technical*) [15C. < French *cicatriser* < *cicatrice* 'scar'] —**cicatrization** /síkə trī záysh'n/ *n*

cicely /síssəli/ *n* PLANTS same as **sweet cicely** [Late 16C. < Latin *seselis*, assimilated to the woman's name *Cicely*]

cicero /síssərō/ *n* a size of printed character slightly larger than the pica [< its first use (1458) for an edition of the works of CICERO]

Cicero /síssərō/, **Marcus Tullius** (106–43 BC) Roman philosopher, writer, and politician. He was Rome's greatest orator during a long political career. His

letters and essays are known for their rich prose style. —**Ciceronian** /síssə rṓni ən/ *adj*

'When you have no basis for an argument, abuse the plaintiff.'
[Marcus Tullius Cicero, *Pro Flacco*; 1st century BC]

cicerone /chíchə rṓni, síssə-/ (*plural* **-nes** or **-ni** /-ni/) *n* a guide for tourists [Early 18C. < Italian, after CICERO; from a guide's knowledge and eloquence]

cichlid /síklid/ *n* a tropical freshwater fish with spiny fins, popular as an aquarium fish. Family: Cichlidae. [Late 19C. < modern Latin *Cichlidae* < Greek *kikhlē*, a kind of fish]

cicisbeo /chíchiz báyō/ (*plural* **-bei** /-báyee/) *n* a married woman's male escort or lover (*archaic or literary*) [Early 18C. < Italian]

Cid /sid/, **El** (1040?–99) Spanish military leader. Legend obscures the true nature of 'The Lord Champion' who fought both for and against Spain's Moorish rulers, and was virtual dictator of Valencia from 1094 to 1099. Born **Vivar, Rodriguez Díaz de**

CID[1] *n* the detective branch of the UK police force. Full form **Criminal Investigation Department**

CID[2] *abbr* ONLINE consider it done (*used in e-mails or text messages*)

-cide *suffix* **1.** killer ○ *fungicide* **2.** killing ○ *tyrannicide* [Via French < Latin *-cida* 'killer', *-cidium* 'killing' < *caedere* 'to kill'] —**-cidal** *suffix*

cider /sídər/ *n* **1.** an alcoholic drink made by pressing and fermenting apples. N Am term **hard cider 2.** *N Am* a nonalcoholic drink made from freshly pressed apples [13C. Via Old French *sidre* < Hebrew *šēkār* 'alcoholic drink']

CULTURAL NOTE *Cider With Rosie*, a memoir (1959) by Laurie Lee. An account of the author's childhood and youth in Gloucestershire, it is noted for its evocative descriptions of rural life and its affectionate portrayal of Lee's family and friends. Among his strongest memories is his first taste of cider, taken in a hay wagon with his friend Rosie.

cider vinegar *n* a light vinegar made from apple juice

ci-devant /see də vaaN/ *adj, adv* used to indicate that what follows was somebody's former name, office, or title (*formal*) [Early 18C. < French, 'before this']

~~cieling~~ incorrect spelling of **ceiling**

Cienfuegos /syen fwáy goss/ city and capital of Cienfuegos Province, central Cuba, situated on Cienfuegos Bay. Population: 132,000 (1996).

CIF, c.i.f. *abbr* cost, insurance, and freight

c.i.f.c.i. *abbr* FREIGHT cost, insurance, freight, commission, and interest (*used in quotes to indicate what is included in the price*)

CIFE *abbr* EDUC colleges and institutes for further education

cig /sig/ *n* same as **cigarette** (*informal*) [Late 19C. Shortening]

cigar /si gáar/ *n* a cylindrical roll of tobacco leaves for smoking, with thin brown paper or a single tobacco leaf as an outer covering [Early 18C. Directly or via French *cigare* < Spanish *cigarro*, probably < Mayan *sik'ar* 'smoking'] ◇ **close but no cigar** *N Am* the answer, response, or result is not good enough (*informal*)

~~cigaret~~ incorrect spelling of **cigarette**

cigarette /síggə rét/ *n* **1.** a cylindrical roll of shredded tobacco leaves for smoking, with an outer covering of thin, usually white, paper **2.** a roll of shredded leaves of any kind for smoking, e.g. marijuana leaves or leaves of herbs ○ *a marijuana cigarette* [Mid-19C. < French, 'small cigar' < *cigare* (see CIGAR)]

cigarette card *n* a small card with a picture and information on it, formerly given away inside a cigarette packet and now considered a collector's item

cigarette lighter *n* same as **lighter**[1] (sense 1)

cigarette pants *npl* women's trousers with straight close-fitting legs

cigarette paper *n* a sheet of thin paper with gum on one edge, used with loose tobacco to roll cigarettes

cigarillo /síggə rílló/ (*plural* **-los**) *n* a slender cigar about the same size as a cigarette [Mid-19C. < Spanish, 'small cigar' < *cigarro* (see CIGAR)]

~~cigerette~~ incorrect spelling of **cigarette**

~~ciggarette~~ incorrect spelling of **cigarette**

ciggy /síggi/ (*plural* **-gies**) *n* same as **cigarette** (*informal*) [Mid-20C. Shortening and alteration]

CII *abbr* Chartered Insurance Institute

cilantro /si lántrō/ *n* coriander leaves. Use: flavouring food in cookery. [Early 20C. Via Spanish < Latin *coriandrum* 'coriander']

cilia MICROBIOL plural of **cilium**

ciliary /sílli əri/ *adj* **1.** describes the short threads (**cilia**) projecting from some cells and the beating movement they make **2.** describes the tissue and muscle that surrounds the lens of the eye [Late 17C. < CILIUM]

ciliary body *n* the ring-shaped part at the front of the eye that connects the pigmented layer (**choroid**) of the eyeball with the iris diaphragm. It also contains the ciliary muscle, which alters the curvature of the lens.

ciliate /sílli ayt, -ət/ *n* a simple microscopic organism with projecting threads that thrash to help it to move along. Phylum: Ciliophora. [Mid-18C. < CILIUM] —**ciliate** *adj* —**ciliated** /-aytid/ *adj*

cilice /sílliss/ *n* **1.** TEXTILES same as **haircloth 2.** a garment made of haircloth [Late 16C. Via French < Greek *Kilikia* 'Cilicia', district of Anatolia; because made of goats' hair from Cilicia]

~~cilinder~~ incorrect spelling of **cylinder**

cilium /sílli əm/ (*plural* **-ia** /-i ə/) *n* **1.** a tiny projecting thread, found with many others on a cell or microscopic organism, that beats rhythmically to aid the movement of a fluid past the cell or movement of the organism through liquid **2.** MED same as **eyelash** (*technical*) [Early 18C. < Latin, 'eyelash']

Cimarosa /cheémə rṓzə/, **Domenico** (1749–1801) Italian composer. The most famous of his 60 operas is the light-hearted *The Secret Marriage* (1792).

cimbalom /símbələm, tsímb-/ *n* a musical instrument resembling a hammered dulcimer, used especially in Hungarian folk music [Late 19C. Via Hungarian < Italian *cimbalo* 'dulcimer']

Cimbri /símbri/ *npl* a Germanic people who lived in parts of Jutland and the Rhine valley during the second century BC. They began to spread southwards, but were routed by the Romans in 101 BC. [< Latin]

cimetidine /sī métti deen/ *n* a drug that decreases production of stomach acid. Use: peptic ulcer treatment. [Late 20C. < CYANO- + METHYL + -IDINE]

cimex /símeks/ (*plural* **cimices** /sími seez/) *n* a bedbug or related insect that feeds on birds, humans, and other mammals. Genus: *Cimex.* [Late 16C. < Latin, 'bedbug']

Cimmerian /si meéri ən/ *adj* dark and gloomy (*literary*) ■ *n* in Greek mythology, a member of a people who lived in a land of perpetual darkness [Late 16C. < Latin *Cimmerius* < Greek *Kimmerios*]

~~cinamon~~ incorrect spelling of **cinnamon**

C in C, C-in-C *abbr* MIL Commander in Chief

cinch /sinch/ (*informal*) *n* **1.** SOMETHING EASILY DONE something that can be done or achieved with very little effort **2.** SOMETHING CERTAIN something that is absolutely certain to happen ■ *vt* (**cinches, cinching, cinched**) **1.** *N Am* GRASP SOMETHING ROUND MIDDLE to grasp something round the middle, as a belt does **2.** ASSURE SOMETHING to make certain of something [Mid-19C. < Spanish *cinche* 'girth' < Latin *cingere* 'gird']

cinchona /sing kṓnə/ *n* **1.** *also* **cinchona bark** the dried bark of a South American tree. Use: source of quinine and some other drugs. **2.** an evergreen tree or bush that produces cinchona. Native to: South America. Genus: *Cinchona.* [Mid-18C. < modern Latin, after the Countess of *Chinchón* (1576–1641), vicereine of Peru] —**cinchonic** /-kónnik/ *adj*

cinchonine /síng kə neen/ *n* a colourless crystalline solid. Source: cinchona bark. Use: treatment of malaria. Formula: $C_{19}H_{22}N_{20}$.

cinchonism /síngkənizəm/ *n* a condition resulting from the excessive use of quinine and other drugs derived from cinchona bark. The symptoms are headache, ringing in the ears, temporary deafness, and dizziness.

Cincinnati /sínssi nátti/ city in southwestern Ohio on the Ohio-Kentucky border, on the Ohio River, southwest of Dayton. Population: 323,885 (2002 estimate).

Cincinnatus /sínssi náttəss/, **Lucius Quinctius** (519?–430 BC) Roman general and politician. Considered a model of republican Roman values, he was twice appointed dictator when Rome was under attack. After defeating the enemy, he refused all honours and retired to his farm.

cincture /síngkchər/ *n* a girdle or belt, especially a cord or sash tied round a priest's, monk's, or nun's habit [Late 16C. < Latin *cinctura* 'girdle' < *cingere* 'gird']

cinder /síndər/ *n* BURNT WOOD OR FUEL a small piece of charred wood or coal, especially one that continues to glow ■ **cinders** *npl* **1.** ASHES the ashes that remain after a fire has burnt out **2.** INDUST SLAG waste material produced by smelting **3.** GEOL FRAGMENTS OF SOLIDIFIED LAVA loose fragments of porous solidified lava that is ejected from a volcano and builds up round the crater [Old English *sinder* 'slag' < Germanic] —**cindery** *adj*

cinder block *n N Am* same as **breeze block**

Cinderella /síndə réllə/ *n* an object of undeserved neglect ■ *adj* achieving sudden recognition or success, or relating to somebody or something achieving this [Mid-19C. After the fairy-tale character *Cinderella*, who is neglected by her stepmother and sisters but enabled by her fairy godmother to attend a ball and meet a prince]

cine- *prefix* film, motion picture ○ *cinephile* [< CINEMA]

cineaste /sínni ast/ *n* **1.** a fan of films and film making **2.** a maker of films [Early 20C. < French < *ciné*, shortening of *cinématographe* (see CINEMA)]

cine camera /sínni-/ *n* a camera used for taking moving pictures rather than still photographs. N Am term **movie camera** [Shortening of *cinematographic*]

cine film *n* photographic film used for making moving pictures rather than still photographs. N Am term **movie film** [Shortening of *cinematographic*]

cinema /sínnəmə, sínni maa/ *n* **1.** PLACE TO WATCH FILMS a building or room where films are shown **2.** CINEMAS COLLECTIVELY cinemas considered collectively **3.** FILM INDUSTRY the film industry, or the business of making films **4.** FILMS COLLECTIVELY films considered collectively [Early 20C. < French *cinéma*, shortening of *cinématographe*, literally 'movement writing' < Greek *kinēma* 'movement']

cinemagoer /sínnəmə gō ər, sínni maa-/ *n* somebody who is watching a film at a cinema or who regularly goes to the cinema. N Am term **moviegoer**

cinematheque /sínnəmə tek/ *n* a small cinema, especially one showing artistic or classic films [Mid-20C. < French < *cinéma* (see CINEMA)]

cinematic /sínnə máttik/ *adj* **1.** typical of the style in which films are made **2.** relating to films or film-making —**cinematically** *adv*

cinematize /sínnəmə tīz/ (**-tizes, -tizing, -tized**), **cinematise** (**-tises, -tising, -tised**) *vt* to adapt a play, novel, or other work for the cinema

cinematograph /sínnə máttə graaf, -graf/ *n* a combined cine camera and projector now rarely used except for optical effects photography [Late 19C. < French *cinématographe* (see CINEMA)]

cinematography /sínnəmə tóggrəfi/ *n* the art or technique of photographing and lighting films —**cinematographer** *n* —**cinematographic** /sínnə matə gráffik/ *adj* —**cinematographically** *adv*

cinéma vérité /sínnəmə vérri tay/ *n* a style of filmmaking characterized by a search for an authentic documentary feel. The term was first applied to a series of French documentary films in the 1960s. [Mid-20C. < French, 'cinema of truth']

cineole /sínni ōl/, **cineol** *n* CHEM same as **eucalyptol** [Late 19C. Reversal of modern Latin *oleum cinae* 'wormseed oil']

cinephile /sínni fīl/ *n* CINEMA same as **cineaste** (sense 1)

cineraria /sínnə ráiri ə/ *n* a plant cultivated as a houseplant for its mass of blue, purple, or red flowers resembling daisies. Native to: Canary Islands. Latin name: *Senecio hybridus.* [Late 16C.

< modern Latin < Latin *ciner-* 'ashes'; from the fluffy grey leaves of the plant originally called this]

cinerarium /sínnə ráiri əm/ (*plural* **-ia** /-i ə/) *n* a place where the ashes of a corpse are stored [Mid-18C. < late Latin < Latin *ciner-* 'ashes']

cinerary /sínnərəri/ *adj* relating to ashes, especially human ashes [Mid-18C. < Latin *cinerarius* < *ciner-* 'ashes']

cinereous /si neéri əss/ (*literary*) *adj* **1.** LIKE OR OF ASHES resembling or consisting of ashes **2.** OF GREY COLOUR of an ash-grey colour ■ *n* GREY COLOUR an ash-grey colour [15C. < Latin *cinereus* < *ciner-* 'ashes']

cinerin /sínnərin/ *n* an oily liquid compound. Source: pyrethrum. Use: insecticides. [Mid-20C. < Latin *ciner-* 'ashes']

cingulum /síng gyŏŏləm/ (*plural* **-la** /-lə/) *n* **1.** a part of the body that surrounds or encircles another part **2.** a band or stripe that encircles a plant or animal [Early 19C. < Latin, 'girdle' < *cingere* 'gird'] —**cingulate** /-lət, -layt/ *adj*

cinnabar /sínnə baar/ *n* **1.** MINERALS MINERAL SOURCE OF MERCURY a reddish-brown mineral consisting of mercuric sulphide. Use: source of mercury. **2.** CHEM RED PIGMENT red mercuric sulphide. Use: pigment. **3.** COLOURS BRIGHT RED a bright red colour tinged with orange [14C. Via Latin < Greek *kinnabari*] —**cinnabar** *adj* —**cinnabarine** /sínnəbə rīn, -baarin/ *adj*

cinnabar moth *n* a large European moth that has orange-red wings. Latin name: *Hypocrita jacobaeae*.

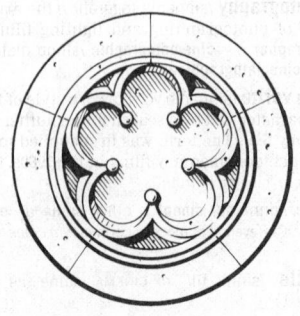

cinnamic acid

cinnamic acid /si námmik-/ *n* a white odourless acid that is insoluble in water. Use: perfume manufacture. Formula: $C_9H_8O_2$. [< its presence in cinnamon oil]

cinnamon /sínnəmən/ *n* **1.** FOOD SPICE OBTAINED FROM BARK a spice that is dried aromatic tree bark, used as strips or ground into powder **2.** TREES ASIAN TREE a tropical evergreen tree that produces cinnamon. Native to: Asia. Genus: *Cinnamomum*. **3.** COLOURS REDDISH-BROWN COLOUR a warm reddish-brown colour [14C. < French *cinnamome*] —**cinnamon** *adj*

cinnamon stone *n* MINERALS same as **essonite** [< its colour]

cinque /singk/ *n* the number five on cards or dice, or a throw of five in a dice game [14C. < French, 'five']

cinquecento /chíngkwi chéntō/ *n* the 16th century, especially with reference to Italian art and architecture [Mid-18C. < Italian, '500', shortening of *mil-cinquecento* '1500']

cinquefoil /síngk foyl, sángk-/ (*plural* **-foils** or *same*) *n* **1.** PLANTS same as **potentilla** **2.** an architectural

design in the form of five arcs joined together [13C. < Latin *quinquefolium* 'five leaves']

Cinque Ports /síngk-/ group of seaports on the southeastern coast of England: Sandwich, Dover, Hythe, Romney and Hastings. They historically supplied the monarch with ships in return for special privileges.

CIO *abbr* **1.** ONLINE check it out (*used in e-mails or text messages*) **2.** N Am Congress of Industrial Organizations **3.** ONLINE cut it out (*used in e-mails or text messages*)

cioppino /chə peénō/ *n* a thick seafood soup or stew with tomatoes, spices, and herbs, popular in the United States [Mid-20C. Origin ?]

Cipango /si páng gō/ *n* in medieval mythology, an island off the eastern coast of Asia, perhaps modern-day Japan

cipher /sífər/, **cypher** *n* **1.** WRITTEN CODE a written code in which the letters of a text are replaced with others according to a system **2.** CODE KEY the key to a cipher **3.** TEXT IN CODE a text written in cipher **4.** DESIGN DESIGN OF INTERLACING INITIALS a decorative design consisting of a set of interlaced initials **5.** MUSIC FAULT IN ORGAN VALVE a fault in an organ valve that causes a pipe to sound continuously without the key having been pressed ■ *v* (**-phers, -phering, -phered**) **1.** *vt* WRITE IN CODE to write a text or message in cipher **2.** *vi* MUSIC SOUND OWING TO FAULT to sound continuously because of a faulty valve (*refers to organs or organ pipes*) [14C. Via Old French *cif(f)re* < Arabic *şifr* 'zero']

cipolin /síppəlin/ *n* Italian marble with green and white streaks [Late 18C. Directly or via French < Italian *cipollino* 'small onion' < *cipolla* 'onion'; because its pattern resembles the layers of an onion]

Cipro /síppro/ *tdmk* a trademark for the antibiotic ciprofloxacin

ciprofloxacin /sípprō flóksəsin/ *n* a powerful antibiotic. Use: in eye drops for treatment of corneal ulcers and surface infections of the eye, treatment of anthrax in humans.

cir. *abbr* **1.** TIME circa **2.** MATHS circle **3.** ELEC circuit **4.** PUBL circulation **5.** MATHS circumference

circa /súrkə/ *prep* used before a date to indicate that it is approximate or estimated [Mid-19C. < Latin < *circus* 'circle']

circadian /sur káydi ən/ *adj* describes a pattern repeated approximately every 24 hours [Mid-20C. < Latin *circa* 'about' + *dies* 'day']

Circassian /sur kássi ən/ *n* a group of languages spoken in southern Russia, northern Georgia, and Turkey, belonging to the Abkhaz-Adyghean branch of North Caucasian languages. Native speakers: 1.5 million. [Mid-16C. < *Circassia*, Latinized form of Russian *Cherkes*] —**Circassian** *adj*

Circe /súrssi/ *n* in Greek mythology, the daughter of Hecate and the Sun, who lured sailors to her island where she made love to them and then turned them into pigs [12C. Via Latin < Greek *Kirkē*] —**Circean** *adj*

circinate /súrssi nayt/ *adj* describes leaves or fronds that are coiled with the tip in the centre, as in most ferns [Early 19C. < Latin *circinatus*, past participle of *circinare* 'make round' < *circinus* 'pair of compasses' < *circus* 'circle'] —**circinately** *adv*

Circinus /súrssinəss/ *n* a small inconspicuous constellation in the southern hemisphere near Centaurus [Early 19C. < Latin *circinus* (see CIRCINATE)]

~~circiut~~ incorrect spelling of **circuit**

circle /súrk'l/ *n* **1.** SHAPE OF PERFECT HOLLOW RING a two-dimensional geometric figure formed of a curved line surrounding a centre point, every point of the line being an equal distance from the centre point **2.** AREA INSIDE CIRCLE the area enclosed by a circle **3.** CIRCLE-SHAPED THING an area or object in the shape of a circle **4.** CIRCLE-SHAPED PATTERN an arrangement or pattern in the shape of a circle **5.** GROUP OF PEOPLE a group of people who share a common interest, profession, activity, or social background **6.** CURVED ROUTE a course or route that follows a curved path **7.** CYCLE a process or series of events that ends at the point at which it began or that repeats itself continuously **8.** THEATRE RAISED THEATRE SEATING a section of tiered seating in a theatre that is above ground level **9.** PREHIST FORMATION OF ANCIENT STONES a ring-shaped formation of large stones that dates from prehistoric times and is thought to have had a

religious or astronomical use ■ *v* (**-cles, -cling, -cled**) **1.** *vti* MOVE ALONG CURVING ROUTE to move, or move round something, following a curving route or path that ends where it began and usually repeats its cycle **2.** *vt* MAKE MARK ROUND SOMETHING to draw a ring round something in order to mark it or draw attention to it **3.** *vt* SURROUND PLACE OR AREA to surround a place or an area with people [Pre-12C. Via French < Latin *circulus* 'small circle' < *circus* 'circle'] —**circler** *n* ◇ **come full circle** to return to an earlier or first position or situation after leaving it ◇ **go** *or* **run round in circles** to be very busy without actually achieving anything ◇ **square the circle** to try to do something extremely difficult or impossible

CULTURAL NOTE *The Caucasian Chalk Circle*, a play (1948) by German dramatist Bertolt Brecht. The central story of this play within a play portrays a dispute for the custody of a young boy between his natural mother and the woman who has raised him at great personal cost. The work examines traditional values and the need to adapt them to changing historical circumstances.

circlet /súrklət/ *n* **1.** a circular decoration, especially a decorative band worn on the head **2.** a small circle (*literary*)

circs /surks/ *npl* same as **circumstances** (*see* **circumstance**) (*informal*) [Mid-19C. Contraction]

circuit /súrkit/ *n* **1.** CIRCULAR PATH a route or path that follows a curved course and finishes at the point at which it began **2.** AREA BOUNDED BY CIRCULAR PATH an area that lies inside a circular route or path **3.** SINGLE JOURNEY ROUND CIRCULAR PATH a single complete journey round a circular route or path **4.** REGULAR JOURNEY a journey that somebody such as a salesperson or circuit judge regularly makes round an area **5.** STOPS ON JOURNEY the places visited by somebody on a regular circuit **6.** ROUND OF EVENTS a series of events or places regularly attended or visited by the same group of people **7.** ONGOING SERIES OF COMPETITIONS an ongoing series of competitions or tournaments in which the same group of players regularly participate **8.** ELEC ROUTE FOR ELECTRICITY a route around which an electrical current can flow, beginning and ending at the same point **9.** MOTOR SPORTS RACETRACK FOR MOTORSPORTS a racetrack for cars or motorcycles **10.** SPORTS SET OF EXERCISES a complete round of exercises in circuit training **11.** ARTS CHAIN OF ARTS VENUES a group of theatres, cinemas, or clubs under the same management or showing the same performances or films in rotation **12.** CHR LOCAL GROUP OF METHODIST CHURCHES a group of Methodist churches that form a local division of the Church's national administration **13.** LAW GEOGRAPHICAL DIVISION OF ENGLISH LEGAL SYSTEM any of the six areas that England is divided into for the purposes of administering the law ■ *vti* (**-cuits, -cuiting, -cuited**) MOVE ROUND ALONG CIRCULAR PATH to follow a circular route surrounding something (*formal*) [14C. Via French < Latin *circuitus* < *circuire* 'go round' < *ire* 'go']

circuit board *n* a thin insulating board on which electronic components and connections are mounted or etched

circuit breaker *n* a device that can automatically stop the flow of electricity in a circuit if there is too much current to operate safely

circuit judge *n* a judge who travels from one court to another within a region on a regular basis

circuitous /sur kyŏŏ itəss/ *adj* lengthy because very indirect [Mid-17C. < medieval Latin *circuitosus* < Latin *circuire* (see CIRCUIT)] —**circuitously** *adv* —**circuitousness** *n*

circuitry /súrkitri/ (*plural* **-ries**) *n* **1.** CIRCUIT COMPONENTS the components of an electric circuit **2.** ELECTRICAL SYSTEM the system of circuits in an electrical or electronic device **3.** LAYOUT OF CIRCUIT the design or layout of an electric circuit

circuit training *n* a form of sports training that involves performing different exercises in rotation

circuity /sur kyŏŏ əti/ (*plural* **-ties**) *n* the indirect and lengthy nature of something, especially the way somebody speaks, argues, or reasons [Mid-16C. < French *circuité* < Latin *circuire* (see CIRCUIT)]

circular /súrkyŏŏlər/ *adj* **1.** SHAPED LIKE CIRCLE having the shape of a perfect circle, or resembling a circle in shape **2.** ENDING WHERE BEGINNING following a curved route or path that ends at the point where it began **3.** CIRCUITOUS indirect and complicated **4.** WIDELY DIS-

TRIBUTED intended for distribution to a large number of people **5.** LOGIC NOT LOGICAL describes an argument that does not move logically to a satisfactory conclusion because it assumes as true something that needs to be proved or demonstrated ■ *n* WIDELY DISTRIBUTED NOTICE a letter, advertisement, or other notice distributed to a large number of people [14C. Via Anglo-Norman < late Latin *circularis* < Latin *circulus* (see CIRCLE)] —**circularly** *adv*

circular breathing *n* the technique of using the cheeks to force air out of the mouth while breathing in through the nose, used by woodwind and brass players to hold long notes

circular function *n* MATHS same as **trigonometric function**

circularise *vt* another spelling of **circularize**

circularity /súrkyŏŏ lárrəti/ *n* **1.** CIRCULAR SHAPE the quality or fact of being circular in shape **2.** COMPLEXITY AND INDIRECTNESS the indirect and complicated nature of something such as a method or route **3.** LOGIC ILLOGICAL NATURE the illogical nature of something such as an argument or piece of reasoning [Late 16C. < medieval Latin *circularitas* < *circularis* (see CIRCULAR)]

circularize /súrkyŏŏlə rīz/ (**-izes, -izing, -ized**), **circularise** (**-ises, -ising, -ised**) *vt* **1.** to publicize something by distributing leaflets or notices widely **2.** to ask people for support or survey public opinion by sending out questionnaires, letters, or leaflets —**circularization** /súrkyŏŏlə rī záysh'n/ *n*

circular measure *n* the measurement of an angle in units (**radians**) that relate it to the angle formed in the centre of a circle by a sector

circular saw *n* an electrically powered saw with a circular toothed blade that rotates at high speed

circulate /súrkyŏŏ layt/ (**-lates, -lating, -lated**) *v* **1.** *vi* MOVE ROUND CIRCULAR SYSTEM to move freely through a circuit or follow a circular route **2.** *vti* PASS ROUND to distribute or pass something from person to person or from place to place, or be passed in this way **3.** *vi* FLOW FREELY to move or flow freely in an enclosed space or defined area **4.** *vi* MINGLE to move from person to person or group to group at a social gathering in order to talk to different people (*informal*) [15C. < Latin *circulat-*, past participle of *circulare* < *circulus* (see CIRCLE)] —**circulatable** *adj* —**circulator** *n*

circulating library /súrkyŏŏ layting-/ *n* LIBRARIES same as **mobile library**

circulating medium *n* anything used as money, e.g. a valuable commodity, banknotes, or illegal drugs

circulation /súrkyŏŏ láysh'n/ *n* **1.** MOVEMENT OF BLOOD ROUND BODY the continuous movement of blood through all parts of the body **2.** FLOW the free movement of something such as air or water in an enclosed space **3.** DISTRIBUTION OR COMMUNICATION the passing or communication of something such as news, information, or money, from place to place or from person to person **4.** PUBL NUMBER DISTRIBUTED OF PUBLICATION the number of copies of a publication that are sold or distributed to readers in a given period **5.** FIN USE AS MONEY valid use as currency **6.** LIBRARIES LIBRARY DEPARTMENT the department of a lending library that oversees the lending and retrieval of books and other items

circulatory /súrkyŏŏ láytəri, súrkyŏŏlətəri/ *adj* relating to the circulation of the blood

circulatory system *n* the system consisting of the heart, blood vessels, and lymph vessels that pumps blood and lymph round the body

circum- *prefix* around ○ *circumlunar* [< Latin *circus* 'circle']

circumambient /súrkəm ámbi ənt/ *adj* surrounding (*literary*) —**circumambiently** *adv*

circumambulate /súrkəm ámbyŏŏ layt/ (**-lates, -lating, -lated**) *v* **1.** *vti* to walk round something, e.g. round a tomb or a sacred site as part of a ritual (*formal or humorous*) **2.** *vi* to avoid the point of a subject or discussion (*formal*) —**circumambulation** /-ambyŏŏ láysh'n/ *n*

circumcise /súrkəm sīz/ (**-cises, -cising, -cised**) *vt* **1.** to remove all or part of the foreskin from the penis of a boy or man, either for hygiene reasons or as part of a religious ritual **2.** to cut away the skin (**prepuce**) covering the clitoris, or remove the clitoris of a girl or woman, usually as part of a religious ritual [13C. < Old French *circonciser* < Latin *circumcis-*, past participle of *circumcidere* 'cut round' < *caedere* 'to cut'] —**circumciser** *n*

circumcision /súrkəm sízh'n/ *n* **1.** REMOVAL OF MALE'S FORESKIN the removal of all or part of the foreskin from the penis **2.** REMOVAL OF CLITORIS OR PREPUCE the cutting away of the skin (**prepuce**) covering the clitoris, or the removal of the clitoris **3.** RELIGIOUS CEREMONY WITH CIRCUMCISION especially in Judaism or Islam, a religious ceremony during which a circumcision is performed on boys

Circumcision *n* a Roman Catholic festival held until 1970 marking the circumcision of Jesus Christ. Date: 1 January.

circumference /sər kúmfrənss/ *n* **1.** DISTANCE AROUND CIRCLE the distance around the edge of a circle **2.** DISTANCE AROUND SOMETHING the distance around the edge of an object or a place that is roughly circular **3.** EDGE OF SOMETHING the edge of a round object or area [14C. < Latin *circumferentia* < *circumferent-*, present participle of *circumferre* 'carry round' < *ferre* 'carry'] —**circumferential** /sər kúmfə rénsh'l/ *adj* —**circumferentially** *adv*

circumflex /súrkəm fleks/, **circumflex accent** *n* in some languages, a mark (ˆ) placed above a letter to indicate a specific pronunciation, usually different from that of the unaccented letter, or a contraction. Circumflexes may be written over vowels as in French or over consonants as in Esperanto. See table at **diacritic** [Late 16C. < Latin *circumflexus*, past participle of *circumflectere* 'bend round' < *flectere* 'bend']

circumfluent /sər kúmmflŏŏ ənt/, **circumfluous** /-flŏŏ əss/ *adj* flowing all around a thing or place (*formal*)

circumlocution /súrkəm lə kyóosh'n/ *n* **1.** the use of more words than necessary to express something, especially to avoid saying it directly **2.** something said using more words than necessary, especially to avoid expressing it directly [15C. Directly or via French < Latin *circumlocution-* 'speaking around' < *locution-* (see LOCUTION)] —**circumlocutory** /-lókyŏŏtəri/ *adj*

circumlunar /súrkəm lóonər/ *adj* around or surrounding the Moon

circumnavigate /súrkəm návvi gayt/ (**-gates, -gating, -gated**) *vt* to sail or fly around something such as the world or an island —**circumnavigable** *adj* —**circumnavigation** /-navi gáysh'n/ *n* —**circumnavigator** *n*

circumpolar /súrkəm pṓlər/ *adj* located or living near one or both poles of Earth or another planet

circumpolar star *n* a star that is always visible above the horizon at a given latitude

circumscribe /súrkəm skrīb/ (**-scribes, -scribing, -scribed**) *v* **1.** to limit the power of something or somebody to act independently (*formal; often passive*) **2.** to draw one geometrical figure around another so that they touch at every corner (**vertex**) of the enclosed figure or at every side of the enclosing figure without cutting across each other [14C. < Latin *circumscribere* 'write round' < *scribere* 'write'] —**circumscribable** *adj* —**circumscriber** *n*

circumscription /súrkəm skrípsh'n/ *n* **1.** RESTRICTION OF POWER the limiting of the power of something or somebody to act independently (*formal*) **2.** MATHS ENCLOSING OF SOMETHING WITHIN GEOMETRICAL SHAPE the act of drawing one geometrical figure around another so that they touch at every corner (**vertex**) of the enclosed figure or at every side of the enclosing figure without cutting across each other **3.** MATHS DRAWN SHAPE a shape drawn or enclosed by circumscription **4.** COINS INSCRIPTION ROUND CIRCULAR EDGE a circular inscription around the edge of a coin or medal —**circumscriptive** *adj* —**circumscriptively** *adv*

circumsolar /súrkəm sṓlər/ *adj* around or surrounding the Sun

circumspect /súrkəm spekt/ *adj* taking into consideration all possible circumstances and consequences before acting [15C. < Latin *circumspect-*, past participle of *circumspicere* 'look around' < *specere* 'look'] —**circumspection** /súrkəm spéksh'n/ *n* —**circumspective** /súrkəm spéktiv/ *adj* —**circumspectly** *adv*

SYNONYMS See ***cautious***.

circumstance /súrkəmstənss, -staanss/ *n* **1.** CONDITION AFFECTING SITUATION a condition that affects what happens or how somebody reacts in a particular situation (*usually used in the plural*) ○ *Circumstances have arisen that make it impossible to continue.* **2.** UNCONTROLLABLE CONDITIONS the conditions that affect somebody's life and that are beyond his or her control ○ *a victim of circumstance* **3.** WAY SOMETHING HAPPENS the way an event happens or develops ○ *Mystery still surrounds the exact circumstances of the accident.* **4.** EVENT an event or occurrence (*formal*) ■ **circumstances** *npl* CONDITIONS the social, financial, material, or spiritual conditions that somebody lives in ○ *Please report any change in your circumstances.* [12C. Directly or via French < Latin *circumstantia* < *circumstant-*, present participle of *circumstare* 'stand around' < *stare* 'stand'] ◇ **under** *or* **in no circumstances** no matter what the situation might be ○ *You must under no circumstances reveal your password.* ◇ **under** *or* **in the circumstances** taking everything into account ○ *She performed very well under the circumstances.*

circumstanced /súrkəm staanst/ *adj* living in a particular state or set of conditions (*formal*) ○ *She came from a family that was happily circumstanced.*

circumstantial /súrkəm stánsh'l/ *adj* **1.** BASED ON INFERENCE containing or based on facts that allow a court to deduce that somebody is guilty without conclusive proof ○ *circumstantial evidence* **2.** SPECIAL related to particular circumstances **3.** FORMAL with a great deal of formality and ceremony **4.** DETAILED thorough and very detailed (*formal*) —**circumstantiality** /súrkəm stanshi álləti/ *n* —**circumstantially** *adv*

circumstantiate /súrkəm stánshi ayt/ (**-ates, -ating, -ated**) *vt* to provide evidence to support an argument or allegation (*formal*) —**circumstantiation** /súrkəm stanshi áysh'n/ *n*

circumstellar /súrkəm stéllər/ *adj* around or surrounding a star

circumterrestrial /súrkəm tə réstri əl/ *adj* around or surrounding Earth

circumvallate /súrkəm vállayt/ (**-lates, -lating, -lated**) *vt* to protect a town or camp by surrounding it with a rampart or a defensive wall (*archaic or formal*) [Mid-17C. < Latin *circumvallat-*, past participle of *circumvallare* 'fortify with a rampart round' < *vallum* 'rampart' < *vallus* 'stake'] —**circumvallation** /-və láysh'n/ *n*

circumvent /súrkəm vént/ (**-vents, -venting, -vented**) *vt* **1.** to find a way of avoiding restrictions imposed by a rule or law without actually breaking it ○ *an attempt to circumvent the ban* **2.** to anticipate and counter somebody's plans [15C. < Latin *circumvent-*, present participle of *circumvenire* 'come round' < *venire* 'come'] —**circumventer** *n* —**circumvention** *n* —**circumventive** *adj*

circumvolution /súrkəm və lóosh'n/ *n* a turning or winding movement around a central axis [15C. < Latin *circumvolut-*, past participle of *circumvolvere* 'turn around' < *volvere* 'turn'] —**circumvolutory** /-və lóotəri/ *adj*

circus /súrkəss/ *n* **1.** TRAVELLING ENTERTAINERS a group of travelling entertainers, including clowns, acrobats, and sometimes animal trainers and their animals **2.** TRAVELLING SHOW a performance given by circus entertainers, or the place where they perform **3.** ROMAN STADIUM an open stadium built by the ancient Romans to stage chariot races or fights between gladiators **4.** ROMAN SHOW a performance staged in a Roman stadium **5.** PLACE WHERE STREETS MEET an open space, approximately circular in shape, where several streets meet ○ *Piccadilly Circus* **6.** SELF-IMPORTANT EVENT a confused, noisy, or overwhelming event or situation, especially one that seems full of self-importance (*informal*) ○ *a media circus* [14C. < Latin, 'ring, circle'] —**circusy** *adj*

ORIGIN The Latin word *circus*, 'ring', 'circle', from which ***circus*** is derived, is also the source of English *circle*, *circular*, *circulate*, and *search*.

Circus Maximus /súrkəss máksiməss/ *n* a stadium in Rome that was used in ancient times to stage chariot races and fights between gladiators [< Latin, 'biggest racetrack']

ciré /séeray/ *adj* SHINY describes fabric with a shiny highly glazed finish ■ *n* **1.** SHINY FINISH a very shiny highly glazed finish achieved by treating a fabric with wax or heat **2.** SHINY FABRIC a fabric with a shiny finish [Early 20C. < French past participle of *cirer* 'to wax' < *cire* 'wax' < Latin *cera*]

Cirencester /sī́rən sestər/ ancient market town in Gloucestershire, west-central England. Population: 15,221 (1991).

cire perdue /séer pair dyŏŏ/ *n* same as **lost wax** (*technical*) [Late 19C. < French, 'lost wax']

cirque /surk/ *n* a semicircular hollow with steep walls formed by glacial erosion on mountains. It often forms the head of a valley. [Mid-19C. Via French < Latin *circus* 'ring']

cirrhosis /sə rṓssiss/ *n* a chronic progressive disease of the liver characterized by the replacement of healthy cells with scar tissue [Early 19C. < modern Latin < Greek *kirrhos* 'orange-coloured'] —**cirrhotic** /sə róttik/ *adj*

cirri METEOROL, ZOOL plural of **cirrus**

cirriform /sírri fawrm/ *adj* shaped like a long slender tendril or tentacle [Early 19C. < Latin *cirrus* 'curl']

cirriped /sírri ped/, **cirripede** /-peed/ *n* a sea crustacean that lives fixed in one spot and draws food by means of slender hairs (**cirri**). Subclass: Cirripedia. [Mid-19C < modern Latin *Cirripedia* 'with curly legs' < Latin *cirrus* 'curl']

cirrocumulus /sírrō kyŏŏmyŏŏləss/ (*plural* **-li** /-lī/) *n* a high-altitude cloud formed of icy particles. It occurs in lines of small rounded clouds often resembling fish scales and sometimes called a mackerel sky.

cirrostratus /sírrō straátəss/ (*plural* **-ti** /-tī/) *n* a cirrus cloud resembling a transparent white veil high in the sky. It indicates wet weather.

cirrus /sírrəss/ (*plural* **-ri** /-rī/) *n* **1.** a thin wispy cloud, occurring as narrow bands of tiny ice particles, that forms at the highest and coldest point of the cloud region **2.** a slender tentacle with sensory or locomotive function, or a part resembling one [Early 18C. < Latin, 'curl, fringe'] —**cirrate** /sírrayt/ *adj*

cis /siss/ *adj* having two atoms or groups on the same side of a double bond between carbon atoms [Late 18C. < Latin (see CIS-)]

CIS *abbr* Commonwealth of Independent States

cis- *prefix* on the near side of ○ *cisatlantic* [< Latin *cis* < Indo-European, 'this']

cisalpine /siss álpīn/ *adj* **1.** situated south of the Alps **2.** relating to a movement in the Roman Catholic Church to limit papal power and encourage the independence of local churches [Mid-16C. < Latin *cisalpinus* 'on this side of the Alps' (as viewed from Rome) < *alpinus* 'alpine']

cisatlantic /síss ət lántik/ *adj* situated on the same side of the Atlantic Ocean as the writer or speaker

CISC /sisk/ *abbr* complex instruction set computer

cisco /sískō/ (*plural* **-coes** or **-cos**) *n* a silvery freshwater whitefish found in deep lakes. Native to: North America. Genus: *Coregonus*. [Mid-19C. Back-formation < Canadian French *ciscoette*, alteration (influenced by *-ette* 'small') of Ojibwa *bemidewiskawed* 'that which has oily skin']

Ciskei /síss kī/ former homeland of South Africa, now part of Eastern Cape Province

cislunar /siss lŏŏnər/ *adj* situated between the Earth and the Moon

cismontane /siss móntayn/ *adj* on the same side of the mountains as the writer or speaker

cispadane /síss pə dayn/ *adj* situated on the southern side of the Po River in northern Italy [Late 18C. < CIS- + Latin *Padus* 'the Po']

cisplatin /siss pláttin/, **cisplatinum** /-plátti nəm/ *n* a drug that adds an alkyl group to DNA. Use: treatment of ovarian and testicular cancer. [Late 20C. < CIS- + *-platin*, INN stem]

cissing /síssing/ *n* the appearance of marks such as bubbles or pits in paintwork. It is a result of failure of the paint to adhere properly to the surface. [Late 20C. Origin ?]

cissy *n, adj* another spelling of **sissy** (*informal offensive insult*)

cist /sist/, **kist** /kist/ *n* a wood or stone coffin, dating from the latter part of the Stone Age [Early 19C. < Welsh, 'chest']

Cistercian /si stúrsh'n/ *adj* relating to an austere contemplative Christian order of monks and nuns founded by reformist Benedictines in 1098 ■ *n* a member of the Cistercian order of monks and nuns [15C. < French *cistercien* < Latin *Cistercium* 'Cîteaux', near Dijon, France]

cistern /sístərn/ *n* **1.** a tank for storing water, especially one in the roof of a house or connected to a toilet **2.** an underground tank for storing rainwater **3.** ANAT same as **cisterna** [13C. Via French < Latin *cisterna* < *cista* 'chest' < Greek *kistē*]

cisterna /si stúrnə/ (*plural* **-nae** /-nee/) *n* a pouch or cavity that contains a body fluid [Late 19C. < Latin *cisterna* (see CISTERN)] —**cisternal** *adj*

cistron /sísstrən, -tron/ *n* a section of DNA containing the genetic code for a short chain of amino acids (**polypeptide**) that is the smallest functional unit carrying genetic information [Mid-20C. < CIS- + TRANS- + -ON [1]] —**cistronic** /siss trónnik/ *adj*

cistus /sístəss/ *n* an evergreen ornamental bush. Flowers: white, red, or yellow. Genus: *Cistus*. [Mid-16C. < Greek *kistos* 'red-flowered bush']

cit. *abbr* **1.** cited **2.** citizen **3.** COMPUT, TELECOM computer-integrated telephony

citadel /síttəd'l, -del/ *n* **1.** a fortress or strongly fortified building in or near a city, used as a place of refuge **2.** an organization or institution that strongly defends a particular way of life or principle [Mid-16C. Directly or via French < Italian *cittadella* 'little city' < obsolete *cittade* 'city' < Latin *civitat-* (see CITY)]

citation /sī táysh'n/ *n* **1.** OFFICIAL ACKNOWLEDGMENT OF MERIT an official document or speech that praises somebody's actions, accomplishments, or character **2.** EXTRACT FROM WORK a quotation from an authoritative source that is used to support an idea or argument **3.** ACT OF CITING SOMETHING the act or process of citing something **4.** LAW REFERENCE TO PREVIOUS DECISION a reference to a previous decision by a court or legal authority **5.** LAW USE OF PRECEDENT the legal practice or process of referring to precedent **6.** *N Am* LAW ORDER TO APPEAR IN COURT a writ for somebody to appear in a court of law —**citational** *adj* —**citatory** /sītətəri, sī táy-/ *adj*

cite /sīt/ *vt* (**cites, citing, cited**) **1.** QUOTE SOMETHING OR SOMEBODY to mention something or somebody as an example to support an argument or help explain what is being said (*formal*) **2.** LAW NAME SOMEBODY to name somebody officially in a court case **3.** *N Am* LAW ORDER TO APPEAR IN COURT to order somebody officially to appear in court **4.** MIL OFFICIALLY PRAISE SOMEBODY to praise the actions of a member of the armed services in an official document (*often passive*) ■ *n* same as **citation** (sense 2) (*informal*) [15C. < Latin *citare* 'summon repeatedly' < *citus*, past participle of *ciere* 'summon']

SPELLCHECK Do not confuse the spelling of ***cite***, ***site***, and ***sight***, which sound similar. ***Cite*** is primarily a verb, indicating mentioning or naming, as in *cite the book in a footnote, cited them in court*. ***Site*** is a noun and verb, and refers to location (*a building site, sited the school outside the village*). ***Sight*** is connected with the faculty of seeing, and is also used as a noun and a verb (*has excellent sight, sighted him in the distance*).

cithara /síthərə/, **kithara** /k-/ *n* a stringed musical instrument played in ancient Greece, resembling a lyre [Late 18C. Via Latin < Greek *kithara*]

citify /sítti fī/ (**-fies, -fying, -fied**) *vt* (*disapproving*) **1.** to develop an area and make it more urban **2.** to make somebody adopt the customs, behaviour, or dress of those who live in cities —**citification** /síttifi káysh'n/ *n* —**citified** *adj*

citizen /síttiz'n/ *n* **1.** LEGAL RESIDENT OF COUNTRY somebody who has the right to live in a country because he or she was born there or has been legally accepted as a permanent resident **2.** COUNTY, TOWN, OR CITY DWELLER a permanent resident of a county, town, or city **3.** CIVILIAN somebody who is not a member of the armed forces, a police officer, or a public official [13C. < Anglo-Norman *citezein* < Old French *citeain* < Latin *civitat-* (see CITY)] —**citizenly** *adj*

CULTURAL NOTE ***Citizen Kane***, a film (1941) by US director Orson Welles. Repeatedly nominated as one of the greatest films of all time, it is the story of the rise and the tormented private life of a fictional media baron, Charles Foster Kane (supposedly based on the life of the billionaire publisher William Randolph Hearst). The film's many stylistic innovations include the use of mock-newsreel footage and striking deep-focus photography.

citizenry /síttiz'nri/ (*plural* **-ries**) *n* the citizens of a place or area collectively (*formal*; *takes a singular or plural verb*)

citizen's arrest *n* an arrest made by an ordinary citizen rather than by a police officer

Citizens' Band *n* radio frequencies used by the general public to talk to one another over short distances

citizenship /síttiz'nship/ *n* **1.** the legal status of being a citizen of a country **2.** the duties and responsibilities that come with being a member of a community

Citlaltépetl /séet lal táy pett'l/ volcanic peak in central Veracruz State, eastern Mexico, and the highest peak in Mexico. Height: 5,610 m/18,406 ft.

citole /síttōl/ *n* MUSIC same as **cittern** [14C. < French, probably diminutive of Latin *cithara* (see CITHARA)]

citral /síttrəl/ *n* a volatile pale yellow liquid with a pleasant odour. Source: lemon grass oil. Use: in perfumes, flavourings. Formula: $C_{10}H_{16}O$.

citrate /síttrayt/ *n* a salt or ester of citric acid

citric /síttrik/ *adj* relating to citrus fruit

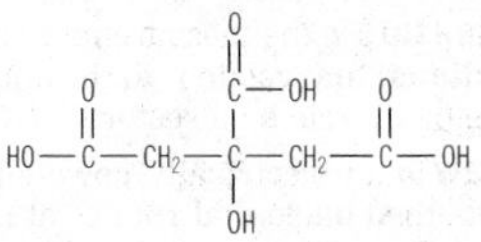

citric acid

citric acid *n* a weak colourless acid. Source: lemon, lime, and pineapple juice, fermentation of sugars. Use: flavourings. Formula: $C_6H_8O_7$.

citric acid cycle *n* CHEM same as **Krebs cycle**

citriculture /síttri kulchər/ *n* the cultivation of citrus fruits [Early 20C. < CITRUS] —**citriculturist** /síttri kúlchərist/ *n*

citrine /síttrin/ *n* **1.** MINERALS YELLOW QUARTZ a brownish-yellow semiprecious stone that is a variety of quartz. Use: gems. **2.** COLOURS GREENISH-YELLOW COLOUR a greenish-yellow colour, like that of a lemon ■ *adj* COLOURS GREENISH-YELLOW of the colour citrine [Late 16C. Via French *citrin(e)* 'lemon-coloured' < medieval Latin *citrinus* < Latin *citrus* 'citrus tree']

citron /síttrən/ *n* **1.** FOOD CITRUS FRUIT LIKE LARGE LEMON the fruit of an evergreen citrus tree, resembling a large lemon in shape and colour and having a thick aromatic rind **2.** FOOD CANDIED RIND the candied rind of a citron. Use: food decoration and flavouring. **3.** TREES THORNY CITRUS TREE a small thorny evergreen citrus tree that bears citrons. Latin name: *Citrus medica*. **4.** PLANTS WATERMELON a small watermelon that has inedible white flesh and a hard rind. Latin name: *Citrullus lanatus* var. citroides. **5.** COLOURS same as **citrine** *n* (sense 2) [Early 16C. < French, alteration (influenced by *limon* 'lemon') of Latin *citrus* 'citrus tree'] —**citron** *adj*

citronella /síttrə néllə/ *n* **1.** a pale yellow aromatic oil. Source: a tropical grass. Use: in perfumes and soaps, as insect repellent. **2.** *also* **citronella grass** a tropical grass that has bluish-green lemon-scented leaves and contains oil. Native to: Asia. Latin name: *Cymbopogon nardus*. [Mid-19C. Via modern Latin < French *citronnelle* 'lemon oil' < *citron* (see CITRON)]

citronellal /síttrə néllal/ *n* a colourless liquid that smells like lemons. Source: citronella oil. Use: perfumes, flavourings. Formula: $C_{10}H_{18}O$.

citronella oil *n* CHEM same as **citronella** (sense 1)

citronellol /síttrə néllol/ *n* an alcohol. Source: citronellal. Formula: $C_{10}H_{20}O$.

citron wood *n* the wood of the citron tree or of the sandarac tree

citrulline /síttrəlin/ *n* an amino acid formed in the liver during the production of urea [Mid-20C.

< medieval Latin *citrullus* 'watermelon' < Latin *citrus* 'citrus tree']

citrus /síttrəss/ *n* oranges, lemons, limes, grapefruit, pomelos, and related fruit collectively (*often used before a noun*) ○ *citrus fruits* [Early 19C. < Latin, 'citron tree, citrus tree']

cittern /síttərn/ *n* a medieval stringed instrument similar to a lute but with wire strings and a flat back [Mid-16C. Probably blend of Latin *cithara* (see CITHARA) + GITTERN]

city /sítti/ (*plural* **-ies**) *n* **1.** VERY LARGE URBAN AREA an urban area where a large number of people live and work **2.** PEOPLE IN CITY the inhabitants of a city collectively **3.** LARGE UK TOWN in the United Kingdom, a large town that has received the title of city from the Crown. It is usually the seat of a bishop, and so often has a cathedral. **4.** US URBAN CENTRE OF GOVERNMENT in the United States, an incorporated urban centre that has self-government, boundaries, and legal rights established by state charter **5.** CANADIAN URBAN AREA in Canada, a town or urban area that has been incorporated and given the title of city by a provincial government **6.** AUSTRALIAN TOWN in Australia, a large town that received the title of city from the British Crown or a colonial government, or more recently, from a state government **7.** AUSTRALIAN URBAN AREA in Australia, an urban area within a larger conurbation, which has been given the title of city by the state government **8.** *N Am* EXTREME THING a thing, place, or situation that is a good or extreme example of its type (*slang; used in combination*) ○ *It was panic city outside.* [12C. Via Old French *cité* < Latin *civitat-* 'citizenship, community' < *civis* 'citizen']

City *n* **1.** the important financial institutions of London. They include the Bank of England, the Stock Exchange, and the major international banks. **2.** same as **City of London**

city academy *n* a state-funded independent secondary school in an inner-city area that receives additional funding from the private or voluntary sectors

City and Guilds (*plural same*) *n* a technical or craft qualification awarded by the City and Guilds Institute (*informal*)

City and Guilds Institute *n* an examination body that awards qualifications for technical and craft skills

City Code *n* a code established in the United Kingdom in 1968 to control takeover bids and mergers

city council *n* a group of elected officials responsible for the government of a city or other municipality

city desk *n* **1.** the newspaper department that deals with financial news **2.** *N Am* a newspaper department that deals with local news

city editor *n* **1.** the newspaper editor in charge of financial news **2.** *N Am* the newspaper editor in charge of local news

city father *n* a member of a city or town council or a civil officer who has limited judicial authority

city hall *n* **1.** *also* **City Hall** CITY COUNCIL BUILDING the building where a city council has its main administrative offices **2.** *N Am* CITY ADMINISTRATORS the administrators and elected officials who run a city **3.** *N Am* BUREAUCRACY the bureaucracy that runs a city, especially when regarded as insensitive or inflexible (*disapproving*)

city manager *n* an administrator appointed by a municipal council to run its affairs

City of London /sítti-/ the oldest part of London, and its business and financial heart. Population: 7,185 (2001). Area: 3 sq. km/1 sq. mi.

cityscape /sítti skayp/ *n* **1.** a view of a city or town landscape **2.** a photograph or painting of part of a city or town

city slicker *n* a worldly resident of a city (*informal disapproving*)

city-state *n* a independent state consisting of a sovereign city and its surrounding territory

city technology college *n* an inner-city secondary school specializing in technical subjects, with close links to and funding partly provided by private industry

citywide /sítti wīd/ *adj* involving the whole of a particular city ■ *adv* so as to involve the whole of a particular city

Ciudad Bolivar /syoo dád bo lée vaar/, **Ciudad Bolívar** river port and capital of Bolívar State, eastern Venezuela, situated on the River Orinoco. Population: 258,112 (1992).

Ciudad Juárez /-hwáa ress/ city in Chihuahua State, northern Mexico, across the Rio Grande from El Paso, Texas. Population: 1,218,818 (2000).

Ciudad Real /-ray áal/ capital of Ciudad Real Province, in the Castile-La Mancha Region, south-central Spain. Population: 65,084 (2002).

Ciudad Victoria /-vik táwri ə/ capital of Tamaulipas State, northeastern Mexico, situated 241 km/150 mi. southeast of Monterrey. Population: 256,900 (2002).

civet /sívvit/ *n* **1.** *also* **civet cat** WILD ANIMAL LIKE CAT a small carnivorous mammal that resembles a cat in appearance. Native to: Africa, Asia. Family: Viverridae. **2.** COSMETICS MUSKY SUBSTANCE a yellow or brown greasy substance smelling strongly of musk, secreted by the anal glands of a civet. Use: perfume manufacture. **3.** FUR the fur of a civet [Mid-16C. Via French *civette* < Italian *zivetto* < medieval Latin *zibethum* < Arabic *zabād* 'civet perfume']

civic /sívvik/ *adj* **1.** relating to the government of a town or city ○ *civic reception* **2.** connected with the duties and obligations of belonging to a community ○ *civic pride* [Mid-17C. < Latin *civicus* < *civis* 'citizen'] —**civically** *adv*

civic centre *n* **1.** a complex containing the public buildings of a town or city e.g. the town hall, library, and recreational facilities **2.** *N Am* a municipal entertainment complex containing an indoor arena that can be used for sports, concerts, and trade shows

civic-minded *adj* taking an active interest in the community needs and affairs of a town or city —**civic-mindedness** *n*

civics /sívviks/ *n* the study of the rights and duties of citizens (*takes a singular verb*)

civil /sívv'l/ *adj* **1.** POLITE polite, but in a way that is cold and formal **2.** RELATING TO CITIZENS relating to what happens within a state or between different citizens or groups of citizens ○ *civil war* **3.** NOT MILITARY connected with ordinary citizens and organizations as opposed to the armed forces ○ *the civil authorities* **4.** AS INDIVIDUAL CITIZEN relating to each citizen as an individual rather than as a member of a community or nation ○ *civil liberties* **5.** NOT RELIGIOUS performed by a state official such as a registrar rather than a member of the clergy ○ *civil marriage* **6.** same as **civic** (sense 2) **7.** LAW HAPPENING BETWEEN INDIVIDUALS involving individual people or groups in legal action other than criminal proceedings ○ *a civil action* [14C. < Latin *civilis* < *civis* 'citizen']

civil code *n* the codified body of statutes in Quebec that derives from Roman and Napoleonic civil law

civil defence *n* **1.** the organization and training of civilian volunteers to help the armed forces, police, and emergency services in the event of a war, a national emergency, or a natural disaster **2.** civilian volunteers who take part in civil defence (*takes a singular or plural verb*)

civil disobedience *n* the deliberate breaking of a law by ordinary citizens, carried out as nonviolent protest or passive resistance

civil engineering *n* the branch of engineering concerned with the planning, design, and construction of such things as roads, bridges, and dams —**civil engineer** *n*

civilian /sə vílli ən/ *n* a citizen who is not a member of the armed forces [Early 14C. < Old French *civilien* 'of civil law' < *civil* 'civil' < Latin *civilis* (see CIVIL)] —**civilian** *adj*

civilianize /sə vílli ə nīz/ (**-izes, -izing, -ized**), **civilianise** (**-ises, -ising, -ised**) *vt* to change something from military to civilian use —**civilianization** /si vílli ə nī záysh'n/ *n*

civilisation *n* another spelling of **civilization, etc**

civilise *vt* another spelling of **civilize**

civilised *adj* another spelling of **civilized**

civility /sə víllәti/ (*plural* **-ties**) *n* **1.** the rather formal politeness that results from observing social conventions **2.** something said or done in a formally polite way

civilization /sívvə lī záysh'n/, **civilisation** *n* **1.** HIGHLY DEVELOPED SOCIETY a society that has a high level of culture and social organization **2.** ADVANCED DEVELOPMENT OF SOCIETY an advanced level of development in society that is marked by complex social and political organization, and material, scientific, and artistic progress **3.** ADVANCED SOCIETY IN GENERAL all the societies at an advanced level of development considered collectively **4.** POPULATED AREAS places where people live, rather than uninhabited areas **5.** CIVILIZING PROCESS the process of creating a high level of culture in a particular society or region **6.** COMFORT the level of material comfort that somebody is used to (*humorous*)

civilize /sívvə līz/ (**-lizes, -lizing, -lized**), **civilise** (**-lises, -lising, -lised**) *vt* **1.** to create a high level of culture and social organization in a society **2.** to teach somebody to behave in a more socially and culturally acceptable way —**civilizable** *adj* —**civilizer** *n* —**civilizing** *adj*

civilized /sívvə līzd/, **civilised** *adj* **1.** CULTURALLY ADVANCED having advanced cultural and social development **2.** DECENT showing high moral development **3.** REFINED refined in tastes

civil law *n* **1.** LAW OF CITIZENS' RIGHTS the law of a state dealing with the rights of private citizens **2.** ANCIENT ROMAN LAW the law of ancient Rome, especially the part concerned with private citizens **3.** LAW BASED ON ROMAN LAW a system of law based on Roman law rather than common law or canon law

civil liberties *npl* the basic rights guaranteed to individual citizens by law, e.g. freedom of speech and action —**civil libertarian** *n*

civil list *n* in the United Kingdom, the money paid each year by the state to support the royal family [Originally for the civil government of the state]

civilly /sívvəli/ *adv* in a polite but not particularly warm or enthusiastic way

civil rights *npl* rights that all citizens of a society are supposed to have, e.g. the right to vote or to receive fair treatment from the law

civil servant *n* an employee in a government department

civil service *n* all the government departments of a state and the people who work in them

civil union *n* a ceremony celebrating the affirmation of a partnership shared by a same-sex couple or a couple who choose not to marry

civil war *n* a war between opposing groups within a country

Civil War *n* **1.** the civil war fought between the Royalist supporters of Charles I and the Parliamentarians led by Oliver Cromwell, between 1642 and 1648 **2.** the civil war fought in the United States from 1861 to 1865 between the North and the slave-owning states of the South

civil year *n* CALENDAR same as **calendar year** [*Civil* 'legally recognized']

civvies /sívviz/ *npl* ordinary clothes as opposed to a military uniform (*informal*) [Late 19C. Shortening and alteration of CIVILIAN, probably after CLOTHES]

civvy /sívvi/ (*plural* **-vies**) *n* MIL same as **civilian** (*informal*) [Early 20C Shortening and alteration]

civvy street *n* civilian life as referred to by military personnel (*informal*)

CIX /kiks/ *abbr* commercial Internet exchange (*used in e-commerce*)

CJ *abbr* **1.** *US* Chief Judge **2.** Chief Justice

CJD *abbr* Creutzfeldt-Jakob disease

ck *abbr* Cook Islands (*used in Internet addresses*) See table at **domain name**

CKD *abbr* COMM completely knocked down (*used of goods that are sold in parts to be assembled later*)

CKO *abbr* BUSINESS chief knowledge officer

cl *abbr* **1.** TRANSP carload **2.** MEASURE centilitre **3.** Chile (*used in Internet addresses*) See table at **domain name** **4.** class **5.** classification **6.** RELIG clergy **7.** FURNITURE closet **8.** CLOTHING cloth

Cl *symbol* CHEM ELEM chlorine

clabbery /klábbəri/ *adj regional* dirty [Late 19C. < Gaelic *clabar* 'mud']

REGIONAL NOTE See *manky*.

clachan /klákhən, -kən/ *n Scotland* a small village [15C. < Gaelic, 'village, burying place']

clack /klak/ (**clacks, clacking, clacked**) *v* 1. *vti* to make a short hard loud noise, or cause something to make such a noise 2. *vi* to chatter constantly or rapidly (*informal*) 3. *vi* same as **cluck** *v* (sense 1) [13C. An imitation of the sound] —**clack** *n* —**clacker** *n*

Clackmannan /klak mánnən/ parish and town in central Scotland, east of Stirling. Population: 3,420 (1991).

Clackmannanshire /klak mánnənshər/ local government unitary council in Scotland, established in 1996. It corresponds to the old county of this name, which was abolished in 1975.

clack valve *n* a valve with a hinged flap that swings open

Clactonian /klak tṓni ən/ *n* a Lower Palaeolithic culture of northwestern Europe that made stone chopping tools [After CLACTON-ON-SEA] —**Clactonian** *adj*

Clacton-on-Sea /kláktən-/ seaside resort on the North Sea coast of Essex, England. Population: 45,065 (1991).

clad[1] /klad/ *past participle, past tense of* **clothe** ■ *adj* 1. wearing particular clothes ○ *clad in blue* 2. covered in a particular thing (*literary; often used in combination*) ○ *iron-clad* [13C. < Old English *clāðed*, past participle of *clāðian* (see CLOTHE)]

clad[2] /klad/ (**clads, cladding, clad**) *vt* 1. to cover a wall or building with cladding 2. to cover or plate a metal with a layer of another metal, especially to make armour plating [Mid-16C. Probably < CLAD[1]]

clad- *prefix* same as **clado-** (*used before vowels*)

Claddagh ring /kláddəkh-, kláddaak-/ *n* a ring usually in the form of two hands clasping a heart surmounted by a crown, originally given in Ireland as a token of affection [Late 20C. After a village near Galway city, Ireland]

cladding /kládding/ *n* 1. **OUTER LAYER ON BUILDING** a layer of stone, tiles, or wood added to the outside of a building to protect it or improve its insulation or appearance 2. **METAL COATING** a protective metal coating bonded onto another metal 3. **COMPUT COVERING FOR OPTICAL FIBRE** a covering for optical fibre that reflects light back to the core and strengthens the cable

clade /klayd/ *n* a group of organisms, e.g. a species, that are considered to share a common ancestor [Mid-20C. < Greek *klados* 'branch']

cladist /kláy dist/ *n* a biologist who classifies organisms according to the principles of cladistics —**cladism** *n*

cladistics /klə dístiks/ *n* a system of biological classification that groups organisms on the basis of their observed shared characteristics in order to deduce the common ancestors (*takes a singular verb*) —**cladistic** *adj* —**cladistically** *adv*

clado- *prefix* branch, shoot ○ *cladogram* [< Greek *klados* < Indo-European, 'to strike']

cladoceran /klə dóssərən/ *n* a tiny freshwater crustacean such as a water flea. Order: Cladocera. [Early 20C. < modern Latin *Cladocera* < Greek *klados* 'branch' + *keras* 'horn'] —**cladoceran** *adj*

cladode /kláddōd/ *n BOT* same as **cladophyll** —**cladodial** /klə dṓdi əl/ *adj*

cladogenesis /kláddō jénnəssiss, kláydō-/ *n* evolutionary change regarded as taking place by the splitting of an ancestral species into two or more different descendant species —**cladogenetic** /-jə néttik/ *adj* —**cladogenetically** *adv*

cladogram /kláydə gram/ *n* a tree-shaped diagram showing evolutionary relationships and the points where species appear to have diverged from common ancestors

cladophyll /kláydə fil/ *n* a flattened stem similar to a leaf

clafoutis /kláffōoti/ (*plural same*) *n* a fruit and batter pastry, typically made with cherries [Late 20C. < French < dialect *clafir* 'to stuff' + standard French *foutre* 'to stuff']

---

claim /klaym/ *v* (**claims, claiming, claimed**) 1. *vt* **MAINTAIN SOMETHING IS TRUE** to say, without proof or evidence, that something is true ○ *He claims we've already met.* 2. *vt* **DEMAND SOMETHING AS ENTITLEMENT** to demand officially something that somebody has a right to or owns 3. *vti* **RECEIVE STATE MONEY** to officially request and receive state money or other benefits 4. *vt* **END SOMEBODY'S LIFE** to cause the loss of somebody's life 5. *vt* **WIN TITLE** to take a title, prize, or record 6. *vt* **DEMAND ATTENTION** to force somebody to give attention ■ *n* 1. **SOMETHING THAT MAY BE TRUE** an assertion that something is true, unsupported by evidence or proof 2. **BASIS FOR GETTING SOMETHING** the basis for demanding or getting something 3. **DEMAND FOR SOMETHING** a demand for something somebody has a right to or owns 4. INSUR, SOC WELFARE **OFFICIAL REQUEST FOR MONEY** an official request for money or other benefits from the state or an organization 5. INSUR, SOC WELFARE **MONEY REQUESTED** the amount of money requested in a claim 6. LAW **LEGAL RIGHT TO LAND** the legal right to own a piece of land and to mine it for minerals 7. LAW **PIECE OF LAND** the piece of land to which somebody claims a legal right [14C. < Old French *clamer* 'to call' < Latin *clamare*] —**claimable** *adj* —**claimer** *n* ◇ **lay claim to something** to say that you have a right to something, or take what you think you have a right to

ORIGIN The Latin word *clamare*, 'to call', from which *claim* is derived, is also the source of English *acclaim*, *clamour*, *exclaim*, and *proclaim*.

claimant /kláymənt/ *n* 1. somebody who claims something such as state benefits or an inheritance 2. somebody who brings a lawsuit in a civil court against a person or organization (**defendant**)

claims adjuster *n* INSUR same as **loss adjuster**

Clair /klair/, **René** (1898–1981) French film director and scriptwriter. *The Italian Straw Hat* (1927) established him as a master of light comedy. Born **Chomette, René-Lucien**

clair de lune /kláir də lóon/ *n* 1. a pale blue or greyish-blue glaze used on porcelain 2. a pale bluish-grey colour [Late 19C < French, 'light of the moon'] —**clair de lune** *adj*

clairvoyance /klair vóyənss/, **clairvoyancy** /-ənssi/ *n* the supposed ability to perceive things that are usually beyond the range of human senses [Mid-19C. < French < *clairvoyant* 'clear-sighted' < *voyant* present participle of *voir* 'see']

clairvoyant /klair vóy ənt/ *n* somebody who is supposedly able to perceive things that are usually beyond the range of human senses [Late 17C. < French (see CLAIRVOYANCE)] —**clairvoyant** *adj* —**clairvoyantly** *adv*

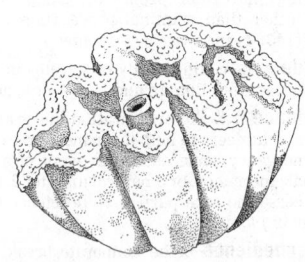

clam

clam[1] /klam/ *n* 1. **BURROWING SHELLFISH** an invertebrate animal with a shell in two parts and a muscular foot to burrow into sand. Many are edible and the largest is nearly 1.5 m / 5 ft long. Native to: seas, rivers, lakes. Class: Pelecypoda. 2. **CLAM FLESH** the soft edible flesh of a clam 3. *US* MONEY same as **dollar** (sense 1) (*slang*) ■ *vi* (**clams, clamming, clammed**) *N Am* **COLLECT CLAMS** to gather clams as food [Early 16C. < obsolete *clam-shell* 'clamp-shell' < Old English *clamm* 'bond, grip' < Indo-European, 'form into a ball']

clam up *vi* to become suddenly secretive or unwilling to talk (*informal*)

clam[2] /klam/ *vti regional* same as **clem**

clamant /kláymənt/ *adj* demanding attention (*literary*) [Mid-17C. < Latin *clamant-*, present participle of *clamare* 'call'] —**clamantly** *adv*

clambake /klám bayk/ *n* 1. a picnic in which seafood

---

such as clams and other foods are cooked and eaten 2. *N Am* a relaxed party or other gathering (*informal*)

clamber /klámbər/ *vi* (**-bers, -bering, -bered**) to climb quickly but awkwardly, using hands and feet ■ *n* a climb that involves clambering [14C. Probably < *clamb*, former past tense of CLIMB + suffix denoting repetition] —**clamberer** *n*

clam chowder *n* a thick soup made from clams and potatoes

clammy /klámmi/ (**-mier, -miest**) *adj* 1. slightly damp and unpleasantly cold 2. warm and damp [14C. Probably < *clam* 'to smear', back-formation < *clamde*, past tense of Old English *clǣman* < Germanic, 'clay'] —**clammily** *adv* —**clamminess** *n*

clamor *vi, n* US spelling of **clamour**

clamorous /klámmərəss/ *adj* 1. **DEMANDING ATTENTION** demanding attention loudly and insistently 2. **LOUD** loud and excited or angry 3. **NOISY** making a loud noise —**clamorously** *adv* —**clamorousness** *n*

clamour /klámmər/ *vi* (**-ours, -ouring, -oured**) 1. **DEMAND NOISILY** to demand something noisily or desperately 2. **SHOUT LOUDLY** to shout at the same time as other people, and make a lot of noise ■ *n* 1. **PERSISTENT DEMAND** a persistent demand for something, made in an excited or angry way 2. **LOUD NOISE** a loud noise, especially one made by people shouting together [14C. Via French < Latin *clamor-* < *clamare* 'to call'] —**clamourer** *n*

clamp /klamp/ *n* 1. **HOLDING DEVICE** a mechanical device with movable jaws. Use: to hold two things firmly together or one object firmly in position. 2. AUTOMOT same as **wheel clamp** ■ *vt* (**clamps, clamping, clamped**) 1. **FASTEN THINGS TOGETHER** to fasten two or more things firmly together using a clamp 2. **HOLD SOMETHING FIRMLY** to hold something firmly and tightly in position 3. **PUT CLAMP ON CAR** to fix a clamp to the wheel of an illegally parked car. *N Am* term **boot**[1] [15C. Probably < assumed Middle Dutch or Middle Low German *klampe*]

clamp down *vi* to take firm action to limit something bad or control somebody doing something bad (*informal*) ○ *Police have clamped down on illegal parking in the area.*

clampdown /klámp down/ *n* firm official action taken to limit something bad or control somebody doing something bad (*informal*)

clamper /klámpər/ *n* a spiked metal frame fastened under a shoe to provide extra grip on ice or snow

clamshell /klám shel/ *n* 1. the shell of a clam 2. *N Am* a dredging bucket that has two hinged jaws (*informal*)

clan /klan/ *n* (*takes a singular or plural verb*) 1. **GROUP OF FAMILIES** a group of families related through a common ancestor or marriage 2. **RELATED SCOTTISH FAMILIES** a group of Scottish families with common ancestors, a common surname, and a single chief 3. **LARGE FAMILY** a group of people who are all members of a particular family (*informal*) 4. **GROUP WITH SHARED AIM** a group of people who act together because they have the same interests or aims (*informal*) [15C. < Gaelic *clann* 'offspring' < Old Irish *cland* < Latin *planta* 'sprout']

clandestine /klan déstin, klán de stīn/ *adj* needing to be concealed, usually because it is illegal or unauthorized [Mid-16C. < Latin *clandestinus* < *clam* 'secretly'] —**clandestinely** *adv* —**clandestinity** /klán de stínnəti/ *n*

SYNONYMS See *secret*.

clang /klang/ *vti* (**clangs, clanging, clanged**) 1. **MAKE LOUD RINGING NOISE** to make the loud sound of two metal objects hitting each other 2. **MOVE MAKING CLANGING SOUND** to move or operate with a clanging sound ■ *n* **LOUD RINGING NOISE** a ringing sound made by two metal objects hitting each other [Late 16C. < Latin *clangere* 'emit a ringing sound']

clanger /klángər/ *n* an unwise or embarrassing mistake (*informal*) ○ *drop a clanger*

clangor *n* US spelling of **clangour**

clangour /klángər/ *n* 1. a clang or repeated loud clanging 2. a din or uproar —**clangorous** *adj* —**clangorously** *adv*

clanjamfry /klan jámfri/ *n Scotland* a rabble or crowd of people

clank /klangk/ *vti* (**clanks, clanking, clanked**) 1. **MAKE METALLIC NOISE** to make the short loud sound of two

---

heavy metal objects hitting each other **2. MOVE MAKING CLANKING SOUND** to move or operate with a clanking sound ■ *n* **METALLIC NOISE** a short loud sound made by two heavy metal objects hitting each other [Mid-17C. Probably an imitation of the sound] —**clankingly** *adv* —**clanky** *adj*

clannish /klánnish/ *adj* inclined to stick together as a group and exclude outsiders —**clannishly** *adv* —**clannishness** *n*

clansman /klánzmən/ (*plural* **-men** /-mən/) *n* a man who is a member of a Scottish clan

clansperson /klánz purss'n/ (*plural* **-people** /-peep'l/) *n* a member of a Scottish clan (*usually used in the plural*)

clanswoman /klánz wŏŏmən/ (*plural* **-women** /-wimin/) *n* a woman who is a member of a Scottish clan

clap[1] /klap/ *v* (**claps, clapping, clapped**) **1.** *vti* **APPLAUD** to hit the hands together repeatedly to express approval **2.** *vti* **HIT HANDS TOGETHER** to hit the hands together quickly and loudly **3.** *vti* **HIT HANDS IN RHYTHM** to hit the hands together repeatedly in time with a beat **4.** *vt* **PUT SOMETHING SOMEWHERE QUICKLY** to move something or somebody to or against something quickly ○ *clapped him in jail* **5.** *vt Scotland* **PAT ANIMAL** to stroke or pat an animal (*informal*) ■ *n* **1. SUDDEN LOUD SOUND** the sound made by striking the palms together once, or a sound resembling this **2. EXPRESSION OF APPROVAL THROUGH APPLAUSE** an expression of approval by loud continuous clapping **3. CLAPPING RHYTHMICALLY** a session of rhythmic clapping **4.** *Scotland* **PAT** the act of stroking or patting an animal (*informal*) [Old English *clæppan* < Germanic, an imitation of the sound]

clap[2] /klap/ *n* MED same as **gonorrhoea** (*slang*) [Late 16C. Origin ?]

clapboard /kláp bawrd/ *n* a long narrow wooden board that has one edge thicker than the other. Use: to clad buildings. [Mid-17C. Alteration, by partial translation, of obsolete *clapholt* < Low German *klappholt* < *klappen* 'clap, split' + *holt* 'wood']

clapped-out /klapt ówt/ *adj* worn out and in very poor condition (*informal*; *not hyphenated when used after a verb*)

clapper /kláppər/ *n* **1. PART MAKING BELL RING** a piece of metal inside a bell that strikes its sides, making it ring **2. SOMEBODY WHO CLAPS** somebody who claps his or her hands ■ **clappers** *npl* **MUSICAL INSTRUMENT** a musical instrument consisting of two flat pieces of wood that are held between the thumb and forefinger and clapped together ◇ **like the clappers** extremely fast, or as fast as possible (*informal*)

clapperboard

clapperboard /kláppər bawrd/ *n* a pair of hinged boards filmed at the start of each take in a film and clapped together to help to synchronize the soundtrack with the film

Clapton /kláptən/, **Eric** (*b.* 1945) British guitarist, singer, and songwriter. The nickname indicating the rock-steady quality of this versatile bluesman graces his album *Slowhand* (1977).

'You were at school and you were pimply and no one wanted to know you. You get into a group and you've got thousands of chicks there.'
[Eric Clapton. Quoted in *Rock 'n' Roll Babylon*, Gary Herman; 1994]

claptrap /kláp trap/ *n* nonsense, especially pompous or important-sounding nonsense (*informal*) [Late

18C. Originally, in the theatre, a device or line to elicit clapping]

claque /klak/ *n* (*takes a singular or plural verb*) **1.** a group of people hired to applaud a performance **2.** a group of people around a rich or famous person whom they praise and support uncritically (*disapproving*) [Mid-19C. < French < *claquer* 'to clap', an imitation of the sound]

claqueur /klákər/ *n* a member of a rich or famous person's entourage who gives uncritical praise or support [Mid-19C. < French, 'clapper' < *claquer* (see CLAQUE)]

clarabella /klárrə béllə/, **claribella** *n* an eight-foot flute stop on an organ [Mid-19C. < Latin *clara bella* 'clear and beautiful']

Clare /klair/ **1.** coastal county in Munster Province, southwestern Republic of Ireland. Population: 94,006 (2002). Area: 3,188 sq. km/1,231 sq. mi. **2.** island off the western coast of Ireland, administratively part of County Mayo. Area: 16 sq. km/6 sq. mi. **3.** river in the northeast of the South Island, New Zealand. Length: 209 km/130 mi.

Clare (of Assisi), **St** (1194–1253) Italian nun. She was a follower of St Francis of Assisi, alongside her sister St Agnes. The three founded the order of the Poor Ladies of Damiano, or Poor Clares. Born **Offreducio, Chiara**

Clare, John (1793–1864) British poet and naturalist. He wrote *Poems Descriptive of Rural Life* (1820) and *The Shepherd's Calendar* (1827).

'I love at eventide to walk alone / Down narrow lanes oerhung with dewy thorn / Where from the long grass underneath the snail / Jet black creeps out and sprouts his timid horn.'
[John Clare, 'Summer Moods', *Selected Poems and Prose of John Clare*; 1966]

clarence /klárrənss/ *n* an enclosed four-wheeled carriage that seats four and has a glass front [Mid-19C. After the Duke of *Clarence*, later WILLIAM IV]

Clarence /klárrənss/ **1.** river in northeastern New South Wales, southeastern Australia. Length: 394 km/245 mi. **2.** river in the northeastern part of the South Island, New Zealand, that rises in the Spenser Mountains and flows into the Pacific Ocean north of Kaikoura. Length: 209 km/130 mi.

Clarenceux /klárrən sŏ́/ *n* the second King-of-Arms in England. The King-of-Arms is the highest rank of heraldic officer. [15C. < Anglo-Norman < English *Clarence*, English dukedom, after *Clare* in Suffolk]

Clarendon /klárrəndən/ *n* a style of boldface roman type [Mid-19C. Probably after the *Clarendon* Press in Oxford]

Clarendon /klárrəndən/, **Edward Hyde, 1st Earl of** (1609–74) English politician and historian. Author of *History of the Rebellion in England* (1702–04), he was impeached for high treason.

Clarendon Code *n* four acts passed by Parliament between 1661 and 1665 to deal with the religious problems caused by the Restoration of Charles II. Although the acts are named after the Earl of Clarendon, he did not support them.

claret /klárrət/ *n* **1.** red wine from the Bordeaux area of southwestern France **2.** a deep purplish-red colour, like that of claret [Early 18C. < Old French *(vin) claret* 'light-coloured (wine)' < Latin *vinum claratum* 'clarified wine', *claratum* form of *clarare* 'clarify' < *clarus* 'clear'] —**claret** *adj*

claret cup *n* an iced summer drink made from claret, brandy, lemon, and sugar, sometimes with sherry or curaçao added

claribella *n* MUSIC another spelling of **clarabella**

clarify /klárri fī/ (**-fies, -fying, -fied**) *v* **1.** *vt* **MAKE SOMETHING CLEARER** to make something clearer by explaining it in greater detail **2.** *vti* **MAKE BUTTER CLEAR** to make butter or fat clear by gently heating it and removing any impurities, or become clear through this process **3.** *vti* **MAKE LIQUID CLEAR** to make a liquid clear and pure, or become clear and pure, usually by filtering [14C. Via Old French < late Latin *clarificare* 'make clear' < Latin *clarus* 'clear'] —**clarification** /klárrifi káysh'n/ *n* —**clarifier** *n*

clarinet /klárrə nét/ *n* a musical instrument of the woodwind family, with a straight body and a single

reed [Mid-18C. < French *clarinette* 'little clarion' < *clarine* 'clarion' < Latin *clarus* 'clear']

clarinettist /klárrə néttist/, **clarinetist** *n* somebody who plays the clarinet

clarion /klárri ən/ *n* **1.** a four-foot organ stop that sounds like a trumpet **2.** a medieval trumpet with a clear high-pitched tone [14C. < medieval Latin *clarion-* < Latin *clarus* 'clear']

clarion call *n* an urgent or inspiring appeal to people to do something [< the use of the clarion as a signal in war]

clarity /klárrəti/ *n* **1. CLEARNESS OF EXPRESSION** the quality of being clearly expressed **2. CLEARNESS OF THOUGHT** clearness in what somebody is thinking **3. CLEARNESS OF REPRODUCTION** the quality of being clear in sound or image **4. TRANSPARENT QUALITY** the quality of being clear, pure, or transparent ○ *wine of great clarity* [Early 17C. < Latin *claritat-* < *clarus* 'clear']

Helen Clark

Clark /klaark/, **Helen Elizabeth** (*b.* 1950) New Zealand politician. She became leader of the New Zealand Labour Party in 1993 and prime minister in 1999. See table at **prime minister**

Clark, Joe (*b.* 1939) Canadian politician. He became the leader of the Conservative Party in 1976 and served as prime minister from 1979 to 1980. Full name **Clark, Charles Joseph.** See table at **prime minister**

'Political freedom is rare enough in the world, but the kind of social and cultural freedom which is the hallmark of Canada is even less common.'
[Joe Clark, *Speech to the Canadian Parliament*; 18 February 1977]

Clark, Manning (1915–91) Australian historian. He wrote the six-volume *A History of Australia* (1962–87). Full name **Clark, Charles Manning Hope**

Clark cell /klaark-/ *n* a standard battery cell with a mercury anode surrounded by a paste of mercury sulphate, and a zinc cathode immersed in saturated zinc sulphate solution [Late 19C. After Josiah Latimer *Clark* (1822–98), British engineer]

Clarke /klaark/, **Sir Arthur C.** (*b.* 1917) British writer and scientist. His works of science fiction include the screenplay of *2001: A Space Odyssey* (1968), written with Stanley Kubrick. Full name **Clarke, Arthur Charles**

'If we relate the life of a star to the life of a man...the Sun is but a week old...Life has existed on this planet for two or three days of the week that has passed; the whole of human history lies within the last second, and there are eighty years to come.'
[Sir Arthur C. Clarke, *By Space Possessed*; 1993]

Clarke, Austin (1896–1974) Irish poet and playwright. He followed William Butler Yeats in promoting verse drama and wrote the autobiographical *Twice Round the Black Church* (1962).

'Burn Ovid with the rest. Lovers will find / A hedge-school for themselves and learn by heart / All that the clergy banish from the mind.'
[Austin Clarke, 'Penal Law', *Collected Poems*; 1974]

Clarke, Jeremiah (1674?–1707) English composer and organist. His best-known work, 'The Prince of Denmark's March', was long attributed to Henry Purcell.

Clarke, John (*fl* 1639) English scholar. He wrote *Paroemiologia Anglo-Latina* (1639), a collection of English and Latin proverbs.

Clarke, Marcus Andrew Hislop (1846–81) British-born Australian writer. He wrote *For the Term of His Natural Life* (1874). See Cultural note at **term**

claro /klaárō/ (*plural* **-ros** or **-roes**) *n* a mild light-coloured cigar [Late 19C. Via Spanish, 'light' < Latin *clarus* 'clear']

clarsach /klaár sakh, -səkh/ *n* a small harp of ancient Scotland and Ireland [15C. < Irish *cláirseach*, Gaelic *clàrsach*]

clarts /klaarts/ *npl N England, Scotland* small lumps of mud, especially those stuck to shoes (*informal*) [Early 19C. Origin ?]

clarty /klaárti/ (**-tier, -tiest**) *adj N England, Scotland* very dirty or muddy (*informal*)

REGIONAL NOTE See ***manky***.

clary /kláiri/ (*plural* **-ies**) *n* a perennial plant of the mint family. Native to: southern Europe. Genus: *Salvia*. [14C. Via obsolete French *clarie* < medieval Latin *sclarea*]

clash /klash/ *v* (**clashes, clashing, clashed**) **1.** *vi* **FIGHT OR ARGUE** to come into verbal or physical conflict with somebody ○ *Demonstrators clashed with police outside the headquarters this morning.* **2.** *vi* **BE AT ODDS WITH SOMETHING** to be incompatible ○ *The conclusions clash with the evidence.* **3.** *vti* **MAKE LOUD NOISE** to make a loud harsh metallic noise, or hit things together to make such a noise **4.** *vi* **NOT HARMONIZE** to look unpleasant or inharmonious when together ○ *The orange of the upholstery clashes with the pink of the paintwork.* **5.** *vi* **CONFLICT WITH SOMETHING ELSE** to conflict with something else in terms of timing or appropriateness (*refers to events*) ○ *The final episode of the serial clashes with one of my husband's favourite programmes.* ■ *n* **1. FIGHT OR ARGUMENT** a short fierce encounter, verbal or physical, with another person or group ○ *There were several clashes between supporters outside the stadium.* **2. LOUD METALLIC SOUND** a loud harsh metallic noise **3. LACK OF HARMONY** a jarring or unpleasant juxtaposition of incompatible colours **4. CONFLICT CAUSED BY DIFFERENCE** a difference of opinions or qualities that causes conflict ○ *a clash of personalities* **5. COINCIDENCE OF CONFLICTING EVENTS** a conflict between two or more events due to occur at the same time [Early 16C. An imitation of the sound] —**clasher** *n*

SYNONYMS See ***fight***.

clasp /klaasp/ *vt* (**clasps, clasping, clasped**) **1. HOLD SOMEBODY OR SOMETHING TIGHTLY** to hold somebody or something tightly with the hands or arms ○ *She clasped the baby tightly to herself in the surging crowd.* ○ *I clasped the handrail as the boat lurched.* **2. FASTEN THINGS** to fasten or hold two things together with a device designed for this purpose ■ *n* **1. SMALL BUCKLE OR FASTENING** a small fastening for holding things such as bags or jewellery closed or together **2. TIGHT HOLD** a firm tight hold with the arms, a hand, or a device for fastening or holding things together **3. IDENTIFYING ATTACHMENT ON MILITARY MEDAL** a small metal bar on the ribbon of a medal that identifies the military action or service for which the honour was awarded [14C. Origin ?]

clasper /klaáspər/ *n* **1.** either of a pair of structures located in the anal region of some male insects and crustaceans and used to grasp a female during copulation **2.** either of a pair of long reproductive organs on the pelvic fins of male sharks and rays

clasp knife *n* a pocket knife with one or more blades and sometimes other devices that can be folded back into the handle

class /klaass/ *n* **1. GROUP TAUGHT TOGETHER** a group of students or pupils who are taught or study together **2. PERIOD OF TEACHING** a period when students meet to be taught a particular subject ○ *When's our next biology class?* **3. SPECIFIC SUBJECT TAUGHT** a particular course of instruction **4.** *N Am* **STUDENTS WHO GRADUATE TOGETHER** the group of students who leave or graduate from an institution in the same year **5. GROUP WITHIN SOCIETY** a group of people within a society who share the same social and economic status **6. SOCIAL GROUP WITH SIMILAR OPPORTUNITIES** a category of people who have a similar level of opportunity to obtain economic resources and prestige **7. STRUCTURE OF SOCIETY** the structure of divisions in a society determined by the social or economic grouping of its members **8. ELEGANCE IN STYLE** elegance in appearance, behaviour, or lifestyle (*informal*) **9. EXCELLENCE** admirable skill or excellence in performance (*informal*) ○ *a player who lacks class* **10. DIVISION ACCORDING TO QUALITY** a categorization of services or goods according to quality ○ *This airline has several classes of seating.* **11. UNIVERSITY HONOURS DEGREE GRADE** a grade assigned to university honours degrees ○ *a first-class honours degree* **12. GROUP OF SIMILAR ITEMS** a group into which things with at least one characteristic in common are classified **13. SET OF RELATED ORGANISMS** a major category in the taxonomic classification of related organisms, comprising a group of orders ○ *Elephants and dolphins both belong to the class Mammalia.* **14.** MATHS, LOGIC same as **set**² *n* (sense 7) ■ *vt* (**classes, classing, classed**) **ASSIGN SOMEBODY OR SOMETHING TO GROUP** to assign somebody or something to a particular category or group ○ *It's not old enough to be classed as a vintage car.* [Mid-16C. < Latin *classis* 'political class']

SYNONYMS See ***type***.

class. *abbr* **1.** ARTS classic **2.** ARTS classical **3.** BIOL, GOV classification **4.** BIOL, GOV classified

class act *n* a person or thing regarded as an example of excellence (*informal*)

class action *n* a legal action brought by several litigants jointly, usually relying on one another to prove each individual's case

class-conscious *adj* overly concerned about people's relative social status —**class-consciousness** *n*

classes CHR plural of **classis**

classic /klássik/ *adj* **1. TOP QUALITY** generally considered to be of the highest quality or lasting value, especially in the arts **2. DEFINITIVE** authoritative and perfect as a standard of its kind ○ *a classic example of a mixed metaphor* **3. ALWAYS FASHIONABLE** always fashionable and elegant, usually because of simplicity and restraint in style ○ *the classic 'little black dress'* **4. GENERALLY ACCEPTED** conforming to generally accepted principles or methods **5. EXTREMELY AND USUALLY COMICALLY APROPOS** apropos to an extreme degree, usually with a comical or ironic twist (*informal*) ○ *It was classic – the way she tripped while she was telling us all to be careful!* ■ *n* **1. WORK OF HIGHEST QUALITY** something created or made, especially a work of art, music, or literature, that is generally considered to be of the highest quality and of enduring value ○ *The novel has become a 20th-century classic.* ○ *a design classic* **2. SIMPLE ELEGANT GARMENT** a piece of clothing of a simple and enduring style **3. OUTSTANDING OR TYPICAL EXAMPLE** something that is an outstanding or typical example of its kind ○ *Last night's show was a classic.* **4. MAJOR SPORTING EVENT** a major sporting event, e.g. a horse race or golf tournament **5. SOMETHING COMICALLY APROPOS** something that is comically or ironically apropos (*informal*)

USAGE classic or **classical**? There is some overlap in the meanings of these words, but essentially ***classic*** describes the value or status of something (*a classic example of Art Deco*), whereas ***classical***, although often implying a judgment of value or worth, is a more factual reference to the literature, art, and culture of the ancient world or to the high period of an art form (*a classical education, classical music, classical ballet*). A ***classic*** is something created or made that is of the highest quality, whereas *classics* is the study of the languages and cultures of ancient Greece and Rome.

classical /klássik'l/ *adj* **1. RELATING TO ANCIENT GREECE OR ROME** relating or belonging to the ancient Greeks or Romans or their cultures ○ *classical literature* ○ *a classical scholar* **2. IN ANCIENT GREEK OR ROMAN STYLE** in the style of ancient Greece or Rome, especially in architecture **3. OF MUSIC CONSIDERED TO BE SERIOUS** describes music that is considered serious or intellectual and is usually written in a traditional or formal style, as opposed to such genres as pop, rock, and folk music **4. OF 18C AND 19C MUSIC** describes the style of music composed in Europe in the 18th and 19th centuries **5. STUDYING LATIN AND GREEK** consisting of or involving the study of the ancient Greek and Latin languages and literature ○ *a classical education* **6. ORTHODOX OR CONSERVATIVE** considered as the traditional or authoritative form of something ○ *classical Freudianism* **7.** same as **classic** *adj* (sense 2) **8.** PHYS **EXCLUDING QUANTUM THEORY AND RELATIVITY** not taking into account quantum theoretical or relativistic effects [Late 16C. < Latin *classicus* 'of the first class' < *classis* 'political class'] —**classicality** /klássi kálləti/ *n*

USAGE See ***classic***.

classical conditioning *n* the teaching of a response to a new stimulus by pairing it repeatedly with a stimulus for which there is a biological reflex. The best-known example is Pavlov's experiment in which dogs heard a bell ring every time food appeared and eventually started salivating at the sound of the bell alone. ◊ **operant conditioning**

classicalism *n* ARTS same as **classicism**

classical Latin *n* the form of the Latin language used between the end of the 1st century BC and the 3rd century AD, when the standard authors of classical literature wrote

classically /klássikli/ *adv* **1. SIMPLY STYLED** in a simple and elegant style **2. AS TRADITIONALLY ACCEPTED OR DONE** in a manner that is traditionally accepted and belongs in the mainstream of the relevant art **3. IN MANNER OF GRAECO-ROMAN CULTURE** in the style of ancient Greece or Rome **4. AS USUALLY OCCURS** used to indicate what usually or typically happens ○ *Classically, cases like this are solved through painstaking investigation.* **5. AS TYPICAL EXAMPLE** as a classic example of something **6. IN CLASSIC WAY** in a classic or classical manner

classicise *vti* another spelling of **classicize**

classicism /klássissizəm/, **classicalism** /klássik'lizəm/ *n* **1. RESTRAINED STYLE IN ARTS** a style of art and architecture based on Greek and Roman models or principles, characterized by regularity of form and restraint of expression **2. GREEK OR LATIN IDIOM** a Greek or Latin phrase or expression **3. STUDY OF GRAECO-ROMAN CULTURE** the study or knowledge of ancient Greece and Rome

classicist /klássissist/ *n* **1.** a scholar of ancient Greek and Latin **2.** a supporter of classicism in the arts

classicize /klássi sīz/ (**-cizes, -cizing, -cized**), **classicise** (**-cises, -cising, -cised**) *vt* to imbue something with classical qualities or characteristics ○ *classicized the design of the windows*

classics /klássiks/ *n* the academic study of the languages, literature, and history of ancient Greece and Rome (*takes a singular verb*) ■ *npl* a body of ancient Greek and Roman literature (*takes a plural verb*)

USAGE See ***classic***.

classification /klássifi káysh'n/ *n* **1. ORGANIZATION INTO GROUPS** the allocation of items to groups according to type ○ *classification of members according to abilities and interests* **2. CATEGORY** a group or category within an organized system ○ *The classification 'history' can be further subdivided.* **3. CATEGORIZATION OF LIVING THINGS** the categorization of organisms into defined groups on the basis of identified characteristics. The Linnaean classification groups organisms into species, genera, families, and higher taxonomic groups on the basis of visible resemblances, while other systems may use other determining factors, e.g. the molecular relationships among the groups. **4. DESIGNATION AS SENSITIVE INFORMATION** the restriction of sensitive government or military information to authorized people [Late 18C. < French < *classe* 'class' < Latin *classis* 'political class'] —**classificatory** *adj*

classification schedule *n* the complete plan and content of a library's cataloguing system

classified /klássi fīd/ *adj* **1. SECRET OR SENSITIVE** available only to authorized people for reasons of national security. The basic categories of classified information are confidential, secret, and top secret. **2. GROUPED BY TYPE** arranged in groups according to a classification system **3. LISTED IN BRITISH ROAD SYSTEM** classed as a motorway, an A-road, or a B-road in the British system of classifying roads ■ **classifieds** *npl* **GROUP OF ADVERTISEMENTS** classified advertisements printed together in a newspaper or magazine (*informal*)

classified advertisement, classified ad *n* a small advertisement positioned with others of similar content in a newspaper or magazine

classify /klássi fī/ (**-fies, -fying, -fied**) vt **1.** to assign things or people to categories **2.** to designate information as being available only to authorized people for reasons of security [Late 18C. Back-formation < CLASSIFICATION] —**classifiable** adj —**classifier** n

class interval n any of the intervals into which adjacent discrete values of a variable are divided

classis /klássiss/ (plural **classes** /kláss seez/) n **1.** in some Reformed churches, a governing body composed of elders and pastors **2.** a district or group of churches governed by a classis [Late 16C. < Latin, 'political class']

classism /klaassizzəm/ n discrimination or prejudice based on social or economic class —**classist** adj, n

classless /klaasslss/ adj **1.** not having social or economic classes **2.** not belonging to or associated with a particular social or economic class —**classlessness** n

class list n a list of the classes of degree awarded in a British university

class mark n LIBRARIES same as **class number**

classmate /klaass mayt/ n a member of the same school class as another person

class number n a series of letters and/or numbers on a book or other publication in a library identifying it, the category of its subject matter, and usually its shelf location

classroom /klaass room, -room/ n a room, especially in a school or college, where classes are held

class struggle n the Marxist principle of a continuous struggle for political and economic power between the ruling and working classes

classwork /klaass wurk/ n school work that pupils do in lessons at school, as opposed to at home or after school

classy /klaassi/ (**-ier, -iest**) adj very stylish and elegant (informal) —**classily** adv —**classiness** n

clast /klast/ n a fragment of rock produced by the breaking down of larger rocks [Mid-20C. Back-formation < CLASTIC]

clastic /klástik/ adj **1.** able to be separated into parts or have parts removed to enable better study ○ Clastic models are often used to teach anatomy. **2.** describes rock that is composed of fragments of other rocks [Late 19C. < French clastique < Greek klastos 'broken in pieces']

clathrate /kláth rayt/ n CRYSTAL WITH EMBEDDED SUBSTANCE a solid compound with a physical structure in which molecules of one substance are fully enclosed within the crystal structure of another ■ adj **1.** WITH CRYSTAL-EMBEDDED SUBSTANCE having molecules of one substance enclosed fully within the crystal structure of another substance **2.** LIKE LATTICE resembling a lattice in structure or appearance [Mid-19C. < Latin clathrat-, past participle of clathrare 'fit with bars' < clathri 'lattice' < Greek klēthra 'bars']

clatter /kláttər/ v (**-ters, -tering, -tered**) **1.** vti MAKE RATTLING NOISE to make, or cause something to make, a loud rattling noise ○ We heard the horses' hooves clattering down the cobbled road. **2.** vi CHATTER NOISILY to chatter or prattle, especially noisily **3.** vt N England, Scotland BOX SOMEBODY'S EARS to hit somebody on the ears, especially as a punishment ■ n **1.** BANGING METALLIC SOUND a loud metallic banging or rattling noise ○ the clatter of pots and pans in the kitchen **2.** NOISY CHATTER noisy chatter and prattling talk **3.** LOUD COMMOTION a noisy disturbance [Assumed Old English clatrian < Germanic, probably an imitation of the sound] —**clatterer** n —**clatteringly** adv

Claudel /klō dél/, **Paul Louis Charles Marie** (1868–1955) French writer and diplomat. His symbolism and devout Catholicism inform such dramas as The Satin Slipper (1928–29).

claudication /kláwdi káysh'n/ n **1.** limping or impaired walking, especially as a result of reduced blood supply to the leg muscles **2.** MED same as **intermittent claudication** [15C. < Latin claudication- < claudicare 'to limp' < claudus 'lame']

Claudius I /kláwdi əss/ (10 BC–AD 54) Roman emperor. His reign (AD 41–54) was notable for the expansion of the Roman empire and the emperor's ambitious building programme. Full name **Tiberius Claudius Drusus Nero Germanicus**

clause /klawz/ n **1.** a group of words consisting of a subject and its predicate **2.** a distinct section of a document, especially a legal document, that is usually separately numbered [13C. < French < assumed Latin clausa 'close of a rhetorical period' < claudere 'to close'] —**clausal** adj

claustrophobe /kláwstrə fōb, klóstrə-/ n PSYCHIAT same as **claustrophobic** [Mid-20C. Back-formation < CLAUSTROPHOBIA]

claustrophobia /kláwstrə fóbi ə, klóstrə-/ n an irrational fear of being in a confined or enclosed space [Late 19C. < modern Latin < claustrum (see CLOISTER)]

claustrophobic /kláwstrə fóbik, klóstrə-/ adj **1.** CONFINED OR CRAMPED unpleasantly or uncomfortably confined ○ The room is claustrophobic but painting the walls a light colour might help. **2.** OF OR HAVING CLAUSTROPHOBIA relating to or having claustrophobia ■ n SOMEBODY WHO FEARS ENCLOSED SPACES somebody who is affected by claustrophobia —**claustrophobically** adv

clavate /kláy vayt/ adj with one end thicker than the other ○ Some protozoa have clavate cilia. [Early 19C. < modern Latin clavatus < Latin clava 'club (for striking)'] —**clavately** adv

clave[1] /klaav, klayv/ n either of a pair of hardwood sticks that are hit together to make a clicking sound [Early 20C. Via American Spanish < Spanish, 'keystone' < Latin clavis 'key']

clave[2] /klayv/ past tense of **cleave**[2]

clavicembalo /klávvi chémbəlō/ (plural **-los**) n MUSIC same as **harpsichord** [Mid-18C. Via Italian < medieval Latin clavicymbalum, literally 'key cymbal']

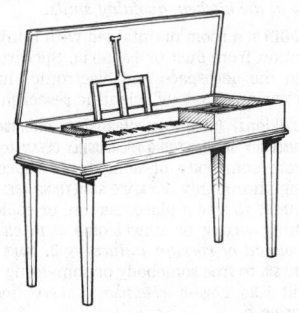

clavichord

clavichord /klávvi kawrd/ n a keyboard instrument of the 15th to 19th centuries, a precursor of the modern piano, in which small wedges strike horizontal strings to produce a soft sound [15C. < medieval Latin clavichordium < Latin clavis 'key' + chorda 'string'] —**clavichordist** n

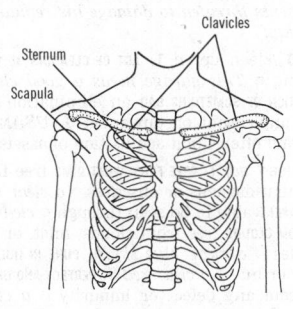

Sternum
Scapula
Clavicles
clavicle

clavicle /klávvik'l/ n **1.** the long curved bone that connects the upper part of the breastbone with the shoulder blade at the top of each shoulder in humans **2.** a bone or structure with a function similar to that of the human clavicle in some other animals. It is reduced or absent in many mammals. [Early 17C. < Latin clavicula 'small key' < clavis 'key'] —**clavicular** /klə víkyōōlər, kla-/ adj

clavier /klə veer, klávvi ər/ n **1.** a stringed keyboard musical instrument **2.** the keyboard of a musical instrument [Early 18C. Directly or via German Klavier < French < medieval Latin claviarius 'key-bearer' < Latin clavis 'key']

Clavius /kláyvi əss/ large walled plain on the Moon near the south pole, approximately 225 km/140 mi. in diameter

claw /klaw/ n **1.** ANIMAL'S SHARP NAIL a pointed curved nail on the end of each toe in birds, some reptiles, and some mammals **2.** PINCER an appendage used for grasping in crabs and other invertebrates **3.** APPENDAGE RESEMBLING CLAW something resembling a claw in shape or function, e.g. a mechanical grabbing device ■ v (**claws, clawing, clawed**) **1.** vti ATTACK WITH CLAWS to scratch or dig at something or somebody with claws, fingernails, or something similar ○ The dogs had clawed at the door. **2.** vt FORM SOMETHING BY SCRATCHING to form something by digging or scratching with claws or something similar ○ Using our bare hands we clawed a hole in the sand. [Old English clawu < Germanic] —**clawed** adj —**clawless** adj

claw back vt **1.** to get something back with difficulty ○ She's slowly clawing back some of the status she used to have. **2.** to recover through taxation money paid out, especially in state benefits

claw off vi to avoid the dangers of a lee shore or other hazard by sailing as close to the wind as possible on alternate tacks

clawback /kláw bak/ n **1.** the recovery of money, especially through taxation **2.** a sum of money recovered, especially through taxation

claw hammer

claw hammer n a hammer with a tapered fork at one end of its head for removing nails

claw setting n a jewellery setting in which a stone or similar item is gripped by small prongs

clay /klay/ n **1.** TYPE OF FINE SOIL OR ROCK a fine-grained material consisting mainly of hydrated aluminium silicates that occurs naturally in soil and sedimentary rock. Use: in making bricks, ceramics, and cement. **2.** MODELLING SUBSTANCE a substance like clay used for modelling **3.** HEAVY STICKY EARTH earth, especially heavy sticky wet earth **4.** HUMAN BODY the physical body of a human being, particularly the matter of which it is composed (literary) ○ From clay we are made. **5.** TENNIS same as **clay court 6.** SPORTS same as **clay pigeon** (sense 1) ■ vt (**clays, claying, clayed**) COVER SOMETHING WITH CLAY to cover or fill something with clay [Old English clǣg < Indo-European] —**clayey** adj

Clay /klay/, **Cassius ▶ Ali, Muhammad**

Clay, Henry (1777–1852) US politician. He long served in the US Congress and was the architect of the Missouri Compromise (1820–21) and the Compromise of 1850 that temporarily averted civil war.

'I had rather be right than be President.'
[Henry Clay, Speech in the Senate; 1850]

clay court n a tennis court with a hard surface made of crushed clay or shale

Claymation /klay máysh'n/ tdmk a trademark for an animated film process using clay figurines that are moved and filmed so as to create lifelike imagery and motion

clay mineral n hydrated aluminium silicate. Source: clay.

claymore /kláy mawr/ n **1.** a large double-edged broadsword formerly used by Scottish Highlanders **2.** ARMS same as **claymore mine** [Early 18C. < Gaelic claidheamh mór 'great sword']

claymore mine n a landmine in the shape of a convex disc that is placed above ground and detonates horizontally. It is designed to kill or maim approaching personnel.

claypan /kláy pan/ *n* a layer of impervious clay close to the surface of the ground that holds water after heavy rain

clay pigeon *n* **1.** a clay disc hurled into the air from a machine and used as a target for shooting **2.** *US* somebody who is vulnerable to attack (*slang*)

claystone /kláy stōn/ *n* a compact fine-grained rock containing primarily clay particles

Clayton's /kláyt'nz/ *adj ANZ* imitation or illusory rather than real (*informal*) [Late 20C. After a soft drink promoted as 'the drink I have when I'm not having a drink']

cld *abbr* FIN called

clean /kleen/ *adj* **1.** NOT DIRTY free from dirt or impurities ○ *clean hands* **2.** UNADULTERATED containing no foreign matter or pollutants ○ *a clean water supply* **3.** FREE OF INFECTION not infected or diseased ○ *a clean wound* **4.** WASHED freshly laundered or washed after use ○ *fetched some clean shirts* **5.** PARTICULAR ABOUT PERSONAL HYGIENE taking pains over personal hygiene or grooming ○ *He is very clean in his habits.* **6.** EMPTY containing nothing at all (*informal*) ○ *The flat was stripped clean by the previous tenants.* **7.** MORALLY UPRIGHT morally pure and upright **8.** FAIR not corrupt or dishonest ○ *a clean verdict* **9.** NOT RUDE not rude or obscene **10.** BLANK without anything on it, especially anything written ○ *a clean sheet of paper* **11.** WITH NO POLICE RECORD having or showing no record of convictions or penalties, e.g. for driving offences ○ *Don's record is clean.* **12.** FREE OF PROBLEMS without problems or difficulties ○ *The doctor gave me a clean bill of health.* **13.** SMOOTH-EDGED without rough or jagged edges ○ *a clean blow of the axe* **14.** STREAMLINED simple and flowing in design, without projections or additions ○ *the aircraft's clean silhouette* **15.** COMPLETE complete and unqualified ○ *made a clean break with the past* **16.** NOT POLLUTING producing the least possible pollution ○ *a clean source of energy* **17.** MINIMALLY RADIOACTIVE producing the least possible radioactive fallout or contamination **18.** WITH NO FLAWS describes a gemstone that is free of flaws **19.** FREE OF WEEDS cleared of weeds and unwanted undergrowth **20.** NOT HEAVILY CORRECTED containing relatively few mistakes or corrections **21.** PERFORMED PRECISELY precisely performed and in accordance with the best technique ○ *a clean jump* **22.** WITH NO FOULS OR RULE-BREAKING played, fought, or won by strict compliance with the rules ○ *a clean victory for our team* **23.** WITH NO ILLEGAL DRUGS not containing or possessing illegal drugs (*slang*) **24.** UNADDICTED free from addiction to narcotic drugs or other substances (*slang*) **25.** WITH NO CONCEALED ARMS not carrying concealed weapons (*slang*) ○ *A body search revealed that the suspect was clean.* **26.** INNOCENT not guilty of a specific crime (*slang*) **27.** JUDAISM RITUALLY UNDEFILED describes somebody who is ritually undefiled according to Jewish law **28.** JUDAISM ABLE TO BE LAWFULLY EATEN describes food that may be eaten according to Jewish law **29.** CHR PURE IN SPIRIT spiritually pure or purified ■ *v* (**cleans, cleaning, cleaned**) **1.** *vti* MAKE SOMETHING FREE OF DIRT to rid something of dirt or impurities ○ *Have you finished cleaning your room?* **2.** *vt* REMOVE DIRT to get rid of unwanted dirt, stains, or marks ○ *cleaned the mud from her boots* **3.** *vi* GET FREE OF DIRT to become free of dirt, chiefly because of a content or structure that easily repels it ○ *This acrylic rug cleans easily.* **4.** *vt* RID SOMETHING OF CORRUPTION to free something of dishonest practices ○ *The commissioners were bent on cleaning the council of nepotism.* **5.** *vt* PREPARE DEAD ANIMAL FOR COOKING to prepare a dead animal for cooking by removing its entrails **6.** *vt* REMOVE CONTENTS OF SOMETHING to use up the contents of something ○ *The children cleaned their plates and asked for more.* ■ *n* SESSION OF CLEANING a spell of removing unwanted dirt or marks ■ *adv* **1.** IN ORDER TO REMOVE DIRT so as to make something free from dirt **2.** IN ORDER TO REMOVE EVIDENCE so as to rid something of incriminating evidence **3.** WITH NO OBSTRUCTION directly, especially without having any obstruction **4.** CLEANLY in a clean way ○ *Does this type of gas burn clean?* ○ *We wanted to play the game clean.* **5.** ENTIRELY completely or utterly (*informal*) ○ *I clean forgot to call.* [Old English *clǣne* < Germanic, 'pure'] —**cleanable** *adj* —**cleanness** *n* ◇ **come clean** to confess or tell the truth about something (*informal*)

clean out *vt* to use up or steal all of somebody's money or belongings (*informal*) ○ *Buying the new bike cleaned me out.*

clean up *v* **1.** *vti* MAKE SOMETHING CLEAN OR TIDY to make somebody or something clean or tidy ○ *Can you just give me a minute to clean up in here?* **2.** *vt* ERADICATE SOMETHING UNPLEASANT to rid a place of something unpleasant such as pollution or crime **3.** *vi* MAKE MONEY to acquire a large amount of money (*slang*) ○ *They really cleaned up in the stock market last year.*

clean and jerk *n* in weightlifting, a movement in which the weight is lifted to shoulder height, held there briefly, and then quickly pushed above the head

clean-cut *adj* **1.** neat in dress or appearance ○ *a clean-cut young officer in a spotless uniform* **2.** distinctly outlined or designed **3.** same as **clear-cut** *adj* (sense 1)

cleaner /kléenər/ *n* **1.** somebody whose job is to clean the interior of a building **2.** a chemical or machine used for cleaning

cleaners /kléenərz/ *n* a shop where clothes and other items are taken to be dry-cleaned ○ *My best suit is at the cleaners.* ◇ **take somebody to the cleaners** to deprive somebody of his or her money or possessions by dishonest means (*slang*)

clean-limbed *adj* having a well-proportioned and youthful-looking body

cleanliness /klénnlinəss/ *n* the degree to which somebody keeps clean or a place is kept clean ○ *a small hotel noted for its cleanliness*

clean-living *adj* never doing anything that might be considered immoral or unhealthy

cleanly /kléenli/ *adv* **1.** EASILY OR EFFICIENTLY with ease or efficiency ○ *a cleanly executed triple jump on the ice* **2.** WITHOUT JAGGED EDGES in a manner that does not leave rough edges ○ *The saw cut cleanly.* **3.** FAIRLY in a fair manner **4.** IN CLEAN WAY in a way that is clean ○ *Work cleanly in the kitchen, avoiding spills.*

clean room *n* a room maintained with minimal contamination from dust or bacteria. Such rooms are used in the aerospace and electronics industries and in various kinds of scientific research.

cleanse /klenz/ (**cleanses, cleansing, cleansed**) *vt* **1.** MAKE SOMEBODY OR SOMETHING THOROUGHLY CLEAN to remove dirt from somebody or something, especially by washing thoroughly **2.** MAKE SOMETHING FREE FROM UNPLEASANTNESS to free a place, person, or society from something wrong or unwelcome ○ *to cleanse the town council of corrupt influences* **3.** MAKE SOMEBODY FREE FROM SIN to free somebody or something from sin or guilt [Old English *clǣnsian* < *clǣne* (see CLEAN)] —**cleansing** *n*

cleanser /klénzər/ *n* **1.** a substance for cleaning something thoroughly, especially cream or another product for cleaning the skin **2.** a cosmetic product for cleaning the face

clean-shaven *adj* with the facial hair shaved off

cleanskin /kléen skin/ *n Aus* **1.** an unbranded farm animal (*dated*) **2.** somebody with no criminal record or record of corruption (*slang*) ○ *The latest developments threaten to damage his reputation as a cleanskin.*

cleanup /kléen up/ *n* **1.** ACT OF CLEANING a thorough cleaning ○ *This garage needs a good cleanup.* **2.** ELIMINATION OF SOMETHING BAD an elimination of something unpleasant or unwanted **3.** *US* LARGE GAIN a large and often illicit acquisition of assets (*slang*)

clear /kleer/ *adj* **1.** FREE FROM WHAT DIMS free from anything that darkens or obscures ○ *a clear stream* **2.** TRANSPARENT able to be seen through ○ *clear glass* **3.** FREE FROM CLOUDS free from clouds, mist, or airborne particles ○ *a clear blue sky* **4.** PURE IN HUE pure in colour or hue ○ *a clear red* **5.** PERFECT AND UNBLEMISHED free from any defect or impurity ○ *a clear complexion* **6.** DISTINCT easily heard or seen ○ *clear outlines* **7.** SOUNDING PLEASANT having a pleasant sound ○ *a clear singing voice* **8.** OUT-AND-OUT completely certain, allowing for no doubt ○ *clear evidence of collusion* **9.** UNAMBIGUOUS easy to understand and without ambiguity ○ *clear instructions* **10.** UNDERSTOOD PRECISELY understood without confusion or uncertainty ○ *Is it clear what you have to do when the bell rings?* **11.** EVIDENT so obvious as to need no further explanation or guidance ○ *After half an hour of trying it was clear that the engine would not work properly.* **12.** MENTALLY SHARP AND DISCERNING able to think without confusion ○ *You'll do better in the exam if you keep your mind clear.* **13.** WITHOUT GUILT free from feelings of guilt or blame ○ *a clear conscience* **14.** UNOBSTRUCTED free from obstructions or hindrances ○ *Keep the aisles clear.* **15.** EMPTY empty, with all movable items removed **16.** NOT ATTACHED TO OR TOUCHING SOMETHING free of, or freed from, connection or contact ○ *must be clear of any moving parts* **17.** NET net of deductions or charges ○ *I earn a clear £500 a week.* **18.** NOT FINANCIALLY OBLIGATED not having any debt or financial obligation **19.** SHOW JUMPING UNPENALIZED without any penalties being incurred ○ *jumped a clear round* ■ *adv* **1.** OUT OF THE WAY completely away from something ○ *Please stand clear of the doors until the vehicle has stopped.* **2.** ALL THE WAY totally or completely (*informal*) ○ *They moved clear across the country.* ■ *v* (**clears, clearing, cleared**) **1.** *vi* DISSIPATE AND DISPERSE to undergo the process of dissolving or dispersing, thereby disappearing ○ *By noon the fog had finally cleared.* **2.** *vi* NO LONGER BE FOGGY OR DULL to brighten and become free of adverse conditions ○ *There will be rain in the morning, but the skies will clear by the early afternoon.* **3.** *vti* MAKE OR BECOME TRANSPARENT to become or make something transparent or translucent ○ *The water cleared as the particles sank to the bottom.* **4.** *vt* RID SOMETHING OF EXTRANEOUS MATTER to free something of impurities or unwanted matter ○ *clear a drain of blockages* **5.** *vt* RID THROAT OF OBSTRUCTIONS to rid the throat of phlegm or other obstructions by coughing **6.** *vt* CLARIFY THOUGHTS to remove confusion or misunderstanding from the mind ○ *I'd like a few minutes to clear my head before going into the meeting.* **7.** *vi* RETURN TO SENSES to become or make the mind free from the dulling effects of alcohol, drugs, illness, or a blow to the head ○ *After my head had cleared I was able to stand up again.* **8.** *vt* PROVE SOMEBODY INNOCENT to free somebody from suspicion or blame ○ *anxious to clear her name* **9.** *vt* REMOVE OBJECTS OR OBSTRUCTIONS FROM SOMETHING to empty a space of objects or obstructions ○ *The room had been cleared.* **10.** *vt* FORM SPACE FOR SOMEBODY OR SOMETHING to make a route for somebody or something by removing obstructions **11.** *vt* REMOVE PEOPLE FROM PLACE to empty a building or place of people, e.g. for security reasons ○ *Police had to clear the area.* **12.** *vt* DISENTANGLE SOMETHING to straighten out something that is snarled or otherwise in disarray or disorder ○ *Hurry up and clear that anchor line!* **13.** *vt* MOVE PAST SOMETHING WITHOUT TOUCHING to move past or over something without touching it ○ *If we stay on this course we should clear the buoy.* **14.** *vti* ALLOW TO UNLOAD OR DEPART to be allowed to unload or depart, or allow a vehicle or cargo to unload or passengers to depart, after customs and other formalities have been dealt with ○ *The plane has been cleared for landing.* **15.** *vt* GIVE SOMEBODY AUTHORIZATION to authorize somebody to do something or go somewhere ○ *You are now cleared to enter the restricted area.* **16.** *vt* GAIN MONEY AS PROFIT to earn or acquire something as profit (*informal*) ○ *We cleared £5,000 on the deal.* **17.** *vt* PAY OFF DEBT to settle a debt **18.** *vi* MOVE BETWEEN ACCOUNTS to be authorized and credited to the account of the payee ○ *Cheques take three days to clear.* **19.** *vti* SETTLE BANKING ACCOUNTS to settle the accounts of a banking transaction through a clearing house **20.** *vt* GET BALL OUT OF DEFENCE AREA to get the ball out of the defence area **21.** *vt* DELETE DATA to delete data from a computer display or storage device ■ *n* OPEN SPACE an empty or open area or space ○ *The deer were standing in the clear.* [13C. Via Old French *cler* < Latin *clarus* 'clear, bright'] —**clearable** *adj* —**clearer** *n* —**clearness** *n* ◇ **in the clear** free from suspicion or blame

ORIGIN The Latin word *clarus*, 'clear', 'bright', from which ***clear*** is derived, is also the source of English *chiaroscuro*, *claret*, *clarify*, *clarion*, and *declare*.

clear away *vti* to remove unwanted objects from a place and leave it tidy

clear off *vi* to go away (*informal*; *often used as a command*) ○ *Clear off and don't come back!*

clear out *v* **1.** *vi* LEAVE FAST to leave a place quickly or urgently (*informal*) ○ *We cleared out as fast as we could.* **2.** *vt* REMOVE CONTENTS OF SOMETHING to remove the contents of something such as a room or cupboard, or to tidy something by removing some of its contents ○ *clearing out the attic* **3.** *vt* USE ALL OF SOMEBODY'S MONEY to leave somebody without money or other resources (*slang*) ○ *It will clear us out if we have to pay all the legal expenses.*

clear up *v* **1.** *vi* BECOME BRIGHTER to become brighter, e.g. after rain **2.** *vti* MAKE OR GET BETTER to alleviate or cure something, or be alleviated or cured **3.** *vti* PUT SOMETHING IN ORDER to tidy something by removing or arranging disorganized contents ○ *Please clear up all this mess before you leave.* **4.** *vt* SOLVE OR EXPLAIN

SOMETHING to solve a mystery or explain a misunderstanding ○ *Here is a big problem that has never been fully cleared up.*

clearance /kléeranss/ *n* **1. REMOVING UNWANTED OBJECTS** the removal of obstructions or unwanted objects such as dilapidated buildings or overgrown bushes before building or cultivating **2. PERMISSION FOR SOMETHING TO HAPPEN** permission to do something or for something to take place ○ *several aircraft awaiting clearance to take off* **3. WIDTH OR HEIGHT OF OPENING** the width or height of an opening or passage **4. CHEAP SALE OF GOODS** a sale of goods at reduced prices in order to clear stock **5. REMOVAL OF PEOPLE FROM LAND** the forcible removal from an area of land of the people who have traditionally lived there **6. PASSAGE OF COMMERCIAL DOCUMENTS** the passage of commercial documents through a clearing house **7. GETTING BALL OUT OF DEFENCE AREA** in games, the process of clearing the ball from the defence area **8.** FORESTRY same as **clearing** (sense 1) **9.** MIL same as **security clearance**

clear-cut *adj* **1.** so definite as to leave no possibility of ambiguity **2.** with a distinct outline or form ○ *a clear-cut silhouette of a naval frigate on the horizon* ■ *vt N Am* FORESTRY same as **clear-fell**

clear-eyed *adj* **1. DISCERNINGLY PERCEPTIVE** able to discern things clearly **2. SHARP-EYED** having sharp sight **3. BRIGHT-EYED** having bright eyes

clear-fell *vt* to cut down and remove all of the trees from a wood or other area of land. N Am term **clear-cut**

clear-headed *adj* able to think clearly and decisively, especially in difficult circumstances —**clear-headedly** *adv* —**clear-headedness** *n*

clearing /kléering/ *n* **1.** a space without trees in an area of land that is wooded or overgrown **2.** exchange between banks of cheques, drafts, and notes, and the settlement of consequent differences

clearing bank *n* any bank that uses a central clearing house for transferring credits and cheques between itself and other banks

clearing house *n* **1.** an institution where financial transactions between member banks are cancelled against each other, leaving only balances to be paid **2.** an agency that collects and distributes information

clearing house interbank payment system *n* an electronic system for international dollar payments and currency exchanges (*used in e-commerce*)

clearly /kléerli/ *adv* **1. WITH NO PROBLEM IN HEARING** in a way that is easy to hear **2. WITH NO PROBLEM IN SEEING** in a way that is easy to see **3. WITH NO PROBLEM IN UNDERSTANDING** in a way that is easy to understand ○ *a clearly phrased piece of legislation* **4. LOGICALLY** in a logical and unconfused manner ○ *a clearly written legal brief* **5. OBVIOUSLY** used to acknowledge that a statement is undeniably true ○ *Clearly, we must take immediate action.*

clear-out *n* a session of removing the contents of something such as a room, or of tidying it by removing some of its contents ○ *We had a great clear-out at the weekend and now we've got room for the new table.*

clear-sighted *adj* **1.** having or showing good perception or judgment **2.** having sharp vision —**clear-sightedly** *adv* —**clear-sightedness** *n*

clearstory *n* ARCHIT same as **clerestory**

clear-up *n* a session of putting something in order

clearway /kléer way/ *n* a section of road where drivers may not normally stop

clearwing /kléer wing/ *n* a moth with scaleless transparent wings that is active during the daytime. Family: Sesiidae.

cleat /kleet/ *n* **1.** NAUT **DEVICE FOR SECURING BOAT** a device with two projections pointing in opposite directions to which a rope can be tied to secure a boat **2. HARD PIECE FIXED UNDER SHOE** a small piece of metal or hard plastic fixed to the sole of a shoe to improve its grip or to reduce wear **3. DEVICE ON BOOT FOR CLIMBING TREES** a device with a blade or set of sharp projections that is attached to a boot to assist in climbing trees or poles **4. WEDGE-SHAPED SUPPORT** a wooden or other wedge attached to a structure in order to support it ■ *vt* (**cleats, cleating, cleated**) **1. PROVIDE SOMETHING WITH CLEATS** to fix a cleat or cleats to something, or support something using a cleat **2. SECURE ROPE TO CLEAT** to tie a rope to a cleat [14C. Ultimately < W Germanic, 'firm lump']

cleavage /kléevij/ *n* **1. CREASE VISIBLE BETWEEN BREASTS** the hollow visible between a woman's breasts when a low-cut garment is worn **2. SPLIT IN SOMETHING** a split, division, or separation of something **3. ACT OF SPLITTING** division or splitting **4.** GEOL, MINERALS **ROCK OR MINERAL FRACTURE** the splitting of minerals or rocks along natural planes of weakness determined by their internal crystal lattice. The angle of cleavage is one of the features used to identify minerals. **5.** BIOL **REPEATED DIVISION OF FERTILIZED EGG** the repeated division of a fertilized ovum (**zygote**) before formation of the early embryo (**blastula**). The zygote does not increase in size during this process because the cells become progressively smaller after each division. **6.** CHEM **SPLITTING OF MOLECULE** the splitting of a molecule into simpler molecules through the breaking of a chemical bond

cleave[1] /kleev/ (**cleaves, cleaving, cleaved** or **clove** /klōv/ or **cleft** /kleft/, **cleaved** or **cloven** /klṓv'n/ or **cleft**) *vti* **1. SPLIT** to split, or make something split, especially along a plane of natural weakness **2. CUT PATH THROUGH SOMETHING** to make a way through something (*literary*) **3. PENETRATE SOMETHING** to penetrate or pierce something deep or dense such as water or heavy undergrowth (*literary*) [Old English *clēofan* < Indo-European] —**cleavable** *adj*

cleave[2] /kleev/ (**cleaves, cleaving, cleaved** or **clave** /klayv/, **cleaved**) *vi* to cling closely, steadfastly, or faithfully to somebody or something (*formal*) ○ *Is it wrong to cleave to such fond memories?* [Old English *cleofian* < Indo-European]

cleaver /kléevər/ *n* a heavy knife with a broad blade, used by butchers

Cleaver /kléevər/, **Eldridge** (1935–98) US political activist. He became minister of information of the Black Panther Party (1967) but left the United States to avoid arrest (1968). He advocated armed revolution, but later became a born-again Christian.

cleavers /kléevərz/ *n N Am* PLANTS same as **goosegrass** [Alteration of Old English *clife*, related to CLEAVE[2]; because its bristles stick to whatever they come in contact with]

cleck /klek/ *Wales vi* (**clecks, clecking, clecked**) to gossip about or inform on somebody ■ *n* a piece of gossip [< Welsh *clecan* 'to gossip', *clec* 'gossip']

Cleese /kleez/, **John** (*b.* 1939) British comic actor and writer. He is best known for the television series *Monty Python's Flying Circus* (1969–74) and *Fawlty Towers* (1975–79). Full name **Cleese, John Marwood**

> 'I find it rather easy to portray a businessman. Being bland, rather cruel and incompetent comes naturally to me.'
> [Attributed to John Cleese]

Cleethorpes /kléé thawrps/ town in Humberside northeastern England, situated at the mouth of the River Humber, southeast of Hull. Population: 32,719 (1991).

clef /klef/ *n* in written or printed music, a symbol placed at the beginning of each staff to indicate the pitch [Late 16C. Via French < Latin *clavis* 'key']

cleft[1] /kleft/ *n* **1.** a small indentation in a surface such as skin or land ○ *The river descends through a cleft in the cliffs.* **2.** a substantial gap or division separating two things (*formal*) ○ *the ever widening cleft between the parties in their approaches to state funding* [Old English *geclyft* < Germanic]

cleft[2] /kleft/ past participle, past tense of **cleave**[1] ■ *adj* having been separated into two or more sections by division

cleft lip *n* an upper lip congenitally divided into two parts that have been only partially reunited by surgery

cleft palate *n* a congenital fissure along the midline of the roof of the mouth. It is caused by a failure of the two sides of the hard palate to meet and fuse during foetal development and is often associated with a cleft lip.

cleg /kleg/ *n N England, Scotland* same as **horsefly** [15C. < Old Norse *kleggi*]

Cleisthenes /klī́sthə neez/ (570?–507 BC) Greek ruler. His constitutional reforms of 507 BC, by which he established a council of 500 citizens, are seen as the foundation of Athenian democracy.

cleistogamous /klī stóggəməss/ *adj* relating to or bearing small flowers that do not open, are self-pollinated in the bud, and appear in addition to brighter flowers on the same plant [Late 19C. < Greek *kleistos* 'closed' < *kleiein* 'to close'] —**cleistogamously** *adv* —**cleistogamy** *n*

Cleland /klélland/, **John** (1709–89) British government official and writer, author of the bawdy *Fanny Hill, the Memoirs of a Woman of Pleasure* (1748–49)

clem /klem/ (**clems, clemming, clemmed**), **clam** /klam/ (**clams, clamming, clammed**) *vti regional* to be hungry, or make a person or animal hungry [Mid-16C. < Old English *beclemman* 'to confine' < Germanic]

CULTURAL NOTE The verb ***clem*** is still found in UK regional dialects, especially in the forms **clemmed** or **clammed**. Like many dialect words, this one is dying out because the hunger associated with it is no longer a regular occurrence for the poor. Rural dialects continue to preserve a number of words meaning 'extremely hungry', including *clemmed out, fammelled, starved*, and *thirly*.

clematis /klémmətiss, klə máytiss/ (*plural* **-tises** or *same*) *n* a climbing plant with fluffy seed heads. Flowers: large, flat, typically blue, purple, pink, or white. Native to: northern temperate regions. Genus: *Clematis*. [Mid-16C. Via Latin, 'clematis, periwinkle' < Greek *klēmatis* < *klēma* 'vine branch']

Clemenceau /klém aNsō/, **Georges** (1841–1929) French journalist and politician. He was prime minister of France (1906–09, 1917–20) and helped to formulate the Treaty of Versailles, which formally ended World War I.

> 'We have won the war: now we have to win the peace, and it may be more difficult.'
> [Georges Clemenceau. Quoted in *Clemenceau*, D. R. Watson; 1974]

clemency /klémmənssi/ *n* **1.** the tendency to show mercy or leniency ○ *appealed for clemency for the imprisoned activists* **2.** mildness or temperateness, especially in the weather ○ *the clemency of areas affected by the Gulf Stream*

Clemens /klémmənz/, **Samuel Langhorne** ➧ **Twain, Mark**

clement /klémmənt/ *adj* **1.** showing or experiencing no extremes in weather conditions **2.** showing mercy or leniency [15C. < Latin *clement-* 'mild, gentle'] —**clemently** *adv*

Clement I /klémmənt/, **St** (*d.* AD 101?) Roman pope (AD 92?–101?). The third or fourth successor to St Peter, he probably wrote the *Epistle to the Corinthians* (AD 95?), a vital document on papal authority. Known as **Clement of Rome**

Clement VII (1478–1534) pope. During his papacy (1523–34), Rome was sacked (1527) by troops of the Holy Roman Emperor and the English church broke with Rome (1533). Born **Giulio de' Medici**

clementine /klémmən tīn, -teen/ *n* an orange-coloured citrus fruit, bred by crossing a tangerine with a Seville orange [Early 20C. < French *clémentine*]

clench /klench/ *v* (**clenches, clenching, clenched**) **1.** *vt* **HOLD TEETH OR FIST TIGHTLY TOGETHER** to close your teeth or fist tightly, e.g. when angry **2.** *vt* **CLUTCH SOMETHING** to hold or grip something tightly ○ *He clenched the rope in his teeth.* **3.** *vti* **CONTRACT** to contract, or cause a muscle to contract, suddenly, often as a result of sudden tension or emotion ○ *His jaw clenched as he waited.* **4.** *vt* NAUT another spelling of **clinch** *v* (sense 4) ■ *n* **1. TIGHT HOLD** a tight hold or grip ○ *She held the steering wheel in a tight clench.* **2. DEVICE THAT GRIPS TIGHTLY** a mechanical device that holds or grips something firmly [Old English *beclencan* < Germanic, 'to stick'] —**clenched** *adj*

cleome /kli ṓmi/ *n* an aromatic plant. Flowers: white or purplish, in clusters. Native to: warm regions. Genus: *Cleome*. [Early 19C. Via modern Latin < Greek, a plant]

Cleon /kléé on/ (*d.* 422 BC) Greek politician and general. As leader of the Athenians, he spurned Spartan peace overtures during the Peloponnesian War (431–404 BC) and was killed in battle.

Cleopatra /kléé ə páttrə/ (69–30 BC) Egyptian monarch. A queen (51–30 BC) of legendary beauty, she and her lover Mark Antony were defeated by Octavian's forces at Actium (31 BC).

Cleopatra's Needle *n* either of two Egyptian obelisks originally erected at Heliopolis about 1500 BC. One was moved to the Thames Embankment, London (1878), the other to Central Park, New York (1880).

clepsydra /klépsidrə/ (*plural* **-dras** or **-drae** /-dree/) *n* an ancient device used for measuring time by noting the amount of water or mercury that passes through a small aperture during a particular period [Mid-17C. Via Latin < Greek *klepsudra* < *kleptein* 'steal' + *hudor* 'water']

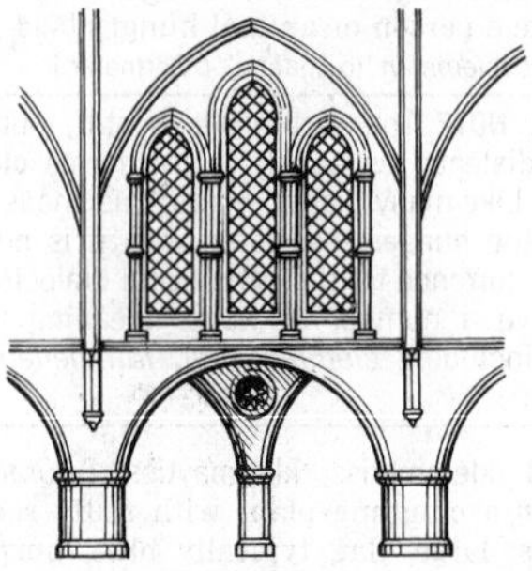

clerestory

clerestory /kleér stawri, -stəri/ (*plural* **-ries**), **clearstory** *n* the upper part of the wall of a building, especially of a church nave, that contains windows [< earlier spelling of CLEAR]

clergy /klúrji/ (*plural* **-gies**) *n* the body of people ordained for religious service, especially in the Christian church (*takes a singular or plural verb*) [13C. Partly < Old French *clergie* (< *clerc* 'cleric'); partly < *clergé* 'body of clerks'; both < ecclesiastical Latin *clericus* (see CLERK)]

clergyman /klúrjimən/ (*plural* **-men** /-mən/) *n* a man who is a member of the clergy

clergywoman /klúrji wŏŏmən/ (*plural* **-women** /-wimin/) *n* a woman who is a member of the clergy

cleric /klérrik/ *n* a member of the clergy [Early 17C. < ecclesiastical Latin *clericus* (see CLERK)]

clerical /klérrik'l/ *adj* **1. OF OFFICE WORK** relating to office work, especially of a routine administrative kind **2. OF CLERGY** relating or belonging to the clergy **3. PROMOTING CLERICALISM** advocating or supporting clericalism —**clerically** *adv*

clerical collar *n* a stiff white collar, continuous at the front, worn by some members of the Christian clergy

clericalism /klérrik'lizəm/ *n* **1.** a policy of supporting the power or views of the clergy **2.** the power or influence of the clergy —**clericalist** *n*

clericals /klérrik'lz/ *npl* the characteristic clothing worn by some members of the clergy

clerihew /klérri hyoo/ *n* a humorous or satirical verse consisting of two rhyming couplets in lines of irregular metre about somebody who is named in the verse [Early 20C. After Edmund *Clerihew* Bentley (1875–1956), British writer]

clerk /klaark/ *n* **1. GENERAL OFFICE WORKER** a worker who performs general office duties such as keeping records or sending out correspondence **2. GOVERNMENT WORKER WHO KEEPS RECORDS** an official who keeps transcripts and other records of a legislative or other body **3.** LAW **ADMINISTRATOR IN COURT OF LAW** an administrator of the business of a court **4.** LAW **COURT LEGAL ADVISER** somebody with legal qualifications who advises lay magistrates on points of law in court **5.** *N Am* OCCUPATIONS, COMM same as **shop assistant 6.** *N Am* **SERVICE DESK WORKER** somebody at a service desk who helps and advises other people **7.** CHR **CLERIC** a member of the clergy (*formal*) [Pre-12C. Via ecclesiastical Latin *clericus* 'of the clergy' < Greek *klērikos* < *klēros* 'heritage'] —**clerk** *vi* —**clerkdom** *n* —**clerkish** *adj* —**clerkship** *n*

clerkly /klaárkli/ *adj* **1.** relating to or characteristic of a clerk ○ *a clerkly attention to detail in the midst of a crisis* **2.** same as **scholarly** (*archaic*) —**clerkliness** *n*

clerk of the works *n* an official who inspects the standard of construction of a new building

Clermont-Ferrand /kláir moN fe raáN/ capital of Puy-de-Dôme Department, Auvergne Region, south-central France. It is an industrial city, with a major rubber industry. Population: 137,140 (1999).

cleveite /kleév īt/ *n* a crystalline form of uraninite [Late 19C. After Per T. *Cleve* (1840–1905), Swedish chemist]

Cleveland /kleévlənd/ **1.** former county of north-eastern England, from 1974 until 1996. Area: 583 sq. km/225 sq. mi. **2.** city and port in northeastern Ohio on the southeastern shore of Lake Erie. Population: 467,851 (2002 estimate).

Cleveland, Grover (1837–1908) 22nd and 24th president of the United States. A Democrat with a reputation for scrupulous honesty, he spent both his terms as president (1885–89, 1893–97) opposing special interests and the political spoils system. Full name **Cleveland, Stephen Grover**. See table at **president**

clever /klévvər/ *adj* **1. INTELLIGENT** having sharp mental abilities **2. SHOWING INTELLIGENCE** demonstrating mental agility and creativity ○ *It's a clever idea, but will it work?* **3. GLIBLY FACILE** showing highly capable mental abilities in a showy or superficial way ○ *Don't give me one of your clever answers.* **4. DEXTEROUS** highly skilled in using the hands **5. UNUSUAL AND EFFECTIVE** produced by skill or ingenuity ○ *What a clever little gadget!* **6.** *regional* **HEALTHY** in a state of good health [13C. Origin ?] —**cleverly** *adv* —**cleverness** *n*

SYNONYMS See ***intelligent***.

clever-clever *adj* affectedly or ostentatiously clever (*informal*)

clever Dick, **clever clogs** (*plural same*) *n* somebody regarded as arrogant or ostentatiously clever (*informal disapproving*)

clevis /klévviss/ *n* a U-shaped device with a hole at the end of each prong through which a pin or bolt can be pushed to secure another part in place [Late 16C. Origin ?]

clew /kloo/ *n* **1. BALL OF THREAD** a wound ball of thread or yarn **2.** SAILING **CORNER OF FORE-AND-AFT SAIL** the rear lower corner of a triangular or four-sided sail set along the length of a boat **3.** SAILING **CORNER OF SAIL SET ACROSS BOAT** either of the two lower corners of a sail such as a square sail or a spinnaker set parallel to the width of a boat ■ **clews** *npl* NAUT **HAMMOCK CORDS** the cords by which a hammock is suspended ■ *vt* (**clews, clewing, clewed**) **ROLL THREAD INTO BALL** to roll thread or yarn into a ball [Old English *cliwen*, probably related to CLAW]

clew up *vt* to furl a square sail by pulling on lines attached to its lower corners

clianthus /kli ánthəss, klī-/ (*plural* **-thuses** or *same*) *n* a plant of the pea family. Flowers: scarlet in drooping clusters. Native to: Australia, New Zealand. Genus: *Clianthus*. [Mid-19C. < modern Latin < Greek *kleos* 'glory' + *anthus* 'flower']

cliché /kleé shay/ *n* **1.** a phrase or word that has lost its original effectiveness or power from overuse **2.** an overused activity or notion [Mid-19C. < French, past participle of *clicher* 'stereotype']

clichéd /kleé shayd/ *adj* having lost all original effectiveness or power as a result of overuse

Clichy /kleé shee/ northern industrial suburb of Paris, France. Population: 50,179 (1999).

click[1] /klik/ *n* **1. SHORT SHARP SOUND** a short sharp sound, often metallic but not resonant **2.** COMPUT **PRESS OF COMPUTER MOUSE BUTTON** a single action of pressing and releasing a button on a computer mouse **3.** MECH ENG **MECHANICAL COMPONENT FOR LOCKING POSITION** a component of a mechanical device that holds a part in a locking position, or the movement of the part between adjacent positions **4.** PHON **SOUND PRODUCED BY SUCKING IN AIR** a consonant sound produced by sucking in air and moving the tongue against the soft palate. It is part of the phonemic system of some African languages such as Xhosa, but in English is used only for the sound represented by 'tut-tut'. Technical name **suction stop** ■ *v* (**clicks, clicking, clicked**) **1.** *vti* **MAKE SHORT SHARP SOUND** to make, or cause something to make, a short sharp sound **2.** *vti* COMPUT **PRESS COMPUTER MOUSE BUTTON** to press and release a button of a computer mouse ○ *Click on 'yes'.* **3.** *vi* **BECOME CLEARLY UNDERSTOOD** to be understood suddenly (*informal*) ○ *It finally clicked where I'd seen him before.* **4.** *vi* **EASILY COMMUNICATE OR WORK TOGETHER** to communicate or work together easily and readily (*informal*) ○ *The partners never clicked.* **5.** *vi* **BE SUCCESS** to be successful or popular (*informal*) ○ *The new show clicked from the very first performance.* [Late 16C. An imitation of the sound]

click[2] /klik/ *n* MEASURE same as **kilometre** (*slang*) ○ *about twenty clicks from here* [Mid-20C. Origin ?]

clickable /klíkəb'l/ *adj* describes an item on a computer screen that may be activated by clicking on it with the mouse

click-and-mortar *adj* BUSINESS same as **clicks-and-mortar**

click art *n* computer clip art for use in illustrating electronic documents

click beetle *n* a beetle that can right itself when inverted by springing into the air with a clicking sound. Family: Elateridae.

clicker /klíkər/ *n* **1.** somebody or something that clicks **2.** a foreman or forewoman at a printing press or shoe factory (*informal*)

click rate *n* the number of times that a site in an Internet advertisement is visited, as a percentage of the number of times the advertisement is viewed (*used in e-commerce*)

clicks-and-mortar, **click-and-mortar** *adj* describes a hybrid business involved in e-commerce that also markets its physical products through a traditional shop or uses other physical structures such as warehouses (*used in e-commerce*) [After *bricks-and-mortar*]

clickstream /klík streem/ *n* the path of mouse clicks that somebody makes in navigating the Internet, sometimes used in marketing research (*used in e-commerce*)

clickthrough /klík throo/ *n* a measure of the effectiveness of an Internet advertisement, based on the number of times the viewer accesses the advertisement (*used in e-commerce*)

client /klī ənt/ *n* **1. SOMEBODY USING PROFESSIONAL SERVICE** a person or organization taking advice from a lawyer, accountant, or other professional person **2. CUSTOMER** a person or organization to whom goods or services are provided and sold **3. USER OF SOCIAL SERVICES AGENCY** a user of the services offered by a social services agency **4. PERSON OR ENTITY HELPED BY ANOTHER** a person or entity dependent on the protection or patronage of another person or entity ○ *the former Soviet Union and its clients in the Middle East* **5.** COMPUT **COMPUTER PROGRAM THAT REQUESTS DATA** a computer program that obtains data from a program on another computer, often one linked on a network. An Internet browser is a specific kind of client. [14C. < Latin *client-* 'dependent' < *cluere* 'obey'] —**cliental** *adj* —**clientless** *adj*

clientage /klī əntij/ *n* a social system in which free commoners receive the patronage of wealthy or influential aristocrats. It was common in ancient Rome and has become a feature of some modern societies.

client-centred therapy *n* a form of psychotherapy in which the therapist seeks to elicit solutions to problems by gaining the trust of the patient through careful questioning. It was founded by Carl Rogers in the 1940s and is still used widely as a counselling method.

clientele /kleé on tél, -ən-/ *n* the clients or customers of a professional organization or business, considered as a group (*takes a singular verb*) ○ *The clientele of our family law firm consists mostly of big corporations.* [Mid-16C. Directly and via French < Latin *clientela* < *client-* (see CLIENT)]

client-server, **client/server** *adj* describes a computer network in which processing is divided between a client program running on a user's machine and a network server program. One server can provide data to, or perform storage-intensive processing tasks in conjunction with, one or more clients.

client state *n* a country that depends on another for economic, political, or military support

cliff /klif/ *n* a high steep rock or ice face, especially a rock face extending along a coastline [Old English *clif* < Germanic] —**cliffy** *adj*

cliff dweller *n* a member of an Anasazi people who constructed dwellings on ledges of cliffs in what is now the southwestern United States

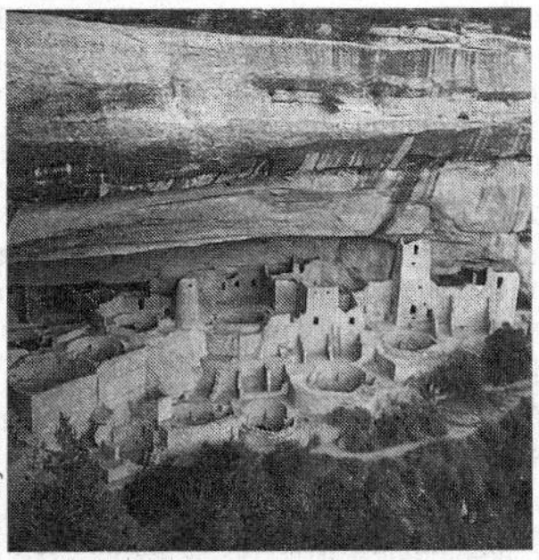

cliff dwelling: Mesa Verde, Colorado, United States

cliff dwelling *n* a building or group of buildings lived in by cliff dwellers

cliffhanger /klíf hangər/ *n* **1. ENDING LEFT TEASINGLY UNRESOLVED** an unresolved ending in a part of a serialized drama or book that leaves the audience or reader eager to know what will happen next **2.** ARTS **DRAMA SERIAL WITH SUSPENSEFUL ENDINGS** a drama serial that has episodes that often end in suspenseful unresolved situations **3. TENSE SITUATION** a situation full of tension or suspense because it is not clear what will happen next [< early serial films in which characters were left hanging off the edge of a cliff at the end of an episode] —**cliffhanging** *adj*

cliff jumping *n* the sport of jumping from a high point such as a cliff into water

Clift /klift/, **Charmian** (1923–69) Australian writer. She wrote *Peel Me a Lotus* (1958). She was married to George Johnston.

climacteric /klī máktərik, klī mak térrik/ *n* **1.** a period in which critically important changes take place **2.** PHYSIOL same as **menopause** (*technical*) **3.** BOT a stage in the ripening of some fruits such as apples when the rate of respiration increases [Mid-16C. < French < Greek *klimaktēr* 'rung of a ladder' < *klimax* 'ladder'] —**climacteric** *adj* —**climacterically** *adv*

climactic /klī máktik/ *adj* **1.** extremely exciting or decisive **2.** relating to or forming a climax [Late 19C. < CLIMAX] —**climactically** *adv*

USAGE climactic or **climatic**? ***Climactic***, coming from *climax*, means 'exciting or decisive' and 'forming a climax', as in *The hard-fought election was climactic* [not *climatic*]. *In a climactic* [not *climatic*] *passage, the author kills off the heroine.* ***Climatic***, coming from *climate*, means 'relating to weather changes', as in *severe climatic* [not *climactic*] *changes caused by global warming.*

climate /klīmət/ *n* **1.** METEOROL **TYPICAL WEATHER IN REGION** the average weather or the regular variations in weather in a region over a period of years **2. PLACE WITH PARTICULAR WEATHER** a place with a particular type of weather ○ *I prefer a warm climate.* **3. INDOOR ENVIRONMENT** the prevailing conditions or environment in an indoor setting such as an office ○ *a climate-controlled building* **4. SITUATION** the situation or atmosphere that prevails at a particular time or place [14C. Via late Latin < Greek *klimat-* 'slope, region of the earth']

climate change *n* long-term alteration in global weather patterns, especially increases in temperature and storm activity, regarded as a potential consequence of the greenhouse effect

climatic /klī máttik/ *adj* relating to, caused, or caused by weather changes —**climatically** *adv*

USAGE See ***climactic***.

climatic zone *n* an area of the Earth's surface that possesses a distinct type of climate. There are eight major climatic zones, roughly demarcated by lines of latitude. These consist of the tropical zone near the equator, two subtropical and two temperate zones, one boreal zone in the northern hemisphere, and the two polar ice caps.

climatology /klīmə tólləji/ *n* the scientific study of climates —**climatologic** /klīmətə lójjik/ *adj* —**climatological** *adj* —**climatologically** *adv* —**climatologist** *n*

climax /klī maks/ *n* **1. KEY MOMENT** the most important or exciting point in something such as an event or a story **2.** PHYSIOL **ORGASM** a sexual orgasm **3.** LITERAT **EVER-INTENSIFYING SEQUENCE OF PHRASES** a sequence of phrases or sentences, each more forceful or intense than the last, or the conclusion of such a sequence **4.** ECOL **FINAL STAGE IN ECOLOGICAL COMMUNITY'S DEVELOPMENT** a late or final stage in the development of an ecological community in which the composition of plants and animals is relatively stable and well matched to environmental conditions ■ *v* (**-maxes, -maxing, -maxed**) **1.** *vti* **REACH KEY POINT** to reach the most important or exciting point in something such as an event or a story, or bring something to its most important or exciting point **2.** *vi* PHYSIOL **HAVE ORGASM** to have a sexual orgasm [Mid-16C. Via late Latin < Greek *klimax* 'ladder, progression']

climb /klīm/ *v* (**climbs, climbing, climbed**) **1.** *vti* **ASCEND USING HANDS AND FEET** to move towards the top of something, especially using the hands and feet ○ *climb a ladder* **2.** *vti* **MOVE UPWARDS** to move upwards, or move towards the top of something, by any means, and typically through continual or gradual effort ○ *climb the stairs* ○ *The plane climbed through a low cloud layer.* **3.** *vi* CLIMBING **BE MOUNTAINEER** to go up mountains or rocks on foot or using hands and feet as a sport **4.** *vi* **MOVE WITH EFFORT** to manoeuvre the body somewhere with effort or difficulty ○ *I managed to climb out of bed.* **5.** *vi* **RISE IN AMOUNT** to rise in value or amount ○ *temperature climbing into the thirties* **6.** *vti* **MOVE HIGHER SOCIALLY OR PROFESSIONALLY** to move to a higher social or professional position **7.** *vti* BOT **GROW UPWARDS ON SOMETHING** to grow upwards by using plants or objects as a support, e.g. by producing shoots or tendrils that cling to them ■ *n* **1. ACT OF CLIMBING** the process of moving to the top of something ○ *It was a steep climb to the top.* **2.** CLIMBING **HILL OR MOUNTAIN** a route used to go up a hill, mountain, or rock, or the hill, mountain, or rock itself **3. RISE IN VALUE OR AMOUNT** a rise in the value or amount of something [Old English *climban*, via W Germanic, 'adhere' < Indo-European, 'form into a ball'] —**climbable** *adj*

SPELLCHECK Do not confuse the spelling of ***climb*** and ***clime*** ('place with a particular climate'), which sound similar.

climb down *vi* to abandon forcefully or publicly expressed views or demands, especially in the face of opposition from somebody else

climb into *vt* to put on clothes, usually easy-to-wear ones (*informal*)

climb out of *vt* to take off clothes, usually easy-to-wear ones (*informal*)

climb-down *n* an abandonment of forcefully or publicly expressed views or demands, especially in the face of opposition from somebody else

climber /klīmər/ *n* **1. SOMEBODY WHO CLIMBS MOUNTAINS** somebody who climbs rocks or mountains as a sport **2.** BOT **PLANT THAT CLINGS** a plant that attaches itself to other plants or objects such as posts and walls as it grows **3. SOMEBODY ADVANCING SOCIALLY** somebody who steadily gains in rank or status, especially somebody who is unscrupulous and ambitious (*disapproving; usually used in combination*) ○ *derided the newcomers as social climbers*

climbing /klīming/ *n* the sport of climbing mountains or rocks

climbing frame *n UK* a framework of interlocking metal, wooden, or plastic bars designed for children to climb on. Aus, US term **jungle gym**

climbing iron *n* same as **crampon**

climbing wall *n* a wall with handholds and footholds, often located indoors, that is designed to provide practice at rock-climbing

clime /klīm/ *n* a place with a particular type of climate (*formal; often used in the plural*) ○ *off to sunnier climes* [Late 16C. Via Latin < Greek *klima* 'slope']

SPELLCHECK See ***climb***.

~~**climing**~~ incorrect spelling of **climbing**

-clinal *suffix* sloping, slanting ○ *isoclinal* [< Greek *klinein* 'to lean']

clinandrium /kli nándri əm/ (*plural* **-dria** /-dri ə/) *n* a hollow in the upper column of the flower of an orchid, containing the anther [Mid-19C. < modern Latin, 'stamen bed' < Greek *klinē* 'couch']

clinch /klinch/ *v* (**clinches, clinching, clinched**) **1.** *vt* **RESOLVE SOMETHING DECISIVELY** to settle in a positive way the outcome of something such as a business deal or an argument **2.** *vi* **PUT ARMS AROUND OPPONENT** in boxing or wrestling, to put your arms around an opponent's body so as to pin the opponent's arms and prevent an exchange of blows **3.** *vt* CONSTR **FLATTEN END OF NAIL** to bend or flatten the protruding end of a nail or rivet, or fasten things together using nails or rivets in this way **4.** *vt* NAUT **FASTEN SOMETHING WITH KNOT** to fasten or secure something with a knot in a rope that is created by making a half hitch ■ *n* **1. PASSIONATE EMBRACE** a tight passionate embrace between lovers (*informal*) **2. TACTIC OF PINNING OPPONENT'S ARMS** in boxing or wrestling, a tactic designed to prevent an exchange of blows in which you put your arms around an opponent's body, pinning the opponent's arms to his or her sides **3.** CONSTR **NAIL WITH END BENT OVER** a nail or rivet with its protruding end bent over, or a fastening made in this way **4.** NAUT **KNOT IN ROPE** a knot in a rope that is created by making a half hitch [Mid-16C. Origin ?]

clincher /klínchər/ *n* **1. DECIDING FACTOR** the factor that decides the outcome of something such as an argument or a contest (*informal*) **2.** CONSTR **NAIL WITH END BENT OVER** a nail or rivet that has its protruding end bent over **3.** CONSTR **TOOL FOR BENDING NAIL** a tool for bending the ends of nails or rivets

cline /klīn/ *n* **1.** a continuum between two extremes **2.** a gradual variation in the characteristics of a plant or animal species that occurs when it is distributed over an area with differing environmental or geographical conditions [Mid-20C. < Greek *klinein* 'to lean'] —**clinal** *adj* —**clinally** *adv*

ORIGIN The Indo-European word from which ***cline*** is ultimately derived, is also the ancestor of English *clinic, decline, enclitic, incline, ladder, lean*[1], and *recline*.

Cline /klīn/, **Patsy** (1932–63) US singer. Her slick, sentimental country songs such as 'Crazy' (1961) attracted huge popular audiences. She died in a plane crash at the peak of her career. Born **Hensley, Virginia Patterson**

-cline *suffix* slope ○ *syncline* [Back-formation < -CLINAL]

cling /kling/ *vi* (**clings, clinging, clung** /klung/) **1. HOLD ONTO SOMEBODY OR SOMETHING TIGHTLY** to hold onto somebody or something tightly with the hands or arms **2. ADHERE TO SOMETHING** to adhere to something by sticking to it or staying very close to it **3. RETAIN IDEAS OR CUSTOMS** to refuse to give up something such as a belief or tradition that you have grown fond of or used to **4. HAVE EMOTIONAL NEED FOR SOMEBODY** to have a strong emotional attachment to somebody **5. LINGER** to linger, usually in the air, resisting dispersion or dissipation ■ *n* **1. STICKING QUALITY** the tendency of something to stick to surfaces **2.** BOT same as **clingstone** [Old English *clingan* 'adhere' < Germanic] —**clinger** *n* —**clingingly** *adv*

cling film *n* a clear plastic film that sticks to itself and to other surfaces. Use: food wrapping.

clingfish /klíng fish/ (*plural same or* **-fishes**) *n* a small fish whose pelvic fins have been modified into a sucking disc that it uses to attach itself to rocks or other objects. Family: Gobiesocidae.

clingstone /klíng stōn/ *n* a fruit with flesh that sticks to the stone. Some varieties of peach, nectarine, and plum have fruit of this type.

clingy /klíngi/ (**-ier, -iest**) *adj* (*informal*) **1.** too dependent on the company or emotional support of other people **2.** sticking closely to the body ○ *a clingy fabric* —**clinginess** *n*

clinic /klínnik/ *n* **1.** HEALTH SERVICES **MEDICAL CENTRE** a medical centre for outpatients, attached to a hospital or forming part of it **2.** HEALTH SERVICES **SPECIALIZED MEDICAL CENTRE** a medical centre that specializes in a particular condition or area of medicine **3.** HEALTH SERVICES **GROUP MEDICAL PRACTICE** an office or suite of offices where a number of doctors practise general medicine as a partnership **4.** HEALTH SERVICES **PRIVATE HOSPITAL** a private hospital that charges patients directly for their treatment **5.** EDUC **BEDSIDE TEACHING SESSION FOR STUDENT DOCTORS** a teaching session during which student doctors are allowed to examine patients in hospital wards **6.** HEALTH SERVICES **SESSION ATTENDED BY PATIENTS** a session in a hospital that patients attend for specialized treatment or advice **7. GROUP INSTRUCTION SESSION** a teaching session in which an expert in a particular field gives practical instruction and advice to a group ○ *a tennis clinic* [Mid-19C. Via French *clinique* < Greek *klinikē*

(tekhnē) '(method of treating) the bedridden' < *klinikos* 'of a bed' < *klinē* 'bed' < *klinein* 'to lean']

-clinic *suffix* having a particular number of obliquely intersecting axes ○ *triclinic* [< Greek *klinein* 'to lean']

clinical /klínnik'l/ *adj* **1.** MED **BASED ON MEDICAL TREATMENT OR OBSERVATION** based on or involving medical treatment, practice, observation, or diagnosis **2.** **UNEMOTIONAL** practical and unemotional **3.** **SEVERE IN DECOR OR DESIGN** plain and severe in design, especially so as to seem uncomfortable —**clinically** *adv*

clinical ecology *n* the branch of medicine dealing with the supposed effects of the modern technological environment on human health, especially the relationship of allergies to the increase in chemicals in the environment

clinical nurse manager *n* the administrative manager of the nursing staff in a hospital

clinical psychology *n* the branch of psychology that deals with the diagnosis and treatment of psychological and behavioural problems —**clinical psychologist** *n*

clinical thermometer *n* a thermometer used for measuring the temperature of somebody's body, which continues to register the observed temperature until reset

clinician /kli níshʹn/ *n* **1.** a medical professional who works directly with patients, as distinct from one working in research **2.** a medical professional who practises or teaches in a clinic

clink[1] /klingk/ (**clinks, clinking, clinked**) *vti* to make, or cause something to make, the short, high-pitched, slightly ringing sound that metal or glass objects make when they knock against each other [14C. Ultimately an imitation of the sound] —**clink** *n*

clink[2] /klingk/ *n* a prison (*dated slang*) [Early 16C. < the *Clink*, former prison in Southwark, borough of London]

clinker /klíngkər/ *n* **1.** **BALL OF COAL RESIDUE** a hard mass of ash and partially fused coal that remains after coal is burnt in a fire or furnace **2.** **HARD BRICK** an overhard brick that has been fired in a kiln for too long ▪ *vi* (**-ers, -ering, -ered**) **FORM LUMPY BURNT RESIDUE** to form hard lumps of ash and partially fused coal after burning [Mid-17C. Alteration of obsolete *clincard* < obsolete Dutch *klinckaerd* 'brick' < *klinken* 'to ring'; from the sound made by a brick when struck]

clinker-built *adj* describes a boat that has a hull made of overlapping planks [< *clinker* 'clinched nail' < *clink* 'secure a rivet', variant of CLENCH]

clinkety-clank /klíngkəti klángk/ *n* the dull short ringing sounds produced when something metallic hits a surface repeatedly [< CLINK[1] + CLANK]

clinkstone /klíngk stōn/ *n* MINERALS same as **phonolite** [Translation of German *Klingstein* 'ringing stone'; from its metallic resonance when struck]

clino- *prefix* slope, slant ○ *clinometer* [< Greek *klinein* 'to lean']

clinometer /klī nómmitər/ *n* an instrument used in surveying or geology to measure the angle of a slope or incline —**clinometric** /klīnə méttrik/ *adj* —**clinometrical** *adj* —**clinometry** *n*

clinopyroxene /klínō pī rók seen/ *n* a silicate mineral of the pyroxene group, containing calcium, iron, and magnesium, and forming monoclinic crystals, e.g. augite

clinostat /klínō stat/ *n* a piece of laboratory equipment with a turntable that allows a plant placed on it to be exposed to a stimulus such as light equally on all sides

-clinous *suffix* **1.** having stamens and pistils in a particular number of flowers ○ *diclinous* **2.** descending from a particular line ○ *matriclinous* [< Greek *klinein* 'to lean']

clint /klint/ *n* a limestone block separated from others by cracks, forming a limestone pavement [14C. Via Danish, Swedish *klint* < Old Swedish *klinter* 'rock']

Clinton /klíntən/, **Bill** (*b.* 1946) 42nd president of the United States (1993–2001). Before his election to the White House he was Democratic governor of Arkansas (1978–80, 1982–92). In 1999 he was impeached and acquitted by the US Senate for perjury and obstruction of justice. Full name **Clinton, William Jefferson**. See table at **president**

'There is nothing wrong with America that cannot be cured by what is right with America.'
[Attributed to Bill Clinton]

Hillary Rodham Clinton and Bill Clinton

The White House

Clinton, Hillary Rodham (*b.* 1947) US lawyer, first lady (1993–2001), and senator. After eight years as first lady, she was elected to the US Senate in 2000.

'"It takes a village to raise a child"…a timeless reminder that children will only thrive if their families thrive and if the whole of society cares enough to provide for them.'
[Hillary Rodham Clinton, *New York Times*; 5 February 1996]

clintonia /klin tóni ə/ *n* a broad-leafed perennial plant of the lily family with blue or purple berries. Flowers: white, yellow, or purplish. Genus: *Clintonia*. [Mid-19C. < modern Latin, after De Witt *Clinton* (1769–1828), US politician]

Clio /klí ō/ *n* in Greek mythology, the Muse of history, one of the nine Muses believed to inspire and nurture the arts

cliometrics /klí ō méttriks/ *n* the study of economic history using statistics, advanced methods of data processing, analysis of mathematical data, and economic modelling (*takes a singular verb*) [Mid-20C. < CLIO] —**cliometric** *adj* —**cliometrician** /klí ō mə trísh'n/ *n*

clip[1] /klip/ *v* (**clips, clipping, clipped**) **1.** *vt* **CUT OR TRIM SOMETHING** to cut or trim something, or cut it off, e.g. with scissors or shears ○ *clipped the dog's hair* **2.** *vt* **CUT SOMETHING OUT** to remove something from something else by cutting ○ *clipping a coupon from the newspaper* **3.** *vt* **SHORTEN TIME TAKEN FOR SOMETHING** to reduce the time taken to complete something, especially travelling time ○ *clipped two minutes off the world record* **4.** *vt* PHON **TRUNCATE SPEECH SOUND** to shorten a speech sound **5.** *vt* LING **ABBREVIATE WORD** to shorten a word or other expression by abbreviating it or dropping a syllable **6.** *vt* **CURTAIL POWER** to reduce or diminish power or influence **7.** *vi* **GO FAST** to move at a brisk pace (*informal*) **8.** *vt* **SIDESWIPE SOMEBODY OR SOMETHING** to make physical contact with somebody or something with a light glancing slapping blow (*informal*) **9.** *vt* **SWINDLE SOMEBODY** to cheat or swindle somebody, especially by overcharging (*slang*) ▪ *n* **1.** CINEMA, MEDIA **FILM OR TV EXTRACT** an extract, especially a short piece, from film or television footage **2.** MEDIA **EXTRACT FROM PRINT MEDIA** a news story or other article cut out of a print publication and used, e.g., as a sample of work **3.** **THING OR AMOUNT CUT** something cut or removed, especially the amount of wool cut from a flock of sheep at one shearing **4.** **GLANCING BLOW** a sideswiping or glancing blow **5.** **RATE OF MOTION** the speed at which somebody or something moves (*informal*) ○ *Food prices shot up at their fastest clip in years.* [13C. Probably < Old Norse *klippa* 'cut short']

clip[2] /klip/ *n* **1.** **GRIPPING DEVICE** a device that grips or clasps loose things together or that holds things firmly (*often used in combination*) **2.** JEWELLERY **PIECE OF JEWELLERY** a piece of jewellery with a gripping device fitted that attaches to clothing **3.** ARMS **BULLET-HOLDER** a container for bullets, slotted directly into an automatic firearm ▪ *vti* (**clips, clipping, clipped**) **HOLD SOMETHING WITH GRIPPING DEVICE** to hold loose things together, or attach one thing to another, using a clip, or be attached in this way [Old English *clyppan* 'embrace, fasten' < W Germanic]

clip art *n* prepackaged artwork, available on software for use in documents produced on a computer [Because originally in the form of *clip sheets*, pages of drawings that graphic designers could cut out]

clipboard /klíp bawrd/ *n* **1.** a small portable board with a clip fitted to the top, used for securing papers and providing a hard writing surface **2.** a part of computer memory where cut or copied data is stored temporarily

clip-clop *n* the rhythmic sound made by a walking horse's hooves as they strike hard ground ▪ *vi* (**clip-clops, clip-clopping, clip-clopped**) to make the sound of hooves striking hard ground [Early 20C. An imitation of the sound]

clip joint *n* a shop or club that habitually overcharges its customers (*slang*) [< CLIP[1] 'swindle']

clip-on *adj* describes something, especially an item of clothing, that is attached by means of a clip ▪ *n* an accessory that is attached with a clip, e.g. an earring or a tie

clipped /klipt/ *adj* **1.** trimmed or cut back neatly **2.** spoken with each word pronounced separately and distinctly in a way that sounds terse or upper-class

clipper

clipper /klíppər/ *n* **1.** **FAST SAILING SHIP** a mid-19th-century tall ship with a sharp bow, designed for travelling at fast speeds **2.** **USER OF CUTTING TOOL** a cutter or shearer of something **3.** ELECTRONICS same as **limiter** (sense 1) ▪ **clippers** *npl* **TOOL FOR CLIPPING SOMETHING** a hand tool for cutting or clipping something

clippie /klíppi/ *n* a female bus or tram conductor (*dated informal*)

clipping /klípping/ *n* N Am MEDIA same as **cutting** (sense 2) ▪ **clippings** *npl* pieces of grass or hair that have been cut or clipped off

clique /kleek/ *n* a close group of friends or colleagues with similar interests and goals, whom outsiders regard as excluding them [Early 18C. < French < *cliquer* 'to click, to clap', an imitation of the sound] —**cliquey** *adj* —**cliquish** *adj* —**cliquishly** *adv* —**cliquishness** *n*

clishmaclaver /klíshmə kláyvər/ *n* Scotland casual chat or gossip (*informal*) [Early 18C. < *clish* (probably < Scottish *clish-clash* 'idle gossip') + *claver* 'to gossip']

clitellum /klī télləm/ (*plural* **-la** /-lə/) *n* a glandular section, similar in shape to a saddle, in the body wall of some worms such as earthworms and leeches, that secretes a sticky substance during copulation. The substance is later used to form a sac in which the eggs are deposited. [Mid-19C. Via modern Latin < Latin *clitellae* 'packsaddle' (from its shape), literally 'little litters']

clitic /klíttik/ *adj* describes a word that cannot be stressed and is pronounced as part of the word that follows or precedes it, e.g. 've' in 'I've' [Mid-20C. Back-formation < ENCLITIC, PROCLITIC] —**clitic** *n*

clitoridectomy /klíttəri déktəmi/ (*plural* **-mies**) *n* the cutting off of all or part of a woman's or girl's clitoris, practised in some societies as a social or cultural rite of passage

clitoris /klíttəriss/ (*plural* **clitorises** or **clitorides** /klíttə rī deez/) *n* a sensitive erectile female sex organ at the front junction of the labia minora in the vulva [Early 17C. Via modern Latin < Greek *kleitoris* 'little hill'] —**clitoral** *adj*

Clive /klīv/, **Robert, Baron Clive of Plassey** (1725–74) British soldier and colonial administrator who was instrumental in establishing British rule in India. He served as governor of Bengal (1765–67) but later became embroiled in scandal and committed suicide. Known as **Clive of India**

Cllr *abbr* Councillor

clm *abbr* column

cloaca /klō áykə/ (*plural* **-cae** /-kee/) *n* the terminal region of the gut in reptiles, amphibians, birds, and many fishes, as well as in some invertebrates. The intestinal, urinary, and genital canals open into it. [Late 16C. < Latin, 'sewer, canal'] —**cloacal** *adj*

cloak /klōk/ *n* **1.** OUTER GARMENT a loose sleeveless outer garment that fastens at the neck **2.** ENSHROUDING OBJECT OR FORCE something that covers or conceals things (*literary*) ○ *left under a cloak of secrecy* ■ *vt* (**cloaks, cloaking, cloaked**) ENSHROUD SOMETHING to cover or conceal something (*often passive*) [13C. Via Old French *cloque* 'bell, cloak' < medieval Latin *clocca*]

cloak-and-dagger *adj* involving secrecy or intrigue, often as part of an espionage operation [Translation of French *de cape et d'épée* 'of cape and sword', symbols of the rank of characters in dramas of intrigue]

cloakroom /klōk room, -room/ *n* **1.** PLACE FOR DEPOSITING BELONGINGS a room in a public building such as a theatre, club, or restaurant, where customers can leave coats, umbrellas, and other belongings during their stay. N Am term **coat check 2.** LAVATORY a lavatory, especially one in a public building, or downstairs in a house with an upstairs bathroom. N Am term **rest room 3.** CUPBOARD FOR COATS a walk-in cupboard in a house, where coats and other outdoor items are stored

clobber /klóbbər/ (*informal*) *vt* (**-bers, -bering, -bered**) **1.** HIT SOMEBODY OR SOMETHING to hit somebody or something with great force **2.** DEFEAT SOMEBODY to defeat somebody decisively **3.** TREAT SOMEBODY OR SOMETHING HARSHLY to deal with somebody or something in a harsh or critical way ○ *The scheme has been clobbered in the national press.* ■ *n* SOMEBODY'S BELONGINGS OR CLOTHES somebody's belongings or clothes, often those intended for a particular activity [Mid-20C. Origin ?]

cloche /klosh/ *n* **1.** a small structure made of glass or clear plastic, placed over cold-sensitive garden plants in cold weather **2.** a woman's or girl's close-fitting hat with a very narrow brim [Late 19C. Via French, 'bell' < medieval Latin *clocca*; from the shape]

clock[1] /klok/ *n* **1.** DEVICE DISPLAYING TIME a freestanding device that measures and records time, which it displays by a pointer on a dial or by a digital read-out **2.** MEASURING INSTRUMENT WITH DISPLAY a measuring instrument with a dial or a digital display, e.g. any of a vehicle's control gauges, especially the mileometer **3.** BUSINESS same as **time clock 4.** ELECTRONIC CIRCUIT THAT SYNCHRONIZES COMPUTER PROCESSES an electronic circuit that generates pulses at a constant rate in order to synchronize the internal operations in a computer **5.** same as **biological clock** (*informal*) **6.** SEED HEAD OF DANDELION the fluffy white seed head of a dandelion ■ *vt* (**clocks, clocking, clocked**) **1.** MEASURE TIME SOMEBODY OR SOMETHING TAKES to measure or record the time somebody or something takes, using a stopwatch or an electronic timing device (*informal*) ○ *a car that was clocked at 95 mph* **2.** PUNCH SOMEBODY to punch somebody (*slang*) ○ *He clocked him one.* **3.** NOTICE SOMETHING to notice something (*slang*) ○ *We clocked him going into the betting shop.* **4.** AUTOMOT TAMPER WITH VEHICLE'S MILEOMETER to turn back the mileometer on a used car so that the mileage appears much lower than it is (*slang*) [14C. Via Middle Dutch, Middle Low German *klocke* < medieval Latin *clocca* 'bell'] ◇ **against the clock** with limited time to finish something ◇ **around** *or* **round the clock** day and night, without stopping ◇ **turn** *or* **put the clock(s) back** to return to the conditions of an earlier time

clock in *or* **on** *vi* to arrive for work, or record arrival for work, by inserting a personalized card into a time clock

clock out *or* **off** *vi* to leave work, or record departure from work, by inserting a personalized card into a time clock

clock up *vt* to reach a particular total (*informal*)

clock[2] /klok/ *n* a design on the ankle or side of a stocking or sock [Mid-16C. Origin ?]

clock golf *n* a putting game in which the ball is played from each of several points on the edge of a circular lawn towards a single hole in the centre

clock radio *n* an electronic device that incorporates a digital clock, an alarm clock, and a radio

clock speed *n* the speed of a microprocessor's internal clock that controls how fast a computer makes calculations, usually measured in megahertz (MHz) or gigahertz (GHz)

---

clock-watcher *n* an employee who is keen to leave work as soon as possible —**clock-watching** *n*

clockwise /klók wīz/ *adv, adj* in the same direction that the hands of a clock move around a clock face

clockwork /klók wurk/ *n* a mechanism consisting of cogs and a wound spring, used to drive a traditional clock or a moving toy ◇ **like clockwork** with unvarying regularity and predictability ○ *Thanks to the volunteers, the event ran like clockwork.*

clod /klod/ *n* **1.** a large lump of soil **2.** somebody regarded as unintelligent and slow-witted (*insult*) [14C. Variant of CLOT] —**cloddish** *adj* —**cloddishly** *adv* —**cloddishness** *n* —**cloddy** *adj*

clodhopper /klód hopər/ *n* somebody regarded as awkward and unsophisticated (*informal insult*) ■ **clodhoppers** *npl* a pair of large heavy shoes or boots (*informal*) [Early 18C. Originally 'ploughman'; from walking over ploughed land with clods of earth]

clofibrate /klō fíbbrayt/ *n* a drug used to reduce blood cholesterol, triglycerides, and uric acid [Mid-20C. < *clofibric acid*, probably < CHLORO- + *fibrate*, INN stem]

clog /klog/ *v* (**clogs, clogging, clogged**) **1.** *vti* BLOCK GRADUALLY to block a tube or opening gradually with dirt or dust, or become gradually blocked with dirt or dust **2.** *vt* TRANSP HINDER MOVEMENT IN SOMETHING to block something such as a road or tunnel, making movement difficult ■ *n* **1.** CLOTHING HEAVY SHOE a heavy shoe traditionally made of wood, or a shoe with a heavy, traditionally wooden, sole **2.** OBSTRUCTION something that works against somebody as an obstacle or hindrance **3.** WEIGHT RESTRICTING ANIMAL'S MOVEMENT a wooden block fastened to an animal's leg to restrict its movement [14C. Origin ?] ◇ **pop your clogs** to die (*slang*)

clog up *vti* same as **clog** *v* (sense 1)

clog dance *n* a dance performed by dancers wearing clogs, who tap or stamp in time to music

cloggy /klóggi/ *adj regional* sticky or dirty —**clogginess** *n*

REGIONAL NOTE See *manky*.

cloisonné /klwaa zónn ay/ *adj* decorated with a pattern formed by pieces of enamel in various colours separated by strips of flattened wire [Mid-19C. < French, 'partitioned', past participle of *cloisonner* < Old French *cloison* 'partition' < Latin *claudere* 'to close'] —**cloisonné** *n*

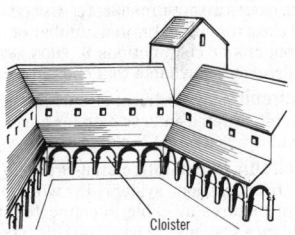

cloister

cloister /klóystər/ *n* **1.** ARCHIT COVERED WALKWAY ROUND COURTYARD a continuous covered outdoor walkway built against buildings surrounding a central courtyard or quadrangle, especially in a monastery or college **2.** RELIG MONASTERY OR CONVENT a place where people live a life of religious seclusion and contemplation, e.g. a monastery or convent **3.** RELIG LIFE OF RELIGIOUS SECLUSION the life of religious seclusion lived by a monk or nun ○ *He chose the cloister rather than the secular world.* **4.** PLACE OF SECLUSION a place where people can be private or secluded ■ *vt* (**-ters, -tering, -tered**) FIND PRIVATE PLACE to find a quiet private place where you can remain undisturbed [13C. Via Old French *cloistre* < medieval Latin *claustrum* < Latin, 'bar, bolt' < *claudere* 'to close'] —**cloistral** *adj*

cloistered /klóystərd/ *adj* **1.** SECLUDED secluded from the ordinary life of the world ○ *had led a cloistered life* **2.** RELIG IN MONASTERY living or occurring in a monastery or convent **3.** ARCHIT WITH CLOISTER having a cloister for walking in

clomiphene /klómi feen/ *n* a drug that induces ovu-

---

lation. Use: infertility treatment. [Mid-20C. < CHLORO- + AMINE + PHENYL]

clomipramine /klō míppə meen/ *n* a tricyclic drug. Use: to treat depression, phobias, and obsessional conditions.

clomp /klomp/ *n, vti* same as **clump**[2]

Cloncurry /klon kúrri/ town in northwestern Queensland, Australia, a centre of mining and cattle grazing. Population: 3,856 (2002 estimate).

clone: first clone of an adult animal ('Dolly'), Roslin Institute, Edinburgh (1997)

clone /klōn/ *n* **1.** GENETICS GENETICALLY IDENTICAL ORGANISM a plant, animal, or other organism that is genetically identical to its parent, having developed by vegetative reproduction from a bulb, cutting, or other part, or, in experimental conditions, from a single cell **2.** GENETICS GROUP OF GENETICALLY IDENTICAL PROGENY a collection of organisms, cells, or molecular segments that are genetically identical direct descendants of a single parent by asexual reproduction, e.g. plant cuttings or grafts **3.** COMPUT NEAR COPY OF HARDWARE OR SOFTWARE a hardware device, e.g. a PC, or a piece of software, that is a functional copy of another, more expensive product developed by another manufacturer ■ *v* (**clones, cloning, cloned**) **1.** *vti* GENETICS PRODUCE GENETICALLY IDENTICAL ORGANISM to produce an organism that is genetically identical to its parent by vegetative reproduction or a laboratory technique, or be produced in this way **2.** *vt* MAKE COPY OF SOMETHING to produce an exact or near copy of an object or product [Early 20C. < Greek *klōn* 'twig'] —**clonal** *adj* —**clonally** *adv* —**cloner** *n*

SYNONYMS See *copy*.

clonidine /klónnə deen, klṓnədin/ *n* a drug that relaxes and widens the arteries. Use: treatment of hypertension, migraine headaches, and heart failure. [Late 20C. < CHLORO- + -*onidine*, INN stem]

clonk /klongk/ *n* DULL HOLLOW SOUND the dull hollow sound of something heavy, usually metal, ceramic, or glass, hitting a hard surface ■ *v* (**clonks, clonking, clonked**) **1.** *vti* MAKE DULL HOLLOW SOUND to make a dull hollow sound, or make something produce such a sound **2.** *vt* HIT SOMEBODY HEAVILY to hit somebody with a heavy blow (*informal*) [Mid-19C. An imitation of the sound]

Clonmel /klon mél/ town and sporting centre in County Tipperary, Republic of Ireland. Population: 15,739 (2002).

clonotypic /klṓnō típpik/ *adj* relating to or characteristic of a clone [Late 20C. < CLONE]

clonus /klṓnəss/ *n* a series of rapid repetitive contractions and relaxations in a muscle during movement, which is characteristic of grand-mal epilepsy seizures [Early 19C. Via Latin < Greek *klonos* 'turmoil, agitation'] —**clonic** /klónnik/ *adj* —**clonicity** /klō níssəti/ *n*

Clooney /klooni/, **George** (b. 1961) US film and television actor. He played Dr Douglas Ross in the US television series *ER* in the 1990s. Full name **Clooney, George Timothy**

cloot /kloot/ *n Scotland* **1.** a hoof, or either of the two halves of a cloven hoof **2.** a cloth [Late 18C. Variant of CLOUT]

clootie dumpling /klooti-/ *n Scotland* a sweet pudding, similar to Christmas pudding, that is boiled in a cloth [< CLOOT]

clop /klop/ *n* the sound that a walking horse's hooves make when they strike hard ground ■ *vi* (**clops,**

---

clopping, clopped) to make the sound of a walking horse's hooves striking hard ground [Mid-19C. An imitation of the sound]

cloque /klo káy, klókay/, **cloqué** *n* a fabric with a raised woven or embossed pattern that makes it look quilted [Early 20C. < French *cloqué* 'blistered' < dialect *cloque* 'bell, bubble' < medieval Latin *clocca* 'bell']

close[1] /klōss/ *adj* **(closer, closest) 1. NEAR** near in space or time ○ *The deadline is getting closer all the time.* **2. ABOUT TO HAPPEN** about to happen, or about to do something ○ *close to collapse* **3. IN FRIENDLY RELATIONSHIP** involved in a very friendly or affectionate relationship ○ *a close friend* **4. CLOSELY RELATED** being a member of somebody's immediate family ○ *invited her parents and other close relatives* **5. INVOLVING REGULAR CONTACT** involving or having regular contact because of a shared interest in something ○ *enjoyed close cooperation* **6. THOROUGH** involving great care and thoroughness ○ *a close inspection* **7. DECIDED BY SMALL MARGIN** decided by, or likely to be decided by, a small margin ○ *a close contest* **8.** TEXTILES **ALLOWING LITTLE SPACE BETWEEN** densely packed or woven with only little spaces between ○ *a close weave* **9. VERY SIMILAR** very similar to an original ○ *a close copy* **10. NEARLY CORRECT** almost correct, but not exact ○ *You're not quite right, but you're pretty close.* **11. NEARLY PARTICULAR NUMBER OR QUANTITY** approximately the same as a particular number or quantity ○ *There were close to 300 people at the rally.* **12. SECRETIVELY SILENT** unwilling to talk about something or to reveal feelings ○ *was close about the cause of the disaster* **13. CUT VERY SHORT** cut so as to be very short **14. NOT GENEROUS WITH MONEY** unwilling to spend or give money **15. HARD TO GET** describes money or credit that is difficult to obtain **16. CLOSELY GUARDED** kept closely guarded **17. STUFFY** oppressively hot and airless **18.** *US* **DEFENSIVE, WITH SHORT PASSES** in team ball and similar games, involving short passes only, so as to retain possession **19.** PHON **PRODUCED WITH TONGUE NEAR PALATE** describes a vowel sound that is produced with the tongue near the palate, e.g. the 'ee' in 'tee' ■ *adv* **(closer, closest) 1. NEAR TO SOMETHING** near in space or time **2. TIGHTLY** in a snug tight way [13C. Via French *clos* < Latin *clausus*, past participle of *claudere* 'close'] —**closeness** *n*

close[2] /klōz/ *v* **(closes, closing, closed) 1.** *vti* **COVER OPENING** to move, or move something, so that an opening or hole is covered or blocked ○ *closing the door* **2.** *vti* **COME OR BRING TOGETHER** to bring the edges or ends of something together, or be brought together ○ *Close your eyes.* **3.** *vti* **SHUT DOWN BUSINESS FOR SHORT TIME** to stop working or operating, or shut a shop or business, for a short period of time or overnight **4.** *vti* COMM same as **close down** (sense 1) **5.** *vt* same as **close off 6.** *vti* **TERMINATE** to come to an end, or end something such as an activity, period of time, or spoken or written text **7.** *vti* **REDUCE DISTANCE** to reduce the distance between two people or things, especially in a race or chase **8.** *vt* COMM **BRING DEAL TO CLOSURE** to complete a transaction successfully, e.g. a business deal or a house purchase **9.** *vi* FIN **HAVE PARTICULAR END-OF-DAY VALUE** to have a particular value at the end of a day's trading on a stock exchange ○ *Share prices closed higher in heavy trading.* **10.** *vt* COMPUT **DEACTIVATE AND STORE FILE OR PROGRAM** to perform the series of operations necessary to deactivate a computer file or program and store it for later use **11.** *vt* ELEC ENG **COMPLETE ELECTRICAL CIRCUIT** to complete an electrical circuit **12.** *vt Malaysia* **SWITCH SOMETHING OFF** to turn or switch something off ■ *n* **1. END** the end of an activity, period of time, or spoken or written text ○ *The applause brought the recital to a close.* **2.** MUSIC same as **cadence** (sense 5) [13C. < French *clos-*, stem of *clore* 'to close' < Latin *claudere*] —**closable** *adj* —**closer** *n*

ORIGIN The Latin word *claudere*, 'to close', from which ***close*** is derived, is also the source of English *clause, cloister, conclude, conclusive, include, preclude, recluse*, and *seclude*.

close down *v* **1.** *vti* to stop operating or trading permanently, or make a factory, business, or school do this **2.** *vi* to stop broadcasting at the end of the day

close in *vi* **1.** to move closer and eventually surround somebody or something **2.** to become progressively shorter, with fewer hours of daylight

close off *vt* to prevent people from reaching a place or using a route by blocking access to it (*often passive*)

close up *v* **1.** *vti* **LOCK BUILDING** to lock the doors of a building at the end of a working or trading session **2.** *vti* **MOVE CLOSER TOGETHER** to move closer together, or make people or things move closer together **3.** *vti* **BRING TOGETHER** to bring the ends or edges of something together, or be brought together ○ *The surgeon closed up the incision.* **4.** *vi* **HIDE EMOTIONS** to hide your true emotions because you do not want somebody to know or understand you

close with *vt* to enter into physical conflict or a fight with somebody ○ *The two boxers closed with one another.*

close[3] /klōss/ *n* **1.** *also* **Close CUL-DE-SAC** a residential road, often a cul-de-sac on a modern housing estate (*often used in street names*) **2. AREA ROUND CATHEDRAL** the area immediately surrounding a cathedral, including the buildings, many of which are often cathedral property **3.** *also* **Close** *Scotland* **COURTYARD** an outdoor area enclosed by buildings, e.g. a courtyard, or a passageway leading to one (*often used in street names*) **4.** *Scotland* **PASSAGEWAY INSIDE TENEMENT BUILDING** in the west of Scotland, especially Glasgow, a passage inside a tenement building that leads from the street to the common stairway [13C. Via French *clos* < Latin *clausum* 'enclosure', neuter of *clausus* (see CLOSE [1])]

close call *n* a dangerous or unpleasant situation, especially one that could have resulted in death or injury, from which somebody just manages to escape

close company *n* a company that is controlled by its directors

close-cropped *adj* cut very short

closed /klōzd/ *adj* **1. NOT OPEN FOR BUSINESS** describes a business or institution where work, operation, or trading has temporarily or permanently stopped **2. DENYING ACCESS** describes a place to which access is denied or through which passage is not permitted ○ *The road is closed for repairs.* **3. NO LONGER TO BE DISCUSSED** no longer to be discussed or investigated ○ *The subject is closed.* **4. RIGIDLY EXCLUDING OTHERS' IDEAS** rejecting the ideas, beliefs, opinions, or influence of others ○ *He has a closed mind to all arguments.* **5. NOT ADMITTING OUTSIDERS** allowing no outsiders in, or tending not to meet with outsiders **6. CONFIDENTIAL AND PRIVATE** carried on or conducted in the strictest confidentiality or secrecy ○ *The bill is being considered by the committee in closed session.* **7.** MATHS **FULLY ENCLOSING AREA OR VOLUME** describes a curve, especially a circle, that fully encloses an area, or to describe a solid every surface of which is such a curve **8.** GRAM **HAVING LIMITED NUMBER OF MEMBERS** describes a word class that has a limited number of members, e.g. pronouns or conjunctions **9.** PHON **ENDING IN CONSONANT** describes a syllable that ends in a consonant

closed circuit *n* an electrical circuit in which there is an uninterrupted endless path for current to flow when voltage is applied —**closed-circuit** *adj*

closed-circuit television, closed-circuit TV *n* a television transmission system in which cameras transmit pictures by cable to connected monitors. Surveillance systems are based on this type of transmission.

closed company *n* BUSINESS same as **close company**

closed couplet *n* a pair of rhymed lines that form a complete sentence or unit of meaning

closed-door *adj* restricted to members or those directly involved, and not open to the general public or the news media

closed-end fund *n* an investment company with a fixed number of shares trading on the stock exchange

closed-end investment company *n US* a corporation whose capitalization is fixed, whose capital is invested in other companies, and whose own shares are traded by outside investors

closed fracture *n* a broken bone that does not protrude through the skin

closed interval *n* a mathematical set consisting of all the numbers between two given numbers (**endpoints**), including the given numbers. All the whole numbers greater than or equal to 5 and less than or equal to 10 constitute a closed interval.

closed loop *n* a system, usually computer-controlled, that adjusts itself to varying conditions by feeding output information back as input

closedown /klṓz down/ *n* **1.** a temporary or permanent stopping of work or operations **2.** the end of a broadcasting day or period

closed season *n US* same as **close season**

closed set *n* a mathematical set that includes the limits by which the set is defined, e.g. all the points within and on a circle

closed shop *n* a place of work in which the employer has agreed to employ only members of a particular trade union

closed stance *n* in sports such as baseball or golf, a stance in which the front foot is closer to the line of play than the rear foot

close-fisted /klṓss fístid/ *adj* reluctant to spend money —**close-fistedness** *n*

close-fitting *adj* fitting tightly on the body

close-grained /klṓss-/ *adj* describes wood that has dense fibres and a smooth texture

close harmony *n* the arrangement of chord tones so that they are as close together as possible, used especially in music for vocal ensembles

close-hauled /klṓss-/ *adj, adv* having the sails set for sailing towards the direction from which the wind is blowing

close-in *adj N Am* **1.** very near to a centre of action or activity **2.** taking place at close range

close-knit *adj* describes a community or group whose members are supportive of and loyal to one another

closely /klṓssli/ *adv* **1. IN VERY SIMILAR WAY** in a way that is very similar or strongly linked to something ○ *She closely resembles you.* **2. CAREFULLY AND THOROUGHLY** in a careful and thorough way ○ *listening closely* **3. SO AS TO BE NEAR** in a way that is near something in space or time ○ *We heard a bang, closely followed by another.* **4. INTIMATELY** in an intimate manner ○ *worked closely with her*

closemouthed /klṓss mówthd, -mówtht/ *adj* unwilling to talk or to reveal anything

close-order drill *n* a military formation or movement that is conducted with soldiers at close intervals

closeout /klṓz owt/ *n N Am* COMM same as **closing-down sale**

close protection officer *n* somebody who is employed to protect somebody, especially a celebrity or public figure, from physical attack

close punctuation *n* punctuation in which a large number of commas, semicolons, and colons are used

close-run *adj* having a very close result

close season *n* **1.** the time of the year when it is illegal to hunt and kill some animals, birds, or fish **2.** the period between the end of one annual seasonal sports competition and the start of the next one, especially in football

close shave *n* same as **close call**

closestool /klṓss stool/ *n* formerly, a stool or chair containing a chamber pot [15C. Literally 'enclosed stool']

closet /klózzit/ *adj* **SECRET** having beliefs or behaviours that are not openly acknowledged but kept secret ■ *vt* **(-ets, -eting, -eted) PUT SOMEBODY IN PRIVATE PLACE** to put somebody in a small room in order to provide privacy (*often passive*) ○ *He closeted himself in the study all morning.* ■ *n* **1.** *N Am* **LARGE CUPBOARD** a walk-in wardrobe or walk-in cupboard in which clothes and linen are stored **2. SMALL PRIVATE ROOM** a small private room (*archaic*) **3.** same as **water closet** (*archaic*) [14C. < Old French, 'small enclosure' < *clos* (see CLOSE [3])] —**closetful** *n* ◇ **come out of the closet** to acknowledge openly something previously kept secret, especially the fact of being gay or lesbian

closet drama *n N Am* a play or plays written to be read rather than performed

close thing *n* same as **close call**

close-up *n* **1.** PHOTOGRAPHY, CINEMA, MEDIA **CLOSE-RANGE PHOTO OR SHOT** a photograph, or a film or television shot, taken from a position very close to the subject **2. DETAILED LOOK AT SOMETHING** a detailed view or examination of something ■ *adj, adv* **AT CLOSE RANGE** from a position very near somebody or something else

closing /klṓzing/ *adj* **FINAL** forming or connected with

the final part of an activity or period of time ○ *in the closing stages of the game* ■ *n* **1.** SOMETHING THAT CLOSES something that closes, e.g. a fastening on clothes **2.** *N Am* TRANSFER OF PROPERTY OWNERSHIP a meeting among principals in a real estate transaction, during which legal papers related to the sale and purchase are signed and financial arrangements are made final and binding

closing date *n* **1.** the final date on which something such as an application for a job can be submitted and be eligible for consideration **2.** a date on which a transaction is concluded, especially when a seller delivers a deed and a buyer pays for it

closing-down sale *n* a sale of all remaining merchandise, at very low prices. N Am term **closeout**

closing price *n* the price of a share or bond on a stock exchange recorded at the official close of trading

closing time *n* the time that an establishment such as a shop, library, or bar closes and people have to leave

clostridium /klo stríddi əm/ (*plural* **-iums** or **-ia** /-i ə/) *n* a rod-shaped, usually motile, Gram-positive bacterium that can cause serious illnesses including botulism, tetanus, and gas gangrene. Genus: *Clostridium*. [Late 19C. < modern Latin, 'little spindle' < Greek *klōstēr* 'spindle'] —**clostridial** *adj*

closure /klózhər/ *n* **1.** PERMANENT END OF BUSINESS the permanent ending of a business or activity **2.** BARRING OF ACCESS blocking the access to a place or blocking a route **3.** SOMETHING THAT CLOSES OPENING a device for closing an opening, e.g. a zip or a cap on a bottle, or the place where the opening closes **4.** CLOSING SOMETHING an act or process of closing something, e.g. closing an opening or terminating an activity **5.** *UK, ANZ, Can* POL PROCEDURE FOR CUTTING DEBATE SHORT a parliamentary procedure that allows a debate to be cut short and a vote to be taken immediately. US term **cloture 6.** PSYCHOL SENSE OF FINALITY the sense of finality and coming to terms with an experience, felt or experienced over time **7.** GEOL VERTICAL DISTANCE OF ROCK FORMATION the distance measured vertically between the top of a rock formation (**anticline**) and the lowest contour **8.** MATHS BEING CLOSED SET IN MATHEMATICS the characteristic of a set in which the application of a given mathematical operation to any member of the set always has another member of the set as its result **9.** PHON CONTACT BETWEEN VOCAL ORGANS PRODUCING SOUND a contact made between vocal organs such as the tongue and the soft palate that produces a speech sound ■ *vt* (**-sures, -suring, -sured**) *UK, ANZ, Can* POL CUT DEBATE SHORT to apply closure to a debate or speaker in parliament. US term **cloture**

clot /klot/ *n* **1.** STICKY LUMP a mass of thickened liquid, especially blood **2.** OFFENSIVE TERM an offensive term for a person considered to be unintelligent (*informal*) ■ *v* (**clots, clotting, clotted**) **1.** *vti* THICKEN AND FORM LUMPS to thicken, or cause a liquid thicken, and form lumps **2.** *vt* IMPEDE to hinder the free movement or accessibility of something ○ *The flow of the film is clotted by obscure arguments.* ○ *streets clotted by traffic jams* [Old English *clott* < Indo-European, 'form into a ball'] —**clottish** *adj*

cloth /kloth/ *n* **1.** FABRIC fabric made by weaving, knitting, or felting thread or fibres **2.** PIECE OF FABRIC a piece of fabric used for a particular purpose, e.g. a dishcloth (*often used in combination*) **3.** CLERGY the clergy, or the clothes worn by its members **4.** SAIL a sail of a boat **5.** PIECE OF FABRIC SCENERY a painted piece of fabric used as scenery in a theatre [Old English *clāp* < Germanic]

clothbound /kloth bownd/ *adj* describes a book that has a cloth-lined hardback cover

cloth cap *n* a flat cap, usually made of tweed, with a stiffened peak. It is regarded as a symbol of the working class.

clothe /klōth/ (**clothes, clothing, clothed** or **clad** /klad/, **clothed** or **clad**) *vt* **1.** DRESS SOMEBODY to put clothes on somebody (*often passive*) **2.** PROVIDE CLOTHING FOR SOMEBODY to provide somebody with clothes **3.** COVER SOMETHING to completely cover an area ○ *The hills were clothed in mist.* **4.** COVER SOMETHING UP to obscure or conceal something as if wrapping something round it **5.** ENDOW SOMEBODY OR SOMETHING to endow or invest somebody or something with some quality (*usually passive*) [Old English *clāpian* < *clāp* (see CLOTH)]

cloth-eared *adj* unable or unwilling to hear (*informal*)

clothes /klōthz/ *npl* **1.** garments that cover the body **2.** sheets and blankets used to cover a bed (*dated*) [Old English *clāpas*, plural of *clāp* (see CLOTH)]

clothes basket *n* **1.** a deep container made of wicker, fabric, or other material, used for storing dirty clothes before they are washed. N Am term **clothes hamper 2.** a wicker or plastic container used for carrying clothes that are to be washed or that have just been washed or dried. N Am term **laundry basket**

clothes hamper *n N Am* same as **clothes basket**

clothes hanger *n* HOUSEHOLD same as **hanger** (sense 1)

clothes hoist *n* a frame of long wooden slats attached to a ceiling and raised and lowered by a pulley, on which wet clothes are hung to dry

clotheshorse /klōthz hawrss/ *n* **1.** a frame on which clothes are hung to dry indoors. ◊ **airer 2.** somebody who wears the latest fashions (*informal*)

clothesline /klōthz līn/ *n* a cord on which clean laundry is hung to dry, usually outdoors

clothes moth *n* any small moth whose larvae feed on wool and fur. Family: Tineidae.

clothes peg *n* a small clip of plastic or wood used to secure laundry to a clothesline. N Am term **clothespin**

clothes press *n* a piece of furniture for storing clothes, with hanging space and sometimes drawers or shelves

clothes prop *n* a long pole for holding a clothesline above the ground

clothier /klōthi ər/ *n* a retail seller of clothes or cloth [14C. Alteration of obsolete *clother* < CLOTH]

clothing /klōthing/ *n* **1.** clothes collectively **2.** a covering for something

Clotho /klō thō/ *n* in Greek mythology, one of the three Fates who influenced human destiny. She held the distaff and spun the thread of life. [< Greek *Klōthō*, literally 'I spin']

cloth of gold *n* a luxury fabric of the Middle Ages woven from silk, or sometimes wool, intermixed with gold thread

clotrimazole /klō trímə zol/ *n* an antifungal drug used to treat yeast and fungal infections

clotted cream /klóttid-/ *n* a thick cream made by removing the cream from the top of heated milk

clotting factor /klótting-/ *n* any substance in the blood that is essential for blood to coagulate

cloture /klóchər/ *US* POL *n* same as **closure** *n* (sense 5) ■ *vt* (**-tures, -turing, -tured**) same as **closure** [Late 19C. < French *clôture* 'closing']

cloud /klowd/ *n* **1.** MASS OF WATER IN SKY a visible mass of water or ice particles in the atmosphere from which rain and other forms of precipitation fall **2.** MASS OF PARTICLES IN AIR a mass of particles in the air, e.g. dust or smoke ○ *a cloud of smoke* **3.** FLYING MASS an airborne mass of insects or birds **4.** DARKER PART a dark or dim area on something such as jewellery **5.** SOMETHING WORRYING something that causes anxiety or fear ○ *Lack of financial independence was a cloud hanging over our future.* **6.** GLOOMY CONDITION a condition of gloom or despondency ○ *a cloud of despair* **7.** COMPUT UNPREDICTABLE PART OF COMPUTER NETWORK an unpredictable or unidentifiable part of a network through which data passes ■ *v* (**clouds, clouding, clouded**) **1.** *vti* BECOME CLOUDY to become covered with clouds or mist, or make something cloudy **2.** *vt* CONFUSE SOMETHING to make something more confusing ○ *cloud the issue* **3.** *vt* DETRACT FROM SOMETHING to make something appear less good ○ *It will cloud her reputation.* **4.** *vt* IMPAIR SOMETHING to diminish a mental faculty ○ *Depression had clouded his judgment.* **5.** *vti* LOOK TROUBLED to become or cause something to become troubled or gloomy ○ *His face clouded with disappointment.* **6.** *vti* BECOME OR MAKE SOMETHING OPAQUE to become or cause something to become opaque or murky ○ *The water was clouded with particles.* [Old English *clūd* 'mass of rock, hill'] ◇ **on cloud nine** extremely happy (*informal*) ◇ **under a cloud** in disgrace
cloud over, cloud up *vi* **1.** to become covered with clouds or mist **2.** to become troubled

cloudberry /klówdbəri/ *n* (*plural* **-ries**) a creeping perennial plant with yellowish edible berries.

cloud

Flowers: white. Native to: Europe, North America, Asia. Latin name: *Rubus chamaemorus.*

cloudburst /klówd burst/ *n* a sudden heavy rain shower

cloud chamber *n* a device in which the movement of high-energy particles is detected as they pass through a chamber of supersaturated vapour. Observable tracks are formed when droplets condense on the ionized molecules left by the high-energy particles

cloud-cuckoo-land *n* an imaginary place in which problems do not exist [Translation of Greek *Nephelokokkugia*, imaginary city in the air in Aristophanes' *Birds*]

clouded /klówdid/ *adj* **1.** appearing troubled **2.** opaque or murky

clouded leopard *n* a rare medium-sized cat with short legs and a greyish to yellowish coat with darker irregular markings. Native to: the area from Nepal to Borneo. Latin name: *Neofelis nebulosa.*

clouded yellow *n* a butterfly that has yellowish wings with brownish or blackish margins and migrates between continental Europe and Britain. Latin name: *Colias croceus.*

cloud forest *n* a high-altitude tropical forest that is usually covered by cloud. Clinging plants (**epiphytes**), especially mosses and ferns, grow on the trees in profusion, encouraged by the moisture.

cloudland /klówd land/ *n* same as **dreamland** (sense 1)

cloudless /klówdləss/ *adj* **1.** bright and sunny without clouds ○ *a cloudless sky* **2.** free of trouble —**cloudlessly** *adv* —**cloudlessness** *n*

cloud rack *n* a group of clouds moving across the sky

cloudscape /klówd skayp/ *n* a view or depiction of clouds

cloud seeding *n* the technique or process of scattering substances such as silver iodide into clouds from an aircraft in order to precipitate rain

cloudy /klówdi/ (**-ier, -iest**) *adj* **1.** WITH CLOUDS covered with or full of clouds **2.** OPAQUE opaque or murky

○ *a cloudy liquid* **3.** RESEMBLING CLOUDS having the appearance of clouds **4.** TROUBLED seeming troubled or gloomy **5.** NOT CLEAR obscure or difficult to understand —**cloudily** *adv* —**cloudiness** *n*

clough /kluf/ *n regional* a ravine, or the sloping side of it [Old English *clōh* < Germanic]

clout /klowt/ *n* **1.** POWER AND INFLUENCE the power to direct, shape, or otherwise influence things (*informal*) **2.** PUNCH a blow with the hand or fist (*informal*) **3.** ARCHERY TARGET in archery, a mark or target, especially at a long distance **4.** *regional* PIECE OF CLOTH a rag or piece of cloth ○ *a dish clout* ■ *vt* (**clouts, clouting, clouted**) HIT SOMEBODY WITH HAND to hit somebody or something hard with the hand [Old English *clūt* 'patch made of cloth']

clove[1] /klōv/ *n* **1.** a dried aromatic flower bud. Use: as a spice. **2.** an evergreen tree with flower buds that are used dried as a spice and other parts that yield aromatic oil of cloves. Native to: the Moluccas. Latin name: *Syzgium aromaticum.* [12C. < Old French *clou (de girofle)* 'nail (of the clove tree)' < Latin *clavus* 'nail'; from the resemblance of a clove-tree bud to a nail]

clove[2] /klōv/ *n* one of the segments of a compound bulb ○ *a clove of garlic* [Old English *clufu* < Germanic]

clove[3] /klōv/ past tense of **cleave**[1]

clove[4] /klōv/ past tense of **cleave**[2]

clove hitch *n* a knot made of two half-hitches. Use: to attach a rope to a post or to another, thicker, rope. [< former past participle of CLEAVE[1]]

cloven /klṓv'n/ past participle of **cleave**[1] ■ *adj* split or divided into two parts (*archaic or literary*)

cloven hoof, **cloven foot** *n* **1.** the divided hoof of such animals as cattle, sheep, and pigs. Order: Artiodactyla. **2.** an indication of the presence of the devil, traditionally represented in Christianity with a cloven hoof —**cloven-hoofed** *adj*

clove oil *n* PHARM same as **oil of cloves**

clove pink *n* PLANTS same as **carnation** (sense 1) [< CLOVE[1]; from its smell]

clover /klṓvər/ *n* **1.** a plant with three-lobed leaves often cultivated as a forage plant, for erosion control, and to provide nectar for bees. Genus: *Trifolium.* **2.** a forage plant similar to clover. Genera: *Meliotus* or *Lespedeza* or *Medicago.* [Old English *clāfre* < Germanic] ◇ **in clover** financially well off (*informal*)

cloverleaf /klṓvər leef/ (*plural* **cloverleaves** /-leevz/) *n* **1.** the three-lobed leaf of a clover plant (*often used before a noun*) ○ *a cloverleaf motif* **2.** an arrangement of major roads resembling a four-leaf clover, with entrance and exit roads enabling traffic to change direction at speed without intersections

Clovis /klṓviss/ *adj* describes a prehistoric North American culture characterized by leaf-shaped flint points that were used as parts of weapons to hunt game [Mid-20C. After *Clovis*, city in New Mexico, United States]

Clovis /klṓviss/ (466?–511) Frankish king (481–511). The first important ruler of the Merovingian dynasty, he enlarged his kingdom until it included most of present-day France and part of Germany.

clown /klown/ *n* **1.** COMIC CIRCUS PERFORMER a comic performer, usually in a circus, who does not speak and wears an outlandish costume and heavy makeup **2.** SOMEBODY FUNNY somebody who behaves comically **3.** PRANKSTER a practical joker **4.** ILL-MANNERED PERSON an ill-mannered or ineffectual person (*informal*) ■ *vi* (**clowns, clowning, clowned**) **1.** BEHAVE COMICALLY to behave in a silly or funny way **2.** PLAY PRANKS to play practical jokes **3.** PERFORM AS CLOWN to perform as a circus clown [Mid-16C. Origin ?] —**clownery** *n* —**clowning** *n*

clown anemone *n* ZOOL same as **anemone fish**

clownish /klównish/ *adj* resembling or characteristic of a clown —**clownishly** *adv* —**clownishness** *n*

cloy /kloy/ (**cloys, cloying, cloyed**) *vti* to sicken somebody or become sickened with too much sweetness from something initially pleasing [Mid-16C. Shortening of obsolete *accloy*, via French *encloer* 'drive in a nail' < medieval Latin *inclavare* < Latin *clavus* 'nail'] —**cloyingly** *adv* —**cloyingness** *n*

clozapine /klṓzə peen/ *n* an antipsychotic drug. Use: to treat schizophrenia. [Mid-20C. Contraction of CHLORO- + BENZODIAZEPINE]

cloze test /klṓz-/ *n* a test of comprehension and grammar in which a language student supplies appropriate missing words omitted from a text [Alteration of CLOSURE]

club /klub/ *n* **1.** THICK STICK USED AS WEAPON a thick heavy stick used as a weapon **2.** STICK FOR HITTING BALL a stick or bat used in some sports, especially golf, to hit a ball ○ *a golf club* **3.** ASSOCIATION FOR PURSUING COMMON INTEREST an association of people with a common interest ○ *a gardening club* **4.** NATIONS SHARING SOMETHING a group of nations or people who have a particular thing in common ○ *the nuclear club* **5.** ORGANIZATION FOR SPORT an organization formed for the pursuit of a sport on an amateur or a professional basis ○ *a football club* **6.** PREMISES OF CLUB the premises where the activities of a club are pursued ○ *See you at the club tonight!* **7.** PLACE FOR DANCING a place where people dance to recorded music, usually with bars and other leisure facilities **8.** LEISURE same as **nightclub** **9.** BUILDING PROVIDING FACILITIES TO MEMBERS a building that offers facilities and refreshment to members of the organization that owns or occupies it ○ *a gentlemen's club* **10.** CARDS CARD WITH CLOVERLEAF SYMBOL a playing card of the suit of clubs **11.** BLACK SYMBOL ON PLAYING CARD a black symbol shaped like a cloverleaf on a playing card **12.** ORGANIZATION GIVING DISCOUNTS a scheme or organization in which members receive price reductions in return for regular purchases ○ *a book club* **13.** SAVINGS SCHEME a savings scheme organized as a means of saving for something ○ *a Christmas club* **14.** ARTS same as **Indian club** ■ *v* (**clubs, clubbing, clubbed**) **1.** *vt* HIT SOMEBODY OR SOMETHING WITH CLUB to hit somebody or something with a club ○ *She clubbed the ball over the fence.* **2.** *vi* FORM CLUB to join or form a club for social purposes or to pursue a common interest **3.** *vi* DRIFT WITH ANCHOR LOWERED to drift with an anchor that drags to reduce the speed of the vessel [12C. < Old Norse *klubba* 'heavy stick'] ◇ **in the (pudding) club** pregnant (*informal*) ◇ **join the club!** used to tell somebody that you are in the same position as he or she is (*informal*)

club together *vi* **1.** to contribute money collectively for some purpose **2.** to collaborate as a group

clubbable /klúbbəb'l/, **clubable** *adj* sociable, or inclined to join groups or organizations —**clubbability** /klúbbə bílləti/ *n*

clubbed /klubd/ *adj* describes an appendage with a swelling at one end, like a club ○ *clubbed antennae*

clubber /klúbbər/ *n* **1.** CLUB GOER somebody who regularly goes to clubs (*informal*) **2.** MEMBER OF CLUB a member of a private club **3.** CLUB WIELDER the wielder of a club

clubbing /klúbbing/ *n* **1.** the activity of going to nightclubs **2.** a medical condition in which the tips of the fingers and toes become thickened, especially at the base of the nail. It may be associated with some lung or heart diseases.

clubby /klúbbi/ (**-bier, -biest**) *adj* **1.** SOCIABLE enjoying the friendliness associated with clubs **2.** TYPICAL OF CLUB typical of a social club **3.** SNOBBISH socially exclusive and snobbish —**clubbily** *adv* —**clubbiness** *n*

club chair *n* a heavily upholstered chair with a low back and thick arms [< its use in gentlemen's clubs]

club class *n* a class of travel on an aircraft between first class and economy class

clubface /klúbb fayss/ *n* the surface of the head of a golf club with which the player strikes the ball

club foot *n* **1.** a congenital condition of the foot, especially one in which the foot is twisted and turned inwards **2.** a foot that is affected by club foot —**club-footed** *adj*

club hand *n* **1.** a congenital condition in which the hand is twisted and turned inwards or outwards **2.** a hand affected by club hand —**club handed** *adj*

clubhaul /klúb hawl/ (**-hauls, -hauling, -hauled**) *vti* to force a sailing vessel to change tack by dropping the lee-anchor and hauling in the anchor cable to swing the stern to windward

clubhouse /klúb howss/ *n* the premises of a club, especially a sports club

clubland /klúb land/ *n* an area in a large city such as London in which many exclusive social clubs and nightclubs are located

clubman /klúb mən/ (*plural* **-men** /-mən/) *n* a man who belongs to one or more exclusive social clubs

club moss *n* a nonflowering plant that typically has creeping stems with small overlapping leaves and reproduces by spores, often borne in club-shaped organs (**strobili**). Order: Lycopodiales.

clubperson /klúb purss'n/ (*plural* **-people** /-peep'l/ or **-persons**) *n* **1.** somebody who belongs to many clubs, especially social or civic organizations **2.** somebody who enjoys going to nightclubs

clubroom /klúb room, -rōōm/ *n* a room in which members of a club meet

clubroot /klúb root/ *n* a disease affecting plants of the cabbage family, in which the roots become swollen and distorted. Latin name: *Plasmodiophora brassicae.*

clubs /klubz/ *n* one of the four suits used in cards, with a black shape similar to a cloverleaf as its symbol (*takes a singular or plural verb*)

club sandwich *n* a sandwich consisting of two layers of fillings between three slices of bread [Origin ?]

club soda *n N Am* BEVERAGES same as **soda water** (sense 1) [< a proprietary name]

cluck /kluk/ *interj* USED TO REPRESENT HEN'S CALL used to imitate the short low clicking sound made by a hen ■ *v* (**clucks, clucking, clucked**) **1.** *vi* MAKE HEN'S SOUND to make natural short low clicking sounds (*refers to hens*) **2.** *vti* EXPRESS SOMETHING WITH CLICKING SOUND to show disapproval or concern by making short clicking sounds ■ *n* **1.** HEN'S CALL a hen's short low clicking call **2.** *N Am* UNINTELLIGENT PERSON somebody who is considered mildly unintelligent (*informal*) [15C. An imitation of the sound]

clucked /klukt/ *adj regional* describes a hen that is ready to sit on eggs and hatch them

clucky /klúki/ (**-ier, -iest**) *adj Aus* keen to have children (*slang*) [< the idea of a broody hen]

clue /kloo/ *n* **1.** AID IN SOLVING MYSTERY something that helps to solve a mystery or crime **2.** AID IN SOLVING CROSSWORD one of the numbered items of information used to solve a crossword puzzle **3.** EXPLANATION FOR BEHAVIOUR an explanation or reason for something that is difficult to understand [Late 16C. Alteration of CLEW] ◇ **not have a clue about something** (*informal*) **1.** to know nothing about something **2.** to be very bad at something

clue in *vt* to provide somebody with useful information ○ *She clued me in about office politics.*

clued-up /klood úp/ *adj* well-informed about somebody or something (*informal; not hyphenated when used after a verb*) ○ *She's quite clued up about food additives.* [Alteration of *clewed up* 'furled up' < CLEW 'corner of a sail']

clueless /kloōləss/ *adj* incompetent or ignorant (*informal*) —**cluelessness** *n*

Cluj-Napoca /kloōzh nə pṓkə/ industrial city and capital of Cluj County in Transylvania, northwestern Romania. Population: 332,297 (1997).

clumber spaniel /klúmbər-/, **clumber** *n* a thickset short-legged spaniel with a dense silky coat, belonging to an English breed [After *Clumber* Park, Nottinghamshire]

clumble-fisted /klúmb'l fistid/ *adj W Country* unable to do something gracefully or tactfully

clump[1] /klump/ *n* **1.** CLUSTER OF THINGS a compact cluster or group of growing things ○ *a clump of moss* **2.** MASS OF SIMILAR THINGS an undifferentiated mass of something **3.** CLUSTER OF CELLS a cluster of cells such as bacteria or red blood cells, especially one formed during an immune response or when blood of incompatible blood groups is mixed ■ *v* (**clumps, clumping, clumped**) **1.** *vti* COMBINE THINGS INTO MASS to be gathered or gather things into a mass **2.** *vt* CAUSE MASSING OF CELLS to cause cells such as bacteria or red blood cells to combine into a mass, especially as part of an immune response [13C. Probably < Low German *klump*]

clump[2] /klump/, **clomp** /klomp/ *n* **1.** THUMPING SOUND a heavy thumping sound **2.** HEAVY BLOW a heavy blow or punch (*informal*) ■ *v* (**clumps, clumping, clumped; clomps, clomping, clomped**) **1.** *vi* MOVE WITH CLUMP to walk or move with a heavy thumping sound **2.** *vt* THUMP SOMEBODY to give somebody a heavy thump or punch (*informal*) [Mid-17C. An imitation of the sound]

clumpy /klúmpi/ (**-ier, -iest**) *adj* **1.** large, heavy, and ungainly **2.** composed of or growing in clumps —**clumpily** *adv* —**clumpiness** *n*

clumsy /klúmzi/ (-sier, -siest) *adj* 1. poorly coordinated physically 2. said or done in an awkward or insensitive way ○ *a clumsy remark* [Late 16C. Origin ?] —**clumsily** *adv* —**clumsiness** *n*

clung past participle, past tense of **cling**

Clunies-Ross /klooniz róss/, **Sir Ian** (1899–1959) Australian veterinary scientist. He was prominent in the development of the Australian sheep industry.

clunk /klungk/ *n* 1. DULL SOUND a dull sound like that of a heavy piece of metal hitting something 2. BLOW OR SOUND IT MAKES a blow, or the sound made by a blow (*informal*) ■ *vti* (**clunks, clunking, clunked**) MAKE DULL SOUND to make, or cause something to make, a dull heavy sound [Late 18C. An imitation of the sound]

clunker /klúngkər/ *n N Am* a dilapidated old motor vehicle or piece of machinery (*informal*)

clunky /klúngki/ (-ier, -iest) *adj* solid, bulky, or heavy

Cluny lace /klooni-/ *n* a strong white lace made of silk, linen, or cotton [Late 19C. After a town in east-central France]

clupeid /kloopi id/ *n* a soft-finned bony fish that has oily flesh, a narrow body, and a forked tail. Herrings, sardines, and shad are clupeids. Family: Clupeidae. [Late 19C. < modern Latin *Clupeidae* < Latin *clupea*, a small river fish]

cluster /klústər/ *n* 1. DENSE BUNCH a small group of people or things that are closely packed together ○ *a cluster of diamonds* ○ *a little cluster of onlookers* 2. STARS THAT APPEAR NEAR EACH OTHER a group of galaxies or stars that are gravitationally interacting in space and appear to an observer on Earth to be close together 3. GROUP OF CONSONANTS a group of consecutive consonants in the same syllable 4. SUBSET IN STATISTICAL SAMPLE a statistically significant subset within a population, used in sampling 5. CHORD OF THREE OR MORE NOTES a chord consisting of three or more notes spaced a semitone apart 6. *US* DESIGN INDICATING MILITARY AWARDS in the US Army, a small metal design indicating that a medal has been awarded before to the same person 7. GROUP OF BOMBS a group of bombs dropped together 8. SET OF MINES a basic unit of mines used in laying a minefield 9. NETWORK OF SMALL COMPUTERS a network of computers under the control of a larger, more powerful computer ■ *vti* (-ters, -tering, -tered) FORM INTO CLUSTER to gather something into or form a small group [Old English *clyster* < Germanic] —**clustered** *adj* —**clustery** *adj*

cluster analysis *n* a statistical technique that compares multiple characteristics of a population to determine whether individuals fall into different groups

cluster ballooning *n* the sport of piloting a cluster of large helium-filled balloons while sitting in a harness suspended from the balloons —**cluster balloonist** *n*

cluster bomb *n* a canister dropped from an aircraft to release a number of small bombs over a wide area

cluster controller *n* a computer that sorts and files data from smaller computers in a network

cluster headache *n* a severe recurring headache associated with the release of histamine in the bloodstream, and marked by sudden sharp pain behind one eye or nostril

clutch[1] /kluch/ *v* (**clutches, clutching, clutched**) 1. *vt* HOLD SOMETHING TIGHTLY to grip something tightly 2. *vi* MAKE GRABBING MOVEMENT to try to grab hold of something ■ *n* 1. MECHANISM THAT CONNECTS SHAFTS a device that enables two rotating shafts to be connected and disconnected smoothly, especially one in a motor vehicle that transmits power from the engine to the gearbox 2. PEDAL ACTIVATING CLUTCH the pedal that activates the clutch in a motor vehicle 3. GRIP ON SOMETHING a tight grip on something 4. CONTROLLING POWER control and influence (*often used in the plural*) ○ *We were plainly in his clutches.* [14C. Variant of obsolete *clitch* 'to bend, grasp' < Old English *clyccan* 'to grasp']

clutch[2] /kluch/ *n* 1. GROUP OF EGGS LAID TOGETHER the number of eggs laid by a bird at one time 2. GROUP OF CHICKENS HATCHED TOGETHER all the chickens hatched together from one clutch of eggs 3. GROUP OF SIMILAR THINGS a number of similar people or things (*informal*) [Early 18C. Probably variant of dialectal *cletch* < *cleck* 'hatch' < Old Norse *klekja*]

clutch bag *n* a handbag that has no strap or handle and is carried under the arm or in the hand. N Am term **clutch purse**

Clutha /klootha/ the longest river in the South Island, New Zealand. It issues from Lake Wanaka and flows southeastwards, reaching the coast southeast of Balclutha. Length: 336 km/209 mi.

clutter /klúttər/ *n* 1. UNTIDY STUFF an untidy collection of objects 2. DISORGANIZED MESS a condition of disorderliness or overcrowding 3. CONFUSING RADAR IMAGES images on a radar screen that hinder observation ■ *vt* (-ters, -tering, -tered) FILL SOMETHING WITH CLUTTER to make a place untidy or overfilled with objects [Mid-16C. Probably variant of obsolete *clotter* 'clot repeatedly' < CLOT]

Clwyd /kloo id/ former county of Wales from 1974 to 1996

Clyde /klīd/ most important river of Scotland. It flows westwards through Glasgow to the Firth of Clyde, where it joins the Atlantic Ocean. Length: 171 km/106 mi.

Clydebank /klīd bangk/ town in western Scotland, on the north bank of the River Clyde. Population: 29,171 (1991).

Clydesdale /klīdz dayl/ *n* a strong heavy horse belonging to a breed originally developed in Scotland as draught animals [Late 18C. After an area of the River CLYDE]

clype /klīp/ *Scotland* (*informal*) *vi* (**clypes, clyping, clyped**) to inform somebody in authority of another person's wrongdoings as a way of getting that person into trouble ■ *n* somebody willing to inform on another person [Early 18C. Probably variant of obsolete *clepe* 'call' < Old English *clipian*]

clyster /klístər/ *n* MED same as **enema** (*archaic*) [14C. Directly or via French < Latin < Greek *klustēr* 'syringe' < *kluzein* 'wash out']

Clytemnestra /klītəm neestrə/ *n* in Greek mythology, Agamemnon's wife and the queen of Mycenae. Clytemnestra and her lover, Aegisthus, killed Agamemnon on his return from Troy. She was later killed by her son Orestes.

cm[1] *symbol* MEASURE centimetre

cm[2] *abbr* Cameroon (*used in Internet addresses*) See table at **domain name**

Cm *symbol* CHEM ELEM curium

c.m. *abbr* 1. PHYS centre of mass 2. MIL court martial

CMA *abbr* 1. Canadian Medical Association 2. certified medical assistant

Cmdr *abbr* MIL Commander

CMEA *abbr* INTERNAT REL Council for Mutual Economic Assistance

CMG *abbr* Companion of the Order of St Michael and St George

cml *abbr* COMM commercial

c'mon /kəm ón/ *contr* come on (*nonstandard*)

CMOS /see moss/ *abbr* COMPUT complementary metal oxide semi-conductor

CMV *abbr* cytomegalovirus

CMYK *n* the standard model for printing in which all colours are described in terms of the quantity of cyan, magenta, yellow, and black they contain

cn *abbr* China (*used in Internet addresses*) See table at **domain name**

C/N *abbr* 1. INSUR cover note 2. COMM credit note

CNAA *abbr* EDUC Council for National Academic Awards

CNAR *abbr* FIN compound net annual rate

CND *abbr* POL Campaign for Nuclear Disarmament

cnidarian /nī daíri ən/ *n* any invertebrate sea animal that has tentacles surrounding the mouth, e.g. sea anemones, corals, and jellyfishes. Phylum: Cnidaria. [Early 20C. < modern Latin *Cnidaria* < Greek *knidē* 'nettle' < *knizein* 'cause to itch'] —**cnidarian** *adj*

CNN *abbr* BROADCAST Cable News Network

C-note *n US* a one-hundred-dollar note (*informal*)

CNS *abbr* ANAT central nervous system

CORBIS/Michael S. Yamashita
CN Tower, Toronto, Canada

CN Tower *n* a tall tower in central Toronto, Canada. It is more than 553 m/1800 ft high and was the world's tallest free-standing structure when it was built in 1976.

Cnut another spelling of **Canute**

co *abbr* Colombia (*used in Internet addresses*) See table at **domain name**

Co *symbol* CHEM ELEM cobalt

CO *abbr* 1. Colorado 2. Commanding Officer 3. Commonwealth Office 4. conscientious objector

Co. /kō/ *abbr* 1. Colorado 2. Company (*used in names of businesses*) 3. County (*used in placenames*)

co- *prefix* 1. together, jointly ○ *coauthor* 2. associate, alternate ○ *copilot* 3. to the same degree ○ *coeternal* 4. complement of an angle ○ *cotangent* [< Latin, variant of *com-* COM-]

coact *vi*	**coinventor** *n*
coaction *n*	**coinvest** *vt*
coactive *adj*	**coinvestigator** *n*
coactively *adv*	**coinvestor** *n*
coactivity *n*	**comaker** *n*
coactor *n*	**comanage** *vt*
coadminister *vt*	**comanagement** *n*
coadministration *n*	**comanager** *n*
coanchor *n, vti*	**comember** *n*
coauthor *n, vt*	**conominee** *n*
coauthorship *n*	**co-official** *adj*
cocaptain *vt, n*	**co-organize** *vt*
co-chair *n, vt*	**co-organizer** *n*
co-chairman *n*	**co-own** *vt*
co-chairperson *n*	**co-owner** *n*
co-chairwoman *n*	**co-ownership** *n*
cochampion *n*	**copresent** *vt*
cocreate *vt*	**copresenter** *n*
codesign *vt*	**copresident** *n*
codesigner *n*	**coprincipal** *n*
codevelop *vt*	**coprisoner** *n*
codeveloper *n*	**coproduce** *vt*
codirect *v*	**coproducer** *n*
codirector *n*	**coproduction** *n*
codiscover *vt*	**copublish** *vt*
codiscoverer *n*	**copublisher** *n*
codrive *vt*	**corecipient** *n*
codriver *n*	**coregent** *n*
coedit *vt*	**corepressor** *n*
coeditor *n*	**coresearcher** *n*
coemperor *n*	**coruler** *n*
coexecutor *n*	**coscript** *vt*
cofinance *vt*	**cosponsor** *n, vt*
cofound *vt*	**cosponsorship** *n*
cofounder *n*	**cotenant** *n*
cofund *vt*	**cotrustee** *n*
coholder *n*	**cowinner** *n*
cohost *vt, n*	**coworker** *n*
cohostess *n*	**cowrite** *vt*
coinvent *vt*	**cowriter** *n*

c/o *abbr* 1. MAIL care of 2. ACCT carried over

CoA *abbr* BIOL coenzyme A

coacervate /kō ássər vayt/ *n* an aggregate of colloidal droplets bound together by electrostatic forces

coach /kōch/ *n* 1. LONG-DISTANCE BUS a bus designed for long-distance travel or sightseeing 2. HORSE-DRAWN CARRIAGE a large enclosed horse-drawn carriage 3. RAILWAY CARRIAGE a railway carriage 4. SOMEBODY WHO TRAINS SPORTS PLAYERS a trainer of sports players and athletes 5. SOMEBODY WHO TRAINS PERFORMERS a trainer of actors or singers 6. TUTOR somebody who instructs a person in a particular subject 7. TUTOR FOR EXAMINATIONS a private tutor who prepares students for

examinations **8.** *N Am* **INEXPENSIVE TRAVEL CATEGORY** an inexpensive class of passenger accommodation on a bus, train, or aircraft ■ *v* **(coaches, coaching, coached) 1.** *vt* **TRAIN ATHLETE** to train somebody in a sport **2.** *vt* **TRAIN PERFORMER** to train somebody in acting or singing **3.** *vt* **TRAIN STUDENT** to give somebody private instruction in a particular subject or prepare somebody for an examination **4.** *vti* **TRANSPORT PEOPLE IN COACH** to carry passengers in a horse-drawn coach, or travel by coach [Mid-16C. Via French *coche* < German *Kutsche* < Hungarian *kocsi (szekér)* '(wagon) of Kocs' (village in Hungary)] —**coachable** *adj*

SYNONYMS See ***teach***.

coach bolt *n* a bolt for timber with a shank that at one end is square in section with a rounded head. This end grips the timber while the nut is turned by a spanner. N Am term **carriage bolt**

coachbuilder /kṓch bildər/ *n* a person or company that builds the bodies of vehicles such as cars, lorries, or railway carriages —**coachbuilding** *n*

coach-built *adj* made as the body for a vehicle according to an individual specification

coaching /kṓching/ *n* **1.** the training of athletes or performers **2.** training in how to deal with emotional problems and interpersonal relationships

coaching inn *n* a roadside inn, often with stables, that was formerly used by horse-drawn coach services to provide refreshments and accommodation for passengers and to change horses

coachload /kṓch lōd/ *n* the total number of people who are travelling in or who fill a coach ○ *coachloads of tourists*

coachman /kṓchmən/ (*plural* **-men** /-mən/) *n* the driver of a horse-drawn coach or carriage

coach screw *n* a screw with a deep, usually square head

coach station *n* a long-distance bus station

coachwood /kṓch wòod/ (*plural* **-woods** or *same*) *n* a medium-sized tree with a straight trunk, small crown, and white flowers that provides a light versatile wood. Use: cabinetmaking. Native to: Australia. Latin name: *Ceratopetalum apetalum*.

coachwork /kṓch wurk/ *n* the painted bodywork of a road vehicle or railway carriage

coadaptation /kṓ a dap táysh'n/ *n* the mutually advantageous development of characteristics in two or more species of organisms —**coadapted** *adj*

coadjutant /kō ájjətənt/ *n* a helper or assistant (*formal*) —**coadjutant** *adj*

coadjutor /kō ájjòotər/ *n* **1.** a helper (*formal*) **2.** a bishop who assists a diocesan bishop [15C. Via French < late Latin, literally 'helper with' < Latin *adjutor* 'helper' < *adjuvare* 'to help']

coagula MED plural of **coagulum**

coagulant /kō ággyòolənt/ *n* a substance that coagulates blood —**coagulant** *adj*

coagulase /kō ággyòo layz, -layss/ *n* an enzyme produced by some bacteria that causes coagulation of the blood [Early 20C. < COAGULATE]

coagulate *vti* /kō ággyòo layt/ **(-lates, -lating, -lated) 1. MAKE OR BECOME SEMISOLID** to thicken, or cause liquid to thicken, into a soft semisolid mass **2. GROUP TOGETHER IN LARGER MASS** to group together as a mass, or cause the particles in a colloid to group together, as egg white does when heated ■ *n* /kō ággyòolət/ **COAGULATED MASS** a soft semisolid mass produced by the grouping together of the particles of a colloid [15C. < Latin *coagulat-*, past participle of *coagulare* < *coagere* 'drive together'] —**coagulability** /kō ággyòolə bílləti/ *n* —**coagulable** *adj* —**coagulation** /kō ággyòo láysh'n/ *n* —**coagulator** *n*

coagulation factor *n* MED same as **clotting factor**

coagulum /kō ággyòoləm/ (*plural* **-la** /-lə/) *n* a clot or coagulated mass of something, especially blood [Mid-16C. < Latin < *coagulare* (see COAGULATE)]

Coahuila /kṓ ə wéelə/ state in north-central Mexico on the border with Texas. Capital: Saltillo. Population: 2,298,070 (2000). Area: 149,510 sq. km/57,725 sq. mi. Full name **Coahuila de Zaragoza**

coal /kōl/ *n* **1. BLACK ROCK USED AS FUEL** a hard black or dark brown sedimentary rock formed by the decomposition of plant material, widely used as a fuel **2. COAL LUMP** a piece of coal ○ *hot coals* **3. SMALL PIECE OF COMBUSTIBLE MATERIAL** any small piece of combustible material **4.** CHEM same as **charcoal** (sense 1) ■ *v* **(coals, coaling, coaled) 1.** *vt* **CONVERT SOMETHING INTO CHARCOAL** to burn something combustible and convert it into charcoal **2.** *vti* **PROVIDE OR TAKE ON COAL** to supply something with coal, or take on coal [Old English *col* < Indo-European, 'glowing ember'] —**coaly** *adj* ◇ **carry** *or* **take coals to Newcastle** to do something superfluous or supply something that is already plentiful ◇ **haul somebody over the coals** to reprimand somebody severely

coal black *adj* **1.** completely black **2.** very dark black in colour —**coal black** *n*

coaler /kṓlər/ *n* a ship or train that transports coal

coalesce /kṓ ə léss/ **(-lesces, -lescing, -lesced)** *vti* to merge or cause things to merge into a single body or group [Mid-16C. < Latin *coalescere* 'grow up together' < *alescere* 'grow up' < *alere* 'nourish'] —**coalescence** *n* —**coalescent** *adj*

coalface /kṓl fayss/ *n* **1.** the newly exposed rock surface in a mine, from which coal is being cut **2.** the site of physical or practical work, as opposed to management or administration

coalfield /kṓl feeld/ *n* an area with coal deposits

coalfish /kṓl fish/ (*plural same* or **-fishes**) *n* a black-backed or dark-coloured edible fish, e.g. a sablefish or pollack

coal gas *n* **1.** a flammable mixture of gases obtained by distilling coal, consisting mainly of methane and hydrogen. Use: fuel. **2.** the gas produced when coal is burned

coalification /kṓlifi káysh'n/ *n* the process in which coal is formed by the action of pressure and heat on buried plant material. The moisture content of the plants is progressively removed and the material remaining is solidified.

coalition /kṓ ə lísh'n/ *n* **1.** a temporary union between two or more groups, especially political parties **2.** the merging of things into one body or mass [Early 17C. < medieval Latin *coalition-* < Latin *coalit-*, past participle of *coalescere* (see COALESCE)] —**coalitionist** *n*

Coalition *n* in Australia, a long-standing political coalition between the Liberal Party and the National Party

coal measures *npl* a series of strata containing economically workable coal deposits, e.g. the upper Carboniferous rocks of northwestern Europe

coalmine /kṓl mīn/ *n* a mine where coal is dug from the ground —**coalminer** *n* —**coalmining** *n*

coalminer's lung *n* MED same as **anthracosis**

Coalport /kṓl pawrt/ *n* a variety of white, strongly patterned bone china made in Coalport, near Shrewsbury, England, in the 19th century

Coalsack /kṓl sak/ *n* **1.** a dark cloud of interstellar dust **(nebula)**, part of the Crux constellation and visible in the southern hemisphere in front of the Milky Way **2.** a dark interstellar cloud **(nebula)** of the northern hemisphere near the constellation Cygnus

coal scuttle *n* a metal container for holding and pouring coal for a domestic fire

coal tar *n* a thick black liquid. Source: by-product in the production of coke. Use: making dyes, drugs, and soap.

coal-tar pitch *n* a by-product of the distillation of coal tar. Use: making road surfaces, in carbon electrodes, in binding fuel briquettes.

coaming /kṓming/ *n* a raised edging round the cockpit or hatchway of a boat for keeping out water [Early 17C. Origin ?]

coapt /kō ápt/ **(-apts, -apting, -apted)** *v* to join or bring displaced parts close together in their correct alignment, e.g. the edges of a wound or broken bone [Late 16C. < late Latin *coaptare* 'fit together' < Latin *aptus* 'fastened, suitable'] —**coaptation** /kṓ ap táysh'n/ *n*

coarctate /kō áark tayt/ *adj* **1.** MED **CONSTRICTED** describes any vessel or canal in the body that has become constricted, narrowed, or pressed together **2.** ZOOL **IN HARD SHELL** describes a pupa that is enclosed in a horny oval case ■ *vi* **(-tates, -tating, -tated) CONSTRICT** to become narrow, constricted, or pressed together (*refers to blood vessels or other body passages*) [15C. < Latin *coar(c)tat-*, past participle of *coar(c)tare* 'press close together' < *artare* 'press close' < *artus* 'confined, narrow'] —**coarctation** /kō aark táysh'n/ *n*

coarse /kawrss/ **(coarser, coarsest)** *adj* **1. ROUGH** harsh or rough to the touch **2. WITH THICK GRAINS OR STRANDS** consisting of large grains or thick strands **3. INDELICATE OR TASTELESS** lacking taste or refinement **4. VULGAR** vulgar or obscene **5. UNREFINED** not refined ○ *coarse metal* **6. INFERIOR** of inferior quality [14C. Origin ?] —**coarsely** *adv* —**coarseness** *n*

SPELLCHECK coarse or **course**? Do not confuse the spelling of ***coarse*** and ***course***, which sound similar. ***Coarse*** is an adjective meaning 'rough' or 'vulgar', as in *coarse fabric, coarse language*. The word ***course*** is chiefly used as a noun, meaning 'a sequence of events', 'a route', 'a programme of study', 'part of a meal', etc. (as in *a course of action, the course of the river*). It can also be used as a verb, meaning 'run swiftly' or 'hunt with dogs': *Tears coursed down his cheeks.*

coarse fish *n* any freshwater fish that does not belong to the salmon family

coarse fishing *n* the sport of fishing for coarse fish

coarse-grained *adj* **1.** having a large or rough grain **2.** vulgar in speech or manner

coarsen /káwrss'n/ **(-ens, -ening, -ened)** *vti* to become or make something coarse or coarser

coast /kōst/ *n* **1. LAND NEXT TO SEA** land beside the sea ○ *sailed along the coast* **2.** same as **seaside 3.** *N Am* **SLOPE FOR SLEDGING** a slope suitable for sledging ■ *v* **(coasts, coasting, coasted) 1.** *vi* **MOVE BY MOMENTUM** to move forwards by momentum, without applying power **2.** *vi* **SUCCEED EFFORTLESSLY** to progress with very little effort **3.** *vti* **TRAVEL ALONG SHORE** to sail along a shore [14C. Via French < Latin *costa* 'rib, side'] —**coastal** *adj*

coasteering /kōsteéring/ *n* a sporting activity that takes place along a coast and combines scrambling, rock climbing, traversing, swimming, and cliff jumping

coaster /kṓstər/ *n* **1. MAT FOR GLASS** a mat placed under a glass in order to protect a surface **2. SHIP TRADING ALONG COAST** a ship that sails along a coast to trade **3. SOMETHING THAT COASTS** something that coasts of its own momentum **4. TRAY FOR PASSING BOTTLE** a small tray, sometimes on wheels, for passing a bottle or decanter round a table

coastguard /kṓst gaard/ *n* **1.** an emergency service that rescues people in difficulties at sea and acts against smuggling **2.** a member of the coastguard

Coast Guard *n* a US military service that enforces maritime laws, acts in emergencies at sea, and maintains navigational aids, in wartime supplementing the navy

coastline /kṓst līn/ *n* the outline of a coast as viewed from the sea or on a map

Coast Mountains /kṓst-/ Canadian range following the Pacific coast from Vancouver into Yukon Territory. The highest peak is Mount Waddington, 3,994 m/13,104 ft. Length: 1,200 km/750 mi.

Coast Ranges long narrow mountain ranges on the western coast of North America, along the Pacific coast from southern Alaska to northwestern Mexico. Highest peak: Mount Logan 5,959 m/19,551 ft.

coast-to-coast *adj* from one coast to another of a continent or a nation ○ *The debate had coast-to-coast coverage on the news media.*

coastwise /kṓst wīz/ *US adv* along the coast ■ *adj* following the direction of the coast

coat /kōt/ *n* **1. WARM OUTER GARMENT** an item of clothing with long sleeves that is usually at least knee-length and is worn outdoors over other clothes **2.** *NZ, US* **SUIT JACKET** a jacket worn as part of a suit, with a skirt or trousers **3. COVERING ON ANIMAL** the fur, wool, or hair that covers an animal **4. THIN COVERING** any thin layer that covers something ■ *vt* **(coats, coating, coated) 1. COVER SURFACE** to cover a surface with a thin layer of something (*often passive*) **2. GIVE COAT TO SOMEBODY** to provide somebody with a coat (*usually used in the passive*) [14C. < Old French *cote* < Germanic] —**coater** *n*

Coatbridge /kṓt brij/ industrial town in south-central Scotland. Population: 43,617 (1991).

coat check *n N Am* same as **cloakroom** (sense 1)

coat dress *n* a tailored dress that is shaped like a coat and fastened at the front from the neck to the hem, usually with buttons

coated /kṓtid/ *adj* **1.** WITH OUTER LAYER covered with a layer of something **2.** PREPARED FOR WRITING OR PRINTING ON describes paper that is treated with a fine layer of a mineral to make it suitable for writing or printing on **3.** TREATED AGAINST MOISTURE describes fabric with a treated surface or plastic coating that resists moisture

coatee /kṓtee, kō teé/ *n* **1.** a baby's knitted coat **2.** a military cutaway coat with shortened coat-tails

Coates /kōts/, **Joseph Gordon** (1878–1943) New Zealand politician. He held several ministerial posts as a Reform Party politician and was prime minister of New Zealand (1925–28). See table at **prime minister**

coat hanger *n* a curved frame with a hook, used to hang clothes

Coat Hanger *n Aus* Sydney Harbour Bridge (*informal humorous*) [< its shape]

coati /kō aáti/ (*plural* **-tis** or *same*), **coatimundi** /kō aáti moóndi/ (*plural* **-dis** or *same*) *n* a South or Central American omnivorous mammal, related to the raccoon, that has a narrow flexible snout and a striped tail. Genus: *Nasua*. [Early 17C. Via Portuguese < Tupi *kua'ti*]

coating /kṓting/ *n* **1.** a thin layer that covers something ○ *a coating of dust* **2.** cloth used to make coats

coat of arms

coat of arms *n* **1.** a design on a shield that signifies a particular family, university, or city **2.** a garment that is decorated with a coat of arms [Translation of French *cote d'armes*]

coat of mail *n* a protective garment of armour worn in medieval times, consisting of linked metal rings

coat stand *n* a stand with hooks for hanging coats on

coat-tail *n* the part below the waist at the back of a coat, especially one of the parts when it is divided into two (*usually used in the plural*) ◇ **on somebody's coat-tails** helped by somebody else rather than succeeding alone

coax /kōks/ (**coaxes, coaxing, coaxed**) *v* **1.** *vti* PERSUADE GENTLY to persuade somebody gently to do something **2.** *vt* OBTAIN SOMETHING BY GENTLE PERSUASION to get something from somebody by gentle persuasion **3.** *vt* GENTLY MAKE SOMETHING WORK to manipulate something patiently until it moves or works ○ *I finally coaxed the sticky drawers open.* [Late 16C. < obsolete *cokes* 'simpleton', origin ?] —**coaxingly** *adv*

coax cable /kṓ aks-/ *n* ELEC same as **coaxial cable** [Shortening]

coaxial /kō áksi əl/ *adj* **1.** having a common axis **2.** belonging or relating to a coaxial cable —**coaxially** *adv*

coaxial cable *n* a cable consisting of an inner core and an outer flexible braided tube, both of conductive material separated by an insulator, used to transmit high-frequency signals at high speeds

cob[1] /kob/ *n* **1.** CORE OF MAIZE EAR the hard core to which individual kernels of maize are attached **2.** ROUND BREAD a rounded loaf of bread **3.** SHORT-LEGGED RIDING HORSE a sturdy short-legged riding horse **4.** FOOD same as **cobnut 5.** MALE SWAN a male swan **6.** SMALL PIECE a small lump or mass of something hard, especially coal [15C. Origin ?]

cob[2] /kob/ *n* a building material consisting of clay, gravel, and straw [Early 17C. Origin ?]

cob[3] /kob/ *n* a crude often irregularly shaped gold or silver coin that circulated in Spanish colonies in the Americas between the 16th and 18th centuries [Late 17C. < Spanish *cabo de barra* 'end of bar'; from the coin-sized planchets sliced from cast bars]

cobalamin /kə bálləmin/ *n* PHARM same as **vitamin B₁₂** [Mid-20C. Blend of COBALT + VITAMIN]

cobalt /kṓ bawlt, -bolt/ *n* a tough brittle silvery-white metallic element. Source: iron, nickel, copper ores. Use: colouring ceramics, alloys. Symbol **Co**. See table at **element** [Late 17C. < German *Kobalt*, variant of *Kobold* 'harmful goblin'; from miners' belief that cobalt ore was harmful to neighbouring silver ores; originally a trademark]

cobalt 60 /kṓbawlt síksti/ *n* a naturally radioactive isotope of cobalt with a mass number of 60 that spontaneously emits strong gamma radiation. Use: in radiotherapy and industry.

cobalt bloom *n* MINERALS same as **erythrite** [Translation of German *Kobaltblüte*]

cobalt blue *adj* deep greenish-blue in colour —**cobalt blue** *n*

cobalt bomb *n* a device containing cobalt 60, used in radiotherapy

cobaltic /kō báwltik, -ból-/ *adj* relating to or containing cobalt, especially with a valency of three

cobaltite /kō báwl tīt, -ból-/ *n* a rare silvery-white or greyish mineral consisting of cobalt sulphide and arsenide. Use: ceramics.

cobaltous /kō báwltəs, -ból-/ *adj* relating to or containing cobalt, especially with a valency of two

cobber /kóbbər/ *n* ANZ a friend or companion (*dated informal*) [Late 19C. Origin ?]

Cobbett /kóbbit/, **William** (1763–1835) British writer, journalist, and reformer. He wrote *History of the Protestant Reformation* (1824–27) and *Rural Rides* (1830).

> 'To be poor and independent is very nearly an impossibility.'
> [William Cobbett, *Advice to Young Men*; 1829]

cobble[1] /kóbb'l/ *n* **1.** ROADS same as **cobblestone 2.** a naturally rounded rock fragment between 64 and 256 mm/2.5 and 10 in in diameter ▪ *vt* (**-bles, -bling, -bled**) to pave a road with cobblestones [Early 17C. Shortening of COBBLESTONE] —**cobbled** *adj*

cobble together *vt* to assemble or make something roughly and quickly

cobble[2] /kóbb'l/ (**-bles, -bling, -bled**) *vt* to make, mend, or patch footwear [15C. Back-formation < COBBLER[1]]

cobbler[1] /kóbblər/ *n* a maker or mender of footwear [13C. Origin ?]

cobbler[2] /kóbblər/ *n* **1.** a baked fruit dessert with a soft thick crust **2.** an iced drink made of wine, rum or whisky, and sugar, often garnished with fruit and mint [Early 19C. Probably < COBBLER[1]]

cobblers /kóbblərz/ (*slang*) *n* an offensive term for something regarded as nonsense ▪ *npl* an offensive term for a man's testicles [Mid-20C. Shortening of *cobbler's awls*, rhyming slang for *balls* 'testicles']

cobbler's wax *n* a resin used to wax thread

cobblestone /kóbb'l stōn/ *n* a small rounded stone used for paving streets [15C. < COB[1]] —**cobblestoned** *adj*

Cobden /kóbdən/, **Richard** (1804–65) British economist and politician. An outstanding orator and advocate of free trade, he formed, with John Bright, the Anti-Corn Law League (1838).

> 'The progress of freedom depends more upon the maintenance of peace, the spread of commerce, and the diffusion of education, than upon the labours of cabinets and foreign offices.'
> [Richard Cobden, *Speech to Parliament*; 26 June 1850]

cobelligerent /kṓ bə líjjərənt/ *n* a person or country that is an ally in a fight or war

cobia /kṓbi ə/ (*plural same* or **-as**) *n* a large bony dark-striped fish that is related to the perch and sea bass. Native to: tropical and subtropical seas. Latin name: *Rachycentron canadum*. [Mid-19C. Origin ?]

coble /kṓb'l/ *n* N *England, Scotland* a small flat-bottomed boat for fishing, usually used near a coast or in an estuary [Pre-12C. Probably < Celtic]

cobnut /kób nut/ *n* a variety of hazelnut [Mid-16C. Alteration of *cobill nut* < COB[1]]

COBOL /kṓ bol/, **Cobol** *n* a high-level computer programming language widely adopted for corporate business applications [Mid-20C. Acronym < *common business-oriented language*]

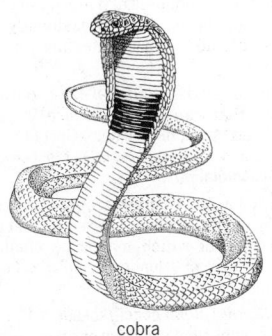

cobra

cobra /kṓbrə/ *n* a venomous snake that, when excited, rears up and spreads the skin behind its head to form a hood. Native to: tropical Asia and Africa. Genera: *Naja* or *Ophiophagus*. [Early 19C. Shortening of *cobra de capello* 'snake with a hood' < Portuguese; *cobra* < Latin *cubra* 'snake']

cobranding /kō bránding/ *n* the display of two or more corporate logos on a product or website in order to give the impression that the product or site is a joint enterprise

coburg /kṓburg/ *n* **1.** a thin fabric made of wool and cotton or silk, twilled on one side. Use: dress fabric, lining cloth. **2.** a round loaf with a cross cut on the top of the dough before baking [Early 19C. After Prince ALBERT of Saxe-*Coburg*]

Coburg /kṓ burg/ city in Bavaria, southeastern Germany, near the Czech border. It was the seat of the Dukes of Saxe-Coburg-Gotha, whose line supplied many of Europe's monarchs. Population: 43,928 (1997).

cobweb /kób web/ *n* **1.** DUSTY SPIDER'S WEB a fine thread or a web of fine threads spun by a spider, especially when covered with dust **2.** SOMETHING LIKE COBWEB something that resembles a cobweb in being flimsy and insubstantial or in acting as a trap or snare ▪ **cobwebs** *npl* SLUGGISH MENTAL STATE mental sluggishness and tiredness ○ *I need to blow the cobwebs away.* [14C. < obsolete *cop* 'spider' < Old English *ātorcoppe*, probably literally 'poison-head'] —**cobwebbed** *adj* —**cobwebby** *adj*

cobweb site *n* a website that has not been updated for a long period of time

coca /kṓkə/ (*plural same*) *n* **1.** the dried leaves of an Andean bush. Use: chewed as a stimulant, processed for cocaine and other alkaloids. **2.** a bush whose leaves yield coca. Native to: Andes. Latin name: *Erythroxylum coca*. [Late 16C. Via Spanish < Aymara *kuka* or Quechua *koka*]

Cocacolonization /kṓkə kollə nī záysh'n/ *n* the spread of western, specifically US, popular culture and commercialism to indigenous societies throughout the world, creating a bland uniformity (*disapproving*) [Mid-20C. < *Coca-Cola*, trademark for a cola-flavoured drink + colonization]

cocaine /kō káyn/ *n* an addictive narcotic drug obtained from the leaves of the coca plant, taken illegally as a stimulant. Formula: $C_{17}H_{21}NO_4$. [Mid-19C. < COCA]

cocainize /kō káy nīz/ (**-izes, -izing, -ized**), **cocainise** (**-ises, -ising, -ised**) *vt* to anaesthetize somebody with a topical application of cocaine in paste form in the nose —**cocainization** /kō kay nī záysh'n/ *n*

cocarcinogen /kṓ kaar sínnəjən, kō kaársin-/ *n* a substance that does not cause cancer on its own but can increase the effect of carcinogenic factors or substances when acting together with them —**cocarcinogenic** /kō kaárssinə jénnik/ *adj*

cocci BIOL plural of **coccus**

coccid /kóksid/ *n* an insect that folds its wings over its back when not flying. Scale insects and mealy

bugs are coccids. Family: Coccidae. [Late 19C. < modern Latin *coccus* (see COCCUS)] —**coccid** *adj*

coccidia ZOOL plural of **coccidium**

coccidioidomycosis /kok síddi óydōmī kőssiss/ *n* a respiratory disease of humans and domestic animals in North America, marked by flu-like symptoms, caused by inhalation of spores from a fungus *Coccidioides immitis*

coccidiosis /kok síddi őssiss/ *n* a disease of domestic animals and birds, and occasionally humans, caused by coccidia in the intestines, and causing diarrhoea

coccidium /kok síddi əm/ (*plural* **-ia** /-i ə/) *n* a parasitic sporozoan that can cause disease in the gut of humans and animals. Order: Coccidia. [Mid-19C. < modern Latin < Greek *kokkid-* 'little berry' < *kokkos* 'berry'] —**coccidial** *adj*

coccolith /kóka lith/ *n* a microscopic calcareous platelet that forms the covering for some marine plankton, one form of which makes up chalk deposits [Mid-19C. < modern Latin *Coccolithus* < Greek *kokkos* 'grain' + *lithos* 'stone']

coccus /kókəss/ (*plural* **cocci** /kóksī/) *n* 1. a spherical or nearly spherical microorganism, especially a bacterium 2. a subdivision of a fruit that contains a single seed and resembles a berry [Early 19C. Via modern Latin < Greek *kokkos* 'grain, berry'] —**coccal** *adj* —**coccoid** *adj* —**coccous** *adj*

-coccus *suffix* a spherical microorganism ○ *pneumococcus* [< COCCUS]

coccyx /kók siks/ (*plural* **-cyges** /-sī jeez/ *or* **-cyxes**) *n* a small triangular bone at the base of the spinal column [Late 16C. Via Latin < Greek *kokkux* 'cuckoo'; from its resemblance to a cuckoo's beak] —**coccygeal** /kok síjji əl/ *adj*

Cochabamba /kócha bámba/ city and capital of Cochabamba Department, central Bolivia, situated northeast of Oruro. Population: 560,284 (1997).

co-channel /kō chán'l/ *adj* relating to a transmission occupying the same frequency band as another

Cochin /kő chin/ major port in Kerala State, southwestern India. Population: 1,355,406 (2001).

cochineal /kóchi neel/ *n* a red dye obtained from the crushed dried bodies of female cochineal insects. Use: food colouring, fabric dye. [Late 16C. < French *cochenille* or Spanish *cochinilla* < Latin *coccinus* 'scarlet' < Greek *kokkos* 'berry', because the dried body of the insect was believed to be a berry]

cochineal insect *n* a small red scale insect that feeds on cacti. Native to: Mexico, Caribbean. Latin name: *Coccus cacti*.

Cochise /kō chéess, -chéez/ (1815?–74) Chiricahua Apache leader. He led fighting against white settlers in Arizona Territory (1862–71).

cochlea /kókli ə/ (*plural* **-ae** /-ī, -ee/ *or* **-as**) *n* a spiral structure in the inner ear that looks like a snail shell and contains tiny hair cells whose movement is interpreted by the brain as sound [Mid-16C. Via Latin *coc(h)lea* 'snail shell, screw' < Greek *kokhlias*] —**cochlear** *adj* —**cochleate** /-li ət, -ayt/ *adj*

cochlear implant *n* a device implanted under the skin that picks up sounds and converts them to impulses transmitted to electrodes placed in the cochlea, restoring some hearing to people with a hearing impairment

Cochran /kókrən/, **Jacqueline** (1910–80) US aviator. She was the first woman pilot to break the sound barrier (1953).

cock /kok/ *n* 1. ADULT MALE CHICKEN an adult male of a domestic fowl, usually only kept for breeding. Cocks have a distinctive crowing call. 2. MALE BIRD the adult male of a bird 3. MALE ANIMAL an adult male salmon, crab, or lobster 4. WEATHERCOCK a weathercock 5. ARMS PART OF GUN the hammer of a gun that, when released by the action of the trigger, makes the gun fire 6. ARMS RAISED POSITION OF HAMMER OF GUN the raised position of the hammer of a gun when it is ready to fire 7. CONSTR same as **stopcock** 8. TILTED POSITION the tilt or angle in the position of somebody's head or hat, often suggesting that he or she is in a good mood 9. TABOO TERM a highly offensive term for a man's penis (*taboo*) 10. *regional* CHUM OR MATE used as a friendly or familiar way of addressing a man, especially among Cockneys (*dated informal*) 11. NONSENSE something considered to be nonsense (*dated*

informal) ■ *vt* (**cocks, cocking, cocked**) 1. ARMS PREPARE GUN FOR FIRING to pull back the hammer of a gun so that it is ready to be fired when the trigger is pulled 2. TURN EAR OR EYES to turn an ear or one or both eyes in a particular direction in order to listen for or look out for somebody or something 3. TILT OR ANGLE SOMETHING to tilt or raise something to one side 4. RAISE LIMB IN AIR to lift or raise a part of the body 5. SET SOMETHING TO OPERATE to set a device or mechanism so that it will release something such as a camera shutter [Pre-12C. Probably < medieval Latin *coccus*, an imitation of a cock's crow]

cockabully /kóka bŏoli/ (*plural* **-lies**) *n* NZ any small freshwater fish (*used especially by children*) [Late 19C. < Maori *kokopu*, partly after BULLY [3]]

cockade /ko káyd/ *n* a rosette, ribbon, or other ornament worn, usually on a hat, as an identifying badge or as part of a livery [Mid-17C. < French *bonnet à la coquarde* 'bonnet worn proudly' < obsolete *coquard* 'proud' < *coq* 'cock'] —**cockaded** *adj*

cock-a-doodle-doo /-dŏo/ *n* used as a description or imitation of the sound a cock makes when it crows —**cock-a-doodle-doo** *vi*

cock-a-hoop *adj* 1. extremely happy or excited about something 2. boastful about something that has been achieved [< *set the cock on the hoop* 'celebrate']

cock-a-leekie /-leeki/, **cockieleekie** /kóki leeki/ *n* a Scottish soup made from a whole chicken and leeks and sometimes containing prunes

cockamamie /kóka maymi/, **cockamamy** *adj* N Am not making any sense or lacking plausibility (*informal*) ○ *a cockamamie excuse* [Mid-20C. Probably alteration of DECALCOMANIA]

cock-and-bull story, **cock-and-bull** *n* a ridiculous and scarcely credible story that somebody tries to convince people is true [Origin ?]

cockatiel /kóka teel/, **cockateel** *n* a small grey parrot with a white patch on its wing and a prominent crest that is yellow in males. Native to: Australia. Latin name: *Nymphicus hollandicus*. [Late 19C. < Dutch *kaktielje*, probably diminutive of *kaketoe* (see COCKATOO)]

cockatoo

cockatoo /kóka tŏo/ (*plural* **-toos**) *n* 1. a parrot with a prominent crest, often with white or light-coloured feathers. Native to: Australia, New Guinea, South and Southeast Asia. Family: Cacatuidae. 2. *Aus* a farmer, especially one with a small farm [Mid-17C. Via Dutch *kaketoe* < Malay *kakatua*; influenced by COCK]

cockatrice /kóka tríss/ *n* a mythological serpent that was supposed to have hatched from a cock's egg and to be able to kill with its stare [14C. Via Old French *cocatris* < medieval Latin *calcatrix* 'tracker' < Latin *calcare* 'to track' < *calx* 'heel']

Cockayne /ko káyn/, **Leonard** (1855–1934) British-born New Zealand botanist. He was a pioneer of field botany and ecology.

cockboat /kók bōt/ *n* a small rowing boat, especially one that belongs to a larger ship. Cockboats are often used to ferry stores and provisions between ship and shore. [15C. *Cock* via Old French *coque* < Latin *codex* 'block of wood']

cockchafer /kók chayfər/ *n* a large European beetle with larvae that destroy trees and other plants. Family: Scarabaeidae.

cockcrow /kók krō/ *n* the time of day when the sun begins to show above the horizon (*archaic or literary*)

cocked hat /kokt-/ *n* a two- or three-cornered hat with a wide turned-up brim that was popular in the

18th century, especially as part of a uniform or livery ◇ **knock somebody** *or* **something into a cocked hat** to be much better than somebody or something else (*informal*)

cocker[1] /kókər/ *n* 1. BREED same as **cocker spaniel** 2. somebody involved in cockfighting either as a breeder or trainer of cocks, or as a regular spectator [Late 17C. < COCK]

cocker[2] /kókər/ *n* used to refer to a close friend (*informal*) ■ *vt* (**-ers, -ering, -ered**) to treat somebody in an excessively protective or indulgent way (*archaic*) [15C. Origin ?]

cockerel /kókərəl/ *n* a young male chicken, usually one that is less than a year old [15C. < COCK + diminutive suffix]

Cockerell /kókərəl/, **Sir Christopher** (1910–99) British radio and marine engineer. His experiments (1953–59) led to the invention of the hovercraft. Full name **Cockerell, Sir Christopher Sydney**

cocker spaniel *n* a small dog with long floppy ears and a soft wavy coat, belonging to a breed of spaniel originally developed for flushing out game [< WOODCOCK]

cockeye /kók ī/ *n* an offensive term for an eye that is turned inwards or outwards from the nose so that parallel vision is impossible

cockeyed /kók īd/ *adj* 1. FOOLISH not sensible or properly thought out (*informal*) 2. NOT ALIGNED positioned at an awkward or crooked angle 3. OFFENSIVE TERM an offensive term meaning having one eye that turns inwards or outwards from the nose 4. VERY DRUNK so drunk that it is impossible to see straight (*informal*)

cock feather *n* the feather on an arrow positioned at right-angles to the notch into which the bow string fits [< COCK 'stick up']

cockfight /kók fīt/ *n* an organized fight between two cocks, each of which is fitted with sharp metal spurs, in front of spectators who often make bets on the outcome

cockfighting /kók fīting/ *n* the practice of setting two cocks to fight each other in front of spectators who often make bets on the outcome. The sport is illegal in many countries.

cockhorse /kók hawrss/ *n* a rocking horse, or a stick with an imitation horse's head on one end

cockie *n* Aus AGRIC another spelling of **cocky**[2] (*informal*) [Late 19C. Shortening of COCKATOO]

cockieleekie *n* FOOD another spelling of **cock-a-leekie**

cockle[1] /kók'l/ *n* 1. SHELLFISH WITH HEART-SHAPED SHELL an invertebrate sea animal with a small rounded or heart-shaped ridged shell in two parts. Family: Cardiidae. 2. *also* **cockleshell** MARINE BIOL SHELL OF COCKLE the small rounded or heart-shaped ridged shell in two parts that a cockle lives in 3. *also* **cockleshell** SMALL BOAT a small lightweight boat 4. WRINKLE a crease or pucker in a piece of material such as paper or cloth ■ *vti* (**-les, -ling, -led**) BECOME OR MAKE WRINKLED to become wrinkled or puckered, or make something such as a piece of material wrinkled or puckered [14C. Via French *coquille* 'shell' < medieval Greek *kokhulion* < Greek *kogkhē* 'conch'] ◇ **warm the cockles of your heart** to give you a feeling of wellbeing or sentimental contentment

cockle[2] /kók'l/ *n* a weedy plant that belongs to the pink family, especially the corn cockle, which grows in cornfields [Pre-12C. Origin ?]

cockleboat /kók'l bōt/ *n* same as **cockboat** [Early 17C. < COCKLE[1]]

cocklebur /kók'l bur/ *n* a coarse annual plant with prickly seed husks that attach easily to people's clothes or animals' fur. Genus: *Xanthium*. [Mid-19C. < COCKLE[2]]

cockleshell /kók'l shel/ *n* MARINE BIOL same as **cockle**[1] *n* (senses 2–3)

cockloft /kók loft/ *n* a small room beneath the roof of a building

cockney /kókni/ (*plural* **-neys**) *n* 1. *also* **Cockney** SOMEBODY FROM LONDON'S EAST END somebody born in London, traditionally within a two-mile radius of the bells of St Mary-le-Bow church in London's East End. Cockneys are considered to be the 'true' Londoners. 2. *also* **Cockney** LONDON DIALECT the accent or dialect of native Londoners from the East End 3. *Aus* FISH YOUNG AUSTRALIAN SNAPPER a young snapper. Native to:

Australia. Latin name: *Chrysophrys guttulatus.* [14C. < *coken,* obsolete genitive plural of COCK + obsolete *ey* 'egg' < Old English *æg* < Germanic] —**cockneyism** *n*

cock-of-the-rock (*plural* **cocks-of-the-rock**) *n* a bird, the male of which has bright orange or red feathers and a crest that extend over the beak. Native to: tropical South America. Genus: *Rupicola.* [Because it nests on rocks]

cockpit /kók pit/ *n* **1.** AVIAT PILOT'S PART OF AIRCRAFT the compartment in an aircraft or spacecraft where the pilot and other crew members sit **2.** MOTOR SPORTS AREA FOR DRIVER IN RACING CAR a space for the driver in a racing car **3.** NAUT ENCLOSURE FOR WHEEL OR TILLER an enclosure at the stern of a boat for the wheel or tiller **4.** SPORTS PLACE FOR COCKFIGHTING an enclosed place where cockfights are held **5.** MIL FREQUENT BATTLEGROUND a place where many battles have been fought

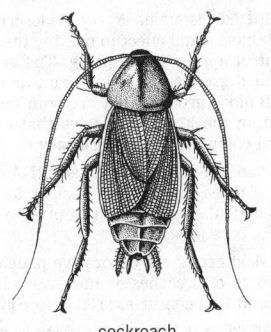
cockroach

cockroach /kók rōch/ *n* a nocturnal insect with a flat oval body, long antennae, and chewing mouthparts, some species of which are household pests. Order: Blattodea. [Early 17C. By folk etymology < Spanish *cucaracha*]

cockscomb /kóks kōm/ *n* **1.** the red fleshy crest that grows on the top of a domestic cock's head **2.** a tropical plant often grown as a houseplant. Flowers: orange or red, appearing as a broad crest or plume resembling a cockscomb. Latin name: *Celosia cristata.* **3.** FASHION another spelling of **coxcomb** (sense 1)

cockshot /kók shot/ *n* LEISURE same as **cockshy** (sense 2) (*dated*)

cockshy /kók shī/ (*plural* **-shies**) *n* (*dated*) **1.** a target or mark for throwing things at in a contest **2.** a throw at a cockshy [Early 19C. Because a cock was formerly the target and prize]

cockspur /kók spur/ *n* a spur on the foot of some male birds

cocksucker /kóksukə/ *n* (*taboo offensive insult*) **1.** a highly offensive term of abuse for a man **2.** a highly offensive term for somebody who performs fellatio

cocksure /kok shoór, -sháwr/ *adj* arrogantly confident and self-assured [Early 16C. < **cock**, euphemism for 'God'] —**cocksurely** *adv* —**cocksureness** *n*

cockswain *n* ROWING another spelling of **coxswain**

cocktail /kók tayl/ *n* **1.** MIXED BEVERAGE a drink that is made up of a mixture of different beverages such as fruit juice or soda and usually alcohol, and served iced or chilled **2.** LIGHT SNACK a light appetizer before a main meal, consisting usually of seafood or fruit served with a sauce (*usually used in combination*) ○ *a prawn cocktail* **3.** MIXTURE OF THINGS a mixture of different features or things ○ *a malicious cocktail of lies and gossip* **4.** MED COMBINATION TREATMENT a combination of two or more drugs or therapeutic agents given as a single treatment ■ **cocktails** *npl* GATHERING TO CONSUME ALCOHOLIC BEVERAGES a gathering where alcoholic beverages are consumed, sometimes with light snacks, often early in the evening before another social event ■ *adj* SMALL small and designed to be eaten as a snack with the fingers or on a cocktail stick ○ *cocktail sausage* [Early 17C. < COCK]

cocktail cabinet *n* a cabinet or cupboard in which alcoholic and other drinks are kept. N Am term **liquor cabinet**

cocktail cabinet game, **cocktail game** *n* a type of early computer arcade game housed in a table with the graphics on a screen in the table-top, and played sitting down

cocktail dress *n* a short dress, often of expensive fabric and semiformal design, worn for an early-evening social occasion such as a cocktail party

cocktail lounge *n* a bar, sometimes a room in a large hotel, where cocktails and other drinks are served

cocktail party *n* a party where cocktails and light snacks are served, often taking place early in the evening before another social event

cocktail shaker *n* a metal container used for mixing different, usually alcoholic, drinks with ice

cocktail stick *n* a small pointed wooden or plastic stick on which olives or cherries are placed in cocktails, or on which small items of food such as sausages or cubes of cheese are served

cock-teaser, **cock-tease** *n* a highly offensive term for somebody who makes sexual advances towards a man without intending to have sex with him (*taboo*)

cockup /kók up/ *n* a blunder or an instance of mismanagement (*informal*)

cocky[1] /kóki/ (**-ier, -iest**) *adj* arrogantly confident and sure of yourself (*informal*) —**cockily** *adv* —**cockiness** *n*

cocky[2] /kóki/ *n Aus* AGRIC same as **cockatoo** (sense 2) (*informal*) [Late 19C. Shortening of COCKATOO]

coco /kố kō/ *n* PLANTS, FOOD same as **coconut** [Mid-16C. < Spanish *coco,* Portuguese *côco,* literally 'grinning face'; from the appearance of the base of the shell]

cocoa /kốkō/ *n* **1.** BROWN POWDER FOR MAKING CHOCOLATE an unsweetened brown powder made from roasted and ground cocoa beans. Use: making chocolate, cooking, hot drink. **2.** HOT DRINK MADE WITH COCOA POWDER a hot drink made with milk or water, cocoa powder, and often sugar **3.** BROWN COLOUR a light to medium brown colour [Early 18C. Alteration of CACAO]

cocoa bean *n* the bean-shaped seed of the cacao tree. Use: making cocoa powder and chocolate.

cocoa butter *n* a thick oily solid obtained from cocoa beans. Use: making chocolate, in cosmetics and suntan oils.

cocoanut *n* FOOD another spelling of **coconut**

cocoa-payol /kốkō pay ól/ *n Carib* somebody of Spanish, usually Venezuelan, ancestry (*informal*) [Early 19C. *Payol* < Spanish *español* 'Spanish']

coco-de-mer /kốkō də máir/ *n* (*plural* **cocos-de-mer** /*pronunc. same*/) *n* **1.** a fan palm, now found only in nature reserves in the Seychelles, that produces the largest seed in the world. Latin name: *Lodoicea maldivica.* **2.** the edible two-lobed fruit of a coco-de-mer palm [Early 19C. < French, 'coco from the sea'; because first known from nuts found floating in the sea]

coconut

coconut /kốkə nut/ *n* (*plural same* or **-nuts**), **cocoanut** *n* **1.** the fruit of the coconut palm, consisting of a hard fibrous husk around a single-seeded nut with firm white flesh that is eaten raw or dried to make copra and a hollow core containing sweet-tasting liquid (**coconut milk**). Use: husk: matting, compost. **2.** the sweet white flesh of the coconut fruit, used widely in cooking and confectionery in the form of small dried flakes **3.** TREES same as **coconut palm 4.** same as **baldhead** (sense 2) (*slang offensive; used in Black English*)

coconut butter *n* solidified coconut oil used in the manufacture of soap and candles

coconut crab *n* a large hermit crab that burrows in the ground and can climb trees. Native to: islands of Pacific and Indian Oceans. Latin name: *Birgus latro.*

coconut matting *n* coarse floor matting made from the fibres that grow on coconut shells

coconut milk *n* the sweet watery juice that is contained within a coconut and is used in drinks and cookery

coconut oil *n* a thick sweet-smelling oil extracted from the flesh of the coconut and used widely in food and cosmetics

coconut palm *n* a tall tropical palm tree with large fruits (**coconuts**). Use: beverages, oil, fibre, utensils, thatch. Latin name: *Cocos nucifera.*

coconut shy (*plural* **coconut shies**) *n* a traditional fairground game or stall at which coconuts are balanced on stands and people have to try to knock them off by throwing balls at them

cocoon /kə koón/ *n* **1.** ZOOL SHEATH FOR CATERPILLAR the silky covering with which a caterpillar or other insect larva encloses itself during its transition to an adult state **2.** ZOOL EGG COVERING a protective covering on the eggs of spiders, leeches, and other invertebrates **3.** ZOOL SHEATH FOR SPIDER'S PREY a sheath in which spiders wrap their prey **4.** INDUST COVERING THAT PROTECTS SOMETHING FROM WATER a cover or protective spray used to seal machinery and make it waterproof, especially military equipment when in storage or transport **5.** SOMETHING SIMILAR TO COCOON something that resembles a cocoon in the way that it provides protection or a sense of safety ■ *v* (**-coons, -cooning, -cooned**) **1.** *vt* WRAP SOMEBODY OR SOMETHING SAFELY to cover or envelop somebody or something in order to provide warmth or protection ○ *cocooned in a pile of bedclothes* **2.** *vt* KEEP SOMEBODY SAFE FROM SOMETHING to protect somebody from unpleasantness or danger **3.** *vi N Am* WITHDRAW INTO PRIVACY to withdraw into a state of personal privacy in order to escape stressful everyday life (*informal*) [Late 17C. < French *cocon* < Latin *coccus* 'berry' (see COCCUS)] —**cocooned** *adj*

coco plum *n* a tropical tree, cultivated for its edible fruit that is usually eaten preserved and, in West Africa, for an oil obtained from its seeds. Native to: tropical America and Africa. Latin name: *Chrysobalanus icaco.*

Cocos Islands /kốkəss-/ group of 27 small islands in the Indian Ocean that belong to Australia, situated approximately 930 km/580 mi. southwest of Java. Population: 595 (1993). Area: 14 sq. km/6 sq. mi.

cocotte /kə kót/ *n* **1.** a promiscuous woman or prostitute (*literary*) **2.** a heat-proof dish in which food can be cooked and served in small portions [Early 20C. Alteration of French *cocasse* < Latin *cucuma* 'cooking-pot']

co-counselling *n* a form of counselling in which participants receive training as counsellors and work alternately as counsellor and client

cocoyam /kốkō yam/ *n* (*plural same* or **-yams**) *n* a plant with edible tubers. Native to: western Africa. Genus: *Colocasia.* [Early 20C. Probably < COCO 'tarot root' (in Caribbean English)]

AKG London

Jean Cocteau

Cocteau /kóktō/, **Jean** (1889–1963) French writer and film director. His works include the novel *Les Enfants terribles* (1929) and the film *La Belle et la bête* (1945).

'Mirrors would do well to reflect a bit more before throwing back images.'
[Jean Cocteau, 'Des beaux-arts considérés comme un assassinat (On the arts considered as an act of murder)', *Essai de*

critique indirecte (Essay of Indirect Criticism); 1932]

cocurricular /kókə ríkyŏŏlər/ *adj US* not forming part of the official curriculum but complementing it

cocuswood /kókəss wŏŏd/ (*plural same*) *n* **1.** a hard wood that turns black with age. Use: musical instruments, backs of brushes, inlays. **2.** a tree that yields cocuswood. Native to: Caribbean. Latin name: *Brya ebenus*. [Mid-17C. Origin ?]

Cocytus /kō kítəss, -sítəss/ *n* in Greek mythology, one of the tributaries of the River Styx that flowed through the underworld [< Greek *Kōkutos*, literally 'wailing']

cod[1] /kod/ (*plural same* or **cods**) *n* **1.** SALTWATER FOOD FISH a saltwater fish that has three dorsal fins and slender feelers like whiskers (**barbels**) on its jaw, and lives close to the seabed. Family: Gadidae. **2.** COD AS FOOD the flesh of a cod used as food **3.** AUSTRALIAN FISH a fish similar to cod, e.g. blue cod or Murray cod [14C. Origin ?]

cod[2] /kod/ *n* (*archaic*) **1.** a bag **2.** the sac of skin that contains the testes of a male mammal [Old English *cod(d)* < Germanic]

cod[3] /kod/ *Ireland n* an offensive term for somebody regarded as mildly unintelligent or silly ■ *vti* (**cods, codding, codded**) to joke or play a trick on somebody [Late 17C. Origin ?]

Cod, Cape /kod/ peninsula in the southeastern part of the US state of Massachusetts. One of the prime tourist destinations of New England, it is between 2 km/1 mi. and 32 km/20 mi. wide and about 105 km/65 mi. long.

COD *abbr* MAIL cash on delivery

coda /kódə/ *n* **1.** in some pieces of music, a final section that adds dramatic energy to the work as a whole, usually through intensified rhythmic activity **2.** an additional section at the end of a text such as a literary work or speech that is not necessary to its structure but gives additional information [Mid-18C. Via Italian < Latin *cauda* 'tail']

coddle /kódd'l/ (**-dles, -dling, -dled**) *vt* **1.** to treat somebody in an excessively protective and indulgent way **2.** to cook an egg in water just below the boiling point [Late 16C. Origin ?] —**coddler** *n*

code /kōd/ *n* **1.** SYSTEM OF LETTERS, NUMBERS, OR SYMBOLS a system of letters, numbers, or symbols into which normal language is converted to allow information to be communicated secretly, briefly, or electronically **2.** INFORMATION SYSTEM OF LETTERS OR NUMBERS a system of letters or numbers that gives information about something such as postal or telephone areas **3.** COMPUT COMPUTER INFORMATION a system of symbols, numbers, or signals that conveys information to a computer **4.** LAW, PUBLIC ADMIN RULES AND REGULATIONS a system of accepted laws and regulations that govern procedure or behaviour in particular circumstances or within a particular profession ○ *the penal code* **5.** WAY OF BEHAVING a set of unwritten rules concerning acceptable standards of behaviour ○ *moral code* ■ *v* (**codes, coding, coded**) **1.** *vt* PUT SOMETHING IN CODE to put a message or text into code **2.** *vt* COMPUT WRITE COMPUTER PROGRAM to write a computer program that provides instructions to a computer **3.** *vi* GENETICS PROVIDE GENETIC INFORMATION to act as or provide the genetic information that enables a polypeptide, RNA molecule, or one of their constituent groups to be produced (*refers to codons or genes*) [Late 16C. < Latin *codex* 'block of wood, book, set of statutes'] —**coder** *n*

code blue, **Code Blue** *n US* a medical emergency, especially in a hospital, when a patient's heart stops beating or his or her lungs stop functioning

codebook /kódbŏŏk/ *n* a book containing a key to a code or codes

codec /kó dek/ *n* a piece of equipment that codes and decodes electronic signals [Late 20C. < shortenings of CODE, DECODE]

codefendant /kó di féndənt/ *n* one of two or more people who are defending a legal charge or claim in a court of law

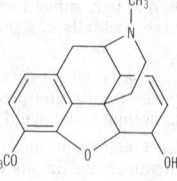

codeine

codeine /kó deen/ *n* an opiate drug. Use: to relieve pain and coughing. Formula: $C_{18}H_{21}NO_3$. [Mid-19C. < Greek *kōdeia* 'poppy head']

code name *n* a name used to disguise the identity or nature of somebody or something such as a military operation —**code-name** *vt*

Code Napoléon /kód na pố lay óN/ *n* the codification of French laws drawn up under Napoleon between 1804 and 1810 and forming the basis of modern French civil law

cod end *n* the narrow end of a purse seine or other trawl net for commercial fishing [< COD[2]]

code of conduct *n* a set of unwritten rules according to which people in a particular group, class, or situation are supposed to behave

code of practice *n* a set of rules according to which people in a particular profession are expected to behave

codependency /kódi péndənsi/, **codependence** /-dənss/ *n* **1.** the dependence of two people, groups, or organisms on each other, especially when this reinforces mutually harmful behaviour patterns **2.** a situation in which a person such as the partner of an alcoholic or a parent of a drug-addicted child needs to feel needed by the other person —**co-dependent** *n, adj*

code red *interj, n* used to indicate that a difficult or dangerous situation has deteriorated drastically so as to constitute an emergency

code-sharing *n* an arrangement between two airlines in which they both sell seats on a flight using their own flight numbers

codetermination /kódi túrmi náysh'n/ *n* cooperation between management and employees in making decisions

code word *n* **1.** SECRET WORD IDENTIFYING SOMEBODY OR SOMETHING a secret word or phrase that is used to identify a person, operation, or organization whose true identity is to be kept hidden **2.** SECRET PASSWORD a secret word or phrase that is used as a password in a secret operation **3.** EUPHEMISM a word or phrase used to describe something in a euphemistic way ○ *corporate re-engineering is often just a code word for layoffs*

codex /kó deks/ (*plural* **-dices** /-di seez/) *n* a collection of ancient manuscript texts, especially of the Biblical Scriptures, in book form [Late 16C. < Latin, 'block of wood, book, set of statutes']

Codex Juris Canonici /kó deks jŏŏriss kə nónni sī/ *n* the official code of canon law of the Roman Catholic Church since 1918, when it replaced the Corpus Juris Canonici. It was revised in 1983. [< ecclesiastical Latin, 'code of canon law']

codfish /kódfish/ (*plural same* or **-fishes**) *n* FISH same as **cod**[1] (sense 1)

codger /kójjər/ *n* a man, especially a man of advanced years who is seen as slightly eccentric or amusing (*informal insult*) [Mid-18C. Origin ?]

codices LITERAT, ANCIENT HIST plural of **codex**

codicil /kódissil/ *n* **1.** an additional part of a will that either modifies it or revokes part of it **2.** an appendix or supplement to a text (*formal*) [15C. < Latin *codicillus*, diminutive of *codex* 'block of wood, book, set of statutes'] —**codicillary** /kódi sílləri/ *adj*

codicology /kódi kólləji/ *n* the study of manuscripts [Mid-20C. < French *codicologie* < Latin *codic-* 'book'] —**codicological** /kódikə lójjik'l/ *adj*

codify /kódi fī/ (**-fies, -fying, -fied**) *vt* to arrange things, especially laws, rules, or principles, into an organized system or code —**codification** /kódifi káysh'n/ *n* —**codifier** *n*

coding theory /kóding/ *n* the branch of mathematics that applies algebra and number theory to the development of ways of representing information in computer systems and data transmission networks

codling /kódling/ (*plural* **-lings** or *same*) *n* a small or young cod

codling moth, **codlin moth** /kóddlin-/ *n* a small moth with a thick body whose larvae feed on apples, pears, and other fruit. Latin name: *Laspeyresia pomonella*.

cod-liver oil *n* an oil rich in vitamins A and D that is extracted from the liver of the cod and is often used as a food supplement

codominant /kō dómminənt/ *adj* **1.** describes genes that each have equal effect in making the character they control appear in offspring. The genes for A and B blood groups are codominant and give rise to the AB blood group if they are both inherited. **2.** determining the kinds of species that exist in an ecological community —**codominance** *n*

codon /kó don/ *n* a unit in messenger RNA consisting of a set of three consecutive nucleotides that specifies a particular amino acid in protein synthesis [Mid-20C. < CODE + -ON[1]]

codpiece /kód peess/ *n* a decorative pouch attached to the crotch of breeches or hose worn by men in the 15th and 16th centuries [15C. < COD[2]]

codswallop /kódz woləp/ *n, interj* same as **nonsense** (sense 1) (*dated informal*) [Mid-20C. Origin ?]

Cody /kódi/, **William Frederick** (1846–1917) US scout and entertainer. He sometimes worked as an army scout in the Western territories, and earned his nickname by killing thousands of buffalo to feed railway workers in the 1860s. From 1883 to 1913 he toured with his own 'Wild West Show'. Known as **Buffalo Bill**

Coe /kō/, **Sebastian, Lord** (*b.* 1956) British athlete and politician. He broke eight world middle-distance track records and was a Conservative MP (1992–97).

co-ed /kó ed/ *adj* EDUCATING MEN AND WOMEN TOGETHER with both male and female students (*informal*) ■ *n* **1.** *N Am* WOMAN AT MIXED COLLEGE a female student who attends a college or university where men and women are educated together (*dated informal*) **2.** SCHOOL FOR BOTH SEXES a school where boys and girls are educated together (*informal*) [Late 19C. Shortening of co-educational]

coedition /kó i dish'n/ *n* a book published by two or more publishers jointly

coeducation /kó eddyŏŏ káysh'n/ *n* the education of both sexes together —**coeducational** *adj* —**coeducationally** *adv*

coef. /kó if/ *abbr* coefficient

coefficient /kó i físh'nt/ *n* **1.** the number placed before a letter that represents a variable in algebra, e.g. the '3' of '3x' in the equation '3x = 6' **2.** a numerical constant that is a measure of a property of a substance [Mid-17C. < modern Latin *coefficient-* 'combining to produce a result' < Latin *efficient-* (see EFFICIENT)]

coefficient of correlation *n* MATHS same as **correlation coefficient**

coefficient of expansion *n* the change in length or area of a material per unit length or unit area that accompanies a change in temperature of one degree

coefficient of friction *n* the ratio of the force needed to make two surfaces slide over each other to the force that holds them together. Symbol μ

-coel *suffix* cavity, chamber ○ *pseudocoel* [Via modern Latin *-coela* < Greek *koilos* 'hollow' < Indo-European]

coelacanth /séelə kanth/ *n* a large fish that varies from bright blue to brownish and has fleshy lobes at the base of its fins and a three-lobed tail. Coelacanths were thought to have been extinct for 70 million years until a living species was discovered in 1938 off the east coast of Africa. Native to: Indian Ocean. Latin name: *Latimeria chalumnae*. Illustration on next page [Mid-19C. < modern Latin *Coelacanthus* < Greek *koilos* 'hollow' + *akantha* 'spine'; because its fins have hollow spines] —**coelacanthine** /séelə kán thin/ *adj* —**coelacanthous** *adj*

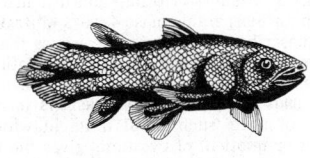

coelacanth

-coele *suffix* same as **-coel**

coelentera ZOOL plural of **coelenteron**

coelenterate /si léntə rayt/ *n* ZOOL same as **cnidarian** [Late 19C. < modern Latin *Coelenterata* < Greek *koilos* 'hollow' + *enteron* 'intestine'] —**coelenteric** /seè len térrik/ *adj*

coelenteron /si léntə ron/ (*plural* **-tera** /-tərə/) *n* the internal body cavity of an invertebrate sea animal (**coelenterate**)

coeliac /seèli ak/ *adj* relating to, involving, or contained in the abdomen [Mid-17C. Via Latin < Greek *koiliakos* < *koilia* 'abdomen' < *koilos* 'hollow']

coeliac disease *n* a disorder caused by a sensitivity to gluten that makes the digestive system unable to deal with fat. Symptoms include diarrhoea and anaemia.

coelom /seèləm, -lōm/ (*plural* **-loms** or **-lomata** /si lōmətə/) *n* the cavity between the body wall and the gut of many animals, formed when the embryonic mesoderm is divided into two layers [Late 19C. Via German *Koelom* < Greek *koilōma* 'a hollow'] —**coelomic** /si lómmik/ *adj*

coelomate /seèlə mayt, si lōmit/ *adj* having a cavity between the body wall and the digestive tract —**coelomate** *n*

coelostat /seèlə stat/ *n* an instrument with a mirror that rotates parallel to the Earth's axis in order to reflect light from an astronomical object onto a second mirror aimed at a fixed telescope [Late 19C. < Latin *caelum* 'sky']

coemption /kō émpsh'n/ *n* the purchase of all available supplies of a particular commodity [14C. < Latin *coemption-* 'buying up' < *emere* 'take, buy']

Coen /koon/, **Jan Pieterszoon** (1587–1629) Dutch colonial administrator. He secured the East Indies for Holland and founded its capital in Batavia, present-day Jakarta (1619).

coen- *prefix* same as **coeno-** (*used before vowels*)

coeno- *prefix* general, common ◇ *coenocyte* [< Greek *koinos* < Indo-European, 'together']

coenobite /seènō bīt/, **cenobite** *n* a member of a religious community [15C. Via French *cénobite* or ecclesiastical Latin *coenobita* < Greek *koinobion* 'common life'] —**coenobitical** /-bíttik'l/ *adj*

coenocyte /seènō sīt/ *n* a cell, part, or organism that contains many nuclei not separated by cell walls, e.g. the threads (**hyphae**) of many fungi or the bodies of some algae —**coenocytic** /seènō síttik/ *adj*

coenosarc /seènō ssaark/ *n* material linking the stems of individuals within a colony of polyps and containing a highly branched canal system with digestive and circulatory functions [Mid-19C. < COENO- + Greek *sark-* 'flesh']

coenzyme /kō én zīm/ *n* a nonprotein compound that combines with a specific protein (**apoenzyme**) to form an active enzyme

coenzyme A *n* a complex compound that acts with specific enzymes in energy-producing biochemical reactions

coenzyme Q *n* BIOCHEM same as **ubiquinone**

coequal /kō eèkwəl/ *adj* equal in size, rank, or status to another [14C. < Latin *coaequalis* 'of the same age' < *aequalis* (see EQUAL)] —**coequal** *n* —**coequality** /kō i kwólləti/ *n* —**coequally** *adv*

coerce /kō úrss/ (**-erces, -ercing, -erced**) *vt* to make somebody do something against his or her will by

using force or threats [15C. < Latin *coercere* 'shut in together' < *arcere* 'shut in'] —**coercible** *adj*

coercion /kō úrsh'n/ *n* **1.** the use of force or threats to make somebody do something against his or her will **2.** force or threats used to make somebody do something against his or her will —**coercionary** *adj* —**coercionist** *n, adj*

coercive /kō úrssiv/ *adj* using force or threats to make somebody do something against his or her will —**coercively** *adv* —**coerciveness** *n*

coercive force *n* the magnetic force necessary to demagnetize a substance

coercivity /kò ur sívvəti/ *n* PHYS same as **coercive force**

coessential /kò i sénsh'l/ *adj* having the same essence or nature [Late 15C. < ecclesiastical Latin *coessentialis* 'of the same substance' < late Latin *essentialis* (see ESSENTIAL)]

coeternal /kò i túrn'l/ *adj* existing together throughout eternity (*formal*) [14C. < ecclesiastical Latin *co-aeternus* < Latin *aeternus* (see ETERNAL)] —**coeternally** *adv*

coeternity /kò i túrnəti/ *n* eternal existence with somebody or something else [Late 16C. < late Latin *co-aeternitas* < Latin *aeternitas* (see ETERNITY)]

Coetzee /kúrt zee/, **J. M.** (*b.* 1940) South African novelist. His works, reflecting turmoil in South Africa, include *The Life and Times of Michael K* (1983) and *Disgrace* (1999), both of which won the Booker Prize. He was awarded the Nobel Prize in literature in 2003. Full name **Coetzee, John Maxwell**

> 'I have never seen anything like it: two little discs of glass suspended in front of his eyes in loops of wire.'
> [J. M. Coetzee, *Waiting for the Barbarians*; 1982]

coeval /kō eèv'l/ *adj* having the same age, duration, or date of origin (*formal*) [Early 17C. < late Latin *coaevus* < Latin *aevum* 'age' < Greek *aiōn*] —**coevality** /kò i válləti/ *n* —**coevally** *adv*

coevolution /kò eevə loòsh'n/ *n* the joint development and adaptation to external changes of two or more interdependent species, e.g. parasites and the animals they live on —**coevolutionary** *adj*

coevolve /kò i vólv/ (**-volves, -volving, -volved**) *vi* to evolve and adapt together, e.g. in the way that parasites and the animals they live on do

coexist /kò ig zíst/ (**-ists, -isting, -isted**) *vi* **1.** to exist together at the same time and in the same place **2.** to occupy the same place in a peaceful way —**co-existence** *n* —**coexistent** *adj*

coextend /kò ik sténd/ (**-tends, -tending, -tended**) *vti* to extend, or make things extend, in or through the same space or length of time —**coextension** *n*

coextensive /kò ik sténssiv/ *adj* sharing the same limits, boundaries, or scope —**coextensively** *adv*

cofactor /kō faktər/ *n* a substance that acts with and is essential to the activity of an enzyme, e.g. a coenzyme or metal ion

C of C *abbr* COMM chamber of commerce

C of E *abbr* CHR Church of England

coffee

coffee /kóffi/ *n* **1.** STRONG CAFFEINE-RICH DRINK a drink containing caffeine and with a mildly stimulating effect that is made from the ground or processed seeds of a tropical tree **2.** SEEDS FOR MAKING COFFEE the roasted seeds (**coffee beans**) of a tropical tree used to make coffee. They are ground, or made into powder or granules that dissolve in hot water. **3.** BUSH YIELDING COFFEE BEANS a bush cultivated for its seeds (**coffee**

beans) that are used to make coffee. Genus: *Coffea*. **4.** PALE BROWN COLOUR a pale brown colour, like that of milky coffee **5.** *US* RICH BROWN COLOUR a medium to dark rich brown colour [Late 16C. Via Turkish *kahve* < Arabic *kahwa*] —**coffee** *adj* ◇ **wake up and smell the coffee** used to tell somebody that he or she is wrong about a particular situation and that it is time to acknowledge reality (*informal*)

coffee bag *n* a small porous bag containing ground coffee powder that is steeped in boiling water to make coffee

coffee bar *n* a small café where coffee, other drinks, and snacks are served

coffee bean *n* a seed of the coffee tree that is roasted and ground, or processed in other ways, to make coffee

coffee break *n* a short break for coffee or other refreshment

coffee cake *n* **1.** a cake flavoured with coffee **2.** *N Am* a sweet cake or roll, often containing nuts and raisins, that is eaten with coffee

coffee cup *n* a cup intended for drinking coffee, usually smaller than a teacup but sometimes much larger and generally with a saucer underneath

coffee grinder *n* an electrical or hand-operated device for grinding roasted coffee beans

coffeehouse /kóffi howss/ (*plural* **-houses** /-howziz/) *n* a place where coffee and other refreshments are served

coffee klatch, **coffee klatsch** *n* *N Am* a small social gathering where people drink coffee and engage in casual conversation [Late 19C. Anglicization of KAF-FEEKLATSCH]

coffee machine *n* **1.** a vending machine that dispenses hot drinks such as coffee, tea, and hot chocolate **2.** a machine in which coffee is made by filtering or forcing heated water at high pressure through coffee grounds into a jug or cup

coffeemaker /kóffi maykər/ *n* a device, usually an electrical appliance, for brewing coffee

coffee mill *n* HOUSEHOLD same as **coffee grinder**

coffee morning *n* an informal social gathering where coffee and snacks are served, often to raise money for charity or a cause

coffeepot /kóffi pot/ *n* a tall narrow pot with a curved spout and lid designed for serving or brewing coffee

coffee shop *n* a place where coffee and snacks are served and coffee beans are sold

coffee table *n* a low table for use in a living room

coffee-table book *n* a large, usually expensive book with lavish illustrations, especially one used for display or casual perusal rather than reading

coffer /kóffər/ *n* **1.** STRONGBOX a strong chest or box used for keeping money or valuables safe **2.** ARCHIT CEILING PANEL an ornamental sunken panel in a ceiling or dome **3.** CONSTR same as **cofferdam** (sense 1) ■ **coffers** *npl* FUNDS a supply or store of money, often belonging to an organization ■ *vt* (**-fers, -fering, -fered**) **1.** STORE SOMETHING VALUABLE IN STRONGBOX to put money or valuables in a coffer **2.** DECORATE CEILING WITH COFFERS to decorate something, especially a ceiling, with coffers [13C. < French *coffre* < Latin *cophinus* (see COFFIN)]

cofferdam /kóffər dam/ *n* **1.** a temporary watertight structure that is pumped dry to enclose an area underwater and allow construction work on a ship, bridge, or rig to be carried out **2.** an empty space that acts as a protective barrier between two floors or bulkheads on a ship

coffin /kóffin/ *n* **1.** BOX FOR CORPSE a long oblong container, usually made of wood, in which a dead body is placed for burial or cremation **2.** PART OF HOOF the horny part of a horse's hoof that contains the coffin bone **3.** PRINTING PRINTING FRAME a frame that holds electrotype or stereotype printing plates ■ *vt* (**-fins, -fining, -fined**) PUT SOMEBODY OR SOMETHING IN COFFIN to place somebody or something in a coffin or in something resembling a coffin [14C. Via Old French *cof(f)in* 'little basket' < Latin *cophinus* 'basket' < Greek *kophinos*]

coffin bone *n* the main bone in a horse's hoof

coffin nail *n* same as **cigarette** (*dated slang*)

Coffs Harbour /kófs-/ coastal city in eastern New South Wales, Australia. It is a tourist resort and

fruit-growing centre. Population: 62,906 (2002 estimate).

C of S *abbr* MIL chief of staff

cog

cog[1] /kog/ *n* **1.** a projection on the edge of a gearwheel that engages with corresponding parts on another wheel to transfer motion from one wheel to the other **2.** somebody regarded as a small and unimportant part of a large organization or system **3.** MECH ENG same as **cogwheel** [13C. Probably < N Germanic] —**cogged** *adj*

cog[2] /kog/ *n* a piece that projects from the end of a timber beam and is designed to fit into an opening in another beam to form a joint ■ *vt* (**cogs, cogging, cogged**) to join two timber beams with a cog [Early 19C. Probably variant of *cock* 'pamper', shortening of COCKER[2]]

cogeneration /kố jenə ráysh'n/ *n* the production of two types of energy such as heat or electricity from one source in such a way that both are usable, instead of one being treated as waste energy —**cogenerator** /kō jénnə raytər/ *n*

cogent /kójənt/ *adj* forceful and convincing to the intellect and reason ○ *a cogent argument* [Mid-17C. < Latin *cogent-*, present participle of *cogere* 'drive together' < *agere* 'drive'] —**cogency** *n* —**cogently** *adv*

SYNONYMS See *valid*.

cogitate /kójji tayt/ (**-tates, -tating, -tated**) *vti* to think deeply and carefully about something (*formal*) [Late 16C. < Latin *cogitat-*, past participle of *cogitare*, literally 'disturb together' < *agitare* (see AGITATE)] —**cogitation** /kójji táysh'n/ *n* —**cogitative** *adj*

cognac /kón yak/ *n* a high-quality brandy distilled from white grapes in Cognac, western France

Cognac /kón yak/ town in Charente Department, western France, north of Bordeaux. It is known for the brandy distilled there. Population: 19,534 (1999).

cognate /kóg nayt/ *adj* **1.** LING having the same linguistic root or origin **2.** related by blood or having an ancestor in common (*formal*) [14C. < Latin *cognatus*, literally 'born together' < *gnatus*, past participle of *(g)nasci* 'be born'] —**cognate** *n* —**cognation** /kog náysh'n/ *n*

cognate object *n* a noun that functions as the object of a verb that is from the same etymological root, as in 'to dream a dream' or 'to think a thought'

~~cognative~~ incorrect spelling of **cognitive**

cognisable, etc. another spelling of **cognizable**, etc.

cognition /kog nísh'n/ *n* **1.** the mental faculty or process of acquiring knowledge by the use of reasoning, intuition, or perception **2.** knowledge acquired through reasoning, intuition, or perception [15C. < Latin *cognition-* < *cognoscere* 'get to know' < *(g)noscere* 'know'] —**cognitional** *adj*

cognitive /kógnitiv/ *adj* **1.** relating to the process of acquiring knowledge by the use of reasoning, intuition, or perception **2.** relating to thought processes [Late 16C. < medieval Latin *cognitivus* < Latin *cognoscere* (see COGNITION)] —**cognitively** *adv*

cognitive dissonance *n* a state of psychological conflict or anxiety resulting from a contradiction between a person's simultaneously held beliefs or attitudes

cognitive map *n* a map of three-dimensional space maintained in the brain

cognitive psychology *n* the branch of psychology concerned with the study of mental states

cognitive science *n* the scientific study of knowledge and how it is acquired, combining aspects of philosophy, psychology, linguistics, anthropology, and artificial intelligence

cognitive therapy *n* a treatment of psychiatric disorders such as anxiety or depression that encourages patients to confront and challenge the distorted way of thinking that characterizes their disorder

cognitivism /kógnitivizəm/ *n* the theory that moral judgments are statements of fact and can therefore be classed as true or false

cognizable /kógnizəb'l/, **cognisable** *adj* **1.** able to be known or perceived by the human mind (*formal*) **2.** LAW falling within the jurisdiction of a particular court of law and therefore able to be tried by that court —**cognizably** *adv*

cognizance /kógnizənss/, **cognisance** *n* **1.** KNOWLEDGE knowledge or awareness of something (*formal*) **2.** SCOPE OF SOMEBODY'S KNOWLEDGE the extent or range of what somebody can know and understand (*formal*) **3.** LAW COURT'S RIGHT TO DEAL WITH SOMETHING the right of a court of law to deal with a particular matter **4.** LAW TAKING NOTICE OF FACT notice of a fact or facts taken by a court of law **5.** HERALDRY DISTINGUISHING SIGN a badge or other sign that is worn to distinguish the wearer [14C. < Old French *conis(s)aunce* < Latin *cognoscere* (see COGNITION)]

cognizant /kógnizənt/, **cognisant** *adj* having knowledge of something (*formal*)

SYNONYMS See *aware*.

cognomen /kog nố men/ (*plural* **-nomens** or **-nomina** /-nómminə/) *n* **1.** a nickname or name that describes somebody, e.g. 'Ethelred the Unready' (*formal*) **2.** a surname or family name, especially the third name given to a citizen of ancient Rome, e.g. 'Cicero' in 'Marcus Tullius Cicero' [Early 17C. < Latin, 'added name' < *(g)nomen* 'name'] —**cognominal** /kog nómmin'l/ *adj*

cognoscenti /kónnyō shénti, kógnə-/ (*singular* **-te** /-tay/) *npl* people who have a refined and superior knowledge of a subject, especially the arts [Mid-18C. < obsolete Italian, 'people who know', < Latin *cognoscent-*, present participle of *cognoscere* (see COGNITION)]

cogon /kố gōn/ *n* a coarse tall grass used, especially in the Philippines, as thatching. Genus: *Imperata*. [Late 19C. Via Spanish < Tagalog *kúgon*]

cog railway *n* US same as **rack railway**

cogwheel /kóg weel/ *n* a wheel with a series of projections around the rim that enable it to engage with projections on another wheel or rack to create traction and so produce motion

cohabit /kō hábbit/ (**-its, -iting, -ited**) *vi* **1.** to live together, especially without being formally married **2.** to coexist with somebody or something else [Mid-16C. < late Latin *cohabitare* < *habitare* (see INHABIT)] —**cohabitant** *n* —**cohabitation** /kố habi táysh'n/ *n* —**cohabitee** /kố habi tee/ *n* —**cohabiter** *n*

cohen /kố in/ (*plural* **-hens** or **-hanim** /-ə neém/), **kohen** (*plural* **-hanim**) *n* in Judaism, a person recognized as a descendant of Aaron. The cohanim were priests in the Temple in ancient Jerusalem, and a man identified as a cohen still retains specific obligations in Orthodox Judaism today. [< Hebrew *kohein* 'priest']

Cohen /kố in/, **Leonard** (*b.* 1934) Canadian poet, novelist, singer, and songwriter. His albums include *Songs of Leonard Cohen* (1968) and *I'm Your Man* (1988).

Cohen, Stanley (*b.* 1922) US biochemist. He co-developed the recombinant DNA techniques that became the basis of genetic engineering and shared the 1986 Nobel Prize in Physiology or Medicine.

cohere /kō héer/ (**-heres, -hering, -hered**) *vi* **1.** STICK TOGETHER to stick to or hold together in a mass that is not easily separated (*formal*) **2.** BE LOGICALLY CONSISTENT to be logically or aesthetically consistent so that all the separate parts fit together and add up to a harmonious or credible whole (*formal*) **3.** PHYS BE HELD TOGETHER BY MOLECULAR FORCES to be held together by the molecular forces of cohesion [Mid-16C. < Latin *cohaerere* < *haerere* 'to stick']

coherent /kō héerənt/ *adj* **1.** LOGICALLY OR AESTHETICALLY CONSISTENT logically or aesthetically consistent and

holding together as a harmonious or credible whole **2.** SPEAKING LOGICALLY able to speak clearly and logically ○ *He was so confused and dazed he was barely coherent.* **3.** PHYS STICKING TOGETHER able to hold together to form an inseparable mass **4.** PHYS WITH SAME WAVELENGTH describes electromagnetic waves that have the same wavelength and a fixed phase relationship. Coherent light is produced by lasers. **5.** MEASURE FORMING UNITS WITHOUT INTRODUCING CONSTANTS forming a system of units such as SI units in which the product or quotient of two units gives the unit of the derived quantity —**coherence** *n* —**coherently** *adv*

cohesion /kō heezh'n/ *n* **1.** the state or condition of joining or working together to form a united whole, or the tendency to do this **2.** the force of attraction by which the molecules of a solid or liquid tend to remain together [Mid-17C. < Latin *cohaes-*, past participle of *cohaerere* (see COHERE)]

cohesive /kō héessiv/ *adj* sticking, holding, or working together as a united whole ○ *welded the team into a cohesive unit* [Early 18C. < Latin *cohaes-* (see COHESION)] —**cohesively** *adv* —**cohesiveness** *n*

cohort /kố hawrt/ *n* **1.** ANCIENT HIST UNIT OF ROMAN ARMY an ancient Roman military unit equal to one tenth of a legion and consisting of 300 to 600 men **2.** SOLDIERS a group of soldiers or warriors **3.** GROUP OF PEOPLE a united group of people **4.** SUPPORTER a supporter, accomplice, or associate of a leader, especially one to whom special treatment and preference is given (*disapproving*) **5.** STATS GROUP WITH STATISTICAL SIMILARITIES a group of people sharing a common factor such as the same age or the same income bracket, especially in a statistical survey [15C. < Latin *cohort-* 'enclosure']

USAGE What is a **cohort**? The common use of **cohort** to mean 'a united group of people' has given rise to a use in which a **cohort** is a single assistant or supporter: *His most trusted cohort was an Englishman, David Hall* (*The Independent*). This use is more common in US English.

cohosh /kố hosh/ *n* PLANTS same as **black cohosh** [Late 18C. < Algonquian *kkwàhas*]

cohousing /kố howzing/ *n* N Am a communal living arrangement by which people share tasks such as crop-growing and childcare, own their private living spaces but share common spaces such as dining areas

cohune /kō hoón/ *n* a palm with feathery leaves that produces a nut that yields an oil similar to coconut oil. Use: soaps and cosmetics. Native to: Central America. Latin name: *Orbignya cohune*. [Mid-18C. < Miskito]

COI *abbr* Central Office of Information

Coiba Island /ko eébə-/ island in the Pacific Ocean off the coast of Panama, site of a national park and penal colony. Population: 850. Area: 494 sq. km/191 sq. mi.

coif *n* /koyf/ **1.** TYPE OF SKULLCAP FOR WOMEN a close-fitting linen cap worn by women in the Middle Ages, now worn by some nuns under their veils **2.** LEATHER SKULLCAP a thick, close-fitting leather cap formerly worn under a hood of chain mail ■ *vt* /kwaaf/ (**coifs, coiffing, coiffed**) **1.** COVER HEAD WITH COIF to cover somebody's head with a coif or with something like a coif **2.** ARRANGE HAIR to arrange or style somebody's hair (*formal*) [14C. Via Old French *coife* 'headdress' < late Latin *cofia* 'helmet' < Germanic]

coiffeur /kwaa fúr/ (*plural* **-feurs**) *n* a man who is a hairdresser (*formal or humorous*) [Mid-19C. < French < Old French *coife* (see COIF)]

coiffeuse /kwaa fúrz/ (*plural* **-feuses** /-fúrz/) *n* a woman who is a hairdresser (*formal or humorous*) [Late 18C. < French, feminine of COIFFEUR]

coiffure /kwaa fyóor/ *n* the way somebody wears his or her hair (*formal or humorous*) [Mid-17C. < French < *coiffer* 'arrange the hair' < Old French *coife* (see COIF)] —**coiffure** *vt* —**coiffured** *adj*

coign, coigne *n* BUILDINGS same as **quoin**

coign of vantage *n* a good position from which to observe somebody or something or to take action

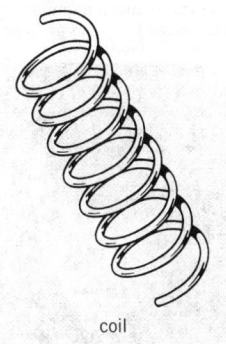

coil

coil /koyl/ *n* **1.** SERIES OF LOOPS a series of connected loops into which something has been wound or gathered **2.** LOOP one of a series of loops into which something has been wound or gathered **3.** SPIRAL something that curls or is curled into a spiral shape **4.** PIPES ARRANGED IN ROWS OR SPIRAL a series of pipes arranged in rows or in a spiral, e.g. in a radiator or condenser **5.** WIRE SPIRAL FOR ELECTRIC CURRENT a spiral of wire through which an electric current is passed to create a magnetic field or to function as an inductor **6.** DEVICE SUPPLYING ELECTRICITY TO SPARKING PLUGS a device that supplies a high voltage to the spark plugs in an internal-combustion engine **7.** CONTRACEPTIVE DEVICE a coil-shaped device made of plastic or metal that is placed inside the womb to prevent a woman from becoming pregnant ■ *v* (**coils, coiling, coiled**) **1.** *vti* WIND SOMETHING INTO LOOPS to wind something into a series of connected loops, or form a series of connected loops ○ *The rope had coiled itself around the propeller.* **2.** *vi* CURVE OR BEND to move in a curving, sinuous way [Early 16C. Via Old French *coillir* 'gather' < Latin *colligere* (see COLLECT¹)] —**coiler** *n*

coil pot *n* a pot formed from a structure of coils or ropes of clay laid one on top of the other in a spiral

coil spring *n* N Am a helical spring made from wire

Coimbatore /kóymbə táwr/ industrial city and administrative headquarters of Coimbatore District, Tamil Nadu State, southeastern India. Population: 1,446,034 (2001).

Coimbra /kwímbrə, kweéNbrə/ historic city and capital of Coimbra District in west-central Portugal. Population: 74,616 (1981).

coin /koyn/ *n* **1.** PIECE OF METAL MONEY a usually circular flat piece of metal stamped with its value as money **2.** METAL MONEY money in the form of coins rather than banknotes or cheques **3.** PAPER OR METAL MONEY money in whatever form, as opposed to such things as cheques ■ *vt* (**coins, coining, coined**) **1.** MINT COINS to make a coin or coins **2.** MAKE METAL INTO COINS to make a metal such as gold or silver into coins **3.** CREATE EXPRESSION to invent or devise a word or phrase [14C. < Old French *coin(g)* 'wedge, (wedge-shaped) die for stamping coins' < Latin *cuneus* 'wedge'] —**coiner** *n* ◇ **coin it (in)** to earn a great deal of money (*informal*)

coinage /kóynij/ *n* **1.** COINS currency in the form of coins **2.** CURRENCY the system or type of coins in use as currency ○ *decimal coinage* **3.** MAKING OF METAL MONEY the act or process of minting coins **4.** INVENTION OF NEW WORD OR PHRASE the invention of a new word or phrase **5.** NEW WORD OR PHRASE a newly used word or phrase ○ *'Cyberspace' was a popular coinage of the 1980s.*

coin box *n* a box into which coins are inserted to get something from a coin-operated machine

coincide /kó in síd/ (**-cides, -ciding, -cided**) *vi* **1.** HAPPEN AT SAME TIME to happen at or around the same time **2.** BE SAME IN POSITION OR FORM to occupy the same place, or be exactly alike in position or form **3.** AGREE to agree exactly [Early 18C. < medieval Latin *coincidere* 'fall upon together' < Latin *incidere* 'fall upon' < *cadere* 'to fall']

coincidence /kó ínssidənss/ *n* **1.** CHANCE HAPPENING something that happens by chance in a surprising or remarkable way **2.** HAPPENING WITHOUT PLANNING the fact of happening by chance ○ *By sheer coincidence, we both ended up at the same restaurant.* **3.** HAVING IDENTICAL FEATURES the fact or condition of happening at the same time or place or being identical

coincident /kó ínssidənt/ *adj* (*formal*) **1.** happening at the same time, or occupying the same position in

space **2.** in exact agreement, or matching exactly —**coincidently** *adv*

coincidental /kó ínssi dént'l/ *adj* **1.** happening by chance rather than intentionally **2.** happening or existing at the same time —**coincidentally** *adv*

coinfection /kó in féksh'n/ *n* infection with two or more diseases or viruses at the same time ○ *TB-HIV coinfection*

coin-operated *adj* describes a device that functions only after the insertion of one or more coins of a specific value

coir /kóyər/ *n* a coarse fibre that comes from the husk of the coconut. Use: matting, rope. [Late 16C. < Malayalam *kayaṟu* 'cord, coir']

coition /kó ísh'n/ *n* MED same as **sexual intercourse** [Mid-16C. < Latin *coition-* < *coire* (see COITUS)]

coitus /kó itəss/ *n* same as **sexual intercourse** (*formal or technical*) [Mid-19C. < Latin, past participle of *coire* 'go together' < *ire* 'go'] —**coital** *adj* —**coitally** *adv*

coitus interruptus /-íntə rúptəss/ *n* during sexual intercourse, the deliberate withdrawal of the penis from the vagina before semen is ejaculated, as an attempted method of contraception [< modern Latin, 'interrupted coitus']

coke¹ /kōk/ *n* a solid residue consisting mainly of carbon, left after the volatile elements have been driven from bituminous coal or other petroleum material. Use: fuel. ■ *vti* (**cokes, coking, coked**) to change something such as bituminous coal into coke, or to become coke or like coke [Mid-17C. Origin ?]

coke² /kōk/ *n* cocaine used as an illegal drug (*slang*) [Early 20C. Contraction]

Coke /kōk/, **Sir Edward** (1552–1634) English lawyer. As Chief Justice of the Court of Common Pleas (1606–13) he defended the common law against the royal prerogative and the privilege of the Church.

cokehead /kók hed/ *n* a frequent user or addict of cocaine (*slang*)

col /kol/ *n* **1.** a low point in a ridge of mountains, often forming a pass between two peaks **2.** a pattern of atmospheric pressure distribution that develops between two anticyclones and two depressions arranged alternately, characterized by light variable winds and often thundery weather in summer or foggy conditions in winter [Mid-19C. Via French < Latin *collum* 'neck']

COL /kol/ *abbr* **1.** COMPUT computer-oriented language **2.** ECON cost of living

col. *abbr* **1.** EDUC college **2.** SOC SCI colony **3.** colour **4.** PRINTING column

Col. *abbr* **1.** MIL Colonel **2.** Colorado **3.** BIBLE Colossians **4.** Columbia **5.** Columbian

col- *prefix* same as **com-** (*used before l*)

cola¹ /kólə/, **kola** *n* **1.** a sweet carbonated drink flavoured with cola nuts **2.** a tropical evergreen tree cultivated for its reddish seeds (**cola nuts**). Genus: *Cola*. [Early 17C. < Temne *k'ola* 'cola nut']

cola² /kólə/ ANAT plural of **colon**²

cola³ /kólə/ LITERAT plural of **colon**¹ (sense 3)

COLA *abbr* cost-of-living adjustment

~~**colaborate**~~ incorrect spelling of **collaborate**

Colac /kó lak/ town in central Victoria, Australia, that is an agricultural and pastoral centre. Population: 10,241 (1991).

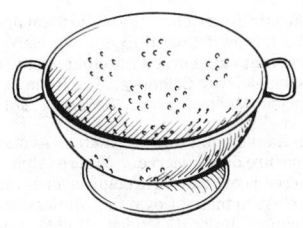

colander

colander /kúlləndər/ *n* a bowl-shaped dish with holes in it. Use: draining food cooked in water and washing vegetables or fruit. [14C. Origin ?]

cola nut *n* the small hard seed of the cola tree, which contains caffeine and theobromine. Use: carbonated drinks, medicines.

~~**colateral**~~ incorrect spelling of **collateral**

colatitude /kō látti tyood/ *n* the difference between a latitude and 90°

Colbert /kól bair/, **Claudette** (1903–96) French-born US film actor. She acted in Hollywood films and won an Academy Award for *It Happened One Night* (1934). Born Chauchoin, Lily Claudette

Colbert, **Jean-Baptiste** (1619–83) French politician. He reformed the French economy as Louis XIV's comptroller general of finance from 1665.

colcannon /kəl kánnən/ *n* an Irish dish made of cabbage and potatoes boiled and mashed together and served with butter or cream [Late 18C. Origin ?]

Colchester /kólchistər/ town in SE England. Population: 155,796 (2001).

colchicine /kólchi seen, kólk-/ *n* a poisonous extract of autumn crocus plants. Use: to inhibit cell division and cause chromosome doubling in plants, to treat gout.

colchicum /kólchikəm, kólk-/ *n* a flowering bulb with pink or white flowers that appear separately from the leaves, especially in the autumn. Native to: Europe. Genus: *Colchicum*. [Late 16C. < Greek *kolkhikon* 'product of Colchis' < *Kolkhis* 'Colchis', home of MEDEA; because it was considered poisonous]

cold /kōld/ *adj* **1.** AT LOW TEMPERATURE at or with a relatively low, uncomfortably low, or unusually low temperature ○ *The weather turned colder.* ○ *a cold drink* **2.** MAKING PLACE SEEM COOLER giving a place a feeling of coolness rather than warmth ○ *Blue is a cold colour.* **3.** COOKED HOT THEN COOLED cooked or prepared as a hot food and then cooled ○ *Serve the pie cold, with ice cream.* **4.** TACITURN AND EMOTIONLESS showing no emotion, sympathy, or kindness **5.** UNFRIENDLY AND UNCARING feeling or exhibiting no friendship or sense of caring **6.** STRONG BUT CONTROLLED intense but expressed or shown in a controlled way ○ *cold fury* **7.** SEXUALLY FRIGID giving or feeling no sexual response **8.** HARD TO FOLLOW no longer recent or fresh and so difficult to track or follow ○ *The trail had gone cold.* **9.** NOT NEAR OBJECT OF SEARCH not close to the correct answer or to something being searched for (*informal*) **10.** DEAD dead, especially from a long time before **11.** METALL PROCESSED AT LOW TEMPERATURE processed at a temperature below that at which recrystallization takes place ○ *cold working of steel* ■ *n* **1.** VIRAL INFECTION OF NOSE AND THROAT a viral infection of the nose, throat, and bronchial tubes, characterized by sneezing, nasal congestion, coughing, and headaches **2.** COLD WEATHER low-temperature weather or conditions ○ *The cold made me shiver.* **3.** CONDITION CAUSED BY LOW TEMPERATURE the state or condition of being subjected to low temperatures ■ *adv* **1.** EXTEMPORANEOUSLY without any preparation ○ *sang the part cold* **2.** N Am COMPLETELY completely and without any possibility of a change of mind ○ *turned the proposal down cold* [Old English *c(e)ald* < Indo-European] —**coldish** *adj* —**coldness** *n* ◇ **blow hot and cold** to display wide extremes of attitude or mood ◇ **catch a cold** to experience financial loss (*informal*) ◇ **come** or **be brought in from the cold** to be allowed to take part in something after being previously excluded ◇ **leave somebody cold** to fail to impress or excite somebody ◇ **out in the cold** ignored or denied benefits that other people are getting ○ *The new funding proposals would leave us out in the cold.* ◇ **out cold** unconscious or in a deep sleep (*informal*)

cold-blooded /-blúddid/ *adj* **1.** describes an animal with an internal body temperature that varies according to the temperature of the surroundings **2.** showing a total lack of kindness, pity, or care for somebody's suffering —**cold-bloodedly** *adv* —**cold-bloodedness** *n*

coldboot /kóld boot/ (**-boots, -booting, -booted**) *vt* to restart a computer by switching it off and on. ◇ **warmboot**

cold call *n* a telephone call or personal visit made to somebody not known to the caller or visitor, in order to try to sell that person goods or services —**cold-call** *vt*

cold chisel *n* a tool consisting of a solid metal shaft with a sharply bevelled point or edge that is struck with a hammer or mallet. Use: to break up or shape hard materials such as metal or stone. [Because it can cut cold metal]

cold comfort *n* something intended to be encouraging or reassuring that does not help in practice

cold cream *n* a thick cream used for cleaning and softening the skin, especially on the face

cold cuts *npl* slices of cooked meat that are served cold

cold drink *n* **1.** a chilled drink of water, juice, or something similar **2.** *S Africa, Southern US* a non-alcoholic drink

cold duck *n* a cocktail made with sparkling burgundy and champagne [Translation of German *kalte Ente*, by folk etymology < *kaltes Ende* 'cold end', supposedly because leftover champagne and burgundy were poured into a single bottle]

cold feet *npl* a loss of nerve about something planned, causing a person not to go ahead as originally intended [Because a soldier with cold or frozen feet is prevented from fighting]

cold fish *n* somebody regarded as unfeeling or unfriendly (*informal*)

cold frame *n* a box with glass or clear plastic sides and an opening roof, used in gardens for protecting seedlings and other plants from cold weather

cold front *n* the boundary zone of an advancing cold-air mass as it replaces warmer air

cold fusion *n* a hypothetical form of nuclear fusion held to take place at room temperature

cold-hearted /-haártid/ *adj* showing no sympathy or warmth to other people —**cold-heartedly** *adv* —**cold-heartedness** *n*

Colditz /kóldits/ site of Colditz Castle, a German prisoner-of-war camp during World War II, from which many prisoners made daring escapes. It is situated about 48 km/30 mi. southwest of Leipzig.

cold light *n* light produced from a low-temperature source such as phosphorescence containing no infrared wavelengths and therefore having no heating effects

coldly /kóldli/ *adv* without emotion, affection, friendliness, or sympathy

cold pack *n* **1.** a bag, cloth, or sheet that is soaked with water or filled with something cold and applied to the body to relieve pain or inflammation **2.** the packing and sterilization of uncooked food in jars or tins

cold-pressed *adj* describes high-grade olive oil produced from the first pressing of the raw olives. The pressed olives are subsequently heated to extract further amounts of oil.

cold-rolled *adj* describes metal that is rolled into sheets under pressure at room temperature in order to retain the crystalline structure of the metal and produce a smooth surface —**cold-rolling** *n*

cold rubber *n* a durable synthetic rubber made through polymerization at low temperature and used for retreading tyres

cold shoulder *n* a refusal to behave in a friendly or pleasant way towards somebody ○ *He gave me the cold shoulder.* [Because unwelcome guests were formerly given only a cold shoulder of mutton] —**coldshoulder** /kóld shōldər/ *vt*

cold snap *n* a sudden short period of very cold weather

cold sore *n* a small painful blister on or near the lips, or sometimes the nose, caused by the virus *Herpes simplex* [Because the sores often accompany colds]

cold storage *n* chilled or refrigerated conditions in which perishable items, especially food, are kept to preserve them ○ **in cold storage** ready to be put into action at some later date, but not currently being used

cold store *n* a refrigerated building or area for keeping goods, especially food or furs, in cold conditions to preserve them

Coldstream /kóld streem/ small town on the River

Tweed in Scottish Borders, Scotland. Population: 1,746 (1991).

cold sweat *n* a very nervous, anxious, or frightened state, often with sweating and cold clammy skin

cold turkey *n* **1.** a method of stopping drug addiction by not taking any further drugs and not having any other treatment to protect the addict from the withdrawal symptoms **2.** the unpleasant symptoms, usually including nausea and shivering, that accompany a sudden withdrawal from an addictive drug [Origin ?]

cold type *n* typesetting that is done without casting metal

cold war *n* a relationship between two people or groups that is unfriendly or hostile but does not involve actual fighting or military combat —**cold warrior** *n*

Cold War *n* the hostile yet nonviolent relations between the former Soviet Union and the United States, and their respective allies, from around 1946 to 1989

cold wave *n* **1.** a sudden fall in temperature associated with the passage of air of continental polar origin **2.** a permanent wave in hair that is produced using chemicals rather than heat (*dated*)

cold-weld (**cold-welds, cold-welding, cold-welded**) *vt* to join two metal surfaces using pressure rather than heat —**cold-welding** *n*

cole /kōl/ *n* a member of the cabbage family. Genus: *Brassica*. (*archaic*) [Pre-12C. < Latin *caulis* 'stem, cabbage']

Cole /kōl/, **Thomas** (1801–48) British-born US artist. He painted North American landscapes and is often considered the forerunner of the Hudson River School.

   'It is generally thought that the liberal arts tend to soften our manners; but they do more—they carry with them the power to mend our hearts.'
[Thomas Cole, 'Essay on American Scenery 2', *The American Monthly Magazine*; January 1836]

colectomy /kō léktəmi/ (*plural* **-mies**) *n* a surgical operation in which part or all of the colon is removed [Late 19C. < COLON²]

colemanite /kólmən īt/ *n* a white or colourless crystalline mineral consisting of hydrous calcium borate. Use: source of borax. [Late 19C. After William T. *Coleman* (1824–93), US mine owner]

coleopteran /kólli óptərən/ *n* an insect with modified forewings that function as tough covers for the membranous hind wings, e.g. beetles. Order: Coleoptera. [Mid-19C. < modern Latin *coleoptera* < Greek *koleopteros* < *koleos* 'sheath' + *pteron* 'wing'] —**coleopterous** *adj*

coleoptile /kólli óp tīl/ *n* the first leaf in some grasses that forms a protective sheath around the stem tip (**plumule**) [Mid-19C. < Greek *koleos* 'sheath' + *ptilon* 'feather']

coleorhiza /kólli ə rízə/ (*plural* **-zae** /-zee/) *n* a protective sheath surrounding the young root of a germinating grass seed [Mid-19C. < Greek *koleos* 'sheath' + *rhiza* 'root']

Coleraine /kōl ráyn/ town and county seat of Coleraine District, Northern Ireland, situated on the River Bann. Population: 20,721 (1991).

Coleridge /kólərij/, **Samuel Taylor** (1772–1834) British poet. His collection *Lyrical Ballads* (1798), published with William Wordsworth, launched romanticism in English poetry. See Cultural note at **mariner**

   'The fair breeze blew, the white foam flew, / The furrow followed free; / We were the first that ever burst / Into that silent sea.'
[Samuel Taylor Coleridge, 'The Rime of the Ancient Mariner', *Lyrical Ballads*; 1798]

   'In Xanadu did Kubla Khan / A stately pleasure-dome decree: / Where Alph, the sacred river, ran / Through caverns measureless to man / Down to a sunless sea.'
[Samuel Taylor Coleridge, 'Kubla Khan'; 1797]

coleslaw /kōl slaw/ *n* a salad made with shredded

raw cabbage usually in a mayonnaise dressing [Late 18C. < Dutch *koolsla* < *kool* 'cabbage' + *sla* 'salad']

AKG London

Colette

Colette /ko lét/ (1873–1954) French novelist. Among the best known of her many novels are *Chéri* (1920) and *Gigi* (1945). Full name **Colette, Sidonie Gabrielle Claudine**

   'It's nothing to be born ugly. Sensibly, the ugly woman comes to terms with her ugliness and exploits it as a grace of nature.'
[Colette, *Journey for Myself*; 1971]

coleus /kố li əss/ *n* a plant grown for its brightly coloured variegated leaves. Genus: *Coleus*. [Mid-19C. Via modern Latin < Greek *koleos* 'sheath'; from the way the plant's filaments are joined]

coley /kốli/ (*plural same* or **-leys**) *n* an edible white-fleshed fish, especially the coalfish [Mid-20C. Probably < COALFISH]

coli- *prefix* same as **colo-** (*used before vowels*)

colic /kólli k/ *n* **1.** PAIN IN ABDOMEN a sudden attack of abdominal pain, often caused by spasm, inflammation, or obstruction **2.** CRYING IN BABIES excessive crying and irritability in infants from a variety of causes, especially stomach or intestinal discomfort **3.** SERIOUS DIGESTIVE DISEASE IN HORSES a serious disease of the digestive system in horses, sometimes leading to fatal intestinal blockage [15C. Via French < Latin *colicus* < Greek *kolikos* 'suffering in the large intestine' < *kolon* 'large intestine'] —**colic** *adj*

colicky /kólliki/ *adj* experiencing bouts of abdominal pain (**colic**)

coliform /kóli fawrm, kólli-/ *adj* describes rod-shaped bacteria that are normally found in the colons of humans and animals and become a serious contaminant when found in the food or water supply [Early 20C. < modern Latin *coli* 'of the large intestine', form of Latin *colon* 'large intestine']

colinear /kố línni ər/ *adj* **1.** with corresponding parts arranged in a regular linear order **2.** MATHS another spelling of **collinear** [Early 20C. < CO- + LINEAR] —**colinearity** /kốlinni árrəti/ *n*

coliseum /kólli seé əm/, **colosseum** /kóllə-/ *n* a large building used as a theatre or for sports events [Early 16C. < medieval Latin, 'something colossal' < Latin *colosseus* 'colossal' < *colossus* 'colossus']

colistin /kə lístin, kō-/ *n* an antibiotic effective against a wide range of organisms. Source: a soil bacterium. Use: to treat gastrointestinal infections. [Mid-20C. < modern Latin (*Bacillus*) *colistinus* < *coli* (see COLIFORM)]

colitis /kə lítiss, ko-/ *n* inflammation of the colon, characterized by lower-bowel spasms and upper abdominal cramps [Mid-19C. < COLON²] —**colitic** /kə líttik, ko-/ *adj*

coll. *abbr* **1.** COMM collateral **2.** colleague **3.** MAIL collect **4.** MAIL collection **5.** MAIL collector **6.** EDUC college **7.** EDUC collegiate **8.** LANGUAGE colloquial

coll- *prefix* same as **collo-** (*used before vowels*)

collaborate /kə lábbə rayt/ (**-rates, -rating, -rated**) *vi* **1.** to work with another person or group in order to achieve something **2.** to betray others by working with an enemy, especially an occupying force [Late 19C. < late Latin *collaborat-*, past participle of *collaborare* 'work together' < Latin *labor* 'toil'] —**collaborative** *adj* —**collaboratively** *adv* —**collaborator** *n*

USAGE collaborate or **corroborate**? *Collaborate* means 'to work with others in order to achieve something': *Two authors collaborated on the biography. Corroborate* means 'to give or represent evidence of the truth of

something': *The results corroborated the success of the new method.* The two words are not interchangeable.

collaboration /kə lábbə ráysh'n/ *n* **1.** the act of working together with one or more people in order to achieve something **2.** the betrayal of others by working with an enemy, especially an occupying force —**collaborationism** *n* —**collaborationist** *n, adj*

collaborative divorce *n N Am* a divorce in which the terms are agreed upon by both spouses and their solicitors prior to presenting the final agreement to a judge without a trial

collage /ko la̋azh, kóllaazh/ *n* **1.** PICTURE WITH PIECES STUCK ON SURFACE a picture made by sticking cloth, pieces of paper, photographs, and other objects onto a surface **2.** ART OF MAKING COLLAGES the art of making pictures by sticking cloth, pieces of paper, photographs, and other objects onto a surface **3.** COMBINATION OF DIFFERENT THINGS a combination of different things [Early 20C. < French *coller* 'to glue' < *colle* 'glue' < Greek *kolla*] —**collage** *vti* —**collagist** *n*

collagen /kólləjən/ *n* a fibrous protein found in skin, bone, and other connective tissues [Mid-19C. < French *collagène* < Greek *kolla* 'glue'] —**collagenic** /kóllə jénnik/ *adj* —**collagenous** /kə lájjənəss/ *adj*

collagenase /kə lájjə nayz, -nayss/ *n* any enzyme that breaks down collagen

collapsar /kə láp saar/ *n* ASTRON same as **black hole** (sense 1) [Late 20C. < COLLAPSE]

collapse /kə láps/ *v* (**-lapses, -lapsing, -lapsed**) **1.** *vi* FALL DOWN to fall down suddenly, generally as a result of damage, structural weakness, or lack of support ○ *A section of cliff had collapsed into the sea.* **2.** *vi* FAIL ABRUPTLY to fail or come to an end suddenly ○ *Their partnership nearly collapsed under the strain.* **3.** *vi* FALL SUDDENLY to fall or faint because of illness, exhaustion, or weakness ○ *He collapsed from overwork.* **4.** *vi* SUDDENLY SIT OR LIE DOWN to sit or lie down suddenly and relax completely, or give way to emotion ○ *I collapsed into an armchair.* **5.** *vi* BEND DOUBLE WITH EMOTION to bend over double or otherwise contort the body, typically in the throes of emotion such as laughter or crying **6.** *vti* DEFLATE to fold up or become flat from lack of pressure or loss of air, or cause something such as a parachute to do this ○ *The left lung had collapsed.* **7.** *vti* FOLD SOMETHING TO MAKE IT SMALLER to fold something up so that it is smaller or takes up less space, or fold up in this way ■ *n* **1.** FAILURE OR END a failure or sudden end to something ○ *the abrupt collapse of the campaign* **2.** FALLING DOWN the act of falling down suddenly, generally as a result of damage, structural weakness, or lack of support ○ *The roof was in danger of collapse.* **3.** DECREASE IN VALUE a sudden reduction or decrease in value ○ *the threatened collapse of the yen* **4.** SUDDEN ILLNESS a sudden onset of severe illness, resulting in hospitalization or bed rest ○ *in a state of nervous collapse* [Mid-18C. Back-formation < *collapsed* < Latin *collapsus*, past participle of *collabi* 'fall together' < *labi* 'to fall'] —**collapsible** *adj*

collar /kóllər/ *n* **1.** GARMENT'S NECKBAND the upright or turned-over neckband of a coat, jacket, dress, shirt, or blouse **2.** BAND ROUND NECK OF ANIMAL a leather, plastic, fabric, or metal band placed round the neck of an animal to identify it or attach it to a lead **3.** AREA RESEMBLING COLLAR an area round the neck of a bird or animal that has a colour or marking different from the rest **4.** AGRIC PART OF HARNESS the cushioned ring or other part of a harness that presses against a draught animal's shoulders **5.** RING-SHAPED DEVICE OR PART a ring-shaped device or part on a shaft that guides, seats, or restricts another mechanical part **6.** NECKLACE a close-fitting necklace or one that lies flat over the shoulders **7.** ORNAMENTAL INSIGNIA OF OFFICE an ornamental chain or band worn round the neck as a badge of office or insignia of knighthood **8.** MEAT FROM NECK a cut of meat, especially bacon, taken from an animal's neck **9.** POLICE ARREST an arrest made by a police officer (*slang*) ■ *vt* (**-lars, -laring, -lared**) **1.** FIND OR STOP SOMEBODY to find or stop somebody you want to talk to (*informal*) **2.** CATCH SOMEBODY to catch somebody and hold him or her to prevent escape (*slang*) **3.** MAKE POLICE ARREST to arrest a criminal suspect (*slang*) **4.** PUT COLLAR ON SOMETHING to put a collar on something such as an animal, a garment, or a machine part **5.** FOOD PICKLE AND ROLL MEAT to pickle meat by soaking it in salt or brine with seasonings and flavouring ingredients, then rolling, boiling, and pressing it [14C. Via Old French *colier* < Latin *collare* < *collum* 'neck'] —**collared** *adj* —**collarless** *adj* ◇ **hot under the collar** angry, irritated, or generally agitated (*informal*)

collarbone /kóllər bōn/ *n* ANAT same as **clavicle** (sense 1)

collard /kóllərd/ *n N Am* a variety of kale with a crown of smooth edible leaves [Mid-18C. Alteration of *colewort*]

collared dove *n* a fawn-coloured bird of the pigeon family that has a black collar round its neck. Native to: Near East, central and northern Europe. Latin name: *Streptopelia decaocto.*

collate /kə láyt, ko-/ (**-lates, -lating, -lated**) *vt* **1.** PUT PAGES IN ORDER to assemble pages in the correct order **2.** COMPARE INFORMATION to bring together pieces of information and compare them in detail **3.** VERIFY PAGE SEQUENCING to verify the correct sequencing and completeness of the pages in a book **4.** ADMIT CLERIC TO BENEFICE to admit a member of the clergy to a benefice [Mid-16C. < Latin *collat-*, past participle of *conferre* 'bring together' < *ferre* 'bring'] —**collator** *n*

collateral /kə láttərəl/ *n* **1.** PROPERTY AS SECURITY AGAINST LOAN property or goods used as security against a loan and forfeited if the loan is not repaid **2.** DESCENDANT FROM DIFFERENT LINE a relative descended from the same ancestor as another person but through a different set of parents, grandparents, and other forebears ■ *adj* **1.** ACCOMPANYING accompanying but secondary ○ *collateral issues* **2.** ADDITIONAL additional to and in support of something ○ *collateral evidence* **3.** WITH PROPERTY AS SECURITY obtained by putting up property or goods as security, to be forfeited if the loan cannot be paid **4.** DESCENDED FROM SAME ANCESTOR having the same ancestor but descended through a different set of parents, grandparents, and other forebears **5.** PARALLEL running side by side in parallel or corresponding in some way, e.g. in size [14C. < medieval Latin *collateralis*, literally 'side by side with' < Latin *lateralis* 'on the side' (see LATERAL)] —**collaterality** /kə láttə rálləti/ *n* —**collaterally** *adv*

collateral damage *n* unintended damage to civilian life or property during a military operation

collateralize /kə láttərə līz/ (**-izes, -izing, -ized**) *vt* to pledge property or goods as security for a loan —**collateralization** /kə láttərə lī záysh'n/ *n*

collation /kə láysh'n/ *n* **1.** COMPARISON OF INFORMATION a detailed comparison between different items or forms of information **2.** ASSEMBLY OF PAGES IN ORDER the assembling of pieces of paper in the right order, particularly the sections of a book prior to binding **3.** TECHNICAL DESCRIPTION OF BOOK the technical description of a book, including its bibliographical details and information about its physical construction, or the act of compiling such a description **4.** LIGHT MEAL a light meal or refreshment ○ *a cold collation* **5.** APPOINTMENT OF CLERGY the appointment of clergy to a benefice **6.** READING OF RELIGIOUS TEXT the reading of a religious text to a gathering of monks [14C. < Latin *collation-* 'a bringing together' < *collat-* (see COLLATE)]

collative /kə láytiv/ *adj* describes an ecclesiastical benefice to which a member of the clergy is appointed

colleague /kólleeg/ *n* a person somebody works with, especially in a professional or skilled job [Early 16C. Via French < Latin *collega* 'person somebody commissions with' < *legare* 'commission, entrust' < *lex* 'law']

collect[1] /kə lékt/ *v* (**-lects, -lecting, -lected**) **1.** *vt* GATHER THINGS IN ONE PLACE to bring things together ○ *I collected up my belongings and left.* **2.** *vt* KEEP THINGS OF SAME TYPE to obtain and keep objects of a similar type because of their interest, value, or beauty **3.** *vt* FETCH SOMEBODY OR SOMETHING to go to get people or objects and bring them somewhere ○ *They collected me from the airport.* **4.** *vt* TAKE MONEY OR PRIZE to take the money or prize to which a person is entitled **5.** *vti* ASK FOR DONATIONS to ask for money from people for a particular purpose **6.** *vti* ACCUMULATE to gather and gradually accumulate in a place **7.** *vi* GRADUALLY ASSEMBLE to come together gradually in a place and form a group or crowd of people ○ *By now an angry crowd had collected.* **8.** **collect yourself** *vr* GET CONTROL OF YOURSELF to gain or regain control of yourself and deliberately calm yourself or prepare yourself psychologically **9.** *vi* GET MONEY to obtain money that is due, e.g. from an insurance policy **10.** *vt ANZ* TRANSP COLLIDE WITH SOMETHING to be in collision with another vehicle or person (*informal*) ■ *adv N Am* same as **reverse charges** ■ *adj N Am* same as **reverse-charge** [Mid-16C. Directly or via French < medieval Latin *collectare* < Latin *collect-*, past participle of *colligere* 'gather together' < *legere* 'gather']

SYNONYMS ***collect, accumulate, gather, amass, assemble, stockpile, hoard***

CORE MEANING: to bring dispersed things together

collect to bring things together, or to make a collection of similar things as a hobby ○ *Our eyes, ears, and noses collect information about distant objects.* ○ *He started collecting stamps at the age of nine.* **accumulate** to obtain a large amount of something over a period of time ○ *Merchants began to accumulate wealth in the form of gold bullion.* ○ *An enormous amount of material about such families has been accumulated over the past century.* **gather** to bring together people or things to form a group, or compile something such as information or ideas from various sources ○ *We gathered the children at the entrance to the exhibition.* ○ *She was gathering flowers as we strolled round the garden.* ○ *They are gathering together more information on the subject.* **amass** to bring a large quantity of things together over time ○ *the growing evidence that is being amassed by investigators* ○ *He is thought to have amassed a fortune of hundreds of millions of dollars.* **assemble** to bring people or things together, or gather together in one place ○ *one of the greatest orchestras ever assembled* ○ *Assemble all the ingredients before starting to cook.* ○ *All the guests will be assembling in the hall at 12.* **stockpile** to collect and store large amounts of things such as equipment or weapons for future use ○ *UN resolutions that banned the country from stockpiling, developing, or using weapons of mass destruction* **hoard** to collect and store, often secretly, large amounts of things such as food or money for future use ○ *She carefully hoarded the extra money she made.* ○ *At the first hint of a supply problem, people start hoarding dry goods.*

collect[2] /kóllekt/ *n* a short formal prayer that can vary according to the day, said before the reading of the epistle in some Christian church services [13C. Via Old French < late Latin *collecta* 'assembly' < Latin *collect-* (see COLLECT[1])]

collectable /kə léktəb'l/, **collectible** *n* an object of a type that is valued or sought after by collectors ■ *adj* good for collecting or popular with collectors and much sought after

collectanea /kóllek tàyni ə/ *npl* a selection of pieces of writing by an author or by several authors [Mid-17C. < Latin, 'things collected' < form of *collectaneus* 'collected' < *collect-* (see COLLECT[1])]

collected /kə léktid/ *adj* **1.** CALM AND COMPOSED calm and in control of yourself **2.** BROUGHT TOGETHER AS WHOLE gathered together in one book or set of volumes as the whole of an author's work or work of a particular type **3.** RIDING CONTROLLED IN GAIT moving with a controlled gait —**collectedly** *adv* —**collectedness** *n*

collectible *n, adj* another spelling of **collectable**

collection /kə léksh'n/ *n* **1.** GROUP OF THINGS OR PEOPLE a group of things or people together in one place **2.** SEVERAL DIFFERENT WORKS TOGETHER a number of different pieces of writing or music together in one book, CD, or record **3.** OBJECTS HELD BY COLLECTOR a set of objects collected for their interest, value, or beauty **4.** PAINTINGS OR OBJECTS IN MUSEUM all the paintings or objects of one kind held by an art gallery or museum **5.** TAKING OF DONATIONS the act of taking money due or given ○ *They took up a collection for him when he was in hospital.* **6.** TAKING OF MONEY IN CHRISTIAN CHURCH the act of accepting money from worshippers in a Christian church service, or the money collected **7.** TAKING the taking of something on a regular basis, e.g. letters from postboxes by the Post Office, or refuse from buildings **8.** GATHERING TOGETHER the act of gathering things together (*formal*) **9.** RANGE OF NEW CLOTHES a range of newly designed clothes for a particular season ○ *the spring collection* [14C. Via French < Latin *collection-* < *collect-* (see COLLECT[1])]

collection agency *n* a business that collects payments on loans that are in arrears or on unpaid bills

collective /kə léktiv/ *adj* **1.** SHARED BY ALL made or shared by everyone in a group **2.** COLLECTED TO FORM WHOLE collected together to form a whole or added up to form a total from different sources or groups **3.**

APPLYING TO MANY applying to a number of individuals taken together ○ *Staff training was the collective responsibility of the three personnel officers.* **4. WORKER-RUN UNDER STATE SUPERVISION** describes a business or other enterprise run by the people who work in it but under the jurisdiction of the state ■ *n* **1. WORKER-RUN ENTERPRISE** an enterprise that is run by its workers under state control, e.g. a farm or factory **2. MEMBERS OF COLLECTIVE** the members of a collective who work in and run the business **3.** GRAM same as **collective noun** —**collectively** *adv* —**collectiveness** *n*

collective agreement *n* a contract of employment negotiated between management and a union

collective bargaining *n* negotiations between management and a union about pay and conditions of employment on behalf of all the workers in the union

collective farm *n* a farm that is state-supervised but operated by its workers

collective noun *n* a noun that refers to a group of people or things considered as a single unit. 'Committee' and 'government' are collective nouns.

USAGE Collective nouns: Examples of collective nouns are *audience, committee, crowd, flock, government, jury,* and *orchestra,* all of which are singular in form but plural in that they refer to groups that are made up of a number of individuals or individual things. Nouns that denote a class of objects, for example *furniture* and *luggage,* are always singular: *My luggage is missing.* Other collective nouns can be treated as singular or plural. Thus *The audience was absolutely silent* but *It was so warm the audience were stripping off their jackets.* It is important to avoid inconsistency in your choice of verb and pronoun number when using collective nouns. For instance, this example contains inconsistencies: *The committee has* [singular] *decided to reject the proposal and will give their* [plural: use *its* instead] *reasons in writing tomorrow.* Some people regard the treatment of collective nouns as plural as wrong and it is especially criticized in the United States.

collective security *n* the maintenance of peace and security through the united action of nations

collective unconscious *n* the inherited part of unconscious thought, memories, and instinct, which, according to Jungian principles, is common to members of a people and is observable through dreams and behaviour

collectivise *vt* POL another spelling of **collectivize**

collectivism /kə léktivizəm/ *n* the system of control and ownership of factories and farms and of the means of production and distribution of products by a nation's people —**collectivist** *n* —**collectivistic** /kə lékti vístik/ *adj* —**collectivistically** *adv*

collectivity /kóllek tívvəti/ (*plural* -ties) *n* **1.** a state or situation in which people or things are together or work together to form a whole **2.** a group regarded as an aggregate, especially a people

collectivize /kə lékti víz/ (-izes, -izing, -ized), **collectivise** (-ises, -ising, -ised) *vt* to run or organize something such as a farm according to principles of collective control —**collectivization** /kə lékti ví záysh'n/ *n*

collector /kə léktər/ *n* **1. SOMEBODY WHO COLLECTS OBJECTS** somebody who accumulates objects for their interest, value, or beauty ○ *a stamp collector* **2. SOMEBODY WHO MAKES COLLECTION** somebody whose job is to collect something such as money owed, tickets, or refuse **3. CONTAINER WHERE THINGS COLLECT** something in which things are collected intentionally or where unwanted things collect **4. TRANSISTOR REGION** the region of a transistor towards or through which charge carriers flow **5.** *S Asia* **SOUTH ASIAN ADMINISTRATOR** the chief administrator of a district

collectorate /kə léktərət/ *n S Asia* the district over which a collector presides

collector's item *n* an object that is sought after or valued highly by collectors

colleen /kə leén, kólleen/ *n* **1.** *Ireland* a girl, especially a young girl **2.** a girl living or born in Ireland or a girl of Irish descent [Early 19C. < Irish *cailín* 'little girl' < *caile* 'girl']

college /kóllij/ *n* **1. INSTITUTION OF HIGHER LEARNING** an educational institution for higher education, especially one offering courses in specialized or practical subjects ○ *a further education college* **2. PART OF BRITISH UNIVERSITY** a division of some of the larger British universities, e.g. Oxford and Cambridge **3. SCHOOL** a school for students after the age of 16 ○ *a sixth form college* **4. BRITISH SCHOOL** used as part of the name of some British public schools ○ *Eton College* **5. PROFESSIONAL BODY** a group of people, usually of the same profession, who have agreed duties and rights **6. COLLEGE BUILDINGS** the building or buildings of a college **7. MEMBERS OF COLLEGE** the staff and students of a college **8.** *N Am* **UNIVERSITY SCHOOL OR DIVISION** a school or a division of a university that usually has its own dean and other administrators and whose faculty teaches and confers degrees in specific academic fields **9. BODY OF CLERGY** a group or body of clergy who live together [14C. Directly or via French < Latin *collegium* 'association, corporation' < *collega* (see COLLEAGUE)]

College of Arms *n* an institution with jurisdiction in England, Wales, and Northern Ireland that specializes in matters relating to heraldry, the granting of arms, and tracing genealogies

College of Cardinals *n* the body of Roman Catholic cardinals who elect popes, assist the pope in church governance, and manage the Holy See in the absence of a living or elected pope

College of Heralds *n* HERALDRY same as **College of Arms**

College of Justice *n* the Scottish Court of Session, Scotland's highest civil court

collegia POL plural of **collegium**

collegial /kə leéji əl/ *adj* **1. OF COLLEGE OR UNIVERSITY** involving, typical of, or belonging to a college or university **2. POWER-SHARING** with power shared equally between colleagues **3. OF POWER-SHARING BY BISHOPS** relating to a situation or system in the Roman Catholic Church in which the bishops share equal power [14C. Directly or via French < late Latin *collegialis* < Latin *collegium* (see COLLEGE)] —**collegiality** /kə leéji álləti/ *n* —**collegially** *adv*

collegian /kə leéji ən/ *n* a college undergraduate, graduate student, or recent graduate [15C. < medieval Latin *collegianus* < Latin *collegium* (see COLLEGE)]

collegiate /kə leéji ət/ *adj* **1.** involving, belonging to, appropriate to, or being a college, including its students and their pursuits **2.** consisting of separate university colleges [15C. < medieval Latin *collegiatus* '(member) of a college' < Latin *collegium* (see COLLEGE)] —**collegiately** *adv*

collegiate church *n* **1. CHURCH WITH CANONS** a Roman Catholic or Anglican church that has a chapter of canons but is not a cathedral **2. CHURCH WITH TWO MINISTERS** in Scotland, a church with two or more ministers of equal seniority **3.** *US* **GROUP OF CHURCHES** a group or association of churches that have pastors in common

collegium /kə leéji əm/ (*plural* -giums or -gia /-ji ə/) *n* **1.** in the former Soviet Union, a committee of equally empowered members in charge of a department or industry **2.** CHR same as **College of Cardinals** [< Latin (see COLLEGE)]

col legno /kol lég nō, -láy nyō/ *adv* to be played by tapping the strings of a stringed instrument with the back of the bow (*used as a musical direction*) [< Italian, 'with the wood']

~~collegue~~ incorrect spelling of **colleague**

collembolan /kə lémbələn/ *n* INSECTS same as **springtail** [Late 19C. < modern Latin *Collembola* < Greek *kolla* 'glue' + *embolon* 'peg'] —**collembolous** *adj*

collenchyma /kə léngkimə/ *n* a layer of supportive plant tissue that consists of elongated living cells that have walls unevenly thickened with cellulose and pectin [Mid-19C. < COLLO-] —**collenchymatous** /kóllən kímmətəss/ *adj*

Colles' fracture /kólliz-/ *n* a fracture of the radius bone in which a piece broken off at the end is displaced towards the back of the wrist. The fracture is commonly caused by falling on the palm of the hand. [Late 19C. After Abraham *Colles* (1773–1843), Irish surgeon]

collet /kóllit/ *n* **1. CONE-SHAPED MECHANICAL PIECE** a slotted cone-shaped piece that encloses and grips a rod or shaft when inserted into the sleeve of a lathe or other machine **2. SETTING FOR GEMSTONE** a band or claw that holds a gemstone **3. BAND ATTACHED TO SPRING IN WATCH** a ring that holds the hairspring in a watch

[15C. < French, 'little collar' < *col* 'collar' < Latin *collum* 'neck']

collide /kə líd/ (-lides, -liding, -lided) *vi* **1.** to hit a person or object moving towards you or a person or object you are moving towards ○ *I collided with her in the corridor.* **2.** to come into conflict with somebody else or another group [Early 17C. < Latin *collidere* 'shatter', literally 'strike together' < *laedere* 'strike']

collider /kə lídər/, **colliding-beam machine** /kə líding-/ *n* a particle accelerator in which two oppositely moving particle beams are made to collide. This allows the particles to use more of their energy to create new particles than when they collide with a fixed target.

collie

collie /kólli/ *n* a dog with a long narrow muzzle, belonging to a breed originally developed to herd sheep. There are short-haired (smooth) and long-haired (rough) collies. [Mid-17C Origin ?]

~~collieflour~~, ~~collieflower~~ incorrect spelling of **cauliflower**

collier /kólli ər/ *n* **1.** somebody who mines coal (*dated*) **2.** a boat designed to transport coal [13C. < COAL]

colliery /kóllyəri/ (*plural* -ies) *n* a coal mine and the buildings associated with it

collinear /ko línni ər/, **colinear** /kō-/ *adj* lying on or passing through a single straight line [Mid-19C. < COL- + LINEAR] —**collinearity** /ko línni árrəti/ *n*

collins /kóllinz/ *n* an iced drink made with spirits such as gin or vodka and fruit juice such as lemon or lime [Mid-19C. Origin ?]

Collins /kóllinz/, **Jackie** (*b.* 1939) British novelist. Her popular novels include *The Bitch* (1978).

Michael Collins

Collins, Michael (1890–1922) Irish politician. A creator of the Irish Free State (1922), he was shot by Republicans who opposed the Anglo-Irish Treaty.

'Think—what have I got for Ireland? Something which she has wanted these past 700 years...I tell you this—early this morning I signed my death warrant.'
[Michael Collins, *Letter to John O'Kane*; 6 December 1921]

Collins, Wilkie (1824–89) British novelist. His *The Woman in White* (1860) and *The Moonstone* (1868) were pioneering mystery novels. Full name **Collins, William Wilkie**. See Cultural note at **moonstone**

'There, in the middle of the broad, bright high road...stood the figure of a solitary Woman, dressed from head to foot in white garments, her face bent in grave inquiry on mine, her hand pointing to the dark

cloud over London, as I faced her.'
[Wilkie Collins, *The Woman in White*; 1860]

Collins Street farmer, **Collins Street cocky** *n Aus* somebody who has money invested in rural properties, often for tax reasons, but who lives and works in the city of Melbourne (*informal*) [After an important business street in Melbourne]

collision /kə lízh'n/ *n* **1.** **CRASH** the action of two moving vehicles, ships, aircraft, or other objects hitting each other **2.** **CONFLICT BETWEEN IDEAS** a conflict between people or their ideas or beliefs **3.** PHYS **EXCHANGE OF ENERGY BETWEEN PARTICLES** an encounter between two or more particles that come together or close to each other, and exchange or transfer energy [15C. < late Latin *collision-* < Latin *collis-*, past participle of *collidere* (see COLLIDE)] —**collisional** *adj*

collision course *n* a path or course of action that inevitably leads to conflict ○ *The two of them were clearly on a collision course.*

collision damage waiver *n N Am* an insurance option available to somebody renting a car that waives the renter's liability for damage to the vehicle as a result of a collision

collision zone *n* an extensive linear feature marking the collision of two continental plates, characterized by young fold mountains and earthquakes

collo- *prefix* glutinous, gelatinous ○ *collotype* [Via modern Latin < Greek *kolla* 'glue']

collocate *v* /kóllə kayt/ (**-cates, -cating, -cated**) **1.** *vi* **OCCUR FREQUENTLY WITH ANOTHER WORD** to occur frequently in conjunction with another word. For example, 'vast' collocates with 'majority' in the phrase 'vast majority'. **2.** *vt* **PUT SOMETHING NEXT TO SOMETHING** to arrange something so that it is next to or close to something else (*formal*) ■ *n* /kólləkət/ **WORD THAT OCCURS WITH ANOTHER** a word that is frequently or typically used with another word [Early 16C. < Latin *collocat-*, past participle of *collocare* 'place together' < *locare* 'to place']

collocation /kóllə káysh'n/ *n* **1.** the association between two words that are typically or frequently used together **2.** an arrangement in which things are placed next to each other or close together

collodion /kə lódi ən/ *n* a thick colourless solution of pyroxylin, ether, and alcohol. Use: to treat wounds and hold surgical dressings, formerly, to make photographic plates. [Mid-19C. < Greek *kollōdēs* 'glue-like' < *kolla* 'glue']

colloid /kólloyd/ *n* **1.** CHEM **SUSPENSION OF SMALL PARTICLES** a suspension of small particles dispersed in another substance **2.** CHEM **PARTICLES IN COLLOID** the particles that are suspended in a colloid solution **3.** PHYSIOL **SUBSTANCE IN THYROID GLAND** a thick gelatinous substance that is produced in the thyroid gland and stores hormones [Mid-19C. < Greek *kolla* 'glue'] —**colloid** *adj* —**colloidal** /kə lóyd'l/ *adj*

collop /kólləp/ *n* **1.** a slice of meat, especially fried bacon **2.** a small piece of something [14C. < N Germanic]

colloq. *abbr* LANGUAGE colloquial

~~colloquail~~ incorrect spelling of **colloquial**

colloquia plural of **colloquium**

colloquial /kə lókwi əl/ *adj* said more usually in informal conversation than in formal speech or writing [Mid-18C. < Latin *colloquium* (see COLLOQUIUM)] —**colloquiality** /kə lókwi álləti/ *n* —**colloquially** *adv* —**colloquialness** *n*

colloquialism /kə lókwi əlizəm/ *n* an informal word or phrase that is more usual in conversation than in formal speech or writing

colloquium /kə lókwi əm/ (*plural* **-quiums** or **-quia** /-kwi ə/) *n* **1.** an academic conference or seminar in which a particular topic is discussed, often with guest speakers **2.** an informal meeting to discuss something [Late 16C. < Latin, 'conversation' < *colloqui* 'speak with' < *loqui* 'speak']

colloquy /kólləkwi/ (*plural* **-quies**) *n* **1.** a formal conversation or discussion (*formal*) **2.** a literary or other written work in the form of a dialogue [15C. < Latin *colloquium* (see COLLOQUIUM)]

~~collosal~~ incorrect spelling of **colossal**

collotype /kóllə tīp/ *n* **1.** a process for making lithographic prints **2.** a print that is made by use of the collotype process

collude /kə lo͞od/ (**-ludes, -luding, -luded**) *vi* to cooperate with somebody secretly in order to do something illegal or undesirable [Early 16C. < Latin *colludere* 'play with' < *ludere* 'play' < *ludus* 'game'] —**colluder** *n*

collusion /kə lo͞ozh'n/ *n* secret cooperation between people in order to do something illegal or underhand [14C. Directly or via French < Latin *collusion-* < *collus-*, past participle of *colludere* (see COLLUDE)]

collusive /kə lo͞ossiv/ *adj* secretly cooperating or involving secret cooperation in order to do something illegal or underhanded [Late 17C. < Latin *collus-* (see COLLUSION)] —**collusively** *adv* —**collusiveness** *n*

colluvium /kə lo͞ovi əm/ *n* loose rock and soil at the base of a cliff or steep slope [Mid-20C. < Latin < *colluvies* < *colluere* 'wash thoroughly' < *lavere* 'to wash'] —**colluvial** *adj*

collywobbles /kólli wob'lz/ *npl* a feeling of nervousness about something (*informal*) [Early 19C. Probably < COLIC + WOBBLE]

Colo. *abbr* Colorado

colo- *prefix* intestine ○ *colorectal* [< COLON [2]]

colobi *npl* ZOOL plural of **colobus**

coloboma /kóllə bōmə/ *n* a malformation of the retina, iris, or other tissue of the eye, usually present at birth [Mid-19C. Via modern Latin < Greek *koloboma* 'part removed in mutilation' < *kolobos* 'docked'] —**colobomatous** *adj*

colobus /kólləbəss/ (*plural* **-buses** or **-bi** /-bī/), **colobus monkey** *n* a large slender monkey that has a long tail and long silky fur but lacks developed thumbs. Native to: Africa. Genus: *Colobus*. [Late 19C. Via modern Latin < Greek *kolobos* 'docked, maimed']

colocation /kō lō káysh'n/ *n* the sharing of the facilities of a hosting centre with other Internet clients

colocynth /kóllə sinth/ *n* **1.** a spongy bitter yellow fruit about the size of a lemon but speckled with green. Use: laxative. **2.** a vine related to the pumpkin and squash that bears colocynths. Native to: Europe. Latin name: *Citrulus colocynthis*. [Mid-17C. Via Latin *colocynthis* < Greek *kolokunthis* < *kolokunthē* 'pumpkin, round gourd']

cologne /kə lōn/ *n* a scented liquid with a lighter scent than perfume [Early 19C. After COLOGNE]

Cologne /kə lōn/ river port and largest city in the North Rhine-Westphalia state of Germany. Population: 963,817 (1997).

Colombia

Colombia /kə lúmbi ə, -lóm-/ country in northwestern South America surrounded by the Caribbean Sea, Venezuela, Brazil, Peru, Ecuador, Panama, and the Pacific Ocean. Language: Spanish. Currency: peso. Capital: Bogotá. Population: 41,662,073 (2003). Area: 1,141,748 sq. km/440,831 sq. mi. Official name **Republic of Colombia** —**Colombian** *n, adj*

Colombo /kə lúmbō/ port and commercial capital of Sri Lanka, situated on the western coast. Population: 615,000 (1995).

colon[1] /kólən, -lon/ *n* **1.** **PUNCTUATION MARK** the punctuation mark (:) used to divide distinct but related sentence components such as clauses in which the second elaborates on the first, or to introduce a list, quotation, or speech. Colons are also used between numbers in statements of proportion or time and Biblical or literary references. **2.** **MARK USED IN PHONETICS** a mark (:) after a vowel in a system of phonetic writing that shows that the vowel is lengthened **3.** (*plural* **cola** /kólə/) **UNIT OF CLASSICAL POETRY** in Greek or Roman verse, a rhythmic unit consisting of two to six metrical feet with one main accent [Mid-16C. Via Latin < Greek *kōlon* 'clause, limb']

USAGE A ***colon*** is used to divide a sentence when the second part explains or elaborates on what has gone before: *They have put forward a different theory: the phenomenon may be caused by movements within the earth's crust.* It is also used to introduce a list: *You will need the following equipment: a rucksack, waterproof clothing, strong walking boots, and a map.* A colon sometimes separates numbers, e.g. in biblical references, ratios, and clock times: *Genesis 13:8; a ratio of 6:4; the train that departs at 17:42.* When a colon is followed by a full sentence, the first word is often capitalized in US English.

colon[2] /kólən, -lon/ (*plural* **-lons** or **-la** /-lə/) *n* the section of the large intestine that runs from the caecum to the rectum [14C. Via Latin < Greek *kolon* 'large intestine']

colón /ko lón/ (*plural* **-lóns** or **-lones** /-lóness/) *n* the main unit of currency in Costa Rica and El Salvador. See table at **currency** [Late 19C. After Cristóbal *Colón*, Spanish name of Christopher COLUMBUS]

Colón /ko lón/ city and capital of Colón Province, central Panama, situated on Limón Bay at the entrance to the Panama Canal. Population: 158,935 (1996).

colonel /kúrn'l/ *n* **1.** **MILITARY RANK IN UK** an officer in the British Army or Royal Marines of a rank above lieutenant colonel **2.** **MILITARY RANK IN UNITED STATES** an officer in the US Army, Marine Corps, or Air Force of a rank above lieutenant colonel **3.** **MILITARY RANK IN CANADA** an officer in the Canadian Army or Air Force of a rank above lieutenant colonel **4.** *US* **HONORARY US TITLE** an honorary title in a state militia, bestowed by the governor in some US states, notably Kentucky [Mid-16C. Via obsolete French *coronel* < Italian *colonnella*, literally 'little column' < *colonna* 'column' < Latin *columna* (see COLUMN)] —**colonelcy** *n* —**colonelship** *n*

SPELLCHECK colonel or **kernel**? Do not confuse the spelling of ***colonel*** and ***kernel***, which sound similar. A ***colonel*** is an officer in the armed forces. A ***kernel*** is the edible part of a nut or the central part of something.

Colonel Blimp /-blímp/ *n* same as **blimp** [2]

colones MONEY plural of **colón**

colonia /kə lóni ə/ *n N Am* a poor Hispanic-American community, especially along the border between the United States and Mexico [Late 20C. < Spanish, 'colony']

colonial /kə lóni əl/ *adj* **1.** **RELATING TO COLONY** possessing, ruling over, living in, or relating to a colony **2.** *also* **Colonial** OF **BRITISH EMPIRE** relating to the colonies of the former British Empire, or to the Empire as a whole **3.** *also* **Colonial RELATING TO BRITISH COLONIES IN AMERICA** relating to the 13 original British colonies in North America before their independence in 1776 **4.** **IN STYLE OF AMERICAN COLONIES** dating from or in a style typical of British North America in the late 17th to the early 19th century **5.** HIST **FROM AUSTRALIAN TIME AS COLONY** dating from or related to the period before the Federation of Australia in 1901 **6.** *NZ* **NEW ZEALAND PRE-1840** in New Zealand, relating to the period before 1840 **7.** **LIVING IN COLONIES** describes animals that live in groups or colonies and are dependent on each other. Some, e.g. corals, are physically joined, while others such as insects show social organization and specialized functions. ■ *n* **1.** **SOMEBODY WHO LIVES IN COLONY** a resident of a colony who comes from the colonizing country **2.** **SOMEBODY FROM COLONY** somebody whose native country is a colony [Late 18C. < COLONY] —**colonially** *adv* —**colonialness** *n*

CULTURAL NOTE ***The Wild Colonial Boy***, an anonymous song from the 1860s. It tells the story of Jack Doolan, an Irish boy transported to Australia for theft, who becomes an outlaw before being hunted down and killed by police. In Australia, the phrase came to mean 'bushranger'.

colonialism /kə lóni əlizəm/ *n* a policy in which a country rules other nations and develops trade for its own benefit —**colonialist** *n* —**colonialistic** /kə lóni ə lístik/ *adj*

colonic /kō lónnik/ *adj* relating to or situated in the colon ■ *n* same as **colonic irrigation**

colonic irrigation, **colonic hydrotherapy** *n* the injection of fluids through the anus into the colon to clean it out

colonise *vt* INTERNAT REL another spelling of **colonize**

colonist /kólllənist/ *n* **1.** SOMEBODY LIVING IN NEW COLONY an immigrant to a new colony, or one of the founders of it **2.** *also* **Colonist** EUROPEAN SETTLER OF AMERICA one of the early European settlers of North America before it became the United States **3.** ORGANISM MOVING INTO NEW ECOSYSTEM an organism, e.g. a plant such as a weed, that moves into and establishes itself in a new ecosystem

colonitis /kólllə nítiss/ *n* MED same as **colitis**

colonize /kólllə nīz/ (-**nizes**, -**nizing**, -**nized**), **colonise** (-**nises**, -**nising**, -**nised**) *v* **1.** *vti* ESTABLISH COLONY to establish a colony in another country or place **2.** *vt* GO TO LIVE IN NEW LAND to go to and live permanently as part of a settlement in a foreign land that was previously sparsely inhabited **3.** *vti* BECOME ESTABLISHED IN NEW ECOSYSTEM to establish plants or animals, or become established, in a biological colony in a new ecosystem **4.** *vt* BECOME DOMINANT to become the most important or influential person or thing in a field of activity ○ *Japan's chefs colonize World Cuisine.* —**colonizable** *adj* —**colonization** /kólllə nī záysh'n/ *n* —**colonizer** *n*

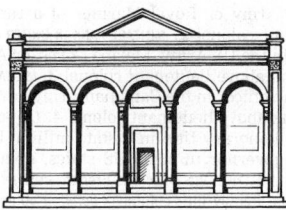

colonnade

colonnade /kólllə náyd/ *n* a row of columns, usually supporting a roof or arches [Early 18C. < French < *colonne* 'column' < Latin *columna* (see COLUMN)] —**colonnaded** *adj*

colonoscope /kə lónnə skōp/ *n* a long flexible instrument (**endoscope**) for viewing the interior of the colon, and often equipped with a device that can remove tissue for biopsy

colonoscopy /kólllə nóskəpi/ (*plural* -**pies**) *n* a medical examination of the colon using a colonoscope [< COLON[2]] —**colonoscopic** /kə lónnə skóppik/ *adj*

colony /kóllləni/ (*plural* -**nies**) *n* **1.** COUNTRY RULED BY ANOTHER a country or area that is ruled by another country **2.** SETTLEMENT IN AMERICA one of the early settled areas in North America that formed the 13 founding states of the United States after independence (*often used in the plural*) **3.** GROUP OF COLONISTS the group of people who have gone to live in a colony **4.** GROUP OF SIMILAR PEOPLE a group of people of the same nationality or ethnic group, doing the same work, or living in the same circumstances, who reside together or near one another ○ *a colony of artists* **5.** AREA WHERE GROUP LIVES the area where a group of people with shared ethnicity, interests, or occupations lives, e.g. in a city **6.** GROUP OF ANIMALS OR PLANTS a group of animals, insects, or organisms of the same kind that are living together and dependent on each other, or a group of plants growing in the same place **7.** MASS OF ORGANISMS a localized mass or growth of organisms such as bacteria in or on a nutrient medium [14C. < Latin *colonia* 'farm, settlement' < *colonus* 'tiller' < *colere* 'cultivate']

colophon /kólllə fon/ *n* **1.** the symbol or emblem that is printed on a book and represents a publisher or publisher's imprint **2.** the details of the title, printer, publisher, and publication date given at the end of a book. Colophons are commonly found in early printed books and in modern private press editions. [Early 17C. Via late Latin < Greek *kolophōn* 'summit, finishing touch']

colophony /ko lóffəni/ *n* INDUST same as **rosin** [14C. < Latin *colophonia* < *Colophonia resina* 'resin of Colophon' (city in Lydia, in what is now Turkey)]

color *n*, *vti* US spelling of **colour**

Colorado /kólllə raadō/ **1.** state in the western United States bordered by Wyoming, Nebraska, Kansas, Oklahoma, New Mexico, Arizona, and Utah. Capital: Denver. Population: 4,506,542 (2002 estimate). Area: 269,618 sq. km/104,100 sq. mi. **2.** major North American river, rising in northern Colorado and flowing southwest through the Grand Canyon. Length: 2,330 km/1,450 mi.

Colorado beetle *n* a small black-and-yellow striped beetle that is a serious agricultural pest and feeds on the leaves of potato plants. Latin name: *Leptinotarsa decemlineata*. N Am term **Colorado potato beetle**

Colorado Desert desert area of southeastern California west of the Colorado River. It includes the Salton Sea and the Imperial Valley.

Colorado Springs city in central Colorado, south of Denver and east of Pikes Peak, home to the United States Air Force Academy. Population: 371,182 (2002 estimate).

Colorado topaz *n* **1.** a brownish-yellow topaz found in the state of Colorado **2.** a type of brownish-yellow quartz that resembles true Colorado topaz

coloration /kólllə ráysh'n/, **colouration** *n* **1.** the appearance or pattern of colour on an object **2.** the pattern of colours naturally occurring on a plant or an insect, bird, or other animal

coloratura /kólllərə tóorə/ *n* a passage or piece of vocal music characterized by florid and demanding ornamentation, usually consisting of a rapid succession of notes. Coloratura passages are frequent in 18th- and 19th-century arias. [Mid-18C. < obsolete Italian, 'colouring']

coloratura soprano *n* a soprano with a light versatile voice capable of performing coloratura roles

colorectal /kólō rékt'l/ *adj* relating to both the colon and rectum

colorific /kúllə ríffik/ *adj* producing or giving colour to something

colorimeter /kúllə rímmitər/ *n* **1.** an instrument for measuring and specifying colours by comparison with an established set of standard colours **2.** an instrument that determines the concentration of a solution of a coloured substance by reference to standard solutions or standard colour slides [Mid-19C. < Latin *color* (see COLOUR)] —**colorimetric** /kúlləri méttrik/ *adj* —**colorimetrically** *adv* —**colorimetry** *n*

colossal /kə lóss'l/ *adj* **1.** VERY LARGE unusually or impressively large ○ *a colossal high-rise office building* **2.** VERY GREAT very great or impressive **3.** SCULPTURE TWICE LIFE SIZE describes sculptures that are twice life size —**colossally** *adv*

colosseum *n* ANCIENT HIST another spelling of **coliseum**

Colosseum, Rome

Colosseum /kólllə seé əm/ *n* a large amphitheatre in Rome, built in the 1st century AD for sport and entertainment

Colossians /kə lósh'nz/ *n* a book of the Bible, originally a letter addressed to the church in the Phrygian city of Colossae, written between AD 55 and 63 and traditionally attributed to St Paul (*takes a singular verb*) See table at **Bible**

colossus /kə lóssəss/ (*plural* -**si** /-sī/ or -**suses**) *n* **1.** a statue that is several times larger than life size **2.** an enormously large or powerful person or thing ○ *a colossus among contemporary fashion designers* [14C. Via Latin < Greek *kolossos*]

colostomy /kə lóstəmi/ (*plural* -**mies**) *n* **1.** a surgical operation that creates an artificial anus through an opening made in the abdomen from the colon **2.** an opening surgically created in the abdomen that functions as an anus

colostrum /kə lóstrəm/ *n* a yellowish fluid rich in antibodies and minerals that a mother's breasts produce after giving birth and before the production of true milk. It provides newborns with immunity to infections. [Late 16C. < Latin]

colour /kúllər/ *n* **1.** PROPERTY CAUSING VISUAL SENSATION the property of objects that depends on the light that they reflect and is perceived as red, blue, green, or other shades **2.** NOT BLACK OR WHITE a manifestation of colour, e.g. red or green, as opposed to black, white, or grey ○ *printed in colour* **3.** ART PIGMENT a pigment used in painting **4.** SOMETHING THAT ADDS COLOUR something that is used to add colour to something, e.g. paint, cosmetics, or dye ○ *She chose an auburn colour to dye her hair.* **5.** NATURAL SHADE OF COMPLEXION the natural shade or colour of somebody's skin as characteristic of race, especially somebody who is not white ○ *We do not discriminate against people on the basis of colour.* **6.** NON-WHITE SKIN COLORATION a skin colour other than that conventionally described as white ○ *people of colour* **7.** HEALTHY LOOK TO SKIN the normal look of somebody's skin, especially in the face, when healthy **8.** EXTRA FACIAL REDNESS an extra redness in somebody's face, e.g. caused by embarrassment or exposure to cold wind **9.** VARIETY OF COLOURS brightness and variety in the colours that something such as a room or picture has **10.** INTEREST OR VIVIDNESS a quality in something that gives it interest or immediacy ○ *The story lacks colour.* **11.** ART USE OF COLOUR IN PAINTING the use of colour in painting, as distinct from line, form, or composition ○ *liked her handling of colour* **12.** MUSIC SOUND QUALITY the quality of a particular sound **13.** LAW CLAIM OF LEGALITY a claim or appearance of legal right ○ *by colour of law* **14.** PHYS HYPOTHETICAL QUANTUM CHARACTERISTIC a hypothetical property of quarks that takes three forms designated red, blue, and green **15.** OPTICS ABILITY TO SEE COLOURS the aspect of visual perception by which an observer recognizes colours **16.** *US* MIN EXTRACT GOLD FOUND IN GRAVEL a particle of gold found in gravel or sand ■ **colours** *npl* **1.** SOMEBODY'S REAL SELF somebody's real beliefs, opinions, ethics, and principles ○ *It showed her up in her true colours.* **2.** NATIONAL OR MILITARY FLAG the flag of a nation or military unit **3.** COLOURS REPRESENTING TEAM OR GROUP the colours that are used to represent a team, school, or other group **4.** CLOTHING WORN IN SPORT the clothing worn by a jockey or an athlete that indicates the horse's owner or the team to which the athlete belongs **5.** SPORTS TEAM MEMBERS' BADGE a badge or other symbol given to members of a sports team ○ *In her second year she got her rowing colours.* **6.** HERALDRY HERALDIC COLOUR the main heraldic colours (**tinctures**) of azure, vert, sable, gules, and purpure ■ *v* (-**ours**, -**ouring**, -**oured**) **1.** *vt* CHANGE COLOUR OF SOMETHING to change or add to the colour of something using paint, dye, cosmetics, or a similar agent **2.** *vi* TAKE ON COLOUR to take on a particular colour or change colour **3.** *vi* BLUSH to have more red in the cheeks or face than usual, generally because of embarrassment **4.** *vt* SKEW OPINION OR JUDGMENT to influence an opinion or judgment, especially so as to make it less objective [13C. Via Old French < Latin *color*] —**colourer** *n* ◇ **nail your colours to the mast** to make your opinions or intentions obvious ○ *They've nailed their colours to the mast and announced that they will not sell their property for redevelopment.* ◇ **with flying colours** to an excellent standard

colour in *vti* to colour shapes or areas that have been left white or blank, especially in a special book of outline drawings for children

colour up *vi* to become red in the face because of embarrassment or annoyance ○ *If you so much as look at him, he colours up.*

colourable /kúllərəb'l/ *adj* (*formal*) **1.** appearing to be reasonable or true, but in fact being neither ○ *a colourable explanation* **2.** feigned or intended to deceive

colourant /kúllərənt/ *n* a dye, pigment, ink, or similar agent that is used to add or change colour

colouration *n* another spelling of **coloration**

colour bar *n* the legal, social, and traditional barriers that separate people of different ethnic groups

colour-blind *adj* **1.** partially or completely unable to distinguish between some colours because of a medical condition **2.** not discriminating between people on the grounds of their ethnic group or the colour of their skin —**colour blindness** *n*

colour-code *vt* to classify different types of thing by different colours

colour contrast *n* the perceived difference in a colour that occurs when it is surrounded by another colour

coloured /kúllərd/ *adj* **1.** HAVING COLOUR having a particular colour or colours (*often used in combination*) ○ *dark coloured* ○ *honey coloured* **2.** OFFENSIVE TERM an offensive term meaning belonging to an ethnic group whose members are predominantly dark-skinned (*dated*) **3.** DISTORTED OR BIASED biased or sensationalized ○ *a highly coloured account of the incident* ■ *n* OFFENSIVE TERM an offensive term for somebody who belongs to an ethnic group that is predominantly dark-skinned (*dated*)

Coloured *S Africa adj* belonging to a group of mixed ethnic origin, formerly a racial classification in the apartheid era ■ *n* somebody whose ancestors were of both African and non-African descent, formerly a racial classification in the apartheid era

colourfast /kúllər faast/ *adj* containing a dye that will not fade or wash out [Early 20C. < FAST[1]] —**colourfastness** *n*

colour filter *n* a filter made of coloured glass or gelatin that absorbs light of a particular colour before it reaches the camera lens. It is used to achieve artistic effects or to compensate for weather conditions.

colourful /kúllərf'l/ *adj* **1.** WITH BRIGHT COLOURS having bright or varied colours **2.** INTERESTING interesting or exciting and sometimes amusing ○ *a colourful period of history* ○ *the colourful characters of 'Alice in Wonderland'* **3.** NOT ORDINARY OR PREDICTABLE characterized by unusual, unconventional, and sometimes illegal behavior ○ *no attempt to hide his colourful past* **4.** FULL OF SWEARWORDS characterized by coarse words or obscenities (*informal; used euphemistically*) —**colourfully** *adv* —**colourfulness** *n*

colouring /kúlləring/ *n* **1.** ACT OF GIVING COLOUR the act of giving colour to something ○ *Children often enjoy colouring.* **2.** COLOURING SUBSTANCE a substance that gives colour to something, e.g. a food dye **3.** COLOUR OF COMPLEXION OR HAIR the shade of somebody's skin or hair colour **4.** CHARACTERISTIC COLOURS OF BIRD OR ANIMAL the characteristic colours of a bird's plumage or an animal's coat

colouring book, colouring-in book *n* a book with drawings for a child to colour

colourise *vt* CINEMA another spelling of **colourize**

colourist /kúllərist/ *n* **1.** a painter whose technique involves special use of colour **2.** somebody whose work involves colouring things —**colouristic** /kúllə rístik/ *adj* —**colouristically** *adv*

colourize /kúllər īz/ (**-izes, -izing, -ized**), **colourise** (**-ises, -ising, -ised**) *vt* to add colour to a black-and-white film, e.g. by using computer techniques

colourless /kúllərləss/ *adj* **1.** WITHOUT COLOUR lacking colour **2.** CHARACTERLESS not interesting or exciting ○ *a colourless personality* **3.** PALE pale or lacking distinctive colour —**colourlessly** *adv* —**colourlessness** *n*

colour line *n US* a separation of ethnic groups, physically or socially, either in law or as the result of discrimination

colour phase *n* **1.** a seasonal variation in the colour of a bird's plumage or an animal's coat **2.** a distinct and permanent colour variation shown by a group of animals within a species

colourpoint /kúllər poynt/ *n UK* a long-haired cat with the markings of a Siamese cat, bred by crossing a Persian cat with a Siamese cat. ANZ, N Am term **Himalayan cat**

colourpoint shorthair /kúllər poynt sháwrt hair/ *n* a domestic cat belonging to a breed with a light-coloured coat and darker markings on the face, ears, feet, and tail

colour scheme *n* a combination of colours used in interior decoration

colour sergeant *n* a sergeant who carries a national, battalion, or regimental flag on parade

colour subcarrier *n* the component of a television signal that transmits colour information to the receiver

colour supplement *n* a magazine printed in colour and forming a section of a newspaper

colourwash /kúllər wosh/ *n* a coloured distemper —**colourwash** *vt*

colourway /kúllər way/ *n* one of a range of possible colours available ○ *The shirt comes in three exciting colourways, taupe, red, and navy.*

colour wheel *n* the spectrum represented as a circular diagram that shows how colours are related to one another

colpitis /kol pítis/ *n* MED same as **vaginitis** (*technical*)

colpo- *prefix* vagina ○ *colposcope* [< Greek *kolpos*]

colposcope /kólpəskōp/ *n* a magnifying and photographic instrument used to examine the vagina —**colposcopic** /kólpə skóppik/ *adj* —**colposcopy** /kol póskəpi/ *n*

colt /kōlt/ *n* a young uncastrated male horse, usually under four years of age ■ **colts** *npl* a team made up of young or inexperienced players, often the junior team representing a club or school [Old English, origin ?]

coltan /kól tan/ *n* a metallic ore in the form of black sand that occurs mainly in eastern Democratic Republic of the Congo. Use: source of tantalum for the capacitors used in electronic devices such as mobile phones and laptop computers. [Late 20C. < COLUMBITE + TANTALITE]

coltish /kṓltish/ *adj* energetic and playful in nature —**coltishly** *adv* —**coltishness** *n*

Coltrane /kol tráyn/, **John** (1926–67) US saxophonist and composer. He was a leading proponent of free-form jazz in the 1960s. His compositions include 'Giant Steps'.

> 'If the music doesn't say it, how can words say it *for* the music?'
> [John Coltrane, *Jazz Is*, Nat Hentoff; 1976]

coltsfoot /kṓltsfoot/ (*plural* **-foots** or *same*) *n* a plant with large hoof-shaped leaves. Flowers: yellow. Use: in herbal medicine to treat coughs. Native to: Europe, Asia, North America. Latin name: *Tussilago farfara.*

colubrid /kóllyoobrid/ (*plural same* or **-brids**) *n* a snake belonging to a family of mostly nonvenomous snakes. Family: Colubridae. [Late 19C. < modern Latin *Colubridae* < Latin *colubrid-*, stem of *coluber* 'snake']

colubrine /kóllyoo brīn/ *adj* **1.** resembling a snake **2.** relating to or belonging to the colubrid snakes [Early 16C. < Latin *colubrinus* < *coluber* 'snake']

colugo /kə loogō/ (*plural* **-gos** or *same*) *n* VERTEB same as **flying lemur** [Early 18C. < Malay]

Colum /kóllәm/, **Padraic** (1881–1972) Irish poet and dramatist. He was an early supporter of Dublin's Abbey Theatre, where his plays, including *The Land* (1905), were presented.

Columba /kə lúmbə/ *n* a small faint constellation of the southern hemisphere between Canis Major and Pictor. See illustration at **constellation**

Columba /kə lúmbə/, **St** (521–597) Irish missionary. He travelled from the monastery he founded on the Hebridean island of Iona to spread Christianity through Scotland.

columbarium /kóllәm báiri əm/ (*plural* **-ia** /-i ə/) *n* **1.** a chamber or wall in which urns containing the ashes of the dead are stored **2.** a niche in which an urn containing funeral ashes is placed in a columbarium [Mid-18C. < Latin *columba* 'dove']

Columbia /kə lúmbi ə/ **1.** river that flows through southwestern Canada and the northwestern United States and empties into the Pacific Ocean below Portland, Oregon. Length: 2,000 km/1,240 mi. **2.** capital of South Carolina, on the eastern bank of the Congaree River, northwest of Charleston. Population: 117,394 (2002 estimate).

Columbian /kəlúmbi ən/ *adj* relating to the United States, or its peoples or cultures

columbine[1] /kóllәm bīn/ (*plural* **-bines** or *same*) *n N Am* PLANTS same as **aquilegia** [14C. Via French < medieval Latin *columbina (herba)* '(plant) like a dove' < Latin *columbinus* (see COLUMBINE[2]); from its resemblance to a cluster of doves]

columbine[2] /kóllәm bīn/ *adj* resembling or relating to doves (*literary*) [14C. Via French < Latin *columbinus* 'like a dove' < *columba* 'dove']

columbite /kə lúmm bīt/ *n* a black, reddish-brown, or transparent mixed oxide mineral containing niobium, iron, and manganese. Use: source of niobium. [Early 19C. < COLUMBIUM]

columbium /kə lúmbi əm/ *n* the element niobium (*not in technical use*) Symbol **Cb** [Early 19C. < modern Latin *Columbia* 'America'; because discovered in ore from Massachusetts] —**columbic** *adj* —**columbous** *adj*

Columbus /kə lúmbəss/ **1.** capital and largest city of Ohio. It is home to Ohio State University. Population: 725,228 (2002 estimate). **2.** city in western Georgia, on the Chattahoochee River, east of Phoenix City, Alabama. Population: 185,948 (2002 estimate).

Columbus, Christopher (1451–1506) Italian explorer. He reached the Caribbean in 1492, thereby opening the Americas to European trade and colonization.

> 'I believe that the earthly Paradise lies here, which no one can enter except by God's leave. I believe that this land which your Highnesses have commanded me to discover is very great, and that there are many other lands in the south of which there have never been reports.'
> [Christopher Columbus, *Narrative of his third voyage*; 1498]

Columbus Day *n* in the United States, a day marking Christopher Columbus's arrival in the New World in 1492. Date: second Monday in October.

columella /kóllyoo méllə/ (*plural* **-lae** /-li/) *n* a tiny bone in the middle ear of all land vertebrates that transmits sound waves from the eardrum to the inner ear and corresponds to the stapes in mammals [Late 16C. < Latin, 'little column' < *columna* (see COLUMN)] —**columellar** *adj* —**columellate** *adj*

column /kólləm/ *n* **1.** ROUND PILLAR an upright support shaped like a long cylinder ○ *a Corinthian column* **2.** SOMETHING SHAPED LIKE COLUMN something resembling a column in form ○ *a column of smoke* **3.** ANAT, BOT PART SHAPED LIKE COLUMN a long part of a plant or animal ○ *spinal column* **4.** LINE OF PEOPLE OR THINGS a long line of people or vehicles **5.** SECTION OF PAGE one of two or more vertical sections of printed material on a page **6.** REGULAR ARTICLE an item in a newspaper or magazine that is always written by the same person or is always about the same subject **7.** VERTICAL ARRANGEMENT OF NUMBERS a vertical arrangement of figures or mathematical terms [15C. Directly or via French < Latin *columna*, probably < *columen* 'top'] —**columnar** /kə lúmnər/ *adj* —**columned** *adj*

columnar jointing *n* the development of parallel prismatic columns in contracting intrusive or extrusive rock undergoing cooling

column inch *n* an area on a page one column wide and one inch deep, used to measure the amount of type that would fill that space

columnist /kólləmnist/ *n* a journalist who writes a regular column for a newspaper or magazine ○ *a gossip columnist*

colure /kə loor/ *n* either of two great circles on the celestial sphere that intersect at the celestial poles, one of which connects the equinoctial points on the ecliptic, while the other connects the solstitial points [14C. Via late Latin *coluri* < Greek *kolourai (grammai)* 'truncated (lines)' < *kolouros* 'truncated' < *kolos* 'docked' + *oura* 'tail']

Colwyn Bay /kólwin-/ coastal resort in Conwy, North Wales. Population: 29,883 (1991).

coly /kṓ li/ (*plural* **-ies** or *same*) *n* a gregarious bird with soft hairy feathers, a crest on its head, and a very long tail. Native to: Africa. Family: Coliidae. [Mid-19C. Via modern Latin *Colius* < Greek *kolios* 'green woodpecker']

colza /kólzə/ *n* PLANTS same as **rape**[2] [Early 18C. Via French (Walloon) < Low German *kōlsāt*, Dutch *koolzaad* < *kool* 'cabbage' + *zaad* 'seed']

colza oil *n* INDUST same as **rape oil**

com *abbr* commercial organization (*used in Internet addresses*) See table at **domain name**

COM /kom/ *n* the process of converting computer

output directly to microfilm. Full form **computer output microfilm**

com. *abbr* **1.** ARTS comedy **2.** comic **3.** COMM commerce **4.** COMM commercial **5.** committee **6.** SOC SCI commune[1]

Com. *abbr* **1.** MIL Commander **2.** NAVY Commodore **3.** POL Communist

com- *prefix* together, with, jointly (*used before b, m, n, or p*) ○ *commingle* [< Latin < Indo-European, 'together']

coma[1] /kṓmə/ *n* a prolonged state of deep unconsciousness [Mid-17C. Via modern Latin < Greek *kōma* 'deep sleep']

coma[2] /kṓmə/ (*plural* **-mae** /-mee/) *n* **1.** a luminous cloud of gas and dust surrounding the head of a comet **2.** a defect in a lens that produces a blurred, comet-shaped image of a point, or the image produced [Early 17C. Via Latin < Greek *komē* 'hair of the head'] —**comal** *adj*

Coma Berenices /kṓmə bérri nī seez/ *n* a faint constellation of the northern hemisphere. See illustration at **constellation** [Mid-16C. < Latin, 'Berenice's hair', after a 3C BC Egyptian queen whose hair, cut off and dedicated as an offering for her husband's safe return from war, is said to have been placed in the stars]

Comanche /kə mán chi/ (*plural same* or **-ches**) *n* **1.** a member of a Native American people who formerly led a nomadic life in areas of Kansas, Oklahoma, and Texas, and who now live mainly in Oklahoma **2.** the Shoshonean language of the Comanche. Native speakers: 500. [Early 19C. Via Spanish < Southern Paiute or a related language] —**Comanche** *adj*

~~**comand**~~ incorrect spelling of **command**

Comaneci /kómmə néch/, **Nadia** (*b.* 1961) Romanian-born US gymnast. At the age of 14, competing for Romania, she was the youngest person to win an Olympic gold medal in gymnastics and the first to attain a perfect 10 mark (1976).

comatose /kṓmətōss/ *adj* **1.** in a coma **2.** in a very tired or drunken state (*informal*) [Late 17C. < Greek *kōmat-* 'deep sleep'] —**comatosely** *adv*

comatulid /kə máttyoŏlid/ (*plural* **-lids** or *same*), **comatula** /-lə/ (*plural* **-lae** /-lee/ or *same*) *n* an invertebrate sea animal that is free-swimming when it reaches maturity, e.g. a feather star. Order: Comatulida. [Late 19C. < modern Latin *Comatulidae* < late Latin *comatulus* 'with neatly curled hair' < Latin *comatus* 'having hair']

comb /kōm/ *n* **1.** INSTRUMENT FOR NEATENING HAIR an instrument with a row of long thin teeth, used to make hair tidy **2.** FASTENING FOR HAIR a piece of plastic or wood with long thin teeth, used to fasten back the hair **3.** TEXTILES TOOL FOR CLEANING WOOL a tool or machine part with long slender teeth, used for cleaning wool or other materials **4.** RIDING same as **currycomb** **5.** NEATENING OF HAIR an act of neatening the hair with a comb (*informal*) **6.** CREST OF COCK the fleshy red growth on the head of a cock or other bird **7.** FOOD same as **honeycomb** *n* (senses 1–2) ■ *vt* (**combs, combing, combed**) **1.** RUN COMB THROUGH HAIR to tidy hair or fur with a comb **2.** TEXTILES CLEAN OR ARRANGE FIBRES to clean or arrange the fibres of wool or other materials using a comb **3.** SEARCH PLACE THOROUGHLY to search an area thoroughly ○ *We combed the house for his keys.* [Old English *camb* < Indo-European, 'tooth'] ◇ **go over** *or* **through something with a fine-tooth(ed) comb** to study or search something extremely carefully

comb. *abbr* **1.** combination **2.** combining **3.** CHEM combustion

combat /kóm bat/ *n* **1.** FIGHTING fighting between two people or groups, especially between soldiers (*often used before a noun*) ○ *He had never seen combat.* ○ *combat troops* **2.** FIGHT OR STRUGGLE a struggle between opposing individuals or forces ○ *a combat between good and evil* ■ **combats** /kóm bats/ *npl* CASUAL CLOTHES WITH MILITARY LOOK loose-fitting casual clothes, especially trousers, with a military style and often in camouflage colours ■ *vt* (**-bats, -bating, -bated**) **1.** TRY TO DESTROY SOMETHING DANGEROUS to attempt to destroy or control something harmful ○ *measures to combat pollution* **2.** RESIST SOMEBODY OR SOMETHING to resist or oppose somebody or something actively [Mid-16C. < French *combattre* 'to fight' (literally 'fight with') < Latin *battuere* 'to beat'] —**combatable** /kom báttəb'l/ *adj* —**combater** /-báttər/ *n*

combatant /kómbətənt/ *n* **1.** a person or group taking part in a war **2.** a participant in a struggle or argument

combat fatigue *n US* same as **battle fatigue**

combative /kómbətiv/ *adj* eager to fight or argue —**combatively** *adv* —**combativeness** *n*

combat trousers *npl* loose-fitting casual trousers with one or more large pockets on each thigh [Because worn by soldiers]

combe /koom/, **coomb, coombe** *n* primarily in southern England, a small valley with steep sides that seldom has running water in it [Pre-12C. < Celtic]

comber /kṓmə/ *n* **1.** a person or machine that combs wool or other materials **2.** *N Am* same as **beach-comber** (sense 2)

combination /kómbi náysh'n/ *n* **1.** MIXTURE an association of different things or factors, or the act of mixing them ○ *We were saved by a combination of skill and good luck.* **2.** COMBINED SET two or more people or things that are combined to form a set ○ *The red shirt and navy waistcoat make a striking colour combination.* **3.** NUMBERS THAT OPEN LOCK a series of numbers or letters needed to open a combination lock **4.** BOXING SERIES OF PUNCHES in boxing, two or more punches quickly delivered one after the other **5.** CHESS SEQUENCE OF MOVES INVOLVING SEVERAL PIECES in chess, a series of tactical moves involving two or more pieces **6.** ALLIANCE an association between people or groups established in order to accomplish something **7.** MATHS ARRANGEMENT OF NUMBERS IN SUBSETS an arrangement of the numbers or symbols in a mathematical set into smaller subsets without regard to the order in which those numbers or symbols appear **8.** MATHS SUBSET a subset containing a specific number of the elements of a particular set, selected without regard to the order in which they were chosen **9.** CHEM FORMATION OF COMPOUND the union of substances in the formation of a chemical compound ■ **combinations** *npl* UNDERWEAR a piece of underwear covering the whole body and with long sleeves and legs (*dated*) —**combinational** *adj*

SYNONYMS See *mixture.*

combination lock *n* a lock that opens only when a set of wheels, each with a sequence of numbers from 0 to 9, are aligned to give a specific sequence of numbers

combinatorial analysis /kómbinə táwr i əl-/ *n* the branch of mathematics dealing with combinations and permutations, especially those relating to probability and statistics

combine *v* /kəm bīn/ (**-bines, -bining, -bined**) **1.** *vti* JOIN OR MIX TOGETHER to be joined or mixed together, or join or mix people or things together ○ *Combine the ingredients in a large mixing bowl.* ○ *All these factors combine to make for a truly successful product.* **2.** *vt* DO THINGS SIMULTANEOUSLY to undertake two or more activities at the same time ○ *It can be difficult to combine having a career with being a mother.* **3.** *vti* CHEM UNITE CHEMICALLY to join together, or make substances join together, to form a chemical compound **4.** *vti* AGRIC HARVEST CROPS WITH MACHINE to harvest crops using a combine harvester ■ *n* /kóm bīn/ **1.** ASSOCIATION an association of business organizations **2.** AGRIC same as **combine harvester** [15C. < late Latin *combinare* 'put two things together' < Latin *bini* 'two at a time' < *bi-* (see BI-)] —**combinable** *adj* —**combinative** /kómbi naytiv, -nətiv/ *adj*

combined /kəm bīnd/ *n* a skiing event consisting of a downhill run and a slalom run that are slightly less arduous than either run as a single event

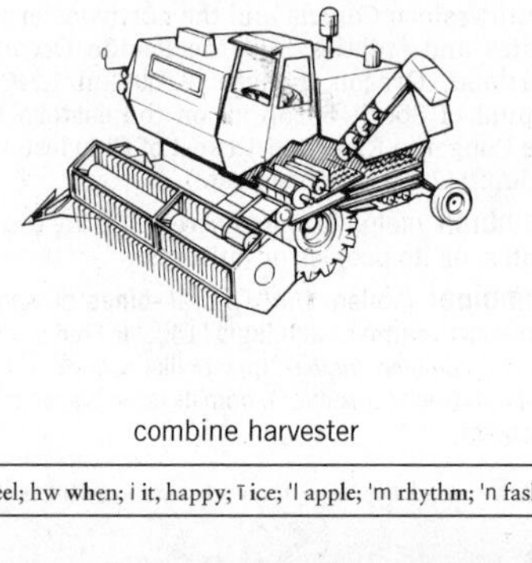

combine harvester

combine harvester /kóm bīn-/ *n* a large farm machine that is used to harvest crops

combings /kṓmingz/ *npl* small loose pieces of hair, wool, or other fibre that are collected during combing

combining form /kəm bī́ning-/ *n* a form of a word in English or another language that is used only in combination with other words to make compound words, e.g. 'Franco-' in 'Franco-British', 'bio-' as in 'biodegradable'

combo /kómbō/ (*plural* **-bos**) *n* **1.** a small jazz or dance band **2.** a combination of several people or components (*informal*) ○ *a burger, fries, and shake combo* [Early 20C. < COMBINATION]

comb-over *n* a man's hairstyle designed to conceal baldness by allowing the hair to grow long on one side of the head and combing it over the top (*informal*)

combust /kəm búst/ (**-busts, -busting, -busted**) *vti* to react vigorously with oxygen to produce heat and light, seen as a flame, or make something do this [15C. Partly < obsolete *combust* 'burnt' < Latin *combustus* (see COMBUSTION); partly back-formation < COMBUSTION]

combustible /kəm bústəb'l/ *adj* **1.** able or likely to catch fire and burn **2.** able to react vigorously with oxygen to produce heat and light, seen as a flame —**combustibility** /kəm bústə bílləti/ *n* —**combustible** *n* —**combustibly** *adv*

combustion /kəm búschən/ *n* **1.** the burning of fuel in an engine to provide power **2.** a chemical process in which a substance reacts vigorously with oxygen to produce heat and light, seen as a flame [15C. < Latin *combustus*, past participle of *comburere* 'burn up' < *urere* 'to burn'] —**combustive** *adj*

combustion chamber *n* an enclosed space in which combustion takes place, e.g. in a jet engine or internal-combustion engine

combustor /kəm bústər/ *n* a combustion system in a jet engine or gas turbine, consisting of the fuel injection system, the igniter, and the combustion chamber

Comdr *abbr* MIL Commander

Comdt *abbr* MIL Commandant

come /kum/ (**comes, coming, came** /kaym/, **come**) CORE MEANING: a basic intransitive verb expressing movement towards a specified place or person. This verb often expresses the concept of movement coupled with the arrival at a place where an activity will take place. ○ *Come and sit by me.* ○ *Come to my house tomorrow.*

1. *vi* REACH PLACE to reach or extend to a particular point or place ○ *Her hair came down to her waist.* **2.** *vi* REACH STATE to reach or be brought into a particular state or situation ○ *It just came apart in my hands.* **3.** *vi* HAPPEN to happen or exist at a particular point or time ○ *I never thought this day would come.* **4.** *vi* OCCUR IN MIND to occur as a thought in the mind ○ *An afterthought came to me while I was shaving.* **5.** *vi* ORIGINATE to originate from a place or thing ○ *The meat came from Canadian herds.* **6.** *vi* RESULT to be the result or consequence of something ○ *comes from eating too much chocolate* **7.** *vi* BE PRODUCED to be produced in a particular size, colour, or style ○ *This model also comes in red.* **8.** *vi* HAVE ORGASM to reach sexual climax (*slang; sometimes considered offensive*) **9.** *vt* ADOPT BEHAVIOUR to adopt a particular kind of attitude or behaviour (*informal*) ○ *Don't come the smart aleck with me, son.* **10.** *prep* PRIOR TO by a particular time in the future ○ *Come July there will be an extra fifty cases to deal with.* **11.** *n* OFFENSIVE TERM an offensive term for a man's semen (*slang*) ◇ **come again?** used to ask someone to repeat or explain something (*informal*) ◇ **come like somebody** *or* **something** to behave or act like somebody or something (*slang; used in Black English*) ◇ **come off it!** used to express contemptuous disbelief (*informal*) ◇ **come to pass** to happen (*archaic or literary*) ◇ **come to think of** *or* **about it** used to introduce a thought that has just occurred to you or something that you have just remembered (*informal*) ◇ **come what may** whatever happens ○ *He swore that, come what may, he would never let her out of his sight again.* ◇ **have it coming (to you)** to be about to receive the punishment or retribution that you deserve ◇ **how come?** used to ask the reason for something (*informal*) ○ *How come you never told me?*

come about *vi* to take place or occur

come across *v* 1. *vt* FIND SOMEBODY OR SOMETHING to find something or meet somebody by chance ○ *I came across a reference to her in the newspaper.* 2. *vi* BE COMMUNICATED to be clearly communicated ○ *The point came across loud and clear: cutbacks are inevitable.* 3. *vi* PRODUCE IMPRESSION to give a particular impression ○ *She comes across as honest and sincere.*

come along *vi* 1. HAPPEN to happen or appear ○ *We'll deal with whatever comes along.* 2. PROGRESS to progress or develop (*only used in continuous tenses, usually in questions or with an adverb*) ○ *How's the new recruit coming along?* 3. ACCOMPANY SOMEBODY to go somewhere with somebody 4. HURRY UP to move or act more quickly ○ *Come along or we'll be late for dinner.* 5. USED TO ENCOURAGE OR REPRIMAND SOMEBODY used to encourage or reprimand somebody who is tired, unhappy, unwilling, or uncooperative (*usually used in the imperative*) ○ *Come along, dry your eyes.*

come apart *vi* to tear or disintegrate ○ *The dress just came apart when I washed it.*

come around *vi US* same as **come round**

come at *vt* 1. ATTACK SOMEBODY to set upon and attack somebody ○ *came at him from behind* 2. ARRIVE AT SOMETHING to reach or discover something with difficulty ○ *The only way to come at the facts is to ask pertinent questions.* 3. *Aus* AGREE TO DO SOMETHING to agree to do something (*slang*) 4. *Aus* TOLERATE SOMETHING BAD to tolerate something bad such as obnoxious behaviour (*slang*) ○ *I can't come at that.* 5. *Aus* ASSUME SOMETHING to assume or suppose something (*slang*)

come away *vi* to become detached from something ○ *The handle came away in my hand.*

come back *vi* 1. REGAIN POPULARITY to become popular again ○ *Seventies fashions came back briefly during the mid-nineties.* 2. RETURN TO MIND to appear or become clear again from somebody's memory ○ *I can't remember the address, but give me a moment and it'll come back to me.* 3. RETORT to reply energetically or aggressively to somebody ○ *She came back at him immediately with a counterblast.*

come back to *vt* 1. to reconsider or refer to something again (*informal*) ○ *I'll come back to that question in a moment.* 2. to speak to somebody again about something at a later time ○ *Do you mind if I come back to you on that one?*

come before *vt* to be submitted for consideration or judgment before a person or group of people with authority ○ *The proposal comes before the committee next week.*

come between *vt* 1. to disrupt a relationship ○ *I won't let anything come between us.* 2. to prevent somebody from having or doing something ○ *He won't let anything come between him and his Saturday football.*

come by *vt* to manage to acquire something ○ *Jobs are not so easy to come by nowadays.*

come down *vi* 1. DECREASE to decrease in value or amount ○ *Prices are coming down.* 2. REACH DECISION to make a decision or judgment ○ *The judge came down in favour of the plaintiff's motion.* 3. BE HANDED DOWN to be passed down from one generation to another ○ *written records that have come down to us from that period* 4. LEAVE UNIVERSITY to leave a university, especially Oxford or Cambridge 5. RETURN TO NORMAL CONSCIOUSNESS to return to a normal state of consciousness after being affected by drugs (*informal*)

come down on *vt* to punish or criticize somebody

come down to *vt* to mean or represent something fundamentally, when all nonessential detail has been disregarded

come down with *vt* to catch a cold, flu, or another minor illness

come for *vt* 1. to arrive at a place to pick somebody or something up 2. to move towards somebody in a threatening way ○ *The dog came for me.*

come forward *vi* to show a willingness to offer help or give information ○ *She came forward with a rather good suggestion.*

come from *vt* 1. to have a particular place of origin or source ○ *She came from Manchester.* 2. be descended from a particular line, family, or stock

come in *vi* 1. FINISH IN PARTICULAR POSITION to finish a race in a particular position ○ *The British yacht came in fifth.* 2. ARRIVE to arrive or be received and become available for use, sale, or communication ○ *The spring fashions will be coming in next month.* 3. BECOME FASHIONABLE to become fashionable or popular ○ *Long hair for men came in during the 1960s.* 4. PARTICIPATE to become involved in something ○ *There are three other companies interested in coming in on the deal.* 5. BEGIN SPEAKING to begin speaking during a discussion or in reply to a radio signal ○ *Perhaps I could ask you to come in on that point, Professor Wilson.* 6. PROVE to turn out to have a particular level of usefulness ○ *That little knife came in very handy when we went camping.* 7. TRANSP APPROACH DESTINATION to approach or arrive at a destination ○ *Her flight is coming in at 4:00.* 8. BECOME HIGHER to become higher, driving water up over the shore (*refers to the tide*)

come in for *vt* to be the object of criticism or scrutiny ○ *The policy has come in for scathing attacks by the media.*

come into *vt* to inherit money or property

come of *vt* to be the result of something

come off *v* 1. *vt* FALL OFF to fall from something ○ *She came off at the water jump.* 2. *vt* COME LOOSE to become detached or be detachable from something ○ *The top comes off easily.* 3. *vi* HAPPEN to take place as planned or predicted (*informal*) ○ *Let's hope the trip comes off.* 4. *vi* SUCCEED to be successful (*informal*) ○ *It was a risky thing to try, but it came off.* 5. *vt* BE DEDUCTED FROM SOMETHING to be deducted from something 6. *vt* STOP TAKING MEDICINE to stop taking a drug or a medicine ○ *When I came off the painkillers, the doctor put me on aspirin.*

come on *v* 1. *vi* START TO OPERATE to become available for use or begin to function (*refers to a power source or machine*) ○ *The street lights come on at dusk.* 2. *vi* HURRY to hurry up (*usually used in the imperative*) ○ *Come on, I haven't got all day!* 3. *vi* USED TO ENCOURAGE SOMEBODY used to encourage somebody who is tired or unwilling (*usually used in the imperative*) ○ *Come on, you can do it if you try.* 4. *vi* USED TO SHOW DISBELIEF used to tell somebody to stop exaggerating or lying (*usually used in the imperative*) ○ *Come on! You don't expect me to believe that, do you?* 5. *vi* TO TELL SOMEBODY TO STOP PRETENDING used to tell somebody to drop a pretence or stop behaving in a superior way (*usually used in the imperative*) ○ *Come on! You know you can't afford that car.* 6. *vi* PROGRESS to develop well or in a particular way ○ *How's the book coming on?* 7. *vi* ADVANCE to move forward, especially in battle ○ *Our cannon fire tore huge holes in their ranks, but still they came on.* 8. *vi* DEVELOP GRADUALLY to develop gradually ○ *It grew chilly as night came on.* 9. *vt* THEATRE ENTER DURING PLAY to go onto the stage as part of the action ○ *The villain doesn't come on until Act 2.* 10. *vt* APPEAR OR SPEAK ON BROADCAST MEDIUM to appear or speak on television, radio, or the telephone ○ *I noticed her voice when she came on the phone.* 11. *vi* BEGIN AT SCHEDULED TIME to begin at a particular time (*refers to radio or television programmes or a stage performer*) ○ *Her favourite show is coming on in an hour, and she never misses it.*

come on to *vt* 1. to begin to deal with something ○ *We now come on to the most controversial item on our agenda.* 2. to make sexual advances to somebody (*slang*)

come out *vi* 1. BECOME KNOWN to be revealed ○ *The true facts only came out when journalists began to dig a little deeper.* 2. PUBL BE PUBLISHED to be published ○ *Her new novel is coming out next month.* 3. DECLARE OPINION to state an opinion or judgment openly ○ *The majority came out in favour of raising the age limit.* 4. REVEAL SECRET ABOUT YOURSELF to reveal to other people something about yourself that you have kept secret 5. ACKNOWLEDGE SEXUALITY to declare openly that you are gay or lesbian 6. HAVE FIRST SAME-SEX RELATIONSHIP to have your first sexual relationship with somebody of the same sex ○ *I think she came out when she was 17, with her best friend.* 7. MAKE DEBUT IN SOCIETY to make a first appearance in society 8. BE UTTERED to be uttered involuntarily or with an unintended effect ○ *We had no intention of revealing the story; it came out by accident.* 9. BECOME VISIBLE IN SKY to become visible in the sky ○ *The sun came out from behind a cloud.* 10. BE REMOVABLE to disappear after cleaning ○ *Even the toughest stains come out with this new detergent.* 11. STRIKE to begin a strike ○ *The train drivers came out in sympathy.*

come out in *vt* to have something such as spots or a rash appear on the skin

come out of *vt* 1. to survive a hazard or illness ○ *I'd say she came out of the ordeal in pretty good shape.* 2. to be deducted from an amount of money ○ *The new window will have to come out of your pocket money.*

come out with *vt* to say something surprising ○ *never know what children will come out with*

come over *v* 1. *vi* CHANGE SIDES to change an opinion or allegiance ○ *She says she'll come over if we guarantee her a seat on the board.* 2. *vi* BE COMMUNICATED to be clearly communicated ○ *The message came over loud and clear: he isn't going to change his mind.* 3. *vi* GIVE IMPRESSION to give a particular impression ○ *She comes over as much less forceful and ambitious than her sister.* 4. *vt* AFFECT SOMEBODY to affect or overcome somebody ○ *A feeling of giddiness came over her.* 5. *vi* DEVELOP PARTICULAR FEELING to begin to feel a particular sensation (*informal*) ○ *I came over all peculiar and had to sit down.*

come round *vi* 1. VISIT to visit somebody ○ *Why don't you come round this evening?* 2. REGAIN CONSCIOUSNESS to regain consciousness, e.g. after being knocked out ○ *When I came round, I was in hospital.* 3. CHANGE YOUR OPINION to change your opinion to that of somebody else ○ *They soon came round to our way of thinking.* 4. RECUR to happen again at the expected time ○ *The same questions come round year after year at these meetings.*

come through *v* 1. *vt* SURVIVE to survive a dangerous or unpleasant experience 2. *vi* BE RECEIVED to be received or heard, usually through a telecommunications medium ○ *A fax has come through from head office.* 3. *vt* MOVE THROUGH PLACE to move between one place and another ○ *The porch was so crowded, we had to come through the kitchen.* ○ *Coming through! Coming through! These plates are hot!*

come to *v* 1. *vi* REGAIN CONSCIOUSNESS to regain consciousness or wake up ○ *The patient came to in the recovery room.* 2. *vi* NAUT SLOW DOWN OR STOP to slow down or stop (*refers to boats*) 3. *vt* TOTAL to amount to a particular total ◇ **come to that** used when adding something to what has just been said ○ *Her job is far from safe – come to that all of our jobs are at risk.*

come together *vi* 1. to meet or gather together in one place 2. to coalesce successfully from disparate parts ○ *It's all finally starting to come together.*

come under *vt* 1. BE CLASSIFIED to be classified under a particular heading ○ *Hawthorne comes under American authors.* 2. BE SUBJECT TO SOMEBODY OR SOMETHING to be subject to the authority of somebody or something ○ *Which department do we come under?* 3. UNDERGO SOMETHING to be subjected to something ○ *She came under attack from members of her own party.*

come up *vi* 1. EMERGE FROM WATER to rise to the surface of water ○ *She'll have to come up for air in a minute.* 2. APPEAR ABOVE HORIZON to appear above the horizon ○ *I enjoy watching the sun come up.* 3. BE MENTIONED to be mentioned or discussed ○ *a topic that came up in conversation* 4. OCCUR UNEXPECTEDLY to happen unexpectedly ○ *I won't be able to make lunch; something's come up at work.* 5. BE HAPPENING SOON to be going to happen in the near future ○ *Coming up next, the news.* 6. APPEAR IN COURT to be tried in a court of law ○ *Her case comes up next week.* 7. BE SELECTED AS WINNER to win a prize in a game involving luck ○ *if my numbers come up*

come up against *vt* to meet with something that has to be faced or dealt with ○ *He has come up against fierce criticism.*

come up for *vt* to become due for something ○ *The case is coming up for review.*

come upon *vt* to meet somebody or find something by chance

come up to *vt* to be as good as a particular standard or level ○ *His performance more than came up to expectations.*

come up with *vt* to produce or discover something, in response to a need or challenge ○ *She's come up with a brilliant solution.*

comeback /kúm bak/ *n* 1. RETURN TO SUCCESS a return to a successful position or activity ○ *Rumour has it that she's planning a comeback.* 2. SHARP REPLY a sharp or witty reply ○ *He's always been one for the quick comeback.* 3. COMPLAINT OR CLAIM FOR COMPENSATION a complaint about something, or a claim for compensation ○ *I don't want any comebacks from dissatisfied customers.*

Comecon /kómi kon/, **COMECON** *n* an organization of the former Soviet Union and satellite Communist countries aimed at encouraging economic development. It existed between 1949 and 1991. Full form **Council for Mutual Economic Assistance**

comedian /kə meédi ən/ *n* 1. COMIC ENTERTAINER a entertainer who amuses an audience with comedy 2. COMIC ACTOR an actor who plays comic roles 3. AMUSING PERSON somebody who is or tries to be amusing (*often*

ironic) ○ *Some comedian put salt in the sugar bowl.* [Late 16C. < French *comédien* < *comédie* (see COMEDY)]

comedienne /kə meedi én/ *n* **1. FEMALE COMIC ENTERTAINER** a female entertainer who tells jokes **2. COMIC ACTRESS** a female actor who takes comic roles **3. AMUSING WOMAN** a woman who is or tries to be amusing (*often ironic*) [Mid-19C. < French, form of *comédien* (see COMEDIAN)]

comedo /kómmidō/ (*plural* **comedones** /kómmi dō neez/ or **comedos**) *n* MED same as **blackhead** (sense 1) (*technical*) [Mid-19C. < Latin, 'glutton, worm' < *comedere* 'devour' (see COMESTIBLE)]

comedogenic /kómmidō jénnik/ *adj* tending to cause or aggravate blackheads

comedown /kúm down/ *n* a decline in status or position (*informal*)

comedy /kómmədi/ (*plural* **-dies**) *n* **1. FUNNY PLAY, FILM, OR BOOK** a play, film, or book depicting amusing events **2. COMIC GENRE** comic works, especially plays, considered as a literary genre **3. COMIC ENTERTAINMENT** entertainment that is amusing **4. COMIC ELEMENTS** the humorous aspects of a situation or work of art [14C. Via French *comédie* < Greek *kōmōidia* < *kōmōidos* 'comic actor' < *kōmos* 'revel' + *aoidos* 'singer' < *aeidein* 'sing'] —**comedic** /kə meedik/ *adj* —**comedically** *adv*

comedy of errors *n* a ludicrous situation in which many mistakes are made and things go wrong

comedy of manners *n* a comedy that satirizes the manners and customs of a section of society, especially fashionable society

come-hither *adj* sexually inviting or provocative (*humorous*)

~~**comeing**~~ incorrect spelling of **coming**

comely /kúmmli/ (**-lier, -liest**) *adj* describes a woman who is good-looking (*archaic or literary*) [13C. Probably shortening of obsolete *becomely* 'becoming' < BECOME] —**comeliness** *n*

come-on *n* **1.** something that arouses interest or desire, e.g. a free gift intended to encourage purchasers (*informal*) **2.** a comment or action intended to indicate sexual interest in somebody

comer /kúmmər/ *n* somebody or something that is likely to succeed (*informal*)

comestible /kə méstəb'l/ (*formal*) *n* something edible, usually a cooked food ■ *adj* edible [15C. Via French < medieval Latin *comestibilis* < Latin *comestus*, past participle of *comedere* 'eat completely' < *edere* 'eat']

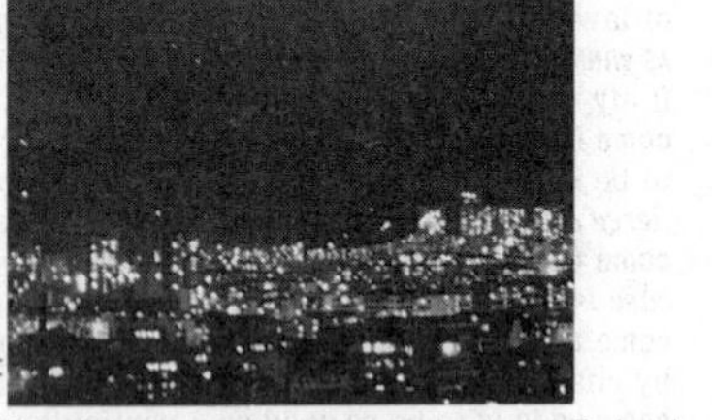
Popperfoto

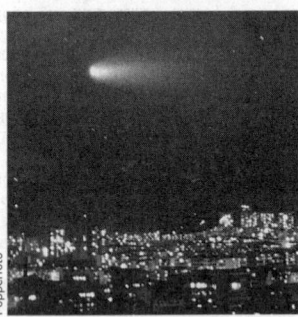

comet: Hale-Bopp comet, photographed over Bulgaria (1997)

comet /kómmit/ *n* an astronomical object that is composed of a mass of ice and dust and has a long luminous tail produced by vaporization when its orbit passes close to the Sun [12C. Directly or via French < Latin (*stella*) *cometa* 'long-haired (star)' < Greek (*astēr*) *komētēs* < *komē* 'hair of the head'] —**cometary** *adj* —**cometic** /kə méttik/ *adj*

comeuppance /kum úppənss/ *n* something unpleasant, regarded as a just punishment for somebody (*informal*) ○ *He got his comeuppance in the end.* [Mid-19C. < *come up*, probably 'be tried before a court']

~~**comfertable**~~ incorrect spelling of **comfortable**

comfit /kúmfit/ *n* a sweet consisting of a piece of fruit, a seed, or a nut in a sugar coating [14C. Via French < Latin *confectum, confecta* < *confectus* (see CONFECT)]

comfort /kúmfərt/ *n* **1. STATE OF BEING COMFORTABLE** conditions in which somebody feels physically relaxed ○ *Enjoy the comfort of your own home.* **2. COMFORTABLE THING** something that makes you feel physically relaxed (*often used in the plural*) ○ *the comforts of home* **3. RELIEF FROM PAIN** relief from pain or anxiety ○ *They brought comfort to the wounded.* **4. SOMEBODY OR SOMETHING PROVIDING RELIEF** somebody or something that provides relief from pain or anxiety ○ *The family has been such a comfort to me since my wife died.* ■ *vt* (**-forts, -forting, -forted**) **1. CHEER SOMEBODY** to bring somebody relief from distress or anxiety ○ *The victim's parents were being comforted at home by relatives.* **2. MAKE SOMEBODY COMFORTABLE** to make somebody feel pleasantly relaxed ○ *She was comforted by the warmth.* [12C. < Old French *confort* < late Latin *confortare* 'strengthen completely' < Latin *fortis* 'strong']

comfortable /kúmftəb'l, -fərtəb'l/ *adj* **1. RELAXED** feeling comfort or ease ○ *Sit down and make yourselves comfortable.* **2. MAKING SOMEBODY RELAXED** making somebody feel physically relaxed ○ *I changed into something more comfortable.* **3. NOT ANXIOUS** free from stress or anxiety ○ *I don't feel comfortable with that idea.* **4.** MED **STABLE PHYSICALLY** in a stable physical condition ○ *The patient is comfortable.* **5. ADEQUATE OR LARGE** large enough to prevent anxiety or risk ○ *The government won by a comfortable majority.* **6. WITH ADEQUATE INCOME** having enough income ○ *They're not what you'd call well-off, but they're certainly comfortable.* —**comfortableness** *n*

comfortably /kúmftəbli, -fərtəbli/ *adv* **1. AT EASE** with a feeling of comfort or ease ○ *Are you sitting comfortably?* **2. WITHOUT PROBLEMS** with enough of something to stave off worry, especially enough money to live on without worrying about providing essentials ○ *We can manage comfortably on what we earn together.* **3. EASILY** by a large margin ○ *The home team won comfortably.*

comfortably off *adj* having an adequate or more than adequate income ○ *They often complain that they can't afford luxuries, but in fact they're quite comfortably off.*

comforter /kúmfərtər/ *n* **1.** somebody who helps to relieve other people's grief or anxieties **2.** *N Am* a warm quilt used as a bed covering **3.** same as **dummy** (*dated*)

Comforter *n* CHR same as **Holy Spirit**

comfort food *n* easily prepared unsophisticated food that is psychologically comforting, especially food that is high in carbohydrates (*informal*)

comforting /kúmfərting/ *adj* relieving anxiety or pain —**comfortingly** *adv*

comfortless /kúmfərtləss/ *adj* affording no comfort ○ *a sterile, comfortless room* —**comfortlessly** *adv* —**comfortlessness** *n*

comfort level *n* the set of physical or psychological circumstances in which somebody feels most at ease and free from physical discomfort or stress (*informal*) ○ *the comfort level of knowing you have enough savings to meet emergencies*

comfort station *n N Am* a public toilet (*used euphemistically*)

comfort zone *n* same as **comfort level**

comfrey /kúmfri/ *n* a plant with hairy leaves and stems. Flowers: pink, white, or blue, in clusters. Native to: Europe, Asia. Genus: *Symphytum*. [13C. Via Anglo-Norman, Old French < Latin *conferva* < *confervere* 'heal', literally 'boil together' < *fervere* (see FERVENT)]

comfy /kúmfi/ (**-fier, -fiest**) *adj* same as **comfortable** (senses 1–2) (*informal*) [Early 19C. Shortened form]

comic /kómmik/ *adj* **1. FUNNY** capable of inducing amusement, smiles or laughter **2.** THEATRE **RELATING TO COMEDY** relating to, characteristic of, or appearing in comedy ○ *a great comic routine* ■ *n* **1.** ARTS **COMEDIAN** a comedian or comedienne ○ *worked as a nightclub comic* **2.** PUBL **MAGAZINE** a magazine that consists of stories told in a series of coloured panels. N Am term **comic book** [Late 16C. Via Latin < Greek *kōmikos* < *kōmos* 'revel']

SYNONYMS See *funny*.

comical /kómmik'l/ *adj* funny to the extent of being absurd, especially if unintentional ○ *comical facial expressions* —**comicality** /kómmi kálləti/ *n* —**comically** *adv*

SYNONYMS See *funny*.

comic book *n N Am* PUBL same as **comic** *n* (sense 2)

comic opera *n* **1.** an opera with a humorous plot and a happy ending **2.** comic operas considered as a musical genre

comic relief *n* **1.** LITERAT, THEATRE **FUNNY SECTION INSERTED IN SERIOUS WORK** relief from tension, or a further heightening of tension by contrast, provided by a comic scene or passage inserted into a serious work **2.** LITERAT, THEATRE **CHARACTERS PROVIDING COMIC INTERVALS** a character or set of characters whose function is to provide intervals of comedy in a serious work **3. FUNNY INCIDENT WITHIN SERIOUS SITUATION** occasion for laughter in the midst of a tense or serious situation

comic strip *n* a series of cartoons that tell a story or a joke

coming /kúmming/ *adj* **1. HAPPENING SOON** about to happen or start ○ *She was dreading the coming winter.* **2. PROBABLY SUCCESSFUL** likely to be successful in the near future ○ *She's the coming power in this company.* ■ *n* **ARRIVAL** the arrival of a person or an event

coming of age *n* **1.** the reaching of the official age of adulthood and legal responsibility **2.** the reaching of an advanced stage of development ○ *the coming of age of the computer*

comings and goings *npl* busy activity in which people arrive and depart frequently

Comintern /kómmin turn/ *n* an international organization of Communist parties set up by Lenin in 1919 and abolished in 1943 [Early 20C. < Russian *Komintern* < *kommunisticheskii internatsional'nyi* 'communist international']

~~**comission**~~ incorrect spelling of **commission**

~~**comitee**~~ incorrect spelling of **committee**

comity of nations /kómmiti-/ *n* the mutual recognition among nations of one another's laws, customs, and institutions [< Latin *comitas* < *comis* 'courteous']

comm. *abbr* **1.** COMM commerce **2.** COMM commercial **3.** committee **4.** POL commonwealth

comma /kómmə/ *n* **1.** GRAM a punctuation mark (,) that represents a slight pause in a sentence or is used to separate words and figures in a list **2.** MUSIC a short pause or interval in a piece of music **3.** INSECTS same as **comma butterfly** [Late 16C. Via Latin < Greek *komma* 'piece cut off' < *koptein* 'to cut']

USAGE ***Commas*** are used in pairs around text that adds extra information and that can be omitted without affecting the structure of the sentence: *He was staying with his sister, a piano teacher, in Paris. The plant, which thrives in acid soils, is grown for its scented foliage.* (An increasingly common error is the omission of the second, closing comma.) A comma may also follow a subordinate clause placed at the beginning of a sentence: *If I miss the train, I will be late for the meeting. Born in 1950, he spent his early childhood in India.* When commas are used to separate items in lists, the final comma (before *and, or,* or *etc.*) is optional: *We invited Sarah, Jack, Kate, and Tom. You can have coffee, tea, cold milk or hot chocolate. They sell books, paper, envelopes, stamps, etc.* Similarly, a series of adjectives used before a noun may or may not be separated by commas: *It was a long, slow, difficult process. She was wearing a long blue knitted scarf.* Commas may also be inserted at appropriate points to break up a lengthy complicated sentence, but it is often better and clearer to split the sentence up into smaller units. A comma should not, however, be used to separate a long subject from a verb: *The girl I used to know many years ago at school was now unrecognizable* (no comma between *school* and *was*).

comma butterfly *n* an orange and brown butterfly that has a comma-shaped white mark on the underside of each hind wing. Latin name: *Polygonia calbum.*

command /kə maand/ *n* **1. ORDER** an order or instruction given by somebody in authority **2. CONTROL** control over somebody or something that is gained by personal power or authority ○ *She sized up the situation and took command.* **3. THOROUGH KNOWLEDGE** thorough knowledge of something, especially a language ○ *a fluent command of French* **4.** COMPUT **OPERATING INSTRUCTION TO COMPUTER** an instruction to a computer to carry out an operation **5.** MIL **MILITARY CONTROL** the ability to control an area militarily ○ *Our primary objective is to gain command of the*

high ground. **6.** MIL **GROUP OF OFFICERS IN CONTROL** a group of officers who control part of an army ○ *the enemy command* **7.** MIL **MILITARY GROUP WITH PARTICULAR FUNCTION** a section of an army or air force that has a particular function ■ *v* **(-mands, -manding, -manded) 1.** *vt* **ORDER SOMEBODY** to give somebody an order or instruction ○ *I command you to let these men go.* **2.** *vt* **BE ABLE TO OBTAIN SOMETHING** to deserve or be entitled to something ○ *With your qualifications you can command a high salary.* **3.** *vt* **LOOK OVER SOMETHING** to be in a position that has a wide view over something ○ *The observation deck commands a breathtaking view of San Francisco Bay.* **4.** *vti* MIL **HAVE AUTHORITY OVER SOMETHING** to control a military unit or a specific area ○ *an officer who commands a special operations battalion* **5.** *vt* MIL **CONTROL OR DOMINATE AREA** to control an area using military force ○ *a fort that commanded the single pass through steep mountains* [13C. Via Anglo-Norman *comaunder*, Old French *comander* < assumed late Latin *commandare* 'enjoin strongly' < Latin *mandare* (see MANDATE)] —**commandable** *adj*

command and control *n* **1.** a system that directs the course of a missile **2.** a military commander's exercise of authority and direction of operations

commandant /kómmən dant/ *n* an officer in command of a military organization

command economy *n* an economy in which resources and business activity are controlled by the government

commandeer /kómmən deér/ **(-deers, -deering, -deered)** *vt* **1. SEIZE SOMETHING FOR MILITARY PURPOSES** to take something from its owner for official or military purposes **2. TAKE SOMETHING OVER** to take or use something, often by force **3.** MIL **FORCE SOMEBODY INTO MILITARY SERVICE** to force somebody to serve in the armed forces [Early 19C. Via Afrikaans *kommandeer* < Dutch *kommanderen* 'to command' < French *commander* (see COMMAND)]

commander /kə maándər/ *n* **1.** MIL **MILITARY OFFICER** an officer commanding a military unit **2.** NAVY **NAVAL RANK** an officer in the Royal, Canadian, or US navies or the US Coast Guard of a rank above lieutenant commander **3.** POLICE **SENIOR POLICE OFFICER** an officer in charge of a police district in London **4. MEMBER WITH HIGH RANK** a high-ranking member of a knightly and fraternal order —**commandership** *n*

commander in chief (*plural* **commanders in chief**) *n* an officer who has supreme command of military forces

Commander in Chief *n* used as an honorific title to denote the president of the United States, as commander of the nation's armed forces

command group *n* a group of officers and security personnel who accompany a military commander

commanding /kə maánding/ *adj* **1. IMPRESSIVE** able to control or dominate ○ *a commanding presence* **2. OVERLOOKING** looking out or over something from a high position ○ *a commanding view* **3. DOMINANT** demonstrating clear superiority ○ *a commanding lead* —**commandingly** *adv*

commanding officer *n* an officer in command of a military unit or establishment

command key *n* **1.** a computer key that gives commands to the computer, expanding the keyboard options **2.** a key on a keyboard that causes a device to initiate a predefined action

command-line *adj* using letters or words instead of codes to give instructions to a computer [Because such instructions are entered on one line after a particular character called the *command prompt*]

commandment /kə maándmənt/ *n* a command from God, especially one of the Ten Commandments

command module *n* the part of a spacecraft that houses the controls and the crew's living quarters

commando /kə maándō/ (*plural* **-dos** or **-does**) *n* **1.** MIL **SPECIALLY TRAINED SOLDIER** a member of a military force specially trained to make dangerous raids **2.** MIL **SPECIALLY TRAINED UNIT** a military unit made up of commandos **3.** HIST, MIL **BOER FIGHTING UNIT** a force of Boer troops during the Boer War [Late 18C. < Portuguese, 'raiding party' < *commandar* 'to command']

command paper *n* a government document presented to Parliament, historically by royal command

command performance *n* a performance of a play or film given by command of a ruler or state

command post *n* **1.** a military headquarters for a command group and its officers during an operation **2.** a temporary headquarters for a team of people involved in an operation

commedia dell'arte /ko máydi ə del aár tay/ *n* an Italian form of popular comedy developed during the 16th and 17th centuries, characterized by the use of stock characters and familiar plots [Late 19C. < Italian, literally 'comedy of art']

commemorate /kə mémmə rayt/ **(-rates, -rating, -rated)** *vt* **1.** to honour the memory of somebody or something in a ceremony ○ *a service held to commemorate the dead* **2.** to serve as a memorial to something [Mid-17C. < Latin *commemorat-*, past participle of *commemorare* 'call to mind clearly' < *memorare* 'remind' < *memor* 'mindful'] —**commemorative** /-rətiv/ *adj, n* —**commemorator** *n* —**commemoratory** *adj*

commemoration /kə mémmə ráysh'n/ *n* **1.** a ceremony or religious service to commemorate a person or an event **2.** the act of honouring the memory of a person or an event —**commemorational** *adj*

commence /kə ménss/ **(-mences, -mencing, -menced)** *vti* to begin happening, or begin something [14C. < Old French *com(m)encier* < Latin *initiare* (see INITIATE)] —**commencer** *n*

commencement /kə ménssmənt/ *n* **1.** the beginning of something (*formal*) ○ *the commencement of open hostilities* **2.** *N Am* a ceremony during which degrees and diplomas are conferred at US high schools, colleges, and universities, or the day on which this ceremony takes place

commend /kə ménd/ **(-mends, -mending, -mended)** *vt* **1. PRAISE SOMEBODY OR SOMETHING** to praise somebody or something in a formal way ○ *She was commended for her bravery.* **2. CAUSE SOMETHING TO BE ACCEPTABLE** to show something to possess worthwhile qualities ○ *The plan has much to commend it.* **3. ENDORSE SOMEBODY OR SOMETHING** to endorse somebody or something as being worthy of approval ○ *I had no hesitation in commending her to them.* **4. SURRENDER SOMEBODY OR SOMETHING FOR SAFEKEEPING** to entrust somebody, yourself, or your soul to somebody's safekeeping (*archaic or formal*) [14C. < Latin *commendare* 'entrust completely' < *mandare* (see MANDATE)] —**commender** *n*

commendable /kə méndəb'l/ *adj* worthy of praise —**commendably** *adv*

commendation /kómmen dáysh'n/ *n* **1.** praise of somebody's abilities **2.** an award or citation given to somebody in recognition of an outstanding achievement —**commendatory** /kə méndətəri/ *adj*

commensal /kə ménss'l/ *adj* describes a relationship between organisms of two different species in which one derives food or other benefits from the association while the other remains unharmed and unaffected [Late 19C. Directly or via French < medieval Latin *commensalis* 'at table together' < Latin *mensa* 'table'] —**commensal** *n* —**commensality** /kómmen sálləti/ *n* —**commensally** *adv*

commensalism /kə méns'lizəm/ *n* the relationship between organisms of two different species in which one derives food or other benefits from the association while the other remains unharmed and unaffected

commensurable /kə ménshərəb'l/ *adj* **1. RELATED BY MEASUREMENT** related by virtue of sharing the same system of measurement or by being measurable using the same units **2. COMMENSURATE** proportionate to something else (*formal*) ○ *His salary is commensurable to his ability.* **3.** MATHS **WITH COMMON FACTOR** divisible by the same unit an even number of times [Mid-16C. < late Latin *commensurabilis* 'completely measurable' < *mensurabilis* (see MENSURABLE)] —**commensurability** /kə ménshərə bílləti/ *n* —**commensurably** *adv*

commensurate /kə ménshərət/ *adj* **1. EQUAL IN SIZE** of the same size or extent **2. IN PROPORTION** appropriately proportionate ○ *The rewards will be commensurate with the efforts made.* **3. MEASURED USING COMPATIBLE UNITS** describes units of measurement that belong to the same system such as feet and inches or centimetres and metres [Mid-17C. < late Latin *commensuratus*, literally 'measured with' < Latin *mensura* 'measure'] —**commensurately** *adv* —**commensuration** /kə ménshə ráysh'n/ *n*

comment /kómment/ *n* **1. REMARK** a remark that states a fact or expresses an opinion ○ *Comments are invited from all participants.* **2. CRITICAL OBSERVATION** an implied or indirect judgment ○ *The film is a comment on the materialism of modern society.* **3. DISCUSSION** written or spoken discussion, analysis, or criticism ○ *The incident attracted a great deal of press comment.* **4. EXPLANATORY NOTE** a note that explains a passage in a text **5.** COMPUT **NOTE EXPLAINING PROGRAM CODE** a note embedded in a computer program that describes how the following programming code works ■ *vti* **(-ments, -menting, -mented) MAKE COMMENT** to state a fact or give an opinion [14C. < Latin *commentum* 'invention' < *comment-*, past participle of *comminisci* 'invent', literally 'think together']

commentary /kómməntəri/ *n* (*plural* **-ies**) **1. SPOKEN DESCRIPTION OF EVENT** a spoken description of an event as it happens, especially of a sporting event being broadcast on radio or television. N Am term **play-by-play** **2. CLARIFICATION OF SITUATION** an example illustrating a situation **3. SERIES OF EXPLANATORY NOTES** a series of notes explaining or interpreting a written text **4. EXPLANATORY ESSAY** an essay or book that explains a text ■ **commentaries** *npl* **RECORD OF EVENTS** a record of events, usually written by somebody who participated in them —**commentarial** /kómmən táiri əl/ *adj*

commentary box *n* a booth at a sports stadium from which a television or radio commentator makes a broadcast

commentate /kómmən tayt/ **(-tates, -tating, -tated)** *vi* to provide a commentary, either in radio or television broadcasting or on texts

commentator /kómmən taytər/ *n* **1.** a broadcaster for radio or television who describes events, especially sporting events, as they happen **2.** a reporter and analyst of the news for radio, television, or a newspaper

commerce /kómmurss/ *n* **1.** the large-scale buying and selling of goods and services **2.** the study of the principles and practices of commerce [Direct or via French < Latin *commercium* 'mutual trade']

commercial /kə múrsh'l/ *adj* **1. RELATING TO COMMERCE** relating to the buying and selling of goods or services **2.** COMM **SUITABLE FOR TRADING** appropriate or sufficient for the purposes of trade **3.** COMM **FOR INDUSTRIAL USE** produced in bulk for industrial use and often unrefined **4.** COMM **DONE FOR PROFIT** done with the primary aim of making money ○ *a commercial venture* **5.** COMM **PAID FOR WITH ADVERTISING** supported by revenue from advertising ○ *commercial radio* ■ *n* BROADCAST, COMM **ADVERTISEMENT ON RADIO OR TELEVISION** an advertisement broadcast on radio or television —**commerciality** /kə múrshi álləti/ *n*

commercial art *n* graphic art produced for purposes such as advertising and packaging —**commercial artist** *n*

commercial bank *n* a bank whose primary business is providing financial services to companies

commercial break *n* an interval during a radio or television programme for the purpose of broadcasting advertisements

commercial college *n* a college that teaches primarily business-related subjects

commercialese /kə múrsh'l eéz/ *n* the language or jargon used by people who work in business

commercial Internet exchange *n* E-COMMERCE a connection point between commercial Internet service providers (*used in e-commerce*)

commercialise *vt* COMM another spelling of **commercialize**

commercialism /kə múrsh'lizəm/ *n* **1.** the principles and methods of commerce **2.** excessive emphasis on profit-making —**commercialist** *n* —**commercialistic** /kə múrsh'l ístik/ *adj*

commercialize /kə múrsh'l īz/ **(-izes, -izing, -ized)**, **commercialise (-ises, -ising, -ised)** *vt* **1.** to apply business principles to something or run it as a business **2.** to exploit something for financial gain —**commercialization** /kə múrsh'l ī záysh'n/ *n*

commercially /kə múrshəli/ *adv* in commercial terms, or from a profit-making point of view

commercial paper *n* short-term negotiable financial documents backed only by the good name of the company

commercial traveller *n* a travelling company sales representative (*dated*)

commercial vehicle *n* a road vehicle designed to transport goods or passengers

commère /kómmair/ *n* a woman who introduces acts on a television, radio, or stage show [Early 20C. < French, 'godmother', literally 'mother with' < Latin *mater* 'mother']

comess /kómmess/ *n Carib* **1.** a commotion or confused situation **2.** in Trinidad, any kind of scandal, conflict, or illegal behaviour [Late 20C. Via French Creole < French *commerce* 'business']

commie /kómmi/, **commy** (*plural* **-mies**) *n* POL same as **Communist** (*informal disapproving*) [Mid-20C. < COMMUNIST] —**commie** *adj*

commination /kómmi náysh'n/ *n* **1.** ACT OF DENOUNCING a formal denunciation of somebody or something (*formal*) **2.** THREAT OF PUNISHMENT a warning of punishment or vengeance, especially punishment by God (*formal*) **3.** CHR LIST OF GOD'S WARNINGS a recital of God's warnings to sinners, read out in the Ash Wednesday service in Anglican churches [15C. < Latin *comminat-*, past participle of *comminari*, literally 'threaten with' < *minari* (see MENACE)] —**comminatory** /kómminətəri/ *adj*

commingle /ko míng g'l/ (**-gles, -gling, -gled**) *v* **1.** *vti* to mix two or more things, or become mixed (*literary*) **2.** *vt* FIN to put a number of funds or properties into a single fund or stock

comminute /kómmi nyoot/ (**-nutes, -nuting, -nuted**) *v* **1.** *vti* BREAK BONE INTO FRAGMENTS to break, or cause a bone to break, into small parts **2.** *vt* PULVERIZE SOMETHING to crush or grind something into a powder **3.** *vt* DIVIDE SOMETHING INTO SMALL PARTS to divide something, especially property, into small parts (*formal*) [Late 16C. < Latin *comminut-*, past participle of *comminuere* 'lessen greatly' < *minuere* 'lessen'] —**comminuted** /kómmi nyootəd/ *adj* —**comminution** /kómmi nyoósh'n/ *n*

comminuted fracture /kómmi nyootid-/ *n* a fracture in which the bone is broken into fragments

commis /kómmi/ (*plural* **-mis** /-mi, -miz/) *n* an agent or deputy [Late 16C. < French < past participle of *commettre* 'entrust' < Latin *committere* (see COMMIT)]

commis chef *n* a trainee chef who has the most junior position in the kitchen

commiserate /kə mízzə rayt/ (**-ates, -ating, -ated**) *vi* to express sympathy or sorrow [Late 16C. < Latin *commiserat-*, past participle of *commiserari*, literally 'lament with' < *miser* 'miserable'] —**commiserative** *adj* —**commiseratively** *adv*

commiseration /kə mízzə ráysh'n/ *n* a feeling of sympathy for and understanding of the troubles of somebody else ■ **commiserations** *npl* expressions of sympathy or sorrow

commissar /kómmi saár/ *n* **1.** in the former Soviet Union, the chief minister in a government department **2.** in the former Soviet Union, a Communist Party official, often attached to a military unit, responsible for providing political education [Early 20C. Via Russian *komissar* < medieval Latin *commissarius* 'officer in charge' < Latin *commiss-*, past participle of *committere* (see COMMIT)] —**commissarial** /kómmi sáiri əl/ *adj*

commissariat /kómmi sáiri ət/ *n* **1.** ARMY ARMY SUPPLY DEPARTMENT an army department responsible for organizing food and supplies **2.** ARMY ARMY SUPPLIES food and other supplies given to soldiers **3.** HIST, GOV FORMER SOVIET GOVERNMENT DEPARTMENT a government department in the former Soviet Union before 1946 [Late 16C. < assumed medieval Latin *commissariatus* < *commissarius* (see COMMISSAR)]

commissary /kómmissəri/ (*plural* **-ies**) *n* a deputy or representative, especially of a bishop —**commissaryship** *n*

commission /kə mísh'n/ *n* **1.** FEE PAID TO AGENT a fee paid to an agent for providing a service, especially a percentage of the total amount of business transacted **2.** TASK a job or task given to a person or a group, especially an order to produce a particular product or piece of work **3.** GROUP WITH TASK a group of people authorized to carry out a duty **4.** AUTHORITY TO ACT AS AGENT the authority granted to a person or organization to act as an agent for another **5.** ACT OF COMMITTING SOMETHING the committing of a crime or other offence **6.** AUTHORITY OR INSTRUCTION the authority or an instruction to do something (*formal*) **7.** GOV GOVERNMENT GROUP a government agency that has judicial, administrative, or legislative powers **8.** MIL APPOINTMENT AS MILITARY OFFICER an appointment to the rank of officer in the armed forces, or a document conferring such a rank ■ *vt* (**-sions, -sioning, -sioned**) **1.** ASSIGN TASK TO SOMEBODY to assign a duty or task to somebody **2.** ORDER SOMETHING SPECIAL to place an order for something that must be specially made or created ○ *have commissioned a new architectural firm to design the building* **3.** BRING EQUIPMENT INTO OPERATION to bring equipment or machinery into operation **4.** START UP PROJECT to bring a new project or facility into operation **5.** MIL MAKE SOMEBODY OFFICER to confer the rank of officer on somebody in the armed forces **6.** NAUT EQUIP SHIP to bring a boat into active service [14C. Directly or via French < Latin *commission-* < *commiss-* (see COMMISSAR)] —**commissional** *adj* —**commissionary** *adj* ◇ **in commission** in operational use or working order ◇ **on commission** with a percentage of the value of sales being full or partial payment for the work of selling ◇ **out of commission** not in operational use or working order

commissionaire /kə míshə náir/ *n* **1.** a uniformed attendant or usher at a cinema, hotel, or theatre **2.** in Canada, a veteran of the armed forces who belongs to the Corps of Commissionaires, an organization whose uniformed members can be hired to protect buildings and property [Mid-17C. < medieval Latin *commissionarius* < Latin *commission-* (see COMMISSION)]

commissioned officer /kə mísh'nd-/ *n* an officer in the armed forces or in the US Coast Guard who is appointed by commission

commissioner /kə mísh'nər/ *n* **1.** COMMISSION MEMBER a member of a commission **2.** SOMEBODY WORKING FOR COMMISSION somebody authorized by a commission to carry out prescribed duties or tasks **3.** GOV GOVERNMENT OFFICIAL a government representative in an administrative area —**commissionership** *n*

commissioner for oaths *n* a solicitor authorized to authenticate oaths for people making affidavits

Commission for Racial Equality *n* the official body appointed by the Home Secretary to enforce the Race Relations Act of 1976

commissure /kómmi syoor/ *n* **1.** ANAT PLACE WHERE CELLS OR ORGANS MEET a line or point where two cells, organs, or body parts meet or connect **2.** ANAT LINKING BAND OF NERVE TISSUE a band of nerve tissue that connects opposite sides of the central nervous system, e.g. the tissue connecting the left and right sides of the brain **3.** BOT PLACE WHERE PLANT PARTS JOIN a junction or seam between two organs or parts, e.g. that between the carpels of a flower [15C. < Latin *commissura* 'juncture' < *commiss-* (see COMMISSAR)] —**commissural** /kə míssyoórəl, kómmi syoórəl/ *adj*

commit /kə mít/ (**-mits, -mitting, -mitted**) *v* **1.** *vi* PROMISE DEVOTION to pledge devotion or dedication to somebody or something ○ *He wasn't yet ready to commit to the relationship.* **2.** *vt* PROMISE RESOURCES to devote or pledge something such as time or money to an undertaking **3.** *vt* DO WRONG to do something wrong or illegal ○ *commit a crime* **4.** *vt* ENTRUST SOMETHING TO SOMEBODY to entrust something or somebody to somebody else for protection **5.** *vt* RECORD SOMETHING FOR FUTURE to consign or record something in order to preserve it ○ *committed the numbers to memory* **6.** *vt* ASSIGN SOMETHING FOR DESTRUCTION to give something over for destruction or disposal **7.** *vt* LAW, PSYCHIAT INSTITUTIONALIZE SOMEBODY to confine somebody legally to an institution, e.g. a prison or mental health facility **8.** *vt* LAW SEND SOMEBODY FOR TRIAL to send somebody for trial in a higher court **9.** *vt* POL REFER PROPOSED LAW FOR REVIEW to refer a bill to a parliamentary committee for review [14C. < Latin *committere* 'put together' < *mittere* 'put, send'] —**committable** *adj* —**committer** *n*

~~**commitee**~~ incorrect spelling of **committee**

commitment /kə mítmənt/ *n* **1.** RESPONSIBILITY something that takes up time or energy, especially an obligation ○ *family commitments* **2.** LOYALTY devotion or dedication, e.g. to a cause, person, or relationship **3.** PREVIOUSLY PLANNED ENGAGEMENT a planned arrangement or activity that cannot be avoided **4.** POL REFERRAL OF BILL FOR REVIEW a referral of a bill to a parliamentary committee for review **5.** LAW, PSYCHIAT INSTITUTIONALIZING SOMEBODY an act of legally confining somebody to prison or a mental health facility

commitment ceremony *n* a formal ceremony, officiated by a member of the clergy or by a chosen friend, that affirms the partnership of a couple who cannot marry or who have chosen not to marry [Late 20C.]

committal /kə mítt'l/ *n* LAW same as **commitment** (sense 5)

committed /kə míttid/ *adj* devoted to somebody or something such as a cause or relationship —**committedly** *adv*

committee *n* **1.** /kə mítti/ a group of people appointed or chosen to perform a function on behalf of a larger group **2.** /kómmi teé/ a person to whom something, e.g. the charge of somebody deemed incapable of looking after himself or herself, is committed (*dated*)

committeeman /kə míttimən/ (*plural* **-men** /-mən/) *n N Am* a man who is a member of one or more committees

committee stage *n* the stage in parliamentary proceedings in which a bill is closely examined by Members of Parliament sitting in relevant committees, between the second and third readings of the bill

committeewoman /kə mítti wŏŏmən/ (*plural* **-women** /-wimən/) *n N Am* a woman who is a member of one or more committees

~~**committment**~~ incorrect spelling of **commitment**

commo /kómmō/ *n US* COMMUNICATION same as **communication** (sense 1) (*informal; often used before a noun*)

commode /kə mṓd/ *n* **1.** CHAIR WITH CHAMBER POT a chair or box-shaped piece of furniture holding a chamber pot covered by a lid **2.** PORTABLE WASHSTAND a movable washstand with a cupboard underneath containing a chamber pot or washbasin **3.** DECORATED CABINET a low cabinet or chest of drawers, usually elaborately decorated [Late 17C. < French, originally 'suitable' < Latin *commodus* 'conforming with due measure' < *modus* (see MODE)]

commodious /kə mṓdi əss/ *adj* pleasantly spacious (*formal*) —**commodiously** *adv* —**commodiousness** *n*

commoditization /kə móddi tī záysh'n/ *n* the process by which a product reaches a point in its development where one brand has no features that differentiate it from other brands, and consumers buy on price alone

commodity /kə móddəti/ (*plural* **-ties**) *n* **1.** an item that is bought and sold, especially a raw material or manufactured item **2.** something that people value or find useful [15C. < Latin *commodus* (see COMMODE)]

commodore /kómmə dawr/ *n* **1.** NAVY NAVAL OFFICER a title for a very senior captain in the Royal Navy or US Navy who is assigned command responsibilities generally lesser than those of a rear admiral but generally greater than those of a captain **2.** NAVY MERCHANT NAVY CAPTAIN a captain in command of a merchant fleet **3.** SAILING PRESIDENT OF YACHT CLUB the head of a yacht or boat club [Late 17C. Probably alteration of Dutch *komandeur* 'commander' < French *commandeur* < Old French *comander* (see COMMAND)]

Commodus /kómmədəss/, **Lucius Aelius Aurelius** (161–192) Roman emperor (180–192). His reign of violence and despotism led to his eventual assassination.

common /kómmən/ *adj* **1.** SHARED belonging to or shared by two or more people or groups ○ *working towards a common goal* ○ *a doctrine common to several religions* **2.** OF OR FOR ALL relating or belonging to the community as a whole ○ *an area of common land* **3.** EVERYDAY often occurring or frequently seen ○ *a common sight in cities* **4.** WIDELY FOUND describes a widely found species of plant or animal **5.** NON-SPECIALIST used by people who have no specialist knowledge ○ *The common name for 'Viscum album' is 'mistletoe'.* **6.** GENERAL done, used, or held by most people ○ *common practice* **7.** ORDINARY without special privilege, rank, or status ○ *the common man* **8.** OF EXPECTED STANDARD of the standard that most people expect ○ *common courtesy* **9.** VULGAR considered to be lower-class, ill-bred, or vulgar ○ *a common accent* **10.** MATHS WITH EQUAL MATHEMATICAL RELATIONSHIP having an equal relationship to two or more mathematical entities **11.** LITERAT OF VARYING STRESS OR LENGTH describes a syllable that, in a line of poetry, can be either long or short, or stressed or unstressed **12.** CHR USEFUL FOR SEVERAL RELIGIOUS FESTIVALS capable of being

used as a service for any of a number of similar religious festivals ■ *n* **1.** PIECE OF PUBLIC LAND an area of land available for anybody to use, e.g. as a public recreation area or, formerly, as pasture for cattle **2.** LAW RIGHT TO USE SOMEBODY'S LAND the legal right to use somebody else's land or waters in a particular way, usually for grazing or fishing **3.** CHR SERVICE FOR SEVERAL RELIGIOUS FESTIVALS a religious service that can be used for any of a number of similar festivals **4.** same as **common sense** (*slang*) [13C. Via French < Latin *communis*] —**commonness** *n*

commonage /kómmənij/ *n* **1.** RIGHT TO USE JOINTLY the legal right to use something, especially a pasture, in common with other people, or the use that is made of it **2.** PUBLIC OWNERSHIP OF LAND the status of something, usually land, that is publicly owned and available **3.** LAND FOR ALL TO USE land that is publicly owned and available **4.** POL same as **commonalty** (sense 1)

commonality /kómmə nálləti/ (*plural* **-ties**) *n* **1.** the sharing of characteristics or qualities with other individuals **2.** a shared characteristic or quality **3.** POL same as **commonalty** (sense 1) [Late 16C. Alteration of COMMONALTY]

commonalty /kómmənəlti/ *n* (*takes a singular or plural verb*) **1.** the ordinary people as distinct from the upper classes, especially when considered as a political class **2.** a group or society or its membership [13C. Via French < medieval Latin *communalitas* < Latin *communis* 'common']

common bile duct *n* the duct formed by the joining of the duct from the liver and that from the gall bladder

common blue *n* a common butterfly, the male of which is blue and the female usually brown with orange markings. Native to: Europe. Latin name: *Polyommatus icarus.*

common carrier *n* a company in the business of transporting goods or passengers

common chord *n* a major or minor musical chord of three notes (**triad**) that contains a perfect fifth

common cold *n* MED same as **cold** *n* (sense 1)

common denominator *n* **1.** a whole number that can be divided exactly by the lower numbers (**denominators**) of two or more fractions. For example, 8 is a common denominator of $\frac{1}{4}$ and $\frac{1}{2}$. **2.** a shared belief or characteristic

common difference *n* the difference between successive terms in an arithmetic series. For example, 3 is the common difference in the series 2, 5, 8, 11.

common divisor *n* ANZ, N Am same as **common factor**

commoner /kómmənər/ *n* **1.** ORDINARY PERSON an ordinary member of society who does not belong to the nobility **2.** STUDENT WITHOUT SCHOLARSHIP in some universities and colleges, a student who does not receive a scholarship **3.** MEMBER OF HOUSE OF COMMONS a member of the House of Commons

Common Era *n* the period after the birth of Jesus Christ (*used in dates*)

USAGE See AD¹.

common factor *n* a number that two or more other numbers can be divided by exactly. For example, 4 is a common factor of 8, 12, and 20. N Am term **common divisor**

common fraction *n* MATHS same as **simple fraction**

common gender *n* **1.** in English, the gender of a noun that can refer to a person or animal of either sex, e.g. 'leader' and 'fox' **2.** in some languages, the gender of those nouns that can be either masculine or feminine but not neuter

common good *n* the advantage or benefit of everyone

common ground *n* something mutually agreed upon, especially as a basis for negotiation

common knowledge *n* something that is generally known

common law *n* **1.** the body of law developed as a result of custom and judicial decisions, as distinct from the law laid down by legislative assemblies. Common law forms the basis of all law that is applied in England and most of the United States. **2.** law that is applied consistently throughout a place and is not subject to regional variations

common-law *adj* **1.** LAW WITHOUT OFFICIAL CEREMONY describes a partner in a marriage that is recognized in some jurisdictions when both parties declare themselves married without an official ceremony. Common-law marriages are recognized in some states in the United States. **2.** OF UNMARRIED COUPLE LIVING TOGETHER describes a partner in a marriage so called because of the length of time the two unmarried people have lived together as husband and wife **3.** OF COMMON LAW based on or relating to common law

common logarithm *n* a logarithm with ten as its base number

common loon *n* N Am BIRDS same as **great northern diver**

commonly /kómmənli/ *adv* by most people or in most circumstances ○ *The measure was commonly held to be a success.*

common market *n* an economic association established, typically between nations, with the aim of removing or reducing trade barriers

Common Market *n* a term used in the 1960s and 1970s to refer to both the European Community and the European Economic Community (*dated*)

common measure *n* **1.** MUSIC same as **common time 2.** LITERAT the stanza form used for ballads, with four iambic lines rhymed 'abab' or 'abac' **3.** MATHS same as **common factor**

common metre *n* **1.** LITERAT same as **common measure** (sense 2) **2.** the verse form used in many hymns, consisting of four-line verses that alternate lines of eight and six syllables

common multiple *n* a number that can be divided exactly by two or more other numbers. For example 12 is a common multiple of 2, 3, and 4.

common noun *n* a noun that refers to any of a class of people or things, e.g. 'singer' and 'place', as distinct from a proper noun, e.g. 'Lennon' or 'Washington'. Common nouns can be preceded by words that modify their meaning, e.g. 'some' and 'any'.

common or garden *adj* of the ordinary everyday kind [Originally of a plant]

commonplace /kómmən playss/ *adj* **1.** EVERYDAY encountered or happening often **2.** DULL uninteresting as a result of being unoriginal ■ *n* **1.** DULL REMARK an unoriginal remark **2.** SOMETHING ORDINARY something that occurs or is encountered often [Mid-16C. Ultimately translation of Greek *koinos topos* 'general theme'] —**commonplaceness** *n*

commonplace book *n* a personal notebook used for copying down quotations and memorable passages from other books

Common Pleas *n* LAW same as **Court of Common Pleas** (*takes a singular verb*)

common prayer, **Common Prayer** *n* standard prayers for public worship in the Church of England, as recorded in the Book of Common Prayer

Common Riding *n* Scotland a traditional ceremony carried out annually in some towns in Scotland, especially in the Borders, when mounted men inspect the boundaries of the common land

common room *n* **1.** a lounge available to everyone living in a residential community or institution **2.** a sitting room in a college or university where staff or students can relax

commons /kómmənz/ *n* **1.** COLLEGE DINING HALL a dining hall in a college or university (*takes a singular verb*) **2.** *also* **Commons** COMMON PEOPLE the common people as distinct from the ruling classes (*takes a singular or plural verb*) ■ *npl* COMPUT SHARED DATA STORE data stored in the memory of one computer that is available to all computers linked to it by a network (*takes a plural verb*)

Commons *n* (*takes a singular or plural verb*) **1.** the politicians who are elected to the lower houses of the UK and Canadian parliaments and represent all the people **2.** GOV same as **House of Commons**

common salt *n* FOOD same as **salt** (sense 1)

common sense *n* sound practical judgment derived from experience rather than study

commonsense /kómmən senss/ *adj* based on common sense —**commonsensical** /kómmən sénssik'l/ *adj* —**commonsensically** *adv*

common stock *n* N Am same as **ordinary shares**

common time *n* a musical metre with four crotchet beats to the bar, commonly referred to as four-four time

common touch *n* the ability of a celebrity, a member of the royal family, or somebody in public life to behave towards ordinary people in a naturally friendly, informal, and uncondescending way

commonwealth *n* **1.** NATION OR ITS PEOPLE a nation or its people considered as a political entity **2.** REPUBLIC a nation or state in which the people govern **3.** ASSOCIATION OF STATES a group of states that have formed an association for the political and economic benefit of all members **4.** PEOPLE WITH COMMON INTEREST a group of people linked by something that they all have in common

Commonwealth *n* **1.** ASSOCIATION OF BRITAIN AND SOVEREIGN STATES a political, educational, and development association of sovereign states, most of which are former British colonies, with the British monarch as its head **2.** POL FEDERATED STATES OF AUSTRALIA the official designation of the federated states of Australia, often used to refer to the federal government as opposed to the state governments **3.** TERRITORY ASSOCIATED WITH UNITED STATES a self-governing territory voluntarily associated with the United States. Puerto Rico and the Northern Mariana Islands are Commonwealths. **4.** TITLE FOR SOME US STATES an official title used by the US states of Kentucky, Massachusetts, Pennsylvania, and Virginia **5.** HIST REPUBLIC IN 17C ENGLAND the state and republican government in England from the death of Charles I in 1649 until the restoration of the monarchy in 1660

Commonwealth Day *n* a holiday in some countries of the Commonwealth. Date: second Monday in March.

Commonwealth Games *npl* a sports contest held every four years involving participants from countries of the Commonwealth

Commonwealth of Independent States *n* an association formed in 1991 by most of the republics of the former Soviet Union, with ceremonial headquarters in Minsk, Belarus

Commonwealth of Nations *n* POL same as **Commonwealth** (sense 1)

common year *n* an ordinary year of 365 days, as distinct from a leap year

commotion /kə mósh'n/ *n* a scene of noisy confusion or activity [14C. < Latin *commotion-* 'intensive motion' < *motion-* (SEE MOTION)] —**commotional** *adj*

comms /komz/ *npl* communications, especially for moving troops and supplies (*informal*) [Shortening]

communal /kómmyoōn'l, kə myoōn'l/ *adj* **1.** SHARED used or owned by all members of a group or community **2.** OF COMMUNITIES relating to communities or to living in communities **3.** OF COMMUNE belonging or relating to a commune **4.** RELATING TO DIFFERENT SOCIAL GROUPS relating to or involving different groups within a society [Early 19C. < late Latin *communalis* < Latin *communis* 'common'] —**communally** *adv*

communal bereavement *n* the phenomenon of widespread distress, e.g. insomnia, depression, and greater susceptibility to heart attacks, seen following a high-profile tragedy among people who have never met those who have died in it

communalise *vt* POL another spelling of **communalize**

communalism /kómmyoōn'lizəm/ *n* **1.** the principles and practices of communal living or ownership, or support for a communal society **2.** a greater loyalty to an ethnic or religious group than to society in general —**communalist** *n* —**communalistic** /kómmyoōn'l ístik/ *adj*

communality /kómmyoō nálləti/ *n* **1.** shared use or ownership **2.** the spirit of cooperation and solidarity that exists among members of a community or commune

communalize /kómmyoōn'l īz/ (**-izes**, **-izing**, **-ized**), **communalise** (**-ises**, **-ising**, **-ised**) *vt* to put something into joint ownership among the members of a community

communard /kómmyoō naard/ *n* somebody living in a commune [Late 19C. < French *commune* (SEE COMMUNE¹)]

Communard *n* a member or supporter of the Paris Commune of 1871

commune[1] /kóm yoon/ *n* **1. COMMUNAL GROUP** a mutually supportive community in which possessions and responsibilities are shared **2. PEOPLE LIVING IN COMMUNE** a group of families or individual people living in a commune **3. SMALL ADMINISTRATIVE DISTRICT** the smallest administrative district of some countries such as France, Italy, and Switzerland, governed by a mayor and a council [Late 17C. Via French < medieval Latin *communia* < Latin *communis* 'common']

commune[2] /kə myóon, kóm yoon/ (**-munes, -muning, -muned**) *vi* to experience a deep emotional or spiritual relationship with something ○ *communing with nature* [14C. < Old French *comuner* 'to share' < *comun* 'common' < Latin *communis*]

Commune *n* **1.** the insurrectionary committee that governed Paris at the height of the French Revolution in 1792, originally the driving force behind the executions of members of the previous ruling classes. More moderate forces gradually gained control and by 1795 it had been suppressed. **2.** same as **Paris Commune**

communicable /kə myóonikəb'l/ *adj* **1.** able to be passed from one person, animal, or organism to another ○ *a communicable disease* **2.** easily communicated, or capable of being communicated [14C. < late Latin *communicabilis* < Latin *communicare* (see COMMUNICATE)] —**communicability** /kə myóonikə bílləti/ *n* —**communicably** *adv*

communicant /kə myóonikənt/ *n* **1.** somebody who receives the Christian sacrament of Communion **2.** somebody or something that provides information [15C. < Latin *communicant-*, present participle of *communicare* (see COMMUNICATE)]

communicate /kə myóoni kayt/ (**-cates, -cating, -cated**) *v* **1.** *vti* **EXCHANGE INFORMATION** to give or exchange information, e.g. by speech or writing ○ *We communicate by e-mail.* **2.** *vt* **CONVEY FEELING OR THOUGHT** to transmit or reveal a feeling or thought by speech, writing, or gesture so that it is clearly understood **3.** *vi* **UNDERSTAND ONE ANOTHER** to share a good personal understanding ○ *siblings who never really communicate* **4.** *vi* **HAVE COMMON ACCESS** to be connected or provide access to each other **5.** *vt* MED **TRANSMIT DISEASE** to pass a disease or infection on to somebody **6.** *vi* CHR **GIVE OR RECEIVE COMMUNION** to give or receive the Christian sacrament of Communion [Early 16C. < Latin *communicat-*, past participle of *communicare* 'share' < *communis* 'common'] —**communicator** *n* —**communicatory** /-kətəri/ *adj*

communication /kə myóoni káysh'n/ *n* **1. EXCHANGE OF INFORMATION** the exchange of information between people, e.g. by means of speaking, writing, or using a common system of signs or behaviour **2. MESSAGE** a spoken or written message **3. ACT OF COMMUNICATING** the communicating of information **4. RAPPORT** a sense of mutual understanding and sympathy **5. ACCESS** a means of access or communication, e.g. a connecting door —**communicational** *adj*

communication cord *n* a cord or handle in a railway carriage that a passenger can pull to stop a train in an emergency. N Am term **emergency cord**

communications /kəmyooni káysh'nz/ *n* **STUDY OF HUMAN COMMUNICATION** the study of the different means people use to communicate with each other, e.g. by gesture, speech, telecommunications, and writing (*takes a singular or plural verb*) ■ *npl* **1. SYSTEMS FOR COMMUNICATING** the technology and systems used for sending and receiving messages, e.g. postal and telephone networks **2.** MIL **TRANSPORTATION OF TROOPS** a system of routes and transportation for moving troops and supplies

communications satellite *n* an artificial satellite used to relay data such as radio, telephone, and television signals around the world. Signals may be reflected, but more often they are strengthened using a solar-powered transponder. Satellites often follow a geostationary orbit, remaining in the same position relative to Earth.

communication theory, communications theory *n* the study of all forms of human communication, including branches of linguistics such as semantics as well as telecommunications and other nonlinguistic forms

communicative /kə myóonikətiv/ *adj* **1. TALKATIVE** inclined or ready to talk **2. OF COMMUNICATION** relating to communication or to systems for communication **3.** EDUC **STRESSING PRACTICAL COMMUNICATION** in foreign language teaching, stressing the importance of language as a tool for communicating information and ideas —**communicatively** *adv* —**communicativeness** *n*

communion /kə myóoni ən/ *n* **1. INTIMACY** a feeling of emotional or spiritual closeness **2. CONNECTION** a relationship, especially one in which something is communicated or shared ○ *What communion can there be between Good and Evil?* ○ *continues to work in communion with the Church to help the needy* **3.** CHR **RELIGIOUS GROUP WITH COMMON FAITH** a religious group with its own set of beliefs and practices, especially a Christian denomination **4.** CHR **FELLOWSHIP BETWEEN RELIGIOUS GROUPS** a sense of shared religious identity and fellowship, especially between members of different Christian denominations [14C. < Latin *communion-* < *communis* 'common'] —**communional** *adj* —**communionally** *adv*

Communion *n* **1. CHRISTIAN SACRAMENT** a Christian sacrament that commemorates Jesus Christ's Last Supper, with the priest or minister consecrating bread and wine that is consumed by the congregation **2. COMMUNION SERVICE** the service containing the sacrament of Communion **3. CONSECRATED BREAD AND WINE** the consecrated bread and wine received by worshippers at a Communion service

communiqué /kə myóoni kay/ *n* an official announcement, especially to the press or public [Mid-19C. < French past participle of *communiquer* 'communicate' < Latin *communicare* (see COMMUNICATE)]

communise *vt* POL another spelling of **communize**

communism /kómmyŏŏnizəm/ *n* the political theory or system in which all property and wealth is owned in a classless society by all the members of that society [Mid-19C. < French *communisme* < *commun* 'common' < Latin *communis*]

Communism *n* **1.** the Marxist-Leninist version of a classless society in which capitalism is overthrown by a working-class revolution that gives ownership and control of wealth and property to the state **2.** any system of government in which a single, usually totalitarian, party holds power, and the state controls the economy

Communism Peak /kómmyŏŏ nizəm-/ former name for **Ismail Samani Peak**

communist /kómmyŏŏnist/ *n* **1.** an advocate or supporter of any type of communism **2.** a participant in communal living [Mid-19C. < French *communiste* < *commun* (see COMMUNISM)] —**communist** *adj* —**communistic** /kómmyŏŏ nístik/ *adj*

Communist *n* a supporter of Communism or a member of an organization that supports or practises Communism —**Communist** *adj*

communitarian /kə myóoni táiri ən/ *n* a member or supporter of a collectivist or cooperative community or system [Mid-19C. < COMMUNITY] —**communitarian** *adj* —**communitarianism** *n*

community /kə myóonəti/ (*plural* **-ties**) *n* **1. PEOPLE IN AREA** a group of people who live in the same area, or the area in which they live ○ *a close-knit fishing community* **2. PEOPLE WITH COMMON BACKGROUND** a group of people with a common background or with shared interests within society ○ *the financial community* **3. NATIONS WITH COMMON HISTORY** a group of nations with a common history or common economic or political interests ○ *the international community* **4. SOCIETY** the public or society in general ○ *a useful member of the community* **5. INTERACTING PLANTS AND ANIMALS** all the plants and animals that live in the same area and interact with one another **6.** ONLINE same as **virtual community** [14C. Via Old French *communeté* < Latin *communitat-* < *communis* 'common']

community centre *n* a building used for a range of community activities

community charge *n* a flat-rate tax levied in Britain from the late 1980s until 1993 on all adults to part-finance local government. It was introduced as a replacement for domestic rates and was replaced by the council tax, based on property value.

community chest *n N Am* a fund raised by voluntary contributions for local charities and social welfare activities (*dated*)

community college *n* **1.** in the UK, an educational centre with recreational facilities available to the whole community **2.** *NZ* in New Zealand, an educational institution that offers both courses in practical or technical subjects for students and general interest courses for members of the local community

community education *n* educational and recreational programmes provided by local governments for people in their communities

community home *n* a home provided by a local authority or voluntary organization for children who cannot live with relatives or foster parents

community medicine *n* the branch of medicine devoted to the provision of public health care

community nurse *n* an experienced nurse with extra training who visits patients in their homes

community of interest *n* a group of diverse people or organizations with a shared concern who have united to campaign for a common cause

community policing *n* policing that seeks to integrate officers into the local community in order to reduce crime and foster good community relations

community relations *npl* **1.** the relationships between different cultural, ethnic, political, or religious groups who live in an area and may come into conflict **2.** mediation between different cultural, ethnic, political, or religious groups living in an area

community school *n* a state primary or secondary school for which a local education authority has staffing, premises, and admissions responsibilities

community service *n* a penalty requiring that an offender convicted of a relatively minor crime do unpaid work that is beneficial to the community as an alternative to imprisonment

community-service order *n* a court order requiring a convicted offender to do community service for a number of hours

communize /kómmyŏŏ nīz/ (**-nizes, -nizing, -nized**), **communise** (**-nises, -nising, -nised**) *vt* **1.** to transfer something such as land or property from private to public ownership **2.** to apply communist principles of organization to a government or people [Late 19C. < Latin *communis* 'common'] —**communization** /kómmyŏŏ nī záysh'n/ *n*

commutate /kómmyŏŏ tayt/ (**-tates, -tating, -tated**) *vt* to convert alternating electric current to direct current or vice versa

commutation /kómmyŏŏ táysh'n/ *n* **1.** LAW **REDUCTION IN SEVERITY OF LEGAL PENALTY** the reduction of a prison sentence or other legal penalty to a less severe one **2. CONVERSION** an exchange or substitution, e.g. the substitution of one kind of payment for another (*formal*) **3.** ELEC **CONVERSION OF ELECTRIC CURRENT** the converting of an electric current from alternating to direct current or vice versa **4.** *N Am* TRANSP **COMMUTER'S TRAVEL** the travelling undertaken by a commuter

commutation ticket *n US* a passenger ticket valid for multiple trips over a given route during a limited period, sold for less than the total cost of tickets purchased separately for each trip

commutative /kə myóotətiv/ *adj* **1.** involving or relating to exchanges or substitutions **2.** in mathematics or logic, giving the same result irrespective of the order in which two or more terms or quantities are placed. Addition and multiplication are commutative processes, while subtraction and division are not. —**commutatively** *adv* —**commutativity** /kə myóotə tívvəti/ *n*

commutator /kómmyŏŏ taytər/ *n* a device that maintains the direction of flow of electric current in a generator or reverses it in an electric motor

commute /kə myóot/ (**-mutes, -muting, -muted**) *v* **1.** *vi* **TRAVEL REGULARLY BETWEEN PLACES** to travel regularly from one place to another, especially between home and work **2.** *vti* **REPLACE WITH SOMETHING ELSE** to be changed or substituted, or change or substitute one thing for another, e.g. one form of payment for another **3.** *vi* **BE REPLACEMENT** to compensate or act as a substitute **4.** *vt* LAW **REDUCE SEVERITY OF PENALTY** to reduce a legal sentence to a less severe one **5.** *vt* ELEC same as **commutate** **6.** *vi* MATHS **GIVE SAME MATHEMATICAL RESULT WITH DIFFERENT ORDER** to give the same mathematical result irrespective of the order in which two or more quantities are placed, as in addition but not subtraction [15C. < Latin *commutare* 'change altogether' < *mutare* 'to change'] —**commutable** *adj*

commuter /kə myóotər/ n 1. somebody who travels regularly between places, especially between home and work 2. N Am an airline that provides short flights between major cities

commuter belt n a residential area from which many people commute

commy n POL another spelling of **commie** (*informal disapproving*)

Como /kṓmō/ resort town and capital of Como Province, Lombardy, northern Italy, on the southwestern shore of Lake Como. Population: 78,680 (2001).

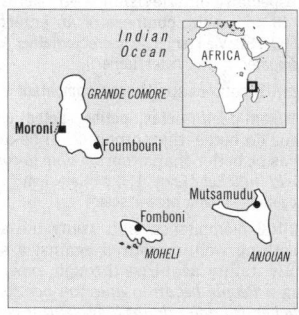

Comoros

Comoros /kómmərōz, kə máwrōz/ an independent state consisting of a group of islands in the Indian Ocean, 290 km/180 mi. from Mozambique and 320 km/200 mi. from Madagascar. Language: French, Arabic. Currency: Comorian Franc. Capital: Moroni. Population: 632,948 (2003). Area: 1,862 sq. km/719 sq. mi. Official name **Federal Islamic Republic of the Comoros** —**Comorian** /kə máwri ən/ n, adj

comp[1] /komp/ (*informal*) n 1. an accompaniment, especially a jazz accompaniment played on piano or guitar 2. MUSIC same as **accompanist** ◼ vti (**comps, comping, comped**) to play a musical accompaniment, especially in jazz, on piano or guitar [Mid-20C. Shortening of ACCOMPANIMENT, ACCOMPANIST]

comp[2] /komp/ (*informal*) n same as **competition** (sense 2) ◼ vi (**comps, comping, comped**) to enter a competition [Early 20C. Shortening of COMPETITION]

comp. abbr 1. companion 2. GRAM comparative 3. compare 4. HR compensation 5. COMPUT compilation 6. COMPUT compiled 7. complete 8. MUSIC composer 9. MATHS, BOT composite 10. composition 11. CHEM, LING compound 12. comprehensive 13. comprising

compact[1] adj /kəm pákt/ 1. SMALL AND EFFICIENTLY ARRANGED small, with efficient use of available space 2. PACKED TIGHTLY closely clustered or packed together ◦ *a compact bundle of papers* 3. SHORT AND STURDY short and stocky 4. CONCISE brief and concise ◼ v /kəm pákt/ (**-pacts, -pacting, -pacted, -pacted** or **-pact**) 1. vti PACK SOMETHING TIGHTLY to become, or make something, more dense or firmly packed 2. vt METALL COMPRESS METAL POWDER to compress metal powder in a die so that it bonds into a single component ready for heat-treatment (**sintering**) ◼ n /kóm pakt/ 1. COSMETICS CASE FOR MAKEUP a small flat case containing makeup, usually face powder, with a mirror inside the lid 2. PHOTOGRAPHY same as **compact camera** 3. N Am SMALLISH CAR a medium-sized car that is economical to run 4. METALL METAL POWDER READY FOR PRESSING a mass of metal powder in a die, ready for the compression and heat-treatment (**sintering**) that will bond it into a single component [14C. < Latin *compactus*, past participle of *compingere* 'fasten together' < *pangere* 'fasten'] —**compactible** adj —**compactly** adv —**compactness** n

compact[2] /kóm pakt/ n an agreement, especially an informal or private agreement [Late 16C. < Latin *compactum* < past participle of *compacisci* 'make an agreement together' < *pacisci* (see PACT)]

compact camera n a small camera with an integral lens

compact disc n a hard plastic disc approximately 12 cm/4 in. in diameter on which information such as music or computer data is digitally encoded in a format readable by laser beam

Compact Disc-Interactive n COMPUT full form of **CDI**

compact disc player n a machine for playing compact discs

compacter n US HOUSEHOLD another spelling of **compactor**

compaction /kəm páksh'n/ n 1. the compression of particles to make a dense mass, or the compressed state of the resulting mass 2. a process in the formation of sedimentary rock in which pressure from overlying sediment forces water from unconsolidated sediment, reducing its volume and yielding solid rock

compactor /kəm páktər/, **compacter** n N Am a machine used in the home to compress rubbish into small bundles for easy disposal

compact video disc n a compact disc that plays both sound and pictures

companion[1] /kəm pánnyən/ n 1. SOMEBODY TO BE WITH somebody who accompanies or shares time with another 2. SOMEBODY WHOSE JOB IS ACCOMPANYING ANOTHER somebody, usually a woman, employed to live with another person, especially in former times 3. MATCHING ARTICLE an object or item that goes with another to make a pair 4. PUBL HANDBOOK a guide or handbook on a particular subject 5. ASTRON FAINTER OF TWO STARS the fainter of the stars that make up a double-star or multiple-star system 6. another spelling of **Companion** [13C. < late Latin *companion-* 'somebody who shares bread' < Latin *panis* 'bread'] —**companion** vt

companion[2] /kəm pánnyən/ n a companionway, or a covering above it [Mid-18C. Alteration of obsolete Dutch *kompanje* 'quarterdeck' < Italian *compagna* '(storeroom for) provisions', < Latin *panis* 'bread']

Companion n the lowest-ranking member in a British order of knighthood

companionable /kəm pánnyənəb'l/ adj friendly, sociable, and good company ◦ *They sat in a companionable silence.* —**companionableness** n —**companionably** adv

companion animal n an animal kept for companionship and enjoyment

companionate /kəm pánnyənət/ adj 1. appropriate for a companion 2. right for each other

companionate marriage n marriage based on mutual affection and shared interests as opposed to purely economic or dynastic considerations

companion cell n in flowering plants, a cell that lies alongside a sap-conducting sieve-tube element, whose function it is thought to influence. Companion cells have a prominent nucleus and dense cytoplasm, and form fine cytoplasmic connections (**plasmodesmata**) with the adjacent sieve-tube element.

companion piece n a work, especially of music or literature, that is closely related to another, often by the same composer or author

companion set n a set of tools used to tend a fire

companionship /kəm pánnyən ship/ n 1. the company of friends and the relationship that exists between them 2. an organized group of people

companionway /kəm pánnyən way/ n a stairway or ladder between decks on a ship

company /kúmpəni/ (*plural* **-nies**) n 1. BUSINESS BUSINESS a business enterprise 2. STATE OF BEING TOGETHER the state of being with other people ◦ *He didn't feel at ease in company.* 3. GROUP a gathering of people 4. COMPANIONS the people that somebody associates with 5. PARTICULAR TYPE OF COMPANION somebody seen as providing a particular type of companionship ◦ *He can be very good company.* 6. GUEST a guest or visitor, especially for a meal or overnight stay ◦ *We're having company this weekend.* 7. BUSINESS BUSINESS PARTNERS the partners of a business enterprise whose names are not included in the firm's title 8. ARTS TROUPE a group of performing artists such as actors 9. MIL GROUP OF TROOPS a unit of soldiers, usually consisting of two or more platoons 10. NAVY, NAUT SHIP'S CREW the crew and officers of a ship 11. YOUTH ORG GROUP OF GUIDES a unit of Girl Guides 12. BUSINESS, HIST TRADE GUILD a medieval trade guild [13C. < Anglo-Norman *compainie* < late Latin *companion-* (see COMPANION[1])]

company car n a car owned or leased by a business for use by an employee, often as a fringe benefit

company doctor n 1. a doctor employed by a company to look after the health of its employees 2. somebody who specializes in making unprofitable businesses efficient and profitable

company-grade officer n MIL same as **company officer**

company man n an employee who puts loyalty to an employer before friendship or personal beliefs (*disapproving*)

company officer n a commissioned officer who holds the rank of captain or below

company town n N Am a town whose residents depend on a single business for employment, housing, and shops

compar. abbr GRAM comparative

comparable /kómpərəb'l/ adj 1. similar enough for a fair comparison to be made ◦ *We ate a meal comparable with that of the finest restaurant.* 2. as good as another or each other ◦ *They both have comparable skills.* —**comparability** /kómpərə bílləti/ n —**comparably** adv

USAGE The most acceptable pronunciation in British English is with the stress on the first syllable, although stress on the second syllable is also heard and is more usual in American usage.

USAGE comparable to or **comparable with**? *Comparable* mimics the verb *compare* in being followed either by *to* or *with*, depending in careful usage on whether unlike or like things are being considered: *The agency provides a service comparable to that of a good library. The air raid was comparable with the ones on Dresden or Hiroshima.* See also **compare**.

comparatist /kəm párrətist/ n somebody who uses a comparative method, e.g. in the study of linguistics [Mid-20C. < French *comparatiste*, < *comparatif* 'comparative']

comparative /kəm párrətiv/ adj 1. COMPARED WITH OTHERS considered relative to something known, mentioned, or expected ◦ *He passed the test with comparative ease.* 2. INVOLVING COMPARISONS based on or using comparisons of different things in the investigation of something ◦ *comparative linguistics* 3. GRAM IN FORM EXPRESSING INCREASE describes the form of an adjective or adverb that expresses an increase in quality, quantity, or degree, e.g. 'quicker' or 'more importantly' ◼ n GRAM COMPARATIVE FORM OF WORD a comparative form of an adjective or adverb [15C. < Latin *comparat-*, past participle of *comparare* (see COMPARE)] —**comparativeness** n

comparatively /kəm párrətivli/ adv in comparison with something else ◦ *The costs were comparatively high.*

comparator /kəm párrətər/ n 1. an instrument used for comparing properties such as colour or shape of a system or object with those of a standard 2. a circuit used for comparing the difference between two electronic signals

compare /kəm páir/ v (**-pares, -paring, -pared**) 1. vt EXAMINE PEOPLE OR THINGS FOR SIMILARITIES to examine two or more people or things in order to discover similarities and differences between them 2. vt LIKEN SOMEBODY OR SOMETHING TO ANOTHER to consider or represent somebody or something as similar to another ◦ '*Shall I compare thee to a summer's day?*' (William Shakespeare, *Sonnet*; 1564–1616) 3. vi BE AS GOOD to be equal or similar in quality or standing, especially to be as good as another ◦ *As an athlete she can compare with the best in the sport.* 4. vi RELATE IN PARTICULAR WAY to have a particular relationship with something or somebody else ◦ *Its performance compares badly with that of rival engines.* 5. vi MAKE COMPARISON to make a comparison between two or more people or things 6. vt GRAM GIVE FORMS OF ADJECTIVE OR ADVERB to give the positive, comparative, and superlative forms of an adjective or adverb ◼ n COMPARISON comparison (*literary*) ◦ *a painting beautiful beyond compare* [15C. < Latin *comparare* < *compar* 'equal with' < *par* 'equal'] —**comparer** n

USAGE Compare to or **compare with**? In careful usage, **compare to** is preferred when two unlike things are being likened: *He compared her skin to ivory.* **Compare with** is used when the comparison is between similar things and implies differences as well as similarities: *Tourists find its hotels poor value compared with those of other European capitals.* When **compare** is used intransitively (i.e. without an object), *with* should always be used: *The new model compares well with others in the same price range.* See also **comparable**.

comparison /kəm párriss'n/ n 1. the act or process of

examining two or more people or things in order to discover similarities and differences between them ○ *Journalists continue to draw comparisons between the two systems.* ○ *The initial outlay seems insignificant in comparison with the potential profits.* **2.** the quality of being similar ○ *There's no comparison between them.* [14C. Via Old French *comparesoun* < Latin *comparation-*, < *comparat-*, past participle of *comparare* (see COMPARE)]

comparison-shop *vi* to compare the prices and features of the same or similar items, especially in different shops, in order to find the best deal —**comparison shopper** *n* —**comparison shopping** *n*

~~**comparitive**~~ incorrect spelling of **comparative**

compartment /kəm paartmənt/ *n* **1. PARTITIONED SPACE** one of the areas into which an enclosed space is divided **2. TRAIN CARRIAGE SECTION** a walled area within a passenger train carriage, with a door and features such as two facing rows of seats or sleeping accommodation **3. SMALLER PART** a separate part of something larger ○ *He liked to divide his life into different compartments.* ○ *a glove compartment* [Mid-16C. < French *compartiment* < late Latin *compartiri* 'divide up' < Latin *partiri* 'divide' < *pars* 'part'] —**compartmental** /kóm paart mént'l/ *adj* —**compartmentally** *adv*

compartmentalize /kóm paart mént'l īz/ (**-izes, -izing, -ized**), **compartmentalise** (**-ises, -ising, -ised**) *vt* to divide something into separate areas, categories, or compartments, often in a way that makes the separate parts too isolated ○ *She had to compartmentalize her home life and work.* —**compartmentalization** /kóm paart mént'l ī záysh'n/ *n*

compass /kúmpəss/ *n* **1. DIRECTION FINDER** a device for finding directions, usually with a magnetized pointer that automatically swings to magnetic north **2. PERSONAL DIRECTION** a sense of personal direction ○ *a leader who was devoid of moral compass* **3. SCOPE** the scope of something such as a subject or area of study ○ *beyond the compass of the enquiry* **4. HINGED DEVICE FOR DRAWING CIRCLES** a device for drawing circles or measuring distances, e.g. on a map, that consists of two rods, one pointed, the other often holding a pencil, joined by an adjustable hinge (*often used in the plural*) ■ *vt* (**-passes, -passing, -passed**) **1. UNDERSTAND SOMETHING** to understand something fully and completely (*formal*) ○ *far more than the average mind can compass* **2.** same as **encompass** (sense 2) **3. ACHIEVE SOMETHING** to achieve or attain something (*literary*) [14C. < French *compas* 'circle', *compasser* 'to measure' < assumed Vulgar Latin *compassare*, literally 'step off' < Latin *passus* 'step'] —**compassable** *adj*

compass card *n* the circular diagram in a direction-finding compass over which the needle rotates

compassion /kəm pásh'n/ *n* sympathy for the suffering of others, often including a desire to help [14C. Via French < ecclesiastical Latin *compassion-* < Latin *compass-*, past participle of *compati* (see COMPATIBLE)] —**compassionless** *adj*

compassionate /kəm pásh'nət/ *adj* showing feelings of sympathy for the suffering of others, often with a desire to help —**compassionately** *adv* —**compassionateness** *n*

compassionate leave *n* exceptional leave granted to somebody, especially in the armed forces, for personal reasons such as the death of a close relative

compassion fatigue *n* a loss of sympathy for the suffering of others experienced by donors or carers as a result of the demands made of them

compass plant *n* a plant with leaves that tend to point north and south. Flowers: yellow, similar to a daisy's. Native to: prairie regions of central United States. Latin name: *Silphium laciniatum.*

compass rose *n* a circular diagram printed on a chart or map to show the direction of north and other main points of the compass [Because its design was thought to resemble a rose]

compass saw *n* a handsaw with a tapering blade, used for cutting curved shapes

compass sense *n* the ability of some birds, fish, and insects to use the Earth's magnetic field to guide them across long distances

compass window *n* a semicircular bay window

~~**compatable**~~ incorrect spelling of **compatible**

compatibilist /kəm páttəb'list/ *n* a person who believes that you can be wholly free and responsible for your actions, even though every one of those actions has already been predetermined by events occurring well before your birth and thereby out of your control (*formal*)

compatible /kəm páttəb'l/ *adj* **1. HARMONIOUS** able to exist, live, or work together without conflict ○ *a highly compatible couple* **2. CONSISTENT** consistent or in keeping with something else ○ *an observation not compatible with the facts* **3.** COMPUT **ABLE TO BE USED TOGETHER** in computing, able to be used together with or substituted for another piece of hardware or software ○ *The software isn't PC-compatible.* **4.** MED **ACCEPTABLE TO BODY** describes blood, organs, or tissue that can be transplanted or transfused into somebody's body without being rejected **5.** BOT **ABLE TO POLLINATE EACH OTHER** describes plant varieties that are able to pollinate each other successfully **6.** BOT **ABLE TO BE GRAFTED** describes plants that are able to be grafted onto each other successfully **7.** FUNGI **ABLE TO MATE** describes fungal strains that are able to mate successfully [Mid-16C. < French < Latin *compati* 'suffer together' < *pati* (see PATIENT)] —**compatibility** /kəm páttə bílləti/ *n* —**compatibly** *adv*

compatriot /kəm páttri ət/ *n* somebody from the same country as another person [Late 16C. Via French < late Latin *compatriota* 'fellow countryman' < *patriota* (see PATRIOT)]

compd *abbr* CHEM compound

compeer /kóm peer/ *n* (*formal*) **1.** the equal or peer of somebody else **2.** somebody who is a close companion or associate of somebody else [14C Via Old French *comper* < Latin *compar* (see COMPARE)]

compel /kəm pél/ (**-pels, -pelling, -pelled**) *vt* **1.** to force somebody to do something ○ *I felt compelled to listen.* **2.** to make something happen by force [14C. < Latin *compellere*, literally 'drive together' < *pellere* 'to beat'] —**compellable** *adj* —**compeller** *n*

compelling /kəm pélling/ *adj* **1.** attracting strong interest and attention ○ *a compelling film about human relationships* **2.** necessitating action or belief ○ *I felt a compelling need to explain my actions.* ○ *some very compelling arguments* —**compellingly** *adv*

compendious /kəm péndi əss/ *adj* containing a wide range of information in a concise form (*formal*) —**compendiously** *adv* —**compendiousness** *n*

compendium /kəm péndi əm/ (*plural* **-diums** or **-dia** /-di ə/) *n* **1. SHORT COMPREHENSIVE ACCOUNT** a comprehensive but brief account of a subject, especially in book form **2. TWO BOOKS IN ONE** a book in which two or more previously published books are brought together **3. COLLECTION** a collection of things, especially several different board games in one box [Late 16C. < Latin < *compendere* 'weigh together' < *pendere* (see PENSIVE)]

compensate /kómpən sayt/ (**-sates, -sating, -sated**) *v* **1.** *vi* **MAKE AMENDS** to make amends or make up for something ○ *Nothing can compensate for the loss of one's home.* **2.** *vt* **PAY SOMEBODY FOR WORK OR LOSS** to pay somebody for work done or for something lost ○ *adequately compensated for their efforts* **3.** *vti* **COUNTERBALANCE** to counterbalance a force or quality **4.** *vi* PSYCHOL **OFFSET PERSONALITY WEAKNESS** to behave in a way that emphasizes a particular ability or personality trait in order to make up for a deficiency in another [Mid-17C. < Latin *compensat-*, past participle of *compensare*, literally 'weigh together' < *pensare* (see PENSIVE)] —**compensable** /kəm pénssəb'l/ *adj* —**compensative** /kómpən saytiv, kəm pénssətiv/ *adj* —**compensator** *n*

compensation /kómpən sáysh'n/ *n* **1. MONEY IN PAYMENT FOR LOSS** an amount of money or something else given to pay for loss, damage, or work done **2. GIVING OF COMPENSATION** the act of giving money or something else to pay for loss, damage, or work done **3. AMENDS** something that makes amends or makes up for something else ○ *one of the compensations of living abroad* **4.** PSYCHOL **BEHAVIOUR THAT OFFSETS WEAKNESS** behaviour that emphasizes a particular ability or personality trait in order to make up for a deficiency in another —**compensational** *adj*

compensation culture *n* the tendency to seek financial compensation for any injustice or wrong done by another, or for any physical or mental suffering caused by the action or negligence of another

compensation order *n* an order from a court instructing somebody convicted of an offence to pay compensation to the victim

compensatory /kómpən sáytəri/ *adj* serving to offset the negative effects or results of something else

compensatory growth *n* the growth in size of one part or organ of the body to make up for the failure or loss of another

compensatory time *n US* additional time off work offered by an employer for additional hours worked by an employee

compere /kóm pair/ *n* the host of an entertainment show, especially on television ■ *vti* (**-peres, -pering, -pered**) to act as the compere of an entertainment show [Mid-18C. Via French *compère* 'godfather' < medieval Latin *compater* < Latin *pater* 'father']

~~**competant**~~ incorrect spelling of **competent**

compete /kəm peet/ (**-petes, -peting, -peted**) *vi* **1.** to try to win or do better than others **2.** to be able to do as well as or better than others ○ *able to compete on the world market* [Early 17C. < late Latin *competere* 'strive together' < Latin *petere* 'seek']

competence /kómpitənss/ *n* **1. ABILITY** the ability to do something well, measured against a standard, especially ability acquired through experience or training ○ *People began to question her competence as a teacher.* ○ *I don't doubt his scientific competence for a moment.* **2. SUFFICIENT INCOME** income that is enough to live on (*formal*) **3.** LAW **STATE OF BEING LEGALLY QUALIFIED** acceptance by a court as legally qualified to be a party or witness **4.** LING **LANGUAGE KNOWLEDGE** knowledge of a language that enables somebody to speak and understand it **5.** BIOL **ABILITY OF CELL TO SPECIALIZE** the ability of embryonic cells to respond to an outside stimulus in a way that affects their development into specialized tissue

SYNONYMS See ***ability.***

competency /kómpitənsi/ (*plural* **-cies**) *n* an ability to do something, especially measured against a standard ○ *core competencies*

competent /kómpitənt/ *adj* **1. ABLE** having enough skill or ability to do something well **2. ADEQUATE** good enough or suitable for something ○ *The graphics test showed the printer to be competent, but no more.* **3.** LAW **LEGALLY CAPABLE** accepted by a court as legally qualified to be a party or witness **4.** MED, BIOL **FUNCTIONING NORMALLY** able to function normally, especially in response to an antigen [14C. Via French < Latin *competent-*, present participle of *competere* (see COMPETE)] —**competently** *adv*

competition /kómpə tísh'n/ *n* **1. PROCESS OF TRYING TO BEAT OTHERS** the process of trying to win or do better than others ○ *Several firms are in competition for the contract.* **2. CONTEST** an activity in which people try to win something or do better than others **3. OPPOSITION** the opposition in a competitive situation, or the level of opposition ○ *keep one step ahead of the competition* ○ *fierce competition* **4.** ECOL **STRUGGLE FOR RESOURCES** the struggle between organisms of the same or different species for limited resources such as food or light ○ *competition between weeds and flowers* [Early 17C. < late Latin *competition-* < Latin *competere* (see COMPETE)]

competitive /kəm péttitiv/ *adj* **1. INVOLVING ATTEMPT TO WIN** involving or decided by competition ○ *a highly competitive sport* **2. WANTING TO BEAT OTHERS** inclined towards wanting to achieve more than others **3. BETTER THAN COMPETITION** as good as or slightly better than others because of being good value or worth more ○ *competitive prices* —**competitiveness** *n*

competitive exclusion *n* the concept that two or more species with identical requirements cannot coexist on the same limited resources because one will compete more successfully than the other

competitive local exchange carrier *n US* a company that offers an alternative service to the established telephone service provider in a particular area

competitively /kəm péttitivli/ *adv* **1.** in a way that involves trying to win or do better than others **2.** in a way that is as good as or slightly better than others because of being good value or worth more ○ *competitively priced*

competitor /kəm péttitər/ *n* **1.** an opponent, especially in a commercial market **2.** a person or animal

taking part in a competition [Early 16C. < Latin *competere* (see COMPETE)]

compilation /kómpi láysh'n/ *n* **1.** something created by putting together things that have been gathered from various places ○ *a compilation of new poems* **2.** the process of bringing things together from various places to form a whole

compile /kəm pīl/ (**-piles, -piling, -piled**) *vt* **1. GATHER THINGS TOGETHER** to bring things together from various places to form a whole **2. CREATE SOMETHING BY COMPILING THINGS** to create something by putting together things that have been gathered from various places ○ *compile statistical data* **3.** COMPUT **TRANSLATE COMPUTER LANGUAGE** to convert a computer program written in a high-level language into an intermediate language (**machine language**) using a special program (**compiler**) [14C. < French *compiler*, probably < Latin *compilare* 'to plunder']

compiler /kəm pīlər/ *n* **1.** somebody who brings things together, especially to create a whole **2.** a computer program that converts another program from a high-level language into an intermediate language (**machine language**)

complacent /kəm pláyss'nt/ *adj* **1.** self-satisfied and unaware of possible dangers **2.** eager to please (*archaic*) [Mid-17C. < Latin *complacent-*, present participle of *complacere* 'please very much' < *placere* 'to please'] — **complacency** *n* —**complacently** *adv*

USAGE complacent or **complaisant**? Both words are used of people and their actions. A ***complacent*** smile is a smile of self-satisfaction, whereas a ***complaisant*** smile is one that is intended to please. It is possible for a smile, or for somebody showing the smile, to be both ***complacent*** and ***complaisant***.

complain /kəm pláyn/ (**-plains, -plaining, -plained**) *vi* **1. EXPRESS UNHAPPINESS** to express discontent or unhappiness about a situation **2. DESCRIBE SYMPTOMS** to describe symptoms that are being experienced, e.g. of an illness ○ *complaining of chest pains* **3. PROTEST** to formally make an accusation of wrongdoing or a crime, or register a protest ○ *The neighbours complained to the police about the noise.* [14C. < French *complaign-*, stem of *complaindre* < Latin *plangere* 'to beat'] —**complainer** *n* —**complainingly** *adv*

SYNONYMS ***complain, object, protest, grumble, grouse, carp, gripe, whine, nag***

CORE MEANING: to indicate dissatisfaction with something

complain to express discontent or unhappiness about a situation ○ *Nearby neighbours had complained about the noise and the mess.* ○ *He complains bitterly that tests were not done years ago.* **object** to be opposed to something, or express opposition to it ○ *We object strongly to the two proposals.* ○ *Sports bodies have objected on the grounds that the scheme would take away space that could be used as a sports field.* **protest** to express strong disapproval or disagreement ○ *a day of action to protest at the government's health policies* ○ *From eight months onwards, babies are likely to protest loudly at being passed around.* **grumble** to complain or mutter in a discontented way, possibly repeatedly or continually ○ *He picked up his brush and, grumbling, got down to work.* ○ *Investors were grumbling about not being told the whole story.* **grouse** to complain regularly and continually, often in a way that is not constructive ○ *grousing about the commercialism of art* ○ *'These talks are leading nowhere', one of the negotiators groused.* **carp** to keep complaining or finding fault, especially about unimportant things ○ *He was a unpleasant employer, carping all the time.* **gripe** (*informal*) to complain continually and irritatingly ○ *griping about the fact that I had not presented him with an advance copy of the book* ○ *You griped when I was in the house all day, and now that I've got a job you are griping at that!* **whine** to complain in an unreasonable, repeated, or irritating way ○ *so-called experts whining about the state of the nation's schools* ○ *whining to me about his problems.* **nag** to find fault with somebody regularly and repeatedly ○ *I was always being nagged about the length of my hair or the untidiness of my room.*

complainant /kəm pláynənt/ *n* a person or organization that takes legal action against another

complaint /kəm pláynt/ *n* **1. STATEMENT OF UNHAPPINESS** a statement expressing discontent or unhappiness about a situation ○ *If you've any complaints, talk to the manager.* **2. SOMETHING MAKING SOMEBODY UNHAPPY** something that makes somebody discontented or unhappy **3. EXPRESSING OF UNHAPPINESS** the act of expressing discontent or unhappiness about a situation ○ *has cause for complaint* **4. AILMENT** a physical disorder, usually something minor **5.** LAW **STATEMENT** a statement setting out the reasons for a legal action [14C. < French *complainte*, feminine past participle of *complaindre* (see COMPLAIN)]

complaisant /kəm pláyz'nt/ *adj* showing a willingness to please others by carrying out, or allowing them to carry out, their wishes [Mid-17C. < French, present participle of *complaire* 'agree in order to please' < Latin *complacere* (see COMPLACENT)] —**complaisance** *n* —**complaisantly** *adv*

USAGE See ***complacent***.

compleat /kəm pleét/ *adj* having or exhibiting full knowledge of a particular field or skill (*archaic*) [14C. Variant of COMPLETE]

complected /kəm pléktid/ *adj N Am* having a particular kind of complexion (*informal; usually used in combination*) [Early 19C. Back-formation < COMPLEXION]

complement *n* /kómplimənt/ **1. COMPLETING PART** something that completes or perfects something else **2. ONE OF TWO** either of two things that form a unit **3. FULL QUANTITY** a quantity of people or things that is considered complete ○ *the full complement of warships and replenishing vessels* **4.** GRAM **SENTENCE PART** a word or group of words, excluding the verb, that complete the predicate of a sentence or clause **5.** MATHS, LOGIC **ITEMS EXCLUDED FROM SUBSET** the elements of a set that are not included in a particular subset of that set **6.** MATHS same as **complementary angle 7.** IMMUNOL **GROUP OF BLOOD PROTEINS** a set of proteins in the bloodstream that, together with antibodies, recognize and attack foreign cells such as bacteria **8.** MUSIC **NOTE INTERVAL** an interval that, when added to a given interval, equals an octave ■ *vt* /kómpli ment/ (**-ments, -menting, -mented**) **COMPLETE SOMETHING** to complete, perfect, or go well with something else ○ *a light dessert that complements a rich meal* [14C. < Latin *complementum* 'something that fills up' < *complere* (see COMPLETE)] —**complemental** /kómpli mént'l/ *adj* —**complementally** *adv*

USAGE complement or **compliment**? The two words are close in spelling but their meanings are quite different. A ***complement*** is something added to perfect a thing and make it complete, whereas a ***compliment*** is an expression of praise: *A fine wine is the perfect complement to good cooking. The cook received many compliments from the guests that evening.* Both words are also used as verbs, and both have adjectival forms: ***complementary*** and ***complimentary***. ***Complimentary*** has the special meaning 'given free', and so a ***complimentary*** copy of a book is one given without charge, whereas a ***complementary*** copy is one that completes a set of books.

complementarity /kómpli men tárrəti/ (*plural* **-ties**) *n* **1.** the condition of things that complement one another **2.** the concept that two different models may be necessary to describe an atomic or subatomic system, e.g. electrons may be regarded as particles or waves in different circumstances

complementary /kómpli méntəri/ *adj* **1. COMPLETING** completing something else **2.** GENETICS **INTERDEPENDENT** describes genes that are interdependent and produce their effect only when present together **3.** MATHS **NOT IN SUBSET** describes the elements of a mathematical set that are not included in a particular subset of that set **4.** MATHS **FORMING PART OF RIGHT ANGLE** describes either of two angles that together make a right angle **5.** ALTERN MED **OF COMPLEMENTARY MEDICINE** used in or using complementary medicine —**complementarily** *adv* —**complementariness** *n*

USAGE See ***complement***.

complementary angle *n* either of two angles that together make up a right angle

complementary colour *n* coloured light or a colour that, when combined with another, produces white or grey

complementary DNA *n* single-stranded DNA made in a laboratory so that its base sequence is complementary to a messenger RNA template. It is assembled by the enzyme reverse transcriptase and may be used in gene cloning or as a gene probe.

complementary gene *n* a gene that produces an observable effect in an organism only in conjunction with another gene

complementary medicine *n* a range of therapies based on the holistic treatment of physical disorders, generally addressing the causes of diseases rather than their symptoms and also taking steps in the prevention of disease. The term embraces therapies such as acupuncture, herbal medicine, and homeopathy.

complementation /kómpli men táysh'n/ *n* **1.** the act or fact of completing, perfecting, or going well with something else **2.** the effect produced when two separate mutations occur together in an organism and partly or wholly cancel out each other's action

complement fixation *n* the process in which a group of blood proteins (**complement**) is bound to a specific combined antibody-antigen pair as part of the immune reaction to foreign cells

complementizer /kómplimən tīzər/ *n* a word introducing a clause that acts as a complement ○ *'For' in 'for Sam to be late is unusual' is a complementizer.*

complete /kəm pleét/ *adj* **1. WHOLE** having every necessary part or everything that is wanted ○ *a complete set of Dickens* **2. FINISHED** having reached the normal or expected end ○ *The washing machine stops when the last spin cycle is complete.* **3. ABSOLUTE** being the greatest degree of something ○ *a complete waste of time* **4. PERFECT** having all the necessary qualities or abilities for a particular role ○ *She is the complete diplomat.* **5.** BOT **HAVING ALL PRINCIPAL FLOWER PARTS** describes flowers that have all the principal flower parts, which are carpels, petals, sepals, and stamens ■ *vt* (**-pletes, -pleting, -pleted**) **1. MAKE SOMETHING WHOLE** to make something whole by including every necessary part or everything that is wanted ○ *one more goblet to complete the set* **2. FINISH SOMETHING** to finish something or bring it to an end ○ *You have 20 minutes to complete the quiz.* **3. ACCOMPLISH SOMETHING** to carry out or accomplish something ○ *The terms of the sale have been completed.* [14C. Directly or via French < Latin *completus*, past participle of *complere* 'fill up' < *plere* 'fill'] —**completeness** *n* ◇ **complete with** including a particular thing as a feature

ORIGIN The Latin word *plere*, 'to fill', from which ***complete*** is derived, is also the source of English *accomplish, complement, compliment, comply, deplete, expletive, implement, replete, supplement,* and *supply.* Its Indo-European ancestor is in turn the source of English *full*[1].

complete blood count *n* a diagnostic test used to identify the levels of all blood-cell types in a quantity of blood

completely /kəm pleétli/ *adv* used to emphasize the extent of something ○ *completely wrong* ○ *I completely forgot about it.*

complete metamorphosis *n* a metamorphosis that involves the four stages of egg, larva, pupa, and adult in insects such as butterflies, beetles, flies, and bees

completion /kəm pleésh'n/ *n* **1. FINISHING OF SOMETHING** the act of finishing something or of bringing it to an end **2. STATE OF BEING FINISHED** the state of being finished or brought to an end ○ *the building is nearing completion* **3.** LAW **FINAL STAGE OF SALE** the final stage of the sale of land or real property, when ownership changes hands **4.** AMERICAN FOOTBALL **CAUGHT PASS** in American football, a forward pass that has been successfully caught

completist /kəm pleétist/ *n* a collector who wants to obtain everything available in his or her speciality

complex *adj* /kóm pleks, kəm pléks/ **1. COMPLICATED** difficult to analyse, understand, or solve **2. HAVING MANY PARTS** made up of many interrelated parts ■ *n* /kóm pleks/ **1. SET OF INTERCONNECTED BUILDINGS** a group of interconnected buildings functioning as a whole ○ *a sports complex* **2. INFLUENCE ON BEHAVIOUR** a set of related feelings, ideas, or impulses that may be repressed but continues to influence thoughts and behaviour ○ *a guilt complex* **3. EXAGGERATED FEELINGS** an exaggerated or obsessive set of feelings about something (*informal*) ○ *He has a complex about eating in restaurants.* **4.** CHEM **COMPOUND OF NONMETAL AND METAL ATOMS** a compound in which nonmetal molecules or ions form weak bonds (**coordinate bonds**) with a central metal atom [Mid-17C. Directly or via French < Latin *complexus*, past participle of *complecti*

'weave together' < *plectere* 'to plait'] —**complexly** *adv* —**complexness** *n*

complex conjugate *n* a complex number in a pair of numbers that have the same real components but opposite imaginary components. The complex conjugate of a + ib is a – ib.

complex fraction *n* a fraction with a mixed number or fraction in its numerator or denominator or in both

complexion /kəm pléksh'n/ *n* **1.** the quality and colour of the skin, especially of the face **2.** the character of something or the way it appears ○ *This development puts an entirely new complexion on the matter.* [14C. < French, 'bodily constitution' < Latin *complecti* (see COMPLEX)] —**complexioned** *adj*

complexity /kəm pléksəti/ (*plural* **-ties**) *n* **1.** COMPLICATED NATURE the condition of being difficult to analyse, understand, or solve **2.** CONDITION OF HAVING MANY PARTS the condition of being made up of many interrelated parts **3.** COMPLICATED THING one of the interrelated problems or difficulties involved in a complicated matter (*often used in the plural*)

complex number *n* a number in the form *a* + *ib*, where i = &√−1, that may be either real or imaginary

complex plane *n* a plane whose coordinates are expressed as single complex numbers

complex sentence *n* a sentence containing one or more subordinate clauses

compliance /kəm plī ənss/, **compliancy** /-ənssi/ *n* **1.** the state or act of conforming with or agreeing to do something ○ *in compliance with the court order* **2.** readiness to conform or agree to do something

compliance documentation *n* the documents that a company issuing shares must publish to comply with regulatory requirements governing new share issues and related matters

compliance legislation *n* legislation enacted to ensure compliance with a legal agreement or requirement such as a treaty or mandate

compliance officer *n* somebody employed by a financial organization to ensure that conflicts of interest do not arise in companies with wide-ranging, complex financial dealings and that regulations are not broken

compliant /kəm plī ənt/ *adj* **1.** ready to conform or agree to do something **2.** made or done according to requirements or instructions (*often used in combination*) ○ *compliant with the general statutes* ○ *Y2K-compliant* —**compliantly** *adv*

complicate *vt* /kómpli kayt/ (**-cates, -cating, -cated**) to make something complex or difficult ○ *Further delay will only complicate matters.* ○ *a complicating factor* ■ *adj* /kómplikət/ describes leaves or insect wings that are folded lengthways [Early 17C. < Latin *complicat-*, past participle of *complicare* 'fold together' < *plicare* 'to fold']

complicated /kómpli kaytid/ *adj* **1.** composed of many interrelated parts or features ○ *a complicated diagram* **2.** difficult to understand, deal with, or explain ○ *Life is complicated enough as it is.* —**complicatedly** *adv*

complication /kómpli káysh'n/ *n* **1.** DIFFICULT STATE a difficult or confused state caused by many interrelated factors **2.** DIFFICULTY something that makes something else more difficult or complex ○ *Far from being helpful, this is just a further complication.* **3.** INTRODUCTION OF DIFFICULTY the act of making something complex or difficult **4.** PLOT DEVICE an event or character whose introduction into a story causes difficulty **5.** MEDICAL PROBLEM a disease or problem that arises in addition to the initial condition or during a surgical operation

complicit /kəm plíssit/ *adj* involved in something illegal or wrong ○ *It was clear that some of the staff were complicit in the attempt to cover up the scandal.* [Late 20C. Back-formation < COMPLICITY]

complicity /kəm plíssəti/ *n* involvement with another in doing something illegal or wrong [Mid-17C. < archaic *complice* (see ACCOMPLICE)]

compliment *n* /kómplimənt/ **1.** STATEMENT OF PRAISE something said to express praise or approval **2.** GESTURE OF RESPECT OR HONOUR something done to show respect or honour ■ *vt* /kómpli ment/ (**-ments, -menting, -mented**) **1.** PRAISE SOMEBODY to express praise or approval of somebody **2.** GIVE SOMETHING TO SOMEBODY to give somebody a gift as a sign of respect or honour **3.** CONGRATULATE SOMEBODY to express congratulations to somebody [Mid-17C. Via French < Italian *complimento* < Latin *complementum* (see COMPLEMENT)] ◇ **return the compliment** to respond to a gesture that somebody has made with a similar gesture

---

USAGE See ***complement***.

---

complimentary /kómpli méntəri/ *adj* **1.** expressing praise or approval ○ *a complimentary glance* **2.** given free as a courtesy or favour ○ *complimentary seats* —**complimentarily** *adv*

USAGE See ***complement***.

---

compline /kómplin, -līn/, **complin** /-lin/ *n* in the Roman Catholic church, the last of the seven separate hours (**canonical hours**) that are set aside for prayer each day [12C. Alteration of Old French *complie* < medieval Latin *(hora) completa* 'final (hour)' < Latin *completus* (see COMPLETE)]

comply /kəm plī/ (**-plies, -plying, -plied**) *vi* to obey or conform to something such as a rule, law, regulation, or wish [Late 16C. Via obsolete French *complire* < Latin *complere* (see COMPLETE)] —**complier** *n*

compo[1] /kóm pō/ *n* a substance that is a mix of various ingredients, e.g. cement or mortar (*slang*) [Early 19C. Shortening of COMPOSITION]

compo[2] /kómpō/ *n* (*informal*) **1.** *Aus* compensation paid to workers for injury at work **2.** *NZ* in New Zealand, a payment for injury under the provisions of an accident compensation scheme funded by general taxation [Mid-20C. Shortening and alteration of COMPENSATION] ◇ **be on compo** *ANZ* to be in receipt of payment for an injury (*informal*)

component /kəm pṓnənt/ *n* **1.** PART a part of something, usually of something bigger ○ *a manufacturer of vehicle components* ○ *one of several major components of our research* **2.** ELEC ELECTRIC PART a device such as a resistor or transistor that is part of an electronic circuit **3.** MATHS VECTOR one of a set of vectors whose combination (**resultant**) is another vector **4.** CHEM CONSTITUENT SUBSTANCE one of the substances necessary to describe each phase of a chemical system ■ *adj* FORMING PART forming part of a whole [Mid-16C. < Latin *component-*, present participle of *componere* 'put together' < *ponere* 'to place'] —**componential** /kómpə nénsh'l/ *adj*

componentize /kəm pṓnən tīz/ (**-izes, -izing, -ized**), **componentise** (**-ises, -ising, -ised**) *vt* **1.** to divide something into smaller, more manageable, or more flexible parts **2.** to divide a large software application into smaller independently functioning parts

compo rations *npl* food in a dried and compressed form, meant for use by soldiers when no fresh food is available [shortening of COMPOSITE]

comport /kəm páwrt/ (**-ports, -porting, -ported**) *v* (*formal*) **1. comport yourself** *vr* to behave in a particular way **2.** *vi* to agree or be consistent with something ○ *This does not comport with the established facts.* [14C. < Latin *comportare* 'bring together' < *portare* 'to carry']

comportment /kəm páwrtmənt/ *n* the way in which somebody behaves (*formal*)

compose /kəm pṓz/ (**-poses, -posing, -posed**) *v* **1.** *vt* BE PARTS OF SOMETHING to be the components or parts that make up something ○ *fertilizer composed of organic compounds* ○ *the nations that compose the alliance* **2.** *vt* PUT ELEMENTS TOGETHER to put things together to form a whole ○ *composed a light lunch, using cold meats and salads* **3.** *vt* ARRANGE ITEMS to arrange things in order to achieve an effect ○ *composing objects for a still life in oils* **4.** *vti* CREATE to create something, especially a piece of music or writing ○ *She is trying to compose a rather difficult letter to her client.* **5.** *vt* CALM SOMEBODY to make somebody become calm ○ *Please compose yourself.* **6.** *vti* SET TYPE to set type in preparation for printing [14C. < French *composer*, alteration (influenced by *poser* 'to place') of Latin *componere* (see COMPONENT)]

USAGE See ***comprise***.

---

composed /kəm pṓzd/ *adj* not agitated or distracted —**composedly** /-zidli/ *adv* —**composedness** /-zidnəss/ *n*

composer /kəm pṓzər/ *n* a creator of something, especially of music

composite /kómpəzit/ *adj* **1.** COMPOUND made up of different parts **2.** BOT WITH COMPLEX FLOWER HEADS describes any plant belonging to a large family that has flower heads resembling a single flower but composed of many smaller flowers. Dandelions and daisies are composite plants. Family: Compositae. ■ *n* **1.** SOMETHING MADE OF PARTS something made from different parts ○ *The new law is a composite of previous suggested legislation.* **2.** BOT COMPOSITE PLANT a composite plant **3.** INDUST BUILDING MATERIAL a building material made up of different ingredients **4.** *N Am* CRIME IMAGE OF SUSPECT an image of a suspect's face that is created by a police artist or photographer, based on input from witnesses (*informal*) ■ *vt* (**-ites, -iting, -ited**) COMBINE PROPOSALS to combine motions from various local branches of an organization such as a political party or a trade union for discussion at a higher level [14C. Directly or via French < Latin *compositus*, past participle of *componere* (see COMPONENT)] —**compositely** *adv* —**compositeness** *n*

Composite *adj* belonging to a classical order of architecture that combines features of the Ionic and Corinthian orders

composite construction *n* a building technique that combines the use of steel and concrete to make supporting columns, resulting in stronger, lighter, and less costly supports

composite photograph *n* an image or scene made up of two or more original images placed side by side, overlapped, or superimposed

composite school *n* in some Canadian provinces, a secondary school in which academic, business, and vocational programmes are offered

composite volcano *n* GEOL same as **stratovolcano**

composition /kómpə zísh'n/ *n* **1.** CONSTITUENTS the way in which something is made, especially in terms of its different parts **2.** ARRANGEMENT the way in which the parts of something are arranged, especially the parts of a visual image ○ *the artist's masterly composition of a group portrait* **3.** PUTTING TOGETHER OF THINGS the act or process of combining things to form a whole **4.** CREATION OF MUSICAL OR LITERARY WORK the act or process of creating something such as a piece of music or writing **5.** ARTS ARTISTIC CREATION something created as a work of art, especially a piece of music **6.** PIECE OF WRITING a short piece of writing, especially a school exercise **7.** PRODUCT something created by combining separate parts **8.** LAW SETTLEMENT a settlement whereby creditors agree to accept partial payment of debts by a bankrupt party, usually in return for a consideration such as immediate payment of a lesser amount **9.** LING WORD FORMATION the formation of compound words from separate words **10.** PRINTING TYPESETTING the setting of type in preparation for printing **11.** LOGIC LOGICAL FALLACY the fallacy of arguing that what is true of parts of a whole is true of the whole [14C. Via French < Latin *composition-* < *composit-*, past participle of *componere* (see COMPONENT)] —**compositional** *adj* —**compositionally** *adv*

compositor /kəm pózzitər/ *n* somebody who sets text in type [Mid-16C. < Latin, 'compiler' < *composit-* (see COMPOSITION)]

compos mentis /kómpəss méntiss/ *adj* sane or of sound mind [< Latin, 'in control of your mind']

compost /kóm post/ *n* **1.** DECAYED PLANT MATTER a mixture of decayed plants and other organic matter used by gardeners for enriching soil **2.** SOIL MIXTURE FOR POT PLANTS a mixture based on peat or soil that is used in pots for growing plants ○ *a rich potting compost* ■ *v* (**-posts, -posting, -posted**) **1.** *vti* DECAY to convert organic matter to compost, or to be converted to compost **2.** *vt* PUT COMPOST ON SOIL to treat soil or an area of ground by adding compost [14C. Via Old French *composte* 'mixture' < Latin *composita* < *composit-* (see COMPOSITION)] —**compostable** *adj*

composter /kóm postər/ *n* a device, often shaped like a box or barrel, used to collect organic materials to be used later in composting

compost heap *n* a pile of organic matter left to rot for use as fertilizer, especially by a gardener or farmer

composure /kəm pṓzhər/ *n* calm and steady control over the emotions

compote /kóm pōt/ *n* fruit cooked in sugar or syrup, served as a hot or cold dessert [Late 17C. Via French, 'mixture' < Old French *composte* (see COMPOST)]

compound[1] *n* /kóm pownd/ **1. MIXTURE** something made by combining two or more things **2.** CHEM **CHEMICAL SUBSTANCE** a substance formed by the chemical combination of elements in fixed proportions **3.** GRAM **WORD MADE UP OF OTHER WORDS** a word that is formed from two or more identifiable words, e.g. 'blackbird', 'cookbook', or 'bullheaded', or, in some analyses, 'mother-in-law' or 'fire drill' ■ *adj* /kóm pownd/ **1. HAVING PARTS** made up of two or more parts **2.** GRAM **MADE FROM TWO OR MORE WORDS** describes a word that is made up of two or more words or word parts **3.** BOT **DIVIDED INTO PARTS** describes a leaf that is divided into two or more parts (**leaflets**) attached to a single stalk ■ *v* /kəm pównd, kom-/ (**-pounds, -pounding, -pounded**) **1.** *vti* **COMBINE THINGS** to add together, or add one thing to another, to form a whole ○ *hatred that was compounded with fear and revulsion* **2.** *vt* **MAKE SOMETHING FROM PARTS** to make something by combining parts ○ *a medication compounded from several constituent elements* **3.** *vt* **INTENSIFY SOMETHING** to make something more extreme or intense by adding something to it ○ *Further financial reverses compounded his despair.* **4.** *vt* LAW **TAKE BRIBE TO IGNORE CRIME** to accept a bribe in return for not prosecuting or informing about a crime **5.** *vti* **SETTLE DEBT** to settle a debt by paying a lesser amount owed, usually immediately and in a lump sum [14C. < Old French *compoun-*, stem of *compondre* < Latin *componere* (see COMPONENT)] —**compoundable** *adj* —**compounder** *n*

SYNONYMS See ***mixture***.

compound[2] /kóm pownd/ *n* **1.** an enclosed group of buildings for the segregation or restraint of a particular group of people **2.** *Malaysia, Singapore* a garden with a fence or wall round it [Late 17C. < Malay *kampong* 'enclosure, village']

compound engine *n* an engine in which potential generated in one stage is augmented in another

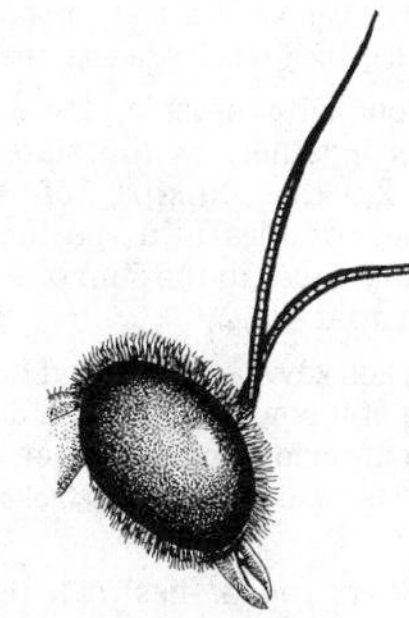

compound eye

compound eye *n* the eye that most insects and some crustaceans have, made up of several separate light-sensitive parts

compound fault *n* a series of geological faults that lie close together, following the same general direction

compound fraction *n* MATHS same as **complex fraction**

compound fracture *n* MED same as **open fracture**

compound interest *n* interest that is calculated on the combined total of the original sum borrowed (**principal**) and the interest it has already accrued

compound meter *n N Am* MUSIC same as **compound time**

compound microscope *n* a microscope consisting of two lenses or lens systems and an eyepiece, mounted in a tube

compound sentence *n* a sentence containing two or more clauses that can stand independently. The clauses are often linked by a conjunction, which is sometimes preceded by a comma, as in 'We waited for over an hour, but she didn't show up'.

compound time *n* MUSIC musical time in which the number of beats to the bar is a multiple of three. N Am term **compound meter**

comprehend /kómpri hénd/ (**-hends, -hending, -hended**) *v* **1.** *vti* to grasp the meaning or nature of something ○ *It was hard to comprehend the sheer scale of the problem.* **2.** *vt* to include something as a part of a larger whole (*formal*) [14C. < Latin *comprehendere* 'grasp fully' < *prehendere* 'seize']

comprehensible /kómpri hénssəb'l/ *adj* capable of being understood [15C. Directly or via French < Latin *comprehensibilis* < *comprehens-*, past participle of *comprehendere* (see COMPREHEND)] —**comprehensibility** /kómpri hénssə bílləti/ *n* —**comprehensibleness** *n* —**comprehensibly** *adv*

comprehension /kómpri hénsh'n/ *n* **1. UNDERSTANDING** the grasping of the meaning of something **2. INTELLECTUAL ABILITY** the ability to grasp the meaning of something ○ *It's beyond my comprehension.* **3.** EDUC **SET OF QUESTIONS ON TEXT** an exercise consisting of a set of questions on a short text, designed to test students' understanding of it [15C. Directly or via French < Latin *comprehension-* < *comprehens-* (see COMPREHENSIBLE)]

comprehensive /kómpri hénssiv/ *adj* **1. INCLUSIVE** covering many things or a wide area ○ *a comprehensive survey of public opinion* **2. INCLUDING ALL** including everything, so as to be complete ○ *comprehensive knowledge of the subject* **3. COVERING MANY EVENTUALITIES** describes insurance policies that provide coverage or benefit in most areas **4.** EDUC **FOR CHILDREN OF ALL EDUCATIONAL ABILITIES** for all children of a local area, no matter what their level of ability ■ *n* EDUC same as **comprehensive school** [Early 17C. Directly or via French < Latin *comprehensivus* < *comprehens-* (see COMPREHENSIBLE)] —**comprehensively** *adv*

comprehensiveness /kómpri hénssivnəss/ *n* the state of including a great deal or everything

comprehensive school *n* a local secondary school for children of all ability levels

compress *v* /kəm préss/ (**-presses, -pressing, -pressed**) **1.** *vti* **SHRINK** to make something smaller by applying pressure or a similar process, or become smaller in this way **2.** *vt* **PRESS THINGS TOGETHER** to press things such as the lips together **3.** *vt* COMPUT **MAKE COMPUTER FILES SHORTER** to reduce the number of bits required to represent computer text, data, or images so as to save storage space or reduce transmission time ■ *n* /kóm pres/ **1.** MED **TREATMENT PAD** a cloth pad, often moistened or medicated, pressed firmly against a part of the body as a treatment, e.g. to stop bleeding **2. MACHINE** a machine for compressing material, especially cotton that is being packed [14C. Via Old French < late Latin *compressare* 'keep pressing together' < Latin *comprimere* 'press together' < *premere* 'to press'] —**compressed** *adj* —**compressibility** /kəm préssə bílləti/ *n* —**compressible** *adj*

compressed air /kəm prést-/ *n* air that is kept in a container under pressure, often used to power machines

compression /kəm présh'n/ *n* **1. REDUCTION IN SIZE** the reduction of the volume or mass of something by applying pressure, or the state of having been treated in this way **2. PHASE IN ENGINE** the phase in the working of an internal-combustion engine in which a combination of fuel and air is compressed in a cylinder before being ignited **3.** COMPUT **REDUCTION OF COMPUTER DATA** a technique for reducing the number of bits required to represent text, data, or images so as to save storage space or reduce transmission time [14C. Via French < Latin *compression-* < *compress-*, past participle of *comprimere* (see COMPRESS)] —**compressional** *adj*

compression chamber *n* a chamber in an internal-combustion engine in which a combination of fuel and air is compressed in a cylinder before being ignited

compression ratio *n* the ratio between the largest and smallest possible volumes in the cylinder of an internal-combustion engine that contains a combination of fuel and air being compressed

compression sack *n* a tubular bag made of synthetic fabric with special straps to compress the bulk of its contents and make it easier for hikers and mountaineers to carry

compression wave *n* a longitudinal wave created in a fluid by a compressing force, e.g. a sound wave in air

compressive /kəm préssiv/ *adj* having the power or tendency to compress [14C. Via French < medieval Latin *compressivus* < Latin *compress-* (see COMPRESSION)] —**compressively** *adv*

compressor /kəm préssər/ *n* **1.** a machine that compresses gas so that the power produced when the gas is released can be used to power another machine such as a pneumatic drill **2.** a muscle that compresses or flattens a part of the body

comprimario /kómpri máiri ō/ *n* a secondary role in an opera or ballet, or somebody who performs such a role [< Italian, 'jointly' + 'primary']

~~**comprimise**~~ incorrect spelling of **compromise**

comprise /kəm príz/ (**-prises, -prising, -prised**) *vt* **1. INCLUDE SOMETHING** to incorporate or contain something **2. CONSIST OF SOMETHING** to be made up of something **3.** ⚠ **CONSTITUTE SOMETHING** to make up the whole of something [15C. < French *compris*, past participle of *comprendre* 'include' < Latin *comprehendere* (see COMPREHEND)] —**comprisable** *adj*

USAGE comprise, consist of, include, compose, or **constitute**? ***Comprise*** and ***consist of*** are concerned with a whole that has a number of parts. They are used in the active voice, with the whole as their subject and the parts as their object: *The house comprises three bedrooms, a bathroom, a kitchen, and a living room. The meal consisted of several small dishes that everybody dipped into and shared.* If some rather than all the parts are mentioned, ***include*** may be used instead: *The house includes a kitchen and a living room on the first floor.* ***Consist of*** is more usual than ***comprise*** when the parts, or some of them, are mass nouns, as opposed to count nouns that can be used with *a* or a number: *Breakfast consists of bread, jam, cereal, and coffee.* ***Compose*** and ***constitute*** are concerned with parts that make up a whole. ***Compose*** is normally used in the passive and ***constitute*** in the active: *The team is composed of several experts in the field. The following commodities constitute the average household diet.*

compromise /kómprə mīz/ *n* **1. AGREEMENT** a settlement of a dispute in which two or more sides agree to accept less than they originally wanted ○ *After hours of negotiations a compromise was reached.* **2. SOMETHING ACCEPTED RATHER THAN WANTED** something that somebody accepts because what was wanted is unattainable **3. POTENTIAL DANGER OR DISGRACE** exposure to danger or disgrace ■ *v* (**-mises, -mising, -mised**) **1.** *vi* **AGREE BY CONCEDING** to settle a dispute by agreeing to accept less than what was originally wanted **2.** *vt* **LESSEN VALUE OF SOMEBODY OR SOMETHING** to undermine or devalue somebody or something by making concessions ○ *Don't compromise your integrity by telling half-truths.* **3.** *vt* **EXPOSE SOMEBODY OR SOMETHING TO DANGER** to expose somebody or something to danger or disgrace ○ *This scandal could compromise his chances of re-election.* ○ *drugs that can compromise the immune system* [15C. Via French *compromis* < Latin *compromissum* 'mutual agreement' < past participle of *compromittere* 'make mutual promises' < *promittere* (see PROMISE)] —**compromiser** *n*

compromising /kómprə mīzing/ *adj* likely to expose somebody to danger or disgrace —**compromisingly** *adv*

comp time *n N Am* HR same as **compensatory time** (*informal*)

Compton /kómptən, kúmp-/, **Sir Denis** (1918–97) British cricketer and footballer. An international player in both his sports, he set an all-time batting record in the 1947 season with 3,816 runs, including 18 centuries.

Compton-Burnett /kómptən bər nét/, **Ivy, Dame** (1884–1969) British novelist. She wrote *Pastors and Masters* (1925) and *Brothers and Sisters* (1929).

> 'There is more difference within the sexes than between them.'
> [Ivy Compton-Burnett, *Mother and Son*; 1955]

Compton effect *n* the decrease in energy and increase in wavelength experienced by a photon after colliding or interacting with an electron [Early 20C. After A. H. *Compton* (1892–1962), US physicist]

comptroller /kən trṓlər/ *n* FIN same as **controller** (sense 2) [15C. Variant influenced by *compt*, older spelling of COUNT [1]]

compulsion /kəm púlsh'n/ *n* **1. FORCE** a force that makes somebody do something **2. COMPELLING** an act of compelling or the state of being compelled ○ *You are under no compulsion to leave.* **3.** PSYCHOL **PSYCHOLOGICAL FORCE** a psychological and usually irrational force that makes somebody do something, often unwillingly ○ *felt an irresistible compulsion* [14C. Via French < late Latin *compulsion-* < Latin *compuls-*, past participle of *compellere* (see COMPEL)]

compulsive /kəm púlssiv/ *adj* **1. DRIVEN TO DO SOMETHING**

driven by an irresistible inner force to do something ○ *a compulsive liar* 2. POWERFULLY INTERESTING exerting a powerful attraction or interest ○ *The TV series was compulsive viewing.* ■ *n* SOMEBODY UNDER PSYCHOLOGICAL COMPULSION somebody whose actions are driven by a usually irrational psychological force —**compulsively** *adv* —**compulsiveness** *n*

compulsory /kəm púlssəri/ *adj* 1. NECESSARY required by law or an authority ○ *Attendance at the lecture is compulsory.* 2. FORCED caused by force, or using force to make somebody do something ■ *n* (*plural* **-ries**) REQUIRED ROUTINE an exercise or routine that participants in a sport such as gymnastics or figure skating must perform as part of a competition (*often used in the plural*) [Early 16C. < medieval Latin *compulsorius* < Latin *compuls-* (see COMPULSION)] —**compulsorily** *adv* —**compulsoriness** *n*

compulsory purchase *n* a situation in which somebody is obliged by law to sell property to the government or a local authority because it is wanted for public use

compunction /kəm púngksh'n/ *n* feelings of shame and regret about doing something wrong [14C. Via French < ecclesiastical Latin *compunction-* < Latin *compunct-*, past participle of *compungere* 'sting strongly' < *pungere* 'to prick, sting'] —**compunctious** *adj* —**compunctiously** *adv*

compurgation /kóm pur gáysh'n/ *n* formerly, a way of proving that somebody is innocent by collecting oaths from friends and colleagues [Mid-17C. < medieval Latin *compurgation-* < Latin *compurgare* 'cleanse completely' < *purgare* 'purify'] —**compurgator** /kóm pur gaytər/ *n*

computation /kómpyoo̅ táysh'n/ *n* 1. the calculating of something, or the result of a calculation 2. the use of a computer, especially for calculation, or something calculated using a computer —**computational** *adj* —**computationally** *adv*

compute /kəm pyóot/ (**-putes, -puting, -puted**) *v* 1. *vt* CALCULATE SOMETHING to calculate an answer or result, especially using a computer 2. *vi* YIELD RESULT to yield a result, especially a correct result, from calculation ○ *These numbers just don't compute.* 3. *vi* USE COMPUTER to use a computer or calculator [Early 17C. < Latin *computare* 'reckon together' < *putare* 'reckon'] —**computable** *adj*

computed tomography /kəm pyóotid-/ *n* a technique for producing images of cross-sections of the body. A computer processes data from X-rays penetrating the body from many directions and projects the results on a screen. This is the technology used when conducting a CT scan.

computer /kəm pyóotər/ *n* 1. an electronic device that accepts, processes, stores, and outputs data at high speeds according to programmed instructions 2. somebody who calculates figures or amounts using a machine

computer-aided design *n* the use of a computer and sophisticated graphics software to design products or systems

computer-aided engineering *n* the use of computers and specialized programs in engineering to automate analysis and testing through simulation of such factors as stress and loads

computer animation *n* COMPUT same as **animation** (sense 3)

computerate /kəm pyóotərit/ *adj* COMPUT same as **computer-literate** [Late 20C. < COMPUTER, after LITERATE]

computer conferencing *n* the use of computers to allow people at distant sites to exchange text and graphic messages as they would at a meeting

computer crime *n* illegal activities carried out on or by means of a computer. Computer crime includes criminal trespass into another computer system, theft of computerized data, and the use of an online system to commit or aid in the commission of fraud.

computer dating *n* the business or practice of putting people's personal details and preferences into a computer that then matches apparently compatible couples

computerese /kəm pyóotə réez/ *n* the technical language used by people involved with computers (*humorous*)

computer game *n* a game in the form of computer software, run on a personal computer or games machine and played by one or more people using a keyboard, mouse, control pad, or joystick. Computer games usually combine sound and graphics and range from traditional games such as chess to fast-moving action games or complex puzzles.

computer graphics *n* the use of a computer and specialized software to produce and manipulate pictorial images for purposes of animation, business presentations, and scientific research (*takes a singular verb*) ■ *npl* the images produced by computer graphics (*takes a plural verb*)

computer-integrated telephony *n* COMPUT, TELECOM same as **computer-telephone integration**

computerize /kəm pyóotə rīz/ (**-izes, -izing, -ized**), **computerise** (**-ises, -ising, -ised**) *vt* 1. to install or start using a computer system to organize, control, or automate something, e.g. a mechanical process 2. to store information in a computer system or process it by computer —**computerizable** *adj* —**computerization** /kəm pyóotə rī záysh'n/ *n* —**computerized** *adj*

computerized axial tomography, computerized tomography *n* MED same as **computed tomography**

computer language *n* COMPUT same as **programming language**

computer-literate *adj* having a good understanding and experience of working with a computer or computer system —**computer literacy** *n*

computer modelling *n* the use of computer graphics and other techniques to create a simplified version of something so as to predict and analyse potential technical problems

computer science *n* the study of the mathematics and technology of computers and their applications

computer-telephone integration *n* a system that allows telephonic resources to be made accessible to and controlled by computers so that the same networks can be shared by voice and data traffic

computer virus *n* COMPUT same as **virus** (sense 3)

computing /kəm pyóoting/ *n* the activity of using computers or computer software

comrade /kóm rayd, -rid/ *n* 1. a close friend or a companion 2. *also* **Comrade** a fellow member of a group, especially a fellow soldier or a fellow supporter of a communist or socialist party [Mid-16C. Via French *camerade, camarade* < Spanish *camarada* 'barracks mate' < *camara* 'room' < Latin *camera* (see CAMERA)] —**comradely** *adj* —**comradeship** *n*

comrade-in-arms (*plural* **comrades-in-arms**) *n* somebody who is fighting on the same side in a war, battle, or other armed struggle

Comrades Marathon, Comrades *n S Africa* a long-distance race held annually between Pietermaritzburg and Durban in South Africa

Comstockery /kóm stokəri, kúm-/ *n US* the removal of, or strong opposition to, anything that could be seen as immoral or obscene in literary, artistic, or broadcast material [Early 20C. After Anthony *Comstock* (1844–1915), US reformer]

con[1] /kon/ *vt* (**cons, conning, conned**) 1. TRICK SOMEBODY to cheat somebody dishonestly, usually out of money or property, by first convincing the victim of something that is untrue 2. LIE TO SOMEBODY to tell somebody something untrue or misleading 3. PERSUADE SOMEBODY to persuade or inveigle somebody to agree to something (*informal*) ○ *See if you can con him into babysitting tonight.* ■ *n* DISHONEST TRICK a dishonest trick or business ploy that takes advantage of somebody's trust, e.g. telling lies in order to get money or property unfairly [Late 19C. Shortening of CONFIDENCE TRICK]

con[2] /kon/ *n* 1. an argument against doing something, or evidence supporting the view that something should not be done ○ *the pros and cons* 2. an opponent of something, or somebody who votes against something [Late 16C. Shortening of Latin *contra* 'against']

con[3] /kon/ *n* CRIME same as **convict** (*slang*) [Late 19C. Shortening]

con[4] /kon/ (**cons, conning, conned**) *vt* (*archaic*) 1. to study something with great care and attention 2. to learn or memorize something [< Old English *cunnan* 'know how', *cunnian* 'explore' < Indo-European]

con[5] /kon/ *vt* (**cons, conning, conned**) to direct the course of a ship ■ *n* control of the course of a ship, or the controls used [Early 17C. Alteration of obsolete *cond* < French *conduire* < Latin *conducere* (see CONDUCE)]

con[6] /kon/ *prep* used to mean 'with' in a musical direction [< Italian, 'with']

con. *abbr* 1. MUSIC concerto 2. LAW conclusion 3. TELECOM, TRANSP connection 4. COMM consolidated 5. continued 6. contra

Con. *abbr* 1. Conformist 2. POL Conservative 3. Consul

Conakry /kónnəkri, kónnəkreé/ capital, largest city, and chief Atlantic port of Guinea, in Western Africa. Population: 705,280 (1983 estimate).

con amore /kón a máw ray, -máwri/ *adv* with tender feeling (*used as a musical direction*) [< Italian, 'with love']

con artist *n* a confidence trickster

conation /kō náysh'n/ *n* in psychology, a mental process involving the will, e.g. impulse, desire, or resolve [Mid-19C. < Latin *conation-* < *conat-*, past participle of *conari* 'try'] —**conational** *adj* —**conative** /kōnətiv, kónnə-/ *adj*

con brio /kon breé ō/ *adv* with spirit or vigour (*used as a musical direction*) [< Italian, 'with vigour']

conc. *abbr* 1. CHEM concentrated 2. CHEM concentration 3. concerning 4. MUSIC concerto 5. concession

concatenate /kon káttə nayt, kən-/ *vt* (**-nates, -nating, -nated**) 1. BRING THINGS TOGETHER to connect separate units or items into a linked system 2. COMPUT LINK UNITS TOGETHER in computing, to link two or more information units, e.g. character strings or computer files, so that they form a single unit ■ *adj* COMPUT LINKED TOGETHER linked together in a sequence or chain [15C. < late Latin *concatenat-*, past participle of *concatenare* 'chain together' < Latin *catena* 'chain']

concatenation /kon káttə náysh'n, kən-/ *n* 1. the linking of things together, or the state of being interconnected 2. the linking of computer characters, strings, or files in a specific order to form a single entity equal to the sum of the lengths of the original entities

concave /kón kayv, kon káyv/ *adj* 1. curved inward like the inner surface of a bowl or sphere 2. describes a polygon with an interior angle greater than 180° [< Latin *concavus* 'hollowed out' < *cavus* 'hollow'] —**concavely** *adv*

concavity /kon kávvəti/ (*plural* **-ties**) *n* 1. the state of being concave 2. a concave part or surface

concavo-concave /kon káyvō-/ *adj* describes a lens that is concave on both surfaces

concavo-convex /kon káyvō-/ *adj* describes a lens that is concave on one surface and convex on the other

conceal /kən seél/ (**-ceals, -cealing, -cealed**) *vt* 1. to put or keep something or somebody out of sight, or prevent the person or thing from being found ○ *The evidence was carefully concealed.* 2. to keep something secret, or prevent it from being known [13C. Via French < Latin *concelare* 'hide well' < *celare* 'hide'] —**concealable** *adj* —**concealment** *n*

concealer /kən seélər/ *n* 1. flesh-coloured makeup that can be applied to the skin to hide blemishes 2. somebody or something that conceals something

concede /kən seéd/ (**-cedes, -ceding, -ceded**) *v* 1. *vt* RELUCTANTLY ACCEPT SOMETHING TO BE TRUE to admit or acknowledge something, often grudgingly or with reluctance 2. *vti* ADMIT FAILURE BEFORE END to accept and acknowledge defeat in a contest, debate, election, or fight, often without waiting for the final result 3. *vt* GIVE SOMETHING AWAY to allow an opponent or opposing team to gain something valuable, usually a goal or points 4. *vt* GRANT RIGHTS TO SOMEBODY to allow or yield something such as a right or privilege to another person or country [15C. Via French < Latin *concedere* 'yield completely' < *cedere* 'yield'] —**conceder** *n*

~~**conceed**~~ incorrect spelling of **concede**

conceit /kən seét/ *n* 1. EXCESSIVE SELF-PRIDE a high opinion of your own qualities or abilities, especially one that is not justified 2. LITERAT EXAGGERATED COMPARISON IN LITERATURE an imaginative poetic image, or writing

that contains such an image, especially a comparison that is extreme or far-fetched **3.** WHIMSICAL OBJECT an object created from the imagination **4.** IMAGINATIVE IDEA an idea, opinion, or theme, especially one that is fanciful or unusual in some way **5.** WITTY EXPRESSION a witty, inventive, or amusing expression (*archaic*) ■ *vt* **(-ceits, -ceiting, -ceited)** *N England* LIKE SOMETHING to like or tolerate something [14C. < CONCEIVE]

conceited /kən seétid/ *adj* **1.** having or showing an excessively high opinion of your own qualities or abilities **2.** imaginative, fanciful, witty, or ingenious (*archaic*) —**conceitedly** *adv* —**conceitedness** *n*

SYNONYMS See ***proud***.

conceivable /kən seévəb'l/ *adj* possible to imagine, understand, or believe ○ *We tried every means conceivable to contact her.* —**conceivability** /kən seévə bílləti/ *n*

conceivably /kən seévəbli/ *adv* possibly, even if only a remote possibility ○ *You could just conceivably be wrong.*

conceive /kən seév/ **(-ceives, -ceiving, -ceived)** *v* **1.** *vti* THINK OF OR IMAGINE SOMETHING to form an idea or concept of something in your mind **2.** *vt* INVENT OR DEVISE SOMETHING to think up something such as a plan or an invention that could be put into action ○ *conceived and written by John Sander* **3.** *vt* START TO EXPERIENCE SOMETHING to produce something from the mind such as an emotion **4.** *vti* BECOME PREGNANT to become pregnant with a child or with young **5.** *vt* UNDERSTAND to understand something [13C. < Old French *conceiv-*, stem of *concevoir* < Latin *concipere* 'take in' < *capere* 'seize, take'] —**conceiver** *n*

concelebrate /kən sélli brayt/ **(-brates, -brating, -brated)** *vti* to celebrate the Christian Mass or Communion jointly with one or more other priests [Late 16C. < Latin *concelebrat-*, past participle of *concelebrare* 'celebrate together' < *celebrare* (see CELEBRATE)] —**concelebrant** *n* —**concelebration** /kən sélli bráysh'n/ *n*

concentrate /kónss'n trayt/ *v* **(-trates, -trating, -trated)** **1.** *vti* THINK INTENSELY ABOUT SOMETHING to focus all of your thoughts or mental activity on one subject or activity, usually in silence ○ *I found myself unable to concentrate on my work.* **2.** *vti* DEVOTE EFFORTS TO ONE THING to direct attention, time, and resources to one particular area or activity, usually over a period of time **3.** *vti* CLUSTER TOGETHER to bring things together in the same place or area, or to come together in the same place **4.** *vt* MAKE SUBSTANCE PURER to make a substance purer by the removal of another substance, especially by removing a liquid **5.** *vti* MAKE SOMETHING THICKER OR STRONGER to remove water from a substance, usually a liquid, leaving a smaller quantity that is thicker in consistency and stronger in flavour, or become thicker and stronger in this way **6.** *vti* ACCUMULATE IN TISSUE to accumulate, or cause a substance to accumulate, in biological tissue over a period of time **7.** *vt* MINERALS PURIFY ORE to remove rock and other material from ore to purify it ■ *n* **1.** PURE SUBSTANCE a substance made purer by the removal of another, especially a liquid **2.** THICK FOOD SUBSTANCE a food substance, especially a liquid, made thicker or stronger in flavour by the removal of liquid [Mid-17C. < CONCENTRE] —**concentrated** *adj* —**concentratedly** *adv* —**concentrative** *adj*

concentration /kónss'n tráysh'n/ *n* **1.** FOCUS OF MIND OR RESOURCES the direction of all thought or effort towards one particular task, idea, or subject **2.** CLUSTER OR NUMBER a large number of things or amount of something collected together in one area ○ *the concentration of computing talent in one part of the country* **3.** STRENGTH OF SOLUTION the amount of a substance dissolved in another. Symbol *c* **4.** MAKING LIQUID THICKER OR STRONGER the removal of water from something, usually a liquid, to make it thicker or stronger

concentration camp *n* **1.** any of the prison camps used for exterminating prisoners under the rule of Hitler in Nazi Germany. Conditions were inhuman, and prisoners, mostly Jewish people, were generally starved or worked to death, or killed immediately, resulting in the extermination of more than six million people. **2.** a prison camp used in war for the incarceration of political prisoners or civilians. An example is the type of camp used by Great Britain during the Boer War to move civilians out of the war zone.

concentrator /kónss'n traytər/ *n* **1.** COMPUT TELECOMMUNICATIONS DEVICE a telecommunications device that combines outgoing messages into one message or extracts individual messages from one transmission into which they have been combined **2.** MINERALS FACTORY THAT PROCESSES MINERAL ORE an industrial plant that produces purified or concentrated mineral ore **3.** INDUST MIRROR SYSTEM FOR PRODUCING SOLAR ENERGY a set of mirrors used to concentrate sunlight in the collection of energy from the sun

concentre /kon séntər/ **(-tres, -tring, -tred)** *vti* to direct things to a common centre, or converge at a common centre [Late 16C. < French *concentrer* < *con-* 'together' + *centre* 'centre']

concentric /kən séntrik, kon-/ *adj* **1.** describes circles and spheres of different sizes with the same middle point **2.** with a common axis or centre line [14C. < medieval Latin *concentricus* 'having the same centre' < Latin *centrum* 'centre'] —**concentrically** *adv* —**concentricity** /kónss'n tríssəti/ *n*

Concepción /kən sépsi ṓn/ **1.** capital city of Bío-Bío Region, central Chile, situated on the River Bío-Bío, 418 km/260 mi. southwest of Santiago. Population: 372,252 (1998). **2.** capital city of Concepción Department, central Paraguay, situated on the River Paraguay. It is the commercial centre of northern Paraguay and serves as a free port for southwestern Brazil. Population: 35,276 (1992).

concept /kón sept/ *n* **1.** SOMETHING THOUGHT OR IMAGINED something that somebody has thought up, or that somebody might be able to imagine **2.** BROAD PRINCIPLE AFFECTING PERCEPTION AND BEHAVIOUR a broad abstract idea or a guiding general principle, e.g. one that determines how a person or culture behaves, or how nature, reality, or events are perceived ○ *the concept of time* **3.** UNDERSTANDING OR GRASP the most basic understanding of something ○ *has little concept of what is involved* **4.** WAY OF DOING OR PERCEIVING SOMETHING a method, scheme, or type of product or design [Mid-16C. < late Latin *conceptus* < past participle of Latin *concipere* (see CONCEIVE)] —**conceptual** /kən séptyoo əl/ *adj*

concept art *n* ARTS same as **conceptual art**

conception /kən sépsh'n/ *n* **1.** BROAD UNDERSTANDING a general understanding of something **2.** SOMETHING CONCEIVED IN MIND a result of thought, e.g. an idea, invention, or plan **3.** BIOL CONCEIVING OF YOUNG the fertilization of an egg by a sperm at the beginning of pregnancy **4.** BIOL FOETUS an embryo or foetus (*technical*) **5.** ORIGIN OR BEGINNINGS the beginnings or origin of something **6.** FORMULATION OF IDEA the process of arriving at an abstract idea or belief or the moment at which such an idea starts to take shape or emerge **7.** same as **concept** (sense 1) [14C. Via French < Latin *conception-* < *concipere* (see CONCEIVE)] —**conceptional** *adj* —**conceptive** *adj* —**conceptively** *adv*

concept product *n* a highly advanced and innovative product that is not yet in commercial production

concept statement *n* an explanation or summary of the overall aims or nature of a project

conceptual art *n* art designed to present an idea rather than to be appreciated for its creative skill or beauty, often making use of unconventional media instead of painting or sculpture —**conceptual artist** *n*

conceptualise *vti* another spelling of **conceptualize**

conceptualism /kən séptyoo əlizəm/ *n* **1.** the philosophical theory that the existence of something is dependent on our having a mental concept of it **2.** a school of art concerned primarily with the ideas behind a work of art rather than the artwork itself —**conceptualistic** /-lístik/ *adj* —**conceptualistically** *adv*

conceptualist /kən séptyoo əlist/ *n* **1.** somebody who believes in conceptualism **2.** somebody who creates conceptual art

conceptualize /kən séptyoo ə līz/ **(-izes, -izing, -ized)**, **conceptualise (-ises, -ising, -ised)** *vti* to arrive at a concept or generalization as a result of things seen, experienced, or believed —**conceptualization** /kən séptyoo ə lī záysh'n/ *n* —**conceptualizer** *n*

conceptus /kən séptəss/ (*plural* **-tuses**) *n* an embryo or foetus along with all the tissues that surround it throughout pregnancy, including the placenta, amniotic sac and fluid, and the umbilical cord (*technical*) [Mid-18C. < Latin, 'something conceived' < past participle of *concipere* (see CONCEIVE)]

concern /kən súrn/ *vt* **(-cerns, -cerning, -cerned)** **1.** MAKE SOMEBODY WORRIED to give somebody an uneasy or anxious feeling **2.** INVOLVE SOMEBODY to require somebody to be involved with something, or get involved with or interested in something **3.** BE INTERESTING OR IMPORTANT TO SOMEBODY to have a direct effect on, or be a matter of significance to, somebody or something **4.** BE ON SUBJECT OF SOMETHING to be about a particular topic ■ *n* **1.** WORRY worry, or a cause of worry ○ *His condition is giving rise to concern.* **2.** RELEVANT AFFAIR a matter that affects somebody or that somebody has the right to be involved with ○ *It's no concern of yours.* **3.** CARING FEELINGS a feeling of worry, compassion, sympathy, or regard for somebody or something **4.** BUSINESS a commercial enterprise **5.** OBJECT a gadget or trivial object (*dated*) [Late 14C. Via French < late Latin *concernere*, literally 'sift together' < Latin *cernere* 'sift']

concerned /kən súrnd/ *adj* **1.** ANXIOUS OR WORRIED worried or apprehensive, particularly about something such as a situation that is developing or that has newly arisen **2.** INTERESTED attentive to and interested in something **3.** INVOLVED having an active role in or related to something ○ *A message was conveyed to the families concerned.* —**concernedly** /-nidli/ *adv*

concerning /kən súrning/ *prep* to do with or involving something or somebody ○ *information concerning her disappearance*

concernment /kən súrnmənt/ *n* (*archaic*) **1.** a concern or matter of interest **2.** importance, relevance, or weight

concert /kónssərt/ *n* **1.** PUBLIC MUSICAL PERFORMANCE an event where an individual musician or a group of musicians, e.g. a choir, band, or orchestra, performs in front of an audience **2.** AGREEMENT harmony or accord, e.g. in purpose or action (*formal*) ○ *a concert of criticism* **3.** UNIFIED PAIR OR GROUP a combination of people or things in agreement or harmony (*formal*) ■ *vti* **(-certs, -certing, -certed)** ACT IN AGREEMENT OR UNITY to do or plan something in cooperation with another person or group (*formal*) [Late 16C. Via French < Italian *concerto* (see CONCERTO)] ◇ **in concert 1.** playing music or singing at a live concert **2.** working or acting together, especially in a united or harmonious way (*formal*) ○ *Jones, in concert with three associates, planned and carried out the attack.*

concertante /kónchər tán tay, -ti/ *adj* **1.** relating to or resembling a concerto, especially one in the baroque style **2.** relating to a symphonic work that highlights individual instruments within the orchestra [Early 18C. < Italian, present participle of *concertare* 'bring into harmony']

concerted /kən súrtid/ *adj* **1.** planned or carried out by two or more people working together or with the same aim **2.** written for several soloists to perform together in an ensemble or within the context of a larger-scale work —**concertedly** *adv* —**concertedness** *n*

concertgoer /kónssərt gō ər/ *n* somebody who is attending a concert, or somebody who often goes to concerts —**concertgoing** *adj*

concert grand *n* the largest size of grand piano, between 2.74 m/9 ft and 3.66 m/12 ft long, designed for use in a concert hall

concert hall *n* a public building designed for performances of music

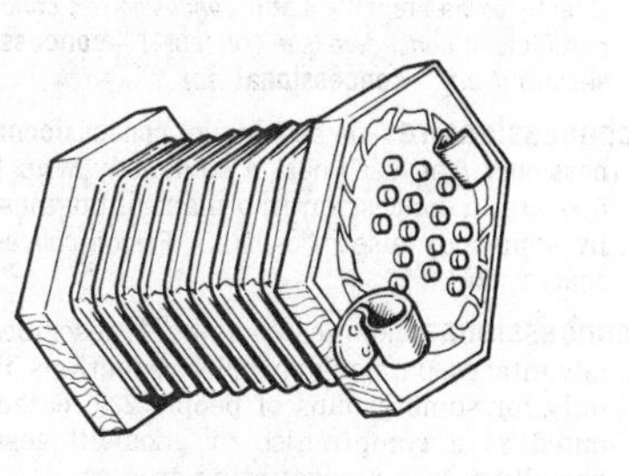

concertina

concertina /kónssər teénə/ *n* a small accordion with button keys ■ *vi* **(-nas, -naing, -naed)** to collapse in a series of folds like an accordion [Mid-19C. < CONCERT + Italian suffix *-ina*] —**concertinist** *n*

concertino /kón chər teénō/ (*plural* **-nos** or **-ni** /-nee/) *n* **1.** the solo instrumental group in a piece of music played by a small group of soloists and a larger ensemble **(concerto grosso) 2.** a small-scale concerto for a single solo instrument [Late 18C. < Italian, 'little concerto' < *concerto* (see CONCERTO)]

concertize /kónssər tīz/ (**-tizes, -tizing, -tized**), **concertise** (**-tises, -tising, -tised**) *vi* to perform in concerts (*refers to soloists or conductors*)

concertmaster /kónssərt maastər/ *n N Am* the leader of the first violin section of an orchestra, usually next in rank below the conductor

concertmistress /kónssərt mistrəss/ *n N Am* a woman who is the leader of the first violin section of an orchestra, usually next in rank below the conductor

concerto /kən cháirtō, -chúrtō/ (*plural* **-tos** or **-ti** /-ti/) *n* **1.** an instrumental work for orchestra that highlights a soloist or group of soloists **2.** in music before 1650, a work for voices with organ or continuo [Early 18C. < Italian < *concertare* 'bring into harmony']

concerto grosso /kən cháirtō gróssō/ (*plural* **concerti grossi** /-tee gróssee/ or **concerto grossos**) *n* a genre of orchestral composition, popular in the 17th century, that contrasts a small group of soloists **(concertino)** with a larger ensemble **(ripieno)** [< Italian, 'big concerto']

concert overture *n* a short orchestral composition similar to an opera overture but intended for concert performance on its own

concert party (*plural* **concert parties**) *n* **1.** a small number of performers working together to entertain the public, e.g. in a seaside town. Concert parties were especially popular in the early 20th century. (*dated*) **2.** a group of people buying shares (*slang*)

concert pitch *n* **1.** MUSIC **STANDARD PITCH TO WHICH INSTRUMENTS TUNED** the internationally agreed standard pitch to which orchestral instruments are tuned, typically using the A above middle C as a reference. In an instrument tuned to concert pitch, the A above middle C is at a pitch of 440 cycles per second. **2.** MUSIC **PITCH OF NOTE IN TRANSPOSED MUSIC** the sounding pitch of a note played by an instrument when transposing a piece of written music to a different key, as opposed to the written pitch **3. READINESS** a state of readiness for action (*informal*)

concession /kən sésh'n/ *n* **1. SPECIAL PRIVILEGE** something, e.g. a privilege, right, or kindness, that is granted to a person or group, usually in view of special circumstances **2. SOMETHING UNWILLINGLY ADMITTED** something acknowledged or admitted, even if unwillingly or grudgingly **3. RELUCTANT YIELDING** an act or an example of conceding, yielding, or compromising in some way, often grudgingly or unwillingly **4. CHEAP TICKET** a special reduced price at which tickets for travel or entertainment are sold to some groups of people, e.g. senior citizens, students, or the unemployed **5.** COMM **SMALL BUSINESS OUTLET INSIDE ANOTHER ESTABLISHMENT** a branch of a business set up and operating in a place belonging to another commercial enterprise, or a business agreement that grants the right to do this **6. RIGHT TO USE LAND** an official licence granted by a landowner or government that allows work such as drilling for oil to be carried out in a specific area of land [Early 17C. Directly or via French < Latin *concession-* < *concess-*, past participle of *concedere* (see CONCEDE)] —**concessible** /kən séssəb'l/ *adj* —**concessional** *adj*

concessionaire /kən sésh'n áir/, **concessionnaire, concessioner** /kən sésh'nər/ *n* somebody who holds or operates a concession in a place of business owned by somebody else [Mid-19C. < French *concession* (see CONCESSION)]

concessionary /kən sésh'nəri/ *adj* **1.** describes special advantages, particularly price reductions, that exist only for some groups of people **2.** created or executed as a compromise or goodwill gesture, especially within a negotiating process

concessioner, **concessionnaire** *n* COMM same as **concessionaire**

concession road, **concession line** *n* in Canada, especially in Ontario and Quebec, a rural road running along the line of the survey of Canada that divided farmland into concessions

concession stand *n US* a stall selling food and drinks run by somebody who is not employed by the owners of the place in which the stall is located

concessive /kən séssiv/ *adj* **1.** describes a word or part of a sentence that expresses concession, e.g. the word 'although' **2.** relating to or containing a concession [Early 18C. < late Latin *concessivus* < Latin *concess-* (see CONCESSION)] —**concessively** *adv*

conch /kongk, konch/ (*plural* **conchs** /kongks/ or **conches** /kónchiz/) *n* **1.** a tropical invertebrate sea animal with a large, often brightly coloured, spiral shell **2.** the large spiral shell of a conch. Use: horn or trumpet, ornament, jewellery. **3.** ANAT same as **concha**[1] [14C. Via Latin *concha* < Greek *kogkhē* 'shell, shellfish']

conch- *prefix* same as **concho-** (*used before vowels*)

concha[1] /kóngkə/ (*plural* **-chae** /-ki/) *n* a part of the body shaped like a conch shell, e.g. the external ear or the central cavity of the ear [Late 16C. < Latin (see CONCH)] —**conchal** *adj*

concha[2] /kónchə/, **concho** (*plural* **-chos**) *n Southwest US* a usually silver, shell-shaped ornament that is attached to a cowboy's hatband, chaps, belt, or saddle [Late 19C. Via American Spanish < Spanish, 'shell']

conchi- *prefix* same as **concho-**

conchie /kónchi/, **conchy** (*plural* **-chies**) *n* POL same as **conscientious objector** (*dated disapproving*) [Early 20C. Shortening]

conchiglie /kon kéeli/ *n* pasta formed into small shell shapes [< Italian, 'little shells' < Latin *concha* (see CONCH)]

conchiolin /kong kī əlin/ *n* a fibrous protein in mollusc shells [Late 19C. < modern Latin *conchiola* 'little shell' < Latin *concha* (see CONCH)]

concho- *prefix* shell ○ *conchology* [< Latin *concha* (see CONCH)]

conchoidal /kong kóyd'l/ *adj* having or being a surface shaped like a bivalve shell with smooth ridges and depressions ○ *conchoidal fracture*

conchology /kong kólləji/ *n* a branch of zoology dealing with sea shells and the animals that inhabit them —**conchological** /kóngkə lójjik'l/ *adj* —**conchologist** *n*

conchy *n* POL another spelling of **conchie** (*dated informal*)

concierge /kónssi airzh, kóN-/ (*plural* **-cierges** /*pronunc. same*/) *n* **1.** especially in France, somebody whose job is to staff or watch the entrance to a large residential building, and who usually also lives on the premises **2.** *N Am* somebody who is employed at a hotel or apartment building to help the guests or residents, e.g. by dealing with luggage, making travel arrangements, or delivering messages [Mid-16C. Via French < Latin *conservus* 'fellow slave' < *servus* 'slave']

~~**concieve**~~ incorrect spelling of **conceive**

conciliar /kən sílli ər/ *adj* belonging to, issued by, or relating to a council, especially a church council [Late 17C. < Latin *concilium* 'council, meeting'] —**conciliarly** *adv*

conciliate /kən sílli ayt/ (**-ates, -ating, -ated**) *vti* **1. BRING DISPUTING SIDES TOGETHER** to work with opposing parties with the aim of bringing them to an agreement or reconciliation, especially in an industrial dispute **2. GET SOMEBODY'S SUPPORT OR FRIENDSHIP BACK** to bring a disagreement with somebody to an end, or overcome somebody's anger, suspicion, or hostility **3. BE CHARMING** to gain something, especially somebody's friendship, goodwill, or respect, by behaving pleasantly [Mid-16C. < Latin *conciliat-*, past participle of *conciliare* < *concilium* 'council, meeting'] —**conciliable** *adj* —**conciliation** /kən sílli áysh'n/ *n* —**conciliative** *adj* —**conciliator** *n* —**conciliatory** /-ətəri/ *adj*

concinnity /kən sínnəti/ (*plural* **-ties**) *n* **1.** a balanced, graceful, polished quality, especially in a literary work **2.** a harmonious structuring of all the parts of something [Mid-16C. < Latin *concinnitas* < *concinnus* 'skilfully put together'] —**concinnous** *adj*

concise /kən sīss/ *adj* using as few words as possible to give the necessary information, or compressed in order to be brief [Late 16C. Directly or via French < Latin *concisus*, past participle of *concidere* 'cut down' < *caedere* 'to cut'] —**concisely** *adv* —**conciseness** *n* —**concision** /kən sízh'n/ *n*

conclave /kóng klayv/ *n* **1. SECRET MEETING** a private gathering of a select group of people, where discussions are kept secret **2.** CHR **MEETING TO SELECT POPE** the secret meeting at which Roman Catholic cardinals elect a new pope **3.** CHR **ROOMS WHERE POPE IS ELECTED** the private rooms in which the college of Roman Catholic cardinals assembles to elect a new pope [14C. Via French < Latin, 'locked room' < *clavis* 'key'] —**conclavist** *n*

conclude /kən klóod/ (**-cludes, -cluding, -cluded**) *v* **1.** *vt* **COME TO CONCLUSION ABOUT SOMETHING** to form an opinion or make a logical judgment about something after considering everything known about it **2.** *vti N Am* **DECIDE SOMETHING** to reach a decision about something (*dated*) **3.** *vt* **SETTLE SOMETHING** to make a formal agreement complete and fixed, especially after detailed or prolonged discussions or arrangements **4.** *vti* **FINISH** to come to an end, or bring something to an end ○ *concluded the discussion* [13C. < Latin *concludere* 'close completely' < *claudere* 'to close'] —**concluder** *n*

SYNONYMS See ***deduce***.

conclusion /kən klóozh'n/ *n* **1. DECISION BASED ON FACTS** a decision made or an opinion formed after considering the relevant facts or evidence **2. FINAL PART OF SOMETHING** the part that brings something to a close (*formal*) **3. FINAL SETTLEMENT OF SOMETHING** the completion of a formal agreement or deal, especially after long or detailed discussions and arrangements **4.** LOGIC **PART OF ARGUMENT DEDUCED FROM EVIDENCE** the portion of an argument for which evidence is presented [14C. Directly or via French < Latin *conclusion-* < *conclus-*, past participle of *concludere* (see CONCLUDE)]

conclusive /kən klóossiv/ *adj* proving a matter beyond all doubt [Late 16C. < late Latin *conclusivus* < Latin *conclus-* (see CONCLUSION)] —**conclusively** *adv* —**conclusiveness** *n*

concoct /kən kókt/ (**-cocts, -cocting, -cocted**) *vt* **1.** to create something by mixing or combining various ingredients in a new way, especially in cooking **2.** to think up a story or plan, especially something imaginative, that is intended to be deceitful or misleading [Mid-16C. < Latin *concoct-*, past participle of *concoquere* 'cook together' < *coquere* 'to cook'] —**concocter** *n* —**concoctive** *adj*

concoction /kən kóksh'n/ *n* **1. NEW AND UNUSUAL MIXTURE** a new and unusual mixture, especially a drink or dish created by mixing together ingredients **2. CONCOCTING OF MIXTURE** the act or process of combining ingredients to create something new and unusual **3. LIE OR TRICK** a story or plan devised to be deceitful

concomitance /kən kómmitənss/ *n* **1. EXISTENCE OR OCCURRENCE TOGETHER** the existence or occurrence of something at the same time as, or in connection with, something else **2. SOMETHING CONNECTED WITH SOMETHING ELSE** something that exists at the same time, or in connection with, something else **3.** CHR **CHRISTIAN BELIEF REGARDING COMMUNION** the belief of some Christians that the body and blood of Jesus Christ are embodied in the bread and wine taken at Communion

concomitant /kən kómmitənt/ *adj* happening or existing along with or at the same time as something else (*formal*) ○ *parenthood and all its concomitant responsibilities* [Early 17C. < late Latin *concomitant-*, present participle of *concomitari* 'accompany' < Latin *comit-* 'companion'] —**concomitant** *n* —**concomitantly** *adv*

concord /kóng kawrd/ *n* **1. PEACEFUL COEXISTENCE** agreement, friendly relations, or peace **2. TREATY** a peace treaty **3.** MUSIC **PLEASING COMBINATION OF SOUNDS** a pleasing sound made when two or more notes are played together (*formal*) **4.** GRAM same as **agreement** (sense 4) [13C. Via French < Latin *concord-* 'of one heart' < *cor* 'heart']

Concord /kóng kawrd/ **1.** city in western California, north of the Oakland-San Francisco area, northeast of Berkeley. Population: 125,225 (2002 estimate). **2.** town in northeastern Massachusetts, west of Boston, on the Concord River. On 19 April 1775, it was the site of the first military encounter of the American War of Independence. Population: 17,028 (2002 estimate). **3.** capital of New Hampshire, in the south of the state, on the Merrimack River. Population: 41,404 (2002 estimate). **4.** city in southwestern North Carolina, northeast of Charlotte. It was a gold-mining town in the 18th century. Population: 58,490 (2002 estimate).

concordance /kən káwrd'nss/ *n* **1.** similarity or agreement between two or more things **2.** an index of words arranged in alphabetical order, e.g. of all the words in a body or bank of text. A concordance often gives information about the meaning and context of a listed word. [14C. Via French < medieval Latin *concordantia* < Latin *concordant-* (see CONCORDANT)]

concordant /kən káwrd'nt/ *adj* showing harmony, unity, or agreement (*formal*) [15C. Via French < Latin *concordant-*, present participle of *concordare* 'bring into harmony' < *concord-* (see CONCORD)] —**concordantly** *adv*

concordat /kon káwr dat, kən-/ *n* an official agreement, especially a formal contract between the pope and a national government concerning the religious affairs of a country [Early 17C. Via French < Latin *concordatum* < past participle of *concordare* (see CONCORDANT)]

concours /kóng koor/, **concours d'élégance** *n* a meeting at which classic or vintage cars are exhibited and prizes awarded

concourse /kóng kawrss/ *n* **1. LARGE OPEN SPACE** a large space where people can gather in a public place or building, e.g. at an airport or train station **2. CROWD** a large number of people who have gathered for a special event (*formal*) **3. GATHERING TOGETHER** the action of coming or moving together, or an example of this (*formal*) [14C. Via French < Latin *concursus* 'assembly' < *concurs-*, past participle of *concurrere* (see CONCUR)]

concrescence /kən kréss'nss/ *n* **1.** the growing or coming together of body parts or organs, especially in the normal early formation of an embryo **2.** MED same as **concretion** (sense 3) [Early 17C. < Latin *concrescent-*, present participle of *concrescere* (see CONCRETE)] —**concrescent** *adj*

concrete /kóng kreet/ *n* **1. HARD CONSTRUCTION MATERIAL** a mixture of cement, sand, aggregate, and water in specific proportions that hardens to a strong stony consistency over varying lengths of time **2.** PHYS **MASS OF COALESCED PARTICLES** a mass formed when particles coalesce ■ *adj* **1. SOLID AND REAL** able to be seen or touched because it exists in reality, not just as an idea **2. DEFINITE** certain and specific rather than vague or general ○ *concrete proposals for reform* **3.** PHYS **SOLIDIFIED** made solid by coalescence ■ *vt* (**-cretes, -creting, -creted**) **PUT CONCRETE SOMEWHERE** to cover an area with concrete [14C. Via French < Latin *concretus*, past participle of *concrescere* 'grow together' < *crescere* 'grow'] —**concretely** *adv* —**concreteness** *n*

concrete jungle *n* an urban area completely covered with walkways, roads, and buildings, and perceived as a hostile environment

concrete music *n* electronic music assembled from recordings of live sounds, usually including natural and mechanical sources, manipulated for effect [Translation of French *musique concrète* 'real music']

concrete noun *n* a noun that refers to a physical, and usually visible or touchable, object or substance, e.g. 'clock' or 'elephant'

concrete poetry *n* verse that uses physical arrangement of the words on the page to add to its meaning and effect

concretion /kən kréesh'n/ *n* **1. FORMATION OF WHOLE FROM PARTS** the process in which separate parts or particles come together into a solid mass **2. SOLID FORMED BY UNIFICATION OF PARTS** a hard solid mass formed by parts uniting into a whole **3.** MED **INORGANIC MASS IN BODY** a mass of inorganic material in a body organ or tissue, usually caused by disease **4.** GEOL **ROUNDED MASS** a rounded mass of compact concentric layers within a sediment, built up round a nucleus such as a fossil [Mid-16C. Directly or via French < Latin *concretion-* < *concret-*, past participle of *concrescere* (see CONCRETE)] —**concretionary** *adj*

concretise *vt* another spelling of **concretize**

concretism /kóng kreet izəm/ *n* the creation of physical things to represent abstract ideas, especially by the use of concrete poetry —**concretist** *n*

concretize /kóng kreet īz/ (**-tizes, -tizing, -tized**), **concretise** (**-tises, -tising, -tised**) *vt* to make something solid, real, or specific —**concretization** /kóng kree tī záysh'n/ *n*

concubinage /kon kyóobinij, kən-/ *n* the state of being or keeping a concubine

concubine /kóng kyoo bīn/ *n* **1.** a woman who is the lover of a wealthy married man but with the social status of a subordinate form of wife, often kept in a separate home, especially in imperial China **2.** a woman who lives with a man and has a sexual relationship with him but is not married to him (*dated*) [13C. Via French < Latin *concubina* 'sharer of somebody's bed' < *cubare* 'lie down'] —**concubinary** /kóng kyóo bīnəri, kon kyóobinəri/ *adj*

concupiscence /kən kyóopiss'nss, kon-/ *n* powerful feelings of physical desire (*formal*) [14C. Via French < late Latin *concupiscentia* < *concupiscere* 'start longing for' < *cupere* 'to desire'] —**concupiscent** *adj*

concur /kən kúr/ (**-curs, -curring, -curred**) *v* **1.** *vti* **AGREE** to have the same opinion as somebody else, or reach agreement independently on a specific point **2.** *vi* **COINCIDE** to happen at the same time **3.** *vi* **COOPERATE OR COMBINE** to work or act together, especially cooperatively [14C. < Latin *concurrere*, literally 'run together' < *currere* 'run'] —**concurringly** *adv*

SYNONYMS See *agree*.

concurrent /kən kúrrənt/ *adj* taking place, existing, or running in parallel at the same time [14C. < Latin *concurrent-*, present participle of *concurrere* (see CONCUR)] —**concurrence** *n* —**concurrently** *adv*

concuss /kən kúss/ (**-cusses, -cussing, -cussed**) *vt* to cause somebody concussion, usually by a blow to the head or a jarring fall or jolt [Late 16C. < Latin *concuss-*, past participle of *concutere* 'strike together' < *quatere* 'to strike']

concussion /kən kúsh'n/ *n* **1.** MED **MILD BRAIN INJURY** an injury to the brain, often resulting from a blow to the head, that can cause temporary disorientation, memory loss, or unconsciousness **2.** MED **INJURY TO BODILY ORGAN** an injury to an organ of the body, usually caused by a violent blow or shaking **3. SUDDEN JOLT OR SHOCK** any sudden violent jolting or shaking —**concussive** /-kússiv/ *adj*

~~condem~~ incorrect spelling of **condemn**

condemn /kən dém/ (**-demns, -demning, -demned**) *vt* **1. SAY SOMEBODY OR SOMETHING IS BAD** to state that somebody or something is in some way wrong or unacceptable **2. GIVE SOMEBODY LEGAL SENTENCE** to make a judicial pronouncement stating what punishment has been imposed on a person found guilty of a crime, especially in the case of a heavy penalty or a death sentence **3. CONSIDER SOMEBODY OR SOMETHING GUILTY** to judge that somebody or something is to blame for something **4. MAKE SOMEBODY EXPERIENCE SOMETHING** to force somebody to experience something very unpleasant, especially something permanent or long-lasting **5. BAN USE OR CONSUMPTION OF SOMETHING** to issue an official order saying that something such as a building is unfit to be used **6. PROVE SOMEBODY GUILTY** to serve as proof of the guilt of somebody [14C. Via French < Latin *condemnare* 'pass final sentence' < *damnare* (see DAMN)] —**condemnable** /kən démnəb'l/ *adj* —**condemnation** /kón dem náysh'n, kóndəm-/ *n* —**condemnatory** /kən démnətəri, kón dem náytəri/ *adj*

SYNONYMS See *criticize*.

condemned cell /kən démd-/ *n* a prison cell where a person who has been sentenced to death is kept before the execution is carried out

condensate /kón den sayt, kóndən sayt, kən dén sayt/ *n* a substance resulting from condensation, especially a liquid from a vapour

condensation /kón den sáysh'n, kóndən sáysh'n/ *n* **1.** PHYS **CONVERSION OF GAS TO LIQUID** the process by which a vapour loses heat and changes into a liquid **2. FILM OF WATER DROPLETS** tiny drops of water that form on a cold surface such as a window when warmer air comes into contact with it **3. MAKING SOMETHING SHORTER** the state of being compressed or made briefer, or the act or result of summarizing or compressing something **4.** CHEM **FORMATION OF DENSER MOLECULES** the bonding of molecules of a substance to form a larger denser molecule, usually with the release of simpler substances such as water —**condensational** *adj*

condensation trail *n* AVIAT same as **vapour trail**

condense /kən déns/ (**-denses, -densing, -densed**) *v* **1.** *vti* **CHANGE FROM GAS TO LIQUID** to lose heat and change from a vapour into a liquid, or make a vapour change to a liquid **2.** *vti* COOK **THICKEN BY REMOVING WATER** to make something, especially a food, denser by removing water, or become denser in this way **3.** *vt* **MAKE TEXT SHORTER** to reduce the length of a text by removing unnecessary words or passages or by expressing the content more concisely **4.** *vti* CHEM **FORM DENSER MOLECULES** to bond together to form a larger denser molecule, or make molecules undergo this process [15C. Via French < Latin *condensare* 'thicken' < *condensus* 'very dense' < *densus* 'thick'] —**condensability** /kən dénssə bílləti/ *n* —**condensable** *adj*

condensed milk /kən dénst-/ *n* milk that is thickened by evaporating most of the water content and then sweetened

condenser /kən dénssər/ *n* **1.** PHYS a device that converts a gas to a liquid to obtain either the substance or the released heat **2.** OPTICS a lens or mirror used to concentrate light, e.g. onto a transparency or specimen **3.** ELEC same as **capacitor**

Conder /kóndər/, **Charles Edward** (1868–1909) British painter. He was trained in Australia, where he was part of the impressionist Heidelberg School. Among his best-known works is *A Holiday at Mentone* (1888).

condescend /kóndi sénd/ (**-scends, -scending, -scended**) *vi* **1.** to behave towards other people as though they are socially or intellectually inferior **2.** to do something regarded as unimportant or demeaning in order to impress or appear generous towards others ○ *She condescended to travel with us.* [14C. Via French < ecclesiastical Latin *condescendere* 'lower yourself' < Latin *descendere* (see DESCEND)]

condescending /kón di sénding/ *adj* behaving towards other people in a way that shows you consider yourself socially or intellectually superior to them —**condescendingly** *adv*

condescension /kón di sénsh'n/ *n* behaviour that implies that somebody is graciously lowering himself or herself to the level of people less important or intelligent [Mid-17C. Via French < ecclesiastical Latin *condescension-* < *condescendere* (see CONDESCEND)]

~~condesending~~ incorrect spelling of **condescending**

condign /kən dīn/ *adj* well deserved and completely appropriate (*formal*) [14C. Via French < Latin *condignus* 'wholly worthy' < *dignus* 'worthy'] —**condignly** *adv*

condiment /kóndimənt/ *n* salt, pepper, mustard, relish, or a similar substance added in small amounts to food, usually at the table, to improve or adjust its flavour [15C. Via French < Latin *condimentum* < *condire* 'to preserve']

condition /kən dísh'n/ *n* **1. STATE OF REPAIR** the particular state of repair or ability to function of an object or piece of equipment ○ *The car is still in good condition.* **2. STATE OF HEALTH** a state of physical fitness or general health ○ *out of condition* **3. DISORDER** a physical disorder **4. WAY OF BEING** a general state or mode of existence, especially one characterized by hardship or suffering **5. SOMETHING NECESSARY** something that must exist for something else to happen, e.g. to bring a situation about or make a contract valid ○ *a condition of the agreement* **6. STATUS** position, rank, or social status (*formal*) **7. STATE OF PREGNANCY** the state of being pregnant (*informal*) ○ *A woman in her condition shouldn't be dancing!* ■ *npl* **1. conditions FACTORS AFFECTING PEOPLE** the factors or circumstances that affect the situation somebody is living or working in ○ *poor working conditions* **2. STATE OF WEATHER** the state of the weather ■ *vt* (**-tions, -tioning, -tioned**) **1. TRAIN SOMEBODY** to make people or animals act or react in a particular way by gradually getting them used to a specific pattern of events **2. MAKE SOMEBODY STRONG OR SOMETHING READY** to give somebody or something a treatment to improve general health, soundness, readiness for use, appearance, or performance **3. IMPROVE CONDITION OF HAIR** to put conditioner or a similar substance on the hair in order to improve its appearance and texture **4. SPECIFY REQUIREMENT** to state a requirement that must be fulfilled, or to make something dependent on a requirement, especially in a legal contract (*formal*) **5. ADAPT SOMETHING** to adapt something to specific conditions or activities **6. COOL AIR** to make air cooler ○ *Heat pumps condition the air on the first floor.* [13C. Via French < Latin *condition-* 'agreement, stipulation' < *condicere* 'talk together' < *dicere* 'say'] —**conditionable** *adj*

conditional /kən dísh'nəl/ *adj* **1. DEPENDENT ON SOMETHING ELSE BEING DONE** describes something that will be done or will happen only if and when another thing is done or happens **2.** GRAM **STATING CONDITION OR LIMITATION** describes a clause, conjunction, verb form, or sen-

tence that expresses a condition or limitation **3.** MATHS **TRUE ONLY FOR CERTAIN MATHEMATICAL VALUES** true only for some values of one or more variables in a mathematical equation **4.** MATHS **DESCRIBES SERIES OF NUMBERS** describes a convergent series of numbers that becomes a divergent series when its terms are converted to their absolute values ■ *n* GRAM **CONDITIONAL FORM** a conditional clause, conjunction, verb form, or sentence —**conditionality** /kən dísh'n állәti/ *n* —**conditionally** *adv*

conditional access *n* the coding of television transmissions in order to limit reception to subscribers who have decoding devices

conditional discharge *n* a judgment of a criminal court that finds somebody guilty but lets the person go unpunished subject to specific conditions such as to keep the peace for a year

conditionalization /kən dísh'n'l ī záysh'n/, **conditionalisation** *n* the process of turning a statement into a conditional statement, e.g. changing 'It will rain' into 'If it is cloudy, then it will rain'

conditionally /kən dísh'nәli/ *adv* with the proviso that all valid conditions be met

conditional probability *n* the probability that one event will occur, given that another event has occurred or is certain to occur

condition code *n* a signal, usually in the form of a number, that indicates the status of a previous arithmetic, logic, or input/output operation

conditioned /kən dísh'nd/ *adj* **1.** having reached a particular or high level of fitness, quality, or performance **2.** brought on unconsciously by a stimulus that triggers a reaction because of a learned association with something else

conditioned response, conditioned reflex *n* a response to a new second stimulus as a result of association with a prior stimulus. The classic example is Pavlov's experiment in which dogs began to salivate at the sound of a bell, having previously been fed when the bell was rung.

conditioned stimulus *n* in classical psychological conditioning, an otherwise ineffective stimulus that, when paired with an unconditioned stimulus, is able to evoke a conditioned response

conditioner /kən dísh'nәr/ *n* **1.** a liquid or cream applied to hair, either after or with shampoo and usually while the hair is still wet, to make it more manageable or healthier **2.** a substance that makes something such as bread dough or soil easier to manage

conditioning /kən dísh'ning/ *n* **1.** a method of controlling or influencing the way people or animals behave or think by using a gradual training process **2.** the work or programme used to bring somebody or something to a good physical state

condo /kóndō/ (*plural* **-dos**) *n N Am* BUILDINGS same as **condominium** (senses 1–2) (*informal*) [Mid-20C. Shortening]

condole /kən dṓl/ (**-doles, -doling, -doled**) *vi* to express sympathy to somebody who is experiencing grief, loss, or pain, especially over a death (*formal*) [Late 16C. < ecclesiastical Latin *condolere* 'grieve together' < *dolere* 'suffer'] —**condolatory** *adj* —**condoler** *n* —**condolingly** *adv*

USAGE condole or **console**? These words are easy to confuse because they are both connected with reassuring people in distress. The more common word is ***console***, which takes an object and means 'to provide comfort to somebody': *She tried to console her father when his mother died.* ***Condole*** is a more formal term meaning 'to express sympathy', and does not take an object but uses *with* instead: *She condoled with her father over the death of his mother.*

condolence /kən dṓlәnss/ *n* an expression of sorrow and sympathy, usually to somebody who is grieving over a death (*often used in the plural*) —**condolent** *adj* —**condolently** *adv*

con dolore /kón do láw ray, -ri/ *adv* in a sad or sorrowful way (*used as a musical direction*) [< Italian, 'with sorrow'] —**con dolore** *adj*

condom /kóndәm, -dom/ *n* a close-fitting rubber covering worn by a man over the penis during sexual intercourse to prevent pregnancy or the spread of sexually transmitted disease [Early 18C. Origin ?]

condominium /kóndә mínni әm/ *n* **1.** *N Am* **INDIVIDUALLY OWNED FLAT** an individually owned unit of property, especially a flat or town house, in a building or on land that is owned in common by the owners of the units **2.** *N Am* **BUILDING CONTAINING CONDOMINIUMS** a building or complex containing condominium flats or town houses **3. STATE RULED BY FOREIGN COUNTRIES** a country governed by two or more different countries with joint responsibility **4. JOINT GOVERNMENT OF TERRITORY** the system under which a country or state is ruled by two or more other nations [Early 18C. < modern Latin, 'joint right of ownership' < Latin *dominium* (see DOMINION)]

condone /kən dṓn/ (**-dones, -doning, -doned**) *vt* to regard something that is considered immoral or wrong in a tolerant way, without criticizing it or feeling strongly about it ○ *condoning violence* [Mid-19C. < Latin *condonare* 'give up' < *donare* (see DONATION)] —**condonable** *adj* —**condonation** /kóndә náysh'n, kóndō-/ *n* —**condoner** *n*

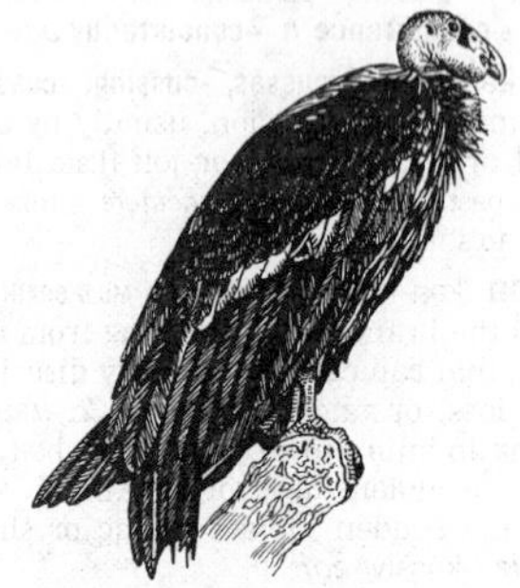

condor

condor /kón dawr, kóndәr/ *n* a large vulture with dull black feathers and white around the neck. Native to: Andes. Latin name: *Vultur gryphus.* [Early 17C. Via Spanish *cóndor* < Quechua *kuntur*]

Condorcet /kon dawr sáy/, **Marie Jean Antoine Nicholas de Caritat, Marquis de** (1743–94) French philosopher, political leader, and mathematician. Among his contributions to French thought are his study of the theory of probability (1785) and his reform of the education system. His best-known work, *Esquisse d'un Tableau Historique des Progrès de l'Esprit Humain (Sketch of the Intellectual Progress of Mankind)* (1795), outlines his belief in human progress.

condottiere /kón doti áir ay, -ri/ (*plural* **-ri** /-ri/) *n* **1.** a man who led a group of hired soldiers, especially during the period of the Italian Renaissance, between the 13th and 16th centuries **2.** a hired soldier [Late 18C. < Italian, 'contractor']

conduce /kən dyóoss/ (**-duces, -ducing, -duced**) *vi* to help, contribute, or lead to bringing about an action or event (*formal*) [14C. < Latin *conducere* 'bring together' < *ducere* 'to lead'] —**conducer** *n* —**conducible** *adj* —**conducingly** *adv*

conducive /kən dyóossiv/ *adj* tending to bring about an intended result ○ *tensions not conducive to a good working relationship*

conduct *v* /kən dúkt/ (**-ducts, -ducting, -ducted**) **1.** *vt* **DO OR RUN SOMETHING** to carry out, manage, or control something ○ *Negotiations were conducted in great secrecy.* **2.** *vr* **BEHAVE** to behave in a particular way ○ *She conducted herself with great dignity.* **3.** *vt* **GUIDE SOMEBODY ALONG** to lead a person or group of people somewhere by going along with them **4.** *vti* **LEAD INSTRUMENTAL OR VOCAL GROUP** to lead a group of musicians or a musical performance by signalling the beat with a baton or hand gestures, giving cues, and offering suggestions for interpretation or expression **5.** *vti* **TRANSMIT ENERGY** to transmit energy such as heat, light, sound, or electricity ■ *n* /kón dukt/ **1. BEHAVIOUR** the way a person behaves, especially in public ○ *language or conduct likely to offend* **2. HOW SOMEBODY MANAGES SOMETHING** the management or execution of matters such as work or official affairs ○ *criticized for his conduct of the campaign* [15C. Directly or via Old French *conduit* < Latin *conduct-*, past participle of *conducere* (see CONDUCE)] —**conductibility** /kən dúktә bíllәti/ *n* —**conductible** *adj*

SYNONYMS See ***guide***.

conductance /kən dúktәnss/ *n* a measure of the ability of an object or substance to transmit electricity, expressed as the reciprocal of resistance. Symbol *G*

conducted tour /kən dúktid-/ *n* a tour of a place of cultural interest, led by a guide who explains the significance of the various sights

conduction /kən dúksh'n/ *n* **1. TRANSMISSION OF ENERGY** the passage of energy, particularly heat or electricity, through something **2. TRANSMISSION THROUGH NERVE FIBRE** the transmission of biochemical or electrical energy through a nerve fibre **3. CONVEYANCE THROUGH PASSAGE** the passage of something through or along something, e.g. water through a pipe

conductive /kən dúktiv/ *adj* **1.** transmitting or able to transmit energy, particularly heat or electricity **2.** describes a cell that allows a physiological disturbance such as a nerve impulse to pass through it

conductive education *n* a system of education that teaches children and adults with motor disorders to function independently

conductive keratoplasty *n* a surgical treatment to correct long-sightedness that involves the use of heat, delivered via a needle, to shrink tissue and reshape the eyeball

conductivity /kón duk tívvәti/ (*plural* **-ties**) *n* **1.** the ability of an object or substance to transmit heat, electricity, or sound **2.** ELEC same as **conductance 3.** the ability of tissue to transmit nerve impulses

conductor /kən dúktәr/ *n* **1.** MUSIC **DIRECTOR OF ORCHESTRA OR CHOIR** somebody in charge of an orchestra or choir who marks time and signals to musicians or singers when and how to play or sing **2.** TRANSP **SOMEBODY WHO COLLECTS FARES** an employee who takes money for tickets on a bus or tram **3.** *N Am* RAIL same as **guard** *n* (sense 3) **4.** PHYS **SOMETHING THAT CONVEYS HEAT OR ELECTRICITY** a substance, body, or medium that allows heat, electricity, light, or sound to pass along it or through it. Metals are good conductors of heat because of the high concentration of free electrons they contain. **5.** TECH same as **lightning conductor** —**conductorial** /kón duk táwri әl/ *adj* —**conductorship** *n*

conduit /kóndyoo it, kóndit/ *n* **1. CHANNEL FOR LIQUID** a pipe or channel that carries liquid to or from a place **2. PROTECTIVE COVER FOR CABLE** a pipe or tube that covers and protects electrical cables **3. CONVEYOR OF INFORMATION** somebody or something that conveys information, especially in secret [14C. Original form of CONDUCT]

condyle /kóndil, -dīl/ *n* a rounded part at the end of a bone that forms a moving joint with a cup-shaped cavity in another bone. The ball part of a ball-and-socket joint such as the hip or shoulder joint is a condyle. [Mid-17C. Via French < Greek *kondulos* 'knuckle'] —**condylar** *adj* —**condyloid** *adj*

condyloma /kóndi lṓmә/ (*plural* **-mas** or **-mata** /-mәtә/) *n* a growth resembling a wart on the skin or a mucous membrane, usually of the genitals or anus [14C. Via Latin < Greek *kondulōma* 'callous knob or lump' < *kondulos* 'knuckle']

cone /kōn/ *n* **1. POINTED OBJECT WITH ROUND BASE** an object or shape that has a circular base and tapers to a point at the top, or has a circular top and tapers to a point at the bottom **2. POINTED FIGURE WITH CURVED FLAT BASE** a three-dimensional geometric figure formed by straight lines through a fixed point (**vertex**) to the points of a fixed curve (**directrix**). A circular cone has a directrix that is a circle. **3. CONE-SHAPED WAFER FOR ICE CREAM** a cone-shaped wafer in which ice cream is sold, or such a wafer with ice cream in it **4. PLASTIC CONE-SHAPED ROAD MARKER** a plastic cone-shaped object used as a temporary road marker or barrier, e.g. to close off part or all of a road during repairs or after an accident **5. CONE-SHAPED PAPER FOR MARIJUANA** a small cone-shaped paper container from which marijuana is smoked **6.** BOT **SEED-BEARING STRUCTURE OF TREE** a tightly packed cluster of scales that bears the reproductive organs of coniferous plants such as pines and firs. Male cones produce pollen, and female cones bear seeds. Technical name **strobilus** (sense 1) **7.** BOT **REPRODUCTIVE PART OF NONFLOWERING PLANTS** a club-shaped, umbrella-shaped, or poker-shaped cluster of fertile leaves that bears the spore-producing organs of a club moss or horsetail **8.** ANAT **LIGHT RECEPTOR CELL IN EYE** a cone-shaped cell sensitive

to light and colour in the retina of the eye of a human being or any other vertebrate animal. There are three different types of cone cell, responding to blue, green, or red light. **9.** MARINE BIOL **SEA SNAIL WITH CONE-SHAPED SHELL** a sea snail with a cone-shaped, vividly marked shell and a poisonous, sometimes fatal, sting. Native to: South Pacific and Indian oceans. Family: Conidae. **10.** GEOG **VOLCANO** a cone-shaped mountain, especially a volcano ■ *vt* **(cones, coning, coned) MAKE SOMETHING INTO CONE SHAPE** to shape something into the form of a cone [15C. Via French < Greek *kōnos* 'pine cone, cone']

cone off *vt* to close off a part of a road with traffic cones because of road repairs or an accident

~~**conection**~~ incorrect spelling of **connection**

coneflower /kōn flowər/ *n* a plant of the daisy family with variously coloured flowers with a brown or black cone-shaped centre. Native to: North America. Genera: *Echinacea* or *Rudbeckia*.

cone shell *n* MARINE BIOL same as **cone** *n* (sense 9)

con espressione /kón ess pressi ṓni/ *adv* with feeling and expression (*used as a musical direction*) [< Italian, 'with expression'] —**con espressione** *adj*

Conestoga wagon /kónni stṓgə-/ *n* a large heavy wagon with a high rounded canvas covering, usually drawn by six horses and used for long-distance freight transportation in North America during the 18th and 19th centuries [Early 18C. After a village in SE Pennsylvania]

coney *n* ZOOL another spelling of **cony**

Coney Island /kṓni-/ amusement area, formerly a resort, in southern Brooklyn, New York City. It was an island, but has become part of Long Island since the silting up of Coney Island Creek.

conf, **conf.** *abbr* **1.** confer **2.** conference **3.** CHR confessor **4.** confidential

confab /kón fab/ (*informal*) *n* a chat or casual discussion ■ *vi* **(-fabs, -fabbing, -fabbed)** to have a chat or discussion about something [Early 18C. Shortening of *confabulation*]

confabulate /kən fábbyoo layt/ **(-lates, -lating, -lated)** *vi* **1.** to discuss or have a chat about something (*formal*) **2.** to give fictitious accounts of past events, believing they are true, in order to cover a gap in the memory caused by a medical condition such as dementia or Korsakoff's syndrome [Early 17C. < Latin *confabulat-*, past participle of *confabulari* 'talk together' < *fabula* (see FABLE)] —**confabulation** /-fábbyoo láysh'n/ *n* —**confabulator** *n* —**confabulatory** /-fábbyoolətəri, -fábbyoo láytəri/ *adj*

confect /kən fékt/ **(-fects, -fecting, -fected)** *vt* **1.** to create something by combining different materials or items ○ *the authority to set up rules and confect and enforce a programme* **2.** to make sweets by combining ingredients such as sugar, fruit, and nuts, or make preserves (*formal*) [14C. < Latin *confect-*, past participle of *conficere* 'put or make together' < *facere* 'make']

confection /kən féksh'n/ *n* **1.** FOOD **SOMETHING SWEET** a sweet food made by combining ingredients such as fruit, nuts, and sugar **2. COMBINATION** the process of combining things, or the result of such combination ○ *a confection of lies and half-truths* **3. ELABORATE CREATION** an often elaborate piece of craftsmanship and skill, e.g. an ornate piece of women's clothing ○ *Her gown was a marvellous confection of lace and tulle.*

confectioner /kən féksh'nər/ *n* somebody who makes or sells sweets

confectioners' sugar *n US* FOOD same as **icing sugar**

confectionery /kən féksh'nəri/ (*plural* **-ies**) *n* **1.** FOOD **CONFECTIONS** sweets considered collectively **2.** COOK **SWEET-MAKING** the skill, technique, or practice of making sweets **3.** COMM **CONFECTIONER'S SHOP** a shop where sweets are sold

confed *abbr* POL **1.** confederate **2.** confederation

confederacy /kən féddərəssi/ *n* **1.** an alliance of people, states, or parties for a common purpose, or the people, states, or parties in an alliance **2.** a group of people who have joined together to do something unlawful

Confederacy *n* HIST same as **Confederate States of America**

confederal /kən féddərəl/ *adj* **1.** relating to a confederation **2.** relating to the activities of two or more nations —**confederalist** *n*

confederate *n* /kən féddərət/ **1. ALLY** one of two or more people, groups, or nations that have formed an alliance for a common purpose **2. ACCOMPLICE** a plotter or conspirator ■ *adj* /kən féddərət/ **ASSOCIATED** joined in common purpose ■ *vti* /kən féddə rayt/ **(-ates, -ating, -ated) UNITE** to form people, groups, or nations into a confederacy, or become part of a confederacy [14C. < late Latin *confoederat-*, past participle of *confoederare* 'league together' < *foeder-* (see FEDERAL)] —**confederative** /-rətiv/ *adj*

Confederate *n* a supporter or soldier of the Confederate States of America during the American Civil War —**Confederate** *adj*

Confederate States of America *n* the confederation of the 11 southern states that seceded from the United States in 1861, an act that started the American Civil War. Alabama, Arkansas, Florida, Georgia, Louisiana, Mississippi, North Carolina, South Carolina, Tennessee, Texas, and Virginia were the states that seceded.

confederation /kən féddə ráysh'n/ *n* **1. GROUP OF LOOSELY ALLIED STATES** a group of states that are allied together to form a political unit in which they keep most of their independence but act together for purposes such as defence **2. BODY REPRESENTING INDEPENDENT ORGANIZATIONS** a body comprising representatives of independent organizations that wish to cooperate for a common beneficial purpose **3. CONFEDERATING** the formation of a confederation, or the state of being a confederation —**confederationism** *n* —**confederationist** *n*

Confederation *n* **1.** the original union of Ontario, Quebec, New Brunswick, and Nova Scotia in 1867 into the federation of Canada, afterwards joined by the six other provinces **2.** the union of the original 13 states of the United States under the Articles of Confederation from 1781 to 1789

confer /kən fúr/ **(-fers, -ferring, -ferred)** *v* **1.** *vi* **DISCUSS SOMETHING WITH SOMEBODY** to talk to somebody in order to compare opinions or make a decision **2.** *vt* **GIVE HONOUR OR TITLE** to give something such as a title, honour, or favour to somebody (*formal*) ○ *The university conferred an honorary degree on the president.* **3.** *vt* **GIVE CHARACTERISTIC** to give somebody or something a status or characteristic ○ *His demeanour conferred a sense of dignity on the whole affair.* ○ *genes that confer resistance to certain infections* [15C. < Latin *conferre* 'bring together' < *ferre* 'bring'] —**conferment** *n* —**conferrable** *adj* —**conferral** *n* —**conferrer** *n*

SYNONYMS See *give*.

~~**confered**~~ incorrect spelling of **conferred**

conferee /kónfə reé/, **conferree** *n* **1.** a participant in a conference **2.** the recipient of a title, honour, or favour

conference /kónfərənss/ *n* **1. MEETING FOR LECTURES AND DISCUSSION** a meeting, sometimes lasting for several days, in which people with a common interest participate in discussions or listen to lectures to obtain information **2. MEETING FOR SERIOUS DISCUSSION** a meeting to discuss serious matters such as policy or business **3. MEETING OF REPRESENTATIVES OF ORGANIZATION** a usually annual gathering of local representatives of an organization, e.g. a political party, trade union, or church, at which policy matters and other issues are discussed or decided ○ *I would ask conference to throw out this motion.* ○ *the Conservative Party Conference* **4.** POL **MEETING OF TWO LEGISLATIVE COMMITTEES** a meeting of select members or committees from two legislative bodies, for the purpose of settling differences between bills they have passed **5.** CHR **AREA ORGANIZATION OF CHURCHES** in some Protestant churches, a regional or national body to which a number of local churches belong ○ *the Friends General Conference* **6. SPORTS LEAGUE** an association or league of sports teams that compete with each other ○ *the Vauxhall Conference*

Conference *n* a cultivated variety of pear with a long, relatively thin shape and dark green-brown skin

conference call *n* a conversation involving three or more people linked together by telephone

conferencing /kónfərənssing/ *n* the holding of a conference, meeting, or discussion in which the participants are linked by telephone (**audio-conferencing**), by telephone and video equipment (**video conferencing**), or by computer (**computer conferencing**)

conferree *n* another spelling of **conferee**

confess /kən féss/ **(-fesses, -fessing, -fessed)** *v* **1.** *vti* **ADMIT HAVING DONE SOMETHING WRONG** to admit a wrongdoing, crime, or error openly ○ *She confessed to having taken the watch.* ○ *interrupted to confess that I had left the door unlocked* **2.** *vt* **ACKNOWLEDGE SOMETHING TO BE TRUE** to admit the truth of something reluctantly ○ *I must confess I didn't really want to come here tonight.* ○ *asked me about ley lines but I had to confess my ignorance* **3.** *vt* **STATE BELIEF ABOUT YOURSELF** to say that you believe something to be the case, especially something about yourself and especially something bad ○ *I confess myself quite unworthy of the honour you are bestowing on me.* **4.** *vti* CHR **ADMIT SINS** to reveal sins to a priest or to God and ask for forgiveness ○ *It had been some months since I had confessed.* **5.** *vt* CHR **HEAR SOMEBODY'S CONFESSION** to listen to a confession of sins by somebody ○ *A priest visited her to confess her every day.* **6.** *vt* **ACKNOWLEDGE FAITH IN SOMETHING** to declare faith or belief in something or somebody (*archaic*) [14C. Via French *confesser* < Latin *confess-*, past participle of *confiteri* 'acknowledge', literally 'declare utterly' < *fateri* 'declare'] —**confessable** *adj*

confessant /kən féss'nt/ *n* somebody who confesses sins to a priest

confessedly /kən féssidli/ *adv* used to indicate that something is admitted to be the case

confession /kən fésh'n/ *n* **1. ADMISSION OF WRONGDOING** an admission of having done something wrong or embarrassing ○ *a confession of weakness on her part* **2.** LAW **ADMISSION OF GUILT** a voluntary written or verbal statement admitting the commission of a crime ○ *made a full written confession* **3. OPEN ACKNOWLEDGMENT OF FEELINGS** a profession of emotions or beliefs such as love, loyalty, or faith **4.** CHR **DECLARATION OF SINS** a formal declaration of sins confidentially to a priest or to God **5.** RELIG **DECLARATION OF BELIEFS OR DOCTRINES** a declaration of the beliefs or doctrines of a religious body **6.** CHR **RELIGIOUS GROUP SHARING BELIEFS** a religious group that has a specific set of beliefs and practices

confessional /kən fésh'nəl/ *adj* suited to, typical of, or resembling an act of confession ■ *n* in the Roman Catholic church, a small wooden stall with a partition behind which a priest sits to hear confession —**confessionally** *adv*

confessor /kən féssər/ *n* **1.** CHR **PRIEST** a priest who hears confessions **2.** CHR **SPIRITUAL ADVISER** a priest who acts as somebody's spiritual adviser as well as hearing his or her confessions **3.** CHR **CHRISTIAN NOT DETERRED BY PERSECUTION** a Christian who demonstrates his or her faith despite persecution for it, but without becoming a martyr (*archaic*) **4. SOMEBODY WHO CONFESSES** somebody who makes a confession

confetti /kən fétti/ *n* small pieces of coloured paper or dried flowers thrown over people at festive occasions, especially over the bride and groom at a wedding ■ *adj* similar to confetti in shape or colour [Early 19C. < Italian, plural of *confetto* 'small sweet thrown at carnivals' < Latin *conficere* (see CONFECT)]

confidant /kónfi dánt, kónfi dant/ *n* a person somebody trusts and discusses personal matters and problems with [Mid-17C. Alteration of CONFIDENT]

confidante /kónfi dánt, kónfi dant/ *n* a woman somebody trusts and discusses personal matters and problems with [Early 18C. Alteration of CONFIDENT]

confide /kən fíd/ **(-fides, -fiding, -fided)** *v* **1.** *vti* to tell somebody something that is to remain secret or private ○ *He later confided to me that he had not wanted the position at all.* ○ *He'd been foolish enough to confide in her.* **2.** *vt* to entrust somebody with something such as a valuable object or an important task (*archaic*) [15C. < Latin *confidere* 'put your trust in' < *fidere* 'to trust' < *fides* 'trust'] —**confider** *n*

confidence /kónfidənss/ *n* **1. BELIEF IN OWN ABILITIES** self assurance or a belief in your ability to succeed ○ *lacked the confidence needed to reach the top* **2. FAITH IN SOMEBODY TO DO RIGHT** belief or trust in somebody or something, or in the ability of somebody or something to act in a proper, trustworthy, or reliable manner ○ *I have total confidence in her judgment.* **3. SECRET** something told to somebody that is to be kept private **4. TRUSTING RELATIONSHIP** a relationship

based on trust and intimacy ○ *She took me into her confidence.* ○ *But I told you it in confidence!*

confidence game *n N Am* same as **confidence trick**

confidence interval *n* a range of statistical values within which a result is expected to fall with a specific probability

confidence level *n* a measure of how reliable a statistical result is, expressed as a percentage that indicates the probability of the result being correct

confidence limit *n* in statistics, the highest and lowest values of a confidence interval

confidence trick *n* a fraud in which somebody obtains something of value by first gaining the trust of the victim, then betraying that person. N Am term **confidence game**

confidence trickster *n* somebody who uses a dishonest trick or business ploy to defraud somebody else

confident /kónfidənt/ *adj* 1. SELF-ASSURED certain of having the ability, judgment, and resources needed to succeed 2. CONVINCED sure about the nature or facts of something ○ *We are confident that the market for our products is expanding.* 3. EXCESSIVELY FORWARD bold and presumptuous in manner [Late 16C. Via French < Latin *confident-*, present participle of *confidere* (see CONFIDE)] —**confidently** *adv*

confidential /kónfi dénsh'l/ *adj* 1. PRIVATE AND SECRET carried out or revealed in the expectation that anything done or revealed will be kept private 2. FOR SELECT GROUP not available to the public, e.g. because it is commercially or industrially sensitive or concerns matters of national security 3. DEALING WITH PRIVATE AFFAIRS entrusted with somebody's personal or private matters 4. SUGGESTING CLOSE RELATIONSHIP suggesting familiarity or intimacy that may or may not exist ○ *a confidential whisper* —**confidentiality** /kónfi denshi álləti/ *n* —**confidentially** *adv*

confiding /kən fíding/ *adj* 1. willing to trust others with the knowledge of private or personal matters 2. in a manner or tone appropriate for telling somebody something secret or that suggests that a secret is being told —**confidingly** *adv*

configuration /kən fíggə ráysh'n, -fíggyə-/ *n* 1. ARRANGEMENT OF PARTS the way the parts of something are arranged and fit together ○ *In terms of boat configuration, deck layouts are all the same.* 2. SHAPE OR OUTLINE the shape or outline of something, determined by the way its parts are arranged ○ *Geese fly in a V-shaped configuration.* 3. COMPUT COMPUTER SYSTEM'S SETUP the way in which the software and hardware components of a computer system are arranged and interconnected 4. PSYCHOL same as **Gestalt** 5. CHEM, PHYS ARRANGEMENT OF ATOMS IN MOLECULE the fixed stable spatial arrangement of atoms within a molecule —**configurational** *adj* —**configurationally** *adv* —**configurative** /kən fíggərətiv, -fíggyŏŏ-/ *adj*

configure /kən fíggər/ (**-ures, -uring, -ured**) *vt* to set up, design, or arrange the parts of something for a specific purpose [14C. < Latin *configurare* 'fashion after a pattern', literally 'form together' < *figura* 'shape']

confine /kən fín/ *vt* (**-fines, -fining, -fined**) 1. KEEP WITHIN LIMITS to keep somebody or something within particular limits or boundaries ○ *Please confine your comments to the matter in hand.* 2. KEEP IN SOME PLACE to prevent somebody or something from leaving an enclosed or limited space such as a prison, room, or bed ○ *confined to quarters for insubordination* ■ **confines** /kón fínz/ *npl* BOUNDARIES the boundaries, limits, or scope restricting somebody or something ○ *seeking emotional fulfilment within the confines of a long-term relationship* [15C. < French *confiner* < *confins* (plural) 'boundaries' < Latin *confinis* 'ending with' < *finis* 'end'] —**confinable** *adj* —**confiner** *n*

confined /kən fínd/ *adj* small, cramped, and completely enclosed ○ *a confined space*

confined aquifer *n* GEOL same as **artesian aquifer**

confinement /kən fínmənt/ *n* 1. restriction or limitation within the boundaries or scope of something 2. the period of time or the process of giving birth, beginning when a woman goes into labour and ending when a child is born (*dated*)

confirm /kən fúrm/ (**-firms, -firming, -firmed**) *v* 1. *vt* PROVE SOMETHING TO BE TRUE to verify the truth or validity of something thought to be true or valid ○ *Similar findings have been confirmed in recent clinical experiments.* 2. *vti* MAKE SOMETHING DEFINITE to make certain that a tentative arrangement or one made earlier is firm ○ *call to confirm the booking* 3. *vt* LEGALLY APPROVE SOMETHING to ratify or make something valid with a formal or legal act ○ *confirmed his appointment to the post with a unanimous vote* 4. *vt* JUD-CHR ADMIT SOMEBODY INTO RELIGIOUS BODY in Judaism and Christianity, to admit somebody into full membership of a religious body or community 5. *vt* STRENGTHEN SOMETHING to make something stronger (*formal*) [13C. Via French < Latin *confirmare*, literally 'strengthen together' < *firmare* 'strengthen'] —**confirmability** /kən fúrmə bílləti/ *n* —**confirmable** *adj* —**confirmatory** /kən fúrmətəri, kónfər máytəri/ *adj* —**confirmer** *n*

confirmation /kónfər máysh'n/ *n* 1. CONFIRMING SOMETHING the act of verifying or ratifying something ○ *sought confirmation of his suspicions* ○ *the appointment is subject to confirmation by the Senate* 2. SOMETHING THAT CONFIRMS SOMETHING ELSE something that supports, validates, or verifies something else ○ *a confirmation of my worst fears* ○ *Send written confirmation of the date of delivery.* 3. CHR ACCEPTANCE INTO CHURCH in Christianity, a religious ceremony that marks somebody's formal acceptance into a church 4. JUDAISM CEREMONY MARKING BEGINNING OF RESPONSIBLE ADULTHOOD in Reform Judaism, a ceremony that marks the completion of somebody's religious training and entry into full adult membership of the community —**confirmational** *adj*

confirmed /kən fúrmd/ *adj* 1. SETTLED AND UNLIKELY TO CHANGE firmly settled in a particular habit and unlikely to change ○ *a confirmed teetotaller* 2. ESTABLISHED AS TRUE having been found or shown to be true or definite ○ *confirmed cases of infection* 3. CHR MADE MEMBER OF CHURCH received into a Christian church as a full member

confirmedly /kən fúrmidli/ *adv* to an extent or in a way that is unlikely to change

confiscate /kónfi skayt/ *vt* (**-cates, -cating, -cated**) 1. TAKE SOMETHING AWAY to take somebody's property with authority, or appropriate property for personal use as if with authority ○ *I'll confiscate that ruler if you don't stop playing with it.* 2. TAKE SOMETHING AS LEGAL PENALTY to seize property legally forfeited to the public treasury as a penalty ○ *The goods were confiscated by customs.* ■ *adj* (*formal*) 1. TAKEN BY AUTHORITY taken legally, or forfeited 2. HAVING FORFEITED PROPERTY having had property taken away legally or by forfeiture [Mid-16C. < Latin *confiscat-*, past participle of *confiscare* 'appropriate for the public treasury' < *fiscus* 'purse, treasury'] —**confiscable** /kən fískəb'l/ *adj* —**confiscation** /kónfi skáysh'n/ *n* —**confiscator** *n* —**confiscatory** /kən fískətəri/ *adj*

confit /kón fee/ *n* meat such as goose, duck, or pork that has been cooked and preserved in its own fat [Mid-20C. < French < Latin *conficere* (see CONFECT)]

Confiteor /kən fítti awr/ *n* a Roman Catholic prayer of confession and plea for forgiveness [13C. < Latin, 'I confess' < the opening words *Confiteor Deo Omnipotenti* 'I confess to Almighty God']

confiture /kónfi tyoor/ *n* fruit jam or preserve

conflagration /kónflə gráysh'n/ *n* a large fire that causes a great deal of damage [15C. < Latin *conflagration-* < *conflagrare* 'burn up' < *flagrare* 'to blaze']

SYNONYMS See ***fire***.

conflate /kən fláyt/ (**-flates, -flating, -flated**) *vti* to join or merge two or more things into a unified whole [15C. < Latin *conflat-*, past participle of *conflare* 'melt together' < *flare* 'to blow'] —**conflation** *n*

conflict *n* /kón flikt/ 1. MIL WAR warfare between opposing forces, especially a prolonged and bitter but sporadic struggle ○ *news that the conflict had reached the outskirts of the capital* 2. DIFFERENCE a disagreement or clash between ideas, principles, or people ○ *The two sides came into conflict over the proposed contract.* 3. PSYCHOL MENTAL STRUGGLE a psychological state resulting from the often unconscious opposition between simultaneous but incompatible desires, needs, drives, or impulses 4. LITERAT PLOT TENSION opposition between or among characters or forces in a literary work that shapes or motivates the action of the plot ■ *vi* /kən flíkt/ (**-flicts, -flicting, -flicted**) DIFFER to be incompatible, in opposition, or in disagreement ○ *The latest findings conflict with those of the original report.* [15C. < Latin *conflictus*, past participle of *confligere* 'strike together, fight' < *fligere* 'strike'] —**confliction** /kən flíksh'n/ *n* —**conflictive** /kən flíktiv/ *adj* —**conflictual** /kən flíkchoo əl/ *adj*

SYNONYMS See ***fight***.

conflict diamonds *npl* diamonds mined illegally and traded on the black market to finance a military campaign

conflicted /kən flíktid/ *adj* ⚠ confused or ambivalent because of competing desires, possibilities, or impulses (*informal*) ○ *I haven't known him when he wasn't conflicted about his relationship with his family.*

USAGE ***Conflicted***, meaning 'confused or ambivalent because of competing desires, possibilities, or impulses', is closely associated with the jargon of psychobabble, and so disliked by many people.

conflicting /kən flíkting/ *adj* 1. inconsistent or contradictory and unable to be reconciled ○ *We've been receiving conflicting reports about the whereabouts of the kidnappers.* 2. requiring different and incompatible actions ○ *In the confusion, the men were given conflicting instructions.* —**conflictingly** *adv*

conflict of interest *n* a conflict between the public and private interests of somebody in an official position, or conflicts between a number of public positions

confluence /kónfloo ənss/ *n* 1. GEOG MEETING OF STREAMS a flowing together of two or more streams, or a point at which streams combine 2. GEOG STREAM a stream formed by others combining 3. MEETING OF TWO OR MORE THINGS a meeting or joining of two or more things, or the place where two or more things meet or join [15C. < late Latin *confluentia* < Latin *confluent-*, present participle of *confluere* 'flow together' < *fluere* 'flow'] —**confluent** *adj, n*

conflux /kón fluks/ *n* GEOG same as **confluence** (senses 1–2) [Early 17C. < Latin *confluxus* 'flowed together' < *confluere* (see CONFLUENCE)]

confocal /kon fṓk'l/ *adj* having the same focus or foci [Mid-19C. < Latin *con-* 'with' + FOCAL] —**confocally** *adv*

conform /kən fáwrm/ (**-forms, -forming, -formed**) *v* 1. *vi* BEHAVE ACCEPTABLY to behave or think in a socially acceptable or expected way ○ *the constant pressure to conform* 2. *vi* FOLLOW STANDARD to comply with a fixed standard, regulation, or requirement ○ *a transformer that doesn't conform to UK standards* 3. *vi* FIT IN to be or fit in with a person's idea of what somebody or something should be like ○ *He certainly doesn't conform with my expectations of a diplomat.* 4. *vti* MATCH to match a pattern or sample, or make somebody or something match a pattern or sample 5. *vti* AGREE to be in accord, or bring something into accord with something else ○ *As soon as possible, the revolutionary government conformed the country's laws with those of the Soviet Union.* 6. *vti* BE OR MAKE SIMILAR to be the same as or very similar to something or somebody, or make something similar ○ *The Assyrian account of the great flood conforms closely with the Biblical account.* 7. *vi* CHR FOLLOW NATIONAL CHURCH to follow the practices of the established church of a country, especially formerly to belong to the Anglican Church in England and Wales (*archaic*) [14C. Via French < Latin *conformare*, literally 'shape after' < *forma* 'shape'] —**conformer** *n*

conformable /kən fáwrməb'l/ *adj* 1. IN AGREEMENT consistent or compatible with something ○ *This gradual increase is conformable with the theory.* 2. SIMILAR similar in form or shape ○ *I think this software is conformable with what you already have on your system.* 3. COMPLIANT eager to obey or comply with the wishes of others (*literary*) 4. GEOL ABOVE PREVIOUS LAYER describes a layer of rock that lies on the stratum that was deposited immediately before it, so there is no break in stratigraphic sequence or intervening erosion —**conformability** /kən fáwrmə bílləti/ *n* —**conformably** *adv*

conformal /kən fáwrm'l/ *adj* 1. describes a mathematical transformation that leaves the angles between intersecting curves unchanged 2. describes a map that shows the correct shape and scale of a small area

conformance /kən fáwrmənss/ *n* the act of conforming or of bringing about accord or compliance

conformation /kón fawr máysh'n/ *n* **1. SOMETHING'S STRUCTURE** the shape, outline, or form of something, especially an animal, determined by the way in which its parts are arranged ○ *the ideal conformation of a young horse suitable as a family mount* **2. SYMMETRY** symmetrical arrangement of parts ○ *That sculpture shows excellent conformation.* **3.** CHEM **MOLECULAR ARRANGEMENT** a spatial arrangement of the atoms of a molecule, especially one that results from rotation around a single bond **4. CREATION OF CONFORMITY** bringing the process of one thing into accord with another —**conformational** *adj* —**conformationally** *adv*

conformist /kən fáwrmist/ *n* **1. FOLLOWER OF CUSTOMS AND RULES** somebody who behaves or thinks in a socially acceptable or expected way **2. MEMBER OF NATIONAL CHURCH** a Christian who belongs to an established national church, especially the Church of England ■ *adj* **SOCIALLY ACCEPTABLE** characterized by adherence to accepted norms of behaviour or thought —**conformism** *n*

conformity /kən fáwrməti/ *n* **1. DOING AND THINKING AS OTHERS** behaviour or thought that is socially acceptable or expected ○ *a certain lack of conformity in his attitudes* **2. FOLLOWING OF STANDARD** compliance with a fixed standard, regulation, or requirement **3. AGREEMENT IN FORM** agreement, correspondence, or similarity in structure, manner, or character **4.** CHR **COMPLIANCE** acceptance and adherence to the doctrines of an established national church, especially the Church of England

confound /kən fównd/ (**-founds, -founding, -founded**) *vt* **1. BEWILDER SOMEBODY** to puzzle or confuse somebody **2. MAKE THINGS WORSE** to cause a confused situation to become even more confused ○ *Shouting at her like that only confounded the problem.* **3. REFUTE SOMETHING** to prove somebody or something to be wrong ○ *confounded the critics and went on to become an international success* **4. PUT SOMEBODY TO SHAME** to cause somebody to feel ashamed or embarrassed ○ *Her presentation confounded everyone who had criticized her.* **5. MIX THINGS UP** to fail to distinguish between two or more things ○ *I am not confounding modesty with bashfulness.* ○ *He often confounds fact and opinion.* **6. EXPRESSING ANGER** used to express anger at something or somebody (*dated*) ○ *Confound his insolence!* **7. RUIN SOMETHING** to ruin or destroy somebody or something (*archaic*) [13C. Via Anglo-Norman *conf(o)undre* < Latin *confundere* 'pour together' < *fundere* 'melt, pour'] —**confounder** *n* —**confoundingly** *adv*

confounded /kən fówndid/ *adj* **1.** puzzled or confused by something ○ *'I don't know what's happened', he spluttered, completely confounded.* **2.** used to express annoyance or irritation (*dated informal*) ○ *Where's that confounded dog?* —**confoundedly** *adv* —**confoundedness** *n*

confraternity /kónfrə túrnəti/ (*plural* **-ties**) *n* a group of people united in a common profession or for a purpose, often a group of Christians who have joined together to perform charitable acts [15C. < French *confraternité* < Latin *confrater*, literally 'brother with somebody' < *frater* 'brother']

confrère /kón frair/ *n* a fellow member of a professional, charitable, or other group (*formal*) [15C. Via French < Latin *confrater* (see CONFRATERNITY)]

confront /kən frúnt/ (**-fronts, -fronting, -fronted**) *vt* **1. CHALLENGE SOMEBODY FACE TO FACE** to come face to face with somebody, especially in a challenge, and usually with hostility, criticism, or defiance **2. MAKE SOMEBODY AWARE OF SOMETHING** to bring something such as contradictory facts or evidence to the attention of somebody, often in a challenging way ○ *confronted her with the evidence* **3. ENCOUNTER DIFFICULTY** to be forced to deal with something, especially an obstacle that must be overcome ○ *This is just one of the difficulties students confront these days.* **4. BE PROBLEM FOR SOMEBODY** to cause difficulty to or present an obstacle for somebody ○ *The hardships that would confront the settlers were blissfully unknown when they started out.* [Mid-16C. Via French < medieval Latin *confrontare* < Latin *front-* 'forehead'] —**confronter** *n*

confrontation /kón frun táysh'n/ *n* **1. ENCOUNTER** a face-to-face meeting or encounter, especially a challenging or hostile one **2. FIGHT** fighting, or a fight or battle **3.** INTERNAT REL **HOSTILITY WITHOUT WARFARE** hostility between nations stopping short of actual warfare, though probably involving armed forces **4. CONFLICT BETWEEN IDEAS OR PEOPLE** conflict between ideas, beliefs, or opinions, or between the people who hold them ○ *This country is headed for a confrontation over the exploitation of natural resources.* **5. ENCOUNTERING OF SOMETHING** the act of encountering or facing up to something such as an obstacle —**confrontational** *adj* —**confrontationist** *n, adj*

Confucian /kən fyóosh'n/ *adj* relating to the teachings of Confucius or his followers, emphasizing personal control, adherence to a social hierarchy, and social and political order —**Confucian** *n* —**Confucianism** *n* —**Confucianist** *n*

Confucius /kən fyóoshəss/ (551?–479? BC) Chinese philosopher, administrator, and moralist. His social and moral teachings, collected in the *Analects*, tried to replace former religious observances.

> 'When you meet someone better than yourself, turn your thoughts to becoming his equal. When you meet someone not as good as you are, look within and examine your own self.'
> [Confucius, *Analects*; 5th century BC]

con fuoco /kon foo ókō/ *adv* with energy, passion, and fire (*used as a musical direction*) [< Italian, 'with fire'] —**con fuoco** *adj*

confuse /kən fyóoz/ (**-fuses, -fusing, -fused**) *vt* **1. MAKE SOMEBODY UNABLE TO THINK INTELLIGENTLY** to make somebody unable to think or reason clearly or act sensibly **2. MAKE SOMETHING PUZZLING** to make something hard or harder to understand ○ *received additional information that only served to confuse the issue* **3. MIX THINGS UP** to mistake one person or thing for another **4. EMBARRASS SOMEBODY** to make somebody feel embarrassed or ill at ease **5. THROW SOMETHING INTO DISARRAY** to cause disorder in something ○ *The dense fog utterly confused traffic on the motorway.* [14C. Via French *confus* 'perplexed' < Latin *confusus* 'mixed up' < *confundere* (see CONFOUND)] —**confusability** /kən fyóozə bílləti/ *n* —**confusable** *adj*

confused /kən fyóozd/ *adj* **1. UNABLE TO THINK INTELLIGENTLY** unable to think or reason clearly or to act sensibly **2. DISORDERED** in no logical or sensible order ○ *got his grammar hopelessly confused* **3. EMBARRASSED** embarrassed and not knowing what to say or how to act **4. NOT DIFFERENTIATED** mistaken for each other **5.** PSYCHIAT **DISORIENTATED** having impaired psychological capacity to the extent of being forgetful and no longer able to carry out simple everyday tasks —**confusedly** /-fyóozidli, -fyóozdli/ *adv* —**confusedness** /-zidnəss/ *n*

confusing /kən fyóozing/ *adj* unclear and difficult to understand —**confusingly** *adv*

confusion /kən fyóozh'n/ *n* **1. BEWILDERMENT** the act of confusing somebody or something, or the state of being confused or perplexed ○ *tried to hide his confusion* **2. LACK OF CLARITY** misunderstanding of a situation or the facts **3. MISTAKING ONE FOR ANOTHER** a failure to distinguish between people or things **4. DISORDER** a chaotic or disordered state **5. EMBARRASSMENT** self-consciousness or embarrassment **6.** PSYCHIAT **DISORIENTATED STATE OF MIND** a psychological state in which somebody is disorientated and no longer able to carry out simple everyday tasks —**confusional** *adj*

confutation /kónfyoo táysh'n/ *n* (*formal*) **1.** the act of proving conclusively that somebody is wrong or that something is false, invalid, or faulty ○ *The lawyer's confutation of the witness's testimony was decisive.* **2.** a fact, observation, or piece of evidence proving that somebody is wrong or that something is false, invalid, or faulty (*often used in the plural*) —**confutative** /kən fyóotətiv/ *adj*

confute /kən fyóot/ (**-futes, -futing, -futed**) *vt* to prove conclusively that somebody is wrong or that something is false, invalid, or faulty (*formal*) [Early 16C. < Latin *confutare* 'restrain, answer conclusively'] —**confutable** *adj* —**confuter** *n*

cong. *abbr* **1.** RELIG congregational **2.** POL congress **3.** POL congressional

Cong. *abbr* **1.** RELIG Congregational **2.** POL Congress **3.** POL Congressional

conga /kóng gə/ *n* **1. DANCE DONE IN LINE** a Latin American dance in which people form a line and, holding the waist of the person ahead, move three steps forward, then kick out a leg **2. MUSIC** the music for a conga **3.** MUSIC same as **conga drum** ■ *vi* (**-gas, -gaing, -gaed**) **DANCE** to dance the conga [Mid-20C. < American Spanish *(danza) Conga* 'dance from the Congo' < Spanish *Congo*]

conga drum *n* a tall tapering drum, played with both hands and used in Latin American and African music

congé /kón zhay, kóN-/ (*plural* **-gés**) *n* **1. PERMISSION** formal permission for somebody to leave (*formal*) **2. LEAVE-TAKING** a departure (*formal*) **3. BOW** a formal bow (*formal*) **4.** ARCHIT **CONCAVE MOULDING** an architectural moulding that is concave in shape [14C. < Old French *congié* < Latin *commeare* 'come and go']

congeal /kən jéel/ (**-geals, -gealing, -gealed**) *vti* **1.** to become thick and solid, or cause a liquid to thicken and solidify **2.** to become firm and strong, or make something firm and strong ○ *Let's act before opposition to our plan congeals.* [14C. Via French < Latin *congelare* 'freeze together' < *gelu* 'frost'] —**congealer** *n* —**congealment** *n*

congelation /kónji láysh'n/ *n* (*technical*) **1.** the process of turning from a liquid into a solid, or the state of being solid as a result of congealing **2.** a liquid that has solidified [15C. Directly or via French < Latin *congelation-* < *congelare* (see CONGEAL)]

congener /kən jéenər, kónjinər/ *n* **1.** somebody or something that belongs to the same class, group, or type, e.g. a plant of the same genus as another, or two chemical elements of the same group **2.** a complex organic molecule that develops in wine and spirits during the fermentation and aging processes, thought to be implicated in causing hangovers [Mid-18C. < Latin *con-* 'with' + *gener-* 'race, kind']

congeneric /kónji nérrik/, **congenerous** /kon jénnərəss, kən-/ *adj* describes organisms belonging to the same class, group, or type

congenial /kən jéeni əl/ *adj* **1. AGREEABLE** pleasant and suited to somebody's character or tastes ○ *found it a very congenial atmosphere* **2. SIMILAR** compatible in tastes, interests, attitudes, or backgrounds ○ *carefree travel with congenial companions* **3. FRIENDLY** having an outgoing pleasant character ○ *Her congenial nature makes her well-loved in the town.* [Early 17C. < Latin *con-* 'with' + GENIAL] —**congeniality** /kən jéeni álləti/ *n* —**congenially** *adv* —**congenialness** *n*

congenic /kən jénnik/ *adj* describes animal cells that are genetically identical except for the arrangement of genes in a single restricted chromosome region (**locus**)

congenital /kən jénnit'l/ *adj* **1.** describes an unusual condition present at birth ○ *a congenital disorder* **2.** firmly established as part of somebody's character or beliefs [Late 18C. < Latin *congenitus* 'born with' < *genitus*, past participle of *gignere* 'beget'] —**congenitally** *adv* —**congenitalness** *n*

congenital anomaly *n* a medically significant condition present at birth and resulting from developmental processes

conger eel /kóng gər-/, **conger** *n* a large scaleless eel. Native to: temperate and tropical coastal waters of the Atlantic Ocean. Latin name: *Conger oceanicus*. [Via French *congre* < Greek *goggros*]

congeries /kən jéereez, kónjə-/ (*plural same*) *n* a collection or assortment of things ○ *made a nation of what had been a far-flung congeries of states* [Mid-16C. < Latin, 'heap, pile' < *congerere* (see CONGEST)]

congest /kən jést/ (**-gests, -gesting, -gested**) *v* **1.** *vti* to overcrowd a street or area so that movement is slow or difficult, or become overcrowded **2.** *vt* to accumulate as excessive fluid in an organ or body part, as a result of disease or infection [15C. < Latin *congest-*, past participle of *congerere* 'collect' < *gerere* 'carry'] —**congested** *adj* —**congestible** *adj* —**congestive** *adj*

congestion /kən jéschən/ *n* **1. EXCESSIVE TRAFFIC OR PEOPLE** a state of overcrowding in a street or other area, making movement slow or difficult **2.** MED **EXCESSIVE ACCUMULATION OF FLUID** the condition of having an excessive amount of blood or fluid accumulate in an organ or body part as a result of disease or infection **3.** COMPUT **HAVING TOO MUCH INFORMATION TO TRANSFER** in computing, a situation in which the amount of information to be transferred is greater than the amount that the data communication path can carry

congestion charge *n* a daily payment made by a motorist for the right to drive into a city centre,

introduced as a means of reducing traffic congestion —**congestion charging** n

congestive heart failure n a form of heart failure in which the heart is unable to pump away the blood returning to it fast enough, causing congestion in the veins

conglomerate n /kən glómmərət/ **1.** BUSINESS ORGANIZATION INVOLVED IN MANY AREAS a large business organization that consists of a number of companies that deal with a variety of different business, manufacturing, or commercial activities **2.** MIX OF THINGS a mass formed from gathering a number of dissimilar materials or parts **3.** GEOL ROCK COMPRISING PIECES OF OTHER ROCKS coarse-grained sedimentary rock containing fragments of other rock larger than 2 mm/0.08 in in diameter, held together with another material such as clay ■ adj /kən glómmərət/ FORMED BY COMBINING DIFFERENT THINGS consisting of a mass or accumulation of dissimilar materials or parts ■ vti /kən glómmə rayt/ (-ates, -ating, -ated) MIX TOGETHER TO FORM MASS to gather materials or parts into a mass, or be gathered into a mass [Late 16C. < Latin conglomeratus 'wound into a ball' < glomer- 'ball'] —**conglomeratic** /kən glómmə ráttik/ adj —**conglomeration** /kən glómmə ráysh'n/ n —**conglomerator** /-raytər/ n —**conglomeritic** /kən glómmə ríttik/ adj

conglomerated /kən glómmə raytid/ adj made up of and controlling many parts of an industry ○ a conglomerated corporation

Congo /kóng gō/ Africa's second longest river, which provides a major transport network. It rises in the south of the Democratic Republic of the Congo and empties into the Atlantic Ocean. Length: 4,374 km/2,718 mi. Former name **Zaire**

Democratic Republic of the Congo

Congo, Democratic Republic of the large equatorial country of Central Africa with a coastline on the Atlantic Ocean. Language: French. Currency: Congo franc. Capital: Kinshasa. Population: 56,625,039 (2003). Area: 2,344,885 sq. km/905,365 sq. mi. Former name **Zaire** (1971–97), **Belgian Congo** (1908–60), **Congo Free State** (1885–1908)

Republic of the Congo

Congo, Republic of the country in west-central Africa, on the coast of the Atlantic Ocean. Language: French. Currency: CFA franc. Capital: Brazzaville. Population: 2,954,258 (2003). Area: 342,000 sq. km/132,000 sq. mi. Former name **People's Republic of the Congo** (1970–92)

congo dye /kóng gō-/ n a dye containing nitrogen [Because associated with the Congo region or African Americans from there]

Congo eel n an amphibian that has a long body with gill slits and two pairs of rudimentary limbs that enable it to travel on land. Native to: southeastern United States. Latin name: Amphiuma means. [See CONGO DYE]

Congo franc n the main unit of currency in the Democratic Republic of the Congo. See table at currency

Congo Free State former name for **Congo, Democratic Republic of the** (1885–1908)

Congolese /kóng gə leéz/ n **1.** somebody who comes from the Democratic Republic of the Congo, the Republic of the Congo, or any of the former countries that they represent **2.** LANG same as **Kongo**[1] (sense 2) [Early 20C. < French Congolais < Congo 'the River Congo'] —**Congolese** adj

Congo red n a dye that is red in alkaline solutions and blue in acid solutions. Use: chemical indicator, biological stain, dye. [See CONGO DYE]

Congo snake n AMPHIB same as **Congo eel**

congou /kóng goo, -gō/ n a fine grade of Chinese black tea, made from the largest leaf gathered from the tip of a shoot on a tea plant [Early 18C. Shortening of Cantonese kungfúch'a, Modern Standard Chinese gōngfu chá 'tea made for refined tastes', literally 'effort tea']

congrats /kən gráts/ npl, interj an expression of congratulations (informal) [Early 20C. Shortening]

congratulate /kən gráttyoo layt, -gráchoo-/ (-lates, -lating, -lated) v **1.** vt to express pleasure or approval to somebody for an achievement or good fortune or on a special occasion **2.** vr to feel self-satisfied in having success or good fortune ○ I was congratulating myself on my driving skills, when I skidded into a snow bank. [Mid-16C. < Latin congratulat-, past participle of congratulari 'rejoice with' < gratus 'thankful'] —**congratulative** adj —**congratulator** n —**congratulatory** adj

congratulation /kən gráttyoo láysh'n, -gráchoo-/ n the act of expressing pleasure to somebody for an achievement or good fortune or on a special occasion ○ made a short speech of congratulation ■ npl, interj **congratulations** an expression of pleasure or acknowledgment of somebody's success or good fortune or on a special occasion

congregant /kóng grigənt/ n a member of a religious congregation, especially in a Jewish synagogue [Late 19C. < Latin congregant-, present participle of congregare (see CONGREGATE)]

congregate vti /kóng gri gayt/ (-gates, -gating, -gated) ASSEMBLE PEOPLE OR ANIMALS to come together in a group, or gather people or animals into a group ■ adj /-gət, -gayt/ (formal) **1.** HAVING COME TOGETHER gathered or assembled in a group **2.** RELATING TO GATHERING relating to an assembled group [15C. < Latin congregat-, past participle of congregare 'collect together' < greg- 'flock'] —**congregative** adj —**congregator** n

congregation /kóng gri gáysh'n/ n **1.** RELIG GROUP OF WORSHIPPERS a group of people who have gathered for a religious service **2.** RELIG MEMBERS OF SAME CHURCH the members of a specific church **3.** CHR ROMAN CATHOLIC RELIGIOUS BODY a Roman Catholic religious body whose members follow a common rule of life and are bound by simple vows (formal) **4.** CHR DIVISION OF ROMAN CATHOLIC CENTRAL ADMINISTRATION a section of the central administrative organization (**curia**) of the Roman Catholic Church **5.** CHR COMMITTEE OF ROMAN CATHOLIC BISHOPS a committee of Roman Catholic bishops responsible for handling the business of a general council (formal) **6.** GATHERING a group of people or things ○ A congregation of reporters waited outside the courthouse. **7.** EDUC SENIOR MEMBERS OF UNIVERSITY STAFF an assembly of the senior members of the academic staff of a university **8.** COMING TOGETHER the act of gathering or assembling (formal) ○ Congregation in the halls is not allowed.

congregational /kóng gri gáysh'nəl/ adj relating to a congregation

Congregational adj relating to Congregationalism or its followers

Congregational Church n a Protestant denomination in which each church is self-governing

congregationalism /kóng gri gáysh'nəlizəm/ n a system of church organization in which each church is self-governing —**congregationalist** n, adj

Congregationalism n the beliefs and practices of the Congregational Church —**Congregationalist** n, adj

congress /kóng gress/ n **1.** a conference or formal meeting of delegates or representatives, e.g. the representatives of a group of nations, to discuss matters of interest or concern **2.** a society or organization of people with common interests and concerns **3.** same as **sexual intercourse** (dated formal) [15C. < Latin congressus, past participle of congredi 'go together' < gradi 'proceed'] —**congressional** /kən grésh'nəl/ adj

Congress n **1.** US PARLIAMENT the national legislative body of the United States, consisting of the House of Representatives and the Senate **2.** SESSION OF CONGRESS a two-year term of the US Congress, or the members of Congress during such a term ○ the 22nd Congress **3.** GOVERNING AND LAW-MAKING BODY the governing body in some countries ○ the National People's Congress **4.** NAME OF POLITICAL PARTY the shortened name of a number of political parties whose name includes the word 'Congress', e.g. the African National Congress or the Indian National Congress —**Congressional** adj

congressional district n a district within a US state that is entitled to elect one representative to the House of Representatives

Congressional Medal of Honor n the highest military decoration in the United States, awarded by Congress for outstanding bravery in action

Congressional Record n a government journal in the United States that records and publishes the proceedings of Congress

congressman /kóng gressmən/ (plural -men /-mən/) n a man who is a member of the US Congress, especially of the House of Representatives

Congress of Industrial Organizations n a federation of industrial trade unions formed in the United States in 1935 and merged with the American Federation of Labor in 1955 to form the AFL-CIO

Congress of Vienna n a congress held in Vienna between 1814 and 1815 to deal with the territorial and jurisdictional problems remaining after the defeat of Napoleon in the Napoleonic Wars

congressperson /kóng gress purss'n/ (plural -people /-peep'l/) n a member of the US Congress, especially of the House of Representatives

congresswoman /kóng gress woomən/ (plural -women /-wimin/) n a woman who is a member of the US Congress, especially of the House of Representatives

Congreve /kóng greev/, **William** (1670–1729) English playwright and poet. He wrote The Double Dealer (1693), Love for Love (1695) and The Way of the World (1700).

'Heaven has no rage like love to hatred turned, / Nor hell a fury like a woman scorned.'
[William Congreve, The Mourning Bride; 1697]

congruent /kóng groo ənt/ adj **1.** IN AGREEMENT corresponding to or consistent with each other or with something else (formal) ○ culturally congruent education **2.** MATHS WITH SAME SHAPE with identical geometric shapes **3.** MATHS DIFFERING BY EXACTLY DIVISIBLE AMOUNT describes two numbers whose difference is exactly divisible by a third number (**modulus**) [15C. < Latin congruent-, present participle of congruere 'meet together' < ruere 'to fall'] —**congruence** n —**congruency** n —**congruently** adv

congruity /kən groo əti/ n (formal) **1.** the state or fact of agreeing or being consistent with each other or with something else **2.** the quality or fact of being suitable or appropriate for something

congruous /kóng groo əss/ adj **1.** appropriate to or suitable for a purpose or situation (formal) **2.** corresponding to or consistent with each other or something else [Late 16C. < Latin congruus 'suitable' < congruere (see CONGRUENT)] —**congruously** adv —**congruousness** n

conic /kónnik/ MATHS adj same as **conical** ■ n same as **conic section** [Late 16C. Via modern Latin < Greek kōnikos < kōnos 'cone']

conical /kónnik'l/ adj **1.** shaped like a cone **2.** relating to or having the form of a geometric cone

conic projection n **1.** a method of making a map by projecting the globe onto a surrounding cone whose point is above one of the poles and then flattening

the cone **2.** a map made by conic projection. On a conic projection, the parallels of latitude appear as concentric circles, and the lines of longitude radiate from the centre as equal radii.

conics /kónniks/ *n* the branch of geometry involving the study of conic sections (*takes a singular verb*)

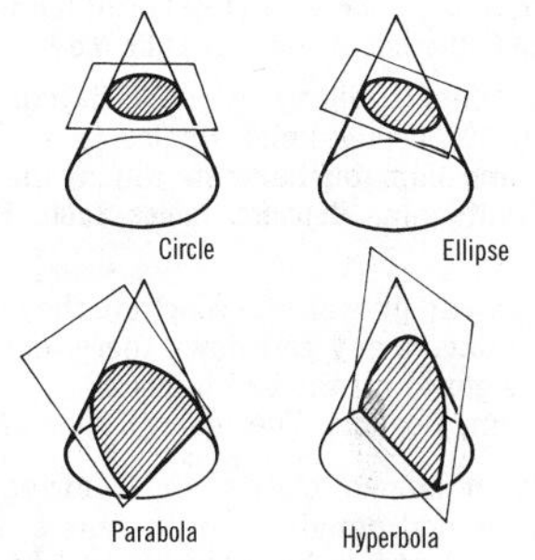

conic section

conic section *n* a curve produced by the intersection of a plane with a circular cone, e.g. a circle, ellipse, hyperbola, or parabola

conidia FUNGI plural of **conidium**

conidiophore /kō níddi ə fawr/ *n* a simple or branched part (**hypha**) of a fungus that produces spores asexually [Late 19C. < CONIDIUM] —**conidiophorous** /kō níddi óffərəss/ *adj*

conidium /kō níddi əm/ (*plural* **-ia** /-i ə/) *n* an asexually produced spore of some types of fungus [Late 19C. < modern Latin < Greek *konis* 'dust'] —**conidial** *adj*

conifer /kónnifər, kṓn-/ *n* any tree that has thin leaves (**needles**) and produces cones. Many types are evergreen. Pines, firs, junipers, larches, spruces, and yews are conifers. Order: Coniferales. [Mid-19C. < Latin, 'cone-bearing' < Greek *kōnos* 'cone'] —**coniferous** /kə níffərəss/ *adj*

coniine /kṓni een, kō neen/ *n* a colourless substance with poisonous properties. Source: hemlock. Formula: $C_8H_{17}N$. [Mid-19C. < *conium* 'hemlock' < Latin]

Coniston Water /kónnistən-/ lake in Cumbria, northern England, where several water speed records have been set. Area: 7 sq. km/3 sq. mi. Depth: 56 m/184 ft.

conj, **conj.** *abbr* **1.** GRAM conjugation **2.** ASTRON, GRAM conjunction **3.** GRAM conjunctive

conjecture /kən jékchər/ *n* **1.** GUESSWORK the formation of judgments or opinions on the basis of incomplete or inconclusive information ○ *The origin of this ritual is a matter of conjecture.* **2.** SOMETHING GUESSED a conclusion, judgment, or statement based on incomplete or inconclusive information **3.** MATHS, SCI UNPROVED THEOREM a theorem in science or mathematics that has still to be proved [14C. Directly or via French < Latin *conjectura* < *conjicere* 'throw together' < *jacere* 'throw'] —**conjecturable** *adj* —**conjectural** *adj* —**conjecture** *vti* —**conjecturer** *n*

conjoin /kən jóyn/ (**-joins, -joining, -joined**) *vti* to join two or more things, or become joined (*formal*) ○ *conjoined in holy matrimony* [14C. Via French *conjoindre* < Latin *conjungere* 'join together' < *jungere* 'join'] —**conjoiner** *n*

conjoined twin /kən jóynd-/ *n* either of twins born physically joined together

conjoint /kən jóynt/ *adj* **1.** done by, involving, or relating to two or more combined entities ○ *a conjoint project* **2.** joined or combined —**conjointly** *adv*

conjugal /kónjŏŏg'l/ *adj* relating to marriage or to husbands and wives [Early 16C. < Latin *conjugalis* < *conjugare* (see CONJUGATE)] —**conjugality** /kónjŏŏ gálləti/ *n* —**conjugally** *adv*

conjugal rights *npl* the rights that a husband or wife is entitled to in a marriage, especially the right to have sexual relations with his or her spouse

conjugal visit *n* a visit to a jail by the husband or wife of a prisoner, during which the couple is allowed some privacy, e.g. to allow them to have sexual relations

conjugant /kónjŏŏgənt/ *n* either of a pair of organisms, cells, or gametes in the process of reproducing [Early 20C. < Latin *conjugant-*, present participle of *conjugare* (see CONJUGATE)]

conjugate *v* /kónjŏŏ gayt/ (**-gates, -gating, -gated**) **1.** *vt* GRAM STATE FORMS OF VERB to state systematically the different forms a verb has according to tense, mood, person, and number **2.** *vi* GRAM HAVE DIFFERENT GRAMMATICAL FORMS to have different grammatical forms according to tense, mood, number, or person (*refers to verbs*) **3.** *vt* CHEM JOIN SUBSTANCES to combine two substances in such a way that they can easily be separated again, especially in chemical reactions **4.** *vi* BIOL REPRODUCE to reproduce by physically joining in order to transfer genetic information (*refers to organisms that normally reproduce by division*) ■ *adj* /kónjŏŏgət, -gayt/ **1.** PAIRED joined in pairs (*formal*) **2.** MATHS ADDING UP TO 360 DEGREES describes a pair of angles that together add up to 360 degrees **3.** CHEM DIFFERING BY ONE PROTON describes substances that have such similar molecular structures that one becomes the other through the gain or loss of a proton **4.** CHEM EXISTING TOGETHER IN EQUILIBRIUM describes a state of chemical equilibrium in which two liquids coexist in separate forms, one being the solute and the other the solvent ■ *n* /kónjŏŏ gət/ **1.** GRAM VERB FORM one of the different forms of a verb according to tense, mood, person, or number **2.** RESULT OF JOINING a product of joining or union **3.** MATHS same as **conjugate complex number** [15C. < Latin *conjugatus*, past participle of *conjugare* 'yoke together' < *jugum* 'yoke'] —**conjugable** *adj* —**conjugately** *adv* —**conjugateness** *n* —**conjugative** *adj* —**conjugator** *n*

conjugate complex number *n* either of a pair of complex numbers that are symmetrically located on either side of an x-axis, differing only in the sign of the imaginary component

conjugated /kónjŏŏ gaytid/ *adj* **1.** containing two or more double or triple chemical bonds in alternation with single bonds **2.** describes a double chemical bond separated by a single bond

conjugated protein *n* a protein attached to a non-protein

conjugation /kónjŏŏ gáysh'n/ *n* **1.** GRAM INFLECTION OF VERB the different patterns of inflection of a given verb **2.** GRAM GROUP OF VERBS WITH SAME INFLECTIONS a group of verbs that use the same patterns of inflection **3.** GRAM SET OF VERB INFLECTIONS the complete set of inflections for a verb **4.** ACT OF JOINING TOGETHER the act of joining or uniting, or the state of being joined **5.** BIOL REPRODUCTION IN SIMPLE ORGANISMS the simplest form of reproduction, in which two single-celled organisms such as bacteria or protozoans link together, exchange genetic information, and then separate **6.** BIOL FUSION OF NUCLEI the fusion of the nuclei of a male and a female gamete in algae and fungi **7.** GENETICS PAIRING OF CHROMOSOMES the distribution of pairs of chromosomes into the four nuclei produced by the division of a parent nucleus **8.** CHEM ALTERNATION OF NUMBER OF BONDS the occurrence of two or more double or triple bonds in alternation with single bonds in a molecule —**conjugational** *adj* —**conjugationally** *adv*

conjunct /kón jungkt/ *adj* **1.** UNITED attached or joined **2.** LING ADJACENT TO CONSONANT describes consonants that are next to each other within a word without a vowel or vowels between **3.** MUSIC CONSISTING OF SINGLE STEPS IN SCALE relating to or consisting of adjacent notes in a musical scale ■ *n* LOGIC EITHER PROPOSITION IN CONJUNCTION in logic, either of the two propositions or formulas in a conjunction [15C. < Latin *conjunctus*, past participle of *conjungere* (see CONJOIN)] —**conjunctly** *adv*

conjunction /kən júngksh'n/ *n* **1.** GRAM CONNECTING WORD a word that is used to link sentences, clauses, phrases, or words, e.g. 'and', 'but', or 'if' **2.** COMBINING OF SEVERAL THINGS the act of joining or combining two or more things **3.** SIMULTANEOUS OCCURRENCE a simultaneous occurrence of events or circumstances **4.** ASTRON ALIGNMENT WITH SUN the position of a planet or the Moon when aligned with the Sun, as seen from Earth **5.** ASTRON CLOSE PROXIMITY OF PLANETS the appearance of two planets very close to each other or in the same place on the celestial sphere **6.** ASTROL ASTROLOGICAL ASPECT in astrology, an aspect of 0° between two planets **7.** LOGIC TYPE OF COMPOUND STATEMENT in logic, a proposition of the form 'A and B' that is true only if both A and B are true [14C. < Latin *conjunction-* < *conjunct-*, past participle of *conjungere* (see CONJOIN)] —**conjunctional** *adj* —**conjunctionally** *adv* ◇

in conjunction with together with or combined with something

conjunctiva /kón jungk tívə/ (*plural* **-vas** or **-vae** /-vee/) *n* a delicate mucous membrane that covers the internal part of the eyelid and is attached to the cornea [14C. < medieval Latin *(tunica) conjunctiva* 'connective (membrane)' < Latin *conjunct-* (see CONJUNCTION)] —**conjunctival** *adj*

conjunctive /kən júngktiv/ *adj* **1.** CONNECTIVE serving to join things **2.** COMBINED joined or combined with something else **3.** GRAM OF GRAMMATICAL CONJUNCTIONS relating to conjunctions or their grammatical function, or consisting of conjunctions [15C. < late Latin *conjunctivus* < Latin *conjunct-* (see CONJUNCTION)] —**conjunctively** *adv*

conjunctive adverb *n* an adverb or adverbial phrase that is used to connect parts or clauses of a sentence

conjunctive eye movement *n* a simultaneous movement of both eyes in the same direction

conjunctivitis /kən júngkti vítiss/ *n* inflammation of the conjunctiva caused by infection, injury, or allergy

conjuration /kónjŏŏ ráysh'n/ *n* **1.** SUPPOSED MAGIC TRICK a supposed magic or supernatural occurrence achieved by pronouncing a spell or chanting **2.** MAGIC SPELL a word or phrase that a magician says when casting a spell (*literary*) **3.** INVOCATION OF SUPPOSED SUPERNATURAL FORCE a summoning or invoking, usually of a supposed supernatural force, by pronouncing a sacred name (*literary*) **4.** PERFORMANCE OF TRICKS the performance of illusions or tricks (*archaic*)

conjure /kúnjər/ (**-jures, -juring, -jured**) *v* **1.** *vi* PERFORM MAGIC TRICKS to perform illusions and magic tricks that require agile hand movements, usually for entertainment **2.** *vti* INVOKE SUPPOSED SUPERNATURAL FORCES to call upon or order a supposed supernatural force or being by reciting a spell ○ *He was struck dumb by the very demons he was conjuring.* **3.** *vt* INFLUENCE SOMETHING WITH SPELL to change or influence something by reciting a spell or invocation **4.** /kən jŏŏr/ *vt* BEG SOMEBODY to implore somebody to do something (*archaic*) ○ *I conjure you to show me mercy.* **5.** *vt* ORDER SOMEBODY to command somebody solemnly to do something (*archaic*) [13C. Via French < Latin *conjurare* 'bind with an oath', literally 'swear together' < *jurare* (see JURY)]

conjure up *vt* **1.** EVOKE SOMETHING to create something in the mind ○ *This music conjures up images of rural scenes.* **2.** PRODUCE SOMETHING AS IF BY MAGIC to produce or create something difficult or unexpected as if by magic ○ *She conjured up a delicious meal from the most basic ingredients.* **3.** SUMMON SUPPOSED SUPERNATURAL BEING to call upon a supposed supernatural force or being by reciting a spell or chanting magic words

conjurer /kúnjərər/, **conjuror** *n* **1.** an entertainer who performs tricks involving manual agility and the illusion of magic **2.** a magician, or somebody who summons supposed supernatural forces or beings

conjuring /kúnjəring/ *n* the performance of tricks that involve manual agility or the illusion of magic, as an entertainment

conjuror *n* another spelling of **conjurer**

conk[1] /kongk/ (*slang*) *n* **1.** HEAD the head or the nose **2.** BLOW TO HEAD a blow, especially on the head or, less commonly, the nose ■ *vt* (**conks, conking, conked**) HIT SOMEBODY to hit somebody, especially on the head or nose [Early 19C. Origin ?]

conk[2] /kongk/ (**conks, conking, conked**) [Early 20C. Origin ?]

conk out *vi* (*informal*) **1.** to stop operating or break down suddenly ○ *The car conked out at the traffic lights.* **2.** to collapse or fall asleep, usually through exhaustion ○ *I conked out the minute I got home.*

conker /kóngkər/ *n UK* a horse chestnut without its spiny outer casing, used in the game of conkers [Mid-19C. Probably blend of CONCH, CONK[1] + CONQUER]

conkers /kóngkərz/ *n* a children's game, usually for two people, in which each player has a conker threaded onto a string and uses it to try to smash the opponent's conker. The game used to be played with snail shells instead of horse chestnuts. (*takes a singular verb*)

con man *n* a confidence trickster (*informal*) [Shortening of CONFIDENCE]

con moto /kon mṓt ṓ/ *adv* in a lively or brisk way

(*used as a musical direction*) [Early 19C. < Italian, 'with movement']

Connacht /kónnawt, -nət/, **Connaught** province comprising the counties of Galway, Leitrim, Mayo, Roscommon, and Sligo on the western coast of the Republic of Ireland. Population: 464,296 (2002). Area: 17,122 sq. km/6,611 sq. mi.

connate /kónn ayt/ *adj* **1.** describes parts that have grown closely joined to a single structure in a plant or animal **2.** describes water, usually very saline, that has been trapped in sedimentary rock since the original deposits were laid down [Mid-17C. < late Latin *connatus*, past participle of *connasci* 'be born with' < Latin *nasci* 'be born'] —**connately** *adv* —**connateness** *n*

Connaught another spelling of **Connacht**

connect /kə nékt/ (**-nects, -necting, -nected**) *v* **1.** *vti* LINK TWO THINGS to join two or more people, things, or parts together ○ *Connect these two wires and it should work.* ○ *A flagstone walk connected the main house with the tool shed.* **2.** *vt* ASSOCIATE SOMEBODY OR SOMETHING WITH ANOTHER to make a psychological or emotional association between people, things, or events ○ *She always connected that house with family celebrations.* **3.** *vi* GET ON WELL to develop a good rapport with somebody ○ *The interview was a disaster – we never really connected.* **4.** *vi* HIT FIRMLY to strike, punch, or kick firmly, with good contact between the striking surface and the object struck (*informal*) ○ *The punch connected, and he sank to the ground.* **5.** *vt* TELECOM ESTABLISH TELECOMMUNICATION LINK FOR SOMEBODY to set up a communication link between people, organizations, or places ○ *connected to the Internet* **6.** *vt* UTIL LINK SOMEBODY OR SOMETHING TO UTILITY to link people or equipment to a source of electricity, water, or gas ○ *Have the gas board connected you yet?* ○ *The appliance should not be connected to the mains.* **7.** *vi* TRANSP ALLOW TIME FOR PASSENGERS TO TRANSFER to arrive shortly before another vehicle or vessel departs, or shortly after another arrives, so as to allow passengers to change from one to the other ○ *This train connects with another one going to the city centre.* **8.** *vi* TRANSP MAKE TRANSPORT CONNECTION to change from one vehicle or vessel to another ○ *those wishing to connect to a long-haul flight* [15C. < Latin *connectere* 'tie together' < *nectere* 'bind'] —**connectible** *adj* —**connector** *n*

connect up *vti* same as **connect** (senses 1, 8)

connected /kə néktid/ *adj* **1.** JOINED TOGETHER joined or linked firmly together **2.** RELATED having something in common ○ *The two incidents are probably connected.* **3.** WITH WEALTHY RELATIVES having upper-class or wealthy relatives (*often used in combination*) ○ *Her husband is well connected.* **4.** WITH BENEFICIAL SOCIAL CONNECTIONS having useful business or social connections (*often used in combination*) **5.** LOGICAL AND INTELLIGIBLE ordered in a logical and intelligible way **6.** MATHS DESCRIBING MATHEMATICAL RELATION describes a mathematical relation for which either the relation or its converse is true for any two members in a set —**connectedly** *adv* —**connectedness** *n*

Connecticut /kə néttikət/ **1.** southernmost state in New England, United States. It is bordered on the north by Massachusetts, on the east by Rhode Island, on the south by the Long Island Sound, and on the west by New York State. Population: 3,460,503 (2002 estimate). Area: 14,359 sq. km/5,544 sq. mi. **2.** longest river of New England, flowing southwards from Massachusetts to enter Long Island Sound. Length: 655 km/407 mi.

Connecticut Wits *npl* LITERAT same as **Hartford Wits**

connecting rod /kə nékting-/ *n* a rod that transmits motion, especially the rod that connects the crankshaft to the piston in an internal-combustion engine

connection /kə néksh'n/, **connexion** *n* **1.** LINKING OF PEOPLE OR THINGS the joining together of two or more people, things, or parts **2.** PHYSICAL LINK something that links two or more things ○ *check for a loose connection* **3.** LOGICAL LINK a linking association between people, things, or events ○ *denied any connection with terrorist organizations* **4.** CONTEXT the relationship of something with its context ○ *In this connection, we need to tighten up safety procedures in general.* **5.** INFLUENTIAL CONTACT a friend, relative, or associate who either has, or has access to, influence or power (*often used in the plural*) ○ *She used her connections to get an interview with the lead singer.* **6.** RELATION a relative, usually a distant relative or by marriage (*often used in the plural*) ○ *The family's English but they have Spanish connections.* **7.** TRANSPORT LINK an occasion when passengers change from one vehicle or vessel to another ○ *If we don't hurry, we'll miss our connection in Paris.* **8.** VEHICLE SCHEDULED TO PERMIT TRANSFER a particular bus, train, ferry, or plane that is scheduled to arrive at such a time as to allow passengers to transfer onto it from another scheduled form of transport ○ *Your connection will arrive on platform ten at 9.15.* **9.** COMMUNICATION LINK a communication link, especially between telephones **10.** SUPPLIER OF ILLEGAL SUBSTANCES a supplier of illegal substances, usually drugs (*slang*) ■ **connections** *npl* CONTROLLERS OF RACEHORSE the owners or controllers of a racehorse [14C. < Latin *connexion-* < *connex-*, past participle of *connectere* (see CONNECT)] —**connectional** *adj*

connectionism /kə néksh'nizəm/ *n* the theory that thoughts and behaviour are based on patterns of stimulus and response that have been either inherited or learnt

connective /kə néktiv/ *adj* LINKING joining two or more people, things, or parts ■ *n* **1.** LINK something that joins two or more people, things, or parts **2.** GRAM LINKING WORD a word that links sentences, phrases, clauses, or words **3.** BOT STAMEN TISSUE the tissue that joins the two lobes of an anther in the stamen of a plant —**connectively** *adv*

connective tissue *n* animal tissue that supports, connects, and surrounds organs and other body parts and consists mainly of collagen, elastic and reticular fibres, fatty tissue, cartilage, or bone

connectivity /kónnek tívvəti/ *n* the ability to communicate with another system or piece of hardware or software, or with an Internet site

connect-the-dots *adj US* (*slang*) **1.** gathering information or facts from different sources to make a coherent whole ○ *The article was a model of connect-the-dots journalism.* **2.** straightforward or obvious ○ *It's a connect-the-dots problem, easily solvable.* [< producing a picture by connecting printed dots]

connect time *n* the period of time a user is logged on to a remote computer, e.g. when browsing the Internet

Connemara /kónnə maárə/ mountainous coastal area of Galway, in the western part of the Republic of Ireland

Connery /kónnəri/, **Sean** (*b.* 1930) Scottish film actor. He played the starring role in several James Bond films and won an Academy Award for best supporting actor for *The Untouchables* (1987). Full name **Connery, Thomas Sean**

> 'My only grumble about the Bond films is that they don't tax one as an actor. All one really needs is the constitution of a rugby player to get through those 19 weeks of swimming, slugging, and necking.'
> [Sean Connery, *Interview, The Sunday Express*; 14 February 1965]

connexion *n* another spelling of **connection**

conning tower /kónning-/ *n* **1.** a structure on the top of a submarine that is used as the navigation bridge and main point of entrance **2.** the armoured pilot house in the shape of a low dome found on the deck of a warship [< CON 5]

conniption /kə nípsh'n/ *n N Am* a hysterical fit caused by extreme excitement or anger (*informal*; *often used in the plural*) [Mid-19C. Origin ?]

connivance /kə nívənss/ *n* **1.** secret joint conspiracy or plotting **2.** unspoken encouragement of or consent to wrongdoing by somebody else

connive /kə nív/ (**-nives, -niving, -nived**) *vi* **1.** to plan secretly to do something, usually something wrong or illegal **2.** to pretend not to know about or do nothing to stop a wrongful or illegal act, thus showing encouragement of or consent to the act ○ *suspected of conniving in the leaking of a sensitive document* [Early 17C. Via French < Latin *connivere* 'close your eyes'] —**conniver** *n* —**connivery** *n*

connivent /kə nív'nt/ *adj* describes insect wings and flower petals or stamens that converge and touch but remain separate and not fused

conniving /kə níving/ *adj* devious and scheming —**connivingly** *adv*

~~**connoiseur**~~ incorrect spelling of **connoisseur**

connoisseur /kónnə súr/ *n* an expert in an area of the fine or domestic arts, or somebody with discriminating taste in such a speciality [Early 18C. < French < *connoistre* 'know' < Latin *cognoscere* (see COGNITION)]

Connolly /kónn'li/, **Maureen** (1934–69) US tennis player. She was the first woman to win all four grand slam tournaments in one year (1953). Full name **Connolly, Maureen Catherine**. Known as **Little Mo**

Connors /kónnərz/, **Jimmy** (*b.* 1952) US tennis player. He won 109 professional singles titles, including eight grand slam tournaments, during the 1970s and 1980s. Full name **Connors, James Scott**. Known as **Jimbo**

> 'They can give all the coaching they want. But once a guy gets down there on court, he's got to hit the ball himself.'
> [Jimmy Connors, *The Times*; 5 June 1984]

connotation /kónnə táysh'n/ *n* **1.** IMPLIED ADDITIONAL MEANING an additional sense or senses associated with or suggested by a word or phrase. Connotations are sometimes, but not always, fixed, and are often subjective. ○ *Patriotism can have some negative connotations for people.* **2.** SUGGESTING OF ADDITIONAL MEANING FOR WORD the implying or suggesting of an additional meaning for a word or phrase apart from the literal or main meaning **3.** DEFINING CHARACTERISTIC in logic, the characteristic or set of characteristics that makes up the meaning of a term and thus defines the objects to which a term can be applied —**connotative** /kónnə taytiv, kə nṓtətiv/ *adj* —**connotatively** *adv*

connote /kə nṓt/ (**-notes, -noting, -noted**) *vt* **1.** to imply or suggest something in addition to the literal or main meaning ○ *The word 'hearth' often connotes cosiness and warmth.* **2.** to imply something else as a condition or a consequence ○ *His reluctance to act connotes cowardice.* [Mid-17C. < medieval Latin *connotare* 'mark along with' < Latin *notare* 'to mark' < *nota* 'sign']

USAGE ***connote*** **or** ***denote*****?** ***Denote*** refers to the literal or main meaning of a word, whereas ***connote*** refers to its implications or associations. The word *family*, for example, *denotes* a group of people related by blood or marriage but *connotes* the bonds of affection, trust, and loyalty that unite them.

---

connubial /kə nyóobi əl/ *adj* relating to marriage (*literary*) [Mid-17C. < Latin *connubialis* 'relating to marriage' < *connubium* 'marriage' < *nubere* 'marry'] —**connubially** *adv*

conodont /kṓnə dont, kónnə-/ *n* a very small tooth-shaped fossil thought to be the remains of a marine organism. Conodonts are commonly found in marine limestone beds from the Palaeozoic era and are used by geologists to date rock layers. [Mid-19C. < Greek *kōnos* 'cone']

conquer /kóngkər/ (**-quers, -quering, -quered**) *v* **1.** *vt* SEIZE AREA BY MILITARY FORCE to take control of a place by force of arms ○ *The Normans conquered England in 1066.* **2.** *vt* DEFEAT PEOPLE IN WAR to win a victory over a people in war **3.** *vt* MASTER SOMETHING DIFFICULT to overcome a difficulty, problem, or illness ○ *conquered his fear of heights* ○ *hoping to show that a zero tolerance policy can conquer street crime* **4.** *vt* CLIMB MOUNTAIN to make a difficult or dangerous mountain ascent ○ *the first woman to conquer Everest* **5.** *vt* WIN SOMEBODY'S ADMIRATION to win somebody's love, affection, or admiration, often through strength of character or seduction, and sometimes somewhat against the person's will ○ *By the end of the last song, she had conquered their hearts.* **6.** *vi* WIN to be victorious [13C. Via Old French *conquerre* < Latin *conquirere* 'seek for, procure' < *quaerere* 'seek'] —**conquerable** *adj*

SYNONYMS See *defeat*.

---

conqueror /kóngkərər/ *n* **1.** a victor in a war **2.** a victor in a competitive event

conquest /kóng kwest/ *n* **1.** SUBJUGATION OF ENEMY the process of taking control of a place or people by force of arms **2.** SOMETHING ACQUIRED BY CONQUERING something that has been acquired through force of arms, e.g. land, people, or goods **3.** SOMEBODY WON OVER somebody whose love, affection, or admiration has been won, often through strength of character or seduction, and sometimes somewhat against the per-

son's will ○ *was another of his many conquests* [13C. Via Old French < Vulgar Latin *conquaesita*, literally 'sought diligently' < Latin *quaerere* 'seek']

conquistador /kon kwístə dawr, -kístə-/ (*plural* **-quistadors** or **-quistadores** /-dáwr áyz) *n* a Spanish conqueror or adventurer, especially one of those who conquered Mexico, Peru, and Central America in the 16th century [Mid-19C. < Spanish < Latin *conquirere* (see CONQUER)]

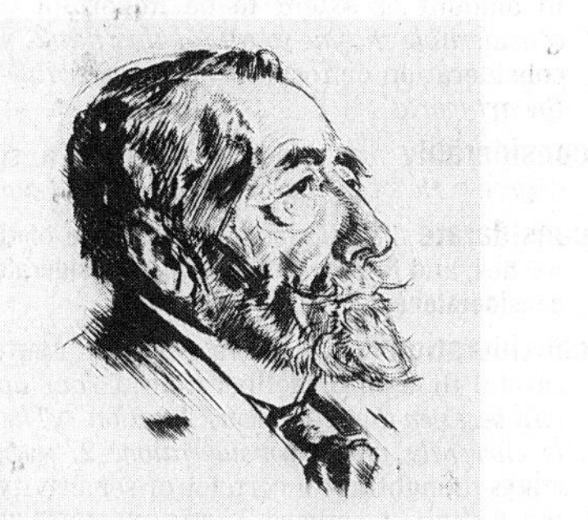
AKG London
Joseph Conrad

Conrad /kón rad/, **Joseph** (1857–1924) Polish-born British writer. His novels and stories include *Nostromo* (1904), *Lord Jim* (1900), and *Heart of Darkness* (1902). See Cultural note at **heart**

> 'You shall judge of a man by his foes as well as by his friends.'
> [Joseph Conrad, *Lord Jim*; 1900]

Conran /kónnrən/, **Sir Terence** (*b.* 1931) British designer and retailer. The opening of his first Habitat shop in 1964 marked a significant change in British attitudes to design and the marketing of household wares. Full name **Conran, Terence Orby**

> 'Design occupies a unique space between art and science. Designers must be sensitive to what is technically possible and what is humanly desirable.'
> [Sir Terence Conran, *Terence Conran on Design*; 1996]

cons. *abbr* **1.** RELIG consecrated **2.** MAIL consigned **3.** MAIL consignment **4.** LING consonant **5.** *also* **cons** POL constitution **6.** POL constitutional

Cons. *abbr* **1.** POL Conservative **2.** POLICE Constable **3.** **Cons** POL Constitution **4.** INTERNAT REL Consul

consanguinity /kón sang gwínnəti/ *n* **1.** relationship by descent from the same ancestor, and not by marriage or affinity **2.** a close relationship or connection —**consanguineous** *adj*

conscience /kónsh'nss/ *n* **1. SENSE OF RIGHT AND WRONG** the sense of what is right and wrong that governs somebody's thoughts and actions, urging him or her to do right rather than wrong ○ *Let your conscience be your guide.* **2. OBEDIENCE TO CONSCIENCE** behaviour according to what your sense of right and wrong tells you is right ○ *campaigning on behalf of prisoners of conscience* **3. SHARED MORAL VIEWPOINT** a shared concern for moral issues ○ *a social conscience* **4.** PSYCHOANAL **PART OF SUPEREGO** the part of the superego that passes judgments on thought and behaviour to the ego for further consideration [13C. Via Old French < Latin *conscientia* 'consciousness' < *conscire* 'be conscious', literally 'know thoroughly' < *scire* 'know'] ◇ **in all** *or* **good conscience 1.** while being fair and reasonable **2.** used to emphasize that what you are saying is truly the case ◇ **on somebody's conscience** causing somebody to feel guilty or anxious about something

USAGE See ***conscientious.***

conscience clause *n* a clause in an act, law, or contract that exempts those who have moral or religious objections from complying

conscience money *n* money paid voluntarily in compensation for a previous act of wrongdoing by which somebody has been harmed

conscience-stricken, conscience-smitten *adj* feeling guilty or anxious about having done something wrong

~~**conscientious**~~ incorrect spelling of **conscientious**

conscientious /kónshi énshəss/ *adj* **1.** showing great care, attention, and industriousness in carrying out a task or role ○ *a conscientious parent* **2.** governed by or done according to somebody's sense of right and wrong ○ *a conscientious decision to dedicate an hour a week to charity* [Early 17C. Via French < medieval Latin *conscientiosus* < Latin *conscientia* (see CONSCIENCE)] —**conscientiously** *adv* —**conscientiousness** *n*

USAGE conscientious or **conscious**? If you are ***conscious*** you are awake or aware: *The patient is conscious. We are conscious of the danger.* ***Conscious*** can also mean 'deliberate, intentional', as in *We made a conscious* [not *conscientious*] *move to win the championship.* If you are ***conscientious*** you are diligent and thorough, or governed by your conscience or own sense of ethics: *Conscientious students study diligently. I made a conscientious* [not *conscious*] *effort to contribute to fund-raising events.* Both these adjectives can modify nouns like *decision* and *effort*, but the writer must ensure that the context is clear. A *conscious decision/effort* is one made intentionally and deliberately (*a conscious decision/effort to disregard all risks*); a *conscientious decision/effort* is one involving an ethical judgment (*a conscientious decision/effort to right wrongs when we see them*).

SYNONYMS See ***careful.***

conscientious objector *n* somebody who, for moral or religious reasons, believes it is wrong to wage war and therefore refuses to join any branch of the armed services

conscious /kónshəss/ *adj* **1. AWAKE** awake and responsive to stimuli ○ *He's been seriously injured but he's still conscious.* **2. KEENLY AWARE** fully appreciating the importance of something ○ *I'm conscious of all that you've done for us.* **3. INTENTIONAL** considered and deliberate, or done with critical awareness ○ *a conscious effort not to lose her temper* **4. WELL-INFORMED** well-informed on issues relating to a particular topic of serious significance (*often used in combination with adverbs*) ○ *environmentally conscious* **5. CONCERNED WITH SOMETHING** aware of and interested in a particular topic (*often used hyphenated in combination*) ○ *fashion-conscious* ○ *health-conscious* **6.** PSYCHOL **FUNCTIONING WITH INDIVIDUAL'S KNOWLEDGE** relating to or concerned with a part of the mind that is capable of thinking, choosing, or perceiving ■ *n* PSYCHOL **AREA OF MIND AWARE OF SURROUNDINGS** the part of the human mind that is aware of the feelings, thoughts, and surroundings [Late 16C. < Latin *conscius* 'knowing' < *scire* 'know'] —**consciously** *adv*

USAGE See ***conscientious.***

SYNONYMS See ***aware.***

consciousness /kónshəssnəss/ *n* **1. AWARENESS OF SURROUNDINGS** the state of being awake and aware of what is going on around you ○ *feelings of dizziness followed by loss of consciousness* **2. SOMEBODY'S MIND** somebody's mind and thoughts ○ *In time, this experience will fade from your consciousness.* **3. SHARED FEELINGS AND BELIEFS** the set of opinions, feelings, and beliefs of a group ○ *national consciousness* **4. AWARENESS OF PARTICULAR ISSUE** awareness of or sensitivity to a particular issue ○ *health consciousness*

USAGE See ***conscientious.***

consciousness-raising *n* **1.** the process of increasing people's awareness of a moral or social issue with a view to encouraging them to take action **2.** the increasing of self-awareness, usually through group therapy —**consciousness-raiser** *n*

conscript *vt* /kən skrípt/ (**-scripts, -scripting, -scripted**) to enrol somebody compulsorily in the armed forces ■ *n* /kón skript/ a recruit who has been compulsorily enrolled, especially in the armed forces [15C. < Latin *conscript-*, past participle of *conscribere* 'enrol' < *scribere* 'write']

conscription /kən skrípsh'n/ *n* the obligatory enrolment of citizens in the armed forces

consecrate /kónssi krayt/ (**-crates, -crating, -crated**) *vt* **1.** RELIG **DECLARE PLACE HOLY** to declare or set apart a building, area of ground, or specific spot as holy ○ *The cathedral was consecrated in the 12th century.* **2. DEDICATE SOMETHING TO PARTICULAR PURPOSE** to dedicate somebody or something to a particular purpose **3. MAKE CUSTOM REVERED** to cause a custom to be revered **4.** CHR **BLESS COMMUNION BREAD AND WINE** to sanctify the bread and wine for use in the Communion service as symbols of the body and blood of Jesus Christ **5.** RELIG **ORDAIN BISHOP** to ordain a priest as a bishop [14C. < Latin *consecrat-*, past participle of *consecrare* 'make sacred' < *sacer* 'sacred'] —**consecrative** *adj* —**consecrator** *n* —**consecratory** /kónssi kráytəri/ *adj*

consecration /kónssi kráysh'n/ *n* the ceremony in which somebody or something is consecrated

Consecration *n* the process or ceremony of sanctifying the bread and wine during Communion

consecutive /kən sékyootiv/ *adj* **1.** following one after another without interruption or break ○ *He's been off work now for three consecutive days.* **2.** following a logical or chronological sequence [Early 17C. Via French < medieval Latin *consecutivus* < Latin *consecut-*, past participle of *consequi* (see CONSEQUENT)] —**consecutively** *adv* —**consecutiveness** *n*

consensual /kən sénssyoo əl/ *adj* **1. BY MUTUAL CONSENT** involving the agreement of all involved **2.** LAW **REQUIRING CONSENT ONLY** used to describe an agreement requiring only the consent of the parties involved to make it binding **3.** PHYSIOL **RESPONDING INVOLUNTARILY TO INDIRECT STIMULUS** describes an involuntary response by one body part to a stimulus to another, e.g. the pupil of one eye constricting when the other eye is exposed to light [Mid-18C. < Latin *consens-*, past participle of *consentire* (see CONSENT)] —**consensually** *adv*

consensus /kən sénssəss/ *n* **1.** general or widespread agreement among all the members of a group ○ *After hours of deliberation, they finally reached a consensus.* **2.** a concept of society in which the absence of conflict is seen as the equilibrium state of society [Mid-17C. < Latin < past participle of *consentire* (see CONSENT)]

USAGE The word ***consensus*** is often misspelt *concensus*, probably from the erroneous influence of the word *census*.

USAGE Since ***consensus*** already means 'a view or opinion that is generally shared', expressions such as *general consensus* and *consensus of opinion* are, strictly speaking, tautologies (i.e. they say the same thing twice), and the modifiers 'general' and 'of opinion' are redundant. However, occasionally a modifier can be justified, as in *There was a consensus of feeling, but no consensus of opinion.* It is always best to begin by considering whether or not the word without modifiers expresses what you mean.

consent /kən sént/ *vi* (**-sents, -senting, -sented**) **1. GIVE PERMISSION** to give formal permission for something to happen ○ *As soon as they met Robert, her parents consented to the marriage.* **2. AGREE** to agree to do something ○ *She consented to appear as a witness.* ■ *n* **1. PERMISSION FOR SOMETHING** acceptance of or agreement to something proposed or desired by another **2. CONSENSUS** agreement on an opinion or course of action ○ *It was by common consent the best.* [13C. Via Old French < Latin *consentire* 'feel with' < *sentire* 'feel'] —**consenter** *n*

SYNONYMS See ***agree.***

consenting adult /kən sénting-/ *n* somebody who is old enough to be allowed to participate legally in something and is willing to do so, especially in a sexual activity

~~**consentrate**~~ incorrect spelling of **concentrate**

consequence /kónssikwənss/ *n* **1. RESULT** something that follows as a result ○ *This is a direct consequence of your negligence.* **2. RELATION BETWEEN CAUSE AND EFFECT** the relation between a result and its cause **3. IMPORTANCE** importance or significance (*formal; often used in negative statements*) ○ *Your opinion is of no consequence whatsoever to me.* **4. LOGICAL CONCLUSION** a conclusion reached through valid deductive reasoning [14C. Via French < Latin *consequentia* < *consequi* (see CONSEQUENT)] ◇ **in consequence** as a result of something (*formal*)

consequences /kónssikwənssiz/ *npl* the unpleasant or difficult results of a previous action (*takes a plural verb*) ■ *n* a game in which each player in turn writes down a line of a story about two people, their meeting, and its consequences, without knowing what the previous lines are. The intention is to produce incongruous and therefore humorous juxtapositions, which are discovered when the completed stories are read out loud. (*takes a singular verb*)

consequent /kónssikwənt/ *adj* **1.** FOLLOWING AS RESULT following as a result or effect ○ *weeks of rain and the consequent flooding* **2.** LOGIC AS LOGICAL CONCLUSION following as a logical conclusion ■ *n* **1.** LOGIC RESULT OF SOMETHING something that follows as a result **2.** LOGIC SECOND HALF OF CONDITIONAL SENTENCE the part of a conditional sentence that expresses the result and is the q clause in a proposition of the form 'if p then q' **3.** MATHS SECOND TERM OF RATIO the second term in a mathematical ratio [15C. Via French < Latin *consequent-*, present participle of *consequi* 'follow along with' < *sequi* 'follow']

consequential /kónssi kwénsh'l/ *adj* **1.** RESULTANT following as a consequence or result of something **2.** IMPORTANT of considerable importance, significance, or value ○ *a consequential figure on the classical music circuit* **3.** TOO SELF-IMPORTANT having an exaggerated opinion of personal qualities or abilities **4.** INSUR ARISING AS INDIRECT COST describes costs, loss, or damage beyond the market value of the object lost or damaged, including other indirect costs arising —**consequentiality** /kónssi kwénshi álləti/ *n* —**consequentially** *adv*

consequentialism /kónsi kwénsh'lizəm/ *n* the tenet by which an action is considered right or wrong depending on whether its outcome is good or bad

consequently /kónssikwəntli/ *adv* as a result or in view of something ○ *The joke backfired and the relationship consequently deteriorated.*

~~**consern**~~ incorrect spelling of **concern**

conservancy /kən súrv'nssi/ (*plural* **-cies**) *n* a commission, court, or board with authority to regulate and protect a waterway, port, or area of countryside, and often also its wildlife

conservation /kónssər váysh'n/ *n* **1.** the preservation, management, and care of natural and cultural resources **2.** the keeping or protecting of something from change, loss, or damage —**conservational** *adj*

conservation area *n* an area of special environmental or historical importance that is protected from casual changes by law

conservationist /kónssər váysh'nist/ *n* a supporter of or advocate for the preservation of the environment, especially the natural world

conservation of charge *n* the principle that the total electric charge of an isolated system remains constant, no matter what internal changes take place

conservation of energy *n* the principle that the amount of energy in an isolated system remains the same, even though the form of energy may change

conservation of mass, conservation of matter *n* the principle that the total mass of an isolated system remains constant, in spite of any physical or chemical changes that may take place

conservation of momentum *n* the principle that the total linear or angular momentum of an isolated system remains the same

conservatism /kən súrvətizəm/ *n* **1.** RELUCTANCE TO ACCEPT CHANGE unwillingness or slowness to accept change or new ideas **2.** RIGHT-WING POLITICAL VIEWPOINT a right-of-centre political philosophy based on a tendency to support gradual rather than abrupt change and to preserve the status quo **3.** DESIRE TO PRESERVE CURRENT SOCIETAL STRUCTURE an ideology that views the existing form of society as worthy of preservation

Conservatism *n* the principles and practice of Conservative politicians or supporters

conservative /kən súrvətiv/ *adj* **1.** RELUCTANT TO ACCEPT CHANGE in favour of preserving the status quo and traditional values and customs, and against abrupt change **2.** OF CONSERVATISM relating to, characteristic of, or displaying conservatism **3.** CAUTIOUS AND ON LOW SIDE cautiously moderate and therefore often less than the final outcome ○ *Several hundred pounds is probably a very conservative estimate.* **4.** CONVENTIONAL IN APPEARANCE conventional or restrained in style and avoiding showiness ○ *a conservative business suit* **5.** USING MINIMUM MEDICAL INTERVENTION designed to help relieve symptoms or preserve health with a minimum of medical intervention ■ *n* **1.** TRADITIONALIST a supporter or advocate of traditional ideas and behaviour **2.** SUPPORTER OF CONSERVATISM somebody who believes in or supports conservatism —**conservatively** *adv* —**conservativeness** *n*

Conservative *adj* **1.** OF CONSERVATIVE PARTY relating to, belonging to, or supporting a Conservative Party **2.** OF CONSERVATIVE JUDAISM relating to, associated with, or characteristic of Conservative Judaism ■ *n* SUPPORTER OF CONSERVATIVE PARTY a member or supporter of a Conservative Party

Conservative Judaism *n* a form of Judaism that accepts most of the principles and practices of traditional Judaism but supports the modification and relaxing of some laws. The movement arose around the turn of the 20th century as a reaction against the more liberal Reform Judaism.

Conservative Party *n* (*takes a singular or plural verb*) **1.** MAIN UK RIGHT-WING POLITICAL PARTY in the United Kingdom, the principal right-of-centre political party. It supports low personal taxation, home ownership, and free-market principles. It was founded in the early 1830s as a successor to the Tory Party. **2.** CANADIAN RIGHT-WING POLITICAL PARTY in Canada, the Conservative Party of Canada, or, formerly, the Progressive Conservative Party **3.** POLITICAL PARTY OPPOSED TO CHANGE in countries other than the United Kingdom and Canada, a political party that is opposed to change

Conservative Party of Canada *n* a Canadian political party established in 2003 when members of the Progressive Conservative Party and the Canadian Alliance voted for union. It believes in a united Canada under the British monarchy, free trade, and emphasis on the rights and responsibilities of individuals.

conservatoire /kən súrvə twaar/ *n* MUSIC same as **conservatory** (sense 2) [Late 18C. Via French < Italian *conservatorio* < late Latin *conservatorium* (see CONSERVATORY)]

conservator /kən súrvətər/ *n* **1.** somebody who preserves or restores works of art or other valued objects in a museum or collection **2.** a person or institution responsible for protecting the interests of a legal incompetent, e.g. under a protective trust —**conservatorial** /kən súrvə táwri əl/ *adj*

conservatorium /kən súrvə táwri əm/ (*plural* **-ums** or **-a** /-ə/) *n Aus* MUSIC same as **conservatory** (sense 2) [Mid-19C. Via German < late Latin (see CONSERVATORY)]

conservatory /kən súrvətəri/ (*plural* **-ries**) *n* **1.** a room with glass walls and roof where plants are grown or displayed, often built onto the side of a house **2.** an institution or school where students are taught one of the arts, most commonly music or drama, to a professional standard [Mid-16C. < late Latin *conservatorium* < Latin *conservare* (see CONSERVE)]

conserve *vt* /kən súrv/ (**-serves, -serving, -served**) **1.** PROTECT SOMETHING FROM HARM OR DECAY to keep something, especially an important environmental or cultural resource, from harm, loss, change, or decay ○ *the importance of conserving our national heritage* **2.** USE SOMETHING SPARINGLY to use something sparingly so as not to exhaust supplies ○ *some drastic measures to conserve water* **3.** PRESERVE FOOD IN SUGAR to preserve food, especially fruit, in sugar **4.** KEEP MATTER OR ENERGY CONSTANT to keep something such as matter or energy constant through physical changes or chemical reactions ■ *n* /kón surv, kən súrv/ FRUIT IN SYRUP a food consisting of fruit in a thick sugar syrup, like jam but less firmly set and usually containing larger pieces of fruit [14C. Via French < Latin *conservare* 'preserve well' < *servare* 'keep'] —**conservable** *adj* —**conserver** *n*

~~**consession**~~ incorrect spelling of **concession**

Consett /kónssit, -set/ former mining and steel town in County Durham, northern England. Population: 20,148 (1991).

consider /kən síddər/ (**-ers, -ering, -ered**) *v* **1.** *vti* REFLECT ON SOMETHING to think carefully about something ○ *You should consider your next move carefully.* ○ *time to consider whether this is what you really want* **2.** *vt* JUDGE SOMETHING to have something as an opinion or point of view ○ *He considers himself lucky to be alive.* ○ *I consider it unlikely that they'll accept our proposal.* **3.** *vt* RESPECT SOMEBODY OR SOMETHING to show respect for or be thoughtful of somebody's feelings or position ○ *They never seem to consider the feelings of others.* **4.** *vt* WEIGH UP POSSIBILITIES BEFORE DECIDING to weigh up the pros and cons of a situation before making a decision on a course of action ○ *I'm considering my options.* ○ *They're considering buying a new house.* **5.** *vt* EXAMINE AND DISCUSS PROBLEM to examine a problem and discuss it in detail ○ *On this week's show, we're going to consider the following question.* **6.** *vt* TAKE SOMETHING INTO ACCOUNT to take something into account, often in a sympathetic way ○ *We've done rather well, all things considered.* **7.** *vt* LOOK CAREFULLY AT SOMETHING to look at something carefully and with concentration (*formal*) [14C. Via French < Latin *considerare*] —**considered** *adj* —**considerer** *n*

considerable /kən síddərəb'l/ *adj* **1.** large enough in amount or extent to be important ○ *needs a considerable income to afford this flat* **2.** worthy of consideration or respect ○ *a considerable figure in the art world*

considerably /kən síddərəbli/ *adv* to a significant degree ○ *He's considerably older than I am.*

considerate /kən síddərət/ *adj* mindful of the needs, wishes, and feelings of others —**considerately** *adv* —**considerateness** *n*

consideration /kən síddə ráysh'n/ *n* **1.** CAREFUL THOUGHT careful thought or deliberation ○ *Your application will be given the fullest consideration.* ○ *The proposal is currently under consideration.* **2.** MINDFULNESS OF OTHERS thoughtful concern for or sensitivity towards the feelings of others **3.** RELEVANT FACTOR IN ASSESSING SOMETHING something to be taken into account when weighing up the pros and cons of a situation before making a decision ○ *Value for money is one of the most important considerations for our customers.* **4.** DETAILED EXAMINATION detailed discussion or scrutiny ○ *The issue for consideration on today's show is cosmetic surgery.* **5.** PAYMENT a payment or fee in return for a service (*formal*) **6.** RESPECT high regard (*formal*) ○ *She has always been held in great consideration by this congregation.* **7.** SOMETHING MAKING CONTRACT BINDING something done by one of the parties as part of a contractual arrangement that makes it binding, e.g. the payment of the price in a contract of sale ◇ **in consideration of** (*formal*) **1.** because of **2.** as payment for ◇ **of little** *or* **no consideration** not important or significant (*formal*) ◇ **take something into consideration** to take account of special circumstances, often in a sympathetic way

considering /kən síddəring/ *prep, conj* taking something into account ○ *It's a tremendous bargain, considering the price and how much we need one.* ■ *adv* taking everything into account, often in a sympathetic way (*usually used at the end of a phrase or sentence*) ○ *We've done a really good job, considering.*

~~**consience**~~ incorrect spelling of **conscience**

consigliere /kón seel yáiri/ (*plural* **-siglieri** /-seel yáiri/) *n N Am* an adviser to the leader of a crime syndicate [Early 17C. < Italian < Latin *consilium* (see COUNSEL)]

consign /kən sīn/ (**-signs, -signing, -signed**) *vt* **1.** ENTRUST SOMEBODY OR SOMETHING to hand somebody or something over to the care of another ○ *The children were consigned to the care of the nanny.* **2.** GET RID OF SOMEBODY OR SOMETHING to dispose of somebody or something, usually for a long time, if not permanently ○ *Before fleeing, they consigned the documents to the flames.* **3.** DELIVER SOMETHING to address, deliver, or hand over for later delivery something for sale, safekeeping, or disposal [15C. Via French < Latin *consignare* 'certify with a seal' < *signum* 'mark'] —**consignable** *adj* —**consignee** /kón sī née/ *n* —**consignor** *n*

consignment /kən sīnmənt/ *n* **1.** DELIVERY a quantity or package of goods delivered or to be delivered **2.** DISPOSAL OF SOMEBODY OR SOMETHING the disposal of somebody or something, usually for a long time, if not permanently **3.** ENTRUSTING OF SOMEBODY OR SOMETHING the handing over of somebody or something to the care of another ◇ **on consignment** on the understanding that payment will be made only when the goods have been sold and that any remaining unsold articles can be returned

~~**consious**~~ incorrect spelling of **conscious**

consist /kən síst/ (**-sists, -sisting, -sisted**) *vi* **1.** to be made up of diverse parts ○ *This dressing consists of oil, lemon juice, and mustard.* **2.** to be based on or defined by something ○ *Her talent consists in her superb musicianship.* [Early 16C. < Latin *consistere* < *sistere* 'make stand' < *stare* 'to stand']

USAGE See ***comprise***.

~~**consistant**~~ incorrect spelling of **consistent**

consistency /kən sístənssi/, **consistence** /-ənss/ *n* **1.**

CONSTANCY the ability to maintain a particular standard or repeat a particular task with minimal variation ○ *Consistency is important in performing this job.* ○*'A foolish consistency is the hobgoblin of small minds.'* (Ralph Waldo Emerson *Self-Reliance*; 1841) **2. COHERENCE** reasonable or logical harmony between parts ○ *The plot lacked consistency.* **3. DEGREE OF THICKNESS OR SMOOTHNESS** the degree of thickness or smoothness of a mixture ○ *Blend the mixture until it reaches the consistency of thick cream.*

consistent /kən sístənt/ *adj* **1. COHERENT** reasonably or logically harmonious ○ *The evidence is consistent with the defendant's statement.* ○ *Their accounts of the incident just aren't consistent.* **2. RELIABLE** able to maintain a particular standard or repeat a particular task with minimal variation ○ *He's one of the most consistent strikers in the league.* **3.** MATHS **WITH COMMON SOLUTIONS** having a set of solutions in common, especially for two or more equations or inequalities **4.** LOGIC **FREE OF CONTRADICTION** containing no provable contradiction [Late 16C. < Latin *consistent-*, present participle of *consistere* (see CONSIST)] —**consistently** *adv*

consistory /kən sístəri/ (*plural* **-ries**) *n* **1.** CHR **ASSEMBLY OF CARDINALS AND POPE** in the Roman Catholic Church, an assembly of cardinals convoked and led by the pope **2.** CHR **ANGLICAN DIOCESAN COURT** in the Anglican Church, the court of any diocese except Canterbury **3.** CHR **CONGREGATIONAL GOVERNING BODY** in some Reformed churches, the governing body of a congregation **4.** CHR **REGULATORY COURT IN LUTHERAN CHURCHES** in Lutheran state churches, a court appointed to regulate ecclesiastical affairs **5. COUNCIL** a council or assembly (*archaic*) [13C. Via Anglo-Norman < late Latin *consistorium* 'place of assembly' < Latin *consistere* (see CONSIST)] —**consistorial** /kónssi stáwri əl/ *adj*

consociate (*formal*) *vti* /kən sṓshi ayt, -sṓssi-/ (**-ates, -ating, -ated**) **JOIN ASSOCIATION** to enter or welcome somebody into a friendly association or alliance ■ *adj* /kən sṓshi ət/ **ASSOCIATED** associated or united ■ *n* /kən sṓshi ət/ **PARTNER** an associate or partner [15C. < Latin *consociat-*, past participle of *consociare* 'associate' < *socius* 'companion']

consociation /kən sṓshi áysh'n, -sṓssi-/ *n* **1. FRIENDLY ASSOCIATION** a friendly association or alliance (*formal*) **2.** ECOL **ECOLOGICAL COMMUNITY WITH ONE MAIN SPECIES** an ecological community that has one dominant species, e.g. a wood consisting predominantly of beech trees **3.** POL **POLITICAL COALITION** a grouping of political parties or pressure groups within a region or country that work together to share power —**consociational** *adj*

consocies /kən sṓsh eez/ (*plural same*) *n* same as **consociation** (sense 2) [Early 20C. Blend of CONSOCIATE + SPECIES]

consolation /kónssə láysh'n/ *n* **1. SOURCE OF COMFORT** a source of comfort to somebody who is upset or disappointed ○ *The fortune she left was little consolation for him.* **2. COMFORT TO SOMEBODY IN DISTRESS** comfort to somebody who is distressed or disappointed ○ *Most of those at the funeral murmured some words of consolation as they left.* **3.** SPORTS, LEISURE **GAME FOR EARLIER LOSERS** a game or contest held for people or teams who have lost earlier in a tournament

consolation prize *n* a prize given to comfort the loser or losers in a game or competition

console[1] /kən sṓl/ (**-soles, -soling, -soled**) *vt* to provide a source of comfort to somebody who is distressed or disappointed [Mid-17C. Via French < Latin *consolare* < *solari* 'to comfort'] —**consolable** *adj* —**consolatory** *adj* —**consoler** *n* —**consolingly** *adv*

USAGE See ***condole.***

console[2] /kón sōl/ *n* **1.** ELECTRONICS **CONTROL PANEL** a desk, table, display, or keyboard onto which the controls of an electronic system or some other machine are fixed **2.** FURNITURE **CABINET FOR TELEVISION OR STEREO** a free-standing cabinet, especially one used to house a television or stereo system **3.** FURNITURE same as **console table** **4.** MUSIC **ORGAN CONTROLS** the part of an organ that houses the keyboards or manuals, pedals, and stops **5.** ARCHIT **ORNAMENTAL BRACKET** an ornamental bracket, often in the shape of a scroll, used for decoration and for supporting wall fixtures **6. PLAYER FOR COMPUTER GAME** an electronic device that connects to a television set on which computer games and DVDs can be played [Mid-17C. < French]

console table /kón sōl-/ *n* a small table with curved legs designed to stand against a wall

consolidate /kən sólli dayt/ (**-dates, -dating, -dated**) *v* **1.** *vti* **UNITE BUSINESS ACTIVITIES** to bring businesses or business activities together, or come together, into a single unit **2.** *vti* **STRENGTHEN POSITION** to increase the strength, stability, or depth of your success or position ○ *This excellent performance has enabled her to consolidate her lead.* **3.** *vti* **COMBINE SOMETHING INTO SINGLE MASS** to combine separate items or scattered material into a single whole or mass **4.** *vt* FIN **COMBINE ACCOUNTS** to combine several sets of financial accounts in a single set of accounts [Early 16C. < Latin *consolidat-*, past participle of *consolidare* 'make solid' < *solidus* 'firm, whole'] —**consolidator** *n*

Consolidated Fund /kən sólli daytid-/ *n* in the United Kingdom, a government fund made up of revenue from taxes, used to cover regular costs, especially interest payments on the national debt

consolidation /kən sólli dáysh'n/ *n* **1. COMBINING OF BUSINESS ACTIVITIES** the bringing together of businesses or business activities into a single unit **2. STRENGTHENING OF POSITION** the increasing of the strength, stability, or depth of a person's or group's success or position ○ *The final six weeks saw a consolidation of their position at the top of the league.* **3. COMBINATION INTO SINGLE MASS** the combination of separate items or scattered material into a single whole or mass **4.** POL **COMBINING OF ACTS INTO SINGLE STATUTE** the combination of two or more Acts of Parliament into a single statute **5.** GEOL **COMPACTING OF LOOSE DEPOSIT INTO ROCK** a process by which a loose deposit is compacted into hard rock **6.** PSYCHOL **PSYCHOLOGICAL PROCESS THAT FIXES MEMORY** the process in the brain that enables somebody to have a lasting memory of a particular event

consols /kón solz, kən sólz/ *npl* in the United Kingdom, government bonds with a fixed interest rate and no date of maturity [Late 18C. Contraction of *consolidated annuities*]

consommé /kon sómmay/ *n* a thin clear soup made from meat stock. It can be eaten hot, or cold in the form of a jelly. [Early 19C. < French < past participle of *consommer* 'use up' < Latin *consummare* (see CONSUMMATE)]

consonance /kónss'nənss/, **consonancy** /kónss'nənssi/ (*plural* **-cies**) *n* **1. AGREEMENT** agreement or harmony (*formal*) **2.** LING **SIMILARITY BETWEEN CONSONANTS** a close similarity between consonants or groups of consonants, especially at the ends of words, e.g. between 'strong' and 'ring' **3.** MUSIC **PLEASANT COMBINATION OF MUSICAL NOTES** a combination of notes that sound pleasing when played simultaneously

consonant /kónss'nənt/ *n* **1.** LING **SPEECH SOUND OTHER THAN VOWEL** a speech sound produced by partly or totally blocking the path of air through the mouth **2. LETTER REPRESENTING CONSONANT** a letter of the alphabet that represents a consonant ■ *adj* **1. IN AGREEMENT WITH SOMETHING** in agreement or harmony with something (*formal*) ○ *delighted to learn that their views were consonant with our own* **2.** MUSIC **PLEASING IN HARMONY** containing chords or harmonies that are pleasing to hear **3.** LING **HAVING SIMILAR SOUNDS** having similar sounds, or showing consonance [14C. Via French < Latin *consonant-* 'sounding together' < *sonare* 'to sound'] —**consonantal** /kónssə nánt'l/ *adj* —**consonantly** *adv*

con sordino /kon sawr deén ō/ *adv* using a mute or the mute pedal (*used as a musical direction*) [Early 19C. < Italian, 'with a mute']

consort *vi* /kən sáwrt/ (**-sorts, -sorting, -sorted**) **ASSOCIATE WITH UNDESIRABLE** to associate with or spend time in the company of somebody undesirable (*formal*) ○ *consorting with known criminals* ■ *n* /kón sawrt/ **1.** *also* **Consort SPOUSE OF MONARCH** the husband or wife of a reigning monarch **2. PARTNER** a partner or companion (*formal*) **3. SHIP THAT ESCORTS ANOTHER** a ship that accompanies another on a journey **4. GROUP SPECIALIZING IN EARLY MUSIC** a small group of musicians specializing in works of the baroque or an earlier period [15C. Via French < Latin *consort-* 'having the same fate' < *sors* 'fortune'] ◇ **in consort with** in association or together with others (*archaic or formal*)

consortium /kən sáwrti əm/ (*plural* **-tia** /-ti ə/) *n* **1.** an association or grouping of institutions, businesses, or financial organizations, usually set up for a common purpose that would be beyond the capabilities of a single member of the group **2.** LAW the right of a husband or wife to the company, affection, and help of, and sexual relations with, his or her spouse (*archaic*) [Early 19C. < Latin, 'fellowship' < *consort-* (see CONSORT)] —**consortial** *adj*

conspecific /kónspə síffik/ *adj* belonging to the same species as another organism —**conspecific** *n*

conspectus /kən spéktəss/ *n* **1.** a general survey or overview of something **2.** an outline or synopsis of something [Mid-19C. < Latin < *conspect-*, past participle of *conspicere* (see CONSPICUOUS)]

conspicuous /kən spíkyoo əss/ *adj* **1.** easily or clearly visible ○ *The building's most conspicuous feature is its dome-shaped roof.* **2.** attracting attention through being unusual or remarkable ○ *He felt uncomfortably conspicuous, since he was the only man in evening dress.* [Mid-16C. < Latin *conspicuus* < *conspicere* 'observe carefully' < *specere* 'look at'] —**conspicuously** *adv* —**conspicuousness** *n*

conspicuous consumption *n* the practice of spending large quantities of money, often extravagantly, to impress others

conspiracist /kən spírrəssist/ *n* somebody who believes that a conspiracy caused an event

conspiracy /kən spírrəssi/ (*plural* **-cies**) *n* CRIME **1. PLAN TO COMMIT ILLEGAL ACT TOGETHER** a secret plan or agreement between two or more people to commit an illegal or subversive act **2. MAKING OF AGREEMENT BY CONSPIRATORS** the making of a secret plan or agreement to commit an illegal or subversive act **3. GROUP OF CONSPIRATORS** a group of people planning or agreeing in secret to commit an illegal or subversive act [14C. < Anglo-Norman *conspiracie*, alteration of Old French *conspiration* < Latin *conspirat-*, past participle of *conspirare* (see CONSPIRE)]

conspiracy of silence *n* an agreement among a group of people to say nothing in public about a matter of public interest or importance, in order to protect or promote selfish interests

conspiracy theory *n* a belief that a particular event is the result of a secret plot rather than the actions of an individual person or chance —**conspiracy theorist** *n*

conspirator /kən spírrətər/ *n* a member of a group of people planning or agreeing in secret to commit an illegal or subversive act

conspiratorial /kən spírrə táwri əl/ *adj* indicating or betraying knowledge of or involvement in a conspiracy ○ *a conspiratorial whisper* —**conspiratorially** *adv*

conspire /kən spír/ (**-spires, -spiring, -spired**) *vi* **1.** to plan or agree in secret with others to commit an illegal or subversive act ○ *In court, the three defendants admitted to conspiring against the government.* **2.** to combine so as to cause a particular result, often one involving harm, inconvenience, or difficulty ○ *Rain and tears conspired to smudge her carefully applied mascara.* [14C. Via French < Latin *conspirare*, literally 'breathe together' < *spirare* 'breathe'] —**conspiringly** *adv*

conspiriologist /kən spírri óllajist/ *n US* somebody who believes in conspiracy theories

con spirito /kon spírritō/ *adv* in a lively or spirited way (*used as a musical direction*) [Late 19C. < Italian, 'with spirit']

const. *abbr* **1.** MATHS, PHYS constant **2.** POL constitution

constable /kúnstəb'l, kón-/ *n* **1. POLICE OFFICER** in the United Kingdom, Canada, Australia, and New Zealand, a police officer of the lowest rank **2. OFFICER BELOW SHERIFF** in some towns or townships in the United States and, historically, in British towns and boroughs, a low-ranking law officer **3. CASTLE WARDEN** the warden of a royal castle or fortress **4. ROYAL HOUSEHOLD OFFICIAL IN MIDDLE AGES** the chief administrative and military officer in a royal household, especially in medieval France and England [12C. Via Old French *conestable* < late Latin *comes stabilis* 'count of the stable'] —**constableship** *n*

Constable /kúnstəb'l/, **John** (1776–1837) British landscape painter. His paintings such as *The Haywain* (1821) came to symbolize rural England.

> 'There is nothing ugly; I never saw an ugly thing in my life: for let the form of an object be what it may, light, shade, and perspective will always make it beautiful.'
> [John Constable. Quoted in *Memoirs of the Life of John Constable*, C. R. Leslie; 1843]

constabulary /kən stábbyŏŏləri/ *n* (*plural* **-ies**) a police force for a city or a district ■ *adj* relating to a police force, or involved in being a police officer

Constance, Lake /kónstənss/ lake in central Europe, in the Alps, on the borders of Austria, Germany, and Switzerland. Area: 540 sq. km/210 sq. mi. Depth: 252 m/827 ft. Length: 74 km/46 mi. German name **Bodensee**

constant /kónstənt/ *adj* **1.** EVER PRESENT always present or available ○ *constant whining* ○ *a constant supply of fresh water* **2.** HAPPENING OR DONE REPEATEDLY occurring or made again and again ○ *constant visits to the doctor* **3.** NOT CHANGING OR VARYING remaining the same and not varying with change in other things ○ *kept at a constant pressure* **4.** FAITHFUL faithful and loyal, especially to a husband, wife, or other loved one ■ *n* **1.** SOMETHING UNCHANGING an object, quality, or fact that is invariable or ever present ○ *This pre-occupation has become a constant in our daily lives.* **2.** MATHS QUANTITY WITH FIXED VALUE a mathematical quantity that retains a fixed value in any circumstances or throughout a particular set of calculations. Pi, the ratio of the circumference to the radius of any circle, is a constant. **3.** PHYS UNVARYING PROPERTY a property, condition, or quantity that is assumed not to vary for the purposes of a theory or experiment, e.g. the speed of light [14C. Via French < Latin *constant-*, present participle of *constare* 'stand together' < *stare* 'to stand'] —**constancy** *n* —**constantly** *adv*

constantan /kónstən tan/ *n* an alloy of copper and nickel whose electrical resistance is unaffected by changes in temperature. Use: resistors, thermocouples. [Early 20C. < CONSTANT]

Constantine II /kónstən tīn, -teen/ (*b.* 1940) **ex-king of Greece** Succeeding to the throne in 1964, he was exiled in 1967 by a military junta and deposed in 1973. A referendum abolished the Greek monarchy in 1974.

Constantine (the Great) (274–337) Roman emperor (306–37). He supported Christianity from 312 and was baptized shortly before his death. He moved his capital to Byzantium, renamed Constantinople in 330. Born **Flavius Valerius Aurelius Constantinus**

Constantinople /kón stanti nōp'l/ former name for **Istanbul**

constative /kónstətiv/ *adj* **1.** relating to a statement that conveys information and is capable of being considered as true or false **2.** relating to verb forms indicating that something has been completed in the past [Early 20C. < Latin *constat-*, past participle of *constare* (see CONSTANT)]

constellate /kónstə layt/ (**-lates, -lating, -lated**) *vti* to form clusters, e.g. in a constellation, or cause something to do this (*literary*) [Late 16C. < late Latin *constellatus* 'with stars together' < Latin *stella* 'star']

constellation /kónstə láysh'n/ *n* **1.** ASTRON GROUP OF STARS FORMING SHAPE a group of stars visible from Earth that forms a distinctive pattern and has a name, often derived from Greek mythology, linked to its shape. There are 88 constellations and the groupings are historical rather than scientific. **2.** ASTRON AREA OF SKY CONTAINING CONSTELLATION the area of the sky within and around a constellation **3.** GATHERING OF CELEBRITIES a gathering of famous or important people ○ *a glittering constellation of Hollywood stars* **4.** GROUP OF RELATED THINGS a group of things felt to be related to each other in some way ○ *Problems tend to occur not singly, but in constellations.* **5.** ASTROL ASTROLOGICAL ARRANGEMENT OF PLANETS the arrangement of the planets in the zodiac at a particular time, believed by astrologers to influence human character or events on Earth —**constellational** *adj* —**constellatory** /kən stéllətəri/ *adj*

consternate /kónstər nayt/ (**-nates, -nating, -nated**) *vt* to fill somebody with alarm, confusion, or dismay [Mid-17C. < Latin *consternat-*, past participle of *consternare* 'make prostrate with fear' < *sternare* 'lay low']

consternation /kónstər náysh'n/ *n* a feeling of alarm, confusion, or dismay, often caused by something unexpected ○ *The news caused worldwide consternation and a panic on the stock exchange.*

constipate /kónsti payt/ (**-pates, -pating, -pated**) *vt* to cause somebody or something to become constipated [Mid-16C. < Latin *constipat-*, past participle of *constipare* 'cram together' < *stipare* 'to press']

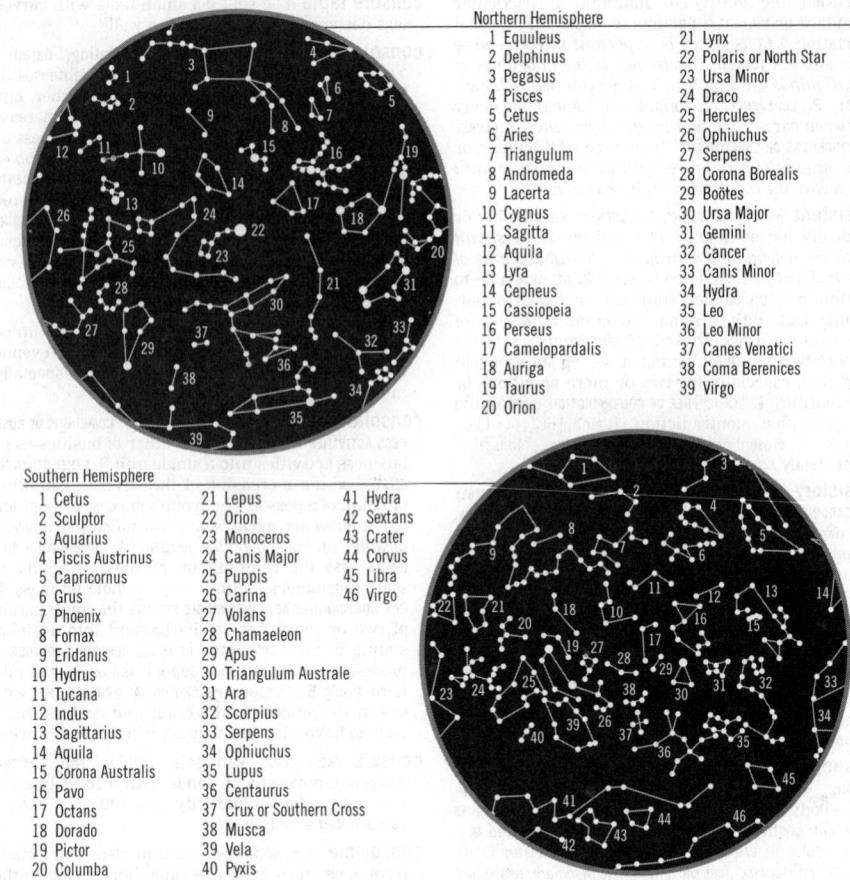

Northern Hemisphere

1 Equuleus	21 Lynx
2 Delphinus	22 Polaris or North Star
3 Pegasus	23 Ursa Minor
4 Pisces	24 Draco
5 Cetus	25 Hercules
6 Aries	26 Ophiuchus
7 Triangulum	27 Serpens
8 Andromeda	28 Corona Borealis
9 Lacerta	29 Boötes
10 Cygnus	30 Ursa Major
11 Sagitta	31 Gemini
12 Aquila	32 Cancer
13 Lyra	33 Canis Minor
14 Cepheus	34 Hydra
15 Cassiopeia	35 Leo
16 Perseus	36 Leo Minor
17 Camelopardalis	37 Canes Venatici
18 Auriga	38 Coma Berenices
19 Taurus	39 Virgo
20 Orion	

Southern Hemisphere

1 Cetus	21 Lepus	41 Hydra
2 Sculptor	22 Orion	42 Sextans
3 Aquarius	23 Monoceros	43 Crater
4 Piscis Austrinus	24 Canis Major	44 Corvus
5 Capricornus	25 Puppis	45 Libra
6 Grus	26 Carina	46 Virgo
7 Phoenix	27 Volans	
8 Fornax	28 Chamaeleon	
9 Eridanus	29 Apus	
10 Hydrus	30 Triangulum Australe	
11 Tucana	31 Ara	
12 Indus	32 Scorpius	
13 Sagittarius	33 Serpens	
14 Aquila	34 Ophiuchus	
15 Corona Australis	35 Lupus	
16 Pavo	36 Centaurus	
17 Octans	37 Crux or Southern Cross	
18 Dorado	38 Musca	
19 Pictor	39 Vela	
20 Columba	40 Pyxis	

constellations

constipated /kónsti paytid/ *adj* **1.** having difficulty in eliminating solid waste from the body, with faeces being hard and dry **2.** unable to flow at the usual rate because of blockage or obstruction

constipation /kónsti páysh'n/ *n* **1.** a condition in which a person or animal has difficulty in eliminating solid waste from the body and the faeces are hard and dry **2.** a state in which the usual flow of something is blocked or obstructed

constituency /kən stíttyoo ənssi, -stíchyoo-/ (*plural* **-cies**) *n* **1.** GOV ELECTORAL DISTRICT one of the areas into which a country is divided for election purposes, and from which a representative is elected to serve in a legislative body **2.** POL VOTERS IN CONSTITUENCY the voters or residents in a particular electoral district **3.** POL GROUP WITH COMMON OUTLOOK a group of people thought to have common aims or views, and therefore sometimes appealed to for support ○ *people outside his usual constituency of young married couples* **4.** COMM CUSTOMERS CONSIDERED AS GROUP a group of people served by an organization, especially a business ○ *enlarging its constituency via a website*

constituent /kən stíttyoo ənt, -stíchyoo-/ *n* **1.** POL RESIDENT OF CONSTITUENCY somebody living in an electoral district, especially somebody entitled to vote **2.** INGREDIENT one of the parts that make up something ○ *one of the constituents of cement* **3.** GRAM WORD, PHRASE, OR CLAUSE a word, phrase, or clause in a larger construction such as a sentence **4.** LAW CLIENT somebody who appoints another to act on his or her behalf (*formal*) ■ *adj* **1.** FORMING PART forming a part of something (*formal*) ○ *the constituent elements of a compound* **2.** POL WITH POWER TO DRAW UP CONSTITUTION having the power to draw up or alter a constitution ○ *a constituent assembly* [15C. Directly or via French < Latin *constituent-*, present participle of *constituere* (see CONSTITUTE)] —**constituently** *adv*

constitute /kónsti tyoot/ (**-tutes, -tuting, -tuted**) *vt* **1.** BE SOMETHING to be, amount to, or have the status of a particular thing ○ *This letter does not constitute an offer of employment.* **2.** BE INGREDIENT OF SOMETHING to make up the whole or a particular part of something ○ *a panel constituted of four individuals* **3.** FORMALLY ESTABLISH SOMETHING to create and establish something formally, especially an official body (*formal*) ○ *constitute an assembly* **4.** FORMALLY APPOINT SOMEBODY to appoint somebody formally to a position (*formal*) [15C. < Latin *constitut-*, past participle of *constituere* 'establish' < *statuere* 'set up'] —**constituter** *n*

USAGE See *comprise*.

constitution /kónsti tyoósh'n/ *n* **1.** POL STATEMENT OF FUNDAMENTAL LAWS a written statement outlining the basic laws or principles by which a country or organization is governed **2.** POL DOCUMENT CONTAINING FUNDAMENTAL LAWS a document or statute outlining the basic laws or principles by which a country or organization is governed **3.** SOMEBODY'S GENERAL HEALTH somebody's general physical and sometimes psychological make up, especially the body's ability to remain healthy and withstand disease or hardship ○ *has the constitution of an ox* **4.** COMPOSITION OF SOMETHING the parts or members of something, or the way in which they combine to form it **5.** ACT OR PROCESS OF ESTABLISHING SOMETHING the formal creation or establishment of something

Constitution *n* the Constitution of the United States, containing seven articles and 26 amendments, that has been in effect since its adoption in 1789

constitutional /kónsti tyoósh'nəl/ *adj* **1.** POL OF COUNTRY'S OR ORGANIZATION'S CONSTITUTION relating to the constitution of a country or an organization ○ *constitutional reform* **2.** POL GOVERNED BY CONSTITUTION governed or regulated by a constitution **3.** POL IN ACCORDANCE WITH CONSTITUTION authorized by a constitution ○ *The US Supreme Court has to decide whether such punishments are constitutional.* **4.** RELATING TO SOMEBODY'S HEALTH relating to, or being part of or a consequence of somebody's general physical and sometimes psychological make up ■ *n* WALK a short walk, taken regularly for health reasons —**constitutionally** *adv*

constitutionalise *vt* POL another spelling of **constitutionalize**

constitutionalism /kónsti tyoósh'nəlizəm/ *n* **1.** the principles or practice of government regulated by

a constitution 2. belief in constitutional government —**constitutionalist** *n, adj*

constitutionality /kónsti tyóosh'n állәti/ *n* the validity or permissibility of something in terms of the provisions or principles of a constitution

constitutionalize /kónsti tyóosh'nә līz/ (**-izes, -izing, -ized**), **constitutionalise** (**-ises, -ising, -ised**) *vt* **1.** to incorporate a piece of legislation into a constitution, or authorize a practice through it **2.** to make a form of government, a country, or an organization subject to a constitution —**constitutionalization** /kónsti tyóosh'nә lī záysh'n/ *n*

constitutional monarchy *n* **1.** a political system in which the head of state is a king or queen ruling to the extent allowed by a constitution **2.** a country with a constitutional monarchy —**constitutional monarch** *n*

constitutive /kәn stíttyóotiv/ *adj* **1.** POL **HAVING POWER TO ESTABLISH INSTITUTION** having the power to create or establish a system of government, legislative body, or other institution, or to appoint members of official bodies **2. FORMING PART** forming a part of something **3. ESSENTIAL** essential to the particular nature or character of something **4.** BIOCHEM **FORMED CONTINUOUSLY** describes enzymes that are formed continuously without an external stimulus —**constitutively** *adv*

constrain /kәn stráyn/ (**-strains, -straining, -strained**) *vt* **1. FORCE SOMEBODY TO ACT** to force somebody to do something, especially through pressure of circumstances or a sense of obligation ○ *Many companies have been constrained to lay off workers.* **2. RESTRICT SOMEBODY OR SOMETHING** to limit or restrict somebody or something, especially to prevent the free expression of something ○ *The industry has been constrained by skill shortages.* **3. RESTRAIN SOMEBODY OR SOMETHING** to hold somebody or something back from an action (*literary*) ○ *We felt constrained by the presence of the others.* [14C. Via Old French *constraindre* < Latin *constringere* 'bind tightly together' < *stringere* 'draw tight'] —**constrainable** *adj* —**constrainer** *n*

constrained /kәn stráynd/ *adj* lacking naturalness or spontaneity because of self-consciousness, reserve, or inhibiting circumstances —**constrainedly** /-nidli/ *adv*

constraint /kәn stráynt/ *n* **1. LIMITING FACTOR** something that limits freedom of action ○ *Even in a free society individual liberty must be subject to certain constraints.* ○ *budgetary constraints* **2. STATE OF RESTRICTION** a state in which freedom of action is severely restricted **3. LACK OF SPONTANEITY** a lack of warmth and spontaneity in somebody's manner or in the atmosphere on a particular occasion [14C. < French *constreinte*, feminine past participle of *constraindre* (see CONSTRAIN)]

constrict /kәn stríkt/ (**-stricts, -stricting, -stricted**) *v* **1.** *vti* **NARROW** to make something, especially a blood vessel, narrower, or become narrower **2.** *vt* **LIMIT OR RESTRICT SOMEBODY OR SOMETHING** to limit the movement of a person or part of the body in an uncomfortable way **3.** *vt* **RESTRICT FLOW OF SOMETHING** to stop or slow down the flow of something such as air, liquid, or blood **4.** *vt* ZOOL **SUFFOCATE PREY BY SQUEEZING** to squeeze animals caught as prey until they suffocate, as many snakes do to their prey [Mid-18C. < Latin *constrict-*, past participle of *constringere* (see CONSTRAIN)] —**constrictive** *adj* —**constrictively** *adv* —**constrictiveness** *n*

constriction /kәn stríksh'n/ *n* **1. PROCESS OF NARROWING** the process of becoming narrower, or of making something narrower **2. NARROW PLACE** a narrow place or part ○ *A constriction in the tube prevents the mercury from returning to the bulb.* **3.** MED **FEELING OF TIGHTNESS** a feeling of tightness or pressure, especially in the chest or throat **4. RESTRICTION** something that severely restricts somebody's freedom of movement, action, or expression **5.** ZOOL **SUFFOCATION BY SQUEEZING** the process of squeezing animals caught as prey until they suffocate, as many snakes do

constrictor /kәn stríktәr/ *n* **1.** REPT **SNAKE THAT SQUEEZES PREY TO DEATH** a large nonvenomous snake that coils itself around its prey and suffocates it, e.g. an anaconda, boa, or python **2.** ANAT **MUSCLE** a muscle that tightens to make a part of the body narrower **3. SOMEBODY OR SOMETHING CONSTRICTING** somebody or something that constricts somebody or something else

construct *vt* /kәn strúkt/ (**-structs, -structing, -structed**) **1. BUILD SOMETHING** to build or assemble something by putting together separate parts in an ordered way **2. CREATE SOMETHING IN MIND** to create something such as a theory as a result of systematic thought **3.** MATHS **DRAW SOMETHING ACCURATELY** to draw something accurately using given measurements ■ *n* /kónstrukt/ **CONSTRUCTED THING OR CONCEPT** something that has been systematically put together, usually in the mind, especially a complex theory or subjective notion ○ *sexual identity viewed as a social construct* [15C. < Latin *construct-*, past participle of *construere* 'pile together' < *struere* 'pile, build'] —**constructible** *adj*

construction /kәn strúksh'n/ *n* **1. ACT OR PROCESS OF CONSTRUCTING** the building of something, especially a large structure such as a house, road, or bridge **2.** BUILDINGS **BUILT STRUCTURE** a structure that has been built **3.** CONSTR **WORKMANSHIP AND MATERIALS** the way in which something has been built, especially with regard to the type and quality of the structure, materials, and workmanship **4.** CONSTR **BUILDING INDUSTRY** the building industry regarded as a whole **5. CREATION OF SOMETHING** the creation of something such as a system or concept from a number of different parts **6. INTERPRETATION** the way in which something is interpreted or explained (*formal*) ○ *put the worst possible construction on the news* **7.** GRAM **COMBINATION OF WORDS** a group of words governed by particular grammatical rules **8.** MATHS **GEOMETRIC SHAPE** a geometric figure drawn accurately in accordance with given measurements **9.** ART **WORK OF ART** a visual work of art that is put together from a variety of different materials, abstract in design, and usually three-dimensional —**constructional** *adj* —**constructionally** *adv*

constructionist /kәn strúksh'nist/ *n US* an interpreter of a legal text or document

construction site *n* an area where a building or group of buildings is being constructed or repaired, often fenced off to prevent access by those not working there

constructive /kәn strúktiv/ *adj* **1. USEFUL** carefully considered and meant to be helpful ○ *constructive criticism* **2.** LAW **BASED ON INFERENCE** based on what somebody infers from other statements or circumstances **3.** CONSTR **STRUCTURAL** relating to or involved in construction, especially forming part of the basic structure of a building —**constructively** *adv* —**constructiveness** *n*

constructive dismissal *n* action by an employer intended to make continuing in a job intolerable for an unwanted employee, thus forcing the employee to resign

constructive engagement *n* the policy of maintaining limited political and business links with a country while continuing to demand political or social reform in that country

constructive margin *n* a boundary between two tectonic plates at which new crust is formed, e.g. the mid-ocean ridges

constructivism /kәn strúktivizәm/ *n* a modern art movement associated with Moscow in the 1920s that produced large nonrepresentational structures made of industrial materials such as plastic, glass, and sheet metal. Its leading figures were Naum Gabo and Antoine Pevsner. —**constructivist** *n*

construe /kәn stróo/ (**-strues, -struing, -strued**) *v* **1.** *vt* **INTERPRET SOMETHING IN PARTICULAR WAY** to interpret or understand the meaning of a word, gesture, or action in a particular way ○ *His silence could be construed as an admission of guilt.* **2.** *vti* GRAM **ANALYSE SYNTAX OF TEXT** to analyse the syntax of a piece of text, especially text that is to be translated **3.** *vt* GRAM **USE WORD IN PARTICULAR WAY** to use a word in a grammatical structure, e.g. by making it singular or plural ○ *'Folk' is construed as plural, except when it means 'folk music'.* [14C. < Latin *construere* (see CONSTRUCT)] —**construability** /kәn stróo ә bíllәti/ *n* —**construable** *adj* —**construal** *n* —**construer** *n*

consubstantial /kónsәb stánsh'l/ *adj* having the same substance as something else, especially another member of the Holy Trinity [14C. < ecclesiastical Latin *consubstantialis*, literally 'substance together' < Latin *substantia* 'substance'] —**consubstantiality** /kónsәb stánshi állәti/ *n*

consubstantiate /kónsәb stánshi ayt/ (**-ates, -ating, -ated**) *vti* to become united, or unite two things, in one single substance, as the body and blood of Jesus Christ are believed to become one with bread and wine in the Christian doctrine of transubstantiation [Late 16C. < late Latin *consubstantiatus* 'united in one substance' < *substantiat-*, past participle of *substantiare* (see SUBSTANTIATE)]

consubstantiation /kónsәb stánshi áysh'n/ *n* **1.** the belief of some Christians that the body and blood of Jesus Christ coexist in the bread and wine consecrated at Communion with the natural elements of which the bread and wine are made. This belief is held mainly by High-Church Anglicans. **2.** the process by which the body and blood of Jesus Christ are believed by some Christians to become present in the bread and wine consecrated at Communion

consuetude /kónswi tyood/ *n* a long-standing custom or right, particularly one that has acquired legal force (*formal*) [14C. Directly or via French < Latin *consuetudo* 'the state of being completely accustomed' < *suescere* 'become accustomed'] —**consuetudinary** /kónswi tyóodinәri/ *adj*

consul /kónss'l/ *n* **1.** GOV, INTERNAT REL **GOVERNMENT OFFICIAL WORKING ABROAD** a government official living in a foreign city to promote the commercial interests of the official's own state and protect its citizens **2.** ANCIENT HIST **ANCIENT ROMAN MAGISTRATE** in ancient Rome, one of the two chief magistrates who were elected to govern annually **3.** HIST **FORMER FRENCH OFFICIAL** one of the three chief magistrates of the first French Republic between 1799 and 1804 [14C. < Latin] —**consular** /kónssyóolәr/ *adj* —**consulship** *n*

consulate /kónssyóolәt/ *n* **1.** INTERNAT REL **CONSUL'S OFFICE** a consul's office or official residence **2.** INTERNAT REL **SCOPE OF CONSUL'S RESPONSIBILITIES** the political office or period of office of a consul, or the jurisdiction of a consul **3.** ANCIENT HIST **ANCIENT ROMAN GOVERNMENT** the ancient Roman system of government administered by consuls

Consulate *n* **1.** the government, consisting of three consuls, that ruled France from 1799 to 1804 **2.** the period from 1799 to 1804 during which France was ruled by three consuls

consulate general (*plural* **consulate generals** or **consulates general**) *n* the building where a consul general lives or works

consul general (*plural* **consul generals** or **consuls general**) *n* a consul of the highest rank, usually based in a major foreign city that is important for trade

consult *v* /kәn súlt/ (**-sults, -sulting, -sulted**) **1.** *vti* **ASK FOR SPECIALIST ADVICE** to ask for specialist advice or information, especially from a professional ○ *If symptoms persist, consult a doctor.* **2.** *vti* **ASK PERMISSION** to ask for somebody's opinion or permission before taking action ○ *You'd be wise to consult the boss before you make any major changes.* **3.** *vt* **REFER TO SOURCE OF INFORMATION** to look at something such as a reference book in order to get information **4.** *vi* **GIVE PROFESSIONAL ADVICE** to provide specialist advice for a fee ○ *After 15 years in computer programming, I now consult from home.* ■ *n* /kәn súlt, kón sult/ **CONSULTATION** a consultation or discussion about something (*informal*) [Early 16C. Via French < Latin *consultare* 'confer' < *consulere* 'seek advice'] —**consultable** *adj* —**consulter** *n*

consultant /kәn súltәnt/ *n* **1.** an expert who charges a fee for providing advice or services in a particular field **2.** a senior doctor who is fully qualified in a particular branch of medicine —**consultancy** *n* —**consultantship** *n*

consultation /kónss'l táysh'n, kónsul-/ *n* **1. EXCHANGE OF OPINIONS** a discussion aimed at ascertaining opinions or reaching an agreement ○ *After a quick consultation with his wife, he signed the paper.* **2. MEETING WITH EXPERT** a meeting with an expert in a particular field to obtain advice ○ *an appointment for a consultation with the heart surgeon* **3. REFERENCE TO SOURCE OF INFORMATION** the act of referring to a book or person for information or advice ○ *Consultation of the manual confirmed the problem was the gearbox.*

consultative /kәn súltәtiv/ *adj* available for consultation, or involved in consultation —**consultatively** *adv*

consulting /kәn súlting/ *adj* **1. PROVIDING SPECIALIST ADVICE** providing specialist advice to other people who work in the same field **2. OF CONSULTANTS OR CONSULTATION**

relating to a consultant or consultation ○ *a consulting fee* ■ *n* BUSINESS OF CONSULTATION the business of being a consultant

consulting room *n* the room in which a doctor sees patients, mainly in a hospital

consumable /kən syoóməb'l/ *adj* able or intended to be discarded after use, rather than reused

consumables /kən syoóməb'lz/ *npl* goods that have to be bought regularly because they wear out or are used up, e.g. food and clothing

~~consumate~~ incorrect spelling of **consummate**

consume /kən syoóm/ (**-sumes, -suming, -sumed**) *v* **1.** *vt* EAT OR DRINK SOMETHING to eat or drink something, especially in large amounts **2.** *vt* USE SOMETHING UP to use something in such a way that it cannot be reused or recovered afterwards ○ *The newer models consume less petrol.* **3.** *vt* ENGROSS SOMEBODY to fill somebody's mind or attention fully (*usually passive*) ○ *consumed by a desire for new experiences* **4.** *vt* DESTROY SOMETHING OR SOMEBODY to destroy something or somebody completely ○ *was consumed by fire* **5.** *vti* BUY FROM OTHERS to buy goods or services produced by other people [14C. Directly or via French < Latin *consumere* 'take up completely' < *sumere* 'take']

consumedly /kən syoómidli/ *adv* extremely or excessively, usually to an annoying or distressing degree (*archaic*)

consumer /kən syoómər/ *n* **1.** BUYER a buyer of goods or services **2.** SOMEBODY OR SOMETHING THAT CONSUMES SOMETHING somebody or something that consumes something by eating it, drinking it, or using it up ○ *The country is one of the largest consumers of paper products.* **3.** ECOL ORGANISM THAT FEEDS ON OTHERS in an ecological community or food chain, an organism that feeds on other organisms, or on material derived from them. Consumers include herbivorous and carnivorous animals, which feed on plants and other animals respectively, and also organisms such as worms, fungi, and bacteria, which feed on nonliving organic material. —**consumership** *n*

consumer confidence *n* a measure of how people feel about the future of the economy and their own financial situation, obtained through polling

consumer credit *n* money lent by financial institutions to enable members of the public to buy consumer goods or services. Hire-purchase agreements, credit cards, and charge accounts are all forms of consumer credit.

consumer durables *npl* items that last a relatively long time and are purchased infrequently, e.g. computers and washing machines

consumer-facing *adj* involving direct contact with, or able to be directly accessed by, consumers ○ *a consumer-facing website*

consumer goods *npl* goods that are bought by consumers and are not used to produce other goods

consumerism /kən syoómərizəm/ *n* **1.** BELIEF IN BENEFITS OF CONSUMPTION the belief that the buying and selling of large quantities of consumer goods is beneficial to an economy or a sign of economic strength **2.** MATERIALISTIC ATTITUDE an attitude that values the acquisition of material goods (*disapproving*) **3.** PROTECTION OF CONSUMERS' RIGHTS the protection of the rights and interests of consumers, especially with regard to price, quality, and safety —**consumerist** *n, adj*

consumer price index *n* **1.** a government-issued list of the retail prices of basic household goods and services **2.** *ANZ* the average cost of a basket of goods during a specific period, used as an indicator of economic inflation

consumer society *n* a society in which the consumption of mass-produced goods is encouraged through mass communication

consumer-to-business *adj* relating to Internet transactions between an individual consumer and a business organization, rather than between businesses

consuming /kən syoóming/ *adj* so intense as to take up all of somebody's attention, time, and energy ○ *a consuming interest in horses* —**consumingly** *adv*

consummate *vt* /kónssə mayt, kónssyoō-/ (**-mates, -mating, -mated**) **1.** COMPLETE MARRIAGE to make a marriage legally complete and fully valid by having sexual intercourse **2.** FULFIL RELATIONSHIP THROUGH SEX to bring a relationship to completion, or gratify a desire, especially by having sexual intercourse (*often passive*) **3.** CONCLUDE SOMETHING to bring something such as a business deal to a conclusion (*formal*) ○ *Leaving her business partner to consummate the deal, she boarded a flight for New York.* **4.** ACHIEVE SOMETHING to achieve or fulfil something, especially something long sought (*formal; often passive*) ○ *Twelve years of effort and struggle were consummated when the foundation stone for the new theatre was laid.* ■ *adj* /kónssəmət, kən súmmət/ **1.** SUPREME OR PERFECT excellent, skilful, or accomplished ○ *with consummate ease* **2.** UTTER OR TOTAL possessing or showing a bad quality to an extreme degree ○ *consummate arrogance* [15C. < Latin *consummat-*, past participle of *consummare* 'accomplish' < *summa* 'the highest thing'] —**consummately** *adv* —**consummative** /kən súmmətiv/ *adj* —**consummator** *n* —**consummatory** /kən súmmətəri/ *adj*

consummation /kónssə máysh'n, kónsyoō-/ *n* **1.** PERFECT ENDING the bringing of something to a satisfying conclusion, or the final satisfying completion or achievement of something ○ *The publication of her book was a consummation of her whole life's work.* **2.** LEGAL COMPLETION OF MARRIAGE BY SEX the legal completion of a marriage by an act of sexual intercourse between the spouses **3.** COMPLETION OF DEAL the finalization of something such as a business deal

consumption /kən súmpsh'n/ *n* **1.** ACT OF EATING OR DRINKING the eating or drinking of something, or the amount that somebody eats or drinks ○ *unfit for human consumption* **2.** ACT OF USING SOMETHING UP the use of natural resources or fuels, or the amount of resources or fuels used ○ *consumption of fossil fuels* **3.** CONSUMER EXPENDITURE the purchase and use of goods and services by consumers, or the quantity of goods and services purchased **4.** WASTING DISEASE any condition that causes progressive wasting of the tissues, especially tuberculosis of the lungs (*dated*) [14C. Via French < Latin *consumption-* < *consumere* (see CONSUME)]

consumptive /kən súmptiv/ *adj* **1.** ENGAGED IN OR CAUSING CONSUMPTION engaged in, causing, or encouraging the consumption of food, materials, or goods, especially in a wasteful or destructive way **2.** AFFECTED BY TUBERCULOSIS affected by a wasting disease, especially tuberculosis of the lungs, or connected with such a disease (*dated*) ■ *n* SOMEBODY WITH TUBERCULOSIS somebody affected by a wasting disease, particularly tuberculosis of the lungs (*dated*) ○ *a chronic consumptive* [Mid-17C. < medieval Latin *consumptivus* < Latin *consumere* (see CONSUME)] —**consumptively** *adv* —**consumptiveness** *n*

cont. *abbr* **1.** containing **2.** PUBL contents **3.** GEOG continent **4.** GEOG continental **5.** continued **6.** GRAM continuous **7.** MED, GRAM contraction **8.** control

contact /kón takt/ *n* **1.** STATE OF COMMUNICATION a state or relationship in which communication happens or is possible ○ *Our only means of contact with the base was a small radio receiver.* ○ *He made contact with his counterpart in the Tokyo office.* **2.** ACT OF COMMUNICATING an act of communicating with somebody ○ *All my contacts with her to date have been about business.* **3.** PHYSICAL CONNECTION a situation in which two or more things or people actually touch or strike against one another ○ *White phosphorus ignites on contact with the air.* **4.** INTERACTION a state in which somebody has access to and can be affected or influenced by people, situations, ideas, or information ○ *You'll come into contact with a variety of people.* **5.** ACCESS ARRANGEMENT the right of a child and a separated or divorced parent to meet regularly **6.** SOMEBODY WHO CAN HELP an acquaintance who may be socially or professionally helpful ○ *I made some very useful contacts at the trade fair.* **7.** DISEASE CARRIER a person or animal seen as a possible carrier of an infectious disease **8.** DEVICE MAKING ELECTRICAL CONNECTION a movable part that can be made to touch another conductive part in order to enable an electrical current to pass, e.g. a component of a switch **9.** ELECTRICAL CONNECTION a connection between or the connection of two or more electrical conductors so that current flows between them ■ **contacts** *npl* CONTACT LENSES a set of contact lenses (*informal*) ■ *v* (**-tacts, -tacting, -tacted**) **1.** *vt* REACH SOMEBODY FOR COMMUNICATION to send a message to somebody, or reach somebody, e.g. by telephone or letter, in order to communicate ○ *You can contact me at this number.* **2.** *vti* TOUCH to touch or strike against something ■ *adj* **1.** USED FOR COMMUNICATING WITH SOMEBODY used as a means to contact somebody ○ *a contact address* **2.** WORKING BY TOUCHING working or happening by touching or being touched by something or somebody **3.** CAUSED BY TOUCH caused by touching something that irritates ○ *contact dermatitis* [Early 17C. < Latin *contactus*, past participle of *contingere*, literally 'touch with' < *tangere* 'to touch'] —**contactable** /kon táktəb'l/ *adj* —**contactual** /kon táktyoō əl/ *adj* —**contactually** *adv*

contact binary *n* a binary star system in which one of the components is transferring matter to its companion star

contact card *n* a smart card with a chip that can be read when touched by a reader

contact flight, contact flying *n* navigation of an aircraft by observing landmarks and other visible guides, without the use of navigational aids

contact group *n* a group of people who are neutral in a dispute and meet both sides to try to resolve disagreements through discussion

contact inhibition *n* the normal cessation of cell division and growth caused by physical contact with other cells. This normal end to cell division does not function when cancer is present, resulting in uncontrolled reproduction of cells.

contact language *n* a simplified language variety that retains features of other languages contributing to it, used for communication in places where most speakers do not share a common language

contact lens *n* a small plastic or glass lens placed directly onto the front of the eye to correct vision or make the iris appear a different colour

contactless card /kón taktləss-/ *n* a smart card with a chip that can be read via radio transmission, e.g. for the collection of road tolls

contact print *n* a photographic print made by placing a negative directly on top of photosensitive paper and exposing it to light. This is usually done to check the images on a roll of film before making enlargements from individual negatives.

contact sport *n* a sport in which physical contact between players is an integral part of the game, e.g. in boxing, rugby, or ice hockey

contagion /kən táyjən/ *n* **1.** SPREAD OF DISEASE BY PHYSICAL CONTACT the transmission of disease, especially by physical contact between people or contact with infected objects such as bedding or clothing **2.** DISEASE SPREAD BY PHYSICAL CONTACT an illness that spreads from one person to another, especially by physical contact between persons or contact with infected objects **3.** HARMFUL INFLUENCE a harmful or corrupting influence with a tendency to spread **4.** SPREAD OF FEELING the spreading of an attitude or emotion from person to person among a number of people (*literary*) ○ *the contagion of happiness* [14C. < Latin *contagion-* < *contingere* (see CONTACT)]

contagious /kən táyjəss/ *adj* **1.** ABLE TO BE PASSED BY CONTACT transmitted from one person to another either by direct contact with the person or by indirect contact, e.g. contact with his or her clothes **2.** CAPABLE OF TRANSMITTING DISEASE affected by or carrying a disease that can be transmitted by direct or indirect contact **3.** LIKELY TO AFFECT OTHERS quickly spread from one person to another ○ *Laughter is contagious.* [14C. < late Latin *contagiosus* < Latin *contingere* (see CONTACT)] —**contagiously** *adv* —**contagiousness** *n*

contagious abortion *n* a contagious or infectious disease of farm animals that is characterized by spontaneous abortion, e.g. brucellosis

contain /kən táyn/ (**-tains, -taining, -tained**) *vt* **1.** HAVE SOMETHING WITHIN to have or hold something inside ○ *This pack contains a training video and set of instructions.* **2.** INCLUDE SOMETHING to include something as part of the contents or makeup ○ *The report contains several inaccuracies.* ○ *drinks that contain caffeine* **3.** CONTROL EMOTION to keep an emotion under control ○ *I couldn't contain myself any longer.* **4.** STOP SOMETHING SPREADING to restrict the movement, spread, or influence of a strong enemy, force, disease, or idea **5.** MATHS BE DIVISIBLE BY NUMBER to be divisible by a number, leaving no remainder **6.** MATHS FORM SIDES OF ANGLE to form the boundaries that define an angle [13C. Via French *contenir* < Latin *continere* 'hold together' < *tenere* 'to hold'] —**containable** *adj*

container /kən táynər/ *n* **1.** an object such as a box, jar, or bottle that is used to hold something, especially when it is being stored or transported **2.** a large metal box of a standard size into which goods are packed so that they can be transported securely and efficiently from departure point to destination by road, sea, or rail, without having to be repacked

containerize /kən táynə rīz/ (**-izes, -izing, -ized**), **containerise** (**-ises, -ising, -ised**) *vt* **1.** to pack something in freight containers for transportation by road, sea, or rail, especially commercially **2.** to convert a port, transport system, or industry so that it can handle standard-sized freight containers —**containerization** /kən táynə rī záysh'n/ *n*

container port *n* a port capable of handling containerized cargo

container ship *n* a ship specially designed to carry cargo that is packed in freight containers

containment /kən táynmənt/ *n* **1.** ATTEMPT TO STOP SPREAD OF SOMETHING action taken to restrict the spread of a hostile element such as an enemy or something undesirable such as a disease **2.** CONTROL MEASURE IN NUCLEAR REACTIONS the use of magnetic fields to prevent the reacting particles from touching the containing vessel's walls in a reactor **3.** ACT OR PROCESS OF CONTAINING SOMETHING the act or process of being contained or of containing something

contaminate /kən támmi nayt/ (**-nates, -nating, -nated**) *vt* **1.** to make something impure, unclean, or polluted, especially by mixing harmful impurities into it or by putting it into contact with something harmful ○ *contaminate blood products* **2.** to make something such as soil unfit for use or exploitation as a result of contact with polluting or harmful substances ○ *land contaminated by heavy industry* [15C. < Latin *contaminat-*, past participle of *contaminare* < *contamen*, literally 'touching with' < *tangere* 'to touch'] —**contaminable** /-nəb'l/ *adj* —**contaminant** *n* —**contaminative** /-nətiv/ *adj* —**contaminator** *n*

contamination /kən támmi náysh'n/ *n* **1.** ACT OF CONTAMINATING SOMETHING the act or process of contaminating something or becoming contaminated, or the unclean or impure state that results from this **2.** SOMETHING THAT CONTAMINATES something that physically contaminates a substance or that corrupts a person morally ○ *The investigators found considerable contamination in the rivers.* **3.** ALTERATION OF WORD OR PHRASE the process by which a word or phrase changes as a result of mistaken association with another word or phrase

contango /kən táng gō, kon-/ *n* (*plural* **-gos**) **1.** INTEREST PAYABLE WHEN DELIVERY DELAYED interest payable by a broker when the delivery of and payment for stock is postponed **2.** POSTPONEMENT OF STOCK DELIVERY formerly, the postponement of the delivery of stock to a broker and payment for it, from one account day to the next ■ *vt* (**-gos, -going, -goed**) ARRANGE CONTANGO to arrange for delivery and payment to be postponed when transferring stock in a stock exchange [Mid-19C. Origin ?]

contd *abbr* continued

conte /koNt/ *n* **1.** LITERAT same as **short story** (*literary*) **2.** a narrative tale from the Middle Ages [Late 19C. < French < Old French *co(u)nter* (see COUNT [1])]

conté /kón tay/ *n* a hard drawing crayon made of clay and graphite [Mid-19C. After Nicolas Jacques *Conté* (1755–1805), French inventor]

contemn /kən tém/ (**-temns, -temning, -temned**) *vt* to view or treat somebody with contempt (*archaic*) [15C. Directly or via French < Latin *contemnere* (see CONTEMPT)] —**contemner** /-témnər/*n* —**contemnible** /-témnəb'l/ *adj* —**contemnibly** /-témnəbli/ *adv*

contemplate /kóntəm playt, -təm-/ (**-plates, -plating, -plated**) *v* **1.** *vt* HAVE SOMETHING AS POSSIBLE INTENTION to think about something as a possible course of action ○ *contemplating moving house* **2.** *vt* CONSIDER SOMETHING to think about something seriously and at length, especially in order to understand it more fully ○ *I sat there, contemplating what she'd said.* **3.** *vi* THINK ABOUT SPIRITUAL MATTERS to think calmly and at length, especially as a religious or spiritual exercise **4.** *vt* LOOK AT SOMETHING THOUGHTFULLY to look at something thoughtfully and steadily ○ *tourists contemplating the restored frescoes* [Late 16C. < Latin *contemplat-*, past participle of *contemplari* 'observe carefully' < *templum* 'space for observing omens'] —**contemplation** /kóntəm pláysh'n, -tem-/ *n* —**contemplator** *n*

contemplative /kən témplətiv/ *adj* calm and thoughtful, or inclined to be this way ■ *n* somebody who practices spiritual contemplation, e.g. a monk or nun —**contemplatively** *adv*

contemporaneous /kən témpə ráyni əss, kon-/ *adj* existing, occurring, or beginning at the same time or during the same period of time as something else [Mid-17C. < Latin *contemporaneus*, literally 'time together' < *tempor-* 'time'] —**contemporaneity** /kən témpərə neé əti, kon-/ *n* —**contemporaneously** *adv* —**contemporaneousness** *n*

contemporary /kən témprəri/ *adj* **1.** OF SAME TIME existing or occurring at or dating from the same period of time as something or somebody else ○ *The Celts were dismissed by contemporary chroniclers as barbarians.* **2.** EXISTING in existence now ○ *problems of contemporary urban society* **3.** MODERN IN STYLE distinctively modern in style ○ *contemporary dance* **4.** OF SAME AGE of the same or approximately the same age as somebody else ○ *She and I are more or less contemporary.* ■ *n* (*plural* **-ies**) **1.** SOMEBODY OR SOMETHING OF SAME TIME somebody or something living or existing during the same period of time as another ○ *This 18th-century table is a contemporary of the Shaker furniture in the other room.* **2.** SOMEBODY OF SAME AGE somebody of about the same age as somebody else ○ *It was nice to spend time with my Dad's contemporaries.* **3.** MODERN PERSON OR THING somebody or something in existence at the present time [Mid-17C. < medieval Latin *contemporarius* < Latin *tempor-* 'time'] —**contemporarily** *adv* —**contemporariness** *n*

contemporize /kən témpə rīz/ (**-rizes, -rizing, -rized**), **contemporise** (**-rises, -rising, -rised**) *vt* **1.** to make something modern or fashionable **2.** to place somebody or something in the same period as somebody or something else [Mid-17C. < late Latin *contemporare* 'make contemporary' < Latin *tempor-* 'time'] —**contemporization** /kən témpə rī záysh'n/ *n*

~~**contempory**~~ incorrect spelling of **contemporary**

contempt /kən témpt/ *n* **1.** a powerful feeling of dislike towards somebody or something considered to be worthless, inferior, or undeserving of respect **2.** LAW same as **contempt of court** [14C. < Latin *contemptus* 'scorn' < *contemnere* 'despise utterly' < *temnere* 'to scorn']

contemptible /kən témptəb'l/ *adj* deserving to be treated with contempt —**contemptibility** /kən témptə bílləti/ *n* —**contemptibleness** *n* —**contemptibly** *adv*

contempt of court *n* the crime of deliberately failing to obey or respect the authority of a court of law or legislative body

contemptuous /kən témptyoo əss/ *adj* feeling, expressing, or demonstrating a strong dislike or utter lack of respect for somebody or something [Early 16C. < medieval Latin *contemptuosus* < Latin *contemnere* (see CONTEMPT)] —**contemptuously** *adv* —**contemptuousness** *n*

contend /kən ténd/ (**-tends, -tending, -tended**) *v* **1.** *vt* STATE SOMETHING to argue or claim that something is true **2.** *vi* COMPETE to compete for something, especially a prize or trophy ○ *the teams contending for the cup* **3.** *vi* STRUGGLE OR DEAL WITH SOMETHING to fight with, struggle against, or deal with somebody or something ○ *Their lawyers have a number of awkward issues to contend with.* **4.** *vi* DEBATE WITH SOMEBODY to debate or dispute with somebody (*literary*) [15C. Directly or via French < Latin *contendere* 'strive together' < *tendere* 'strive']

contender /kən téndər/ *n* a competitor, especially somebody who has a good chance of winning

SYNONYMS See ***candidate***.

content[1] /kón tent/ *n* **1.** AMOUNT OF SOMETHING IN CONTAINER the amount of something contained in something else ○ *fruit with a high vitamin C content* **2.** SUBJECT MATTER the various issues, topics, or questions dealt with in speech, discussion, or a piece of writing ○ *a speech that was highly emotive in both tone and content* **3.** MEANING OR MESSAGE the meaning or message contained in a creative work, as distinct from its appearance, form, or style **4.** INFORMATION AVAILABLE ELECTRONICALLY information made available by an electronic medium or product **5.** CAPACITY the capacity of a container ■ **contents** *npl* **1.** SOMETHING CONTAINED everything that is inside a particular container ○ *picked up the file and emptied its contents onto the desk* **2.** SUBJECT OF TEXT the subject matter of a document or publication ○ *revealed the contents of the letter* **3.** LIST OF SUBJECT OR CHAPTER HEADINGS a list at the front of a publication that gives the title and number of the first page of each new chapter, article, or part [15C. < medieval Latin *contentum* 'something contained', form of Latin *contentus*, past participle of *continere* (see CONTAIN)]

content[2] /kən tént/ *adj* **1.** QUIETLY SATISFIED AND HAPPY reasonably happy and satisfied with the way things are **2.** READY TO ACCEPT SOMETHING willing to accept a situation or comply with a proposed course of action ○ *He had to be content with third place in the race.* ■ *v* (**-tents, -tenting, -tented**) **1.** *vt* CAUSE SOMEBODY TO FEEL CONTENT to make somebody feel happy or satisfied with something **2.** *vr* ACCEPT OR MAKE DO WITH SOMETHING to accept or make do with something, rather than taking further action or making more demands ○ *He contented himself with a few cutting remarks about lack of discipline and did not take the matter further.* ■ *n* same as **contentment** (sense 1) ■ *interj* HOUSE OF LORDS EXPRESSION OF AGREEMENT used by a member of the House of Lords to express formal agreement to a bill. Disagreement is expressed by the phrase 'not content'. (*formal*) [15C. Via French < Latin *contentus* (see CONTENT [1])] —**contently** *adv*

contented /kən téntid/ *adj* peacefully happy and satisfied with the way things are or with what has been done —**contentedly** *adv* —**contentedness** *n*

contention /kən ténsh'n/ *n* **1.** ASSERTION IN ARGUMENT an opinion or claim stated in the course of an argument ○ *It is my contention that the scheme was bound to fail.* **2.** DISAGREEMENT angry disagreement between people ○ *a lot of contention over the quality of the goods* **3.** RIVALRY competition between rivals or opponents ○ *fierce contention for the title* [14C. Directly or via French < Latin *contention-* < *contendere* (see CONTEND)]

contentious /kən ténshəss/ *adj* **1.** CREATING DISAGREEMENT causing or likely to cause disagreement and disputes between people with differing views ○ *It should have been possible to word the statement in a less contentious way.* **2.** ARGUMENTATIVE frequently engaging in and seeming to enjoy arguments and disputes **3.** LAW SUBJECT TO LITIGATION contested by another interested party ○ *a contentious will* [15C. Via French < Latin *contentiosus* < *contendere* (see CONTEND)] —**contentiously** *adv* —**contentiousness** *n*

contentment /kən téntmənt/ *n* **1.** a feeling of calm satisfaction **2.** a circumstance, or a feature or characteristic of something, that gives rise to satisfaction (*formal or literary*)

content provider /kón tent-/ *n* a website containing mainly news or information rather than commercial facilities such as shopping or banking, or a business supplying the information for such a website

content word /kón tent-/ *n* a word that primarily conveys meaning rather than grammatical function, e.g. a noun, verb, or adjective

conterminous /kon túrminəss, kən-/, **coterminous** /kō-/ *adj* **1.** INSIDE SAME BOUNDARY enclosed inside a common boundary **2.** ADJACENT next to and sharing a common boundary with something **3.** MEETING IN TIME OR PLACE meeting end to end, so that where or when one finishes the next begins [Mid-17C. < Latin *conterminus*, literally 'boundary with' < *terminus* 'boundary'] —**conterminously** *adv*

contessa /kon téssə/ *n* an Italian countess [Early 19C. Via Italian < medieval Latin *comitissa*, feminine of *comit-* 'companion']

contest *n* /kón test/ **1.** COMPETITION TO FIND BEST an organized competition for a prize or title, especially one in which the entrants appear or demonstrate their skills individually and the winner is chosen by a group of judges **2.** STRUGGLE FOR CONTROL a struggle between opposing individuals, organizations, or forces for victory or control ■ *vt* /kən tést/ (**-tests, -testing, -tested**) **1.** CHALLENGE SOMETHING to challenge or question something **2.** TAKE PART IN CONTEST to take part in a contest or competition, especially an election [Late 16C. Directly or via French < Latin *contestari* 'begin a lawsuit by calling witnesses together' < *testari* 'be a witness'] —**contestable** /kən téstəb'l/ *adj* —**contestably** *adv* —**contester** *n*

contestant /kən téstənt/ *n* **1.** a competitor in a contest or competition **2.** somebody who challenges something such as a will, verdict, or decision

SYNONYMS See *candidate.*

context /kón tekst/ *n* **1. TEXT SURROUNDING WORD OR PASSAGE** the words, phrases, or passages that come before and after a particular word or passage in a speech or piece of writing and help to explain its full meaning **2. SURROUNDING CONDITIONS** the circumstances or events that form the environment within which something exists or takes place ○ *The dispute needs to be viewed in its historical context.* **3.** E-COMMERCE **DATA TRANSFER STRUCTURE** a data structure used to transfer electronic data to and from a business management system [15C. < Latin *contextus* 'connected' < *contexere* 'weave together' < *texere* 'weave'] —**contextless** *adj* —**contextual** /kən tékstyoo əl/ *adj* —**contextually** *adv*

contextualize /kən tékstyoo ə līz/ (**-izes, -izing, -ized**), **contextualise** (**-ises, -ising, -ised**) *vt* to place a word, phrase, or idea within a suitable context —**contextualization** /kən tékstyoo ə lī záysh'n/ *n*

Conti /kónti/, **Tom** (*b.* 1941) Scottish-born British stage and film actor. He is a versatile character actor whose success dates from his Tony award for the Broadway production of *Whose Life Is It Anyway?* (1979).

contig /kən tíg/ *n* a continuous series of overlapping cloned DNA segments derived from the genetic material of a chromosome and used in mapping the physical order of bases along the chromosome [Late 20C. Shortening of CONTIGUOUS]

contiguity /kónti gyóo əti/ (*plural* **-ties**) *n* (*formal*) **1.** closeness in space or time to something, or actual contact with it along one side **2.** a continuous line, mass, or series ○ *a contiguity of roofs*

contiguous /kən tíggyoo əss/ *adj* (*formal*) **1. ADJOINING** sharing a boundary or touching each other physically **2. NEIGHBOURING** situated next to something else or to each other **3. CONTINUOUS** connected together so as to form an unbroken sequence in time or an uninterrupted expanse in space [Early 16C. < Latin *contiguus* 'touching together' < *contingere* (see CONTACT)] —**contiguously** *adv* —**contiguousness** *n*

continent[1] /kóntinənt/ *n* **1.** any of the seven large continuous land masses that constitute most of the dry land on the surface of the Earth. They are Africa, Antarctica, Asia, Australia, Europe, North America, and South America. **2.** the part of the Earth's crust that rises above the oceans [Mid-16C. < Latin *terra continens* 'continuous land' < the present participle of *continere* (see CONTAIN)]

continent[2] /kóntinənt/ *adj* **1.** able to exercise control over urination and bowel movements **2.** restrained, especially abstaining from sexual activity (*formal*) [14C. < Latin *continent-*, present participle of *continere* (see CONTAIN)] —**continence** *n*

Continent *n* the mainland of Europe, not including the British Isles

continental /kónti nént'l/ *adj* **1.** relating to, typical of, or belonging to the continents of the Earth **2.** another spelling of **Continental** *adj* (sense 1) ■ *n* another spelling of **Continental** *n* (sense 1) —**continentalism** *n* —**continentalist** *n* —**continentally** *adv*

Continental *adj* **1. OF MAINLAND EUROPE** from or relating to mainland Europe **2. OF ORIGINAL 13 AMERICAN COLONIES** from or relating to the 13 colonies that later became the United States ■ *n* **1. MAINLAND EUROPEAN** somebody from mainland Europe (*informal*) **2. AMERICAN SOLDIER DURING REVOLUTION** a soldier in the American army during the American War of Independence

continental breakfast *n* a light breakfast usually consisting of fruit juice, a roll, croissant, or pastry with jam and butter, and coffee or tea [Because it is common on the Continent]

continental climate *n* the climate characteristic of the interior of a continent, with hot summers, cold winters, and little rainfall

continental code *n US* COMMUNICATION same as **International Morse code**

Continental Congress *n* the congress of delegates from the American colonies held before, during, and after the American War of Independence. It issued the Declaration of Independence (1776) and drafted the Articles of Confederation (1777).

continental crust *n* the part of the outer shell of Earth that constitutes the continents and the rocks beneath them down to the level of the mantle. It is approximately 35 km/22 mi. thick in most areas and is composed of sedimentary rocks near the surface and metamorphic rocks at a lower depth.

continental divide *n* a massive area of high ground in the interior of a continent, from either side of which a continent's river systems flow in different directions

Continental Divide series of mountain ridges running from Alaska to Mexico and including the Rocky Mountains that forms the main watershed of North America

continental drift *n* a theory that explains the formation, alteration, and extremely slow movement of the continents across the Earth's crust. The continents are thought to have been formed from one large land mass that split, drifted apart, and in places collided again.

continental margin *n* the region of ocean between the deep sea and shore, consisting of the continental rise, slope, and shelf

continental quilt *n* HOUSEHOLD same as **duvet** (sense 1)

continental rise *n* the transitional area of the continental margin between the continental slope and abyssal plain

continental shelf *n* the gently sloping undersea area surrounding a continent at depths of up to 200 m/ 656 ft, at the edge of which the continental slope drops steeply to the ocean floor

continental slope *n* the steep slope from the continental shelf down to the ocean floor

contingence /kən tínjənss/ *n* **1.** physical contact between objects **2.** same as **contingency** (sense 1)

contingency /kən tínjənssi/ (*plural* **-cies**) *n* **1. SOMETHING THAT MAY HAPPEN** an event that might occur in the future, especially a problem, emergency, or expense that might arise unexpectedly and therefore must be prepared for **2. SOMETHING SET ASIDE FOR UNFORESEEN EMERGENCY** provision made against future unforeseen events, e.g. an allocation of funds in a budget **3. DEPENDENCE UPON CHANCE** dependence upon chance or factors and circumstances that are presently unknown **4. CHANGE IN MEANING PRODUCED BY CLAUSE** in systemic grammar, a change in the meaning of the main clause brought about by the addition of a bound clause introduced by 'if', 'when', 'though', or 'since'

contingency fee (*plural* **contingency fees** or **contingent fees**) *n* a payment for professional services such as those of a lawyer that is made only if the client receives a satisfactory result

contingency plan *n* a plan designed to deal with a particular problem, emergency, or state of affairs if it should occur

contingent /kən tínjənt/ *adj* **1. DEPENDENT ON WHAT MAY HAPPEN** dependent on or resulting from a future and as yet unknown event or circumstance ○ *Payment is contingent upon winning the case.* **2. POSSIBLE BUT NOT CERTAIN** possible, but not certain to happen ○ *'...all the advantages of a long slow ramble with Elfride, without the contingent possibility of the enjoyment being spoilt by her becoming weary.'* (Thomas Hardy, *A Pair of Blue Eyes*; 1889) **3. CHANCE** happening by chance **4.** LOGIC **TRUE ONLY UNDER CERTAIN CONDITIONS** true only under some conditions or under existing conditions, and therefore not universally true or valid ■ *n* **1. GROUP OF PEOPLE** a group of people representing a particular organization or belief, or from a particular region or country, and forming part of a larger group **2. GROUP OF MILITARY PERSONNEL** a group of soldiers forming part of a larger force **3.** same as **contingency** (sense 1) [14C. < Latin *contingent-*, present participle of *contingere* (see CONTACT)] —**contingently** *adv*

contingent fee *n* COMM same as **contingency fee**

contingent worker *n US* a temporary employee, often employed for a specific task

~~**continous**~~ incorrect spelling of **continuous**

continual /kən tínnyoo əl/ *adj* **1.** happening again and again, especially regularly **2.** ⚠ continuing almost without interruption or ending [14C. < French *continuel* < *continuer* (see CONTINUE)] —**continualness** *n*

USAGE continual or **continuous**? Something ***continual*** continues, with breaks, over a period of time, whereas something ***continuous*** goes on without stopping. So a ***continual*** noise is one that is constantly repeated, like a dog's barking, and a ***continuous*** noise is one that continues without stopping, like the roar of a waterfall. The same distinction applies to the adverbs ***continually*** and ***continuously***: *The speaker was continually interrupted by hecklers. She drove continuously for three hours.* In popular usage, however, ***continual*** and ***continually*** are now frequently used to mean 'without stopping'.

continually /kən tínnyoo əli/ *adv* **1.** with great frequency or regularity **2.** ⚠ all the time, almost without interruption or ending ○ *hard to think with the kids continually screaming*

USAGE See *continual.*

continuance /kən tínnyoo ənss/ *n* **1. CONTINUATION OF SOMETHING** the fact or quality of continuing into the future **2. LENGTH OF TIME SOMETHING LASTS** the period of time that something lasts or continues **3.** *N Am* **ADJOURNMENT** a postponement of legal proceedings until a later date

continuant /kən tínnyoo ənt/ *n* a speech consonant made with the vocal passage partly open for breath to pass through, thus enabling the sound to be prolonged at will, e.g. 'l', 'f', or 's'

continuation /kən tínnyoo áysh'n/ *n* **1. PROCESS OF CONTINUING** the process of continuing something without interruption **2. ADDITION OR EXTENSION** an additional part that extends something that already exists or has already begun **3. STARTING AGAIN AFTER INTERRUPTION** the renewal of an action, event, or process after it has been interrupted

continuative /kən tínnyoo ətiv/ *adj* **1. AIDING CONTINUITY** causing or helping something to continue (*formal*) **2.** GRAM **EXPRESSING CONTINUATION** expressing the continuation of an action, or indicating that a discourse is moving on to another point ■ *n* GRAM **WORD EXPRESSING CONTINUATION** a continuative clause, phrase, or word —**continuatively** *adv*

continuator /kən tínnyoo aytər/ *n* somebody who continues something, especially work started by somebody else, or somebody or something that maintains continuity

continue /kən tínnyoo/ (**-ues, -uing, -ued**) *v* **1.** *vti* **KEEP GOING** to last, or make something last, beyond the present or throughout a period of time ○ *pledge to continue campaigning against the ban* ○ *Talks between the two sides continued during May.* **2.** *vti* **NOT STOP** to keep up an activity or state already begun ○ *were able to continue broadcasting without interruption* **3.** *vti* **START SOMETHING AGAIN** to start doing something again after an interruption or pause ○ *We'll continue this discussion later.* **4.** *vti* **BEGIN SPEAKING AGAIN** to begin speaking again, or say something, after an interruption or pause **5.** *vti* **MAKE SOMETHING LONGER** to extend, or extend something, beyond a particular point or beyond its original length **6.** *vi* **MOVE FARTHER** to move or travel farther in a particular direction ○ *Continue east along the coast path.* **7.** *vt Scotland, N Am* **POSTPONE CASE** to postpone legal proceedings [14C. Via French < Latin *continuare* 'make continuous' < *continere* (see CONTAIN)] —**continuable** *adj* —**continued** *adj* —**continuer** *n*

continued fraction *n* a fraction with a whole number as numerator, and a number plus a fraction as denominator, the denominator in turn having a number plus a fraction as its denominator. If there is a finite number of terms, it is said to be terminating, otherwise it is nonterminating.

continuing /kən tínnyoo ing/ *adj* having existed for some time, currently in existence, and likely to remain so in the future —**continuingly** *adv*

continuing education *n* **1.** adult education, usually in the form of short or part-time courses, continuing throughout a person's life **2.** *N Am* regular courses or training designed to bring professionals up to date with the latest developments in their particular field

continuity /kónti nyóo əti/ (*plural* **-ties**) *n* **1. UNCHANGING QUALITY** the fact of staying the same, of being consistent throughout, or of not stopping or being interrupted ○ *measures to ensure continuity of supply* ○ *the stability and continuity of traditional rural life* **2. CONSISTENT WHOLE** something that remains consistent or uninterrupted throughout ○ *stressed the continuities with the past* **3. CONSISTENCY BETWEEN FILM OR BROADCAST PARTS** consistency in the details from one part of a film or broadcast to another ○

discrepancies in continuity **4. SEAMLESSNESS OF NARRATIVE** smoothness in the narrative flow in a film or broadcast **5. DETAILED SCRIPT** a comprehensive script that includes full details of the contents of each shot or scene, including such items as camera positions and costume features **6. SPOKEN LINK IN BROADCASTING** commentary by a television or radio broadcaster that fills the time between the end of one programme or programme segment and the beginning of the next

continuo /kən tínnyoo ō/ (*plural* **-os**) *n* an instrumental bass accompaniment, usually played on a keyboard, with numbers written beneath the notes so that musicians can improvise and provide harmony [Early 18C. < Italian, 'continuous' < Latin *continuus* (see CONTINUOUS)]

continuous /kən tínnyoo əss/ *adj* **1. UNCHANGED OR UNINTERRUPTED** continuing without changing, stopping, or being interrupted ○ *three days of continuous rain* **2. UNBROKEN** having no gaps, holes, or breaks ○ *a continuous line* **3.** GRAM same as **progressive** *adj* (sense 6) **4.** MATHS **RELATING TO DIFFERENCE OF FUNCTION VALUES** relating to a line or curve along which the difference between function values at any two points within a given interval will approach zero if the interval is decreased sufficiently **5. RELATING TO UNINTERRUPTED CHEMICAL MANUFACTURING** relating to chemical manufacturing in which material is processed in an uninterrupted stream. Continuous processes are usually advantageous for large-scale chemical production. [Mid-17C. < Latin *continuus* 'uninterrupted' < *continere* (see CONTAIN)] —**continuously** *adv* —**continuousness** *n*

USAGE See *continual.*

continuous assessment *n* assessment of pupils' progress based on work they do or tests they take throughout the term or year, rather than on a single examination

continuous creation theory *n* ASTRON same as **steady-state theory**

continuous spectrum *n* a sequence of frequencies that is without breaks over a relatively wide range of wavelengths

continuous wave *n* an electromagnetic wave generated as an unbroken train of constant frequency and amplitude, rather than in pulses

continuum /kən tínnyoo əm/ (*plural* **-a** /-yoo ə/ or **-ums**) *n* **1.** a link between two things, or a continuous series of things, that blend into each other so gradually and seamlessly that it is impossible to say where one becomes the next ○ *A rainbow forms a continuum of colour.* **2.** a set of real numbers between any two of which a third can always be found, and in which there are no gaps [Mid-17C. < Latin, form of *continuus* (see CONTINUOUS)]

contort /kən táwrt/ (**-torts, -torting, -torted**) *v* **1.** *vti* to become so twisted as to take on an unnatural or grotesque shape, or to twist something, especially a part of the body, in this way ○ *Fear had contorted their faces.* **2.** *vt* to change something so greatly that it becomes unrecognizable [15C. < Latin *contort-*, past participle of *contorquere* 'twist violently' < *torquere* 'to twist'] —**contortive** *adj*

contorted /kən táwrtid/ *adj* **1.** greatly or violently twisted out of shape **2.** describes plant parts such as sepals or leaves whose margins overlap in the bud like playing cards in a hand, so that they appear to be twisted —**contortedly** *adv* —**contortedness** *n*

contortion /kən táwrsh'n/ *n* **1.** a twisting of something, especially a part of the body, out of its natural shape **2.** a bewilderingly complex manoeuvring or manipulation of something ○ *verbal contortions that tie his opponents in knots*

contortionist /kən táwrsh'nist/ *n* **1.** somebody who bends his or her own body into unusual shapes as an entertainment ○ *You'd have to be a contortionist to get into those jeans.* **2.** somebody who twists or distorts something such as a statement ○ *a debater skilled as a logical contortionist* —**contortionistic** /kən táwrsh'n ístik/ *adj*

contour /kón toor/ *n* **1. SHAPE'S OUTLINE** an outline, especially of something curved or irregular (*often used in the plural*) ○ *The contours of the hills were characteristically rounded.* **2. GENERAL NATURE** the general character or nature of something ○ *scenes that establish the contour of the play* **3.** GEOG same as **contour line** ■ *adj* **1. SHAPED OR FITTED** shaped to fit something, especially the shape of somebody's body ○ *contour furniture* **2. FOLLOWING LAND'S SHAPE** following the lie of the land, rather than cutting through or across it ○ *contour farming* ■ *vt* (**-tours, -touring, -toured**) **1. SHAPE SOMETHING TO FIT** to shape one thing so that it fits the outlines of another ○ *furniture that is contoured to the human body* **2. PUT CONTOUR LINES ON MAP** to mark contour lines on something such as a map **3. MAKE SOMETHING FOLLOW SHAPE OF LAND** to build or operate something so that it follows the natural shape of the land ○ *roads that are sensitively contoured* [Mid-17C. < French < Italian *contornare* 'draw in outline', literally 'turn with' < Latin *tornare* (see TURN)]

contour feather *n* a medium-sized feather of a bird that forms part of its external body covering and determines its shape, excluding the wings and tail

contour interval *n* the interval between contour lines on a map, or the altitude the interval represents ○ *at contour intervals of 10 metres*

contour line *n* a line on a map connecting points on a land surface that are the same elevation above sea level

contour map *n* a map that uses contour lines to show the shapes and elevations of land surfaces

contr. *abbr* **1.** GRAM contraction **2.** MUSIC contralto **3.** control

Contra /kóntrə/ *n* a member of the United States-backed counter-revolutionary force that tried to overthrow the Nicaraguan government in the 1980s [Late 20 C. < Spanish *contrarevolucionario* 'counter-revolutionary']

contra- *prefix* **1.** against, opposite, contrasting ○ *contraindicate* **2.** lower in pitch ○ *contrabass* [< Latin *contra* 'against' < Indo-European, 'together']

contraband /kóntrə band/ *n* **1. ILLEGAL IMPORTS AND EXPORTS** goods that are illegally imported or exported, e.g. goods that evade duty or are prohibited by law from being taken into or out of a country ○ *dealers in contraband* **2. ILLEGAL TRADE** illegal trade, especially the illegal importing or exporting of goods **3. SUPPLIES FORBIDDEN TO WARRING SIDES** goods that a neutral country must not supply to either side in a war ■ *adj* **1. ILLEGALLY TRADED** bought or sold, especially imported or exported, illegally ○ *truckloads of contraband cigarettes* **2. FORBIDDEN FROM BEING IMPORTED OR EXPORTED** forbidden by law from being traded, especially as an import or export [Late 16C. Via Spanish *contrabanda* < Italian *contrabbando*, literally 'against proclamation' < *bando* 'proclamation' < Germanic] —**contrabandist** *n*

contrabass /kóntrə bayss/ *n* **1.** MUSIC same as **double bass 2. INSTRUMENT PITCHED LOWEST OF ITS FAMILY** an instrument pitched an octave below the usual range for that family of instruments **3. CONTRABASSIST** an instrumentalist in an orchestra or band who plays the contrabass ■ *adj* **PITCHED OCTAVE BELOW** pitched an octave below the usual range of that instrument ○ *contrabass clarinet* [Early 19C. < Italian *contrabbasso* < *basso* 'bass'] —**contrabassist** /kóntrə báyssist/ *n*

contrabassoon /kóntrə bə sóon/ *n* **1.** a U-shaped woodwind instrument that is the largest in the oboe family and has a pitch an octave below the bassoon **2.** an instrumentalist in an orchestra or chamber group who plays the contrabassoon —**contrabassoonist** *n*

contraception /kóntrə sépsh'n/ *n* **1.** the prevention of pregnancy using artificial methods such as condoms and contraceptive pills or natural methods such as avoiding sex during the woman's known fertile periods **2.** a method or device used to prevent pregnancy [Late 19C. < CONTRA- + CONCEPTION]

contraceptive /kóntrə séptiv/ *n* **DEVICE PREVENTING FERTILIZATION** a device used to prevent fertilization of an egg, e.g. a condom worn by a man during intercourse, or a pill taken regularly by a woman ■ *adj* **1. OF CONTRACEPTION** relating to contraception ○ *contraceptive advice* **2. PREVENTING INSEMINATION** designed to prevent sperm from fertilizing an egg ○ *various contraceptive methods and devices*

contraceptive ring *n* a plastic ring inserted into the vagina that releases a constant flow of a contraceptive drug

contract *n* /kón trakt/ **1. FORMAL AGREEMENT** a formal or legally binding agreement, e.g. one for the sale of property, or one setting out terms of employment ○ *Such actions would be in breach of contract.* **2. DOCUMENT RECORDING AGREEMENT** a document that records a formal or legally binding agreement ○ *sign a contract* **3. AGREEMENT TO MARRY** a formal agreement to marry (*dated*) **4. PAID ASSASSIN'S ASSIGNMENT** a hiring of an assassin to kill somebody (*informal*) ○ *a contract killing* **5. HIGHEST BRIDGE BID IN ONE HAND** in bridge, a winning bid in a single hand, in which partners agree regarding the number of tricks they can take **6. NUMBER AND SUIT OF CONTRACT** in bridge, the number and suit of the tricks agreed on by the highest bidders **7.** CARDS same as **contract bridge** ■ *v* /kən trákt/ (**-tracts, -tracting, -tracted**) **1.** *vti* **SHRINK OR LESSEN** to shrink or become smaller, or make something shrink or become smaller ○ *metals expanding and contracting as temperatures change* **2.** *vti* **TIGHTEN OR DRAW TOGETHER** to become tighter or draw together, or make something tighter or draw something together ○ *see the muscles contracting under the skin* **3.** *vt* **FORMALLY OR LEGALLY AGREE TO DO SOMETHING** to make a formal or legally binding agreement with somebody to do something, especially work (*often passive*) ○ *I'm not contracted to work on Sundays.* **4.** *vt* **GET ILLNESS** to become affected by an illness or disease **5.** *vt* **SHORTEN WORD OR PHRASE** to shorten a word by leaving out letters or syllables, or a phrase by leaving out words **6.** *vt* **ARRANGE MARRIAGE** to arrange a marriage formally (*dated*) [14C. Directly or via French < Latin *contractus*, past participle of *contrahere* 'draw together' < *trahere* 'to draw'] —**contractible** /kən tráktəb'l/ *adj*

contract out /kón trakt ówt/ *v* **1.** *vt* to offer work to other companies or workers outside the organization that is commissioning the work **2.** *vi* to withdraw from something by making a formal or legally binding declaration ○ *employees contracting out of the state pension scheme*

contract bridge *n* the most common variety of bridge, in which points are awarded only for tricks bid and won

contractile /kən trákt īl/ *adj* able or tending to shrink, tighten, or become narrower —**contractility** /kón trak tílləti/ *n*

contractile vacuole *n* a membrane-surrounded cavity within a cell that regulates the water content of the cell by absorbing water and then contracting to expel it

contraction /kən tráksh'n/ *n* **1. REDUCTION IN SIZE** a shrinking or reducing ○ *alternate expansion and contraction* **2. CONTRACTING OF BODY PART** a tightening or narrowing of a muscle, organ, or other body part **3. TIGHTENING OF WOMB MUSCLES EFFECTING CHILDBIRTH** a tightening of the muscles of the womb that occurs at increasingly frequent intervals immediately before childbirth and eventually pushes the baby out of the womb **4. SHORTENED WORD** a shortened form or shortening of a word or phrase, e.g. 'he'll' for 'he will'. In English, the omitted letter or letters may be marked with an apostrophe, depending on the type of contraction. —**contractional** *adj* —**contractionary** *adj* —**contractive** *adj*

contractor /kən tráktər/ *n* **1. COMPANY OR PERSON UNDER CONTRACT** a company or person with a formal contract to do a specific job, supplying labour and materials and providing and overseeing staff if needed **2. THING THAT CONTRACTS** something that contracts, e.g. a muscle **3. SOMEBODY WHO MAKES CONTRACT** one of the parties to a contract

contracts /kón trakts/ *n* the branch of law that deals with contracts (*takes a singular verb*) ○ *She made a career in contracts.*

contractual /kən trákchoo əl/ *adj* contained in, arising from, or in the form of a formal or legally binding agreement ○ *fulfilling your contractual obligations* —**contractually** *adv*

contracture /kən trákchər/ *n* a permanent tightening or shortening of a body part such as a muscle, tendon, or the skin, often affecting its shape

contradance *n* DANCE another spelling of **contredanse**

contradict /kóntrə díkt/ (**-dicts, -dicting, -dicted**) *vt* **1.** to argue against the truth or correctness of somebody's statement or claim **2.** to show that something is not true or that the opposite is true ○ *The results contradicted all previously held theories.* [Late 16C. < Latin *contradict-*, past participle of *contradicere* 'speak against' < *dicere* 'speak'] —**contradictable** *adj* —**contradicter** *n* —**contradictive** *adj* —**contradictively** *adv*

SYNONYMS See *disagree*.

contradiction /kóntrə díksh'n/ *n* **1.** something that has aspects that are illogical or inconsistent with each other ○ *a contradiction in terms* **2.** a statement, or the making of a statement, that opposes or disagrees with somebody or something ○ *I can say without fear of contradiction that she is our best worker.*

contradictory /kóntrə díktəri/ *adj* **1. INCONSISTENT** inconsistent either within itself or in relation to others **2. OPPOSING** holding or consisting of an opposite view **3. ARGUMENTATIVE** tending to take opposite views —**contradictorily** *adv* —**contradictoriness** *n*

contradistinction /kóntrədi stíngksh'n/ *n* differentiation between two things by identifying their contrasting qualities —**contradistinctive** *adj* —**contradistinctively** *adv*

contraflow /kóntrəflō/ *n* a temporary two-way traffic system on one carriageway of a motorway or dual carriageway

contrail /kón trayl/ *n* AVIAT same as **vapour trail** [Mid-20C. Contraction of *condensation trail*]

contraindicate /kóntrə índi kayt/ (**-cates, -cating, -cated**) *vt* to state something to be inadvisable while taking particular medication because of a likely adverse reaction ○ *Taking aspirin with this drug is contraindicated.* —**contraindicant** *n* —**contraindication** /kóntrə índi káysh'n/ *n* —**contraindicative** /kóntrə in díkətiv/ *adj*

contralateral /kóntrə láttərəl/ *adj* describes a body part that is on the opposite side of the body, or that acts in conjunction with such a part

contralto /kən tráltō/ (*plural* **-tos**) *n* **1. LOWEST FEMALE VOCAL RANGE** the lowest vocal range for women's voices, below soprano and mezzo-soprano **2. SOMEBODY WITH CONTRALTO SINGING VOICE** a singer, usually a woman, with a contralto voice **3. PART FOR CONTRALTO** a singing part for a contralto [Mid-18C. < Italian, 'below alto']

contraposition /kóntrəpə zísh'n/ *n* **1.** a position opposite to or against something ○ *took up a stand in contraposition to government policy* **2.** in logic, the relation of a proposition to its contrapositive [Mid-16C. < late Latin *contraposition-* < Latin *contraponere* 'place opposite' < *ponere* 'to place']

contrapositive /kóntrə pózzətiv/ *n* in logic, a conditional proposition that negates another conditional proposition and also reverses its clauses. The proposition 'if not q then not p' is the contrapositive of the proposition 'if p then q'.

contrapposto /kóntrə póstō/ (*plural* **-tos**) *n* a relaxed asymmetrical pose of the human body in art, especially sculpture, in which the shoulders and hips are turned in different planes [Early 20C. < Italian, past participle of *contrapporre* < Latin *contraponere* (see CONTRAPOSITION)]

contraption /kən trápsh'n/ *n* a device or machine, especially one that appears strange or improvised ○ *They'd rigged up a contraption for opening the door.* [Early 19C. Origin ?]

contrapuntal /kóntrə púnt'l/ *adj* describes polyphonic music with very active and strongly differentiated parts [Mid-19C. < Italian *contrapunto* 'counterpoint' < *punto* 'point' < Latin *punctum* (see POINT)] —**contrapuntally** *adv*

contrapuntist /kóntrə púntist/ *n* a composer of music in counterpoint or in a contrapuntal style [Late 18C. < Italian *contrapuntista* < *contrapunto* (see COUNTERPOINT)]

contrarian /kən tráiri ən/ *n* **1.** a habitual opponent of accepted policies, opinions, or practices ○ *a thoroughgoing contrarian, accepting nothing anyone says* **2.** an investor who goes against current market trends, e.g. by buying shares that most other investors are selling

contrariety /kóntrə rí əti/ (*plural* **-ties**) *n* **1. OPPOSITENESS** the state or quality of opposing or being contrary **2. POINT OF DIFFERENCE** a point of difference or inconsistency **3. OBSTACLE TO PROGRESS** something that obstructs or hinders progress ○ *battling against the contrarieties of the weather*

contrariwise /kən tráiri wīz/ *adv* **1. IN OPPOSITE WAY** in the opposite way or direction or on the opposite side **2. ON OTHER HAND** used to introduce a statement in direct opposition to what has already been said **3. UNHELPFULLY** in a way that obstructs or hinders progress ○ *Unfortunately, things turned out contrariwise, and we had to give up the idea.*

contrary /kóntrəri/ *adj* **1. CONFLICTING** not at all in agreement with something ○ *Such arrangements were contrary to his moral code.* **2. OPPOSITE** opposite in direction ○ *flew in a direction contrary to the rest of the aeroplanes* **3. OBSTRUCTING OR HINDERING PROGRESS** making forward motion extremely hard ○ *slowed by contrary winds* **4.** /kən tráiri/ **DELIBERATELY DISOBEDIENT** wilfully disobedient or uncooperative ○ *a contrary child* **5.** LOGIC **UNABLE TO BE TRUE AT ONCE** describes a pair of propositions that cannot both be true, though they may both be false ■ *n* **THE OPPOSITE** the opposite of something ○ *Actually, the contrary is true.* [13C. Via Anglo-Norman < Latin *contrarius* < *contra* 'against'] —**contrarily** /kən tráirəli/ *adv* —**contrariness** /kən tráirinəss/ *n* ◇ **contrary to** differently from ◇ **on** *or* **to the contrary** quite the reverse is true

contrast *n* /kón traast/ **1. MARKED DIFFERENCE** a difference, or something that is different ○ *in stark contrast to the luxury they formerly enjoyed* **2. JUXTAPOSITION OF DIFFERENT THINGS** an effect created by placing or arranging very different things such as colours, shades, or textures next to each other **3. DEGREE OF LIGHTNESS AND DARKNESS** the difference, or the use of differences, between the lightest and the darkest parts of something, e.g. to create a special effect in a painting, photograph, or television image ■ *vti* /kən tráast/ (**-trasts, -trasting, -trasted**) **SEEM OR MAKE THINGS SEEM DIFFERENT** to compare different things or arrange them in a way that highlights their differences, or be markedly different when compared with something ○ *These poems have a mature voice when contrasted with her earlier work.* [15C. Via French < Italian *contrastare* 'stand against' < Latin *stare* 'to stand'] —**contrastable** /kən tráastəb'l/ *adj* —**contrastably** *adv* —**contrasting** *adj* —**contrastingly** *adv*

contrastive /kən tráastiv/ *adj* forming a contrast, or using contrasting colours, tones, or textures —**contrastively** *adv* —**contrastiveness** *n*

contrast medium *n* a substance opaque to X-rays that is used to fill a body cavity, making the outline of the body part easier to see on an X-ray photograph. Barium is frequently used as a contrast medium.

contrasty /kón traasti/ *adj* showing sharp contrast between the lightest and darkest areas in a photograph or television or movie image

contravene /kóntrə veén/ (**-venes, -vening, -vened**) *vt* **1.** to break a rule or law ○ *outdated equipment that contravenes the safety regulations* **2.** to disagree with or oppose a statement or decision ○ *There was no question of contravening the committee's findings.* [Mid-16C. < late Latin *contravenire* 'come against' < Latin *venire* 'come'] —**contravener** *n* —**contravention** /-vénsh'n/ *n*

~~**contraversial**~~ incorrect spelling of **controversial**

contrecoup /kóntrə koo/ *n* an injury to one side of an organ, especially the brain, as a result of a blow that causes it to swing inside the retaining cavity [Mid-18C. < French, 'a blow opposite' < *coup* (see COUP)]

contredanse /kóntrə daanss/, **contradance** *n* **1.** a folk dance in which two pairs of partners face each other **2.** the music for a contredanse [Early 19C. < French, by folk etymology (influenced by *contre* 'against') < English *country dance*]

contretemps /kóntrə ton/ *n* (*formal*) **1.** a dispute or minor disagreement **2.** a mishap, especially an awkward or embarrassing one [Late 17C. < French, literally 'against the time']

contrib. *abbr* **1.** contribution **2.** contributor

contribute /kən tríbbyoot, kóntri byoot/ (**-utes, -uting, -uted**) *v* **1.** *vti* **DONATE MONEY OR TIME** to give something such as money or time to a common fund or for a specific purpose ○ *contributed generously to environmental causes* **2.** *vi* **BE PARTIAL CAUSE OF SOMETHING** to be one of the factors that causes something ○ *a heart condition that contributed to his early death* **3.** *vti* **OFFER OPINION** to offer opinions or advice in a meeting or discussion ○ *I felt I had nothing new to contribute to the debate.* **4.** *vti* **PROVIDE WORKS FOR PUBLICATION** to supply material for a publication or broadcast [Mid-16C. < Latin *contribut-*, past participle of *contribuere* 'bring in together' < *tribuere* 'to grant'] —**contributive** *adj*

USAGE The traditional pronunciation of ***contribute*** is with the stress on the first syllable; however stress on the first syllable is now more widespread and considered standard.

contribution /kóntri byóosh'n/ *n* **1. DONATION** something such as money or time that is given, especially to a common fund or for a specific purpose **2. REGULAR PAYMENT** a regular fixed amount paid, e.g. to a pension fund, often deducted from somebody's wage ○ *national insurance contributions* **3. ROLE PLAYED IN ACHIEVING SOMETHING** the part played by somebody or something in causing a result ○ *She recognized the contribution of her parents to her success.* **4. MATERIAL SUPPLIED FOR PUBLICATION OR BROADCAST** a piece of material that forms part of a publication or broadcast

contributor /kən tríbbyŏŏtər/ *n* **1. ONE OF THOSE GIVING SOMETHING** somebody who gives time or money to a common fund, project, or purpose **2. SOMEBODY SUPPLYING MATERIAL PUBLISHED OR BROADCAST** one of the people supplying material for a publication or broadcast **3. CAUSE** one of the causes of something ○ *Smoking is also a major contributor to heart disease.*

contributory /kən tríbbyŏŏtəri/ *adj* **1. HELPING SOMETHING HAPPEN** partly responsible for something ○ *Poor diet is often a contributory factor.* **2. GIVEN IN COMMON WITH OTHERS** given along with others to a common fund or project **3. REQUIRING EMPLOYEE TO PAY IN PART** describes an insurance or pension scheme in which the employee shares the cost of the premiums with the employer ■ *n* (*plural* **-ries**) **SOMEBODY WHO MAKES CONTRIBUTION** somebody who donates money or time

contributory negligence *n* a victim's share in the responsibility for an accident, when care to prevent it could have been taken by the victim as well as the other party

con trick *n* same as **confidence trick** (*informal*)

contrite /kón trīt, kən trít/ *adj* **1.** deeply sorry for having behaved wrongly **2.** done or said out of a sense of guilt or remorse ○ *full of contrite promises* [13C. Via French < Latin *contritus*, past participle of *conterere* 'rub together' < *terere* 'rub'] —**contritely** *adv* —**contriteness** *n*

contrition /kən trísh'n/ *n* **1.** deep and genuine feelings of guilt and remorse **2.** in the Roman Catholic Church, repentance for past sins and a firm resolve not to sin in future ○ *acts of contrition*

contrivance /kən trívnss/ *n* **1. DEVIOUS PLOT** a plan intended to deceive **2. SCHEMING** the making of clever or deceitful schemes **3. GADGET** a cleverly made device or machine to fulfil a need ○ *a contrivance for keeping your back straight*

contrive /kən trív/ (**-trives, -triving, -trived**) *v* **1.** *vti* **DO SOMETHING CREATIVELY** to accomplish something by being clever and creative ○ *She contrived a meeting between the warring factions.* **2.** *vt* **MAKE SOMETHING INGENIOUS** to make something in a skilful or ingenious way ○ *A tree house had been contrived from bits of scrap.* **3.** *vt* **MANAGE TO DO SOMETHING** to accomplish something difficult or unexpected ○ *She somehow contrived to be both an effective and a well-liked teacher.* **4.** *vti* **PLOT** to formulate clever or deceitful schemes ○ *The gang contrived a way to hack into the main computer system.* [13C. Via Old French *contro(u)ver* 'invent' < medieval Latin *contropare* 'compare' < Latin *tropus* 'turn, manner' < Greek *tropos*] —**contrivable** *adj* —**contriver** *n*

contrived /kən trívd/ *adj* **1.** not natural and spontaneous ○ *Her apology was very contrived.* **2.** unrealistic and unconvincing ○ *a film with a contrived ending* —**contrivedly** /-vidli/ *adv*

control /kən trṓl/ *vt* (**-trols, -trolling, -trolled**) **1. MANAGE** to exercise power or authority over something such as a business or nation ○ *The company is controlled largely by foreign interests.* **2. OPERATE MACHINE** to work or operate something such as a vehicle or machine ○ *Computers control many of the safety features on board.* **3. RESTRAIN OR LIMIT SOMETHING** to limit or restrict somebody or something, e.g. in expression, occurrence, or rate of increase ○ *The government set out to control inflation.* ○ *her inability to control her temper* **4.** FIN **OVERSEE FINANCIAL AFFAIRS** to regulate the financial affairs of a business or other large organization **5.** ACCT **VERIFY ACCOUNTS** to examine financial accounts and verify them as correct ■ *n* **1. ABILITY TO MANAGE SOMETHING** ability or authority to manage or direct something ○ *circumstances beyond*

our control **2. OPERATING SWITCH** a mechanical or electronic device used to operate a vehicle or machine ○ *Turn down the heat control.* **3. SKILL** skill in using something or in performing (*often used in combination*) ○ *players with excellent ball control* **4. LIMITS AND RESTRICTIONS** the process of limiting or restricting somebody or something, or the methods used in this ○ *an era of price and wage control* **5. PLACE OF INSPECTION OR DIRECTION** a place at which something is checked or inspected or from which something is directed (*usually used in combination*) ○ *passengers filing through passport control* **6. COMPARATIVE STANDARD IN EXPERIMENT** a subject taking part in an experiment or survey but not involved in the procedures affecting the rest of the experiment, thus acting as the standard against which the results are compared **7. SUPERVISING PERSON OR GROUP** a person or group that supervises or monitors operations or operatives ○ *Their intelligence agents report to control twice a week.* **8.** COMPUT same as **control key** **9.** PARANORMAL **SPIRIT THAT SUPPOSEDLY GUIDES SEANCE** a spirit that is believed to help a medium gain access to other spirits being called up in a seance ■ **controls** *npl* **1. MEANS OF CONTROLLING** the means by which a machine is operated ○ *nobody at the controls* **2. RULES** the regulations governing a system ○ *import controls* [15C. Via Anglo-Norman *contreroller* < medieval Latin *contrarotulare* 'check against a duplicate register' < *rotul-* 'little roll' (see ROLL)] —**controllability** /kən trṓlə bílləti/ *n* —**controllable** *adj* —**controllably** *adv*

control freak *n* somebody who exerts an excessive control over others and his or her own life (*slang*)

control gene *n* a gene that regulates the development and specialization of cells

control grid *n* ELECTRONICS same as **grid** (sense 6)

control group *n* in an experiment, the group of test subjects left untreated or unexposed to some procedure and then compared with treated subjects in order to validate the results of the test

control key *n* a computer key pressed together with other keys to perform specific functions

~~**controll**~~ incorrect spelling of **control**

controlled /kən trṓld/ *adj* **1. KEPT UNDER CONTROL** kept in check and not expressed fully or at all ○ *She spoke with scarcely controlled fury.* **2. CAREFULLY REGULATED** carefully measured and regulated, especially in relation to medical treatments or scientific experiments ○ *They tested the effectiveness of controlled doses of the drug.* **3. DONE WITH SKILL AND DISCIPLINE** showing the skill, judgment, and discipline needed in order to achieve a desired result, without doing too little or too much ○ *His controlled performance as Lear was masterful.*

controlled substance *n* a substance subject to statutory control, especially a drug that can be obtained legally only with a doctor's prescription

controlled user *n* a drug addict who is able to maintain an otherwise normal way of life

controller /kən trṓlər/ *n* **1. SOMEBODY WHO CONTROLS OR ORGANIZES SOMETHING** somebody in a managing, supervising, or monitoring position **2.** FIN **FINANCIAL SUPERVISOR** somebody whose job is to oversee financial matters in a business or government department **3. CONTROLLING DEVICE** a device or mechanism that controls something —**controllership** *n*

controlling interest *n* ownership of enough of a company's shares to allow the holder to control the business

control panel *n* the collection of lights, digital displays, and switches used to monitor and control the operation of a vehicle, device, or machine

control rod *n* a rod or cylinder made of or containing neutron-absorbing material such as graphite, used to control the rate of fission in a nuclear reactor

control room *n* a room from which an organization coordinates the activities of a large group of people or the operation of a number of machines

control surface *n* a movable surface that controls the direction of an aircraft, rocket, or missile, e.g. a rudder or elevator

control tower *n* a high building at an airport, from which air-traffic controllers organize the movements of incoming and outgoing aircraft by radioing to their pilots

controversial /kóntrə vúrsh'l/ *adj* **1.** provoking strong disagreement or disapproval, e.g. in public debate ○ *controversial policies* **2.** enjoying or habitually engaging in controversy —**controversialist** *n* —**controversially** *adv*

controversy /kóntrə vurssi, kən tróvvərsi/ (*plural* **-sies**) *n* disagreement on a contentious topic, strongly felt or expressed by all those concerned, or an instance of this [14C. < Latin *controversia* < *controversus* 'disputed', literally 'turned against' < *vertere* 'to turn']

USAGE The traditional pronunciation of ***controversy*** is with the stress on the first syllable (on the analogy of words such as *acrimony* and *matrimony*); however stress on the second syllable is increasingly heard although not considered standard.

controvert /kóntrə vúrt/ (**-verts, -verting, -verted**) *vt* to argue strongly against something [Mid-16C. < Latin *contro-*, form of *contra-* 'against' + *vertere* 'to turn'] —**controverter** *n* —**controvertible** *adj* —**controvertibly** *adv*

contumacious /kóntyoo máyshəss/ *adj* **1.** flagrantly disobedient or rebellious **2.** persistently refusing to appear in court or to obey a court order without good reason —**contumaciously** *adv* —**contumaciousness** *n*

contumacy /kóntyoomәssi/ *n* **1.** flagrant disobedience or rebelliousness **2.** persistent refusal to appear in court or to obey a court order without good reason [13C. < Latin *contumacia* < *contumac-* 'insolent']

contumelious /kóntyoo méeli əss/ *adj* having or showing an insulting, scornful, or contemptuous attitude (*archaic or literary*) —**contumeliously** *adv*

contumely /kón tyoomli/ (*plural* **-lies**) *n* (*archaic or literary*) **1.** insulting, scornful, or contemptuous language or treatment **2.** an openly insulting, scornful, or contemptuous remark [14C. Via French < Latin *contumelia*]

contuse /kən tyóoz/ (**-tuses, -tusing, -tused**) *vt* to bruise a body part (*technical*) [14C. < Latin *contus-*, past participle of *contundere* 'beat small' < *tundere* 'to beat']

contusion /kən tyóozh'n/ *n* an injury to the body in which skin and bone are not broken but damage is done to tissues under the skin, causing a bruise (*technical*)

conundrum /kə núndrəm/ *n* **1.** something that is puzzling or confusing **2.** a riddle, especially one with an answer in the form of a play on words [Early 17C. Origin ?]

SYNONYMS See ***problem***.

conurbation /kón ur báysh'n/ *n* a large urban area created when neighbouring towns spread into and merge with each other [Early 20C. < *con-*, variant of COM- + Latin *urb-* 'city']

Conv. *abbr* Conventual

convalesce /kónvə léss/ (**-lesces, -lescing, -lesced**) *vi* to spend time recovering from an illness or the effects of medical treatment, especially by resting [15C. < Latin *convalescere* < *valescere* 'grow strong' < *valere* 'be strong']

convalescent /kónvə léss'nt/ *n* a patient who is recovering from an illness or the effects of medical treatment —**convalescence** *n* —**convalescent** *adj*

convection /kən véksh'n/ *n* **1.** circulatory movement in a liquid or gas, resulting from regions of different temperatures and different densities rising and falling in response to gravity **2.** heat transfer within the atmosphere involving the upward movement of huge volumes of warm air, leading to subsequent condensation and cloud formation [Mid-19C. < late Latin *convection-* < Latin *convehere* 'bring together' < *vehere* 'carry'] —**convectional** *adj* —**convective** *adj* —**convectively** *adv*

convection oven *n* an oven with a fan that circulates heat throughout the oven, so that food on all levels cooks uniformly

convector /kən véktər/ *n* a heater that depends on convection of air to transfer heat from the heating element [Early 20C. < CONVECTION]

convene /kən véen/ (**-venes, -vening, -vened**) *v* **1.** *vt* **ARRANGE MEETING** to call people together for a formal meeting ○ *A meeting of the working group has been convened for tomorrow.* **2.** *vi* **GATHER FOR MEETING** to come together for a formal meeting **3.** *vt* **CALL BEFORE COURT** to order somebody to appear before a court, tribunal, or other decision-making body [15C. < Latin *convenire* 'come together' < *venire* 'come'] —**convenable** *adj*

convener /kən véenər/, **convenor** *n* **1.** somebody who chairs formal meetings, especially somebody elected or appointed to do so in a trade union in a specific workplace **2.** *Scotland* the chairperson and civic head of some Scottish local councils

~~**conveniant**~~ incorrect spelling of **convenient**

convenience /kən véeni ənss/ *n* **1. QUALITY OF BEING CONVENIENT** the quality of being or making things easy, useful, or suitable ○ *have the convenience of working at home* **2. SOMEBODY'S PERSONAL COMFORT** personal comfort, or circumstances that promote somebody's personal comfort ○ *All rooms have cooking facilities, for our guests' convenience.* **3. SOMETHING PROVIDING EASE OR COMFORT** something that makes life easier or more comfortable, especially a labour-saving device ○ *apartments supplied with every modern convenience* **4. LAVATORY** a lavatory, especially in a public place

convenience food *n* packaged food that can be prepared quickly and easily, e.g. tinned foods and cook-chill meals

convenience store *n* a small shop near a residential area that stocks food and general household goods and is open long hours

convenient /kən véeni ənt/ *adj* useful or suitable, because it makes things easier, is close by, or does not involve much effort or trouble ○ *Choose a time convenient for you.* [14C. < Latin *convenient-*, present participle of *convenire* (see CONVENE)] —**conveniently** *adv*

convenor *n* HR, PUBLIC ADMIN another spelling of **convener**

convent /kónvənt/ *n* **1.** a community of women who live a life devoted largely to religious worship **2.** the building occupied by a community of religious women [13C. Via Anglo-Norman *covent* < Latin *conventus* 'assembly' < *convenire* (see CONVENE)]

conventicle /kən véntik'l/ *n* **1.** an unlawful or secret religious gathering **2.** a building where a conventicle is held [14C. < Latin *conventiculum* 'small assembly' < *convenire* (see CONVENE)] —**conventicler** *n*

convention /kən vénsh'n/ *n* **1. GATHERING** a gathering of people who have a common interest or profession ○ *He's attending a sales convention in Manchester.* **2. PEOPLE ATTENDING FORMAL MEETING** the people present at a convention **3. FORMAL AGREEMENT** an agreement between groups, especially an international agreement slightly less formal than a treaty ○ *under the terms of the Geneva Convention* **4. USUAL WAY OF DOING THINGS** the customary way in which things are done within a group ○ *designs that flout convention* **5. FAMILIAR DEVICE** a standard technique or well-used device, especially in the arts ○ *Her style does not follow the usual literary conventions.* **6.** CARDS **CODED BID** in bridge, a bid intended for a partner to understand differently from its face value, because of a prearranged bidding system [15C. Via French < Latin *convention-* < *convenire* (see CONVENE)]

conventional /kən vénsh'nəl/ *adj* **1. SOCIALLY ACCEPTED** conforming to socially accepted customs of behaviour or style, especially in a way that lacks imagination ○ *the conventional white wedding dress* **2. USUAL OR ESTABLISHED** using well-established methods or styles ○ *conventional cooking in an oven rather than a microwave* **3. OF GATHERING OF PEOPLE** relating to a large gathering of people with a common interest or purpose **4.** ARMS **WITHOUT NUCLEAR ENERGY** not involving the use of nuclear weapons or energy **5.** LAW **BASED ON CONSENT** in law, based or dependent on the consent of the various parties —**conventionalism** *n* —**conventionalist** *n* —**conventionally** *adv*

conventionalise *vt* another spelling of **conventionalize**

conventionality /kən vénshənálləti/ (*plural* **-ties**) *n* **1.** adherence to social conventions in behaviour, tastes, or methods **2.** a socially accepted way of behaving or of doing something ○ *the conventionalities of a formal occasion*

conventionalize /kən vénsh'nə līz/ (**-izes, -izing, -ized**), **conventionalise** (**-ises, -ising, -ised**) *vt* to make something conventional, especially in style or taste ○ *His flights of fancy had become conventionalized as the Gothic style.* —**conventionalization** /kən vénsh'nə lī záysh'n/ *n*

conventional wisdom *n* general or widespread belief ○ *Conventional wisdom dictates that such skills merit high rewards.*

convention bounce *n US* an increase in the support for a presidential candidate following nomination at a party convention (*informal*)

conventioneer /kən vénshənéer/ *n N Am* a participant in a convention

convent school *n* a school for girls in which some or all of the teachers are nuns

conventual /kən vénchoo əl/ *adj* relating to or resembling a convent in quietness, simplicity, or discipline ○ *living a quiet conventual life* ■ *n* a woman who lives in a convent —**conventually** *adv*

Conventual *n* a member of a branch of a Franciscan order of friars who live a less austere life than in other branches

converge /kən vúrj/ (**-verges, -verging, -verged**) *vi* **1. MEET** to reach the same point coming from different directions ○ *the place where the roads converge* **2. BECOME SAME** to become gradually less different and eventually the same ○ *political beliefs that were rapidly converging* **3. ARRIVE AT SAME DESTINATION** to gather or meet at the same destination ○ *Delegates from all over the world are converging on the city of New York.* **4.** MATHS **APPROACH FINITE LIMIT** to approach a finite limit as the number of terms in an infinite series increases **5.** BIOL **DEVELOP SIMILAR CHARACTERISTICS** to develop, independently of other species, superficially similar characteristics in response to a set of environmental conditions, e.g. the development of wings in birds and insects [Late 17C. < late Latin *convergere* 'lean together' < Latin *vergere* 'to bend']

convergence /kən vúrjənss/, **convergency** /kən vúrjənsi/ (*plural* **-cies**) *n* **1. COMING TOGETHER** a coming together from different directions, especially a uniting or merging of groups or tendencies that were originally opposed or very different **2.** MATHS **CONDITION OF CONSTANT OR INCREASING DIFFERENCES** the characteristic of a series or sequence of numbers in which the difference between each term and the following term remains constant or increases **3.** BIOL **SIMILAR EVOLUTIONARY DEVELOPMENT** the tendency of different species to develop similar characteristics in response to a set of environmental conditions **4.** METEOROL **MEETING OF AIR MASSES** the meeting of different air masses, often resulting in vertical air currents **5.** OPHTHALMOL **TURNING OF EYES INWARDS** the turning inwards of both eyes in order to look at something nearer than the previous object viewed **6.** COMPUT **INTEGRATION OF IT SERVICES** automated mapping and integration of information technology environments available to a user —**convergent** *adj*

convergent evolution *n* BIOL same as **convergence** (sense 3)

convergent margin *n* a boundary between two tectonic plates that are moving together, one dipping under the other

conversant /kən vúrss'nt/ *adj* knowing about or familiar with something from experience or study ○ *not conversant with local customs* [14C. < French, present participle of *converser* (see CONVERSE[1])] —**conversance** *n* —**conversantly** *adv*

conversation /kónvər sáysh'n/ *n* **1. CASUAL TALK** an informal talk with somebody, especially about opinions, ideas, feelings, or everyday matters ○ *a telephone conversation* **2. TALKING** the activity of talking to somebody informally ○ *in conversation with one of the cleaners* **3.** COMPUT **REAL-TIME INTERACTION WITH COMPUTER** an interaction with a computer carried on in real time **4. NONVERBAL EXCHANGE** a nonverbal exchange or interaction ○ *Critics spoke of the conversation between the new building and its neighbours.* [14C. Via French < Latin *conversation-* < *conversari* 'turn yourself about' < *conversare* (see CONVERSE[1])]

conversational /kónvər sáysh'nəl/ *adj* **1.** relating to informal talking, especially to the ability to say interesting things ○ *conversational skills* **2.** informal in language and style, and usually dealing with or suitable for simple subjects ○ *She writes in an easy conversational style.* ○ *conversational German* —**conversationally** *adv*

conversationalist /kónvər sáysh'nəlist/, **conversationist** /-sáysh'nist/ *n* somebody who enjoys engaging in conversation and can converse in an enjoyable way ○ *Her husband's not much of a conversationalist.*

conversation piece *n* **1.** something that attracts people's interest and leads to conversation ○ *I don't think much of the sculpture in their front garden, but it makes a good conversation piece.* **2.** a portrait painting of a group of stylish people in a domestic or landscape setting

conversazione /kónvə satsi óni/ (*plural* **-ni** /-ni/ or **-nes**) *n* a social gathering to hear a talk on or discuss a topic related to the arts (*formal*) [Mid-18C. < Italian, 'conversation' < Latin *conversare* (see CONVERSE[1])]

converse[1] *vi* /kən vúrss/ (**-verses, -versing, -versed**) **1.** to have a conversation ○ *a place where they can converse uninterrupted* **2.** COMPUT to interact with a computer in real time, as if engaged in a dialogue ■ *n* /kón vurss/ same as **conversation** (sense 2) (*archaic*) ○ *They were deep in converse with one another.* [14C. Via French *converser* < Latin *conversare* 'live with' < *versari* 'occupy yourself' < *vertere* 'to turn'] —**converser** *n*

converse[2] /kón vurss/ *n* **1. OPPOSITE** the opposite of something ○ *Actually, the converse is true.* **2.** LOGIC **REVERSED CATEGORICAL SENTENCE** a categorical sentence in which the subject and predicate have been reversed, e.g. 'all dogs are collies' from 'all collies are dogs' ■ *adj* **OPPOSITE** opposite or reverse [14C. < Latin *conversus*, past participle of *convertere* (see CONVERT)] —**conversely** *adv*

conversion /kən vúrsh'n/ *n* **1. ALTERATION** a change in the nature, form, or function of something ○ *a conversion of waste land into a sports field* **2. SOMETHING ALTERED** something that has been changed in nature, form, or function, especially a building or room ○ *a loft conversion* **3. CHANGE OF MEASURING SYSTEM** a change from one measuring or calculating system to another, or a calculation done to bring about the change ○ *the conversion from miles to kilometres* **4. CHANGING OF SOMEBODY'S BELIEFS** an adoption of new opinions or beliefs, especially in religion ○ *his conversion to Islam* **5.** RUGBY **CONVERTING OF TRY** in rugby, a kicking of the ball over the crossbar following a try, or the score made with a successful kick **6.** LOGIC **REVERSING TERMS IN CATEGORICAL SENTENCE** the reversing of the subject and predicate in a categorical sentence, forming a new sentence, e.g. 'all dogs are collies' from 'all collies are dogs' **7.** LAW **UNLAWFUL HOLDING OF ANOTHER'S PROPERTY** unlawful treating of somebody else's property as your own **8.** LAW **CHANGING OF PROPERTY CLASSIFICATION** the changing of one type of property to another, e.g. from joint to separate property [14C. Via French < Latin *conversion-* < *convers-*, past participle of *convertere* (see CONVERT)] —**conversional** *adj* —**conversionary** *adj*

conversion disorder *n* a neurosis marked by the appearance of physical symptoms such as partial loss of muscle function without physical cause but in the presence of psychological conflict

convert *v* /kən vúrt/ (**-verts, -verting, -verted**) **1.** *vti* **CHANGE SOMETHING'S CHARACTER** to change something from one character, form, or function to another, or be changed in character, form or function ○ *a process for converting waste into usable fuel* **2.** *vti* **CHANGE SOMETHING'S FUNCTION** to change the function or use of something, or be able to change in function or use ○ *sofas that convert into beds* **3.** *vt* **CHANGE MEASURING OR CALCULATING UNITS** to change units of one measuring or calculating system into units of another ○ *the formula for converting litres into gallons* **4.** *vti* **CHANGE SOMEBODY'S BELIEFS** to adopt new opinions or beliefs, especially religious beliefs, or change the opinions or beliefs of somebody ○ *His wife converted to Judaism.* **5.** *vti* RUGBY **KICK TO ADD ON POINTS** in rugby, to add to the points awarded for a try by following it with a successful kick of the ball over the crossbar **6.** *vt* LOGIC **REVERSE TERMS IN CATEGORICAL SENTENCE** to reverse the subject and predicate in a categorical sentence, forming a new sentence, e.g. 'all dogs are collies' from 'all collies are dogs' **7.** *vt* LAW **UNLAWFULLY HOLD ANOTHER'S PROPERTY** to treat somebody else's property as your own unlawfully **8.** *vt* LAW **CHANGE CLASSIFICATION OF PROPERTY** to change the classification of property, e.g. from joint to separate property, in the course of a transaction ■ *n* /kón vurt/ **SOMEBODY WITH CHANGED BELIEFS** somebody who has chosen a new way of life or a new set of beliefs ○ *ex-conservative converts to liberalism* [13C. Via French < Latin *convertere* 'turn around' < *vertere* 'to turn'] ◇ **preach to the converted** to advocate a viewpoint to people who already have it

SYNONYMS See *change*.

converter /kən vúrtər/, **convertor** *n* **1.** TECH **DEVICE THAT CONVERTS** a device that converts something, e.g. an electrical device that converts alternating current into direct current **2.** PHYS **FREQUENCY CHANGER** an electronic component for changing one frequency to another **3.** METALL **FURNACE** a furnace for refining molten metal **4.** COMPUT **DATA CODE CHANGER** in computing, a device for changing data from one form to another, e.g. from analogue to digital **5.** INDUST same as **converter reactor**

converter reactor *n* a nuclear reactor that converts one nuclear fuel into another, especially fertile into fissile material

convertible /kən vúrtəb'l/ *adj* **1. CAPABLE OF BEING CONVERTED** capable of being changed from one form, function, or use to another ○ *Nationalism, as history demonstrates, is too easily convertible into bitterness and selfishness.* **2.** FIN **EXCHANGEABLE FOR GOLD OR ANOTHER CURRENCY** able to be legally exchanged for gold or for another currency **3.** FIN **EXCHANGEABLE FOR STOCK** exchangeable for other assets, especially a fixed number of shares in ordinary stock ■ *n* **CAR WITH REMOVABLE ROOF** a car with a roof that can be folded back or taken off ○ *a flashy red convertible* —**convertibility** /kən vúrtə bílləti/ *n* —**convertibly** *adv*

convertor *n* TECH, SCI another spelling of **converter**

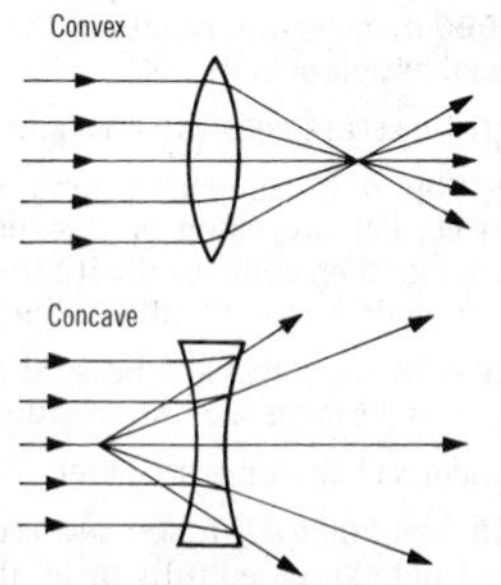

convex: convex and concave lenses

convex /kón veks, kon véks/ *adj* **1. OUTWARDLY CURVING** having a surface that curves outwards rather than inwards **2.** OPTICS **SHAPED LIKE SPHERE'S EXTERIOR** shaped like the exterior of a sphere, paraboloid, ellipsoid, or other outwardly curved surface ○ *a convex lens* **3.** MATHS **CONTAINING NO ANGLE ABOVE 180°** describes a polygon with no interior angle greater than 180° ■ *vti* (**-vexes, -vexing, -vexed**) **CURVE OUTWARDS** to curve outwards, or make something curve outwards [Late 16C. < Latin *convexus* 'vaulted, arched'] —**convexly** /kón veksli/ *adv*

convexity /kon véksəti/ (*plural* **-ties**) *n* **1.** the quality of curving outwards **2.** an outwardly curving surface or part

convexo-concave /kon véksō-/ *adj* describes a lens that is convex on one side and concave on the other

convexo-convex /kon véksō-/ *adj* describes a lens that is convex on both sides

convey /kən váy/ (**-veys, -veying, -veyed**) *vt* **1. COMMUNICATE SOMETHING** to communicate or express something ○ *a look that conveyed all the tenderness he felt for her* **2. MEAN SOMETHING** to have something as a meaning or connotation ○ *'Majesty' conveys grandeur.* **3. TRANSFER SOMETHING THROUGH CARRIER** to transfer or transmit something along a wire, pipe, tube, or other carrier **4. TAKE SOMEBODY SOMEWHERE** to take somebody or something somewhere (*formal*) **5.** LAW **CHANGE OWNERSHIP OF SOMETHING** to transfer ownership of something ○ *The title to the property was conveyed last June.* [14C. Via Old French *conveier* < medieval Latin *conviare* 'go together on the road' < Latin *via* 'road'] —**conveyable** *adj*

conveyance /kən váy ənss/ *n* **1. MOVING OF SOMETHING** the conveying of something, especially the transportation or transmission of something from one place to another ○ *the conveyance of information from the mainland to the islands* **2. VEHICLE** a vehicle or other means of transportation (*formal*) ○ *public conveyances* **3.** LAW **TRANSFER OF OWNERSHIP** a document that legally transfers ownership, or the transfer itself —**conveyancer** *n* —**conveyancing** *n*

conveyor /kən váy ər/, **conveyer** *n* **1.** a device that transports or transmits something, especially a conveyor belt **2.** a person or thing that transmits something, especially news ○ *a conveyor of good tidings*

conveyor belt *n* a device that consists typically of a continuous wide flat rubber loop moved by electrically operated rollers, used to move objects from one place to another nearby

convict *v* /kən víkt/ (**-victs, -victing, -victed**) **1.** *vt* DECLARE SOMEBODY GUILTY to declare somebody guilty of a crime in a court of law (*often passive*) ○ *had been previously convicted of fraud* **2.** *vi* ARRIVE AT GUILTY VERDICT to reach a verdict of guilty ○ *juries who will convict on the slimmest evidence* **3.** *vt* SHOW SOMEBODY TO BE AT FAULT to show that somebody is in the wrong in some respect ○ *actions that convicted her of selfishness* ■ *n* /kón vikt/ SOMEBODY IN PRISON somebody serving a prison sentence ○ *an escaped convict* [14C. < Latin *convict-*, past participle of *convincere* (see CONVINCE)] —**convictable** *adj*

conviction /kən víksh'n/ *n* **1.** FIRMLY HELD BELIEF a belief or opinion that is held firmly ○ *It's my conviction that they are lying.* **2.** FIRMNESS OF BELIEF firmness of belief or opinion ○ *said with complete conviction* **3.** GUILTY VERDICT an act of finding somebody guilty of a crime, or an instance of being found guilty ○ *The accused has no previous convictions.* —**convictional** *adj*

USAGE conviction or **persuasion**? ***Conviction*** is 'a firmly held belief' and 'firmness of belief': *It is my conviction* [not *persuasion*] *that the defendant's rights have been violated. I say this with total conviction* [not *persuasion*]: *we are headed for a recession.* ***Persuasion*** is 'the act of or ability to get someone else to accept your opinion, belief, or viewpoint', 'a set of beliefs', and 'a group of people with particular beliefs', as in *she used great persuasion in conveying her position to the voters; a politician of the conservative persuasion.*

convince /kən vínss/ (**-vinces, -vincing, -vinced**) *vt* **1.** to make somebody sure or certain of something ○ *We are convinced of his guilt.* **2.** to persuade somebody to believe or do something ○ *Nothing would convince them to invest in such a scheme.* [Mid-16C. < Latin *convincere* 'prove wrong' < *vincere* 'overcome'] —**convincer** *n* —**convincible** *adj*

USAGE convince or **persuade**? Traditionally, to ***convince*** somebody is to make him or her certain of something, and to ***persuade*** somebody is to induce him or her to act: *She convinced him that he had talent and persuaded him to study music.* Because of this distinction, some people object to the use of an infinitive after ***convince***, pointing out that *She convinced him to...* will tend to involve action. Nonetheless, the distinction is quickly disappearing by force of widespread usage, and constructions like this one are increasingly seen in the work of reputable writers: *After a long series of tests I was convinced to go ahead with the surgery despite the risks.*

convincing /kən vínssing/ *adj* **1.** PERSUASIVE able to persuade somebody to believe that something is true or to act ○ *convincing arguments* **2.** ABLE TO PERSUADE PEOPLE skilled at making people believe something ○ *a convincing impostor* **3.** BEYOND DOUBT impressively clear or definite ○ *a convincing victory* —**convincingly** *adv*

SYNONYMS See ***valid***.

convivial /kən vívvi əl/ *adj* **1.** enjoyable because of its friendliness ○ *spent many a convivial evening at the pub* **2.** fond of the company of others ○ *He was famously convivial.* [Mid-17C. < Latin *convivialis* < *convivium* 'feast' < *vivere* 'to live'] —**convivialist** *n* —**conviviality** /kən vívvi állәti/ *n* —**convivially** *adv*

convocation /kónvə káysh'n/ *n* **1.** a large formal assembly, e.g. the senior members of a church or the members of a university council **2.** the arranging or calling of a formal meeting [14C. < Latin *convocation-* < *convocare* (see CONVOKE)] —**convocator** /kónvə kaytər/ *n*

convoke /kən vṓk/ (**-vokes, -voking, -voked**) *vt* to call a formal meeting, or call people together for a meeting [Late 16C. < Latin *convocare* 'call together' < *vocare* 'to call'] —**convocative** /-vókətiv/ *adj* —**convoker** *n*

convolute /kónvə loot/ *vti* (**-lutes, -luting, -luted**) to twist or coil something in folds ○ *The snake's coils were tightly convoluted.* ■ *adj* describes petals or leaves that are rolled from the sides so that one side is wrapped around the other [Late 17C. < Latin *convolut-*, past participle of *convolvere* 'twist round' < *volvere* 'to roll'] —**convolutely** *adv*

convoluted /kónvə lootid/ *adj* **1.** too complex or intricate to understand easily ○ *convoluted sentences* **2.** having many twists, coils, or whorls ○ *the brain's convoluted surface* —**convolutedly** *adv* —**convolutedness** *n*

convolution /kónvə lóosh'n/ *n* **1.** TWISTED SHAPE a curve, coil, or twist **2.** TWISTED RIDGE ON BRAIN SURFACE a ridged fold on the surface of the brain **3.** INTRICACY a complexity or intricacy, especially one of many ○ *The plot had so many convolutions it was difficult to follow.* —**convolutional** *adj* —**convolutionary** *adj*

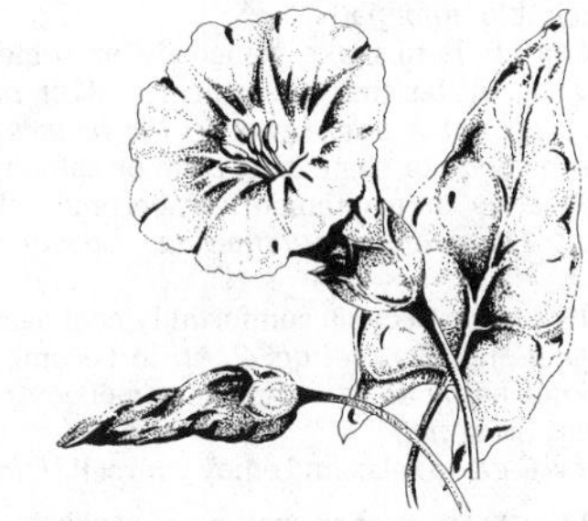

convolvulus

convolvulus /kən vólvyŏŏləss/ (*plural* **-luses** or **-li** /-lī/) *n* a plant of the morning-glory family, many of which have a twining growth habit, including bindweed. Flowers: trumpet-shaped. Genus: *Convolvulus*. [Mid-16C. < Latin < *convolvere* (see CONVOLUTE)]

convoy /kón voy/ *n* **1.** VEHICLES OR SHIPS TRAVELLING TOGETHER a group of vehicles or ships travelling together, often with an escort for protection ○ *travelling in convoy* **2.** VEHICLES' OR SHIPS' ESCORT a protective escort for a group of vehicles or ships ■ *vt* (**-voys, -voying, -voyed**) ESCORT VEHICLES OR SHIPS to travel as an escort to protect a group of vehicles or ships [14C. < French *convoi* < Old French *conveier* (see CONVEY)]

convulsant /kən vúlss'nt/ *adj* causing convulsions ■ *n* a drug that causes convulsions

convulse /kən vúlss/ (**-vulses, -vulsing, -vulsed**) *v* **1.** *vti* SHAKE UNCONTROLLABLY to jerk or shake violently and uncontrollably, or make a muscle or body part go into repetitive spasm **2.** *vt* CAUSE TO SHAKE to make somebody shake with laughter or a strong emotion (*often passive*) ○ *convulsed with panic* **3.** *vt* DISRUPT SOMETHING to cause extreme disruption or disturbance in something ○ *Problems in the Asian economies convulsed the London markets.* [Mid-17C. < Latin *convuls-*, past participle of *convellere* 'pull violently' < *vellere* 'pull']

convulsion /kən vúlsh'n/ *n* (*often used in the plural*) **1.** UNCONTROLLABLE SHAKING a violent shaking of the body or limbs caused by uncontrollable muscle contractions, which can be a symptom of brain disorders and other conditions **2.** DISTURBANCE an extreme disruption or disturbance (*literary*) ■ **convulsions** *npl* LAUGHTER fits of laughter —**convulsionary** *adj*

convulsive /kən vúlssiv/ *adj* **1.** sudden, jerky, or uncontrollable **2.** undergoing or producing uncontrollable jerking of the body or limbs —**convulsively** *adv*

Conway /kón way/, **Jill Ker** (*b.* 1934) Australian-born US historian and writer. She is noted for her autobiography *The Road from Coorain* (1989).

con woman *n* a woman swindler who uses a confidence game to cheat or defraud people (*informal*)

Conwy /kónwi/ town and local government district in North Wales. Population: 3,627 (1991).; district 109,596 (2001).

cony /kṓni/ (*plural* **-nies**), **coney** (*plural* **-neys**) *n* **1.** rabbit fur used for coats and other articles of clothing **2.** *N Am* ZOOL a rabbit, especially the common domesticated European rabbit **3.** ZOOL same as **hyrax** **4.** ZOOL same as **pika** [14C. Via Anglo-Norman < Latin *cuniculus* 'rabbit, burrow']

coo /koo/ *v* (**coos, cooing, cooed**) **1.** *vi* MAKE SOUND OF PIGEON to make the deep hooting sound that is characteristic of pigeons **2.** *vti* SPEAK VERY TENDERLY to speak with affected or exaggerated admiration, or say something in this way ■ *n* BIRD'S SOUND the deep hooting sound that pigeons make ■ *interj* EXPRESSING SURPRISE used to express surprise or wonder (*informal*) ○ *Coo! Look at all that money!* [Mid-17C. An imitation of the sound]

COO *abbr* BUSINESS chief operating officer

Coober Pedy /kóobər péedi/ town in South Australia, a centre of opal mining. It is noted for its underground dwellings, built by miners seeking to escape the heat. Population: 2,321 (2002 estimate).

co-occur *vi* **1.** to happen at the same time and place **2.** to appear together in the same contexts (*refers to speech sounds and other linguistic elements*) —**co-occurrence** *n*

cooee /kóo ee/ *interj, n* a call used to attract somebody's attention (*informal*) [Late 18C. An imitation of a high-pitched cry used by Australian Aboriginals] ◇ **within cooee of** *ANZ* near

cook /kŏŏk/ *v* (**cooks, cooking, cooked**) **1.** *vti* PREPARE FOOD to prepare food for a meal **2.** *vti* MAKE OR BECOME HOT to make food safe and appetizing by heating it, or undergo heating in order to become ready to eat ○ *The onions have been cooking for a while.* ○ *Cook the beef until it is tender.* **3.** *vi* HAPPEN to be happening or developing (*informal*) ○ *I had the feeling that something was cooking.* **4.** *vi* BE UNCOMFORTABLE IN HEAT to feel extreme discomfort in hot conditions (*informal*) ○ *cooking in an overcrowded bus* **5.** *vt* CHANGE SOMETHING IN ORDER TO DECEIVE to alter or tamper with information or evidence fraudulently (*slang*) **6.** *vt* HEAT ILLEGAL DRUG to heat an illegal drug such as heroin (*slang*) ■ *n* SOMEBODY WHO PREPARES FOOD somebody who prepares and cooks food, usually as a job or in a particular way ○ *an excellent cook* [Pre-12C. Via assumed Vulgar Latin *cocus* 'cook' < Latin *coquus* < *coquere* 'to cook'] —**cookable** *adj* ◇ **too many cooks spoil the broth** the help or involvement of too many people can do more harm than good

cook up *vt* **1.** to prepare or improvise a meal quickly **2.** to invent something untrue or dishonest such as an excuse (*informal*) **3.** DRUGS same as **cook** *v* (sense 6) (*slang*)

Cook, Mount /kŏŏk/ **1.** highest mountain in New Zealand, situated in the Southern Alps on the South Island. Height: 3,754 m/12,316 ft. Maori name **Aoraki** **2.** peak of the St Elias Range in southwestern Yukon Territory. Height: 4,194 m/13,760 ft.

Cook /kŏŏk/, **James, Captain** (1728–79) British explorer and cartographer. During three great voyages (1768–71, 1772–75, 1776–79) he charted New Zealand and Australia and explored the Antarctic and the northwestern coast of North America.

> 'At daylight in the morning we discovered a bay which appeared to be tolerably well sheltered from all winds, into which I resolved to go with the ship.'
> [Attributed to James Cook. Recording his arrival at Botany Bay; 20 April 1770]

Cook, Sir Joseph (1860–1947) British-born Australian politician and diplomat. He was a Liberal Party politician and prime minister of Australia (1913–14). See table at **prime minister**

Cook, Peter (1937–95) British actor and comedian. He became famous as a writer and performer in *Beyond the Fringe* (1959–64) and as the owner of the satirical magazine *Private Eye*. Full name **Cook, Peter Edward**

> 'I am very interested in the Universe—I am specializing in the universe and all that surrounds it.'
> [Peter Cook, *Beyond the Fringe*; 1959–64]

Cook, Thomas (1808–92) British travel agent. In 1841 he organized a railway excursion for a temperance group which began tourism in its modern form.

cookbook /kŏŏk bŏŏk/ *n ANZ, N Am* same as **cookery book**

cook-chill *adj* describes food that is cooked, packaged, and refrigerated, and then reheated before serving ■ *n* the preparation of cook-chill food

cooker /kŏŏkər/ *n* **1.** *UK* APPLIANCE FOR COOKING a box-shaped kitchen appliance for cooking food, powered by electricity, gas, oil or solid fuel, and including

an oven, grill, and hob. ANZ, N Am term **stove** [1] **2.** **DEVICE FOR COOKING** a device that cooks food, especially in a particular way ○ *a slow cooker* **3. APPLE FOR COOKING** a type of apple, usually large and sour, that is more suitable for cooking than for eating raw (*informal*)

cookery /kóokəri/ *n* **1.** COOK same as **cooking** *n* (sense 1) **2.** a type or style of cooking ○ *Mediterranean cookery* ○ *vegetarian cookery*

cookery book *n UK* a book containing recipes for preparing food. ANZ, N Am term **cookbook**

cookie /kóoki/, **cooky** (*plural* **-ies**) *n* **1.** *N Am* FOOD same as **biscuit** (sense 1) **2.** ONLINE a computer file containing information about a user that is sent to the central computer with each request. The server uses this information to customize data sent back to the user and to log the user's requests. **3.** somebody who is regarded as being of a particular type or disposition (*informal*) ○ *She's a tough cookie.* [Early 18C. < Dutch *koekje* 'little cake' < *koek* 'cake'] ◇ **that's the way the cookie crumbles** that is the way things tend to happen (*informal*)

cookie cutter *n N Am* a shaped template with a sharp edge. Use: pressing into a sheet of dough to make biscuit shapes.

cookie-cutter *adj N Am* seemingly mass-produced without distinctive features

cookie sheet *n N Am* HOUSEHOLD same as **baking tray**

cooking /kóoking/ *n* **1. PREPARATION OF FOOD** the process or activity of preparing food for eating **2. PREPARED FOOD** food that has been prepared for eating ○ *She doesn't like my cooking.* ■ *adj* **USED IN COOKING** intended for use in cooking rather than for consumption raw or on its own

Cook Islands group of predominantly volcanic islands in the South Pacific, lying approximately 4,500 km/2,800 mi. south of Hawaii and 2,600 km/1,600 mi. northeast of New Zealand. They are self-governing in free association with New Zealand. Population: 20,611 (2001). Area: 237 sq. km/92 sq. mi.

Cookson /kóoks'n/, **Dame Catherine Ann** (1906–98) British novelist. Her novels of working-class life in northeastern England have become worldwide bestsellers. Pseudonym **Merchant, Catherine, Fawcett, Catherine**

Cook's tour /kóoks-/ *n* a quick tour or survey, with attention only to the main features (*informal*) ○ *The book doesn't aim to give anything more than a Cook's tour of European history.* [After Thomas Cook]

Cookstown /kóoks town/ local government district in County Tyrone, Northern Ireland. Population: 32,581 (2001). Area: 622 sq. km/240 sq. mi.

Cook Strait area of ocean separating the North Island and the South Island of New Zealand, noted for its treacherous currents. At its narrowest it is 22 km/14 mi. wide.

cooktop /kóok top/ *n N Am* a flat cooking unit that includes hot plates or burners and a surface that can be used for food preparation, fixed on top of a cabinet or other fitment or appliance

Cooktown /kóok town/ coastal town in northern Queensland, Australia. Formerly a mining town, it is now a tourist centre. Population: 1,344 (1991).

cook-up *n* a Caribbean dish of mixed meats, seafood, and rice

cookware /kóok wair/ *n* utensils used in cooking, e.g. pots, pans, and dishes

cooky *n* another spelling of **cookie**

cool /kool/ *adj* **1. FAIRLY COLD** somewhat cold, usually pleasantly so **2. KEEPING TEMPERATURE LOW** made of fabric that keeps the body at a pleasant temperature when it is hot **3. SEEMING COLD** giving an impression of coldness ○ *a cool mint green* **4. STAYING CALM** staying calm or not showing emotions, especially nervousness or fear **5. UNFRIENDLY** unfriendly or unenthusiastic ○ *They gave us a rather cool reception.* **6. FASHIONABLE** fashionable and sophisticated (*informal*) ○ *looking cool* **7. EXCELLENT** used to indicate approval or admiration (*slang*) ○ *a cool idea* **8. OK** used to indicate agreement or acceptance (*slang*) ○ *That's cool, no problem.* **9. EMPHASIZING SUM OF MONEY** used to emphasize how large a sum of money is (*slang*) ○ *a cool £3.2 million* ■ *vti* (**cools, cooling, cooled**) **1. MAKE OR BECOME LESS WARM** to become less warm, or cause somebody or something to become less warm ○ *Wait until the mixture cools.* ○ *The room was cooled by a large fan.* **2. MAKE OR BECOME LESS INTENSE** to make somebody or something less intense, or become less intense ○ *anything that might cool his anger* ■ *n* **1. SLIGHT CHILL** moderate coldness, especially in relation to greater heat or coldness ○ *We were glad to come back into the cool of our hotel room.* **2. CALMNESS** the ability to remain calm in difficult circumstances (*informal*) **3. STYLISHNESS** stylishness that is attractive without being ostentatious (*informal*) ■ *adv* **CALMLY** in a calm self-controlled way (*informal*) ○ *Just act cool.* ■ *interj* **EXPRESSING PLEASURE** used to express pleasure, or excitement at a prospect or event (*slang*) ○ *You're coming too? Cool!* [Old English *cōl* < Indo-European, 'cold'] —**coolness** *n* ◇ **be cool with** to agree with or be willing to accept something ○ *I'm cool with that.* ◇ **keep your cool** to remain calm (*informal*) ◇ **lose your cool** to become angry and excitable (*informal*)

cool down *vti* **1.** to make somebody or something less warm, or become less warm ○ *Wait till the engine cools down before you lift the bonnet.* **2.** to make somebody or something calm or calmer after strong feeling or excitement, or become calm or calmer ○ *The political situation has cooled down a lot.*

cool off *v* **1.** *vi* to become comfortably cool again ○ *I went for a swim to cool off.* **2.** *vti* to become calm again after being angry, or make somebody regain calmness (*informal*)

cool out *vi Carib* to relax and enjoy yourself (*informal*)

coolabah *n* TREES another spelling of **coolibah**

coolamon /kóolə mon/ *n Aus* an oblong wooden container used by Australian Aboriginals for holding food or water [Mid-19C. < Kamilaroi *gulaman*]

Coolangatta /kóolən gáttə/ coastal town in southeastern Queensland, Australia, a commercial centre and tourist resort. Population: 3,778 (1996).

coolant /kóolənt/ *n* a substance, usually a liquid, used to prevent overheating in an engine or other mechanism

cool bag, cool box *n UK* a portable insulated container used to keep food cool outdoors. ANZ, N Am term **cooler**

cooldrink /kóol dringk/ *n S Africa* BEVERAGES same as **soft drink**

cooler /kóolər/ *n* **1.** *ANZ, N Am* same as **cool bag** **2. COOL PLACE OR CONTAINER** a compartment or container in which something is cooled or kept cool **3. COLD DRINK** a refreshing drink, e.g. an iced mixture of wine, fruit juice, and soda water or a chilled nonalcoholic drink such as an iced coffee **4. PRISON** a prison or prison cell (*slang*)

Coolgardie /kool gaárdi/ gold-mining town in southern Western Australia. It was once the third largest town in the state. Population: 4,176 (2001).

cool head *n* **1.** an ability to remain calm and sensible in dangerous or difficult situations **2.** somebody who has a cool head

cool-headed *adj* staying calm in tense situations

coolibah /kóolə baa/ (*plural* **-bahs** or *same*), **coolabah** *n* a smooth-barked eucalyptus tree with long leaves containing oil glands, that grows near water sources. Native to: Australia. Latin name: *Eucalyptus microtheca.* [Late 19C. < Kamilaroi *gulubaa*]

Coolidge /kóolij/, **Calvin** (1872–1933) 30th president of the United States. A pro-business Republican president (1923–29), he presided over a period of prosperity, but refused renomination in 1928 following the economic collapse that led to the Great Depression. Full name **Coolidge, John Calvin.** See table at **president**

> 'Patriotism is easy to understand in America; it means looking out for yourself while looking out for your country.'
> [Attributed to Calvin Coolidge]

coolie /kóoli/ *n* in South Asia, China, and parts of East and Southeast Asia, an offensive term for a local man hired cheaply to do manual labour (*offensive*) [Mid-17C. < Hindi *kūlī*]

cooling /kóoling/ *adj* **1.** making you feel cooler in a pleasant way **2.** *Malaysia, Singapore* used in some Asian medical systems to describe foods or food preparation techniques that are believed to make the body cool and affect conditions such as fever and high blood pressure —**coolingly** *adv*

cooling-off period /kóoling-/ *n* **1.** an agreed pause in a dispute to allow tempers to cool and peaceful solutions to be examined **2.** a period of reflection allowed before making a legally binding commitment

cooling tower *n* a tall open-topped structure in which the steam produced by an industrial process is condensed

Coolin Hills ➧ **Cuillin Hills**

cool jazz *n* jazz with a light tone and relaxed character, popular in the mid-20th century, especially on the West Coast of the United States

coolly /kóol li/ *adv* **1.** in a calm or relaxed way ○ *She coolly marched up to the desk and demanded to see the manager.* **2.** without friendliness or enthusiasm ○ *He greeted her coolly.*

coolth /koolth/ *n* pleasant coolness or coldness relative to greater heat or cold (*informal or humorous*) [Mid-16C. < COOL]

coom /koom/ *n regional* dusty or greasy dirt, e.g. coal dust [Late 16C. Origin ?]

Cooma /kóomə/ town in southeastern New South Wales, Australia. Formerly the administrative centre of the Snowy Mountains Hydroelectric Scheme, it is the gateway to the New South Wales ski slopes. Population: 9,416 (2002 estimate).

Coomaraswamy /koo maárə swaámi/, **Ananda Kentish** (1877–1947) Sri Lankan-born Indian orientalist. His many works on Asian culture, including *The Transformation of Nature in Art* (1934), stimulated scholarship in Asian studies.

Coomassie /koo mássi/ former name for **Kumasi**

coomb, coombe *n* GEOG another spelling of **combe**

Coombs /koomz/, **Nuggett** (1906–97) Australian economist. The head of Australia's Reserve Bank (1959–68), he was an active supporter of environmental causes and Aboriginal land rights. Born **Coombs, Herbert Cole**

coon /koon/ *n* **1.** *N Am* ZOOL same as **raccoon** (*informal*) **2.** a highly offensive term for a Black person (*taboo*) **3.** *Aus* a highly offensive term for an Australian Aboriginal (*taboo*) **4.** a highly offensive term for somebody from the islands of the Pacific (*taboo*) [Mid-18C. < RACCOON]

Coonabarabran /kóonə bárrə bran/ town in northern New South Wales, Australia, near the Siding Spring Anglo-Australian Observatory. Population: 6,833 (2002 estimate).

coon-ass /kóon ass/, **coonass** *n Southern US* a term for a person of French Acadian ancestry, used chiefly in Louisiana, northeastern and southeastern Texas, and parts of Mississippi and southern Tennessee (*sometimes offensive*) ○ *'... she was (he'd said) "the prettiest little coon-ass gal you ever saw".'* (Donna Tartt, *The Little Friend*; 2003) [Mid-20C. Folk etymology of French *conasse*, 'female genitals']

cooncan /kóon kan/ *n* a card game from Mexico that is similar to rummy and played with one or two packs [Late 19C. By folk etymology < American Spanish *conquián* < Spanish *con quién?* 'with whom?']

coonskin /kóon skin/ *n N Am* **1.** the pelt of a raccoon **2.** an item of clothing made from coonskin

coop[1] /koop/ *n* **1. ENCLOSURE FOR POULTRY** an enclosure or hut in which poultry is kept **2. FISHING BASKET** a wicker basket used for catching fish **3. PRISON** a prison or prison cell (*slang*) [13C. Origin ?] ◇ **fly the coop** to escape or leave a place (*informal*)

coop up *vt* to keep somebody in a confined space

coop[2] *abbr* **1.** business cooperative (*used in e-mails*) **2.** non-profit-making cooperative (*used in Internet addresses*) See table at **domain name**

co-op /kō op/, **coop** *n* a cooperative organization or venture, especially a marketing enterprise (*informal*) [Mid-19C. Shortening of COOPERATIVE]

cooper /kóopər/ *n* somebody skilled in making and repairing wooden barrels ■ *vti* (**-ers, -ering, -ered**) to make or repair wooden barrels [15C. < Middle Dutch *kūper* < *kūpe* 'cask']

Cooper /kóopər/, **Gary** (1901–61) US film actor. He starred in Westerns, winning Academy Awards for *Sergeant York* (1941) and *High Noon* (1952).

Cooper, Sir Henry (*b.* 1934) British boxer. British and sometime European heavyweight champion (1959–69, 1970–71), he was noted for his powerful left hook, ''Enry's 'ammer'. Full name **Cooper, Henry William**

Cooper, James Fenimore (1789–1851) US writer. Among his *Leather-Stocking Tales* about frontier life is the novel *The Last of the Mohicans* (1826).

> 'History, like love, is apt to surround her heroes with an atmosphere of imaginary brightness.'
> [James Fenimore Cooper, *The Last of the Mohicans*; 1826]

Cooper, Samuel (1609–72) English miniaturist. His portraits in oils, including those of Oliver Cromwell and John Milton, brought new vivacity and realism to the miniature style.

cooperage /kóopərij/ *n* **1. COOPER'S CRAFT** the craft of making and repairing wooden barrels **2. COOPER'S WORKPLACE** a place where wooden barrels are made and repaired **3. COOPER'S FEE** the fee charged by a cooper for making or repairing barrels

cooperate /kō óppə rayt/ **(-ates, -ating, -ated)** *vi* **1.** to work or act together to achieve a common aim **2.** to do what is asked or required [Late 16C. < ecclesiastical Latin *cooperat-*, past participle of *cooperari* 'work together' < Latin *operari* 'to work'] —**cooperator** *n*

cooperation /kō óppə ráysh'n/ *n* **1.** the act of working or acting together to achieve a common aim ○ *working in cooperation with international aid agencies* **2.** help provided by doing what is asked or required —**cooperationist** *n*

cooperative /kō óppərətiv/ *adj* **1. WILLING TO HELP** doing or willing to do what is asked or required ○ *She's a good worker and very cooperative.* **2. WORKING TOGETHER** working or acting together with others, or done by people working or acting together ○ *a cooperative effort* **3.** BUSINESS **OPERATED COLLECTIVELY** owned jointly by all its members or workers, who share all profits equally ○ *a cooperative farm* ■ *n* **BUSINESS OWNED BY WORKERS** a business that is jointly owned by the people who run it, with all profits shared equally ○ *a workers' cooperative* —**cooperatively** *adv* —**cooperativeness** *n*

cooperative society *n* a commercial organization distributing goods to its members who participate in profit-sharing schemes

Cooper Creek /kóopər-/ river in central Australia that runs from the junction of the Barcoo and Thomson rivers in Queensland to Lake Eyre in South Australia. Length: 800 km/500 mi.

co-opt /kō ópt/ **(co-opts, co-opting, co-opted)** *vt* **1. APPOINT SOMEBODY BY AGREEMENT** to appoint somebody to a body by agreement with the other members **2. INVOLVE OPPONENT IN LARGER GROUP** to absorb an opponent or opposing group into a larger group or society by making promises and concessions **3. ADOPT SOMETHING** to adopt or appropriate something such as a political issue or idea as your own [Mid-17C. < Latin *cooptare* 'choose mutually' < *optare* 'choose'] —**co-optation** /kō op táysh'n/ *n* —**co-optative** *adj* —**co-option** *n* —**co-optive** *adj*

coordinate *v* /kō áwrdi nayt/ **(-nates, -nating, -nated) 1.** *vt* **ORGANIZE SOMETHING COMPLEX** to organize a complex enterprise in which numerous people are involved and bring their contributions together to form a coherent or efficient whole ○ *responsible for coordinating the campaign* **2.** *vti* **MAKE PARTS MOVE TOGETHER** to make moving parts such as parts of the body work together in sequence or in time with one another, or work together in this way ○ *hand and eye coordinating perfectly for the overhead shot* **3.** *vt* **PUT THINGS TOGETHER** to place or class things together ○ *Before we can proceed, all our files have to be coordinated.* **4.** *vi* **WORK TOGETHER** to work together as a unit ○ *members of the team coordinating brilliantly* **5.** *vti* **GO WELL TOGETHER** to make a pleasing combination or match ○ *outfit and accessories that coordinate stylishly* ■ *n* /kō áwrdinət/ **1.** MATHS, MAPS **NUMBER SPECIFYING POSITION** each of a set of numbers that together describe the exact position of something such as a place on a map with reference to a set of axes ○ *Did you receive the coordinates for your target?* **2. SOMEBODY OR SOMETHING EQUAL** somebody or something that is equal in rank or importance (*formal*) ○ *We need the faculties of the college as coordinates in this endeavour.* **3.** CHEM, PHYS **VARIABLE** a variable used with others to describe the state of a physical or chemical system ■ **coordinates** *npl* **MATCHING CLOTHES** clothes that are designed to be worn together ■ *adj* /kō áwrdinət/ **1. EQUAL** equal in rank or importance ○ *The district offices should work as coordinate elements of the company.* **2.** CHEM, PHYS **INVOLVING SET OF VARIABLES** involving the use of coordinates [Mid-17C. < CO- + Latin *ordinat-*, past participle of *ordinare* 'set in order'] —**coordinated** *adj* —**coordinately** /-nətli/ *adv* —**coordinateness** /-nətnəss/ *n* —**coordinative** /-nətiv/ *adj*

coordinate bond *n* a chemical bond between two atoms created by the sharing of a pair of electrons, both supplied by one atom. A coordinate bond is a type of covalent bond.

coordinate clause *n* a clause in a sentence that has the same grammatical function or status as another clause and is usually joined to it by a coordinating conjunction such as 'and' or 'but'

Coordinated Universal Time *n* TIME same as **Greenwich Mean Time**

coordinate geometry *n* MATHS same as **analytical geometry**

coordinating conjunction /kō áwrdi nayting-/ *n* a word that joins two words or clauses with the same grammatical function or status, e.g. 'and' or 'but'

coordination /kō áwrdi náysh'n/ *n* **1.** the combining of diverse parts or groups to make a unit, or the way these parts work together **2.** the skilful and balanced movement of different parts, especially parts of the body, at the same time

coordination complex, coordination compound *n* a chemical compound containing one or more ions, atoms, or molecules bound by coordinate bonds to a central metallic atom

coordination number *n* the number of ions, atoms, or molecules attached by coordinate bonds to the metallic atom in a complex

coordinator /kō áwrdi naytər/ *n* **1.** somebody responsible for organizing diverse parts of an enterprise or groups into a coherent or efficient whole **2.** GRAM same as **coordinating conjunction**

Coorong /koo róng/ long narrow salt lagoon on the southeastern coast of South Australia. It was declared a national park in 1966. Area: 4,000 sq. km/1,500 sq. mi.

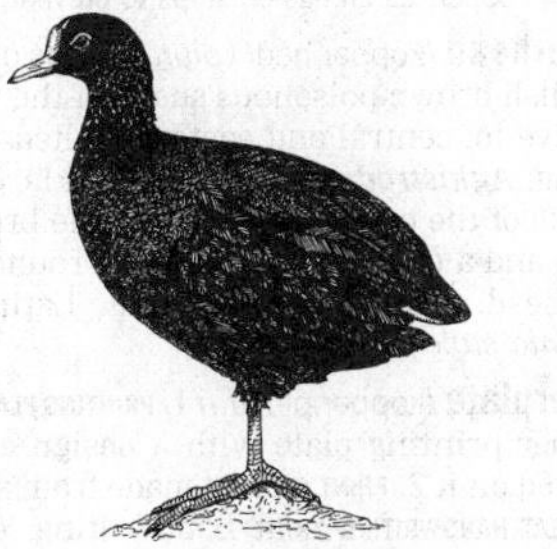

coot

coot /koot/ (*plural* **coots** or *same*) *n* **1.** a water bird with long lobed toes, black feathers, and a white beak and forehead. Native to: Europe, Asia, North America. Genus: *Fulica*. **2.** somebody regarded as odd, eccentric, or unreasonably stubborn (*informal insult*) [13C. Origin ?]

Cootamundra /kóotə múndrə/ town in New South Wales, Australia, northwest of Canberra. Population: 7,667 (2002 estimate).

cooter /kóotər/ *n* a large freshwater turtle. Native to: eastern United States. Genus: *Chrysemys*. [Early 19C. < Gullah]

cootie /kóoti/ *n NZ, N Am* a louse of the kind that infests people (*informal*) [Early 20C. Probably < Malay *kutu*]

cop[1] /kop/ *n* same as **police officer** (*informal*) ■ *vt* **(cops, copping, copped) 1. CATCH SOMEBODY** to catch or arrest somebody for an offence (*informal*) ○ *was copped for driving without a licence* **2. RECEIVE PUNISHMENT** to get into trouble, be blamed, or be punished (*informal*) ○ *If they find out, you'll really cop it.* **3.** *US* **STEAL** to steal something, especially by snatching it hurriedly (*slang*) **4.** *US* **TOUCH OR GLIMPSE SOMEBODY OR SOMETHING** to touch or look at somebody or something quickly and furtively (*slang*) ○ *copped a look at the answers to the quiz* **5.** *US* **OBTAIN DRUGS** to obtain illegal drugs (*slang*) **6.** *US* **GET SOMETHING DESIRABLE** to come into possession of something considered desirable (*slang*) ○ *managed to cop two tickets to the game* [Early 18C. Probably variant of *cap* 'to catch', via French *caper* < Latin *capere* 'seize'; noun partly < the verb, partly shortening of COPPER[2]] ◇ **a fair cop** a fair or just arrest (*informal*) ◇ **cop a plea** *N Am* to negotiate with a prosecutor in order to avoid prosecution for a serious crime by agreeing to plead guilty to a lesser crime (*slang*) ◇ **cop it sweet** *ANZ* to accept a penalty or punishment without resisting or complaining (*informal*) ◇ **not much cop** not very good or useful (*informal*)

cop off *vi* to have a sexual encounter or begin a sexual relationship with somebody (*slang*)

cop out *vi* to withdraw from an activity because of lack of nerve or inclination (*slang*)

cop[2] /kop/ *n* a cone-shaped roll of thread on a spindle [Old English *coppe* 'summit', origin ?]

Copacabana /kṓpə kə bánnə/ beach resort and residential area in southern Rio de Janeiro, Brazil

copacetic /kṓpə séetik/, **copasetic** *adj N Am* excellent or very good (*slang*) [Early 20C. Origin ?]

copal /kṓp'l/ *n* a hard resin obtained from various tropical trees. Use: making varnish. [Late 16C. Via Spanish < Nahuatl *copalli*]

Copán /kō pán/ ancient city of the Maya people, in northwestern Honduras. It is an important archaeological site.

coparenting /kō páirənting/ *n* **1.** the care and bringing up of children by two people who have divorced or separated **2.** shared responsibility for bringing up children between two people who are not legally married, especially a same-sex couple —**coparent** *n*

copartner /kō paátnər/ *n* a close partner or associate, especially one who has an equal stake in a company —**copartnership** /kō paátnəship/ *n*

copasetic *adj N Am* another spelling of **copacetic** (*slang*)

copayment /kō páymənt/ *n* an arrangement by which two or more parties make matching payments on a loan or other financial obligation, or a payment made in this way

cope[1] /kōp/ **(copes, coping, coped)** *vi* to deal successfully with a difficult problem or situation [14C. < Old French *co(l)per* 'to strike' < Greek *kolaphos* 'blow'] —**coper** *n*

cope[2] /kōp/ *n* **1. PRIEST'S CLOAK** a long sleeveless ceremonial cape worn by priests in some Christian churches **2.** ARCHIT same as **coping** ■ *vt* **(copes, coping, coped) 1. PROVIDE WALL WITH COPING** to lay a protective top course of brick or stone (**coping**) on a wall **2. JOIN TIMBER** to join two pieces of moulded timber [13C. Via medieval Latin *capa* 'cloak, hood' < late Latin *cappa*] —**coped** *adj*

copeck *n* MONEY another spelling of **kopek**

Copenhagen /kṓpən háygən, -haágən/ capital and largest city of Denmark, situated on the eastern coast of Sjælland Island and the northern coast of Amager Island. Population: 491,148 (2001). Danish name **København**

Copenhagen blue *adj* of a greyish-blue colour —**Copenhagen blue** *n*

copepod /kṓpə pod/ (*plural* **-pods** or *same*) *n* a tiny crustacean that lives among plankton and is an important food source for many fish. Native to: seas, lakes. Subclass: Copepoda. [Late 19C. < modern Latin *Copepoda* < Greek *kōpē* 'oar' + *-pod* 'foot'; from its paddle-shaped feet]

coper /kṓpər/ *n* a trader or merchant, especially one who deals in horses [Mid-16C. < obsolete *cope* 'buy' < Middle Dutch or Low German *kōpen*]

Copernican /kə púrnikən/ *adj* **1.** relating to Nicolaus Copernicus or the Copernican system **2.** profoundly important or far-reaching (*literary*) ○ *a Copernican change in attitudes*

Copernican system *n* the theory of Nicolaus Copernicus regarding the mechanics of the solar system, which postulates that the Earth and other planets revolve around the Sun. This theory challenged the Ptolemaic system of astronomy that had prevailed since the 2nd century.

Copernicus /kə púrnikəss/ large crater on the Moon in the northwestern quadrant, 93 km/58 mi. in

diameter. It is the centre of a major system of rays on the lunar surface.

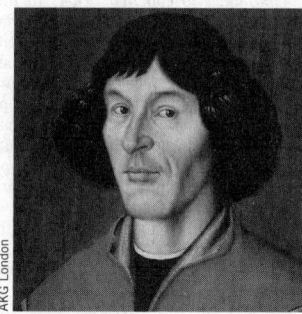

Nicolaus Copernicus

Copernicus, **Nicolaus** (1473–1543) Polish astronomer. His major work, *On the Revolutions of the Celestial Spheres* (1543), postulated that the Earth and other planets revolve around the Sun, and laid the foundations of modern astronomy. Born **Kopernik, Mikołaj**

copestone /kốp stōn/ *n* any of the stones that form the top edge of a wall [Mid-16C. < COPE ²]

copier /kóppi ər/ *n* a device that makes copies of something such as software or recordings

copilot /kố pīlət/ *n* a second pilot in an aircraft, who shares the flying but is not in command

coping /kốping/ *n* the top, often sloping, course of brick or stone on top of a wall that forms a protective cap against the weather [Mid-16C. < COPE ² *v* (sense 1)]

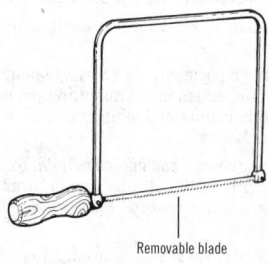

Removable blade

coping saw

coping saw *n* a saw with a thin flexible blade held tight in a U-shaped frame. Use: cutting curves in wood.

copious /kópi əss/ *adj* produced or existing in large quantities [14C. < French *copieux* or Latin *copiosus* < *copia* 'abundance'] —**copiously** *adv* —**copiousness** *n*

copita /kố peétə/ *n* a traditional Spanish tulip-shaped sherry glass, or a drink of sherry served in one [Mid-19C. < Spanish, 'little cup']

coplanar /kố pláynər/ *adj* lying in the same plane —**coplanarity** /kố play nárrəti/ *n*

Aaron Copland

Copland /kốplənd/, **Aaron** (1900–90) US composer whose music was often based on folk themes. He won the Pulitzer Prize in music for *Appalachian Spring* (1944).

'Music is in a continual state of becoming.'

[Aaron Copland, *Music and Imagination*; 1952]

copolymer /kō póllimər/ *n* a substance with a high molecular weight that results from chemically combining two or more monomers —**copolymeric** /kố poli mérrik/ *adj*

copolymerize /kō póllimə rīz/ (**-izes**, **-izing**, **-ized**), **copolymerise** (**-ises**, **-ising**, **-ised**) *vt* to unite two or more monomers chemically to form a copolymer — **copolymerization** /kō póllimə rī záysh'n/ *n*

cop-out *n* (*slang*) **1.** EXCUSE FOR NOT TAKING ACTION a feebly transparent excuse or explanation for refusing to face up to something **2.** EVASION OF RESPONSIBILITY a feeble avoidance of a responsibility or commitment **3.** SOMEBODY WHO BACKS OUT OF SOMETHING somebody who avoids an obligation or a commitment ○ *What a bunch of cop-outs!*

copper¹ /kóppər/ *n* **1.** REDDISH-BROWN METAL a malleable, reddish-brown metallic element that is a good conductor of electricity and heat. Source: ores such as chalcopyrite. Use: wiring, coatings, alloys. Symbol **Cu**. See table at **element** **2.** REDDISH-BROWN COLOUR a reddish-brown colour, like that of polished copper **3.** SMALL COIN a low-value coin made of copper or brass (*informal*) ○ *a pocketful of coppers* **4.** POT FOR BOILING WATER a large pot used to boil water (*dated*) **5.** INSECTS REDDISH-BROWN BUTTERFLY a small reddish-brown butterfly. Genera: *Lycaena* or *Heodes*. ■ *vt* (**-pers**, **-pering**, **-pered**) COVER SOMETHING WITH COPPER to cover or coat something with copper (*often passive*) [Pre-12C. < late Latin *cuprum* < Greek *Kupros* 'Cyprus', important ancient source of copper] —**copper** *adj* —**coppery** *adj*

copper² /kóppər/ *n* same as **police officer** (*dated informal*) [Mid-19C. < COP ¹ *n* (verb)]

copperas /kóppərəss/ *n* MINERALS same as **ferrous sulphate** [15C. Via French < medieval Latin *cuperosa*]

copper beech *n* a beech tree with dark reddish leaves. Native to: Europe.

Copper Belt *n* an area in Central Africa that has rich deposits of copper ore

copper-bottomed *adj* **1.** having a copper coating on the base **2.** certain or reliable, especially financially

copper-fasten *vt* to make an agreement binding [< the use of copper fastenings on ships to prevent corrosion]

copperhead /kóppər hed/ (*plural* **-heads** or *same*) *n* **1.** a reddish-brown poisonous snake of the viper family. Native to: central and eastern United States. Latin name: *Agkistrodon contortrix*. **2.** a large poisonous snake of the cobra family with pale brown to black skin and a copper-coloured band round the back of its head. Native to: Australia. Latin name: *Denisonia superba*.

copperplate /kóppər playt/ *n* **1.** PRINTING PLATE a polished copper printing plate with a design etched or engraved on it **2.** PRINT a print made from a copperplate **3.** NEAT HANDWRITING neat handwriting, especially in the style of copybooks produced from copperplates

copper pyrites *n* MINERALS same as **chalcopyrite**

coppersmith /kóppər smith/ *n* **1.** somebody who makes or repairs copper objects **2.** a small greenish bird with a distinctive metallic call. Native to: Southeast Asia. Latin name: *Megalaima haemacephala*.

copper sulphate *n* a poisonous blue compound containing copper and sulphur. Use: textile dyeing, electroplating, fungicides, wood preservatives. Formula: $CuSO_4$.

coppice /kóppiss/ *n* an area of densely growing small trees, especially one in which the trees are regularly cut back to encourage more growth ■ *vt* (**-pices**, **-picing**, **-piced**) to cut back trees periodically to encourage young growth [Mid-14C. < Old French *copeïz* < *coper* (see COPE ¹)]

Coppola /kóppələ/, **Francis Ford** (b. 1939) US film director. He directed the *Godfather* trilogy (1972, 1974, 1990).

'*Apocalypse Now* is not about Vietnam, it is Vietnam. We were in the jungle; there were too many of us; we had access to too much money, too much equipment; and, little by little, we went insane.'

[Francis Ford Coppola. Quoted in *Films Illustrated*; October 1979]

Francis Ford Coppola

copra /kópprə/ *n* the dried flesh of a coconut, from which coconut oil is obtained [Late 16C. Via Portuguese < Malayalam *koppara*]

Coprates /kópprə teez/ giant canyon on Mars running east–west to the equatorial region. It is over 800 km/500 mi. long and 95 km/60 mi. wide in places.

copro- *prefix* dung, excrement ○ *coprophilous* [< Greek *kopros*]

coprocessor /kố prố sessər/ *n* a second processor in a computer, improving performance by handling specialized tasks

coprolalia /kópprə láyli ə/ *n* the uncontrolled use of violent and obscene language, especially as a result of an illness such as Tourette's syndrome

coprolite /kópprə līt/ *n* a piece of fossilized dung from which information about eating patterns in prehistoric times can be discovered —**coprolitic** /kópprə líttik/ *adj*

coprology /ko prólləji/ *n* an obsession with defecation, especially as expressed in art and literature

coprophagy /ko próffəji/ *n* the eating of dung by some species of insects or animals —**coprophagous** *adj*

coprophilia /kópprə fílli ə/ *n* an obsessive and often sexual interest in faeces and defecation —**coprophiliac** *n* —**coprophilic** *adj*

coprophilous /kə próffiləss/ *adj* describes organisms that live on or in dung, as some insects or fungi do

copse /kops/ *n* TREES same as **coppice** [Late 16C. Contraction]

cop shop *n* a police station (*informal*)

Copt /kopt/ *n* **1.** a member of the Coptic Church **2.** an Egyptian of non-Arab descent [Early 17C. Via French or modern Latin < Arabic *al-kibṭ* 'the Copts' < Coptic *Gyptios* 'Egyptian' < Greek *Aiguptios*]

copter /kóptər/ *n* AVIAT same as **helicopter** (*informal*) [Mid-20C. Shortening]

Coptic /kóptik/ *n* a language formerly spoken in Egypt, a later form of ancient Egyptian and one of the Afro-Asiatic languages. Coptic survives as the liturgical language of Egyptian Monophysite Christians. ■ *adj* relating or belonging to the Copts, Coptic, or the Egyptian Monophysite Christian Church

Coptic Church *n* the Egyptian Christian Church, established in the 6th century and adhering to the doctrine of the Monophysites

copula /kóppyoolə/ (*plural* **-las** or **-lae** /-lee/) *n* **1.** GRAM LINKING VERB a verb that links the subject of a sentence with an adjective or noun phrase (**complement**) relating to it, e.g. 'be' or 'seem' **2.** LOGIC LINK BETWEEN SUBJECT AND PREDICATE a form of the verb 'to be' linking the subject and the predicate in some propositions, e.g. 'are' in 'Some dogs are poodles' **3.** LINK BETWEEN TWO THINGS anything that provides a link between two things (*formal*) [Early 17C. < Latin, 'link'] —**copular** *adj*

copulate /kóppyoo layt/ (**-lates**, **-lating**, **-lated**) *vi* to have sexual intercourse [Early 17C. < Latin *copulat-*, past participle of *copulare* 'join together' < *copula* 'link'] —**copulation** /kóppyoo láysh'n/ *n* —**copulatory** /kóppyoo láytəri/ *adj*

copulative /kóppyoolətiv/ *adj* **1.** linking or joining (*formal*) **2.** relating to a verb that links the subject with its complement or to the function of such a verb (*technical*) —**copulatively** *adv*

copy /kóppi/ *n* (*plural* **-ies**) **1.** REPRODUCTION something

that is made exactly like something else in appearance or function **2. ONE OF MANY** one of many identical specimens of something produced in large numbers, especially something printed or published **3. WRITTEN TEXT** the written text to be published in a book, newspaper, or magazine, as distinct from visual material or graphics ■ *v* (**-ies, -ying, -ied**) **1.** *vt* **MAKE IDENTICAL VERSION OF SOMETHING** to make another example or specimen that is exactly the same as something else **2.** *vt* **DO SAME AS SOMEBODY** to do exactly what somebody else does **3.** *vti* **CHEAT BY DOING SAME** to reproduce the work of another person fraudulently [14C. Via French < Latin *copia* 'abundance'] —**copyable** *adj*

SYNONYMS *copy, reproduce, duplicate, clone, replicate, re-create*

CORE MEANING: to make something that resembles something else to a greater or lesser degree

copy to make another example or specimen that is exactly the same as something else ○ *Please complete this coupon or carefully copy all the details on to a plain sheet of paper.* **reproduce** to make a copy of something by technical means ○ *an attempt to reproduce human speech digitally* ○ *No part of this publication may be reproduced without the prior permission of the publisher.* **duplicate** to make an identical version of something one or more times ○ *Give the notes to my assistant so they can be duplicated.* ○ *She had duplicated in adult life the pattern of behaviour she had learned as a child.* **clone** to make a near or exact copy, especially of a piece of equipment or biological material. ○ *the scientist who first cloned sheep* ○ *The gene has been cloned and sequenced.* **replicate** to make an identical version of something repeatedly and exactly, or do something again in exactly the same way ○ *anecdotal evidence which cannot be replicated in the laboratory* ○ *The original findings have been replicated by other investigators.* **re-create** to make something that appears to be the same as something that no longer exists, or that exists in a different place ○ *The company has gone all-out to re-create the play's 1970s atmosphere.* ○ *At their best, gardens can re-create a corner of paradise.*

copy down *vt* to make a written copy of something ○ *Journalists copied down his every word.*

copy in *v* to send a copy to somebody, especially a copy of a letter or other document

copybook /kóppi book/ *n* **BOOK OF HANDWRITING SPECIMENS** a book containing models of handwriting for young students to copy ■ *adj* **1. EXCELLENT** so good that it could be used as a model for others to copy **2. UNORIGINAL** following guidelines slavishly and showing no originality ◇ **blot your copybook** to do something that spoils your previously good record or reputation

copycat /kóppi kat/ (*informal*) *n* somebody, especially a child, who slavishly imitates another ■ *adj* done in close imitation of somebody or something else

copy clothing *n* Hong Kong clothes that are copies of designer garments, usually passed off as genuine

copy desk *n* a desk at which written material is edited for publication

copy-edit *vti* to read written material and correct it for publication

copy editor *n* a reader and corrector of written texts for publication

copyhold /kóppi hōld/ *n* a tenure of land held at the will of a landowner, originally a lord [15C. Because recorded in a transcript of the manorial court rolls]

copyholder /kóppi hōldər/ *n* **1. DOCUMENT STAND** a stand that holds documents upright while they are being read or keyed **2. ASSISTANT TO PROOFREADER** somebody who reads written material aloud to a proofreader **3. HOLDER OF ESTATE** a holder of a tenement (**copyhold**) that consisted of an estate held at the will of a landowner, originally a lord (*dated*)

copyist /kóppi ist/ *n* **1.** somebody who makes copies of handwritten documents or music **2.** a mere imitator of others

copy machine *n* US same as **photocopier**

copy protection *n* a means of preventing unauthorized duplication of computer software —**copy-protected** *adj*

copyreader /kóppi reedər/ *n* N Am same as **subeditor** (sense 2)

copyright /kóppi rīt/ *n* **CREATIVE ARTIST'S CONTROL OF ORIGINAL WORK** the legal right of creative artists or publishers to control the use and reproduction of their original works ■ *adj* **PROTECTED BY COPYRIGHT** controlled or restricted by a copyright ■ *vt* (**-rights, -righting, -righted**) **GET COPYRIGHT OF SOMETHING** to secure the copyright on a creative work —**copyrightable** *adj* —**copyrighter** *n*

copyright deposit library, **copyright library** *n* a library that receives a free copy of every book published in the British Isles, belonging to a group of six in England, Scotland, Wales, and the Republic of Ireland

copy typist *n* a typist who works from written or typed drafts, rather than from dictation

~~copywright~~ incorrect spelling of **copyright**

copywriter /kóppi rītər/ *n* somebody who writes advertisements or promotional material —**copywriting** *n*

coq au vin /kók ō váN, -ván/ (*plural* **coqs au vin** /kók-/ or **coq au vins** /-váNz, -vánz/) *n* a dish of chicken cooked in red wine with other ingredients [< French, 'cock in wine']

coquet /ko két/ (*literary*) *vi* (**-quets, -quetting, -quetted**) **1. FLIRT** to act coyly and flirtatiously **2. ACT FRIVOLOUSLY** to act casually or frivolously ■ *n* **MAN WHO FLIRTS** a flirtatious man [Late 17C. < French, 'little cock' < *coq* 'cock'] —**coquetry** /kókitri/ *n*

coquette /ko két/ *n* a flirtatious woman [Mid-17C. < French, feminine of *coquet* (see COQUET)] —**coquettish** *adj* —**coquettishly** *adv* —**coquettishness** *n*

coquille /ko kée/ *n* **1. SEAFOOD DISH** a dish of seafood baked and served in a scallop shell or a scallop-shaped dish **2. SHELL OR SHELL-SHAPED DISH** a scallop shell or a scallop-shaped dish **3. FENCING GUARD ON FOIL** a bell-shaped guard on a fencing foil [< French (see COCKLE[1])]

coquina /kō kéenə/ *n* **1.** a soft limestone formed largely from crushed shells and coral. Use: building material in the Caribbean and the southeastern United States. **2.** a small clam common off the coasts of the eastern and southern United States. Genus: *Donax*. [Mid-19C. < Spanish, 'cockle shell']

coquito /ko kéetō/ (*plural* **-tos** or *same*) *n* a palm tree with edible nuts and sweet sap that is used to make wine. Native to: Chile. Latin name: *Jubaea chilensis*. [Mid-19C. < Spanish, 'little coco shell' < Portuguese *côco* (see COCO)]

cor /kawr/ *interj* used to express amazement or admiration (*informal*) [Mid-20C. Shortening of COR BLIMEY]

cor. *abbr* **1.** corner **2.** MUSIC cornet **3.** correction **4.** COMMUNICATION correspondence **5.** MEDIA correspondent

Cor. *abbr* BIBLE Corinthians

coracle /kórrək'l/ *n* a small round boat made from animal skins stretched over a wicker frame [Mid-16C. < Welsh *corwgl* < Middle Irish *curach*]

coracoid /kórrə koyd/ *n* a bony projection on the shoulder blade in most mammals [Mid-18C. Via modern Latin < Greek *korakoeidēs* 'like a crow' (from its resemblance to a crow's beak) < *korax* 'crow, raven']

Barnaby's

coral

coral /kórrəl/ *n* **1. MARINE ORGANISM** a marine organism that lives in colonies and has an external skeleton. Class: Anthozoa. **2. HARD MARINE DEPOSIT** a hard deposit consisting of the skeletons of coral, often forming ocean reefs **3. SOMETHING MADE OF CORAL** a piece of coral, especially red coral or an object made from one **4. DEEP PINKISH-ORANGE COLOUR** a deep pinkish-orange colour **5. LOBSTER'S OR CRAB'S EGGS** the unfertilized eggs

of a lobster or crab that turn pinkish-orange when cooked [14C. Via French < Greek *korallion*] —**coral** *adj* —**coralloid** *adj*

coralberry /kórrəl berri/ (*plural* **-ries** or *same*) *n* **1.** a bush that produces dark red berries that persist into winter. Native to: North America. Latin name: *Symphoricarpos orbiculatus*. **2.** an evergreen bush. Native to: eastern Asia. Genus: *Ardisia*.

coralline /kórrə līn/ *adj* **1. OF OR LIKE CORAL** relating to or resembling coral **2. PINKISH** of a pinkish-red or pinkish-orange colour ■ *n* **1. CALCIUM-COVERED RED ALGA** a red alga whose fronds are covered or impregnated with calcium deposits. Genus: *Corallina*. **2. ORGANISM THAT RESEMBLES CORAL** a sponge or other organism that resembles coral

coral reef *n* an ocean reef composed of the skeletons of living coral, together with minerals and organic matter

coralroot /kórrəl root/ (*plural* **-roots** or *same*) *n* a leafless orchid with small insignificant flowers that feeds through roots that resemble coral. Genus: *Corallorhiza*.

Coral Sea /kórrəl-/ sea in the southwestern Pacific Ocean bounded by Australia, New Guinea, the Solomon Islands, and Vanuatu

Coral Sea Islands Territory island group and external dependency of Australia, lying in the South Pacific, east of Queensland

coral snake *n* **1.** a poisonous and mainly nocturnal snake that is strikingly marked with red, black, and yellow or white bands. Native to: North and South America. Genera: *Micrurus* or *Micruroides*. **2.** a poisonous snake that is red with yellow and black bands. Native to: eastern Australia. Latin name: *Brachyurophis australis*.

coral tree *n* a thorny bush or small tree with brightly coloured seeds growing in long pods and flowers that are pollinated by birds. Flowers: large, red or orange. Native to: tropical and subtropical regions. Genus: *Erythrina*.

coral trout *n* a fish that has a scarlet body covered with blue spots. Native to: northern Australia. Latin name: *Plectropoma maculatum*.

cor anglais /káwr óng glay/ (*plural same* or **cors anglais** /káwrz-/) *n* UK, ANZ, Can a woodwind instrument like an oboe but larger and lower-pitched. US term **English horn** [< French, 'English horn']

coranto /ko rántō/ (*plural* **-tos** or *same*) *n* DANCE same as **courante** (sense 2) [Mid-16C. Alteration of French *courante* 'running']

corban /káwr ban/ *n* **1.** an offering to God made by the ancient Hebrew people **2.** an offering made to the Temple of Jerusalem [14C. Via Greek < Hebrew *qorbān* 'offering' < *qārab* 'approach']

corbeil /káwrb'l/, **corbeille** *n* a stone carving of a basket of fruit or flowers as a feature on a building [Mid-18C. Via French *corbeille* < late Latin *corbicula* 'small basket' < Latin *corbis* 'basket']

corbel

corbel /káwrb'l/ *n* **SUPPORTING STONE BRACKET** a bracket of brick or stone that juts out of a wall to support a structure above it ■ *vt* (**-bels, -belling, -belled**) **1. LAY MASONRY UNITS TO FORM PROJECTION** to lay stones or bricks in layers so that each juts out above the one below to form a supporting bracket **2. SUPPORT SOMETHING WITH CORBELS** to support a cornice or other structure on corbels [14C. < Old French, 'little raven' < *corp* 'raven' < Latin *corvus*; from its original profile resembling a beak from being cut slantways]

corbelling /káwrbəling/ *n* a structural system using corbels as supports

corbel step *n* CONSTR same as **corbie step**

Corbett /káwrbit/ *n Scotland* a Scottish mountain between 762 m/2500 ft and 914.4 m/3000 ft [After J. R. *Corbett*, who listed such mountains]

Corbett /káwrbit/, **James John** (1866–1933) US boxer. He was the world heavyweight boxing champion from 1892 to 1897. Known as **Gentleman Jim**

corbie /káwrbi/ (*plural* **-bies** or *same*) *n Scotland* a crow, especially a raven [15C. < Old French *corbin* < late Latin *corvinus* (see CORVINE)]

corbie gable *n* a gable with top edges shaped like a series of steps [< CORBIE STEP]

corbie step *n* each of a series of decorative steps going up the side of a gable [< the idea that only crows can reach them]

cor blimey /káwr blīmi/, **gorblimey** /gáwr blīmi/ *interj* used to express amazement or admiration (*dated informal*) [Alteration of *God blind me!*]

Corbusier ▸ **Le Corbusier**

Corby /káwrbi/ former steel town in Northamptonshire, central England. It was designated a new town in 1950. Population: 53,174 (2001).

cord /kawrd/ *n* **1.** STRING OR ROPE thick strong string or thin rope ○ *hands and feet tied with cords* **2.** FASTENING OR BELT a length of material used as a fastening or belt **3.** ELECTRICAL CABLE flexible insulated electric cable **4.** BODY PART RESEMBLING ROPE a part of the body resembling cord, e.g. the spinal cord or the umbilical cord **5.** RIBBED FABRIC any fabric with a ribbed surface, especially corduroy **6.** UNIT OF VOLUME FOR CUT TIMBER a unit of volume for cut timber, equal to 128 cu. ft (approximately 3.6 cu. m) ■ **cords** *npl* TROUSERS corduroy trousers (*informal*) ○ *a pair of cords* ■ *vt* (**cords, cording, corded**) **1.** TIE SOMETHING WITH CORD to fasten or tie something with cord or rope ○ *Are the packages corded and ready to ship?* **2.** STACK WOOD IN CORDS to stack wood in units with a volume of one cord [13C. Via Old French *corde* < Latin *chorda* < Greek *khordē* 'string'] —**corder** *n*

USAGE See *chord* [1].

cordage /káwrdij/ *n* **1.** ropes or cords collectively, especially the lines and rigging of a ship **2.** the amount of wood in a stack, measured in cords

cordate /káwrd ayt/ *adj* describes a leaf that is heart-shaped [Mid-18C. < modern Latin *cordatus* < Latin *cord-* 'heart'] —**cordately** *adv*

Corday /káwrd ay/, **Charlotte** (1768–93) French assassin. She supported the moderate Girondins during the French Revolution, and was guillotined after murdering the Jacobin extremist Jean Paul Marat. Full name **Corday d'Armont, Marie Anne Charlotte**

corded /káwrdid/ *adj* **1.** TIED UP securely tied up with string or rope **2.** RIBBED describes a fabric with a ribbed surface **3.** WITH TIGHT MUSCLES having tensed or well-developed muscles visible as ridges or ripples

Cordelia /kawr déeli ə/ *n* a small natural satellite of Uranus, discovered in 1986 by the Voyager 2 planetary probe. Its gravitational influence appears to help stabilize the outer ring of Uranus.

cord grass *n* a coarse grass found on coastal salt marshes or mudflats. Genus: *Spartina*.

cordial /káwrdi əl/ *adj* **1.** HOSPITABLY WARM friendly and affectionate **2.** DEEPLY FELT sincere or profound (*literary*) ○ *has a cordial dislike for dogs* **3.** REFRESHING stimulating or invigorating (*literary*) ■ *n* **1.** FRUIT DRINK a fruit drink, especially one sold in concentrated form and diluted with water **2.** TONIC a stimulating or medicinal drink [14C. < medieval Latin *cordialis* 'of the heart' < Latin *cord-* 'heart'] —**cordially** *adv* —**cordialness** *n*

cordiality /káwrdi álləti/ *n* friendliness and affection ○ *We were surprised by the cordiality of their response.*

cordierite /káwrdi ə rīt/ *n* a purplish-blue or grey aluminosilicate mineral containing magnesium and iron. Source: metamorphic rocks. [Early 19C. After Pierre L. *Cordier* (1777–1861), French geologist]

cordillera /káwdil yáirə/ (*plural* **-ras**) *n* a system of mountain ranges consisting of approximately parallel ridges [Early 18C. < Spanish < *cordilla* 'small cord' < *cuerda* 'cord' < Latin *chorda* (see CORD)]

Cordilleras /káwdil yáirəz/, **Cordillera** system of mountain ranges in western North America, including the Sierra Nevada, the Coast and Cascade ranges, and the Rocky Mountains. Highest peak: Mount McKinley 6,194 m/20,320 ft.

cordite /káwrd īt/ *n* a smokeless explosive, usually made of gunpowder and nitroglycerine [Late 19C. < CORD; from its stringy appearance]

cordless /káwrdləss/ *adj* powered by an internal battery and not needing to be continuously attached by a cable to an external electricity supply

cordless telephone *n* a telephone, powered by a recharging battery, with a portable handset that can be removed from its base unit and has a short-range radio link to it

córdoba /káwrdəbə/ *n* the main unit of Nicaraguan currency. See table at **currency** [Early 20C. After Francisco Fernández de *Córdoba* (1475–1526), Spanish explorer]

Cordoba /káwrdəbə/, **Córdoba, Cordova** /káwrdəvə/ **1.** city and capital of Córdoba Province in central Argentina. It is the site of the National University of Córdoba, founded in 1613. Population: 1,157,507 (1991). **2.** city in Andalusia, southern Spain. It is the capital of Córdoba Province. Population: 314,805 (2002).

cordon /káwrd'n/ *n* **1.** PEOPLE OR VEHICLES ENCIRCLING AREA a line of police officers or soldiers, or their vehicles, surrounding an area to control access to it **2.** RIBBON a piece of ribbon worn for decoration or as a sign of rank or a mark of honour **3.** GARDENING FRUIT TREE WITH SHORT SIDE SHOOTS a fruit tree grown as a single stem at an angle against a support, with its side branches pruned back close to the stem **4.** ARCHIT same as **string course** [Late 16C. < Old French, 'small cord' < *corde* (see CORD)]

cordon off (**cordons off, cordoning off, cordoned off**) *vt* to surround an area with a line of police officers, soldiers, or their vehicles, to control access to it

cordon bleu /káwr don blúr/ *adj* **1.** OF HIGHEST CLASS describes a cook or cooking of the highest class **2.** WITH CHEESE AND HAM describes a way of preparing meat, especially veal, by rolling a thin slice around cheese and ham and then coating in breadcrumbs ■ *n* (*plural* **cordon bleus**) **1.** MASTER CHEF a cook of the very highest class, especially a master chef **2.** KNIGHT'S RIBBON a blue ribbon worn by knights of the highest order in Bourbon France [Early 18C. < French, 'blue ribbon']

cordon sanitaire /káwr don sani táir/ *n* **1.** a barrier erected to control the spread of a disease by restricting movement to and from the infected area **2.** a neutral state, or a string of neutral states, lying between two states that are hostile to each other [Mid-19C. < French, 'sanitary line']

Cordova ▸ **Cordoba**

cordovan /káwrdəvən/ *n* a fine soft leather originally made from goatskin and now usually made from horsehide [Late 16C. < Spanish *cordován*, after CORDOBA]

corduroy /káwdə roy, -dyoo-/ *n* a heavy cotton fabric with a ribbed nap running lengthways ■ **corduroys** *npl* trousers made of corduroy [Late 18C. Probably < CORD + *duroy*, a coarse woollen fabric]

corduroy road *n* a road made of logs across muddy or swampy ground [Because its surface resembles corduroy]

cordwainer /káwrd waynər/ *n* somebody who made shoes and other articles from fine soft leather (**cordovan**) (*archaic*) —**cordwainery** *n*

cordwood /káwrd wòod/ *n* wood in stacks with a volume of one cord, or cut into lengths of 1.2 m/4 ft for stacking in cords

core /kawr/ *n* **1.** ESSENTIAL PART the central or most important part of something ○ *the core of the argument* **2.** CENTRAL PART OF FRUIT the fibrous central part of some fruit, containing the seeds **3.** GEOL CENTRE OF EARTH the central part of Earth, or the corresponding part of another astronomical object. Earth's core is molten in parts and is composed of an alloy of iron and nickel. **4.** INDUST CENTRAL PART OF NUCLEAR REACTOR the central part of a nuclear reactor in which fission takes place **5.** ELEC IRON IN TRANSFORMER a block of iron in a coil or transformer, used to intensify and direct the magnetic field produced by a current in surrounding coils **6.** GEOL SAMPLE OBTAINED BY DRILLING a tubular segment of rock, ice, or other material obtained as a study sample by drilling **7.** PREHIST STONE USED TO MAKE TOOLS a block of stone from which tools or flakes are chipped **8.** COMPUT PIECE OF COMPUTER MEMORY formerly, a ring-shaped piece of magnetic material used to store digital data in a computer, each core representing one binary digit (**bit**) **9.** COMPUT COMPUTER MEMORY the main memory of a computer, which was composed of arrays of ring-shaped magnets before the introduction of semiconductor memories ■ *adj* ESSENTIAL of central or fundamental importance ○ *The company's core business is steel manufacturing.* ○ *core competencies* ■ *vt* (**cores, coring, cored**) TAKE CORE OUT OF FRUIT to remove the core from a piece of fruit [13C. Origin ?] —**corer** *n*

CORE /kawr/ *abbr* Congress of Racial Equality

core competency *n* an area of expertise that is fundamental to a particular job or function

core curriculum *n* the subjects that all students are required to study at school

core dump *n* **1.** a transfer of data from the main memory of a computer, usually to external storage **2.** a long-winded response to a simple question (*informal humorous*)

coreferential /kō refə rénsh'l/ *adj* referring to the same person or thing ○ *In the sentence 'Mary lost her purse', 'Mary' and 'her' are coreferential.*

~~**corelate**~~ incorrect spelling of **correlate**

coreligionist /kō ri lijjənist/ *n* somebody of the same religion as another person

corella /kə rélə/ *n* a white cockatoo with some pink face feathers, blue skin around the eyes, and a long beak. Native to: Australasia. Genus: *Cacatua*. [Late 19C. < an Aboriginal language]

Corelli /kə rélli, ko-/, **Arcangelo** (1653–1713) Italian composer and violinist. He was a virtuoso violinist. His chamber music set a baroque style that influenced Johann Sebastian Bach.

core memory *n* COMPUT same as **core** *n* (sense 9)

coreq /kōrék/ *n US* EDUC same as **corequisite** (*informal*)

corequisite /kō rékwizit/ *n N Am* a course of study that must be taken along with another

~~**corespondence**~~ incorrect spelling of **correspondence**

co-respondent, corespondent /kō ri spóndənt/ *n* somebody named in a divorce suit as the alleged adulterous sexual partner of the respondent ■ **co-respondents** *npl* CLOTHING same as **co-respondent shoes** (*humorous*) —**co-respondency** *n*

co-respondent shoes *npl* men's two-tone shoes, usually black or brown and white (*humorous*)

core subject *n* a subject that all students are required to study at school, e.g. English or mathematics

core time *n* the part of the working day during which workers on flexitime must be present at work

corf /kawrf/ (*plural* **corves** /kawrvz/) *n* a wagon used inside a mine for transporting mined coal or ore [15C. Via Middle Dutch or Middle Low German *korf* 'basket' < Latin *corbis*]

Corfu /kawr fóo, -fyóo/ most northerly island in the Ionian Islands, west of Greece. It is a major tourist centre. Population: 107,592 (1991). Area: 641 sq. km/247 sq. mi.

corgi /káwrgi/ (*plural* **-gis**) *n* a small dog with short legs and smooth hair, belonging to one of two breeds, the Cardigan Welsh corgi and the Pembroke Welsh corgi [Early 20C. < Welsh < *cor* 'dwarf' + *ci* 'dog']

CORGI /káwrgi/ *abbr* Council for Registered Gas Installers

coriaceous /kórri áyshəss/ *adj* like leather in texture or appearance (*technical*) [Late 17C. < late Latin *coriaceus* < Latin *corium* 'leather']

coriander /kórri ándər/ *n* **1.** the leaves or seeds of an aromatic plant, or a powder made from the crushed seeds. Use: food seasoning. **2.** the annual aromatic plant from which coriander is taken. Native to: Asia, Mediterranean. Latin name: *Coriandrum sativum*. [13C. Via French < Greek *koriandron*]

Corinth /kórrinth/ ancient Greek city and modern town 5 km/3 mi. to its northeast. The ruins of the ancient city are about 80 km/50 mi. west of Athens. Population: 27,412 (1991). Greek name **Kórinthos**

Corinthian /kə rínthi ən/ *adj* **1.** OF CORINTH relating to the ancient Greek city or modern Greek town of Corinth **2.** ARCHIT SLENDER AND ORNATE AT TOP describes a

a at; aa father; aw all; ay day; ai hair; ə about, item, edible, common, circus; e egg; ee eel; hw when; i it, happy; ī ice; 'l apple; 'm rhythm; 'n fashion; o odd; ō open; oo good; oo pool; ow owl; oy oil; th thin; th this; u up; ur urge;

slender architectural column with an ornate capital **3. DEBAUCHED** debauched or ostentatiously luxurious (*literary*) **4.** SPORTS **OF SPORTS CLUB** used in the name of sports clubs and competitions ○ *The Essex Sunday Corinthian League* ■ *n* **1. SOMEBODY FROM CORINTH** somebody from Corinth in Greece **2.** SPORTS **WEALTHY SPORTSPERSON** a wealthy amateur sportsperson (*archaic*)

Corinthian order *n* an ancient Greek order of architecture characterized by a slender column with an ornate capital [< its origin in CORINTH]

Corinthians /kə rínthi ənz/ *n* either of two books of the Bible, originally letters addressed to the church at Corinth and traditionally attributed to St Paul (*takes a singular verb*) See table at **Bible**

Coriolanus /kórri ō láynəss/ *n* in Roman legend, the defeater of the Volsci in the 5th century BC

Coriolis effect /kórri ṓliss-/ *n* the observed deflection of something such as a missile in flight relative to the surface of Earth, caused by Earth's rotation beneath the object. The deflection is to the right in the northern hemisphere and to the left in the southern hemisphere. [After Gaspard de *Coriolis* (1792–1843), French mathematician]

Coriolis force /kóri ṓlis-/ *n* an apparent but nonexistent force used to describe the effect of Earth's rotation on the motion of moving objects [See CORIOLIS EFFECT]

corium /káwri əm/ (*plural* **-ria** /-ri ə/) *n* **1.** MED same as **dermis 2.** the leathery middle part of the forewing of some insects [Early 19C. < Latin, 'hide, leather']

cork /kawrk/ *n* **1. BOTTLE STOPPER** a usually cylindrical piece of material used as a bottle stopper **2. OUTER BARK OF CORK OAK** the light flexible outer bark of the cork oak tree. Use: for bottle stoppers, as an insulator. **3.** FISHING **FLOAT USED IN ANGLING** a small float used in angling to maintain a hook or net suspended in the water **4.** BOT **LAYER OF PLANT TISSUE** dead tissue that forms a protective outer layer on plants and is part of the bark in woody plants ■ *vt* (**corks, corking, corked**) **1. SEAL CONTAINER WITH CORK** to stop or seal something, especially a bottle, with a cork **2. RESTRAIN FEELINGS** to restrain feelings, especially strong negative ones such as anger or grief (*informal*) [13C. Probably via Middle Dutch < Arabic dialect *kurk* 'cork-soled sandal']

Cork /kawrk/ **1.** county town of County Cork, southern Ireland. It is a port on the River Lee and the second largest city in the Republic of Ireland. Population: 123,062 (2002). **2.** coastal county in Munster Province, southwestern Republic of Ireland. Population: 420,510 (2002). Area: 3,188 sq. km/1,231 sq. mi.

corkage /káwrkij/ *n* a fee charged at some restaurants for serving wine and other alcoholic drinks that customers bring in from elsewhere

corkboard /káwrk bawrd/ *n* a thin sheet made from compressed cork granules, typically used as a floor covering and as wall insulation before plastic was available

cork cambium *n* a zone of actively dividing tissue near the outer surface of a woody plant that produces cork

corked /kawrkt/ *adj* **1.** sealed or stopped with a cork or other object **2.** given an unpleasant flavour by substances from a tainted cork ○ *Waiter, this wine's corked!*

corker /káwrkər/ *n* **1.** somebody or something particularly striking or special (*informal*) ○ *It was a corker of a day.* **2.** a person or machine that fits corks, especially into bottles

corking /káwrking/ *adj* excellent or splendid (*dated informal*)

cork oak *n* an evergreen oak whose thick bark is a source of cork. Native to: Mediterranean. Latin name: *Quercus suber*.

corkscrew /káwrk skroo/ *n* **DEVICE FOR REMOVING CORKS FROM BOTTLES** a device for taking corks out of bottles, usually a pointed spiral of metal attached to a handle or simple lever ■ *v* (**-screws, -screwing, -screwed**) **1.** *vi* **MOVE IN SPIRAL PATH** to move in a spiral path ○ *watched anxiously as the plane corkscrewed towards the ground* **2.** *vt* **WIND SOMETHING IN SPIRAL** to wind or twist something in a spiral ■ *adj* **SPIRAL-SHAPED** shaped like a spiral ○ *corkscrew curls*

corkwood /káwrk wŏŏd/ (*plural* **-woods** or *same*) *n* a deciduous bush or small tree that grows in wetlands and has light porous wood. Native to: southeastern United States. Latin name: *Leitneria floridana*.

corky /káwrki/ (**-ier, -iest**) *adj* **1.** made from or resembling cork **2.** having the taste or smell of cork —**corkiness** *n*

corm /kawrm/ *n* a short swollen underground stem base in some plants such as crocuses and gladioli that stores food over the winter and produces new foliage in the spring. New corms often form on top of old ones and are used as a means of propagating new plants. [Mid-19C. Via modern Latin < Greek *kormos* 'lopped-off tree trunk'] —**cormous** *adj*

cormorant

cormorant /káwrmərənt/ *n* a large diving bird with webbed feet, a hooked beak, and a long neck that can expand to swallow fish. Native to: coastal waters. Family: Phalacrocoracidae. [13C. Alteration of Old French *cormaran* 'sea raven' < *corp* 'raven' + *marenc* 'of the sea' (< Latin *marinus*)]

corn[1] /kawrn/ *n* **1.** *UK, Ireland* **WHEAT, BARLEY, OR OATS** any cereal crop, especially wheat, barley, or oats **2.** *UK, Ireland* **GRAIN OF CORN** the grains produced by corn plants, especially when collected together by harvesting **3.** *N Am* same as **maize** (sense 2) **4.** *N Am* same as **maize** (sense 1) **5.** BEVERAGES same as **corn whisky 6. CORNY ITEM OR MATERIAL** something trite or overly sentimental (*informal*) [Old English < Indo-European, 'grain']

corn[2] /kawrn/ *n* a hardened or thickened, often painful, area of skin, usually on a toe, caused by friction or pressure [14C. Via French < Latin *cornu* 'horn']

Corn. *abbr* Cornwall

cornball /káwrn bawl/ (*informal*) *n US* somebody regarded as naively sentimental ■ *adj N Am* trite or overly sentimental ○ *a cornball movie* [Mid-20C. Originally 'sweet ball of popcorn', often sold at carnivals and regarded as unsophisticated]

corn borer *n* a moth whose larvae bore into and feed on maize. There are different species, including the European corn borer and the southern corn borer. Family: Pyralidae.

cornbraid /káwrn brayd/ *n* HAIR same as **cornrow**

corn bread *n N Am* bread made from maize flour

corn chip *n* a crisp thin piece of fried maize flour batter, eaten as a savoury snack food

corn circle *n* AGRIC same as **crop circle**

corncob /káwrn kob/ *n* **1.** an ear of sweetcorn or maize **2.** the hard core of an ear of maize, on which the kernels grow

corncockle /káwrn kok'l/ (*plural* **-les** or *same*) *n* an annual plant with poisonous seeds, once common as a weed in cornfields. Flowers: reddish-purple. Native to: Mediterranean. Latin name: *Agrostemma githago*. [Early 18C. < CORN[1] + COCKLE[2]]

corncrake /káwrn krayk/ *n* a speckled bird with a harsh call, a short beak, and reddish wings. Native to: fields and meadows of Europe and Asia. Latin name: *Crex crex*.

corncrib /káwrn krib/ *n N Am* a ventilated building used for the storage and drying of maize ears

corn dog *n N Am* a hot dog on a stick, coated in maize-flour batter and deep-fried, typically sold at fairs and carnivals

corndogging /káwrn doging/ *n US* a surfing initiation ritual in which a surfer is rolled in sand after surfing by his or her fellow surfers (*slang*)

corn dolly *n* a small ornamental object made from plaited straw

cornea /káwrni ə, kawr née ə/ (*plural* **-as** or **-ae** /-ni ee/) *n* the transparent convex membrane that covers the pupil and iris of the eye [14C. < medieval Latin *cornea tela* 'horny tissue' < Latin *cornu* 'horn'; from its fibrous consistency] —**corneal** *adj*

corn earworm *n* a large striped American moth larva that feeds destructively on maize, tomatoes, cotton bolls, and many other plants. Latin name: *Heliothis zea*.

corned /kawrnd/ *adj* cooked and then preserved in salt or brine ○ *corned mutton* [Early 17C. < CORN[1] 'preserve with salt']

corned beef *n* beef that has been cooked, preserved in salt or brine, and often canned

Corneille /kawr náy/, **Pierre** (1606–84) French playwright. His plays include the tragedies *Le Cid* (1637), *Horace* (1640), and *Polyeucte* (1643).

> 'Who is all-powerful should fear all things.'
> [Pierre Corneille, *Cinna*; 1641]

cornel /káwrn'l/ (*plural* **-nels** or *same*) *n* any plant related to dogwood. Genus: *Cornus*. [15C. < Old French *corneille* < Latin *cornus*]

cornelian *n* MINERALS same as **carnelian**

cornelian cherry /kawr néeli ən-/ *n* a small deciduous tree cultivated for its clusters of bright yellow spring flowers and small red sour fruits. Native to: southern Europe. Latin name: *Cornus mas*.

corner /káwrnər/ *n* **1. MEETING OF LINES OR SURFACES** the angle formed where two or more lines or surfaces meet ○ *the four corners of a square* **2. AREA ENCLOSED BY CONVERGING LINES** the area enclosed where two lines or surfaces meet ○ *the corner of the room* **3. PROJECTING PART OF SOMETHING** a projecting angular part of something ○ *She bumped her knee on the corner of the table.* **4. PLACE WHERE TWO ROADS MEET** the place where two roads or streets meet ○ *the shop on the corner* **5. DIFFICULT SITUATION** a difficult or embarrassing position, especially one from which there is no easy way of escape ○ *got himself into a corner about his previous statements* **6. QUIET PLACE** a secluded, peaceful, or secret place ○ *Let's find a quiet corner where we can sit and talk.* **7. REMOTE PLACE** an area or place, especially one that is remote ○ *Explorers then voyaged to every corner of the world.* **8. OBJECT PUT OVER CORNER** an object made to fit over a corner of something, especially to protect it ○ *a diary with metal corners* **9.** COMM **CONTROL OF MARKET** a monopoly of a particular commodity acquired in order to control its market price **10.** SPORTS **PART OF PLAYING FIELD OR SURFACE** in various sports, part of the playing field or surface where two boundaries meet **11.** HOCKEY, FOOTBALL **KICK OR SHOT FROM CORNER** in some sports, a free kick or shot from a corner of the field given to the attacking team when a defending player plays the ball over the goal line **12.** BOXING, WRESTLING **PART OF RING** in boxing and wrestling, any of the four parts of a ring where the ropes are attached to the posts, especially the two where the competitors rest between rounds ■ *adj* **1. LOCATED ON CORNER** situated on a street corner ○ *a corner shop* **2. INTENDED FOR CORNER** intended to be put in a corner ○ *a corner cabinet* **3. SITUATED AT CORNER** at or in a corner of something ○ *sat at a corner table* ■ *v* (**-ners, -nering, -nered**) **1.** *vt* **FORCE SOMEBODY INTO DIFFICULT POSITION** to force a person or an animal into a position from which escape is difficult **2.** *vt* **PUT SOMEBODY OR SOMETHING IN CORNER** to place somebody or something in a corner **3.** *vt* **PROVIDE SOMETHING WITH CORNERS** to give corners to something **4.** *vt* COMM **ACQUIRE MONOPOLY WITHIN COMMERCIAL MARKET** to acquire a monopoly of a particular commodity and so be able to control its market price ○ *an attempt to corner the soya bean market* **5.** *vi* **TURN CORNER** to drive around a corner (*refers to vehicles or their drivers*) **6.** *vti* HOCKEY, FOOTBALL **TAKE CORNER** in some sports, to take a free kick or hit from a corner of the field on the opponents' goal line [13C. < Anglo-Norman < Latin *cornua*, plural of *cornu* 'horn, point'] ◇ **cut corners** to do something in a quicker, cheaper, or less careful way than is desirable or wise ◇ **turn the corner** to get past the worst part of a difficult or dangerous situation

Corner *n Aus* the part of Australia where the borders of Queensland, New South Wales, and South Australia meet

cornerback /káwrnər bak/ *n* in American football, either of two defensive halfbacks placed behind the linebackers and near the sidelines

Corner Country *n* same as **Corner**

cornered /káwrnərd/ *adj* **1. IN DIFFICULT POSITION** in a difficult or embarrassing position, especially when there is no easy way of escape **2. WITH CORNERS** with a particular number or type of corners (*usually used in combination*) **3. WITH NUMBER OF CONTENDERS** with a particular number of contenders ○ *a three-cornered struggle for the championship*

corner kick *n* in football, a free kick from a corner of the field given to the attacking team when a defending player plays the ball over the goal line

cornerman /-man/ (*plural* **-men** /-men/) *n US* an adviser, especially to a political candidate (*slang*)

corner shop *n* a small shop, especially one at the corner of two streets, where a limited range of groceries and general goods is sold

cornerstone /káwrnər stōn/ *n* **1. VITAL PERSON OR THING** somebody or something fundamentally important **2. STONE AT CORNER OF TWO WALLS** a stone joining two walls where they meet at a corner **3. FIRST STONE OF NEW BUILDING** the first stone laid at a corner where two walls begin and form the first part of a new building

cornerwise /káwrnər wīz/, **cornerways** /-wayz/ *adv, adj* diagonal or diagonally, or with a corner at the front

cornet /káwrnit/ *n* **1. MUSIC BRASS INSTRUMENT LIKE TRUMPET** a three-valved brass instrument shaped like a compressed trumpet. Its tubing is more conical than a trumpet and it has a softer warmer sound. **2. MUSIC** same as **cornetist 3. CONICAL WAFER FOR ICE CREAM** a wafer shaped into a cone for holding ice cream, or one of these filled with ice cream **4. FOOD INDUST PAPER CONE FOR HOLDING SWEETS** a piece of paper folded into a cone shape and used to hold small edible things, especially sweets **5. MIL OBSOLETE CAVALRY RANK** formerly, a commissioned officer in a cavalry regiment of the lowest rank **6. CLOTHING WOMAN'S HEADDRESS** a headdress of starched cloth worn by women in the 12th to 15th centuries **7. CLOTHING NUN'S HEADDRESS** a large white headdress worn by some Christian nuns in the 12th and 13th centuries **8. S Africa ARMY** same as **field cornet** [14C. < French, 'small horn' < *corne* 'horn' < Latin *cornu*]

cornetfish /káwrnit fish/ (*plural same* or **-fishes**) *n* a sea fish that has a long tubular snout ending in a small mouth and a forked tail with a long trailing extension from its centre. Native to: tropical or subtropical waters. Family: Fistulariidae.

cornetist /kawr néttist/, **cornettist** *n* somebody who plays a cornet

cornett /kawr nétt/ *n* a Renaissance and baroque wooden horn with six keys and a cup mouthpiece [Late 19C. Variant of CORNET]

cornettist *n* MUSIC another spelling of **cornetist**

corn exchange *n* a market where corn was bought or sold, or the building where such transactions took place

corn-fed *adj* fed or fattened on cereal grains

cornfield /káwrn feeld/ *n* a field in which cereal crops such as wheat, barley, or oats are growing

cornflakes /káwrn flayks/ *npl* a breakfast cereal consisting of small pieces of toasted maize, usually eaten with cold milk

cornflour /káwrn flow ər/ *n* FOOD fine-grained starchy flour made from maize. Use: especially, thickener in sauces and soups. N Am term **cornstarch**

cornflower /káwrn flow ər/ *n* an annual plant, formerly common as a blue-flowered weed in cultivated fields. Flowers: blue, pink, white, or purple when cultivated. Native to: Europe, Asia, naturalized in North America. Latin name: *Centaurea cyanus*.

cornflower blue *n* a deep brilliant purplish-blue colour —**cornflower-blue** *adj*

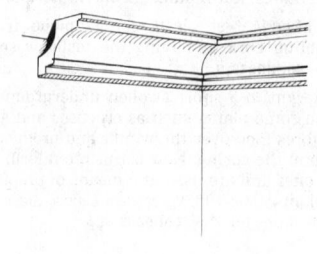

cornice

cornice /káwrniss/ *n* **1. PROJECTING MOULDING ALONG WALL** a projecting horizontal moulding along the top of a wall or building **2. DECORATIVE PLASTER MOULDING** a decorative plaster moulding around a room where the walls and ceiling meet **3. ARCHIT PART OF CLASSICAL BUILDING** the top projecting section of the part of a classical building that is supported by the columns (**entablature**) **4.** CLIMBING **OVERHANG OF SNOW** an overhanging mass of snow or ice formed by wind action ■ *vt* (**-nices, -nicing, -niced**) ARCHIT **PUT CORNICE ON WALL** to decorate or finish a wall or building with a cornice [Mid-16C. Via obsolete French < Italian]

corniche /kawr nèesh/ *n* a coast road, especially one cut into a cliff [Mid-19C. < French, modern form of *cornice* (see CORNICE)]

cornification /káwrnifi káysh'n/ *n* the conversion of skin cells into keratin or other horny material such as nails or scales [Mid-19C. < Latin *cornu* 'horn']

Cornish /káwrnish/ *adj* OF CORNWALL relating to Cornwall or its extinct Celtic language ■ *npl* PEOPLE OF CORNWALL the people of Cornwall ■ *n* EXTINCT CELTIC LANGUAGE an extinct Celtic language spoken in Cornwall until the late 18th century. Breton is the living language most closely related to Cornish.

LANGUAGE HERITAGE See *Celtic*.

Cornishman /káwrnishmən/ (*plural* **-men** /-mən/) *n* a man who comes from Cornwall

Cornish pasty *n* a baked food made of a circle of pastry filled with beef and vegetables, with the pastry edges pinched together over the filling, eaten as a savoury snack or light meal

Cornishwoman /káwrnish wŏŏmən/ (*plural* **-women** /-wimin/) *n* a woman who comes from Cornwall

Corn Laws *npl* a group of laws introduced in Great Britain in 1804 and repealed in 1846 that were designed to restrict the importation of foreign corn by imposing duty on it. This caused bread prices to rise and led to riots.

corn lily *n* a plant of the iris family. Flowers: various colours, resembling lilies, on tall, wiry stems. Native to: southern Africa. Genus: *Ixia*.

corn marigold *n* an annual plant that was formerly a common weed in cultivated fields. Flowers: resembling yellow daisies. Latin name: *Chrysanthemum segetum*. [Because it grows in cornfields]

cornmeal /káwrn meel/ *n* flour made from maize

corn oil *n* oil extracted from maize. Use: cooking, margarine, salad oil, soaps.

corn on the cob *n* an ear of maize that is cooked and served whole

cornpone *n* Southern US fried or baked bread made with maize meal ■ *adj* N Am relating to country life and people in being simple, unpretentious, and homely (*informal*)

cornrow /káwrn rō/ *n* a narrow parallel plait of hair in a set of plaits covering the head and made close against the scalp ■ *vt* (**-rows, -rowing, -rowed**) to style hair in cornrows [Late 20C. Because the braids resemble kernels of maize]

corn salad *n* N Am same as **lamb's lettuce**

corn snow *n* N Am fallen snow that has a grainy surface because it has thawed and refrozen

cornstarch /káwrn staarch/ *n* N Am same as **cornflour**

corn syrup *n* N Am syrup made from cornflour. Use: sweetener in many foods.

cornu /káwrnyoo/ (*plural* **-nua** /-nyŏŏ ə/) *n* a part that resembles a horn or has a horn-shaped pattern [Late 17C. < Latin, 'horn'] —**cornual** *adj*

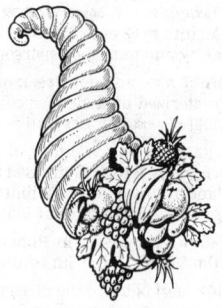

cornucopia

cornucopia /káwrnyŏŏ kṓpi ə/ *n* **1. ABUNDANCE** a great abundance of something **2. ARTS GOAT'S HORN OVERFLOWING WITH PRODUCE** a painting or other representation of a goat's horn overflowing with fruits, flowers, and vegetables, used to symbolize plenty or prosperity **3. HORN-SHAPED CONTAINER** an ornament or container shaped like a goat's horn **4.** MYTHOL **HORN OF GOAT THAT SUCKLED ZEUS** in Greek mythology, the horn of the goat that suckled Zeus [Early 16C. Via late Latin < Latin *cornu copiae* 'horn of plenty'] —**cornucopian** *adj*

cornute /kawr nyoot/, **cornuted** /-nyṓotid/ *adj* relating to a horn or horns [Early 17C. < Latin *cornutus* 'horned' < *cornu* 'horn']

Cornwall /káwrnwəl, -wawl/ county in the extreme southwest of England, bordered on three sides by the sea. Population: 499,114 (2001). Area: 3,515 sq. km/1,357 sq. mi.

corn whisky *n* whisky distilled from mash made mostly of maize

corny /káwrni/ (**-ier, -iest**) *adj* unsophisticated and trite ○ *a corny love scene* [Late 16C. < CORN¹] —**cornily** *adv* —**corniness** *n*

corolla /kə rṓllə/ *n* the petals of a flower collectively, forming a ring around the reproductive organs and surrounded by an outer ring of sepals [Mid-18C. < Latin, 'garland', literally 'little crown' < *corona* 'crown']

corollary /kə rṓlləri/ *n* (*plural* **-ies**) **1. NATURAL CONSEQUENCE** something that is a natural consequence of or accompaniment to something else **2. LOGIC STATEMENT EASILY PROVED FROM ANOTHER** a proposition that follows, with little or no further reasoning, from the proof of another **3.** LOGIC **OBVIOUS DEDUCTION** something that is very obviously or easily deduced from something already proven **4. SOMETHING ADDED** something added to something else, e.g. something appended to a document ■ *adj* FOLLOWING following as a consequence or result [14C. < Latin *corollarium* 'money paid for a garland' < *corolla* (see COROLLA)]

coromandel /kórrə mánd'l/ *n* INDUST same as **calamander** [Mid-19C. After the COROMANDEL COAST]

Coromandel Coast /kór ə mánd'l-/ southern part of the eastern Indian coastline in the states of Tamil Nadu and Andhra Pradesh, on the Bay of Bengal

Coromandel Peninsula peninsula on the northeastern coast of the North Island, New Zealand. Rugged and heavily forested, it is 112 km/70 mi. long and, on average, 32 km/20 mi. wide.

corona /kə rṓnə/ (*plural* **-nas** or **-nae** /-nee/) *n* **1. ASTRON RING OF LIGHT AROUND MOON** a ring of light visible around a luminous body, especially the Moon, typically as a result of optical effects caused by thin cloud, water droplets, or ice in the Earth's atmosphere **2. ASTRON PART OF SUN'S ATMOSPHERE** the outermost part of the Sun's atmosphere **3. BOT LIP OF FLOWER TRUMPET** the prominent, sometimes frilly lip of the petal tube or trumpet corolla of some flowers such as daffodils and narcissi **4. ANAT TOP OF BODY PART** the top of a part of the body, e.g. the crown of the head or a tooth **5.** PHYS same as **corona discharge 6.** ARCHIT **PART OF CORNICE** the flat vertical surface of a cornice just above the bottom surface (**soffit**) **7. LONG CIGAR** a long cigar with a blunt rounded mouth end **8. CIRCULAR CHANDELIER** a circular hanging chandelier, especially in a church [Mid-16C. < Latin, 'crown'] —**coronal** /kórrən'l/ *adj*

Corona Australis /-o stráyliss/ *n* a constellation of the southern hemisphere. See illustration at **constellation**

Corona Borealis /-báwri áyliss/ *n* a constellation of the northern hemisphere. See illustration at **constellation**

coronach /kórrənəkh/ *n Ireland, Scotland* a dirge or funeral lament sung or played on bagpipes [Early 16C. < Gaelic *corranach*, literally 'outcry together' < *rànach* 'outcry']

corona discharge *n* a luminous discharge from the surface of an object that is highly charged electrically, caused by ionization of the surrounding gas

Coronado /kórrō naádō/, **Francisco Vásquez de** (1510–54) Spanish explorer. He led the first European expeditions to what is now the southwestern United States.

coronagraph /kə rŏnnə graaf, -graf/, **coronograph** *n* a telescope that masks the bright disc of the Sun so that the Sun's corona can be studied

coronal suture *n* a junction extending side-to-side across the crown of the skull between the two parietal bones and the frontal bone

coronary /kórrənəri/ *n* (*plural* **-ies**) MED **1.** same as **coronary thrombosis 2.** same as **heart attack** (sense 1) (*informal*) ■ *adj* **1.** describes the arteries that supply blood to the muscle tissue of the heart, or the veins that take blood away from it **2.** relating to disease of the coronary arteries and veins, and conditions associated with it ○ *coronary care* [Early 17C. < Latin *coronarius* 'crown shaped' < *corona* 'crown']

coronary artery *n* an artery supplying blood to the muscles of the heart, either of a pair arising from the aorta. The left artery divides into two almost immediately, giving rise to the common assumption that there are three coronary arteries.

coronary bypass *n* an operation in which a new blood vessel is grafted onto the heart to replace a blocked coronary artery

coronary thrombosis *n* the blocking of a coronary artery by a blood clot, which obstructs the blood supply to the heart muscle, resulting in death of the muscle and, often, a heart attack

coronary vein *n* a vein of the group that drains blood from the muscles of the heart

coronation /kórrə náysh'n/ *n* the ceremony or act of crowning a monarch [14C. Via French < medieval Latin *coronation-* < Latin *corona* 'crown']

coronavirus /kə rŏnə vīrəss/ *n* a single-stranded RNA virus that causes major illnesses in animals and humans and is a cause of the common cold. Family: Coronaviridae.

coroner /kórrənər/ *n* a public official responsible for investigating deaths that appear not to have natural causes [13C. < Anglo-Norman *coruner* 'officer of the crown' < *corune* (see CROWN)] —**coronership** *n*

coronet /kórrənit/ *n* **1.** SMALL CROWN a small crown, especially one worn by a prince or a peer rather than a reigning monarch **2.** WOMAN'S HEAD DECORATION a circular ornamental band worn by women on the head **3.** VET TOP OF HORSE'S HOOF the upper part of a horse's hoof, where the horn of the hoof meets the skin of the pastern **4.** ZOOL BASE OF DEER'S ANTLER the rosette of bone at the base of a deer's antler [14C. < French, 'little crown' < *corone* (see CROWN)]

coronograph *n* ASTRON same as **coronagraph**

Corot /kórrō/, **Jean-Baptiste Camille** (1796–1875) French landscape and portrait painter. His freely handled landscapes influenced the Barbizon School and impressionism. Postimpressionists admired the tonal contrasts of his earlier, classical work.

corotate /kṓ rō táyt/ (**-tates, -tating, -tated**) *vi* to turn in conjunction with another turning object —**corotation** /kṓ rō táysh'n/ *n* —**corotational** *adj*

corp. *abbr* BUSINESS corporation

Corp. *abbr* MIL corporal²

~~**corperation**~~ incorrect spelling of **corporation**

corpora plural of **corpus**

corporal¹ /káwrpərəl/ *adj* relating to or affecting the body [14C. Via French < Latin *corporalis* < *corpus* 'body'] —**corporally** *adv*

USAGE corporal or **corporeal**? ***Corporal*** means 'relating to the body' and is mainly used in *corporal punishment*, in reference to the inflicting of physical hurt. ***Corporeal*** means 'material or physical rather than spiritual': *The gods of antiquity were not just spirits but were believed to enjoy a corporeal existence.*

corporal² /káwrpərəl/ *n* **1.** a noncommissioned officer in various armed forces, of a rank immediately below sergeant, or, in Canada, a master corporal **2.** an officer in the Royal Navy, immediately junior to the master-at-arms [Mid-16C. Via French < Italian *caporale* 'of the head' < *capo* (see CAPO ²)]

corporal³ /káwrpərəl/, **corporale** /káwrpə rávli/ *n* a white, usually linen, cloth on which the consecrated bread and wine are placed in the Christian sacrament of Communion [14C. Directly or via French < medieval Latin *(pallium) corporale* '(cloth) for the body']

corporality /káwrpə rálləti/ *n* the state of being in physical or bodily form rather than spiritual form

Corporal of Horse *n* a noncommissioned officer in the Household Cavalry of a rank above sergeant

corporal punishment *n* the striking of a somebody's body as punishment

corporate /káwrpərət/ *adj* **1.** INVOLVING CORPORATION relating or belonging to a corporation **2.** OF CORPORATION'S EMPLOYEES designed for, suitable for, or associated with people who work for large corporations ○ *corporate fashions* **3.** INCORPORATED legally united to form a body that can act as a unit **4.** OF GROUP AS WHOLE relating to or involving a group as a whole (*formal*) ■ *n* BUSINESS same as **corporation** (sense 1) (*informal*) [16C. < Latin *corporatus*, past participle of *corporare* 'form a body' < *corpus* 'body'] —**corporately** *adv*

corporate bond *n* a bond issued by a company rather than by a national or local government

corporate hospitality *n* free entertainment offered by a company to customers or trading partners, e.g. at major sporting events, as a way of winning their favour

corporate killing *n* a proposed criminal offence under which companies and similar organizations, and their directors, would be held responsible for the deaths of employees, clients, or passengers occurring as a result of the company's negligence

corporate raider *n* a company or person who attempts to take control of a business by acquiring a substantial number of its shares or by manipulating proxies

corporate social responsibility *n* the belief that a company should take into account the social, ethical, and environmental effects of its activities on its staff and the community around it

corporate tax *n ANZ, N Am* FIN same as **corporation tax**

corporation /káwrpə ráysh'n/ *n* **1.** GROUP REGARDED AS INDIVIDUAL BY LAW a company recognized by law as a single body with its own powers and liabilities, separate from those of the individual members. Corporations perform many of the functions of private business, governments, educational bodies, and the professions. **2.** LOCAL GOVERNING AUTHORITY the governing authority of a municipality such as a city or town ○ *working for the corporation* ○ *corporation transport* **3.** GROUP ACTING AS SINGLE ENTITY a group of people acting as a single entity **4.** STOMACH a paunch, especially a large one (*dated informal humorous*) [15C. < late Latin *corporation-* < Latin *corporatus* (see CORPORATE)]

corporation tax *n UK* a tax on the profits of a company. ANZ, N Am term **corporate tax**

corporatism /káwrpərətizəm/ *n* a system of running a state using the power of organizations such as businesses and trade unions that act, or claim to act, for large numbers of people —**corporatist** *adj, n*

corporeal /kawr páwri əl/ *adj* **1.** relating to or involving the physical body rather than the mind or spirit **2.** material or physical rather than spiritual [Early 17C. < late Latin *corporealis* < Latin *corpus* 'body'] —**corporeality** /kawr páwri álləti/ *n* —**corporeally** *adv*

USAGE See ***corporal¹***.

corporeity /káwrpə reé əti/ *n* the condition of existing as something material or physical [Early 17C. < French *corporéité* < Latin *corpus* 'body']

corps /kawr/ (*plural* **corps** /kawrz/) *n* **1.** MIL SPECIALIZED MILITARY FORCE a military force that carries out specialized duties **2.** MIL TACTICAL UNIT a tactical military unit that is made up of two or more divisions with additional supporting services **3.** GROUP OF ASSOCIATED PEOPLE a group of people who work together or are associated ○ *the press corps* [Late 16C. Via French < Latin *corpus* 'body']

corps de ballet /káwr də bállay/ (*plural* **corps de ballet** /*pronunc. same*/) *n* the dancers of a ballet company who perform as a group rather than individually [< French, 'dance company']

corps diplomatique /káwr dipplō ma teék/ (*plural* **corps diplomatiques** /káwr dípplō ma teék/) *n* INTERNAT REL same as **diplomatic corps** [< French]

corpse /kawrps/ *n* a dead body, especially of a human being ■ *vti* (**corpses, corpsing, corpsed**) to become unable to speak lines because of involuntary laughing, or make an actor on stage unable to speak his or her lines because of involuntary laughing (*slang*) [14C. Directly or via French < Latin *corpus* 'body']

corpsman /káwrmən/ (*plural* **-men** /-mən/) *n* in the US armed forces, an enlisted person with training in giving first aid and basic medical treatment

corpulent /káwrpyoōlənt/ *adj* somewhat overweight [15C. < Latin *corpulentus* < *corpus* 'body'] —**corpulence** *n* —**corpulently** *adv*

cor pulmonale /káwr pulmə naáli/ *n* enlargement and failure of the right ventricle of the heart, caused by disease of the lungs or pulmonary blood vessels [< modern Latin, 'pulmonary heart']

corpus /káwrpəss/ (*plural* **-pora** /-pərə/) *n* **1.** BODY OF WRITINGS a body of writings by a particular person, on a particular subject, or of a particular type ○ *one of the most popular works in the Shakespearean corpus* **2.** MAIN PART the main part of something **3.** ANAT PART OF ORGAN the main portion of something such as an organ or other body part, or a mass of tissue with a distinct function ○ *the corpus of the uterus* **4.** FIN CAPITAL the capital or principal of a sum of money **5.** LING COLLECTION OF LANGUAGE EXAMPLES a large collection of written, and sometimes spoken, examples of the usage of a language, employed in linguistic analysis [Early 18C. < Latin, 'body']

corpus albicans /-ál bikanz/ (*plural* **corpora albicantia** /-albi kánti ə/) *n* an area of white scar tissue formed in an ovary by the decay of the corpus luteum when implantation of a fertilized egg fails to occur [< modern Latin, 'whitening body']

corpus callosum /káwrpəss kə lóssəm/ (*plural* **corpora callosa** /káwrpərə kə lóssə/) *n* the thick band of nerve fibres that connects the two hemispheres of the brain in higher mammals and allows the hemispheres to communicate [< modern Latin, 'callous body']

Corpus Christi¹ /káwrpəss krísti/ *n* a mainly Roman Catholic festival honouring the institution of Communion. Date: Thursday after Trinity Sunday. [< medieval Latin, 'body of Christ']

Corpus Christi² /káwrpəss krísti/ city and port in southeastern Texas, on the southern shore of Corpus Christi Bay. Population: 278,520 (2002 estimate).

corpuscle /káwr puss'l/ *n* **1.** UNATTACHED CELL a small independent body, especially a cell in blood or lymph **2.** PARTICLE a discrete particle, especially a photon **3.** SMALL PARTICLE a very small particle of anything [Mid-17C. < Latin *corpusculum* 'small body' < *corpus* 'body'] —**corpuscular** /kawr púskyoōlər/ *adj*

corpuscular theory *n* the theory that light consists of a stream of particles. It was originally introduced by Isaac Newton, and has applications in quantum physics. The theory cannot be used to explain all the properties of light.

corpus delicti /káwrpəss di lík tī/ *n* the body of facts that show that a crime has been committed, including physical evidence such as a corpse [< modern Latin, 'body of the crime']

corpus luteum /káwrpəss loóti əm/ (*plural* **corpora lutea** /káwrpərə loóti ə/) *n* a yellow mass of tissue that forms in a part of the ovary (**Graafian follicle**) after ovulation in mammals and secretes the hormone progesterone. If no pregnancy is established, the corpus luteum degenerates, but it continues to secrete the hormone if pregnancy occurs. [< modern Latin, 'yellow body']

corpus striatum /káwrpəss strī áytəm/ (*plural* **corpora striata** /káwrpərə strī áytə/) *n* a mass of striped grey and white nervous tissue, in each hemisphere of the brain [< modern Latin, 'striated body']

corr. *abbr* **1.** correct **2.** corrected **3.** correction **4.** COMMUNICATION correspondence **5.** MEDIA correspondent

corral /kə ráal/ *N Am n* **1.** AGRIC **PLACE FOR LIVESTOCK** a fenced area in which livestock or horses are kept **2.** HIST **CIRCLE OF WAGONS** a temporary defensive enclosure formed by wagons arranged in a circle, formerly used by people travelling through North America ■ *vt* (**-rals, -ralling, -ralled**) **1.** AGRIC **PUT ANIMALS IN CORRAL** to gather animals together and drive them into a corral **2.** HIST **PUT WAGONS IN CIRCLE** to form wagons into a temporary defensive circle **3. ACQUIRE THINGS** to gather together and take control of people or things (*informal*) ○ *hopes to corral sufficient funding for the project* [Late 16C. < Spanish]

corrasion /kə ráyzh'n/ *n* the mechanical erosion of a surface by fragments of rock carried by water, wind, or ice [Late 19C. < Latin *corras-*, past participle of *corradere* 'scrape together' < *radere* 'to scrape'] —**corrasive** /kə ráyssiv/ *adj*

correct /kə rékt/ *vt* (**-rects, -recting, -rected**) **1. REMOVE ERRORS FROM SOMETHING** to take the errors out of something **2. INDICATE ERRORS IN SOMETHING** to point out or mark the errors in something **3. RECTIFY IMPERFECTION** to rectify an imperfection in something, or counteract something wrong or undesirable ○ *wears glasses to correct his astigmatism* **4. MODIFY SOMETHING** to modify something such as behaviour in order to make it acceptable or bring it up to a standard **5. PUNISH SOMEBODY TO GAIN IMPROVEMENT** to punish or scold somebody, especially a child, to bring about improvement or reform (*dated*) ■ *adj* **1. ACCURATE** accurate or without errors ○ *the correct time* **2. ACCEPTABLE** acceptable, or meeting a required standard ○ *correct dress* [14C. < Latin *correct-*, past participle of *corrigere* 'rule completely' < *regere* 'to rule'] —**correctable** *adj* —**correctly** *adv* —**correctness** *n* —**corrector** *n*

correction /kə réksh'n/ *n* **1. ALTERATION THAT CORRECTS SOMETHING** an alteration that removes an error **2. WRITTEN COMMENT ON ERROR** something written beside an error in a text to point out what should be there instead **3. REMOVAL OF ERRORS** the removal of errors from something, or the indication of errors in something **4. MODIFICATION TO CALCULATION** an adjustment made to a calculation or measurement to compensate for an observed deviation from ideal conditions **5. PUNISHMENT TO REFORM SOMEBODY** punishment, especially when meant to improve or reform the person punished (*dated*) —**correctional** *adj*

correctional facility *n N Am* a prison or other institution where criminals are confined

correction fluid *n* an opaque liquid used to paint over a written or printed error and provide a surface for adding a correction

corrections officer *n N Am* somebody employed in a prison to guard and supervise the inmates

correctitude /kə rékti tyood/ *n* the fact of being correct, especially in behaviour and manners [Late 19C. Blend of CORRECT + RECTITUDE]

corrective /kə réktiv/ *adj* acting or intended to correct something ○ *corrective action* ■ *n* something that corrects or is meant to correct something —**correctively** *adv*

corrective shoe *n N Am* same as **surgical boot**

Correggio /ko réjji ō/ (1489–1534) Italian painter. His work is characterized by sensuous nude figures, skilful use of light and shadow, and luminous colours. Born **Antonio Allegri**

Corregidor /kə réggi dawr/ island at the entrance to Manila Bay in the Philippines. During World War II, it was the scene of intense fighting by US and Filipino forces against Japanese troops until its capture by the Japanese in May 1942. It was recaptured by US forces in 1945. Area: 5 sq. km/2 sq. mi.

correlate /kórrə layt/ *v* (**-lates, -lating, -lated**) **1.** *vti* **HAVE OR SHOW MUTUAL RELATIONSHIP** to have a mutual or complementary relationship, or show that two or more things such as a cause and an effect have a mutual or complementary relationship ○ *How do these results correlate with your findings?* **2.** *vt* **GATHER AND COMPARE THINGS** to gather together and compare related things such as results or reports ○ *Her job is to correlate the statistics from a range of sources and prepare a report.* ■ *adj* **HAVING SHARED PROPERTIES** having mutual or complementary properties ■ *n* **1. COMPLEMENTARY THING** something that shares mutual or complementary properties with something else **2.** STATS **VARIABLE RELATED TO ANOTHER VARIABLE** either of two variables that are related with the result that a variation in one is accompanied by a linear variation of the other [Mid-18C. Back-formation < CORRELATION] —**correlatable** *adj* —**correlator** *n*

correlation /kórrə láysh'n/ *n* **1. MUTUAL OR COMPLEMENTARY RELATIONSHIP** a relationship in which two or more things are mutual or complementary, or one thing is caused by another ○ *the close correlation between the two factors* **2. ACT OF CORRELATING** the act of correlating, or the condition of being correlated **3.** STATS **RELATEDNESS OF VARIABLES** the degree to which two or more variables are related and change together [Mid-16C. < medieval Latin *correlation-* 'mutual relationship' < Latin *relation-* (see RELATION)] —**correlational** *adj*

correlation coefficient *n* a number or function indicating the degree of correlation between two variables. It ranges between 1 for high positive correlation to –1 for high negative correlation, with 0 indicating a purely random relationship.

correlative /kə réllətiv/ *adj* **1. BEING CORRELATES** in a mutual or complementary relationship **2.** GRAM **TOGETHER BUT NOT ADJACENT** functioning together but not usually adjacent, as the conjunctions 'either' and 'or' ■ *n* **1.** same as **correlate** *n* (sense 1) **2.** GRAM **CORRELATIVE WORD** a word, especially a conjunction, that functions with another but is not usually adjacent to it —**correlatively** *adv* —**correlativeness** *n* —**correlativity** /kə réllə tívvəti/ *n*

correspond /kórri spónd/ (**-sponds, -sponding, -sponded**) *vi* **1. CONFORM OR BE CONSISTENT** to conform, be consistent, or be in agreement with something else **2. BE SIMILAR** to be similar or equivalent **3. WRITE TO ONE ANOTHER** to communicate with somebody by exchanging written messages [Early 16C. Via French < medieval Latin *correspondere* 'respond to each other' < Latin *respondere* (see RESPOND)]

correspondence /kórri spóndənss/ *n* **1. WRITTEN COMMUNICATION** communication by means of exchanged written messages such as letters or e-mail **2. WRITTEN MESSAGES** written messages, especially letters **3. CONFORMITY** conformity, consistency, or agreement between two or more things **4. SIMILARITY** similarity or equivalence between two or more things

correspondence column *n* a part of a newspaper or magazine where letters from readers are printed

correspondence course *n* an educational course in which the teaching organization sends lessons and tests to students by post or e-mail and students return completed work in the same way

correspondence school *n* an educational organization that teaches through correspondence courses

correspondent /kórri spóndənt/ *n* **1. SOMEBODY COMMUNICATING IN WRITING** somebody who communicates in writing, e.g. by letter or e-mail ○ *Most of my correspondents have e-mail now.* **2. SOMEBODY PROVIDING SPECIAL REPORTS** somebody employed by a news organization, especially a newspaper or broadcasting company, to provide reports from a particular place or on a particular subject ○ *our Paris correspondent* **3.** BUSINESS **SOMEBODY DEALING WITH DISTANT BUSINESS** a person or company that regularly does business with another, especially one that is distant **4. SOMETHING THAT CORRESPONDS** something that conforms or agrees with, or is similar to, something else (*formal*) ■ *adj* same as **corresponding** (sense 2)

corresponding /kórri spónding/ *adj* **1. CONSISTENT** consistent, conforming, or in agreement with something else ○ *Line up the prongs on one half with the corresponding sockets on the other.* **2. ANALOGOUS** similar or equivalent to something else in one or more important respects ○ *the corresponding word in her own language* **3. WORKING FROM DISTANCE** interacting or contributing from a distance, e.g. by post ○ *a corresponding member based in China* **4. DEALING WITH CORRESPONDENCE** handling or assigned to handle correspondence

corresponding angles *npl* the angles formed on the same side of two lines and a third line (**transversal**) that intersects them, each of the four angles at each intersection corresponding to the four angles at the other

correspondingly /kórri spóndingli/ *adv* in a way that is consistent, equivalent, or similar ○ *A large company has correspondingly large problems.*

corrida /ko réedə/ *n* a programme of bullfights [Late 19C. < Spanish, 'running' (of bulls) < Latin *currere* 'to run']

corridor /kórri dawr/ *n* **1. PASSAGE INSIDE BUILDING** a passage between parts of a building, often with a series of rooms opening onto it **2.** RAIL, NAUT **PASSAGEWAY IN RAILWAY CARRIAGE** a passageway in a railway carriage giving access to compartments **3.** INTERNAT REL **STRIP OF LAND** a narrow strip of land belonging to one country and projecting through another, e.g. to give a landlocked country access to a port **4.** AVIAT **REGION OF AIRSPACE FOR AIR TRAFFIC** a region of airspace designated for use by air traffic **5.** AEROSP **SPACECRAFT FLIGHT PATH** a predetermined flight path that a spacecraft follows upon re-entry into the Earth's atmosphere [Late 16C. Via French < Italian *corridore* < Latin *currere* 'to run']

corrie /kórri/ *n* GEOG same as **cirque** [Mid-16C. Via Scottish Gaelic *coire* 'a hollow' < Old Irish, 'cauldron']

Corriedale /kórri dayl/ (*plural* **-dales** or *same*) *n* a sheep belonging to a breed without horns developed in New Zealand. Kept for: wool, meat. [Early 20C. After an estate in New Zealand]

corrigenda /kórri jén də/ *n* PUBL same as **errata** (*see* **erratum**) (*takes a singular or plural verb*) ■ plural of **corrigendum**

corrigendum /kórri jéndəm/ (*plural* **-da** /-də/) *n* an error to be corrected [Early 19C. < Latin, 'thing to be corrected']

corroborate /kə róbbə rayt/ (**-rates, -rating, -rated**) *vt* to give or represent evidence of the truth of something ○ *The photographs corroborate the verbal account.* [Mid-16C. < Latin *corroborat-*, past participle of *corroborare* 'strengthen together' < *roborare* 'strengthen'] —**corroboration** /kə róbbə ráysh'n/ *n* —**corroborative** /-rətiv/ *adj* —**corroboratively** *adv* —**corroborator** *n* —**corroboratory** /kə róbbə ráytəri/ *adj*

USAGE See ***collaborate***.

corroboree /kə róbbəri/ *n Aus* **1.** a gathering of an Aboriginal people **2.** a noisy gathering of people, especially a party (*informal*) [Late 18C. < Dharuk *garaabara*]

corrode /kə rṓd/ (**-rodes, -roding, -roded**) *v* **1.** *vti* to destroy something progressively by chemical action, or be destroyed in this way **2.** *vt* to undermine or destroy something gradually ○ *The constant criticism has corroded the candidate's public image.* [14C. < Latin *corrodere* 'gnaw away' < *rodere* 'gnaw'] —**corrodant** *n* —**corroder** *n* —**corrodibility** /kə rōdə bílləti/ *n* —**corrodible** *adj*

~~**correlary**~~ incorrect spelling of **corollary**

corrosion /kə rṓzh'n/ *n* **1.** CHEM **DESTRUCTION BY CHEMICAL ACTION** a process by which something, especially a metal, is destroyed progressively by chemical action, as iron is when it rusts **2. CORRODED MATERIAL** material produced by corrosion, e.g. rust **3. GRADUAL DESTRUCTION** the gradual destruction or undermining of something ○ *a steady corrosion of the public trust* **4. RESULT OF CORROSION** the condition produced by corrosion [14C. < late Latin *corrosion-* < Latin *corros-*, past participle of *corrodere* (see CORRODE)] —**corrosible** /kə rṓssəb'l/ *adj*

corrosive /kə rṓssiv/ *adj* **1.** CHEM **CHEMICALLY DESTRUCTIVE** able to destroy something progressively by chemical action **2. GRADUALLY DESTRUCTIVE** destroying or undermining something gradually **3. VERY SARCASTIC** very strongly sarcastic or bitter ○ *a corrosive review* ■ *n* CHEM **DESTRUCTIVE SUBSTANCE** a substance that is able to destroy something progressively by chemical action, e.g. an acid [14C. Via French < medieval Latin *corrosivus* < Latin *corros-* (see CORROSION)] —**corrosively** *adv* —**corrosiveness** *n*

corrosive sublimate *n* CHEM same as **mercuric chloride**

corrugate /kórrə gayt/ *vti* (**-gates, -gating, -gated**) to fold into parallel ridges and troughs, or fold something such as a sheet of cardboard into parallel ridges and troughs ■ *adj* same as **corrugated** [Early 17C. < Latin *corrugat-*, past participle of *corrugare* 'wrinkle

completely' < *rugare* 'to wrinkle'] —**corrugation** /kórrə gáysh'n/ *n*

corrugated /kórrə gaytid/ *adj* **1.** folded into parallel ridges and troughs **2.** made from a corrugated material ○ *a shed with a corrugated roof*

corrugator /kórrə gaytər/ *n* a muscle that wrinkles the skin when it contracts

corrupt /kə rúpt/ *adj* **1.** IMMORAL OR DISHONEST immoral or dishonest, especially as shown by the exploitation of a position of power or trust for personal gain **2.** DEPRAVED extremely immoral or depraved **3.** COMPUT CONTAINING ERRORS describes computer data or software that is unusable or unreliable because of the presence of errors that have been introduced unintentionally ○ *a corrupt computer file* **4.** CONTAINING COPYING ERRORS containing undesirable changes in meaning or errors made in copying ○ *a corrupt transcription of the manuscript* **5.** CONTAMINATED contaminated or tainted by something else (*archaic*) **6.** ROTTEN putrid or decomposing (*archaic*) ■ *v* (**-rupts, -rupting, -rupted**) **1.** *vti* BECOME OR MAKE SOMEBODY DISHONEST to become dishonest, or destroy or compromise somebody's morality or honesty **2.** *vti* BECOME OR MAKE SOMEBODY DEPRAVED to become immoral or depraved, or cause somebody to become immoral or depraved **3.** *vt* COMPUT INTRODUCE ERRORS INTO COMPUTER DATA to introduce unintentional errors into computer data or software, making it unusable or unreliable **4.** *vt* SPOIL TEXT WITH COPYING ERRORS to make undesirable changes in meaning or introduce other errors into a text during copying **5.** *vt* CONTAMINATE SOMETHING to contaminate something or taint somebody (*archaic*) **6.** *vt* ROT SOMETHING to make something rot or become putrid (*archaic*) [14C. < Latin *corruptus*, past participle of *corrumpere* 'break completely' < *rumpere* 'to break'] —**corrupter** *n* —**corruptible** *adj* —**corruptly** *adv* —**corruptness** *n*

corruption /kə rúpsh'n/ *n* **1.** DISHONESTY FOR PERSONAL GAIN dishonest exploitation of power for personal gain **2.** DEPRAVITY extreme immorality or depravity **3.** UNDESIRABLE CHANGE an undesirable change in meaning or another error introduced into a text during copying **4.** CORRUPTING OF SOMETHING the corrupting of something or somebody, or the state of being corrupt **5.** LING ALTERED WORD OR PHRASE a word or phrase that has been altered from its original form **6.** ROTTING rotting or putrefaction, or the state of being rotten or putrid (*archaic*) [14C. Via French < Latin *corruption-* < *corruptus* (see CORRUPT)]

corruptive /kə rúptiv/ *adj* having a bad effect on somebody's character or behaviour —**corruptively** *adv*

corsage /kawr saázh, káwrss aazh/ *n* **1.** a small bouquet worn on the bodice of a dress or the lapel of a jacket **2.** the bodice of a dress (*archaic*) [Early 19C. < French < Old French *cors* 'body']

corsair /káwrss air, kawr sáir/ *n* **1.** NAUT, HIST PIRATE a pirate, especially one based on the North African coast between the 16th and 19th centuries **2.** HIST PRIVATE SHIP COMMISSIONED BY GOVERNMENT a privately owned ship commissioned by a government to attack foreign ships, especially one based on the coast of North Africa **3.** HIST OWNER OF PRIVATEER the owner of a ship commissioned by a government to attack ships of other countries [Mid-16C. Via French < medieval Latin *cursarius* < Latin *cursus* 'hostile incursion' < past participle of *currere* 'to run']

corselet /káwrsslət, -lit/ *n* **1.** *also* **corselette** /káwrssə lét/ a garment combining a corset and a bra **2.** *also* **corslet** armour covering the upper body [15C. < French < Old French *cors* 'body']

corset /káwrssit/ *n* **1.** STIFF GARMENT a stiffened garment worn by women to shape the waist and breasts **2.** STIFF UNDERGARMENT a stiff undergarment with laces to fasten it tightly, formerly worn to shape and support the body **3.** MED INJURY SUPPORT a stiffened garment worn by men or women for back support when injured [13C. < French < Old French *cors* 'body'] —**corseted** *adj*

corsetière /káwrss eti áir/ *n* somebody who makes or fits women's corsets [Mid-19C. < French < *corset* (see CORSET)]

corsetry /káwrssitri/ *n* **1.** corsets collectively **2.** the process or business of making corsets

Corsica /káwrssikə/ mountainous island in the Mediterranean Sea, an administrative region of France. Population: 249,737 (1990). Area: 8,680 sq. km/3,350 sq. mi. —**Corsican** *adj, n*

corslet *n* ARMS another spelling of **corselet** (sense 2)

Cortázar /káwrtə zaar, kawr tá/, **Julio** (1914–84) Belgian-born Argentinian writer, known for his surrealist works, including the novel *Hopscotch* (1963)

> 'The unusual is only found in a very small percentage, except in literary creations, and that is exactly what makes literature.'
> [Julio Cortázar, *The Winners*; 1960]

cortege /kawr táyzh, -tézh/, **cortège** *n* **1.** a procession, especially a funeral procession **2.** a retinue of servants or attendants [Mid-17C. Via French < Italian *corteggio* < *corteggiare* 'attend court' < *corte* 'court' < Latin *cohort-* 'enclosed space']

Cortés, Sea of /kawr téz/ former name for **California, Gulf of**

Cortés /káwr tez/, **Hernán** (1485–1547) Spanish explorer. He conquered Mexico in 1521 for Spain, and served as its governor (1523–28).

cortex /káwr teks/ (*plural* **-tices** /-ti seez/ or **-texes**) *n* **1.** the outer layer of a solid organ or part of the body, e.g. the outer covering of the kidney or brain (**cerebral cortex**) **2.** the tissue in plant stems and roots between the outer layer (**epidermis**) and the central core (**stele**) [Mid-17C. < Latin, 'bark'] —**cortical** /káwrtik'l/ *adj*

cortic- *prefix* same as **cortico-** (*used before vowels*)

cortico- *prefix* cortex, cortical ○ *corticospinal* [< Latin *cortic-* 'bark']

corticoid /káwrti koyd/ *n* a drug that acts in a similar way to the hormone produced by the outer layer of the adrenal gland

corticospinal /káwrtikō spín'l/ *adj* relating to or connecting the outer covering of the brain (**cerebral cortex**) and the spinal cord

corticosteroid /káwrtikō stérroyd, -stéer-/ *n* **1.** an adrenal steroid hormone involved in metabolism and immune response **2.** a synthetic drug similar to a natural corticosteroid. Use: reduction of inflammation and allergic reactions, prevention of graft rejection.

corticotrophin /káwrtikō trṓfin/, **corticotropin** /-pin/ *n* BIOCHEM same as **ACTH** [Mid-20C. Contraction of *adrenocorticotrophic hormone*]

cortisol /káwrti sol, -zol/ *n* BIOCHEM same as **hydrocortisone** (sense 1) [Mid-20C. < CORTISONE]

cortisone /káwrti zōn/ *n* a steroid hormone secreted by the adrenal cortex [Mid-20C. Contraction of *corticosterone*, a type of corticosteroid]

Cortona ♦ **Pietro da Cortona**

corundum /kə rúndəm/ *n* a hard mineral form of alumina that crystallizes in a range of colours. Use: gems, abrasives. [Early 18C. < Tamil *kuruntam*]

coruscate /kórrə skayt/ (**-cates, -cating, -cated**) *vi* (*literary*) **1.** to give off flashes of bright light **2.** to show brilliance or virtuosity [Early 18C. < Latin *coruscat-*, past participle of *coruscare* 'to glitter'] —**coruscant** /kə rúskənt/ *adj*—**coruscating** *adj*—**coruscation** /kórrə skáysh'n/ *n*

corvée /káwr vay/ *n* **1.** in feudal times, a day of unpaid labour required of a serf for a manorial lord **2.** a period of labour formerly sometimes required by a state in lieu of taxes, especially in pre-Revolutionary France [14C. Via French < Latin *corrogata*, past participle of *corrogare* 'summon together' < *rogare* 'ask']

corves MIN EXTRACT plural of **corf**

corvette /kawr vét/ *n* **1.** an armed naval escort vessel, smaller than a destroyer **2.** formerly, a small wooden sailing ship with one tier of guns [Mid-17C. < French < Dutch *korf* 'small ship', literally 'basket' < Latin *corbis*]

corvid /káwrvid/ *n* a bird of the family that includes crows, jays, and magpies. Family: Corvidae. [Mid-20C. < modern Latin *Corvidae* < Latin *corvus* 'raven']

corvina /kawr véenə/ *n* a red grape variety from northeastern Italy. Use: making light red wine.

corvine /káwr vīn/ *adj* relating to crows or the crow family (*literary*) [Mid-17C. < Latin *corvinus* < *corvus* 'raven']

Corvus /káwrvəss/ *n* a small constellation of the southern hemisphere. See illustration at **constellation**

Corybant /kórri bant/ (*plural* **-bants** or **-bantes** /-bán teez/) *n* in the religion of ancient Phrygia, a priest of the goddess Cybele who performed wild ecstatic dances [15C. < Latin *Corybant-* < Greek *Korubas*] —**Corybantic** /kórri bántik/ *adj*

corymb /kórrimb, -im/ *n* a flat flower head consisting of flowers whose stalks grow from different points on the flower stem but reach approximately the same height [Early 18C. Via French < Greek *korumbos* 'summit'] —**corymbed** *adj* —**corymbose** /kórrimbōss/ *adj*—**corymbous** /kórrimbəss/ *adj*

coryphée /kórri fáy/ *n* a leading ballet dancer who usually performs with a small group of other dancers [Early 19C. Via French < Greek *koruphaios* 'chorus leader' < *koruphē* 'head']

coryza /kə rízə/ *n* **1.** MED NASAL CONGESTION severe nasal congestion **2.** MED COLD a common cold (*technical*) **3.** VET BIRD DISEASE a respiratory disease of chickens and turkeys, caused by bacteria [Early 16C. Via Latin < Greek *koruza* 'nasal mucus, catarrh'] —**coryzal** *adj*

cos[1] /koss/ (*plural* **coses** or *same*) *n* a lettuce with long crisp leaves. N Am term **romaine** [Late 17C. After COS]

cos[2] /koz/ *abbr* MATHS cosine

'cos /kəz, koz/ *conj* same as **because** (*informal*) [Early 19C. Shortening and alteration]

Cos /koss/ second largest of the Greek Dodecanese Islands, lying off the coast of Turkey in the Aegean Sea. Population: 20,350 (1981). Area: 287 sq. km/111 sq. mi. Greek name **Kos**

COS *abbr* **1.** FREIGHT cash on shipment **2.** MIL chief of staff

Cosa Nostra /kṓssə nóstrə, kṓzə-/ *n* in the United States, an organized crime organization linked with the Mafia of Sicily [Mid-20C. < Italian, 'our concern']

COSATU /kō sáttoo/, **Cosatu** *abbr* Congress of South African Trades Unions

cosec /kṓ sek/ *abbr* MATHS cosecant

cosecant /kō séekənt/ *n* for a given angle in a right-angled triangle, a trigonometric function equal to the length of the hypotenuse divided by that of the side opposite the angle

coseismal /kō sízm'l/ *n* a line on a map that connects places where the effects of an earthquake were felt at the same time

Cosenza /kō zénzə, -zéntsə/ capital of Cosenza Province, Calabria Region, southern Italy. Population: 72,998 (2001).

Cosgrave /kóz grayv/, **Liam** (*b.* 1920) Irish politician and lawyer. The son of William Thomas Cosgrave, he led the Fine Gael party from 1965 to 1977 and was prime minister of Ireland from 1973 to 1977.

Cosgrave, William Thomas (1880–1965) Irish politician. A republican, he co-founded Sinn Fein (1905), fought in the Easter Rising (1916), and became the first president of the Irish Free State (1922–32).

cosh /kosh/ *n* a blunt weapon usually made of rubber or metal ■ *vt* (**coshes, coshing, coshed**) to attack somebody using a cosh [Mid-19C. Origin ?]

COSHH regulations /kósh-/ *npl* legal requirements concerning the storage and use of hazardous chemicals in the workplace [Acronym < *control of substances hazardous to health*]

cosign /kṓ sīn, kō sín/ (**-signs, -signing, -signed**) *vt* **1.** to sign something jointly with one or more other people or representatives of other bodies **2.** to guarantee a loan, lease, or other contractual agreement undertaken by another person by signing the contract along with that person —**cosigner** *n*

cosignatory /kō sígnətəri/ (*plural* **-ries**) *n* a person, government, or organization that signs a document or treaty jointly with others

cosine /kṓ sīn/ *n* for a given angle in a right-angled triangle, a trigonometric function equal to the length of the side adjacent to the angle divided by the hypotenuse

cosmeceutical /kózmə syóotik'l/ *n* a product that falls between the categories designated as pharmaceuticals and cosmetics, especially in terms of marketing [Late 20C. Blend of COSMETIC + PHARMACEUTICAL]

cosmetic /koz méttik/ *n* **1.** BEAUTIFYING SUBSTANCE a preparation that is applied to the face or the body to make it more attractive, e.g. lipstick (*often used in the plural*) **2.** *N Am* SUPERFICIALLY ATTRACTIVE ASPECT something added or done to something else to cover

up defects ■ *adj* **1.** INTENDED TO BEAUTIFY intended to improve somebody's physical appearance ○ *cosmetic surgery* **2.** DONE ONLY FOR APPEARANCES done to make something seem better but having no real value ○ *The changes to the code of conduct were purely cosmetic, since attitudes remained fundamentally the same.* **3.** DECORATIVE designed or added for decorative purposes rather than to have any real function [Early 17C. Via French *cosmétique* < Greek *kosmētikos* 'skilled in ornamenting' < *kosmein* 'arrange' < *kosmos* 'order'] —**cosmetically** *adv*

cosmetician /kózmə tísh'n/ *n* somebody who makes or sells cosmetics, or who applies them professionally

cosmetic surgery *n* plastic surgery that is intended to improve the appearance of a part of the body, e.g. the shape of the nose or the size of the breasts

cosmetology /kózmə tólləji/ *n* the study of cosmetics, or the art or profession of using cosmetics [Mid-19C. < French *cosmétologie* < *cosmétique* (see COSMETIC)] —**cosmetologist** *n*

cosmic /kózmik/ *adj* **1.** OF WHOLE UNIVERSE relating to the whole universe **2.** ASTRON OF UNIVERSE APART FROM EARTH describes outer space or a part of the universe other than the Earth **3.** ENORMOUS very great in size or significance ■ *interj* EXPRESSING AMAZEMENT used to express amazement or wonder (*slang*) [Mid-17C. < Greek *kosmikos* < *kosmos* 'universe'] —**cosmically** *adv*

cosmic dust *n* small particles of solid matter found in outer space, often collected in clouds

cosmic radiation *n* radiation consisting of cosmic rays

cosmic ray *n* a stream of high-energy radiation that reaches Earth from outer space

cosmic string *n* an extremely long and thin astronomical object thought to be a space–time defect formed when the universe began

cosmo- *prefix* the universe, space ○ *cosmology* [< Greek *kosmos* 'universe']

cosmochemistry /kózmō kémmistri/ *n* the scientific study of the chemical composition of the universe — **cosmochemical** *adj*

cosmogony /koz móggəni/ (*plural* -**nies**) *n* **1.** the study of the origin of the universe or of a part of it **2.** a theory that seeks to explain the origin of the universe [Late 17C. < Greek *kosmogonia* 'creation of the world' < *kosmos* 'universe'] —**cosmogonic** /kózmə gónnik/ *adj* —**cosmogonical** *adj* —**cosmogonically** *adv* —**cosmogonist** *n*

cosmography /koz móggrəfi/ (*plural* -**phies**) *n* the study and description or mapping of the entire world or of the universe [14C. Via late Latin < Greek *kosmographia* < *kosmos* 'universe'] —**cosmographer** *n* —**cosmographic** /kózmə gráffik/ *adj* —**cosmographical** *adj* —**cosmographically** *adv*

cosmological argument *n* a logical argument that tries to prove the existence of God from empirical information about the universe

cosmological principle *n* the principle that the universe would look the same to observers at any point in it as it does to us

cosmology /koz mólləji/ *n* **1.** the philosophical study of the nature of the universe **2.** the scientific study of the origin and structure of the universe [Mid-17C. < modern Latin *cosmologia* < Greek *kosmos* 'universe'] —**cosmologic** /kózmə lójjik/ *adj* —**cosmological** *adj* —**cosmologically** *adv* —**cosmologist** *n*

cosmonaut /kózmə nawt/ *n* an astronaut in the space programmes of Russia and the former Soviet Union [Mid-20C. Blend of COSMOS[1] + ASTRONAUT, after Russian *kosmonavt*]

cosmopolis /koz móppəliss/ *n* a large city where people from many different countries and cultures live [Mid-19C. < Greek *kosmos* 'universe' + *polis* 'city']

cosmopolitan /kózmə póllitən/ *adj* **1.** MADE UP OF DIVERSE PEOPLES composed of or containing people from different countries and cultures **2.** SHOWING CULTURAL DIVERSITY showing the influence of many countries and cultures ○ *the city's cosmopolitan atmosphere* **3.** INTERNATIONAL IN SCOPE having worldwide relevance or scope ○ *events of national and cosmopolitan importance* **4.** UNPREJUDICED free from national prejudices **5.** KNOWLEDGEABLE AND REFINED showing a breadth of knowledge and refinement from having travelled widely ○ *his wide-ranging and cosmopolitan interests*

6. ECOL OCCURRING WORLDWIDE describes plants or animals growing or occurring in many different parts of the world ■ *n* **1.** WELL-TRAVELLED PERSON a sophisticated traveller to many different countries **2.** COCKTAIL a cocktail consisting of vodka, orange-flavoured liqueur, cranberry juice, and lime juice [Mid-17C. < COSMOPOLITE]

cosmopolite /koz móppə līt/ *n* TRAVEL same as **cosmopolitan** *n* (sense 1) [Early 17C. Via French < Greek *kosmopolitēs* 'citizen of the world' < *kosmos* 'universe' + *polis* 'city'] —**cosmopolitism** *n*

cosmos[1] /kóz moss/ *n* **1.** the universe considered as an ordered and integrated whole **2.** an ordered system or harmonious whole [13C. < Greek *kosmos* 'order, universe']

cosmos[2] /kóz moss/ (*plural* -**moses** or *same*) *n* a tall plant with flowers of various colours that resemble large daisies. Native to: tropical America. Genus: *Cosmos.* [Early 19C. Via modern Latin < Greek *kosmos* 'order, universe, ornament']

Cossack /kóss ak/ *n* **1.** a peasant of Polish or Russian descent living in southeastern Russia or in Siberia or Ukraine. Cossacks are noted for their skill in horsemanship. **2.** a member of a Russian army unit whose soldiers are or were Cossacks [Late 16C. Via Russian *kazak* < Turkic, 'nomad, adventurer']

cosset /kóssit/ (-**sets**, -**seting**, -**seted**) *vt* to give somebody or something excessive care and protection (*disapproving*) [Mid-16C. Origin ?]

cossie /kózzi/, **cozzie** *n* CLOTHING same as **swimsuit** (*informal*) [Early 20C. Shortening and alteration]

cost /kost/ *v* (**costs, costing, cost**) **1.** *vt* HAVE PARTICULAR PRICE to require the payment of a particular sum **2.** *vti* BE EXPENSIVE to require payment of a large sum of money by somebody (*informal*) **3.** *vt* CAUSE LOSS OF SOMETHING to cause somebody or something to lose, sacrifice, or suffer something **4.** (*past and past participle* **costed**) *vt* CALCULATE MONEY REQUIRED FOR SOMETHING to calculate the price or expense of something ■ *n* **1.** AMOUNT PAID FOR SOMETHING the amount of money required to be paid for something **2.** MONEY SPENT DOING SOMETHING the amount of money spent in producing or doing something **3.** LOSS OR EFFORT the loss, sacrifice, suffering, or effort involved in doing something **4.** same as **cost price** ■ **costs** *npl* **1.** LEGAL EXPENSES the amount of money that is spent pursuing a legal action, especially those expenses that a losing party may be required to pay **2.** TOTAL SUM OF MONEY the calculated amount of money needed for something ○ *housing costs* [14C. Via Old French *co(u)ster* < Latin *constare* 'stand firm' < *stare* 'to stand'] —**costless** *adj*

costa /kóstə/ (*plural* -**tae** /-tee/) *n* **1.** ANAT same as **rib** (sense 1) (*technical*) **2.** a part of something such as a leaf or a wing that resembles a rib [Mid-19C. < Latin, 'rib'] —**costal** *adj*

Costa Brava /kóstə braávə/ resort region on the Mediterranean coast of northeastern Spain, north of Barcelona

cost accountant *n* an accountant who calculates and provides detailed information on the cost of producing something or carrying out an operation in a business, and compares actual costs with expected costs

cost accounting *n* accounting that is concerned with providing detailed information on the cost of producing something or carrying out an operation in a business

Costa del Sol /kóstə del sól/ resort region on the Mediterranean coast of southern Spain

costae plural of **costa**

co-star *n* JOINT LEAD ACTOR an actor who shares prominence with another actor in a production ■ *v* **1.** *vi* TOP THE BILL WITH OTHERS to share prominence with another actor or actors in a production **2.** *vt* FEATURE SOMEBODY AS LEAD ACTOR to include or feature somebody as one of the lead actors

costard /kústərd, kós-/ *n* a large English cooking apple [13C. < Anglo-Norman < *coste* 'rib' < Latin *costa*]

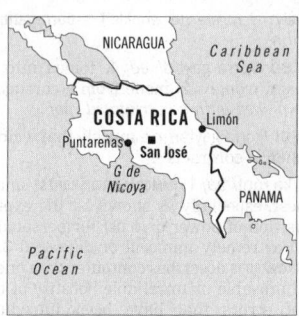
Costa Rica

Costa Rica /kóstə reekə/ country in southern Central America between the Caribbean Sea and the Pacific Ocean. Language: Spanish. Currency: colón. Capital: San José. Population: 3,896,092 (2003). Area: 51,060 sq. km/19,714 sq. mi. Official name **Republic of Costa Rica** —**Costa Rican** *n, adj*

costate /kóst ayt/ *adj* describes a leaf that has ridges or is ribbed [Early 19C. < Latin *costatus* < *costa* 'rib']

cost-benefit analysis *n* a method of project evaluation that compares the potential benefits with the anticipated costs

cost centre *n* a section of a business to which costs can be assigned in an analysis of the relationship of costs and the value of benefits arising from them

cost-cutting *n* the taking of action to reduce costs, especially in a business, or the actions taken (*often used before a noun*) ○ *a cost-cutting exercise*

cost-effective *adj* economically worthwhile in terms of what is achieved for the amount of money spent —**cost-effectively** *adv* —**cost-effectiveness** *n*

costermonger /kóstər mung gər/, **coster** /kóstər/ *n* a seller of fruit and vegetables or other things from a barrow or stall in the street (*archaic*) [Early 16C. < COSTARD + *monger* 'seller']

costing /kósting/ *n* **1.** the process of calculating the cost involved in undertaking a project **2.** the cost that has been calculated for undertaking a project (*often used in the plural*)

costive /kóstiv/ *adj* **1.** constipated, or causing constipation (*technical*) **2.** slow to act or speak (*literary*) [14C. Via French < Latin *constipatus*, past participle of *constipare* (see CONSTIPATE)] —**costively** *adv* —**costiveness** *n*

costly /kóstli/ (-**lier**, -**liest**) *adj* **1.** EXPENSIVE costing large sums of money to buy **2.** LUXURIOUS using expensive and luxurious materials **3.** INVOLVING EFFORT OR TIME involving a great deal of effort, time, or sacrifice **4.** DAMAGING causing great loss, damage, or suffering —**costliness** *n*

cost of living *n* the amount of money spent on food, clothing, accommodation, and other basic necessities (*hyphenated when used before a noun*)

cost-of-living adjustment *n* an increase in wages or salary to compensate for an increase in the cost of living

cost-of-living index *n* ECON same as **consumer price index** (sense 1)

cost-plus *n* a pricing system that calculates the price of a product by adding a fixed percentage as profit to the production cost

cost price *n* the price that somebody selling something paid for it

cost-push, cost-push inflation *n* inflation in which price rises result from increased production costs or similar factors rather than from customer demand

costume /kós tyoom/ *n* **1.** THEATRICAL CLOTHES clothes worn to make a person look like somebody or something else, especially in a theatrical performance **2.** REGIONAL OR HISTORICAL DRESS clothes traditionally worn in a particular place or during a particular period in the past ○ *national costume* ○ *18th-century costume* **3.** CLOTHES FOR PARTICULAR ACTIVITY the clothing appropriate for a particular activity (*dated*) **4.** WOMEN'S OUTFIT a set of women's clothes comprising a matching jacket and skirt (*dated*) ■ *vt* (-**tumes**, -**tuming**, -**tumed**) **1.** PUT SOMEBODY IN COSTUME to provide

somebody with a costume **2.** **PROVIDE COSTUMES FOR SHOW** to provide clothes for a theatrical production [Early 18C. Via French < Italian *costume*, literally 'custom, fashion' < Latin *consuetudin-* (see CUSTOM)]

costume drama *n* a dramatic production in which the actors wear clothes appropriate for the period during which the drama takes place

costume jewellery *n* decorative jewellery that does not contain precious stones or metals

costume party *n* US a party at which guests wear clothing suggestive of a historical period, a character from a film, or some other theme

costumier /ko styoomi ər, -i ay/, **costumer** /kós tyoomər/ *n* a maker or supplier of costumes for a play, show, or festivity [Mid-19C. < French < *costumer* 'provide with a costume' < *costume* (see COSTUME)]

co-survivor *n* a close relative or friend of somebody who has experienced a traumatizing event, e.g. a rape victim, Aids patient, or victim of a disaster

cosy /kṓzi/ *adj* (**-sier, -siest**) **1.** **SNUG** warm, comfortable, and snug **2.** **FRIENDLY** friendly and intimate **3.** **UNETHICALLY CLOSE** close and friendly, but for mutually beneficial or underhand purposes (*disapproving*) ■ *n* (*plural* **-sies**) **COVERING TO KEEP SOMETHING WARM** a covering, often knitted or padded, put over something, especially a teapot, to keep it or its contents warm [Early 18C. Origin ?] —**cosily** *adv* —**cosiness** *n*

cosy up *v* **1.** *vi* to sit or lie as close as possible to somebody for warmth or affection **2.** to try to ingratiate yourself, or become friendly or intimate, with somebody

cot[1] /kot/ *n* **1.** a small bed designed for a baby or young child, often with high sides. N Am term **crib** **2.** N Am same as **camp bed 3.** a hammock with a stiff frame, used on board ship [Mid-17C. < Hindi *khāt* 'framework strung with rope and used as a bed', via Sanskrit *khatvā* < Tamil *kaṭṭu* 'tie']

cot[2] /kot/ *n* **1.** a cover for an injured finger, shaped like the finger of a glove **2.** a small cottage (*archaic or literary*) [Old English < Germanic]

cot[3] /kot/ *abbr* MATHS cotangent

cot[4] *n* AGRIC another spelling of **cote**

CoT *abbr* college of technology

cotan /kṓ tan/ *abbr* MATHS cotangent

cotangent /kō tánjənt/ *n* for a given angle in a right-angled triangle, a trigonometric function equal to the length of the side adjacent to the angle divided by that of the side opposite the angle —**cotangential** /kṓ tan jénsh'l/ *adj*

cot case *n* **1.** *ANZ* **VERY DRUNK PERSON** an intoxicated person who is capable only of sleep (*informal*) **2.** *NZ* **SICK PERSON** somebody who is very sick or injured **3.** *NZ* **PERSON CONFINED TO BED** a patient who must stay in bed because of illness

cotch /koch/ (**cotches, cotching, cotched**) *vt* same as **catch** (*slang; used in Black English*)

cot death *n* MED the sudden and unexplained death of a baby while sleeping. N Am term **crib death**

cote /kōt/, **cot** /kot/ *n* a small shelter, especially one for birds or animals (*usually used in combination*) [Old English < Germanic]

Côte d'Azur /kṓt da zyoor/ part of the French Riviera near the Italian border, including Cannes, Nice, and Monaco

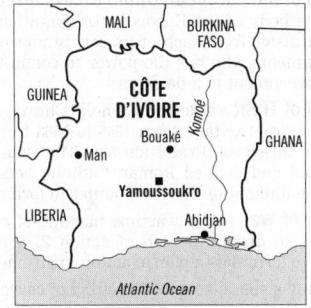

Côte d'Ivoire

Côte d'Ivoire /-dee vwaár/ country in West Africa, situated north of the Gulf of Guinea and east of Liberia. Language: French. Currency: CFA franc.

Capital: Yamoussoukro. Population: 16,962,491 (2003). Area: 322,462 sq. km/124,503 sq. mi. Official name **Republic of Côte d'Ivoire**. Former name **Ivory Coast**

Côte d'Or /-dáwr/ administrative region and major wine-producing area in Burgundy, east-central France. The main city in the region is Dijon. Population: 506,755 (1999). Area: 8,763 sq. km/3,383 sq. mi.

coterie /kṓtəri/ *n* a small exclusive group of people who share the same interests [Early 18C. < French < Middle Low German *kote* 'cottage']

coterminous *adj* same as **conterminous**

Côtes d'Armor /kōt daar máwr/ department of northwestern France in Brittany. Population: 538,594 (1991). Area: 6,876 sq. km/2,655 sq. mi.

Côtes-du-Nord /kṓt dyoo náwr/ former name for **Côtes d'Armor**

Côtes du Rhône /kōt dyoo rṓn/ *n* a red or white wine from a region of southeastern France

coth /koth/ *abbr* hyperbolic cotangent [Late 19C. < *cot*, shortening of COTANGENT + *h* for HYPERBOLIC]

cotidal /kō tīd'l/ *adj* describes a line that joins together locations on a coastal map where tides occur simultaneously

cotillion /kə tíllyən, kō-/, **cotillon** *n* **1.** **FRENCH DANCE** a complex French dance popular in the 18th century **2.** *US* **DANCE LIKE QUADRILLE** a dance similar to a quadrille **3.** **MUSIC** the music for a cotillion **4.** *US* **FORMAL DANCE** a formal evening ball or semiformal afternoon dance [Early 18C. < French *cotillon*, literally 'petticoat' < Old French *cote* (see COAT)]

cotinga /kō tíng gə, kə-/ *n* a bird with a broad beak and rounded wings, the male of some species having brightly coloured plumage and unusual modified wing and head feathers. Native to: Central and South America. Family: Cotingidae. [Late 18C. Via French < Tupi *cutinga*]

Cotman /kótmən/, **John Sell** (1782–1842) British painter, etcher, and leading member of the Norwich School of landscape artists. Most of his watercolours show Norfolk landscapes.

cotoneaster /kə tōni ástər/ *n* a bush with small oval leaves, cultivated for its red or orange berries that often remain throughout the winter. Native to: Europe, South Asia. Genus: *Cotoneaster*. [Mid-18C. < modern Latin < Latin *cotoneum* (see QUINCE)]

Cotonou /kṓtə noō/ port and capital of Atlantique Province, southern Benin. Population: 750,000 (1994).

Cotopaxi /kṓtə páksi/ volcano in central Ecuador, in the Andes. It is the highest active volcano in the world. Height: 5,897 m/19,347 ft.

co-trimoxazole /kṓtri móksə zōl/ *n* a compound anti-bacterial agent. Use: treatment of urinary-tract infections. [Late 20C. < CO- + blend of *trimethoprim* + *sulfamethoxazole*]

Cotswold /kóts wold/ *n* a sheep with fine long wool belonging to a breed originating in the Cotswolds ■ *adj* relating to the Cotswolds [Mid-19C. < COTSWOLDS]

Cotswolds /kóts wōldz/ range of limestone hills in southwestern England, extending 80 km/50 mi. from near Bath to northern Oxfordshire

cotta /kóttə/ *n* in the Roman Catholic Church and in some Anglican and Lutheran churches, a short surplice reaching to just above the waist, worn by clergy, acolytes, and choristers [Mid-19C. < Italian < Germanic]

cottage /kóttij/ *n* **1.** **SMALL RURAL HOUSE** a small house, usually situated in the countryside **2.** *N Am* **HOLIDAY HOME** a small holiday home in the country or beside the sea **3.** *N Am* **SMALL RESIDENTIAL UNIT** a small residential unit, e.g. at a camp, in which residents can be housed in groups **4.** **PUBLIC TOILET** a public toilet, especially one used by gay men for sexual encounters (*slang*) [14C. < Anglo-Norman *cotage* or Anglo-Latin *cotagium* < Germanic] —**cottagey** *adj*

cottage cheese *n* a soft white low-fat cheese with a distinctive lumpy texture and mild flavour

cottage hospital *n* a small rural hospital that does not have any resident medical staff

cottage industry *n* a small-scale business involving people who mostly work at home

cottage loaf *n* a loaf of bread consisting of a large round piece with a smaller one on top

cottage pie *n* a baked dish made from minced meat in gravy with a topping of mashed potato

cottager /kóttijər/ *n* **1.** **OCCUPANT OF COTTAGE** somebody who lives in a cottage **2.** **GAY MAN WHO FREQUENTS TOILETS** a gay man who has sex or looks for sexual partners in public toilets (*slang*) **3.** N Am **SOMEBODY AT HOLIDAY HOME** a holidaymaker at a small holiday home in the country or beside the sea

cottaging /kóttijing/ *n* gay sex or a search for gay partners in public toilets, a practice that was especially prevalent in the years when gay sex was a criminal offence (*slang*)

cottar /kóttər/, **cotter** *n* **1.** formerly in Scotland, a farm worker who was allowed to occupy a cottage in return for labour **2.** AGRIC, HIST same as **cottier** [Mid-16C. Origin ?]

Cottbus /kót booss/ city in Cottbus District, Brandenburg, Germany, near the Polish border. Population: 125,643 (1997).

cotter /kóttər/ *n* **1.** a wedge, key, or bolt used to keep two parts of something such as machinery together **2.** MECH same as **cotter pin** [14C. Origin ?] —**cottered** *adj* —**cotterless** *adj*

cotter pin *n* a split pin inserted through corresponding holes in machine parts such as a nut and a shaft, and then bent so that it holds the parts in place

cottier /kótti ər/ *n* formerly in Ireland, a tenant who farmed land he had acquired as the highest bidder [14C. < Old French *cotier*]

cotton[1] /kótt'n/ *n* **1.** **FABRIC MADE FROM COTTON** fabric woven or knitted from spun cotton fibre **2.** **YARN OR THREAD** yarn or thread made from cotton or a synthetic substitute **3.** **SOMETHING MADE OF COTTON** something made of cotton fabric (*often used in the plural*) **4.** **SOFT FIBRE** a soft white downy fibre that grows in seed pods. Use: textiles. **5.** **PLANTS BUSH PRODUCING DOWNY FIBRE** the tropical or subtropical bush that produces cotton. Genus: *Gossypium*. **6.** **SUBSTANCE LIKE COTTON** a substance that resembles cotton fibre but is produced by another plant such as kapok [14C. Via French *coton* < Arabic *kutun*]

cotton[2] /kótt'n/ (**-tons, -toning, -toned**) [< obsolete *cotton* 'prosper', probably < COTTON[1], from the realization that raising a nap increased its value]

cotton on *vi* to grasp the meaning of what is being said or done (*informal*)

cotton ball *n* US a small ball of cotton wool, used for removing makeup or cleansing the skin or a wound

Cotton Belt *n* an extensive agricultural area in the southeastern United States where cotton is the main crop

cotton bud *n* a short stick with a small amount of cotton wool wound tightly onto one or both ends, e.g. used in cleaning ears or applying makeup

cotton bush *n Aus* a downy bush used to feed livestock in Australia. Latin name: *Kochia aphylla*.

cotton cake *n* compressed cottonseed produced from the residue remaining after the extraction of oil. Use: livestock feed.

cotton candy *n* N Am same as **candyfloss**

cotton gin *n* a machine for separating seeds, husks, and other unwanted material from cotton fibre

cotton grass *n* a reedy bog plant that has white tufted cottony flower heads. Native to: northern temperate areas. Genus: *Eriophorum*.

cottonmouth /kótt'n mowth/ (*plural* **-mouths** /-thz, -ths/) *n* REPT same as **water moccasin** (sense 1) [Mid-19C. < the whitish colour inside its mouth]

cotton-picking *adj* N Am used to indicate disapproval, annoyance, or emphasis (*slang*) [Because cotton-picking was done by only the poorest labourers]

cotton reel *n* a spool on which thread is wound

cottonseed /kótt'n seed/ *n* the seed of the cotton plant. Use: source of oil, meal.

cotton stainer *n* an insect that pierces cottonseed pods (**bolls**) and stains the fibres. Genus: *Dysdercus*.

cotton swab *n* US COSMETICS same as **cotton bud**

cottontail /kótt'n tayl/ *n* a small rabbit with brown or grey fur and a tail with a white cottony underside. Native to: North America. Genus: *Sylvilagus*.

cotton waste *n* waste cotton yarn. Use: cleaning material.

cottonwood /kótt'n wŏŏd/ (*plural* **-woods** *or same*) *n* a poplar tree that has seeds with cottony tufts. Native to: North America. Latin name: *Populus deltoides*.

cotton wool *n* **1.** soft fluffy cotton fibre that has been purified and bleached. Use: cleaning skin, removing makeup. (*hyphenated when used before a noun*) N Am term **absorbent cotton 2.** raw unprocessed cotton

cottony /kótt'ni/ *adj* looking or feeling like cotton

cottony-cushion scale *n* a small sap-sucking insect that damages citrus crops in California and elsewhere. Native to: Australia. Latin name: *Icerya purchasi*.

COTW *n* the countries that opposed Saddam Hussein in the Iraq War of 2003. Full form **Coalition of the Willing**

-cotyl *suffix* cotyledon ○ *hypocotyl* [< COTYLEDON]

cotyledon /kótti léed'n/ *n* **1.** the first leaf, or one of the first pair of leaves, produced by the seed of a flowering plant. They may serve as food stores, remaining in the seed at germination, or produce food by photosynthesis. **2.** a tuft of projections (**villi**) on the placenta of a mammal [Mid-16C. Via Latin, 'navelwort' < Greek *kotulēdōn* 'cup-shaped cavity' < *kotulē* 'cup'] —**cotyledonal** *adj* —**cotyledonary** *adj* —**cotyledonous** *adj*

cotylosaur /kóttilə sawr, kə tíllə-/ *n* an extinct reptile with a heavy body and short legs, probably the first land vertebrate. Order: Cotylosauria. [Early 20C. < Greek *kotulē* 'cup' + *sauros* 'lizard']

coucal /kóo kal, -k'l/ *n* a tropical bird of the cuckoo family with a large hooked beak and long broad tail. Native to: Africa, South Asia, Australasia. Genus: *Centropus*. [Early 19C. < French, probably blend of *coucou* 'cuckoo' + *alouette* 'lark']

couch[1] /kowch/ *n* **1.** LONG SEAT a piece of upholstered furniture on which two or more people can sit side by side **2.** DOCTOR'S LONG SEAT a long seat with a headrest that a patient lies on when visiting a doctor, especially a psychiatrist **3.** BARLEY MALTING FRAME a frame on which barley grain is spread during malting **4.** FIRST COAT OF PAINT a layer of paint or varnish applied to a canvas as a first coat ■ *v* (**couches, couching, couched**) **1.** *vt* PHRASE SOMETHING IN PARTICULAR WAY to express something using a particular style or choice of words **2.** *vti* LIE OR LAY DOWN to lie down, or lay somebody or something down (*archaic or literary; often passive*) **3.** *vt* FOOD INDUST SPREAD BARLEY FOR MALTING to spread barley on a frame for malting **4.** *vt* ARMS LOWER LANCE to lower a lance into position for an attack **5.** *vt* SURG REMOVE CATARACT to remove a cataract by pushing down the lens of the eye **6.** *vt* HANDICRAFT EMBROIDER BY HOLDING DOWN THREAD to embroider a pattern by holding down threads with other threads passed through the material [14C. < French *couche* (noun), *coucher* 'lie down' < Latin *collocare* (see COLLOCATE)] —**coucher** *n*

couch[2] /kówch, kooch/ *n* PLANTS same as **couch grass**

couchant /kówchənt/ *adj* in heraldry, used to describe an animal lying down with its head raised [15C. < French, present participle of *coucher* (see COUCH [1])]

couchette /koo shét/ *n* **1.** a seat in a compartment on a continental European train that can be converted into a sleeping berth **2.** a compartment of a train containing couchettes [Early 20C. < French, 'small bed' < *couche* (see COUCH [1])]

couch grass /kówch-, kóoch-/, **couch** *n* a grass with rapidly spreading underground roots that is a troublesome weed in gardens. Latin name: *Agropyron repens*. [Late 16C. Variant of QUITCH GRASS]

couch potato *n* an inactive person who spends too much time sitting watching television (*slang disapproving*) [< the idea that somebody who watches the 'boob tube' (television) is a 'tuber'; also with reference to potato crisps]

coudé /koo dáy/, **coudé telescope** *n* an astronomical telescope that reflects light from a main mirror onto a detector to one side [Late 19C. < French, past participle of *couder* 'bend at right angles' < *coude* 'elbow' < Latin *cubitum*]

cougar /kóogər, -gaar/ (*plural* **-gars** *or same*) *n* same as **puma** [Late 18C. Via French *couguar* < Guarani *cuguaçuarana*]

cough /kof/ *v* (**coughs, coughing, coughed**) **1.** *vi* EXPEL AIR FROM LUNGS NOISILY to release air through the windpipe and mouth sharply and noisily **2.** *vt* EXPEL SOMETHING BY COUGHING to expel something from the lungs or windpipe by coughing **3.** *vi* MAKE SHARP NOISE to make a noise that is similar to the sound of somebody coughing ■ *n* **1.** ACT OR SOUND OF COUGHING a sudden noisy release of air through the windpipe and mouth, often expelling an obstruction **2.** ILLNESS CAUSING COUGHING an illness causing coughing because of an infection in the lungs [14C. Ultimately < Germanic, an imitation of the sound] —**cougher** *n*

cough up *vti* to give something reluctantly, e.g. money or information (*slang*)

cough drop *n* a medicated sweet for soothing a cough or sore throat

cough mixture *n* a medicated syrup that soothes or suppresses a cough

~~**cought**~~ incorrect spelling of **caught**

co.uk *abbr* UK commercial organization (*used in Internet addresses*) See table at **domain name**

could /kŏŏd, kəd/ CORE MEANING: a modal verb used as the past tense of 'can' ○ *My mother did the best she could for my brother and me.* ○ *She could perform on the trapeze.* ○ *His feet were so swollen that he could hardly walk.* ○ *We were so tired we couldn't stay awake.*

1. *modal v* EXPRESSING POSSIBILITY used to indicate that something is possibly true or happening in the future ○ *She thinks that medical technology could be the field for her.* **2.** *modal v* EXPRESSING REQUEST used when making polite requests ○ *Could you close the window please?* **3.** *modal v* INDICATING POSSIBLE PAST SITUATION used to indicate a possible situation in the past that did not happen ○ *We could have gone.* **4.** *modal v* EXPRESSING POLITE OFFER used to make polite offers and suggestions ○ *You could stay at my place.* **5.** *vi* FOR EMPHASIS used in questions to emphasize strong feelings about something ○ *How could you do that?* [Old English *cūþe*, past tense of *cunnan* 'know' (see CAN [1]); altered after SHOULD, WOULD]

couldn't /kŏŏdd'nt/ *contr* could not

couldst /kŏŏdst/ 2nd person singular past of **could** (*archaic*)

could've /kŏŏddəv/ *contr* could have (*informal*)

USAGE See *of*.

---

coulee /kóoli, -lay/ *n* **1.** a thick short flow of viscous molten lava **2.** *Can, Northwest US* a deep gully formed by rain or melting snow and usually dry in the summer [Early 19C. < French, 'flow' < feminine past participle of *couler* 'to flow' < Latin *colare* 'to strain']

coulibiac, **coulibiaca** *n* FOOD another spelling of **koulibiac**

coulis /kóoli/ *n* a thin purée of fruit or vegetables used as a garnish [Late 20C. Via French < Old French *coleïs* 'flowing']

coulisse /koo léess/ *n* in a theatre, a piece of side scenery on a stage or the space between two of these pieces (*often used in the plural*) [Early 19C. < French < *(porte) coulisse* 'sliding (door)' < Old French *(porte) coleïce* (see PORTCULLIS)]

couloir /kóol waar/ *n* a broad mountain gully, especially one prone to avalanches [Early 19C. < French, 'channel' < *couler* (see COULEE)]

coulomb /kóo lom/ *n* the SI unit of electric charge equal to the amount of charge transported by a current of one ampere in one second. Symbol **C** [Late 19C. After Charles Augustin de *Coulomb* (1736–1806), French physicist]

Coulomb's law /kóo lomz-/ *n* a law of electricity stating that the force of attraction or repulsion between two electric charges is proportional to their product and inversely proportional to the square of the distance between them [See COULOMB]

coulometry /koo lómmətri/ *n* a means of analysing the results of a process of electrolysis by measuring the amount of electricity used in the process to determine the amount of the substance produced [Mid-20C. < COULOMB] —**coulometric** /kóolə méttrik/ *adj* —**coulometrically** *adv*

coulter /kóltər/, **colter** *n* a vertical blade attached to a plough that cuts into the soil in front of a ploughshare [Pre-12C. < Latin *culter* 'knife']

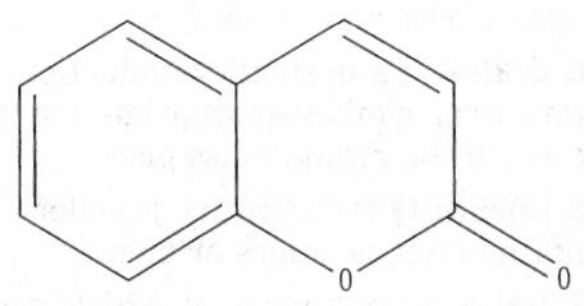

coumarin

coumarin /kóomərin/ *n* a fragrant compound. Source: plants or made synthetically. Use: in perfumes and medicine. Formula: $C_9H_6O_2$. [Mid-19C. < French *coumarine* < Tupi *cumarú* 'tonka bean tree', a source of coumarin] —**coumaric** *adj*

coumestan /kóomi stan/ *n* a phytoestrogen found especially in red clover and bean sprouts [Late 20C. < COUMARIN]

coumestrol /koo méstrol/ *n* a phytoestrogen found especially in alfalfa [Mid-20C. < COUMARIN]

~~**councelor**~~ incorrect spelling of **counsellor**

council /kównss'l/ *n* **1.** PEOPLE RUNNING LOCAL AFFAIRS a group of people elected to run the administrative affairs of a local district **2.** COMMITTEE an appointed or elected body of people with an administrative, advisory, or representative function **3.** CHURCH ASSEMBLY an assembly of church representatives who meet to decide matters of discipline and doctrine **4.** COUNCIL MEETING a meeting of a council **5.** MEETING FOR DISCUSSION a meeting to discuss or decide something **6.** *Aus* UPPER HOUSE OF STATE PARLIAMENT in Australia, the upper house of a state parliament [Pre-12C. Via Anglo-Norman *cuncile* < Latin *concilium* 'calling together']

USAGE council or **counsel**? ***Council*** is a noun only, meaning a body of people, especially in an advisory or administrative context. ***Counsel*** is both a noun and a verb, and has to do with advice, particularly of a professional nature, and the giving of it. The noun ***counsel*** most often means a lawyer or lawyers, whereas a *counsellor* gives some other kind of professional advice, as in *debt counsellor* or *marriage guidance counsellor.* The verb describes the activity of such advisers: *The company psychologist counsels employees having stress problems. International financial analysts counselled caution.*

---

council area *n* the geographical or administrative area under the control of a local council

council chamber *n* a room where a council gathers for discussion

councillor /kównsələr/ *n* **1.** a member of a council elected to run the administrative affairs of a local district **2.** an elected or appointed member of an advisory council —**councillorship** *n*

councilman /kównss'lmən/ (*plural* **-men** /-mən/) *n US* a man who is a member of a council, especially of a local authority

Council of Europe *n* an organization of European states founded in 1949 to further political unity

Council of the European Union *n* the main decision-making body of the European Union, attended by one minister from each of its constituent national governments who has the power to commit his or her government to a decision

Council of Trent *n* a Roman Catholic Church council held in Trento, Italy, from 1545 to 1563 to respond to the threat of Protestantism. The council reaffirmed and defined Roman Catholic beliefs and laid the foundation for the Counter-Reformation.

council of war *n* **1.** a wartime meeting of military officers to discuss a plan of action **2.** a meeting called to formulate a plan of action in an emergency

councilor *n* PUBLIC ADMIN US spelling of **councillor**

councilperson /kównss'l purss'n/ (*plural* **-persons** or **-people** /-peep'l/) *n US* a member of a council, especially of a local authority

council tax *n* in the United Kingdom, a local tax that is levied on the basis of the estimated value of a

property. The tax was introduced in 1993 to replace the short-lived community charge and the earlier rates system.

councilwoman /kównss'l wŏŏmən/ (*plural* **-women** /-wimin/) *n US* a female member of a council, especially of a local authority

counsel /kównss'l/ *n* **1. COURT LAWYER** a lawyer or group of lawyers who conduct cases in court or give legal advice (*takes a singular or plural verb*) **2. SOMEBODY WHO GIVES ADVICE** somebody whose advice is sought or who acts as an official adviser **3. ADVICE** advice sought from or given by somebody, especially somebody who is wise or knowledgeable (*formal; often used in the plural*) **4. CONSULTATION** consultation with others (*archaic or literary*) ■ *vt* (**-sels, -selling, -selled**) **1. ADVISE SOMEBODY TO DO SOMETHING** to advise somebody on a particular course of action (*formal*) **2. ADVISE SOMEBODY ON PERSONAL PROBLEMS** to give somebody advice and support on personal or psychological matters, usually in a professional context [12C. Via Old French *conseil* < Latin *consilium* 'consultation' < *consulere* 'seek advice'] ◇ **keep your own counsel** to keep your thoughts and intentions secret

USAGE See ***council***.

SYNONYMS See ***recommend***.

counseling *n* US spelling of **counselling**

counsellee /kównss'l ée/ *n* somebody who receives counselling

counselling /kównss'ling/ *n* **1.** help with personal or psychological matters usually given by a professional **2.** meetings with a counsellor to receive help with personal or psychological problems

counsellor /kównss'lər/ *n* **1. ADVISER ON PERSONAL PROBLEMS** somebody, usually a professional, who helps others with personal, social, or psychological problems **2. ADVISER ON SPECIAL SUBJECT** a professional who gives advice on such matters as careers, education, or health **3. SOMEBODY WHO GIVES ADVICE** somebody such as a friend who gives advice **4.** *also* **counsellor-at-law** (*plural* **counsellors-at-law**) *US* **LAWYER** a lawyer, especially one who acts for a client in a trial **5.** *also* **counsellor-at-law** (*plural* **counsellors-at-law**) *Ireland* **ADVISORY BARRISTER** in Ireland, a barrister who acts in an advisory capacity **6. SENIOR DIPLOMAT** an officer of senior grade in the diplomatic service **7.** *N Am* **HIGH-RANKING DIPLOMAT** a diplomat ranking below an ambassador or minister **8.** *N Am* **CHILDREN'S SUPERVISOR** a supervisor of young people at a summer camp —**counsellorship** *n*

counselor *n* US spelling of **counsellor**

count[1] /kownt/ *v* (**counts, counting, counted**) **1.** *vti* **SAY NUMBERS** to say numbers in order, usually starting at one **2.** *vti* **ADD UP** to add things up to see how many there are or to find the value of an amount of money **3.** *vt* **INCLUDE SOMEBODY OR SOMETHING** to include somebody or something in a calculation ○ *If you count me and Jodie, there will be 15 people.* **4.** *vti* **CONSIDER OR BE CONSIDERED** to consider somebody or something, or be considered, in a particular way or as a particular thing **5.** *vi* **BE OF IMPORTANCE** to be of importance or value **6.** *vi* **HAVE VALUE** to have a specific value **7.** *vti* **KEEP TIME** to keep musical time by counting beats ■ *n* **1. SAYING OF NUMBERS** an act of saying numbers in order **2. FINDING OF TOTAL** an addition of people or things to find a total **3. TOTAL OF SOMETHING** a total that is reached by adding things up **4. ONE OF MANY POINTS** any one of a number of points, e.g. in a discussion **5. CHARGE AGAINST SOMEBODY** a charge against somebody who is on trial **6. BOXING REFEREE'S COUNT** in boxing, a count to ten by the referee during which a boxer who has been knocked down must stand up or lose the match [14C. < Old French *conte* (noun), *co(u)nter* 'reckon' < Latin *computare* 'reckon together'] ◇ **keep count** to count and remember the number of people or things counted ◇ **lose count** to fail to count accurately or remember the number of people or things counted ◇ **out for the count 1.** unconscious or deeply asleep and unlikely to wake again for some time (*slang*) **2.** BOXING unable to stand up, after being knocked down, within the ten-second count given by the referee in a boxing match, and therefore losing the match

count against *vt* to be damaging to somebody's interests or prospects

count down *vi* to count backwards from a number to zero or from a given time to something such as the launch of a rocket

count in *vt* to include somebody in a plan

count on, count upon *vt* **1.** to rely on somebody to do something **2.** to be sure that something will happen

count out *vt* **1. COUNT THINGS ONE BY ONE** to count something such as money one item at a time **2. NOT INCLUDE SOMEBODY** to exclude somebody from a plan **3. DECLARE BOXER DEFEATED BY COUNTING TEN** to disqualify a boxer who has been knocked down and fails to get up within ten seconds

count towards *or* **toward** *vt* to be included as part of something

count upon *vt* same as **count on**

count[2] /kownt/ *n* a nobleman in some European countries, of a rank equal to that of a British earl [14C. Via Old French *conte* < Latin *comit-* 'companion', literally 'somebody who goes with']

countable /kówntəb'l/ *adj* **1.** able to be counted **2.** used to describe a noun that can be preceded by 'a' or 'an' followed by a plural verb, and usually has a distinct plural form —**countability** /kówntə bílləti/ *n* —**countably** *adv*

countdown /kównt down/ *n* **1. BACKWARDS COUNT** a count in descending order before an event such as a rocket launch **2. ACTIVITIES BEFORE EVENT** the activities carried on during the period of time before something such as a rocket launch **3. PREPARATORY PERIOD** the period immediately preceding an important event

countenance /kówntənənss/ (*formal*) *n* **1. FACE OR EXPRESSION** somebody's face, or the expression on it **2. COMPOSURE** composure or self-control ■ *vt* (**-nances, -nancing, -nanced**) **TOLERATE OR APPROVE SOMETHING** to tolerate, accept, or give approval to something [13C. < Old French *contenance* 'demeanour', literally 'contents' < *contenir* (see CONTAIN)] —**countenancer** *n*

counter[1] /kówntər/ *n* **1. FLAT SURFACE** a flat surface on which food or drink is served, goods are displayed, or business is transacted **2. FLAT SURFACE IN KITCHEN** a kitchen worktop **3. SMALL MARKER** in board games a small object, often a flat disc, used to mark a player's position or to keep score **4. IMITATION COIN** an object, usually a flat disc, used as a substitute for a coin [14C. Via Anglo-Norman *counteor* < medieval Latin *computatorium* 'place for counting' < Latin *computare* 'reckon together'] ◇ **under the counter** secretly and unofficially, usually because there is something illegal about what is being done

counter[2] /kówntər/ *vti* (**-ters, -tering, -tered**) **1. CONTRADICT OR OPPOSE SOMETHING** to say something that contradicts or opposes what somebody has said **2. DO SOMETHING IN OPPOSITION** to do something in opposition to what somebody else is doing, so as to make it less effective **3. PUNCH OPPONENT IN RETURN** in boxing, to defend yourself against a punch from an opponent, and deliver a punch in return ■ *adv* **1. OPPOSITE** in the opposite direction **2. CONTRARILY** in a contrary manner ■ *adj* **CONTRADICTING** contradicting or opposing something ○ *a counter blow* ■ *n* **1. RESPONSE** a response made in retaliation to something that has been said **2. OPPOSITE OF SOMETHING** something that is the opposite of something else or that is done in opposition to something else **3.** BOXING **RETURNING PUNCH** in boxing, a punch that counters a punch aimed by an opponent **4.** FENCING **PARRY** in fencing, a parry in which the foils make a circular movement **5.** NAUT **END OF SHIP'S STERN** the part of the stern of a ship or boat that juts out above the water line **6.** PRINTING **HOLLOW PART OF TYPEFACE** a hollow part of a piece of type, e.g. the inner parts of the letters 'p' and 'd' [14C. < COUNTER-] ◇ **run counter to something** to be in direct contrast or opposition to something

counter[3] /kówntər/ *n* **1.** a device that counts automatically **2.** somebody whose job is to count something such as votes [14C. Partly via Anglo-Norman *count(e)our*, Old French *conteor* < Latin *computator* < *computare* 'reckon together'; partly < COUNT [1]]

counter- *prefix* **1.** contrary, opposing ○ *counterattack* **2.** complementary, corresponding ○ *counterpart* [Via Anglo-Norman *countre-* < Latin *contra* (see CONTRA-)]

counteraccusation *n*
counteragent *n*
counteraggression *n*
counterargue *vi*
counterassault *n*
counterbid *n*
counterblockade *n*
counterblow *n*
counterbrace *vt*
countercampaign *n*
countercomplaint *n*
counterconspiracy *n*
countercoup *n*
countercriticism *n*
counterdemand *n*
counterdeployment *n*
countereffort *n*
counterevidence *n*
counterfire *n*
counterforce *n*
counterhypothesis *n*
counterinflation *n*
counterinflationary *adj*
counterinfluence *n*
counterorder *n*
counterplay *n*
counterplot *n, vi*
counterploy *n*
counterproposal *n*
counterprotest *n*
counterquestion *n*
counterraid *n*
counterrally *n*
counterreaction *n*
counterreform *n*
counterresponse *n*
counterretaliation *n*
countershot *n*
counterspy *n*
counterstatement *n*
counterstep *n*
counterstrategy *n*
counterstrike *n*
counterstroke *n*
countersuggestion *n*
countersuit *n*
countersurveillance *n*
countertactics *npl*
counterthreat *n*
counterthrust *n*
countertrend *n*
counterview *n*

counteract /kówntər ákt/ (**-acts, -acting, -acted**) *vt* to prevent something having an effect, or lessen its effect —**counteraction** *n* —**counteractive** *adj* —**counteractively** *adv*

counterargument /kówntər aargyŏŏmənt/ *n* a fact or opinion that challenges the reasoning behind somebody's proposal and shows that there are grounds for taking an opposite view

counterattack /kówntər ə tak/ *n* an attack made in response to an attack by an enemy or opponent

counterattraction /kówntər ə tráksh'n/ *n* something set up to draw people away from another attraction

counterbalance /kówntər bal ənss/ *vt* (**-ances, -ancing, -anced**) **1. HAVE OPPOSING EFFECT ON SOMETHING** to be or have an equal and opposing force or effect on something **2. BALANCE SOMETHING WITH EQUAL WEIGHT** to make something balance by putting equal weight on the opposite side ■ *n* **1. COUNTERBALANCING PERSON OR THING** somebody or something that has an equal and opposing force or effect on somebody or something else **2. BALANCED STATE** a state of balance with an equal and opposing force or effect **3. WEIGHT THAT BALANCES ANOTHER** a weight that exactly balances another weight

counterbattery fire /kówntər battəri-/ *n* firing weapons with the aim of destroying enemy artillery

counterblast /kówntər blaast/ *n* **1.** an attack on somebody in speech or writing, made in response to an attack by that person **2.** a blast that counters the effect of a preceding blast

counterchange /kówntər chaynj/ (**-changes, -changing, -changed**) *v* **1.** *vti* to interchange the parts or positions of two things **2.** *vt* to chequer or dapple something with colours (*literary*)

countercharge /kówntər chaarj/ *n* **1. ACCUSATION AGAINST ACCUSER** an accusation made against the person or group who has accused another of something **2.** MIL **CHARGE AGAINST AGGRESSORS** a charge made by police or military forces against a group of aggressors ■ *vt* (**-charges, -charging, -charged**) **CHARGE ACCUSER WITH SOMETHING** to bring a charge against an accuser

countercheck /kówntər chek/ *n* **1. SECOND CHECK** a check made to ensure that a previous check was correct **2. RESTRAINT ON SOMETHING** something that acts to block or restrain something else ■ *v* (**-checks, -checking, -checked**) **1.** *vti* **CHECK AGAIN** to carry out a second check on something, in order to ensure that the first was accurate **2.** *vt* **RESTRAIN SOMETHING** to act in order to block the force or action of something

counterclaim /kówntər klaym/ *n* a claim entered by the defendant in a court of civil law, as a response to the original claim that was entered against the defendant by the plaintiff ■ *vi* (**-claims, -claiming, -claimed**) to make a claim in response to, or as a defence against, an earlier claim —**counterclaimant** /kówntər kláymənt/ *n*

counterclockwise /kówntər klók wīz/ *adv, adj N Am* same as **anticlockwise**

counterconditioning /kówntər kən dísh'ning/ *n* a process of psychological conditioning that attempts to replace somebody's undesired habitual response to a particular situation with a desired learned response

counterculture /kówntər kulchər/ *n* a culture that has ideas and ways of behaving that are consciously and deliberately very different from the cultural values of the larger society that it is part of —

countercultural /kówntər kúlchərəl/ *adj* —**counterculturist** *n*

countercurrent /kówntər kurrənt/ *n* **1.** CURRENT FLOWING OPPOSITE WAY a current that flows in the opposite direction to another current **2.** CONTRARY TREND a trend that is contrary to the prevailing one ■ *adj* **1.** FLOWING IN OPPOSITE DIRECTION flowing in the opposite direction to another current **2.** USING OPPOSING CURRENTS involving the flow of two currents in opposite directions —**countercurrently** *adv*

counterdemonstration /kówntər demən stráysh'n/ *n* a public demonstration that is held to oppose the purpose of another demonstration that was recently held or is currently being held —**counterdemonstrator** /-démmən straytər/ *n*

counterespionage /kówntər éspi ə naazh/ *n* government activity designed to detect and prevent spying by an enemy

counterexample /kówntər ig zaamp'l/ *n* a fact or argument that indicates that a theory, scientific hypothesis, or mathematical theorem is not true

counterfactual /kówntər fákchoo əl/ *adj* **1.** CONTRARY TO FACTS not reflecting or considering the facts **2.** EXPRESSING WHAT MIGHT HAVE HAPPENED expressing what has not actually happened but might have happened in other circumstances ■ *n* STATEMENT OF WHAT MIGHT HAVE HAPPENED a statement expressing something that did not happen but might have

counterfeit /kówntərfit/ *adj* **1.** FORGED made as a copy of something, especially money, in order to defraud or deceive people **2.** FALSE pretended in order to deceive somebody ○ *counterfeit geniality* ■ *v* (**-feits, -feiting, -feited**) **1.** *vti* FORGE to make realistic copies of something, especially money, in order to defraud or deceive people **2.** *vt* PRETEND TO FEEL SOMETHING to pretend to have an emotion in order to deceive somebody ■ *n* FORGERY a copy of something, especially money, made in order to defraud or deceive people [14C. < Anglo-Norman *countrefet*, past participle of *countrefaire* 'counterfeit' < medieval Latin *contrafacere* < Latin *contra-* 'against' + *facere* 'make, do'] —**counterfeiter** *n*

~~counterfit~~ incorrect spelling of **counterfeit**

counterfoil /kówntər foyl/ *n* the part of a cheque, ticket, or other paper used in a financial transaction that is detached and kept by the issuer as a record

counterfort /kówntər fawrt/ *n* a buttress that sticks out at right angles from a wall [Late 16C. < French *contrefort* < Old French *contreforcier* 'buttress']

counterglow /kówntər glō/ *n* ASTRON same as **gegenschein** [Mid-19C. Translation of German *Gegenschein*]

counterhegemonic /kówntər hejjə mónnik/ *adj US* contrary to the prevailing fashion, especially in intellectual matters

counterinsurgency /kówntər in súrjənssi/ *n* military and political activities undertaken by a government to defeat a rebellion or guerrilla movement —**counterinsurgent** *n*

counterintelligence /kówntər in téllijənss/ *n* government and military activities designed to gather information about enemy spies, thwart their activities, and supply them with false information

counterintuitive /kówntər in tyóo itiv/ *adj* not in accordance with what would naturally be assumed or expected ○ *I know it's counterintuitive, but the highest grade in this system is D and the lowest is A.* —**counterintuitively** *adv*

counterirritant /kówntər írritənt/ *n* a skin cream that produces an irritation to reduce underlying tissue inflammation —**counterirritation** /kówntər irri táysh'n/ *n*

counterleak /kówntər leek/ *n* exposure to a reporter, by an anonymous source, of somebody else's leaking of information, with the result that the reporter may then suspect a conspiracy

counter lunch *n Aus* same as **counter meal** (*informal*)

countermagnet /kówntər magnət/ *n S Asia* something that exercises an equal power of attraction in drawing people away from another attractive thing ○ *The towns were intended to be countermagnets to Delhi.*

countermand /kówntər maánd, kówntər maand/ *vt* (**-mands, -manding, -manded**) **1.** CANCEL COMMAND to give an order or instruction that a previous order or instruction should not be followed **2.** CALL SOMEBODY OR SOMETHING BACK to recall somebody or something sent somewhere by a previous order ■ *n* ORDER CANCELLING ANOTHER an order cancelling a previous order [15C. < French *contremander* < Latin *mandare* (see MANDATE)]

countermarch /kówntər maarch/ *n* **1.** RETURN MARCH a march, especially one undertaken by soldiers, back from a position following the same route as that taken on the outward march **2.** CHANGE IN MARCHING DIRECTION a marching manoeuvre in which soldiers change the direction they are marching in while retaining their positions within a formation **3.** COMPLETE CHANGE OF APPROACH a complete change in somebody's behaviour or way of doing things ■ *v* (**-marches, -marching, -marched**) **1.** *vti* MARCH BACK to return from a position by marching back along the same route, or make soldiers do this **2.** *vi* CHANGE DIRECTION OF MARCHING to change the direction of a formation of marching soldiers without altering the positions of the individual soldiers

counter meal *n Aus* a meal eaten at the bar in a café or pub (*informal*)

countermeasure /kówntər mezhər/ *n* something that is done in reaction to and as a defence against a hostile action by somebody else, or something that is done in order to deal with a threat

countermine /kówntər mīn/ *v* (**-mines, -mining, -mined**) **1.** *vti* EXPLODE ENEMY'S MINES IN AREA to place explosive mines in an area in order to explode mines placed there by an enemy **2.** *vti* DIG TUNNELS AGAINST ENEMY'S TUNNELS to dig underground tunnels in order to intercept or destroy tunnels dug by an enemy **3.** *vt* SECRETLY FOIL PLOT to take secret action against somebody's plans ■ *n* **1.** TUNNEL DUG AGAINST ENEMY'S TUNNELS a tunnel dug to intercept or destroy tunnels dug by an enemy **2.** SECRET ACTION TO FOIL PLOT a secret action designed to undermine or destroy a plot or scheme

countermove /kówntər moov/ *n* a move made in response to an opponent's move, e.g. in a game ■ *vi* (**-moves, -moving, -moved**) to act in response to an opponent's action, e.g. in a game —**countermovement** *n*

counteroffensive /kówntər ə fenssiv/ *n* a major attack or series of attacks made by a military force in response to the attacks made by an enemy

counteroffer /kówntər offər/ *n* an offer made by somebody selling something, usually a reduction in what was first asked, made to persuade the buyer to improve a previous unsatisfactory offer

counterpane /kówntər payn/ *n* a cover for a bed and its bedding (*dated*) [15C. Alteration of *counterpoint*, via French < medieval Latin *culcita puncta* 'stitched quilt']

counterpart /kówntər paart/ *n* **1.** SOMEBODY OR SOMETHING CORRESPONDING TO ANOTHER somebody or something that resembles another or functions similarly in a different system or group **2.** MATCHING PART OR THING either of two parts that fit together or are complementary ○ *I identified bolt A but could not find its counterpart, socket B.* **3.** ACTOR PLAYING OPPOSITE ANOTHER an actor who plays opposite somebody else in a play or film **4.** COPY OF LEGAL DOCUMENT a copy of a lease, contract, or other legal document that is held by one party to a transaction and that duplicates the copy held by the other party

counterparty /kówntər paarti/ (*plural* **-ties**) *n* one of the two people, companies, or organizations involved in a business transaction, as referred to by the other participant in the transaction

counterplan /kówntər plan/ *n* **1.** a plan made to defeat or respond to another plan **2.** a plan prepared as an alternative or substitute for the primary plan

counterplea /kówntər plee/ *n* a plea made by the plaintiff in a court of law in response to the plea made by the defendant

counterpoint /kówntər poynt/ *n* **1.** SOUNDING TOGETHER OF MELODIES in a piece of music, the sounding together of two or more melodic lines each of which displays an individual and differentiated melodic contour and rhythmic profile **2.** MELODY COMBINED WITH ANOTHER in a piece of music, a melodic line or part that is sung or played at the same time as another **3.** CONTRASTING ELEMENT in a work of art, a theme or element that forms a contrast with another ■ *vt* (**-points, -pointing, -pointed**) **1.** CONTRAST WITH SOMETHING to make an effective contrast with something, especially in a work of art ○ *Richard's social ease counterpoints his sister's awkwardness.* **2.** ARRANGE MUSIC IN COUNTERPOINT to add one or more melodic lines in counterpoint in a piece of music [15C. Via French < medieval Latin (*cantus*) *contrapunctus* '(song) with notes marked opposite (the melody)']

counterpoise /kówntər poyz/ *n* **1.** COUNTERACTING WEIGHT a weight that balances another weight **2.** COMPENSATING FACTOR something that has the effect of diminishing or compensating for the effect of something else ○ *The government had covertly encouraged the fascists as a counterpoise to the reformers.* **3.** BALANCED STATE a state of equilibrium ■ *vt* (**-poises, -poising, -poised**) **1.** OPPOSE AND BALANCE SOMETHING to counteract or compensate for something by providing an equal force, influence, or weight **2.** MAKE SOMETHING BALANCED to bring something into a state of balance [15C. Alteration of French *contrepeis* 'counterweight']

counterproductive /kówntər prə dúktiv/ *adj* producing problems or difficulties instead of helping to achieve a goal ○ *A direct challenge to her authority is likely to be counterproductive.* —**counterproductively** *adv* —**counterproductivity** /kówntər prodduk tívvəti/ *n*

counterproof /kówntər proof/ *n* an impression taken from a new print of an engraving while it is still wet, producing a reversed image of the print

counterpunch /kówntər punch/ *n* a punch made by a boxer in response to an opponent's punch —**counterpunch** *vi* —**counterpuncher** *n*

counter-reformation *n* a reform or reform movement that seeks to reverse the effects of earlier reforms

Counter-Reformation *n* the movement of reform and regeneration instituted by the Roman Catholic Church in 1545 to counter the increasing strength of Protestantism in Europe as a result of the Reformation

counter-revolution *n* subversive activity with the aim of undoing the effects of a previous revolution and overthrowing the government or social system that it produced —**counter-revolutionist** *n*

counter-revolutionary *n* (*plural* **counter-revolutionaries**) **1.** SOMEBODY FIGHTING REVOLUTIONARY GOVERNMENT somebody, especially a member of a military force, who seeks to overthrow a national government or social system established by a revolution **2.** SOMEBODY OPPOSED TO REVOLUTION an opponent of a revolution as a means of political and social change ■ *adj* OPPOSED TO REVOLUTION opposed to a specific revolution or to revolution as a means of political and social change

countersank past tense of **countersink**

counterscarp /kówntər skaarp/ *n* the slope or bank on the outer side of the ditch outside a fort [Late 16C. Via French *contrescarpe* < Italian *controscarpa* < *scarpa* 'scarp']

countershading /kówntər shayding/ *n* a pattern of colouring on an animal's skin or coat where the upper parts are darker than the lower, counteracting the effects of sun and shade and camouflaging the animal

countershaft /kówntər shaaft/ *n* an intermediate shaft that transmits power from the main shaft to a working part but rotates in the opposite direction, especially in a belt drive or gear drive

countersign /kówntər sīn/ *vt* (**-signs, -signing, -signed**) to sign a document that somebody else has signed, e.g. as a witness to the signature or to confirm an authorization ■ *n* **1.** an agreed and secret sign, word, or signal given as a password to a military sentry in order to pass **2.** LAW same as **countersignature**

countersignature /kówntər signəchər/ *n* a signature added to a document that has already been signed, e.g. to witness the first signature or to confirm an authorization

countersink /kówntər singk/ *vt* (**-sinks, -sinking, -sank** /-sangk/, **-sunk** /-sungk/) **1.** MAKE HOLE TO INCLUDE SCREW HEAD to widen the top of the hole for a screw or bolt so that the head will fit into the hole and be level with or below the surface **2.** MAKE SCREW HEADS LEVEL WITH SURFACE to place screws, bolts, or nails in wood or another material so that their heads are level with or below the surface of the material ■ *n* **1.** HOLE THAT ACCEPTS SCREW HEAD a hole for a screw or bolt that

is wider at the top so that the head will fit into the hole and be level with or below the surface **2. COUNTERSINKING TOOL** a special drill bit or other tool for countersinking holes for screws or bolts

counterstain /kówntər stayn/ *n* an additional stain applied to a specimen to be examined under a microscope, in order to bring out features not revealed by the primary stain ■ *vt* (**-stains, -staining, -stained**) to use a counterstain on a microscope specimen

countersubject /kówntər sub jekt/ *n* a second theme or melodic line that contrasts with the main one in a fugue or other piece of music employing counterpoint

countersue /kówntər soo/ (**-sues, -suing, -sued**) *vti* to bring a lawsuit against somebody who is suing you

countersunk past participle of **countersink**

countertenor /kówntər tenər/ *n* **1.** an adult male singing voice that is higher than tenor and covers the alto range, produced by singing in falsetto **2.** a man whose singing voice is a countertenor [14C. Via French *contrateneur* < obsolete Italian *contratenore* 'against the tenor']

counterterrorism /kówntər térrərizəm/ *n* **1.** military or political activities intended to combat or prevent terrorism **2.** terrorist activities undertaken in revenge for or in retaliation against terrorism —**counterterrorist** *adj, n*

countertop /kówntər top/ *n N Am* the surface of a worktop, especially in a kitchen, or of the top of a counter in a shop

countertrade /kówntər trayd/ *n* a system of international trade in which countries exchange goods or services, rather than pay for imports with currency —**countertrader** *n*

countertransference /kówntər tránsfərənss/ *n* a process that sometimes occurs in psychoanalytic therapy where repressed emotions in the therapist are awakened by identification with the experiences and feelings of the patient

countertype /kówntər tīp/ *n* **1.** a type that is the complete opposite of another type **2.** a type that corresponds with or is equivalent to another type

countervail /kówntər váyl/ (**-vails, -vailing, -vailed**) *v* **1.** *vti* to exert a counteracting power or influence against something, especially against a harmful force, idea, or influence **2.** *vt* to offset or compensate for something [14C. < Anglo-Norman *contrevaloir*, literally 'be worth against']

countervailing duty (*plural* **countervailing duties**) *n* an import duty on commodities that can be produced very cheaply in their country of origin, e.g. because of a subsidy, imposed in order to protect domestic producers

counterweigh /kówntər wáy/ (**-weighs, -weighing, -weighed**) *vt* to counterbalance something

counterweight /kówntər wayt/ *n* **1.** a weight that balances another weight **2.** something such as a force, idea, or influence that counteracts or compensates for something else —**counterweighted** *adj*

counterwork /kówntər wurk/ *n* **1.** work or action undertaken to counteract other work or another action **2.** fortifications against an attack

countess /kówntiss, -ess, kown téss/ *n* **1.** the wife or widow of a count or earl **2.** a woman who holds the rank of count or earl [12C. Via Old French *contesse* < medieval Latin *comitissa* < Latin *comit-* 'companion']

counting /kównting/ *prep* taking a particular person or thing into consideration in a total ○ *We were thirteen in all, not counting the children in the party.*

counting house *n* the place where the financial work of a business is done or where its accounts are kept (*archaic*)

countless /kówntləss/ *adj* many more than it is possible or convenient to count ○ *I've told him countless times to be more careful.* —**countlessly** *adv*

count noun *n* a noun that refers to one thing rather than a mass of something and that can be used with 'a' or 'an', with a number, and in the plural. Examples of English count nouns are 'cat', 'sheep', and 'child'.

count palatine (*plural* **counts palatine**) *n* **1. LOCAL RULER IN HOLY ROMAN EMPIRE** a count who ruled over his own domain (**county palatine**) in the Holy Roman

Empire, or an official who ruled an area of the empire as the emperor's representative **2. SOMEBODY WITH JUDICIAL POWER OVER COUNTY** in former times, an earl or other nobleman in England or Ireland who held the highest judicial authority and other supreme powers within his own domain (**county palatine**) **3. ROMAN PALACE OFFICIAL** in the late Roman Empire, a palace official with judicial authority

countrified /kúntri fīd/, **countryfied** *adj* **1.** having a style or quality appropriate to the country ○ *a pretty, countrified row of houses* **2.** not fashionable or sophisticated and of a style or quality considered typical of rural areas

country /kúntri/ *n* (*plural* **-tries**) **1. SEPARATE NATION** a nation or state that is politically independent, or a land that was formerly independent and remains separate in some respects **2. HOMELAND** the nation or state where somebody was born or is a citizen **3. GEOGRAPHICALLY DISTINCT AREA** a large area of land regarded as distinct from other areas, e.g. because of its natural boundaries or because it is inhabited by a specific group of people **4. FARMED AND UNDEVELOPED AREA** an area that is farmed or remains in a relatively undeveloped state, as distinct from cities, towns, and other built-up areas ○ *a house in the country* **5. REGION WITH SPECIAL CHARACTER** a region that is distinguished by particular characteristics or is associated with a particular activity, person, or group of people ○ *This was chapel country, and all the pubs were closed.* **6. NATION'S PEOPLE** the people of a nation or state, especially when affected as a group by political or other events ○ *a scandal that rocked the country* **7.** MUSIC same as **country music** ■ *adj* **1. CHARACTERISTIC OF RURAL AREAS** characteristic of rural areas or the people living there **2. OF COUNTRY MUSIC** characteristic of, similar to, or performing country music [13C. < Old French *cuntrée* < assumed Vulgar Latin *(terra) contrata* '(land) lying opposite' < Latin *contra* 'against'] —**countryish** *adj* ◇ **go to the country** to hold a general election

country and western *n* MUSIC same as **country music** (*hyphenated when used before a noun*)

country bumpkin *n* same as **bumpkin**[1]

country club *n* a club for social and leisure activities with facilities for golf, tennis, or other outdoor sports, usually located in the suburbs or the country

country code *n* a code of conduct for people spending leisure time in the country, suggesting how to respect the natural environment and avoid causing damage or harm

country cousin *n* somebody from the country whose unsophisticated reactions to town life are considered amusing (*dated*)

country dance *n* a folk dance in which several couples move within a square, a circle, or two lines —**country dancing** *n*

countryfied *adj* another spelling of **countrified**

country gentleman *n* a man who owns an estate in the country

country house *n* a large house in the country, often with a large area of land attached

country-made *adj S Asia* made by hand ○ *a country-made pistol*

countryman /kúntrimən/ (*plural* **-men** /-mən/) *n* **1.** a citizen by birth or adoption of the same nation as somebody else **2.** a rural resident, especially a man brought up in the country who is familiar with rural life

country music *n* US popular music, based on the traditional music of the rural South and the cowboy music of the West, whose songs express strong personal emotions. Country musicians typically play such instruments as the guitar and fiddle. —**country musician** *n*

country park *n* an area of countryside in the United Kingdom that has been set aside for public recreational use through the agency of the Countryside Commission

Country Party *n* a former name for the National Party of Australia

countryperson /kúntri purss'n/ (*plural* **-people** /-peep'l/ or **-persons**) *n* **1.** a rural resident, especially somebody brought up in the country who is familiar with rural life **2.** a citizen by birth or adoption of the same nation as somebody else

country risk *n* the likelihood that a country will be unable or unwilling to repay its debts

country rock[1] *n* rock music that is strongly influenced by US country music

country rock[2] *n* rock that has been intruded by magma or that surrounds veins of mineral ore

country seat *n* an estate or a large house in the country that is a family's hereditary property

countryside /kúntri sīd/ *n* **1.** an area of land that is farmed or in a relatively undeveloped state ○ *a village set in wooded countryside* **2.** the people who live in a country area ○ *The entire countryside was up in arms against the proposed development.*

Countryside Commission *n* a British organization concerned with the preservation of the countryside in England and Wales and with setting up country parks for public recreation

Countryside Commission for Scotland *n* a UK organization concerned with the preservation of the countryside in Scotland and with setting up country parks for public recreation

countrywide /kúntri wīd/ *adj, adv* throughout an entire nation ○ *a countrywide organization for professional women* ○ *rates that were increased countrywide*

countrywoman /kúntri wŏŏmən/ (*plural* **-women** /-wimin/) *n* **1.** a woman who is a citizen by birth or adoption of the same nation as somebody else **2.** a woman who lives in the country, especially one brought up there who is familiar with rural life

county /kównti/ *n* (*plural* **-ties**) **1. LOCAL GOVERNMENT AREA** a unit of local government and one of the administrative subdivisions that the states of the United States and, excepting major cities, all of England and Wales are divided into **2. PEOPLE OF COUNTY** the people who live in a county ■ *adj* **SUGGESTIVE OF RICH COUNTRY FAMILIES** belonging to or associated with long-established British upper-class or wealthy families who live in the country (*informal*) ○ *girls from county families* [13C. Via Anglo-Norman *counté* < Latin *comitatus* 'group of companions' < *comit-* 'companion']

county borough *n* any town with a local government that is independent of the surrounding county, including many towns in England and Wales before 1974 and the four largest boroughs in the Republic of Ireland

county council *n* a local government body administering a county in the United Kingdom and some parts of the United States

county court *n* a local court in England and Wales with limited powers to decide civil cases, usually those concerning less than a given amount of money

county palatine (*plural* **counties palatine**) *n* **1.** the lands governed by a nobleman or imperial official with the rank of count palatine in the Holy Roman Empire **2.** formerly in England and Ireland, the lands administered by an earl or other nobleman who exercised judicial authority

county seat *n N Am* same as **county town**

county town *n* a town that is the seat of local government in a county. N Am term **county seat**

countywide /kównti wīd/ *adj, adv* throughout an entire county

coup /koo/ *n* **1.** the sudden violent overthrow of a government and seizure of political power, especially by the army **2.** a success that is unexpected and achieved with exceptional skill ○ *Getting the author to come and speak was quite a coup.* [Late 18C. Via French, 'blow' < medieval Latin *colpus* < Greek *kolophos* 'blow with the fist']

coup de foudre /kóo də fóodrə/ (*plural* **coups de foudre** /pronunc. same/) *n* something that happens suddenly and is overwhelming, especially love at first sight [< French, 'stroke of lightning']

coup de grâce /kóo də graáss/ (*plural* **coups de grâce** /pronunc. same/), **coup de grace** (*plural* **coups de grace**) *n* **1.** a final blow or shot that kills a person or animal, especially one intended to end suffering **2.** the final action that assures victory or success, especially in a sporting event [< French, 'blow of mercy']

USAGE Pronunciation trap: ***Coup de grâce*** is often mistakenly pronounced /kòo də graá/, as people, perhaps having heard words such as *bourgeois, esprit de corps,* and *foie gras* pronounced without their final consonants, imagine the expression should be pronounced in French. But the correct French pronunciation is more like the correct English pronunciation: /kòo də graáss./

coup de main /kòo də máN/ (*plural* **coups de main** /*pronunc. same*/) *n* a sudden, fierce, and successful surprise attack against an enemy [< French, 'blow of the hand']

coup d'état /kòo day taá/ (*plural* **coups d'état** /*pronunc. same*/) *n* POL same as **coup** (sense 1) [< French, 'stroke of state']

coup de théâtre /kòo də tay aátrə/ (*plural* **coups de théâtre** /*pronunc. same*/) *n* **1.** SURPRISING TURN OF EVENTS something that occurs in a very dramatic way, especially a sensational and unexpected turn of events **2.** EFFECTIVE PIECE OF THEATRE a strongly dramatic moment in a play or other theatrical production, produced by an exceptional piece of writing, performance, or staging **3.** SUCCESSFUL PLAY a play or other theatrical performance that is very successful [< French, 'stroke of theatre']

coup d'oeil /koo dőy/ (*plural* **coups d'oeil** /*pronunc. same*/) *n* a quick look at something, especially one that provides an overall general impression [< French, 'stroke of the eye']

coupe[1] /koop/ *n* **1.** a dessert of ice cream and fruit **2.** a small shallow glass bowl, often with a stem, for fruit and ice cream [Late 19C. Via French, 'goblet' < late Latin *cuppa* (see CUP)]

coupe[2] /koop, kòo pay/ *n N Am* same as **coupé** (sense 1) [Early 20C. Variant of COUPÉ]

coupé /kòo pay/ *n* **1.** CAR WITH TWO DOORS a car with two doors, a sloping back, and a hard fixed roof. N Am term **coupe**[2] **2.** TWO-SEATER CARRIAGE a closed four-wheeled carriage that has two inside seats for passengers and a driver's seat outside at the front **3.** END COMPARTMENT IN RAILCAR an end compartment in an old type of European railway carriage, with seats on one side only [Mid-19C. < French *(carrosse) coupé* 'cut-down (carriage)' (because smaller than earlier models), past participle of *couper* 'cut' (see COPE [1])]

Couperin /kòopə ran, -raN/, **François** (1668–1733) French composer and organist. The best-known member of a musical family, his baroque keyboard compositions greatly influenced Johann Sebastian Bach. Known as **Le Grand**

couple /kúpp'l/ *n* **1.** TWO SIMILAR THINGS two things of the same kind that are together or are considered as a pair ○ *found a couple of mugs in the cupboard* **2.** SEVERAL a few things of the same kind ○ *There are a couple of questions I'm not sure about.* **3.** TWO PEOPLE SHARING LIVES two people who are married, are living together, or have an intimate relationship **4.** TWO PEOPLE DOING SOMETHING TOGETHER two people, especially a man and a woman, who are sitting, walking, dancing, or working together ○ *There were only a few couples on the dance floor.* **5.** SOMETHING THAT JOINS something that links or joins two similar things **6.** MECH ENG SYSTEM OF OPPOSING FORCES in mechanics, a system of two equal forces that are parallel and operate in opposite directions **7.** FIELD SPORTS PAIR OF DOGS a pair of hunting dogs attached to each other by a leash, or the double collar and leash on which they are held **8.** PHYS, ELEC ELECTRICAL CONTACT a connection of two dissimilar metals that develops an electric current in the presence of an electrical conductor **(electrolyte)** ■ *v* **(-ples, -pling, -pled) 1.** *vt* ASSOCIATE TWO THINGS to associate or combine one person or thing with another ○ *High prices coupled with poor living conditions made their lives difficult.* **2.** *vt* JOIN TWO THINGS to join or link two things or people ○ *to couple freight cars* **3.** *vi* HAVE SEX to have sexual intercourse (*formal*) [13C. Via French < Latin *copula* 'link'] —**coupledom** *n*

USAGE When ***couple*** refers to two partners or married people, it may be treated as either singular or plural: *The couple wants to be married before the end of the year. The couple have not been reconciled, and continue to live apart.* However, if a pronoun refers to the word, it is almost always plural (*they, them, their*), and so the verb should be plural as well: *The couple have repeatedly asked that their privacy be respected.* In other uses, ***couple*** is often followed by *of* and a plural noun, in which case it is treated as plural: *A couple of books were on the table.* In informal uses the strict sense of 'two' may be expanded to 'several'. The use of ***couple*** without *of* in such contexts (*I bought a couple CDs*) is increasingly heard but should be avoided in formal writing.

coupler /kúpplər/ *n* **1.** on an organ or harpsichord, a mechanical or electronic device that connects two keyboards so that all the keys can be played from one keyboard **2.** something or somebody that joins or combines two things **3.** ENG same as **coupling** (sense 4) **4.** *US* same as **coupling** (sense 5)

couplet /kúpplət/ *n* two lines of verse that form a unit alone or as part of a poem, especially two that rhyme and have the same metre [Late 16C. < French, 'little couple' < *couple* (see COUPLE)]

coupling /kúppling/ *n* **1.** SOMETHING THAT JOINS TWO THINGS something that joins two things, especially a device for connecting two pieces of pipe, hose, or tube **2.** JOINING TWO THINGS TOGETHER a joining together or linking of two persons or things ○ *a disastrous coupling of two very different singers* **3.** SEX ACT an act of sexual intercourse **4.** MECH ENG LINK THAT TRANSFERS POWER a part of a mechanical system by which power is transmitted from one rotating part to another part **5.** *UK, ANZ, Can* RAIL CONNECTOR FOR RAILWAY CARRIAGES a device on railway carriages that is used to link them in a train. US term **coupler 6.** ZOOL TRUNK OF ANIMAL'S BODY the part of the body of a four-legged animal between the forequarters and hindquarters **7.** ELEC CONNECTION OF ELECTRICAL CIRCUITS a means of connecting two electrical circuits so that power can be passed between them, or the process of connecting electrical circuits in this way

coupon /kòo pon/ *n* **1.** VOUCHER REDEEMED BY STORE OR COMPANY a voucher that entitles somebody to a discount, refund, gift, or place in a draw, typically issued as a sales promotion **2.** ORDER FORM a printed form, e.g. in an advertisement, that may be filled in and returned to order a product or request information **3.** FORM FOR PAYMENT BY INSTALMENTS a form or card showing the payment due on a specific date for something that was bought by hire purchase. The card is returned with the payment. **4.** CERTIFICATE OF INTEREST ON BOND a detachable part of a bond that indicates a date and the amount of interest paid on that date. The holder must present it in order to receive payment of the interest. **5.** TICKET IN RATIONING SYSTEM a ticket issued in a rationing system that entitles somebody to an amount of a rationed item and that must be handed over in exchange for that item **6.** ENTRY FORM FOR FOOTBALL POOLS an entry form for the football pools, with lists of fixtures against which entrants can mark their bets of a draw or a home or away win [Early 19C. < French, 'piece cut off' < *couper* (see COPE [1])]

couponing /kòopəning/ *n* the use of coupons as a means of promoting a product's sales or of saving money on purchases

courage /kúrrij/ *n* the ability to face danger, difficulty, uncertainty, or pain without being overcome by fear or being deflected from a chosen course of action ○ *She showed great courage throughout this difficult time.* [13C. < Old French *corage* < Latin *cor* 'heart'] —**courageous** /kə ráyjəss/ *adj* —**courageously** *adv* —**courageousness** *n*

CULTURAL NOTE ***The Red Badge of Courage***, a novel by US writer Stephen Crane (1895). Set during the American Civil War, it tells the story of an idealistic soldier, Henry Fleming, who panics in battle and temporarily deserts. During a scuffle with another deserter, he receives a minor wound. Returning to battle bearing this 'badge of courage', he performs with heroism but is wracked by guilt.

SYNONYMS ***courage, bravery, valour, fearlessness, nerve, guts, pluck, mettle***

CORE MEANING: personal resoluteness in the face of danger or difficulties

courage the ability to face danger, difficulty, uncertainty, or pain without being overcome by fear or being deflected from a chosen course of action ○ *a supreme act of courage under fire* ○ *She must pluck up courage and tell him the truth.* **bravery** courage in the face of danger, difficulty, or pain ○ *A friend paid tribute to his bravery throughout his long illness.* **valour** courage, especially that shown in war or battle ○ *He was awarded the George Medal for his valour.* ○ *He praised the valour and determination of our troops.* **fearlessness** resoluteness in the face of dangers or challenges ○ *a police officer displaying determination, fearlessness, and devotion to duty* ○ *We walked on the high Wells Road viaduct with the fearlessness of the young.* **nerve** coolness, steadiness, and self-assurance ○ *He didn't have the nerve to upset his boss's plans.* ○ *She almost lost her nerve and backed out.* **guts** (*slang*) strength of character and boldness ○ *It takes a lot of guts to get back to normal activities after such a terrible injury.* ○ *Why don't they have the guts to tackle the government?* **pluck** courage and determination in meeting danger or difficulty ○ *Very few people have had the pluck to stand up to their mother.* ○ *It took pluck to face up to her critics.* **mettle** spirited determination ○ *Only time will tell if she has the mettle to rise to the challenge.* ○ *He showed his mettle in putting on the show against the odds.*

~~**courageous**~~ incorrect spelling of **courageous**

courante /kòo raánt/ *n* **1.** a musical composition in quick triple time, often part of a baroque suite **2.** a dance of French and Italian origin in triple time with short quick steps [Late 16C. < French, 'running']

Courbet /kòor bay/, **Gustave** (1819–77) French painter. He was a leading French realist with such controversial works as *Burial at Ornans* (1850). A supporter of the Paris Commune (1871), he died in exile.

> 'To record the manners, ideas, and aspect of the age as I myself saw them—to be a man as well as a painter—in short to create a living art—that is my aim.'
> [Gustave Courbet, *Realism*; 1855]

coureur de bois /koo rúr də bwaá/ (*plural* **coureurs de bois** /*pronunc. same*/) *n* somebody of French or French and Native American descent who trapped and traded furs in the 18th and 19th centuries in the north and northwest of what is now Canada [Early 18C. < French, 'woods runner']

courgette /kawr zhét/ *n UK* PLANTS, FOOD a small vegetable marrow eaten cooked or sometimes raw in salads. ANZ, N Am term **zucchini** [Mid-20C. < French, 'small gourd', via Old French *cohourde* < Latin *cucurbita*]

courier /kòorri ər/ *n* **1.** SOMEBODY PROVIDING DELIVERY SERVICE a person or company that delivers documents or small and valuable packages by hand **2.** OFFICIAL MESSENGER a diplomat, soldier, or other person with the responsibility of carrying and delivering official documents **3.** SECRET MESSENGER a smuggler or illicit carrier of something such as illegal drugs **4.** TRAVELLERS' GUIDE a paid guide and helper who accompanies a group of travellers and makes arrangements for them, especially somebody employed by a travel agency to do this ■ *vt* **(-ers, -ering, -ered)** SEND SOMETHING BY COURIER to send a document or package by a commercial courier service [14C. < French, 'runner' < Latin *currere* 'to run']

Courrèges /kòo rézh, -ráyzh/, **André** (*b.* 1923) French fashion designer. Alongside Pierre Cardin and Mary Quant, he was a creator of the space-age look of the 1960s, characterized by miniskirts (1964), white boots, and trouser suits.

course /kawrss/ *n* **1.** PROGRAMME OF STUDY a programme of study or training, especially one that leads to a qualification from an educational institution **2.** UNIT IN EDUCATIONAL PROGRAMME one of several distinct units that together form a programme of study leading to a qualification such as a degree ○ *a short course in comparative literature* **3.** DIRECTION TRAVELLED the direction or route along which something travels **4.** PATH OF RIVER the route followed by a river or stream or by something very long such as a road or boundary **5.** ACTION CHOSEN an action or series of actions that somebody decides to take ○ *The simplest course of action would be to say nothing.* **6.** SEQUENCE OF EVENTS the progression or development of a sequence of events, especially a development that is normal or expected ○ *events that changed the course of history* **7.** PERIOD OF TIME the progression or development of a period of time ○ *in the course of the afternoon* **8.** PART OF MEAL one of two or more different dishes or types of food that are served in sequence during a meal **9.** ESTABLISHED SEQUENCE OF TREATMENT a sequence of medical treatment, exercise, or medi-

cation that is followed over a period of time ○ *on a course of antidepressants* **10.** **PLACE FOR RACE OR SPORT** an area where a race is run or where a sport in which players progress over the area is played ○ *a golf course* **11.** **ONWARD MOVEMENT** swift onward movement ○ *Nothing could interrupt his headlong course.* **12.** **GREYHOUND CHASE** a chase or race by dogs such as greyhounds **13.** **LAYER OF BRICKS** one of the layers of bricks that make up a wall **14.** **LOWEST SAIL ON SHIP** the lowest sail or row of sails on a square-rigged ship ■ *v* (**courses, coursing, coursed**) **1.** *vi* **RUN FAST** to flow or run swiftly **2.** *vti* **HUNT ANIMALS WITH GREYHOUNDS** to hunt animals, especially hares, with greyhounds or other dogs that hunt by sight **3.** *vt* **USE GREYHOUNDS FOR HUNTING** to use greyhounds or other dogs that hunt by sight [13C. Via French *cours* < Latin *cursus*, past participle of *currere* 'to run'] ◇ **in due course** after the lapse of an appropriate period of time ◇ **of course** **1.** without any question or doubt ○ *Of course you must go!* **2.** used to show that the speaker has just understood something or agrees with something ○ *'We must tell nobody about this'. 'Of course'.* **3.** used to point out a possibility that somebody may not have considered **4.** as may be expected ○ *Of course, we were hoping it would never happen to us.* ◇ **off course** away from the direction that you were going in ○ *The boat was blown off course.* ◇ **on course** in the right direction, or in a favourable position to achieve what you want to do ○ *We were on course to complete the project on time.*

SPELLCHECK See *coarse.*

course book *n* a book that is used by students and teachers as the basis of a course of study

courser[1] /káwrssər/ *n* **1.** a dog that is trained to hunt its quarry by sight instead of by scent **2.** a hunter who uses coursers [Early 17C. < COURSE]

courser[2] /káwrssər/ *n* a strong swift horse (*literary*) [13C. < Old French *corsier* < Latin *cursus* (see COURSE)]

courser[3] /káwrssər/ *n* a bird related to plovers that is a swift runner. Native to: dry regions of Africa and Asia. Subfamily: Glariolidae. [Mid-18C. Anglicization of modern Latin *Cursorius* < Latin *cursor* (see CURSORY)]

courseware /káwrss wair/ *n* software and data used in computer-based training [Late 20C. < COURSE + SOFTWARE]

coursework /káwrss wurk/ *n* work that is assigned to students as part of an educational course and counts towards the assessment given for the course

coursing /káwrssing/ *n* the sport of hunting with dogs such as greyhounds that follow their quarry using sight instead of scent

court[1] /kawrt/ *n* **1.** **MEETING WHERE LEGAL JUDGMENTS ARE MADE** a session of an official body that has authority to try cases, resolve disputes, or make other legal decisions ○ *She's threatening to take us to court over this.* **2.** *also* **Court** **JUDGE** the constituted authority presiding over a court of law ○ *The court heard opening arguments on Tuesday.* **3.** **COURTROOM OR COURTHOUSE** a place where a court of law is held **4.** **PEOPLE IN COURTROOM** all those present in a courtroom ○ *The court shall rise.* **5.** **OPEN SPACE WITHIN WALLS** an open space partly or completely surrounded by buildings and walls **6.** **OPEN AREA INSIDE BUILDING** a large open or roofless area within a building **7.** **AREA FOR BALL GAME** an area marked out for playing a sport such as tennis or basketball **8.** **MONARCH'S ATTENDANTS** the ministers, courtiers, and officials of the royal household who attend a king or queen **9.** **MEETING OF MONARCH AND ATTENDANTS** an occasion when a king or queen and the ministers, courtiers, and officials of the royal household are assembled **10.** **MONARCH'S RESIDENCE** the place where a king or queen and the court are usually in residence **11.** **IMPORTANT PERSON'S FOLLOWERS** a group of people who devote their time to the service and flattery of a noble, rich, or important person **12.** **SHORT STREET** a short street of houses that is closed at one end **13.** **GROUP OF HOUSES** a group of houses built around an open space **14.** **BLOCK OF FLATS** a large building containing many flats or offices **15.** **LARGE HOUSE** a large and imposing house and the land surrounding it (*often used in placenames*) **16.** **GOVERNING BODY** the governing body or council of an organization such as a corporation or academic institution [13C. Via Anglo-Norman < Old French *cort* < Latin *cohort-* 'enclosed space'] ◇ **be laughed out of court** to be ridiculed so severely that what you have to say is not considered seriously (*informal*) ◇ **pay court to somebody** **1.** to try to win influence with somebody or to win somebody's approval or favour through flattery or attentiveness **2.** to try to gain somebody's love (*dated*) ◇ **rule something out of court** to refuse absolutely to allow something to take place

court[2] /kawrt/ (**courts, courting, courted**) *v* **1.** *vt* **BE ATTENTIVE TO SOMEBODY** to try to win influence with somebody or to win somebody's approval or favour through flattery or attentiveness **2.** *vt* **TRY TO GAIN SOMETHING** to try to gain something such as somebody's attention or admiration by behaving in ways that are intended to attract or encourage it **3.** *vt* **RISK EXPERIENCING SOMETHING BAD** to behave in a way that increases the likelihood of failure, injury, or other misfortune ○ *courted disaster* **4.** *vt* **WOO SOMEBODY** to try to gain somebody's love (*dated*) **5.** *vi* **BE SWEETHEARTS** to spend time together in a romantic relationship as a prelude to getting married (*dated*) ○ *We used to come here when we were courting.* **6.** *vt* ZOOL **TRY TO ATTRACT MATE** to engage in behaviour that is designed to attract another animal or bird as a mate [Early 16C. < Old Italian *corteare* < Latin *cohort-* 'enclosed space']

Court /kawrt/, **Margaret Jean** (*b.* 1942) Australian tennis player. She was the winner of the Wimbledon women's singles championship in 1963, 1965, and 1970. In 1970 she also completed the grand slam. She has a record 62 grand slam victories. Born **Smith, Margaret Jean**

court bouillon /káwrt bōō yon/ *n* a liquid used for poaching fish, made with water flavoured with vegetables, herbs, and wine or vinegar. The liquid is discarded after the fish has been poached. [< French, 'short broth']

court card *n* any of the kings, queens, and jacks in a pack of playing cards. N Am term **face card**

court case *n* LAW same as **case**[1] *n* (sense 5)

court circular *n* an account of what a country's monarch will be doing that day, along with other news of the royal family, published in a leading national newspaper

court cupboard *n* a sideboard or cabinet with some open shelves for display, used especially in the 16th and 17th centuries

court dress *n* the type and style of clothing that is officially approved for wear at a royal court

Courtenay /káwrtni/, **Bryce** (*b.* 1933) South African-born Australian writer. He wrote the bestselling novel *The Power of One* (1989). Full name **Courtenay, Arthur Bryce**

courteous /kúrti əss/ *adj* polite in a way that shows consideration of others or good manners [13C. < Old French *corteis* 'courtly' < *cort* (see COURT[1])] —**courteously** *adv* —**courteousness** *n*

courtesan /káwrti zán, káwrti zan/ *n* a prostitute or mistress, especially one associated with a rich, powerful, or upper-class man who provides her with luxuries and status [Mid-16C. Via French *courtisane* < Italian *cortigiana* 'female courtier' < *corte* 'court' < Latin *cohort-* 'enclosed space']

courtesy /kúrtəssi/ *n* (*plural* **-sies**) **1.** **POLITE OR CONSIDERATE BEHAVIOUR** consideration for other people, or good manners ○ *He didn't even have the courtesy to offer me a seat.* **2.** **POLITE OR CONSIDERATE ACTION** something done out of politeness or consideration for another person ○ *We should certainly go, if only as a courtesy to Helen.* ■ *adj* **1.** **FOR SAKE OF POLITENESS** given or done as a courtesy ○ *a courtesy call* **2.** **PROVIDED FREE** provided free of charge ○ *Your courtesy limousine will take you to the airport.* [13C. < Old French *curtesie* < *corteis* 'courtly' < Latin *cohort-* 'enclosed space'] ◇ **(by) courtesy of somebody** through somebody's generosity or help

courtesy card *n* a card given to customers of a supermarket or other business that entitles them to special benefits or privileges

courtesy light *n* a light inside the passenger compartment of a vehicle that turns on automatically when the door is opened

courtesy title *n* a personal title that is used to address somebody out of politeness or as a social convention even though the person is not professionally or socially entitled to it

court hand *n* a style of handwriting formerly used by legal clerks

courthouse /káwrt howss/ (*plural* **-houses** /-howziz/) *n* a building where a court of law is held

courtier /káwrti ər/ *n* **1.** an aristocrat who frequents a royal court or attends a king or queen **2.** somebody who flatters a more important person [13C. < Anglo-Norman *courteour* < Old French *courtoyer* 'be at court' < *cort* (see COURT[1])]

~~**courtious**~~ incorrect spelling of **courteous**

court leet (*plural* **courts leet**) *n* LAW, HIST same as **leet**[1]

courtly /káwrtli/ (**-lier, -liest**) *adj* **1.** **WITH REFINED MANNERS** showing great delicacy and refinement in behaviour **2.** **OF HIGHEST QUALITY** rich or fine and suitable for a royal court **3.** **INSINCERELY POLITE** insincerely polite or deferential in order to win somebody's favour —**courtliness** *n*

courtly love *n* a medieval European code of behaviour that idealized the love of a knight for a usually married noblewoman and prescribed how they should act towards each other

court martial (*plural* **courts martial** or **court martials**) *n* **1.** a military court that tries members of the armed forces and others for offences under military law **2.** a trial by court martial

court-martial (**court-martials, court-martialling, court-martialled**) *vt* to try somebody by a military court for an offence under military law

Court of Appeal *n* a branch of the Supreme Court in England and Wales that hears civil and criminal appeals from other courts

court of chancery *n* in the United States, a court of equity, ruling on matters not covered by common law

Court of Chancery *n* a division of the High Court in England and Wales, presided over by the Lord Chancellor

court of claims *n* a US federal court that has jurisdiction over claims brought against the government

Court of Common Pleas *n* a former higher court with jurisdiction over civil cases in England and Wales

court of enquiry *n* **1.** a group specially set up to investigate a matter of public concern such as the cause of a disaster **2.** a military tribunal that investigates a matter of concern, especially in order to determine whether official charges should be brought

court of equity *n* a court in England and Wales belonging to a court system organized under the Lord Chancellor that dispenses judgments on the basis of principles of equity, e.g. in cases of wills and trusts

Court of Exchequer *n* a former civil court with jurisdiction over revenue cases

court of first instance *n* a court in which legal proceedings are started, in particular one attached to the European Court of Justice

court of honour *n* a military court that investigates questions involving personal honour

Court of Justiciary *n* LAW same as **High Court of Justiciary**

court of law *n* a court that hears legal cases and issues rulings based on legal statutes or common law

court of record *n* a court that has its proceedings placed on an official permanent record and has the power to give penalties for contempt of court

Court of Saint James's *n* the court of the monarch of the United Kingdom, to which ambassadors are accredited

Court of Session *n* the highest civil court in Scotland

court of summary jurisdiction (*plural* **courts of summary jurisdiction**) *n* **1.** a court, especially a magistrate's court, that tries minor offences without a jury **2.** a magistrate's court in an Australian state or territory

court order *n* an official order issued by the judge of a court, requiring or forbidding somebody to do something

court plaster *n* cloth treated on one side with isinglass or another adhesive substance, formerly

used to bandage small cuts, hide skin blemishes, and simulate beauty spots [< its use by ladies at court]

Courtrai /koor tráy/ city in West Flanders, western Belgium. It is known for its textile industries. Population: 75,099 (1999).

court recorder *n UK* somebody who records the proceedings of a law court and prepares a verbatim report of them. ANZ, N Am term **court reporter**

court reporter *n ANZ, N Am* same as **court recorder**

court roll *n* the register of the lands held by a medieval manor

courtroom /káwrt room, -ro͝om/ *n* a room used for holding a session of a court of law

courtship /káwrt ship/ *n* **1.** TRYING TO GAIN SOMEBODY'S LOVE the act of paying attention to somebody with a view to developing a more intimate relationship **2.** PRELUDE TO MARRIAGE the period of a romantic relationship before marriage **3.** INGRATIATING BEHAVIOUR friendly and often ingratiating attention for the purpose of winning a favour or establishing an alliance or other relationship **4.** ZOOL MATING BEHAVIOUR behaviour designed to attract another animal or bird as a mate, or the time during which an animal or bird engages in this

court shoe *n* a woman's shoe that is plain and cut low in front and has a moderately high heel. N Am term **pump**[2]

courtside /káwrt sīd/ *adj, adv* at the side of an athletics court where a match or game such as tennis or basketball is being played

court tennis *n N Am* same as **real tennis**

courtyard /káwrt yaard/ *n* an area of ground that is surrounded by buildings, lies inside a large building, or is adjacent to a building and enclosed by walls

couscous /ko͝oss kooss/ *n* **1.** a food resembling tiny grains, made from semolina and cooked by steaming or soaking in boiling water **2.** a North African dish consisting of a spicy stew of meat and vegetables served with couscous [Late 16C. Via French < Arabic *kuskus* < *kaskasa* 'pulverize']

cousin /kúzz'n/ *n* **1.** UNCLE'S OR AUNT'S CHILD a child of somebody's uncle or aunt **2.** DISTANT RELATIVE somebody to whom somebody else is related through the brother or sister of a grandparent, great-grandparent, or an even older ancestor **3.** SOMEBODY WITH MUCH IN COMMON somebody with whom another feels connected because of similar ancestry, ethnic background, or interests ○ *our Canadian cousins* **4.** RELATED THING something that is similar to or connected with something else ○ *The new idea is a cousin of chaos theory.* **5.** TERM OF ADDRESS BETWEEN SOVEREIGNS used by European sovereigns as a term of address for another sovereign or a member of a royal family [13C. Via French < Latin *consobrinus* 'mother's sister's child' < *sobrinus* 'maternal cousin'] —**cousinhood** *n* —**cousinly** *adj*

Cousin /koo záN/, **Victor** (1792–1867) French philosopher. He wrote studies of Blaise Pascal and Immanuel Kant. His original works include *Philosophical Fragments* (1826).

> 'Art for art's sake.'
> [Victor Cousin, 'Cours de philosophie', *Du Vrai, du beau et du bien (Lectures on the True, the Beautiful, and the Good)*; 1853]

cousin german (*plural* **cousins german**) *n* same as **cousin** (sense 1) (*dated*) [14C. < French *cousin germain*; *germain* < Latin *germanus* (see GERMAN)]

Cousteau /koostṓ/, **Jacques** (1910–97) French film director and underwater explorer. He invented the aqualung (1943). His films include the Oscar-winning *The Golden Fish* (1959).

> 'The sea is the universal sewer.'
> [Jacques Cousteau. Quoted in *Speaking Freely*, Stuart Berg Flexner and Anne H. Soukhanov; 1997]

couth /kooth/ *adj* showing very good manners or great social sophistication (*humorous*) [Late 19C. Back-formation < UNCOUTH]

couthie /ko͝othi/, **couthy** (**-ier, -iest**) *adj Scotland* **1.** FRIENDLY acting in a friendly or sociable way **2.** COMFORTABLE comfortable and homely **3.** HOMESPUN without pretensions or complications [Early 18C. < Scots *couth* 'kind, agreeable' < Old English *cūþ* (see UNCOUTH)]

couture /koo tyo͝or/ *n* **1.** the design and production of fashionable high-quality custom-made clothes **2.** high-quality clothing made to order by a fashion designer [Early 20C. Via French < late Latin *consutura* 'sewing together' < Latin *suere* 'sew']

couturier /koo tyo͝ori ay/ *n* a designer of fashionable high-quality custom-made clothes [Late 19C. < French, 'dressmaker' < *couture* (see COUTURE)]

couturière /koo tyo͝ori áir/ *n* a female designer of fashionable high-quality custom-made clothes [Early 19C. < French, feminine of *couturier* (see COUTURIER)]

couturify /koo tyo͝ori fī/ (**-fies, -fying, -fied**) *vt* to make a garment stylish by using fine fabrics, unusual colours, or other features of designer clothing (*informal*) [Late 20C. < COUTURE]

couvade /koo vaád/ *n* the mimicking of childbirth by the father while it is taking place, a custom in some Native South American societies [Mid-19C. < French, 'hatching' < *couver* 'to hatch' < Latin *cubare* 'lie down']

Cov., cov. *abbr* STATS covariance

covalence /kō váylənss/ *n N Am* CHEM same as **covalency**

covalency /kō váylənssi/ *n* chemical valency involving the sharing of electrons

covalent /kō váylənt/ *adj* describes a chemical bond in which the attractive force between atoms is created by the sharing of electrons —**covalently** *adv*

covariance /kō váiri ənss/ *n* a statistical measure of the tendency of two variables to change in conjunction with each other. It is equal to the product of their standard deviations and correlation coefficients.

covariant /kō vairi ənt/ *adj* exhibiting a tendency to change in conjunction with another statistical variable

cove[1] /kōv/ *n* **1.** BAY IN SHORELINE a small bay on the shore of the sea or a lake, especially one that is enclosed by high cliffs **2.** NOOK IN CLIFF a small semicircular recessed valley in the side of a hill or cliff **3.** CURVE AT TOP OF WALL an inwardly curved surface at the point where a wall meets a ceiling **4.** CURVED MOULDING a moulding that curves inwards ■ *vti* (**coves, coving, coved**) HAVE OR GIVE INWARD CURVE to have a cove, or design or build a wall with a cove [Old English *cofa* 'bedchamber, alcove' < Germanic, 'hollow place providing shelter']

cove[2] /kōv/ *n* same as **man** *n* (sense 1) (*dated slang*) [Mid-16C. Probably < Romany *kova* 'person, thing']

covellite /kō vél īt/ *n* a purple mineral consisting of thin sheets of copper sulphide [Mid-19C. After Niccolò *Covelli* (1790–1829), Italian mineralogist]

coven /kúvv'n/ *n* a meeting or group of witches, usually 13 in number [Mid-17C. Variant of obsolete *covin* 'company, agreement', via French < medieval Latin *convenium* < Latin *convenire* (see CONVENE)]

covenant /kúvvənənt/ *n* **1.** SOLEMN AGREEMENT a solemn agreement that is binding on all parties **2.** LAW LEGALLY BINDING AGREEMENT a formal and legally binding agreement or contract such as a lease, or one of the clauses in an agreement of this kind. A covenant is often used to require an owner or user of a piece of land to do or refrain from doing something. **3.** LAW LAWSUIT FOR BREACH OF AGREEMENT a lawsuit for damages that is brought because of the breaking of a legal covenant **4.** BIBLE MUTUAL PROMISES OF GOD AND ISRAELITES in the Bible, the promises that were made between God and the Israelites, who agreed to worship no other gods ■ *vt* (**-nants, -nanting, -nanted**) PROMISE LEGALLY TO DO SOMETHING to promise something in a covenant, especially, formerly, regular payments of a stated amount to a charity in a deed of covenant [13C. < Old French, present participle of *convenir* 'agree' (see CONVENE)] —**covenantal** /kúvvə nánt'l/ *adj* —**covenantally** *adv*

Covenant *n* an agreement by which Scottish Presbyterians united to defend their church on several occasions in the 17th century

covenantee /kúvvənən teé/ *n* somebody to whom something is promised in a covenant

covenanter /kúvvənəntər/, **covenantor** *n* somebody who undertakes a covenant

Covenanter *n* a defender of the Scottish Presbyterian Church who joined its Covenant during the 17th century

covenant marriage *n* in the United States, a form of marriage contract whose statute imposes stricter than usual conditions for couples wishing to marry or get divorced, e.g. premarital counselling and a two-year separation prior to divorce

covenantor *n* LAW another spelling of **covenanter**

Coventry /kóvvəntri/ historic cathedral city in Warwickshire, England, and the home of Warwick University. It has also been a car manufacturing centre. Population: 301,900 (2000). ◇ **send somebody to Coventry** to refuse to speak to or associate with somebody as a punishment or mark of disapproval

coventure /kō vénchər/, **co-venture** *vti* (**-tures, -turing, -tured**) to undertake a business venture in partnership with another person or company ■ *n* a business agreement, deal, or partnership involving two or more companies

cover /kúvvər/ *v* (**-ers, -ering, -ered**) **1.** *vt* PUT SOMETHING OVER SOMETHING ELSE to put something over the whole of or the upper surface of something, e.g. in order to hide, protect, or decorate it **2.** *vt* BE ALL OVER SOMETHING to lie across or in a layer over the whole of or the upper surface of something ○ *rocks covered with seaweed* **3.** *vt* KEEP SOMEBODY WARM to put something such as a blanket over or around somebody for warmth ○ *She covered him with the quilt.* **4.** *vt* BE WRAPPED AROUND SOMETHING to be lying over or wrapped around somebody to provide warmth ○ *She was covered only by a thin blanket.* **5.** *vt* PUT CLOTHING ON to put a piece of clothing on part of your own or somebody else's body ○ *Keep your head covered if you're going out.* **6.** *vt* BE WORN ON BODY to be worn on part of the body **7.** *vt* PUT LID ON SOMETHING to put a lid or protective covering over something **8.** *vt* TALK OR WRITE ABOUT SOMETHING to deal with a subject in a discussion, speech, book, or article ○ *His talk covered several aspects of company law.* **9.** *vt* PROVIDE NEWS OF SOMETHING to be responsible for reporting, videotaping, or photographing an event or a particular class of events for a newspaper or a broadcasting company ○ *covers foreign affairs for a cable channel* **10.** *vt* INCLUDE INSTANCE to take something into account and provide an adequate treatment of it ○ *The law only covers commercial vehicles.* **11.** *vt* EXTEND OVER AREA to include the whole of an area, either physically or as a field of operations or responsibility ○ *an office complex covering three blocks* ○ *a long-term development blueprint covering the whole of the city* **12.** *vt* TRAVEL DISTANCE to travel a particular distance **13.** *vt* HIDE SOMETHING to conceal a feeling, action, or situation by presenting a different appearance or directing attention elsewhere ○ *covered my mistake by changing the subject* **14.** *vt* INSUR INSURE SOMEBODY to provide insurance protection to somebody **15.** *vt* INSUR INSURE AGAINST SOMETHING to provide insurance protection against a type of hazard or risk **16.** *vt* PAY FOR SOMETHING to be sufficient to pay for something ○ *£20 should cover it.* **17.** *vt* PROTECT SOMEBODY OR SOMETHING FROM ATTACK to protect somebody, a part of an army, or a piece in chess or another game from attack by occupying a position nearby **18.** *vt* AIM GUN AT SOMEBODY OR SOMETHING to have a person or place in the aim or range of a gun, especially in order to provide protection against a possible attack **19.** *vt* WATCH SOMEBODY OR SOMETHING to maintain a watch on or a patrol of something, e.g. to track somebody's movements ○ *covered the rear exit to block their escape* **20.** *vt* INFUSE SOMEBODY to bring an overwhelming amount of some quality upon yourself or somebody else (*often passive*) ○ *was covered in confusion* **21.** *vi* DO SOMEBODY'S JOB to do the work of somebody who is absent for a time ○ *He's covering for me while I'm away.* **22.** *vi* TELL LIES FOR SOMEBODY to keep people from learning the real truth about somebody ○ *covered for him by lying* **23.** *vt* ZOOL COPULATE WITH FEMALE to copulate with a female animal, especially a mare (*refers especially to stallions*) **24.** *vt* CARDS PLAY HIGHER CARD to play a card that has a higher value than one already played by somebody else **25.** *vti* FIN BUY REPLACEMENT STOCK to buy shares of stock or commodities in order to replace others that have been borrowed from a broker and sold with the expectation that the price will fall **26.** *vt* GAMBLING MATCH ANOTHER GAMBLER'S BET to match the amount of money bet by another gambler **27.** *vt*

MUSIC **RECORD NEW VERSION OF SONG** to record a new version of a song that was first sung or made popular by another performer **28.** *vt* SPORTS **DEFEND AREA AGAINST OPPONENT** to play in defence against a particular opponent or in a particular position or area on a playing surface ■ *n* **1. SOMETHING THAT COVERS SOMETHING** one thing that hides, protects, or covers something else, or is used to cover something **2. LID** something that covers the top of a container, e.g. a lid **3. BINDING OF BOOK OR MAGAZINE** the protective binding, thick paper, or boards at the front and back of a book or magazine **4. CLOTH THAT COVERS FURNITURE** a cloth or plastic covering for bedding or a piece of furniture **5. SHELTER FROM WEATHER** shelter from the weather, or the providing of shelter from the weather **6. SHELTER FROM DANGER** concealment or protection, especially that provided by undergrowth where animals can hide or by a shelter from attack ○ *took cover under the trees* **7. VEGETATION** the plants that cover an area of land **8. DEFENCE AGAINST ATTACK** protection provided, especially to an attacking force, by other forces located nearby or in the air ○ *air cover* **9. PROTECTIVE PRETENCE** a false identity or a pretext that provides protection for somebody such as a spy or detective **10. SUBSTITUTES FOR WORKERS** people who are available to do other people's jobs when they are absent ○ *24-hour emergency cover* **11. PLACE LAID AT TABLE** a place laid at table, e.g. in a restaurant ○ *covers laid for 16 guests* **12.** COMM same as **cover charge 13.** CRICKET same as **cover point 14.** INSUR **INSURANCE PROTECTION** the amount or type of protection provided by an insurance policy. Aus, N Am term **coverage 15.** FIN **ENOUGH MONEY** sufficient funds or guaranteed income to meet a liability or cover a planned expenditure **16.** MUSIC **NEW RECORDING OF WELL-KNOWN SONG** a recording by a performer of a song that was first sung or popularized by another performer **17.** MUSIC **UNDERSTUDY** an understudy for a musical role **18.** STAMPS **ENVELOPE** a postmarked envelope ■ **covers** *npl* **1. COVERINGS ON BED** the sheets, blankets, and other coverings on a bed **2. WATERPROOF SHEETS PROTECTING SPORTS FIELD** sheets of waterproof material spread over a playing surface to protect it against rain **3.** CRICKET **OFF-SIDE FIELD** the area of a cricket field in front of the batsman on the off side that is between cover point and extra cover [13C. Via Old French *covrir* < Latin *cooperire* 'cover completely' < *operire* 'to cover'] —**coverable** *adj* —**coverer** *n* —**coverless** *adj* ◇ **blow somebody's cover** to expose a disguise, lie, or pretence that somebody has been using to conceal something ◇ **under cover of something** hidden or protected by something ◇ **under separate cover** in another envelope or package

cover up *v* **1.** *vt* **COVER SOMETHING COMPLETELY** to cover somebody or something completely **2.** *vt* **CONCEAL SOMETHING BAD** to try to conceal that something illegal, immoral, or undesirable has happened or how or why it happened **3.** *vi* BOXING **PROTECT HEAD AND UPPER BODY** to hide the head and upper body behind the arms as protection against another boxer's blows

coverage /kúvvərij/ *n* **1.** MEDIA **ATTENTION** the attention given to an event or topic by newspapers, radio, and television in their reporting ○ *extensive news coverage* **2.** MEDIA **AUDIENCE** the percentage of all the people in a given area who are reached by a newspaper or radio or television station **3.** DEGREE OF COVERING the degree to which something is covered by something else ○ *Thicker paint will give better coverage.* **4.** FIN **AVAILABLE FUNDS** the amount of funds available to cover financial liabilities or commitments **5.** *Aus, N Am* INSUR same as **cover** *n* (sense 14)

coveralls /kúvvər awlz/ *npl N Am* a one-piece outer garment that covers and protects the clothes

cover charge *n* a fixed charge that is added per head to the cost of drinks and food in a nightclub or restaurant, e.g. for bread or entertainment

cover crop *n* a crop planted between main crops to prevent erosion or to be ploughed in to enrich the soil

covered wagon /kúvvərd-/ *n N Am* a large wagon with a canvas roof stretched over arched supports, formerly used by pioneers crossing the plains of North America

cover girl *n* a young woman, usually a glamorous model, whose picture is on the cover of a magazine

cover glass *n Aus, US* same as **cover slip**

covering /kúvvəring/ *n* something that protects, hides, or covers something

covering fire *n* weapon fire used to protect friendly troops from direct fire from the enemy's weapons

covering letter *n* a letter sent with another document or a package, providing necessary or additional information. N Am term **cover letter**

coverlet /kúvvərlət/ *n* a usually decorative cover for a bed, placed over the other bedclothes when the bed is not being used [13C. < Old French *couvre lit* 'bed cover']

cover letter *n N Am* same as **covering letter**

covermount /kúvvər mownt/ *n* a gift fixed to the cover of a magazine, e.g. a diary or recipe book

cover note *n* a document given by an insurance company to somebody who has taken out a policy, acting as a temporary certificate of insurance until the full policy is issued

cover page, **cover sheet** *n* a form sent along with a fax that gives information about the sender, e.g. the name, address, telephone number, and fax number

cover point *n* in cricket, a position in the covers to the right of the fielder at point, or a fielder who takes up this position

cover sheet *n* TELECOM same as **cover page**

cover slip *n UK, NZ, Can* a piece of thin glass used to cover a specimen on a microscope slide. Aus, US term **cover glass**

cover story *n* **1.** a magazine feature that is illustrated on the front cover and is the most important article in the issue **2.** a story made up to deceive somebody, e.g. to provide a false identity for an undercover investigator

covert /kúvvərt, kóvurt/ *adj* SECRET not intended to be known, seen, or found out ■ *n* **1. UNDERGROWTH PROVIDING COVER** a thicket, or undergrowth, in which game can shelter or hide **2. SHELTER** a shelter or hiding place **3. SMALL FEATHER** a small feather around the base of a quill on the wing or tail of a bird **4.** *also* **covert cloth** TEXTILES **TWILLED CLOTH** a hard-wearing twilled cloth. Use: suits. [13C. < Old French, past participle of *covrir* (see COVER)] —**covertly** *adv* —**covertness** *n*

SYNONYMS See *secret*.

coverture /kúvvərchər/ *n* **1.** a shelter or covering **2.** the condition of being a married woman [13C. < Old French < *covrir* (see COVER)]

cover-up *n* **1.** a concealment of something illegal, immoral, or undesirable **2.** a loose item of clothing worn over another garment, e.g. a wrap over an evening dress or a T-shirt over a swimsuit

cover version *n* MUSIC same as **cover** *n* (sense 16)

covet /kúvvət/ (**-ets, -eting, -eted**) *v* **1.** *vti* to have a strong desire to possess something that belongs to somebody else **2.** *vt* to want to have something very much (*formal*) [13C. < Old French *coveitier* < Latin *cupiditas* (see CUPIDITY)] —**covetable** *adj* —**coveter** *n* —**covetingly** *adv* —**covetous** *adj* —**covetously** *adv* —**covetousness** *n*

SYNONYMS See *want*.

covey /kúvvi/ (*plural* **-eys**) *n* **1.** a small group of game birds such as partridge, grouse, or quail **2.** a small group of people or things [14C. < French *covée* 'brood' < Latin *cubare* 'lie down']

Covic /chóvich/, **Dragan** (*b.* 1956) Croat representative of the presidency of Bosnia and Herzegovina (2002–), which rotates among a Serb, a Bosnian Muslim, and a Croat

coving /kóving/ *n* a prefabricated curved moulding used as a decorative cover for the join between a wall and a ceiling

COW

cow[1] /kow/ *n* **1. LARGE FEMALE QUADRUPED** an adult female grazing quadruped. Kept for: milk, meat, breeding. Genus: *Bos.* **2. MALE OR FEMALE OF DOMESTIC CATTLE** an animal of either sex and any age belonging to any breed of domestic cattle. Genus: *Bos.* **3. LARGE FEMALE MAMMAL** an adult female of large mammal species such as whales, elephants, seals, or moose **4. OFFENSIVE TERM** an offensive term that deliberately insults a woman (*slang*) **5.** ANZ **SOMETHING UNPLEASANT** something unpleasant or disagreeable (*dated informal*) [Old English *cū* < Indo-European] ◇ **have a cow** *N Am* to become suddenly and greatly excited or angry (*slang*) ◇ **till the cows come home** until an extremely long time has elapsed (*informal*)

cow[2] /kow/ (**cows, cowing, cowed**) *vt* to frighten somebody into submission or obedience [Late 16C. Probably < Old Norse *kúga* 'oppress']

cowal /ków əl/ *n Aus* a small swampy hollow in the Australian interior [Late 19C. < Kamilaroi]

Cowan /ków ən/ salt lake in southern Western Australia. Area: 940 sq. km/359 sq. mi.

coward /ków ərd/ *n* **1.** somebody regarded as fearful and uncouraged **2.** somebody who harms or attacks people who are weaker or unable to defend themselves [13C. < Old French *cuard* < Latin *cauda* 'tail']

Coward /ków ərd/, **Sir Noel** (1899–1973) British dramatist, actor, and songwriter. He was the author of *Private Lives* (1930), *Blithe Spirit* (1941), and *Brief Encounter* (1946).

> 'We have no reliable guarantee that the afterlife will be any the less exasperating than this one, have we?'
> [Sir Noel Coward, *Blithe Spirit*; 1941]

cowardice /ków ərdiss/ *n* an absence of courage, or behaviour that is cowardly

cowardly /ków ərdli/ *adj* **1.** showing a lack of physical or moral courage, or too scared to do a particular thing ○ *a cowardly attempt to avoid blame* **2.** showing meanness or cruelty to people who are weaker or unable to defend themselves and fear of those who are equal or stronger ○ *a cowardly attack on an undefended village* —**cowardliness** *n* —**cowardly** *adv*

SYNONYMS *cowardly, faint-hearted, spineless, gutless, pusillanimous, craven, chicken*

CORE MEANING: lacking in courage

cowardly showing a lack of physical or moral courage, or too scared to do a particular thing ○ *a wicked and cowardly attack* ○ *too cowardly to admit his mistake* **faint-hearted** lacking resolve, boldness, or enthusiasm ○ *The gift trade's huge International Spring Fair is not for the faint-hearted.* **spineless** seriously lacking in willpower or strength of character ○ *Workers at the plant have criticized their leaders as spineless.* ○ *their spineless acceptance that nothing can be done to improve the service* **gutless** seriously lacking in resolve and determination ○ *They're too gutless to oppose the measure in public.* **pusillanimous** (*formal*) showing a contemptible lack of boldness and resolve ○ *The head teacher, while personally pusillanimous, was always ready to follow up the action of others.* ○ *She condemns the country's foreign policy and her own pusillanimous government's backing of it.* **craven** so weak and lacking in courage as to be worthy of contempt ○ *an act of craven stupidity* ○ *a craven surrender to pressure from big business* **chicken** (*informal*, often used by children and young people) showing a lack of courage, or too scared to do a particular thing ○ *The boy got called*

chicken by the other kids. ○ *I'll show him who's chicken!* ○ *too chicken to tell him face to face*

cow bail *n ANZ* a frame placed around a cow's head to keep it still during milking

cowbane /ków bayn/ (*plural same*) *n* **1.** a poisonous plant of the parsley family. Native to: marshy areas of Europe. Genus: *Cicuta*. **2.** a poisonous marsh plant. Native to: North America. Latin name: *Oxypolis rigidior*.

cowbell /ków bel/ *n* **1.** a bell fastened to a collar round a cow's neck that clangs as the cow moves, making the animal easier to find **2.** a bell without a clapper, played as a percussion instrument by being struck with a drumstick

cowberry /ków bəri/ *n* **1.** (*plural* **cowberries**) a small red fruit with a smooth skin and a tart taste **2.** (*plural* **cowberries** or *same*) a creeping flowering bush that produces cowberries. Native to: northern temperate areas. Latin name: *Vaccinium vitis-idaea*.

cowbird /ków burd/ *n* a blackbird that lays its eggs in the nests of other birds and often feeds alongside grazing cattle. Native to: North America. Genus: *Molothrus*.

cowboy /ków boy/ *n* **1.** MAN WHO LOOKS AFTER CATTLE a man employed to look after cattle, especially in the western United States. Cowboys traditionally work on horseback, but now also use motor vehicles. **2.** MALE CHARACTER IN WESTERNS a male character in stories and films about the western United States in the late 1800s, often shown fighting Native Americans or outlaws **3.** UNRELIABLE WORKER an unskilled or unscrupulous person working in a trade or business who carries out inferior work (*informal*)

cowboy boot *n* a high-heeled boot, like those originally worn by cowboys, usually with pointed toes and ornamental stitching

cowboy hat *n* a hat, usually felt, with a high crown and a wide brim, originally worn by cowboys and now widely worn in the southwestern and midwestern United States

cowboys and Indians *n* a children's game involving two sides pretending to be cowboys and Native Americans fighting against each other (*takes a singular verb*)

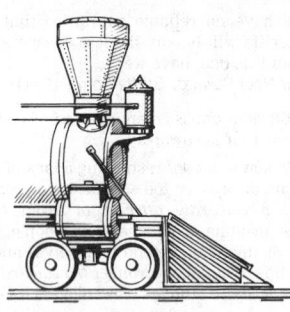
cowcatcher

cowcatcher /ków kachər/ *n* an angled metal frame formerly fixed to the front of a steam railway engine to clear animals and other obstructions from the track

Cowdrey /ków dri/, **Colin, Baron Cowdrey of Tonbridge** (1932–2000) Indian-born British cricketer. As a batsman, he scored 107 centuries in a playing career spanning almost 25 years. He played for England 114 times, 27 times as captain. Full name **Cowdrey, Michael Colin**

Cowen /ków ən/, **Sir Zelman** (*b*. 1919) Australian lawyer and politician. He was a professor of law and governor general of Australia (1977–82).

cower /ków ər/ (*-ers, -ering, -ered*) *vi* to cringe or move backwards defensively in fear [13C. < Middle Low German *kūren* 'lie in wait']

Cowes /kowz/ resort and yachting centre on the Isle of Wight. A regatta is held there every August. Population: 16,335 (1991).

cowfish /ków fish/ (*plural same* or *-fishes*) *n* **1.** a small brightly coloured warm-water sea fish with spines that resemble horns above the eyes. Family:

Ostraciidae. **2.** a sea mammal such as some species of dolphin or porpoise, or a manatee

cowgirl /ków gurl/ *n* **1.** FEMALE CHARACTER IN WESTERNS a female character in stories and films about the western United States in the late 1800s, usually accompanying or assisting a cowboy in his exploits **2.** *N Am* WOMAN WHO LOOKS AFTER CATTLE a woman employed to look after cattle, especially in the western United States **3.** *US* FEMALE RODEO PERFORMER a woman who performs or competes in shows such as rodeos

cowhand /ków hand/ *n N Am* somebody employed to look after cattle

cowherd /ków hurd/ *n* somebody who tends cattle, usually on foot (*archaic or literary*)

cowhide /ków hīd/ *n* **1.** SKIN OF COW the skin of a cow or bull, removed and processed **2.** LEATHER leather made from a cowhide **3.** LEATHER WHIP a whip made of braided leather or rawhide ■ *vt* (*-hides, -hiding, -hided*) WHIP SOMEBODY to beat somebody with a whip made of braided leather or rawhide

Cowichan sweater /ków ichan-/ *n* a heavy homespun jersey, originally black and white and knitted with symbolic designs by Native American peoples of the Pacific Northwest coast [After a people of Canada]

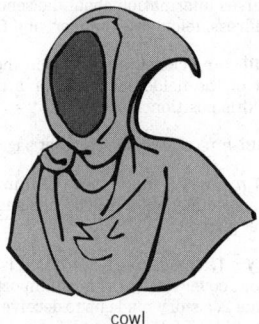
cowl

cowl /kowl/ *n* **1.** CLOTHING, CHR MONK'S HOOD the hood on a monk's cloak, or a monk's hooded cloak **2.** CLOTHING same as **cowl neck 3.** HOOD FOR CHIMNEY a hood-shaped, sometimes revolving, cover fitted to a chimney or vent to improve ventilation and prevent downward draughts **4.** PART OF VEHICLE BODY the part of the body of a motor vehicle to which the windscreen, bonnet, and dashboard are attached **5.** ENG same as **cowling** [Pre-12C. Via Germanic < Latin *cucullus* 'hood']

cowled /kowld/ *adj* fitted with or wearing a hood or hooded cloak

Cowley /ków li/, **Abraham** (1618–67) English poet. He was a Royalist secret agent and author of *The Mistress* (1647) and *Pindarique Odes* (1656).

> 'A mighty pain to love it is, / And 't is a pain that pain to miss; / But of all pains, the greatest pain / It is to love, but love in vain.'
> [Abraham Cowley, 'Gold', *Anacreon*; 1656]

cowlick /ków lik/ *n* a tuft of hair growing in a different direction from the rest of the hair on somebody's head and usually sticking up [< its resemblance to a ridge of hair on a cow's hide that is thought to be caused by the animal licking itself]

cowling /ków ling/ *n* a streamlined removable metal covering for an aircraft engine, fuselage, or nacelle

cowl neck *n* a collar on a woman's garment such as a jersey that drapes in large folds around the neck (*hyphenated when used before a noun*)

cowman /ków mən/ (*plural* **-men** /-mən/) *n* **1.** a man who tends cattle, especially one who is responsible for the milking and other aspects of managing a dairy herd **2.** *N Am* a man who owns cattle or a cattle ranch **3.** *US* AGRIC same as **cowboy** (sense 1)

cow parsley *n* a tall perennial plant that grows beside roads and in hedgerows. Flowers: white, in umbrella-shaped clusters. Native to: Europe. Latin name: *Anthriscus sylvestris*.

cow parsnip *n* a tall perennial plant with a thick stem. Flowers: tiny, white and purple, in flattened clusters. Native to: northern temperate regions. Genus: *Heracleum*.

cowpat /ków pat/ *n* a circular flat mass of dung excreted by a cow

cowpea /ków pee/ *n* PLANTS same as **black-eyed bean**

Cowper /kóopər, ków-/, **William** (1731–1800) British poet. His works include the ballad 'John Gilpin' (1783) and the rural idyll *The Task* (1785).

> 'God moves in a mysterious way / His wonders to perform; / He plants his footsteps in the sea, / And rides upon the storm.'
> [William Cowper, 'Light Shining out of Darkness', *Olney Hymns*; 1779]

Cowper's gland /kóopərz-, ków-/ *n* either of two small glands, just below the prostate, that secrete into the urethra a lubricant fluid that is released just prior to ejaculation of semen [Mid-18C. After William *Cowper* (1666–1709), English anatomist]

cow pillow *n S Asia* a large cotton-stuffed cylindrical pillow used for reclining rather than sleeping [*Cow* suggesting something big and bulky]

cowpoke /ków pōk/ *n N Am* a cowboy or cowgirl (*informal*)

cowpox /ków poks/ *n* a mild viral skin disease in cattle, usually affecting the udder with a pustular rash. Cowpox virus was once used to inoculate humans against smallpox. Technical name **vaccinia**

cowpuncher /ków punchər/ *n N Am* a cowboy or cowgirl (*informal*)

Cowra /ków rə/ town and agricultural centre on the Lachlan River in central New South Wales, Australia. Population: 13,108 (2002 estimate).

cowrie /ków ri/, **cowry** (*plural* **-ries**) *n* **1.** a tropical invertebrate sea animal that has a glossy brightly coloured shell with a long central toothed opening. Family: Cypraeidae. **2.** the shell of a cowrie, formerly used as money in parts of Africa, South Asia, and the South Pacific [Mid-17C. < Hindi *kaurī*]

cow shark *n* a large flabby bottom-dwelling shark that has a weak jaw and small teeth. Native to: warm and temperate seas. Family: Hexanchidae.

cowshed /ków shed/ *n* a building in which cattle are housed

cowslip /ków slip/ *n* a small plant of the primrose family. Flowers: long-stemmed, drooping, fragrant, yellow. Native to: grassy areas in temperate regions of Europe, Africa, Asia. Latin name: *Primula veris*. [Old English *cūslyppe* 'cow dung', probably from a belief that it grew where a cowpat had fallen]

cox /koks/ *n* the member of a rowing crew who faces forward, steers the boat, and directs the speed and rhythm of the rowers ■ *vti* (**coxes, coxing, coxed**) to act as the cox of a rowing boat, especially in a race [Late 19C. Shortening of COXSWAIN] —**coxless** *adj*

Cox /koks/ *n* same as **Cox's Orange Pippin** (*informal*)

Cox /koks/, **David** (1783–1859) British artist. He is known for his watercolours of landscapes in northern Wales, characterized by broad washes and atmospheric effects.

Cox, Paul (*b*. 1940) Dutch-born Australian film director. He wrote and directed *Man of Flowers* (1983) and *Cactus* (1986).

Cox, Philip (*b*. 1939) Australian architect. He is noted for his use of awnings and curved steel frames in buildings such as the Yulara Resort at Uluru and the Sydney Exhibition Centre.

coxa /kóksə/ (*plural* **-ae** /-see/) *n* **1.** the base segment of the leg of most insects and other arthropods **2.** the hipbone or hip joint (*technical*) [Early 19C. < Latin, 'hip'] —**coxal** *adj*

coxalgia /kok sálji ə, -jə/ *n* pain in the hip, or disease of the hip —**coxalgic** *adj*

Cox and Box *npl* same as **Box and Cox**

coxcomb /kóks kōm/ *n* (*archaic*) **1.** a conceited man with an excessive interest in clothes and fashion **2.** the cap worn by a medieval jester, shaped like a cockscomb [Mid-16C. Alteration of COCKSCOMB] —**coxcombry** *n*

Coxsackie virus /kok sáki-, kŏok saáki-/, **coxsackie virus** *n* a virus belonging to a group that occurs in the human intestinal tract and causes respiratory, neurological, and muscular diseases such as viral

meningitis and a condition similar to poliomyelitis [Mid-20C. After a place in New York State]

Cox's Orange Pippin *n* a small variety of eating apple with a yellowish-green skin flecked or patched with red [Mid-19C. After Richard Cox (c.1776–1845), amateur British fruit-grower]

coxswain /kóks'n, -swayn/**, cockswain** *n* **1.** ROWING same as **cox 2.** somebody who oversees a lifeboat and its crew, and who usually steers it **3.** the senior petty officer of a small ship ◼ *vti* (**-swains, -swaining, -swained**) ROWING same as **cox** *v* [14C. < *cock* 'ship's boat' + SWAIN]

coy /koy/ *adj* **1.** PRETENDING TO BE SHY pretending, in a teasing or provocative way, to be reserved or modest **2.** SHY shy or reserved in social situations **3.** UNCOMMUNICATIVE unwilling to reveal information about somebody or something, especially in a way that teases or annoys somebody who wants the information [14C. Via French *coi* 'quiet' < Latin *quietus*] —**coyish** *adj* —**coyly** *adv* —**coyness** *n*

Coy. *abbr* MIL company

coyote /kóy ōt, koy ōti/ (*plural* **-tes** or *same*) *n* **1.** a carnivorous canine mammal, similar to but smaller than the wolf. Native to: North America. Latin name: *Canis latrans.* **2.** a smuggler who brings illegal immigrants into the United States (*slang*) [Mid-18C. Via Mexican Spanish < Nahuatl *coyotl*]

coyotillo /kóyō teé lyō/ (*plural* **-los**) *n* a thorny bush with small green flowers and poisonous black berries. Native to: Mexico, southwestern United States. Latin name: *Karwinskia humboldtiana.* [Late 19C. < Mexican Spanish, 'little coyote']

coypu

coypu /kóy poo/ (*plural* **-pus** or *same*) *n* a large rodent with webbed feet for swimming and a long tail. Kept for: fur. Native to: South America. [Late 18C. < Araucanian]

coz /kuz/ *n* same as **cousin** (*archaic*) [Mid-16C. Shortening]

cozen /kúzz'n/ (**-ens, -ening, -ened**) *vti* to deceive, cheat, or defraud somebody (*archaic*) [Late 16C. Origin ?] —**cozener** *n*

cozenage /kúzz'n ij/ *n* trickery or deception (*archaic*)

cozy *adj*, *n* US spelling of **cosy**

cozzie *n* CLOTHING another spelling of **cossie** (*informal*)

CP *abbr* **1.** MEDIA Canadian Press **2.** Cape Province **3.** ONLINE chat post (*used in e-mails*) **4.** CHEM chemically pure **5.** command post **6.** POL Communist Party **7.** *Aus* Country Party

cp. *abbr* compare

CPA *abbr* COMPUT critical path analysis

cpd *abbr* CHEM compound

CPI *abbr* ECON consumer price index

Cpl *abbr* MIL Corporal

CPO *abbr* NAVY Chief Petty Officer

CPR *abbr* **1.** RAIL Canadian Pacific Railway **2.** MED cardiopulmonary resuscitation

cps *abbr* **1.** COMPUT characters per second **2.** PHYS cycles per second

CPS *abbr* Crown Prosecution Service

CPSA *abbr* PUBLIC ADMIN Civil and Public Services Association

CPSU *abbr Aus* Community and Public Service Union

Cpt., CPT *abbr* MIL Captain

CPU *abbr* COMPUT central processing unit

CQ[1] *n* a set of code letters transmitted at the start of a radio message indicating that the message is meant for all receivers and requesting a response

CQ[2] *abbr* MIL charge of quarters

cr *abbr* Costa Rica (*used in Internet addresses*) See table at **domain name**

Cr[1] *symbol* CHEM ELEM chromium

Cr[2] *abbr* Councillor

CR *abbr* **1.** Community of the Resurrection **2.** PSYCHOL conditioned reflex **3.** PSYCHOL conditioned response **4.** Costa Rica

cr. *abbr* **1.** FIN credit **2.** FIN creditor **3.** creek

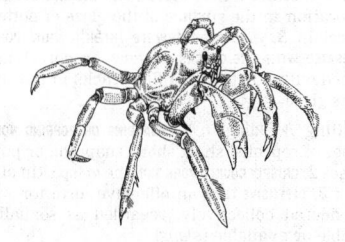

crab

crab[1] /krab/ *n* **1.** FLAT CRUSTACEAN a crustacean with a broad flat shell, antennae, a small abdomen, and five pairs of legs, the front two of which are in the form of grasping pincers. Suborder: Brachyura. **2.** CRUSTACEAN LIKE CRAB an animal similar or related to the true crab, e.g. the hermit crab, horseshoe crab, or king crab **3.** FLESH OF CRAB the flesh of a crab used as food **4.** PARASITIC LOUSE IN PUBIC HAIR a parasitic louse resembling a tiny crab that infests the pubic hair of humans, causing inflammation and itching of the skin. Latin name: *Phthirius pubis.* **5.** MECH ENG CRANE a machine similar to a crane designed to lift and move heavy weights **6.** AVIAT FLYING MANOEUVRE a flying manoeuvre in which an aircraft is steered slightly into a crosswind to compensate for drifting off course ◼ **crabs** *npl* LICE INFESTATION an infestation of crab lice (*informal*) ◼ *v* (**crabs, crabbing, crabbed**) **1.** *vti* SCURRY SIDEWAYS to move sideways as a crab does, or cause something to move in this way **2.** *vi* CATCH CRABS to go fishing or hunting for crabs **3.** *vti* AVIAT FLY INTO CROSSWIND to steer an aircraft slightly into a crosswind to compensate for drifting off course **4.** *vi* NAUT SAIL WITH SIDEWAYS DRIFT to sail forwards with a slight sideways drift caused by a current [Old English *crabba* < Indo-European, 'scratch'] —**crabber** *n* —**crab-like** *adj* ◇ **catch a crab** in rowing, to make a faulty stroke by failing to make contact with the water or plunging the oar blade in too deeply

crab[2] /krab/ *n* TREES same as **crab apple** [15C. Origin ?]

crab[3] /krab/ *n* OFFENSIVE TERM an offensive term for somebody regarded as bad-tempered or disagreeable (*informal insult*) ◼ *v* (**crabs, crabbing, crabbed**) (*informal*) **1.** *vi* CRITICIZE SOMEBODY OR SOMETHING to criticize or grumble about somebody or something **2.** *vt* SPOIL SOMETHING to ruin or spoil something through interference [Late 16C. Probably back-formation < CRABBED]

Crab *n* ZODIAC same as **Cancer** (senses 2–3) [CRAB[1]]

crab apple *n* **1.** a small sour fruit. Use: in preserves. **2.** a tree that produces crab apples. Genus: *Malus.* [< CRAB[2]]

Crabbe /krab/**, George** (1754–1832) British poet and clergyman. He was the author of *The Village* (1783), *The Parish Register* (1807), and *The Borough* (1810).

'Habit with him was all the test of truth, / "It must be right: I've done it from my youth".'

[George Crabbe, *Letter 3*, 'The Vicar', *The Borough*; 1810]

crabbed /krabd, krábbid/ *adj* **1.** GROUCHY bad-tempered, irritable, or disagreeable by nature **2.** HARD TO READ hard to read, because the words and letters are compressed **3.** COMPLICATED complicated and hard to follow (*dated*) ◦ *crabbed logic* [13C. < CRAB[1] because

the way crabs threaten with their claws and their sideways walk suggest bad temper; reinforced by the idea of 'sourness' found in CRAB[2]] —**crabbedly** *adv* —**crabbedness** *n*

crabbing /krábbing/ *n* fishing or hunting for crabs [Mid-17C. < CRAB[1]]

crabby /krábbi/ (**-bier, -biest**) *adj* bad-tempered or irritable in character (*informal*) [Mid-16C. < CRAB[1], CRAB[2]] —**crabbily** *adv* —**crabbiness** *n*

crab grass *n* a coarse grass that grows in warm regions, has creeping stems that root freely, and is considered a weed in lawns and gardens. Genus: *Digitaria.* [< CRAB[1]]

crab louse *n* ZOOL same as **crab**[1] (sense 4) [< CRAB[1]]

crabmeat /kráb meet/ *n* the flesh of a crab used as food [< CRAB[1]]

Crab Nebula *n* the gaseous remains of an exploded star in the constellation Taurus, about 5,000 light-years from Earth

crab stick *n* a stick-shaped piece of processed fish that has been flavoured and coloured to resemble crabmeat [< CRAB[1]]

crabstick /kráb stik/ *n* **1.** somebody bad-tempered or irritable (*informal*) **2.** a stick or club made from the wood of a crab apple [< CRAB[2], CRAB[3]]

crabwise /kráb wīz/ *adv, adj* **1.** sideways, as crabs usually move **2.** in a roundabout and cautious way [Early 20C. < CRAB[1]]

crachach /krákh akh/ *npl Wales* upper-class people (*informal*) [Late 20C. < Welsh]

crack /krak/ *v* (**cracks, cracking, cracked**) **1.** *vti* BREAK WITHOUT COMING FULLY APART to break in such a way that a fine split or splits appear but the split sections do not come apart, or make something break in this way ◦ *cracked a rib in falling* **2.** *vti* BREAK INTO PIECES to break into pieces, or break something into pieces **3.** *vti* BREAK WITH SHARP NOISE to break with a sudden sharp noise, or make something break in this way ◦ *cracked some eggs into a saucepan* **4.** *vti* MAKE SHARP NOISE to make a loud sharp sound, or cause something such as a whip or a rifle to make a loud sharp sound ◦ *thunder cracked overhead* **5.** *vt* HIT SOMETHING HARD to hit something with a powerful impact ◦ *cracked his head on the beam* **6.** *vti* BREAK OPEN UNDER PRESSURE to break open because of pressure, or make something such as a nut break or open by pressure **7.** *vti* FAIL OR MAKE SOMETHING FAIL to fail, give way, or break down, or make somebody or something do so ◦ *The champion was two sets down, but he didn't crack.* **8.** *vti* BREAK DOWN PSYCHOLOGICALLY to break down psychologically, or cause somebody to break down psychologically, e.g. under stress or torture **9.** *vi* BECOME HOARSE OR CHANGE IN PITCH to become slightly hoarse or suffer from uncontrollable changes in pitch, especially because of emotion or stress (*refers to voices*) **10.** *vti* DECODE OR SOLVE SOMETHING to decipher or solve something such as a code, puzzle, or problem (*informal*) ◦ *Police are under pressure to crack the case.* **11.** *vt* BREAK INTO SOMETHING to force a way into something, especially a safe (*informal*) **12.** *vi Scotland* TO CHAT to chat or gossip ◦ *We haven't got time to crack with you just now.* **13.** *vt* INDUST BREAK MOLECULES DOWN INTO SMALLER MOLECULES to break down something, especially the heavier hydrocarbons in petroleum, into smaller molecules by using heat or catalysis **14.** *vt* COMPUT DISABLE COPY PROTECTION to defeat the copy protection that is intended to prevent somebody from illegally copying and distributing a software product, music CD, or DVD (*slang*) **15.** *vt* COMPUT BREAK INTO COMPUTER SYSTEM to gain unauthorized access to a computer system with the intention of doing damage or committing a crime (*slang*) ◼ *n* **1.** THIN BREAK a break or flaw in something such as a mirror that is visible as a fine line ◦ *cracks in the ice* **2.** LONG NARROW OPENING a relatively long narrow break, hole, or opening in something ◦ *peeked through a crack in the fence* **3.** SHARP NOISE a sudden loud sharp noise ◦ *the crack of a rifle* **4.** WEAKNESS a flaw, defect, or weak spot **5.** UNEVEN VOICE TONE a hoarseness or uncontrollable change in pitch in somebody's voice **6.** PURIFIED FORM OF COCAINE a purified and extremely addictive form of cocaine **7.** BLOW a hard blow from somebody or something (*informal*) ◦ *a crack over the head* **8.** SARCASTIC COMMENT a sarcastic, funny, or rude remark, especially at somebody else's expense (*informal*) **9.** ATTEMPT an attempt at something (*informal*) **10.**

SOMEBODY OR SOMETHING THAT EXCELS somebody or something that is outstandingly good, talented, or skilled (*informal*) **11.** *Ireland, Scotland* CONVERSATION chat, conversation, gossip, or news **12.** *also* **craic** *Ireland* ENJOYMENT entertainment, fun, or enjoyment, especially when experienced in a group or in a specific place ○ *The crack was fierce in Heraghty's last night!* ○ *We took turns at driving, and the crack was great all the way down.* ■ *adj* EXCELLENT excellent, expert, or trained to a high degree of efficiency ○ *She's a crack shot.* [Old English *cracian* < Germanic, 'make a loud noise'] ◇ **a fair crack of the whip** a reasonable chance to attempt something ◇ **be not all he's** *or* **she's** *or* **it's cracked up to be** to be not as good as promised or reputed ◇ **crack a bottle** to open a bottle of alcoholic drink ◇ **crack a joke** to tell a joke ◇ **crack it** to achieve something or be successful (*informal*) ◇ **fall between** *or* **through the cracks** to be overlooked or forgotten ◇ **paper over the cracks** to try to hide the fact that something is wrong rather than dealing with the problem ◇ **the crack of doom** the moment when the world ends and God's final judgment of humankind (**the Last Judgment**) begins (*literary*)

crack down *vi* to take strong and decisive action against something undesirable or illegal or against somebody involved in such activity (*informal*)

crack on *vi* to continue to work, travel, or do something, especially quickly or energetically

crack onto *vt Aus* to try to start a sexual relationship with somebody (*informal*)

crack up *v* **1.** *vi* HAVE BREAKDOWN to experience a psychological or, sometimes, physical breakdown, usually because of stress (*informal*) **2.** *vi* BREAK INTO PIECES to crack and break into pieces **3.** *vti* LAUGH UNCONTROLLABLY to laugh uncontrollably, or cause somebody to laugh uncontrollably (*informal*)

crackbrained /krák braynd/ *adj* extremely irrational or eccentric (*informal*) ○ *a crackbrained idea*

crack cocaine *n* DRUGS same as **crack** *n* (sense 6)

crackdown /krák down/ *n* a strong and decisive measure taken against an undesirable or illegal activity or against somebody involved in such activity (*informal*)

cracked /krakt/ *adj* **1.** HAVING CRACKS marked with a crack or cracks ○ *dry cracked lips* **2.** COARSELY CRUSHED broken or crushed into coarse pieces ○ *cracked ice* **3.** HOARSE sounding rough or hoarse vocally, often because of emotion or stress **4.** IRRATIONAL extremely irrational (*informal*)

cracked wheat *n* whole grains of wheat that have been chopped into little pieces

cracker /krákər/ *n* **1.** DECORATED TUBE WITH TRINKET a cardboard tube, containing a small toy, trinket, joke, or paper hat, and wrapped in coloured paper, that opens with an explosive noise when both its ends are pulled **2.** LEISURE same as **firecracker** **3.** FLAT CRISP BISCUIT a thin crisp biscuit, usually unsweetened and sometimes salted, often eaten with cheese **4.** SOMEBODY OR SOMETHING EXCELLENT somebody or something that is excellent or a fine example of its kind (*informal*) **5.** INDUST DEVICE FOR CRACKING PETROLEUM COMPOUNDS a device in which petroleum oils and tars are broken down to yield more valuable light fuels **6.** COMPUT SOMEBODY WHO DISABLES COPY PROTECTION somebody who defeats the copy protection of a software product, music CD, or DVD (*slang*) **7.** COMPUT SOMEBODY WHO BREAKS INTO COMPUTER SYSTEM somebody who gains unauthorized access to a computer system with the intention of doing damage or committing a crime (*slang*)

cracker-barrel *adj US* expressing unsophisticated but practical sense or wisdom of the kind often associated with a rural community [< the idea of the village store as a social centre]

crackerjack /krákər jak/ *adj* outstanding in quality or ability (*dated informal*) [Late 19C. < CRACKER 'excellent' + JACK [1] 'man'] —**crackerjack** *n*

crackers /krákərz/ *adj* mildly irrational or eccentric (*informal*)

crackhead /krák hed/ *n* an addict of crack cocaine (*slang*)

crack house *n* a house or flat where crack cocaine is sold to addicts and where, sometimes, it is also made (*slang*)

cracking /kráking/ *adj* (*informal*) **1.** QUICK very fast ○ *at a cracking pace* **2.** EXCELLENT excellent or impressive ■ *adv* same as **extremely** (*informal*) ○ *did a cracking good job* ■ *n* BREAKING DOWN INTO SMALLER MOLECULES the breaking down of something, especially the heavier hydrocarbons in petroleum, into smaller molecules using heat or catalysis ◇ **get cracking** to start moving or doing something quickly or more quickly (*informal*)

crackle /krák'l/ *v* (**-les, -ling, -led**) **1.** *vi* MAKE RAPID SNAPPING NOISE to make repeated short sharp snapping or popping noises such as dry wood makes when burning, or cause something to make such noises **2.** *vi* SCINTILLATE to be lively, energetic, or scintillating ○ *The play crackles with wit.* **3.** *vt* DECORATE POTTERY WITH CRACKS to decorate a piece of pottery or porcelain with a network of fine cracks in the surface of its glaze ■ *n* **1.** REPEATED SNAPPING NOISES a series of repeated short sharp snapping or popping noises **2.** FINE DECORATIVE CRACKS a network of fine cracks created as decoration in the surface of the glaze of pottery or porcelain **3.** *also* **crackleware** /krák'l wair/ PORCELAIN DECORATED WITH FINE CRACKS pottery or porcelain decorated with a network of fine cracks in the surface of its glaze

crackling /krákling/ *n* **1.** SNAPPING OR POPPING NOISES a series of repeated short sharp snapping or popping noises **2.** CRISPLY COOKED PORK SKIN the crisp skin of roast pork **3.** OFFENSIVE TERM an offensive term for women considered collectively, regarded as sexually desirable or available (*slang*)

crackly /krákli/ (**-lier, -liest**) *adj* **1.** brittle or crisp **2.** making or consisting of a series of repeated short sharp snapping or popping noises

cracknel /krákn'l/ *n* a hard light brittle biscuit [14C. Via Old French *craquelin* < Middle Dutch *krākeline*, a small cake < *krāken* 'to crack']

Cracknell /krákn'l/, **Ruth Winifred** (1925–2002) Australian actor. She is noted for her performances in classic theatrical works as well as television dramas and situation comedies.

crackpot /krák pot/ *n* somebody regarded as eccentric or wildly imaginative (*informal insult*) ■ *adj* extremely eccentric or unrealistic (*informal*) ○ *another of his crackpot money-making schemes*

cracksman /kráksmən/ (*plural* **-men** /-mən/) *n* a burglar, especially one who breaks into safes (*slang*)

crack-up *n* (*informal*) **1.** a psychological or sometimes physical breakdown **2.** a motor vehicle or aircraft crash

Cracow another spelling of **Kraków**

-cracy *suffix* rule, government, power ○ *technocracy* [< French *-cratie* < Greek *kratos* 'power, strength' < Indo-European, 'hard']

cradle /kráyd'l/ *n* **1.** BABY'S BED a small bed for a baby, usually on rockers and with enclosing sides **2.** STARTING PLACE the place where something begins or develops in its early stages ○ *the cradle of civilization* **3.** AUTOMOT MECHANIC'S BOARD ON WHEELS a flat board on wheels or casters on which a mechanic can slide under a vehicle **4.** CIV ENG SUPPORTING FRAMEWORK a framework for supporting something such as a ship that is being built or repaired **5.** CIV ENG HANGING PLATFORM a movable platform or cage hung on the side of something such as a building or ship, to hold a worker **6.** SUPPORT FOR TELEPHONE HANDSET the part of a telephone on which the handset rests or hangs **7.** MED PROTECTIVE FRAME SUPPORTING BEDCLOTHES a frame placed beneath bedclothes covering a patient to keep them from touching a sensitive part of the body, e.g. after an injury or operation **8.** MIN EXTRACT PANNING DEVICE a rocking device like a box used in panning for gold ■ *vt* (**-dles, -dling, -dled**) **1.** HOLD SOMEBODY OR SOMETHING CAREFULLY to hold or support somebody or something tenderly, carefully, or protectively, especially in a hollow formed with the arms or hands **2.** PUT SOMEBODY OR SOMETHING INTO CRADLE to put somebody or something into a cradle or something like a cradle **3.** CIV ENG SUPPORT SOMETHING IN FRAMEWORK to support something such as a ship that is being built or repaired in a framework **4.** NURTURE SOMEBODY OR SOMETHING to look after a young child or support something in the early stages of its development **5.** HANG UP PHONE to put the handset of a telephone on its cradle **6.** MIN EXTRACT WASH SOIL FOR GOLD to wash gold-bearing soil in a cradle [Old English *cradol*] —**cradler** *n* ◇ **rob the cradle** *N Am* to be romantically or sexually involved with somebody who is much younger (*informal*)

cradle cap *n* a skin condition that commonly affects the scalp of young babies, causing scaling and flaking

Cradle Mountain /kráyd'l-/ mountain in central Tasmania, Australia, now part of Cradle Mountain-Lake St Clair National Park. Height: 1,545 m/5,069 ft.

cradle snatcher *n* somebody who has a romantic or sexual relationship with a much younger person (*disapproving*) N Am term **cradle-robber**

cradlesong /kráyd'l song/ *n* MUSIC same as **lullaby** *n* (sense 1)

cradling /kráydling/ *n* a wooden or iron framework, especially one used to support a ceiling while it is being installed

Crafers-Bridgewater /kráyfərz bríj wawtər/ town in South Australia, near Adelaide, in the Mount Lofty Ranges. Population: 11,879 (1991).

craft /kraaft/ *n* **1.** SKILFUL CREATIVE ACTIVITY a profession or activity involving the skilful making of decorative or practical objects by hand, e.g. weaving, pottery, or woodcarving (*often used in combination*) **2.** OBJECT PRODUCED BY SKILFUL HANDIWORK something produced skilfully by hand, especially in a traditional manner, e.g. a piece of pottery or carving (*often used in the plural*) **3.** SKILL skill in making or doing things, especially by hand **4.** SKILLED PROFESSION OR ACTIVITY a profession or activity that requires skill and training, or experience or specialized knowledge (*often used in combination*) ○ *his love for the craft of film making* **5.** TRADE ASSOCIATION the people engaged in a skilled trade or profession, considered as a group (*dated*) **6.** DEVIOUSNESS skill in trickery or deceiving others (*archaic*) **7.** (*plural same*) VESSEL a vessel used for travelling, e.g. a boat, ship, aeroplane, or space vehicle (*often used in combination*) ■ *vt* (**crafts, crafting, crafted**) MAKE SOMETHING WITH SKILL to produce or create something with skill and care [Old English *cræft* 'strength, power' < Germanic] —**crafter** *n*

craft-brewed *adj US* made by a small-scale brewery in small quantities

craft food *n* food for sale to consumers that is prepared carefully using high-quality ingredients, especially as contrasted with fast food

craftsman /kraáftsmən/ (*plural* **-men** /-mən/) *n* **1.** a man who works at a skilled trade or profession **2.** a man who does something with great skill and expertise —**craftsmanlike** *adj* —**craftsmanly** *adj* —**craftsmanship** *n*

craftsperson /kraáfts purss'n/ (*plural* **-persons** or **-people** /-peep'l/) *n* a skilful maker of decorative or practical objects by hand

craftswoman /kraáfts wŏŏmən/ (*plural* **-women** /-wimin/) *n* **1.** a woman who works at a skilled trade or profession **2.** a woman who does something with great skill and expertise

craft union *n* a labour union for people who work at a specific skilled trade, as distinct from an organization for those employed in a specific industry

craftwork /kraáft wurk/ *n* **1.** activity that involves the skilful making of decorative or practical objects by hand, e.g. weaving, pottery, or woodcarving **2.** objects that are the products of manual skill —**craftworker** *n*

crafty /kraáfti/ (**-ier, -iest**) *adj* using or involving cunning or trickery to deceive other people —**craftily** *adv* —**craftiness** *n*

crag /krag/ *n* a steep rough mass of rock forming part of a cliff or mountain peak [14C. < Celtic, probably Welsh *craig* or Gaelic *creagh*] —**cragged** *adj*

craggy /krággi/ (**-gier, -giest**) *adj* **1.** steep and rocky, and forming part of a cliff or mountain peak **2.** rugged-looking with strong prominent masculine features —**craggily** *adv* —**cragginess** *n*

cragsman /krágzmən/ (*plural* **-men** /-mən/) *n* a skilled and experienced rock climber

craic *n Ireland* another spelling of **crack** *n* (sense 12) (*informal*)

Craig /krayg/, **Sir Edward Henry Gordon** (1872–1966) British actor, director, and stage designer. He was the author of *On the Art of the Theatre* (1911) and

published the theatrical journal *The Mask* (1908–29).

> 'Farce is the essential theatre. Farce refined becomes high comedy; farce brutalized becomes tragedy.'
> [Sir Edward Henry Gordon Craig, *The Story of my Days*; 1957]

Craigavon /krayg ávv'n/ administrative district in County Armagh, Northern Ireland. Population: 80,671 (2002).

Craigieburn /kráygi burn/ town in central Victoria, Australia. It is an industrial and residential centre. Population: 12,919 (1996).

Craiova /krī óvə/ city and capital of Dolj County, southwestern Romania. It is an important industrial centre. Population: 310,838 (1997).

crake /krayk/ *n* a marsh bird with a short beak. Native to: Europe, Asia, Africa. [14C. < Old Norse *kráka* 'crow', *krákr* 'raven' < an imitation of its sound]

cram /kram/ *v* (**crams, cramming, crammed**) **1.** *vt* **FORCE SOMETHING INTO SMALL SPACE** to force objects or people into a space or container that is too small to hold them comfortably **2.** *vt* **EAT FOOD GREEDILY** to eat food hastily and greedily **3.** *vt* **FORCE SOMEBODY TO EAT** to encourage or force a person or animal to eat more than is necessary **4.** *vti* **STUDY INTENSIVELY** to study a subject intensively, e.g. for an imminent examination (*informal*) **5.** *vt* **TUTOR SOMEBODY INTENSIVELY** to tutor somebody intensively for an examination (*informal*) ■ *n* **1.** **TIGHTLY PACKED STATE** a situation in which a group of people or things are crushed, crowded, or tightly packed together **2.** **PERIOD OF INTENSIVE STUDY** a period of intensive study, e.g. for an imminent examination (*informal*) [Old English *(ge)crammian* < Germanic]

Cram /kram/, **Steve** (*b.* 1960) British middle-distance runner. In 1984 he was Olympic silver medallist in the 1,500 metres. Over 19 days in 1985, he set new world records for the mile, the 1,500 metres, and the 2,000 metres. Full name **Cram, Steven**

crambo /krámbō/ (*plural* **-boes**) *n* a game in which one player gives a word or a line of verse for which the other players must find a rhyming word or line (*dated*) [Mid-17C. Alteration of obsolete *crambe* 'cabbage, distasteful repetition', via Latin < Greek *krambē* 'cabbage']

cram-full *adj* completely filled with something

crammer /krámmər/ *n* a school or tutor that prepares students intensively for an examination, especially one that they have failed before

cramp[1] /kramp/ *n* **1.** **PAINFUL MUSCLE CONTRACTION** a sudden painful involuntary contraction of a muscle **2.** **MUSCLE PARALYSIS** temporary loss of function in a muscle or muscle group caused by repetitive use or overexertion ○ *writer's cramp* ■ **cramps** *npl* **ABDOMINAL PAIN** severe pain in the abdomen or adjoining areas, usually of gastrointestinal or uterine origin ■ *vi* (**cramps, cramping, cramped**) **BE AFFECTED WITH CRAMP** to experience muscular cramp [14C. Via French < Middle Dutch *krampe*]

cramp[2] /kramp/ *n* **1.** **DEVICE FOR HOLDING THINGS TOGETHER** an adjustable clamp for temporarily holding or pressing objects together **2.** **RESTRICTION** something that confines, restricts, or restrains, e.g. a set of shackles **3.** **CONFINED PLACE** a confined or restricted position or place **4.** **BAR WITH BENT ENDS** a metal bar with ends bent at right angles, used in building to hold objects such as bricks or timbers together ■ *vt* (**cramps, cramping, cramped**) **1.** **HOLD THINGS TOGETHER** to fasten, hold, or press objects together with a cramp **2.** **CONFINE SOMEBODY OR SOMETHING** to confine or enclose somebody or something in a small space (*usually passive*) **3.** **HAMPER SOMEBODY OR SOMETHING** to hamper or obstruct somebody or something [14C. < Middle Dutch *krampe*]

cramped /krampt/ *adj* **1.** **LACKING SPACE** inconveniently or uncomfortably small and confining **2.** **PACKED IN** packed into too small a space for comfort **3.** **HARD TO READ** written or printed in small characters that are close together and hard to read [Late 17C. < CRAMP[2]]

cramp iron *n* CONSTR same as **cramp**[2] *n* (sense 4)

crampon /krám pon, krámpən/ *n* a framework of metal spikes fastened to the sole of a boot or shoe to provide better traction on ice or snow (*usually used in the plural*) [13C. Via French < Frankish]

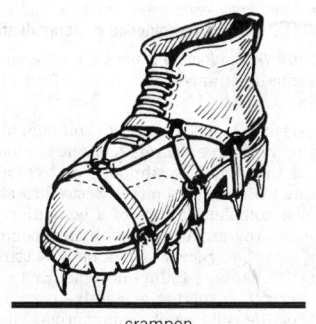
crampon

Cranach /kráə nakh/, **Lucas, the Elder** (1472–1553) German painter and engraver. He was known for paintings of stylized sensuous nudes; he was also a friend of Martin Luther, whose portrait he painted, as well as a propagandist for the Reformation. Born **Müller or Sunder, Lucas**

cranage /kráynij/ *n* the use of a crane, or the fee paid for such use

cranberry /kránbəri/ (*plural* **-ries**) *n* **1.** a sour red or reddish berry. Use: fruit juice, sauce for roast turkey. **2.** a low-growing evergreen plant of the heath family that yields cranberries. Genus: *Vaccinium*. [Mid-17C. < German *Kranbeere* 'crane berry', because the stamens are said to look like a crane's beak]

Cranborne Chase /krán bawrn-/ ancient royal forest in Wiltshire and Dorset, southern England, that is still partly wooded. It forms part of an Area of Outstanding Natural Beauty along with West Wiltshire Downs. Area: 983 sq. km/379 sq. mi.

Cranbourne /krán bawrn/ town in southeastern Australia. It is a suburb of Melbourne. Population: 18,886 (1991).

crane (sense 4)

crane /krayn/ *n* **1.** **LIFTING MACHINE** a large machine used to lift and move heavy objects by means of a hook attached to cables suspended from a supporting, usually movable, beam **2.** **MOVING SUPPORT FOR CAMERA** a moving platform with a long support for a film or television camera **3.** **MOVABLE SUPPORT WITH LONG ARM** a device with a long arm for supporting something, e.g. one for swinging and holding a pot or kettle over a fire **4.** **BIRDS LONG-LEGGED BIRD** a bird with long legs and a long neck that lives on plains and in marshes. Family: Gruidae. ■ *v* (**cranes, craning, craned**) **1.** *vti* **STRETCH NECK** to stretch the neck in order to get a better view of something **2.** *vt* **MOVE SOMETHING BY CRANE** to lift or move something using a crane [Old English *cran* < Indo-European, probably an imitation of the bird's cry]

Crane /krayn/, **Hart** (1899–1932) US poet. He celebrated modern civilization in poems such as *The Bridge* (1930). Full name **Crane, Harold Hart**

> 'We have all seen / The moon in lonely alleys make / A grail of laughter of an empty ash can.'
> [Hart Crane, 'Chaplinesque'; 1926]

Crane /krayn/, **Stephen** (1871–1900) US writer. He is known for his novel *The Red Badge of Courage* (1895) and other fiction and poetry.

> 'A singular disadvantage of the sea lies in the fact that after successfully surmounting one wave you discover that

there is another behind it just as important and just as nervously anxious to do something effective in the way of swamping boats.'
> [Stephen Crane, 'The Open Boat', *The Open Boat and Other Stories*; 1898]

Crane, **Walter** (1845–1915) British painter and illustrator. A leading member of the Arts and Crafts movement, he is known for his illustrations of children's books and his watercolours of mythological scenes.

crane fly *n* ANZ, N Am a large two-winged fly with a long thin body and long legs. Family: Tipulidae. UK term **daddy longlegs**

cranesbill /kráynz bil/ *n* PLANTS same as **geranium** (sense 2)

crani- *prefix* same as **cranio-** (*used before vowels*)

crania ANAT plural of **cranium**

cranial /kráyni əl/ *adj* relating to, involving, or located in the skull, especially the part covering the brain

cranial index *n* ANTHROP same as **cephalic index**

cranial nerve *n* either of a pair of nerves that originate in the brain stem and pass out of the skull to the surface of the body. There are 12 pairs of cranial nerves in mammals, birds, and reptiles, and usually 10 in fish and amphibians.

cranial osteopathy *n* gentle manipulation of the bones of the cranium and face to relieve tension and headache. It is also used for relieving pressure on the brain in newborn babies.

craniate /kráyni it, -ayt/ *adj* having a skull or cranium

cranio- *prefix* cranium, skull ○ *craniometry* [< CRANIUM]

craniofacial /kráyni ō fáysh'l/ *adj* relating to or involving both the cranium and the face

craniology /kráyni ólləji/ *n* the scientific study of the shapes, sizes, and other characteristics of human skulls —**craniological** /kráyni ə lójjik'l/ *adj* —**craniologically** *adv* —**craniologist** *n*

craniometry /kráyni ómmətri/ *n* the scientific measurement of skulls —**craniometer** *n* —**craniometric** /-ə méttrik/ *adj* —**craniometrical** *adj* —**craniometrically** *adv* —**craniometrist** *n*

craniosacral /kráyni ō sáykrəl, -sák-/ *adj* ANAT same as **parasympathetic**

craniosacral therapy *n* gentle manipulation of the bones of the face, skull, and spine, intended to relieve conditions including migraine, sinusitis, and musculoskeletal problems

craniotomy /kráyni óttəmi/ (*plural* **-mies**) *n* cutting open the skull to expose the brain, especially for brain surgery

cranium /kráyni əm/ (*plural* **-niums** or **-nia** /-ni ə/) *n* the skull of a vertebrate, especially the part that covers the brain [15C. Via medieval Latin < Greek *kranion*]

crank[1] /krangk/ *n* **1.** **MECHANICAL DEVICE FOR TRANSMITTING MOTION** a device consisting of an arm or handle that is connected to a shaft at right angles, enabling the transmission of motion to or from the shaft. A crank may be used for changing rotary motion to reciprocating motion or vice versa. **2.** *also* **crank handle** **HANDLE FOR STARTING MOTOR** a handle with two or four right-angled bends, used to start an engine **3.** **ECCENTRIC PERSON** an offensive term for somebody regarded as having unusual ideas and opinions (*informal insult*) **4.** US DRUGS **ILLEGAL DRUG** powdered methamphetamine used as an illegal drug (*slang*) ■ *v* (**cranks, cranking, cranked**) **1.** *vti* **USE CRANK ON SOMETHING** to start, move, or operate something by turning a crank **2.** *vt* **FORM SOMETHING INTO CRANK SHAPE** to form something into the right-angled shape of a crank ■ *adj* **ECCENTRIC** associated with or done by somebody who has unusual, often strongly held, ideas and opinions (*disapproving*) [Old English *cranc* < Germanic, 'crooked']

crank out *vt* to produce something quickly, mechanically, regularly, and in large quantities (*informal*)

crank up *v* **1.** *vti* **START SOMETHING WITH CRANK** to start something, especially an engine, with a crank **2.** *vt* **INCREASE SOMETHING** to increase the force, volume, or intensity of something (*informal*) **3.** *vt* **START SOMETHING** to get something to begin to operate or happen

(*informal*) **4.** *vi* INJECT DRUG to take or inject an illegal drug (*slang*)

crank[2] /krangk/ *adj* describes a vessel that is unsteady on the water and likely to capsize [Early 17C. Origin ?]

crankcase /krángk kayss/ *n* the metal casing that encloses the crankshaft in some engines, especially internal-combustion engines

crank handle *n* MECH ENG same as **crank**[1] *n* (sense 2)

crankpin /krángk pin/ *n* a short cylindrical bearing piece in the arm of a crank, attached to a connecting rod

crankshaft /krángk shaaft/ *n* a shaft that drives or is driven by a crank, e.g. one attached to a connecting rod in an internal-combustion engine

cranky[1] /krángki/ (-ier, -iest) *adj* **1.** ECCENTRIC eccentric or obsessive (*informal*) **2.** NOT IN WORKING ORDER not in good working order and likely to break down or operate unreliably **3.** *N Am* IRRITABLE disagreeable and easily irritated (*informal*) **4.** CROOKED characterized by twists and turns **5.** *regional* UNWELL unwell or infirm —**crankily** *adv* —**crankiness** *n*

cranky[2] /krángki/ *adj* NAUT same as **crank**[2]

Cranmer /kránmər/, **Thomas** (1489–1556) English archbishop. He became Archbishop of Canterbury (1533) and was largely responsible for compiling the *Book of Common Prayer* (1549, 1552). He annulled Henry VIII's marriages to Catherine of Aragon and Anne Boleyn, and divorced him from Anne of Cleves. Under Queen Mary he was burnt at the stake.

crannog /kránnəg/ *n* an ancient Celtic settlement in Scotland or Ireland, built on a natural or constructed island in a lake or bog and usually fortified [Early 17C. < Irish *crannóg* or Gaelic *crannag* 'timber structure' < *crann* 'tree']

cranny /kránni/ (*plural* -nies) *n* a small narrow crack, hole, or opening in a wall or rock [15C. < French *crané* 'notched' < popular Latin *crena* 'small notch'] —**crannied** *adj*

crap[1] /krap/ (*slang*) *n* **1.** an offensive term for rubbish, nonsense, or something worthless or annoying **2.** an offensive term for an act of passing solid waste matter out of the body through the anus **3.** an offensive term for excrement ■ *adj* an offensive term meaning worthless, useless, or lacking in ability ■ *v* (craps, crapping, crapped) **1.** *vti* an offensive term meaning to pass solid waste matter out of the body through the anus **2.** *vt* an offensive term meaning to be afraid of doing something [15C. Probably < Middle Dutch]

crap[2] /krap/ *n N Am* **1.** a losing throw at craps **2.** GAMBLING same as **craps** (sense 1) (*usually used before a noun*) [Late 19C. Back-formation < CRAPS]

crap out *vi* (*slang*) **1.** to avoid or discontinue an activity, especially out of fear **2.** *N Am* to make a losing throw in the game of craps

crape /krayp/ *n* **1.** TEXTILES same as **crêpe** (sense 1) **2.** black silk formerly used for mourning clothes **3.** a band of crape worn as a sign of mourning round the arm or, formerly, round a hat [Early 16C. < French *crêpe* (see CRÊPE)]

crape myrtle *n* a deciduous bush or tree, cultivated for its white, pink, or red flowers. Native to: Asia. Latin name: *Lagerstroemia indica*.

crapper /kráppər/ *n* an offensive term for a toilet (*slang*) [Mid-20C. < CRAP[1]]

crappie /kráppi/ (*plural* -pies or same) *n* a freshwater sunfish with equal-sized anal and dorsal fins. Native to: lakes and ponds in North America. Genus: *Pomoxis*. [Mid-19C. Origin ?]

crappy /kráppi/ (-pier, -piest) *adj* an offensive term meaning worthless, useless, of poor quality, or badly made or done (*slang*)

craps /kraps/ *n N Am* **1.** a US gambling game played with two dice **2.** GAMBLING same as **crap**[2] [Early 18C. Probably < French, variant of *crabs* 'score of two ones at dice' < English, plural of CRAB[1]]

crapshoot /kráp shoot/ *n* **1.** *US* something that is a matter of chance or is risky (*informal*) **2.** *N Am* a game of craps —**crapshooter** *n*

crapulent /krápyoolənt/, **crapulous** /-ləss/ *adj* regularly overindulging in food or alcohol (*literary*) [Mid-17C.

< late Latin *crapulentus* 'very drunk' < Greek *kraipalē* 'drunken headache'] —**crapulence** *n* —**crapulently** *adv*

craquelure /krákə loor/ *n* a network of small cracks that sometimes appear on the surface of an oil painting as it ages [Early 20C. < French]

crash[1] /krash/ *n* **1.** VEHICLE COLLISION a collision involving a moving vehicle or aircraft **2.** LOUD NOISE a loud noise such as that made by thunder or by something breaking violently into pieces **3.** COMPUTER BREAKDOWN a sudden complete failure of a computer system, device, or program, usually with an accompanying loss of data ○ *a system crash* **4.** FINANCIAL COLLAPSE the financial collapse or failure of something such as a stock market, involving a massive drop in share prices, or the collapse of a commercial business ■ *v* (crashes, crashing, crashed) **1.** *vti* COLLIDE VIOLENTLY to strike against something with great force, causing damage or destruction, or cause something such as a car to strike against something in this way **2.** *vti* MAKE LOUD NOISE to make a loud noise, or cause something to make a loud noise **3.** *vti* BREAK INTO PIECES to break into pieces violently and noisily, or break an object in this way **4.** *vti* MOVE NOISILY to move noisily, destructively, or violently, or cause something to move in this way **5.** *vti* HAVE OR CAUSE COMPLETE COMPUTER FAILURE to experience a sudden complete failure, or cause a computer system to have a sudden complete failure **6.** *vi* COLLAPSE FINANCIALLY to suffer financial collapse or failure **7.** *vi* DROP SHARPLY to decrease in value rapidly and steeply ○ *Share prices crashed.* **8.** *vi* BE HEAVILY DEFEATED to be heavily defeated, e.g. in a sports match (*informal*) **9.** *vti* ATTEND UNINVITED to attend an event such as a party without an invitation (*informal*) **10.** *vi* SLEEP to sleep, especially somewhere other than usual when exhausted, or stay temporarily somewhere other than at home (*slang*) ■ *adj* **1.** RAPID AND INTENSIVE done intensively over a short period of time in order to achieve the desired results quickly ○ *crash course* ○ *crash diet* **2.** SUDDEN AND STRONG abrupt and forceful ○ *a perfectly timed crash tackle* [14C. Origin ?] —**crasher** *n*

crash out *vi* (*informal*) **1.** same as **crash**[1] *v* (sense 10) **2.** to fall asleep suddenly

crash[2] /krash/ *n* a coarse linen or cotton cloth. Use: towels, curtains, book bindings. [Early 19C. < Russian *krashenina* 'dyed coarse linen']

crash axe *n* a tool similar to an axe, used by aircrews to cut an escape route through the skin of a commercial aircraft cockpit in case of an emergency occurring on the ground

crash barrier *n* a safety barrier at the edge of a road or racetrack or between the carriageways of a motorway

crash box *n* a theatrical sound-effects device consisting of a box filled with various objects that, when shaken or dropped, will simulate the sound of a crash

crash course *n* a course of study or training done intensively over a short period of time in order to learn the basics of a subject, skill, or activity quickly

crash diet *n* a strict and intensive diet carried out over a short period of time in order to lose weight quickly

crash dive *n* a steep rapid dive from the surface of a body of water by a submarine

crash-dive *vti* **1.** to dive steeply through the air and crash, or cause an aircraft to do this **2.** to make a steep rapid descent from the surface of a body of water, or cause a submarine to do this

crash gearbox *n* a gearbox without synchromesh that demands considerable skill and care by the driver to ensure that engine and wheel speed are aligned during gear changes

crash helmet *n* a hard padded helmet worn by cyclists, racing drivers, and others to protect the head in case of an accident

crash hot *adj Aus* excellent or of high quality (*informal*; hyphenated before a noun) ○ *a crash-hot tennis player*

crashing /kráshing/ *adj* complete and utter (*informal*) ○ *a crashing bore*

crash landing *n* an emergency landing by an aircraft,

usually causing damage to the aircraft —**crashland** /krásh land/ *vti*

crash pad *n* **1.** padding inside a vehicle that is designed to protect the occupants in a crash **2.** a place other than home where somebody sleeps or stays temporarily (*dated informal*)

crash-test *vt* **1.** to test a vehicle by deliberately crashing it into a wall to learn how it and its occupants will be affected in an accident **2.** to establish the safety and reliability of something by subjecting it to tests, e.g. using heat, pressure, or strain, until it reaches its breaking point

crashworthy /krásh wurthi/ *adj* able to withstand a crash —**crashworthiness** *n*

crass /krass/ *adj* **1.** so thoughtless, vulgar, and insensitive as to lack all refinement or delicacy **2.** extreme or flagrant ○ *crass stupidity* [15C. < Latin *crassus* 'thick'] —**crassitude** *n* —**crassly** *adv* —**crassness** *n*

-crat *suffix* a supporter or member of a particular form of government or hierarchy ○ *technocrat* [< French *-crate* < Greek *kratos* 'strength']

cratch /krach/ *n* a rack for hay or other livestock fodder [13C. < Old French *creche* 'manger, crib' < Germanic]

crate /krayt/ *n* **1.** BOX OR BASKET a large basket or a large open sturdy box used to carry or store objects **2.** OLD VEHICLE an old rickety aeroplane, car, or lorry (*dated informal*) ■ *vti* (crates, crating, crated) PUT SOMETHING IN CRATE to put or pack something in a crate [14C. Origin ?]

crater (sense 4)

crater /kráytər/ *n* **1.** VOLCANO SUMMIT a circular funnel-shaped depression produced by volcanic eruption **2.** EXPLOSION HOLE a large hole in the ground or a surface caused by an explosion **3.** METEORITE IMPACT AREA a bowl-shaped hole on the surface of the Moon or a planet caused by the impact of a meteorite **4.** ANCIENT GREEK WINE BOWL in ancient Greece, a large shallow bowl with two handles, used to mix wine and water. US spelling **krater** ■ *vti* (-ters, -tering, -tered) FORM CRATERS to form craters, or make craters form in something [Early 17C. Via Latin < Greek *kratēr* '(mixing) bowl']

Crater *n* a small constellation of the southern hemisphere. See illustration at **constellation**

craton /kráy ton/ *n* the extensive interior of a large block of the Earth's crust that has been relatively stable for many millions of years [Mid-20C. Either alteration of *kratogen* < Greek *kratos* 'strength'; or < German *Kraton*, alteration of Greek *kratos*] —**cratonic** /krə tónnik/ *adj*

cratur /kráytər/ *n Ireland, Scotland* **1.** whisky, often distilled illegally (*informal*) ○ *a drop of the cratur* **2.** same as **person** (sense 1) (*slang*) [Variant of CREATURE]

cravat /krə vát/ *n* a scarf or band of fabric worn around a man's neck, usually inside a shirt, and tied at the front [Mid-17C. < French *cravate* < *Cravate* 'Croatian' < German *Krabat(e)* < Serbo-Croat *Hrvāt* 'a Croat']

crave /krayv/ (craves, craving, craved) *v* **1.** *vti* to have a strong desire for something **2.** *vt* to beg somebody to give or do something (*archaic*) [Old English *crafian* 'to demand' < Germanic] —**craver** *n* —**cravingly** *adv*

SYNONYMS See **want**.

craven /kráyv'n/ *adj* so lacking in courage as to be worthy of contempt ■ *n* a despicable coward (*archaic*) [12C. Origin ?] —**cravenly** *adv* —**cravenness** *n*

SYNONYMS See *cowardly*.

craving /kráyving/ *n* a strong desire for something

craw /kraw/ *n* **1.** ZOOL, INSECTS same as **crop** *n* (senses 7–8) **2.** the stomach of an animal (*informal*) **3.** *Ireland* the throat or gullet [14C. Related to Middle Low German *krage* or Middle Dutch *crāghe* 'neck, throat']

crawfish /kráw fish/ *n* (*plural same* or **-fishes**) MARINE BIOL same as **crayfish** (sense 1) ■ *vi US* to withdraw from an undertaking or enterprise (*informal*) [Early 17C. Variant]

Joan Crawford

Crawford /kráwfərd/, **Joan** (1908–77) US actor. She starred in over 70 films and won an Academy Award for *Mildred Pierce* (1945). Born **LeSueur, Lucille**

'I think that the most important thing a woman can have – next to talent of course – is her hairdresser.'
[Joan Crawford, *Esquire*; April 1957]

crawl /krawl/ *vi* (**crawls, crawling, crawled**) **1.** MOVE CLOSE TO GROUND to move slowly along on hands and knees or with the body close to the ground or a surface **2.** MOVE VERY SLOWLY to move forward at a slow pace **3.** BE SERVILE to try to please somebody by behaving in a servile way (*informal*) **4.** BE OVERRUN to be filled with large numbers of moving people or things ○ *The place was crawling with reporters.* **5.** FEEL CREEPY to feel a sensation of being covered with moving insects, usually in reaction to something frightening or disgusting ○ *made his skin crawl* ■ *n* **1.** SLOW SPEED a very slow pace **2.** OVERARM SWIMMING STROKE a fast swimming stroke in which the swimmer lies face down and uses a flutter kick and an overarm stroke **3.** PROGRESS ON HANDS AND KNEES slow movement on hands and knees or with the body close to the ground or a surface [14C. Probably < Old Norse *krafla* 'paw with the hands'] —**crawlingly** *adv*

crawler /kráwlər/ *n* **1.** SOMEBODY ACTING INGRATIATINGLY somebody regarded as servile or sycophantic (*informal*) **2.** SOMETHING THAT CRAWLS an insect or other animal that crawls **3.** VEHICLE WITH TRACKS a vehicle that has continuous tracks of linked plates instead of wheels **4.** ONLINE, COMPUT PROGRAM COLLECTING ONLINE DOCUMENTS a computer program that collects online documents and reference links

crawler lane *n* an extra lane on an uphill section of a main road for slow-moving vehicles

Crawley /kráwli/ town in West Sussex, southeastern England. It was designated a new town in 1947. Population: 99,744 (2001).

crawling peg /kráwling-/ *n* a method of controlling exchange rates or prices by limiting their fluctuation for a time and later allowing them to change in small increments

crawl space *n* a low unfinished space under a floor or above a ceiling in a building that gives access to plumbing, wiring, and ductwork

crawly /kráwli/ (**-ier, -iest**) *adj* causing a shuddery disgust or unease (*informal*)

craw-thumper *n Ireland* an offensive term for somebody who makes a great show of being very pious (*insult*)

Craxi /kráksi/, **Bettino** (1934–2000) Italian politician. He was Italy's first socialist prime minister (1983–87). Indicted for corruption in 1993, he was convicted and sentenced to 14 years' imprisonment.

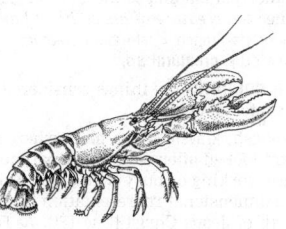

crayfish

crayfish /kráyfish/ (*plural same* or **-fishes**) *n* **1.** a freshwater crustacean with large claws like those of a lobster. It is prized for its tail meat. Superfamily: Astacoidea. **2.** MARINE BIOL same as **spiny lobster 3.** a crayfish used as food [14C. By folk etymology < French *crevice* < Indo-European, 'to scratch']

crayon /kráy on/ *n* **1.** COLOURED DRAWING STICK a stick of coloured wax, chalk, or charcoal, used for drawing and colouring **2.** DRAWING a drawing made using crayons ■ *vti* (**-ons, -oning, -oned**) USE CRAYONS to draw or colour something with crayons [Mid-17C. < French, 'pencil' < *craie* 'chalk' < Latin *creta* 'chalk, clay'] —**crayonist** *n*

craze /krayz/ *n* **1.** FAD a fashion that is extremely popular for a short time **2.** PERSONAL OBSESSION a short-lived obsession or enthusiasm that somebody has for something **3.** CERAMICS FINE CRACK a fine crack in the glaze of pottery. It happens when the glaze cools and contracts at a different temperature from the clay. ■ *vti* (**crazes, crazing, crazed**) **1.** BECOME OR MAKE IRRATIONAL to become, or make somebody become, irrational or highly excited (*often considered offensive*) **2.** CERAMICS PRODUCE OR SUSTAIN CRACKS to produce fine cracks in the glaze of pottery, or become covered with such cracks [14C. Probably < assumed Old Norse *krasa* 'shatter'] —**crazed** *adj*

crazing /kráyzing/ *n* fine cracks in the glaze of a piece of pottery, produced when the glaze cools and contracts at a different temperature from the clay. When the effect is deliberate, it is often called 'crackle'.

crazy /kráyzi/ *adj* (**-zier, -ziest**) (*informal*) **1.** OFFENSIVE TERM an offensive term meaning affected by a psychiatric disorder **2.** RIDICULOUS not showing good sense or practicality **3.** VERY FOND extremely fond of somebody or something ○ *crazy about tennis* ■ *n* (*plural* **-zies**) *N Am* OFFENSIVE TERM an offensive term for somebody with a psychiatric disorder —**crazily** *adv* —**craziness** *n*

Crazy Horse /kráyzi háwrss/ (1849?–77) Oglala Sioux leader. He opposed and fought against white settlement. Born **Tashunca Witco**

'It is a good day to fight! It is a good day to die! Strong hearts, brave hearts to the front! Weak hearts and cowards to the rear!'
[Crazy Horse, Address to Sioux warriors at the Battle of Little Bighorn; 25 June 1876]

crazy paving *n* a pavement of irregularly shaped pieces of paving stone fitted together, often used for garden paths

crazy quilt *n* a quilt made of irregularly shaped and patterned pieces of cloth sewn together

CRB *abbr* GOV Criminal Records Bureau

CRE *abbr* Commission for Racial Equality

creak /kreek/ *vi* (**creaks, creaking, creaked**) **1.** SQUEAK to make a prolonged squeaking noise **2.** MOVE WITH SQUEAKING to move along while making prolonged squeaking noises ■ *n* PROLONGED SQUEAK a prolonged squeaking noise [14C. An imitation of the sound] —**creakingly** *adv*

SPELLCHECK Do not confuse the spelling of *creak* and *creek* ('a narrow tidal inlet'), which sound similar.

creaky /kréeki/ (**-ier, -iest**) *adj* **1.** CREAKING making a prolonged squeaking noise **2.** STIFF not able to move easily, especially as a result of ageing (*informal*) **3.** OLD OR OLD-FASHIONED showing signs of having

deteriorated over time or of being old-fashioned (*informal*) —**creakily** *adv* —**creakiness** *n*

cream /kreem/ *n* **1.** FATTY PART OF MILK a high-fat liquid product separated from milk. Use: in cooking, accompaniment to desserts. **2.** CREAMY FOOD a food that contains cream or has a consistency like cream **3.** CREAMY LOTION a cosmetic or medicinal preparation that has a thick smooth consistency like cream **4.** BEST PART the best part of something ○ *the cream of society* **5.** YELLOW-TINGED WHITE an off-white colour with a yellow tinge **6.** SOFT-CENTRED CHOCOLATE a chocolate with a soft smooth filling ■ *v* (**creams, creaming, creamed**) *vt Aus* DEFEAT SOMEBODY to defeat somebody thoroughly in a competition or fight ■ *adj* WHITE WITH SOME YELLOW of a yellowish-white colour ■ *v* (**creams, creaming, creamed**) **1.** *vt* COMBINE INGREDIENTS to mix ingredients together to soften and combine them **2.** *vt* PREPARE SOMETHING WITH CREAM to add cream to something while cooking it or on serving it **3.** *vti* FORM FOAM ON TOP to form a frothy layer resembling cream on the surface of a liquid, or cause such a layer to form **4.** *vt* REMOVE CREAM FROM MILK to separate the cream from milk **5.** *vti* FORM CREAM to form cream, or allow milk to form cream **6.** *vt Aus, N Am* DEFEAT SOMEBODY to defeat somebody thoroughly (*slang*) ○ *We creamed them!* **7.** *vti* TABOO TERM a highly offensive term meaning to ejaculate (*taboo*) [14C. < French *creme*, blend of late Latin *cramum* + ecclesiastical Latin *chrisma* 'ointment' (< Greek *khrisma*)]

cream off *vt* **1.** to take away the best part of something **2.** *US* to take and use something for an illicit or unintended purpose (*informal*)

cream cheese *n* a soft white unmatured cheese with a high fat content

cream cracker *n* a crisp savoury biscuit usually eaten with cheese

creamer /kréemər/ *n* **1.** a cream substitute, used especially in coffee or tea **2.** a small jug for serving cream

creamery /kréeməri/ (*plural* **-ies**) *n* **1.** a place at which milk is processed and dairy products are produced **2.** a business that sells dairy products

cream of tartar *n* potassium bitartrate, when used as a leavening agent in cooking

cream puff *n* **1.** CREAM-FILLED PASTRY a sweet pastry made of a flaky shell filled with whipped cream and dusted with icing sugar **2.** OFFENSIVE TERM an offensive term for a man regarded as effeminate (*slang*) ■ *adj US* UNIMPORTANT of little consequence or difficulty

cream sherry *n* a smooth sweet sherry

cream soda *n* a carbonated soft drink flavoured with vanilla

cream tea *n* an afternoon meal of tea served with scones, jam, and thick, traditionally clotted, cream

creamware /kréem wair/ *n* glazed earthenware of a deep creamy colour, first produced in Britain in about 1720

creamy /kréemi/ (**-ier, -iest**) *adj* **1.** with a texture, colour, taste, or consistency like cream **2.** containing a large amount of cream —**creamily** *adv* —**creaminess** *n*

Crean /kreen/, **Simon** (b. 1949) Australian politician. He was elected to parliament as an Australian Labor Party MP in 1990 and was the leader of the Australian Labor Party from 2001 to 2003. Full name **Crean, Simon Findlay**

crease /kreess/ *n* **1.** FOLD PUT IN FABRIC a straight line formed in clothing or fabric by pressing **2.** UNWANTED FABRIC FOLD an unwanted line in clothing or fabric that has been crushed or folded **3.** SKIN WRINKLE a line or wrinkle on the skin **4.** LINE NEAR WICKET in cricket, a line that marks the position of the bowler or batsman **5.** ICE HOCKEY ICE HOCKEY GOAL AREA the rectangular area in front of an ice hockey goal **6.** SPORTS GOAL AREA the semicircular area surrounding a lacrosse goal ■ *v* (**creases, creasing, creased**) **1.** *vti* MAKE OR ACQUIRE CREASES to form lines, folds, or wrinkles in something, or become lined, folded, or wrinkled ○ *This fabric creases badly.* ○ *His face creased into a smile.* **2.** *vt* GRAZE SKIN to graze the skin and inflict a superficial wound [Late 16C. Probably < CREST] —**creaser** *n* —**creasy** *adj*

crease up *vti* to laugh, or make somebody laugh, uncontrollably (*informal*)

create /kri áyt/ (-ates, -ating, -ated) *v* 1. *vt* MAKE SOMETHING to bring something into existence 2. *vt* GIVE RISE TO SOMETHING to result in something or make something happen 3. *vti* PRODUCE INVENTIONS OR ART to use imagination to invent things or produce works of art 4. *vt* APPOINT SOMEBODY to give somebody a new title, role, or office 5. *vt* ARTS PERFORM ROLE FOR FIRST TIME to be the first person to perform a particular role in a theatrical production 6. *vi* CAUSE TROUBLE to become upset and make a fuss (*informal*) [14C. < Latin *creat-*, past participle of *creare* 'bring forth']

creatine

creatine /krée ə teen/, **creatin** /-tin/ *n* an amino acid that provides energy to muscles, usually as phosphocreatine. Formula: $C_4H_9N_3O_2$. [Mid-19C. < assumed Greek *kreat-* 'flesh']

creatine kinase *n* an enzyme that breaks down phosphocreatine into creatine and phosphoric acid, releasing energy

creatine phosphate *n* BIOCHEM same as **phosphocreatine**

creatinine /kri áttə neen/ *n* a derivative of creatine found in muscle, blood, and urine. Formula: $C_4H_7ON_3$. [Mid-19C. < CREATINE]

creation /kri áysh'n/ *n* 1. MAKING SOMETHING the bringing of something into existence 2. EARTH AND ITS INHABITANTS the world and everything in it 3. SOMETHING CREATED BY SOMEBODY a product of human imagination or invention 4. ELABORATE GARMENT an elaborate or striking item of clothing —**creational** *adj*

Creation *n* 1. according to the Bible, the act of God that brought the universe and all living beings into existence 2. according to the Bible, the universe as created by God

creationism /kri áysh'nizəm/ *n* the belief that God created the universe —**creationist** *adj*, *n*

creation science *n* the attempt to provide scientific proof for the account of God's creation of the world that is described in the Bible

creative /kri áytiv/ *adj* 1. NEW AND ORIGINAL using or showing use of the imagination to create new ideas or things ○ *a creative approach to the problem of lack of space* 2. ABLE TO CREATE able to create things ○ *Humans are a creative species.* 3. RESOURCEFUL making imaginative use of the limited resources available ○ *a creative cook* 4. FIN DECEPTIVE IN PRESENTING FINANCIAL INFORMATION employing deceptive methods to distort financial records (*ironic*) ○ *creative accounting* ○ *creative bookkeeping* ■ IDEAS PERSON a creator of new ideas and concepts for sales campaigns (*informal*) ○ *ad agency creatives hard at work on a TV infomercial* —**creatively** *adv* —**creativeness** *n*

creative writing *n* 1. the writing of fiction, poetry, or drama, often as an exercise 2. works of fiction, poetry, or drama

creativity /krée ay tívvəti/ *n* 1. the ability to use the imagination to develop new and original ideas or things, especially in an artistic context 2. the quality of being creative

creator /kri áytər/ *n* somebody who produces or initiates something —**creatorship** *n*

Creator *n* God regarded as creator of the universe

creature /kréechər/ *n* 1. LIVING BEING any living person or animal 2. UNPLEASANT ANIMAL an unpleasant or frightening living thing 3. CREATED THING somebody or something that has been created ○ *a creature of your imagination* 4. TYPE OF PERSON somebody of a particular type ○ *He's a harmless creature.* 5. SUB-

SERVIENT PERSON somebody who owes his or her status to another person and is thereby subject to undue influence ○ *a creature of his political handlers* [13C. Directly or via French < late Latin *creatura* < Latin *creat-* (see CREATE)] —**creatural** *adj*

creature comforts *npl* things considered necessary for a comfortable life

crèche /kresh, kraysh/ *n* 1. a place where small children are looked after while their parents or guardians are working or busy with other tasks 2. N Am a three-dimensional representation of the scene at the birth of Jesus Christ [Late 18C. Via French, 'crib' < assumed Vulgar Latin *creppia* < Germanic]

cred /kred/ *n* same as **credibility** (sense 3) (*informal*) [Late 20C. Shortening]

credence /kréed'nss/ *n* 1. ACCEPTANCE acceptance based on the degree to which something is believable 2. TRUSTWORTHINESS the power to inspire belief or trust 3. *also* **credence table** CHR CHURCH TABLE FOR BREAD AND WINE a small shelf or table in a church where the bread, wine, and containers used for Communion are kept [14C. Directly or via French < medieval Latin *credentia* 'belief' < Latin *credent-*, present participle of *credere* 'believe']

credential /krə dénsh'l/ *n* 1. PROOF OF ABILITY OR TRUSTWORTHINESS a certificate, letter, or experience that qualifies somebody to do something 2. AUTHENTICATION anything that provides authentication for a claim ■ **credentials** *npl* OFFICIAL IDENTIFICATION a letter, badge, or other official identification that confirms somebody's position or status [15C. < medieval Latin *credentialis* 'entitling confidence' < *credentia* (see CREDENCE)]

credentialled /krə dénsh'ld/ *adj* 1. trained and licensed in a particular profession ○ *a credentialled medical practitioner* 2. having or carrying credentials that allow somebody to do something or participate in something (*informal*) ○ *spoke to all the credentialled reporters at the event*

credenza /krə dénzə/ *n* a low sideboard, usually without legs [Late 19C. Via Italian < medieval Latin *credentia* (see CREDENCE)]

credibility /kréddə bílləti/ *n* 1. BELIEVABILITY the ability to inspire belief or trust 2. WILLINGNESS TO BELIEVE a willingness to accept something as true 3. STATUS somebody's status as an acceptable person among a group of people

USAGE See **credible**.

credibility gap *n* 1. DISTRUST OF OFFICIAL STATEMENTS a situation in which the public distrusts the accuracy of official statements 2. LACK OF TRUST any situation in which a lack of trust exists between two groups 3. DISCREPANCY BETWEEN CLAIM AND TRUTH an apparent difference between what is claimed to be true and what is in fact true

credible /kréddəb'l/ *adj* 1. easy to believe 2. inspiring trust and confidence [14C. < Latin *credibilis* < *credere* 'believe'] —**credibly** *adv*

USAGE **credible**, **creditable**, or **credulous**? These three adjectives, and the corresponding nouns *credibility*, *credit*, and *credulity*, are sometimes confused. Somebody or something is **credible** when he, she, or it can be easily or readily believed: *My story may sound barely credible but I assure you it's true.* **Credible** also has the newer meaning 'inspiring confidence': *The government needs to develop a credible monetary policy.* Somebody is **credulous** when he or she is all too ready to believe: *Only the most credulous person would believe such a feeble excuse.* **Creditable** is connected with the word *credit* and means 'bringing credit': *An excellent squash player, she plays a creditable game of tennis as well.*

credit /kréddit/ *n* 1. DELAYED PAYMENT an arrangement by which a buyer can take possession of something now and pay for it later or over time ○ *offer credit* ○ *buy on credit* 2. TIME TO PAY the time allowed for payment of something by credit 3. SPENDING ENTITLEMENT AT SHOP money that a customer is owed by a shop and is entitled to spend there 4. MONEY PAID INTO ACCOUNT an amount of money paid into an account 5. AMOUNT BANK WILL LEND the amount of money that a financial institution is prepared to lend somebody 6. FINANCIAL STATUS somebody's financial status or reputation 7. RECOGNITION praise or recognition for something done 8. SOURCE OF PRIDE a source of pride or honour 9. ACKNOWLEDGMENT OF SOMEBODY'S ROLE a

mention of the role that somebody played in an endeavour, especially an artistic one 10. DEDUCTION OF PAYMENT FROM OWED AMOUNT the deduction from a business account of an amount owed that has been paid 11. ACCOUNT PAYMENTS COLUMN the right-hand side of an account record, where payments to the account are recorded 12. PAYMENT RECORDED a payment recorded against an amount owed 13. COURSE UNIT a completed unit of study in a course of higher education 14. N Am RECOGNITION OF COURSE COMPLETION official recognition that a student has successfully completed a course of study ○ *get credit for a course* 15. EXAMINATION GRADE a mark above a basic pass in an exam 16. EXAM MARK a mark awarded in one examination that counts towards an overall grade ■ **credits** *npl* CINEMA, MEDIA LIST OF ACKNOWLEDGMENTS a listing of the people involved in a film or television production, together with their roles or jobs ■ *vt* (-its, -iting, -ited) 1. BELIEVE SOMETHING to accept that something is true 2. RECOGNIZE SOMEBODY AS RESPONSIBLE to recognize somebody as the person responsible for an achievement 3. ATTRIBUTE SOMETHING TO SOMEBODY to ascribe something such as a personal quality to somebody 4. ADD MONEY TO BANK ACCOUNT to add an amount of money to somebody's bank or savings account 5. RECORD PAYMENT OF MONEY to record an amount of money as a payment in an accounting record 6. US EDUC SAY OFFICIALLY THAT STUDENT PASSED to award a credit to a student for successful completion of a course of study [Mid-16C. Via French < Latin *creditum* 'loan' < past participle of *credere* 'entrust, believe'] ◇ **to somebody's credit** something for which somebody should be commended

USAGE See **credible**.

ORIGIN The Latin word *credere*, 'to believe', from which **credit** is derived, is also the source of English *credible*, *creed*, *grant*, and *miscreant*.

creditable /krédditəb'l/ *adj* bringing credit, or worthy of praise —**creditability** /kréddítə bílləti/ *n* —**creditableness** *n* —**creditably** *adv*

USAGE See **credible**.

credit account *n* UK an account that allows a customer to buy goods and services and pay for them later. ANZ, N Am term **charge account**

credit bureau *n* US FIN same as **credit-reference agency**

credit card *n* a card issued by a bank or business that allows somebody to purchase goods and services and pay for them later, often with interest

credit line *n* 1. same as **line of credit** 2. a printed acknowledgment of the author or source of material that was included in a publication

credit note *n* UK, ANZ, Can FIN a slip of paper stating that somebody is owed an amount of money by a shop and is entitled to goods to that value. US term **credit slip**

creditor /kréddítər/ *n* a person or organization owed money by another

credit rating *n* an estimate of somebody's ability to repay money given on credit

credit-reference agency *n* a business that provides information concerning somebody's creditworthiness to companies or banks

credit slip *n* US same as **credit note**

credit squeeze *n* a reduction in the availability of credit or an increase in the interest charged for credit

credit standing *n* the reputation that somebody has for paying off financial obligations

credit transfer *n* a transfer of money between bank accounts

credit union *n* a cooperative savings association that makes loans to its members at reduced interest rates

creditworthy /kréddit wurthi/ *adj* considered to be financially reliable enough to be given credit or lent money —**creditworthiness** *n*

credo /kráydō/ (*plural* -dos) *n* a statement of principles or beliefs, especially one that is professed formally [12C. < Latin, 'I believe' (first words of the Apostles' and Nicene creeds), form of *credere* 'believe']

Credo (*plural* -dos) *n* 1. the Apostles' Creed or Nicene Creed, both of which are ancient statements of the

basic doctrines of Christianity **2.** a musical setting, especially in a Mass, of the Credo

credulity /krə dyóoləti/ *n* the tendency to believe something too readily

USAGE See ***credible***.

credulous /kréddyŏoləss/ *adj* **1.** too easily convinced that something is true **2.** resulting from a tendency to believe things too readily [Late 16C. < Latin *credulus* < *credere* 'believe'] —**credulously** *adv* —**credulousness** *n*

USAGE See ***credible***.

Cree /kree/ (*plural same* or **Crees**) *n* **1.** a member of a Native North American people who live in central Canada and Montana. The Cree are the largest group of the Native Americans in Canada. **2.** the Algonquian language of the Cree people. Native speakers: 62,000. [Mid-18C. < Canadian French *Cris*, shortening of *C(h)ristinaux*, alteration of an Algonquian word (modern *kinistiono*)] —**Cree** *adj*

creed /kreed/ *n* **1. STATEMENT OF BELIEFS** a formal summary of the principles of the Christian faith **2. RELIGION** a set of religious beliefs **3. SET OF PRINCIPLES** any set of beliefs or principles [Pre-12C. < Latin *credo* (see CREDO)]

creek /kreek/ *n* **1.** a narrow tidal inlet or bay on a sea coast, especially in a salt marsh **2.** *ANZ, N Am* a stream, especially one that flows into a river [15C. Directly or via French *crique* < Old Norse *kriki* 'nook, corner'] ◇ **up the creek (without a paddle)** in a difficult situation, or in trouble (*informal*)

creel /kreel/ *n* **1. WICKER BASKET FOR FISH** a wicker basket used by anglers for holding fish **2. WICKER FISH TRAP** a wicker trap for catching fish or lobsters **3. BOBBIN HOLDER** a framework in a spinning machine that holds the bobbins [14C. Origin ?]

creep /kreep/ *vi* (**creeps, creeping, crept** /krept/ or **creeped**) **1. MOVE QUIETLY** to move along silently and stealthily **2. MOVE NEAR GROUND** to move along with the body close to the ground **3. PROCEED SLOWLY** to move along very slowly **4. GRADUALLY DEVELOP** to appear, approach, or develop gradually **5. SHIVER WITH DISGUST** to tingle uncomfortably as if covered with crawling insects, especially from fear or disgust **6. SPREAD OVER SURFACE** to grow along a surface by sending out tendrils, suckers, or roots **7. BE DISPLACED SLIGHTLY** to move slightly from the original or proper position **8. BE OBSEQUIOUS** to behave in a servile manner to somebody in authority (*informal*) **9.** INDUST **DEFORM FROM STRESS OR HEAT** to become deformed over a period of time due to stress or heat ■ *n* **1. CREEPING MOVEMENT** a slow or stealthy pace or movement **2. SOMEBODY REPELLENT** somebody considered obnoxious or disliked (*informal*) **3. OBSEQUIOUS PERSON** somebody regarded as servile to those in authority (*informal*) **4. SLIGHT DISPLACEMENT** the slight movement of something **5.** GEOL **MOVEMENT OF ROCK** a gradual movement of rock and debris down a slope **6.** GEOL **DEFORMATION OF ROCKS UNDER STRESS** a slow deformation of rocks and minerals in response to prolonged stress **7.** METALL **DEFORMATION OF METAL UNDER STRESS** a gradual deformation of a hard material, especially metal, as a result of heat or stress ■ **creeps** *npl* **UNEASY FEELING** an uneasy or unnerving feeling usually caused by fear or disgust (*informal*) [Old English *crēopan* < Germanic]

creep up on *vt* **1.** to approach somebody or something stealthily **2.** to enter somebody's consciousness or feelings gradually

creepback /kreép bak/ *n* the tendency for employers to recruit new staff surreptitiously after making unnecessary redundancies

creeper /kreépər/ *n* **1. CLINGING PLANT** a plant that grows by means of tendrils, suckers, or roots that anchor it to a surface **2. SMALL CLIMBING BIRD** a small climbing bird with a slender curved beak and short legs. Native to: forests of North America, Europe, Asia, and Africa. Family: Certhiidae. **3. SOMEBODY OR SOMETHING THAT CREEPS** a person or animal that moves by creeping **4.** AUTOMOT same as **cradle** *n* (sense 3) **5. UNDERWATER GRAPPLING DEVICE** a device with hooks that is used to drag for submerged objects in deep water

creeping /kreéping/ *adj* **1.** developing or advancing gradually over a period of time **2.** growing and spreading by sending out tendrils, suckers, or roots

creeping eruption *n* a skin disease caused by hookworm or roundworm larvae, producing itching and eruptions in the form of spreading red lines on the skin

creeping Jennie /-jénni/, **creeping Jenny** *n UK, NZ, Can* an evergreen creeping plant with round leaves. Flowers: yellow. Native to: Europe, eastern North America. Latin name: *Lysimachia nummularia*. Aus, US term **moneywort**

creeping thistle *n* a thistle that grows 90 cm/3 ft tall. Flowers: pinkish-purple to white. Latin name: *Cirsium arvense*. N Am term **Canada thistle**

creepy /kreépi/ (**-ier, -iest**) *adj* unsettling because of causing fear, disgust, or uneasiness (*informal*) —**creepily** *adv* —**creepiness** *n*

creepy-crawly (*plural* **creepy-crawlies**) *n* a crawling insect or small animal (*informal*)

cremains /kri máynz/ *npl US* the ashes that remain after a corpse has been cremated [Mid-20C. Contraction of *cremated remains*]

cremate /krə máyt/ (**-mates, -mating, -mated**) *vt* to burn a corpse until only ashes are left [Late 19C. Either < Latin *cremat-* (see CREMATION), or back-formation < CREMATION] —**cremator** *n*

cremation /krə máysh'n/ *n* **1.** the burning of a corpse until only ashes are left **2.** a funeral ceremony during which a cremated person's ashes are interred [Early 17C. < Latin *cremation-* < *cremat-*, past participle of *cremare* 'burn']

crematorium /krémmə táwri əm/ (*plural* **-riums** or **-ria** /-ri ə/) *n* a building or furnace where corpses are incinerated [Late 19C. < modern Latin < Latin *cremat-* (see CREMATION)]

crematory /krémmətəri/ *n* (*plural* **-ries**) *N Am* same as **crematorium** ■ *adj* relating to or used for cremation

crème brûlée /krém broo láy/ (*plural* **crème brûlées** /-láyz/ or **crèmes brûlées** /krém broo láy/) *n* a rich baked custard with caramelized sugar on top [< French, 'burnt cream']

crème caramel /krém kárrə mél/ (*plural* **crème caramels** or **crèmes caramel** /krém -/) *n* a custard coated with caramelized sugar, which forms a sauce, cooked in a mould. It is chilled and removed from the mould before serving. [< French, 'caramel cream']

crème de cacao /krém də kə kaá ō/ (*plural* **crème de cacaos** or **crèmes de cacao** /krém-/) *n* a sweet chocolate-flavoured liqueur [< French, 'cream of cacao']

crème de la crème /krém də la krém/ *n* the very best of a group of people or things [< French, 'cream of the cream']

crème de menthe /krém də maánth/ (*plural* **crème de menthes** or **crèmes de menthe** /krém-/) *n* a sweet mint-flavoured liqueur [< French, 'cream of mint']

crème fraîche /krém frésh/ *n* a thickened French soured cream, used in cooking or served with other foods [< French, 'fresh cream']

Cremona /kri mṓnə/ capital of Cremona Province, Lombardy, northern Italy. It is situated on the River Po, southeast of Milan. Population: 70,887 (2001).

crenate /kreé nayt/, **crenated** /-naytid/ *adj* having a scalloped edge or a surface with rounded projections (*technical*) [Late 18C. < modern Latin *crenatus* < Latin *crena* 'small notch'] —**crenately** *adv*

crenation /kri náysh'n/ *n* **1. ROUNDED PROJECTION** a rounded projection from the edge or surface of something such as a plant leaf or a coin **2. SCALLOPED EDGE OR SURFACE** a scalloped edge, or a surface with rounded projections **3. SHRINKAGE OF RED BLOOD CELLS** a medical condition in which the red blood cells shrink and develop multiple indentations and protrusions

crenel /krénn'l/, **crenelle** /krə nél/ *n* **1.** a gap in the top of a castle wall or parapet, used for firing missiles or shooting **2.** a rounded protrusion from an edge or surface [15C. < Old French, 'small notch' < Latin *crena*]

crenelate *adj* ARCHIT US spelling of **crenellate**

crenellate /krénə layt/ (**-lates, -lating, -lated**) *vt* **1.** to provide a structure with battlements or decorative features resembling battlements **2.** to make something with square indentations like the openings (**crenels**) of a battlement [Early 19C. < French *créneler* < Old French *crenel* (see CRENEL)] —**crenellated** *adj* —**crenellation** *n*

crenelle *n* ARCHIT another spelling of **crenel**

crenulate /krénnyŏo layt/, **crenulated** /-laytid/ *adj* describes plant leaves or shorelines that have a finely scalloped or notched wavy edge (*technical*) [Late 18C. < modern Latin *crenulatus* < *crenula* 'small notch' < Latin *crena*]

crenulation /krénnyŏo láysh'n/ *n* (*technical*) **1.** a very small notch or indentation, e.g. on a plant's leaf **2.** the condition of having very fine notching or indentations along an edge

creodont /kreé ə dont/ (*plural* **-donts** or **-donta** /-dóntə/) *n* an extinct carnivorous mammal that lived during the Tertiary period. Suborder: Creodonta. [Late 19C. < modern Latin *Creodonta* 'flesh-toothed ones' < Greek *kreas* 'flesh' + *odont-* 'tooth']

creole /kreé ōl/ *n* **LANGUAGE OF MIXED ORIGIN** a language that has evolved from the mixture of two or more languages and has become the first language of a group. See panel on next page ■ *adj* **1. COOKED AS IN NEW ORLEANS** cooked in a spicy highly flavoured way associated with the French Creoles of New Orleans. Tomatoes, hot peppers, onions, and rice are characteristic ingredients. **2. OF CREOLE** relating to or belonging to a creole language [Late 19C. < CREOLE]

Creole *n* **1. SOMEBODY OF FRENCH ANCESTRY** somebody who comes from the southern United States, especially southern Louisiana, and is descended from early French settlers **2. LANGUAGE OF LOUISIANA** the creolized French language spoken by the Creoles of New Orleans and southern Louisiana **3. LANGUAGE OF CARIBBEAN ISLANDS** a group of creolized languages, based on English and French, spoken on some islands of the Caribbean **4. CARIBBEAN PERSON OF EUROPEAN ANCESTRY** somebody who comes from a Caribbean or Latin American country and is of European, especially Spanish descent **5. CREOLE SPEAKER** somebody of both European and African ancestry who speaks a form of Creole ▶ See panel on next page [Mid-18C. < French < Spanish *criollo* 'native' < Portuguese *crioulo* < *criar* 'bring up' < Latin *creare* 'bring forth'] —**Creole** *adj*

creolize /kreé ə līz/ (**-lizes, -lizing, -lized**), **creolise** (**-lises, -lising, -lised**) *vt* to form a new mixed language from two or more other languages —**creolization** /kreé ə lī záysh'n/ *n* —**creolized** *adj*

Creon /kreé ən/ *n* in Greek mythology, the brother of Jocasta and the successor of Oedipus as king of Thebes. He was also the uncle of Antigone and issued an edict forbidding the burial of the body of her brother Polynices, which she defied.

creosol /kreé ə sol/ *n* a pale yellow or colourless oily liquid. Source: creosote. Formula: $C_8H_{10}O_2$. [Mid-19C. < CREOSOTE]

creosote /kreé ə sōt/ *n* **1. WOOD PRESERVATIVE** a thick yellowish to brown oily substance. Source: coal tar. Use: wood preservative. **2. ANTISEPTIC** a yellow to colourless oily substance. Source: wood tar. Use: antiseptic. ■ *vt* (**-sotes, -soting, -soted**) **APPLY CREOSOTE TO SOMETHING** to apply creosote to wood as a preservative [Mid-19C. < German *Kreosote* < Greek *kreas* 'flesh' + *sōtēr* 'preserver'; from its antiseptic properties]

creosote bush *n* a resinous evergreen bush with leaves that smell like creosote. Native to: deserts of southwestern United States and Mexico. Latin name: *Larrea tridentata*.

crêpe /krayp/, **crepe** *n* **1.** TEXTILES a light fine fabric with a crinkled surface **2.** FOOD a thin pancake usually served rolled up or folded with a filling **3.** PAPER same as **crepe paper 4.** INDUST same as **crepe rubber** [Late 18C. < French < Old French *crespe* 'curled' < Latin *crispus*] —**crêpy** *adj*

crêpe de Chine /kráyp də sheén/, **crepe de Chine** *n* a light smooth silk fabric. Use: delicate articles of clothing. [< French, 'crêpe of China']

crepe paper, **crêpe paper** *n* a thin, slightly stretchy, crinkled coloured paper, used for wrapping presents or making decorations (*hyphenated when used before a noun*)

crêperie /kráypəri, krép-/, **creperie** *n* a restaurant that specializes in thin pancakes (**crêpes**) with fillings [< French *crêperie* < *crêpe* (see CRÊPE)]

crepe rubber, **crêpe rubber** *n* rubber in the form of thin crinkled sheets, used especially for the soles of shoes

crêpe suzette /krayp soo zét/ (*plural* **crêpes suzettes** /kráyp soo zét/) *n* a pancake prepared with orange sauce and flambéed with an orange-flavoured

WORLD ENGLISH ***Creole*** languages are found in communities where a pidgin language earlier served as a useful lingua franca. Creoles are often the sole language of a community and so are capable of fulfilling all their speakers' linguistic needs. In being transformed into a creole, a pidgin's vocabulary is expanded and its structures made increasingly subtle, flexible, and precise.

Creoles, which involve a language shift, are often caused by the disruption of normal speech communities. The best-known examples are found in the Caribbean. Caribbean creoles evolved as a result of the slave trade, when as many as ten million Africans, speaking perhaps 500 different mother tongues, were sold into slavery. Africans working on plantations were obliged to relinquish their ancestral languages and communicate in pidgin forms of a European tongue. Children born into slave communities used the pidgin for all their communication needs and thus transformed it into a creole.

More recently, creoles related to English have developed in many other places including Cameroon, Nigeria, Hawaii, and Papua New Guinea. In such areas, speakers found that the pidgin lingua franca helped communication between different groups so much that it was increasingly spoken at home and children acquired it as a mother tongue.

The name *creole* comes from Spanish *criollo* meaning 'native'. In the 16th century, a 'creole' was a person of European ancestry born in the New World. Over the next two centuries, it was applied to children of mixed race and then to Africans born in the Americas. By the early 1800s, 'creole' could be applied to a language.

Creoles develop differently depending on whether they coexist with the language from which they draw their vocabulary. In parts of the world like Jamaica, for example, where the Creole or *Patwa*coexists with Standard English, most speakers are adept at using a spectrum of forms depending on such factors as the occasion, the degree of intimacy between speakers, and the level of education.

The study of contemporary creoles indicates that the life cycle of pidgin to creole may be a regular feature of language contact. Latin probably developed into a pidgin form in many regions of the Roman Empire. Some versions undoubtedly died but others became standardized and eventually developed into the related Romance languages. There is evidence, too, that contemporary English has undergone similar processes because of contacts with the Vikings and Normans. When compared with Old English, Chaucer's language shows many features that indicate it had developed into a pidgin language.

Here is an example of Hawaiian Creole English: 'God, you our Fadda./ You stay inside da sky./ We like all da peopo know fo shua how you stay,/ An dat you stay good and spesho,/ An we like dem give you plenny respeck. Da Jesus Book, Matthew 6:9–10' (Joseph E. Grimes *et al.*)

(God, you are our Father./ You are in heaven./ We want everyone to be certain how you are, and that you are good and special,/ and we want them to give you plenty of respect.)

See also ***pidgin***.

liqueur or brandy [< French, probably after *Suzanne* Reichenberg (1853–1924), French actress]

crepitate /kréppi tayt/ (**-tates, -tating, -tated**) *v* **1.** *vi* to make a crackling or grating sound (*formal or literary*) **2.** to make the crackling or grating sound of crepitus [Early 17C. < Latin *crepitat-*, past participle of *crepitare* 'crackle' < *crepare* 'to rattle', an imitation of the sound] —**crepitant** *adj* —**crepitation** /kréppi táysh'n/ *n*

crepitus /kréppitəss/ *n* **1.** the grating sound heard when the broken ends of a bone rub together **2.** a crackling sound heard in the chest of somebody who has a lung disease such as pneumonia [Early 19C. < Latin, 'rattling' < *crepare* (see CREPITATE)]

crept past participle, past tense of **creep**

crepuscular /kri púskyŏolər/ *adj* **1.** relating to or resembling the fading light of dusk (*literary*) **2.** describes fish and land mammals that are active at dusk and dawn, when the light level is low (*technical*) [Mid-17C. < Latin *crepusculum* 'twilight']

Cres. *abbr* Crescent (*used in addresses*)

cresc. *abbr* MUSIC crescendo

crescendo /krə shéndō/ *n* (*plural* **-dos** or **-does** or **-di** /-dee/) **1.** MUSIC **INCREASE IN LOUDNESS** a gradual increase in the volume of a passage of music **2.** MUSIC **MUSIC PLAYED INCREASINGLY LOUDLY** a passage of music in which there is a gradual increase in volume **3. INTENSIFICATION** an increase in volume or intensity similar to a crescendo in music **4.** ⚠ **CLIMAX** the climax of an increase in volume or intensity ■ *adj* **BECOMING LOUDER OR MORE INTENSE** gradually increasing in volume or intensity ■ *adv* MUSIC **WITH INCREASING LOUDNESS** with a gradual increase in volume ■ *vi* (**-does, -doing, -doed**) **BECOME LOUDER OR STRONGER** to increase in volume or intensity [Late 18C. < Italian, present participle of *crescere* 'increase' < Latin, 'grow']

USAGE A ***crescendo*** is properly a process and not the end of a process. This is usually well understood in musical contexts, where the word is a technical term. In figurative uses, however, it tends to be used as an alternative for *climax*, which is indeed the end point or culmination of a process. In careful usage, noise or feeling can increase *to* a climax but it does so *in a* ***crescendo***. Correct: *The bird's calls rose in a crescendo.* Avoid: *The abusive phone calls reached a crescendo the following week.*

crescent /kréss'nt, krézz'nt/ *n* **1. LESS THAN HALF VISIBLE MOON** the Moon or a planet before and after it is full, when it has less than half its disc illuminated **2. ARC SHAPE** a curved shape like that of the Moon when it is less than half illuminated **3. ARC-SHAPED THING** something shaped like a crescent **4.** *also* **Crescent ARC-SHAPED STREET** a curved street, especially one that opens onto the same street at each end **5.** *also* **Crescent ISLAMIC SYMBOL** the emblem of Islam or Turkey, shaped like a crescent moon **6.** *also* **Crescent ISLAMIC POWER** Islamic or Turkish power **7. HERALDIC SYMBOL FOR SECOND SON** in heraldry, a crescent moon, used to signify a second son ■ *adj* **1. ARC-SHAPED** shaped like a crescent **2. GROWING** gradually increasing in size (*literary*) [14C. Via Anglo-Norman < Latin *crescent-*, present participle of *crescere* 'grow'] —**crescentic** /krə séntik, krə zéntik/ *adj*

ORIGIN The Latin word *crescere*, 'to grow', from which ***crescent*** is derived, is also the source of English *accrete, concrete, create, crescendo, crew*[1], *croissant, increase,* and *recruit.*

cresol /kreé sol/ *n* a colourless compound. Source: wood or coal tar. Use: antiseptic, disinfectant. Formula: C_7H_8O. [Mid-19C. Alteration of CREOSOL]

cress /kress/ (*plural same* or **cresses**) *n* **1.** small pungently flavoured leaves. Use: in salads, as a garnish. **2.** a plant of the mustard family whose leaves are cress [Old English *cressa* < Germanic]

cresset /kréssit/ *n* a metal cup or basket mounted on a pole and filled with oil or pitch that was burned to give light [14C. < Old French < *craisse* 'oil, grease' < Latin *crassus* 'fat']

Cressida /kréssidə/ *n* **1.** in medieval retellings of the Trojan War, a Trojan woman captured by the Greeks who was unfaithful to her Trojan lover, Troilus, by giving herself to the Greek Diomedes **2.** a small natural satellite of Uranus, discovered by the Voyager 2 planetary probe in 1986

crest /krest/ *n* **1. TOP OF CURVE OR SLOPE** the top part of something that slopes or rises upwards, e.g. a wave or a hill **2. CULMINATION** the highest stage or culminating point in an activity or achievement **3.** ZOOL **TUFT ON ANIMAL'S HEAD** a tuft or other growth on the top of the head of a bird or other animal **4. SOMETHING RESEMBLING HEAD TUFT** something resembling the crest of a bird or other animal **5.** ZOOL **NECK RIDGE** a ridge along the neck of a horse, lion, or other mammal, from which hair grows **6.** ARMS **HELMET ORNAMENT** a plume or other decoration on the top of a helmet **7.** HERALDRY **SYMBOL OF FAMILY OR OFFICE** a small animal, bird, or other heraldic symbol of a family or office, placed above the shield in a coat of arms or used alone on a helmet ■ *v* (**crests, cresting, crested**) **1.** *vi* **RISE UP TO TOP** to reach or rise to a crest **2.** *vt* **REACH TOP OF SOMETHING** to reach the crest of something such as a hill **3.** *vt* **TOP SOMETHING** to be at the top of something [14C. Via French *creste* < Latin *crista* 'tuft'] —**crested** *adj*

crestfallen /krést fawlən/ *adj* disappointed or humiliated, especially after being enthusiastic or confident [Late 16C. < the drooping of somebody's head when disappointed]

cresting /krésting/ *n* **1.** an ornamental ridge on a roof **2.** an ornamental carving or rail on the top of a piece of furniture

cresylic acid /kri síllik-/ *n* CHEM same as **cresol** [< *cresyl*, isomeric radical < CRESOL]

cretaceous /kri táyshəss/ *adj* consisting of or resembling chalk (*technical*) [Late 17C. < Latin *cretaceus* 'chalky' < *creta* 'chalk'] —**cretaceously** *adv*

Cretaceous *n* the period of geological time, 144 million to 65 million years ago, during which the dinosaurs became extinct, layers of chalk were laid down, and flowering plants arose —**Cretaceous** *adj*

Crete /kreet/ largest Greek island in the southern Aegean Sea. The chief town is Heraklion. Population: 540,054 (1991). Area: 8,261 sq. km/3,190 sq. mi. —**Cretan** /kreét'n/ *adj, n*

cretic /kreétik/ *n* LITERAT same as **amphimacer** [Late 16C. Via Latin, 'Cretan' < Greek *krētikos* < *Krētē* 'Crete']

cretin /kréttin/ *n* **1.** an offensive term for somebody considered unintelligent (*insult*) **2.** an offensive term for somebody affected by congenital myxoedema (*dated insult*) [Late 18C. Via French < Swiss French *creitin* 'mentally disabled person' < Latin *Christianus* (see CHRISTIAN)] —**cretinism** *n* —**cretinoid** *adj* —**cretinous** *adj*

cretonne /kre tón/ *n* a heavy cotton, linen, or rayon fabric, usually printed with a colourful design. Use: upholstery. [Late 19C. < French, after *Creton*, village in Normandy]

Creutzfeldt-Jakob disease /króyts felt yák ob-/ *n* a rare fatal brain disease, a form of spongiform encephalopathy, that develops slowly, causing dementia and loss of muscle control. A transmissible protein particle (**prion**) is the suspected cause. A new variant of the disease, which develops rapidly and affects younger people, appeared in the late 1980s. [Late 20C. After H. G. *Creutzfeldt* (1885–1964) and A. M. *Jakob* (1884–1931), German neurologists]

crevalle jack (*plural same* or **crevalle jacks**) *n* FISH same as **jack crevalle**

crevasse /krə váss/ *n* **1. DEEP CRACK** a deep crack, e.g. in the ice of a glacier **2.** *US* **CRACK IN EMBANKMENT** a crack in a river embankment or dyke ■ *vti* (**-vasses, -vassing, -vassed**) **FORM CREVASSES** to develop crevasses, or make something develop crevasses [Early 19C. < French, modern form of Old French *crevace* (see CREVICE)]

crevice /krévviss/ *n* a narrow crack or opening, especially in rock [14C. < Old French *crevace* 'a burst' < *crever* 'to burst' < Latin *crepare* 'to rattle', an imitation of the sound] —**creviced** *adj*

crew[1] /kroo/ *n* **1. ONBOARD STAFF** the people who work on a ship, aircraft, or spacecraft **2.** NAUT **SHIP'S STAFF EXCLUDING OFFICERS** the members of a ship's staff who are not officers **3. SPECIALIZED STAFF ON CRAFT** a smaller group within the overall staff of a ship, aircraft, or spacecraft who are assigned a particular task ○ *cabin crew* **4. PEOPLE WORKING TOGETHER** a group of people who work together on a project or task **5. GROUP OF FRIENDS** a group of people who spend much time together or are somehow associated with one another (*informal*) **6. ROWERS** the rowers and cox of a racing boat ■ *v* (**crews, crewing, crewed**) **1.** *vi* **BE ON CREW** to be a member of a crew **2.** *vt* **BE ON STAFF OF VESSEL** to serve as a member of the personnel of a ship, aircraft, or spacecraft (*often passive*) [15C. < French *creüe* 'increase, recruit' < the past participle of *croistre* 'grow' < Latin *crescere*]

crew[2] past tense of **crow**[2]

crew chief *n US* a noncommissioned officer in the US Air Force who is in charge of the maintenance and ground handling of an aircraft

crew cut *n* a haircut, usually worn by men and boys, with the hair cut close to the head [Probably because adopted by boat crews at the US universities of Harvard and Yale in the mid-20C]

Crewe /kroo/ town and major rail junction in Cheshire, northwestern England. Population: 63,351 (1991).

a at; aa father; aw all; ay day; air hair; ə about, item, edible, common, circus; e egg; ee eel; hw when; i it, happy; ī ice; 'l apple; 'm rhythm; 'n fashion; o odd; ō open; ŏŏ good; oo pool; ow owl; oy oil; th thin; th this; u up; ur urge;

crewed /krood/ *adj* operated by onboard personnel ○ *a crewed mission to the Moon*

crewel /kroō əl/ *n* **1.** a loosely twisted woollen yarn used in embroidery **2.** HANDICRAFT same as **crewelwork** [15C. Origin ?]

crewelwork /kroō əl wurk/ *n* embroidery work done with crewel yarn

crewmate /kroō mayt/ *n* a fellow member of a crew, especially on board a ship or spacecraft

crew neck *n* **1.** a close-fitting round neckline on a sweater, sweatshirt, or other garment **2.** a sweater with a close-fitting round neck [< the sweaters with such a neckline worn by boat crews] —**crew-neck** *adj*

crib /krib/ *n* **1.** AGRIC **HAY RACK** a trough or box for hay or other fodder from which livestock can feed **2.** CHR **MODEL OF MANGER** a model of the manger in which, according to the Bible, Jesus Christ slept after his birth **3.** *N Am* FURNITURE same as **cot**[1] (sense 1) **4.** AGRIC **ANIMAL'S STALL** a stall for cattle or horses **5.** EDUC same as **crib sheet** (*informal*) **6. PLAGIARISM** a theft of material from an intellectual or artistic work **7.** *NZ* **SMALL HUT** in the Otago and Southland regions of New Zealand, a small cabin **8. PROSTITUTE'S ROOM** a rundown house or room used by a prostitute (*slang*) **9. BASKET** a wicker basket **10.** CARDS **DEALER'S CARDS** in cribbage, the cards used by the dealer consisting of cards discarded by the other players **11.** CARDS same as **cribbage** (*informal*) **12.** *ANZ* **SNACK** a light snack (*informal*) ■ *v* (**cribs, cribbing, cribbed**) **1.** *vti* **PLAGIARIZE** to steal somebody's ideas or work (*informal*) **2.** *vi* EDUC **USE CRIB SHEET** to use a crib sheet in an examination (*informal*) **3.** *vt* **PUT SOMEBODY OR SOMETHING IN CRIB** to put somebody or something such as an infant or hay into a crib **4.** *vt* **PROVIDE CRIB FOR SOMETHING** to construct or provide a crib for something [Old English *crib(b)* 'manger, trough' < Germanic] —**cribber** *n*

cribbage /kríbbij/ *n* a card game for two to four players in which the score is kept by moving pegs along rows of holes in a small board (**cribbage board**) [Mid-17C. Probably < CRIB + -AGE]

cribbing /kríbbing/ *n* **1.** EDUC the use of a crib sheet to cheat in an examination (*informal*) **2.** CONSTR the timbers used for a framework, e.g. of a mineshaft or foundation **3.** VET same as **crib-biting**

crib-biting *n* a behavioural pattern that develops in horses kept in stables, marked by chewing of the stalls and salivating excessively. The disorder is partly an inherited condition and partly an expression of boredom. —**crib-biter** *n*

crib death *n N Am* MED same as **cot death**

cribellum /kri béllәm/ (*plural* **-la** /-lә/) *n* an oval perforated plate just in front of the silk-secreting organs (**spinnerets**) in some spiders, through which the emerging silk is combed [Late 19C. < late Latin, 'small sieve' < *cribrum* 'sieve']

cribriform /kríbbri fawrm/ *adj* describes a part with small holes like a sieve, especially the top part (**cribriform plate**) of the ethmoid bone forming the roof of the nasal cavity (*technical*) [Mid-18C. < Latin *cribrum* 'sieve']

crib sheet *n* a list of answers or a translation of a foreign text used for cheating in examinations or lessons

cricetid /krī séetid/ (*plural* **-tids** or *same*) *n* a small rodent of the family that includes the hamster, gerbil, muskrat, and vole. Family: Cricetidae. [Mid-20C. < modern Latin *Cricetidae* < *Cricetus* (genus name of hamsters) < medieval Latin *cricetus* 'hamster'] —**cricetid** *adj*

crick /krik/ *n* a painful stiffness or muscle spasm in the neck or back ■ *vt* (**cricks, cricking, cricked**) to cause a painful stiffness or muscle spasm in the neck or back [15C. Origin ?]

Crick /krik/, **Francis H. C.** (*b.* 1916) British biophysicist. He worked with James D. Watson and Maurice Wilkins in exploring the structure of the DNA molecule, for which they shared the Nobel Prize in physiology or medicine (1962). Full name **Francis Henry Compton Crick**

Popperfoto

cricket: a batsman is bowled

cricket[1] /kríkit/ *n* an outdoor sport played by two teams of 11 players using a flat bat, a small hard ball, and wickets. A player scores by batting the ball and running, while the defenders can get a player out by bowling and hitting the wicket, catching a hit ball, or running the player out. ■ *vi* (**-ets, -eting, -eted**) to play cricket [Late 16C. Origin ?] —**cricketer** *n* ◇ **not cricket** not fair or honourable (*dated informal*)

cricket[2] /kríkit/ *n* a leaping insect that has biting mouthparts, long legs, and antennae. The male produces a chirping sound by rubbing its forewings together. Family: Gryllidae. [14C. < French *criquet* 'grasshopper, locust' < Old French *criquer* 'to click', an imitation of the sound]

cricket[3] /kríkit/ *n* a wooden footstool [Mid-17C. Origin ?]

cricoid /krī́k oyd/ *adj* relating to or in the region of the lowermost cartilage of the larynx [Mid-18C. Via modern Latin, 'ring-shaped' < Greek *krikoeidēs* < *krikos* 'ring']

cricoid cartilage *n* the lowermost cartilage of the larynx, which has a shape like a signet ring

cri de coeur /krée dә kúr/ (*plural* **cris de coeur** /*pronunc. same*/) *n* a heartfelt, usually anguished appeal [< French, 'cry from the heart']

crier /krī́ әr/ *n* **1. CRYING PERSON OR ANIMAL** a person or animal that cries **2.** PUBLIC ADMIN same as **town crier** **3. LAW COURT ANNOUNCER** an official who makes public announcements of the orders of a court of law **4. VENDOR SHOUTING WARES** a pedlar who makes public announcements about the goods that he or she has for sale (*archaic*)

crim /krim/ *n ANZ* same as **criminal** (*informal*) [Early 20C. Shortening]

Crimbo /krímbō/ *n UK* same as **Christmas** (*informal*) [Late 20C. Alteration]

crime /krīm/ *n* **1. ILLEGAL ACT** an action prohibited by law or a failure to act as required by law **2. ILLEGAL ACTIVITY** activity that involves breaking the law ○ *measures to combat crime* **3. IMMORAL ACT** an act considered morally wrong **4. UNACCEPTABLE ACT** a shameful, unwise, or regrettable act (*informal*) ○ *It's a crime the way some people waste food.* [13C. Via French < Latin *crimen* (stem *crimin-*) 'judgment' < *cernere* 'decide'] —**crimeless** *adj*

CULTURAL NOTE ***Crime and Punishment***, a novel (1866) by Russian writer Fyodor Dostoyevsky. Set in St Petersburg, it describes how a young student, Raskolnikov, plans and carries out the murder of a woman pawnbroker, ostensibly for money, but in reality to prove that some individuals are above the law. Ultimately, however, his conscience forces him to confess his crime.

Crimea /krī mée ә/ peninsula in southeastern Ukraine between the Black Sea and the Sea of Azov. Area: 25,993 sq. km/10,036 sq. mi. —**Crimean** *n, adj*

crime against humanity *n* a cruel and immoral act such as torture, murder, or expulsion, committed against a large number of people

crime of passion *n* a crime that is motivated by an extreme emotion, especially sexual jealousy

crime passionnel /kréem pássi ә nél/ (*plural* **crimes passionnels** /*pronunc. same*/) *n* CRIME same as **crime of passion** [< French]

crime sheet *n* a record that lists somebody's breaches of military regulations

crime wave *n* a period during which more crimes than usual are committed

criminal /krímminәl/ *n* **SOMEBODY ACTING ILLEGALLY** somebody who has committed a crime ■ *adj* **1. PUNISHABLE AS CRIME** punishable as a crime under the law **2. PROSECUTING CRIMINALS** relating to or involved in the prosecution and punishment of people accused of committing crimes **3. RELATING TO CRIMINALS** relating to or done by criminals **4. MORALLY WRONG** morally wrong, whether illegal or not **5. UNACCEPTABLE** shameful, unwise, or regrettable (*informal*) ○ *a criminal waste of resources* [15C. Directly or via French < late Latin *criminalis* 'of crime' < Latin *crimin-* (see CRIME)] —**criminally** *adv*

criminal conversation *n* adultery considered as a legal breach of the marriage contract (*technical*)

criminalise *vt* LAW another spelling of **criminalize**

criminality /krímmi nállәti/ (*plural* **-ties**) *n* **1. CRIMINAL QUALITY** a criminal character or quality **2. TENDENCY TO BREAK LAW** a tendency to commit crimes **3. CRIME** a criminal act or practice (*often used in the plural*)

criminalize /krímminә līz/ (**-izes, -izing, -ized**), **criminalise** (**-ises, -ising, -ised**) *vt* **1.** to make an action punishable as a crime under the law **2.** to make somebody become a criminal or treat somebody as a criminal —**criminalization** /krímminә lī záysh'n/ *n*

criminal negligence *n* the crime of causing injury or harm to a person or property as the result of doing something or failing to provide a proper or reasonable level of care

criminal record *n* a record of somebody's previous convictions for crime

criminol. *abbr* criminology

criminology /krímmi nóllәji/ *n* the sociological study of crime, criminals, and the punishment of criminals —**criminological** /krímminә lójjik'l/ *adj* —**criminologically** *adv* —**criminologist** *n*

crimp /krimp/ *vt* (**crimps, crimping, crimped**) **1. FOLD OR PRESS ENDS TOGETHER** to fold or press the ends or edges of something together **2. PLEAT SOMETHING** to press or gather something such as a piece of fabric into small folds **3. CURL HAIR** to make somebody's hair wavy, usually with curling tongs **4. PINCH EDGES AS DECORATION** to pinch or press together the edges of pastry to form a seal or for decoration **5.** MANUF **MOULD LEATHER** to mould or form leather into a shape **6. JOIN METAL INTO SEAM** to bend or fold the edges of sheet metal to form a seam for a tube or between two pieces ■ *n* **1. CRIMPING** an act of crimping something **2. TIGHT HAIR WAVE** a tight artificial wave in somebody's hair, usually made with curling tongs **3. PINCHED EDGE** a fold or crease made by pinching together two edges, e.g. of fabric or pastry **4.** INDUST **CREASE FORMED BY BENDING** a fold or crease formed by bending something such as sheet metal **5. CURL OF WOOL FIBRES** the curl or wave of wool fibres [Late 17C. Probably < Dutch or Low German *krimpen* 'shrink, crimp' < Germanic] —**crimper** *n*

Crimplene /krím pleen/ *tdmk* a trademark for a crease-resistant synthetic clothing fabric

crimpy /krímpi/ (**-ier, -iest**) *adj* having many small waves, folds, or wrinkles

crimson /krímz'n/ *n* **DEEP RED COLOUR** a deep rich purplish-red colour ■ *v* (**-sons, -soning, -soned**) **1.** *vti* **BECOME OR MAKE CRIMSON** to become a deep rich purplish-red colour, or make something become this colour **2.** *vi* **REDDEN IN FACE** to blush with embarrassment, shyness, or shame [15C. Via Old Spanish *cremesín* < Arabic *ḳirmizī* 'red colour' < *ḳirmīz* 'kermes insect'] —**crimson** *adj*

cringe /krinj/ *vi* (**cringes, cringing, cringed**) **1. CROUCH OR MOVE BACK SUDDENLY** to pull the head and body quickly away from somebody or something in a frightened or servile way **2. BE EMBARRASSED OR UNCOMFORTABLE** to react to something with embarrassment or discomfort, often by physically flinching (*informal*) ○ *We always cringe at his jokes.* **3. ACT HUMBLY** to behave in a very humble or servile way (*disapproving*) ■ *n* **1. FRIGHTENED OR SERVILE MOVEMENT** a quick pulling away of the head and body from somebody or something in a frightened or servile way **2. EMBARRASSED REACTION** an embarrassed or uncomfortable reaction, often shown by a physical flinch (*informal*) [13C. Probably < Old English *crincan* 'to yield'] —**cringer** *n*

cringe-making *adj* embarrassing or painful in a way that causes a wincing reaction (*informal*)

cringle /kríng g'l/ *n* a piece of rope with a metal ring (**thimble**) in it, fitted into the main rope (**boltrope**) around the edge of a sail [Early 17C. < Low German *kringel* 'small ring']

crinkle /kríngk'l/ *vti* (**-kles, -kling, -kled**) **1. CREASE UP** to become, or make something become, finely folded, wrinkled, or wavy, e.g. by crushing or pressing it **2. MAKE SOFT CRACKLING SOUND** to make little crunching or rustling noises, like the sound of paper being crushed, or cause something to make these noises ■ *n* **TINY CREASE OR WAVE** a little crease, fold, or wave, especially in paper or cloth [14C. Origin ?]

crinklecut /kríngk'l kut/ *adj* cut in wavy shapes or with wavy edges

crinkly /kríngkli/ *adj* (**-klier, -kliest**) **1. WAVY OR CREASED UP TIGHTLY** covered in or full of fine creases, folds, or waves ○ *made of an unusual crinkly material* **2. MAKING RUSTLING NOISES** making little crunching or rustling noises ■ *n* (*plural* **-klies**) **OFFENSIVE TERM** an offensive term for somebody of advanced years (*slang*) —**crinkliness** *n*

crinoid /krī́ noyd, krínnoyd/ *n* a primitive invertebrate sea animal (**echinoderm**) with a cup-shaped body and five feathery radiating arms, related to starfish and sea urchins. Class: Crinoidea. [Mid-19C. < Greek *krinoeidēs* 'like a lily' < *krinon* 'lily'] —**crinoid** *adj*

crinoline /krínnəlin/ *n* **1. FABRIC FOR STIFFENING THINGS** a stiff fabric made of horsehair and cotton or linen. Use: formerly, linings, petticoats. **2. STIFF PETTICOAT** a petticoat of crinoline fabric or net, worn to expand a skirt **3. HOOPED SKIRT** a skirt or petticoat containing wire hoops, worn to expand the skirt [Mid-19C. Via French < Italian *crinolino* < *crino* 'horsehair' + *lino* 'flax'] —**crinolined** *adj*

crinum /krī́nəm/ (*plural same* or **-nums**) *n* a plant that grows from a bulb and has long thin leaves and clusters of flowers in various colours. Native to: tropics. Genus: *Crinum*. [Via modern Latin < Greek *krinon* 'lily']

criollo /kri ṓlō/ (*plural* **-los**) *n* **1.** somebody who comes from a Latin American country and is of European, especially Spanish, descent **2.** a domestic mammal such as a horse belonging to a Latin American breed [Late 19C. < Spanish (see CREOLE)] —**criollo** *adj*

criosphinx /krée ō sfingks/ (*plural* **-sphinxes** or **-sphinges** /-sfín jeez/) *n* in Egyptian mythology and art, a figure that is like a sphinx in having a lion's body but has the head of a ram instead of a human head [Mid-19C. < Greek *krios* 'ram']

cripes /krīps/ *interj* used to express surprise or concern (*dated slang*) [Early 20C. Alteration of CHRIST]

Crippen /kríppin/, **Hawley Harvey** (1862–1910) US-born British dentist and murderer. He poisoned his wife and fled to Canada with his lover. The first British police use of an early form of radio communication resulted in his arrest, trial, and execution.

cripple /krípp'l/ *n* **1. OFFENSIVE TERM** an offensive term for somebody whose use of a limb or limbs is impaired **2. OFFENSIVE TERM** an offensive term for somebody who is challenged in a particular area or aspect, e.g. financially ■ *vt* (**-ples, -pling, -pled**) **1. OFFENSIVE TERM** an offensive term meaning to impair the ability of somebody to move, e.g. as a result of an accident or medical condition **2. IMPAIR FUNCTIONING OR PROGRESS** to impair the functioning or progress of something such as a machine or project ○ *Dissent has crippled corporate decision-making.* [Old English *crypel* < Germanic, 'bent'] —**crippled** *adj* —**crippling** *adj* —**cripplingly** *adv*

cris de coeur plural of **cri de coeur**

crisis /krī́ siss/ (*plural* **crises** /krī́ seez/) *n* **1. DANGEROUS OR WORRYING TIME** a situation or period in which things are very uncertain, difficult, or painful, especially a time when action must be taken to avoid complete disaster or breakdown **2. CRITICAL MOMENT** a time when something very important for the future happens or is decided **3.** MED **TURNING POINT IN DISEASE** a point in the course of a disease when the patient suddenly begins to get worse or better [15C. Via Latin < Greek *krisis* 'decisive moment' < *krinein* 'decide']

crisis centre *n* a place where people can go in a time of personal difficulty or distress for advice and support, often from voluntary staff

crisis management *n* the business or process of working through a crisis to solve or cope with problems as they arise

crisp /krisp/ *adj* **1. HARD BUT EASILY BROKEN** dry and firm, and of a texture that breaks easily ○ *The snow had frozen overnight and was crisp underfoot.* **2. FRESH AND CRUNCHY** fresh and firm enough to snap when bitten into ○ *a crisp apple* **3. STIFF AND CLEAN** with a stiff, uncreased, or unspoiled surface ○ *a crisp white tablecloth* **4. DISTINCT** distinct and clear, without ambiguity or distortion ○ *She was pleased with the crisp image of the print.* **5. SHARP AND CONCISE** sharp and concise, often to the point of brusqueness ○ *a crisp reply* **6. INVIGORATING** invigorating and fresh ○ *It was a beautiful crisp frosty morning.* ■ *n* **1.** *UK* **FRIED POTATO SLICE** a very thin slice of fried potato, eaten as a snack, usually salted and often flavoured ○ *cheese-and-onion flavoured crisps* ANZ, N Am term **potato chip 2.** *N Am* FOOD same as **crumble** ■ *vti* (**crisps, crisping, crisped**) **BECOME OR MAKE CRISP** to become or make something crisp or crisper, usually in an oven [Mid-16C. < Latin *crispus* 'curled' (the original sense in English)] —**crisply** *adv* —**crispness** *n* ◇ **to a crisp** until hard and crunchy, usually excessively so (*informal*) ○ *toast burnt to a crisp*

crispate /kríss payt/ *adj* describes leaves that have curled or wavy edges (*technical*) [Mid-19C. < Latin *crispatus*, past participle of *crispare* 'curl' < *crispus* 'curled']

crispation /kriss páysh'n/ *n* **1.** the act of curling, or the condition of being curled (*formal*) **2.** a minor convulsive muscle contraction that produces a creeping feeling in the skin [Early 17C. < Latin *crispat-*, past participle of *crispare* (see CRISPATE)]

crispbread /krísp bred/ *n* a flat crisp usually rectangular cracker or biscuit made from rye, wheat, corn, or other grain

crisper /kríspər/ *n* a covered compartment in a refrigerator, where fruits and vegetables are placed to keep them fresh and crisp

crispy /kríspi/ (**-ier, -iest**) *adj* having a pleasantly light, crunchy texture ○ *Do you like your bacon crispy?* —**crispily** *adv* —**crispiness** *n*

crissa ZOOL plural of **crissum**

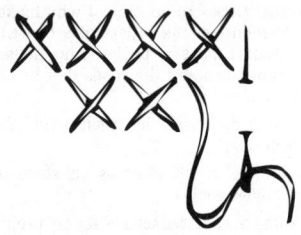

crisscross

crisscross /kríss kross/ *n* **CROSS OR LATTICE ARRANGEMENT** a pattern of lines that cross each other ■ *adj* **HAVING VERTICAL AND HORIZONTAL CROSSED LINES** running in different directions across each other, or made up of lines like this ■ *adv* **BACK AND FORTH** in a way that makes a crisscross pattern of crossing lines ■ *v* (**-crosses, -crossing, -crossed**) **1.** *vti* **MAKE PATTERN OF CROSSED LINES** to create a crisscross pattern on something **2.** *vt* **GO TO AND FRO ACROSS SOMETHING** to travel or move backwards and forwards or in all different directions over something [Early 17C. Alteration of obsolete *Christcross*, the figure of a cross, contraction of *Christ's cross*]

crissum /kríssəm/ (*plural* **-sa** /-sə/) *n* the feathers beneath the tail of a bird [Late 19C. < modern Latin < Latin *crissare* 'wiggle the hips'] —**crissal** *adj*

crista /krístə/ (*plural* **-tae** /-tee/) *n* **1.** a crest or ridge, e.g. the border of a bone **2.** a fold in the inner membrane of a mitochondrion, providing a large surface area over which the enzymes responsible for energy metabolism are located [Mid-19C. < Latin, 'tuft of hair, ridge'] —**cristate** *adj*

cristobalite /kris tṓbəlīt/ *n* a white form of quartz. Source: volcanic rocks. [Late 19C. After the hill of San *Cristóbal*, near Pachuca de Soto, Mexico]

crit[1] /krit/ *n* ARTS same as **critique** *n* (sense 1) (*informal*) ○ *I haven't seen the film but I've read a couple of crits.* [Early 20C. Shortening]

crit[2] /krit/ *n regional* the smallest or weakest piglet in a litter [Origin ?]

REGIONAL NOTE See ***underling***.

crit. *abbr* **1.** ARTS critic **2.** MED critical **3.** ARTS criticism

criterion /krī téeri ən/ (*plural* **-ria** /-ri ə/) *n* an accepted standard used in making a decision or judgment about something (*often used in the plural*) [Early 17C. < Greek *kritērion* < *kritēs* (see CRITIC)] —**criterial** *adj*

USAGE criterion or **criteria**? ***Criterion*** is singular and ***criteria*** is plural; it is generally regarded as incorrect to use ***criteria*** as a singular noun (with *criterias* as a bogus plural), although this is commonly seen and heard in the print and electronic media, and in some law contexts as well. The phrase *set of criteria* may be used when a singular expression is required.

critic /kríttik/ *n* **1. SOMEBODY JUDGING SOMETHING** somebody who judges or appraises somebody or something ○ *an eminent critic of postwar government* **2. WRITER OF REVIEWS** somebody, especially a journalist, who writes or broadcasts opinions on the quality of things such as drama productions, art exhibitions, literary works, and society as a whole ○ *the newspaper's TV critic* **3. FAULT-FINDER** somebody who habitually finds fault [Mid-16C. Via Latin < Greek *kritikos* 'discerning' < *kritēs* 'judge' < *krinein* 'decide']

critical /kríttik'l/ *adj* **1. NOT APPROVING** tending to find fault with somebody or something, or with people and things in general **2. GIVING COMMENTS OR JUDGMENTS** containing or involving comments and opinions that analyse or judge something, especially in a detailed way ○ *a critical analysis of modern economic theory* **3. CRUCIAL** extremely important because of being or happening at a time of special difficulty, trouble, or danger, when matters could quickly get either worse or better ○ *The decision was a critical one for the country.* **4. ESSENTIAL** absolutely necessary for the success of something ○ *Their support is critical to our campaign.* **5. LIFE-THREATENING** medically life-threatening or in danger ○ *a patient in a critical condition* **6. UNDERGOING CHANGE** relating to a property of a system that is undergoing a sudden change ○ *critical temperature* **7. SUSTAINING NUCLEAR CHAIN REACTION** designed or having the mass to sustain a nuclear chain reaction —**critically** *adv* —**criticalness** *n*

critical angle *n* **1.** the angle between a ray of light and a surface at which the ray will be completely reflected by the surface **2.** AEROSP same as **stalling angle**

critical care *n* the highest level of monitoring and intensive care in hospital of patients with life-threatening failure of several organs or body systems. ◊ **intensive care** (sense 2)

criticality /krítti kálləti/ *n* **1.** the condition of being crucial, decisive, or extremely serious **2.** the point in an intensifying nuclear reaction at which it becomes self-sustaining

critical list *n* the list of those patients in a hospital who are in a medically life-threatening condition

critical mass *n* **1. NECESSARY SIZE OR AMOUNT** the size or amount of something that is required before an activity or event can take place **2. AMOUNT OF FISSIONABLE MATERIAL** the smallest amount of fissionable material needed to maintain a nuclear chain reaction **3.** BUSINESS **NECESSARY NUMBER OF CUSTOMERS** the number of customers or size of market share that allows a business enterprise to become profitable **4.** COMPUT **POINT OF EXCESSIVE SOFTWARE FEATURES** the point in software development at which a piece of software acquires so many features that it ceases to be useful

critical point *n* **1.** the point at which two or more phases of a substance such as liquid and gas are identical or in equilibrium **2.** *N Am* MATHS same as **stationary point**

critical region *n* the possible results of a statistical test that are outside the range of acceptable probabilities and, if observed, would lead to their rejection

critical section *n* in surfing, the most difficult part of a wave to surf

critical state *n* CHEM same as **critical point** (sense 1)

critical temperature *n* the temperature of a substance at the critical point when it is between liquid and vapour phases

critical thinking *n* disciplined intellectual criticism that combines research, knowledge of historical context, and balanced judgment

criticise *vti* another spelling of **criticize**

criticism /kríttissizəm/ *n* 1. ACT OF CRITICIZING a spoken or written opinion or judgment of what is wrong or bad about somebody or something 2. DISAPPROVAL spoken or written opinions that point out one or more faults of somebody or something 3. ASSESSMENT OF CREATIVE WORK considered judgment of or discussion about the qualities of something, especially a creative work 4. MEDIA same as **critique** (sense 1)

criticize /krítti sīz/ (-cizes, -cizing, -cized), **criticise** (-cises, -cising, -cised) *vti* 1. to express disapproval of or dissatisfaction with somebody or something 2. to make a considered assessment of the qualities of something, especially a creative work —**criticizable** *adj* —**criticizer** *n* —**criticizingly** *adv*

SYNONYMS *criticize, censure, castigate, blast, condemn, find fault with, pick holes in, nitpick*

CORE MEANING: to express disapproval of or dissatisfaction with somebody or something

criticize to express disapproval of or dissatisfaction with somebody or something ○ *The new policy was strongly criticized by environmental groups.* ○ *He has criticized the Government for not launching an investigation.* **censure** to make a formal, often public or official statement of disapproval of somebody or something ○ *The three ministers were censured by investigation committees.* ○ *It is not known whether the player will be censured for his gesture as he left the field.* **castigate** (*formal*) to criticize or rebuke somebody or somebody's behaviour severely ○ *She castigated her political opponent on Tuesday for exaggerating the problem.* ○ *He was castigated as an alarmist by the country's president.* **blast** (*informal*) to criticize somebody or something severely ○ *She blasts homeowners who waste water during droughts.* ○ *The Olympic champion yesterday blasted critics of the British team's performance at the Games.* **condemn** to state that something or somebody is in some way wrong or unacceptable ○ *When is the Councillor going to condemn the rioters' actions?* ○ *This breach of medical confidentiality was strongly condemned by the Health Minister.* **find fault with** to criticize somebody or something, often unfairly ○ *He finds fault with everything I do.* ○ *It is difficult to find fault with this eccentric and lively account.* **pick holes in** to look for and find minor mistakes in something, particularly in an argument ○ *It's almost impossible to pick holes in their claim.* **nitpick** to find insignificant details of something unsatisfactory, often unjustifiably. ○ *Moira said her brother was still nitpicking over the contract.* ○ *We're just nitpicking – both proposals are generally sensible and workable.*

critique /kri téek/ *n* 1. a written or broadcast assessment of something, usually a creative work, with comments on its good and bad qualities 2. MEDIA same as **criticism** (sense 3) ■ *vt* (-tiques, -tiquing, -tiqued) to discuss or comment on something such as a creative work, giving an assessment of its good and bad qualities [Mid-17C. Via French < Greek *kritikē* (*tekhnē*) 'art of criticism' < *kritikos* (see CRITIC)]

~~**critism**~~ incorrect spelling of **criticism**

critter /kríttər/ *n N Am* a living thing, especially an animal (*informal or regional*) ○ *That dog was a funny old critter.* [Early 19C. Alteration of CREATURE]

CRO *abbr* 1. PHYS cathode-ray oscilloscope 2. HR Community Relations Officer 3. LAW Criminal Records Office

Croagh Patrick /krō páttrik/ mountain in County Mayo, western Republic of Ireland. It is traditionally thought to have been visited by St Patrick and is regarded by some Christians as a holy mountain. Height: 765 m/2,510 ft.

croak /krōk/ *n* 1. CRY OF ANIMAL OR BIRD a rough, usually low-pitched, vibrating sound, especially the characteristic cry of a frog or crow 2. ROUGH VOICE OF PERSON a rough low uneven sound or voice of somebody with a dry or sore throat ■ *v* (croaks, croaking, croaked) 1. *vi* MAKE LOW-PITCHED CALL to make a rough,

usually low-pitched, vibrating sound, especially the characteristic cry of a frog or crow 2. *vti* SPEAK HOARSELY to speak or say something in a rough low uneven voice because of a dry or sore throat 3. *vi* GRUMBLE to grumble or mutter gloomily (*informal*) 4. *vti* KILL OR DIE to kill somebody, or be killed (*slang*) [Mid-16C. Probably an imitation of the sound] —**croakily** *adv* —**croaky** *adj*

croaker /krōkər/ *n* 1. a fish that makes croaking or grunting noises. Family: Sciaenidae. 2. a bird or other animal that croaks when it calls

Croat /krō at/ *n* 1. somebody who comes from Croatia 2. LANG same as **Croatian** (sense 1) [Mid-17C. Via modern Latin *Croata* < Serbo-Croatian *Hrvāt*] —**Croat** *adj*

Croatia

Croatia /krō áyshə/ country in southeastern Europe, on the Balkan Peninsula, bordering the Adriatic Sea. Language: Croatian. Currency: kuna. Capital: Zagreb. Population: 4,422,248 (2003). Area: 56,510 sq. km/21,819 sq. mi. Official name **Republic of Croatia**

Croatian /krō áysh'n/ *n* 1. the Slavic language that is the official language of Croatia, closely related to Bosnian and Serbian. Native speakers: 5 million. 2. PEOPLES same as **Croat** (sense 1) —**Croatian** *adj*

croc /krok/ *n* REPT same as **crocodile** (sense 1) (*informal*) [Late 19C. Shortening]

Croce /krō chay/, **Benedetto** (1866–1952) Italian philosopher, historian, and political leader. He opposed fascism and made important contributions to idealistic philosophy.

crocein /krōssi in/ *n* a red or orange acid azo dye [20C. < Latin *croceus* 'saffron-coloured' < *crocus* (see CROCUS)]

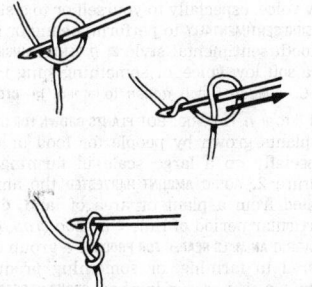

crochet: hooked needle is used to catch thread (top), which is twisted and pulled to create loop (centre and bottom)

crochet /krō shay/ *n* a form of needlework used to make clothes or decorative items from wool or thread by looping the wool or thread through itself with a hooked needle (**crochet hook**) ■ *vti* (-chets /-shayz/, -cheting /-shaying/, -cheted /-shayd/) to make something using the technique of crochet [Mid-19C. < French, literally 'little hook' < *croche* 'hook' < Germanic] —**crocheter** /krō shayər/ *n*

croci PLANTS plural of **crocus**

crocidolite /krō síddə līt/ *n* a fibrous purplish-blue form of the mineral riebeckite [Mid-19C. < Greek *krokid-* 'nap of woollen cloth']

crock¹ /krok/ *n* 1. CLAY POT a pot made of clay 2. POTTERY FRAGMENT a fragment of clay pottery 3. *N Am* FALSEHOOD something, especially a story, that is ridiculous or untrue (*slang*) ○ *His story about working until midnight is just a crock!* [Old English *crocc* < Germanic]

crock² /krok/ *n* a worn-out person, vehicle, or machine (*informal*) ■ *vt* (crocks, crocking, crocked) to injure or weaken somebody or something (*slang*) [15C. Origin ?]

crock³ /krok/ *n* regional dirt or soot [Mid-17C. Origin ?]

crocked /krokt/ *adj* (*slang*) 1. physically incapacitated by an injury ○ *I'm too crocked to play this week.* 2. *N Am* same as **drunk** *adj* (sense 1) [Early 20C. Origin ?]

crockery /krókəri/ *n* plates, cups, saucers, and other household items made of china or earthenware [Early 18C. < *crocker* 'potter' < CROCK¹]

crocket /krókit/ *n* a leaf shape carved as a decoration in Gothic architecture [Late 17C. < Old French dialect *croquet* 'shepherd's crook', variant of Old French *crochet* (see CROCHET)]

Crockett /krókit/, **Davy** (1786–1836) US frontiersman. He fought against the Creek Native Americans and joined Congress in 1827. A member of the Texas revolutionaries fighting against Mexico, he died at the battle of the Alamo. Full name **Crockett, David**

> 'I leave this rule for others when I'm dead,/Be always sure you're right—then go ahead.'
> [Davy Crockett, *Narrative of the Life of David Crockett, of the State of Tennessee*; 1834]

crocodile

crocodile /krókə dīl/ (*plural* -diles *or* same) *n* 1. LARGE REPTILE WITH STRONG JAWS a large carnivorous reptile that lives near water, and has a long thick-skinned body and a broad head with strong jaws. Native to: tropical or subtropical regions. Family: Crocodylidae. 2. REPT same as **crocodilian** 3. LEATHER FROM CROCODILE SKIN leather made from the skin of a crocodile ○ *crocodile shoes* 4. LINE OF CHILDREN a procession of schoolchildren walking in pairs (*informal*) ○ *A neat crocodile of schoolchildren filed into the museum.* [13C. Via Old French *cocodril* < Greek *krokodilos*, a small lizard]

crocodile bird *n* same as **Egyptian plover**

crocodile clip *n UK* ELEC ENG a metal clip with serrated jaws held closed by a spring, used for making temporary electrical connections. Aus, N Am term **alligator clip**

crocodile tears *npl* false tears or an insincere show of grief [Because crocodiles were believed to make sounds like weeping to attract prey, and to shed hypocritical tears over their victims]

crocodilian /krōkə dílli ən/ *n* a large predatory reptile belonging to a group that includes the alligator, cayman, crocodile, gavial, and related extinct animals. Order: Crocodylia. —**crocodilian** *adj*

crocoite /krókō īt, krō kō-/, **crocoisite** /krō kṓ i sīt/ *n* a rare orange or red mineral consisting of lead chromate. Formula: PbCrO₄. [Mid-19C. Alteration of French *crocoise* < Greek *krokoeis* 'saffron-coloured' < *krokos* 'saffron']

crocosmia /krō kózmi ə/ (*plural* -as *or* same) *n* a plant cultivated for its orange-to-red ornamental flower sprays. Native to: southern Africa. Genus: *Crocosmia*. [< modern Latin < Greek *krokos* 'saffron, crocus']

crocus /krṓkəss/ (*plural* -cuses *or* -ci /-kī, -kee/) *n* 1. a small perennial spring-flowering plant that grows from a corm. Flowers: white, red, purple, or yellow. Genus: *Crocus*. 2. a plant that has a flower like a true crocus, e.g. the autumn crocus 3. ANZ, US CHEM same as **jeweller's rouge** [14C. Via Latin < Greek *krokos* 'saffron, crocus']

Croesus /kréessəss/ *n* a very wealthy man [After CROESUS]

Croesus /kréessəss/ (*fl* 6th century BC) king of Lydia. A proverbially wealthy ruler, he reigned from about 560 BC to 546 BC when he was defeated and probably captured by Cyrus the Great.

croft /kroft/ *n* a small plot of land, often with a house on it, that the owner or occupier works, especially in Scotland [Old English, origin ?] —**crofter** *n*

crofting /krófting/ *n* the occupation of working a small plot of land, especially in Scotland, or the system of using land in this way

Crohn's disease /krōnz-/ *n* a chronic inflammatory disease, usually of the lower intestinal tract, marked by scarring and thickening of the intestinal wall and obstruction [Mid-20C. After B. B. *Crohn* (1884–1983), US pathologist]

croissant /krwáss oN/ *n* a piece of baked dough or pastry shaped into a crescent, usually moist, flaky, and very rich in fat, originally made in France [Late 19C. < French, 'crescent']

Croix de Guerre /krwaá də gáir/ (*plural same*) *n* a French military medal awarded for bravery in war [< French, 'war cross']

Cro-Magnon /krō mágnən, -mánn yon/ *n* the earliest known form of modern human being found in Europe, dating from about 50,000 to 30,000 years ago [Mid-19C. After a hill in the Dordogne, France]

Crome /krōm/, **John** (1768–1821) British landscape painter. He was instrumental in forming the Norwich School of landscape artists (1803) that flourished until the 1830s. Most of his works depict the Norfolk countryside.

cromlech /króm lek/ *n* **1.** a group of prehistoric standing stones arranged in a circle **2.** an ancient stone burial chamber [Late 17C. < Welsh < *crwm* 'arched' + *llech* 'flat stone']

Crompton /krómptən/, **Richmal** (1890–1969) British writer. She was the author of the popular *William* series of children's books.

Crompton, Samuel (1753–1827) British inventor. His 'spinning mule' (1779) greatly improved muslin manufacture, but he failed to patent it and made little profit from it.

Cromwell /króm wel/, **Oliver** (1599–1658) English soldier and politician. He led the Parliamentarians to victory in the English Civil War (1642–49) and, after the execution of Charles I, ruled as Lord Protector of England (1653–58).

> 'A few honest men are better than numbers.'
> [Oliver Cromwell, *Letter to Sir W. Spring*; September 1643]

Cromwell, Thomas, Earl of Essex (1485?–1540) English politician. He carried out the dissolution of the monasteries for Henry VIII during the Reformation, but was later beheaded.

crone /krōn/ *n* **1.** an offensive term that deliberately insults a woman's age, appearance, and temperament (*insult*) **2.** *N Am* a woman aged over 40 (*approving; used by one woman to another*) [14C. < Old N French *carogne* 'withered old woman', literally 'carrion' < Latin *caro* 'flesh']

USAGE See *insult*.

~~**cronic**~~ incorrect spelling of **chronic**

Cronin /krōnin/, **A. J.** (1896–1981) Scottish novelist and physician. His bestsellers, including *The Stars Look Down* (1935), drew on his medical background, as did the television series *Dr Finlay's Casebook* (1960s). Full name **Cronin, Archibald Joseph**

Cronkite /krón kīt, króng-/, **Walter** (*b.* 1916) US broadcast journalist. He made his name covering World War II and the Nuremberg trials. As the longtime presenter of the nightly 'CBS Evening News' (1962–81) his sound journalism and reportage through the controversial Vietnam War and the Watergate scandal led him to be voted the man most trusted by Americans. Full name **Cronkite, Jr, Walter Leland**

> 'And that's the way it is.'
> [Walter Cronkite, sign-off signature, *CBS Evening News*; 1962–81]

~~**cronology**~~ incorrect spelling of **chronology**

Cronus /krōnəss/, **Cronos, Kronos** *n* in Greek mythology, a Titan who ruled the world until his son Zeus dethroned him. Roman equivalent **Saturn**

crony /krōni/ (*plural* **-nies**) *n* a close friend, sometimes one to whom special treatment and preference is given (*disapproving*) [Mid-17C. < Greek *khronios* 'long-lasting' < *khronos* 'time']

crony capitalism *n* the flow of wealth to a small group of people who are already wealthy and well connected

cronyism /krōni izəm/ *n* special treatment and preference given to friends or colleagues, especially in politics (*disapproving*)

crook /kro͝ok/ *n* **1.** DISHONEST PERSON a thief, cheat, or criminal (*informal*) **2.** BEND IN SOMETHING a bent or curved part of something, e.g. the curve made by somebody's arm when the elbow is bent **3.** HOOK-SHAPED DEVICE a curved or hooked tool, instrument, or part in a mechanism **4.** AGRIC SHEPHERD'S HOOKED STICK a long stick with a curved end used by a shepherd to catch or guide a sheep **5.** CHR same as **crosier** (sense 1) **6.** TUBE INSERTED IN INSTRUMENT a tube inserted into a brass instrument to increase its length and lower its fundamental pitch ■ *vti* (**crooks, crooking, crooked**) FORM BEND to curve, or make something such as a finger take on a hooked or curved shape ■ *adj ANZ* (*informal*) **1.** UNWELL ill or unwell ○ *I'm feeling a bit crook today.* **2.** NOT WORKING PROPERLY not working properly or in need of repair ○ *The door's a bit crook: it doesn't shut properly.* **3.** UNPLEASANT nasty or unpleasant ○ *It was real crook that time we had our money stolen.* [12C. < Old Norse *krókr* 'hook'] —**crookery** *n* ◇ **go crook on somebody** *ANZ* to break down, fail, or deteriorate (*informal*) ◇ **go off crook on somebody** *ANZ* to become angry with or rebuke somebody (*informal*)

crooked /kro͝okid/ *adj* **1.** WITH BENT SHAPE sharply curved, bent, or twisted, often in more than one place **2.** ALIGNED INCORRECTLY not aligned properly or set at an angle ○ *That picture is crooked.* **3.** NOT LEGAL illegal or dishonest (*informal*) —**crookedly** *adv* —**crookedness** *n*

Crookes /kro͝oks/, **Sir William** (1832–1919) British chemist and physicist. His work on the vacuum electron tube furthered the development of X-rays, television, and radar. He discovered the metal thallium.

croon /kroon/ *vti* (**croons, crooning, crooned**) **1.** SING OR MURMUR GENTLY to sing or murmur something in a soft low voice, especially to yourself or to a sleepy child **2.** SING SENTIMENTALLY to perform a song or songs in a smooth sentimental style ■ *n* GENTLE SINGING singing in a soft low voice, or something sung in this way [15C. < Middle Dutch *krōnen* 'to lament'] —**crooner** *n*

crop /krop/ *n* **1.** AGRIC, BOT PLANTS GROWN FOR USE a group of plants grown by people for food or other use, especially on a large scale in farming or horticulture **2.** AGRIC AMOUNT HARVESTED the amount harvested from a plant or area of land, during one particular period of time ○ *a good crop of tomatoes* **3.** AGRIC ANIMALS REARED FOR PRODUCE a group of animals reared in farming, or something produced from them ○ *a poor crop of lambs* **4.** GROUP OF PEOPLE OR THINGS a number of people or things doing something or being done at the same time ○ *last year's crop of students* **5.** WHIP HANDLE the handle of a whip **6.** SHORT HAIRSTYLE a short hairstyle, usually for a woman **7.** POUCH IN BIRD'S THROAT a pouch in the throat of many birds in which they store food before regurgitating it to feed their young **8.** POUCH IN DIGESTIVE SYSTEM a pouch in the digestive tract of an insect or earthworm ■ *v* (**crops, cropping, cropped**) **1.** *vt* CUT SOMETHING SHORT to cut something short, e.g. hair or a lawn **2.** *vti* AGRIC GRAZE to eat the top parts of growing plants, especially grass **3.** *vti* AGRIC GATHER PRODUCE to cut or gather the produce of plants or of a cultivated area ○ *crop a field* **4.** *vti* AGRIC PRODUCE CROP to produce a crop, or make an area of land produce a crop ○ *The tomatoes cropped well this summer.* **5.** *vt* CUT PART OF PHOTO to cut off or conceal unwanted parts of an image, especially a photograph [Old English *cropp* 'ear of grain' < Germanic, 'round mass']

crop out *vi* GEOL same as **outcrop**

crop up *vi* to appear or arrive, especially unexpectedly or from time to time (*informal*) ○ *Her name keeps cropping up in conversation.*

crop circle *n* an area in a field of crops where the plants have been mysteriously flattened, usually overnight, into the shape of a circle or a more complex pattern

crop-dusting *n* the spraying of powdered fungicide or insecticide onto crops from the air

crop pants /krópt-/, **cropped pants** *npl* trousers that end between the knee and the ankle

cropper /króppər/ *n* **1.** a plant described in terms of its ability to yield produce ○ *a heavy cropper* **2.** *US* AGRIC same as **sharecropper** ◇ **come a cropper** (*informal*) **1.** to experience a hurtful or embarrassing fall **2.** to fail completely

crop rotation *n* a system of farming in which a piece of land is planted with different crops in succession, in order to improve soil fertility and control crop pests and diseases

crop top *n* a piece of clothing for women or girls, covering the upper body but cut short to end above the navel

croquembouche /krók om bo͝osh/ *n* a tall cone-shaped cake or dessert constructed from balls of choux pastry filled with custard and coated with a hard caramel glaze [< French *croque en bouche* 'crunch in the mouth']

croque monsieur /krók mə syúr/ *n* a toasted, grilled, or fried cheese and ham sandwich [< French, 'bite (a) man']

croquet /krō kay, -ki/ *n* **1.** LAWN GAME WITH BALLS AND MALLETS an outdoor game, usually played on a lawn, in which the players use long-handled wooden mallets to hit large wooden balls through a series of hoops (**wickets**) **2.** STROKE IN LAWN GAME a stroke played in the game of croquet whereby a player knocks away an opponent's ball by hitting his or her own ball when the two are touching ■ *vti* (**-quets** /-kayz, -kiz/, **-queting** /-kay ing, -ki ing/, **-queted** /-kayd, -kid/) KNOCK SOMEBODY'S CROQUET BALL AWAY to knock away an opponent's ball in the game of croquet by hitting your own ball when the two are touching [Mid-19C. Origin ?]

croquette /kro két/ *n* a little flat cake, cylinder, or ball of savoury mixture coated in egg and breadcrumbs, and fried [Early 18C. < French < *croquer* 'to crunch', an imitation of the sound]

crore /krawr/ (*plural* **crores** or *same*) *n S Asia* ten million, especially ten million rupees or the equivalent, one million pounds, in sterling [Early 17C. Via Hindi *kror* < Sanskrit *koṭiḥ*]

Crosby /krózbi/, **Bing** (1904–77) US singer and actor. Famous for songs such as 'White Christmas' (1942), he also starred in many films, including *High Society* (1956). Born **Crosby, Harry Lillis**

crosier /krōzi ər, -zhər/, **crozier** *n* **1.** a staff with a hooked end like a shepherd's crook, carried by Christian bishops, archbishops, or abbots, symbolizing their roles of caring for their congregations as shepherds tend flocks **2.** a part of a plant that has a curled end, e.g. the frond of a fern [13C. < Old French *crosier* 'crook bearer' < *croce* 'crook']

cross /kross/ *n* **1.** TWO INTERSECTING LINES a sign or mark (X) made of two straight lines that bisect each other, used to mark or cancel something, or as a signature by people who cannot write **2.** CHRISTIAN SYMBOL a long vertical bar intersected at right angles, usually about two-thirds up, by a shorter horizontal bar, used as a symbol of Christianity or the Crucifixion. The shape refers to the cross on which Jesus Christ was crucified. **3.** *also* **Cross** WOODEN STRUCTURE JESUS CHRIST DIED ON the wooden cross on which, according to the Bible, Jesus Christ was crucified and died **4.** CROSS-SHAPED SYMBOL a symbol or emblem in the form of a stylized cross. A cross is usually formed by two intersecting lines or bands, of any length and meeting at any angle, but sometimes by a main line or band intersected by shorter ones. (*often used in combination*) **5.** CROSS-SHAPED DECORATION a medal or insignia shaped like a cross **6.** WOODEN EXECUTION POST WITH CROSSBAR an upright wooden post with a shorter post fixed across it at right angles towards the top, on which, formerly, people were nailed or hanged in public executions **7.** STONE MONUMENT an upright stone or structure in the shape of a cross or holding a cross, erected to commemorate somebody or something (*often used in placenames*)

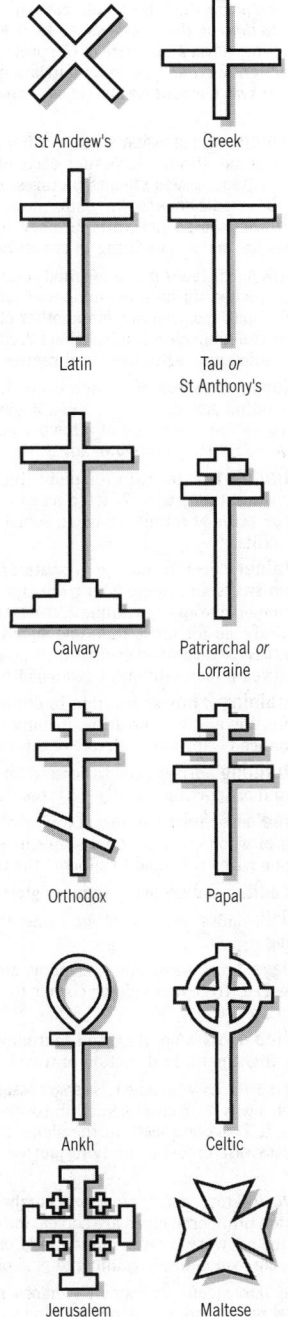

St Andrew's — Greek

Latin — Tau *or* St Anthony's

Calvary — Patriarchal *or* Lorraine

Orthodox — Papal

Ankh — Celtic

Jerusalem — Maltese

cross

8. DIFFICULTY a difficulty in somebody's personal life that is particularly testing, troubling, or painful ○ *His daughter's death was a particularly difficult cross to bear.* **9. MIXTURE** somebody or something that is a blend of two different types or characteristics ○ *a cross between a mystery and a historical novel* **10. GENETICS HYBRID INDIVIDUAL** an animal or plant produced by interbreeding two genetically different individuals **11. SOCCER, HOCKEY PASS ACROSS PITCH** in football or hockey, a pass sent across the pitch, usually in the air **12. BOXING SIDEWAYS BLOW** a punch thrown at a boxing opponent from the side, in response to and evading the opponent's jab or lead **13. SPORTS PASS ACROSS GOAL** a pass that sends the ball across the field in a team game such as hockey **14. CONSTR PIPE CONNECTION** a cross-shaped joint used to connect four pipes **15. SOMETHING DISHONEST** something dishonest or fraudulent, especially a sports contest in which the outcome has been dishonestly decided before it begins (*slang*) ■ *v* (**crosses, crossing, crossed**) **1.** *vti* **GO ACROSS** to move or move somebody or something from one side of something to the other ○ *We've already crossed the border.* ○ *The river's too*

swift to cross the horses here. **2.** *vti* **MEET AT ONE POINT** to meet at a particular place or time and then continue separately again ○ *A settlement grew up where two trade routes crossed.* **3.** *vt* **PLACE THINGS ONE ACROSS OTHER** to put two things so that one lies across the other ○ *crossed her legs* **4.** *vt* **BANKING MAKE CHEQUE PAYABLE ONLY THROUGH BANK** to draw two parallel lines across the front of a cheque, diagonally or vertically, meaning that it has to be paid into a bank account **5.** *vi* **MAIL BE EN ROUTE AT ONE TIME** to be travelling in opposite directions between the same two correspondents at the same time (*refers to letters and other forms of communication*) **6.** *vti* **TELECOM CONNECT TELEPHONE LINES WRONGLY AND CONFUSINGLY** to make an incorrect connection between telephone numbers or lines, so that two or more conversations intermingle with each other, or be connected in this way (*often passive*) **7.** *vt* **GENETICS INTERBREED PLANTS OR ANIMALS** to interbreed or hybridize plants or animals that are genetically different **8.** *vt* **CHR MAKE CHRISTIAN BLESSING GESTURE WITH HAND** to draw the shape of a Christian cross in the air over somebody or something as a symbol of God's blessing **9.** *vti* **SPORTS PASS BALL ACROSS PITCH** in football and some other games, to make a pass that sends the ball across, rather than up or down, the field **10.** *vt* **THWART SOMEBODY** to do something that goes against somebody's wishes or that annoys or frustrates somebody ○ *I wouldn't cross her unless you want to make life difficult for yourself.* **11.** *vt* **WRITE LINE ACROSS LETTER 'T'** to draw a horizontal line across the vertical line of a letter 'T', to complete the letter ■ *adj* **ANGRY** feeling or indicating anger ○ *exchanged a few cross words* [Pre-12C. Via Old Norse *kross* < Old Irish *cros* < Latin *crux*] —**crosser** *n* —**crossly** *adv* —**crossness** *n*

cross off *vt* to remove something, especially a name or item written on a list, by drawing a line through it

cross out *vt* to cancel something, especially a word or item that is wrong or not wanted, by drawing a line through it

cross- *prefix* **1.** crossing ○ *crossover* **2.** opposing, opposite ○ *crosscurrent* **3.** reciprocal, mutual ○ *crosslink* [< CROSS]

cross action *n* a legal proceeding brought by somebody who has been sued against the person who brought the original action or against a codefendant

crossbar /króss baar/ *n* **1.** a bar that runs horizontally between two vertical posts, e.g. between goalposts or the uprights of a jump **2.** a horizontal metal bar that runs from below the handlebars to below the saddle on a man's or boy's bicycle

crossbeam /króss beem/ *n* a beam that passes between two supports in the structure of a building

crossbearer /króss bairər/ *n* somebody who bears a cross in front of a bishop or archbishop in a ceremonial procession

cross bedding *n* **1.** layers of geological strata in which deposits were laid down at an angle with respect to those above and below, commonly seen in sandstone deposited as dunes **2.** the layering of geologic strata transverse to the main beds of stratified rock —**cross-bedded** *adj*

cross bench *n* one of the benches in a parliament where members sit if they belong to neither the governing party nor one of the main opposition parties (*hyphenated when used before a noun*) ○ *a cross-bench MP* [Mid-19C. < its position at right angles to the government and opposition benches] —**crossbencher** /króss benchər/ *n*

crossbill /króss bil/ *n* a large finch that has a beak with crossed tips that it uses to extract seeds from conifer cones. Native to: coniferous forests. Genus: *Loxia*.

crossbones /króss bōnz/ *npl* a representation of two human thighbones crossing each other in the middle, traditionally placed beneath a skull as a symbol of death. The image of crossbones lying below a skull was traditionally used by pirates on their flag (**Jolly Roger**) and in modern times is used to show that something is poisonous.

crossbow /króss bō/ *n* a medieval weapon, or its modern sports successor, consisting of a bow attached crosswise to a stock with a cranking mechanism and a trigger. A crossbow fires short heavy arrows called bolts or quarrels. —**crossbowman** *n*

crossbreed /króss breed/ *vti* (**-breeds, -breeding, -bred** /-bred/) to breed new strains of plants or animals from genetically different individuals ■ *n* an animal or plant produced by crossbreeding —**crossbred** /-bred/ *adj, n*

cross-buttock *n* a wrestling throw in which the hip is used to pivot an opponent

cross-Channel *adj* going across the English Channel ○ *cross-Channel ferries*

crosscheck /króss chék/ (**-checks, -checking, -checked**) *vt* **1.** to make sure that something such as a fact or figure is correct by looking it up in other sources or asking another person **2.** in hockey, ice hockey, and lacrosse, to obstruct an opposing player by using both hands to thrust a playing stick across his or her body —**crosscheck** *n*

cross-claim *n* a claim made against another party on the same side of a lawsuit such as a codefendant

cross-country *adj* **1. NOT ON ROAD OR TRACK** done over fields or hills, or through woods, not on roads or a specially prepared area ○ *a cross-country run* **2. ACROSS WHOLE COUNTRY** from one side of a country to another, or throughout a country ○ *The band embarked on a cross-country tour.* **3. OPERATING OFF ROADS** designed or able to operate without roads ○ *a cross-country vehicle* ■ *n* **RACING OVER FIELDS** a sporting activity or event such as running, cycling, or racing that is done off the roads

cross-country skiing *n* skiing on long narrow skis across open countryside on fairly level ground

crosscourt /króss kawrt/ *adj* hit or thrown from one side of a playing court towards the other, especially in tennis or basketball

cross cousin *n* a cousin who is related to somebody through a brother and sister, being either a father's sister's child or a mother's brother's child

cross-cultural *adj* relating to or comparing two or more different cultures ○ *cross-cultural research on community activism* —**cross-culturally** *adv*

crosscurrent /króss kurrənt/ *n* **1.** a current that flows across another current, mainly in water but also in air **2.** a movement or trend that conflicts with the general one, especially a trend in people's ideas or opinions

crosscut /króss kut/ *adj* **1. CUT AT ANGLE** describes something such as wood, meat, or fabric that is cut across its main grain **2. FOR CUTTING ACROSS** made or used for cutting across the grain of wood ■ *vti* (**-cuts, -cutting, -cut**) **CINEMA ALTERNATE FILM SHOTS** to alternate repeatedly brief scenes from one filmed sequence with scenes from another to give the impression that the events they show are happening at the same time ■ *n* **1. CUT MADE ACROSS** a cut made across something such as a long piece of timber **2. TUNNEL ACROSS VEIN OF ORE** a tunnel in a mine that cuts across a vein of ore **3. CINEMA EXAMPLE OF FILM ALTERNATING SHOTS** an example of the film technique in which short segments of two or more scenes are alternated **4. SHORT CUT** a shorter and more direct route to a place

crosscut saw *n* a saw used for cutting wood across the grain

crosscutting /króss kutting/ *n* repeated alternation between brief filmed sequences to give the impression that the events they show are happening at the same time

cross-dress *vi* to wear clothes usually worn by somebody of the opposite sex —**cross-dresser** *n* —**cross-dressing** *n*

crosse /kross/ *n* a wooden stick used in the game of lacrosse, curved at the top into a triangular frame that supports a tough leatherwork net [Mid-19C. < French, 'bishop's crook']

cross-examine *vt* **1.** to question a witness for the opposing side in a hearing or trial **2.** to ask somebody a lot of detailed questions in a persistent or aggressive way (*informal*) —**cross-examination** *n* —**cross-examiner** *n*

SYNONYMS See *question*.

cross-eyed *adj* an offensive term meaning having an eye alignment that makes one or both eyes turn in towards the nose

cross-fade *vti* in film or television editing, to grad-

ually introduce a new sound or picture while causing another one to disappear

cross-fertilization *n* **1.** the fertilization of a female sex cell (**gamete**) of one individual by a male sex cell from a different individual, usually of the same species **2.** BOT same as **cross-pollination 3.** the exchange of ideas between two groups, especially cultures, that produces benefits for both —**cross-fertile** *adj* —**cross-fertilize** *vti*

crossfield /króss feeld/ *adj* kicked or thrown from one side of a playing field towards the other, especially in football or rugby ○ *a crossfield pass*

crossfire /króss fīr/ *n* **1.** gunshots that come from more than one place, in such a way that the lines of fire converge **2.** heated or lively conversation, with different and opposing views and ideas being put forward, or an example of this

cross-grained *adj* **1.** with an irregular grain or a grain that runs across the length **2.** difficult to deal with because of stubbornness, contrariness, or bad temper (*informal*)

cross hairs, **crosshairs** /króss hairz/ *npl* a pair of fine lines or wires that cross at right angles inside a lens or sight, e.g., used in focusing an optical instrument or aiming a rifle

crosshatch /króss hátch/ (**-hatches, -hatching, -hatched**) *vti* to draw parallel or intersecting lines across part of a drawing or diagram, usually diagonally, especially to give the effect of shadow or different texture —**crosshatching** *n*

crosshead /króss hed/ *n* a sliding metal block securing one end of a piston rod to a connecting rod

cross-hedging *n* the process of securing a future financial position against unfavourable economic events by taking out a position in a different financial transaction that would benefit by the same unfavourable events

cross-index *v* **1.** *vt* to give a particular item one or more additional entries in an index, under different headings, as cross-references to it **2.** *vti* to supply cross-references in something

crossing /króssing/ *n* **1.** SOMEWHERE WHERE SOMEBODY CAN CROSS a place that has been specially constructed, chosen, or marked out as somewhere where something such as a road or a border may be crossed **2.** POINT WHERE ROUTES CROSS a place where a railway line and a road, or two railway lines, roads, or similar routes go across each other **3.** JOURNEY ACROSS WATER a journey across a body of water **4.** CENTRAL AREA OF CROSS-SHAPED CHURCH the place in a cross-shaped church where the nave and the transept meet

crossing-over *n* the interchange of segments between homologous chromosomes during cell division (**meiosis**), resulting in new combinations of gene types (**alleles**) and therefore variability in inherited characteristics

crossjack /króss jak/ *n* a sail on the mizzenmast of a ship

cross-legged /-légd, -léggid/ *adj* in a sitting position with the legs bent so that the knees are apart and the ankles are crossed in front ■ *adv* with one leg lying over the other ○ *sitting cross-legged*

crosslet /krósslit/ *n* on coats of arms, a cross that has a smaller cross at the end of each of its arms

cross-link *n also* **cross-linkage** a transverse connecting element, e.g. an atom, chemical group, or covalent bond between parallel chains of a complex organic molecule, especially a polymer or protein ■ *vt* to join polymer chains by a cross-link

cross matching *n* the process of testing for the compatibility of a donor's and recipient's tissues before blood transfusion or tissue transplantation —**cross-match** *vt*

cross-multiply *vi* to multiply each numerator of two fractions by the denominator of the other —**cross-multiplication** *n*

cross of Lorraine *n* a cross with two horizontal bars (**patriarchal cross**) that was adopted as the symbol of the duchy of Lorraine [After LORRAINE]

Cross of Valour *n* the highest Canadian decoration for courage

crossopterygian /kro sópta ríjji ən/ (*plural* **-ans** or *same*) *n* a bony fish with paired fleshy pectoral fins like limbs that is thought to be ancestral to amphibians and other land vertebrates. All except the coelacanth are extinct. Subclass: Crossopterygii. [Mid-19C. < modern Latin *Crossopterygii* < Greek *krossoi* 'fringe' + *pterux* 'wing'] —**crossopterygian** *adj*

crossover /króss ōvər/ *n* **1.** CROSSING OR TRANSFER POINT a place for crossing from one side of something to the other, or from one line, system, or vehicle to another **2.** SOMETHING NOW POPULAR WITH DIFFERENT AUDIENCE an artist, musician, artistic creation, or piece of music that has become popular outside one original category **3.** WIDENING OF POPULARITY the process by which an artistic work becomes popular outside the category in which it originated **4.** GENETICS same as **crossing-over 5.** *US* AUTOMOT same as **sport tourer** ■ *adj* MIXING TWO DIFFERENT STYLES resulting from a mixture of two different artistic categories or styles, or from aspects of one category becoming popular in another

cross-party *adj* involving two or more political parties ○ *Members of both government and opposition are arriving for cross-party talks.*

crosspatch /króss pach/ *n* somebody who is considered to be bad-tempered and touchy (*dated informal*) [Late 17C. < CROSS 'annoyed' + PATCH 'fool']

crosspiece /króss peess/ *n* a piece that crosses a structure or implement from one side to the other, e.g. a beam in a building or part of the handle of a tool

cross-platform *adj* available for more than one type of computer or operating system

cross-ply *adj* describes tyres made with the strands of the fabric crossing each other diagonally. N Am term **bias-ply**

cross-pollination *n* the transfer of pollen from an anther of one flower to the stigma of another —**cross-pollinate** *vti*

cross-post *vti* to post a single electronic message or article simultaneously to multiple newsgroups, an action generally considered a serious breach of netiquette

cross product *n* MATHS same as **vector product**

cross-purpose *n* a conflicting or contrary purpose ◇ **at cross-purposes** not understanding each other, usually through not realizing that the other person means or intends something different

cross-question *vt* LAW same as **cross-examine** (sense 1) ■ *n* a lawyer's question to a witness being cross-examined in a court case —**cross-questioning** *n*

cross-reaction *n* the immunological reaction of one antigen with the antibodies developed against another similar antigen —**cross-react** *vi* —**cross-reactive** *adj* —**cross-reactivity** *n*

cross-refer *vti* to give a note that tells a reader of a book, index, or library catalogue to look in another specified part or on another page of the same work

cross-reference *n* a note, especially one printed in a book, index, or library catalogue, that tells a reader to look in another specified place for information ■ *v* **1.** *vt* to provide a text, index, or library catalogue with cross-references **2.** *vti* INFO SCI same as **cross-refer**

cross-resistance *n* resistance developed by an organism to the effects of a toxin as a result of being exposed to a similar toxin

crossroad /króssrōd/ *n N Am* a road that runs across another one or that links two main roads

crossroads /króss rōdz/ (*plural same*) *n* **1.** a place where two or more roads meet or cross each other **2.** a time when an important decision must be made

crossruff /króss ruf/ *n* in whist and bridge, a tactic in which two partners alternately trump each other's first card (**lead**) in each round ■ *vti* (**-ruffs, -ruffing, -ruffed**) in whist or bridge, to play a crossruff, or trump a card in a crossruff [Late 16C. < CROSS- + RUFF 2]

cross section *n* **1.** PLANE CUTTING THROUGH OBJECT a plane surface formed by cutting through an object at right angles to an axis, especially the longest axis **2.** SOMETHING CUT IN CROSS SECTION a piece cut as part of a cross section, or an image of such a piece ○ *draw a cross section of a cone* **3.** REPRESENTATIVE SAMPLE a sample of something that represents all or most of the different parts that the whole contains ○ *polled a cross section of the residents* **4.** PHYS PROBABILITY OF PARTICLE INTERACTION a measure of the probability of an interaction such as fission or ionization occurring between two elementary particles —**cross-sectional** *adj*

cross-stitch *n* **1.** EMBROIDERY STITCH a stitch made up of two diagonal stitches crossing each other **2.** EMBROIDERY IN CROSS-SHAPED STITCHES pictures, designs, or items of needlework sewn using cross-stitches ■ *vti* SEW USING CROSS-STITCH to embroider using cross-stitches, or make something in cross-stitch

crosstalk /króss tawk/ *n* **1.** unwanted sounds or other signals picked up by one channel of an electronic communications system from another channel, e.g. between telephones or loudspeakers **2.** conversation full of quick and witty lines and replies (*informal*)

cross-town, **crosstown** /króss town/ *adj* **1.** travelling or extending across a city or town **2.** situated in or relating to the other side of a town ○ *playing their cross-town rivals* —**crosstown** *adv*

cross-train *v* **1.** *vi* to train for more than one competitive sport at a time **2.** *vti* to learn one or more tasks or skills at a time, or teach somebody one or more skills

crosstrainer /króss traynər/ *n* **1.** SOMEBODY TRAINING FOR DIFFERENT SPORTS an athlete who trains for more than one competitive sport at a time **2.** SPORTS SHOE a sports shoe designed for more than one sporting activity **3.** EXERCISING MACHINE an exercise machine intended to help develop many different groups of muscles

cross training *n* fitness training in different sports, e.g. running and weightlifting, usually undertaken to enhance performance in one of the sports

cross-training *adj* designed to be used for more than one kind of sporting activity ○ *a cross-training bike*

crosstree /króss tree/ *n* either of a pair of horizontal pieces of wood or metal on a ship's mast to which ropes or wires are fixed to support the mast

cross vault, **cross vaulting** *n* same as **groin vault**

crosswalk /króss wawk/ *n N Am* same as **pedestrian crossing**

crossways /króss wayz/ *adv* **1.** same as **crosswise** *adv* (sense 1) **2.** from one side or corner to another, in a slanting line

crosswind /króss wind/ *n* a wind that blows across a route, flight path, or direction of travel

crosswise /króss wīz/ *adv* **1.** SIDEWAYS ACROSS SOMETHING in such a way as to cross something or be positioned across it **2.** IN CROSS SHAPE in the shape of a cross ■ *adj* TRANSVERSE crossing or lying across something else

crossword /króss wurd/, **crossword puzzle** *n* a puzzle in which numbered clues are solved and words that form the answers entered horizontally or vertically into a correspondingly numbered grid of squares

crostini /kro steéni/ *npl* small canapés made from toasted bread with a savoury topping such as olive paste or mushrooms [< Italian, 'little crusts']

crotch /kroch/ *n* **1.** PLACE WHERE LEGS JOIN BODY the part of the human body where the legs join the trunk **2.** PART OF GARMENT COVERING GENITALS the area of a pair of trousers or underpants that covers the wearer's genitals **3.** PLACE WHERE TREE DIVIDES a part of a tree where it forks into two branches **4.** FORKED STICK a pole or stick with a forked end **5.** FORK IN STICK a fork in a pole or stick [Mid-16C. Probably variant of CRUTCH] —**crotched** *adj*

crotchet /króchit/ *n* **1.** a musical note with the time value of a quarter of a semibreve. A crotchet lasts half as long as a minim and twice as long as a quaver and is written as a filled note head with a stem. N Am term **quarter note 2.** a whim, or a perverse idea or opinion (*dated*) [14C. < Old French *crochet* (see CROCHET)]

crotchet rest *n* a musical rest with the time value of a crotchet. N Am term **quarter rest**

crotchety /króchəti/ *adj* irritable and difficult to please (*informal*) —**crotchetiness** *n*

croton /krṓt'n/ (*plural same* or **-tons**) *n* **1.** a bush or tree of the spurge family, some types of which are noted for their medicinal properties. Native to:

tropics. Genus: *Croton.* **2.** an evergreen plant grown for its leathery variegated foliage. Native to: tropics. Latin name: *Codiaeum variegatum.* [Mid-18C. Via modern Latin < Greek *krotōn* 'sheep-tick'; from the shape of its seeds (sense 1)]

crotonic acid /krō tónnik-/ *n* a colourless crystalline organic acid. Use: organic synthesis, manufacture of drugs and resins. Formula: $C_4H_6O_2$. [< CROTON]

croton oil *n* a yellowish-brown oil extracted from the seeds of a croton tree. Use: formerly, purgative, counterirritant.

crouch /krowch/ *vi* (**crouches, crouching, crouched**) **1.** **BEND DOWN LOW** to squat down on the balls of the feet with knees bent and body hunched over ○ *I had to crouch to get under the table.* **2.** **BEND IN PREPARATION TO POUNCE** to stay down close to the ground with legs bent, waiting to spring or run forwards (*refers to animals*) ■ *n* **CROUCHING POSITION** the position of a human squatting with back and knees bent or of an animal with the body pressed low to the ground in readiness to spring [14C. Probably < variant of Old French *crochir* 'be crooked' < *croche* (see CROCHET)]

croup[1] /kroop/ *n* an inflammatory condition of the larynx and trachea, especially in young children, marked by a cough, hoarseness, and difficulty in breathing [Mid-18C. < *croup* 'to croak', probably an imitation of the sound] —**croupous** *adj* —**croupy** *adj*

croup[2] /kroop/, **croupe** *n* the hindquarters of a four-legged animal, especially a horse [13C. < French *croupe*]

croupier /kroopi ay, -ər/ *n* somebody in charge of a gaming table who collects and pays out the players' money and chips, and deals the cards or spins the roulette wheel [Mid-18C. < French, 'person who rides behind' < *croupe* 'rump']

croustade /kroo staád/ *n* an edible casing for a savoury filling [Mid-19C. < French < Latin *crusta* 'rind']

crouton /kroo ton/ *n* a small piece, usually a cube, of fried bread used as a garnish for soups, salads, and other dishes (*usually used in the plural*) [Early 19C. < French *croûton*, 'little crust' < *croûte* 'crust' < Latin *crusta* 'rind, shell']

crow[1] /krō/ *n* **1.** a large bird with shiny black feathers and a raucous cry, of a family whose members include rooks and ravens. Native to: found worldwide. Genus: *Corvus.* **2.** an offensive term for a woman that deliberately insults the pitch of her voice (*dated slang*) [Old English *crāwe* < Germanic] ◇ **as the crow flies** in a straight line ◇ **eat crow** *N Am* to be forced to admit that you have been wrong or have been humiliatingly defeated (*informal*)

crow[2] /krō/ *vi* (**crows, crowing, crowed** or **crew** /kroo/, **crowed**) **1.** **CRY LIKE COCK** to give the loud shrill cry of a cock **2.** **CRY OUT HAPPILY** to cry out with pleasure in the way that babies do **3.** **BRAG ABOUT SOMETHING** to boast about personal success or celebrate about something another person has failed to do in a noisy and exuberant way ■ *n* **COCK'S LOUD CRY** a long shrill call made by a bird, especially a cock [Old English *crāwan* < Germanic]

Crow /krō/ (*plural same* or **Crows**) *n* **1.** a member of a Native North American people who once lived on the plains of North Dakota and who now live in southern Montana and Wyoming **2.** the Siouan language of the Crow people. Native speakers: 5,000. [Early 19C. Translation of French *(gens de) corbeaux* 'raven people', translation of a Native American name] —**Crow** *adj*

crowbar /krō baar/ *n* an iron or steel bar with one flattened end, often also bent or forked. Use: as a lever for raising or moving things. ■ *vt* (**-bars, -barring, -barred**) to prise or force something using a crowbar (*informal*) [Mid-18C. Because the flattened end resembles a crow's foot]

crowberry /krōbəri/ (*plural* **-ries**) *n* **1.** a low-growing evergreen bush with edible black berries. Native to: colder regions. Latin name: *Empetrum nigrum.* **2.** the flavourless edible berry of the crowberry bush

crowd[1] /krowd/ *n* **1.** **PEOPLE GATHERED TOGETHER** a large group of people gathered in one place **2.** **AUDIENCE OR SPECTATORS** a group of people attending the same public event or entertainment ○ *performing in front of a sell-out crowd* **3.** **SET OF PEOPLE** a group of people with something in common **4.** **MASSES** the mass or majority of people **5.** **LARGE GROUP OF THINGS** a large number of things put or found together ■ *v* (**crowds, crowding, crowded**) **1.** *vi* **THRONG TOGETHER** to assemble or move in large numbers **2.** *vti* **HERD OR CRAM** to urge, herd, or force a closely packed group of people, animals, or things into a place, or move into a place in a closely packed group **3.** *vti* **ADVANCE BY SHOVING** to move forward by pushing and shoving, or shove past a person or barrier **4.** *vt* **FILL OR PACK SOMETHING** to fill or cover something or a place in large numbers or to capacity **5.** *vti* **PRESS NEAR SOMEBODY** to stand or move uncomfortably close to somebody or something **6.** *vt* **PRESSURIZE SOMEBODY** to put pressure on somebody to do something, or make somebody feel forced into an act [Old English *crūdan* 'to press' < W Germanic] —**crowded** *adj* —**crowdedness** *n* —**crowder** *n*
crowd out *vt* to exclude or push out somebody or something by force of numbers

crowd[2] /krowd/ *n* an ancient Celtic stringed instrument that was bowed or plucked [14C. < Welsh *crwth*]

crowd pleaser *n* a person, object, event, or occasion that has great popular appeal (*informal*) —**crowd-pleasing** *adj*

crowd puller *n* a person, object, or event that is popular enough to draw a large audience or body of spectators

Crowe /krō/, **Russell** (*b.* 1964) New Zealand-born Australian actor. He came to prominence in *Romper Stomper* (1992) and won an Academy Award for best actor for *Gladiator* (2000). Full name **Crowe, Russell Ira**

crow eater *n Aus* an offensive term for a person who comes from South Australia [Origin ?]

crowfoot /krō foot/ *n* **1.** **PLANT WITH LEAVES LIKE CROW'S FOOT** a plant related to the buttercup that has divided leaves resembling the feet of a crow. Flowers: small, yellow or white. Genus: *Ranunculus.* **2.** **PLANT LIKE CROWFOOT** a plant that has leaves resembling a bird's foot **3.** (*plural* **crowfeet** /-feet/) NAUT **ROPES SUPPORTING AWNING** a set of ropes to support an awning on a boat

crown /krown/ *n* **1.** **HEADDRESS SYMBOLIZING ROYALTY** an ornate headdress worn as a symbol of sovereignty, often made of gold and set with gems **2.** **SYMBOL OF ACHIEVEMENT** a wreath or circlet worn on the head as a symbol of victory, success, or high achievement **3.** *also* **Crown** POL **MONARCH** the reigning monarch of a country **4.** *also* **Crown** POL **MONARCH'S POWER** the power or authority vested in a monarch **5.** **EMBLEM LIKE CROWN** an emblem or ornament resembling or representing a crown **6.** **TOP-RANKING TITLE** a title or distinction that signifies victory or supreme achievement **7.** **PINNACLE** the highest point of quality, achievement, or fame **8.** **UPPERMOST PART** the top part of something, especially a hill **9.** ANAT **TOP OF HEAD** the top part of the head **10.** CLOTHING **TOP OF HAT** the top part of a hat **11.** DENT **VISIBLE PART OF TOOTH** the visible part of a tooth, covered by enamel **12.** DENT **ARTIFICIAL TOOTH** an artificial replacement for the visible part of a tooth that has decayed or been damaged **13.** BOT **UPPER PART OF PLANT** the upper part of a tree or bush, consisting of the foliage and branches **14.** BOT **ROOTS AND LOWER STEM OF PLANT** the roots and lower stem of a plant, or a plant consisting only of these parts, used especially for propagation **15.** BIRDS **TOP OF BIRD'S HEAD** the top part of the head of a bird **16.** **TOP OF GEMSTONE** the upper part of a cut gemstone **17.** NAUT **JUNCTION OF ANCHOR ARMS AND SHANK** the junction where the arms of an anchor join the shank **18.** ROADS **CENTRE OF ROAD** the middle of a road, especially a cambered one **19.** **WINDING KNOB ON WATCH** a ridged winding knob on a watch **20.** HIST, COINS **BRITISH COIN** a former British coin worth five shillings, now issued only to commemorate special events **21.** COINS **EUROPEAN COIN** a European coin whose name is translated as 'crown', e.g. the Norwegian and Danish krone or the Swedish krona **22.** BOT same as **corona** (sense 3) **23.** **SIZE OF PAPER** a size of paper equal to 38 by 51 cm/15 by 20 in ■ *vt* (**crowns, crowning, crowned**) **1.** **CONFER ROYAL STATUS ON SOMEBODY** to make a person a monarch, or place a crown on a person's head to symbolize monarchy **2.** **REWARD SOMEBODY WITH CROWN** to place a crown on somebody's head, especially in recognition of a victory, success, or achievement **3.** **RANK SOMEBODY HIGHEST** to confer the top rank on somebody ○ *crowned him champion* **4.** **BE SUMMIT OF SOMETHING** to be or form the top of something **5.** **PUT FINISHING TOUCH TO SOMETHING** to complete or be the consummation or confirmation of something **6.** DENT **FIT CROWN TO TOOTH** to fit an artificial crown to a damaged or decayed tooth **7.** BOARD GAMES **MAKE INTO KING IN DRAUGHTS** to promote an ordinary draughts piece to the status of king **8.** **TOP SOMETHING WITH SOMETHING ELSE** to put something on or at the top of something else **9.** **HIT SOMEBODY ON HEAD** to hit somebody over the head (*informal*) [12C. Via Anglo-Norman *corune*, Old French *corone* < Latin *corona* 'wreath, garland' < Greek *korōnē* 'something curved' < *korōnis* 'curved']

Crown Agent *n* **1.** somebody appointed by the Minister for Overseas Development to sit on a board that provides financial, commercial, and other services to some foreign governments and international organizations **2.** a solicitor in Scotland engaged to prepare prosecution cases

crown cap *n* a metal cap with a corrugated edge, used to seal bottles of beer and other drinks

Crown Colony *n* a British colony in which the Crown has a whole or partial governing power

Crown Court *n* a court presided over by circuit judges that hears criminal cases in England and Wales

Crown Derby *n* a soft-paste porcelain manufactured in the city of Derby from 1784 to 1848 and usually marked with the letter 'D' surmounted by a crown

crowned head /krównd-/ *n* a reigning monarch

crown gall *n* a disease of fruit and roses that results in swellings on the roots or stems and is caused by the bacterium *Agrobacterium tumefaciens*

crown glass *n* **1.** high-quality glass with a low refractive index. Use: lenses. **2.** a traditional window glass made by spinning a bubble of molten glass on the end of a rod until it forms a flat disc

crown green *n* a bowling green that is higher in the middle than it is at the edges

crown imperial (*plural* **crown imperials** or *same*) *n* a garden plant with a strong musky smell that grows from a bulb. Flowers: bell-shaped, orange or yellow, in a cluster at the top of a single tall stem. Latin name: *Fritillaria imperialis.*

crowning /krówning/ *adj* **1.** **ULTIMATE IN ACHIEVEMENT** representing supreme achievement or the ultimate moment in something **2.** **FORMING SUMMIT** forming a crown or summit ■ *n* **1.** POL **INVESTITURE OF MONARCH** the process or ceremony of making somebody a monarch **2.** MED **STAGE IN LABOUR** the stage in giving birth at which an infant's head passes through the vaginal opening

crowning glory *n* **1.** the most impressive feature or achievement of a particular person or thing **2.** somebody's hair (*humorous*)

Crown jewels *npl* **1.** the jewellery and regalia that a monarch wears on state occasions **2.** *also* **crown jewels** the male genitals, especially the testicles (*humorous slang*)

crown lens *n* a lens made of crown glass, especially the converging component of an achromatic lens

Crown Office *n* an office of the Queen's Bench Division of the High Court, responsible for administration

crown of thorns *n* **1.** MARINE BIOL **SPINY STARFISH** a spiny starfish that feeds on live coral. Native to: Pacific. Latin name: *Acanthaster planci.* **2.** PLANTS **THORNY BUSH WITH SCARLET BRACTS** a thorny spurge bush with scarlet bracts grown as a house plant or as a hedge in tropical regions. Native to: Madagascar. Latin name: *Euphorbia milii.* **3.** **HEAVY BURDEN** a painful or onerous burden (*literary*) [< the biblical accounts of the wreath of thorns placed on the head of Jesus Christ]

crownpiece /krówn peess/ *n* **1.** a part that fits over or forms the top of something **2.** a bridle strap that fits over a horse's head behind the ears

crown prince *n* the principal male heir in a monarchy

crown princess *n* **1.** the principal female heir in a monarchy **2.** the wife of a crown prince

Crown Prosecution Service *n* an independent body set up in 1986 to determine whether cases prepared by the police in England and Wales should be brought to trial

crown roast *n* a meat joint consisting of two rib sections sewn together to form a circle

crown saw *n* a cylindrical saw with a row of teeth along one edge, designed for cutting round holes

crown vetch *n* a leguminous plant with small pink or white flowers. Native to: Europe. Latin name: *Coronilla varia.*

crown wheel *n* a wheel in a clock or watch next to the winding knob, formed from two sets of teeth at right angles to each other

crow's feet *npl* a network of wrinkles radiating from the outer corner of the human eye [Because they resemble the footprints of crows]

crow's foot *n* **1.** HANDICRAFT a sewing stitch with three points, used especially for finishing off a seam **2.** AVIAT a set of short ropes that redistributes the pull of a single rope, used in airships and ballooning **3.** MIL same as **caltrop** (sense 1) [< the shape]

crow's-nest *n* **1.** a lookout point consisting of a railed platform at the top of a ship's mast or superstructure **2.** a high enclosed lookout point on land

crow step *n* ARCHIT same as **corbie step** [Because only a small or perching animal could use it]

Croydon /króyd'n/ borough in South London. At one time it had London's main airport. Population: 330,587 (2001).

croze /krōz/ *n* **1.** a groove at the top of a barrel or cask into which the flat surface is fitted **2.** a cooper's tool used to cut grooves at the top of barrels and casks [Early 17C. < French *creux* 'hollow, groove', probably < Celtic]

crozier *n* CHR, BOT another spelling of **crosier**

CRP *abbr S Asia* Central Reserve Police

CRT[1] *n* a computer monitor containing a cathode-ray tube [< CRT [2]]

CRT[2] *abbr* ELECTRONICS cathode-ray tube

cru /kroo/ *n* **1.** a vineyard or wine-growing area in France that meets specific standards of quality **2.** an official grade of French wine [Early 19C. < French *crû*, past participle of *croître* 'grow' < Latin *crescere*]

cruces plural of **crux**

crucial /kro͞osh'l/ *adj* **1.** DECISIVE most vital and of the greatest significance in determining an outcome **2.** ⚠ IMPORTANT very important or significant (*informal*) **3.** EXCELLENT great or excellent (*slang*) [Early 18C. < French < Latin *cruc-* 'cross'] —**cruciality** /kro͞oshi álləti/ *n*

USAGE ***Crucial*** has the core meaning of decisive: *Her tie-breaking vote was crucial.* However, ***crucial*** has been trivialized to the point that it often means nothing more than 'important'. This is especially true in media reports: *If proportional representation is adopted, it is crucial (= important) to choose the best method.* Avoid overusing ***crucial*** in formal writing; it is better reserved for something decisive.

crucially /kro͞osh'li/ *adv* in a way that determines the outcome of something or has great impact and importance

crucian /kro͞osh'n/ (*plural* **-cians** or *same*), **crucian carp** *n* a carp that has a dark-green back, golden-yellow sides, and reddish fins. Native to: Europe, Asia. Latin name: *Carassius carassius.* [Mid-18C. Alteration of Low German *karu(s)se* < Latin *coracinus*, a black fish of the Nile < Greek *korax* 'raven']

cruciate /kro͞oshi ət, -ayt/ *adj* **1.** same as **cruciform 2.** describes insect wings that form a cross shape when at rest [Late 17C. < medieval Latin *cruciata* < Latin *crux* 'cross']

crucible /kro͞ossib'l/ *n* **1.** METALL CONTAINER FOR MELTING SOMETHING a heat-resistant container in which ores or metals are melted **2.** METALL BOTTOM OF FURNACE the hollow part at the bottom of a furnace where molten metal collects **3.** TESTING CIRCUMSTANCES a place or set of circumstances where people or things are subjected to forces that test them and often make them change **4.** ORDEAL a severe trial or ordeal [15C. < medieval Latin *crucibulum* 'nightlight, crucible']

CULTURAL NOTE ***The Crucible***, a play (1953) by US dramatist Arthur Miller. Intended as a metaphor for the 'un-American' McCarthy hearings of the 1950s, the play is set in Salem, Massachusetts, in 1692 and describes how the social fabric of a small town is ripped apart when a group of young girls starts to denounce townsfolk as witches. It was made into a film by Nicholas Hytner in 1996.

crucible steel *n* a high-grade steel made by mixing steel and additives in a furnace

crucifer /kro͞ossifər/ *n* **1.** a plant with long narrow seed pods, e.g. the cabbage, turnip, broccoli, or wallflower. Flowers: with four petals in the shape of a cross. Family: Cruciferae. **2.** somebody who bears a cross, especially in a Christian ceremony [Mid-16C. < ecclesiastical Latin < Latin *cruc-* 'cross' + *-fer* 'bearer'] —**cruciferous** /kroo síffərəss/ *adj*

~~**crucifiction**~~ incorrect spelling of **crucifixion**

crucifix /kro͞ossifiks/ *n* a model or image of Jesus Christ on the cross [12C. Via French < ecclesiastical Latin *crucifixus* < Latin *cruci fixus* 'fixed to a cross']

crucifixion /kro͞ossi fíksh'n/ *n* **1.** EXECUTION BY HANGING ON CROSS a form of execution used in ancient times that involved binding or nailing the victim to an upright cross until death **2.** EXECUTION an execution involving crucifixion **3.** ORDEAL a painful ordeal or victimization

Crucifixion *n* **1.** the agony and death of Jesus Christ on the cross at Calvary **2.** a depiction of Jesus Christ on the cross

cruciform /kro͞ossi fawrm/ *adj* shaped like a cross [Mid-17C. < Latin *cruc-* 'cross'] —**cruciformly** *adv*

crucify /kro͞ossi fī/ (**-fies, -fying, -fied**) *v* **1.** *vt* EXECUTE SOMEBODY ON CROSS to execute somebody by crucifixion **2.** *vt* CRITICIZE SOMEBODY HARSHLY to criticize somebody unsparingly **3.** *vt* TREAT SOMEBODY CRUELLY to defeat, torment, or victimize somebody in a thorough or cruel way **4. crucify yourself** *vr* SEVERELY DISCIPLINE YOUR BODY to subject yourself to hard physical discipline [14C. Via French *crucifier* < ecclesiastical Latin *crucifigere* < Latin *cruci figere* 'fix to a cross'] —**crucifier** *n*

cruck /kruk/ *n* either of a pair of curved wooden timbers that supported the roof of some medieval English buildings [Late 16C. Probably variant of CROOK]

crud /krud/ *n* **1.** FILTH a messy, dirty, or sticky substance (*slang*) **2.** SOMEBODY OR SOMETHING CONTEMPTIBLE a person or thing that is considered disgusting or worthless (*slang*) **3.** NONSENSE absolute nonsense (*slang*) **4.** INDUST WASTE PRODUCT an unwanted by-product, especially in the nuclear industry **5.** SKIING SLUSHY SNOW slushy snow that is unfit for good skiing (*informal*) [14C. Earlier form of CURD] —**cruddy** *adj*

crude /krood/ *adj* (**cruder, crudest**) **1.** UNSKILFUL roughly or unskilfully made or conceived ○ *a crude model of a ship* **2.** VULGAR vulgar or obscene ○ *a crude gesture* **3.** IN RAW STATE in an unprocessed condition ○ *crude ore* **4.** APPROXIMATE not precisely accurate ○ *a crude estimate* **5.** UNCORRECTED OR UNEMBELLISHED describes numerical results or collected data that have not been organized, adjusted, or altered in any way ○ *crude data* ○ *crude facts* ■ *n* INDUST same as **crude oil** [14C. < Latin *crudus* 'raw, rough'] —**crudely** *adv* —**crudeness** *n* —**crudity** *n*

crude oil *n* petroleum that has not yet been refined

crudités /kro͞odi tay/ *npl* small pieces of raw vegetables e.g. carrots and cucumber, eaten as an appetizer or snack, often served with a dip [Mid-20C. < French, plural of *crudité* < Latin *cruditas* < *crudus* 'raw']

cruel /kro͞o əl/ *adj* (**-eller, -ellest**) **1.** MERCILESS deliberately and remorselessly causing pain or anguish **2.** BRINGING ABOUT PAIN bringing about pain and distress ■ *vt* (**-els, -elling, -elled**) *Aus* RUIN CHANCE OF SOMETHING to spoil an opportunity of doing something (*informal*) ○ *The scandal could cruel the Minister's re-election.* [12C. Via French < Latin *crudelis*] —**cruelly** *adv* —**cruelness** *n*

cruelty /kro͞o əlti/ (*plural* **-ties**) *n* **1.** CONDITION OF BEING CRUEL the quality or condition of being cruel **2.** DELIBERATELY CRUEL ACT an act that deliberately causes pain and distress **3.** LAW PSYCHOLOGICAL OR PHYSICAL PAIN the infliction of pain, distress, or anguish, especially when it is long-term and considered extreme enough to be grounds for divorce [13C. Via Old French *crualté* < Latin *crudelitas* < *crudelis* 'cruel']

cruelty-free *adj* describes manufactured goods, especially cosmetics, that have been developed without being tested on animals

cruet /kro͞o it/ *n* **1.** CONDIMENT CONTAINER a small container for holding salt, pepper, oil, or vinegar **2.** CONDIMENT SET a set of matching cruets on a stand **3.** SMALL BOTTLE USED IN COMMUNION either of two containers that hold the water and wine used in the Christian Communion service [13C. < Anglo-Norman, 'little flask' < Old French *crue* 'flask' < Germanic]

Cruikshank /kro͝ok shangk/, **George** (1792–1878) British caricaturist and illustrator. He was famous for his satirical etchings and wood engravings. He also illustrated works by Charles Dickens and William Thackeray, among others.

cruise /krooz/ *v* (**cruises, cruising, cruised**) **1.** *vti* TRAVEL BY SEA to travel by ship over a sea or other large body of water, usually calling at several places **2.** *vi* TRAVEL AT EASY RATE to travel at a steady efficient rate, below top speed **3.** *vi* PROCEED CASUALLY to proceed in a leisurely casual way or with no particular destination ○ *We've just been cruising around in the car.* **4.** *vi* ACHIEVE OBJECTIVE IN SPORT to progress or achieve a goal with very little effort, especially in sport ○ *cruised to the semifinals* **5.** *vti* SEEK SEXUAL PARTNER to go out looking for a sexual partner, or frequent a public place in search of one (*slang*) **6.** *vi* NAVY PATROL SEA to patrol an area of sea on the lookout for enemy vessels ■ *n* TRIP BY SEA a journey by ship for pleasure or for naval purposes [Mid-17C. < Dutch *kruisen* 'to cross' < *kruis* 'cross' < Latin *crux*]

Cruise /krooz/, **Tom** (*b.* 1962) US actor. He has starred in many Hollywood films, including *Jerry Maguire* (1996). Born **Mapother IV, Thomas Cruise**

cruise control *n* an electronic device in a motor vehicle that allows a selected speed to be maintained consistently

cruise liner *n* same as **cruise ship**

cruise missile *n* a long-range jet-propelled guided missile that flies low

cruiser /kro͞ozər/ *n* **1.** SMALL WARSHIP a fast and easily manoeuvrable warship that is smaller and less heavily armoured than a battleship **2.** same as **cabin cruiser 3.** SOMETHING OR SOMEBODY THAT CRUISES a vehicle that cruises, e.g. a ship, aircraft, or motor vehicle, or a person who cruises **4.** SOMEBODY SEEKING SEXUAL PARTNER somebody who seeks a sexual partner in a public place (*slang*) [Late 17C. < Dutch *kruiser* < *kruisen* (see CRUISE)]

cruiserweight /kro͞ozər wayt/ *n* **1.** in professional boxing, a weight category for competitors whose weight does not exceed 86 kg/190 lb **2.** a professional boxer who competes at cruiserweight level

cruise ship *n* a large luxurious passenger ship equipped with many leisure facilities, used for going on cruises

cruising radius /kro͞ozing-/ *n* the maximum distance that a vessel or aircraft can travel without needing to refuel

cruller /krúllər/, **kruller** *n N Am* a small ring-shaped deep-fried cake [Early 19C. < Dutch *kruller* < *krullen* 'to curl']

crumb /krum/ *n* **1.** SMALL FRAGMENT OF BAKED FOOD a very small fragment of bread, cake, biscuit, or similar food **2.** SMALL AMOUNT a tiny amount of something **3.** INNER PART OF LOAF the soft middle part of a loaf of bread **4.** CONTEMPTIBLE PERSON somebody regarded as contemptible (*dated slang*) ■ *v* (**crumbs, crumbing, crumbed**) **1.** *vt* COOK PUT CRUMBS ON OR IN FOOD to coat or thicken food with crumbs, especially breadcrumbs **2.** *vti* COOK CRUMBLE to break bread, cake, or biscuits into small bits, or be broken in this way **3.** *vt* CLEAN CRUMBS FROM SOMETHING to clear away crumbs from something [Old English *cruma* < Germanic]

crumble /krúmb'l/ *v* (**-bles, -bling, -bled**) **1.** *vti* REDUCE TO TINY BITS to break up into tiny bits, or make something break into tiny bits **2.** *vi* DISINTEGRATE to disintegrate or fall apart ■ *n* PUDDING WITH CRUMB TOPPING a baked pudding made from fruit topped with a crumbly mixture of flour, fat, and sugar baked until the top is crunchy. N Am term **crisp** [15C. Probably < Old English *gecrymmian* 'break into crumbs' < *cruma* (see CRUMB)]

crumbly /krúmbli/ *adj* (**-blier, -bliest**) **1.** EASILY CRUMBLED tending to crumble readily **2.** WITH MANY CRUMBS containing or covered with many crumbs ■ *n* (*plural* **-blies**) OLDER PERSON a mildly insulting term for an older person (*offensive*) —**crumbliness** *n*

crumbs /krumz/ *interj* used to express dismay or shock (*dated informal*) [Late 19C. Alteration of CHRIST]

crumby /krúmmi/ (**-ier, -iest**) *adj* **1.** full of or covered with crumbs **2.** soft and spongy in texture, like the inside of a loaf of bread **3.** same as **crummy** (*informal*)

crumhorn /krúm hawrn/, **krummhorn** *n* a medieval double-reed woodwind instrument with an upward-curving tube [Late 17C. < German *Krummhorn* 'crooked horn']

crummy /krúmmi/ (**-mier, -miest**) *adj* (*informal*) **1.** inferior or of little worth ○ *a crummy hotel* **2.** miserable or unwell ○ *had a headache and felt crummy* [Mid-19C. Variant of CRUMBY]

crump /krump/ *n* **SOUND OF BURSTING BOMB** the thudding sound of an exploding shell or bomb ■ *vi* (**crumps, crumping, crumped**) **1. MAKE THUDDING NOISE** to make a thudding noise like the sound of an exploding shell or bomb **2. MAKE CRUNCHING NOISE** to make a crunching noise like the sound of footsteps in crisp snow [Mid-17C. An imitation of the sound]

Crump /krump/, **Barry John** (1935–96) New Zealand writer. He is author of the comic novel *A Good Keen Man* (1960).

crumpet /krúmpit/ *n* **1. CAKE COOKED ON GRIDDLE** a solid cake with a slightly elastic texture and small holes that is eaten toasted with butter **2.** *Scotland* **THIN PANCAKE** a large thin pancake **3. OFFENSIVE TERM** an offensive term for a woman, or women collectively, regarded as sexually desirable or available (*slang*) [Late 17C. Origin ?]

crumple /krúmp'l/ *v* (**-ples, -pling, -pled**) **1.** *vti* **CREASE AND WRINKLE** to become full of irregular creases and wrinkles, or make something full of creases **2.** *vti* **COLLAPSE** to collapse, or make something collapse **3.** *vi* **LOOK UPSET OR DISAPPOINTED** to lose the appearance of equanimity and control, especially when upset or disappointed and close to tears ■ *n* **WRINKLE** a crease or wrinkle in something [14C. < Old English *crump* 'crooked, curled up'] —**crumply** *adj*

crumple zone *n* a part of a motor vehicle designed to absorb the impact of a collision by crumpling easily

crunch /krunch/ *v* (**crunches, crunching, crunched**) **1.** *vt* **MUNCH FOOD NOISILY** to crush crisp foods audibly with the teeth **2.** *vti* **MAKE CRUSHING SOUND** to make a noisy crushing sound, or cause something to make such a sound **3.** *vt* COMPUT **RAPIDLY PROCESS DATA** to process data or numbers at high speed (*informal*) ■ *n* **1. CRUSHING NOISE** a loud short sound made when something is crushed ○ *the crunch of footsteps on gravel* **2. DECISIVE MOMENT** a critical time or situation, especially one when a decision or action must be taken ○ *when it comes to the crunch* **3.** FITNESS **SIT-UP EXERCISE** a form of sit-up in which the body is only partially raised, intended to strengthen the abdominal muscles ■ *adj* **NEEDING DECISIVE ACTION** requiring a decision or action [Early 19C. An imitation of the sound] —**cruncher** *n*

crunchy /krúnchi/ (**-ier, -iest**) *adj* crisp and making a crunching sound when eaten or walked upon —**crunchily** *adv* —**crunchiness** *n*

crupper /krúppər/ *n* **1.** a strap that passes under the tail of a horse and is attached to a saddle or harness to prevent it from sliding forwards **2.** the hindquarters of a horse [14C. < Anglo-Norman *cropere*, Old French *cropiere*]

crus /kruss, krooss/ (*plural* **crura** /kroórə/) *n* **1.** the leg between the knee and ankle **2.** a body part shaped like a leg or pair of legs [Late 16C. < Latin, 'leg'] —**crural** /kroórəl/ *adj*

crusade /kroo sáyd/ *n* **1. CONCERTED EFFORT** a vigorous concerted action to promote or eliminate something **2. RELIGIOUSLY MOTIVATED EFFORT** a war or campaign that is religiously motivated, e.g. one with papal sanction **3.** *also* **Crusade RELIGIOUS WAR** in the 11th, 12th, and 13th centuries, a military expedition by European Christians to retake areas in the Holy Land captured by Muslim forces ■ *vi* (**-sades, -sading, -saded**) **1. CAMPAIGN VIGOROUSLY** to make a vigorous or concerted effort to promote or eliminate something **2. FIGHT FOR RELIGION** to fight in a religious crusade [15C. < medieval Latin *cruciata* < Latin *crux* 'cross']

crusader /kroo sáydər/ *n* **1.** a vigorous campaigner for or against something **2.** *also* **Crusader** a soldier who took part in any of the crusades to the Holy Land

crusado /kroo sáydō, -zaádō/ (*plural* **-does** or **-dos**) *n* a gold or silver coin with a cross imprinted on it that was a unit of currency in Portugal between the 15th and 20th centuries [Mid-16C. < Portuguese *cruzado* (see CRUZADO)]

cruse /krooz/ *n* a small earthenware container used to hold liquids (*archaic*) [Old English *crūse* < Germanic]

crush /krush/ *v* (**crushes, crushing, crushed**) **1.** *vti* **COMPRESS** to compress somebody or something, causing injury, damage, or distortion, or become compressed in this way **2.** *vti* **CREASE** to crease a fabric or item of clothing, or become creased **3.** *vti* **GRIND** to grind something into small pieces, or be ground in this way **4.** *vt* **QUELL PROTEST** to put down a protest or movement using force **5.** *vt* **OVERWHELM SOMEBODY OR SOMETHING** to defeat, subdue, or suppress somebody or something overwhelmingly **6.** *vt* **MASH FRUIT** to reduce fruit or vegetables to juice and pulp by pressing **7.** *vt* **PHYSICALLY PRESS SOMEBODY HARD** to exert physical pressure on somebody by hugging, pressing, or pushing **8.** *vt* **OPPRESS SOMEBODY** to oppress or burden somebody severely **9.** *vt* **HUMILIATE SOMEBODY** to humiliate somebody by the force of a remark, criticism, or argument **10.** *vi* **CROWD TOGETHER** to move in a mass or crowd ■ *n* **1. CROWD OF PEOPLE** a crowd or mass, especially of people **2. CROWDED SITUATION** a crowded situation, or an action that results in this **3.** BEVERAGES **FRUIT DRINK** a drink containing the juice from crushed fruit **4. SHORT-LIVED LOVE** a temporary romantic attraction, especially in teenagers and young people (*informal*) **5. OBJECT OF SOMEBODY'S TEMPORARY ROMANTIC ATTRACTION** the person who is the object of somebody's temporary romantic infatuation (*informal*) [14C. < Anglo-Norman *crussier*, Old French *croissir*] —**crushable** *adj* —**crusher** *n* —**crushing** *adj* —**crushingly** *adv*

SYNONYMS See ***love***.

crush bar *n* a bar in a theatre where drinks are served before performances and during intervals

crush barrier *n* a barrier, especially a temporary one, put up to restrain crowds and prevent people from being crushed

crushed /krusht/ *adj* **1.** extremely upset, saddened, or depressed ○ *was totally crushed upon hearing the news of the accident* **2.** describes a fabric or material that has been manufactured or treated to create permanent creases in it ○ *crushed velvet*

crushproof /krúsh proof/ *adj* made to resist being crushed, creased, or wrinkled

crust /krust/ *n* **1. OUTER PART OF BREAD** the thin, usually hard or crisp outer part of a loaf or slice of bread **2. PIECE OF BREAD** a piece of bread that is mostly crust or is stale and dry **3. PASTRY FOR PIE** the pastry that wholly or partly encases a pie or tart **4. HARD UPPER LAYER** a crisp, hard, or thick outer layer or coating that develops on something **5.** MED **SCAB** a dry hardened outer layer of blood, pus, or other bodily secretion that forms over a cut or sore **6.** GEOL **SOLID OUTER LAYER OF EARTH** the thin outermost layer of Earth, approximately one per cent of Earth's volume, that varies in thickness and has a different composition from the interior. Other terrestrial planets are believed to have crusts. **7.** WINE **LAYER OF POTASSIUM TARTRATE** a thin layer of potassium tartrate that forms on the inside of some wine and port bottles as the contents mature **8.** BIOL **BODY COVERING** the hard outermost body covering in some living organisms, such as lichens and crustaceans **9. INCOME** a living (*informal*) ○ *just trying to earn a crust* ■ *v* (**crusts, crusting, crusted**) **1.** *vi* **DEVELOP AS CRUST** to form into a crust **2.** *vti* **MAKE OR BECOME ENCRUSTED** to cover something with a crust or become covered with a crust [14C. Via Old French *crouste* < Latin *crusta* 'rind, shell']

crustacean /kru stáysh'n/ *n* an invertebrate animal with several pairs of jointed legs, a hard protective outer shell, two pairs of antennae, and eyes at the ends of stalks. Lobsters, crabs, shrimps, crayfish, water fleas, barnacles, and wood lice are crustaceans. Subphylum: Crustacea. [Mid-19C. < modern Latin *Crustacea* (plural) '(things) having a shell' < Latin *crusta* 'shell'] —**crustacean** *adj* —**crustaceous** *adj*

crustal /krúst'l/ *adj* describes the crust of Earth or another astronomical object [Mid-19C. < Latin *crusta* 'shell']

crustie *n* another spelling of **crusty** (*slang*)

crustose /krústōss/ *adj* describes lichens or algae that resemble a crust on the surface they adhere to [Late 19C. < Latin *crustosus* < *crusta* 'shell']

crusty /krústi/ *adj* (**-ier, -iest**) **1. HAVING CRUST** having a crisp crust ○ *crusty bread* **2. CURT** gruff, curt, and candid in speech ■ *n also* **crustie** (*plural* **-ies**) **UNKEMPT PERSON** a dirty, unkempt person who leads an unconventional, unmaterialistic life, often in borrowed or temporary accommodation (*slang*) —**crustily** *adv* —**crustiness** *n*

crutch /kruch/ *n* **1. SOMETHING PROVIDING HELP OR SUPPORT** something that sustains or supports somebody or something that is otherwise liable to collapse, fail, or falter **2.** MED **WALKING AID** a staff with a handgrip and a rest for the forearm or armpit, used to help a person who is unable to walk unassisted **3.** ANAT same as **crotch** (sense 1) **4.** NAUT **FORKED SUPPORT** a forked supporting piece for a boom, oar, or spar ■ *vt* (**crutches, crutching, crutched**) **HOLD SOMETHING UP WITH CRUTCH** to support something with a crutch or similar object [Old English *cryc(c)* < Germanic]

crux /kruks/ (*plural* **cruxes** or **cruces** /kroó seez/) *n* **1. CRUCIAL POINT** an essential or deciding point or element in something, e.g. in an argument **2. PUZZLING PROBLEM** an extremely difficult or puzzling problem **3.** CLIMBING **ARDUOUS PART OF CLIMB** the most demanding part of a climb up a mountain or rocks [Mid-17C. < Latin, 'cross']

Crux *n* ASTRON same as **Southern Cross**. See illustration at **constellation**

crux ansata /krúks an sáatə/ (*plural* **cruces ansatae** /kroó seez an sáatee/) *n* ANCIENT HIST same as **ankh** [< Latin, 'cross with a handle']

Cruyff /kroyf/, **Johan** (*b.* 1947) Dutch footballer. As captain of the Netherlands' national team and the Dutch team Ajax, he led them respectively to the World Cup final in 1974 and three European Cups (1971–73).

Manuel Zambrana/Corbis

Celia Cruz

Cruz /krooz/, **Celia** (1924–2003) Cuban-born US vocalist. She was one of the leading singers of the popular Latin dance music called salsa. Known as **the Queen of Salsa**

cruzado /kroo zaádō/ (*plural* **-does** or **-dos**) *n* **1.** a unit of currency used in Brazil between 1986 and 1990, equivalent to 100 centavos **2.** a coin or note worth one cruzado **3.** MONEY another spelling of **crusado** [Mid-16C. < Portuguese < past participle of *cruzar* 'mark with a cross' < Latin *crux* 'cross']

Crvenkovski /kurv'n kóvski/, **Branko** (*b.* 1962) prime minister of the Former Yugoslav Republic of Macedonia. He was elected as Macedonia's first prime minister in 1992, lost office in 1998, and was re-elected in 2002.

cry /krī/ *v* (**cries, crying, cried**) **1.** *vti* **SHED TEARS** to shed tears as the result of a strongly felt emotion **2.** *vti* **SHOUT** to call or shout out loudly **3.** *vi* ZOOL **MAKE DISTINCTIVE SOUND** to make a natural high-pitched characteristic call (*refers to birds or animals*) **4.** *vt* **GIVE SOMETHING AS REASON** to plead or profess something as a reason or explanation ○ *cry hardship* **5.** *vt* **ANNOUNCE FOR SALE** to proclaim something publicly as being for sale (*archaic*) ■ *n* (*plural* **cries**) **1. INARTICULATE SOUND** a loud inarticulate expression of rage, pain, or surprise **2. SHOUT** a loud call or shout **3. CALL OF BIRD OR ANIMAL** the natural high-pitched characteristic call of a bird or animal **4. PERIOD OF WEEPING** an act or period of shedding tears **5. PUBLIC DEMAND** a public demand, especially an urgent one **6.** FIELD SPORTS **BAYING OF HOUNDS** the sound of hounds baying as they chase their quarry **7.** FIELD SPORTS **HOUNDS** a pack of

hounds **8. PROCLAMATION** an announcement or advertisement called out in public (*archaic*) [13C. Via French *crier* < Latin *quiritare* 'raise a public outcry' < *Quirites* 'Roman citizens'] ◇ **for crying out loud!** used to express annoyance, impatience, frustration, or surprise (*informal*) ◇ **in full cry** in enthusiastic pursuit of something

CULTURAL NOTE *Cry, the Beloved Country*, a novel (1948) by South African writer Alan Paton. It tells of a Black man's search for his sister and his son in Johannesburg, where he encounters the underside of life and the racial hatred that divides the country. His sister has become a prostitute and his son is condemned to death for the murder of a white farmer's son. The novel ends on a note of optimism on the issue of racial harmony, as the two fathers are reconciled.

cry down *vt* to say disparaging or belittling things about somebody or something

cry off *vi* to withdraw from an arrangement or activity previously agreed to (*informal*)

cry out *v* **1.** *vti* to exclaim something loudly because of pain, shock, or fear **2.** *vi* to be in obvious and urgent need

cry up *vt* to praise somebody or something highly

crybaby /krī baybi/ (*plural* **-bies**) *n* an offensive term for somebody, especially a child, who cries or complains a lot (*insult*)

crying /krī ing/ *adj* desperate or deplorable and demanding a remedy ◇ *a crying shame*

cryo- *prefix* freezing, cold ◇ *cryosurgery* [< Greek *kruos* 'icy cold' < Indo-European, 'freeze over']

cryobank /krī ō bangk/ *n* a place where biological material such as semen and body tissue can be stored at extremely low temperatures

cryobiology /krī ō bī ólləji/ *n* the branch of biology that studies how extremely low temperatures affect organisms —**cryobiological** /krī ō bī ə lójjik'l/ *adj* —**cryobiologically** *adv* —**cryobiologist** *n*

cryogen /krī ō jen/ *n* a substance such as liquid nitrogen used in producing extremely low temperatures

cryogenic /krī ō jénnik/ *adj* relating to extremely low temperatures —**cryogenically** *adv*

cryogenics /krī ō jénniks/ *n* the branch of physics that studies the causes and effects of extremely low temperatures (*takes a singular verb*)

cryolite /krī ə līt/ *n* an uncommon white fluoride mineral containing sodium and aluminium. Use: source of aluminium. [Early 19C. < CRYO-; because first found in Greenland]

cryometer /krī ómmitər/ *n* a thermometer that measures very low temperatures —**cryometry** *n*

cryonics /krī ónniks/ *n* the study or practice of keeping a newly dead body at an extremely low temperature in the hope of restoring it to life later with the help of future medical advances (*takes a singular verb*) ■ *npl* the collective techniques involved in cryogenics (*takes a plural verb*) [Mid-20C. Contraction of CRYOGENICS] —**cryonic** *adj*

cryophilic /krī ō fíllik/ *adj* capable of living at low temperatures

cryophyte /krī ə fīt/ *n* an organism that can live or grow on snow or ice, e.g. an alga

cryoprecipitate /krī ō pri síppitət/ *n* a substance that is precipitated at low temperatures, especially a precipitate of blood containing a blood-clotting factor

cryopreservation /krī ō prézzər váysh'n/ *n* the process of storing semen, ova, corneas, embryos, or body tissue at extremely low temperatures for future use —**cryopreserve** /-pri zúrv/ *vt*

cryoprobe /krī ō prōb/ *n* an instrument used in cryosurgery for cooling body tissue to low temperatures

cryoprotectant /krī ō prə téktənt/ *n* a substance such as glycerol used to protect stored living tissue from the effects of freezing

cryoscope /krī ə skōp/ *n* an instrument used for determining the temperature at which a liquid freezes

cryoscopy /krī óskəpi/ *n* the study or practice of determining the freezing point of liquids —**cryoscopic** /krī ə skóppik/ *adj*

cryostat /krī ə stat/ *n* a regulating device for maintaining a constant low temperature

cryosurgery /krī ō súrjəri/ *n* surgery in which low temperatures are applied, e.g. to destroy diseased tissue or to seal down detached retinas —**cryosurgeon** /krī ō surjən/ *n* —**cryosurgical** *adj*

cryotherapy /krī ō thérrəpi/ (*plural* **-pies**) *n* medical treatment that involves cooling the body, especially by applying ice packs

crypt /kript/ *n* **1.** an underground room or vault, often below a church, used as a burial chamber or chapel, or for storing religious artefacts **2.** a small recess, tubular gland, or follicle in the body [Late 18C. Via Latin < Greek *kruptē* 'vault', feminine of *kruptos* 'hidden']

crypt- *prefix* same as **crypto-** (*used before vowels*)

cryptanalysis /kríptə nálləssiss/ *n* the process or science of deciphering coded texts or messages —**cryptanalyst** /krip tánnəlist/ *n* —**cryptanalytic** /krípt ənə líttik/ *adj* —**cryptanalytical** *adj*

cryptic /kríptik/ *adj* **1. AMBIGUOUS OR OBSCURE** deliberately mysterious and seeming to have a hidden meaning **2. SECRET** secret or hidden in some way **3. INDICATING SOLUTION INDIRECTLY** describes crossword puzzles, clues, or anagrams with an indirect solution **4. USING CODES** relating to or using codes or similar techniques **5.** ZOOL **PROTECTIVE** describes body markings or colouring that camouflages an animal [Early 17C. Via late Latin < Greek *kruptikos* < *kruptē* (see CRYPT)] —**cryptically** *adv*

SYNONYMS See *obscure*.

cryptic crossword *n* a crossword which uses obscure clues to indicate the solutions indirectly

crypto- *prefix* secret, hidden ◇ *cryptogram* ◇ *cryptanalysis* [< Greek *kruptos* < *kruptein* 'to hide']

cryptoclastic /kríptə klástik/ *adj* describes rock composed of microscopic mineral fragments

cryptococcosis /kríptōkə kṓssiss/ *n* an infectious disease that affects parts of the body, especially the brain and central nervous system, with lesions or abscesses caused by the fungus *Cryptococcus neoformans* [Mid-20C. < CRYPTOCOCCUS]

cryptococcus /kríptō kókəss/ (*plural* **-ci** /-kókī/) *n* a fungus that resembles a yeast, some types of which cause illnesses such as cryptococcosis. Genus: *Cryptococcus*. [Early 20C. < modern Latin, 'hidden coccus']

cryptocrystalline /kríptō krístəlīn/ *adj* describes rocks that are composed of crystals too small to be seen with a petrological microscope

cryptogam /kríptə gam/ *n* an organism such as a fern, moss, alga, or fungus that reproduces by means of spores instead of seeds [Late 18C. Via French < modern Latin *cryptogamus* 'hidden marriage'; because the means of reproduction is not apparent] —**cryptogamic** /kríptə gámmik/ *adj* —**cryptogamous** /krip tóggəməss/ *adj*

cryptogenic /kríptō jénnik/ *adj* MED same as **idiopathic**

cryptogram /kríptə gram/ *n* **1.** a text or message that is in code or cipher **2.** a symbol with a secret meaning or significance

cryptographic /kríptə gráffik/ *adj* relating to or using cryptography —**cryptographical** *adj* —**cryptographically** *adv*

cryptographic key *n* a parameter that determines the transformation of computer data to encrypted format, measured in bits (*used in e-commerce*)

cryptography /krip tóggrəfi/ *n* **1.** the study or analysis of codes and coding methods **2.** coded or secret writing —**cryptograph** /kríptə graaf, -graf/ *n* —**cryptographer** *n*

cryptology /krip tólləji/ *n* COMMUNICATION **1.** same as **cryptography** (sense 1) **2.** same as **cryptanalysis** —**cryptologic** /kríptə lójjik/ *adj* —**cryptological** *adj* —**cryptologist** *n*

cryptomeria /kríptō meéri ə/ *n* UK, Can a tall coniferous tree with curved needle-shaped leaves arranged in spirals. Native to: China, Japan. Latin name: *Cryptomeria japonica*. ANZ, US term **Japanese cedar** [Mid-19C. < modern Latin, 'hidden part', because its seeds are hidden by scales]

cryptorchid /krip táwrkid/ *n* a man, boy, or male animal with one or both testicles that have failed to descend into the scrotum [Late 19C. < CRYPTORCHISM]

cryptorchism /krip táwrkizəm/, **cryptorchidism** /-táwrkidizəm/ *n* a developmental condition affecting some men, boys, or male animals in which one or both testicles fail to descend into the scrotum [Late 19C. < CRYPTO- + Latin *orchis* 'testicle' < Greek *orkhis*]

cryptosporidiosis /kríptōspə ríddi ṓssiss/ *n* an infectious condition of humans and domestic animals, characterized by fever, diarrhoea, and stomach cramps, and spread by a protozoan of the genus *Cryptosporidium* [< CRYPTOSPORIDIUM]

cryptosporidium /kríptōspə ríddi əm/ (*plural* **-dia** /-di ə/) *n* a water-borne protozoan parasite that contaminates drinking water supplies, causing intestinal infections in human beings and domestic animals [Late 20C. < modern Latin < Greek *kruptos* 'hidden' + *sporidium* 'little spore' < *spora* 'seed']

cryptozoic /kríptō zṓ ik/ *adj* describes invertebrates that live in dark or concealed places such as under stones or in caves or holes

Cryptozoic *adj* GEOL same as **Precambrian** —**Cryptozoic** *n*

cryptozoite /kríptō zṓ īt/ *n* a malarial parasite at the stage in its life cycle when it is present in the host's body tissue but before it invades the red blood cells [< CRYPTO- + Greek *zōion* 'animal']

cryptozoology /kríptō zoo ólləji/ *n* the study of imaginary creatures or fabled creatures such as the Loch Ness monster or the yeti —**cryptozoological** /kríptō zoo ə lójjik'l/ *adj* —**cryptozoologist** *n*

cryst. *abbr* CHEM, MINERALS, ELECTRONICS **1.** crystalline **2.** crystallography

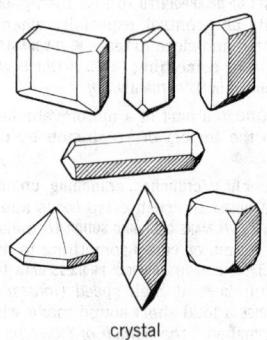

crystal

crystal /kríst'l/ *n* **1.** MINERALS **QUARTZ** a clear colourless mineral, especially quartz **2.** MINERALS **PIECE OF CRYSTAL** a piece of a mineral in crystal form **3.** CHEM **SOLID WITH REPETITIVE INTERNAL STRUCTURE** a solid containing an internal pattern of atoms, molecules, or ions that is regular, repeated, and geometrically arranged **4.** OBJECT LIKE **CRYSTAL** something that has the form of a crystal, e.g. a frozen snowflake or a grain of salt ◇ *snow crystals* ◇ *crystals of salt* **5.** GLASS **HEAVY GLASS** a heavy transparent sparkling glass **6.** HOUSEHOLD **CRYSTAL GLASS OBJECTS** objects made from heavy transparent sparkling glass **7.** ELECTRONICS **ELECTRONIC COMPONENT** a crystalline substance that has semiconducting or piezoelectric properties and is used as an electronic component, or the electrical device using it **8.** *N Am* JEWELLERY same as **watch glass** (sense 1) **9.** *US* DRUGS same as **crystal meth** (*slang*) ■ *adj* VERY CLEAR clear and sparkling [Pre-12C. Via French < Latin *crystallum* < Greek *krustallos* 'ice']

crystal ball *n* **1.** a clear solid sphere of glass or rock crystal that is used by a fortune teller for supposedly predicting the future **2.** a means of supposedly predicting future events

crystal clear *adj* **1.** clear or obvious to the understanding **2.** clean and sparkling

crystal gazing *n* the prediction of future events by questionable means, most commonly by staring into a crystal ball in the belief that images of future events will appear there —**crystal gazer** *n*

crystal healing *n* the use of pieces of crystal in the belief that they can promote health and increase well-being

crystall- *prefix* same as **crystallo-** (*used before vowels*)

crystal lattice *n* the regular array of points in space that are occupied by the atoms, ions, or molecules that make up a crystal

crystalliferous /krístə líffərəss/, **crystalligerous** /krístə líjjərəss/ *adj* forming or containing crystals

crystalline /krístə līn/ *adj* **1.** relating to, made of, containing, or resembling crystals **2.** clear and sparkling —**crystallinity** /krístə línnəti/ *n*

crystalline lens *n* the transparent lens behind the iris in the eyes of vertebrates

crystallise *vti* another spelling of **crystallize**

crystallite /krístə līt/ *n* a tiny rudimentary crystal, e.g. of a type found in some igneous rocks —**crystallitic** /krístə líttik/ *adj*

crystallize /krístə līz/ (**-lizes, -lizing, -lized**), **crystallise** (**-lises, -lising, -lised**) *vti* **1.** MAKE OR BECOME WELL-DEFINED to make an idea or feeling become fixed or definite, or become fixed or definite **2.** FORM CRYSTALS to form crystals, or make something do this **3.** COOK COAT WITH SUGAR CRYSTALS to coat or impregnate something with crystals, especially sugar crystals, or become coated or impregnated in this way —**crystallizability** /krístə līzə bílləti/ *n* —**crystallizable** *adj* —**crystallization** /krístə lī záysh'n/ *n* —**crystallizer** *n*

crystallo- *prefix* crystal, crystalline ○ *crystallography* ○ *crystalliferous* [< Greek *krustallos* 'ice']

crystallography /krístə lóggrəfi/ *n* the branch of science dealing with the formation and properties of crystals —**crystallographer** *n* —**crystallographic** /krístələ gráffik/ *adj* —**crystallographically** *adv*

crystalloid /krístə loyd/ *adj* RESEMBLING CRYSTAL having the structure, properties, or appearance of a crystal ■ *n* **1.** PHYS SUBSTANCE PASSING THROUGH SEMIPERMEABLE MEMBRANE a substance that in solution can pass through a semipermeable membrane **2.** BOT PROTEIN IN PLANT CELL a mass of protein resembling a crystal that commonly occurs in seeds and other storage organs —**crystalloidal** /krístə lóyd'l/ *adj*

crystal meth *n US* powdered methamphetamine used as an illegal drug (*slang*)

Crystal Palace *n* a large glass building designed for the Great Exhibition in Hyde Park, London, in 1851, later moved to south London and destroyed by fire in 1936

crystal pleat *n* any of a series of permanently pressed pleats of varying widths, often in a sheer fabric

crystal set *n* an early form of radio receiver that used a quartz crystal as a detector

Cs *symbol* CHEM ELEM caesium

CS *abbr* **1.** FIN capital stock **2.** CIV ENG chartered surveyor **3.** MIL chief of staff **4.** CHR Christian Science **5.** CHR Christian Scientist **6.** POL civil service **7.** LAW Court of Session

CSA *abbr* Child Support Agency

csardas *n* DANCE, MUSIC another spelling of **czardas**

CSB *abbr* chemical stimulation of the brain

csc *abbr* MATHS cosecant

CSC *abbr* POL Civil Service Commission

CSE *n* a school-leaving certificate in England and Wales that was replaced in 1988 by the GCSE. Full form **Certificate of Secondary Education**

CSEU *abbr* Confederation of Shipbuilding and Engineering Unions

CSF *abbr* MED cerebrospinal fluid

CS gas *n* a gas that causes tears, salivation, and painful breathing. Formula: $C_9H_5ClN_2$. [Abbreviation of *Corson-Stoughton*, after B. B. *Corson* (b. 1896) and R. W. *Stoughton* (1906–57), US chemists]

CSH /kash/ *n US* a military field hospital. Full form **Combat Support Hospital**

CSIRO *abbr* Commonwealth Scientific and Industrial Research Organization

CSM *abbr* Company Sergeant-Major

CSO *abbr* Central Statistical Office

C-SPAN /see span/ *n* a US cable TV channel that focuses chiefly on public affairs such as Congressional hearings and cultural and social issues [Acronym < *Cable Satellite Public Affairs Network*]

CSR *abbr* BUSINESS corporate social responsibility

CSS *abbr* Certificate in Social Service

CST *abbr* **1.** TIME Central Standard Time **2.** PSYCHIAT convulsive shock treatment

CSU *abbr* Civil Service Union

CSYS *abbr Scotland* EDUC Certificate of Sixth Year Studies

ct *abbr* **1.** FIN cent **2.** EDUC certificate

CT *abbr* **1.** TIME Central Time **2.** MED computed tomography **3.** Connecticut

Ct. *abbr* Count (*used in titles*)

CTC *abbr* **1.** City Technology College **2.** Cyclists' Touring Club

CTD *abbr US* MED cumulative trauma disorder

ctenidium /ti níddi əm/ (*plural* **-ia** /-i ə/) *n* a gill found in molluscs that has a central axis with a fringe of filaments on each side. It is used in gas exchange and filter feeding. [Late 19C. Via modern Latin < Greek *ktenidion* 'little comb' < *kteis* 'comb']

ctenoid /téen oyd, ténnoyd/ *adj* describes fish scales that have tiny projections like the teeth of combs, or fish that have such scales [Mid-19C. < Greek *kten-* 'comb']

ctenophore /ténnə fawr, téenə-/ *n* a invertebrate sea animal resembling a jellyfish, with eight rows of undulating filaments used for swimming. Sea gooseberries and sea walnuts are ctenophores. Phylum: Ctenophora. [Late 19C. < modern Latin *ctenophorus* < Greek *kten-* 'comb'] —**ctenophoran** /ti nóffərən/ *adj, n*

CTI *abbr* COMPUT, TELECOM computer-telephony integration

ctn *abbr* **1.** HOUSEHOLD carton **2.** MATHS cotangent

CTO *adj* describes stamps that are bought by private collectors and postmarked in sheets. Full form **cancelled to order**

C to C, **C2C** *adj* **1.** between two centres. Full form **centre to centre 2.** relating to Internet transactions between two consumers. Full form **consumer-to-consumer**

CTRL, **Ctrl** *abbr* COMPUT control key

CTRL-ALT-DEL, **Ctrl-Alt-Del** *n* a combination of three computer keys, labelled control (CTRL), alternate (ALT), and delete (DEL), that are struck together to reboot a computer

CT scan *n UK* a diagnostic medical scan in which cross-sectional images of a body part are formed through computerized axial tomography and shown on a computer screen. ANZ, N Am term **CAT scan**

CT scanner *n UK* a radiological diagnostic scanning machine used to make a CT scan. ANZ, N Am term **CAT scanner**

CTV *abbr* Canadian Television Network Limited

cu *abbr* Cuba (*used in Internet addresses*) See table at **domain name**

Cu *symbol* CHEM ELEM copper[1]

CU *abbr* **1.** close-up **2.** ONLINE see you (*used in e-mails or text messages*)

cu. *abbr* MEASURE cubic

cuadrilla /kwaa dréeyə/ *n* a group of three banderilleros and two picadors who assist a matador in the bullring [Mid-19C. < Spanish, 'little square' (from a formation used) < *cuadra* 'square' < Latin *quadr-*]

cuatro /kwáttrō/ *n Carib* a small four-stringed guitar [Mid-20C. < Spanish, 'four']

cub /kub/ *n* **1.** YOUNG OF CARNIVOROUS MAMMAL an offspring of a carnivorous mammal such as a bear, lion, or tiger **2.** YOUNG PERSON a cheeky young person (*dated*) **3.** *Ireland, regional* same as **boy** (sense 1) (*informal*) ■ *vi* (**cubs, cubbing, cubbed**) **1.** PRODUCE YOUNG to give birth to an animal cub **2.** HUNT FOX CUBS to hunt fox cubs [Mid-16C. Origin ?] —**cubbish** *adj* —**cubbishly** *adv*

Cub *n* YOUTH ORG same as **Cub Scout**

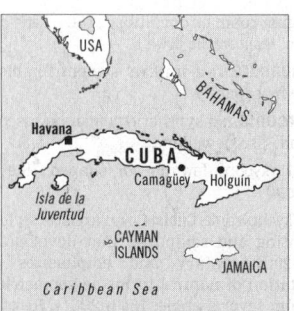
Cuba

Cuba /kyóobə/ country in the Caribbean Sea comprising two main islands and over 1,000 islets. Language: Spanish. Currency: peso. Capital: Havana. Population: 11,263,429 (2003). Area: 114,525 sq. km/44,218 sq. mi. Official name **Republic of Cuba** —**Cuban** *adj, n*

cubage /kyóobij/ *n UK, NZ* the cubic content or volume of a solid. Aus, N Am term **cubature**

Cuba libre /kyóobə leébray/ *n* a drink made by mixing rum, cola, ice, and lime juice [< American Spanish, 'free Cuba' (a toast used during the Cuban War of Independence, 1895–98)]

Cuban heel *n* a straight broad heel of medium height for a shoe

cubature /kyóobəchər/ *n* **1.** the process of working out the cubic content or volume of a solid **2.** *Aus, N Am* MEASURE same as **cubage** [Late 17C. < CUBE[1]]

cubbyhole /kúbbi hōl/, **cubby** /kúbbi/ (*plural* **-bies**) *n* **1.** a small space or room **2.** a small storage compartment

cubbyhouse /kúbbi howss/ (*plural* **-houses** /-howziz/) *n Aus* a playhouse for a child. UK term **Wendy house**

cube[1] /kyoob/ *n* **1.** SOLID FIGURE OF SIX EQUAL SIDES a three-dimensional geometric figure formed of six equal square plane faces, each set at right angles to the four sides adjacent to it **2.** CUBE-SHAPED OBJECT a solid shaped like a cube **3.** PRODUCT OF THREE EQUAL NUMBERS the product of three equal numbers or quantities multiplied together, usually written in mathematical notation as a raised 3, e.g. 4^3 means $4 \times 4 \times 4$ ■ *vt* (**cubes, cubing, cubed**) **1.** MULTIPLY ITEM BY ITSELF TWICE to multiply a number or quantity by itself twice, e.g. 6 cubed is $6 \times 6 \times 6$ **2.** DICE FOOD to cut or shape food into cubes **3.** WORK OUT CUBIC CONTENT OF SOMETHING to calculate the cubic content of something [Mid-16C. Directly or via French < Latin *cubus* < Greek *kubos* 'cube, pelvis'] —**cuber** *n*

cube[2] /kyóo bay, kóo-/, **cubé** *n* **1.** a root extract containing rotenone. Use: insecticides, fish poison. **2.** a leguminous woody plant. Use: source of rotenone. Native to: tropical America. Genus: *Lonchocarpus*. [Early 20C. < American Spanish]

cubeb /kyóo beb/ *n* **1.** a small unripe brownish spicy berry of a climbing plant. Use: formerly, to treat respiratory and urinary disorders. **2.** a climbing plant with heart-shaped leaves, spikes of small flowers, and brownish spicy berries. Native to: Southeast Asia. Latin name: *Piper cubeba*. [13C. Via French *cubèbe* < Arabic *kubāba*]

cube root *n* a number or quantity that, when multiplied by itself twice, equals a given number or quantity

cubic /kyóobik/, **cubical** /-ik'l/ *adj* **1.** THREE-DIMENSIONAL having three measurable dimensions **2.** EQUAL TO VOLUME OF CUBE describes a volume or capacity that is equal to that of a particular cube **3.** CUBE-SHAPED shaped like a cube **4.** MATHS RELATING TO OR CONTAINING CUBED VARIABLE describes a mathematical expression or equation in which at least one variable is cubed but no variable is to be multiplied by itself more than two times ○ *a cubic equation* **5.** CRYSTALS HAVING THREE EQUAL AXES describes a crystal that has three equal perpendicular axes. Symbol **c** ■ *n* MATHS MATHEMATICAL EXPRESSION a cubic expression, equation, or curve —**cubically** *adv*

cubicle /kyóobik'l/ *n* a small partitioned area for private use in a larger, more public room such as

a changing room or dormitory [15C < Latin *cubiculum* 'bedroom' < *cubare* 'lie down']

cubic measure *n* a unit or system for measuring volume or capacity

cubic zirconia *n* a synthetic gemstone resembling a diamond. Use: jewellery.

cubiform /kyoóbi fawrm/ *adj* shaped like a cube (*technical*)

cubism /kyoóbizəm/, **Cubism** *n* an artistic style, chiefly in painting and sculpture, that developed in the early 20th century and emphasizes the representation of natural forms as geometric shapes seen from several angles [Early 20C. < French *cubisme* < *cube* (see CUBE¹)] —**cubist** *n*

cubit /kyoóbit/ *n* an ancient unit of length, equal to the distance from the elbow to the tip of the middle finger, approximately 43–56 cm/17–22 in [14C. < Latin *cubitum* 'elbow, forearm']

cubital /kyoóbit'l/ *adj* relating to the elbow, ulnar bone, or forearm [15C. < Latin *cubitalis* < *cubitum* 'elbow, forearm']

cuboid /kyoó boyd/ *n* **1.** MATHS SOLID FIGURE OF SIX RECTANGULAR PLANES a three-dimensional geometric figure formed of six rectangular plane faces, each set at right angles to the four sides adjacent to it **2.** ANAT BONE IN FOOT the outermost tarsal bone of the foot in vertebrates ■ *adj* MATHS CUBE-SHAPED shaped like a cube —**cuboidal** /kyoo bóyd'l/ *adj*

cub reporter *n* an inexperienced young newspaper reporter

Cub Scout *n* a member of the branch of the Scout Association for younger children, generally 8 to 11 years of age

cucking stool /kúking-/ *n* a punishment used in medieval times in which somebody was tied to a stool and pelted with rotting food [< obsolete *cuck* 'defecate' < N Germanic; because a commode was sometimes used]

cuckold /kúkold/ *n* a husband whose wife has been unfaithful to him ■ *vt* (**-olds, -olding, -olded**) to make a cuckold of a husband [Pre-12C. < Old N French, variant of Old French *cucuault* < *cucu* 'cuckoo'] —**cuckoldry** *n*

cuckoo

cuckoo /koókoo/ *n* (*plural* **-oos**) **1.** BIRD LAYING IN OTHERS' NESTS a bird that lays its eggs in the nests of other birds that bring the nestlings up as their own. Native to: Europe. Latin name: *Cuculus canorus*. **2.** BIRD RELATED TO TRUE CUCKOO a bird that is a member of the cuckoo family **3.** CUCKOO'S CALL the characteristic two-note call of the European cuckoo **4.** SOMEBODY REGARDED AS ECCENTRIC somebody regarded as eccentric or unconventional (*informal*; *sometimes offensive*) ■ *adj* ECCENTRIC eccentric or unconventional (*informal*) ■ *vi* (**-oos, -ooing, -ooed**) GIVE CALL OF CUCKOO to make the characteristic two-note call of the cuckoo [13C. < Old French *cucu*, an imitation of its call]

CULTURAL NOTE *One Flew Over the Cuckoo's Nest*, a film (1975) by US director Milos Forman. Based on Ken Kesey's 1962 novel, it describes how mischievous convict Randle McMurphy inspires his fellow inmates in a psychiatric hospital to rebel against the disciplinarian Nurse Ratched. The film can be seen as a metaphor for the conflict between individuality and creativity and society's pressure to conform.

cuckoo clock *n* a clock that indicates the hour with sounds like a cuckoo's call, usually accompanied

by the appearance of a mechanical bird from behind a door

cuckooflower /koó koo flowər/ *n* a plant often found in moist meadows. Flowers: light purple or occasionally white, with yellow anthers. Latin name: *Cardamine pratensis*. [Late 16C. Because the plant is in flower at about the time of year when the European cuckoo is first heard]

cuckoopint /koó koo pīnt/ *n* a perennial plant with leaves shaped like arrowheads and flowering stems consisting of a yellowish-green cone around a reddish-purple spike that later carries poisonous scarlet berries. Native to: Europe. Latin name: *Arum maculatum*. [15C. Shortening of *cuckoo pintle* 'cuckoo penis'; from the shape of the spadix]

cuckoo shrike *n* a songbird with a long rounded tail that feeds on insects and is often noisy. Native to: Africa, Asia, Australasia. Family: Campephagidae.

cuckoo spit *n* a white frothy secretion found on the stems and leaves of plants, produced by the larvae of insects such as the frog-hopper [Because it was believed to have been spat out by cuckoos]

cucumber /kyoó kumbər/ *n* **1.** a long fruit with dark green peel and crisp white watery flesh that is usually eaten raw in salads and sandwiches or pickled **2.** a climbing or trailing annual plant of the gourd family that produces cucumbers. Latin name: *Cucumis sativus*. [14C. < Latin *cucumer-*, by association with Old French *cocombre*] ◇ **cool as a cucumber** calm and composed, especially under pressure

cucurbit /kyoo kúrbit/ *n* a climbing or trailing plant of the gourd family with large, fleshy, tough-skinned or hard-skinned fruits, e.g. the cucumber, watermelon, or pumpkin. Native to: tropical or subtropical regions. Family: Cucurbitaceae. [14C. Via French < Latin *cucurbita* 'gourd']

Cúcuta /koókətə/ city in northeastern Colombia and the capital of Norte de Santander Department, situated near the Venezuelan frontier. Population: 624,000 (1999).

cud /kud/ *n* partly digested food that cows and other ruminants return to the mouth, after it has passed into the first stomach, to chew again as an aid to digestion [Old English *cudu* < Indo-European, 'sticky substance']

cuddle /kúdd'l/ *v* (**-dles, -dling, -dled**) **1.** *vti* TENDERLY HUG OR NESTLE to nestle together or hold somebody or something close for affection, warmth, or comfort **2.** *vi* ASSUME COMFORTABLE POSITION to get into a warm comfortable position ■ *n* TENDER HUG a prolonged hug or embrace given to comfort or show affection [Early 16C. Origin ?] —**cuddler** *n*
cuddle up *vi* to assume a relaxed comfortable position alone or close to another person

cuddly /kúdd'li/ (**-dlier, -dliest**) *adj* **1.** pleasant to hold because of being soft, warm, or endearingly attractive **2.** given to or fond of cuddling

cuddy¹ /kúddi/ *n* **1.** SMALL CABIN ON BOAT a small cabin or galley on a boat **2.** OFFICERS' MESS the officers' mess on a ship **3.** SMALL ROOM a small room or closet [Mid-17C. Probably via early modern Dutch *kajute* < French *cahute* 'shanty']

cuddy² /kúddi/ *n* (*plural* **-dies**) *n Scotland* a donkey or horse (*informal*) [Early 18C. Origin ?]

cudgel /kújjəl/ *n* a heavy stick used as a weapon ■ *vt* (**-els, -elling, -elled**) to beat somebody with a cudgel [Old English *cycgel*, origin ?] ◇ **take up the cudgels** to defend or support a person or cause actively and energetically

cudweed /kúd weed/ (*plural* **-weeds** or *same*) *n* a plant of the daisy family that has woolly leaves. Flowers: white or yellow, in clusters. Native to: temperate regions worldwide. Genera: *Gnaphalium* or *Filago*.

cue¹ /kyoo/ *n* **1.** SIGNAL TO SPEAK OR ACT something said or done that provides the signal for somebody, especially an actor or performer, to say or do something **2.** PROMPT OR REMINDER something that prompts or reminds somebody to do something ○ *I took my cue from my brother and said nothing*. **3.** PSYCHOL RESPONSE-PRODUCING STIMULUS a stimulus or pattern of stimuli, often not consciously perceived, that results in a specific learned behavioural response ■ *vt* (**cues, cueing, cued**) GIVE SIGNAL OR PROMPT TO SOMEBODY

to give somebody, especially an actor or performer, a signal to say or do something [Mid-16C. Origin ?]

SPELLCHECK cue or **queue**? Do not confuse the spelling of **cue** and **queue**, which sound similar. **Cue** is a noun denoting a signal or reminder to do something (as in *the actor's cue to enter*) or a long stick used in games such as snooker; it can also be used as a verb, meaning 'give a cue to'. **Queue** is a noun denoting a line of waiting people, a list of waiting computer tasks, or a plait of hair; it can also be used as a verb, meaning 'wait or put in a queue': *We had to queue for two hours to get the tickets*.

cue in *vt* **1.** GIVE SIGNAL TO SOMEBODY to signal that it is time for somebody, especially a performer, to say or do something ○ *The conductor will cue you in.* **2.** INSTRUCT OR REMIND SOMEBODY to give somebody information, instructions, or a reminder **3.** INSERT SOMETHING INTO PERFORMANCE to insert something such as a speech or song into a performance

cue² /kyoo/ *n* **1.** CUE GAMES STICK USED TO KNOCK BALL in games such as billiards, snooker, and pool, a long tapering stick used to strike the cue ball **2.** HAIR, HIST same as **queue** *n* (sense 4) ■ *vt* (**cues, cueing, cued**) **1.** CUE GAMES STRIKE BALL WITH CUE in games such as billiards, snooker, and pool, to strike a cue ball with a cue **2.** TIE HAIR IN PLAIT to tie the hair at the back of the head in a plait [Mid-18C. Variant of QUEUE]

cue ball *n* in games such as billiards, snooker, and pool, the white ball struck with the cue so that it strikes the object ball in turn

cue bid *n* in bridge, a bid made to show a partner that the bidder has either an ace or no cards in a particular suit

cue card *n* in broadcasting, a large card containing the words that somebody is to say, held up out of sight of the viewing audience

cued speech /kyood speéch/ *n* a series of hand movements used to differentiate ambiguous mouth positions as an aid in lip reading

cue game *n* a game such as billiards, snooker, or pool in which a long tapering stick is used to strike a cue ball

Cuenca /kwéngkə/ city in a valley of the Andes Mountains in southern Ecuador. It is the capital of Azuay Province. Population: 278,035 (2000).

Cuernavaca /kwáirnə vaákə/ tourist resort and capital city of Morelos State, south-central Mexico. Population: 338,706 (2000).

cuesta /kwéstə/ *n* a ridge with a steep face on one side and a gentle slope on the other, especially in the southwestern United States [Early 19C. Via Spanish, 'slope' < Latin *costa* 'rib, side']

cuff¹ /kuf/ *n* **1.** END OF SLEEVE NEAREST WRIST the part of a sleeve that covers the wrist, either turned back or with a band of fabric attached **2.** ANZ, N Am FOLD AT BOTTOM OF TROUSER LEG a turned-up fold at the bottom of a trouser leg **3.** PART OF GLOVE COVERING LOWER ARM the part of a glove or gauntlet that extends up the arm beyond the wrist **4.** MED BAND USED IN MEASURING BLOOD PRESSURE an inflatable band fastened around a patient's arm when measuring blood pressure ■ **cuffs** *npl* HANDCUFFS a pair of handcuffs (*informal*) ■ *vt* (**cuffs, cuffing, cuffed**) **1.** ANZ, N Am PUT TURN-UPS ON TROUSERS to put turned-up folds on the bottom of a pair of trousers **2.** HANDCUFF SOMEBODY to put handcuffs on somebody (*informal*) [14C. Origin ?]

cuff² /kuf/ *vt* (**cuffs, cuffing, cuffed**) to hit somebody lightly with an open hand ■ *n* a light blow with an open hand [Mid-16C. Probably an imitation of the sound of hitting]

cuff link *n* an ornamental fastener for a shirt cuff, used as an alternative to a button (*often used in the plural*)

Cufic *adj*, *n* LANGUAGE another spelling of **Kufic**

Cuiabá /koóyə baá/ city in southwestern Brazil on the River Cuiabá. It is the capital of Mato Grosso State. Population: 433,355 (1996).

cui bono /kwee bónō/ *n* **1.** the legal principle that somebody who would gain something from a particular action or event is probably responsible for it **2.** the usefulness of something used to measure its value [Early 17C. < Latin, 'to whom is the benefit']

Cuillin Hills /ko͝olin-/, **Coolin Hills** range of hills on the Isle of Skye, northwestern Scotland. The highest peak is Sgurr Alasdair, 1,009 m./3,309 ft.

cuirass /kwi ráss/ *n* **1. ARMOUR FOR UPPER BODY** a piece of body armour made of metal or leather, covering the chest and sometimes the back **2. PROTECTION** a protective covering, or a means of protection **3.** ZOOL **ANIMAL'S HARD PROTECTIVE COVERING** a protective outer covering on some animals, e.g. scales or a shell [15C. Via Old French *cuirace* < Latin *coriaceus* 'made of leather' < *corium* 'leather']

cuirassier /kwírrə seér/ *n* a mounted soldier wearing a cuirass, especially in 16th-century Europe [Mid-16C. < French < *cuirasse*, modern form of Old French *cuirace* (see CUIRASS)]

cuish *n* ARMS same as **cuisse**

cuisine /kwi zeén/ *n* **1.** a style of cooking, especially one that is notable for high quality **2.** the range of food prepared by a restaurant, country, or person [Late 18C. Via French, 'kitchen' < Latin *coquina* < *coquere* 'to cook']

cuisine minceur /-maN súr/ *n* a low-calorie form of cooking originating in France [< French, 'slimness cooking']

cuisse /kwiss/, **cuish** /kwish/ *n* a piece of armour formerly worn in battle to protect the thigh [13C. < Old French *cuiss(i)eus*, plural of *cuissel* < late Latin *coxale* < Latin *coxa* 'hip']

cuke /kyook/ *n* FOOD same as **cucumber** (*informal*) [Early 20C. Shortening]

CUL *abbr* see you later (*used in e-mails or text messages*)

CUL8R *abbr* see you later (*used in e-mails or text messages*)

culchie /kúlchi/ *n Ireland* an offensive term for a farm labourer (*informal insult*) [Mid-20C. Origin ?]

cul-de-sac /kúl-, ko͝ol-/ (*plural* **culs-de-sac** /*pronunc. same*/ or **cul-de-sacs**) *n* **1. STREET CLOSED AT ONE END** a road with no exit at one end, often in a residential area **2. IMPASSE** a situation in which further progress is impossible **3.** ANAT **BODY CAVITY RESEMBLING POUCH** a body cavity or tubular structure open at one end only [< French, 'bottom of a sack']

Culebra, Isla de /koo lébbrə/ island and wildlife refuge off the eastern coast of Puerto Rico. Area: 26 sq. km/10 sq. mi. Population: 1,542

culet /kyo͞olət/ *n* the flat face at the base of a faceted gemstone [Late 17C. < French, 'little base' < *cul* (see CULOTTES)]

Culiacán /ko͞olyə kaán/ city in western Mexico, the capital of Sinaloa State. Population: 745,537 (2000).

culinary /kúllinəri/ *adj* relating to food or cooking [Mid-17C. < Latin *culinarius* < *culina* 'kitchen'] —**culinarily** *adv*

cull /kul/ *vt* (**culls, culling, culled**) **1. REMOVE ANIMAL FROM HERD** to remove an animal, especially a sick or weak one, from a herd or flock **2.** VET **REDUCE SIZE OF GROUP BY KILLING** to reduce the size of a herd, flock, or population by killing some of the animals in it **3. REMOVE SOMEBODY OR SOMETHING AS WORTHLESS** to remove an inferior person or thing from a group **4. SELECT SOMEBODY OR SOMETHING** to select or gather people or things, especially those that are good examples of their kind ○ *The following cases are culled from the police reports.* ■ *n* **1. SOMETHING WITHOUT VALUE** something regarded as worthless, especially an unwanted or inferior animal removed from a herd **2.** VET **REDUCTION OF ANIMAL NUMBERS** a reduction of the numbers of an animal population achieved by killing some of its members [12C. < Old French *coillier* < Latin *colligere* 'gather together' < *legere* 'gather']

cullet /kúlit/ *n* broken or waste glass returned for recycling [Early 19C. Variant of COLLET 'glass left on the end of a blowing iron']

Culloden /kə lódd'n/ moor near Inverness, in northeastern Scotland. It was the scene of a battle in 1746 that ended the second Jacobite Rebellion.

cully /kúlli/ (*plural* **-lies**) *n* same as **friend** (*slang*) [Mid-17C. Origin ?]

culm[1] /kulm/ *n* **1.** waste from a coal mine **2.** anthracite coal of poor quality [14C. Probably < Old English *col* (see COAL)]

culm[2] /kulm/ *n* the jointed hollow stem of a grass or similar plant [Mid-17C. < Latin *culmus*]

culminant /kúlminənt/ *adj* **1.** describes a planet or other astronomical object that is at its highest altitude **2.** reaching a climax or point of highest development (*formal*) [Early 17C. < late Latin *culminant-*, present participle of *culminare* (see CULMINATE)]

culminate /kúlmi nayt/ (**-nates, -nating, -nated**) *v* **1.** *vti* **COME OR BRING TO HIGHEST POINT** to reach a climax or point of highest development, or make something do this ○ *a general feeling of dissatisfaction that culminated in his resignation* **2.** *vti* **FINISH SPECTACULARLY** to come or bring something to an end, especially a climactic one ○ *The festivities culminated in a procession through the town.* **3.** *vi* **HAVE SOMETHING AT HIGHEST END** to have something at the apex ○ *The tower culminates in a point.* **4.** *vi* ASTRON **REACH HIGHEST OR LOWEST POINT** to reach the highest or, less commonly, the lowest point in the sky relative to an observer's horizon (*refers to astronomical objects*) [Mid-17C. < late Latin *culminat-*, past participle of *culminare* 'exalt' < *culmen* 'summit']

culmination /kúlmi náysh'n/ *n* **1. HIGHEST POINT** the highest, most important, or final point of an activity **2. ACT OF CULMINATING** the arrival at, or the bringing of something to, a climax **3.** ASTRON **HIGHEST OR LOWEST ALTITUDE** the highest or, less commonly, the lowest point in the sky that an astronomical object reaches relative to an observer's horizon

culottes /kyoo lóts/ *npl* a pair of women's knee-length shorts, cut to resemble a skirt [Mid-19C. < French, 'knee breeches', literally 'small bottom' < *cul* 'bottom, rump' < Latin *culus*]

culpable /kúlpəb'l/ *adj* deserving blame or punishment for a wrong [13C. Via French < Latin *culpabilis* < *culpare* 'to blame' < *culpa* 'fault, blame'] —**culpability** /kúlpə bílləti/ *n* —**culpably** *adv*

culpable homicide *n Scotland* the crime of manslaughter

Culpeper /kúl pepər/, **Nicholas** (1616–54) English physician and astrologer. He was a Puritan and compiled an influential manual on herbal medicine, *The English Physician Enlarged* (1653).

Culpeper, Thomas, 2nd Baron Culpeper (1635–89) English-born colonial administrator. He was the governor of Virginia (1680–83).

culprit /kúlprit/ *n* **1. WRONGDOER** somebody who is responsible for or guilty of an offence or misdeed **2. ACCUSED PERSON** somebody charged with a crime and awaiting trial, especially somebody who has pleaded not guilty **3. ORIGIN OF PROBLEM** a cause of a problem (*informal*) ○ *A faulty connection proved to be the culprit.* [Late 17C. Probably misunderstanding of *cul. prist* < Anglo-Norman *Culpable: prest d'averrer* 'You are guilty; we are ready to prove it']

cult /kult/ *n* **1. RELIGION** a system of religious or spiritual beliefs, especially an informal and transient belief system regarded by others as misguided, unorthodox, extremist, or false, and directed by a charismatic, authoritarian leader **2. RELIGIOUS GROUP** a group of people who share religious or spiritual beliefs, especially beliefs regarded by others as misguided, unorthodox, extremist, or false **3. IDOLIZATION OF SOMEBODY OR SOMETHING** an extreme or excessive admiration for a person, philosophy of life, or activity (*often used before a noun*) ○ *the cult of youth* ○ *a cult hero* **4. OBJECT OF IDOLIZATION** a person, philosophy, or activity regarded with extreme or excessive admiration **5. FAD** something popular or fashionable among a devoted group of enthusiasts (*often used before a noun*) ○ *has taken on cult status* **6.** CULTL ANTHROP **SYSTEM OF SUPERNATURAL BELIEFS** a body of organized practices and beliefs supposed to involve interaction with and control over supernatural powers **7.** SOCIOL **ELITE GROUP** a self-identified group of people who share a narrowly defined interest or perspective [Early 17C. Directly or via French < Latin *cultus* 'worship' < *colere* 'cultivate'] —**cultic** *adj* —**cultish** *adj* —**cultism** *n* —**cultist** *n*

culti RELIG plural of **cultus**

cultivar /kúlti vaar/ *n* a variety of a cultivated plant that is developed by breeding and has a designated name [Early 20C. Blend of CULTIVATE + VARIETY]

cultivate /kúlti vayt/ (**-vates, -vating, -vated**) *vt* **1. PREPARE LAND FOR CROPS** to work land or prepare soil for growing crops **2. GROW PLANT** to grow a plant or crop **3. LOOSEN SOIL** to break up soil with a tool or machine, especially before sowing or planting **4. NURTURE SOMETHING** to improve or develop something, usually by study or education ○ *cultivating her interest in science* **5. DEVELOP ACQUAINTANCE WITH SOMEBODY** to develop an acquaintance or intimacy with somebody, often for personal advantage **6. MAKE SOMEBODY CULTURED** to civilize or educate a person or group [Mid-17C. < medieval Latin *cultivat-*, past participle of *cultivare* < *cultivus* 'cultured' < Latin *cult-* (see CULTURE)] —**cultivable** *adj* —**cultivatable** *adj* —**cultivated** *adj*

Cultivated Australian *n* the prestige form of Australian English, spoken with a standard British English accent

WORLD ENGLISH See ***Australian English***.

cultivation /kúlti váysh'n/ *n* **1. PREPARATION OF LAND OR GROWING CROPS** the planting, growing, and harvesting of crops or plants, or the preparation of land for this purpose **2. IMPROVEMENT** improvement or development, especially through study or education **3. SOPHISTICATION** educated taste or sophistication

cultivator /kúlti vaytər/ *n* **1.** somebody who grows, nurtures, or encourages something ○ *an enthusiastic cultivator of roses* ○ *a cultivator of useful political contacts* **2.** a gardening or farm tool or machine for breaking up soil

cultural /kúlchərəl/ *adj* **1.** relating to a culture or civilization **2.** relating to the arts and intellectual activity —**culturally** *adv*

cultural anthropology *n* the scientific study of human culture or the culture of specific societies, including social structure, language, religion, art, and technology —**cultural anthropologist** *n*

cultural cringe *n Aus* a sense of embarrassment caused by a feeling that your national culture is inferior to others

cultural diversity *n* ethnic variety, as well as socioeconomic and gender variety, in a group, society, or institution

cultural lag *n* a slower rate of change in one part of a culture or one society compared with another

cultural materialism *n* the anthropological theory that environment, resources, technology, and other material things are the major influences on cultural change

cultural relativism *n* the principle that people should not judge the behaviour of others using the standards of their own culture, and that each culture must be analysed on its own terms

Cultural Revolution *n* a political and cultural reform movement in the People's Republic of China from 1965 to 1968 that was intended to revolutionize political opinion and behaviour. It was characterized by social upheaval. The Red Guard played a prominent role in the movement, which was aimed at restoring principles associated with Mao Zedong.

cultural studies *n* (*takes a singular verb*) **1.** the study of culture from a sociological rather than an aesthetic viewpoint. It draws on the social sciences such as politics and semiotics, rather than traditional forms of literary, artistic, or musical criticism. **2.** a wide-ranging educational course, especially at college or university level, covering all aspects of culture, the arts, sciences, and social science. It is often intended as a foundation for other courses.

cultural weapon *n S Africa* a traditional African weapon sometimes carried by participants at political rallies

culture /kúlchər/ *n* **1. ARTS COLLECTIVELY** art, music, literature, and related intellectual activities, considered collectively ○ *Culture is necessary for a healthy society.* ○ *popular culture* **2. KNOWLEDGE AND SOPHISTICATION** enlightenment and sophistication acquired through education and exposure to the arts ○ *They are people of culture.* **3. SHARED BELIEFS AND VALUES OF GROUP** the beliefs, customs, practices, and social behaviour of a particular nation or people ○ *Southeast Asian culture* **4. PEOPLE WITH SHARED BELIEFS AND PRACTICES** a group of people whose shared beliefs and practices identify the particular place, class, or time

to which they belong **5. SHARED ATTITUDES** a particular set of attitudes that characterizes a group of people ○ *The company tries hard to avoid a blame culture.* **6. DEVELOPMENT OF TOOLS AND LANGUAGE** the development and use of artefacts and symbols in the advancement of a society **7. GROWING OF BIOLOGICAL MATERIAL** the growing of biological material, especially plants, microorganisms, or animal tissue, in a nutrient substance (**culture medium**) in specially controlled conditions for scientific, medical, or commercial purposes **8. BIOTECH BIOLOGICAL MATERIAL GROWN IN SPECIAL CONDITIONS** biological material, especially plants, microorganisms, or animal tissue, grown in a nutrient substance (**culture medium**) in specially controlled conditions for scientific, medical, or commercial purposes **9. TILLAGE** the cultivation of the land or soil in preparation for growing crops or plants **10. IMPROVEMENT** the development of a skill or expertise through training or education ○ *physical culture* ■ *vt* (**-tures, -turing, -tured**) **1. GROW BIOLOGICAL MATERIAL IN SPECIAL CONDITIONS** to grow biological material, especially plants, microorganisms, or animal tissue, in a nutrient substance (**culture medium**) in specially controlled conditions, for scientific, medical, or commercial purposes **2. AGRIC CULTIVATE PLANTS** to cultivate plants or crops **3. NURTURE SOMEBODY OR SOMETHING** to nurture somebody or something, especially in order to advance your own interests ○ *She spent a great deal of time culturing new contacts on Capitol Hill.* [13C. Via French < Latin *cultura* 'tillage' < *cult-*, past participle of *colere* 'inhabit, cultivate']

cultured /kúlchərd/ *adj* **1. EDUCATED AND SOPHISTICATED** educated and informed about the arts and related intellectual activity **2. GROWN IN NUTRIENT SUBSTANCE** grown in a nutrient substance (**culture medium**) in a laboratory **3. ARTIFICIALLY PRODUCED** created artificially, and not by natural or organic processes

cultured pearl *n* a pearl created artificially by introducing a foreign body into an oyster or clam shell to attract layers of mother-of-pearl around it

culture lag *n* SOCIOL same as **cultural lag**

culture medium (*plural* **culture media** or **culture mediums**) *n* a nutrient substance such as a broth or an agar gel in which scientists grow selected microorganisms, fungi, cells, or tissue in a laboratory

culture shock *n* the feelings of confusion and anxiety experienced by somebody suddenly encountering an unfamiliar cultural environment

culture vulture *n* somebody who has a strong or obsessive interest in the arts (*informal*)

culture war *n* public debate reflecting the division over religious, educational, political, and moral issues within a multicultural society —**culture warrior** *n*

cultus /kúltəss/ (*plural* **-tuses** or **-ti** /-tī/) *n* a religious group, especially a cult and its system of beliefs (*formal*) [Early 17C. < Latin *cultus* (see CULT)]

culverin /kúlvərin/ *n* **1.** a long-range cannon used between the 15th and 17th centuries **2.** a musket used in the 15th and 16th centuries [15C. < French *coulevrine* < *couleuvre* 'snake' < Latin *colubra*]

culvert /kúlvərt/ *n* **1.** a covered channel that carries water or cabling under a road or railway, or through an embankment **2.** an arch, bridge, or part of a road that covers a culvert [Late 18C. Origin ?]

cum /kum/ *prep* together with, along with, in combination with, or functioning as (*informal*) ○ *He lives and works in an apartment cum office.* [Late 19C. < Latin, 'with']

Cumb. *abbr* Cumbria

cumber /kúmbər/ *vt* (*archaic or literary*) **1.** to hamper or hinder somebody or something **2.** to burden or encumber somebody or something [14C. Probably shortening of ENCUMBER]

Cumberland /kúmbərlənd/ former county in northwestern England on the Scottish border, now part of Cumbria

Cumberland Gap pass through the Cumberland Mountains near the meeting point of Tennessee, Virginia, and Kentucky. Height: 503 m/1,650 ft.

Cumberland sausage *n* a large sausage containing coarse-cut pork, originally made in Cumberland

Cumbernauld /kúmbər náwld/ town and former local government region in central Scotland, now in North Lanarkshire. It was built as a new town in 1955. Population: 48,762 (1991).

cumbersome /kúmbərsəm/ *adj* **1.** awkward to carry or handle because of weight, size, or shape **2.** difficult to use or deal with because of length or complexity —**cumbersomely** *adv* —**cumbersomeness** *n*

Cumbria /kúmbri ə/ county in northwestern England, formed in 1974, incorporating mainly the former counties of Cumberland and Westmorland. Carlisle is the county town. Population: 487,607 (2001). Area: 6,810 sq. km/2,629 sq. mi. —**Cumbrian** *n, adj*

cumbrous /kúmbrəss/ *adj* large and unwieldy (*archaic or literary*) ○ '*this cumbrous and creaking structure*' (Thomas Hardy, *Tess of the d'Urbervilles*; 1891) [14C. < *cumber* 'encumbrance, hindrance, obstruction', probably < CUMBER] —**cumbrously** *adv* —**cumbrousness** *n*

cum div. *abbr* FIN cum dividend

cum dividend *adv* with a right to the current dividend when buying a security

cumene /kúmmeen/ *n* an oily colourless liquid hydrocarbon. Use: fuel additive, synthesis of chemicals. Formula: $C_6H_5CH(CH_3)_2$. [Mid-19C. Via French < Latin *cuminum* (see CUMIN)]

cumin /kúmmin/, **cummin** *n* **1.** the aromatic seeds of a plant of the carrot family. Use: whole or ground as a spice. **2.** the plant that produces cumin seeds. Native to: Mediterranean. Latin name: *Cuminum cyminum*. [Pre-12C. Via Latin *cuminum* < Greek *kuminon* < Semitic]

cum laude /kúm lów day/ *adv, adj N Am* with academic honours [< Latin, 'with praise']

cummerbund /kúmmər bund/ *n* a pleated sash, often brightly coloured, worn around the waist by men as part of formal dress [Early 17C. < Urdu *kamar-band* 'loin-band, waistband']

cummin *n* PLANTS, COOK another spelling of **cumin**

cummings /kúmmingz/, **e. e.** (1894–1962) US poet. He is known for his experimental poetry, which was written mostly in lowercase letters. Full name **Cummings, Edward Estlin**

    '*The churches are drowning with stars, everywhere stars blossom, frank and gold and keen...Now (touched by a resonance of sexually celestial forms) the little murdered adventure called Humanity becomes a selfless symbol.*'
    [e. e. cummings, *Eimi*; 1933]

Cummings /kúmmingz/, **Bart** (*b.* 1927) Australian racehorse trainer. He has won 11 Melbourne Cups and numerous classic races including the Caulfield Cup and the Golden Slipper Stakes. Full name **Cummings, James Bartholomew**

cum new *adv* with a right to any shares that may be issued free or on favourable terms to existing shareholders when buying a security

cumquat *n* TREES, FOOD another spelling of **kumquat**

cumulate /kyóomyoo layt/ *v* (**-lates, -lating, -lated**) **1.** *vti* same as **accumulate 2.** *vt* to combine two or more items into one ■ *adj* heaped up in a pile or mass [Mid-16C. < Latin *cumulat-*, past participle of *cumulare* 'gather in a heap' < *cumulus* 'heap, pile'] —**cumulation** /kyóo myoo láysh'n/ *n*

cumulative /kyóomyoolətiv/ *adj* **1. GRADUALLY BUILDING UP** becoming successively larger, stronger, or more effective ○ *Many drugs have a cumulative effect on the body.* **2. CREATED BY GRADUAL ADDITIONS** resulting from successive additions **3. FIN ADDED TO NEXT PAYMENT** describes an interest or dividend payment that is added to the next payment rather than being paid out when it falls due **4. FIN ENTITLING SHAREHOLDER TO CLAIM DIVIDEND ARREARS** describes preferred shares whose holder has the right to claim dividend arrears before dividends are distributed to holders of common shares **5. LAW MORE SEVERE FOR REPEAT OFFENDER** describes a more severe punishment imposed on somebody who has previously committed the same crime **6. LAW CONSECUTIVE** used to describe a sentence or prison term that follows another consecutively

7. STATS INCLUDING ALL GIVEN VALUES OF VARIABLE relating to the sum of the number of times a variable has a specific value totalled over all the values of the variable that are less than a given value **8. STATS INCREASING WITH SUCCESSIVE MEASUREMENTS** describes an error that increases as more measurements are taken —**cumulatively** *adv* —**cumulativeness** *n*

cumulative distribution function *n* a procedure that assigns to each possible value of a random variable the probability that this value will be found. If each value is equally likely to be found, the distribution is said to be uniform.

cumulative trauma disorder *n US* same as **RSI**

cumuli METEOROL plural of **cumulus**

cumulonimbus /kyóomyoo lō nímbəss/ (*plural* **-bi** /-bī/ or **-buses**) *n* a tall dark cumulus cloud in the shape of an anvil, often bringing thunderstorms [Late 19C. < CUMULUS]

cumulus /kyóomyoōləss/ (*plural* **-li** /-lī/) *n* **1.** a large white or grey cloud with a flat base and a rounded fluffy top, or a mass of such clouds, developing as a result of rising hot air currents **2.** a mass or heap [Mid-17C. < Latin, 'heap, pile'] —**cumulous** *adj*

Cuna /kóonə/ (*plural same* or **-nas**), **Kuna** *n* **1.** a member of a Native Central American people of the isthmus of Panama and northwestern Colombia **2.** the Chibchan language of the Cuna people. Native speakers: 30,000 to 50,000. [Mid-19C. < Cuna] —**Cuna** *adj*

cuneal /kyoóni əl/ *adj* having the shape of a wedge (*technical*) [Late 16C. Directly or via modern Latin < medieval Latin *cunealis* < Latin *cuneus* 'wedge']

cuneate /kyoóni ət, -ayt/ *adj* describes a leaf that is more or less triangular with the narrowest point of the triangle forming the tip [Early 19C. < Latin *cuneus* 'wedge'] —**cuneately** *adv*

AKG London

cuneiform: Sumerian clay tablet (18th century BC)

cuneiform /kyoóni fawrm/ *adj* **1. USED IN ANCIENT WRITING SYSTEM** relating or belonging to a writing system in which wedge-shaped impressions were made in soft clay. There were several such writing systems in ancient Southwest Asia, including one for Sumerian. **2. USED FOR CUNEIFORM WRITING** describes the clay tablets on which cuneiform script was written **3. WEDGE-SHAPED** with the narrowly triangular shape of a wedge **4. ANAT OF ANKLE** describes any of three wedge-shaped bones of the ankle ■ *n* **1. CUNEIFORM SCRIPT** writing that uses small wedge-shaped characters **2. ANAT WEDGE-SHAPED ANKLE BONE** any of the three cuneiform bones of the ankle [Late 17C. < French *cunéiforme* or modern Latin *cuneiformis* < Latin *cuneus* 'wedge']

cunjevoi /kúnjə voy/ *n Aus* MARINE BIOL same as **sea squirt** [Early 19C. < an Australian Aboriginal language, probably of New South Wales]

cunner /kúnnər/ (*plural same* or **-ners**) *n* a small fish of the wrasse family. Native to: North Atlantic Ocean. Latin name: *Tautogolabrus adspersus*. [Early 17C. Origin ?]

cunnilingus /kúnni líng gəss/ *n* sexual stimulation of a woman's genitals using the tongue and lips [Late 19C. < Latin, 'vulva-licker']

cunning /kúnning/ *adj* **1. CRAFTY AND DECEITFUL** clever or artful in a way that is intended to deceive **2. CLEVERLY THOUGHT OUT** showing skill, shrewdness, and ingenuity in planning or doing something **3. N Am CUTE** attractive in a pleasant delicate way (*dated informal*) ■ *n* **1. CRAFTINESS AND DECEITFULNESS** the ability to deceive in a clever subtle way **2. SKILFUL PERFORMANCE** skilful

ingenuity or grace in doing something [13C. Probably < Old Norse *kunna* 'know'] —**cunningly** *adv* —**cunningness** *n*

Cunningham /kúnningəm/, **Allan** (1791–1839) British-born Australian botanist and explorer. An early collector of Australian plants, he was the first European to explore the Darling Downs region of eastern Australia.

> 'While the hollow oak our palace is, / Our heritage the sea.'
> [Allan Cunningham, 'A Wet Sheet and a Flowing Sea', *The Songs of Scotland*; 1825]

Charles E. Rothin/Corbis

Merce Cunningham

Cunningham, Merce (*b*. 1919) US dancer and choreographer. He formed his own dance company in 1953 and has played an important role in the development of avant-garde dance.

> 'I compare...dance...to water...Everyone knows what water is or what dance is, but...fluidity makes them intangible ...Music at least has a literature, a notation.'
> [Merce Cunningham. Quoted in *The Dancer and the Dance*, in conversation with Jacqueline Lesschaeve; 1991]

cunt /kunt/ *n* **1.** a highly offensive term for a woman's genitals (*taboo*) **2.** a highly offensive term for a woman (*taboo*) **3.** a highly offensive term for somebody who is viewed with great dislike or contempt, especially a man (*taboo insult*) **4.** a highly offensive term for sexual intercourse with a woman (*taboo*) [13C. Ultimately < Germanic]

cup /kup/ *n* **1.** DRINKING CONTAINER a small container, usually with a handle, used to hold liquids for drinking **2.** AMOUNT CUP HOLDS the contents of a cup ○ *Will you have another cup?* **3.** MEASURE **MEASURE USED IN COOKING** a unit of volume used especially in cooking, equal to 284 ml/8 fl oz **4.** WINNER'S PRIZE an ornamental trophy, typically a large two-handled silver goblet, awarded as a prize in a competition, especially a sports competition **5.** SPORTS CONTEST a sporting competition in which the winner's prize is a large ornamental goblet **6.** BOWL-SHAPED OBJECT something that has an open hollow rounded shape **7.** CLOTHING PART OF BRA either of the shaped sections of a bra that support and cover the breasts **8.** BOT, ANAT BOWL-SHAPED PLANT OR BODY PART an open hollow rounded part or structure in a plant or in the body **9.** BEVERAGES PARTY PUNCH a mixed drink with a particular ingredient as its base, usually served from a large bowl at parties ○ *a champagne cup* **10.** FOOD DISH SERVED IN CUP-SHAPED CONTAINER a dessert or appetizer served in a small bowl or glass dish **11.** CHR COMMUNION CHALICE OR WINE the vessel from which the consecrated wine is drunk during the Christian service of Communion, or the wine itself **12.** GOLF HOLE ON GOLF COURSE the hole on a green that is the target in golf, or the metal lining of a golf hole **13.** SOMEBODY'S LOT IN LIFE what a person is destined to receive, suffer, or enjoy in life (*literary*) ■ *vt* (**cups, cupping, cupped**) **1.** MAKE HANDS INTO CUP to form one or both of the hands into an open hollow rounded shape, usually to hold or receive something such as water **2.** HOLD SOMETHING IN HANDS to hold something in cupped hands **3.** DRAW BLOOD TO SKIN'S SURFACE formerly, to use a cupping glass to increase the blood supply to an area of the skin [Pre-12C. < late Latin *cuppa*, probably < Latin *cupa* 'tub'] ◇ **in your cups** drinking or having drunk too much alcohol (*archaic or humorous*)

cup-and-saucer plant *n* a climbing plant. Flowers: large, brightly coloured. Native to: Mexico. Latin name: *Cobaea scandens.*

cupbearer /kúp bairər/ *n* a servant who pours wine, especially one employed in a royal household

cupboard /kúbbərd/ *n* a piece of furniture, either built-in or freestanding, or a small room used for storing food and other kitchen necessities

cupboard love *n* affection that is motivated by self-interest [< CUPBOARD in the obsolete sense 'food']

cupcake /kúp kayk/ *n* a small individual iced cake, baked in a paper or foil case or in a cup-shaped mould

cupel /kyoóp'l/ *n* a small container in which precious metals are refined, especially one in which gold and silver are separated from base metals during assaying ■ *vt* (**-pels, -pelling, -pelled**) to separate gold or silver from a base metal using a cupel [Early 17C. < French *coupelle* 'little cup' < *coupe* 'cup' < late Latin *cuppa* (see CUP)] —**cupellation** /kyoópə láysh'n/ *n* —**cupeller** *n*

Cup Final, cup final *n* the final match in a knockout sports competition, especially the FA Cup or the Scottish Cup

cupful /kúpfoöl/ *n* **1.** the amount held by a cup ○ *There's only about a cupful of water left.* **2.** *Aus, N Am* MEASURE same as **cup** *n* (sense 3)

cup fungus *n* an often bright red, orange, or yellow fungus with a cup-shaped spore-bearing structure on its surface. Subdivision: *Ascomycotina.*

cup holder *n* **1.** BEVERAGE HOLDER a device for holding a container for drinks to keep it from tipping, especially one installed in a vehicle **2.** CD DRIVE the tray of a compact disc drive in a computer, or the drive itself **3.** SPORTS PREVIOUS WINNER OF CUP a team that won the cup in the previous staging of a sporting competition or tournament

cupid /kyoópid/ *n* a representation of the god Cupid as a symbol of love in painting or sculpture [Early 17C. < CUPID]

Cupid /kyoópid/ *n* in Roman mythology, the god of love, the son of Venus, usually represented as a young boy with wings and a bow and arrow. Greek equivalent **Eros** [14C. < Latin *Cupido*, literally 'desire' < *cupere* 'to desire']

cupidity /kyoo píddəti/ *n* greed, especially for money or possessions (*formal*) [15C. Directly or via French < Latin *cupiditas* < *cupere* 'to desire']

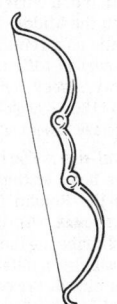

Cupid's bow (sense 2)

Cupid's bow *n* **1.** a double curve, especially the curves of the upper lip **2.** a bow with two curves used in archery [< the traditional representation of the bow used by Cupid]

cup of tea *n* (*informal*) **1.** what somebody likes or prefers ○ *This is more my cup of tea.* **2.** *US* something to be dealt with

cupola /kyoópələ/ *n* **1.** ARCHIT DOME-SHAPED ROOF a roof or ceiling in the form of a dome **2.** ARCHIT STRUCTURE ON ROOF a small structure on a roof, sometimes made of glass and providing natural light inside **3.** MIL GUN TURRET a domed structure protecting a gun, e.g. on a warship **4.** MIL, RAIL SMALL OBSERVATION DOME a glass observation dome on the roof of an armoured vehicle or railway van **5.** METALL BLAST FURNACE a cylindrical blast furnace used in foundries for remelting iron or other metals [Mid-16C. Via Italian < late Latin *cupula* 'little cask, vault' < *cupa* 'cask']

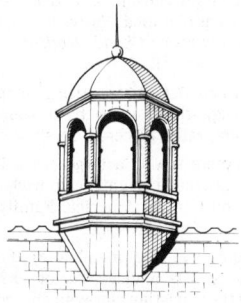

cupola

cuppa /kúppə/ *n* a cup of tea (*informal*) ○ *Let's have a cuppa.* [Mid-20C. < an informal pronunciation of *cup of*]

cupped /kupt/ *adj* formed into the open hollow shape of a cup

cupping /kúpping/ *n* a historical medical practice in which a cupping glass was used to increase the blood supply to an area of the skin

cupping glass *n* a glass container in which a partial vacuum is created by heat or suction that is applied to the skin to increase the blood supply in the tissues below

cuppy /kúppi/ (**-pier, -piest**) *adj* **1.** with the shape of a cup **2.** with many small shallow hollows in the surface

cupr- *prefix* same as **cupro-** (*used before vowels*)

cuprate /kyoó prayt/ *n* a salt containing an anionic grouping of copper and oxygen

cupreous /kyoópri əss/ *adj* **1.** consisting of or containing copper **2.** of a reddish-brown colour [Mid-17C. < late Latin *cupreus* < *cuprum* (see COPPER [1])]

cupric /kyoóprik/ *adj* containing copper with a valency of 2 [Late 18C. < late Latin *cuprum* (see COPPER [1])]

cupriferous /kyoo prífferəss/ *adj* having copper as a constituent [Late 18C. < late Latin *cuprum* (see COPPER [1])]

cuprite /kyoó prīt/ *n* a reddish-brown or black mineral that is an ore of copper and consists of copper oxide [Mid-19C. < late Latin *cuprum* (see COPPER [1])]

cupro- *prefix* copper ○ *cupronickel* [< late Latin *cuprum* (see COPPER [1])]

cupronickel /kyoó prō ník'l/ *n* a corrosion-resistant alloy of copper containing up to 40 per cent nickel

cuprous /kyoóprəss/ *adj* containing copper with a valency of 1 [Mid-17C. < late Latin *cuprum* (see COPPER [1])]

cup tie *n* a match in a knockout competition for which the prize is a cup

cup-tied *adj* **1.** unable to play in a cup tie for some reason such as disqualification or injury **2.** not free to play another fixture because of participation in a cup tie

cupule /kyoó pyool/ *n* a cup-shaped body part or plant part, e.g. that enclosing the base of an acorn [15C. < late Latin *cupula* 'little cask, vault' < *cupa* 'cask']

Cuquenan Waterfall /koó kay nán-/ waterfall in Venezuela, one of the highest in the world. Height: 610 m/2,000 ft.

cur /kur/ *n* **1.** a mixed-breed dog, especially one that is ill-natured or in poor condition **2.** an offensive term for somebody regarded as mean, cowardly, or otherwise unpleasant (*dated insult*) [12C. Originally in *cur-dog*, origin ?]

curable /kyoórəb'l/ *adj* **1.** describes a condition that is capable of being treated by medical procedures **2.** having a condition that can be treated by medical procedures —**curability** /kyoórə bílləti/ *n* —**curably** *adv*

curaçao /kyoórə sō/ *n* an orange-flavoured liqueur that originated on the Caribbean island of Curaçao [Early 19C. < CURAÇAO]

Curaçao /kyoórə sō/ island in the Netherlands Antilles, in the Caribbean Sea, and the largest of the island group. Area: 444 sq. km/171 sq. mi.

curacy /kyoórəssi/ (*plural* **-cies**) *n* the position or term of office of a curate [15C. < CURATE [1]]

curare /kyoo raári/, **curari** *n* **1.** a dark resin from some South American plants. Use: muscle relaxant,

traditional arrow poison. **2.** a tropical vine from which curare is obtained. Native to: South America. Genera: *Strychnos* or *Chondodendron.* [Late 18C. Via Spanish, Portuguese < Carib *kurarí*]

curarize /kyŏŏrə rīz/ (**-rizes, -rizing, -rized**), **curarise** (**-rises, -rising, -rised**) *vt* to treat somebody with curare —**curarization** /kyŏŏrə rī záysh'n/ *n*

curassow /kyŏŏrə sow/ *n* a large crested game bird with a long tail and a brightly coloured beak. Native to: South and Central America. Family: Cracinae. [Late 17C. Alteration of CURAÇAO]

curate[1] /kyŏŏrət/ *n* **1.** a member of the Christian clergy who assists a vicar, rector, or priest **2.** a member of the Christian clergy in charge of a parish [14C. < medieval Latin *curatus* 'somebody who cares for a parish' < Latin *cura* 'care']

curate[2] /kyoo ráyt/ (**-rates, -rating, -rated**) *v* **1.** *vti* to be the curator of a museum, gallery, or other collection **2.** *vt* to organize and choose the items in an exhibition at a museum or gallery (*usually passive*) [Early 18C. Back-formation < CURATOR]

curate's egg *n* something that may be described as only partly bad, especially when this makes the whole thing unacceptable [< a cartoon in *Punch* magazine, 1895, in which a curate, when served a bad egg at the bishop's table, assured his host that 'parts of it are excellent']

curative /kyŏŏrətiv/ *adj* able to restore health ■ *n* a substance or treatment that can restore health —**curatively** *adv* —**curativeness** *n*

curator /kyoo ráytər/ *n* **1.** HEAD OF MUSEUM OR OTHER COLLECTION the administrative head of a museum, gallery, or other collection **2.** EXHIBITION ORGANIZER somebody who organizes and chooses the items in an exhibition at a museum or gallery **3.** *Scotland* LAW MINOR'S GUARDIAN the legal guardian of a minor [14C. < Latin < *curare* (see CURE)] —**curatorial** /kyŏŏrə táwri əl/ *adj* —**curatorship** *n*

curb /kurb/ *n* **1.** IMPOSED LIMITATION something that controls or limits something else ○ *sought a curb on drug trafficking* **2.** RIDING HORSE'S BIT AND ATTACHED CHAIN a horse's bit with a chain or strap attached, passed under the horse's jaw **3.** EDGING FOR LAWN a line of stones that forms the edge of an area of lawn **4.** RAISED PART THAT SURROUNDS SOMETHING an enclosing frame or raised margin, e.g. around a skylight or a well **5.** *N Am* ROADS US spelling of **kerb** ■ *vt* (**curbs, curbing, curbed**) **1.** HOLD SOMETHING BACK to restrain, control, or limit something ○ *hope to curb inflation* **2.** *N Am* ROADS US spelling of **kerb** [15C. Probably variant of *courb* 'to curve', via French *courber* < Latin *curvare*]

curb bit *n* RIDING same as **curb** *n* (sense 2)

curb roof *n* a roof that has two or more different angles of slope on each side, e.g. a mansard or gambrel roof

curculio /kur kyŏŏli ō/ (*plural* **-os**) *n* a weevil that damages fruit trees, vegetables, and other plants. Genus: *Conotrachelus.* [Mid-18C. < Latin, 'corn weevil']

curcuma /kúrkyŏŏmə/ *n* a tropical plant from which turmeric and zedoary are obtained. Native to: South Asia. Genus: *Curcuma.* [15C. Via medieval Latin < Arabic *kurkum* 'turmeric' < Sanskrit *kuṇkuma* 'saffron']

curd /kurd/ *n* **1.** SOLID PART OF SOUR MILK the solid substance formed when milk coagulates. Use: for making cheese. **2.** SUBSTANCE LIKE MILK CURD a food substance with a consistency similar to milk curd ■ *vti* (**curds, curding, curded**) CURDLE to turn something into curd, or to become curd [14C. Origin ?] —**curdy** *adj*

curd cheese *n* a mild soft cheese made from skimmed milk curds

curdle /kúrd'l/ (**-dles, -dling, -dled**) *vti* **1.** to separate into curds and whey, or cause a liquid such as milk to separate into curds and whey, e.g. by permitting or encouraging bacterial action **2.** to go bad or wrong, or spoil something (*informal*) [Late 16C. < CURD]

cure /kyoor, kyawr/ *v* (**cures, curing, cured**) **1.** *vti* HEAL SOMEBODY to restore a sick person or animal to health ○ *Six months later she was completely cured.* **2.** *vt* TREAT ILLNESS SUCCESSFULLY to bring an end to an illness, disorder, or injury by medical treatment ○ *Diseases like this are not easily cured.* **3.** *vt* RESOLVE PROBLEM to bring an end to a problem ○ *curing unemployment* **4.** *vti* PRESERVE FOOD to preserve food, especially meat or fish, usually by smoking, drying, or salting it, or be preserved by one of these methods **5.** *vt* PRESERVE SOMETHING BY DRYING to preserve a substance, especially leather or tobacco, by drying it **6.** *vt* MANUF FINISH SOMETHING WITH CHEMICAL PROCESS to finish a material by applying chemicals **7.** *vt* INDUST MAKE RUBBER STRONGER to strengthen rubber with additives in the presence of heat and pressure **8.** *vti* CONSTR HARDEN SOMETHING to make a material, especially concrete or cement, harden ■ *n* **1.** SOMETHING THAT RESTORES HEALTH a medication or treatment that brings about a full recovery from an illness or injury ○ *working to find a cure for the disease* **2.** RECOVERY restoration or return to health ○ *I managed to achieve a complete cure.* **3.** PROBLEM'S SOLUTION something that resolves a problem **4.** FOOD PRESERVATION PROCESS the preservation of meat or fish, especially by smoking, drying, or salting **5.** SPIRITUAL CARE in the Christian Church, the spiritual and pastoral responsibility of the clergy for laypeople **6.** *N Ireland* FOLK REMEDY a folk practice supposed to cure an illness, and handed down as a secret in a family [13C. Via French < Latin *curare* 'care for' < *cura* 'care, concern'] —**curer** *n*

ORIGIN The Latin word *cura*, 'care', 'concern', from which ***cure*** is derived, is also the source of English *curate*[1], *curious, scour*[1], *secure,* and *sinecure.*

---

curé /kyŏŏr ay/ *n* a parish priest in a French-speaking country [Mid-17C. Via French < medieval Latin *curatus* (see CURATE[1])]

cure-all *n* a treatment or remedy that is believed to be able to cure every ailment or problem

~~**currency**~~ incorrect spelling of **currency**

curet *n*, *vt* SURG another spelling of **curette**

curettage /kyŏŏrə taa<u>zh</u>, kyoo réttij/ *n* a surgical procedure that involves scraping the inside surface of a body cavity with an instrument shaped like a spoon (**curette**) to remove unwanted growths or other tissue [Late 19C. < French < *curette* (see CURETTE)]

curette /kyoo rét/, **curet** *n* a spoon-shaped surgical instrument used to remove tissue from the inner surface of a body cavity ■ *vt* (**-rettes, -retting, -retted; -rets**) to scrape tissue from the inner surface of a body cavity using a curette [Mid-18C. < French < *curer* 'clean out' < Latin *curare* (see CURE)]

curettement /kyoo rétmənt/ *n* SURG same as **curettage**

curfew /kúr fyoo/ *n* **1.** RESTRICTION ON PEOPLE'S MOVEMENTS an official restriction on people's movements, requiring them to remain indoors after a specific time **2.** TIME OR SIGNAL FOR CURFEW the time at which a curfew takes effect, or the signal given at this time **3.** LENGTH OF CURFEW the duration of a curfew **4.** MEDIEVAL REMINDER TO EXTINGUISH LIGHTS in the Middle Ages, the ringing of a bell in the evening as a reminder to put out fires and lights ○ *'The curfew tolls the knell of parting day'* (Thomas Gray, *Elegy written in a Country Churchyard*; 1751) [13C. < Anglo-Norman *coeverfu*, Old French *cuevrefeu*, literally 'cover fire']

curia /kyŏŏri ə/ (*plural* **-riae** /ky'oo ri ee/) *n* **1.** PAPAL COURT the administrative body at the Vatican, by which the pope governs the Roman Catholic Church **2.** SUBDIVISION OF ANCIENT ROMAN TRIBE in ancient Rome, a subdivision of each tribe, or the place where it met **3.** ANCIENT ROMAN SENATE the senate or senate house in an ancient Roman city **4.** MEDIEVAL COURT a medieval monarch's court of justice [Early 17C. < Latin, 'council'] —**curial** *adj*

~~**curiculum**~~ incorrect spelling of **curriculum**

curie /kyŏŏri/ *n* a unit of radioactivity equal to 3.7 times 10^{10} disintegrations per second [Early 20C. After Pierre CURIE and Marie CURIE]

Curie /kyŏŏri/, **Irène** ♦ **Joliot-Curie, Irène**

Curie, Marie (1867–1934) Polish-born French chemist and physicist. She pioneered research into radioactivity and was twice awarded the Nobel Prize (in Physics in 1903 and in Chemistry in 1911). Her husband Pierre Curie collaborated with her and was jointly awarded the 1903 Nobel Prize in physics. Born **Skłodowska, Marja**

> 'All my life through, the new sights of Nature made me rejoice like a child.'
> [Attributed to Marie Curie]

Curie, Pierre (1859–1906) French physicist. A professor of physics at the Sorbonne in Paris, his research with his wife, Marie Curie, on radioactivity led to the discovery of polonium and radium. They shared the Nobel Prize in physics (1903).

AKG London

Marie Curie

Curie point *n* the temperature at which in some substances such as iron there is a change in the magnetic characteristics from ferromagnetic to paramagnetic behaviour [After Pierre CURIE]

Curie's law *n* the law of physics stating that there is an inverse proportionality between the effect of a magnetic field on a paramagnetic material and its absolute temperature [After Pierre CURIE]

Curie temperature *n* PHYS same as **Curie point**

Curie-Weiss law /-vīss-/ *n* a variation of Curie's law in which the temperature term is reduced by an amount equal to the Curie point [After Pierre CURIE and Pierre Ernest *Weiss* (1865–1940) French physicist]

curio /kyŏŏri ō/ (*plural* **-os**) *n* an object that is valued and often collected for its interest or rarity [Mid-19C. Shortening of CURIOSITY]

curiosa /kyŏŏri ṓssə, -ṓzə/ *npl* **1.** books or other texts dealing with unusual topics, especially erotica **2.** interesting and unusual objects [Late 19C. < Latin, neuter plural of *curiosus* (see CURIOUS)]

curiosity /kyŏŏri óssəti/ (*plural* **-ties**) *n* **1.** DESIRE TO KNOW SOMETHING eagerness to know about something or to get information **2.** TENDENCY TO PRY an excessive interest in other people's affairs **3.** SOMEBODY OR SOMETHING THOUGHT STRANGE an interesting and unusual object, person, or phenomenon [14C. Via French < Latin *curiositas* < *curiosus* (see CURIOUS)]

curious /kyŏŏri əss/ *adj* **1.** EAGER TO KNOW SOMETHING eager to know about something or to get information ○ *I'm curious to know how they found out about the party.* **2.** TOO INQUISITIVE excessively eager to find out about other people's affairs **3.** ODD strange, unexpected, or hard to explain ○ *several curious events* **4.** VERY INTRICATE intricate or detailed (*archaic or literary*) [14C. Via French < Latin *curiosus* 'careful, inquisitive' < *cura* 'care'] —**curiously** *adv* —**curiousness** *n*

~~**curiousity**~~ incorrect spelling of **curiosity**

Curitiba /kŏŏri téebə/ city in southern Brazil. It is the capital of Paraná State. Population: 1,476,253 (1996). Former name **Curityba**

curium /kyŏŏri əm/ *n* a silvery white metallic radioactive element. Source: produced artificially from plutonium. Symbol **Cm**. See table at **element** [Mid-20C. After Pierre CURIE and Marie CURIE]

curl /kurl/ *v* (**curls, curling, curled**) **1.** *vti* MAKE HAIR CURLY to put hair into waves, coils, or spirals, or be naturally like this **2.** *vti* MAKE SOMETHING CURVED OR COILED to bend, twist, or wind something into a curved or spiral shape, or become curved or coiled ○ *He curled the silver ribbon into spirals.* ○ *The paper had begun to curl at the edges.* **3.** *vi* MOVE IN SPIRAL MOTION to move in a curve or spiral ○ *Smoke curled into the sky.* **4.** *vi* SPORTS PARTICIPATE IN CURLING to play the game of curling ■ *n* **1.** CURVED OR COILED HAIRS a lock of hair curved into a round or spiral shape (*often used in the plural*) **2.** TENDENCY TO CURL the tendency of hair to grow or stay in ringlets ○ *My hair doesn't have much curl.* **3.** CURVED OR COILED THING something with a curved or coiled shape, e.g. a wood shaving or the crest of a breaking wave **4.** ADOPTION OF CURVED SHAPE the formation of something into a curved or round shape **5.** GYM WEIGHTLIFTING MANOEUVRE a weightlifting move in which a barbell is held at thigh height with the underarms facing outwards, then raised to the

chest, and lowered without moving the shoulders, upper arms, or legs **6.** MARKING ON WOOD a curved or spiral marking in wood grain [14C < Middle Dutch *krul* 'curly' < Germanic]

curl up *v* **1.** *vi* CURVE BODY AND DRAW UP LEGS to sit or lie with the body curved and the legs tucked up ○ *curl up in bed with a good novel* **2.** *vti* COIL to become curved or coiled, or bend, twist, or wind something into a curved or spiral shape ○ *The paper curled up in the fire before it burst into flames.* **3.** *vi* FEEL EXTREMELY EMBARRASSED to be overcome with embarrassment, revulsion, or some other strong feeling (*informal*) ○ *When I realized my mistake I just wanted to curl up and disappear.*

Curl /kurl/, **Robert Floyd** (*b.* 1933) US chemist. Together with Richard Smalley and Harold Kroto, he discovered the family of carbon molecules called fullerenes, and shared a Nobel Prize in chemistry (1996).

curled paperwork /kúrld-/ *n* ART same as **rolled paperwork**

curler /kúrlər/ *n* **1.** a roller or other device used to curl hair **2.** somebody who plays the game of curling

curlew

curlew /kúr lyoo/ *n* a large shorebird with brownish feathers, long legs, and a long slender beak that curves downwards. Genus: *Numenius*. [14C. < Old French *courlieu*, variant of *courlis*, an imitation of its cry]

Curlewis /kur lóo iss/, **Sir Adrian Herbert** (1901–85) Australian judge. He was a prominent figure in the development of lifesaving services for swimmers.

curlicue /kúrli kyoo/ *n* an ornamental twist, especially in calligraphy or design [Mid-19C. < CURLY + CUE[2] 'pigtail'] —**curlicued** *adj*

curling /kúrling/ *n* a team game played on an ice rink, in which a heavy polished stone with a handle is slid towards a circular target (**tee**) [Early 17C. < the curving path of the stone as it reaches the target]

curling iron *n ANZ, N Am* same as **curling tongs**

curling stone *n* a heavy polished stone with a handle used in the game of curling

curling tongs *npl UK* HAIR a device consisting of a heated rod round which the hair is twisted to form a curl. ANZ, N Am term **curling iron**

curlpaper /kúrl paypər/ *n* a small piece of paper rolled round a lock of hair, which is then twisted and left to set into a curl

curly /kúrli/ (**-ier, -iest**) *adj* **1.** WITH CURLS arranged in curls, or curling naturally **2.** CURVED OR COILED bent or twisted into a wavy, curved, or spiral shape ○ *The paper has gone all curly.* **3.** TRICKY difficult to answer or deal with (*informal*) ○ *had to fend off a few curly questions* **4.** WOODWORK WITH CURVES IN GRAIN describes wood that has irregular curved or wavy markings in the grain —**curliness** *n*

curly bracket *n* PRINTING, MATHS same as **brace**[1] *n* (sense 4)

curly endive *n* PLANTS same as **endive** (sense 1)

curly top *n* a viral disease of beets, tomatoes, beans, and other plants that makes the leaves curl

curmudgeon /kur mújjən/ *n* somebody considered to be bad-tempered, disagreeable, or stubborn [Late 16C. Origin ?] —**curmudgeonly** *adj* —**curmudgeonry** *n*

Curnow /kúr now/, **Allen** (1911–2001) New Zealand poet. He wrote *Valley of Decision* (1933). Full name **Curnow, Thomas Allen**

currach /kúrrəkh, -rə/, **curragh** *n Ireland, Scotland* a boat like a coracle, formerly used on Scottish and Irish lakes and rivers [15C. < Irish, Gaelic *curach* 'small boat']

currant /kúrrənt/ *n* **1.** SMALL DRIED GRAPE a small dark dried seedless grape. Use: in cookery. Native to: Mediterranean. **2.** SMALL JUICY FRUIT a small round juicy fruit of a small deciduous bush, especially a redcurrant or blackcurrant **3.** FRUIT-BEARING BUSH the bush, cultivated in temperate regions, that produces currants, especially redcurrants or blackcurrants. Genus: *Ribes*. [Early 16C. Shortening of Anglo-Norman *raisins de Corauntz*, variant of Old French *raisins de Corinthe* 'grapes from Corinth', where they originated]

SPELLCHECK currant or **current**? Do not confuse the spelling of ***currant*** and ***current***, which sound similar. The word ***currant*** is used only as a noun, denoting a small dried grape (as in *currant bun*), or a fruit or plant such as a blackcurrant or redcurrant. The word ***current*** can be used as a noun, denoting a flow of water, air, or electricity, or as an adjective, meaning 'of the present' (as in *current affairs*).

currawong /kúrrə wong/ *n* a large bird with black and white feathers and a strong pointed beak that feeds on carrion and lives in noisy flocks. Native to: Australia. Genus: *Strepera*. [Early 20C. < Yagara *garraway* (also found in neighbouring languages)]

currency /kúrrənssi/ (*plural* **-cies**) *n* **1.** MONEY a system of money, or the notes and coins themselves, used in a country. See table on next page **2.** ACCEPTANCE OF IDEA OR TERM widespread acceptance or use of an idea, theory, word, or phrase **3.** CIRCULATION the transmitting of something, especially money, from person to person **4.** TIME WHEN SOMETHING IS CURRENT the period of time during which something is current **5.** *Aus* INDIGENOUS AUSTRALIAN an Australian-born resident of Australia, as opposed to a British-born immigrant (*dated slang*) [Mid-17C. < CURRENT]

current /kúrrənt/ *adj* **1.** EXISTING NOW happening, existing, or in force at the present ○ *In my current job, I am in charge of 25 people.* **2.** VALID accepted as legally valid **3.** PRESENTLY ACCEPTED widely known, accepted, or believed ○ *The theory is no longer current.* ■ *n* **1.** FLOW OF WATER OR AIR a steady flow of water or air in one direction **2.** STREAM a mass of water or air flowing steadily in one direction **3.** FLOW OF ELECTRIC CHARGE the flow of electricity through a cable, wire, or other conductor **4.** RATE OF FLOW OF ELECTRICITY the rate of flow of an electric charge through a conductor **5.** TENDENCY a trend or tendency ○ *going against the current and moving out of the city to a farm* [13C. < Old French *corant*, present participle of *courre* 'run' < Latin *currere*]

SPELLCHECK See ***currant***.

ORIGIN The Latin word *currere*, 'to run', from which ***current*** is derived, is also the source of English *corridor*, *courier*, *course*, *occur*, and *succour*.

current account *n UK, ANZ, Can* an account at a bank or building society from which money may be drawn on demand. US term **checking account**

current affairs *npl* important political and social events or issues of the present time (*often used before a noun*) US term **current events**

current assets *npl* available cash and other assets that could be converted to cash within a year

current-cost accounting *n* a method of accounting that assesses the value of assets as the cost of replacing them rather than as their original cost

current density *n* the ratio of the amount of current flowing through a conductor to the cross-sectional area of the conductor. Symbol *j*, *J*

current efficiency *n* in an electrolytic process, the mass of the substance liberated by a current divided by the theoretical mass, as predicted by Faraday's law

current events *npl N Am* same as **current affairs**

current liabilities *npl* business liabilities that are due to be cleared before the end of the financial year

currently /kúrrəntli/ *adv* at the present time ○ *They are currently living abroad.*

current ratio *n* the ratio of current assets to current liabilities

curricle /kúrrik'l/ *n* a light two-wheeled open carriage drawn by a pair of horses side by side [Mid-18C. < Latin *curriculum* 'racing chariot']

curriculum /kə ríkyŏŏləm/ (*plural* **-la** /-lə/ or **-lums**) *n* the subjects taught at an educational institution, or the topics taught within a subject [Early 19C. < Latin, 'running, course' < *currere* 'to run'] —**curricular** *adj*

curriculum vitae /kə ríkyŏŏləm vée tī, -vī tee/ (*plural* **curricula vitae** /kə ríkyŏŏlə-/) *n* full form of **CV**[2] [Early 20C. < Latin, 'course of life']

currier /kúrri ər/ *n* somebody who dresses and finishes leather after it has been tanned [14C. Via Old French *corier* < Latin *coriarius* < *corium* 'leather']

currish /kúrish/ *adj* having a hostile or disagreeable disposition (*literary*) [15C. < CUR] —**currishly** *adv* —**currishness** *n*

curry[1] /kúrri/ *n* (*plural* **-ries**) **1.** HIGHLY SPICED SAVOURY DISH a dish containing meat, fish, or vegetables in a highly spiced sauce ○ *chicken curry* **2.** SEASONING FOR CURRY a mixture of spices used to prepare curry. It may be a sauce, paste, powder, or other form. (*often used before a noun*) ○ *curry paste* ■ *vt* (**-ries, -rying, -ried**) PREPARE FOOD IN SPICY SAUCE to cook meat, fish, or vegetables in a highly spiced sauce [Late 16C. < Tamil *kari* 'sauce']

curry[2] /kúrri/ (**-ries, -rying, -ried**) *vt* **1.** to groom a horse **2.** to make leather flexible and waterproof as the final stage in its processing [13C. < Old French *correier* 'prepare' < Latin *con* 'with' + Germanic ancestor of READY]

currycomb /kúrri kōm/ *n* a comb with metal or rubber teeth, used to groom horses ■ *vt* (**-combs, -combing, -combed**) to groom a horse with a currycomb [Late 16C. < CURRY[2]]

curry powder *n* a mixture of finely ground spices, usually turmeric, cumin, coriander, chilli, and ginger, used to make curry [< CURRY[1]]

curse /kurss/ *n* **1.** SWEARWORD a swearword, obscenity, or blasphemous oath **2.** EVIL PRAYER a malevolent appeal to a supernatural being for harm to come to somebody or something, or the harm that is thought to result from this **3.** SOURCE OF HARM a cause of unhappiness or harm ○ *the curse of poverty* **4.** MENSTRUATION menstruation or a menstrual period (*dated slang*) **5.** CHR, HIST RELIGIOUS BAN an ecclesiastical pronouncement of censure or excommunication ■ *interj* CURSES USED AS OATH used to express irritation or annoyance ■ *v* (**curses, cursing, cursed**) **1.** *vti* SWEAR to utter swearwords or obscenities at somebody **2.** *vt* WISH EVIL ON SOMEBODY to appeal malevolently to a supernatural being for harm to come to somebody or something [Old English *curs*, origin ?] —**curser** *n*

cursed /kúrssid, kurst/ *adj* **1.** HAVING BEEN WISHED EVIL afflicted with harm thought to result from a curse **2.** WICKED OR HATEFUL evil to the point of being despicable **3.** ANNOYING OR FRUSTRATING stubborn to the point of causing irritation or annoyance (*informal*) —**cursedly** /kúrssidli/ *adv* —**cursedness** /kúrssidnəss/ *n*

cursive /kúrssiv/ *adj* WRITTEN IN FLOWING STYLE describes writing or a style of writing in a flowing style with the letters joined together ■ *n* **1.** FLOWING SCRIPT cursive writing, or a cursive script **2.** MANUSCRIPT WRITTEN IN FLOWING STYLE an ancient manuscript or other piece of writing in a flowing hand **3.** PRINTING TYPEFACE a typeface in which the letters are joined together [Late 18C. < medieval Latin *cursivus* < Latin *currere* 'to run'] —**cursively** *adv* —**cursiveness** *n*

cursor /kúrssər/ *n* a moving marker on a computer screen that marks the point at which keyed characters will appear or be deleted ■ *vi* (**-sors, -soring, -sored**) to move the cursor in a particular direction on a computer screen ○ *Cursor down to 'properties'.* [14C. < Latin (see CURSORY)]

cursorial /kur sáwri əl/ *adj* having a body or body parts particularly well-adapted for running [Mid-19C. < Latin *cursor* (see CURSORY)]

cursory /kúrssəri/ *adj* done in a quick or superficial way [Early 17C. < Latin *cursorius* < *cursor* 'runner' < *currere* 'to run'] —**cursorily** *adv* —**cursoriness** *n*

curt /kurt/ *adj* **1.** rude or abrupt **2.** using few words [14C. < Latin *curtus* 'cut short'] —**curtly** *adv* —**curtness** *n*

ALPHABETICAL CURRENCY TABLE

Unit	Country
afghani	Afghanistan
agora	Israel
avo	Macau
baht	Thailand
baisa	Oman
balboa	Panama
ban	Moldova
	Romania
birr	Ethiopia
bolivar	Venezuela
boliviano	Bolivia
butut	Gambia
cedi	Ghana
cent	Antigua and Barbuda
	Australia
	Austria
	Bahamas
	Barbados
	Belgium
	Belize
	Brunei
	Canada
	Cyprus
	Dominica
	Ecuador
	Eritrea
	Ethiopia
	Fiji
	Finland
	France
	Germany
	Greece
	Grenada
	Guyana
	Hong Kong
	Ireland
	Italy
	Jamaica
	Kenya
	Kiribati
	Liberia
	Luxembourg
	Malta
	Marshall Islands
	Mauritius
	Micronesia
	Namibia
	Nauru
	Netherlands
	New Zealand
	Palau
	Portugal
	St Kitts and Nevis
	St Lucia
	St Vincent and the Grenadines
	Seychelles
	Sierra Leone
	Singapore
	Solomon Islands
	Somalia
	South Africa
	Spain
	Sri Lanka
	Suriname
	Swaziland
	Taiwan
	Tanzania
	Trinidad and Tobago
	Tuvalu
	Uganda
	United States
	Zimbabwe
centas	Lithuania
centavo	Argentina
	Bolivia
	Brazil
	Cape Verde
	Chile
	Colombia
	Cuba
	Dominican Republic
	El Salvador
	Guatemala
	Honduras
	Mexico
	Mozambique
	Nicaragua
	Philippines
centesimo	Panama
	Uruguay
centime	Algeria
	Benin
	Burkina Faso
	Burundi
	Cameroon
	Central African Republic
	Chad
	Comoros
	Congo (Dem. Rep. of the)
	Congo (Rep. of the)
	Côte d'Ivoire
	Djibouti
	Equatorial Guinea
	Gabon
	Guinea
	Guinea-Bissau
	Haiti
	Liechtenstein
	Madagascar
	Mali
	Monaco
	Morocco
	Niger
	Rwanda
	Senegal
	Switzerland
	Togo
centimo	Costa Rica
	Paraguay
	Peru
	São Tomé and Príncipe
	Venezuela
CFA franc	Benin
	Burkina Faso
	Cameroon
	Central African Republic
	Chad
	Congo (Rep. of the)
	Côte d'Ivoire
	Equatorial Guinea
	Gabon
	Guinea-Bissau
	Mali
	Niger
	Senegal
	Togo
chetrum	Bhutan
chon	North Korea
	South Korea
colón	Costa Rica
	El Salvador
Congo franc	Congo (Dem. Rep. of the)
cordoba	Nicaragua
dalasi	Gambia
denar	Macedonia, Former Yugoslav Rep. of
dinar	Algeria
	Bahrain
	Iraq
	Jordan
	Kuwait
	Libya
	Serbia and Montenegro
	Sudan
	Tunisia
dinar	Iran
dirham	Morocco
	United Arab Emirates
dirham	Libya
	Qatar
dobra	São Tomé and Príncipe
dollar	Antigua and Barbuda
	Australia
	Bahamas
	Barbados
	Belize
	Brunei
	Canada
	Dominica
	Ecuador
	Fiji
	Grenada
	Guyana
	Hong Kong
	Jamaica
	Kiribati
	Liberia
	Marshall Islands
	Micronesia
	Namibia
	Nauru
	New Zealand
	Palau
	St Kitts and Nevis
	St Lucia
	St Vincent and the Grenadines
	Singapore
	Solomon Islands
	Taiwan
	Trinidad and Tobago
	Tuvalu
	United States
	Zimbabwe
dong	Vietnam
dram	Armenia
escudo	Cape Verde
euro	Austria
	Belgium
	Finland
	France
	Germany
	Greece
	Ireland
	Italy
	Luxembourg
	Netherlands
	Portugal
	Spain
eyrir	Iceland
filler	Hungary
fils	Bahrain
	Iraq
	Jordan
	Kuwait
	United Arab Emirates
	Yemen
forint	Hungary
franc	Burundi
	Comoros
	Djibouti
	Guinea
	Liechtenstein
	Madagascar
	Monaco
	Rwanda
	Switzerland
gourde	Haiti
grosz	Poland
guarani	Paraguay
guilder	Suriname
halala	Saudi Arabia
haler	Czech Republic
halier	Slovakia
hao	Vietnam
hryvnia	Ukraine
jiao	China
khoum	Mauritania
kina	Papua New Guinea
kip	Laos
kobo	Nigeria
kopek	Russia
kopiyka	Ukraine
koruna	Czech Republic
	Slovakia
krona	Faroe Islands
	Iceland
	Sweden
krone	Denmark
	Norway
kroon	Estonia
kuna	Croatia
kwacha	Malawi
	Zambia
kwanza	Angola
kyat	Myanmar
laari	Maldives
lari	Georgia
lat	Latvia
lek	Albania
lempira	Honduras
leone	Sierra Leone
leu	Moldova
	Romania
lev	Bulgaria
lilangeni	Swaziland
lipa	Croatia
lira	Malta
	Turkey
litas	Lithuania
loti	Lesotho
lumma	Armenia
lwei	Angola
manat	Azerbaijan
	Turkmenistan
marka	Bosnia and Herzegovina
markka	Finland
metical	Mozambique
millime	Tunisia
mongo	Mongolia
naira	Nigeria
nakfa	Eritrea
ngultrum	Bhutan
ngwee	Zambia
øre	Denmark
	Norway
öre	Sweden
ouguiya	Mauritania
pa'anga	Tonga
paisa	India
	Nepal
	Pakistan
para	Yugoslavia
pataca	Macau
penny	United Kingdom
peseta	Andorra
pesewa	Ghana
peso	Argentina
	Chile
	Colombia
	Cuba
	Dominican Republic
	Mexico
	Philippines
	Uruguay
piaster	Egypt
	Jordan
	Lebanon
	Syria
poisha	Bangladesh
pound	Cyprus
	Egypt
	Lebanon
	Syria
	United Kingdom
pound	Sudan
pul	Afghanistan
pula	Botswana
pya	Myanmar
qindar	Albania
quetzal	Guatemala
rand	South Africa
real	Brazil
rial	Iran
	Oman
	Yemen
riel	Cambodia
ringgit	Malaysia
riyal	Qatar
	Saudi Arabia
rubel	Belarus
ruble	Russia
	Tajikistan
rufiyaa	Maldives
rupee	India
	Mauritius
	Nepal
	Pakistan
	Seychelles
	Sri Lanka
rupiah	Indonesia
santim	Latvia
satang	Thailand
sen	Cambodia
	Indonesia
	Japan
	Malaysia
sene	Samoa
seniti	Tonga
sent	Estonia
sente	Lesotho
shekel	Israel
shilling	Kenya
	Somalia
	Tanzania
	Uganda
sol	Peru
som	Kyrgyzstan
	Uzbekistan
stotin	Slovenia
stotinka	Bulgaria
taka	Bangladesh
tala	Samoa
tambala	Malawi
tenge	Kazakhstan
tetri	Georgia
thebe	Botswana
toea	Papua New Guinea
tolar	Slovenia
tughrik	Mongolia
tyiyn	Kyrgyzstan
vatu	Vanuatu
won	North Korea
	South Korea
yen	Japan
yuan	China
zloty	Poland

= main unit
= subunit

a at; aa father; aw all; ay day; ai hair; ə about, item, edible, common, circus; e egg; ee eel; hw when; i it, happy; ī ice; 'l apple; 'm rhythm; 'n fashion; o odd; ō open; o͝o good; o͞o pool; ow owl; oy oil; th thin; th this; u up; ur urge;

curtail /kur táyl/ (**-tails, -tailing, -tailed**) *vt* to reduce the length or duration of something [15C. Alteration of CURTAL] —**curtailment** *n*

curtail step /kúr tayl-/ *n* a wider lowest step on some flights of stairs, often rounded at one or both ends [Mid-18C. Origin ?]

curtain /kúrt'n/ *n* **1. CLOTH HUNG TO COVER SOMETHING** a piece of cloth hung at a window, in a doorway, or round a bed, usually for privacy or to exclude light or draughts **2. CLOTH AT FRONT OF STAGE** in a theatre, a hanging cloth that is raised and lowered or pulled back and forth at the front of the stage **3. BEGINNING OR END OF SHOW** the beginning or end of a performance, act, or scene, as marked by the raising or lowering or opening and closing of the curtain **4. BARRIER OR SCREEN** something that acts as a barrier or screen to divide, protect, or conceal something **5. SOMETHING LIKE CURTAIN** something that resembles a curtain in appearance ○ *a curtain of water* **6.** BUILDINGS **WALL CONNECTING OTHER STRUCTURES** a length of wall, especially one that connects two towers or gates ■ *vt* (**-tains, -taining, -tained**) **1. HIDE OR DIVIDE SOMETHING WITH CURTAIN** to surround, separate, or conceal something with a curtain **2. FIT SOMETHING WITH CURTAINS** to provide something, especially a window, with curtains [13C. Via French < late Latin *cortina*, translating Greek *aulaia*] ◇ **bring down the curtain on something** to bring an end to something (*informal*)

curtain call *n* an appearance by actors, dancers, or singers at the front of the stage to receive the audience's applause at the end of a performance

curtain lecture *n* a private reprimand given to a man by his wife (*dated*) [Because originally delivered within the privacy of drawn bed curtains]

curtain raiser *n* **1.** a short performance put on immediately before the main performance **2.** a smaller or less important event that takes place before the main event

curtain speech *n* **1.** a speech addressed to the audience by somebody in front of the curtain after a play has ended **2.** the speech before the final curtain of an act or play

curtain wall *n* **1.** an external wall that does not bear any of the load of the building it is attached to **2.** a low wall outside a castle built for defence

curtal /kúrt'l/ *n* an animal whose tail has been docked (*archaic*) [Early 16C. < obsolete French *courtault* < *court* 'short' + *-ault*, pejorative suffix]

~~**curtesy**~~ incorrect spelling of **courtesy**

curtilage /kúrtəlij/ *n* an enclosed area occupied by a dwelling, grounds, and outbuildings [14C. < Old French *co(u)rtillage* < *co(u)rtil* 'kitchen garden', literally 'small court' < *cort* 'court']

Curtin /kúrtin/, **John Joseph** (1885–1945) Australian journalist and politician. He was an Australian Labor Party politician and prime minister of Australia (1941–45). See table at **prime minister**

~~**curtious**~~ incorrect spelling of **courteous**

Curtiz /kúrtiz/, **Michael** (1888–1962) Hungarian-born US film director. He won an Academy Award for *Casablanca* (1942) and directed over 160 films.

curtsy /kúrtsi/, **curtsey** *vi* (**-sies, -sying, -sied; -seys, -seying, -seyed**) to bend the knees, with one foot behind the other, as a gesture of respect. Women curtsy in formal situations where men bow, e.g. when acknowledging the applause of an audience after performing on stage, or when meeting royalty. ■ *n* (*plural* **-sies;** *plural* **-seys**) a movement made by a woman as a sign of respect for somebody in which she bends her knees with one foot behind the other [Early 16C. Variant of COURTESY]

curule /kyo͝or ool/ *adj* in ancient Rome, having the status to sit on an official chair (**curule chair**) and the privileges associated with this status [Mid-16C. < Latin *curulis* < *currus* 'chariot' < *currere* 'to run'; because the chief Roman magistrate was conveyed in a chariot]

curule chair *n* a folding chair with heavy legs and no back, used by high officials of ancient Rome

curvaceous /kur váyshəss/ *adj* having an attractive body with rounded hips and breasts —**curvaceously** *adv* —**curvaceousness** *n*

curvature /kúrvəchər/ *n* **1. BEING CURVED** the quality of being curved **2. DEGREE OF CURVE** the degree of curving in a line or surface ○ *the slight curvature of the land* **3.** MATHS **RECIPROCAL OF RADIUS** the reciprocal of the radius of the circle that best matches a curve at a given point [15C. < Latin *curvatura* 'bending' < *curvus* 'curved']

curve /kurv/ *n* **1. ROUNDED LINE** a line that bends smoothly and regularly from being straight or flat, like part of a circle or sphere **2. SOMETHING SHAPED IN CURVE** something with a smooth round shape, e.g. a rounded part of a woman's body or a bend in a road **3.** STATS **PLOTTED LINE** a line plotted on a graph from statistical data **4.** MATHS **LINE REPRESENTING EQUATION** a line whose points are defined by an equation and whose coordinates are functions of an independent variable **5.** BASEBALL same as **curveball** ■ *vti* (**curves, curving, curved**) **MOVE IN CURVE** to move or bend in a curve, or make something move or bend in a curve [15C. < Latin *curvus* 'curved, crooked'] —**curved** *adj* ◇ **ahead of the curve** forward-thinking and ahead of a trend or trends ◇ **behind the curve** reacting, or slow to react, to a trend or trends

curveball /kúrv bawl/ *n* in baseball, a ball that when pitched drifts to the left if thrown by a right-handed pitcher and to the right if thrown by a left-handed pitcher

curvet /kur vét/ *n* a leap by a horse in dressage in which its hind legs are raised just before the forelegs touch the ground ■ *vti* (**-vets, -veting** or **-vetting, -veted** or **-vetted**) to perform a curvet in dressage, or make a horse perform a curvet [Late 16C. < Italian *corvetta* 'small curve' < *corve* 'curve' < Latin *curvus* 'curved']

curvilinear /kúrvi línni ər/, **curvilineal** /kúrvi línni əl/ *adj* **1.** being a curve, or having a curved part or parts ○ *a curvilinear polygon* **2.** moving along a curved path or line ○ *The ball followed a curvilinear trajectory.* [Early 18C. < Latin *curvus* 'curved', after RECTILINEAR] —**curvilinearity** /kúrvilinni árrəti/ *n* —**curvilinearly** *adv*

curvy /kúrvi/ (**-ier, -iest**) *adj* **1.** with a rounded shape **2.** having many curves or bends

Curzon /kúrz'n/, **Clifford, Sir** (1907–82) British concert pianist. His repertoire ranged from Wolfgang Amadeus Mozart to Alan Rawsthorne. He also gave recitals with Benjamin Britten. Full name, **Clifford Michael, Sir**

Curzon, George Nathaniel, Lord (1859–1925) British politician. As viceroy of India (1898–1905), he partitioned Bengal. He was Lord Privy Seal during World War I.

> 'The British flag has never flown over a more powerful or a more united empire...Never did our voice count for more in the councils of nations; or in determining the future destinies of mankind.'
> [George Nathaniel Curzon, *Speech to the House of Lords*; 18 November 1918]

Cusack /kyo͞oss ak, kyo͞oz-/, **Cyril** (1910–93) South African-born Irish actor and stage director. He made his name at Dublin's Abbey Theatre (1932–45), toured with his own company (1946–61), acted with major British companies, and appeared in many films.

cuscus /kúss kuss/ *n* a tree-dwelling nocturnal marsupial with a round head, large eyes, large curved claws, and thick fur. Native to: rain forests of northeastern Australia and New Guinea. Genus: *Phalanger*. [Mid-17C. Via French *couscous* or modern Latin *cuscus* < Dutch *koeskoes* < a language of New Guinea]

cusec /kyo͞o sek/ *n* a unit of flow equal to one cubic foot per second, no longer in common use [Early 20C. Shortening of *cubic foot per second*]

CUSeeMe /see yo͞o see mée/ *n* a computer program that enables users to engage in real-time video conferencing over the Internet [Late 20C. < play on abbreviation of *Cornell University*, Ithaca, New York, where it was developed]

Cush /ko͝osh/, **Kush** *n* **1.** in the Bible, the oldest son of Ham and brother of Canaan (Genesis 10:6) **2.** a region of northeastern Africa thought to be where the descendants of Cush settled. It is roughly equivalent to modern Ethiopia, part of northern Sudan, and southern Egypt.

cushat /kúshət/ *n Scotland* BIRDS same as **wood pigeon** [Old English *cuscute*, origin ?]

Cushing /ko͝oshing/, **Peter** (1913–94) British actor. He was noted for his Baron Frankenstein and other roles in Hammer Studio's Gothic horror films (1957–73).

Cushing's disease *n* a form of Cushing's syndrome caused by excessive production of the hormone ACTH by the pituitary gland [Mid-20C. After Harvey *Cushing* (1869–1939), US surgeon]

Cushing's syndrome *n* a condition caused by excessive production of corticosteroids by the adrenal cortex or pituitary gland and marked by obesity, muscular weakness, hypertension, striated skin, and fatigue [Mid-20C. See CUSHING'S DISEASE]

cushion /ko͝osh'n/ *n* **1. SOFT FILLED BAG FOR SITTING ON** a fabric case filled with soft material, used to sit or lean on **2. SOFT PROTECTIVE PAD** a pad that is used for support, to rest against, to protect against damage, or as a shock absorber **3. SOMETHING SOFT AND YIELDING** something that gives slightly when pressed ○ *a cushion of moss at the foot of the tree* **4. SOMETHING HELPFUL** something that limits the effect of an unpleasant situation ○ *An unexpected legacy provided a cushion when her savings ran out.* **5.** CUE GAMES **BILLIARD TABLE RIM** the raised rim around the top of a snooker or billiard table that borders its playing surface **6.** TRANSP same as **air cushion** (sense 1) **7.** HANDICRAFT **ACCESSORY FOR MAKING LACE** a pillow for supporting the tools used in making lace ■ *vt* (**-ions, -ioning, -ioned**) **1. PROTECT SOMEBODY OR SOMETHING AGAINST IMPACT** to protect somebody or something against the effects of physical impact ○ *A pile of sand cushioned his fall.* **2. REDUCE UNPLEASANTNESS** to lessen the effect of an unpleasant situation, especially one involving money ○ *a generous pension to cushion the blow of early retirement* **3. SUPPORT SOMETHING WITH CUSHION** to support or rest something on a cushion or other soft object **4. PAD SOMETHING** to pad something with cushions or some other soft spongy material [14C. < French *coussin*, literally '(support for the) hip' < Latin *coxa* 'hip'] —**cushiony** *adj*

Cushitic /ko͝o shíttik/ *n* a branch of the Afro-Asiatic family of languages spoken in Ethiopia, Somalia, and Kenya. Native speakers: 13 million. [Early 20C. < CUSH] —**Cushitic** *adj*

cushy /ko͝oshi/ (**-ier, -iest**) *adj* requiring little or no hard work, and often providing a good salary and many perks (*informal*) ○ *a cushy job* [Early 20C. < Hindi *khūsh* 'pleasant'] —**cushily** *adv* —**cushiness** *n*

cusk /kusk/ (*plural same* or **cusks**) *n* FISH **1.** *N Am* same as **torsk 2.** *US* same as **burbot** [Early 17C. Origin ?]

cusp /kusp/ *n* **1.** ASTROL **BORDER BETWEEN ZODIAC SIGNS** the border between two astrological star signs **2.** ASTRON **POINTED END OF CRESCENT MOON** either of the pointed ends of a crescent moon or of any astronomical object appearing with the same curved shape **3.** DENT **RIDGE ON MOLAR TOOTH** a ridge on the grinding surface of a molar tooth that helps in grinding and chewing food **4.** ANAT **FLAP OF VALVE** a triangular fold or flap of a valve in the heart or in lymph vessels that allows the flow of blood or lymph in one direction only **5.** BOT **POINTED END** a pointed end of a leaf or other plant part **6.** ARCHIT **POINTED PROJECTION IN GOTHIC ARCHITECTURE** a pointed projection formed by the intersection of two arcs, found especially in Gothic architecture **7.** MATHS **POINT OF INTERSECTION** a point where two arcs or branches of a curve intersect and the two tangents to the curve coincide [Late 16C. < Latin *cuspis* 'point'] —**cusped** *adj* —**cuspidate** /kúspi dayt/ *adj*

cuspid /kúspid/ *n* DENT same as **canine** *n* (sense 1) [Mid-18C. < Latin *cuspid-* 'point']

cuspidor /kúspi dawr/ *n N Am* same as **spittoon** [Mid-18C. < Portuguese < *cuspir* 'to spit' < Latin *conspuere* < *spuere*]

cuss /kuss/ (*informal*) *vti* (**cusses, cussing, cussed**) same as **curse** *v* (sense 1) ■ *n* **1.** somebody with a particular, usually irritating, trait ○ *an awkward cuss* **2.** an instance of vulgar or offensive language [Late 18C. Variant of CURSE]

cussed /kússid/ *adj* (*informal*) **1.** causing annoyance and anger, especially by being uncooperative **2.** same as **cursed** (senses 1–2) [Mid-19C. Variant of CURSED] —**cussedly** *adv* —**cussedness** *n*

cussword /kúss wurd/ *n N Am* same as **swearword** (*informal*)

custard /kústərd/ *n* **1.** a sweet sauce made with eggs, milk, sugar, and a thickening agent, or with milk and custard powder **2.** a cooked mixture of sugar, eggs, and milk [15C. < Anglo-Norman *crustade* < Old French *crouste* 'crust'] —**custardy** *adj*

ORIGIN A *custard* was originally an open pie of meat or fruit (the name referred to the pie's pastry shell or crust). The filling included stock or milk, often thickened with eggs. By around 1600 the term indicated a dish in its own right made of eggs beaten into milk and cooked.

custard apple *n* **1.** HEART-SHAPED GREEN FRUIT a large heart-shaped fruit with large black seeds and soft whitish flesh inside a green skin **2.** CARIBBEAN TREE a tree that bears custard apples. Native to: Caribbean. Latin name: *Annona reticulata*. **3.** TREE RELATED TO CUSTARD APPLE a fruit-bearing tree related to a true custard apple tree, e.g. the pawpaw or sweetsop

custard pie *n* a pie filled with custard, whipped cream, or a substance resembling either of these. Custard pies are traditionally thrown at people in slapstick comedy routines.

custard powder *n* a powder containing cornflour, colouring, and sugar, used as a basis for making custard

Custer /kústər/, **George Armstrong** (1839–76) US soldier. He was killed fighting against Native Americans at the Battle of Little Bighorn (1876).

custodial /ku stṓdi əl/ *adj* **1.** INVOLVING DETENTION involving or consisting of detention in a prison ○ *a custodial sentence* **2.** RELATING TO LEGAL CUSTODY relating to the legal custody of, and responsibility for, a child ○ *a custodial parent* **3.** RELATING TO CUSTODIAN connected with the work of a custodian ■ *n* FIN same as **custodian** (sense 2)

custodian /ku stṓdi ən/ *n* **1.** PERSON RESPONSIBLE FOR SOMETHING VALUABLE somebody responsible for holding or looking after valuable property on behalf of a company or another person **2.** PROTECTOR OF VALUABLE COLLECTION an overseer of the contents of a museum, library, or other public institution **3.** SAFEGUARDER OF INVESTORS' FUNDS an organization, e.g. a bank, that holds in safekeeping the securities and other assets of an investment company or individual investor **4.** UPHOLDER OF SOMETHING VALUABLE a protector and upholder of something seen as valuable and endangered such as traditions or moral values **5.** CARETAKER somebody who looks after a building [Late 18C. < CUSTODY] —**custodianship** *n*

custody /kústədi/ *n* **1.** RIGHTS OVER CHILD the legal right to look after a child **2.** DETENTION detention by the police or other authorities ○ *arrested and in custody* ○ *Police have taken a man into custody.* **3.** PROTECTION the state of being held in another person's care or protection [15C. < Latin *custodia* 'guarding' < *custos* 'guardian']

custom /kústəm/ *n* **1.** TRADITION something that people always do or always do in a particular way by tradition **2.** USUAL BEHAVIOUR the way somebody usually or routinely behaves in a particular situation **3.** LAW TRADITION LIKE LAW a traditional practice that is so long-established and universal that it has acquired the force of law **4.** COMM REGULAR BUYING FROM SHOP the regular buying of goods from a particular shop or business ○ *The manager and staff would like to thank you for your custom.* N Am term **patronage 5.** SHOP'S CUSTOMERS all the customers of a particular shop or business **6.** HIST FEUDAL RENT a tribute, rent, or other obligation paid by a feudal vassal to a lord ■ *adj* **1.** MADE TO ORDER made or built to order **2.** MAKING GOODS TO ORDER making, building, or selling goods to order ○ *a custom tailor* **3.** CHANGED TO SUIT BETTER altered in order to fit somebody's requirements better [12C. Via Old French *costume* 'habitual practice' < Latin *consuetudin-* < *consuescere*, literally 'accustom completely' < *suescere* 'become accustomed']

SYNONYMS See ***habit***.

customable /kústəməb'l/ *adj* liable to import or export duties

customary /kústəməri/ *adj* **1.** USUAL conforming to what is usual or normal **2.** CHARACTERISTIC usual for somebody or characteristic of somebody's usual behaviour ○ *his customary good humour* **3.** LAW BASED ON CUSTOM based on custom and tradition rather than written law ■ *n* (*plural* **-ies**) LAW BODY OF USUAL PRACTICES a listing of customary practices that have the force of law —**customarily** *adv* —**customariness** *n*

SYNONYMS See ***usual***.

custom-built *adj* designed and built to meet the requirements of an individual customer —**custom-build** *vt*

custom drug *n* a drug that targets a specific condition, especially a drug that is tailored to an individual patient's genetic requirements

customer /kústəmər/ *n* **1.** a person or company that buys goods or services **2.** somebody who interacts with others in a particular way (*informal*) ○ *a cool customer* [15C. < the idea of 'customary business practice']

customer rage *n* extreme frustration and anger on the part of a consumer-caller with the quality of a product or service, exhibited by aggressive behaviour towards a customer-service representative, e.g. over the telephone

customer service, customer services *n* a department of a business that deals with routine enquiries and complaints from or disputes with customers ○ *You can call customer service free.*

custom house, customhouse /kústəm howss/ (*plural* **-houses** /-howziz/), **customs house** *n* an office at a port where customs are collected and where ships are given permission to enter or leave

customize /kústə mīz/ (**-izes, -izing, -ized**), **customise** (**-ises, -ising, -ised**) *vt* to alter something in order to make it fit somebody's requirements better ○ *She has customized the software to suit our needs.* —**customization** /kústə mī záysh'n/ *n* —**customizer** *n*

custom-made *adj* designed and made to meet the requirements of an individual customer ○ *custom-made shoes*

customs /kústəmz/ *n* (*takes a singular or plural verb*) **1.** *also* **Customs** PLACE WHERE DUTIABLE GOODS ARE EXAMINED a place where goods and baggage are examined on entering a country to see what duty is payable on them and to check for smuggled goods ○ *pass through customs* **2.** *also* **Customs** GOVERNMENT AGENCY a government department responsible for collecting taxes on imports and for preventing illegal imports **3.** DUTIES ON GOODS taxes payable on imports and exports [14C. < CUSTOM 'customary tax']

Customs and Excise *n* in the United Kingdom, the department of government responsible for collecting customs and VAT and for preventing the import of illegal goods

customs house *n* FIN, SHIPPING same as **custom house**

customs union *n* an association of countries that enjoy free trade among themselves and agree on tariffs for nonmembers

cut /kut/ *v* (**cuts, cutting, cut**) **1.** *vti* DIVIDE SOMETHING WITH SHARP TOOL to divide something into pieces using a knife, scissors, or a similar sharp-edged tool **2.** *vt* SEVER PART USING SHARP TOOL to sever something or separate a part of something using a sharp-edged tool such as a knife, scissors, or a saw ○ *cut a slice of bread* **3.** *vti* MAKE HOLE IN SOMETHING to pierce or make a hole in something using a sharp instrument **4.** *vi* BE SHARP to be sharp enough to slice or pierce things easily ○ *These scissors won't cut.* **5.** *vt* INJURE SOMEBODY WITH SHARP EDGE to injure somebody or yourself with something sharp, usually enough to draw blood **6.** *vt* SHORTEN SOMETHING WITH SHARP TOOL to make something shorter by removing some of it with a sharp tool such as scissors ○ *I'm having my hair cut this afternoon.* **7.** *vt* SHAPE GARMENT to shape fabric in a particular way in order to fashion a garment ○ *You can tell a jacket that has been nicely cut.* **8.** *vt* REDUCE QUANTITY to reduce an amount, e.g. of money or time, or remove an amount from something ○ *cut a budget* **9.** *vt* STOP PROVIDING SOMETHING to stop providing a service or supply of something ○ *cut the supply of water to the farmers* **10.** *vt* SWITCH SOMETHING OFF to stop something operating ○ *cut the engine* **11.** *vi* TAKE OR BE SHORT-CUT to cross, travel, or make a line through or across an area, especially in order to save time ○ *This path cuts through the woods.* **12.** *vti* INTERSECT to cross something or cross each other at a particular point ○ *The road cuts the river in three places.* **13.** *vi* CHANGE DIRECTION SHARPLY to make a sharp change in direction ○ *You need to cut to the right here.* **14.** *vti* DELETE DATA to delete data on a computer, often in order to insert it somewhere else. ◊ **paste**[1] *v* (sense 3) **15.** *vt* SHORTEN SOMETHING BY EDITING to make something such as a film, text, or speech shorter by removing parts of it, or remove a part to make it shorter **16.** *vti* CINEMA, BROADCAST EDIT FILM OR VIDEO to edit a film or other work intended for performance or broadcast **17.** *vi* CINEMA STOP FILMING to stop filming a particular scene (*usually used as a command*) **18.** *vi* CINEMA CHANGE SCENE to switch suddenly from one scene to another when filming or showing a film **19.** *vt* MAKE RECORDING to make a recording of a song or group of songs (*informal*) ○ *The band cut 12 new tracks for the album.* **20.** *vt* CASTRATE ANIMAL to castrate or geld a male animal **21.** *vti* DIVIDE PACK OF CARDS to divide a pack of cards in two, usually after shuffling them **22.** *vt* DILUTE to add a substance to another, especially to a drug or an alcoholic drink, usually in order to make it weaker or cheaper **23.** *vti* REMOVE GRIME to dissolve something such as dirt or grease from something else in the process of cleaning it **24.** *vt* GROW TEETH THROUGH GUMS to produce a tooth through the surface of the gums ○ *The baby's cutting a tooth.* **25.** *vt* SNUB SOMEBODY to pay no attention to somebody in a public place or in an obvious way **26.** *vti* UPSET SOMEBODY to hurt somebody's feelings ○ *a cruel remark that cut me deeply* **27.** *vt* STOP DOING SOMETHING to stop doing something that is annoying somebody (*informal*) ○ *Cut that racket!* **28.** *vt* NOT ATTEND EVENT to fail to attend a scheduled event as expected, e.g. not go to school (*informal*) ○ *expelled for cutting classes* **29.** *vt* RACKET GAMES HIT BALL SO IT SPINS to hit a ball with a racket in such a way that it spins as it flies through the air **30.** *vt* CRICKET HIT CRICKET BALL WITH BAT HORIZONTAL to strike a cricket ball square on the offside with the bat more or less parallel to the ground ■ *n* **1.** WOUND IN SKIN an injury made when something sharp pierces the skin **2.** INCISION an incision made in something with a knife or other sharp-edged tool **3.** REDUCTION a reduction in the amount of something ○ *cuts in taxes and interest rates* **4.** STOPPING OF SUPPLY a stopping of a supply, e.g. of electricity or water ○ *power cuts* **5.** HAIRCUT a haircut or hairstyle **6.** GARMENT STYLE the way of cutting a garment from fabric that determines its shape and fit ○ *a dress with a flattering cut* **7.** PRUNING OF TEXT a removal of a section of something such as a film, text, or speech in order to make it shorter or improve it, or a section removed ○ *The editor advised me to make some cuts in the final chapter.* **8.** CINEMA VERSION a particular edited version of a film ○ *the director's final cut of the film* **9.** RECORDING SINGLE RECORDING a track on a musical recording **10.** PIECE OF MEAT FOR COOKING a piece of meat cut in a standard way, ready to be cooked ○ *buys the cheapest cuts* **11.** SHARE a share of an amount of money or something else to be divided (*informal*) **12.** RACKET GAMES SPIN ON BALL the spin given to a ball struck by a racket **13.** BASEBALL SWING OF BAT a swing of a baseball bat **14.** CRICKET CRICKET STROKE a cricket stroke square on the offside where the bat is swung more or less parallel to the ground **15.** CARDS DIVIDING OF PACK OF CARDS the action of dividing a pack of cards in two **16.** PRINTING PRINTING DEVICE a block for printing that has a design engraved, incised, or cut in relief on it (*often used in combination*) **17.** HURTFUL STATEMENT OR ACTION a statement or action intended to insult or hurt **18.** ITEMS FOR DRAWING LOTS one of several pieces of paper or straws used to draw lots **19.** CIV ENG CANAL a stretch of canal or a channel made for a river **20.** same as **snub** (*archaic*) **21.** *Ireland* LOOKS somebody's personal appearance (*informal*) **22.** *Ireland* MESS a messy condition ■ *adj* **1.** INJURED WITH SOMETHING SHARP injured or damaged by something sharp, usually enough to draw blood ○ *nursing a cut finger* **2.** SEPARATED WITH KNIFE separated or severed using a knife, scissors, or similar sharp tool ○ *cut flowers* **3.** DRUNK totally drunk (*informal*) **4.** BOT DIVIDED describes a leaf that is divided into segments [13C. < assumed Old English *cytan*] —**cuttable** *adj* ◇ **a cut above** somebody *or* something superior to somebody or something ◇ **cut and run** to leave a place quickly to avoid being caught or detained ◇ **cut both ways** to have both advantages and disadvantages ◇ **cut it fine** to allow barely enough of something, often time, for what has to be

done ◇ **cut loose** (*informal*) **1.** to break away from the influence or control of somebody or something **2.** to behave in an unrestrained and relatively uncontrolled way ◇ **cut somebody dead** to ignore somebody deliberately and completely ◇ **cut somebody short** to interrupt somebody who is speaking ◇ **cut somebody some slack** *US* to allow somebody a degree of freedom or latitude to do something ◇ **cut something short** to end something earlier than expected or desired ◇ **not (be able to) cut it** to fall short of requirements, or be unable to cope with a situation (*informal*) ○ *His usual excuses just don't cut it with me.* ◇ **the cut of somebody's jib** somebody's manner and general appearance

cut across *vt* to affect a widely differing group of people or things equally

cut along *vi* go somewhere promptly (*dated informal*; *usually used as a command*)

cut back *vti* **1.** to reduce the amount of something ○ *cut back on spending* **2.** *vt* to cut the tops or all of the stems or branches off a plant in order to remove dead growth or produce bushier growth ○ *cut back the roses*

cut down *v* **1.** *vti* REDUCE SOMETHING to consume, use, or do less of something, especially because it is considered harmful ○ *The doctor says I have to cut down on fried foods.* **2.** *vt* FELL OR CLEAR AWAY PLANTS to cut through the trunk or stem of a plant so that it can be removed or harvested **3.** *vt* KILL SOMEBODY to kill somebody, especially suddenly or unexpectedly (*usually passive*) **4.** *vt* MAKE CLOTHING SMALLER to alter a piece of clothing so that it will fit somebody smaller **5.** *vt* AUTOMOT REMODEL CAR BY REMOVING EXTRAS to remodel a car by removing unnecessary extras, especially in order to make it more suitable for racing

cut in *v* **1.** *vti* INTERRUPT to interrupt when somebody is speaking **2.** *vi* JOIN TRAFFIC DANGEROUSLY to join a lane of traffic too close in front of another car so that it has to brake sharply **3.** *vti* JOIN MIDDLE OF QUEUE to enter a queue of people by pushing in front of others who have been waiting **4.** *vi* START TO OPERATE to start working as part of a machine or electrical device **5.** *vt* ALLOW SOMEBODY TO SHARE to allow somebody to have a share in something, especially money ○ *cut us in on the profits* **6.** *vi* PARTNER SOMEBODY ALREADY DANCING to interrupt a dancing couple and take one of them as your own partner **7.** *vi* CARDS REPLACE CARD PLAYER to take the place of a person who has abandoned a card game **8.** *vt* COOK MIX FAT WITH FLOUR to mix fat into flour using a metal blade

cut off *v* **1.** *vt* REMOVE PART OF SOMETHING to remove something that is part of something else by cutting it **2.** *vt* STOP SUPPLY to stop supplying something ○ *cut off the electricity* **3.** *vt* ISOLATE SOMEBODY OR SOMETHING to separate a person, group, or place from usual communication or contact ○ *a town cut off by the blizzard* **4.** *vt* STOP SOMEBODY TALKING to interrupt what somebody is saying and stop him or her talking ○ *cut him off in mid-sentence* **5.** *vt* DISCONNECT SOMEBODY ON TELEPHONE to disconnect somebody who is talking on the telephone **6.** *vt* DISINHERIT SOMEBODY to exclude somebody from an inheritance ○ *They cut their son off without a penny.* **7.** *vti* BRING SOMETHING TO ABRUPT END to bring something to an abrupt end, or be brought to an abrupt end ○ *The noise cut off suddenly.* **8.** *vt* MAKE SOMEBODY DIE PREMATURELY to bring somebody to an early death (*usually passive*) ○ *She was cut off in her prime.*

cut out *v* **1.** *vt* REMOVE SOMETHING BY CUTTING to remove part of something using a cutting tool **2.** *vt* CUT SHAPE FROM SOMETHING to cut a shaped piece from a larger part or whole **3.** *vt* STOP DOING SOMETHING to stop doing something, especially because it is considered harmful ○ *I've cut out all dairy products.* **4.** *vt* REMOVE PART FROM TEXT to remove part of a text or broadcast **5.** *vt* OMIT SOMETHING to exclude, eliminate, or omit something ○ *I followed the recipe but cut out the walnuts.* **6.** *vt* EXCLUDE SOMEBODY to exclude or eliminate somebody from a group or activity ○ *cut them out of future negotiations* **7.** *vt* DISINHERIT SOMEBODY to change a will so that somebody will no longer inherit **8.** *vi* CEASE FUNCTIONING to stop functioning suddenly, especially to stop providing power ○ *The engine cut out.* **9.** *vt* SEPARATE ANIMAL FROM HERD to separate an animal, especially a cow, from a herd **10.** *vi* END to finish or come to an end (*informal*) ○ *The road cuts out at the creek.* **11.** *vt* STOP SOMETHING ANNOYING to stop doing something that is annoying somebody

(*informal*; *often used as a command*) ○ *Cut out the wisecracks.* ■ *adj* NATURALLY SUITED naturally suited for a particular activity or profession ○ *I wasn't cut out to be a driving instructor.*

cut over *vt* to transfer existing data, functions, or users of a computer system to new facilities or equipment in a synchronized manner

cut through *vt* to deal with a problem or obstacle in a way that reduces or eliminates it ○ *Can't we cut through the formalities?*

cut up *v* **1.** *vt* CUT SOMEBODY OR SOMETHING INTO PIECES to divide somebody or something into pieces by cutting **2.** *vt* INJURE SOMEBODY to injure somebody, especially enough to draw blood **3.** *vt* ENDANGER TRAFFIC to endanger fellow road users by driving suddenly in front of them or across their path **4.** *vt* UPSET SOMEBODY to upset and distress somebody greatly (*informal*; *usually passive*) ○ *He was cut up over his mother's death.* **5.** *vt* CRITICIZE SOMEBODY to criticize somebody severely (*dated informal*) **6.** *vi* N Am MISBEHAVE to behave in a humorous and disruptive way (*slang*) ○ *cutting up in class* ◇ **cut up rough** to become very angry or unpleasant (*dated informal*)

cut-and-cover *adj* describes a method of constructing a tunnel by digging a trench down from ground level and then roofing it

cut-and-dried *adj* **1.** clear, settled, and not needing changes or causing further problems ○ *The ethics of organ transplants aren't exactly cut-and-dried.* **2.** obvious or conforming to what is expected ○ *a cut-and-dried press conference* [Originally of herbs on sale]

cut-and-paste *n* a facility of computers allowing data to be deleted in one place and inserted in another ○ *Use cut-and-paste to move that paragraph into the new document.* —**cut-and-paste** *vt*

cut-and-shut *n* a car created by welding together the bodies of two cars that have been damaged in an accident (*slang*) —**cut-and-shut** *vt*

cut and thrust *n* fast, aggressive, or dramatic exchanges between people ○ *the cut and thrust of parliamentary debate* ■ *adj* describes swords designed for use with both the blade and the tip

cutaneous /kyoō táyni əss/ *adj* relating to the skin [Late 16C. < modern Latin *cutaneus* < Latin *cutis* 'skin'] —**cutaneously** *adv*

cutaneous anthrax *n* skin ulceration caused by anthrax bacteria

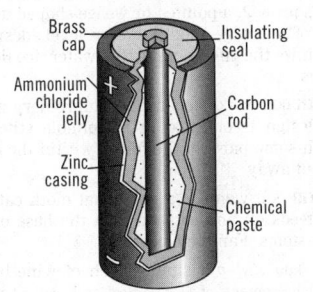

cutaway: cutaway view of a battery

cutaway /kúttə way/ *n* **1.** MODEL WITH INSIDE VIEW a drawing or model of something with part of its outside removed to give a view of the inside **2.** CINEMA, MEDIA SECONDARY SHOT WITH CAMERA in a filmed sequence, a short shot that shows an action separate from the main action ■ *adj* **1.** GIVING INSIDE VIEW constructed or represented so as to give a view of the inside **2.** CLOTHING CUT DIAGONALLY having the front cut diagonally away from the centre, e.g. in the part of a tail coat below the waist

cutback /kút bak/ *n* a reduction in the amount of something ○ *cutbacks in public spending*

cutch /kuch/ *n* TREES same as **catechu** [Mid-18C. < Malay *kachu* 'astringent vegetable extract' < Dravidian]

cute /kyoot/ (**cuter, cutest**) *adj* **1.** ATTRACTIVE IN CHILDLIKE WAY endearingly attractive in the way that some children and young animals are **2.** PHYSICALLY ATTRACTIVE young and physically attractive **3.** SHREWD sharply clever or wily [Early 18C. Shortening of ACUTE] —**cutely** *adv* —**cuteness** *n* ◇ **get cute (with somebody)** to show insolence to somebody (*informal*)

cutes ANAT plural of **cutis**

cutesy /kyoōtsi/ (**-sier, -siest**) *adj* too obviously attempting to be charming (*informal*) —**cutesiness** *n*

cutey *n* another spelling of **cutie** (*informal*)

cut glass *n* glass with a decorative pattern cut into its surface

cut-glass *adj* **1.** made of glass with a decorative pattern cut into its surface **2.** sounding extremely upper-class ○ *a cut-glass accent*

Cuthbert /kúthbərt/, **St** (630?–687) English missionary. He preached throughout Northumbria and lived as a hermit on Farne Island for over a decade. Many miracles are attributed to him.

Cuthbert, Betty (*b.* 1938) Australian sprinter. Her three gold medals at the 1956 Olympics and another at the 1964 Olympics gained her the nickname of 'the Golden Girl'.

cuticle /kyoōtik'l/ *n* **1.** SKIN AT BASE OF NAILS an edge of hard skin at the base of a fingernail or toenail **2.** ANAT same as **epidermis** (sense 1) **3.** ANAT DEAD EPIDERMIS dead or hardened epidermis **4.** ZOOL HARD COVERING OF INVERTEBRATES a hardened noncellular layer secreted by and covering the epidermis in many invertebrates **5.** BOT PROTECTIVE PLANT LAYER the thin outermost noncellular layer covering the parts of plants that are above the ground and helping to prevent water loss [15C. < Latin *cuticula* 'little skin' < *cutis* 'skin'] —**cuticular** /kyoo tíkyōōlər/ *adj*

cutie /kyoōti/, **cutey** (*plural* **-eys**) *n* an endearingly or physically attractive person (*informal*)

cutin /kyoōtin/ *n* a waxy mixture of fats and soaps forming the protective layer (**cuticle**) of plants [Mid-19C. < CUTIS]

cut-in *n* in a filmed sequence, a camera shot that focuses in on a smaller portion of a scene already established

cutinize /kyoōti nīz/ (**-izes, -izing, -ized**), **cutinise** (**-ises, -ising, -ised**) *vti* to deposit cutin in the cell walls of the parts of plants that are above the ground —**cutinization** /kyoōti nī záysh'n/ *n*

cutis /kyoōtiss/ (*plural* **-tes** /-teez/) *n* ANAT same as **dermis** [Early 17C. < Latin, 'skin']

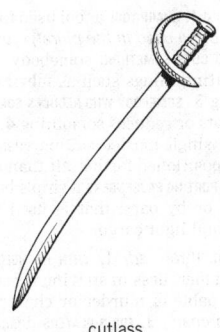

cutlass

cutlass /kúttləss/ *n* a short thrusting sword with a flat and slightly curved blade, used in the past especially by sailors [Late 16C. Via French *cutelas* 'large knife' < Latin *cultellus* 'small knife' < *culter* (see COULTER)]

cutler /kúttlər/ *n* **1.** somebody who makes cutlery for a living **2.** somebody whose job is to make, repair, or sell knives and other bladed tools (*archaic*) [14C. < French *coutelier* < Old French *coutel* < Latin *cultellus* (see CUTLASS)]

cutlery /kúttləri/ *n* **1.** UK, ANZ, Can EATING UTENSILS knives, forks, and spoons used for eating. US term **flatware 2.** TOOLS WITH BLADES knives and other instruments with a blade **3.** JOB OF CUTLER the job of making knives and other bladed instruments (*dated*)

cutlet /kúttlət/ *n* **1.** a piece of lamb or veal taken from the neck of an animal **2.** a mixture of chopped meat, fish, nuts, vegetables, or other foods, made into a flat round shape, covered with breadcrumbs, and fried [Early 18C. < French *côtelette* 'little rib' < Latin *costa* 'rib']

cut lunch *n* ANZ FOOD same as **packed lunch** (*informal*)

cutoff /kút of/ *n* **1.** LIMIT a limit or date beyond which

something is stopped **2. END OF SUPPLY** an end to the supply of something ○ *a cutoff in oil imports* **3. ENG VALVE** a valve that controls the flow of fluid or gas through a pipe **4. MUSIC BREAK IN MUSIC** the end of a note, passage, or piece of music, especially when indicated by a sign from the conductor **5. MUSIC SIGNAL FROM MUSIC CONDUCTOR** a sign given by a conductor to indicate a break in the music **6. ELECTRONICS ELECTRICAL THRESHOLD** the value of voltage, frequency, or other variable that represents a minimum or maximum for effective operation **7. GEOG NEW RIVER CHANNEL** a short channel cut by a river across a bend in the river, forming an oxbow lake ■ **cutoffs** *npl* **SHORTS MADE FROM TROUSERS** shorts made by cutting off the legs of a pair of trousers, especially jeans

cutout /kút owt/ *n* **1. SILHOUETTE SHAPE** a two-dimensional shape of somebody or something, usually made from stiff cardboard **2. SOMETHING CUT OUT** something that has been cut out from something else **3. ELEC SAFETY DEVICE FOR ELECTRICAL CIRCUIT** a device that switches off an electrical circuit or supply, e.g. to a machine, as a safety measure **4. UNORIGINAL PERSON** an unoriginal or characterless person or an unimaginative imitation of somebody ○ *a cardboard cutout* **5. RECORDING OUTDATED AUDIO RECORDING** a recording sold at a discount because it is out-of-date and supply exceeds demand

cutover /kút ōvər/ *n* the transfer of a system such as a computer network to new facilities or equipment including the transitional period when old and new systems are operating concurrently

cut-price *adj* **1.** offered for sale for less than the standard price **2.** selling goods or services at a cheaper price than is standard ○ *a cut-price chemist*

cutpurse /kút purss/ *n* **CRIME** same as **pickpocket** (*archaic*)

cut-rate *adj* selling for less than the standard price, and often regarded as shoddy

CUTS /kuts/ *abbr* **COMPUT** Computer Users' Tape System

Cuttack /kúttək/ city in eastern Orissa State, eastern India. It is situated at the head of a delta formed by the River Mahanadi on the Bay of Bengal. Population: 587,637 (2001).

cutter /kúttər/ *n* **1. SHARP TOOL** a tool used to cut through something (*often used in the plural*) ○ *wire cutters* **2. SOMEBODY WHO CUTS SOMETHING** somebody whose work involves cutting things such as fabrics to be made into clothing **3. SOMEBODY WHO REDUCES SOMETHING** somebody who cuts or reduces something **4. SINGLE-MASTED SAILING BOAT** a single-masted sailing vessel on which the mast is positioned farther aft than on a sloop **5. BOAT FOR TRANSPORTING PASSENGERS** a ship's boat, powered by a motor or by oars, that is used to transport passengers and light cargo

cutthroat /kút thrōt/ *adj* **1. WITH NO HOLDS BARRED** aggressive and merciless in striving for supremacy **2. MURDEROUS** capable of murder or characteristic of a murderer (*archaic*) **3. FOR 3 PLAYERS** describes games for three players that are adapted from games for four partnered players ○ *cutthroat bridge* ■ **1. DANGEROUS PERSON** a murderer or an aggressive dangerous person **2. HOUSEHOLD** same as **cutthroat razor 3.** (*plural same* or **cutthroats**) **FISH** same as **cutthroat trout**

cutthroat razor *n* a razor with a long blade and a handle that the blade can be folded into. N Am term **straight razor**

cutthroat trout *n* a trout that resembles the rainbow trout but has reddish-orange markings on each side of the throat. Native to: western North America. Latin name: *Salmo clarkii*.

cut time *n* N Am same as **alla breve**

cutting /kútting/ *n* **1. PART OF PLANT FOR PROPAGATION** a piece taken from a stem, leaf, or root that will grow into a new plant **2. MEDIA ARTICLE CUT FROM NEWSPAPER** an article or photograph that has been cut out of a newspaper or magazine. N Am term **clipping 3. CIV ENG OPEN TRENCH THROUGH HIGH GROUND** an open trench cut through a hill or high ground to avoid a steep incline for a railway, road, or canal **4. EDITING PROCESS** the process of editing a text, film, or recording **5. CINEMA CHANGING OF SHOTS IN FILM** the technique of changing from one shot to another in the editing of

a film ■ **cuttings** *npl* **PILE OF SMALL FRAGMENTS** small fragments that are brought up during rock drilling or that accumulate during coal cutting ■ *adj* **1. ABRASIVE AND HURTFUL** sharply expressed and likely to upset somebody's feelings ○ *a cutting remark* **2. VERY COLD** piercingly cold ○ *a cutting wind* —**cuttingly** *adv*

cutting board *n* N Am **HOUSEHOLD** same as **chopping board**

cutting edge *n* the most advanced and modern stage of something (*hyphenated when used before a noun*)

cutting room *n* a room where cinema film is edited, usually by hand and by being physically cut

cuttlebone /kútt'l bōn/ *n* the white internal shell of a cuttlefish. Use: whole as a mineral supplement for caged birds, in powdered form for polishing. [Late 16C. < Old English *cudele* (see CUTTLEFISH)]

cuttlefish

cuttlefish /kútt'l fish/ (*plural same* or **-fishes**) *n* an invertebrate sea animal that lives on the seabed and has ten arms, a flattened body, and an internal shell. Cuttlefish eject a dark inky fluid as a defence mechanism. Genus: *Sepia*. [Late 16C. < Old English *cudele*, related to COD² 'bag'; from its shape]

cutty /kútti/ (*plural* **-ties**) *n* N Ireland, Scotland an offensive term for a woman [Early 19C. < CUT]

cutty grass *n* a grass with sharp-edged leaves. Native to: New Zealand. Latin name: *Cyperus ustulatus*. [< CUT]

cutup /kút up/ *n* N Am somebody known for telling jokes, showing off, and playing pranks (*informal*)

cutwater /kút wawtər/ *n* **1.** the foremost part of a ship's prow **2.** a pointed or wedge-shaped upstream face of a bridge pier at water level, designed to minimize the effects of moving water, ice floes, and debris

cutwork /kút wurk/ *n* openwork embroidery in which the design is outlined in buttonhole stitch, after which some parts of the fabric within the outlines are cut away

cutworm /kút wurm/ *n* a nocturnal moth caterpillar that feeds on and eats through the base of young plant stems. Family: Noctuidae.

cuvée /koo váy/ *n* a single batch of wine [Mid-19C. < French, 'contents of a vat' < *cuve* 'cask, vat' < Latin *cupa*]

cuvette /koo vét/ *n* a transparent tubular laboratory vessel or dish for holding a liquid [Late 17C. < French, 'small cask' < *cuve* (see CUVÉE)]

Cuvier /kyoóvi ay/, **Georges, Baron** (1769–1832) French zoologist and anatomist. He devised animal classification systems and established the fields of comparative anatomy and palaeontology. Full name **Georges Léopold Chrétien Frédéric Dagobert, Baron Cuvier**

cuz /kəz/ *conj* same as **because** (*nonstandard*)

Cuzco /koóss kō, koóss-/ city in southern Peru, and capital of Cuzco Department. It was the capital of the Inca empire until 1533. Population: 278,590 (1998).

CV *abbr* Cape Verde (*used in Internet addresses*) See table at **domain name**

CV¹ *abbr* **1.** Cape Verde **2. MIL** Cross of Valour

CV², **cv** *n* a summary of a person's educational qualifications, skills, and professional history. Full form **curriculum vitae**

CVA *abbr* **MED** cerebrovascular accident

CVE *abbr* Certificate of Vocational Education

CVO *abbr* **MIL** Commander of the Royal Victorian Order

CVS *abbr* **1. MED** chorionic villus sampling **2.** Council of Voluntary Service

CW *abbr* **PHYS** continuous wave

CW *abbr* **1. MIL** chemical warfare **2. ARMS** chemical weapons **3. PHYS** continuous wave

cwm /kōom, koom/ *n* **1. Wales GEOG** same as **valley** (sense 1) (*often used in placenames*) **2. GEOL** same as **cirque** [Mid-19C. < Welsh, 'valley']

Cwmbran /kōom braán/ town in Monmouthshire, Wales. It was designated as a new town in 1949. Population: 46,021 (1991).

CWO *abbr* **1. MAIL** cash with order **2. MIL** Chief Warrant Officer **3. BUSINESS** chief Web officer

CWS *abbr* **COMM** Cooperative Wholesale Society

cwt *abbr* **MEASURE** hundredweight [*C* the roman numeral for 'hundred']

CX *abbr* Christmas Island (*used in Internet addresses*) See table at **domain name**

cXML *abbr* **E-COMMERCE** commerce XML (*used in e-commerce*)

cy *abbr* Cyprus (*used in Internet addresses*) See table at **domain name**

-cy *suffix* **1.** condition, quality ○ *buoyancy* **2.** action ○ *advocacy* **3.** rank, office ○ *baronetcy* [Via Old French *-cie, -tie* < Latin *-cia, -tia*, Greek *-k(e)ia, -t(e)ia*]

CYA *abbr* **ONLINE** see ya (*used in e-mails or text messages*)

cyan /sī ən, -an/ *n* a deep greenish-blue colour that, together with yellow and magenta, is one of the three subtractive colours [Late 19C. < Greek *kuanos* 'dark blue'] —**cyan** *adj*

cyan- *prefix* same as **cyano-** (*used before vowels*)

cyanamide /sī ánnə mīd/, **cyanamid** /-mid/ *n* **1.** a white crystalline caustic compound. Formula: CH_2N_2. **2. CHEM** same as **calcium cyanamide**

cyanate /sī ə nayt/ *n* a salt or ester of cyanic acid

cyanic /sī ánnik/ *adj* of a greenish-blue colour

cyanic acid *n* a weak colourless unstable acid. Formula: HOCN.

cyanide /sī ə nīd/ *n* **1. COMPOUND CONTAINING CARBON AND NITROGEN** a compound containing carbon and nitrogen as a CN group or CN⁻ ion **2. CHEM** same as **potassium cyanide 3. CHEM** same as **sodium cyanide** ■ *vt* (**-nides, -niding, -nided**) **1. METALL HARDEN METAL WITH CYANIDE** to treat something such as a metal surface with cyanide in order to increase its hardness **2. MIN EXTRACT TREAT ORE WITH SODIUM CYANIDE** to treat ore with a weak solution of sodium cyanide in order to remove gold or silver [Early 19C. < CYANOGEN] —**cyanidation** /sī ə nī dáysh'n/ *n*

cyanide process *n* a process for extracting gold or silver from ore by treating the ore with a weak solution of sodium cyanide and recovering the metal particles from the resulting solution

cyanine /sī ə neen/ *n* a chemical belonging to a group of blue dyes. Use: improving the sensitivity of photographic film to green, yellow, red, and infrared light.

cyanite /sī ə nīt/ *n* **MINERALS** another spelling of **kyanite**

cyano- *prefix* **1.** blue ○ *cyanosis* **2.** cyanide ○ *cyanogenesis* **3.** cyanogen ○ *cyanic acid* [< Greek *kuanos* 'dark blue']

cyanoacrylate /sī ə nō ákri layt/ *n* a liquid acrylate monomer belonging to a group with adhesive properties. Use: industry and medicine.

cyanobacteria /sī ənō bak teéri ə/ *npl* bacteria belonging to a large group that have a photosynthetic pigment and carry out photosynthesis. They were formerly classified as blue-green algae. Family: Cyanophyta.

cyanocobalamin /sī ə nō kō bálləmin/ *n* **BIOCHEM** same as **vitamin B$_{12}$**

cyanogen /sī ánnəjən/ *n* **1.** a flammable colourless poisonous gas. Use: organic synthesis. Formula: C_2N_2. **2.** a univalent radical. Source: cyanide compounds. Formula: CN. [Early 19C. < French *cyanogène*

< Greek *kuanos* 'dark blue'; from its being a constituent of Prussian blue]

cyanogenesis /sī ə nō jénnississ/ *n* the natural generation and release of hydrogen cyanide that occurs in some plants —**cyanogenetic** /sī ə nō ji néttik/ *adj*—**cyanogenic** *adj*

cyanohydrin /sī ə nō hī́drin/ *n* an organic compound belonging to a group that contain both nitrile and hydroxyl groups

cyanosis /sī ə nṓssiss/ *n* a condition in which the skin and mucous membranes take on a bluish colour because there is not enough oxygen in the blood [Mid-19C. Via modern Latin < Greek *kuanōsis* 'blueness' < *kuanos* 'dark blue'] —**cyanotic** /sī ə nóttik/ *adj*

cyanotype /sī́ ánnə tī́p/ *n* PRINTING same as **blueprint** *n* (sense 1)

Cybele /síbbəli/ *n* in the mythology of ancient Phrygia, the goddess of nature. She was worshipped by the Romans as the Great Mother of the Gods.

cyber- *prefix* **1.** computers and information systems ○ *cyberlaw* **2.** virtual reality ○ *cyberspace* **3.** the Internet ○ *cybercafé* [< CYBERNETICS, CYBERSPACE]

cyberart *n*	**cybermasses** *npl*
cyberartist *n*	**cybernaut** *n*
cyberattack *n*	**cyberphobia** *n*
cyberbabble *n*	**cyberphobic** *n, adj*
cyberbank *n*	**cyberprophet** *n*
cyberbanking *n*	**cybersafety** *n*
cyberbrain *n*	**cybersales** *npl*
cybercommerce *n*	**cybersecurity** *n*
cybercrime *n*	**cybersex** *n*
cyberculture *n*	**cybershopper** *n*
cyberdate *n*	**cybershopping** *n*
cyberdating *n*	**cybersnooper** *n*
cyberfeminism *n*	**cybersnooping** *n*
cyberfeminist *n, adj*	**cybersuit** *n*
cyberforensics *n*	**cybertheft** *n*
cyberfraud *n*	**cyberthief** *n*
cyberhacker *n*	**cyberthriller** *n*
cyberhacking *n*	**cybervandalism** *n*
cyberinsurance *n*	**cyberwar** *n*
cyberinvestor *n*	**cyberwarfare** *n*
cyberland *n*	**cyberwidow** *n*
cybermarketing *n*	**cyberworld** *n*

cybercafé /síbər kaffay/ *n* **1.** a coffee house where people can browse the Internet for a fee **2.** an area on the Internet where people communicate using a chat program or a bulletin board

cybercast /síbər kaast/ *n* a broadcast of an event transmitted via the Internet, in either sound or vision or in both [Blend of CYBER- + BROADCAST] —**cybercast** *vti*

cyber dhaba /-daába/ *n* S Asia in South Asia, a roadside stall where people can use computers or the Internet to find out information, send e-mail, or engage in commercial transactions [*Dhaba* < Hindi, 'roadside eating place']

cyberlaw /síbər law/ *n* the body of laws relating to computers, information systems, and networks —**cyberlawyer** *n*

cyber mall *n* a shared portal on the Internet providing information and links for a number of online businesses

cybermediary /síbər meédi əri/ (*plural* **-ies**) *n* an organization that facilitates online transactions without owning the products or services [Late 19C. Blend of CYBER- + INTERMEDIARY]

cybernate /síbər nayt/ (**-nates, -nating, -nated**) *vt* to control a manufacturing process with a servomechanism or computer [Mid-20C. < CYBERNETICS] —**cybernated** *adj* —**cybernation** /síbər náysh'n/ *n*

cybernetics /síbər néttiks/ *n* (*takes a singular verb*) **1.** the science or study of communication in organisms, organic processes, and mechanical or electronic systems **2.** the replication or imitation of biological control systems with the use of technology [Mid-20C. < Greek *kubernētēs* 'steersman' < *kubernan* 'to steer'] —**cybernetic** *adj* —**cybernetical** *adj* —**cybernetically** *adv* —**cybernetician** /síbərni tísh'n/ *n* —**cyberneticist** *n*

cyberpunk /síbər pungk/ *n* science fiction featuring characters living in a darkly frightening futuristic world dominated by computer technology

cyberself /síbər self/ (*plural* **-selves** /-selvz/) *n* a false identity assumed by somebody in an Internet chat room or in interactive Internet role-play

cyberspace /síbər spayss/ *n* **1.** the notional realm in which electronic information exists or is exchanged ○ *an e-mail message lost in cyberspace* **2.** the imagined world of virtual reality

cybersquatting /síbər skwoting/ *n* the registering of an Internet domain name containing a trademark with the intention of selling it to the trademark owner —**cybersquatter** *n*

cyberstalker /síbər stáwkər/ *n* **1.** a paedophile who uses the Internet to seek sex with children **2.** a stalker who uses the Internet to harass a victim —**cyberstalking** *n*

cybersurfer /síbər surfər/ *n* somebody who spends a lot of time surfing the Internet (*slang*) —**cybersurfing** *n*

cyberterrorism /síbər térrərizəm/ *n* the use of techniques that disrupt or damage computer-based information systems to cause fear, injury, or economic loss —**cyberterrorist** *n, adj*

cybertraveller /síbər travvələr/ *n* ONLINE same as **cybersurfer**

cyberwoozling /síbər woozling/ *n* the gathering of data from the computer of a visitor to a website without his or her knowledge or authorization (*slang*) [Late 20C. < CYBER- + *woozle*, after a scary animal in the Winnie the Pooh stories of A. A. MILNE]

cyborg /sī́ bawrg/ *n* a fictional being that is part human, part robot [Mid-20C. Blend of CYBERNETICS + ORGANISM]

cybrary /síbrəri/ (*plural* **-ies**) *n* a guide to the information available on the World Wide Web on a particular topic, or an information-gathering service using the Internet [Late 20C. Blend of CYBER- + LIBRARY] —**cybrarian** /sībráiri ən/ *n*

cycad /sī́ kad/ *n* a tropical tree that has a thick trunk, sharp-pointed leaves like palm leaves, and cones. Order: Cycadales. [Mid-19C. < modern Latin *Cycad-* < Greek *kukas*, miswriting of *koikas*, plural of *koix*, a palm tree]

cycl- *prefix* same as **cyclo-** (*used before vowels*)

Cyclades /síklə deez/ large group of Greek islands in the southern Aegean Sea. The largest island is Naxos and the chief town is Hermoupolis on the island of Syros. Population: 88,485 (1981). Area: 2,572 sq. km/993 sq. mi.

cyclamate /síklə mayt/ *n* a salt or ester of cyclamic acid, especially sodium cyclamate. Use: artificial sweetener. [Mid-20C. Contraction of *cyclohexylsulphamate*]

cyclamen /síkləmən/ *n* **1.** a small plant with heart-shaped leaves that grows wild under trees in parts of Europe, and is also cultivated. Flowers: white, pink. Genus: *Cyclamen*. **2.** a bright deep pink colour [Mid-16C. Via Latin *cyclaminos* < Greek *kuklaminos*, probably < *kuklos* 'circle'; from its bulbous root] —**cyclamen** *adj*

cyclamic acid /síkləmik-/ *n* a synthetic crystalline acid. Use: production of cyclamates, food additive. Formula: $C_6H_{13}NO_3S$. [Contraction of *cyclohexylsulphamic acid*]

cyclase /-klayz, -klayss/ *n* an enzyme that aids the formation of hydrocarbon rings (**cyclization**) in a compound

cycle /sík'l/ *n* **1.** REPEATED SEQUENCE OF EVENTS a sequence of events that is repeated again and again, especially a causal sequence ○ *breaking the cycle of violence and bloodshed* **2.** TIME BETWEEN REPEATED EVENTS a period of time during which one complete sequence of a recurring series of events occurs ○ *a seven-year economic cycle* **3.** COMPLETE PROCESS a complete process or sequence of processes in a machine or electronic device, or the time that this takes **4.** PHYS ONE COMPLETE OSCILLATION one complete continuous change in the magnitude of an oscillating quantity or system that brings the system back to its original energy state ○ *running at 100 cycles per second* **5.** ARTS LINKED ARTWORKS a series of linked songs, poems, stories, plays, or operas that deal with the same story,

events, or characters ○ *Wagner's Ring cycle* **6.** TIME LONG TIME a very long period of time **7.** ASTRON ORBIT one complete orbit of an astronomical object **8.** COMPUT SET OF OPERATIONS a set of instructions completed as a unit by a computer, or the time that completion takes **9.** BICYCLE a bicycle or tricycle **10.** BICYCLE RIDE a ride on a bicycle or tricycle ○ *go for a cycle* **11.** *US* AUTOMOT same as **motorcycle** ■ *v* (**-cles, -cling, -cled**) **1.** *vi* RIDE BICYCLE to ride a bicycle or tricycle **2.** *vti* GO THROUGH CYCLE to put something through or go through a sequence of events ○ *programmed to cycle every hour* [14C. Directly or via French < Latin *cyclus* < Greek *kuklos* 'circle']

cycle lane *n* a lane of a road for the use of cyclists

cycle of erosion *n* the development of landforms from mountains to plains

cycle path *n* ROADS a route or path for the use of cyclists. N Am term **bikeway**

cycle rickshaw *n* a three-wheeled vehicle like a large tricycle with a wide back seat for passengers, used as hired transport

cyclic /síḱlik, síḱ-/, **cyclical** /-iḱ'l/ *adj* **1.** IN CYCLES occurring or repeated in cycles **2.** CHEM ARRANGED IN RING describes organic compounds that are composed of a closed ring of atoms **3.** MUSIC WITH RECURRENT THEME describes music containing a recurrent theme or motif —**cyclicality** /síkli kálləti, síḱ-/ *n* —**cyclically** *adv* —**cyclicity** /sī klíssəti, si-/ *n*

cyclical unemployment *n* the fluctuation in the level of unemployment that coincides with a business cycle

cyclic AMP *n* a cyclic form of AMP that activates enzymes in many hormone-induced biochemical reactions

cyclic GMP *n* a cyclic form of GMP that is responsible for aspects of cell division and growth

cyclisation *n* CHEM another spelling of **cyclization**

cyclist /síḱlist/ *n* somebody who rides a bicycle or tricycle

cyclization /sī klī záysh'n, síklī́-/, **cyclisation** *n* the formation of one or more hydrocarbon rings in an organic compound

cyclo- *prefix* **1.** circle, cycle ○ *cyclometer* **2.** cyclic compound ○ *cyclopropane* [< Greek *kuklos* 'circle']

cycloaddition /síklō ə dísh'n/ *n* the creation of a ring structure in a chemical compound

cycloalkane /síklō ál kayn/ *n* CHEM an alicyclic hydrocarbon

cyclo-cross /síklō-/ *n* the sport of racing bicycles across rough country, or a race of this kind [< CYCLE + MOTOCROSS]

cyclogenesis /sī klō jénnəssiss, sī klṓ-/ *n* the formation and development of a cyclone [Mid-20C. < CYCLONE]

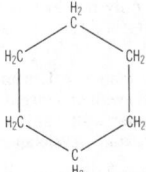

cyclohexane

cyclohexane /sī klō hék sayn, sī klṓ-/ *n* a colourless, pungent, flammable liquid hydrocarbon. Source: benzene. Use: paint thinner, solvent, in organic synthesis. Formula: C_9H_{12}.

cyclohexanone /síklō héksənōn/ *n* a colourless liquid ketone. Use: solvent, organic synthesis. Formula: $C_6H_{10}O$.

cycloheximide /sī klō héksə mīd/ *n* a colourless crystalline compound. Source: the bacterium *Streptomyces griseum*. Use: fungicide. Formula: $C_{15}H_{23}NO_4$.

cycloid /sī kloyd/ *adj* **1.** LIKE CIRCLE resembling a circle **2.** FISH CIRCULAR AND THIN describes fish scales that are circular and thin with smooth edges **3.** PSYCHOL MOODY changing between states of depression and elation (*technical*) ■ *n* **1.** MATHS GEOMETRIC CURVE a geometric curve formed by a point on the circumference of a circle that rolls along a straight line **2.** FISH FISH WITH CYCLOID SCALES a fish with scales that are circular and thin with smooth edges —**cycloidal** *adj* —**cycloidally** *adv*

cyclometer /sī klómmitər/ *n* an instrument that counts the number of times a wheel rotates and can, therefore, show the distance a vehicle has travelled —**cyclometric** /sīklō méttrik/ *adj* —**cyclometry** *n*

cyclone /sīklōn/ *n* **1.** METEOROL LARGE-SCALE STORM SYSTEM a large-scale storm system with winds that rotate anticlockwise in the northern hemisphere and clockwise in the southern hemisphere around and towards a low-pressure centre **2.** METEOROL VIOLENT STORM a violent rotating windstorm or tornado **3.** TECH ROTATING DEVICE a device that rotates rapidly, using centrifugal force to separate materials, e.g. particles from a gas [Mid-19C. < Greek *kuklōma* 'wheel, coil' < *kuklos* 'circle'] —**cyclonic** /sī klónnik/ *adj* —**cyclonical** *adj* —**cyclonically** *adv*

Cyclone /sīklōn/ *tdmk ANZ, US* a trademark for a type of fence made from panels of wire grid

cyclopaedia *n* PUBL another spelling of **cyclopedia**

cyclopean /sī klō peé ən, sī klṓpi ən/, **Cyclopean** *adj* **1.** MYTHOL LIKE CYCLOPS relating to or resembling a Cyclops **2.** ARCHIT MADE OF BIG STONES constructed of massive irregular stone blocks without mortar **3.** OPTICS DESCRIBING VISION describes the phenomenon of apparent unity in binocular vision

cyclopedia /sī klō peédi ə/, **cyclopaedia** *n* PUBL same as **encyclopedia** [Early 18C. Shortening] —**cyclopedic** *adj* —**cyclopedist** *n*

cyclopentane /sī klō pén tayn, sí klō pén tayn/ *n* a colourless, flammable, pungent, liquid cycloalkane. Use: paint remover, fuel, solvent. Formula: C_5H_{10}.

cyclopes ZOOL plural of **cyclops**

Cyclopes MYTHOL plural of **Cyclops**

cyclophosphamide /sīklō fósfə mīd/ *n* a toxic drug that suppresses immunity. Use: treatment of leukaemia, lymphoma, Hodgkin's disease, tumours.

cycloplegia /sī klō pleéjə, sí klō-/ *n* loss of movement in the eye muscles that adjust the size of the lens and are used for focusing —**cycloplegic** *adj*

cyclopropane /sī klō prṓ payn, sí klō-/ *n* a flammable hydrocarbon gas. Use: general anaesthetic, in organic synthesis. Formula: C_3H_6.

cyclops /sī klops/ (*plural* **cyclopes** /sī klṓ peez/ or *same*) *n* a freshwater crustacean (**copepod**) with a single eye. Genus: *Cyclops.* [Mid-19C. < modern Latin < Latin 'Cyclops' (see CYCLOPS)]

Cyclops /sī klops/ (*plural* **Cyclopes** /sī klṓ peez/ or *same* or **Cyclopses**) *n* in Greek mythology, of a race of giants who had only one eye in the middle of the forehead [Early 16C. Via Latin < Greek *Kuklōps* < *kuklos* 'circle' + *ōps* 'eye']

cyclorama /sī klō raámə/ *n* **1.** a picture painted all the way round the wall of a circular room **2.** a large concave curtain or wall behind a stage [Mid-19C < CYCLO- after PANORAMA] —**cycloramic** /-rámmik/ *adj*

cyclosis /sī klṓssiss/ *n* the rotary flow of protoplasm within some cells and protozoans [Mid-19C. < Greek *kuklōsis* 'encirclement' < *kuklos* 'circle']

cyclosporin /sī klō spáwrin/, **cyclosporine** /-reen, -rin/ *n* a drug obtained from a soil fungus. Use: suppression of tissue rejection following transplant surgery. [Late 20C. < CYCLO- + *polysporum*, fungus that produces the drug]

cyclostome /síklə stōm, síklə-/ *n* a jawless fish with a circular sucking mouth and without true teeth. Lampreys and hagfish are cyclostomes. Class: Cyclostomata. [Mid-19C. < CYCLO- + Greek *stoma* 'mouth'] —**cyclostomate** /sī klóstəmət/ *adj* —**cyclostomatous** /sīklō stómmətəss, -stṓmətəss, síklō-/ *adj*

cyclostyle /sīklō stīl/ *n* a now obsolete duplication method using perforated stencils, or a special pen used in this process. The pen had a tiny toothed perforating wheel and was used to create stencils on sheets of waxed paper. [Late 19C. < CYCLO- + STYLE 'stylus'] —**cyclostyled** *adj*

cyclothymia /sī klō thīmi ə, sí-/ *n* a psychiatric disorder in which the patient has frequent, relatively mild mood swings between elation and depression —**cyclothymic** *adj*

cyclotron /sī klō tron/ *n* a circular particle accelerator in which charged particles are confined by a vertical magnetic field and accelerated by an alternating high-frequency applied voltage. It is used to study the way particles interact.

cyder /sīdər/ *n* same as **cider** (*archaic*) [16C. Variant]

cygnet /sígnət/ *n* a young swan [15C. Old French *cigne* 'swan' < Greek *kuknos*]

Cygnus /sígnəss/ *n* a constellation of the northern hemisphere containing the star Deneb. See illustration at **constellation**

CYL *abbr* ONLINE see you later (*used in e-mails or text messages*)

cyl. *abbr* **1.** cylinder **2.** cylindrical

cylinder /síllindər/ *n* **1.** OBJECT SHAPED LIKE TUBE an object or shape with straight sides and circular ends of equal size **2.** MATHS GEOMETRICAL SOLID a three-dimensional geometrical solid bounded by two equal parallel circles and a curved surface formed by moving a straight line so that its ends lie on the circles **3.** MATHS GEOMETRICAL SURFACE a three-dimensional geometric surface formed by a straight line moving in a circle round and parallel to a fixed straight line, forming a hollow tube shape **4.** LONG THIN CONTAINER a long thin sealed container, e.g. one in which gas is kept under pressure **5.** HOUSEHOLD TANK FOR HOT WATER a closed container, usually insulated, for storing and supplying domestic hot water **6.** MECH ENG CHAMBER FOR PISTON a chamber in an internal-combustion engine or a pump within which a piston moves back and forth **7.** PRINTING ROTATING PART OF PRINTING PRESS a revolving drum of a printing press that produces or receives the impression **8.** ARMS ROTATING PART OF REVOLVER the rotating part of a revolver, containing chambers into which cartridges are loaded **9.** ARCHAEOL ANCIENT CYLINDRICAL CLAY OBJECT a hollow barrel-shaped object of baked clay covered in cuneiform script **10.** HIST same as **cylinder seal** [Late 16C. Via Latin < Greek *kulindros* 'roller' < *kulindein* 'to roll'] —**cylindered** *adj*

cylinder block *n* AUTOMOT a metal casting enclosing the cylinders of an internal-combustion engine. N Am term **engine block**

cylinder head *n* the closed detachable end of a cylinder in an internal-combustion engine

cylinder press *n* a printing press in which a flat bed holding the type moves under a revolving cylinder carrying the paper

cylinder seal *n* an engraved cylindrical clay or stone object used in ancient times, especially in Mesopotamia, as a seal that was rolled in wet clay to leave an impression

cylindrical /si líndrik'l/, **cylindric** /-drik/ *adj* having straight sides, circular ends of equal size, and a constant circular cross section —**cylindricality** /si líndri kálləti/ *n* —**cylindrically** *adv*

cylindrical projection *n* a method of making a map by projecting the globe onto a surrounding cylinder. The Mercator projection is a type of cylindrical projection.

cyma /sīmə/ (*plural* **-mae** /-mee/ or **-mas**) *n* a projecting moulding with an S-shaped profile [Mid-16C. Via modern Latin < Greek *kuma* 'swelling, wave' < *kuein* 'become pregnant']

cymbal /símb'l/ *n* a circular brass percussion instrument played with a stick or in pairs by striking them together [Pre-12C. Directly or via French < Latin *cymbalum* < Greek *kumbalon* < *kumbē* 'bowl, cup'] —**cymbaleer** /símbə leér/ *n* —**cymbaler** *n* —**cymbalist** *n*

SPELLCHECK cymbal or **symbol**? Do not confuse the spelling of ***cymbal*** and ***symbol***, which sound similar. A ***cymbal*** is a round brass percussion instrument, as in *play the cymbals.* ***Symbol***, the more frequent of the two words, denotes an object, sign, or character that represents something else, as in *mathematical symbols.*

cymbidium /sim bíddi əm/ (*plural* **-bidia** /-di ə/ or **-diums**) *n* an orchid with long narrow leaves. Flowers: brightly coloured with boat-shaped lower petals. Native to: tropical Asia, Australia. Genus: *Cymbidium.* [Early 19C. < modern Latin < Greek *kumbē* 'cup']

cyme /sīm/ *n* a flower cluster in which each flower stem ends in a single flower and other flower stems form below and to the side [Early 18C. Via French, 'summit' < Latin *cyma* (see CYMA)] —**cymiferous** /sī míffərəss/ *adj* —**cymoid** *adj*

cymene /sīmeen/ *n* a colourless liquid benzene derivative, existing in three isomers. Use: solvents, manufacture of resins. Formula: $(CH_3)_2CHC_6H_4CH_3$. [Mid-19C. < Greek *kummon* 'cumin']

cymophane /sīmə fayn/ *n* an opalescent variety of chrysoberyl. Use: gems. [Early 19C. < Greek *kuma* (see CYMA) + *-phanēs* 'showing']

cymose /sī mōss, -mōz, sī mṓss/, **cymous** /sīməss/ *adj* relating to, like, or being a cyme —**cymosely** *adv*

Cymric /kímmrik/ *adj* **1.** relating to Wales **2.** relating to the Welsh language (*dated*) ■ *n* LANG same as **Welsh** (*dated*) [Mid-19C. < Welsh *Cymry* 'the Welsh' < *Cymru* 'Wales']

Cymru /kúmri, kŏomri/ ➧ **Wales**

Cynewulf /kínniwŏolf/, **Cynwulf** /kín-/ (*fl* 750?) English poet and probable author of four important Old English poems. He may have been a Northumbrian monk.

cynic /sínnik/ *n* **1.** somebody who believes that human actions are insincere and motivated by self-interest **2.** somebody sneering and sarcastic [Late 16C. < CYNIC]

Cynic /sínnik/ *n* a member of a group of ancient Greek philosophers who believed that virtue is the only good and that the only means of achieving it is self-control. The sect was founded by Antisthenes in the 4th century BC. ■ *adj* belonging to, characteristic of, or relating to the Cynics [Mid-16C. Via Latin < Greek *Kunikos*]

cynical /sínnik'l/ *adj* **1.** DISTRUSTFUL OF HUMAN NATURE doubting or contemptuous of human nature or the motives, goodness, or sincerity of others ○ *Many people have developed a cynical distrust of politicians.* **2.** SARCASTIC mocking, scornful, or sneering ○ *They were made the butt of many cynical jokes.* **3.** IGNORING ACCEPTED STANDARDS OF BEHAVIOUR acting with disregard or contempt for accepted standards of behaviour ○ *a cynical disregard for the welfare of employees* —**cynically** *adv* —**cynicalness** *n*

cynicism /sínnissizəm/ *n* **1.** the state or fact of having cynical attitudes or beliefs, or a cynical character or quality **2.** a cynical action, comment, or idea

Cynicism *n* the beliefs or philosophy of the ancient Greek Cynics

cynosure /sīnə syoor, sínnə-, -zyoor/ *n* (*formal*) **1.** the centre of admiration, attention, or attraction **2.** somebody or something acting as a guide or used for direction ○ *Guidebooks are the cynosure of the inexperienced traveller.* [Late 16C. Via Latin *Cynosura* 'Ursa Minor' (which contains Polaris) < Greek *kunosoura*, literally 'dog's tail'] —**cynosural** /sīnə syŏorəl, sínnə-, -zyŏorəl/ *adj*

Cynthia /sínthi ə/ *n* **1.** the Moon personified as a goddess (*literary*) **2.** MYTHOL same as **Diana** [Late 16C. After Mount *Cynthus* in Delos, where the goddess Diana was supposedly born]

Cynwulf ➧ **Cynewulf**

cypher *n* COMMUNICATION another spelling of **cipher**

cypherpunk /sīfər pungk/ *n* an experienced computer hacker who breaks codes and enters secure computer systems [Late 20C. < CYPHER, after CYBERPUNK]

cy pres /seé práy/ *adv* in law, as nearly as possible to the will or intention of a person whose wishes cannot be executed literally [Via Anglo-Norman < French *si près* 'as near as']

cypress

cypress[1] /síprəss/ n **1.** CONIFER a coniferous evergreen tree with dark green leaves resembling scales. Native to: Europe, Asia, North America. Genus: *Cupressus*. **2.** TREE OR BUSH LIKE CYPRESS a coniferous tree or bush that is similar to a true cypress, e.g. a bald or swamp cypress **3.** WOOD the hard wood of a cypress tree **4.** SYMBOL OF MOURNING the branches or branches of a cypress tree as a symbol of mourning [12C. Via French < late Latin *cypressus* < Greek *kuparissos*]

cypress[2] /síprəss/, **cyprus** n a fine silk or cotton fabric, usually black. Use: mourning clothes. [15C. Via Anglo-Norman *cipres* < Old French *Cipre* 'Cyprus']

cypress pine n a conifer that is grown for timber. Native to: Australia. Genus: *Callitris*. [< CYPRESS[1]]

Cyprian /sípri ən/, **St** (200?–258) African-born Roman lawyer, bishop, and martyr. He was a Carthaginian bishop, and his works, including *On the Unity of the Catholic Church* (251), influenced St Augustine. Full name **Caecilius Cyprianus, Thascius**

cyprinid /si prínid, sípprinid/ (plural same or **-nids**) n a freshwater fish of the family that includes the carps and minnows, typically with rounded scales, soft fins, and toothless jaws. Family: Cyprinidae. [Late 19C. < Latin *cyprinus* (see CYPRINOID)] —**cyprinid** adj

cyprinodont /si prínnə dont, -prīnə-/ n a small freshwater fish with soft fins and a toothed jaw, e.g. a killifish or guppy. Native to: North America, Europe, Asia, Africa. Family: Cyprinodontidae. [Mid-19C. < CYPRINOID] —**cyprinodont** adj

cyprinoid /síppri noyd/ n any fish belonging to a large group that includes carp [Mid-19C. < Latin *cyprinus* 'carp' < Greek *kuprinos*] —**cyprinoid** adj

Cypriot /sípri ət/, **Cypriote** n SOMEBODY FROM CYPRUS somebody who comes from Cyprus ■ adj **1.** OF CYPRUS relating to Cyprus **2.** OF LANGUAGES OF CYPRUS relating to the dialects of Greek and Turkish that are spoken on Cyprus [Late 16C. < Greek *Kupriōtēs* < *Kupros* 'Cyprus']

cyproheptadine /sípro hépta deen/ n an antihistamine drug. Use: treatment of asthma, allergies, skin disorders. [Late 20C. < CYCLIC + HEPTA- + PIPERIDINE]

cyprus n TEXTILES another spelling of **cypress**[2]

Cyprus

Cyprus /síprəss/ island country in the eastern Mediterranean Sea. Since 1974, it has been partitioned between the Greek Cypriot south and the officially unrecognized Turkish Republic of Northern Cyprus. It became an independent member of the Commonwealth in 1961 and a member of the European Union in 2004. Principal language: Greek. Currency: Cyprus pound, Turkish lira. Capital: Nicosia. Population: 771,657 (2003). Area: 9,251 sq. km/3,572 sq. mi. Official name **Republic of Cyprus**

cypsela /sípsilə/ (plural **-lae** /-lee/) n a small hard one-seeded fruit with an attached calyx that does not split during seed dispersal, as in the daisy and dandelion. Family: Compositae. [Late 19C. Via modern Latin < Greek *kupselē* 'hollow vessel']

Cyrano de Bergerac /sírrənō də búrzhə rak/, **Savinien** (1619–55) French poet and dramatist. He fought in over 1,000 duels, often on account of insults relating to his extraordinarily long nose. His satirical accounts of journeys to the Sun and the Moon suggested the character of Lemuel Gulliver to Jonathan Swift.

> 'Perish the Universe, provided I have my revenge.'
> [Savinien Cyrano de Bergerac, *La Mort d'Agrippine* (The Death of Agrippina); 1654]

Cyrenaic /sírə náy ik/ adj **1.** PEOPLES OF CYRENE relating to ancient Cyrene or Cyrenaica **2.** PHILOSOPHY OF PHILOSOPHY OF PLEASURE relating to or advocating the philosophical doctrines of Aristippus of Cyrene, who believed pleasure is the supreme good ■ n **1.** PEOPLES SOMEBODY FROM CYRENE somebody who came from ancient Cyrene or Cyrenaica **2.** PHILOSOPHY BELIEVER IN CYRENAIC PHILOSOPHY an adherent of the Cyrenaic school of philosophy **3.** PHILOSOPHY HEDONIST somebody who believes that pleasure is the sole good in life [Late 16C. Via Latin < Greek *Kurēnaikos* < *Kurēnē* 'Cyrene'] —**Cyrenaicism** /-issizəm/ n

Cyrenaica /sírə náy ikə, sírrə-/ historic region settled by the ancient Greeks that occupied the eastern half of Libya

Cyrene /sī reéni/ ancient Greek town in Libya and the original capital of Cyrenaica, founded in about 630 BC. The ruins are situated about 225 km/140 mi. from Benghazi in northeastern Libya.

Cyril /sírrəl/, **St** (827–869) Greek missionary. With his brother Methodius he brought Christianity to the Slavs of southeastern Europe, and is said to have devised the Cyrillic alphabet.

Cyrillic /si ríllik/ adj relating to an old alphabet derived from Greek script and attributed to St Cyril, or a modified form used in writing modern Slavic languages such as Bulgarian and Russian. The Cyrillic alphabet is also used in writing the non-Slavic languages of some republics of the former Soviet Union. ■ n the Cyrillic alphabet [Early 19C. After St CYRIL]

Cyrus II /sírəss/ (600?–529 BC) king of Persia (550–529 BC). He founded the Persian Empire and was known for his tolerance, allowing the Jews to return from exile in Babylon.

cyst /sist/ n **1.** SPHERICAL SWELLING a closed, usually spherical, membranous sac that develops in human or other animal tissue and contains fluid or semisolid material. Some types of cyst form when glands are blocked, and most cysts are benign. **2.** ANAT HOLLOW ORGAN OR CAVITY a thin-walled bladder, sac, or vesicle in an animal **3.** BOT, FUNGI RESTING SPORE in some algae and fungi, a spore that is not undergoing cell division **4.** BOT AIR-FILLED CAVITY IN SEAWEEDS a small air-filled cavity resembling a bladder that occurs in some seaweeds such as the bladder wrack **5.** ZOOL PROTECTIVE SAC ENCLOSING ORGANISM a sac or capsule that encloses and protects some organisms in a dormant or larval stage **6.** ZOOL PROTECTIVE COVERING AROUND PARASITE a protective covering around a parasite, produced by a host or by the parasite itself [Early 18C. Via late Latin < Greek *kustis* 'bladder, cyst'] —**cystoid** adj, n

cyst- prefix same as **cysto-** (used before vowels)

cystectomy /si stéktəmi/ (plural **-mies**) n **1.** surgical removal of a cyst **2.** surgical removal of the urinary bladder

cysteine /sísti een, -tayn/ n a sulphur-containing amino acid that is converted to cystine during metabolism. Formula: $C_3H_7NO_2S$. [Late 19C. < CYSTINE + -eine, variant of -EIN]

cystic /sístik/ adj **1.** FORMING CYST forming, of the nature of, or consisting of a cyst **2.** CONTAINING CYST containing a cyst or cysts **3.** WITHIN CYST enclosed within a cyst **4.** RELATING TO BLADDER relating to a bladder, especially the urinary bladder

cystic duct n the duct of the gall bladder that joins

the bile duct from the liver to form the common bile duct

cysticercus /sísti súrkəss/ (plural **-ci** /-sī/) n the larva of some tapeworms that consists of a folded inverted head encapsulated in a fluid-filled sac. It is found in the body tissues of infested people and animals. [Mid-19C. < modern Latin *cysticercus* < Greek *kustis* 'bladder' + *kerkos* 'tail']

cystic fibrosis /-fī brốssiss/ n a hereditary disease starting in infancy that affects various glands and results in secretion of thick mucus that blocks internal passages, including those of the lungs, causing respiratory infections. The pancreas is also affected, resulting in a deficiency of digestive enzymes and impaired nutrition.

cystine /sís teen/ n an amino acid found in many proteins, especially keratin [Mid-19C. < Greek *kustis* 'bladder']

cystinuria /sísti nyoóri ə/ n the excessive excretion of cystine in the urine and the formation of cystine stones in the kidney, characteristic of an inherited disorder of the metabolism

cystitis /si stítiss/ n inflammation of the urinary bladder, often caused by infection

cysto- prefix hollow structure, sac, cyst ∘ *cystocarp* [Via modern Latin, 'bladder' < Greek *kustis*]

cystocarp /sístə kaarp/ n the reproductive body of red algae produced after fertilization and consisting of a mass of asexual spores borne on filaments

cystocoele /sístə seel/ n a hernia of a woman's urinary bladder that protrudes through the vaginal wall

cystography /si stóggrəfi/ n X-ray examination of the urinary bladder after the introduction of a liquid that is partially opaque to X-rays

cystolith /sístə lith/ n **1.** a hard mineral deposit, usually of calcium carbonate, that occurs in the epidermal cells of some plants such as figs or stinging nettles **2.** a stone that occurs in the bladder

cystoscope /sístə skōp/ n a narrow tubular instrument that is passed through the urethra to examine the interior of the urethra and the urinary bladder —**cystoscopic** /sístə skóppik/ adj —**cystoscopy** /si stóskəpi/ n

cystostomy /si stóstəmi/ (plural **-mies**) n the surgical construction of an opening into the urinary bladder to permit the removal of stones

cyt- prefix same as **cyto-** (used before vowels)

-cyte suffix cell ∘ *phagocyte* [Via modern Latin *-cyta* < Greek *kutos* 'hollow vessel']

Cytherea /síthə reé ə/ n MYTHOL same as **Aphrodite**

Cytherean /síthə reé ən/ adj **1.** relating to Cytherea **2.** relating to the planet Venus

cytidine /sítti deen/ n a compound (**nucleoside**) formed from cytosine and ribose. Formula: $C_9H_{13}N_3O_5$. [Early 20C. < CYTO- + -IDINE]

cytidylic acid /sítti díllik-/ n a nucleotide derived from cytosine and found in DNA and RNA. Formula: $C_9H_{14}N_3O_8P$. [Mid-20C. < CYTIDINE]

cyto- prefix cell ∘ *cytotoxin* [< Greek *kutos* 'hollow vessel' < Indo-European, 'thing that hides']

cytochalasin /sítō kə láyzin/ n a substance derived from fungi that inhibits the formation of microscopic filaments within living cells, thereby interfering with various cell activities, as in the cleavage

of cytoplasm following nuclear division. Cytochalasins are used in cell biology to investigate phenomena such as cytoplasmic movement and cell motility. [Mid-20C. < CYTO- + Greek *khalasis* 'dislocation']

cytochemistry /sītō kémmistri/ *n* a branch of biochemistry dealing with the chemistry of the cells of organisms —**cytochemical** *adj* —**cytochemically** *adv*

cytochrome /sītō krōm/ *n* a protein belonging to a group that contains iron and plays a role in cell respiration

cytochrome oxidase *n* an enzyme complex that is involved in the electron transport phase of cell respiration

cytogenesis /sītō jénnəssiss/ *n* the origin, development, and variation of living cells

cytogenetics /sītō jə néttiks/ *n* the study of the relationship between inheritance and the structure and function of cell components (*takes a singular verb*) —**cytogenetic** *adj* —**cytogenetically** *adv* —**cytogeneticist** *n*

cytogeny /sī tójjəni/ *n* BIOL same as **cytogenesis**

cytokine /sītō kīn/ *n* any protein secreted by lymph cells that affects cellular activity and controls inflammation [Mid-20C. < CYTO- + Greek *kinein* 'to move']

cytokinesis /sītō kī neéssiss, -ki-/ *n* division of the cytoplasm of a cell during mitosis or meiosis —**cytokinetic** /sītō kī néttik, -ki-/ *adj*

cytokinin /sītō kínin/ *n* a plant growth hormone that encourages cell division

cytology /sī tólləji/ *n* **1.** a branch of biology dealing with the study of cells, especially their structures and functions **2.** the examination of cells obtained from body tissue or fluids, especially to establish if they are cancerous —**cytologic** /sītə lójjik/ *adj* —**cytological** *adj* —**cytologically** *adv* —**cytologist** *n*

cytolysis /sī tólləssiss/ *n* the destruction or dissolution of cells, e.g. by the immune system —**cytolytic** /sītō líttik/ *adj*

cytomegalic /sītō mə gállik/ *adj* characterized by, producing, or relating to enlarged cells [Mid-20C. < CYTO- + MEGALO-]

cytomegalic inclusion disease *n* a serious disease of newborn babies affecting the brain, liver, kidneys, and lungs. It is caused by cytomegalovirus infection of pregnant mothers and leads to enlargement of the affected cells.

cytomegalovirus /sītō méggəlō vīrəss/ *n* a virus that causes enlargement of epithelial cells, usually resulting in mild infections but causing more serious disorders in Aids patients and in newborn babies

cytopathogenic /sītō pathə jénnik/, **cytopathic** /-páthik/ *adj* relating to or causing damage or disease to cells —**cytopathogenicity** /-pathəjə nísseti/ *n*

cytopathology /sītō pə thólləji/ (*plural* **-gies**) *n* **1.** a branch of pathology dealing with cell disease and damage **2.** the set of features or conditions associated with a diseased cell or cells —**cytopathologic** /-pathə lójjik/ *adj* —**cytopathological** *adj* —**cytopathologist** *n*

cytopathy /sī tóppəthi/ *n* deterioration or disease in a living cell

cytopharynx /sītō fárringks/ (*plural* **-pharynges** /-fə rín jeez/ or **-pharynxes**) *n* a tube in some protozoans extending from the cytoplasm into the endoplasm

cytophotometer /sītō fə tómmitər/ *n* an instrument that uses the variations in light intensity produced by stained cell cytoplasm to identify and locate chemical compounds within cells —**cytophotometric** /sītō fōtō méttrik/ *adj* —**cytophotometrically** *adv* —**cytophotometry** *n*

cytoplasm /sītō plazəm/ *n* the complex of chemical compounds and structures within a plant or animal cell excluding the nucleus. Cytoplasm contains the cytosol, organelles, vesicles, and cytoskeleton. —**cytoplasmic** /sītō plázmik/ *adj* —**cytoplasmically** *adv*

cytoplasmic inheritance *n* the inheritance of genes from the female parent that are not in the nucleus but in organelles such as mitochondria that are found in the cytoplasm. This type of inheritance is not controlled by Mendel's laws.

cytoplasmic streaming *n* the movement of cytoplasm within living cells resulting in the transport of nutrients and enzymes, and in the case of one-celled organisms, locomotion of the cell itself

cytoplast /sītō plaast, -plast/ *n* a plant or animal cell that has had the nucleus removed —**cytoplastic** /sītō plástik/ *adj*

cytosine /sītə seen/ *n* a pyrimidine base that pairs with guanine in DNA and RNA. Symbol **C** [Late 19C. < CYTO- + -OSE [1]]

cytoskeleton /sītō skéllitən/ *n* the internal network of protein filaments and microtubules in an animal or plant cell that controls the cell's shape and movement —**cytoskeletal** *adj*

cytosol /sītə sol/ *n* the fluid component of a cell's cytoplasm excluding organelles and other structures —**cytosolic** /sītə sóllik/ *adj*

cytosome /sītəsōm/ *n* the cytoplasm in a cell, excluding the nucleus

cytostatic /sītə státtik/ *adj* suppressing cell growth and multiplication ■ *n* a cytostatic agent —**cytostatically** *adv*

cytotaxis /sītō táksiss/ *n* the movement of cells or cell masses in relation to one another

cytotaxonomy /sītō tak sónnəmi/ *n* the classification of organisms according to cell structure, especially the number, structure, and shape of chromosomes —**cytotaxonomic** /-taksə nómmik/ *adj* —**cytotaxonomically** *adv* —**cytotaxonomist** *n*

cytotechnologist /sītō tek nóllejist/ *n* somebody trained to prepare cell samples and identify irregularities —**cytotechnology** *n*

cytotoxic /sītō tóksik/ *adj* **1.** describes a drug that prevents cell division **2.** describes a type of cell in the immune system that destroys other cells —**cytotoxicity** /-tok sísseti/ *n*

cytotoxic T cell *n* BIOL same as **killer cell** (*technical*)

cytotoxin /sītō tóksin/ *n* any substance that kills living cells

cytotropic /sītō tróppik/ *adj* describes motile cells that are mutually attracted to each other

cytotropism /sītō trŏpizəm/ *n* the movement or turning of cells or cell masses towards or away from one another

czar, etc. *n* HIST another spelling of **tsar, etc.**

czardas /chaárdash/, **csardas** *n* **1.** a Hungarian dance with a slow section followed by a faster one **2.** the music for a czardas [Mid-19C. < Hungarian *csárdás* < *csárda* 'inn']

Czech /chek/ *n* **1.** SOMEBODY FROM CZECH REPUBLIC somebody who comes from the Czech Republic **2.** SOMEBODY FROM CZECHOSLOVAKIA somebody who came from the former Czechoslovakia **3.** LANGUAGE OF CZECH REPUBLIC the official language of the Czech Republic, belonging to the West Slavonic group of Indo-European languages. Native speakers: 10 million. [Early 19C. Via Polish < Czech *Čech*] —**Czech** *adj*

Czechoslovak /chékō slóvak/ *n* same as **Czech** (sense 2) [Early 20C. Back-formation < CZECHOSLOVAKIA] —**Czechoslovak** *adj*

Czechoslovakia /chékəslə vaáki ə, -váki ə, chékō slō váki ə/ *former country in central Europe that was divided into the Czech Republic and the Slovak Republic, or Slovakia, on 1 January 1993 —**Czechoslovakian** *n, adj*

Czech Republic

Czech Republic /chék-/ country in central Europe created in 1993 when the former Czechoslovakia was divided into the Czech Republic and the Slovak Republic, or Slovakia. It became a member of the European Union in 2004. Language: Czech. Currency: Czech koruna. Capital: Prague. Population: 10,249,216 (2003). Area: 78,864 sq. km/30,450 sq. mi.

Czerny /chúrni/, **Karl** (1791–1857) Austrian pianist and composer. He was a pupil of Ludwig van Beethoven and the teacher of Franz Liszt. Of his many compositions, his teaching studies for the piano are best known.

Częstochowa /chéNstə khŏva, chénstə kŏva/ city in south-central Poland, north of Katowice. It is famous for the Jasna Góra monastery, which many Roman Catholic pilgrims visit every year to see the famous painting of 'Our Lady of Częstochowa', also called 'The Black Madonna'. Population: 258,100 (1997).

Dd

d[1] /dee/ (*plural* **d's**), **D** (*plural* **D's** or **Ds**) *n* **1.** 4TH LETTER OF ENGLISH ALPHABET the fourth letter of the English alphabet, representing a consonant sound **2.** LETTER 'D' WRITTEN a written representation of the letter 'd' **3.** ROMAN NUMERAL the Roman numeral for 500

d[2] *symbol* **1.** PHYS deuteron **2.** PHYS relative density **3.** CHESS FOURTH VERTICAL ROW OF CHESSBOARD used to refer to the fourth vertical row of squares from the left on a chessboard

d[3] *abbr* **1.** ZOOL dam[2] **2.** CALENDAR date **3.** daughter **4.** TIME day **5.** MEASURE degree **6.** MONEY denarius *or* denarii (*used of old-style currency in Great Britain before 1971*) **7.** TRAVEL departs **8.** depth **9.** MATHS, PHYS diameter **10.** died **11.** dollar **12.** drachma

'd *contr* **1.** did ○ *Where'd she get that hat?* **2.** had ○ *We'd already finished supper.* **3.** should **4.** would ○ *I'd like to stop at the shop.*

d', **D'** see also under surname

D[1] /dee/ (*plural* **D's** or **Ds**) *n* **1.** 'D'-SHAPED OBJECT something shaped like a letter 'D' **2.** MUSIC 2ND NOTE IN C MAJOR the second note of a scale in C major **3.** MUSIC SOMETHING THAT PRODUCES D a string, key, or pipe tuned to produce the note D **4.** MUSIC SCALE BEGINNING ON D a scale or key that starts on the note D **5.** MUSIC WRITTEN SYMBOL OF D a graphic representation of the tone of D **6.** EDUC 4TH HIGHEST GRADE the fourth highest grade in a series, e.g. a below-average grade for academic work **7.** HOCKEY SEMICIRCLE ROUND HOCKEY GOAL in hockey, the semicircle surrounding the goal, from which a player may try to score **8.** SOC SCI SEMISKILLED OR UNSKILLED WORKER in the market research system that classifies people according to their occupation, somebody in a semiskilled or unskilled manual job

D[2] *symbol* **1.** CHEM deuterium **2.** OPTICS dioptre **3.** PHYS dispersion **4.** AEROSP drag **5.** MATHS used to refer to the first derivative of a function

D[3] *abbr* **1.** CALENDAR December **2.** Department **3.** JUD-CHR Deus **4.** PHYS, MATHS diameter **5.** dinar **6.** Director **7.** JUD-CHR Dominus **8.** Don **9.** CARS drive (*used on gear levers of automatic transmissions*) **10.** Duchess **11.** Duke

da[1] *symbol* MEASURE deca-

da[2] see also under surname

DA[1] *abbr* **1.** COMM deed of arrangement **2.** ARMS delayed action **3.** BANKING deposit account **4.** COMPUT digital-to-analogue **5.** LAW district attorney **6.** COMM documents against acceptance

DA[2] *n* a man's hairstyle popular in the 1950s in which the hair is slicked back and drawn into a point at the back of the neck (*informal*) [Abbreviation of *duck's arse*; because it looks like a duck's tail]

d.a. *abbr* **1.** BANKING deposit account **2.** COMM documents against acceptance

D/A *abbr* **1.** COMM days after acceptance **2.** COMM delivery on acceptance **3.** BANKING deposit account **4.** COMPUT digital-to-analogue **5.** COMM documents against acceptance

dab[1] /dab/ *vt* (**dabs, dabbing, dabbed**) **1.** TAP SOMETHING GENTLY to pat or touch something lightly or gently ○ *She dabbed the tears from her eyes.* **2.** APPLY SOMETHING GENTLY to apply a substance using a quick light tapping action ○ *The nurse dabbed some ointment on the cut.* ■ *n* **1.** SMALL QUANTITY a small quantity, especially of a moist or soft substance ○ *a dab of butter* **2.** GENTLE TAP a light gentle tap, e.g. with the hand or a soft material **3.** CRIME FINGERPRINT a fingerprint, especially of a suspected criminal (*slang;*

often used in the plural) [14C. Suggestive of the action]

dab[2] /dab/ (*plural* **dabs** or *same*) *n* **1.** a small brown flatfish. Native to: Europe. Latin name: *Limanda limanda.* **2.** the flesh of a dab as food [15C. Origin ?]

dab[3] /dab/ *n* same as **dab hand** (*informal*) [Late 17C. Origin ?]

dabber /dábbər/ *n* a pad used by engravers and printers to apply ink or colour [Late 18C. < DAB[1]]

dabble /dább'l/ (**-bles, -bling, -bled**) *v* **1.** *vi* BECOME INVOLVED SUPERFICIALLY to have a casual or superficial interest in something ○ *He dabbled in local politics for a few years.* **2.** *vi* SPLASH to paddle, play, or splash in water **3.** *vt* DIP SOMETHING to wet something by dipping it in a liquid ○ *We sat by the pool, dabbling our feet in the water.* **4.** *vt* SPLASH SOMETHING WITH LIQUID to daub, splash, or spatter somebody or something with a liquid **5.** *vi* ZOOL MOVE UNDER WATER FOR FOOD to move the bill to the bottom of shallow water in order to reach food (*refers to ducks*) [Mid-16C. Probably < Dutch *dabbelen* 'keep tapping' < *dabben* 'to tap'] —**dabbler** *n*

dabchick /dáb chik/ *n* a small diving water bird, the smallest of the European grebes. Latin name: *Tachybaptus ruficollis.* [Mid-16C. Origin ?]

dab hand *n* somebody with a special ability to perform some activity (*informal*) [Early 19C. < DAB[3]]

dabster /dábstər/ *n* regional somebody with a special talent in some activity [Early 18C. < DAB[3]]

da capo /daa ka'apō/ *adv* to be played or sung again from the beginning of the passage or piece (*used as a musical direction*) [Early 18C. < Italian, 'from the head'] —**da capo** *adj*

Dacca ♦ Dhaka

dace /dayss/ (*plural same* or **daces**) *n* **1.** a small freshwater fish with a slim olive-green body. Native to: Europe. Latin name: *Leuciscus leuciscus.* **2.** a small freshwater fish. Native to: North America. Family: Cyprinidae. [15C. < Old French *dars* 'dace, dart']

dacha /dáchə/, **datcha** *n* a Russian cottage or house in the suburbs or countryside [Mid-19C. < Russian, 'grant of land']

Dachau /dákow, dákh-/ site of a World War II Nazi concentration camp (1933–45) in Bavaria, about 16 km/10 mi. northwest of Munich, southwestern Germany. It is now a memorial to those who died there.

dachshund

dachshund /dáksənd, dásh-, -hoǒnd/ *n* a small dog belonging to a breed that has a long body, short legs, and drooping ears [Late 19C. < German, 'badger dog']

~~dachsund~~ incorrect spelling of **dachshund**

dack /dak/ *n regional* the smallest or weakest piglet in a litter [Origin ?]

REGIONAL NOTE See *underling*.

---

dacks *n ANZ* another spelling of **daks**

dacoit /də kóyt/, **dakoit** *n* a member of a gang of armed robbers in South Asia and Myanmar [Late 18C. < Hindi *dakait* < *dākā* 'gang robbery']

dactyl /dáktil/ *n* **1.** a metrical foot of one long syllable followed by two short syllables in classical verse or one stressed syllable followed by two unstressed syllables in modern verse **2.** a finger, toe, or related body part [14C. Via Latin < Greek *daktulos* 'finger']

dactyl- *prefix* same as **dactylo-** (*used before vowels*)

-dactyl *suffix* an animal with fingers or toes of a particular kind or number ○ *polydactyl* [< Greek *daktulos* 'finger'] —**-dactylous** *suffix*

dactylic /dak tíllik/ *adj* relating to a metrical dactyl, or containing dactyls ■ *n* LITERAT same as **dactyl** (sense 1) —**dactylically** *adv*

dactylic hexameter *n* a line of verse consisting of six feet, the fifth of which is a dactyl, the first four dactyls or spondees, and the sixth a spondee or trochee. It is the metre of Greek and Roman epic poetry.

dactylo- *prefix* finger, toe ○ *dactylology* [< Greek *daktulos* 'finger']

dactylography /dákti lóggrəfi/ *n* the scientific examination of fingerprints for identification purposes —**dactylographic** /dak tíllə gráffik/ *adj*

dactylology /dákti lólləji/ *n* communication using signs made with the hands, often used by hearing-impaired people

dad /dad/ *n* a person's father (*informal; often used as a form of address*) [Mid-16C. Origin ?]

Dada /daá daa/, **dada**, **Dadaism** /daá daa izəm/, **dadaism** *n* a European artistic and literary movement of the early 20th century whose work was characterized by anarchy, irrationality, and irreverence [Early 20C. < French, 'hobbyhorse'] —**Dadaist** *n, adj*

daddy /dáddi/ (*plural* **-dies**) *n* **1.** (*informal*) a person's father, especially a young child's (*often used as a form of address*) **2.** Aus, N Am the earliest or finest example of something ○ *He was a fine trumpet player, the daddy of them all.*

daddy longlegs /-lóng legz/ (*plural same*) *n* **1.** UK a fly with long legs and slender wings. Family: Tipulidae. ANZ, N Am term **crane fly 2.** N Am an arachnid with long legs and an oval body. Order: Opiliones.

dado /dáydō/ *n* (*plural* **-does** or **-dos**) **1.** CONSTR LOWER PART OF INTERIOR WALL the lower part of an interior wall, decorated or faced in a different manner from the upper part, usually with panels, paint, or wallpaper **2.** ARCHIT same as **die**[2] (sense 5) **3.** CONSTR RECTANGULAR GROOVE IN BOARD a rectangular groove cut into a board so that a matching piece can be fitted into it to form a joint ■ *vt* (**-does, -doing, -doed**) CONSTR **1.** PUT DADO ON WALL to fit a wall with a dado **2.** CUT DADO IN SOMETHING to cut a rectangular groove in something so that a matching piece can be fitted into it to form a joint **3.** INSERT SOMETHING INTO DADO to insert something into a rectangular groove to form a joint [Mid-17C. < Italian, 'die (of a pedestal), cube']

dado rail *n* a decorative rail fitted round an interior wall, usually at middle height

Dadra and Nagar Haveli /daàdrə ən naàgər haa váylee/ Union Territory in western India, between the states of Maharashtra and Gujarat. Capital: Silvassa. Population: 220,451 (2001). Area: 491 sq. km/189 sq. mi.

daedal /deéd'l/, **dedal** *adj* (*literary*) **1.** INTRICATE complex or intricate **2.** INGENIOUS skilful or ingenious ■ *n* INGENIOUS INVENTOR an expert or ingenious inventor [Late 16C. Via Latin < Greek *daidalos* 'skilful']

Daedalus /deéd ələs/ *n* in Greek mythology, a craftsman and inventor who built a labyrinth on the island of Crete to house the Minotaur. He made wings so that he could escape from Crete with his son Icarus, but his son perished during the flight. — **Daedalian** /di dáyli ən/ *adj*

daemon /deémən, dĭ-, dáy-/ *n* **1.** *also* **daimon** /dĭ mŏn/ MYTHOL DEMIGOD a mythological being that is part-god and part-human **2.** *also* **daimon** MYTHOL GUARDIAN SPIRIT a spirit supposed to look after a person or place **3.** COMPUT SOFTWARE a piece of software that carries out background tasks such as filtering or debugging, at fixed intervals or in response to specific events **4.** same as **demon** (sense 1) (*archaic*) [Variant of DEMON] — **daemonic** /di mónnik/ *adj*

daff /daf/ *n* PLANTS same as **daffodil** (sense 1) (*informal*) [Early 20C. Shortening]

daffodil

daffodil /dáffədil/ *n* **1.** a plant with long slender leaves growing from a bulb. Flowers: yellow, trumpet-shaped. Native to: Europe. Latin name: *Narcissus pseudonarcissus*. **2.** a brilliant yellow colour, like that of a daffodil [Mid-16C. < medieval Latin *affodilus* 'asphodel'] — **daffodil** *adj*

daffy /dáffi/ (**-fier, -fiest**) *adj* silly in an amusing or harmless way (*informal*) [Late 19C. < alteration of DAFT] — **daffily** *adv* — **daffiness** *n*

daft /daaft/ *adj* **1.** NOT SENSIBLE obviously silly or unreasonable (*informal*) ○ *a daft idea* **2.** VERY ENTHUSIASTIC extremely enthusiastic about something (*informal*) **3.** *Scotland* FRIVOLOUS thoughtless or frivolous [Old English *gedæfte* 'fitting' < Germanic, 'fit, suitable'] — **daftly** *adv* — **daftness** *n*

REGIONAL NOTE See *addle-headed*.

Dafydd ap Gwilym /dávvith ap gwíllim/ (1320?–80?) Welsh poet. Considered one of the greatest medieval poets, he wrote poems about love and the beauty of nature.

dag /dag/ *n* **1.** ANZ DUNG-COATED WOOL a lock of dung-coated wool on a sheep's hindquarters **2.** ANZ SLOVENLY PERSON a dirty or untidy person (*informal*) **3.** ANZ UNFASHIONABLE PERSON somebody who is considered unfashionable (*informal*) **4.** ANZ UNUSUAL CHARACTER somebody who is regarded as odd, often with amusing characteristics or unconventional habits (*informal*) **5.** DECORATIVE EDGING a decorative edging for garments, used especially in medieval times ■ *vti* (**dags, dagging, dagged**) ANZ REMOVE SOILED WOOL FROM SHEEP to cut off dung-coated wool from a sheep's coat [Early 17C. Shortening of DAGLOCK]

da Gama /də gaámə/ ➧ **Gama, Vasco da**

Dagan /daáagən/ *n* in Babylonian mythology, the god of the Earth

Dagestan /dági staán/ autonomous republic in the Caucasus region of southern Russia, bordered by Kalmykia to the north, the Caspian Sea to the east, Azerbaijan to the south, and Chechnya and Georgia

to the west. The administrative centre is Makhachkala. Area: 50,300 sq. km/19,400 sq. mi. Population: 2,121,000 (1997).

Dagestanian /daágə stáyni ən/ *n* **1.** a group of North Caucasian languages spoken in Dagestan. Native speakers: 3,000. **2.** somebody who comes from Dagestan — **Dagestanian** *adj*

dagga /dúkhə, daágə/ *n S Africa* same as **cannabis** (sense 1) [Late 17C. Via Afrikaans < Nama *daxa*]

dagger /dággər/ *n* **1.** SHORT POINTED KNIFE a short pointed knife used as a weapon **2.** IRRITATION something that torments or wounds somebody ○ *Such cutting words were a dagger to my heart.* **3.** PRINTING SIGN USED AS REFERENCE MARK a sign (†) that is used as a reference mark, especially to a footnote ■ *vt* (**-gers, -gering, -gered**) PRINTING MARK SOMETHING WITH REFERENCE SIGN to mark text with a dagger sign [14C. Origin ?] ◇ **be at daggers drawn** to be hostile to each other and ready to defend a strongly held opposing view ◇ **look daggers at somebody** to look at somebody in an angry or hostile way

daggy /dággi/ (**-gier, -giest**) *adj* (*informal*) **1.** ANZ UNFASHIONABLE unfashionable, especially from a young person's point of view **2.** ANZ MESSY untidy, dirty, and unpleasant ○ *Her bedsit was so daggy.* **3.** *Aus* UNCONVENTIONAL different from other people, or unwilling to conform

dago /dáygō/ (*plural* **-gos** or **-goes**), **Dago** *n* a highly offensive term for somebody of Italian, Spanish, or Portuguese birth or descent (*taboo*) [Mid-19C. Variant of the name *Diego*]

dagoba /daágəbə/ *n* a dome-shaped shrine that contains Buddhist relics [Early 19C. Via Sinhalese *dāgaba* < Pali *dhātu-gabbha* 'receptacle for relics']

Dagon /dáygən/ *n* in Philistine mythology, the chief god, often depicted as half man and half fish

Daguerre /da gáir/, **Louis Jacques** (1789–1851) French painter and inventor. Originally a scene painter, he became a pioneer photographer who, working initially with French physicist Joseph Niépce (1829), perfected the daguerreotype process (1837). Full name **Daguerre, Louis Jacques Mandé**

daguerreotype /də gérrō tīp/, **daguerrotype** *n* **1.** EARLY PHOTOGRAPHIC PROCESS an early photographic process in which an image was produced on a light-sensitive silver or silver-coated plate and developed in mercury vapour **2.** EARLY PHOTOGRAPH a photograph produced by the daguerreotype process ■ *vt* (**-types, -typing, -typed**) PHOTOGRAPH SOMEBODY OR SOMETHING to make a daguerreotype of something or somebody [Mid-19C. < French *daguerréotype*, after L. J. DAGUERRE]

Dagupan /da goó pan/ port and city on Luzon island in the northwestern Philippines. Population: 116,211 (1990).

dah /daa/ *n* the spoken representation of a dash in Morse code and other telegraphic codes [Mid-20C. An imitation of the sound made by a Morse code transmitter]

dahabeah /daáhə beé ə/, **dahabeeyah, dahabiah** *n* a shallow-bottomed passenger boat or houseboat with sails and sometimes an engine, used on the Nile [Mid-19C. < Arabic *dahabīya* 'golden (boat)']

dahi /daáhi/ *n S Asia* FOOD same as **yoghurt** [< Hindi *dahī* 'curds']

dahi vada /-vaádə/ *n* in South Asian cooking, a dish of cooked lentils shaped in balls, deep-fried, and served in yoghurt [< Hindi *vaḍā* 'ball of dried lentils']

Dahl /daal/, **Roald** (1916–90) British writer. He is best known for his many children's books, including *James and the Giant Peach* (1961) and *Charlie and the Chocolate Factory* (1964). His books for adults include *Kiss, Kiss* (1960).

'Do you *know* what breakfast cereal is made of? It's made of all those little curly wooden shavings you find in pencil sharpeners!'
[Roald Dahl, *Charlie and the Chocolate Factory*; 1964]

dahlia

dahlia /dáyli ə/ *n* a tall perennial plant with tuberous roots. Flowers: large, brightly coloured. Genus: *Dahlia*. [Early 19C. After Andreas *Dahl* (1751–89), Swedish botanist]

Dahomey /də hŏmi/ former name for **Benin** (until 1975)

daidzein /dĭdzin/ *n* an isoflavone found in soya products that is a possible natural cancer preventative

daikon /dĭkən/ *n ANZ, N Am* a long sweet white radish used in Asian cuisines. Latin name: *Raphanus sativus longipinnatus*. UK term **mooli** [Late 19C. < Japanese < *dai* 'big' (< Middle Chinese *daj*) + *kon* 'root' (< Middle Chinese *k@n*)]

Dáil Éireann /dóyl áirən, daál-/, **Dáil** *n* the lower house of the parliament of the Republic of Ireland [Early 20C. < Irish, 'Irish Assembly']

daily /dáyli/ *adj* **1.** DONE EVERY DAY done or occurring every day **2.** FOR EACH DAY for each day, or for a period of a day **3.** LASTING ONE DAY for the duration of a day, or during a day ■ *adv* EVERY DAY on each day ■ *n* (*plural* **-lies**) MEDIA NEWSPAPER PUBLISHED EVERY DAY a newspaper published every day or every day except Sunday (*often used in the plural*) ■ **dailies** *npl* CINEMA DAY'S SHOOTING OF FILM SCENES unedited prints of a day's shooting of scenes from a film, prepared each day for the director to view the following day [15C. < DAY]

daily double *n* **1.** a bet, e.g. in horseracing, won by correctly choosing the winners of two specified races taking place on the same day **2.** the two races specified for a daily double bet

daily dozen *n* a set of physical exercises done each day (*informal*)

daimio *n* HIST another spelling of **daimyo**

Daimler /dáymlər/, **Gottlieb** (1834–1900) German engineer and inventor. His high-speed petrol-burning internal-combustion engine powered the first motorcycle and one of the earliest successful cars (1887).

daimon *n* MYTHOL another spelling of **daemon** (senses 1–2)

daimyo /dĭmyō/ (*plural* same or **-os**), **daimio** *n* a great Japanese feudal lord who was a vassal of the emperor [Early 18C. < Japanese, 'great name']

Daintree /dáyn tree/ river in northern Queensland, Australia, that rises near the town of Mossman and flows into the Pacific Ocean near Cape Tribulation. Length: 108 km/67 mi.

Daintree National Park national park in northeastern Queensland, Australia, that forms part of the Wet Tropics of Queensland World Heritage Area. Area: 7,080 sq. km/2,734 sq. mi.

dainty /dáynti/ *adj* (**-tier, -tiest**) **1.** PRETTY delicate and pretty ○ *dainty slippers* **2.** TASTY choice, delicious, or tasty ○ *a dainty morsel* **3.** REFINED IN TASTE having refined taste or manners **4.** OVERLY FASTIDIOUS excessively fastidious or particular ■ *n* (*plural* **-ties**) DELICACY something delicious, especially a small piece of food [13C. Via Anglo-Norman *dainte*, Old French *daintie* < Latin *dignitas* (see DIGNITY)] — **daintily** *adv* — **daintiness** *n*

daiquiri /dĭkəri, dák-/ (*plural* **-ris**) *n* an iced cocktail made from rum, lemon or lime juice, and sugar or syrup [Early 20C. After *Daiquiri*, Cuba]

dairy /dáiri/ *n* (*plural* **-ies**) **1.** PLACE TO STORE MILK AND CREAM a room or building where milk and cream and sometimes other perishables are stored **2.** FARM FOR MILK PRODUCTION a farm that produces milk and milk

products **3. PLACE TO MAKE BUTTER AND CHEESE** a room or building where butter and cheese are made **4. ESTABLISHMENT THAT SELLS OR PROCESSES MILK** a commercial establishment that processes, sells, or distributes milk and milk products **5. DAIRY PRODUCTS** dairy products collectively **6.** *NZ* **GROCERY STORE** a small local grocery store that sells milk, newspapers, and other provisions **7.** *US regional* **DUG-OUT HOLE** a space dug out in the side of a hill ■ *adj* **1. RELATING TO MILK PRODUCTS** relating to, producing, or containing milk or milk products **2.** JUDAISM **CONCERNING FOODS IN JEWISH DIETARY LAW** relating to those foods, including milk products, eggs, fish, and vegetables, that Jewish dietary law allows on occasions when milk is consumed [13C. < obsolete *deie* 'woman servant, dairy worker' < Old English *dæge* 'kneader (of bread)']

SPELLCHECK dairy or **diary**? Do not confuse the spelling of *dairy* and *diary*. The word *dairy* is a noun and adjective referring to milk, cream, butter, etc., as in *buy milk from the dairy, dairy farming, cheese and other dairy products*. The word *diary* is a noun denoting a personal record of events or appointments, or a book used for this purpose.

---

dairy cattle *npl* cattle bred and raised for milk production

dairying /dáiri ing/ *n* the business of operating a dairy or dairy farm

dairyman /dáiriman, -man/ (*plural* **-men**) *n* a man who owns or is employed at a dairy

dairyperson /dáiri purss'n/ (*plural* **-persons** or **-people** /-peep'l/) *n* an owner or employee of a dairy

dairywoman /dáiri wŏŏman/, **dairywoman** /-wimin/ *n* a woman who owns or is employed at a dairy

dais /dáy iss, dayss/ *n* a raised platform at the end of a hall or large room [13C. Via French < Latin]

daishiki *n* CLOTHING another spelling of **dashiki**

daisy

daisy /dáyzi/ (*plural* **-sies**) *n* **1.** a low-growing wild plant, with cultivated varieties. Flowers: white or pinkish-white petals, yellow centre. Native to: Europe. Latin name: *Bellis perennis*. **2.** a tall flowering plant. Flowers: large white petals around a yellow centre. Native to: Europe, Asia, North America. Latin name: *Chrysanthemum leucanthemum*. [Old English *dæges eage* 'day's eye'; because the flower opens in daylight and closes at night]

daisy bush *n* a bush or tree with clusters of white flowers resembling daisies. Native to: Australia, New Zealand, New Guinea. Genus: *Olearia*.

daisy chain *n* **1.** a garland made by threading the stems of daisies together **2.** a series of connected things, events, or people (*slang*)

daisycutter /dáyzi kutar/ *n* **1.** a bomb that detonates just above ground level, used against personnel and to destroy vegetation in order to create a landing zone for helicopters **2.** in cricket, a ball bowled or struck so that it skims the ground

daisy wheel *n* in some electronic typewriters and printers, a wheel with type elements at the ends of spokes radiating from a central hub

dak /daak, dak/, **dawk** *n* **1.** formerly in South Asia, a system of mail delivery or passenger transport using relays of horses or bearers **2.** *S Asia* letters, parcels, and other mail [Early 18C. < Hindi *dāk* < Sanskrit *drāk* 'quickly']

Dakar /dák aar, -ər/ capital and largest city of Senegal. It is situated on Cape Verde Peninsula, close to the westernmost tip of mainland Africa, and is one of

West Africa's leading ports. Population: 1,708,000 (1995).

dak bungalow *n* in South Asia, a house for travellers, originally on the route of a dak

dakoit *n* CRIME another spelling of **dacoit**

Dakota[1] /də kŏtə/ (*plural* **-tas** or *same*) *n* **1.** a member of the Sioux people, especially the Santee branch **2.** a Siouan language spoken in the United States and the Canadian province of Manitoba. Native speakers: 10,000–20,000. [Early 19C. < Dakota *Dakhŏta* 'allies'] —**Dakota** *adj*

Dakota[2] /də kŏtə/ ♦ **North Dakota, South Dakota** — **Dakotan** *n, adj*

daks /daks/, **dacks** *npl* ANZ trousers (*informal*) [< proprietary name]

dal[1] *n* FOOD another spelling of **dhal**

dal[2] *symbol* MEASURE decalitre

Dalai Lama /dálī laámə/ *n* in Tibetan Buddhism, the highest priest and, until the Chinese occupation of Tibet in 1959, the traditional spiritual and secular ruler of Tibet [Late 17C. < Mongolian, 'ocean lama']

dalasi /də laássi/ (*plural* **-sis**) *n* the main unit of Gambian currency. See table at **currency** [Late 20C. < name of an earlier Gambian coin]

dale /dayl/ *n* a broad lowland valley, especially in northern England ○ *walked over hill and dale* [Old English *dæl* < Indo-European, 'bend, curve']

Dale /dayl/, **Sir Henry Hallett** (1875–1968) British physiologist and pharmacist. With Otto Loewi, he established the role of the chemical acetylcholine in the transmission of nerve impulses. He and Loewi were joint Nobel laureates (1936).

daled *n* same as **daleth**

Dalek /daá lek/, **dalek** *n* an alien being in a metal casing, similar to a robot and with a harsh monotonous voice, from the British science-fiction television series *Dr Who* [Mid-20C. Invented word]

Dales, Yorkshire ♦ **Yorkshire Dales**

dalesman /dáylzmən/ (*plural* **-men** /-mən/) *n* somebody, especially a man, who comes from a dales region, especially the Yorkshire Dales in England

daleswoman /dáylz wŏŏmən/ (*plural* **-women** /-wimin/) *n* a woman who comes from a dales region, especially the Yorkshire Dales in England

daleth /daá lit/, **daled** /-lid/, **dalet** /-lit/ *n* the fourth letter of the Hebrew alphabet, represented in the English alphabet as 'd'. See table at **alphabet**

Daley /dáyli/, **Richard J.** (1902–76) US politician. He was the Democratic mayor of Chicago (1955–76) and was known for exerting strong personal control over local Democratic Party politics. Full name **Daley, Richard Joseph**

Dalgarno /dal gaárnō/, **George** (1626?–87) Scottish educationalist. His *Didascalocophus* (1680) was perhaps the first attempt at codifying a sign language for deaf people.

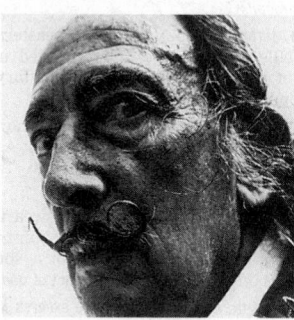

Salvador Dali

Dali /daá ali/, **Dalí, Salvador** (1904–89) Spanish surrealist painter. He is known for the dreamlike imagery and almost photographic realism of his work. After settling in New York (1940), he adopted other styles and wrote *The Secret Life of Salvador Dali* (1942). — **Daliesque** /daá ali ésk/ *adj*

> 'Those who do not want to imitate anything, produce nothing.'
> [Salvador Dali, *Dalí by Dalí*; 1970]

dalia incorrect spelling of **dahlia**

Dalian /daá li án/ industrial seaport on the southern peninsula in Liaoning Province, northeastern China. Population: 2,560,000 (1995).

Dalit /daá alit/ *n* in parts of South Asia, a member of the lowest caste within the traditional Hindu caste system [Via Hindi < Sanskrit *dalita* 'oppressed']

Dallapiccola /dálla píkələ/, **Luigi** (1904–75) Italian composer and teacher. His works, including the opera *The Prisoner* (1948), blend traditional Italian lyricism with modern serial techniques.

Dallas /dálləss/ city in northeastern Texas, on the Trinity River, east of Fort Worth. It is an important commercial, financial, and distribution centre. Population: 1,211,467 (2002 estimate).

dalliance /dálli ənss/ *n* (*literary*) **1.** a flirtation or flirtatious episode **2.** the frivolous or idle wasting of time

Dall sheep /dawl-/, **Dall's sheep** *n* a wild mountain sheep with curved horns and a coat varying from white to black. Native to: Alaska, Canada. Latin name: *Ovis dalli*. [After William H. *Dall* (1845–1927), US naturalist]

dally /dálli/ (**-lies, -lying, -lied**) *vi* **1. FLIRT** to act in an amorous, flirtatious, or playful manner **2. TOY** to trifle or deal lightly with something or somebody **3. WASTE TIME** to dawdle, loiter, or waste time [14C. < Anglo-Norman *dalier* 'amuse yourself'] —**dallier** *n*

Dalmatia /dal máyshə/ region of Croatia, consisting of a coastal area and offshore islands. It is bordered inland by the Dinaric Alps and includes the major cities of Dubrovnik and Split. Area: 12,950 sq. km/5,000 sq. mi.

Dalmatian /dal máysh'n/ *n* **1.** *also* **dalmatian** SPOTTED DOG a dog belonging to a breed that has a white coat with black or brown spots **2. SOMEBODY FROM DALMATIA** somebody who comes from Dalmatia **3. EXTINCT ROMANCE LANGUAGE** an extinct Romance language formerly spoken along the Adriatic coast in the region of Dubrovnik —**Dalmatian** *adj*

Dalmatian coast *n* a coastline characterized by chains of islands close to the mainland, formed when rising sea levels flood a series of valleys and ridges parallel to the coast

dalmatic /dal máttik/ *n* **1.** a vestment with slit sides and wide sleeves, worn by a priest or deacon of the Roman Catholic Church **2.** a robe with slit sides and wide sleeves, worn by British sovereigns at their coronation [15C. Directly or via Old French *dalmatique* < Latin *dalmatica* '(robe) made of Dalmatian wool' < *Dalmaticus* 'of Dalmatia']

d'Alpuget /dal pyóo zhay/, **Blanche** (*b.* 1944) Australian writer. She wrote the novel *Turtle Beach* (1981) and *Robert J. Hawke: A Biography* (1982). Full name **d'Alpuget, Josephine Blanche**

dal segno /dal sényō/ *adv* to be played or sung again from the point marked with the sign ‰ to the point marked 'fine' (*used as a musical direction*) [Late 19C. < Italian, 'from the sign']

dalton /dáwltən/ *n* CHEM same as **atomic mass unit** [Mid-20C. After John DALTON]

Dalton /dáwltən/, **John** (1766–1844) British physicist and meteorologist. His experiments with gases (1803) laid the foundations of modern atomic theory. He also first described colour blindness (1794).

daltonism /dáwltənizəm/, **Daltonism** *n* colour blindness, especially an inability to distinguish between red and green [Mid-19C. < French *daltonisme*, after John DALTON] —**daltonic** /dawl tónnik/ *adj*

Dalton plan /dáwltən-/, **Dalton system** *n* a system of teaching and learning whereby the student is free to continue without interruption on any subject that may arise in the course of his or her study [Early 20C. After *Dalton*, Massachusetts, US]

Dalton's law *n* the principle that mixed gases in a given volume exert a pressure equal to the sum of the pressures they would exert individually in the same volume [After John DALTON]

Dalton system *n* EDUC same as **Dalton plan**

dam: Hoover dam (completed 1936), Arizona/Nevada,
United States

dam[1] /dam/ *n* **1.** BARRIER CONTROLLING FLOW OF WATER a barrier of concrete or earth that is built across a river or stream to obstruct or control the flow of water, especially in order to create a reservoir **2.** RESERVOIR CONFINED BY DAM a reservoir of water created, confined, or controlled by a dam **3.** SOMETHING LIKE DAM a barrier that resembles or acts as a dam ■ *vt* (**dams, damming, dammed**) **1.** CONFINE SOMETHING WITH DAM to confine, provide, or restrain something with a dam **2.** OBSTRUCT SOMETHING to obstruct or restrict something [14C. < Middle Dutch]

dam[2] /dam/ *n* the female parent of an animal, especially of four-legged domestic livestock [14C. Variant of DAME]

dam[3] *symbol* MEASURE decametre

Dam /dam/, **Henrik** (1895–1976) Danish biochemist. Working with Edward A. Doisy, he isolated vitamin K, a fat-soluble substance necessary for blood coagulation. The pair shared a Nobel Prize (1943). Full name **Dam, Carl Peter Henrik**

damage /dámmij/ *n* **1.** HARM OR INJURY physical injury that makes something less useful, valuable, or able to function ○ *Damage to the vehicle was slight.* **2.** ADVERSE EFFECT a harmful effect on somebody or something ○ *did untold damage to her standing in the community* ○ *suffered psychological damage as a result of the harassment* **3.** COST the cost or price of something (*informal*) ○ *What's the damage?* ■ **damages** *npl* LAW MONEY PAID AS COMPENSATION money paid or claimed as compensation for harm, loss, or injury ■ *v* (**-ages, -aging, -aged**) **1.** *vt* HARM SOMEBODY OR SOMETHING to cause damage to somebody or somebody **2.** *vi* BE HARMED to suffer damage ○ *Soft fruit damages easily.* [13C. < Old French, 'loss through injury' < *dam* 'loss, damage' < Latin *damnum*]

SYNONYMS See *harm*.

damage control *n* **1.** containment and neutralization of difficulties caused by an event, e.g. public relations problems caused by a scandal, legal case, or other controversial matter (*informal*) ○ *As soon as the scandal broke, the Party's damage control kicked in.* **2.** shipboard measures to control, contain, and offset damages to a vessel, e.g. by collision, attack, fire, or an explosion

damaging /dámmijing/ *adj* causing or capable of causing harm, injury, or loss ○ *a damaging report* — **damagingly** *adv*

Daman /də máan/ capital of the Union Territory of Daman and Diu, western India. Population: 26,905 (1991).

Daman and Diu /-deé oo/ Union Territory of western India, comprising the coastal town of Daman and the island of Diu off the coast of Gujarat. Capital: Daman. Population: 158,059 (2001). Area: 112 sq. km/43 sq. mi.

damar *n* INDUST another spelling of **dammar**

Damara /də máarə/ (*plural* **-as** or *same*) *n* **1.** a member of a people living in southwestern Africa, mainly in Namibia **2.** a dialect of the Nama language spoken in Namibia. Native speakers: 160,000. [Early 19C. < Nama] —**Damara** *adj*

Damaraland /də máarə land/ historical region in north-central Namibia, named after the Damara people

damascene /dámmə seen, -seén/ *vt* (**-cenes, -cening, -cened**) DECORATE METAL WITH WAVY PATTERNS to decorate

metal such as iron or steel with wavy patterns of etching or inlays of precious metals, especially gold or silver ■ *n* DESIGN OR OBJECT CREATED BY DAMASCENING a design or object created by the process of damascening ■ *adj* **1.** RELATING TO DAMASCENING relating to the art or process of damascening metal **2.** OF OR LIKE DAMASK made of or resembling damask [Mid-19C. < DAMASCENE (adj)] —**damascener** *n*

Damascene /dámmə seen, -seén/ *n* somebody who comes from Damascus ■ *adj* relating to Damascus [15C. < Via Latin *Damascenus* 'of Damascus' < Greek *damaskēnos*]

Damascus /də máskəss, -maáskəss/ capital city of Syria on the River Baradá in the southwestern part of the country. Thought to have been inhabited since 2000 BC, it is one of the oldest cities in the world. Population: 2,036,000 (1995).

damask /dámməsk/ *n* **1.** PATTERNED FABRIC a reversible cotton, linen, or silk fabric with a pattern woven into it. Use: table linen. **2.** TABLE LINEN table linen made from damask **3.** GREYISH-PINK COLOUR a greyish-pink colour, like that of the damask rose ■ *vt* (**-asks, -asking, -asked**) DECORATE FABRIC WITH PATTERN to decorate or weave a fabric with an elaborate pattern [14C. < Latin *Damascus* 'Damascus'] —**damask** *adj*

damask rose *n* a large hardy rose. Flowers: fragrant, pink or red. Use: essential oil. Native to: Asia. Latin name: *Rosa damascena*. [< *Damask* 'of Damascus']

Damavand /dámmə vand/ mountain in Iran, northeast of Tehran. It is the highest peak in the Elburz Mountains and in the country. Height: 5,670 m/18,602 ft.

Dama wallaby /dámmə-/ *n* ZOOL same as **tammar** [< early variant]

Dam Busters *npl* a squadron of the Royal Air Force that bombed dams in Germany during World War II

dame /daym/ *n* **1.** N Am WOMAN OR GIRL a term for a woman or girl (*often considered offensive*) **2.** WOMAN IN CHARGE OF HOUSEHOLD the woman in charge of a household (*archaic*) **3.** WOMAN a married or matronly woman who is no longer young (*archaic*) **4.** SENIOR NUN used as the formal title of the superior of a convent **5.** THEATRE same as **pantomime dame** [13C. Via Old French and late Latin *domna* < Latin *domina* 'woman in charge of the house']

Dame *n* **1.** the title of a woman awarded any of various orders of chivalry or merit such as the Order of the British Empire by a sovereign or government **2.** the official title of the wife of a baronet or knight

dame school *n* formerly, a small school, often in a rural area, where children were taught the basics of reading, writing, and arithmetic by a woman of advanced years, usually in her home

dame's violet, **dame's rocket** *n* a perennial plant of the mustard family. Flowers: fragrant, purple or white. Native to: Europe, Asia. Latin name: *Hesperis matronalis*. [Translation of the Latin name in old herbals, *Viola matronalis*]

Damietta /dámmi éttə/ city in the northeastern corner of the Nile delta, Egypt. It is situated near the mouth of the River Damietta, a tributary of the Nile. Population: 89,498 (1986).

dammar /dámmər/, **damar**, **dammer** *n* a hard resin obtained from various trees of Southeast Asia. Use: inks, lacquers, oil paints, varnishes. [Late 17C. < Malay *damar* 'resin']

dammit /dámmit/ *interj* used as a swearword to express irritation, displeasure, disappointment, or frustration with somebody or something (*sometimes offensive*) [Mid-19C. Variant of *damn it*]

damn /dam/ *interj, adj, adv* USED TO EXPRESS ANNOYANCE used emphatically or as a swearword to express annoyance, disappointment, or frustration with somebody or something (*informal; sometimes considered offensive*) ■ *v* (**damns, damning, damned**) **1.** *vt* SAY SOMEBODY OR SOMETHING IS BAD to express disapproval of somebody or something, especially in public **2.** *vt* DOOM SOMEBODY OR SOMETHING TO FAILURE to cause somebody or something to fail **3.** *vt* CONDEMN SOMEBODY TO HELL in Christian belief, to condemn somebody to hell or to eternal punishment **4.** *vti* SWEAR AT SOMEBODY OR SOMETHING to curse or swear at somebody or something, using the word 'damn' [13C. Via Old French

damner 'condemn' < Latin *damnare* < *damnum* 'damage'] — **damner** *n* ◇ **damn all** nothing at all (*slang*) ◇ **not give or care a damn** to be not at all concerned or worried about something ◇ **not worth a damn** completely worthless

damnable /dámnəb'l/ *adj* **1.** detestable, hateful, or extremely bad **2.** in Christian belief, deserving divine condemnation or damnation (*dated*) —**damnability** /dámnə bílləti/ *n* —**damnably** *adv*

damnation /dam náysh'n/ *n* **1.** CONDEMNATION in Christian belief, condemnation to hell or eternal punishment **2.** SIN in Christian belief, something that causes condemnation to hell or eternal punishment **3.** PUNISHMENT in Christian belief, eternal punishment in hell ■ *interj* ANGRY EXCLAMATION used as a swearword to express anger or disappointment

damnatory /dámnətəri/ *adj* causing, expressing, or threatening condemnation (*formal*)

damned /damd/ *adj* **1.** CONDEMNED in Christian belief, condemned to hell or to eternal punishment **2.** EXPRESSION OF ANNOYANCE used emphatically or as a swearword to express annoyance (*informal*) ■ *adv* VERY extremely (*informal*) ○ *a damned good saxophone player* ■ *npl* PEOPLE CONDEMNED TO HELL in Christian belief, those condemned to hell or doomed to suffer eternal punishment

damnedest /dámdist/ *n* everything possible (*informal*) ○ *She did her damnedest to persuade them to stay.* ■ *adj* most amazing or extraordinary (*dated informal*) ○ *It was the damnedest thing I'd ever seen.*

damnify /dámni fī/ (**-fies, -fying, -fied**) *vt* to cause damage or loss to somebody or something [Early 16C. Via Old French *damnifier* < Latin *damnificare* 'injure, condemn' < *damnare* (see DAMN)] —**damnification** /dámnifi káysh'n/ *n*

damning /dámming/ *adj* **1.** proving or showing that somebody or something is guilty, wrong, or very bad **2.** very critical or unfavourable ○ *The reviewer made some very damning comments about the show.* —**damningly** *adv*

Damocles /dámmə kleez/ (*fl* 4th century BC) Syracusan Greek courtier. Dionysius of Syracuse, tired of his envious flattery, had him seated beneath a sword hanging from a hair in order to show him the perils that the powerful had to endure. —**Damoclean** /dámmə kleé ən/ *adj*

Damodar /dámmə daar/ river that rises in the Chota Nagpur plateau in the Indian state of Bihar, flows through Bangla, then joins the River Hoogly southwest of Korkata. Length: 592 km/368 mi.

damp /damp/ *adj* **1.** MOIST slightly wet ○ *damp laundry* **2.** HALF-HEARTED unenthusiastic or indifferent ■ *n* **1.** SLIGHT WETNESS humidity, moisture, or slight wetness ○ *patches of damp* **2.** MIN EXTRACT HARMFUL GAS poisonous gas or rank air, especially in a mine **3.** DEPRESSING FEELING a feeling of gloom or melancholy (*archaic*) ■ *vt* (**damps, damping, damped**) **1.** DAMPEN SOMEBODY OR SOMETHING to make somebody or something slightly wet **2.** EXTINGUISH OR SLOW DOWN FIRE to extinguish a fire or make it burn more slowly by reducing its supply of air **3.** MUSIC REDUCE VIBRATION OF STRING to reduce the vibration of a string on a piano **4.** MUSIC MUFFLE BRASS OR WOODWIND INSTRUMENT to muffle the sound of a brass or woodwind instrument **5.** DISCOURAGE SOMEBODY OR SOMETHING to discourage somebody or stifle a feeling ○ *Rain damped the picnickers' enthusiasm.* **6.** PHYS REDUCE OSCILLATION to decrease the amplitude of an oscillation or wave [14C. < Middle Low German < Germanic] —**damply** *adv* —**dampness** *n*

SYNONYMS See *wet*.

damp down *vt* **1.** MAKE FIRE BURN MORE SLOWLY to cause a fire to burn more slowly by adding ash or by reducing the flow of air **2.** REDUCE INTENSITY OF SOMETHING to control, restrain, or reduce the intensity of something **3.** FLATTEN SOMETHING USING SLIGHTLY WET OBJECT to flatten something by pressing or smoothing it with a slightly wet object ○ *Bill damped down his hair.*

damp off *vi* to decline in power, wealth, or strength

dampcourse /dámp kawrss/ *n* a layer of waterproof material near the ground in a brick wall that prevents damp from rising

dampen /dámpən/ (**-ens, -ening, -ened**) *vti* **1.** to make something slightly wet, or become slightly wet **2.** to deaden or stifle something, or become deadened or stifled —**dampener** *n*

dampen down *vt* same as **damp down**

dampen off *vi* same as **damp off**

damper /dámpər/ *n* **1.** SOMEBODY OR SOMETHING DISCOURAGING somebody or something that causes discouragement or inhibition **2.** PLATE TO CONTROL FIRE a metal plate that controls the draught in a furnace or stove **3.** MUSIC PIANO MUTE a felt-covered block in a piano that stops the vibration of strings **4.** MUSIC HORN OR WOODWIND MUTE a mute to muffle the sound of a brass or woodwind instrument **5.** ELEC ENG DEVICE TO CONTROL VIBRATION a device for controlling the excessive vibration of a suspended magnetic needle **6.** ELEC ENG DEVICE IN ELECTRIC MOTOR a piece of copper embedded in or near the poles of an electric motor to reduce any tendency to pulsate to speeds above or below its intended speed **7.** *Aus* FOOD UNLEAVENED BREAD bread made from a simple flour and water dough and often cooked over an open fire. It is a traditional bush food in Australia. ◇ **put a damper on something** to make something less fun and more inhibited ○ *The sudden arrival of the adults put a damper on the kids' party.*

Dampier /dámpi ər/ coastal town in northwestern Western Australia that serves as a port for nearby mining and industrial centres. Population: 1,819 (1991).

Dampier, William (1652–1715) English explorer. He was one of the first Europeans to visit Australia and published numerous surveys, logs, and charts of his voyages around the world.

damping off /dámping-/ *n* a fatal disease of seedlings grown under very damp conditions that is caused by various fungi

damp-proof *adj* impervious or resistant to damp or moisture ■ *vt* to make something such as a building damp-proof

damp-proof course *n* CONSTR same as **dampcourse**

damp squib *n* something that is intended or expected to be effective or impressive but fails or disappoints (*informal*)

damsel /dámz'l/ *n* a girl or young unmarried woman, originally one of noble birth (*archaic or literary*) [13C. < Old French *dameisele*, alteration (after *dame*) of *donsele* < Vulgar Latin *dominicella* 'little lady' < Latin *domina* 'woman in charge of the house']

damselfish /dámz'l fish/ (*plural same* or **-fishes**) *n* a small brightly-coloured sea fish that lives along coral reefs. Native to: tropics. Family: Pomacentridae.

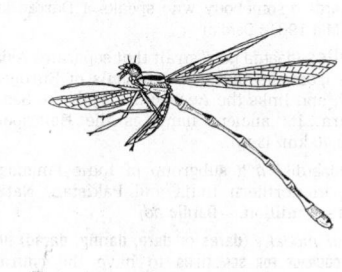

damselfly

damselfly /dámz'l flī/ (*plural* **-flies**) *n* a slender insect, related to the dragonfly but smaller in size, that folds its wings together above its body when resting and has eyes facing sideways. Suborder: Zygoptera.

damson /dámz'n/ *n* **1.** a small sour dark purple fruit, usually eaten cooked or made into jam **2.** a fruit tree related to the plum that produces damsons. Latin name: *Prunus insititia*. [15C. Alteration of DAMASCENE (adj)]

dan[1] /dan/, **Dan** *n* **1.** one of the numbered black-belt levels of proficiency in martial arts such as judo and karate **2.** somebody who has achieved a dan [Mid-20C. Via Japanese < Middle Chinese *nam* 'male']

dan[2] /dan/ *n* a small buoy, often with a flag attached, used as a marker [Late 17C. Origin ?]

Dan /dan/ *n* in the Bible, the son of Jacob and Bilhah and the founder of the tribe of Dan (Genesis 30:6)

Dan. *abbr* **1.** BIBLE Daniel **2.** Danish

Dana /dáynə/, **Richard Henry** (1815–82) US writer and lawyer. He is known for his maritime narrative *Two Years Before the Mast* (1840).

'There is not so pitiable an object in the world as a landsman beginning a sailor's life.'
[Richard Henry Dana, *Two Years Before the Mast*; 1840]

Danaides /də náy i deez/, **Danaïdes** *npl* in Greek mythology, the 50 daughters of Danaüs, king of Argos, who were ordered by their father to kill their bridegrooms, but one, Hypermnestra, refused

Da Nang /də náng/, **Danang** city and port in east central Vietnam. It was a major US military base during the Vietnam War. Population: 382,674 (1992).

dan buoy *n* NAVIG same as **dan**[2]

Danby /dánbi/, **Francis** (1793–1861) Irish-born British painter. He is known for his dramatic biblical and historical subjects as well as his romantic landscapes.

dance /daanss/ *v* (**dances, dancing, danced**) **1.** *vi* MOVE RHYTHMICALLY TO MUSIC to move the feet and body rhythmically, usually in time to music **2.** *vt* PERFORM PARTICULAR STEPS TO MUSIC to perform or participate in a particular series of rhythmic steps and movements, usually to music ○ *to dance a lively polka* **3.** *vt* MAKE SOMEBODY DANCE to cause somebody to dance ○ *He danced her across the floor.* **4.** *vi* JUMP UP AND DOWN to leap or skip, especially in an emotional manner ○ *The children danced with glee.* **5.** *vi* MOVE ABOUT QUICKLY to bob up and down or move quickly about ○ *The leaves danced across the lawn.* **6.** *vt* ACHIEVE SOMETHING BY DANCING to achieve or proceed through something by dancing ○ *She danced her way to fame and adulation.* **7.** *vi* BOARD GAMES FAIL TO ROLL RE-ENTRY NUMBER in backgammon, to fail to roll a number that re-enters a piece from the bar ○ *He rolled a 6–6 and danced.* ■ *n* **1.** RHYTHMIC BODY MOVEMENTS TO MUSIC a series of rhythmic steps and movements, usually performed to music **2.** PERIOD OF DANCING a session of dancing **3.** OCCASION FOR DANCING a social gathering for dancing **4.** ART OF DANCING dancing as a performance art **5.** MUSIC MUSIC FOR DANCING a piece of music for a dance **6.** ZOOL PATTERN OF ANIMAL MOVEMENTS a pattern of animal movements used, e.g. by birds in courtship or by bees in giving information about food ■ *adj* OF OR FOR DANCING relating to, involving, or created for dancing [13C. < Old French] —**danceable** *adj* —**dancer** *n*

dance band *n* a band that plays music for dancing

dance floor *n* an area of bare floor for dancing

dance hall *n* **1.** an enclosed space where public dances are held **2.** *N Am* electronically produced dance music combining different musical styles with a disc jockey talking or rapping to the rhythm

dance music *n* **1.** music suitable for dancing **2.** pop music that uses repeated electronic rhythms

dance of death, **Dance of Death** *n* an allegorical representation in medieval art, literature, and music of a dance in which Death, personified as a skeleton, leads people to the grave

dancercise /daʹanssər sīz/ *n* aerobic exercise in the form of dance [Mid-20C. Blend of DANCE + EXERCISE]

dancing /daʹanssing/ *n* the performance of or participation in a dance ■ *adj* performing, used for, or participating in dance or a dance ○ *my dancing partner* ○ *dancing shoes*

dancing dervish *n* a member of an ascetic Muslim religious group known for very energetic dancing

D and C *n* a gynaecological surgical procedure in which the cervix is widened and some of the womb lining is scraped out for diagnostic or treatment purposes or in an abortion. Full form **dilatation and curettage**

dandelion /dándi lī ən/ *n* a weed with bright yellow flowers on hollow stalks that produce fluffy white seed heads. Use: leaves in salads, medicine, winemaking. Latin name: *Taraxacum officinale*. [15C. < French *dent de lion* 'lion's tooth']

Dandenong Ranges /dándə nong-/ densely forested range of hills near Melbourne in Victoria, Australia. Its highest peak is Mount Dandenong, 634 m./2,080 ft.

dandelion

dander[1] /dándər/ *n* **1.** minute particles or scales shed from the feathers, hair, or skin of various animals **2.** *Ireland* same as **dandruff** [Late 18C. Origin ?] ◇ **get somebody's dander up** to make somebody angry

dander[2] /dándər/, **daunder** /dáwndər/ *N England, Scotland n* a saunter or stroll ■ *vi* (**-ders, -dering, -dered**) to saunter or stroll [Late 16C. Origin ?]

Dandie Dinmont

Dandie Dinmont /dándi dínmont/, **Dandie Dinmont terrier** *n* a small terrier belonging to a breed from the Scottish Borders with a long body, short legs, drooping ears, and a long, wiry, greyish or brownish coat [Early 19C. After the fictional owner of such dogs in *Guy Mannering* by Sir Walter Scott]

dandify /dándi fī/ (**-fies, -fying, -fied**) *vt* to dress somebody as or cause somebody to resemble a dandy —**dandification** /dándifi káysh'n/ *n* —**dandified** *adj*

dandle /dánd'l/ (**-dles, -dling, -dled**) *vt* **1.** to move a baby or small child gently up and down in your arms or on your knees **2.** to fondle or pet somebody or something [Mid-16C. Origin ?] —**dandler** *n*

dandruff /dándrəf, -druf/ *n* loose dry scales of dead skin that are shed from the scalp [Mid-16C. < *dand-*, origin ? + *-ruff*, origin ?] —**dandruffy** *adj*

dandy /dándi/ *n* (*plural* **-dies**) **1.** MAN TOO CONCERNED WITH APPEARANCE a man who is excessively concerned with his elegant appearance (*dated*) **2.** *N Am* EXCELLENT PERSON OR THING somebody or something considered to be very good or the best in its class (*informal*) **3.** SAILING BOAT same as **dandy roll** ■ *adj* (**-dier, -diest**) **1.** *N Am* EXCELLENT very good, excellent, or first-rate (*informal*) **2.** CHARACTERISTIC OF DANDY dressed or acting like a dandy (*dated*) [Late 18C. Shortening of Scottish *Jack-a-dandy* 'affected man'] —**dandily** *adv* —**dandyish** *adj* —**dandyism** *n*

dandy brush *n* a stiff coarse brush for grooming animals, especially horses

dandy roll, **dandy roller** *n* a wire cylinder used in paper manufacture to produce a watermark

Dane /dayn/ *n* somebody who comes from Denmark [14C. < Old Norse *Danir* (plural) 'Danes']

Danegeld /dáyn geld/, **Danegelt** /-gelt/ *n* **1.** an annual tax first levied in the 10th century in England to buy off Danish invaders. It continued until the 12th century as a land tax. **2.** a payment made in order to avoid trouble or to prevent attack from a stronger enemy [Pre-12C. < assumed Old Norse *Danagiald* < *Danir* (plural) 'Danes' + *giald* 'payment']

Danelaw /dáyn law/ *n* **1.** the body of laws established in the parts of England settled in the 9th century by Danish invaders **2.** the parts of Anglo-Saxon

England that came under Danish law and where Danish customs were observed [Old English *Dena lagu* 'Danes' law']

dang /dang/ *interj, adj, adv N Am* same as **damn** (*informal; euphemistic*) [Late 18C. Alteration]

danged /dangd/ *adj, adv US* same as **damned** *adj* (sense 2), *adv* (*informal; euphemistic*)

danger /dáynjər/ *n* **1.** exposure or vulnerability to harm, injury, or loss ○ *Their lives were in danger.* ○ *His reckless behaviour had put them all in danger.* **2.** somebody or something that may cause harm, injury, or loss (*often used in the plural*) ○ *the dangers of smoking* [13C. Via Anglo-Norman *daunger* < assumed Vulgar Latin *domniarium* 'power to do harm' < Latin *dominium* 'sovereignty' < *dominus* 'lord']

danger money *n* additional payment made for doing a job that involves danger. N Am term **hazard pay**

dangerous /dáynjərəss/ *adj* **1.** likely to cause or result in harm or injury **2.** involving risk or difficulty ○ *The business is in a dangerous financial position.* —**dangerously** *adv* —**dangerousness** *n*

dangle /dáng g'l/ *v* (**-gles, -gling, -gled**) **1.** *vti* HANG LOOSELY to swing or hang loosely, or cause something to swing or hang loosely ○ *The children dangled their legs over the side of the swimming pool.* **2.** *vt* OFFER SOMETHING AS INDUCEMENT to offer or display something as an enticement or inducement ○ *The possibility of promotion was dangled before her.* ■ *n* DANGLING THING something that dangles [Late 16C. Probably suggesting the action] —**dangler** *n* —**dangly** *adj*

dangling participle *n* a participle that is not grammatically linked to the word it is intended to modify. In 'Driving down the street, the house came into view', 'driving' is a dangling participle.

USAGE *Dangling participles*, also called 'hanging participles' or 'misplaced modifiers', typically occur at the beginning of sentences and modify either the wrong thing or nothing in particular: *Startled by the noise, her book fell to the floor* (but it was she, not her book, who was startled). *Lying in the sun, it was hard to imagine the winter back home* (who was lying in the sun?). Correct such mismatches by changing the wording: *Startled by the noise, she dropped her book* and *Lying in the sun, he found it hard to imagine the winter back home.* A number of dangling participles, however, are well established and idiomatic, for example *given, granting,* and *speaking*: *Given that dividends depend on earnings, what determines earnings?* Other similar words, including *considering* and *regarding*, are so well established in such contexts that they are generally thought of as independent of the verbs from which they sprang and are now said to be prepositions.

dan grade *n* MARTIAL ARTS same as **dan** [1] (sense 1)

Daniel /dánnyəl/ *n* **1.** BIBLICAL PROPHET in the Bible, a prophet whose faith in God protected him in the lion's den **2.** BOOK OF BIBLE the book of the Bible that tells the story of Daniel. See table at **Bible** **3.** WISE PERSON a wise and honourable person

Daniel /dánnyəl/, **Samuel** (1562–1619) English poet. His works include the sonnet collection *Delia* (1592) and his famous masque *Hymen's Triumph* (1615).

> 'Unless above himself he can / Erect himself, how poor a thing is man!'
> [Samuel Daniel, 'To the Ladie Margret, Countesse of Cumberland'; 1600?]

danio /dáyni ō/ (*plural* **-os**) *n* a brightly-coloured freshwater fish that is kept as an aquarium fish. Native to: India, Sri Lanka. Genera: *Danio* or *Brachydanio*. [Late 19C. < modern Latin]

Danish /dáynish/ *adj* OF DENMARK relating to Denmark or its people, language, or culture ■ *n* LANG LANGUAGE OF DANES the official language of Denmark, also an official language of the Faroe Islands and Greenland, belonging to the North Germanic group of Indo-European languages. Native speakers: 5 million. ■ *npl* PEOPLES PEOPLE FROM DENMARK people who come from Denmark [14C. < Anglo-Norman *Danes* (plural) 'Danes' < Old Icelandic *Danir*]

LANGUAGE HERITAGE See ***Scandinavian***

Danish blue *n* a blue-veined cheese with a strong taste, originally produced in Denmark

Danish pastry *n* a rich puff pastry made from a yeast dough with a sweet filling containing fruit or nuts

dank /dangk/ *adj* unpleasantly damp and cold [14C. Probably < N Germanic] —**dankly** *adv* —**dankness** *n*

SYNONYMS See *wet*.

Dankworth /dángk wurth/, **Johnny** (*b.* 1927) British jazz musician, bandleader, and composer. From traditional jazz in the 1950s, he moved through bebop to chamber jazz. With his wife, the singer Cleo Laine, he established the Wavendon All Music Plan (1969). Full name **Dankworth, John Philip William**

D'Annunzio /da nóonssi ō/, **Gabriele** (1863–1938) Italian novelist, poet, and playwright. A supporter of Italian fascism, he headed an unofficial Italian occupation of Fiume, now called Rijeka, in Croatia (1919–20).

danse macabre /daanss mə kaábrə/ (*plural* **danses macabres** /*pronunc. same*/) *n* ARTS same as **dance of death** [Late 19C. < French, 'macabre dance']

danseur /doN súr, daan súr, daaN sőr/ *n* a male ballet dancer [Early 19C. < French, 'male dancer']

danseuse /doN súrz, daan súrz, daaN sőrz/ *n* a female ballet dancer [Early 19C. < French, 'woman dancer']

danshiki /dan sheeki/ (*plural* **-kis**) *n* a brightly coloured loose-fitting garment resembling a long shirt without buttons, worn mainly by men in West Africa [Mid-20C. < Hausa]

Dante /dánti/ (1265–1321) Italian poet. One of the greatest poets in world literature, he is best known for his epic masterpiece *The Divine Comedy*, which he began writing in 1307 and completed shortly before his death. He was involved in the political struggles of his time, and his involvement in politics forced him to leave his native Florence. He finally settled in Ravenna. See Cultural note at **inferno**. Full name **Alighieri, Dante** —**Dantean** /dánti ən, dan tée ən/ *adj, n*

> 'Consider your origins: you were not made to live as brutes, but to follow virtue and knowledge.'
> [Dante, 'Inferno', *The Divine Comedy*; 1307?–21?]

Dantesque /dan tésk/ *adj* in the style of the works of Dante Alighieri

danthonia /dan thóni ə/ *n* a perennial tufted grass that has narrow leaves and small flowers growing closely together along the stem. Native to: Australia, New Zealand. Genus: *Danthonia*. [Early 20C. < modern Latin, after Étienne *Danthoine*, 19C French botanist]

Danton /dántən, daaN toN/, **Georges Jacques** (1759–94) French lawyer. Minister of justice in Revolutionary France, he was overthrown in the Reign of Terror (1793) and guillotined the following year.

> 'Thou wilt show my head to the people: it is worth showing.'
> [Georges Jacques Danton. Quoted in *The French Revolution*, Thomas Carlyle; 1837]

Danube /dán yoob/ longest river in western Europe. It rises in the Black Forest in southwestern Germany and flows through Austria, the Czech Republic, Slovakia, Hungary, Croatia, Yugoslavia, Bulgaria, Romania, and Ukraine. It empties into the Black Sea. Length: 2,850 km/1,770 mi. —**Danubian** /də nyóobi ən/ *adj*

Danville /dánvil/ city in southern Virginia near the North Carolina border. It was the last capital of the Confederacy. Population: 47,596 (2002 estimate).

Danzig /dánssig/ ♦ **Gdansk**

dap /dap/ (**daps, dapping, dapped**) *v* **1.** *vi* FISH WITH BOBBING BAIT to fish by bobbing the bait lightly on the surface of the water **2.** *vi* DIP QUICKLY to dip gently or quickly into water **3.** *vti* BOUNCE OR SKIP to bounce or skip, or cause something to bounce or skip, especially across the surface of water **4.** *vt* JOIN WITH NOTCH to cut a notch in timber in order to join it to another piece [Mid-17C. Probably suggesting the action]

daphne /dáfni/ (*plural* **-nes** or *same*) *n* a cultivated bush with glossy evergreen leaves. Flowers: fragrant, bell-shaped, pink or purplish. Native to: Europe, Asia. Genus: *Daphne*. [15C. < Greek *daphnē* 'laurel, bay tree']

daphnia /dáfni ə/ (*plural* **-as** or *same*) *n* a tiny freshwater flea with a transparent shell and branched antennae for swimming. Some types are used as food for aquarium fish. Genus: *Daphnia*. [Mid-19C. < modern Latin < *Daphne*, nymph in Greek mythology]

Da Ponte /da pónti/, **Lorenzo** (1749–1838) Italian librettist and poet. He wrote the librettos for Wolfgang Amadeus Mozart's *Don Giovanni* (1787) and other operas. He moved to New York City in 1805. Born **Conegliano, Emanuele**

dapper /dáppər/ *adj* **1.** TRIM describes a man who is neat and elegant in dress and manner **2.** LIVELY alert and lively or brisk **3.** NIMBLE small and active or nimble [15C. < Middle Dutch or Middle Low German, 'bold, heavy'] —**dapperly** *adv* —**dapperness** *n*

dapple /dápp'l/ *vti* (**-ples, -pling, -pled**) MARK SOMETHING WITH PATCHES OF COLOUR to mark something with patches or spots of a different colour or with light and shade, or be marked in this way ○ *Sunlight dappled the path through the trees.* ■ *adj* same as **dappled** ■ *n* **1.** COLOURED MARKINGS spots or patches of a different colour, especially on a horse, or of light and shade **2.** SPOT OF COLOUR an individual spot or patch of colour, light, or shade **3.** DAPPLED ANIMAL an animal, especially a horse, with a dappled coat [Late 16C. Back-formation < DAPPLED]

dappled /dápp'ld/ *adj* marked with spots or patches of a different colour or with light and shade ○ *in the dappled shade of the chestnut tree* [15C. Origin ?]

dapple-grey *adj* describes a horse or pony of a light-grey or white colour with darker grey spots or patches ■ *n* (*plural* **dapple-greys**) a dapple-grey horse or pony [14C. Origin ?]

daps /daps/ *npl SW England* light shoes for gymnastics or sport with canvas uppers and rubber soles [Early 20C. Origin ?]

dapsone /dáp sōn/ *n* an antibacterial drug containing sulphur. Use: treatment of leprosy and dermatitis. [Mid-20C. Contraction of *dipara-amino-phenylsulphone*]

darbies /daárbiz/ *npl* a pair of handcuffs (*archaic slang*) [Late 16C. Shortening of *Father Darby's bands*, a restraint for those arrested for debt]

Darby and Joan /daárbi ən jōn/ *n* a man and woman who are devoted to each other and have long lived together in domestic harmony [Late 18C. < a couple in a poem published in the *Gentleman's Magazine* in 1735]

Darby and Joan club *n* a social club for people of advanced years

Darcy /daárssi/, **Les** (1895–1917) Australian boxer. He was a winner of the Australian lightweight, middleweight, and heavyweight championships. Full name **Darcy, James Leslie**

Dard /daard/ *n* somebody who speaks a Dardic language [Mid-19C. < Dardic]

Dardanelles /daárdə nélz/ strait that separates Asian Turkey from the Gallipoli peninsula of European Turkey, and links the Aegean Sea with the Sea of Marmara. Its ancient name is the Hellespont. Length: 70 km/43 mi.

Dardic /daárdik/ *n* a subgroup of Indic languages spoken in northern India and Pakistan. Native speakers: 7 million. —**Dardic** *adj*

dare /dair/ *modal v* (**dares** or **dare, daring, dared**) HAVE ENOUGH COURAGE FOR SOMETHING to have the courage needed to do something ○ *wanted to ask but then didn't dare* ○ *'We must dare to think about "unthinkable things" because when things have become unthinkable, thinking stops and action becomes mindless.'* (William Fulbright *US Senate Speech*; 27 March 1965) ■ *v* **1.** *vti* HAVE AUDACITY TO DO SOMETHING to do something that angers or outrages somebody (*sometimes used as an auxiliary*) ○ *Don't you dare do that!* ○ *How dare you?* **2.** *vt* CHALLENGE SOMEBODY to challenge somebody to do something, usually something dangerous or frightening ○ *daring each other to jump first* ■ *n* CHALLENGE a challenge to somebody to do something dangerous or frightening, or a response to such a challenge ○ *did it for a dare* [Old English *darr, dearr*, forms of *durran* 'dare' < Germanic] —**darer** *n*

daredevil /dáir dev'l/ *n* RISK-TAKER a daring risk-taker, especially somebody who performs dangerous stunts ■ *adj* **1.** UNMINDFUL OF DANGER showing a carefree disregard for risk or danger, especially by performing dangerous stunts **2.** DANGEROUS involving a high degree of risk or danger ○ *a daredevil stunt*

daredevilry /dáir devv'lri/, **daredeviltry** /dáir devv'ltri/ *n* 1. a carefree disregard for risk or danger 2. dangerous acts or stunts performed by a daring person

Dar el-Baida /daár el bídə/ ➧ **Casablanca**

daresay /dáir sáy/ ◇ **I daresay, I dare say** 1. used, often in an irritable tone, to express the fact that the speaker considers something to be likely or possible ○ *And that, I daresay, is the last we'll see of him.* 2. used angrily or impatiently to dismiss something that is true but irrelevant ○ *'That's what they told me at the office'. – 'I daresay, but they often get things wrong'.*

Dar es Salaam /daár ess sə laám/ largest city, leading port, and former capital of Tanzania. The name means 'haven of peace'. Population: 2,545,000 (1999).

darg /daarg/ *n* 1. *Scotland* a day's work (*informal*) 2. *Aus* a specific amount of work [Mid-16C. Shortening and alteration of *daywork*]

dargah /daárgə/ *n* 1. a site where a Muslim holy man was buried or cremated 2. a shrine built at a dargah [< Persian]

daring /dáiring/ *adj* 1. **BRAVE AND ADVENTUROUS** showing a courageous or reckless disregard for danger ○ *The officer led a daring assault on the enemy machine-gun post.* 2. **RISKY** involving an element of risk or danger ○ *a daring move* 3. **SHOCKING** unconventional, different, or innovative in a way that is likely to shock, upset, or offend ■ *n* **BOLDNESS** courage combined with a willingness to take risks or attempt difficult or unconventional things —**daringness** *n*

daringly /dáiringli/ *adv* in a way that involves taking a risk and is likely to be exciting or shocking ○ *She daringly decided to break with tradition.*

dariole /dárri ōl/ *n* 1. *also* **dariole mould** a small cup-shaped mould in which individual portions of a dish can be cooked and then served 2. a dish cooked and served in a dariole [14C. < French, 'custard tart']

Darius I /də rí əss/ (558–486 BC) king of Persia. He reorganized the administration of the Persian Empire during his reign (521–486 BC). His army invaded Greece in 490 but was defeated at the battle of Marathon.

Darius III (380?–330 BC) king of Persia. He was defeated by Alexander the Great at the battles of Issus (333 BC) and Guagamela (331 BC), and was assassinated by one of his own satraps.

Darjeeling[1] /daar jéeling/ *n* a high-quality black tea grown around Darjeeling in India, or a hot drink made from its leaves

Darjeeling[2] /daar jéeling/ town in northern Bangla, India, close to the border with Nepal. Under British rule, it was the summer capital of the government of Bengal. It is famous for its tea estates. Population: 73,062 (1991).

dark /daark/ *adj* 1. **NOT LIGHT OR LIT** having little or no light ○ *It's getting dark; do you mind if I put the light on?* ○ *It was a dark and stormy night.* 2. **NOT LIGHT IN COLOUR** reflecting less light than other colours or shades and therefore appearing deeper, richer, or more sombre ○ *The curtains are dark green.* 3. **BROWNISH OR BLACKISH** not pale or fair, but brown to black in hair or eye colour ○ *She has darker eyes than her brother.* 4. **MISERABLE** characterized by unhappiness, misfortune, or pessimism ○ *in the dark days after her brother's death* 5. **ANGRY** suggesting hostility or anger ○ *dark looks* 6. **NASTY** evil or wicked ○ *the dark side of his character* 7. **MYSTERIOUS** little known or kept hidden from others ○ *dark secrets* 8. **UNENLIGHTENED** lacking enlightenment, learning, and artistic or scientific achievement (*formal*) 9. THEATRE **CLOSED** not open for the presentation of theatrical performances 10. **MELLOW** deep and rich in sound ■ *n* 1. **LACK OF LIGHT** a place, time, or situation in which there is too little light to see properly ○ *I don't like driving in the dark.* 2. **NIGHTFALL** the beginning of night ○ *We left early to be home before dark.* 3. **SHADED AREA** a darker colour or a darker-coloured or shaded part ○ *the contrast between the darks and the lights in the picture* [Old English *deorc* < Indo-European] ◇ **in the dark** ignorant, unaware, or not informed about something ○ *She kept everyone in the dark about her plans.* ◇ **whistle in the dark** to attempt to or pretend to keep up your courage when afraid

Dark /daark/, **Eleanor** (1901–85) Australian writer. She wrote a trilogy of historical novels about the early years of European settlement in Australia, the first of which was *The Timeless Land* (1941). Born **O'Reilly, Eleanor**

dark adaptation, **dark adaption** *n* the reflex changes that enable the eye to continue to see in dim light, e.g. dilation of the pupil and increased sensitivity of the retina —**dark-adapted** *adj*

Dark-Age *adj* relating to, dating from, belonging to, or typical of the Dark Ages

Dark Ages *npl* 1. the period of European history between the fall of the Roman Empire in AD 476 and about AD 1000, for which there are few historical records and during which life was comparatively uncivilized 2. an undeveloped state, way of life, or way of doing things (*informal*) ○ *Computers were in their Dark Ages a few decades ago.*

dark chocolate *n* chocolate that has no added milk and is darker and less sweet than milk chocolate

darken /daárkən/ (**-ens, -ening, -ened**) *vti* 1. to become darker, or make something darker ○ *I mixed a little blue and brown with the red to darken it.* 2. to become unhappy, less hopeful, or angry, or cause such a change in somebody or something ○ *The outlook has darkened considerably since the last update.* —**darkener** *n*

dark energy *n* a hypothetical force that opposes the attraction of gravity throughout the universe and causes the expansion of the universe to accelerate

dark fibre *n* a fibre optic cable that is not transmitting a signal

dark-field illumination *n* the lighting of a specimen in a microscope from the side so that it can be seen against a dark background

dark-field microscope *n* OPTICS same as **ultra-microscope**

dark glasses *npl* spectacles with dark-tinted lenses, especially sunglasses

dark horse *n* 1. **LITTLE-KNOWN PERSON** somebody about whom very little is known or who tends to be reticent, especially somebody who subsequently reveals unexpected talents 2. SPORTS **UNEXPECTEDLY SUCCESSFUL CONTESTANT** a little-known competitor who achieves unexpected success in a race or other sporting contest 3. *N Am* POL **UNEXPECTEDLY SUCCESSFUL CANDIDATE** a candidate who gains an unexpected amount of support in an electoral campaign [< the idea of a little-known racehorse making a surprisingly good showing in a race]

darkie *n* another spelling of **darky** (*dated taboo offensive*)

darkish /daárkish/ *adj* fairly dark in colour or shading ○ *a woman with darkish hair*

dark lantern *n* a lantern with a sliding panel that is used to dim or hide its light

darkle /daárk'l/ (**-kles, -kling, -kled**) *vi* (*archaic or literary*) 1. to grow dark 2. to appear indistinctly [Early 19C. Back-formation < DARKLING]

darkling /daárkling/ (*archaic or literary*) *adv* **IN DARKNESS** in the dark ○ *'Darkling I listen, and full many a time...'* (John Keats, *Ode to a Nightingale*; 1820) ■ *adj* 1. **LACKING CLARITY** dark, dim, or obscure 2. **OCCURRING IN DARKNESS** done or happening in the night [15C. < DARK + -LING[2]]

darkling beetle *n* a beetle with a hard black or brown body whose larvae feed on decaying vegetable matter, living plants, and grain. Family: Tenebrionidae.

darkly /daárkli/ *adv* 1. in a way that conveys a threat or a sense of foreboding 2. in or with black or as a dark-coloured shape ○ *trees darkly outlined against the horizon*

dark matter *n* matter postulated to exist in the universe because of observed gravitational effects. It is thought to comprise a substantial part of the mass of the universe but remains as yet undetected by direct observation.

dark meat *n* meat from the legs and thighs of poultry, which is a darker colour than the meat of the breast

darkness /daárknəss/ *n* 1. the absence or lack of light ○ *He flicked a switch and the room was plunged into darkness.* 2. same as **nighttime** 3. the comparative depth of a colour or its closeness to black

dark reaction *n* the second phase of photosynthesis, which does not require light

darkroom /daárk room, -rŏŏm/ *n* a room from which natural light is excluded so that light-sensitive photographic materials can be safely handled and photographs can be developed

dark rum *n* rum that is brown in colour

darksome /daárksəm/ *adj* lacking light and therefore gloomy or unpleasant (*archaic or literary*) ○ *doomed to die in a darksome dungeon*

dark star *n* a star that is not visible and is usually detectable only by its radio or infrared emissions or by its gravitational effect on other astronomical objects. It is often a component of a binary star and can cause the brightness of its visible partner to vary periodically.

darky /daárki/ (*plural* **-ies**), **darkie** *n* a highly offensive term for a Black person (*dated taboo*)

darling /daárling/ *n* 1. **LOVING TERM OF ADDRESS** used as an affectionate form of address to a loved one, or as a general, informal, and sometimes slightly affected form of address to a social acquaintance 2. **SOMEBODY CONSIDERATE** somebody who is kind, helpful, or likable 3. **INFORMAL TERM OF ADDRESS** an extremely informal and usually suggestive term of address, often to a stranger (*informal*) 4. **FAVOURITE** somebody who is especially popular with somebody else or a group ○ *She's the darling of the literary reviews.* 5. **BELOVED PERSON** a much-loved person or sweetheart (*dated*) ○ *She is my darling.* ■ *adj* 1. **DEARLY LOVED** loved very much 2. **NICE** pretty and charming (*informal*) 3. *also* **darlin'** *Ireland* **SWEET-NATURED** lovable, kind, pleasant, or sweet-natured (*informal*) [Old English *deorling* 'dear person, dear one' < DEAR]

Darling /daárling/ river in southeastern Australia that rises near Toowoomba in southern Queensland and joins the Murray River in New South Wales, forming the country's longest river system. Length: 2,739 km/1,702 mi.

Darling, Grace (1815–42) British hero. The daughter of a lighthouse keeper on the Farne Islands off the coast of Northumberland, she rowed with her father in a storm to rescue shipwrecked sailors (1838). Full name **Darling, Grace Horsley**

Darling Downs fertile tableland in southeastern Queensland, Australia, east of Brisbane. Area: 72,520 sq. km/28,000 sq. mi.

Darling Range range of hills near Perth in Western Australia. Its highest peak is Mount Cooke, 582 m/1,910 ft.

Darlington /daárlingtən/ city and borough in County Durham, northern England. The Stockton and Darlington Railway, the world's first public steam railway line, opened there in 1825. Population: 97,838 (2001).

darmstadtium /daarm státti əm/ *n* a highly unstable radioactive chemical element, produced artificially by nuclear fusion. Symbol **Ds**. See table at **element**

darn[1] /daarn/ *vti* (**darns, darning, darned**) to mend a hole in a piece of clothing or fabric using long interwoven stitches to fill the gap ○ *sat there darning socks* ■ *n* a repair to a piece of clothing or fabric using long interwoven stitches [Early 17C. Probably < French dialect *darner* 'mend' < *darne* 'piece'] —**darner** *n*

darn[2] /daarn/ (*informal*; *euphemistic*) *interj* **EXCLAMATION** used instead of a swearword to express irritation, displeasure, or surprise ■ *adj, adv* **EMPHATIC TERM** used instead of a swearword to give emphasis or to indicate irritation or displeasure with somebody or something ○ *a darn good movie* ■ *vt* (**darns, darning, darned**) **CONDEMN SOMEBODY OR SOMETHING** used to express annoyance or frustration with somebody or something ○ *Darn it, I told you not to go in there.* [Late 18C. Alteration of DAMN]

darned /daarnd/ *adj* used instead of a swearword to express annoyance, surprise, or refusal (*informal*; *euphemistic*) ○ *I'll be darned if I know.* ○ *The darned car won't start.*

darnedest /daárndist/ *adj* most amazing or extraordinary (*informal*; *euphemistic*)

darnel /daárn'l/ *n* a grass commonly found growing as a weed in grain fields. Native to: Europe, Asia. Genus: *Lolium*. [Early 14C. Origin ?]

darning /da´arning/ n **1.** the work of repairing holes in clothing or fabric with long interwoven stitches **2.** clothing or fabric that needs to be darned

darning egg, **darning mushroom** n a piece of wood or plastic shaped like an egg or mushroom, used to support the fabric around a hole that is being darned

darning needle n a long needle with a large eye, used in darning

Darnley /da´arnli/, **Henry Stewart, Lord** (1545–67) Scottish nobleman. He was the second husband of Mary, Queen of Scots, and father of James VI of Scotland, who later became James I of England.

darogha /da´rrōga/ n S Asia somebody in charge of a group of police officers [Mid-17C. < Persian, Urdu *daroga* 'governor']

dart /daart/ n **1.** DARTS MISSILE USED IN GAME a short weighted arrow with a long slender point, a tapered tubular body, and plastic or metal fins that is thrown at a dartboard in the game of darts **2.** ARMS MISSILE USED AS WEAPON a small arrow with a point at one end and feathers or fins at the other that can be thrown, shot from a blowgun, or scattered by an exploding bomb **3.** ZOOL POINTED PROJECTING PART OR ORGAN a pointed projecting body part used, e.g. to penetrate tissue, or, in some species of snail, in mating **4.** FAST MOVE a sudden quick movement ○ *He made a dart for the door.* **5.** HANDICRAFT STITCHED TAPERING FOLD a tapering fold sewn into a garment to make it fit, e.g. at the waist or bust ■ v (**darts, darting, darted**) **1.** vi MOVE SWIFTLY to move suddenly and quickly ○ *The little fish darted under a stone.* **2.** vt MAKE SOMETHING MOVE QUICKLY to move, extend, or direct something suddenly and quickly ○ *She darted a meaningful glance at her press secretary during the meeting with reporters.* [14C. < Old French < Germanic < Indo-European, 'sharp']

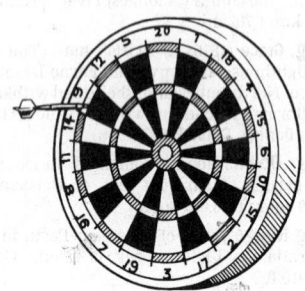

dartboard

dartboard /da´art bawrd/ n a round piece of wood or similar material marked with 20 radiating numbered segments and a bull's eye in the centre, used as a target in the game of darts. The bull's eye has an inner and an outer ring, and the radiating segments have concentric bands representing a triple and a double score.

darter /da´artər/ n **1.** N AMERICAN FISH a brightly-coloured fast-moving freshwater fish of the perch family. Native to: eastern North America. Family: Percidae. **2.** UK, Aus, Can TROPICAL FISH-EATING BIRD a fish-eating diving bird with a long neck and sharp beak. Native to: warmer freshwater regions of the Americas, Africa, Asia, and Australia. Family: Anhingidae. US term **anhinga** **3.** SOMEBODY OR SOMETHING THAT DARTS somebody or something that moves suddenly and quickly

Dartford /da´artfərd/ town and local government district in Kent, southern England. Population: 85,911 (2001).

darting /da´arting/ adj swift and sudden, or making swift and sudden movements ○ *His darting runs down the left flank frequently opened up the Scottish defence.* —**dartingly** adv

Dartmoor /da´art moor/ area in Devon, Southwestern England The highest point is High Wilhays, 621 m/2,038 ft. Area: 954 sq. km/368 sq. mi. [Mid-19C. See DARTMOOR NATIONAL PARK]

Dartmoor National Park national park in Devon, southwestern England, established in 1951

Dartmoor pony n a hardy long-haired pony belonging to a breed originating on Dartmoor in Devon

Dartmouth /da´artməth/ town and seaport in Devon, England. The Royal Naval College is located there. Population: 28,503 (1998).

darts /daarts/ n an indoor game in which players take turns throwing arrow-shaped missiles (**darts**) from a set distance at a circular board (**dartboard**) placed at about eye level on a wall (*takes a singular verb*)

Darwin /da´arwin/ coastal city in northern Australia, capital of the Northern Territory. Population: 86,600 (1998).

Darwin, Charles (1809–82) British naturalist. He laid the foundation of modern evolutionary theory and wrote *On the Origin of Species by Means of Natural Selection* (1859). He wrote many other books on the natural sciences, including *The Volcanic Islands* (1844) and *The Descent of Man* (1871). Full name **Darwin, Charles Robert**

'We must, however, acknowledge, as it seems to me, that man with all his noble qualities...still bears in his bodily frame the indelible stamp of his lowly origin.'
[Charles Darwin, *The Descent of Man*; 1871]

Darwinian /daar winni ən/ adj **1.** RELATING TO DARWIN OR HIS THEORY relating to the 19th-century British naturalist Charles Darwin or his theory of evolution **2.** OF DARWIN, AUSTRALIA relating to the city of Darwin, Australia ■ n **1.** DARWINIST somebody who believes in or advocates Charles Darwin's theory of evolution **2.** also **Darwinite** /da´arwi nīt/ SOMEBODY FROM DARWIN somebody who comes from the city of Darwin, Australia

Darwinian theory n the theory, first developed by the 19th-century British naturalist Charles Darwin, that species of living things originate, evolve, and survive through natural selection in response to environmental forces

Darwinism /da´arwinizəm/ n **1.** BIOL same as **Darwinian theory** **2.** belief in or advocacy of Charles Darwin's theory of evolution —**Darwinist** n, adj

Darwinite /da´arwi nīt/ n PEOPLES same as **Darwinian** n (sense 2)

Darwin's finches npl the birds of the Galapagos Islands on which Charles Darwin based his theory of natural selection through observation of their feeding habits and corresponding differences in beak structure. Subfamily: Geospizinae.

dash /dash/ n **1.** RUSHING MOVEMENT a quick purposeful movement by a person or a group of people in a particular direction ○ *There was a dash for the exit as soon as the alarm was raised.* **2.** SMALL QUANTITY ADDED a small quantity of something added to something else, e.g. to improve the flavour of food or drink or to enliven speech or writing ○ *A dash of common sense would make the arguments a lot more convincing.* **3.** VIGOUR AND VERVE a combination of vigour, daring, and style in the way somebody acts ○ *She carried it off with a certain amount of dash.* **4.** QUICK STROKE a quick and often violent movement, blow, or stroke ○ *with a dash of her arm* **5.** ATHLETICS RACE a short-distance running race **6.** GRAM PUNCTUATION MARK a short horizontal line (–) used as a punctuation mark, often in place of a comma or colon, or as a sign that a letter or word has been omitted **7.** COMMUNICATION MORSE SYMBOL a short horizontal line representing a long sound or flash of light in written transcriptions of Morse code **8.** AUTOMOT DASHBOARD the instrument panel of a car (*informal*) ■ v (**dashes, dashing, dashed**) **1.** vi HURRY OFF to run, move, or travel fast or hastily ○ *He dashed off to catch his plane.* **2.** vt KNOCK OR THROW SOMETHING VIOLENTLY to knock or throw something with a sudden violent sweep or blow (*formal*) ○ *She dashed the papers down on the desk in anger.* **3.** vti SMASH SOMETHING to break or throw something, or be broken or thrown, usually against a hard surface (*formal*) ○ *The waves were dashing against the sea wall.* **4.** vt RUIN SOMETHING to frustrate or destroy something (*often passive*) ○ *The new crisis has dashed all hopes of a speedy return to democratic government.* **5.** vt DISCOURAGE SOMEBODY to make somebody feel discouraged or intimidated (*usually passive*) ○ *I felt more than a little dashed by the ease with which she had refuted my arguments.* **6.** vt ADD SMALL AMOUNT TO SOMETHING to alter, improve, or flavour something

with a small amount of another substance (*often passive*) ○ *tonic water dashed with bitters* **7.** vt EXPRESS IRRITATION WITH SOMEBODY OR SOMETHING used to express annoyance or dissatisfaction with somebody or something (*dated informal*) ○ *Dash it, I've already paid the man!* [13C. Origin ?] ◇ **cut a dash** to be dressed smartly and stylishly so as to attract attention (*dated*) ◇ **do your dash** Aus to use up all your energy in an effort or attempt at something (*informal*)

USAGE **Dashes** are used in pairs around text that adds extra information and can be omitted without affecting the structure of the sentence: *He drives to Portland and back—a round trip of 600 miles—at least once a week.* **Commas** and **brackets** can be used for the same purpose, and are often preferable in formal contexts, but dashes (used sparingly) are a stronger means of separating and have the effect of drawing attention to the extra information. Similarly, a dash may be used instead of a *colon* to introduce something that explains or elaborates on what has gone before: *Unemployment in the town has fallen to 3,000—a drop of almost 20%.* In contexts like these there are no spaces between the dashes and the text they interrupt. A dash can also be used in place of omitted letters, e.g., to avoid mentioning a person's full name: *Mr J— accused Ms D— of lying.* The long dash is also called an *em dash*. A shorter *en dash* is used to separate dates: *2010–20.*

dash off vt to write, draw, or compose something in a great hurry (*informal*) ○ *She dashed off a note to her secretary before leaving the office.*

dashboard /dash´bawrd/ n **1.** a panel in front of the driver of a vehicle or the pilot of a small aircraft or boat that contains various indicator dials, switches, and controls **2.** a board, panel, or screen to protect the driver of a horse-drawn carriage from being splashed with mud [Mid-19C. < DASH in the obsolete sense 'splash, spatter']

dashed /dasht/ past participle, past tense of **dash** ■ adv used to add emphasis to an adjective or adverb (*dated informal*) ○ *You see it's dashed awkward, because I've already promised to take Emmy.* ■ adj used to express annoyance or dissatisfaction (*dated informal*) ○ *It's a dashed shame they lost.*

dasheen /da shéen/ n Carib **1.** tubers of the taro plant, usually boiled for eating **2.** PLANTS same as **taro** [Late 19C. Origin ?]

dasheki n CLOTHING another spelling of **dashiki**

dasher /dash´ər/ n a device that agitates or stirs the contents of a churn or ice-cream maker

dashi /da´shi/ n a clear broth or stock, usually made from fish [Mid-20C. < Japanese]

dashiki /də shéeki/, **daishiki**, **dasheki** n a brightly coloured loose-fitting garment resembling a long shirt without buttons, worn mainly by men in Africa, the Caribbean, and the United States [Mid-20C. Probably < Yoruba *danshiki*]

dashing /da´shing/ adj (*dated*) **1.** smartly dressed and stylish ○ *That's a rather dashing outfit, if I may say so.* **2.** confident and full of bravado and spirit ○ *a dashing young officer* —**dashingly** adv —**dashingness** n

dashpot /dash´ pot/ n a device consisting of a piston inside a fluid-filled cylinder that absorbs or dampens vibrations in a mechanism

Dassera n HINDUISM same as **Dussehra**

dassie /da´ssi/ n **1.** ZOOL same as **rock hyrax 2.** S Africa a silvery fish with a black stripe on its tail. Native to: southern Africa. Latin name: *Diplodus sargus capensis.* [Late 18C. Via Afrikaans < Dutch *dasje* 'small badger' < *das* 'badger']

dastardly /da´stərdli/ adj nasty, treacherous, or cowardly (*dated or humorous*) ○ *a dastardly deed* [Late 16C. < *dastard*, probably < *dast*, a past participle of DAZE] —**dastardliness** n

dasyure /da´ssi yoor/ n a small usually carnivorous marsupial. Native to: Australia, Tasmania, neighbouring islands. Subfamily: Dasyurinae. [Mid-19C. Via French < modern Latin *dasyurus* < Greek *dasus* 'rough, hairy' + *oura* 'tail']

DAT /de´e ay te´e, dat/ abbr COMPUT digital audio tape

data /da´ytə, da´atə/ n (*takes a singular or plural verb*) **1.** △ information, often in the form of facts or figures obtained from experiments or surveys, used as a

basis for making calculations or drawing conclusions **2.** ⚠ information, e.g. numbers, text, images, and sounds, in a form that is suitable for storage in or processing by a computer ■ plural of **datum** [Mid-17C. < plural of Latin *datum*, neuter past participle of *dare* 'give, grant']

USAGE Data – singular or plural? Because the meaning of ***data*** is much like that of the singular noun *information*, and because its Latin *-a* plural announces the word's plural status less plainly than a final *s* would, ***data*** is often treated as if it were singular. This use is extremely common, and few perceive it as wrong these days, especially given the word's connotation of a collection or single unit made up of many informational subunits. All the same, in formal or technical contexts, *Our data have been assembled over a number of years* would be regarded as correct, and constructions such as *very little data, the data shows...*, and *a great deal of data* would be regarded as incorrect.

data bank *n* **1.** a large store of information, especially kept in or available to a computer, sometimes consisting of several databases **2.** COMPUT same as **database**

database /dáytə bayss/ *n* a systematically arranged collection of computer data, structured so that it can be automatically retrieved or manipulated ■ *vt* to input data into a database

database management system *n* a computer program devised to create, store, and manipulate databases

data capture *n* the collecting and entering of data in a computer, or the conversion of data into a form compatible with computers

data compression *n* the encoding of data so that it requires less disk space for storage and less time for transmission

data element *n* the smallest meaningful piece of information in an electronic business transaction (*used in e-commerce*)

data fusion *n* the integration of data and knowledge collected from disparate sources by different methods into a consistent, accurate, and useful whole

dataglove /dáytə gluv/ *n* a glove with sensors that feed spatial and tactile data to a computer, allowing the wearer to manipulate and explore virtual reality

data mining *n* the locating of previously unknown patterns and relationships within data using a database application, e.g. the locating of customers with common interests in a retail establishment's database

dataport /dáytə pawrt/ *n* a socket for connecting a laptop computer to the Internet

data processing *n* the entering, storing, updating, and retrieving of information using a computer

data protection *n* **1.** legal safeguards to prevent misuse of information stored on computers, particularly information about individual people **2.** the adoption of administrative, technical, or physical deterrents to safeguard computer data

data set *n* a computer file

datasheet /dáytə sheet/ *n* a document accessible on the Internet that gives a detailed description of something, especially a product

data warehouse *n* a database used for analysing overall business strategy rather than routine operations

datcha *n* BUILDINGS another spelling of **dacha**

date[1] /dayt/ *n* **1.** DAY, MONTH, AND YEAR a phrase or string of numbers that denotes a specific day of the month or year. It usually consists of the number of the day, the name or number of the month, and the number of the year. **2.** TIME OF EVENT a date used to locate a past or future event in time ○ *The concert has been postponed to a later date.* **3.** VISUAL REPRESENTATION OF DATE the words or numbers of a date in the form of a written statement or inscription, e.g. on a document or coin ○ *There's no date on this letter.* **4.** PERIOD OF TIME the period during which something such as a work of art was created ○ *This has much in common with other artefacts of the same date.* **5.** APPOINTMENT an appointment to meet somebody for a social or business activity ○ *I've got a dinner date with a client.* **6.** ROMANTIC APPOINTMENT a romantic engagement with somebody ○ *I thought we had a date tonight.* **7.** PARTNER ON DATE somebody with whom a date has been arranged ○ *My date stood me up.* **8.** ARTS COMMITMENT TO PERFORM an engagement to give a performance ○ *Our band has a date to play at the Coliseum.* ■ **dates** *npl* DATES OF BIRTH AND DEATH the years of somebody's birth and death ○ *Do you happen to know Van Gogh's dates?* ■ *v* (**dates, dating, dated**) **1.** *vt* PUT DATE ON SOMETHING to mark something with a date, usually the current date ○ *Please sign and date the contract.* **2.** *vt* ASSIGN DATE TO SOMETHING to find out or state the time or period when something was made ○ *The early works of Shakespeare are rather difficult to date precisely.* **3.** *vi* ORIGINATE to have an origin in a particular time in the past ○ *We have family records dating back to the 16th century.* **4.** *vi* GO OUT OF STYLE to become old-fashioned ○ *This is a classic style and won't date.* **5.** *vt* MAKE SOMEBODY OR SOMETHING SEEM OLD to reveal the age of somebody or something, or make somebody or something seem old-fashioned ○ *The shape of the headlights dates the car.* **6.** *vti* GO ON DATES WITH SOMEBODY to go out regularly with somebody as a romantic partner ○ *We dated for a few months.* [14C. < medieval Latin *data* < past participle of Latin *dare* 'give, grant'; from uses such as *(epistola) data Romae* '(letter) given at Rome', with the day and month appended] —**datable** *adj* ◇ **to date** up to the present time

date[2] /dayt/ *n* **1.** a dark-coloured oval fruit that has sweet flesh and a single hard narrow seed **2.** TREES same as **date palm** **3.** *Aus* a highly offensive term for the anus (*taboo*) [13C. Via Old French < Greek *daktulos* 'finger or toe, date']

datebook /dáyt bòòk/ *n N Am* a diary in which social engagements and other things to be remembered are noted

dated /dáytid/ *adj* **1.** no longer used or in vogue, often having been current or fashionable in the recent past **2.** marked with a date

dateless /dáytləss/ *adj* **1.** unlikely to become old-fashioned or obsolete **2.** limitless in time (*archaic or literary*) ○ *'For precious friends hid in death's dateless night'* (William Shakespeare, *Sonnets*; 1609)

dateline /dáyt līn/ *n* a line at the head of a newspaper article or similar item giving the date and place of writing

Date Line *n* TIME same as **International Date Line**

date palm *n* a tall palm tree with feathery fronds, cultivated for its fruit. Native to: North Africa, western Asia. Latin name: *Phoenix dactylifera.*

date rape *n* an act of rape committed against somebody during or after a date —**date-rape** *vt*

date stamp *n* a rubber stamp used to mark the date on something, or the date marked by such a stamp —**date-stamp** *vt*

Datin /daátin/ *n* in Malaysia, the title of a woman member of a senior order of chivalry [< Malay]

dating agency /dáyting-/ *n* a business that finds potential romantic partners for people

dating service *n* LEISURE same as **dating agency**

dative /dáytiv/ *n* **1.** a grammatical form (**case**) that identifies the source, agent, or instrument of action of the verb in some inflected languages and that affects nouns, pronouns, and adjectives **2.** a word or phrase in the dative [15C. < Latin *dativus* 'of giving' < *dat-*, past participle of *dare* 'give, grant'] —**dative** *adj*

dative bond *n* CHEM same as **coordinate bond** [Because one atom gives up electrons to another]

datolite /dáttə līt/ *n* a hydrated silicate containing calcium and boron. Source: igneous rocks. [Early 19C. < Greek *dateisthai* 'divide'; from the divisions between its crystals]

Datuk /daátək/ *n* in Malaysia, the title of a man who is a member of a senior order of chivalry [Mid-19C. < Malay *datok*]

datum /dáytəm, daá-/ (*plural* **-ta** /-tə/) *n* **1.** ITEM OF INFORMATION a piece of information **2.** LOGIC GIVEN FACT a known or assumed fact that is used as the basis for a theory, conclusion, or inference **3.** (*plural* **datums**) MAPS POINT OF REFERENCE a point, line, or surface used as a basis for measurement or calculation in mapping or surveying [Mid-18C. < Latin (see DATA)]

datum line, datum level, datum plane *n* the horizontal line or plane from which all other heights and depths are measured or calculated on a map or chart

DATV /dáy tee veé/ *abbr* MEDIA digitally assisted television

daub /dawb/ *v* (**daubs, daubing, daubed**) **1.** *vt* APPLY SOMETHING BLOTCHILY to put or spread a semiliquid substance such as mud, paint, or cream, on a surface in a crude, hurried, or irregular way ○ *They had daubed slogans all over the walls.* **2.** *vti* PAINT CRUDELY to paint or apply paint crudely and inexpertly ■ *n* **1.** BLOTCH OF SUBSTANCE a patch, splash, or smear of a semiliquid substance applied to something in a crude, hurried, or irregular way **2.** BAD PAINTING a painting that is considered to be crudely or inexpertly done ○ *'When he first came to Rome he painted worthless daubs and gave no promise of talent.'* (Henry James, *Roderick Hudson*; 1876) **3.** CONSTR SUBSTANCE FOR DAUBING a mixture of clay, lime, and chopped straw plastered onto interwoven rods or twigs to make a wall [14C. Via Old French *dauber* < Latin *dealbare* 'whiten over, plaster' < *albare* 'whiten' < *albus* 'white'] —**dauber** *n* —**dauby** *adj*

daube /dōb/ *n* in French cookery, a dish of braised meat or vegetables, especially a traditional French dish of beef braised in wine [Early 18C. < French, via Italian *dobba* < Catalan *a la adoba* 'stewed' < Germanic, 'to strike']

Daubigny /dṓbinyi/, **Charles-François** (1817–78) French painter and etcher. He was a landscape painter associated with the Barbizon School whose work influenced the impressionists.

daud /dawd/ *Scotland n* a lump, chunk, or stiff dollop of something ■ *vt* (**dauds, dauding, dauded**) to knock or thump something [Late 16C. Probably an imitation of a thumping sound]

Daudet /dṓ day/, **Alphonse** (1840–97) French writer. His works include *Lettres de mon moulin* (1869). Full name **Daudet, Louis Marie Alphonse**

> 'During the day beings live, at night things live.'
> [Alphonse Daudet, 'Les Étoiles' '(The Stars)', *Lettres de mon moulin (Letters from my Mill)*; 1869]

daughter /dáwtər/ *n* **1.** FEMALE CHILD somebody's female child **2.** WOMAN OR GIRL CONNECTED WITH PLACE a woman or girl considered as a product of a place or institution (*formal*) ○ *daughter of the church* **3.** PRODUCT OF SOMETHING something produced by or issuing from something else (*literary*) ○ *Truth is the daughter of time.* **4.** DESCENDANT a woman or girl descendant (*literary*) ○ *a daughter of Eve* **5.** PHYS NUCLIDE FORMED BY RADIOACTIVE DECAY a nuclide formed from an element by radioactive decay ■ *adj* **1.** FORMED FROM SOMETHING ELSE formed by or from a similar thing, usually retaining close links with it and sometimes remaining subordinate to it **2.** BEING OFFSPRING produced by a process of reproduction, replication, or division [Old English *dohtor* < Indo-European] —**daughterless** *adj*

daughterboard /dáwtər bawrd/ *n* a printed circuit board that plugs into a motherboard, usually to improve the performance of a system or add function

daughter cell *n* either of the identical cells produced when a living cell divides

daughter-in-law (*plural* **daughters-in-law**) *n* the wife of somebody's son

daughterly /dáwtərli/ *adj* typical or expected of a daughter ○ *She came to regard the distinguished professor with an almost daughterly affection.* —**daughterliness** *n*

Daughters of the American Revolution *npl* in the United States, a women's patriotic society founded in 1890 by descendants of those who fought in the War of American Independence. It has about 200,000 members and is based in Washington, DC.

Daumier /dṓ mi ay/, **Honoré** (1808–79) French painter and caricaturist. He is known for his satirical caricatures of contemporary society and politics.

daunder *n, vi N England, Scotland* same as **dander**[2]

daunt /dawnt/ (**daunts, daunting, daunted**) *vt* to make somebody feel anxious, intimidated, or discouraged (*usually passive*) ○ *The scale of the task would have daunted even the most experienced organizer.* [13C.

Via Anglo-Norman *daunter* < Latin *domitare* 'to tame'] — **daunter** *n*

daunting /dáwnting/ *adj* likely to discourage, intimidate, or frighten somebody ○ *You'll find the task less daunting if you divide it up into manageable sections.* —**dauntingly** *adv*

dauntless /dáwntless/ *adj* unlikely or unable to be frightened or discouraged ○ *We remember with admiration their dauntless courage and optimism.* —**dauntlessly** *adv* —**dauntlessness** *n*

dauphin /dáwfin, dṓ-/ *n* in former times, the eldest son of the king of France and the direct heir to the throne [15C. < French, in Old French *daulphin* (see DOLPHIN); because of dolphins on a relevant coat of arms]

ORIGIN The title *dauphin* originally belonged to the lords of the Viennois, an area in the southeast of France, whose coat of arms incorporated three dolphins. After the Viennois province of Dauphiné was sold by Charles of Valois to the French crown in 1343, the king gave it to his eldest son, and from then on all eldest sons of the French monarch inherited it, along with the title *dauphin*.

dauphine /dáw feen, dṓ-/, **dauphiness** /dáwfi ness, dṓ-/ *n* (plural **-phines** /-feen/; plural **-esses**) the wife of the dauphin ■ *adj* prepared by mixing mashed potato with choux pastry dough and forming the mixture into balls or cylinders, which are then coated with breadcrumbs and deep-fried ○ *dauphine potatoes* [Mid-19C. < French, feminine form of *dauphin* (see DAUPHIN)]

dauphinois /dṓfin waaz/, **dauphinoise** *adj* thinly sliced and baked in milk or cream, sometimes with garlic or cheese ○ *potatoes dauphinois* [< French, 'from the Dauphiné province']

Davao /də vów/ city on Mindanao island in the southern Philippines. Population: 1,191,000 (1995)

daven /daá ven/ (**davens, davening, davened**) *vti* to recite prayers from the Jewish liturgies [Mid-20C. < Yiddish *davnen* 'pray']

Davenant, **Sir William** (1606–68) English poet and dramatist. His works include the comic play *The Wits* (1633) and the epic poem *Gondibert* (1651). His notable theatrical innovations include an early English opera, movable scenery, and the introduction of women actors. He was appointed poet laureate in 1638.

davenport /dávv'n pawrt/ *n* **1.** an ornamental writing desk with a sloping top and drawers in its sides **2.** *N Am* a large well-upholstered sofa, especially one that can be converted into a bed [Mid-19C. Origin ?]

David /dáyvid/, **St** (520?–589?) patron saint of Wales. A missionary in Wales and southwestern England, he is thought to have founded 12 monasteries, including Glastonbury in Somerset.

David (d. 962 BC) king of Judah. During his reign (1000–962 BC), he defeated the Philistines, conquered Jerusalem, and became the ruler of Israel.

David, **Sir Edgeworth** (1858–1934) Welsh-born Australian geologist and explorer. He was a member of Ernest Henry Shackleton's 1907 Antarctic expedition and leader of the first party to reach the South Magnetic Pole (1908). Full name **David, Sir Tannatt William Edgeworth**

David, **Elizabeth** (1913–92) British food researcher and writer. Her many books include *Mediterranean Food* (1950) and *English Bread and Yeast Cookery* (1977).

David /da veéd/, **Jacques-Louis** (1748–1825) French painter. His neoclassical romantic style, as displayed in his *Death of Marat* (1793), made him the favoured painter of French Revolutionary leaders and of Napoleon I.

'To give a body and a perfect form to your thought, this alone is what it is to be an artist.'
[Jacques-Louis David, *Statement to his pupils, Le peintre Louis David 1748–1825: Souvenirs et documents inédits*; 1880]

Davies /dáyviss/, **Paul Charles William** (b. 1946) British-born Australian physicist. He was professor of natural philosophy at the University of Adelaide, Australia, and author of *The Mind of God* (1992).

'Chaos evidently provides us with a bridge

between the laws of physics and the laws of chance.'
[Paul Charles William Davies, *New Scientist Guide to Chaos*; 1991]

Davies, **Sir Peter Maxwell** (b. 1934) British composer and conductor. His works, which include the operas *The Lighthouse* (1980) and *Resurrection* (1987), often deal with apocalyptic themes.

Davies, **Robertson** (1913–95) Canadian novelist, essayist, and playwright. His books include *The Salterton Trilogy* (1951–58), *The Deptford Trilogy* (1970–75), and *The Cornish Trilogy* (1981–88). *What's Bred in the Bone* (1985) was short-listed for the Booker Prize.

'Our age has robbed millions of the simplicity of ignorance, and has so far failed to lift them to simplicity of wisdom.'
[Robertson Davies, *A Voice from the Attic*; 1960]

Davies, **W. H.** (1871–1940) British poet. His works include *The Soul's Destroyer* (1905) and *The Autobiography of a Super Tramp* (1907). As a young man, he spent some years living on the road in Britain and the United States before settling down to writing. Full name **Davies, William Henry**

'What is this life if, full of care, / We have no time to stand and stare?'
[W. H. Davies, 'Leisure', *Songs of Joy*; 1911]

da Vinci ▸ **Leonardo da Vinci**

Bette Davis

Davis /dáyviss/, **Bette** (1908–89) US film actor. She won the Academy Award for best actress for *Dangerous* (1985) and *Jezebel* (1938). Full name **Davis, Ruth Elizabeth**

Davis, **Jefferson** (1808–89) US politician. He was the first and only president of the Confederate States of America (1861–65).

'All we ask is to be let alone.'
[Jefferson Davis, *Inaugural Address as president of the Confederate States of America*; 18 February 1861]

Davis, **Davys, John** (1550?–1605) English navigator. While searching for a northwestern route between Europe and the Indies, he sailed through the present-day Davis Strait (1587).

Davis, **Judy** (b. 1955) Australian actor. She is noted for her performances on stage and in films including *My Brilliant Career* (1979) and *Husbands and Wives* (1992).

Miles Davis

Davis, **Miles** (1926–91) US jazz trumpeter and composer. A consummate improviser, he pioneered a

more understated form of bebop known as 'cool jazz'. He was also noted for incorporating electronic instruments into jazz and combining jazz and rock. Full name **Miles Dewey Davis III**

'You can tell the way I play by the way I stand.'
[Miles Davis. Quoted in *Black Talk*, Ben Sidan; 1971]

Davis, **Sammy, Jr.** (1925–90) US singer, actor, and dancer. One of the most popular and successful US entertainers of his time, he was well known for his exuberant performances on stage and in films such as *Ocean's Eleven* (1960), as well as for his encounters with racism.

Davis Cup *n* **1.** an annual international men's tennis competition for which a trophy is awarded to the winning nation **2.** the trophy awarded to the winning nation in the Davis Cup competition [Early 20C. After Dwight Filley *Davis*, who donated the trophy]

Davison /dáyviss'n/, **Emily** (1872–1913) British suffragette. Protesting against women's exclusion from the franchise, she died from injuries sustained when trying to catch the reins of a racehorse owned by King George V during the Epsom Derby.

Davis Strait body of water separating Baffin Island, Canada, from Greenland, and forming the entrance to Baffin Bay. Depth: 3,660 m/11,900 ft.

davit /dávvit/ *n* a small crane at the side of a ship's deck, especially one of a pair of curved metal posts with tackle attached for suspending and lowering a lifeboat [15C. < Anglo-Norman *daviot, daviet* < the name *Davi* 'David']

Davitt /dávvit/, **Michael** (1846–1906) Irish nationalist leader. He was imprisoned (1870–77) for nationalist activities, and founded the Land League (1879), which opposed absentee landlords.

Davos /dávvoss/ mountain resort in Graubünden Canton, eastern Switzerland. Population: 11,325 (1998).

Davy /dáyvi/, **Sir Humphry** (1778–1829) British chemist. He is best known as the inventor of the miner's safety lamp (**Davy lamp**)(1815). He also discovered the use of nitrous oxide as an anaesthetic and identified several metallic elements.

Davy Jones *n* the personification of the sea

Davy Jones's locker *n* the bottom of the sea, especially considered as the final resting place of drowned sailors or sunken ships (*informal*)

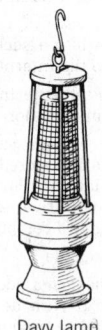
Davy lamp

Davy lamp /dáyvi-/ *n* a portable oil-burning lamp, formerly used by miners, in which the flame is protected by metal gauze to prevent it from igniting explosive gases underground [Early 19C. After Sir Humphry DAVY]

Davys ▸ **Davis, John**

daw /daw/ *n* BIRDS same as **jackdaw** (*archaic or regional*) [15C. Probably < assumed Old English *dawe* < Germanic]

dawdle /dáwd'l/ (**-dles, -dling, -dled**) *vi* **1.** to walk or move slowly and reluctantly or idly ○ *We'll get there in time if you don't dawdle.* **2.** to spend far more time than is necessary in doing something ○ *We dawdled over lunch.* [Mid-17C. Origin ?] —**dawdler** *n* —**dawdling** *n, adj* —**dawdlingly** *adv*

Dawkins /dáwkinz/, **Richard** (b. 1941) British evolutionary biologist. He is best known for his book *The Selfish Gene* (1976), which describes the gene's

strategy for survival. He developed his arguments in *The Blind Watchmaker* (1986).

> 'It is raining DNA outside. On the bank of the Oxford canal at the bottom of my garden is a large willow tree, and it is pumping downy seeds into the air...It is raining instructions out there; it's raining programs; it's raining tree-growing, fluff-spreading algorithms. That is not a metaphor, it is the plain truth. It couldn't be any plainer if it were raining floppy disks.'
> [Richard Dawkins, *The Blind Watchmaker*; 1986]

dawl /dawl/ *n regional* the smallest or weakest piglet in a litter [Origin ?]

REGIONAL NOTE See ***underling***.

dawn /dawn/ *n* **1. DAYBREAK** the first appearance of light in the sky as the Sun rises at the beginning of a new day **2. BEGINNING** the beginning of something, especially a period of time or history ○ *the dawn of the industrial era* ■ *vi* (**dawns, dawning, dawned**) **1. BEGIN** to begin, as the sun rises and light appears in the sky (*refers to a new day*) ○ *The day dawned cloudy and wet.* **2. BECOME APPARENT** to begin to be perceived ○ *The realization dawned that few would survive.* **3. START TO EXIST** to begin to develop or exist (*literary*) [15C. Back-formation (as verb) < DAWNING]
dawn on *vt* to come into the mind or consciousness of somebody ○ *It was some time before the seriousness of the situation dawned on them.*

dawn chorus *n* **1.** the loud singing of many birds as the first light of day appears in the sky **2.** any loud sound, especially from a number of different sources, occurring very early in the morning (*humorous*) ○ *a dawn chorus of power drills and hammering*

dawning /dáwning/ *n* the beginning of a new day or of a new period of time or history ○ *with the dawning of the computer age* ■ *adj* beginning to appear, develop, or be perceived [13C. Alteration of obsolete *dawing* < Old English *dagian* 'dawn, become day' < Germanic]

dawn raid *n* **1.** a surprise attack on enemy troops at dawn **2.** a surprise attempt to buy a large number of a company's shares at the start of a day's trading, especially as a first stage in a takeover bid

dawn redwood *n* a deciduous tree with flat leaves and small round cones, widely grown as an ornamental. Native to: China. Latin name: *Metasequoia glyptostroboides*.

Dawson /dáwss'n/ river in eastern Queensland, Australia, that rises in the Carnarvon Range and flows into the Mackenzie and Fitzroy rivers near the town of Duaringa. Length: 640 km/398 mi.

DAX /daks/ *n* a share index on the Frankfurt Stock Exchange. Full form **Deutsche Aktienindex**

day /day/ *n* **1. 24 HOURS** a period of 24 hours, usually beginning and ending at midnight **2. SUNRISE TO SUNSET** the part of a 24-hour period when it is light, between sunrise and sunset **3. TIME OF ACTIVITY** the part of a 24-hour period when somebody is working or active ○ *I work an 8-hour day.* **4. INDEFINITE PERIOD OR POINT IN TIME** a time or period of time in the past, present, or future ○ *One of these days we'll get round to painting the house.* **5. TIME OF FAME** the time when a particular person or thing is well known, popular, successful, or effective ○ *In her day she was one of our best-known Shakespearean actors.* **6. LIFE OR EXISTENCE** the time when a particular person or thing is active or in existence ○ *In my day we had to work on Saturday mornings.* **7. PERIOD OF EARTH'S ROTATION ABOUT AXIS** a unit of time equal to the Earth's period of rotation about its axis, measured either relative to the Sun (**solar day**) or the stars (**sidereal day**) **8.** ASTRON **PERIOD OF PLANET'S ROTATION ABOUT AXIS** the period of time in which a planet revolves once on its axis [Old English *dæg* < Indo-European] ◇ **call it a day** to finish work or stop doing something ◇ **carry** *or* **win the day** to gain a victory ◇ **day after day** for several or many days in a row ◇ **day by day 1.** each consecutive day **2.** progressively ◇ **day in, day out** every day without exception and all day long ◇ **have a nice day** *US* used for wishing somebody well when parting ◇ **have seen better days** to be in a less prosperous or less good condition than previously ◇ **in this day and age** nowadays, as opposed to past times and customs ◇ **it's early days** things are at an early stage and it is uncertain how they will develop or turn out ◇ **make somebody's day** to make somebody very happy ◇ **name the day** to set a date for something, typically a wedding ◇ **save the day** to prevent defeat or disaster ◇ **somebody's** *or* **something's days are numbered** expresses the opinion that somebody or something will not survive much longer ◇ **that'll be the day!** expresses the opinion that something is most unlikely to happen (*informal*) ○ *You think they'll offer me Mike's job? That'll be the day!* ◇ **the other day** not long ago ◇ **those were the days!** expresses affection and nostalgia for past times

Day /day/, **Doris** (*b.* 1924) US film actor and singer. She came to fame in the late 1950s with roles in light musicals and romantic comedies such as *Calamity Jane* (1953) and *Pillow Talk* (1959), for which she received an Academy Award nomination. Born **Kappelhoff, Doris von**

Dayak *n* PEOPLES another spelling of **Dyak**

Dayan /dī án/ *n* the judge of the Beth Din, a Jewish religious court [Late 19C. < Hebrew < *dān* 'to judge']

Dayan /dī án/, **Moshe** (1915–81) Israeli general and politician. He was chief of Israel's general staff (1953–58) and defence minister (1967–74). He resigned after criticism over the Yom Kippur War (1973–74), but became foreign minister in 1977, resigning again in 1979 in protest at Menachem Begin's policies concerning the West Bank.

> 'Whenever you accept our views we shall be in full agreement with you.'
> [Moshe Dayan, *Observer*; 14 August 1977]

day bed *n* a couch or bed for reclining on during the day

day blindness *n* the inability to see clearly in bright light with comparatively good vision in dim light. Technical name **hemeralopia**

daybook /dáy bòok/ *n* a book in which financial transactions are recorded day by day

dayboy /dáy boy/ *n* a boy who is a pupil at a residential school but lives at home

daybreak /dáy brayk/ *n* the time when light first appears in the sky at the beginning of a day

daycare /dáy kair/ *n* daytime supervision and recreational or medical facilities for preschool children, disabled people, or elderly people wanting special assistance

day centre *n* a place providing nonresidential care or recreation for senior citizens, people with physical disabilities, or people with psychiatric disorders

daydream /dáy dreem/ *n* **1. DREAM EXPERIENCED WHILE AWAKE** a series of often distracting and usually pleasant thoughts and images that pass through the mind while awake **2. UNREALIZABLE HOPE OR FANTASY** a pleasant wish or hope that is unlikely to be fulfilled ■ *vi* (**-dreams, -dreaming, -dreamt** /-dremt/ *or* **-dreamed**) **THINK DISTRACTING THOUGHTS** to have or indulge in daydreams —**daydreaming** *n* —**daydreamy** *adj*

daydreamer /dáy dreemər/ *n* somebody regarded as inattentive or unrealistic

dayflower /dáy flowər/ *n* a tropical plant with narrow pointed leaves. Flowers: blue or purplish, soon wilting. Genus: *Commelina*. [Late 17C. Because the flowers last for only one day]

dayfly /dáy flī/ (*plural* **-flies**) *n* INSECTS same as **mayfly** (sense 1) [Early 17C. Because it lives for only one day]

daygirl /dáy gurl/ *n* a girl who is a pupil at a residential school but lives at home

Day-Glo /dáy glō/ *tdmk* a trademark for fluorescent dyes and colouring agents

day hospital *n* a nonresidential hospital or part of a hospital where patients go for treatment or therapy during the daytime

day job *n* a job that somebody does merely to earn an income while trying to achieve success in another field, especially the arts

day labourer *n* a manual worker who is hired and paid on a day-to-day basis —**day labour** *n*

Day-Lewis /day lòo iss/, **Cecil** (1904–72) Irish-born British poet and novelist. His poetry includes *A Time to Dance* (1935) and *Poems in Wartime* (1940). The poet laureate (1968–72), he also wrote works of literary criticism, and published detective stories under the name Nicholas Blake.

> 'Now the peak of summer's past, the sky is overcast / And the love we swore would last for an age seems deceit.'
> [Cecil Day-Lewis, *Hornpipe*; 1943]

Day-Lewis, Daniel (*b.* 1957) British-born Irish stage and film actor. He won an Academy Award for best actor in *My Left Foot* (1989).

daylight /dáy līt/ *n* **1. SUNLIGHT** natural light from the sun ○ *Open the curtains and let in a bit of daylight.* **2. DAYTIME** the part of the day when it is light **3. DAYBREAK** the time when light first appears in the sky at the beginning of a day **4. PUBLIC AWARENESS** public knowledge, notice, or scrutiny ○ *There are some secrets that they would prefer not to have exposed to daylight.* **5. VISIBLE GAP** a visible gap between competitors in a race, showing the lead that one has over the other ○ *There's definitely daylight now between the two boats as they approach the halfway mark.* ◇ **beat** *or* **knock** *or* **scare** *or* **frighten the living daylights out of somebody** to beat or frighten somebody very severely (*informal*) ◇ **in broad daylight** in open daylight for all to see

daylight lamp *n* a lamp that gives light with a range of wavelengths similar to natural light

daylight robbery *n* the charging of prices that seem far too high (*informal*) N Am term **highway robbery**

daylight-saving time *n* an adjustment of clock time to allow more hours of normal daylight. Clocks are usually set one hour ahead of standard time to achieve this.

day lily *n* a perennial summer flowering plant with long slender leaves. Flowers: large yellow, red, or orange, resembling those of the lily, usually dying after one day. Genus: *Hemerocallis*.

daylong /dáy long/ *adj, adv* throughout the entire day

day-neutral *adj* used to describe plants that mature and flower unaffected by the length of the daylight period they grow in

day-night match *n* a one-day cricket match that begins in the early afternoon in natural light and continues into the evening under artificial light

day nursery *n* a place where preschool children are looked after during the daytime, usually while their parents are at work

Day of Atonement *n* JUDAISM same as **Yom Kippur**

day off (*plural* **days off**) *n* a day on which somebody does not have to work

Day of Judgment *n* JUD-CHR same as **Judgment Day**

day of reckoning *n* a time when somebody is made to answer for crimes or mistakes

day one *n* the first day or the very beginning of something (*informal*) ○ *It's day one of the electoral campaign.*

day out (*plural* **days out**) *n* a day of leisure spent away from home

daypack /dáy pak/ *n* a small rucksack or bag for carrying things needed during the day

day release *n* a system that allows employees to take days off work without loss of pay to continue their education or training (*hyphenated when used before a noun*)

day return *n* a ticket, or the fare charged, to travel to a place and back again on the same day, usually at a reduced price ○ *Two day returns to Glasgow, please.*

day room *n* a communal recreation room in an institution such as a hospital or barracks

days /dayz/ *adv* during the day or every day ○ *I work days one week and nights the next.*

day sailer *n* a small sailing boat without sleeping accommodation

day school *n* **1.** a private school that does not take boarders **2.** a school that holds classes during the daytime but not during the evening

day shift *n* **1.** a shift that is worked during the day or part of the day **2.** a group of employees who work during the day at a place where others work during the night

dayside /dáy sīd/ n the side of a planet that faces the Sun

Days of Awe npl JUDAISM same as **High Holidays**

days of grace npl the extra days, customarily three, allowed for the settlement of a note or bill after it falls due

day spa n US HEALTH same as **health spa** (sense 2)

dayspring /dáy spring/ n the first light of day (literary)

daystar /dáy staar/ n ASTRON 1. same as **morning star** (literary) 2. same as **sun** n (sense 1) (archaic or literary)

day student n a student at a school, college, or university who does not board there

daytime /dáy tīm/ n the part of the day when there is natural light ■ adj occurring, done, or used during the daytime

day-to-day adj 1. occurring or tending to be the same every day ○ the day-to-day business of earning a living 2. planning or providing for one day at a time ○ We do everything on a day-to-day basis – we can never plan ahead

Dayton /dáyt'n/ city in Ohio on the Great Miami River, southwest of Columbus and northeast of Cincinnati. Population: 162,669 (2002 estimate).

Daytona Beach /day tônə-/ city and resort on the Atlantic coast of northeastern Florida, situated on the Halifax River. Its hard white-sand beach, long the site of car speed trials and races, is a popular spring holiday destination for students. Population: 64,605 (2002 estimate).

Dayton Accords npl an agreement signed by the presidents of Bosnia, Croatia, and Serbia in 1995, containing measures to end hostilities in the former Yugoslavia [< DAYTON, where the agreement was reached]

day trading n the purchase and subsequent sale of securities on the same day, used as a way of making quick profits on price movements —**day trader** n

day trip n a journey or outing to and from a place within a day —**day tripper** n

day trousers npl comfortable loose-fitting trousers for casual wear, usually made of hard-wearing fabric such as denim or corduroy

daywear /dáy wair/ n clothes for wearing during the day

daze /dayz/ n CONFUSED STATE a state of confusion and unclear thinking, often the result of a blow or shock ○ Things happened so quickly I was left in a daze. ■ vt (dazes, dazing, dazed) 1. STUN SOMEBODY to leave somebody wholly or partly unconscious or unable to think clearly, especially as a result of a blow or shock ○ The blow seemed to have dazed her. 2. BEWILDER SOMEBODY to leave somebody feeling confused or amazed [14C. Back-formation < dazed < Old Norse dasaðr 'weary from cold or exertion'] —**dazed** adj

dazzle /dázz'l/ vti (-zles, -zling, -zled) 1. DEPRIVE OF SIGHT TEMPORARILY to make somebody temporarily unable to see ○ The glare of the oncoming headlights dazzled me. 2. AMAZE SOMEBODY to amaze somebody with brilliance or skill or with a wonderful spectacle or display (often passive) ○ She dazzled the spectators with a triple somersault. ■ n LIGHT THAT DAZZLES very bright light that deprives somebody of sight temporarily ○ a lot of dazzle from the white-painted walls of the house [15C. < DAZE]

dazzle up vt to make something more attractive and colourful (informal)

dazzling /dázzling/ adj 1. bright enough to deprive somebody of sight temporarily 2. spectacularly skilful or impressive ○ a dazzling line-up of stars —**dazzlingly** adv

dB symbol MEASURE decibel

Db symbol CHEM ELEM dubnium

DB, **D/B** abbr ACCT daybook

DBA abbr Doctor of Business Administration

DB connector n a connector that facilitates serial and parallel input and output. Full form **data bus connector**

DBE abbr Dame Commander of the Order of the British Empire

DBMS abbr COMPUT database management system

DBS abbr BROADCAST 1. direct broadcasting by satellite 2. direct broadcasting satellite

DC abbr 1. MUSIC da capo 2. PUBLIC ADMIN Detective Constable 3. ELEC ENG direct current 4. PUBLIC ADMIN District Commissioner 5. also **D.C.** District of Columbia

DCA abbr Department for Constitutional Affairs

DCB abbr Dame Commander of the Order of the Bath

DCC abbr RECORDING digital compact cassette

DCD abbr RECORDING digital compact disc

DCL abbr Doctor of Civil Law

DCM abbr MIL Distinguished Conduct Medal

DCMG abbr Dame Commander of the Order of St Michael and St George

DCVO abbr Dame Commander of the Royal Victorian Order

dd abbr 1. dated 2. delivered

DD abbr 1. BANKING demand draft 2. BANKING direct debit 3. MIL dishonourable discharge 4. CHR, EDUC Doctor of Divinity

D/D abbr BANKING direct debit

D-day n 1. BEGINNING OF LIBERATION OF EUROPE 6 June 1944, the day on which Allied forces landed in northern France to begin the liberation of occupied Europe in World War II 2. DAY WHEN OPERATION IS TO BEGIN a day chosen for the beginning of a military operation or other major venture 3. MIL START OF 2003 IRAQ GROUND WAR 19 March 2003, the day on which ground operations began during the War in Iraq, involving invading coalition forces of the United States, the United Kingdom, Spain, and some other countries

DDR abbr HIST Deutsche Demokratische Republik

DDR SDRAM abbr COMPUT double data rate synchronous dynamic random-access memory

DDS abbr 1. LIBRARIES Dewey decimal system 2. DENT, EDUC Doctor of Dental Science 3. DENT, EDUC Doctor of Dental Surgery

DDSc abbr DENT, EDUC Doctor of Dental Science

DDT n an insecticide effective especially against malaria-carrying mosquitoes. It has been banned in many countries since 1974 because of its toxicity, its persistence in the environment, and its ability to accumulate in living tissue. Formula: $C_{14}H_9Cl_5$. Full form **dichlorodiphenyltrichloroethane**

de[1], **De** see also under surname

de[2] abbr Germany (used in Internet addresses) See table at **domain name**

DE abbr Delaware[2] (sense 1)

de- prefix 1. opposite, reverse ○ decertify 2. remove ○ decaffeinate ○ delist 3. derived from ○ denominative 4. reduce ○ declass 5. get off ○ deplane 6. formed by removing one or more atoms from a particular element ○ deoxy- [Via Old French de-, des- < Latin de-, dis- 'apart, away']

deaccession /deé ək sésh'n/ (-sions, -sioning, -sioned) vti to remove a book or work of art from the collection of a library or museum and sell it

deacidify /deé ə síddi fī/ (-fies, -fying, -fied) vt to remove the acid from something, or reduce the acid content of something —**deacidification** /dee ə síddifi káysh'n/ n

deacon /deékən/ n 1. in the Roman Catholic, Orthodox, and Anglican Churches, an ordained member of the clergy who ranks below a priest 2. in many Protestant churches, a lay person who is appointed or elected to assist the minister [Pre-12C. Via Latin diaconus < Greek diakonos 'servant, messenger']

deaconess /deékənəss/ n 1. a woman who ranks below a priest 2. a woman who is appointed to assist a minister (dated)

deaconry /deékənri/ (plural -ries) n 1. the position or rank of deacon 2. deacons considered as a group

deactivate /dee ákti vayt/ (-vates, -vating, -vated) vt 1. MAKE SOMETHING INACTIVE to prevent something that is active or live, especially an explosive device, from operating 2. STOP ACTIVE COMPOUND FROM WORKING to render a biologically active compound such as an enzyme inactive or ineffective 3. US END ACTIVE MILITARY STATUS to make a military unit no longer active —**deactivation** /dee ákti váysh'n/ n —**deactivator** n

dead /ded/ adj 1. NO LONGER ALIVE having passed from the living state to being no longer alive ○ a dead bird 2. INANIMATE never having been alive and having none of the characteristics of a living thing 3. WITHOUT LIVING THINGS having no living things, or unable to support life ○ a dead planet 4. WITHOUT PHYSICAL SENSATION having lost normal sensitivity to touch or pain, e.g. from the effects of cold, disease, or anaesthesia ○ My fingers have gone completely dead. 5. INSENSITIVE unable or unwilling to respond to, understand, or appreciate something ○ She seemed completely dead to her surroundings. 6. LACKING ANY SIGNS OF LIFE showing little indication of feeling or vitality ○ His eyes were dead. 7. LIKE CORPSE having the appearance of a dead person 8. LACKING ACTIVITY OR INTEREST without human activity or anything interesting or entertaining ○ This town is dead after seven o'clock at night. 9. NO LONGER CURRENT no longer in use, or no longer relevant, appropriate, or important ○ That issue is now dead, despite attempts to revive it. 10. BROKEN DOWN no longer able to operate because of a fault, breakdown, or loss of power ○ The phone went dead. 11. NOT BURNING no longer burning or able to burn 12. NONRESONANT not resonant or producing sounds that are not resonant ○'To where Saint Mary Woolnoth kept the hours / With a dead sound on the final stroke of nine' (T. S. Eliot, The Waste Land; 1922) 13. TOTAL sudden, abrupt, and complete ○ came to a dead stop in the middle of the road ○ There was a dead silence for a few seconds. 14. EXACT precise or exact in position or character ○ dead centre 15. EXHAUSTED very tired or completely without energy (informal) 16. DOOMED certain to face a very unpleasant fate (informal) ○ If I don't get this report in by tomorrow, I'm dead. 17. EMPTY empty and ready to be cleared away (informal) 18. WITH NO RETURN producing or yielding no return ○ dead capital 19. SPORTS OUT OF PLAY in some sports, used to describe a ball that has crossed the boundary of the playing area 20. GOLF LANDING CLOSE TO GOLF HOLE in golf, used to describe a shot in which the ball comes to rest so close to the hole that the next shot cannot miss ■ npl DEAD PEOPLE people who have died or been killed ○ respect for the dead ■ adv 1. PRECISELY emphasizes that an approximate-sounding description or instruction, e.g. concerning a time, a position, or a straight line, is in fact precise or to be followed precisely ○ Keep going dead ahead for another 300 yards. 2. ENTIRELY completely or absolutely ○ You can be sure that he won't make the same mistake again. 3. WITH SUDDENNESS abruptly or immediately ○ stopped dead in her tracks 4. VERY used in informal contexts to add emphasis to an adjective or adverb (informal) ○ I was dead scared. [Old English dēad <Germanic, 'died'] —**deadness** n ◇ **the dead of night** or **winter** the most extreme point of night or winter

SYNONYMS dead, deceased, departed, late, lifeless, defunct, extinct

CORE MEANING: no longer living, functioning, or in existence

dead having passed from the living state to being no longer alive ○ He was dead before his body hit the floor. ○ A father of four was shot dead by soldiers last night. ○ The dead fox had been hit on the road and run over. **deceased** (formal, of people only, especially in legal or other technical contexts, or as a euphemism) no longer living ○ the heirs of a deceased partner ○ His grandmother, now deceased, came from Glasgow. **departed** (literary, restricted to people) no longer living ○ sweet departed spirit ○ the soul of our dear brother here departed **late** (of people) having died recently or within living memory ○ the late Iranian leader Ayatollah Khomeini **lifeless** not living, or apparently not living ○ She lay lifeless in the snow. ○ They found the baby cold and seemingly lifeless. **defunct** no longer operative, valid, or functional, or no longer in existence ○ attempts to revive a defunct ceasefire ○ former editor-in-chief of a now defunct newspaper **extinct** no longer in existence, or no longer active ○ an animal that was declared extinct in 1936 ○ small houses clinging to the lower slopes of extinct volcanoes

dead air n an unintentional period of silence during a broadcast

dead-air space n a space that is sealed or has no ventilation

dead-and-alive adj without any interest or vitality (informal) ○ something more than this dead-and-alive existence

dead beat *adj* completely exhausted (*informal*)

deadbeat /déd beet/ *n* **1.** LOAFER somebody regarded as irresponsible, lazy, and disreputable (*slang insult*) **2.** *N Am* SOMEBODY WHO DOES NOT PAY DEBTS a debtor who does not repay money that is owed (*slang*) ■ *adj* PHYS DAMPED AND NOT OSCILLATING describes an instrument that gives a true reading without oscillation

dead bolt *n* a bolt that is operated directly by the turning of a key or knob and not by a spring mechanism

dead cat bounce *n* an apparent recovery from a major decline in share prices resulting from speculators rebuying stock that they previously sold rather than from a genuine upturn in the market (*slang*)

dead centre *n* **1.** MIDDLE the exact centre of something **2.** TOP OR BOTTOM OF PISTON STROKE the position at the top or bottom of a piston stroke in a reciprocating engine or pump, at which point the piston and the connecting rod are in a straight line **3.** POINTED ROD IN LATHE a nonrotating pointed shaft mounted at both ends or one end of a lathe to support the workpiece and hold it in place

dead duck *n* something or somebody with no chance of success or survival (*slang*)

deaden /dédd'n/ (**-ens, -ening, -ened**) *vt* **1.** MAKE SOMETHING LESS INTENSE to lessen the intensity of something such as pain or sound ○ *The snow deadened the sound of their footsteps.* **2.** DESENSITIZE SOMEBODY OR SOMETHING to make something or somebody less sensitive to pain or other stimuli ○ *A local anaesthetic will deaden the nerves.* **3.** MAKE SOMETHING LESS RESONANT to make an area soundproof or less resonant —**deadener** *n*

dead end *n* **1.** POINT AT WHICH BECOMES ABRUPTLY an end of a street, path, road, or passage beyond which it is impossible to proceed **2.** PASSAGE THAT ENDS ABRUPTLY a street, path, or passage beyond which somebody or something cannot proceed ○ *Our road is a dead end, so we don't get much traffic.* **3.** SITUATION THAT LEADS NOWHERE a situation or course of action in which further progress or development is impossible ○ *a line of research that proved to be a dead end*

dead-end *adj* **1.** WITH CLOSED END with no exit at one end **2.** WITHOUT PROSPECTS offering no prospects of progress, development, or improvement ○ *stuck in a dead-end job* **3.** *N Am* WITH NO PROSPECTS describes young people, usually from underprivileged backgrounds, whose behaviour makes them unlikely to succeed in life (*informal*)

deadening /dédd'ning/ *n* material used to make a room or building soundproof or less resonant

deadeye /déd ī/ *n* **1.** a rounded block of wood, pierced by three holes with a groove around its edge, used to tighten shrouds on sailing vessels **2.** *N Am* a skilled marksman or markswoman (*informal*)

deadfall /déd fawl/ *n* a simple trap consisting of a heavy weight that falls on and crushes its victim when a support is removed

dead fingers *n* a condition that can affect people who work with pneumatic drills, causing loss of sensation and reduced blood circulation in the fingers (*takes a singular verb*)

dead hand *n* **1.** a negative or oppressive influence exerted over an activity or a group of people ○ *remove the dead hand of bureaucracy* **2.** LAW same as **mortmain**

deadhead /déd hed/ *n* **1.** SOMEBODY INCOMPETENT somebody regarded as unintelligent, useless, or ineffectual (*informal insult*) **2.** SOMEBODY WITH FREE TICKET somebody who uses a free ticket for travel or to attend an event (*informal*) **3.** *US* VEHICLE WITH NO PASSENGERS a vehicle or aircraft that is carrying no passengers or freight (*informal*) ■ *v* (**-heads, -heading, -headed**) **1.** *vt* REMOVE DEAD FLOWERS FROM PLANT to remove dead flower heads from a plant to improve its appearance or stimulate further flowering **2.** *vti N Am* DRIVE EMPTY VEHICLE to drive or pilot a vehicle or aircraft that is carrying no passengers or freight ○ *Williams deadheaded it from New Jersey to California last weekend.*

dead heat *n* a race or other competition in which two or more contestants finish together or with the same score

dead-heat (**dead-heats, dead-heating, dead-heated**) *vi* to finish a race or other competition together or with the same score

dead letter *n* **1.** LETTER THAT CANNOT BE DELIVERED a letter that the postal service cannot deliver, usually because the address is inadequate or the addressee does not claim it **2.** UNENFORCED OR INEFFECTIVE RULE a law or regulation that still applies but is not enforced or uniformly obeyed **3.** SOMETHING NOW IRRELEVANT OR UNIMPORTANT something that is no longer considered relevant or important

dead letter box, **dead letter drop** *n* a place where a message or other item can be left in secret by one person and collected later by another, so that the two people do not meet

dead lift *n* a weightlifting event in which a weight is raised from the floor to the level of the hips and lowered again in a controlled manner

deadlight /déd līt/ *n* **1.** a protective shutter or plate fastened over a porthole or cabin window in bad weather **2.** a thick glass window set in the deck or side of a ship to let light into a cabin

deadline /déd līn/ *n* **1.** the time by which something must be done or completed **2.** formerly, a line in a prison or prison camp marking a boundary beyond which prisoners were forbidden to go on pain of death

dead load *n* the permanent weight of a structure such as a bridge, exclusive of its load

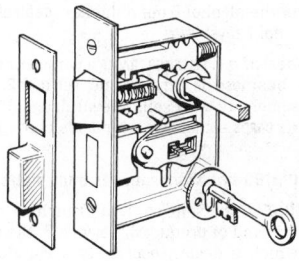

deadlock (sense 3)

deadlock /déd lok/ *n* **1.** STALLED SITUATION a situation in which no further progress is possible in a dispute, usually because the people involved are unwilling to change their positions or to compromise ○ *try to break the deadlock in negotiations* **2.** DRAW in sport, a draw **3.** TYPE OF LOCK a lock that can only be opened or closed with a key —**deadlock** *vti*

dead loss *n* **1.** something or somebody that is completely useless and not worth spending any further time, effort, or money on (*informal*) **2.** a complete loss for which no form of compensation is available

deadly /déddli/ *adj* (**-lier, -liest**) **1.** CAUSING DEATH able or likely to cause death **2.** PRECISE very accurate, especially in shooting ○ *deadly aim* **3.** EXTREMELY HOSTILE involving or having an intense desire for the defeat, downfall, or death of somebody ○ *deadly enemies* **4.** CAUSING OFFENCE causing or intended to cause great offence to another person ○ *a deadly insult* **5.** COMPLETE used to emphasize the intensity of something ○ *in deadly earnest* **6.** DULL extremely boring (*informal*) ○ *back to the deadly routine of daily life* ■ *adv* **1.** same as **deathly** ○ *deadly pale* **2.** COMPLETELY to the greatest extent possible ○ *I was being deadly serious when I made that suggestion.* —**deadliness** *n*

SYNONYMS **deadly, fatal, mortal, lethal, terminal**
CORE MEANING: causing death

deadly likely or designed to cause death ○ *Cannons are extremely deadly weapons.* ○ *a killer bee whose sting is ten times more deadly than the common-or-garden varieties* **fatal** used to describe accidents or illnesses that result in death ○ *a fatal road accident* ○ *an acute form of pneumonia which may prove fatal* **mortal** causing death ○ *mortal wounds* ○ *His face was drawn as if he realized the mortal danger they were now in.* **lethal** certain to or intended to cause death ○ *sentenced to death by lethal injection* ○ *Any sharply pointed object is potentially a lethal weapon.* **terminal** used to describe illnesses that result in death ○ *diagnosed with terminal cancer*

deadly nightshade *n UK* a poisonous plant with small black berries, commonly found in hedgerows. Flowers: drooping, purplish. Native to: Europe, Asia. Latin name: *Atropa belladonna*. ANZ, N Am term **belladonna**

deadly sins *npl* according to some Christian beliefs, the sins that lead to damnation, specifically the seven deadly sins of anger, avarice, envy, gluttony, lechery, pride, and sloth

deadman /déd man/ (*plural* **-men** /-men/) *n* **1.** a heavy block or plate buried in the ground that serves as an anchor to a connected structure such as a retaining wall **2.** a belaying point for use in firm snow, consisting of a metal plate with a wire loop attached to it [Mid-19C. Because buried securely, like a coffin]

dead man's float *n* a floating position in which a swimmer is face down with arms extended forward and legs kept together

dead man's handle, **dead man's pedal** *n* a safety device on an electric or diesel train that automatically cuts off the power and applies the brakes when the driver releases pressure on it

dead march *n* a piece of solemn music played to accompany a procession at a funeral, especially a military funeral

dead men's shoes *npl* a situation in which the only prospect of promotion is the death or retirement of more senior employees

dead nettle *n* a flowering plant that resembles a nettle but does not sting. Genus: *Lamium*.

dead-on *adj* very accurate or correct (*informal; not hyphenated when used after a verb*) ○ *a dead-on prediction*

deadpan /déd pan/ *adj* PURPOSELY IMPASSIVE deliberately expressing no emotion ■ *adv* EXPRESSIONLESS without showing any expression or emotion ○ *delivered the line absolutely deadpan* ■ *n* EXPRESSIONLESS FACE OR PERFORMER an expressionless face, or a performer with an expressionless face ■ *vti* (**-pans, -panning, -panned**) SPEAK OR ACT IN DEADPAN MANNER to speak or do something in a deliberately expressionless way [Early 20C. < US slang *pan* 'face']

dead reckoning *n* a simple method of determining the position of a ship or aircraft by charting its course and speed from a previously known position

dead ringer *n* **1.** somebody or something that exactly resembles another (*informal*) **2.** an automatically dialled telemarketing call that cuts off when answered because there is nobody at the sender's end available to deal with it

Dead Sea /déd-/ salt lake on the border between Israel and Jordan, in southwestern Asia. Its surface, at 400 m/1,312 ft below sea level, marks the lowest point on Earth. Area: 1,020 sq. km/394 sq. mi.

Dead Sea Scrolls *npl* a collection of ancient manuscripts, discovered in caves near the Dead Sea, that provide important evidence for biblical scholars and historians. They were discovered between 1947 and 1956, and are generally held to have been written between 100 BC and AD 68.

dead set *n* the rigid motionless position of a hunting dog pointing with its muzzle at game ■ *interj Aus* used to show surprise and ask for confirmation (*informal*)

dead shot *n* an expert shooter

dead spot *n* an area within the range of a radio transmitter where reception of the signal is weak or dead

deadstart /déd staart/ *vti* COMPUT same as **coldboot**

dead time *n* an interval during which an electrical device or component, having just responded to one stimulus, is unable to respond to another

dead weight *n* **1.** HEAVY WEIGHT a heavy motionless weight bearing down on something or somebody ○ *a foundation slab carrying the dead weight of the building* **2.** OPPRESSIVE BURDEN somebody or something that weighs somebody else down or hinders progress **3.** TOTAL WEIGHT the total weight of everything carried on a ship, equal to the difference between the laden and unladen weight **4.** CIV ENG same as **dead load**

Dead White European Male, **Dead White Male** *n* a conventionally important historical figure, especially one of the writers and thinkers whose works have traditionally formed the basis of academic study in Europe and North America (*informal disapproving*)

deadwood /déd wŏŏd/ *n* **1.** DEAD TREE PARTS dead trees and branches **2.** SOMEBODY OR SOMETHING UNNECESSARY people or things regarded as useless or superfluous **3.** PLANKS BETWEEN KEEL AND STERN vertical planks filling the gap between the keel and the stern of a sailing vessel

dead zone *n* an area in which mobile phone users are unable to receive signals

deaf /def/ *adj* **1.** HARD OF HEARING completely or partially unable to hear in one or both ears **2.** UNRESPONSIVE OR INDIFFERENT unwilling to respond to something as if unable to hear it ○ *They remained deaf to all our entreaties.* ■ *npl* PEOPLE WHO CANNOT HEAR people who are hard of hearing [Old English *dēaf* < Indo-European] —**deafness** *n*

deaf aid *n* MED same as **hearing aid**

deafblind /déf blīnd/ *adj* unable either to hear or to see

deafen /déff'n/ (**-ens, -ening, -ened**) *vt* **1.** to make somebody temporarily or permanently unable to hear ○ *I was momentarily deafened by the noise of the explosion.* **2.** to soundproof a room, wall, or building

deafening /déff'ning/ *adj* extremely or unbearably loud ○ *She turned up the volume until the noise was absolutely deafening.* —**deafeningly** *adv*

deaf-mute (*dated*) *adj* ⚠ an offensive term meaning unable to hear or speak ■ *n* an offensive term for somebody who is unable to hear or speak

USAGE ***Deaf-mute*** and ***mute*** in reference to people who are unable to hear or speak are highly offensive and should be avoided. Preferred substitutes are *hearing-impaired* or *hearing-and-speech-impaired*.

deaf without speech *adj* hearing-impaired and able to utter sounds but not words, usually because of being born hearing-impaired or having become so before learning how to talk

Deák /dáy aak/, **Ferenc** (1803–76) Hungarian politician. He oversaw the restoration of Hungary's constitution and the establishment of the dual monarchy of Austria-Hungary (1867).

Deakin /déekin/, **Alfred** (1856–1919) Australian Liberal politician. He was prime minister of Australia (1903–04, 1905–08, and 1909–10). See table at **prime minister**

deal[1] /deel/ *n* **1.** BUSINESS TRANSACTION an agreement, arrangement, or transaction, usually one that benefits all the parties involved **2.** BARGAIN something offered for sale on favourable terms (*informal*) **3.** TREATMENT the particular treatment given to somebody or received from somebody (*informal*) ○ *They got a pretty raw deal from their employer.* **4.** DISTRIBUTION OF CARDS the distribution of the cards needed to play a card game **5.** PLAYER'S TURN TO DISTRIBUTE CARDS a particular player's right or turn to distribute the cards for a card game ○ *Whose deal is it?* **6.** ROUND OF GAME a round of a card game following a specific distribution of the cards **7.** CARDS DISTRIBUTED OR RECEIVED the cards distributed or received for a particular round of a card game ■ *v* (**deals, dealing, dealt** /delt/) **1.** *vti* DISTRIBUTE CARDS to distribute the cards for a round of a card game ○ *You deal seven cards to each player.* **2.** *vti* GIVE OUT PARTICULAR CARD to give a particular card or cards to a player when distributing them ○ *I was dealt five clubs and no hearts.* **3.** *vti* SELL SOMETHING to sell something, especially illegal drugs **4.** *vt* MAKE SOMEBODY EXPERIENCE SOMETHING to cause somebody to experience or suffer something, often as a reward or punishment ○ *The latest opinion poll has dealt a severe blow to her hopes of re-election.* [Old English *dǣl* 'part, share, amount', *dǣlan* 'divide' < Germanic] ◇ **a done deal** something that has already been settled or finalized ◇ **cut a deal** to negotiate an agreement ◇ **make a big deal out of something** to make a fuss about something unimportant (*informal*) ◇ **the real deal** the ultimate example of its kind, or somebody regarded as the epitome of a particular trait or characteristic

deal in *vt* **1.** to buy and sell something as a business ○ *We deal mainly in second-hand goods.* **2.** to let somebody join in a card game or some other form of joint activity (*informal*) ○ *Deal me in.*

deal out *vt* to give something, or a share of something, to each of a number of people ○ *She dealt out compliments to all the actors.*

deal with *vt* **1.** HANDLE SOMETHING to take action with regard to something or somebody, e.g. to solve a problem or to help somebody **2.** BE ABOUT SOMETHING to write or speak about something or to have something as the subject of written or spoken material ○ *I was intending to deal with the Metaphysical poets in my next lecture.* **3.** TREAT SOMEBODY IN PARTICULAR WAY to treat or behave towards somebody in a particular way, especially in a business context ○ *People who break the regulations will be dealt with severely.* **4.** HAVE BUSINESS DEALINGS WITH SOMEBODY to do business with somebody or an organization

deal[2] /deel/ *n* **1.** fir or pine wood, especially when cut to a standard size **2.** a plank or board of deal [15C. < Middle Low German or Middle Dutch *dele* 'plank']

Deal /deel/ fishing port in Kent on the English Channel, southeastern England. Population: 28,504 (1991).

dealate /dée ay layt, -lit/, **dealated** /-laytid/ *adj* used to describe an insect such as an ant or termite that has lost or shed its wings, usually after mating —**dealation** /dée ay láysh'n/ *n*

dealcoholize /dee álkə hol īz/ (**-izes, -izing, -ized**), **dealcoholise** (**-ises, -ising, -ised**) *vt* to remove some or all of the alcohol from a drink —**dealcoholization** /di álkə hol ī záysh'n/ *n*

dealer /déelər/ *n* **1.** SELLER OR TRADER a person or company whose business is buying and selling **2.** SELLER OF DRUGS somebody who sells illegal drugs **3.** SOMEBODY WHO DEALS CARDS somebody who deals cards in a card game

dealer plates *npl N Am* same as **trade plates**

dealership /déelərship/ *n* **1.** a franchise to sell a specific brand of product or service **2.** the premises from which a dealer, especially a car dealer, operates

dealfish /déel fish/ (*plural same* or **-fishes**) *n* a deep-sea fish with a long flat silvery body. Native to: northeastern Atlantic. Genus: *Trachipterus*. [Mid-19C. < DEAL[2]; because it resembles a thin plank]

dealing /déeling/ *n* conduct towards or treatment of other people, especially in business matters ○ *The firm's reputation for fair dealing is at stake.* ■ **dealings** *npl* contact and interaction with other people or organizations for business purposes

dealing room *n* a room at a stock exchange where the buying and selling of stocks and shares takes place

dealmaker /déel maykər/ *n* somebody who arranges deals, especially in business or politics —**dealmaking** *n*

dealt past participle, past tense of **deal**[1]

deaminase /di ámmə nayss, -nayz/ *n* an enzyme that breaks down amino compounds such as amino acids

deaminate /dee ámmə nayt/ (**-nates, -nating, -nated**), **deaminize** /dee ámmə nīz/ (**-nizes, -nizing, -nized**), **deaminise** (**-nises, -nising, -nised**) *vt* to remove an amino group from a molecule —**deamination** /dee ámmə náysh'n/ *n* —**deaminization** /dee ámmə nī záysh'n/ *n*

dean /deen/ *n* **1.** ACADEMIC ADMINISTRATOR a senior member of the academic staff of a university or college who manages the whole institution or a department, faculty, or group of students **2.** COLLEGE ADVISER OR RULE-ENFORCER a member of the academic staff of a university or college responsible for the counselling and welfare of students, and sometimes, as at Oxford and Cambridge universities, for discipline **3.** SENIOR CLERIC a senior member of the clergy who holds an administrative position in a cathedral or collegiate church, or in a division in a diocese [14C. Via Old French *deien* < late Latin *decanus* 'person in charge of ten others' < Latin *decem* 'ten'] —**deanship** *n*

Dean, Forest of /deen/ wooded area and national park in western Gloucestershire. Population: 79,982 (2001).

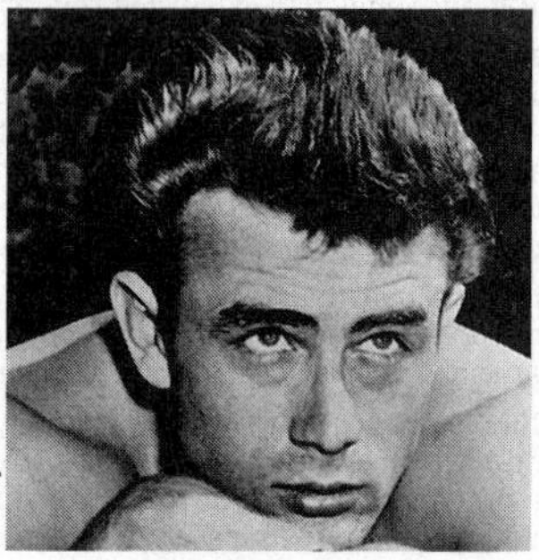
Barnaby's

James Dean

Dean /deen/, **James** (1931–55) US film actor. He became a symbol of misunderstood youth through his roles in *East of Eden* (1955) and *Rebel Without a Cause* (1955).

deanery /déenəri/ (*plural* **-ies**) *n* **1.** a dean's jurisdiction, office, or residence **2.** a group of parishes administered by a rural dean

Dean of Faculty *n* **1.** the president of the Faculty of Advocates in Scotland **2.** the administrator of a university or college faculty

dean's list *n* in the United States, a list of students who have achieved a high standard in their work at a secondary school, college, or university

dear /deer/ *adj* **1.** BELOVED loved or especially valued ○ *a dear friend* **2.** COSTLY high in price ○ *Prices are dear at that shop.* **3.** CHARGING A LOT charging high prices ○ *That's a dear place for food.* ■ *n* **1.** SOMEBODY BELOVED somebody who is loved or valued, especially for being kind or thoughtful **2.** TERM OF ENDEARMENT used as an affectionate term of address ■ *interj* EXPRESSES SHOCK used to express shock or consternation ○ *Oh dear!* ■ *adv* DEARLY at a high cost ○ *This will cost you dear.* [Old English *deore* < Germanic] —**dearness** *n*

SPELLCHECK Do not confuse the spelling of ***dear*** and ***deer***, which sound similar. The word ***dear*** as a noun denotes somebody loved. The noun ***deer*** denotes a widespread animal notable for the male's branched antlers.

Dear *adj* used before a name or title to begin a letter

dearie /déeri/, **deary** (*plural* **-ies**) *n* used to address somebody in an affectionate way (*informal*)

Dear John letter, **Dear John** *n* a letter from a woman ending a romantic or sexual relationship (*informal*) [< the salutation opening such a letter, *John* being a common man's forename]

dearly /déerli/ *adv* **1.** with great affection or intensity **2.** at a high cost ○ *He paid dearly for his mistake.*

dearth /durth/ *n* a scarcity of something ○ *a dearth of new ideas* [13C. < DEAR]

SYNONYMS See ***lack***.

deasil /déss'l, dyésh'l/ *adv Scotland* in a clockwise direction [Late 18C. < Gaelic *deiseil*]

death /deth/ *n* **1.** END OF BEING ALIVE the ending of all vital functions or processes in an organism or cell **2.** WAY OF DYING a manner of dying ○ *an easy death* **3.** SOMEBODY'S DYING an instance of somebody's dying **4.** END OF SOMETHING the destruction or extinction of something ○ *Losing the job marked the death of his ambitions.* **5.** CONDITION OF BEING DEAD the condition or quality of being dead ○ *In death she looked peaceful and composed.* [Old English *dēaþ* < Germanic] ◇ **at death's door** so ill or injured as to be almost dead ◇ **be in at the death** to be present at the end or culmination of something ◇ **be the death of somebody** to cause somebody's death (*often used figuratively for emphasis*) ○ *All this homework will be the death of me!* ◇ **catch your death (of cold)** to get a very bad cold ◇ **flog something to death** to repeat something, such as a story or idea, so often that people become bored with it ◇ **hold on for grim death, hang on like grim death** to keep hold of somebody or something very tightly and determinedly (*informal*) ◇ **like death warmed up** looking very ill ◇ **put somebody to death** to kill somebody, especially in accordance with a legal death sentence ◇ **sick to death of something** tired of hearing about something or having to deal with it ◇ **to death 1.** until somebody or something

dies **2.** used to add emphasis ○ *bored to death* ◇ **to the death** until one opponent in a fight is killed

SYNONYMS See *kill.*

Death *n* a personification of death, usually represented as a ghostly form or skeleton holding a scythe

death adder *n* a poisonous snake with a body like an adder. Native to: Australia. Latin name: *Acanthopis antarcticus.*

death angel *n* FUNGI same as **death cap**

deathbed /déth bed/ *n* the bed on which somebody dies ■ *adj* said, done, or made by somebody while near death ○ *deathbed confessions*

death benefit *n* a sum of money that is paid to the beneficiary of a life insurance policy after the death of the insured

deathblow /déth blṓ/ *n* **1.** an action or event that destroys or ends something **2.** a blow that kills somebody

death camp *n* a place where prisoners are systematically killed or where harsh conditions make survival unlikely

death cap *n* a poisonous fungus that has a pale cap and a structure resembling a cup at its base. Native to: European and North American woodlands. Latin name: *Amanita phalloides.*

death cell *n* a prison cell in which somebody who has been sentenced to death is kept before execution

death certificate *n* an official document completed and signed by a doctor, stating that somebody is dead and giving the cause of death if known

death chamber *n* a room where prisoners condemned to death are executed

death-dealing *adj* causing or liable to cause death

death-defying *adj* taking the risk of being killed

death duty *n* the former name for a tax paid in the United Kingdom on inherited property. Now called **inheritance tax**

death futures *npl* a financial investment in the form of the purchase at a reduced rate of the life insurance of somebody who has a terminal illness. This both provides necessary income for the dying person to meet medical costs and guarantees a good return for the purchaser. (*hyphenated when used before a noun*)

death grant *n* a sum of money formerly paid under the British National Insurance scheme when somebody died, in order to cover funeral expenses

death house *n* a building where prisoners condemned to death are housed prior to execution

death instinct *n* an inherent and unconscious tendency, proposed in some theories of the mind, towards self-destruction

death knell *n* **1.** a sign that something is dead, destroyed, or coming to an end ○ *The bankruptcy notice was the company's death knell.* **2.** the ringing of a bell to announce that somebody has died

deathless /déthləss/ *adj* immortal, usually because of being excellent (*literary or humorous*) —**deathlessly** *adv* —**deathlessness** *n*

deathly /déthli/ *adj* **1.** LIKE DEATH resembling death or somebody who is dead ○ *deathly pallor* **2.** EXTREME high in degree or intensity ○ *a deathly hush* ■ *adv* EXTREMELY extremely or intensely —**deathliness** *n*

death mask: 'Mask of Agamemnon', discovered in a grave at Mycenae, Greece, in 1876

death mask *n* a cast made of somebody's face soon after death

deathmatch /déth mach/ *n* in a computer game, a fight that ends in the death of a character

death metal *n* heavy metal music characterized by satanic and horror film iconography

death penalty *n* LAW same as **capital punishment**

death rate *n* the proportion of deaths to the population of an area or group

death rattle *n* a rough gurgling noise that sometimes comes from somebody's throat at the moment of death, caused by breath passing through mucus

death ray *n* an imaginary power beam that can kill

death row /-rṓ/ *n* a row of prison cells, or an area in a prison, housing prisoners that have been sentenced to death

death seat *n Aus, US* the seat next to the driver in a motor vehicle, considered to be especially dangerous (*informal*)

death sentence *n* **1.** the punishment of death, received in a court of law **2.** an event or decision that has a fatal effect

death's head *n* a human skull or its representation in art, often a symbol of mortality

death's head moth, **death's head hawkmoth** *n* a large moth with pale markings on the back of its thorax that look like a human skull. Native to: Europe. Latin name: *Acherontia atropos.*

death squad *n* an unofficial but organized group of people who seek out and murder political opponents or other people they consider as enemies (*takes a singular or plural verb*)

death stroke *n* same as **deathblow**

death toll *n* the total number of people killed as a result of an event such as a road accident or natural disaster

deathtrap /déth trap/ *n* a building, structure, or vehicle that is extremely unsafe (*informal*)

Death Valley /déth-/ low-lying desert region in southeastern California. It contains the lowest point in the United States, 86 m/282 ft below sea level.

Death Valley National Park national park in southeastern California and southwestern Nevada that includes Death Valley and the surrounding mountains. Area: 13,628 sq. km/5,262 sq. mi.

death warrant *n* **1.** an official document that authorizes somebody's execution **2.** something that ends hope or expectation

deathwatch /déth woch/ *n* **1.** a vigil near a dead or dying person, sometimes a traditional or religious custom **2.** INSECTS same as **deathwatch beetle**

deathwatch beetle *n* a small beetle whose larva bores into wood and makes a ticking sound. Latin name: *Xestobium rufovillosum.*

death wish *n* **1.** a desire to die or, less commonly, a desire for the death of somebody else **2.** a desire for self-destruction or personal misery

deattribution /di áttri byóosh'n/ *n* a change in an official or agreed opinion about the attribution of a work of art

deave /deev/ (**deaves, deaving, deaved**) *vt* (*informal*) **1.** *Ireland, N England, Scotland* to make somebody tired or confused, especially by making a lot of noise or fuss **2.** to cause somebody to be unable to hear, especially temporarily [Old English *dēafian* 'deafen' < DEAF]

REGIONAL NOTE *Deave* meaning 'to deafen' was once widespread, but is now confined to the north of England, Scotland, and Ireland. The *v* is a vestige of a feature of English pronunciation from earliest times. When *f* occurred before a vowel, it was pronounced /v/. We have relics of this in *hoof* and *hooves, wife* (once *wif*) and *wives,* and *wolf* and *wolves.*

deb /deb/ *n* same as **debutante** (*informal*) [Early 20C. Shortening]

deb. *abbr* **1.** FIN debenture **2.** BANKING debit

debacle /day baak'l, di-/ *n* **1.** a sudden disaster, defeat, or humiliating failure **2.** a sudden breakup of river ice in the spring thaw, causing a violent rush of

water and ice [Early 19C. < French < *débâcler* 'unbar' (of ice breaking on a river) < Latin *bacculus* 'stick']

debag /dee bág/ (**-bags, -bagging, -bagged**) *vt* to remove the trousers from somebody by force as a joke or humiliation (*slang*) [Early 20C. < BAGS (sense 2; *see* **bag**)]

debar /di baar/ (**-bars, -barring, -barred**) *vti* to exclude somebody from entering or taking part in something [15C. < Old French *desbarrer* < *barrer* 'to bar'] —**debarment** *n*

debark[1] /di baark/ (**-barks, -barking, -barked**) *v* **1.** *vi* TRANSP same as **disembark** (senses 1–2) **2.** *vt US* to unload something from a vehicle (*formal*) [Mid-17C. < French *débarquer* 'get out of a boat'] —**debarkation** /dee baar káysh'n/ *n*

debark[2] /dee baark/ (**-barks, -barking, -barked**) *vt* to remove the bark from wood [Mid-18C. < DE- + BARK[2]]

debase /di báyss/ (**-bases, -basing, -based**) *vt* **1.** to reduce something in value or quality **2.** to reduce somebody in status, significance, or moral worth —**debasedness** /di báyssidnəss/ *n* —**debasement** *n* —**debaser** *n*

debatable /di báytəb'l/ *adj* **1.** liable to be questioned or disputed ○ *Whether it's actually an improvement is debatable.* **2.** claimed by more than one country or party (*formal*)

debatably /di báytəbli/ *adv* used to show that the speaker or writer is aware that some people might disagree with the statement about to be made ○ *He was, debatably, the best orator of his generation.*

debate /di báyt/ *vti* (**-bates, -bating, -bated**) **1.** TALK OR ARGUE ABOUT SOMETHING to talk about something at length and in detail, especially as part of a formal exchange of opinion **2.** THINK ABOUT SOMETHING to ponder something carefully ■ *n* **1.** PUBLIC MEETING FOR DISCUSSION an organized or public discussion of something **2.** CONSIDERATION a prolonged consideration of something **3.** ARGUMENT argument or prolonged discussion ○ *The matter is not open to debate.* [13C. < Old French *debat* < Latin *battere* 'to fight'] —**debater** *n*

debating society /di báyting-/ *n* an organization whose main purpose is to hold regular formal debates on different topics

debauch /di báwch/ (*formal*) *vt* (**-bauches, -bauching, -bauched**) **1.** LEAD SOMEBODY INTO IMMORAL BEHAVIOUR to persuade somebody to behave in an immoral way **2.** SEDUCE SOMEBODY to seduce somebody sexually ■ *n* EPISODE OF DISSIPATION a period of indulgence in immoral behaviour [Late 16C. < French *débaucher*] —**debaucher** *n*

debauched /di báwcht/ *adj* unrestrainedly and immorally self-indulgent —**debauchedly** /di báwchtli, -chidli/ *adv* —**debauchedness** /di báwchtnəss, -chidnəss/ *n*

debauchee /débbaw chée/ *n* somebody regarded as immoral, unrestrained, and self-indulgent

debauchery /di báwchəri/ (*plural* -**ies**) *n* unrestrained self-indulgent immoral behaviour, or an instance of this

de Beauvoir, Simone ♦ Beauvoir, Simone de

debenture /di bénchər/ *n* **1.** *also* **debenture bond** UNSECURED BOND a bond backed only by the credit standing of the issuer, sometimes convertible into stock **2.** CERTIFICATE OF DEBT a certificate that acknowledges the existence of a debt of a particular amount owed to somebody **3.** CUSTOMS REFUND CERTIFICATE a certificate issued by customs officials that provides for a refund of duty previously paid [15C. < Latin *debentur* 'they are owed', form of *debere* 'owe'] —**debentured** *adj*

debilitate /di bílli tayt/ (**-tates, -tating, -tated**) *vt* to sap the strength or energy of somebody or something [Mid-16C. < Latin *debilitat-*, past participle of *debilitare* 'weaken' < *debilitas* 'weakness' (see DEBILITY)] —**debilitation** /di bílli táysh'n/ *n* —**debilitative** *adj*

debilitated /di bílli taytid/ *adj* with reduced strength or energy as a result of illness or physical exertion

SYNONYMS See *weak.*

debilitating /di bílli tayting/ *adj* reducing somebody's strength or energy

debility /di bílləti/ (*plural* -**ties**) *n* a general lack of strength or energy [15C. Via French < Latin *debilitas* < *debilis* 'weak']

debit /débbit/ n **1.** RECORDED DEBT OR EXPENSE an entry showing a debt or expense in a record of accounts **2.** SUM OF MONEY DEDUCTED an amount of money taken out of an account **3.** TOTAL OF DEBTS OR EXPENSES the total of individual debit entries in an account **4.** COLUMN FOR RECORDING DEBTS OR EXPENSES a column on the left of an accounting statement where debts and expenses are recorded **5.** DRAWBACK something that is disadvantageous or unfavourable ○ *The pay's better, but on the debit side there's a lot more work to do.* ■ *vt* **(-its, -iting, -ited) 1.** RECORD DEBIT to make, enter, or record a debit in an account **2.** CHARGE SOMEBODY MONEY to remove a sum of money from somebody's account in payment for something [15C. < Latin *debitum* (see DEBT)]

debit card n a plastic card that the holder can use to pay for purchases, the money being transferred directly from the holder's account to the seller

debonair /débbə náir/ adj **1.** looking well-dressed, sophisticated, and at ease **2.** characterized by ease of manner, elegance, or confidence [13C. < Old French < *de bon aire* 'of good disposition'] —**debonairly** adv

debone /deé bón/ **(-bones, -boning, -boned)** vt to remove the bones from meat or fish

debouch /di bówch, di boósh, deé-/ **(-bouches, -bouching, -bouched)** vi **1.** to move from an enclosed or confined area into more open terrain **2.** to widen out, or flow out, from a valley or ravine into a broader area (*refers to a geographical feature such as a valley or a flow of water*) [Mid-18C. < French *déboucher* 'come out of the mouth' < Latin *bucca* 'cheek, mouth'] —**debouchment** n

débouché /débboo sháy/ n an exit or outlet for troops in fortifications [Mid-18C. < French < past participle of *déboucher* (see DEBOUCH)]

Debrecen /débbrə tsen/ capital of Hajdú-Bihar County, eastern Hungary. Population: 205,032 (1999).

Debrett /də brét/, **Debrett's Peerage** n a publication that lists members of the British aristocracy [Mid-19C. After John *Debrett* (1705–1822), publisher]

débridement /di breédmənt, day breéd moN/ n the removal of dead, damaged, or infected tissue from a wound [Mid-19C. < French, 'unbridling'] —**débride** vti

debrief /dee breéf/, **(-briefs, -briefing, -briefed)** vt **1.** to question somebody closely about a task, mission, or event after it has ended **2.** to supply somebody with information about a task, mission, or event after it has ended —**debrief** n

debriefing /dee breéfing/ n an interview in which somebody is asked about or reports on a task, mission, or event after it has ended

debris /déb ree, dáy bree/, **débris** n fragments of something that has been destroyed or broken into pieces [Early 18C. < French *débris* 'broken up' < Old French *brisier* 'break']

de Broglie wavelength /də brógli-, də bróli-/ n the wavelength of the wave associated with the motion of an atomic or subatomic particle (**de Broglie wave**) that produces diffraction. The de Broglie wavelength is given by Planck's constant divided by the mass and velocity of the particle. [Early 20C. After Louis Victor *de Broglie* (1892–1987), French physicist]

debt /det/ n **1.** SOMETHING OWED an amount of money, a service, or an item of property that is owed to somebody **2.** STATE OF OWING SOMETHING the condition of owing something to somebody **3.** OBLIGATION an obligation or borrowing ○ *Her poetry shows a great debt to the works of Lorca.* **4.** SIN a sin or trespass (*archaic*) [13C. Via French *dette* < Latin *debitum* < past participle of *debere* 'owe'] —**debtless** adj —**debtor** /déttər/ n

ORIGIN The Latin word *debere* 'to owe', from which **debt** is derived, is also the source of English *debenture*, *debit*, *due*, *duty*, and *endeavour*.

debt collector n somebody who is employed to recover money owed to somebody else

debt of honour n a debt that somebody is morally, but not legally, obliged to pay

debt relief n a policy that advocates the cancellation of debts owed by poorer developing countries to richer countries

debt swap n an exchange of financial obligations, especially between corporations or governments, in order to gain profit or a more convenient repayment schedule

debud /deé búd/ **(-buds, -budding, -budded)** vt BOT same as **disbud** (sense 1)

debug /dee búg/ **(-bugs, -bugging, -bugged)** vt **1.** FIND AND REMOVE ERRORS FROM SOMETHING to find and remove errors in a system, especially a computer program or device **2.** REMOVE SECRET LISTENING DEVICES FROM PLACE to find and take away any electronic listening devices that are concealed in a place **3.** CLEAR PLACE OF INSECTS to remove or destroy insects that are in a place (*informal*)

debugger /dee búggər/ n a computer utility program that helps find software errors by allowing the user to access the source code

debunk /dee búngk/ **(-bunks, -bunking, -bunked)** vt to show that something is wrong or false [Early 20C. < BUNK²] —**debunker** n

deburr /deé búr/ **(-burrs, -burring, -burred)** vt to remove rough edges (**burrs**) from a piece of machined metal

debus /deé búss/ **(-busses** or **-buses, -bussing** or **-busing, -bussed** or **-bused)** vti to leave a bus, or unload people or supplies from a bus

Debussy /də byoóssi/, **Claude** (1862–1918) French composer. His works include the opera *Pelléas et Mélisande* (1902) and the orchestral poem *La mer* (1905). He developed a style known as musical impressionism. Full name **Debussy, Achille Claude**

> 'Music is the arithmetic of sounds as optics is the geometry of light.'
> [Claude Debussy. Quoted in *The Penguin Dictionary of Modern Quotations*, J. M. Cohen (ed.); 1971]

debut /dáybyoo, débb-/ n **1.** FIRST PUBLIC APPEARANCE the first public appearance or presentation of a performer, programme, or performance **2.** YOUNG WOMAN'S FIRST OFFICIAL SOCIAL ENGAGEMENT a young woman's first appearance in public at a formal social event ■ *vti* **(-buts, -buting, -buted)** MAKE FIRST FORMAL PUBLIC APPEARANCE to show or perform formally and publicly for the first time, or make something do this [Mid-18C. < French < *débuter* 'lead off' < *de-* 'from' + *but* 'goal, target']

debutante /débbyoo taant/ n a young woman who is being introduced formally into society by appearing at a formal social event such as a dance or party for the first time [Early 19C. < French, 'leading off' < present participle of *débuter* (see DEBUT)]

debye /də bí/ n a unit of electric dipole moment [After Peter J. *Debye* (1884–1966), US chemical physicist]

dec. abbr **1.** deceased **2.** declaration **3.** GRAM declension **4.** ASTRON declination **5.** decrease

Dec. abbr December

dec- prefix same as **deca-** (*used before vowels*)

deca-, deka- prefix ten ○ *decagram* [< Greek *deka* < Indo-European, 'ten']

decade /dék ayd, di káyd/ n **1.** a period of ten years **2.** a group, set, or series of ten [15C. Via French < late Latin *decad-* < Greek *deka* 'ten'] —**decadal** /dékəd'l/ adj

USAGE The pronunciation of **decade** with a stress on the second syllable is increasingly heard, but the traditional pronunciation puts the stress on the first syllable.

decadence /dékədənss/, **decadency** /-dənssi/ n **1.** PROCESS OF CIVILIZATION'S DECLINE a process of decline or decay in a society, especially in its morals **2.** STATE OF DECLINE the condition of a civilization in decline **3.** IMMORALITY a state of uninhibited immoral self-indulgence [Mid-16C. Via French *décadence* < medieval Latin *decadentia* < Latin *decidere* 'fall down or away' (see DECAY)]

decadent /dékədənt/ adj **1.** IN DECLINE undergoing a process of decline or decay, especially in morals **2.** IMMORAL showing uninhibitedly or immorally self-indulgent behaviour ■ n IMMORAL PERSON somebody who is uninhibitedly or immorally self-indulgent [Mid-19C. < French < *décadence* (see DECADENCE)] —**decadently** adv

decaf /deé kaf/ (*informal*) n **1.** a decaffeinated drink, especially coffee **2.** N Am decaffeinated coffee ■ adj BEVERAGES same as **decaffeinated** [Late 20C. Shortening]

decaffeinated /dee káffi naytid, di-/ adj having had all or most of the caffeine taken out ■ n a drink from which all or most of the caffeine has been removed —**decaffeinate** vt —**decaffeination** /dee káffi náysh'n, di-/ n

decagon /dékəgən, -gon/ n a polygon with ten straight sides and ten angles [Mid-17C. Via medieval Latin < Greek *dekagōnos* 'ten-angled'] —**decagonal** /də kággən'l/ adj —**decagonally** adv

decahedron /déka heédrən/ n a three-dimensional geometric figure formed of ten flat outer surfaces —**decahedral** adj

decal /di kál, deé kal/ n **1.** a picture or design on specially treated paper that allows it to be transferred to a surface such as glass, wood, or metal **2.** N Am a decorative paper or plastic sticker [Mid-20C. Shortening of DECALCOMANIA]

decalcify /dee kálssi fí/ **(-fies, -fying, -fied)** vti to lose calcium or a calcium compound, or remove calcium or a calcium compound from bones or teeth —**decalcification** /dee kálssifi káysh'n/ n —**decalcifier** n

decalcomania /di kálkə máyni ə/ n **1.** the process of fixing a picture or design to the surface of something such as glass, wood, or metal by transferring it from specially treated paper **2.** DESIGN same as **decal** [Mid-19C. < French *décalcomanie* < *décalquer* 'transfer a tracing' + *-manie* 'mania, craze'; from its popularity in the 19C]

decalescence /deéka léssənss/ n the absorption of heat without temperature increase at specific conditions during the heating of a metal, caused by changes in the crystalline composition [Late 19C. < *calescence* 'increasing warmth or heat'] —**decalescent** adj

decalitre /déka leetər/ n a unit of volume equal to ten litres. Symbol **dal** [Early 19C. < French *décalitre*]

Decalogue /déka log/ n BIBLE same as **Ten Commandments** [14C. Directly or via French < ecclesiastical Latin *decalogus* < Greek *dekalogos (biblos)* '(book of) ten pronouncements' < *deka* 'ten' + *logos* 'word, pronouncement']

decametre /déka meetər/ n a unit of length equal to ten metres. Symbol **dam** [Early 19C. < French *décamètre*]

decametric /déka méttrik/ adj having radio waves of high frequency, between 10 and 100 metres

decamp /di kámp/ **(-camps, -camping, -camped)** vi **1.** to leave a place abruptly or secretly **2.** to pack up and leave a camp or camping site [Late 17C. < French *décamper* < *camp* 'camp'] —**decampment** n

decanal /di káyn'l, dékənəl/ adj relating to a dean or deanery (*formal*) [Early 18C. < medieval Latin *decanalis* < late Latin *decanus* (see DEAN)]

decane /dék ayn/ n an isomeric liquid alkane. Formula: $C_{10}H_{22}$. [Late 18C. < DECA- + -ANE]

decani /di káyn í/ adj relating to or sung by the half of a church choir that sits on the south side of the chancel. ◊ **cantoris** [Mid-18C. < late Latin, form of *decanus* (see DEAN), referring to the side of the church the dean usually sits on]

decanoic acid /déka nó ik-/ n CHEM same as **capric acid** [< *decane*, liquid hydrocarbon]

decant /di kánt/ **(-cants, -canting, -canted)** vt **1.** to pour a liquid gently and carefully from one container to another so as not to disturb sediment **2.** to move people temporarily from their houses or areas in order to allow work to be done on their houses or areas [Mid-17C. < medieval Latin *decanthare* < Latin *canthus* 'lip of a jug' < Greek *kanthos* 'corner of the eye' (from the supposed similarity in shape)]

decanter

decanter /di kántər/ *n* a decorative bottle with a stopper, used for holding and serving alcoholic drinks. See illustration on previous page

decapitate /di káppi tayt/ (**-tates, -tating, -tated**) *vt* to cut off the head of somebody or something [Early 17C. < late Latin *decapitat-*, past participle of *decapitare* < Latin *caput* 'head'] —**decapitation** /di káppi táysh'n/ *n* —**decapitator** *n*

decapod /dékə pod/ *n* **1.** an invertebrate animal with stalked eyes and five pairs of legs, one or more with pincers, attached to the thorax. Many decapods are marine crustaceans and they include shrimps, lobsters, and crabs. Order: Decapoda. **2.** a sea mollusc with ten tentacles, e.g. a cuttlefish or squid. Class: Cephalopoda. [Early 19C. Via French *décapode* < modern Latin *Decapoda*, literally 'ten legs'] —**decapodal** /də káppəd'l/ *adj* —**decapodan** /də káppədən/ *adj* —**decapodous** /də káppədəss/ *adj*

decapsulate /dee kápsyoŏ layt/ (**-lates, -lating, -lated**) *vt* to remove a capsule from a body part or organ such as the kidney —**decapsulation** /dee kápsyoŏ láysh'n/ *n*

decarbonate /dee kaárbə nayt/ (**-ates, -ating, -ated**) *vt* to remove carbon dioxide or carbonic acid from something —**decarbonation** /dee kaárbə náysh'n/ *n* —**decarbonator** *n*

decarbonize /dee kaárbə nīz/ (**-izes, -izing, -ized**), **decarbonise** (**-ises, -ising, -ised**) *vt* to remove the carbon from something, e.g. the carbon deposits from an internal-combustion engine —**decarbonization** /dee kaárbə nī záysh'n/ *n* —**decarbonizer** *n*

decarboxylase /dée kaar bóksi layz, -layss/ *n* an enzyme that removes a carboxyl group from a molecule

decarboxylation /dée kaar bóksi láysh'n/ *n* the removal or loss of a carboxyl group from an organic compound —**decarboxylate** /dée kaar bóksi layt/ *vt*

decarburize /dee kaárbyoŏ rīz, -kaárbə-/ (**-rizes, -rizing, -rized**), **decarburise** (**-rises, -rising, -rised**) *vt* CHEM, ENG same as **decarbonize**

decastyle /dékə stīl/ *n* a portico that has ten columns ■ *adj* consisting of or having ten columns [Early 18C. < Greek *dekastulos* 'having ten columns']

decasyllable /dékə siləb'l/ *n* a line of verse or a word made up of ten syllables —**decasyllabic** /dékə si lábbik/ *adj*

decathlete /di káth leet/ *n* an athlete who competes in a decathlon

decathlon /di káth lon, -lən/ *n* a contest in which athletes compete in ten different events and are awarded points for each to find the best all-round athlete. The events are long jump, high jump, pole vault, shot put, discus, javelin, 110-metre hurdles, and running over 100 metres, 400 metres, and 1,500 metres. [Early 20C. < DECA- + Greek *athlon* 'contest']

decay /di káy/ *v* (**-cays, -caying, -cayed**) **1.** *vti* GO ROTTEN to decompose and become soft, crumbly, or liquefied, or make something do this **2.** *vti* DECLINE OR CAUSE DECLINE to decline in quality gradually and steadily, or make something do this **3.** *vi* PHYS DISINTEGRATE to undergo spontaneous disintegration (*refers to radioactive material*) **4.** *vi* PHYS DECREASE to decrease gradually in magnitude (*refers to a physical quantity or effect*) **5.** *vi* ASTRON DESCEND to decrease gradually in altitude (*refers to an artificial satellite in orbit*) ■ *n* **1.** REDUCTION a decline in quality ○ *'A state too extensive in itself, or by virtue of its dependencies, ultimately falls into decay.'* (Simón Bolívar, *Letter from Jamaica*; 1815) **2.** PROCESS OF BIOLOGICAL DETERIORATION the process of decomposition that affects plant material and the bodies of animals after they die and are invaded by bacteria or fungi **3.** ROTTEN OR SPOILED PART the areas of something that are decomposed or rotted ○ *cut out the decay* **4.** PHYS DISINTEGRATION OF RADIOACTIVE MATERIAL the spontaneous disintegration of a radioactive material along with the emission of one or more elementary particles or radiation **5.** PHYS GRADUAL DECREASE a gradual decrease in the magnitude of a physical quantity or effect such as current, stored charge, or phosphorescence **6.** ASTRON DESCENT OF ARTIFICIAL SATELLITE the gradual decrease in altitude of an orbiting artificial satellite **7.** MUSIC DECLINE IN SOUND OF NOTE the fading away of a musical note [15C. Via French *decair* < Latin *decidere* 'fall off or away' < *cadere* 'to fall'] —**decayable** *adj*

decay constant *n* the probability that an unstable radioactive nucleus will decay in a standard unit of time

Deccan /dékən/ triangular plateau that makes up much of southern India, south of the Sātpura Range. It is bordered by the mountainous Eastern and Western Ghats ranges.

decease /di séess/ (*formal*) *n* same as **death** ■ *vi* (**-ceases, -ceasing, -ceased**) same as **die**[1] [14C. Via French < Latin *decessus* 'death, departure' < past participle of *decedere* 'go away' < *cedere* 'give way']

deceased /di séest/ (*formal*) *n* somebody who has died recently ■ *adj* no longer living

SYNONYMS See *dead.*

decedent /di séed'nt/ *n US* LAW same as **deceased** [Late 16C. < Latin *decedent-*, present participle of *decedere* (see DECEASE)]

deceit /di séet/ *n* **1.** the act or practice of deceiving or misleading somebody **2.** something that is done to deceive or mislead somebody [13C. < Old French < *deceveir* (see DECEIVE)]

deceitful /di séetf'l/ *adj* intentionally misleading or fraudulent —**deceitfully** *adv* —**deceitfulness** *n*

deceive /di séev/ (**-ceives, -ceiving, -ceived**) *v* **1.** *vt* INTENTIONALLY TRICK OR MISLEAD SOMEBODY to mislead or deliberately hide the truth from somebody **2.** **deceive yourself** *vr* FOOL YOURSELF to convince yourself of something that is not true **3.** *vt* BE SEXUALLY UNFAITHFUL TO SOMEBODY to be sexually unfaithful to a spouse or sexual partner [13C. Via Old French *deceveir* < Latin *decipere* 'ensnare, take in' < *capere* 'take, seize'] —**deceivability** /di séevə bílləti/ *n* —**deceivable** *adj* —**deceiver** *n*

deceiving /di séeving/ *adj* liable or meant to deceive or mislead —**deceivingly** *adv*

decelerate /dee séllə rayt/ (**-ates, -ating, -ated**) *vti* to reduce speed, or make something do this [Late 19C. < DE- + ACCELERATE] —**deceleration** /dee séllə ráysh'n/ *n* —**decelerator** *n*

December /di sémbər/ *n* in the Gregorian calendar, the 12th month of the year, lasting 31 days. See table at **calendar** [13C. Via French < Latin < *decem* 'ten'; because the tenth month of the Roman year]

Decembrist /di sémbrist/ *n* a member of a group of Russian officers who tried unsuccessfully to overthrow Tsar Nicholas I of Russia in December 1825

decemvir /di sémvər/ (*plural* **-virs** or **-viri** /-və ree, -və rī/) *n* **1.** in ancient Rome, one of a group of ten magistrates, especially those who drew up the laws of the Twelve Tables in 451–450 BC **2.** a member of an official body that consists of ten people (*archaic*) [15C. < Latin *decem viri* 'ten men'] —**decemviral** *adj*

decemvirate /di sémvərət/ *n* a group of ten people who hold power or office together

decency /déess'nssi/ *n* (*plural* **-cies**) **1.** CONFORMITY WITH MORAL STANDARDS behaviour or an attitude that conforms to the commonly accepted standards of what is right and respectable **2.** MODESTY modesty or propriety ■ **decencies** *npl* MORAL BEHAVIOUR the commonly accepted standards of good behaviour (*formal*)

decennary /di sénnəri/ *n* (*plural* **-ries**) a ten-year period (*formal*) ■ *adj* CALENDAR same as **decennial** [Early 19C. < DECENNIUM]

decennia /di sénni ə/ *n* plural of **decennium**

decennial /di sénni əl/ *adj* lasting for, consisting of, or happening every ten years ■ *n* an anniversary celebrated ten years after something or every ten years —**decennially** *adv*

decennium /di sénni əm/ (*plural* **-niums** or **-nia** /-ni ə/) *n* a ten-year period [Late 17C. < Latin < *decennis* < *decem* 'ten' + *annus* 'year']

decent /déess'nt/ *adj* **1.** MORAL conforming to accepted standards of moral behaviour ○ *It was decent of her to apologise.* **2.** GOOD above average in quality or quantity ○ *one of the few decent restaurants around here* **3.** SATISFACTORY adequate or sufficient in quality ○ *did a decent job* **4.** KIND kind, considerate, or generous **5.** SUFFICIENTLY DRESSED fully dressed, as opposed to being naked or wearing underwear only (*informal*) ○ *Don't come in; I'm not decent!* [Mid-16C. Directly or via French < Latin *decent-*, present participle of *decere* 'be fitting'] —**decentness** *n*

decently /déess'ntli/ *adv* in a way that conforms to accepted standards of moral behaviour or appearance

decentralize /dee séntrə līz/ (**-izes, -izing, -ized**), **decentralise** (**-ises, -ising, -ised**) *vti* to reorganize something such as a political unit so that power is shifted from a central or upper location to another less central place, or be reorganized in this way —**decentralization** /dée sentrə lī záysh'n/ *n*

deception /di sépsh'n/ *n* **1.** the practice of deliberately making somebody believe things that are not true **2.** an act, trick, or device intended to deceive or mislead somebody [15C. Directly or via French < Latin *deception-* < *decept-*, past participle of *decipere* (see DECEIVE)]

Deception Bay /di sépsh'n-/ coastal town near the city of Brisbane in southeastern Queensland, Australia. It is located on the bay of the same name. Population: 10,352 (1991).

deceptive /di séptiv/ *adj* **1.** liable or meant to deceive or mislead somebody **2.** capable of being mistaken for something else ○ *a deceptive barking noise* [Early 17C. Directly or via French < late Latin *deceptivus* < Latin *decept-* (see DECEPTION)] —**deceptiveness** *n*

deceptively /di séptivli/ *adv* in a way that deceives or misleads, or is contrary to appearances ○ *a deceptively easy task*

USAGE Although *deceptively simple* almost invariably means 'complex, despite apparent simplicity', that is not a model from which to generalize about the meaning of ***deceptively.*** When people are asked whether, for example, *a deceptively dangerous place to stand* is a place that is more or less dangerous than it appears, they respond variously, with a substantial minority admitting they have no idea what ***deceptively*** is intended to convey. Sometimes context clarifies the meaning: *It was a small house, but it had deceptively large rooms.* Unless the context makes the meaning clear, ***deceptively*** is best avoided.

decerebrate /dee sérri brayt/ *adj* having lost all cerebral function, vision, hearing, and other senses, and voluntary motor activity, e.g. as a result of a severe stroke ■ *vt* (**-brates, -brating, -brated**) to remove the cerebrum or brain stem from an animal surgically [Late 19C. < DE- + CEREBRUM] —**decerebration** /dee sérri bráysh'n/ *n*

decern /di súrn/ (**-cerns, -cerning, -cerned**) *vti* in Scots law, to state or impose something as a binding decree ○ *They decern and decree the said John Smith to be returned to prison.* [15C. Via French < Latin *decernere* 'decide, pronounce a decision' < *cernere* 'separate, sift']

decertify /dee súrti fī/ (**-fies, -fying, -fied**) *vt* to withdraw certification from somebody or something —**decertification** /dee súrtifi káysh'n/ *n*

dechannelize /dee chánn'l īz/ (**-izes, -izing, -ized**), **dechannelise** (**-ises, -ising, -ised**) *vt* to reroute a river to its original location and configuration of flow

deci- *prefix* a tenth ○ *decigram* Symbol **d** [< French < Latin *decimus* (see DECIMAL)]

decibel /déssi bel, déssib'l/ *n* a unit of relative loudness, electric voltage, or current equal to ten times the common logarithm of the ratio of two readings. For sound, the decibel scale runs from zero for the least perceptible sound to 130 for sound that causes pain. Symbol **dB**

decide /di sīd/ (**-cides, -ciding, -cided**) *v* **1.** *vti* CHOOSE to make a choice or come to a conclusion about something ○ *We decided not to go in the end.* **2.** *vt* LEAD SOMEBODY TO CHOOSE to make somebody choose what to do or come to a conclusion about something (*informal*) ○ *His encouraging letter decided me against giving up the course.* **3.** *vt* END SOMETHING CLEARLY to bring something to an end in a definite or obvious way ○ *The final goal decided the contest.* **4.** *vi* ARRIVE AT VERDICT to come to a verdict or judgment [14C. Directly or via French *décider* < Latin *decidere* 'cut off' < *caedere* 'cut'] —**decidable** *adj*

decided /di sīdid/ *adj* **1.** clearly seen, felt, or noticed ○ *a decided slant* **2.** free of uncertainty or doubt ○ *a person of decided opinions* —**decidedness** *n*

decidedly /di sī́didli/ *adv* without any doubt or question

decider /di sī́dər/ *n* something that settles the outcome of a contest or argument, especially, in sport, a game played to determine the ultimate winner

deciding /di sī́ding/ *adj* acting to settle the result of a contest or debate, or to make clear what must be done next

decidua /di síddyoo ə/ (*plural* **-as** or **-ae** /-ee/) *n* a specialized part of the mucous membrane (**endometrium**) that lines the womb during pregnancy and is shed with the placenta at birth [Late 18C. < modern Latin *decidua (membrana)* 'deciduous (membrane)'] —**decidual** *adj* —**deciduate** *adj*

deciduous /di síddyoo əss/ *adj* **1.** SHEDDING LEAVES IN AUTUMN describes trees and bushes that shed their leaves in the autumn **2.** OF DECIDUOUS TREES describes a forest or wood that is composed mostly of deciduous trees **3.** SHED AFTER DEVELOPMENTAL STAGE describes the teeth, antlers, or wings of animals and birds that are shed after a stage of development **4.** SHED EASILY OR AT INTERVALS describes the scales of fish that are shed easily or at intervals [Mid-17C. < Latin *deciduus* < *decidere* 'fall down' < *cadere* 'fall, die'] —**deciduously** *adv* —**deciduousness** *n*

deciduous tooth *n* DENT same as **milk tooth**

~~**decieve**~~ incorrect spelling of **deceive**

decigram /déssi gram/, **decigramme** *n* a metric unit of mass equal to one tenth of a gram. Symbol **dg** [Early 19C. < French *décigramme*]

decile /déss īl, -il/ *n* **1.** one of ten groups containing an equal number of the items that make up a frequency distribution **2.** one of the nine values that divide the total number of items in a frequency distribution into ten groups, each containing an equal number of items

decilitre /déssi leetər/ *n* a unit of volume equal to 0.1 litre. Symbol **dl** [Early 19C. < French *décilitre*]

decimal /déssim'l/ *adj* relating to the number ten as a base and counted or ordered in units of ten ■ *n* a number expressed in a counting system that uses units of 10, especially a decimal fraction [Early 17C. < modern Latin *decimalis* < Latin *decimus* 'tenth' < *decem* 'ten'] —**decimally** *adv*

decimal classification *n* LIBRARIES same as **Dewey decimal system**

decimal currency *n* currency based on units of ten or multiples of ten

decimal fraction *n* a numerical fraction with ten as its denominator, written showing the fractional elements after a decimal point

decimalize /déssimə līz/ (**-izes, -izing, -ized**), **decimalise** (**-ises, -ising, -ised**) *vti* to convert something such as a country's currency or measurement system into a decimal or metric system, or convert to a decimal or metric system —**decimalization** /déssimə lī záysh'n/ *n*

decimal place *n* the place or a specific number of digits to the right of the decimal point in a line of numbers

decimal point *n* a printed or written dot in a decimal number that divides the whole numbers from the tenths, hundredths, and smaller divisions of ten

decimal system *n* a numerical system that has the number ten as the basic unit with other units as powers or multiples of ten. The metric system of measurement and most currency systems are based on a decimal system.

decimate /déssi mayt/ (**-mates, -mating, -mated**) *vt* **1.** ⚠ DESTROY LARGE PROPORTION OF SOMETHING to kill off or remove a large proportion of a group of people, animals, or things **2.** ⚠ ALMOST DESTROY SOMETHING to inflict so much damage on something that it is seriously reduced in effectiveness ○ *Current prices will decimate the present level of service provision.* **3.** KILL ONE PERSON IN 10 to kill one out of every ten people in a group, especially in a body of mutinous soldiers (*archaic*) [Late 16C. < Latin *decimat-*, past participle of *decimare* 'take a tenth' < *decimus* (see DECIMAL)] —**decimation** /déssi máysh'n/ *n* —**decimator** *n*

USAGE The popular meaning of ***decimate***, 'to destroy', now predominates because the need for a word meaning 'to kill one person in ten' has greatly diminished. Even so, the popular meaning is not accepted by everyone, and it is often better to use *annihilate, exterminate, destroy,* or *devastate*.

---

decimetre /déssi meetər/ *n* a unit of length equal to 0.1 metre. Symbol **dm**

decipher /di sī́fər/ (**-phers, -phering, -phered**) *vt* **1.** to succeed in establishing what a word or piece of writing says when it is difficult or almost impossible to read **2.** to study something that is written in code or in an unknown form of writing until it can be understood and read normally —**decipherable** *adj* —**decipherer** *n* —**decipherment** *n*

decision /di sízh'n/ *n* **1.** SOMETHING SOMEBODY HAS CHOSEN something that somebody chooses or makes up his or her mind about, after considering it and other possible choices ○ *made a final decision on the guest list* **2.** FIRMNESS IN CHOOSING SOMETHING the ability to choose or decide about things in a clear and definite way without too much hesitation or delay ○ *a man of decision* **3.** PROCESS OF CHOOSING the process of coming to a conclusion or determination about something **4.** BOXING VICTORY DECIDED ON POINTS a win in a boxing match that is awarded to the fighter who is given the higher total of points by the judges ○ *He won a 10-round decision.* [15C. Directly or via French < Latin *decision-* < past participle of *decidere* (see DECIDE)] —**decisional** *adj*

decision-making *n* the process of making choices or reaching conclusions, especially on important political or business matters —**decision-maker** *n*

decision theory *n* the study of the best possible outcomes for decisions made under varying conditions

decision tree *n* a diagram set out like the branches of a tree that shows the consequences of a decision, each decision entailing a course of action that requires various other decisions

decisive /di sī́ssiv/ *adj* **1.** settling or ending something such as a debate, controversy, or contest ○ *a decisive victory* **2.** showing an ability to make decisions quickly, firmly, and clearly [Early 17C. Via French < medieval Latin *decisivus* < past participle of Latin *decidere* (see DECIDE)] —**decisively** *adv* —**decisiveness** *n*

deck /dek/ *n* **1.** FLOOR SURFACE ACROSS SHIP a level surface that runs from one side of a ship to the other, forming a floor **2.** LEVEL OF SHIP OR VEHICLE a floored, self-contained area of a ship or a passenger vehicle such as a bus or tram **3.** *N Am* LEVEL OF STRUCTURE a tier or level of a building or other structure **4.** *N Am* BUILDINGS same as **sun deck** ○ *They had a barbecue on the deck.* **5.** FLOOR OF ROADWAY OR BRIDGE the floor or platform of a roadway or bridge **6.** AUDIO UNIT a wide flat piece of audio equipment that contains a player for compact discs, records, cassettes, or tapes **7.** *N Am* PACK OF CARDS a pack of playing cards **8.** GROUND the ground or floor (*informal*) ■ *vt* (**decks, decking, decked**) **1.** KNOCK SOMEBODY DOWN to strike and knock somebody down deliberately (*informal*) **2.** DECORATE SOMEBODY OR SOMETHING to decorate or ornament somebody or something (*literary*) ○ *deck the halls with boughs of holly* **3.** BUILD DECK FOR SOMETHING to make a deck for a ship or other structure ■ *n* SKATEBOARD PLATFORM the platform of a skateboard on which the rider stands (*slang*) ■ *adj* TRENDSETTING very fashionable or trendsetting (*slang*) [15C. < Middle Dutch *dec* 'roof, covering, cloak' < Germanic] —**decked** *adj* —**decker** *n* ◇ **clear the deck** *or* **decks** to get rid of all obstacles, especially pending work, prior to beginning a new task ◇ **hit the deck** (*informal*) **1.** to fall on the floor or ground, often as self-protection **2.** *US* to get out of bed ◇ **on deck 1.** on the top external surface of a ship or boat **2.** *N Am* scheduled to appear next ◇ **play with a full deck** *N Am* to be rational and intelligent (*informal*)

deck out *vt* to decorate something, or dress somebody up in fancy clothes

deck over *vt* to complete the construction of an upper deck on a ship

deck bridge *n* a bridge designed so that the roadway or track is supported by the upper horizontal part of the structural framework

deck chair *n* a collapsible adjustable outdoor chair with a wooden framework and a seat made from strong fabric

deck hand *n* a labourer on a ship, yacht, or other vessel

deckhouse /dék howss/ (*plural* **-houses** /-howziz/) *n* a structure built on the main deck of a ship or other vessel

decking /déking/ *n* planking or other flooring material used for the deck of a ship or a seating area in a garden

deckle /dék'l/ *n* **1.** a metal frame used to contain pulp in a mould during the making of handmade paper **2.** PAPER same as **deckle edge** [Mid-18C. < German *Deckel* 'little covering' < *Decke* 'covering']

deckle edge *n* a rough, irregular, or feathery edge on handmade paper —**deckle-edged** *adj*

deck officer *n* an officer responsible for tasks such as navigation that take place on a ship's main deck

deck shoe *n* a flat canvas shoe with a thick nonslip sole, typically worn on a yacht

deck tennis *n* a game based on lawn tennis, using a small court with a net and a ring made of rubber or rope that the players throw back and forth

declaim /di kláym/ (**-claims, -claiming, -claimed**) *v* **1.** *vti* to make a formal or theatrical speech or statement about something **2.** *vi* to deliver a recitation [14C. Directly or via French < Latin *declamare* 'cry out' < *clamare* 'cry, call'] —**declaimer** *n*

declamation /déklə máysh'n/ *n* **1.** a speech or presentation spoken in a formal or theatrical style **2.** the art or process of declaiming ○ *'The air of the New World seems favourable to the art of declamation.'* (Joseph Conrad, *Nostromo*; 1904) [15C. Directly or via French < Latin *declamation-* < past participle of *declamare* (see DECLAIM)]

declamatory /di klámmətəri/ *adj* **1.** spoken or written in a formal or theatrical style **2.** loud and rhetorical but without very meaningful content —**declamatorily** *adv*

declarant /di kláirənt/ *n* somebody who makes a legal or formal, statement [Late 17C. < French *déclarant*, present participle of *déclarer* 'declare']

declaration /déklə ráysh'n/ *n* **1.** FORMAL STATEMENT a formal document giving explicit details such as the terms of a business agreement or plan, or information on goods or assets for tax purposes **2.** OFFICIAL PROCLAMATION an emphatic formal public statement, especially by a government or public body **3.** MAKING OF DECLARATION the process or act of declaring something in an official or public way **4.** LAW UNSWORN BUT SOLEMN LEGAL STATEMENT a formal statement of facts that is allowed in a legal case in place of a statement made under oath **5.** LAW PLAINTIFF'S OFFICIAL WRITTEN CLAIM a formal document in which a plaintiff lays out precise details of the circumstances leading to the legal action being taken **6.** LAW RULING ON QUESTION OF LAW a ruling by a judge or court on the legal position of contesting parties **7.** CARDS ANNOUNCEMENT OF BID in bridge, the act of naming a suit as trumps or of declaring no-trumps by the player who makes the final bid [14C. < Latin *declaration-* < past participle of *declarane* (see DECLARE)]

Declaration of Human Rights *n* a United Nations document approved on 10 December 1948, by the General Assembly, affirming the rights of all human beings. It proclaimed their right to free movement in search of truth and justice and their right to live their lives in dignity.

declaration of independence *n* a proclamation by which a country, group, or people asserts publicly that it has become independent of a governing power

Declaration of Independence *n* a written statement, issued and adopted by the Continental Congress in 1776, proclaiming that the 13 North American colonies henceforward would govern themselves instead of being ruled by Great Britain. The Declaration of Independence was formally endorsed on 4 July 1776.

declarative /di klárrətiv/ *adj* **1.** containing a statement **2.** in the form of a statement ○ *a declarative sentence* —**declarative** *n* —**declaratively** *adv*

declarator /di klárrətər/ *n* in Scotland, a legal action

brought by somebody who wants a right or status to be clarified and stated judicially

declaratory /di klárrətəri/ *adj* **1.** stating and clarifying something, especially a legal right, status, decree, or judgment **2.** same as **declarative** —**declaratorily** *adv*

declare /di kláir/ (**-clares, -claring, -clared**) *v* **1.** *vti* **ANNOUNCE SOMETHING CLEARLY OR LOUDLY** to state something in a plain, open, or emphatic way **2.** *vt* **STATE SOMETHING FORMALLY OR OFFICIALLY** to make an official or public announcement about somebody or something, especially on a legal or medical matter ○ *The doctors declared her fit to work.* ○ *The chairperson declared the meeting open.* **3.** *vt* **REVEAL SOMETHING AS TAXABLE** to inform customs or tax authorities about goods on which duty is owed or about income that is taxable **4.** *vt* **ANNOUNCE ACTION OR STATUS** to make an official statement that a particular course of action or status is in effect ○ *to declare independence* **5.** *vi* **MAKE DECISION KNOWN** to announce a choice or decision formally and publicly (*formal*) **6. declare yourself** *vr* **PROPOSE MARRIAGE** to make a formal or open statement of love for and a wish to marry somebody (*archaic*) **7.** *vi* CRICKET **CHOOSE TO END INNINGS** in cricket, to end an innings before all the batsmen have been dismissed, having decided, as the batting side or the captain of it, that the team has probably made enough runs **8.** *vti* CARDS **SAY WHICH SUIT IS TRUMPS** in bridge, to announce to the other players the suit that has been chosen as trumps or no-trumps for the next hand **9.** *vti* CARDS **LAY CARDS ON TABLE** in a card game such as bezique, to show that you have a specific score by displaying the cards face up on the table and claiming your score [14C. < Latin *declarare* 'make clear' < *clarus* 'clear'] —**declarable** *adj* ◇ **declare war 1.** to make a formal public announcement that the country represented is now at war with another country and will begin military action against it ○ *'Older men declare war, but it is the youth that must fight and die.'* (Herbert Hoover, *Speech, Republican National Convention*; 27 June 1944) **2.** to begin a fierce campaign to get rid of or defeat something, or start fighting it in earnest

declass /deé klaás/ (**-classes, -classing, -classed**) *vt* to give somebody a lower status or class in society

déclassé /day kláss ay, -klaáss-, dáy kla sáy/ *adj* reduced to a lower class or status in society [Late 19C. < French, past participle of *déclasser* 'declass']

declassify /dee klássi fī/ (**-fies, -fying, -fied**) *vt* to remove something from an official list of confidential or top-secret material so that anyone may see it —**declassifiable** *adj* —**declassification** /dee klássifi káysh'n/ *n*

declaw /deé kláw/ (**-claws, -clawing, -clawed**) *vt* to remove the claws from the paws of an animal

declension /di klénsh'n/ *n* **1.** GRAM **SET OF WORDS THAT BEHAVE SIMILARLY** a group of nouns, adjectives, or pronouns that all change their form or word-endings in the same way according to gender, number, or grammatical case **2.** GRAM **PROCESS OF ENDING WORDS** the process by which some sets of nouns, adjectives, and pronouns vary in form to show gender, number, or grammatical case **3. WORSENING OR FALLING AWAY** the process of gradually declining or deteriorating (*formal*) **4.** GEOL **DOWNWARD SLOPE** a downward slope, especially of terrain [15C. Via French *déclinaison* < Latin *declination-* < *declinare* 'bend away' (see DECLINE), from the idea of inflections deviating from the pure form] —**declensional** *adj* —**declensionally** *adv*

declinable /di klīnəb'l/ *adj* used to describe a noun, adjective, or pronoun having different grammatical forms according to number, case, or gender [Mid-16C. Via French < Latin *declinabilis* < *declinare* (see DECLINE)]

declination /dékli náysh'n/ *n* **1.** the angular distance of an astronomical object measured in degrees from the celestial equator along the great circle passing through it and the celestial poles **2.** PHYS, GEOG same as **magnetic declination** —**declinational** *adj*

decline /di klīn/ *v* (**-clines, -clining, -clined**) **1.** *vti* **REFUSE INVITATION** to give a polite refusal to an invitation **2.** *vi* **REFUSE PARTICIPATION** to refuse to respond or take part in something **3.** *vi* **DIMINISH** to decrease in number, amount, value, or quality ○ *shares declining in value* **4.** *vi* **GET WEAKER** to become physically or mentally less vigorous, especially because of illness or advancing years ○ *His health had declined.* **5.** *vt* GRAM **LIST VARIOUS FORMS** to state the grammatical forms of a noun, adjective, or pronoun **6.** *vi* GRAM **HAVE INFLECTIONS** to exist in various inflected forms according to number, case, or gender (*refers to a noun, adjective, or pronoun*) **7.** *vi* **SLOPE DOWN** to bend something downwards, or slope downwards ■ *n* **1. DETERIORATION OR REDUCTION** a decrease in number, amount, value, or quality **2. PERIOD NEAR END** the terminal period of somebody or something, ending in death or disappearance ○ *at the decline of the empire* **3. DOWNWARD SLOPE** a downward slope or movement [14C. Directly or via French < Latin *declinare* 'turn aside, bend away' < *clinare* 'bend'] —**decliner** *n* ◇ **be on the decline 1.** to show a gradual decrease in number, amount, value, or quality **2.** to show a gradual worsening of health

declinometer /dékli nómmitər/ *n* an instrument that measures the difference between magnetic north or south and true north or south at a specific point on the Earth's surface [Mid-19C. < DECLINATION]

declivitous /di klívvətəs/ *adj* sloping downwards

declivity /di klívvəti/ (*plural* **-ties**) *n* **1.** a surface, especially a piece of land, that slopes downwards **2.** a downward inclination, especially of a piece of land [Early 17C. < Latin *declivitas* < *clivus* 'slope']

declutch /deé klúch/ (**-clutches, -clutching, -clutched**) *vi* to disengage the clutch of a motor vehicle (*technical*)

Deco /dékō/, **deco** *adj* DESIGN same as **art deco** [Mid-20C. Shortening]

decoct /di kókt/ (**-cocts, -cocting, -cocted**) *vt* to extract the essence or active ingredient from a substance by boiling it [15C. < Latin *decoct-*, past participle of *decoquere* 'boil down' < *coquere* 'cook']

decoction /di kóksh'n/ *n* **1.** the extraction of an essence or active ingredient from a substance by boiling **2.** a concentrated substance that results from decoction

decode /dee kṓd/ (**-codes, -coding, -coded**) *v* **1.** *vt* **DECIPHER CODE** to transform an encoded message into an understandable form **2.** *vt* **TRANSFORM ELECTRONIC SIGNAL FOR USE** to transform an electronic signal into a usable form **3.** *vt* **FIND MEANING OF INDIRECT LANGUAGE** to find the direct meaning of cryptic or indirect language **4.** *vt* **DISCOVER UNDERLYING MEANING OF IMAGE** to understand the underlying meaning of something such as a painting **5.** *vti* **TRANSLATE FOREIGN LANGUAGE** to understand the meaning of a word or phrase in a foreign language —**decodable** *adj* —**decoder** *n*

decoder /dee kṓdər/ *n* a person, device, or computer program that decodes something

decoke /deé kṓk/ (**-cokes, -coking, -coked**) *vt* to remove the carbon deposits from an internal-combustion engine

decollate /deé kə láyt, dékə layt/ (**-lates, -lating, -lated**) *vt* to separate continuous paper into single sheets —**decollation** /deékə láysh'n, dékə-/ *n* —**decollator** *n*

décolletage /dáy kol taázh, day kóllə taázh/ *n* **1.** the top front part of a woman's low-cut garment **2.** a piece of women's clothing with a décolletage [Late 19C. < French < *décolleté* (see DÉCOLLETÉ)]

décolleté /day kól tay, -kóllə tay/ *n* **CHEST AREA** the upper part of a woman's chest, below the neck ■ *adj* **1. WITH LOW NECKLINE** having a low-cut front neckline ○ *a décolleté dress* **2. WEARING LOW-CUT GARMENT** wearing a décolleté garment [Mid-19C. < French, past participle of *décolleter* 'lower the neckline' < *collet* 'collar' < Latin *collum* 'neck']

decolonize /dee kóllə nīz/ (**-nizes, -nizing, -nized**), **decolonise** (**-nises, -nising, -nised**) *vt* to grant independence to a colony —**decolonization** /dee kóllə nī záysh'n/ *n*

decolorant /dee kúllərənt/ *n* a chemical that removes the colour from a fabric or other substance —**decolorant** *adj*

decolorize /dee kúllə rīz/ (**-izes, -izing, -ized**), **decolorise** (**-ises, -ising, -ised**) *vt* to remove the colour from a fabric or other substance, e.g. by chemical means —**decolorization** /dee kúllə rī záysh'n/ *n*

decolour /dee kúllər/ (**-ours, -ouring, -oured**) *vt* INDUST same as **decolorize** —**decoloration** /dee kúllə ráysh'n/ *n*

decommission /deékə mísh'n/ (**-sions, -sioning, -sioned**) *vt* to remove something such as a ship, nuclear power station, machinery, or weapons from service

decompensation /deé kom pen sáysh'n/ *n* **1.** the failure of the heart to maintain adequate circulation because of various stresses upon it **2.** the deterioration of existing psychological defences in a patient already exhibiting pathological behaviour

decompiler /deékəm pīlər/ *n* a computer program that translates basic machine code back into high-level source code

decompose /deékəm pṓz/ (**-poses, -posing, -posed**) *vti* **1. ROT** to break down organic matter from a complex to a simpler form, mainly through the action of fungi and bacteria, or be broken down in this way **2. BREAK DOWN INTO PIECES** to break something down into smaller or simpler parts, or be broken down in this way **3.** CHEM **BREAK DOWN INTO CONSTITUENT PARTS** to separate into constituent parts, or cause something to separate into its constituent parts —**decomposability** /deékəm pōzə bílləti/ *n* —**decomposable** *adj* —**decomposer** *n* —**decomposition** /deé kompə zísh'n/ *n*

decompress /deékəm préss/ (**-presses, -pressing, -pressed**) *v* **1.** *vti* **REDUCE PRESSURE** to cause a reduction in the atmospheric pressure of an enclosed space, or experience such a reduction **2.** *vti* **ALLOW EXPANSION** to allow a substance to expand to normal dimensions or volume by the removal of pressure, or undergo this process **3.** *vt* COMPUT **EXPAND COMPUTER DATA** to expand compressed electronic data to its normal extent, or undergo this process —**decompressive** *adj*

decompression /deékəm présh'n/ *n* **1. PRESSURE DECREASE** a decrease in surrounding or inherent pressure, especially the controlled decrease in pressure that divers undergo to prevent decompression sickness **2.** COMPUT **COMPUTER DATA EXPANSION** the expansion to full size of compressed electronic data ○ *decompression must precede installation* ○ *decompression software* **3.** SURG **SURGERY TO REDUCE PRESSURE IN ORGAN** a surgical procedure to reduce pressure in an organ or part of the body caused, e.g. by fluid on the brain, or to reduce the pressure of tissues on a nerve

decompression chamber *n* a sealed room where divers undergo decompression

decompression sickness, **decompression illness** *n* a condition marked by joint pain, nausea, loss of motion, and breathing difficulties experienced by divers and others who emerge too quickly from a pressurized environment. It is caused by the formation of nitrogen bubbles in the blood and tissues.

decon /dee kon/ (**-cons, -conning, -conned**) *vt* same as **decontaminate** (*informal*) [Late 19C. [shortening]]

decondition /deékən dísh'n/ (**-tions, -tioning, -tioned**) *v* **1.** *vt* to cause or teach a person or animal to stop exhibiting a conditioned response **2.** *vti* to lose physical fitness through lack of exercise, illness, or a period of weightlessness in space flight, or cause somebody to do this

decongest /deé kənjést/ (**-gests, -gesting, -gested**) *vt* **1.** to loosen mucus in the nasal passages, sinuses, or bronchi **2.** to increase the flow in something that is compacted or congested

decongestant /deékən jéstənt/ *n* an agent that relieves nasal congestion —**decongestant** *adj* —**decongestive** *adj*

deconsecrate /dee kónssi krayt/ (**-crates, -crating, -crated**) *vt* to convert a sacred place, building, or object to secular use —**deconsecration** /deé konssi kráysh'n/ *n*

deconstruct /deékən strúkt/ (**-structs, -structing, -structed**) *vt* to subject a text to critical analysis using the theories of deconstruction

deconstruction /deékən strúksh'n/ *n* a method of analysing texts based on the ideas that language is inherently unstable and shifting and that the reader rather than the author is central in determining meaning. It was introduced by the French philosopher Jacques Derrida in the late 1960s. —**deconstructionism** *n* —**deconstructionist** *n, adj*

decontaminate /deékən támmi nayt/ (**-nates, -nating, -nated**) *vt* to remove unwanted chemical, radioactive, or biological impurities or toxins from

a person, object, or place —**decontaminant** *n* —**decontamination** /dee̅kən támmi náysh'n/ *n* —**decontaminative** *adj* —**decontaminator** *n*

decontrol /dee̅kən trṓl/ (**-trols, -trolling, -trolled**) *vt* to remove official restraints or regulations on something, especially rents

decor /dáy kawr, dék-/, **décor** *n* **1.** the style of furniture and furnishings chosen for a room or house **2.** the scenery of a stage [Late 19C. < French < *décorer* 'decorate' < Latin *decorare* (see DECORATE)]

decorate /dékə rayt/ (**-rates, -rating, -rated**) *v* **1.** *vt* MAKE SOMETHING ATTRACTIVE to make something more attractive by adding ornate or stylish features to it **2.** *vti* CHANGE APPEARANCE OF ROOM to paint or wallpaper a building or a room **3.** *vt* AWARD MEDAL TO SOMEBODY to give a medal or other honour or award to somebody to acknowledge bravery, dedication, or achievement [Mid-16C. < Latin *decorat-*, past participle of *decorare* 'beautify' < *decus* 'ornament']

Decorated architecture /dékə raytid-/, **Decorated style** *n* the second, more ornate stage of English Gothic architecture, characterized by an increased use of geometric tracery and floral motifs

decoration /dékə ráysh'n/ *n* **1.** ATTRACTIVE ITEM an item, usually one of a group, attached to something to make it look more attractive or to mark a special occasion **2.** ORNAMENTATION the addition of ornaments to make something more attractive **3.** PAINTING AND PAPERING the painting and wallpapering in a room or building **4.** AWARD a medal or other honour or award given to somebody to acknowledge bravery, dedication, or achievement

decorative /dékərətiv/ *adj* **1.** ATTRACTIVE serving merely to look attractive rather than having a functional purpose **2.** ORNAMENTAL serving to make something look more attractive, especially by the addition of nonfunctional embellishments **3.** OF DECORATION relating to the decoration of a room or home ○ *added some nice decorative touches* —**decoratively** *adv* —**decorativeness** *n*

decorative art *n* art concerned with the design and production of functional but decorative items for home use such as ceramics, furniture, and fabrics (*often used in the plural*)

decorator /dékə raytər/ *n* **1.** SOMEBODY WHO PAINTS AND WALLPAPERS somebody whose job is painting and wallpapering houses and other buildings **2.** *US* INTERIOR DECORATOR somebody whose job is to plan the decoration and furnishings of a room or building **3.** SOMEBODY WHO DECORATES somebody whose job is to decorate something (*often used in combination*)

decorous /dékərəss/ *adj* **1.** conforming to what is acceptable or expected in formal or solemn settings, especially in dress or behaviour ○ *'They began to talk politely, in decorous half-completed sentences, with little gasps of agreement.'* (William Faulkner, *Sanctuary*; 1931) **2.** understated and dignified [Mid-17C. < Latin *decorus* 'seemly' < *decor* 'attractiveness'] —**decorously** *adv* —**decorousness** *n*

decorticate /dee káwrti kayt/ *vt* (**-cates, -cating, -cated**) **1.** BOT REMOVE OUTER LAYER FROM PLANT to remove an outer layer such as bark, rind, or a husk from a plant or part of a plant **2.** SURG SURGICALLY REMOVE LAYER FROM ORGAN to remove surgically the outer layer of an organ or structure such as the brain or kidney ■ *adj* MED WITHOUT CORTEX FUNCTION describes a brain that has lost the function of its cerebral cortex as a result of disease or surgery [Early 17C. < Latin *decorticat-*, past participle of *decorticare* < *cortex* (see CORTEX)] —**decortication** /dee káwrti káysh'n/ *n* —**decorticator** *n*

decorum /di káwrəm/ *n* **1.** dignity or good taste that is appropriate to a specific occasion **2.** the compatibility of an element such as character, form, style, or plot in a literary or artistic work with the work as a whole [Mid-16C. < Latin < *decorus* (see DECOROUS)]

decoupage /dáy koo paa͟zh/, **découpage** *n* **1.** a decorative technique in which a design is made of cut-out pieces of printed paper glued onto a flat base and then varnished **2.** a picture or other form of decoration made using decoupage [Mid-20C. < French < *découper* 'cut up, cut out' < *couper* 'cut']

decouple /dee kúpp'l/ (**-ples, -pling, -pled**) *vt* **1.** to separate or disengage one thing from another **2.** to remove or weaken the interaction between two electronic circuits, subsystems, or systems so that there is little or no transfer or feedback of energy between them —**decoupler** *n*

decoy *n* /dee̅ koy, di kóy/ **1.** DISTRACTOR somebody or something used to deceive or divert attention, especially in order to lure somebody into a trap **2.** FIELD SPORTS LURE TO ATTRACT ANIMAL a bird or other animal, or a realistic replica, used by hunters to attract wildlife to a place for trapping or shooting **3.** MIL FAKE EQUIPMENT a fake tank, ship, aircraft, or other military apparatus meant to deceive the enemy **4.** FIELD SPORTS ENTRAPMENT AREA an enclosed area or stretch of water that game or fowl are driven or lured into so that they can be easily shot or captured ■ *vt* /di kóy/ (**-coys, -coying, -coyed**) DECEIVE to deceive or entrap a person or animal by using a decoy [Mid-16C. < Dutch *de kooi* 'the cage' < Latin *cavea* 'cage']

decoy duck /dee̅ koy-/ *n* **1.** a wild duck that has been tamed so it can be used for attracting other ducks **2.** a model duck, usually carved from wood, for use as a decoy or decoration

decrease *vti* /di kree̅ss/ (**-creases, -creasing, -creased**) DIMINISH to lessen in size, strength, or amount, or cause something to do this ■ *n* /dee̅ kreess/ **1.** PROCESS OF DIMINISHING the process of diminishing in size, strength, or amount ○ *street crime is on the decrease* **2.** REDUCTION a reduction in the size, strength, or amount of something ○ *a 2% decrease in revenue* [14C. Via Old French *decreiss-* < Latin *decrescere* < *crescere* 'grow'] —**decreasing** *adj* —**decreasingly** *adv*

decree /di kree̅/ *n* **1.** OFFICIAL ORDER an order with the power of legislation issued by a ruler or other person or group with authority **2.** LAW COURT RULING a ruling given by a court, especially a divorce court **3.** RELIG DIVINE WILL in Christian belief, the will or purpose of God, interpreted through events considered to be God's doing ■ *vt* (**-crees, -creeing, -creed**) ISSUE ORDER FOR SOMETHING TO HAPPEN to make an official order, pronouncement, or legal ruling to effect something [14C. Via Old French *decré*, variant of *decret* < Latin *decretum*, neuter past participle of *decernere* 'decide, pronounce a decision'] —**decreeable** *adj* —**decreer** *n*

decree absolute (*plural* **decrees absolute**) *n* the final divorce court ruling that officially ends a marriage, leaving both parties free to marry again

decree nisi /-nī sī/ (*plural* **decrees nisi**) *n* an interim ruling of a divorce court that will become absolute in the absence of objections arising

decreet /di kree̅t/ *n* in Scots law, the final judgment in a court case [14C. < Old French *decret* (see DECREE)]

decrement /dékrimənt/ *n* **1.** the amount by which a quantity or quality gradually decreases **2.** the process by which a quantity or quality gradually decreases (*formal*) [Late 16C. < Latin *decrementum* < *decrescere* (see DECREASE)] —**decremental** /dékri mént'l/ *adj* —**decrementally** *adv*

decrepit /di kréppit/ *adj* **1.** in poor condition, especially as a result of being old, overused, or not working efficiently **2.** with strength lessened by the effects of age (*informal*) [15C. < Latin *decrepitus* < *crepitus*, past participle of *crepare* 'crack, creak'] —**decrepitly** *adv* —**decrepitude** *n*

SYNONYMS See ***weak***.

decrepitate /di kréppi tayt/ (**-tates, -tating, -tated**) *vti* to heat a substance, especially a salt, until it crackles or stops crackling, or be heated in this way (*technical*) [Mid-17C. < DE- + Latin *crepitare* 'crackle' < *crepitus* 'cracked' (see DECREPIT)] —**decrepitation** /di kréppi táysh'n/ *n*

decresc. *abbr* MUSIC decrescendo

decrescendo /dee̅kra shéndō/ MUSIC *adv* same as **diminuendo** ■ *n* (*plural* **-dos**) same as **diminuendo** [Early 19C. < Italian, 'decreasing'] —**decrescendo** *adj*

decrescent /di kréss'nt/ *adj* describes the moon when it is waning (*technical*) [Early 17C. < Latin *decrescent-*, present participle of *decrescere* (see DECREASE)] —**decrescence** *n*

decretal /di kree̅t'l/ *n* a papal decree or edict that relates to an aspect of Roman Catholic law or doctrine [14C. < late Latin *decretale* < Latin *decret-*, past participle of *decernere* (see DECERN)] —**decretal** *adj*

decretory /di kree̅təri/ *adj* relating to or having the force of a decree [Late 16C. < Latin *decretorius* < *decret-* (see DECRETAL)]

decriminalize /dee krímminə līz/ (**-izes, -izing, -ized**), **decriminalise** (**-ises, -ising, -ised**) *vt* to make legal an action or substance that was formerly illegal —**decriminalization** /dee̅ krimminə lī záysh'n/ *n* —**decriminalized** *adj*

SYNONYMS See ***legal***.

decry /di krī/ (**-cries, -crying, -cried**) *vt* to express strong disapproval of or openly criticize somebody or something ○ *critics decrying lowered standards in education* [Early 17C. After French *décrier* 'cry down'] —**decrial** *n* —**decrier** *n*

decrypt /dee krípt/ (**-crypts, -crypting, -crypted**) *vt* same as **decode** (senses 1, 3) [Mid-20C. < DE- + CRYPTOGRAM] —**decryption** *n*

decubitus /di kyoo̅bitəss/ *n* the position of a person's body when he or she is lying down, usually on the front, back, or side (*technical*) [Late 19C. < modern Latin < Latin *decumbere* (see DECUMBENT)] —**decubital** *adj*

decubitus ulcer *n* MED same as **bedsore** (*technical*)

decumbent /di kúmbənt/ *adj* **1.** describes plants that lie along the ground but have a tip growing upwards **2.** describes hair or bristles that lie or grow flat along a surface [Early 17C. < Latin *decumbent*, present participle of *decumbere* 'lie down' < *cubare* 'lie down'] —**decumbence** *n* —**decumbently** *adv*

decurion /de kyoo̅ri ən/ *n* **1.** in ancient Rome, an officer in command of ten soldiers **2.** a councillor in the Roman Empire [14C. < Latin *decurion-* < *decuria* (see DECURY), after *centurion*]

decurrent /di kúrrənt/ *adj* describes plant leaves that curve down at the edges, or trees with a rounded shape [15C. < Latin *decurrent-*, present participle of *decurrere* 'run down' < *currere* 'run'] —**decurrently** *adv*

decury /dékyoori/ (*plural* **-ies**) *n* in ancient Rome, a company of ten soldiers [Mid-16C. < Latin *decuria* < *decem* 'ten', after *centuria* 'century']

decussate /di kússayt/ *adj* **1.** having the shape of a cross **2.** describes leaves that form pairs opposite each other and at right angles to the pair above and the pair below, as in the horse chestnut [Early 19C. < Latin *decussatus*, past participle of *decussare* 'divide crosswise' < *decussis*, the numeral ten (written 'X') < *decem* 'ten' + *assis*, a coin] —**decussately** /-aytli, -ətli/ *adv* —**decussation** /dee̅ ku sáysh'n/ *n*

dedans /də daaN/ *n* (*plural same*) in real tennis, the open end of the court just behind the serving area where spectators can watch the match ■ *npl* the spectators who watch from the dedans [Early 18C. < French, 'inside, interior']

Dedham Vale /déddəm-/ Area of Outstanding Natural Beauty on the border of Essex and Suffolk, eastern England. Area: 90 sq. km/35 sq. mi.

dedicate /déddi kayt/ (**-cates, -cating, -cated**) *vt* **1.** DEVOTE ATTENTION TO SOMETHING to spend time or energy doing something **2.** COMMIT YOURSELF TO SOMETHING to commit yourself or your life to something **3.** ADDRESS WORK OF ART TO SOMEBODY to associate a book, piece of music, or other art form with somebody as a token of friendship or esteem or as an acknowledgment of help received **4.** PLAY MUSIC ADDRESSED TO SOMEBODY to play a piece of music, or request the playing of a piece of music, as a tribute, especially on the radio **5.** SET SOMETHING ASIDE FOR PURPOSE to set something aside for a particular purpose ○ *an entire TV series dedicated to birds* **6.** SET SOMETHING APART AS HOLY to set something apart for a sacred purpose or to the memory of a holy person, saint, or god, especially in a ceremony for this purpose ○ *'We cannot dedicate – we cannot consecrate – we cannot hallow – this ground. The brave men...who struggled here have consecrated it.'* (Abraham Lincoln, *Gettysburg Address*; 19 November, 1863) [15C. < Latin *dedicat-*, past participle of *dedicare* 'consecrate' < *dicare* 'proclaim'] —**dedicatee** /déddikə tee̅/ *n* —**dedicative** /-kətiv, -kaytiv/ *adj* —**dedicator** *n* —**dedicatory** /-kətəri, -kaytəri/ *adj*

dedicated /déddi kaytid/ *adj* **1.** wholeheartedly devoted or committed to an aim, cause, or job **2.** designed to carry out only one task, or set aside for a specific purpose ○ *relayed via a dedicated satellite link* —**dedicatedly** *adv*

dedicated line *n* a telephone line assigned to a designated user, usually to provide a permanent connection to the Internet

dedication /déddi káysh'n/ *n* 1. DEVOTION the quality of being devoted or committed to something ○ *her dedication to duty* 2. INSCRIPTION a short printed text at the beginning of a written or musical work associating it with somebody esteemed by the author 3. PIECE OF MUSIC a piece of music played or requested as a tribute, especially on the radio 4. SETTING ASIDE an act of setting something aside for a purpose, often in a special ceremony —**dedicational** *adj*

dedifferentiation /dee difə renshi áysh'n/ *n* BIOL same as **anaplasia**

deduce /di dyóoss/ (**-duces, -ducing, -duced**) *vt* 1. to come to a conclusion, often without all the necessary or relevant information, but using what is known in a logical way 2. to come to a conclusion by inference from a general principle [15C. < Latin *deducere* 'lead out' < *ducere* 'to lead'] —**deducible** *adj*

SYNONYMS ***deduce, infer, assume, reason, conclude, work out, figure out***

CORE MEANING: to reach a logical conclusion on the basis of information

deduce to come to a conclusion, often without all the necessary or relevant information, but using what is known in a logical way ○ *While it is relatively easy to deduce a cause from an effect, it is more difficult to predict effects from causes.* ○ *It didn't take a rocket scientist to deduce that they were having an affair.* **infer** to come to a conclusion or form an opinion about something on the basis of evidence or reasoning ○ *It has been inferred from his poetry that he was homosexual.* ○ *Negligence may be inferred from the fact that the product left the manufacturer in a defective state.* **assume** to accept something as true without checking or confirming it ○ *She had always assumed that her mother was born in Paris.* ○ *He could reasonably have assumed from what was said that his employment prospects were good.* **reason** to consider information and use it to reach a conclusion in a logical way ○ *Scott reasoned that if Annabel were having a heart attack, she wouldn't be able to talk on the telephone.* ○ *Either, he reasoned, there was no burglar, or else the burglar was not interested in diamonds.* **conclude** to form an opinion or make a logical judgment about something after considering everything known about it ○ *The report concluded that a world recession was unlikely.* ○ *They were forced to conclude from the evidence that the case had been mishandled.* **work out** to solve a problem or find an answer to a question by reasoning or calculation ○ *Try and work out what the poem is about.* ○ *Nobody could work out which speaker was which.* **figure out** to find a solution or reach a conclusion by careful thought or reasoning ○ *Your task is to figure out what this answer means in terms of likely delay.* ○ *I can't figure out why he got into foreign investment.*

deduct /di dúkt/ (**-ducts, -ducting, -ducted**) *vt* to subtract an amount for some purpose [15C. < Latin *deduct-*, past participle of *deducere* (see DEDUCE)]

deductible /di dúktəb'l/ *adj* 1. *N Am* allowed by tax authorities as a legitimate expense not liable to tax 2. capable of being, or liable to be, subtracted from something for some purpose ■ *n N Am* INSUR same as **excess** *n* (sense 4) —**deductibility** /di dúktə bílləti/ *n*

deduction /di dúksh'n/ *n* 1. AMOUNT DEDUCTED an amount that is subtracted from something, especially as an allowance against tax 2. SUBTRACTION OF AMOUNT the act of subtracting an amount for a purpose 3. CONCLUSION DRAWN a conclusion drawn from available information 4. DRAWING CONCLUSION the process of drawing a conclusion from available information 5. LOGIC LOGICAL CONCLUSION a conclusion reached by applying the rules of logic to a premise 6. LOGIC REASONING the forming of conclusions by applying the rules of logic to a premise

deductive /di dúktiv/ *adj* based on logical or reasonable deduction —**deductively** *adv*

deed /deed/ *n* 1. SOMETHING DONE an intentional act ○ *'The last temptation is the greatest treason / To do the right deed for the wrong reason.'* (T. S. Eliot, *Murder in the Cathedral*; 1935) 2. NOTEWORTHY ACTION an action that is outstanding in a particular way 3. DOCUMENT a signed document that outlines the terms of an agreement, especially one that details a change in ownership of property 4. LAW same as **title deed** ■ **deeds** *npl* ACTIONS action in general, especially as contrasted with speech ■ *vt* (**deeds, deeding, deeded**) *N Am* LAW TRANSFER PROPERTY TO SOMEBODY to sign over or transfer something, especially property, to another person [Old English *dēd* < Germanic, 'a doing' < Indo-European]

deed box *n* a lockable strongbox where deeds and other important documents can be safely kept

deeded /deédid/ *adj N Am* associated with a deed that shows clear ownership ○ *a ranch consisting of 640 deeded acres*

deed of covenant *n* a signed document by which somebody formally agrees to make payments for a period of several years to a person in specific circumstances or especially, formerly, to a charity. For charitable donations deeds of covenant have been superseded by Gift Aid.

deed poll *n* an official document, especially one that makes a change in somebody's name, that is signed and executed by one person only [< POLL 'cut off cleanly', as opposed to notched at the edge as with a contract drawn up in multiple copies]

deejay /deé jay/ *n* same as **DJ**[1] (sense 1) (*informal*) [Mid-20C. Respelling] —**deejay** *vi*

deem /deem/ (**deems, deeming, deemed**) *vt* to judge or consider something in a particular light (*formal; often used in the passive*) ○ *a plan that was deemed impractical from the very start* [Old English *dēman* < Germanic, 'to judge']

de-emphasize /dee émfə sīz/, **de-emphasise** *vt* to make something seem or be less important or central — **de-emphasis** /-fəssiss/ *n*

deemster /deémstər/, **dempster** /démpstər/ *n* either of the two justices serving on the Isle of Man — **deemstership** *n*

de-energize /dee énnər jīz/, **de-energise** *v* 1. *vt* to cut off an electrical circuit from its source of power 2. *vti* to have less energy or vitality, or cause somebody to have less energy or vitality —**de-energization** /deé ennər jī záysh'n/ *n*

deep /deep/ *adj* 1. DOWN FROM SURFACE extending from a surface downwards or inwards ○ *a deep wound* 2. FAR FROM TOP TO BOTTOM extending a long way from top to bottom ○ *a deep well* ○ *'The deep dark-shining / Pacific leans on the land.'* (Robinson Jeffers, *Night*; 1925) 3. FAR FROM FRONT TO BACK extending a long way from front to back ○ *a cupboard with deep shelves* 4. FAR FROM EDGE extending a long way from a surface or boundary inwards ○ *deep wood* 5. MADE UP OF UNITS standing or lining up in a particular number of rows ○ *people six deep on the pavement* 6. FAR DOWN OR IN relatively far down, in, or inside something ○ *a nagging pain deep in his chest* 7. COMING FROM OR REACHING INSIDE BODY coming from or reaching far down inside the body ○ *take a deep breath* 8. LOW IN PITCH low in pitch and rounded in tone ○ *a deep booming voice* 9. DARK IN COLOUR relatively dark, rich, or intense in colour ○ *deep purple* 10. EXTREME extreme, severe, or intense ○ *deep suspicion* 11. PROFOUND intellectually profound ○ *no evidence of deep thinking* ■ *adj, adv* 1. SPORTS NEAR OWN GOAL in sports such as football, nearer to the goal a team is defending than the goal it is attacking ○ *Aberdeen played with two deep defenders.* ○ *deep in their own territory* 2. CRICKET NEAR BOUNDARY in cricket, playing or played near the boundary of the playing area, farther from home plate or one of the bases than is usual, relatively far from the batsman ○ *deep mid-on* ■ *adv* FAR far, especially from a surface or point of entry ○ *The expedition went deep into the jungle.* ■ *n* 1. SEA the ocean depths 2. CRICKET POSITION FAR FROM BATSMAN in cricket, the fielding position relatively far from the batsman 3. INTENSE PART the middle or most intense part of something (*literary*) ○ *the deep of night* [Old English *dēop* < Indo-European, 'deep, hollow'] —**deepness** *n* ◇ **deep down (inside)** in your innermost being ◇ **deep in something** completely overwhelmed by or absorbed in something ○ *deep in a new novel* ○ *She sat silent, deep in thought.* ◇ **in deep** very involved

deep-discount bond *n* a bond sold at a large discount because it bears little or no interest although it provides a capital gain on redemption

deep-dish *adj* baked in a deep dish and so thicker than normal ○ *deep-dish pizza*

deep-dyed *adj* 1. describes fabric that has been dyed with a concentrated fade-resistant dye 2. same as **dyed-in-the-wool** (sense 1)

deepen /deépən/ (**-ens, -ening, -ened**) *vti* 1. to become deep or deeper, or make something deep or deeper ○ *Torrential rain caused the potholes to widen and deepen.* 2. to become more intense, or make something more intense ○ *the recession was deepening* —**deepener** *n*

deep end *n* the part of a swimming pool, lake, or other body of water where the water is deepest ◇ **be thrown in at the deep end** to have to learn something new or difficult with very little experience or warning ◇ **go off (at) the deep end** to fly into a rage or lose your emotional equilibrium

deep-fat fryer *n* same as **deep fryer**

deep-freeze *vt* 1. FREEZE SOMETHING QUICKLY to freeze something such as food quickly in order to prolong its freshness or nutritional value 2. KEEP SOMETHING VERY COLD to store something at very low temperatures 3. SUSPEND ACTIVITY to put off or suspend activity (*informal*) —**deep-frozen** *adj*

deep-fry *vt* to cook food in fat or oil that is deep enough to cover the food completely —**deep-fried** *adj*

deep fryer *n* an electrical appliance for deep-frying food

deep-laid *adj* carefully worked out and highly confidential ○ *a deep-laid plan*

deep-litter *adj* 1. using a thick layer of straw or other natural material for farm animals, especially poultry, to move about in 2. from or produced by animals raised in deep-litter conditions

deeply /deépli/ *adv* 1. profoundly or intensely ○ *deeply offended* 2. far down inside ○ *breathe deeply* ○ *deeply felt pain*

deep-pan *adj* describes a pizza with a deep filling baked in a dish with raised sides

deep-rooted *adj* 1. firmly held or established, usually over a long period of time, and so unlikely to change 2. having roots that grow deep in the soil

deep-sea *adj* relating to the deep waters of the ocean far away from land

deep-seated *adj* firmly established and difficult to change or eradicate ○ *deep-seated fear*

deep-set *adj* describes eyes with deep sockets

Deep South /deep sówth/ a part of the southeastern United States, usually considered to comprise Alabama, Georgia, Louisiana, Mississippi, and South Carolina, regarded as the heartland of traditional Southern culture

deep space *n* space beyond the Earth's gravitational influence or beyond the orbit of the Moon

deep structure *n* the underlying form of a language, conceived as containing all the information needed to make any sentence in that language

deep vein thrombosis *n* a potentially fatal condition in which a blood clot forms in a vein or artery and may partially or completely block blood flow. It is often the result of long periods of immobility.

deep-water *adj* 1. describes a harbour or anchorage that is deep enough to accommodate large ocean-going vessels 2. *US regional* designed or trained to travel on the sea

deer /deer/ (*plural same*) *n* an animal distinguished by the branched antlers on males. More than forty species of deer exist, of different sizes and with different markings, and they are found wild on all continents except Australia and Antarctica. Family: Cervidae. [Old English *dēor* 'animal' < Germanic, 'breathing creature' < Indo-European, 'breath, vapour']

SPELLCHECK See ***dear***.

deer-culler *n NZ* a professional hunter of wild deer

deer fly *n* a biting fly that infests deer and other animals, sucking blood and spreading the infectious disease tularemia. It also delivers a stinging bite to humans. Genus: *Chrysops.*

deergrass /deér graass/ (*plural same*) *n* a perennial flowering plant that grows in thick tufts. Native to:

temperate peat bogs. Latin name: *Trichophorum caespitosum*.

deerhound /deer hownd/ *n* a large long-legged dog with a very shaggy coat, belonging to a breed developed in Scotland as a hunting dog from a Mediterranean strain of greyhound

deer lick *n* a naturally occurring or artificial salty patch of ground where deer come to lick

deer mouse *n* a mouse that lives in natural surroundings rather than buildings, often making its nest in a tree or tree stump. Native to: North and Central America. Genus: *Peromyscus*.

deerskin /deer skin/ *n* the treated hide of a deer used as a fabric

deerstalker /deer stawkər/ *n* **1.** *also* **deerstalker hat** a tweed hat with peaks at the front and back and earflaps that can either be tied together on its crown or fastened under the chin **2.** a deer hunter on foot

deerstalking /deer stawking/ *n* the activity of hunting wild deer by stealthily following them on foot

deer tick *n* a tick that is a parasite of humans and other animals and transmits the bacterium that causes Lyme disease. Latin name: *Ioxides dammini*.

de-escalate /dee éskə layt/ *vt* to reduce the level or intensity of a difficult or dangerous situation —**de-escalation** /dee eskə láysh'n/ *n*

Deeside and Lochnagar /dee sīd ənd lókhnə gaar/ National Scenic Area in Scotland, situated on the banks of the River Dee in Aberdeenshire. Area: 400 sq. km/250 sq. mi.

deet /deet/ *n* an oily colourless chemical that is the active ingredient in the most widely used insect repellents applied to the skin. Formula: $C_{12}H_{17}NO$. [Mid-20C. Contraction and alteration of DIETHYL TOLUAMIDE]

def /def/ *adj* excellent (*slang*) [Late 20C. Shortening of DEFINITIVE]

def. *abbr* **1.** MIL, SPORTS, LAW defence **2.** LAW defendant **3.** FIN deferred **4.** GRAM definite **5.** LING definition

deface /di fáyss/ (**-faces, -facing, -faced**) *vt* to spoil the appearance of something, especially intentionally [14C. < French *défacer* < *face* (see FACE)] —**defaceable** *adj* —**defacement** *n* —**defacer** *n*

de facto /day fáktō/ *adv* **IN FACT** in fact, whether with a legal right or not ■ *adj* **1. AS THOUGH RIGHTFUL** acting or existing in fact but without legal sanction ○ *the de facto rules of the country* **2.** *ANZ* **COHABITING** living together as if married ○ *a de facto couple* ■ *n* (*plural* **de factos**) *ANZ* **PARTNER** somebody who is living with another person as if they were married (*informal*) [Early 17C. < Latin, 'in fact', literally 'from what is done']

defaecate *vi* another spelling of **defecate**

defalcate /dee fal kayt, -fawl-/ (**-cates, -cating, -cated**) *vt* to misuse something, especially money or property, that belongs to somebody else and is held in trust [Mid-16C. < medieval Latin *defalcat-*, past participle of *defalcare* 'deduct' < Latin *falx* 'scythe'] —**defalcation** /dee fal káysh'n, -fawl-/ *n* —**defalcator** *n*

defame /di fáym/ (**-fames, -faming, -famed**) *vt* to attack somebody or somebody's reputation, character, or good name by making slanderous or libellous statements [14C. Via Old French *deffamer* < Latin *diffamare* 'spread about as an insulting report' < *fama* 'talk, report, reputation'] —**defamation** /déffə máysh'n/ *n* —**defamatory** /di fámmətəri/ *adj* —**defamer** *n*

SYNONYMS See *malign*.

defang /dee fáng/ (**-fangs, -fanging, -fanged**) *vt* to remove the fangs from a snake or other animal

defat /dee fát/ (**-fats, -fatting, -fatted**) *vt* to remove the fat or fats from something

default /di fáwlt/ *n* **1. PRESET OPTION** an option that will automatically be selected by a computer if the user does not choose one **2. FAILURE TO DO SOMETHING** a failure to meet an obligation, especially a financial one **3.** LAW **NONAPPEARANCE IN COURT** a failure to make a summoned court appearance **4.** SPORTS **NON-PARTICIPATION IN COMPETITION** a failure to appear for or complete a competition ■ *vi* (**-faults, -faulting, -faulted**) **1. FAIL TO PAY DEBT** to fail to pay a debt or other financial obligation **2.** LAW **FAIL TO APPEAR IN COURT** to fail to make an appearance in court although summoned to do so **3.** SPORTS **FAIL TO COMPETE** to fail to appear for a match or contest **4.** COMPUT **USE PRESET OPTION** to use a device, command, or file when no other is specified [13C. < Old French *defaute*, past participle of *defaillir* 'fail' < *faillir* (see FAIL)] ◇ **by default 1.** having come about because some other thing, often something expected, did not happen **2.** having come about because somebody failed to appear as expected **3.** according to a computer's preset configuration ◇ **in default of something** *or* **somebody** because of a lack of something or the absence of somebody (*formal*)

defaulter /di fáwltər/ *n* **1. NONPAYER** a debtor who defaults on a financial obligation **2.** LAW **ABSENTEE FROM COURT** somebody who fails to respond to a court summons **3.** SPORTS **ABSENTEE FROM COMPETITION** a person or team failing to appear for a match or contest **4.** MIL **MILITARY OFFENDER** a soldier who commits a military offence

defeasance /di feez'nss/ *n* **1. ACT OF MAKING SOMETHING VOID** the declaration of something as null and void **2. LEGAL CLAUSE** a clause in a legal document that states that, in the event of a condition being fulfilled, the document will become null and void **3. LEGAL DOCUMENT** a document containing a defeasance [15C. < Old French *defesance* < *defaire* < medieval Latin *disfacere* (see DEFEAT)]

defeasible /di feezəb'l/ *adj* **1.** capable of being made or declared null and void **2.** liable to be forfeited —**defeasibility** /di feezə bílləti/ *n*

defeat /di feet/ *vt* (**-feats, -feating, -feated**) **1. BEAT ENEMY** to win a victory over enemy forces in a battle or war **2. BEAT COMPETITOR** to win a victory over a competitor, e.g. in sport or business **3. WIN VOTE** to win a victory over another person or group in a debate or vote **4. CAUSE FAILURE OF SOMETHING** to cause something to fail or to fall short of realization ○ *The truck defeated all my attempts to get it to start.* **5. BAFFLE SOMEBODY** to leave somebody in a baffled or uncomprehending state ○ *His logic defeats me.* **6.** LAW **MAKE SOMETHING VOID** to make or declare something null and void ■ *n* **1. FACT OF LOSING TO OPPONENT** the fact or an instance of losing to an enemy in battle or an opponent in a competition ○ *the home team's humiliating defeat* **2. FAILURE** failure to win or to realize a goal ○ *She refused to admit defeat and appealed.* [14C. Via Anglo-Norman *defeter* 'disfigure, destroy' < medieval Latin *disfacere* 'unmake' < Latin *facere* 'do, make'] —**defeater** *n* ◇ **defeat the object** *or* **purpose of something** make the desired or expected outcome ridiculous or possible

SYNONYMS ***defeat, beat, conquer, vanquish, overcome, triumph, thrash, trounce***

CORE MEANING: to win a victory

defeat to win a victory over an enemy or competitor, or to cause somebody or something to fail ○ *The Spartans succeeded in defeating their enemies.* ○ *She played a major role in defeating the proposal.* **beat** to defeat somebody in a contest, or to succeed in the face of difficulty ○ *'I am the champion of the world and will beat him again', he said.* ○ *After a paralysing accident a month ago, his goal is to walk again, though he realizes he will have to beat some big odds to do it.* **conquer** to defeat and take control of a people in war, or to succeed despite difficulty ○ *their vow to retake their conquered land* ○ *He's already conquered his toughest challenge.* **vanquish** to defeat somebody decisively in a battle or competition ○ *The visitors emerge victorious and the home team are once again vanquished.* **overcome** to defeat somebody or something, especially in a conflict or competition ○ *The French quickly overcame the opposing forces* ○ *The home team overcame their longtime rivals to move to the top of the league* **triumph** to be successful, especially against an adversary or against difficult odds ○ *Foreknowledge will help a wise general to triumph over his enemies.* ○ *It seemed that scientific investigation was triumphing over ignorance.* **thrash** to defeat a person or team decisively, especially in a sporting competition ○ *Spurs, who were previously thrashed by United, took the lead.* **trounce** to defeat an opponent or team convincingly ○ *In the first round match the Japanese player fired powerful and well-placed ground strokes to trounce the American veteran.*

defeatist /di feetist/ *adj* showing a tendency to expect failure or accept it too readily ■ *n* somebody who consistently expects or accepts failure —**defeatism** *n*

defecate /déffə kayt/ (**-cates, -cating, -cated**), **defaecate** *v* **1.** *vi* to expel faeces from the bowel through the rectum (*formal or technical*) **2.** *vt* to remove impurities from a solution, especially a solution that contains sugar [15C. < Latin *defaecat-*, past participle of Latin *defaecare* 'remove waste' < *faex* 'dregs, waste'] —**defecation** /déffə káysh'n/ *n* —**defecator** *n*

defect *n* /dee fekt/ **1. FLAW IN SOMETHING** a physical problem in a machine, structure, or system, especially one that prevents it from functioning correctly **2. INADEQUATE FEATURE** a feature of something that is regarded as inadequate **3. IMPERFECTION IN CRYSTAL** an imperfection in the internal structure of a crystal, e.g. an atom of a different substance ■ *vi* /di fékt/ (**-fects, -fecting, -fected**) **1. REJECT HOMELAND** to leave your native country or the country you are living in and refuse to return there, usually for political or moral reasons **2. ABANDON ALLEGIANCE** to abandon allegiance to a cause or party, especially when this also involves supporting something previously opposed [15C. < Latin *defect-*, past participle of *deficere* 'be wanting, desert' < *facere* 'do, make'] —**defection** *n* —**defector** *n*

SYNONYMS See *flaw*[1].

defective /di féktiv/ *adj* **1. FAULTY** imperfect or faulty, so not functioning properly or at all **2. OFFENSIVE TERM** an offensive term that means having learning difficulties or problems in coping with emotions (*insult*) **3.** GRAM **INCOMPLETE** lacking the usual or expected range of grammatical inflections ■ *n* **OFFENSIVE TERM** an offensive term for somebody who has learning difficulties or problems in coping with emotions (*insult*) —**defectively** *adv* —**defectiveness** *n*

USAGE defective or deficient? ***Defective*** is normally used in reference to processes, machines, or other functional things such as the human senses: *If the workmanship is defective, they'll replace the shoes with a new pair. As he grew older his hearing became defective.* ***Deficient*** describes things that lack a quality, element, or ingredient, without this amounting to actual failure to work or function: *Her voice is beautiful but a little deficient in power. Their diet is deficient in vitamin D.*

defeminize /dee fémmi nīz/ (**-nizes, -nizing, -nized**), **defeminise** (**-nises, -nising, -nised**) *vt* to remove or diminish characteristics of somebody or something that are traditionally regarded as associated with women or girls

defence /di fénss/ *n* **1. PROTECTION** the protection of something, especially from attack by an enemy **2. SOMETHING THAT PROTECTS** a method or object for protecting something ○ *Prevention is our strongest defence against the disease.* **3. ARMED FORCES** a country's armed forces **4. JUSTIFICATION** an excuse or justification for something ○ *spoke in defence of the motion* **5.** LAW **REASONS OFFERED** the set of reasons that a defendant offers in court in denial of a charge **6.** LAW **DEFENDANT'S CASE** the facts and their presentation as they relate to the defendant in a court case **7.** LAW **LAWYER AND DEFENDANT** the lawyer or lawyers and the defendant in a court case **8.** SPORTS **DEFENSIVE PLAY** in sports, the method or manoeuvres that prevent the other team from scoring **9.** SPORTS **DEFENSIVE PLAYERS** the sports team members who have responsibility for defence ■ **defences** *npl* **1. PROTECTIVE QUALITIES** the qualities of the body or mind that protect somebody from attack, injury, or illness **2. FORTIFICATIONS** the fortifications that protect a place from enemies or the forces of nature ○ *Roman defences that are now a tourist attraction* ○ *sea defences* [14C. < Old French *defens(e)* < Latin *defens-*, past participle of *defendere* (see DEFEND)]

defenceless /di fénssləss/ *adj* lacking any form of protection and therefore vulnerable ■ *npl* people who are unable to defend themselves and their interests ○ *working as a shield for the defenceless* —**defencelessly** *adv* —**defencelessness** *n*

defenceman /di fénss man/ (*plural* **-men** /-men/) *n N Am* a team member who plays in a defensive position, especially in ice hockey

defence mechanism *n* **1.** any means of avoiding emotional distress, destructive impulses, or a threat to self-esteem, especially the suppression of unwanted thoughts or memories **2.** a natural protective response to danger or attack used by an organism, e.g. when faced with a predator or invaded by a disease agent

defence-minded *adj* giving emphasis to building a team with strong defensive skills

defend /di fénd/ (**-fends, -fending, -fended**) *v* **1.** *vt* PROTECT SOMEBODY OR SOMETHING to protect somebody or something from attack, harm, or danger **2.** *vti* REPRESENT SOMEBODY IN COURT to represent and speak on behalf of an accused person in court **3.** *vt* SUPPORT POSITION to offer support for something or somebody, especially by arguing against the objections or criticism of others **4.** *vi* RESIST OPPONENT in sport, to resist the attacks of an opposing side and try to prevent them from scoring **5.** *vt* TRY TO KEEP TITLE to try to retain a title, especially a sporting one, by competing in the relevant competitions **6.** *vt* PROTECT GOAL in sports, to protect the goal and goal area from the attacks of the opposition [13C. Via French < Latin *defendere* 'ward off' < Indo-European, 'strike, kill'] —**defendable** *adj*

SYNONYMS See *safeguard*.

defendant /di féndənt/ *n* a person or company required to answer charges in a court

~~**defendent**~~ incorrect spelling of **defendant**

defender /di féndər/ *n* **1.** DEFENSIVE PLAYER in sport, somebody whose role is to try to prevent the opposition from scoring or getting into a scoring position **2.** SUPPORTER somebody who supports or justifies something or somebody **3.** PROTECTOR a protector of a person or place against attack **4.** HOLDER OF TITLE the holder of a title that is challenged recurrently

Defender of the Faith *n* a title given by Pope Leo X in 1521 to King Henry VIII and held by English and British monarchs ever since. It was bestowed after the king wrote a pamphlet denouncing Martin Luther's doctrines and supporting the sacraments of the Roman Catholic Church.

defending /di fénding/ *adj* holding a title that is subject to recurring competition ○ *the defending champions*

defenestrate /dee fénni strayt/ (**-trates, -trating, -trated**) *vt* to throw something or somebody out of a window (*formal or humorous*) [Early 17C. < DE- + Latin *fenestra* 'window'] —**defenestration** /dee fénni stráysh'n/ *n*

defense *n* US spelling of **defence**

defensible /di fénssəb'l/ *adj* **1.** capable of being protected from attack **2.** able to be explained, justified, or excused —**defensibility** /di fénssə bílləti/ *n* —**defensibleness** *n* —**defensibly** *adv*

defensin /di fénssin/ *n* a peptide in a set of three present in human white blood cells that appear to play a role in the prevention or elimination of infection

defensive /di fénssiv/ *adj* **1.** QUICK TO JUSTIFY aiming to deflect or avoid perceived criticism **2.** SERVING TO PROTECT designed for protection or defence **3.** FAVOURING DEFENCE AS PLAYING STRATEGY concentrating more on preventing an opponent from gaining an advantage than on scoring **4.** *N Am* OF DEFENCE PLAYER relating to those players who have responsibility for defence —**defensiveness** *n* ◇ **on the defensive 1.** expecting criticism or aggression and prepared to respond **2.** having assumed a position that indicates readiness to play defensively

defensively /di fénssivli/ *adv* **1.** in a defensive way **2.** as regards defence, especially defensive play ○ *Defensively they played well, but they couldn't manage to score.*

defensive medicine *n* US medical treatment that involves carrying out extensive diagnostic testing in order to minimize the chances of a patient's suing the doctor or hospital for negligence

defer[1] /di fúr/ (**-fers, -ferring, -ferred**) *vti* to put something off until a later time [14C. < French *différer* 'put aside, differ'] —**deferment** *n* —**deferrable** *adj* —**deferral** *n* —**deferrer** *n*

defer[2] /di fúr/ (**-fers, -ferring, -ferred**) *vi* to give way to, and usually acknowledge the merit of, somebody else's judgment, opinion, wishes, or action ○ *I defer to your superior knowledge.* [15C. Via French < Latin *deferre* 'carry away' < *ferre* 'carry' (see FERTILE)] —**deferrer** *n*

~~**defered**~~ incorrect spelling of **deferred**

deference /défférənss/ *n* **1.** polite respect, especially putting another person's interests first **2.** submission to the judgment, opinion, or wishes of another person [Mid-17C. < DEFER [2]] ◇ **in deference to** out of respect or courtesy to somebody or something

deferent[1] /défférənt/ *adj* same as **deferential** [Early 19C. < DEFER [2], DEFERENCE]

deferent[2] /défférənt/ *adj* describes a duct, nerve, or vessel in the body that is capable of carrying impulses or fluid away, down, or outwards [Early 17C. Via French < Latin *deferent-*, present participle of *deferre* (see DEFER [2])]

deferential /défff rénsh'l/ *adj* showing or expressing polite respect or courtesy [Early 19C. < DEFERENCE] —**deferentially** *adv*

deferred annuity /di fúrd-/ *n* an investment that does not pay out until at least one year after the final premium has been paid

deferred month *n* a more distant month in which futures or options trading is taking place, as opposed to a month that is nearer in time

deferred sentence *n* a sentence that is not passed until a specific period has elapsed in order to allow the court time to assess the behaviour of the convicted person

defervescence /deéfər véss'nss/ *n* **1.** a decrease in a fever **2.** the stage of an illness during which fever subsides [Early 18C. < Latin *defervescere* 'stop boiling' < *fervere* 'be hot, boil'] —**defervesce** *vti* —**defervescent** *adj*

~~**deffered**~~ incorrect spelling of **deferred**

defiance /di fí ənss/ *n* open, bold, or hostile refusal to obey or conform ◇ **in defiance of** with complete disregard for a rule, law, or person in authority

defiant /di fí ənt/ *adj* **1.** deliberately and openly disobedient **2.** tending to confront and challenge [Late 16C. < French *défiant*, present participle of *défier* < assumed Vulgar Latin *disfidare* 'renounce your faith'] —**defiantly** *adv*

defibrillate /dee fíbbri layt/ (**-lates, -lating, -lated**) *vt* to apply an electric shock to the chest, or sometimes directly to the heart itself, in order to restore a regular heartbeat after a critically irregular beat has developed —**defibrillation** /dee fíbbri láysh'n/ *n*

defibrillator /dee fíbbri laytər/ *n* a machine that administers a controlled electric shock to the chest or heart to correct a critically irregular heartbeat that cannot drive the circulation

deficiency /di físh'nssi/ (*plural* **-cies**) *n* **1.** SHORTAGE an inadequate supply of something necessary, especially a nutrient **2.** POOR PROVISION a weakness in the provision or performance of something ○ *serious deficiencies in the provision of cleaning services* **3.** AMOUNT LACKING the amount by which something falls short of being complete

SYNONYMS See *lack*.

deficiency disease *n* a disease resulting from lack of a nutrient or other substance required by a human being or other animal or a plant for growth, development, or general health. The deficiency may be caused either by an inadequate supply of the required substance or by an inability to process it.

deficient /di físh'nt/ *adj* **1.** lacking a particular quality, element, or ingredient, especially one that is expected or necessary ○ *deficient in tact* **2.** inadequate or not good enough [Late 16C. < Latin *deficient-*, present participle of *deficere* 'leave undone, fail' < *facere* 'do, make'] —**deficiently** *adv*

USAGE See *defective*.

deficit /déffəssit/ *n* **1.** the amount by which expenditure exceeds income or budget **2.** the amount by which a total is less than it should be [Late 18C. < French *déficit* < Latin *deficit* 'it is lacking' < *deficere* (see DEFICIENT)]

SYNONYMS See *lack*.

deficit financing *n* the practice of deliberately allowing government spending to exceed its revenues in order to try to boost economic activity and lower unemployment

deficit spending *n* government spending that is financed by borrowing money rather than through money raised by taxation

defilade /déffi láyd/ *n* fortifications or protection against enemy gunfire that might be aimed at a line of troops ■ *vt* (**-lades, -lading, -laded**) to set up protective fortifications to protect troops or a position [Early 19C. < French *défiler* (see DEFILE [2]), after ENFILADE]

defile[1] /di fíl/ (**-files, -filing, -filed**) *vt* **1.** CORRUPT SOMETHING to corrupt or ruin something (*formal*) ○ *'The dust is his original sin and inward corruptions, that have defiled the whole man.'* (John Bunyan, *The Pilgrim's Progress*; 1678) **2.** DAMAGE REPUTATION to damage somebody's reputation or good name **3.** DESTROY SANCTITY OF SOMETHING to make a holy or sacred thing or place no longer fit for ceremonial use **4.** POLLUTE SOMETHING to make something dirty or polluted (*formal*) **5.** DEPRIVE WOMAN OF VIRGINITY to be the first man to have sexual intercourse with a woman, usually outside marriage (*archaic*) [14C. Alteration of French *defouler* 'trample' < *fouler* 'trample under foot'] —**defilement** *n* —**defiler** *n*

defile[2] /di fíl/ *n* **1.** MOUNTAIN PASS a narrow pass between mountains **2.** PASSAGE a passage only wide enough for people to pass single-file ■ *vi* (**-files, -filing, -filed**) MARCH SINGLE-FILE to march or go in single file, especially when the way is too narrow to march in any other formation [Late 17C. < French *défiler* 'march in a line' < *file* (see FILE [1])]

~~**definate**~~ incorrect spelling of **definite**

~~**definately**~~ incorrect spelling of **definitely**

define /di fín/ (**-fines, -fining, -fined**) *v* **1.** *vt* STATE SOMETHING to state or describe something exactly ○ *clearly defined objectives* **2.** *vt* CHARACTERIZE SOMEBODY OR SOMETHING to identify somebody or something by a distinctive characteristic quality or feature ○ *The age we live in is defined by a deep sense of uncertainty.* **3.** *vt* SHOW SOMETHING CLEARLY to show something clearly, especially in shape or outline (*usually passive*) ○ *The tyre marks were clearly defined in the snow.* **4.** *vt* MARK LINE to mark a boundary, edge, or limit ○ *That row of trees defines the eastern boundary of the estate.* **5.** *vti* GIVE MEANING OF WORD to give the precise meaning of a word or expression [14C. Via French < Latin *definire* 'limit, determine' < *finis* 'final moment, end'] —**definability** /di fínə bílləti/ *n* —**definable** *adj* —**definably** *adv* —**definer** *n*

definiendum /di fínni éndəm/ (*plural* **-da** /-də/) *n* the word or expression defined by a definition, e.g. in a dictionary or glossary (*technical*) [Late 19C. < Latin, 'thing to be defined' < *definire* (see DEFINE)]

definiens /di fínni enz/ (*plural* **-entia** /-énshə/) *n* the words used to define a word or expression, e.g. in a dictionary or glossary (*technical*) [Late 19C. < medieval Latin, 'something that defines' < present participle of Latin *definire* (see DEFINE)]

defining /di fíning/ *adj* giving a distinctive character to something or encapsulating its character ○ *That was the defining act of his election campaign.*

definite /déffənət/ *adj* **1.** CLEAR precise and distinct ○ *a definite age range* ○ *the definite outline of a building among the trees* **2.** FIXED fixed, certain, and not to be altered ○ *Have we got a definite date for the meeting?* **3.** ABSOLUTELY SET ON SOMETHING certain about something and unlikely to have a change of mind ○ *I'm definite about this.* **4.** OBVIOUS unquestionable and unmistakable ○ *a definite turn for the better* **5.** BOT WITH TERMINAL FLOWER describes a flower head in which the first-formed flower is at the stalk's end with subsequent flowers developing lower down on one or both sides of the stalk [Mid-16C. < Latin *definitus*, past participle of *definire* (see DEFINE)] —**definiteness** *n*

USAGE **definite** or **definitive**? ***Definite*** describes something as being distinct or precise without making any strong judgment about it: *He has definite ideas on the subject.* ***Definitive*** denotes something authoritative, conclusive, or decisive, and is therefore a more evaluative word: *She wrote the definitive book on the subject.*

definite article *n* a word that designates a noun as being specific and identifiable, e.g. 'the'

definite integral *n* a determination of the difference in values of an integral between two limits, expressed using symbols

definitely /déffənətli/ *adv* **1.** CERTAINLY without a doubt ○ *He definitely had a Swedish accent.* **2.** FINALLY AND UNCHANGEABLY as a conclusion after some thought or hesitation ○ *Once she had definitely decided to go,*

she started packing. **3.** EXACTLY in a precise way ○ *Without knowing definitely what it was, he just felt that something was wrong.* **4.** OBVIOUSLY in a distinct and unmistakable way ○ *Her attitude suddenly became more definitely critical.* **5.** ABSOLUTELY with no exceptions ○ *The notice said 'Definitely no bikers'.* ■ *interj* YES used to say 'yes' in an emphatic and enthusiastic way ○ *'Are you going to come to the party?' 'Definitely!'*

definition /déffə nísh'n/ *n* **1.** MEANING OF WORD a brief precise statement of what a word or expression means, e.g. in a dictionary **2.** ACT OF DEFINING WORD the act or process of defining what a word or expression means, e.g. in writing a dictionary **3.** CLARIFICATION the act of describing or stating something clearly and unambiguously **4.** MEDIA, PHOTOGRAPHY CLARITY the degree of clarity of an image. It is related to the sharpness and degree of contrast in the image. **5.** EMBODIMENT OF SOMETHING somebody or something believed to represent or embody a particular idea or quality (*formal*) ○ *His behaviour has always seemed to me the very definition of courtesy.* **6.** SHARPNESS OF SOUND the degree of distinctiveness of a sound [14C. Via French < Latin *definition-* < *definire* (see DEFINE)] —**definitional** *adj* ◇ **by definition** used to emphasize that somebody or something is considered to have a particular intrinsic quality

definitive /di fínnətiv/ *adj* **1.** CONCLUSIVE AND FINAL providing a final decision that will not be questioned or changed ○ *We need a definitive answer.* **2.** MOST AUTHORITATIVE recognized as being the most authoritative and of the highest standard ○ *the definitive study of the subject* **3.** STAMPS SOLD FOR LONG TIME describes postage stamps sold for an extended or indefinite period, often as part of a set sharing common design elements **4.** BIOL FULLY GROWN fully formed or completely developed ■ *n* STAMPS DEFINITIVE STAMP a postage stamp sold for an extended or indefinite period [14C. < French *définitif* < Latin *definire* (see DEFINE)] —**definitively** *adv* —**definitiveness** *n*

USAGE See ***definite***.

definitive host *n* the plant or animal in or on which a parasitic organism reaches sexual maturity

~~**definitly**~~ incorrect spelling of **definitely**

deflagrate /défflə grayt/ (**-grates, -grating, -grated**) *vti* to burn violently, or make something burn violently (*technical*) [Early 17C. < Latin *deflagrat-*, past participle of *deflagrare* 'burn up' < *flagrare* 'burn'] —**deflagration** /défflə gráysh'n/ *n*

deflate /di fláyt/ (**-flates, -flating, -flated**) *v* **1.** *vti* LET AIR OUT to let out air or gas from an inflatable object with the result that it shrinks or collapses, or lose air or gas **2.** *vt* MAKE SOMEBODY LESS CONFIDENT to destroy somebody's confidence or make somebody less self-assured or conceited **3.** *vt* DESTROY THEORY to show that a theory or argument is wrong **4.** *vt* ECON CAUSE DEFLATION IN ECONOMY to bring about deflation in the economy or the money supply [Late 19C. < DE- + INFLATE] —**deflated** *adj* —**deflator** *n*

deflation /di fláysh'n/ *n* **1.** COLLAPSE BECAUSE OF AIR LOSS the release or escape of air or gas from something, resulting in its shrinking or collapsing **2.** LOSS OF SELF-ESTEEM a sudden loss of confidence, self-assurance, or conceit **3.** ECON REDUCED ECONOMIC ACTIVITY the reduction of general economic activity, including lower prices and a reduced supply of money and credit **4.** GEOL EROSION the erosion of land by wind

deflationary /di fláysh'nəri/ *adj* **1.** undergoing or creating a lower level of general economic activity **2.** serving to reduce or destroy somebody else's self-assurance or confidence

deflationist /di fláysh'nist/ *adj* in favour of economic deflation —**deflationist** *n*

deflect /di flékt/ (**-flects, -flecting, -flected**) *v* **1.** *vti* CHANGE COURSE to change course because of hitting something, or change something's course by coming into contact with it **2.** *vt* DIRECT ATTENTION AWAY to direct people's attention or criticism away from a subject or issue to something else **3.** *vt* FORCE ALTERATION OF PLANS to force somebody to change what he or she is doing or planning to do [Mid-16C. < Latin *deflectere* 'bend away' < *flectere* 'bend'] —**deflectable** *adj* —**deflective** *adj* —**deflector** *n*

deflection /di fléksh'n/, **deflexion** *n* **1.** CHANGE OF COURSE a change of course that results from hitting somebody or something **2.** AMOUNT SOMETHING DEFLECTS the amount or distance by which something is deflected **3.** ACT OF DIVERTING ATTENTION the act of directing people's attention or criticism away from something **4.** MOVEMENT OF NEEDLE AWAY FROM ZERO a definite movement of the indicator on a measuring instrument **5.** ENG MOVEMENT OF STRUCTURE UNDER LOAD the movement of a structure or a part of a structure when it is bearing a load

deflexed /di flékst, dée-/ *adj* describes petals or leaves that bend sharply downwards [Late 18C. < Latin *deflexus*, past participle of *deflectere* (see DEFLECT)]

deflexion *n* another spelling of **deflection**

defloration /dée flaw ráysh'n, défflə-/ *n* an act of having sex with a woman and so ending her virginity (*literary*) [14C. Directly or via French < late Latin *defloration-* < *deflorare* (see DEFLOWER)]

deflower /dee flówər/ (**-ers, -ering, -ered**) *vt* **1.** to have sex with a woman and so end her virginity (*literary*) **2.** to remove some or all of the flowers from a plant [14C. Via Old French *defflourer* < late Latin *deflorare* < Latin *flos* 'flower'] —**deflowerer** *n*

defocus /dee fṓkəss/ *v* (**-cuses** or **-cusses, -cusing** or **-cussing, -cused** or **-cussed**) **1.** *vt* SOFTEN PICTURE to soften or blur an image by focusing away from the exact plane of focus of the object in the image **2.** *vti* STOP FOCUSING to stop focusing on something, or cause the eyes to stop focusing on something ■ *n* CONDITION OF DEFOCUSING the condition or state caused by defocusing, e.g. the blurring of a photographic image

Defoe /di fṓ/, **Daniel** (1660?–1731) English novelist and journalist. His novels were among the earliest in the English language, and include *Robinson Crusoe* (1719) and *Moll Flanders* (1722). Born **Daniel Foe**

> 'He bade me observe it, and I should always find, that the calamities of life were shared among the upper and lower part of mankind; but that the middle station had the fewest disasters.'
>
> [Daniel Defoe, *Robinson Crusoe*; 1719]

defog /dee fóg/ (**-fogs, -fogging, -fogged**) *vti* **1.** to remove condensation from the lens of a camera or other optical equipment, especially by allowing it to warm up, or lose condensation in this way **2.** *N Am* same as **demist** —**defogger** *n*

defogger /dee fóggər/ *n N Am* **1.** same as **demister 2.** a liquid used to clean and remove condensation from goggles or eyeglasses

defoliant /dee fṓli ənt/ *n* a chemical that strips trees and plants of their leaves and is sometimes used in warfare to deny cover to enemy forces

defoliate /dee fṓli ayt/ (**-ates, -ating, -ated**) *vti* to strip trees and plants of their leaves, e.g. by using chemicals or through pollution or attack by pests, or lose leaves in any of these ways [Late 18C. < late Latin *defoliat-*, past participle of *defoliare* < Latin *folium* 'leaf, page'] —**defoliation** /dee fṓli áysh'n/ *n* —**defoliator** *n*

deforce /dee fáwrss/ (**-forces, -forcing, -forced**) *vt* to keep the rightful owner of property away from it, or keep the property away from its owner, by force or violence (*formal*) [14C. < Anglo-Norman *deforcer* 'force away from' < *forcier* < Latin *fortis* 'strong'] —**deforcement** *n*

deforest /dee fórrist/ (**-ests, -esting, -ested**) *vt* to remove the trees from an area of land —**deforestation** /dee fórri stáysh'n/ *n* —**deforester** *n*

deform /di fáwrm/ (**-forms, -forming, -formed**) *vti* **1.** DISTORT to become, or make something become, distorted, damaged, or disfigured **2.** SPOIL to spoil the appearance of something and make it ugly, or become spoiled and ugly ○ *The new office buildings have deformed the whole area.* **3.** PHYS CHANGE SHAPE to change the shape of something through stress, or become changed in this way [15C. Via French < Latin *deformare* < *forma* 'mould, shape, beauty'] —**deformability** /di fáwrmə bíllәti/ *n* —**deformable** *adj* —**deformed** *adj* —**deformer** *n*

deformalize /dee fáwrmə līz/ (**-izes, -izing, -ized**), **deformalise** (**-ises, -ising, -ised**) *vt* to make something such as a meeting or report less formal —**deformalization** /dee fáwrmə lī záysh'n/ *n*

deformation /dée fawr máysh'n/ *n* **1.** ACT OF DEFORMING OR BEING DEFORMED the act or process of damaging, disfiguring, or spoiling the look of something, or the condition of being damaged, disfigured, or spoiled **2.** CHANGE IN SHAPE a change in the shape of something, especially one that suggests damage or disfigurement **3.** UNPLEASANT RESULT OF CHANGE the harmful or disfiguring result of a change in form **4.** CHANGE IN SHAPE BECAUSE OF STRESS a change in shape resulting from the application of stress

deformity /di fáwrməti/ (*plural* **-ties**) *n* **1.** DISFIGUREMENT the condition of being disfigured or badly formed ○ *the deformity of the pine trees at such a high altitude in the mountains* **2.** STRUCTURAL CHANGE FROM NORMAL a permanent change from normal body structure **3.** SOMETHING WITH SHAPE FAR FROM NORMAL something that has a shape not normal for its kind or nature

Defra /déffrə/ *abbr UK* Department of Environment, Food and Rural Affairs

defrag /dee frag/ (**-frags, -fragging, -fragged**) *vt* COMPUT same as **defragment** (*informal*) [Late 20C. Shortening]

defragment /dee frag mént/ (**-ments, -menting, -mented**) *vt* to reorganize the storage space on a hard disk and optimize its performance by consolidating related files

defraud /di fráwd/ (**-frauds, -frauding, -frauded**) *vt* to deprive somebody of money or property by dishonest means [14C. Directly or via French < Latin *defraudare* < *fraudare* 'to cheat'] —**defraudation** /dee fraw dáysh'n/ *n* —**defrauder** *n* —**defraudment** *n*

defray /di fráy/ (**-frays, -fraying, -frayed**) *vt* to provide money to pay for part or all of the cost of something ○ *The company will defray the cost of your training course.* [Mid-16C. < French *défrayer* < *frais* 'expenses'] —**defrayable** *adj* —**defrayal** *n* —**defrayer** *n* —**defrayment** *n*

defrock /dee frók/ (**-frocks, -frocking, -frocked**) *vt* to take away the status, job, and authority of a priest or other member of the clergy, especially as a punishment for wrongdoing [Early 17C. < French *défroquer* < *froc* 'frock']

defrost /di fróst, dee-/ (**-frosts, -frosting, -frosted**) *vti* **1.** to remove frost or ice from something, or become free of frost or ice **2.** to thaw frozen food, or become thawed

deft /deft/ *adj* **1.** moving or acting in a quick, smooth, and skilful way **2.** showing good sense and skill in achieving or acquiring things [13C. Variant of DAFT] —**deftly** *adv* —**deftness** *n*

defunct /di fúngkt/ *adj* **1.** no longer operative, valid, or functional **2.** no longer alive or in existence (*humorous*) [Mid-16C. < Latin *defunctus*, past participle of *defungi* 'finish' < *fungi* 'perform'] —**defunctness** *n*

SYNONYMS See ***dead***.

defuse /dee fyóoz/ (**-fuses, -fusing, -fused**) *vt* **1.** to make a situation less tense, dangerous, or uncomfortable ○ *The diplomats tried to defuse the escalating crisis.* **2.** to make a bomb or mine harmless by removing its detonating device

SPELLCHECK **defuse** or **diffuse**? Do not confuse the spelling of ***defuse*** and ***diffuse***, which sound similar. ***Defuse*** is only used as a verb, meaning 'make something less dangerous or less tense', as in *defuse a bomb, defuse the situation.* ***Diffuse*** can be used as a verb or, with a slightly different pronunciation, as an adjective. The verb ***diffuse*** means 'spread or scatter' or 'make less intense', as in *diffuse propaganda, diffuse the light.*

defy /di fī/ (**-fies, -fying, -fied**) *vt* **1.** OPENLY RESIST SOMEBODY OR SOMETHING to challenge openly somebody's or something's authority or power by refusing to obey a command or regulation ○ *He defied all orders from head office.* **2.** CHALLENGE SOMEBODY to challenge or dare somebody to do something ○ *I defy you to find a better deal than this.* **3.** NOT BE EXPLAINED BY SOMETHING to fail to be explained or clarified by something such as logic or analysis ○ *a decision that defies all logic* [14C. Via French *défier* < assumed Vulgar Latin *disfidare* 'renounce your faith' < Latin *fides* 'trust, belief'] —**defier** *n*

dégagé /dáy gaa zháy/ *adj* (*formal*) **1.** casual and relaxed **2.** detached and without emotional involvement [Late 17C. < French, 'disengaged']

degas /dee gáss/ (**-gases** or **-gasses, -gassing, -gassed**) *vt* to remove gas from a liquid or solid or from a vacuum system

a at; aa father; aw all; ay day; ai hair; ə about, item, edible, common, circus; e egg; ee eel; hw when; i it, happy; ī ice; 'l apple; 'm rhythm; 'n fashion; o odd; ō open; ŏŏ good; oo pool; ow owl; oy oil; th thin; th this; u up; ur urge;

Edgar Degas: self-portrait (1854–5)

AKG London

Degas /dáy gaa, də gaá/, **Edgar** (1834–1917) French painter and sculptor. A leading impressionist, he often depicted the human figure in movement, particularly ballet dancers. Full name **Degas, Hilaire Germain Edgar**

'It is very good to copy what one sees; it is much better to draw what you can't see any more but is in your memory. It is a transformation in which imagination and memory work together. You only reproduce what struck you, that is to say the necessary.'
[Edgar Degas. Quoted in *Degas by Himself: Drawings, Prints, Paintings, Writings*, Richard Kendall (ed.); 1987]

Charles de Gaulle

AKG London

de Gaulle /də góll/, **Charles, General** (1890–1970) French general and politician. He became leader of the Free French in London after the fall of France in World War II, taking over as head of the provisional government in 1945. He served as French president from 1959 to 1969. Full name **de Gaulle, Charles André Joseph Marie**

'The French will only be united under the threat of danger. Nobody can simply bring together a country that has 265 kinds of cheese.'
[Charles de Gaulle, *Election speech*; 1951]

degauss /deé gówss/ (**-gausses, -gaussing, -gaussed**) *vt* to remove or counteract a magnetic field in something such as electrical equipment or a ship's hull —**degausser** *n*

degearing /di geéring/ *n* reduction of the amount of debt that a company owes, usually by laying off workers, selling off unprofitable divisions, and other cost-cutting measures

degedege /dégge dégge/ *adj* only one (*slang; used in Black English*) ○ *Is a one degedege banana you come give me!* [Probably < a W African language]

degenderize /dee jéndə rīz/ (**-izes, -izing, -ized**), **degenderise** (**-ises, -ising, -ised**), **degender** /dee jéndər/ (**-ders, -dering, -dered**) *vt* to remove references to people's gender from language or a text in order to make it more neutral or less biased —**degenderization** /dee jéndə rī záysh'n/ *n*

degeneracy /di jénnərəssi/ *n* 1. (*plural* **degeneracies**) BAD BEHAVIOUR immoral, depraved, or corrupt behaviour, or an instance of this 2. WORSENED CONDITION a condition that is worse than normal or worse than before 3. WORSENING OF CONDITION the process of becoming physically, morally, or mentally worse 4. QUANTUM PHYS STATE OF EQUAL ENERGY the condition of two or more quantum states that have the same energy

degenerate *vi* /di jénnə rayt/ (**-ates, -ating, -ated**) 1. BECOME WORSE to develop into a condition that is worse than before, worse than normal, or not as good as it should be 2. BIOL BECOME USELESS to become less specialized or lose the ability to function (*refers to organisms or body parts*) ■ *adj* /di jénnə rət/ 1. IN WORSENED CONDITION in a condition that is worse than normal or worse than before 2. INFERIOR in a condition that is worse than an original or previous state 3. QUANTUM PHYS EQUAL IN ENERGY describes a system in which different quantum states have equal energy 4. BIOL WITH REDUCED OR ABSENT PART describes a part, or an organism with a part, that has become reduced in size or function or lost completely during the history of its species or compared to related species ■ *n* /di jénnə rət/ SOMEBODY IMMORAL somebody regarded as immoral or corrupt [15C. < Latin *degenerat-*, past participle of *degenerare* 'depart from your own kind' < *genus* 'race, kind'] —**degenerately** /-ətli/ *adv* —**degenerateness** /-ətnəss/ *n*

degenerate matter *n* highly compressed matter consisting of elementary particles that are not combined to form atoms, occurring in the final stage of a star's development into a white dwarf

degeneration /di jénnə ráysh'n/ *n* 1. WORSENING OF CONDITION the process of becoming physically, morally, or mentally worse 2. MED DETERIORATION a disease process that causes a gradual deterioration in the structure of a body part with a consequent loss of the ability to function 3. BIOL LOSS OF FUNCTION the gradual loss of the biological function, specialization, or adaptation of a part of the body over many generations

degenerative /di jénnərətiv/ *adj* causing or showing a gradual deterioration in the structure of a body part with a consequent loss of the part's ability to function

degenerative joint disease *n* MED same as **osteoarthritis**

deglamorize /dee glámmə rīz/ (**-izes, -izing, -ized**), **deglamorise** (**-ises, -ising, -ised**) *vt* to make something less attractive or exciting than it sometimes appears —**deglamorization** /dee glámmə rī záysh'n/ *n*

deglaze /dee gláyz/ (**-glazes, -glazing, -glazed**) *vt* 1. to remove the glaze from pottery to leave a dull finish 2. to dissolve fragments remaining in a frying or roasting pan by heating them and adding a liquid so as to make a sauce

deglutinate /dee gloóti nayt/ (**-nates, -nating, -nated**) *vt* to remove the gluten from cereal or flour [Late 19C. < DE- + Latin *glutin-*, stem of *gluten* 'glue'] —**deglutination** /dee gloóti náysh'n/ *n*

deglutition /deé gloo tísh'n/ *n* the act or process of swallowing (*technical*) [Mid-17C. < French *déglutition* < Latin *degluttire* 'swallow down' < *gluttire* (see GLUTTON)]

degradable /di gráydəb'l/ *adj* 1. able to undergo chemical or biological decomposition 2. able to be degraded in any way —**degradability** /di gráydə bílləti/ *n*

degradation /déggrə dáysh'n/ *n* 1. GREAT HUMILIATION great humiliation brought about by loss of status, reputation, or self-esteem ○ *suffered the degradation of overwhelming defeat at the polls* 2. ACT OF HUMILIATING SOMEBODY the act of humiliating somebody, causing him or her a loss of status, reputation, or self-esteem ○ *the constant degradation and undermining of other members of staff* 3. BAD LIVING CONDITIONS a way of life without dignity, health, or social comforts 4. LOSS OF QUALITY a decline in the quality or performance of something ○ *a rapid degradation in the engine's horsepower* 5. PROCESS OF DECLINE the process by which a decline in quality or performance is brought about 6. GEOL, GEOG EROSION erosion of the Earth's land surface by water, wind, or ice 7. CHEM BREAKDOWN OF COMPOUND the breakdown of a chemical compound into atoms or simpler compounds 8. PHYS DECREASE OF ENERGY the process by which the energy available for doing work is irreversibly decreased

degrade /di gráyd/ (**-grades, -grading, -graded**) *v* 1. *vt* TREAT SOMEBODY HUMILIATINGLY to cause somebody a humiliating loss of status, self-esteem, or reputation 2. *vti* WORSEN to become worse, or make something become worse, especially in quality or performance ○ *Using the wrong fuel had significantly degraded*

the engine's power. 3. *vt* LOWER SOMEBODY IN GRADE to lower somebody in rank, grade, or level 4. *vti* GEOL, GEOG ERODE to erode the land surface or a river bed, or be eroded by the action of wind, ice, or water 5. *vt* ENVIRON DESTROY OR DAMAGE ENVIRONMENT to cause damage or destruction to part of the environment as a result of human activity 6. *vti* PHYS REDUCE AVAILABLE ENERGY to reduce irreversibly the energy available in matter, or be reduced irreversibly [14C. Via French < ecclesiastical Latin *degradare* 'reduce in rank' < Latin *gradus* 'step, stage'] —**degraded** *adj* —**degrader** *n*

degrading /di gráyding/ *adj* causing somebody to feel shame and humiliation —**degradingly** *adv*

degrease /dee greéss/ (**-greases, -greasing, -greased**) *vt* to remove grease from something such as an engine, especially using chemicals —**degreaser** *n*

degree /di greé/ *n* 1. EXTENT OR AMOUNT the relative extent, amount, intensity, or level of something, especially when compared with other things ○ *showed a high degree of awareness of the issues* 2. EDUCATIONAL QUALIFICATION a qualification awarded by a university or college following successful completion of a course of study or period of research, or a similar qualification granted as an honour 3. UNIT OF TEMPERATURE MEASUREMENT a unit of measurement for temperature on a scale such as Celsius or Fahrenheit ○ *degrees Celsius* Symbol ° 4. UNIT FOR MEASURING ANGLES a unit of measurement for planar angles, equal to a 360th of a full revolution. Symbol ° 5. UNIT OF LATITUDE OR LONGITUDE a unit of latitude or longitude, equal to 1/360 of a circle, used to locate and designate places on the Earth ○ *27 degrees north* Symbol ° 6. MED SEVERITY OF BURNS ON BODY a level of classification of the seriousness of the damage to tissue caused by a burn, third-degree burns being the most serious 7. MEASURE UNIT OF MEASUREMENT ON SCALE a unit on any of various measurement scales, e.g. that used to measure specific gravity or that used to specify the alcohol content of drinks. Symbol ° 8. *N Am* LAW CLASSIFICATION OF MURDER a level of classification of murder according to its seriousness, first-degree murder being the most serious 9. GRAM STATE OF ADJECTIVE OR ADVERB a state of an adjective or adverb, either the positive, the comparative, or the superlative 10. SOC SCI CLOSENESS OF RELATIONSHIP an indication of the genealogical closeness of a relationship within a family 11. SOC SCI STATUS rank, position, or status in society (*formal or literary*) ○ *of high degree* 12. MUSIC POSITION OF NOTE ON MUSICAL SCALE the relative position of a note on a musical scale 13. MATHS HIGHEST EXPONENT OF DERIVATIVE in a differential equation, the exponent of the derivative of highest order, e.g. $4x^2y^2$ is of degree four 14. MATHS SUM OF POLYNOMIAL VARIABLE EXPONENTS in a polynomial equation, the sum of the exponents of the variables in the term with the highest power, e.g. $4x^3y^2 + 3y^2 + 2$ is of degree five [13C. Via French *degré* < assumed Vulgar Latin *degradus*, literally 'step down' < Latin *gradus* 'step, stage']

degree day *n* the day on which students receive their degrees at a university award ceremony

degree-day *n* a unit of measurement for heating systems, used to estimate fuel requirements and representing one degree of variation from the mean daily temperature out of doors

degree of freedom *n* 1. STATS INDEPENDENT VARIABLE an independent variable in a statistical measure or frequency distribution 2. PHYS, CHEM VARIABLE SPECIFYING ENERGY an independent variable needed to specify the energy state of an atom, molecule, or system 3. CHEM VARIABLE SPECIFYING STATE any of the independent variables such as pressure that are needed to specify the state of a system according to the phase rule

degression /di grésh'n/ *n* 1. a gradual decrease or downward movement (*formal*) 2. a gradual lowering of the tax rate on sums below a specific amount [15C. < medieval Latin *degression-* < Latin *degress-*, past participle of *degredi* 'step down' < *gradus* 'step, stage'] —**degressive** *adj*

deh /de/ *vi* to be somewhere (*slang; used in Black English*)

de Havilland /di hávvilənd/, **Olivia** (b. 1916) British-born US film actor. She won Academy Awards for *To Each His Own* (1946) and *The Heiress* (1949). Full name **de Havilland, Olivia Mary**

De Havilland /di hávvilənd/, **Sir Geoffrey** (1882–1965) British aviation pioneer and aircraft designer. Aircraft designed by him include the Tiger Moth (1931), Mosquito (1940), and Comet airliner (1952).

dehisce /di híss/ (-hisces, -hiscing, -hisced) vi 1. to burst open, releasing seeds, pollen, or spores (refers to dry fruits, seed pods, anthers, or spore-bearing structures) 2. to open along the joined edges (technical; refers to a wound that has been stitched) [Mid-17C. < Latin dehiscere 'open up' < hiscere 'begin opening' < hiare 'gape'] —**dehiscence** n —**dehiscent** adj

dehorn /dee háwrn/ (-horns, -horning, -horned) vt to remove or prevent the growth of the horns of an animal by surgery or cauterization —**dehorner** n

Dehra Dun /dáirə doón/, **Dehra Dūn** capital city of Uttaranchal state in northern India. Population: 527,859 (2001).

dehumanize /dee hyoómə nīz/ (-izes, -izing, -ized), **dehumanise** (-ises, -ising, -ised) vt 1. **MAKE SOMEBODY LESS HUMAN** to make somebody less human by taking away his or her individuality, the creative and interesting aspects of his or her personality, or his or her compassion and sensitivity towards others 2. **REMOVE PEOPLE-FRIENDLY FEATURES OF SOMETHING** to take away the qualities or features of something that make it able to meet human needs and desires or enhance people's lives ○ The very design of these tower blocks dehumanizes them. 3. **MAKE SOMETHING BORINGLY ROUTINE** to remove creativity and interest from a process and make it dull, routine, and mechanical —**dehumanization** /dee hyoómə nī záysh'n/ n —**dehumanized** adj —**dehumanizing** adj

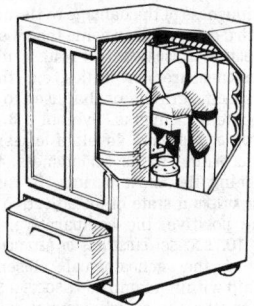

dehumidifier: cutaway view showing filters for removal of moisture from the air

dehumidifier /dee hyoo míddi fīr ər/ n an electrical appliance for removing excess humidity from the air in a room or building

dehumidify /dee hyoo míddi fī/ (-fies, -fying, -fied) vt to remove excess humidity from the air in a room or building —**dehumidification** /dee hyoo míddifi káysh'n/ n

dehydrate /dee hī drayt, dee hī dráyt, dee hī drayt/ (-drates, -drating, -drated) v 1. vt FOOD INDUST **PRESERVE FOOD BY DRYING** to remove moisture from food as a way of preserving it 2. vti MED **LOSE BODY FLUIDS** to lose water or fluids from the body or its tissues, or cause the body or its tissues to do this 3. vt CHEM **TAKE AWAY WATER FROM COMPOUND** to deprive a chemical compound of water molecules or of the proportion of hydrogen and oxygen atoms present in water

dehydrated /dee hī draytid, dee hī dráytid, dee hī draytid/ adj 1. FOOD INDUST **DRIED** preserved by the removal of all moisture 2. MED **EXPERIENCING FLUID LOSS** lacking water in the body, as the result of loss of bodily fluids or from being deprived of liquid 3. CHEM **WITH WATER MOLECULES REMOVED** describes a chemical compound that has had water molecules removed or the proportion of hydrogen and oxygen atoms that would be present in a water molecule removed

SYNONYMS See dry.

dehydration /dee hī dráysh'n/ n 1. FOOD INDUST **REMOVAL OF MOISTURE FROM FOOD** the removal of moisture from food as a way of preserving it 2. MED **LOSS OF BODY FLUID** a dangerous lack of water in the body resulting from inadequate intake of fluids or excessive loss through sweating, vomiting, or diarrhoea 3. CHEM **LOSS OF WATER BY CHEMICAL COMPOUND** the process by which a chemical compound loses water molecules or the

---

proportion of hydrogen and oxygen atoms present in water

dehydrator /dee hī draytər, dee hī dráytər, dee hī draytər/ n an electrical appliance for drying food, consisting of a stack of interlocking trays through which heated air is circulated

dehydrochlorinase /dee hī drō kláwri nayz, -nayss/ n an enzyme that removes hydrogen and chlorine from compounds. Its presence accounts for the resistance shown by some insects to DDT.

dehydrochlorinate /dee hīdrō kláwri nayt/ (-ates, -ating, -ated) vt to chemically remove hydrogen and chlorine or hydrogen chloride from a substance —**dehydrochlorination** /dee hīdrō kláwri náysh'n/ n

dehydrogenase /dee hī drójjə nayz, -nayss, dee hīdrəjə-/ n an enzyme that speeds up the transfer of hydrogen between compounds

dehydrogenate /dee hī drójjə nayt, dee hīdrəjə nayt/ (-ates, -ating, -ated) vt to remove hydrogen from a compound, e.g. by means of a catalyst or in an enzyme-controlled process in cells —**dehydrogenation** /dee hī drójjə náysh'n, dee hīdrəjə-/ n

dehydrogenize /dee hī drójjə nīz, dee hīdrəjə nīz/ (-izes, -izing, -ized), **dehydrogenise** (-ises, -ising, -ised) vt CHEM same as **dehydrogenate** —**dehydrogenization** /dee hī drójjə nī záysh'n, dee hīdrəjə nī-/ n

dehypnotize /dee hípnə tīz/ (-tizes, -tizing, -tized), **dehypnotise** (-tises, -tising, -tised) vt to bring somebody out of a hypnotic state —**dehypnosis** /dee hip nóssiss/ n —**dehypnotization** /dee hípnə tī záysh'n/ n

de-ice /dee íss/ (de-ices, de-icing, de-iced) vt to remove ice from something such as a windscreen, or prevent ice from forming on it

de-icer /dee íssər/ n a device or chemical substance that removes ice or prevents it forming, e.g. on the windscreen of a motor vehicle or the wings of an aircraft. One of the commonest de-icers is ethylene glycol, which is used in antifreeze.

deicide /dee i sīd, dáy-/ n 1. the act of killing a god or goddess 2. somebody who kills a god or goddess [Early 17C. Partly < ecclesiastical Latin deicida 'god-killer', partly < Latin deus 'god' + -CIDE] —**deicidal** /dáy i sīd'l, dee i-/ adj

deictic /díktik/ adj describes a word or expression such as 'you', 'this', 'now', and 'there' that depends for its full meaning on the context in which it is used [Early 19C. < Greek deiktikos < deiknunai 'to show'] —**deictically** adv

deid /deed/ adj Scotland same as **dead** [15C. Variant]

deify /dee i fī, dáy-/ (-fies, -fying, -fied) vt 1. to make somebody into a god 2. to honour or adore somebody or something as if he, she, or it were divine [14C. Via French déifier < ecclesiastical Latin deificare < Latin deus 'god'] —**deification** /dee ifi káysh'n, dáy-/ n —**deifier** n

Deighton /dáyt'n/, **Len** (b. 1929) British writer. He is best known for spy thrillers, including The Ipcress File (1962). He has also written on cookery and military history. Full name **Deighton, Leonard Cyril**

deign /dayn/ (deigns, deigning, deigned) vi to do something in a way that shows that it is considered a great favour ○ I don't suppose he'll deign to accept our invitation. [13C. Via Old French deignier < Latin dignare 'deem worthy' < dignus 'worthy']

Dei gratia /dáy i gráati ə, dee ī gráyshə/ adv by the grace of God [< Latin]

deil /deel/ n Scotland same as **devil** [15C. Variant]

Deimos /dáy moss/ n the outermost of the two natural satellites of Mars, both of which are small. It was discovered in 1877 and there is evidence suggesting that it is a captured asteroid. [After one of the sons of Ares in Greek mythology]

deindustrialise vti INDUST another spelling of **deindustrialize**

deindustrialization /dee in dústri ə lī záysh'n/, **deindustrialisation** n the removal or reduction of industrial activity in a country or region, especially heavy industry or manufacturing industry

deindustrialize /dee in dústri ə līz/ (-izes, -izing, -ized), **deindustrialise** (-ises, -ising, -ised) vti to take away or lose industries, especially the heavy industries and manufacturing industries, from a country or region

---

deinstitutionalize /dee insti tyóosh'nə līz/ (-izes, -izing, -ized), **deinstitutionalise** (-ises, -ising, -ised) vt to discharge a patient or client from institutional care, often in order to treat the person in his or her community —**deinstitutionalization** /dee insti tyóosh'nə lī záysh'n/ n

deionize /dee í ə nīz/ (-izes, -izing, -ized), **deionise** (-ises, -ising, -ised) v to remove ions from a solution —**deionization** /dee í ə nī záysh'n/ n —**deionizer** n

deism /dee izəm, dáy-/ n a belief in God based on reason rather than revelation and involving the view that God has set the universe in motion but does not interfere with how it runs. Deism was especially influential in the 17th and 18th centuries. [Late 17C. < Latin deus 'god'] —**deist** n —**deistic** /dee ístik, dáy-/ adj —**deistically** adv

deity /dee iti, dáy-/ (plural -ties) n 1. **GOD OR GODDESS** a god, goddess, or other being regarded as divine 2. **SOMEBODY OR SOMETHING RESEMBLING GOD** somebody or something that is treated like a god 3. **DIVINE STATE** the condition or status of a god or goddess [14C. Via French < ecclesiastical Latin deitas 'divine nature' < Latin deus 'god']

Deity n in monotheistic belief, God

deixis /díksiss/ n the use of a word or expression such as 'he', 'that', 'now', or 'here', whose full meaning depends on the context in which it is used [Mid-20C. < Greek, 'reference' < deiknunai 'to show']

déjà vu /dáy zhaa voó, -vyoó/ n 1. a feeling of having experienced something before, although in fact it is the first time that it has been experienced 2. a state of boring familiarity or repetitiveness [Early 20C. < French, 'already seen']

USAGE Déjà vu once referred exclusively to the illusion of having experienced something before: Entering the house for the first time, she had an eerie sense of déjà vu. Recently, however, it has come to encompass as well the reality of repetitiveness in events or actions: As they began to discuss which route was best, he had a distinct sense of déjà vu.

dejected /di jéktid/ adj feeling or showing sadness and lack of hope, especially because of disappointment [Late 16C. < archaic deject < Latin deject-, past participle of dejicere 'throw down' < jacere 'throw'] —**dejectedly** adv —**dejectedness** n

dejection /di jéksh'n/ n 1. **GREAT UNHAPPINESS** sadness and lack of hope, especially as a result of disappointment 2. **DEFECATION** the act of passing solid waste matter out of the anus (technical) 3. **EXCREMENT** solid waste matter passed out through the anus (technical)

de jure /dee joóri, day yoó ray/ adv, adj by right according to the law [Mid-16C. < Latin, 'from the law']

deka- prefix another spelling of **deca-**

Dekker /dékər/, **Thomas** (1572?–1632) English dramatist and pamphleteer. He wrote over 40 plays, including The Honest Whore (1604; part II 1630). He also wrote in collaboration with other Elizabethan dramatists including Philip Massinger, Thomas Middleton, and William Rowley.

'Golden slumbers kiss your eyes, / Smiles awake you when you rise.'
[Thomas Dekker, Patient Grissil; 1603]

dekko /dékō/ (plural -kos) n a quick look or glance (informal) ○ Come and have a dekko at this! [Late 19C. < Hindi dekho 'look!']

de Klerk /də klúrk/, **F. W.** (b. 1936) South African politician. He introduced reforms during his presidency (1989–94) that led to the end of apartheid. He shared the Nobel Peace Prize with Nelson Mandela (1993). Full name **de Klerk, Frederik Willem**

'There is no such thing as a nonracial society in a multiracial country.'
[F. W. de Klerk, Time; 1994]

de Kooning /də koóning/, **Willem** (1904–97) Dutch-born US artist. He is known for his abstract expressionist paintings, including the series of six paintings entitled Woman (1953).

'The trouble with being poor is that it takes up all your time.'
[Attributed to Willem de Kooning]

---

del *abbr* COMPUT, PRINTING delete

del. *abbr* 1. delegate 2. POL delegation 3. POL delete

de la see also under surname

Delacroix /déllə krwaa/, **Eugène** (1798–1863) French painter and lithographer. His romantic works, e.g. *Liberty Guiding the People* (1830), are characterized by melodrama and vivid colour. Full name **Delacroix, Ferdinand Victor Eugène**

> 'Painting is only a bridge linking the painter's mind with that of the viewer.'
> [Eugène Delacroix, *Journal*; 1893–95]

Delagoa Bay /déllə gṓ ə-/ bay on the southern Mozambique coast. Mozambique's capital, Maputo, is situated near the head of the bay.

delaine /di láyn/ *n* a fine woollen or woollen and cotton fabric resembling muslin [Mid-19C. Shortening of MOUSSELINE DE LAINE]

de la Mare /də la máir/, **Walter** (1873–1956) British poet, anthologist, and novelist. The works of this prolific writer include *The Listeners and Other Poems* (1912) and *Memoirs of a Midget* (1921).

> 'This Prince of Commerce spent his days / In crafty, calm, cold, cozening strife: / He thus amassed a million pounds, / And bought a pennyworth of life.'
> [Walter de la Mare, 'Hard Labour', *The Complete Poems of Walter de la Mare*; 1969]

delaminate /dee lámmi nayt/ (**-nates, -nating, -nated**) *vti* to separate or peel off in thin layers, or cause something to do this —**delamination** /dee lámmi náysh'n/ *n*

~~**delapidated**~~ incorrect spelling of **dilapidated**

de la Roche /déllə rósh/, **Mazo** (1885–1961) Canadian writer. She is known for her series of novels about the Whiteoak family, the first being *Jalna* (1927).

Delaroche /déllə rósh/, **Paul** (1797–1856) French painter. His historical subjects, e.g. his huge mural (1834–41) in the École des Beaux-Arts, Paris, are painstaking classical-romantic works. Full name **Delaroche, Hippolyte-Paul**

de la Tour, Georges ➧ **La Tour, Georges de**

Delaunay /də láw nay/, **Robert** (1885–1941) French painter. A cubist-influenced painter, he developed the style of Orphism. He was later a pioneer of pure abstract art, as shown in his *Windows* series (1912).

Delaunay, Sonia (1885–1980) Russian-born French painter and designer. Her paintings and designs for textiles, bookbindings, and theatrical costumes in the 1920s were characterized by bright colours and geometric forms. Born **Terk, Sonia**

> 'If you are an artist...You must do what you want and be ready not to sell. You can't be too ambiguous for money.'
> [Sonia Delaunay. Quoted in *Art Talk: Conversations with 15 Women Artists*, Cindy Nemser; 1975]

Delaware[1] /déllə wair/ (*plural same* or **-wares**) *n* a member of a group of Native North American peoples who once lived between the Delaware and Hudson rivers, and now live mostly in Oklahoma, Wisconsin, Kansas, and Ontario [Early 18C. After the *Delaware* River, E United States] —**Delaware** *adj*

Delaware[2] /déllə wair/ 1. first US state, bordered by the Atlantic Ocean, Maryland, Pennsylvania, and New Jersey. Capital: Dover. Population: 807,385 (2002 estimate). Area: 6,206 sq. km/2,396 sq. mi. 2. major river of the eastern United States, with its source in southern New York State. Length: 630 km/390 mi.

De la Warr /déllə wáir/, **Thomas West, 3rd Baron** (1577–1618) English-born colonial governor. In 1610 he arrived at Jamestown in time to save the settlement of Virginia from being disbanded. The state of Delaware is named after him. Known as **Lord Delaware**

delay /di láy/ *v* (**-lays, -laying, -layed**) 1. *vti* PUT SOMETHING OFF UNTIL LATER to postpone something, or wait until later before doing something 2. *vt* MAKE SOMEBODY OR SOMETHING LATE to make somebody or something late or slow ○ *I was delayed at the office.* 3. *vi* PROCRASTINATE to hesitate or fail to do something quickly enough ○ *Don't delay: book today.* ■ *n* 1. LATENESS a failure to happen or to do something at the intended or expected time ○ *All services are subject to delay or cancellation.* 2. EXTENT OF LATENESS the extent of the period of time by which somebody or something is made late or slowed down ○ *long delays on the M1* 3. PROCRASTINATION procrastination or failure to do something quickly enough ○ *This must be done without delay.* [13C. < Anglo-Norman *delaier* 'leave off' < *laier* 'leave'] —**delayer** *n*

delay action *n* MECH ENG same as **delayed action** (sense 1)

delayed /di láyd/ *adj* 1. made to happen later than intended or expected 2. happening after a period of time ○ *causing delayed damage to the kidneys*

delayed action *n* 1. the activation of a mechanism a short time after it has been set (*hyphenated when used before a noun*) 2. a mechanism used to produce delayed action

delayed neutron *n* a neutron emitted after a measurable time delay in the process of nuclear fission

delayed-release *adj* formulated to release an active ingredient gradually to prolong its effect

delayering /dee láy ə ring/ *n* the process of simplifying the structure of an organization to make it more efficient —**delayer** *vti*

delaying action, delaying operation *n* a manoeuvre used to gain time or allow a retreat when there are not enough resources to confront an opponent directly

delaying tactic *n* a deliberate attempt to delay something in order to gain time or another advantage

delay line *n* a device designed to cause a delay in transmitting an electronic signal

Delbrück /dél broȯk/, **Max** (1906–81) German-born US biologist. He shared the Nobel Prize in physiology or medicine (1969) for his work on the replication of viruses and their genetic structure.

dele /deéli/ (*informal*) *n* a mark used in the margin of printed material to show that something is to be deleted ■ *vt* (**-les, -leing, -led**) to mark a passage of printed material for deletion [Early 18C. < Latin, 'delete!']

delectable /di léktəb'l/ *adj* 1. DELICIOUS having a delicious taste 2. DELIGHTFUL absolutely delightful, very pleasing, or very attractive ■ *n* SOMETHING VERY TASTY an appetizing food or dish [14C. < French *délectable* < Latin *delectare* (see DELIGHT)] —**delectability** /di léktə bíllәti/ *n* —**delectably** *adv*

delectation /deé lek táysh'n/ *n* pleasure or enjoyment (*formal*) [14C. < Old French < Latin *delectare* (see DELIGHT)]

delegate *n* /délligət, -gayt/ 1. REPRESENTATIVE OR DEPUTY somebody who is chosen to represent or given the authority to act on behalf of another person, group, or organization, e.g. at a meeting or conference 2. MEMBER OF HOUSE OF DELEGATES a member of a US House of Delegates, the lower house of the legislature in Maryland, Virginia, or West Virginia 3. REPRESENTATIVE OF US TERRITORY a representative of a territory or of the District of Columbia in the US House of Representatives, who may speak on issues but not vote ■ *vti* /délli gayt/ (**-gates, -gating, -gated**) 1. GIVE TASK TO SOMEBODY ELSE to give a task to somebody else with responsibility to act on your behalf ○ *She delegates that responsibility to her assistant.* 2. GIVE AUTHORITY TO SOMEBODY ELSE to give somebody else the power to act, make decisions, or allocate resources on your behalf ○ *an executive who was unafraid to delegate* ■ *n* /délligət, -gayt/ SOMEBODY ASSIGNED A TASK somebody to whom a task or responsibility is delegated (*informal*) [15C. < Latin *delegat-*, past participle of *delegare* 'send away' < *legare* 'send'] —**delegable** *adj* —**delegator** *n*

delegation /déllə gáysh'n/ *n* 1. GIVING OF RESPONSIBILITY TO SOMEBODY ELSE the giving of some power, responsibility, or work to somebody else 2. CONDITION OF BEING GIVEN RESPONSIBILITY the condition of being given to somebody else as a duty or responsibility 3. GROUP REPRESENTING SOMEBODY a group of people chosen to represent or act on behalf of somebody 4. STATE REPRESENTATIVES all the members of the US Congress who represent one state

delegitimize /deélə jíttə mīz/ (**-mizes, -mizing, -mized**), **delegitimise** (**-mises, -mising, -mised**) *vt* to take away the legitimacy or legal status of somebody or something —**delegitimization** /deélə jíttə mī záysh'n/ *n*

~~**delemma**~~ incorrect spelling of **dilemma**

delete /di leét/ *vt* (**-letes, -leting, -leted**) 1. to score out or erase something that is printed or written 2. to erase or remove something from a computer file or disk ■ *n* same as **delete key** ○ *Click on the icon for that file and then hit delete.* [15C. < Latin *delet-*, past participle of *delere* 'blot out, efface']

delete key *n* a computer key that moves the cursor to erase characters, or removes highlighted text

deleterious /délli teéri əss/ *adj* having a harmful or damaging effect on somebody or something [Mid-17C. Via medieval Latin < Greek *dēlētērios* 'noxious'] —**deleteriously** *adv* —**deleteriousness** *n*

deletion /di leésh'n/ *n* 1. REMOVAL OR ERASURE OF SOMETHING the action or process of erasing, scoring out, or removing something written, printed, or shown or stored on a computer 2. SOMETHING REMOVED OR ERASED something erased, scored out, or removed from a text or a computer file or directory 3. GENETICS ABSENCE OF GENETIC MATERIAL the loss or absence of part of a chromosome, ranging from a pair of chemicals (**base pair**) to a whole chromosomal arm. Some medical conditions are the result of deletion.

deleverage /dee leévərij/ (**-ages, -aging, -aged**) *vti* to reduce the amount of debt that a company owes, usually by laying off workers, selling off unprofitable divisions, and other cost-cutting measures

delft /delft/, **Delft, delftware** /délft wair/, **Delftware** *n* earthenware with an opaque white glaze, usually with blue decoration [Late 17C. After DELFT]

Delft /delft/ city in the province of Zuid-Holland, in the western Netherlands, known as a centre of production of glazed earthenware. Population: 96,370 (2000).

delftware /délft wair/, **Delftware** *n* CERAMICS same as **delft**

Delgado, Cape /del gaádō/ cape in northeastern Mozambique, just south of the border with Tanzania

Delhi /délli/ city in northern India. It is a major political, transport, commercial, and industrial centre, and contains New Delhi, the national capital. Population: 13,782,976 (2001).

deli /délli/ (*plural* **-is**) *n* FOOD same as **delicatessen** (sense 1) (*informal*) [Mid-20C. Shortening]

Delian /deéljən/ *adj* relating to the Greek island of Delos ■ *n* somebody who comes from Delos [Late 16C < Latin *Delios* 'of Delos']

Delian League, Delian Confederacy *n* an alliance of Greek states set up in 477 BC to oppose Persia

deliberate *adj* /di líbbərət/ 1. INTENTIONAL carefully thought out and done intentionally 2. CAREFUL slow, careful, and methodical ■ *vti* /di líbbə rayt/ (**-ates, -ating, -ated**) THINK to consider something carefully and in detail [15C. < Latin *deliberatus*, past participle of *deliberare* 'weigh carefully' < *librare* 'weigh' < *libra* 'balance'] —**deliberately** *adv* —**deliberateness** *n* —**deliberator** *n*

deliberation /di líbbə ráysh'n/ *n* (*formal*) 1. CAREFUL THOUGHT long careful consideration of something 2. DISCUSSION formal or official discussion or debate ○ *The planning committee's deliberations went on all night.* 3. CARE slowness and methodical carefulness

deliberative /di líbbərətiv/ *adj* (*formal*) 1. involved in or organized for careful discussion and debate 2. relating to or resulting from discussion and debate —**deliberatively** *adv* —**deliberativeness** *n*

Delibes /də leéb/, **Léo** (1836–91) French composer. His works include the grand opera *Lakmé* (1883) and the ballet *Coppélia* (1870). Full name **Delibes, Clément Philibert Léo**

delicacy /déllikəssi/ (*plural* **-cies**) *n* 1. SOMETHING NICE TO EAT a delicious, rare, or highly prized item of food 2. SENSITIVITY sensitivity to the feelings of others 3. NEED FOR TACT the quality of requiring great tact or sensitivity ○ *a matter of extreme delicacy* 4. GREAT SENSITIVITY IN FEELINGS excessive sensitivity with regard to something offensive or embarrassing ○ *his delicacy on matters of a medical nature* 5. SUBTLETY AND REFINEMENT pleasing subtlety in something such as taste, smell, or colour ○ *the delicacy of her perfume* 6. FINENESS fineness and subtlety of feeling, observation, or execution ○ *the delicacy of the brushwork in his later paintings* 7. FRAGILITY the

quality of being easily damaged or broken **8. LACK OF PHYSICAL STRENGTH** lack of physical strength or health **9. SENSITIVITY OF RESPONSE IN EQUIPMENT** sensitivity in the way something such as scientific equipment or a musical instrument responds to use

delicate /déllikət/ *adj* **1. FRAGILE** having a fine structure that is easily damaged or broken **2. FRAIL** not having much resistance to illness or injury ○ *in delicate health* **3. SUBTLE** mild, gentle, pale, or soft, and pleasant to the senses ○ *a delicate shade of blue* **4. FINE** finely made and containing small parts or details ○ *delicate tracery* **5. SKILFUL** showing or characterized by great skill or craft, especially in producing or containing finely detailed intricate work or gentle or adroit movements ○ *a filigree of delicate shimmering brushstrokes* **6. NEEDING TACT** needing to be dealt with using tact and sensitivity ○ *The negotiations were at a delicate stage.* **7. REFINED** having or showing a refined and sensitive taste **8. EASILY OFFENDED** easily shocked or upset by offensive or embarrassing things **9. ACCURATE** describes instrumentation that is very precise and able to give exact readings **10. NOT WELL** uncomfortable as the result of over-indulgence (*humorous*) ○ *I'm feeling a bit delicate this morning.* ■ **delicates** *npl* **CLOTHES NEEDING SPECIAL WASHING AND DRYING** clothes that need careful washing and drying, e.g. using a special washing machine programme [14C. Directly or via French < Latin *delicatus*, related to *delicere* (see DELIGHT)] —**delicateness** *n*

SYNONYMS See *fragile*.

delicately /déllikətli/ *adv* **1. FINELY** in a way that shows skill in producing fine detail **2. SUBTLY** in a pleasingly mild and subtle way ○ *delicately flavoured* **3. GENTLY AND CAREFULLY** gently and carefully, with no rough or sudden movements **4. WITH TACT** tactfully and sensitively ○ *a matter that must be handled very delicately* **5. PRECARIOUSLY** in a way that seems precarious or sensitive to even a slight change or disturbance ○ *delicately balanced on its edge*

delicatessen /déllikə téss'n/ *n* **1.** a shop specializing in imported or unusual foods and ingredients such as cooked meats, cheeses, and pickles **2.** prepared food sold in a delicatessen, e.g. cooked meats, cheeses, pickles, and salads [Late 19C. Via German and French < Italian *delicatezza* 'delicacy' < Latin *delicatus* (see DELICATE)]

delicious /di líshəss/ *adj* **1.** having an appealing or enjoyable taste or smell **2.** highly amusing, pleasing, or enjoyable [13C. < Old French < Latin *delicia* 'pleasure' < *delicere* (see DELIGHT)] —**deliciousness** *n*

deliciously /di líshəssli/ *adv* **1. TASTILY** in a way that appeals to the sense of taste or smell ○ *a deliciously sweet and crunchy apple* **2. APPETIZINGLY** in an appetizing way ○ *king prawns sizzling away deliciously on the barbecue* **3. ENJOYABLY** in an amusing, pleasing, or enjoyable way

delict /di líkt/ *n* in Scottish civil law, a wrong or injury done to somebody [Early 16C. < Latin *delictum*, neuter past participle of *delinquere* 'offend' (see DELINQUENT)]

delight /di lít/ *n* **1. JOY** great enjoyment and pleasure ○ *To my delight, he accepted.* **2. SOMEBODY OR SOMETHING GIVING JOY** somebody or something that brings somebody great enjoyment and pleasure ○ *That's one of the delights of travelling to interesting places.* ■ *v* (**-lights, -lighting, -lighted**) **1.** *vti* **GIVE JOY TO SOMEBODY** to give somebody great enjoyment and pleasure **2.** *vi* **DERIVE JOY FROM SOMETHING** to gain great enjoyment and pleasure from something ○ *She delighted in outwitting her competitors.* [13C. < Old French *delit* < Latin *delectare* 'keep enticing' < *delicere* 'allure' < *lacere* 'entice'] —**delighted** *adj* —**delightedly** *adv* —**delighter** *n*

delightful /di lítf'l/ *adj* giving great enjoyment and pleasure, especially by being pleasant, good to look at, or amusing —**delightfully** *adv* —**delightfulness** *n*

Delilah /di lílə/ *n* in the Bible, the mistress of Samson who betrayed him to the Philistines. Having discovered that the source of his strength was his hair, she cut it off while he slept.

DeLillo /də leélō/, **Don** (*b.* 1936) US novelist. One of the foremost postmodernist writers in the United States, he is author of *White Noise* (1985), which won the National Book Award for Fiction, and *Underworld* (1997).

'I've come to think of Europe as a hard-cover book, America as the paperback version.'
[Don DeLillo, *The Names*; 1982]

delimit /di límmit/ (**-its, -iting, -ited**), **delimitate** /di límmi tayt/ (**-tates, -tating, -tated**) *vt* to set out or establish the limits or boundaries of something (*formal*) [Mid-19C. Via French < Latin *delimitare* < *limit-* (see LIMIT)] —**delimitation** /di límmi táysh'n/ *n* —**delimitative** *adj*

delimiter /di límmitər/ *n* a character or space marking the beginning or end of a data element

delineate /di línni ayt/ (**-ates, -ating, -ated**) *vt* **1. DESCRIBE SOMETHING** to describe or explain something in detail (*formal*) **2. DRAW SOMETHING** to sketch or draw something in outline **3. PORTRAY SOMETHING VISUALLY** to represent something visually using something such as a chart or graph **4. DEMARCATE BOUNDS OF SOMETHING** to indicate the physical boundaries of something [Mid-16C. < Latin *delineat-*, past participle of Latin *delineare* 'sketch out' < *linea* (see LINE¹)] —**delineable** *adj* —**delineation** /di línni áysh'n/ *n* —**delineative** *adj*

delineator /di línni aytər/ *n* **1.** an adjustable pattern that a tailor uses to cut garments of different sizes **2.** somebody or something that outlines or describes something

delinquency /di língkwənssi/ *n* **1. UNLAWFUL BEHAVIOUR** antisocial or illegal behaviour or acts, especially by young people **2. NEGLECT OF DUTY** failure to fulfil a duty, commitment, or responsibility (*formal*) **3.** *US* **FIN SOMETHING OVERDUE** something that is overdue for payment, e.g. a debt or tax (*formal*)

delinquent /di língkwənt/ *n* **YOUTHFUL OFFENDER** somebody, especially a young person, who has acted antisocially or broken the law ■ *adj* **1. ANTISOCIAL OR UNLAWFUL** relating to antisocial behaviour or law-breaking **2. IGNORING DUTY** neglecting a duty, commitment, or responsibility (*formal*) **3.** **FIN UNPAID** unpaid and overdue for payment [15C. < Latin *delinquent-*, past participle of *delinquere* 'offend' < *linquere* 'leave'] —**delinquently** *adv*

deliquesce /délli kwéss/ (**-quesces, -quescing, -quesced**) *vi* **1. CHEM DISSOLVE** to dissolve gradually by absorbing moisture from the air **2. BOT FORM BRANCHES** to form many branches without a main stem **3. FUNGI BECOME LIQUID** to become soft or liquid after the release of spores [Mid-18C. < Latin *deliquescere* 'start melting away' < *liquere* 'be liquid'] —**deliquescence** *n* —**deliquescent** *adj*

delirious /di lírri əss/ *adj* **1.** irrational as a temporary result of a physical condition such as fever, poisoning, or brain injury **2.** extremely excited or emotional ○ *delirious with joy* [Late 16C. < DELIRIUM] —**deliriousness** *n*

deliriously /di lírri əssli/ *adv* **1.** as a result of being delirious, e.g. because of poisoning, fever, or brain injury ○ *muttering and shouting out deliriously* **2.** in an extremely excited or emotional way ○ *deliriously happy at passing her driving test*

delirium /di lírri əm/ (*plural* **-iums** *or* **-ia** /-i ə/) *n* **1.** a state marked by extreme restlessness, confusion, and sometimes hallucinations, caused by fever, poisoning, or brain injury **2.** a state of extreme excitement or emotion [Mid-16C. < Latin < *delirare* 'be deranged', literally 'be out of your track' < *lira* 'ridge between furrows']

delirium tremens /-trémmenz, -treé menz/ *n* agitation, tremors, and hallucinations caused by alcohol dependence and withdrawal [< Latin, 'trembling delirium']

delish /di lísh/ *adj* same as **delicious** (*informal*) [Early 20C. Shortening]

delist /dee líst/ (**-lists, -listing, -listed**) *vt* **1.** to remove somebody or something from an official list **2.** *N Am* to remove a security from a listing on a stock exchange

Delius /deéli əss/, **Frederick** (1862–1934) British composer. His music is characterized by rich orchestration and the subtle evocation of moods, e.g. as in *On Hearing the First Cuckoo in Spring* (1912).

deliver /di lívvər/ (**-ers, -ering, -ered**) *v* **1. CARRY SOMETHING TO SOMEBODY** to take something such as mail, goods that have been bought, or a message to a person or an address **2.** *vt* **HELP BABY TO BE BORN** to give medical help to a baby human or animal when it is being born **3.** *vt* **PRODUCE BABY** to give birth to a baby (*often passive*) **4.** *vt* **MAKE SPEECH** to make a speech or give a talk to an audience **5.** *vt* **ANNOUNCE SOMETHING** to announce something formally such as an opinion, decision, or judgment ○ *The jury delivered its verdict.* **6.** *vt* **THROW BALL** to toss or throw a ball to somebody or at something **7.** *vt* **INFLICT BLOW** to inflict a blow on somebody or something **8.** *vi* **DO THING PROMISED** to do what has been promised ○ *He has yet to deliver anything that was promised in his speeches.* **9.** *vt* *US* **POL ACHIEVE SUPPORT FOR SOMEBODY** to organize and obtain the support of a place or people for a candidate or political party (*informal*) **10.** *vt* **PROVIDE SOMETHING** to provide or produce something ○ *Note the total dosage of antibiotics delivered.* **11.** *vt* **RELEASE SOMEBODY** to free or save somebody from captivity, hardship, or evil (*literary*) **12.** *vt* **GIVE SOMEBODY SOMETHING** to hand somebody or something over to somebody else ○ *You have 48 hours to deliver the payment.* [13C. Via French *délivrer* < Latin *deliberare* 'free completely' < *liberare* (see LIBERATE)] —**deliverability** /di lívvərə bílləti/ *n* —**deliverer** *n*

deliverable /di lívvərəb'l/ *adj* able to be delivered as promised ■ *n* something that has been promised to a customer or client, especially a piece of work that is part of a larger project, often contractually identified both in time and content (*usually used in the plural*)

deliverance /di lívvərənss/ *n* **1.** rescue from captivity, hardship, or domination by evil (*formal*) ○ *He sought deliverance from his imprisonment.* **2.** a formal announcement of a decision, judgment, or opinion

CULTURAL NOTE *Deliverance*, a film (1972) by British director John Boorman. Based on the novel by James Dickey (1972), it is the story of a canoe trip through the Appalachian Mountains undertaken by four city businessmen. The journey turns into a struggle for survival when the men are exposed to unexpected dangers and harried by sinister mountain people.

delivery /di lívvəri/ (*plural* **-ies**) *n* **1. TAKING OF SOMETHING TO SOMEBODY** the carrying of something such as mail, goods that have been bought, or a message to a person or address ○ *We can arrange delivery of any items purchased.* **2. VISIT BY SOMEBODY BRINGING SOMETHING** a visit made regularly to a person or address by a postal worker or a vendor's vehicle ○ *We only get one delivery a day.* **3. ITEM BROUGHT TO SOMEBODY** something brought by a postal worker or a vendor, e.g. the post or goods that have been bought **4. BIRTH PROCESS** the process of giving birth to a baby **5. MANNER OF SPEAKING** the action or manner in which somebody speaks to an audience ○ *She needs to work on her vocal delivery.* **6. RESCUE OF VICTIM** the rescue or saving of somebody from captivity, hardship, or evil ○ *He prayed for delivery from his oppressors.* **7. WAY OF PUTTING BALL IN MOTION** the action or manner of throwing, tossing, or rolling a ball or aiming a punch **8. LAW ACTION NEEDED TO EFFECT PROPERTY TRANSFER** a formal action needed to accomplish a transfer of property

delivery room *n* a specially equipped room in a hospital where women give birth

dell /del/ *n* a small, usually wooded valley or hollow [Old English < Germanic]

Della Falls /déllə/ waterfall, located in central Vancouver Island, British Columbia, Canada. Height: 440 m/1,445 ft. Flowing from a glacier-fed lake, Della Falls are Canada's highest waterfall.

Della Robbia /déllə róbbi ə/, **Luca** (1400?–82) Italian sculptor and ceramicist. He is best known for his early Renaissance panels in Florence Cathedral. He invented a technique for making glazed terracotta figures.

Delmarva Peninsula /del maárvə-/ peninsula in the US states of Delaware, Maryland, and Virginia. Length: 290 km/180 mi.

delocalize /dee lōkə līz/ (**-izes, -izing, -ized**), **delocalise** (**-ises, -ising, -ised**) *vt* to remove something from its locality —**delocalization** /dee lōkə lī záysh'n/ *n*

Delon /də lóN/, **Alain** (*b.* 1935) French actor, producer, director, and screenwriter. His notable films include the film noir classic *The Godson* (1967).

Delors /də láwr/, **Jacques** (*b.* 1925) French politician. As president of the European Commission (1985–94), he oversaw moves towards a free European

Community market in 1992. Full name **Delors, Jacques Lucien Jean**

'Europe is not just about material results, it is about spirit. Europe is a state of mind.'
[Jacques Delors, *Independent*; 19 May 1994]

Delos /dée loss/ island of Greece, the smallest island of the Cyclades group in the southern Aegean Sea, now almost uninhabited. In classical times it was considered sacred to Apollo and believed to be the birthplace of Apollo and Artemis. Area: 5 sq. km/2 sq. mi.

delouse /dee lówss/ (**-louses, -lousing, -loused**) vt to give a person or animal treatment to remove lice

Delphi /délfi/ ancient Greek town on the southern slopes of Mount Parnassus, about 9.5 km/6 mi. north of the Gulf of Corinth. It is the site of the Temple of Apollo and the Delphic oracle.

Delphic adj **1. Delphic** /délfik/, **Delphian** /délfi ən/ relating to Delphi or its temple or oracle **2. also delphic** obscure and open to more than one interpretation

Delphic oracle n in ancient Greece, an oracle of great authority and notorious ambiguity at Delphi, where it was believed the god Apollo spoke through a priestess

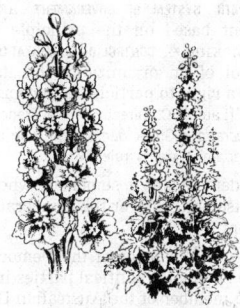

delphinium

delphinium /del fínni əm/ (*plural* **-iums** or **-ia** /-i ə/) n a tall ornamental plant. Flowers: blue or white in long spikes. Genus: *Delphinium*. [Early 17C. Via modern Latin < Greek *delphinion* 'larkspur' < *delphis* 'dolphin'; from the shape of the flower]

Delphinus /del fínəss/ n a small faint constellation of the northern hemisphere lying on the Milky Way, situated between Pegasus and Aquila. See illustration at **constellation**

Delphi technique n a process used in business forecasting of reaching a consensus by the anonymous solicitation and comparison of the views of experts [< the oracle at DELPHI]

delta /déltə/ n **1. TRIANGULAR LAND AREA AT RIVER MOUTH** a triangular deposit of sand and soil at the mouth of a river or inlet **2. also Delta AREA IN RIVER DELTA** an area in or around the delta of a river **3. 4TH LETTER OF GREEK ALPHABET** the fourth letter of the Greek alphabet, represented in the English alphabet as 'd'. See table at **alphabet 4. SOMETHING TRIANGULAR** something shaped like a triangle or delta **5. MATHS CHANGE IN VARIABLE** a change in the value of a variable. Symbol Δ [Pre-12C. Via Latin < Greek < Phoenician]

Delta n **1. CODE WORD FOR LETTER 'D'** a code word for the letter 'D', used in international radio communications **2. FOURTH BRIGHTEST STAR** the fourth brightest star in a constellation (*followed by the Latin genitive*) **3. AEROSP US ROCKET** a rocket used by the United States to launch satellites into orbit above Earth

Delta Force n the US Army 1st Special Forces Operational Detachment, a military and counterterrorist force similar to the SAS

delta ray n a low-energy particle, e.g. an electron, emitted by matter when subjected to ionizing radiation

delta wave, **delta rhythm** n a slow brain wave that is produced by adults in deep sleep. Delta waves are produced in the front of the brain and have a frequency of 3.5 cycles per second.

delta wing n an aeroplane wing that has a triangular swept-back shape

deltiology /délti ólləji/ n the collection and study of postcards [Mid-20C. < Greek *deltion* 'little writing tablet' < *deltos* 'writing tablet'] —**deltiologist** n

deltoid /dél toyd/ n a thick triangular muscle that covers the shoulder joint ■ adj triangular in shape (*technical*) [Mid-18C. Directly or via French < modern Latin *deltoides* 'delta-shaped' < Greek *delta*]

delts /delts/ npl the deltoid muscles (*informal*) [Shortening]

delude /di lood/ (**-ludes, -luding, -luded**) vt to persuade somebody to believe something that is untrue or unreal [15C. < Latin *deludere* 'play to your detriment' < *ludere* 'play' (see LUDIC)] —**deludable** adj —**deluded** adj —**deluder** n —**deludingly** adv

deluge /déllyooj/ n **1. SUDDEN HEAVY DOWNPOUR** a sudden heavy downpour of rain or torrent of water **2. VAST QUANTITY** an overwhelming amount of something ■ vt (**-uges, -uging, -uged**) **1. INUNDATE SOMEBODY WITH SOMETHING** to overwhelm somebody with a large amount of something **2. OVERWHELM SOMEBODY OR SOMETHING WITH WATER** to flood or soak somebody or something with heavy rain or a sudden torrent of water [15C. < Old French < Latin *diluere* 'wash away' < *lavare* 'wash']

Deluge n BIBLE same as **Flood**

delusion /di loozh'n/ n **1.** a persistent false belief held in the face of strong contradictory evidence, especially as a symptom of a psychiatric condition **2.** a false or mistaken belief or idea about something [15C. < Latin *delusion-* < past participle of *deludere* (see DELUDE)] —**delusional** adj

USAGE See **allusion**.

delusions of grandeur npl gross and false overestimation of personal worth, importance, powerfulness, or attractiveness

delusive /di loossiv/ adj leading to a belief in something untrue or unreal [Early 17C. < Latin *delus-*, past participle of *deludere* (see DELUDE)] —**delusively** adv —**delusiveness** n

delusory /di loossəri/ adj deceptive in nature or character and likely to mislead or delude somebody [15C. < late Latin *delusorius* < past participle of Latin *deludere* (see DELUDE)]

deluxe /də lúks/, **de luxe** adj of a luxurious standard and surpassing all others of the same type [Early 19C. < French *de luxe* 'of luxury']

delve /delv/ (**delves, delving, delved**) v **1.** vi **DIG INTO SOMETHING AND SEARCH AROUND** to thrust your hand deeply into something in order to find a hidden or hard-to-reach item or items **2.** vi **DIG FOR INFORMATION** to investigate or research something thoroughly in order to obtain information **3.** vti **EXCAVATE SOMETHING** to dig something such as a ditch, hole, or burrow (*archaic*) [Old English *delfan* < Germanic] —**delver** n

dem /dem/ pron *Carib* same as **them** ◇ an or and **dem** or an them *Carib* **1.** used to form a plural ○ *di man an dem a come* **2.** and others

Dem /dem/ n US POL same as **Democrat** (*informal*) [Late 19C. Shortening]

dem. abbr GRAM demonstrative

Dem. abbr POL **1.** Democrat **2.** Democratic

demagnetize /dee mágnə tīz/ (**-izes, -izing, -ized**), **demagnetise** (**-ises, -ising, -ised, -ised**) vt to remove the magnetic properties from something —**demagnetization** /dee mágnə tī záysh'n/ n —**demagnetizer** n

demagog n US POL US spelling of **demagogue**

demagogic /démmə góggik/, **demagogical** /-ik'l/ adj making an appeal to people's emotions, instincts, and prejudices in a way that is considered to be politically manipulative and dangerous [Mid-19C. < Greek *dēmagōgikos* < *dēmagōgos* (see DEMAGOGUE)] —**demagogically** adv

demagogue /démmə gog/ n **1.** a political leader who gains power by appealing to people's emotions, instincts, and prejudices in a way that is considered manipulative and dangerous **2.** in ancient times, a popular leader who represented the ordinary people [Mid-17C. < Greek *dēmagōgos* 'leader of the people' < *agōgos* 'leader' < *agein* 'lead'] —**demagoguery** n —**demagoguism** n

de Man /də mán/, **Paul** (1919–83) Belgian-born US philosopher and theorist. He moved to the United

States in 1947 and taught at Cornell, Johns Hopkins, and Yale universities. He is most famous for his essays on deconstructionism, e.g. *Blindness and Insight: Essays in the Rhetoric of Contemporary Criticism* (1971).

demand /di máand/ n **1. FORCEFUL REQUEST** a clear and firm request that is difficult to ignore or deny **2. CUSTOMER INTEREST IN ACQUIRING SOMETHING** the level of desire or need that exists for particular goods or services ○ *Demand for that model is outstripping supply.* **3. NEED FOR RESOURCES OR ACTION** an urgent requirement for time, facilities, resources, or action **4. LAW LEGALLY ENFORCEABLE REQUEST** a formal request that must be complied with by law ■ v (**-mands, -manding, -manded**) **1.** vt **REQUEST SOMETHING FORCEFULLY** to request something clearly and firmly in a way that is difficult to ignore or deny **2.** vt **ASK FORCEFULLY FOR ANSWER** to ask for an answer to a question in an extremely forceful way **3.** vti **CALL FOR RESOURCES** to require something such as time, facilities, resources, or action in order to function or succeed [14C. Via French < Latin *demandare* 'entrust completely' < *mandare* 'entrust, order' (see MANDATE)] —**demandable** adj —**demander** n ◇ **in demand** wanted or sought by many people ◇ **on demand** promptly, whenever a request is received

demand deposit n a bank deposit that can be withdrawn at any time without notice

demand feeding n the practice of feeding a baby when it cries to be fed, rather than at set times

demanding /di máanding/ adj requiring a lot of time, attention, energy, or resources

demandingly /di máandingli/ adv in a highly insistent manner

demand loan n FIN same as **call loan**

demand-pull, **demand-pull inflation** n inflation caused by demand for goods and services outstripping supply

demand-side adj relating to an economic policy that emphasizes the importance of demand and consumption

demantoid /di mán toyd/ n a transparent green variety of garnet. Use: gems. [Late 19C. < German, 'diamond-shaped' < *Demant* 'diamond']

demarcate /dée maar kayt/ (**-cates, -cating, -cated**) vt **1.** to decide on and set the boundaries of a piece of land **2.** to state in a clear way where something begins and ends [Early 19C. Back-formation < DEMARCATION] —**demarcator** n

demarcation /dée maar káysh'n/ n **1. SETTING OF BORDERS** the process of deciding on and setting the boundaries of a piece of land **2. IDENTIFIABLE SEPARATION OF THINGS** the division of something so that its divided parts are separate and identifiable **3. CLEAR DIVISION OF WORK DUTIES** the division of work duties into clearly identifiable parts to be carried out by different workers [Early 18C. < Spanish *demarcación* 'marking off' < *marcar* 'to mark' < Germanic]

demarcation dispute n **1.** in industrial relations law, a dispute as to which workers are to perform which tasks, especially when different trade unions are involved **2.** a disagreement over where a land boundary lies

démarche /dáy maarsh/ (*plural* **-marches** /-maarsh/) n **1. DIPLOMATIC REPRESENTATION** a diplomatic representation, especially a move, manoeuvre, or protest made orally **2. CITIZENS' PROTEST STATEMENT** a statement of protest made by or on behalf of the citizens of a nation to their government or to a controlling authority **3. MOVE OR COUNTERMOVE** a move, step, or countermove [Mid-17C. < French *démarcher* 'take steps' < *marcher* 'march']

De Maria /də ma rée ə/, **Walter** (b. 1935) US artist. A prominent conceptual artist and pioneer of the Land Art movement, he is best known for *New York Earth Room* (1977) and for his large-scale sculpture on a plateau in New Mexico *The Lightning Field* (1977).

dematerialize /dée mə teéri ə līz/ (**-izes, -izing, -ized**), **dematerialise** (**-ises, -ising, -ised**) vti to disappear, or cause something to disappear —**dematerialization** /deé mə teéri ə lī záysh'n/ n

deme /deem/ n **1.** a township in Attica in ancient Greece **2.** a local population of closely related inter-

breeding species [Mid-19C. < Greek *dēmos* (see DEMOS)]

demean /di meén/ (**-means, -meaning, -meaned**) *vt* to reduce somebody to a much lower status in a humiliating way [Early 17C. < DE- 'down' + MEAN[2] 'inferior in rank'] —**demeaning** *adj*

demeanor *n* US spelling of **demeanour**

demeanour /di meénər/ *n* somebody's behaviour, manner, or appearance, especially as it reflects on character

demented /di méntid/ *adj* **1.** completely unreasonable or lacking any sense of the consequences of actions taken (*informal*) **2.** affected by the loss of intellectual functions that is associated with dementia [Mid-17C. Past participle of obsolete *dement* 'deprive of reason' < Latin *dementare* < *ment-* 'mind'] —**dementedly** *adv* —**dementedness** *n*

dementia /di ménshə/ *n* the usually progressive deterioration of intellectual functions such as memory that can occur while other brain functions such as those controlling movement and the senses are retained [Late 18C. < Latin < *dement-* < *de-* 'away' + *ment-* 'mind']

dementia praecox /-preé koks/ *n* PSYCHIAT same as **schizophrenia** (sense 1) (*archaic*) [< Latin, 'premature loss of mind']

demerara /démmə ráirə/, **demerara sugar** *n* sugar with yellowish-brown crystals that feel slightly moist [Mid-19C. < *Demerara*, region of Guyana]

Demerara window *n Carib* a louvred window, hinged at the top and pushed up and held with a stick

demerger /deé múrjər/ *n* a merger between two or more companies that is dissolved, or the separation of one company from a larger company or group —**demerge** *vti*

demerit /dee mérrit/ *n* **1.** a negative feature or disadvantage of something, especially when contrasted with its positive features or advantages (*often used in the plural*) **2.** *N Am* a mark against somebody such as a student or cadet for a deficiency or misconduct [14C. Directly or via French < Latin *demeritum* < *demereri* 'deserve thoroughly' < *mereri* 'deserve'] —**demeritorious** /dee mérri táwri əss/ *adj* —**demeritoriously** *adv*

demersal /di múrss'l/ *adj* living or found in the deepest part of a body of water [Late 19C. < Latin *demersus*, past participle of *demergere* 'submerge' < *mergere* 'plunge']

demesne /di máyn/ *n* **1.** POSSESSION OF OWN LAND the possession and use of your own land, as opposed to the ownership of land that is occupied by tenants (*formal*) **2.** ESTATE an extensive landed property (*formal*) **3.** REALM OF MONARCH the realm under the rule of a monarch (*formal*) **4.** PRIVATE GROUNDS OF MANSION the estate attached to a mansion for the private use of the owner (*archaic*) **5.** FEUDAL MANORIAL LAND manorial land that a feudal lord kept for his own private use (*archaic*) [14C. Via Old French *demeine* 'belonging to a lord' < Latin *dominicus* < *dominus* 'lord']

Demeter /di meétər/ *n* in Greek mythology, the goddess of corn and the harvest, daughter of Cronus and Rhea and mother of Persephone. Roman equivalent **Ceres** (sense 1)

demi- *prefix* **1.** half ○ *demivolte* **2.** partly ○ *demigod* [Via Old French < Latin *dimidius* 'split in two' < *dis-* 'apart' + *medius* 'half']

demibastion /démmi básti ən/ *n* a two-sided fortification that consists of a wall facing forwards and a wall facing a flank

demigod /démmi god/ *n* **1.** MAN TREATED LIKE GOD an important or revered man who is treated like a god **2.** HUMAN WITH POWERS OF GOD a mythological being who is half human and half god **3.** MINOR GOD a god regarded as minor in a hierarchy of other gods

demigoddess /démmi goddess/ *n* **1.** an important or revered woman who is treated like a goddess **2.** a mythological being who is half woman and half goddess

demijohn /démmi jon/ *n* a large bottle that has a short narrow neck and is often used for making wine. Demijohns may also be made of earthenware and are sometimes encased in a wickerwork covering. [Mid-18C. By folk etymology < French *dame-jeanne* 'Lady Jane', its popular name in France]

demilitarize /dee míllitə rīz/ (**-rizes, -rizing, -rized**), **demilitarise** (**-rises, -rising, -rised**) *vt* to remove or prohibit the presence of soldiers, weapons, and military installations in an area after an agreement has been made to stop fighting —**demilitarization** /deé millitə rī záysh'n/ *n*

demilitarized zone *n* an officially recognized area from which all soldiers, weapons, and military installations have been removed after an agreement to stop fighting

DeMille /də míl/, **Cecil B.** (1881–1959) US film director and producer. He was known for his lavish epic films. Full name **DeMille, Cecil Blount**

demimondaine /démmi mon dáyn/ *n* a woman who is financially supported by a wealthy lover [Late 19C. < French < *demi-monde* 'half world']

demimonde /démmi mónd/ *n* (*literary*) **1.** people who are not considered to be entirely respectable **2.** a class of women who were financially supported by wealthy lovers, especially in the 19th and early 20th centuries [Mid-19C. < French *demi-monde* 'half world']

demineralize /dee mínnərə līz/ (**-izes, -izing, -ized**), **demineralise** (**-ises, -ising, -ised**) *vt* to remove minerals or mineral salts from something such as bone or a liquid —**demineralization** /dee mínnərə lī záysh'n/ *n* —**demineralizer** *n*

demi-pension /démmi paáN syoN/ *n* TRAVEL same as **half board**

Demirel /démmi rél/, **Süleyman** (*b.* 1924) Turkish politician. He served four terms as prime minister (1965–93) and was the ninth president of Turkey (1993–2000).

demirelief /démmiri leef/ *n* same as **half relief**

demise /di mīz/ (*formal*) *n* **1.** SOMEBODY'S DEATH the death of somebody, especially when it happens slowly and predictably **2.** END OF SOMETHING the end of something that used to exist, especially when it happens slowly and predictably ■ *vti* (**-mises, -mising, -mised**) TRANSFER LEGALLY to transfer something through a line of descent or according to a will, or be transferred in this way [15C. < Anglo-Norman < Old French *demis* 'sent away' < Latin *dimittere* (see DEMIT)] —**demisable** *adj*

demi-sec /démmi sék/ *adj* describes champagne or sparkling wine that is more sweet than dry [< French, 'half dry'] —**demi-sec** *n*

demisemiquaver /démmi semi kwayvər/ *n* a musical note with the time value of one thirty-second of a semibreve. It is written as a filled note head with a stem and three tails. N Am term **thirty-second note**

demission /di mísh'n/ *n* resignation from an important official post [Mid-16C. Via French < Latin *dimission-* 'dismissal' < past participle of *dimittere* (see DEMIT)]

demist /dee míst/ *vti* to remove mist or condensation from something, especially a car windscreen, or lose surface mist or condensation. N Am term **defog**

demister /dee místər/ *n* a piece of equipment that clears away mist or condensation, especially a device that channels warm air over the inside of a car windscreen. N Am term **defogger**

demit /di mít/ (**-mits, -mitting, -mitted**) *vti* to resign from or give up an important official post (*formal*) [15C. Via French < Latin *dimittere* 'send away' < *mittere* 'send']

demitasse /démmi tass/ *n* a small cup of coffee, or the cup in which such coffee is served [Mid-19C. < French, 'half cup']

demiurge /démmi urj/ *n* **1.** a very strong, driving, and influential force or personality (*formal*) **2.** a public magistrate in some ancient Greek states [Early 17C. Via ecclesiastical Latin < Greek *dēmiourgos* 'skilled person' < *dēmios* 'of the people' + *-ergos* 'working'] —**demiurgeous** *adj* —**demiurgic** *adj* —**demiurgical** *adj* —**demiurgically** *adv*

Demiurge *n* in Gnostic and Platonic philosophies, the creator and controller of the material world

demivierge /démmi vi áirzh/ *n* a young woman who takes part in sexual activity without ending her virginity [Early 20C. < French, 'half virgin']

demivolte /démmi volt/, **demivolt** *n* in dressage, a half turn made by a horse with its forelegs raised [Mid-17C. < French, 'half turn']

demiworld /démmi wurld/ *n* same as **demimonde** (sense 1)

demo /démmō/ *n* (*plural* **demos**) **1.** PUBLIC PROTEST a public event in which people protest against something, often by marching through the streets (*informal*) **2.** MUSIC MUSIC SAMPLE a recorded sample of music produced for promotional purposes (*informal*) **3.** COMPUT TRIAL SOFTWARE a trial version of software that demonstrates its principle features (*informal*) **4.** *N Am* COMM same as **demonstrator** (sense 3) **5.** DEMONSTRATION OF PRODUCT a demonstration, especially of a new product (*informal*) ■ *vt* (**demos, demoing, demoed**) SHOW HOW SOMETHING WORKS to explain, describe, or give a demonstration of how something works or how to do something (*informal*) [Mid-20C. Shortening of DEMONSTRATION]

demob /dee mób/ (**-mobs, -mobbing, -mobbed**) *vti* same as **demobilize** (*informal*) [Early 20C. Shortening]

demobilize /di mṓbə līz/ (**-izes, -izing, -ized**), **demobilise** (**-ises, -ising, -ised, -ised**) *vti* to discharge somebody from the armed forces and send him or her home, usually after a war, or be discharged in this way —**demobilization** /di mṓbə lī záysh'n/ *n*

democracy /di mókrəssi/ (*plural* **-cies**) *n* **1.** REPRESENTATION OF PEOPLE the right to a form of government in which power is invested in the people as a whole, usually exercised on their behalf by elected representatives **2.** DEMOCRATIC NATION a country with a democratically elected government **3.** DEMOCRATIC SYSTEM OF GOVERNMENT a system of government based on the principle of majority decision-making **4.** CONTROL OF ORGANIZATION BY MEMBERS the control of an organization by its members, who have a right to participate in decision-making processes [Late 16C. Directly or via French < medieval Latin *democratia* < Greek *dēmokratia* 'rule of the people' < *dēmos* 'people' + *kratos* 'rule']

democrat /démmə krat/ *n* somebody who believes in or supports democracy or the democratic system of government

Democrat *n* **1.** a member of the Democratic Party, one of the two major political parties in the United States **2.** a member of the Australian Democrats, a centre-left minority political party

democratic /démmə kráttik/ *adj* characterized by democracy in government or in the decision-making processes of an organization or group —**democratically** *adv*

Democratic *adj* relating to or associated with the Democratic Party of the United States or the Australian Democrats

democratic deficit *n* a situation in which political structures, organizations, or decision-making processes lack democratic legitimacy, especially as discussed in the European Union

Democratic Party *n* one of the two major political parties in the United States, formed after a split in the former Democratic-Republican Party under Andrew Jackson in 1828

Democratic Unionist Party *n* a Northern Ireland political party, established by the Reverend Ian Paisley in 1971, and strongly committed to the maintenance of the union between Great Britain and Northern Ireland

democratize /di mókrə tīz/ (**-tizes, -tizing, -tized**), **democratise** (**-tises, -tising, -tised**) *vt* **1.** GIVE CONTROL OF COUNTRY TO PEOPLE to make a country into a democracy **2.** INTRODUCE DEMOCRACY TO STATE to take steps towards establishing the features of liberal democracy in a state **3.** GIVE CONTROL OF ORGANIZATION TO MEMBERS to put an organization under the control of its members by giving them free and equal decision-making powers **4.** GIVE SOMETHING POPULAR APPEAL to make something accessible to everybody —**democratization** /di mókrə tī záysh'n/ *n*

Democritus /di mókritəss/ (460?–370? BC) Greek philosopher. A prolific writer, he first propounded the atomic theory of the universe. Only a few fragments of his work remain.

> 'In reality we apprehend nothing for certain, but only as it changes according to the condition of our body, and of the things that impinge or offer resistance to it.'
> [Attributed to Democritus]

démodé /day mṓd ay/ *adj* no longer fashionable [Late

19C. < French, past participle of *démoder* 'go out of fashion' < *mode* 'fashion']

demodulate /dée móddyoo layt/ (**-lates, -lating, -lated**) *vt* to extract a signal carrying information from a radio wave (**carrier**) —**demodulation** /dée modyoo láysh'n/ *n* —**demodulator** *n*

demographic /démmə gráffik/ *adj* OF HUMAN POPULATIONS relating to demography or demographics ■ *n* MARKETING PART OF POPULATION a part of a population identified as a group, especially as a target for sales or advertising ■ **demographics** *npl* CHARACTERISTICS AND STATISTICS OF HUMAN POPULATION the characteristics of a human population or part of it, especially its size, growth, density, distribution, and statistics regarding birth, marriage, disease, and death —**demographical** *adj* —**demographically** *adv*

demography /di móggrəfi/ *n* **1.** the study of human populations, including their size, growth, density, and distribution, and statistics regarding birth, marriage, disease, and death **2.** the makeup of a particular human population [Late 19C. < Greek *dēmos* 'people'] —**demographer** *n* —**demographist** *n*

demoiselle /dém waa zél/ *n* **1.** a young woman or girl, especially one who is French (*literary*) **2.** *also* **demoiselle crane** BIRDS a small crane with a slender grey body, black plumes, and white ear tufts. Native to: northern Africa, Asia. Latin name: *Anthropoides virgo*. **3.** FISH same as **damselfish 4.** INSECTS same as **damselfly** [Early 16C. < French, modern form of Old French *dameisele* (see DAMSEL)]

demolish /di móllish/ (**-ishes, -ishing, -ished**) *vt* **1.** WRECK STRUCTURE to destroy a building or other structure completely **2.** DAMAGE SOMETHING IRREPARABLY to damage something so severely that it cannot be repaired or restored **3.** BEAT OPPONENT SOUNDLY to beat an opponent very convincingly, especially in sport or debate (*informal*) **4.** EAT FOOD FAST to eat a large amount of food very quickly (*informal*) [Mid-16C. < Old French *démoliss-*, stem of *démolir* < Latin *demolire* 'undo construction of a mass' < *moles* 'mass'] —**demolisher** *n*

demolition /démmə lísh'n/ *n* **1.** DESTRUCTION OF BUILDING the complete destruction of a building or other structure ○ *The old hospital is scheduled for demolition.* **2.** ANNIHILATION the destruction or annihilation of somebody or something ■ **demolitions** *npl* EXPLOSIVES explosives, especially those used by the armed forces [Mid-16C. Via French < Latin *demolition-* < *demolire* (see DEMOLISH)]

demolition derby *n N Am* an entertainment and sports event held at a fair or on a speedway at which drivers crash old cars, the winner being the driver of the last car running

demolitionist /démmə lísh'nist/ *n* a person or company whose job it is to demolish buildings

demon /déemən/ *n* **1.** SUPPOSED EVIL SPIRIT a supposed ghost or spirit regarded as evil **2.** PERSONAL FEAR OR ANXIETY a fear or anxiety that torments somebody ○ *We all have our own personal demons.* **3.** EXPERT somebody who is very skilled at something (*informal*) [13C. Via Latin *daemon*, medieval Latin *demon* 'evil spirit' < Greek *daimōn* 'divine power, guiding spirit']

demonetize /dee múnni tīz/ (**-tizes, -tizing, -tized**), **demonetise** (**-tises, -tising, -tised**) *vt* **1.** to stop using a particular metal to make coins **2.** to withdraw units of money from circulation [Mid-19C. < French *démonétiser* 'refrain from using money' < Latin *moneta* 'money'] —**demonetization** /dee múnni tī záysh'n/ *n*

demoniac /di mṓni ak/, **demoniacal** /déemə nī́ ək'l/ *adj* **1.** resembling or characteristic of a supposed evil spirit **2.** evil or wicked in character or nature **3.** same as **demonic** (sense 2) [14C. < late Latin *daemoniacus* < Latin *daemon* (see DEMON)]

demonic /di mónnik/ *adj* **1.** relating to or resembling a demon, especially in wickedness **2.** intense, frantic, or wild, as if driven or possessed by a demon —**demonically** *adv*

demonise *vt* another spelling of **demonize**

demonism /déemənizəm/ *n* **1.** the worship of or belief in demons **2.** RELIG same as **demonology** —**demonist** *n*

demonize /déemə nīz/ (**-izes, -izing, -ized**), **demonise** (**-ises, -ising, -ised**) *vt* to cause somebody or something to appear evil or threatening in the eyes of others —**demonization** /déemə nī záysh'n/ *n*

demonolatry /déemə nóllətri/ *n* the worship of demons or of the devil —**demonolater** *n*

demonology /déemə nólləji/ *n* the study of demons, especially those that are frequent in the folklore of some societies —**demonological** /déemənə lójjik'l/ *adj* —**demonologist** *n*

demonstrable /di mónstrəb'l/ *adj* **1.** so obvious as to be readily recognized ○ *a demonstrable need for rail service* **2.** capable of being shown to exist or be true ○ *demonstrable proof* [14C. Directly or via French < Latin *demonstrabilis* < *demonstrare* (see DEMONSTRATE)] —**demonstrability** /di mónstrə bílləti/ *n* —**demonstrably** *adv*

demonstrate /démmən strayt/ (**-strates, -strating, -strated**) *v* **1.** *vt* EXPLAIN WORKINGS OF SOMETHING to explain or describe how something works or how to do something **2.** *vt* SHOW VALIDITY OF SOMETHING to show or prove something clearly and convincingly **3.** *vi* PROTEST OR SUPPORT SOMEBODY OR SOMETHING to make a public show as a group for or against an issue, cause, or person, often by marching through the streets [Mid-16C. < Latin *demonstrat-*, past participle of *demonstrare* < *monstrare* 'show' < *monstrum* 'omen']

demonstration /démmən stráysh'n/ *n* **1.** DISPLAY SHOWING HOW TO DO SOMETHING a presentation to others of the way in which something works or is done **2.** GROUP DISPLAY OF OPINION a public show as a group for or against an issue, cause, or person **3.** MIL SHOW OF MILITARY PREPAREDNESS a show of military force or readiness for combat **4.** CONCLUSIVE PROOF evidence or proof that allows no doubt as to the validity or soundness of something

demonstration sport *n* a sport that is contested in the Olympics on a trial basis and has yet to be accepted as a permanent medal sport

demonstrative /di mónstrətiv/ *adj* **1.** OBVIOUSLY AFFECTIONATE unrestrained in showing love and affection towards somebody **2.** PROVING serving as proof ○ *demonstrative evidence* **3.** GRAM SPECIFYING WHICH PERSON OR THING describes a word such as 'this' or 'those' specifying which person or thing is being referred to ■ *n* GRAM WORD SPECIFYING WHICH PERSON OR THING a demonstrative word or phrase, e.g. 'this', 'that', 'these', or 'those' —**demonstratively** *adv* —**demonstrativeness** *n*

demonstrator /démmən straytər/ *n* **1.** SUPPORTER OR PROTESTER a public protester or supporter of something, usually a member of a group **2.** EXPLAINER OF DEVICES somebody who shows or explains how to do something, or how something works **3.** SOMETHING DEMONSTRATING FEATURES something made available for testing by potential buyers, e.g. a motor vehicle, electrical appliance, or power tool. N Am term **demo**

demoralize /di mórrə līz/ (**-izes, -izing, -ized**), **demoralise** (**-ises, -ising, -ised**) *vt* **1.** ERODE MORALE OF SOMEBODY to erode or destroy the courage, confidence, or hope of a person or group **2.** CAUSE CONFUSION IN SOMETHING to throw something into disorder or chaos **3.** RUIN SOMEBODY MORALLY to corrupt somebody morally —**demoralization** /di mórrə lī záysh'n/ *n* —**demoralizer** *n* —**demoralizingly** *adv*

demos /déemoss/ *n* **1.** the ordinary people of a community or nation (*formal*) **2.** the common people in an ancient Greek city-state [Late 18C. < Greek *dēmos* 'district, people living in a district']

Demosthenes /di mósthə neez/ (384–322 BC) Greek orator. His reputation as the greatest Greek orator is based mainly on the *Philippics* (351, 344, 341 BC), a series of orations urging the Athenians to oppose the growing power of Philip II of Macedon.

demote /dee mṓt/ (**-motes, -moting, -moted**) *vt* to reduce somebody or something to a lower rank, status, or position [Late 19C. < DE- + PROMOTE]

demotic /di móttik/ *adj* **1.** relating to or involving ordinary people (*formal*) **2.** relating to a simplified form of Egyptian hieroglyphics [Early 19C. < Greek *dēmotikos* 'popular, common' < *dēmos* 'people']

Demotic *n* **1.** the colloquial form of modern Greek, adopted as the official variety of the language **2.** the later form of the ancient Egyptian language, written in the demotic script that was current in the first millennium BC —**Demotic** *adj*

demotion /dee mṓsh'n/ *n* a reduction in the rank, status, or position of somebody or something

demotivate /dee mṓti vayt/ (**-vates, -vating, -vated**) *vt* to make somebody feel less keen to work or study effectively —**demotivation** /dee mṓti váysh'n/ *n*

demount /dee mównt/ (**-mounts, -mounting, -mounted**) *vt* **1.** to take a piece of equipment away from its supports **2.** to take something apart, usually with the intention of reassembling it later —**demountable** *adj*

Dempsey /démpsi/, **Jack** (1895–1983) US boxer. He won the world heavyweight title in 1919, which he lost to Gene Tunney in 1926. Full name **Dempsey, William Harrison**. Known as **the Manassa Mauler**

> 'Kill the other guy before he kills you.'
> [Jack Dempsey, *Times*; 2 June 1983]

dempster *n* LAW same as **deemster**

demulcent /di múls'nt/ *n* a substance that soothes irritated or inflamed skin or mucous membranes. Lanoline and glycerin are demulcents. [Mid-18C. < Latin *demulcent-*, present participle of *demulcere* 'soothe down' < *mulcere* 'soothe'] —**demulcent** *adj*

demulsify /di múlssi fī/ (**-fies, -fying, -fied**) *vti* to break an emulsion down permanently into its components, or be broken down permanently —**demulsification** /di múlssifi káysh'n/ *n* —**demulsifier** *n*

demur /di múr/ (**-murs, -murring, -murred**) *v* **1.** *vi* SHOW RELUCTANCE to delay or try to avoid doing something because of personal reservations or objections ○*'While I acknowledged it might come to that [the use of force in the Persian Gulf], I demurred, saying it was too early to contemplate such action.'* (George Bush, *A World Transformed*; 1998) **2.** *vi* OBJECT SOMEWHAT to object mildly to something that you do not want to do but have been asked to do **3.** *vti* LAW MAKE LEGAL OBJECTION to admit the facts of an opposing argument, but object that those facts alone are not by themselves adequate to make the case **4.** *vt* SAY SOMETHING AS OBJECTION to state something as a mild objection or a legal demurrer [13C. Via Old French *demorer* 'delay, stay' < Latin *demorare*] —**demurrable** *adj* —**demurral** /di múrrəl/ *n*

SYNONYMS See ***object***.

demure /di myoór/ (**-murer, -murest**) *adj* **1.** looking or behaving in a modest manner, with reserve or seriousness **2.** acting in an affectedly shy or modest way [14C. < past participle of Old French *demorer* (see DEMUR)] —**demurely** *adv* —**demureness** *n*

demurrage /di múrrij/ *n* **1.** detention or delay of a cargo carrier during its loading or unloading process, beyond its scheduled time of departure **2.** compensation paid when there is a delay in loading or unloading a carrier causing a delay in the carrier's departure [Mid-17C. < Old French *demo(u)rage* < *demorer* (see DEMUR)]

demurrer /di múrrər/ *n* a legal objection that admits the facts of an opposing argument but asserts that those facts alone are not adequate to make the case [Early 16C. < French *demorer* (see DEMUR)]

demutualize /dee myoóchoo ə līz/ (**-izes, -izing, -ized**), **demutualise** (**-ises, -ising, -ised, -ised**) *vti* to convert a mutual organization such as a building society or an insurance company to a public company, or be converted in this way —**demutualization** /dee myoóchoo ə lī záysh'n/ *n*

demy /di mī́/ *adj* describes printing paper that is 444.5 mm/17.5 in. by 571.5 mm/22.5 in. or writing paper that is 393.7 mm/15.5 in. by 508 mm/20 in. [15C. Alteration of DEMI-]

demyelination /dee mī́ əli náysh'n/ *n* the loss of the fatty covering (**myelin**) of nerve fibres —**demyelinate** /dee mī́ əli nayt/ *vt*

demystify /dee místi fī/ (**-fies, -fying, -fied**) *vt* to remove the mystery surrounding something, e.g. by explaining it in simple language —**demystification** /dee místifi káysh'n/ *n* —**demystifier** *n*

demythologize /déemi thóllə jīz/ (**-gizes, -gizing, -gized**), **demythologise** (**-gises, -gising, -gised**) *vt* to reveal and understand the true character, nature, or meaning of something by ridding it of all mythical or mysterious aspects —**demythologization** /déemi thóllə jī záysh'n/ *n* —**demythologizer** *n*

den /den/ *n* **1.** WILD ANIMAL'S LAIR the hidden home of a wild animal **2.** PLACE OF CRIME a place where illegal or secret activities take place **3.** CHILDREN'S HIDEOUT a secret place where children play **4.** SQUALID ROOM a

squalid small room or place to live **5. QUIET ROOM** a small quiet retreat in a house, especially a study (*dated*) **6.** *N Am* **ROOM FOR RELAXING** a room in a house where family members and guests relax **7.** *N Am* **CUB SCOUT GROUP** a group of Cub Scouts typically made up of eight to ten youths [Old English *denn* 'wild animal's lair' < Indo-European, 'flat surface']

DEN *abbr* District Enrolled Nurse

Denali /də naáli/ **♦ McKinley, Mount**

denar /deénar/ *n* the main unit of currency in the Former Yugoslav Republic of Macedonia. See table at **currency** [Late 20C. Alteration of Serbo-Croatian *dinar* 'dinar' after Latin *denarius* (see DENARIUS)]

denarius /di náiri əss/ (*plural* **-ii** /-i ī/) *n* **1.** an ancient Roman silver coin originally worth ten asses **2.** an ancient Roman gold coin worth 25 silver denarii [14C. < Latin, literally 'containing ten' < *deni* 'ten at a time']

denary /deénəri/ *adj* relating to a number system that has ten as its base, as in the decimal system [Mid-19C. < Latin *denarius* (see DENARIUS)]

denationalize /dee násh'nə līz/ (**-izes, -izing, -ized**), **denationalise** (**-ises, -ising, -ised**) *vt* **1.** to sell an industry or other major asset owned by the state to private investors **2.** to deprive a people or nation of national rights or characteristics —**denationalization** /dee násh'nə līˈ záysh'n/ *n*

denaturalize /dee náchərə līˈz/ (**-izes, -izing, -ized**), **denaturalise** (**-ises, -ising, -ised**) *vt* **1.** to take away a naturalized citizen's citizenship, e.g. for having entered the country illegally **2.** to take away the original nature of something ○ *once-verdant jungles that were denaturalized by defoliants* —**denaturalization** /dee náchərə līˈ záysh'n/ *n*

denature /dee náychər/ (**-tures, -turing, -tured**) *vt* **1. MAKE SOMETHING UNPALATABLE** to make food or drink, especially alcohol, unsuitable for human consumption, by adding poison, dye, or unpleasant flavours **2.** BIOCHEM **MODIFY MOLECULE'S STRUCTURE** to change the molecular structure and characteristics of a molecule by chemical or physical means **3.** INDUST **REMOVE WEAPON POTENTIAL OF NUCLEAR MATERIAL** to make nuclear material unsuitable for use in a weapon by adding an isotope that cannot be split —**denaturant** *n* —**denaturation** /dee náychə ráysh'n/ *n*

denazify /dee naátsi fīˈ/ (**-fies, -fying, -fied**) *vt* to remove something or somebody connected to Nazis or Nazism —**denazification** /dee naátsifi káysh'n/ *n*

Denbighshire /dénbishər/ county in north Wales. It was divided between the counties of Clwyd and Gwynedd between 1974 and 1994. Population: 93,065 (2001).

Dench /dench/, **Dame Judi** (*b.* 1934) British actor. She has played leading roles with Britain's major stage companies and in award-winning films such as *Mrs Brown* (1997). She won an Academy Award for her performance in *Shakespeare in Love* (1999). Full name **Dench, Dame Judith Olivia**

dendr- *prefix* same as **dendro-** (*used before vowels*)

dendri- *prefix* same as **dendro-**

dendriform /déndri fawrm/ *adj* shaped like a tree

dendrimer /déndrimər/ *n* a copolymer with a regular branching structure attached to a central chain of carbon atoms —**dendrimeric** /déndri mérrik/ *adj*

dendrite /dén drīt/ *n* **1.** a branched extension of a nerve cell (**neuron**) that receives electrical signals from other neurons and conducts those signals to the cell body **2.** a mineral crystallized in the shape of a tree [Early 18C. Directly or via French < Greek *dendritēs* 'of a tree' < *dendron* 'tree'] —**dendritic** /den dríttik/ *adj* —**dendritical** *adj* —**dendritically** *adv*

dendro- *prefix* tree, resembling a tree ○ *dendrology* ○ *dendrite* [< Greek *dendron* < Indo-European, 'be solid']

dendrochronology /déndrō krə nóllaji/ *n* the study of the annual growth rings in trees, wood, or wooden objects, especially as a way of dating wooden remains or determining past climatic conditions —**dendrochronological** /déndrō krónnə lójjik'l/ *adj* —**dendrochronologist** *n*

dendrogram /déndrə gram/ *n* a diagram showing the relationships of items arranged like the branches of a tree

dendroid /dén droyd/, **dendroidal** /den dróyd'l/ *adj* **1.** **WITH STEM RESEMBLING TREE TRUNK** describes plants with

an erect main stem like a tree trunk **2.** **MULTIBRANCHED** describes plants with many branches, like those of a tree **3.** **RESEMBLING TREE** generally resembling a tree in shape or form

dendrology /den drólləji/ *n* the study of trees and other woody plants —**dendrologic** /déndrə lójjik/ *adj* —**dendrological** *adj* —**dendrologist** *n* —**dendrologous** *adj*

dendron /dén dron/ *n* ANAT same as **dendrite** (sense 2) (*dated*) [Late 19C. < DENDRITE + -ON [2]]

dene /deen/ *n* a narrow wooded valley (*often used in placenames*) [Old English *denu* < Germanic]

Dene /dénni, dénnay/ *npl* a group of Athabaskan-speaking Native North Americans who live in northern Canada, chiefly in the Northwest Territories [Late 19C. Via Canadian French < Athabaskan]

Deneb /dénneb/ *n* the brightest star in the constellation Cygnus. Deneb is a white giant located over 1600 light-years from Earth.

denervate /dee núr vayt, dénnər-/ (**-vates, -vating, -vated**) *vt* to deprive an organ or body part of nerves, either by cutting them or by blocking them with drugs, e.g. to control pain —**denervation** /deé nur váysh'n/ *n*

Deneuve /də nőv/, **Catherine** (*b.* 1943) French film actor. Her films include *Repulsion* (1965) and *Belle de Jour* (1967). Born **Dorléac, Catherine**

dengue /déng gi, -gay/, **dengue fever** *n* a tropical disease caused by a virus that is transmitted by mosquitoes and marked by high fever and severe muscle and joint pains [Early 19C. < Caribbean Spanish]

Deng Xiaoping

Deng Xiaoping /dúng show píng/ (1904–97) Chinese political leader. Purged twice from the Communist Party, he was reinstated in 1977 and was the undisputed leader of China until his death. He introduced reforms that led to greater economic freedom in China.

> 'No individual in the present Chinese leadership can determine any of our policies on his own. All important decisions are made through collective discussions.'
> [Deng Xiaoping, *Interview with Robert Maxwell;* 1984]

deni /dénee/ (*plural same*) *n* a subunit of currency in the Former Yugoslav Republic of Macedonia. See table at **currency** [Late 20C. < Macedonian]

deniable /di nīˈ əb'l/ *adj* **1.** able to be disclaimed or declared untrue ○ *deniable allegations* **2.** describes an activity planned and carried out in such a way that disavowal of it would probably be believed ○ *deniable covert operations* —**deniably** *adv*

denial /di nīˈ əl/ *n* **1.** **DISAVOWAL** a statement saying that something is not true or not correct ○ *her continued denial of the story* **2.** **REFUSAL TO ALLOW SOMEBODY SOMETHING** a refusal to grant something desired or believed to be a right ○ *a denial of justice* **3.** **REFUSAL TO ACKNOWLEDGE EXISTENCE OF SOMETHING** a refusal to believe in something or admit that something exists **4.** PSYCHOL **REFUSAL TO FACE UNPLEASANT FACTS** a state of mind marked by a refusal or an inability to recognize and deal with a serious personal problem ○ *She's in denial.* **5.** LAW **OPPOSITION TO ALLEGATION** in a court of law, a statement denying an accusation of wrongdoing

denial-of-service attack *n* an illegal attempt to put a computer system out of action by overloading it with data from many sources simultaneously

denier [1] /dénni ər/ *n* **1.** a unit of fineness of silk and some artificial fibres such as nylon equal to one

gram per 9,000 m of yarn. It is now largely superseded by other units. **2.** /də neér/ a silver coin, formerly used in several European countries [15C. Via French < Latin *denarius* (see DENARIUS)]

denier [2] /di nírˈ/ *n* somebody who denies something [15C. < DENY]

denigrate /dénni grayt/ (**-grates, -grating, -grated**) *vt* **1.** to attack somebody's character or reputation **2.** ⚠ to disparage or criticize somebody or something, or make something seem unimportant [15C. < Latin *denigrat-*, past participle of *denigrare* 'blacken completely' < *niger* 'black'] —**denigration** /dénni gráysh'n/ *n* —**denigrator** *n*

> **USAGE** In its best-established sense **denigrate** means 'attack somebody's reputation'. However, it is now often found in sentences like *I don't mean to denigrate the problem*, where its meaning has become closer to 'disparage or belittle somebody or something'. In this, it is following in the footsteps of *deprecate*, whose traditional meaning is 'express condemnation of somebody or something', but which in *self-deprecating* has taken on the additional sense of 'belittle'.

denim /dénnim/ *n* a durable woven cotton cloth. Use: clothing, especially jeans. ■ **denims** *npl* clothes made of denim, especially jeans, jackets, shirts, or skirts [Late 17C. < French *(serge) de Nîmes* '(serge) of Nîmes', France]

De Niro /də neérō/, **Robert** (*b.* 1943) US actor. He won Academy Awards for *The Godfather II* (1974) and *Raging Bull* (1980).

> 'Are you talking to me? / Are you talking *to me*? / Are you talking to me? / …Well, I'm the only one here.'
> [Robert De Niro. Words of lines for a main character, *Taxi Driver*; 1976]

denitrate /dee nīˈ trayt/ (**-trates, -trating, -trated**) *vti* to remove a nitro or nitrate group, nitrogen compound, or nitrous acid from a chemical compound, or lose such components —**denitration** /deé nī tráysh'n/ *n*

denitrify /dee nítri fīˈ/ (**-fies, -fying, -fied**) *vt* **1.** to remove nitrogen or a nitrogen compound from a substance **2.** to convert nitrates into nitrites and ammonia —**denitrification** /dee nítrifi káysh'n/ *n*

denizen /dénniz'n/ *n* **1.** **RESIDENT** a resident of a specific country or area **2.** **HABITUAL VISITOR** a habitual visitor to a place ○ *denizens of cyberspace chat rooms* **3.** **FOREIGNER WITH RIGHTS OF RESIDENCE** a new resident in a foreign country who is given some legal rights there **4.** ECOL **NON-NATIVE PLANT OR ANIMAL** a non-native plant or animal that grows or lives in an area [15C. < Anglo-Norman *deinzein* < Old French *deinz* 'inside' < Latin *de intus* 'from inside']

Denmark

Denmark /dén maark/ southernmost and smallest country in Scandinavia, comprising the Jutland peninsula and about 480 islands. Language: Danish. Currency: krone. Capital: Copenhagen. Population: 5,384,384 (2003). Area: 43,094 sq. km/16,639 sq. mi. Official name **Kingdom of Denmark**

Denning /dénning/, **Alfred, Baron Denning of Whitchurch** (1899–1999) British judge. He issued a number of controversial judicial decisions during a long and distinguished career, and was Master of the Rolls (1962–82).

> 'When a diplomat says yes, he means perhaps. When he says perhaps, he means no. When he says no, he is not a diplomat.

When a lady says no, she means perhaps.
When she says perhaps, she means yes.
But when she says yes, she is no lady.'
[Alfred Denning, *Speech to the Magistrates Association*; 14 October 1982]

Dennis /dénniss/, **C. J.** (1876–1938) Australian writer. He was the author of humorous verse written in colloquial language. His best-known work is *The Songs of a Sentimental Bloke* (1915). Full name **Dennis, Clarence Michael James**

denom. *abbr* RELIG denomination

denominal /di nómminəl/ *adj* describes parts of speech that are formed from or have the same form as a noun, e.g. the verb 'to butter' —**denominal** *n*

denominate /di nómmi nayt/ (**-nates, -nating, -nated**) *vt* **1.** to define something in terms of a particular unit of currency **2.** to give something a particular name or description (*formal*) [Mid-16C. < Latin *denominat-*, past participle of *denominare*, literally 'name completely' < *nominare* 'to name'] —**denominable** *adj*

denomination /di nómmi náysh'n/ *n* **1.** RELIGIOUS GROUPING a religious grouping within a faith that has its own system of organization **2.** UNIT OF VALUE OR MEASURE a unit in a scale of value, especially monetary value, weight, measure, or size **3.** NAME OR DESIGNATION a name or designation given to a class, group, or type [14C. Directly or via French < Latin *denomination-* < *denominat-* (see DENOMINATE)] —**denominational** *adj*

denominative /di nómminətiv/ *adj* GRAM same as **denominal** [Late 16C. < late Latin *denominativus* < Latin *denominat-* (see DENOMINATE)] —**denominative** *n* —**denominatively** *adv*

denominator /di nómmi naytər/ *n* **1.** NUMBER BELOW LINE IN FRACTION the number below the line in a simple fraction, which indicates the number of parts making up the whole **2.** COMMON CHARACTERISTIC something held in common **3.** AVERAGE LEVEL an average standard, degree, or level of quality or taste

de nos jours /də nō zhoor/ *adj* of our time [< French]

denotation /deenō táysh'n/ *n* **1.** BASIC MEANING the most specific or literal meaning of a word, as opposed to its figurative senses or connotations **2.** INDICATOR OF SOMETHING a sign, symbol, or indication of something **3.** REFERENCE OF TERM in logic, the reference of a term

denote /di nōt/ (**-notes, -noting, -noted**) *vt* **1.** MEAN SOMETHING to have something as a meaning, especially a specific or literal one **2.** REFER TO SOMEBODY OR SOMETHING to designate or refer to somebody or something **3.** SIGNIFY SOMETHING to be a sign or indication of something [Late 16C. Via French < Latin *denotare*, literally 'mark completely' < *notare* 'to mark'] —**denotative** /deenō taytiv/ *adj* —**denotive** *adj*

USAGE denote or **represent**? Use **denote** when you want to say 'to mean', 'to refer to', or 'to signify': *That word denotes 'life' in Spanish. For our purposes, the word 'corporation' will denote the XYZ Foundation. The tiny points of light in the sky denote the Plough.* It is preferable to use **represent** when you mean 'to symbolize something else': *The red maple leaf represents* [not *denotes*] *Canada.*

USAGE See **connote**.

denouement /day noo moN/ *n* **1.** a final part of a story or drama in which everything is made clear and no questions or surprises remain **2.** the final stage or climax of a series of events ○ *the gripping denouement of the championship* [Mid-18C. < French < *dénouer* 'untie' < *nouer* 'to tie' < Latin *nodus* 'knot']

denounce /di nównss/ (**-nounces, -nouncing, -nounced**) *vt* **1.** CRITICIZE SOMETHING PUBLICLY to criticize or condemn something publicly and harshly **2.** CHARGE SOMEBODY WITH WRONGDOING to accuse somebody publicly of something such as disloyalty, or inform against somebody **3.** ANNOUNCE TERMINATION OF AGREEMENT to make a formal announcement of the end of a treaty or other agreement (*formal*) [14C. Via Old French *denoncier* < Latin *denuntiare* < *nuntiare* 'proclaim, announce' < *nuntius* 'messenger'] —**denouncement** *n* —**denouncer** *n*

SYNONYMS See **disapprove**.

de novo /di nōvō/ *adv* anew, afresh, or over again from the beginning [Mid-16C. < Latin, 'from new']

Denpasar /den paá saar/ city in Indonesia and capital

of the island province of Bali, located near Bali's southernmost point. Population: 373,272 (1997).

dense /denss/ (**denser, densest**) *adj* **1.** TIGHTLY PACKED so close together that there is little sense of open or unoccupied space ○ *a dense jungle* ○ *a dense population of 2 million* **2.** VERY THICK so thick that it is difficult or impossible to see through ○ *dense summer haze* **3.** HARD TO PENETRATE INTELLECTUALLY so complex and intricate that it is difficult to assimilate and understand **4.** SLOW TO LEARN OR UNDERSTAND considered to lack the ability to learn or understand quickly (*informal insult*) **5.** WITH HIGH MASS with a relatively high mass per unit volume [15C. Directly or via French < Latin *densus* 'thick, dense'] —**densely** *adv* —**denseness** *n*

densimeter /den símmitər/ *n* an instrument that measures density or specific gravity [Mid-19C. < Latin *densus* 'thick, dense'] —**densimetric** /dénssi méttrik/ *adj* —**densimetry** *n*

densitometer /dénssi tómmitər/ *n* **1.** an instrument for measuring optical density, e.g. that of a photographic negative **2.** PHYS same as **densimeter** [Early 20C. < DENSITY] —**densitometric** /dénssitə méttrik/ *adj* —**densitometry** *n*

density /dénssəti/ (*plural* **-ties**) *n* **1.** the concentration of people or things within an area in relation to its size **2.** PHYS a measure of a quantity such as mass or electric charge per unit volume. Symbol ρ **3.** ELEC same as **charge density 4.** ELEC same as **current density**

density function *n* STATS same as **probability density function** (sense 2)

dent /dent/ *v* (**dents, denting, dented**). **1.** *vti* MAKE DEPRESSION IN SOMETHING BY HITTING to make a shallow depression in the surface of something by hitting it or putting pressure on it, or receive a depression through pressure **2.** *vt* HARM SOMETHING ABSTRACT to do nonphysical, usually minor, damage to something ○ *dented their championship hopes* ■ *n* **1.** AREA IN DEPRESSED SURFACE a shallow depression in the surface of something that is made by hitting it or putting pressure on it **2.** NONPHYSICAL DAMAGE nonphysical, usually minor, damage, e.g. to somebody's reputation or pride **3.** ADVANCE progress in reaching a goal (*informal*) ○ *make a dent in the backlog* **4.** REDUCTION a reduction in an amount of something such as resources (*informal*) ○ *a dent in the budget* [13C. Variant of DINT]

dent. *abbr* DENT **1.** dental **2.** dentistry

dental /dént'l/ *adj* **1.** OF DENTISTRY relating to or used in dentistry **2.** OF TEETH relating or belonging to the teeth **3.** DENT NEAR TOOTH affecting or located in or near a tooth ○ *dental abscess* **4.** PHON MADE BY TONGUE AND TEETH describes a consonant that is formed by placing the tongue against the back of the top front teeth ■ *n* PHON DENTAL CONSONANT a consonant formed by placing the tongue against the back of the top front teeth [Late 16C. < late Latin *dentalis* < Latin *dent-* 'tooth']

dental caries *n* decay of teeth caused by the action of acid-forming bacteria and improper dental care

dental floss *n* thread that is used to remove food and plaque from between the teeth

dental hygiene *n* the care people take of their teeth and gums to prevent tooth and gum disease

dental hygienist *n* somebody who provides routine dental care, especially cleaning and scaling teeth

dental nurse *n* a dentist's assistant, who prepares materials and equipment and helps the dentist during the treatment of a patient

dental surgeon *n* DENT same as **dentist**

dental technician *n* somebody trained to make dental appliances such as caps, dentures, and bridges

dentate /dén tayt/ *adj* edged with pointed or tooth-shaped projections [15C. < Latin *dentatus* < *dent-* 'tooth'] —**dentately** *adv* —**dentation** /den táysh'n/ *n*

denti- *prefix* tooth, dental ○ *dentiform* [< Latin *dent-* 'tooth' < Indo-European]

denticle /déntik'l/ *n* **1.** a small tooth or tooth-shaped projection **2.** a small tooth-shaped scale with a projecting spine, typical of cartilaginous fish [15C. < Latin *denticulus* 'small tooth' < *dent-* 'tooth'] —**denticular** /den tíkyoŏlər/ *adj*

denticulate /den tíkyoŏlət, -layt/ *adj* **1.** with fine teeth or pointed projections **2.** describes a building or part of a building decorated with small rectangular blocks (**dentils**) that look like a row of teeth [Mid-17C. < Latin *denticulatus* < *denticulus* (see DENTICLE)] —**denticulately** *adv*

dentiform /dénti fawrm/ *adj* shaped like a tooth

dentifrice /déntifriss/ *n* a paste or similar compound for cleaning teeth [15C. Via French < Latin *dentifricium* < *dent-* 'tooth' + *fricare* 'rub']

dentil /déntil/ *n* a small rectangular block that is arranged with others to look like a row of teeth, used as a form of architectural decoration [Late 16C. < Italian *dentello* or obsolete French *dentille* 'small tooth' < Latin *dent-* 'tooth']

dentilingual /dénti líng gwəl/ *adj* describes a speech sound pronounced or articulated with the tongue touching the teeth on the top jaw

dentine /dén teen/, **dentin** /-tin/ *n* the hard part of a tooth that lies underneath the enamel and surrounds the pulp and root canals [Mid-19C. < Latin *dent-* 'tooth'] —**dentinal** /-tin'l/ *adj*

dentist /déntist/ *n* somebody trained and licensed to practise general dentistry or a branch of dentistry such as orthodontics or dental surgery [Mid-18C. < French *dentiste* < *dent* 'tooth' < Latin *dent-*]

dentistry /déntistri/ *n* the medical science concerned with the prevention and treatment of tooth and gum disorders and diseases

dentition /den tísh'n/ *n* **1.** the type, number, and arrangement of a set of teeth **2.** the process of developing and cutting new teeth [Late 16C. < Latin *dent-* 'tooth']

Denton /déntən/ city in northern Texas, north of Fort Worth and northwest of Dallas. Population: 90,349 (2002 estimate).

denture /dénchər/ *n* a partial or complete set of artificial teeth for the upper or lower jaw, usually attached to a plate [Late 19C. < French < *dent* 'tooth' (see DENTIST)]

denturist /déncharist/ *n* N Am a dental technician who makes and fits dentures that are sold directly to the public rather than through a dentist

denuclearize /dee nyoókli ə ríz/ (**-izes, -izing, -ized**), **denuclearise** (**-ises, -ising, -ised**) *vt* to remove, ban, or eliminate nuclear weapons or nuclear power sources from a place, industry, or organization —**denuclearization** /dee nyoókli ə rī záysh'n/ *n*

denude /di nyoŏd/ (**-nudes, -nuding, -nuded**) *vt* **1.** REMOVE SOMEBODY'S OR SOMETHING'S COVERING to strip somebody or something bare **2.** ENVIRON DESTROY GROUND COVER OF PLACE to strip away the covering vegetation from an area **3.** GEOL STRIP AREA BY EROSION to remove soil from an area, or expose underlying layers of rock by weathering and erosion [15C. < Latin *denudare* 'strip away' < *nudare* 'strip' < *nudus* 'nude'] —**denudation** /deé nyoo dáysh'n/ *n*

denumerable /di nyoómərəb'l/ *adj* in mathematics, able to form a one-to-one correspondence with the positive integers [Early 20C. < late Latin *denumerare* 'count out' < Latin *numerare* (see NUMERATE)] —**denumerability** /di nyoómərə bílləti/ *n* —**denumerably** *adv*

denunciation /di núnssi áysh'n/ *n* a public accusation or condemnation of something or somebody [15C. Directly or via French < medieval Latin *denunciation-* < past participle of Latin *denuntiare* (see DENOUNCE)]

Denver /dénvər/ capital city and commercial centre of the US state of Colorado, in the Rocky Mountains. It is home to the Denver campus of the University of Colorado. Population: 560,415 (2002 estimate).

Denver boot *n* N Am same as **wheel clamp**

deny /di nī/ (**-nies, -nying, -nied**) *v* **1.** *vt* SAY SOMETHING IS NOT TRUE to declare that something is not true or not the case **2.** *vt* REFUSE REQUEST to refuse to let somebody have or do something **3.** *vt* DISAVOW SOMEBODY to refuse to acknowledge somebody **4. deny yourself** *vr* NOT ALLOW YOURSELF SOMETHING to refuse to gratify your own needs or desires [13C. Via Old French *deneier* < Latin *denegare* 'negate completely' < *negare* 'deny']

deoch an doruis /dyókh ən dórriss/, **doch an doris** /dókh ən dórriss/ *n* Scotland a parting drink [Late 17C. < Scottish Gaelic *deoch an doruis* 'a drink at the door']

deodar /dée ō daar/ (*plural* **-dars** or *same*) *n* **1.** the hard sweet-smelling wood of a Himalayan tree. Use: timber. **2.** a cedar tree with dark blue-green leaves and drooping branches that is the source of deodar wood. Native to: Himalayan range. Latin name: *Cedrus deodara*. [Early 19C. Via Hindi *deodār* < Sanskrit *devadāru* 'divine wood']

deodorant /dee ṓdərənt/ *n* **1.** a substance applied to the body, especially under the arms, to mask or prevent body odour **2.** a substance that is used to disguise unpleasant smells [Mid-19C. < DE- + Latin *odor* 'smell']

deodorize /dee ṓdə rīz/ (**-izes, -izing, -ized**), **deodorise** (**-ises, -ising, -ised**) *vt* to disguise or eliminate unpleasant smells in a place [Mid-19C. < DE- + Latin *odor* 'smell'] —**deodorization** /dee ṓdə rī záysh'n/ *n* —**deodorizer** *n*

Deo gratias /dáy ō graáti əss/ *interj* thanks be to God (*used in various Christian choral and liturgical contexts*) [< Latin]

deontic /di óntik/ *adj* relating to the concept of moral obligation [Mid-19C. < Greek *deont-*, present participle of *dein* 'be wanting, be needful']

deontological /di óntə lójjik'l/ *adj* relating to philosophical theories that state that the moral content of an action is not wholly dependent on its consequences —**deontologically** *adv*

deontology /dée on tólləji/ *n* the study of what is morally obligatory, permissible, right, or wrong [Early 19C. < Greek *deont-* (see DEONTIC)] —**deontologist** *n*

deorbit /dee áwrbit/ (**-bits, -biting, -bited**) *vti* to put something out of orbit, or go out of orbit

Deo volente /dáy ō və lénti/ *interj* God willing [< Latin]

deoxidize /dee óksi dīz/ (**-dizes, -dizing, -dized**), **deoxidise** (**-dises, -dising, -dised**) *vt* **1.** to remove the oxygen from a compound or molecule **2.** CHEM same as **reduce** (sense 12) —**deoxidization** /dee óksi dī záysh'n/ *n* —**deoxidizer** *n*

deoxy- *prefix* containing less oxygen than a related compound ○ *deoxyribose*

deoxygenate /dee óksijə nayt/ (**-ates, -ating, -ated**) *vt* to remove dissolved oxygen from a substance —**deoxygenation** /dee óksijə náysh'n/ *n*

deoxygenize /dee óksijə nīz/ (**-izes, -izing, -ized**), **deoxygenise** (**-ises, -ising, -ised**) *vt* CHEM same as **deoxygenate**

deoxyribonuclease /dée oksi rībō nyóokli ayz/ *n* GENETICS full form of **DNase** [Mid-20C. < DEOXYRIBONUCLEIC ACID]

deoxyribonucleic acid /dée oksi rībō nyoo kláyik-, -kláy-/ *n* GENETICS full form of **DNA**[1] (sense 1) [Mid-20C. < DEOXYRIBOSE]

deoxyribonucleotide /dée oksi rībō nyóokli ə tīd/ *n* a nucleotide containing deoxyribose that is a component of DNA [Mid-20C. < DEOXYRIBOSE]

deoxyribose /dée oksi rībōss/ *n* a five-carbon simple sugar that is a structural component of DNA

dep. *abbr* **1.** GOV, BUSINESS department **2.** TRANSP departs **3.** TRANSP departure **4.** GRAM deponent **5.** LAW deposed **6.** FIN deposit **7.** TRANSP depot **8.** *also* **Dep.** deputy

Depardieu /dé paar djő/, **Gérard** (*b.* 1948) French actor. His films include *The Last Metro* (1980), *Cyrano de Bergerac* (1990), and *Green Card* (1990).

> 'I appreciate teamwork. I don't like a one-man show. I'm an interpreter, a sort of tool—I don't mean an object. The right tool is quite essential. Try pounding a nail in with a screwdriver.'
> [Attributed to Gérard Depardieu]

depart /di paárt/ (**-parts, -parting, -parted**) *v* **1.** *vi* SET OFF to leave, especially at the beginning of a journey **2.** *vi* CHANGE to change or vary from a pattern **3.** *vt* DIE to reach the end of your life (*literary*) ○ *depart this life* [13C. < French *départir* 'end your life' < Latin *partire* 'divide into parts' < *pars* 'part']

departed /di paártid/ *n* somebody who has died, especially recently (*formal or literary*) ■ *adj* having died (*archaic or literary*)

SYNONYMS See *dead*.

department /di paártmənt/ *n* **1.** SECTION OF ORGANIZATION a division of a large organization such as a university or store that has its own function **2.** PART OF GOVERNMENT a major division of government that is responsible for dealing with a specific area of policy or administration **3.** SPECIALITY somebody's speciality or area of responsibility (*informal*) **4.** CATEGORY a particular quantifiable or qualifiable category (*informal*) **5.** POL FRENCH DISTRICT an administrative district in France

departmental /dée paart mént'l/ *adj* relating to a department in a government or an organization —**departmentally** *adv*

departmentalise *vt* another spelling of **departmentalize**

departmentalism /dée paart mént'lizəm/ *n* **1.** the division of organizations into departments, particularly as a deliberate policy that is taken to excess **2.** the tendency of government departments to follow their own interests

departmentalize /dée paart mént'l īz/ (**-izes, -izing, -ized**), **departmentalise** (**-ises, -ising, -ised**) *vt* to divide an organization into departments, especially as a policy or to an excessive degree —**departmentalization** /dée paart mént'l ī záysh'n/ *n*

Department for Constitutional Affairs *n* a UK government department whose role is to ensure effective justice for all and protect and extend democratic rights

Department for Culture, Media and Sport *n* a UK government department responsible for the arts, cultural activities and heritage, sport, tourism, and press freedom and regulation

Department for Education and Skills *n* a UK government department responsible for education at all levels and ages, and training people for work

Department for Environment, Food and Rural Affairs *n* a UK government department responsible for the natural and developed environment, safe food supplies, rural communities, and the sustainable use of natural resources

Department for International Development *n* a UK government department responsible for policies aimed at reducing global poverty and promoting sustainable development

Department for Transport *n* a UK government department responsible for overseeing the transport system

Department for Work and Pensions *n* a UK government department responsible for Jobcentres, the Child Support Agency, pensions, services for people with disabilities, and other matters relating to individual people's needs

Department of Health *n* a UK government department with the responsibility of improving the health and well-being of the population

Department of Social Security *n* a former UK government department responsible for unemployment benefits and other matters of social welfare. Its functions were taken over by the Department for Work and Pensions in 2001.

Department of Trade and Industry *n* a UK government department that promotes UK business, invests in science, engineering and technology, and protects the rights of working people and consumers

department store *n* a large store that sells a wide range of goods in separate departments

departure /di paárchər/ *n* **1.** SETTING OFF the action of setting off on a journey **2.** CHANGE FROM USUAL a change from the usual or expected way **3.** COURSE a course of action, or the beginning of one **4.** NAUT EAST OR WEST TRAVEL the distance travelled due east or west by a ship, as a change in longitude

departure lounge *n* an area where departing passengers can wait until their aircraft or other transport is ready

depasture /dée paáschər/ (**-tures, -turing, -tured**) *vt* **1.** AGRIC same as **overgraze** **2.** to allow animals to graze on an area

depauperate /di páwpərət/ *adj* **1.** lacking or depleted in the variety of plant or animal species **2.** less than fully grown or developed [Mid-19C. < medieval Latin *depauperatus*, past participle of *depauperare* 'impoverish' < Latin *pauper* (see PAUPER)]

depend /di pénd/ (**-pends, -pending, -pended**) *vi* **1.** BE CONTINGENT to be affected or decided by other factors **2.** VARY to vary according to the circumstances **3.** HANG DOWN to hang down or be suspended from something (*archaic*) [15C. Via French < Latin *dependere* 'hang down' < *pendere* 'hang']

USAGE The verb ***depend*** should be followed by *on* when it introduces a clause beginning with *how, what, where, whether, who,* or *why*: *It depends on how you interpret the word 'liberal'. The amount you pay depends on what you earn.* The omission of *on* in sentences of this type is more acceptable in speech than in writing, as in *'Are you planning to go?' 'It just depends'.*

depend on, depend upon *vt* **1.** to need something in order to exist or survive **2.** to have complete confidence in somebody or something

dependable /di péndəb'l/ *adj* able to be trusted or depended on ○ *a dependable employee* ○ *a dependable source of power* —**dependability** /di péndə bílləti/ *n*

dependably /di péndəbli/ *adv* **1.** used to indicate that somebody or something is behaving as usual or expected ○ *Sam was, dependably, the last to arrive.* **2.** in a way that inspires trust or confidence

dependant /di péndənt/ *n* a family member or other person who is supported financially by another, especially one living in the same house. US term **dependent**

USAGE dependant or **dependent**? The adjective derived from the verb *depend* is always spelt ***dependent***, in both British and US English: *The young birds are still dependent on their parents.* The noun meaning 'somebody who is supported financially by another', as in *an unmarried woman with no dependants*, is usually spelt ***dependant*** in British English and ***dependent*** in US English. The US spelling of the noun is gaining ground, but is still widely regarded as incorrect, in Britain.

dependence /di péndənss/ *n* **1.** RELIANCE ON SOMEBODY OR SOMETHING reliance on or trust in somebody or something for help or support ○ *dependence on public transport* ○ *mutual dependence* **2.** STATE OF BEING CONTINGENT the state of being affected or decided by particular factors or circumstances ○ *agriculture's dependence on the weather* **3.** PHYSICAL OR PSYCHOLOGICAL NEED a physical or psychological need to use a drug or other substance regularly, despite the fact that it is likely to have a damaging effect

dependency /di péndənssi/ (*plural* **-cies**) *n* **1.** a country or state that belongs to another nonadjacent country **2.** a building near to and associated with a larger main building **3.** same as **dependence**

dependency theory *n* a theory of international relations holding that major states influence other states though their economic power

dependent /di péndənt/ *adj* **1.** NOT SELF-RELIANT needing to rely on or trust in somebody or something for help or support, especially financial support ○ *countries dependent on oil revenues* ○ *dependent children* **2.** NEEDING SOMETHING having a physical or psychological need to use a drug or other substance regularly (*usually used in combination*) ○ *alcohol-dependent* **3.** CONTINGENT affected or decided by particular factors or circumstances (*often used in combination*) ○ *age-dependent* ■ *n US* same as **dependant** —**dependently** *adv*

USAGE See ***dependant***.

dependent clause *n* GRAM same as **subordinate clause**

dependent variable *n* an element in a mathematical expression that changes its value according to the value of other elements present

depersonalize /dée púrss'nəl īz/ (**-izes, -izing, -ized**), **depersonalise** (**-ises, -ising, -ised**) *vt* **1.** to take away or omit the qualities from something that make a person feel welcome or important ○ *a depersonalized workplace* **2.** to make somebody lose his or her sense of personal identity and external reality —**depersonalization** /dee púrss'nəl ī záysh'n/ *n*

depict /di píkt/ (**-picts, -picting, -picted**) *vt* **1.** to describe or portray something in words **2.** to show something in a picture, painting, or sculpture [15C. < Latin *depict-*, past participle of *depingere* 'portray' < *pingere* 'to paint'] —**depicter** *n* —**depictive** *adj*

depiction /di píksh'n/ *n* a picture, description, or other representation of something

depigmentation /deè pígmən táysh'n/ *n* partial or total absence in the body of the pigment melanin, especially in the skin, hair, and eyes

depilate /déppi layt/ (**-lates, -lating, -lated**) *vti* to remove hair from the body, usually from the legs or underarms [Mid-16C. < Latin *depilat-*, past participle of Latin *depilare* < *pilus* 'hair'] —**depilator** *n*

depilation /déppi láysh'n/ *n* the removal of hair, including its roots, from the body or from hides or leather

depilatory /di píllətəri/ *adj* used for removing hair from the body ■ *n* (*plural* **-ries**) a substance that removes hair from the body

deplane /dee pláyn/ (**-planes, -planing, -planed**) *vi N Am* to disembark from an aeroplane

deplete /di pleèt/ (**-pletes, -pleting, -pleted**) *vt* **1.** to use up or reduce something such as supplies, resources, or energy **2.** to use up or remove all the contents of something [Early 19C. < Latin *deplet-*, past participle of *deplere* 'empty out' < *plere* 'fill'] —**depletable** *adj* —**depletion** /di pleèsh'n/ *n* —**depletive** *adj*

depleted uranium /di pleètid-/ *n* uranium containing an unusually low amount of the U-235 isotope, usually as a result of having been used as fuel in a nuclear reactor

depletion layer *n* a layer in a semiconductor that has few charge carriers transporting electric charge between zones of different conductivity

deplorable /di pláwrəb'l/ *adj* **1.** worthy of severe condemnation **2.** wretched because of neglect, poverty, or other misfortune —**deplorability** /di pláwrə bílləti/ *n* —**deplorably** *adv*

deplore /di pláwr/ (**-plores, -ploring, -plored**) *vt* **1.** to disapprove of something very strongly **2.** to regret or feel grief about something [Mid-16C. Via French or Italian < Latin *deplorare* 'lament, regret' < *plorare* 'wail'] —**deploringly** *adv*

SYNONYMS See ***disapprove***.

deploy /di plóy/ (**-ploys, -ploying, -ployed**) *v* **1.** *vti* to position troops, weapons, or resources in a specific area in readiness for action, or take up position in this way **2.** *vt* to put something to use [15C. Via French *déployer* < Latin *displicare* 'unfold' < *plicare* 'to fold'] —**deployable** *adj* —**deployer** *n* —**deployment** *n*

deplume /dee ploòm/ (**-plumes, -pluming, -plumed**) *vt* to remove the feathers from a bird [15C. Via French < medieval Latin *deplumare* < Latin *pluma* 'down, feather'] —**deplumation** /deè ploo máysh'n/ *n*

depolarize /dee pṓlə rīz/ (**-izes, -izing, -ized**), **depolarise** (**-ises, -ising, -ised**) *vti* to remove or reduce the polarization or polarity of something, or lose polarization or polarity —**depolarization** /dee pṓlə rī záysh'n/ *n* —**depolarizer** *n*

depoliticize /deèpə lítti sīz/ (**-cizes, -cizing, -cized**), **depoliticise** (**-cises, -cising, -cised**) *vt* to remove the political aspect of something —**depoliticization** /deèpə lítti sī záysh'n/ *n*

depollution /deèpə loòsh'n/ *n* the removal of pollution from something —**depollute** *vt*

depolymerize /dee póllimə rīz/ (**-izes, -izing, -ized**), **depolymerise** (**-ises, -ising, -ised**) *vti* to break down a polymer into simpler monomers, or undergo this process —**depolymerization** /dee póllimə rī záysh'n/ *n*

depone /di pṓn/ (**-pones, -poning, -poned**) *vti* to testify or declare something under oath [15C. < medieval Latin *deponere* (see DEPOSE)]

deponent /di pṓnənt/ *adj* GRAM **PASSIVE AND ACTIVE** describes a verb that inflects like a passive verb but is active in meaning ■ *n* **1.** GRAM **ACTIVE VERB WITH PASSIVE FORM** a verb that inflects like a passive verb but is active in meaning **2.** LAW **TESTIFYING WITNESS** somebody who signs an affidavit or testifies under oath [15C. < Latin *deponent-*, present participle of *deponere* (see DEPOSE)]

depopulate /dee póppyoò layt/ (**-lates, -lating, -lated**) *vt* to cause a reduction in the number of residents in an area, e.g. through disease, war, famine, or enforced relocation [Mid-16C. < Latin *depopulat-*, past participle of *depopulare* 'ravage completely, reduce in population' < *populari* 'lay waste' < *populus* 'people'] —**depopulation** /dee póppyoò láysh'n/ *n* —**depopulator** *n*

deport[1] /di páwrt/ (**-ports, -porting, -ported**) *vt* **1.** to force a foreign national to leave a country **2.** to expel or banish somebody from his or her own country [Mid-17C. Via French < Latin *deportare* 'carry off' < *portare* 'carry'] —**deportable** *adj* —**deportation** /deè pawr táysh'n/ *n*

deport[2] /di páwrt/ (**-ports, -porting, -ported**) *vr* **deport yourself** to conduct yourself in a particular way ○ *deports herself with dignity* [15C. < Old French *deporter* 'behave, conduct yourself' < *porter* < Latin *portare* 'carry']

deportee /deè pawr teè/ *n* somebody subject to deportation

deportment /di páwrtmənt/ *n* the manner in which a person behaves, especially in respect of physical bearing [Early 17C. < French *déportement* < Old French *deporter* (see DEPORT [2])]

depose /di pṓz/ (**-poses, -posing, -posed**) *v* **1.** *vt* to remove somebody from office or from a position of power **2.** *vti* to give evidence or testify on oath, either in a written or verbal form [13C. < French *déposer*, alteration (influenced by *poser* 'put') of Latin *deponere* 'put down', in medieval Latin 'testify' < *ponere* 'to place'] —**deposable** *adj* —**deposal** *n* —**deposer** *n*

deposit /di pózzit/ *v* (**-its, -iting, -ited**) **1.** *vt* **PUT SOMETHING SOMEWHERE** to put or drop something somewhere ○ *She deposited her coat on the couch.* **2.** *vt* **LEAVE SOMETHING IN SAFE PLACE** to leave something somewhere for safekeeping ○ *deposit valuables in the hotel safe* **3.** *vt* **PUT MONEY IN BANK** to pay money into an account in a bank or other financial institution **4.** *vt* **GIVE PAYMENT AS SECURITY** to give a sum of money as part-payment or security ○ *deposited £500 as a down payment* **5.** *vti* **FORM LAYER** to leave or form a layer of sand, sediment, or other substance, as a gradual process in one place, or be left in this way ○ *layers of silt deposited by the river* ■ *n* **1. PUTTING MONEY IN BANK** an act of placing money or a valuable item in a bank or other financial institution ○ *make a monthly deposit* **2. MONEY IN BANK** an amount of money or a valuable item that is paid into or left in a bank or other financial institution ○ *Deposits made after 2 pm are credited the following day.* **3. SECURITY MONEY** a partial payment or security on something that is going to be bought ○ *You need to pay a deposit.* **4. SURETY MONEY** money that is given as security against possible damage or loss, e.g. on something rented **5. ELECTION CANDIDATE'S MONEY** money that candidates in a parliamentary election must deposit to show that their standing is serious and which they forfeit if they fail to win a given percentage of votes **6. COATING** a coating or crust that is left on a surface by a process such as evaporation or electrolysis **7. ACCUMULATION OF NATURAL MATERIALS** an accumulation of sand, sediment, minerals, or other substances that has built up over a period of time through a natural process ○ *a land rich in mineral deposits* **8. DEPOSITED THING** something put or left in a place [Late 16C. < Latin *depositum* < *deposit-*, past participle of *deponere* (see DEPOSE)] —**depositor** *n*

deposit account *n* a bank account that earns interest

depositary /di pózzitəri/ (*plural* **-ies**) *n* **1.** a person or institution that is entrusted with something for safekeeping **2.** same as **depository** (sense 1)

deposition /déppə zísh'n, deèpə-/ *n* **1. WITNESS'S TESTIMONY** testimony that is given under oath, especially a statement given by a witness that is read out in court in the witness's absence **2. OUSTING FROM OFFICE** the act of removing somebody from high office or power **3. DEPOSIT** something that has been deposited somewhere **4. BUILD-UP OF DEPOSITS** the accumulation of natural materials by a gradual process [14C. Via French < Latin *deposition-* < *deponere* (see DEPOSE)] —**depositional** *adj*

depository /di pózzitəri/ (*plural* **-ries**) *n* **1.** a place where something is kept for safekeeping or storage, e.g. a warehouse or store for furniture or valuables **2.** same as **depositary** (sense 1)

deposit slip *n ANZ, N Am* a form for listing the contents of a bank deposit. UK term **paying-in slip**

depot /déppō/ *n* **1. WAREHOUSE** a warehouse or other place used for storing things **2.** TRANSP **VEHICLE BASE** a building where buses, trains, or lorries are based and serviced **3.** *N Am* TRANSP **STATION** a railway or bus station **4.** MIL **MILITARY STORE** a place where military supplies are stored **5.** MIL **MILITARY TRAINING BASE** a place where military recruits are gathered together and trained [Late 18C. Via French *dépôt* < Latin *depositum* (see DEPOSIT)]

deprave /di práyv/ (**-praves, -praving, -praved**) *vt* to have a morally bad or corrupting influence on somebody (*often passive*) [14C. Directly or via French < Latin *depravare* 'to corrupt' < *pravus* 'crooked'] —**depraver** *n*

depraved /di práyvd/ *adj* showing great moral corruption or wickedness —**depravedly** /di práyvidli, -práyvd-/ *adv*

depravity /di právvəti/ (*plural* **-ties**) *n* **1.** a state of moral corruption **2.** a morally corrupt or wicked act [Mid-17C. Alteration (after DEPRAVE) of obsolete *pravity* < Latin *pravitas* < *pravus* 'crooked']

deprecate /déppri kayt/ (**-cates, -cating, -cated**) *vt* **1.** to express condemnation of something or somebody ○ *The spokesman deprecated the use of violence.* **2.** ⚠ same as **depreciate** (sense 3) **3.** COMPUT to state that a computational method or computer feature is superseded [Early 17C. < Latin *deprecat-*, past participle of *deprecari*, literally 'pray against' < *precari* (see PRAY)] —**deprecation** /déppri káysh'n/ *n* —**deprecator** *n*

USAGE deprecate or **depreciate**? Traditionally, to ***deprecate*** something is to condemn it as wrong in itself: *We deprecate the use of public money for nonessential purposes.* To ***depreciate*** something is to belittle or disparage it, even though it may not be wrong or bad in itself: *They were constantly depreciating our attempts to speak Italian.* This use is increasingly rare, with ***deprecate*** sometimes used instead. Admittedly, *self-deprecate* goes a long way towards blurring the distinction, for it means 'belittle yourself', not 'condemn yourself'; in this sense it is well established, but it may be best regarded as the exception rather than the rule. Both words have more common synonyms: *condemn, deplore,* and *disapprove of* for ***deprecate***, and *belittle, disparage,* and *decry* for ***depreciate***. ***Depreciate*** is also commonly used intransitively (without an object), in financial contexts, to mean 'lose value': *The value of the yen has depreciated 20 per cent in real terms.*

deprecating /déppra kayting/ *adj* showing or expressing disapproval —**deprecatingly** *adv*

deprecatory /déppri kaytəri, -kətəri/, **deprecative** /-kətiv/ *adj* **1.** disapproving and critical **2.** showing or expressing apology —**deprecatorily** *adv*

depreciate /di preèshi ayt/ (**-ates, -ating, -ated**) *v* **1.** *vti* **LOSE VALUE** to become less valuable, or lessen the value of something **2.** *vt* **TREAT SOMETHING AS DECREASINGLY VALUABLE** to consider something as having less value each year over a fixed period, for the calculation of income tax **3.** *vt* **BELITTLE SOMETHING OR SOMEBODY** to speak critically or disparagingly about something or somebody [15C. < late Latin *depreciat-*, past participle of *depreciare*, alteration of Latin *depretiare* 'lower the price of' < *pretium* 'price, money'] —**depreciable** *adj* —**depreciatingly** *adv* —**depreciator** *n*

USAGE See ***deprecate***.

depreciation /di preèshi áysh'n/ *n* **1. DROP IN VALUE** the decrease in value of an item over time **2. AMOUNT OF DECREASE** the amount or percentage by which something decreases in value over time, usually one year **3. BELITTLEMENT** critical commentary or strong disparagement of somebody or something

depreciative /di preèshi ətiv/ *adj* **1.** reducing or tending to reduce something in value **2.** losing or tending to lose value

depreciatory /di preèshi ətəri/ *adj* **1.** FIN same as **depreciative 2.** belittling or critical

depredation /déppra dáysh'n/ *n* an attack involving plunder and pillage [15C. Via French < late Latin *depraedation-* < past participle of Latin *depraedari*, literally 'plunder thoroughly' < *praedari* (see PREDATORY)]

depress /di préss/ (**-presses, -pressing, -pressed**) *vt* **1. MAKE SOMEBODY UNHAPPY** to make somebody feel very sad or hopeless ○ *'There's nothing that depresses me more than seeing a planet being destroyed.'* (Douglas Adams, *Life, The Universe, and Everything*; 1982) **2. WEAKEN SOMETHING** to weaken something, or make something less active **3. DEVALUATE SOMETHING** to decrease the value of something **4. PUSH ON SOMETHING** to press something such as a button or lever [14C. Via French < Latin *depress-*, past participle of *deprimere* 'press down' < *premere* 'press'] —**depressible** *adj*

depressant /di préss'nt/ *n* a drug or agent that slows the body's vital functions ■ *adj* able to sedate or lower the rate of the body's vital functions

depressed /di prést/ *adj* **1. SAD** unhappy or hopeless **2. HAVING DEPRESSION** having the psychiatric disorder depression **3. ECONOMICALLY LACKING** lacking economic resources or activities ○ *a depressed area* **4. WEAK** less active or strong than usual ○ *the depressed dollar* **5. LOWER** lower than the surrounding area **6. BIOL FLATTENED** flattened, as if from downward pressure

depressing /di préssing/ *adj* making somebody feel sad or disheartened —**depressingly** *adv*

depression /di présh'n/ *n* **1. SADNESS** a state of unhappiness and hopelessness **2. PSYCHIATRIC DISORDER** a psychiatric disorder showing symptoms such as persistent feelings of hopelessness, dejection, poor concentration, lack of energy, inability to sleep, and, sometimes, suicidal tendencies **3. ECONOMIC SLUMP** a period in which an economy is greatly affected by unemployment, low output, and poverty **4. REDUCED ACTIVITY** a lowering of activity, quality, vitality, or force **5. HOLLOW** an area on the surface of something that is lower than the surface surrounding it **6. METEOROL LOW PRESSURE AREA** an area of low barometric pressure that often brings rain

depressive /di préssiv/ *adj* **1. CAUSING DEPRESSION** relating to or causing depression ○ *the depressive atmosphere of a grey, cold marshland* **2. PSYCHIAT HAVING DEPRESSION** experiencing or with a history of depression ■ *n* PSYCHIAT **DEPRESSED PERSON** a habitually depressed person —**depressively** *adv* —**depressiveness** *n*

depressor /di préssər/ *n* **1. MEDICAL INSTRUMENT** a medical or surgical instrument that is used to move aside or press down an organ or part of the body **2. PULLING MUSCLE** a muscle that acts to pull down a part of the body **3. APPLIER OF PRESSURE** somebody or something that presses down

depressor nerve *n* a nerve that, when stimulated, decreases activity in an organ, lowers blood pressure, or slows the heart

depressurize /dee préshə rīz/ (**-izes, -izing, -ized**), **depressurise** (**-ises, -ising, -ised**) *vt* to reduce the pressure of air or gas within a container, cabin, or other enclosed space —**depressurization** /de préshə rī záysh'n/ *n*

deprivation /déppri váysh'n/ *n* **1.** the state of being without or denied something, especially of being without adequate food or shelter **2.** the act of taking something away from somebody or preventing somebody from having something

deprive /di prīv/ (**-prives, -priving, -prived**) *vt* **1.** to prevent somebody from having something **2.** to take something away from somebody ○ *They have no right to deprive you of your own property.* [14C. Via French < medieval Latin *deprivare* 'deprive completely' < Latin *privare* (see PRIVATION)] —**deprivable** *adj* —**depriver** *n*

deprived /di prīvd/ *adj* lacking the things needed for a comfortable or successful life

de profundis /dáy prə fóŏndiss/ *adv* out of the depths of misery or despair [13C. < Latin, 'out of the depths', first words of Psalm 130]

deprogramme /dee prṓ gram/ (**-grammes, -gramming, -grammed**) *vt* to undo the effects of indoctrination on somebody, especially somebody under the influence of a religious group —**deprogrammer** *n*

dept *abbr* department

depth /depth/ *n* **1. HOW DEEP SOMETHING IS** the distance or measurement from the top of something to its bottom, from front to back, or from the outside in **2. BEING DEEP** the quality of being deep **3. INTENSITY** the strength of a feeling **4. COMPLEXITY** complexity or profundity of character or thought ○ *a woman of great depth* ○ *the depths of knowledge* **5. BREADTH** wideness in scope **6. COLOUR QUALITY** the richness of a colour **7. LOWNESS** the low tone or pitch of a sound ■ **depths** *npl* **1. LOWEST POINT** the lowest or worst point or moment ○ *the depths of despair* **2. DEEP PART** a deep or remote part of something ○ *the ocean depths* **3. MIDDLE PART** the middle part of something long, monotonous, and possibly unpleasant ○ *in the depths of tedious research* **4. DEBASEMENT** a state of great moral debasement ○ *having fallen to such depths* [14C. < DEEP] ◇ **hidden depths** interesting or

serious aspects of somebody's character that are not immediately obvious ◇ **out of your depth 1.** unable to stand because the water is too deep **2.** unable to understand or do something because it is outside the range of your knowledge or skills

depth charge, **depth bomb** *n* a bomb that is designed to explode at a particular depth under water, often used against submarines

depth gauge, **depth finder** *n* an instrument that measures the depth of water or other liquid

depth of field *n* the total focused area in front of and behind an object held in the focus of a camera or lens

depth of focus *n* the distance that a camera lens can be moved closer to or further from the film, without the resulting image being blurred

depth perception *n* the ability to perceive objects and their spatial relationship in three dimensions

depth psychology *n* the study and psychology of the unconscious mind

depth sounder *n* an ultrasonic instrument that measures the depth of water under a ship

depurate /déppyoŏ rayt/ (**-rates, -rating, -rated**) *vt* to cleanse or purify something, especially by removing toxins [Early 17C. < medieval Latin *depurat-*, past participle of *depurare* < Latin *purus* 'pure'] —**depuration** /déppyoŏ ráysh'n/ *n* —**depurative** *adj* —**depurator** *n*

deputation /déppyoŏ táysh'n/ *n* **1.** a group of people who have been chosen to represent a larger group of people and act on their behalf **2.** the act of appointing a deputy or deputation

depute /di pyoŏt/ (*formal*) *vt* (**-putes, -puting, -puted**) **1. CHOOSE REPRESENTATIVE** to choose somebody to be your agent, substitute, or representative **2. DELEGATE SOMETHING** to delegate work, authority, or duties to somebody else ■ *adj Scotland* DEPUTY acting as deputy ○ *headmaster depute* [14C. Via French *députer* < Latin *deputare* 'assign' < *putare* 'consider']

deputize /déppyoŏ tīz/ (**-tizes, -tizing, -tized**), **deputise** (**-tises, -tising, -tised**) *v* **1.** *vi* to act as somebody's deputy **2.** *vt* to choose somebody to act as a deputy —**deputization** /déppyoŏ tī záysh'n/ *n*

deputy /déppyoŏti/ (*plural* **-ties**) *n* **1. SOMEBODY'S REPRESENTATIVE** somebody fully authorized or appointed to act on behalf of somebody else **2. SECOND-IN-COMMAND** an assistant who is authorized to act in a superior's place **3. MEMBER OF PARLIAMENT** a parliamentary representative in some countries, e.g. in France, Germany, or Italy **4.** *US* POLICE same as **deputy sheriff** [15C. < French *député*, past participle of *députer* (see DEPUTE)]

SYNONYMS See *assistant*.

deputy head *n* a senior member of a school staff, second in status to the head teacher

deputy sheriff *n* a sheriff's assistant in the United States, authorized to take charge when the sheriff is absent

de Quincey /də kwínssi/, **Thomas** (1785–1859) British essayist and critic. He was a friend of William Wordsworth and Samuel Taylor Coleridge, and author of *Confessions of an English Opium Eater* (1821).

> 'All that is literature seeks to communicate power; all that is not literature, to communicate knowledge.'
> [Thomas de Quincey, 'Letters to a Young Man Whose Education has been Neglected', *London Magazine*; 1823]

deracinate /dee rássi nayt/ (**-nates, -nating, -nated**) *vt* to remove somebody or something from a natural environment, especially people from their native culture (*literary*) [Late 16C. < French *déraciner* < *racine* 'root' < late Latin *radicina* < Latin *radix*] —**deracination** /dee rássi náysh'n/ *n*

derail /dee ráyl/ (**-rails, -railing, -railed**) *vti* **1.** to make a train or tram come off the rails, or come off the rails **2.** to send something off course, or go off course ○ *plans to derail the election campaign* [Mid-19C. < French *dérailler* < *rail* (see RAIL¹)] —**derailment** *n*

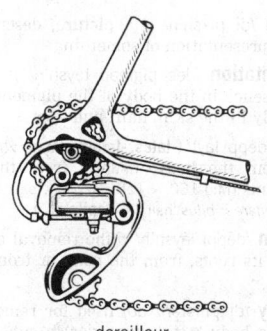
derailleur

derailleur /di ráylyər/ *n* a device for changing gears on a bicycle that lifts the chain from one sprocket wheel to another [Mid-20C. < French *dérailleur* < *dérailler* (see DERAIL)]

Derain /də ráN/, **André** (1880–1954) French painter, illustrator, and stage designer. A leader in several art movements of the early 20th century, he is particularly noted for the paintings of his Fauve period (1905–08).

derange /di ráynj/ (**-ranges, -ranging, -ranged**) *vt* **1. MAKE SOMEBODY IRRATIONAL** to make somebody irrational or extraordinarily angry **2. DISTURB ROUTINE** to disturb the normal way in which something works **3. THROW SOMETHING INTO DISORDER** to throw something into disorder and confusion [Late 18C. < French *déranger* 'put out of line' < *rang* 'line'] —**deranged** *adj* —**derangement** *n*

derate /dee ráyt/ (**-rates, -rating, -rated**) *vt* **1.** to lower the rated capability of an electrical apparatus **2.** to lower or abolish the rates on a property

deration /dee rásh'n/ (**-tions, -tioning, -tioned**) *vt* to stop rationing a commodity, usually because the supply has become adequate

derby /daárbi/ (*plural* **-bies**) *n* **1. IMPORTANT LOCAL CONTEST** an important contest, especially between local teams **2. HORSE RACE** a horse race run annually, usually for three-year-olds **3. RACE** any race or contest open to qualified competitors **4.** *N Am* same as **bowler hat** [Late 19C. After DERBY¹]

Derby¹ *n* a flat horse race for three year olds, run annually at Epsom Downs, Surrey, England, or one held each spring at Churchill Downs in Louisville, Kentucky, in the United States [Early 19C. After the 12th Earl of *Derby*, who founded the English race]

Derby² *n* a close-textured pale-coloured cheese, sometimes flavoured with sage [After DERBYSHIRE]

Derby³ /daárbi/ **1.** cathedral city in Derbyshire, England. Population: 221,708 (2001). **2.** port in north-western Western Australia, situated on King Sound near the mouth of the River Fitzroy. Population: 8,517 (2002 estimate).

Derby, **23rd Earl of** (1799–1869) British politician. Three times prime minister (1852, 1858–59, and 1866–68), he carried the second Reform Act for the emancipation of West Indian slaves (1867) through Parliament. Full name **Stanley, Edward George Geoffrey Smith**

Derbyshire /daárbishər/ *n* county in central England, including most of the Peak District. Matlock is the administrative centre. Population: 734,585 (2001). Area: 2,631 sq. km/1,016 sq. mi.

derecognize /dee rékəg nīz/ (**-nizes, -nizing, -nized**), **derecognise** (**-nises, -nising, -nised**) *vt* to stop accepting the legitimacy of something, especially a trade union or diplomatic mission —**derecognition** /dee rekəg nísh'n/ *n*

deregister /dee réjjistər/ (**-ters, -tering, -tered**) *vti* to remove a name or other item from a register or official list —**deregistration** /dee réjji stráysh'n/ *n*

deregulate /dee réggyoŏ layt/ (**-lates, -lating, -lated**) *vt* to free something such as an organization or industry from regulation —**deregulation** /dee réggyoŏ láysh'n/ *n* —**deregulator** *n* —**deregulatory** *adj*

derelict /dérrəlikt/ *adj* **1. DESERTED** no longer lived in **2. NEGLECTED** in poor condition because of neglect **3. LAW ABANDONING DUTY** neglectful of duty or obligations ■ *n* **1. HOMELESS PERSON** somebody without a home or

employment **2.** ABANDONED PROPERTY a building, ship, or other property that has been abandoned **3.** LAW NEGLECTFUL PERSON somebody who is neglectful of duty or obligations [Mid-17C. < Latin *derelictus*, past participle of *derelinquere* 'abandon utterly' < *relinquere* (see RELINQUISH)]

dereliction /dérrə líksh'n/ *n* **1.** LAW NEGLECT OF DUTY deliberate neglect of duty or obligations **2.** ABANDONMENT the act of abandoning a building **3.** STATE OF NEGLECT a state of abandonment or neglect **4.** LAW LAND GAINED FROM SEA land gained because water has receded from it

derepress /deé ri préss/ (**-presses, -pressing, -pressed**) *vt* to activate a gene by deactivating the repressor — **derepression** *n*

derepressor /deé ri préssər/ *n* an agent, e.g. a protein, that begins or enhances gene transcription by removing the repression of an operon

derequisition /dee rékwi zísh'n/ (**-tions, -tioning, -tioned**) *vt* to return something to civilian use that was earlier requisitioned by the military or a government

derestrict /deé ri stríkt/ (**-stricts, -stricting, -stricted**) *vt* to remove the restrictions from something — **derestriction** *n*

Derg, Lough /durg/ stretch of water in western Ireland, in counties Tipperary, Galway, and Clare. Area: 96 sq. km/37 sq. mi. Depth: 36 m/118 ft. Length: 32 km/20 mi.

deride /di ríd/ (**-rides, -riding, -rided**) *vt* to show contempt for somebody or something [Mid-16C. < Latin *deridere* 'laugh down' < *ridere* 'laugh'] — **derider** *n* —**deridingly** *adv*

SYNONYMS See *ridicule*.

~~de rigeur~~ incorrect spelling of **de rigueur**

de rigueur /də ri gúr/ *adj* strictly required by the current fashion or by etiquette [Mid-19C. < French, 'of strictness']

derision /di rízh'n/ *n* contempt and mockery [14C. < French *dérision* < Latin *deridere* (see DERIDE)] —**derisible** /di rízzəb'l/ *adj*

derisive /di ríssiv, -ziv/ *adj* showing contempt or ridicule [Mid-17C. < DERISION] —**derisively** *adv* —**derisiveness** *n*

USAGE **derisive** or **derisory**? *Derisive* means 'showing contempt or ridicule': *He gave a derisive laugh*. *Derisory* means 'so small or inadequate as to deserve contempt or ridicule' (*a derisory offer*), though it sometimes is used as a synonym of **derisive**, as in *looked at me with a derisory smile*. Careful writers do try to maintain the distinction and the use of **derisory** where **derisive** is appropriate is best avoided.

derisory /di ríssəri, -ríz-/ *adj* **1.** so small or inadequate as to deserve contempt or ridicule **2.** ⚠ same as **derisive** [Early 17C. < late Latin *derisorius* < Latin *deridere* (see DERIDE)]

USAGE See *derisive*.

deriv. *abbr* **1.** LING, MATHS, LOGIC derivation **2.** LING, MATHS, CHEM derivative

derivate /dérrivət/ *n, adj* same as **derivative** [15C. < Latin *derivatus*, past participle of *derivare* (see DERIVE)]

derivation /dérri váysh'n/ *n* **1.** SOURCE the origin or source of something such as a word or somebody's name **2.** LING WORD FORMATION the formation of a word or term from another word or from a basic form **3.** MATHS, LOGIC PROOF a mathematical or logical argument whose steps show that the conclusion follows necessarily from initial assumptions **4.** ACT OF DERIVING SOMETHING the act of obtaining something from a source or issuing from a source —**derivational** *adj*

SYNONYMS See *origin*.

derivative /di rívvətiv/ *adj* UNORIGINAL copied from somewhere and not original ■ *n* **1.** DERIVED THING an idea, language, term, or other thing that has developed from something else that is similar to it **2.** LING DERIVED WORD a word that is formed from another word, e.g. 'quickly' from 'quick' **3.** CHEM RELATED CHEMICAL PRODUCT a chemical substance that is formed from a related substance ○ *an opium derivative* **4.**

MATHS CHANGE OF FUNCTION the limit approached in the ratio of a function and its variable, as the variable is changed ever more infinitesimally **5.** FIN FINANCIAL PRODUCT a tradable financial product whose value depends on the value of some other asset or combination of assets —**derivatively** *adv* —**derivativeness** *n*

derive /di rív/ (**-rives, -riving, -rived**) *v* **1.** *vti* GET OR COME FROM SOMETHING to obtain something from a source, or come from a source **2.** *vt* LOGIC DEDUCE SOMETHING to reach a conclusion about something by reasoning **3.** *vi* LING COME FROM SOURCE to develop from another word or a source word or term **4.** *vt* LING FORM ONE WORD FROM ANOTHER form a word or term from another, or state that a word or term developed from another **5.** *vt* CHEM MAKE COMPOUND to create a chemical substance from another **6.** *vt* MATHS OBTAIN FUNCTION to obtain a function by differentiation [14C. Directly or via French < Latin *derivare* 'draw off water through a channel' < *rivus* 'stream'] —**derivable** *adj* —**deriver** *n*

derived unit *n* a unit of measurement that is a multiple or fraction of a base unit

derm- *prefix* same as **derma-** (*used before vowels*)

-derm *suffix* skin ○ *ectoderm* [< Greek *derma*]

derma /dúrmə/ *n* same as **kishke** [Probably via Yiddish *gederem* 'intestines' < Old High German *darm* 'gut']

derma- *prefix* skin ○ *dermatome* [Early 18C. Via modern Latin < Greek, 'skin']

dermabrasion /dúrmə bráyzh'n/ *n* a surgical process that removes scars or other imperfections of the skin by scraping the skin's surface with wire brushes or very fine sandpaper [Mid-20C. < Greek *derma* 'skin' + ABRASION]

dermal /dúrm'l/, **dermic** /-mik/ *adj* involving, located in, or made up of skin or its main layer (**dermis**) [Early 19C. < Greek *derma* 'skin']

dermapteran /dur máptərən/ *n* an insect that has strong sharp sensory appendages coming from the end of its abdomen, e.g. an earwig [Late 19C. < modern Latin *Dermaptera* < Greek *derma* 'skin' + *pteron* 'wing'] —**dermapteran** *adj*

dermat- *prefix* same as **dermato-** (*used before vowels*)

dermatitis /dúrmə títiss/ *n* inflammation of the skin from any cause, resulting in a range of symptoms such as redness, swelling, itching, or blistering

dermato- *prefix* skin ○ *dermatoplasty* [< Greek *dermat-*, stem of *derma* 'skin']

dermatoglyphics /dúrmətō glíffiks/ *npl* the lines that form a pattern on the skin, e.g. on the fingers and palms of the hands (*takes a plural verb*) ■ *n* the study of dermatoglyphics (*takes a singular verb*) [Early 20C. < DERMATO- + Greek *gluphē* 'carving' (see GLYPH)] —**dermatoglyphic** *adj*

dermatoid /dúrmə toyd/ *adj* resembling skin

dermatology /dúrmə tóllэji/ *n* the branch of medicine that deals with the skin and diseases affecting the skin —**dermatological** /dúrmətə lójjik'l/ *adj* —**dermatologically** *adv* —**dermatologist** *n*

dermatome /dúrmətōm/ *n* **1.** an area of skin that has nerve fibres coming from a single spinal nerve **2.** an instrument used to slice thin layers of skin for skin grafting —**dermatomic** /dúrmə tómmik/ *adj*

dermatopathology /dúrmətō pə thóllэji/ *n* the medical study of the skin and its reaction to disease and pathogens at the cellular level —**dermatopathologic** /-pəthə lójjik/ *adj* —**dermatopathological** /-lójjik'l/ *adj*

dermatophyte /dur máttə fīt/ *n* a parasitic fungus that affects the skin, hair, or nails —**dermatophytic** /dur máttə fíttik/ *adj*

dermatophytosis /dúrmətō fī tōsiss/ *n* a fungal infection of the skin, hair, or nails

dermatoplasty /dúrmətō plasti/ *n* any operation on the skin, especially skin grafting (*technical*) —**dermatoplastic** /dúrmətō plástik/ *adj*

dermatosis /dúrmə tóssiss/ (*plural* **-toses** /-tō seez/) *n* any disease affecting the skin

-dermatous *suffix* having a particular kind of skin ○ *sclerodermatous* [< Greek *dermat-* (see DERMATO-)]

dermestid /dur méstid/ *n* a beetle with clubbed antennae that eats organic materials, e.g. cabinet and carpet beetles. Family: Dermestidae. [Late 19C.

< modern Latin *Dermestidae* < Greek *derma* 'skin' + *esthiein* 'eat']

dermic *adj* BIOL same as **dermal**

dermis /dúrmiss/ *n* the thick sensitive layer of skin or connective tissue beneath the epidermis that contains blood, lymph vessels, sweat glands, and nerve endings [Mid-19C. < modern Latin, back-formation < EPIDERMIS]

-dermis *suffix* skin ○ *endodermis* [Back-formation < EPIDERMIS]

dermoid /dúr moyd/, **dermoid cyst** *n* a benign tumour that contains skin or skin derivatives, found in the ovaries or on the face, especially round the eyes [Early 19C. < Greek *derma* 'skin']

dernier cri /dúrni ay kreé/ *n* the latest thing in fashion [Late 19C. < French, 'latest cry']

dero /dérrō/ (*plural* **-os**), **derro** (*plural* **-ros**) *n* ANZ an offensive term for somebody who is unemployed, poor, and homeless [Shortening of DERELICT]

derogate /dérrə gayt/ (**-gates, -gating, -gated**) *v* **1.** *vi* DEVIATE FROM CONDITIONS to deviate from a norm, rule, law, or set of conditions, e.g. by refusing to be bound by part of a treaty **2.** *vi* MAKE SOMETHING SEEM INFERIOR to make something seem inferior or less significant (*formal*) ○ *conduct that will derogate from your good name* **3.** *vt* CRITICIZE SOMEBODY OR SOMETHING to criticize somebody or something severely **4.** *vt* REPEAL LAW PARTIALLY to repeal or abolish part of a law or decree [15C. < Latin *derogat-*, past participle of *derogare* 'repeal a law, detract from, impair' < *rogare* 'ask, propose a law']

derogation /dérrə gáysh'n/ *n* **1.** DEVIATION a deviation from a rule or law, especially one specifically provided for **2.** EXEMPTION FROM RULE an exemption from a law or ruling given to a state **3.** DISPARAGEMENT the act of belittling or criticizing somebody or something — **derogative** /di róggətiv/ *adj*

derogatory /di róggətəri/ *adj* expressing criticism or a low opinion —**derogatorily** *adv* —**derogatoriness** *n*

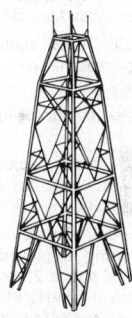

derrick (sense 2)

derrick /dérrik/ *n* **1.** a simple crane that is typically used for moving cargo onto or from a ship **2.** a structure placed over an oil well that is used to raise and lower piping, drills, and other boring equipment [Early 17C. After a London hangman called *Derrick*; originally 'hangman, gallows']

Derrida /de reédə/, **Jacques** (b. 1930) Algerian-born French philosopher. He introduced deconstruction, a controversial technique for textual analysis.

> 'The writer writes *in* a language and *in* a logic whose proper system, laws, and life his discourse by definition cannot dominate absolutely.'
> [Jacques Derrida, *Of Grammatology*; 1967]

derrière /dérri air, dérri áir/ *n* somebody's bottom (*humorous*) [Late 18C. < French, 'behind']

derring-do /dérring doó/ *n* boldness or acts of great daring (*dated*) [Late 16C. Alteration and misinterpretation of *dorring don* 'daring to do']

derringer /dérrinjər/ *n* a pocket-sized, short-barrelled, large-calibre pistol [Mid-19C. After Henry *Deringer* (1786–1868), US gunsmith]

derris /dérriss/ *n* **1.** an insecticide made from a tropical plant. It contains the natural toxin rotenone. **2.** a woody climbing plant with a tuberous root that produces derris. Native to: South Asia. Genus:

Derris. [Mid-19C. Via modern Latin < Greek, 'leather covering']

derry /dérri/ (*plural* **-ries**) *n* a derelict house (*dated slang*) [Mid-20C. Shortening]

Derry /dérri/ district council in County Londonderry, Northern Ireland. Population: 105,066 (2002).

derv /durv/ *n* diesel oil used as a fuel for road vehicles [Mid-20C. Acronym < *diesel-engined road vehicle*]

dervish /dúrvish/ *n* **1.** a member of any of several ascetic Muslim religious groups, some of which are known for their practices of very energetic dancing, whirling, chanting, or singing. They are known as whirling, dancing, or howling dervishes according to the group they belong to. **2.** a very energetic person [Late 16C. Via Turkish *derviş* < Persian *darvīš* 'poor, mendicant']

Derwent /dúrwent/ river in southern Tasmania, Australia, that rises in Lake St Clair and flows southwestwards to the Tasman Sea at Storm Bay near Hobart. Length: 190 km/118 mi.

Derwentwater /dúrwənt wawtər/ lake in Cumbria, northwestern England. Length: 4.8 km/3 mi.

DES *abbr* **1.** E-COMMERCE data encryption standard **2.** PHARM diethylstilbestrol

desacralize /deé sákrə līz/ (**-izes, -izing, -ized**), **desacralise** (**-ises, -ising, -ised**) *vt* to remove the sacred, religious, or supernatural qualities or status from something

Desai /də sī/, **Anita** (*b.* 1937) Indian writer. Her novels include *Cry, the Peacock* (1963) and *In Custody* (1984).

Desai /de sī/, **Morarji Ranchhodji** (1896–1995) Indian politician. Five times imprisoned under British rule, and in 1975–77 by Indira Gandhi, he was prime minister of India (1977–79), heading the Janata Party.

desalinate /dee sálli nayt/ (**-nates, -nating, -nated**) *vt* to remove the salt from something —**desalination** /dee sálli náysh'n/ *n* —**desalinator** *n*

desalinize /dee sálli nīz/ (**-nizes, -nizing, -nized**), **desalinise** (**-nises, -nising, -nised**) *vt* CHEM same as **desalinate** —**desalinization** /dee sálli nī záysh'n/ *n*

desalt /dee sáwlt, -sólt/ (**-salts, -salting, -salted**) *vt* CHEM same as **desalinate** —**desalter** *n*

desaturation /dee sáchə ráysh'n/ *n* the addition of white to a saturated colour in order to achieve a paler shade

descale /dee skáyl/ (**-scales, -scaling, -scaled**) *vt* to remove the lime scale that has accumulated in a household appliance such as a kettle

descant /déss kant, díss-/, **discant** /díss-/ *n* **1.** HIGH MELODY a melody that is sung or played above the basic melody of a piece of music **2.** COMMENT a comment, remark, or criticism on a particular subject (*literary*) ■ *vi* (**-cants, -canting, -canted**) DISCOURSE ON SOMETHING to comment at length on a particular subject (*literary*) [14C. Via Anglo-Norman *descaunt* < medieval Latin *discantus* 'part song, refrain' < Latin *cantus* 'song'] —**descanter** /de skántər, di-/ *n*

Descartes /dáy kaart/, **René** (1596–1650) French philosopher and mathematician. He is often called the father of modern philosophy, and his *Discourse on Method* (1637) introduced his technique of philosophical enquiry. His work on analytical geometry resulted in the Cartesian system of coordinates.

 'There is a great difference between the mind and the body, inasmuch as the body is by its very nature always divisible, while the mind is utterly indivisible.'
 [René Descartes, *Meditations on First Philosophy*; 1641]

descend /di sénd/ (**-scends, -scending, -scended**) *v* **1.** *vti* GO DOWN to go down a staircase, hill, valley, or other downward incline **2.** *vi* COME NEARER GROUND to come nearer the ground, especially in an aircraft in preparation for landing **3.** *vi* SLOPE to slope downwards **4.** *vti* BE RELATED to be connected by blood to an ancestor ○ *be descended from Vikings* **5.** *vi* BE INHERITED to be inherited from or passed down by parents or ancestors **6.** *vi* ARRIVE SUDDENLY to arrive at a place suddenly, especially in large numbers ○ *tourists descending on unspoiled areas* **7.** *vi* BECOME ESTABLISHED to become more evident or established, suddenly or by degrees ○ *An atmosphere of gloom descended on the assembled crowd.* **8.** *vi* LOWER ONESELF to behave in a way that is disappointing and below somebody's usual standards [14C. Via French *descendre* < Latin *descendere* 'climb down' < *scandere* 'climb'] —**descendable** *adj*

descendant /di séndənt/ *n* **1.** a person, animal, or plant related to one that lived in the past **2.** something that is based in design, form, or concept on an earlier thing ■ *adj* another spelling of **descendent**

SPELLCHECK **descendant** or **descendent**? Do not confuse the spelling of *descendant* and *descendent*, which sound similar. *Descendant* is the only spelling of the noun, denoting somebody or something related to an ancestor, or something based on an earlier thing. *Descendent* is the usual spelling of the adjective, which means 'going downwards'.

descendent /di séndənt/ *adj* moving downwards

SPELLCHECK See *descendant*.

descender /di séndər/ *n* **1.** the tail part of a letter that extends below the baseline of other letters, e.g. on a 'y' or 'g' **2.** somebody or something that descends

descendeur /déssaaN dúr/ *n* a mechanical device that can be tightened or loosened on a rope, enabling a climber to control the speed of his or her descent [Late 20C. < French, 'descender' < *descendre* (see DESCEND)]

descendible /di séndəb'l/ *adj* **1.** able to be inherited **2.** allowing descent or downward movement

descending /di sénding/ *adj* going or arranged from highest to lowest, greatest to smallest, or latest to earliest ○ *in descending order*

descent /di sént/ *n* **1.** GOING DOWN an act of going from the top to the bottom or from a higher position to a lower position **2.** WAY DOWN a path or other way down something such as a mountain **3.** DECLINE a decline or change from something better to something worse **4.** SUDDEN ARRIVAL the sudden arrival of a person or group of people **5.** ANCESTRAL BACKGROUND the connection somebody has to an ancestor or group of ancestors **6.** INHERITED DEVELOPMENT characteristics or developments that can be traced to an earlier source **7.** ONE GENERATION a step of one generation in a lineage **8.** LAW INHERITANCE the transmission of property by inheritance [13C. < French *descente* < *descendre* (see DESCEND)]

SPELLCHECK **descent** or **dissent**? Do not confuse the spelling of *descent* and *dissent*, which sound similar. The word *descent* is only used as a noun, meaning 'the act of descending', 'a way down', 'ancestral background', 'a decline', etc., as in *a steep descent, people of Spanish descent*. The word *dissent* can be a noun or a verb, referring to disagreement or nonconformity, as in *dissent from official party policy, to dissent from orthodox religious doctrine*.

Deschamps /day shaaN/, **Eustache** (1340?–1407?) French poet. He wrote many ballads and poems, and the first treatise on French versification.

 'Who will bell the cat?'
 [Eustache Deschamps, 'Ballade: Le Chat et les souris' ('Ballad: The Cat and the Mice'); 14th century]

deschool /deé skoól/ (**-schools, -schooling, -schooled**) *v* **1.** *vt* to remove children from school to educate them at home **2.** *vti* to reduce somebody's involvement with education within the school system, or undergo this process —**deschooling** *n*

descramble /deé skrámb'l/ (**-bles, -bling, -bled**) *vt* to make intelligible a message transmitted in code form —**descrambler** *n*

describe /di skrī́b/ (**-scribes, -scribing, -scribed**) *vt* **1.** EXPLAIN SOMETHING to give an account of something by giving details of its characteristics **2.** CHARACTERIZE SOMEBODY OR SOMETHING to label or typify somebody or something **3.** DRAW SHAPE to make a shape or outline in the air (*formal*) ○ *The plane described a perfect figure of eight.* **4.** REPRESENT SOMETHING to represent something pictorially or with a model [15C. < Latin *describere* 'write down' < *scribere* 'write'] —**describable** *adj* —**describer** *n*

description /di skrípsh'n/ *n* **1.** EXPLANATION a written or verbal account, representation, or explanation of something **2.** PROCESS OF DESCRIBING the process of giving an account or explanation of something **3.** SORT a kind or variety of something ○ *cars of every description* [14C. Via French < Latin *description-* < *descript-*, past participle of *describere* (see DESCRIBE)]

descriptive /di skríptiv/ *adj* **1.** BEING DESCRIPTION containing or consisting of description **2.** CLASSIFYING serving mainly to label, describe, or classify **3.** ATTRIBUTIVE expressing an attribute or quality of a noun ○ *descriptive adjective* [Mid-18C. < late Latin *descriptivus* < Latin *descript-* (see DESCRIPTION)] —**descriptively** *adv* —**descriptiveness** *n*

descriptive clause *n* GRAM same as **nonrestrictive clause**

descriptive linguistics *n* the study of a language limited to a comprehensive account of its grammar at a given time, omitting historical or comparative features and not attempting to formulate prescriptive rules (*takes a singular verb*)

descriptivism /di skríptivizəm/ *n* **1.** adherence to the practices and tenets of descriptive linguistics **2.** the notion or thesis that descriptive statements can be true and accurate reflections of phenomena —**descriptivist** *n, adj*

descriptor /di skríptər/ *n* a word or phrase used to categorize records in a database so that all records containing the key can be retrieved together [Mid-20C. < Latin, 'describer' < *descript-* (see DESCRIPTION)]

descry /di skrī́/ (**-scries, -scrying, -scried**) *vt* to catch sight of something (*literary*) [14C. < Old French *descrier* 'cry out, proclaim' < *crier* (see CRY)] —**descrier** *n*

Desdemona /dézdi mṓnə/ *n* a small satellite of Uranus, discovered in 1986 by Voyager 2

~~**desease**~~ incorrect spelling of **disease**

desecrate /déssi krayt/ (**-crates, -crating, -crated**) *vt* **1.** to damage something sacred, or do something that is offensive to the religious nature of something **2.** to damage something that is held dear or revered [Late 17C. < DE- + CONSECRATE] —**desecrater** *n* —**desecration** /déssi kráysh'n/ *n* —**desecrator** /déssi kraytər/ *n*

deseed /dee seéd/ (**-seeds, -seeding, -seeded**) *vt* to remove the seeds from a fruit, vegetable, or plant

desegregate /dee séggri gayt/ (**-gates, -gating, -gated**) *vti* to put an end to a customary or enforced separation of ethnic or racial groups in a place or institution, e.g. in a workplace or school —**desegregation** /dee séggri gáysh'n/ *n* —**desegregationist** *n*

deselect /deé si lékt/ (**-lects, -lecting, -lected**) *vt* **1.** REMOVE SELECTION to remove selection status from an option or data on a menu or list on a computer screen **2.** REJECT POLITICIAN to refuse to select a serving MP, councillor, or party member for re-election **3.** *US* LET TRAINEE GO to end the training of an unsuitable trainee before the training program is completed —**deselection** *n*

~~**desend**~~ incorrect spelling of **descend**

desensitize /dee sénssə tīz/ (**-tizes, -tizing, -tized**), **desensitise** (**-tises, -tising, -tised**) *vt* **1.** MAKE SOMEBODY LESS ALLERGIC to make somebody less sensitive to a known allergen by injecting increasing amounts of the allergen over time, building up resistance **2.** MAKE SOMEBODY LESS SENSITIVE TO FEAR to make somebody less responsive to an overwhelming fear by repeated exposure to the feared situation or object, either in natural or artificial circumstances **3.** MAKE SOMEBODY OR SOMETHING LESS SENSITIVE to make somebody or something less sensitive in other respects —**desensitization** /dee sénssə tī záysh'n/ *n* —**desensitizer** *n*

~~**desent**~~[1] incorrect spelling of **decent**

~~**desent**~~[2] incorrect spelling of **descent**

desert[1] /dézzərt/ *n* **1.** DRY AREA an area of land, usually in very hot climates, that consists only of sand, gravel, or rock with little or no vegetation, no permanent bodies of water, and erratic rainfall. See table on next page **2.** DEPRIVED PLACE a place or situation that is devoid of some desirable thing or overwhelmed by an undesirable thing ○ *a cultural desert* **3.** LIFELESS PLACE a place devoid of life [12C. Via French *désert* < late Latin *desertum* 'abandoned place' < Latin *desert-* (see DESERT[2])]

WORLD'S LARGEST DESERTS

	Desert	Area	Location
1	Sahara Desert	[3.5 million sq. mi./9.1 million sq. km]	North Africa
2	Gobi Desert	[0.5 million sq. mi./1.3 million sq. km]	Central Asia/Mongolia
3	Patagonian Desert	[0.26 million sq. mi./0.67 million sq. km]	South America/Argentina
=4	Rub' al-Khali Desert	[0.25 million sq. mi./0.65 million sq. km]	Southwestern Asia/Arabia
=4	Great Victoria Desert	[0.25 million sq. mi./0.65 million sq. km]	Australia
6	Great Basin Desert	[0.21 million sq. mi./0.54 million sq. km]	North America
7	Kalahari Desert	[0.2 million sq. mi./0.5 million sq. km]	Southwestern Africa
8	Great Sandy Desert	[0.15 million sq. mi./0.39 million sq. km]	Australia
9	Garagum Desert	[0.14 million sq. mi./0.35 million sq. km]	Central Asia/Turkmenistan
10	Sonoran Desert	[0.12 million sq. mi./0.31 million sq. km]	Mexico and United States

USAGE desert or dessert? *Dessert* is a noun, pronounced with the stress on the second syllable, and it has only one modern meaning: 'a sweet course eaten at the end of a meal'. *Desert* is pronounced with the stress on the first syllable when it is a noun meaning 'a dry area', and with the stress on the second syllable when it is a noun meaning 'something somebody deserved', as in *just deserts* and similar expressions. The stress is also on the second syllable when *desert* is used as a verb, meaning 'abandon something' or 'run away'.

desert[2] /di zúrt/ (-serts, -serting, -serted) v 1. vt ABANDON PLACE to leave a place with no one staying behind 2. vt ABANDON PERSON to leave or abandon somebody, especially somebody to whom a duty or obligation is owed 3. vti MIL LEAVE ARMY WITHOUT PERMISSION to run away from an armed force or military post without permission and intending never to go back 4. vt BE UNAVAILABLE TO SOMEBODY to be absent from somebody when needed ○ *Her sense of humour appeared to have deserted her.* [14C. Via French *déserter* < Latin *desert-*, past participle of *deserere* 'abandon' < *serere* 'join'] —**deserted** adj —**deserter** n

USAGE See *desert*[1].

desert[3] /di zúrt/ n something deserved, either punishment or reward (*usually used in the plural*) ○ *He'll get his just deserts.* [13C. < Old French, 'what is deserved' < past participle of *deservir* (see DESERVE)]

USAGE See *desert*[1].

desert boot n a laced ankle boot of beige or brown suede with a crepe-rubber sole

desertification /di zúrtifi káysh'n/ n a process by which land becomes increasingly dry until almost no vegetation grows on it, making it a desert

desertion /di zúrsh'n/ n the act or an instance of deserting from the armed forces

desert island n a small isolated unpopulated tropical island

desert pavement n a layer of gravel that remains when the finer-grained particles of a desert soil have been blown away

desert pea n a trailing plant with bright red flowers. Native to: Australia. Latin name: *Clianthus formosus.*

desert rat n 1. any rodent that lives in a desert 2. a soldier who served in the British 7th Armoured Division in North Africa during World War II (*informal*)

desert varnish n a very thin dark surface coating of iron and manganese oxides that forms on exposed rock surfaces in deserts

deserve /di zúrv/ (-serves, -serving, -served) vt to have earned or be worthy of something [13C. Via Old French *deservir* < Latin *deservire* 'serve well' < *servire* (see SERVE)] —**deserved** adj —**deserver** n

deservedly /di zúrvidli/ adv in a way that is justly and fully earned or merited ○ *She was deservedly popular as a teacher.*

deserving /di zúrving/ adj worthy to receive something because of need, merit, or justice ○ *The charity was thought to be a deserving cause.* —**deservingly** adv —**deservingness** n

desex /dee séks/ (-sexes, -sexing, -sexed) vt 1. to remove the sex organs from an animal or person 2. BIOL, SOC SCI same as **desexualize**

desexualize /dee sékshoo ə līz/ (-izes, -izing, -ized), **desexualise** (-ises, -ising, -ised) vt to suppress or diminish the sexual characteristics of an animal or person —**desexualization** /dee sékshoo ə lī záysh'n/ n

deshabille /dáyssə beél/, **dishabille** /díssə-/ n a state in which somebody is partially undressed or dressed very casually or incompletely (*formal*) [Late 17C. < French *déshabillé*, past participle of *déshabiller* 'undress' < *habiller* 'dress']

desi /dáyssi/, **deshi** /dáyshi/ adj S Asia 1. produced or made locally 2. characteristic of rural areas, especially those considered to be unsophisticated [< Hindi]

De Sica /də seékə/, **Vittorio** (1901–74) Italian film director and actor. He made Italian neorealism internationally known through his *Bicycle Thieves* (1948).

desiccant /déssikənt/ n a substance that absorbs water. Use: removal of moisture. [Late 17C. < Latin *desiccant-*, present participle of *desiccare* (see DESICCATE)]

desiccate /déssi kayt/ (-cates, -cating, -cated) v 1. vt to remove the moisture from something, or become free of moisture 2. to preserve food by removing its moisture [Late 16C. < Latin *desiccat-*, past participle of *desiccare* 'dry out' < *siccus* 'dry'] —**desiccation** /déssi káysh'n/ n —**desiccative** /déssikətiv, -kaytiv/ adj —**desiccator** n

desiccated /déssi kaytid/ adj 1. free from moisture, or preserved by drying (*used of products, especially food*) 2. lacking in energy or vitality

SYNONYMS See *dry*.

desiderata plural of **desideratum**

desiderative /di zídderətiv, -sídd-/ adj 1. having a desire for something (*formal*) 2. describes a verb that, in some languages, expresses a desire to perform the action indicated by a related verb

desideratum /di zíddə ráatəm, -síddə-/ (*plural* -ta /-tə/) n something that is desired or felt to be essential (*formal*) [Mid-17C. < Latin, neuter past participle of *desiderare* 'desire, wish for']

design /di zín/ v (-signs, -signing, -signed) 1. vti CREATE DETAILED PLAN OF SOMETHING to make a detailed plan of the form or structure of something, emphasizing features such as its appearance, convenience, and efficient functioning ○ *a well-designed car interior* 2. vti PLAN AND MAKE SOMETHING to plan and make something in a skilful or artistic way 3. vt INTEND SOMETHING FOR PARTICULAR USE to intend something for a particular purpose ○ *The scholarship was designed to aid foreign students.* 4. vt INVENT SOMETHING to contrive, devise, or plan something ○ *They designed a scheme to get rich quick.* ■ n 1. PICTURE OF SOMETHING'S FORM AND STRUCTURE a drawing or other graphical representation of something that shows how it is to function or be made 2. WAY SOMETHING IS MADE the way in which something is planned and made ○ *the elegant design of the aircraft's wings* 3. DECORATIVE PATTERN a pattern or shape, sometimes repeated, used for decoration ○ *a geometric design* 4. PROCESS OF DESIGNING the process, techniques, or art of designing things ○ *studied architecture and design* 5. INTENTION an underlying sense of purpose or planning (*formal*) ■ **designs** npl SELFISH OR DISHONEST PLAN a secretive plan undertaken for selfish or dishonest motives [14C.

< Latin *designare* (see DESIGNATE)] ◇ **by design** intentionally or on purpose

designate /dézzig nayt/ vt (-nates, -nating, -nated) 1. DESCRIBE SOMEBODY OR SOMETHING FORMALLY to give somebody or something a formal description or name (*often passive*) 2. CHOOSE SOMETHING FOR USE to choose something for a particular purpose (*usually passive*) 3. NAME SOMEBODY TO POSITION to formally choose somebody for a job, position, or duty 4. MARK SOMETHING to mark or indicate something ○ *Coloured pins on the map designated the new buildings.* ■ adj CHOSEN FOR FUTURE POST chosen for a particular position, while not yet actually in office [Late 18C. < Latin *designat-*, past participle of *designare* 'mark out' < *signum* 'mark'] —**designative** /dézzig naytiv/ adj —**designator** /dézzig náytəri, -nətəri/ adj —**designatory** /dézzig náytəri, -nətəri/ adj

designated driver n a driver of a motor vehicle who abstains from alcoholic drinks on a social occasion in order to drive people home safely

designated hitter n a player in baseball who does not play defensively but substitutes for a pitcher in the batting order

designation /dézzig náysh'n/ n 1. a name, label, or description given to something or somebody 2. the act or process of being named or specified

designedly /di zínidli/ adv intentionally or on purpose

designer /di zínər/ n SOMEBODY WHO DESIGNS somebody who designs things, especially fashionable and expensive clothes ■ adj 1. DESIGNED BY SOMEBODY FAMOUS created or produced by a famous designer 2. FASHIONABLE trendy, popular, and usually expensive ○ *designer foods* 3. SPECIALLY MADE created for a specific purpose, requirement, or need

designer baby n a baby preselected at the embryo stage for desirable characteristics (*informal*)

designer drug n a drug that has been chemically altered to enhance its properties or to evade a legal prohibition

designer gene n a gene that is introduced into an organism to control the presence or absence of a specific characteristic

designer label n a label attached to clothing to display the name of the designer

designer stubble n beard growth that is kept deliberately short to create a look that suggests a nonchalant attitude to grooming that belies the effort taken to achieve it (*informal*)

designing /di zíning/ adj tending to scheme and make secret plans for personal benefit —**designingly** adv

desinence /déssinənss/ n an ending or suffix of a word (*technical*) [Late 16C. Via French *désinence* < medieval Latin *desinentia* < Latin *desinere* 'leave off, end' < *sinere* 'leave'] —**desinential** /déssi nénsh'l/ adj

desirable /di zírəb'l/ adj 1. WORTHY OF DESIRE worth having or doing 2. ATTRACTIVE sexually attractive or pleasing ■ n SOMEBODY OR SOMETHING DESIRED somebody who or something that is desired —**desirability** /di zírə bílləti/ n —**desirably** adv

desire /di zír/ vt (-sires, -siring, -sired) 1. WISH FOR SOMETHING to want something very strongly 2. FIND SOMEBODY SEXUALLY ATTRACTIVE to want to have sexual relations with somebody 3. REQUEST SOMETHING to wish for and request something (*formal*) ■ n 1. CRAVING a wish, craving, or longing for something 2. SOMETHING WISHED FOR something that or somebody who is wished for (*formal*) 3. SEXUAL CRAVING a strong wish for sexual relations with somebody (*formal*) ○ *'Is it not strange that desire should so many years outlive performance?'* (William Shakespeare, *Henry IV, Part 2*) [13C. Via French *désirer* < Latin *desiderare*] —**desirer** n

SYNONYMS See *want*.

desireable incorrect spelling of **desirable**

desirous /di zírəss/ adj seeking or wishing for something very much (*formal*) —**desirously** adv —**desirousness** n

desist /di síst, -zíst/ (-sists, -sisting, -sisted) vi to stop doing something [15C. Via French < Latin *desistere* < *sistere* 'bring to a standstill' < *stare* 'stand'] —**desistance** n

desk /desk/ n 1. TABLE USED FOR WORK a table with a broad flat or sloping top, often with drawers and compartments, used for writing, reading, drawing,

or computing **2. COUNTER OFFERING SERVICE TO CUSTOMERS** a counter where a service is provided, e.g. in a hotel or an airport **3. DEPARTMENT OF ORGANIZATION** a division of a communications company or other organization that specializes in a particular area of interest **4. STAND FOR SUPPORTING MUSIC** a stand for supporting a musical score that is shared by two players in an orchestra, or the two players who share it **5. BOOK STAND IN CHURCH** a stand for the book from which a service is read in church ■ *adj* **OF DESK** done at a desk, or designed to be kept on a desk ○ *a desk diary* [14C. Via medieval Latin *desca* < Latin *discus* 'disc, dish, tray' (see DISH)]

deskbound /désk bownd/ *adj* working at a desk rather than at a physically active or practical task

desk clerk *n N Am* a hotel receptionist

desk dining *n* eating lunch at your desk at your place of work, in order to save time (*informal*)

desk editor *n* somebody who prepares text for typesetting or publishing

deskfast /désk fəst/ *n* breakfast eaten while at work, especially at a desk in an office (*informal*)

deskill /dee skíl/ (**-skills, -skilling, -skilled**) *vt* to remove the need for skill or judgment in the performance of a task, often because of increasingly sophisticated production methods

desk job *n* a job in which most duties or tasks are undertaken while sitting at a desk in an office

desk organizer *n N Am* COMM same as **desk tidy**

desk sergeant *n* a police sergeant who works in administration at a police station

desk study *n* an investigation of the available facts and figures relevant to a specific issue, often before starting a new or more detailed study of it

desk tidy *n* a small container with several compartments used on a desk to keep pens, paper clips, and other small items of office stationery tidy and handy for use. N Am term **desk organizer**

desktop /désk top/ *n* **1. GRAPHICAL COMPUTER REPRESENTATION OF OFFICE DESK** a display on a computer screen comprising background and icons representing equipment, programs, and files **2. SURFACE OF DESK** the working surface of a desk ■ *adj* **USABLE ON TOP OF DESK** small and compact enough for the top of a desk

desktop publishing *n* the use of a personal computer and specialist software to lay out and produce typeset-quality documents for printing. Desktop publishing systems can mix text and graphics on the same page and are used to produce a variety of documents from flyers and newsletters to brochures and books.

desm- *prefix* same as **desmo-** (*used before vowels*)

desman /déssmən/ *n* **1.** an amphibious mammal resembling a mole that has dense fur, webbed feet, and a flat scaly tail. Native to: Pyrenees. Latin name: *Galemys pyrenaicus*. **2.** an amphibious mammal related to the Pyrenean desman. Native to: Russia. Latin name: *Desmana moschata*. [Late 18C. Shortening of Swedish *desmanråtta* 'muskrat' < *desman* 'musk' + *råtta* 'rat']

desmid /déssmid, déz-/ *n* a green, usually one-celled, freshwater alga composed of two symmetrical half-cells. It forms branching colonies like mats and is found in unpolluted water. Family: Desmidiaceae. [Mid-19C. < modern Latin *Desmidium* < Greek *desmos* 'bond, chain'] —**desmidian** /dess míddi ən, dez-/ *adj*

desmo- *prefix* ligament, bond ○ *desmosome* [< Greek *desmos* < *dein* 'bind']

Des Moines /di móyn/ capital, largest city, and commercial centre of the US state of Iowa, situated where the Raccoon River meets the Des Moines River in the south-central part of the state. Population: 198,076 (2002 estimate).

desmosome /dézmə sōm/ *n* a small patch of interlocking fibres between the outer membranes of adjacent cells that helps to hold cells together in tissues such as skin

Desmoulins /dáy moo láN/, **Camille** (1760–94) French revolutionary and journalist. An effective pamphleteer and orator, he incurred the wrath of Maximilien Robespierre and was guillotined. Full name **Desmoulins, Lucie-Simplice-Camille-Benoist**

desolate *adj* /déssələt/ **1. EMPTY** bare, uninhabited, and deserted **2. ALONE** solitary, joyless, and without hope ○ *'And I was desolate and sick of an old passion'* (Ernest Dowson, *Non Sum Qualis Eram Bonae Sub Regno Cynarae*; 1896) **3. GRIM** dismal and gloomy ■ *vt* /déssə layt/ (**-lates, -lating, -lated**) **1. DEVASTATE PLACE** to make a place barren or deserted **2. MAKE SOMEBODY WRETCHED** to make somebody feel sad and lonely [14C. < Latin *desolatus*, past participle of *desolare* 'leave alone' < *solus* 'alone'] —**desolately** *adv* —**desolateness** *n* —**desolater** *n* —**desolation** /déssə láysh'n/ *n*

desorption /dee sáwrpsh'n, -záwrp-/ *n* the action or process of releasing an absorbed substance from something, e.g. gas from rocks [Early 20C. < DE- + ABSORPTION]

de Soto /də sṓtō/, **Hernando** (1500?–42?) Spanish explorer. He explored parts of South America (1519–32) and southeastern North America (1539–42).

despair /di spáir/ *n* **1. FEELING OF HOPELESSNESS** a profound feeling that there is no hope **2. CAUSE OF HOPELESSNESS** somebody or something that makes somebody feel hopeless or exasperated ■ *vi* (**-spairs, -spairing, -spaired**) **LOSE HOPE** to feel that there is no hope [14C. Via French < Latin *desperare* 'stop hoping' < *sperare* 'to hope' < *spes* 'hope']

despairing /di spáiring/ *adj* feeling or showing loss of hope ○ *a despairing look* —**despairingly** *adv*

~~desparate~~ incorrect spelling of **desperate**

despatch *vti, n* another spelling of **dispatch**

desperado /déspə raádō/ (*plural* **-does** or **-dos**) *n* a reckless and violent criminal [Early 17C. Alteration of obsolete *desperate* 'desperate person', after Spanish *desesperado*]

desperate /désspərət/ *adj* **1. DESPAIRING** overwhelmed with urgency and anxiety, to the point of losing hope ○ *Desperate because of his financial situation, he took his own life.* **2. AS LAST RESORT** so drastic or reckless as to be suitable only for a last resort ○ *The firefighters made a last desperate attempt to rescue the children.* **3. EXTREME** extremely difficult, serious, or dangerous ○ *a desperate shortage of food and water* **4. IN GREAT NEED** wanting or needing something very much ○ *Desperate for an answer, she phoned again.* **5. BEYOND HOPE** so wicked as to allow no hope of redemption **6. AWFUL** extremely bad (*informal*) ○ *The food was desperate!* [14C. < Latin *desperatus*, past participle of *desperare* (see DESPAIR)] —**desperately** *adv* —**desperateness** *n*

desperation /déspə ráysh'n/ *n* **1.** recklessness brought on by great urgency and anxiety ○ *In desperation people were jumping from the windows of the blazing building.* **2.** a condition of being without hope

~~desperatly~~ incorrect spelling of **desperately**

despicable /di spíkəb'l/ *adj* fully deserving of contempt [Mid-16C. < late Latin *despicabilis* < Latin *despicari* 'look down on'] —**despicability** /di spíkə bílləti/ *n* —**despicably** *adv*

Despina /de speénə/ *n* a small natural satellite of Neptune, discovered in 1989 by the Voyager 2 planetary probe

despise /di spī́z/ (**-spises, -spising, -spised**) *vt* to look down on and feel contempt for somebody or something [13C. < Old French *despis-*, stem of *despire* < Latin *despicere* 'look down on' < *specere* 'look'] —**despiser** *n*

despite /di spī́t/ *prep* **1.** although it might have been prevented by something ○ *The mission blasted off today despite bad weather.* **2.** indicates that something is done unexpectedly or unintentionally ○ *She blushed deeply despite herself.* [13C. Via Old French *despit* 'spite' < Latin *despect-*, past participle of *despicere* (see DESPISE)] ◇ **in despite of** in spite of or notwithstanding (*archaic*)

despoil /di spóyl/ (**-spoils, -spoiling, -spoiled**) *vt* to rob a place of everything of value ○ *Thieves had despoiled the palace.* [13C. Via Old French *despoillier* < Latin *despoliare* 'strip entirely of booty' < *spolium* 'booty'] —**despoiler** *n* —**despoilment** *n* —**despoliation** /di spṓli áysh'n/ *n*

despond /di spónd/ (*archaic or literary*) *vi* (**-sponds, -sponding, -sponded**) to become discouraged or lose hope ■ *n* a feeling of extreme unhappiness and hopelessness [Mid-17C. < Latin *despondere* 'give up (your vitality)' < *spondere* 'to promise'] —**despondingly** *adv*

despondent /di spóndənt/ *adj* extremely unhappy and discouraged —**despondence** *n* —**despondency** *n* —**despondently** *adv*

despot /déss pot, -pət/ *n* **1. POWERFUL RULER** a tyrant or ruler with absolute powers **2. TYRANNICAL PERSON** somebody who behaves in a tyrannical way towards other people **3. ROMAN, BYZANTINE, OR OTTOMAN RULER** a minor emperor or prince of the later Roman, Byzantine, or Ottoman empires [Mid-16C. Via French < Greek *despotēs* 'absolute ruler']

despotic /di spóttik/, **despotical** /-k'l/ *adj* relating to, carried out by, or behaving like a despot —**despotically** *adv*

despotism /déspətizəm/ *n* **1.** rule by a despot or tyrant **2.** cruel and arbitrary use of power

despumate /di spyoó mayt, désspyoō-/ (**-mates, -mating, -mated**) *v* **1.** *vi* to form froth or scum on the surface **2.** *vt* to remove the scum or froth on the surface of a liquid [Mid-17C. < Latin *despumat-*, past participle of *despumare* 'skim off (scum)' < *spuma* 'foam, scum'] —**despumation** /désspyoō máysh'n/ *n*

desquamate /déskwə mayt/ (**-mates, -mating, -mated**) *v* **1.** *vi* to flake or peel off naturally in small pieces (*refers especially to skin*) **2.** *vt* to remove a thin layer of skin, especially as a treatment for acne [Early 18C. < Latin *desquamat-*, past participle of *desquamare* 'scale off' < *squama* 'scale'] —**desquamation** /déskwə máysh'n/ *n*

des res /déz réz/ *n* a house or flat that is considered, especially by an estate agent, as highly desirable (*informal*) [Late 20C. Shortening of *desirable residence*]

Dessau /déss ow/ industrial city in Halle District, Saxony-Anhalt State, east-central Germany. It is situated north of Leipzig. Population: 92,535 (1997).

dessert /di zúrt/ *n* **1.** a sweet course eaten at the end of a meal **2.** fresh or dried fruit and nuts served at the end of a meal (*dated*) [Mid-16C. < French, '(course following) clearing the table' < past participle of *desservir* 'remove what has been served' < *servir* (see SERVE)]

USAGE See *desert*[1].

dessertspoon /di zúrt spoon/ *n* **1.** a medium-sized spoon, larger than a teaspoon but smaller than a tablespoon, used for eating dessert **2.** *also* **dessertspoonful** the amount a dessertspoon contains

dessert wine *n* a sweet wine served with dessert or after a meal

~~dessicated~~ incorrect spelling of **desiccated**

destabilize /dee stáybə līz/ (**-lizes, -lizing, -lized**), **destabilise** (**-lises, -lising, -lised**) *vt* to make something, especially a government or economy, unstable in order to impair its functioning or bring about its collapse —**destabilization** /dee stáybə lī záysh'n/ *n*

De Stijl /də stī́l/ *n* an artistic movement founded in the Netherlands in 1917 that advocated the reduction of forms to geometric shapes and the use of primary colours along with black and white [Mid-20C. < Dutch, 'the style', title of the periodical that represented the movement]

destination /désti náysh'n/ *n* **1. PREDETERMINED END OF TRIP** the place to which somebody or something is going or must go **2. INTENDED OR DESTINED END** a purpose for which somebody or something is intended ■ *adj* **INVOLVING PARTICULAR PLACE** involving or relating to an establishment such as a restaurant or shop that people make a point of going to, usually because of its reputation (*informal*) ○ *destination dining* [14C. < Latin *destination-* 'appointment' < *destinare* (see DESTINE)]

destination wedding *n* a wedding for which the couple travel to a far-off location to have their marriage ceremony

destine /déstin/ (**-tines, -tining, -tined**) *vt* to intend or decide that somebody will have a particular fate or something will have a particular use [14C. Via French < Latin *destinare* 'set up, decree, determine' < *-stinare* 'cause to stand']

destined /déstind/ *adj* **1.** sure, preordained, or intended ○ *From an early age he was destined to follow his father in the family business.* **2.** travelling towards a particular destination

destiny /déstini/ (*plural* **-nies**) *n* **1. SOMEBODY'S PREORDAINED FUTURE** the apparently predetermined and inevitable series of events that happen to somebody or

something ○ *No one could have foreseen that the child's destiny was to rule an empire.* **2.** **INNER REALIZABLE PURPOSE OF LIFE** the inner purpose of a life that can be discovered and realized ○ *He decided that his destiny was to go into show business.* **3.** *also* **Destiny** **SOMETHING THAT PREDETERMINES EVENTS** a force or agency that predetermines what will happen ○ *Destiny had decided her future.* [14C. < Old French *destinee* < Latin *destinare* (see DESTINE)]

destitute /désti tyoot/ *adj* **1.** lacking all money, resources, and possessions necessary for subsistence **2.** lacking a particular quality [14C. < Latin *destitutus*, past participle of *destituere* 'set down, abandon' < *statuere* 'set' < *status* 'position']

destitution /désti tyoósh'n/ *n* lack of the necessary means of subsistence

destrier /déstri ər/ *n* a warhorse or charger, especially of a medieval knight (*archaic*) [14C. Via Anglo-Norman *destrer*, Old French *destrier* < Latin *dexter* 'right' (because led by the right hand)]

destroy /di stróy/ (**-stroys, -stroying, -stroyed**) *v* **1.** *vti* **DEMOLISH** to demolish something or reduce something to fragments **2.** *vti* **RUIN** to ruin something or make something useless **3.** *vti* **ABOLISH** to abolish, rescind, or end something **4.** *vt* **DEFEAT SOMEBODY** to defeat somebody in a crushing way **5.** *vt* **KILL ANIMAL** to kill something or somebody, especially an animal (*usually passive*) ○ *Afterwards, the dog could not be cured and so had to be destroyed.* [12C. Via Old French *destruire* < Latin *destruere* 'undo results of building' < *struere* 'build'] —**destroyable** *adj*

destroyer /di stróy ər/ *n* **1.** a fast highly manoeuvrable warship, smaller than a cruiser and bigger than a frigate, that is used to escort convoys and attack submarines **2.** somebody or something that causes destruction

destroying angel *n* a highly poisonous large white mushroom with a frill near the top of its stalk. It grows in moist woodlands in temperate regions. Latin name: *Amanita virosa.*

destruct /di strúkt/ *n* the intentional destruction of a malfunctioning missile or rocket after its launch ■ *vti* (**-structs, -structing, -structed**) to intentionally destroy a malfunctioning missile or rocket after its launch, or be destroyed in this way [Mid-20C. Back-formation < DESTRUCTION]

destructible /di strúktəb'l/ *adj* capable of being destroyed or liable to be destroyed [Mid-18C. Via French < late Latin *destructibilis* < Latin *destruct-* (see DESTRUCTION)] —**destructibility** /di strúktə bílləti/ *n*

destruction /di strúksh'n/ *n* **1.** **PROCESS OF DESTROYING** the act or process of destroying something **2.** **DESTROYED STATE** the condition of having been destroyed **3.** **MEANS OF DESTROYING** a cause or means of destroying something ○ *A love of fast cars was his destruction.* [13C. < Latin *destruction-* < *destruct-*, past participle of *destruere* (see DESTROY)]

destructive /di strúktiv/ *adj* **1.** causing or capable of causing destruction **2.** intended to damage or hurt rather than be helpful or instructive [15C. Via French < late Latin *destructivus* < Latin *destruct-* (see DESTRUCTION)] —**destructively** *adv* —**destructiveness** *n* —**destructivity** /di strúk tívvəti, deé struk-/ *n*

destructive distillation *n* the process of heating solid substances in the absence of air to decompose them in order to obtain useful products from the vapour and residues

destructor /di strúktər/ *n* **1.** an incinerator used to burn rubbish **2.** an onboard explosive device used to destroy a missile or rocket if it malfunctions dangerously after its launch

desuetude /désswi tyood/ *n* the condition of not being in use (*formal*) [Early 17C. Via French < Latin *desuetudo* < *desuescere* 'become unaccustomed' < *suescere* 'be accustomed']

desulfurize *vti* INDUST US spelling of **desulphurize**

desulphurize /dee súlfə rīz/ (**-izes, -izing, -ized**), **desulphurise** (**-ises, -ising, -ised**) *vti* to remove sulphur and its compounds from something, typically from petroleum products or from flue gases when coal or another fuel is burned, or lose sulphur in this way —**desulphurization** /dee súlfə rī záysh'n/ *n* —**desulphurizer** *n*

desultory /déss'ltəri/ *adj* **1.** aimlessly passing from one thing to another **2.** happening in a random, disorganized, or unmethodical way ○ *The soldiers were subject to desultory fire from the enemy position.* [Late 16C. < Latin *desultorius* 'leaping' < *desilire* 'leap down' < *salire* 'leap'] —**desultorily** *adv* —**desultoriness** *n*

det., **det** *abbr* GRAM determiner

detach /di tách/ (**-taches, -taching, -tached**) *v* **1.** *vti* to separate, disconnect, or unfasten something, or become separated, disconnected, or unfastened **2.** *vt* to separate a military unit or an individual person from a larger unit for special duties [Late 17C. Via French *détacher* < Old French *destachier* < *attachier* (see ATTACH)] —**detachable** *adj* —**detacher** *n*

detached /di tácht/ *adj* **1.** **NOT ATTACHED** not attached to something **2.** **SEPARATE** describes a building that stands on its own and is not joined to another building **3.** **FREE FROM EMOTIONAL INVOLVEMENT** unaffected by emotional involvement or any form of bias —**detachedly** /di táchidli, di táchtli/ *adv*

detached retina *n* an eye condition in which the retina becomes separated from the eyeball, causing loss of vision

detachment /di táchmənt/ *n* **1.** **ALOOFNESS** lack of interest in or involvement with other people or with worldly concerns **2.** **DISINTERESTEDNESS** a lack of bias, prejudice, or emotional involvement **3.** **SEPARATION** the condition of being separated from something, or the process of separating one thing from another **4.** **MILITARY UNIT** a military unit separated from its normal, larger unit for special duties **5.** **SPECIALIZED GROUP** any specialized and separately employed unit of a group or organization

detail /deé tayl/ *n* **1.** **INDIVIDUAL PART** an individual separable part of something, especially one of several items of information ○ *No details of the proposed legislation are available yet.* **2.** **EVERY ELEMENT OF WHOLE** all of the individual parts that together make up a whole ○ *attention to detail* **3.** **INCLUSION OF ALL ELEMENTS** the treatment and inclusion of all of the individual parts that make up something ○ *Your description of the item needs more detail.* **4.** **INSIGNIFICANT PART** something that is insignificant or a minor part of something else ○ *Safety in the sport is not a mere detail.* **5.** ARTS, ARCHIT **SMALL ELEMENT OF ARTWORK OR STRUCTURE** a small element of a work of art or building structure, considered separately **6.** **GROUP WITH SPECIAL TASK** a group of people, especially in the armed services, given a specific task ■ **details** *npl* **PERSONAL FACTS** facts about somebody, e.g. his or her name and address ■ *vt* (**-tails, -tailing, -tailed**) **1.** **LIST THINGS** to list or enumerate a series of items or events ○ *Please detail all the things that were stolen.* **2.** MIL **GIVE MILITARY UNIT SPECIALIZED ASSIGNMENT** to assign a military unit to a specialized task (*often passive*) **3.** **DECORATE SOMETHING** to add refinements or decorations to something [Early 17C. < French *détail* 'piece cut off' < *détaillir* 'cut up' < *taillier* 'cut'] —**detailer** *n* ◇ **go into detail** to be very specific and include all of the particulars ◇ **in detail** covering every item or particular

detail drawing *n* a large-scale drawing that shows part of a machine, device, or building

detailed /deé tayld/ *adj* including all or many of the distinguishing features of something

detailing /deé tayling/ *n* details or small decorative features added to something such as a garment or piece of artwork ○ *exquisite detailing*

detain /di táyn/ (**-tains, -taining, -tained**) *vt* **1.** to hold back or delay somebody or something **2.** to restrain or keep somebody or something in custody [15C. Via Old French *detenir* < Latin *detinere* 'hold back' < *tenere* 'hold, keep'] —**detainable** *adj* —**detainment** *n*

detainee /deé tay neé, di-/ *n* somebody who is held in custody

detainer /di táynər/ *n* **1.** a writ authorizing that somebody in custody may be confined for a further period **2.** the wrongful withholding of somebody's property or freedom

detect /di tékt/ (**-tects, -tecting, -tected**) *vt* **1.** to notice or discover the existence of something **2.** ELECTRONICS same as **demodulate** [15C. < Latin *detect-*, past participle of *detegere* 'uncover' < *tegere* 'cover'] —**detectability** /di téktə bílləti/ *n* —**detectable** *adj* —**detectably** *adv*

detection /di téksh'n/ *n* **1.** **PERCEPTION OF SOMETHING'S EXISTENCE** the act of noticing or discovering the existence of something, or the state of having been noticed or discovered **2.** **DETECTIVE WORK** the work of a detective in investigating crime or wrongdoing **3.** TELECOM **SIGNAL EXTRACTION** the extraction of a signal carrying information from a radio wave (**carrier**)

detective /di téktiv/ *n* somebody who investigates and gathers evidence about possible crimes or wrongdoing ■ *adj* acting to detect something ○ *detective devices*

detector /di téktər/ *n* **1.** a device for sensing the presence of or changes in something such as radiation or pressure **2.** somebody or something that detects

detent /di tént/ *n* a locking device that permits movement of a machine part in one direction only, e.g. a lever or spring-loaded catch [Late 17C. < French *détente* 'release' < Latin *tendere* 'to stretch']

détente /day tónt, -taánt/ *n* a relaxation of tension or hostility between nations [Early 20C. < French, 'relaxation' (see DETENT)]

detention /di ténsh'n/ *n* **1.** the act of keeping somebody in custody, or the state of being kept in custody **2.** a form of punishment for school students in which they are made to stay in class at a break or at school after normal hours [15C. < late Latin *detention-* < Latin *detinere* (see DETAIN)]

detention centre *n* **1.** in Canada and formerly in the United Kingdom, a place where young offenders can be detained to serve a court sentence or while on remand accused of a crime **2.** a place where people wishing to enter a country without prior approval can be held until their claim is processed

detention home *n* in the United States, a remand centre for young offenders

deter /di túr/ (**-ters, -terring, -terred**) *vti* to discourage somebody from taking action or prevent something from happening, especially by making somebody feel afraid or anxious ○ *New laws to deter speeding will be enforced at the end of the month.* [Mid-16C. < Latin *deterrere* 'scare off' < *terrere* 'scare'] —**determent** *n*

deterge /di túrj/ (**-terges, -terging, -terged**) *vt* to cleanse something, especially a wound (*technical*) [Early 17C. Directly or via French < Latin *detergere* 'wipe off' < *tergere* 'wipe']

detergent /di túrjənt/ *n* a cleansing substance, especially a synthetic liquid that dissolves dirt and oil ■ *adj* having the properties of a detergent —**detergency** *n*

deteriorate /di teéri ə rayt/ (**-rates, -rating, -rated**) *vti* to become or make something worse in quality, value, or strength [Late 16C. < late Latin *deteriorat-*, past participle of *deteriorare* < Latin *deterior* 'worse'] —**deterioration** /di teéri ə ráysh'n/ *n* —**deteriorative** *adj*

determinable /di túrminəb'l/ *adj* **1.** able to be worked out, decided, or found **2.** able to be terminated (*technical*) —**determinability** /di túrminə bílləti/ *n* —**determinably** *adv*

determinant /di túrminənt/ *n* **1.** **CAUSE** a factor that causes or influences something **2.** MATHS **ARRAY OF MATHEMATICAL ELEMENTS** a square array of elements that itself has a numerical value, used in various mathematical processes such as solving simultaneous equations and studying linear transformations ■ *adj* **CAUSAL** causing or influencing something

determinate /di túrminət/ *adj* **1.** having exact and definite limits **2.** same as **determined** (*formal*) **3.** BOT describes a pattern of flowering in which primary and secondary stems end in a flower bud and stop growing —**determinacy** /di túrminəssi/ *n* —**determinately** *adv* —**determinateness** *n*

determination /di túrmi náysh'n/ *n* **1.** **FIRMNESS OF PURPOSE** firmness of purpose, will, or intention ○ *full of ambition and determination* **2.** **FIXED PURPOSE** a fixed purpose or resolution ○ *her determination to succeed* **3.** **ACT OF DISCOVERING SOMETHING** an act of finding out or ascertaining something, especially as a result of investigation or research (*formal*) ○ *determination of the cause of death* **4.** **DECISION ON COURSE OF ACTION** the process of deciding on or establishing a course of action (*formal*) ○ *They were entrusted with the determination of future policy.* **5.** **SETTLEMENT OF DISPUTE OR CONTEST** the authoritative settlement of a dispute, especially by a judicial body **6.** **END OF ESTATE, INTEREST, OR RIGHT** the conclusion or termination of an estate,

interest, or right **7.** LOGIC QUALIFYING OF CONCEPT the qualifying of a concept or proposition by defining its attributes **8.** BIOL STAGE IN DEVELOPMENT OF EMBRYONIC TISSUE the stage in the development of embryonic tissue after which it can only develop as one specific type of tissue and no longer has the potential to develop into different types

determinative /di túrminətiv/ adj able to determine something ■ n **1.** a factor that determines something **2.** GRAM same as **determiner** (sense 1)

determine /di túrmin/ (-mines, -mining, -mined) v **1.** vt DECIDE SOMETHING to decide or settle something conclusively **2.** vt FIND OUT SOMETHING to find out or ascertain something, usually after investigation **3.** vt INFLUENCE SOMETHING to influence or form something **4.** vt FIX LIMITS OF SOMETHING to fix the limits or form of something **5.** vti ADOPT PURPOSE to adopt a set purpose, or make somebody do this ○ determined to leave as soon as possible **6.** vti END to end something, or come to an end [14C. Via French < Latin determinare 'set the limits of' < terminus 'limit, boundary']

determined /di túrmind/ adj feeling or showing firmness or a fixed purpose —**determinedly** adv —**determinedness** n

determiner /di túrminər/ n **1.** a word that appears before any descriptive adjective and decides the kind of reference that a noun has, e.g. 'a', 'the', 'this', 'each', 'some', 'either', 'my', and 'your' **2.** somebody or something that determines something

determining /di túrmining/ adj causing or deciding something

determinism /di túrminizəm/ n the doctrine or belief that everything, including every human act, is caused by something and that there is no real free will —**determinist** n —**deterministic** /di túrmi nístik/ adj

deterrent /di térrənt/ n **1.** SOMETHING THAT DETERS something that deters somebody or something **2.** WEAPONS THAT DETER ATTACK weapons, particularly nuclear weapons, held as a retaliatory threat ■ adj ACTING TO DETER capable of deterring somebody or something —**deterrence** n

detest /di tést/ (-tests, -testing, -tested) vt to dislike somebody or something very much [15C. Via French < Latin detestari 'bear witness against, denounce' < testis 'witness'] —**detester** n

detestable /di téstəb'l/ adj causing or deserving intense dislike —**detestability** /di téstə bílləti/ n —**detestably** adv

detestation /déé te stáysh'n/ n **1.** an intense dislike of somebody or something **2.** somebody or something that is detested ○ Apples are a real detestation for him.

dethrone /dee thrón/ (-thrones, -throning, -throned) vt **1.** to remove a ruler, especially a monarch, from power **2.** to remove somebody from a high or powerful position —**dethronement** n —**dethroner** n

detinue /détti nyoo/ n a legal action to reclaim wrongfully withheld personal property [15C. < Old French 'detention' < detenir (see DETAIN)]

detonate /détta nayt/ (-nates, -nating, -nated) vti to explode, or make something explode [Early 18C. < Latin detonat-, past participle of detonare 'thunder down' < tonare 'to thunder'] —**detonative** adj

detonation /détta náysh'n/ n **1.** an explosion, or an act of making something explode **2.** a premature spontaneous burning of a fuel-air mixture inside an internal-combustion engine

detonator /détta naytər/ n a device or small quantity of explosive used to make a bomb or larger quantity of explosive explode

detour /déé toor, day tóór/ n **1.** a deviation from a shorter, more direct route **2.** N Am ROADS same as **diversion** (sense 2) ■ vti (-tours, -touring, -toured) to deviate from a shorter route, or make somebody or something do this [Mid-18C. < French détour < Old French destorner 'turn away' < torner < Latin tornare (see TURN)]

detox /déé toks/ (informal) n **1.** a medical facility in which alcoholics or drug addicts are detoxified **2.** the detoxification of an alcoholic or drug addict ■ vti (-toxes, -toxing, -toxed) MED same as **detoxify** (sense 1) [Late 20C. Shortening of DETOXIFICATION, DETOXIFY]

detoxicate /dee tóksi kayt/ (-cates, -cating, -cated) vt MED same as **detoxify** (sense 1) —**detoxicant** n, adj

detoxification /dee tóksifi káysh'n/, **detoxication** /dee tóksi káysh'n/ n **1.** the process of removing a toxic substance from something or counteracting its toxic effects **2.** the process of subjecting somebody or yourself to withdrawal from a toxic or addictive substance such as alcohol or drugs

detoxify /dee tóksi fí/ (-fies, -fying, -fied) v **1.** vti to subject somebody or yourself to withdrawal from a toxic or addictive substance such as alcohol or drugs **2.** vt to remove a toxic substance from something or counteract its toxic effects [Early 20C. < DE- + TOXIC]

detract /di trákt/ (-tracts, -tracting, -tracted) vi to reduce the quality, value, or importance of something by taking something away from it [15C. < Latin detract-, past participle of detrahere 'take or pull away' < trahere 'pull'] —**detractingly** adv —**detractive** adj —**detractively** adv —**detractory** adj

detraction /di tráksh'n/ n **1.** the act of damaging somebody's reputation, especially by making discrediting comments (formal) **2.** somebody or something that detracts from the quality, value, or importance of something

detractor /di tráktər/ n somebody who disparages or devalues somebody or something

detrain /dee tráyn/ (-trains, -training, -trained) vti to get out of or remove people from a railway train —**detrainment** n

detribalize /dee tríbə līz/ (-izes, -izing, -ized), **detribalise** (-ises, -ising, -ised) vti to abandon tribal practices, usually as a result of exposure to another culture, or make somebody do this —**detribalization** /dee tríbə līẓ záysh'n/ n

detriment /déttrimənt/ n **1.** damage, harm, or disadvantage **2.** something that causes damage, harm, or disadvantage (formal) [15C. Via French < Latin detrimentum < deterere 'wear away' < terere 'rub, wear']

detrimental /déttri mént'l/ adj causing damage, harm, or disadvantage —**detrimentally** adv

detrition /di trísh'n/ n the process of wearing something away by friction [Late 17C. < medieval Latin detrition- < Latin deterere (see DETRIMENT)]

detritivore /di tríta vawr/, **detritovore** n an organism that feeds on decaying animal or plant material. Detritivores such as bacteria, earthworms, and many insects aid in breaking down soil. [Mid-20C. < DETRITUS]

detritus /di trítəss/ n **1.** DEBRIS debris or discarded material **2.** GEOL ROCK FRAGMENTS fragments of rock that have been worn away **3.** ECOL ORGANIC MATTER organic debris formed by the decomposition of plants or animals [Late 18C. < Latin < past participle of deterere (see DETRIMENT)] —**detrital** adj

Detroit /di tróyt/ city in southeastern Michigan, United States, on the Detroit River and Lake St Clair. It is one of the most important car manufacturing centres in the world. Population: 925,051 (2002 estimate).

de trop /də tró/ adj superfluous or excessive (literary) [Mid-18C. < French]

detumescence /déé tyoo méss'nss/ n a gradual reduction in a swelling, especially of a penis [Late 17C. < Latin detumescere 'stop swelling' < tumere 'swell'] —**detumesce** vi —**detumescent** adj

deuce[1] /dyooss/ n **1.** in tennis, badminton, and other racket games, a situation in which a player must score two successive points to win after the score is tied **2.** a playing card with two pips or the face of a die with two spots [15C. Via Old French deus 'two' < Latin duos]

deuce[2] /dyooss/ (dated slang) interj used instead of a swearword to show displeasure, irritation, or surprise ■ n something that is bad or unpleasant [Mid-17C. Via Dutch or Low German duus 'throw of two on two dice' (the lowest score) < Latin duos 'two']

deuced /dyoóssid, dyoost/ (dated slang) adj used instead of a swearword to give emphasis or to show displeasure, irritation, or surprise ■ adv decidedly or extremely —**deucedly** adv

Deus /dáyooss/ n JUD-CHR same as **God** [13C. < Latin]

deus ex machina /dáyooss eks mákinə/ n **1.** an improbable character or unconvincing event used to resolve a plot **2.** in ancient Greek and Roman

theatre, a god introduced to resolve a complicated plot [< modern Latin, 'god from the machinery' (used in Greek theatre to lower actors onto the stage)]

Deut. abbr BIBLE Deuteronomy

deuter- prefix same as **deutero-** (used before vowels)

deuteragonist /dyoóta rággənist/ n a character second in importance to the leading character (**protagonist**) in ancient Greek drama [Mid-19C. < Greek deuteragōnistēs < deuteros 'second' + agōnistēs 'actor' (see PROTAGONIST)]

deuteranopia /dyoótərə nōpi ə/ n colour blindness in which red and green are confused —**deuteranopic** /-nóppik/ adj

deuterate /dyoóta rayt/ (-ates, -ating, -ated) vt to add deuterium to a chemical compound [Mid-20C. < DEUTERIUM] —**deuteration** /dyoóta ráysh'n/ n

deuteride /dyoóta ríd/ n a compound of hydrogen (**hydride**) in which hydrogen has been replaced by its heavier isotope deuterium [Mid-20C. < DEUTERIUM]

deuterium /dyoo teéri əm/ n an isotope of hydrogen that has double the mass of ordinary hydrogen because it contains a neutron in its nucleus. Use: tracer in experiments. Symbol **D** [Mid-20C. < Greek deuteros 'second']

deuterium oxide n CHEM same as **heavy water**

deutero- prefix second, secondary ○ deuterocanonical [< Greek deuteros]

deuterocanonical /dyoótərōkə nónnik'l/ adj relating or belonging to a secondary, less well-regarded, or disputed collection of religious scripture, especially the Apocrypha

deuteron /dyoóta ron/ n the nucleus of a deuterium atom, consisting of one proton and one neutron. It is used mainly as a bombarding particle in particle accelerators such as cyclotrons. Symbol **D**⁺ [Mid-20C. < DEUTERO-, after PROTON]

Deuteronomy /dyoóta rónnəmi/ n a book of the Bible that repeats the Ten Commandments and records much of mosaic law. It is the fifth book of the Pentateuch. See table at **Bible** [14C. Via late Latin < Greek Deuteronomion 'second law'; because the book contains a repetition of the Decalogue and of parts of Exodus] —**Deuteronomic** /dyoótərə nómmik/ adj

deuterostome /dyoótərō stōm/ n an animal whose mouth develops from a second opening in the early embryo, opposite to the initial opening (**blastopore**) of the rudimentary gut. Chordates and echinoderms are deuterostomes.

deutoplasm /dyoóta plazzəm/ n nutrient matter contained in some reproductive cells, e.g. the yolk in a bird's egg —**deutoplasmic** /dyoóta plázmik/ adj

Deutschmark /dóych maark/, **Deutsche Mark** /dóychə-/ n the main unit of the former German currency. Symbol **DM** [Mid-20C. < German, 'German mark' < deutsch 'German' + Mark (see MARK²)]

deutzia /dyoótsi ə/ (plural -as or same) n a bush with clusters of white to pink or lavender flowers. Native to: Asia, Central America. Genus: Deutzia. [Mid-19C. < modern Latin, after Johann van der Deutz, 18C Dutch patron of botany]

deva /dáyvə/ n a Hindu or Buddhist god [Early 19C. < Sanskrit, 'god']

Eamon De Valera

De Valera /dévvə láirə/, **Eamon** (1882–1975) US-born Irish politician. He was a key figure in establishing the Irish Republic. He formed a dissident faction of Sinn Fein, the Fianna Fáil party (1926), was prime

minister (1932–48, 1951–54, and 1957–59), and served as president (1959–73).

'Whenever I wanted to know what the Irish people wanted, I had only to examine my own heart and it told me straight off what the Irish people wanted.'
[Eamon De Valera, *Speech to the Irish Parliament*; 6 January 1922]

devaluate /deé válybo ayt/ (**-ates, -ating, -ated**) ECON same as **devalue** (sense 1)

devalue /dee vállyoo/ (**-ues, -uing, -ued**) *vti* **1.** to lower the value of a nation's currency by government action, or become lowered in value **2.** to cause the value or importance of somebody or something to be reduced, or to become reduced in value or importance —**devaluation** /deé valyoo áysh'n/ *n*

Devanagari /dáyvə naágəri/ *n* the alphabet that is used to write Hindi, Marathi, Nepali, and several languages of northern India, as well as classical Sanskrit [Late 18C. < Sanskrit < *deva* 'god' + *Nāgarī*, earlier name for the script]

devastate /dévvə stayt/ (**-tates, -tating, -tated**) *vt* **1.** to cause severe or widespread damage to something ○ *an area devastated by floods* **2.** to shock or upset somebody greatly (*often passive*) ○ *We were devastated by the news of his death.* [Mid-17C. < Latin *devastat-*, past participle of *devastare* 'lay waste completely' < *vastare* 'lay waste' < *vastus* 'waste'] —**devastation** /dévvə stáysh'n/ *n* —**devastative** *adj* —**devastator** *n*

devastating /dévvə stayting/ *adj* **1.** DAMAGING causing severe or widespread damage ○ *policies that have a devastating effect on economic growth* **2.** VERY UPSETTING causing great shock or upset ○ *The news was devastating.* **3.** SHARPLY CRITICAL containing criticism that is very sharp and very effective or damaging, often as a result of its precise detail or caustic wit **4.** REMARKABLE startlingly impressive or attractive (*informal*) ○ *the devastating speed of her forehand return* —**devastatingly** *adv*

devein /deé váyn/ (**-veins, -veining, -veined**) *vt* to remove the dark thready gut (**vein**) from the back of the tail meat of a prawn

develop /di vélləp/ (**-ops, -oping, -oped**) *v* **1.** *vti* CHANGE AND GROW to change and become larger, stronger, or more impressive, successful, or advanced, or cause somebody or something to change in this way ○ *The business has developed from humble beginnings into a multinational concern.* **2.** *vi* ARISE AND INCREASE to arise and then increase or progress to a more complex state ○ *Tension was developing between the two nations.* **3.** *vt* ADOPT OR ACQUIRE SOMETHING to acquire a feature, habit, or illness that then becomes more marked or extreme ○ *The baby is developing a cold.* **4.** *vt* ENLARGE ON SOMETHING to add details to a basic plan or idea **5.** *vti* PRESENT OR BE REVEALED IN STAGES to present the sequential events or successive stages of a story or argument, or have such events or stages revealed ○ *The theory is developed at length in her new book.* **6.** *vt* USE RESOURCES FOR HUMAN PURPOSES to use or make available land, minerals, or other natural resources for human purposes such as housing **7.** *vt* BUILD STRUCTURES to plan and construct buildings, roads, or other technological structures ○ *develop a global communications system* **8.** *vt* TURN FILM INTO NEGATIVES OR PRINTS to treat photographic film with chemicals in order to produce a negative or print (*often passive*) ○ *Send the films off to be developed.* **9.** *vi* ACHIEVE SEXUAL MATURITY to become sexually mature **10.** *vt* CHESS BRING PIECE INTO PLAY to bring a chess piece into play **11.** *vt* MUSIC VARY MUSICAL THEME to add to a musical theme by using variation or ornamentation, especially by breaking it down into motifs and using other musical techniques [Mid-17C. < French *développer* 'unwrap' < Old French *voloper* 'wrap'] —**developable** *adj*

~~develope~~ incorrect spelling of **develop**

developed /di vélləpt/ *adj* wealthy and technologically advanced, with sophisticated manufacturing and service industries

~~developement~~ incorrect spelling of **development**

developer /di vélləpər/ *n* **1.** SOMEBODY WHO DEVELOPS somebody or something that develops something ○ *the developer of a new manufacturing process* **2.** BUYER OF LAND FOR BUILDING a person or company that buys land in order to build on it or sell it to others who want to build on it **3.** PHOTOGRAPHY CHEMICAL FOR MAKING NEGATIVES OR PRINTS a chemical used to turn exposed film into negatives or prints

developing /di vélləping/ *adj* using or involving small-scale agriculture and industry of the kind that characterized the earlier economic stages of technologically advanced nations

developing agent *n* PHOTOGRAPHY same as **developer** (sense 3)

development /di vélləpmənt/ *n* **1.** EVENT CAUSING CHANGE an incident that causes a situation to change or progress (*often used in the plural*) ○ *Have there been any political developments since last week?* **2.** PROCESS OF CHANGE the process of changing and becoming larger, stronger, or more impressive, successful, or advanced, or of causing somebody or something to change in this way ○ *sustained economic development* **3.** INCOMPLETE STATE a state in which the developing of something is not yet completed ○ *The prototype is in development.* **4.** GROUP OF BUILDINGS a group of buildings of the same kind that are built as a single construction project **5.** MUSIC VARIATION OF MUSICAL THEME the process of varying and ornamenting a musical theme **6.** MUSIC MUSICAL SECTION WHERE THEME IS DEVELOPED one of the three main sections of the sonata form, in which the musical themes presented in the exposition are rhythmically and melodically elaborated **7.** CHESS BRINGING OF PIECE INTO PLAY the bringing of a chess piece into play —**developmental** /di vélləp mént'l/ *adj* —**developmentally** *adv*

developmental psychology *n* the branch of psychology that deals with the ways that personality, cognitive ability, and behaviour change during somebody's life span, with particular concentration on childhood development

development area *n* an area of high unemployment that receives government money to help develop new industry there

développé /dáyvvəllə pay, di véll ə-/ *n* a ballet movement in which the foot of one leg is drawn up to the knee of the other and then extended slowly out into the air [Early 20C. < French, past participle of *développer* (see DEVELOP)]

deverbative /dee vúrbətiv/, **deverbal** /dee vúrb'l/ *adj* derived from a verb, e.g. as the noun 'driver' is derived from the verb 'drive', and the adjective 'clingy' from the verb 'cling' [Early 20C. After DENOMINATIVE]

Devi /dáyvi/ *n* the supreme Hindu goddess, wife of the god Shiva, manifested in the different forms and characters of Durga, Kali, Parvati, and Sati [Late 20C. < Sanskrit, 'goddess']

deviance /deévi ənss/, **deviancy** /-ənssi/ *n* behaviour that is sharply different from a customary, traditional, or generally accepted standard

deviant /deévi ənt/ *adj* diverging sharply from a customary, traditional, or generally accepted standard, or displaying such divergent behaviour ○ *abstract paintings, once thought deviant, now worth millions* ■ *n* an offensive term for somebody whose behaviour is different from a customary, traditional, or generally accepted standard [14C. < late Latin *deviant-*, present participle of *deviare* (see DEVIATE)]

deviate *vi* /deévi ayt/ (**-ates, -ating, -ated**) **1.** to be different or behave differently **2.** to turn off from a course or path ■ *adj* /deévi ət/ PSYCHOL same as **deviant** ■ *n* /deévi ət/ PSYCHOL same as **deviant** [Mid-17C. < late Latin *deviat-*, past participle of *deviare* 'depart from the way' < Latin *via* 'way, road'] —**deviator** *n* —**deviatory** *adj*

deviation /deévi áysh'n/ *n* **1.** CHANGE OR DIFFERENCE a change or difference from what is usual, accepted, expected, or planned ○ *These rituals represented a deviation from established practices.* **2.** PSYCHOL UNACCEPTABLE BEHAVIOUR OR ATTITUDE behaviour or an attitude that is sharply different from a customary, traditional, or generally accepted standard **3.** STATS DIFFERENCE FROM STATISTICAL AVERAGE the difference between any individual value and a fixed value such as the average of all the other values in its series **4.** NAVIG COMPASS ERROR an error in a compass reading caused by local magnetic fields, especially on a ship at sea

deviationism /deévi áysh'nizəm/ *n* departure from accepted or established political views, especially from orthodox communism —**deviationist** *n, adj*

device /di víss/ *n* **1.** TOOL OR MACHINE a tool or machine designed to perform a particular task or function **2.** PLOY a way of achieving something, especially a clever or dishonest way **3.** EXPLOSIVE OBJECT a bomb or something that causes an explosion or fire **4.** LITERARY OR DRAMATIC TOOL something designed to create a particular effect in a literary or dramatic work, or to evoke a particular response from a reader, listener, or viewer ○ *a familiar cinematic device* **5.** EMBLEM OR MOTTO an emblem or motto, or a combination of the two, especially when used in heraldry ○ *a heraldic device* **6.** ORNAMENTAL DESIGN an ornamental pattern or design, e.g. in embroidery [13C. < Old French *devis* 'division, contrivance', *devise* 'plan' < Latin *dividere* (see DIVIDE)] ◇ **leave somebody to his** *or* **her own devices** to let somebody do as he or she wishes, instead of giving the person direction or assistance

~~devide~~ incorrect spelling of **divide**

devil /dévv'l/ *n* **1.** *also* **Devil** GOD'S ENEMY in Christianity and some other religions, the enemy of God, who rules Hell, tempts people to sin, and personifies the spirit of evil as Satan **2.** EVIL SPIRIT an evil spirit, particularly a subordinate of Satan **3.** OFFENSIVE TERM somebody who is regarded as evil, unpleasant, or violent (*insult*) **4.** MISCHIEVOUS PERSON OR ANIMAL a mischievous, troublesome, or high-spirited person or animal **5.** PERSON OR ANIMAL a person or animal of the sort described ○ *You lucky devil!* **6.** NAME FOR TOOL a name given to various tools or machines, especially ones that cut or tear **7.** METEOROL same as **dust devil** **8.** DIFFICULT OR UNPLEASANT CASE an extremely difficult or unpleasant instance of something (*informal*) **9.** INTENSIFIER used as an intensifier in questions and exclamations (*informal*) ○ *Who the devil does he think he is?* **10.** PRINTING same as **printer's devil** (*archaic*) **11.** JUNIOR BARRISTER somebody who works as an assistant for a barrister in order to gain experience (*archaic informal*) ■ *vt* (**-ils, -illing, -illed**) **1.** MAKE FOOD SPICY to cook or prepare a food with spicy seasonings **2.** *N Am* PESTER SOMEBODY to annoy, worry, or pester somebody, especially by making repeated requests for something (*informal*) ○ *He's been devilling me with requests for an interview.* [Old English *dēofol*, via Latin *diabolus* < Greek *diabolos* 'devil, Satan'] ◇ **between the devil and the deep blue sea** faced with two equally undesirable choices ◇ **the devil is in the details** although a plan or project sounds good in theory, implementation of it may be difficult because of complexities inherent in it ○ *Although the initial marketing strategy is impressive, the devil is in the details.*

devilfish /dévv'l fish/ (*plural same or* **-fishes**) *n* a fish that is thought to have an evil or frightening appearance, e.g. a manta ray or octopus

devilish /dévv'lish/ *adj* **1.** SINISTER OR CRUEL sinister, cruel, or evil in a way that is considered like or worthy of the devil ○ *some devilish scheme to get what they want* **2.** MISCHIEVOUS full of or indicating mischievousness ○ *a devilish grin* **3.** GREAT extremely great or intense (*informal*) ○ *the devilish midday heat* ■ *adv* VERY extremely (*dated informal*) —**devilishly** *adv* —**devilishness** *n*

devil-may-care *adj* **1.** foolishly lighthearted about risk or danger **2.** tending to enjoy the present and not think or worry about the future

devilment /dévv'lmənt/ *n* troublesome, mischievous, or devilish behaviour ○ *always getting up to some devilment or other*

devilry /dévv'lri/ (*plural* **-ries**) *n* **1.** cruel or evil behaviour or actions **2.** evil act or acts supposedly performed by calling on the powers of the devil or evil spirits

devil's advocate *n* **1.** somebody who argues about something merely to provoke discussion **2.** a Roman Catholic official appointed to argue against the canonization or beatification of a candidate

devil's coach-horse *n* a large fierce black beetle with long jaws. Family: Staphylinidae. [< the rearing and defiant attitude that it assumes when disturbed]

devil's darning needle *n* INSECTS same as **damselfly** (*informal*) [< its long thin body]

devil's food cake *n* a rich dark chocolate cake [< the contrast with the paleness of ANGEL FOOD CAKE]

zh vision. In foreign words: kh German Bach; aN French vin; aaN French blanc; ö German schön, French feu; oN French bon; öN French un; ü as in French rue. Stress marks: ´ as in secret /seékrət/, academic /ákə démmik/

Devil's Island /dévv'lz-/ rocky islet off the coast of French Guiana in the Atlantic Ocean. It was used as a penal colony from 1852 to 1946.

Devil's Marbles mound of granite boulders and sacred Aboriginal site in central Australia, near Tennant Creek in the Northern Territory. The boulders are about 1,500 million years old.

devious /deévi əss/ *adj* **1.** SECRETIVE AND CALCULATING not straightforward, sincere, or honest about intentions or motives **2.** UNFAIR OR UNDERHAND not adhering to the right or usual course, procedures, or standards **3.** RAMBLING circuitous and roundabout, usually changing direction many times ○ *got here by a devious route* [Late 16C. < Latin *devius* 'out of the way' < *via* 'way, road'] —**deviously** *adv* —**deviousness** *n*

devisal /di víz'l/ *n* **1.** the inventing or contriving of something **2.** the handing down of property through a will

devise /di víz/ *vt* (**-vises, -vising, -vised**) **1.** THINK SOMETHING UP to conceive of the idea for something and work out how to make it or put it into practice **2.** PASS ON PROPERTY to pass on property through a will ■ *n* **1.** CLAUSE BEQUEATHING PROPERTY a clause in a will stating that an item of property is to be given to somebody or something **2.** LAW BEQUEATHING OF PROPERTY the bequeathing of an item of property **3.** LAW SOMETHING BEQUEATHED an item of property bequeathed through a will [13C. < French *deviser* 'divide, order, form a plan' < Latin *dividere* (see DIVIDE)] —**devisable** *adj* —**deviser** *n*

devisee /di vī zeé/ *n* somebody to whom property has been bequeathed in a will

devisor /di vízər/ *n* somebody who bequeaths property in a will [15C. < Anglo-Norman *devisour*, Old French *deviseor* < Old French *deviser* (see DEVISE)]

devitalize /dee vítə līz/ (**-izes, -izing, -ized**), **devitalise** (**-ises, -ising, -ised**) *vt* to deprive something of its strength or vigour —**devitalization** /dee vítə lī záysh'n/ *n*

devitrify /dee vítri fī/ (**-fies, -fying, -fied**) *vti* to change from a glassy to a crystalline state and become brittle and opaque, or cause a material to do this —**devitrification** /deé vitrifi káysh'n/ *n*

Devizes /di vízіz/ market town in Wiltshire, southern England. Population: 13,205 (1991).

devocalize /dee vṓkə līz/ (**-izes, -izing, -ized**), **devocalise** (**-ises, -ising, -ised**) *vt* PHON same as **devoice** —**devocalization** /deévōkə lī záysh'n/ *n*

devoice /dee vóyss/ (**-voices, -voicing, -voiced**) *vt* to pronounce a usually voiced speech sound without vibration of the vocal cords

devoid /di vóyd/ *adj* completely lacking in something ○ *a house devoid of charm* [14C. < past participle of obsolete *devoid* 'remove, vacate' < Old French *devoidier* 'empty out' < *vuidier* 'to empty' < Latin *vacare* 'be empty']

devoirs /də vwaá/ *npl* expressions or acts of courtesy and respect (*archaic or literary*) [15C. < Old French *deveir* 'owe' < Latin *debere*]

devolatilize /dee vóllətə līz/ (**-izes, -izing, -ized**), **devolatilise** (**-ises, -ising, -ised**) *vt* to remove volatile material from a substance, usually by means of heat or a vacuum and sometimes by both —**devolatilization** /dee vóllətə lī záysh'n/ *n*

devolution /deévə lóosh'n/ *n* **1.** DELEGATION OF POWER the transfer of power from a central to a subordinate level or organization, particularly from a central government to regional or local governments **2.** DELEGATING OF RESPONSIBILITIES the delegation of responsibilities from a superior to a subordinate, deputy, or substitute **3.** INHERITANCE OF PRIVILEGES the transfer or inheritance of authority, rights, or property, e.g. from a monarch to his or her successors **4.** BIOL same as **degeneration** (sense 3) [15C. < late Latin *devolution-* < Latin *devolvere* (see DEVOLVE)] —**devolutionary** *adj*

devolutionist /deévə lóosh'nist/ *n* somebody who favours transferring power from a central government to smaller political units —**devolutionist** *adj*

devolve /di vólv/ (**-volves, -volving, -volved**) *v* **1.** *vti* TRANSFER OR BE TRANSFERRED TO ANOTHER to transfer power, responsibility, or rights to somebody or something, e.g. from a central government to a regional government, or be transferred in this way ○ *the government's pledge to devolve powers to local communities* **2.** *vi* BECOME SOMEBODY ELSE'S OBLIGATION to become the duty or responsibility of somebody else ○ *Many child-care responsibilities have devolved on husbands.* **3.** *vi* RELY OR DEPEND to be decided by something or depend on something for its validity (*formal*) ○ *Their case devolved on witnesses' willingness to testify.* **4.** *vi* LAW BE GIVEN OR BEQUEATHED to be given to somebody under the terms of a will or other legal instruction [15C. < Latin *devolvere* 'roll down' < *volvere* 'roll'] —**devolvement** *n*

USAGE devolve on or **to?** The traditional distinction is that powers, authority, etc. ***devolve*** or are ***devolved on*** (or ***upon***) somebody, whereas a right or benefit ***devolves to*** somebody. However, this is not widely observed in current usage. The two constructions are used more or less interchangeably, though the use of *to* is somewhat more common: *The point of devolving power to provincial assemblies ... was to give these provinces some control over their own affairs* (*Economist*). *On* or *upon* is used when the right or authority is regarded as a kind of inheritance (actually or figuratively): *In 1912 the leadership of the expedition's remnant at Cape Evans devolved upon Atkinson, the sole remaining officer* (*Dictionary of National Biography*).

devon /dévv'n/ *n Aus* a bland processed meat in the form of a large sausage, usually sold in slices [Mid-19C. Probably < *Devon*, breed of cattle, after DEVON]

Devon /dévv'n/ county in southwestern England, bordered on the north by the Bristol Channel and on the south by the English Channel. It is a popular holiday area. Population: 704,493 (2001). Area: 6,711 sq. km/2,591 sq. mi.

Devonian /de vṓni ən/ *n* **1.** SOMEBODY FROM DEVON somebody who comes from the county of Devon **2.** GEOLOGICAL PERIOD the geological period, 410 million to 360 million years ago, during which amphibians first appeared and fish became abundant. See table at **geological time** ■ *adj* **1.** BELONGING TO GEOLOGICAL PERIOD relating to the Devonian period of geological time **2.** CHARACTERISTIC OF DEVON relating to Devon, or its people or culture [Early 17C. < medieval Latin *Devonia* < Old English *Defenascīr* 'Devonshire', former name of DEVON]

Devonport /dévv'n pawrt/ city on the northern coast of Tasmania, Australia. It is a busy cargo and ferry port. Population: 24,207 (2002 estimate).

Devonshire cream /dévv'nshər-/ *n* FOOD same as **clotted cream** [Because a speciality of DEVON, formerly *Devonshire*]

devoré /də váw ray/, **dévoré** *n* **1.** the use of a chemical paste to create patterns in fabrics such as velvet by dissolving the natural fibres and revealing the synthetic warp and weft threads **2.** fabric created using the devoré technique [< French, past participle of *dévorer* (see DEVOUR)]

devote /di vṓt/ (**-votes, -voting, -voted**) *vt* to commit yourself to, or allot or use something for, a particular activity, aim, or purpose ○ *She devoted her whole life to the cause.* [Late 16C. < Latin *devot-*, past participle of *devovere* 'dedicate by a vow' < *vovere* 'to vow']

devoted /di vṓtid/ *adj* **1.** feeling or showing great love, commitment, or loyalty to somebody or something, especially over a long period of time **2.** feeling or showing great dedication to something —**devotedly** *adv* —**devotedness** *n*

devotee /dévvō teé/ *n* **1.** a very keen enthusiast or follower of something **2.** a dedicated member of a religious or spiritual group

devotion /di vṓsh'n/ *n* **1.** COMMITTED LOVE deep love and commitment **2.** DEDICATION great dedication and loyalty **3.** ENTHUSIASM strong enthusiasm and admiration for somebody or something **4.** RELIGIOUS FERVOUR fervent religious or spiritual feeling **5.** ACT OF DEVOTING the act of devoting something or being devoted to a particular purpose ■ **devotions** *npl* PRAYERS prayers or other religious observances, especially somebody's private prayers or observances —**devotional** *adj*

devour /di vów ər/ (**-vours, -vouring, -voured**) *vt* **1.** EAT SOMETHING QUICKLY to eat something quickly and hungrily ○ *They devour in minutes what it's taken you all afternoon to prepare.* **2.** TAKE SOMETHING IN EAGERLY to read, look at, watch, or listen to something eagerly ○ *Young children seem to devour her stories.* **3.** DESTROY SOMETHING to destroy something rapidly and completely (*literary*; *often passive*) ○ *a house devoured by the flames* **4.** WASTE SOMETHING to use up something unwisely or wastefully (*literary*) **5.** OVERWHELM SOMEBODY to become an overwhelming and destructive passion or obsession for somebody (*literary*; *usually passive*) ○ *was devoured by jealousy* [14C. Via Old French *devour-*, stressed stem of *devorer* < Latin *devorare* 'swallow down' < *vorare* 'swallow'] —**devourer** *n* —**devouring** *adj* —**devouringly** *adv*

devout /di vówt/ *adj* **1.** VERY RELIGIOUS deeply religious **2.** DEVOTED TO SOMETHING devoted to a particular personal interest or cause ○ *a devout sports fan* **3.** VERY SINCERE deeply and sincerely felt or meant (*formal*) [12C. Via French < Latin *devotus*, past participle of *devovere* (see DEVOTE)] —**devoutly** *adv* —**devoutness** *n*

De Vries /də vreéss/, **Hugo** (1848–1935) Dutch botanist and geneticist. He independently discovered the laws of heredity and introduced the theory of mutation in plant evolution. Full name **De Vries, Hugo Marie**

dew /dyoo/ *n* **1.** WATER DROPLETS ON COOL OUTDOOR SURFACES moisture from the air that has condensed as tiny drops on outdoor objects and surfaces that have cooled, especially during the night **2.** SMALL DROPS drops of moisture of any kind, e.g. tears or sweat (*literary*) **3.** FRESHNESS AND PURITY a fresh and pure or refreshing quality in something (*literary*) ■ **dews** *npl* DEWDROPS drops of dew (*literary*) ■ *vt* (**dews, dewing, dewed**) COAT SOMETHING WITH DEW to coat or moisten something with drops of dew (*literary*) [Old English *dēaw* < Germanic]

SPELLCHECK dew or **due?** Do not confuse the spelling of ***dew*** and ***due***, which sound similar. ***Dew*** is chiefly used as a noun, denoting droplets of moisture, as in *the morning dew on the grass*. ***Due*** is used as an adjective, meaning 'expected', 'ready', 'appropriate', or 'owed' (as in *due for promotion, after due consideration*), or as a noun denoting something due (as in *give him his due, pay your dues*).

dewan *n* POL another spelling of **diwan**

Dewar /dyóo ər/, **Donald** (1937–2000) Scottish politician and first First Minister of Scotland (1999–2000). A member of parliament for the Labour party since 1966, he served as shadow Scottish Secretary (1983–92) before overseeing the Scottish devolution process as secretary of state for Scotland (1997–99). Full name **Dewar, Donald Campbell**

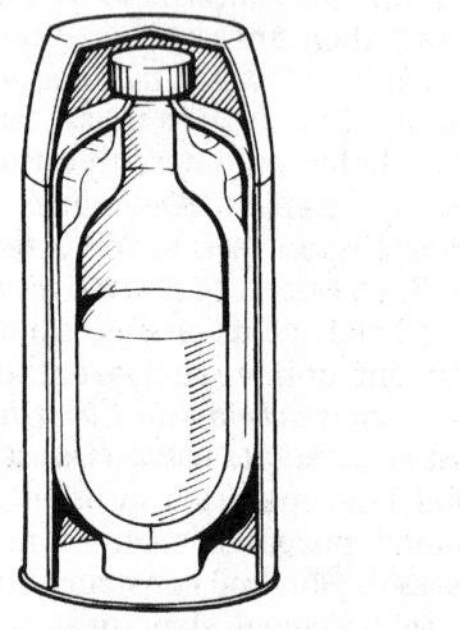

Dewar flask

Dewar flask /dyóo ər-/, **Dewar vacuum flask** *n* a double-walled silvered glass or metal flask with a vacuum between the walls, providing thermal insulation. It is frequently used to store liquefied gases. [Mid-20C. After Sir James *Dewar* (1824–1923), British physicist and chemist]

dewater /dee wáwtər/ (**-ters, -tering, -tered**) *vt* to remove water from a substance, especially sewage or crude oil, or from a place

dewberry /dyóobəri/ (*plural* **-ries**) *n* **1.** an edible bluish-black blackberry **2.** a variety of the bramble with trailing stems and bluish-black fruit. Genus: *Rubus*.

dewclaw /dyóo klaw/ *n* a functionless shorter digit or claw on the foot of a dog or other mammal [Late 16C. Origin ?] —**dewclawed** *adj*

dewdrop /dyóo drop/ *n* **1.** a drop of water that has condensed on a cool outdoor surface **2.** a drop of mucus hanging from somebody's nostril (*informal*; *euphemistic*)

De Wet /də vét/, **Christiaan** (1854–1922) South African

general and politician. He was a guerrilla leader in both Anglo-Boer Wars (1880–81,1899–1902) and helped form the National Party in South Africa (1912–13). Full name **De Wet, Christiaan Rudolph**

Dewey /dyoo i/, **John** (1859–1952) US philosopher, psychologist, and educator. He developed the philosophy of pragmatism and was a leading educational theorist.

> 'In the traditional method the child must say something that he has merely learned. There is all the difference in the world between having something to say, and having to say something.'
> [John Dewey, *Dewey on Education*; 1959]

Dewey, Melvil (1851–1931) US librarian and educator. He formulated the Dewey decimal system (1876), which revolutionized the way books were catalogued.

Dewey decimal system, Dewey decimal classification *n* a system of classifying library books that divides them into ten main classes, divided in turn into categories with three-digit numbers and subcategories with numbers after a decimal point [After Melvil DEWEY]

dewfall /dyoo fawl/ *n* **1.** the formation of dew, or the time when dew begins to form **2.** the amount of dew that has condensed on objects and surfaces

de Wint /də wint/, **Peter** (1784–1849) British painter. His watercolour landscapes and architectural and genre studies recorded contemporary life in eastern England.

De Witt /də wit/, **Jan** (1625–72) Dutch politician. The chief minister of the Netherlands (1653–72) and a leading republican, he secured Dutch victory in the Second Anglo-Dutch War (1664–67).

dewlap /dyoo lap/ *n* **1.** a loose fold of skin hanging from the neck of some animals such as cows **2.** a loose fold of skin on somebody's throat, often forming later in life [14C. < obsolete *dew*, origin ? + LAP[1] 'loose piece'] —**dewlapped** *adj*

DEW line /dyoo-/ *n* a line of radar stations across the Arctic regions of North America, designed to give early warning of approaching enemy aircraft and missiles [Acronym < *distant early warning*]

deworm /dee wúrm/ (-**worms, -worming, -wormed**) *vt* to cure an animal of an infestation of worms —**dewormer** *n*

dew point *n* the temperature at which the air cannot hold all the moisture in it and dew begins to form. If objects and surfaces have cooled to below freezing point when the moisture in the air begins to condense, frost is formed instead.

dew pond *n* a small shallow pond on high ground that is regularly refreshed by heavy rainfall and condensing fog

dew worm *n N Am* a common earthworm used as fishing bait

dewy /dyoo i/ (-**ier, -iest**) *adj* **1.** COVERED WITH DEW covered with dew or characterized by the presence of dew **2.** MOIST moist or moist-looking **3.** LIKE DEW like dew, especially in having a fresh, pure, or refreshing quality (*literary*) —**dewily** *adv* —**dewiness** *n*

dewy-eyed *adj* childishly innocent, inexperienced, or trusting ○ *full of dewy-eyed optimism*

dex /deks/ *n* dexamphetamine, or a tablet containing it (*slang*) [Mid-20C. Shortening]

dexamethasone /déksə méthəsōn/ *n* a synthetic steroid. Use: treatment of inflammatory conditions and hormonal imbalances. [Mid-20C. < *dexa*- (blend of HEXA- + DECA-) + -*methasone*, INN stem]

dexamfetamine /déksam féttə meen/ *n* PHARM same as **dexamphetamine** (*technical*)

dexamphetamine /déksam féttə meen/ *n* a form of amphetamine. Use: stimulant, antidepressant. N Am term **dextroamphetamine**

dexie /déksi/ *n* a tablet containing dexamphetamine (*slang*) [Mid-20C. Shortening]

dexiotropic /déksi ō trópik/ *adj* describes the cleavage of a fertilized egg in which the newly dividing cells form a pattern that spirals to the right when viewed from above [Late 19C. < Greek *dexios* 'on the right side']

dexter /dékstər/ *adj* placed on the right-hand side of

a coat of arms, that is, on the left from the point of view of somebody looking at it (*technical; usually used after nouns*) [Mid-16C. < Latin, 'on the right']

dexterity /dek stérrəti/ *n* **1.** ease and skill in physical movement, especially in using the hands and manipulating objects ○ *manual dexterity* **2.** sharpness or quickness of mind

dexterous /dékstərəss/, **dextrous** /dékstrəss/ *adj* **1.** characterized by ease and skill in physical movement, especially in using the hands and manipulating objects **2.** mentally sharp or quick [Early 17C. < Latin *dexter* 'skilful, on the right'] —**dexterously** *adv* —**dexterousness** *n*

dextr- *prefix* same as **dextro-** (*used before vowels*)

dextral /dékstrəl/ *adj* (*technical*) **1.** on or relating to the right-hand side, especially of the body **2.** same as **right-handed** *adj* (sense 1) **3.** describes the clockwise spiralling of the shell of an invertebrate sea animal [Mid-17C. < medieval Latin *dextralis* < Latin *dextra* 'right hand' < *dexter* 'on the right'] —**dextrality** /dek strálləti/ *n* —**dextrally** *adv*

dextran /dékstrən/ *n* a branched polysaccharide produced by the action of bacteria on sucrose. Use: blood plasma substitute, food additive. [Late 19C. < DEXTRO- + -AN[2]]

dextrin /dékstrin/, **dextrine** /-streen, -strin/ *n* a product that is an intermediate in the formation of maltose. Source: heating of starch. Use: adhesive, size, in syrups and beers. Formula: $(C_6H_{10}O_5)_n$. [Mid-19C. < DEXTRO-]

dextro /dékstrō/ *adj* CHEM same as **dextrorotatory** [Early 20C. Shortening]

dextro- *prefix* **1.** right, on the right ○ *dextrocardia* **2.** dextrorotatory ○ *dextroglucose* [< Latin *dexter* 'on the right']

dextroamphetamine /dékstrō am féttə meen/, **dextroamfetamine** *technical n N Am* PHARM same as **dexamphetamine**

dextrocardia /dékstrō kaárdi ə/ *n* a medical condition in which the heart inclines to the right side of the centre of the chest instead of the left, often with a similar reversal of all abdominal organs

dextroglucose *n* BIOCHEM same as **dextrose**

dextrorotary *adj* CHEM same as **dextrorotatory**

dextrorotation /dékstrō rō táysh'n/ *n* a rotation to the right or clockwise, particularly of the plane of polarization of light passing through a crystal or solution. Substances that cause dextrorotation are said to be optically active.

dextrorotatory /dékstrō rō táytəri/, **dextrorotary** /-rōtəri/ *adj* rotating the plane of polarization of light passing through it to the right or clockwise

dextrose /dékstrōz/ *n* a sugar produced during cellular metabolism in plant and animal tissue. It is found in many fruits, especially grapes, and is a major component of honey.

dextrous *adj* same as **dexterous**

dey /day/ (*plural* **deys**) *n* **1.** the governor of Algiers under the Ottoman Empire **2.** a title sometimes used for ruling officials in Tunis and Tripoli in North Africa under the Ottoman Empire [Mid-17C. Via French < Turkish *dayi* 'maternal uncle', also a courtesy title]

DF *abbr* **1.** HIST Defender of the Faith **2.** TELECOM direction finder

D/F *abbr* TELECOM direction finder

DFC *abbr* MIL Distinguished Flying Cross

DfES *abbr* GOV Department for Education and Skills

DfID /dífid/ *abbr* GOV Department for International Development

DFM (*plural* **DFMs**) *n* a medal awarded to members of the RAF below officer rank for bravery while flying but not in combat. Full form **Distinguished Flying Medal**

DfT *abbr* GOV Department for Transport

dg *symbol* MEASURE decigram

DG *abbr* **1.** CHR Deo gratias **2.** director-general

DH *abbr* **1.** GOV Department of Health **2.** *US* BASEBALL designated hitter

DHA[1] *n* a polyunsaturated essential fatty acid found in cold-water fish and some algae that has been

linked to the reduction of cardiovascular disease and other health benefits. Full form **docosahexaenoic acid**

DHA[2] *abbr* District Health Authority

dhaba /daábə/ *n S Asia* a roadside stall where food is sold [< Hindi]

Dhaka /dákə/, **Dacca** capital and largest city of Bangladesh. It is situated in the centre of the country, on the Buriganga, one of the tributary rivers of the Ganges delta. Population: 3,368,940 (1991).

dhal /daal/, **dal** *n* a thick stew made from lentils, onions, and spices, originating in South Asia [Late 17C. < Hindi *dāl*]

dhansak /dún saak, dán-/ *n* a curry made from meat or vegetables mixed with lentils, originating in South Asia [Late 20C. < Gujarati]

dharma /daármə/ *n* **1.** in Hinduism, somebody's duty to behave according to strict religious and social codes, or the righteousness earned by performing religious and social duties **2.** in Buddhism, the truth about the way things are and will always be in the universe or in nature, especially when contained in scripture [Late 18C. < Sanskrit, 'something established, decree, custom'] —**dharmic** *adj*

dharmashala /daármə shaálə/ (*plural* -**las**), **dharmsala** /-saálə/ *n* in South Asia, a building that has a religious or charitable purpose, often used as a place where travellers may rest without payment [Early 19C. < Sanskrit *dharmaśālā* 'virtue house']

dharna /daárnə/, **dhurna** /dúrnə/ *n* in parts of South Asia, the practice of protesting against an injustice by sitting and fasting outside the door of the offender [Late 18C. < Hindi, 'placing, act of sitting in restraint']

Dharuk /dúrrŏŏk/ (*plural same* or -**uks**) *n* **1.** a member of an Australian Aboriginal people that formerly inhabited the area around present-day Sydney **2.** the language of the Dharuk people, now extinct [Probably < an Aboriginal language] —**Dharuk** *adj*

Dhaulagiri /dówlə geéri/ one of the world's highest mountains. It is situated in the Himalayan range in northern Nepal. Height: 8,172 m/26,811 ft.

dhobi /dóbi/ *n* in South Asia, some other parts of Asia, and East Africa, somebody who washes laundry [Mid-19C. < Hindi < *dhob* 'washing']

dhobi itch *n UK* a fungal infection of the skin in the groin area, especially in men in the tropics. Technical name **tinea cruris**. ANZ, N Am term **jock itch**

dhobiwallah /dóbi wolə/ *n S Asia* same as **dhobi**

dhol /dōl/ *n* a large, barrel-shaped, often double-ended drum used in South Asian music [Mid-19C. < Hindi *dhol*]

dholak /dólək/ *n* a small barrel-shaped drum used in South Asian music [Mid-19C. < Hindi *dholak*]

dhole /dōl/ *n* a wild dog with a reddish coat and bushy tail that hunts large animals in packs. Native to: South Asia. Latin name: *Cuon alpinus*. [Early 19C. Probably < Kannada *tōla* 'wolf']

dhoney /dóni/ (*plural* -**neys**) *n* a small sailing boat formerly used in South Asia [Late 16C. < Telugu *doni*, or < Kannada]

dhoti /dóti/, **dhootie** /dóoti/, **dhotie** /dóti/, **dhuti** /dóoti/ *n* **1.** a loincloth worn by some Hindu men **2.** the cotton cloth used to make the loincloths worn by some Hindu men [Early 17C. < Hindi]

dhow

dhow /dow/ *n* a low-sided ship with one or two masts and triangular curving sails, used by Arab sailors in the Indian Ocean. See illustration on previous page [Late 18C. Probably < Persian]

Dhu al-Hijjah /dŏŏ əl híjjaa/ *n* in the Islamic calendar, the 12th month of the year, during which the holiday of Yom Arafat is celebrated. See table at **calendar** [Late 18C. < Arabic, 'the one of the pilgrimage']

Dhu al-Qa'dah /dŏŏ əl ka̓a daa/ *n* in the Islamic calendar, the 11th month of the year. See table at **calendar** [Late 18C. < Arabic, 'the one of the sitting']

Dhurga /dúrgə/ *n* an Australian Aboriginal language of New South Wales, now extinct or almost extinct [Mid-20C. < Dhurga] —**Dhurga** *adj*

dhurna *n* another spelling of **dharna**

dhurrie /dúrri/, **durrie** *n* **1.** a flat-woven cotton rug made in South Asia **2.** a heavy woven cotton rug, traditionally from India [Late 19C. < Hindi *darī*]

dhuti *n* CLOTHING, TEXTILES another spelling of **dhoti**

Dhuwal-Dhuwala *n* an Australian Aboriginal language spoken in eastern Arnhem Land. Native speakers: 1,390.

di-[1] *prefix* **1.** two, twice, double ○ *dicephalous* **2.** containing two atoms, radicals, or groups ○ *dimethyl* [< Greek. < Indo-European 'two']

di-[2] *prefix* same as **dia-** (*used before vowels*)

dia. *abbr* diameter

dia- *prefix* through, across ○ *diachronic* ○ *diadromous* [< Greek *dia*]

diabase /dī̓ə bayss/ *n* US GEOL same as **dolerite** [Mid-19C. < French] —**diabasic** /dī̓ə báyssik/ *adj*

Diabesity /dī̓ə beė̓ səti/ *tdmk US* a trademark for diabetes caused by obesity

diabetes /dī̓ə beė̓ teez/ *n* a medical disorder, especially diabetes mellitus, that causes the body to produce an excessive amount of urine [Mid-16C. Via Latin < Greek, 'passer through, siphon' < *diabainein* 'go through']

diabetes insipidus /-in síppidəss/ *n* a disorder of the pituitary gland that causes the body to produce large amounts of urine [< modern Latin, 'bland diabetes']

diabetes mellitus /-mə lítəss/ *n* a disorder in which there is no control of blood sugar, through inadequate insulin production (**Type 1**) or decreased sensitivity to insulin (**Type 2**), causing kidney, eye, and nerve damage. Type 1 usually develops in childhood and requires lifelong injection of insulin, while Type 2 typically develops in middle age and can usually be controlled by diet and drugs. [< modern Latin, 'honey-sweet diabetes']

diabetic /dī̓ə béttik/ *adj* **1.** HAVING DIABETES having diabetes, especially diabetes mellitus **2.** RELATING TO DIABETES relating to or caused by diabetes, especially diabetes mellitus ○ *diabetic symptoms* **3.** INTENDED FOR SOMEBODY WITH DIABETES made without sugar and therefore suitable for somebody who has diabetes mellitus ■ *n* SOMEBODY WITH DIABETES somebody who has diabetes, especially diabetes mellitus

diablerie /di a̓ablə ri/ *n* **1.** witchcraft or magic **2.** stories, traditions, and practices associated with magic or devil worship **3.** same as **mischief** (*literary*) [Mid-18C. < French < *diable* 'devil' < Latin *diabolus* (see DEVIL)]

diabolical /dī̓ə bóllik'l/ *adj* **1.** *also* **diabolic** OF DEVIL connected with the devil or devil worship **2.** *also* **diabolic** EVIL extremely cruel or evil **3.** VERY BAD extremely bad or unpleasant (*informal*) **4.** USED FOR EMPHATIC DISAPPROVAL used for emphasis when disapproving of something, especially somebody's behaviour (*slang*) [14C. < French *diabolique* < late Latin *diabolicus* < Latin *diabolus* (see DEVIL)] —**diabolically** *adv*

diabolise *vt* another spelling of **diabolize**

diabolism /dī̓ ábbəlizəm/ *n* **1.** worship of the devil or devils **2.** evil behaviour or character (*literary*) — **diabolist** *n*

diabolize /dī̓ ábbə līz/ (**-lizes, -lizing, -lized**), **diabolise** (**-lises, -lising, -lised**) *vt* **1.** to cause somebody or something to appear evil **2.** to make somebody or something evil

diabolo /dī̓ ábbəlō/ (*plural* **-los**) *n* **1.** the game of spinning a top with a narrow waist and two heads

on a string tied to two sticks held in the hands **2.** a top designed to be used in the game of diabolo [Early 20C. Via Italian, literally 'devil' < Latin *diabolus* (see DEVIL)]

diacetylmorphine /dī̓ ássətil máwr feen/ *n* DRUGS same as **heroin** (*technical*)

diachronic /dī̓ ə krónnik/ *adj* relating to or involving the study or development of something, especially a language, through time ○ *diachronic linguistics* [Mid-19C. < DIA- + Greek *khronos* 'time'] —**diachronically** *adv*

diachronism /dī̓ ákrənizəm/ *n* the existence within a single geological formation of regions of rock that were laid down at different times, e.g. by a sea that gradually covered a landmass —**diachronous** *adj*

diachrony /dī̓ ákrəni/ *n* change or development over time

diacid /dī̓ ássid/ *adj* having two acidic hydrogen atoms that may be replaced by metal or acid ions to form a salt or an ester ■ *n* an acid that has two acidic hydrogen atoms

diaconal /dī̓ ákənəl/ *adj* relating to a deacon or deaconess or to the position of deacon or deaconess [Early 17C. < late Latin *diaconalis* < Latin *diaconus* (see DEACON)]

diaconate /dī̓ ákə nayt/ *n* the position of deacon or deaconess, or the term of office of a deacon or deaconess [Early 18C. < late Latin *diaconatus* < Latin *diaconus* (see DEACON)]

COMMON DIACRITICS

Name	Mark		Word/Phrase
grave	À	à	à la mode
acute	Á	á	Cádiz
circumflex	Â	â	château
tilde	Ã	ã	São Paulo
umlaut	Ä	ä	Fräulein
angstrom	Å	å	Århus
cedilla	Ç	ç	façade
grave	È	è	crèche
acute	É	é	purée
circumflex	Ê	ê	fête
dieresis	Ë	ë	Noël
grave	Ì	ì	Forlì
acute	Í	í	Valparaíso
circumflex	Î	î	maître d'hôtel
dieresis	Ï	ï	faïence
haček	Ň	ň	Plzeň
tilde	Ñ	ñ	mañana
acute	Ó	ó	Kraków
circumflex	Ô	ô	maître d'hôtel
umlaut	Ö	ö	rösti
haček	Ř	ř	Dvořák
acute	Ú	ú	Setúbal
circumflex	Û	û	crêpe
krouzek	Ů	ů	domů ('home')
umlaut	Ü	ü	gemütlich

diacritic /dī̓ ə kríttik/ *adj* indicating a change or modification in something, especially in the way a printed letter is to be pronounced or stressed ■ *n* a mark above or below a printed letter that indicates a change in the way it is to be pronounced or stressed. Acute and grave accents, tildes, and cedillas are examples of diacritics. [Late 17C. < Greek *diakritikos* 'that distinguishes or separates' < *krinein* 'separate, decide'] —**diacritically** *adv*

diacritical /dī̓ ə kríttik'l/ *adj* LING same as **diacritic**

diacritical mark *n* LANGUAGE same as **diacritic**

diacylglycerol /dī̓ ássil glíssə rol/ *n* an intermediate signalling molecule produced during intracellular processes

diadelphous /dī̓ ə délfəss/ *adj* describes stamens or flowers that have the stamen filaments grouped into

two bundles [Early 19C. < DI-[1] + Greek *adelphos* 'brother']

diadem /dī̓ ə dem/ *n* **1.** CROWN a jewelled headband used as a royal crown **2.** JEWELLED HEADBAND any jewelled headband **3.** REGAL POWER royal power or dignity (*literary*) [14C. Via French < Greek *diadēma* '(regal) headband' < *diadein* 'bind around' < *dein* 'bind']

diadem spider *n* a garden spider that spins orbed webs. Native to: Europe, Asia. Latin name: *Araneus diadematus*. [< its webs]

Diadochi /dī̓ áddəki/ *npl* the six Macedonian generals who divided up and then fought over the empire of Alexander the Great after his death [Mid-19C. < Greek *diadokhoi* 'successors' < *diadekhesthai* (see DIADOCHY)]

diadochy /dī̓ áddəki/ *n* the replacement of one element by another within the structure of a crystal [Early 18C. < Greek *diadokhē* 'succession' < *diadekhesthai* 'succeed one another' < *dekhesthai* 'take, accept']

diadromous /dī̓ áddrəməss/ *adj* describes fish that migrate between fresh and salt water [< Greek *dia* 'through, across' + *dromos* 'running']

diaeresis /dī̓ eérəssiss/ (*plural* **-ses** /-seez/), **dieresis** (*plural* **-ses** /dī̓ eérəssiss/) *n* **1.** a mark (¨) placed above a vowel to show that it should be pronounced. It may be above the second of two adjacent vowels to show that it is a separate syllable, as in the word 'naïve', or above a single vowel, as in the name 'Brontë'. See table at **diacritic 2.** a pause in a line of poetry that occurs when the end of a metrical foot coincides with the end of a word [Late 16C. Via Latin < Greek *diairesis* < *diairein* 'separate, divide' < *hairein* 'take'] —**diaeretic** /dī̓ ə réttik/ *adj*

diag. *abbr* MATHS **1.** diagonal **2.** diagram

diagenesis /dī̓ ə jénnəssiss/ *n* the changes that take place in a sediment as a result of increased temperatures and pressures, causing solid rock to form, e.g. as sand becomes sandstone —**diagenetic** /dī̓ ə je néttik/ *adj*

diageotropism /dī̓ əji óttrəpizəm/ *n* a response of a plant to gravity in which a part of the plant adopts a horizontal position —**diageotropic** /-jee ə tróppik/ *adj*

Diaghilev /di ággə lef/, **Sergei** (1872–1929) Russian ballet impresario. His Ballets Russes company, founded in Paris in 1909, revolutionized ballet as an art, unifying dance, music, drama, and painting. Full name **Diaghilev, Sergei Pavlovich**

diagnose /dī̓ əgnōz/ (**-noses, -nosing, -nosed**) *vt* **1.** to identify an illness or disorder in a patient through an interview, physical examination, and medical tests and other procedures ○ *The doctor diagnosed rheumatism.* **2.** to identify the nature or cause of something, especially a problem or fault [Mid-19C. Back-formation < DIAGNOSIS] —**diagnosable** /dī̓ əg nōzəb'l/ *adj*

diagnosis /dī̓ əg nóssiss/ (*plural* **-noses** /-nósseez/) *n* **1.** IDENTIFICATION OF ILLNESS the identifying of an illness or disorder in a patient through physical examination, medical tests, or other procedures ○ *a doctor with vast experience of diagnosis* **2.** IDENTIFICATION OF PROBLEM the identifying of the nature or cause of something, especially a problem or fault ○ *mechanics specializing in fault diagnosis* **3.** DECISION REACHED BY DIAGNOSIS a decision or conclusion reached by medical or other diagnosis ○ *The diagnosis is flu.* [Late 17C. Via modern Latin < Greek *diagnōsis* < *diagignōskein* 'distinguish' < *gignōskein* 'know, perceive']

diagnostic /dī̓ əg nóstik/ *adj* identifying, or used in identifying, the nature or cause of an illness, disorder, or problem ■ *n* a test, procedure, or instrument used to identify the nature or cause of an illness, disorder, or problem —**diagnostically** *adv* — **diagnostician** /dī̓ əg no stísh'n/ *n*

diagnostics /dī̓ əg nóstiks/ *n* the art of identifying illnesses or disorders in patients through diagnosis, or procedures for diagnosis (*takes a singular verb*)

diagonal /dī̓ ággənəl/ *adj* **1.** SLANTING OR OBLIQUE running from one side to another in a slanting or oblique way **2.** WITH SLANTING LINES having slanting lines or markings **3.** MATHS JOINING ANGLES OR CORNERS describes a line that joins two opposite or nonadjacent angles or corners of a straight-sided geometric figure ■ *n* **1.** SLANTING LINE a slanting line or direction **2.** MATHS LINE JOINING ANGLES a line that joins two opposite or nonadjacent angles or corners of a straight-sided geometric figure **3.** PRINTING same as **slash** *n* (sense

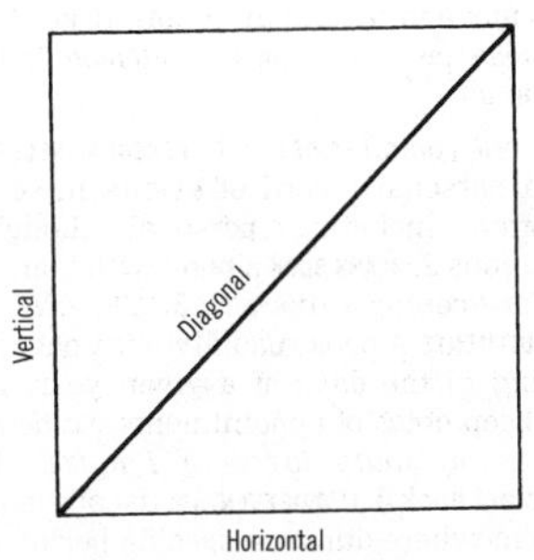

diagonal

4) [Mid-16C. < Latin *diagonalis* < Greek *diagōnios* 'from angle to angle' < *gōnia* 'angle'] —**diagonally** *adv*

diagram /dī́ ə gram/ *n* **1.** SIMPLE EXPLANATORY DRAWING a simple drawing showing the basic shape, layout, or workings of something **2.** CHART a chart or graph that illustrates something such as a statistical trend **3.** MATHS MATHEMATICAL DRAWING a line drawing that presents mathematical information ■ *vt* (**-grams, -gramming, -grammed**) INFO SCI, MATHS ILLUSTRATE SOMETHING to make a diagram that represents or illustrates something [Early 17C. Via Latin < Greek *diagramma* 'geometric figure, written list, scale in music' < *diagraphein* 'mark out by lines, draw' < *graphein* 'write']

diagrammatic /dī́ əgrə máttik/ *adj* in the form of an explanatory drawing or chart —**diagrammatically** *adv*

diagraph /dī́ ə graf, -graaf/ *n* a mechanical instrument used for producing scale copies of diagrams and maps [Late 19C. < French *diagraphe* < Greek *diagraphein* (see DIAGRAM)]

diakinesis /dī́ əki nee̅ssiss, -kī-/ *n* the final stage in cell reduction division (**meiosis**), during which the paired chromosomes begin to shorten, thicken, and separate [Early 20C. < modern Latin < Greek *dia* 'through, across' + *kinēsis* 'motion' (see KINESIS)] —**diakinetic** /-néttik/ *adj*

dial /dī́ əl/ *n* **1.** INDICATOR WITH MOVABLE POINTER an instrument with a movable pointer that displays a measurement such as the current speed of a vehicle or the level of steam pressure inside a boiler **2.** CONTROL KNOB a round control knob or disc turned with the fingers to adjust a piece of electrical or mechanical equipment such as a radio **3.** STATION INDICATOR ON RADIO a numbered panel with a movable pointer on a radio, used for tuning in to different stations **4.** CLOCK FACE the round face of a traditional clock **5.** DISC WITH HOLES ON TELEPHONE a disc with numbered finger holes on the front of an old telephone, turned with a finger to select the required telephone number **6.** *Aus* same as **face** *n* (sense 1) (*slang*) **7.** SUNDIAL a sundial or its face (*dated or literary*) ■ *vti* (**-als, -alling, -alled**) CONTACT SOMEBODY ON TELEPHONE to contact a number or a person by telephone ○ *She must have dialled the wrong number.* [14C. < Old French, 'wheel in clockwork that makes a revolution once a day' < Latin *dies* 'day'] —**dialler** *n*

dial. *abbr* LING **1.** dialect **2.** dialectal

dial-a-ride *n* a bus service that can be called to the door by telephone, generally intended for people in need of assistance in moving about

dialect /dī́ ə lekt/ *n* LING **1.** REGIONAL VARIETY OF LANGUAGE a regional variety of a language, with differences in vocabulary, grammar, and pronunciation **2.** LANGUAGE SPOKEN BY CLASS OR PROFESSION a form of a language spoken by members of a social class or profession **3.** NONSTANDARD SPEECH nonstandard spoken language **4.** MEMBER OF LANGUAGE FAMILY one of a family of related languages ○ *Romance dialects such as French and Italian* [Mid-16C. Directly or via French < Latin *dialectus* 'way of speaking, dialect' < Greek *dialektos* 'conversation, language, local speech' < *dialegesthai* (see DIALOGUE)] —**dialectal** /dī́ ə lékt'l/ *adj* —**dialectally** *adv*

REGIONAL NOTE The word ***dialect*** has been used in so many different ways that linguists often prefer to avoid it and use a term such as *lect*, which has no class, social, regional, or ethnic overtones. Many speakers use ***dialect*** when they mean 'accent', forgetting that a dialect comprehends pronunciation, vocabulary, and grammar. Somebody who says 'boot' for 'but' is speaking with a local accent. Somebody who says 'I were reet chuffed tha come, lass' is speaking dialect.

SYNONYMS See ***language***.

dialectic /dī́ ə léktik/ *n* **1.** TENSION BETWEEN CONFLICTING IDEAS the tension that exists between two conflicting or interacting forces, elements, or ideas **2.** INVESTIGATION OF TRUTH THROUGH DISCUSSION the investigation of the truth through discussion, or the art of investigating truths through discussion **3.** *also* **dialectics** DEBATE RESOLVING CONFLICT debate intended to resolve a conflict between two contradictory or apparently contradictory ideas or parts logically, establishing truths on both sides rather than disproving one argument (*takes a singular verb*) **4.** HEGELIAN PROCESS the process, in Hegelian and Marxist thought, in which two apparently opposed ideas, the thesis and antithesis, become combined in a unified whole, the synthesis **5.** SOCRATIC METHOD FOR REVEALING TRUTH the methods used in Socratic philosophy to reveal truth through disputation [Late 16C. Via Latin *dialectica* < Greek *dialektikē (tekhnē)* '(art) of discussion or debate' < *dialektikos* 'of conversation' < *dialektos* (see DIALECT)] —**dialectician** /dī́ ə lek tísh'n/ *n*

dialectical /dī́ ə léktik'l/ *adj* **1.** PHILOSOPHY ACHIEVED BY DIALECTIC achieved or attempted by dialectic **2.** PHILOSOPHY INVOLVING DIALECTIC involving or depending upon dialectic **3.** LING DIALECTAL relating to or belonging to a dialect —**dialectically** *adv*

dialectical materialism *n* the Marxian concept of reality in which material things are in the constant process of change brought about by the tension between conflicting or interacting forces, elements, or ideas —**dialectical materialist** *n*

dialectics /dī́ ə léktiks/ *n* PHILOSOPHY same as **dialectic** (sense 3)

dialectology /dī́ ə lek tólləji/ *n* the study of the dialects of a language —**dialectological** /dī́ ə lektə lójjik'l/ *adj* —**dialectologically** *adv* —**dialectologist** *n*

dial gauge *n* a sensitive measuring device that indicates small displacements of a plunger by means of a pointer moving over a circular scale. It is usually used for measuring pressure or a vacuum.

dialling code /dī́ ə ling-/ *n* digits indicating a specific area or country that are dialled before the local number in calls made from outside that area or country

dialling tone *n UK* a continuous sound that is heard when a telephone receiver is lifted, signalling that a number can be dialled. ANZ, N Am term **dial tone**

dialog box *n* COMPUT US spelling of **dialogue box**

dialogic /dī́ ə lójjik/ *adj* **1.** written in the form of a conversation **2.** relating to dialogues

dialogist /dī álləjist/ *n* **1.** a writer of dialogue for films, television, or radio **2.** a participant in a dialogue —**dialogistic** /dī́ alə jístik/ *adj*

dialogue /dī́ ə log/ *n* **1.** CHARACTERS' WORDS the words spoken by characters in a book, film, or play, or a section of a work that contains spoken words ○ *pages of dialogue* **2.** FORMAL DISCUSSION a formal discussion or negotiation, especially between opposing sides in a political or international context **3.** CONVERSATION talk of any kind between two or more people (*formal*) **4.** LITERARY WORK IN CONVERSATION FORM a work of literature in the form of a conversation ■ *vi* (**-logues, -loguing, -logued**) TAKE PART IN TALK to take part in a conversation, discussion, or negotiation [12C. Via French < Greek *dialogos* < *dialegesthai* 'speak with each other' < *legein* 'speak'] —**dialoguer** *n*

dialogue box *n* a small rectangular window displayed on a computer screen that conveys information to, or requires a response from, the user

dial tone *n ANZ, N Am* same as **dialling tone**

dial-up *adj* requiring a computer modem and telephone line to establish communication with another computer or a network

dialyse /dī́ ə līz/ (**-lyses, -lysing, -lysed**) *vti* **1.** to remove the accumulated waste products of metabolism from the blood of a patient whose kidneys are not functioning, or undergo such a procedure **2.** to separate dissolved substances from a solution by diffusing it through a semipermeable membrane, or be subjected to this process [Mid-19C. < DIALYSIS, after ANALYSE] —**dialysability** /dī́ ə līzə bílləti/ *n* —**dialysable** *adj* —**dialysation** /dī́ ə lī záysh'n/ *n* —**dialyser** *n*

dialysis /dī állәssiss/ *n* **1.** the process of filtering the accumulated waste products of metabolism from the blood of a patient whose kidneys are not functioning properly, using a kidney machine **2.** the separation of dissolved substances from a solution by allowing the solution to diffuse through a semipermeable membrane [Mid-19C. Via Latin, 'set of propositions without a connecting conjunction' < Greek *dialusis* 'separation, loosening' < *luein* 'loosen'] —**dialytic** /dī́ ə líttik/ *adj* —**dialytically** *adv*

dialyze *vti* MED, CHEM US spelling of **dialyse**

diamagnet /dī́ ə magnət/ *n* a substance that is repelled by magnetic fields, e.g. a noble gas, halogen, and alkali or alkaline earth metal —**diamagnetic** /dī́ ə mag néttik/ *adj* —**diamagnetically** *adv*

diamagnetism /dī́ ə mágnətizəm/ *n* a tendency in materials with a relative permeability of less than one to be repelled by a magnetic field and align themselves at right angles to it

diamanté /dee̅ ə mónt ay, dī́ ə-/ *adj* COVERED WITH IMITATION DIAMONDS decorated with colourless imitation gems (**rhinestones**) that look like diamonds ■ *n* **1.** IMITATION DIAMONDS colourless imitation gems that look like diamonds. Use: jewellery. **2.** CLOTHES WITH IMITATION DIAMONDS clothing or fabric decorated with diamanté [Early 20C. < French, past participle of *diamanter* 'set with diamonds' < *diamant* (see DIAMOND)]

Diamantina /dī́ əmən tee̅nə/ river in eastern Australia that rises near the town of Cloncurry in Queensland and flows southwards into Lake Eyre in South Australia. Length: 900 km/560 mi.

diamantine /dī́ ə mán tīn/ *adj* **1.** resembling diamonds **2.** made of diamond or consisting of diamonds [Early 17C. < French *diamantin* < *diamant* (see DIAMOND)]

diameter /dī ámmitər/ *n* **1.** a straight line running from one side of a circle or other rounded geometric figure through the centre to the other side, or the length of this line **2.** the width or thickness of something, especially something circular or cylindrical ○ *10 cm in diameter* [14C. Via French < Latin *diametrus* < Greek *diametros (grammē)* '(line) that measures through' < *metron* 'measure'] —**diametral** *adj*

diametric /dī́ ə méttrik/, **diametrical** /dī́ ə méttrik'l/ *adj* complete in respect of being opposite or different

diametrically /dī́ ə méttrikli/ *adv* used to emphasize that a difference or contrast is as great as it can be ○ *diametrically opposite concepts*

diamine /dī́ ə meen/ *n* an organic chemical compound that contains two amino groups

diamond /dī́ əmənd/ *n* **1.** MINERALS HARD COLOURLESS MINERAL a hard transparent precious stone that is a variety of carbon. Use: gems, abrasives, cutting tools. **2.** MATHS SHAPE LIKE SQUARE RESTING ON CORNER a two-dimensional geometric figure formed of four sides, like a square standing on one of its corners **3.** CARDS CARD WITH DIAMOND-SHAPED SYMBOL a playing card with a diamond-shaped symbol on it **4.** BASEBALL PART OF PLAYING AREA the area of a baseball field bounded by home plate and the three bases **5.** BASEBALL PLAYING AREA an area for playing baseball including the infield and the outfield **6.** *N Ireland* IRISH MARKET SQUARE the market square of a town in Northern Ireland (*regional*) ■ *vt* (**-monds, -monding, -monded**) DECORATE SOMETHING WITH DIAMONDS to decorate something with diamonds or similar gemstones [13C. Via French *diamant* 'hardest metal' < medieval Latin *diamant-*, alteration of Latin *adamant-* (see ADAMANT)]

diamond anniversary *n* an anniversary celebrating 60, or sometimes 75, years of something such as marriage [< the custom of marking the occasion with gifts containing diamonds]

diamondback /dī́ əmənd bak/ *n* **1.** a large poisonous rattlesnake with diamond-shaped markings on its back. Native to: southwestern United States, Mexico. Latin name: *Crotalus adamantus* or *Crotalus atrox*. **2.** a terrapin with diamond-shaped markings on its shell. Native to: salt marshes of the Atlantic and the Gulf coasts of North America. Genus: *Malaclemys*.

diamondback moth *n* a brightly coloured moth with diamond-shaped markings on the underside of the front wings, visible when the wings are folded. Family: Plutellidae.

diamondiferous /dī əmən díffərəss/ *adj* containing diamond or diamonds that can be extracted

diamond in the rough *n N Am* same as **rough diamond** (sense 2)

diamond jubilee *n* same as **diamond anniversary**

diamond point *n* a cutting tool in which two cutting edges meet at an acute angle, forming a diamond shape

diamond python *n* a greenish-yellow python with yellow diamond-shaped markings along its side. Native to: Australia, New Zealand, New Guinea. Latin name: *Morelia argus*.

diamonds /dī əməndz/ *n* one of the four suits used in cards, with a red diamond shape as its symbol (*takes a singular or plural verb*)

diamond wedding *n* the celebration of 60 years of marriage. N Am term **diamond anniversary** [< the custom of marking the occasion with gifts containing diamonds]

diamorphine /dī ə máwr feen/ *n* PHARM same as **heroin** (*technical*) [Early 20C. Contraction of DIACETYLMORPHINE]

Diana /dī ánnə/ *n* in Roman mythology, the goddess of hunting, virginity, and the moon. Greek equivalent **Artemis**

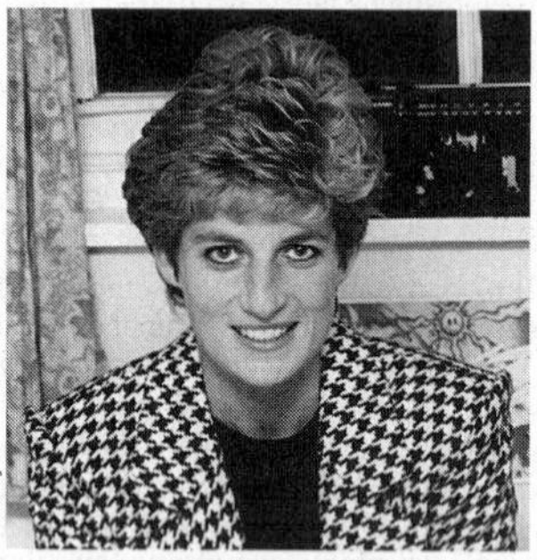

Diana, Princess of Wales

Diana /dī ánnə/, **Princess of Wales** (1961–97) British princess. She married Prince Charles in 1981, had two sons, and was divorced in 1996. She was killed in a car crash in Paris. Born **Spencer, Diana Frances**

> 'The vicious circle of fear, prejudice and ignorance has increased the spread of Aids to an alarming level. Due to fear and prejudice, many still do not want to listen. After all, Aids is a killer.'
> [Diana, *Independent*; 17 February 1993]

diandrous /dī ándrəss/ *adj* describes flowers that have two stamens, or fungi and nonseeding plants that have two antheridia [Late 18C. < DI-[1] + Greek *andr-* 'man']

dianthus /dī ánthəss/ *n* a flowering plant belonging to the group that includes carnations, pinks, and sweet william. Genus: *Dianthus*. [Late 18C. < modern Latin < Greek *Dios* 'of Zeus' + *anthos* 'flower']

diapason /dī ə páyz'n, -páyss'n/ *n* MUSIC **1. PIPE ORGAN'S MAIN STOP** one of two main stops on a pipe organ that control the organ's tone and characteristic sound **2. MUSICAL RANGE** the range of a musical instrument or of somebody's singing voice (*technical*) **3. TUNING DEVICE** a tuning fork or pitch pipe (*technical*) [14C. Via Latin < Greek *dia pasōn khordōn* 'across all the notes of the scale'] —**diapasonal** *adj* —**diapasonic** /dī ə pay zónnik, -sónnik/ *adj*

diapause /dī ə pawz/ *n* a period during which the metabolism of some animals or insects slows down, temporarily suspending their bodily development and growth. Such periods are linked to seasonal or environmental changes.

diapedesis /dī əpə deésiss/ *n* a condition in which blood leaks through the apparently unruptured walls of blood vessels into surrounding tissue, as a reaction to severe inflammation or injury [Early 17C. < modern Latin < Greek *dia-* 'through' + *pēdan* 'to leap'] —**diapedetic** /-déttik/ *adj*

diaper /dī əpər/ *n* **1.** *N Am* same as **nappy 2. PATTERN OF SMALL MOTIFS** a pattern woven into or printed on fabric, consisting of a small motif, often a diamond, repeated to cover an entire surface **3.** TEXTILES **FABRIC WITH DIAPER PATTERN** cotton or linen fabric with a diaper pattern woven into or printed on it ■ *vt* (**-pers, -pering, -pered**) **1.** *N Am* **DRESS BABY IN NAPPY** to put a nappy on a baby **2. PUT DIAPER PATTERN ON SOMETHING** to decorate something, especially fabric, with a diaper pattern [14C. Via Old French *diapre* 'ornamental cloth' < medieval Greek *diaspros* 'thoroughly white']

diaper rash *n N Am* same as **nappy rash**

diaphanous /dī áffənəss/ *adj* **1.** delicate or gauzy, so as to be transparent ○ *the insect's diaphanous wings* **2.** fragile or insubstantial because extremely faint or slight (*literary*) ○ *diaphanous breezes* [Early 17C. Via Latin *diaphanus* < Greek *diaphanēs* 'shown through' < *phainein* 'to show'] —**diaphaneity** /dī əfə neé əti/ *n* —**diaphanously** *adv* —**diaphanousness** *n*

diaphone /dī ə fōn/ *n* **1.** a set of all the different ways that a speech sound is pronounced in all the dialects of a language, or a member of this set **2.** a foghorn with a two-note sound

diaphoresis /dī əfə reéssiss/ *n* sweating, especially sweating induced for medical reasons (*technical*) [Late 17C. < late Latin < Greek *diaphorein* 'dissipate by sweating' < *phorein* 'carry']

diaphoretic /dī əfə réttik/ *adj* describes agents that induce sweating, or their effect —**diaphoretic** *n*

diaphragm /dī ə fram/ *n* **1.** ANAT **MUSCULAR WALL BELOW RIB CAGE** a curved muscular membrane in humans and other mammals that separates the abdomen from the area around the lungs **2.** MED **DOME-SHAPED CONTRACEPTIVE** a dome-shaped rubber or plastic contraceptive device for women, placed inside the vagina over the entrance to the womb to prevent sperm from entering **3.** PHOTOGRAPHY **CAMERA'S MECHANISM CONTROLLING OPENING FOR LIGHT** a disc with a fixed or variable opening that controls the amount of light that enters a camera or other optical instrument **4.** ACOUSTICS **VIBRATING DISC IN SOUND EQUIPMENT** a thin disc in a microphone, telephone receiver, or other sound device that vibrates in response to sound waves or electrical signals, converting one into the other **5. THIN MEMBRANE** a thin separating membrane, e.g. the porous plate dividing the sections of an electrolytic cell or the plate of cells across the stems of some water plants [14C. < late Latin *diaphragma* < Greek *diaphrassein* 'to barricade' < *phrassein* 'fence in'] —**diaphragmatic** /dī ə frag máttik/ *adj* —**diaphragmatically** *adv*

~~diaphram~~ incorrect spelling of **diaphragm**

diaphysis /dī áffəssiss/ (*plural* **-yses** /-ə seez/) *n* the central section of a long bone, between the growth areas at each end [Mid-19C. < Greek *diaphusis* 'growing through' < *phusis* 'growth'] —**diaphysial** /dī ə fízzi əl/ *adj*

diapir /dī ə peer/ *n* a dome-shaped body of rock that migrates upwards through denser overlying rock, e.g. a salt deposit [Early 20C. < Greek *diapeirainein* 'pierce through' < *peirainein* 'pierce'] —**diapiric** /dī ə pírrik/ *adj*

diapositive /dī ə pózzitiv/ *n* PHOTOGRAPHY same as **transparency** (sense 2)

diarchy /dī aarki/ (*plural* **-chies**), **dyarchy** *n* **1.** a form of government in which power is held by two supreme rulers or two governing bodies **2.** a country ruled or run by two supreme rulers or two governing bodies [Mid-19C. < DI-[1] after MONARCHY] —**diarchal** /dī áark'l/ *adj* —**diarchic** /dī áarkik/ *adj* —**diarchical** *adj*

~~diarhea~~ incorrect spelling of **diarrhoea**

diarise *v* another spelling of **diarize**

diarist /dī ərist/ *n* the writer of a diary, especially one that is published

diarize /dī ərīz/ (**-rizes, -rizing, -rized**), **diarise** (-rises, -rising, -rised) *v* **1.** *vt* to enter an appointment or date to remember in a diary **2.** *vi* to keep a record of events in a diary (*archaic*)

diarrhoea /dī ə reé ə/, **diarrhea** *n* **1.** frequent and excessive discharging of the bowels producing thin watery stools, usually as a symptom of gastro-intestinal upset or infection **2.** thin watery faeces [Early 16C. Via Latin < Greek *diarrhoia* < *diarrhein* 'flow through' < *rhein* 'to flow'] —**diarrhoeal** *adj* —**diarrhoeic** *adj*

diarthrosis /dī aar thróssiss/ (*plural* **-throses** /-thró seez/) *n* **1.** a joint of the body that is able to move freely in various directions, e.g. the shoulder, hip, knee, or elbow **2.** the ability of some joints of the body to move in several directions [Late 16C. < Greek < *diarthroun* 'fasten by a joint' < *arthroun* 'fasten'] —**diarthrodial** *adj*

diary /dī əri/ (*plural* **-ries**) *n* **1. PERSONAL RECORD OF LIFE'S EVENTS** a personal record of events in somebody's life, often including personal thoughts and observations **2. BLANK BOOK** a book with blank or lined paper for keeping a diary in **3.** *UK, ANZ, Can* **BOOK FOR APPOINTMENTS** a book, usually with pages labelled according to the days of a given year, in which people keep notes of appointments ○ *a desk diary* ○ *I'll check my diary to see if I'm free.* US term **appointment book 4. LIST OF EVENTS** a list of events taking place somewhere during a specific period of time ○ *a diary of October's events* [Late 16C. < Latin *diarium* < *dies* 'day']

SPELLCHECK See *dairy*.

Dias /deé ass/, **Diaz, Bartolomeu** (1450?–1500) Portuguese navigator and explorer. He was the first European to round the Cape of Good Hope (1488), establishing a sea route from Europe to Asia.

diaspora /dī áspərə/ *n* a dispersion of a people, language, or culture that was formerly concentrated in one place ○ *the African diaspora* [Late 19C. < Greek < *diaspeirein* 'disperse' < *speirein* 'sow, scatter']

Diaspora *n* **1.** the dispersion of the Jews from Palestine following the Babylonians' conquest of the Judaean Kingdom in the 6th century BC and again following the Romans' destruction of the Second Temple in AD 70 **2.** the Jewish communities living outside either the present-day state of Israel or the ancient biblical kingdom of Israel

diaspore /dī ə spawr/ *n* **1.** a white, grey, or pink form of aluminium oxide mineral. Source: bauxite. Use: abrasives, heat-resistant materials. **2.** a seed or spore that is dispersed from a plant [Early 19C. < Greek *diaspora* (see DIASPORA); from its dispersion when heated]

diastase /dī ə stayz, -stayss/ *n* BIOCHEM former name for **amylase** [Mid-19C. < modern Latin *diastasis* (see DIASTASIS) + -ASE] —**diastasic** /dī ə stáyzik, -stáysik/ *adj*

diastasis /dī ástəssiss/ (*plural* **-tases** /-tə seez/) *n* the dislodging of the end **(epiphysis)** of a long bone from its shaft without a fracturing of the bone itself (*technical*) [Early 18C. Via modern Latin < Greek, 'separation' < *stasis* 'placing'] —**diastatic** /dī ə státtik/ *adj*

diastema /dī ə steémə/ (*plural* **-mata** /-mətə/) *n* a larger than usual gap between two adjacent teeth (*technical*) [Mid-19C. Via late Latin < Greek, 'gap' < *diistanai* 'place apart' < *histanai* 'to place'] —**diastematic** /dī əstə máttik/ *adj*

diastereoisomer /dī ə stérri ō íssəmər/, **diastereomer** /dī ə stérriəmər/ *n* a molecule that has the same formula and structure as another **(stereoisomer)**, but is arranged differently in space and is therefore not a mirror image

diastole /dī ásstəli/ *n* the rhythmic expansion of the chambers of the heart at each heartbeat, during which they fill with blood [Late 16C. Via late Latin < Greek, 'separation, expansion' < *diastellein* 'to place apart' < *stellein* 'to place'] —**diastolic** /dī ə stóllik/ *adj*

diastyle /dī ə stīl/ *adj* describes classical buildings with columns set at intervals equal to three or sometimes four times the diameter of a column, slightly farther apart than in the Doric order ■ *n* a diastyle building or colonnade [Mid-16C. Directly or via Latin < Greek *diastulos* 'between columns' < *stulos* 'column']

diathermia /dī ə thúrmi ə/ *n* MED same as **diathermy** [Early 20C. < modern Latin < Greek *dia* 'across, through' + *thermē* 'heat']

diathermic /dī ə thúrmik/ *adj* **1.** relating to diathermy **2.** able to conduct or transmit heat or infrared radiation [Early 20C. < French *diathermique* < Greek *dia* 'across, through' + *thermē* 'heat']

diathermy /dī ə thurmi/ *n* the treatment of organs or tissues by passing high-frequency electric currents through them in order to generate heat, thus increasing circulation [Early 20C. < modern Latin *diathermia* (see DIATHERMIA)]

diathesis /dī áthississ/ (*plural* **-eses** /-is seez/) *n* a susceptibility to a disease or set of diseases such as allergies or gout [Mid-17C. < modern Latin < Greek

diatithenai 'arrange, dispose' < *tithenai* 'put'] —**diathetic** /dī ə théttik/ *adj*

diatom /dī ə tom/ *n* a microscopic one-celled alga that has silica-filled cell walls or shells divided into two halves. Diatoms are responsible for the formation of diatomite in water. Class: Bacillariophyceae. [Mid-19C. < modern Latin *Diatoma* < Greek *diatomos* 'cut in two' < *diatemnein* 'to cut through' < *temnein* 'to cut'] —**diatomaceous** /dī ətə máyshəss/ *adj*

diatomaceous earth *n* **1.** GEOL same as **diatomite 2.** a form of unrefined diatomite. Use: insecticide.

diatomic /dī ə tómmik/ *adj* having two atoms per molecule —**diatomicity** /dī atə míssəti/ *n*

diatomite /dī áttə mīt/ *n* a soft powdery porous rock. Source: accumulated shells of diatoms. Use: in fireproof cements, insulating materials, dynamite, as insecticide.

diatonic /dī ə tónnik/ *adj* relating to or based on musical scales consisting of five tones and two semitones, e.g. a major or minor scale with no extra sharps or flats added ■ *n* the interval between any two notes of a diatonic scale [Early 17C. Via French or late Latin < Greek *diatonikos* 'at intervals of a tone' < *tonos* 'tone'] —**diatonically** *adv* —**diatonicism** /-sizəm/ *n*

diatribe /dī ə trīb/ *n* a bitter verbal or written attack on somebody or something ○ *a diatribe against falling standards* [Late 16C. Via French < Greek *diatribē* 'act of spending time (in discourse)']

diatropism /dī áttrəpizəm/ *n* the tendency of a plant or plant part to grow at right angles in response to an external stimulus such as light —**diatropic** /dī ə tróppik/ *adj*

Diaz another spelling of **Dias**

diazepam /dī áyzə pam, -ázzə-/ *n* a tranquillizer that has habit-forming potential. Use: short-term relief of anxiety or tension, muscle relaxant. [Mid-20C. < *di-* + *-azepam*, INN stem]

diazine /dī ə zeen/, **diazin** /dī ə zin, dī ázzin/ *n* a chemical compound in which the molecules contain a hexagonal ring of four carbon atoms and two nitrogen atoms, existing in three isomeric forms. Formula: $C_4N_2H_4$.

diazo /dī áy zō/ *adj* describes an organic compound containing two adjacent nitrogen atoms, e.g. an azo compound or a diazonium salt ■ *n* (*plural* **-zos** or **-zoes**) a photograph or photocopy made using the diazotype process

diazole /dī áy zōl/ *n* an organic chemical compound with a five-sided ring structure containing three carbon atoms and two nitrogen atoms

diazonium salt *n* a salt containing two adjacent nitrogen atoms as an (**azo**) group. Use: manufacture of azo dyes.

diazotize /dī áyzə tīz/ (**-tizes, -tizing, -tized**), **diazotise** (**-tises, -tising, -tised**) *vt* to transform an amine into a diazo compound using nitrous acid —**diazotization** /dī áyzə tī záysh'n/ *n*

diazotype /dī áyzə tīp/ *n* a printing or photographic process that exploits the light-sensitive properties of diazo compounds

dib /dib/ (**dibs, dibbing, dibbed**) *vi* to fish by causing the bait to bob on the surface of the water [Early 17C. Alteration of DAB [1]]

dibasic /dī báyssik/ *adj* **1.** describes an acid that has two replaceable hydrogen atoms **2.** describes a salt or an acid that is formed with two atoms of a monovalent metallic element —**dibasicity** /dī bay síssəti/ *n*

dibber /díbbər/ *n* a small pointed gardening tool used to make holes in the soil for planting seeds, bulbs, or seedlings [Mid-18C. < *dib*, related to DIBBLE]

dibble /díbb'l/ *n* GARDENING same as **dibber** ■ *vt* (**-bles, -bling, -bled**) to make planting holes in soil with a pointed tool, or put plants or seeds in such holes [14C. Origin ?] —**dibbler** *n*

dibbuk *n* JUDAISM another spelling of **dybbuk**

dibbydibby /díbbee díbbee/ *adj* (*slang*; *used in Black English*) **1.** WITH UNPLEASANT TASTE having an unpleasant taste or flavour ○ *Is a one dibbydibby banana you come give me!* **2.** DUBIOUS likely to be dishonest, untrustworthy, or immoral **3.** MINOR of minor importance or influence

dibromide /dī brṓ mīd/ *n* a chemical compound whose molecules contain two bromine atoms

dibs /dibz/ *npl* a claim of exclusive rights to take or use something (*informal*; (*takes a singular verb*)) ○ *called dibs on the front seat* ■ *n* money, especially in small amounts (*dated informal*) ■ *npl* LEISURE same as **jacks** [Early 19C. < shortening of *dibstones* 'game played with pebbles']

dicarboxylic acid /dī kaar bok síllik-/ *n* any acid that contains two carboxyl groups

dice /dīss/ *n* **1.** (*plural same*) NUMBERED CUBE USED IN GAMES a small cube with the numbers 1 to 6 marked in dots on the sides, used in gambling and in a wide variety of games of chance **2.** GAME PLAYED WITH DICE a gambling game played with dice, e.g. craps (*takes a singular or plural verb*) ■ *npl* CHUNKS cube-shaped pieces, especially of meat (*takes a plural verb*) ■ *v* (**dices, dicing, diced**) **1.** *vt* CUT UP FOOD to cut food into cubes ○ *diced carrots* **2.** *vti* PLAY WITH DICE to gamble using dice, or win or lose something playing dice **3.** *vi* TAKE RISKS to challenge or take risks with somebody or something dangerous ○ *dicing with death* **4.** *vt* DECORATE SOMETHING WITH SQUARE PATTERN to decorate something with a pattern of squares or cubes **5.** *vt Aus* ABANDON SOMETHING to abandon or discard something (*informal*) [14C. < French *dé* (plural *dés*) < Latin *datum*, past participle of *dare* 'give, play'] —**dicer** *n* ◇ **load the dice 1.** to manipulate a situation unfairly in order to obtain a desired result **2.** to add weight to a dice so that it always falls on the same side (*informal*) ◇ **no dice** used to indicate that there is no chance of something happening (*informal*)

USAGE Dice – singular or plural? The singular form *die*, of which *dice* was originally the plural, is now seldom used other than in the idiom *The die is cast*. ***Dice***, used with a singular verb, means 'a small cube with the numbers 1 to 6 marked in dots on its sides used in gambling' (its plural in this use is ***dice***), or a gambling game in which these cubes are used. ***Dice*** (plural) can also refer to cube-shaped pieces, especially of food.

dicentra /dī séntrə/ *n* a perennial plant that grows best in shade. Flowers: small, drooping, in arching sprays. Genus: *Dicentra*. [Mid-19C. < modern Latin < Greek *dikentros* 'two-pointed' < *kentron* 'centre, point'; from the shape of its leaves]

dicephalous /dī séffələss, dī kéffələss/ *adj* having two heads

dicey /dīssi/ (**-ier, -iest**), **dicy** *adj* uncertain and involving danger or risk (*informal*)

dichasium /dī káyzi əm/ (*plural* **-sia** /-zi ə/) *n* a flowering stem that has a single flower growing on the end (**cyme**) and later sprouts two single-flower branches, one on each side of and below the first flower [Late 19C. < Greek *dikhasis* 'division' < *dikha* 'apart'] —**dichasial** *adj* —**dichasially** *adv*

dichlorodifluoromethane /dī kláwr ō dī flóor ō méeth ayn/ *n* a colourless, nonflammable, gaseous CFC. Use: propellant in aerosols, refrigerant, in fire extinguishers. Formula: CCl_2F_2.

dichlorodiphenyltrichloroethane /dī kláwr ō dī féen īl trī kláwr ō ée thayn/ *n* CHEM full form of **DDT**

dichloromethane /dī kláwr ō méeth ayn/ *n* a colourless, nonflammable, toxic gas. Use: in paint strippers, degreasing, plastics processing. Formula: CH_2Cl_2.

dichlorophenoxyacetic acid /dī kláwrō fə nóksi ə séetik ássid/ *n* CHEM same as **2,4-D**

dichogamy /dī kóggəmi/ *n* a plant's production of male and female parts at different times, in order to prevent self-pollination and ensure cross-fertilization [Mid-19C. < Greek *dikho-* 'apart' + *gamos* 'marriage'] —**dichogamic** /dī kō gámmik/ *adj* —**dichogamous** *adj*

dichotic /dī kóttik/ *adj* involving or relating to the simultaneous stimulation of each ear with different sounds [Mid-20C. < Greek *dikho-* 'apart' + *ōt-* 'ear']

dichotomize /dī kóttə mīz/ (**-mizes, -mizing, -mized**), **dichotomise** (**-mises, -mising, -mised**) *vti* to divide something into two classes or groups, or become divided into two —**dichotomization** /dī kóttə mī záysh'n/ *n*

dichotomy /dī kóttəmi/ (*plural* **-mies**) *n* **1.** SEPARATION OF DIFFERENT OR CONTRADICTORY THINGS a separation into two divisions that differ widely from or contradict each other **2.** BOT BRANCHING OF PLANTS the division of each of a plant's branches into two more branches **3.** ASTRON MOON PHASE WHEN HALF VISIBLE the phase of the Moon or a planet when half of its surface appears illuminated by the Sun [Late 16C. Via modern Latin < Greek *dikhotomia* 'cutting in two' < *dikho-* 'apart, in two' + *temnein* 'to cut'] —**dichotomic** /dī kō tómmik/ *adj* —**dichotomous** *adj* —**dichotomously** *adv*

dichroic /dī krṓ ik/ *adj* describes a crystal that appears to be a different colour when viewed along a different axis [Mid-19C. < Greek *dikhroos* 'two-coloured' < *khrōs* 'colour'] —**dichroism** *n*

dichroite /dī krō īt/ *n* MINERALS same as **cordierite** [Early 19C. < Greek *dikhroos* (see DICHROIC)]

dichroitic /dī krō íttik/ *adj* CHEM same as **dichroic**

dichromate /dī krṓ mayt/ *n* a salt of dichromic acid, characteristically orange-red in colour

dichromatic /dī krō máttik/ *adj* **1.** WITH TWO COLOURS having two colours **2.** OPHTHALMOL PARTIALLY COLOUR-BLIND able to distinguish only two of the three primary colours and their combinations **3.** ZOOL WITH DIFFERENT COLOUR PHASES describes animals, especially birds, that have two different colours in phases that are not associated with the normal variations in colour that occur with sex and age

dichromatism /dī krṓmətizəm/ *n* **1.** the presence of only two colours in something **2.** colour-blindness in which only two of the three primary colours and their combinations can be distinguished

dichromic /dī krṓmik/ *adj* OPHTHALMOL same as **dichromatic** (sense 2) [Mid-19C. < Greek *dikhrōmos* 'two-coloured' < *khrōma* 'colour']

dichromic acid *n* an unstable acid found only in solution and in the form of dichromate salts. Formula: $H_2Cr_2O_7$.

dichromism /dī krṓm izəm/ *n* OPHTHALMOL same as **dichromatism** (sense 2)

dicht /di<u>kh</u>t/ *Scotland vti* to wipe or rub dirt or dust from something ■ *n* a wipe or rub to clean dirt or dust away [Late 17C. Variant of DIGHT]

~~**dicision**~~ incorrect spelling of **decision**

dick[1] /dik/ *n* (*slang*) **1.** an offensive term for the penis **2.** an offensive term for a boy or man regarded as very thoughtless [Mid-16C. < the male first name *Dick*]

dick[2] /dik/ *n N Am* same as **detective** (*dated slang*) [Early 20C. Origin ?]

Dick and Jane /dík ənd jáyn/ *npl US* the stereotypes of middle-class white Americans (*informal*; *hyphenated when used before a noun*)

dickens /díkinz/ *n* used for emphasis in a variety of expressions, especially expressions of surprise or annoyance (*informal*) ○ *What the dickens is going on here?* ○ *scared the dickens out of me* [Late 16C. Probably < the surname *Dickens*]

Dickens /díkinz/, **Charles** (1812–70) British novelist. His career began with magazine sketches, written under the pseudonym 'Boz', before *Pickwick Papers* (1837) brought him greater popularity. His many subsequent novels, appearing in monthly instalments and often depicting poverty and social injustice in Victorian England, have remained popular. Full name **Dickens, Charles John Huffam**. See Cultural note at **bleak, carol, expectation, hard, twist**

> 'It was the best of times, it was the worst of times.'
> [Charles Dickens, *A Tale of Two Cities*; 1859]

> 'In the little world in which children have their existence, whosoever brings them up, there is nothing so finely perceived and so firmly felt, as injustice.'
> [Charles Dickens, *Great Expectations*; 1860–66]

Dickensian /di kénzi ən/ *adj* **1.** OF CHARLES DICKENS relating to the 19th-century British novelist Charles Dickens **2.** REMINISCENT OF POVERTY-STRICKEN VICTORIAN BRITAIN typical or reminiscent of the harsh poverty-stricken living conditions described in the works of Dickens **3.** JOLLY AND GENIAL jolly and cordial, like some of the scenes and characters featured in the novels of Dickens **4.** FULL OF TWISTS AND AMAZING COINCIDENCES full of twists and remarkable coincidences, like the plots of some of the novels of Dickens ○ *an*

episode too Dickensian for most modern audiences to swallow

dicker /díkər/ *vi* (**-ers, -ering, -ered**) to bargain for goods or services (*informal*) ○ *collectors dickering at antique sales* ■ *n* bargaining in general, or something settled, achieved, or obtained through bargaining [Early 19C. Probably < Latin *decuria* 'group of ten, ten hides for sale' < *decem* 'ten' + *vir* 'man']

dickey *n* another spelling of **dicky**²

dickhead /dík hed/ *n* an offensive term for a man who is regarded as unintelligent or annoying (*slang insult*)

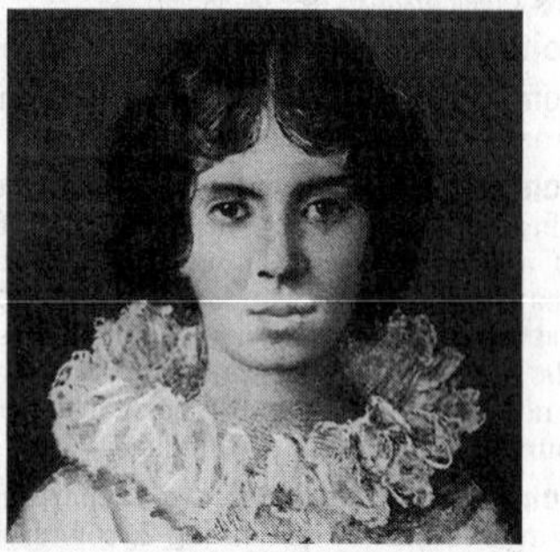

CORBIS/Bettmann

Emily Dickinson

Dickinson /díkinss'n/, **Emily** (1830–86) US poet. She is considered one of America's greatest writers. Most of her poems were published posthumously. Full name **Dickinson, Emily Elizabeth**

dicky¹ /díki/ (**-ier, -iest**) *adj* (*informal*) **1.** not well in health **2.** faulty or unreliable ○ *The doctor says I have a dicky heart.* [Late 18C. Origin ?]

dicky² /díki/ (*plural* **-ies**), **dickey** (*plural* **-eys**) *n* **1.** FALSE SHIRT FRONT OR NECK a garment that is only the front or neck of a shirt, worn under a shirt, jacket, or jumper **2.** OUTSIDE CAR SEAT a folding outside seat on the back of some early cars **3.** *regional* DONKEY a donkey, especially a male [Mid-18C. Origin ?]

dicky bird /díki-/ *n* **1.** a small bird (*baby talk*) **2.** a single word (*slang*) ○ *did not say a dicky bird* [Late 18C. Probably < *Dicky*, pet form of the name *Richard*; in sense 2 rhyming slang for WORD]

dicky bow *n* CLOTHING same as **bow tie** (*informal*) [Origin ?]

diclinous /dīklinəss, dī klīnəss/ *adj* describes plants that have stamens and pistils in separate flowers, rather than in the same flower [Early 19C. < modern Latin *diclines* 'two beds' < Greek *klinē* 'bed'] —**diclinism** /dī klinnizəm/ *n* —**dicliny** *n*

dicotyledon /dī kotti leéd'n/ *n* a flowering plant that produces two seed leaves (**cotyledons**) when it germinates and whose subsequent leaves have a network of veins. Most herbaceous plants, trees, and bushes are dicotyledons. Subclass: Dicotyledonae. [Early 18C. < modern Latin *Dicotyledonae*, literally 'two cotyledons'] —**dicotyledonous** *adj*

dicrotism /dīkrətizəm/ *n* a physiological condition in which each heartbeat produces a double pulse, occurring in typhoid fever and other conditions [Mid-19C. < Greek *dikrotos* 'double-beating'] —**dicrotal** *adj* —**dicrotic** /dī króttik/ *adj*

dict. *abbr* **1.** dictation **2.** POL dictator **3.** PUBL dictionary

dicta plural of **dictum**

Dictaphone /díktəfōn/ *tdmk* a trademark for a small hand-held tape recorder used for dictation

dictate *v* /dik táyt/ (**-tates, -tating, -tated**) **1.** *vti* SPEAK ALOUD WORDS TO BE WRITTEN to speak the words of a text or letter to be written, either to somebody writing it down as it is spoken, or into a tape recorder for later transcription **2.** *vti* RULE OR CONTROL OTHER PEOPLE to rule over or make decisions for others with absolute authority, or attempt to do so ○ *dictates their every move* **3.** *vt* CONTROL SOMETHING to have control over something (*usually passive*) ○ *The decision to go will be dictated by the weather conditions.* ■ *n* /dík tayt/ **1.** COMMAND GIVEN an order telling people what they must do ○ *dictates received from their superiors* **2.** GOVERNING PRINCIPLE a rule or principle that governs how people behave ○ *the dictates of fashion* [Late 16C. < Latin *dictat-*, past participle of *dictare* 'say often' < *dicere* 'to say']

dictation /dik táysh'n/ *n* **1.** the act of dictating a text or letter, or of writing down what is being dictated **2.** a test or exercise of language comprehension in which pupils write down words spoken aloud by a teacher ○ *a French dictation* —**dictational** *adj*

dictator /dik táytər/ *n* **1.** POL POWERFUL RULER a leader who rules a country with absolute power, usually by force **2.** BOSSY PERSON somebody who is regarded as behaving in an autocratic or domineering way **3.** AUTHORITY ON SUBJECT somebody whose opinions on a subject are listened to and followed by society at large ○ *one of the great dictators of modern music* **4.** ANCIENT HIST TEMPORARY ROMAN RULER in ancient Rome, a temporary appointed leader with absolute power to deal with a crisis or an emergency

dictatorial /díktə táwri əl/ *adj* **1.** fond of telling others what to do or of using power or authority to make them do it **2.** relating to or ruled by dictators —**dictatorially** *adv*

dictatorship /dik táytər ship/ *n* **1.** DICTATOR'S POWER OR RULE a dictator's power or authority, or the period of time during which a dictator rules **2.** GOVERNMENT BY DICTATOR government by a dictator, usually by force **3.** COUNTRY RULED BY DICTATOR a state ruled by a dictator **4.** ABSOLUTE AUTHORITY absolute power or authority

diction /díksh'n/ *n* **1.** the clarity with which somebody pronounces words when speaking or singing **2.** choice of words to fit their context ○*'a tendency to identify the poetic impulse with melancholy moods and sonorous diction'* (Northrop Frye, *The Bush Garden*; 1972) [Mid-16C. < Latin *diction-* < *dicere* 'to say'] —**dictional** *adj* —**dictionally** *adv*

ORIGIN The Latin word *dicere* 'to say', from which ***diction*** is derived, is also the source of English *addict, condition, dictate, dictionary, ditto, ditty, edict, judge, predict*, and *verdict*. Its derivative *dicare* 'to state, proclaim' also gave rise to English *abdicate, indicate, preach*, and *predicate*.

dictionary /díksh'nəri/ (*plural* **-ies**) *n* **1.** BOOK OF WORD MEANINGS a reference book that contains alphabetically ordered words, with explanations of their meanings, often with information about grammar, pronunciation, and etymology **2.** FOREIGN-LANGUAGE REFERENCE BOOK OF WORDS a reference book that alphabetically arranges and translates words and phrases in two or more languages ○ *a Spanish-English dictionary* **3.** SPECIALIZED REFERENCE BOOK a reference book that alphabetizes and explains terms relating to a subject or topic ○ *a dictionary of music* **4.** LIST OF INFORMATION a book that lists examples or information arranged alphabetically or in some other way, e.g. by author ○ *a dictionary of quotations* **5.** COMPUT WORD-PROCESSING REFERENCE a file used as a reference by a word-processing program for correct spelling and hyphenation **6.** COMPUT ALPHABETICAL LIST OF COMPUTER CODES an alphabetized list of keys or code names used in a program, each briefly defined [Early 16C. < medieval Latin *dictionarius* 'of words' < Latin *diction-* (see DICTION)]

dictum /díktəm/ (*plural* **-tums** or **-ta** /-tə/) *n* **1.** an authoritative saying, statement, or pronouncement **2.** a popular saying **3.** LAW same as **obiter dictum** (sense 1) [Late 16C. < Latin < past participle of *dicere* 'say']

dictyopteran /díkti óptərən/ *n* an insect with, typically, a flattened body, long legs, and leathery front wings held flat over the membranous hind wings, e.g. a cockroach or mantis. Order: Dictyoptera. [< modern Latin *Dictyoptera* < Greek *diktuon* 'net' + *pteron* 'wing']

dicy *adj* another spelling of **dicey** (*informal*)

dicynodont /dī sínnə dont/ *n* an extinct plant-eating reptile with teeth like tusks. Suborder: Dicynodontia. [Mid-19C. < modern Latin *Dicynodontia*, literally 'two canine teeth' < Greek *kun-* 'dog' + *odont-* 'tooth']

did past tense of **do**¹

DID *abbr* PSYCHIAT dissociative identity disorder

didactic /dī dáktik, di-/ *adj* **1.** containing a political or moral message ○ *didactic theatre* **2.** tending to give instruction or advice, even when it is not welcome or not needed [Mid-17C. < Greek *didaktikos* < *didaskein* 'teach'] —**didactically** *adv*

didacticism /dī dáktisizəm, di-/ *n* the instructional quality of something such as a piece of writing, or the attitude of somebody who likes to instruct others or give them advice ○ *the welcome absence of didacticism in modern poetry*

didactics /dī dáktiks, di-/ *n* the science or profession of teaching (*takes a singular verb*)

diddle¹ /dídd'l/ (**-dles, -dling, -dled**) *vt* (*informal*) **1.** CHEAT SOMEBODY to cheat or swindle somebody (*often passive*) **2.** COMPUT MANIPULATE DATA ILLEGALLY to manipulate computer data illegally **3.** COMPUT MANIPULATE PROGRAM to manipulate a computer program in an informal or a not particularly serious manner [Early 19C. Probably < Jeremy *Diddler*, character who constantly borrowed and failed to repay money in *Raising the Wind* (1803) by James Kenney (1780–1849)] —**diddler** *n*

diddle² /dídd'l/ (**-dles, -dling, -dled**) *v* **1.** *vi* SPEND TIME IDLY to spend time doing nothing in particular (*informal*) ○ *spent the morning diddling about* **2.** *vi* TOUCH OR PLAY WITH SOMETHING REPEATEDLY to spend time touching, fiddling with, or adjusting something repeatedly (*informal*) **3.** *vt* JERK REPEATEDLY to jerk something up and down or back and forth (*informal*) **4.** *vt N Am* OFFENSIVE TERM an offensive term meaning to have sexual intercourse with a woman (*slang*) [Mid-17C. Origin ?] —**diddler** *n*

diddlysquat /díddli skwot/, **diddly** *n N Am* nothing at all (*informal*) ○ *And what did I get? Diddlysquat!* [Mid-20C. Probably alteration of *doodlysquat*, origin ?]

diddy /díddi/ (**-dier, -diest**) *adj* very small (*informal*) ○ *a diddy little travelling manicure set* [Mid-20C. Probably alteration of *tiddy* 'small']

~~**dident**~~ incorrect spelling of **didn't**

Diderot /deédərō/, **Denis** (1713–84) French encyclopedist and philosopher. He was the chief editor of the 35-volume *Encyclopédie* (1751–80), one of the major works of the Enlightenment.

> 'No man has received from nature the right to give orders to others. Freedom is a gift from heaven, and every individual of the same species has the right to enjoy it as soon as he is in enjoyment of his reason.'
> [Denis Diderot, 'Political Authority', *Encyclopédie*; vol. 1, 1751]

didgeridoo /díjjəri dóo/ (*plural* **-doos**), **didjeridoo** *n* an Aboriginal musical instrument with a long thick wooden pipe that is blown to create a deep reverberating humming sound [Early 20C. < an Aboriginal language, an imitation of the sound]

didi /deé dee/ *n S Asia* **1.** somebody's older sister or female cousin (*often used as a form of address*) **2.** used as a form of address for an older woman [< Hindi]

didn't /díd'nt/ *contr* did not ○ *I didn't want to go.*

Dido /dīdō/ *n* in Roman mythology, the queen and founder of Carthage who killed herself when abandoned by her lover, Aeneas

Didrikson /dídriks'n/, **Babe** ♦ **Zaharias, Babe Didrikson**

didst /didst/ *vti* second person present singular of 'did', used with 'thou' (*archaic*)

didymium /dī dímmi əm/ *n* a mixture of metallic elements from the rare-earth, or lanthanide, series of elements, consisting chiefly of neodymium and praseodymium. Use: production of coloured glass, optical filters. [Mid-19C. < Greek *didumos* 'twin']

die¹ /dī/ (**dies, dying, died**) *v* **1.** *vi* STOP LIVING to cease to be alive (*refers to a person, plant, or animal*) **2.** *vi* STOP EXISTING to cease to exist, especially gradually ○ *feelings I thought had died long ago* **3.** *vi* STOP WORKING to stop functioning ○ *The engine suddenly died.* **4.** *vti* DIE AS STATED to experience a particular kind of death ○ *The villain, of course, dies a gruesome death.* **5.** *vi* EMPHASIZING DESIRE used to indicate how strongly the speaker wishes to do or have something ○ *I'm dying to tell them!* [12C. Probably < Old Norse *deyja* < Indo-European] ◇ **die hard** to give up or come to an end only after long, difficult, and sustained resistance ◇ **to die for** highly desirable and hence worth sacrificing something to obtain (*informal*)

SPELLCHECK die or **dye**? Do not confuse the spelling of ***die*** and ***dye***, which sound similar. ***Die*** is a verb meaning 'stop living or existing': *Her mother died last year. The*

sound died away. There is also a noun spelt *die*, which is used in the saying *the die is cast* and which denotes a dice, a mould, or a stamping or cutting tool. *Dye* is a noun or verb referring to a substance used to change the colour of something, as in *vegetable dyes, to dye your hair, a dyed-in-the-wool conservative.* Note also that the present participle of *die* is spelt *dying*, whereas the present participle of *dye* is spelt *dyeing.*

USAGE A person can *die of* an illness, or *die in* an earthquake or a fire. In careful usage, *die from* should be reserved for indirect causes of death, for example refusal to leave a flooded area or failure to wear a seat belt.

die away *vi* to fade or grow faint
die back *vi* to wither or die from the tips of new shoots back to the established stem or old wood of the plant, as a result of disease, seasonal change, or poor conditions
die down *vi* to become quieter, weaker, or less intense
die off *vi* to die gradually one by one, until none is left
die out *vi* **1.** to become extinct, or gradually cease to exist ○ *entire species that have died out in our century* **2.** to fade and finally disappear gradually ○ *Over the years, opposition to the plan had died out.*

die[2] /dī/ *n* **1.** (*plural* **dice** /dīss/) LEISURE same as **dice** *n* (sense 1) (*formal*) **2.** ENG **STAMPING OR PRESSING TOOL** the metal tool on a stamping or pressing machine that gives the finished object its shape and design **3.** ENG **MOULD** a tool for moulding substances such as metal or plastic **4.** ENG **TOOL FOR CUTTING** a tool that cuts screw threads on metal rods, consisting of a metal block with an internally threaded hole into which blank rods are screwed to cut external threads **5.** ARCHIT **PART OF PEDESTAL** the part of a pedestal that lies between the base and the cornice, especially when it is cubic in shape [12C. < French *dé* (see DICE)] ◇ **as straight as a die** completely honest and trustworthy (*informal*)

dieback /dī bak/ *n* gradual decay that sets in at a plant's young shoots then works back to established stems or old wood, as a result of disease, seasonal change, or poor conditions

die-cast *vt* to make a metal or plastic object by pouring or forcing molten metal or plastic into a mould —**die-cast** *adj*

diecious *adj* PLANTS another spelling of **dioecious**

Diefenbaker /dee'fən baykər/, **John George** (1895–1979) Canadian politician. He headed the Progressive Conservative Party (1956–67) and served as prime minister of Canada (1957–63). See table at **prime minister**

    'Freedom is the right to be wrong, not the right to do wrong.'
    [John George Diefenbaker. Quoted in *Reader's Digest*; September 1979]

dieffenbachia /deef'n báki ə/ *n* an evergreen plant with poisonous sap, widely cultivated as a house plant for its large many-coloured leaves. Native to: tropical America. Genus: *Dieffenbachia.* [Late 19C. < modern Latin, after Ernst *Dieffenbach* (1794–1855), German botanist]

~~**diegn**~~ incorrect spelling of **deign**

Diego Garcia /dee áygō gaar see ə/ largest island in the disputed island territory of the Chagos Archipelago, in the central Indian Ocean. It is the site of a US communications centre and naval base. Area: 27 sq. km/11 sq. mi.

diehard /dī haard/ *adj* resistant to any kind of change, and reluctant to give up beliefs, positions, or attitudes ○ *diehard fans* ■ *n* somebody who resists change or stubbornly persists in a belief or opinion ○ *with the old diehards holding out to the bitter end* —**diehardism** *n*

~~**dieing**~~ incorrect spelling of **dying**

dieldrin /dee'ldrin/ *n* an insecticide based on a chlorinated naphthalene derivative, now widely banned. Formula: $C_{12}H_8OCl_6$. [Mid-20C. After Otto *Diels* (1876–1954), German chemist + *aldrin*, toxic insecticide, after Kurt *Alder* (see DIELS-ALDER REACTION)]

dielectric /dī iléktrik/ *adj* not able to conduct direct electric current, and therefore useful as an insulator ■ *n* a dielectric substance [Mid-19C. < DIA-] —**dielectrically** *adv*

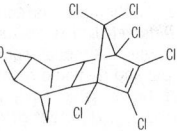

dieldrin

dielectric constant *n* PHYS same as **relative permittivity**

dielectric heating *n* the heating of an insulating material by placing it in a rapidly changing electric field. The technique is used in the manufacture of foam rubber, plastics, and other materials.

dielectric lens *n* a lens made of insulating material that deflects radio waves passing through it in the way that a glass lens deflects light. Use: to shape beams emitted from radar and microwave antennas.

Diels-Alder reaction /dee'lz áwldər-/ *n* a chemical reaction in which an organic compound with two double bonds between carbon atoms (**diene**) and a compound containing a double or triple bond combine to form a ring compound [Mid-20C. After Otto *Diels* (see DIELDRIN) and Kurt *Alder* (1902–58), German chemist]

Diem /dyem/, **Ngo Dinh** (1901–63) Vietnamese politician. He was supported by the United States as the first president of South Vietnam (1955–63). He was assassinated after large antigovernment demonstrations.

diencephalon /dī en séffə lon, -kéffə-/ *n* the area in the centre of the brain just above the brain stem that includes the thalamus and hypothalamus [Late 19C. < DIA- + Greek *enkephalos* 'brain'] —**diencephalic** /dī enssə fállik/ *adj*

diene /dī een/ *n* an unsaturated hydrocarbon (**alkene**) containing two carbon-to-carbon double bonds

Dieppe /di ép/ seaport and resort on the English Channel in the Seine-Maritime department, Haute-Normandie region, in northwestern France. It is situated about 97 km/60 mi. west of Amiens. Population: 34,653 (1999).

dieresis *n* LING, LITERAT another spelling of **diaeresis**

Dieri /dee'ri/, **Diyari** *n* an Aboriginal language of South Australia, now almost extinct [Late 19C. < *Dieri*] —**Dieri** *adj*

diesel /dee'z'l/ *n* **1.** AUTOMOT same as **diesel engine 2.** a vehicle, e.g. a car or train, that is powered by a diesel engine **3.** AUTOMOT same as **diesel oil** [Late 19C. After Rudolf *Diesel* (1858–1913), German engineer]

diesel-electric *n* a locomotive in which a diesel engine drives an electric generator that provides current to the traction motors driving the wheels

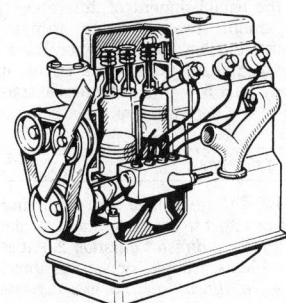

diesel engine: cutaway view showing compression chambers

diesel engine *n* an internal-combustion engine that ignites diesel oil using compression alone, rather than using an electrical spark

diesel fuel *n N Am* same as **diesel oil**

diesel-hydraulic *n* a locomotive primarily powered by a diesel engine but with power transmitted through an oil-filled torque converter or infinitely variable gear

diesel oil *n* a thick oily fuel that is obtained from the distillation of petroleum. It has an ignition temperature of 540°C and is ignited by the heat of compression. N Am term **diesel fuel**

Dies Irae /dee'ayz eér ī/ *n* **1.** a 13th-century Latin hymn that describes the Last Judgment, used in a Christian Mass for the dead **2.** a musical setting of the Dies Irae, usually as part of a Requiem Mass [< Latin, 'day of wrath']

diesis /dī əsiss/ (*plural* **-eses** /-ə seez/) *n* PRINTING same as **double dagger** [14C. Via Latin < Greek, 'quarter tone' (which the symbol originally indicated)]

dies non /dī eez nón/ *n* a day on which no legal business is done [Early 19C. Shortening of Latin *dies non juridicus* 'day not judicial']

diestock /dī stok/ *n* a device for holding the dies that are used for cutting threads on screws [Mid-19C. < DIE[2]]

diestrus *n* ZOOL US spelling of **dioestrus**

diet[1] /dī ət/ *n* **1.** WHAT PERSON OR ANIMAL EATS the food that a person or animal usually consumes **2.** CONTROLLED INTAKE OF FOOD a controlled intake of food and drink designed for weight loss, for health or religious reasons, or to control or improve a medical condition ○ *a wheat-free diet* **3.** REGULAR INTAKE OF SOMETHING a continuous or daily experience of, or indulgence in, something other than food ○ *living on a diet of soap operas and game shows* ■ *adj* DESIGNED OR PROMOTED FOR WEIGHT LOSS describes a food or drink that is intended for people trying to lose weight, usually because it is low in calories or fat, or contains a sugar substitute ○ *a diet soda* ■ *vi* (**-ets, -eting, -eted**) EAT LESS to follow a restricted pattern of eating or drinking in order to lose weight [Pre-12C. Via Old French *diete* < Greek *diaita* 'course of life'] —**dietary** *adj* —**dieter** *n*

diet[2] /dī ət/ *n* **1.** LAW COURT SESSION IN SCOTLAND in Scotland, a session of a court, or the date fixed for a court hearing **2.** POL PARLIAMENT a legislative assembly in some countries such as Japan **3.** HIST ASSEMBLY IN HOLY ROMAN EMPIRE a general assembly of the estates of the Holy Roman Empire [15C. < medieval Latin *dieta* 'day's journey, work', (by association with Latin *dies* 'day') 'day for a meeting (of legislators)', probably < Greek *diaita* 'course of life']

dietary fibre *n* same as **fibre** (sense 7)

dietary laws *npl* the rules governing which items of food practising Jews are permitted to eat, derived from Leviticus 11 and Deuteronomy 14

dietetic /dī ə téttik/ *adj* **1.** relating to what people eat and drink **2.** prepared to suit the requirements of a special diet —**dietetically** *adv*

dietetics /dī ə téttiks/ *n* the study of food and nutrition and its relation to people's health (*takes a singular verb*)

diethylcarbamazine /dī éthil kaar bámmə zeen-, dī ee thīl-/ *n* a white water-soluble substance in the form of crystals. Use: to treat worms in humans, dogs, and cats. [< DI-[1] + ETHYL + CARBO- + AMIDE + AZINE]

diethyl ether /dī éthil-, dī ee thīl-/ *n* CHEM same as **ether** (sense 1)

diethylstilbestrol /dī éthil stil bee'strol/, **diethylstilboestrol** *n* a synthetic oestrogen. Use: formerly, for hormone replacement. [Mid-20C. < DI-[1] + ETHYL + STILBENE + OESTROGEN + -OL[1]]

diethyl toluamide /dī éthil tólyoo ámmīd, dī ee thīl-/ *n* CHEM same as **deet**

~~**dieties**~~ incorrect spelling of **deities**

dietitian /dī ə tísh'n/, **dietician** *n* a specialist in the study of food and nutrition in relation to health

Marlene Dietrich

Dietrich /dée trik/, **Marlene** (1901–92) German-born US singer and film actor. She starred in films from the 1930s to the 1970s, including *The Devil is a Woman* (1935) and *Witness for the Prosecution* (1957). Full name **von Losch, Maria Magdalene Dietrich**

'Once a woman has forgiven her man, she must not reheat his sins for breakfast.'
[Marlene Dietrich, *Cosmopolitan*; February 1980]

Dieu et mon droit /dyő ay mon drwáa/ *n* 'God and my right', the motto written under the coat of arms of the British Royal Family [< French]

~~**diferent**~~ incorrect spelling of **different**

diff. *abbr* **1.** difference **2.** different

differ /díffər/ (**-fers, -fering, -fered**) *vi* **1.** to be dissimilar or unlike ○ *new models that differ greatly from the early prototypes* **2.** to have different opinions about something ○ *We agreed to differ.* [14C. Via French, 'differ, defer' < Latin *differre* 'differ' < *ferre* 'carry']

SYNONYMS See ***disagree.***

difference /díffrənss/ *n* **1.** STATE OF BEING UNLIKE OTHERS the quality of being different from or unlike something or somebody else ○ *There's no real difference between going by train and going by car.* **2.** DISTINGUISHING FEATURE a feature that distinguishes one person or thing from another ○ *Can you spot the differences between the two?* **3.** SIGNIFICANT CHANGE a change that has an effect ○ *a noticeable difference in her moods* **4.** DISAGREEMENT a disagreement, argument, or divergence of opinions ○ *settle our differences* **5.** MATHS ANSWER TO SUBTRACTION EQUATION the amount by which one quantity is greater or smaller than another ○ *What's the difference between 16 and 6?* **6.** LOGIC DEFINING FEATURE a distinguishing feature that marks out a thing being defined or discussed from others that are more general ○ *being divisible by two is the difference between even numbers and other whole numbers* **7.** HERALDRY ADDITION TO COAT OF ARMS an addition to a family's coat of arms that represents a younger branch of the family ◇ **make all the difference** to have an enormous, usually positive, effect or influence ◇ **make no difference** to be of no importance or not matter ◇ **split the difference** to take the average of two amounts, or agree on something that is halfway between two extremes ◇ **tell the difference** to distinguish or figure out the features that make things unlike each other

USAGE difference or **differentiation**? These two words do not share a single meaning, so careful writers avoid using them interchangeably. ***Difference*** denotes the quality of being different, or an instance of this. ***Differentiation*** denotes becoming different in the course of development. *My paper explores the difference* [not *differentiation*] *between the world of the adult and the world of the child.* Conversely, do not use ***difference*** when ***differentiation*** is called for: *studied the history of the differentiation* [not *difference*] *of Latin into vernaculars.*

different /díffrənt/ *adj* **1.** UNLIKE SOMETHING OR SOMEBODY ELSE not the same as something or somebody else ○ *This is certainly different from anything I've ever experienced before.* **2.** DISTINCT separate or distinct from another or others ○ *She wore a different pair of shoes every day.* **3.** UNUSUAL contrary to norms or expectations ○ *What do you think of my hat? – Well, it's certainly different.* [14C. Via French < Latin *different-*, present participle of *differre* (see DIFFER)] —**differently** *adv*

USAGE different from, different to, or **different than**? No one objects to ***different from*** (on the analogy of *differ from*): *His attitude towards women was quite different from that of his contemporaries.* ***Different to*** is not so generally accepted, although it is commonly used in British English. ***Different than*** is also seen and heard, especially in US English. Although some object to it as a matter of principle and it should be avoided in formal writing, it can at times serve as a useful shortcut. Compare *The book has a different title from the one I thought it had* with *The book has a different title than I thought.*

differentia /díffə rénshi ə/ (*plural* **-tiae** /-shi ee/) *n* an element that separates one thing from another, especially a trait that distinguishes one subclass from another, e.g. one species from another in the same genus

differential /díffə rénsh'l/ *n* **1.** DIFFERENCE BETWEEN POINTS ON SCALE a difference between two values on a scale, e.g. a difference in the rates of pay for different jobs in the same line of work **2.** AUTOMOT same as **differential gear 3.** MATHS CHANGE IN VARIABLE an infinitesimal change in a variable ■ *adj* **1.** OF DIFFERENCES relating to or based on differences **2.** MATHS RELATING TO CHANGE IN VARIABLES relating to or involving infinitesimal changes in a variable with respect to another variable

differential calculus *n* the branch of mathematics dealing with continuously varying quantities, with applications in the determination of maximum and minimum points, and with rates of change through the use of derivatives and differentials

differential coefficient *n* MATHS same as **derivative** *n* (sense 4)

differential equation *n* a mathematical equation that relates functions and their derivatives

differential gear *n* an arrangement of gears that allows two shafts driven by a third to turn at different speeds, e.g. in a motor vehicle

differentiate /díffə rénshi ayt/ (**-ates, -ating, -ated**) *v* **1.** *vti* SEE DIFFERENCES BETWEEN THINGS to see or show the differences between two or more things **2.** *vt* BE DIFFERENCE to establish a difference between two things or among several things **3.** *vti* MAKE OR BECOME DIFFERENT to make something different or specialized by modifying it, or become different or specialized by being modified **4.** *vti* EDUC PROVIDE ACTIVITIES MATCHED TO ABILITY to provide school work and activities that are suited to the individual abilities of each student **5.** *vi* BIOL BECOME SPECIALIZED to change from a generalized form into a form specialized for a tissue, organ, or other body part (*refers to embryo cells*) **6.** *vt* MATHS CALCULATE DERIVATIVE OF FUNCTION to calculate the mathematical derivative of a function [Early 19C. < medieval Latin *differentiat-*, past participle of *differentiare* < Latin *differre* (see DIFFER)] —**differentiable** *adj* —**differentiator** *n*

differentiation /díffə renshi áysh'n/ *n* **1.** DEVELOPMENT FROM ONE INTO MANY a developmental process from a single unit or whole into many other derived things, or from a simple to a complex state **2.** VISIBLE DIFFERENCES the complex of visible differences exhibited among two or more things **3.** ESTABLISHMENT OF DIFFERENCES the establishment of differences or a difference among two or more things **4.** BIOL SPECIALIZATION change from a generalized form to another, specialized, form for a tissue, organ, or other body part **5.** MATHS CALCULATION OF DERIVATIVE calculation of the derivative of a mathematical function

USAGE See ***difference.***

difficult /díffik'lt/ *adj* **1.** HARD TO DO requiring a lot of planning or effort to do, understand, or deal with ○ *a difficult job* ○ *a difficult question* **2.** FULL OF PROBLEMS full of problems, trouble, or aspects that are hard to endure ○ *a difficult birth* **3.** HARD TO PLEASE hard to please or control ○ *a difficult audience* **4.** HARD TO CONVINCE hard to convince or persuade ○ *If they're difficult, offer them more.* **5.** FULL OF HARDSHIP containing great hardship, especially of a financial kind [14C. Back-formation < DIFFICULTY] —**difficultness** *n*

SYNONYMS See ***hard.***

difficulty /díffik'lti/ *n* (*plural* **-ties**) **1.** QUALITY OF BEING DIFFICULT the quality of being hard to do, understand, or deal with **2.** SOMETHING NOT EASILY DONE something that is hard to do, understand, or deal with **3.** EFFORT a great effort or struggle to do something **4.** DISPUTE a dispute or controversy ■ **difficulties** *npl* **1.** TROUBLE a situation full of trouble, danger, or embarrassment ○ *Even a strong swimmer can get into difficulties in this river.* **2.** OBJECTIONS objections or attempts to prevent the progress of something ○ *You're supposed to be here to help, not make difficulties.* [14C. < Latin *difficultas* < *difficilis* 'not easy' < *facilis* (see FACILE)]

diffident /díffidənt/ *adj* **1.** lacking self-confidence and rather shy **2.** reserved or restrained in behaviour [15C. < Latin *diffident-*, present participle of *diffidere* 'to distrust' < *fidere* 'to trust'] —**diffidence** *n* —**diffidently** *adv*

diffract /di frákt/ (**-fracts, -fracting, -fracted**) *vti* to produce diffraction in waves such as light or sound waves, or undergo diffraction [Early 19C. < Latin *diffract-*, past participle of *diffringere* 'to break apart' < *frangere* 'to break'] —**diffractive** *adj* —**diffractively** *adv* —**diffractiveness** *n*

diffraction /di fráksh'n/ *n* the bending or spreading out of waves, e.g. of sound or light, as they pass round the edge of an obstacle or through a narrow aperture

diffraction grating *n* a glass plate or metal mirror engraved with a large number of parallel lines or grooves, used to produce a spectrum by diffraction or interference

diffraction ring *n* a circular pattern of light that surrounds a particle under a microscope, resulting from diffraction

diffractometer /díffrak tómmitər/ *n* an instrument that uses diffraction, usually of X-rays or electrons by crystals, to investigate the atomic structure of a material

~~**diffrent**~~ incorrect spelling of **different**

diffuse[1] /di fyóoz/ (**-fuses, -fusing, -fused**) *vti* **1.** SPREAD THROUGH to spread something throughout something else, or become spread throughout something else **2.** SCATTER OR BECOME SCATTERED to scatter something over an area, or become scattered over an area **3.** MAKE SOMETHING LESS INTENSE to make something, especially light, less bright or intense, or become less bright or intense **4.** UNDERGO OR SUBJECT TO DIFFUSION to subject something to diffusion, or undergo diffusion [14C. < Latin *diffus-*, past participle of *diffundere* 'pour in every direction' < *fundere* 'pour'] —**diffusible** *adj*

SPELLCHECK See ***defuse***

diffuse[2] /di fyóoss/ *adj* **1.** spread throughout a wide area **2.** lacking organization and conciseness, especially in writing or speech [15C Directly or via French < Latin *diffusus* 'spread out', past participle of *diffundere* (see DIFFUSE [1])] —**diffusely** *adv* —**diffuseness** *n*

SPELLCHECK See ***defuse***

SYNONYMS See ***wordy.***

diffuser /di fyóozər/, **diffusor** *n* **1.** HAIR DRYER ATTACHMENT an attachment for a hair dryer that slows down and spreads the air flow, making the drying action gentler **2.** DEVICE THAT DIFFUSES LAMP LIGHT a piece of translucent or reflective material fixed to a light source such as a lamp in order to soften or spread the light over a wide area **3.** PHOTOGRAPHY, CINEMA DEVICE THAT SOFTENS PHOTOGRAPHER'S LIGHT a cloth screen, piece of frosted glass, or other material that is used to soften the brightness of the lighting in photography or cinematography **4.** ACOUSTICS CONE TO DISPERSE SOUND WAVES a device, e.g. a cone or wedge, fixed inside a loudspeaker to diffuse sound waves

diffusion /di fyóozh'n/ *n* **1.** PROCESS OF DIFFUSING a process during which something diffuses or is diffused **2.** RESULT OF DIFFUSING the result of something diffusing or being diffused **3.** CULTL ANTHROP SPREAD OF CULTURAL FEATURES the spread of tools, practices, or other features from one culture to another **4.** PHYS SCATTERING OF LIGHT the scattering of light in many directions as the result of reflection from an uneven surface or passage though a translucent material **5.** PHYS INTERMINGLING OF SUBSTANCES the random movement of atoms, molecules, or ions from one site in a medium to another, resulting in complete mixing —**diffusional** *adj*

diffusionism /di fyo͞ozh'nizəm/ *n* the anthropological theory that similarities in tools, practices, or other features between cultures result from their being spread from one culture to another rather than being arrived at independently —**diffusionist** *adj, n*

diffusive /di fyo͞ossiv/ *adj* **1.** relating to, involving, or characteristic of diffusion **2.** same as **diffuse**[2] (sense 2) —**diffusively** *adv*

diffusor *n* another spelling of **diffuser**

~~**dificult**~~ incorrect spelling of **difficult**

dig /dig/ *v* (**digs, digging, dug** /dug/) **1.** *vti* **BREAK UP OR REMOVE EARTH** to break up, turn, or remove something, especially soil, with the hands, paws, a tool, or a machine ○ *The excavator dug the rock out of the hole.* **2.** *vt* **CREATE SOMETHING BY DIGGING** to make something by removing material, especially earth, with the hands, paws, a tool, or a machine ○ *digging a hole* **3.** *vti* **OBTAIN OR FREE BY DIGGING** to obtain, uncover, or free something by removing the material covering it using the hands, paws, a tool, or a machine ○ *dig the car out of the snow* **4.** *vi* **SEARCH BY DIGGING** to try to find something by digging ○ *dig for buried treasure* **5.** *vti* **MOVE THROUGH SOMETHING BY DIGGING** to move through something by digging a way through it **6.** *vti* **DISCOVER SOMETHING BY RESEARCH** to find out something by research or questioning ○ *See what you can dig up about her past.* **7.** *vi* **SEARCH CAREFULLY** to search carefully or persistently ○ *digging through the papers in the file* **8.** *vti* **PUSH INTO SOMETHING FORCEFULLY** to push something into something else with force, or be pushed with force into something ○ *dug his teeth into the steak* ○ *dug her elbow into my side* **9.** *vti* **UNDERSTAND SOMETHING** to understand something fully or with sympathy (*dated slang*) ○ *I dig what you're saying.* **10.** *vt* **LIKE SOMEBODY OR SOMETHING** to like or appreciate somebody or something (*dated slang*) ○ *They don't dig jazz.* ■ *n* **1. PROD** a push with something fairly sharp ○ *a dig in the ribs* **2. CUTTING REMARK** a remark intended to hurt or make fun of somebody ○ *a dig about her new hairstyle* **3. ACT OF DIGGING** the act of digging or excavating something **4.** ARCHAEOL **ARCHAEOLOGICAL EXCAVATION** an archaeological or palaeontological excavation ○ *a dig in Egypt* **5.** SOCCER **POWERFUL BLOW** a powerful blow, especially a kick at a football (*informal*) ○ *It was a well-placed free kick and he really gave it quite a dig.* ■ **digs** *npl* **LODGINGS** a room or rooms that somebody rents in another person's house (*dated informal*) [12C. Origin ?]

dig in *v* **1.** *vti* **TAKE UP DEFENSIVE POSITIONS** to prepare trenches or other defensive structures, or establish a force or equipment in a defensive position **2.** *vi* **RESIST ATTACK** to put up a stubborn resistance to an attack **3.** *vi* **MAINTAIN OPINION STUBBORNLY** to stick to an established position, e.g. in an argument, and fight stubbornly to maintain it **4.** *vi* **START EATING** to start eating, especially in an enthusiastic way (*informal*) **5.** *vt* **BURY PLANTS** to cover plants or the remains of a crop by turning over the soil in which they are growing and burying them

dig out *vt* **1. UNCOVER SOMETHING** to obtain, uncover, or free something by removing the material covering it using the hands, paws, a tool, or a machine **2. RETRIEVE SOMETHING** to retrieve something from where it is kept (*informal*) **3. DISCOVER SOMETHING** to find something out by research or questioning (*informal*)

dig up *vt* **1. TAKE SOMETHING OUT OF GROUND** to dig for something that is buried in the ground and remove it **2. TURN OVER EARTH** to dig into and turn over the soil in an area **3. INVESTIGATE SOMETHING** to find out something by research or investigation (*informal*)

digamma /dī gamə/ *n* a letter of the ancient Greek alphabet that became obsolete in the classical period, represented in the English alphabet as 'w'. See table at **alphabet** [Late 17C. Via Latin < Greek, 'double gamma'; from its resemblance to two capital gammas, one above the other]

digamy /díggəmi/ (*plural* **-mies**) *n* a second marriage that, unlike bigamy, is legal because the first husband or wife is dead or has been divorced (*formal*) [Early 17C. Via late Latin < Greek *digamia*, < *digamos* 'married to two people' < *gamos* 'marriage'] —**digamous** *adj*

digastric /dī gástrik/ *adj* describes a muscle, especially the muscle on either side of the lower jaw, in which two fleshy parts are connected by a tendon [Early 18C. < modern Latin *digastricus* < *gastricus* (see GASTRIC); from an analogy between 'fleshy parts' and 'stomachs']

digerati /díjjə raáti/, **digiterati** /díjjitə raáti/ *npl* people with expertise in computers, the Internet, or the World Wide Web (*informal*) [Late 20C. < DIGITAL after LITERATI]

digest *v* /dī jést, di-/ (**-gests, -gesting, -gested**) **1.** *vt* **PROCESS FOOD** to process food in the body into a form that can be absorbed and used or excreted **2.** *vt* **ABSORB SOMETHING MENTALLY** to think about something and come to understand or appreciate what it means **3.** *vt* **ORGANIZE SOMETHING SYSTEMATICALLY** to organize something into a system, often through selective condensing of the various items **4.** *vt* **ABRIDGE SOMETHING** to make a summary of something, often a written work **5.** *vti* CHEM **BREAK DOWN** to soften or break down a substance through exposure to heat, water, chemicals, enzymes, or bacteria, or be broken down in this way ■ *n* /dī jest/ **1. SUMMARY** a shortened version of a work that contains the most important or interesting information from the original version **2. COLLECTION OF ABRIDGED PIECES** a magazine, book, or broadcast that contains shortened versions of articles or stories originally from different sources **3.** LAW **COLLECTION OF LEGAL OPINIONS** a systematic compilation of laws or legal opinions [14C. < Latin *digest-*, past participle of *digerere* 'carry apart' < *gerere* 'carry']

digester /dī jéstər, di-/ *n* **1.** somebody or something that digests something **2.** a vessel or device in which chemical digestion takes place

digestible /dī jéstəb'l, di-/ *adj* easily digested —**digestibility** /dī jéstə bílləti, di-/ *n* —**digestibly** *adv*

digestif /di zhe steéf/ *n* an alcoholic drink, e.g. a brandy or liqueur, drunk after a meal, supposedly to help the digestion of food [Early 20C. < French, 'digestive' < Latin *digestivus* < *digerere* (see DIGEST)]

digestion /dī jéschən, di-/ *n* **1. PROCESSING OF FOOD IN BODY** the breaking down of foodstuffs in the body into a form that can be absorbed and used or excreted **2. ABILITY TO DIGEST FOOD** the ability to process food in the body into a form that can be absorbed and used or excreted **3. ABILITY TO ABSORB IDEAS** the ability to think about something and come to understand or appreciate what it means, or the process of doing so **4.** CHEM **BREAKING DOWN** the softening or breaking down of a substance through exposure to heat, water, chemicals, enzymes, or bacteria —**digestional** *adj*

digestive /dī jéstiv, di-/ *adj* relating to or aiding in the digestion of food ■ *n* **1.** something that aids or promotes the digesting of food **2.** FOOD same as **digestive biscuit** —**digestively** *adv*

digestive biscuit *n* a semisweet round biscuit that is made from wholemeal flour

digestive gland *n* a gland that secretes digestive enzymes, e.g. the pancreas in vertebrates

digestive tract *n* ANAT same as **alimentary canal**

digger /díggər/ *n* **1.** somebody or something that digs **2.** a tool, machine, or part of a machine that is used for digging or excavation **3.** another spelling of **Digger**

Digger (*plural* **Diggers** or **diggers**) *n* **1. SOMEBODY FROM AUSTRALIA OR NEW ZEALAND** somebody from Australia, especially a soldier who served in World War I, or somebody from New Zealand, especially a soldier who served in World War I or II (*informal*) **2.** *Aus* **MAN IN LATER LIFE** a man of advanced years (*informal*) **3.** *ANZ* **FORM OF ADDRESS** used as a friendly form of address between men (*informal*) **4. MEMBER OF RELIGIOUS GROUP** a member of the English Puritan religious group, the Diggers, active in 1649 and 1650, who believed in communal land ownership

diggings /díggingz/ *n* **MINING LOCATION** a place where something is mined, especially precious metals or gems ■ *npl* **1. MATERIAL EXCAVATED** material that has been dug out of a hole or mine **2. LODGINGS** a room or rooms that somebody rents in somebody else's house (*dated informal*)

dight /dīt/ (**dights, dighting, dight** or **dighted**) *vt* to equip, dress, or adorn somebody (*archaic*) [Old English *dihtan*, via Germanic < Latin *dictare* 'say often', (see DICTATE)]

digicam /díji kam/ *n* PHOTOGRAPHY same as **digital camera**

digit /díjjit/ *n* **1.** MATHS **NUMERAL IN DECIMAL SYSTEM** one of the ten Arabic numerals, 0 to 9, that are used to represent numbers in the decimal system **2.** MATHS **NUMERAL IN ANY NUMBER SYSTEM** in any system of numbering, a symbol that represents a number **3.** ANAT **HUMAN FINGER OR TOE** a finger or toe of a human **4.** ZOOL **ANIMAL FINGER OR TOE** a finger, toe, or similar part on a terrestrial vertebrate [14C. < Latin *digitus* 'finger, toe']

digital: clock displaying the time in numerical form

digital /díjjit'l/ *adj* **1. REPRESENTING DATA AS NUMBERS** processing, storing, transmitting, representing, or displaying data in the form of numerical digits, as in a digital computer **2. REPRESENTING SOUND/LIGHT WAVES AS NUMBERS** representing a varying physical quantity such as sound or light waves by means of discrete signals interpreted as numbers, usually in the binary system, as in a digital recording or digital television **3.** ECON **OF E-COMMERCE** relating to, used in, or characterized by e-commerce **4. LIKE FINGER** like a finger or toe **5. DONE WITH FINGERS** using or operated by a finger or fingers [15C. < Latin *digitalis* < *digitus* 'finger, toe'] —**digitally** *adv*

digital audio tape *n* a magnetic tape used in the digital recording of music

digital camera *n* a camera that records and stores photographic images in digital form. The images can be viewed and manipulated by the camera, loaded onto a computer, and printed as a photograph or e-mailed as an image.

digital cash *n* credit in the form of an encoded bank authorization that can be used for buying goods or services on the Internet

digital certificate *n* a unique code assigned to a buyer, merchant, or bank in online business transactions that allows the recipient to verify the sender's identity and encrypt a response

digital coins *npl* electronic payment in small denominations (*used in e-commerce*)

digital computer *n* a computer that stores and performs a series of mathematical and logical operations on data expressed as discrete signals interpreted as numbers, usually in the form of binary notation

digital display *n* a video display that renders a limited number of colours and shades of grey

digital divide *n* the difference in opportunities available to people who have access to modern information technology and those who do not

digital encryption standard *n* a standard for private key data encryption that uses 56-bit encryption (*used in e-commerce*)

digital imagery, **digital imaging** *n* the process of altering a digital image on a computer

digitalis /díjji táyliss/ (*plural* **-ises** or *same*) *n* **1.** a drug containing glycoside, prepared from dried foxglove leaves. Use: heart stimulant. **2.** a plant such as the foxglove. Native to: Europe, Asia. Genus: *Digitalis*. [Early 17C. Via modern Latin, 'foxglove' < Latin, 'of or like a finger' (see DIGITAL); from the shape of the flowers]

digitalize[1] /díjjitə līz/ (**-izes, -izing, -ized**), **digitalise** (**-ises, -ising, -ised**) *vt* COMPUT same as **digitize** [Mid-20C. < DIGITAL] —**digitalization** /díjjitə lī záysh'n/ *n*

digitalize[2] /díjjitə līz/ (**-izes, -izing, -ized**) **digitalise** (**-ises, -ising, -ised**) *vt* to treat somebody with digitalis [Mid-20C. < DIGITAL]

digital logic *n* the use of digital circuitry to determine if a condition is true or false

digital object identifier *n* an identifying symbol for a web file that redirects users to any new Internet location for that file

digital recording *n* **1.** audio recording in which sounds are stored as numbers, producing purer sound **2.** a recording made using the digital method

digital signature *n* a digital signal or pattern that identifies the user or the user's habits

Digital Subscriber Line *n* full form of **DSL**

digital tablet *n* COMPUT same as **graphics tablet**

digital television *n* **1.** television broadcasting in which the picture is transmitted as discrete signals represented as numbers **2.** a television set specially constructed or adapted for receiving such signals

digital video disc, **digital versatile disc** *n* TECH full form of **DVD**

digital video disc-ROM *n* TECH full form of **DVD-ROM**

digital wallet *n* an item of software that stores information about an online shopper's payment options and may contain credit in the form of digital cash, or credit card or bank information

digital watch *n* a watch that shows the time in numerical form, instead of by hands on a dial

digitate /díjji tayt/, **digitated** /-taytid/ *adj* **1.** having fingers or toes, or having parts that are like fingers or toes **2.** describes leaves that have divisions or parts arrayed from a central point like the spread fingers of a hand —**digitately** *adv* —**digitation** /díjji táysh'n/ *n*

digiterati *npl* COMPUT same as **digerati** (*informal*)

digitigrade /díjjiti grayd/ *adj* describes the gait of animals such as cats and deer that walk with only the tips of the digits touching the ground, the rest of the foot being raised ◼ *n* an animal such as a cat or deer that walks with its weight on its digits and the back of its foot raised [Mid-19C. < French < Latin *digitus* 'finger, toe' + *gradus* 'step']

digitize /díjji tīz/ (**-tizes, -tizing, -tized**), **digitise** (**-tises, -tising, -tised**) *vt* to convert an image, graph, or other data into digital form for processing on a computer —**digitization** /díjji tī záysh'n/ *n* —**digitizer** *n*

digitizing tablet /díjji tīzing-/ *n* COMPUT same as **graphics tablet**

digitoxin /díjji tóksin/ *n* a bitter white glycoside found in foxglove leaves. Use: heart stimulant. Formula: $C_{41}H_{64}O_{13}$. [Late 19C. Blend of DIGITALIS + TOXIN]

digizine /díjji zeen/ *n* a magazine that is delivered in digital form either on the Internet or on a CD-ROM (*informal*) [Blend of DIGITAL + MAGAZINE]

diglossia /dī glóssi ə/ *n* the existence of a formal literary form of a language, considered more prestigious, along with a colloquial form used by most speakers and considered of lower status [Mid-20C. < Greek *diglōssos* 'bilingual' < *glōssa* 'language']

dignified /dígni fīd/ *adj* showing self-respect or behaving in a proper and respectable way —**dignifiedly** *adv*

dignify /dígni fī/ (**-fies, -fying, -fied**) *vt* **1.** GIVE DISTINCTION TO SOMETHING to give honour or an aura of importance to something **2.** GIVE UNDESERVED ATTENTION TO SOMETHING to treat somebody or something as honourable or worthy of attention when this treatment is undeserved ○ *I won't dignify his insult with a response.* **3.** ENNOBLE SOMEBODY to award an honour to somebody, or raise somebody to noble rank [15C. Via obsolete French *dignifier* < late Latin *dignificare* 'make worthy' < Latin *dignus* 'worthy']

dignitary /dígnitəri/ (*plural* **-ies**) *n* somebody who holds a high rank or position

dignity /dígnəti/ (*plural* **-ties**) *n* **1.** SELF-RESPECT a proper sense of pride and self-respect **2.** SERIOUSNESS IN BEHAVIOUR seriousness, respectfulness, or formality in somebody's behaviour and bearing **3.** WORTHINESS the condition of being worthy of respect, esteem, or honour **4.** DUE RESPECT the respect or honour that a high rank or position should be shown **5.** HIGH OFFICE a high rank, position, or honour [12C. Via French < Latin *dignitas* < *dignus* 'worthy']

ORIGIN The Latin word *dignus* 'worthy', from which *dignity* is derived, is also the source of English *condign*, *dainty*, *deign*, *disdain*, and *indignant*.

digoxin /dī jóksin/ *n* a glycoside extracted from foxglove leaves. Use: heart stimulant. [Mid-20C. Contraction of DIGITOXIN, a similar glycoside]

digraph /dí graaf, -graf/ *n* **1.** a pair of letters that represents a single speech sound, e.g. 'ng' in 'ring' or 'ch' in 'child' **2.** PRINTING same as **ligature** (sense 5) —**digraphic** /dī gráffik/ *adj* —**digraphically** *adv*

digress /dī gréss/ (**-gresses, -gressing, -gressed**) *vi* to move away from the central topic or line of argument in speaking or writing, usually temporarily [Early 16C. < Latin *digress-*, past participle of *digredi* 'step aside' < *gradus* 'step']

digression /dī grésh'n/ *n* **1.** an act or instance of departing from the central topic or line of argument while speaking or writing, usually temporarily **2.** a part of something spoken or written that departs from the central topic or line of argument, usually temporarily —**digressional** *adj* —**digressionary** *adj*

digressive /dī gréssiv/ *adj* tending to depart from the central topic or line of argument —**digressively** *adv* —**digressiveness** *n*

dihedral /dī heedrəl/ *n* **1.** *also* **dihedral angle** the angle contained between two planes that intersect, measured by the angle made by any two lines at right angles to the two planes **2.** the angle between an upwardly inclined aircraft wing and a horizontal line [Late 18C. < DI-[1] + Greek *hedra* 'seat, base']

dihybrid /dī híbrid/ *n* an organism that is heterozygous for two genes, so that each gene is represented by two variant forms (**alleles**) — **dihybridism** *n*

dihydric /dī hídrik/ *adj* containing two hydroxyl groups

Dijon /deé zhoN/ capital of the Côte d'Or Department in east-central France. It is situated at the foot of the Côte d'Or hills, about 249 km/155 mi. southeast of Paris. Population: 149,867 (1999).

dik-dik

dik-dik /dík dik/ (*plural* **dik-diks** or *same*) *n* a small long-muzzled antelope. Native to: dry regions of eastern Africa. Genus: *Madoqua*. [Late 19C. An imitation of the animal's cry]

dike[1] *n*, *vt* CONSTR, GEOL another spelling of **dyke**[1]

dike[2] *n* SOC SCI another spelling of **dyke**[2] (*slang offensive*)

diktat /dík taat/ *n* **1.** a statement or order that cannot be opposed **2.** a harsh settlement imposed on a defeated opponent or enemy [Mid-20C. Via German < Latin *dictatum* < past participle of *dictare* (see DICTATE)]

dilapidate /di láppi dayt/ (**-dates, -dating, -dated**) *vti* to become, or make something become, partly ruined or decayed, especially through neglect [Early 16C. < Latin *dilapidat-*, past participle of *dilapidare* 'squander' < *lapis* 'stone'] —**dilapidation** /di láppi dáysh'n/ *n*

dilapidated /di láppi daytid/ *adj* partly ruined or decayed, especially as a result of neglect

dilatancy /dī láyt'nssi, di-/ *n* the tendency of a substance to become more viscous or solid when affected by an outside force or agitation

dilatant /dī láyt'nt, di-/ *adj* **1.** ABLE TO EXPAND able or likely to expand **2.** CHEM BECOMING MORE VISCOUS tending to become more viscous or solid when affected by an outside force or agitation ◼ *n* SUBSTANCE CAUSING EXPANSION a substance that causes another to expand

dilatation /dílə táysh'n, díllə-/ *n* **1.** same as **dilation** (senses 1–2) **2.** a lengthy detailed explanation or discussion of a subject by a speaker or writer — **dilatational** *adj*

dilatation and curettage *n* SURG full form of **D and C**

dilatator /dílə taytər, díllə-/ *n* MED same as **dilator** (sense 2)

dilate /dī láyt, di-/ (**-lates, -lating, -lated**) *v* **1.** *vti* to become, or cause something to become, wider, larger, or stretched **2.** *vi* to talk or write at great length [14C. Via French < Latin *dilatare* 'spread widely apart' < *latus* 'wide'] —**dilatable** *adj* —**dilative** *adj*

dilation /dī láysh'n, di-/ *n* **1.** EXPANDING OF SOMETHING the act or process of widening or being widened, enlarging or being enlarged, or stretching or being stretched **2.** EXPANDED CONDITION a condition in which something is widened, enlarged, or stretched **3.** EXPANDED THING something, especially a part of something else, that has become widened, enlarged, or stretched **4.** MED ENLARGEMENT OF BODY PART the stretching or enlargement of a hollow organ or body cavity

dilatometer /dílllə tómmitər/ *n* an instrument used to measure expansion, e.g. in the volume of a liquid — **dilatometric** /dílllətə méttrik/ *adj* —**dilatometry** *n*

dilator /dī láytər, di-/ *n* **1.** a muscle or muscle group that expands a part of the body **2.** something that makes something else wider or larger, especially a medical instrument used to widen a body passage

dilatory /dílllətəri/ *adj* **1.** tending to waste time or move slowly **2.** intended to cause a delay or waste time [15C. < late Latin *dilatorius* < Latin *dilat-*, past participle of *differre* 'to delay'] —**dilatorily** *adv* —**dilatoriness** *n*

dildo /díldō/ (*plural* **-dos**), **dildoe** (*plural* **-does**) *n* an object shaped like a penis, used in sexual activity [Late 16C. Origin ?]

~~dilema~~ incorrect spelling of **dilemma**

dilemma /di lémmə, dī-/ *n* **1.** a situation in which somebody must choose one of two or more unsatisfactory alternatives **2.** in logic, a form of reasoning that, though valid, leads to two undesirable alternatives [Early 16C. Via Latin < Greek *dilēmma* 'double proposition' < *lēmma* 'proposition']

dilettante /dílli tánti, -taánti/ *n* (*plural* **-tantes** or **-tanti** /-ti/) **1.** DABBLER IN ART OR KNOWLEDGE somebody who takes up a subject or interest in a superficial or desultory way **2.** ART LOVER somebody who is very interested in the fine arts (*dated*) ◼ *adj* SUPERFICIAL relating to somebody who has only a superficial understanding of something [Mid-18C. < Italian < *dilettare* 'to delight' < Latin *delectare* (see DELIGHT)] —**dilettantish** *adj* —**dilettantism** *n*

diligence[1] /díllijənss/ *n* **1.** persistent and hardworking effort in doing something **2.** the care or attention expected by the law in doing something such as fulfilling the terms of a contract [14C. Via French < Latin *diligentia* < *diligent-* (see DILIGENT)]

diligence[2] /dílllijənss/ *n* a stagecoach, especially in France [Late 17C. < French, shortening of *carrosse de diligence* 'coach of speed']

diligent /dílllijənt/ *adj* showing persistent and hardworking effort in doing something [14C. Via French < Latin *diligent-*, present participle of *diligere* 'value highly, love' < *legere* 'choose'] —**diligently** *adv*

dill

dill[1] /dil/ *n* **1.** the leaves or seeds of an aromatic herb. Use: as flavouring or garnish. **2.** a herb with fine feathery leaves and flat flower heads that produces dill. Latin name: *Anethum graveolens*. [Old English *dile*, origin ?] —**dilly** *adj*

dill[2] /dil/ *n* ANZ an offensive term that deliberately insults somebody's intelligence or foresight

(*informal insult*) [Mid-20C. Back-formation < *dilly* 'fool', origin ?]

dill pickle *n* a cucumber that has been pickled in dill-flavoured vinegar or brine

dilly bag /dílli-/ *n Aus* a bag traditionally made of plaited grass or reeds, used by Aboriginals for carrying food and other belongings [< Aboriginal *dili* 'coarse grass']

dilly-dally /dílli-/ (**dilly-dallies, dilly-dallying, dilly-dallied**) *vi* to waste time by being too slow, doing nothing, or being unable to decide what to do (*informal*) [Doubled < DALLY]

diluent /dílyoo ənt/ *n* a substance that dilutes another substance ■ *adj* used for diluting something [Early 18C. < Latin *diluent-*, present participle of *diluere* (see DILUTE)]

dilute /dī loót, -lyoót/ *v* (**-lutes, -luting, -luted**) **1.** *vt* MAKE OR BECOME THINNER to make something thinner or weaker by adding water or another liquid, or to become thinner or weaker in this way **2.** *vti* LESSEN STRENGTH to reduce the strength or effect of something, or become reduced in strength or effect **3.** *vt* FIN REDUCE VALUE OF STOCK to decrease the value of a stock by issuing additional shares ■ *adj* THINNED thinner or weaker than at full concentration because of the addition of water or another liquid [Mid-16C. < Latin *dilut-*, past participle of *diluere* 'to wash away' < *lavare* 'to wash'] —**diluteness** *n* —**diluter** *n*

dilution /dī loósh'n, -lyoósh'n/ *n* **1.** ACT OF THINNING OR WEAKENING a thinning or weakening of a substance, usually a liquid, by the addition of another substance such as water **2.** LESS CONCENTRATED LIQUID a substance, especially a liquid, that has been made thinner or weaker by the addition of water or another liquid **3.** LESSENING OF STRENGTH a lessening of the strength or effect of something **4.** THINNED OR WEAKENED STATE a thinned or weakened condition **5.** FIN DECREASE IN STOCK VALUE a decrease in the value of a stock caused by the issue of additional shares

diluvial /dī loóvi əl, di-/, **diluvian** /-vi ən/ *adj* relating to the great Flood described in the Bible [Mid-17C. < late Latin *diluvialis* < Latin *diluvium* 'flood' < *diluere* (see DILUTE)]

dim /dim/ *adj* (**dimmer, dimmest**) **1.** NOT WELL LIT not easy to see in or into because of inadequate light **2.** PRODUCING LITTLE LIGHT not producing very much light, or less bright than is usual **3.** DULL IN COLOUR dull or subdued in colour or brightness **4.** NOT CLEARLY VISIBLE not clearly visible or distinct **5.** NOT EASY TO PERCEIVE difficult to understand or perceive with the senses **6.** NOT CLEAR TO MIND not clearly recalled or perceived **7.** NOT SEEING CLEARLY not able to see clearly **8.** IMPROBABLE unlikely to be successful or fulfilled **9.** UNINTELLIGENT regarded as lacking in intelligence or mental sharpness (*informal*) ■ *v* (**dims, dimming, dimmed**) **1.** *vti* MAKE OR BECOME DIM to make something less bright, clear, or keen, or become less bright, clear, or keen **2.** *vt N Am* AUTOMOT same as **dip** *v* (sense 7) [Old English < Germanic] —**dimly** *adv* —**dimmable** *adj* —**dimness** *n*

dim. *abbr* **1.** dimension **2.** MUSIC diminuendo **3.** GRAM diminutive

DiMaggio /di májji ō/, **Joe** (1914–99) US baseball player. Considered one of the greatest hitters and centre fielders of all time, he played with the New York Yankees from 1936 to 1951 and was elected to the Baseball Hall of Fame in 1955. Full name **DiMaggio, Joseph Paul**. Known as **Joltin' Joe, Yankee Clipper**

> 'A ball player's got to be kept hungry to become a big-leaguer. That's why no boy from a rich family ever made the big leagues.'
> [Attributed to Joe DiMaggio]

Dimbleby /dímb'lbi/, **Richard** (1913–65) British broadcaster and journalist. He was a war correspondent on British radio during World War II and later became a television presenter and commentator specializing in state occasions. Full name **Dimbleby, Richard Frederick**

dime /dīm/ *n N Am* a US or Canadian coin worth ten cents [14C. Via French, 'tithe, tenth part' < Latin *decima*, form of *decimus* 'tenth' < *decem* 'ten'] ◇ **a dime a dozen** very numerous or common, and therefore of little value (*informal*)

dimenhydrinate /dī men hídri nayt/ *n* an antihistamine drug. Use: treatment of travel sickness. [Mid-20C. < DIMETHYL + HYDR- + AMINE]

dimension /di ménsh'n, dī-/ *n* **1.** MEASUREMENT OF SIZE OF SOMETHING a measurement of something in one or more directions such as length, width, or height ○ *the dimensions of the room* **2.** SIZE the size or extent of something (*usually used in the plural*) ○ *discussed the dimensions of the problem* **3.** ASPECT a feature or distinctive part of something ○ *the spiritual dimension of life* **4.** LIFELIKE QUALITY the artistic quality of appearing to be convincing and lifelike ○ *The characters in this novel lack dimension.* **5.** LEVEL OF REALITY a level of consciousness, existence, or reality **6.** MATHS COORDINATE FOR SPACE AND TIME a coordinate used with others to locate a point in space and time **7.** PHYS PROPERTY DEFINING PHYSICAL QUANTITY one of a group of properties or magnitudes such as mass or time that collectively define a physical quantity ■ *vt US* **1.** MAKE SOMETHING TO REQUIRED SIZE to cut or make something to a specific size **2.** INDICATE SIZE OF SOMETHING to specify the size of something [14C. Via French < Latin *dimension-* < *dimetiri* 'to measure out' < *metiri* 'to measure'] —**dimensional** *adj* —**dimensionality** /di ménshə nálləti, dī-/ *n* —**dimensionally** *adv* —**dimensionless** *adj*

dimensional analysis *n* **1.** the procedure of checking or ensuring that the terms in a physical equation have the same dimensions **2.** the application of knowledge of the physical dimensions of a system to infer information mathematically too complex to calculate

dimer /dímər/ *n* a molecule made up of two simpler identical molecules [Early 20C. < DI-[1] + -MER] —**dimeric** /dī mérrik/ *adj*

dimercaprol /dímər ká prol/ *n* a colourless oily substance with an unpleasant smell. Use: antidote to heavy metal poisoning. [Mid-20C. < DI-[1] + MERCAPTAN + PROPANE]

dime store *n N Am* a shop that sells a range of inexpensive goods [The maximum price of goods sold there being, originally, one dime]

dime-store *adj N Am* **1.** not costing very much money **2.** of low or second-rate quality

dimeter /dímmitər/ *n* **1.** a line of verse consisting of two metrical feet **2.** verse made up of lines consisting of two metrical feet [Late 16C. < late Latin < Greek *dimetros* 'having two measures' < *metron* 'measure']

dimethoate /dī méthō ayt/ *n* a white crystalline compound. Use: insecticide. Formula: $C_5H_{12}NO_3PS_2$. [Mid-20C. < DIMETHYL + THIO-]

dimethyl /dī meé thīl, -méth'l/ *adj* having two methyl groups in a molecule

dimethylamine /dī meé thīl áy meen, -méth'l-/ *n* a soluble flammable gas with an odour like ammonia. Use: solvent, in drugs, synthesis of chemicals. Formula: C_2H_7N.

dimethylglyoxime /dī meé thīl glī ók seem, -méth'l-/ *n* a white powdery or crystalline substance soluble in alcohol. Use: reagent, biochemical research.

dimethylnitrosamine /dī meé thīl nītrōsə meén, dī méth'l-, dī meé thīl nī tróss áy meen/ *n* a yellow carcinogenic compound. Source: tobacco smoke, some foods. Formula: $C_2H_6N_2O$.

dimethylsulphoxide /dī meé thīl sul fók sīd, -méth'l-/ *n* CHEM full form of **DMSO**

dimidiate /di míddi it, -ayt/ *adj* **1.** DIVIDED IN TWO divided into halves **2.** BIOL ASYMMETRICAL having one part or side developed more than, or differently from, the other ■ *vt* (**-ates, -ating, -ated**) HERALDRY HALVE HERALDIC EMBLEM to halve each of two heraldic emblems so that both can appear on one shield [Late 16C. < Latin *dimidiat-*, past participle of *dimidiare* 'halve' < *dimidium* 'half' < *medium* 'middle'] —**dimidiation** /di míddi áysh'n/ *n*

dimin. *abbr* **1.** MUSIC diminuendo **2.** GRAM diminutive

diminish /di mínnish/ (**-ishes, -ishing, -ished**) *v* **1.** *vti* MAKE OR BECOME SMALLER to make something smaller or less important, or become smaller or less important **2.** *vti* SEEM OR MAKE SEEM SMALLER to appear smaller, or make something appear smaller **3.** *vti* ARCHIT TAPER FROM BOTTOM TO TOP to taper from the lower part to the upper part, or make something taper in this way **4.** *vt* MUSIC CONTRACT MUSICAL INTERVAL to contract a perfect or minor musical interval by one semitone [15C. Blend of obsolete *diminue* (< Latin *minuere* 'lessen') + *minish* 'diminish' (< Latin *minutia* 'smallness')] —**diminishable** *adj* —**diminishingly** *adv* —**diminishment** *n*

diminished /di mínnisht/ *adj* **1.** reduced in quantity, size, or importance **2.** describes a musical interval or chord reduced by one semitone

diminished responsibility *n* in criminal law, a partial defence where the defendant seeks to argue reduced culpability on the grounds that a psychiatric disorder reduced responsibility for his or her actions

diminishing returns /di mínnishing-/ *npl* additional increases in something such as profits or benefits that do not rise in proportion to the additional effort or investment necessary to produce them

diminuendo /di mínnyoo éndō/ *adv* with a gradual decrease in volume (*used as a musical direction*) ■ *n* (*plural* **-dos**) a piece of music, or a section of a piece, played diminuendo [Late 18C. < Italian, present participle of *diminuire* 'diminish' < Latin *diminuere* (see DIMINUTION)] —**diminuendo** *adj*

diminution /dímmi nyoósh'n/ *n* **1.** a lessening, decreasing, or reduction of something, or the result of such a reduction **2.** the repetition of a musical phrase, using notes that are of a shorter duration than in the original phrase [14C. < Latin *diminut-*, past participle of *diminuere* 'break into small pieces' < *minuere* 'lessen'] —**diminutional** *adj*

diminutive /di mínnyootiv/ *adj* **1.** VERY SMALL very small or much smaller than is usual **2.** INDICATING SMALLNESS describes a suffix such as '-ette' or '-let' that indicates small size, youth, familiarity, or fondness or a word or name formed with such a suffix ■ *n* **1.** WORD INDICATING SMALLNESS a word or name that indicates small size, youth, familiarity, or fondness, e.g. 'kitchenette' or 'booklet' **2.** SUFFIX INDICATING SMALLNESS a suffix, e.g. '-ette', or '-let', that indicates small size, youth, familiarity, or fondness **3.** VERY SMALL PERSON OR THING a person or thing that is very small or much smaller than is usual [14C. < French *diminutif* < Latin *diminut-* (see DIMINUTION)] —**diminutively** *adv* —**diminutiveness** *n*

dimity /dímmiti/ *n* a thin cotton fabric with a striped or checked texture produced by weaving together yarn of different thicknesses [15C. < medieval Latin *dimitum* < Greek *dimitos* 'of double thread' < *mitos* 'warp thread']

DIMM /dim/ *n* a plug-in module that adds random-access memory to a computer. Full form **dual in-line memory module**

dimmer /dímmər/ *n* **1.** *also* **dimmer switch** a device, e.g. a variable resistor, that can be used to vary the brightness of a light by regulating the amount of current supplied to it **2.** *N Am* AUTOMOT same as **dip switch**

dimorphism /dī máwrfizəm/ *n* **1.** BIOL EXISTENCE OF DIFFERENT FORMS WITHIN SPECIES the existence of two or more different forms within a biological species. In sexual dimorphism, male and female may vary in colour, size, or some other trait. **2.** BOT EXISTENCE OF DIFFERENT PLANT PART FORMS the existence in a plant of two different forms of the same organ or part, as when there are two forms of flower **3.** CHEM EXISTENCE OF DIFFERENT CRYSTALLINE FORMS the existence of a substance in two different crystalline forms —**dimorphic** *adj* —**dimorphous** *adj*

dimple /dímp'l/ *n* **1.** INDENTED AREA IN SKIN a naturally occurring slightly indented area in the skin and flesh of the cheek, chin, or other part of the body **2.** INDENTED SURFACE AREA an indented, hollowed, or depressed area in the surface of something ■ *v* (**-ples, -pling, -pled**) **1.** *vti* FORM DIMPLE to form a dimple or dimples in something, or have a dimple or dimples ○ *This mould dimples the surface of the golf ball.* **2.** *vt* PRODUCE DIMPLES IN CHEEKS to cause dimples to appear in the cheeks by smiling [14C. < assumed Old English *dympel* < Germanic] —**dimply** *adj*

dim sum /dím súm/ *n* dumplings, spring rolls, and various other traditional Chinese dishes served in small portions as a meal (*takes a singular or plural verb*) [< Chinese (Cantonese) *tím sam* 'small centre']

dimwit /dím wit/ *n* an offensive term that deliberately insults somebody's intelligence (*informal*) —**dimwitted** /dím wíttid/ *adj* —**dimwittedly** *adv* —**dimwittedness** *n*

din /din/ *n* LOUD PERSISTENT NOISE a loud persistent noise, especially one composed of confused sounds ■ *v* (**dins, dinning, dinned**) **1.** *vi* BE NOISY to make a loud persistent noise **2.** *vt* SUBJECT TO LOUD NOISE to subject somebody to a loud persistent noise **3.** *vt* INSTIL SOMETHING THROUGH REPETITION to fix something in somebody's mind by repeating it over and over again [Old English *dyne* < Indo-European]

Din *symbol* MONEY dinar

DIN /din/ *n* **1.** a system of numbers used to express the speed of a photographic film **2.** a system of standard electrical connections, used especially in television and audio equipment [Acronym < German *Deutsche Industrie-Norm* 'German industry standard']

dinar /dée naar/ *n* a currency unit in some North African, southwestern Asian, and southeastern European countries. See table at **currency** [Mid-17C. Via late Greek < Latin *denarius* (see DENARIUS)]

Dinaric Alps /di nárrik-, dī-/ southeastern extension of the Eastern Alps that runs parallel to the Adriatic coast through Slovenia, Croatia, Bosnia-Herzegovina, and Yugoslavia, as far south as Albania. Highest peak: Bobotov Kuk 2,522 m/8,274 ft.

DIN connector *n* a multi-pin device for making an electrical connection

D'Indy /dáN dee/, **Vincent** (1851–1931) French composer, teacher, and writer. He was a disciple of César Franck, whose ideals guided his influential direction of the Schola Cantorum, the Paris conservatory that d'Indy co-founded in 1894. Full name **d'Indy, Paul Marie Théodore Vincent**

dine /dīn/ (**dines, dining, dined**) *v* **1.** *vi* EAT DINNER to eat the main meal of the day ○ *We dine early.* **2.** *vi* EAT to have a particular food or type of food in a meal ○ *We dined on vegetables and rice.* **3.** *vt* PROVIDE DINNER FOR SOMEBODY to provide dinner for somebody, or take somebody out to dinner (*informal*) [13C. < Old French *di(s)ner*]

dine out *vi* to eat dinner somewhere other than at home, especially in a restaurant

diner /dínər/ *n* **1.** somebody eating a meal, especially dinner **2.** *N Am* a small inexpensive restaurant where customers eat at the counter or in booths

dinero /di náirō/ *n* same as **money** (*informal*) [Mid-19C. < Spanish]

Dinesen /dínniss'n/, **Isak** (1885–1962) Danish writer. A much-travelled author, she is best known for her short stories such as *Seven Gothic Tales* (1934) and her semi-autobiographical work, *Out of Africa* (1938). Pseudonym of **Blixen-Finecke, Karen Christence, Baroness.** Born **Dinesen, Karen Christence**

'What is man, when you come to think upon him, but a minutely set, ingenious machine for turning, with infinite artfulness, the red wine of Shiraz into urine?' [Isak Dinesen, 'The Dreamers', *Seven Gothic Tales*; 1934]

dinette /dī nét/ *n* an alcove or part of a room where meals are eaten, especially in or near a kitchen

ding¹ /ding/ *v* (**dings, dinging, dinged**) **1.** *vti* to ring with a high-pitched sound, or make something do this **2.** *vt* same as **din** *v* (sense 3) ■ *n* a ringing sound, especially one made by a bell [Mid-16C. An imitation of the sound]

ding² /ding/ (*informal*) *v* (**dings, dinging, dinged**) **1.** *vti* regional STRIKE SOMETHING to strike something up against something **2.** *vt* Aus, N Am MAKE DENT IN SOMETHING to make a dent or cause other surface damage in something ■ *n* Aus, N Am DENT a dent or other surface damage in something [14C. Probably < Old Norse]

ding³ /ding/ *n* Aus an offensive term for an Italian or Greek person (*slang*) [Mid-20C. Shortening of DINGBAT]

ding⁴ /ding/ *n* Aus a party or celebration (*informal*) [Mid-20C. Origin ?]

ding-a-ling /díngə líng/ *n* **1.** the sound of a bell, especially a small hand-held bell **2.** somebody who is considered odd, irrational, or incapable of serious or organized thought (*informal insult*) [Late 19C. An imitation of the sound]

dingbat /díng bat/ *n* **1.** PRINTER'S SYMBOL a symbol or ornamental character used in a printed work, e.g.

a star or pointing hand **2.** SILLY PERSON somebody who is considered silly or lacking in intelligence (*informal insult*) **3.** *US* THING WHOSE NAME IS NOT KNOWN an object whose name has been forgotten or is not known (*slang*) [Mid-19C. Origin ?]

dingbats /díng bats/ (*slang*) *n* Aus same as **delirium tremens** ■ *adj* behaving in a way thought to be strange or irrational [Mid-20C. Plural of DINGBAT] ◇ **give somebody the dingbats** Aus to make somebody nervous or annoyed (*slang*)

ding-dong *n* **1.** SOUND OF BELL the sound of a bell being struck two or more times **2.** SOUND IMITATIVE OF BELL SOUND a ringing or repeated sound that is similar to that made by a bell **3.** ARGUMENT a fierce argument (*informal*) **4.** *N Am* IRRATIONAL PERSON somebody considered as odd, irrational, silly, or lacking in intelligence (*informal insult*) ■ *adj* FIERCELY CONTESTED fiercely contested, with advantage shifting continually from one side to another (*informal*) ○ *a ding-dong battle of wills* ■ *vi* (**ding-dongs, ding-donging, ding-donged**) MAKE RINGING SOUND to make a ringing sound like a bell [Mid-16C. An imitation of the sound]

dinge /dinj/ *n* a dingy state or condition [Early 19C. Probably back-formation < DINGY]

dinghy

dinghy /díngi, díng gi/ (*plural* **-ghies**) *n* **1.** a small boat, especially one with one mast and sails, used for recreation or racing **2.** an inflatable life raft [Early 19C. < Hindi *dīgī* 'small boat', < *dēgā* 'boat']

dingle /díng g'l/ *n* a wooded valley (*literary*) [13C. Origin ?]

dingo /díng gō/ (*plural* **-goes**) *n* a wild dog with a reddish-brown coat. Native to: Australia. Latin name: *Canis dingo.* [Late 18C. < Aboriginal *dingu*]

Dingo /díng gō/, **Ernie** (*b.* 1956) Australian actor and television presenter. His films include *The Fringe Dwellers* (1986).

dingy /dínji/ (**-gier, -giest**) *adj* **1.** DARK lacking light in a gloomy or unpleasant way **2.** DIRTY OR FADED dirty-looking, discoloured, or faded **3.** SHABBY shabby and uninviting [Mid-18C. Origin ?] —**dingily** *adv* —**dinginess** *n*

dining car /díning-/ *n* ANZ, N Am a railway carriage where meals are served to a train's passengers. UK term **restaurant car**

dining leaf *n* S Asia a banana leaf used as a plate for serving food

dining room *n* a room where meals are eaten, especially in a home or hotel

dining table *n* a table on which meals are served, usually in a dining room

dinitrobenzene /dī nī trō bén zeen/ *n* a yellow crystalline compound that occurs in three isomeric forms. Use: manufacture of dyes and plastics. Formula: $C_6H_4(NO_2)_2$.

dink /dingk/ *n* SPORTS same as **drop shot** [Mid-20C. An imitation of the sound of the ball being hit]

DINK /dingk/, **dink** *n* ANZ, N Am SOCIOL same as **dinky**² (*informal*) [Late 20C. Acronym < dual (or double) income, no kids]

Dinka /díngkə/ (*plural* **-kas** or same) *n* **1.** a member of a people who live in the Nile Valley in southern Sudan **2.** a language of the Nilo-Saharan family, spoken in southern Sudan. Native speakers: 1.4 million. [Mid-19C. < Dinka *Jieng* 'people'] —**Dinka** *adj*

dinkie *n* SOCIOL another spelling of **dinky**²

dinkum /díngkəm/ *adj* ANZ believed to be genuine, real, or honest (*informal*) [Late 19C. Origin ?]

dinkum oil *n* ANZ the truth (*informal*)

dinky¹ /díngki/ (*informal*) *adj* (**-kier, -kiest**) regional small and compact or neat ■ *n* (*plural* **-kies**) S Africa a small bottle of wine, usually containing 250 ml [Late 18C. < Scots dialect *dink* 'finely dressed, trim', origin ?]

REGIONAL NOTE See *itsy-bitsy*.

dinky² /díngki/ (*plural* **-kies**), **dinkie** *n* UK a member of a couple who both have careers, usually in well-paid fields, and who have no children (*informal*) ANZ, N Am term **DINK** [Late 20C. < DINK]

dinky-di /-dí/ *adj* Aus believed to be genuine, real, or typical (*informal*) [Early 20C. Alteration of DINKUM]

dinna /dínnə/, **dinnae** /dínni/ *v* regional do not

dinner /dínnər/ *n* **1.** MAIN MEAL the main meal or one of the main meals of the day, eaten either at midday or in the evening **2.** BANQUET a formal evening meal given in honour of somebody or something **3.** RESTAURANT MEAL a meal that is eaten in a restaurant and consists of several courses, often offered together for a set price **4.** FOOD FOR DINNER the food served during or for a dinner [13C. < Old French *di(s)ner* 'dine']

dinner-dance *n* a formal social occasion at which dancing follows a dinner

dinner jacket *n* a man's jacket without tails that is worn on formal occasions, especially in the evening. N Am term **tuxedo**

dinner lady *n* a woman who serves food and supervises children during the midday meal break in a school (*informal*)

dinner party *n* a social gathering where dinner is served at somebody's home

dinner service, **dinner set** *n* a matching set of all the plates, dishes, cups, and saucers needed to serve a meal to a number of people

dinner table *n* **1.** a table at which meals are eaten, often large and capable of seating a group of people **2.** the occasion at which people are seated at a table to eat a meal together

dinnertime /dínnər tīm/ *n* the time of the day when dinner is usually eaten

DIN number *n* a number that indicates the speed of a photographic film, as expressed in the DIN system

dinoflagellate /dí nō flájjələt/ *n* a tiny single-celled sea organism with two long slender appendages (**flagella**), occurring in large numbers in plankton. Some types are luminescent and some are toxic, especially when they multiply prolifically to cause a brownish-red discoloration (**red tide**). Latin name: *Dinoflagellata.* [Late 19C. < modern Latin *Dinoflagellata* < Greek *dinos* 'a whirling' + Latin *flagellum* 'whip' (see FLAGELLUM)]

dinosaur /dínə sawr/ *n* **1.** an extinct, chiefly terrestrial reptile that lived in the Mesozoic Era. Some dinosaurs were the largest known land animals. Order: Ornithischia or Saurischia. **2.** somebody or something that is hopelessly out of date or incapable of adapting to change [Mid-19C. < modern Latin *dinosaurus* < Greek *deinos* 'terrible' + *sauros* 'lizard'] —**dinosaurian** /dínə sáwri ən/ *adj*

dint /dint/ *n* same as **dent** ■ *vt* (**dints, dinting, dinted**) same as **dent** [Old English *dynt* 'blow, stroke (especially of a weapon)' < Germanic] ◇ **by dint of** using something, or by the force of something

diocese /dí əsiss/ *n* the Christian churches that are under the authority of one bishop, or the district containing them [14C. < Greek *dioikēsis* 'administration' < *dioikein* 'manage' < *oikos* 'house'] —**diocesan** /dī óssiss'n/ *adj*

Diocletian /dí ə kléesh'n/ (AD 245–313) emperor of Rome. Proclaimed emperor in 284, he instituted successful administrative reforms, but his attempt to restore traditional religion by persecuting Christians failed. He abdicated in 305. Full name **Gaius Aurelius Valerius Diocletianus**

diode /dí ōd/ *n* an electronic device that has two electrodes and is used to convert alternating current to direct current

dioecious /dī éeshəss/, **diecious**, **dioicous** /dī óykəss/ *adj* having male and female flowers on different

plants of the same species [Mid-18C. < modern Latin *Dioecia*, literally 'two houses' < Greek *oikos* 'house'] — **dioeciously** *adv* —**dioecism** /-éesizəm/ *n*

dioestrus /dī éestrəss/ *n* a stage of the oestrous cycle, following oestrus, in which the ovary is functional and the predominant ovarian hormone produced is progesterone —**dioestrous** *adj*

Diogenes /dī ójjə neez/ (412?–323 BC) Greek philosopher. He was a founder of Cynicism, an ancient school of philosophy. He is said to have lived in a tub in Athens and to have wandered the streets with a lamp, seeking an honest man.

> 'The mountains too, at a distance, appear airy masses and smooth, but seen near at hand they are rough.'
> [Diogenes. Quoted in 'Pyrrho', *Lives of the Philosophers*, Diogenes Läertius; 3rd century AD]

diol /dī ol/ *n* an alcohol with two hydroxyl groups in each molecule

Diomedes /dī ə meédeez/ *n* in Greek mythology, a former suitor of Helen of Troy who joined the Greek army and became a hero of the Trojan War

Dione /dī óni/ *n* a natural satellite of Saturn discovered in 1684. It has a radius of 560 km/348 mi. and the surface exhibits several distinct terrain types.

Dionysiac *adj* MYTHOL same as **Dionysian**

dionysian /dī ə nízzi ən, -níssi-/ *adj* 1. relating to or involving drunkenness and sexual activity 2. in the philosophical writings of Nietzsche, spontaneous and intuitive rather than rational

Dionysian /dī ə nízzi ən, -níssi-, **Dionysiac** /dī ə nízzi ak, -níssi-/ *adj* 1. relating to the Greek god Dionysus 2. relating to the worship of the Greek god Dionysus [Early 17C. < Greek *Dionusos* 'Dionysus']

Dionysius Exiguus /dī ə níssi əss eg zíggyoŏ əss/ (AD 500?–556) Scythian Roman scholar. He introduced the Christian era of dating in his *Cyclus Paschalis* (525). He adopted the name *Exiguus*, 'little', as a token of humility.

Dionysius the Areopagite /-árri óppə gīt/ (*fl* 1st century AD) Greek religious leader. He converted to Christianity through the preaching of St Paul, as recorded in the Bible in Acts 17:34, and is thought to have been the first bishop of Athens. He was formerly thought to be the author of influential theological texts that were actually written in about AD 500.

Dionysus /dī ə níssəss/ *n* in Greek mythology, the god of wine, identified with Bacchus

Diophantine equation /dī ō fán tīn-/ *n* an algebraic equation that contains two or more variables, has only whole-number (**integral**) coefficients, and has integral solutions for the variables [After DIOPHANTUS]

Diophantus /dī ə fántəss/ (*fl* 3rd century AD) Greek mathematician. His *Arithmetica* was the first work to apply algebraic rather than geometrical methods to solving mathematical problems.

diopside /dī óp sīd/ *n* a pale green mineral consisting of calcium magnesium silicate. Source: igneous rocks. [Early 19C. < DI-¹ + Greek *opsis* 'aspect']

dioptre /dī óptər/ *n* a unit of measurement for the power of a lens, especially a spectacle lens, equal to the reciprocal of the focal length of the lens in metres. Symbol **D** [Late 19C. Via French < Latin *dioptra* 'instrument for measuring angles' < Greek < *dia-* 'through' + *optos* 'visible'] —**dioptral** *adj*

dioptric /dī óptrik/, **dioptrical** /-óptrik'l/ *adj* 1. relating to the study of how images are formed by lenses 2. relating to the refractive powers of light or the measurement of the refractive power of a lens [Mid-17C. < Greek *dioptrikos* < *dioptra* (see DIOPTRE)] —**dioptrically** *adv*

dioptrics /dī óptriks/ *n* the branch of optics that studies the refraction of light by lenses or within the eye (*takes a singular verb*)

Dior /dee awr/, **Christian** (1905–57) French couturier. In 1946 he founded the fashion house bearing his name. He achieved worldwide fame by introducing the 'New Look' in 1947, which featured narrow shoulders and calf-length skirts.

> 'My models—they're the life of my dresses,

and I want my dresses to be happy.'
> [Christian Dior. Quoted in *Dior*, Françoise Giroud; Stewart Spencer, tr.; 1987]

diorama /dī ə raámə/ *n* 1. a three-dimensional representation of a scene in which objects or models are arranged in a natural setting against a realistic background, e.g. in a museum 2. a representation of a scene that is made to appear three-dimensional, e.g. one in which the viewer looks through a hole at objects painted on layers of translucent material [Early 19C. < French, literally 'sight through'; < Greek *dia-* 'through' after *panorama*] —**dioramic** /dī ə rámmik/ *adj*

diorite /dī ə rīt/ *n* a dark granular igneous rock that consists of plagioclase and a ferromagnesian mineral such as hornblende. Use: surfacing roads. [Early 19C. < Greek *diorizein* 'distinguish' < *orizein* 'to limit'] —**dioritic** /dī ə ríttik/ *adj*

Dioscuri /dī óskyoŏri, -óskyoŏ rī, dī o skyoŏri, -skyoŏr ī/ *npl* in Greek mythology, the twin gods Castor and Pollux, who were the sons of Zeus and Leda [Early 20C. < Greek *Dioskouroi* < *Dios* 'of Zeus' + *kouros* 'boy, son']

dioxane /dī ók sayn/, **dioxan** /dī óks'n/ *n* a toxic flammable colourless liquid. Use: solvent for waxes and resins, paints, lacquers, cosmetics, deodorants, textile manufacture. Formula: $C_4H_8O_2$.

dioxide /dī ók sīd/ *n* an oxide that has two oxygen atoms in each molecule

dioxin /dī óksin/ *n* a heterocyclic hydrocarbon that is a carcinogen and toxic environmental pollutant. Source: by-product of combustion processes, manufacture of herbicides and bactericides, chlorine bleaching of paper.

dip /dip/ *v* (**dips, dipping, dipped**) 1. *vt* PUT SOMETHING BRIEFLY IN LIQUID to put something briefly into a liquid and take it out again ○ *She dipped her fingers in the water.* 2. *vi* MOVE DOWNWARDS to sink to a lower level ○ *The plane dipped and then flew on.* 3. *vt* LOWER SOMETHING to lower something and raise it again ○ *The horse dipped its head.* 4. *vi* BECOME LESS to fall to a lower level or amount, especially for a short time ○ *Prices dipped at the beginning of October.* 5. *vti* PUT YOUR HAND IN to put your hand into something in order to take something out ○ *He dipped his hand into his pocket.* 6. *vt* SCOOP SOMETHING to take up liquid or small pieces of a substance with something such as a spoon or cup ○ *She was dipping soup from the pot.* 7. *vt* LOWER HEADLIGHTS to alter a car's headlights so that they shine downwards and slightly towards the kerb in order to avoid dazzling oncoming drivers. N Am term **dim** 8. *vt* DISINFECT ANIMAL to put an animal such as a sheep or dog into a bath of disinfectant 9. *vi* SLOPE DOWNWARDS to slope downwards from the horizontal ○ *The road dipped towards the river.* 10. *vt* MAKE CANDLE FROM WAX to make a candle by repeatedly putting a wick into melted wax ○ *dip a candle* ■ *n* 1. LOWERING an act of sinking lower, of lowering something, or of putting something in liquid ○ *She acknowledged him with a dip of her head.* 2. PUTTING HAND IN the action of putting the hand into something to take something out or of scooping up liquid or small pieces of a substance 3. SWIM a quick swim ○ *There's time for a dip before lunch.* 4. SLIGHT DECREASE a temporary decrease in the amount or level of something ○ *a dip in sales* 5. LOWER PLACE a place where the ground slopes, especially to form a hollow ○ *We came to a dip in the road.* 6. MIXTURE FOR DIPPING FOOD INTO a creamy mixture into which pieces of food can be dipped, often served with crisps ○ *an avocado dip* 7. CANDLE a candle made by dipping a wick repeatedly in wax 8. DISINFECTANT FOR ANIMALS a mixture of chemicals used to disinfect animals ○ *sheep dip* 9. LIQUID CHEMICAL PREPARATION a chemical mixture in which something can be immersed, e.g. a dye or preservative 10. *N Am* OFFENSIVE TERM an offensive term that deliberately insults somebody's intelligence or common sense (*slang insult*) 11. THIEF WHO PICKS POCKETS a pickpocket (*slang*) 12. GEOG ANGLE OF MAGNETIC NEEDLE the angle that a magnetic needle makes with the horizontal plane 13. GEOL ANGLE OF ROCK LAYER the angle a sloping rock layer makes to the horizontal ○ *The rock bed has a dip of ten degrees.* 14. GYMNASTICS PARALLEL BARS EXERCISE an exercise on parallel bars in which the elbows are bent until the gymnast's chin is level with the bars, and the body is raised by straightening the arms [Old English *dyppan* < Germanic]

dip into *vt* 1. to read parts of a text such as a book

or magazine rather than the whole of it 2. to use some of the money that has been saved

dip out *vi Aus* (*informal*) 1. OPT OUT to choose not to participate in something ○ *I think I'll dip out on this tutorial.* 2. MISS OUT to fail to be given an opportunity to do something ○ *He was in the pool, but when it came to the final selection he dipped out.* 3. NOT PASS EXAM OR COURSE to fail in an examination or course of study ○ *He dipped out of uni in his first year.*

dip., Dip. *abbr* EDUC diploma

DipEd /dip éd/ *abbr* EDUC Diploma in Education

dipeptidase /dī pépti dayz, -dayss/ *n* an enzyme that breaks down dipeptides in the final stage of protein digestion

dipeptide /dī pép tīd/ *n* a compound composed of two amino acids

diphasic /dī fáyzik/, **diphase** /dī fayz/ *adj* describes parasites that have an independent stage in their life cycle

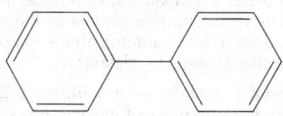

diphenyl

diphenyl /dī feén'l, -fénn'l/ *n* a white crystalline substance. Use: fungicide, in organic synthesis, as a heat transfer agent. Formula: $C_{12}H_{10}$.

diphenylamine /dī feén'l ə meen, -fénn'l-/ *n* a colourless toxic crystalline substance. Use: in solid rocket propellants, dyes, manufacture of plastics. Formula: $(C_6H_5)_2NH$.

diphenylketone /dī feén'l keéton, -fénn'l-/ *n* CHEM same as **benzophenone**

diphosgene /dī fóz jeen/ *n* a colourless oily liquid with an extremely poisonous vapour. Use: in gas warfare during World War I. Formula: $ClCOOCCl_3$.

diphosphate /dī fóss fayt/ *n* a chemical compound that contains two phosphate groups per molecule

diphosphoglyceric acid /dī fósfō gli sérrik-/ *n* a compound in red blood cells that allows the release of oxygen from haemoglobin

diphtheria /dif theéri ə, dip-/ *n* a serious infectious disease, caused by a bacterium, *Corynebacterium diphtheriae*, that attacks the membranes of the throat and releases a toxin that damages the heart and the nervous system. The main symptoms are fever, weakness, and severe inflammation of the affected membranes. [Mid-19C. < modern Latin < Greek *diphthera*, *diphtheris* 'hide, skin', indicating the tough membrane developed in the throat] —**diphtherial** *adj* — **diphtheric** /-thérrik/ *adj* —**diphtheritic** /dífthə ríttik, díp-/ *adj* —**diphtheroid** /dífthə royd, díp-/ *adj*

diphthong /díf thong, díp-/ *n* 1. a complex vowel sound in which the first vowel gradually moves towards a second vowel so that both vowels form one syllable, e.g. 'a' and 'i' in 'rail' 2. a character formed by joining the two letters 'a' and 'e' as 'æ' or the two letters 'o' and 'e' as 'œ' [15C. Via French < Latin *diphthongus* 'two sounds' < Greek *phthoggos* 'sound'] —**diphthongal** /dif thóng g'l, díp-/ *adj*

diphthongize /díf thong īz, díp-/ (**-izes, -izing, -ized**), **diphthongise** (**-ises, -ising, -ised**) *vti* to become a diphthong, or make a vowel into a diphthong —**diphthongization** /dif thong ī záysh'n, díp-/ *n*

diphycercal /díffi súrk'l/ *adj* describes a tail fin, on young fish and some adult fish such as lampreys and lungfish, that is found above and below the backbone. See illustration on next page [Mid-19C. < Greek *diphu-* 'of double form' + *kerkos* 'tail']

diphyodont /dī fī ə dont/ *adj* describes a mammal that

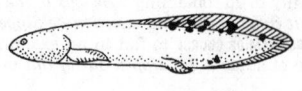

diphycercal

grows two sets of teeth in a lifetime [Mid-19C. < Greek *diphu-* 'double form' + *odont-* 'tooth']

dipl. *abbr* 1. diplomat 2. diplomatic

dipl- *prefix* same as **diplo-** (*used before vowels*)

diplegia /dī plééjə/ *n* inability to move corresponding parts on both the right and left sides of the body [Late 19C. < DI-¹ after PARAPLEGIA] —**diplegic** *adj, n*

diplex /dī pleks/ *adj* capable of simultaneously transmitting or receiving two signals in the same direction along a telecommunications channel [Late 19C. Alteration of DUPLEX] —**diplexer** *n*

diplo- *prefix* 1. double, twin ○ *diplopod* 2. having twice the basic number of chromosomes ○ *diplont* [< Greek *diploos* 'double']

diploblastic /dípplə blástik/ *adj* used to describe an invertebrate animal in which the adult tissues are derived from just two layers of embryonic germ tissue, namely endoderm and ectoderm. Cnidarians are diploblastic.

diplodocus /di plóddəkəss, dípplō dókəss/ *n* a large herbivorous dinosaur of the late Jurassic Period that had four legs and a very long neck and tail. It had nostrils near the top of the head, indicating that it spent time in deep water. Genus: *Diplodocus*. [Late 19C. < modern Latin < Greek *diploos* 'double' + *dokos* 'beam']

diploë /dípplō ee/ *n* a layer of spongy bone tissue found between the harder inside and outside bone layers of the cranium [Late 16C. < Greek *diploē* 'doubling' < *diploos* 'double']

diploid /díp loyd/ *adj* possessing two matched sets of chromosomes in the cell nucleus, one set from each parent. There is a characteristic diploid number of chromosomes for each species. —**diploidic** /di plóydik/ *adj* —**diploidy** *n*

diploma /di plṓmə/ *n* 1. a certificate given by a college, university, or professional organization, indicating that somebody has completed a course of education or training and reached the required level of competence 2. a written document or charter, especially one that confers specific rights or privileges [Mid-17C. Via Latin < Greek, 'folded paper' < *diploun* 'fold, make double' < *diploos* 'double']

diplomacy /di plṓməssi/ *n* 1. INTERNATIONAL RELATIONS the management of communication and relationships between nations by members and employees of each nation's government 2. SKILL IN INTERNATIONAL DEALINGS skill in managing communication and relationships between nations 3. TACT skill and tact in dealing with other people

diplomat /dípplə mat/ *n* 1. a member or employee of a government who represents his or her country in dealings with other nations, especially by working in an embassy or consulate abroad 2. somebody who is tactful and sensitive in dealings with other people [Early 19C. < French *diplomate*, back-formation < *diplomatique* (see DIPLOMATIC)]

diplomate /dípplə mayt/ *n* somebody who holds a professional diploma

diplomatic /dípplə máttik/ *adj* 1. INVOLVING DIPLOMACY concerned with or involving international diplomacy or the work of diplomats 2. TACTFUL showing tact and skill in dealing with people 3. RELATING TO DIPLOMATICS relating to the study of old documents 4. COPIED ACCURATELY accurately reproducing an original document or printed text [Early 18C. < French *dip-*

lomatique and modern Latin *diplomaticus* < Latin *diploma* (see DIPLOMA)] —**diplomatically** *adv*

diplomatic bag *n* a bag in which official correspondence travels between a government office and an embassy of that government in another country, carried by a special messenger. The bag is not subject to the regulations governing ordinary mail.

diplomatic corps *n* all the diplomats from other countries who reside in another nation

diplomatic immunity *n* the legal status of diplomats, who are not subject to the legal and taxation systems of a country in which they are resident as accredited representatives

diplomatics /dípplə máttiks/ *n* the study and verification of very old documents (*takes a singular verb*)

diplomatist /di plṓmətist/ *n* a professional diplomat

diplont /dī plont/ *n* an organism whose cells, other than reproductive cells, have a diploid number of chromosomes in their nuclei —**diplontic** /di plóntik/ *adj*

diplopia /di plṓpi ə/ *n* OPHTHALMOL same as **double vision** (*technical*) —**diplopic** /di plóppik/ *adj*

diplopod /dípplə pod/ *n* a millipede that has two pairs of legs on each body segment. Class: Diplopoda. [Mid-19C. < modern Latin *Diplopoda* < Greek *diploos* 'double' + *pod-* 'foot'] —**diplopodous** /di plóppədəss/ *adj*

diplotene /dípplō teen/ *n* a stage in the first part of reproductive cell division (**meiosis**) in which paired chromosomes start to move apart from one another but remain connected at points. At these connecting points, genetic information is exchanged. [Early 20C. < DIPLO- + Greek *tainia* 'band, ribbon']

dipody /díppədi/ *n* (*plural* **-dies**) a line of verse consisting of two stressed units or feet [Late 19C. < Greek *dipod-* 'two-footed']

dipole /dī pōl/ *n* two equal and opposite magnetized or electrically charged poles that are separated by a short distance —**dipolar** /dī pṓlər/ *adj*

dipole moment *n* 1. the product of one of the equal but opposite charges on two atoms in a molecule, and the distance separating them 2. the product of two equal and opposite magnetic poles or electric charges that are separated by a short distance

dipper /díppər/ *n* 1. SCOOP a cup or ladle for dipping into liquid 2. SMALL WATER BIRD a small plain-coloured bird that lives beside rivers and can swim and dive. Family: Cinclidae. 3. SOMETHING THAT DIPS somebody or something that dips objects in a liquid, e.g. a machine operating an industrial process. 4. SMALL PAINT HOLDER a small container to hold paint on an artist's palette

dippy /díppi/ (**-pier, -piest**) *adj* silly or eccentric, especially in an amusing or harmless way (*informal*) [Early 20C. Origin ?] —**dippily** *adv* —**dippiness** *n*

dipropellant /dīprə péllənt/ *n* AEROSP same as **bipropellant**

diprotic /dī próttik/ *adj* with two transferable hydrogen protons [< DI-¹ + PROTON]

diprotodont /dī prṓtə dont/ *adj* describes a marsupial that has the first pair of incisor teeth in each jaw enlarged ■ *n* a marsupial with enlarged incisors, e.g. a kangaroo or a wallaby. Order: Diprotodontia.

dipshit /díp shit/ *n* an offensive term that deliberately insults somebody's intelligence or value (*slang insult*)

dipso /dípsō/ (*plural* **-sos**) *n* same as **alcoholic** (*slang insult*) [Late 19C. Shortening of DIPSOMANIAC]

dipsomania /dípsō máyni ə/ *n* a habitual and uncontrollable craving for alcohol (*dated*) [Mid-19C. < Greek *dipsa* 'thirst']

dipsomaniac /dípsō máyni ak/ *n* somebody with a habitual and uncontrollable craving for alcohol (*dated*) —**dipsomaniacal** /dípsō mə nī ək'l/ *adj*

dipstick /díp stik/ *n* 1. a measuring rod that is dipped into a container to indicate the depth of liquid in it, especially one used to measure the amount of oil in a car's engine 2. an offensive term that deliberately insults somebody's intelligence or competence (*informal insult*)

dip switch *n* a control used to dip a car's headlights or raise them to full beam. N Am term **dimmer**

DIP switch /díp-/, **dip switch** *n* a switch that turns optional settings on or off on a computer component. Full form **dual in-line package switch**

dipteran /díptərən/, **dipteron** /-ron/ *n* a two-winged insect. Flies, gnats, mosquitoes, and midges are dipterans. Order: Diptera. [Mid-19C. < modern Latin *Diptera* < Greek *dipteros* 'two-winged'] —**dipteral** *adj* —**dipterous** *adj*

~~diptheria~~ incorrect spelling of **diphtheria**

~~dipthong~~ incorrect spelling of **diphthong**

diptych /díptik/ *n* 1. a pair of paintings, especially religious paintings on two hinged panels 2. a pair of writing tablets joined by a hinge and having wooden backs and waxed writing surfaces, used especially in ancient Greece and Rome [Early 17C. Via Latin < late Greek *diptukha* 'pair of writing tablets', plural of *diptukhos* 'folded in two' < *ptukhē* 'fold']

dipyridamole /dī pī ríddə mōl/ *n* a drug that widens the blood vessels. Use: treatment of angina, prevention of blood clots. [Mid-20C. < DI-¹ + PYRIMIDINE + PIPERIDINE + AMINO- + -OL ¹]

diquat /dī kwot/ *n* a biodegradable herbicide used to control weeds in water [Mid-20C. < DI-¹ + QUATERNARY; because based on a quaternary amine]

Dirac /di rák/, **Paul** (1902–84) British theoretical physicist. He worked on quantum theory and predicted the existence of the positron, the first particle of antimatter to be established experimentally. He shared the Nobel Prize in physics (1933). Full name **Dirac, Paul Adrien Maurice**

'God is a mathematician of a very high order, and He used very advanced mathematics in constructing the universe.'
[Paul Dirac, *Scientific American*; May 1963]

Dirac constant *n* a constant used in quantum mechanics that is Planck's constant divided by 2π

Dirac equation *n* an equation in quantum mechanics that describes the wave behaviour of an electron in an electromagnetic field, in a manner consistent with special relativity

dire /dīr/ (**direr, direst**) *adj* 1. characterized by severe, serious, or desperate circumstances 2. warning of a future disaster or serious consequences [Mid-16C. < Latin *dirus* 'fearful, awful, boding ill'] —**direly** *adv* —**direness** *n*

direct /di rékt, dī-/ *v* (**-rects, -recting, -rected**) 1. *vt* SUPERVISE SOMEBODY to organize and control the work of an organization or a group of people ○ *I found her directing a team of rescue workers.* 2. *vt* INSTRUCT SOMEBODY to tell somebody to do something (*formal*) ○ *The medicine should be taken only as directed.* 3. *vt* FOCUS ATTENTION ON SOMETHING to focus attention or concentrate activities on something ○ *Please direct your attention towards the figures at the right of the screen.* 4. *vt* AIM OR SEND SOMETHING to aim, point, or send something in a particular direction ○ *Direct the extinguisher at the base of the flames.* 5. *vt* ADDRESS LETTER to write an address on something to be delivered ○ *The envelope was directed to our offices.* 6. *vt* GIVE SOMEBODY DIRECTIONS to tell somebody how to get to a place ○ *Can you direct me to the station?* 7. *vt* ADDRESS COMMENTS TO SOMEBODY to say something to somebody specifically ○ *The remarks were directed to his sister.* 8. *vti* SUPERVISE FILMS OR PLAYS to be responsible for supervising the creative aspects of a film, play, or television programme, giving instructions and guidance to the actors and other people involved ○ *He has directed several films.* 9. *vt* N Am MUSIC same as **conduct** *v* (sense 4) ■ *adj* 1. NOT STOPPING OR DEVIATING going straight from one place or point to another ○ *a direct flight from Paris to Miami* 2. IMMEDIATE lacking the influence of any other factors ○ *No direct link between the two events has been established.* 3. PERSONAL in which no person, action, or process intervenes ○ *We are in direct contact with them.* 4. STRAIGHTFORWARD easy to understand or respond to ○ *The author makes a direct appeal to our emotions.* 5. PRECISE having the characteristics of accuracy and precision ○ *a direct quotation* 6. IMMEDIATELY RELATED connected by a straight and unbroken line of descent from parent to child ○ *a direct descendant of George Washington* 7. COMPLETE OR EXACT showing complete contradiction or opposition ○ *Their conclusions were in direct contradiction to ours.* 8. POL DIRECTLY INVOLVING ELECTORATE

involving participation in government from the electorate rather than through electoral representatives ○ *direct democracy* **9.** MATHS, LOGIC **WORKING FROM PREMISE TO CONCLUSION** working immediately from the premise to the conclusion in proving something **10.** ASTRON **MOVING WEST TO EAST** moving from west to east as observed from celestial north ■ *adv* **1. STRAIGHT, WITHOUT DIVERSION** straight from one place or person to another, without a stop or diversion ○ *You can fly direct from Amsterdam to Chicago.* **2. DIRECTLY** by an immediate connection, without somebody or something intervening ○ *You can dial Calcutta direct.* [14C. < Latin *directus*, past participle of *dirigere* 'set straight, guide'] —**directness** *n*

ORIGIN The Latin word *dirigere* 'to set straight, guide' from which ***direct*** is derived, is also the source of English *address, dirge, dirigible*, and *dress*.

SYNONYMS See ***guide***.

direct access *n* the ability to retrieve information directly from any part of a storage device without referring to the preceding data

direct action *n* a political or industrial action intended to have an immediate and noticeable effect that will influence a government or employer, e.g. a strike, a boycott, or civil disobedience

direct connection *n* a fast permanent connection linking a computer or system to a network such as the Internet. It can be used at any time and is much faster than a dial-up connection.

direct cost *n* a business cost that can be linked directly with a specific project or activity

direct coupling *n* direct connection of one part of a circuit to another without the use of transformers or capacitors, allowing both direct current and alternating current to flow along the connection —**direct-coupled** *adj*

direct current *n* electrical current that flows in only one direction and has a fairly constant average value

direct debit *n* an arrangement by which sums of money of varying amounts that are owed at regular intervals are paid to the creditor directly from the payer's bank account

direct deposit *n US* a method of transferring a payment such as a salary electronically directly from the payer's bank account into the payee's

direct discourse *n N Am* same as **direct speech**

direct dye *n* a dye that can be used directly on a fabric without needing an extra chemical (**mordant**) to fix the colour

directed speech *n* LING same as **motherese**

direct elections *npl* government elections in which the electorate consists of the people of a country rather than a small group of selected representatives

direct evidence *n* evidence that provides direct factual information in a trial, e.g. a photograph, a document, or a witness's account

direct free kick *n* in football, a free kick that is awarded as compensation for a foul and can be taken as a direct shot at the opponent's goal

direct injection *n* the injection of fuel in liquid form into the cylinders of an internal-combustion engine, without previously passing it through a carburettor

direction /di réksh'n, dī-/ *n* **1. MANAGEMENT** instructions given by somebody who controls something or somebody **2. WAY** the way in which somebody or something goes, points, or faces ○ *They shook hands and walked off in opposite directions.* **3. SUPERVISION OF SOMETHING** the control and supervision of a group, person, or organization **4. DEVELOPMENT** the way in which something develops ○ *The organization has begun to take a new direction.* **5. SENSE OF PURPOSE** a feeling of having a definite goal or purpose ○ *He's a nice boy, but seems to lack a sense of direction.* **6.** ARTS **ART OF DIRECTING** the art or practice of directing a film or play **7.** MUSIC **INSTRUCTION IN MUSIC** an instruction in a piece of music that shows how it should be played **8.** MUSIC **CONDUCTING PERFORMERS** the process of conducting an orchestra or choir ■ **directions** *npl* **INSTRUCTIONS** instructions on how to get to a place or how to do something ○ *I need to stop the car and ask for directions.* —**directionless** *adj*

directional /di réksh'nəl, dī-/ *adj* **1. RELATING TO DIRECTION** showing, concerned with, or dependent on direction ○ *Use your directional lights to indicate the way you plan to turn.* **2. RELATING TO CONTROL OF SOMETHING** showing or relating to the management or control of somebody's work, behaviour, or way of thinking **3. INDICATING TREND** showing the future direction in which something might go **4.** ELECTRONICS **MORE EFFICIENT IN ONE DIRECTION** more efficient in a specific direction for transmitting and receiving sound waves, nuclear particles, light, or radio waves ○ *a directional aerial* —**directionality** /di rékshə nálləti, dī-/ *n*

directional drilling *n* a method of drilling for oil or gas or for installing underground utilities in which special assemblies are used to drill at any angle and around obstacles

direction finder *n* a device used especially in navigation to determine the direction of a transmitted radio signal —**direction finding** *n*

directive /di réktiv, dī-/ *n* **1. ORDER** an order or official instruction **2.** LAW **EU LAW PASSED IN MEMBER COUNTRIES** a law passed by the European Union that is then applied through the domestic law of its member states ■ *adj* **1. PROVIDING GUIDANCE** giving explicit guidance or instructions ○ *directive utterances* **2. SHOWING DIRECTION** indicating a direction ○ *directive signals* —**directiveness** *n*

direct labour *n* labour that is directly involved in the production of goods or the provision of services rather than, e.g. in administration or sales

direct lighting *n* a method of lighting in which a large percentage, usually not less than 90 per cent, of the emitted light is directed downwards

directly /di réktli, dī-/ *adv* **1. STRAIGHT** straight to a place or a person, or straight in a particular direction ○ *She went directly to the filing cabinet.* ○ *Your letter was sent directly to me.* **2. WITH NOTHING IN BETWEEN** without any person, thing, or event intervening ○ *I prefer to deal directly with senior management.* **3. COMPLETELY** in every respect ○ *I am directly opposed to everything that they stand for.* **4. CLEARLY** in a clear and unambiguous manner ○ *She refuses to say directly what the trouble is.* **5. IMMEDIATELY** at once (*dated*) ○ *I'll deal with it directly.* **6.** *US regional* **SOON** in a short while ○ *Please take a seat, and I'll be with you directly.* ■ *conj* **IMMEDIATELY AFTER** as soon as something happens ○ *I left directly I heard the news.*

direct mail *n* the use of mail addressed to potential customers as a way of advertising, or the promotional material that is mailed —**direct mailer** *n*

direct-mail shot *n* a mailing of promotional literature to a number of potential customers directly

direct marketing *n* methods of marketing by which a company deals directly with its end customers, including mail order by catalogue, direct mail, telephone sales, or the advertising of goods

direct object *n* the word or phrase in a sentence that indicates somebody or something directly affected by the action of the verb, e.g. 'cat' in 'she fed the cat'

director /di réktər, dī-/ *n* **1. HEAD OF MANAGEMENT** a manager of an organized group or a programme of activity **2. SOMEBODY WHO RUNS COMPANY** a member of the board that controls the affairs of a company. A board may be made up of executive directors, who manage the company, and nonexecutive directors, who contribute advice. **3. FILMMAKER** a supervisor of the actual making of a film or television programme **4. MUSICAL CONDUCTOR** a supervisor of the work of a group of musicians, especially an orchestra conductor [15C. Via Anglo-Norman < late Latin < Latin *directus* (see DIRECT)] —**directorial** /dī rek táwri əl, di rék-/ *adj* —**directorially** *adv* —**directorship** *n*

directorate /di réktərət, dī-/ *n* a board of directors, e.g. of a company

director-general (*plural* **directors-general**) *n* the title given to the head of some large public organizations, e.g. the BBC in Britain

Director of Public Prosecutions *n* **1.** the head of the Crown Prosecution Service, which is responsible for the conduct of all criminal prosecutions in England and Wales **2.** in Australian states and at a federal level, the government official responsible for prosecutions on behalf of the Crown

director's chair *n* **1.** the chair used by the director on the set of a film **2.** a light folding chair with a wooden or metal frame with arms, and a canvas back and seat

director's cut *n* a cut of a film that has not been altered by a studio and that its director has complete artistic control over, often not the version that is released commercially

directory /di réktəri, dī-/ *n* (*plural* **-ries**) **1. BOOK OF NAMES** a book alphabetically listing persons and organizations, usually with information about how to contact them **2.** COMPUT **INDEX OF COMPUTER FILES** an index of files stored on a computer disk. A disk may have many separate directories containing different types of file. **3. RULE BOOK** a book of rules or instructions **4.** BUSINESS **GROUP OF DIRECTORS** a board of company directors **5. LIST OF TENANTS** a listing in the lobby of a building of those who live or work in the building, with their floor or room numbers ■ *adj* **GIVING DIRECTION** providing direction or advice

directory assistance *n ANZ, N Am* same as **directory enquiries**

directory enquiries *n UK* a service provided by a telephone company that provides the telephone number of anyone in the country who has agreed to have his or her number listed. ANZ term **directory assistance**. N Am term **information, directory assistance**

direct primary *n* a primary election in the United States in which the candidates who will seek office as nominees of a political party are chosen directly by popular vote

direct question *n* **1.** a question directed to a specific person and requiring a response **2.** a question repeated in the exact words that were spoken, placed inside quotation marks in writing

direct-reading *adj* allowing the immediate reading of a measurement, without intervening calculations

directrix /di rékt riks, dī-/ (*plural* **-trixes** or **-trices** /-triseez/) *n* a fixed line used in constructing a curve or conic section, the distance from the line divided by the distance from a fixed point being identical for all points on the figure [Early 16C. < medieval Latin, feminine form of late Latin *director* (see DIRECTOR)]

direct selling *n* MARKETING same as **direct marketing**

direct speech *n UK, ANZ, Can* the repeating of speech by giving the exact words that were spoken, and in writing, conventionally shown inside quotation marks. US term **direct discourse**

direct tax *n* a tax that is levied directly on the income or capital of a person or organization, rather than as part of the price of goods or services

dire straits *npl* a situation of emergency or desperate need

dire wolf *n* a large extinct mammal of the Pleistocene Epoch, similar to a wolf. Native to: North America. Latin name: *Canis dirus.*

dirge /durj/ *n* **1. FUNERAL HYMN** a song of mourning or lament, especially one about death or intended for a funeral **2. MOURNFUL MUSIC** a song or piece of music that sounds sad or depressing **3. FUNERAL SERVICE** a funeral service that is sung [Early 15C. < Latin *dirige* 'guide!' (first word of Psalm 5:8, used as the antiphon in a funeral service)]

dirham /deer ram, deerrəm/ *n* a unit of currency in some North-African and Middle-Eastern countries. See table at **currency** [Late 18C. Via Arabic < Greek *drachmē* 'number of coins one hand can hold']

dirigible /dírrijəb'l/ *n* AVIAT same as **airship** ■ *adj* able to be steered or navigated [Late 16C. < Latin *dirigere* 'direct, guide'; because an airship (unlike a balloon) can be steered] —**dirigibility** /dírrijə bílləti/ *n*

dirigisme /dírri zhizəm/ *n* full and direct state control of a country's economy and social institutions [Mid-20C. < French < *diriger* 'to direct' < Latin *dirigere*] —**dirigiste** /dírri zheest/ *adj*

diriment /dírrimənt/ *adj* invalidating a marriage in canon law [Mid-19C. < Latin *diriment-* < *dirimere* 'take apart']

dirk /durk/ *n* a dagger with a long straight blade, formerly used by Scottish Highlanders ■ *vt* (**dirks, dirking, dirked**) to stab somebody with a dagger [Mid-16C. Origin ?]

Dirk Hartog Island /dúrk haár tog-/ uninhabited island off the western coast of Australia. It is the westernmost point on the continent, and in 1616 was the site of the first landing by a European. Area: 613 sq. km/234 sq. mi.

dirndl /dúrnd'l/ *n* **1.** *also* **dirndl skirt** a full skirt that is gathered at the waist **2.** a dress with a full gathered skirt and a tight, low bodice that is worn over a short-sleeved blouse and is part of German and Austrian national costume [Mid-20C. < German dialect, 'little girl']

dirt /durt/ *n* **1.** UNCLEAN SUBSTANCE a substance that spoils the cleanness of somebody or something ○ *There was a smear of dirt on his shirt.* **2.** EARTH earth, soil, or mud ○ *Children were playing in the dirt by the side of the road.* **3.** HARD-PACKED EARTH soil packed down to make a firm surface, especially mixed with gravel and cinders to make a racetrack for motor cycles or for horse racing ○ *dirt floors* **4.** SCANDALOUS FACTS scandalous or damaging facts about somebody ○ *The local paper may have some dirt on the candidates.* **5.** CORRUPTING INFLUENCE something that is considered to have a corrupting influence, e.g. pornography or bad language [13C. < Old Norse *drit* 'excrement' < Germanic] ◇ **dig the dirt on somebody** *or* **something** to search for scandalous information about somebody or something in order to make it public ◇ **treat somebody like dirt** to treat somebody with the utmost contempt (*informal*)

dirt bike *n* a motorcycle designed to be ridden across country or on dirt roads

dirtboarding /dúrt bawrding/ *n* EXTREME SPORTS same as **mountainboarding**

dirt-cheap *adj, adv* extremely cheap or cheaply (*informal*)

dirt-poor *adj* having so little money that the basic needs of life can scarcely be satisfied

dirt road *n* a road that is not surfaced, but consists of hard-packed earth

dirt track *n* **1.** a narrow road or path that is not surfaced, but consists of earth **2.** a track of earth mixed with gravel and cinders that is used for horse racing or motorcycle racing

dirty /dúrti/ *adj* (**-ier, -iest**) **1.** NOT CLEAN marked by or covered in dirt ○ *dirty fingernails* **2.** CAUSING DIRT creating dirt or pollution ○ *a battered truck with a dirty engine* **3.** MAKING SOMEBODY GRIMY likely to cause somebody to be filthy or grimy ○ *Working on cars is a dirty job.* **4.** NOT HONEST OR LEGAL lacking honesty or moral integrity, especially if the rules of a game or law have been broken ○ *dirty tactics* **5.** MALICIOUS characterized by extreme meanness and cruelty ○ *a dirty lie* **6.** SEXUALLY SUGGESTIVE concerned with sex, especially in a way that is rude or suggestive **7.** ANGRY expressing anger, displeasure, or disapproval ○ *a dirty look* **8.** LACKING BRIGHTNESS OR CLARITY lacking in lustre or clarity (*often used in combination*) ○ *The walls were a dirty green.* **9.** STORMY characterized by heavy rain and strong winds ○ *dirty weather* **10.** RADIOACTIVE producing radioactive contamination **11.** DESPICABLE behaving in a nasty or despicable way (*informal*) ○ *a dirty rascal* **12.** *US* RELATING TO ILLEGAL DRUGS relating to the use or sale of illegal drugs by somebody (*slang*) ■ *adv* (**-ier, -iest**) **1.** UNFAIRLY in an unfair or dishonest way ○ *You have to fight dirty if you want to win.* **2.** SUGGESTIVELY in a sexually suggestive or indecent way ■ *v* (**-ies, -ying, -ied**) **1.** *vti* MAKE OR BECOME DIRTY to make something or somebody dirty, or become dirty ○ *He wouldn't want to dirty his hands with that kind of work.* **2.** *vt* DISHONOUR SOMETHING to make something seem less honest or honourable ○ *to dirty their reputation* —**dirtily** *adv* —**dirtiness** *n* ◇ **get your hands dirty 1.** to perform menial or manual labour or work very hard **2.** to perform or participate in a degrading or unpleasant act

CULTURAL NOTE ***Dirty Harry***, a film (1971) by US director Don Siegel. It is the story of San Francisco policeman Harry Callahan (Clint Eastwood), known as 'Dirty' because he always gets the worst jobs, and his attempts to apprehend a serial killer, Scorpio. Famous lines spoken by the Callahan character have also made their way into mainstream US English. An example is 'Go ahead, make my day!' from *Sudden Impact* (1983).

SYNONYMS ***dirty, filthy, grubby, grimy, soiled, squalid, unclean***

CORE MEANING: not clean

dirty marked by or covered in dirt ○ *Diesel engines have very dirty exhaust emissions.* ○ *Each year, over a million children die from diarrhoea spread by dirty water.* **filthy** extremely or disgustingly dirty ○ *Just look at your shoes – they're filthy!* ○ *I was taken into a filthy room with little furniture.* **grubby** slightly dirty ○ *a rather grubby handkerchief* ○ *Travelling always made her feel grubby.* **grimy** heavily ingrained with accumulated dirt ○ *the faint light from a grimy window* ○ *The rescue workers' faces were tired and grimy.* **soiled** stained or marked, especially during normal use ○ *soiled bed linen* ○ *His white shirt was a little soiled.* **squalid** neglected, insanitary and unpleasant ○ *living in squalid conditions* ○ *She died alone in a squalid bed-sit.* **unclean** dirty and insanitary, or impure in moral or religious contexts ○ *unclean water supplies* ○ *After such violent experiences, the victims often say they feel unclean.* ○ *People with leprosy were regarded as ritually unclean.*

dirty bomb *n* a bomb containing radioactive nuclear waste dispersed by means of conventional explosives

dirty denim *n* denim that is given a dirty or discoloured appearance, usually by weaving brown yarn into the fabric during the manufacturing process. Use: clothing, especially jeans.

dirty linen, **dirty laundry** *n* personal matters that it would be embarrassing or disadvantageous to let other people know about ○ *Don't wash your dirty linen in public.*

dirty old man *n* an older man who shows an interest in sex that is perceived as immoral, perverted, or generally unpleasant (*informal insult*)

dirty trick *n* UNFAIR ACTION something unfair or dishonest that is done to gain an advantage ■ **dirty tricks** *npl* **1.** UNFAIR POLITICAL TACTICS tactics used in a political campaign to discredit an opponent in a way that is not completely fair or honest **2.** SPY TACTICS secret activities carried out by the spies of one government in order to disrupt or destroy the internal functioning of another nation (*informal*) **3.** COMMERCIAL ESPIONAGE the activity of stealing secret products or processes from one company and selling them to rival companies (*informal*)

dirty word *n* **1.** a swearword or offensive word **2.** something that is disapproved of ○ *Delay seems to be a dirty word in this office!*

dirty work *n* something that somebody wants to be done that is unpleasant, unfair, unkind, dishonest, or illegal

dis /diss/ (**disses, dissing, dissed**), **diss** *vt* (*slang*) **1.** to treat somebody without respect, e.g. by talking back or being purposely rude **2.** to criticize somebody or something [Late 20C. Origin ?]

Dis /diss/ *n* **1.** MYTHOL same as **Pluto** (sense 2) **2.** in Roman mythology, the region of the dead. Greek equivalent **Hades**

dis- *prefix* **1.** to undo, do the opposite ○ *disapprove* **2.** opposite or absence of ○ *discourtesy* **3.** to deprive of, remove from ○ *dishonour* **4.** not ○ *disobedient* **5.** to free from ○ *disburden* **6.** completely ○ *dissever* [Directly or via French < Latin < *dis* 'apart']

disability /dissə bílləti/ (*plural* **-ties**) *n* **1.** RESTRICTED CAPABILITY TO PERFORM PARTICULAR ACTIVITIES an inability to perform some or all of the tasks of daily life **2.** MEDICAL CONDITION RESTRICTING ACTIVITIES a medically diagnosed condition that makes it difficult to engage in the activities of daily life **3.** LEGAL DISQUALIFIER something that causes somebody to be regarded in law as ineligible to perform a specific transaction

disability clause *n* a clause in a life insurance policy indicating the conditions that will apply if the holder becomes unable to work, including release from payment of further premiums

disable /diss áyb'l/ (**-bles, -bling, -bled**) *vt* **1.** RESTRICT SOMEBODY IN SOME ACTIVITIES to make somebody unable to perform the activities needed to earn a living or carry out the basic tasks of daily life without difficulty **2.** STOP SOMETHING FROM WORKING to prevent a device or system from working by disconnecting a part of it **3.** DISQUALIFY SOMEBODY LEGALLY to make somebody ineligible in law to perform a specific transaction —**disablement** *n*

disabled /diss áyb'ld/ *adj* **1.** UNABLE TO PERFORM PARTICULAR ACTIVITIES describes somebody with a condition that makes it difficult to perform some or all of the basic tasks of daily life **2.** UNABLE TO OPERATE incapable of performing or functioning ■ *npl* DISABLED PEOPLE people with disabilities

USAGE Although the adjective ***disabled*** has a long history of use by those so affected, *people with disabilities* is preferred over the adjective and noun forms of ***disabled***.

disabuse /díssə byoóz/ (**-buses, -busing, -bused**) *vt* to tell somebody or make somebody realize that an idea is not true ○ *I was quickly disabused of my idealistic notions about the campaign.* ○ *She disabused him of many old prejudices.* [Early 17C. < ABUSE in the obsolete sense 'a delusion'] —**disabusal** *n*

disaccharide /dī sákə rīd/ *n* a sugar consisting of two linked monosaccharide units

disaccord /díssə káwrd/ (*formal*) *n* lack of harmony or agreement ■ *vi* (**-cords, -cording, -corded**) to disagree or not be in accordance with one another

disadvantage /díssəd vaántij/ *n* **1.** BAD QUALITY something that makes a situation less good or that makes somebody or something less effective or desirable **2.** BAD SITUATION a situation that is unfavourable to somebody ○ *He was at a disadvantage, having only received the documents that morning.* **3.** LOSS injury, loss, or damage (*formal*) ■ *vt* (**-tages, -taging, -taged**) CAUSE PROBLEM FOR SOMEBODY to put somebody or something at a disadvantage

disadvantaged /díssəd vaántijd/ *adj* in a worse position than somebody else or other people

disadvantageous /díss advən táyjəss, diss ádvən-/ *adj* not helpful or favourable —**disadvantageously** *adv* —**disadvantageousness** *n*

disaffect /díssə fékt/ (**-fects, -fecting, -fected**) *vt* to make somebody dissatisfied with somebody or something, especially somebody to whom respect or loyalty is owed —**disaffected** *adj* —**disaffectedly** *adv* —**disaffectedness** *n* —**disaffection** *n*

disaffiliate /díssə fílli ayt/ (**-ates, -ating, -ated**) *v* **1.** *vti* to end the affiliated status of a subsidiary group ○ *The group was formally disaffiliated from its parent body at the end of 1985.* **2.** *vi* to withdraw from affiliation or association with a larger group or organization —**disaffiliation** /díssə fílli áysh'n/ *n*

disaffirm /díssə fúrm/ (**-firms, -firming, -firmed**) *vt* **1.** to say that something is not true or that the opposite of it is true (*formal*) **2.** to alter a legal decision, or refuse to recognize or acknowledge something formally —**disaffirmance** *n* —**disaffirmation** /díss affər máysh'n/ *n*

disaggregate /diss ággrəgət, -gayt/ (**-gates, -gating, -gated**) *vti* to separate something into its component parts, or break apart —**disaggregation** /díss agrə gáysh'n/ *n*

disagree /díssə greé/ (**-grees, -greeing, -greed**) *vi* **1.** NOT AGREE to have or put forward a different view or opinion ○ *She strongly disagrees with you on this point.* **2.** NOT MATCH to fail to be in accordance with something, or to show a different result **3.** AFFECT SOMEBODY BADLY to have an unpleasant effect on somebody ○ *I love oysters, but they disagree with me.* **4.** DISAPPROVE to be opposed to a rule, law, or idea [15C. < French *désagréer* < *agréer* 'agree']

SYNONYMS ***disagree, differ, argue, dispute, take issue with, contradict, agree to differ, be at odds***

CORE MEANING: to have or express a difference of opinion with somebody

disagree to have or put forward a different view or opinion ○ *He strongly disagrees with what was said.* ○ *I disagree with Neil about keeping the plan quiet – it often does less damage to be completely open from the start.* **differ** to have different opinions about something ○ *People may well differ on the issue of whether this development is a good or a bad thing.* ○ *Accounts differ as to who was present and how many vehicles they had.* **argue** to express disagreement, especially continuously or angrily ○ *My husband and I argue about football all the time.* ○ *She knew better than to argue with him when he used that tone of voice.* **dispute** to disagree or argue about something ○ *For years, scholars have disputed over this text.* ○ *The two*

brothers had been disputing about the terms of their parents' will. **take issue with** to disagree strongly with somebody about something ○ *I would take issue with her view.* ○ *It is with regret that I have had to take issue with a fellow member of our committee.* **contradict** to argue against the truth or correctness of a statement or claim ○ *Let her tell her story and don't contradict her.* ○ *Important witnesses are contradicting each other's accounts.* **agree to differ** to stop arguing and accept that the opposing viewpoints are irreconcilable ○ *We might as well agree to differ and get along as well as we can.* ○ *If after discussion the social worker and client agree to differ with respect to the report's content, both versions will be recorded.* **be at odds** to be in disagreement, especially over a period of time or about a particular issue ○ *The Mayor seems to be at odds with his own officials over this question.*

disagreeable /díssə grée əb'l/ *adj* **1.** causing feelings that are not pleasant or enjoyable **2.** lacking courtesy or constantly finding a reason to disagree with somebody —**disagreeability** /díssə gree ə bílləti/ *n* —**disagreeableness** *n* —**disagreeably** *adv*

disagreement /díssə greémənt/ *n* **1.** FAILURE TO AGREE ABOUT SOMETHING the fact of having or expressing a different opinion and failing to agree about something **2.** SLIGHT ARGUMENT a situation in which a number of people or groups argue **3.** DIFFERENCE failure to be in accordance with something

disallow /díssə lów/ (**-lows, -lowing, -lowed**) *vt* **1.** to refuse to accept something because it is not true, valid, or correctly done **2.** to cancel a privilege or entitlement, or refuse to allow something that was previously allowed —**disallowable** *adj* —**disallowance** *n*

~~disallusion~~ incorrect spelling of **disillusion**

disambiguate /díss am bíggyoo ayt/ (**-ates, -ating, -ated**) *vt* to establish the true meaning of an expression, regulation, or ruling that is confusing or that could be interpreted in more than one way —**disambiguation** /díss am bíggyoo áysh'n/ *n*

~~disapear~~ incorrect spelling of **disappear**

~~disapointed~~ incorrect spelling of **disappointed**

disappear /díssə peér/ (**-pears, -pearing, -peared**) *v* **1.** *vi* VANISH FROM SIGHT to cease to be seen, e.g. by moving away or going behind or into something **2.** *vi* NOT BE FOUND to be gone from or no longer be seen in a place without any explanation **3.** *vi* CEASE TO EXIST to no longer exist **4.** *vt* CAUSE OPPONENT TO DISAPPEAR to make a political opponent disappear by arresting or killing the person without due process of law ○ *It wasn't the first time they had disappeared someone who was in the way.* —**disappearance** *n*

disappeared /díssə peérd/ *npl* people who have been arrested by a regime that they opposed and whose subsequent fate is not known [Late 20C. Translation of Spanish *desaparecido*]

disappearing act ◇ **do a disappearing act** to be unable to be found or contacted when needed (*humorous*)

disapplication /díss appli káysh'n/ *n* a special exemption from the National Curriculum given to a school

disappoint /díssə póynt/ (**-points, -pointing, -pointed**) *v* **1.** *vi* to be less good, attractive, or satisfactory than was hoped or expected **2.** *vt* to let somebody down by not doing something or by not happening as hoped or expected [15C. < French *désappointer* 'deprive of an appointment']

disappointed /díssə póyntid/ *adj* unhappy because something was not as good, attractive, or satisfactory as expected, or because something hoped for or expected did not happen —**disappointedly** *adv*

disappointing /díssə póynting/ *adj* not as good, attractive, or satisfactory as hoped or expected —**disappointingly** *adv*

disappointment /díssə póyntmənt/ *n* **1.** FEELING OF BEING LET DOWN a feeling of sadness or frustration because something was not as good, attractive, or satisfactory as expected, or because something hoped for did not happen **2.** SOMETHING DISAPPOINTING something or somebody that disappoints somebody, or an occasion when somebody is disappointed **3.** FRUSTRATION the frustration of hopes or wishes

Disappointment, Lake /díssə póyntmənt/ dry salt lake in Western Australia, once thought to have incorporated a lagoon, hence its name. Area: 330 sq. km/130 sq. mi.

disapprobation /diss ápprə báysh'n/ *n* the expression of moral or social disapproval (*formal*)

disapproval /díssə pro͞ov'l/ *n* a negative judgment of something based on personal standards

disapprove /díssə pro͞ov/ (**-proves, -proving, -proved**) *v* **1.** *vi* to give a negative judgment of something based on personal standards **2.** *vt* to refuse to approve or agree to something (*formal*) —**disapproving** *adj* —**disapprovingly** *adv*

SYNONYMS ***disapprove, frown on, object, criticize, condemn, deplore, denounce, censure***

CORE MEANING: to have an unfavourable opinion of something or somebody

disapprove to give a negative judgment of something based on personal standards ○ *Why do you disapprove so strongly of my leisure pursuits?* ○ *Her parents will disapprove if they find out where she spent the evening.* **frown on** to dislike and disapprove of something ○ *a practice which would be frowned on today* ○ *They were brought up in an era when ease and convenience were frowned on.* **object** to be opposed to something, or express opposition ○ *a petition strongly objecting to the proposals* ○ *I don't object to people smoking in the open air.* **criticize** to express disapproval of or dissatisfaction with somebody or something ○ *The ministers have been sharply criticized for their conduct.* ○ *I feel that the role of the media is to criticize the government, not to defend it.* **condemn** to state that something or somebody is in some way wrong or unacceptable ○ *The present system has been widely condemned as unfair and archaic.* ○ *The rebels were forced to sign statements condemning their own actions.* **deplore** to disapprove of something very strongly ○ *We deplore all use of violence.* ○ *I deeply deplore the government's action.* **denounce** to criticize or condemn something publicly and harshly ○ *a letter denouncing the government's economic approach as ruinous* ○ *The hierarchy publicly denounced any attack on ecclesiastical privileges.* **censure** to make a formal, often public or official statement of disapproval ○ *A partner in the firm was officially censured for unprofessional conduct.* ○ *The Press Complaints Commission has censured the newspaper for a story it printed.*

disarm /diss áarm/ (**-arms, -arming, -armed**) *v* **1.** *vti* GIVE UP WEAPONS to give up a supply of weapons or reduce the strength of armed forces, or force another nation to do this **2.** *vt* DEFUSE BOMB to make a bomb unable to explode, or make a weapon incapable of being fired **3.** *vt* WIN SOMEBODY OVER to make somebody less hostile or suspicious and more inclined to act in a friendly way ○ *They disarmed us with their confidence and skill.* —**disarmer** *n*

disarmament /diss áarmәmənt/ *n* **1.** the process of reducing a nation's supply of weapons or the strength of its armed forces ○ *a believer in negotiated mutual disarmament* **2.** the condition of having given up weapons ○ *Disarmament brought peace to the troubled region.*

disarming /diss áarming/ *adj* making somebody feel more friendly or trusting —**disarmingly** *adv*

disarrange /díssə ráynj/ (**-ranges, -ranging, -ranged**) *vt* to disturb the order or arrangement of something —**disarrangement** *n*

disarray /díssə ráy/ *n* **1.** DISORGANIZED STATE a disorganized and confused state ○ *The meeting was thrown into disarray by the surprise announcement.* **2.** UNTIDINESS a state of untidiness, especially in dress ■ *vt* (**-rays, -raying, -rayed**) **1.** MAKE SOMETHING DISORGANIZED to make something confused and disorganized **2.** UNDRESS SOMEBODY to remove somebody's clothes (*archaic*)

disarticulate /díss aar tíkyo͝o layt/ (**-lates, -lating, -lated**) *vti* to separate something at the joints, or come apart at the joints —**disarticulation** /díss aar tíkyo͝o láysh'n/ *n* —**disarticulator** *n*

disassemble /díssə sémb'l/ (**-bles, -bling, -bled**) *vt* to take something such as a piece of machinery apart —**disassembly** *n*

disassociate /díssə sṓshi ayt, -sṓssi-/ (**-ates, -ating, -ated**) *vt* **1.** to end an association with another person or group **2.** to deny any connection or involvement with somebody or something ○ *In a press conference, the MP attempted to disassociate himself from the scandal.*

disassociation /díssə sōshi áysh'n, -sōssi-/ *n* **1.** the termination of an association with another person or group **2.** the denial of any connection or involvement with somebody or something else

USAGE disassociation or **dissociation**? Both these words, and the verbs (*disassociate, dissociate*) from which they come, share the meaning 'separation from a relationship with another', and in this sense they are interchangeable: *sought disassociation/dissociation from the scandal; sought to dissociate/disassociate themselves from the scandal.* ***Dissociation***, however, does have two senses not shared by ***disassociation***: in psychology and psychiatry, 'separation of emotions as a defence mechanism' and in chemistry, 'the breaking up of a molecule into simpler components'. Do not confuse the two words.

disaster /di záastər/ *n* **1.** an event that causes serious loss, destruction, hardship, unhappiness, or death **2.** somebody or something that fails completely, especially in a way that is distressing, embarrassing, or laughable (*informal*) [Late 16C. Via French < Italian *disastro*, literally 'ill-starred' < Latin *astrum* 'star' < Greek *astron*]

disaster area *n* **1.** a place that is officially declared to be in a state of emergency and in need of special assistance after a natural disaster ○ *The southern half of the state has been declared a disaster area.* **2.** a very untidy or disorganized place or situation (*informal*)

disaster movie *n* a film that deals with a disaster such as an earthquake or plane crash in a dramatic and spectacular way

~~disasterous~~ incorrect spelling of **disastrous**

disastrous /di záastrəss/ *adj* **1.** having seriously damaging results **2.** performed in an incompetent or awkward way [Late 16C. < French *désastreux* < Italian *disastro* (see DISASTER)] —**disastrously** *adv* —**disastrousness** *n*

~~disatisfied~~ incorrect spelling of **dissatisfied**

disavow /díssə vów/ (**-vows, -vowing, -vowed**) *vt* to deny any knowledge of, responsibility for, or association with somebody or something —**disavowable** *adj* —**disavowal** *n* —**disavowedly** /-idli/ *adv* —**disavower** *n*

disband /diss bánd/ (**-bands, -banding, -banded**) *vti* to break up as a group or organization, or cause a group or organization to break up —**disbandment** *n*

disbar /diss báar/ (**-bars, -barring, -barred**) *vt* to take away officially the right of a barrister to practise law —**disbarment** *n*

disbelief /díss bi leéf/ *n* the feeling of not believing or of not being able to believe somebody or something

disbelieve /díss bi leév/ (**-lieves, -lieving, -lieved**) *v* **1.** *vt* to think that something somebody has said is untrue **2.** *vi* to have no belief in something, especially in God or religion —**disbeliever** *n* —**disbelieving** *adj* —**disbelievingly** *adv*

disbenefit /diss bénnifit/ *n* something that makes a situation disadvantageous or unfavourable

disbud /diss búd/ (**-buds, -budding, -budded**) *vt* **1.** to remove buds or shoots from a plant so that the remaining ones will be larger and stronger **2.** to remove the horns from a young animal

disburden /diss búrd'n/ (**-dens, -dening, -dened**) *vt* **1.** to gain relief by telling somebody about something that is causing anxiety or guilt **2.** to free somebody or something from a burden or constraint —**disburdenment** *n*

disburse /diss búrss/ (**-burses, -bursing, -bursed**) *vt* to pay out money, especially from a fund (*formal*) [Mid-16C. < Old French *desbourser* 'remove from the purse' < *bourse* 'purse'] —**disbursable** *adj* —**disbursement** *n* —**disburser** *n*

SPELLCHECK disburse or **disperse**? Do not confuse the spelling of ***disburse*** and ***disperse***, which sound similar. ***Disburse*** is largely restricted to formal contexts and refers specifically to paying out money: *All the funds have been disbursed.* ***Disperse***, the more frequent of the two verbs, means 'scatter', 'cause to go away', or 'disappear': *The crowds dispersed.*

disc /disk/, **disk** *n* **1.** ROUND FLAT OBJECT an object that is thin, flat, and circular **2.** MECH ENG BRAKE PART a circular piece of metal around the hub of a vehicle wheel, against which the pads of a disc brake press **3.** AGRIC STEEL BLADE a circular steel blade with a sharpened edge that is used on a disc harrow or plough **4.** ANAT PART BETWEEN BONES OF SPINE a flat round structure in the skeleton of a person or animal that separates the bones of the spine **5.** BOT CENTRE OF FLOWER HEAD the central part of the flower head of a composite plant, made up of tiny tubular flowers **6.** COMPUT COMPUTER STORAGE DEVICE a device consisting of one or more thin magnetically or optically etched plates, used in a computer to store information **7.** MUSIC MUSICAL RECORDING a gramophone record (*dated informal*) [Mid-17C. Directly or via French < Latin *discus* (see DISH)] —**disc-like** *adj*

disc. *abbr* **1.** COMM discount **2.** discovered

disc- *prefix* same as **disco-** (*used before vowels*)

discalced /diss kálst/ *adj* wearing sandals or going barefoot in accordance with the rules of some orders of monks, friars, or nuns [Mid-17C. Shortening of obsolete *discalceated* 'with shoes removed' < Latin *calceare* 'to shoe' < *calceus* 'shoe']

discant *n, vi* MUSIC same as **descant** —**discanter** *n*

discard /diss kaárd/ *v* (**-cards, -carding, -carded**) **1.** *vt* THROW SOMETHING AWAY to get rid of something that is not wanted or needed **2.** *vt* REJECT CARD in some card games, to put down a card from a hand and not play it **3.** *vti* PLAY CARD in a card game such as bridge or whist, to play a card so that it has no value, because it is neither in the required suit nor a trump ■ *n* **1.** /díss kaard/ ACT OF DISCARDING the act of discarding a playing card **2.** SOMETHING DISCARDED somebody or something that has been discarded —**discardable** *adj* —**discarder** *n*

discarnate /diss kaárnət, -nayt/ *adj* lacking a physical body [Mid-17C. < DIS- + Latin *carn-* 'flesh']

disc brake *n* a brake that works by the friction of a caliper or pads against a rotating disc

disc camera *n* a camera that uses film on a disc rather than a spool or cartridge

discern /di súrn, -zúrn/ (**-cerns, -cerning, -cerned**) *v* **1.** *vt* SEE OR NOTICE SOMETHING UNCLEAR to see or notice something that is not very clear or obvious **2.** *vt* UNDERSTAND SOMETHING to understand something that is not immediately obvious **3.** *vti* DISTINGUISH to be able to tell the difference between two or more things [14C. Directly or via French < Latin *discernere* 'separate off' < *cernere* 'separate, determine'] —**discerner** *n* —**discernible** *adj*

discernibly /di súrnəbli, -zúrnəbli/, **discernably** *adv* in an obvious way or to a noticeable extent ○ *not discernibly different*

discerning /di súrning, -zúrning/ *adj* showing good judgment and good taste —**discerningly** *adv*

discernment /di súrnmənt, -zúrnmənt/ *n* good taste and judgment

disc flower, **disc floret** *n* a tiny tubular flower that is one of the group that forms the centre disc of the flower head of some composite plants, e.g. the daisy

discharge *v*/diss chaárj/ (**-charges, -charging, -charged**) **1.** *vt* DISMISS SOMEBODY FROM INSTITUTIONAL SETTING to arrange for or allow somebody to leave an institution, especially a hospital, or make the decision yourself to leave such a place after being an inpatient **2.** *vt* RELEASE SOMEBODY FROM ARMED FORCES to release somebody from service in the armed forces formally, or formally end your service **3.** *vt* RELEASE OR ACQUIT SOMEBODY to release a prisoner, or acquit somebody in a court of law **4.** *vti* EMIT OR DUMP LIQUID OR GAS to emit, give off, or dispose of a gas or liquid, or be emitted or disposed of **5.** *vt* CARRY SOMETHING OUT to complete a duty, responsibility, or promise successfully (*formal*) **6.** *vt* RELEASE SOMEBODY FROM DUTY to excuse somebody from a duty or obligation **7.** *vt* DISMISS EMPLOYEE to dismiss somebody from a job (*formal*) **8.** *vt* PAY DEBT to pay a debt in full (*formal*) **9.** *vti* SHOOT OR GO OFF to fire a weapon or missile, or be fired (*formal*) **10.** *vt* CANCEL COURT ORDER to cancel or annul a court order **11.** *vti* OFFLOAD SHIP'S CARGO to unload cargo or passengers from a ship **12.** *vti* LOSE ELECTRIC CHARGE to lose or release electric charge by the addition or loss of electrons from a stationary body, e.g. in static electricity, or be released in this way **13.** *vi* SPARK to give off electricity suddenly in the form of a spark or arc, e.g. in the release of stored energy in a capacitor **14.** *vti* DRAIN ELECTRICITY to drain slowly of electricity, or make the electricity in a battery drain slowly **15.** *vt* RELEASE PRESSURE ON BUILDING to release the pressure on part of a building by spreading it over adjacent parts **16.** *vt* BLEACH FABRIC to remove the colour from fabric by bleaching it **17.** *vi* RUN OR BLUR to undergo a running or blurring of dyes ■ *n* /díss chaarj/ **1.** DISMISSAL FROM INSTITUTION permission or orders to leave an institution, especially a hospital, after being a patient **2.** SEPARATION FROM ARMED FORCES formal and official release of somebody from the armed forces, or a document certifying this **3.** PRISONER'S RELEASE the release of a prisoner from custody **4.** MUCUS a flow of fluid from the body, especially an unusual or large flow of mucus from the bodily orifices or pus from a wound **5.** EMISSION OF SUBSTANCES the emission of gases, liquids, or chemicals **6.** RATE OF EMISSION the rate at which a gas or liquid is being emitted **7.** PERFORMANCE OF DUTY the carrying out of a duty, obligation, responsibility, or promise (*formal*) **8.** DEBT PAYMENT the payment of a debt (*formal*) **9.** FIRING the firing of a gun (*formal*) **10.** PRODUCTION OF ELECTRICITY the process of converting chemical energy into electrical energy, e.g. in a battery **11.** CONTINUOUS FLOW OF ELECTRICITY THROUGH AIR the continuous flow of electric energy through air or a gas as a result of ionization, as occurs when a spark jumps a gap, or, at a reduced pressure, as in a fluorescent lamp **12.** CARGO OFFLOADING the unloading of cargo **13.** VOLUME OF RIVER WATER FLOW the volume of water in a river flowing past a point during a specific time interval [14C. Via Old French *descharger* < late Latin *discar(r)icare* 'unload' < Latin *car(ri)care* 'to load'] —**dischargeable** *adj* —**discharger** *n*

SYNONYMS See ***perform***.

discharged bankrupt /dis chaárjd-/ *n* somebody whose period of bankruptcy has come to an end and who is no longer bound by the restrictions that apply to people who have been declared bankrupt

discharge lamp *n* an electric lamp that glows as a result of electricity passing through a gas

discharge tube *n* a tube filled with low-pressure gas that glows when it conducts electricity at a given voltage. Use: neon and fluorescent lights.

disc harrow *n* a harrow with a series of discs set at an angle on one or more axles that loosen the soil when moved over ploughed land

disci ATHLETICS plural of **discus**

disciple /di sīp'l/ *n* **1.** somebody who believes in and follows the teachings of a leader, a philosophy, or a religion **2.** in the Bible, one of the 12 original followers of Jesus Christ [Pre-12C. < Latin *discipulus* 'learner' < *discere* 'learn'] —**discipleship** *n* —**discipular** /di síppyŏŏlər/ *adj*

Disciple *n* **1.** CHR another spelling of **disciple** (sense 2) **2.** a member of the Disciples of Christ

Disciples of Christ *n* a Protestant denomination of the Christian Church whose congregations regard the Bible as the sole rule of faith and living, and practise baptism by total immersion. It was founded in the United States in 1809 by Thomas and Alexander Campbell. (*takes a singular or plural verb*)

disciplinarian /díssəpli náiri ən/ *n* somebody who believes in or enforces strictly defined rules of behaviour ■ *adj* same as **disciplinary**

disciplinary /díssəplinəri/ *adj* **1.** relating to the enforcement and punishment of rules of behaviour **2.** relating to an academic subject ○ *Teachers tried to cut across traditional disciplinary boundaries in their lessons.* —**disciplinarily** *adv* —**disciplinarity** /díssəpli nárrəti/ *n*

discipline /díssəplin/ *n* **1.** TRAINING TO ENSURE PROPER BEHAVIOUR the practice or methods of teaching and enforcing acceptable patterns of behaviour **2.** ORDER AND CONTROL a controlled orderly state, especially in a class of school children **3.** CALM CONTROLLED BEHAVIOUR the ability to behave in a controlled and calm way even in a difficult or stressful situation **4.** CONSCIOUS CONTROL OVER LIFESTYLE mental self-control used in directing or changing behaviour, learning something, or training for something **5.** EDUC ACTIVITY OR SUBJECT a subject or field of activity, e.g. an academic subject **6.** PUNISHMENT punishment designed to teach somebody obedience **7.** CHR CHURCH RULES the system of rules used in a religious denomination or order ■ *v* (**-plines, -plining, -plined**) **1.** *vr* MAKE YOURSELF DO SOMETHING REGULARLY to make yourself act or work in a controlled or systematic way **2.** *vt* PUNISH SOMEBODY to punish somebody as a way of enforcing obedience **3.** *vt* TEACH SOMEBODY OBEDIENCE to teach somebody to obey rules or to behave in an acceptable way [13C. Directly or via French < Latin *disciplina* 'instruction given to a learner' < *discipulus* (see DISCIPLE)] —**disciplinable** *adj* —**disciplinal** /díssə plīn'l/ *adj* —**disciplined** *adj* —**discipliner** *n*

disc jockey *n* MUSIC, MEDIA full form of **DJ**[1] (sense 1)

disclaim /diss kláym/ (**-claims, -claiming, -claimed**) *v* **1.** *vt* DENY CONNECTION WITH SOMETHING to deny that you know about something or that you are responsible for something **2.** *vt* DENY VALIDITY OF SOMETHING to refuse to accept the validity or authority of something **3.** *vti* RENOUNCE LEGAL RIGHT to renounce a legal claim or right to something [15C. < Anglo-Norman *disclaimer* 'not to claim' < Old French *clamer* 'to claim'] —**disclamation** /dískla máysh'n/ *n*

disclaimer /diss kláymər/ *n* LAW **1.** REFUSAL TO ACCEPT RESPONSIBILITY a statement refusing to accept responsibility for something, e.g. a denial of legal liability for any injury associated with a product **2.** STATEMENT RENOUNCING LEGAL RIGHT a statement saying that somebody gives up a legal right or claim to something such as damages arising from an accident **3.** DENIAL OF KNOWLEDGE a statement denying knowledge of something

disclose /diss klṓz/ (**-closes, -closing, -closed**) *vt* **1.** to reveal something that has been kept a secret **2.** to reveal something that has been covered or hidden [15C. < Old French *desclos-*, present stem of *desclore* < medieval Latin *disclaudere* 'to open' < Latin *claudere* 'to close'] —**disclosable** *adj* —**discloser** *n*

disclosing agent /dis klṓzing-/ *n* a dye in liquid or tablet form that colours something, especially the teeth to show plaque

disclosure /diss klṓzhər/ *n* **1.** the revelation of information that was previously kept secret **2.** a piece of information that is revealed after being secret

disco /dískō/ *n* (*plural* **-cos**) **1.** CLUB OR PARTY WITH DANCING a club or party where people dance to recorded pop music, often introduced by a DJ **2.** STEADY-BEAT POP MUSIC FOR DANCING a style of pop music with a steady pronounced beat, popular in the 1970s for dancing. It developed from soul music, in response to the growing popularity of discos. **3.** DANCE DONE TO DISCO MUSIC popular dancing with hips and arms moving to the repetitive beat of disco music **4.** EQUIPMENT PLAYING RECORDED MUSIC FOR DANCERS the audio equipment used to play records for crowds of people to dance to, usually consisting of amplifiers, speakers, and a record, tape, or CD deck, often with lighting equipment ■ *vi* (**-cos, -coing, -coed**) TAKE PART IN DISCO DANCING to dance to disco music (*informal*) [Mid-20C. Shortening of DISCOTHEQUE]

disco- *prefix* **1.** disc ○ *discoid* **2.** gramophone record ○ *discography* [Via Latin < Greek *diskos* (see DISH)]

discobolus /diss kóbbələss/ (*plural* **-li** /-lī/), **discobolos** *n* a discus thrower in ancient Greece [Early 18C. Via Latin < Greek *diskobolos* 'disc-throwing' < *diskos* (see DISH) + *-bolos* 'throwing' < *ballein* 'to throw']

discography /di skóggrəfi/ (*plural* **-phies**) *n* a list of the recordings made by a performer, group, or of a specific category of music —**discographer** *n* —**discographic** /dískə gráffik/ *adj*

discoid /dísk oyd/ *n* a disc-shaped object or part ■ *adj also* **discoidal** /diss kóyd'l/ shaped like a disc [Late 18C. < Greek *diskoeidēs* < *diskos* (see DISH)]

discolour /diss kúllər/ (**-ours, -ouring, -oured**) *vti* to change from the original or proper colour and take on an unpleasant, faded, darkened, or dirty appearance, or make something change in this way [14C. Directly or via French < medieval Latin *discolorare* < Latin *colorare* 'to colour'] —**discoloration** /diss kúllə ráysh'n/ *n* —**discoloured** *adj* —**discolourment** *n*

discombobulate /dískəm bóbbyŏŏ layt/ (**-lates, -lating, -lated**) *vt N Am* to throw somebody into a state of confusion (*informal; often passive*) [Mid-19C. Probably alteration of DISCOMPOSE or DISCOMFIT] —**discombobulation** /dískəm bóbbyŏŏ láysh'n/ *n*

discomfit /diss kúmfit/ (**-fits, -fiting, -fited**) *vt* **1.** to make somebody feel confused, uneasy, or embarrassed **2.** to frustrate somebody's plans (*formal*) [13C. < Old French *desconfit*, past participle of *desconfire* 'destroy' < *confire* 'make' < Latin *conficere* (see CONFECT)] —**discomfiter** *n* —**discomfiture** *n*

discomfort /diss kúmfərt/ *n* **1.** STATE OF PHYSICAL UNEASE very mild pain, or a feeling of being physically uncomfortable **2.** EMBARRASSMENT the state of feeling awkward, embarrassed, or uneasy **3.** CAUSE OF LACK OF COMFORT something that makes somebody feel physically or mentally uncomfortable ■ *vt* (**-forts, -forting, -forted**) MAKE SOMEBODY UNCOMFORTABLE to make somebody feel physically or mentally uncomfortable [14C. < Old French *desconfort* < *desconforter* 'deprive of comfort' < *conforter* 'to comfort'] —**discomfortable** *adj* —**discomforting** *adj* —**discomfortingly** *adv*

discommode /dískə mṓd/ (**-modes, -moding, -moded**) *vt* to cause problems or inconvenience to somebody (*formal*) [Early 18C. < obsolete French *discommoder* 'deprive of convenience' < Latin *commodus* 'suitable'] —**discommodious** *adj* —**discommodiously** *adv*

discompose /dískəm pṓz/ (**-poses, -posing, -posed**) *vt* to make somebody lose his or her composure —**discomposedly** /dískəm pṓzidli/ *adv*

discomposure /dískəm pṓzhər/ *n* loss of the ability to remain calm and self-assured, especially under difficult or emotional circumstances

disconcert /dískən súrt/ (**-certs, -certing, -certed**) *vt* **1.** to make somebody feel ill at ease, slightly confused, or taken aback **2.** to upset or frustrate plans (*formal*) [Mid-17C. < French *desconcerter* 'bring out of agreement' < Old Italian *concertare* 'bring into agreement'] —**disconcerted** *adj* —**disconcertion** *n* —**disconcertment** *n*

disconcerting /dískən súrting/ *adj* making somebody feel ill at ease, slightly confused, or taken aback —**disconcertingly** *adv*

disconfirm /dískən fúrm/ (**-firms, -firming, -firmed**) *vt* to show that something such as a theory cannot be right —**disconfirmation** /díss konfər máysh'n/ *n*

disconformity /dískən fáwrməti/ (*plural* **-ties**) *n* **1.** same as **nonconformity** (*archaic*) **2.** in geology, a break in the sedimentary record in which the rock layers remain parallel

disconnect /dískə nékt/ *v* (**-nects, -necting, -nected**) **1.** *vt* SHUT OFF SUPPLY OF PUBLIC UTILITY to shut off a telephone line or the supply of water, gas, or electricity to a building or customer **2.** *vti* DETACH POWER FROM APPLIANCE to break the connection between an appliance and its source of power **3.** *vt* BREAK TELEPHONE CONNECTION BETWEEN SPEAKERS to break or lose the telephone connection between two people during a conversation (*usually passive*) **4.** *vt* DETACH ONE PART FROM ANOTHER to detach something that was connected to something else **5.** *vti* BREAK OFF EMOTIONAL OR SPIRITUAL RELATIONSHIP to end, forget, or lose an emotional or spiritual connection with something or somebody ■ *n* DISCONNECTION a disconnection of joined parts or things ○ *a disconnect between his words and his acts* —**disconnecter** *n* —**disconnective** *adj*

disconnected /dískə néktid/ *adj* **1.** not connected or joined **2.** showing no logical connection or relationship ○ *rambling disconnected prose* —**disconnectedly** *adv* —**disconnectedness** *n*

disconnection /dískə néksh'n/, **disconnexion** *n* **1.** the disconnecting of a telephone line or a supply of gas, water, or electricity **2.** the separation of things that were formerly linked or connected

disconsolate /diss kónssələt/ *adj* miserable or disappointed and unable to be cheered up [15C. < medieval Latin *disconsolatus* 'comfortless' < Latin *consolatus*, past participle of *consolare* (see CONSOLE [1])] —**disconsolately** *adv* —**disconsolateness** *n* —**disconsolation** /diss kónssə láysh'n/ *n*

discontent /dískən tént/ *n* **1.** DISSATISFIED UNHAPPINESS a feeling of mild unhappiness and dissatisfaction **2.** LONGING FOR BETTER THINGS a restless desire for something better (*literary*) **3.** DISCONTENTED PERSON somebody who is mildly unhappy and dissatisfied (*literary or formal*) ■ *adj* same as **discontented** —**discontentment** *n*

discontented /dískən téntid/ *adj* feeling mildly unhappy and dissatisfied —**discontentedly** *adv* —**discontentedness** *n*

discontinue /dískən tínnyoo/ (**-ues, -uing, -ued**) *v* **1.** *vti* to come to an end after happening regularly, or end something that has been happening regularly **2.** *vt* to stop manufacturing something, usually a particular model or type of product [15C. Via French < medieval Latin *discontinuare* 'not to continue' < Latin *continuare* 'continue'] —**discontinuance** *n* —**discontinuation** /dískən tínnyoo áysh'n/ *n* —**discontinued** *adj* —**discontinuer** *n*

discontinuity /díss konti nyóo əti/ (*plural* **-ties**) *n* **1.** BREAK IN OTHERWISE CONTINUOUS PROCESS a break or gap in a process that would normally be continuous **2.** MATHS POINT OF CHANGE the point or value of a variable at which a curve or mathematical function shows an abrupt change as the variable smoothly increases or decreases **3.** MATHS LACK OF MATHEMATICAL CONTINUITY the characteristic of being discontinuous **4.** MATHS MATHEMATICAL VALUE a value of a variable for which a function is not continuous **5.** GEOL BOUNDARY BETWEEN ROCK TYPES a boundary between rock types deep within the Earth's crust that is detected as a change in the speed of seismic waves

discontinuous /dískən tínnyoo əss/ *adj* **1.** having breaks or gaps in an otherwise continuous process or line **2.** describes variables and functions that have mathematical discontinuity —**discontinuously** *adv*

discord /díss kawrd/ *n* **1.** LACK OF AGREEMENT disagreement or strife between people, or incompatibility or conflict between things or situations **2.** UNPLEASANT MUSICAL COMBINATION inharmonious combination of sounds, especially musical sounds **3.** MUSIC UNHARMONIOUS CHORD a musical chord or interval that is conventionally regarded as unpleasant or requiring resolution [13C. Via French < Latin *discordia* < *discord-*, stem of *discors* < *cors* 'heart']

discordant /diss káwrd'nt/ *adj* **1.** in disagreement, or incompatible **2.** consisting of sounds, usually musical notes, that are harsh, unpleasant, or clashing —**discordance** *n* —**discordantly** *adv*

discotheque /dískə tek/ *n* LEISURE same as **disco** *n* (sense 1) [Mid-20C. < French *discothèque* < *disque* 'disc, record' + *-thèque* 'library']

discount *n* /díss kownt/ **1.** REDUCTION IN PRICE a reduction in the usual price of something **2.** FIN same as **discount rate 3.** FIN INTEREST DEDUCTED FROM FINANCIAL INSTRUMENT the interest deducted from the face value of a financial instrument or promissory note before a sale or loan is completed **4.** FIN DEDUCTION FROM PAR VALUE OF SHARES the amount by which the par value of shares exceeds the market price actually paid by purchasers ■ *v* /diss kównt/ (**-counts, -counting, -counted**) **1.** *vt* REDUCE PRICE OF SOMETHING to offer something for sale at less than the usual price **2.** *vt* FIN TRADE INVESTMENT AT REDUCED PRICE to buy or sell a financial instrument at a reduced price that is calculated according to the interest rate and risk on the investment **3.** *vti* FIN MAKE SECURED LOAN AT REDUCED RATE to lend money on a negotiable long-term financial instrument at a reduced price that is calculated according to the instrument's risk and the interest due before its maturity **4.** *vt* DISMISS SOMETHING AS UNTRUE OR TRIVIAL to decide that something can be disregarded as unimportant, irrelevant, or untrue ○ *We had already discounted the theory that they were involved.* **5.** *vt* ANTICIPATE SOMETHING AND ALLOW FOR IT to foresee something and make adjustments to lessen or absorb its impact ○ *Tax cuts in the next budget have already been discounted by the City.* ■ *adj* /díss kownt/ WITH REDUCED PRICE for sale at less than the usual price, or selling goods for less than the usual price ○ *a discount warehouse* [Early 17C. < French *descompte* (noun) and Italian *discontare* (verb) < medieval Latin *discomputare*, literally 'count away' < Latin *computare* 'reckon together'] —**discountable** /diss kówntəb'l, díss kowntəb'l/ *adj*

discount broker *n* **1.** an agent who buys and sells bills or other commercial paper at a discount **2.** *N Am* a stockbroker who executes trades for customers, but who in exchange for low commissions offers little advice or investment research —**discount brokerage** *n*

discount card *n* a plastic card entitling the holder to a reduction on the price of goods or services bought at a specific place

discounted cash flow /diss kówntid-/ *n* a method of valuing an investment by calculating what future cash returns will be worth at the time they are received, based on estimates of future inflation and interest rates

discountenance /diss kówntinənss/ (*formal*) *vt* (**-nances, -nancing, -nanced**) **1.** EMBARRASS SOMEBODY to make somebody embarrassed **2.** DISAPPROVE OF SOMEBODY OR SOMETHING to discourage or disapprove of somebody or something ■ *n* DISFAVOUR disapproval of somebody or something

discounter /díss kowntər/; *except commerce* /diss kówntər/ *n* **1.** COMM same as **discount store 2.** FIN SOMEBODY WHO DISCOUNTS FINANCIAL INSTRUMENTS somebody who buys, sells, or lends money on financial instruments at a reduced price **3.** SOMEBODY WHO DISMISSES SOMETHING somebody who discounts something as unimportant, irrelevant, or untrue **4.** ANTICIPATOR somebody who discounts something to lessen or absorb its impact

discount house *n* **1.** a financial institution that buys and sells negotiable bills of exchange at discounted rates **2.** *N Am* COMM same as **discount store**

discount market *n* the part of the financial market trading in discounted commercial bills, including banks, brokers, and discount houses

discount rate *n* the rate at which expected cash returns from a security are converted into the security's market price

discount store *n* a shop that sells goods at prices that are reduced from those recommended by the manufacturers

discourage /diss kúrrij/ (**-ages, -aging, -aged**) *vt* **1.** TEND TO STOP SOMETHING to tend to prevent something from happening by making it more difficult or unpleasant ○ *dirty beaches that discourage sunbathing* **2.** TRY TO DETER SOMEBODY to try to stop a person or animal from doing something **3.** MAKE SOMEBODY LESS OPTIMISTIC to make somebody feel less motivated, confident, or optimistic [15C. < Old French *descoragier* 'deprive of courage' < *corage* 'courage'] —**discouragement** *n* —**discourager** *n*

discouraging /dis kúrrijing/ *adj* making somebody feel less motivation, confidence, or optimism about something —**discouragingly** *adv*

discourse *n* /díss kawrss/ **1.** SERIOUS SPEECH OR PIECE OF WRITING a serious and lengthy speech or piece of writing about a topic **2.** SERIOUS CONVERSATION serious discussion about something between people or groups **3.** LING LANGUAGE language, especially the type of language used in a particular context or subject ○ *political discourse* **4.** LING MAJOR UNIT OF LANGUAGE a unit of language, especially spoken language, that is longer than the sentence. The term is used by linguists when investigating features of language that extend beyond sentences. ■ *vi* /diss káwrss/ (**-courses, -coursing, -coursed**) **1.** SERIOUSLY SPEAK OR WRITE ON TOPIC to speak or write about a subject in a formal context and at length ○ *In the second part, the author discourses on ethics.* **2.** CONVERSE to have a conversation (*formal*) [15C. < Latin *discursus* 'running to and fro' < *discurrere* 'to run apart' < *currere* 'to run'] —**discourser** /diss káwrssər/ *n*

discourse analysis *n* the analysis of features of language that extend beyond the limits of a sentence

discourtesy /diss kúrtəssi/ (*plural* **-sies**) *n* behaviour or an action that is bad-mannered or impolite —**discourteous** /diss kúrti əss/ *adj* —**discourteously** *adv* —**discourteousness** *n*

discover /diss kúvvər/ (**-ers, -ering, -ered**) *vt* **1.** FIND OUT ABOUT SOMETHING to find out information that was not previously known ○ *We discovered she'd known all along.* **2.** BE FIRST TO FIND OR LEARN SOMETHING to be the first person to find or learn something previously unknown ○ *Researchers discovered a new genetic link to the causes of the disease.* **3.** FIND SOMEBODY OR SOMETHING to find somebody or something unexpectedly or after a search ○ *was discovered living in Florida* **4.** FIRST NOTICE INTEREST IN SOMETHING to realize for the first time that you enjoy or have a talent for something ○ *Having discovered painting in her 50s, she ended up making a living by it.* **5.** RECOGNIZE SOMEBODY'S POTENTIAL FOR SUCCESS to realize that a musician, actor, performer, or other person has exceptional talent or unusual beauty, and help to bring him or her to prominence [14C. Via Old French *descovrir* < late Latin *discooperire* 'to uncover' < Latin *cooperire* 'to cover'] —**discoverable** *adj* —**discoverer** *n*

discovered check /dis kúvvərd-/ *n* a move in chess that creates a check previously blocked by the piece moved

discovery /diss kúvvəri/ (*plural* **-ies**) *n* **1.** SOMETHING LEARNT OR FOUND something new that has been learnt or found ○ *These dinosaur remains were one of the most important discoveries of the century.* **2.** PROCESS OF LEARNING SOMETHING the fact or process of finding out about something for the first time ○ *the discovery of DNA* ○ *a voyage of discovery* **3.** PROCESS OF FINDING SOMETHING the process or act of finding something or somebody unexpectedly or after searching ○ *The discovery of the abandoned car provided new clues.* **4.** SOMEBODY RECOGNIZED AS POTENTIALLY SUCCESSFUL a previously unknown musician, actor, performer, or other person who has been identified by somebody as having exceptional talent or unusual beauty **5.** RECOGNITION OF POTENTIAL FOR SUCCESS the recognition of somebody's exceptional talent or beauty, leading to that person's fame **6.** LAW MUTUAL DISCLOSING OF DATA OR DOCUMENTS the stage of a legal proceeding during which each side must provide data and documents to the other side **7.** LAW DISCLOSABLE DATA AND DOCUMENTS data or materials that a party in a legal proceeding must disclose to another party before or during the proceeding

Discovery Bay /di skúvvəri-/ bay on the southern Victoria coast, Australia, southwest of Melbourne. It is 80 km/50 mi. wide.

disc plough *n* an agricultural implement with a cutting disc fixed in a frame, which cuts furrows in the soil and turns it up. It is drawn by a tractor.

discredit /diss kréddit/ *vt* (**-its, -iting, -ited**) **1.** HARM REPUTATION OF SOMEBODY to make somebody or something appear untrustworthy or wrong **2.** CAUSE SOMETHING TO SEEM DOUBTFUL to cast doubt on the validity or accuracy of something **3.** NOT BELIEVE SOMETHING to not accept that something is accurate or true ○ *Scientists generally discredit the theory of canals on Mars.* ■ *n* **1.** LOSS OF REPUTATION the loss of somebody's or something's good name or reputation ○ *brought the game into discredit* **2.** CAUSE OF BAD REPUTATION somebody or something who causes the loss of a good name or reputation ○ *a discredit to his profession* **3.** DOUBT OR SUSPICION doubt about the validity or accuracy of something —**discreditable** *adj*

discreet /di skreét/ *adj* **1.** TACTFUL careful to avoid embarrassing or upsetting others **2.** GOOD AT KEEPING SECRETS careful not to speak about anything that should be secret or confidential **3.** SUBTLE AND UNOBTRUSIVE subtle and circumspect, ensuring that no undue attention is attracted ○ *wearing discreet makeup* **4.** MODEST modest, and not ostentatious or flashy [14C. Via French < Latin *discretus* 'distinct', past participle of *discernere* 'distinguish' (see DISCERN)] —**discreetness** *n*

SPELLCHECK discreet or **discrete**? Do not confuse the spelling of ***discreet*** and ***discrete***, which sound similar. ***Discreet*** is the more frequent word in general use and means 'tactful', 'good at keeping secrets', or 'subtle and unobtrusive': *I made a few discreet enquiries.* ***Discrete*** is a more formal or technical word meaning 'separate, unconnected, and distinct': *Several discrete strands of evidence were pursued.*

discreetly /di skreétli/ *adv* taking care to avoid upsetting or embarrassing people, giving away anything confidential, or appearing immodest or flashy

discrepancy /di skréppənssi/ (*plural* **-cies**) *n* a distinct difference between two things such as sets of figures that should match or correspond ○ *found a discrepancy in the figures* [Early 17C. < Latin *discrepantia* < *discrepare* 'differ' < *crepare* 'to rattle'] —**discrepant** *adj*

discrete /di skreét/ *adj* **1.** completely separate and unconnected **2.** describes mathematical elements or variables that are distinct, unrelated, and have a finite number of values [14C. < Latin *discretus* (see DISCREET)] —**discretely** *adv* —**discreteness** *n*

SPELLCHECK See ***discreet***.

discretion /di skrésh'n/ *n* **1.** TACT the good judgment and sensitivity needed to avoid embarrassing or upsetting others **2.** FREEDOM TO DECIDE the freedom or authority to judge something or make a decision about it ○ *Tipping is left to the customer's discretion.* **3.** CONFIDENTIALITY the ability to keep sensitive information secret [14C. Via French < Latin *discretion-* 'separation, discernment' < *discret-*, past participle of *discernere* (see DISCERN)]

discretionary /di skrésh'nəri/ *adj* **1.** GIVING SOMEBODY AUTHORITY TO DECIDE giving somebody the freedom to make a decision according to individual circumstances **2.** GIVEN OR REFUSED ACCORDING TO CIRCUMSTANCES given according to the merits of an individual case, rather than being provided or awarded automatically **3.** USABLE AS WANTED able to be used as desired without any stipulations ○ *a discretionary fund* —**discretionarily** *adv*

discretionary account *n* a securities account in which the broker has been given the authority to make decisions about buying and selling without the customer's prior permission

discretionary income *n* income that is left over after necessary expenditure

discretionary trust *n* a trust in which somebody other than its founder, e.g. a trustee, determines the beneficiaries' shares

discriminant /di skrímminənt/ *n* a relation between the coefficients *a*, *b*, and *c* of a mathematical expression of the form $ax^2 + bx + c = 0$, used in the study of roots and other properties of the expression [Mid-19C. < Latin *discriminant-*, present participle of *discriminare* (see DISCRIMINATE)]

discriminant function *n* a statistical method used to place an item that could belong to any of two or more sets of variables in the correct set, with a minimal probability of error

discriminate *v* /di skrímmi nayt/ (**-nates, -nating, -nated**) **1.** *vi* TREAT GROUP UNFAIRLY BECAUSE OF PREJUDICE to treat one person or group worse than others or better than others, usually because of a prejudice about race, ethnicity, age, religion, or gender **2.** *vti* DISCERN DIFFERENCE to recognize or identify a difference ○ *could not discriminate between red and green* **3.** *vi* BE AWARE OF DIFFERENCES to pay attention to subtle differences and exercise judgment and taste ■ *adj* /di skrímmi nət/ SHOWING DISCRIMINATION showing the ability to appreciate quality or notice differences (*formal*) [Early 17C. < Latin *discriminat-*, past participle of *discriminare* 'to divide' < *discrimin-* 'division' < *discernere* (see DISCERN)] —**discriminable** *adj* —**discriminately** /-nətli/ *adv* —**discriminative** /-nətiv/ *adj*

discriminating /di skrímmi nayting/ *adj* **1.** able to identify subtle differences and appreciate good quality or taste ○ *Discriminating customers prefer these handmade linens.* **2.** describes tariffs that are set at different rates for different importers —**discriminatingly** *adv*

discrimination /di skrímmi náysh'n/ *n* **1.** TREATING PEOPLE DIFFERENTLY THROUGH PREJUDICE unfair treatment of one person or group, usually because of prejudice about race, ethnicity, age, religion, or gender **2.** ABILITY TO NOTICE AND VALUE QUALITY the ability to appreciate good quality or taste **3.** AWARENESS OF SUBTLE DIFFERENTIATION the ability to notice subtle differences **4.** ELECTRONICS SIGNAL SELECTION the selection of a transmitted signal with a specific characteristic, e.g. frequency, by elimination of signals with other characteristics, using a discriminator —**discriminational** *adj*

discriminator /di skrímmi naytər/ *n* a device or circuit that translates phase or frequency variations into amplitude variations in a modulated signal such as a radio signal, used to select signals with specific characteristics

discriminatory /di skrímminətəri/ *adj* **1.** treating a person or group unfairly, especially because of prejudice about race, ethnicity, age, religion, or gender **2.** describes a statistical test that is unbiased because the sampling procedure avoided the systematic distortion that could be introduced by an unrepresentative population —**discriminatorily** *adv*

~~**discription**~~ incorrect spelling of **description**

disc sander *n* an electrically powered tool with a revolving abrasive disc. Use: sanding, grinding, polishing irregular surfaces.

discursive /diss kúrssiv/ *adj* **1.** lengthy and including extra material that is not essential to what is being written or spoken about ○ *One book is concise and snappy, while the other has a more relaxed, discursive style.* **2.** using logic rather than intuition to reach a conclusion [Late 16C. < medieval Latin *discursivus* < *discurs-*, past participle of *discurrere* (see DISCOURSE)] —**discursively** *adv* —**discursiveness** *n*

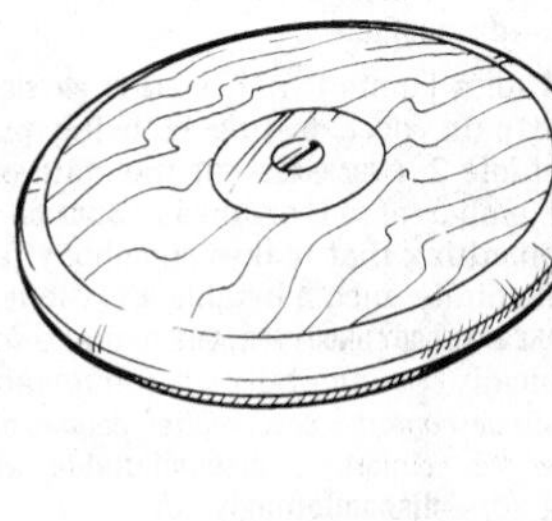

discus

discus /dískəss/ (*plural* **-cuses** or **-ci** /-kī/) *n* **1.** DISC THROWN IN ATHLETICS a weighted disc thrown in competitions by an athlete who spins with outstretched arms to launch it from the flat of his or her hand. The ancient Greek Olympic games included the throwing of a bronze discus. **2.** ATHLETICS EVENT an athletics event in which the contestants compete to throw a discus as far as possible **3.** COLOURFUL AQUARIUM FISH a small colourful freshwater fish that has a compressed disc-shaped body and is popular as an aquarium fish. Native to: South America. Latin name: *Symphysodon discus.* [Mid-17C. < Latin (see DISH)]

discuss /di skúss/ (**-cusses, -cussing, -cussed**) *vt* **1.** to talk about a subject with others ○ *need to discuss it with them first* **2.** to consider a topic in speaking or writing ○ *Chapter 3 discusses the events leading up to the War of Independence.* [14C. < Latin *discuss-*, past participle of *discutere* 'dash to pieces' < *quatere* 'to shake'] —**discussant** *n* —**discusser** *n*

discussion /di skúsh'n/ *n* **1.** a talk between two or more people about a subject, usually to exchange ideas or reach a conclusion, or talk of this kind ○ *deep in a discussion about what to do next* ○ *My decision is not open to discussion.* **2.** a detailed consideration or examination of a topic in writing or speech

disc wheel *n* a car wheel with a continuous flat outer surface instead of spokes

disdain /diss dáyn/ *n* extreme contempt or disgust for something or somebody ■ *vt* (**-dains, -daining, -dained**) to regard somebody or something as not worthy of respect [14C. Probably < Old French *desdeignier* 'treat as unworthy' < late Latin *dedignare* < *dignare* 'treat as worthy'] —**disdainful** *adj* —**disdainfully** *adv* —**disdainfulness** *n*

disease /di zéez/ *n* **1.** MEDICAL CONDITION a condition in humans, plants, or animals that results in pathological symptoms and is not the direct result of physical injury **2.** SPECIFIC DISORDER a disorder in humans, animals, or plants with recognizable signs and often having a known cause **3.** PROBLEM IN SOCIETY a serious problem in society or with a group of people [14C. < Old French *desaise* 'lack of ease' < *aise* 'ease'] —**diseased** *adj*

diseconomy /díssi kónnəmi/ (*plural* **-mies**) *n* something that contributes to increased costs

disembark /díssim baárk/ (**-barks, -barking, -barked**) *v* **1.** *vi* to get off a passenger vehicle, especially a ship, aircraft, or train **2.** *vt* to let passengers off a ship, bus, train, or aircraft, or unload cargo (*formal*) [Late 16C. < French *désembarquer*, Spanish *desembarcar*, or Italian *disimbarcare*, < French *embarquer* or the equivalent (see EMBARK)] —**disembarkation** /diss ém baar káysh'n, díss im-/ *n* —**disembarkment** *n*

disembarrass /díssim bárrəss/ (**-rasses, -rassing, -rassed**) *vt* to free somebody from something embarrassing, unpleasant, or burdensome (*formal*) —**disembarrassment** *n*

disembodied /díssim bóddid/ *adj* coming from somebody who cannot be seen in a way that may be eerie or frightening ○ *a disembodied voice whispering in the darkness*

disembody /díssim bóddi/ (**-ies, -ying, -ied**) *vt* in some beliefs, to free the soul or spirit from the body —**disembodiment** *n*

disembowel /díssim bów əl/ (**-els, -elling, -elled**) *vt* **1.** to cut open the stomach of a person or animal and remove the internal organs, especially the intestines **2.** to remove the internal substance, elements, or parts of something (*literary*) —**disembowelment** *n*

disembroil /díssim bróyl/ (**-broils, -broiling, -broiled**) *vt* to free yourself or somebody else from a difficult situation (*archaic or literary*)

disempower /díssim pów ər/ (**-ers, -ering, -ered**) *vt* to take power or influence away from somebody or from yourself —**disempowerment** *n*

disenable /díssi náyb'l/ (**-bles, -bling, -bled**) *vt* to prevent something, or make something unable to operate or perform a function ○ *disenabled the weapons system on the aircraft prior to landing* —**disenablement** *n*

disenchant /díssin chaánt/ (**-chants, -chanting, -chanted**) *vt* **1.** to make somebody stop believing that something or somebody is worthwhile, right, or deserving of support **2.** to free somebody from an enchantment or magic spell (*literary*) [Late 16C. < French *désenchanter* 'undo enchantment' < *enchanter* 'enchant'] —**disenchanted** *adj* —**disenchanter** *n* —**disenchanting** *adj* —**disenchantingly** *adv* —**disenchantment** *n*

disencumber /díssin kúmbər/ (**-bers, -bering, -bered**) *vt* to relieve somebody or something of a burden or problem —**disencumberment** *n*

disendow /díssin dów/ (**-dows, -dowing, -dowed**) *vt* to withdraw an endowment, especially a gift of money —**disendower** *n* —**disendowment** *n*

disenfranchise /díssin fránch īz/ (**-chises, -chising, -chised**) *vt* to deprive a person or organization of a privilege, immunity, or legal right, especially the right to vote —**disenfranchisement** /-izmənt/ *n*

disengage /díssin gáyj/ (**-gages, -gaging, -gaged**) *v* **1.** *vti* PHYSICALLY DISCONNECT OR BECOME DISCONNECTED to disconnect one thing from another, or become disconnected from something **2.** *vt* MENTALLY DETACH YOURSELF OR ANOTHER to withdraw or mentally separate yourself or somebody else from a situation or difficulty **3.** *vti* MIL STOP FIGHTING IN WAR to bring troops out of a war or combat, or withdraw from a war or combat **4.** *vti* FENCING MOVE SWORD FROM OPPONENT'S to move the point of your sword around an opponent's sword in order to open a new line of attack

disengagement /díssin gáyjmənt/ *n* **1.** the release of somebody or something from a physical or mental attachment **2.** the withdrawal of troops or an army from a war or combat

disentail /díssin táyl/ (**-tails, -tailing, -tailed**) *vt* to lift the restrictions on who may inherit specific property —**disentailment** *n*

disentangle /díssin táng g'l/ (**-gles, -gling, -gled**) *vt* **1.** UNTANGLE JUMBLE to untangle and free things that are muddled, tied, or knotted together **2.** STRAIGHTEN OUT CONFUSION to clarify something confusing, or separate and analyse a confusion of ideas ○ *It was hard to disentangle fact from fiction in his account.* **3.** EXTRICATE SOMEBODY FROM SITUATION to free somebody or yourself from a relationship or complicated situation —**disentanglement** *n*

disentomb /díssin to͞om/ (**-tombs, -tombing, -tombed**) *vt* to take a body out of a tomb or from a place like a tomb

disequilibrium /díss eekwi líbbri əm/ *n* a state of instability or imbalance, especially in an economy

disestablish /díssi stáblish/ (**-lishes, -lishing, -lished**) *vt* **1.** to undo or change something that has been established for a long time **2.** to end the official relationship between the state and a nation's established church or religion —**disestablishment** *n*

disesteem /díssi ste͞em/ (*formal*) *vt* (**-teems, -teeming, -teemed**) to have a low opinion of somebody or something ■ *n* lack of respect or esteem ○ *held in disesteem*

diseur /dee zúr/ *n* a man, usually an actor, who is an accomplished reciter of dramatic monologues. Such recitals, often accompanied by music, were once a popular form of theatrical entertainment. [< French, 'talker' < *dire* 'to say' < Latin *dicere*]

diseuse /dee zúrz/ *n* a woman, usually an actor, who is an accomplished reciter of dramatic monologues. Such recitals, often accompanied by music, were once a popular theatrical entertainment. [Late 19C. < French, feminine of *diseur* (see DISEUR)]

disfavour /diss fáyvər/ *n* **1.** CONDITION OF DISAPPROVAL the state of being disapproved of ○ *This fell into disfavour years ago.* **2.** DISRESPECT OR DISAPPROVAL a feeling of disapproval or lack of respect ○ *They were looked on with disfavour.* ■ *vt* (**-ours, -ouring, -oured**) DISLIKE OR DISAPPROVE OF SOMETHING to regard something with dislike or disapproval (*formal*)

disfigure /diss fíggər/ (**-ures, -uring, -ured**) *vt* to mar the appearance of somebody or something [14C. < Old French *desfigurer* 'deprive something of its figure' < Latin *figura* 'figure'] —**disfiguration** /diss fíggə ráysh'n/ *n* —**disfigurement** *n*

disforest /diss fórrist/ (**-ests, -esting, -ested**) *vt* FORESTRY same as **deforest**

disfranchise /dis fránch īz/ (**-chises, -chising, -chised**) *vt* POL same as **disenfranchise** —**disfranchisement** /-izmənt/ *n*

disfrock /dis frók/ (**-frocks, -frocking, -frocked**) *vt* CHR same as **defrock**

disgorge /diss gáwrj/ (**-gorges, -gorging, -gorged**) *vt* **1.** POUR SUBSTANCES OUT to pour out liquid, gas, or other contents in a gushing stream ○ *disgorged the contents of her purse* **2.** LET PEOPLE OUT to let a large number of people come out of a building or vehicle at the same time ○ *a cruise ship disgorging thousands of passengers* **3.** REGURGITATE OR VOMIT FOOD to vomit or regurgitate food that has been eaten or partly eaten, as some birds and mammals do to feed their young [15C. < Old French *desgorger* 'expel from the throat' < *gorge* 'throat'] —**disgorgement** *n*

disgrace /diss gráyss/ *n* **1.** STATE OF BEING DISAPPROVED OF shame or loss of respect arising from bad behaviour ○ *She was sent home in disgrace.* **2.** CAUSE OF SHAME OR DISRESPECT a cause of shame or loss of respect ○ *She's a disgrace to the family.* ■ *vt* (**-graces, -gracing, -graced**) CAUSE SOMEBODY TO LOSE RESPECT to bring shame or loss of respect on yourself or others who are associated with you by bad behaviour ○ *He disgraced himself by forgetting the wedding.* [Mid-16C. Via French *disgracier* < Italian *disgraziare* < *disgrazia* 'disfavour' < Latin *gratia* (see GRACE)] —**disgracer** *n*

disgraceful /diss gráyssf'l/ *adj* so bad or unacceptable that it should be something to be ashamed of ○ *The way they were treated was disgraceful.* —**disgracefully** *adv* —**disgracefulness** *n*

disgruntle /diss grúnt'l/ (**-tles, -tling, -tled**) *vt* to make somebody feel dissatisfied and irritated [Mid-17C. < obsolete *gruntle* 'to grumble, grunt' < GRUNT[1]] —**disgruntled** *adj* —**disgruntlement** *n*

disguise /diss gīz/ *vt* (**-guises, -guising, -guised**) **1.** CHANGE SOMEBODY'S APPEARANCE FOR CONCEALMENT to make changes in the appearance of somebody or something to avoid recognition ○ *He fled the besieged city disguised as a woman.* **2.** HIDE SOMETHING TO PREVENT OTHERS KNOWING to hide feelings or facts from other people ○ *She couldn't disguise her horror.* **3.** CHANGE SOMETHING TO PREVENT RECOGNITION to change something so that it cannot be recognized ○ *His voice has been disguised during the interview to conceal his identity.* ■ *n* **1.** SOMETHING DONE TO PREVENT RECOGNITION something worn or done in order to change somebody's appearance and prevent recognition ○ *Anyone would have seen through such a flimsy disguise.* **2.** ALTERATION OR CONCEALMENT TO PREVENT RECOGNITION the alteration or concealment of something in order to prevent it being seen or recognized by others ○ *a plot that relies on disguise* **3.** ALTERED APPEARANCE an altered appearance intended to conceal somebody's identity or make somebody look like somebody else ○ *went to the ball in disguise* [14C. < Old French *desguis(i)er* 'remove your appearance' < *guise* 'appearance'] —**disguisable** *adj* —**disguised** *adj* —**disguiser** *n*

disgust /diss gúst/ *n* **1.** STRONG DISAPPROVAL OR REVULSION a feeling of horrified disapproval of something ○ *viewed the tawdry scandal with unconcealed disgust* **2.** IMPATIENT IRRITATION a feeling of impatient irritation ○ *Much to my disgust, I was compelled to hand over the documents.* ■ *vt* (**-gusts, -gusting, -gusted**) MAKE SOMEBODY FEEL REVOLTED to make somebody feel sickened or revolted [Late 16C. < French *desgoust* or Italian *disgusto* 'have a distaste for' < Latin *gustus* 'taste'] —**disgusted** *adj* —**disgustedly** *adv* —**disgustedness** *n*

SYNONYMS See *dislike*.

---

disgusting /diss gústing/ *adj* **1.** tending to repel and sicken people ○ *a disgusting smell* **2.** completely unacceptable or disgraceful ○ *a disgusting waste of money* —**disgustingly** *adv* —**disgustingness** *n*

dish /dish/ *n* **1.** SERVING BOWL a container for serving food **2.** SERVING OF FOOD a serving or plateful of food, especially one that forms only part of a larger meal **3.** SPECIAL RECIPE OR STYLE food prepared to a recipe or in a recognized style ○ *a Mediterranean dish* **4.** SCI SHALLOW OPEN CONTAINER a shallow open container as used in laboratories or hospitals **5.** ELECTRONICS RADIO OR TELEVISION AERIAL a dish-shaped aerial transmitting and receiving radio or television signals, as used in radar and satellite broadcasting **6.** GEOL HOLLOW PLACE a shallow depression, e.g. in rock **7.** ATTRACTIVE PERSON a good-looking person (*slang*) ■ **dishes** *npl* DIRTY PLATES, CUTLERY, AND PANS the plates, eating utensils, and pans that are dirtied during the cooking and eating of a meal ○ *my turn to wash the dishes* ■ *vt* (**dishes, dishing, dished**) **1.** HOLLOW SOMETHING OUT to make or form a concave shape in something **2.** RUIN SOMETHING to ruin or thwart something (*informal*) ○ *The rejection letter dished her hopes of a university place.* [Pre-12C. Via Latin *discus* 'dish, platter' < Greek *diskos* 'disc, quoit, platter' < *dikein* 'to throw']

dish out *vt* **1.** to serve food to people ○ *dishing out mashed potatoes* **2.** to give something out freely, especially criticism, money, punishment, or advice (*informal*) ◇ **dish it out (but not be able to take it)** to criticize others freely (while not being able to accept criticism) (*informal*) ○ *She can really dish it out but she surely can't take it.*

dishabille *n* CLOTHING another spelling of **deshabille**

dish aerial *n* a transmitting and receiving aerial in the form of a dish-shaped reflector, as used in radar and in satellite broadcasting. N Am term **dish antenna**

disharmony /diss haármәni/ *n* **1.** CONFLICT BETWEEN PEOPLE disagreement or conflict between people or groups who cannot get along with each other **2.** LACK OF MUSICAL HARMONY lack of agreement in music or sounds, resulting in unpleasant sound combinations **3.** IMBALANCE lack of balance in something such as the body or the environment —**disharmonious** /díss haar mṓni əss/ *adj* —**disharmoniously** *adv*

dishcloth /dísh kloth/ *n* **1.** HOUSEHOLD same as **tea towel** **2.** a cloth used for washing dishes

dishearten /diss haárt'n/ (**-ens, -ening, -ened**) *vt* to make somebody lose hope and enthusiasm —**disheartenment** *n*

disheartening /diss haárt'ning/ *adj* making somebody lose hope or enthusiasm —**dishearteningly** *adv*

dished /disht/ *adj* **1.** CONCAVE hollowed out in a shape like a dish **2.** POINTING IN TOWARDS EACH OTHER describes pairs of vehicle wheels that are set at an angle so that the bottoms are closer together than the tops **3.** DEFEATED completely exhausted, beaten, or thwarted (*informal*)

dishevel /di shévv'l/ (**-els, -elling, -elled**) *vt* to disarrange somebody's clothes or hair [Late 16C. Probably back-formation < DISHEVELLED] —**dishevelment** *n*

disheveled *adj* US spelling of **dishevelled**

dishevelled /di shévv'ld/ *adj* **1.** with untidy hair or clothes **2.** disordered and untidy [14C. < Old French *deschevelé*, past participle of *descheveler* 'disarrange the hair' < *des-* 'apart' + *chevel* 'hair']

dishonest /diss ónnist/ *adj* meaning or meant to deceive, defraud, or trick people [14C. Via Old French *deshoneste* < Latin *dehonestus* < *honestus* 'honourable']

dishonestly /diss ónnistli/ *adv* in a lying or deceitful way

dishonesty /diss ónnisti/ (*plural* **-ties**) *n* **1.** the use of lies or deceit, or the tendency to be deceitful **2.** a dishonest act

dishonour /diss ónnər/ *n* **1.** LOSS OF OTHER PEOPLE'S RESPECT the loss of a good reputation **2.** CAUSE OF SHAME a cause of shame or loss of respect **3.** FIN FAILURE TO PAY CHEQUE failure or refusal by a bank or other financial institution to pay a cheque, bill of exchange, or other financial document (*formal*) ■ *vt* (**-ours, -ouring, -oured**) **1.** BRING SHAME ON SOMEBODY to do something that

brings shame on yourself or on people associated with you **2.** **BREAK AGREEMENT** to fail to keep a promise or agreement **3.** **TREAT SOMEBODY DISRESPECTFULLY** to treat somebody without any respect (*formal*) **4.** FIN **FAIL TO PAY CHEQUE** to fail to pay a cheque, bill of exchange, or other financial document **5.** **DISGRACE WOMAN BY SEDUCTION OR RAPE** to bring shame on a woman by having sexual intercourse with her before marriage or by raping her (*archaic or literary*) [14C. Via French < medieval Latin *dishonorare* 'not to honour' < *honorare* 'to honour'] —**dishonourer** *n*

dishonourable /diss ónnərəb'l/ *adj* **1.** morally unacceptable and liable to make somebody lose the respect of others **2.** behaving in a dishonest or morally unacceptable way —**dishonourableness** *n* —**dishonourably** *adv*

dishonourable discharge *n* dismissal from the armed forces as punishment for a serious offence such as desertion

dishpan /dísh pan/ *n* N Am a large pan or plastic tub used for washing dishes

dishpan hands *n* a condition of the hands in which the skin is dry, scaly, and reddened because of sensitivity or overexposure to cleaning materials such as detergent (*takes a singular or plural verb*)

dishrag /dísh rag/ *n* HOUSEHOLD same as **dishcloth** (sense 2)

dishtowel /dísh towəl/ *n* N Am same as **tea towel**

dishwasher /dísh woshər/ *n* **1.** an electrically operated machine that washes, rinses, and dries crockery and kitchen utensils **2.** somebody who washes dishes, especially in a restaurant

dishwashing liquid /dísh woshing-/ *n* N Am same as **washing-up liquid**

dishwater /dísh wawtər/ *n* **1.** water that is or has been used for washing crockery or kitchen utensils **2.** a weak or tasteless drink

dishy /díshi/ (**-ier, -iest**) *adj* very good-looking (*informal*)

~~**disign**~~ incorrect spelling of **design**

disillusion /díssi lóozh'n/ *vt* (**-sions, -sioning, -sioned**) to cause somebody to realize that an ideal is false or a belief is mistaken (*often passive*) ■ *n* same as **disillusionment** —**disillusioned** *adj* —**disillusive** /-lóossiv/ *adj*

disillusionment /díssi lóozh'nmənt/ *n* disappointment caused by a frustrated ideal or belief

disincentive /díssin séntiv/ *n* something that deters somebody from taking an action

disinclination /díssinkli náysh'n/ *n* an unwillingness to do something

disincline /díssin klīn/ (**-clines, -clining, -clined**) *vt* to make somebody unwilling to do something (*often passive*)

disinclined /díssin klīnd/ *adj* without a strong motivation to do something ○ *Seeing the lack of unity among the team he felt disinclined to pursue the issue.*

SYNONYMS See *unwilling*.

disincorporate /díssin káwrpə rayt/ (**-rates, -rating, -rated**) *vti* to end the corporate status of a company, organization, or community, or undergo such a process —**disincorporation** /díssin káwrpə ráysh'n/ *n*

disinfect /díssin fékt/ (**-fects, -fecting, -fected**) *vt* to clean something so as to destroy disease-carrying microorganisms and prevent infection [Late 16C. < French *désinfecter* < *infecter* 'infect'] —**disinfection** *n* —**disinfector** *n*

disinfectant /díssin féktənt/ *n* a chemical that destroys or inhibits the growth of microorganisms that cause disease

disinfest /díssin fést/ (**-fests, -festing, -fested**) *vt* to free a place, person, or animal of small pests such as rodents or insects —**disinfestation** /díssin fe stáysh'n/ *n*

disinflation /díssin fláysh'n/ *n* a slowdown in the rate at which prices increase, e.g. during a recession —**disinflationary** *adj*

disinformation /díssinfər máysh'n/ *n* false or deliberately misleading information, often put out as propaganda

disingenuous /díssin jénnyoo əss/ *adj* **1.** withholding or not taking account of known information **2.** giving a false impression of sincerity or simplicity —**disingenuously** *adv* —**disingenuousness** *n*

disinherit /díssin hérrit/ (**-its, -iting, -ited**) *vt* **1.** to change a will so as to deprive somebody of an inheritance **2.** to deprive somebody of a natural or established right or privilege —**disinheritance** *n*

disinhibit /díssin híbbit/ (**-its, -iting, -ited**) *vt* to free somebody from inhibitions (*technical*)

disinhibition /díssinhi bísh'n/ *n* **1.** **LOSS OF INHIBITION** a loss of inhibition, e.g. through the influence of alcohol or drugs (*technical*) **2.** PSYCHOL **TEMPORARY LOSS OF INHIBITION** a temporary loss of inhibition caused by an outside stimulus such as a loud noise **3.** CHEM **REMOVAL OF INHIBITOR** the removal of a substance that slows or stops a chemical reaction

disintegrate /diss ínti grayt/ (**-grates, -grating, -grated**) *vti* **1.** **BREAK INTO FRAGMENTS** to break into components or fragments, or break something into small pieces or constituent parts **2.** **LOSE WHOLENESS** to destroy the cohesion, unity, or wholeness of something, or undergo such destruction **3.** PHYS **SPLIT ATOM** to split the nucleus of an atom, or undergo atomic fission —**disintegrable** *adj* —**disintegrative** /-grətiv/ *adj*

disintegration /diss ínti gráysh'n/ *n* **1.** **BREAKING INTO PIECES** irreversible breaking into components or fragments **2.** **LOSS OF UNITY** the loss of unity, cohesion, or integrity **3.** PHYS **BREAK-UP OF NUCLEUS** the break-up of an atomic nucleus or an unstable elementary particle into smaller parts, either by radioactive decay or through bombardment with high-energy particles

disintegration constant *n* PHYS same as **decay constant**

disintegrator /diss ínti graytər/ *n* **1.** a machine in which atoms are split as a result of being hit by accelerated particles **2.** a person, machine, or force that destroys or disintegrates something

disinter /díssin túr/ (**-ters, -terring, -terred**) *vt* **1.** to dig up or remove a dead body from a grave or tomb **2.** to expose something that was hidden (*formal*) [Early 17C. < French *désenterrer* < *enterrer* 'inter'] —**disinterment** *n*

disinterest /diss íntrəst/ *vt* (**-ests, -esting, -ested**) **MAKE SOMEBODY LOSE BIAS OR INTEREST** to cause somebody to lose interest or partiality ■ *n* **1.** **IMPARTIALITY** lack of bias or self-interest **2.** ⚠ **ABSENCE OF INTEREST** a lack of interest

USAGE See *disinterested.*

disinterested /diss íntrəstid/ *adj* **1.** free from bias or self-interest **2.** ⚠ indifferent, not interested, or no longer interested —**disinterestedly** *adv* —**disinterestedness** *n*

USAGE **disinterested** or **uninterested**? ***Disinterested*** means 'free from bias or self-interest', and also has a widely used but much criticized meaning 'indifferent or not interested'. In formal writing you should avoid using ***disinterested*** with the meaning 'not interested'.

disintermediation /díssintər meedi áysh'n/ *n* the elimination of intermediaries such as wholesalers or retailers in business transactions between producers and consumers

disintoxicate /díssin tóksi kayt/ (**-cates, -cating, -cated**) *vt* MED same as **detoxify** (sense 1) —**disintoxication** /díssin tóksi káysh'n/ *n*

disinvent /díssin vént/ (**-vents, -venting, -vented**) *vt* to undo the invention of something ○ *Nuclear weapons cannot be disinvented.*

disinvest /díssin vést/ (**-vests, -vesting, -vested**) *vti* to withdraw or reduce an investment —**disinvestment** *n*

disinvite /díssin vīt/ (**-vites, -viting, -vited**) *vt* to withdraw an invitation to somebody (*humorous*) —**disinvitation** /dis ínvi táysh'n/ *n*

~~**disipline**~~ incorrect spelling of **discipline**

disjoin /diss jóyn/ (**-joins, -joining, -joined**) *vti* to disconnect parts, things, or ideas, or become disconnected [15C. < Old French *desjoign-*, stem of *desjoindre* < Latin *disjungere* < *jungere* 'to join'] —**disjoinable** *adj*

disjoint /diss jóynt/ (**-joints, -jointing, -jointed**) *v* **1.** *vti* **SEPARATE AT JOINTS** to separate something at the joints, or come apart at the joints **2.** *vti* **DISLOCATE** to force or move something out of its usual position, or be moved out of the usual position **3.** *vt* **DESTROY UNITY OF SOMETHING** to destroy the unity or coherence of something **4.** *vt* same as **disjoin** [15C. < Old French *desjoint*, past participle of *desjoindre* (see DISJOIN)] —**disjoint** *adj*

disjointed /diss jóyntid/ *adj* not connected in an easily understandable way —**disjointedness** *n*

disjointedly /diss jóyntidli/ *adv* in a way that makes connections or order unclear

disjunct /diss júngkt/ *adj* **1.** **SEPARATED** discontinuous or separated in time or space **2.** MUSIC **SEPARATED BY ONE SECOND** describes consecutive notes that are separated by an interval of a second **3.** MUSIC **WITH MELODIC LEAPS** describes a melody in which leaps are the dominant feature rather than smooth progression ■ *n* LOGIC **CLAUSE** either the p clause or the q clause in a logical proposition of the form 'p or q' [15C. < Latin *disjunctus*, past participle of *disjungere* (see DISJOIN)]

disjunction /diss júngksh'n/ *n* **1.** **DISCONNECTION** a disconnection of joined parts or things **2.** LOGIC **PROPOSITION WITH 'OR'** a proposition of the form 'p or q' that is false if both p and q are false, but true if at least one of them is true **3.** LOGIC same as **disjunct** **4.** GENETICS **CHROMOSOME SEPARATION** the separation of like chromosomes during cell division

disjunctive /diss júngktiv/ *adj* **1.** **DIVIDING** serving to divide things, or having the effect of dividing things (*technical*) **2.** GRAM **SHOWING CONTRAST** describes a word such as 'or' that establishes a contrast between two words or linguistic elements **3.** LOGIC **OF LOGICAL DISJUNCTION** relating to or having the form of a proposition of the type 'p or q' ■ *n* **1.** GRAM **CONTRAST WORD** a conjunction or other word that establishes a contrast **2.** LOGIC same as **disjunction** (sense 2) —**disjunctively** *adv*

disjuncture /diss júngkchər/ *n* same as **disjunction** (sense 1)

disk /disk/ *n* **1.** a device consisting of one or more magnetically or optically etched thin plates, used in a computer to store information **2.** another spelling of **disc** [Variant of DISC]

disk drive *n* a computer device that reads data from and writes data to spinning magnetic or optical disks

diskette /di skét/ *n* COMPUT same as **floppy disk**

disk operating system *n* an operating system for personal computers that uses disks and diskettes for storage of programs and data

disk pack *n* a removable data storage device used in minicomputers and mainframes, consisting of a stack of magnetic or optical disks

dislike /diss līk/ *vt* (**-likes, -liking, -liked**) **NOT LIKE SOMEBODY OR SOMETHING** to consider something or somebody disagreeable or unpleasant ■ *n* **1.** **DISAPPROVING FEELING** an attitude or feeling of disapproval or lack of enjoyment **2.** **SOMETHING NOT LIKED** something that is considered disagreeable —**dislikable** *adj*

SYNONYMS ***dislike, distaste, hatred, hate, disgust, loathing, repugnance, abhorrence, animosity, antipathy, aversion, revulsion***

CORE MEANING: a feeling of not liking somebody or something

dislike an attitude or feeling of disapproval or lack of enjoyment ○ *a dislike of sudden change* ○ *She took a dislike to the dress and refused to wear it.* ○ *He didn't try to hide his dislike of his brother's wife.* **distaste** disapproval of something or somebody's behaviour ○ *He wrinkled his nose in distaste at the acrid smell.* ○ *a distaste for inactivity* **hatred** *or* **hate** intense hostility towards somebody or something ○ *violent verbal expressions of hatred* ○ *Even the children's hearts were full of hate.* **disgust** a feeling of horrified disapproval ○ *I like to go poking about in charity shops, much to my husband's disgust.* ○ *He took early retirement from the university in disgust at the drop in standards.* **loathing** intense dislike of somebody or something ○ *A passionate loathing of materialism is evident in his writing.* ○ *I developed an irrational loathing for the man sent to meet me.* **repugnance** a very strong feeling of disgust, mainly for behaviour and activities ○ *He*

expressed his repugnance at the assault. ○ *international repugnance of the past week's violence* **abhorrence** a feeling of intense disapproval, mainly of behaviour and activities ○ *our deep and abiding abhorrence of the current system* ○ *They declared an absolute abhorrence of receiving money from gambling in any form.* **animosity** a feeling or spirit of hostility and resentment ○ *a nation with a history of animosity towards rival exporters* ○ *There was no personal animosity between my sister and me.* **antipathy** strong hostility or opposition towards somebody or something ○ *his well-known antipathy to the nationalist cause* ○ *These rumours fuelled the crowd's antipathy towards the government.* **aversion** strong hostility or opposition towards somebody or something ○ *had always shown a total aversion to most forms of exercise* ○ *his instinctive aversion to being ordered about* **revulsion** a sudden violent feeling of disgust ○ *The case sent a wave of revulsion against political corruption through the country.*

---

dislocate /díssla kayt/ (**-cates, -cating, -cated**) *vt* **1. PUT SOMETHING OUT OF PLACE** to put or force something out of its usual place or position **2. DISPLACE BODY PART** to move or force a bone out of the joint into which it fits **3. THROW SOMETHING INTO CONFUSION** to disrupt, upset, or disturb the order of something [Late 16C. Probably back-formation < DISLOCATION] —**dislocated** *adj*

dislocation /díssla káysh'n/ *n* **1. DISLOCATING OR BEING DISLOCATED** the displacement of something from its usual or proper position **2.** MED **DISPLACEMENT OF BODY PART** the displacement of a body part, especially of a bone from its usual fitting in a joint **3.** CHEM **IMPERFECTION IN CRYSTAL** an irregularity in the fine structure (**lattice**) of an otherwise normal crystal [14C. Directly or via French < medieval Latin *dislocation-* < Latin *locat-* (see LOCATE)]

dislodge /diss lój/ (**-lodges, -lodging, -lodged**) *vti* to force something or somebody from a previously fixed or secure position, or leave such a position [15C. < Old French *dislogier* < *logier* < *loge* 'hut'] —**dislodgment** *n*

disloyal /diss lóy əl/ *adj* showing a lack of faith in or loyalty to somebody or something [15C. < Old French *desloial* < *loial* (see LOYAL)] —**disloyally** *adv*

disloyalty /diss lóyəlti/ (*plural* **-ties**) *n* **1.** a lack of loyalty to a person, vow, organization, or state **2.** a disloyal or unfaithful act

dismal /dízm'l/ *adj* **1. DEPRESSING** depressing to the spirit or outlook **2. HOPELESS** showing a lack or failure of hope **3. OF POOR QUALITY** very poor or inadequate ○ *a dismal performance* [14C. < obsolete noun, 'unlucky days', via Anglo-Norman < medieval Latin *dies mali*] —**dismally** *adv* —**dismalness** *n*

dismal science *n* SOC SCI same as **economics** (*humorous*)

dismantle /diss mánt'l/ (**-tles, -tling, -tled**) *v* **1.** *vt* **BREAK SOMETHING DOWN INTO PARTS** to take something apart in a way that causes it to stop working **2.** *vi* **COME APART** to be able to be separated into components **3.** *vt* **DESTROY SOMETHING BY REMOVING KEY ELEMENTS** to destroy something such as an institution or system by removing essential parts **4.** *vt* **EMPTY PLACE OF EQUIPMENT** to strip a room or building of furniture or equipment [Late 16C. < Old French *desmanteler* 'tear down a fortress wall' < *emmanteler* 'shelter, fortify' < *mantel* 'cloak' (see MANTLE)] —**dismantlement** *n* —**dismantler** *n*

dismast /díss maást/ (**-masts, -masting, -masted**) *vt* to break off or remove the mast or masts of a boat or ship —**dismastment** *n*

dismay /diss máy/ *vt* (**-mays, -maying, -mayed**) (*usually passive*) **1. DISCOURAGE SOMEBODY** to cause somebody to feel discouraged or disappointed **2. ALARM SOMEBODY** to fill somebody with alarm, apprehension, or distress ■ *n* **1. FEELING OF DISCOURAGEMENT** a feeling of hopelessness, disappointment, or discouragement **2. LOSS OF COURAGE** a sudden loss of courage or confidence [14C. < assumed Anglo-Norman *desmaiier*] —**dismayingly** *adv*

dismember /diss mémbər/ (**-bers, -bering, -bered**) *vt* **1. REMOVE LIMB FROM BODY** to cut off or remove a limb or other part of a person or animal **2. DIVIDE SOMETHING UP** to cut or tear something into pieces **3. DESTROY SOMETHING BY TAKING IT APART** to destroy something by taking it apart ○ *dismembered the alliance* [14C. Via French < assumed Vulgar Latin *dismembrare* < Latin *membrum* 'limb, part'] —**dismemberer** *n* —**dismemberment** *n*

dismiss /diss míss/ (**-misses, -missing, -missed**) *vt* **1. REFUSE TO CONSIDER SOMETHING** to refuse to give consideration to something **2. REJECT SOMEBODY OR SOMETHING** to consider somebody or something as unsuitable for a particular reason ○ *dismissed the idea as ridiculous* **3. END EMPLOYMENT OF SOMEBODY** to stop employing somebody, e.g. because of unsatisfactory work or wrongdoing **4. SEND SOMEBODY AWAY** to order or allow somebody to leave **5.** LAW **REFUSE CASE FURTHER HEARING IN COURT** to refuse to give further hearing to a case in court **6.** CRICKET **PUT PLAYER OR TEAM OUT** in cricket, to end the innings of a batsman or a team [15C. < medieval Latin *dismiss-*, past participle of *dismittere* 'send away' < Latin *mittere* 'send off'] —**dismissible** *adj*

dismissal /diss míss'l/ *n* **1. TERMINATION OF SOMEBODY'S EMPLOYMENT** the removal of somebody from employment or service **2. NOTICE OF TERMINATION** an order or notice of termination from employment or service **3. ACT OF SENDING AWAY** the formal sending away of a person or group ○ *didn't report the incident till after the class's dismissal* **4. REJECTION FROM CONSIDERATION** the rejection of something from consideration **5.** CRICKET **PUTTING PLAYER OR TEAM OUT** the ending of a batsman's or team's innings

dismissive /diss míssiv/ *adj* indicating rejection, especially in a contemptuous or indifferent way —**dismissively** *adv* —**dismissiveness** *n*

dismount /diss mównt/ *v* (**-mounts, -mounting, -mounted**) **1.** *vi* **GET OFF ANIMAL** to get down from the back of an animal such as a horse or camel **2.** *vi* **GET OFF CYCLE** to get off a bicycle or motorcycle **3.** *vt* **REMOVE ITEM FROM FRAME** to remove something from a frame, mounting, stand, or support ■ *n* **ACT OF DISMOUNTING** an act of dismounting or of being dismounted —**dismountable** *adj*

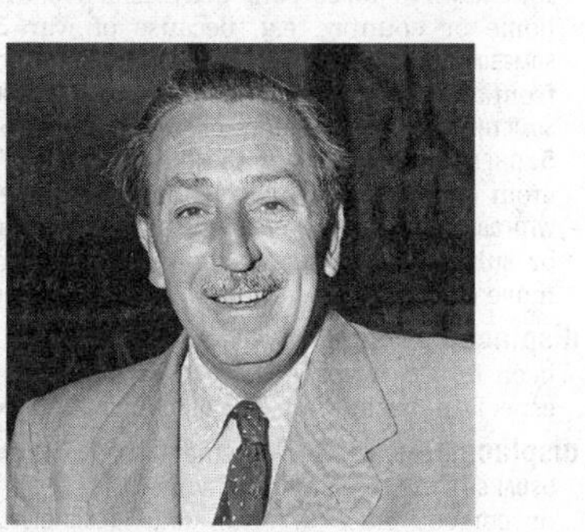
CORBIS/Bettmann

Walt Disney

Disney /dízni/, **Walt** (1901–66) US animator and producer. He created Mickey Mouse and Donald Duck, and originated the feature-length cartoon with *Snow White and the Seven Dwarfs* (1937). Full name **Disney, Walter Elias**

> 'Too many people grow up. That's the real trouble with the world, too many people grow up. They forget. They don't remember what it's like to be 12 years old. They patronise, they treat children as inferiors. Well I won't do that.'
> [Attributed to Walt Disney]

Disneyesque /dízni ésk/ *adj* reminiscent of or in the style of the sometimes whimsical films and cartoons created by Walt Disney or the Disney studios

disobedience /díssə beédi ənss/ *n* a refusal or failure to obey

disobedient /díssə beédi ənt/ *adj* refusing or failing to obey, especially habitually [15C. Via French < assumed Vulgar Latin *desobedient-* < Latin *oboedient-*, present participle of *oboedire* (see OBEY)] —**disobediently** *adv*

disobey /díssə báy/ (**-beys, -beying, -beyed**) *vti* to refuse or fail to obey a rule, instruction, or authority, or somebody giving an instruction or in authority [14C. Via French *désobéir* < assumed Vulgar Latin *desobedir* < Latin *oboedire* (see OBEY)] —**disobeyer** *n*

disoblige /díssə blíj/ (**-bliges, -bliging, -bliged**) *vt* to be unwilling to help somebody [Late 16C. < French *désobliger* < Latin *obligare* (see OBLIGE)]

disobliging /díssə blíjing/ *adj* selfishly or rudely unwilling to help —**disobligingly** *adv*

~~**disolve**~~ incorrect spelling of **dissolve**

disomic /dī sṓmik/ *adj* having chromosomes occurring in pairs [Early 20C. < DI-[1] + -SOME[1]] —**disomy** *n*

disorder /diss áwrdər/ *n* **1. ILLNESS** a medical condition involving a disturbance to the usual functioning of the mind or body **2. LACK OF ORDER** a lack of systematic or orderly arrangement **3. UNTIDINESS** a state of untidiness ○ *found the room in complete disorder* **4.** LAW **UNRULY BEHAVIOUR** a public disturbance or breach of the peace ■ *vt* (**-ders, -dering, -dered**) **UPSET ARRANGEMENT** to disarrange or disturb the order of something

disordered /diss áwrdərd/ *adj* **1.** marked by confusion or disarray **2.** affected by a disturbance to the usual physical functioning or the mind or body ○ *disordered sleep* —**disorderedness** *n*

disorderly /diss áwrdərli/ *adj* **1. LACKING ORDER** lacking order or organization **2. UNRULY** unruly and resisting authority **3.** LAW **DISTURBING PEACE** disturbing the peace or violating public order —**disorderliness** *n*

disorderly conduct *n* a minor offence likely to cause a breach of the peace

disorderly house *n* an establishment where activities take place that may become unruly or violate public order or decency, e.g. a brothel or gaming club (*formal*)

disorganise *vt* another spelling of **disorganize**

disorganization /diss áwrgə nī záysh'n/, **disorganisation** *n* **1.** a lack of organization or orderly arrangement **2.** the destruction or disruption of the organization, system, or unity of something

disorganize /diss áwrgə nīz/ (**-izes, -izing, -ized**), **disorganise** (**-ises, -ising, -ised**) *vt* to destroy or disrupt the organization, system, or unity of something [Late 18C. < French *désorganiser* < *organiser* (see ORGANIZE)] —**disorganized** *adj* —**disorganizer** *n*

disorientate /diss áwri ən tayt/ (**-tates, -tating, -tated**), **disorient** /diss áwri ənt/ (**-ents, -enting, -ented**) *vt* **1.** to cause somebody to feel lost or confused, especially with regard to direction or position **2.** to confuse somebody by giving misleading information —**disorientated** *adj* —**disorientation** /diss áwri ən táysh'n/ *n*

disown /diss ṓn/ (**-owns, -owning, -owned**) *vt* to refuse or no longer acknowledge a connection with somebody or something —**disowner** *n* —**disownment** *n*

~~**dispair**~~ incorrect spelling of **despair**

disparage /di spárrij/ (**-ages, -aging, -aged**) *vt* to refer disapprovingly or contemptuously to somebody or something —**disparagement** *n* —**disparager** *n*

disparaging /di spárrijing/ *adj* showing or expressing disapproval or contempt —**disparagingly** *adv*

disparate /díspərət/ *adj* describes people or things so completely unlike one another that they cannot be compared [15C. < Latin *disparatus*, past participle of *disparare* 'separate' < *parare* 'prepare'] —**disparately** *adv* —**disparateness** *n*

~~**disparitry**~~ incorrect spelling of **disparity**

disparity /di spárrəti/ (*plural* **-ties**) *n* **1.** a lack of equality between people or things **2.** dissimilarity or incongruity [Mid-16C. Via French < late Latin *disparitas* < *paritas* (see PARITY[1])]

dispassion /diss pásh'n/ *n* the state of not being influenced by emotion or personal feelings ○ *viewed the chaos round her with dispassion*

dispassionate /diss pásh'nət/ *adj* not influenced by emotion or personal feelings —**dispassionately** *adv* —**dispassionateness** *n*

dispatch /di spách/, **despatch** *vt* (**-patches, -patching, -patched**) **1. SEND SOMETHING TO PLACE** to send off something such as a letter or parcel to a destination **2. SEND SOMEBODY AWAY TO DO SOMETHING** to instruct somebody to go somewhere in order to carry out a task **3. DEAL WITH SOMETHING QUICKLY** to complete or deal with something quickly or efficiently **4. EAT SOMETHING UP** to eat food quickly (*informal*) **5. KILL SOMEBODY** to kill a person or animal ■ *n* **1. SEND-OFF** the sending of somebody or something such as a messenger or a letter **2. EFFICIENT SPEED** speed and efficiency ○ *carried out her duties with dispatch* **3. OFFICIAL MESSAGE** a message or report, especially an official communication from a diplomat or an officer in the armed forces **4.** MEDIA **NEWS REPORT** a news item or

report sent by a journalist or news agency ○ *dispatches from the scene of the fire* **5. ACT OF KILLING** the killing of a person or animal [Early 16C. Via Italian *dispacciare* < negative form of assumed Vulgar Latin *impactare* 'impede' < Latin *impact-*, past participle of *impingere* (see IMPINGE)] —**dispatcher** *n*

dispatch box *n* a case for carrying documents, especially a red case of the kind used by British government ministers

Dispatch Box *n* either of two boxes in each side of the chamber in the House of Commons that are used as lecterns by ministers when they address Parliament

dispatch case *n* a case for carrying papers or documents (*dated*)

dispatch rider *n* a messenger who travels by motorcycle or on horseback (*dated*)

dispel /di spél/ (**-pels, -pelling, -pelled**) *vt* **1.** to rid somebody's mind of a thought or an idea, especially an erroneous one **2.** to disperse or drive away something ○ *clouds and mist that the sun soon dispelled* [15C. < Latin *dispellere* 'drive away' < *pellere* 'beat'] —**dispeller** *n*

dispensable /di spénssəb'l/ *adj* able to be dispensed with or replaced —**dispensability** /di spénssə bílləti/ *n*

dispensary /di spénssəri/ (*plural* **-ries**) *n* **1.** a place where medical supplies are stored and distributed to patients by a pharmacist **2.** a place where temporary medical treatment is provided

dispensation /díspən sáysh'n/ *n* **1. EXEMPTION** exemption or release from a rule or obligation, especially a religious one **2. DOCUMENT GIVING EXEMPTION** an official document authorizing dispensation, especially religious dispensation **3. RELIGIOUS SYSTEM** in Christian belief, a divinely ordained religious system **4. DIVINE ORDERING** in Christian belief, a divine ordering or management of affairs and events in the world **5. RELIGIOUS EPOCH** the time during which a religious doctrine or practice is believed to be in force **6. DISTRIBUTION OF THINGS** the distribution or giving out of something ○ *dispensation of emergency supplies* —**dispensational** *adj* —**dispensatory** /di spénsətəri/ *adj*

dispense /di spénss/ (**-penses, -pensing, -pensed**) *vt* **1. PROVIDE SERVICE** to give a service or advice to several recipients **2. SUPPLY PRODUCT** to supply something such as food, drink, or money automatically on insertion of payment or a card **3.** PHARM **SUPPLY MEDICINES** to supply medicine according to a prescription [14C. Via French < Latin *dispensare* < *dispendere* 'weigh out' < *pendere* 'weigh']

SYNONYMS See ***share***[1].

dispense with *vt* **1.** to manage without something ○ *Since it's sunny, we can dispense with the rain gear.* **2.** to get rid of something not wanted or needed ○ *Let's dispense with all these convoluted rules and regulations.*

dispenser /di spénssər/ *n* **1. DEVICE FOR DISPENSING GOODS** a device that releases its contents in convenient or measured quantities when operated (*usually used in combination*) **2. PROVIDER OF SOMETHING** somebody or something that distributes something **3.** PHARM **MEDICINE SUPPLIER** somebody who supplies medicine according to a prescription

~~**dispensible**~~ incorrect spelling of **dispensable**

dispensing chemist /di spénssing-/ *n* a pharmacist, especially one who runs a chemist's shop

dispensing optician *n* OPHTHALMOL same as **optician** (sense 3)

dispersal /di spúrss'l/ *n* **1. DISTRIBUTION** the distribution or scattering of people or things over an area **2.** BIOL **NATURAL SPREAD OF SEED** the natural distribution of plant seeds and the offspring of organisms that are not mobile over a wide area by various methods **3.** BIOL **MOVEMENT OF ORGANISMS** the movement of organisms away from their place of birth or from centres of population density **4. DISAPPEARANCE** disappearance as a result of scattering or going away in different directions

dispersant /di spúrss'nt/ *n* a liquid or gas that facilitates or improves the dispersion of small particles or droplets, e.g. in an aerosol —**dispersant** *adj*

disperse /di spúrss/ (**-perses, -persing, -persed**) *vti* **1. SCATTER** to cause something to scatter in different directions, or scatter in this way **2. DISTRIBUTE WIDELY** to distribute something over a wide area, or become widespread **3. CAUSE TO DISAPPEAR** to cause something to disappear, or disappear **4.** CHEM **DISTRIBUTE EVENLY** to distribute particles evenly throughout a medium, or become distributed in this way **5.** PHYS **SEPARATE INTO COLOURS** to separate white light into the component colours of the spectrum, or undergo this process [14C. < Old French *disperser* < Latin *dispers-*, past participle of *dispergere* 'scatter around' < *spargere* 'scatter'] —**disperser** *n*

SPELLCHECK See ***disburse***

dispersion /di spúrsh'n/ *n* **1. DISPERSAL** the scattering or distribution of something within an area or space **2. CONDITION OF BEING DISPERSED** the fact or state of being spread, scattered, or distributed **3.** STATS **DISTRIBUTION OF VALUES** the distribution of a statistical frequency distribution about an average or median **4.** CHEM **MEDIUM WITH DISPERSED PARTICLES** a chemical system consisting of a gas, liquid, or colloid containing dispersed particles

Dispersion *n* JUDAISM same as **Diaspora** (sense 1)

dispersive /di spúrssiv/ *adj* tending to cause dispersion —**dispersively** *adv* —**dispersiveness** *n*

dispirit /di spírrət/ (**-its, -iting, -ited**) *vt* to discourage or dishearten somebody —**dispirited** *adj* —**dispiritedly** *adv* —**dispiritedness** *n*

dispiriting /di spírriting/ *adj* discouraging or disheartening —**dispiritingly** *adv*

displace /diss pláyss/ (**-places, -placing, -placed**) *vt* **1. MOVE SOMETHING FROM USUAL PLACE** to move something from its usual or correct place **2. FORCE SOMEBODY TO LEAVE HOME** to force somebody to leave his or her home or country, e.g. because of war **3. REMOVE SOMEBODY FROM POST** to discharge or remove somebody from an office, position, or job **4. REPLACE SOMEBODY OR SOMETHING** to take the place of somebody or something **5.** CHEM **TAKE PLACE OF ATOM** to take the place of another atom or group in a compound **6.** PHYS **REPLACE FLUID WITH OBJECT** to replace a volume of fluid with a floating or submerged object, forcing the original fluid to move elsewhere —**displaceable** *adj* —**displacer** *n*

displaced person /diss pláyst-/ *n* somebody who has been forced to leave his or her home or country, especially because of war or political oppression

displacement /diss pláyssmənt/ *n* **1. MOVEMENT FROM USUAL SITE** the movement of something from its usual or correct place **2.** PHYS, NAUT **FLUID DISPLACED** the amount of fluid such as water that is forced to move by an object floating on or submerged in it, often used as a measure of a ship's size **3.** PHYS **AMOUNT OF MOVEMENT IN PARTICULAR DIRECTION** the amount of movement of an object measured in a particular direction **4.** CHEM **CHEMICAL REPLACEMENT** a chemical reaction in which one atom or chemical group takes the place of another in a compound **5.** PSYCHOL **TRANSFER OF EMOTIONS OR BEHAVIOUR** the transfer of emotion from the original focus to another less threatening person or object, or the substitution of one response or piece of behaviour for another **6.** GEOL **MOVEMENT OF GEOLOGICAL FAULT** the distance that a point on one side of a geological fault has moved, relative to a corresponding point on the other side **7.** AUTOMOT **ENGINE VOLUME** the total volume displaced by the pistons in an internal combustion engine

displacement ton *n* a unit of measure for the displacement of a floating ship, equivalent to 0.99 cu m/35 cu ft. or 2,240 lb

display /di spláy/ *v* (**-plays, -playing, -played**) **1.** *vt* **MAKE SOMETHING VISIBLE** to make something visible or available for others to see **2.** *vt* **MAKE SOMETHING EVIDENT** to reveal or make evident a quality or feeling **3.** *vti* COMPUT **SHOW DATA** to show messages, data, or graphics on a monitor, or appear on a monitor **4.** *vti* ZOOL **SHOW STYLIZED BEHAVIOUR** to show a pattern of animal behaviour, e.g. to attract a mate or defend a territory ■ *n* **1. VISUAL ARRANGEMENT** a collection of things arranged or done for others to see, especially something considered attractive, interesting, or entertaining (*often used in combination*) **2. STATE OF BEING VIEWABLE** the state of being clearly and easily visible or placed for people to view ○ *new work on display* **3. SHOW OF FEELING OR QUALITY** an act of showing a feeling or quality ○ *a display of courage* **4.** PRINTING, MARKETING **GRAPHIC ADVERTISING** printed advertising that uses attractive pictures, typography, or other features **5. ELECTRONIC SCREEN** an electronic device that presents visual information **6. INFORMATION ON SCREEN** the information shown on a computer monitor or other electronic device **7.** ZOOL **STYLIZED BEHAVIOUR** a pattern of animal behaviour used to produce a response in other animals, especially of the same species, e.g. when courting or defending territory ■ *adj* **INTENDED FOR ADVERTISING** describes typefaces that are designed for prominent use in advertising [Late 16C. Via Old French *despleier* < Latin *displicare* 'unfold' < *plicare* 'to fold'] —**displayer** *n*

display cabinet, **display case** *n* a case or stand with glass panels, used for showing items of interest

displease /diss pléez/ (**-pleases, -pleasing, -pleased**) *vti* to annoy or dissatisfy somebody [14C. < Old French *desplais-*, stem of *desplaire* < assumed Vulgar Latin *displacere* < Latin *placere* 'to please'] —**displeased** *adj*

displeasing /diss pléezing/ *adj* causing annoyance or dissatisfaction —**displeasingly** *adv*

displeasure /diss plézhər/ *n* a feeling of annoyance or dissatisfaction [15C. < Old French *desplaisir* 'displease, displeasure' < *plaisir* 'pleasure']

disport /di spáwrt/ *vi* (**-ports, -porting, -ported**) to behave in a playful manner (*archaic or humorous*) ■ *n* a form of lively entertainment or diversion [14C. < Old French *desporter* 'divert' < *des-* 'apart' + *porter* 'carry']

disposable /di spṓzəb'l/ *adj* **1. THROWAWAY** designed to be thrown away after use **2. AVAILABLE FOR USE** describes money or assets that are available for use ■ *n* **SOMETHING TO BE USED ONLY ONCE** something that is designed to be thrown away after use, e.g. a paper cup (*often used in the plural*) —**disposability** /di spṓzə bílləti/ *n* —**disposableness** *n*

disposable income *n* **1.** income that remains available for spending after deductions for taxes and other obligations **2.** the total amount of money that a country or community has available for spending

disposal /di spṓz'l/ *n* **1. PROCESS OF GETTING RID OF SOMETHING** the process of throwing away or getting rid of something **2. ORDERLY ARRANGEMENT** an orderly arrangement, distribution, or placement **3. TRANSFERENCE OF SOMETHING TO SOMEBODY ELSE** the transferring of something valuable to somebody else by sale or gift

dispose /di spṓz/ (**-poses, -posing, -posed**) *v* **1.** *vt* **MAKE SOMEBODY WILLING** to make somebody willing or receptive to something (*often passive*) ○ *The President is not disposed to sign the bill.* **2.** *vt* **INCLINE SOMEBODY** to make somebody likely to experience something **3.** *vt* **PUT SOMETHING IN PLACE** to arrange or position something for use or for a particular purpose (*formal; often passive*) ○ *The commander disposed his forces along the coast.* **4.** *vti* **SETTLE MATTER** to settle a matter by putting it into its correct or definitive form (*formal*) ○ *an outcome to be disposed by the court* [14C. < French *disposer*, alteration (after *poser* 'to place') of Latin *disponere* 'set out' < *ponere* 'to place'] —**disposer** *n*

dispose of *vt* **1. GET RID OF SOMETHING** to throw away or get rid of something **2. TRANSFER SOMETHING** to transfer something to the ownership of somebody else, by sale or gift **3. KILL SOMEBODY OR SOMETHING** to kill a person or animal **4. ATTEND TO MATTER** to deal with a matter in order to settle it (*formal*)

disposed /di spṓzd/ *adj* **1.** inclined or tending to something **2.** having a particular attitude towards somebody or something ○ *favourably disposed to us*

disposition /díspə zísh'n/ *n* **1. PERSONALITY** somebody's usual mood or temperament **2. BEHAVIOURAL TENDENCY** an inclination or tendency to act in a particular way **3. SETTLEMENT** settlement of a business or legal matter (*formal*) **4.** same as **disposal** (senses 2–3) [14C. Via French < Latin *disposition-* < *disponere* (see DISPOSE)] —**dispositional** *adj*

dispositive /diss pózzətiv/ *adj* deciding the final outcome of a court case [Early 17C. Directly or via French < medieval Latin *dispositivus* < *disposit-*, past participle of Latin *disponere* (see DISPOSE)]

dispossess /díspə zéss/ (**-sesses, -sessing, -sessed**) *vt* to deprive somebody of the possession or occupancy of something, especially property [15C. < Old French *despossesser* < *possesser* (see POSSESS)] —**dispossessor** *n* —**dispossessory** *adj*

dispossessed /díspə zést/ *adj* deprived of property or rights ■ *npl* people who have been deprived of their property or rights ○ *defended the rights of the dispossessed*

dispossession /díspə zésh'n/ *n* 1. the act of depriving somebody of what he or she owns, especially land or money 2. the state of being deprived of what you own, especially land or money

dispraise /diss práyz/ (*literary*) *vt* (**-praises, -praising, -praised**) to express disapproval of somebody ■ *n* disapproval, or an instance or expression of it ○'*Praise and dispraise play their part in the quality control of literary journalism...*' (Martin Amis *Atlantic Monthly*; December 2003) —**dispraiser** *n*

disproof /diss proof/ *n* 1. the disproving of a legal argument or point 2. evidence that disproves something

disproportion /díspra páwrsh'n/ *n* something that is out of proportion or unequal ■ *vt* (**-tions, -tioning, -tioned**) to make something disproportionate

disproportionate /díspra páwrsh'nət/, **disproportional** /-sh'nəl/ *adj* unequal or out of proportion in quantity, shape, or size —**disproportionally** *adv* —**disproportionately** *adv* —**disproportionateness** *n*

disproportionation /díspra páwrsh'n áysh'n/ *n* a chemical reaction in which a single substance acts as both oxidizing and reducing agent, resulting in the production of dissimilar substances

disprove /diss proov/ (**-proves, -proving, -proved**) *vt* to show that something is not true or correct [14C. < Old French *desprover* < *prover* (see PROVE)] —**disprovable** *adj* —**disproval** *n*

Dispur /diss poor/ capital city of Assam state, northeastern India. Population: 584,342 (1991).

disputable /di spyóotəb'l/ *adj* not definitely true or valid and therefore debatable or open to argument —**disputability** /di spyóotə bílləti/ *n* —**disputableness** *n*

disputably /di spyóotəbli/ *adv* used to suggest that the speaker or writer thinks that something is true and could defend that view against those who disagree

disputant /di spyóot'nt/ *n* somebody involved in an argument or a legal dispute ■ *adj* involved in an argument or a legal dispute

disputation /díspyōo táysh'n/ *n* (*formal*) 1. argumentation or disagreement 2. a formal academic debate in defence of a thesis

disputatious /díspyōo táyshəss/, **disputative** /di spyóotətiv/ *adj* tending to argue or disagree without adequate cause (*formal*) —**disputatiously** *adv* —**disputatiousness** *n*

dispute /di spyóot/ *v* (**-putes, -puting, -puted**) 1. *vti* QUERY SOMETHING to question or doubt the truth or validity of something 2. *vi* DISAGREE ABOUT SOMETHING to disagree or argue about something 3. *vt* STRUGGLE FOR SOMETHING to fight for or strive to win something (*formal*) 4. *vt* OPPOSE SOMETHING to strive against or resist something (*formal*) ■ *n* 1. /di spyóot, díss pyoot/ ARGUMENT a serious argument or disagreement 2. INDUSTRIAL DISAGREEMENT a prolonged disagreement between management and workers or a trade union, often involving industrial action ○ *a labour dispute* [Late 16C. Via French < Latin *disputare*, literally 'argue out' < *putare* 'consider'] —**disputed** *adj* —**disputer** *n*

USAGE The traditional pronunciation of both the noun and the verb uses of *dispute* is with the stress on the second syllable. More recently, a stress on the first syllable has been increasingly heard in the case of the noun.

SYNONYMS See *disagree*.

disqualification /diss kwóllifi káysh'n/ *n* 1. INELIGIBILITY the condition of being or becoming ineligible to do or take part in something 2. ACT OF BEING DISQUALIFIED an instance of being disqualified 3. SOMETHING THAT DISQUALIFIES something that makes somebody ineligible to do or take part in something

disqualify /diss kwólli fī/ (**-fies, -fying, -fied**) *vt* 1. to make or declare somebody unfit, unqualified, or ineligible to do or take part in something 2. to deprive somebody of a legal or other right or privilege —**disqualifiable** *adj* —**disqualified** *adj* —**disqualifier** *n*

disquiet /diss kwī ət/ *n* a feeling of anxiety or uneasiness ■ *vt* (**-ets, -eting, -eted**) to make somebody anxious or uneasy (*archaic or literary*) —**disquietly** *adv* —**disquietness** *n*

disquieting /diss kwī əting/ *adj* causing a feeling of anxiety or uneasiness —**disquietingly** *adv*

disquietude /diss kwī ə tyood/ *n* same as **disquiet**

disquisition /dískwi zísh'n/ *n* a long formal essay or discussion on a subject (*formal*) [Early 17C. Via French < Latin *disquisition-* < *disquirere* 'enquire' < *quaerere* 'seek, ask'] —**disquisitional** *adj*

Benjamin Disraeli

Disraeli /diz ráyli/, **Benjamin, 1st Earl of Beaconsfield** (1804–81) British politician and novelist. He was Conservative prime minister (1868, 1874–80), and author of *Coningsby* (1844) and *Sybil* (1845).

'I repeat...that all power is a trust—that we are accountable for its exercise—that, from the people, and for the people, all springs, and all must exist.'
[Benjamin Disraeli, *Vivian Grey*; 1826]

'There are three kinds of lies: lies, damned lies, and statistics.'
[Attributed to Benjamin Disraeli]

disrate /díss ráyt/ (**-rates, -rating, -rated**) *vt* to demote a naval officer to a lower rank

disregard /díssri gaárd/ *vt* (**-gards, -garding, -garded**) 1. IGNORE SOMEBODY OR SOMETHING to ignore or pay no attention to somebody or something 2. TREAT SOMEBODY OR SOMETHING DISRESPECTFULLY to treat somebody or something with contempt or without respect ■ *n* NEGLECT a lack of attention or respect —**disregarder** *n* —**disregardful** *adj*

disrelish /diss réllish/ (**-ishes, -ishing, -ished**) *vt* to dislike something, or find something distasteful (*archaic*) —**disrelish** *n*

disremember /díssri mémbər/ (**-bers, -bering, -bered**) *vti* to forget or fail to remember something (*informal*)

disrepair /díssri páir/ *n* poor working order or condition as a result of neglect

disreputable /diss réppyōotəb'l/ *adj* 1. lacking respectability on the basis of past or present actions 2. untidy, dirty, or worn in appearance (*humorous*) —**disreputableness** *n* —**disreputably** *adv*

disrepute /díssri pyóot/ *n* a lack or loss of good reputation or respect

disrespect /díssri spékt/ *n* a lack of respect ■ *vt* (**-spects, -specting, -spected**) to show a lack of respect for somebody or something —**disrespectful** *adj* —**disrespectfully** *adv*

disrobe /diss rṓb/ (**-robes, -robing, -robed**) *vti* to remove clothing from yourself or somebody else (*formal*) [Late 16C. < Old French *desrober* < *robe* (see ROBE)] —**disrobement** *n* —**disrober** *n*

disrupt /diss rúpt/ (**-rupts, -rupting, -rupted**) *vt* 1. to interrupt the usual course of a process or activity 2. to destroy the order or orderly progression of something [15C. < Latin *disrupt-*, past participle of *disrumpere* 'break apart' < *rumpere* 'break']

disruption /diss rúpsh'n/ *n* 1. UNWANTED BREAK an unwelcome or unexpected break in a process or activity 2. SUSPENSION the interruption or suspension of usual activity or progress 3. STATE OF DISORDER a state of disorder caused by outside influence

Disruption *n* a split in the Church of Scotland in 1843, leading to the formation of the Free Church.

At issue was the question of patronage versus the choice of a minister by the congregation.

disruptive /diss rúptiv/ *adj* interrupting usual order or progress —**disruptively** *adv* —**disruptiveness** *n*

diss *vt* another spelling of **dis** (*slang*)

~~**dissapear**~~ incorrect spelling of **disappear**

~~**dissapointed**~~ incorrect spelling of **disappointed**

dissatisfaction /díss satiss fáksh'n, di sáttiss-/ *n* 1. a state or feeling of not being satisfied 2. something that causes a feeling of not being satisfied

dissatisfactory /díss satiss fáktəri/ *adj* not satisfactory

dissatisfy /díss sáttiss fī/ (**-fies, -fying, -fied**) *vt* to fail to satisfy somebody —**dissatisfied** *adj*

dissect /dī sékt, di-/ (**-sects, -secting, -sected**) *v* 1. *vti* to cut and separate the parts of animal or plant specimens for scientific or medical study 2. *vt* to examine or analyse a person or subject in detail ○ *dissected the speech* [Late 16C. < Latin *dissect-*, past participle of *dissecare* 'cut apart' < *secare* 'cut'] —**dissectible** *adj* —**dissector** *n*

dissected /dī séktid, di-/ *adj* 1. describes a leaf that is divided into narrow lobes or segments 2. describes a landscape that has been eroded into hills and valleys

dissecting aortic aneurysm *n* an aneurysm, often fatal, that leaks or ruptures, causing sharp stabbing pain in the middle of the back, sweating, and vomiting

dissection /dī séksh'n, di-/ *n* 1. CUTTING AND EXAMINING the cutting and separating of the parts of animal or plant specimens for scientific or medical study 2. DISSECTED SPECIMEN something that has been dissected, e.g. an anatomical specimen 3. EXAMINATION a thorough and detailed analysis or examination of something such as a policy or plan

disseise /diss seéz/ (**-seises, -seising, -seised**), **disseize** (**-seizes, -seizing, -seized**) *vi* to deprive somebody wrongfully of possession of land [14C. < Anglo-Norman *disseisir*, variant of Old French *dessaisir* 'dispossess' < *saisir* (see SEIZE)] —**disseisor** *n*

disseisin /diss seézin/, **disseizin** *n* the act of wrongfully depriving somebody of land [14C. < Anglo-Norman *disseisine*, variant of Old French *dessaisine* < *dessaisir* (see DISSEISE)]

disseize, etc. *v* LAW another spelling of **disseise, etc.**

dissemble /di sémb'l/ (**-bles, -bling, -bled**) *v* 1. *vi* PUT ON FALSE APPEARANCE to put on a false appearance in order to conceal facts, feelings, or intentions 2. *vt* GIVE APPEARANCE OF SOMETHING to put on the appearance of something not actually felt or true (*formal*) 3. *vt* HIDE SOMETHING BY PRETENCE to hide real beliefs, feelings, or intentions through misleading speech or behaviour (*formal*) [15C. < Old French *dessembler* 'be different' < *sembler* 'seem'] —**dissemblance** *n* —**dissembler** *n*

dissembling /di sémbling/ *n* the creation or adoption of a false appearance in order to conceal facts, feelings, or intentions ■ *adj* feigning or pretending —**dissemblingly** *adv*

disseminate /di sémmi nayt/ (**-nates, -nating, -nated**) *vti* to distribute or spread something, especially information, widely, or become widespread [15C. < Latin *disseminat-*, past participle of *disseminare* 'sow abroad' < *semin-* 'seed'] —**dissemination** /di sémmi náysh'n/ *n* —**disseminative** *adj* —**disseminator** *n*

dissension /di sénsh'n/ *n* disagreement or difference of opinion, especially when leading to open conflict [14C. Via French < Latin *dissension-* < *dissentire* (see DISSENT)]

dissensus /diss sénsəss/ *n* disagreement or difference of opinion [Mid-20C. Blend of DISSENT + CONSENSUS]

dissent /di sént/ *vi* (**-sents, -senting, -sented**) 1. DISAGREE to disagree with a widely held or majority opinion 2. ISSUE MINORITY COURT OPINION to disagree with a majority court opinion and put those views into writing (*refers to judges*) ○ *Two Supreme Court justices dissented.* 3. CHR NOT SUPPORT RELIGIOUS PRACTICES to refuse to conform to the authority, doctrines, or practices of an established church 4. WITHHOLD ASSENT to withhold assent or approval ■ *n* 1. DISAGREEMENT disagreement from a widely held or majority opinion 2. CHR RELIGIOUS NONCONFORMITY refusal to conform to the authority, doctrines, or practices of an established church 3. LAW MINORITY OPINION an

opinion of a judge that is not in agreement with that of other judges **4.** POL **REFUSAL TO ACCEPT POLITICAL RULES** opposition to the laws, norms, and structures of a political regime, especially on moral grounds [15C. < Latin *dissentire* 'feel differently' < *sentire* 'feel']

SPELLCHECK See ***descent.***

dissenter /di séntər/ *n* somebody who disagrees with the beliefs or opinions of a majority

Dissenter *n* somebody who rejects the authority, doctrines, or practices of an established church, especially a Protestant who did not accept the Church of England in the 17th and 18th centuries

dissentient /di sénshi ənt/ *adj* showing or expressing disagreement with the beliefs or opinions of a majority (*formal*) [Early 17C. < Latin *dissentient-*, present participle of *dissentire* (see DISSENT)] —**dissentience** *n* —**dissentiency** *n* —**dissentient** *n* —**dissentiently** *adv*

dissenting /di sénting/ *adj* **1.** **EXPRESSING OR SHOWING DISAGREEMENT** disagreeing with the beliefs or opinions of a majority **2.** *also* **Dissenting** CHR **OF DISSENTERS** relating or belonging to a group of religious nonconformists, especially an English Protestant denomination of the 17th and 18th centuries **3.** LAW **DISAGREEING WITH OTHER JUDGES** disagreeing with the majority verdict or opinion of other judges —**dissentingly** *adv*

dissepiment /di séppimənt/ *n* a dividing wall or membrane separating an organ such as a plant ovary, into distinct chambers [Early 18C. < Latin *dissaepimentum* < *dissaepire* 'make separate' < *saepire* 'divide off' < *saepes* 'hedge'] —**dissepimental** /di séppi mént'l/ *adj*

dissertation /díssər táysh'n/ *n* **1.** a lengthy formal written treatment of a subject, especially a long essay submitted as a requirement for a university degree **2.** a formal spoken or written discourse —**dissertational** *adj* —**dissertationist** *n*

disservice /diss súrviss/ *n* an action that causes harm or difficulty

dissever /di sévvər/ (**-ers, -ering, -ered**) *v* (*formal*) **1.** *vt* **SEPARATE SOMETHING** to separate or sever something **2.** *vt* **BREAK UP SOMETHING** to break up or divide something **3.** *vi* **COME APART** to come apart or become disunited [13C. Via Anglo-Norman *desseverer* < late Latin *disseparare* 'split apart' < Latin *separare* (see SEPARATE)] —**disseverance** *n* —**disseveration** /díss sevə ráysh'n/ *n* —**disseverment** *n*

dissidence /díssidənss/ *n* disagreement with authority or with prevailing opinion

dissident /díssidənt/ *n* somebody who publicly disagrees with an established political or religious system or organization [Mid-16C. < Latin *dissident-*, present participle of *dissidere* 'sit apart' < *sedere* 'sit'] —**dissident** *adj* —**dissidently** *adv*

dissimilar /di símmilər/ *adj* differing in one or more respects —**dissimilarly** *adv*

dissimilarity /díssimi lárrəti/ (*plural* **-ties**) *n* **1.** the fact or state of being different in one or more respects **2.** a point of difference or distinction

dissimilate /di símmi layt/ (**-lates, -lating, -lated**) *vti* **1.** to make something dissimilar, or become dissimilar **2.** to undergo linguistic dissimilation, or change a consonant or consonants by this process [Mid-19C. < DIS- + ASSIMILATE] —**dissimilative** *adj* —**dissimilatory** *adj*

dissimilation /di símmi láysh'n/ *n* **1.** the process of becoming dissimilar **2.** the development of a dissimilarity between two consonant sounds in a word that were originally identical

dissimilatory /di símmi láytəri/ *adj* describes a chemical process involving the production of an inorganic compound or element from an organic one, or a product resulting from this process

dissimilitude /díssi mílli tyood/ *n* the condition or quality of differing in one or more respects from something else (*formal*) [15C. < Latin *dissimilitudo* < *dissimilis* 'unlike' < *similis* 'like, similar']

dissimulate /di símmyoŏ layt/ (**-lates, -lating, -lated**) *vti* to disguise or hide true feelings, thoughts, or intentions [15C. < Latin *dissimulat-*, past participle of *dissimulare* 'disguise completely' < *simulare* (see SIMULATE)] —**dissimulation** /di símmyoŏ láysh'n/ *n* —**dissimulative** *adj* —**dissimulator** *n*

dissipate /díssi payt/ (**-pates, -pating, -pated**) *v* **1.** *vti* **CAUSE SOMETHING TO DISAPPEAR** to fade or disappear, or make something do this ○ *storm clouds dissipating* **2.** *vt* **WASTE SOMETHING** to spend or use something wastefully **3.** *vi* **OVERINDULGE** to indulge excessively or extravagantly in the pursuit of physical pleasure [15C. < Latin *dissipat-*, past participle of *dissipare* 'scatter around'] —**dissipater** *n* —**dissipative** *adj* —**dissipator** *n*

dissipated /díssi paytid/ *adj* **1.** overindulging in the pursuit of physical pleasure **2.** resulting from or suggesting overindulgence in the pursuit of physical pleasure ○ *dissipated features* —**dissipatedly** *adv* —**dissipatedness** *n*

dissipation /díssi páysh'n/ *n* **1.** **OVERINDULGENCE** overindulgence in the pursuit of physical pleasures **2.** **WASTEFUL USE** the squandering of resources such as money or fuel (*formal*) **3.** **DISPERSAL** the scattering or dispersal of something ○ *dissipation of early morning fog* **4.** **ABATING OF FEELING OR EMOTION** the disappearance of a feeling or emotion such as anger or anxiety

dissociate /di sṓshi ayt, -sṓssi-/ (**-ates, -ating, -ated**) *v* **1.** *vt* **REGARD SOMEBODY OR SOMETHING AS DISTINCT** to treat somebody or something as distinct from or unconnected with somebody or something else **2.** *vt* same as **disassociate 3.** *vti* CHEM **SPLIT SOMETHING INTO SIMPLER PARTS** to cause the molecules of a compound to break down into simpler molecules, atoms, or ions, usually in a reversible reaction, or break down in this way **4.** *vi* PSYCHIAT **SEPARATE OFF AREAS OF MIND** to separate a group of mental processes from the rest of the mind, causing them to lose their usual relationship with it [Mid-16C. < Latin *dissociat-*, past participle of *dissociare*, literally 'separate from fellowship' < *sociare* 'join together' < *socius* 'companion'] —**dissociable** *adj* —**dissociative** *adj*

dissociation /di sṓshi áysh'n, -sṓssi-/ *n* **1.** **TREATMENT OF SOMETHING AS UNCONNECTED** the treatment of somebody or something as distinct or unconnected, or the fact of being treated in this way **2.** same as **disassociation 3.** CHEM **DIVISION OF MOLECULE** the breaking up of a molecule into simpler components **4.** PSYCHIAT **SEPARATION OF EMOTIONS** the separation of a group of usually connected mental processes such as emotion and understanding from the rest of the mind as a defence mechanism

USAGE See ***disassociation.***

dissociative identity disorder *n* PSYCHIAT same as **multiple personality disorder**

dissoluble /di sóllyoŏb'l/ *adj* able to be dissolved, separated, or ended [Mid-16C. Directly or via French < Latin *dissolubilis* < *dissolvere* (see DISSOLVE)] —**dissolubility** /di sóllyoŏ bílləti/ *n* —**dissolubleness** *n*

dissolute /díssə loot/ *adj* overindulging in physical pleasures in a way that is considered immoral or harmful [14C. < Latin *dissolutus*, past participle of *dissolvere* (see DISSOLVE)] —**dissolutely** *adv* —**dissoluteness** *n*

dissolution /díssə lóosh'n/ *n* **1.** **ACT OF BREAKING SOMETHING DOWN** the separating, decomposing, or disintegrating of something into smaller or more basic constituents **2.** **BREAKING UP OF SOMETHING** the process of breaking up or destroying an organization or institution **3.** **FORMAL ENDING OF MEETING** the formal closing of a meeting or assembly, especially the formal ending of the current parliament's jurisdiction before a general election **4.** LAW **TERMINATION OF LEGAL RELATIONSHIP** the termination of a legal relationship such as a business partnership or a marriage **5.** **DEMISE** somebody's death (*formal*)

dissolve /di zólv/ *v* (**-solves, -solving, -solved**) **1.** *vti* **BECOME ABSORBED IN LIQUID** to become absorbed in a liquid solution, or make a solid do this ○ *Dissolve two tablets in a glass of water.* **2.** *vti* **DISAPPEAR** to fade away gradually and disappear, or make something do this ○ *All his fears dissolved.* **3.** *vti* **BREAK UP** to break up into smaller or more basic parts, or make something do this **4.** *vi* **START LAUGHING OR CRYING** to begin to laugh or cry uncontrollably ○ *He dissolved into tears.* **5.** *vt* **CLOSE FORMALLY** to bring something such as a meeting or a political assembly to a formal close, especially to end the jurisdiction of a current parliament before a general election **6.** *vt* LAW **END LEGAL RELATIONSHIP** to bring a legal relationship such as a business partnership or a marriage formally to an end **7.** *vi* CINEMA, MEDIA **SIMULTANEOUSLY FADE OUT AND IN** to fade out slowly as a second image fades in, briefly merging one with the other ■ *n* CINEMA, MEDIA **SIMULTANEOUS FADE-IN AND FADE-OUT** a change from one scene to another, with the first scene gradually fading out and the next one gradually fading in over it [14C. < Latin *dissolvere*, literally 'loosen asunder' < *solvere* 'loosen'] —**dissolvable** *adj* —**dissolvent** *adj* —**dissolver** *n*

dissonance /díssənənss/ *n* **1.** **UNPLEASANT NOISE** a combination of sounds that is unpleasant to listen to **2.** **INCONSISTENCY** lack of consistency or compatibility between actions or beliefs **3.** MUSIC **UNSTABLE COMBINATION OF MUSICAL NOTES** a combination of notes that, when played simultaneously, sounds displeasing and needs to be resolved to a consonance

dissonant /díssənənt/ *adj* **1.** **UNPLEASANT TO HEAR** making or involving a combination of sounds that is unpleasant to listen to **2.** **CONFLICTING** incompatible or inconsistent (*formal*) **3.** MUSIC **CONTAINING UNPLEASANT COMBINATION OF NOTES** containing unpleasant combinations of notes that need to be resolved to a consonance [15C. < Latin *dissonant-*, present participle of *dissonare* 'be apart in sound' < *sonare* 'to sound'] —**dissonantly** *adv*

dissuade /di swáyd/ (**-suades, -suading, -suaded**) *vt* to persuade somebody not to do something [Early 16C. < Latin *dissuadere* 'advise against' < *suadere* 'advise, persuade'] —**dissuadable** *adj* —**dissuader** *n*

dissuasion /di swáyzh'n/ *n* persuasion not to do something [15C. Directly or via French < Latin *dissuasion-* < *dissuas-*, past participle of *dissuadere* (see DISSUADE)]

dissuasive /di swáyssiv/ *adj* convincing enough to persuade somebody not to do something [Early 16C. < Latin *dissuas-* (see DISSUASION)] —**dissuasively** *adv* —**dissuasiveness** *n*

dissyllable *n* LING, LITERAT another spelling of **disyllable**

dissymmetric /díss si méttrik, díssi-/, **dissymmetrical** /-méttrik'l/ *adj* **1.** same as **asymmetrical** (sense 1) **2.** showing the sort of symmetry possessed by things that are mirror images of each other —**dissymmetrically** *adv*

dissymmetry /diss símmitri, di-/ (*plural* **-tries**) *n* **1.** same as **asymmetry** (sense 1) **2.** the symmetry possessed by things that are mirror images of each other

dist. *abbr* **1.** distance **2.** PUBLIC ADMIN district

distaff /dí staaf/ (*plural* **-taffs** or **-taves** /-stayvz/) *n* **1.** work or other matters regarded as the concern of women (*literary; sometimes considered offensive*) **2.** a rod on which wool or flax is wound for somebody to use when spinning by hand, or the corresponding rod on a spinning wheel [Old English *distæf* < Germanic, 'bunch of flax' + STAFF [1]]

distaff side *n* the wife's or mother's side of a family (*literary*)

distal /díst'l/ *adj* describes a body part situated away from a point of attachment or origin. For example, the elbow is distal to the shoulder. [Early 19C. < DISTANT + -AL [1]] —**distally** *adv*

distance /dístənss/ *n* **1.** **LENGTH BETWEEN TWO THINGS** the length of the space separating two people, places, or things ○ *What's the distance between Paris and New York?* **2.** **FAR-OFF PLACE** a place or position far away or not very close ○ *It's best seen from a distance.* **3.** **CLOSENESS ALLOWING SOME ACTIVITY** the space between two people, places, or things with regard to activity carried on between the two ○ *We can do nothing until they're within hailing distance.* **4.** **AMOUNT OF SEPARATION** the amount by which two places are separated, especially when thought of in terms of the time or inconvenience of a journey between the two ○ *She lives some distance away.* **5.** **COOLNESS OR ALOOFNESS** a cool or slightly aloof response to another person or group ○ *He suddenly felt the need to put some distance between himself and his friends.* **6.** **INTERVAL OF TIME** the interval between one point in time and another, especially a long interval ○ *You can't expect to remember all the details at a distance of more than 20 years.* **7.** **AMOUNT OF PROGRESS** the amount of progress that has been made or that is still to be made ○ *still some distance to go before we can reach an agreement* **8.** **IDEOLOGICAL GULF** difference of opinion or ideology ○ *There's still some distance between us with regard to the basic issues.* **9.** HORSERACING **SPACE**

GREATER THAN 20 LENGTHS a space of more than twenty lengths between two racehorses, usually the winner and the horse finishing second ○ *win by a distance* ■ *v* (**-tances, -tancing, -tanced**) **1.** *vt* RESTRAIN SOMEBODY FROM EMOTIONAL INVOLVEMENT to stop yourself or somebody else from becoming emotionally involved in something ○ *Try to distance yourself from past experiences.* **2. distance yourself** *vr* AVOID GIVING SUPPORT to deny that you support or are involved with somebody or something, or withdraw support from somebody or something ○ *He was trying to distance himself from the allegations.* **3.** *vt* HORSERACING BEAT HORSE BY DISTANCE to beat another racehorse by more than twenty lengths [13C Directly or via French < Latin *distantia* < *distant-* 'standing apart' (see DISTANT)] ◇ **go the distance** to continue until you have completed something

distance learning *n* education for students working at home, with little or no face-to-face contact with teachers and with material provided remotely, e.g. by e-mail, television, or post

distant /dístənt/ *adj* **1.** NOT PHYSICALLY CLOSE situated, living, or happening far away ○ *a distant galaxy* **2.** REMOTE IN TIME remote in time, either in the future or the past ○ *at some time in the distant future* **3.** REMOTE IN RELATIONSHIP remote in relationship or connection ○ *a distant relative* **4.** ALOOFLY RESERVED showing that somebody does not want to be friendly or intimate **5.** HARD TO DISTINGUISH CLEARLY so slight as to be hard to discern, see, or distinguish ○ *a distant resemblance* [14C. Directly or via French < Latin *distant-*, present participle of *distare* 'stand apart' < *stare* 'to stand']

distantly /dístəntli/ *adv* **1.** FAR AWAY from far away and therefore usually not clear or loud ○ *We could distantly make out figures dancing in the village square.* **2.** FAR AWAY MENTALLY not concentrating on the immediate surroundings **3.** ALOOFLY in a detached, cold, or formal way ○ *He smiled at her distantly as she walked past.* **4.** NOT CLOSELY not closely in terms of family or blood relations ○ *distantly related*

distaste /diss táyst/ *n* a feeling of dislike, disapproval, or mild disgust

SYNONYMS See *dislike*.

distasteful /diss táystf'l/ *adj* provoking dislike, disapproval, or mild disgust —**distastefully** *adv* —**distastefulness** *n*

distemper[1] /di stémpər/ *n* a viral disease that affects various animals, especially dogs and cats [Mid-16C. < obsolete verb < late Latin *distemperare* 'combine awry' (referring to an imbalance of bodily 'humours') < Latin *temperare* (see TEMPER)]

distemper[2] /di stémpər/ *n* **1.** paint in which the colouring material is mixed with water and a substance such as glue or size instead of with oil. Distemper is often used for painting walls, theatrical scenery, and posters. **2.** the use of distemper in painting posters and murals [14C. Directly or via Old French *destremper* 'soak, mix' < late Latin *distemperare* (see DISTEMPER [1])] —**distemper** *vt*

distend /di sténd/ (**-tends, -tending, -tended**) *vti* to expand, swell, or inflate as if by pressure from within, or cause something to do this [14C. < Latin *distendere* 'stretch apart' < *tendere* 'stretch'] —**distender** *n* —**distensibility** /di sténssə bílləti/ *n* —**distensible** /di sténssəb'l/ *adj* —**distension** /di sténsh'n/ *n*

distich /dí stik/ *n* two lines of poetry, sometimes rhyming, that form a complete unit in themselves [Early 16C. Via Latin < Greek *distikhon*, form of *distikhos* 'of two rows or verses' < *stikhos* 'row, line of verse'] —**distichal** *adj*

distichous /dístikəss/ *adj* describes leaves that grow in vertical rows on opposite sides of a stem —**distichously** *adv*

distil /di stíl/ (**-tils, -tilling, -tilled**) *v* **1.** *vt* MAKE ALCOHOLIC SPIRITS to produce alcoholic spirits using the process of boiling liquid and condensing its vapour **2.** *vti* PURIFY LIQUID WITH HEAT to purify a liquid by boiling it and then condensing its vapour, or undergo purification in this way **3.** *vt* CREATE SOMETHING FROM ESSENTIAL ELEMENTS to create something from the essential or most important parts of something larger or longer **4.** *vi* EMERGE SLOWLY to be emitted slowly or in small quantities ○*'Then slowly from the silence there distilled drops of music'* (John Buchan, *Greenmantle*; 1916) [14C. < Latin *distillare*, alteration of *destillare*, literally 'drip apart' < *stillare* 'to drip' < *stilla* 'drop'] —**distillable** *adj*

distill *vti* US spelling of **distil**

distillate /dístələt, -ayt/ *n* **1.** a concentrated liquid produced by boiling a liquid mixture and then condensing its vapour **2.** the concentrated essence of something

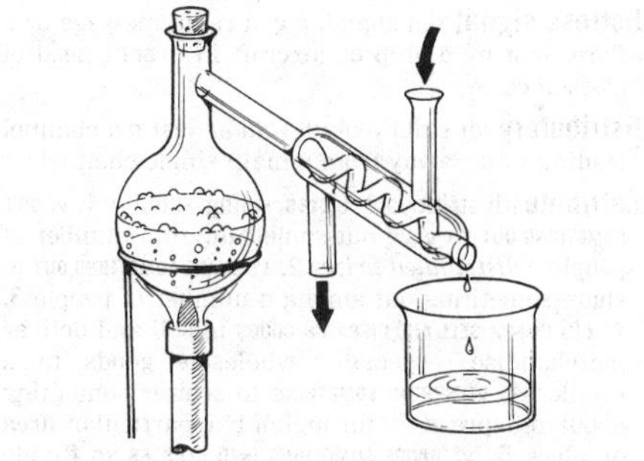

distillation: liquid is boiled (left) and the resulting vapour condensed (right)

distillation /dístə láysh'n/ *n* **1.** the process of separating, concentrating, or purifying liquid by boiling it and condensing the resulting vapour. Alcoholic spirits, such as whisky and vodka are made in this way. **2.** something that consists of the essential points, aspects, or implications of something larger or longer **3.** CHEM same as **distillate** (sense 1) —**distillatory** /di stíllətəri/ *adj*

distillation column *n* a hollow vertical column, fitted inside with perforated trays or packing material, in which liquid mixtures are separated into their components by boiling the mixture and condensing the resulting vapour

distilled /di stíld/ *adj* **1.** derived from or encapsulating a wider experience or larger set of ideas **2.** describes liquids that have been purified or concentrated by distillation

distiller /di stíllər/ *n* a person or company that produces alcoholic spirits such as whisky, vodka, and gin

distillery /di stílləri/ (*plural* **-ies**) *n* a place where strong alcoholic drinks such as whisky, vodka, and gin are made by distillation

distinct /di stíngkt/ *adj* **1.** CLEARLY DIFFERENT clearly different and separate from others ○ *The word has two distinct senses.* **2.** APPARENT TO SENSES easy to hear, see, smell, or understand ○ *I have a very distinct memory of that day.* **3.** CERTAIN definite or undeniable ○ *I had the distinct impression they'd been arguing.* **4.** NOTICEABLE strong enough, large enough, or definite enough to be noticed ○ *There's a distinct smell of petrol in the car.* **5.** EMPHATIC very great in degree, e.g. as an honour felt or experienced ○ *a distinct privilege* [14C. Directly or via French < Latin *distinctus*, past participle of *distinguere* 'to separate' (see DISTINGUISH)] —**distinctly** *adv* —**distinctness** *n*

distinction /di stíngksh'n/ *n* **1.** DIFFERENCE a difference between two or more people or things, or the recognition of such a difference **2.** HIGH QUALITY excellence in quality or talent ○ *tailors of distinction* **3.** SOMETHING TO BE PROUD OF something done or given as a mark of respect or honour ○ *I had the distinction of giving the opening address.* **4.** DISTINGUISHING FEATURE a feature or quality that characterizes or singles out somebody or something ○ *She has the dubious distinction of being the government's staunchest defender.* **5.** EDUC HIGH EXAMINATION GRADE a high mark in an examination

distinctive /di stíngktiv/ *adj* **1.** uniquely characteristic of a person, group, or thing **2.** describes a feature of a phoneme that can distinguish it from other similar phonemes, e.g. the fact that it is labial, fricative, or nasal —**distinctively** *adv* —**distinctiveness** *n*

distingué /di stáng gay/ *adj* having the confidence and dignity of somebody who is used to being respected (*formal*) [Early 19C. < French, past participle of *distinguer* (see DISTINGUISH)]

distinguish /di stíng gwish/ (**-guishes, -guishing, -guished**) *v* **1.** *vti* RECOGNIZE DIFFERENCES BETWEEN PEOPLE OR THINGS to be aware of a difference between two or more people, groups, or things, or show that they are different from each other ○ *to distinguish between fact and fiction* **2.** *vt* BE DIFFERENCE BETWEEN PEOPLE OR THINGS to be the feature or characteristic that shows that one person, group, or thing is different from another ○ *What distinguishes dogs from wolves?* **3.** *vt* MAKE SOMEBODY OR SOMETHING OUT to be able to recognize or identify somebody or something ○ *I could barely distinguish people's faces in the fog.* **4. distinguish yourself** *vr* PERFORM WELL AND ACHIEVE RECOGNITION to make yourself well known because of excellence, especially in a profession, art, or organization ○ *He distinguished himself on the field of battle.* [Late 16C. < French *distinguer* or Latin *distinguere* 'to separate' < *stinguere* 'quench'] —**distinguishable** *adj* —**distinguishably** *adv* —**distinguisher** *n*

distinguished /di stíng gwisht/ *adj* **1.** RECOGNIZED FOR EXCELLENCE well known and respected for an achievement, skill, knowledge, or talent ○ *a distinguished composer* **2.** CONFIDENT AND DIGNIFIED showing the confident and dignified appearance and manners of somebody who is used to respect **3.** SUCCESSFUL showing or involving a great deal of skill, talent, or success

Distinguished Conduct Medal *n* a medal awarded to noncommissioned officers, warrant officers, and ordinary soldiers and airmen and women in the British Army and Royal Air Force for distinguished conduct in action

Distinguished Flying Cross *n* **1.** a Royal Air Force medal awarded to noncommissioned and warrant officers for distinguished conduct when flying in action **2.** a US military medal awarded for extraordinary achievement or for heroism in air combat

Distinguished Service Cross *n* **1.** a British medal awarded in all branches of the armed forces for distinguished service in action **2.** a US Army medal awarded for extraordinary heroism against an enemy. It is the US Army's second highest award for bravery, the highest being the Congressional Medal of Honor.

Distinguished Service Medal *n* a British medal awarded for distinguished conduct in action to noncommissioned officers and ordinary seamen and women in the Royal Navy and Royal Marines

Distinguished Service Order *n* a British medal awarded to commissioned officers in all branches of the armed forces for distinguished service in action

distinguishing /di stíng gwishing/ *adj* allowing one person, group, or thing to be told apart from another ○ *distinguishing characteristics*

distort /di stáwrt/ (**-torts, -torting, -torted**) *v* **1.** *vti* ALTER SHAPE to bend, twist, stretch, or force something out of its usual or natural shape, or be made to do this **2.** *vt* GIVE INACCURATE REPORT OF SOMETHING to describe or report something in an inaccurate or misleading way **3.** *vt* MAKE SOMETHING UNCLEAR OR UNRECOGNIZABLE to change something such as an image in such a way that it becomes unclear or unrecognizable **4.** *vt* ELECTRONICS REPRODUCE SIGNAL INACCURATELY to amplify or reproduce something such as a radio or television signal inaccurately to the extent that it becomes unclear or unrecognizable [15C. < Latin *distort-*, past participle of *distorquere* 'twist completely' < *torquere* 'twist'] —**distorted** *adj* —**distorter** *n* —**distortive** *adj*

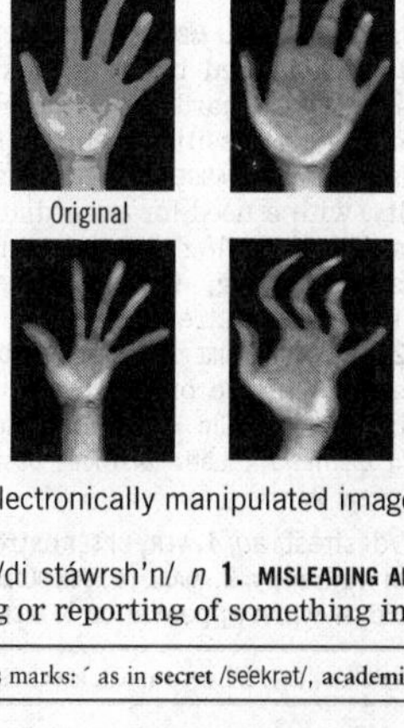

distortion: electronically manipulated images of a hand

distortion /di stáwrsh'n/ *n* **1.** MISLEADING ALTERATION the describing or reporting of something in a way that

is inaccurate or misleading **2.** **RECONFIGURATION FROM CORRECT SHAPE** the bending, twisting, stretching, or forcing of something out of its usual or natural shape **3.** **MISSHAPEN PART** a part of something that has been bent, twisted, stretched, or forced out of its usual or natural shape **4.** **ALTERATION FROM CLARITY** the altering of something such as a radio or television signal to the extent that it becomes unclear or unrecognizable **5.** OPTICS **ALTERATION IN OPTICAL IMAGE** an alteration in an image in which the original proportions are changed, resulting from a defect in a lens or optical system —**distortional** *adj* —**distortionary** *adj*

distr. *abbr* **1.** COMM, STATS, LOGIC distribution **2.** COMM, STATS, MATHS distributor

distract /di strákt/ (**-tracts, -tracting, -tracted**) *vt* **1.** **CATCH SOMEBODY'S ATTENTION** to take somebody's attention away from what he or she is doing or thinking or from what is happening **2.** **AMUSE SOMEBODY** to amuse or entertain somebody, especially as a means of taking his or her mind off something unpleasant **3.** **MAKE SOMEBODY UNEASY** to unsettle somebody's mind with disturbing, confusing, or conflicting emotions (*archaic*) ○ *'O Husband, Husband, my Heart long'd to see thee; but to see thee thus distracts me.'* (John Gay, *The Beggar's Opera*; 1728) [14C. < Latin *distract-*, past participle of *distrahere* 'draw away' < *trahere* 'draw, drag'] —**distractibility** /di stráktə bíllәti/ *n* —**distractible** *adj* —**distractive** *adj* —**distractively** *adv*

distracted /di stráktid/ *adj* **1.** showing a lack of concentration **2.** so worried or upset as to be unable to think clearly or act sensibly —**distractedly** *adv* —**distractedness** *n*

distracting /di strákting/ *adj* **1.** taking somebody's attention away from what he or she wants to do or ought to be doing **2.** helping somebody to relax and forget work or worries —**distractingly** *adv*

distraction /di stráksh'n/ *n* **1.** **SOMETHING THAT DIVERTS ATTENTION** something that interferes with concentration or takes attention away from something else **2.** **AMUSEMENT** something providing entertainment or amusement, especially something that takes the mind off work or worries and helps relaxation **3.** **EMOTIONAL UPSET** a state of great mental upset or emotional intensity ○ *Those pop-up Internet ads drive me to distraction.*

distractor /di stráktər/ *n* **1.** an incorrect option shown as a possible answer to a multiple-choice question **2.** a person or thing that distracts somebody's attention

distrain /di stráyn/ (**-trains, -training, -trained**) *vt* to seize somebody's moveable property either in lieu of payment of a debt or in order to force the person to pay [14C. < Old French *destreign-*, present stem of *destreindre* < Latin *distringere* 'draw asunder'] —**distrainable** *adj* —**distrainee** /di stráy neé/ *n* —**distrainer** *n* —**distrainment** *n*

distraint /di stráynt/ *n UK, Can* the seizing of somebody's movable property either in lieu of payment of a debt or in order to force the person to pay. ANZ, US term **distress** [Mid-18C. < DISTRAIN, after CONSTRAINT]

distrait /di stráy, dí stray/ *adj* inattentive and slightly distracted or absent-minded (*literary*) [14C. < French < past participle of Old French *destraire* 'distract' < Latin *distrahere* (see DISTRACT)]

distraught /di stráwt/ *adj* extremely upset and distressed [14C. Alteration of archaic *distract* 'perplexed' < Latin *distractus*, past participle of *distrahere* (see DISTRACT)] —**distraughtly** *adv*

distress /di stréss/ *n* **1.** **MENTAL SUFFERING** mental suffering, e.g. that caused by grief, anxiety, or unhappiness **2.** **HARDSHIP** hardship or problems caused by a lack of basic necessities **3.** **PHYSICAL PAIN** physical pain or discomfort **4.** **DANGER OR DIFFICULTY** great danger or difficulty, with a need for immediate assistance ○ *a ship in distress* **5.** *ANZ, US* LAW same as **distraint** ■ *vt* (**-tresses, -tressing, -tressed**) **1.** **UPSET SOMEBODY** to make somebody extremely upset, anxious, or alarmed **2.** **MAKE FURNITURE OR FABRIC LOOK OLD** to give a new piece of furniture or fabric an old or worn appearance [13C. Via Old French *destresce* < assumed Vulgar Latin *districtia* < Latin *district-*, past participle of *distringere* 'draw asunder']

distressed /di strést/ *adj* **1.** **VERY UPSET** extremely upset, anxious, or unhappy **2.** **MADE TO LOOK OLDER** artificially given an old or worn appearance **3.** **LACKING MONEY** not having enough money to live on (*dated*) **4.** *US* LAW **REPOSSESSED FROM BAD DEBTOR** repossessed by a bank or other lender from the borrower and offered for sale at a reduced price ○ *foreclosures and other distressed properties*

distressing /di stréssing/, **distressful** /-stréssf'l/ *adj* causing somebody to feel extremely upset —**distressingly** *adv*

distress signal *n* a signal, e.g. a radio message or a flare, sent by a ship or aircraft in urgent need of assistance

distributary /di stríbbyoŏtəri/ (*plural* **-ies**) *n* a channel leading water away from a main single channel

distribute /di stríbbyoot/ (**-utes, -uting, -uted**) *v* **1.** *vt* **GIVE SOMETHING OUT** to give out something to a number of people ○ *distributed prizes* **2.** *vt* **SHARE SOMETHING OUT** to share something out among a number of people **3.** *vt US* COMM **SELL AND DISPATCH GOODS** to sell and deliver merchandise, especially wholesale goods to a retailer **4.** *vt* **SPREAD SOMETHING** to scatter something about or spread it throughout a particular area or place **5.** *vt* **DIVIDE SOMETHING INTO CLASSES** to divide something up into different classes or categories **6.** *vt* LOGIC **MAKE TERM APPLY TO ALL** to apply a term to all the members of the class it designates **7.** *vti* MATHS **MAKE MATHEMATICAL OPERATION APPLY THROUGHOUT** to make an operation such as multiplication or division apply to each part of a mathematical expression [15C. < Latin *distribut-*, past participle of *distribuere* 'assign separately' < *tribuere* (see TRIBUTE)] —**distributable** *adj*

distributed /di stríbbyoŏtid/ *adj* describes computer systems in which two or more computers have a telecommunications link to each other but can also operate independently

distributer *n* another spelling of **distributor**

distribution /dístri byoósh'n/ *n* **1.** **GIVING OUT** the handing out or delivery of things to a number of people ○ *the distribution of leaflets* **2.** **SHARING OUT** the process of dividing up and giving out something shared by a number of people ○ *the distribution of wealth* **3.** **SCATTERING** the scattering or spreading of something over an area **4.** COMM **SELLING AND DELIVERY** the selling and delivery of goods to retailers **5.** COMPUT **SET OF RECIPIENTS** a topic-orientated controlled subset of the total number of potential recipients to which a message, article, or posting to a mailing list or newsgroup is sent **6.** ECOL **ENTIRE AREA WHERE SPECIES IS FOUND** the area or areas taken together where something is located or where a species lives and reproduces **7.** STATS **SPREAD OF STATISTICS** the spread of statistics within known or possible limits, especially in relation to the norm or to expectations **8.** LAW **SHARING OUT OF SOMEBODY'S ESTATE** the dividing up of the estate of somebody who has died intestate among people who are entitled to receive a share **9.** LOGIC **RECOMBINING OF TWO PROPOSITIONS** the recombining of two operations from one proposition in another equivalent proposition, e.g. 'p and (q or r)' is equivalent to '(p and q) or (p and r)' —**distributional** *adj*

distributive /di stríbbyoŏtiv/ *adj* **1.** **INVOLVING DISTRIBUTION** relating to or involving the handing out, sharing out, or scattering about of things **2.** GRAM **REFERRING TO EACH MEMBER OF GROUP** referring to each member of a set or group individually and separately. 'Each', 'every', and 'either' are examples of distributive words in English. **3.** LOGIC **REFERRING TO INDIVIDUALS, NOT CLASSES** referring to an individual member of a class, or to each member individually **4.** MATHS **PRODUCING EQUAL RESULTS** describes a mathematical expression with two operators whose expansion produces the same results whether operated on as a whole or as a sum of the parts ■ *n* GRAM **DISTRIBUTIVE WORD** a word that refers to every member of a set or group individually and separately —**distributively** *adv*

distributor /di stríbbyoŏtər/, **distributer** *n* **1.** **SOMEBODY WHO DISTRIBUTES SOMETHING** a person, organization, or device that distributes something **2.** COMM **WHOLESALER** a wholesaler who sells goods to retailers, usually within a specific geographical area **3.** AUTOMOT **DEVICE CONVEYING ELECTRICITY TO SPARK PLUGS** the device in a motor vehicle's engine that transfers electric current from the induction coil to the spark plugs **4.** CINEMA **ORGANIZATION ARRANGING SCREENING OF FILMS** an organization that advertises films and arranges with owners of cinemas to have them shown

district /dístrikt/ *n* **1.** an area of a town or country, especially one with a distinguishing feature or one that is an administrative division ○ *a fruit-growing district* **2.** the area around a place, e.g. the area around somebody's home or around a town [Early 17C. Via French < medieval Latin *districtus* '(area of) jurisdiction' < Latin *district-* (see DISTRESS)]

district attorney *n* in the United States, the prosecuting officer of a jurisdiction

district court *n* **1.** **SCOTTISH MAGISTRATES' COURT** in Scotland, a magistrates' court dealing with minor offences such as parking fines and nonpayment of debts **2.** **US DISTRICT TRIAL COURT** in the United States, the trial court in either a state or a federal district **3.** **AUSTRALIAN LOWER COURT** in some states of Australia, a court dealing with cases that are not important enough to be tried in a high court

district nurse *n* HEALTH SERVICES same as **community nurse** (*dated*)

District of Columbia /dístrikt əv kə lúmbi ə/ federal district of the United States, situated on the Potomac and Anacostia rivers, coextensive with the city of Washington, DC, the nation's capital. It was created in 1790–91. Area: 176 sq. km/68 sq. mi.

distringas /di stríng gəss, -gass/ *n* in former times, a court order instructing a sheriff to repossess somebody's property [15C. < medieval Latin, 'you shall distrain' (opening word of the writ), form of *distringere* 'draw asunder']

~~**distroy**~~ incorrect spelling of **destroy**

distrust /diss trúst/ *n* a feeling that somebody or something is dishonest or unreliable and does not deserve to be trusted ■ *vt* (**-trusts, -trusting, -trusted**) to have a feeling that somebody or something is dishonest or unreliable and does not deserve to be trusted —**distruster** *n* —**distrustful** *adj*

disturb /di stúrb/ (**-turbs, -turbing, -turbed**) *vt* **1.** **INTERRUPT SOMEBODY** to interrupt or distract somebody when he or she is doing something **2.** **UPSET SOMEBODY** to make somebody feel anxious or slightly troubled **3.** **CHANGE SHAPE OR POSITION** to move something so that it is not in its usual, expected, or correct position or shape ○ *Nothing on my desk had been disturbed.* **4.** **SPOIL PEACE AND QUIET** to spoil the quietness, stillness, or peacefulness of something **5.** **WAKEN SOMEBODY OR SOMETHING** to rouse a person or animal from sleep [12C. Directly or via French < Latin *disturbare* 'disturb completely' < *turbare* 'disturb'] —**disturber** *n* —**disturbing** *adj* —**disturbingly** *adv*

SYNONYMS See ***bother***.

disturbance /di stúrbənss/ *n* **1.** **COMMOTION** noisy and violent behaviour in a public place, or an incident involving such behaviour **2.** **DISRUPTION OF PEACE** the disruption of a peaceful or ordered environment, or something that causes such disruption **3.** **DISRUPTION OF CONCENTRATION** the disruption of somebody's concentration, or something that disrupts somebody's ability to get on with a task in hand **4.** **MOVEMENT FROM USUAL PLACE** the act of altering or moving something so that it is not in its usual, expected, or correct position or shape ○ *visible disturbance of the archaeological site* **5.** **MENTAL UPSET** psychological or emotional upset **6.** GEOL **EARTH TREMOR** a minor movement of the earth that falls short of an earthquake **7.** METEOROL **LOW-PRESSURE AREA** a small area of low pressure **8.** LAW **INTERFERENCE WITH SOMEBODY'S RIGHTS** an act that causes disruption to others or hinders them from pursuing normal legal activities

disturbance of the peace *n* a violation of public order that disrupts or destroys public tranquillity

disturbed /di stúrbd/ *adj* **1.** **ANXIOUS** worried or concerned **2.** **TROUBLED** unsettled and unhappy, with many troubles and upsets **3.** **AFFECTED BY PSYCHIATRIC DISORDER** affected by or displaying symptoms of psychiatric disorder

disulfiram /dī súlfi ram/ *n* a drug used in the treatment of alcoholism [Mid-20C. < *disulfide*, US spelling of DISULPHIDE + *thiuram*, a radical]

disulphide /dī súlfīd/ *n* a chemical compound that has two atoms of sulphur combined with one or more other elements

disunion /diss yoónyən/ *n* **1.** the splitting up of something into separate smaller parts or groups **2.** disagreement or discord

disunite /díssyoō nīt/ (**-nites, -niting, -nited**) *v* **1.** *vt* to create or be a source of disagreement between different people or factions within a group **2.** *vti* to divide something into smaller parts or groups, or become divided in this way —**disunited** *adj* —**disuniter** *n* —**disunity** *n*

disuse /diss yoōss/ *n* the fact or condition of not being used, applied, or followed, especially for a long time

disused /díss yoōzd/ *adj* no longer in use, or no longer used for its original purpose ○ *a disused airfield*

disvalue /diss vállyoo/ *vt* (**-ues, -uing, -ued**) same as **undervalue** (sense 1) ■ *n* negative worth or value

disyllable /dī síllab'l, di-/, **dissyllable** *n* **1.** a word composed of two syllables **2.** a two-syllable unit of rhythm in poetry —**disyllabic** /dī si lábbik, dí-/ *adj*

dit /dit/ *n* the spoken form of the short sound used in Morse and other telegraphic codes [Mid-20C. An imitation of the sound]

ditch /dich/ *n* **1.** NARROW CHANNEL a long narrow channel dug in the ground, usually used for drainage or irrigation but sometimes used as a boundary marker **2.** SMALL BROOK a small natural stream or brook ■ *v* (**ditches, ditching, ditched**) **1.** *vti* DIG DITCHES to enclose, drain, or irrigate an area with ditches **2.** *vti* MAKE EMERGENCY LANDING ON WATER to land, or make an aircraft land, on water in an emergency (*informal*) **3.** *vt* ABANDON SOMETHING OR SOMEBODY to abandon something or somebody as no longer wanted, liked, or needed (*informal*) [Old English *dīc* < Germanic, 'hole and mound produced by digging'] —**ditcher** *n*

ditchwater /dích wawtər/ *n* the dirty stagnant water found in ditches ○ *as dull as ditchwater*

ditheism /dīthi izəm, dī thée-/ *n* **1.** belief in two equal gods **2.** the belief that the world is ruled by two equal and opposing forces or gods, one good and one evil —**ditheist** *n* —**ditheistic** /dīthi ístik/ *adj*

dither /díthər/ *vi* (**-ers, -ering, -ered**) **1.** BE AGITATED AND INDECISIVE to behave in a nervous and indecisive way **2.** *regional* TREMBLE to tremble or quiver, e.g. with cold ■ *n* AGITATED OR INDECISIVE STATE a state of nervous agitation or indecisiveness [Mid-17C. Alteration of obsolete *didder* 'tremble, shake', origin ?] —**ditherer** *n* —**dithery** *adj*

dithering /díthəring/ *n* **1.** nervously confused indecisiveness in the face of alternative possible actions **2.** the mixing of pixels of several colours on a computer display to create the illusion of extra colours or shading

dithyramb /díthi ram, -ramb/ *n* **1.** a passionately emotional speech or piece of writing (*formal*) **2.** in ancient Greece, a wild and impassioned choral hymn, originally addressed to the god Dionysus [Early 17C. Via Latin < Greek *dithurambos*] —**dithyrambic** /díthi rámbik/ *adj*

ditransitive /dī tránssətiv/ *adj* describes a verb that requires both a direct and an indirect object, e.g. 'give' as in 'give the dog a bone'

ditsy /dítsi/ (**-sier, -siest**), **ditzy** (**-zier, -ziest**) *adj N Am* regarded as silly or scatterbrained (*slang*) [Late 20C. Origin ?]

dittany /díttəni/ (*plural* **-nies** or *same*) *n* **1.** an aromatic plant related to oregano and marjoram and cultivated as an ornamental and for its medicinal properties. Flowers: pink. Native to: southern Europe. Latin name: *Origanum dictamnus.* **2.** an aromatic plant cultivated in the United States as a kitchen herb. Latin name: *Cunila origanoides.* **3.** PLANTS same as **gas plant** [12C. < Old French *ditain*, medieval Latin *ditaneum* < Greek *diktamnon*]

ditto /díttō/ *interj* SAME HERE used instead of repeating something that has just been said to indicate that the same thing applies to you (*informal*) ○ *'I'm bored'. 'Ditto!'* ■ *adv* THE SAME THING APPLIES ELSEWHERE indicating that whatever has just been said about one person or thing applies equally to somebody or something else ○ *The car will need to be cleaned; ditto the children.* ■ *n* (*plural* **-tos**) SYMBOL REPRESENTING REPEATED MATTER a pair of marks (") that together represent matter that is repeated directly from what appears above them ■ *vt* (**-tos, -toing, -toed**) REPEAT SOMETHING to repeat or imitate something that somebody else has said or done [Early 17C. Via Tuscan dialect variant of Italian *detto* 'said' < Latin *dictus*, past participle of *dicere* 'say']

ditty /dítti/ (*plural* **-ties**) *n* a short simple popular song [14C. Via Old French *dité* 'composition' < Latin *dictatum* 'thing dictated' < *dictat-* (see DICTATE)]

ditty bag *n* **1.** a small canvas or leather bag used by men for holding small personal belongings **2.** *N Am* same as **sponge bag**

ditzy *adj* another spelling of **ditsy**

diuresis /dīyoō reésiss/ *n* increased excretion of urine caused by excessive intake of fluids, a drug, or a disease [Late 17C. < modern Latin, literally 'urination through' < Greek *ourēsis* 'urination']

diuretic /dīyoō réttik/ *adj* causing increased flow of urine [14C. Via late Latin < Greek *diourētikos* < *diourein*, literally 'urinate through' < *ourein* 'urinate'] —**diuretic** *n* —**diuretically** *adv*

diurnal /dī úrn'l/ *adj* **1.** IN DAYTIME happening during the day as opposed to at night **2.** DAILY happening every day **3.** SCI VARYING WITHIN DAY varying within the course of a single day **4.** ZOOL ACTIVE IN DAYTIME describes animals that are active during the day rather than at night **5.** BOT OPEN ONLY IN DAYTIME describes flowers that open during the day and close at night ■ *n* CHR ROMAN CATHOLIC BOOK FOR WORSHIP in the Roman Catholic Church, a book containing the prayer and worship material for all the set daily services except matins [14C. < late Latin *diurnalis* < Latin *diurnus* 'daily' < *dies* 'day'] —**diurnally** *adv*

diurnal parallax *n* the change in an astronomical object's apparent position caused by the change in the observer's position because of the motion of Earth during a day

div /div/ *n* an offensive term that deliberately insults somebody's intelligence (*slang insult*) [Late 20C. Origin]

div. *abbr* **1.** MIL diversion **2.** MATHS divide **3.** FIN dividend **4.** MATHS division **5.** SOC SCI divorced

diva /deévə/ (*plural* **-vas** or **-ve** /-vay/) *n* **1.** a distinguished woman singer, especially one who sings in operas **2.** a successful woman performer [Late 19C. Via Italian < Latin, 'goddess']

divagate /dīvə gayt/ (**-gates, -gating, -gated**) *vi* (*literary*) **1.** to wander off the subject under discussion **2.** to wander about somewhere [Mid-16C. < Latin *divagat-*, past participle of *divagari* 'wander about' < *vagari* 'wander'] —**divagation** /dīvə gáysh'n/ *n*

divalent /dī váylənt/ *adj* having a valency of 2

Divali *n* HINDUISM another spelling of **Diwali**

divan /di ván/ *n* **1.** BED a bed with no headboard or footboard, especially one with solid sides fitted with feet or castors instead of legs **2.** BACKLESS SOFA a sofa without a back, and sometimes without arms **3.** ISLAMIC COURTROOM OR OTHER CHAMBER in some Islamic countries, a courtroom, council chamber, or other official hall **4.** SMOKING ROOM in former times, a smoking room attached to a coffee shop or cigar shop **5.** LITERAT ARABIC POEMS a collection of poems written in Persian or Arabic, often by a single poet [Late 16C. Via French or Italian < Turkish *dīvān* < Persian *dīvān*]

divaricate /dī várri kayt, di-/ (**-cates, -cating, -cated**) *vi* to branch or fork at a wide angle [Early 17C. < Latin *divaricat-*, past participle of *divaricare* 'stretch apart' < *varicus* 'straddling'] —**divaricate** *adj* —**divaricately** *adv* —**divaricatingly** *adv*

divarication /dī várri káysh'n, di-/ *n* **1.** WIDE BRANCHING separation into widely spread parts or branches **2.** FORK the point at which something forks or branches **3.** DISAGREEMENT a difference of opinion (*formal*)

dive /dīv/ *v* (**dives, diving, dived**) **1.** *vi* JUMP HEAD FIRST INTO WATER to jump or throw yourself into water head first, especially with your arms stretched out above your head **2.** *vi* PERFORM ACROBATIC JUMPS INTO WATER to perform a pattern of acrobatic movements in the air ending in a headfirst plunge into water, especially as a sport **3.** *vi* SWIM UNDER WATER to swim below the surface of a stretch of water, often with special breathing apparatus **4.** *vi* GO TOWARDS BOTTOM OF WATER to go down steeply and quickly towards the bottom of a body of water, sometimes in search of something **5.** *vi* DESCEND STEEPLY AND RAPIDLY to fly or make an aircraft fly steeply and rapidly in the direction of the ground or the sea **6.** *vi* THROW YOURSELF TO GROUND to jump quickly to one side or throw yourself forwards or sideways to the ground ○ *dive out of the way* **7.** *vi* MOVE FAST to move quickly and in a rush in a particular direction ○ *dive for the door* **8.** *vti* PUT HAND IN SOMETHING to put your hand or hands quickly into something such as a pocket or a cupboard, in order to get something out of it ○ *dived into the drawer to retrieve her ID card* **9.** *vi* BEGIN SOMETHING ENTHUSIASTICALLY to undertake or start on some activity with great enthusiasm ○ *He dived into the project.* **10.** *vti* CAUSE SUBMARINE TO DESCEND to cause a submarine to go below the surface of the sea **11.** *vi* DROP IN VALUE to fall sharply in value ■ *n* **1.** HEADLONG JUMP INTO WATER a jump into water head first, especially with your arms stretched out above your head **2.** ACROBATIC PLUNGE an acrobatic plunge into water performed as a sport or in a competition **3.** ACT OF SWIMMING UNDER WATER a swim below the surface of a stretch of water, often with special breathing apparatus **4.** DESCENT TOWARDS BOTTOM OF WATER a steep and usually rapid descent in the direction of the bottom of a body of water **5.** STEEP DESCENT THROUGH AIR a bird's or aircraft's rapid and steep fall or flight in the direction of the ground or the sea **6.** SUBMARINE'S DESCENT a submarine's descent below the surface of the sea **7.** QUICK MOVEMENT SIDEWAYS OR DOWN a quick jump or movement to one side, forwards, or sideways to the ground **8.** FAST MOVEMENT a rapid movement in a particular direction **9.** SHARP FINANCIAL DROP a sharp fall in value **10.** DISREPUTABLE ESTABLISHMENT a dirty, shabby, or disreputable place, e.g. a bar or club (*informal*) **11.** SOCCER FOOTBALLER'S FALL in football, a feigned dramatic fall by a player to try to gain a free kick or penalty (*informal*) **12.** SOCCER GOALKEEPER'S SAVE in football, a goalkeeper's attempt to stretch horizontally to save a shot (*informal*) **13.** BOXING BOXER'S FEIGNED FALL in boxing, a fall or injury feigned by a fighter in order to lose a fight dishonestly (*slang*) ■ ARTS plural of **diva** [Old English *dūfan* 'to sink', *dȳfan* 'to dip' < Germanic]

dive in *vi* to begin eating quickly and with gusto (*informal*)

dive-bomb *vt* to descend steeply in a military aircraft and deliver bombs onto a target —**dive-bomber** *n* —**dive-bombing** *n*

dive brake *n* same as **air brake** (sense 2)

Divehi /dívvè i/ *n* LANG same as **Maldivian** (sense 2) [< Divehi] —**Divehi** *adj*

diver /dīvər/ *n* **1.** SOMEBODY WHO DIVES IN WATER somebody who goes under the surface of water for work or recreation **2.** NORTHERN WATER BIRD a water bird belonging to a family that is skilled in swimming and diving. Native to: northern hemisphere. Family: Gaviidae. N Am term **loon**[1] **3.** DIVING WATER BIRD any water bird noted for its diving skills

diverge /dī vúrj/ (**-verges, -verging, -verged**) *vi* **1.** SEPARATE to separate and go in a different direction or different directions **2.** DIFFER to differ to some extent **3.** NOT CONFORM to deviate from or not fit in with something such as a typical pattern or expressed wish [Mid-17C. < medieval Latin *divergere* 'bend apart' < Latin *vergere* 'bend'] —**diverging** *adj*

divergence /dī vúrjənss/, **divergency** /-jənssi/ (*plural* **-cies**) *n* **1.** DIFFERENCE OR DISPARITY a difference between two or more things such as opinions or attitudes **2.** FAILURE TO CONFORM OR MATCH deviation from something such as a typical pattern or expressed wish **3.** MOVING APART the process of separating or moving apart to follow different paths or different courses **4.** AMOUNT OF DIFFERENCE the amount by which something differs from something else, especially where such a difference is not expected **5.** OPHTHALMOL DEVIATION OF EYE FROM SIGHT LINE a condition in which only one eye is directed at the object of interest and the other is directed outwards **6.** BIOL DIFFERENT DEVELOPMENT OF RELATED ORGANISMS the development of different characteristics by organisms that come from the same ancestor, caused by the influence of different environments **7.** MATHS SEQUENCE OF NUMBERS WITHOUT LIMIT the characteristic of a series or sequence of numbers in which the value of the last term and the sum of the series are without limit **8.** METEOROL MOVEMENT OF AIR CURRENTS a set of meteorological conditions in a given area in which the air expands and the net flow of air is out of the area, usually resulting in fair dry conditions

divergent /dī vúrjənt/ *adj* **1.** MOVING APART following paths or courses that become increasingly different or separate **2.** DIFFERING showing or having differences

3. NOT MATCHING SOMETHING deviating from something such as a typical pattern or an expressed wish **4.** MATHS **INCREASING WITHOUT LIMIT** describes a series or sequence of numbers in which each term is equal to or greater than the preceding term, and the value of the last term and the sum of the series are without limit **5.** MATHS **RADIATING FROM POINT** describes lines radiating from a single point —**divergently** *adv*

diverging lens /dī vúrjing-/ *n* a lens, usually concave, that causes a parallel beam of light to spread

divers /dīvərz/ *adj* more than one, and of various types (*literary*) [13C. Via French < Latin *diversus*, past participle of *divertere* 'separate' (see DIVERT)]

diverse /dī vúrss, dí vurss/ *adj* **1.** made up of many differing parts ○ *culturally diverse* **2.** very different or distinct from one another ○ *a person with diverse interests* [13C. Variant of DIVERS] —**diversely** *adv* —**diverseness** *n*

diversify /dī vúrssi fī/ (**-fies, -fying, -fied**) *vti* **1.** to become more varied, or make something more varied **2.** to expand into new areas of business, or expand a commercial organization into new areas [15C. Via Old French *diversifier* < medieval Latin *diversificare* 'make unlike' < Latin *diversus* (see DIVERS)] —**diversifiability** /dī vúrssi fī ə bílləti/ *n* —**diversifiable** *adj* —**diversification** /dī vúrssifi káysh'n/ *n* —**diversified** *adj* —**diversifier** *n*

diversion /dī vúrsh'n/ *n* **1.** **DISTRACTION** something that takes somebody's attention away from something else **2.** **ALTERNATIVE ROUTE** a route to be taken by traffic as an alternative to the normal route, when the normal route cannot be used. N Am term **detour 3.** **CHANGE OF PURPOSE** a change in the purpose or use of something from what was intended or from what it was previously **4.** **CHANGE OF DIRECTION** a change in the direction or path of something **5.** **PASTIME** an activity or interest that takes somebody's mind off more routine or serious things **6.** MIL **MOCK ATTACK** a mock attack aimed at drawing enemy attention and troops away from the place of the intended main attack [15C. Directly or via French < late Latin *diversion-* 'turning away' < Latin *diversus* (see DIVERS)] —**diversional** *adj*

diversionary /dī vúrsh'nəri/ *adj* designed or carried out to divert somebody's attention away from something

diversity /dī vúrssəti/ (*plural* **-ties**) *n* **1.** a variety of something such as opinion, colour, or style ○ *a city of great cultural diversity* **2.** discrepancy, or a difference from what is normal or expected [14C. Via French < Latin *diversitas* < *diversus* (see DIVERS)]

divert /dī vúrt/ (**-verts, -verting, -verted**) *vt* **1.** **CHANGE SOMETHING'S PATH** to change the route or path taken by something such as traffic or a river **2.** **DRAW ATTENTION FROM SOMETHING** to take somebody's mind off something and draw attention to something else **3.** **CHANGE PURPOSE OR USE** to change the purpose or use of something from what it was previously **4.** **AMUSE SOMEBODY** to amuse or entertain somebody [15C. Via French *divertir* < Latin *divertere* 'turn aside' < *vertere* 'turn'] —**diverter** *n*

diverticula ANAT plural of **diverticulum**

diverticulitis /dīvər tikyoō lītiss/ *n* inflammation of protrusions (**diverticula**) of the lining of the large intestine, causing severe abdominal pain, often with fever and constipation

diverticulosis /dīvər tikyoō lṓsiss/ *n* the presence of protrusions (**diverticula**) in the bowel, caused when the bowel muscles rupture the bowel wall

diverticulum /dīvər tíkyoōləm/ (*plural* **-la** /-lə/) *n* a pouch or sac in the lining of the mucous membrane of a hollow organ, especially one produced in the bowel when the bowel muscle ruptures the bowel wall [Mid-17C. < medieval Latin, 'byway', variant of Latin *deverticulum* < *vertere* 'to turn'] —**diverticular** *adj*

divertimento /di vúrti méntō/ (*plural* **-ti** /-ti/) *n* a piece of light classical instrumental music composed in several movements for an ensemble [Mid-18C. < Italian, 'diversion' < *divertire* 'divert' < Latin *divertere* (see DIVERT)]

diverting /dī vúrting/ *adj* amusing or entertaining, and acting as a temporary distraction from more routine or serious matters —**divertingly** *adv*

divertissement /di vúrtiss moN/ *n* **1.** BALLET **SERIES OF UNTHEMED DANCES** in a ballet, a dance highlighting a dancer's skill rather than developing the story **2.** DANCE **DANCE INTERLUDE** a dance interlude in a play or opera **3.** MUSIC **TUNES DERIVED FROM FAMOUS MELODIES** a set of tunes that are based on well-known melodies [Early 18C. < French < *divertiss-*, stem of *divertir* 'divert' (see DIVERT)]

divest /dī vést/ (**-vests, -vesting, -vested**) *vt* **1.** **TAKE SOMETHING AWAY FROM SOMEBODY** to take away something, especially status or power, from somebody or something (*often passive*) ○ *The report divested the organization of its mystique.* **2.** **MAKE SOMEBODY GIVE UP SOMETHING** to rid somebody or yourself of something, especially a belief or idea ○ *divested herself of the notion* **3.** **MAKE SOMEBODY TAKE SOMETHING OFF** to remove something, usually clothes, from somebody or yourself (*formal or humorous*) ○ *divested himself of his coat* **4.** LAW **GIVE AWAY PROPERTY RIGHTS** to lose or give away rights to the possession of property, or deprive somebody of them [Early 17C. Alteration of obsolete *devest* 'deprive' < Old French *de(s)vester* 'undress' < *vestir* 'clothe' < Latin *vestire*] —**divestment** *n* —**divesture** *n*

divestiture /dī véstichər/ *n* **1.** the removal or deprivation of something **2.** *US* the sale of one or more of a company's subsidiaries, divisions, or holdings, or of its stock in those holdings

divi *n* FIN another spelling of **divvy**[2] *n* (sense 1)

divide /di vīd/ *v* (**-vides, -viding, -vided**) **1.** *vti* **SPLIT INTO PARTS** to separate or split something into two or more parts, or be separated or split into parts ○ *a dormitory divided into cubicles* **2.** *vi* **GO IN DIFFERENT DIRECTIONS** to split into two or more parts that go off in different directions **3.** *vti* **SHARE SOMETHING** to share something between two or more people or groups, or be shared ○ *divide the spoils of war* **4.** *vt* **SEPARATE TWO PLACES** to be a barrier or boundary between one place or thing and another ○ *The river divides the north of the island from the south.* **5.** *vt* **CAUSE DISAGREEMENT BETWEEN PEOPLE** to be the cause or subject of disagreement between people ○ *The zoning proposals are dividing the community.* **6.** *vt* **SEPARATE SOMEBODY FROM ANOTHER** to cause somebody to be apart from somebody else, or cause people to be apart ○ *The war divided them from their parents.* **7.** *vt* MEASURE **MARK SOMETHING OFF** to mark units or sections of a particular size on a measuring instrument such as a ruler **8.** *vt* MATHS **CALCULATE OCCURRENCE OF ONE NUMBER IN ANOTHER** to calculate how many times one number contains another **9.** *vi* MATHS **BE DIVISIBLE** to be able to be divided by a particular number without a remainder **10.** *vi* POL **VOTE** to vote on an issue by separating into two groups, one for and one against, inside a legislative chamber ■ *n* **1.** **BOUNDARY OR GAP** a boundary or gap that stands between two things, conditions, or groups **2.** *N Am* GEOG same as **watershed** (sense 1) [14C. < Latin *dividere* 'separate apart' < *-videre* 'to separate'] —**dividable** *adj*

divide up *vti* to divide, or divide something, into several parts

SYNONYMS See *share*[1].

divided /di vīdid/ *adj* **1.** **SEPARATED** separated into two or more parts or groups **2.** **IN TWO MINDS** drawn towards two or more different and often incompatible purposes or groups ○ *divided loyalties* **3.** **IN DISAGREEMENT** in a state of internal discord, strife, or disagreement ○ *remained deeply divided over the issue* **4.** BOT **SEPARATED INTO SECTIONS** describes leaves that are split into separate sections —**dividedly** *adv* —**dividedness** *n*

divided highway *n N Am* same as **dual carriageway**

divided road *n Aus* same as **dual carriageway**

divided skirt *n* CLOTHING same as **culottes**

dividend /dívvi dend/ *n* **1.** **BONUS** something good or desirable that is gained as a bonus along with something else **2.** FIN **SHAREHOLDER'S SHARE OF PROFIT** company profits paid pro rata to shareholders, either in cash or in more shares **3.** FIN **PAYMENT TO COOPERATIVE'S CUSTOMER** a payment made periodically to the members of a cooperative commercial organization, usually in proportion to the amount the member spends **4.** MATHS **NUMBER DIVIDED BY ANOTHER** a number or quantity that is to be divided by another number or quantity **5.** LAW **PROPORTION OF BANKRUPT'S ESTATE** the proportion of a bankrupt party's estate that is to be divided among the creditors [15C. Via Anglo-Norman < Latin *dividendum* 'thing to be divided', form of *dividere* (see DIVIDE)]

divider /di vīdər/ *n* a device that separates something into sections, e.g. a screen that partitions a room or a sheet of card that separates the sections of a loose-leaf binder ■ **dividers** *npl* an instrument with two movable pointed legs hinged at one end, used for measuring distances on maps and charts and for transferring measurements from one map or chart to another

dividing line /di vīding-/ *n* something that marks a change or distinction between two states or qualities

divi-divi /dívvi dívvi/ (*plural* **divi-divis** or *same*) *n* **1.** a long seed pod that has a high tannin content. Use: tanning leather. **2.** a small tropical American tree that produces divi-divis. Latin name: *Caesalpinia coriaria*. [Mid-19C. Via American Spanish < Carib]

divination /dívvi náysh'n/ *n* **1.** **SEEKING KNOWLEDGE BY SUPERNATURAL MEANS** the methods or practice of attempting to foretell the future or discovering the unknown through omens, oracles, or supernatural powers **2.** **PROPHECY** a prophecy or prediction **3.** **PREMONITION** a premonition or feeling of foreboding about something that is going to happen —**divinatory** /di vínnətəri/ *adj*

divine /di vīn/ *adj* **1.** **HAVING GODLIKE NATURE** being God or a god or goddess **2.** **RELATING TO GOD, GODS, OR GODDESSES** connected with, coming from, or caused by God or a god or goddess **3.** **CONNECTED WITH WORSHIP** relating to the worship or service of God or a god or goddess **4.** **LOVELY** pleasing, attractive, or well performed (*informal*) ■ *v* (**-vines, -vining, -vined**) **1.** *vt* **REALIZE SOMETHING** to come to understand or realize something **2.** *vt* **DISCOVER SOMETHING AS IF SUPERNATURALLY** to learn or discover something by intuition, inspiration, or other apparently supernatural means **3.** *vt* **PREDICT SOMETHING AS IF SUPERNATURALLY** to predict something by apparently supernatural means **4.** *vti* **SEARCH WITH DIVINING ROD** to search for underground water, metal, or minerals using something such as a divining rod ■ *n* **1.** **THEOLOGIAN** a member of the clergy, especially one who is knowledgeable about theology **2.** *also* **Divine GOD** God, or an underlying creative and sustaining force in the universe [14C. Via French < Latin *divinus* < *divus* 'god'] —**divinable** *adj* —**divinely** *adv* —**divineness** *n* —**diviner** *n*

CULTURAL NOTE ***The Divine Comedy***, an epic poem (1307?–20?) by Italian poet Dante Alighieri. Generally considered to be Dante's masterpiece, it is an account of the poet's journey through Hell, Purgatory, and Paradise, rich in historical, scientific, and philosophical allusion. The poet Virgil, representing Reason, is Dante's guide in the first two sections of the work; in the final section his guide is Beatrice, an idealization of the girl he loved in his youth.

divine right *n* the belief that the monarch's authority comes directly from God rather than from the people

diving beetle /dīving-/ *n* a predatory water beetle adapted for swimming that has flattened hind legs and the capacity to breathe air trapped under its wings. Family: Dytiscidae.

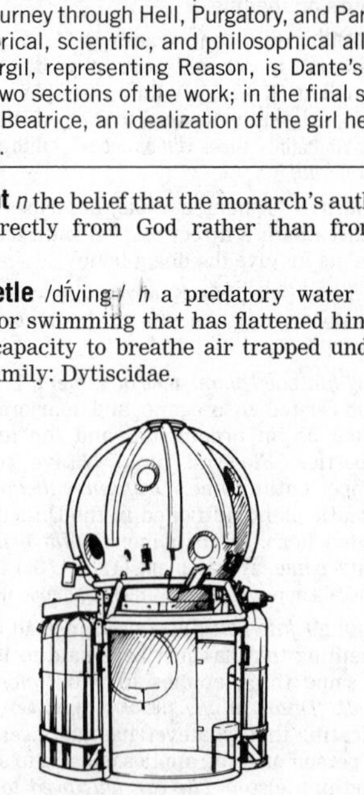

diving bell

diving bell *n* a metal device used for working underwater that has an open bottom and is supplied with compressed air

diving board *n* a raised board at the edge of a swimming pool from which to dive into the water

diving dress *n* SWIMMING same as **diving suit**

diving duck *n* a duck that dives for food and swims under water

diving reflex *n* a reflex in mammals in which the heart rate slows and blood vessels of the skin narrow on immersion in cold water to conserve oxygen. The reflex is strongest in water animals such as seals, but is still present to a minor extent in nonaquatic animals, including humans.

diving suit *n* a waterproof suit, often including a helmet and an air supply, worn by divers

divining rod /di víning-/ *n* a forked stick used as a device for sensing underground water sources or minerals. The diviner holds an end of the rod in each hand, and the rod is said to dip sharply downwards when the diviner walks over a water source or minerals.

divinise *vt* RELIG another spelling of **divinize**

divinity /di vínnəti/ (*plural* **-ties**) *n* **1. QUALITY OF BEING GOD** the quality associated with being God, a god, or a goddess **2.** *also* **Divinity GOD** God, a god, or a goddess **3. THEOLOGY** the study of religion, especially the Christian religion [13C. Via French < Latin *divinitas* 'godhead, divinity' < *divinus* (see DIVINE)]

divinize /dívvi nīz/ (**-izes, -izing, -ized**), **divinise** (**-ises, -ising, -ised**) *vt* to regard a person, being, or object as a god or goddess —**divinization** /dívvi nī záysh'n/ *n*

divisible /di vízzəb'l/ *adj* **1.** able to be divided, especially without leaving a remainder **2.** capable of being separated into different parts [15C. Directly or via French < late Latin *divisibilis* < Latin *divis-* (see DIVISION)] —**divisibility** /di vízzə bílləti/ *n* —**divisibly** *adv*

division /di vízh'n/ *n* **1. SPLITTING INTO PARTS** the act of separating or splitting something into parts, or an instance of this ○ *the division of the region into smaller administrative districts* **2. SHARING OUT OF SOMETHING** the separation of something into parts to be shared out among people or groups ○ *the division of work among members of the group* **3. DISAGREEMENT** a disagreement or strong difference of opinion, especially when this leads to a split in a group ○ *Deep divisions exist within senior management about dealing with the problem.* **4. SOMETHING SEPARATING** something that separates things by forming a boundary between them **5. SEPARATE PART** one of the parts created when something is split **6.** MATHS **DIVIDING ONE NUMBER BY ANOTHER** an operation used to calculate the number of times one number is contained in another **7. SECTION OF ORGANIZATION** a section of a large organization that has a specific task or function ○ *the sales division* **8.** SPORTS **GROUP OF TEAMS** a group of teams of roughly similar standard in a sports league **9.** MIL **ARMY UNIT** a self-contained military unit capable of sustained operations, including a headquarters and two or more brigades in an army or several regiments in the Marines **10.** NAVY **NAVAL UNIT** a self-contained unit in a navy including a group of ships of the same class **11.** AIR FORCE **AIR FORCE UNIT** a self-contained unit in an air force including two or more fighter wings **12.** PUBLIC ADMIN **GOVERNMENT UNIT** a small unit of government **13.** PUBLIC ADMIN **ADMINISTRATIVE AREA** an area administered by a particular government unit **14.** POL **PARLIAMENTARY VOTE** a vote in the British Parliament or a similar legislative body **15.** BOT **CATEGORY IN PLANT CLASSIFICATION** a major category in the taxonomic classification of plants, comprising a group of classes. The corresponding category in animal classification is the phylum. **16.** BOT **SPLITTING OF ROOTS FOR PROPAGATION** the process of separating the root mass of a perennial plant into smaller pieces that are used to grow new plants **17.** BIOL same as **cell division 18.** LOGIC **LOGICAL FALLACY** a fallacy in which it is argued that what is true of a whole collectively is true of any of its parts. An example is the argument that because a car is expensive, so is its windscreen wiper. **19.** MUSIC **GROUP OF ORGAN STOPS** a group of organ stops played on the same manual [14C. Via French < Latin *division-* < *divis-*, past participle of *dividere* (see DIVIDE)] —**divisional** *adj* —**divisionally** *adv* —**divisionary** *adj*

division bell *n* a bell rung in the House of Commons when it is time for Members of Parliament to vote

divisionism /di vízhənizəm/ *n* a late-19th-century style of painting in which unmixed colour is applied to the canvas in small dots that from a distance form recognizable shapes and colour tones. Like pointillism, which it closely resembles, divisionism was a development of the impressionist style. —**divisionist** *n, adj*

division lobby *n* POL same as **lobby** *n* (sense 3)

division of labour *n* a system of organizing production by giving separate tasks to separate workers or groups of workers

division sign *n* a sign (÷) placed between two numbers to show that the first number is divided by the second

divisive /di víssiv/ *adj* causing disagreement or hostility within a group so that it is likely to split [Late 16C. < late Latin *divisivus* < Latin *divis-* (see DIVISION)] —**divisively** *adv* —**divisiveness** *n*

divisor /di vízər/ *n* a number divided into another number [15C. Directly or via French < Latin < *divis-* (see DIVISION)]

divorce /di váwrss/ *n* **1. OFFICIAL ENDING OF MARRIAGE** an ending of a marriage by an official decision in a court of law **2. SEPARATION** a complete separation or split ○ *a divorce between theory and practice* ■ *v* (**-vorces, -vorcing, -vorced**) **1.** *vti* **OFFICIALLY END MARRIAGE** to end a marriage to somebody by an official decision in a court of law **2.** *vt* **SEPARATE SOMETHING** to separate or distinguish something from something else ○ *divorced truth from speculation* [14C. Via French < Latin *divortium* < *divortere*, variant of *divertere* 'part, turn aside' (see DIVERT)] —**divorced** *adj*

divorcé /di váwr sée, -váwrss ay/ *n US* a man who is divorced [Late 19C. < French < past participle of *divorcer* 'divorce' < Latin *divortium* (see DIVORCE)]

divorcee /di váwr sée/ *n* somebody who is divorced [Late 19C. < DIVORCE + -EE]

divorcée /di váwr sée, -váwrss ay/ *n US* a woman who is divorced [Early 19C. < French < feminine of *divorcé* (see DIVORCÉ)]

divot /dívvət/ *n* a small lump of grass and earth accidentally dug out of the ground while playing a sport, especially golf [Early 16C. Origin ?]

divulge /dī vúlj/ (**-vulges, -vulging, -vulged**) *vt* to reveal information, especially information that was previously secret [15C. < Latin *divulgare* 'make widely known to the masses' < *vulgus* 'masses'] —**divulgement** *n* —**divulgence** *n* —**divulger** *n*

divvy[1] /dívvi/ (*plural* **-vies**) *n* an offensive term that deliberately insults somebody's intelligence (*slang insult*) [Late 20C. Origin ?]

divvy[2] /dívvi/ (*informal*) *vt* (**-vies, -vying, -vied**) same as **divvy up** ■ *n* (*plural* **-vies**) **1.** *also* **divi** (*plural* **divis**) a dividend or share of the profits given to members of a cooperative **2.** *N Am* somebody's share of something [Late 19C. Shortening of DIVIDEND]

divvy up *vt* to divide something up and share it out among a group of people (*informal*)

Diwali /di wáali/, **Divali** *n* a Hindu festival associated with Lakshmi, the goddess of prosperity, during which lamps are lit. Date: autumn. [Late 17C. Via Hindi *diwālī* < Sanskrit *dīpāvalī* 'row of lights' < *dīpa* 'light, lamp']

diwan /di wáan/, **dewan** *n S Asia* a senior government official in India, especially the prime minister of a state [Late 17C. Via Urdu < Persian *dīwān* 'fiscal register']

Dix /diks/, **Otto** (1891–1969) German painter and etcher. His work depicts the horrors of World War I and the decadence of German society in its aftermath.

> 'I have never made written confessions, since, as you will see if you inspect them, my pictures are confessions of the most candid sort such as you will rarely find in this age...He who has eyes to see, let him see!'
> [Otto Dix. Quoted in *Otto Dix: Life and Work*, Fritz Löffler; 1982]

dixie /díksi/ *n* a metal cooking pot used for making tea, e.g. by soldiers [Early 20C. < Hindi *degcī*]

Dixie /díksi/ *n US* the southern states that were members of the Confederacy during the American Civil War (*informal*) [Mid-19C. Origin ?]

Dixieland /díksi land/, **dixieland** *n* a style of jazz, originally from New Orleans, characterized by a fast two-beat rhythm and simultaneous improvisation [Early 20C. < *Original Dixieland Jazz Band*, the first jazz band to record commercially]

Dixon /díks'n/, **Sir Owen** (1886–1972) Australian lawyer. He was the chief justice of the High Court of Australia (1952–64) and an authority on constitutional law.

DIY[1], **d.i.y.** *n* the activity of doing repairs and alterations in the home yourself, especially as a hobby, instead of employing tradespeople to do the work. Full form **do-it-yourself** —**DIYer** *n*

DIY[2] *abbr* ONLINE do it yourself (*used in e-mails or text messages*)

diya /dée yə/ *n S Asia* a small oil lamp made from baked clay [< Hindi *dīyā*]

Diyarbakir /di yáar bu keer/ city and capital of Diyarbakir Province in southeastern Turkey. Population: 479,884 (1997).

Diyari *n, adj* LANG another spelling of **Dieri**

dizygotic /dī zī góttik/, **dizygous** /dī zígəss/ *adj* describes twins derived from two separately fertilized eggs (**zygotes**). ◊ **monozygotic**

dizzy /dízzi/ *adj* (**-zier, -ziest**) **1. UNSTEADY AND GIDDY** unsteady, as if about to lose balance, and slightly giddy **2. EXTREME** so high as to make somebody giddy ○ *the dizzy height of the tower* **3. CONFUSED AND BEWILDERED** confused, overwhelmed, and unable to think clearly **4. FAST** extremely fast ○ *dizzy speeds* **5. FUN-LOVING BUT THOUGHTLESS** fun-loving and rather silly or empty-headed (*informal*) ■ *vt* (**-zies, -zying, -zied**) **CAUSE SOMEBODY TO FEEL DIZZY** to cause somebody to feel unsteady, giddy, confused, or bewildered [Old English *dysig* 'foolish, stupid' < Germanic] —**dizzily** *adv* —**dizziness** *n* —**dizzying** *adj* —**dizzyingly** *adv*

dj *abbr* Djibouti (*used in Internet addresses*) See table at **domain name**

DJ[1] *n* **1.** somebody who plays records or other recorded music, e.g. at a live dance or on the radio. Full form **disc jockey 2.** somebody who composes rap or techno music using samples of recorded music [Abbreviation of DISC JOCKEY] —**DJ** *vi*

DJ[2] *abbr* CLOTHING dinner jacket (*informal*)

djebel *n* GEOG another spelling of **jebel**

djellaba /jə láabə/, **djellabah** *n* a long loose-fitting robe with sleeves and a hood, worn especially in Islamic countries [Early 19C. < Moroccan Arabic *jellāb(a)*, *jelläbiyya*]

Djerba /júrbə/ island in southeastern Tunisia, lying in the Gulf of Gabes in the Mediterranean Sea. Population: 92,269 (1984). Area: 510 sq. km/197 sq. mi.

DJIA *abbr* FIN Dow Jones Industrial Average

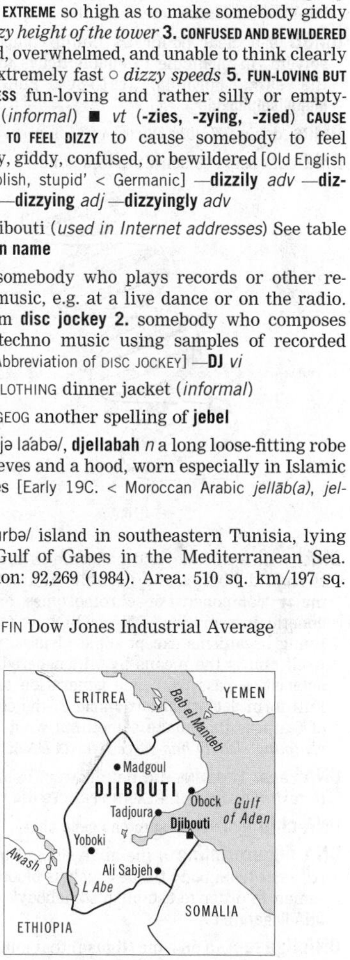

Djibouti

Djibouti /ji bóoti/ **1.** country in the Horn of Africa, bordered by the Gulf of Aden, Somalia, Ethiopia, and Eritrea. Language: Arabic, French. Currency: Djibouti franc. Capital: Djibouti. Population: 457,130 (2003). Area: 23,200 sq. km/8,958 sq. mi. Official name **Republic of Djibouti 2.** the capital of the Republic of Djibouti. Population: 383,000 (1995 estimate).

djinn, **djinni** MYTHOL another spelling of **jinni**

dk *abbr* **1.** dark **2.** NAUT deck **3.** Denmark (*used in Internet addresses*) See table at **domain name 4.** SHIPPING dock[1]

DK *abbr* ONLINE don't know (*used in e-mails or text messages*)

dl *symbol* MEASURE decilitre

DL *abbr* **1.** ONLINE download (*used in e-mails or text messages*) **2.** Down Low (*slang*)

D/L *abbr* BANKING demand loan

D layer *n* **1.** METEOROL same as **D region** (sense 1) **2.** the lower layer of the Earth's mantle, from 720 km/450 mi. deep down to the boundary with the core

DLitt /dee lít/, **DLit** *abbr* **1.** Doctor of Letters **2.** Doctor of Literature

dm[1] *symbol* MEASURE decimetre

dm[2] *abbr* Dominica (*used in Internet addresses*) See table at **domain name**

DM *abbr* MONEY, HIST Deutschmark

DMAC /dée mak/ *n* a coding system used for broadcasting colour television programmes via satellite. Full form **duobinary multiplexed analogue component**

DMD *abbr* DENT, EDUC Doctor of Dental Medicine [Latin *Dentariae Medicinae Doctor*]

DMK *n* in Tamil Nadu, India, a political party advocating the promotion of Tamil society and culture. Full form **Dravida Munnetra Kazgham**

DMS *abbr* **1.** COMPUT data management system **2.** EDUC Diploma in Management Studies

DMSO *n* a clear odourless liquid compound. Use: solvent, in medicine to enable drugs to penetrate the skin. Formula: $(CH_3)_2SO$. Full form **dimethylsulphoxide**

DMus /dee múz/ *abbr* Doctor of Music

DMZ *abbr* MIL, POL demilitarized zone

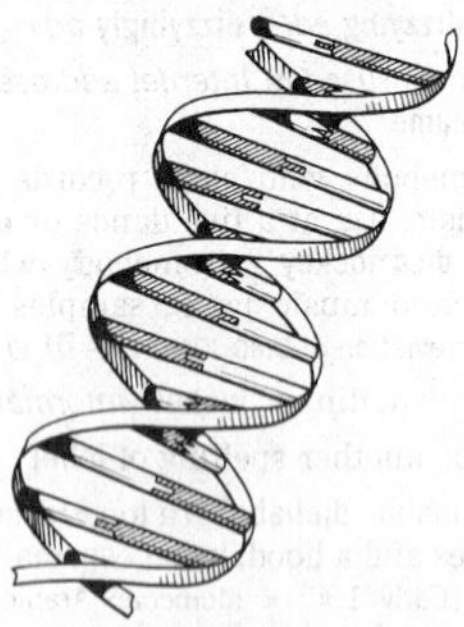

DNA

DNA[1] *n* **1.** a nucleic acid molecule in the form of a twisted double strand (**double helix**) that is the major component of chromosomes and carries genetic information. DNA, which is found in all living organisms except some viruses, reproduces itself and is the means by which hereditary characteristics pass from one generation to the next. Full form **deoxyribonucleic acid** **2.** the combination of features that make something what it is ○ *The company clearly has success in its DNA.*

DNA[2] *abbr* **1.** ONLINE did not answer (*used in e-mails or text messages*) **2.** HEALTH SERVICES did not attend

DNA chip *n* GENETICS same as **gene chip**

DNA fingerprinting *n* the analysis and use of DNA patterns from body tissues such as blood, saliva, or semen in order to establish somebody's identity — **DNA fingerprint** *n*

DNA ligase *n* an enzyme (**ligase**) that joins two DNA strands during replication, repair, and recombination

DNA polymerase *n* an enzyme that uses single-stranded DNA to reproduce and repair DNA

DNA profiling *n* GENETICS same as **DNA fingerprinting** — **DNA profile** *n*

DNase /dée en áyz/ *n* an enzyme that aids the breakdown of DNA into smaller molecules. Full form **deoxyribonuclease**

DNA sequencing *n* the process of determining the exact sequence of the bases along a section length of DNA

DNA virus *n* a virus with a genome containing DNA

Dnepr another spelling of **Dnieper**

Dnestr another spelling of **Dniester**

Dnieper /néepər, dnée-/, **Dnepr** third longest river in Europe after the Volga and Danube. It rises west of Moscow and flows southwards and westwards through Russia, Belarus, and Ukraine before emptying into the Black Sea. Length: 2,290 km/1,420 mi.

Dniester /néestər, dnée-/, **Dnestr** river that rises in the Carpathian Mountains and flows through Ukraine and Moldova before emptying into the Black Sea near Odessa. Length: 1,400 km/870 mi.

D-notice *n* an official government communication to news editors advising them against publishing specific information for security reasons [< its administrative classification letter]

DNR *abbr* MED do not resuscitate

DNS *abbr* COMPUT domain name system

do[1] /doo/ (**does** *stressed* /duz/; *unstressed* /dəz/, **doing**, **did** /did/, **done** /dun/) CORE MEANING: a verb indicating that somebody performs an action, an activity, or a task. It is often used as an informal equivalent of more specific and less frequent verbs, e.g. 'do your nails' instead of 'paint your nails'. ○ *He usually did the cleaning on a Sunday morning.* ○ *Why won't you let me do your hair for you?* ○ *Assuming that your terminal is properly set, here is what you have to do to connect it.*
1. *vt* USE SOMETHING to use something in a particular way ○ *She's done absolutely nothing with the money she inherited.* **2.** *vt* TAKE ACTION to take action in a situation in order to change it or solve a problem ○ *Companies must decide what to do about their chemical waste.* **3.** *vt* CAUSE SOMETHING to cause or produce an effect or result ○ *These disputes do little to help the peace process.* ○ *I could see what the divorce was doing to him.* **4.** *vt* WORK AT SOMETHING to work at something, especially as a job or profession, or as a course of study ○ *What does your mother do at the bank?* **5.** *vt* BE OCCUPIED WITH SOMETHING to be occupied or busy with something ○ *Are you doing anything this evening?* **6.** *vti* CONDUCT SELF to behave in a particular manner ○ *Do what you want.* ○ *Do as you please.* **7.** *vi* FARE to be successful or unsuccessful to a particular extent ○ *Automobile insurance firms are doing well this year.* **8.** *vt* PROVIDE SOMETHING to prepare or provide something ○ *I'm sorry but we don't do a lunch menu.* **9.** *vt* ACHIEVE SPEED OR RATE to achieve a particular speed or rate ○ *We were doing 55 down the motorway.* ○ *We did about 400 miles a day.* **10.** *vt* STUDY SOMETHING to study or work at doing something ○ *Have you done Nabokov yet?* ○ *I've never been able to do algebra.* **11.** *vt* PERFORM SOMETHING to perform or act a play, role, or accent ○ *They're doing 'Macbeth'.* ○ *I'm not very good at doing accents.* **12.** *vt* VISIT OR EXPLORE PLACE to visit or explore a country or city as a tourist (*informal*) ○ *We're doing London tomorrow.* **13.** *vti* BE ADEQUATE to be adequate in quantity or quality for somebody or something ○ *A paper cup does just as well.* ○ *Just an orange juice will do me.* **14.** *vt* SERVE TIME IN PRISON to serve a period of time in prison (*slang*) ○ *He's doing time for cheating on his taxes.* **15.** *vt* EXHAUST SOMEBODY to wear somebody out (*informal*) **16.** *vt* ADAPT SOMETHING to translate or adapt a play, book, or other work (*informal*) ○ *The novel was done into a feature film.* **17.** *vt* CHEAT SOMEBODY to cheat or trick somebody (*informal*) ○ *They did her out of her lunch money.* **18.** *vt* ROB SOMEBODY to rob a person or place (*slang*) ○ *They got caught while they were doing the post office.* **19.** *vt* ARREST SOMEBODY to arrest somebody on suspicion of a crime (*slang*) ○ *The police did her for possession.* **20.** *vt* CONVICT SOMEBODY to prosecute and convict somebody of a crime (*slang*) ○ *He got done for breaking and entering.* **21.** *vt* TAKE DRUGS to take or use a narcotic drug (*slang*) **22.** *vt* HAVE SEX WITH SOMEBODY to have sexual intercourse with somebody (*slang*) **23.** *vt* MURDER SOMEBODY to kill somebody deliberately (*slang*) **24.** *vt Aus* SPEND MONEY to spend or lose all your money (*slang*) ○ *Have you done your money?* **25.** *aux v* FORMS QUESTIONS AND NEGATIVES used with simple present and simple past tenses in the formation of questions and negative sentences. 'Do' and 'did' are often contracted to 'don't' and 'didn't' in negative structures. ○ *What did he want?* ○ *Don't sit there!* ○ *It doesn't matter if you can't come.* **26.** *aux v* GIVES EMPHASIS used to emphasize a positive statement or command, often as a way of politely inviting or persuading somebody to do something ○ *Yes, I do realize you can't finish the work today.* ○ *Please do be quiet!* **27.** *aux v* CHANGES EMPHASIS used to form inverted sentences in order to change the emphasis of a statement ○ *She hopes to go to college, as do her brothers.* **28.** *aux v* REPLACES ANOTHER VERB used to replace an earlier verb or verb phrase to avoid repetition, usually when comparing two things ○ *I want to have a break just as much as you do.* **29.** *n UK, NZ, US* SOCIAL GATHERING a formal social gathering, e.g. a wedding reception (*informal*) ○ *attended a big do at the White House* **30.** *n* same as **excrement** (*informal; used euphemistically*) ○ *a pile of doggy do* [Old English *dōn* < Indo-European, 'to place'] ◇ **could do with** to want or need something ○ *I could do with some help.* ◇ **have to do with somebody** *or* **something 1.** to be connected with somebody or something **2.** to concern somebody or something **3.** to involve contact or a relationship with somebody or something ◇ **that does it!** used to indicate that you are not prepared to tolerate any more (*informal*) ○ *That does it! I'm calling my lawyer!* ◇ **the dos and don'ts** the correct way to proceed or behave in a particular situation ○ *a list of dos and don'ts for the first-time investor* ◇ **to do with** related to or about somebody or something ○ *The lecture was to do with road safety.*

USAGE do ... have or **have ... got**? Both these constructions are used in questions and in negative statements: *Do you have change for a ten-pound note?* or *Have you got change for a ten-pound note? I don't have any change* or *I haven't got any change.* Some consider the first wording in each pair to be more correct, perceiving ***have... got*** as colloquial and even redundant, and pointing out that *have* alone is sufficient to signify possession. But *Have you change?* is not idiomatic, and ***do ... have*** has just as many syllables as ***have ... got***. Therefore, it is hard to see what reasonable basis exists for preferring ***do ... have*** to ***have ... got***.

USAGE did you... or **have you...**? A distinction that arises in connection with questions and negative statements is represented by the wordings *Did you see the show?* and *Have you seen the show? I didn't see the show* and *I haven't seen the show.* In informal conversation, the two are used almost interchangeably. In strict usage, however, there is a difference in time perspective: the first wording in each pair (*Did you...?*) refers to a particular point in the past, whereas the second wording (*Have you...?*) has to do with any time in the past (thus, *ever* could be added to the second sentence in each pair without substantially changing its meaning).

SYNONYMS See ***perform***.

do away with *vt* **1.** to abolish something so that it no longer happens or exists **2.** to kill somebody (*informal*)

do down *vt* **1.** to suggest that somebody or something is insignificant or unimportant (*informal*) **2.** to treat somebody unfairly in order to gain an advantage

do for *vt* **1.** CHARGE OR CONVICT SOMEBODY OF OFFENCE to charge somebody with an offence, or convict somebody of a crime (*informal*) **2.** KILL SOMEBODY to kill somebody (*informal*) Same as **kill** *v* (sense 1) **3.** HARM SOMEBODY OR SOMETHING to cause serious difficulties for somebody or serious damage to something (*dated informal*) **4.** EXHAUST SOMEBODY to make somebody feel so exhausted that he or she has no more energy or enthusiasm to continue (*dated informal*) **5.** WORK AS DOMESTIC CLEANER FOR SOMEBODY to be employed to clean and tidy a house for somebody (*dated informal*)

do in *vt* (*informal*) **1.** to kill or severely beat somebody **2.** to make somebody feel exhausted

do out *vt* to clean or tidy a place such as a room or cupboard (*informal*)

do over *vt* **1.** to clean or redecorate a place such as a house or room (*informal*) **2.** to subject somebody to a violent beating (*slang*)

do up *vt* **1.** FASTEN SOMETHING to fasten a piece of clothing, or be fastened ○ *did up the buttons* **2.** MAKE SOMETHING USABLE AGAIN to make something fit to use again by repairing or decorating it **3.** GIVE SOMETHING DECORATIVE WRAPPING to wrap or cover something with decorative material (*often passive*) **4.** DRESS SMARTLY to dress somebody or yourself in smart clothes (*informal*)

do without *vti* to manage or survive without something that you want, need, or normally have

do[2] /dō/ *n* MUSIC another spelling of **doh**

do[3] *abbr* ONLINE Dominican Republic (*used in Internet addresses*) See table at **domain name**

DO[1] *abbr* **1.** OPHTHALMOL, EDUC Doctor of Optometry **2.** EDUC, MED Doctor of Osteopathy

DO[2] *n* a certification for Spanish wine that guarantees

its origin [Abbreviation of Spanish *denominación de origen*]

D/O *abbr* COMM **1.** delivery order **2.** direct order

DOA *abbr* **1.** MED dead on arrival **2.** DRUGS drug of abuse

doable /dóŏ əb'l/ *adj* able to be done or achieved (*informal*)

dob /dob/ (**dobs, dobbing, dobbed**) [Mid-20C. Variant of DAB[1]]
dob in *vt* (*informal*) **1.** to report damaging or incriminating information about somebody to an authority ○ *You dob her in to the cops and we'll all be in trouble.* ○ *I broke the neighbour's window and my sister went and dobbed me in to mum.* **2.** Aus to contribute money to a collection for a particular purpose ○ *If we all dob in ten bucks, we can get her a great present.*

DOB, d.o.b. *abbr* date of birth

dobber /dóbbər/ *n* same as **informer** (*informal*)

dobbin /dóbbin/, **Dobbin** *n* a horse, especially a large heavy working horse [Late 16C. < *Dobbin*, personal name, alteration of *Robin*]

dobby /dóbbi/ (*plural* **-bies**) *n* a part of a loom that allows small figures to be woven on it [Late 17C. Origin ?]

Dobell /dō bél/, **Sir William** (1899–1970) Australian painter. Noted for his portraits, he was an official war artist during World War II.

Doberman pinscher

Doberman pinscher /dóbərmən pínshər/, **Dobermann pinscher, Doberman** *n* a medium-sized to large powerful dog with a smooth black or dark brown coat, often used as a guard dog or for police work and belonging to a breed originating in Germany [Early 20C. After Ludwig *Dobermann*, 19C German dog breeder; *pinscher* < German, breed name]

dobra /dóbrə/ *n* the main unit of currency of São Tomé and Principe. See table at **currency** [Late 20C. Via Portuguese < Latin *duplus* 'double']

dobsonfly /dóbsən flī/ (*plural* **-flies**) *n* N Am a very large winged insect that has long slender mouthparts in the male. Its larva (**hellgrammite**) is a voracious predator of small water animals and is used by anglers as bait. Native to: North America. Latin name: *Corydalus cornutus*.

doc /dok/ *n* same as **doctor** *n* (sense 1) (*informal*) [Mid-19C. Shortening]

DOC *n* a certification for Italian wine that guarantees its origin [Abbreviation of Italian *denominazione di origine controllata*]

doc. *abbr* LAW document

DOCa *n* a certification for Spanish wine that guarantees its origin and verifies that it meets production regulations [< abbreviation of Spanish *Denominación de Origen Calificada*]

docent /dóss'nt/ *n* **1.** US a university lecturer or teacher, especially one who is not a full-time member of the faculty **2.** N Am a tourist guide working in some museums or cathedrals [Late 19C. < obsolete German < Latin *docent-*, present participle of *docere* 'teach'] —**docentship** *n*

Docetism /dō seétizəm, dósit-/ *n* in Christianity, an early heresy that claimed that Jesus Christ was not a real person [Mid-19C. < *Docete* 'Docetist', via medieval Latin *Docetae* (plural) 'Docetists' < patristic Greek *Dokētai* < Greek *dokein* 'seem, appear'] —**Docetist** *n*

DOCG *n* a certification for Italian wine that guarantees its origin and verifies that it meets production regulations [Abbreviation of Italian *Denominazione di Origine Controllata e Garantita*]

doch an doris *n* Scotland BEVERAGES another spelling of **deoch an doruis**

docile /dó sīl/ *adj* quiet, easy to control, and unlikely to cause trouble [15C. < Latin *docilis* < *docere* 'teach'] — **docilely** *adv* —**docility** /dō sílləti/ *n*

dock[1] /dok/ *n* **1.** PLACE FOR SHIPS TO MOOR an area of water between two piers or next to a pier, where ships can be moored safely for loading and repair **2.** BUILDINGS CONNECTED WITH SHIPPING all the offices, workshops, and other buildings associated with the loading and repair of ships, together with the nearby areas of water (*usually used in the plural*) Aus, N Am term **dockyard 3.** N Am PIER OR WHARF a long narrow structure stretching out into a body of water, or a raised area of land alongside water where ships can load and unload **4.** ENCLOSED AREA OF WATER FOR SHIP an enclosed area of water for a ship in which the water level can be adjusted **5.** NAUT same as **dry dock** ■ *vti* (**docks, docking, docked**) **1.** MOOR to steer a ship into a dock and tie it up, or be steered in and tied up there **2.** AEROSP LINK UP WITH SPACECRAFT to link a spacecraft up with another in space, or be linked up in this way [14C. < Middle Low German *docke* or Middle Dutch *docke*]

dock[2] /dok/ *n* the area in a law court where the accused person stands during a trial [Late 16C. Probably < Flemish *dok* 'fowl pen, rabbit hutch']

dock[3] /dok/ (*plural* **docks** or *same*) *n* **1.** a plant of the buckwheat family with long broad leaves and a long taproot. Flowers: greenish or reddish. Genus: *Rumex.* **2.** a broad-leafed weedy plant [Old English *docce* < Germanic]

dock[4] /dok/ *vt* (**docks, docking, docked**) **1.** REDUCE WAGES to deduct a sum of money from somebody's wages, especially as a punishment **2.** REMOVE TAIL OF ANIMAL to remove the tail of a dog, sheep, or other animal, leaving a short stump ■ *n* **1.** SOLID PART OF TAIL the solid part of an animal's tail **2.** STUMP OF TAIL the stump left when an animal's tail has been docked [14C. Origin ?]

dockage /dókij/ *n* **1.** MOORING CHARGE a charge payable for mooring at a dock **2.** FACILITIES FOR MOORED SHIPS the facilities for ships moored at a dock **3.** DOCKING PROCESS the process of docking a ship [Mid-17C. < DOCK[1]]

docken /dókən/ (*plural* **-ens** or *same*) *n* Scotland **1.** PLANTS same as **dock**[3] **2.** something worthless or unimportant [Old English *doccan*, form of *docce* (see DOCK[3])]

docker /dókər/ *n* somebody whose job is to load and unload ships. N Am term **longshoreman** [Mid-18C. < DOCK[1]]

docket /dókit/ *n* **1.** DOCUMENT LISTING CONTENTS OF PARCEL a short document listing the contents of a parcel or the goods being delivered **2.** SUMMARY OF COURT CASE a summary of the proceedings of a court case **3.** N Am LAW LIST OF FUTURE COURT CASES a list of pending cases in a court **4.** N Am LIST OF THINGS TO DO a list of things to do **5.** DOCUMENT SUMMARY a summary of a document **6.** CUSTOMS CERTIFICATE a customs certificate confirming payment of duty ■ *vt* (**-ets, -eting, -eted**) **1.** US LAW PUT LEGAL CASE IN CALENDAR to enter a legal case in the calendar of future cases **2.** LAW SUMMARIZE COURT CASE to summarize a court case and enter the summary in the appropriate register **3.** LABEL PACKAGE to label a package with a document giving the contents or delivery details **4.** SUMMARIZE SOMETHING to attach or give a summary of something [15C. Origin ?]

docking station /dóking-/ *n* a piece of hardware into which a portable computer is inserted for recharging or expanded operations [< DOCK[1]]

dockland /dók land/ *n* the area surrounding a city's docks or port (*often used in the plural*) [Early 20C. < DOCK[1]]

dockside /dók sīd/ *n* the area of ground alongside the moorings in a dock or harbour [Late 19C. < DOCK[1]]

dockworker /dók wurkər/ *n* SHIPPING same as **docker** [< DOCK[1]]

dockyard /dók yaard/ *n* Aus, N Am SHIPPING same as **dock**[1] *n* (sense 2) [Early 18C. < DOCK[1]]

doco /dókō/ (*plural* **-cos**) *n* Aus MEDIA same as **documentary** (*informal*) [Late 20C. Shortening]

docosahexaenoic acid /dókóssə heksə nō ik-/ *n* BIOCHEM full form of **DHA**[1] [<; Greek *do-*, form of *duo* 'two' + shortening of *eikosi* 'twenty' + *hexa* 'six' + -ANE]

doctor /dóktər/ *n* **1.** HEALTH SERVICES SOMEBODY MEDICALLY QUALIFIED somebody qualified and licensed to give people medical treatment **2.** N Am HEALTH SERVICES DENTIST, VET, OR OSTEOPATH a title used before the names of health professionals such as dentists, vets, and osteopaths **3.** EDUC SOMEBODY WITH HIGHEST UNIVERSITY DEGREE a title given to somebody who has been awarded a doctorate, the highest level of degree awarded by a university **4.** SOMEBODY WHO CAN MEND THINGS a skilled practitioner of something, especially mending or improving something ○ *a play doctor* **5.** CHR ROMAN CATHOLIC THEOLOGIAN in the earlier history of the Roman Catholic Church, an eminent and influential theologian **6.** EDUC TEACHER OR SCHOLAR a teacher or somebody very knowledgeable (*archaic*) ■ *v* (**-tors, -toring, -tored**) **1.** *vt* CHANGE SOMETHING IN ORDER TO DECEIVE to change something in order to make it appear different from the facts or the truth ○ *doctored the figures* **2.** *vt* ADD SOMETHING TO SUBSTANCE to add something, especially a drug, alcohol, or poison, to food or drink **3.** *vt* VET REMOVE SEX ORGANS FROM ANIMAL to spay or castrate an animal to prevent it from producing young **4.** *vti* MED TREAT ILL PEOPLE to treat people when they are ill **5.** *vt* MEND SOMETHING to mend something, especially in a rather rough or hurried way [14C. Via French < Latin, 'teacher' < *doct-*, past participle of *docere* 'teach'] —**doctorly** *adj* ◇ **go for the doctor** Aus to make every effort to achieve something, especially to win a race ◇ **just what the doctor ordered** something that is very welcome, pleasing, or refreshing (*informal*)

doctoral /dóktərəl/, **doctorial** /dok táwri əl/ *adj* written or done in order to obtain a doctorate, the highest degree awarded by a university

doctor-assisted suicide *n* UK the suicide of somebody with an incurable disease carried out with the help of a doctor. Doctor-assisted suicide is illegal in most countries. ANZ, N Am term **physician-assisted suicide**

doctorate /dóktərət/ *n* the highest level of university degree, usually awarded for a lengthy piece of original research, but sometimes for other outstanding achievements

Doctor of Letters, Doctor of Literature *n* the highest level of university doctorate, awarded to somebody who has made a substantial scholarly contribution to a subject, or as an honorary degree to somebody for exceptional achievement [Translation of Latin *Litterarum Doctor*]

Doctor of Philosophy *n* the highest level of university degree, awarded to somebody who has successfully completed a lengthy piece of original research. A Doctor of Philosophy may be awarded in any subject except law, theology, or medicine.

Doctor of Veterinary Medcine *n* the highest level of university degree, awarded to somebody who has successfully completed a lengthy piece of original research in the field of veterinary medicine

Doctor's Commons *npl* the building in London that housed courts for the Church of England and the Admiralty between 1572 and 1867 [< the common table or dining hall]

doctrinaire /dóktri náir/ *adj* determined to use a specific theory or method and refusing to accept that there might be a better approach —**doctrinaire** *n* —**doctrinairism** *n* —**doctrinarian** *n*

doctrine /dóktrin/ *n* **1.** a rule or principle that forms the basis of a belief, theory, or policy **2.** a body of ideas, particularly in religion, taught to people as truthful or correct [14C. Directly or via French < Latin *doctrina* 'teaching, learning' < *doctor* (see DOCTOR)] —**doctrinal** /dok trīn'l, dóktrin'l/ *adj* —**doctrinality** /dóktri nálləti/ *n* —**doctrinally** /dok trīn'li/ *adv*

docudrama /dókyoō draamə/ *n* a dramatized film or television version of a true story [Mid-20C. Blend of DOCUMENTARY + DRAMA] —**docudramatic** /dókyoōdrə máttik/ *adj*

document *n* /dókyoōmənt/ **1.** FORMAL PIECE OF WRITING a formal piece of writing that provides information or acts as a record of events or arrangements **2.** LAW

OBJECT CONTAINING INFORMATION an object such as a film, photograph, or audio recording that contains information and can be used as evidence **3.** COMPUT **COMPUTER FILE** a computer file created using an applications program, e.g. a database, spreadsheet, illustration, or text file ■ *vt* /dókyoŏ ment/ (**-ments, -menting, -mented**) **1. RECORD INFORMATION** to make a record of something by writing about it or by filming or photographing it **2. SUPPORT SOMETHING WITH EVIDENCE** to provide evidence for a statement or claim by supplying supporting information [15C. Via French < Latin *documentum* 'lesson, example' (in medieval Latin, 'instruction, official paper') < *docere* 'teach'] —**documentable** /dókyoŏ méntəb'l/ *adj* —**documental** /dókyoŏ mént'l/ *adj* —**documenter** /dókyoŏ mentər/ *n*

documentalist /dókyoŏ mént'list/ *n* a specialist in documentation

documentary /dókyoŏ méntəri/ *n* (*plural* **-ries**) **FACTUAL FILM OR TV PROGRAMME** a film or TV programme presenting facts and information, especially about a political, historical, or social issue ■ *adj* **1. GIVING FACTS** giving facts and information rather than telling a fictional story **2. CONSISTING OF DOCUMENTS** in the form of documents, or collected from documents —**documentarily** *adv*

documentation /dókyoŏ men táysh'n/ *n* **1. EVIDENTIAL OR REFERENCE DOCUMENTS** documents provided or collected together as evidence or as reference material **2. PROCESS OF PROVIDING WRITTEN INFORMATION** the process of providing written details or information about something **3.** COMPUT **COMPUTER SOFTWARE INFORMATION** the instructions, tutorials, and reference information provided to explain how to install and use software or a computer system

document feeder *n* the part of a printer, scanner, or fax machine that holds a stack of papers and feeds them through the machine so that something can be printed on them

document holder *n* a stand that holds papers in a vertical position so that they can be read easily by somebody working at a desk

docusoap /dókyoŏ sōp/ *n* a television programme that combines documentary style with aspects of soap opera, e.g. by showing the personal lives of people at their workplace [Late 20C. Blend of DOCUMENTARY + SOAP OPERA]

docutainment /dókyoo táynmənt/ *n US* MEDIA same as **infotainment** [Late 20C. Blend of DOCUMENTARY + ENTERTAINMENT]

Dodd /dod/, **Charles Harold** (1884–1973) Welsh biblical scholar. He was a Congregational pastor and sometime lecturer at Oxford and Cambridge universities. From 1949 he directed the *New English Bible* project.

dodder[1] /dóddər/ (**-ders, -dering, -dered**) *vi* **1.** to tremble or shake slightly as a result of age **2.** to walk slowly and unsteadily with shaking limbs as a result of age [Early 17C. Variant of obsolete and dialect *dadder* 'quake, tremble', origin ?] —**dodderer** *n*

dodder[2] /dóddər/ (*plural* **-ders** or *same*) *n* a leafless rootless parasitic plant of the morning glory family that lacks chlorophyll and has a reddish twining stem. Flowers: small, white. Genus: *Cuscuta*. [14C. Origin ?]

doddering /dóddəring/, **doddery** /-əri/ *adj* walking unsteadily, especially as a result of age —**dodderingly** *adv*

doddle /dódd'l/ *n* something very easy to do (*informal*) ○ *I'm sure I'll pass the test – it'll be a doddle.* [Mid-20C. Origin ?]

dodeca- *prefix* twelve ○ *dodecasyllable* [< Greek *dōdeka* < *duō* 'two' + *deka* 'ten']

dodecahedron /dō dekə heédrən/ (*plural* **-drons** or **-dra** /-drə/) *n* a three-dimensional geometric figure formed of 12 equal pentagonal faces meeting in threes at 20 vertices [Late 16C. < Greek *dōdekaedron* < *dōdeka* 'twelve' + *hedra* 'seat, face'] —**dodecahedral** *adj*

Dodecanese /dō dekə neéz/ group of islands in the southeastern Aegean Sea that form a department of Greece. They are a major tourist destination. Capital: Rhodes. Population: 145,071 (1981). Area: 2,663 sq. km/1,028 sq. mi.

dodecanoic acid /dō dekə nō ik-/ *n* CHEM same as **lauric acid** [Mid-20C. < *dodecane* '(kind of) paraffin' < DODECA-]

dodecaphonic /dō dekə fónnik/ *adj* MUSIC same as **twelve-tone** —**dodecaphonism** *n* —**dodecaphonist** *n* —**dodecaphony** *n*

dodecasyllable /dō dekə síllәb'l/ *n* a line of verse of 12 syllables —**dodecasyllabic** /-si lábbik/ *adj*

dodge /doj/ *v* (**dodges, dodging, dodged**) **1.** *vti* **MOVE QUICKLY TO AVOID SOMETHING** to move quickly and suddenly to one side to avoid being caught or hit by somebody or something ○ *He dodged the punch.* **2.** *vt* **AVOID SOMETHING UNPLEASANT** to avoid doing something regarded as unpleasant **3.** *vt* PHOTOGRAPHY **MASK AREA OF PRINT** to mask an area of a photographic print during exposure to prevent light reaching it ■ *n* **1. TRICK TO AVOID DOING SOMETHING** a clever trick or tactic to avoid doing something ○ *a tax dodge* **2. QUICK AVOIDING MOVEMENT** a sudden quick movement to one side to avoid being caught or hit by somebody or something [Mid-16C. Origin ?]

dodge ball *n* a children's game in which opponents try to avoid being hit by a large rubber ball

Dodge City /dój-/ city in southern Kansas, on the northern bank of the Arkansas River, southwest of Great Bend. Population: 25,345 (2002 estimate).

Dodgem /dójjəm/ *tdmk* a trademark for a bumper car

dodger /dójjər/ *n* **1. SOMEBODY AVOIDING DUTY** somebody who avoids a duty or responsibility, especially by using dishonest or deceitful methods **2. SOMEBODY DISHONEST** somebody cunning and untrustworthy **3. SHELTERING SCREEN ON SHIP** a canvas screen on a ship or yacht to protect the person at the helm from spray

Dodgson /dójs'n/, **Charles Lutwidge** ➧ **Carroll, Lewis**

dodgy /dójji/ (**-ier, -iest**) *adj* (*informal*) **1. SUSPECT OR DISHONEST** suspect, dishonest, or untrustworthy **2. RISKY** dangerous or risky **3. LIKELY TO BREAK DOWN** unreliable and likely to break down or stop working —**dodgily** *adv* —**dodginess** *n*

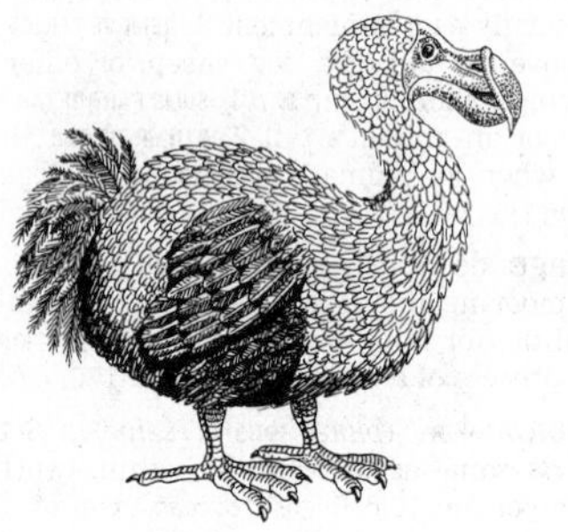

dodo

dodo /dōdō/ (*plural* **-dos** or **-does**) *n* **1. EXTINCT FLIGHTLESS BIRD** a large flightless bird with a hooked beak, extinct since the 17th century. Native to: formerly, Mauritius and neighbouring Indian Ocean islands. Latin name: *Raphus cucullatus*. **2. OLD-FASHIONED PERSON** somebody regarded as old-fashioned and conservative (*informal insult*) **3. UNINTELLIGENT PERSON** somebody regarded as unintelligent (*informal insult*) [Early 17C. < Portuguese *doudo* 'fool, simpleton'] —**dodoism** *n* ◇ **(as) dead as a dodo** no longer existing, functioning, flourishing, or popular

Dodoma /dōdəmə/ official capital of Tanzania since 1983. It is situated in Dodoma Region, west of the former capital, Dar es Salaam. Population: 189,000 (1995).

doe /dō/ *n* a mature female of several animals, including the deer, kangaroo, rabbit, hare, and goat [Old English *dā*, origin ?]

SPELLCHECK doe or **dough**? Do not confuse the spelling of ***doe*** and ***dough***, which sound similar. A ***doe*** is a female animal such as a deer or rabbit. ***Dough*** is used to make bread or pastry.

doe-eyed *adj* having large appealing eyes that convey an impression of gentleness or naive innocence

Doenitz another spelling of **Dönitz**

doer /doŏ ər/ *n* **1.** somebody who does a particular thing (*often used in combination*) ○ *a doer of good* **2.** somebody who takes action instead of just thinking or talking about it

does 3rd person singular present of **do**[1]

doeskin /dō skin/ *n* **1. SKIN OF DEER** the skin of various animals, including a doe, deer, and goat **2. LEATHER** light supple leather made from doeskin that is particularly suitable for gloves **3. SMOOTH WOOLLEN CLOTH** a densely woven smooth woollen cloth

doesn't /dúzz'nt/ *contr* does not

~~**does'nt**~~ incorrect spelling of **doesn't**

doest /doŏ əst/ 2nd person singular present of **do**[1] (*archaic*)

doeth /doŏ əth/ 3rd person singular present of **do**[1] (*archaic*)

doff /dof/ (**doffs, doffing, doffed**) *vt* **1.** to take off or lift and tilt a hat as a greeting or a mark of respect **2.** to take off a coat or another piece of clothing [14C. Contraction of archaic *do off* 'take off'] —**doffer** *n*

dog /dog/ *n* **1. DOMESTIC ANIMAL** a domestic carnivorous animal with a long muzzle, a fur coat, and a long fur-covered tail, whose characteristic call is a bark. Latin name: *Canis familiaris*. **2. MALE DOG** a male dog, wolf, fox, or other member of the dog family **3. WILD ANIMAL** a wild animal such as a wolf, fox, dingo, or coyote that resembles a domestic dog and belongs to the same family. Family: Canidae. **4. CONTEMPTIBLE PERSON** somebody regarded as unpleasant or contemptible (*insult*) **5. OFFENSIVE TERM** an offensive term that deliberately insults somebody's looks (*slang insult*) **6. PERSON** somebody of a particular type (*informal*) ○ *You lucky dog!* **7.** *N Am* **SOMETHING USELESS OR INFERIOR** something useless or of a very poor standard (*informal*) **8.** *Aus* **BETRAYER** somebody who betrays his or her associates (*informal*) **9.** HOUSEHOLD same as **andiron 10.** METEOROL same as **fogbow 11.** MECH ENG **GRIPPING TOOL** a device for gripping or holding things ■ **dogs** *npl* **1.** SPORTS **DOG RACING** greyhound racing in general, or a greyhound race meeting (*informal*) **2. FEET** somebody's feet (*dated informal*) ■ *vt* (**dogs, dogging, dogged**) **1. BOTHER SOMEBODY PERSISTENTLY** to bother or trouble somebody persistently (*often passive*) ○ *was dogged by bad luck* **2. FOLLOW SOMEBODY CLOSELY** to follow somebody closely in a determined way ○ *continued dogging her footsteps* **3.** MECH ENG **GRIP SOMETHING WITH MECHANICAL DEVICE** to grip or hold something firmly with a mechanical device [Old English *docga*, origin ?] —**dog-like** *adj* ◇ **dog in the manger** somebody who tries to prevent somebody else from having or doing something that he or she cannot have or do ◇ **a dog's breakfast** *or* **dinner** something that is messy, disorganized, or badly done (*informal*) ◇ **a dog's life** a wretched existence ◇ **dog eat dog** ruthlessly competitive ◇ **go to the dogs** to be in the final stages of a gradual decline in standards (*informal*) ◇ **let sleeping dogs lie** to take no action in a situation that is currently peaceful but potentially troublesome ◇ **put on the dog** *Aus, N Am* to make a display of wealth or knowledge ostentatiously or pretentiously (*dated informal*)

dog-and-pony show *n N Am* an elaborate business presentation or promotional event (*informal*)

dogbane /dóg bayn/ *n* a plant that bears dogberries with pungent milky juice and a bitter root. Flowers: small, bell-shaped, white or pink. Genus: *Apocynum*.

dogberry[1] /dóg beri, -bəri/ (*plural* **-ries**) *n* **1.** a berry of any of various plants, including dogwood **2.** a plant that produces dogberries [Mid-16C. < DOG implying inferior or inedible]

dogberry[2] /dóg beri, -bəri/ (*plural* **-ries**), **Dogberry** *n* an unintelligent but self-important official [Mid-19C. After *Dogberry*, constable in *Much Ado About Nothing* by Shakespeare] —**dogberryism** *n*

dog biscuit *n* a hard biscuit made for dogs to eat

dogcart /dóg kaart/ *n* a two-wheeled vehicle drawn by a horse and seating two people back to back

dogcatcher /dóg kachər/ *n ANZ, N Am* OCCUPATIONS same as **dog warden**

dog chew *n* a hard piece of leather or compressed edible material given to a dog to chew on, either as a treat or to keep its teeth in good condition

dog collar *n* **1.** a piece of leather or fabric worn around a dog's neck, often with the dog's name attached to it **2.** CHR same as **clerical collar** (*informal*) **3.** JEWELLERY a necklace that fits closely round the neck

dog days *npl* **1.** the hottest period of the summer **2.** a lazy or inactive period of time [Because in ancient times heralded by the simultaneous rising of the Dog Star and the Sun]

doge /dōj, dōzh/ *n* the chief magistrate in Renaissance Venice or Genoa [Mid-16C. Via French < Venetian Italian *doze* < Latin *ducem* 'leader'] —**dogeship** *n*

dog-eared *adj* **1.** having worn and well-thumbed pages that have been creased or folded over to mark the place reached in reading **2.** shabby or well-used

dog-end *n* the discarded end of a cigarette after the rest of it has been smoked (*informal*)

dogey *n N Am* AGRIC another spelling of **dogie**

dogfight /dóg fīt/ *n* **1.** COMBAT BETWEEN FIGHTER PLANES an aerial combat involving two or more fighter planes **2.** FIERCE FIGHT a fierce violent fight **3.** FIGHT INVOLVING DOGS a fight between dogs —**dogfighting** *n*

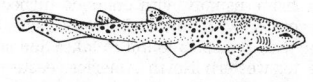

dogfish

dogfish /dóg fish/ *n* (*plural* **-fishes** or *same*) *n* **1.** a small long-tailed shark, either spiny or smooth-skinned. Native to: Pacific, Atlantic, Mediterranean waters. Families: Squalidae or Carcharhinidae or Scyliorhinidae. **2.** FISH same as **bowfin**

dogged /dóggid/ *adj* determined to continue without giving up in spite of difficulties —**doggedly** *adv* —**doggedness** *n*

dogger[1] /dóggər/ *n* a Dutch fishing vessel [14C. < Middle Dutch]

dogger[2] /dóggər/ *n* a large mass of calcium-containing sandstone or ironstone occurring in sedimentary rock [Late 17C. Origin ?]

doggerel /dóggərəl/, **doggrel** /dóggrəl/ *n* **1.** poetry that does not scan well and is often not intended to be taken seriously **2.** something that is badly written or makes no sense at all [14C. Probably < DOG (with its pejorative connotations)]

Doggett /dóggit/, **Thomas** (1660?–1721) Irish actor and playwright. Praised for his performances in William Congreve's plays, he also endowed Doggett's Coat and Badge, a trophy still annually contested by River Thames rowers.

doggie *n* another spelling of **doggy**

doggish /dóggish/ *adj* **1.** resembling a dog, or possessing the qualities of a dog **2.** bad-tempered and aggressive —**doggishly** *adv* —**doggishness** *n*

doggo /dóggō/ *adv* not moving or making any sound in order not to be discovered (*dated informal*) ◦ *lying doggo* [Late 19C. Because dogs can lie in this manner]

doggone /dóggon/, **doggoned** /dóggond/ *N Am* (*informal*) *adv*, *adj* used to emphasize how bad or annoying something is ■ *interj* used to express annoyance or irritation [Early 19C. Probably alteration of *God damn*]

doggrel *n* LITERAT another spelling of **doggerel**

doggy /dóggi/, **doggie** *n* (*plural* **-gies**) same as **dog** (sense 1) (*baby talk*) ■ *adj* **1.** resembling or typical of a dog in behaviour or appearance **2.** fond of or interested in dogs (*informal*)

doggy bag *n* a bag that can be used by a customer at a restaurant to take home any leftover food from his or her meal [< giving the food to a dog]

doggy paddle *UK n* a swimming stroke in which you lie on your front and make rapid downward movements with your arms and legs underneath your body. This stroke is often used by people learning to swim and is not used in competitions. ■ *vi* to swim using the doggy paddle ▶ ANZ, N Am term (all senses) **dog paddle**

dog handler *n* a police officer or security guard who is in charge of a specially trained working dog

doghouse /dóg howss/ (*plural* **-houses** /-howziz/) *n N Am* same as **kennel** *n* (sense 1) ◇ **in the doghouse** in disgrace (*informal*)

dogie /dógi/, **dogy** (*plural* **-gies**), **dogey** (*plural* **-geys**) *n N Am* a calf with no mother [Late 19C. Origin ?]

dog Latin *n* Latin that is incorrect in some way, especially a word or phrase that is falsely made to look or sound like Latin for humorous or satirical effect

dogleg /dóg leg/ *n* **1.** SHARP BEND a sharp bend or angle in something, especially in a road **2.** GOLF BEND IN GOLF COURSE in golf, a sharp bend in a fairway before a hole ■ *vi* (**-legs**, **-legging**, **-legged**) FORM SHARP BEND to form a sharp bend or angle [< the bent form of a dog's hind leg] —**doglegged** /-léggid, -légd/ *adj*

dogma /dógmə/ (*plural* **-mas** or **-mata** /-mətə/) *n* **1.** a belief or set of beliefs that a religion holds to be true **2.** a belief or set of beliefs that a political, philosophical, or moral group holds to be true [Mid-16C. Via late Latin < Greek *dogma, dogmat-* 'opinion, tenet' < *dokein* 'seem good, think']

dogmatic /dog máttik/, **dogmatical** /-ik'l/ *adj* **1.** prone to expressing strongly held beliefs and opinions **2.** relating to or expressing a religious, political, philosophical, or moral dogma —**dogmatically** *adv*

dogmatics /dog máttiks/ *n* the study of religious dogmas, especially Christian dogmas (*takes a singular verb*)

dogmatic theology *n* same as **dogmatics**

dogmatise *vti* another spelling of **dogmatize**

dogmatism /dógmətizəm/ *n* the tendency to express strongly held opinions in a way that suggests they should be accepted without question

dogmatist /dógmətist/ *n* **1.** somebody who expresses strongly held opinions and expects them to be accepted without question **2.** somebody who devises a new religious, political, philosophical, or moral dogma

dogmatize /dógmə tīz/ (**-tizes**, **-tizing**, **-tized**), **dogmatise** (**-tises**, **-tising**, **-tised**) *vi* to express strongly held opinions in a way that suggests they should be accepted without question —**dogmatization** /dógmə tī záysh'n/ *n* —**dogmatizer** *n*

dognap /dóg nap/ (**-naps**, **-napping**, **-napped**) *vt* to steal a dog, especially in order to sell it for use in medical research —**dognapper** *n*

Dogon /dō gon/ *n* a Niger-Congo language of Mali and Burkina Faso. Native speakers: 500,000. —**Dogon** *adj*

do-gooder /-goŏddər/ *n* somebody who sincerely tries to help others, but whose actions may be unwelcome (*informal*) —**do-goodery** *n* —**do-gooding** *n, adj*

dog paddle *ANZ, N Am* SWIMMING *n* same as **doggy paddle** ■ *vi* same as **doggy paddle**

dog racing *n* the sport of greyhound racing in which dogs chase a mechanical hare round a track and spectators may bet on which dog will win

dog rose *n* a wild rose. Flowers: delicate, pink or white. Native to: Europe. Latin name: *Rosa canina*.

dogsbody /dógz bodi/ (*plural* **-ies**) *n* a worker who does boring tasks that others do not want to do (*informal*)

dogsled /dóg sled/ *n* a vehicle mounted on runners and pulled by dogs, designed to travel over snow and ice

dog's-tail *n* a grass that has flowers along a narrow spike. Native to: Europe. Genus: *Cynosurus*.

Dog Star *n* ASTRON **1.** same as **Sirius 2.** same as **Procyon**

dog's-tooth check *n* TEXTILES same as **houndstooth check**

dog tag *n* **1.** a metal disc, attached to a dog's collar, that gives the name and address of the dog's owner and often the name of the dog **2.** *N Am* a metal identification tag for a member of the military, worn on a chain around the neck (*informal*)

dogteeth DENT, ARCHIT plural of **dogtooth**

dog-tired *adj* completely exhausted (*informal*)

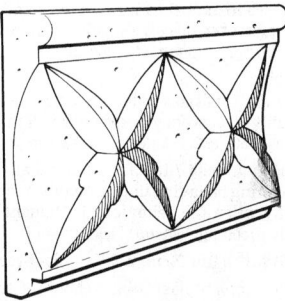

dogtooth (sense 2)

dogtooth /dóg tooth/ (*plural* **-teeth** /-teeth/) *n* **1.** DENT same as **canine** *n* (sense 1) (*informal*) **2.** in 13th-century English architecture, a small raised ornamental feature on a building consisting of four leaf-shaped parts arranged to form an X-shape

dogtooth check *n* TEXTILES, CLOTHING same as **houndstooth check**

dogtooth violet *n* a small spring-flowering bulbous plant with red-speckled leaves. Flowers: drooping, yellow or purple, like small lilies. Genus: *Erythronium*. [< the toothed inner segments of the perianth]

dogtrot /dóg trot/ *n* **1.** a gentle trot at a steady pace **2.** *also* **dog-trot** *Southern US* a roofed corridor that connects two sections of a building, or a main building with a smaller one

dog tucker *n NZ* parts of a slaughtered sheep used as dog food

dog violet *n* a type of violet. Flowers: purple. Native to: Europe, Asia. Latin name: *Viola canina*.

dog warden *n UK* somebody employed to catch stray dogs. ANZ, N Am term **dogcatcher**

dogwatch /dóg woch/ *n* on a ship, the late afternoon watch from 4.00 p.m. to 6.00 p.m. or the early evening watch from 6.00 p.m. to 8.00 p.m.

dogwood /dóg woŏd/ (*plural* **-woods** or *same*) *n* a tree or bush with clusters of small white flowers surrounded by four large white or reddish leaves (**bracts**). Genus: *Cornus*.

dogy *n N Am* another spelling of **dogie**

doh /dō/, **do** *n* a syllable that represents the first note in a scale when singing solfeggio. In fixed solfeggio it represents the note C. [Mid-18C. < Italian *do*] ◇ **be up to high doh** *Scotland* to be extremely agitated or anxious (*informal*)

d'oh /dō/ *interj* used in humorous acknowledgment of a stupid act or remark (*informal*) [Late 20C. Origin ?]

Doha /dō haa, dō ə/ capital and largest city of Qatar, on the Persian Gulf. Population: 392,384 (1995).

doily

doily /dóyli/ (*plural* **-lies**), **doyly** /n/ a decorative lacy mat that is put on plates under cakes or party food to display the food attractively [Late 18C. After *Doiley* or *Doyley*, 17C London draper]

doing /doŏ ing/ present participle of **do**[1] ■ *n* **1.** the act of performing or carrying out something ◦ *It's all your doing.* **2.** a beating or rebuke given as a punishment (*dated informal*)

doings /doŏ ingz/ *n* WHATSIT OR THINGUMMY something whose name has been forgotten or is not known (*informal; takes a singular or plural verb*) ■ *npl* **1.**

DEEDS OR ACHIEVEMENTS the things that somebody has done **2. EXCREMENT** faeces, especially those of a dog (*informal*; *used euphemistically*) **3.** HOUSEHOLD same as **andiron**

doit /doyt/ *n* a small low-value silver coin that was a Dutch unit of currency between the 15th and 17th centuries [Late 16C. < Middle Low German *doyt*]

doited /dóytid/, **doitit** /-tit/ *adj Scotland* an offensive term meaning behaving unreasonably or childishly, especially when the behaviour is thought to result from advanced age (*insult*) [15C. Origin ?]

do-it-yourself *n* full form of **DIY**[1] —**do-it-yourselfer** *n*

dojo /dójō/ (*plural* **-jos**) *n* a school or room for practising judo [Mid-20C. < Japanese < *dō* 'way, art' + -*jō* 'ground']

dol. *abbr* dollar

dolabriform /dō lábbri fawrm/, **dolabrate** /-láb rayt/ *adj* having a shape like an axe head [Mid-18C. < Latin *dolabra* 'mattock, pickaxe']

dolce /dólchi/ *adv* sweetly and gently (*used as a musical direction*) [Early 19C. Via Italian, 'sweet' < Latin *dulcis*] —**dolce** *adj*

dolce far niente /-faar nyén ti/ *n* pleasant idleness and relaxation [Early 19C. < Italian, 'sweet doing nothing']

Dolcelatte /dól chay látt ay/ *n* a soft creamy Italian blue cheese with a mild flavour, made from cow's milk [< Italian, literally 'sweet milk']

dolce vita /-veéta/ *n* a life of luxury and idle self-indulgence [Mid-20C. < Italian, 'sweet life']

doldrums /dóldrəmz, dól-/ *npl* **1.** STAGNATION a sluggish state in which no development or improvement occurs **2.** GLOOMINESS a state of gloominess or lack of energy **3.** METEOROL **AREA NORTH OF EQUATOR** an area with no wind or light variable winds just north of the equator in the Atlantic and Pacific oceans, situated between the trade winds **4.** METEOROL, NAUT **WEATHER CONDITIONS IN DOLDRUMS** the weather conditions prevailing in the doldrums that cause sailing ships to become becalmed [Late 18C. Origin ?]

dole[1] /dōl/ *n* **1.** STATE UNEMPLOYMENT PAYMENT a regular sum of money paid by the state to somebody who is unemployed (*informal*) **2.** CHARITY the giving of clothes, money, or food to somebody who is in need **3.** SOMEBODY'S FATE somebody's fate in life (*archaic*) ■ *vt* (**doles, doling, doled**) DISTRIBUTE SOMETHING AS CHARITY to distribute something as charity to somebody who is in need [Old English *dāl* 'portion' < Germanic]

dole out *vt* to give something to each of a group of people (*informal*)

SYNONYMS See *share*[1].

dole[2] /dōl/ *n* grief, sadness, or misery (*archaic*) [13C. Via Old French *dol* 'mourning' < Vulgar Latin *dolus* < Latin *dolere* 'grieve, suffer pain']

dole bludger *n Aus* an offensive term for somebody who receives benefit payments and is perceived as making no obvious effort to find work (*informal*)

doleful /dólf'l/ *adj* sad and mournful —**dolefully** *adv* —**dolefulness** *n*

dolente /do lénti/ *adv* in a sorrowful manner (*used as a musical direction*) [< Italian, present participle of *dolere* 'feel grief' < Latin] —**dolente** *adj*

dole queue *n* the part of the population that is unemployed and claiming money from the state (*informal*)

dolerite /dólla rīt/ *n* a medium-grained basic igneous rock, usually forming a minor intrusion such as a sill or dyke. US term **diabase** [Mid-19C. < French *dolérite* < Greek *doleros* 'deceptive' < *dolos* 'deceit'; because difficult to distinguish from diorite] —**doleritic** /dólla ríttik/ *adj*

dolichocephalic /dólliko si fállik/, **dolichocephalous** /-séffələss/ *adj* having a head disproportionately longer than it is wide, specifically one with a cephalic index of less than 75 [Mid-19C. < Greek *dolikhos* 'long'] —**dolichocephalism** /dólliko séffəlizəm/ *n*

dolichosaurus /dólliko sáwrəss/ *n* an extinct long-necked water reptile that was common 65 million years ago [< Greek *dolikhos* 'long' + *sauros* 'lizard']

Dolin /dóllin/, **Sir Anton** (1904–83) British dancer and choreographer. A soloist with Sergei Diaghilev's Ballets Russes (1924), he formed his own company in 1927 with his principal partner, Alicia Markova.

He later led the London Festival Ballet (1950–61). Pseudonym of **Kay, Sydney Francis Patrick Chippindall Healey**

doline /də leéna, də leén/, **dolina** /-nə/ *n* a large, often roughly circular basin of valley-sized proportions formed as a result of water dissolving surface limestone [Late 19C. Via German < Slovene *dolina* 'valley']

D'Oliveira /dólli veéra/, **Basil** (b. 1931) South African-born British cricketer. Controversy over his inclusion in the England team for the 1968–69 South African tour led to South Africa being excluded from international cricket from 1970 to 1992. Full name **D'Oliveira, Basil Lewis**

doll /dol/ *n* **1.** a child's toy in the shape of a person or baby **2.** a woman or girl who is pleasant to look at (*informal*; *sometimes considered offensive*) [Mid-16C. < form of the woman's name *Dorothy*] —**dollish** *adj* —**dollishly** *adv* —**dollishness** *n*

doll up *vt* to make yourself or somebody else such as a child look particularly smart or stylish, usually for a special occasion (*informal*)

dollar /dóllər/ *n* **1.** a unit of currency used in the United States, Canada, Australia, New Zealand, and several other countries. See table at **currency 2.** a former British coin worth five shillings (*informal*) [Mid-16C. Via early Flemish *daler* or Low German < German *Taler*, shortening of *Joachimst(h)aler*, after the silver mine of *Joachimsthal*, now Jáchymov, Czech Republic] ◇ **like a million dollars** extremely well, good-looking, or happy (*informal*) ○ *You look like a million dollars!*

dollarbird /dóllər burd/ *n* a blue-grey bird with pale round patches on its wings the size of a dollar coin. Native to: Indonesia and New Guinea, migrating to Australia. Latin name: *Eurystomus orientalis*.

dollar cost averaging *n* the periodic and systematic purchase of a security regardless of the security price

dollar diplomacy *n US* **1.** the use of financial resources to facilitate foreign relations **2.** in the United States, a policy aimed at encouraging and protecting US investment abroad

dollarization /dóllər ī záysh'n/, **dollarisation** *n* **1.** USE BY COUNTRY OF US DOLLARS the use of US dollars by a country as its own currency **2.** LINKING OF CURRENCY TO DOLLAR the linking of a currency's value to that of the US dollar **3.** ACCOUNTING IN US DOLLARS the use of the US dollar for accounting purposes

dollars-and-cents *adj US* considering finance as the determining factor

dollar sign *n* the symbol ($) that represents a dollar

Dollfuss /dól fooss/, **Engelbert** (1892–1934) Austrian politician. A Christian Socialist leader who suppressed socialism, he was chancellor of Austria (1932–34). He was murdered by Austrian Nazis.

dollhouse /dól howss/ (*plural* **-houses** /-howziz/) *n N Am* LEISURE same as **doll's house**

dollop /dólləp/ (*informal*) *n* a spoon-sized quantity of a thick liquid or a soft solid such as ice cream or cream ■ *vt* (**-lops, -loping, -loped**) to spoon a quantity of a thick liquid or a soft solid [Late 16C. Origin ?]

doll's house *n* a toy house containing miniature furniture. N Am term **dollhouse**

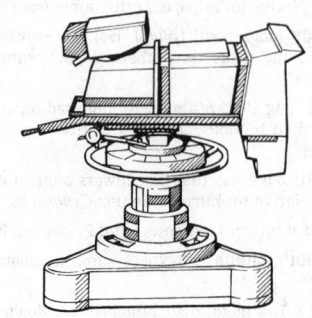
dolly: television camera on dolly

dolly /dólli/ *n* (*plural* **-lies**) **1.** same as **doll** (sense 1) (*baby talk*) **2.** MEDIA, CINEMA **MOVING PLATFORM FOR CAMERA OPERATOR** a platform with wheels on which a camera operator and camera are placed in order to film moving shots for a film or television programme **3.**

MECH ENG **WHEELED PLATFORM FOR MOVING THINGS** a platform on wheels used to move heavy weights **4.** CIV ENG **WEIGHT DROPPED ON POST** a heavy weight dropped on a stake or pile to force it into the ground **5.** CONSTR **TOOL FOR HOLDING RIVET** an anvil that holds one end of a rivet while the other end is being hammered **6.** METALL **HEAVY BLOCK HELD BEHIND HAMMERED METAL** a heavy block held behind sheet metal that is being hammered **7.** CRICKET **EASY BALL** an easy catch (*informal*) ■ *vti* (**-lies, -lying, -lied**) MOVE CAMERA ON DOLLY to move a camera on a dolly in order to film moving shots

dolly bird *n* a young woman thought to be good-looking (*dated informal*; *sometimes considered offensive*)

dolly drop *n* in cricket, a ball bowled high and slowly that reaches the batsman without touching the ground

dolly mixtures *npl* small sweets of various colours, sold as a mixture

dolly shot *n* a shot filmed from a camera mounted on a wheeled platform

Dolly Varden /dólli vaárd'n/ *n* **1.** a woman's hat with a large brim, usually with one side turned down, and decorated with flowers **2.** (*plural same*) a trout or char with red spots found in lakes and streams. Native to: western North America, eastern Asia. Latin name: *Salvelinus malma*. [Late 19C. After a woman of colourful dress in the novel *Barnaby Rudge* by Charles Dickens]

dolma /dólma/ (*plural* **-mas** or **-mades** /dol maá thez, -deez/) *n* a Greek or Turkish dish consisting of a vine or cabbage leaf with a stuffing, usually of meat and rice [Late 17C. < Turkish, 'something stuffed']

dolman /dólmən/ *n* **1.** a woman's coat with large sleeves cut in one piece with the body of the garment **2.** a long Turkish robe [Late 16C. Via French *dol(i)man* < Turkish *dolama(n)* 'robe']

dolman jacket *n* a style of riding jacket, usually worn like a cloak over the shoulders with the sleeves hanging loose

dolman sleeve *n* a sleeve cut in one piece with the body of a garment such as a jacket or dress, particularly one fitting tightly at the wrist and wide at the armhole

dolmen

dolmen /dólmən/ *n* a prehistoric structure thought to have been used as a tomb that consists of a large horizontal slab of stone supported by two or more vertical slabs [Mid-19C. < French]

dolomite /dólla mīt/ *n* **1.** a white, reddish, or greenish mineral consisting of calcium magnesium carbonate. Source: sedimentary rocks. Use: building stone, cement, fertilizers. **2.** a sedimentary rock consisting mainly of the mineral dolomite [Late 18C. < French, after Déodat de *Dolomieu* (1750–1801), French geologist]

Dolomites /dólla mīts/ mountain group in the eastern part of the northern Italian Alps. The highest peak is Marmolada, 3,342 km/10,964 ft.

dolor *n US* spelling of **dolour**

doloroso /dólla róssō/ *adv* sadly or sorrowfully (*used as a musical direction*) [Early 19C. Via Italian < late Latin *dolorosus* (see DOLOROUS)] —**doloroso** *adj*

dolorous /dóllərəss/ *adj* showing, causing, or involving sorrow (*literary*) [14C. Via French < late Latin *dolorosus* < Latin *dolor* (see DOLOUR)] —**dolorously** *adv* —**dolorousness** *n*

dolostone /dólle stōn/ n a form of limestone having more than 50% dolomite [Mid-20C. < DOLOMITE]

dolour /dóllər/ n intense sadness (literary) [13C. Via French < Latin dolor 'pain, grief, sorrow' < dolere 'feel pain']

dolphin

dolphin /dólfin/ (plural **-phins** or same) n **1.** an intelligent sea mammal (**cetacean**) that resembles a large fish and has teeth and a snout similar to a beak. Found almost worldwide, dolphins are related to whales, but are smaller. Family: Delphinidae. **2.** a large sea fish of the perch family, popular as a game fish, that has a long dorsal fin, high blunt forehead, and a brilliant green, blue, and yellow body. Latin name: Coryphaena hippurus or Coryphaena equisetis. [14C. Via Old French daulphin < Greek delphin-]

dolphinarium /dólfi naíri əm/ (plural **-ariums** or **-aria** /-aíri ə/) n a large pool in which dolphins are kept, either for research or for public displays

dolphinfish /dólfin fish/ (plural same or **-fishes**) n FISH same as **dolphin** (sense 2)

dolphin striker n a strut extending from the front of a sailing vessel that helps to prevent upward movement of a beam such as a bowsprit

dolt /dōlt/ n an offensive term that deliberately insults somebody's intelligence (dated informal insult) [Mid-16C. Origin ?]

doltish /dóltish/ adj an offensive term meaning having or showing little or no intelligence (dated informal) —**doltishly** adv —**doltishness** n

Dom /dom/, **dom** n **1.** a title used before the name of some Roman Catholic monks, especially Benedictines **2.** formerly, a title used before the names of some members of the aristocracy and royalty in Portugal and Brazil [Late 17C. Shortening of Latin dominus 'lord']

DOM abbr CHR to God, the best, the greatest [Latin Deo Optimo Maximo]

dom. abbr **1.** domestic **2.** MUSIC dominant

-dom suffix **1.** status, condition ○ martyrdom **2.** office, rank, domain ○ dukedom **3.** people associated with a status or rank ○ fandom [Old English -dōm < Indo-European, 'put, place']

domain /dō máyn, də-/ n **1.** SCOPE the scope of a subject **2.** SPHERE OF INFLUENCE an area of activity over which somebody has influence **3.** TERRITORY GOVERNED a territory ruled by a government or a leader **4.** LAND OWNED an area of land owned and controlled by a person, family, or organization **5.** LAW RIGHTS OF OWNERSHIP rights relating to the ownership of land **6.** ONLINE same as **domain name 7.** MATHS SET OF VALUES OF VARIABLE the set of possible values specified for a given mathematical function **8.** PHYS REGION OF UNIFORM MAGNETISM a region in a ferromagnetic material within which all the atoms are magnetically oriented in the same direction. Increasing the magnetic field increases the size and number of the domains. **9.** ANZ PUBLIC SPACE a public recreation area [15C. < French domaine, alteration of demeine (see DEMESNE)]

domain name n the sequence of words, phrases, abbreviations, or characters that serves as the Internet address of a computer or network

dome /dōm/ n **1.** HEMISPHERICAL ROOF a hemispherical roof, e.g. on a palace or cathedral **2.** HEMISPHERICAL TOP something that resembles a dome in shape and position, e.g. the cover of a furnace or the top of somebody's head ○ the dome of the sky **3.** HEMISPHERICAL

INTERNET DOMAINS

Top-level domains in Internet addresses are the final letters of the address. They indicate the country – except for the United States, where no country code is used – or type of organization, or both.

Selected Organization Domains

Domain	Organization
.ac	academic organization
.aero	aviation industry
.biz	business
.com	commercial organization
.coop	nonprofit cooperative
.edu	educational organization
.gov	government organization
.info	general use
.int	international organization
.mil	military organization
.museum	museum
.name	private individual
.net	networking organization
.org	noncommercial organization
.pro	professional practice

For countries other than the United States, country domains can be combined with organization domains, for example:

.co.uk	United Kingdom organization
.edu.au	Australian educational organization

Selected Country Domains

Domain	Country
.au	Australia
.bd	Bangladesh
.ca	Canada
.gh	Ghana
.hk	Hong Kong
.id	Indonesia
.ie	Ireland
.in	India
.ke	Kenya
.my	Malaysia
.nz	New Zealand
.ng	Nigeria
.pk	Pakistan
.sg	Singapore
.za	South Africa
.lk	Sri Lanka
.ug	Uganda
.uk	United Kingdom
.zm	Zambia
.zw	Zimbabwe

BUILDING STRUCTURE a hemispherical or convex structure, especially a building ○ the Millennium Dome **4.** CRYSTAL FORMATION RESEMBLING ROOF a crystal form in which two inclined surfaces intersect to form an edge like a roof **5.** LARGE STATELY BUILDING a large grand building (archaic) **6.** GEOL CURVED ROCK LAYER a hemispherical topographic feature that slopes in all directions from a central point, formed by upward folding of sediments **7.** GEOL LAVA MASS a mass of solidified viscous lava formed above the vent of a volcano by the build-up of magma ■ v (**domes**, **doming**, **domed**) **1.** vti FORM HEMISPHERICAL SHAPE to rise in a hemispherical shape, or form something into this shape **2.** vt PUT DOME OVER SOMETHING to cover something with a dome [Mid-17C. Via French dôme < Italian duomo 'house, house of God, cathedral' < Latin domus 'house'] —**domed** adj

Dome of the Rock /dōm əv thə rók/ n a domed shrine in Jerusalem, which for Muslims is the second most holy place after the Kaaba at Mecca. It is built on the rock from which Muhammad is believed to have ascended to heaven, and where Abraham is believed to have offered the sacrifice of Isaac.

domesday /doomz day/ n CHR same as **doomsday** (sense 1) (archaic)

Domesday Book, **Doomsday Book** n a record of all the land in England, its value, and its ownership, commissioned by William the Conqueror in 1085 [Because the ultimate authority]

domestic /də méstik/ adj **1.** RELATING TO HOME relating to or used in the home or everyday life within a household **2.** RELATING TO FAMILY relating to or involving a family or the people living together within a household **3.** NOT WILD kept as a farm animal or as a pet **4.** COMM NOT FOREIGN produced, distributed, sold, or occurring within a country ○ domestic oil producers **5.** POL OF NATION'S INTERNAL AFFAIRS relating to the internal affairs of a nation or country ○ domestic issues such as elections **6.** ENJOYING HOME enjoying home and family life ■ n **1.** HOUSEHOLD SERVANT somebody employed to do housework in somebody else's home or other duties in a large household **2.** COMM PRODUCT NOT ORIGINATING ABROAD a product manufactured within

---

a country [15C. Via French < Latin domesticus < domus 'house'] —**domestically** adv

domesticate /də mésti kayt/ (**-cates, -cating, -cated**) vt **1.** TAME ANIMAL to accustom an animal to living with or near people, usually as a farm animal or pet **2.** ACCUSTOM SOMEBODY TO HOUSEHOLD LIFE to accustom somebody to home life or housework (humorous) **3.** BIOL ADAPT PLANTS OR ANIMALS FOR HUMANS to cultivate plants or raise animals, selectively breeding them to increase their suitability for human requirements [Mid-17C. < medieval Latin domesticat-, past participle of domesticare < Latin domesticus (see DOMESTIC)] —**domesticable** adj —**domesticated** adj —**domestication** /də mésti káysh'n/ n —**domesticator** n

domesticity /dóm e stíssəti, dóm-/ n **1.** HOME LIFE life as it is lived at home **2.** FONDNESS FOR HOME LIFE a liking for or familiarity with home life ■ **domesticities** npl HOUSEHOLD MATTERS the concerns of the home and family

domestic prelate n a Roman Catholic priest with honorary membership of the papal household

domestic violence n physical violence between members of a family, especially between spouses or partners

Domett /dómmit/, **Alfred** (1811–87) British-born New Zealand politician and poet. He was premier of New Zealand (1862–63). His poetic works include Ranolf and Amohia (1872).

domette /dō mét/ n a soft fleecy wool and acrylic fabric. Use: lightweight interlining. [Early 19C. Origin ?]

domical /dómmik'l/ adj **1.** shaped like a dome **2.** having a dome or domes

domicile /dómmi sīl/ n **1.** LAW SOMEBODY'S PLACE OF RESIDENCE somebody's true, fixed, and legally recognized place of residence, especially in cases of prolonged absence that require them to prove a continuing and significant connection with the place **2.** N Am SOMEBODY'S HOME the house, flat, or other place where somebody lives (formal) **3.** COMM PLACE FOR PAYMENT the place at which a bill of exchange is to be paid ■ vt (**-ciles, -ciling, -ciled**) GIVE SOMEBODY HOME to establish

---

somebody in or provide somebody with a place of residence (*formal*) ○ *The authorities domiciled the family in a nearby town.* [15C. Directly or via French < Latin *domicilium* < *domus* 'house']

domiciled /dómmi sīld/ *adj* resident in a particular place (*formal*)

domiciliary /dómmi sílli əri/ *adj* 1. relating to a home or homes 2. provided for or attending to people in their own homes [Late 19C. Via French *domiciliaire* < medieval Latin *domiciliarius* < Latin *domicilium* (see DOMICILE)]

domiciliary care *n* personal, domestic, or nursing care provided for people at home rather than in an institution

domiciliate /dómmi sílli ayt/ (-ates, -ating, -ated) *vt* same as **domicile** (*formal*) [Late 18C. < Latin *domicilium* (see DOMICILE)]

dominance /dómminənss/ *n* 1. POWER EXERTED OVER OTHERS control or command wielded over others 2. FIRST IMPORTANCE prime importance, effectiveness, or prominence 3. GENETICS EXPRESSION OF GENETIC FEATURE the property of a gene that causes a parental characteristic it controls to occur in any offspring 4. ECOL PREPONDERANCE OF ONE SPECIES the preponderance of a single plant or animal species in a specific community or over a specific period

dominance hierarchy *n* BIOL same as **hierarchy** (sense 3)

dominant /dómminənt/ *adj* 1. IN CONTROL in control or command over others 2. MORE IMPORTANT more important, effective, or prominent than others 3. GENETICS EXPRESSING SAME CHARACTERISTIC IN OFFSPRING describes a gene that causes a parental characteristic it controls to occur in any offspring, or describes the characteristic itself 4. ECOL PREPONDERANT IN COMMUNITY OR PERIOD relating to a single plant or animal species that is preponderant within a specific community or over a specific period 5. MUSIC RELATING TO 5TH NOTE OF SCALE relating to the fifth note of a musical scale or the harmony based around that note ■ *n* MUSIC 1. 5TH NOTE OF SCALE the fifth note of a musical scale 2. CHORD BASED ON 5TH NOTE a chord or key based on the fifth note of a musical scale [15C. Via French < Latin *dominant-*, present participle of *dominari* (see DOMINATE)] — **dominantly** *adv*

dominant estate *n* N Am same as **dominant tenement**

dominant hemisphere *n* the half of the brain that tends to exercise greater control over functions such as language or movement of the left or right side of the body

dominant tenement *n* property that gives its owner some rights over other property such as the right to cross land belonging to somebody else in order to reach your own house. N Am term **dominant estate**

dominate /dómmi nayt/ (-nates, -nating, -nated) *vti* 1. CONTROL to have control, power, or authority over somebody or something 2. BE PROMINENT to be the most important aspect or element of something 3. BE INFLUENTIAL to have a prevailing influence on somebody or something 4. TOWER ABOVE AREA to overlook an area from a prominent and usually elevated position [Early 17C. < Latin *dominat-*, past participle of *dominari* 'be lord, rule' < *dominus* 'lord'] — **dominative** *adj* — **dominator** *n*

ORIGIN The Latin word *dominus* 'lord', from which **dominate** is derived, is also the source of English *danger*, *demesne*, *domain*, *domineer*, *dominion*, *don¹* (a person), and *dungeon*.

domination /dómmi náysh'n/ *n* 1. control, power, or authority over others or another 2. an angel of the sixth of the nine orders of angels in the traditional Christian hierarchy [14C. Via French < Latin *domination-* < *dominari* (see DOMINATE)]

dominatrix /dómmi náytriks/ (*plural* -trices /-tri seez/) *n* a dominant woman partner in a sadomasochistic relationship [Mid-16C. < Latin, 'woman ruler' < *dominari* (see DOMINATE)]

dominee /dómmi neé/ *n* S Africa CHR same as **predikant** [Mid-20C. Via Afrikaans or Dutch < Latin *dominus* 'lord']

domineer /dómmi neér/ (-neers, -neering, -neered) *vti* to rule over others tyrannically, or behave in an overbearing way [Late 16C. Via Dutch *domineren* < Latin *dominari* (see DOMINATE)]

domineering /dómmi neéring/ *adj* showing a desire or tendency to exercise excessive control or authority over others —**domineeringly** *adv*

~~**dominent**~~ incorrect spelling of **dominant**

Domingo /də míng gō/, **Plácido** (*b.* 1941) Spanish-born opera singer. He is regarded by many people as the greatest tenor voice of his time. Starting in 1990, he often appeared with José Carreras and Luciano Pavarotti as one of the 'Three Tenors'.

Dominic /dómminik/, **St** (1170?–1221) Spanish priest and theologian. The founder of the Dominican order, he established priories in France, Italy, and Spain where special emphasis was placed on education. He was canonized in 1234. Born **de Guzman, Domingo**

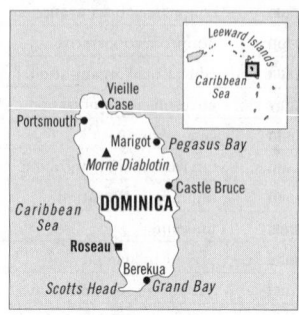

Dominica

Dominica /dómmi neékə, də mínnikə/ island country in the Windward Islands, in the eastern Caribbean Sea. It became an independent member of the Commonwealth in 1978. Language: English. Currency: Eastern Caribbean dollar. Capital: Roseau. Population: 69,655 (2003). Area: 751 sq. km/290 sq. mi. Length: 47 km/29 mi. Official name **Commonwealth of Dominica**

dominical /də mínnik'l/ *adj* (*formal*) 1. relating to Jesus Christ as the Lord 2. in Christianity, relating to Sunday as the day of the Lord [15C. Directly or via French < late Latin *dominicalis* < Latin *dominus* 'lord']

Dominican¹ /də mínnikən/ *n* 1. somebody who comes from the Dominican Republic 2. somebody who comes from Dominica [Early 19C. In sense 1 < Spanish *Dominicana*, after *Santo Domingo*, early settlement and later capital of the Dominican Republic; in sense 2 < DOMINICA] — **Dominican** *adj*

Dominican² /də mínnikən/ *n* a member of the order of friars founded by St Dominic in 1215 ■ *adj* relating or belonging to St Dominic or his order of friars [Late 16C. < medieval Latin *Dominicanus*, after St DOMINIC]

Dominican Republic

Dominican Republic /də mínnikən-/ independent country on Hispaniola Island, off the coast of Puerto Rico in the Caribbean Sea. It was proclaimed a republic in 1844. Language: Spanish. Currency: Dominican peso. Capital: Santo Domingo. Population: 8,715,602 (2003). Area: 48,734 sq. km/18,816 sq. mi. Length: 380 km/235 mi.

dominion /də mínnyən/ *n* 1. RULING CONTROL ruling power, authority, or control 2. SPHERE OF INFLUENCE somebody's area of influence or control 3. LAND RULED the land governed by a ruler (*often used in the plural*) ○ *the monarch's dominions beyond the sea* 4. *also* **Dominion** SELF-GOVERNING TERRITORY a self-governing part of the British Commonwealth or, formerly, the British

Empire [15C. Via French < medieval Latin *dominion-* < Latin *dominium* 'property, right of ownership' < *dominus* 'lord']

dominium /də mínnyəm/ *n* the right of ownership of property, especially land and buildings [Mid-18C. < Latin (see DOMINION)]

domino /dómminō/ (*plural* -noes) *n* 1. SMALL TILE USED IN GAME any one of a set of small oblong blocks with its face divided into two sections, each section either blank or marked with a number of spots, used in playing a game 2. HOODED CLOAK AND MASK formerly, a hooded cloak and eye mask worn as a disguise at a party (**masquerade**), the cloak or mask alone, or the wearer of any of these 3. COUNTRY AFFECTED BY DOMINO THEORY a country thought likely to be affected by political events in another country, particularly by the spread of Communism [Late 17C. < French, 'priest's winter hood, masked cloak worn at masquerades']

ORIGIN The use of *domino* for a small oblong block used in games (or *dominoes* for the game) is not found until the late 18C, probably as an independent borrowing from French (certain French prisoners of war being thought to have brought the game to England). Why the game is so called is uncertain, but it might come from a likening of the gaming pieces (which often originally had white faces with ebony backs) to the pale faces of priests within dark hoods.

domino effect *n* an inevitable succession of related and usually undesirable events, each caused by the preceding one [Because dominoes set up in a row fall in sequence once the first has fallen]

dominoes /dómminōz/ *n* a game played using dominoes (*takes a singular verb*)

domino theory *n* a theory that political events are interrelated and that one can trigger off a chain of others. The theory was developed by US President Dwight D. Eisenhower to warn of the spread of Communism in Southeast Asia.

Domitian /də mísh'n/ (AD 51–96) Roman emperor (81–96). Although he was popular with the army and consolidated the boundaries of the Roman empire, his rule was punctuated by clashes with the senate and the aristocracy. His murder, thought to have been instigated by his wife, ended the Flavian dynasty. Full name **Titus Flavius Domitianus**

dompas /dóm paass/, **dompass** *n* S Africa an identity document carried by Black people in South Africa during the apartheid era, used to restrict their movement within the country (*disapproving*) [Mid-20C. < Afrikaans < *dom* 'stupid' + *pas* 'pass']

don¹ /don/ *n* 1. UNIVERSITY OR COLLEGE TEACHER a university or college teacher, especially one at Oxford or Cambridge 2. SPANISH MAN OF RANK a Spanish gentleman or aristocrat 3. LEADER OF ORGANIZED CRIME FAMILY a head of an organized crime family, especially in the Mafia 4. CRIMINAL a criminal, especially a gang leader, gunman, or drug dealer (*slang; used in Black English*) [Late 16C. Via Spanish < Latin *dominus* 'lord']

don² /don/ (**dons, donning, donned**) *vt* to put on a garment [14C. Contraction of *do on* 'put on']

Don¹ /don/, **don** *n* a title used before a man's first name in Spain and other Spanish-speaking countries [Early 16C. < Spanish (see DON ¹)]

Don² /don/ river rising southeast of Moscow, Russia, flowing through Volgograd and into the Sea of Azov. Length: 1,870 km/1,160 mi.

Dona /dónnə/ *n* a title used before a married woman's first name in Portugal and other Portuguese-speaking countries [Early 17C. Via Portuguese < Latin *domina* 'lady']

Doña /dónnyə/ *n* a title used before a married woman's first name in Spain and other Spanish-speaking countries [Early 17C. Via Spanish < Latin *domina* 'lady']

Donaldson /dónn'lds'n/, **Roger** (*b.* 1945) Australian-born New Zealand filmmaker. He directed *The Bounty* (1984) and *White Sands* (1992).

donate /dō náyt/ (-nates, -nating, -nated) *v* 1. *vti* GIVE OR PRESENT SOMETHING to a contribution to a charitable organization or other good cause 2. *vt* GIVE BODY PART to give your own blood, tissue, organs, or reproductive material to be used in the treatment of another person, either while you are alive or after your death 3. *vt* CHEM TRANSFER ELECTRONS to transfer

electrons to another atom or molecule in a chemical reaction [Late 18C. Back-formation < DONATION]

SYNONYMS See *give*.

Donatello /dónnə téllō/ (1386?–1466) Italian sculptor. In his bronze statue *David* (1430–35) and other works, he revived the classical art of portraying independent functional human figures. Full name **Donato di Niccolò di Betto Bardi**

donation /dō náysh'n/ *n* **1.** a gift or contribution, especially a sum of money given to a charity ○ *All donations will be gratefully received.* **2.** the act of giving something, especially money to a charity [15C. Via French < Latin *donation*- < Latin *donare* 'give' < *donum* 'gift']

Donatist /dónətist/ *n* a member of a Christian group of the 4th and 5th centuries, originating in North Africa, that placed great emphasis on sanctity [Late 16C. < late Latin *Donatista*, after *Donatus*, regarded by Donatists as the first bishop of Carthage] —**Donatism** *n*

donative /dónətiv/ *n* **1.** OFFICIAL DONATION a donation, especially a formal or official one (*formal*) **2.** CHR CHURCH POSITION GIVEN AS GIFT a church office (**benefice**) that is or can be presented as a gift without reference to the bishop, as opposed to one received as a right ■ *adj* MADE AS GIFT given or presented as a gift (*formal*) [15C. < Latin *donativum* < *donare* 'give' (see DONATION)]

donator /dō náytər/ *n* a donor of something, especially money to a charity [15C. Directly or via French < Latin < *donare* 'give' (see DONATION)]

Doncaster /dóngkəstər/ town on the River Don in South Yorkshire, northern England. Population: 286,866 (2001).

done /dun/ past participle of **do**[1] ■ *adj* **1.** CONCLUDED completed or finished **2.** COOKED THROUGH cooked as thoroughly as required ○ *I like my steak well done.* **3.** SOCIALLY ACCEPTABLE acceptable according to the established rules and expectations of a society ○ *It's just not done.* **4.** EXHAUSTED worn out or used up (*informal*) **5.** CHEATED cheated or tricked (*informal*) **6.** US PREORDAINED having been decided already, therefore permitting no changes (*slang*) ○ *It's a done deal, and you can't fight it.* ■ *interj* AGREED used to confirm acceptance of a deal ■ *v Carib, Southern US* ALREADY used as an auxiliary verb to express the sense of 'already' (*nonstandard*) ○ *He done leave.* ■ *adv Carib, Southern US* TRULY OR INDEED used for emphasis ○ *He's done dead.* ◇ **have done with something** to be finished with something and never return to it ○ *Why don't we just sell the house and have done with it?* ◇ **the done thing** the polite and proper thing to do in accordance with social etiquette ◇ **well done** used to express praise or approval of something somebody has done

donee /dō neé/ *n* the recipient of a gift [Early 16C. < DONOR]

done for *adj* (*informal*) **1.** NEAR DEATH close to the point of dying **2.** EXHAUSTED extremely tired **3.** ABOUT TO BE RUINED facing defeat, ruin, or destruction

Donegal /dónni gawl/ county in northwestern Ireland. The Atlantic Ocean lies to the west, Northern Ireland to the east. Population: 129,994 (2002). Area: 4,830 sq. km/1,865 sq. mi. Irish name **Dœn Na nGall**

Donegal tweed *n* a rough tweed characterized by white flecks

doneness /dún nəss/ *n* the state of being fully cooked or ready to serve

doner kebab /dónnər-/, **donner kebab** *n* pitta bread filled with slices cut from a block of spiced meat, usually lamb, grilled on a spit. Based on a Turkish dish, it is usually eaten as a takeaway. N Am term **gyro** [< Turkish *döner kebap* 'rotating kebab']

Donets /də néts, -nyéts/ river in Russia and Ukraine that flows into the River Don northeast of Rostov in southwestern Russia. Length: 1,020 km/631 mi.

Donets Basin major coalfield and industrial region in southeastern Ukraine. The basin extends across the Russian border into the Rostov region.

Donets'k /də nyétsk/ industrial city in southeastern Ukraine. Population: 1,065,000 (1998).

done with *adj* completely finished and no longer an issue of importance

dong[1] /dong/ *n* **1.** DEEP TOLL a deep ringing sound **2.** ANZ PUNCH a heavy blow or punch (*informal*) ■ *vi* (**dongs, donging, donged**) TOLL DEEPLY to make a deep ringing sound [Late 16C. An imitation of the sound]

dong[2] /dong/ *n* a highly offensive term for a penis (*taboo slang*) [Mid-20C. Origin ?]

dong[3] /dong/ *n* the main unit of Vietnamese currency. See table at **currency** [Early 19C. < Vietnamese]

donga /dóng gə/ *n ANZ, S Africa* a steep-sided gully formed by soil erosion [Late 19C. < Nguni]

Dongen /dóngən, Kees van** (1877–1968) Dutch painter. The bright colours and freedom of form of his early Fauvist paintings gave way to more muted tones in his later paintings, e.g. *Aux acacias* (1916–29). Full name **Dongen, Cornelis Theodorus Marie van**

dongle /dóng g'l/ *n* a small hardware device that, when plugged into a computer, enables a specific copy-protected program to run, the program being disabled on that computer if the device is not present. The device is effective against software piracy. [Late 20C. Probably arbitrary]

dong quai /dóng kwí/ *n* **1.** a herb used in traditional Chinese medicine as a treatment for menstrual irregularities **2.** a plant of the celery family whose root is used for dong quai. Native to: China. Latin name: *Angelica sinensis*. [< Chinese]

Dong Yuan /dóng yoŏ án/ (*fl* late 10th century) Chinese artist. He is noted for his monumental, richly coloured landscapes.

Dönitz /dónits/, **Doenitz, Karl** (1891–1980) German naval officer. He was commander of the German submarine fleet (1936–43), naval commander in chief (1943–45), and chancellor of Germany (April–May 1945) after Adolf Hitler's suicide.

Donizetti /dónni zétti/, **Gaetano** (1797–1848) Italian composer. He wrote 65 operas, ranging from dramas such as *Lucia di Lammermoor* (1835) to comic works such as *Don Pasquale* (1843).

donjon /dónjən, dúnj-/ *n* a fortified central tower in a medieval castle [14C. Form of DUNGEON]

Don Juan /dón joŏ ən, -wáan/ *n* a man who has a reputation for having casual sexual relationships with numerous women [Mid-19C. After *Don Juan* Tenorio, legendary Spanish nobleman]

donkey

donkey /dóngki/ (*plural* **-keys**) *n* **1.** a small domesticated member of the horse family with a grey or brown coat, long ears, and a large head. Latin name: *Equus asinus*. **2.** somebody thought of as lacking intelligence (*informal insult*) [Late 18C. Origin ?] ◇ **donkey's years** a very long time (*informal*) ○ *I haven't seen Jack for donkey's years.* ◇ **talk the hind legs off a donkey** to chatter interminably (*slang*)

donkey derby *n* a race for people riding on donkeys, usually as a fundraising event or amusement, e.g. at a country fête

donkey engine *n* a small auxiliary steam engine used either to start a larger engine or independently, e.g. for pumping water on a ship

donkey jacket *n UK* a dark blue or black heavy woollen jacket, typically worn by people working outdoors

donkey vote *n Aus* at an election based on the preferential voting system, a vote in which the preferences are marked simply in the order that they appear on the ballot sheet. In Australia, where voting is compulsory, this is often a way of registering a protest vote or abstention.

donkeywork /dóngki wurk/ *n* (*informal*) **1.** hard or boring work **2.** basic preparation or groundwork

Donleavy /don leévi/, **J. P.** (*b.* 1926) US-born Irish novelist, short-story writer, and playwright. His first novel, *The Ginger Man* (1955), was hailed as a comic masterpiece. Among his other novels are *A Singular Man* (1963) and *The Beastly Beatitudes of Balthazar B* (1968). Full name **Donleavy, James Patrick**

'To more than a few, Ireland remains a glowingly sweet emerald vision having the fifteenth beer over some bereft bar counter at three a.m., in some outskirt corner of San Francisco, Hawaii, Boston, or the Bronx.'
[J. P. Donleavy, *J. P. Donleavy's Ireland*; 1986]

Donna /dónnə/ *n* a title used before a married woman's name in Italy [Early 17C. Via Italian < Latin *domina* 'lady']

Donne /dun/, **John** (1572–1631) English poet, prose writer, and cleric, considered the greatest of the Metaphysical poets. An author of passionate love poetry, he was later ordained and appointed Dean of St Paul's (1621). His verse includes the love poems *Songs and Sonnets*, two *Satires* (both dating from the 1590s), and *Divine Poems* (1607).

'No man is an Island, entire of itself; every man is a piece of the Continent, a part of the main; if a clod be washed away by the sea, Europe is the less, as well as if a promontory were, as well as if a manor of thy friends or of thine own were; any man's death diminishes me, because I am involved in Mankind; And therefore never send to know for whom the bell tolls; It tolls for thee.'
[John Donne, 'Meditation XVII', *Devotions upon Emergent Occasions*; 1624]

donnée /dónnay/, **donné** *n* **1.** a basic fact or assumption on which something else such as a literary or theatrical work is based and from which it develops **2.** a theme or subject, e.g. of a literary or theatrical work [Late 19C. < French, form of *donner* 'give']

donner kebab /dónnər-/ *n* FOOD another spelling of **doner kebab**

donnert /dónnərt/ *adj Scotland* **1.** an offensive term meaning unintelligent (*insult*) **2.** very surprised [Early 18C. < past participle of Scots dialect *donner* 'daze, stun', origin ?]

donnish /dónnish/ *adj* resembling the stereotypical image of a university professor, e.g. in displaying erudition or being absent-minded —**donnishly** *adv* —**donnishness** *n*

donnybrook /dónni broŏk/ *n Aus, N Am* a riotous brawl [Mid-19C. After Donnybrook, suburb of Dublin, Ireland]

donor /dónər/ *n* **1.** SOMEBODY WHO GIVES SOMETHING somebody who gives something, especially money **2.** SOMEBODY GIVING BLOOD OR BODY ORGAN somebody who voluntarily gives blood, a body organ or tissue, or reproductive material for the medical treatment of somebody else **3.** ELECTRONICS IMPURITY ADDED TO SEMICONDUCTOR an impurity (**dopant**) such as arsenic or antimony that is added to a pure semiconductor material such as silicon in order to increase its conductivity by increasing the number of carriers of negative electrical charge (**free electrons**) **4.** CHEM ATOM PROVIDING ELECTRONS FOR BOND an atom, molecule, or group that provides the pair of electrons necessary to form a chemical bond [15C. Via Anglo-Norman, Old French < Latin *donator* < *donare* 'give' (see DONATION)] —**donorship** *n*

donor card *n* a card stating that specific organs, or sometimes the entire body, of the person carrying it may be used for the treatment of others after the donor's death

donor insemination *n* the introduction into a woman's vagina of sperm from a man who is not the woman's sexual partner with the intention of making the woman pregnant

do-nothing *n* somebody who is regarded as lazy or idle (*informal insult*)

Don Quixote /dón kwíksət, -kee hóti/ *n* an impractical idealist who champions hopeless causes [Mid-17C.

After the hero of the satirical romance *Don Quixote de la Mancha* (1605, 1615) by Cervantes]

don't /dōnt/ *contr* do not

don't know *n* a voter or respondent who is undecided about an issue, e.g. during an election campaign or in an opinion survey (*informal*)

donzi /dónzi/ *n* same as **money** (*slang; used in Black English*) [Origin ?]

doo /dōō/ (*plural* **doos**) *n Scotland* **1.** BIRDS same as **dove**[1] *n* (sense 1) (*informal*) **2.** used as a term of endearment [14C. Variant of DOVE[1]]

doocot /dóokit, dōó-/, **dooket** *n Scotland* BUILDINGS same as **dovecote**

doodad /dōó dad/ *n ANZ, N Am* same as **doodah** (*informal*) [Early 20C. Origin ?]

doodah /dōó daa/ *n UK* a thing whose name somebody cannot remember or does not know (*informal*) ANZ, N Am term **doodad** [Early 20C. Probably < *dooda(h)* in the refrain to the song *Camptown Races*]

doodle /dōód'l/ (**-dles**, **-dling**, **-dled**) *vti* to draw something aimlessly or absent-mindedly, usually while doing something else such as having a telephone conversation or attending a meeting [Early 17C. < Low German *dudel-* in *dudeltopf* 'fool'] —**doodle** *n* —**doodler** *n*

doodlebug /dōód'l bug/ *n* **1.** the V-1 flying bomb (*informal*) **2.** *N Am* the large-jawed larva of an ant lion or a similar insect larva

doo-doo /dōó dōō/ *n* **1.** *N Am* human or animal excrement (*slang humorous*) **2.** *Carib* another spelling of **dou-dou** [Mid-20C. Probably < repetition of DO[1]]

doofa /dōófə/ (*plural* **-as**) *n Aus* same as **doofer** (*slang*)

doofer /dōófər/ *n* an object or gadget whose name you cannot remember or do not know (*slang*) [Mid-20C. Probably < *do for*]

doohickey /dōó hiki/ (*plural* **-eys**) *n N Am* an object or gadget whose name you cannot remember or do not know (*informal*) [Early 20C. Blend of DOODAD + HICKEY]

dook /dōōk/ *Scotland n* a wooden plug that is forced into a wall to provide loadbearing support for a nail or screw ■ *vt* (**dooks, dooking, dooked**) to force a wooden plug into a wall to support a nail or screw [Early 19C. Origin ?]

dooket *n Scotland* another spelling of **doocot**

doolally /dōō lálli/ *adj* an offensive term meaning irrational (*informal*) [Early 20C. Alteration of *Deolali*, town near Mumbai (Bombay), India, where British soldiers awaited their return home]

doolie /dōóli/ (*plural* **-ies**) *n S Asia* a stretcher used, especially in the past, to carry a single ill or wounded person [Early 17C. < Hindi *doli* 'small cradle or litter']

Doolittle /dōólitt'l/, **Hilda** (1886–1961) US poet. Known for her imagist poetry, she wrote *Sea Garden* (1916) and *Bid Me to Live* (1960). Pseudonym **H. D., Imagiste**

doom /dōōm/ *n* **1.** DISASTROUS DESTINY a dreadful fate, especially death or utter ruin **2.** OFFICIAL JUDGMENT an official judgment on somebody (*formal*) **3.** *also* **Doom** CHR same as **Judgment Day** (*archaic*) ■ *vt* (**dooms, dooming, doomed**) DESTINE SOMEBODY OR SOMETHING TO DISASTER to condemn somebody or something to a dreadful fate [Old English *dōm* 'judgment, sentence, law' < Indo-European, 'set, put']

doomed /dōōmd/ *adj* **1.** condemned to suffer a dreadful fate, especially one that is imminent and inescapable ○ *From that time, the creature was doomed to extinction.* **2.** bound to fail or suffer something unpleasant ○ *The partnership was doomed from the start.*

doom-laden *adj* suggesting impending disaster or ruin

doom palm *n* TREES same as **doum**

doomsayer /dōóm say ər/ *n* somebody who frequently predicts disasters

doomsday /dōómz day/ *n* **1.** *also* **Doomsday** a day of final reckoning, especially, in Christian theology, the day of the Last Judgment **2.** the final destruction or dissolution of the world

Doomsday Book *n* HIST another spelling of **Domesday Book**

doomster /dōómstər/ *n* same as **doomsayer** (*informal*)

doomwatch /dōóm woch/ *n* the expectation or prediction of imminent disaster, especially environmental disaster —**doomwatcher** *n*

doomy /dōómi/ (**-ier, -iest**) *adj* (*informal*) **1.** not hopeful about the future **2.** causing feelings of imminent disaster

Doona /dōónə/ *tdmk Aus* a trademark for a duvet or continental quilt

door /dawr/ *n* **1.** MOVABLE PANEL AT ENTRANCE a movable barrier used to open and close the entrance to a building, room, cupboard, or vehicle, usually a solid panel, hinged to or sliding in a frame **2.** GAP FORMING ENTRANCE the gap that forms the entrance to a building or room **3.** BUILDING OR ROOM a building or room considered in relation to those on either side ○ *She lives two doors down the street.* [Old English *duru* 'door', *dor* 'gate' < Indo-European, 'entrance to the enclosure around a house'] —**doorless** *adj* ◇ **close** *or* **shut the door on something** to disallow the possibility of something happening ◇ **lay something at somebody's door** to blame something on somebody ◇ **out of doors** in the open air ◇ **show somebody the door** to tell somebody to leave

doorbell /dawr bel/ *n* a bell placed on or beside a door, to be rung by visitors as a sign of their arrival

door bundle *n* a bundle of equipment pushed out of an aircraft by hand before parachutists exit

doorcase /dawr kayss/ *n* CONSTR same as **doorframe**

do-or-die *adj* involving the determination to risk everything in an effort to succeed

doorframe /dawr fraym/ *n* the frame constructed around the entrance to a building or room and into which a door is set

door furniture *n* all the fittings used on doors, e.g. handles, locks, knockers, and letter boxes

doorjamb /dawr jam/ *n* CONSTR same as **doorpost**

doorkeeper /dawr keepər/ *n* somebody on duty at a door or gate, especially somebody who guards the entrance

doorknob /dawr nob/ *n* a round handle used to open or close a door

doorknocker /dawr nokər/ *n* **1.** a metal fixture attached with hinges to the door of a house, used for knocking on the door **2.** somebody who visits people's homes in order to canvas for votes or sell goods or services (*informal*)

doorman /dawrmən/ (*plural* **-men** /-mən/) *n* a man on duty at the door of a building such as a nightclub or hotel, usually employed to assist customers, e.g. by calling cabs

doormat /dawr mat/ *n* **1.** a mat to wipe your shoes on immediately before or after entering a building **2.** a passive person who submits to being treated inconsiderately (*informal*)

~~**doormouse**~~ incorrect spelling of **dormouse**

doornail /dawr nayl/ *n* a nail with a large head formerly used to decorate or reinforce a door

doorperson /dawr purss'n/ (*plural* **-persons** *or* **-people** /-peep'l/) *n* somebody on duty at the door of a building such as a nightclub or hotel, usually employed to assist customers, e.g. by calling cabs

doorplate /dawr playt/ *n* a plate or plaque attached to the door of a building or room, usually giving information about the person associated with the building or room

doorpost /dawr pōst/ *n* either of the vertical side pieces of a doorframe

doorsill /dawr sil/ *n* same as **threshold** (sense 3)

doorstep /dawr step/ *n* **1.** STEP IN FRONT OF DOOR a step at the entrance to a building **2.** THICK BREAD a very thick slice of bread, or a sandwich made from thickly cut bread (*informal*) ■ *v* (**-steps, -stepping, -stepped**) **1.** *vti* CANVASS ALL HOUSES IN AREA to make door-to-door visits to members of the public to ask for their support during an election campaign **2.** *vt* WAIT AT DOOR OF FAMOUS PERSON to wait outside the home or workplace of a politician or celebrity in the hope of interviewing him or her —**doorstepping** *n* ◇ **on your (own) doorstep** very near where you live

doorstop /dawr stop/ *n* **1.** a movable device, e.g. a wedge or heavy object, used to hold a door open **2.** a rubber stud or rubber-tipped projection on a wall,

floor, or door that prevents damage to the wall when the door is opened

door to door *adv* **1.** going from one house to the next, usually in order to sell things, to collect money for charity, or to canvass support in an election **2.** from the place of departure to the place of arrival ○ *The trip took three hours door to door.*

door-to-door *adj* **1.** done or going from one house to the next (*not hyphenated when used after a verb*) **2.** from the point of departure to the point of arrival (*not hyphenated after a verb*)

doorway /dawr way/ *n* **1.** an entrance to a building or room, especially one that has a door **2.** a means of achieving or escaping from something

doorwoman /dawr wŏŏmən/ (*plural* **-women** /-wimin/) *n* a woman on duty at the door of a building such as a nightclub or hotel, usually employed to assist customers, e.g. by calling cabs

doover /dōóvər/ *n Aus* same as **doofer** (*slang*)

dooverlackie /dōóvər laki/, **dooverlacky** *n Aus* same as **doofer** (*slang*)

doo-wop /dōó wop/ *n* harmonized singing of nonsense syllables, with a rhythm-and-blues melody on top, popularized by street singers in the 1950s [Mid-20C. An imitation of the sound]

doozey /dōózi/ (*plural* **-zeys**) *n Aus* same as **doozy** (*slang*)

doozy /dōózi/ (*plural* **-zies**) *n* a remarkable or excellent thing (*slang*) [Early 20C. Origin ?]

dop /dop/ *n S Africa* a small drink (*informal*) [Late 19C. Origin ?]

dopa /dṓpə/ *n* a natural precursor of adrenaline and dopamine. Use: in synthetic form, treatment of Parkinson's disease. [Early 20C. Acronym < DI-[1] + OXY- + PHENYL + ALANINE]

dopamine /dṓpə meen/ *n* a neurotransmitter that is also a precursor of adrenaline [Mid-20C. Blend of DOPA + AMINE]

dopant /dṓpənt/ *n* a substance such as arsenic or antimony that is added in small quantities to a semiconductor material in order to change its electrical characteristics. Dopants are added during the manufacture of semiconducting diodes and transistors.

dope /dōp/ *n* **1.** ILLEGAL DRUG an illegal drug, especially cannabis (*slang*) **2.** DRUG AFFECTING PERFORMANCE a drug given illegally, e.g. to racehorses or athletes, to affect performance **3.** INSIDE INFORMATION confidential information about somebody or something (*slang*) **4.** FOOL somebody who is regarded as unintelligent (*informal insult*) **5.** CHEM VISCOUS LIQUID a viscous liquid. Use: lubrication, waterproofing and strengthening fabrics, coating aircraft wings, improving the combustion of engine fuels. **6.** CHEM ABSORBENT MATERIAL an absorbent material. Use: manufacture of dynamite. **7.** ELECTRONICS same as **dopant** ■ *vt* (**dopes, doping, doped**). **1.** ADD DRUG TO FOOD OR DRINK to add a drug to food or drink secretly in order to affect performance or consciousness **2.** ELECTRONICS ADD IMPURITY TO SEMICONDUCTOR to add a substance such as arsenic or antimony to a semiconductor material like silicon or germanium during the manufacturing process in order to increase its conductivity ■ *adj* EXTREME SPORTS COOL in snowboarding, cool, hip, or generally good or stylish (*slang*) [Early 19C. < Dutch *doop* 'thick dipping sauce' < *doopen* 'dip, mix'] —**doper** *n*

dope up *vt* to make somebody drowsy or semiconscious by administering a drug such as an anaesthetic or an illegal narcotic (*slang*)

dope dog *n US* a dog specially trained to locate by scent contraband narcotics hidden in luggage or packages or concealed on a person's body (*informal*)

dopehead /dōp hed/ *n* somebody who takes illegal drugs regularly or who is physiologically or mentally dependent on them (*slang*)

dope sheet *n* a booklet that gives information about the horses entered for races (*slang*)

dopester /dṓpstər/ *n N Am* somebody who is able to supply information and analysis about current events and forecasts for the future, especially in the fields of sport and politics (*informal*)

dopey /dṓpi/ (**-ier, -iest**), **dopy** *adj* **1.** half-asleep or drowsy **2.** showing a lack of good sense or in-

telligence (*informal insult*) —**dopily** *adv* —**dopiness** *n*

dopiaza /dṓpi azə/ *n* a mildly spiced dish of meat or fish cooked with onions and tomatoes, originating in South Asia [< Hindi *do* 'two' + *pyāz* 'onion']

doping agent /dṓping-/ *n* ELECTRONICS same as **dopant**

doppelgänger /dópp'l gangər, -geng-/ *n* **1.** somebody who closely resembles somebody else **2.** an apparition in the form of a double of a living person [Mid-19C. < German, literally 'double-goer']

Doppler effect /dópplər-/, **Doppler shift** *n* a perceived change in the frequency of a wave as the distance between the source and the observer changes. For example, the sound of a siren on a moving vehicle appears to change as it approaches and passes an observer. [Early 20C. After Christian J. *Doppler* (1803–53), Austrian physicist]

Doppler radar *n* a means of detecting a moving target that uses electromagnetic radiation and relies on a change in the frequency of microwave signals reflected from the target [Mid-20C. < its use of the DOPPLER EFFECT]

Doppler shift *n* PHYS same as **Doppler effect**

dopy *adj* another spelling of **dopey**

dor /dawr/ *n* a European dung beetle that makes a droning sound as it flies. Latin name: *Geotrupes stercorarius*. [Old English *dora* 'bumblebee', origin ?]

dorado /də raáadō/ (*plural* **-dos** or *same*) *n* **1.** FISH same as **dolphin** (sense 2) **2.** a fish resembling a salmon. Native to: South America. Genus: *Salminus*. [Early 17C. Via Spanish, literally 'gilded' < late Latin *deauratus*, past participle of *deaurare* (see DORY[2])]

Dorado *n* an inconspicuous constellation of the southern hemisphere containing part of the Large Magellanic Cloud. See illustration at **constellation**

Doráti /də raáti/, **Antal** (1906–88) Hungarian-born US conductor and composer. He championed Hungarian music and conducted many of the world's major orchestras.

'When I was 25, Bartók needed me, a young man who would get up on the podium, play his music and be whistled at for it.'
[Antal Doráti, *Remark*; April 1986]

dorbeetle /dáwr beet'l/ *n* INSECTS same as **dor**

Dorcas society /dáwrkəss-/ *n* a Christian women's charitable organization that gives clothes to the poor [Mid-19C. After a Christian woman in the Bible (Acts 9:36, 39) who made clothes for the poor]

Dorchester /dáwrchistər/ *n* historic county town of Dorset, southern England. Population: 15,037 (1991).

Dordogne /dawr dóyn, -dónnyə/ river in southwestern France. It rises in the Massif Central and flows generally westwards to join the Garonne north of Bordeaux. Length: 483 km/300 mi.

Dordrecht /dáwr drekt, -drekht/ city and port in Zuid-Holland Province, southwestern Netherlands. An ancient city with many medieval buildings, it is also an important industrial centre. Population: 119,811 (2000).

Doré /dáw ray/, **Gustave** (1833–83) French illustrator, painter, and sculptor. He is best known for his vivid wood engravings, which were used as illustrations for the works of Dante, Edgar Allan Poe, and John Milton, among others. Full name **Doré, Paul Gustave**

Dorian /dáwri ən/ *n* a member of a Greek-speaking people who overthrew the Mycenaean civilization on mainland Greece about 1100 BC. They subsequently colonized the Peloponnese and other parts of the Mediterranean area. [Mid-16C. < Latin *Dorius* 'of Doris' (region of ancient Greece) < Greek *Dōrios* < *Dōris* 'Doris'] —**Dorian** *adj*

Dorian mode *n* a scale of notes originating in ancient Greek music and consisting of the eight notes of the diatonic scale rising from D to D

Doric /dórrik/ *n* **1.** ANCIENT GREEK DIALECT a dialect of ancient Greek spoken in the area of the modern Peloponnese **2.** DIALECT OF SCOTS a rural dialect of Scots spoken in parts of northeastern Scotland ■ *adj* **1.** IN SIMPLE CLASSICAL ARCHITECTURAL STYLE relating to or built in a style of architecture characterized by fluted columns with a rounded moulding at the top and no base **2.** OF DORIANS relating to the Dorians of ancient Greece **3.** OF DORIC relating to Doric dialect

[Mid-16C. Via Latin, 'of Doris' (region of ancient Greece) < Greek *Dōrikos* < *Dōris* 'Doris']

Doric order *n* the first of the five classical orders of architecture, characterized by fluted columns with a rounded moulding at the top and no base. It was developed in Greece in the 7th century BC.

dork /dawrk/ *n* an offensive term that deliberately insults somebody's intelligence, physical appearance or social skills (*slang insult*) [Mid-20C. Origin ?]

Dorking[1] /dáwrking/ *n* a heavy domestic fowl belonging to a breed originating in England. Kept for food. [Late 18C. After DORKING[2]]

Dorking[2] /dáwrking/ town in Surrey, southeastern England. Population: 15,658 (1991).

dorky /dáwrki/ (**-ier**, **-iest**) *adj* regarded as being unintelligent, physically unattractive, or useless (*slang insult*)

dorm /dawrm/ *n* EDUC, TRAVEL same as **dormitory** (*informal*) [Early 20C. Shortening]

dormant /dáwrmənt/ *adj* **1.** NOT ACTIVELY GROWING in an inactive state, when growth and development slow or cease, in order to survive adverse environmental conditions **2.** TEMPORARILY INACTIVE temporarily inactive or not in use **3.** NOT ERUPTING describes a volcano that is not erupting, but not extinct **4.** LATENT latent and able to be aroused ○ *dormant feelings of uneasiness* **5.** HERALDRY SLEEPING in a heraldic device, portrayed in a sleeping posture [14C. < French, present participle of *dormir* 'sleep' < Latin *dormire*] —**dormancy** *n*

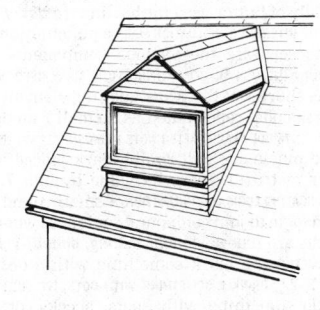

dormer

dormer /dáwrmər/, **dormer window** *n* a window for a room within the roof space that is built out at right angles to the main roof and has its own gable [Late 16C. < Old French *dormëor* 'sleeping room' < *dormir* (see DORMANT)]

dormice ZOOL plural of **dormouse**

dormie /dáwrmi/ *adj* in golf, as many holes up on an opponent as there are holes left to play ○ *dormie four* [Mid-19C. Origin ?]

Dormition of the Blessed Virgin /dawr míssh'n-/ *n* CHR same as **Assumption** (sense 2) [Via French < Latin *dormition-* 'a sleeping' < *dormire* 'to sleep']

dormitory /dáwrmitəri/ (*plural* **-ries**) *n* **1.** a large room in which many people sleep, e.g. at a boarding school or in a hostel **2.** *N Am* EDUC same as **hall of residence 3.** *Aus* SOCIOL same as **dormitory suburb** [15C. < Latin *dormitorium* < *dormire* 'to sleep']

dormitory suburb *n* a suburb whose residents commute to work in the city centre. N Am term **bedroom community**

dormitory town *n* a small town whose residents commute to work in a nearby city. US term **bedroom community**

Dormobile /dáwrmō beel/ *tdmk* a trademark for a motor vehicle equipped for living and sleeping in as well as travelling

dormouse /dáwr mowss/ (*plural* **-mice** /-mīss/) *n* a small nocturnal rodent resembling a mouse with reddish-brown fur and a hairy tail. Dormice feed on nuts, berries, and seeds, and hibernate during the winter. Family: Gliridae. [15C. Origin ?]

Dornoch Firth /dáwr nok-, -nəkh-/ inlet of the North Sea in Highland District, Scotland. It is a National Scenic Area.

Dorothy bag /dórrəthi-/ *n* a small handbag tied by

dormouse

drawstrings that are looped over the wrist [Early 20C. < the woman's name *Dorothy*]

Dorothy Dixer /-díksər/, **dorothy dixer** *n Aus* a question, usually asked in parliament, that allows a minister or other politician to give a prepared answer [Mid-20C. After a popular advice column *Dear Dorothy Dix* by E. M. Gilmer (1870–1951), US journalist suspected of making up many enquiries herself]

dorp /dawrp/ *n S Africa* a village or small country town, sometimes one perceived as backward or unappealing [Mid-19C. < Dutch]

Dors. *abbr* Dorset

dorsa ANAT plural of **dorsum**

dorsal /dáwrss'l/ *adj* **1.** relating to or situated on the back of the body **2.** describes the underside of a leaf or other surface that faces away from the stem [15C. Directly or via French < late Latin *dorsalis* < Latin *dorsum* (see DORSUM)] —**dorsally** *adv*

dorsal fin *n* a single fin on the back of a fish or other water animal such as a dolphin that gives it stability while swimming

Dorset /dáwrssit/ county on southern coast of England. Dorchester is the county town. Population: 390,980 (2001). Area: 2,654 sq. km/1,025 sq. mi.

dorsi- *prefix* same as **dorso-**

dorsiflexion /dáwrssi fléksh'n/ *n* the bending back of a hand or foot or of the fingers or toes

dorsiventral /dáwrssi véntrəl/ *adj* **1.** describes something such as a leaf or a flatworm that is flat, with distinct upper and lower surfaces **2.** ANAT same as **dorsoventral** (sense 1) —**dorsiventrality** /-ven trálləti/ *n* —**dorsiventrally** *adv*

dorso- *prefix* back, upper surface ○ *dorsolateral* [< Latin *dorsum*]

dorsolateral /dáwrssō láttərəl/ *adj* relating to or involving both the back and the side of the body —**dorsolaterally** *adv*

dorsoventral /dáwrssō véntrəl/ *adj* **1.** extending from the back of the body to the front **2.** BIOL same as **dorsiventral** (sense 1)

dorsum /dáwrssəm/ (*plural* **-sa** /-sə/) *n* the back or upper surface of a part of the body such as the hand or foot (*technical*) [Late 18C. < Latin, 'the back']

Dortmund /dáwrtmənd, -mŏŏnd/ city and inland port in North Rhine-Westphalia State in northwestern Germany. A major industrial centre, it is situated in the Ruhr district, about 32 km/20 mi. east of Essen. Population: 600,918 (1997).

dory[1] /dáwri/ (*plural* **-ries**) *n* **1.** a small boat used for various purposes such as patrolling a harbour or transporting people from a larger vessel to the shore **2.** *N Am* a narrow flat-bottomed fishing boat with high sides [Early 18C. Origin ?]

dory[2] /dáwri/ (*plural* **-ries**) *n* a fish with a deep flat body, spiny fins, and an extendable mouth, found near the ocean bottom. Family: Zeidae. [14C. < French *dorée* < form of *dorer* 'gild' < late Latin *deaurare* 'gild over' < Latin *aurum* 'gold']

DOS /doss/ *abbr* COMPUT **1.** denial-of-service **2.** disk operating system

dosa /dṓssə/ (*plural* **-sas** or **-sai** /dṓssī/) *n* a pancake made with rice and lentil flour that is usually stuffed with spiced vegetables and eaten with chutney, originating in South India [< Tamil *tōcai*]

dos-à-dos /dṓ zaa dṓ, dṓssi dṓ/ *n* (*plural same*) a seat on which two or more people can sit back to back, or a vehicle fitted with such a seat (*dated*) ■ *n, interj* DANCE same as **do-si-do** [Mid-19C. < French, 'back to back']

dosage /dṓssij/ *n* **1. DOSE OF DRUG** the amount and frequency of drug administration ○ *Do not exceed the recommended dosage.* **2. ADMINISTRATION OR DETERMINATION OF DOSE** the administration of a measured amount of a drug, or the determination of the correct amount **3. ADDING OF EXTRA INGREDIENT** the addition of an extra ingredient to something, especially wine

dose /dōss/ *n* **1. PRESCRIBED AMOUNT OF MEDICATION** a measured quantity of medication administered once or at specific intervals **2. SHORT PERIOD OF SOMETHING UNPLEASANT** a bout of something unpleasant, especially a minor illness (*informal*) **3. EXPOSURE TO RADIATION** the amount of radiation to which somebody or something is exposed during a specific time, either accidentally or as part of an experiment or medical treatment **4. EXTRA INGREDIENT** an additional ingredient such as syrup added to wine to fortify it **5. VENEREAL DISEASE** an infection with a sexually transmitted disease (*slang*) ■ *vt* (**doses, dosing, dosed**) **1. GIVE MEDICINE TO SOMEBODY** to administer medication to somebody ○ *I've been dosing myself up with flu remedies all week.* **2. MEASURE OUT MEDICATION** to prescribe or administer the required amount of medication **3. ADD INGREDIENT TO SOMETHING** to add an extra ingredient to something [15C. Via French < Greek *dosis* 'prescribed portion' < *didonai* 'give'] ◇ **go through something like a dose of salts** to do and finish something very quickly (*informal*) ◇ **in small doses** no more than a little at a time (*informal*) ○ *I can take their music only in small doses.*

dosemeter /dṓss meetər/ *n* MEASURE same as **dosimeter**

dosh /dosh/ *n* same as **money** (sense 1) (*informal*) [Mid-20C. Origin ?]

do-si-do /dṓssi dṓ/ *n* (*plural* **do-si-dos**) a movement in square dancing in which two dancers pass each other and circle back to back ■ *interj* used to instruct dancers to perform a do-si-do [Early 20C. Alteration of DOS-À-DOS] —**do-si-do** *vti*

dosimeter /dō símmitər/ *n* an instrument for measuring the amount of radiation absorbed by somebody or something, often fixed in a working area or worn by personnel who might be exposed to radiation [Late 19C. < DOSE] —**dosimetric** /dṓssi méttrik/ *adj*—**dosimetrician** /dṓssi-/ *n*—**dosimetrist** *n*—**dosimetry** *n*

Dos Passos /doss páss oss/, **John** (1896–1970) US writer. He is best known for his *U.S.A.* trilogy (1930–36), a critical portrait of US life. Full name **Dos Passos, John Roderigo**

> 'They wrapped me in the stars and stripes.
> I never remembered whether they brought
> me home or buried me at sea but anyway
> I was wrapped up in Old Glory.'
> [John Dos Passos, *The 42nd Parallel*; 1930]

doss /doss/ *vi* (**dosses, dossing, dossed**) **SLEEP ON MAKESHIFT BED** to sleep or settle down to sleep, especially on an improvised bed (*slang*) ○ *Can I doss down on your floor tonight?* ■ *n* **1. IMPROVISED OR BASIC BED** a bed for the night or a place to sleep, especially a makeshift one or one in a dosshouse **2. PERIOD OF SLEEP** a period of sleep (*slang*) **3. EASY TASK** an easy job or activity (*slang*) [Late 18C. Origin ?]

dossal /dóss'l/, **dossel** *n* a rich hanging for the back of an altar or the sides of a chancel in a church [Mid-17C. < medieval Latin *dossale* < Latin *dorsum* 'the back']

dosser /dóssər/ *n* **1.** an offensive term for somebody who sleeps on the street or in a cheap lodging house because he or she has no private dwelling (*slang*) **2.** *Ireland* an offensive term for somebody perceived as lazy and unwilling to work (*insult*)

dosshouse /dóss howss/ *n* a cheap and very basic lodging house for homeless people (*informal*) N Am term **flophouse**

dossier /dóssi ay, -ər/ *n* a collection of documents relating to a person or topic [Late 19C. < French (originally 'bunch of papers with a label on the back') < *dos* 'the back' < Latin *dorsum*]

dost /dust/ 2nd person singular present of **do**[1] (*archaic*)

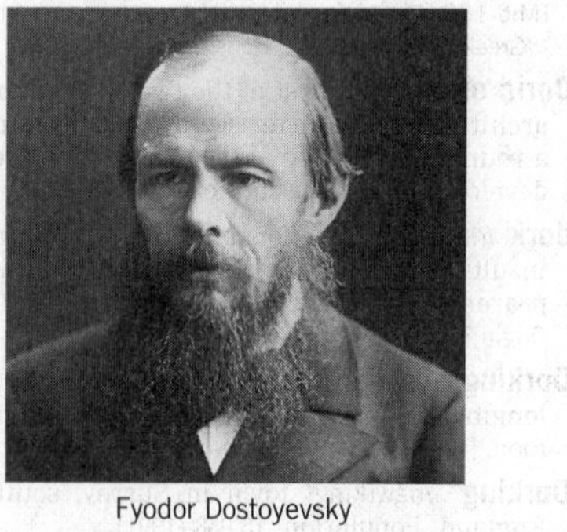

AKG London

Fyodor Dostoyevsky

Dostoyevsky /dóst oy éfski/, **Fyodor** (1821–81) Russian novelist. He is author of *Crime and Punishment* (1866) and *The Brothers Karamazov* (1879–80). Full name **Dostoyevsky, Fyodor Mikhaylovich**

> 'If the devil doesn't exist but man has created him, he has created him in his own image and likeness.'
> [Fyodor Dostoyevsky, *The Brothers Karamazov*; 1879–80]

dot[1] /dot/ *n* **1. WRITTEN OR PRINTED POINT** a small round written or printed mark that placed above the body of the lowercase letter 'i' or one of a set of three replacing missing text **2. SPOT OR SPECK** a small round mark, spot, or speck ○ *The ship was just a dot on the horizon.* **3. SMALL AMOUNT** a very small amount, especially of butter used for basting ○ *a dot of butter* **4.** ONLINE **INTERNET PUNCTUATION MARK** a punctuation mark used to separate the various components of an Internet address **5.** COMMUNICATION **MARK USED IN MORSE CODE** the shorter of the two signalling elements used in Morse code, represented as a small round mark **6.** MUSIC **SYMBOL PLACED AFTER NOTE IN MUSIC** in written or printed music, a small round mark placed after a note or rest to increase its value by half **7.** LOGIC **MARK INDICATING LOGICAL CONJUNCTION** a small round mark used in logic to join compound sentences when both elements are true ■ *vt* (**dots, dotting, dotted**) **1. PUT DOT OVER SOMETHING** to mark something with a dot ○ *dot your i's* **2. SPRINKLE SOMETHING WITH DOTS** to scatter or sprinkle something with spots, specks, or small amounts of something ○ *Dot the fish with butter.* [Old English *dott* 'head of a boil', probably < Germanic, 'lump, plug'] —**dotter** *n* ◇ **on the dot (of)** exactly at the specified time ○ *arrived on the dot* ○ *was expected to get here on the dot of nine*

dot[2] /dot/ *n* in law, a woman's dowry [Mid-19C. Via French < Latin *dot-* 'dowry'] —**dotal** /dṓt'l/ *adj*

dot address *n* the common notation for Internet addresses in the form A.B.C.D., each letter representing, in decimal notation, one byte of a four-byte address

dotage /dṓtij/ *n* an offensive term for the lack of strength or concentration sometimes believed to be characteristic of old age [14C. < DOTE]

dotard /dṓtərd/ *n* an offensive term for somebody who is thought to be unable to think clearly, especially when the inability is attributed to the person's age (*insult*) [14C. < DOTE] —**dotardly** *adj*

dot bomb *n* a failed Internet business (*humorous*)

dotcom /dot kóm/, **dot.com** *n* a company that does business on the Internet or that provides Internet services [< the domain identification *.com* of company Internet addresses] —**dot-com** *adj*

dot-comer /dot kómmər/, **dotcomer, dot.comer** *n* **1.** somebody who works in a dotcom **2.** somebody who does business on the Internet or who consistently buys high-tech shares

dote /dōt/ (**dotes, doting, doted**) *vi* to be very fond of somebody or something ○ *They dote on their grandchildren.* [12C. Origin ?] —**doter** *n*

doth /duth/ 3rd person singular present of **do**[1] (*archaic*)

doting /dṓting/ *adj* demonstrating great love and fondness for somebody or something ○ *doting parents of two new babies* —**dotingly** *adv*

dot matrix *n* a grid of dots selectively lit or coloured to display or print letters, numbers, and other symbols

dot pitch *n* a measure of the clarity of a computer image, based on the amount of white space between the pixels or dots forming the image. The smaller the dot pitch, the greater the clarity.

dot product *n* MATHS same as **scalar product**

dots per inch *n* full form of **dpi**

dotted /dóttid/ *adj* **1. WITH DOTS** marked or patterned with dots **2. COVERED WITH SPECKS** scattered or sprinkled with small things or larger things seen from a distance ○ *a sky dotted with stars* **3. RANDOMLY ARRAYED** spread randomly over a wide area ○ *a lawn dotted with hoop-skirted belles* **4.** MUSIC **INCREASED IN VALUE BY HALF** describes a note or rest in written or printed music increased in value by half

dotted line *n* a printed line formed from dots or dashes, especially one on which somebody is to write something such as a signature

dotted swiss *n* a cotton fabric patterned with raised dots [Shortening of *Swiss muslin*]

dotterel /dóttrəl/ (*plural* **-els** or *same*), **dottrel** (*plural* **-trels** or *same*) *n* **1. REDDISH-BROWN BIRD** a reddish-brown bird of the plover family with white markings on the head and neck. Native to: Europe, Asia. Latin name: *Eudromias morinellus.* **2. BIRD FOUND IN WETLANDS AND GRASSLANDS** a bird of the plover family found in grasslands or near water. Native to: Australia, Andes. Family: Charadriidae. **3.** (*plural* **dotterels** or **dottrels**) **GULLIBLE PERSON** somebody regarded as easily deceived (*archaic*) [15C. < DOTE + *-rel* (< Old French *-erel*); because the plover is easy to catch]

dottle /dótt'l/ *n* the plug of tobacco that is left in a pipe after it has been smoked [15C. < DOT[1]]

dottrel *n* another spelling of **dotterel**

dotty /dótti/ (**-tier, -tiest**) *adj* (*informal*) **1. SILLY** regarded as being irrational or impractical, often endearingly so **2. UNCONVENTIONAL** behaving in a manner that seems amusingly strange to others **3. ABSURD** illogical, impractical, or absurd **4. INFATUATED** very fond of or passionately interested in somebody or something [Late 19C. Origin ?] —**dottily** *adv* —**dottiness** *n*

Douai /doo áy/ city in Nord Department, Nord-Pas-de-Calais Region, northwestern France. A coal-mining and industrial centre, it is situated south of Lille. Population: 42,796 (1999).

Douala /doo áalə/, **Duala** chief port in Cameroon and chief city of Littoral Province, situated west of the capital Yaoundé. Population: 1,500,000 (1997).

Douay Bible /dóo ay-/, **Douay Version** *n* **1.** a Roman Catholic translation of the Latin Vulgate version of the Bible into English, written in the early 17th century **2.** a copy of the Douay Bible [Mid-19C. After *Douay* (modern DOUAI)]

double /dúbb'l/ *adj* **1. BEING TWICE AS MUCH OR MANY** being twice as much in size, number, or value **2. HAVING TWO SIMILAR PARTS** consisting of two identical, similar, or equal parts **3. MEANT FOR TWO PEOPLE** designed or intended for two people ○ *booked a double room* **4. FITTING DOUBLE BED** describes bedding of a size that will fit onto a double bed **5. TWO-LAYERED** consisting of two layers **6. FOLDED OVER ONCE** folded in two, or bent over **7. OF TWO ELEMENTS** consisting of two different parts ○ *a phrase with a double meaning* **8. ACTING IN CONTRASTING OR OPPOSING WAYS** acting one way while feeling very differently, especially when this involves hypocrisy or deceit ○ *led a double life* **9.** BOT **HAVING EXTRA PETALS** describes flowers that have more petals than normal or plants that have flowers of this type **10.** MUSIC **SOUNDING OCTAVE BELOW** sounding an octave of a musical instrument lower than the written music indicates ■ *adv* **1. TWICE AS MUCH** twice as much as normal ○ *had to pay double to get in* **2. IN TWO LAYERS** so as to form two layers ■ *n* **1. TWO TOGETHER** two viewed or regarded together **2. TWICE NORMAL AMOUNT** twice the normal or standard amount ○ *He offered me double.* **3. TWO MEASURES OF DRINK** a drink containing two single measures, especially of spirits (*informal*) **4. DUPLICATE IN APPEARANCE** somebody or something that looks very like another, especially a living person bearing a strong resemblance to somebody else **5. ROOM FOR TWO PEOPLE** a hotel room for two people **6. GHOST IDENTICAL TO LIVING PERSON** an apparition that closely resembles a living person **7. STAND-IN FOR FILM STAR** a replacement for a film actor, e.g. in scenes that involve danger, special skill, or nudity **8. BET ON TWO**

RACES a bet on two races, in which any winnings from the first become the stake for the second (*informal*) **9. SUCCESS IN TWO EVENTS** success in two events or competitions in the same year or series or against the same opponent **10. ABRUPT DIRECTIONAL CHANGE** a sharp change of direction **11. DARTS DART THAT LANDS IN OUTER RING** a throw of a dart that lands within the narrow outer ring of the dartboard, scoring twice the nominal value **12. CARDS CALL INCREASING SCORE** in an auction at bridge, a call that increases the score for succeeding or failing in a contract **13. CUE GAMES STROKE THAT MAKES BALL REBOUND** in cue games, a stroke that makes the ball rebound against a cushion and land in the opposite pocket **14. TENNIS** same as **double fault** (*informal*) **15. MIL FAST MARCHING PACE** a fast marching pace at twice the usual speed **16. PRINTING** same as **doublet** (sense 3) ■ *v* (*-bles, -bling, -bled*) **1.** *vti* **INCREASE TWOFOLD** to make something twice as large or numerous, or become twice as much or many ○ *We doubled our profits the following year.* **2.** *vt* **FOLD SOMETHING IN TWO** to fold or bend something in two **3.** *vt* **MAKE FIST** to clench the fist (*informal*) **4.** *vi* **HAVE SECOND FUNCTION** to have a second or secondary function ○ *His felt hat doubled as a water pail.* **5.** *vi* **ACT AS STAND-IN** to replace a film actor in scenes such as those that include danger, special skill, or nudity **6.** *vi* **PLAY SECOND ROLE** to play an additional part in the same performance **7.** *vt* **MUSIC DUPLICATE MUSICAL PART** to duplicate a musical part, either at the same pitch or an octave above or below **8.** *vi* **MUSIC PLAY MORE THAN ONE MUSICAL INSTRUMENT** to play one or more musical instruments, in addition to the principal one ○ *a violinist who doubles on cello* **9.** *vi* **CARDS ANNOUNCE BRIDGE DOUBLE** in an auction at bridge, to announce a double as a bid **10.** *vti* **CUE GAMES REBOUND** in cue games, to rebound off a cushion, or make a ball rebound off a cushion **11.** *vt* **CHESS PLACE PIECES NEXT TO EACH OTHER** to place two chess pieces of the same type and colour together ○ *double your opponent's pawns* **12.** *vi* **BASEBALL HIT DOUBLE** in baseball, to make a hit that gives the batter time to run to second base **13.** *vt* **NAUT ROUND HEADLAND** to sail around a headland [12C. Via Old French *do(u)bler* < Latin *duplare* < *duplus* 'twofold' < *duo* 'two'] —**doubleness** *n* ◇ **at** *or* **on the double** straight away and as quickly as possible ○ *told the children to form lines at the double*

double back *vi* to turn around and retrace your steps
double over *vi* to bend deeply from the waist, especially in response to pain or laughter
double up *vi* **1.** to share something with somebody else ○ *There weren't enough beds, so some of the children had to double up.* **2.** to bend the body over sharply from the waist, especially in response to pain or laughter

double act *n* two entertainers who regularly perform together

double-acting *adj* **1.** with one or more pistons that move in both directions, giving two strokes per cycle **2.** acting in opposite directions from a central point

double agent *n* a spy for one government who supplies secret information about that government to its rival

double-bank *vti* ANZ to ride with or carry a second person on a bicycle or horse (*informal*)

double bar *n* a symbol, ‖, that marks the end of a piece of music or the end of its principal sections

double-barrelled *adj* **1. WITH TWO BARRELS** describes a gun that has two barrels **2. WITH TWO NAMES TOGETHER** formed from two names, usually hyphenated **3. WITH TWO PURPOSES OR INTERPRETATIONS** serving two purposes, or open to two possible interpretations

double bass *n* the largest and lowest in pitch of the instruments of the violin family, used in the modern symphony orchestra. It is also commonly found in jazz and dance bands, where it is usually plucked rather than bowed.

double-bass *adj* describes an instrument that is larger and lower in pitch than others of its group

double bassoon *n* MUSIC same as **contrabassoon** (sense 1)

double bed *n* a bed intended for two people

double bill *n* a programme of entertainment that has two main items, especially a cinema programme showing two full-length films

double bind *n* **1.** an unresolvable situation from which there is no escape without undesirable consequences **2.** a situation in which conflicting demands make it impossible to do the right thing

double-blind *adj* describes an experiment in which neither the experimenters nor the subjects know which of two similar treatments is genuine and which is a control procedure

double bluff *n* a deception in which somebody tells the truth while assuming that he or she will not be believed

double boiler *n* a pair of cooking pots, one fitting on top of and partly inside the other. Food cooks gently in the upper pot while water simmers in the lower pot.

double bond *n* a chemical bond in which two atoms share two pairs of electrons

double-book *vti* to wrongly make the same reservation, especially for a hotel room or aeroplane seat, for two separate customers

double-breasted *adj* describes a coat or jacket that has a large overlap at the front, usually with two sets of buttons

double bridle *n* a bridle with four reins and a bit with two rings on each side

double check *n* **1.** a second examination to make sure of something **2.** a situation in chess in which a king is in check from two pieces at once

double-check *vti* to check something twice or for a second time ○ *I double-checked that the windows were locked.*

double chin *n* a fold of flesh or loose skin under the chin —**double-chinned** *adj*

double-click *vti* to press and release a mouse button twice in rapid succession in order to invoke a specific command

double-clutch *vi* N Am AUTOMOT same as **double-declutch**

double concerto *n* a concerto for two solo instruments

double cream *n* UK thick cream with a high fat content

double cross *n* the production of a new hybrid from parents, each of which is a first-generation hybrid of pure strains, or the hybrid produced

double-cross *vt* to betray or cheat somebody who believes that he or she is a partner or associate in the same, often criminal enterprise ■ *n* an act of double-crossing a partner or associate —**double-crosser** *n* —**double-crossing** *adj*

double dagger *n* the printed character (‡), used to mark a cross-reference, especially to a footnote

double date *n* an arrangement for two couples to go out together socially as a foursome

double-date *vi* to go out socially as a couple with another couple

double-dealing *n* deliberately deceitful behaviour, especially when involving the betrayal of a partner or associate —**double-dealer** *n* —**double-dealing** *adj*

double-decker

double-decker /-dékər/ *n* **1.** a bus with an upper and a lower deck **2.** something that has two layers, levels, or tiers ○ *a double-decker sandwich*

double-declutch *vi* to use the clutch twice when changing gear in a motor vehicle, first to put the gear lever into neutral and rev the engine, then to engage the new gear. N Am term **double-clutch**

double decomposition *n* a chemical reaction in which two compounds exchange one or more of their components so that two new compounds are formed

double-density *adj* describes a floppy or hard disk that can hold twice the amount of information as a standard disk

double descent *n* the use in some societies of sometimes the mother's and sometimes the father's ancestry in establishing specific features of social identity or status

double digging *n* the process of digging a plot of ground to twice the normal depth and transferring soil from the lower level to the top in order to revitalize it before planting

double-digit *adj* being between 10 and 99 ○ *double-digit inflation*

double digits *npl* US same as **double figures**

double-dip *n* **1.** N Am an ice cream consisting of a cone with two balls of ice cream in it **2.** ANZ, N Am an act of fraudulently receiving income from two different sources such as a pension fund and government social security (*informal*)

double dipping *n* (*informal*) **1.** N Am the fraudulent receipt of two incomes from the government, e.g. by holding a government job and collecting a government pension at the same time **2.** ANZ the fraudulent practice of receiving income from a pension fund as well as social security payments —**double dipper** *n*

double dissolution *n* in Australia, the dissolution of both houses of the federal parliament by the governor general when the upper house repeatedly refuses to pass legislation already passed by the lower house

double doors *npl* two full-length doors that meet in the middle of the doorway when closed

double-dotted *adj* **1.** describes a musical note or rest that has two dots following it to indicate that its length is to be increased by three quarters **2.** characterized by the use of double-dotted notes

double dribble *n* in basketball, an illegal move in which the player dribbles the ball with both hands simultaneously or, having stopped, starts to dribble again

double Dutch *n* speech or writing that cannot be understood at all (*informal*)

double-dyed *adj* **1.** completely and permanently imbued with a particular characteristic or opinion (*literary*) **2.** describes fabrics that are dyed twice in order to make sure that the colour does not run when they are wet

double eagle *n* **1.** a former US gold coin worth 20 dollars **2.** N Am GOLF same as **albatross** (sense 3)

double-edged *adj* **1. HAVING TWO CUTTING EDGES** having a blade sharpened on both edges **2. AMBIGUOUS** having two possible meanings or interpretations, especially one that is apparently innocuous and another that is intentionally unkind or malicious **3. DOING TWO THINGS** achieving two purposes or having two effects

double-edged sword *n* a situation or event that has negative as well as positive consequences

double effect *n* the ethical principle that intentionally doing wrong is impermissible, even if the action has good consequences, and that intentionally doing right is permissible, even if the action has bad consequences

double entendre /dóob'l on tóndrə/ (*plural* **double entendres** /-on tóndrə/) *n* **1.** a remark that is ambiguous and sexually suggestive **2.** ambiguity in which one meaning is sexually suggestive [Late 17C. < obsolete French, 'double understanding']

double entry *n* a bookkeeping system that records each transaction as a credit to one account and a debit from another (*hyphenated before a noun*)

double exposure *n* **1.** the exposure of two separate images on a single piece of photographic film **2.** a photograph that contains one image superimposed on another

double-faced *adj* **1.** FINISHED ON BOTH SIDES describes fabrics that are finished on both sides **2.** HAVING TWO USABLE SIDES having two faces or sides that can be used ○ *a double-faced tape* **3.** TWO-FACED behaving insincerely or deceitfully

double fault *n* in tennis, two consecutive serves that land outside the service box or in the net, with the result that the server loses a point

double-fault *vi* in tennis, to make two consecutive faulty serves and lose a point as a result

double feature *n N Am* a programme consisting of two full-length films shown consecutively

double figures *npl UK, ANZ, Can* the numbers with two digits, from 10 to 99. US term **double digits** —**double-figure** *adj*

double first *n* a first-class honours degree in two subjects studied simultaneously

double flat *n* **1.** a symbol, ♭♭, placed in front of a musical note to indicate that the pitch of the note is to be lowered by two semitones (*hyphenated before a noun*) **2.** a musical note marked with a double flat

double-glaze *vt* to fit a window or building with double glazing

double glazing *n* windows consisting of two layers of glass separated by a space, designed to provide improved heat and sound insulation (*hyphenated before a noun*)

Double Gloucester *n* a hard English cheese that is slightly orange in colour [< production in Gloucestershire]

double-header *n* a train pulled by two engines coupled together

double helix *n* the molecular structure of DNA, consisting of a pair of polynucleotide strands connected by a series of hydrogen bonds and wound in opposing spirals

double-hung *adj* describes a window that has two sashes, each sliding vertically in its own track

double indemnity *n N Am* the guaranteed payout of double the face value of a life insurance policy if the policyholder dies in an accident

double jeopardy *n* the prosecution of somebody a second time for something that he or she has already been tried for

double-jointed *adj* **1.** describes a joint or limb that has unusual flexibility and can bend in the direction opposite to the usual one **2.** describes somebody with double-jointed joints or limbs —**double-jointedness** *n*

double knit *n* a thick knitted fabric (*hyphenated before a noun*)

double knitting *n* knitting wool of medium thickness (*hyphenated before a noun*)

double life *n* a situation in which somebody is simultaneously involved in two sets of circumstances or relationships and keeps each completely separate, and usually secret, from the other

double magnum *n* a wine bottle containing the equivalent of four standard bottles, used mainly for Bordeaux

double negation *n* in logic, the principle that a proposition and the negation of its negation mean one and the same thing

double negative *n* a phrase containing two negatives

USAGE *Double negatives* of the type *I don't know nothing*, in which two negatives close together are intended to reinforce each other, are considered poor style in current standard English, acceptable though they were in earlier usage. These are to be distinguished from the acceptable, if somewhat uncommon, construction *That's not a good idea, I don't think*, in which the reinforcing negatives appear in different clauses. The more usual type of acceptable double negative is seen in *It is not impossible* (= it is distinctly possible), in which the negatives are intended to cancel each other out. This is a figure of speech called *litotes*, a form of understatement.

double obelisk *n* PRINTING same as **double dagger**

double occupancy *n* the use of a hotel room or other accommodation by two people (*hyphenated before a noun*)

double or quits *n* a bet in gambling where a player who owes money has the debt doubled or cancelled depending on the outcome of the next play. US term **double or nothing**

double-page spread *n* a feature or article that fills two facing pages of a newspaper or magazine

double-park *vti* to park a vehicle alongside another already parked and so cause an obstruction — **double-parker** —**double-parking** *n*

double play *n* in baseball, a play in which two players are put out

double pneumonia *n* pneumonia affecting both lungs

double-quick *adj, adv* extremely fast (*informal*)

double quote *n* a quotation mark that consists of two marks ("), not one

doubler /dúbb'lər/ *n* an electronic device that doubles an input frequency or voltage

double reed *n* **1.** a reed in the oboe, cor anglais, or bassoon consisting of two halves that vibrate against each other when air passes through them **2.** a woodwind instrument that has a double reed

double refraction *n* OPTICS same as **birefringence**

double rhyme *n* a two-syllable rhyme, e.g. 'cooking' and 'looking'

doubles /dúbb'lz/ (*plural same*) *n* **1.** a racket game played between two pairs of players **2.** *Carib* a popular and cheap fast food consisting of a sandwich of curried chickpeas in two fried seasoned batter patties (*informal*)

double salt *n* a salt that dissolves in solution as two substances, but crystallizes as one, e.g. alum

double saucepan *n* HOUSEHOLD same as **double boiler**

double sculls *n* a race between boats crewed by two rowers who sit one behind the other and pull two oars each

double sharp *n* **1.** a symbol, 𝄪, placed in front of a musical note to indicate that the pitch of the note is to be raised by two semitones (*hyphenated before a noun*) **2.** a musical note marked with a double sharp

double-sided *adj* used or usable on both sides

double-space *vt* to type or print text with a blank line between each typed or printed line

doublespeak /dúbb'l speek/ *n* same as **double talk** (sense 1)

double spread *n* PUBL same as **double-page spread**

double standard *n* a principle, rule, or expectation that is applied unfairly to different groups, one group usually being condemned for the slightest offence while the other is treated far more leniently

double star *n* ASTRON **1.** same as **binary star** **2.** same as **optical double star**

double-stop *vi* to draw the bow of a stringed instrument simultaneously across two strings, producing two tones ■ *n* a musical chord of two notes played on a stringed instrument —**double-stopping** *n*

doublet /dúbb'lət/ *n* **1.** CLOTHING MAN'S JACKET a man's close-fitting jacket, with or without sleeves, popular in Europe between the 15th and 17th centuries **2.** LING WORD WITH SAME ROOT AS ANOTHER either of two similar words in a language that have the same historical root but have arrived at their current forms via different languages, e.g. 'mood' and 'mode' **3.** PRINTING REPEATED PRINTED LETTER, WORD, OR LINE a letter, word, or line that is printed a second time in error **4.** OPTICS PAIR OF LENSES USED TOGETHER a pair of lenses designed to be used together so that one lens cancels out the distortions in the other **5.** MINERALS FAKE GEM a fake gem made by sticking a coloured layer between two pieces of glass or by sticking a thin layer of a gem on a glass base [14C. < French, 'something doubled']

double tackle *n* a pair of double pulleys for lifting or pulling

double take *n* a reaction of surprise or astonishment after an initial hesitation

double talk *n* **1.** intentionally ambiguous or confusing talk **2.** speech that includes a mixture of real words and nonsense syllables

double taxation *n* taxation applied in one country to foreign income received by a company when this income has already been taxed in the other country

double-team *vt N Am* in various team games such as basketball or American football, to use two players to mark an opponent —**double team** *n*

double teeth *npl regional* the back teeth [< their two points or cusps]

doublethink /dúbb'l thingk/ *n* the conscious or unconscious holding of two opposing beliefs at the same time [Coined by George Orwell in *1984* (1949)]

double time *n* **1.** FIN DOUBLE PAY double the usual rate of pay **2.** MUSIC DOUBLY FAST MUSICAL TEMPO a tempo twice as fast as the basic tempo of a piece of music, or a passage played at that speed **3.** US MIL FAST MARCHING PACE a fast marching pace of 180 steps per minute

double-time *vi US* to march at the fast pace of 180 steps per minute

doubleton /dúbb'ltən/ *n* two cards of the same suit that are the only cards of that suit dealt to a player [Early 20C. After SINGLETON]

double-tonguing *n* the production of a rapid series of staccato notes on a wind or brass instrument by using rapid movements of the tongue —**double-tongue** *vti*

double top *n* in darts, a score of double 20

doubletree /dúbb'l tree/ *n* a bar used to harness two horses to a carriage or other vehicle [After SINGLETREE]

doublets /dúbblats/ *npl* a pair of dice thrown simultaneously, each showing the same number of spots ■ *n* a word game in which one word is transformed into another by substituting letters, the object being to achieve this in the minimum number of substitutions (*takes a singular verb*)

double-u *n US* the letter w

double vision *n* a condition in which two images of the same object are seen simultaneously because the eyes are not focusing properly. Technical name **diplopia**

double whammy *n* two setbacks or unpleasant experiences occurring very close together (*informal*)

double yellow line *n* two lines painted in yellow at the edge of a road, indicating that parking is not permitted at most times of the day

double-zero option *n* an offer to limit the number of intermediate- and short-range nuclear missiles or remove them altogether if an opposing side agrees to do the same

doubloon /du blóon/ *n* a former Spanish gold coin [Early 17C. < Spanish *doblón* < *dobla* 'double' < Latin *duplus*]

doublure /də blóor, doo-/ *n* a lining, especially one made of leather or highly decorated, inside the cover of a book [Late 19C. < French, 'lining']

doubly /dúbb li/ *adv* **1.** in two different ways **2.** to twice the usual degree or extent

doubt /dowt/ *vt* (**doubts, doubting, doubted**) **1.** THINK SOMETHING UNLIKELY to feel unconvinced or uncertain about something, or think that something is unlikely ○ *I doubt if he'll come.* **2.** NOT TRUST SOMEBODY OR SOMETHING to suspect that somebody is not sincere or trustworthy, or that something is not true, likely, or genuine ○ *no reason to doubt her* **3.** *Scotland* EXPECT SOMETHING to tend to believe something ■ *n* **1.** UNCERTAINTY OR MISTRUST a feeling or state of uncertainty, especially as to whether somebody is sincere or trustworthy, or as to whether something is true, likely, or genuine **2.** PHILOSOPHY METHOD OF PHILOSOPHICAL QUESTIONING a method of questioning claims to knowledge, especially in the philosophy of Descartes [13C. Via Old French *doter* < Latin *dubitare* 'be uncertain' < *dubius* 'uncertain'] —**doubtable** *adj* —**doubtably** *adv* —**doubter** *n* —**doubtingly** *adv* ◇ **beyond doubt** completely certain ◇ **no doubt** almost definitely ◇ **in doubt 1.** not feeling confident or sure about something **2.** unlikely or improbable ◇ **open to** *or* **in doubt** not certain, settled, foreseeable with confidence, or finally proved

USAGE doubt whether, if, or that? The verb *doubt* is normally followed by *whether* or *if*, or by *that* if it is in the negative: *I doubt whether/if it's true* but *I don't doubt that it's true*. In recent usage, *that* has been used

in positive contexts too: *I doubt that it's true.* This use remains disputed.

SYNONYMS See ***doubtful.***

doubtful /dówtf'l/ *adj* **1. HESITANT** not feeling sure about something **2. UNLIKELY** not likely to happen or be successful **3. INVITING SUSPICION** probably not true, honest, reputable, or genuine —**doubtfulness** *n*

SYNONYMS *doubtful, uncertain, unsure, in doubt, dubious, sceptical*

CORE MEANING: feeling doubt or uncertainty

doubtful not feeling sure about something ○ *The council was doubtful whether the public would want to pay the charges.* ○ *Oliver felt rather doubtful about having such a friend.* **uncertain** or **unsure** lacking clear knowledge or a definite opinion ○ *She seemed uncertain of her English, and asked for everything to be repeated.* ○ *Some of the biggest names in investment banking are unsure about the future.* **in doubt** not feeling confident or sure about something ○ *When in doubt, the jury often tend to acquit and not convict.* ○ *If the umpires are in any doubt about what to do, they consult with the referee.* **dubious** not sure about an outcome or conclusion ○ *The mayor was dubious about councils being asked to fund the alliance.* ○ *Agencies are dubious as to whether they should take action on behalf of a client.* **sceptical** tending not to believe or accept things but to question them ○ *Most people are fairly sceptical about the efficacy of this treatment.* ○ *In general, viewers tend to be highly sceptical of broadcasters' motives.*

doubtfully /dówtf'li/ *adv* with or expressing doubt

doubting Thomas /dówting-/ *n* somebody who doubts something, especially until given proof [After Jesus Christ's apostle who doubted (John 20:24–9)]

doubtless /dówtləss/ *adv* **1. CERTAINLY** certainly or almost certainly ○ *That was doubtless their intention, as these documents show.* **2. PROBABLY** probably or presumably ○ *You would doubtless have been informed in due course.* ■ *adj* (*formal*) **1. CERTAIN** impossible to doubt or deny **2. HAVING NO DOUBT** having no doubts or suspicions

douc /dook/ *n* a rare yellow-faced monkey of the langur family. Native to: Southeast Asia. Latin name: *Pygathrix nemaeus.* [Late 18C. < Vietnamese]

douce /dooss/ *adj regional* quiet, serious, and undemonstrative in character or expression [13C. < French (see DOUCEUR)] —**doucely** *adv* —**douceness** *n*

douceur /doo súr/ *n* something given as a tip or a bribe (*used euphemistically*) [14C. < French, 'sweetness, favour' < *douce* 'sweet' < Latin *dulcis*]

douche /doosh/ *n* **1. CLEANING OF BODY BY SQUIRTING WATER** the cleaning of a part of the body or a body cavity with a jet of water or air **2. EQUIPMENT PRODUCING CLEANSING WATER JET** a piece of equipment that produces a jet of water or air for a douche ■ *vti* (**douches, douching, douched**) **CLEAN BODY WITH WATER JET** to clean a part of the body or body cavity with a jet of water or air [Mid-18C. Via French < Italian *doccia* 'water pipe' < Latin *duction-* 'leading (through a pipe)']

dou-dou /do͝o doo/, **doo-doo** *n Carib* used as a term of endearment [< French *doux* 'sweet']

dough /dō/ *n* **1. MIXTURE OF FLOUR AND WATER** a soft elastic mixture of flour and water, often with other ingredients such as yeast, oil, butter, salt, and sugar, that becomes bread or pastry when baked **2. MONEY** cash and other financial assets (*slang*) **3. SOFT MASS** a soft elastic substance similar to baking dough, used as children's modelling clay [Old English *dāg* < Indo-European, 'to form']

SPELLCHECK See ***doe.***

dough boy, Dough Boy *n* a US infantryman in World War I

doughboy /dṓ boy/ *n US* a ball of bread dough boiled, steamed, or fried as a dumpling (*slang*)

doughnut /dṓ nut/ *n* **1. ROUND CAKE WITH HOLE OR FILLING** a small sugar-coated cake of sweet dough, fried or baked, and either spherical with a filling of cream or jam, or ring-shaped with no filling **2.** MECH ENG **RING-SHAPED OBJECT** an object in the shape of an inflated ring, e.g. an accelerating tube in a nuclear reactor or a baby's floor cushion for sitting in ■ *vt* (**-nuts, -nutting, -nutted**) **1. CROWD AROUND MP BEING FILMED** to surround a Member of Parliament who is speaking and being filmed for television in order to give the impression that the chamber is fuller than it really is **2. CROWD TELEVISION STUDIO AUDIENCE TOGETHER** to crowd members of a television studio audience together to give viewers the impression that the audience is much larger than it really is

REGIONAL NOTE The terms *bun, cake, cookie,* or *gateau* are a good illustration of the fact that regions often have very different names for the same item of food. The ***doughnut*** seems to have had its origins in the United States in the early 19th century, but whilst ***doughnut*** is the commonest name for this delicacy, it is eaten under the name of *gravy ring* in Northern Ireland.

~~**doughter**~~ incorrect spelling of **daughter**

doughty /dówti/ (**-tier, -tiest**) *adj* brave and determined (*archaic or humorous*) [Old English *dohtig, dyhtig* 'worthy, virtuous' < Indo-European, 'be fit, prosper'] —**doughtily** *adv* —**doughtiness** *n*

Doughty /dówti/, **Charles Montagu** (1843–1926) British travel writer and poet. His masterpiece is *Travels in Arabia Deserta* (1888).

doughy /dṓ i/ (**-ier, -iest**) *adj* **1.** soft, sticky, and elastic, like dough **2.** unhealthily pale and slightly flabby —**doughiness** *n*

Douglas /dúggləss/ capital of the Isle of Man. It is a popular holiday resort. Population: 20,368 (1991).

Douglas, Gawin (1474?–1522) Scottish poet and bishop. His works include *The Palace of Honour* (1501?), and a translation of the *Aeneid* (1513?).

> 'And all small fowlys singis on the spray:
> / Welcum the lord of lycht and lamp of day.'
> [Gawin Douglas, *Eneados (Aeneid)*; 1513?]

Douglas, Sir James, 4th Earl of Morton (1516?–81) Scottish courtier. As lord high chancellor of Scotland (1563) he secured the abdication of Mary, Queen of Scots. He was regent for James VI (1572–78) but was ousted and finally executed.

Douglas, Kirk (*b.* 1916) US film actor. He has starred in over 70 Hollywood films, including *The Bad and the Beautiful* (1952). In 1995 he received a special Academy Award for his contribution to motion pictures. Born **Danielovitch, Issur**

Douglas, Lord Alfred Bruce (1870–1945) British writer and poet. He was at the centre of the scandal that led to the imprisonment of Oscar Wilde. He wrote *The City of the Soul* (1899) and a verse collection, *Sonnets and Lyrics* (1935). Full name **Douglas, Alfred Bruce, Lord**

> 'I am the Love that dare not speak its name.'
> [Lord Alfred Bruce Douglas, 'Two Loves'; 1896]

Douglas, Michael (*b.* 1944) US television and film actor. He won an Academy Award for *Wall Street* (1987). His father is Kirk Douglas.

Douglas, Norman (1868–1952) British writer. His novels include *South Wind* (1917). His travel books *Siren Land* (1911) and *Old Calabria* (1928) were also popular. Full name **Douglas, George Norman**

> 'It is the drawback of all sea-side places that half the landscape is unavailable for purposes of human locomotion, being covered by useless water.'
> [Norman Douglas, 'Mentone', *Alone*; 1921]

Douglas, William O. (1898–1980) associate justice of the US Supreme Court (1939–75). Of strongly held liberal views, he championed individual rights, especially free speech. Full name **Douglas, William Orville**

> 'The right to be let alone is indeed the beginning of all freedom.'
> [William O. Douglas, *An Almanac of Liberty*; 1954]

Douglas fir *n* **1.** a tall pine tree with distinctive rough bark and shaggy-looking cones. Use: timber, Christmas trees. Native to: northwestern North America. Latin name: *Pseudotsuga menziesii.* **2.** the strong durable wood of the Douglas fir tree [After David *Douglas* (1798–1834), Scottish botanist]

Douglas-Home /-hyo͞om/, **Sir Alec, 14th Earl of Home** (1903–95) British prime minister. He was foreign secretary (1960–63) and renounced his hereditary title to succeed Harold Macmillan as prime minister (1963–64). He was made a life peer in 1974. Full name **Douglas-Home, Alexander Frederick**. See table at **prime minister**

> 'There are two problems in my life. The political ones are insoluble and the economic ones are incomprehensible.'
> [Sir Alec Douglas-Home, *Speech*; January 1964]

Douglas spruce *n* TREES, INDUST same as **Douglas fir**

Doukhobor /do͞okō bawr/, **Dukhobor** *n* a member of an 18th-century Russian Christian group that rejected state and church authority and emigrated to western Canada at the end of the century to escape persecution [Late 19C. < Russian *Dukhobar* < *dukh* 'spirit, Holy Ghost' + *-bor* 'fighter']

doula /do͞olə/ *n* a woman who is experienced in childbirth and who provides physical, emotional, and informational assistance and support to a mother before, during, or after childbirth [< Greek *doulē* 'woman slave']

doum /doom/, **doum palm, doom palm** *n* an Egyptian palm tree with egg-shaped fruits that have a gingery taste. Latin name: *Hyphaene thebaica.* [Early 18C. < Arabic *dūm*]

dour /door/ *adj* **1.** severe or gloomy, and unfriendly and unresponsive towards others **2.** grimly and stubbornly determined [14C. Probably via Gaelic *dūr* 'obstinate' < Latin *durus* 'hard'] —**dourly** *adv* —**dourness** *n*

Douro /do͞orō/ river that rises in north-central Spain and flows westwards across Spain and northern Portugal, reaching the Atlantic Ocean near Porto. Length: 895 km/556 mi. Spanish name **Duero**

douroucouli /do͞o roo ko͞oli, do͞orə-/ (*plural* **-lis**) *n* a fairly small, large-eyed, nocturnal monkey with an inflatable sac under its neck that amplifies its calls. Native to: South America. Genus: *Aotus.* [Mid-19C. Probably < language of a people of S Venezuela]

douse[1] /dowss/, **dowse** *vt* (**douses, dousing, doused; dowses, dowsing, dowsed**) **1. IMMERSE SOMEBODY OR SOMETHING IN WATER** to plunge or submerge somebody or something in water **2. PUT LIQUID ON SOMEBODY OR SOMETHING** to put a lot of water or other liquid on somebody or something **3. EXTINGUISH SOMETHING** to put out a light, fire, or flame, especially with water ■ *n* **DRENCHING** a thorough wetting or soaking [Early 17C. Origin ?] —**douser** *n*

douse[2] /dowss/ (**douses, dousing, doused**) *vt* to lower a sail, especially at speed [Mid-16C. Origin ?]

DOVAP /dṓ vap/ *n* a system for measuring the speed and position of objects in flight that is based on the frequency of sound waves. Full form **Doppler velocity and position**

dove[1] /duv/ *n* **1. BIRD OF PIGEON FAMILY** a small bird of the pigeon family, with a cooing call. Family: Columbidae. **2. SUPPORTER OF PEACE** somebody who supports peace and the use of peaceful measures to avoid confrontation or war **3. TERM OF ENDEARMENT** used as an affectionate name for a loved one ■ *adj, n* COLOURS same as **dove-grey** [Assumed Old English *dūfe*, originally 'dark-coloured bird' < Indo-European, 'darken']

dove[2] /dōv/ *N Am* past tense of **dive**

Dove /duv/ *n* in Christianity, a manifestation or representation of the Holy Spirit

dovecote /dúvkōt/, **dovecot** /-kot/ *n* a structure with many separate entrances and compartments, used for housing domestic pigeons

dove-grey *adj* of a mid-grey colour with a tinge of pink or blue —**dove grey** *n*

dovekie /dúvki/ (*plural* **-kies**), **dovekey** (*plural* **-keys**) *n N Am* BIRDS same as **little auk** [Early 19C. Diminutive of DOVE [1]]

Dover /dṓvər/ **1.** city on the southern coast of Kent, southeastern England. It is England's busiest port and the one nearest to France. Population: 104,566 (2001). **2.** city and state capital of Delaware, in the central part of the state, south of Wilmington. Population: 32,581 (2002 estimate). **3.** city in southeastern New Hampshire, situated on the Cocheco

River, northwest of Portsmouth. It is an industrial centre. Population: 27,784 (2002 estimate).

Dover, Strait of the narrowest part of the English Channel, between Dover, England, and Calais, France. Length: 34 km/21 mi.

Dover sole *n* **1.** **EUROPEAN FLATFISH** a flat-bodied fish. Native to: Europe. Latin name: *Solea solea*. **2.** **FLATFISH OF N AMERICAN PACIFIC** a brownish mottled flat-bodied fish. Native to: Pacific coast of North America. Latin name: *Microstomus pacificus*. **3.** **DOVER SOLE AS FOOD** the flesh of a Dover sole used as food [Early 20C. Probably after DOVER, England]

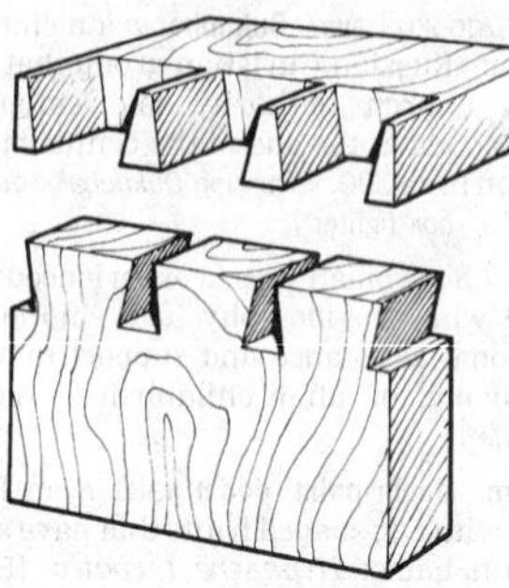

dovetail

dovetail /dúv tayl/ *v* (**-tails, -tailing, -tailed**) **1.** *vti* **FIT TOGETHER** to fit neatly together or combine smoothly and efficiently, or fit or combine things in this way **2.** *vt* **JOIN PIECES OF WOOD** to join wooden boards with interlocking V-shaped tenons ■ *n* **1.** **V-SHAPED TENON** a V-shaped projection on the end of a piece of wood that fits into a similarly shaped opening in another piece to form a strong joint **2.** *also* **dovetail joint** **JOINT WITH DOVETAILS** a joint made using dovetails [< its shape]

dovetail saw *n* a small saw with a reinforced back, slightly smaller than a tenon saw and used for fine woodworking

dovish /dúvvish/ *adj* advocating peaceful solutions and the avoidance of confrontation or war —**dovishness** *n*

Dovzhenko /dov zhéngkō/, **Aleksandr** (1894–1956) Ukrainian film director. His films include *Earth* (1930) and *Ivan* (1932).

dowager /dów əjər/ *n* **1.** a woman who has inherited a title or property from her deceased husband **2.** a rich-looking or respected woman of advanced years [Mid-16C. < Old French *douagere* < Latin *dos* 'dowry']

dowager's hump *n* a marked curving of the spine around the area of the shoulder blades, especially in women with osteoporosis

dowdy /dówdi/ (**-dier, -diest**) *adj* **1.** unattractively plain and unfashionable **2.** wearing plain unfashionable clothes [Late 16C. < *dowd* 'poorly dressed woman', origin ?] —**dowdily** *adv* —**dowdiness** *n*

dowel /dów əl/ *n* a short wooden or metal peg used to join two pieces of wood or metal by fitting tightly at each end into specially drilled holes in the two pieces to be joined ■ *vt* (**-els, -elling, -elled**) to join pieces of wood or metal using dowels [13C. Origin ?]

Dowell /dów əl/, **Anthony** (*b.* 1943) British ballet dancer. He was a leading interpreter of classical and modern roles, notably in partnership with Antoinette Sibley. He became director of the Royal Ballet, London, in 1986.

dower /dów ər/ *n* **1.** **WIDOW'S INHERITANCE** a dead man's estate, or part of his estate, inherited by his widow **2.** CULTL ANTHROP same as **dowry** (sense 1) (*archaic*) **3.** **NATURAL GIFT** something, especially a skill or talent, with which somebody is endowed (*literary*) ■ *vt* (**-ers, -ering, -ered**) **ENDOW SOMEBODY** to endow somebody with something (*literary*) [13C. < Old French *douaire* < Latin *dotare* 'endow' < *dos* 'marriage portion']

dower house *n* a house originally built by a rich landowner for his widow to live in after his death, especially a house on a country estate

Dow Jones Average /dów-/ *tdmk* a trademark for an index of the prices of selected industrial, transport, and utilities stocks that is based on a formula developed and revised periodically by Dow Jones & Company, Inc.

Dowland /dówlənd/, **John** (1562–1626?) English composer and musician. A widely travelled lutenist, he influenced the development of Western vocal music through his *First Book of Songs or Ayres* (1597).

down[1] /down/ (**downs, downing, downed,** *plural* **downs**) CORE MEANING: a grammatical word used to indicate movement or position towards a lower level or the ground ○ (prep) *He ran down the stairs and opened the door.* ○ (prep) *The sheep was caught in brambles 50 ft down the hillside.* ○ (prep) *Tears were pouring down her cheeks.* ○ (adv) *I was numb from the waist down.* ○ (adv) *They all watched the sun go down.* ○ (adv) *She pressed a button and the window slid down.*

1. *prep* **TO LOWER LEVEL IN SOMETHING** towards or at a lower level in something ○ *I dropped my keys down a hole.* **2.** *prep* **ALONG** towards or at a position farther along the length of something and usually at a somewhat lower level ○ *halfway down the street* **3.** *adv* **AT OR TO LOWER LEVEL** at or to a physically lower level or position ○ *down in the basement* **4.** *adv* **ONTO SURFACE** out of the hand and onto a surface ○ *She calmly put her fork down.* **5.** *adv* **AWAY FROM PRESENT LOCATION** to another place away from the current location or base ○ *go down to the beach* **6.** *adv* **TO MORE SOUTHERLY PLACE** to a place in the south or to the south of the current location ○ *going down to Spain for the summer* **7.** *adv* **TO OR AT LOWER AMOUNT** to or at a lower amount or price ○ *to get interest rates down* **8.** *adv* **SHORT BY PARTICULAR AMOUNT** short of, having lost, or losing by a particular amount ○ *They were two goals down at half time.* **9.** *adv* **HAVING ONLY SO MUCH LEFT** having only a particular amount left ○ *I'm down to my last pound.* **10.** *adv* **IN PART PAYMENT** in part payment for something or as a deposit ○ *You put 5% down, and pay the rest in instalments.* **11.** *adv* **INCLUDING EVERYONE OR EVERYTHING** including everyone or everything, from highest to lowest, within a group or hierarchy of people or things, or even including the person or thing mentioned ○ *everyone from the managing director down* ○ *account for everything down to the last farthing* **12.** *adv* **TO LATER PERIOD** from an earlier to a later time or person ○ *The piano had been handed down to him by his grandmother.* **13.** *adv* **IN INFERIOR POSITION** in or to an inferior, less free, or less privileged position or condition ○ *holding political opponents down* **14.** *adv* **TO REDUCED CONDITION** to a lower level of intensity or activity ○ *wind down after work* **15.** *adv* **INTO LESS SOLID STATE** into a different and less solid state ○ *The hot butter will melt down.* **16.** *adv* **ON PAPER** in writing on paper, as a record ○ *wrote it down* **17.** *adv* **CHOSEN OR ARRANGED** chosen for or assigned to something, or arranged or scheduled for a particular time or date ○ *We're down for two sessions next month.* **18.** *adv* LEISURE **VERTICALLY IN CROSSWORD** in a vertical position in a crossword ○ *the solution to 10 down* **19.** *adv* EDUC **AWAY FROM UNIVERSITY** away from, or no longer at, a university ○ *down from Cambridge* **20.** *adv* NAUT **TO WINDWARD** having the rudder to windward **21.** *adj* **UNHAPPY** unhappy and gloomy **22.** *adj* COMPUT **NOT IN OPERATION** describes a computer system that is temporarily not in operation **23.** *adj* **MADE IN PART PAYMENT** made or given in part payment for something or as a deposit ○ *a down payment on the car* **24.** *adj* AMERICAN FOOTBALL **NOT IN PLAY** no longer in play **25.** *adj* BASEBALL **PUT OUT** eliminated from a game **26.** *adj* **ON GROUND** lying on the ground ○ *a down tree* **27.** *adj US* **AGREEABLE TO SOMETHING** ready and willing to do something (*slang*) ○ *Great! I'm down for that.* **28.** *interj* **INSTRUCTION TO DOG** used as an instruction to a dog to stop jumping up or to lie or sit ○ *Down boy!* **29.** *vt* **EAT OR DRINK SOMETHING** to eat food or drink liquid, especially quickly or greedily **30.** *vt* **BRING SOMEBODY OR SOMETHING TO GROUND** to cause somebody or something to fall to the ground through being hurt or damaged **31.** *vt* AMERICAN FOOTBALL **DECLARE BALL OUT OF PLAY** in American football, to declare a ball as no longer in play **32.** *n* AMERICAN FOOTBALL **MOVE MADE IN AMERICAN FOOTBALL** in American football, one of four consecutive plays within which a team must either score or advance the ball at least ten yards [Old English *dūn(e)*, shortened < *adūn(e)* 'from the hill' < *dūn* (see DOWN[3])] ◇ **be down on somebody** *or* **something, have a down on somebody** *or* **something** to show dislike or hostility towards somebody or something, often giving him, her, or it unfair treatment (*informal*) ◇ **be down to somebody** to be the responsibility of somebody ◇ **be down to something** to be the result of something ◇ **down at heel** shabby and neglected ◇ **down under** to or in Australia or New Zealand (*informal*) ◇ **down with somebody** *or* **something!** used to express disapproval of, opposition to, or a desire to get rid of, somebody or something ◇ **go down with something** to become ill with something

down[2] /down/ *n* **1.** **SOFT FLUFFY FEATHERS** the soft fluffy feathers that are a young bird's first plumage **2.** BIRDS **SOFT INNER FEATHERS** the soft feathers that lie beneath the outer feathers in some adult birds **3.** **FEATHERS AS STUFFING** the soft breast feathers of a duck or goose, especially the female eider duck. Use: filling for pillows and quilts. **4.** **COVERING OF SOFT HAIRS** a covering of fine fluffy hairs, e.g. on a child's skin or on the skin of some fruits [14C. < Old Norse *dúnn*]

down[3] /down/ *n* a grassy treeless hill or ridge (*often used in placenames*) ■ **downs** *npl* an area of gently rolling, treeless, grassy upland, used mainly as pasture [Old English *dūn*, origin ?]

Down[1] /down/ *n* a sheep belonging to a southern English breed, e.g. the South Down or Dorset Down [Late 18C. < the DOWNS]

Down[2] /down/ former county in southeast Northern Ireland. Population: 63,828 (2001). Area: 2,448 sq. km/945 sq. mi.

down-and-dirty *adj N Am* crude and often unpleasant (*slang*) ○ *the down-and-dirty truth*

down-and-out *adj* **1.** **JOBLESS AND POOR** having no money or job, often no home, and little hope of things getting better (*informal*) **2.** **UNABLE TO CARRY ON** completely incapacitated and unable to carry on ■ *n* **JOBLESS POOR PERSON** somebody who lacks money, a job, and often a home (*informal*)

down-at-heel *adj* **1.** worn-out or rundown from use or neglect **2.** shabbily dressed as a result of being poor

downbeat /dówn beet/ *adj* **1.** **PESSIMISTIC** showing or expressing pessimism and hopelessness **2.** **CASUAL** deliberately casual and relaxed (*informal*) **3.** **UNDERSTATED** carefully or deliberately understated or restrained ■ *n* **1.** **FIRST BEAT IN BAR** the first beat in a bar of music **2.** **MUSIC CONDUCTOR'S DOWNWARD GESTURE** the downward movement made by a conductor to indicate the downbeat of a bar of music **3.** MUSIC same as **downtempo**

down-bow *n* the action of drawing a bow from its heel towards its point across a stringed instrument

downburst /dówn burst/ *n* a powerful downward wind, often part of a thunderstorm system, that creates strong horizontal winds in all directions when it strikes the ground and is a danger to aircraft

downcast /dówn kaast/ *adj* **1.** sad and pessimistic **2.** looking or directed towards the ground ○ *with downcast eyes*

downcountry /dówn kuntri/ *ANZ, US adj* coming from, associated with, or located in a low-lying, usually more populated region of a country as opposed to an upland area ■ *adv* in, to, or towards a low-lying region of a country

downcourt /dówn kawrt/ *adj, adv* in, to, or towards the opposite end of a basketball or similar court

downdraught /dówn draaft/ *n* a downward movement of air, e.g. on the lee side of a mountain range or down a chimney

downer /dównər/ *n* **1.** **GLOOMY PERSON OR THING** a gloomy person, situation, or experience (*informal*) **2.** **SEDATIVE DRUG** a drug, especially a barbiturate, that induces calmness or sleepiness (*slang*) **3.** **GLOOMY MOOD** a gloomy and pessimistic mood (*informal*) ○ *was on a real downer*

downfall /dówn fawl/ *n* **1.** **FAILURE OR RUIN** the failure or ruin of a previously successful person, group, or organization **2.** **CAUSE OF RUIN** an action or situation responsible for the failure or ruin of a previously successful person, group, or organization **3.** METEOROL **FALL OF RAIN OR SNOW** a sudden heavy fall of rain or snow

downfallen /dówn fawlən/ *adj* **1.** in a seriously neglected or ruined condition **2.** *US* fallen from a position of fame, power, or wealth

downfield /dówn feeld/ *adj, adv N Am* in or towards the opponents' half of a field of play

downforce /dówn fawrss/ *n* a force, produced by a

combination of air resistance and gravity, that exerts a downward pressure on a moving vehicle and helps to counteract loss of control at high speeds

downgrade /dówn grayd/ vt (-grades, -grading, -graded) **1.** LOWER STATUS OF SOMETHING to lower the status, value, or rating of something ○ *The hurricane was downgraded to a tropical storm.* **2.** MOVE SOMEBODY TO LESS IMPORTANT JOB to move somebody from one post or job to another with less responsibility, status, or pay **3.** DISPARAGE SOMEBODY OR SOMETHING to speak or write disparagingly about somebody or something ■ *n* N Am DOWNWARD SLOPE a downward slope on a road

downhaul /dówn hawl/ *n* a rope for pulling down or fixing down a sail, line, or boom to the deck ■ vt to pull a sail, line, or boom down and fix it to the deck

downhearted /dówn haártid/ adj discouraged and unhappy —**downheartedly** adv —**downheartedness** n

downhill adv /down híl/ TOWARDS BOTTOM OF HILL towards the bottom of a hill or slope ■ adj /down híl/ SLOPING DOWN sloping down or taking place on a downward slope ■ n /down híl/ RACE DOWN MOUNTAINSIDE COURSE a skiing race against the clock down a long mountainside course with several hundred yards between marker flags ◇ **go downhill** to decline or deteriorate

downhole /dówn hól/ adj describes equipment used inside an oil well

downhome /dówn hóm/ adj N Am appealingly simple, informal, and unpretentious, and therefore considered characteristic of ordinary people, especially the country people of the southern United States (*informal*) ○ *downhome cooking*

Downing Street /dówning-/ n **1.** the street off Whitehall in Westminster, central London, where the official residences of the British prime minister and chancellor of the exchequer are located **2.** the British prime minister or the British government ○ *Downing Street sources*

downland /dówn land/ n undulating grass-covered hills in southern England, or similar, often flatter grassland in Australia and New Zealand

downlight /dówn līt/, **downlighter** /-lītər/ n a lamp or bulb whose light is directed straight downwards

downlink /dówn lingk/ n a path for the transmission of signals and data between a vehicle or satellite in space and Earth —**downlink** vti

download /dówn lód/ COMPUT vti (-loads, -loading, -loaded) TRANSFER DATA to transfer or copy data from one computer to another, or to a disk or peripheral device, or be transferred or copied in this way ■ n **1.** INSTANCE OF DOWNLOADING an instance or the process of downloading data **2.** DOWNLOADED DATA an amount of data downloaded in a single operation

Down Low, **down low** n US among some young Black men who regard themselves as gay, a clandestine culture that involves secret gay relationships, but rejects the suggestion that the participants are themselves gay, effeminate, or bisexual (*slang*) [Late 20C. Originally popularized by the hip-hop singers TLC and R. Kelly, with the meaning 'secret']

downmarket /dówn maarkit/ adj cheap, appealing to mass taste, and regarded as being of low quality ■ adv towards the part of the market that deals in cheap, low-quality goods that appeal to mass taste

Downpatrick /down páttrik/ town in County Down, Northern Ireland. Its name comes from the 'dun' or large mound where St Patrick is traditionally believed to be buried. Population: 10,257 (1991).

down payment n a part of the full price of something paid at the time it is bought, with the remaining part to be paid later

downpipe /dówn pīp/ n a pipe that carries rainwater from a roof gutter down to a drain or to the ground. N Am term **downspout**

downplay /dówn pláy/ (-plays, -playing, -played) vt to make something seem less important, significant, or serious than it really is

downpour /dówn pawr/ n a heavy and sustained fall of rain

down quark n a quark with an electric charge of $-\frac{1}{3}$, zero strangeness, and zero charm

downrange /down ráynj/ adj, adv away from where a missile was fired

downrigger /dówn riggər/ n a fishing line attached to a weighted cable so that the baited line trails at or near the bottom of the water

downright /dówn rīt/ adj **1.** ABSOLUTE complete and utter ○ *a downright lie* **2.** STRAIGHTFORWARD frank in expressing opinions ■ adv ABSOLUTELY completely and utterly ○ *downright unfair* —**downrightly** adv —**downrightness** n

downriver /dówn rívvər/ adv, adj towards or nearer the mouth of a river, or following the direction of its current

Downs /downz/ either of two chalk uplands in southern England, the North Downs in Surrey and Kent, and the South Downs in Hampshire and Sussex

downscale /down skáyl/ N Am adj same as **downmarket** ■ vti (-scales, -scaling, -scaled) /dówn skayl/ to reduce the scale or extent of something, especially a business

downshift /dówn shift/ (-shifts, -shifting, -shifted) vi **1.** N Am same as **change down 2.** to move from a highly paid but stressful job to one that makes it possible to improve quality of life in other respects —**downshift** n

downside /dówn sīd/ n a negative side to something that also has positive aspects

downsize /dówn sīz/ (-sizes, -sizing, -sized) vti to reduce the size of a business or organization, especially by cutting the workforce

downslide /dówn slīd/ n a downwards trend or course

downspout /dówn spowt/ n N Am CONSTR same as **downpipe**

Down's syndrome /dównz-/ n a genetic disorder characterized by a broad skull, blunt facial features, short stature, and learning difficulties. It is caused by the presence of an extra copy of a specific chromosome. [Mid-20C. After J. H. L. Down (1828–96), English physician]

downstage /dówn stáyj/ adv, adj towards or at the front of a theatre stage ■ n the front half of a theatre stage

downstairs /dówn stáirz/ adv TO LOWER FLOOR down the stairs, or to a lower floor ■ adj ON LOWER FLOOR relating to or situated on a lower or the lowest floor ○ *a downstairs bathroom* ■ n **1.** LOWER FLOOR the lower floor of a building **2.** HOUSE'S SERVANTS the servants of a large household, considered collectively (*informal*)

downstate /dówn stáyt/ adj, adv US **1.** in or to the southerly part of a US state **2.** away from the big cities and in or into the more rural parts of a US state whose major metropolitan area is to the north ○ *downstate Illinois* —**downstate** n —**downstater** n

downstream /dówn streem/ adj **1.** SITUATED TOWARDS MOUTH OF RIVER situated towards or nearer the mouth of a river **2.** MANUF OF LATER PRODUCTION STAGES relating to or occurring in the later stages of production ■ adv **1.** GENETICS FURTHER FORWARD ON DNA MOLECULE further forward on a DNA molecule, in the direction in which the sequence is being read during replication **2.** GEOG TOWARDS MOUTH OF RIVER towards or nearer the mouth of a river, or following the direction of the current ■ n COMPUT TRANSMISSION AWAY FROM CENTRAL NETWORK the transmission of data on a network away from a central distribution point

downstroke /dówn strók/ n a stroke moving or made in a downwards direction

downswing /dówn swing/ n **1.** a downwards trend or course **2.** the downwards part of a golfer's swing

Down syndrome /dówn-/ n US MED same as **Down's syndrome**

downtempo /dówn tempó/ n electronic music that is for listening to instead of dancing to

down-the-line adj US unwavering in support of or adherence to rules or policy

downthrow /dówn thró/ n the relative vertical displacement of rocks on one side of a fault

downtime /dówn tīm/ n **1.** time during which work or production is stopped, e.g. because machinery is not working **2.** a period of relaxation or play between periods of work

down-to-earth adj practical and realistic

downtown /dówn tówn/ NZ, N Am adj, adv in or to the centre of a city, especially its business centre ■ n the centre of a city, especially its business centre —**downtowner** n

downtrend /dówn trend/ n a downward trend or tendency

downtrodden /dówn tród'n/ adj made submissive by constant harsh treatment

downturn /dówn turn/ n a period or trend in which business or economic activity is reduced or is less successful

downward /dównwərd/ adj **1.** MOVING TO LOWER PLACE moving or directed to the ground or to a lower place ○ *a downwards glance* **2.** MOVING TO LOWER LEVEL moving to a lower level or condition **3.** COMING FROM ORIGIN OR SOURCE descending from a source, origin, or beginning ■ adv same as **downwards** —**downwardly** adv —**downwardness** n

downwardly mobile adj moving to a lower status, social class, or income bracket

downward mobility n movement to a lower status, social class, or income bracket

downwards /dównwərdz/ adv **1.** TOWARDS LOWER PLACE towards the ground or a lower place **2.** TO LOWER STATE to a lower level or condition **3.** TO AND INCLUDING EVERYONE to and including all the members of an organization, even the most junior ○ *everyone from the managing director downwards* **4.** TO LATER TIME to a later time or generation

downwash /dówn wosh/ n a downwards wind, e.g. the wind created by an aircraft wing

downwind /dówn wínd/ adv, adj **1.** in the direction that the wind is blowing **2.** in or into a position further along the line of the direction of the wind

downy /dówni/ (-ier, -iest) adj **1.** SOFT soft and fluffy **2.** COVERED WITH SOFT HAIRS covered with soft fine hairs **3.** FEATHER-FILLED filled with feathers [Mid-16C. < DOWN²] —**downiness** n

downy mildew n a disease of plants that produces grey velvety patches on lower leaf surfaces, caused by various fungi. Family: Peronosporaceae.

dowry /dówri/ (plural -ries) n **1.** BRIDE'S FAMILY'S GIFT TO BRIDEGROOM an amount of money or property given in some societies by a bride's family to her bridegroom or his family when she marries **2.** MAN'S GIFT TO BRIDE an amount of money or property transferred by a man to his bride when they marry **3.** CHR MONEY PAID TO ENTER NUNS' ORDER a sum of money required for a woman to enter some monastic orders **4.** TALENT a natural talent (*literary*) [14C. Via Anglo-Norman *dowarie* < Old French *douarie* (see DOWER)]

dowry death n S Asia the death of a married woman by murder or suicide arising from a dispute over her dowry

dowse¹ /dowz/ (dowses, dowsing, dowsed) vi to use a divining rod to search for underground water or minerals [Late 17C. Origin ?] —**dowser** n

dowse² vt, n another spelling of **douse¹**

dowse³ /dowss/ vt SAILING another spelling of **douse²**

dowsing rod /dówzing-/ n PARANORMAL same as **divining rod**

Dowson /dówss'n/, **Ernest** (1867–1900) British poet. A friend of W. B. Yeats and Oscar Wilde, he published two collections of poems in 1896 and 1899 which include his most famous works, 'Cynara' (1891) and 'Vitae summa brevis' (1896). Full name **Dowson, Ernest Christopher**

'They are not long, the days of wine and roses.'
[Ernest Dowson, 'Vitae Summa Brevis Spem Nos Vetat Incohare Longam' ('The shortness of life prevents us from entertaining far-off hopes'); 1896]

Dow theory /dów-/ n a theory that states that stock-market prices can be forecast on the basis of the movements of a selected group of stocks [After Charles Dow (1851–1902), US financial journalist and joint founder of Dow Jones and Company]

doxastic /dok sástik/ n the branch of logic that deals with belief [Early 19C. < Greek *doxa* 'opinion'] —**doxastic** adj

doxie n RELIG another spelling of **doxy¹**

doxology /dok sóllə ji/ (*plural* **-gies**) *n* in Christian religious services, a hymn, prayer, or formula of worship in praise of God [Mid-17C. < medieval Latin *doxologia* 'science of opinion' < Greek *doxa* 'opinion'] —**doxological** /dóksə lójjik'l/ *adj* —**doxologically** *adv*

doxorubicin /dóksō rо́obissin/ *n* an antibiotic obtained from a bacterium. Use: treatment of some tumours. [Late 20C. < *dioxo-* + Latin *rubus* 'red' + -MYCIN]

doxy[1] /dóksi/ (*plural* **-ies**), **doxie** *n* a set of beliefs, especially religious beliefs (*informal*) [Mid-18C. Extracted < such words as ORTHODOXY, HETERODOXY]

doxy[2] /dóksi/ (*plural* **-ies**) *n* (*archaic slang offensive*) **1.** an offensive term for a prostitute **2.** an offensive term for a woman involved in extramarital sexual relationships [Mid-16C. Origin ?]

doxycycline /dóksi sí kleen/ *n* an antibiotic derived from tetracycline. Use: treatment of many diseases. [Mid-20C. Contraction of *deoxytetracycline*]

doyen /dóy ən/ *n* a man who is the most experienced and respected member of a group or profession [15C. Via French < Latin *decanus* 'person in charge of ten others' (see DEAN)]

doyenne /doy énn/ *n* a woman who is the most experienced and respected member of a group or profession [Mid-19C. < French, form of *doyen* (see DOYEN)]

Doyle /doyl/, **Sir Arthur Conan** (1859–1930) British writer and physician. He was author of the Sherlock Holmes detective novels, including *The Hound of the Baskervilles* (1902).

> 'It is an old maxim of mine that when you have excluded the impossible, whatever remains, however improbable, must be the truth.'
> [Sir Arthur Conan Doyle, *The Sign of Four*, 1889]

Doyle, Roddy (*b.* 1958) Irish novelist, playwright, and screenwriter. He won the 1993 Booker Prize with *Paddy Clarke Ha Ha Ha*, building on the success of his first two novels *The Commitments* (1987) and *The Snapper* (1990), both made into films.

> 'Soul is the rhythm o' sex. It's the rhythm o' the factory too. The workin' man's rhythm. Sex an' factory. Not the factory I'm in, said Natalie. There isn't much rhythm guttin' fish.'
> [Roddy Doyle, *The Commitments*, 1987]

doyly *n* HOUSEHOLD another spelling of **doily**

D'Oyly Carte /dóyli kaárt/, **Richard** (1844–1901) British theatrical agent, manager, and producer. He founded an eponymous opera company in 1875 to perform the operettas of W. S. Gilbert and Arthur Sullivan. From 1881 these operettas were staged at his own Savoy Theatre, London.

doz. *abbr* dozen

doze[1] /dōz/ (**dozes, dozing, dozed**) *vi* **1.** to sleep lightly for a short time, especially during the day **2.** to spend time lazily or in a daydream [Mid-17C. Probably < N Germanic] —**doze** *n*

doze off *vi* to fall into a light sleep, especially unintentionally

doze[2] /dōz/ (**dozes, dozing, dozed**) *vt* CONSTR same as **bulldoze** (sense 1) (*slang*) [Mid-20C. Back-formation < DOZER [1]]

dozed /dōzd/ *adj Ireland* describes wood that is rotten or rubber that is perished [Late 18C. Past participle of DOZE [1]]

dozen /dúzz'n/ *n* (*plural same*) **GROUP OF 12** a group of 12 people or objects ■ *det* **MANY** a large number of (*informal*) ○ *I've told you a dozen times already!* ■ **dozens** *npl* **A LARGE NUMBER** a large quantity or a great many (*informal*) ○ *has dozens of friends* ○ *gave away dozens more* [13C. Via Old French *dozeine* < Latin *duodecim* 'twelve' < *duo* 'two' + *decem* 'ten'] —**dozenth** *adj* ◇ **by the dozen** in large quantities ◇ **somebody's daily dozen** somebody's regular regime of physical exercises

dozer[1] /dṓzər/ *n* CONSTR same as **bulldozer** (*slang*) [Mid-20C. Shortened form]

dozer[2] /dṓzər/ *n* somebody sleeping lightly [Early 18C. < DOZE [1]]

dozy /dṓzi/ (**-zier, -ziest**) *adj* **1.** half asleep or tending to fall asleep or doze **2.** slow in understanding (*informal*) —**dozily** *adv* —**doziness** *n*

REGIONAL NOTE See ***addle-headed***.

---

dp *abbr* **1.** COMPUT data processing **2.** PHYS dew point

DP *abbr* **1.** COMPUT data processing **2.** PHYS dew point **3.** SOC WELFARE displaced person

D/P *abbr* COMM **1.** documents against payment **2.** documents against presentation

DPB *n NZ* a state benefit payable to somebody with family responsibilities who has little or no other income. Full form **Domestic Purposes Benefit**

DPhil /dee fíl/, **DPh** *abbr* EDUC Doctor of Philosophy

dpi *n* a measure of the density of the image produced by a computer screen or printer. Full form **dots per inch**

DPP *abbr* LAW Director of Public Prosecutions

DPS *abbr* FIN dividends per share

dpt *abbr* **1.** department **2.** GRAM deponent

DPT *abbr* IMMUNOL diphtheria, pertussis, tetanus (vaccine)

dr *abbr* **1.** FIN debtor **2.** dining room (*used in advertisements*) **3.** MEASURE dram [1] **4.** drawer

Dr *abbr* **1.** Doctor **2.** ROADS drive *n* (sense 3) (*used in addresses*)

DR *abbr* **1.** NAVIG dead reckoning **2.** dining room (*used in advertisements*) **3.** CONSTR dry riser

dr. *abbr* **1.** FIN debit **2.** MONEY, HIST drachma **3.** MEASURE dram [1]

drab[1] /drab/ *adj* (**drabber, drabbest**) **1. LACKING COLOUR OR BRIGHTNESS** uninteresting to look at because of a lack of colour or brightness **2. BORING** lacking interest, enthusiasm, or excitement **3. OF PALE GREYISH-BROWN COLOUR** of a dull pale greyish-brown colour ■ *n* **1. PALE GREYISH-BROWN COLOUR** a dull pale greyish-brown colour **2.** TEXTILES **DULL-COLOURED FABRIC** a grey or brown fabric [Early 16C. < Old French *drap* 'cloth' (see DRAPE)] —**drably** *adv* —**drabness** *n*

drab[2] /drab/ *n* **1. OFFENSIVE TERM** an offensive term that deliberately insults a woman's appearance or cleanliness (*archaic insult*) **2. OFFENSIVE TERM** an offensive term for a prostitute (*archaic*) ■ *vi* (**drabs, drabbing, drabbed**) **USE PROSTITUTES** to have sex with prostitutes (*archaic*) [Early 16C. Origin ?]

drabbet /drábbit/ *n* coarse undyed linen fabric [Early 19C. < DRAB [1]]

drabble /drább'l/ (**-bles, -bling, -bled**) *vti* to become wet and dirty, or make something wet and dirty (*archaic*) [14C. < Low German *drabbeln* 'splash in water']

Drabble /drább'l/, **Margaret** (*b.* 1939) British novelist, editor, and critic. Her novels explore the dilemmas of women in contemporary society and include *The Needle's Eye* (1972) and *The Radiant Way* (1987). She edited *The Oxford Companion to English Literature* (1985).

> 'When nothing is sure, everything is possible.'
> [Margaret Drabble, *The Middle Ground*, 1980]

dracaena /drə seénə/, **dracena** *n* **1.** a tropical evergreen plant with long, strap-shaped, often variegated leaves, popular as a house plant. Genus: *Dracaena*. **2.** a plant with long narrow leaves resembling a true dracaena. Genus: *Cordyline*. [Early 19C. Via modern Latin < Greek *drakaina*, feminine of *drakōn* 'dragon'; from the supposed resemblance of the juice of one species to dragon's blood]

drachm /dram/ *n* **1.** a unit of liquid capacity in the apothecary system, equal to $\frac{1}{8}$ of a fluid ounce. N Am term **fluid dram 2.** MONEY, HIST same as **drachma** (sense 1) [14C. Via French < Greek *drakhmē* 'number or amount one hand can hold' < assumed *drakh-* 'grasp']

drachma /drákmə/ (*plural* **-mas** or **-mae** /-mi/) *n* **1.** the main unit of the former Greek currency, before the euro **2.** an ancient Greek silver coin [Early 16C. Via Latin < Greek *drakhmē* (see DRACHM)]

drack /drak/, **drac** *adj Aus* an offensive term used to describe a woman's appearance as unattractive [Mid-20C. Origin ?] —**drack** *n*

Draco[1] /dráykō/ *n* a large faint constellation of the northern hemisphere. See illustration at **constellation** [Late 17C. < Latin *draco, dracon-* (see DRAGON)]

Draco[2] /dráykō/ (*fl* 7th century BC) Athenian political leader and legislator. His legal code, established in Athens in 621 BC, was considered to be unduly harsh and was later replaced by Solon's more moderate laws.

draco lizard /dráykō-/ *n* REPT same as **flying lizard** [< Latin *draco, dracon-* (see DRAGON)]

dracone /drákōn/ *n* a large flexible container for transporting liquids by towing them on the surface of the sea [Mid-20C. < Greek *drakōn* 'snake']

draconian /drə kṓni ən/ *adj* **1.** unjustly harsh or severe **2.** relating to the Athenian legislator Draco or his wide-ranging and harsh code of laws [Late 19C. < Greek *Drakōn-* 'Draco'] —**draconianism** *n*

draconic /drə kónnik/ *adj* **1.** relating to or like a dragon or dragons **2.** same as **draconian** [In sense 1 < Latin *draco, dracon-* (see DRAGON); in sense 2 < Greek *Drakō* 'Draco'] —**draconically** *adv*

draff /draf/ *n* a residue left in brewing after the grain has been fermented. Use: cattle feed. [13C. Origin ?] —**draffy** *adj*

draft /draaft/ *n* **1. PRELIMINARY VERSION** a preliminary version of a piece of writing such as a speech, essay, or report **2. PRELIMINARY SKETCH** a preliminary sketch or plan **3.** FIN **CHEQUE** a written order to pay money from an account to a person or to another account **4.** CONSTR **LEVELLING LINE ON STONE** a line chiselled on the surface of a building stone as a guide to laying it level **5.** *N Am* MIL **CONSCRIPTION** the order to join the armed services in time of war ■ *n, adj* US spelling of **draught** ■ *v* (**drafts, drafting, drafted**) **1.** *vt* **WRITE PRELIMINARY VERSION OF SOMETHING** to write a preliminary version of something such as a speech, essay, or report **2.** *vt* **MAKE PLAN** to make a preliminary plan or sketch of something, before all the required information is to hand **3.** *vt* **TRANSFER SOMEBODY SOMEWHERE FOR DUTY** to move or send somebody somewhere to carry out a particular task or general work and duties **4.** *vt N Am* MIL **CALL SOMEBODY UP FOR MILITARY SERVICE** to select somebody for compulsory service in the armed forces **5.** *vt US* POL **COMPEL SOMEBODY TO RUN FOR OFFICE** to compel a candidate to run for elective office **6.** *vt US* FIN **WITHDRAW MONEY** to move money from one account to another as a way of effecting payment for something **7.** *vi US* TRANSP, SPORTS **FOLLOW PERSON OR VEHICLE CLOSELY** to follow closely behind another fast-moving competitor or vehicle, taking advantage of the reduced resistance to movement **8.** *vt ANZ* **SORT LIVESTOCK INTO SMALLER GROUPS** to divide or sort livestock into smaller groups according to age, sex, or a specific characteristic [Mid-16C. Form of DRAUGHT] —**drafter** *n*

draft dodger *n US* somebody who seeks to avoid being called up for military service

draftee /draaf teé/ *n N Am* somebody who has been drafted for military service

draftsman, etc. DESIGN US spelling of **draughtsman, etc.**

drafty *adj* US spelling of **draughty**

drag /drag/ *v* (**drags, dragging, dragged**) **1.** *vt* **PULL SOMETHING ALONG WITH EFFORT** to move something, especially something that is too large, heavy, or cumbersome to carry, by pulling it along the ground or across a surface ○ *dragged the fallen tree out of the road* **2.** *vt* **PULL SOMEBODY OR SOMETHING BY FORCE** to move or remove somebody or something that resists, usually by pulling at the person or object with considerable force or violence **3.** *vt* **PERSUADE SOMEBODY TO COME AWAY** to cause, persuade, or force an unwilling person to stop doing something or to leave a place ○ *I'm sorry to drag you away from your work.* **4.** *vti* **TRAIL ALONG GROUND** to be in continuous contact with the ground while moving across it, or allow something to do this ○ *He dragged his feet as he walked.* **5.** *vti* **MOVE** to move, or move yourself or your feet, slowly and with difficulty or great reluctance ○ *I was so tired that I could scarcely drag myself up the stairs.* **6.** *vi* **PASS OR PROCEED SLOWLY** to pass or proceed at a very slow and boring pace ○ *The afternoon was beginning to drag.* **7.** *vt* COMPUT **MOVE ICON WITH MOUSE** to move an icon or other selected item on a computer screen by clicking on it with the mouse and pulling it to a new location **8.** *vt* **SEARCH UNDERWATER AREA** to search a river bed, pond, or other area of water using a net or hook in an attempt to find something or some-

body **9.** *vi* **PUFF ON SMOKING MATERIAL** to put a cigarette, pipe, or cigar to the mouth and suck in the smoke (*informal*) ■ *n* **1.** **HINDRANCE** somebody or something that slows down physical movement or progress in an area or activity ○ *High interest rates have been a drag on the economy.* **2.** AVIAT, PHYS **RESISTANCE TO MOTION** the resistance experienced by a body moving through a fluid medium, especially by an aircraft when travelling through the air. Symbol **D 3.** **SOMEBODY OR SOMETHING BORING** a person, task, duty, or event that is held to be extremely boring and irritating (*informal*) ○ *It was such a drag going alone.* **4.** **PUFF** a puff on a cigarette, pipe, or cigar (*informal*) **5.** **CLOTHING OF OPPOSITE SEX** clothing characteristic of one sex worn by a member of the other, especially women's clothing when worn by men (*slang*) **6.** N Am **STREET** a street or road (*slang*) ○ *the main drag* **7.** **SLOW AND LABORIOUS MOVEMENT OR ACTION** an action or movement carried out slowly and with great effort or difficulty **8.** **DRAGGING MOVEMENT** a sound, movement, or act of dragging **9.** **LINE USED FOR DRAGGING RIVER** a line, chain, or hook that is used for searching or dredging the bottom of an area of water such as a river or pond **10.** VEHICLES **MACHINE OR VEHICLE THAT IS DRAGGED** a vehicle such as a cart or sledge that is pulled along the surface of the ground **11.** TRANSP **BRAKING DEVICE** a braking device, especially a horseshoe-shaped piece of metal fitted on the underside of the wheel of a horse-drawn vehicle **12.** MOTOR SPORTS same as **drag race 13.** FIELD SPORTS **FOX SCENT** the scent left by a fox or other animal that is hunted by dogs **14.** FIELD SPORTS **ARTIFICIAL SCENT** an artificial scent put on the ground for hunting dogs to follow **15.** FIELD SPORTS same as **drag hunt 16.** VEHICLES, HIST **HORSE-DRAWN COACH** a large coach, similar to a stagecoach but privately owned, with seats inside and on top and usually drawn by four horses [14C. < either a form of DRAW or < related Old Norse *draga* < Germanic] ◇ **drag and drop** to click onto an item on a computer screen, move it with the mouse, and release it on an icon ◇ **drag your feet** *or* **heels** to be slow to act, usually because you would prefer to avoid doing anything ○ *dragging their feet on implementing the plan*

SYNONYMS See *pull.*

drag down *vt* **1.** to reduce somebody or something to a lower level or an inferior status by force or pressure ○ *Don't allow yourself to be dragged down by a timid banker.* **2.** to make somebody feel listless, uninterested, or physically weak and tired ○ *Sitting at home alone drags me down.*

drag in *vt* **1.** to insist on introducing an irrelevant topic into a conversation ○ *always drags in his own accomplishments* **2.** to involve an unwilling person in a particular situation ○ *Liz was going to the reunion and dragged me in.*

drag into *vt* **1.** to involve somebody in something dishonest, disreputable, or otherwise undesirable ○ *What are you trying to drag me into?* ○ *They were dragged into the scandal.* **2.** to insist on introducing an irrelevant topic or name into a conversation ○ *always drags his political opinions into our conversations*

drag on *vi* to continue for a very long time, especially past the expected or desired finishing time

drag out *vt* to make something last longer than is necessary or desirable

drag out of *vt* to force somebody to reveal or admit something ○ *Are you going to tell me, or do I have to drag it out of you?*

drag up *vt* **1.** to mention something that somebody does not want discussed or known, especially something unpleasant, upsetting, or embarrassing from that person's past **2.** to bring somebody up in a lazy or undisciplined way (*informal humorous; usually passive*) ○ *Where were you dragged up?*

dragée /dra zháy/ *n* **1.** **HARD-COATED SWEET** a sweet consisting of a nut, piece of fruit, or other centre covered in a hard sugar coating **2.** **TINY CONFECTIONERY BALL** a tiny silver-coated ball used for decorating cakes **3.** **SWEETENED PILL** a medicinal pill covered with a sugar coating to make it taste better [Late 17C. < French, modern form of Old French *dragie* (see DREDGE²)]

draggle /drágg'l/ (**-gles, -gling, -gled**) *v* **1.** *vti* to make something wet and dirty by trailing it along the ground, or become wet and dirty by being trailed along the ground **2.** *vi* to follow along behind somebody else in a slow and usually undisciplined or slovenly fashion [Early 16C. Probably < DRAG]

draggy /drággi/ (**-gier, -giest**) *adj* (*informal*) **1.** slow-moving ○ *a draggy musical* **2.** boring or otherwise annoying ○ *spent a draggy afternoon weeding the garden*

draghound /drág hownd/ *n* a hound used in a drag hunt to follow an artificial scent trail

drag hunt *n* a hunt in which a pack of hounds follows an artificial scent trail

drag-hunt *vti* to hunt a lure that leaves an artificial scent trail with a pack of hounds

draglift /drág lift/ *n* a ski lift with metal bars or ropes that people hold onto as they are pulled up to the top of a slope on their skis

dragline /drág līn/ *n* **1.** an excavating machine with a digging bucket attached by cables to a long jib and operated by being dragged back towards the machine by another cable **2.** a line that is used for dragging, e.g. when hauling a load or dragging a river or pond

drag link *n* a link that conveys motion from the crank of one shaft to the crank of another. In motor vehicles, it is used to connect the steering gear to the steering arm.

dragnet /drág net/ *n* **1.** **POLICE HUNT FOR CRIMINAL** a systematic and coordinated search for a wanted person made by police **2.** **WEIGHTED NET USED UNDERWATER** a net with weights on it used when trawling for fish at sea or when searching for something at the bottom of a river or pond **3.** **NET FOR CATCHING GAME** a net that is drawn across the ground and used to trap small game

dragoman /drággəmən/ (*plural* **-mans** or **-men** /-mən/) *n* a guide or interpreter in some Arabic-, Turkish-, or Farsi-speaking countries (*archaic*) [16C. Via French, Italian, and medieval Greek < Arabic *targumān* < Aramaic *tūrgemānā* < Akkadian *targumānu* 'interpreter']

dragon

dragon /drággən/ *n* **1.** **SCALY GREEN MONSTER** a mythical creature that has green scaly skin, wings, and a long tail, and breathes fire **2.** REPT **LARGE LIZARD** a large lizard, e.g. the Komodo dragon **3.** **OFFENSIVE TERM** an offensive term for a woman regarded as fierce and formidable (*insult*) [13C. Via French < Latin *dracon-* < Greek *drakōn* 'snake'] ◇ **chase the dragon** to take heroin by heating it and breathing in the fumes (*slang*)

Dragon *n* ASTRON same as **Draco**

dragon arum *n* PLANTS same as **dragonroot** (sense 1)

dragon boat *n* a long narrow boat decorated like a dragon, used especially by Chinese people when taking part in annual boat races celebrating the lunar year

dragonet /drággənit/ (*plural* **-ets** or same) *n* a small brightly coloured spiny sea fish with a flat head, narrow body, and large pectoral fins, living near the bottom of warm shallow waters. Family: Callionymidae. [14C. < DRAGON]

dragonfly /drággən flī/ (*plural* **-flies**) *n* an insect with a large head and eyes, a long thin body, and two pairs of iridescent often blue wings that usually remain outstretched when the insect is at rest. Suborder: Anisoptera.

dragonroot /drággən root/ (*plural* **-roots** or same) *n* **1.** a tuberous, foul-smelling, and poisonous perennial plant belonging to the arum family. Latin name: *Dracunculus vulgaris.* **2.** PLANTS same as **green dragon**

dragon's blood *n* a red resinous substance. Source:

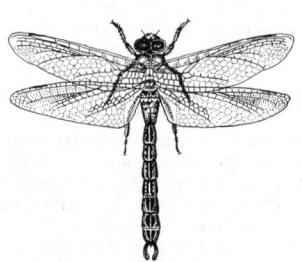

dragonfly

various trees including the dragon tree. Use: colouring varnishes, lacquers.

dragon tree *n* an evergreen tree that has a trunk that grows very thick clusters of spiky leaves, orange fruit, and resin that is a source of dragon's blood. Native to: Canary Islands. Latin name: *Dracaena draco.*

dragoon /drə goón/ *n* **1.** **MOUNTED INFANTRYMAN** in European armies of the 17th and 18th centuries, a mounted infantryman armed with a carbine **2.** **CAVALRYMAN** in armies of the late 18th and 19th centuries, a cavalryman, especially a heavily armed cavalryman. The word is retained in the names of some modern regiments that were originally cavalry regiments. ■ *vt* (**-goons, -gooning, -gooned**) **1.** **FORCE SOMEBODY** to involve somebody in an activity against his or her will, or force somebody to do something ○ *was dragooned into joining the chorus for the show* **2.** **SUBJUGATE SOMEBODY** to persecute or subjugate somebody using military troops [Early 17C. < French *dragon* 'carbine, musket', literally 'dragon']

drag queen *n* a man who dresses as a woman, especially a performer who dresses in a flamboyant women's costume and traditionally affects feminine mannerisms for comic effect (*informal*)

drag race *n* a race between cars with specially modified bodies and engines on a straight track to discover which has the fastest acceleration —**drag racer** *n* —**drag racing** *n*

dragster /drágstər/ *n* **1.** a car that is specially designed for and used in drag racing **2.** a driver who takes part in a drag race

drag strip *n* a short straight track, usually a quarter of a mile in length, used for drag racing

drain /drayn/ *n* **1.** **SEWAGE PIPE** a pipe or channel that carries water or sewage away from a place **2.** **SOMETHING THAT USES UP RESOURCES** something that diminishes or uses up resources or energy ○ *a serious drain on our cash reserves* **3.** **LOSS OR DIMINISHING** the gradual loss, withdrawal, or diminishing of something regarded as an important resource ○ *the drain of trained personnel from the industry* **4.** MED **DEVICE TO REMOVE FLUID FROM WOUND** a tube or other device placed in a wound or incision to draw off fluids such as blood, pus, or water **5.** AGRIC **ARTIFICIAL WATERWAY** an artificial waterway that allows for land drainage ■ *v* (**drains, draining, drained**) **1.** *vti* **FLOW OUT** to flow out of something, often leaving it empty or dry, or allow a liquid to do this **2.** *vti* **EMPTY** to empty or dry something by allowing the water to flow out of or off it, or become empty or dry in this way ○ *drained and refilled the pool* **3.** *vt* AGRIC **DRY OUT LAND** to make marshy land drier by laying pipes, digging ditches or channels, or by any other means that removes the excess water **4.** *vt* GEOG **CHANNEL WATER AWAY FROM LAND** to be a channel for leading water off land ○ *The river Loire drains most of central France.* **5.** *vi* GEOG **DISCHARGE INTO SOMETHING** to discharge surface water or flow into a river or larger body of water (*refers to geographical areas or watercourses*) ○ *The Mississippi River drains into the Gulf of Mexico.* **6.** *vt* **DRINK SOMETHING UP** to empty a cup, glass, or other container by drinking all its contents ○ *drained his tea in one gulp* **7.** *vt* **USE SOMETHING UP** to use up or deplete something gradually, especially somebody's energy and resources, by making constant demands on it ○ *draining the company's financial resources* **8.** *vi* **WANE** to disappear gradually, or become less strong or intense ○ *The colour drained from her cheeks.* **9.**

vt **EXHAUST SOMEBODY** to leave somebody feeling physically or emotionally exhausted ○ *Working with toddlers really drains my energy.* [Old English *dreahnian* < Germanic] —**drainable** *adj* ◇ **down the drain** (*informal*) **1.** wasted or squandered with no hope of retrieval **2.** towards or in a state of total failure or ruin, especially financial failure

drainage /dráynij/ *n* **1. DRAINING PROCESS** the process of draining liquid from something **2. SEWAGE SYSTEM** a system of pipes or channels that carries water or sewage away from a place **3.** MED **FLUID REMOVAL FROM BODY** the removal of fluid such as water, blood, or pus from a wound or part of the body, usually by means of a tube **4. FLUID REMOVED BY DRAINING** water, sewage, or another fluid removed by draining

drainage basin, drainage area *n* GEOG same as **catchment area** (sense 2)

drainboard /dráyn bawrd/ *n N Am* same as **draining board**

drainer /dráynər/ *n* a rack or container in which things are put so that liquid can drain off them

draining board /dráyning-/ *n* a slightly sloping metal, wooden, or plastic surface next to a sink, with shallow grooves on it to allow water to drain off drying dishes into the sink. N Am term **drainboard**

drainpipe /dráyn pīp/ *n* a pipe that carries off rainwater, waste water, or sewage to or through the drains, especially a downpipe attached to the side of a house ■ **drainpipes, drainpipe trousers** *npl* trousers with very narrow legs that were particularly popular in the 1950s, and again in the 1970s and 1980s in punk fashion

drake /drayk/ *n* a male duck [13C. Probably < Germanic]

Drake /drayk/, **Sir Francis** (1540?–96) English navigator and admiral. He was the first English person to circumnavigate the globe, and he later helped to defeat the Spanish Armada (1588).

> 'The advantage of time and place in all practical actions is half a victory; which being lost is irrecoverable.'
> [Sir Francis Drake, *Letter to Queen Elizabeth I*; 1588]

Drakensberg /dráakənz burg/ mountain range extending through southeastern South Africa and Lesotho. The highest peaks include Thabana-Ntlenya, 3,482 m/11,424 ft.

Drake Passage stretch of water between South America and the Antarctic Peninsula that separates the South Atlantic and South Pacific oceans. Length: 800 km/500 mi.

dram[1] /dram/ *n* **1.** a unit of mass in the avoirdupois system equal to $\frac{1}{16}$ of an ounce (or approximately 1.77 grams) **2.** a small amount of an alcoholic drink, particularly whisky or brandy ○ *How about a wee dram before you go?* [15C. Via Old French *drame* or medieval Latin *drama* < Greek *drakhmē* (see DRACHM)]

dram[2] /dram/ *n* the main unit of Armenian currency. See table at **currency** [Via Armenian < Greek *drakhmē* (see DRACHM)]

dram[3] *abbr* dramatic

DRAM /dee ram/ *abbr* dynamic random access memory

drama /dráamə/ *n* **1.** THEATRE **PERFORMED PLAY** a serious play written for performance on stage, television, or radio **2.** ARTS **PLAYS AS GENRE** works written for performance on the stage, radio, or television, considered as a literary genre ○ *17th-century French drama* **3.** THEATRE **PRODUCING OR PERFORMING PLAYS** the performance, production, or writing of plays considered as a job, activity, or subject to be studied **4. EXCITING EVENT** a real-life event or situation that is particularly exciting or emotionally involving ○ *the drama of the trapped climbers* **5. DRAMATIC EVENTS OR QUALITY** exciting, tense, and gripping events and actions, or an exciting, tense, and gripping quality, either in a work of art or in a real-life situation ○ *an evening full of drama* [Early 16C. Via late Latin < Greek, 'play, deed' < *dran* 'do']

drama documentary *n* a documentary work, usually on television or radio, in which real events are reenacted by actors, or in which real events and characters are mingled with fictional ones

Dramamine /drámmə min/ *tdmk* a trademark for a motion-sickness remedy

drama queen *n* somebody who likes to make a drama out of a situation by acting in an emotional way (*informal*)

dramatic /drə máttik/ *adj* **1. SUDDEN AND MARKED** large in degree or scale, and often occurring with surprising suddenness ○ *a dramatic jump in prices* **2. STRIKING** bold, vivid, or strikingly impressive in appearance, colour, or effect ○ *a dramatic view of the Alps* **3. EXCITING AND INTENSE** characterized, in real life or in art, by the kind of intense and gripping excitement, startling suddenness, or larger-than-life impressiveness associated with drama and the theatre ○ *the dramatic sequence of events leading to his escape* **4. FOR THEATRE** written for the theatre, or relating to the theatre, plays, or acting **5. HAVING POWERFUL EXPRESSIVE VOICE** having a powerful singing voice especially suited to the expression of intense emotion, e.g. in tragic or villainous roles in opera ○ *a dramatic tenor* [Late 16C. Via late Latin < Greek *drāmatikos* < *drama* (see DRAMA)]

dramatically /drə máttikli/ *adv* **1.** in a way that grabs the attention and causes an excited, shocked, or startled reaction ○ *flung the papers dramatically to the floor* **2.** to a very noticeable degree and often with surprising suddenness ○ *Things have improved dramatically since your last visit.*

dramatic irony *n* a situation, or the irony arising from a situation, in which the audience has a fuller knowledge of what is happening in a drama than a character does

dramatic monologue *n* a poem or other literary work consisting of words supposedly spoken by a character, often in a specific situation, either directly to the reader or to a listener

dramatics /drə máttiks/ *n* the performance and production of plays for the theatre, especially in a nonprofessional context (*takes a singular verb*) ■ *npl* theatrical and exaggerated behaviour (*takes a plural verb*) ○ *Spare us the dramatics, for goodness sake, and tell us what happened!*

dramatise *vt* THEATRE another spelling of **dramatize**

dramatis personae /drámmətiss pər sṓ nī/ *n* **LIST OF CHARACTERS** a list of the names of the characters who appear in a play, usually printed in the text of a play or in a theatre programme (*takes a singular verb*) ■ *npl* (*formal; takes a plural verb*) **1. CHARACTERS IN PLAY** the characters who appear in a play **2. PEOPLE IN SITUATION** the people involved in a specific situation [< Latin, 'persons of the drama']

dramatist /drámmətist/ *n* a writer of plays for the stage, television, or radio

dramatize /drámmə tīz/ (**-tizes, -tizing, -tized**), **dramatise** (**-tises, -tising, -tised**) *v* **1.** *vt* to turn a literary work or a real event into a drama for presentation on the stage, television, or radio **2.** *vti* to make something more dramatic, especially to exaggerate the importance or seriousness of a situation in an attention-seeking and theatrical way —**dramatizable** *adj* —**dramatization** /drámmə tī záysh'n/ *n* —**dramatizer** *n*

dramaturge /drámmə turj/ *n* **1.** *also* **dramaturgist** /-turjist/ a playwright, particularly one who works with a specific theatre or company **2.** *also* **dramaturg** a member of the staff of a theatre with mainly literary responsibilities, e.g. choosing the plays for performance, editing and adapting texts, and writing programme notes [Mid-19C. Via French < Greek *dramatourgos* 'worker in drama' < *drama* (see DRAMA)]

dramaturgy /drámmə turji/ *n* the art of the theatre, especially with regard to the techniques involved in writing plays —**dramaturgic** /drámmə túrjik/ *adj* —**dramaturgical** *adj* —**dramaturgically** *adv*

Drammen /drámmən/ city and seaport in southern Norway, situated southwest of Oslo. Population: 53,680 (1998).

drank past tense of **drink**

drape /drayp/ *v* (**drapes, draping, draped**) **1.** *vt* **PLACE FABRIC OVER SOMETHING** to hang a piece of fabric over something so that it falls in folds around it or covers it ○ *draped a scarf over her shoulders* **2.** *vt* **COVER SOMETHING WITH FABRIC** to cover something with a piece of fabric, usually so that the fabric hangs down around it in folds ○ *a chair draped in a dust sheet* **3.** *vi* **HANG IN FOLDS** to hang or be able to hang in loose folds on or over something ○ *a heavy fabric that will drape well* **4.** *vt* **REST PART OF BODY CASUALLY** to place part of the body on or over something such as the back of a chair, in a relaxed and casual way ○ *She draped herself elegantly over the sofa.* ■ *n* **1.** *N Am* HOUSEHOLD same as **curtain** *n* (sense 1) (*usually used in the plural*) **2. PIECE OF DRAPING FABRIC** a piece of fabric used to drape over something **3. WAY FABRIC HANGS** the way in which fabric hangs and forms folds, especially when made into a garment ○ *adjusting the drape of the dress* [15C. < Old French *draper* < *drap* 'cloth' < late Latin *drappus* < Celtic]

draper /dráypər/ *n* a dealer in fabric and sewing materials (*dated*) [14C. < Old French *drapier* < *drap* (see DRAPE)]

drapery /dráypəri/ (*plural* **-ies**) *n* **1. CLOTH ARRANGED TO HANG IN FOLDS** cloth or clothing that has been arranged to hang in elegant or decorative folds **2. PIECE OF ELEGANTLY HANGING FABRIC** a piece of fabric used as a decorative cover or garment and usually hanging in loose elegant folds **3. FABRICS AND SEWING MATERIALS** fabrics and sewing materials collectively, especially as goods sold in a shop ○ *the drapery department* N Am term **dry goods 4. DRAPER'S OCCUPATION** the occupation of selling fabrics and sewing materials (*dated*) **5.** *N Am* HOUSEHOLD same as **curtain** *n* (sense 1) (*usually used in the plural*) [14C. < Old French *draperie* < *drap* (see DRAPE)]

drastic /drástik/ *adj* **1.** having a powerful effect or far-reaching consequences ○ *a crisis calling for drastic remedies* **2.** very noticeable, significant, and usually worrying because of its amount or degree ○ *drastic budget cuts* [Late 17C. < Greek *drastikos* 'effective, active' < *dran* 'do']

drastically /drástikli/ *adv* to a very great and usually very worrying degree

drat /drat/ *interj* used to express annoyance or frustration (*informal*) [Early 19C. Alteration of *od rot*, shortening of *God rot*]

dratted /dráttid/ *adj* used to express annoyance or frustration with something or somebody (*informal*) ○ *Where is that dratted pen?*

draught /draaft/ *n* **1. CURRENT OF COLD AIR** a current of uncomfortably cold air penetrating a room or other space **2. CURRENT OF AIR IN ENCLOSED SPACE** a current of air, especially one that is moving through an enclosed space such as a chimney or tunnel **3.** ENG **REGULATING DEVICE** a valve that regulates the flow of air to or from a pipe such as a chimney **4. PULLING ALONG OR DRAWING IN** the act of pulling something along, of drawing something in, or of breathing or drinking something **5. MOUTHFUL OF AIR, LIQUID, OR SMOKE** the amount of air, liquid, or smoke taken in in a single breath or swallow **6.** MED **DOSE OF LIQUID MEDICINE** a dose of medicine in liquid form (*dated*) **7.** BEVERAGES **BEER IN BARRELS** beer that is stored in and served from barrels or casks rather than bottles **8. QUANTITY OF FISH FOUND IN NET** the amount of fish found in a net when it is hauled in **9.** NAUT **DEPTH NEEDED BY SHIP TO FLOAT** the distance between the water line of a ship and the lowest part of its hull, which is the minimum depth of water it requires in order to float **10.** BOARD GAMES **DRAUGHT PIECE** any one of the 24 flat round pieces used in the game of draughts. N Am term **chequer** ■ *adj* **1.** BEVERAGES **SERVED FROM BARREL** stored in and served from a barrel rather than a bottle **2.** AGRIC **PULLING HEAVY LOADS** used to pull heavy loads ○ *a draught animal* [12C. < Old Norse *dráttr* < Germanic] ◇ **feel the draught** to be exposed to dangers or difficulties, especially through a shortage of money (*informal*) ◇ **on draught** available for serving from the barrel

draughtboard /dráaft bawrd/ *n* a game board with eight rows of eight alternate black and white squares on it, used for playing draughts. N Am term **checkerboard**

draughts /draafts/ *n* a game played with 12 black and 12 white pieces on a chequered board. Pieces can only move diagonally, and are taken when enemy pieces jump over them. (*takes a singular verb*) N Am term **checkers**

draughtsman /dráaftsmən/ (*plural* **-men** /-mən/) *n* **1. TECHNICAL DESIGNER** a man who makes detailed plans or drawings for buildings, ships, aircraft, or machines before they are built. This job is now done mainly by computer-aided design. **2. MAN WHO DRAWS WELL** a

LANGUAGE HERITAGE ***Dravidian*** Much of English is made up of words from other languages, and Dravidian, a group of languages spoken in southern India and northeastern Sri Lanka, including Tamil, Telugu, Kannada, and Malayalam, is a small but significant contributor in this respect. From southern South Asia English has received especially names for foods, plants and materials from plants, and terms of music and dance.

From the cuisine of the region have come ***curry*** (late 16th century, from Tamil *kari* 'sauce'), ***dosa*** (a pancake, from Tamil), ***mango*** (late 16th, via Portuguese and Malay from Tamil), ***mulligatawny*** (late 18th, from Tamil *miḷaku-taṇṇi* 'pepper-water'), ***poppadom*** (early 19th, from Tamil), and ***sambhar*** (a spiced vegetarian stew, mid-20th, via Tamil from Sanskrit *sambhāra* 'collection'). Malayalam has given people the ***cachou*** to sweeten the breath (late 16th century, via French) and the ***jak*** fruit (late 16th, via Portuguese).

Names of plants and their products include ***areca*** (late 16th century, via Portuguese from Malayalam), ***betel*** (mid-16th, via Portuguese from Malayalam *verrila*, itself from Tamil), ***coir*** (coconut fibre, late 16th, from Malayalam), ***copra*** (dried coconut, late 16th, from Malayalam via Portuguese), ***patchouli***, source of an aromatic oil (mid-19th, from Tamil), ***poon*** (late 17th, via Sinhalese from Malayalam or Tamil), ***teak*** (late 17th, via Portuguese from Tamil or Malayalam *tēkku*), and ***vetiver*** (mid-19th, via French from Tamil *veṭṭivēr*, from *vēr* 'root'). Migrating animals include the ***bandicoot*** (late 18th, from Telugu *pandikokku*, literally 'pig-rat') and the ***dhole*** (a wild dog, early 19th, probably from Kannada *tōḷa* 'wolf').

In the arts have come ***Kathakali***, a form of drama combining dance and mime (from a Malayalam compound formed from Sanskrit *kathā* 'story' + Malayalam *kaḷi* 'play'), ***mridanga***, a kind of drum (from Tamil), and perhaps the ***tom-tom*** (from an imitative form in either Telugu or Hindi). A migrant with an unexpected musical connection is ***pariah***: hereditary drummers in southern India belonged to a low caste, and the word comes from Tamil *paraiyan* 'drummer'.

Some of the less obvious Dravidian migrants fall into no particular category: ***catamaran*** (early 17th century, from Tamil *kaṭṭumaram* 'tied wood'), ***cheroot*** (late 17th, via French from Tamil), ***cot*** (mid-17th, from Hindi *khāṭ* 'framework strung with rope and used as a bed', via Sanskrit from Tamil *kaṭṭu* 'tie'), and ***godown*** ('warehouse', late 16th), which looks like a word formed from English elements but in fact came via Portuguese *gudao* from Tamil *kitanku*, Kannada *gadangu* 'store'.

man who is skilled at drawing ○ *He's an excellent draughtsman.* **3.** BOARD GAMES **PIECE USED IN DRAUGHTS** a piece used in the game of draughts —**draughtsmanship** *n*

draughtsperson /dra̋afts purss'n/ (*plural* **-persons** or **-people** /-pe̋ep'l/) *n* **1.** a maker of detailed plans or drawings for buildings, ships, aircraft, or machines before they are built. This job is now done mainly by computer-aided design. **2.** somebody who is skilled at drawing

draughtswoman /dra̋afts wŏŏmən/ (*plural* **-women** /-wimmin/) *n* **1.** a woman who makes detailed plans or drawings for buildings, ships, aircraft, or machines before they are built. This job is now done mainly by computer-aided design. **2.** a woman who is skilled at drawing

draughty /dra̋afti/ (**-tier, -tiest**) *adj* chilly and uncomfortable because of flowing currents of cold air —**draughtily** *adv* —**draughtiness** *n*

Drava /dra̋avə/ tributary of the River Danube in south-central Europe. It rises in the Italian Alps, flows through Austria and Slovenia, and then forms part of Croatia's frontier with Hungary. Length: 719 km/447 mi.

Dravidian /drə víddi ən/ *n* a family of languages spoken in southern India and northeastern Sri Lanka. Native speakers: 200 million. [Mid-19C. < Sanskrit *Drāvida* 'relating to the southern group (roughly the Tamils)'] —**Dravidian** *adj*

draw /draw/ *v* (**draws, drawing, drew** /droo/, **drawn** /drawn/) **1.** *vti* **MAKE PICTURE** to make a line, picture, or plan on a surface using a pencil, pen, or crayon rather than paints ○ *She drew a picture of a flower.* **2.** *vt* **DESCRIBE SOMETHING** to depict or describe something in words ○ *He drew a vivid picture of life in 18th-century London.* **3.** *vi* **MOVE** to move in a particular direction, often alongside, towards, or away from something else, and with a smooth steady motion ○ *Another car drew alongside ours.* **4.** *vi* **APPROACH** to approach through time, or move towards a point or stage in something, especially its end ○ *The meeting was drawing to a close.* **5.** *vt* **PULL SOMEBODY OR SOMETHING** to pull something, or lead or pull somebody, in a particular direction, especially towards or away from something ○ *She drew him towards the door.* **6.** *vt* TRANSP **PULL VEHICLE** to pull a vehicle along ○ *a carriage drawn by six horses* **7.** *vt* **OPEN OR CLOSE CURTAIN** to pull a curtain or blind across a window so that it covers or uncovers it **8.** *vt* **PULL ON STRING** to pull on a string, rope, or cord, usually in order to tighten it around something **9.** *vt* ARCHERY **PULL BACK STRING OF BOW** to pull back the string of a bow prior to shooting an arrow **10.** *vt* **TAKE SOMETHING OUT** to take or pull an object out of something in which it has been enclosed or embedded ○ *drew the letter out of the envelope* **11.** *vti* **PULL WEAPON FROM SHEATH** to pull a weapon from a holster or sheath in order to use it **12.** *vt* **REMOVE LIQUID** to remove liquid from a large container such as a barrel by means of a tap **13.** *vt* MED **DRAIN WOUND** to drain a liquid such as blood, pus, or water from a wound or incision **14.** *vt* **HAUL UP WATER** to haul up water from a well or other source using a bucket on a rope **15.** *vt* **ELICIT RESPONSE** to cause somebody or something to make a response or sound ○ *drew hoots of derision from the crowd* **16.** *vt* **OBTAIN SOMETHING FROM SOURCE** to obtain a physical or a moral resource from a place or thing ○ *drew courage from her example* **17.** *vt* **OBTAIN INFORMATION FROM SOMEBODY** to obtain information, a secret, or an opinion from somebody by questioning or persuasion (*often passive*) ○ *She refused to be drawn on the subject.* **18.** *vt* **ATTRACT ATTENTION OR INTEREST** to cause somebody's attention, eye, or interest to be directed towards somebody or something ○ *draw admiring glances* **19.** *vt* **ATTRACT PEOPLE** to attract a person or group to come to see something or somebody ○ *The performance always drew crowds.* **20.** *vt* **SUCK SOMETHING IN** to suck something in, especially air into the lungs ○ *I drew a long breath.* **21.** *vi* **SMOKE CIGARETTE OR PIPE** to suck smoke in from a cigarette or pipe **22.** *vi* **ALLOW AIR THROUGH** to allow a current of air to flow through, removing smoke or gases **23.** *vt* **WITHDRAW MONEY** to take money out of a bank, savings account, or similar source ○ *You can draw up to £200 a day with this card.* **24.** *vt* FIN **RECEIVE MONEY** to receive money regularly from a source ○ *draws a regular salary* **25.** *vt* **WRITE CHEQUE** to write a cheque, bill of exchange, or promissory note **26.** *vt* LAW **WRITE OUT LEGAL DOCUMENT** to compose or write out a legal document in the proper form **27.** *vt* **ARRIVE AT CONCLUSION** to arrive at a conclusion or inference by examining the evidence for something ○ *You'll have to draw your own conclusions.* **28.** *vt* **FORMULATE SOMETHING** to formulate or state a distinction, comparison, or parallel between two or more things ○ *drew a distinction between the causes of the two events* **29.** *vt* **CHOOSE SOMETHING AT RANDOM** to choose or be given something at random, usually in order to ensure that all participants are treated fairly ○ *They drew lots to see who would have to go.* **30.** *vt* CARDS **TAKE PLAYING CARD** in card games, to take a card from a stack, the pack, or the dealer **31.** *vt* CARDS **MAKE PLAYERS PLAY PARTICULAR SUIT** in card games, to make the other players play the cards they have in a specific suit by repeatedly leading that suit ○ *drew trumps and played twelve tricks* **32.** *vti* **FINISH EQUAL** to finish a game with the scores for the opposing sides level or with neither side having won ○ *drew 1–1 in the semifinal* **33.** *vt* NAUT **NEED PARTICULAR DEPTH OF WATER** to need a particular depth of water in which to float **34.** *vti* COOK **STEEP IN BOILING WATER** to steep tea leaves in water to extract the flavour, or steep in this way ○ *Let the tea draw for five minutes.* **35.** *vt* MANUF **MAKE WIRE** to make wire by pulling a length of metal through a conical hole **36.** *vt* **REMOVE INNARDS FROM CARCASS** to remove the innards from a carcass before cooking it **37.** *vt* **DISEMBOWEL SOMEBODY** to disembowel a hanged person **38.** *vt* CUE GAMES **GIVE BACKSPIN TO BALL** in cue games, especially billiards, to give a backward spin to a ball when making a stroke **39.** *vt* GOLF **MAKE BALL CURVE** in golf, to hit a ball so that it curves in flight following the direction of the golfer's swing instead of travelling straight. The ball is drawn to the left by a right-handed player and to the right by a left-handed player. **40.** *vt* BOWLING **SEND BOWL IN CURVE** in bowling, to make the bowl travel along a curved path to the point aimed at ■ *n* **1. ACT OF DRAWING OR PULLING** the act of pulling or sucking on something or otherwise drawing something **2.** GAMBLING **LOTTERY** a lottery, raffle, or other competition where the winner is decided by selecting a ticket at random **3.** GAMBLING **CHOOSING LOTTERY WINNER** the choosing of a winner in a lottery, raffle, or other competition by selecting a ticket at random ○ *The draw will be held next Wednesday.* **4. SELECTION OF OPPONENTS** the act of selecting at random which contestants are to play each other in a sporting contest, or the resulting list of matches to be played ○ *the draw for the third round of the competition* **5.** CARDS, GAMBLING **SOMETHING CHOSEN AT RANDOM** something chosen at random, e.g. a ticket in a lottery or a playing card or cards taken from a stack or the dealer **6. ATTRACTION** something or somebody that interests a lot of people and attracts them as spectators, visitors, or customers ○ *The rock band will be a huge draw for the local fair.* **7. CONTEST THAT NEITHER SIDE WINS** a contest that ends with both sides having the same score or with neither side having won **8. DRAWING OF GUN** the action of pulling a gun from its holster in order to fire it, especially in a gunfight **9.** CARDS **SECOND OR FURTHER DEAL** in draw poker, the deal made to improve the players' hands after they have discarded [Old English *dragan* < Germanic, 'carry'] —**drawable** *adj*

SYNONYMS See ***pull.***

draw back *vi* **1.** pull back suddenly, e.g. in fear **2.** to decide not to continue with some contemplated, planned, or agreed action ○ *They drew back from the deal at the last moment.*

draw in *v* **1.** *vi* **BEGIN EARLIER** to begin earlier, so that darkness comes sooner (*refers to nights or evenings in autumn*) **2.** *vi* **BECOME SHORTER** to become shorter, so that darkness comes sooner (*refers to days in autumn*) **3.** *vt* **INVOLVE SOMEBODY** to get somebody involved in something unwillingly (*often passive*) ○ *I got drawn in before I realized what the argument was really about.* **4.** *vt* **SUCK SOMETHING IN** to breathe or suck something in

draw off *vt* to remove a small amount of liquid from a larger amount by means of a tube or pipe

draw on *v* **1.** *vt* **USE SOMETHING** to make use of a resource for personal benefit ○ *The novel draws on her experiences in Alaska.* **2.** *vi* **ENTER LATER STAGE** to enter a later stage, or move towards an end ○ *as the day drew on* **3.** *vt* **TAKE IN SMOKE** to inhale the smoke from a cigarette or pipe ○ *He drew on his pipe.* **4.** *vt* **WITHDRAW MONEY FROM ACCOUNT** to take money out of a bank or savings account

draw out *v* **1.** *vt* **PROLONG SOMETHING** to make something continue longer than is usual, necessary, or desirable ○ *I drew the conversation out as long as I could.* **2.** *vi* **GROW LONGER** to have more hours of daylight (*refers to days*) **3.** *vt* **GET SOMEBODY TO TALK** to encourage a shy, hostile, or reserved person to talk at length or in detail, or to become more forthcoming in a social or legal situation ○ *drew the witness out during cross-examination* **4.** *vi* **MOVE AWAY FROM SOMETHING** to move away from a close or inner position ○ *The car drew out unexpectedly and hit the passing cyclist.*

draw up *v* **1.** *vt* **WRITE SOMETHING OUT** to prepare or write out a plan, list, or other document ○ *drawing up the terms of the contract* **2.** *vti* **COME TO STOP** to arrive at a point or place in a vehicle or on a horse and stop, or bring a vehicle or horse to a halt ○ *saw the bus draw up* **3.** *vt* **BRING SOMETHING NEARER** to place a chair or seat near something or somebody and sit down on it **4.** *vr* **STRAIGHTEN UP** to straighten the body in order to reach full height and look as imposing or dignified as possible ○ *drew herself up proudly before speaking*

drawback /dráw bak/ *n* **1.** something that causes problems or is a disadvantage or hindrance ○ *The only drawback is the size of the machine.* **2.** a refund of tax or import duty on goods that are later exported

drawbar /dráw baar/ *n* a strong metal bar fitted across the back of a tractor, locomotive, or other vehicle,

with a coupling on it to which machinery or a trailer can be hitched

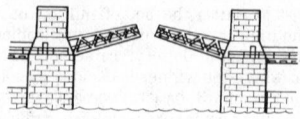

drawbridge

drawbridge /dráw brij/ *n* a bridge that is hinged at one end or in the middle and can be lifted up to cut off access to a place or allow something to pass beneath it

drawdown /dráw down/ *n* a lowering of the level of the water in a reservoir

drawee /draw ée/ *n* the person or organization from whose account money is taken when a cheque or other order for payment is drawn

drawer /drawr/ *n* **1. STORAGE COMPARTMENT IN FURNITURE** a storage compartment in a piece of furniture such as a desk, chest, or table that slides in and out and is usually shaped like a shallow rectangular box **2. SOMEBODY WHO WRITES CHEQUE** somebody who draws a cheque or money order **3. SOMEBODY OR SOMETHING THAT DRAWS** somebody or something that draws, especially somebody who draws pictures or plans ■ **drawers** *npl* **UNDERPANTS** large old-fashioned underpants with short legs, worn by men or women

drawgate /dráw gayt/ *n* a barrier that can be raised or lowered to control the flow of water in a sluice

draw gear *n* the couplings and other equipment used to join railway carriages and trucks together

draw hoe *n* a tool for working soil that has a flat blade set at right angles to the handle, allowing soil or other material to be drawn towards the user

drawing /dráw ing/ *n* **1.** a picture of something made with a pencil, pen, or crayon, usually consisting of lines, often with shading, but generally without colour **2.** the art, activity, or practice of making pictures using a pencil, crayon, or pen ○ *I never was very good at drawing.*

drawing board *n* a large flat board used for drawing and design work, usually attached to a frame with legs and adjustable to different heights and angles ◇ **back to the drawing board** back to the beginning or the planning stage of a failed operation or project, ready to start all over again (*informal*) ○ *Since all else has failed, we're now back to the drawing board.*

drawing pin *n* a short pin with a wide round top used for pinning paper or cardboard to a noticeboard, wall, or other surface. N Am term **thumbtack**

drawing room *n* a large formal room in a house, in which guests are entertained [Mid-17C. Shortening of *withdrawing room*]

drawknife /dráw nīf/ (*plural* **-knives** /-nīvz/) *n* a tool consisting of a narrow rectangular blade with a handle at either end fixed at right angles to it. Use: shaving the surface of wood.

drawl /drawl/ *vti* (**drawls, drawling, drawled**) to draw out the vowel sounds and pronounce words with a slow inflection when speaking ■ *n* a way of speaking in which the speaker draws out the vowel sounds and pronounces words slowly [Late 16C. Probably < Middle Dutch *dralen* 'linger, delay' < *dragan* 'to draw'] —**drawler** *n* —**drawlingly** *adv* —**drawly** *adj*

drawn /drawn/ past tense of **draw** ■ *adj* appearing tired and careworn, usually as a result of anxiety, grief, or illness ○ *He looked pale and drawn.*

drawn butter *n* melted butter that has had the solids removed, served as a sauce, sometimes with herbs and seasoning

drawn-out *adj* continuing longer than is intended or desired

drawn-thread work, **drawn work** *n* embroidery in which some threads are pulled from the fabric and stitches are worked on the remaining threads to produce decorated open areas

drawplate /dráw playt/ *n* a plate pierced by conical holes through which metal is drawn in wire-making

draw poker *n* a form of poker in which each player is dealt five cards face down and after the first round of betting can draw replacements for any discards

drawshave /dráw shayv/ *n* WOODWORK same as **drawknife**

draw shot *n* in cue games, a shot in which the cue ball is hit below centre so that the backspin makes it bounce back when it hits another ball

drawstring /dráw string/ *n* a cord threaded through a hem, piping, or eyelets around the opening in a bag or a garment so that it can be tightened or the opening can be closed

drawtube /dráw tyoob/ *n* a tube that slides inside another tube, e.g. one of the extending tubes in a telescope

dray /dray/ *n* a large low horse-drawn cart with no fixed sides, designed for heavy loads, or a similar motorized vehicle, used especially by breweries [14C. < Old English *dragan* 'to draw']

drayhorse /dráy hawrss/ *n* a large horse used for pulling a dray

Drayton /dráyt'n/, **Michael** (1563–1631) English poet. His *England's Heroical Epistles* (1597) and *Polyolbion* (1612) sang the praises of England. His *Harmonie of the Church* (1591) offended the Archbishop of Canterbury, and was publicly burnt.

'Ill news hath wings, and with the wind doth go, / Comfort's a cripple and comes ever slow.'
[Michael Drayton, *The Barons' Wars*; 1603]

dread /dred/ *vti* (**dreads, dreading, dreaded**) **1. FEEL EXTREMELY FRIGHTENED** to feel extremely frightened or worried about something that may happen in the future **2. BE RELUCTANT** to be reluctant or frightened to do something because it is unpleasant, upsetting, or annoying ■ *n* **1. TERROR** a feeling of great fear or terror, especially at the thought of experiencing or encountering something unpleasant **2. SOURCE OF DREAD** something that is dreaded **3.** also **dred** RASTAFARIAN somebody who is considered a genuine Rastafarian (*slang; used in Black English*) ■ *adj* **1. FEARED** causing fear and extreme anxiety (*literary*) ○ *The dread day arrived.* **2. AWE-INSPIRING** inspiring fear and respect or awe in equal measure (*literary*) **3.** also **dred** GOOD good or excellent (*slang; used in Black English*) ■ *interj* also **dred** EXPRESSES APPROVAL used to express approval (*slang; used in Black English*) [12C. Shortened < Old English *adrædan, ondrædan* 'counsel against' < *rædan* (see REDE)]

dread disease *n* a serious and potentially fatal disease (*hyphenated when used before a noun*) ○ *dread-disease insurance*

dreaded /dréddid/ *adj* inspiring great fear (*sometimes used humorously*)

dreadful /dréddf'l/ *adj* **1. EXTREMELY BAD** extremely unpleasant, harmful, or serious in its effects ○ *a dreadful mistake* **2. EXTREME** extreme in character or degree ○ *a dreadful shame* **3. AWE-INSPIRING** inspiring awe (*literary*) **4.** also **dreadfull** WONDERFUL very good or pleasing (*slang; used in Black English*) —**dreadfulness** *n*

dreadfully /dréddf'li/ *adv* **1.** to a very great extent **2.** in a very unsatisfactory or unpleasant way ○ *He behaved dreadfully.*

dreadlocks: Bob Marley

dreadlocks /dréd loks/, **dredlocks** *npl* long strands of hair that have been twisted closely from the scalp down to the tips in a style made popular by Rastafarians [Mid-20C. Because of a supposed fear of the power of faithful Rastafarians] —**dreadlocked** *adj*

dreadnought /dréd nawt/, **dreadnaught** *n* a heavily armed battleship whose main guns are all of the same calibre [Early 20C. After the British battleship *Dreadnought*]

dreads /dredz/, **dreds** *npl* HAIR same as **dreadlocks** [Late 20C. Contraction]

dream /dreem/ *n* **1. SEQUENCE OF MENTAL IMAGES DURING SLEEP** a sequence of images that appear involuntarily to the mind of somebody who is sleeping, often a mixture of real and imaginary characters, places, and events **2. DAYDREAM** a series of images, usually pleasant ones, that pass through the mind of somebody who is awake **3. SOMETHING HOPED FOR** something that somebody hopes, longs, or is ambitious for, usually something difficult to attain or far removed from present circumstances **4. IDLE HOPE** an idea or hope that is impractical or unlikely ever to be realized **5. VAGUE STATE** a state of inattention owing to preoccupation with thoughts or fantasies ○ *walks around in a dream* **6. SOMETHING BEAUTIFUL** somebody or something that seems particularly good-looking or wonderful ■ *v* (**dreams, dreaming, dreamt** or **dreamed**) **1.** *vti* HAVE DREAM WHILE SLEEPING to experience vivid mental images of something while sleeping **2.** *vi* DAYDREAM to let the mind dwell on pleasant scenes and images while awake, often resulting in inattention **3.** *vi* WISH to want something very much and imagine having or doing it, though it may be unlikely ○ *dreamt of living abroad* **4.** *vi* CONSIDER to think of or consider doing something regarded as wrong or inappropriate ○ *How could you even dream of doing such a thing?* ■ *adj* **1. OCCURRING IN DREAM** occurring in or reminiscent of a dream ○ *a dream sequence* **2. IDEAL** perfect and wonderful in every way ○ *a dream holiday* [13C. Origin ?] —**dreamful** *adj* ◇ **in your dreams** used to indicate that somebody's hope or expectation is completely unrealistic (*informal*)
dream up *vt* to devise or invent something, especially a complicated, ingenious, or ridiculous plan

dreamboat /dreem bōt/ *n* somebody considered to be very good-looking (*informal*)

dreamcatcher /dreem kachər/ *n* a hoop-shaped hanging ornament of beads and feathers made by some Native North Americans, typically hung in the home, especially above a bed

dreamer /dreemər/ *n* **1.** somebody who is absorbed by fantasies or unrealistic plans **2.** somebody who dreams or is dreaming

Dreaming /dreem ing/ *n* in the mythology of Australian Aboriginals, the period during which Earth was formed, the landscape shaped, and living things created

dreamland /dreem land/ *n* **1.** an imaginary, very pleasant, or perfect sphere of existence that exists only in dreams **2.** a state of sleep or unconsciousness (*informal*)

dreamless /dreemləss/ *adj* deep, peaceful, and undisturbed by dreams ○ *a dreamless sleep* —**dreamlessly** *adv* —**dreamlessness** *n*

dreamlike /dreem līk/ *adj* resembling a dream or the images in a dream, especially in seeming unreal or strange

dreamscape /dreem skayp/ *n* a scene, setting, or picture that has the unreal or strange qualities usually associated with images in dreams

dreamt past participle, past tense of **dream**

dream team *n* the best possible combination of people to perform a task (*informal*)

dream ticket *n* a team of candidates standing for associated political offices who seem to have between them all the qualities needed for electoral success (*informal*)

Dreamtime /dreem tīm/ *n* MYTHOL same as **Dreaming**

dream world *n* a world that bears little resemblance to reality and exists only in the mind

dreamy /dreemi/ (**-ier, -iest**) *adj* **1. VAGUE** caused by dreaming or by thinking about something very pleasant and absorbing **2. GIVEN TO DAYDREAMING** having a tendency to spend time daydreaming or lost in

thought **3.** UNREAL strange, vague, or ethereal, like an image in a dream **4.** GORGEOUS extremely good-looking or desirable (*informal*) —**dreamily** *adv* —**dreaminess** *n*

drear /dreer/ *adj* dark, foreboding, and gloomy (*literary*) ○ *a cold, drear day* [Mid-16C. Back-formation < DREARY]

dreary /dréeri/ (**-rier, -riest**) *adj* gloomy, unexciting, and certain to have a wearying and depressing influence ○ *the dreary routine of prison life* [Old English *drēorig* 'dripping with blood' < Germanic] —**drearily** *adv* —**dreariness** *n*

dreck /drek/ *n US* worthless trashy stuff, especially low-quality merchandise [Early 20C Via Yiddish *drek* 'filth, dung' < Middle High German *drec*] —**drecky** *adj*

dred /dred/ *n, adj, interj* another spelling of **dread** *n* (sense 3), *adj* (sense 3), *interj* (*slang; used in Black English*)

dredge[1] /drej/ *n* **1.** MACHINE FOR DIGGING UNDERWATER a machine equipped with a continuous revolving chain of buckets, a scoop, or a suction device for digging out and removing material from under water **2.** SHIPPING same as **dredger**[1] (sense 1) **3.** FISHERIES SHELLFISH NET a net on a frame dragged along the bottom of the sea or a river to gather shellfish ■ *v* (**dredges, dredging, dredged**) **1.** *vt* DIG SOMETHING UP WITH DREDGE to remove or recover material from under water by means of a dredge **2.** *vti* SHIPPING CLEAR CHANNEL to clear, deepen, or widen a waterway, especially one intended for shipping, using a dredge **3.** *vti* USE DREDGE IN SEARCHING SOMETHING to search something, or search for something, using a dredge or a similar device [Early 16C. Origin ?]

dredge up *vt* to bring something to light from an obscure source, e.g. to recall something bad that happened long ago or unearth some scandalous information

dredge[2] /drej/ (**dredges, dredging, dredged**) *vt* to sprinkle or cover food with a coating of icing sugar, flour, or sugar [Late 16C. Via Old French *dragie* 'sugar-plum, sugar almond' < Latin *tragemata* < Greek *tragēmata* 'spices, sweets']

dredger[1] /dréjjər/ *n* **1.** a boat or barge with a dredge on it, used mainly for clearing or deepening waterways **2.** CONSTR same as **dredge**[1] *n* (sense 1) [Early 16C. < DREDGE[1]]

dredger[2] /dréjjər/ *n* a container with small holes in the top used for sprinkling icing sugar, flour, or sugar onto food [Mid-17C. < DREDGE[2]]

dredlocks *npl* another spelling of **dreadlocks**

dreds *npl* another spelling of **dreads**

dree /dree/ (**drees, dreeing, dreed**) *vt Scotland* to bear something unpleasant [Old English *drēogan* 'work, suffer' < Germanic]

D region *n* **1.** the lowest part of the ionosphere above the Earth's surface **2.** a short sequence of various amino acids in an immunoglobulin that contributes to antibody diversity

dregs /dregz/ *npl* **1.** GRITTY PARTICLES IN LIQUID small solid particles found in liquids such as coffee or wine that sink to the bottom of a container and are most in evidence when the container is nearly empty **2.** LEAST VALUABLE PART the least valuable or most unpleasant part of something, especially a group of people ○ *the dregs of society* **3.** LAST REMAINING PART the last remaining, and often least attractive part of something (*literary*) ○ *sat through the dregs of a long boring evening* [14C. Probably < Old Norse *dregg* 'sediment']

dreich /dreekh/ *adj Scotland* describes weather that is dull and depressing [Old English *gedrēog* 'patient, serious' < Germanic]

dreidel /dráyd'l/, **dreidl** *n* a toy that looks like a spinning top, used to play games during Hanukkah [Mid-20C. < Yiddish *dreydl* < Middle High German *dræhen* 'turn']

Dreiser /drīssər, drīzər/, **Theodore** (1871–1945) US novelist and journalist. He is known for his naturalist novels, including *An American Tragedy* (1925). Full name **Dreiser, Theodore Herman Albert**

> 'Art is the stored honey of the human soul, gathered on wings of misery and travail.' [Theodore Dreiser, *Life, Art and America*; 1917]

drench /drench/ *vt* (**drenches, drenching, drenched**) **1.** SOAK SOMEBODY OR SOMETHING to make somebody or something completely wet ○ *got absolutely drenched in the storm* **2.** COVER WITH SOMETHING to cover or surround somebody or something with a large amount of something ○ *drenched in sunlight* **3.** VET GIVE LIQUID MEDICINE TO ANIMAL to give an animal a large dose of medicine in liquid form by mouth ■ *n* VET DOSE OF ANIMAL MEDICINE a large dose of medicine given to an animal in liquid form by mouth [Old English *drencan* 'give to drink' < Germanic] —**drencher** *n* —**drenching** *adj, n*

Dresden /drézdən/ capital of the state of Saxony in east-central Germany. Almost completely destroyed during World War II, it has been largely rebuilt and restored. Population: 474,443 (1997).

Dresden china *n UK, ANZ, Can* fine and delicate porcelain as made in Meissen near Dresden in Germany since the early 18th century. US term **Meissen**[1]

dress /dress/ *v* (**dresses, dressing, dressed**) **1.** *vti* PUT CLOTHES ON to put clothes on somebody or yourself, or put on clothes **2.** *vi* WEAR PARTICULAR CLOTHING to wear clothes of a particular type or in a particular way ○ *She usually dresses in black.* **3.** *vi* PUT ON APPROPRIATE CLOTHES to put on clothes appropriate to a particular occasion, especially formal clothes ○ *We need to dress for the theatre.* **4.** *vt* DECORATE SOMETHING to make a place or object look festive by putting special decorations on it ○ *They dressed the big house for the holidays.* **5.** *vt* COMM ARRANGE GOODS IN WINDOW to arrange goods in a shop window as an attractive display ○ *windows that were dressed for spring* **6.** *vt* MED COVER WOUND to put a bandage or other protective covering on a wound **7.** *vt* COOK PUT SAUCE ON SALAD to put mayonnaise, vinaigrette, or a similar sauce on a salad **8.** *vt* COOK, FIELD SPORTS CLEAN FISH AND GAME to clean and prepare fish, poultry, or meat for cooking or selling **9.** *vt* ARRANGE HAIR to arrange hair, e.g. by combing, clipping, or oiling it **10.** *vti* MIL COME OR BRING INTO ALIGNMENT to come, or bring troops, into a correct alignment with one another for a parade formation **11.** *vt* AGRIC SPREAD FERTILIZER ON SOIL to spread manure or fertilizer over the surface of an area of land **12.** *vt* FINISH MATERIAL to apply a finishing process to a material such as stone or timber, usually in order to give it a smooth attractive surface ■ *n* **1.** WOMAN'S ONE-PIECE GARMENT a one-piece garment for women and girls combining a bodice, with or without sleeves, and a skirt, and covering most of the body **2.** PARTICULAR CLOTHES clothes of a particular type or style ○ *national dress* **3.** CLOTHES IN GENERAL clothes and clothing in general (*often used before nouns*) ○ *He has no interest in matters of dress.* ○ *a dress allowance* **4.** CLOTHES FOR PARTICULAR OCCASION the clothing required for a particular occasion ○ *casual dress* ○ *evening dress* **5.** *S Asia* SET OF CLOTHES an outfit or set of clothes for men or women **6.** OUTWARD APPEARANCE the outward appearance or covering of a thing, especially a living thing, or the way in which something is presented (*literary*) **7.** THEATRE same as **dress rehearsal** (sense 1) (*informal*) ■ *adj* **1.** FORMAL describes clothes that are only worn on formal occasions ○ *dress uniform* **2.** REQUIRING FORMAL ATTIRE describes an event to which formal clothes must be worn ○ *a dress banquet* [14C. Via Old French *dresser* 'arrange, prepare' < Vulgar Latin *directiare* < Latin *directus* 'straight' (see DIRECT)] ◇ **dressed to kill** wearing very glamorous clothes, especially in order to impress somebody (*informal*)

dress down *v* (*informal*) **1.** *vi* to dress in a deliberately understated or casual way for an occasion **2.** *vt* to scold somebody severely

dress up *v* **1.** *vi* DRESS FORMALLY to put on formal or especially elegant clothes, usually for a special occasion such as a party **2.** *vi* PUT ON COSTUMES to put on a special costume or different clothes from those normally worn in order to look like or pretend to be somebody else **3.** *vt* DISGUISE SOMETHING to disguise something unpleasant and try to make it look more pleasant

dressage /dréss aazh/ *n* **1.** the training of a horse to carry out a series of precise controlled movements in response to minimal signals from its rider **2.** a competitive event in which horse and rider are judged on the elegance, precision, and discipline of the horse's movements [Mid-20C. < French, 'training' < *dresser* (see DRESS)]

dress circle *n* a separate raised section of the auditorium of a theatre, concert hall, or opera house, usually the first seating gallery above ground level

dress coat *n* a coat, forming part of a man's full evening dress, that is usually black with a cutaway skirt and tails

dress code *n* a set of requirements as to how people should dress, e.g. when at school or attending a function

dress-down day *n* a day, usually a Friday or during the summer months, on which office workers wear casual clothing to work

dresser[1] /dréssər/ *n* **1.** a piece of furniture consisting of a set of shelves on top of a chest containing cupboards and drawers, often used for storing crockery and cutlery in traditional kitchens ○ *a Welsh dresser* **2.** *N Am* a chest of drawers used in a bedroom for storing clothes, sometimes with a mirror on top [Early 15C. < Old French *dresseur* < *dresser* (see DRESS)]

dresser[2] /dréssər/ *n* **1.** SOMEBODY WHO DRESSES IN PARTICULAR WAY somebody who wears clothes in a particular way **2.** ACTOR'S ASSISTANT somebody who helps an actor to put on or change a costume before and during a performance **3.** PERSONAL GROOMING ASSISTANT somebody whose job it is to ensure that somebody else's wardrobe is in order **4.** SURGEON'S ASSISTANT somebody who assists a surgeon during operations [14C. < DRESS]

dress form *n* an adjustable dummy, used by tailors

dressing /dréssing/ *n* **1.** SALAD SAUCE a sauce used on salads, usually with an oil and vinegar or mayonnaise base **2.** MED WOUND COVERING a bandage, plaster, or other sterile covering put on a wound to protect it from infection or further damage **3.** *N Am* STUFFING a stuffing for poultry or meat **4.** AGRIC FERTILIZER a natural or artificial fertilizer for spreading on the soil **5.** TEXTILES STIFFENING FOR FABRIC size used to stiffen fabrics

dressing-down *n* a scolding or severe reprimand, often in public (*informal*)

dressing gown *n* a coat made of soft light material that is worn over nightclothes or before or after a bath

dressing room *n* **1.** ACTORS' ROOM TO PUT ON COSTUMES a room in a theatre where actors can prepare for a performance by putting on their make-up and costumes **2.** ROOM TO CHANGE CLOTHES IN a small room in a house, hotel suite, or other place for people to change clothes **3.** *US* ROOM FOR TRYING ON CLOTHES a small room in a shop for trying on clothes before making a decision about buying them

dressing station *n* a first-aid station near a combat area

dressing table *n* a low table with drawers and a mirror on top, usually placed in a bedroom so that somebody can sit at it while applying make-up

dressmaker /dréss maykər/ *n* somebody who makes women's clothes, especially professionally —**dressmaking** *n*

dress parade *n* a military parade in which formal dress uniform is worn

dress rehearsal *n* **1.** the final rehearsal of something such as a play, opera, or ballet in full costume and with lights, music, and effects, before it is given its first public performance **2.** a full-scale practice before any important event

dress sense *n* the ability to choose clothes well and coordinate colours and styles effectively

dress shield *n* a small fabric pad worn around the armpits of a piece of clothing to prevent sweat from showing or staining it

dress shirt *n* a man's shirt worn with formal evening wear, usually white and with either a stiff collar or a ruffle down the front

dress suit *n* a man's suit worn as part of formal evening wear, especially with a tail coat

dress uniform *n* a ceremonial uniform worn by members of the armed forces for formal occasions

dressy /dréssi/ (**-ier, -iest**) *adj* **1.** ELEGANT stylish and elegant **2.** WITH GUESTS DRESSED FORMALLY describes a social event at which stylish and elegant clothes are worn ○ *a very dressy buffet luncheon* **3.** OVERDRESSED

dressed in an inappropriately elaborate or showy way —**dressily** *adv* —**dressiness** *n*

drew past tense of **draw**

Drewe /droo/, **Robert Duncan** (*b.* 1943) Australian writer. He wrote the novel *The Savage Crows* (1976).

drey /dray/ *n* a squirrel's nest [Early 17C. Origin ?]

Dreyer /drāy ər/, **Carl Theodor** (1889–1968) Danish film director and screenwriter. His silent films include *The Passion of Joan of Arc* (1928).

Dreyfus /dráyfəss/, **Alfred** (1859–1935) French soldier. He was a Jewish army officer whose imprisonment for treason (1894–95) divided French public opinion. He was officially declared innocent in 1906.

drib /drib/ *n* a very small amount, usually a tiny drop of liquid or a fragment of material ○ *a drib of paint* [Early 18C. Origin ?] ◇ **in dribs and drabs** in very small amounts or stages, and usually in a rather haphazard way ○ *People were beginning to arrive in dribs and drabs.*

dribble /dríbb'l/ *v* (**-bles, -bling, -bled**) **1.** *vi* **PRODUCE SALIVA** to let saliva spill out of the mouth **2.** *vti* **FLOW IN DROPS** to flow in drops or a small stream, or allow a liquid to flow or spill out in this way **3.** *vti* **MOVE BALL** to move a ball along using small repeated movements of the foot, the hand, or a stick **4.** *vti* BASKETBALL **BOUNCE BALL ON COURT** in basketball, to propel the ball in any direction on the court by bouncing it with the hands ■ *n* **1. TINY AMOUNT OF LIQUID** a small amount of liquid falling in drops or a thin stream **2. MOVEMENT WHILE DRIBBLING BALL** a movement or run made while dribbling a ball, especially in football or basketball [Mid-16C. < *drib*, alteration of DRIP] —**dribbler** *n* —**dribbly** *adj*

driblet /dríbblət/, **dribblet** *n* a tiny amount of a liquid [Late 16C. < *drib*, alteration of DRIP]

drier[1] /drī ə/ comparative of **dry**

drier[2] *n* another spelling of **dryer**[2]

driest superlative of **dry**

drift /drift/ *v* (**drifts, drifting, drifted**) **1.** *vi* **BE CARRIED ALONG** to be carried along by the flow of water or air **2.** *vi* **MOVE AIMLESSLY** to move in a slow, smooth, gentle, and unforced way, usually without any direction or purpose ○ *The crowd gradually drifted away.* **3.** *vi* **WANDER AIMLESSLY** to go from one place to another, never staying anywhere for very long and seeming to have little purpose **4.** *vi* NAVIG **WANDER FROM SET COURSE OR POSITION** to deviate from a set course or move gradually away from a fixed position **5.** *vi* **MOVE FROM ONE STATE TO ANOTHER** to move gradually from one state or situation to another in an unintentional, casual, or aimless way ○ *drifted into debt* **6.** *vi* **CHANGE GRADUALLY** to change or develop gradually, or move slowly from one point or position to another ○ *Prices have drifted downwards in recent weeks.* **7.** *vti* **FORM HEAPS** to build up and form heaps as a result of the action of the wind or water currents, or cause something such as snow, sand, or leaves to do this ■ *n* **1. PILED-UP DEPOSITS** a heap, pile, or bank of something such as snow, sand, or leaves created by the action of the wind or water currents **2. DRIFTING MOVEMENT** a slow gentle movement in which something is carried along on a current of air or water **3. MATERIAL CARRIED ALONG** an amount of something carried along on a current of air or water ○ *drifts of smoke coming from the chimneys* **4. MOVEMENT OF PEOPLE** a gradual movement over a period of time of groups of people or animals towards or away from a place ○ *the drift of young people away from rural areas* **5. GRADUAL CHANGE** a broad and gradual change or development, e.g. in people's opinions or behaviour ○ *a drift back to larger cars* ○ *a downward drift in prices* **6. GENERAL MEANING** the general meaning of an argument, opinion, or statement ○ *She used a lot of technical jargon but I managed to get the drift of her argument.* **7. INACTIVITY** a state of inactivity or indecision in which a person or group is carried along by events **8.** NAVIG **DEVIATION** the distance or extent to which a ship or aircraft deviates from its set course because of the action of wind or water currents **9.** GEOL **DEPOSIT OF GRAVEL** a loose deposit of sand, gravel, or rock left by a glacier or ice sheet **10.** GEOG **CURRENT** the motion of a river or broad ocean current **11.** MIN EXTRACT **HORIZONTAL MINESHAFT** a horizontal or almost horizontal mineshaft that follows a vein of ore **12.** MIN EXTRACT **CONNECTING PASSAGE IN MINE** a small passage in a mine connecting two main shafts or tunnels **13.** ELEC ENG **UNCONTROLLED CHANGE IN SETTING** a slow uncontrolled change in a previously adjusted setting, e.g. in the frequency to which an electronic device has been set **14.** MECH ENG **TAPERING STEEL TOOL** a tapering steel tool used to enlarge or align holes in pieces of metal before they are bolted or riveted **15. CONTROLLED SKID** a controlled slide used by racing drivers as a method of cornering at high speed **16.** *S Africa* **SHALLOWS OR FORD** a shallow part of a river, or a ford across it [14C. < Old Norse *drift* 'snowdrift' < Germanic] —**drifty** *adj*

driftage /dríftij/ *n* **1.** material that has drifted along on and been deposited by air or water currents **2.** the distance by which a ship or aircraft has deviated from its set course owing to winds or currents

drifter /dríftər/ *n* **1.** somebody who does not stay in the same place or job for long, but is always moving on, apparently without aim, from place to place **2.** a fishing vessel that fishes with a drift net

drift ice *n* large areas of ice floating in the open sea

drift net *n* a large fishing net supported by floats that is allowed to drift along with the current or is attached to a vessel

driftwood /dríft wŏŏd/ *n* broken pieces of wood that are found washed up on a beach or riverbank or floating in the sea or a river

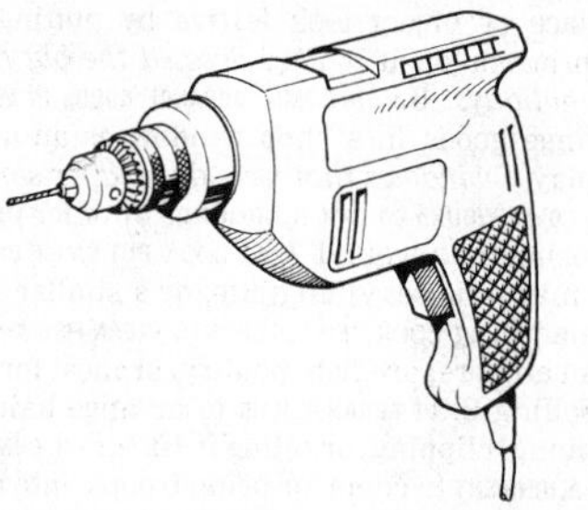

drill (sense 2)

drill[1] /dril/ *n* **1. PART OF TOOL THAT BORES HOLES** a long pointed piece of metal that is held in a machine and rotated at high speed to bore holes in hard substances such as wood, metal, masonry, or rock **2. BORING TOOL WITH DRILL** a tool or machine that holds, drives, and bores holes with a drill **3.** MIL **TRAINING BY REPETITION** a type of military training, particularly in marching manoeuvres and weapons handling, that involves the constant repetition of a set pattern of movements or tasks **4.** EDUC **REPEATED EXERCISE** a sequence of tasks, exercises, or words repeated over and over until they can be performed faultlessly, as used in teaching military skills, languages, or basic arithmetic **5. SAFETY ROUTINE** a sequence of actions practised repeatedly so that people know what to do in an emergency to ensure their safety **6. ROUTINE** a set procedure or routine for doing something (*informal*) **7.** MARINE BIOL **PREDATORY MOLLUSC** a invertebrate sea animal that preys on oysters by boring into their shells. Latin name: *Urosalpinx cinerea.* ■ *v* (**drills, drilling, drilled**) **1.** *vti* **MAKE HOLE WITH DRILL** to bore a hole in something with a drill **2.** *vti* MIL **PRACTISE MARCHING** to practise marching manoeuvres repeatedly on a parade ground as a form of military training and discipline, or make troops do this **3.** *vt* EDUC **TEACH SOMEBODY BY ROTE** to make somebody repeat a sequence of exercises or procedures over and over again in order to learn it **4.** *vt* **SHOOT SOMEBODY OR SOMETHING** to shoot somebody with bullets, or shoot bullets into something (*informal*) **5.** *vt* **HIT BALL HARD** to hit a ball or shot with great force in a straight line towards somebody or something (*informal*) [Early 16C. < Middle Dutch *drillen* 'make a hole, whirl'] —**drillable** *adj* —**driller** *n*

SYNONYMS See *teach.*

drill down *vi* to access data or information organized in hierarchical form by starting from general information and moving through increasingly detailed data

drill[2] /dril/ AGRIC *n* **1. FURROW FOR SEEDS** a shallow furrow in which seeds are sown **2. SEED-PLANTING MACHINE** a machine for planting seeds in furrows **3. PLANTED ROW OF SEEDS** a row of seeds planted along a small furrow ■ *vt* (**drills, drilling, drilled**) **PLANT SEEDS WITH DRILL** to plant seeds with a drill [Early 18C. Origin ?]

drill[3] /dril/ *n* a tough cotton twill. Use: working clothes, uniforms. [Mid-18C. < German *Drillich* < Latin *trilix* 'with three threads' < *licium* 'thread']

drill[4] /dril/ *n* a baboon with a black face and brown fur, similar to a mandrill, though smaller in size. Native to: West Africa. Latin name: *Papio leucophaeus.* [Mid-17C. < W African name]

drilldown /dríl down/ *n* an act of accessing data or information organized in hierarchical form, starting from general information and moving through increasingly detailed data

drilling platform *n* a structure used in offshore oil drilling that supports drilling equipment and is either fixed to the seabed or floats independently

drilling rig /drílling-/ *n* INDUST same as **rig**[1] *n* (sense 2)

drill instructor *n N Am* MIL same as **drillmaster** (sense 1)

drillmaster /dríll maastər/ *n* **1.** a noncommissioned officer who trains soldiers in drill. N Am term **drill instructor 2.** somebody who trains people in a very strict and militaristic way

drill pipe *n* INDUST same as **drill string**

drill press *n* a machine consisting of a powered drill on a vertical stand that is brought down onto the work automatically or by a hand lever

drill sergeant *n* MIL same as **drillmaster** (sense 1)

drillstock /dríll stok/ *n* the part of a drilling tool or machine that holds the shank of the drill

drill string *n* a long metal pipe, progressively built up from lengths of steel tubing, that is attached above the drill when drilling for oil or gas and eventually forms the bore of the well

drily /drīli/, **dryly** *adv* with subtle irony or humour

drink /dringk/ *vti* (**drinks, drinking, drank** /drangk/, **drunk** /drungk/) **1. SWALLOW LIQUID** to take in liquid through the mouth **2. DRINK ALCOHOL** to drink an alcoholic beverage, especially habitually ○ *Don't drink and drive.* ■ *n* **1. DRINKABLE LIQUID** liquid that can be drunk, usually in a container ○ *There isn't much food or drink in the house.* **2. AMOUNT OF LIQUID** an amount of liquid that somebody drinks ○ *Could I have a drink of water?* **3. ALCOHOLIC BEVERAGE** alcoholic drink, especially an individual serving in a glass, bottle, or can **4. EXCESSIVE CONSUMPTION OF ALCOHOL** excessive consumption of alcohol **5. BODY OF WATER** the sea or a large body of water, e.g. a lake or swimming pool (*informal*) ○ *in the drink* ■ **drinks** *npl* **INFORMAL PARTY WITH DRINKS** an informal party at which alcoholic or other drinks are served, but no meal [Old English *drincan* < Germanic]

drink in *vt* **1.** to absorb as much liquid as is available ○ *The plants drank in the welcome rain.* **2.** to absorb eagerly every aspect of something with the mind and senses ○ *She stood silently on the beach, drinking in the beauty.*

drink to *vti* to wish somebody or something happiness, luck, success, or good health by raising a glass and then drinking from it ○ *Let's drink to the success of the venture.* ○ *We drank a toast to absent friends.*

drink up *vt* **1.** to drink all of something **2.** to absorb a liquid completely ○ *The dry earth drank up the rain.*

drinkable /dríngkəb'l/ *adj* **1.** safe for humans or animals to drink **2.** pleasant or enjoyable to drink ○ *a very drinkable local fruit juice*

drink-driving *n* the offence of driving a vehicle while having a higher blood-alcohol content than the law allows. N Am term **drunk-driving** —**drink-driver** *n*

drinker /dríngkər/ *n* **1.** somebody who drinks alcoholic beverages, especially to excess **2.** somebody who drinks a particular type of beverage (*used in combination*) ○ *I'm not a coffee drinker.*

drinking fountain *n* a device attached to a wall that produces a jet of water that people can drink

drinking song *n* a song, often rowdy or suggestive, sung by people drinking alcohol together

drinking-up time *n* a period allowed in a public house after official closing time, when drinks already bought may be finished

a at; aa father; aw all; ay day; air hair; ə about, item, edible, common, circus; e egg; ee eel; hw when; i it, happy; ī ice; 'l apple; 'm rhythm; 'n fashion; o odd; ō open; ŏŏ good; oo pool; ow owl; oy oil; th thin; th this; u up; ur urge;

drinking water *n* water intended for people to drink, especially when free of harmful contents such as industrial waste, chemicals, or animal waste

drink problem *n* an addiction to alcoholic beverages that requires outside assistance to help control it

drinks cabinet *n* an upright piece of furniture with shelves and compartments for storing alcoholic beverages. N Am term **liquor cabinet**

drinks party (*plural* **drinks parties**) *n* an informal party at which alcoholic or other drinks are served, but no meal

Drinkwater /dríngk wawtər/, **John** (1882–1937) British playwright, poet, and actor. He was co-founder of Birmingham Repertory Theatre (1907), where he acted in his own verse dramas, including *Abraham Lincoln* (1918).

drip /drip/ *v* (**drips, dripping, dripped**) **1.** *vti* FALL OR LET FALL IN DROPS to fall as drops of liquid, or let liquid fall as drops ○ *The tap is dripping.* **2.** *vt* LET SOMETHING OUT COPIOUSLY to let out something, particularly an emotion, in great quantity ○ *His voice positively dripped malice.* ■ *n* **1.** SMALL AMOUNT OF LIQUID a drop of liquid or moisture ○ *a bucket to catch the drips* **2.** DRIPPING OF LIQUID an instance or the process of a liquid falling in drops **3.** SOUND OF FALLING DROPS the sound of drops of liquid falling onto something ○ *the steady drip of a leaking tap* **4.** MED MEDICAL PROCEDURE FOR INJECTING LIQUID a medical procedure whereby a therapeutic fluid such as blood, plasma, saline, or glucose is injected continuously into somebody's vein at an adjustable rate. A plastic bag containing the fluid is hung above the patient on a stand. N Am term **drip feed 5.** MED FLUID IN DRIP the therapeutic fluid used in a drip ○ *Add 2 cc of morphine to the drip.* N Am term **drip feed 6.** MED EQUIPMENT FOR DRIP the equipment used to administer a drip (*informal*) N Am term **drip feed 7.** OFFENSIVE TERM an offensive term for somebody regarded as weak and ineffectual (*informal insult*) **8.** ARCHIT PROTECTIVE GROOVE a protective groove cut in a sill or other overhang of a wall or building to cause water to drip freely [Old English *dryppan* < Indo-European, 'to drop']

drip with *vt* **1.** HAVE DROPS FALLING CONTINUOUSLY to have liquid falling in a continuous stream of drops ○ *dripping with sweat* **2.** HAVE TOO MUCH OF SOMETHING to have too much of something, especially some kind of adornment, usually in a way that is considered to be bad taste ○ *a woman dripping with jewels* **3.** GIVE VENT TO EMOTION to give continuous expression to an emotion, especially a negative one such as spite, malice, or sarcasm ○ *Her voice dripped with sarcasm.*

drip coffee *n Aus, N Am* same as **filter coffee** (sense 1)

drip-dry *adj* describes clothes or materials that do not wrinkle or crease as they dry, and so do not needing ironing ○ *a drip-dry shirt* ■ *vti* (**drip-dries, drip-drying, drip-dried**) to dry without creases when hung up wet, or cause something to dry in this way

drip feed *n N Am* MED **1.** same as **drip** *n* (senses 4–5) **2.** same as **drip** *n* (sense 6) (*informal*)

drip-feed /dríp feed/ *vt* **1.** ADMINISTER DRIP TO SOMEBODY to pass a liquid, especially a sugar solution, directly into somebody's vein using a drip **2.** PROVIDE PLANTS WITH CONTINUOUS WATER SUPPLY to provide water or liquid nutrients to indoor plants or field crops continuously in small quantities **3.** PROVIDE MONEY IN INSTALMENTS to give money to a new business in instalments at various stages of its development instead of giving the entire sum at the beginning (*informal*)

dripless /drípləss/ *adj US* designed or made not to drip ○ *This teapot has a dripless spout.*

drip pan *n* a shallow pan or baking sheet used in the oven to catch the juices of roasting meat

dripping /drípping/ *n* FAT FROM COOKING MEAT the fat that melts off meat when it is being cooked and hardens when cold, used for frying, basting, and making pastry. It was formerly also used as a spread on bread. ■ **drippings** *npl US* JUICES FROM COOKING MEAT the juices, including melted fat, produced by roasting or frying meat ■ *adj also* **dripping wet** VERY WET completely soaked ○ *She hurried in, cold and dripping wet from the storm.*

dripping pan *n* HOUSEHOLD same as **drip pan**

dripping wet *adj* same as **dripping**

drippy /dríppi/ (**-pier, -piest**) *adj* **1.** silly and extremely sentimental (*informal*) ○ *a drippy love story* **2.** an offensive term meaning weak and ineffectual (*informal insult*) —**drippily** *adv* —**drippiness** *n*

dripstone /dríp stōn/ *n* **1.** a protective stone drip in the overhang above a door or window **2.** calcium carbonate deposits in the form of stalactites or stalagmites

drissy /dríssi/ *adj Wales* same as **frantic** (*informal*)

drive /drīv/ *v* (**drives, driving, drove** /drōv/, **driven** /drívv'n/) **1.** *vti* TRANSP CONTROL MOVEMENT OF VEHICLE to operate a vehicle, controlling its speed and direction, or be operated in this way ○ *He's learning to drive.* **2.** *vti* TRANSP TRAVEL OR CONVEY IN VEHICLE to travel somewhere in a vehicle, or take somebody somewhere in a vehicle ○ *I'll drive you to the airport.* **3.** *vt* ENG PROVIDE POWER FOR SOMETHING to supply the power that makes something work (*often passive*) ○ *The lawn mower is driven by a petrol engine.* **4.** *vt* STEER PROGRESS OF SOMETHING to provide momentum towards the successful operation or functioning of something ○ *This company is driven by a concern for quality.* **5.** *vt* FORCE SOMEBODY OR SOMETHING INTO CONDITION to force somebody or something into a particular state or condition, often an extremely negative one ○ *Her son's behaviour drove her to despair.* **6. drive yourself** *vr* FORCE YOURSELF TO WORK to force yourself to work too hard or for too long at something ○ *You drive yourself too hard.* **7.** *vt* MOVE PEOPLE OR ANIMALS to force a person or animal to go somewhere ○ *Rain drove them indoors.* **8.** *vt* FORCE SOMETHING IN OR OUT to push, knock, or hammer something forcefully into a particular position ○ *He drove the stakes into the ground.* **9.** *vti* MOVE OR PROPEL FORCEFULLY to move or be blown or thrown with great force against something, or provide the force that does this ○ *The wind drove the snow into huge drifts.* **10.** *vt* MAKE HOLE to make a hole or tunnel in something using great force **11.** *vt* SPORTS HIT BALL HARD in some sports, to kick or hit a ball forcefully **12.** *vti* GOLF HIT LONG SHOT in golf, to hit a long shot from either a tee or a fairway when covering the principal distance between holes ○ *He drove into the rough.* **13.** *vti* BASKETBALL DRIBBLE THROUGH COURT AREA in basketball, to dribble the ball through a particular area of the court towards the basket ○ *She's unstoppable when she drives the baseline.* **14.** *vt* CRICKET STRIKE BALL WITH FORCE in cricket, to strike the ball very hard and straight with the bat held vertically **15.** *vt* FIELD SPORTS CHASE GAME INTO OPEN to chase a hunted animal into the open where it can be killed **16.** *vt NZ* FELL TREES BY CUTTING ONE DOWN to cut down a tree in such a way that it falls on other trees and makes them fall **17.** *vt NZ* FORESTRY FLOAT LOGS DOWNSTREAM to move a mass of floating logs downstream by opening a flood dam ■ *n* **1.** TRANSP RIDE TAKEN IN VEHICLE a trip in a car or other vehicle ○ *go for a drive* **2.** ROADS ROAD LINKING HOUSE TO STREET a paved or surfaced area or private road that goes between a house or garage and the street. N Am term **driveway 3.** *also* **Drive** ROADS WIDE ROAD a street or road that can be used for vehicles, especially one that has pleasant views (*often used in placenames*) **4.** ENG TRANSMISSION OF POWER the means of converting power into motion in a machine such as a motor vehicle ○ *a car with four-wheel drive* **5.** COMPUT same as **disk drive 6.** HARD HIT OF BALL in some sports, a forceful shot or stroke in hitting a ball ○ *She has a good backhand drive.* **7.** GOLF LONG SHOT in golf, a long shot played from either a tee or fairway, when covering the principal distance between two holes **8.** BASKETBALL FAST MOVEMENT TOWARDS BASKET in basketball, a fast direct run towards the basket while dribbling the ball ○ *Our players are having trouble scoring off drives.* **9.** FOCUSED ENERGY energy and determination that helps somebody achieve what he or she wants to do ○ *Do you have the drive to achieve your ambitions?* **10.** PSYCHOL MOTIVATING NEED a powerful need or instinct that motivates behaviour, e.g. hunger or sex **11.** MAJOR PLANNED EFFORT an organized effort made by a lot of people working together to achieve a goal ○ *a recruitment drive* **12.** LEISURE PARTY FOR PLAYING CARD GAME a social event for the purpose of playing a game such as whist, often organized in order to raise funds (*used in combination*) ○ *a beetle drive* **13.** MIL SUSTAINED MILITARY ATTACK a major sustained attack on an enemy, usually including armoured vehicles and large guns **14.** ELECTRONICS VOLTAGE voltage applied to the grid of a transmitting or amplifying valve or to the base of a transistor **15.** AUTOMOT FORWARD POSITION IN AUTOMATIC TRANSMISSION in an automatic transmission, the principal shift position that moves the vehicle forwards [Old English *drīfan* < Indo-European] —**drivable** *adj* ◇ **drive somebody up the wall** to cause somebody to become extremely irritated or annoyed (*informal*)

drive at *vt* to be trying to say or intending to make understood (*informal*) ○ *It was hard to tell what she was driving at.*

drive out *vt* FORESTRY same as **drive** *v* (senses 16–17)

drive-by *n* CRIME same as **drive-by shooting** (*informal*)

drive-by shooting *n* the illegal act of firing a firearm at somebody or something from a moving vehicle

drive chain *n* an endless chain that transmits power from one toothed wheel to another in a mechanical system

drive-in *n* a commercial establishment, e.g. a cinema, that provides services or products to customers while they remain in their cars (*often used before a noun*)

drivel /drívv'l/ *n* **1.** SILLY TALK silly and irrelevant or inaccurate talk ○ *They're talking drivel.* **2.** DROOLED SALIVA saliva dribbling from the mouth ■ *vi* (**-els, -elling, -elled**) **1.** TALK NONSENSE to talk silly and irrelevant or inaccurate nonsense **2.** DROOL to let saliva dribble from the mouth [Old English *dreflian*, origin ?] —**driveller** *n* —**drivelling** *n*

driven /drívv'n/ past participle of **drive** ■ *adj* **1.** striving to achieve personal goals because of a strong need or inner compulsion ○ *Driven people are often overachievers.* **2.** having a particular thing as a principal cause (*used in combination*) ○ *a demand-driven economy*

driver /drīvər/ *n* **1.** TRANSP SOMEBODY WHO CAN DRIVE somebody who operates a motor vehicle, or who is capable of operating one **2.** TRANSP CHAUFFEUR somebody who drives a car or limousine for other people ■ *n*, *n* GOLF CLUB WITH WOODEN HEAD a golf club with a wide wooden head, deep face, and a long shaft, used to drive the ball from the tee down the fairway ■ *n* **1.** MECH ENG MACHINE PART THAT TRANSMITS MOVEMENT a part of a machine that causes another part to move **2.** TOOL THAT APPLIES PRESSURE a tool, e.g. a screwdriver or drill, that exerts heavy pressure on something else **3.** ELECTRONICS ELECTRONIC CIRCUIT an electronic circuit that produces an output used to control another circuit **4.** COMPUT CONTROLLING SOFTWARE a piece of computer software that controls the input and output of a device ○ *a printer driver* **5.** STRONG FORCE something that provides impetus or motivation, e.g. within an organization

driver ant *n* INSECTS same as **army ant**

driverless /drīvərləss/ *adj* **1.** LACKING DRIVER WHILE MOVING moving out of control without a driver **2.** HAVING NO DRIVER not having a driver on a specific occasion ○ *Looks like we're driverless tonight.* **3.** NEEDING NO DRIVER capable of being operated without a driver ○ *driverless transit systems*

driver's licence *n ANZ* AUTOMOT same as **driving licence**

driver's license *n US* TRANSP same as **driving licence**

driver's seat *n US* AUTOMOT same as **driving seat**

driver's side *n* the side of a car on which the steering wheel is located, where the driver sits when operating a vehicle

drive shaft *n* **1.** a rotating shaft that transmits the power from a motor or engine to another part of the machine, e.g. from the engine to the propeller of an aircraft **2.** the shaft that transmits power from the transmission to the differential in a rear-wheel drive vehicle

drive-through *n* a business such as a fast-food restaurant or bank that provides goods or services through a special window to customers who remain in their cars (*often used before a noun*)

drive time *n* a time during the morning or afternoon when commuters are driving to and from work in their cars and listening to the radio

drive train *n* a mechanical part of a vehicle, including the drive shaft and universal joint, that connects the transmission with the axles and transmits power, torque, and motion

drive-up *n US* a place in a commercial establishment such as a restaurant or bank where customers are served while remaining in their cars (*often used before a noun*)

driveway /drīv way/ *n N Am* ROADS same as **drive** *n* (sense 2)

driving /drīving/ *adj* **1.** **FALLING HARD** falling, blowing, or being blown very hard and forcefully ○ *driving rain* **2.** **ABLE TO MAKE SOMETHING HAPPEN** having the ability or influence to make something new or different happen ○ *She is the driving force behind the new development.* ○ *driving ambition* ■ *n* AUTOMOT **PROCESS OF OPERATING VEHICLE** the act or process of operating a motor vehicle, especially with regard to how skilful somebody is ○ *Your driving is even worse than usual today.* —**drivingly** *adv*

driving chain *n* MECH ENG same as **drive chain**

driving examiner *n* an official who conducts a test to decide whether somebody is able to drive sufficiently well to be granted a driving licence

driving gloves *npl* gloves worn while driving a vehicle. They are usually made of leather or have leather palms and knitted fabric backs.

driving iron *n* an iron golf club that can be used instead of a driver

driving licence *n UK* a document obtained after somebody has passed a test demonstrating that he or she knows how to drive safely and within the law. ANZ term **driver's licence**. US term **driver's license**

driving range *n* a place or facility where golfers can practise their drive strokes, usually consisting of a row of small tees fronting an open area of ground

driving seat *n* the seat in which the driver sits when operating a motor vehicle. US term **driver's seat** ◇ **in the driving seat 1.** in a position to determine the course or direction of something **2.** in charge of what is going on

driving test *n* a test of driving skills and knowledge, usually consisting of both a written and a practical test that somebody must pass before driving without supervision on public roads

driving wheel *n* a wheel that causes other wheels to rotate

drizzle /drízz'l/ *n* METEOROL **LIGHT RAIN** light steady rain ■ *v* (**-zles, -zling, -zled**) **1.** *vi* METEOROL **RAIN LIGHTLY** to rain lightly and steadily **2.** *vt* COOK **DRIBBLE LIQUID OVER FOOD** to pour very small quantities of a liquid in a thin stream over food ○ *Lightly drizzle the dressing over the vegetables.* [Mid-16C. Origin ?] —**drizzly** *adj*

Dr Martens /dok maártənz/ *tdmk* a trademark for a type of sturdy lace-up ankle-length boot or shoe with an air-cushioned sole

drogue /drōg/ *n* **1.** NAUT same as **sea anchor 2.** AEROSP same as **drogue parachute 3.** AIR FORCE a cylindrical target towed behind an aircraft, used for firing practice **4.** AVIAT a funnel-shaped receptacle attached to the refuelling hose of a tanker aircraft that locates the probe of the receiving aircraft and fits over it, ensuring firm connection during refuelling **5.** METEOROL same as **windsock** (*technical*) [Early 18C. Origin ?]

drogue parachute /drōg-/ *n* **1.** a small parachute, used on a spacecraft or satellite re-entering the atmosphere, that is released before a larger one to slow the object and stabilize it **2.** a small parachute used to release a larger one from its pack

droit /drwaa/ *n* a right or claim, either legal or moral, that is due to somebody and must be acknowledged [15C. Via French < late Latin *directum* 'rule' < Latin *directus* 'straight' (see DIRECT)]

droit de seigneur /drwaa də say nyúr/, **droit du seigneur** /-dyoo-/ *n* the supposed former legal right of a feudal lord to have sexual intercourse with the bride or daughter of an inferior, usually a serf, on the night of her wedding [< French, 'lord's right']

droll /drōl/ *adj* amusing in a wry or odd way ○ *a droll aside* [Early 17C. < French *drôle* 'buffoon, comical'] —**drollness** *n* —**drolly** *adv*

SYNONYMS See *funny*.

drollery /drōləri/ (*plural* **-ies**) *n* **1.** **QUIRKY HUMOUR** slightly wry or odd humour **2.** **TALKING OR BEHAVING AMUSINGLY** speech or behaviour that is wryly or oddly amusing **3.** **SOMETHING FUNNY** an act or story that is wryly or oddly amusing

dromaeosaur /drōmi ə sawr/ *n* a medium-sized fast-running dinosaur of the Cretaceous Period that had strong hind legs with a long sharp talon on each foot and long three-clawed hands [Late 20C. < modern Latin *Dromaeosaurus* < Greek *dromaios* 'swift-running' + *sauros* 'lizard']

-drome *suffix* racecourse, field ○ *hippodrome* ○ *cosmodrome* [Via Latin < Greek *dromos* 'racecourse' < Indo-European, 'walk, run']

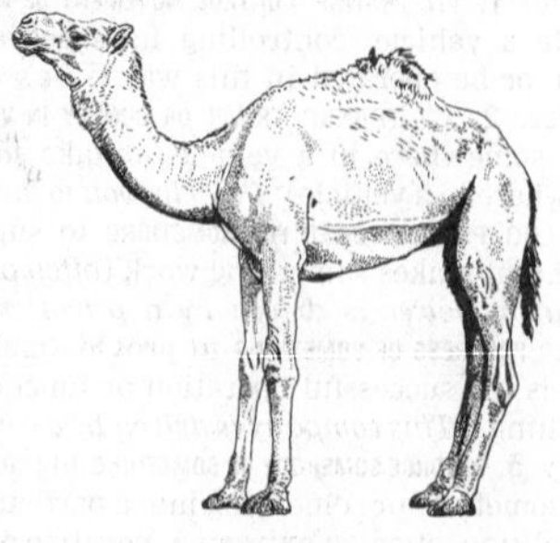

dromedary

dromedary /drómmədəri, drúmmə-/ (*plural* **-ies**) *n* a camel with one hump. Kept for: working, racing. Native to: North Africa, Southwest Asia. Latin name: *Camelus dromedarius*. [13C. < Old French *dromedaire*, late Latin *dromedarius* < Latin *dromad-* 'dromedary' < Greek *dromad-* 'running']

dromond /drómmənd, drúmm-/, **dromon** /-ən/ *n* a sailing galley used in the Middle Ages [14C. Via Anglo-Norman *dromund* < late Latin *dromon-* < Greek *dromō* 'swift ship' < *dromos* 'running']

-dromous *suffix* moving, migrating ○ *catadromous* [< modern Latin *-dromus* < Greek *dromos* 'running']

drone[1] /drōn/ *v* (**drones, droning, droned**) **1.** *vi* **MAKE LOW HUMMING SOUND** to make a continuous low humming sound **2.** *vti* **TALK IN BORING VOICE** to talk or say something in a boring voice, usually for a long time ○ *I could hear his voice droning on in the background.* ■ *n* **1.** **LOW HUMMING SOUND** a continuous low humming sound **2.** MUSIC **UNCHANGING NOTE HELD DURING MELODY** a single note or chord that is held through a melodic part **3.** MUSIC **PIPE IN BAGPIPES PRODUCING CONTINUOUS NOTE** the pipe in a set of bagpipes that produces a single continuous note [Early 16C. < DRONE [2]] —**droningly** *adv*

drone[2] /drōn/ *n* **1.** INSECTS **NONWORKER MALE BEE** a male bee that has no sting, does not gather pollen, and exists only to mate with the queen bee **2.** **LAZY PERSON** somebody who does not work or contribute anything, but relies on the work or energy of others (*insult*) **3.** AVIAT **AIRCRAFT WITH NO PILOT** an aircraft whose flight is controlled from the ground [Old English *drān* < Indo-European, 'to buzz'] —**dronish** *adj*

drongo /dróng gō/ (*plural* **-gos**) *n* **1.** a bird that is usually black with a strong beak, glossy feathers, and a long forked tail. Native to: tropical Africa, Asia, Australia. Family: Dicruridae. **2.** an offensive term that deliberately insults somebody's intelligence or ability to learn (*informal insult*) [Mid-19C. < Malagasy]

droob /droob/ *n* **1.** *Aus* an offensive term for somebody who is thought to be ineffectual (*informal insult*) **2.** a very small amount of something (*informal*) [Mid-20C. Origin ?]

drool /drool/ *v* (**drools, drooling, drooled**) **1.** *vi* **DRIBBLE SALIVA** to let saliva dribble from the mouth ○ *The dog lay drooling at his feet.* **2.** *vi* **SHOW EXAGGERATED APPRECIATION** to show excessive appreciation of somebody or something **3.** *vti* **TALK NONSENSE** to talk nonsense or foolishness ■ *n* **SALIVA DRIBBLING FROM MOUTH** saliva dribbling from the mouth [Early 19C. Origin ?] —**droolingly** *adv*

droop /droop/ *v* (**droops, drooping, drooped**) **1.** *vti* **HANG OR BEND DOWN LIMPLY** to move lower, hang down, or sag limply, or make something do this ○ *Her eyelids drooped with weariness.* **2.** *vi* **BE DISPIRITED** to become discouraged or dejected ○ *His spirits drooped at the prospect of the long and arduous journey.* ■ *n* **SAGGING** a lowered, sagging, or slumped position ○ *The droop of her shoulders suggested her disappointment.* [13C. < Old Norse *drūpa*] —**droopily** *adv* —**droopiness** *n* —**droopingly** *adv* —**droopy** *adj*

droop nose, **droop snoot** *n* an aircraft nose section that can be tilted downwards to increase the pilot's range of vision during landing and takeoff

drop /drop/ *v* (**drops, dropping, dropped**) **1.** *vt* **LET GO OF SOMETHING** to let go of something and cause it to fall, either accidentally or intentionally ○ *He dropped the bowling ball on my foot.* ○ *Somebody had dropped a glove in the street.* **2.** *vi* **FALL** to fall from a higher place to a lower place **3.** *vti* **MOVE TO LOWER POSITION** to move into a lower position, or move the body or part of the body lower ○ *He dropped into a chair.* **4.** *vti* **FALL IN DROPS** to fall in drops of liquid, or make something do this ○ *We listened to the rain dropping on the roof.* **5.** *vti* **LESSEN** to decrease to a lower level, rate, or number, or make something do this ○ *The temperature dropped sharply overnight.* **6.** *vi* **SLOPE DOWNWARDS** to slope downwards, often in a particular way **7.** *vti* **LOWER VOICE** to lower the voice to a quieter level, or be lowered in this way ○ *She dropped her voice to a whisper.* **8.** *vt* **TAKE SOMEBODY OR SOMETHING SOMEWHERE** to take somebody or something to a place, usually by car, and leave the person or thing there ○ *Can you drop me at the bus station?* **9.** *vt* **WRITE SOMETHING TO SOMEBODY** to write and send an informal message or greeting to somebody ○ *Drop me a line when you get there.* **10.** *vt* **STOP DOING OR PLANNING SOMETHING** to abandon a plan or course of action ○ *The council have dropped plans to build a major new leisure centre.* **11.** *vt* **STOP TALKING ABOUT SOMETHING** to stop talking about something, or stop being talked about ○ *Can we drop the subject please?* **12.** *vt* **END RELATIONSHIP WITH SOMEBODY** to end a close or intimate relationship with somebody (*informal*) **13.** *vt* **REMOVE SOMEBODY** to remove somebody from a group of which she or he was formerly a member ○ *She may be dropped from the team.* **14.** *vt* **OMIT LETTER OR WORD** to leave out a letter, word, or phrase ○ *You can drop the 'Sir': just call me Max.* **15.** *vi* **COLLAPSE FROM EXHAUSTION** to collapse in a state of complete exhaustion ○ *I'm ready to drop.* **16.** *vi* **COLLAPSE** to lose consciousness or die, especially suddenly or unexpectedly (*informal*) ○ *People were dropping like flies from the extreme heat.* **17.** *vt* **LOSE MATCH OR GAME** to lose a match, game, or part of a game ○ *He got through to the finals without dropping a set.* **18.** *vt* **SAY SOMETHING CASUALLY** to say something with an air of pretended casualness ○ *She's dropping hints about what she wants for her birthday.* **19.** *vt US* **SPEND OR LOSE MONEY** to spend or lose a particular amount of money on something expensive or in gambling (*informal*) **20.** *vti* **HIT BALL INTO TARGET HOLE** to make the ball go into a target such as a hole or net, or go into a target hole or net **21.** *vt* VET **GIVE BIRTH TO OFFSPRING** to give birth to young, especially a foal **22.** *vt* DRUGS **TAKE ILLEGAL DRUGS** to take an illegal drug by mouth, especially in pill form (*slang*) **23.** *vt* HANDICRAFT **LOWER HEM OF SOMETHING** to lower the hem of something such as a garment or curtain **24.** *vt* AVIAT **DELIVER SOMEBODY OR SOMETHING BY PARACHUTE** to deliver somebody or something such as soldiers or supplies by parachute from an aircraft **25.** *vt* **UNLOAD SOMETHING** to unload something from a ship or vehicle ■ *n* **1.** **SMALL ROUND PORTION OF LIQUID** a very small amount of liquid that becomes a rounded or pear shape as it falls **2.** **SMALL AMOUNT OF LIQUID** a small amount of a liquid ○ *There's not a drop of milk in the house.* **3.** **TINIEST AMOUNT** a very small amount of a feeling or quality (*used in negative statements*) ○ *I swear there isn't a drop of sympathy in that man.* **4.** **DECREASE IN SOMETHING** a decrease in quantity or amount ○ *a drop in salary* **5.** **DISTANCE BETWEEN HIGH POINT AND GROUND** the distance between a higher level and a lower level or the ground **6.** **DESCENT** a slope or fall in ground level, usually sharp or sudden **7.** FOOD **SMALL ROUND SWEET** a small round or oval sweet (*used in combination*) ○ *cough drops* **8.** JEWELLERY **ROUND EARRING OR PENDANT** an earring or pendant, usually round or pear-shaped **9.** MIL, AIR FORCE **DESCENT BY PARACHUTE** a descent from an aircraft by parachute **10.** **GOODS DELIVERED BY PARACHUTE** goods or equipment that an aircraft delivers by parachute, or people dropped by parachute (*often used in combination*) **11.** **DELIVERY** a delivery of goods ○ *make a drop every two weeks* **12.** **SECRET REPOSITORY FOR MESSAGES** a secret place where somebody leaves letters or messages to be picked up by somebody else **13.** **ACT OF LEAVING SECRET COMMUNICATION** the act of leaving a

letter, message, or goods at a prearranged secret location ○ *It's too dangerous to make the drop tonight.* **14.** THEATRE same as **drop curtain** (sense 1) **15.** ELECTRONICS **CONNECTION ON LINE** a point on a transmission line where data can be put in or taken out **16.** MEDIA **SHORT SPUR** a short line that feeds signals to an individual house or flat from a cable television trunk line **17.** TRAPDOOR **UNDER GALLOWS** a trapdoor under a gallows on which somebody who is to be hanged stands **18.** HANDICRAFT **CURTAIN LENGTH** the measured length for a curtain, from the top of a window to its sill or to the floor ■ **drops** npl PHARM **LIQUID MEDICINE APPLIED IN SMALL QUANTITIES** liquid medicine delivered by a dropper to the ear, nose, or eye [< Old English *dropa* (noun), *droppian* < Indo-European] ◇ **a drop in the ocean** just a tiny part of the full quantity that is required, and thus insignificant ◇ **at the drop of a hat** without needing persuasion or prompting ◇ **drop a clanger** *or* **brick** to say something tactless, inappropriate, or mistaken that will cause embarrassment (*informal*) ◇ **let something drop** to reveal information to somebody, often casually or accidentally

drop away vi **1.** same as **drop** v (sense 6) **2.** to leave a group or formation gradually, either on purpose or not ○ *One by one, each jet banked and dropped away from the formation.* **3.** to disappear gradually

drop back *or* **behind** vi to move more slowly than other people and gradually fall farther behind them

drop by 1. vi to visit somebody casually or without having agreed on a time **2.** vt to deliver somebody or something to a specific place ○ *Just drop the laundry by some time this afternoon.*

drop in vi **1.** to visit somebody casually or without having agreed on a time **2.** *Aus* to cut in front of another surfer who has right of way (*slang*)

drop into vt to go from a more active into a less active state of consciousness

drop off v **1.** vi to fall asleep (*informal*) **2.** vi to decline or fall to a lower level (*informal*) ○ *Sales tend to drop off during the summer.* **3.** vt same as **drop** v (sense 8)

drop out vi **1.** to abandon a project or activity without finishing it ○ *He dropped out of college in his final year.* **2.** to reject conventional society and live in an alternative way (*informal*)

drop over *or* **round** vi to visit somebody casually and without having agreed on a time ○ *Drop round any time.*

drop box n *US* a secure container attached to the outside of an office in which letters or packages may be deposited during periods when the office is closed

drop cloth n **1.** THEATRE same as **drop curtain** (sense 1) **2.** *N Am* HOUSEHOLD same as **dustsheet**

drop curtain n **1.** an unframed curtain that can be lowered to a theatre stage from the flies, usually providing background scenery **2.** a theatre curtain that is raised or lowered on stage, instead of being opened or closed by moving sideways

drop-dead adv used to add emphasis (*informal*) ○ *drop-dead gorgeous*

drop-down menu n a vertical list of options that appears on clicking on an item in a computer screen. It remains visible until one of the options has been selected by clicking on it.

~~**droped**~~ incorrect spelling of **dropped**

drop forge n a machine used to shape or stamp molten metal by placing it between two dies and dropping a weight on it —**drop-forge** vt

drop front n a part of a writing desk that can be lowered to provide a writing surface and then raised to conceal the inner part of the desk (*hyphenated when used before a noun*) ○ *a drop-front desk*

drop goal n in rugby, a goal scored by dropping the ball and then kicking it

drop hammer n METALL same as **drop forge**

drop handlebars npl on a racing bicycle, handlebars that curve downwards, enabling the rider to adopt a more aerodynamic posture

drophead coupé /dróp hed-/ n a two-door car that has a folding top and a sloping back, and seats four people

drop-in centre n a place that people can visit without

an appointment to get advice or information, or to meet others

drop kick n **1.** in rugby or American football, a method of kicking a ball on the half-volley by dropping it from the hands **2.** in amateur wrestling, an illegal move in which one wrestler attacks another by leaping into the air and striking an opponent with both feet —**drop-kick** vti

drop leaf n an extension on the end of a table that can be folded down when not needed (*hyphenated when used before a noun*) ○ *a drop-leaf table*

droplet /dróplət/ n a very small drop of liquid

droplight /dróp līt/ n an electric light that can be raised or lowered by using a rope, cord, or pulley

drop lock n in international financial markets, a variable-rate bank loan that is automatically converted to a fixed-rate bond when long-term interest rates fall to a specific level

drop-off n a fall in the level of something

dropout /dróp owt/ n **1.** EDUC **SOMEBODY WHO LEAVES WITHOUT COMPLETING COURSE** a student who withdraws from an educational course, usually at a college or university **2.** **UNCONVENTIONAL PERSON** somebody who chooses an unconventional way of life (*informal*) **3.** RUGBY **DROP KICK TO RESTART GAME** a drop kick performed by a defending rugby team in order to restart a game **4.** COMPUT **SECTION WITHOUT DATA** a small section on a magnetic tape or disk that is missing data

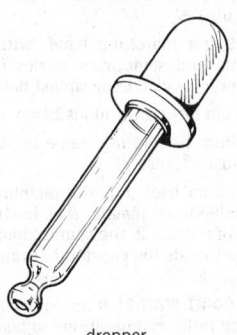

dropper

dropper /dróppər/ n **1.** a small glass or plastic tube with a rubber bulb at one end that is used to suck up liquid and release it one drop at a time (*often used in combination*) ○ *an eye dropper* **2.** a short piece of monofilament line, used by anglers to attach a fly above the tail fly

droppings /dróppingz/ npl animal or bird excrement left on the ground or another surface

drop scone n a small round flat cake made by dropping a spoonful of batter onto a heated pan or griddle

drop shipment n something sold by a retailer to a consumer that is shipped directly from the manufacturer or wholesaler to the consumer

drop shot n in racket games, a shot in which the ball drops abruptly to the ground just after passing over the net or hitting the wall

dropsided lorry /dróp sídid-/ n an open lorry with hinged sides that can be lowered to allow loading or unloading

dropsonde /dróp sond/ n an instrument, dropped from an aircraft and carried down by a parachute, that transmits information about temperature, pressure, and humidity [Mid-20C. < DROP + RADIOSONDE]

dropsy /drópsi/ n MED same as **oedema** (*dated*) [13C. Shortening of *hydropsy*, via Old French < medieval Latin *hydropisia* < Greek *hudrōps* 'somebody with oedema' < *hudōr* 'water'] —**dropsical** adj —**dropsied** adj

dropwort /dróp wurt/ (*plural* **-worts** *or* *same*) n **1.** a plant with finely divided leaves. Flowers: small, white or red, in clusters. Native to: Europe, Asia. Latin name: *Filipendula vulgaris.* **2.** a marsh plant with flower heads shaped like an opened umbrella. Genus: *Oenanthe.* [< its tuberous root fibres]

drop zone n an area where troops or goods such as

military equipment or medical supplies are to be landed, usually by parachute

droshky /dróshki/ (*plural* **-kies**), **drosky** /dróski/ n an open four-wheeled carriage drawn by horses, formerly used in Russia and Poland [Early 19C. < Russian *drozhki* 'small wagon' < *drogi* 'wagon']

drosometer /dro sómmitər/ n a device for measuring dew deposits [Early 19C. < Greek *drosos* 'dew']

drosophila /dro sóffilə, drə-/ (*plural* **-las** *or* *same* or **-lae** /-lee/) n a small two-winged fruit fly that is frequently used in genetic research. Genus: *Drosophila.* [Early 19C. < modern Latin < Greek *drosos* 'dew' + *-philos* 'loving']

dross /dross/ n **1.** **SOMETHING WORTHLESS** something that is worthless, or of a low standard or quality ○ *I considered her early fiction to be pure dross.* **2.** **SCUM ON METAL** the scum formed on molten metals, usually caused by oxidation **3.** *Scotland* **SMALL COALS** small coals or coal dust [Old English *drōs* < Indo-European, 'dark, muddy'] —**drossy** adj

drought /drowt/ n **1.** a long period of extremely dry weather when there is not enough rain for the successful growing of crops **2.** a lengthy and serious lack of something ○ *She experienced a period of creative drought.* [Old English *drūgaþ* 'dryness' < Germanic, 'dry'] —**droughty** adj

drouth /drowth, drooth/ n **1.** *Ireland, Scotland* METEOROL same as **drought** (sense 1) **2.** *regional* same as **thirst** n (sense 1) —**drouthy** adj

drove[1] /drōv/ past tense of **drive**

drove[2] /drōv/ n **1.** **GROUP OF ANIMALS MOVING** a large number of animals, especially cattle, moving in the same direction, e.g. when being driven to a new grazing area **2.** **TYPE OF STONE CHISEL** a broad-edged chisel used for dressing stone ■ **droves** npl **CROWDS OF PEOPLE** very large numbers of people ○ *They came out of the football ground in droves.* ■ vti (**droves, droving, droved**) **MOVE ANIMALS ALONG** to move a herd or flock of animals from one place to another, usually over long distances, e.g. to new pastures or to market [Old English *drāf* < *drīfan* (see DRIVE)] —**drover** n

drove road n *Scotland* a road or track along which cattle or sheep were formerly driven on foot to market

drown /drown/ (**drowns, drowning, drowned**) v **1.** vti to die by immersion and usually suffocation in water or other liquid, or kill a person or animal in this way. Death occurs either from lack of oxygen or as a result of cardiac arrest from the lowered body temperature. ○ *death by drowning* **2.** vt same as **drown out** (*often passive*) **3.** vt to cover or soak something, usually an item of food, with too much liquid ○ *He served us pancakes drowned in syrup.* [13C. Probably < N Germanic] —**drowned** adj —**drowner** n **drown out** vt to make so much noise that it is impossible to hear another sound (*often passive*)

drowse /drowz/ (**drowses, drowsing, drowsed**) vi to be in a state partway between sleeping and waking [Late 16C. Back-formation < DROWSY] —**drowse** n

drowsy /drówzi/ (**-ier, -iest**) adj **1.** **ALMOST ASLEEP** almost asleep or very lightly asleep **2.** **CAUSING SLEEPINESS** tending to make somebody feel sleepy ○ *a drowsy summer afternoon* **3.** **SLUGGISH** sluggish and dull [15C. < Old English *drūsian* 'be sluggish' < Germanic] —**drowsily** adv —**drowsiness** n

drub /drub/ vt (**drubs, drubbing, drubbed**) **1.** **DEFEAT SOMEBODY** to defeat an opponent comprehensively ○ *Their team really drubbed us last year.* **2.** **BEAT SOMEBODY WITH STICK** to beat somebody using a heavy stick or club **3.** **STAMP YOUR FEET** to stamp the feet hard on the ground ■ n **BLOW WITH STICK** a blow made using a heavy stick or club [Early 17C. Origin ?] —**drubber** n —**drubbing** n

drudge /druj/ n a worker who performs dull and laborious tasks [15C. Origin ?] —**drudge** vi —**drudger** n —**drudgingly** adv

drudgery /drújjəri/ n exhausting, boring, unpleasant work

SYNONYMS See **work**.

drug /drug/ n **1.** **MEDICINAL SUBSTANCE** a natural or artificial substance given to treat or prevent disease or to lessen pain **2.** **ILLEGAL SUBSTANCE** an often illegal and sometimes addictive substance that causes changes in behaviour and perception and is taken

for the effects 3. PHARM **MEDICAL SUBSTANCE** a substance given to treat or prevent illness that is officially listed in a medical pharmacopoeia ■ *vt* (**drugs, drugging, drugged**) 1. **GIVE SOMEBODY DRUG** to give a drug to somebody 2. **ADD DRUG TO SOMETHING** to mix a drug with somebody's food or drink to make him or her fall asleep or become unconscious [14C. < French *drogue*]

drug abuse *n* deliberate use of an illegal drug or of too much of a prescribed drug

drug baron *n* CRIME same as **drug lord**

drugged /drugd/ *adj* 1. heavily asleep, unconscious, or unable to function after being given drugs 2. extremely tired and unable to concentrate ○ *drugged with sleep*

drugget /drúggit/ *n* 1. **CARPETING FABRIC** a thick heavy woollen or cotton and wool blend fabric. Use: floor coverings. 2. **RUG** a coarse rug made of wool or cotton and wool 3. **WOOLLEN FABRIC** a woollen or woollen mix fabric. Use: formerly, clothing. [Mid-16C. < French *droguet*]

druggie /drúggi/, **druggy** (*plural* **-gies**) *n* a drug addict (*slang*)

druggist /drúggist/ *n N Am* same as **pharmacist**

druggy /drúggi/ *adj* (**-gier, -giest**) characteristic of somebody who takes drugs regularly (*slang*) ○ *a druggy stupor* ■ *n* another spelling of **druggie**

drug holiday *n* a period when somebody does not take medication normally given every day

drug lord *n* a controller of an international network for the production, processing, and sale of illegal drugs (*informal*)

drug misuse *n* HEALTH same as **drug abuse**

drug of abuse *n* any substance or medication that is misused as a recreational drug

drug pusher *n* somebody who sells illegal drugs

drug runner *n* a smuggler of illegal drugs, usually by ship or plane

drugs squad *n* the department of a police force that investigates the use and sale of illegal drugs

drugstore /drúg stawr/ *n N Am* same as **chemist** (sense 1)

drug tsar *n* a senior official appointed to supervise the detection and suppression of illegal drug dealing (*informal*)

Druid /droō id/, **druid** *n* 1. **PRIEST IN ANCIENT CELTIC RELIGION** a priest of an ancient religion practised in Britain, Ireland, and Gaul until the people of those areas were converted to Christianity 2. **MODERN FOLLOWER OF ANCIENT CELTIC RELIGION** a man who worships and celebrates the forces of nature 3. **OFFICER OF WELSH GORSEDD** an officer of the Gorsedd, who administers eisteddfods in Wales [Mid-16C. Directly or via French < Latin *druides* 'Druids' < Celtic] —**druidic** /droo íddik/ *adj* —**druidical** *adj*

Druidess /droō idəss/ *n* 1. a female priest of an ancient religion practised in Britain, Ireland, and Gaul until the people of those areas were converted to Christianity 2. a woman who worships and celebrates the forces of nature

Druidism /droō idizəm/ *n* an ancient Celtic religion in which the forces of nature were worshipped, and the priests were also prophets and poets, or the modern religion said to derive from it

drum /drum/ *n* 1. **PERCUSSION INSTRUMENT** a musical instrument usually consisting of a membrane stretched across a hollow frame and played by striking the stretched membrane. Other hollow objects are also used as drums. 2. **TAPPING SOUND** a regular tapping sound made by something striking a surface ○ *the drum of rain on the roof* 3. **CYLINDRICAL CONTAINER** a large cylindrical container used for storing liquids such as oil or chemicals 4. **SPOOL** a large spool around which wire, cable, or rope is wound for storage 5. **HOLLOW PART IN MACHINE** a cylindrical hollow part in a machine such as a washing machine 6. ANAT same as **eardrum** 7. **FISH THAT MAKES RHYTHMIC SOUND** a large bony saltwater or freshwater fish that emits a repeated rhythmic sound. Family: Sciaenidae. 8. **CYLINDRICAL STONE BLOCK** one of the cylindrical stone blocks used to make an architectural column 9. **SUPPORT FOR DOME** a band or other structure around the bottom of a dome or circular ceiling that supports it 10. *Aus* same as **brothel** (*dated slang*) ■ *vi* (**drums, drumming, drummed**) 1. **PLAY DRUM** to play a drum or drums 2. **TAP SURFACE** to tap repeatedly and rhythmically on a surface ○ *The rain was drumming on the roof.* 3. **MAKE SOUND WITH BEAK OR WINGS** to produce a short burst of sound like a drum roll by rapidly beating with the beak or wings (*refers to birds*) [Mid-16C. Probably < Middle Dutch *tromme* 'instrument making a loud noise', an imitation of the sound] —**drumming** *n* ◇ **bang** *or* **beat the drum (for somebody** *or* **something)** to try to attract support and favourable attention for somebody or something (*informal*)

drum into *vt* to tell somebody something repeatedly and persistently until the person has learned it or will always remember it (*often passive*)

drum out *vt* (*usually passive*) 1. to force somebody to leave a group or an organization, usually in disgrace 2. to force somebody to stop doing something

drum up *vt* 1. to try actively to get more of something such as business or support 2. to create or think up an explanation ○ *What excuse can I drum up this time?*

drum and bass, drum 'n' bass *n* popular music originating in the United Kingdom in the 1990s that has a fast rhythm, complex percussion, and very low bass lines

drumbeat /drúm beet/ *n* heavy unending criticism, typically public criticism ○ *a steady drumbeat of accusations*

drum brake *n* a brake on vehicles that operates by applying pressure to the inner part of the wheel **(brake drum)**

drum corps *n* a marching band, with percussion instruments and sometimes bugles or fifes, that performs precisely choreographed field drills

drumfire /drúm fīr/ *n* continuous heavy gunfire

drumfish /drúm fish/ (*plural* *same* or **-fishes**) *n* FISH same as **drum** *n* (sense 7)

drumhead /drúm hed/ *n* 1. the membrane, usually made of calfskin or plastic, that is stretched over the frame of a drum 2. the round topmost part of a capstan that holds the capstan bars in position for turning

drumhead court-martial *n* an informal brief trial held during military operations to hear charges of serious offences committed by soldiers while in action [Because an upturned drum serves as the magistrate's bench]

drum kit *n UK, ANZ, Can* a set of percussion instruments used in bands, usually consisting of one or more snare drums, tom-toms, bass drums, and various cymbals. US term **drum set**

drumlin /drúmlin/ *n* a long narrow ridge of gravel and rock deposited by a moving glacier, one end of which is blunt and the other end tapering [Mid-19C. < *drum* 'ridge' < Irish *druim* 'back, ridge']

drum machine *n* an electronic synthesizer that can reproduce drum and percussion sounds in various rhythms and combinations

drum major *n* a leader and conductor of a marching band who moves a baton up and down and twirls it rhythmically

drum majorette *n N Am* MUSIC same as **majorette**

drummer /drúmmər/ *n* 1. **DRUM PLAYER** somebody who plays a drum 2. *N Am* **TRAVELLING SALESPERSON** a travelling salesperson 3. (*plural* **drummers** or *same*) **AUSTRALIAN FISH** a fish that frequents rocky shores. Native to: Australia. Family: Kyphosidae.

Drummond /drúmmənd/, **William** (1585–1649) Scottish poet. As well as poetry, he wrote Royalist pamphlets. *Poems* (1616) was his major work. Known as **Drummond of Hawthornden**

> 'Not to be born, or, being born, to die.'
> [William Drummond, *Poems*; 1616]

drum 'n' bass *n* MUSIC same as **drum and bass**

drum roll *n* a very fast regular beating on a drum that sounds like one long sound

drum set *n US* same as **drum kit**

drumstick /drúm stik/ *n* 1. the stick used to beat a drum 2. the lower half of the leg of a bird such as a chicken when prepared for eating, so called because of its shape

drunk /drungk/ past participle of **drink** ■ *adj* 1. **INTOXICATED WITH ALCOHOL** having drunk too much alcohol and lost control over behaviour, movement, and speech 2. **EMOTIONALLY INTOXICATED** overwhelmed with and judgmentally impaired by an intense emotion ○ *drunk with power* 3. **LONG-SOAKED** describes a meat dish in Chinese cooking in which the meat, usually chicken, has been immersed in a liquid and boiled or marinated overnight ○ *drunk chicken* ■ *n* 1. same as **drunkard** 2. **DRINKING BOUT** a bout of drinking too much alcohol (*slang*) ○ *One more drunk, and I divorce you.*

drunkard /drúngkərd/ *n* somebody who habitually drinks too much alcohol

drunk-driver *n* a driver of a motor vehicle who drives after having drunk more than the legal limit of alcohol

drunk-driving *n N Am* same as **drink-driving**

drunken /drúngkən/ *adj* 1. **INVOLVING EXCESS OF ALCOHOL** involving too much alcohol, or occurring while people have had too much alcohol ○ *a drunken quarrel* 2. **AFFECTED BY ALCOHOL** drunk or frequently drunk 3. **INTOXICATED** overly excited by or as if by having consumed too much alcohol [Old English, old past participle of DRINK] —**drunkenly** *adv* —**drunkenness** *n*

~~drunkeness~~ incorrect spelling of **drunkenness**

drupe /droop/ *n* a fruit with a thin outer skin, soft pulpy middle, and hard stony central part that encloses a seed. Apricots, plums, cherries, and almonds are drupes. [Mid-18C. Via modern Latin < Latin *drupa* 'overripe olive' < Greek *druppa* 'olive']

drupelet /droōplət/, **drupel** /droōp'l/ *n* a small fruit enclosing a single seed that, with many other small sections, makes up a compound fruit such as a blackberry or raspberry

Druze /drooz/ (*plural* *same* or **Druzes**), **Druse** (*plural* *same* or **Druses**) *n* a member of a religion similar to Islam that is found mainly in Israel, Lebanon, and Syria [Late 18C. Directly or via French < Arabic *durūz*, plural of *durzī*, after the religion's founder, Muḥammad ibn Ismā'īl *ad-Darazī* (d. 1019)] —**Druzean** *adj*

dry /drī/ *adj* (**drier** or **dryer, driest** or **dryest**) 1. **NOT WET** not wet, or no longer wet 2. **LACKING MOISTURE IN AIR** having little or no rain, or low humidity ○ *a dry climate* 3. **LACKING USUAL MOISTURE** lacking natural oiliness or moistness ○ *dry skin* 4. **DRAINED OF WATER** having no water because it has evaporated, drained away, or been depleted ○ *a dry riverbed* 5. **LACKING CUSTOMARY MOISTURE** not producing or accompanied by associated moisture in the form of phlegm, tears, or vomit ○ *a dry cough* 6. **NOT REQUIRING LIQUID FOR USE** made to be used without water ○ *dry shampoo* 7. **WITHOUT FLESH ATTACHED** having no meat attached ○ *dry bones* 8. **THIRSTY** thirsty and dehydrated 9. BEVERAGES **LACKING SWEETNESS** describes wines that are not sweet because the sugar has been broken down during fermentation 10. **SERVED WITHOUT FAT OR LIQUID** served without moist accompaniments such as butter or jam ○ *dry toast* 11. **STALE AND FLAVOURLESS** lacking appetizing moistness, e.g. because of being stale or overcooked 12. **SHREWDLY AMUSING** witty in a shrewd, subtle, or sarcastic way 13. **BORING AND ACADEMIC** dense and academic in style 14. **MATTER-OF-FACT** plain and without unnecessary ornamentation ○ *a dry, matter-of-fact account of the incident* 15. **NOT ALLOWING ALCOHOL SALES** not allowing legal sale of alcoholic beverages 16. ZOOL **NO LONGER GIVING MILK** describes a female animal that no longer produces milk 17. **CONTAINING NO MOISTURE** from which the liquid or moisture has been removed ○ *dry weight* 18. ELECTRONICS **POORLY SOLDERED** describes a solder joint on a circuit board that has not completely adhered to the surface and therefore will not conduct electricity ■ *v* (**dries, drying, dried**) 1. *vti* **MAKE SOMETHING DRY** to make something dry, or become dry ○ *It's your turn to dry the dishes.* 2. *vt* FOOD INDUST **PRESERVE FOOD BY EXTRACTING MOISTURE** to preserve food, especially fruit, vegetables, and meat, by extracting most of the moisture from it 3. *vi* **FORGET LINES IN PERFORMANCE** to forget lines during a performance or rehearsal ■ *n* (*plural* **drys** or **dries**) 1. **DRY PLACE** a place that is dry or sheltered from the rain (*informal*) ○ *stay in the dry* 2. *also* **Dry** *Aus* **N AUSTRALIAN DRY SEASON** in northern Australia, the dry season lasting from May to November (*informal*) 3. **RIGHT-WING POLITICIAN** a politician who is a member of the right wing of the British Conservative Party

(*informal dated*) [Old English *drȳge* < Germanic] —**dryable** *adj*—**dryness** *n*

SYNONYMS *dry, dehydrated, desiccated, arid, parched, sere*

CORE MEANING: lacking moisture

dry not wet, or having little or no moisture ○ *prolonged periods of hot, dry weather* ○ *Use an exfoliating cream to remove patches of dry skin.* **dehydrated** lacking sufficient water, or having had water removed ○ *They were seriously dehydrated after five days without food or water.* ○ *instant foods such as dehydrated soups and canned meat* **desiccated** (used of products, especially food) free from moisture, or preserved by drying ○ *a biscuit covered in desiccated coconut* **arid** used of climate or a region that has a very low rainfall ○ *a plant that grows in hot, arid climates* ○ *the arid Red Sea coast* **parched** completely lacking in moisture because of hot conditions or lack of rainfall ○ *the recent floods in this usually parched region* **sere** (*literary*) dry and withered ○ *the sere grasses about the old well*

dry off *vti* to become drier, or make something drier
dry out *vti* 1. to become completely dry, or make something completely dry ○ *It will take a while for the plaster to dry out.* 2. to purge alcohol or other drugs from the body, or put somebody through such a process (*informal*)
dry up *v* 1. *vti* LOSE OR REMOVE MOISTURE to lose water or moisture over a period, or make a river or pool lose its water over a period ○ *The river dried up centuries ago.* 2. *vi* STOP BEING AVAILABLE to stop being available as a resource ○ *The project ended because our sources of funding dried up.* 3. *vt* DRY DISHES to dry plates, dishes, pans, and cutlery with a cloth after they have been washed 4. *vi* STOP TALKING to stop talking, or forget lines during a performance or rehearsal (*informal; often used as a command*) ○ *Oh, just dry up, will you? I'm trying to think!* 5. *vi* RUN OUT OF IDEAS to be unable to perform as usual or as expected ○ *His ideas have dried up.*

dryad /drī́ ad, -əd/ (*plural* **-ads** or **-ades** /-ə deez/) *n* in Greek mythology, a spiritual being believed to live in trees and forests [14C. Via Latin < Greek *Druad-* < *drus* 'tree'] —**dryadic** /drī áddik/ *adj*

dry battery *n* an electric battery that has more than one dry cell

dry-bone ore *n* a type of smithsonite that has many holes, found near the surface of the Earth's crust

dry cell *n* a current-generating electric cell that cannot be regenerated and contains an electrolyte in the form of a paste or within a porous material to keep it from spilling

dry-clean *vt* to clean clothes or fabrics with a chemical solvent

dry-cleaner's (*plural same*) *n* a shop that cleans clothes and household fabrics using a chemical solvent

dry-cleaning *n* 1. the professional cleaning of clothes and fabrics using a chemical solvent 2. clothes and other fabrics that require dry-cleaning or have just been dry-cleaned

dry cough *n* a cough that does not produce phlegm

Dryden /drī́d'n/, **John** (1631–1700) English poet, dramatist, and critic. His works include the play *Marriage à la Mode* (1672) and the verse satire *Absalom and Achitophel* (1681). He was made poet laureate by Charles II (1668), but having become a Catholic in 1685, was deprived of the office on the accession of William of Orange.

'Happy the Man, and happy he alone, / He who can call today his own: / He who, secure within, can say, / Tomorrow do thy worst, for I have liv'd for today.'
[John Dryden, *Translation of Horace's Odes*; 1685]

'Reason to rule, but mercy to forgive: / The first is law, the last prerogative.'
[John Dryden, *The Hind and the Panther*; 1687]

dry distillation *n* CHEM same as **destructive distillation**

dry dock *n* an enclosed dock from which the water can be removed so that construction or repairs can be carried out below the water line of a boat or ship —**dry-dock** *vti*

dryer[1] /drī́ ər/, **drier** *n* 1. a machine or device for drying things 2. a substance added to paint or ink to speed up the drying process

dryer[2] /drī́ ər/ comparative of **dry**

dryest /drī́ist/ superlative of **dry**

dry-eyed *adj* unable or unwilling to shed tears ○ *He remained dry-eyed throughout the trial.*

dry farming *n* a method of growing crops in dry areas by selecting plants that are drought-resistant and using mulch to retain moisture in the soil, so making irrigation unnecessary —**dry farmer** *n*

dry fly *n* an artificial lure used in fly-fishing that remains on the surface of the water instead of sinking

dry ginger *n* BEVERAGES same as **ginger ale**

dry goods *npl* N Am same as **drapery** (sense 3)

dry hole *n* an oil well that has been drilled but that produces no oil, or not enough to make it economically profitable

dry ice *n* cold solid carbon dioxide at the temperature of −78.5°C/−110°F. Use: refrigeration, production of an artificial fog effect.

drying oil *n* an organic oil, e.g. linseed or cottonseed oil, used as a base in paints and varnishes because it reduces drying time. Such oils form a tough thin film when exposed to air.

dry kiln *n* a large oven used to season cut timber

dry land *n* the land as distinct from the sea or a body of water

dryland /drī́ land/ *n* areas prone to severe drought, e.g. deserts and savannas (*often used in the plural*) —**dryland** *adj*

dryly *adv* another spelling of **drily**

dry martini *n* a cocktail that contains a little dry vermouth mixed with gin or vodka

dry measure *n* a system of units used to measure dry products such as grains and fruits by volume, or a unit in such a system

dry nurse *n* a nurse employed to look after somebody's young baby but not to breast-feed it (*archaic*) —**dry-nurse** *vt*

dryopithecine /drī́ ō píthə seen/ (*plural* **-cines** or *same*) *n* an extinct ape of the Miocene and Pliocene epochs, believed by some scientists to be the ancestor of modern apes and humans. Genus: *Dryopithecus*. [Mid-20C. < modern Latin *Dryopithecus* < Greek *drus* 'tree' + *pithēkos* 'ape']

dry point *n* 1. METHOD OF ENGRAVING a technique of engraving in intaglio on a metal, usually copper, plate that produces a feathery effect in the lines of the print 2. STEEL NEEDLE a hard steel needle used to engrave a metal plate 3. PRINT MADE BY DRY POINT an engraving or print made by using dry point

dry riser *n* a waterless pipe that runs vertically, with connections on different levels of a building to which a firefighter's hose can be attached in case of fire

dry-roasted *adj* describes shelled nuts that have been roasted without any oil

dry rot *n* 1. CRUMBLING DECAY IN WOOD dry crumbling decay in wood caused by various fungi 2. PLANT DISEASE a disease caused by various fungi that invade plant stems, bulbs, and fruits, causing them to dry out and decay 3. DESTRUCTIVE FUNGUS a fungus that causes dry rot. Genus: *Merulius*.

dry run *n* a rehearsal of a planned action or activity (*informal*) ○ *Let's have a dry run to make sure it's going to work.*

dry-salt *vt* to use salt to dry and preserve food

dry-salter *n* a dealer in chemical products such as dyes, and also salted, dried, and tinned foods (*archaic*) —**dry-saltery** *n*

Drysdale /drīz dayl/ (*plural* **-dales** or *same*) *n* NZ a sheep belonging to a breed raised commercially in New Zealand for its fleece, which is used in carpeting

Drysdale /drīz dayl/, **Sir Russell** (1912–81) British-born Australian landscape painter. Many of his best-

known works portray the harshness of life in rural Australia. Full name **Drysdale, Sir George Russell**

dry socket *n* a painful condition caused when the blood left by an extracted tooth fails to clot or the clot is dislodged

dry-stone *adj* built with pieces of stone that are fitted together without mortar ○ *a dry-stone wall*

drywall /drī́ wawl/, **dry wall** *n* N Am 1. CONSTR same as **plasterboard** 2. a wall constructed with sheets of plasterboard 3. a wall constructed of stone or masonry without mortar —**dry-wall** *vt*

ds, **DS** *abbr* MUSIC dal segno

d.s. *abbr* 1. BUSINESS days after sight 2. document signed

DSc *abbr* Doctor of Science

DSC *abbr* NAVY Distinguished Service Cross

DSL *n* high-speed telephone line supplying telephony, television, and Internet access. Full form **digital subscriber line**

DSM *abbr* MIL Distinguished Service Medal

DSO *abbr* MIL Distinguished Service Order

dsp *abbr* died without issue

DSS *abbr* 1. Director of Social Services 2. HIST Department of Social Security

DST *abbr* daylight-saving time

DT *abbr* daylight time

DTI *abbr* GOV Department of Trade and Industry

DTP *abbr* COMPUT desktop publishing

DTs *npl* MED same as **delirium tremens** (*informal*)

DTV *abbr* BROADCAST digital television

du /doo/, **Du** see also under surname

DU *abbr* MIL, PHYS depleted uranium

dual /dyoo̅ əl/ *adj* 1. HAVING TWO SIMILAR ELEMENTS having two parts, functions, aspects, or items of a similar kind ○ *dual citizenship* 2. HAVING TWO DISTINCT ASPECTS made up of two distinct, often opposite, parts ○ *serve a dual purpose* 3. SPECIFYING TWO in various languages, used to describe a grammatical number category, in addition to singular and plural, that specifies two people or things ■ *n* GRAM DUAL NUMBER OR INFLECTED FORM dual number, or, in various languages, the inflected form of a noun, pronoun, adjective, or verb that refers to dual number [Early 17C. < Latin *dualis* < *duo* 'two'] —**dually** *adv*

SPELLCHECK dual or **duel**? Do not confuse the spelling of *dual* and *duel*, which sound similar. *Dual* is chiefly used as an adjective, meaning 'having two elements or aspects' or 'double', as in *dual citizenship*, *a dual-purpose device*, *a dual carriageway*. *Duel* is chiefly used as a noun, denoting a fight between two people: *He took offence at this remark and challenged the man to a duel.*

Duala[1] /doo̅ áalə, doo̅ aa laa/ (*plural same* or **-las**) *n* 1. a member of an African people who live in Cameroon 2. the language of the Duala people, belonging to the Bantu group of Niger-Congo languages —**Duala** *adj*

Duala[2] another spelling of **Douala**

dual carriageway *n* a road with two or more lanes of traffic in each direction divided by a central reservation or barrier. Aus term **divided road**. N Am term **divided highway**

dual economy *n* an economy in which different sectors are growing at different rates. Manufacturing and service industries or rural and urban areas may show significant differences in economic performance.

dual in-line package *n* a rectangular housing for components such as integrated circuits or toggle switches that has a row of pins along the base of two opposite sides that can be plugged or soldered into a circuit board

dualism /dyoo̅ əlizəm/ *n* 1. STATE OF HAVING TWO PARTS a state in which something has two distinct parts or aspects, which are often opposites 2. THEORY OF TWO OPPOSING CONCEPTS a philosophical theory based on the idea of opposing concepts, especially the theory that human beings are made up of two independent constituents, the body and the mind or soul 3. DOCTRINE OF OPPOSING PRINCIPLES the religious doctrine

that two opposed and antagonistic forces of good and evil determine the course of events **4.** RELIG **DUAL NATURE OF PEOPLE** the religious idea that people are inherently dual in nature, both spiritual and physical —**dualist** *n* —**dualistic** /dyoo ə lístik/ *adj* —**dualistically** *adv*

duality /dyoo álləti/ (*plural* **-ties**) *n* **1. SOMETHING CONSISTING OF TWO PARTS** a situation or nature that has two states or parts that are complementary or opposed to each other **2. THEORY OF MATTER** in microphysics, the theory that both wave and particle theory account for the behaviour of matter and energy under different conditions **3. MATHEMATICAL SYMMETRY OF OBJECTS OR OPERATIONS** a mathematical symmetry in which some objects or operations can be interchanged without invalidating a relationship, e.g. the interchange of points and lines in a plane in projective geometry

dual-purpose *adj* capable of performing two functions satisfactorily ○ *a dual-purpose cleaner*

dual signature *n* the linking of two discrete parts of a single message allowing a cardholder to communicate with a merchant and a payment gateway simultaneously (*used in e-commerce*)

dual trading *n* the entering by somebody into a securities transaction both on a personal basis and for a customer, giving rise to a conflict of interest

Duarte /dwaár tay/, **José Napoleón** (1925–90) Salvadorean politician. He was twice president of El Salvador (1980–82, 1984–89).

dub[1] /dub/ *vt* (**dubs, dubbing, dubbed**) **1. GIVE SOMEBODY OR SOMETHING NICKNAME** to give a descriptive nickname to somebody or something ○ *The press dubbed him the King of Chess.* **2.** POL **CONFER KNIGHTHOOD ON SOMEBODY** to give somebody a knighthood by tapping the person on the shoulder with a sword as part of a formal ceremony **3.** INDUST **MAKE SOMETHING SMOOTH OR EVEN** to dress a material such as leather or timber to make it smooth or even **4. DECORATE ARTIFICIAL FLY** to add material such as hair or fur to an artificial fly, to give body and a natural look ■ *n* **SOUND OF DRUM** the sound a drum makes [Pre-12C. < Anglo-Norman *duber*, variant of Old French *adober* 'equip with armour'] —**dubber** *n*

dub[2] /dub/ *vt* (**dubs, dubbing, dubbed**) **1. ADD NEW SOUNDTRACK** to add a new soundtrack to a film or television show with the dialogue in a different language but synchronized as closely as possible with the actors' lips ○ *The film was dubbed into Italian.* **2. ADD SOUNDS TO FILM** to add sounds that have been recorded separately to a film soundtrack **3. COPY SOMETHING ONTO NEW MEDIUM** to copy something already recorded onto a different recording medium **4. MAKE COPY** to make a copy of a record or tape ■ *n* **1. SOMETHING ADDED BY DUBBING** new sounds added by dubbing **2. COPY OF RECORDING** a copy made of a tape or recording **3. STYLE OF MUSIC** a style of popular music, originating in reggae in the 1970s, involving remixing records to bring some instruments into the foreground and causing others to echo [Early 20C. Shortening of DOUBLE] —**dubber** *n*

dub[3] /dub/ *n N England, Scotland* a puddle or small pool of water on the ground, especially in the road [15C. Origin ?]

Dubai /doo bī/, **Dubayy** city in the northeastern United Arab Emirates, and the capital city of Dubai state. Population: 674,100 (1995).

Du Barry /doo bárri, dyoo-/, **Marie Jeanne Bécu, Comtesse** (1743?–93) French courtier and mistress of Louis XV. A patron of the arts, she is reputed to have exercised considerable influence over Louis XV until his death in 1774. After the outbreak of the French Revolution (1792), she was tried and guillotined on charges of conspiracy.

Dubayy another spelling of **Dubai**

dubbin /dúbbin/ *n* a mixture of oil and tallow rubbed into leather to soften it and make it waterproof [Early 19C. Alteration of *dubbing*, present participle of DUB[1]]

dubbing /dúbbing/ *n* **1. PROCESS OF ADDING NEW SOUNDTRACK** the process of providing a new soundtrack for a film or television show with the dialogue in a different language but synchronized as closely as possible with the actors' lips **2. SOUNDTRACK** a soundtrack recorded for a film or television show after the photography is finished **3. FINAL SOUNDTRACK** a final mix of all the soundtracks for a film

dubbo /dúbbō/ *adj Aus* an offensive term meaning unintelligent (*slang insult*) [Origin ?] —**dubbo** *n*

Dubbo /dúbbō/ town in central New South Wales, Australia, located on the River Macquarie at the heart of an agricultural region. Population: 38,902 (2002 estimate).

Dubček /dóop chek, dóob-/, **Alexander** (1921–92) Czech politician. His liberal reforms as leader of the Communist party led to Soviet invasion in 1968. Shortly afterwards, he was ousted from power. He re-emerged as a popular figure in 1989.

> 'Socialism with a human face must function again for a new generation. We have lived in the darkness for long enough.'
> [Alexander Dubček, *Speech, Wenceslas Square, Prague*; 4 November 1989]

dubiety /dyoo bī əti/ (*plural* **-ties**) *n* (*formal*) **1.** a feeling of uncertainty about something **2.** something about which you are unsure [Mid-18C. < late Latin *dubietas* < Latin *dubius* 'doubtful']

dubious /dyóobi əss/ *adj* **1. UNSURE ABOUT OUTCOME** not sure about an outcome or conclusion ○ *I was a little dubious about whether or not to trust him.* **2. POSSIBLY DISHONEST OR IMMORAL** likely to be dishonest, untrustworthy, or morally worrying in some way ○ *It's a dubious proposition.* **3. OF UNCERTAIN QUALITY** of uncertain quality, intention, or appropriateness ○ *The thesis is based on several dubious assumptions.* [Mid-16C. < Latin *dubius* 'doubtful'] —**dubiously** *adv* —**dubiousness** *n*

SYNONYMS See ***doubtful***.

dubitable /dyóobitəb'l/ *adj* causing or leading to doubt or uncertainty (*formal*) [Early 17C. < Latin *dubitabilis* < *dubitare* 'be uncertain'] —**dubitably** *adv*

Dublin /dúbblin/ **1.** city and capital of the Republic of Ireland. It is situated on the River Liffey in east-central Ireland, at the head of Dublin Bay on the Irish Sea. Population: 481,854 (2002). Irish name **Baile Átha Cliath 2.** coastal county in Leinster Province in the Republic of Ireland. Population: 1,058,264 (2002). Area: 922 sq. km/356 sq. mi. —**Dubliner** *n*

Dublin Bay prawn *n* a large prawn that is usually used to make scampi

dubnium /dúbni əm/ *n* an extremely rare, unstable element. Source: high-energy bombardment of californium. Symbol **Db**. See table at **element**

Du Bois /doo bóyss/, **W. E. B.** (1868–1963) US historian, sociologist, and civil rights leader. He conducted the first research on the experience of African Americans in the United States and fought for racial equality, becoming the most influential African American intellectual of his time. Full name **Du Bois, William Edward Burghardt**

> 'I believe that all men, black and brown and white, are brothers, varying through time and opportunity, in form and gift and feature, but differing in no essential particular, and alike in soul and the possibility of infinite development.'
> [W. E. B. Du Bois, 'Credo', *Darkwater: Voices from Within the Veil*; 1920]

dub poetry *n* **1.** performance poetry using the rhythms and speech styles of Caribbean English **2.** poetry spoken to a background of dub music (*used in Black English*) [< disc jockeys dubbing their own words onto records]

Dubrovnik /doo bróvnik/ city, port, and holiday resort on the Dalmatian coast in southeastern Croatia. It suffered damage during ethnic conflict in the 1990s. Population: 49,728 (1991).

Dubuffet /dyoo boo fay/, **Jean** (1901–85) French painter and sculptor. He was an avant-garde artist who rejected traditional techniques, often working with found objects and materials such as sand and plaster. Full name **Dubuffet, Jean Philippe Arthur**

ducal /dyóok'l/ *adj* belonging to, relating to, or like a duke or dukedom ○ *a ducal palace* [15C. < French < *duc* (see DUKE)] —**ducally** *adv*

ducat /dúkət/ *n* a gold or silver coin formerly used in some European countries, e.g. Italy and the Netherlands ■ **ducats** *npl* money or cash (*informal dated*) [14C. Via French < medieval Latin *ducatus* 'duchy' (see DUCHY); because the word appeared on early coins]

Duccio di Buoninsegna /dúchi ō di bwónnin sénnyə/ (1260–1320) Italian painter. A precursor of the Renaissance style, he endowed his subjects with humanity and emotion, most notably in his only signed work, the *Maestà* altarpiece (1308–11).

duce /dóo chay, dóochi/ *n* an Italian term for 'leader'. The Italian Fascist leader Mussolini was called 'Il Duce'. [Early 20C. Via Italian < Latin *dux* 'leader']

Duchamp /dyoo shaaN/, **Marcel** (1887–1968) French-born US artist. He displayed everyday objects as works of art, and helped to introduce Cubism to the United States. He became a citizen of the United States in 1955, and later his work became an inspiration for the pop art movement.

> 'Art may be bad, good or indifferent, but, whatever adjective is used, we must call it art, and bad art is still art in the same way as a bad emotion is still an emotion.'
> [Marcel Duchamp, 'The Creative Act', *Art News*; Summer 1957]

Duchenne muscular dystrophy /doo shén-/, **Duchenne's muscular dystrophy** /doo shénz-/, **Duchenne dystrophy, Duchenne's dystrophy** *n* a form of muscular dystrophy that attacks the muscles of the upper respiratory and pelvic areas, usually affecting boys and causing death before maturity [Late 19C. After G. B. A. *Duchenne* (1806–75), French neurologist]

duchess /dúchəss/ *n* **1. HIGH-RANKING NOBLEWOMAN** a noblewoman of high rank. In the British Isles, this is the highest hereditary title of nobility. **2. WIFE OR WIDOW OF DUKE** the wife or widow of a duke ■ *vt* (**-esses, -essing, -essed**) *Aus* **FLATTER SOMEBODY** to treat somebody like royalty, especially in an obsequious or fawning manner (*dated informal*) [14C. Via Old French *duchesse* < medieval Latin *ducissa*, feminine form of *dux* 'leader']

duchesse potatoes /dyoo shéss-, duch éss-/ *npl* a mixture of mashed potatoes, egg, and butter that is piped into the shape of a pyramid or nest and baked [< French, 'duchess']

duchesse satin /dyoo shéss-/ *n* a firm heavy satin with a glossy finish. Use: formal gowns.

duchy /dúchi/ (*plural* **-ies**) *n* the territory over which a duke or duchess has jurisdiction [14C. Via Old French *duche* < medieval Latin *ducatus* < Latin *duc-*, stem of *dux* 'leader']

duck[1] /duk/ *n* **1.** (*plural* **ducks** or *same*) **COMMON WATER BIRD** a common water bird with webbed feet, short legs, and a broad flat beak. It is found all over the world, with the exception of Antarctica. Family: Anatidae. **2. FEMALE DUCK** a female duck **3. DUCK AS FOOD** the flesh of a duck when eaten as a food **4.** *also* **ducks** *regional* **DEAR** used when addressing somebody in a friendly way ○ *Can I help you, duck?* **5. ODD PERSON** somebody regarded as mildly unconventional [Old English *dūce*, origin ?] ◇ **get** *or* **have your ducks all in a row** to have organized your life or a specific task so that it runs smoothly ◇ **take to something like a duck to water** to have a natural talent for something (*informal*)

duck[2] /duk/ *v* (**ducks, ducking, ducked**) **1.** *vti* **BEND QUICKLY** to bend or move the head down quickly, especially to avoid being hit by something **2.** *vi* **MOVE QUICKLY** to move somewhere very quickly, often to avoid being seen ○ *I ducked behind a desk and kept as still as possible.* **3.** *vti* **PLUNGE UNDER WATER** to push somebody under water, or move quickly so as to go below the surface of water **4.** *vt* **AVOID SOMETHING** to avoid dealing with something that ought to be dealt with ○ *The candidate ducked all the questions about her past.* **5.** *vi* CARDS **DELIBERATELY LOSE TRICK** to play a card lower than an opponent's on purpose in order to lose a trick ■ *n* **QUICK DOWNWARD MOVEMENT** a movement downwards with the head, especially to avoid being hit by something [13C. Probably < assumed Old English *dūcan* < W Germanic, 'dive, dip'] —**ducker** *n* ◇ **duck and run** to avoid meeting somebody face to face

duck out *vi* to avoid or dodge doing something (*informal*) ○ *She's trying to duck out of paying her part of the bill.*

duck[3] /duk/ *n* strong, fairly stiff, closely-woven cotton or canvas cloth. Use: protective clothing, furnishings. ■ **ducks** *npl* a pair of trousers, usually

white, or like those worn by sailors [Mid-17C. < Dutch *doek* 'linen']

duck[4] /duk/ *n* a score of zero by a batsman or batswoman [Shortening of *duck's egg* 'zero'] ◇ **break your duck** have your first success or victory after several failures

duck-billed platypus

duck-billed platypus, **duckbill** /dúk bil/ *n* an egg-laying water mammal with a snout shaped like a duck's bill and webbed feet. Native to: Australia. Latin name: *Ornithorynchus anatinus*.

duckboard /dúk bawrd/ *n* a temporary walkway made of wooden boards laid over a wet or muddy area to form a raised path

duck-egg blue *n* a pale greenish-blue colour —**duck-egg blue** *adj*

duckie *n*, *adj* another spelling of **ducky** (*dated informal*)

ducking and diving /dúking-/ *n* 1. erratic moving or running, e.g. in order to avoid being shot or hit 2. in an inefficient business, actions taken in a way that will avert immediate commercial difficulties

ducking stool /dúking-/ *n* formerly, in Europe and New England, a chair or stool in which an offender was tied and then immersed in water as a punishment

duckling /dúkling/ *n* a duck that has not reached maturity

ducks *n* same as **duck**[1] (sense 4)

ducks and drakes *n* a game in which flat stones are bounced across water by throwing them almost parallel to its surface (*takes a singular verb*) [Because suggestive of a waterfowl's movements]

duck's arse *n* an offensive term for a man's hairstyle, popular in the 1950s, in which the hair is slicked back and drawn into a point at the back of the neck to look like a duck's tail

duck soup *n N Am* something that is accomplished easily (*slang*)

duckweed /dúk weed/ *n* a free-floating water plant with small rounded leaves and without a stem that is found on still temperate waters. Genus: *Lemna*.

ducky /dúki/, **duckie** (*dated informal*) *n* (*plural* -**ies**) DARLING used as an affectionate way of addressing somebody ■ *adv US* SATISFACTORY very good or excellent ○ *Everything's just ducky at the moment.* ■ *adj US* CHARMING charmingly pretty ○ *a ducky little cottage*

duco /dyóokō/ *n Aus* the paintwork on a motor vehicle [< a trade name]

duct /dukt/ *n* 1. CHANNEL a tube, pipe, or channel through which something can flow or be carried, e.g. in air-conditioning equipment 2. TUBE IN BODY ORGAN a narrow tubular exit passageway in a gland or bladder through which fluid passes 3. TUBE FOR CABLES a tube or channel containing electrical cables ■ *vt* (**ducts**, **ducting**, **ducted**) 1. FIT SOMETHING WITH DUCTS to supply or equip something such as a building with a duct or a system of ducts 2. ROUTE SOMETHING THROUGH CHANNEL to make a fluid or gas pass through a tube, pipe, or channel ○ *Exhaust fumes are ducted out of the workshop.* [Mid-17C. < Latin *ductus* < *ducere* 'to lead'] —**ductal** *adj* —**ductless** *adj*

ORIGIN The Latin word *ducere* 'to lead', from which **duct** is derived, is also the source of English *aqueduct*, *conduct*, *deduce*, *deduct*, *douche*, *duke*, *educate*, *introduce*, *produce*, *reduce*, *seduce*, and *subdue*.

ductile /dúk tīl/ *adj* 1. MALLEABLE ENOUGH TO BE WORKED able to be drawn out into wire or hammered into very thin sheets ○ *ductile metal* 2. READILY SHAPED able to be moulded or shaped without breaking 3. READILY INFLUENCED easily persuaded or influenced [14C. Directly or via French < Latin *ductilis* 'that may be led' < *ducere* 'to lead'] —**ductility** /duk tílləti/ *n*

SYNONYMS See *pliable*.

ducting /dúkting/ *n* 1. a duct or system of ducts 2. materials, e.g. pipes and tubing, that can be used as ducts

ductless gland *n* ANAT same as **endocrine gland**

ductwork /dúkt wurk/ *n* a system of ducts that has been constructed, or its design

dud /dud/ *n* 1. FAILURE AT SOMETHING somebody or something considered ineffective or a failure (*informal*) 2. SHELL THAT DOES NOT EXPLODE a munition that fails to fire or explode ■ *adj* (**dudder, duddest**) USELESS useless for the intended purpose (*informal*) ○ *a dud cheque* [Early 19C. Origin ?]

dude /dyood, dood/ *n N Am* (*slang*) 1. MAN a man or boy ○ *He's one cool dude.* ○ *Hey, dude, what's up?* 2. CITY DWELLER ON RANCH HOLIDAY an American who lives in a city and takes holidays on a dude ranch in the West 3. FLASHILY DRESSED MAN a man who wears flashy, highly stylish clothes [Late 19C. Origin ?]

dudeen /doo deén/ *n* a clay tobacco pipe with a short stem [Mid-19C. < Irish *dúidín* 'small pipe' < *dúd* 'pipe']

dude ranch *n N Am* a holiday resort offering outdoor activities that is or resembles a typical ranch of the western United States —**dude rancher** *n*

dudgeon /dújjən/ *n* a fit of anger and irritation [Late 16C. Origin ?] ◇ **in high dudgeon** in a very angry or irritated mood

Dudley /dúddli/ industrial town near Birmingham in the West Midlands, England. Population: 305,155 (2001).

Dudley, Robert ♦ **Leicester, Robert Dudley**

duds /duds/ *npl* articles of clothing and accessories (*informal*) [15C. Origin ?]

due /dyoo/ *adj* 1. EXPECTED TO ARRIVE expected to arrive imminently ○ *The baby is due in three weeks.* 2. READY awaiting an event, as part of a normal chain or progression of other events ○ *due for a long-awaited promotion* 3. CAUSED BY SOMEBODY OR SOMETHING caused by or attributable to somebody or something ○ *The delay was due to bad weather.* 4. PAYABLE payable at once and on demand or at a stipulated time ○ *Payment is due in 30 days.* 5. PROPER AND APPROPRIATE meeting all the necessary requirements and thus proper and appropriate to the situation ○ *after due consideration* 6. OWED owed as a debt because of a right or an obligation ○ *Our deep gratitude is due to all those who have helped over the last few months.* ■ *n* SOMEBODY'S RIGHT something that somebody has deserved or is owed ○ *I'll give you your due – you were absolutely right.* ■ **dues** *npl* MEMBERSHIP FEES fees for membership of an organization or use of a facility ■ *adv* DIRECTLY AND EXACTLY in a direct exact way or course ○ *due west* [13C. Via Old French *deu* 'owed' < Latin *debitus* < *debere* 'owe']

SPELLCHECK See *dew*.

USAGE Some people object to the use of the phrase *due to* in sentences like these: *The concert has been cancelled due to circumstances beyond our control* and *The flight was delayed due to bad weather.* Their objection is based on the fact that *due* is an adjective and should be used with a noun, as in *The delay was due to bad weather*, where *due* modifies *delay*. You can avoid using *due to* with a verb by replacing it with *owing to* or *because of*: *The concert has been cancelled owing to circumstances beyond our control. The match was postponed because of bad weather.*

due date *n* the date that something such as the payment of a bill or the birth of a baby is expected to occur

due diligence *n* 1. the degree of care that a prudent person would exercise, which is a legally relevant standard for establishing liability 2. the disclosure to potential buyers of all relevant information that applies to a security issue

duel /dyóo əl/ *n* 1. a prearranged combat, especially

in former times, between two people armed with lethal weapons, usually to settle a disagreement over a matter of honour 2. a struggle or conflict between two people or groups [15C. < medieval Latin *duellum* 'combat between two people' < (influenced by Latin *duo* 'two') Latin *duellum*, archaic form of *bellum* 'war'] —**duel** *vi* —**dueller** *n* —**duellist** *n*

SPELLCHECK See *dual*.

duelling pistol /dyóo əling-/ *n* a pistol specifically designed for fighting a duel, usually more finely manufactured than a normal pistol and often made in sets of two

~~**duely**~~ incorrect spelling of **duly**

duenna /dyoo énnə/ *n* a woman acting as a chaperone or governess to a younger woman, especially in Spain and Portugal in former times [Mid-17C. Via Spanish, 'married lady' < Latin *domina* 'lady']

due-on-sale clause *n* a condition in a mortgage agreement stating that the outstanding amount will be repaid if the related property is sold, the borrower dies, or the property is refinanced

due process of law *n* legal procedures carried out in accordance with established rules and principles

Duero /dwáirō/ Spanish name for **Douro**

duet /dyoo ét/ *n* 1. an instrumental or vocal composition written for two performers of equal importance 2. a pair of people, animals, or things [Mid-18C. < Italian *duetto*, literally 'little duo' or German *Duett* < Latin *duo* 'two'] —**duettist** *n*

duff[1] /duf/ *adj* useless, broken, or of very low quality (*informal*) ■ *vt* (**duffs, duffing, duffed**) to play a bad shot in golf by hitting the ground behind the ball (*informal*) ■ *n Scotland, N Am* same as **litter** *n* (sense 6) [Mid-19C. Origin ?]

duff[2] /duf/ (**duffs, duffing, duffed**) [Mid-20C. Origin ?] **duff up** *vt* to hit or kick somebody repeatedly so as to cause injury (*slang*)

duff[3] /duf/ *n* a heavy pudding that is usually made with suet and dried fruit and is steamed or boiled in a cloth ○ *plum duff* [Mid-19C. Variant of DOUGH]

duff[4] /duf/ *n* an offensive term for the buttocks (*slang*) [Late 19C. Origin ?] ◇ **up the duff** an offensive term meaning pregnant

Duff /duf/, **Alan** (*b.* 1950) New Zealand writer. He wrote *Once Were Warriors* (1990).

duffel /dúff'l/, **duffle** *n* 1. woollen material with a nap on both sides 2. *US* gear, including clothing and equipment, used by campers and hikers [Late 17C. < Dutch, after *Duffel*, Belgium]

duffel bag *n* a cylindrical bag for personal belongings that is fastened with a drawstring

duffel coat

duffel coat *n* a heavy medium-length coat with a hood and toggles for fastening it that is made from duffel

duffer /dúffər/ *n* 1. UNINTELLIGENT PERSON somebody regarded as a slow learner or not competent at something (*informal dated insult*) 2. SOMETHING WORTHLESS something worthless or useless (*dated informal*) 3. *regional* PEDLAR a pedlar of goods, especially cheap or worthless merchandise (*archaic*) [Mid-18C. Origin ?]

duffle *n* TEXTILES, CAMPING another spelling of **duffel**

Dufy /dyóofi/, **Raoul** (1877–53) French painter, illustrator, and designer. Known for his paintings of the French Riviera in a popularized Fauvist style, he also designed textiles and pottery.

dug[1] /dug/ past participle, past tense of **dig**

dug[2] /dug/ *n* **1.** an udder, teat, nipple, or breast of a female mammal **2.** the breast of a human being, especially when regarded with distaste (*literary*) [Mid-16C. Origin ?]

Duggan /dúggən/, **Maurice** (1922–74) New Zealand writer. He was noted for his short stories, and his *Collected Short Stories* was published in 1981.

dugong

dugong /doʻo gong/ *n* a large plant-eating sea mammal, related to the manatee. It has a two-lobed tail, a cleft upper lip, forelimbs resembling flippers, and tusks in the male. Native to: shallow tropical coastal waters. Latin name: *Dugong dugon*. [Early 19C. < Malay *duyung*]

dugout /dúg owt/ *n* **1.** SHELTER ON SPORTS PITCH either of two shelters beside a sports field, especially a soccer pitch, for team officials such as the manager and trainer and team members who are not on the field **2.** CANOE MADE FROM HOLLOWED LOG a canoe or boat hollowed out from a log or tree trunk **3.** SOLDIERS' SHELTER a hole dug in the ground that is covered and used as a shelter, especially by soldiers

duh /də/ *interj* N Am (*slang*) **1.** said as an ironic response to being told something obvious or well known ○ *'Billy asked me to the party, I think he really likes me!' – 'Duh.'* **2.** used in humorous acknowledgment of your own stupidity ○ *'What did you do with the keys?' – 'Duh'.*

Duhamel /dyoʻo ə mel/, **Georges** (1884–1966) French writer and physician. His books include *Civilisation* (1918) and the *Salavin* cycle of novels (1920–32).

    'I hold that the novelist is the historian of the present, just as the historian is the novelist of the past.'
    [Georges Duhamel, *Chronique: La Nuit de Saint-Jean*; 1937]

Duigan /díʹgən/, **John** (*b.* 1949) British-born Australian filmmaker. He wrote and directed *The Year My Voice Broke* (1987) and *Flirting* (1991).

duiker /díʹkər/, **duyker** *n* a small African antelope with short backward-pointing horns. Genera: *Cephalophus* or *Sylvicapra*. [Late 18C. < Afrikaans, literally 'diver' < Middle Dutch *dūken* 'dive']

duikerbok /díʹkər bok/ *n* a common duiker often found close to human settlements. Native to: Africa. Latin name: *Silvicapra grimma*. [Late 18C. < Afrikaans ≺ *duiker* (see DUIKER) + *bok* 'buck']

Duisburg /dyoʻossburg/ city in North Rhine-Westphalia State, northwestern Germany, at the junction of the Rhine and Ruhr rivers. It is a major inland port. Population: 536,106 (1997).

du jour /dyoo zhoʹor/ *adj* **1.** offered or served today ○ *the soup du jour* **2.** being the latest in a series, sequence, or trend [< French, 'of the day']

Dukas /dyoo kaʹa/, **Paul Abraham** (1865–1935) French composer and teacher. His few works include the popular symphonic poem *The Sorcerer's Apprentice* (1897).

duke /dyook/ *n* **1.** HIGH-RANKING NOBLEMAN a nobleman of high rank **2.** RULER OF PRINCIPALITY a prince who rules a duchy, principality, or other small state **3.** FIST a hand or fist, especially a fist clenched for fighting or a boxer's fist raised as an indication of victory (*slang; often used in the plural*) [12C. Via Old French *duc* < Latin *dux* 'leader' < *ducere* 'to lead'] —**dukedom** *n*

duke-the-beetle *n* N Ireland somebody who avoids something unpleasant (*humorous*)

Dukhobor *n* CHR another spelling of **Doukhobor**

dukuna /doʻokoʻo naa/ *n* Carib a pudding made from cornmeal, coconut, grated sweet potatoes, raisins, and sugar, wrapped in leaves and steamed [Late 20C. < Akan]

dulahin /doo laʹa hin/ *n* a Hindu bride (*often used to address a new daughter-in-law*) [< Hindi]

dulcet /dúlssit/ *adj* pleasant to hear, especially because of being soft or soothing [15C. < Old French *doucet* 'small sweet (thing)' < *doux* 'sweet' < Latin *dulcis*]

dulciana /dúlssi áʹanə/ *n* an organ stop or pipe of the diapason type, characterized by a soft sweet tone [Late 18C. < medieval Latin < Latin *dulcis* 'sweet']

dulcimer /dúlssimər/ *n* a zither played with light-weight hammers or sometimes by plucking [15C. < French *doulcemer*]

dulfer /dúlfər/ *n* in mountaineering, a classic method of abseiling using a rope wrapped around the body [Probably < the name of a mountaineer]

dulia /dyoʻo li ə, doʻo-, dyoo líʹ ə/ *n* the veneration of saints and angels, as in the Roman Catholic and Eastern churches [Early 17C. Via medieval Latin, 'service, work done' < Greek *douleia* 'slavery']

dull /dul/ *adj* **1.** BORING arousing no interest or excitement **2.** NOT VIVID lacking vividness or brightness of hue **3.** OVERCAST not bright because of weather conditions such as thick clouds or mist **4.** NOT INTENSELY FELT not acutely or intensely felt or experienced, but prolonged ○ *a dull ache* **5.** MUFFLED muffled and not resonant ○ *a dull thud* **6.** BLUNT lacking sharpness or the ability to cut cleanly **7.** UNINTELLIGENT slow to understand or learn **8.** SLOW TO RESPOND lacking in alertness or speedy responsiveness ○ *dull reflexes* **9.** NOT BUSY without the usual or desirable number of transactions ○ *Trading was dull this morning.* **10.** LISTLESS lacking in energy or enthusiasm ○ *dull, scattered applause* ■ *vti* (**dulls, dulling, dulled**) **1.** REDUCE IN LOUDNESS to become quieter, or cause something to become quieter **2.** BECOME OR MAKE LESS ACUTE to become less acute or intensely felt, or cause something to become less acute or intensely felt ○ *Sleepiness had dulled his hunger.* **3.** BECOME OR MAKE BLUNT to become less sharp, or cause something to become less sharp **4.** BECOME OR MAKE LESS BRIGHT to become less bright or intense, or cause something to become less bright or intense **5.** BECOME OR MAKE LESS BUSY to become less brisk or busy, or cause something to become less brisk or busy [Old English *dol* 'slow-witted' < Germanic] —**dullish** *adj* —**dullness** *n* —**dully** *adv*

dullard /dúllərd/ *n* somebody regarded as unintelligent or slow to comprehend (*literary*)

Dulles /dúlliss/, **John Foster** (1888–1959) US politician and diplomat. He was US secretary of state (1953–59), and delegate to the United Nations, which he helped to form.

    'The ability to get to the verge without getting into the war is the necessary art. If you cannot master it, you inevitably get into war. If you try to run away from it, if you are scared to go to the brink, you are lost.'
    [John Foster Dulles, *Life*; 16 January 1956]

dullsville /dúlz vil/, **Dullsville** *n* (*slang*) **1.** N Am a place, thing, or activity that is boring or unexciting ○ *This town is dullsville in the evening.* **2.** the condition of being bored or uninterested ○ *I sat there in dullsville during the entire eight-hour flight.* [Mid-20C. After place names]

dulse /dulss/ (*plural* **dulses** *or* same) *n* a red alga with edible fronds that grows in the intertidal zone and near the low-water mark in northern temperate seas. Latin name: *Palmaria palmata*. [Early 17C. < Irish and Gaelic *duileasg*]

Duluth /də loʻoth/ major port and city in northeastern Minnesota, at the southern end of Lake Superior, northeast of Minneapolis. Population: 86,419 (2002 estimate).

duly /dyoʹoli/ *adv* **1.** in a proper, correct, or suitable way ○ *duly grateful* **2.** at the proper or expected time ○ *A signal was given and our coach duly departed.*

Duma /doʻomə/ *n* **1.** the parliament of modern Russia, established in 1993 after the dissolution of the former Soviet Union **2.** a Russian council or parliament during the time of tsarist rule, set up around 1905 but quickly deprived of power [Late 19C. < Russian]

Dumas[1] /dyoʻo maa/, **Alexandre** (1802–70) French novelist and dramatist. He wrote the celebrated novels *The Three Musketeers* (1844) and *The Count of Monte Cristo* (1844). Known as **Dumas père**. See Cultural note at **musketeer**

    'Business? It's quite simple: it's other people's money.'
    [Alexandre Dumas, *The Money Question*; 1857]

Dumas[2], **Alexandre** (1824–95) French playwright and novelist. He wrote *The Lady of the Camellias* (1848), on which Verdi based *La Traviata*. Known as **Dumas fils**

du Maurier /dyoo mórri ay/, **Dame Daphne** (1907–89) British novelist. Her books include *Jamaica Inn* (1936), *Rebecca* (1938), and *My Cousin Rachel* (1951).

    'Last night I dreamt I went to Manderley again.'
    [Dame Daphne du Maurier, *Rebecca*; 1938]

du Maurier, **Sir Gerald** (1873–1934) British actor-manager. He ran Wyndham's (1910–25) and the St James's (1926–34) theatres in London. Full name **du Maurier, Sir Gerald Hubert Edward Busson**

dumb /dum/ *adj* **1.** OFFENSIVE TERM an offensive term meaning unable to speak, because of deafness or congenital physical impairment **2.** TEMPORARILY SPEECHLESS temporarily unable to speak because of shock, fear, surprise, or anger **3.** DONE WITHOUT SPEECH performed or expressed without using speech **4.** INTENTIONALLY SILENT deliberately not speaking or refusing to speak **5.** LACKING HUMAN SPEECH lacking the power of speech because not human **6.** PRODUCING NO SOUND designed or adapted to produce no sound **7.** UNINTELLIGENT regarded as having or showing a low level of intelligence (*informal insult*) ■ *vt* (**dumbs, dumbing, dumbed**) MAKE SOMEBODY TEMPORARILY SPEECHLESS to make somebody temporarily unable to speak, especially by using shock or surprise (*literary*) [Old English < Indo-European, 'sensory or mental impairment'] —**dumbly** *adv* —**dumbness** *n*

dumb down *vti* to make something less intellectually challenging (*informal*) ○ *Parents and teachers were adamantly opposed to dumbing down science courses.*

Dumbarton /dum báʹart'n/ town on the River Clyde in West Dunbartonshire, Scotland. Population: 21,962 (1991).

dumb-ass *adj* US an offensive term meaning regarded as having or showing a low level of intelligence (*taboo*)

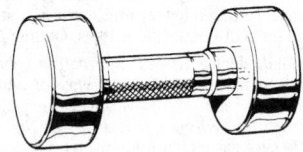

dumbbell

dumbbell /dúm bel/ *n* **1.** an exercise weight in the form of a metal bar with a metal disc or ball at each end **2.** an offensive term that deliberately insults somebody's intelligence or common sense (*slang insult*)

dumb blonde *n* an offensive term for a blonde woman stereotyped as being good-looking but unintelligent

dumb bomb *n* a conventional bomb without guidance or targeting systems

dumb cane *n* a poisonous plant that if chewed can lead to loss of speech in adults or death in children and small animals. Native to: tropical America. Latin name: *Dieffenbachia seguine*.

~~dumbell~~ incorrect spelling of **dumbbell**

dumbfound /dúm fównd/ (-founds, -founding, -founded), **dumfound** vti to make somebody temporarily speechless with astonishment [Mid-17C. < DUMB + CONFOUND]

dumb luck n US good fortune that occurs unexpectedly (informal)

dumbo /dúmbō/ (plural -bos) n an offensive term that deliberately insults somebody's intelligence or common sense (slang insult) [Mid-20C. After JUMBO]

DUMBO /dúmbō/ area of Brooklyn, New York, beneath and near the Brooklyn and Manhattan bridges. Its many warehouses were renovated into artists' lofts, homes, and shops in the late 20th century. [Acronym < down under the Manhattan Bridge overpass]

dumb show n 1. communication without words by actors using gesture or facial expressions 2. a play or part of a play presented in mime form

dumbstruck /dúm strúk/ adj made temporarily speechless by astonishment or shock

dumb terminal n a terminal without an internal microprocessor and therefore without independent processing capability that can enter, transmit, and display alphanumeric data. Typically consisting of a keyboard and display screen, it responds to simple control codes from a computer to which it is connected.

dumbwaiter /dúm wáytər/ n 1. a small lift used for moving food, crockery, and cutlery between the floors of a building 2. a movable stand for food, often with revolving shelves, that is placed near a table 3. same as **lazy Susan**

dumdum bullet /dúm dum-/, **dumdum** n a bullet with a soft core or vertical cuts made in its point that expands on impact and inflicts a severe wound. The use of dumdum bullets is contrary to the Geneva Convention. [Late 19C. After Dum Dum, Calcutta, India]

dumfound vti another spelling of **dumbfound**

Dumfries /dum freéss/ market town in Dumfries and Galloway Region, Scotland, on the River Nith. The poet Robert Burns is buried there. Population: 38,000 (1996).

Dumfries and Galloway council area in southwestern Scotland. Population: 14,805 (2001). Area: 6,369 sq. km/2,459 sq. mi.

Dumfriesshire /dum freéss shər/ former county of Scotland until 1975, now part of Dumfries and Galloway

dummel-headed /dúmm'l héddid/ adj regional an offensive term meaning regarded as unintelligent [Late 19C. < dummel 'stupid' < DUMB]

REGIONAL NOTE See **addle-headed**.

dummy /dúmmi/ n (plural -mies) 1. MANNEQUIN IN SHOP a model of a human used for making or displaying clothes 2. MODEL USED BY VENTRILOQUIST a model of a human, as used by a ventriloquist 3. IMITATION an imitation of something, especially one lacking a feature or function of the original and deceivingly substituted for it ○ A lot of the system's switches are just dummies. 4. UK, ANZ, Can SMALL OBJECT FOR BABY TO SUCK a small rubber or plastic object with a teat that a baby is given to suck for comfort. US term **pacifier** 5. FEIGNED PASS in football, rugby, or a similar game, a feigned pass or other move intended to deceive an opponent, especially a tackler 6. PERSON OR ORGANIZATION ACTING AS FRONT a person or organization serving as a front for another while pretending to be independent ○ a dummy company 7. OFFENSIVE TERM an offensive term that deliberately insults somebody's intelligence or credulity (informal insult) 8. TACITURN PERSON a silent or uncommunicative person (informal) 9. ARMS NONEXPLOSIVE FORM OF MUNITION a nonexplosive form of an explosive munition 10. PUBL MODEL PAGE a page that looks like the final product but is a computer-generated or pasted-up facsimile showing general design specifications 11. PUBL MODEL BOOK a set of model pages, often blank or containing only one group of printed pages (**signature**), that have been bound and jacketed to give an idea of the final book 12. CARDS SET OF CARDS SHOWN an exposed hand of cards in bridge, consisting of the cards held by the player partnering the player who attempts to make the final contract, or the player who exposes his or her cards ■ vt (-mies, -mying, -mied) PUBL MAKE FACSIMILE OF PAGES to make up

a dummy of a page, or make up a set of pages into a dummy ○ dummied several pages for the sales conference [Late 16C. < DUMB + -Y[1]] ◇ **spit the dummy** Aus to lose composure and throw a tantrum (informal)

dummy up vi to remain or become silent (slang)

dummy run n a practice or try-out of a process or procedure

dummy variable n a mathematical variable that can be replaced by another arbitrarily

dumortierite /dyoo máwrti ə rīt/ n a hard fibrous bright blue, bluish-green, or pink aluminosilicate mineral containing boron [Late 19C. < French, after Eugène Dumortier, French palaeontologist]

dump /dump/ vt (dumps, dumping, dumped) 1. DROP OR PUT DOWN SOMETHING CARELESSLY to deposit something on a surface in a careless and usually noisy manner ○ dumped the reports on my desk 2. THROW SOMETHING OUT AS UNWANTED to get rid of something that is unwanted, especially by taking it and leaving it somewhere 3. DISPOSE OF WASTE to dispose of waste by moving it to a prearranged site 4. TERMINATE RELATIONSHIP WITH SOMEBODY to end a romantic or sexual relationship with somebody, especially abruptly and hurtfully (informal) 5. REMOVE SOMEBODY UNDESIRABLE to remove somebody deemed undesirable or a liability from a position such as leadership in a group, especially abruptly and unceremoniously (informal disapproving) 6. LEAVE SOMEBODY TO BE CARED FOR to entrust the care of somebody, e.g. a child or a person of advanced years, to somebody else or to an institution (informal disapproving) 7. COMM OFFLOAD CHEAP MERCHANDISE ON MARKET to offer large quantities of cheaply priced merchandise for sale in a market often in order to maintain a higher price for the goods elsewhere 8. FIN GET RID OF STOCKS to sell off large quantities of stock all at once, thereby driving the price down 9. PSYCHOL CONFIDE NEGATIVE FEELINGS to talk to somebody, especially a friend or therapist, about your negative feelings in order to relieve yourself of them ○ I'm sorry to dump all this on you, but I've got no one else to talk to. 10. COMPUT TRANSFER DATA WITHOUT PROCESSING to transfer computer data from one site to another without processing it ■ n 1. WASTE DISPOSAL SITE a place where waste materials can be left 2. MIL MUNITIONS AND SUPPLY AREA a place for the temporary storage of munitions, food, water, fuel, and other supplies for distribution to troops 3. UNPLEASANT PLACE an unpleasant or dirty place (informal) ○ The hotel was a real dump. 4. COMPUT TRANSFER OF UNPROCESSED DATA a large-scale transfer of unprocessed data from one place to another 5. ACT OF THROWING SOMETHING AWAY an act of discarding something 6. OFFENSIVE TERM an offensive term for an act of evacuating the bowels (slang) [14C. Origin ?]

dump on vt N Am to insult, criticize, or otherwise denigrate somebody else severely (slang)

dumpbin /dúmp bin/ n a large open container used in a shop to display items casually, especially those offered at bargain prices

dumper /dúmpər/ n 1. a person who or machine that disposes of waste by taking it to a prearranged site 2. VEHICLES same as **dumper truck** 3. Aus a large wave able to fling a surfer onto the beach

dumper truck n UK a heavy lorry with an open bed that can be tilted up and back to unload cargo such as gravel, dirt, or refuse from construction sites. ANZ term **tip truck**. N Am term **dump truck**

dumpie /dúmpi/ n S Africa a small bottle of beer containing 340 ml/11.9 fl oz

dumping /dúmping/ n the activity of depositing waste in an area or place

dumping ground n 1. a place where waste materials or unwanted items can be left 2. a place regarded as housing people rejected by the rest of society (disapproving)

dumpling /dúmpling/ n 1. SMALL BALL OF DOUGH a small dough ball cooked and served with a stew or soup 2. DESSERT a baked dessert consisting of pastry wrapped round fruit 3. AFFECTIONATE TERM OF ADDRESS used as an affectionate term of address (informal) 4. SOMEBODY PLUMP somebody who is regarded as short and plump (informal insult) [Early 17C. Origin ?]

dump orbit n an orbit that a communications satellite is moved into at the end of its useful life in which it will not collide with operational satellites

dumps /dumps/ npl a state of sadness and hopelessness (informal) ○ feeling down in the dumps [Early 16C. Plural of obsolete dump, origin ?]

dump truck n N Am same as **dumper truck**

dumpy /dúmpi/ (-ier, -iest) adj having a short and plump shape (informal disapproving) [Mid-18C. Origin ?] —**dumpily** adv —**dumpiness** n

dumpy level n a surveying instrument for taking levels with a short fixed horizontal telescope

dun[1] /dun/ n 1. COLOURS BROWNISH-GREY COLOUR a brownish-grey colour 2. RIDING BROWNISH-GREY HORSE a horse with a brownish-grey coat, black mane, tail, and legs, and usually a dark stripe on its back 3. FISHING DARK FISHING LURE a fishing fly of a grey to brown colour ■ adj (dunner, dunnest) 1. COLOURS BROWNISH-GREY of a dun colour 2. GLOOMY darkly bleak and depressing (literary) ○ a dun and bare prairie [Old English dunn < Indo-European]

dun[2] /dun/ vt (duns, dunning, dunned) HARASS SOMEBODY FOR DEBT REPAYMENT to press or harass somebody persistently for the settlement of a debt ■ n 1. PAYMENT DEMAND a pressing, usually written, demand for payment 2. DEBT COLLECTOR somebody whose job is to collect debts owed to other people [Early 17C. Origin ?]

Dunant /dyoo naáN/, **Jean Henri** (1828–1910) Swiss philanthropist. He founded the International Red Cross (1862–64) and shared the first Nobel Peace Prize (1901).

Dunbar /dun baár/, **William** (1460?–1520?) Scottish poet and priest. He was attached to the court of James IV, and his poetry includes The Thistle and the Rose (1503).

'I that in heill wes and gladnes / Am trublit now with gret seiknes / And feblit with infirmitie: / Timor mortis conturbat me.' [William Dunbar, 'Lament for the Makaris'; 1507?]

Dunbartonshire /dun baárt'nshər/ former county of central Scotland until 1975, now divided into East Dunbartonshire and West Dunbartonshire

AKG London

Isadora Duncan

Duncan /dúngkən/, **Isadora** (1877–1927) US dancer. She laid the foundation for modern dance, basing her ideas on the dances of the ancient Greeks. Full name **Duncan, Dora Angela**

'I have sometimes been asked whether I consider love higher than art, and I have replied that I cannot separate them, for the artist is the only lover, he alone has the pure vision of beauty, and love is the vision of the soul when it is permitted to gaze upon immortal beauty.' [Isadora Duncan, My Life; 1927]

dunce /dunss/ n somebody who is regarded as slow to learn to learn or as generally unintelligent (insult) [Mid-16C. < Duns in John DUNS SCOTUS, whose writings were regarded by Renaissance thinkers as obscure and obtuse]

dunce's cap, **dunce cap** n a conical paper hat formerly worn as a punishment by a pupil who was considered to be slow to learn or lazy at school

Dundalk /dun dáwk/ town in County Louth in the Republic of Ireland. It is situated close to the border with Northern Ireland. Population: 27,385 (2002).

Dundee /dun deé/ 1. city in eastern Scotland on the Firth of Tay. Population: 149,751 (2001). 2. City of

Dundee council area in eastern Scotland. Area: 65 sq. km/25 sq. mi. —**Dundonian** /dun dṓni ən/ *n, adj*

Dundee cake *n* a heavy rich fruitcake decorated on the top with almonds

dunderhead /dúndər hed/ *n* an offensive term that deliberately insults somebody's intelligence or capacity to learn (*informal insult*) [Early 17C. Origin ?] —**dunderheaded** *adj*—**dunderheadedness** *n*

dune /dyoon/ *n* a mound or ridge of sand formed by wind or water action, typically seen on coasts and in deserts [Late 18C. Via French < Middle Dutch *dūne*]

dune buggy *n N Am* same as **beach buggy**

Dunedin /dun eédin/ city and port on the southeast coast of the South Island, New Zealand, situated on Otago Harbour. Population: 107,088 (2001).

Dunfermline /dun fúrmlin/ manufacturing town in Fife, Scotland. Population: 55,083 (1991).

dung /dung/ *n* **1.** the solid excrement of animals, especially large animals such as cattle or horses **2.** AGRIC same as **manure** *n* (sense 1) ■ *vt* (**dungs, dunging, dunged**) to cover land with dung or manure [Old English, origin ?] —**dungy** *adj*

Dungannon /dun gánnən/ town and local government district in County Tyrone, Northern Ireland. Population: 47,735 (2001).

dungaree /dúng gə reé/ *n* STRONG CLOTH a sturdy hard-wearing blue-denim fabric ■ **dungarees** *npl* **1.** WORK GARMENT OF TROUSERS AND BIB a garment made from strong material consisting of loose-fitting trousers with an attached bib and shoulder straps, intended to be worn over ordinary clothing for protection while working **2.** CASUAL GARMENT OF TROUSERS AND BIB a casual garment consisting of trousers with an attached bib front, usually made from denim and worn especially by women and children [Late 17C. < Hindi *dungrī* 'kind of coarse cloth', after a village near Mumbai (Bombay)]

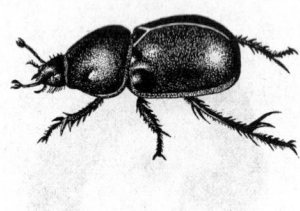
dung beetle

dung beetle *n* a scarab beetle that rolls large balls of dung into tunnels to feed the larvae that hatch from the eggs it lays there. Subfamily: Coprinae.

Dungeness /dúnjə néss/ shingle headland on the southern coast of Kent, southeastern England. It is home to two nuclear power stations.

dungeon /dúnjən/ *n* **1.** a prison cell, often underground, especially beneath a castle **2.** the secure main tower of a castle (*archaic*) [14C. Via Old French *donjon* 'castle keep' (later 'secure underground cell') < Latin *dominus* 'lord']

dungeon-crawl *vi* in computer games, to engage in role-play that generally involves killing monsters and taking their treasure, frequently from underground lairs —**dungeon-crawl** *n*

dunghill /dúng hil/, **dungheap** /-heep/ *n* a pile of solid animal excrement

dungpressor /dúng pressər/ *n* an oppressor (*slang; used in Black English*) [< dung, form of DOWN[1] + OPPRESSOR]

dunite /dúnīt/ *n* a coarse-grained dark igneous rock consisting mainly of a magnesium-rich olivine [Mid-19C. After Mt *Dun*, New Zealand] —**dunitic** /də níttik/ *adj*

dunk /dungk/ *vt* (**dunks, dunking, dunked**) **1.** to dip food into a liquid before eating it **2.** to submerge something in liquid, especially quickly and for a short time ■ *n US* BASKETBALL same as **dunk shot** [Early 20C. Via Pennsylvanian German *dunke* 'dip' < Old High German *dunkōn*] —**dunker** *n*

Dunker /dúngkər/, **Dunkard** /-ərd/ *n* a member of a group of German-American Baptists, the German Baptist Brethren [Mid-18C. < Pennsylvanian German < *dunke* 'dip']

Dunkirk /dun kúrk/ port in northern France, in the Nord Department, Nord-Pas-de-Calais Region, near Calais. In World War II over 330,000 Allied troops were evacuated from the town by sea, under constant enemy fire. Population: 70,850 (1999).

Dunk Island /dúngk-/ island situated off the eastern coast of Queensland, Australia, south of Cairns

dunk shot *n N Am* in basketball, a basket made by putting the ball through the hoop from above

Dún Laoghaire /dun leéri, doon-/ seaport on Dublin Bay on the eastern coast of the Republic of Ireland. Population: 55,540 (1991).

dunlin /dúnnlin/ (*plural* **-lins** or *same*) *n* a small wading bird with a beak that curves downwards. Native to: North America, Europe, Africa, Asia. Latin name: *Calidris alpina*. [Mid-16C. < DUN[1]]

Dunlop /dún lop/, **John Boyd** (1840–1921) British inventor. He invented the pneumatic tyre in about 1887, used at first for bicycles and later for cars.

Dunlop, **Weary** (1907–93) Australian surgeon and war hero. During World War II, he was taken prisoner in Java (1942). He kept a diary until the end of the war, revealing the appalling conditions that he and his companions endured on the Burma-Thailand Railway (1942–45). Full name **Dunlop, Sir Ernest Edward**

dunnage /dúnnij/ *n* packing material used to cushion cargo on a ship [14C. Origin ?]

dunnakin /dúnnəkin/ *n regional* a toilet, especially an outside one without plumbing [Late 18C. Origin ?]

Dunnet Head /dúnnət-/ peninsula and northernmost point of mainland Scotland

dunnite /dúnnīt/ *n* an explosive that contains ammonium picrate [Early 20C. After Col. B. W. *Dunn* (1860–1936), US army officer]

dunno /də nṓ, du-/ *contr* (I) don't know (*nonstandard*) ○ *'Who broke the glass?' 'Dunno'.*

dunnock /dúnnək/ *n* a woodland and garden bird distinguished from the house sparrow by its thin beak and grey head and breast. Native to: Europe. Latin name: *Prunella modularis*. [15C. Probably < DUN[1]]

dunny[1] /dúnni/ (*plural* **-nies**) *n* **1.** *UK regional, ANZ* same as **toilet** (senses 1–2) **2.** *Scotland* a basement or cellar [Early 19C. < DUNNAKIN]

dunny[2] /dúnni/ *n* same as **money** (*slang; used in Black English*) [Origin ?]

Dunoon /də noón/ resort town on the western shore of the Firth of Clyde, Scotland. Population: 9,038 (1991).

Dunsinane /dun sínnən/ hill in central Scotland, near Perth. It figures in Shakespeare's play *Macbeth*. Height: 308 m/1,012 ft.

Duns Scotus /dúnz skótəss/, **John** (1266?–1308) Scottish philosopher and theologian. A deeply influential figure of the Middle Ages, he emphasized religious individuality and defended the doctrine of the Immaculate Conception. He founded the school of scholasticism known as Scotism.

Dunstable /dúnstəb'l/ industrial town in Bedfordshire, central England. Population: 49,666 (1991).

Dunstable, **Dunstaple** /dúnstəp'l/, **John** (1390?–1453) English composer. He wrote sacred and secular pieces that significantly advanced counterpoint and harmony. He was also a noted mathematician and astronomer.

Dunstan /dúnstən/, **St** (909?–988) Anglo-Saxon prelate and reformer. As abbot of Glastonbury (940), he insisted on the strict observance of the Benedictine Rule, which heralded the reform of English monasticism. He became Archbishop of Canterbury (960–88).

dunt /dunt/ *regional n* **1.** INJURY FROM BLOW the injury or damage caused by a hit or a blow **2.** ACT OF HITTING a hit or blow ■ *vt* (**dunts, dunting, dunted**) HIT SOMEBODY OR SOMETHING to strike somebody or something [15C. Variant of DINT]

Duntroon /dun troón/ suburb of Canberra, Australian Capital Territory, Australia. Population: 1,906 (1996).

duo /dyoó ō/ (*plural* **-os**) *n* **1.** PAIR OF CLOSELY ASSOCIATED PEOPLE two people who are considered to be closely connected in some way **2.** SET OF TWO CLOSELY RELATED THINGS a set of two items considered to be closely connected **3.** PLAYERS OF DUET a pair of musicians who play together **4.** DUET a duet, especially one for two instruments [Late 16C. Via Italian, 'two' < Latin]

duo- *prefix* two ○ *duopoly* [< Latin < Indo-European]

duodecimal /dyoo ō déssim'l/ *adj* BASED ON 12 using units of 12 as a basis for counting or ordering. Although duodecimal systems are no longer commonly used, vestiges of them remain in such units as the foot, which is equal to 12 inches. ■ *n* **1.** DUODECIMAL NUMBER a number used to count or order in units of 12 **2.** 12TH a 12th part [Early 18C. < Latin *duodecimus* 'twelfth'] —**duodecimally** *adv*

duodecimo /dyoó ō déssi mō/ (*plural* **-mos**) *n* a book size traditionally created by folding a single sheet of standard-sized printing paper to give 12 leaves or 24 pages [Mid-17C. < Latin *in duodecimo* 'in twelfth']

duodenum /dyoó ō deénəm/ (*plural* **-na** /-nə/ or **-nums**) *n* the first short section of the small intestine immediately beyond the stomach [14C. < medieval Latin *intestinum duodenum digitorum* 'intestine twelve finger-breadths long' < Latin *duodecim* 'twelve'] —**duodenal** *adj*

duologue /dyoó ə log/ *n* **1.** a play or part of a play in which only two actors speak **2.** a dialogue between two actors, or a conversation between two people [Mid-18C. Blend of DUO + MONOLOGUE]

duomo /dwṓmō/ (*plural* **-mos** or **-mi** /-mi/) *n* a cathedral in Italy [Mid-16C. Via Italian < Latin *domus* 'house']

duopoly /dyoo óppəli/ (*plural* **-lies**) *n* an economic situation in which two powerful groups or organizations dominate commerce in one business market or commodity [Early 20C. After MONOPOLY] —**duopolistic** /dyoo óppə lístik/ *adj*

duopsony /dyoo ópsəni/ (*plural* **-nies**) *n* a situation in which two competing buyers exert controlling influence over many sellers [< DUO + -opsony < Greek *opsōnia* 'purchasing of food']

Dupain /dyoo páyn/, **Max** (1911–92) Australian photographer. He is best known for his images of Australian beach culture, e.g. in his work *Sunbaker* (1937). Full name **Dupain, Maxwell Spencer**

dupatta /doō púttə/ *n S Asia* a scarf or covering for the head and upper body worn by women [< Hindi]

dupe /dyoop/ *vt* (**dupes, duping, duped**) to persuade or induce somebody to do something by trickery or deception ○ *He was duped into thinking that they intended to pay.* ■ *n* an object of trickery or deceit [Late 17C. < French] —**dupability** /dyoópə bílləti/ *n* —**dupable** *adj*—**duper** *n*—**dupery** *n*

dupion /dyoópi on/ *n* a rough silk fabric woven from threads of a double cocoon [Early 19C. Via French *doupion* < Italian *doppione* < *doppio* 'double']

duple /dyoóp'l/ *adj* in music, consisting of two beats to the bar or measure [Mid-16C. < Latin *duplus* 'double']

Duplessis /dyoo pléssi/, **Maurice Le Noblet** (1890–1959) Canadian politician. He was premier of Quebec (1936–39 and 1944–59) as the leader of the Union Nationale Party.

duplet /dyoóplət/ *n* **1.** a group of two musical notes played in the time usually required by three **2.** a pair of electrons shared between two atoms that are joined in a chemical bond [Mid-17C. After DOUBLET]

duple time *n* a musical metre in which there are two beats to the bar, e.g. 2/4

duplex /dyoó pleks/ *n* **1.** *Aus, N Am* BUILDINGS **2-FAMILY DWELLING** a house that is divided into two halves and is inhabited by two separate families or tenants with separate entrances **2.** ELECTRONICS **TRANSMISSION IN BOTH DIRECTIONS** transmission of signals along a communications channel in both directions at the same time, e.g. over a telephone line **3.** ONLINE same as **full duplex** ■ *adj* **1.** TWOFOLD consisting of two parts, especially two identical or equivalent parts **2.** ENG HAVING TWO PARTS PERFORMING ONE OPERATION consisting of pairs of units or components that perform the same machine function but operate independently [Mid-

16C. < Latin, 'twofold' < *plicare* 'to fold'] —**duplexity** /dyoo pléksəti/ *n*

duplicate *vt* /dyoópli kayt/ (**-cates, -cating, -cated**) **1.** COPY SOMETHING to make an identical version of something one or more times **2.** REPEAT SOMETHING to do something more than once, especially unknowingly or unnecessarily ■ *n* /dyoópli kət/ **1.** COPY MADE an exact copy, especially of a document **2.** ANOTHER OF SAME a spare of the same kind **3.** REPEATED ACTION a repeat of an earlier action or achievement ■ *adj* /dyoópli kət/ **1.** COPIED EXACTLY being an exact copy of something ○ *a duplicate key* **2.** HAVING TWO CORRESPONDING PARTS consisting of or existing in two corresponding parts [15C. < Latin *duplicat-*, past participle of *duplicare* 'make twofold, double' < *duplus* 'twofold'] —**duplicable** /yoóplikəb'l/ *adj* —**duplicately** /-kətli/ *adv* —**duplicative** *adj* ◇ **in duplicate** so as to create or consist of two exact copies

SYNONYMS See *copy*.

duplicate bridge *n* contract bridge in which the same hand is played by different consecutive players

duplication /dyoópli káysh'n/ *n* **1.** REPETITION OR COPYING the action or an act of duplicating something **2.** EXACT COPY an exact copy of something **3.** GENETICS REPETITION OF GENES a chromosome mutation in which a section of a chromosome, along with the genes it carries, occurs twice

duplicator /dyoópli kaytər/ *n* something that makes copies, especially a machine for copying printed matter

duplicity /dyoo plíssəti/ *n* **1.** the fact of being deceptive, dishonest, or misleading **2.** the state of being double or in a pair (*formal*) ○ *the duplicity of the stars of the constellation* [15C. Directly or via French < late Latin *duplicitas* < Latin *duplic-*, stem of *duplex* (see DUPLEX)] —**duplicitous** /dyoo plíssitəss/ *adj*

duppy /dúppi/ (*plural* **-pies**) *n* Carib a ghost or spirit (*used in Black English*) [Late 18C. Origin ?]

du Pré /dyoo práy/, **Jacqueline** (1945–87) British cellist and teacher. She is particularly famous for her interpretations of cello concertos. Her playing, though not her teaching, was halted in 1972 by multiple sclerosis.

Dupré /dyoo práy/, **Marcel** (1886–1971) French musician and composer. He was for many years the organist at Notre Dame Cathedral, Paris, and was director of the Paris Conservatoire (1954–56).

durable /dyoórəb'l/ *adj* lasting for a long time, especially without sustaining damage or wear ○ *durable materials* ○ *a durable peace* [14C. Via French < Latin *durabilis* < *durare* 'last, harden'] —**durability** /dyoórə bílləti/ *n* —**durableness** *n* —**durably** *adv*

durable goods, **durables** /dyoórəb'lz/ *npl* long-lasting products, e.g. motor vehicles and cookers, refrigerators, and similar large domestic appliances

durables /dyoórəb'lz/ *n* same as **durable goods**

Durack /dyoór ak/ river in Western Australia that rises in the Kimberley Plateau and flows into the Timor Sea in the Cambridge Gulf. Length: 230 km/143 mi.

Durack, Dame Mary (1913–94) Australian writer. She wrote *Kings in Grass Castles* (1959), a historical account of her pioneering pastoralist forebears.

dura mater /dyoórə máytər/ *n* the tough outermost membrane of the three that cover the brain and spinal cord [14C. < medieval Latin, literally 'hard mother', translation of Arabic *al-'umm al-jāfiya* 'coarse mother'] —**dural** /dyoórəl/ *adj*

duramen /dyoŏ ráymən/ *n* heartwood (*technical*) [Mid-19C. < Latin, 'hardness' < *durare* 'last, harden']

durance /dyoórənss/ *n* forcible confinement or imprisonment (*archaic or literary*) [15C. < Old French < Latin *durare* 'last, harden']

Durance /dyoo raánss/ river in southeastern France, rising in the French Alps and flowing to its junction with the River Rhône, near Avignon. Length: 813 km/505 mi.

Durango /dyoŏ ráng gō/ **1.** state in Northwestern Mexico. Capital: Durango. Population: 1,448,661 (2000). Area: 121,775 sq. km/47,020 sq. mi. **2.** capital of Durango State, in the Sierra Madre Mountains,

northwestern Mexico. Population: 491,436 (2000). Full name **Victoria de Durango**

Durante /də ránti/, **Jimmy** (1893–1980) US comic entertainer. Known for his prominent nose and raspy voice, he performed in cabaret, film, and television. Full name **Durante, James Francis**

Duras /dyoo raa/, **Marguerite** (1914–96) Vietnamese-born French novelist, playwright, film director, and screenwriter. Her works include the screenplay for *Hiroshima, mon amour* (1960) and the novel *The Lover* (1984).

duration /dyoo ráysh'n/ *n* the period of time that something lasts or exists ○ *an interval of 15 minutes' duration* [14C. Via French < medieval Latin *duration-* < Latin *durare* 'last, harden'] —**durational** *adj* ◇ **for the duration 1.** for the entire period of time that something is going on or will continue to go on **2.** for the foreseeable future ○ *The house is yours for the duration; stay as long as you like.*

durative /dyoórətiv/ *adj* describes a verb in a continuous tense or aspect or a verb indicating a continuous action

Durban /dúrbən/ city, seaport, and tourist resort in KwaZulu-Natal Province in eastern South Africa. Population: 3,090,126 (1995).

durbar /dúr baar/ *n* formerly, an official reception or audience held by a local prince or British governor in colonial India, or by a local chief or British official in colonial Africa [Early 17C. < Urdu *darbār* < Persian *dar* 'door' + *bār* 'court']

Dürer /dyoórər/, **Albrecht** (1471–1528) German painter and engraver. The clarity of his paintings, e.g. in *Self Portrait* (1498), made him one of the most influential artists of the Reformation.

> 'The Creator fashioned men once and for all as they must be, and I hold that the perfection of form and beauty is contained in the sum of all men.'
> [Albrecht Dürer. Quoted in 'Four Books on Human Proportion', *The Painter's Manual*, Walter L. Strauss (tr.); 1977]

duress /dyoŏ réss/ *n* **1.** the use of force or threats to make somebody do something **2.** illegal force or coercion, as used against a criminal suspect or a prisoner in lawful custody before trial [14C. Via Old French *duresse* < Latin *duritia* 'hardness' < *durus* 'hard']

Durex /dyoŏr eks/ *tdmk* **1.** *UK* a trademark for a condom **2.** *Aus* a trademark for a type of transparent adhesive tape

Durey /dyoo ráy/, **Louis Edmond** (1888–1979) French composer. He was a member of the Paris-based group of composers known as 'Les Six', but left the group in 1921 to concentrate on more popular music that could express his communist ideals.

Durga /doórgə/ *n* in Hinduism, a goddess who is one of the most important deities, embodying for many the supreme manifest form of godhead

Durgapur /dúrgə poor/, **Durgāpur** city in Bangla State, eastern India. It is a major steel-producing centre. Population: 425,836 (1991).

Durham[1] /dúrrəm/ **1.** historic cathedral city in northeastern England. It is the county town and cultural centre of County Durham. Population: 87,709 (2001). **2.** county in northeastern England. The city of Durham is the administrative centre. Population: 493,470 (2001). Area: 2,435 sq. km/940 sq. mi.

Durham[2] /dúrrəm/ *n* a shorthorn beef or dairy cow belonging to a hardy breed originating in northeastern England [After DURHAM[1]]

durian /dyoóri ən/ *n* **1.** a foul-smelling but deliciously flavoured fruit **2.** the tree that bears durians. Native to: tropical rain forests of Southeast Asia. Latin name: *Durio zibethinus*. [Late 16C. < Malay < *duri* 'thorn, prickle']

duricrust /dyoóri krust/ *n* a hard crust formed on the surface of the soil by the precipitation of soluble minerals from mineral waters, particularly during the dry season in semiarid climates [Early 20C. < Latin *durus* 'hard']

during /dyoóring/ *prep* **1.** throughout a period or event, either continuously or several times between the beginning and the end ○ *There was not even a whisper during the service.* **2.** at some point or

moment within a period or event ○ *I can't remember the date, but it was during the winter.* [14C. Present participle of obsolete *dure* 'last' < Old French *durer* < Latin *durus* 'hard']

Durkheim /dúrk hīm/, **Émile** (1858–1917) French social theorist. His rigorous methodology, manifested in *Suicide* (1897) and other works, set the pattern for modern sociological studies.

durmast oak /dúr maast-/, **durmast** *n* an oak tree that has lobed leaves and yields a heavy flexible wood. Use: cabinet-making. Native to: Europe, Asia Minor. Latin name: *Quercus petraea*. [Late 18C. Origin ?]

durn /durn/ *interj, adj, adv, vt* (**durns, durning, durned**) *Southern US* used to indicate frustration or mild anger (*informal*) ○ *Durn that cat, he just bit me!* [Variant of DARN[2]]

duro /doórō/ (*plural* **-ros**) *n* in some Latin American countries, a coin worth a peso or a dollar, or formerly in Spain, a coin worth five pesetas [Late 18C. < Spanish *peso duro* 'hard or solid piastre']

durra /doórrə/, **dourra** *n* a type of sorghum cultivated for its grain. Use: food grain, animal feed. Latin name: *Sorghum bicolor*. [Late 18C. < Arabic *dura*]

Durrell /dúrrəl/, **Gerald** (1925–95) British naturalist and writer, brother of Lawrence Durrell. His books include the autobiographical *My Family and Other Animals* (1956) about his childhood on Corfu, as well as such books as *The Stationary Ark* (1976), which concerns his zoo and wildlife conservation trust in Jersey.

> 'The sneeze in English is the harbinger of misery, even death. I sometimes think the only pleasure an Englishman has is in passing on his cold germs.'
> [Gerald Durrell, *My Family and Other Animals*; 1956]

Durrell, Lawrence (1912–90) British novelist, poet, and travel writer. The *Alexandria Quartet* novels (1957–60) established his reputation. Later works include *Tunc* (1968), *Nunquam* (1970), and the *Avignon Quintet* (1974–85). Full name **Durrell, Lawrence George**

> 'There are only three things to be done with a woman. You can love her, you can suffer for her, or you can turn her into literature.'
> [Lawrence Durrell, *Justine*; 1957]

Dürrenmatt /dyoórrən mat/, **Friedrich** (1921–90) Swiss writer. He wrote plays, including *The Physicists* (1961), existentialist detective novels, and critical essays.

> 'What was once thought can never be unthought.'
> [Friedrich Dürrenmatt, *The Physicists*; 1962]

Durrës /dúrrəss/ city and seaport in western Albania, on the Adriatic Sea. The capital of Durrës District, it is situated about 30 km/20 mi. west of the national capital Tirana. Population: 125,000 (1995).

durrie *n* TEXTILES another spelling of **dhurrie**

durst /durst/ past tense of **dare** (*archaic*)

durum wheat /dyoórəm/, **durum** *n* a wheat that produces the type of flour used to make pasta and couscous. Latin name: *Triticum durum*. [Early 20C. < Latin, form of *durus* 'hard']

Duryea /doóryay, doór i ay/, **Charles Edgar** (1861–1938) US car manufacturer and inventor. Together with his brother, James Frank Duryea, he built one of the first cars in the United States (1893).

durzi /dúrzi/ (*plural* **-zis**) *n* S Asia same as **tailor** *n* (sense 1) [Early 19C. Via Urdu < Persian *darzi*]

Duse /doóz ay/, **Eleonora** (1858–1924) Italian actress. The emotional power of her acting, especially in dramas by her longtime lover Gabriele D'Annunzio, was equalled in her time only by that of Sarah Bernhardt.

Dushanbe /doo shaánbi/ capital city of Tajikistan, in the west of the country in the Gissar Valley. Population: 562,000 (2001).

dusk /dusk/ *n* **1.** PERIOD AFTER DAY BUT BEFORE NIGHT the period of the day after the sun has gone below the horizon but before the sky has become dark **2.** ABSENCE OF DAYLIGHT partial or almost complete darkness (*literary*) ■ *adj* DIM having little or insufficient

light (*literary*) ■ *vti* (**dusks, dusking, dusked**) **DARKEN** to become dark, or make something dark (*literary*) [Old English *dox* 'dark in colour' < Indo-European]

dusky /dúski/ (**-ier, -iest**) *adj* **1. DARK-COLOURED** rather dark in colour **2. DIM** having little or insufficient light **3. OFFENSIVE TERM** an offensive term meaning having a rather dark skin or complexion (*dated*) —**duskily** *adv* —**duskiness** *n*

Dusky Sound /dúski-/ coastal inlet in the southwestern part of the South Island, New Zealand. At 32 km/20 mi. long it is the country's largest fiord.

Dussehra /dússərə/, **Dasehra, Dassera** *n* a Hindu festival that celebrates the victory of good over evil [Late 18C. Via Hindi *dasahrā* < Sanskrit *daśaharā*]

Düsseldorf /dŏŏss'l dawrf/ capital of North Rhine-Westphalia, west-central Germany. Situated on the River Rhine, about 32 km/20 mi. north of Cologne, it is the commercial and cultural centre of the greater Ruhr area. Population: 572,638 (1997).

dust /dust/ *n* **1. SMALL DRY PARTICLES** very small dry particles of a substance such as sand or coal, either in the form of a deposit or a cloud **2. HOUSEHOLD DIRT** the small particles of dirt that settle on horizontal surfaces in buildings **3. REMOVAL OF DUST** an act of removing small particles of dirt from something, usually by wiping with a cloth **4. REMAINS FROM DECAY** the small particles that something, especially a human body, is thought to be reduced to by decay after death **5. EARTH AS BURIAL PLACE** earth, particularly that of somebody's grave (*literary*) **6.** MED **MINERS' DISEASE** silicosis or another respiratory disease affecting miners (*informal*) ■ *v* (**dusts, dusting, dusted**) **1.** *vti* **CLEAN DIRT PARTICLES OFF SOMETHING** to remove small particles of dirt from something, usually by wiping with a cloth **2.** *vt* **SPRINKLE SOMETHING OVER SOMETHING** to sprinkle a powdery substance over something ○ *dust the cake with powdered sugar* [Old English *dūst* < Germanic] —**dustless** *adj* ◇ **(as) dry as dust** so scholarly and devoid of humour as to be arid in tone and content ◇ **bite the dust** (*informal*) **1.** to die, especially in or as a result of a fight **2.** to suffer total failure ◇ **gather dust** to remain unused over a period of time ◇ **kick up** *or* **raise a dust** to cause a controversy or loud disturbance (*informal*) ◇ **shake the dust (of something) from your feet** to leave somewhere forever, especially when glad to do so

dust down *vt* **1.** *also* **dust off RECYCLE SOMETHING OLD** to prepare something for reuse or further consideration **2.** *also* **dust off WIPE OR BRUSH SOMETHING** to clean something, especially by wiping or brushing it **3. REPRIMAND SOMEBODY** to tell somebody off severely (*dated*)

dust up *vt* to attack somebody verbally or physically (*slang*)

dust-bath *n* a form of grooming behaviour in animals, especially birds, that consists in rolling or making agitated movements in the dust on the ground in order to remove parasites

dustbin /dúst bin/ *n* a large outdoor container for household rubbish, usually cylindrical in shape and with a lid. Aus term **garbage bin.** N Am term **garbage can**

dustbin man *n UK* same as **dustman**

dust bowl *n* an area in a semiarid environment in which the topsoil is exposed and dust storms are likely to occur

Dust Bowl *n* a large area in the southern part of the central United States that suffered badly from wind erosion during the 1930s

dustcart /dúst kaart/ *n UK* a large motor vehicle used to collect and compact waste materials left bagged or in containers outside buildings. ANZ, N Am term **garbage truck**

dust cloth *n US* same as **duster** (sense 1)

dust cover *n* **1.** a cover, often made from transparent plastic, for protecting a piece of equipment **2.** PUBL same as **dust jacket 3.** HOUSEHOLD same as **dustsheet**

dust devil *n* a rising or travelling funnel of dust, dirt, or sand that occurs on hot days, especially in desert or dry areas. Dust devils are smaller than tornadoes and are generally not dangerous.

duster /dústər/ *n* **1.** *UK, ANZ, Can* **CLEANING CLOTH** a piece of cloth used for removing dust, especially from household objects and surfaces. US term **dust cloth** **2.** CLOTHING **LONG LOOSE COAT** a long loose coat, sometimes one without buttons or lapels **3.** *US* CLOTHING **HOUSECOAT** a woman's loose housecoat **4.** AGRIC **DEVICE FOR SPREADING AGROCHEMICALS** a machine or device for spreading powdered fungicide, insecticide, or fertilizer over crops or other plants **5.** *US* METEOROL same as **dust storm**

dustily /dústili/ *adv* in an abrupt and impolite manner

dustiness /dústinəss/ *n* **1.** the state of being covered with dust or containing dust **2.** curtness and impoliteness

dusting /dústing/ *n* **1. REMOVAL OF DUST** the act of removing small particles of dirt from something, usually by wiping with a cloth **2. THIN POWDERY COVERING** a thin, sometimes patchy covering of a powdery substance ○ *a dusting of snow on the ground* **3. DEFEAT** a defeat or setback (*slang*) ○ *a candidate who took a real dusting at the polls*

dusting down *n* a severe telling-off

dusting powder *n* fine powder, e.g. talcum powder, especially for use on the skin

dust jacket *n* a paper book cover that protects the hardbound binding and can be discarded

dustman /dústmən/ (*plural* **-men** /-mən/) *n UK* somebody employed to remove rubbish, especially from dustbins outside people's houses. ANZ, N Am term **garbageman**

dust mite *n* a microscopic insect that lives in furnishings and bedding, feeding on dead skin particles shed by humans and other animals and that may cause allergies in some people

dustpan /dúst pan/ *n* a container with a flat base and an open front into which dirt and dust can be swept

dustsheet /dúst sheet/ *n* a large piece of cloth placed over furniture or furnishings to protect them from dust, dirt, or paint. N Am term **drop cloth**

dust storm *n* a strong hot dry wind laden with dust

dust trap *n* a place where dust tends to accumulate

dust-up *n* a violent argument or physical altercation, often one that starts and stops quickly (*slang*)

dusty /dústi/ (**-ier, -iest**) *adj* **1. FULL OF DUST** covered with or containing dust **2.** COLOURS **TINGED WITH GREY** containing tinges of grey with other colours ○ *dusty pink* **3. BORING** uninteresting or uninspiring, especially through being outdated ○ *dusty political slogans* **4. LIKE DUST** resembling dust ○ *a dusty gold powder*

Dusty /dústi/, **Slim** (1927–2003) Australian singer and songwriter. He was a country and western performer, whose 1957 single 'The Pub with No Beer' became one of the bestselling records in the history of Australian popular music. Born **Kirkpatrick, David Gordon**

dusty answer *n* a reply that is unhelpful and curt or impolite (*dated*)

dusty miller *n* **1.** a plant with grey or white leaves covered with a down resembling dust. Latin name: *Senecio cineraria* or *Cerastium tomentosum.* **2.** PLANTS same as **rose campion**

dutch /duch/ *n Cockney* a man's wife (*slang*) [Late 19C. Shortening of DUCHESS]

Dutch /duch/ *n* the official West Germanic language of the Netherlands and the Republic of Suriname. Native speakers: 20 million. See panel on next page ■ *npl* the people of the Netherlands collectively [14C. < Middle Dutch *dutsch* < Germanic, 'people'] —**Dutch** *adj* ◇ **go Dutch** to pay for your own part of the cost of a meal or entertainment

Dutch auction *n* an auction in which the price is lowered gradually until somebody makes a bid

Dutch barn *n* a farm building with a curved roof, open sides, and two levels. Hay, straw, and grain are stored on the upper level and animals are kept below. Dutch barns are usually built into a slope to provide easy access to the upper storey.

Dutch cap *n* a contraceptive diaphragm with triangular flaps, of a type no longer used (*informal*)

Dutch clover *n* PLANTS same as **white clover**

Dutch courage *n* the temporary confidence supposedly obtained from drinking alcohol (*informal*)

Dutch doll *n* a wooden doll with jointed limbs and body

Dutch East Indies /dúch-/ the islands of Indonesia during the period of Dutch colonial government from the late 18th century until independence in 1949

Dutch elm *n* a cultivated hybrid elm tree introduced to Great Britain from the Netherlands in the 17th century and now common in northeastern France and parts of western Great Britain and Ireland. Latin name: *Ulmus x hollandica.*

Dutch elm disease *n* a disease of elm trees caused by a fungus, *Ceratocystis ulmi*, carried by a bark beetle [Because identified by Dutch scientists]

Dutch Guiana /-gi áanə/ former name for **Suriname** (until 1948)

Dutch hoe *n* a hoe used for weeding that is pushed instead of pulled

Dutchman /dúchmən/ (*plural* **-men** /-mən/) *n* **1.** a man who comes from the Netherlands **2.** a piece of building material used to repair or conceal faulty construction ◇ **I'm a Dutchman** used to express complete disbelief in the statement that precedes it ○ *If that's a genuine antique, I'm a Dutchman.*

Dutchman's breeches *n* a woodland plant that has creamy white flowers with two spurs. Native to: eastern United States. Latin name: *Dicentra cucullaria.*

Dutchman's pipe *n* a woody climbing vine that has mottled greenish-brown flowers shaped like the bowl and stem of an old-fashioned tobacco pipe. Native to: eastern United States. Latin name: *Aristolochia sipho.*

Dutch oven *n* **1.** an iron or earthenware container with a lid, used for cooking stews or casseroles **2.** a metal box with an open front placed beside an open fire so that food can be cooked inside it

Dutch treat *n* an outing, e.g. to a restaurant or theatre, where each person pays for himself or herself (*informal*)

Dutch uncle *n* somebody, typically a mentor, who criticizes or advises in a frank, sometimes harsh manner (*informal*)

Dutch wife *n* a firm bolster or framework used in bed to support the upper knee while somebody is sleeping on his or her side

Dutchwoman /dúch wŏŏmən/ (*plural* **-women** /-wimin/) *n* a woman who comes from the Netherlands

duteous /dyŏŏti əss/ *adj* obedient or showing a strong sense of duty (*archaic*) —**duteously** *adv* —**duteousness** *n*

dutiable /dyŏŏti əb'l/ *adj* subject to customs or other duties —**dutiability** /dyŏŏti ə bílləti/ *n*

dutiful /dyŏŏtif'l/ *adj* **1.** done to fulfil obligations, often with little enthusiasm ○ *made a dutiful attempt at conversation* **2.** acting according to obligations ○ *a dutiful and hard-working employee* —**dutifully** *adv* —**dutifulness** *n*

Dutton /dútt'n/, **Geoffrey Piers Henry** (1922–98) Australian writer and editor. He wrote *Antipodes in Shoes* (1958).

duty /dyŏŏti/ (*plural* **-ties**) *n* **1. OBLIGATION** something that somebody is obliged to do for moral, legal, or religious reasons ○ *your duties as a parent* **2. ALLOCATED TASK** a task or service allocated to somebody, especially in the course of work **3. NEED TO MEET OBLIGATIONS** the urge to meet moral or religious obligations ○ *a strong sense of duty* **4.** ECON **TAX** a tax on goods, especially imports and exports **5. QUALITY** suitability for a particular grade of use (*usually used in combination*) ○ *heavy-duty shoes* **6.** MECH ENG **MACHINE'S WORKLOAD** the amount of work that a machine is designed to do, or a measure of a machine's efficiency **7.** AGRIC **VOLUME OF WATER FOR IRRIGATION** the volume of water needed to irrigate an area of land in order to cultivate a crop from planting to harvest [13C. < Anglo-Norman *dueté* < Old French *deu* 'owed' (see DUE)] ◇ **off duty** not at work (*hyphenated before nouns*) ○ *an off-duty police officer* ◇ **on duty** at work

SYNONYMS See ***job***.

duty-bound *adj* required to do something because it is morally or legally right

LANGUAGE HERITAGE ***Dutch*** Much of English is made up of words from other languages, and Dutch is a significant contributor in this respect, especially through seafaring and commerce and through colonies established in North America, southern Africa, and in what is now Indonesia.

Dutch maritime traditions introduced English to many nautical terms, from the command ***avast*** (an alteration of Dutch *hou'vast*, a shortening of *houd vast* 'hold fast') to the ***yacht*** (from obsolete Dutch *jaghte*, a shortening of *jaghtschip* 'chasing ship'), by way of ***boom*** ('beam at the bottom of a sail'), ***cruise***, ***marline***, ***skipper***, and ***taffrail***. Well-travelled Dutch-speakers described the ***dune*** (immediately from French, but ultimately from Middle Dutch), ***iceberg***, ***maelstrom***, and ***reef***. Individual fish are identified by Dutch names – ***houting***, ***lumpfish*** (from Middle Dutch *lumpe* 'cod'), ***whiting*** – as is the collective ***school*** and the ***walrus***. Dutch transported words from the languages of far-off lands: from Malay, for example, ***bamboo***, ***cockatoo***, and ***gingham*** (from Malay *genggang* 'striped'), and from Arabic ***monsoon*** (obsolete Dutch *monssoen*, via Portuguese *monção* from Arabic *mawsim* 'season').

In the earliest period of borrowings, the source is often identified more generally as Low German, the group of West Germanic languages and dialects to which Dutch belongs (as indeed does English). Among early words specified as from Dutch are: (from the 13th century) ***booze*** and ***marten***; (from the 14th) ***bundle***, ***curl***, ***dam***, ***Dutch*** itself, ***groove***, ***rack***, ***scum***, and ***spout***; (from the 15th) ***bung***, ***croon***, ***mart***, ***prop***, ***snack***, and ***wagon***.

After the medieval period Dutch continued to penetrate all areas of English vocabulary, but one distinct strand relates to art: ***easel*** and ***landscape***, for example, recorded in the late 16th century; ***etch*** and ***sketch***, recorded in the mid-17th. Other areas include: cold-weather activities, for example ***skate***, ***sled***, and ***sleigh***; food and drink, for example ***advocaat***, ***brandy*** (originally *brandy-wine*, from Dutch *brandewijn* 'burnt (i.e. distilled) wine'), ***coleslaw***, and ***rijsttafel*** (a Dutch meal of Indonesian origin); arms and the military, for example ***blunderbuss*** (an alteration of Dutch *donderbus* 'thunder gun'), ***cashier*** ('dismiss somebody from the armed forces because of misconduct'), ***tattoo*** ('call to soldiers to return to quarters', from Dutch *taptoe* 'shut the tap, i.e. of the beer barrel', a signal at closing time in taverns), and ***trigger***. One Dutch military term whose meaning and origin have been obscured by folk etymology is ***forlorn hope***; this came from Dutch *forloren hoop* 'lost troop', originally 'group of soldiers sent on a hopeless mission'.

In North America the Dutch colony of New Amsterdam, later New York, had a distinct influence on American English. Though now in widespread use, ***boss*** was originally a North American term; the geographical feature the ***bluff*** is particularly North American, as is the ***stoop*** at the entrance to a house (the original Dutch ***stoep*** is similarly used in South Africa). Food terms of Dutch origin include ***cookie***, ***cruller***, and ***waffle***. ***Santa Claus*** visits children at Christmas because of the Dutch.

Settlers took Dutch to southern Africa in the 17th century. Their descendants were given the name ***Boer*** (from Dutch *boer* 'farmer', the source also of ***boor***), and the form of Dutch spoken in southern Africa, known as Cape Dutch, developed into ***Afrikaans*** ('African'). Dutch or Afrikaans names were naturally given to unfamiliar animals, birds, and fishes (***blesbok***, ***dassie***, ***eland***, ***kabeljou***, ***mossie***, ***snoek***), and to the land's characteristic geographical features (***kloof***, ***krans***, ***platteland***, ***vlei***, and, more widely familiar, ***veld***). Historical terms include ***outspan*** and ***Voortrekker***. Within modern South African English many terms of Dutch or Afrikaans are used, from the informal adjective ***lekker*** ('enjoyable and pleasing') through the form of address ***oom*** (literally 'uncle') and the domestic ***voorkamer*** ('front room') to political ***toenadering*** ('rapprochement between political parties'). Familiar outside South Africa are ***apartheid*** and, no longer particularly associated with the country, ***commandeer*** (via Afrikaans *kommandeer* from Dutch *kommanderen* 'to command'), ***spoor*** ('visible trail of an animal'), and ***trek***.

duty-free *adj* **EXEMPTED FROM EXCISE DUTIES** on or at which no customs or excise duties have to be paid ■ *adv* **WITHOUT CUSTOMS AND EXCISE DUTIES** without paying or charging customs or excise duties ■ *n* **SHOP SELLING DUTY-FREE ITEMS** a shop, especially at an airport or on board ship, that sells duty-free goods ■ **duty-frees** *npl* **DUTY-FREE ITEMS** duty-free goods, especially the allowance of duty-free goods that a person is allowed to bring into his or her own country

duty of care *n* the legal duty of everybody who has control of waste to ensure that it is managed safely and transferred only to somebody authorized to take it

duty officer *n* an officer who is present in an office or headquarters and responsible for handling situations that may arise during a given period, especially a period when others are off duty

duumvir /dyoo úmvər/ (*plural* **-virs** or **-viri** /-və ree/) *n* **1.** either of two people who share a position of authority equally between them **2.** a joint holder of a paired post in the ancient Roman government or judiciary [Early 17C. < Latin < *duo* 'two' + *vir* 'man'] —**duumvirate** *n*

Duvalier /dyo͞o válli ay/, **François** (1907–71) Haitian national leader and doctor. He was elected president in 1957 and declared himself president for life in 1964, instituting a dictatorial regime known for its violent purges and mass executions. Known as **Papa Doc**

> 'My government has not been all that I had hoped for.'
> [François Duvalier. Quoted in *Papa Doc, Baby Doc*, James Ferguson; 1987]

Duvalier, Jean-Claude (*b.* 1951) Haitian national leader. He succeeded his father François Duvalier as president (1971–86). Known as **Baby Doc**

duvet /do͞o vay, dyo͞o-/ *n* **1.** a bed quilt made up of broad channels stuffed with down or synthetic material, usually used inside a removable washable cover in place of or together with sheets and blankets **2.** a quilted jacket constructed from channels filled with down, intended for outdoor wear in severe weather conditions [Mid-18C. < French, '(feather) down' < Old Norse *dúnn*]

duvet day *n* any one of an agreed number of days that some employees can take as leave at short notice in addition to their official holiday allowance [< the idea of wanting to remain under the duvet rather than go to work]

duvet jacket *n* CLOTHING same as **duvet** (sense 2)

duvetyn /dyo͞ovə teen/, **duvetyne, duvetine** *n* a soft velvety silk, cotton, woollen, or rayon fabric with a nap [Early 20C. < French *duvetine* < *duvet* (see DUVET)]

du Vigneaud /doo veenyō, dyoo-/, **Vincent** (1901–78) US biochemist. For his work on pituitary hormones, he won the Nobel Prize in Chemistry (1955).

dux /duks/ *n Scotland* the student whose academic achievements are highest in a school, subject, or class [Mid-18C. < Latin, 'leader']

duxelles /do͝ok sél, duk-/ *n* a paste made from mushrooms sautéed with shallots and herbs in butter and used with stuffings, sauces, and soups, or as a garnish [Late 19C. After the Marquis *d'Uxelles*, 17C French nobleman]

duyker *n* ZOOL another spelling of **duiker**

DV *abbr* CHR Deo volente

dvandva /dvaan dvaa/ *n* a compound word made up of two parts of equal status that would make sense if joined by 'and' instead of being compounded, e.g. 'push-pull' and 'Marxist-Leninist' [Mid-19C < Sanskrit, doubling of *dva* 'two']

DVD *n* an optical compact disc that can store a large quantity of video, audio, or other information. Full form **digital video disc**

DVD-A *n* an audio DVD

DVD-R, DVD+R *n* a DVD that can be used to record something but cannot be erased. Full form **digital video disc recordable**

DVD-ROM *n* a high-capacity optical disc on which data can be stored but not altered. Full form **digital video disc read only memory**

DVD-RW, DVD+RW *n* a DVD that can have its contents erased and something else recorded onto it many times. Full form **digital video disc rewritable**

DVI *abbr* COMPUT digital video imaging

Dvina /dveenə/ river in northeastern Europe, comprising the Northern Dvina and the Western Dvina. Length: 1,020 km/634 mi.

DVLA *abbr* PUBLIC ADMIN Driving and Vehicle Licensing Agency

DVM *abbr* VET, EDUC Doctor of Veterinary Medicine

Dvořák /dváwr zhak/, **Antonín** (1841–1904) Bohemian Czech composer. An ardent nationalist, he based many of his musical themes on Czech folk songs. His ninth symphony, *From the New World* (1893), incorporates US folk music.

Dvorak keyboard /dváwr zhak-/ *n* a keyboard with frequently used keys placed near the centre for quicker typing [After August *Dvorak*, 20C US inventor]

DVR *abbr* MEDIA digital video recorder

DVT *abbr* MED deep vein thrombosis

D/W *abbr* LAW dock warrant

dwaal /dwaal/ *n S Africa* a state of inattention or confusion and bewilderment (*informal*) [< Afrikaans]

dwam /dwaam/ (**dwams, dwamming, dwammed**) *vi Scotland* to become ill, especially suddenly, or feel faint [Early 16C. Ultimately < Germanic]

dwarf /dwawrf/ *n* (*plural* **dwarves** /dwawrvz/ or **dwarfs**) **1. SMALL IMAGINARY HUMANOID** a small stocky imaginary being resembling a human, associated with mountains, mines, and buried treasures. Fictional dwarves were often believed to have magic powers and to be sometimes malevolent. **2. PERSON SMALL FOR MEDICAL REASONS** somebody of small stature due to medical reasons, usually somebody with an average-sized body but unusually short limbs, or somebody with growth hormone deficiency **3.** BIOL **SMALL PLANT OR ANIMAL** a plant or animal that is much smaller than others of its species, usually as a result of selective breeding (*often used before a noun*) ○ *a dwarf conifer* **4.** ASTRON same as **dwarf star** ■ *vt* (**dwarfs, dwarfing, dwarfed**) **1. MAKE SOMEBODY OR SOMETHING SEEM SMALL** to make somebody or something else seem very small or very unimportant by comparison ○ *The cathedral is dwarfed by the enormous tower blocks surrounding it.* **2. STUNT SOMEBODY'S OR SOMETHING'S GROWTH** to stunt the growth of somebody or something [Old English *dweorg* < Germanic] —**dwarfish** *adj* —**dwarfishly** *adv* —**dwarfishness** *n*

dwarf bean *n* **1.** a thin green edible bean pod from a type of French bean **2.** a short bushy type of French bean plant. Latin name: *Phaseolus vulgaris*. N Am term **bush bean**

dwarf cornel *n* a widely cultivated plant with scarlet berries that grows only about 20 cm/8 in. high. Flowers: purple, surrounded by white bracts resembling petals. Native to: Arctic and alpine regions. Latin name: *Cornus suecica*.

dwarf galaxy *n* a small galaxy that does not shine brightly and contains no more than a few million stars

dwarfism /dwáwrfizəm/ *n* the condition of being a dwarf

dwarf star *n* a star with relatively low mass, size, and luminosity. The Sun is a dwarf star.

dwarves plural of **dwarf**

dweeb /dweeb/ *n US* somebody considered boring, silly, or socially inept (*slang insult*) [Late 20C. Origin ?]

dwell /dwel/ *vi* (**dwells, dwelling, dwelt** /dwelt/ or **dwelled**) to live and have a home in a particular place (*literary*) ■ *n* the portion of a cam's surface that permits a machine's operation to pause for a period of time at a given position [Old English *dwellan* 'lead astray' < Indo-European, 'rise in a cloud'] —**dweller** *n*
dwell on, dwell upon *vt* to think, write, or talk about something at considerable length

dwelling /dwélling/ *n* a house or other building or place in which somebody lives (*formal*) ■ *adj* living in a particular type of place or environment (*usually used in combination*) ○ *bottom-dwelling fishes*

dwelt past participle, past tense of **dwell**

DWEM /dwem/, **dwem** *abbr* full form **dead white European male**

dwindle /dwínd'l/ (**-dles, -dling, -dled**) *vti* to decrease little by little in size, number, or intensity and approach zero, or make something decrease in this

way ○ *Supplies were dwindling.* [Late 16C. < obsolete *dwine* 'waste away' < Indo-European, 'become exhausted']

dwindler /dwíndlər/ *n regional* the smallest or weakest piglet in a litter

REGIONAL NOTE See *underling*.

DWP *abbr* Department for Work and Pensions

dwt *abbr* MEASURE dead weight tonnage

DX *symbol* TELECOM long-distance

Dy *symbol* CHEM ELEM dysprosium

dyad /dī ad/ *n* **1.** COUPLE two individual units, things, or people linked as a pair (*formal*) **2.** CHEM ATOM WITH VALENCY OF TWO an atom or chemical group with a valency of two **3.** MATHS VECTOR OPERATOR a mathematical operator consisting of two vectors expressed without a multiplication sign between them **4.** MUSIC TWO-NOTE CHORD a musical chord consisting of two notes [Late 17C. Via late Latin < Greek *duad-* < *duo* 'two'] —**dyadic** /dī áddik/ *adj*—**dyadically** *adv*

Dyak /dī ak/ (*plural* **-aks** or *same*), **Dayak** *n* a member of a Malaysian people who live in the interior of Borneo and are noted for their communal long houses [Mid-19C. < Malay, 'up-country'] —**Dyak** *adj*

dyarchy *n* POL another spelling of **diarchy**

dybbuk /díbbək/ (*plural* **-buks** or **-bukim** /-kim/), **dibbuk** *n* in Jewish folklore, a malevolent spirit of a dead person, believed able to take over a living person's body and control his or her behaviour unless exorcized [Early 20C. Via Yiddish *dibek* < Hebrew *dibbūq* < *dābaq* 'cling']

Dyck /dīk/, **Sir Anthony van** (1599–1641) Flemish painter. He was active in Belgium, Italy, and England, and is noted for his sumptuous, large-scale portraits of English royalty and aristocrats.

dye /dī/ *v* (**dyes, dyeing, dyed**) **1.** *vt* COLOUR SOMETHING BY SOAKING to colour or stain something, e.g. fabric or hair, by soaking it in a colouring solution so that it takes on the new colour permanently or semi-permanently **2.** *vi* COLOUR WELL OR BADLY to respond to being treated with a colouring agent and take its colour in a particular way ■ *n* **1.** COLOURING AGENT a natural or synthetic substance that can be used to colour something, e.g. a textile or hair, and is most often applied as a liquid **2.** COLOURING SOLUTION a colouring solution containing a dye **3.** COLOUR PRODUCED the colour produced on something by a dye [Old English *dēah* 'colour, colour that hides' < Germanic] —**dyable** *adj*—**dyer** *n*

SPELLCHECK See *die*[1].

dyed-in-the-wool *adj* **1.** wholeheartedly and stubbornly attached to a set of beliefs, political party, or philosophy and totally convinced of its merits **2.** dyed before weaving into cloth

dyeline /dī līn/ *n* PRINTING same as **diazo**

dyer's greenweed /dī ərz gréen weed/ *n* a small bush, similar to broom, with flowers that were formerly used to produce a yellow dye. Native to: Europe, Asia. Latin name: *Genista tinctoria*.

dyer's rocket *n* a plant of the mignonette family with flowers that were formerly used to produce a yellow dye. Native to: Europe, Asia. Latin name: *Reseda luteola*.

dyer's-weed *n* any plant that yields a dye, e.g. dyer's greenweed or dyer's rocket

dyestuff /dī stuf/ *n* INDUST same as **dye** *n* (sense 1)

dyewood /dī wood/ *n* any wood that can produce a dye

Dyfed /dúvvid/ former county in southwestern Wales. Carmarthen was its administrative centre. Population: 351,500 (1993). Area: 5,768 sq. km/2,227 sq. mi.

dying /dī ing/ *adj* **1.** ABOUT TO DIE on the point of death **2.** OCCURRING JUST BEFORE DEATH carried out, spoken, or occurring at or just before the point of death **3.** FINAL occurring as something is about to reach its end ○ *in the dying seconds of the game*

dyke[1] /dīk/, **dike** *n* **1.** EMBANKMENT TO PREVENT FLOODS an embankment built along the shore of a sea or lake or beside a river to hold back the water and prevent flooding **2.** BARRIER a barrier or obstacle meant to keep something out **3.** CAUSEWAY a raised roadway across a swamp or body of water **4.** DITCH a drainage

ditch or other artificial watercourse **5.** *Scotland* DRY-STONE WALL an enclosing or dividing wall, usually made of stone, often without mortar **6.** GEOL LONG MASS OF IGNEOUS ROCK a vertical or near-vertical mass of igneous rock that has forced its way upwards through overlying strata **7.** *ANZ* same as **lavatory** (sense 1) (*informal*) ■ *vt* (**dykes, dyking, dyked**; **dikes, diking, diked**) **1.** PROTECT LAND WITH DYKES to enclose or protect an area of land with a dyke or series of dykes **2.** DRAIN LAND WITH DITCHES to drain an area of land using ditches [13C. Probably < Old Norse *dík* < Germanic, 'hole and mound resulting from digging'] —**dyker** *n*

dyke[2] /dīk/, **dike** *n* an offensive term for a lesbian (*slang*) [Mid-20C. Origin ?]

dyke swarm *n* a series of parallel or linear dykes [< DYKE[1]]

Bob Dylan

Dylan /díllən/, **Bob** (*b.* 1941) US singer and songwriter. One of the most influential popular musicians of the 20th century, he first established his reputation with protest songs such as 'Blowin' in the Wind' (1962) and 'The Times They Are A-Changin'' (1964). Born **Zimmerman, Robert**

> 'Money doesn't talk, it swears.'
> [Bob Dylan, 'It's Alright, Ma'; 1965]

> 'Ah, but I was so much older then / I'm younger than that now.'
> [Bob Dylan, 'My Back Pages', *Another Side of Bob Dylan*; 1964]

dyn *symbol* PHYS dyne

dynamic /dī námmik/ *adj* **1.** VIGOROUS AND PURPOSEFUL full of energy, enthusiasm, and a sense of purpose and able both to get things going and to get things done **2.** ACTIVE AND CHANGING characterized by vigorous activity and producing or undergoing change and development ○ *a dynamic economy* **3.** PHYS RELATING TO ENERGY AND MOTION involving or relating to energy and forces that produce motion **4.** PHYS RELATING TO DYNAMICS involved in or connected with the study of dynamics **5.** MUSIC RELATING TO LOUDNESS IN MUSIC relating to or indicating variations in the loudness of musical sounds **6.** PHYS CHANGING OVER TIME describes any system that changes over time **7.** COMPUT WHILE PROGRAM IS RUNNING performed while a computer program is running ■ *n* DRIVING FORCE a driving or energizing force, especially one involved in a process of social or psychological change [Early 19C. Via French < Greek *dunamikos* < *dunamis* 'force'] —**dynamical** *adj*—**dynamically** *adv*

dynamic markings, **dynamic marks** *npl* the symbols and words that indicate the degree of loudness or softness with which a piece, passage, or note of music should be played

dynamic range *n* **1.** the range of volume used within a single piece of music **2.** the range over which an electronic audio system can operate to a set standard of performance based on given limits for noise and distortion

dynamics /dī námmiks/ *n* PHYS STUDY OF MOTION the branch of mechanics that deals with motion and the way in which forces produce motion (*takes a singular verb*) ■ *npl* **1.** CHANGE-PRODUCING FORCES the forces that tend to produce activity and change in any situation or sphere of existence **2.** PERSONAL RELATIONSHIPS the relationships of power between the people in a group **3.** MUSIC LOUDNESS AND SOFTNESS IN MUSICAL PIECE the different levels of loudness and softness in a piece of music, and the way in which

a performer reproduces them in performance **4.** MUSIC same as **dynamic markings**

dynamism /dī nəmizəm/ *n* **1.** a vigorously active, forceful, and energizing quality, especially as the hallmark of somebody's personality or approach to a task **2.** a philosophical or scientific theory stressing the role of dynamic forces in explaining phenomena, especially by interpreting events as an expression of forces residing within the object or person involved —**dynamist** *n* —**dynamistic** /dīnə místik/ *adj*

dynamite /dī nə mīt/ *n* **1.** POWERFUL EXPLOSIVE a powerful explosive consisting of a porous material such as wood pulp or sawdust, combined with ammonium or sodium nitrate, or nitroglycerine, and an antacid such as calcium carbonate. Use: blasting. **2.** VERY EXCITING THING something that or somebody who is exceptionally exciting or has an extremely powerful effect (*slang*) ○ *This music is absolute dynamite.* **3.** VERY HARMFUL THING something that or somebody who is potentially very dangerous or harmful (*slang*) ○ *news stories that were political dynamite* ■ *vt* (**-mites, -miting, -mited**) BLOW SOMETHING UP WITH DYNAMITE to blast or destroy something with dynamite [Mid-19C. < Greek *dunamis* 'force'] —**dynamiter** *n*

dynamo /dī nəmō/ (*plural* **-mos**) *n* **1.** a machine that converts mechanical energy into electrical energy, usually in the form of direct current **2.** a hardworking, tirelessly energetic person (*informal*) [Late 19C. Shortening of *dynamo-electric machine*]

dynamo- *prefix* power, energy ○ *dynamometer* [< Greek *dunamis* 'force']

dynamoelectric /dī nəmō i léktrik/, **dynamoelectrical** /-trik'l/ *adj* involved in or relating to the production of electrical from mechanical energy or of mechanical energy from electrical

dynamometer /dī ni mómmitər/ *n* an instrument used to measure mechanical force or power such as the power output of an engine —**dynamometric** /dīnəmō méttrik/ *adj* —**dynamometry** *n*

dynamotor /dī nə mōtər/ *n* an electrical device combining a motor and generator. Use: to convert alternating current to direct current, and vice versa. [Early 20C. < Greek *dunamis* 'force']

dynast /dī nn ast, -əst/ *n* **1.** a ruler, especially a hereditary monarch **2.** a member or founder of a dynasty [Mid-17C. Via Latin < Greek *dunastēs* 'lord' < *dunasthai* 'be able']

dynasty /dínnəsti/ (*plural* **-ties**) *n* **1.** a succession of rulers from the same family **2.** a prominent and powerful family or group of people whose members retain their power and influence through several generations [14C. Directly or via French < late Latin *dynastia* < Greek *dunastēs* 'lord' (see DYNAST)] —**dynastic** /di nástik/ *adj* —**dynastically** *adv*

dyne /dīn/ *n* the centimetre-gram-second unit of force equal to the force that will accelerate a mass of one gram one centimetre per second per second. 1 dyne is equivalent to 10^{-5} newton. Symbol **dyn** [Late 19C. < Greek *dunamis* 'force']

dynein /dī nin/ *n* a protein that uses chemical energy from ATP to create movement within microtubules such as cilia and flagella [Mid-20C. < DYNE]

dynode /dī nōd/ *n* an electrode in an electron tube that produces electrons through secondary emission [Mid-20C. < Greek *dunamis* 'force' (see DYNAMIC) + -ODE]

dys- *prefix* bad, impaired, pathological ○ *dysplasia* [Via Latin < Greek *dus-*]

dysarthria /diss aárthri ə/ *n* difficulty in speech articulation caused by a lack of muscle control resulting from damage to the central nervous system [Late 19C. < modern Latin < Latin *dys-* 'bad' + Greek *arthron* 'joint']

dyscrasia /diss krázi ə/ *n* an unusual condition of the blood cells [14C. Via late Latin < Greek *duskrasia* 'bad mixture' < *krasis* 'mixing']

dysentery /díss'ntəri/ *n* a disease of the lower intestine caused by infection with bacteria, protozoans or parasites and marked by severe diarrhoea, inflammation, and the passage of blood and mucus [14C. Directly or via French < Latin *dysenteria* < Greek *dusenteros* 'having bad intestines' < *enteron* 'intestine'] —**dysenteric** /díss'n térrik/ *adj*

~~dysentry~~ incorrect spelling of **dysentery**

dysfunction /diss fúngksh'n/ *n* **1.** a disturbance in the usual pattern of activity or behaviour ○ *a characteristic dysfunction of petty officialdom* **2.** an irregularity in the functioning of an organ or other part or system of the body

dysfunctional /diss fúngksh'nəl/ *adj* **1.** RELATING BADLY characterized by an inability to function emotionally or as a social unit ○ *a dysfunctional family* ○ *dysfunctional behaviour* **2.** NOT PERFORMING AS EXPECTED failing to perform an expected function ○ *a dysfunctional bureaucracy* **3.** AFFECTED BY DISEASE OR IMPAIRMENT describes an organ or other part or system of the body that is unable to function regularly as a result of disease or impairment

dysgenic /diss jénnik/ *adj* affecting later generations detrimentally by passing on undesirable characteristics

dysgenics /diss jénniks/ *n* the study of factors relating to or causing a decrease in the survival of the genetically well-adapted members of a line of descent (*takes a singular verb*)

dysgraphia /diss gráffi ə/ *n* impairment of writing ability, arising from brain injury or disease [Mid-20C. < DYS- + Greek *graphia* 'writing']

dyskinesia /díss ki neezi ə/ *n* impairment of control over ordinary muscle movement, often resulting in spasmodic movements or tics [Early 18C. Via modern Latin < Greek *duskinēsia* 'difficulty in moving' < *kinēsis* 'movement']

dyslexia /diss léksi ə/ *n* a learning disorder marked by a severe difficulty in recognizing and understanding written language, leading to spelling and writing problems. It is not caused by low intelligence or brain damage. [Late 19C. < DYS- + Greek *lexis* 'speech' < *legein* 'speak'] —**dyslexic** *adj*, *n*

dysmenorrhea *n* MED US spelling of **dysmenorrhoea**

dysmenorrhoea /díss menə ree ə/ *n* severe pain or cramps in the lower abdomen during menstruation —**dysmenorrhoeal** *adj* —**dysmenorrhoeic** *adj*

dyspareunia /díspar yóoni ə/ *n* pain occurring during sexual intercourse [Late 19C. < DYS- + Greek *pareunos* 'lying with somebody' < *para* 'beside' + *eunē* 'bed']

dyspepsia /diss pépsi ə/ *n* acid indigestion (*technical*) [Early 18C. Via Latin < Greek *duspepsia* 'difficult digestion' < *peptein* 'cook, digest']

dyspeptic /diss péptik/ *adj* **1.** having acid indigestion **2.** easily angered [Late 17C. < Greek *duspeptos* 'difficult of digestion' < *peptein* 'cook, digest'] —**dyspeptic** *n*

dysphagia /diss fáyji ə/ *n* difficulty in swallowing, with a variety of possible causes —**dysphagic** /-fáyjik, -fájjik/ *adj*

dysphasia /diss fáyzi ə/ *n* difficulty in speaking and understanding spoken or written language, caused by brain injury or disease —**dysphasic** *adj*

dysphemism /dísfimizəm/ *n* **1.** the deliberate substitution of an offensive expression for a neutral one **2.** an offensive expression deliberately substituted for a neutral one [Late 19C. < DYS- after *euphemism*] —**dysphemistic** /dísfə místik/ *adj*

dysphonia /diss fóni ə/ *n* hoarseness or difficulty in speaking as a result of dysfunction of the vocal cords, caused by brain injury, brain disease, or chemical poisoning [Early 18C. Via modern Latin < Greek *dusphōnia* 'roughness of sound' < *phōnē* 'sound'] —**dysphonic** /-fónnik/ *adj*

dysphoria /diss fáwri ə/ *n* a state of feeling acutely hopeless, uncomfortable, and unhappy [Mid-19C. < Greek *dusphoria* 'discomfort' < *pherein* 'to bear'] —**dysphoric** /-fórrik/ *adj*

dysplasia /diss pláyzi ə/ *n* unusual development or growth of a part of the body such as an organ, bone, or cell, including the total absence of such a part —**dysplastic** /-plástik/ *adj*

dyspnea *n* MED US spelling of **dyspnoea**

dyspnoea /disp nee ə/ *n* difficulty in breathing, often caused by heart or lung disease [Mid-17C. Via Latin < Greek *duspnoia* 'difficulty in breathing' < *pnein* 'breathe'] —**dyspnoeal** *adj* —**dyspnoeic** *adj*

dyspraxia /diss práksi ə/ *n* **1.** poor coordination displayed by some children, diagnosed by illegible handwriting and inability to catch a ball and clap while the ball is in the air. It sometimes accompanies dyslexia. **2.** same as **apraxia** [< Greek *duspraxia* 'ill success' < *praxis* 'action'] —**dyspraxic** *adj*

dysprosium /diss prózi əm/ *n* a soft silvery element of the rare-earth group that is paramagnetic and highly reactive. Source: monazite, bastnaesite. Use: laser materials, nuclear research. Symbol **Dy**. See table at **element** [Late 19C. < Greek *dusprositos* 'difficult to approach' < *ienai* 'go']

dysrhythmia /diss ríthmi ə/ *n* an irregularity in a rhythm, especially of heartbeats or brain waves [Early 20C. < modern Latin, 'bad rhythm' < Greek *rhuthmos* 'rhythm']

dystocia /diss tóshə/ *n* unusually difficult childbirth [Early 18C. < Greek *dustokia* 'difficult childbirth' < *tokos* 'childbirth'] —**dystocial** *adj*

dystonia /di stóni ə/ *n* a neurological disorder that causes involuntary muscle spasms and twisting of the limbs

dystopia /diss tópi ə/ *n* **1.** an imaginary place where everything is as bad as it possibly can be **2.** a vision or description of a dystopia [Mid-20C. < DYS- + UTOPIA] —**dystopian** *adj*

dystrophia *n* MED same as **dystrophy**

dystrophic /diss tróffik/ *adj* **1.** relating to or affected by dystrophy **2.** describes a pond or lake containing unusually acidic brown water, lacking in oxygen, and unable to support much plant or animal life because of an excessive humus content

dystrophin /dístrəfin/ *n* a protein found in muscle that is missing in people with muscular dystrophy

dystrophy /dístrəfi/ (*plural* **-phies**), **dystrophia** /diss trófi ə/ *n* **1.** progressive degeneration of a body tissue such as muscle, caused by inadequate nourishment of the affected part, as a result of some unknown cause **2.** a condition in which pond or lake water is unable to support much plant or animal life because of an excessive humus content [Late 19C. < DYS- + -TROPHY]

dysuria /diss yóori ə/ *n* pain or difficulty in urinating —**dysuric** *adj*

Dyula /dee óola, dyóolə/ (*plural same* or **-las**) *n* **1.** a member of an African people who live mainly in the rainforests of the Ivory Coast **2.** a Mande language spoken in parts of the Ivory Coast, Burkina Faso, and Ghana. Native speakers: 1 million. —**Dyula** *adj*

dz *abbr* Algeria (*used in Internet addresses*) See table at **domain name**

Dzerzhinsk /dər zhínsk/ city in central European Russia on the River Oka. It is a chemical-manufacturing centre. Population: 359,740 (1995).

dziggetai *n* ZOOL another spelling of **chigetai**

dzo /zō/ (*plural* **dzos** or *same*), **zo** (*plural* **zos** or *same*), **zho** (*plural* **zhos** or *same*) *n* the offspring of a cow and a yak [Mid-19C. < Tibetan *mdso*]

Dzongkha /zóngkə/, **Dzongka** *n* a dialect of Tibetan that is the official language of Bhutan. Native speakers: 1 million. [Early 20C. < Tibetan, 'language of the fortress'] —**Dzongkha** *adj*

Dzungaria /jóong gáiri ə/ ♦ **Junggar Pendi**

E e

e[1] /ee/ (*plural* **e's**), **E** (*plural* **E's** or **Es**) *n* **1.** the fifth letter of the English alphabet, representing a vowel sound **2.** a written representation of the letter 'e'

e[2] *symbol* **1.** PHYS electron **2.** MATHS used to refer to the transcendental number 2.718 282… **3.** CHESS used to refer to the fifth vertical row of squares from the left on a chessboard

e[3] *abbr* **1.** engineer **2.** engineering

E[1] *symbol* **1.** *E* PHYS electric field strength **2.** *E* PHYS electromotive force **3.** MEASURE exa- **4.** PHYS internal energy **5.** LOGIC a negative categorical proposition

E[2] /ee/ (*plural* **E's** or **Es**) *n* **1.** 'E'-SHAPED OBJECT something shaped like a letter 'E' **2.** MUSIC 3RD NOTE IN C MAJOR the third note of a scale in C major **3.** MUSIC SOMETHING THAT PRODUCES E a string, key, or pipe tuned to produce the note E **4.** MUSIC SCALE BEGINNING ON E a scale or key that starts on the note E **5.** MUSIC WRITTEN SYMBOL OF E a graphic representation of the tone of E **6.** EDUC 5TH HIGHEST GRADE the fifth highest grade in a series, e.g. a grade indicating that a student's work is of very low quality **7.** DRUGS ECSTASY the drug ecstasy, or a tablet of the drug (*slang*) **8.** SOC SCI CASUAL WORKER in the market research system that classifies people according to their employment, a casual worker or somebody who is dependent on the state

E[3] *abbr* **1.** earl **2.** ELEC earth **3.** east **4.** eastern **5.** TELECOM e-mail (*used to contrast with T, telephone number, and F, fax number*) **6.** TELECOM e-mail address (*used to contrast with T, telephone number, and F, fax number*) **7.** LANG English

e- *prefix* **1.** electronic ○ *e-mail* **2.** electronic data transfer via the Internet ○ *e-commerce* [Abbreviation of ELECTRONIC]

e-bank *n*	**e-news** *n*
e-banking *n*	**e-newspaper** *n*
e-brochure *n*	**e-newsroom** *n*
e-bulletin *n*	**e-office** *n*
e-bulletin board *n*	**e-payment** *n*
e-cash *n*	**e-publishing** *n*
e-catalogue *n*	**e-purse** *n*
e-commerce *n*	**e-shop** *n*
e-conference *n*	**e-shopper** *n*
e-conferencing *n*	**e-shopping** *n*
e-copy *n*	**e-signature** *n*
e-data *n*	**e-system** *n*
e-democracy *n*	**e-tagging** *n*
e-document *n*	**e-text** *n*
e-failure *n*	**e-ticket** *n*
e-fraud *n*	**e-ticketing** *n*
e-frontier *n*	**e-toll** *n*
e-funds *npl*	**e-tolling** *n*
e-gift *n*	**e-trader** *n*
e-journal *n*	**e-trading** *n*
e-journalism *n*	**e-transfer** *n*
e-journalist *n*	**e-voting** *n*
e-magazine *n*	**e-war** *n*
e-money *n*	**e-warfare** *n*

E- *prefix* a food additive that conforms to an EU standard, specified by a number [Abbreviation of EUROPEAN]

E111 *n* a form that entitles citizens of the EU to free health care when visiting other EU countries

ea. *abbr* each

EAC *abbr* ECON East African Community

each /eech/ *det, pron, adv* used to refer to every member of a group of people or things, considered individually ○ *With each victory we get closer to the championship.* ○ *Is a VCR that can be connected to more than one TV better than buying one for each?* ○ *Environmental health officers were supervising an average of 40 cases each.* [Old English ǣlc < Germanic, 'ever alike']

USAGE each or **every**? In some contexts these two words are nearly interchangeable, as in *I examined each puppy in the litter* and *I examined every puppy in the litter*. Here the only difference is a slight shift in perspective from considering the animals individually, with **each**, to considering them collectively, with **every**. Either of the words, placed before the noun, requires the noun and the verb to be singular: *Each puppy is affectionate. Every puppy is affectionate.* **Each**, though not **every**, may also be placed after a plural noun, and then the plural governs the verb: *The puppies each have their own toys.* **Each** can also refer to two or more, whereas **every** must refer to three or more. **Each** can be a determiner (*each puppy*), a pronoun (*each of them*), and an adverb (*Give them a bowlful each*), whereas **every** is a determiner only (*every puppy*). The expression *each and every* relates to a singular noun only, and therefore takes a singular verb only: *Each and every passenger is required to present two photo IDs.* Avoid use of this expression in formal writing, because it is objected to by some people as unnecessarily wordy.

each other *pron* each one of two or more persons or things reciprocally

USAGE each other or **one another**? The traditional rule is that **each other** refers to two entities and **one another** refers to more than two: *Joe and Lee respect each other deeply. All the people at the party knew one another already.* This distinction is not supported by the weight of usage, however, and there is no good reason to reject the alternatives *Joe and Lee respect one another deeply* and *All the people at the party knew each other already.*

each way *adv* on the same horse to come first or be placed in the first three in a race ○ *had £5 each way on number 6* —**each-way** *adj*

eager /éegər/ *adj* **1.** enthusiastic and excited about something and impatiently waiting to do or get it ○ *eager to help* ○ *eager for praise* **2.** expressing enthusiastic interest and expectation or an impatient desire to do something ○ *an eager face* [13C. Via Anglo-Norman *egre* < Latin *acer* 'sharp'] —**eagerly** *adv* —**eagerness** *n*

eager beaver *n* an enthusiastic worker or volunteer (*informal*) [< the perceived industriousness of beavers]

eagle /éeg'l/ *n* **1.** LARGE BIRD OF PREY a large bird of prey with a hooked beak and broad wing span that hunts by day. Family: Accipitridae. **2.** EAGLE AS SYMBOL OF POWER the figure of an eagle used as a symbol of military or political power, e.g. on the standards carried by Roman legions **3.** GOLF SCORE OF 2 UNDER PAR in golf, a score of two under par for a single hole ■ *vti* (-**gles**, -**gling**, -**gled**) GOLF SCORE 2 UNDER PAR in golf, to complete a hole in two strokes under par [14C. Via Anglo-Norman *egle* < Latin *aquila*]

eagle eye *n* **1.** extremely keen eyesight **2.** the ability to notice what other people might miss —**eagle-eyed** *adj*

eagle owl *n* a large owl with brownish plumage and tufts of feathers on its head that look like horns. It is the largest species of owl in the world. Native to: Europe, Asia. Latin name: *Bubo bubo.*

eagle ray *n* a large fish with a projecting snout, massive jaws, and pectoral fins shaped like wings that propel it with a soaring motion. Native to: tropical and subtropical seas. Family: Myliobatidae.

eaglet /éeglət/ *n* a young eagle, especially before it leaves the nest

eaglewood /éeg'l wŏŏd/ (*plural* -**woods** or *same*) *n* **1.** a tree with fragrant resinous timber. Use: perfumes. Native to: Asia. Latin name: *Aquilaria agallocha.* **2.** INDUST same as **aloes** (sense 2)

eagre /éegər/ *n* GEOG same as **bore**[3] [Early 17C. Origin ?]

ealdorman /áwldərmən/ (*plural* -**men** /-mən/) *n* in Anglo-Saxon England, the principal magistrate and commander of the military forces of a shire [Old English *ealdormann*, early form of ALDERMAN]

Eales /eelz/, **John** (*b.* 1970) Australian rugby union player. He played 86 Tests, 55 as captain. He led Australia to victory in the 1999 World Cup and the 2000 and 2001 Tri Nations competitions.

Ealing /éeling/ borough in West London, England. Population: 300,9487 (2001).

Ealing comedy *n* a British comedy film of a series made at Ealing Studios between the 1930s and 1950s

Ealing Studios *n* the film studios in Ealing, West London, where a number of popular and highly regarded British comedy films were made between the 1930s and 1950s

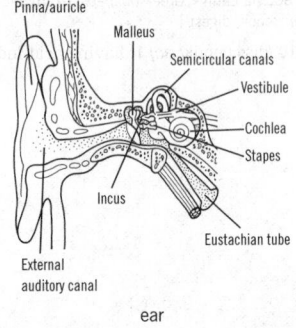

Pinna/auricle
Malleus
Semicircular canals
Vestibule
Cochlea
Stapes
Incus
Eustachian tube
External auditory canal

ear

ear[1] /eer/ *n* **1.** ORGAN OF HEARING the organ of hearing and balance in vertebrates. In mammals it is divided into three parts, the external, middle, and inner ear. The external ear collects sound, the middle ear contains small bones that amplify and transmit it, while the inner ear maintains balance and contains sensory nerve endings for detecting sound. **2.** EXTERNAL PART OF HEARING ORGAN the external part of an ear, visible in humans and most mammals on each side of the head as a flap of cartilage with skin surrounding or covering it **3.** INVERTEBRATE SENSORY ORGAN a sensory organ in invertebrates that is able to sense vibrations and perform a similar function to a vertebrate ear **4.** BIRDS same as **ear tuft 5.** EAR SHAPE something shaped like an ear, especially a handle on a jug or jar **6.** ABILITY TO TELL SOUNDS APART the ability to distinguish accurately between different sounds, e.g. in speech or music ○ *She has a good ear for languages.* **7.** ATTENTION somebody's attention, especially when it is sympathetic or favourable ○ *lend an ear* [Old English *ēare* < Indo-European, 'ear'] —**earless** *adj* ◇ **all ears** listening, or ready to listen, attentively or enthusiastically to something

(*informal*) ◇ **go in one ear and out the other** to be forgotten as soon as heard and so have absolutely no effect on somebody ◇ **have somebody's ear** to be a trusted adviser to somebody, especially somebody powerful or influential ◇ **have** or **keep your ear to the ground** to remain continuously alert to discover new developments or information ◇ **out on your ear** unceremoniously thrown out or dismissed from a place or position you previously occupied (*informal*) ○ *You'll be out on your ear if you're late again.* ◇ **prick up your ears** to begin listening or paying attention to something ◇ **set somebody** or **something by the ears** to cause conflict or disagreement among people or within an organization ◇ **set somebody on his** or **her ear, set something on its ear** to send somebody or something into a state of excited agitation, shock, or confusion ◇ **wet behind the ears** very inexperienced or naive

ear[2] /eer/ n the grain-bearing part at the top of the stalk of a cereal plant such as barley, maize, or sweetcorn ■ vi (**ears, earing, eared**) to form the part of a cereal plant that contains the grains [Old English *ēar* < Indo-European, 'sharp']

earache /eer ayk/ n pain in the middle or inner ear. Technical name **otalgia**

earbash /eer bash/ (**-bashes, -bashing, -bashed**) v (*informal*) **1.** vt to scold or reprimand somebody at length ○ *always earbashing me about the state of the garden* **2.** vi ANZ to talk continuously ○ *Will you two stop earbashing and give me a hand?* —**earbasher** n

earbashing /eer bashing/ n a lengthy scolding or reprimand (*informal*) ○ *copped a right earbashing for getting home late*

ear bone n BIOL same as **otolith**

ear clip n **1.** a metal band or other ornament clipped to the upper part of the ear **2.** a clip-on earring

eardrop /eer drop/ n a pendant earring ■ **eardrops** npl liquid medicine for the ear, usually inserted with a dropper

eardrum /eer drum/ n a membrane of thin skin and fibrous tissue that vibrates in response to sound waves, located between the external and the middle ear. Technical name **tympanic membrane**

eared /eerd/ adj with ears or with ears of a particular type (*usually used in combination*) ○ *long-eared*

eared seal n a seal with conspicuous external ears and independent hind limbs or flippers that it uses to move on land. sea lions and fur seals are eared seals. Family: Otariidae.

earflap /eer flap/ n a piece of fabric or fur on a hat that can be let down to keep the ear warm (*often used in the plural*)

earful /eer fool/ n **1.** a severe scolding or lecture from somebody (*informal*) **2.** a large quantity of sound, conversation, or gossip that somebody hears or overhears

Amelia Earhart
Barnaby's

Earhart /áir haart/, **Amelia** (1898–1937) US aviator. She was the first woman to fly solo over both the Atlantic (1932) and part of the Pacific (1935). She disappeared over the Pacific in 1937 while attempting a round-the-world flight.

'Courage is the price that Life exacts for granting peace.'
[Amelia Earhart, *Courage*; 1927]

earhole /eer hōl/ n the opening in the side of the head that leads into the ear, or the ear itself (*informal*)

---

earing /eering/ n a small rope by which the upper corner of a sail is attached to a yard [Early 17C. Origin ?]

earl /url/ n a British nobleman of a rank above a viscount and below a marquess. The title corresponds to 'count' in continental Europe, which is not used in the United Kingdom, although a woman of equivalent rank is called a 'countess'. [Old English *eorl* 'warrior, nobleman'. Origin ?] —**earldom** n

Earle /url/, **Augustus** (1793–1838) British painter. He is known for his vivid landscapes and paintings of early colonial life in Australia.

earless seal n a seal that does not have conspicuous external ears and has short front and hind flippers that are adapted for swimming rather than moving on land. Family: Phocidae.

Earl Grey n a tea flavoured with bergamot to produce a light-coloured brew with a musky taste [Probably after Charles Grey, the second *Earl Grey* (1764–1845), British prime minister]

Earl Marshal n an officer of the English peerage who presides over the College of Heralds and organizes important ceremonial occasions

earlobe /eer lōb/ n the soft fleshy lower part of the outer ear

early /úrli/ adv (**-lier, -liest**) **1.** BEFORE EXPECTED TIME before the expected or arranged time ○ *They arrived early.* **2.** NEAR BEGINNING OF SOMETHING at or near the beginning of a period of time, process, or sequence of events ○ *early in the interview* **3.** DURING FIRST STAGES at a time when something was not far advanced or developed or when somebody was at a comparatively young age ○ *She decided early that she wanted to become a teacher.* **4.** SOON without delay or before long ○ *Post early for Christmas.* **5.** BEFORE OTHERS before others of the same type ○ *early-flowering tulips* ■ adj (**-lier, -liest**) **1.** OCCURRING NEAR BEGINNING occurring at or near the beginning of a period of time, process, or sequence of events ○ *Early reports indicate a high level of interest.* **2.** OCCURRING BEFORE EXPECTED TIME occurring before the expected or arranged time ○ *early retirement* **3.** PRODUCED NEAR BEGINNING produced at, characteristic of, or representing a not very advanced stage in the development of somebody or something ○ *looking forward to an early end to the deadlock* **4.** IN NEAR FUTURE due, expected, or requested to happen in the very near future **5.** RIPENING BEFORE OTHERS flowering or ripening before other plant varieties of the same type ○ *an early bloomer* ○ *early peaches* [Old English *ǣrlīce* < Indo-European, 'day'] —**earliness** n ◇ **early on** at the beginning or start of something such as a chain of events or a period of time ○ *We should have realized early on that financing would be a major problem.*

early adopter n somebody who embraces a new product, technology, or idea as soon as it becomes available or known. ◊ **late adopter**

early bird n (*informal*) **1.** an early riser **2.** somebody who arrives or acts earlier than the expected or arranged time [< the proverb *The early bird catches the worm*]

early closing n the regular closing of most of the shops in a town or part of a town on one particular afternoon in the week

early day motion n a parliamentary motion tabled for future discussion in the British Parliament on any day when business finishes early. Its main purpose is to draw Parliament's attention to a particular topic.

Early English adj belonging to or typical of the style of early Gothic architecture used between the late 12th and late 13th centuries in England, characterized by sharply pointed arches and arched windows —**Early English** n

early mark n Aus an occasion when permission is given to leave school before the usual time for the end of lessons ◇ **take an early mark** to leave school, work, a gathering, or an event before the usual time

early modern adj relating to or typical of the period in European and world history from 1485 to the late 18th century

early music n music written during the medieval and Renaissance periods, sometimes also including the music of the baroque and early classical periods

---

■ adj typical of a way of performing early music that aims to be as authentic as possible, using period instruments, the contemporary performing style, and a carefully researched score

early retirement n retirement from work before the usual age, often offered, with special inducements, by employers as a way of reducing staff numbers

early riser n somebody who gets up early, especially on a regular basis

early warning n advance notice that something, especially something dangerous or threatening, is going to happen

early warning system n a network of radar, satellites, or other sensing devices designed to give advance warning of an enemy attack, especially in time to take countermeasures

earlywig /úrli wig/ n regional same as **earwig** [Probably alteration]

REGIONAL NOTE See *earwig*.

earmark /eer maark/ vt (**-marks, -marking, -marked**) **1.** DESIGNATE SOMETHING FOR PARTICULAR PURPOSE to select and reserve something to be used for a particular purpose ○ *That money's already been earmarked for upgrading the computer system.* **2.** PUT IDENTIFICATION MARK ON ANIMAL'S EAR to mark the ear of a farm animal with an identifying symbol, notch, or hole ■ n **1.** US IDENTIFYING CHARACTERISTIC a characteristic that makes it possible to recognize the nature or origins of something (*often used in the plural*) ○ *The crime seemed to have all the earmarks of an inside job.* **2.** IDENTIFICATION MARK ON ANIMAL'S EAR an identifying symbol, notch, or hole on or in the ear of a farm animal

earmuffs /eer mufs/ npl ear covers attached to an adjustable headband, worn in cold weather

earn /urn/ (**earns, earning, earned**) v **1.** vti MAKE MONEY BY WORKING to receive money or payment of some other kind in return for work done ○ *earn enough to live on* **2.** vt DESERVE SOMETHING to acquire something as a result of personal actions or behaviour ○ *earn praise* ○ *The remark earned him a stern rebuke.* **3.** vt FIN PRODUCE DIVIDENDS to produce interest or dividends from money invested [Old English *earnian* < Germanic, 'harvest']

USAGE The past tense and past participle of the verb *earn* is *earned*. There is no alternative form ending in *-t*. The word is often heard pronounced /urnt/ and *earnt* is increasingly seen in written English, but it is not a standard form. This error may have arisen through confusion with the verb *learn*, which has the past forms *learned* or *learnt*.

Earn /urn/ river in central Scotland that flows into the River Tay. Length: 74 km/46 mi.

earned income /úrnd-/ n income from paid employment, not from investments

earner /úrnər/ n **1.** somebody who earns a particular level of income ○ *tax incentives for high earners* **2.** an activity, job, product, or transaction that generates money ◇ **a nice little earner** a job or activity that earns somebody a lot of money (*informal*)

earnest[1] /úrnist/ adj **1.** intensely or excessively serious and grave in manner or attitude ○ *an earnest expression* ○ *earnest discussions about privacy and propriety* **2.** undertaken or made in a spirit of deep sincerity and conviction, or with deep feeling ○ *He interrupted me with an earnest assurance of help and support.* [Old English *eornost* < Germanic] —**earnestly** adv —**earnestness** n ◇ **in earnest 1.** serious and sincere in your actions, words, or intentions ○ *Is she in earnest?* **2.** in a determined and purposeful way ○ *Now the campaign would begin in earnest.*

earnest[2] /úrnist/ n **1.** also **earnest money** a small advance payment that confirms a contract (*dated*) **2.** a sign, foretaste, or pledge of something to come (*literary*) [13C. Probably alteration of Old French *erres* 'pledges' < Latin *arra* < Greek *arrabōn* 'pledge' < Hebrew *'ērābhôn* < *'ārab* 'to pledge']

earnings /úrningz/ npl money earned through paid employment, as profit, or from investments

EAROM /ee rom/ abbr electrically alterable read-only memory

Earp /urp/, **Wyatt** (1848–1929) US frontiersman and law

enforcement officer. He was based in Dodge City, Kansas, and later in Tombstone, Arizona, where he participated in the gunfight at the OK Corral (1881). Full name **Earp, Wyatt Berry Stapp**

earphone /eér fōn/ *n* a device that converts electrical signals into audible sound and is worn on or held close to the ear (*often used in the plural*)

earpiece /eér peess/ *n* **1.** the part of a device such as a telephone, radio, or hearing aid that is held in, or close to, the ear **2.** the part of the frame of a pair of spectacles that fits over and round the ear

ear-piercing *n* the making of a hole through the earlobe with a sterilized needle, so that an earring can be attached through the hole ■ *adj* extremely or painfully loud and shrill

earplug /eér plug/ *n* a piece of something soft such as wax or foam rubber that is placed in the ear to keep out noise, water, or cold (*often used in the plural*)

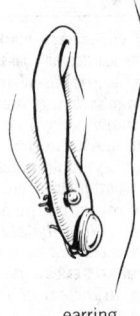

earring

earring /eér ring/ *n* a piece of jewellery worn on the ear, usually either clipped to the earlobe or attached through a hole pierced in it (*often used in the plural*)

earset /eér set/ *n* a piece of equipment attached to a computer or mobile phone that enables the user to speak on the telephone without using the hands

ear shell *n* MARINE BIOL same as **abalone**

earshot /eér shot/ *n* the distance within which sound is audible to somebody ○ *within earshot* [Early 17C. After words such as BOWSHOT]

earsplitting /eér splitting/ *adj* extremely loud or shrill —**earsplittingly** *adv*

ear stone *n* BIOL same as **otolith**

earth /urth/ *n* **1.** ASTRON another spelling of **Earth 2. LAND** the solid dry land surface of Earth, as opposed to the sea or sky **3. SOIL** the soft workable material in which plants grow **4. HUMAN INHABITANTS OF EARTH** all the human inhabitants of Earth (*formal*) **5. PURSUITS OF EVERYDAY LIFE** the pursuits of everyday human life, especially as opposed to matters of the spirit **6. BURROW** the hole or underground lair of a fox or other burrowing animal **7.** ELEC ENG **ELECTRICAL CONNECTION TO GROUND FOR SAFETY** an electrical connection to the ground intended to carry current safely away from a circuit in the event of a fault, or a wire that makes such a connection. N Am term **ground**[1] **8.** COLOURS same as **earth colour 9.** PHILOSOPHY, HIST **ONE OF FOUR ELEMENTS** in ancient and medieval philosophy, one of the four elements, earth, air, fire, and water, from which it was believed everything was made ■ *vt* (**earths, earthing, earthed**) ELEC ENG **CONNECT APPLIANCE SAFELY TO GROUND** to equip an electrical circuit or appliance with a connection to the ground so that current is carried safely away in the event of a fault. N Am term **ground**[1] [Old English *eorþe* < Germanic] ◇ **come** *or* **be brought back (down) to earth** to return to reality after a period of happiness or unrealistic hopes ◇ **cost** *or* **charge the earth** to cost *or* charge a great deal of money ◇ **on earth** used to add intensity to a question, often indicating surprise or disbelief on the part of the questioner (*informal*) ○ *What on earth have you done to the computer now?* ◇ **run somebody** *or* **something to earth** to find somebody or something after a long and difficult search

earth up *vt* to cover part of a plant, especially the lower stem, with soil, in order to protect it against frost or light, or in order to prevent it from turning green

Earth *n* the third planet in order from the Sun with

an orbital period of 365.26 days, a diameter of 12,756 km/7,926 mi., and an average distance from the Sun of 149,600,000 km/93,000,000 mi. Surrounded by an atmosphere composed primarily of nitrogen and oxygen, it is the only planet in the universe known to support life.

earthborn /urth bawrn/ *adj* born on or originating from Earth, and therefore human, mortal, or earthly (*literary*)

earthbound /urth bownd/ *adj* **1. CONFINED TO EARTH** unable to leave Earth **2. MUNDANE AND UNIMAGINATIVE** exclusively concerned with *or* confined to ordinary everyday or worldly matters and lacking in imagination or spirituality **3. HEADING TOWARDS EARTH** heading or moving towards Earth

earth closet *n* a toilet in which soil is used to cover the faeces, often consisting of a seat placed over a deep hole in the ground inside a small outdoor building

earth colour *n* a pigment obtained from earth, e.g. umber or ochre

earthed /urtht/ *adj* connected to the ground by an electrical earth

earthen /urth'n/ *adj* made of earth or baked clay

earthenware /urth'n wair/ *n* pottery made of fairly coarse-textured baked clay that is fired at a very low temperature

Earth Liberation Front *n* an environmental movement that stages demonstrations and takes direct action to defend forests and land from logging companies and developers

earthlight /urth līt/ *n* ASTRON same as **earthshine**

earthling /urthling/ *n* especially in science fiction, a human being, as opposed to an extraterrestrial or supernatural being

earthly /urthli/ (**-lier, -liest**) *adj* **1.** belonging to or characteristic of the physical world, especially as opposed to a spiritual realm or heaven **2.** used to add intensity to a negative or question ○ *no earthly use*

earthman /urth man/ (*plural* **-men** /-men/) *n* in science fiction, a resident of Earth, especially a man, as referred to by an extraterrestrial

earth mother *n* **1. WOMAN FAVOURING NATURAL WAY OF LIFE** a woman who is dedicated to nature and to natural, organic, and environmentally friendly ways of doing things, often rejecting social conventions (*informal*) **2. SENSUAL AND MOTHERLY WOMAN** a woman who conveys a warm combination of sensuality and motherliness **3. FERTILITY GODDESS** a goddess worshipped as a source of life and fertility

earthmover /urth moovər/ *n* a vehicle such as a bulldozer that is designed to move earth, especially in large quantities —**earthmoving** *adj*

earth pillar *n* a pillar of soft material capped by a boulder of more resistant rock that protects it from erosion

earthquake /urth kwayk/ *n* **1.** a violent shaking of the Earth's crust that may cause destruction to buildings and results from the sudden release of tectonic stress along a fault line or from volcanic activity **2.** an event that causes an upheaval in society, politics, or somebody's life

earthrise /urth rīz/ *n* the rising of Earth above the Moon's horizon, as seen from space or from the Moon itself

earth science *n* a science that deals with the Earth's physical properties, structure, or development, e.g. geology

earthshattering /urth shattəring/, **earthshaking** /urth shayking/ *adj* extremely great or important, or having an extremely powerful effect —**earthshatteringly** *adv*

earthshine /urth shīn/ *n* sunlight reflected from Earth that illuminates the part of the Moon not receiving light directly from the Sun

earth sign *n* each of the three signs of the zodiac, Taurus, Virgo, and Capricorn, traditionally associated with stability and consistency

earthstar /urth staar/ *n* a woodland fungus with a

round outer surface that splits open in a star-shaped pattern to release spores. Genus: *Geastrum*.

earth station *n* a system for relaying radio signals between one or more satellites and other communications networks. Earth stations may be on the ground, at sea, or in aircraft.

earth tone *n* a colour with an element of deep rich brown in it, e.g. gold or russet

earthward /urthwərd/ *adj* directed or facing towards Earth or the ground ■ *adv* same as **earthwards**

earthwards /urthwərdz/ *adv* in the direction of the earth or the ground

earth wax *n* INDUST, GEOL same as **ozocerite**

earthwoman /urth woomən/ (*plural* **-women** /-wimmin/) *n* especially in science fiction, a female resident of Earth as referred to by an extraterrestrial

earthwork /urth wurk/ *n* **1.** a fortification made of earth (*often used in the plural*) **2.** construction work involving excavating, earthmoving, and building embankments

earthworm /urth wurm/ *n* a worm that burrows in the soil and helps to aerate and improve it. Family: Lumbricidae.

earthy /urthi/ (**-ier, -iest**) *adj* **1. LIKE SOIL** relating to or consisting of soil **2. NOT SQUEAMISH OR PRETENTIOUS** having or showing a hearty, cheerful, no-nonsense acceptance of the realities and facts of life **3. RATHER INDECENT** crude and coarse ○ *earthy humour* —**earthily** *adv* —**earthiness** *n*

ear trumpet *n* an early type of hearing aid consisting of a trumpet-shaped device that was held to the ear

ear tuft *n* a tuft of feathers above the eyes of some owls and other birds, causing the bird to look larger or blend in with foliage, but not used in hearing

earwax /eér waks/ *n* a yellowish waxy substance secreted by glands in the external ear to protect the delicate lining of the outer ear. Technical name **cerumen**

earwig /eér wig/ *n* SLENDER INSECT WITH PINCERS a common insect with a slender shiny body, small forewings, antennae, and pincers at the end of its abdomen. Order: Dermaptera. ■ *v* (**-wigs, -wigging, -wigged**) **1.** *vti* EAVESDROP to eavesdrop, or eavesdrop on something (*humorous*) **2.** *vt* TRY TO INFLUENCE SOMEBODY to try to influence somebody, e.g. a judge, privately or clandestinely [Old English *ēarwicga* < *ēare* 'ear' + *wicga* 'insect']

REGIONAL NOTE From the proliferation of existing forms, *earwigs* must have been very familiar in all parts of the British Isles. Among the synonyms are *battle-twigs*, *cat-o'-two-tails*, *earlywigs*, *earywigs*, *harry-wiggles*, *skutchy-bells*, and *urrins*. Many of these names, like the insect, are no longer common.

earywig /eéri wig/ *n regional* INSECTS same as **earwig** [Alteration]

REGIONAL NOTE See *earwig*.

ease /eez/ *n* **1. LACK OF DIFFICULTY** lack of difficulty in doing or achieving something ○ *defeated the challenger with ease* **2. LACK OF AWKWARDNESS** lack of awkwardness, stiffness, or self-consciousness in social situations ○ *He felt totally at ease with her.* **3. COMFORT AND AFFLUENCE** a comfortable and leisured state free from worries, problems, and restrictions, especially those affecting somebody's financial situation ○ *a life of ease* ■ *v* (**eases, easing, eased**) **1.** *vt* MAKE LESS UNPLEASANT to make something less unpleasant, difficult, or restrictive **2.** *vti* RELIEVE OR ABATE to become, or to cause something to become, less strong or intense ○ *The rain eased.* ○ *The medication soon started to ease the pain.* **3.** *vti* MANOEUVRE GENTLY to manoeuvre gently and carefully, especially in a tight space, or to manoeuvre something in this way ○ *eased the truck into the space* **4.** *vt* LOOSEN SOMETHING to slacken something that is tied or held tightly **5.** *vt* MAKE EASIER to enable something to take place more easily ○ *This would certainly ease the measure's passage through Parliament.* [12C. < French *aise* 'comfort']

ease off *v* **1.** *vi* to lessen in intensity ○ *The rain had begun to ease off.* **2.** *vt* to slacken a rope or cable

easeful /ēēzfʹl/ adj giving relief from pain, suffering, or distress (literary)

easel /ēēzʹl/ n a freestanding upright support for a painter's canvas or a school blackboard, usually made of wood and having movable clamps [Late 16C. Via Dutch ezel 'donkey' < Latin asinus]

easement /ēēzmənt/ n a limited right to make use of a property owned by another, e.g. a right of way across the property [14C. < Old French aisement < aise 'comfort']

easily /ēēzili/ adv **1.** WITHOUT DIFFICULTY without difficulty, effort, or strain ○ We can easily be there by lunchtime. **2.** QUICKLY quickly and after comparatively little effort, stress, or provocation ○ She doesn't give up easily. **3.** BY FAR without doubt and by a large margin ○ She's easily the best. **4.** PROBABLY used to show that something might probably or could almost certainly happen ○ He could easily have forgotten, so I'd better check. **5.** AT LEAST not less and probably far more than a particular number or amount ○ There were easily 200 people at the meeting. **6.** CALMLY in a relaxed and untroubled way ○ We talked easily, like old friends.

east /ēēst/ n **1.** DIRECTION IN WHICH SUN RISES the direction that lies directly ahead of somebody facing the rising sun or that is located towards the right-hand side of a conventional map of the world **2.** COMPASS POINT OPPOSITE WEST the compass point that lies directly opposite west **3.** AREA IN EAST the part of an area, region, or country that is situated in or towards the east **4.** POSITION EQUIVALENT TO EAST the position equivalent to east in any diagram consisting of four points at 90 degree intervals **5.** another spelling of **East** ■ adj **1.** SITUATED IN EAST situated in, facing, or coming from the east of an area, region, or country **2.** BLOWING FROM EAST describes a wind that blows from the east ■ adv TOWARDS EAST in or towards the east [Old English ēast- < Indo-European, 'to shine']

East /ēēst/ n **1.** ASIA the countries of Asia, especially East Asia **2.** FORMER COMMUNIST COUNTRIES the communist countries of Eastern Europe and Asia during the Cold War **3.** EASTERN REGION OF US the region of the United States that includes the states east of the Mississippi River and north of the Mason-Dixon Line

East Africa /ēēst-/ region in east-central Africa, usually taken to comprise Burundi, Kenya, Rwanda, Somalia, Tanzania, and Uganda —**East African** n, adj

East Anglia /-áng gli ə/ mainly agricultural region in eastern England. It covers Norfolk, Suffolk, Cambridgeshire, and Essex, and includes the Norfolk Broads and the Fens. —**East Anglian** n, adj

East Asia the countries, territories, and regions of China, Hong Kong, Japan, North Korea, South Korea, Macau, Mongolia, parts of Russia, and Taiwan. ◊ **Far East**

East Ayrshire council area in the former Strathclyde Region of west-central Scotland. The administrative centre is Kilmarnock. Area: 1,252 sq. km/483 sq. mi.

East Bengal former region created in 1905 when Bengal Province in northeastern British India was divided into Hindu West Bengal (now Bangla) and the mainly Muslim East Bengal. The division was reversed in 1912 and when British India was partitioned in 1947, East Bengal became East Pakistan. It became the People's Republic of Bangladesh in 1971. ◊ **West Bengal**

East Berlin capital of East Germany from 1949 until 1990, when both Berlin and Germany were reunified —**East Berliner** n

eastbound /ēēst bownd/ adj, adv going or leading towards the east

Eastbourne /ēēst bawrn/ seaside resort and conference centre in East Sussex, southeastern England. Population: 89,667 (2001).

east by north n the direction or compass point midway between east and east-northeast —**east by north** adj, adv

east by south n the direction or compass point midway between east and east-southeast —**east by south** adj, adv

East Cape peninsular region in the eastern part of the North Island, New Zealand, that forms the easternmost part of the country. Most of the region is used for grazing sheep.

East China Sea arm of the northwestern Pacific Ocean between the eastern coast of China and the Ryukyu Islands. It is bounded to the north by the Yellow Sea and to the south by Taiwan. Area: 1,249,200 sq. km/482,300 sq. mi.

East Coast easternmost part of the United States, consisting of the states along its eastern seaboard from Maine to Florida, especially the oldest, most urban part of this area: New England, New York, New Jersey, Pennsylvania, Maryland, Virginia, and Washington, DC.

East Dunbartonshire council area in the former Strathclyde Region of central Scotland. Area: 172 sq. km/66 sq. mi.

East End n an area in the east of London, England, traditionally inhabited by working-class people, now undergoing regeneration —**East Ender** n

Easter /ēēstər/ n **1.** CHRISTIAN FESTIVAL IN SPRING a Christian festival marking the resurrection of Jesus Christ. Date: the Sunday following the full moon on or after 21 March. **2.** SUNDAY OF EASTER FESTIVAL the Sunday on which Easter is celebrated **3.** EASTER WEEKEND the period from the Friday before Easter to the Monday after [Old English Ēastre < Germanic dawn-goddess whose festival was celebrated at the vernal equinox < Indo-European, 'to shine']

Easter bonnet n a woman's hat, often elaborately decorated, traditionally worn for the first time at Easter

Easter bunny (plural **Easter bunnies**) n **1.** an imaginary rabbit that traditionally hides coloured Easter eggs for children to find at Easter **2.** a rabbit, traditionally associated with spring and used as a motif on cards and gifts given at Easter

Easter Day n CALENDAR same as **Easter** (sense 2)

Easter egg n **1.** CHOCOLATE EGG AS EASTER GIFT a chocolate egg given as a gift to children at Easter **2.** N Am COLOURED HEN'S EGG FOR EASTER a hen's egg that has been dyed, painted, or decorated for Easter, often hidden for children to find in an Easter egg hunt **3.** HIDDEN ELEMENT OF A COMPUTER PROGRAM a secret message, graphic, animation, or sound effect hidden in a computer program and activated by a specific undocumented sequence of keystrokes. An Easter egg is typically intended as a harmless joke or as a way to display the credits of the program's development team.

Easter Island

Easter Island /ēēstər-/ island in the South Pacific Ocean belonging to Chile. It is noted for its huge carved stone heads and hieroglyphic tablets. Population: 2,095 (1989). Area: 117 sq. km/45 sq. mi. —**Easter Islander** n

Easter lily n a cultivated spring-flowering lily. Flowers: large, white.

easterly /ēēstərli/ adj **1.** IN EAST situated in or towards the east **2.** BLOWING FROM EAST describes a wind that blows from the east ■ n (plural **-lies**) WIND FROM EAST a wind that blows from the east —**easterly** adv

Easter Monday n the Monday at the end of the Christian festival of Easter

eastern /ēēstərn/ adj **1.** SITUATED IN EAST situated in the east of a region or country **2.** TOWARDS EAST facing the east **3.** another spelling of **Eastern** (sense 1) **4.** EAST OF GREENWICH MERIDIAN lying east of the Greenwich meridian **5.** BLOWING FROM EAST describes a wind that blows from the east

Eastern adj **1.** relating or belonging to the countries of Asia as viewed from Europe or North America **2.** relating or belonging to the Eastern Orthodox Church

Eastern Cape /ēēstərn-/ province in South Africa, in the southeastern part of the country. Capital: Bisho. Population: 6,436,756 (2001). Area: 169,580 sq. km/65,475 sq. mi.

Eastern Church n the Christian churches of Southwest Asia, North Africa, and Eastern Europe seen as a group, including the Coptic Church and the Orthodox Church

Eastern Empire n HIST same as **Byzantine Empire**

easterner /ēēstərnər/, **Easterner** n somebody who comes from the eastern part of a geographical area

Eastern Europe region comprising the countries of east and central Europe that had close ties with the former Soviet Union, e.g. Poland, the Czech Republic, Slovakia, Hungary, Romania, Bulgaria, Albania, and the former Yugoslavia

Eastern European Time n the standard time in the time zone centred on longitude 30°E, which includes Finland and Greece. It is two hours later than Universal Time.

Eastern Ghats /-gaáts/ mountain range in southeastern India, running parallel to the Coromandel Coast, with an average elevation of 600 m/2,000 ft

eastern grey kangaroo n a large silver-grey kangaroo. Native to: forests and scrub of eastern Australia and Tasmania. Latin name: Macropus giganteus.

eastern hemisphere n **1.** the half of the Earth that lies east of the Greenwich meridian and contains Asia, Australasia, and most of Europe and Africa **2.** the countries within the eastern hemisphere, especially the countries of Asia

easternmost /ēēstərn mōst/ adj **1.** farthest to the east **2.** located at the most eastern extreme of an area, region, or country

Eastern Orthodox Church n CHR same as **Orthodox Church** (sense 2)

Eastern Standard Time, **Eastern Time** n **1.** the standard time in the time zone centred on longitude 75° W, which includes the eastern part of North America. It is five hours later than Universal Time. **2.** the standard time in the time zone centred on longitude 150° E, which includes the eastern part of Australia. It is ten hours later than Universal Time.

Eastern Townships /-tówn ships/ group of settlements in southern Quebec Province, Canada, east of Montreal and south of the St Lawrence River

Eastern Transvaal former name for **Mpumalanga**

Easter Rising n an armed rebellion against British rule that took place in Dublin on Easter Day in 1916

Easter Sunday n CALENDAR same as **Easter** (sense 2)

Easter term n the term at the High Court that follows Hilary term

Eastertide /ēēstər tīd/, **Eastertime** /-tīm/ n the period around Easter [12C. < Old English eastertīd]

East Germanic n a group of extinct languages that were formerly spoken in parts of Eastern Europe. It is one of the three groups that form the Germanic branch of Indo-European. Gothic is the only language in this group that has any known written form. —**East Germanic** adj

East Germany ♦ German Democratic Republic —**East German** n, adj

East India Company n a trading company established in England in 1600 to trade with the East Indies, and later with India, which it effectively governed for many years. Similar companies were also founded in the Netherlands and France.

East Indies /-ín deez/ collective name formerly applied to India, Southeast Asia, and the Malay Archipelago, especially Indonesia —**East Indian** adj, n

easting /ēēsting/ n **1.** DISTANCE TRAVELLED EAST the net distance eastwards that a boat travels when making

for the east **2.** PART OF MAP REFERENCE the first part of a map reference that shows how far east a point lies from a reference line running from north to south **3.** NORTH-SOUTH GRID LINE ON MAP a grid line on a map running north to south

East Kilbride /-kil bríd/ manufacturing town in south-central Scotland near Glasgow, designated a new town in 1947. Population: 70,422 (1991).

East London city in southeastern South Africa, a seaport and holiday resort. Population: 102,325 (1991).

East Lothian council area in southeastern Scotland, bordering the Firth of Forth and the North Sea. Area: 678 sq. km/262 sq. mi.

Eastman /éestmən/, **George** (1854–1932) US inventor and philanthropist. He perfected the box camera (1888), the first camera designed specifically for roll film.

east-northeast *n* the direction or compass point midway between east and northeast ■ *adj, adv* in, from, facing, or towards the east-northeast —**east-northeasterly** *adj, adv*

East Pakistan one of the two areas that made up Pakistan following the partition of British India in 1947. It became the independent People's Republic of Bangladesh in 1971.

East Prussia former German province on the Baltic Sea that was divided between Poland and Russia in 1945 —**East Prussian** *n, adj*

East Renfrewshire council area in central Scotland, formerly part of the Strathclyde Region. Area: 173 sq. km/67 sq. mi.

East Riding of Yorkshire /-rīding-/ **1.** historic division of the county of Yorkshire in northeastern England **2.** council area in northeastern England, established in 1996, covering largely the same area as the historic division. Population: 594,440 (1996). Area: 1,819 sq. km/704 sq. mi.

East River strait in southeastern New York State, separating Manhattan Island from Long Island. Length: 24 km/15 mi.

East Sea ➧ **Japan, Sea of**

east-southeast *n* the direction or compass point midway between east and southeast ■ *adj, adv* in, from, facing, or towards the east-southeast —**east-southeasterly** *adj, adv*

East Stewartry Coast /-styoó artri-/ National Scenic Area in southwestern Scotland. Area: 45 sq. km/17 sq. mi.

East Sussex county in southeastern England. Its administrative centre is Lewes. Area: 1,795 sq. km/693 sq. mi.

East Timor former name for **Timor-Leste**

eastward /éestwərd/ *adj* towards or in the east ■ *n* a direction towards the east or a point in the east ■ *adv* same as **eastwards** —**eastwardly** *adj, adv*

USAGE eastward or **eastwards**? ***Eastward*** is the only form available for the adjective (*in an eastward direction*), while ***eastwards*** is commonly used as well as ***eastward*** for the adverb: *The ship was moving slowly eastward/eastwards.*

eastwards /éestwərdz/ *adv* in an easterly direction

Eastwood /éestwŏŏd/, **Clint** (*b.* 1930) US film actor and director. He is known for his westerns such as *The Good, the Bad and the Ugly* (1966) and *Unforgiven* (1992) and for his action films such as *Dirty Harry* (1971). Born **Eastwood, Clinton, Jr.**

> 'Every actor should direct at least once. It gives you a tolerance, an understanding of the problems involved in making a film. In fact every director should act.'
> [Clint Eastwood, *Playboy*; February 1974]

easy /éezi/ *adj* (**-ier, -iest**) **1.** NOT DIFFICULT not causing problems or difficulty, or not requiring much effort, work, or thought ○ *Answer the easy questions first.* ○ *It's easy to see why they chose him.* ○ *always taking the easy way out* **2.** RELAXED AND INFORMAL relaxed, informal, and without awkwardness or self-consciousness, especially in social situations ○ *had an easy manner* **3.** GOOD-NATURED good-natured and tolerant ○ *an easy disposition* **4.** FINANCIALLY PROSPEROUS characterized by financial prosperity and security and the comfort and peace of mind that goes with them ○ *easy living* **5.** NOT HARSH not severe or harsh ○ *received an easy sentence for the crime* **6.** GULLIBLE not difficult to catch, acquire, take advantage of, or exploit ○ *unscrupulous sellers looking for easy targets* **7.** LOOSE not tight or close-fitting ○ *jeans that are an easy fit* **8.** UNHURRIED comfortable, unhurried, and not too fast ○ *took an easy pace up the trail* **9.** NOT STEEP not steep or difficult to climb up or down ○ *It's an easy slope to the top.* **10.** NOT ANXIOUS free from unpleasant feelings such as anxiety, guilt, or worry ○ *Rest easy; we'll be there soon.* **11.** LACKING PREFERENCES having no strong preferences (*informal*) ○ *We can do either: I'm easy.* **12.** OFFENSIVE TERM an offensive term meaning sexually promiscuous or too willing to become sexually involved (*slang*) **13.** ECON READILY OBTAINABLE readily obtainable, because demand is lower than usual ○ *easy credit* **14.** ECON MARKED BY LOW DEMAND AND PRICES characterized by low demand or overproduction and hence low prices ○ *an easy market* ■ *adv* WITHOUT DIFFICULTY OR EFFORT without difficulty or the need for hard work ○ *Everything comes easy to her.* [12C. < Old French *aisié*, past participle of *aisier* 'put at ease' < *aise* 'comfort'] —**easiness** *n* ◇ **go easy on somebody** to treat or deal with somebody gently, leniently, or without harsh criticism or reproach (*informal*) ◇ **go easy on something** to avoid using, eating, or drinking too much of something (*informal*) ◇ **take it easy 1.** to relax, avoid effort, or not work too hard **2.** to calm down and avoid becoming upset or angry

SYNONYMS ***easy, simple, straightforward, uncomplicated***

CORE MEANING: not difficult to do or achieve

easy not causing problems or difficulty, or not requiring much effort, work, or thought ○ *a computer designed to be easy to use* ○ *There is no easy way to answer this question.* **simple** able to be done or understood quickly or with very little effort ○ *Selecting different fonts is a simple process.* ○ *It's a basic concept, simple to grasp.* **straightforward** not difficult to understand or carry out ○ *It was a perfectly straightforward job.* **uncomplicated** readily understood, or easy to deal with ○ *We have made the process as clear and uncomplicated as possible to encourage you to invest.*

easybeat /éezi beet/ *n Aus* a competitor who is easily beaten in a sport or other endeavour

easy-care *adj* describes fabrics or clothes that are easy to wash and iron

easy chair *n* a comfortably upholstered chair, especially an armchair

~~**easyer**~~ incorrect spelling of **easier**

easy game *n* same as **easy meat** (*informal*)

easygoing /éezi gṓ ing/ *adj* **1.** having a relaxed, informal, and tolerant attitude and reluctant to make heavy demands or enforce strict discipline on people **2.** unhurried and comfortable

easy listening *n* popular music in an undemanding style, usually with a lyrical or romantic tune, gentle rhythms, and soft soothing orchestration

~~**easyly**~~ incorrect spelling of **easily**

easy meat, easy game, easy mark *n* somebody who can be easily taken advantage of (*informal*)

easy money *n* **1.** money made with little effort, and often dishonestly (*informal*) **2.** money that can be borrowed at a low rate of interest

easy-peasy /-péezi/ (**easy-peasier, easy-peasiest**) *adj* extremely easy (*informal*) [Reduplication]

easy street *n* a situation in which somebody has no worries, especially no financial worries (*informal*) ○ *For three successful years we were living on easy street.*

easy terms *npl* a form of credit involving payment by instalments

easy virtue *n* lax sexual morals and promiscuous sexual habits (*dated*)

easy wicket *n* **1.** in cricket, a pitch on which the ball bounces predictably and a batsman can score runs relatively easily **2.** *Aus* a task or job that requires little effort (*informal*)

eat /eet/ (**eats, eating, ate** /et, ayt/, **eaten** /éet'n/) *v* **1.** *vti* CONSUME AS SUSTENANCE to take something into the mouth as food and swallow it ○ *They hadn't eaten for three days.* **2.** *vt* CONSUME SOMETHING USUALLY to include something as a usual or fundamental part of a diet ○ *Do dogs eat fish?* **3.** *vi* DINE to have a meal ○ *Are you ready to eat?* **4.** *vti* PENETRATE to penetrate the surface of something by corrosive or mechanical action ○ *Rust had eaten into the chrome.* **5.** *vt* BOTHER SOMEBODY to bother or annoy somebody (*informal*) ○ *What's eating her?* **6.** *vt* USE LARGE QUANTITY OF SOMETHING to use or consume something in large quantities (*informal*) ○ *a big car that eats petrol* **7.** *vt* TABOO TERM a highly offensive term meaning to perform oral sex on somebody (*taboo*) [Old English *etan* < Indo-European] —**eater** *n*

eat away *vt* to consume or destroy something gradually ○ *The surface has been eaten away in parts by acid rain.*

eat away at *vt* **1.** to worry or be a continual source of distress to somebody ○ *Guilt had been eating away at him all day.* **2.** to deplete or use up something gradually by taking small amounts regularly ○ *medical expenses eating away at our income*

eat in *vi* to consume a meal at home ○ *Would you rather eat in or go to a restaurant?*

eat into *vt* to use up part of something, especially in a wasteful or nonproductive way ○ *ate into their savings*

eat out *vi* to consume a meal away from home, usually in a restaurant or similar establishment ○ *Let's eat out tonight.*

eat up *v* **1.** *vti* EAT COMPLETELY to consume food completely or with great appetite **2.** *vt* OBSESS SOMEBODY to absorb or obsess somebody (*usually passive*) ○ *hard to avoid being eaten up by envy* **3.** *vt* RECEIVE SOMETHING ENTHUSIASTICALLY to receive something with enthusiasm or pleasure (*informal*) ○ *The reading public eats up everything she writes.* **4.** *vt* CONSUME SOMETHING QUICKLY to consume or deal with something quickly (*informal*) ○ *Commuting eats up my time.*

eatable /éetəb'l/ *adj* fit, suitable, or pleasant to eat ■ *n* something that is fit, suitable, or pleasant to eat (*informal; usually used in the plural*) ○ *If you organize the liquid refreshments, we'll bring the eatables.*

USAGE eatable or **edible**? ***Eatable*** is used to refer to food that can be eaten with enjoyment, whereas ***edible*** refers to any substance in respect of its suitability as food. If something is ***eatable*** it is also ***edible***, but a substance can be ***edible*** without being ***eatable*** (for example, raw potatoes). Informally, however, ***edible*** is often used to mean ***eatable*** (though not usually the other way round): *The vegetables were overcooked but just about edible.* The same distinction applies to the negative forms of these words: *The meal was uneatable. Toadstools are inedible.*

eaten past participle of **eat**

eatery /éetəri/ (*plural* **-ies**) *n* a place where food is cooked and sold (*informal*)

eating /éeting/ *adj* **1.** SUITABLE AS FOOD suitable for human consumption, especially uncooked ○ *eating apples* **2.** INVOLVING FOOD relating to or used for the consumption of food ○ *eating utensils* ■ *n* FOOD something that can be eaten, especially of a particular quality ○ *These apples are good eating.*

eating disorder *n* an emotional disorder that manifests itself in an irrational craving for, or avoidance of, food, e.g. bulimia

eats /eets/ *npl* same as **food** (sense 2) (*informal*) ○ *What do you do for eats around here?* [Late 19C. < EAT]

Eau Claire /ō kláir/ city in western Wisconsin, at the confluence of the Chippewa and Eau Claire rivers. Population: 62,361 (2002 estimate).

eau de cologne /ṓ də kə lṓn/ *n* COSMETICS same as **cologne** [Early 19C. < French, 'water of Cologne']

eau de nil /ṓ də néel/ *adj* of a pale yellowish-green colour [Late 19C. < French, 'water of the Nile'] —**eau de nil** *n*

eau de toilette /ṓ də twaa lét/ *n* COSMETICS same as **toilet water** [< French]

eau de vie /ṓ də vée/ *n* a strong alcoholic spirit, especially brandy [Mid-18C. < French, 'water of life']

a at; aa father; aw all; ay day; ai hair; ə about, item, edible, common, circus; e egg; ee eel; hw when; i it, happy; ī ice; 'l apple; 'm rhythm; 'n fashion; o odd; ō open; ŏŏ good; oo pool; ow owl; oy oil; th thin; th this; u up; ur urge;

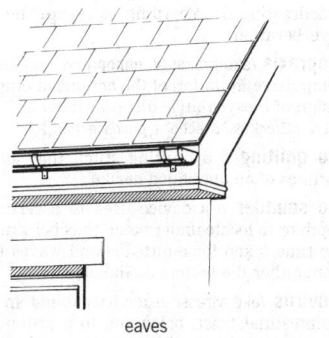

eaves

eaves /eevz/ *npl* the part of a roof that projects beyond the wall that supports it [Old English *efes* < Germanic]

eavesdrop /eevz drop/ (**-drops, -dropping, -dropped**) *vi* to listen to a conversation without the speakers being aware of it [Early 17C. Probably back-formation < *eavesdropper* < obsolete *eavesdrop* 'ground on which rainwater thrown off by eaves falls'; from standing in this area trying to hear private conversations] —**eavesdropper** *n*

Ebadi /i baádi/, **Shirin** (*b.* 1947) Iranian lawyer, teacher, human rights activist, and one of the first woman judges in Iran. Known for promoting peaceful, democratic solutions to social problems, she was awarded the Nobel Peace Prize (2003).

Eban /ee ban/, **Abba** (1915–2002) South African-born Israeli politician. He worked for the United Nations in Palestine (1946) and later held diplomatic and ministerial posts in Israel. These include being Israel's ambassador to the UN (1948–59) and to the United States (1950–59), and deputy prime minister (1963–66). Born **Solomon, Aubrey**

'History teaches us that men and nations behave wisely once they have exhausted all other alternatives.'
[Abba Eban, *Speech, Times*; 17 December 1970]

ebb /eb/ *vi* (**ebbs, ebbing, ebbed**) **1. RECEDE FROM SHORE** to recede from the land, as the tide falls (*refers to the sea or tide*) **2. DIMINISH** to diminish or lessen in intensity ○ *The pain gradually ebbed away.* ■ *n* **1. TIDAL MOVEMENT AWAY FROM LAND** the movement of a receding tide away from the land **2. DIMINUTION** a diminution or lessening in intensity ○ *the ebb and flow of the company's fortunes* [Old English *ebbian* < Germanic] ◇ **at a low ebb 1.** lacking hope and energy **2.** in a depleted condition

ebb tide *n* a receding tide, or the time when a tide recedes

Ebbw Vale /ébboŏ-/ industrial town in southeastern Wales. Population: 19,484 (1991).

EBCDIC /éb see dik/ *n* a binary computer character code, representing 256 standard letters, numbers, symbols, and control characters by means of eight binary digits. Full form **extended binary coded decimal interchange code**

e-beam *n* a stream of high-energy electrons. Use: food irradiation, sterilization, welding, imaging.

e-biz *n* BUSINESS same as **e-business** (sense 2) (*informal*)

e-blocker *n* an employer who uses special software to prevent employees from visiting particular websites while at work

E-boat *n* a fast torpedo boat used by the German navy in World War II [Abbreviation of ENEMY]

Ebola /i bốlə/, **Ebola virus** *n* a virus transmitted by blood and body fluids that causes the linings of bodily organs and vessels to leak blood and fluids, usually resulting in death [Late 20C. After the River *Ebola*, Democratic Republic of the Congo]

e-bomb, **E-bomb** *n* a weapon that creates a brief pulse of microwaves powerful enough to disable electronically operated systems, e.g. in computers, aircraft, and radar

ebon /ébbən/ *n* COLOURS same as **ebony** (sense 3) (*literary*) [14C. Via French < Greek *ebenos* < Semitic] —**ebon** *adj*

Ebonics /e bónniks/ *n* LANG same as **African American Vernacular English** (*takes a singular verb*) [Late 20C. Blend of EBONY + PHONICS]

ebonise *vt* MANUF another spelling of **ebonize**

ebonite /ébbənīt/ *n* MANUF same as **vulcanite**

ebonize /ébbə nīz/ (**-izes, -izing, -ized**), **ebonise** (**-ises, -ising, -ised**) *vt* to stain something black so that it resembles ebony

ebony /ébbəni/ (*plural* **-ies**) *n* **1. DARK HARD WOOD** a hard blackish wood **2. ASIAN TREE** a tree that yields ebony. Native to: tropical Asia. Genus: *Diospyros*. **3. BROWNISH-BLACK COLOUR** black tinged with olive or brown [15C. < EBON, probably after IVORY] —**ebony** *adj*

e-book *n* a battery-powered portable reading device displaying text on a high-resolution screen. E-books can be updated either from a book store or a website that sells digital texts.

Eboracum /i bórrəkəm, ée baw raákəm/ Roman name for the city of York

ebracteate /i brákti ayt, -ti ət/ *adj* describes plants that have no bracts [Mid-19C. < modern Latin *ebracteatus* 'without bracts']

EBRD *abbr* European Bank for Reconstruction and Development

Ebro /éebrō/ river in northeastern Spain. It rises in the Cantabrian Mountains near Reinosa and flows to its delta on the Mediterranean coast, south of Tarragona. Length: 910 km/565 mi.

ebullient /i búlliyənt, i boŏll-/ *adj* **1.** full of cheerful excitement or enthusiasm **2.** boiling or bubbling vigorously (*formal*) [Late 16C. < Latin *ebullient-*, present participle of *ebullire* 'bubble out' < *bullire* 'to bubble'] —**ebullience** *n* —**ebulliently** *adv*

ebullioscopy /i búlli óskəpi, i boŏll-/ *n* a process for determining the molecular weight of a substance by measuring the change it produces in the boiling point of a solution [Early 20C. < Latin *ebullire* (see EBULLIENT)] —**ebullioscope** /i búlli ə skōp/ *n*

ebullition /ébbə lísh'n/ *n* **1.** a state of bubbling up or boiling (*formal*) **2.** a sudden outbreak of violent emotion (*literary*) [14C. Via French < late Latin *ebullition-* < Latin *ebullire* (see EBULLIENT)]

eburnation /éebər náysh'n, ébbər-/ *n* a hardening of the surfaces of bones in a joint as a result of the loss of their cartilage covering, occurring in such medical conditions as osteoarthritis [Mid-19C. < Latin *eburnus* 'made of ivory' < *ebur* 'ivory']

e-business *n* **1.** a company that exists on the Internet, or the marketplace of such businesses collectively **2.** the conduct of business using Internet technology to create links between customers, suppliers, employees, and business partners (*used in e-commerce*)

EBV *abbr* MED Epstein-Barr virus

EB virus *n* MED same as **Epstein-Barr virus**

EC *abbr* **1.** European Commission **2.** European Community

écarté[1] /ay kaár tay/ *n* a card game for two people played with 32 cards in which cards may be discarded in exchange for others [Early 19C. < French, literally 'discarded']

écarté[2] /ay kaár tay/ *n* a ballet position in which the arm on one side of the body are extended [Early 20C. < French, literally 'spread out']

ECB *abbr* BANKING European Central Bank

ecce homo /é kay hốmō, éksi-/ *n* a portrayal of Jesus Christ crowned with thorns [< Latin, literally 'behold the man' (John 19:5)]

eccentric /ik séntrik, ek-/ *adj* **1. UNCONVENTIONAL** unconventional, especially in a whimsical way ○ *an eccentric mode of dress* **2.** TECH **AWAY FROM CENTRE** away from the centre or axis **3.** MATHS **HAVING DIFFERENT CENTRES** describes circles with different centres **4.** ASTRON **ELLIPTICAL** describes an orbit that is elliptical rather than circular ■ *n* **1. UNCONVENTIONAL PERSON** an unconventional person who has unusual habits **2.** MECH ENG **MECHANICAL DEVICE** a mechanical device with an off-centre axis of revolution that converts the rotary motion of one component of a mechanism to reciprocating motion in another [Mid-16C. < late Latin

eccentricus < Greek *ekkentros* 'out of centre' < *kentron* (see CENTRE)] —**eccentrically** *adv*

eccentricity /ék sen tríssəti/ (*plural* **-ties**) *n* **1. ECCENTRIC QUALITY** a quality of being unconventional, especially in a whimsical way **2. ECCENTRIC ACT** an example or instance of unconventional whimsical behaviour **3.** MECH ENG **DISTANCE BETWEEN MAIN AND SECONDARY AXIS** the distance between the axis about which a body rotates and a secondary axis on the object at which a device such as a rod could be attached **4.** ASTRON **DEVIATION** the deviation of the path of an orbiting body from a true circle **5.** MATHS **GEOMETRIC CONSTANT** a constant that describes the shape of a conic section. It is equal to the ratio of the distance from a fixed point of any point on the curve to the distance of that point from the corresponding fixed straight line.

ecchymosis /éki mốssiss/ (*plural* **-moses** /-mốseez/) *n* bleeding from broken blood vessels into surrounding tissue (*technical*) [Mid-16C. Via modern Latin < Greek *ekkhumōsis* < *ekkhumonothai* 'pour out']

Eccles /ék'lz/, **Sir John** (1903–97) Australian physiologist. He was joint winner of the Nobel Prize in physiology or medicine (1963) for his studies of the transmission of impulses between nerve cells. Full name **Eccles, Sir John Carew**

eccles. *abbr* **1.** ecclesiastic **2.** ecclesiastical

Eccles. *abbr* BIBLE Ecclesiastes

Eccles cake /ék'lz-/ *n* a pastry filled with dried fruit [After a town in NW England]

Ecclesiastes /i kleézi áss teez/ *n* a book of the Bible that discusses the futility of life and how to be a God-fearing person. See table at **Bible**

ecclesiastic /i kleézi ástik/ *n* a member of the clergy ■ *adj* CHR same as **ecclesiastical** [15C. Via French or ecclesiastical Latin < Greek *ekklēsiastikos* < *ekklēsiastēs* 'member of an assembly' < *ekklēsia* 'assembly, (later) church']

ecclesiastical /i kleézi ástik'l/ *adj* belonging to or involving the Christian Church or clergy —**ecclesiastically** *adv*

ecclesiasticism /i kleézi ástisizəm/ *n* **1.** excessive regard for the principles and customary practices of the Christian Church **2.** the principles or body of thought constituting organized Christianity

Ecclesiasticus /i kleézi ástikəss/ *n* a book of teachings in the Roman Catholic Bible and the Protestant Apocrypha. See table at **Bible**

ecclesiology /i kleézi ólləji/ *n* **1.** the study of the history and theology of the Christian Church **2.** the study of the architecture and decoration of Christian churches

eccoccino /ékō cheénō/ (*plural* **-nos**) *n* Aus in Australia, a drink similar to cappuccino made with a barley- and chicory-based powder (**Ecco**) instead of coffee [Late 20C. Blend of *Ecco*, name of the powder + CAPPUCCINO]

eccrine /ékrīn, ékrin/ *adj* describes sweat glands that are distributed all over the body, especially on the hands and feet, that do not secrete organic matter, and that are important in regulating body temperature [Mid-20C. < German *Ekkrin* < Greek *ekkrinein* 'secrete']

ecdysiast /ek dízzi ast/ *n* a performer of striptease (*humorous*) [Mid-20C. < ECDYSIS, after *gymnast*]

ecdysis /ékdississ, ek dī-/ *n* the regular moulting of an outer layer by arthropods such as insects and crustaceans, and by reptiles [Mid-19C. < Greek *ekdusis* < *ekduein* 'put off, shed']

ecdysone /ékdi sōn/ *n* a hormone that promotes metamorphosis and ecdysis in insects and crustaceans [Mid-20C. < ECDYSIS]

ecesis /i seéssiss/ *n* the successful establishment of a plant or animal species in a new environment [Early 20C. < Greek *oikēsis* 'an inhabiting' < *oikos* 'house']

ECG *abbr* MED **1.** echocardiograph **2.** electrocardiogram **3.** electrocardiograph

ECGD *abbr* COMM Export Credits Guarantee Department

Echegaray y Eizaguirre /éch ay ga rí ee ay tha gírray/, **José** (1832–1916) Spanish playwright and politician. As well as writing poetic dramas, which won him a

shared Nobel Prize in 1904, he also held ministerial office (1868–74 and 1905).

echelon /éshə lon/ *n* **1.** LEVEL IN HIERARCHY a level of authority or rank in an organization or system ○ *the lower echelons of society* **2.** AIRCRAFT FORMATION WITH OFFSET POSITIONS a group of aircraft flying in positions behind and to one side of the aircraft in front **3.** MIL FORMATION WITH OFFSET POSITIONS a formation in which individuals or units are positioned behind and to one side of those in front to give a stepped effect and allow each a clear view ahead **4.** PHYS DEVICE FOR STUDYING SPECTRA a series of glass plates of equal thickness arranged like steps, used in spectroscopy for studying the fine structure of spectral lines ■ *vti* (**-lons, -loning, -loned**) FORM ECHELON to arrange something in or form an echelon [Late 18C. < French, 'rung' < *échelle* 'ladder' < Latin *scala* 'stair']

ORIGIN *Echelon* derives from French, and comes from the same Latin word as English *scale*².

echeveria /échə veeri ə/ *n* a low-growing cultivated plant with rosettes of fleshy leaves. Flowers: tubular, bell-shaped. Native to: tropical America. Genus: *Echeveria*. [Mid-19C. < modern Latin, after Atanasio *Echeverría* (1766–1811), Mexican botanical illustrator]

echidna /i kídnə/ *n* a spiny insect-eating mammal with a long snout and strong claws. Native to: Australia, New Guinea. Family: Tachyglossidae. [Mid-19C. Via modern Latin, 'viper' < Greek *ekhidna* < *ekhis* 'viper']

echin- *prefix* same as **echino-** (*used before vowels*)

echinacea /éki náyssi ə/ *n* **1.** a herbal remedy prepared from the pulverized leaves and stems of purple coneflowers, thought to bolster the immune system **2.** PLANTS same as **coneflower** [< modern Latin < Greek *ekhinos* 'hedgehog, sea urchin']

echinate /éki nayt/, **echinated** /-naytid/ *adj* describes plant and animal parts that have spines or similar outgrowths [Late 17C. < Latin *echinatus* < Greek *ekhinos* 'hedgehog, sea urchin']

echini ARCHIT, MARINE BIOL plural of **echinus**

echino- *prefix* **1.** spiny ○ *echinoderm* **2.** echinoderm ○ *echinoid* [Via Latin < Greek *ekhinos* 'hedgehog, sea urchin']

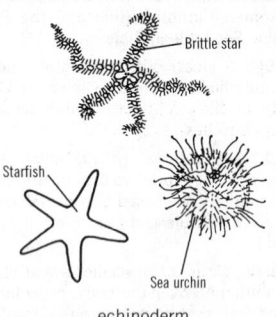

echinoderm

echinoderm /i kínə durm/ *n* an invertebrate sea animal with a radially symmetrical body, tube feet, and a system of calcareous plates under the skin. Starfish, sea urchins, sea lilies, and sea cucumbers are echinoderms. Phylum: Echinodermata. [Mid-19C. < ECHINO- + Greek *derma* 'skin']

echinoid /i kí noyd, ékə-/ *n* an invertebrate sea animal with a hard ovoid body and movable spines. Sea urchins and sand dollars are echinoids. Class: Echinoidea. —**echinoid** *adj*

echinus /i kínəss/ (*plural* **-ni** /-nī/) *n* **1.** a rounded moulding beneath the flat upper part (**abacus**) of a Doric or Tuscan column **2.** MARINE BIOL same as **sea urchin** [14C. < Latin (see ECHINO-)]

echo /ékō/ *n* (*plural* **-oes**) **1.** REPEATED SOUND the repetition of a sound caused by the reflection of sound waves from a surface **2.** SOMETHING SIMILAR something that repeats, imitates, or is reminiscent of something else ○ *Her songs found an echo in the hearts of thousands.* ○ *the current style with its echoes of the 1920s* **3.** PHYS RETURNED SIGNAL the signal reflected by an object struck by a radar transmission, or the

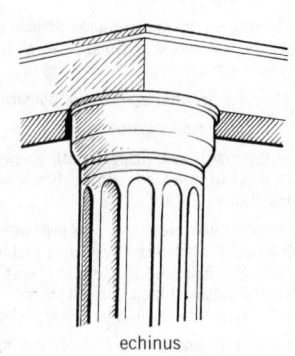

echinus

image of this on a radar screen **4.** LITERAT REPETITION OF SOUNDS the repetition of sounds within a sequence of verse or prose **5.** MUSIC REPEATED MUSIC the repetition, usually more quietly, of a phrase or note in music **6.** MUSIC ELECTRONIC SOUND REPETITION the repetition of sound created electronically for effect or by accident **7.** MUSIC ORGAN CONTROL a device on some organs that gives the effect of an echo coming from a distance ■ *v* (**-oes, -oing, -oed**) **1.** *vt* REFLECT SOUND to make a sound repeat by the reflection of sound waves ○ *The surrounding peaks echoed the eagle's cry.* **2.** *vi* RESOUND to resound by the reflection of sound waves ○ *Their footsteps echoed down the tunnel.* **3.** *vi* BE FULL OF SOUND to be full of the repeated noise of a sound ○ *The auditorium echoed with cheering.* **4.** *vt* REPEAT SOMETHING SAID to repeat a statement or opinion, especially in agreement or imitation ○ *The completed report echoed the initial assessment.* **5.** *vt* IMITATE SOMETHING to imitate or be reminiscent of something else ○ *The building's design echoes the surrounding Georgian terraces.* **6.** *vt* COMPUT DISPLAY CHARACTER AS CHECK to return a character back to its source after a computer or communications device receives it, as an accuracy check. A common example is the display of a character on a computer monitor after it has been entered from a keyboard. [14C. Via French or Latin < Greek *ēkhō*] —**echoingly** *adv*

echo boomer *n* SOC SCI same as **millennial** [After BABY BOOMER]

echocardiogram /ékō kaárdi ə gram/ *n* the visual record produced by an echocardiograph

echocardiograph /ékō kaárdi ə graaf, -graf/ *n* an ultrasound device used to examine the working heart and display moving images of its action —**echocardiographic** /ékō kaárdi ə gráffik/ *adj* —**echocardiography** /ékō kaárdi óggrəfi/ *n*

echo chamber *n* a room with sound-reflecting walls, used in making acoustic measurements or generating sound effects

echoencephalogram /ékō en séffələ gram/ *n* the visual record produced by an echoencephalograph

echoencephalograph /ékō en séffələ graaf, -graf/ *n* an ultrasound device used to examine the structures of the brain —**echoencephalographic** /ékō en séffələ gráffik/ *adj* —**echoencephalography** /ékō en séffə lóggrəfi/ *n*

echogram /ékō gram/ *n* PHYS same as **sonogram**

echography /e kóggrəfi/ *n* PHYS same as **ultrasonography**

echoic /e kó ik/ *adj* **1.** resembling or relating to an echo **2.** LITERAT same as **onomatopoeic**

echoic memory *n* the ability to remember and reproduce a sound in the two or three seconds after it is heard

echoism /ékō izəm/ *n* **1.** a process by which the sound of a vowel changes to imitate the sound of a preceding vowel **2.** LITERAT same as **onomatopoeia**

echolalia /ékō láyli ə/ *n* the compulsive repetition of words spoken by somebody else, often a sign of a psychiatric disorder

echolocation /ékō lō káysh'n/ *n* a means of locating an object based on an emitted sound and the reflection back from it, used naturally by some animals, e.g. bats, and electronically by humans

echo plate *n* an electromechanical device used in

broadcasting or recording to create the effect of reverberation

echopraxia /ékō práksi ə/, **echopraxis** /-práksiss/ *n* the compulsive imitation of the actions of others, often a sign of a psychiatric disorder [Early 20C. < modern Latin < Greek *ēkhō* 'echo' + *praxis* 'action']

echo quilting *n* a quilting stitch that follows the outlines of an appliquéd design

echo sounder *n* a device used to ascertain water depth or to locate underwater objects by measuring the time taken for emitted sound waves to return from either the bottom or the object

echovirus /ékō vírəss/ *n* a virus found in the gastrointestinal tract, belonging to a group of retroviruses associated with intestinal and respiratory infections and meningitis [Mid-20C. Acronym < *enteric cytopathogenic human orphan*]

Echuca /e choŏkə/ town in northern Victoria, Australia, located on the River Murray. Population: 6,486 (1991).

Eckert /ékərt/, **John Presper** (1919–95) US electronics engineer. He worked with John Mauchly on the ENIAC project (1943–46) that developed the first general-purpose electronic digital computer. They then set up a company (1946) that produced the first commercially available computer, UNIVAC.

Eckhart /ék haart/, **Johannes** (1260?–1328?) German philosopher and Christian theologian. His writings set him among the founders of German philosophical mysticism. He was influenced both by the teachings of St Thomas Aquinas and by the doctrines of neo-Platonism. Known as **Eckhart, Meister**

> 'The greatest power available to man is not to use it.'
> [Johannes Eckhart. Quoted in *The Jingle Bell Principle*, Miroslav Holub; 1992]

éclair /ay kláir, i-/ *n* **1.** a long thin cylinder of choux pastry filled with whipped cream and topped with chocolate or coffee icing **2.** a hard toffee sweet with a soft filling, usually chocolate [Mid-19C. < French, literally 'lightning']

éclaircissement /ay kláir seess maáN/ *n* a clearing up of something puzzling [Mid-17C. < French, 'clearing up']

eclampsia /i klámpsi ə/ *n* an illness that sometimes occurs during the later stages of pregnancy and involves high blood pressure and convulsions, sometimes followed by a coma [Mid-19C. Via modern Latin < French *éclampsie* < Greek *eklampsis* 'sudden development' < *eklampein* 'shine out'] —**eclamptic** *adj*

éclat /ay klaá, áy klaa/ *n* **1.** brilliant success ○ *The show came off with éclat.* **2.** ostentatious display [Late 17C. < French, literally 'splinter, fragment']

eclectic /i kléktik/ *adj* **1.** made up of parts from various sources ○ *an eclectic collection of paintings* **2.** choosing what is best or preferred from a variety of sources or styles ○ *an eclectic taste in music* [Late 17C. < Greek *eklektikos* 'picking out, selecting' < *eklegein* 'pick out' < *legein* 'choose'] —**eclectic** *n* —**eclectically** *adv*

eclecticism /i klékti sizəm/ *n* the theory or use of an eclectic approach

eclipse /i klíps/ *n* **1.** OBSCURING OF ASTRONOMICAL OBJECT the partial or complete hiding from view of an astronomical object, e.g. the Sun or Moon, when another astronomical object comes between it and the observer. See illustration on next page **2.** LOSS OF LIGHT a loss or blocking of light **3.** DECLINE a loss of status, power, or favour ○ *the eclipse of the aristocracy* ■ *vt* (**eclipses, eclipsing, eclipsed**) **1.** OUTDO SOMEBODY OR SOMETHING to become more successful, powerful, or popular than something or somebody ○ *a performance that eclipsed all that went before* **2.** ASTRON HIDE ASTRONOMICAL OBJECT to cause a total or partial obscuring of another astronomical object **3.** CAST SHADOW ON SOMETHING to block the light falling on something, or cast a shadow on it [13C. Via French and Latin < Greek *ekleipsis* < *ekleipein* 'no longer to appear or be present' < *leipein* 'leave']

eclipse plumage *n* dull feathers grown for a short period by some birds, especially male ducks, to replace the brightly coloured breeding plumage

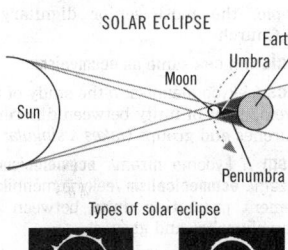

SOLAR ECLIPSE

Sun — Moon — Umbra — Earth — Penumbra

Types of solar eclipse

Total eclipse (full shadow)

Annular eclipse

Partial eclipse (partial shadow)

LUNAR ECLIPSE

Sun — Earth — Umbra — Moon — Penumbra

Types of lunar eclipse

Total eclipse (full shadow)

Partial eclipse (partial shadow)

eclipse: solar and lunar eclipses

eclipsing binary *n* a binary star whose orbit places it between its companion and the observer, resulting in an eclipse

ecliptic /i klíptik/ *n* the apparent path of the Sun's annual motion relative to the stars, shown as a circle passing through the centre of the imaginary sphere (**celestial sphere**) containing all the astronomical objects. Eclipses of the Sun or Moon can occur only when the Moon crosses the ecliptic. ■ *adj* relating to, involving, or typical of an eclipse [14C. Via Latin < Greek *ekluptikos* < *ekleipein* (see ECLIPSE)]

eclogue /ék log/ *n* a pastoral poem, usually in the form of a dialogue between shepherds [15C. Via Latin < Greek *eklogē* 'selection (of poems)' < *eklegein* (see ECLECTIC)]

eclosion /i klṓzh'n/ *n* the emergence of an insect from its pupal case, or the hatching of a larva from an egg [Late 19C. < French *éclosion* < *éclore* 'hatch, open' < Latin *excludere* 'hatch']

ECML *abbr* E-COMMERCE electronic commerce modelling language

Eco /ékō/, Umberto (*b.* 1932) Italian novelist and academic. His novels include *The Name of the Rose* (1980), *Foucault's Pendulum* (1988), and *The Island of the Day Before* (1995). He has written numerous critical works on literature and aesthetics.

> 'The good of a book lies in being read.'
> [Umberto Eco, *The Name of the Rose*; 1980]

eco- *prefix* environment, ecology ○ *ecofriendly* [Shortened < ECOLOGY]

ecoagriculture /éekō ággri kulchər, ékō-/ *n* the practice of agriculture using ecologically beneficial methods that maintain natural resources, biodiversity, and the landscape —**ecoagricultural** /-agri kúlchərəl/ *adj*

eco-architect *n* an architect who specializes in building environmentally friendly energy-efficient buildings —**eco-architecture** *n*

ecocatastrophe /éekōkə tástrəfi, ékō-/ *n* an event, usually caused by human actions, that results in very severe damage to the environment

eco-efficiency *n* the ability to manufacture goods efficiently and at competitive prices without harming the environment —**eco-efficient** *adj*

ecofreak /éekō freek, ékō-/ *n* somebody who is preoccupied or obsessed with the state of the environment (*slang insult*)

ecofriendly /éekō frendli, ékō-/ *adj* intended or perceived to have no harmful effect on the natural environment and its inhabitants

ecol. *abbr* 1. ecological 2. ecology

ecolabelling /éekō layb'ling, ékō-/ *n* the identification and labelling of products and services that are perceived as less harmful to the environment than similar products or services —**ecolabel** *n*

E. coli /ee kṓ līˈ/ *n* a bacterium found in the colon of human beings and animals that becomes a serious contaminant when found in the food or water supply [Late 20C. Abbreviated < modern Latin *Escherichia coli*, after T. *Escherich* (1857–1911), German physician; *coli* 'of the colon']

e-collaboration *n* collaboration among people or organizations made possible by means of electronic technologies such as the Internet, video conferencing, and wireless devices

ecology /i kólləji/ *n* 1. the study of the relationships between living organisms and their interactions with their natural or developed environment ○ '*A land ethic...should be as honest as Thoreau's Walden, and as comprehensive as the sensitive science of ecology.*' (Stewart Udall, *The Quiet Crisis*; 1963) 2. SOC SCI same as **human ecology** [Late 19C. < Greek *oikos* 'house, habitation'] —**ecological** /éekə lójjik'l, ékə-/ *adj* —**ecologically** *adv* —**ecologist** *n*

econ. *abbr* 1. economics 2. economist 3. economy

econometrics /i kónnə méttriks/ *n* the application of mathematical and statistical techniques to economic data and problems (*takes a singular verb*) —**econometric** *adj* —**econometrically** *adv* —**econometrician** /i kónnəmə trísh'n/ *n*

economic /ékə nómmik, éekə-/ *adj* 1. OF ECONOMY OR ECONOMICS relating to economics, or the economy or business activities of a country ○ *economic policy* ○ *the economic outlook is bleak* 2. PROFITABLE producing or capable of producing a satisfactory profit ○ *The planned expansion of the company is no longer an economic proposition.* 3. FINANCIAL relating to or affecting material goods and financial resources ○ *There were economic benefits in delaying the sale.* 4. same as **economical** (sense 4) [Late 16C. Directly or via French < Latin *oeconomicus* < Greek *oikonomikos* < *oikonomos* (see ECONOMY)]

USAGE economic or **economical**? The adjective *economic* denotes economics or the economy, and is concerned with aspects of the production, distribution, and consumption of goods and services: *a Nobel Laureate's economic theories*. The adjective *economical*, on the other hand, has to do with the prudent management of resources and attempts to reduce expenditure: *It is much more economical to buy in bulk. Public transport is economical, compared with hiring a limousine*. But the two adjectives can overlap in one sense, 'efficient in terms of avoiding unnecessary expenditure': *an economical* [or *economic*] *use of electricity*.

economical /ékə nómmik'l, éekə-/ *adj* 1. RESOURCEFULLY FRUGAL careful in making the best use of resources ○ *an economical cook* 2. INEXPENSIVE costing relatively little in comparison with other things in the same class ○ *a home that's economical to run* 3. AVOIDING WASTE efficient in terms of avoiding unnecessary waste ○ *provides an economic alternative to recycling* 4. EFFICIENT efficient in terms of avoiding unnecessary expenditure of time or energy ○ *an economical gesture*

USAGE See *economic*.

economically /ékə nómmikli, éekə-/ *adv* 1. WITH REGARD TO ECONOMY OR ECONOMICS with regard to economics, the economy of a country, or financial matters in general ○ *economically and socially developing societies* 2. PROFITABLY in such a way as to produce a profit 3. FRUGALLY in a thrifty or careful manner

economic determinism *n* the belief that the eco-

nomic organization of a society determines the nature of all other aspects of its life

economic geography *n* a branch of geography that deals with the distribution and use of an area's economic resources

economic geology *n* the study of geological deposits from the viewpoint of their value as resources

economic growth *n* growth in an economy as verified by recognized factors and indexes

economic indicator *n* a quantity expressed statistically and taken as a measure of an economic variable

economic migrant *n* a travelling worker who goes to an area where work or an easier life is available

economic rent *n* 1. a level of housing rent that is enough to make letting profitable for the owner 2. the payment received for a factor of production such as labor or machinery in excess of the amount needed to produce a good

economics /ékə nómmiks, éekə-/ *n* the study of the production, distribution, and consumption of goods and services (*takes a singular verb*) ■ *npl* the financial element of something (*takes a plural verb*) ○ *the economics of running a business* [Late 18C. Probably < French *économique*]

economic union *n* a merging of the economies of two or more states to function as a unit that shares a common financial policy and currency

economise *vi* another spelling of **economize**

economism /i kónnə mizəm/ *n* 1. the belief that economics is the most important element in a society 2. the belief that bringing about an improvement in the living standards of its members is the chief goal of a political organization or trade union organization

economist /i kónnəmist/ *n* a student or expert in the field of economics

economize /i kónnə mīz/ (-mizes, -mizing, -mized), **economise** (-mises, -mising, -mised) *vi* to reduce expenditure, or use resources less wastefully ○ *We had to economize on fuel.* —**economizer** *n*

economy /i kónnəmi/ *n* (*plural* -mies) 1. FINANCIAL AFFAIRS the production and consumption of goods and services of a community regarded as a whole ○ *a gradual shift from an agricultural to an industrial economy* 2. THRIFT the prudent managing of resources to avoid extravagant expenditure or waste 3. REDUCED EXPENDITURE a financial saving, or an attempt to reduce expenditure ○ *need to make economies* 4. EFFECTIVENESS efficiency and conservation of effort in the operation or achievement of something ○ *a graceful economy of movement* 5. TRAVEL same as **economy class** ■ *adj* ECON, FIN CHEAPER intended to be cheaper or give better value for money [15C. Directly or via French < Latin *oeconomia* < Greek *oikonomia* < *oikonomos* 'steward of a household' < *oikos* 'house' + *nemein* 'manage']

economy class *n* a class of travel, especially on airlines, that is relatively low in price and carries the majority of passengers

economy class syndrome *n* thrombosis believed to be caused by a prolonged period of restricted movement and dehydration such as occurs during air travel

economy drive *n* an organized attempt to reduce expenditure and waste

economy of scale *n* a reduction in unit cost achieved by increasing the amount of production

e-consulting *n* the business of providing services such as webpage design and marketing advice to companies doing business on the Internet —**e-consultant** *n*

écorché /é kawr sháy/ (*plural* -chés) *n* an anatomical model of part or all of the human body with the skin removed, to allow study of the muscle structure [Mid-19C. < French, past participle of *écorcher* 'flay']

ecospecies /éekō spee sheez, ékō-/ (*plural same*) *n* a species made up of several subgroups (**ecotypes**) and characterized by its ecological traits

ecosphere /éekō sfeer, ékō-/ *n* ECOL same as **biosphere**

écossaise /áy ko sáyz/ n a lively folk dance in 2/4 time, or the music for this dance [Mid-19C. < French, 'Scottish']

ecosystem /éekō sistəm, ékō-/ n a localized group of interdependent organisms together with the environment that they inhabit and depend on

ecoterrorism /éekō térrərizəm, ékō-/ n 1. the sabotage of the activities of people or corporations, e.g. industrial companies, considered to be polluting or destroying the natural environment 2. deliberate destruction of the environment —**ecoterrorist** n

ecotone /éeka tōn, éka-/ n a zone of transition between two different ecosystems, e.g. where the sea meets the land [Early 20C. < ECO- + Greek tonos 'tension']

ecotourism /éekō toórizəm, ékō-/ n a form of tourism that strives to minimize ecological or other damage to areas visited for their natural or cultural interest

ecotoxic /éekō tóksik, ékō-/ adj causing severe damage to the environment —**ecotoxicity** /éekō tok síssəti, ékō-/ n

ecotoxicology /éekō tóksi kólləji, ékō-/ n the study of how organisms are affected by chemicals released into the environment by human activities —**ecotoxicological** /éekō toksikə lójjik'l, ékō-/ adj

ecotype /éekō tīp, ékō-/ n a subgroup of a species of organism whose members show genetically determined adaptations to some environmental conditions in their habitat

ecowarrior /éekō worri ər, ékō-/ n an activist who takes direct, often unlawful, action on an environmental issue

ecru /ékroo, áy-/ adj of a pale brown colour, like unbleached linen [Mid-19C. < French écru 'raw, unbleached' < Latin crudus 'raw'] —**ecru** n

ECS abbr TELECOM European Communications Satellite

ECSC abbr ECON, INDUST European Coal and Steel Community

~~ecstasy~~ incorrect spelling of **ecstasy**

ecstasy /ékstəssi/ (plural -sies) n 1. INTENSE DELIGHT a feeling of intense delight ○ an evening of pure ecstasy ○ went into ecstasies over the photos 2. INTENSE FEELING OR ACTIVITY a feeling or activity characterized by its extreme intensity ○ an ecstasy of remorse 3. also **Ecstasy** ILLEGAL RECREATIONAL DRUG an illegal drug used as a stimulant and relaxer of inhibitions. Formula: C₁₁H₁₅NO₂. 4. PSYCHOL LOSS OF SELF-CONTROL a mental state, usually caused by intense religious experience, sexual pleasure, or drugs, in which somebody is so dominated by an emotion that self-control and sometimes consciousness are lost [14C. Via French < Greek ekstasis < existanai 'displace, drive out (of your mind)' < histanai 'put']

CULTURAL NOTE *The Ecstasy of St Theresa*, a sculpture (1645–52) by Italian artist Gianlorenzo Bernini. An altarpiece in the Cornaro Chapel in the church of Santa Maria Della Vittoria in Rome, it depicts a vision experienced by the Spanish saint Theresa during which an angel pierced her heart with a golden arrow, causing pain but also intense religious rapture.

ecstatic /ik státtik, ek-/ adj 1. DELIGHTED showing or feeling great pleasure or delight 2. DOMINATED BY EMOTION completely dominated by an intense emotion ■ n SOMEBODY SUBJECT TO TRANCES somebody who experiences spells of intense emotion —**ecstatically** adv

ECT abbr MED electroconvulsive therapy

ectasia /ek tázi ə/, **ectasis** /éktəssiss/ n a swelling or dilation of a part of the body (technical) [Late 19C. < modern Latin < Greek ektasis < ekteinein 'stretch out']

ecto- prefix external, outside ○ ectotherm [< Greek ektos < ek 'out']

ectocommensal /éktə kə méns'l/ n a plant or animal that lives on the outer surface or skin of another organism, causing its host no harm

ectoderm /éktə durm/ n the outermost of three cell layers of an embryo, from which the epidermis, nervous tissue, and sense organs develop

ectogenesis /éktō jénnəssiss/ n the development of an organism in an artificial environment, e.g.

outside the body in which it would normally be found —**ectogenous** /ek tójjənəss/ adj

ectomere /éktə meer/ n a cell (**blastomere**) produced during the division of a fertilized egg that develops with others into the outer cell layer (**ectoderm**) of an embryo

ectomorph /éktə mawrf/ n somebody who belongs to a physiological type that is tall with long lean limbs. ◊ **endomorph** (sense 1), **mesomorph** —**ectomorphic** /éktə máwrfik/ adj

-ectomy suffix surgical removal of a part of the body ○ iridectomy [< modern Latin -ectomia 'cutting out' < Greek ek- 'out' + -tomia (see -TOMY)]

ectoparasite /éktə párrə sīt/ n a parasite that lives on the outside of its host, e.g. on the skin or in the hair. Fleas are ectoparasites. —**ectoparasitic** /-parə síttik/ adj—**ectoparasitism** /-párrəsitizəm/ n

ectophyte /éktə fīt/ n a parasitic plant that lives on the outer surface of its host —**ectophytic** /éktə fíttik/ adj

ectopia /ek tópi ə/ n a change from the usual positioning of an organ or body part [Mid-19C. < modern Latin < Greek ektopos 'out of place' < topos 'place']

ectopic /ek tóppik/ adj describes an organ or body part occurring in an unusual position or form

ectopic pregnancy n the development of a fertilized egg outside the womb, e.g. in a fallopian tube

ectoplasm /éktə plazəm/ n 1. the dense outer layer of the substance (**cytoplasm**) that surrounds the nucleus of a cell 2. the substance believed by spiritualists to issue from a medium who is communicating with spirits —**ectoplasmic** /éktə plázmik/ adj

ectotherm /éktə thurm/ n an animal that maintains its body temperature by absorbing heat from its environment. All animals other than birds and mammals are ectotherms. ◊ **poikilotherm** [Mid-20C. < ECTO- + Greek therme 'heat'] —**ectothermic** /éktə thúrmik/ adj

ectotrophic /éktə tróffik, -trófik/ adj describes an association (**mycorrhiza**) between a fungus and the roots of a plant, in which the fungus obtains its nourishment by enveloping the roots in a sheath. ◊ **endotrophic**

écu /áy kyoo/ n a silver or gold coin of a number formerly used in France [Late 16C. < French, later form of Old French escu < Latin scutum 'shield' (in their design)]

ECU /é kyoo/, **ecu** n the official monetary unit of the European Union from 1979 to 1999. Full form **European Currency Unit**

Ecuador

Ecuador /ékwə dawr/ country in northwestern South America, bordered on the north by Colombia, on the south and east by Peru, and on the west by the Pacific Ocean. Language: Spanish. Currency: sucre. Capital: Quito. Population: 13,710,234 (2003). Area: 272,045 sq. km/105,037 sq. mi. Official name **Republic of Ecuador** —**Ecuadorian** /ékwə dáwri ən/ n, adj

ecumenical /éekyoo ménnik'l/, **ecumenic** /-ménnik/ adj 1. relating to, involving, or promoting the unity of different Christian churches and groups 2. involving all people or groups [Late 16C. Via late Latin 'general, universal' < Greek oikoumenikos < oikoumenē (gē) 'inhabited (world)' < oikos 'house'] —**ecumenically** adv

ecumenicalism n CHR same as **ecumenism**

ecumenical patriarch n the Archbishop of Con-

stantinople, the most senior dignitary of the Eastern Church

ecumenicism n CHR same as **ecumenism**

ecumenics /éekyoo ménniks/ n the study of the aims and development of unity between different Christian churches and groups (takes a singular verb)

ecumenism /i kyóomə nizəm/, **ecumenicism** /éekyoo ménnisizəm/, **ecumenicalism** /éekyoo ménnik'lizəm/ n a movement promoting unity between different Christian churches and groups

eczema /éksəmə/ n an inflammation of the skin characterized by reddening and itching and the formation of scaly or crusty patches that may leak fluid [Mid-18C. Via modern Latin < Greek ekzema 'eruption' < zein 'to boil' < Indo-European]

ed. abbr 1. PUBL edited 2. PUBL edition 3. PUBL editor 4. education

-ed[1] suffix 1. used to form the past participle of regular verbs ○ wasted 2. used to form the past tense of regular verbs ○ nicked ○ landed [Old English -ed, -od < Germanic]

-ed[2] suffix having, characterized by, like ○ redheaded ○ bigoted [Old English -ede, -ode < Germanic]

edacious /i dáyshəss/ adj frequently consuming a great deal of food or drink (formal) [Early 19C. < Latin edac- 'voracious, gluttonous' < edere 'eat'] —**edacity** /i dássəti/ n

Edam[1] /ée dam/ n a mild Dutch cheese with a slightly rubbery texture, typically formed into balls covered with red wax [Early 19C. After EDAM [2]]

Edam[2] /ée dam/ town in the western Netherlands, near Amsterdam, best known for the manufacture of the cheese to which it gives its name. Population: 7,153 (1994).

edaphic /i dáffik/ adj describes the effect of soil characteristics, especially chemical or physical properties, on plants and animals [Late 19C. < Greek edaphos 'floor, ground, soil']

edaphic climax n a stable ecological community that results from the content or properties of the soil rather than the climate

Edberg /éd burg/, **Stefan** (b. 1966) Swedish tennis player. He progressed from a junior grand slam in 1983 to winning Wimbledon and US Open singles championships (1988, 1990, 1991, and 1992).

EDC abbr 1. BUSINESS electronic data capture 2. MIL European Defence Community

Edda /éddə/ n 1. an early 13th-century collection of Old Norse poems 2. a 13th-century collection compiled by Snorri Sturluson containing Norse myths, poems, and a treatise on poetry [Late 17C. Probably < Old Norse ōðr 'spirit, mind, passion, song, poetry'] —**Eddic** adj

Eddington /éddingtən/, **Sir Arthur** (1882–1944) British astronomer. He confirmed Einstein's general theory of relativity and wrote the popular The Expanding Universe (1933). Full name **Eddington, Sir Arthur Stanley**

'We used to think that if we knew one, we knew two, because one and one are two. We are finding that we must learn a great deal more about "and".'
[Sir Arthur Eddington. Quoted in Mathematical Maxims and Minims, N. Rose; 1988]

eddo /éddō/ (plural -does) n PLANTS same as **taro** [Late 17C. Of W African origin]

eddy /éddi/ n (plural -dies) 1. SMALL WHIRL a movement in a flowing stream of liquid or gas in which the current doubles back to form a small whirl 2. DIVERGENCE a relatively unimportant divergence from or movement contrary to the mainstream of something ○ negotiated a few political eddies ■ vi (-dies, -dying, -died) FLOW AGAINST CURRENT to flow contrary to the main current, or make something flow in this way ○ He waded out, the stream eddying around his legs. [15C. Origin ?]

Eddy /éddi/, **Mary Baker** (1821–1910) US religious leader. She founded the Church of Christ, Scientist, and the associated Christian Science movement, in Boston in 1879. Born **Baker, Mary**

'Sin brought death, and death will disappear with the disappearance of sin.'
[Mary Baker Eddy, *Science and Health with Key to the Scriptures*; 1875]

eddy current *n* an electric current set up by an alternating magnetic field

Eddystone Rocks /éddistən-/ dangerous rocks in the English Channel, near Plymouth, England. Four lighthouses have successively been built on or near the rocks since 1698.

edelweiss

edelweiss /áyd'l vīss/ *n* a small plant with white woolly leaves. Flowers: small, yellow bracts surrounded by white modified leaves. Native to: Alps, mountains of Asia. Latin name: *Leontopodium alpinum*. [Mid-19C. < German, 'noble white']

edema *n* MED US spelling of **oedema**

Eden[1] /éed'n/ *n* 1. in the Bible, the garden where Adam and Eve first lived 2. any place seen as being perfect, highly pleasing, or happy ○ *The first explorers saw America as an Eden.* —**Edenic** /ee dénnik/ *adj*

Eden[2] /éed'n/ coastal town in southern New South Wales, Australia. Population: 3,280 (1991).

Eden, Anthony, 1st Earl of Avon (1897–1977) British politician. He resigned as foreign secretary in 1938 over his opposition to British appeasement of the Nazis, but served again as Winston Churchill's wartime foreign secretary (1940–45). He became prime minister in 1955 but resigned in 1957 after authorizing controversial military action against Egypt during the Suez Crisis of 1956. See table at **prime minister**

'We must face the fact that the United Nations is not yet the international equivalent of our own legal system and the rule of law.'
[Anthony Eden, *Speech to Parliament, Hansard*; 1 November 1956]

edentate /ee dén tayt/ *n* a mammal with a placenta and few or no teeth, e.g. a sloth or armadillo. Native to: tropical America. Order: Edentata. ■ *adj* DENT same as **edentulous** (*technical*) [Early 19C. < Latin *edentatus* < *dent-* 'tooth']

edentulous /ee déntyŏŏləss/, **edentulate** /-lət, -layt/ *adj* with no teeth (*technical*) [Early 18C. < Latin *edentulus* < *dent-* 'tooth']

Edgar /édgər/ (944–975) king of the English. His rule, from 959 to 975, was marked by legal, judicial, and administrative reforms. Known as **The Peaceful**

'Nevertheless, this measure is to be common to all the nation, whether Englishmen, Danes or Britons...to the end that poor men and rich may possess what they rightly acquire and that a thief may not find a place to bring what he has stolen.'
[Attributed to Edgar]

Edgbaston /éj bastən/ district in Birmingham, England

edge /ej/ *n* 1. BORDER a line or area that is the outermost part or the part farthest away from the centre of something ○ *a tablecloth with embroidered edges* 2. PART ABOVE DROP the area where land suddenly falls away steeply ○ *the cliff edge* 3. BRINK the point or moment just before a marked change or event ○ *on the edge of victory* 4. MEETING SURFACES the line where two surfaces of something solid meet ○ *A cube has*

6 faces and 12 edges. 5. SHARP SIDE the cutting side of a blade ○ *a razor's edge* 6. SHARPNESS sharpness of a blade ○ *a knife with a fine edge* 7. SHARP QUALITY a piercing, cutting, or wounding quality, e.g. of language or expression ○ *There was an unmistakable edge to her remarks.* 8. VIGOUR noticeable vigour and energy ○ *After the timeout there was a new edge to the team's play.* 9. ADVANTAGE an advantage over somebody, e.g. a competitor (*informal*) ○ *Their strategy still has the edge over more recent approaches.* 10. RIDGE a ridge, crest, or cliff (often used in placenames) 11. PROVOCATIVE RISKY MANNER an audacious, provocative, original quality or manner ■ *v* (**edges, edging, edged**) 1. *vi* MOVE GRADUALLY to move gradually sideways, or make something move in this direction by pushing it ○ *just room enough to edge through* 2. *vt* SHARPEN SOMETHING to give a sharp edge to a blade 3. *vt* SPORTS STRIKE BALL WITH SIDE OF SOMETHING to strike a ball or other object with the side of a cricket bat or football boot ○ *The batsman edged the first ball for four.* 4. *vt* SKIING LEAN ON PART OF SKI to put weight down on the outer or inner side of a ski so that its edge cuts into the snow 5. *vt* TRIM SOMETHING to cut, shape, or trim the border of something ○ *a tool for edging the lawn* 6. *vt* ADD BORDER TO SOMETHING to add a border to something, especially a decorative one ○ *a handkerchief edged with lace* ■ *adj* PROVOCATIVELY RISKY AND DARING operating or behaving in an intense, provocative, daring, and innovative fashion ○ *working in an edge business like cable television* [Old English *ecg* 'corner, edge, sword' < Indo-European, 'be sharp or pointed'] —**edger** *n* ◇ **live on the edge** to be habitually in highly stressful and demanding situations, often involving physical risk and danger ◇ **on edge** in an irritated or nervous state ◇ **take the edge off something** 1. to reduce the intensity or strength of something ○ *The snack took the edge off my hunger.* 2. to do something that makes a situation or person less tense

edge out *vt* 1. to move somebody or something gradually out of position ○ *trying to edge him out of the presidency* 2. to defeat a competitor by a narrow margin (*informal*) ○ *She was edged out of the championship.*

edge city *n* 1. a small city or urban development that exists next to a major conurbation 2. *US* a highly urbanized, yet officially unincorporated community adjacent to a major established city, with homes, varied businesses, entertainment districts, and large shopping areas (*informal*) ○'*Edge City...is the creation of a new world, being shaped by the free in a constantly reinvented land.*' (Joel Garreau, *Washington Post*; 19 September 1991)

Edgehill /éj híl/ ridge in Warwickshire, central England, where the first battle of the English Civil War was fought in 1642

edge tool *n* an implement that has at least one cutting edge

edgeways /éj wayz/, **edgewise** /-wīz/ *adv*, *adj* with the edge or side foremost ○ *fit in edgeways* ○ *with an edgeways motion*

Edgewood /éjwŏŏd/ town in northeastern Maryland, northeast of Baltimore. Population: 23,903 (1990).

Edgeworth /éj wurth/, **Maria** (1767–1849) British novelist. Her best-known work, *Castle Rackrent* (1800), set in rural Ireland, influenced the development of the historical and regional novel in English.

'Business was his aversion; pleasure was his business.'
[Maria Edgeworth, *The Contrast*; 1804]

edging /éjjing/ *n* 1. BORDER something used as a border or trim, usually for decoration or protection 2. FORMING OF EDGE the formation of an edge ■ *adj* USED TO FORM EDGE used in forming an edge

edgy /éjji/ (**-ier, -iest**) *adj* 1. ON EDGE nervous and irritable 2. INTENSE having an intense or energetic quality or atmosphere ○ *an edgy district* 3. TRENDSETTING stylish in an extreme or provocative way ○ *edgy clothes* —**edgily** *adv* —**edginess** *n*

edh /eth/, **eth** *n* a character (ð) used in the runic alphabet and in modern phonetics to represent the 'th' sound that is found in the English words 'this' and 'other' [Mid-19C. < Danish]

EDI *abbr* E-COMMERCE electronic data interchange

edible /éddəb'l/ *adj* suitable for eating by human beings [Early 17C. < Latin *edibilis* 'eatable' < *edere* 'eat'] —**edibility** /éddə bílləti/ *n* —**edibleness** *n*

USAGE See **eatable**.

edibles /éddəb'lz/ *npl* things to eat

edict /éedikt/ *n* 1. a formal proclamation, especially one issued by a government, ruler, or other authority 2. a formal or authoritative command [15C. < Latin *edictum* < past participle of *edicere* 'proclaim' < *dicere* 'say']

Edict of Nantes /-naant/ *n* a law signed by Henry IV in 1598 and revoked by Louis XIV in 1685 that allowed civil and religious tolerance to French Protestants

edification /éddifi káysh'n/ *n* instruction or enlightenment, especially when it is morally or spiritually uplifting

edifice /éddifiss/ *n* 1. a building, especially a large or impressive one 2. a large or complex structure or organization ○ *the edifice of government* [14C. Via French < Latin *aedificium* < *aedificare* 'build' (see EDIFY)]

edify /éddifī/ (**-fies, -fying, -fied**) *vt* to improve the morals or knowledge of somebody [14C. Via French *édifier* < Latin *aedificare* 'build, construct, instruct' < *aedis* 'building, temple' + *facere* 'make'] —**edifier** *n*

edifying /éddi fī ing/ *adj* providing morally useful knowledge or information

Edinburgh /éddinbərə/ 1. capital city of Scotland, situated on the southern shore of the Firth of Forth. It is home to a cathedral, a castle, Holyroodhouse, three universities, and the headquarters of the Scottish Parliament. Population: 418,748 (2001). 2. **City of Edinburgh** council area in southeastern Scotland. Area: 262 sq. km/101 sq. mi.

Edinburgh, Duke of ♦ **Philip, Prince**

Edinburgh rock *n* a Scottish confectionery in the form of pastel-coloured sticks with a powdery texture, made of sugar, cream of tartar, and flavourings

Edirne /e deérnə/ city of northwestern Turkey, northwest of Istanbul. Population: 102,345 (1990).

Thomas Alva Edison

Edison /éddiss'n/, **Thomas Alva** (1847–1931) US inventor. He invented the light bulb (1879), the microphone (1877), the phonograph (1877), and many other devices.

'Genius is one per cent inspiration and ninety-nine per cent perspiration.'
[Thomas Alva Edison. Quoted in *Harper's Magazine*; September 1932]

edit /éddit/ *vt* (**-its, -iting, -ited**) 1. PREPARE TEXT FOR PUBLICATION to prepare a text for publication by correcting errors and ensuring clarity and accuracy 2. DECIDE CONTENT OF PUBLICATION to be in overall charge of the publication of a newspaper, magazine, or broadcast programme 3. CUT MATERIAL to remove material from something such as a publication, broadcast item, recording, or film, e.g. because it is lengthy or offensive ○ *was edited for bad language* ○ *has been edited down from 5 hours of live recording* ■ *n* TEXT PREPARATION the preparation of a text for publication or release, or a stage in this process ○ *Look out for any errors missed in the first edit.* [Late 18C. Back-formation < EDITOR] —**edited** *adj*

edit out *vt* to delete an unwanted part of a text, film,

or recording ○ *Her walk-on part was eventually edited out.*

edit. *abbr* PUBL **1.** edited **2.** edition **3.** editor

edition /i dísh'n/ *n* **1.** PRINTED VERSION one version of a publication issued serially, periodically, or in multiple formats ○ *the morning edition of the newspaper* **2.** BROADCAST VERSION a version or instalment of a broadcast for a particular time or purpose ○ *last week's edition of the show* **3.** PRINTED BATCH a batch of identical copies of a publication all printed at the same time **4.** BATCH OF ITEMS a batch or number of items all produced at the same time **5.** SIMILAR THING a version or copy of something ○ *a smaller edition of his father* [15C. < Latin *edition-* < *edit-*, past participle of *edere* 'give out' < *dare* 'give']

editio princeps /i díshi ō prín seps/ (*plural* **editiones principes** /i díshi ō neez prínssi peez/) *n* the first printed edition of a piece of writing (*literary*) [< modern Latin, 'first edition']

editor /édditər/ *n* **1.** PUBLISHING SUPERVISOR the overall supervisor of content for a book, newspaper, or magazine **2.** CHIEF JOURNALIST the supervisor of content in a part of a newspaper or magazine **3.** TEXT CORRECTOR somebody who prepares a text for publication **4.** CONTROLLER OF PROGRAMME CONTENT somebody who supervises the content of a broadcast programme **5.** FILM EDITOR somebody who prepares the final version of a film, determining the length and the order of shots and scenes **6.** COMPUT same as **text editor** [Mid-17C. < late Latin, 'producer, publisher' < Latin *edit-* (see EDITION)] —**editorship** *n*

editorial /éddi táwri əl/ *adj* relating to, involving, or concerned with the editing of a text or broadcast ○ *editorial control* ○ *made editorial comments in the margins* ■ *n* an article in a newspaper or magazine that expresses the opinion of its editor or publisher —**editorialist** *n* —**editorially** *adv*

editorialize /éddi táwri ə līz/ (**-izes, -izing, -ized**), **editorialise** (**-ises, -ising, -ised**) *vi* **1.** to express an opinion or view in an editorial in a publication **2.** to introduce personal opinions or views, especially inappropriately ○ *He couldn't resist the opportunity, when reporting on a burglary, to editorialize on security systems.*

editor in chief (*plural* **editors in chief**) *n* the overall editor of a publication, publishing house, or set of publications

e-division *n* a part of an organization set up to do business on the Internet

Edmonton /édməntən/ capital city of Alberta, Canada, located in the centre of the province, on the North Saskatchewan River. Population: 782,101 (2001).

Edmund /édmənd/, **St** (841?–870) king of East Anglia. After defeat in battle by the Danes, he is said to have been martyred for refusing to deny Christianity.

Edmund I (921–946) king of the English. He made war on the Vikings, expelling them from England, and carried out legal reforms.

Edmund II (981?–1016) king of the English. He reigned for only a few months in 1016, until defeated in battle by Canute. He was allowed to keep control of the south of England, but died a month later. Known as **Edmund Ironside**

Edmund (of Abingdon), St (1175?–1240) English cleric and scholar. He was Archbishop of Canterbury from 1234 to 1240, and was canonized in about 1249.

Edo /éddō/ (*plural same* or **-os**) *n* **1.** a member of a people living in the Benin region of Nigeria **2.** the language of the Edo people, belonging to the Kwa branch of the Niger-Congo family of languages. Native speakers: 1 million. [Late 19C. < Edo name for BENIN CITY] —**Edo** *adj*

Edom /éedəm/ ancient kingdom situated south of the Dead Sea. According to the Bible, it was given to Esau.

Edomite /éedə mīt/ *n* **1.** a member of an ancient people who lived in the kingdom of Edom in pre-Christian times **2.** an extinct language formerly spoken in the kingdom of Edom. It is one of the Semitic group of Afro-Asian languages, and is related to Hebrew. —**Edomitic** /éedə míttik/ *adj*

EDP *abbr* electronic data processing

e-dress *n* ONLINE same as **e-mail address**

EDT *abbr* **1.** TIME Eastern Daylight Time **2.** E-COMMERCE electronic depository transfer

EDTA *n* a colourless compound that reacts with metals. Use: food preservative, anticoagulant, treatment of lead poisoning. Formula: $C_{10}H_{16}N_2O_8$. Full form **ethylene diamine tetra-acetate**

edu *abbr* US educational organization (*used in Internet addresses*) See table at **domain name**

educ. *abbr* **1.** education **2.** educational

educate /éddyōō kayt/ (**-cates, -cating, -cated**) *v* **1.** *vti* TEACH SOMEBODY to give knowledge to or develop the abilities of somebody by teaching ○ *had been educated at a state school* **2.** *vt* ARRANGE SCHOOLING FOR SOMEBODY to arrange or provide schooling for somebody ○ *They educated their daughters at home.* **3.** *vt* TRAIN SOMEBODY to train somebody, or improve somebody's awareness in a particular field ○ *need to educate people on environmentally safe procedures* **4.** *vt* DEVELOP SOMETHING to develop or improve a faculty or sense ○ *educate the palate* [15C. < Latin *educat-*, past participle of *educare* 'bring up, rear', related to *educere* 'lead out' < *ducere* 'lead'] —**educable** /-kəb'l/ *adj* —**educative** /-kətiv/ *adj* —**educatory** /éddyōōkə tawri, éddyōō káytəri/ *adj*

SYNONYMS See *teach*.

educated /éddyōō kaytid/ *adj* **1.** WELL-TAUGHT having had a good education ○ *This is the writing of an educated person.* **2.** CULTURED showing good taste or refinement ○ *a quiet educated manner* **3.** KNOWLEDGEABLE having the benefit of experience or knowledge ○ *an educated opinion* ○ *cast an educated eye over the antiques*

educated guess *n* a guess that is based on a degree of experience, knowledge, or information

education /éddyōō káysh'n/ *n* **1.** EDUCATING the imparting and acquiring of knowledge through teaching and learning, especially at a school or similar institution ○ *'After all, what is education but a process by which a person begins to learn how to learn?'* (Peter Ustinov, *Dear Me*; 1977) **2.** KNOWLEDGE the knowledge or abilities gained through being educated **3.** INSTRUCTION training and instruction in a particular subject, e.g. health matters **4.** STUDY OF TEACHING the study of the theories and practices of teaching ○ *a degree in education* **5.** SYSTEM FOR EDUCATING PEOPLE the system of educating people in a community or society ○ *jobs in education* **6.** LEARNING EXPERIENCE an informative experience ○ *Spending a weekend in their house was a real education.*

education action zone *n* in England, a cluster of about 20 primary and secondary schools that work together to meet educational targets for improvement. They receive extra funding for three to five years and are run by a forum including businesses, parents, and community organizations.

educational /éddyōō káysh'nəl/ *adj* **1.** giving knowledge, instruction, or information **2.** relating to or concerned with education —**educationally** *adv*

educationalist *n* EDUC same as **educationist**

educational psychology *n* a branch of applied psychology that studies children in an educational setting and is concerned with the assessment of ability and aptitude and the evaluation of teaching and learning methods. Practitioners also deal with problems experienced by some children at school and in other learning situations. —**educational psychologist** *n*

Educational Welfare Officer *n* somebody employed by a local education authority to investigate the home background of children with difficulties at school, identify any problems there, and help to find solutions

educationist /éddyōō káysh'nist, -káysh'nəlist/ *n* an expert in the theories or administration of education

educator /éddyōō kaytər/ *n* **1.** a professional teacher **2.** an expert in the theories or administration of education

educe /i dyooss/ (**educes, educing, educed**) *vt* (*formal*) **1.** to elicit or derive something such as a conclusion **2.** to make something latent develop or appear [15C. < Latin *educere* (see EDUCATE)]

eduction /i dúksh'n/ *n* **1.** the derivation or development of something, or something derived or developed (*formal*) **2.** the exhaust of an engine, especially an internal-combustion or steam engine (*technical*) [Mid-17C. < Latin *eduction-* < past participle of *educere* (see EDUCATE)]

edulcorate /i dúlkə rayt/ (**-rates, -rating, -rated**) *vt* to remove soluble impurities from something by washing (*technical*) [Mid-17C. < medieval Latin *edulcorat-*, past participle of *edulcorare* 'sweeten' < Latin *dulcis* 'sweet']

edutainment /éddyōō táynmənt/ *n* television programmes, computer software, or other media content intended both to entertain and educate users [Late 20C. Blend of EDUCATION + ENTERTAINMENT]

Edward /éddwərd/ (b. 1964) **Prince, Earl of Wessex** Third son of Queen Elizabeth II and Prince Philip, Duke of Edinburgh, he married Sophie Rhys-Jones in 1999

Edward I (1239–1307) king of England. His reign (1272–1307) was marked by the development of parliamentary government and by conflicts with the Welsh, the Scots, and France. Known as **Edward Longshanks**

> 'By God, Sir Earl, either go or hang.'
> [Edward I. To the earl of Norfolk in 1297 on his refusal to go to war in Gascony, *The Chronicle of Walter of Guisborough*]

Edward II (1284–1327) king of England. He was defeated by the Scots at the Battle of Bannockburn in 1314 and his reign (1307–27) ended in his forced abdication and murder. He was the first future king to be styled Prince of Wales (1301). Known as **Edward of Caernarvon**

> 'There is no one who is sorry for me; none fights for my right against them.'
> [Edward II. Referring to the barons, *Vita Edwardi Secundi (The Life of Edward II)*; 1312]

Edward III (1312–77) king of England. He ruled from 1327 until 1377. Through his mother, Isabella of France, he claimed the French throne, starting the Hundred Years' War.

> 'Also say to them, that they suffre hym this day to wynne his spurres, for if god be pleased, I woll this journey be his, and the honoure therof.'
> [Edward III, *The Chronicle of Froissart*, Sir John Bourchier, Lord Berners (tr.); 1523–25]

Edward IV (1442–83) king of England. As an outcome of the Wars of the Roses (1455–85), he became the first king of the House of York (1461–83). He was briefly deposed in 1470–71 by Lancastrian supporters of Henry VI.

> 'The reason why I have called and summoned this my parliament is that I intend to live on my own, and not to charge my subjects except for great and urgent causes, which concern rather their own welfare, and the defence of this my kingdom, than my own pleasure.'
> [Edward IV. Address to the House of Commons, *Rotuli Parliamentorum*; 1467]

Edward V (1470–83?) king of England. On his accession in 1483, he was imprisoned by the future Richard III in the Tower of London and is thought to have been assassinated. With his brother he is often referred to as one of the 'Princes in the Tower'.

Edward VI (1537–53) king of England. He was the son of Henry VIII and Jane Seymour. His reign (1547–53) saw a rapid advancement of Protestantism in England.

Edward VII (1841–1910) king of the United Kingdom. Son of Queen Victoria, he was a keen sportsman and traveller, promoting good relations abroad. His reign (1901–10) is known as the Edwardian period.

Edward VIII (1894–1972) king of the United Kingdom. His brief reign (January–December 1936) ended in abdication after the British Government refused to agree to his marrying US divorcée Wallis Simpson.

> 'I have found it impossible to carry the heavy burden of responsibility and to dis-

charge my duties as King as I would wish to do without the help and support of the woman I love.'
[Edward VIII, *Times*; 12 December 1936]

Edward (the Black Prince) (1330–76) Prince of Wales. The eldest son of Edward III, he commanded English armies against France in the Hundred Years' War, distinguishing himself at Crécy (1346) and Poitiers (1356). He was the father of Richard II.

Edward (the Confessor) (1002?–66) saint and king of the English (1042–66). He was canonized in 1161, but his reign was troubled by political conflict between Norman and English groups.

Edward (the Martyr) (963?–978) saint and king of the English (975–978). He was advised throughout his reign by the Archbishop of Canterbury, St Dunstan. His assassination is thought to have been instigated by his stepmother Elfrida.

Edward, Lake lake in the Great African Rift Valley straddling the border between the Democratic Republic of the Congo and Uganda. Area: 2,150 sq. km/830 sq. mi. Former name **Albert Edward Nyanza**

Edwardian /ed wáwrdi ən/ *adj* relating to, belonging to, or characteristic of British society during the reign of Edward VII in the first decade of the 20th century ■ *n* somebody who was alive or active during Edward VII's reign

Edwin /éddwin/, **St and king of Northumbria** (585?–633) He was converted to Christianity in 627. His reign (616–633) ended with his death in battle against the pagan Penda of Mercia.

ee[1] /ee/ (*plural* **een** /een/) *n Scotland* same as **eye** [Variant]

ee[2] *abbr* Estonia (*used in Internet addresses*) See table at **domain name**

EE *abbr* **1.** Early English **2.** electrical engineer **3.** electrical engineering

-ee *suffix* **1.** somebody who receives or benefits from an action ○ *consignee* **2.** somebody who is the subject of a thing ○ *biographee* **3.** somebody who performs an action ○ *attendee* **4.** somebody connected with ○ *bargee* **5.** a kind of, especially a small one ○ *vestee* [Via Anglo-Norman < Latin *-atus*; sometimes Anglicization of French *-é*, or associated with -Y [1]]

EEA *abbr* LAW European Economic Area

EEC *abbr* POL European Economic Community

EECA *abbr* **1.** E-COMMERCE end entity certificate authority **2.** LAW Eastern Europe and Central Asia

EEG *abbr* MED **1.** echoencephalograph **2.** electroencephalogram **3.** electroencephalograph

eejit /ée jit/ *n Ireland, Scotland* an offensive term that deliberately insults somebody's intelligence or foresight (*informal insult*) [Late 19C. Representing a pronunciation of IDIOT]

eel /eel/ (*plural* **eels** or *same*) *n* **1.** LONG THIN FISH a fish with a long thin body resembling that of a snake, smooth skin without scales, and reduced fins. Freshwater eels typically migrate to the sea to spawn. Order: Anguilliformes. **2.** FISH LIKE EEL any fish similar to a true eel in appearance, e.g. an electric eel **3.** DEVIOUS PERSON an untrustworthy or evasive person [Old English *æl* < Germanic]

eelgrass /éel graass/ *n* **1.** a perennial plant with long narrow dark-green leaves that grows submerged in shallow seawater. Genus: *Zostera*. **2.** PLANTS same as **tape grass**

eelpout /éel powt/ (*plural* **-pouts** or *same*) *n* **1.** a sea fish with a long thin body like an eel. Family: Zoarcidae. **2.** FISH same as **burbot**

eelworm /éel wurm/ (*plural* **-worms** or *same*) *n* ZOOL same as **nematode**

een /een/ *Scotland* plural of **ee**[1]

e'en /een/ (*literary*) *n* evening ■ *adv* even

eena /éenə/ *prep* same as **in** (*slang*; *used in Black English*)

eensy /éenssi/, **eensy-weensy** /-wéenssi/, **incy** /ínssi/, **incy-wincy** /-wínssi/ *adj* extremely small (*informal*) ○ *just an eensy bit more* [Alteration of TEENSY]

eeny[1] /éeni/ *adj* same as **eensy** [Alteration of TEENY]

eeny[2] /éeni/ *adj, n regional* the number one in old counting systems [Origin ?]

REGIONAL NOTE Many children's rhymes are not as nonsensical as they might at first appear. It has been suggested that the four words ***eeny, meeny, miney, mo*** may be a recollection of an extremely old counting system. There is an Austrian rhyme beginning 'Eine, meine, mine, mu', and East Anglian shepherds are reputed to count one to four as *Ina, mina, tethra, methera*. The 'Hickory, Dickory, Dock' rhyme may contain a relic of 8, 9, and 10, which are *hevera, devera, dick* in a Westmorland counting system.

e'er /air/ *adv* same as **ever** (*literary*) [Late 16C. Contraction]

-eer *suffix* **1.** a person engaged in or concerned with ○ *auctioneer* ○ *charioteer* **2.** a contemptible person or act ○ *profiteer* [Via French *-ier* < Latin *-arius*]

eerie /éeri/ (**-rier, -riest**) *adj* unnerving or unusual in a way that suggests a connection with the supernatural ○ *an eerie old house* [13C. Probably < Old English *earg* 'cowardly'] —**eerily** *adv* —**eeriness** *n*

~~**eery**~~ incorrect spelling of **eerie**

EFA *abbr* HEALTH essential fatty acid

eff /ef/ *vti* an offensive term used to express strong feelings by similarity in sound to other offensive terms (*slang*) [Mid-20C. Spelling of first letter of FUCK] ◇ **eff and blind** to swear or use offensive language (*slang*)

efface /i fáyss/ (**-faces, -facing, -faced**) *v* **1.** *vt* to remove or obliterate something by wearing away or rubbing out or some analogous process **2.** *vr* to act in an inconspicuous manner, especially because of shyness or modesty ○ *always effaces himself in company* [15C. < French *effacer* 'wipe out, destroy' < *face* 'face, appearance'] —**effaceable** *adj* —**effacement** *n* —**effacer** *n*

effect /i fékt/ *n* **1.** RESULT a change or changed state occurring as a direct result of action by somebody or something else ○ *showing the effects of prolonged malnutrition* **2.** POWER TO INFLUENCE success in bringing about a change in somebody or something, or the ability to achieve this ○ *I pleaded with them, but to no effect.* **3.** BEING IN FORCE OR OPERATION the state of being in force or operation, or of being the case, often from a particular point in time ○ *The new law doesn't come into effect until next month.* ○ *Much-needed changes were now being put into effect.* ○ *You have to wait for the medicine to take effect.* **4.** IMPRESSION an impression produced in the mind of somebody who sees, hears, or reads something, especially one that is deliberately intended or engineered ○ *The overall effect of the new decor was light and spacious.* **5.** CAUSE OR PRODUCTION OF IMPRESSION something that produces an impression, or the process of causing a special feeling or impression ○ *a grand little speech made merely for effect* **6.** SPECIAL SOUND OR LIGHTING something done to produce a desired response or to add to the realism or theatricality of a film, play, or broadcast (*often used in the plural*) **7.** SCIENTIFIC PHENOMENON a scientifically observed and described phenomenon ○ *the Doppler effect* ■ **effects** *npl* BELONGINGS somebody's personal belongings, or the things that somebody is carrying about him or her (*formal*) ○ *Compensation will be paid for damage to or loss of personal effects.* ■ *vt* (**-fects, -fecting, -fected**) DO OR MAKE SOMETHING to succeed in making or doing something (*formal*) ○ *They effected their escape through a rear window.* [14C. Directly or via French < Latin *effectus* < *efficere* 'accomplish' < *facere* 'make, do'] —**effecter** *n* —**effectible** *adj* ◇ **in effect** used to indicate that what is being said represents the truth of the matter, even though the words used may not be those that other people would choose ○ *In effect, this means that the program is shut down.* ◇ **to that effect** having or indicating approximately the same meaning ○ *She objected and replied to that effect the next day.* ○ *The answer was 'No' – or words to that effect.*

USAGE See *affect*[1].

effective /i féktiv/ *adj* **1.** PRODUCING RESULT causing a result, especially the desired or intended result ○ *an effective remedy for headaches* **2.** PRODUCING FAVOURABLE IMPRESSION successful, especially in producing a strong or favourable impression on people ○ *effective use of imagery* **3.** ACTUAL actual or in practice, even if not officially or theoretically so ○ *was the effective leader during the premier's illness* **4.** OFFICIALLY IN FORCE officially in force, operative, or applicable ○ *a regulation effective as of next month* **5.** READY FOR ACTION fully equipped and ready for military action ■ *n* MILITARY PERSONNEL OR EQUIPMENT a soldier, military unit, or piece of military equipment that is ready for action —**effectiveness** *n* —**effectivity** /éffek tívvəti/ *n*

SYNONYMS ***effective, efficient, effectual, efficacious***
CORE MEANING: producing a result
effective causing a result, especially the desired or intended result ○ *an effective solution to the water supply problem* **efficient** capable of achieving the desired result with the minimum use of resources, time, and effort ○ *an efficient use of personnel* **effectual** (*formal*) potentially successful in producing a desired or intended result ○ *This idea exerts a direct and effectual influence on his thinking.* **efficacious** (*formal*) having the power to achieve a desired result, especially an improvement ○ *Diet may be as efficacious as medication in controlling the condition.*

effectively /i féktivli/ *adv* **1.** in a way that produces a desired result **2.** in fact or in practical terms, though not usually directly or technically ○ *She was effectively barred from seeking another position with the firm.*

effector /i féktər/ *n* **1.** a body part, e.g. a muscle or organ, that is activated by a stimulus, particularly a nerve impulse **2.** a substance, procedure, or agent that produces an effect, e.g. a nerve ending activating a muscle or a molecule affecting enzyme activity

effects-based *adj* describes a military operation or plan aimed at producing a specific outcome or event rather than destroying an enemy by attrition

effectual /i fékchoo əl/ *adj* (*formal*) **1.** potentially successful in producing a desired or intended result **2.** valid, or legally in force [14C. < medieval Latin *effectualis* < Latin *effectus* (see EFFECT)] —**effectuality** /i fékchoo álləti/ *n* —**effectually** *adv* —**effectualness** *n*

SYNONYMS See ***effective***.

effectuate /i fékchoo ayt/ (**-ates, -ating, -ated**) *vt* to do, cause, or accomplish something (*formal*) [Late 16C. < medieval Latin *effectuat-*, past participle of *effectuare* < Latin *effectus* (see EFFECT)] —**effectuation** /i fékchoo áysh'n/ *n*

effeminate /i fémminət/ *adj* **1.** an offensive term used to describe a man whose behaviour, appearance, or speech is considered to be similar to that traditionally associated with women or girls **2.** weak through overrefinement or an absence of vigorous qualities (*disapproving*) [14C. < Latin *effeminatus*, past participle of *effeminare* 'make feminine' < *femina* 'woman'] —**effeminacy** *n* —**effeminately** *adv* —**effeminateness** *n*

effendi /e féndi/ (*plural* **-dis**) *n* **1.** in Southwest Asia and North Africa, an important or well-educated man **2.** a title of respect that is the Turkish equivalent of such English terms as 'Mr' and 'Sir' [Early 17C. Via Turkish *efendi* < modern Greek *aphentēs* < Greek *authentēs* 'lord, master']

efferent /éffərənt/ *adj* describes nerves that carry impulses away from the brain or spinal cord, or blood vessels that carry blood away from an organ. ◊ **afferent** [Mid-19C. < Latin *efferent-*, present participle of *efferre* 'bring out' < *ferre* 'bring, carry'] —**efferent** *n*

efferent neuron *n* ANAT same as **motor neuron**

effervesce /éffər véss/ (**-vesces, -vescing, -vesced**) *vi* **1.** PRODUCE TINY GAS BUBBLES to give off gas in tiny bubbles, often producing foam and a hissing sound (*refers to liquids*) **2.** ESCAPE AS TINY BUBBLES to be given off by a liquid in the form of tiny bubbles (*refers to gases*) **3.** BE LIVELY to behave in a lively, high-spirited, or highly excited way [Early 18C. < Latin *effervescere* < *fervescere* 'come to the boil' < *fervere* 'be hot, boil']

effervescent /éffə véssn't/ *adj* **1.** producing gas in the form of tiny bubbles **2.** behaving in a lively, high-spirited, or highly excited way —**effervescence** *n* —**effervescently** *adv*

effete /i féet/ *adj* **1.** characterized by decadence, over-

refinement, or overindulgence **2.** lacking the strength or ability to get things done [Early 17C. < Latin *effetus* 'worn out by bearing young' < *fetus* 'breeding'] —**effetely** *adv* —**effeteness** *n*

efficacious /èffi káyshəss/ *adj* having the power to produce a desired result, especially an improvement (*formal*) [Early 16C. < Latin *efficac-* < *efficere* (see EFFECT)] —**efficaciously** *adv* —**efficaciousness** *n*

SYNONYMS See ***effective***.

efficacy /éffikəssi/, **efficacity** /èffi kássəti/ *n* the ability to produce the desired result [Early 16C. < Latin *efficacia* < *efficac-* (see EFFICACIOUS)]

efficiency /i físh'nssi/ (*plural* **-cies**) *n* **1. COMPETENCE** the ability to do something well or achieve a desired result without wasted energy or effort **2. PRODUCTIVE USE OF RESOURCES** the degree to which something is done well or without wasted energy **3. MEASURE OF MACHINE'S ENERGY EFFECTIVENESS** the ratio of the amount of energy used by a machine to the amount of work done by it. For example, the measurement of the amount of heat produced per unit of fuel when all of a fuel has been burned is a measure of a heating unit's efficiency. **4.** *N Am* same as **efficiency apartment**

efficiency apartment *n N Am* a small, usually furnished flat consisting of one room that includes kitchen facilities and a separate bathroom

efficient /i físh'nt/ *adj* **1.** performing tasks in an organized and capable way ○ *an efficient worker* **2.** capable of achieving the desired result with the minimum use of resources, time, and effort ○ *an efficient use of fuel* [14C. < Latin *efficient-*, present participle of *efficere* (see EFFECT)] —**efficiently** *adv*

SYNONYMS See ***effective***.

efficient cause *n* something that acts directly to initiate or produce changes in something else

effigy /éffiji/ (*plural* **-gies**) *n* **1.** a dummy, often roughly made and intentionally amusing or insulting, representing somebody disliked or despised **2.** a carved representation of a person, used as an architectural decoration or a monument [Mid-16C. < Latin *effigies* < *effingere* 'portray, form' < *fingere* 'fashion, shape']

effing /éffing/ *adj* an offensive term expressing strong feelings through its similarity in sound to other offensive terms (*slang*)

effloresce /èfflə réss/ (**-resces, -rescing, -resced**) *vi* **1.** BOT **BLOOM** to bloom or develop, like a flower coming into blossom (*literary*) **2.** CHEM **LOSE WATER FROM CRYSTAL** to lose water (**water of crystallization**) and become a powder (*refers to crystals*) **3.** CHEM **BECOME ENCRUSTED WITH POWDERY DEPOSIT** to become encrusted with a powdery deposit or crystals as a result of chemical change or the evaporation of a solution [Late 18C. < Latin *efflorescere* < *florescere* 'come into flower' < *flos* 'flower']

efflorescence /èfflə réss'nss/ *n* **1. UNFOLDING AND FLOURISHING** a process or time of development and unfolding (*literary*) **2. CULMINATION** the highest point of a process of development (*literary*) **3.** CHEM **LOSS OF WATER FROM CRYSTAL** the loss of water (**water of crystallization**) from a crystal **4.** GEOL **POWDERY SUBSTANCE ON ROCK SURFACE** a powdery substance that forms on the surface of rocks and brickwork —**efflorescent** *adj*

effluence /éffloo ənss/ *n* **1.** the act or process of flowing out **2.** something, often an immaterial substance or intangible influence, that flows out from a source (*literary*)

effluent /éffloo ənt/ *n* **1.** liquid waste discharged from a sewage system, factory, nuclear power station, or other industrial plant **2.** a stream or river that flows out of a larger body of water such as a lake or a larger stream [15C. < Latin *effluent-*, present participle of *effluere* 'flow out' < *fluere* 'flow']

effluvium /i flóovi əm, e-/ (*plural* **-via** /-vi ə/) *n* an unpleasant smell or harmful fumes usually given off by waste or decaying matter (*often used in the plural*) [Mid-17C. < Latin < *effluere* (see EFFLUENT)] —**effluvial** *adj*

efflux /éff luks/ *n* **1. INSTANCE OR ACT OF FLOWING OUT** the act or process of flowing out **2. SOMETHING THAT FLOWS OUT** something that flows out of something else (*formal*) **3. PASSING AWAY OF SOMETHING** the passing away of something, e.g. time (*formal*) [Mid-16C. < medieval Latin *effluxus* < Latin *efflux-*, past participle of *effluere* (see EFFLUENT)] —**effluxion** /i flúksh'n, e-/ *n*

effort /éffərt/ *n* **1. ENERGY** mental or physical energy that is exerted in order to achieve a purpose ○ *I wish they'd put a bit more effort into it.* **2. ACTIVITY DIRECTED TOWARDS PARTICULAR END** activities undertaken by a group of people in order to achieve a particular goal or overcome a particular difficulty ○ *the peacekeeping effort* **3. ATTEMPT** an attempt to do something, especially one that involves a considerable amount of exertion, work, or determination ○ *He made an effort to improve things.* **4. RESULT OF ATTEMPT** the result of a sincere attempt to do or make something ○ *It's not bad for a first effort.* **5.** PHYS **APPLIED FORCE** the force (**input force**) applied to a simple machine that produces an effect (**output force**) on the load [15C. < French < Old French *esforcier* 'exert power' < Latin *fortis* 'strong'] —**effortful** *adj* —**effortfully** *adv*

effortless /éffərtləss/ *adj* involving or appearing to involve little or no effort —**effortlessly** *adv* —**effortlessness** *n*

effrontery /i frúntəri/ (*plural* **-ies**) *n* behaviour or an attitude that is so bold or arrogant as to be insulting [Late 17C. < French *effronterie* < late Latin *effront-* 'barefaced' < Latin *front-* 'forehead']

effulgence /i fúljənss, -fóol-/ *n* brightness or a brilliant light radiating from something (*literary*) [Mid-17C. < late Latin *effulgentia* < Latin *effulgere* 'shine brightly' < *fulgere* 'shine'] —**effulgent** *adj*

effuse (*formal*) *v* /i fyóoz/ (**-fuses, -fusing, -fused**) **1.** *vti* **POUR OUT WORDS AND IDEAS** to pour out words and ideas, or to speak profusely about something, generally in an excited way **2.** *vti* **POUR OUT** to flow out, or make something such as a liquid, gas, or light flow out **3.** *vi* **RADIATE** to spread out or radiate from something ■ *adj* /i fyóoss/ BOT **IRREGULARLY SPREAD** tending to spread loosely or irregularly ○ *effuse lichens* [15C. < Latin *effus-*, past participle of *effundere* 'pour out' < *fundere* 'pour']

effusion /i fyóozh'n/ *n* **1. UNRESTRAINED OUTPOURING OF FEELINGS** an extravagant and sometimes excessive expression of feelings in speech or writing **2. ACT OF POURING OUT** the pouring out of something such as a liquid, gas, or light **3. SOMETHING POURED OUT** something such as a liquid, gas, or light that is poured out **4.** MED **MOVEMENT OF BODY FLUIDS** the oozing of fluids from blood or lymph vessels into body cavities or tissues as a result of inflammation **5.** MED **FLUID IN BODY CAVITIES OR TISSUES** lymph or blood present in body cavities or tissues as a result of inflammation **6.** PHYS **FLOW OF GAS THROUGH SMALL OPENING** the flow of a gas through a small aperture under pressure, particularly when the aperture is so small that the distance between molecules is significant

effusive /i fyóossiv/ *adj* giving or involving an extravagant and sometimes excessive expression of feelings in speech or writing ○ *effusive thanks* —**effusively** *adv* —**effusiveness** *n*

~~**eficient**~~ incorrect spelling of **efficient**

Efik /éffik/ (*plural same* or **-iks**) *n* **1.** a member of an Ibibio people who live in southeastern Nigeria **2.** a Niger-Congo language spoken in Nigeria. Native speakers: 4 million. [Mid-19C. < Efik] —**Efik** *adj*

E-FIT /ée fit/ *tdmk* a trademark for software that creates a likeness of the face of a police suspect on the basis of a witness's description

EFL *abbr* EDUC English as a Foreign Language

EFRA /éffrə/ *abbr* E-COMMERCE electronic forms routing and approval

eft /eft/ *n* **1.** an immature newt in the terrestrial phase, usually reddish-orange in colour. Latin name: *Notophthalmus viridescens*. **2.** *regional* same as **newt** [Old English *efeta*. Origin ?]

REGIONAL NOTE See ***newt***.

EFT *abbr* E-COMMERCE electronic funds transfer

EFTA /éftə/ *abbr* ECON European Free Trade Association

EFTPOS /éft poss/ *abbr* E-COMMERCE electronic funds transfer at point of sale

EFTS /efts/ *abbr* E-COMMERCE electronic funds transfer system

eg *abbr* Egypt (*used in Internet addresses*) See table at **domain name**

e.g., eg, eg. *abbr* for or as an example [Latin *exempli gratia*]

USAGE e.g. or **i.e.**? Do not confuse these two abbreviations, which mean different things and have different origins. The abbreviation ***e.g.***, meaning 'for or as an example', comes from the Latin expression *exempli gratia* ('for example'). Use it when you want to list a few typical examples of the thing mentioned: *I have the laboratory equipment, e.g.* [not *i.e.*] *beakers, thermometers, and test tubes, that we need.* Do not end a list that starts with ***e.g.*** with *etc.* The abbreviation ***i.e.***, meaning 'that is, that is to say', comes from the Latin expression *id est* ('that is'). Use it when you want to be more precise about the thing mentioned: *The tribunal, i.e.* [not *e.g.*] *the industrial tribunal, is set for noon on Friday.* Two full stops punctuate ***e.g.*** and ***i.e.*** in US English, whereas they may be unpunctuated in British English.

EGA *abbr* COMPUT enhanced graphics adapter

egad /i gád, ee-/ *interj* used to express surprise (*archaic*) [Late 17C. < alteration of AH + *gad*, euphemism for GOD]

egalitarian /i gàlli táiri ən/ *adj* maintaining, relating to, or based on a belief that all people are, in principle, equal and should enjoy equal social, political, and economic rights and opportunities [Late 19C. < French *égalitaire* < *égal* 'equal' < Latin *aequalis* (see EQUAL)] —**egalitarian** *n* —**egalitarianism** *n*

Egeria /i jéeri ə/ *n* a woman who acts as a trusted adviser or loyal companion (*literary*) [Early 17C. After a Roman goddess and adviser to the early Roman king Numa Pompilius]

egest /i jést/ (**egests, egesting, egested**) *vt* to excrete something from a cell or organism (*formal*) [15C. < Latin *egest-*, past participle of *egerere* 'carry out' < *gerere* 'carry'] —**egestion** *n* —**egestive** *adj*

egesta /i jéstə/ *npl* waste materials excreted from a cell or organism (*formal*) [Early 18C. < Latin, neuter plural of *egestus*, past participle of *egerere* 'carry out' < *gerere* 'carry']

egg[1] /eg/ *n* **1. ANIMAL REPRODUCTIVE STRUCTURE** a large sex cell produced by birds, fish, insects, reptiles, and amphibians, enclosed in a protective covering that allows the fertilized embryo to continue developing outside the mother's body until it hatches **2. HARD-SHELLED OBJECT LAID BY BIRD** the hard-shelled oval object laid by hens and other birds **3. BIRD'S EGG AS FOOD** a bird's egg, especially a hen's egg, used as food ○ *scrambled eggs* **4. SOMETHING SHAPED LIKE HEN'S EGG** something that resembles a hen's egg in shape, e.g. a carved or moulded ornament or chocolate made in an egg shape **5. REPRODUCTIVE CELL** a female reproductive cell **6.** same as **person** (*informal dated*) [14C. < Old Norse] —**eggy** *adj* ◇ **have egg on your face** to be left in an embarrassing or humiliating situation, especially because of having made an obvious mistake ◇ **put all your eggs in one basket** to rely entirely on one person or thing, or on the outcome of one plan or course of action

egg[2] /eg/ (**eggs, egging, egged**) *vt US* to incite somebody to do something ○ *was egged into making rash promises* [12C. < Old Norse *eggja* 'urge' < Germanic]

egg on *vt* to encourage somebody to do something, especially something wrong, foolish, or dangerous ○ *She never would have done it herself, but the girls were egging her on.*

egg-and-dart *n* an ornamental pattern, commonly used in mouldings on buildings or furniture, in which egg-shaped figures alternate with slightly tapered bars, arrows, or anchors. See illustration on next page

eggar /éggər/, **egger** *n* a moth with a brown body and wings whose larvae spin egg-shaped cocoons in the branches of trees. Family: Lasiocampidae. [Early 18C. Probably because of its egg-shaped cocoon]

eggbeater /ég beetər/ *n* **1.** a kitchen utensil used for beating or blending ingredients such as raw eggs or cream, especially one with two sets of spaced

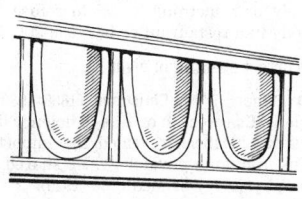

egg-and-dart

vertical blades rotated by turning a handle **2.** *N Am* a rotary-wing aircraft (*slang*)

eggcase /ég kayss/ *n* a protective covering containing eggs, especially one produced by organisms such as insects and molluscs

eggcup /ég kup/ *n* a small bowl-shaped container, often with a short neck and wide base below the bowl, used for holding a boiled egg while it is being eaten

egg custard *n* FOOD same as **custard** (sense 2)

egger *n* INSECTS another spelling of **eggar**

egg flip *n* a drink made by mixing beaten egg, sugar, and an alcoholic beverage, usually sherry, brandy, or port

egg foo yung *n US* FOOD same as **foo yung**

egghead /ég hed/ *n* an intellectual or bookish person (*informal*) [Early 20C. < the idea that a high forehead indicates brains] —**eggheaded** /ég héddid/ *adj*

egg lifter *n Aus* HOUSEHOLD same as **egg slice**

eggnog /égg nóg, ég nog/ *n* a drink made of milk or cream, eggs, sugar, spice, and sometimes an alcoholic beverage such as brandy or rum, traditionally served in the winter, especially at Christmas [Early 19C. < *nog*, a strong beer, origin ?]

eggplant /ég plaant/ *n* **1.** *ANZ, N Am* FOOD VEGETABLE a large fruit with shiny purple skin, eaten cooked as a vegetable **2.** *ANZ, N Am* PLANT WITH LARGE EDIBLE FRUIT a plant of the nightshade family that produces eggplants. Native to: South and East Asia. Latin name: *Solanum melongena*. **3.** *US* COLOURS BLACKISH PURPLE a very dark purple colour. ANZ, Can term **aubergine** ▶ UK term **aubergine**

egg roll *n N Am* a Chinese-American snack similar to a spring roll

egg sac *n* the pouch or cocoon that a female spider spins to protect its eggs

eggs Benedict *n* ham and a poached egg in hollandaise sauce on a slice of toast or a split toasted muffin (*takes a singular or plural verb*) [Late 19C. Origin ?]

eggshell /ég shel/ *n* **1.** HARD COVER OF EGG the brittle protective covering of the egg of a bird, or the similar tough covering of the eggs of animals such as crocodiles and turtles **2.** YELLOWISH-WHITE COLOUR a pale yellowish-white colour ■ *adj* **1.** SLIGHTLY GLOSSY having a slight sheen, with a finish between that of gloss and matt paint **2.** FRAGILE fragile, thin, or delicate ○ *eggshell china* **3.** YELLOWISH-WHITE pale yellowish-white in colour ◇ **walk on eggshells** to proceed with extreme wariness, caution, and tact

eggshell blue *adj* having a delicate pale blue colour —**eggshell blue** *n*

egg slice *n* a flat-bladed kitchen utensil for lifting fried eggs or omelettes out of a frying pan

egg timer *n* **1.** a small hourglass or clockwork device used to time the boiling of an egg **2.** COMPUT same as **hourglass** (sense 2)

egg tooth *n* a small projection on the beak of a baby bird or the upper jaw of a baby reptile, used to cut through the eggshell when hatching, and later shed

egg white *n* the clear viscous liquid found in an egg that turns solid and white when cooked

e-giving /eé giving/ *n* charitable giving carried out exclusively over the Internet by accessing a particular charity's website and using a credit card to make the donation (*informal*)

eglantine /égglǝn tīn/ (*plural* **-tines** or *same*) *n* PLANTS same as **sweetbriar** [14C. Via French *églantine* < Latin *aculentus* 'spiny' < *acus* 'needle']

EGM *abbr* extraordinary general meeting

Egmont, Mount /ég mont/ ▶ **Taranaki, Mount**

ego /eégō, éggō/ (*plural* **egos**) *n* **1.** SELF-ESTEEM somebody's idea of his or her own importance or worth, usually of an appropriate level ○ *The climb left us with frostbite and bruised egos.* **2.** INFLATED OPINION OF SELF an exaggerated sense of self-importance and a feeling of superiority to other people **3.** PSYCHOANAL PART OF MIND CONTAINING CONSCIOUSNESS in Freudian psychology, one of three main divisions of the mind, containing consciousness and memory and involved with control, planning, and conforming to reality ○ '*The poor ego has a still harder time of it; it has to serve three harsh masters, and has to do its best to reconcile the claims and demands of all three.*' (Sigmund Freud, *The Anatomy of the Mental Personality, Lecture 31*) ◊ **id** [1], **superego 4.** PHILOSOPHY SELF the individual self, as distinct from the outside world and other selves [Early 19C. < Latin, 'I']

egocentric /eégō séntrik, éggō-/ *adj* **1.** SELFISH interested only in personal needs and wants, and not caring about other people **2.** LIMITED OR CONFINED IN OUTLOOK limited in outlook or confined to things mainly relating to yourself **3.** PHILOSOPHY CENTRED ON SELF centred on the individual self, and considering it to be the hub of all experience —**egocentric** *n* —**egocentrically** *adv* —**egocentricity** /eégō sen tríssǝti, éggō-/ *n* —**egocentrism** *n*

ego ideal *n* in Freudian psychoanalysis, a person's ideal image of what he or she could or should be, built up from observation of parents or other admired people

egoism /eégō izǝm, éggō-/ *n* **1.** PHILOSOPHY the practice of making personal welfare and interests a primary or sole concern, sometimes at the expense of others **2.** ETHICS the ethical doctrine that the correct basis for morality is self-interest **3.** same as **egotism** (sense 1)

USAGE egoism or **egotism**? These two words, which are equally common, are often used interchangeably, though a distinction can be made. *Egoism* refers, in terms of philosophy, to theories in which self-interest is regarded as the principal motivating factor. And so an *egoist* believes an individual should seek as an end only his or her own welfare: *His conduct was characterized by ruthless egoism. Egotism* implies a vain self-absorption as a matter of behaviour rather than an ethical principle, and an *egotist* is somebody who behaves in a selfish or self-centred way: *Her egotism makes her ignore other people's concerns.*

egoist /eégō ist, éggō-/ *n* **1.** somebody who believes that the correct basis for morality is self-interest **2.** same as **egotist** (sense 1) —**egoistic** /eégō ístik, éggō-/ *adj* —**egoistical** *adj* —**egoistically** *adv*

egomania /eégō máyni ǝ, éggō-/ *n* a dangerously obsessive preoccupation with the self —**egomaniac** *n* —**egomaniacal** /-mǝ nÍ ǝk'l/ *adj* —**egomaniacally** *adv*

ego psychology *n* a psychological theory based on the idea that the ego is an independent part of the personality that develops self-identity through conflict and its resolution over a lifetime

ego surf (**ego surfs, ego surfing, ego surfed**) *vi* to devote time looking for one's name or links to one's webpages, often to see who shares the same name —**egosurfer** *n* —**egosurfing** *n*

egotism /eégōtizǝm, éggō-/ *n* **1.** INFLATED SENSE OF SELF-IMPORTANCE the possession of an exaggerated sense of self-importance and superiority to other people **2.** PREOCCUPATION WITH SELF the tendency to speak or write too much about yourself **3.** SELFISHNESS selfishness or self-centredness [Early 18C. < EGO + *t* + -ISM]

USAGE See *egoism*.

egotist /eégōtist, éggō-/ *n* **1.** somebody with an exaggerated sense of his or her own importance, especially somebody who tends to speak or write about himself or herself excessively **2.** somebody who is selfish or self-centred —**egotistic** /eégō tístik, éggō-/ *adj* —**egotistical** *adj* —**egotistically** *adv*

ego trip *n* a course of action or an experience that boosts somebody's sense of his or her own importance (*informal*) —**ego-trip** *vi* —**ego-tripper** *n*

egregious /i greéjǝss, -ji ǝss/ *adj* conspicuously bad or offensive (*formal*) ○ *an egregious violation of privacy* [Mid-16C. < Latin *egregius* 'illustrious' < *greg-* 'flock'] —**egregiously** *adv* —**egregiousness** *n*

egress /eé gress/ *n* **1.** COMING OR GOING OUT the act of coming or going out of a place (*formal*) **2.** RIGHT TO LEAVE the right to leave a place (*formal*) **3.** EXIT an exit from a place (*formal*) **4.** ASTRON same as **emersion** (sense 2) ■ *vt* (**egresses, egressing, egressed**) *US* LEAVE SOMEWHERE to come or go out of a place (*formal*) [Mid-16C. < Latin *egressus* < *egredi* 'go out' < *gradi* 'proceed, step']

egret /eégrǝt/ *n* a small, mainly white heron that produces long drooping ornamental feathers on the lower part of the back at the start of the breeding season. Egrets' feathers were once popular as decorations for women's hats, so that the birds were hunted almost to extinction. Family: Ardeidae. [14C. Via Anglo-Norman *egrette* < Provençal *aigreta* < *aigron* 'heron' < Germanic]

egusi /e goóssi/ *n* **1.** in West Africa, a mildly spiced stew that is thickened with blended melon seeds and contains fresh vegetable leaves and smoked fish **2.** the bean of a plant of the watermelon family, used in cooking. Latin name: *Citrullus lanatus.* [Early 20C. < Yoruba]

Egypt

Egypt /eéjipt/ country in northeastern Africa bordering the Mediterranean Sea and the Red Sea. It became a republic in 1952. Language: Arabic. Currency: Egyptian pound. Capital: Cairo. Population: 74,718,797 (2003). Area: 997,739 sq. km/385,229 sq. mi. Official name **Arab Republic of Egypt**

Egyptian /i jípsh'n/ *n* **1.** SOMEBODY FROM EGYPT somebody who comes from Egypt **2.** LANGUAGE OF ANCIENT EGYPT the extinct Afro-Asiatic language of ancient Egypt that developed into Coptic around AD 200 **3.** DIALECT OF ARABIC SPOKEN IN EGYPT the dialect of Arabic spoken in modern Egypt. Native speakers: 65 million. —**Egyptian** *adj*

Egyptian plover *n* a black-and-grey bird with long legs that lives on sandy banks of rivers and lakes. Native to: Africa. Latin name: *Pluvianus aegyptius.*

Egyptology /eéjip tóllǝji/ *n* the study of the history, archaeology, culture, and language of ancient Egypt —**Egyptologist** *n*

eh[1] /ay, e/ *interj* (*informal*) **1.** PARDON? used to ask somebody to repeat something **2.** WHAT? used to express surprise at something that has been said **3.** ISN'T THAT SO? used to invite somebody to respond to something that has been said, especially to agree with it or confirm that it is correct or accurately sums up a previous statement **4.** *Can* ARE YOU WITH ME? used to maintain or regain a listener's interest or to establish that what is being said is understood [Mid-16C. Natural exclamation]

eh[2] *abbr* Western Sahara (*used in Internet addresses*) See table at **domain name**

EHO *abbr* SOC WELFARE Environmental Health Officer

Ehrlich /áirlik, -li**kh**/, **Paul** (1854–1915) German bacteriologist and immunologist. He shared a Nobel Prize in physiology or medicine (1908) for his work on immunology and also pioneered chemotherapy, developing a successful treatment for syphilis.

EIA *abbr* environmental impact assessment

EIB *abbr* BANKING European Investment Bank

Eichendorff /íkən dawrf, íkhən-/, **Joseph, Freiherr von** (1788–1857) German poet. His lyrical poems were set to music by Robert Schumann, Felix Mendelssohn, and others. He also wrote a popular novel, *Memoirs of a Good-for-Nothing* (1826). Full name **Eichendorff, Joseph Karl Benedikt von**

Eichmann /íkmən, íkh-/, **Adolf** (1906–62) German Nazi official and war criminal. Responsible for carrying out anti-Semitic policy during World War II, he was captured in Argentina in 1960 by Israeli agents, tried in Israel for crimes against humanity, and hanged two years later. Full name **Eichmann, Karl Adolf**

eicosapentaenoic acid /íkōsə péntinō ik-/ *n* BIOCHEM full form of **EPA** [< Greek *eikosi* 'twenty' + *penta-* 'five']

Eid /eed/, **Id** *n* **1.** ISLAM same as **Eid al-Adha 2.** any Islamic religious festival [Late 17C. Via Arabic *'īd* 'festival' < Aramaic]

Eid al-Adha /-al aádə/, **Eid ul-Adha** /-ōōl-/ *n* an Islamic festival marking the sacrifice made by Abraham and the end of the annual pilgrimage to Mecca, traditionally celebrated by the sacrifice of sheep. Date: 10th-13th days of Dhu al-Hijjah. [Arabic *al-adha* 'festival of the sacrifice']

Eid al-Fitr /-al feétər/, **Eid ul-Fitr** /-ōōl-/ *n* an Islamic festival marking the end of Ramadan. Date: 1st day of Shawwal. [< Arabic *'īd al-fiṭr* 'festival of the breaking of the fast']

eider /ídər/ (*plural* **-ders** or *same*), **eider duck** *n* a large sea duck, the male of which has distinctive black-and-white feathers. The female, the source of eiderdown, has mottled brown feathers. Native to: northern hemisphere. Genus: *Somateria*. [Late 17C. Via Icelandic *æður* < Old Norse *æðr*]

eiderdown /ídər down/ *n* **1.** a warm bed covering consisting of a fabric container filled with feathers or artificial fibres **2.** the soft fluffy breast feathers of the female eider duck, used for stuffing pillows and bed coverings

eider duck *n* BIRDS same as **eider**

eidetic /ī déttik/ *adj* (*formal*) **1.** able to recall or reproduce things previously seen, with startling accuracy, clarity, and vividness ○ *an eidetic memory* **2.** recalled or reproduced with startling accuracy, clarity, and vividness ○ *eidetic images* [Early 20C. < Greek *eidētikos* < *eidos* 'form'] —**eidetically** *adv*

eidolon /ī dólən/, **ī dó** lon/ (*plural* **-lons** or **-la** /-lə/) *n* (*literary*) **1.** a ghostly figure or image **2.** an idealized image of somebody or something [Mid-17C. < Greek *eidōlon* 'idol' (see IDOL)]

Eid ul-Adha *n* ISLAM same as **Eid al-Adha**

Eid ul-Fitr *n* ISLAM same as **Eid al-Fitr**

Eiffel /ífl/, **Gustave** (1832–1923) French engineer. A specialist in metal structures, he is best known as the designer of the Eiffel Tower (1889) and architect of the inner structure of the Statue of Liberty (1885). Full name **Eiffel, Alexandre Gustave**

Eiffel Tower, Paris, France

Eiffel Tower *n* a 300-metre-/984-foot-high iron tower in central Paris. It was designed by Gustave Eiffel for the 1889 Paris Exposition.

eigenvalue /ígən valyoo/ *n* a value of a variable in an equation giving a solution that complies with the conditions that exist at a system's boundaries [Early

20C. < German *eigen* 'own, particular' + VALUE, after German *Eigenwert*]

Eiger /ígər/ mountain peak in the Bernese Alps, southeast of Bern, Switzerland. The north face of the mountain is notorious for the number of mountaineers who have died attempting to climb it. Height: 3,970 m/13,025 ft.

Eigg /eg/ island of the Inner Hebrides, northwestern Scotland. Population: 69 (1991). Area: 67 sq. km/26 sq. mi.

eight /ayt/ *n* **1. 8** the number 8 **2.** SOMETHING WITH VALUE OF 8 something in a numbered series, e.g. a playing card, with a value of eight **3.** GROUP OF 8 a group of eight objects or people **4.** SOMETHING WITH 8 PARTS something composed of eight parts or members, e.g. an eight-cylinder engine **5.** ROWING CREW OF 8 a crew of eight rowers **6.** ROWING RACING BOAT a long narrow rowing boat crewed by eight rowers ■ *symbol* **8** SYMBOL TO REPRESENT 'ATE' OR 'EAT' a figure '8' used to replace '-ate-' or '-eat-' in words (*used in e-mails or text messages*) ○ *see U L8R* ○ *gr8* [Old English *e(a)hta* < Indo-European] —**eight** *adj, pron* ◇ **have one over the eight** to have too much to drink and get drunk (*dated informal*)

eight ball *n* N Am **1.** in pool, the black ball, which has the number 8 on it **2.** a form of pool in which a player must pocket a given 7 of the 15 balls, and then pocket the eight ball, before his or her opponent does ◇ **behind the eight ball** N Am in a difficult or awkward position (*slang*)

eighteen /ay teén, áyt een/ *n* **1. 18** the number 18 **2.** SOMETHING WITH VALUE OF 18 something in a numbered series with a value of 18 **3.** GROUP OF 18 a group of 18 objects or people **4.** Aus AUSTRALIAN FOOTBALL TEAM a team of 18 players in Australian Rules football **5. 18** CINEMA, MEDIA UK FILM RATING in the United Kingdom, a rating given to films and videos considered unsuitable for people under the age of 18 [Old English *e(a)hatēne* < Germanic] —**eighteen** *adj, pron*

18 certificate *n* in the United Kingdom, a certificate designating a film or video considered unsuitable for people under the age of 18

eighteenmo /ay teén mō/ (*plural* **-mos**) *n* PRINTING same as **octodecimo**

eighteenth /ay teénth/ *n* **1.** one of 18 equal parts of something **2.** the birthday of somebody who has just reached 18 years of age —**eighteenth** *adj, adv*

eightfold /áyt fōld/ *adj* **1.** MULTIPLYING BY 8 multiplying the original figure by eight **2.** WITH 8 PARTS consisting of eight parts ■ *adv* BY 8 by eight, or to an amount eight times greater than the original

eightfold path *n* in Buddhism, the means of achieving nirvana, emphasizing adherence to truth and moral values and comprising eight aspects. These are right understanding, right thought, right speech, right action, right livelihood, right effort, right mindfulness, and right concentration.

eighth /aytth/ *n* one of eight equal parts of something —**eighth** *adj, adv*

eighth note *n* N Am MUSIC same as **quaver** *n* (sense 2)

eighth rest *n* N Am MUSIC same as **quaver rest**

eightieth /áyti əth/ *n* **1.** one of 80 equal parts of something **2.** the birthday of somebody who has just reached 80 years of age —**eightieth** *adj, adv*

eightsome reel /áytsəm-/ *n* a Scottish dance performed by sets of four couples, each in circles

802.11 *n* a set of specifications for wireless local area networks

eightvo /áyt vō/ (*plural* **-vos**) *n* PRINTING same as **octavo** (sense 2) [< *8vo*, written abbreviation of OCTAVO]

eighty /áyti/ *n* (*plural* **-ies**) **1. 80** the number 80 **2.** GROUP OF 80 a group of 80 objects or people ■ **eighties** *npl* **1.** NUMBERS 80 TO 89 the numbers 80 to 89, especially as a range of Fahrenheit temperatures **2.** YEARS FROM 80 TO 89 the years from 80 to 89 in a century **3.** PERIOD FROM AGE 80 TO 89 the period of somebody's life from the age of 80 to 89 [13C. Shortening of Old English *hundeahtatig* < *hund-* 'hundred' + *e(a)hta* 'eight' + *-tig* 'group of ten'] —**eighty** *adj, pron*

Eighty-Mile Beach /áyti mīl-/ beach in northwestern Western Australia, located 300 km/185 mi. northeast of Port Hedland. Length: 137 km/85 mi.

eighty-six (**eighty-sixes, eighty-sixing, eighty-sixed**), **86** (**86es, 86ing, 86ed**) *vt* (*slang*) **1.** N Am to dispose of somebody or something **2.** US to refuse to serve somebody in a restaurant or bar [Mid-20C. Origin ?]

eigth incorrect spelling of **eight**

Eijkman /íkmən, íkh-/, **Christiaan** (1858–1930) Dutch physician. His research on diet-deficiency diseases, particularly beriberi, revealed the importance of vitamins in human physiology. He shared a Nobel Prize in physiology or medicine (1929).

EIL *abbr* English as an international language

Eilat /ay laát/, **Elat** seaport, tourist resort, and leading oil port in southern Israel, situated at the head of the Gulf of Aqaba. Population: 38,200 (1999).

Eildon and Leaderfoot /eéldən ənd leédərfòōt/ National Scenic Area in the Scottish Borders council area in southern Scotland. Area: 36 sq. km/14 sq. mi.

-ein *suffix* a chemical compound related to one whose name ends in '-in' or '-ine' ○ *fluorescein* [Alteration of -IN]

eina /áy naa/ S Africa *interj* used to express sudden pain ■ *n* a wound or a pain [Early 20C. < Afrikaans]

Eindhoven /índ hōv'n/ city and industrial centre in the southern Netherlands. Population: 193,000 (1991).

Albert Einstein

Einstein /ín stīn/, **Albert** (1879–1955) German-born US physicist. His theory of general relativity revolutionized scientific thought and served as the theoretical foundation for later exploitation of atomic energy. He won a Nobel Prize in physics in 1921 for his work explaining the photoelectric effect. He became a Swiss (1905) and later a US citizen (1940). In 1939 he joined other physicists in writing to President Franklin Roosevelt to warn him that Germany could possibly make an atomic bomb.

'When you are courting a nice girl, an hour seems like a second. When you sit on a red-hot cinder a second seems like an hour. That's relativity.'
[Albert Einstein, *News Chronicle*; 14 March 1949]

'Everything should be made as simple as possible, but not simpler.'
[Attributed to Albert Einstein]

einsteinium /īn stíni əm/ *n* a synthetic radioactive element. Source: irradiated plutonium and other elements. Symbol **Es**. See table at **element** [After Albert EINSTEIN]

Einthoven /ínt hōv'n/, **Willem** (1860–1927) Dutch physiologist. His most important invention was the string galvanometer, which recorded precise measurements of electrical activity in the heart. He won a Nobel Prize in physiology or medicine (1924).

Eire /áirə/ former name for **Ireland** (sense 2) (1937–49)

eirenicon /ī reéni kon/, **irenicon** *n* a proposal made in order to achieve peace or harmony (*formal*)

EIS *abbr* environmental impact statement

EISA *abbr* COMPUT extended industry standard architecture

Dwight D. Eisenhower

US Military Academy

Eisenhower /íz'n how ər/, **Dwight D.** (1890–1969) 34th president of the United States. He was supreme commander of Allied forces in Europe during World War II. As president, he adopted a policy of containing Communism throughout the world. Full name **Eisenhower, Dwight David.** Known as **Ike**

> 'A people that values its privileges above its principles soon loses both.'
> [Dwight D. Eisenhower, *Inaugural address, Washington, DC*; 20 January 1953]

Eisenstein /íz'n stīn/, **Sergey** (1898–1948) Soviet film director. His innovative cinematographic techniques in films such as *The Battleship Potemkin* (1925) made him a pioneering figure in the history of cinema.

eish /aysh/, **aysh** *interj S Africa* used especially by young urban Black people to express surprise, pleasure, or amazement (*informal*) [Late 20C. Origin uncertain *Isicamtho*?]

eisteddfod /ī stédfəd, ī stéth vod/ (*plural* **-fods** or **-fodau** /ī stéth vodī/) *n* a traditional Welsh festival at which competitions are held for performers and composers of music and poetry [Early 19C. < Welsh, 'session, sitting']

Eiswein /íss vīn/ *n* a sweet white wine produced in Germany and Austria from grapes that have frozen on the vine, so that the sugar content is concentrated [Mid 20C. < German, 'ice wine']

either /íthər, ee´thər/ CORE MEANING: a grammatical word used to indicate or connect two situations, one of which may include or exclude the other ○ *It won't make much difference either way.* ○ (pron) *I refuse to meet either of them.* ○ (conj) *Either there's a problem or there isn't.* ○ (adv) *I don't want to go either.*
1. *det, pron* ONE OR OTHER one or the other, when it does not matter which ○ (det) *You can execute commands on either machine.* ○ (pron) *If either fell behind, the other would help him to catch up.* ○ (pron) *You can get this information from either of the two addressees.* ○ *either of them* **2.** *det, pron* INDICATES NEGATIVE used to refer negatively to each of two situations, where the negative includes them both ○ (det) *You cannot send e-mails to either address at the moment.* ○ (pron) *I'm not interested in either of them.* **3.** *det* BOTH both of two things ○ *The red and yellow patches on either side of the Sun are radiation from the dust ring.* **4.** *conj* INDICATES ALTERNATIVES used preceding alternatives joined by 'or' to indicate that there is a choice between two or more options ○ *Data sources may be either digital or analogue.* **5.** *adv* INDICATES CONNECTION used in a negative statement that indicates a connection or a partial agreement with a previous statement (*at the end of a second statement*) ○ *You won't find the conditions exactly spartan, but don't expect luxury hotels either.* [Old English ǣgþer, contraction of ǣg(e)hwæþer < Germanic, 'always each of two']

USAGE Singular or plural after **either**? *Either* is normally used with a singular verb: *Has either of you been to Paris? Either Lee or David is responsible.* Informally, however, the plural is used when the choices are regarded collectively rather than individually, and it is quite natural to say *Have either of you been to Paris?*, which caters for the possibility that both the people addressed have done so. When *either...or...* occurs with a mixture of singular and plural subjects, the verb trad-

itionally agrees with the subject that is closer to it: *Either David or his parents are at home.*

either-or *adj* offering a choice strictly limited to two options ○ *It's an either-or situation – either you accept or you refuse.*

ejaculate *v* /i jákyoŏ layt/ (**-lates, -lating, -lated**) **1.** *vti* EJECT SEMEN DURING ORGASM to eject semen from the penis during orgasm **2.** *vt* EXCLAIM SOMETHING SUDDENLY to exclaim something suddenly and usually forcefully (*literary*) ■ *n* /-lət/ EJACULATED SEMEN semen that has been ejected from the penis during orgasm [Late 16C. < Latin *ejaculat-*, past participle of *ejaculari* 'throw out' < *jacere* 'throw'] —**ejaculation** /i jákyoŏ láysh'n/ *n* —**ejaculatory** /-lətəri/ *adj*

eject /i jékt/ (**ejects, ejecting, ejected**) *v* **1.** *vt* PUSH SOMETHING OUT WITH FORCE to cause something to burst out from something else with considerable force **2.** *vt* COMPEL SOMEBODY TO LEAVE to force somebody to leave a place or give up a position, e.g. a job or membership ○ *They were forcibly ejected from the meeting.* **3.** *vi* AVIAT LEAVE AIRCRAFT IN ESCAPE DEVICE to escape from an aircraft in an emergency by means of an ejector seat or special capsule **4.** *vt* LAW EVICT SOMEBODY to remove somebody, especially a tenant, from a property by taking legal action [15C. < Latin *eject-*, past participle of *e(j)icere* < *jacere* 'throw'] —**ejectable** *adj* —**ejection** /i jéksh'n/ *n* —**ejective** *adj*

ejecta /i jéktə/ *n* substances ejected from something, especially the material thrown out by a volcanic eruption or from a star (*formal; takes a singular or plural verb*) [Late 19C. < Latin, neuter plural of past participle of *e(j)icere* (see EJECT)]

ejection seat *n N Am* AVIAT same as **ejector seat**

ejectment /i jéktmənt/ *n* **1.** the act or process of ejecting somebody or something, or of being ejected from somewhere (*formal*) **2.** a legal action brought by somebody to recover possession of land that is being held by somebody else

ejector /i jéktər/ *n* **1.** a device for ejecting something from something else, especially a mechanism for ejecting an empty cartridge or shell from a gun **2.** a jet pump device that uses water, steam, or air to remove a gas, fluid, or powder from a space

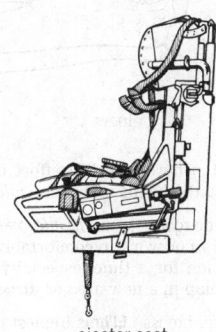

ejector seat

ejector seat /i jéktər-/ *n* a seat in the cockpit of an aircraft that in an emergency propels the occupant clear of the craft by means of a rocket or explosive device. N Am term **ejection seat**

ekdam /ek dúm/ *adv S Asia* in a complete way or to the fullest extent (*informal*) [Late 19C. < Hindi < *ek* 'one' + Urdu *dam* 'breath']

eke /eek/ (**ekes, eking, eked**) [Old English ēacan, ēacian 'increase, add' < Germanic]
eke out *vt* **1.** MAKE SOMETHING LAST WITH SPARING USE to make a supply of something last by using it as slowly and economically as possible **2.** SUPPLEMENT SOMETHING INSUFFICIENT OR INADEQUATE to supplement something that is insufficient or inadequate, usually with difficulty and by hard work **3.** GET SOMETHING ONLY WITH EFFORT to manage to achieve something but only on a small scale and with a great deal of effort ○ *eked out a bare existence*

ekistics /i kístiks/ *n* the study of human settlements in all their aspects, including the origin and development of towns and town planning (*takes a singular verb*) [Mid-20C. < Greek *oikistikos* < *oikizein* 'settle' < *oikos* 'house'] —**ekistic** *adj*

el /el/ *n US* an elevated railway in a city (*informal*) [Early 20C. Shortening]

el. *abbr* GEOG elevation

elaborate *adj* /i lábbərət/ **1.** COMPLEX having many different parts or a lot of detail, and organized in a complicated way ○ *an elaborate system* **2.** FINELY OR RICHLY DECORATED made with a lot of intricate detail or extravagant ornamentation ○ *an elaborate head-dress* **3.** DETAILED AND THOROUGH thought out or organized with thoroughness and careful attention to detail ○ *elaborate preparations* ■ *v* /-rayt/ (**-rates, -rating, -rated**) **1.** *vi* GIVE MORE DETAIL ABOUT SOMETHING to go into greater detail about something that has already been spoken about or described in broad terms ○ *Would you care to elaborate on that?* **2.** *vt* WORK OUT SOMETHING IN DETAIL to work out the details of something **3.** *vti* MAKE OR BECOME MORE COMPLEX to make something more complex or ornate, or become more complex or ornate [15C. < Latin *elaborat-*, past participle of *elaborare* 'produce by effort or labour' < *labor* 'labour'] —**elaborately** *adv* —**elaborateness** *n* —**elaboration** /i lábbə ráysh'n/ *n* —**elaborator** *n*

El 'Alamein /el állə mayn/ coastal town in northern Egypt. It was the site of two important World War II battles in which British forces defeated German troops in 1942. Population: 980 (2001).

Elam /eeləm/ ancient kingdom in southwestern Iran, east of the River Tigris. It was established before 4000 BC and corresponds to the present-day Khuzistan Province, Iran.

Elamite /eeləm īt/ *n* **1.** somebody from the ancient kingdom of Elam **2.** an extinct language formerly spoken in the ancient kingdom of Elam. Elamite has been attested by important discoveries of pictographic and cuneiform inscriptions dating from the third millennium BC through to the first millennium AD. —**Elamite** *adj* —**Elamitic** /eelə míttik/ *adj*

élan /ay lóN, ay lán/, **elan** *n* vigour and enthusiasm, often combined with self-confidence and style [Mid-19C. < French, < *élancer* 'dart, throw' < *lance* (see LANCE)]

eland

eland /eeland/ (*plural* **elands** or *same*) *n* an antelope with humped shoulders, a dewlap, and tightly spiralling horns. It is the largest living antelope. Native to: central and southern Africa. Genus: *Taurotragus*. [Late 18C. Via Afrikaans < Dutch, 'elk' < Lithuanian *élnis*]

élan vital /ay lóN vee taál, ay lán-/ *n* in the philosophy of Henri Bergson, a creative life force present in all living things and responsible for evolution [< French, 'vital ardour']

elapid /éllapid/ *n* a venomous snake with short fangs at the front of the upper jaw, e.g. a cobra, coral snake, or mamba. Family: Elapidae. [Late 19C. < modern Latin *Elapidae* < Greek *elaps*, variant of *el(l)ops*, kind of fish and sea serpent] —**elapid** *adj*

elapse /i láps/ *vi* (**elapses, elapsing, elapsed**) to pass or go by, especially in a gradual, slow, or imperceptible way ○ *Before we knew it, several hours had elapsed.* ■ *n* the passing of a period of time (*formal*) [Late 16C. < Latin *elaps-*, past participle of *elabi* 'slip away' < *labi* 'glide, fall']

Elara /éllərə/ *n* a small natural satellite of Jupiter, discovered in 1905. It is approximately 80 km/50 mi. in diameter and occupies an intermediate orbit.

elasmobranch /i lássmə brangk, -lázmə-/ *n* a fish with a cartilaginous skeleton, e.g. a shark, ray, or skate. Subclass: Elasmobranchii. [Late 19C. < modern Latin

Elasmobranchii < Greek *elasmos* 'beaten metal' + *bragkhia* 'gills'] —**elasmobranch** *adj*

elastic /i lástik/ *n* **1.** STRETCHY MATERIAL strips or threads of rubber or similar stretchable material, or fabric or tape with a stretchy material woven into it so that it can fit tightly round something **2.** N Am same as **rubber band** ■ *adj* **1.** MADE OF ELASTIC made of or containing elastic **2.** STRETCHY AND FLEXIBLE describes an object or substance that can return quickly to its original shape and size after being bent, stretched, or squashed **3.** EASILY CHANGED able to incorporate changes or adapt to new circumstances easily **4.** SPRINGY light and springy, especially in movement ○ *an elastic gait* [Mid-17C. Via modern Latin < Greek *elastikos* 'driving, propelling' < *elaunein* 'drive'] —**elastically** *adv*

SYNONYMS See *pliable.*

elasticate /i lásti kayt/ (**-cates, -cating, -cated**) *vt* UK to put strips or threads of rubber or a similar material into a fabric in order to make it stretchy. ANZ, N Am term **elasticize** —**elasticated** /i lásti kaytid/ *adj*

elastic band *n* same as **rubber band**

elastic collision *n* a collision between two perfectly elastic bodies so that the final kinetic energy of the system is the same as the initial kinetic energy of the system

elastic fibre *n* a smooth long thin fibre in connective tissue, composed mainly of the fibrous protein elastin

elasticity /ée lass tíssəti/ *n* **1.** ABILITY TO RETURN TO SHAPE the ability of an object or substance to return quickly to its original shape and size after being bent, stretched, or squashed **2.** FLEXIBILITY the ability to incorporate changes or adapt to new circumstances easily **3.** ECON RELATIVE CHANGE IN ECONOMIC VARIABLE the relative change in an economic variable, e.g. demand, that occurs in reaction to changes in other variables, e.g. price or advertising input

elasticize /i lásti sīz/ (**-cizes, -cizing, -cized**), **elasticise** (**-cises, -cising, -cised**) *vt* **1.** ANZ, N Am same as **elasticate 2.** to make something elastic or more elastic —**elasticized** /i lásti sīzd/ *adj*

elastic limit *n* the maximum stress that can be applied to a material without the material becoming permanently deformed

elastic wave *n* a wave propagated in a medium in which particles become temporarily displaced, transfer motion to other particles, and then return to their original state

elastin /i lástin/ *n* a fibrous protein resembling collagen that is the main constituent of the elastic fibres of connective tissue [Late 19C. < ELASTIC]

elastomer /i lástəmər/ *n* a natural material such as rubber or a synthetic material such as polyvinyl that has elastic properties [Mid-20C. < ELASTIC] —**elastomeric** /i lástə mérrik/ *adj*

Elastoplast /i lástə plaast/ *tdmk* a trademark for a range of plasters, bandages, and dressings

Elat another spelling of **Eilat**

elate /i láyt/ (**elates, elating, elated**) *vt* to make somebody very happy and excited [Late 16C. < Latin *elat-*, past participle of *efferre* 'carry away' < *ferre* 'carry'] —**elate** *adj* —**elated** *adj*

elater /éllətər/, **elaterid** /i láttərid/ *n* a beetle that belongs to the click beetle family. Family: Elateridae. [Mid-17C. < Greek *elatēr* 'driver' < *elaunein* 'drive']

elation /i láysh'n/ *n* a feeling of great happiness and excitement

Elba /élbə/ mountainous island off the western coast of Italy, the place of Napoleon's first period of exile (1814–15)

Elbe /elb/ river in central Europe that rises in the northern Czech Republic and flows about 1,167 km/725 mi. northwest to the North Sea

Elba

Elbert, Mount /élbərt/ mountain in central Colorado. It is the highest peak in the state and the highest of the Rocky Mountains. Height: 4,399 m/14,433 ft.

elbow /élbō/ *n* **1.** JOINT IN ARM the joint between the upper and lower parts of the human arm **2.** PART OF SLEEVE the part of a sleeve that covers the elbow **3.** JOINT IN ANIMAL LEG the joint in an animal's forelimb corresponding to the elbow in a human **4.** BEND a bend in something such as a river, road, or pipe **5.** SOMETHING BENT something, especially a piece of pipe, made with a bend in it ■ *vti* (**-bows, -bowing, -bowed**) **1.** PUSH SOMEBODY WITH ELBOW to push or hit somebody or something with an elbow **2.** MAKE WAY THROUGH CROWD to progress through a crowd by pushing with the elbow or elbows [Old English *el(n)boga* 'arm bend' < Germanic] ◇ **bend the** *or* **your elbow** to drink alcohol often (*informal*) ◇ **get** *or* **be given the elbow** to be dismissed or rejected (*informal*) ◇ **out at elbow(s) 1.** poorly dressed **2.** short of money

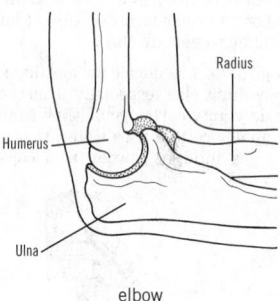

elbow

elbow grease *n* hard physical effort or work, especially using the hands and arms (*informal*)

elbowroom /élbō room, -rōom/ *n* (*informal*) **1.** space to move around in or work in comfortably **2.** freedom from restriction for a time, especially freedom to move or develop in a new area or direction

Elbrus, Mount /el brōoss/, **El'brus** highest mountain in Europe, in the Caucasus Mountains in southern Russia, near the border with Georgia. Height: 5,642 m/18,510 ft.

Elburz Mountains /el bōorz-/ mountain range in northern Iran, near the southern shore of the Caspian Sea. The highest peak is Damavand, 5,604 m/18,386 ft.

elder[1] /éldər/ *adj* **1.** BORN EARLIER born before another, especially within a family, or having more seniority **2.** SUPERIOR superior to others, either by rank or experience ■ *n* **1.** SOMEBODY BORN EARLIER somebody who was born before somebody else ○ *She is five years my elder.* **2.** SOMEBODY WITH SENIORITY somebody who is higher in rank **3.** SENIOR MEMBER OF CHURCH in some Christian churches, a senior lay member responsible for some aspects of church administration, the pastoral care of church members, and sometimes for teaching and preaching **4.** SENIOR MEMBER OF COMMUNITY a member of a family, tribal group, or village who is advanced in years and has influence and authority within the community [Old English *(i)eldra* < Germanic] —**eldership** *n* ◇ **the Elder** used after a person's name to indicate that he or she is the first-born person of a name shared by another ○ *Pitt the Elder*

elder[2] /éldər/ *n* a bush or tree with flat clusters of white flowers and purplish-black berries. Latin name: *Sambucus nigra.* [Old English *ellærn*, origin ?]

elderberry /éldər berri, -bəri/ (*plural* **-ries**) *n* **1.** the purplish-black fruit of the elder, sometimes used to make wine **2.** TREES same as **elder**[2]

Elder Edda *n* LITERAT same as **Edda** (sense 1)

elderly /éldərli/ *adj* **1.** PAST MIDDLE AGE past middle age and approaching the later stages of life (*sometimes considered offensive*) **2.** CHARACTERISTIC OF OLDER PEOPLE characteristic of or relating to older people **3.** OLD-FASHIONED old and somewhat old-fashioned ■ *npl* OLDER PEOPLE AS GROUP older people considered as a group (*sometimes considered offensive*) —**elderliness** *n*

elder statesman *n* somebody advanced in years and experience, especially a politician or former politician, who is respected and whose advice is still valued and unofficially sought

elder stateswoman *n* a woman advanced in years and experience, especially a politician or former politician, who is respected and whose advice is still valued and unofficially sought

eldest /éldist/ *adj* first, either in age or seniority [Old English *(i)eldest* < Germanic]

USAGE See *elder*[1].

ELDO /éldō/ *abbr* AEROSP European Launch Development Organization

Eldon /éldən/, **1st Earl of** (1751–1838) British judge and politician. A judicially brilliant and strongly conservative Lord Chancellor (1801–06 and 1807–27), he was a leading opponent of the parliamentary Reform Bill (1832). Born **Scott, John**

El Dorado /él də raadō/ *n* **1.** a legendary place in South America where the streets were said to be paved with gold, and wealth and riches were to be had in abundance **2.** a place of great wealth or where great wealth can be acquired [Early 19C. < Spanish, literally 'the gilded']

Eleanor of Aquitaine /éllinər əv ákwi tayn/ (1122?–1204) French-born queen of France (1137–52) and England (1154–89). After the annulment of her marriage to King Louis VII of France, she married the future King Henry II of England.

e-learning *n* the acquisition of knowledge and skill using electronic technologies such as computer- and Internet-based courseware and local and wide area networks

Eleatic /élli áttik/ *adj* relating to an ancient Greek school of philosophy that flourished in the 5th and 6th centuries BC. It argued that philosophical reflection was more important than sensory observation. [Late 19C. < Latin *Eliaticus* < *Elea*, ancient Greek city in SW Italy] —**Eleatic** *n* —**Eleaticism** /-áttisizəm/ *n*

elec. *abbr* **1.** electric **2.** electrical **3.** electricity

elecampane /élli kam páyn/ (*plural* **-panes** or *same*) *n* a tall perennial plant related to daisies and dandelions that has large toothed hairy leaves. Flowers: yellow. Use: herbal remedy made from roots for treating coughs and fevers. Latin name: *Inula helenium.* [14C. Contraction of medieval Latin *enula campana* 'elecampane of the fields' < *enula* 'elecampane', via Latin *inula* < Greek *helenion*]

elect /i lékt/ *v* (**elects, electing, elected**) **1.** *vt* CHOOSE SOMEBODY BY VOTE to choose somebody by a vote, e.g. for public office, an official role, or membership of a group ○ *She was elected leader of the commission.* **2.** *vt* DECIDE TO DO SOMETHING to make a decision to do something ○ *elected to stay* **3.** *vt* RELIG CHOOSE SOMEBODY FOR SALVATION especially in Christianity, to choose somebody by divine will for salvation **4.** *vti* US

CHOOSE SOMETHING to choose or select something, particularly a subject or course of study at university ■ *adj* **1. CHOSEN BUT NOT YET IN OFFICE** chosen by a vote but not yet formally installed in office (*used after the noun*) ○ *the president elect* **2. RELIG CHOSEN BY GOD** chosen by God for special favour, salvation, or a task ○*'Samson has assumed that, as an elect instrument, he must be always actively engaged in God's service.'* (John Spencer Hill, *John Milton: Poet, Priest, and Prophet;* 1979) ■ *npl* **1. SELECT GROUP** a specially privileged or gifted group (*literary*) ○ *World-class opera singers are among today's elect.* **2. RELIG PEOPLE CHOSEN BY GOD** people believed to be specially chosen or favoured by God, e.g. those chosen by God for salvation [15C. < Latin *electus* < *eligere* 'pick out' < *legere* 'choose'] —**electable** *adj*

election /i léksh'n/ *n* **1. EVENT AT WHICH PEOPLE VOTE** an organized event at which somebody is chosen by vote for something, especially a public office ○ *held an election* **2. CHOOSING OR BEING CHOSEN BY VOTE** the process of choosing somebody or of being chosen by vote ○ *He stood for election.* **3. SELECTION OF SOMETHING** the act or process of choosing something, e.g. a course of action or subject (*formal*) **4. RELIG SELECTION BY GOD FOR SOMETHING** especially in Christianity, the fact of being chosen by God, or God's act of choosing somebody, for special favour, salvation, or a task

Election Day *n* in the United States, a day designated by law for the election of people to public office

electioneer /i lékshə néer/ *vi* (**-eers, -eering, -eered**) **1. CAMPAIGN IN ELECTION** to take an active part in an election campaign, especially as, or on behalf of, a candidate for political office **2. DO SOMETHING JUST TO WIN VOTES** to attempt to win votes in an election by being insincere and unscrupulous (*disapproving*) ■ *n also* **electioneerer** /i lékshə néerər/ **CAMPAIGN WORKER** a worker on behalf of a candidate or party in an election

elective /i léktiv/ *adj* **1. REQUIRING ELECTION** chosen by a vote, or held by somebody who is chosen by a vote ○ *The monarchy at that time was elective not hereditary.* **2. RELATING TO VOTING** relating to or involving voting ○ *elective office* **3. VOTING** empowered to vote **4. EDUC NOT COMPULSORY** describes a course of study that is optional, and not essential or compulsory ■ *n* **EDUC OPTIONAL SUBJECT OF STUDY** an optional course that a student may select from among several alternatives —**electively** *adv* —**electiveness** *n*

elective mutism *n* PSYCHIAT same as **mutism**

elector /i léktər/ *n* **1. SOMEBODY WHO VOTES** a voter in an election **2. *also* Elector GERMAN RULER WHO ELECTED EMPEROR** a ruler of a German state within the Holy Roman Empire who was entitled to vote in the election of the emperor (*often used as a title*) **3. MEMBER OF ELECTORAL COLLEGE** a member of an electoral college or the US Electoral College

electoral /i léktərəl/ *adj* relating to or involving elections or electors —**electorally** *adv*

electoral college *n* a select body of people who elect somebody to an office on behalf of a larger group

Electoral College *n* in the United States, the formal body elected by voters to choose the president and vice president. Although US voters in effect choose a president and vice president, they are formally voting for members of the Electoral College, who make the choice on their behalf.

electoral quota *n* in Australia, the number of representatives of a state or territory that can be elected to the House of Representatives. The number is proportionate to the population of the state or territory, approximately one for every 70,000 inhabitants.

electoral roll, electoral register *n* an official list of the names and addresses of the people in a specific area who are entitled to vote in an election

electorate /i léktərət/ *n* **1.** all the officially qualified voters within a particular country or area, or for a particular election **2.** *ANZ* an area represented by a member of parliament

electr- *prefix* same as **electro-** (*used before vowels*)

Electra /i léktrə/ *n* in Greek mythology, the daughter of Agamemnon and Clytemnestra. She helped her brother Orestes to avenge their father's murder by killing their mother and Clytemnestra's lover. [< Greek *Ēlektra*, literally 'bright, beaming' < *ēlektōr* 'sun']

Electra complex *n* in psychoanalysis, a daughter's unconscious unresolved sexual attraction to her father

Electra paradox *n* a logical paradox arising from the possibility of somebody's knowing that something is true when it is described in one way but not when it is described in another [< a Greek myth in which Electra is said to recognize her brother Orestes from a description but not by sight]

electret /i léktrit/ *n* a piece of insulating material that is permanently polarized and has a permanent electric field. Use: microphones and telephones. [Late 19C. Blend of ELECTRICITY + MAGNET]

electric /i léktrik/ *adj* **1. INVOLVING OR CAUSED BY ELECTRICITY** relating to, involving, or caused by electricity ○ *electric power* **2. FOR ELECTRICITY** carrying or conveying electricity ○ *electric cables* **3. USING ELECTRICITY** powered or operated by electricity ○ *an electric guitar* ○ *electric vehicles* **4. TENSE OR EXCITED** full of tension or excitement and anticipation ○ *an electric atmosphere* **5. BRIGHT** extremely bright in colour ○ *electric orange* ■ *n* **1. ELECTRICITY** electricity, or the electricity supply, e.g. to a house (*informal*) **2. SOMETHING OPERATED BY ELECTRICITY** a vehicle, machine, or other device that is powered by electricity ■ **electrics** *npl* ELECTRICAL EQUIPMENT OR PARTS the parts of a device or system that are operated by, carry, or generate electricity, or electrically powered equipment [Mid-17C. < modern Latin *electricus* < *electrum* 'amber' < Greek *elektron*]

USAGE electric or **electrical?** *Electric* is more commonly used to describe a device that works by electricity or is involved in producing or carrying electricity: *an electric oven; an electric socket. Electrical* is applied to more general things and to areas of study or activity that are concerned with electricity: *electrical appliances; electrical engineering. Electric* is usual in the figurative meaning 'tense or excited': *The atmosphere at the meeting was electric.*

electrical /i léktrik'l/ *adj* **1.** same as **electric** *adj* (senses 1–3) **2. INVOLVING APPLICATION OF ELECTRICITY** involved in or involving the application of electricity in technology ○ *electrical energy* **3. RELATING TO ELECTRIC FUNCTIONING** involving or concerned with electric cables or circuits, or parts powered by electricity ○ *You'll need an electrician for the electrical work.* **4. CAUSED BY ELECTRICITY** caused by electricity or something that uses or conveys electricity ■ **electricals** *npl* FIN ELECTRICITY COMPANY SHARES shares in electricity companies —**electrically** *adv*

USAGE See *electric*.

electrical engineering *n* the branch of engineering that studies the practical applications of electricity in science and technology —**electrical engineer** *n*

electric blanket *n* a blanket containing an insulated electric heating element, used to warm a bed

electric-blue *adj* of a bright metallic blue colour — **electric blue** *n*

electric chair *n* **1.** a chair used to execute people sentenced to die by electrocution, especially in parts of the United States **2.** a sentence of death by electrocution in an electric chair

electric constant *n* the absolute permittivity of free space, equal to 8.854 x 10^{-12} farad per metre. Symbol v_0

electric eel *n* a long air-breathing fish resembling a true eel that can release a strong discharge of electricity from specialized organs in the tail region. Native to: South American rivers. Latin name: *Electrophorus electricus.*

electric eye *n* a device that converts light into electrical energy or uses it to regulate a flow of current, often incorporated into automatic control systems for doors and lighting

electric fence *n* a wire fence carrying an electric current that gives a mild electric shock to any person or animal that touches it

electric field *n* a field of force surrounding a charged body or associated with a fluctuating magnetic field, with which charged particles interact

electric fire *n* a heater with an element that is made hot by an electric current passing through it, used to heat a room

electric guitar *n* a guitar, often with a solid body, that has an electrical device for picking up sound fitted below the strings and connected to an amplifier and loudspeaker

electrician /i lek trísh'n, éllek-/ *n* somebody who installs, maintains, or repairs electrical wiring or electrical goods

electricity /i lek tríssəti, éllek-/ *n* **1. PHYS ENERGY CREATED BY MOVING CHARGED PARTICLES** a fundamental form of kinetic or potential energy created by the free or controlled movement of charged particles such as electrons, positrons, and ions **2. ELECTRIC CURRENT** electric current, especially when used as a source of power **3. ANTICIPATION OR TENSION** a feeling or atmosphere of excited anticipation or tension

electric jazz *n* jazz produced using electronic instruments or other electronic devices

electric light *n* **1.** a light operated by electricity, e.g. one with an electric bulb or a fluorescent tube **2.** the illumination produced by electricity

electric motor *n* a machine that converts energy from electricity into mechanical energy

electric organ *n* **1.** a musical instrument that is a type of organ whose sound is produced or amplified by means of electricity **2.** in some fish, a specialized muscle tissue that creates an electric field used for finding enemies, obstacles, and food in murky water, and, in some species, for defence against attack

electric piano *n* an electronic keyboard instrument that produces a sound similar to that of a piano

electric potential *n* the work required to bring a unit of positive electric charge from infinity to a specific point in an electric field. Symbol *V*

electric ray *n* a fish that can emit a strong electric discharge from organs in its enlarged pectoral fins. Native to: tropical or temperate seas. Family: Torpedinidae.

electric razor *n* a small electrically powered device used for shaving hair on the face or body

electric shock *n* a sudden painful physical reaction consisting of nerve stimulation and muscle contraction, caused by an electric current flowing through the body

electric storm *n* a thunderstorm, especially one with a great deal of lightning

electrify /i léktri fī/ (**-fies, -fying, -fied**) *vt* **1. CONVERT SOMETHING TO USING ELECTRICITY** to convert something such as a railway line or a piece of machinery so that it can operate on electric power **2. CHARGE SOMETHING ELECTRICALLY** to charge something with electricity or pass an electric current through something **3. THRILL SOMEBODY** to cause somebody to feel a sudden and surprising shock, thrill, or sense of excitement **4. MUSIC AMPLIFY SOUNDS ELECTRICALLY** to amplify electrically the sounds produced by a musical instrument —**electrifiable** *adj* —**electrification** /i léktrifi káysh'n/ *n* —**electrified** *adj* —**electrifier** *n*

electro /i léktrō/ *n* **1.** MUSIC same as **electronic music 2.** *also* **electro-funk** a style of electronic music with African American, urban, rap, and funk influences that became popular in the 1980s and itself influenced hip-hop and techno

electro- *prefix* **1.** electric, electricity, electronic ○ *electromyogram* **2.** electrolysis ○ *electrometallurgy* **3.** electron ○ *electropositive* [< modern Latin *electrum* (see ELECTRIC)]

electroacoustic /i léktrō ə koóstik/ *adj* describes a device that converts sound into electrical signals or vice versa

electroacoustics /i léktrō ə koóstiks/ *n* a branch of electronics that is concerned with the way in which electricity is converted into sound (*takes a singular verb*) —**electroacoustically** *adv*

electroanalysis /i léktrō ə nálləssiss/ (*plural* **-yses** /-ə seez/) *n* the use of electrolysis to perform chemical analysis —**electroanalytic** /i léktrō anə líttik/ *adj* —**electroanalytical** *adj* —**electroanalytically** *adv*

electrocardiogram /i léktrō kaárdi ə gram/ *n* a visual record of the heart's electrical activity made using an electrocardiograph

electrocardiograph /i léktrō kaárdi ə graaf, -graf/ n a device that records the electrical activity of the heart muscle via electrodes placed on the chest, and displays it as a visual record —**electrocardiographic** /-kaardi ə gráffik/ adj —**electrocardiography** /-kaardi óggrəfi/ n

electrocautery /i léktrō káwtəri/ n the process of destroying unwanted tissue, e.g. warts and polyps, or sealing blood vessels, by means of an electrically heated needle

electrochemical /i léktrō kémmik'l/ adj of or relating to electrochemistry —**electrochemically** adv

electrochemical series n a series in which the chemical elements are arranged in order of decreasing tendency to lose electrons

electrochemistry /i léktrō kémmistri/ n a branch of chemistry that studies chemical change associated with electrons and electricity —**electrochemist** n

electrocoagulation /i léktrō kō agyoŏ láysh'n/ n the use of an electrical device that burns tissue to stop bleeding from small blood vessels during surgery or to destroy small tumours

electroconvulsive therapy /i léktrō kən vúlssiv-/ n the passing of a small electric current through the brain to induce a seizure, used in the treatment of severe psychiatric disorders

electrocute /i léktrə kyoot/ (-cutes, -cuting, -cuted) vt 1. to cause injury or death with an electric shock 2. to execute somebody by means of the electric chair [Late 19C. < ELECTRO- + EXECUTE] —**electrocution** /i léktrə kyoŏsh'n/ n

electrode /i lék trōd/ n a conductor through which electricity enters or leaves something such as a battery or a piece of electrical equipment

electrodeposit /i léktrō di pózzit/ vt (-its, -iting, -ited) to deposit a substance, especially a metal, on an electrode by using electrolysis ■ n a substance deposited by using electrolysis —**electrodeposition** /-depə zísh'n/ n

electrode potential n the potential difference produced between an electrode composed of a given chemical element and the solution in which it is immersed

electrodialysis /i léktrō dī álləssiss/ (plural -yses /-ə seez/) n a form of dialysis in which the separation of substances is accelerated by an electric current applied to the electrodes. The desalination of seawater is an example of a use of electrodialysis.

electrodynamics /i léktrō dī námmiks/ n a branch of physics that studies how electric currents interact with magnetic and mechanical forces (takes a singular verb) —**electrodynamic** adj

electrodynamometer /i léktrō dīnə mómmitər/ n a device for measuring the strength of an electric current by the magnetic force it induces in a coil

electroencephalogram /i léktrō in séffələ gram/ n a record of the electrical activity of the brain that is produced by an electroencephalograph

electroencephalograph /i léktrō in séffələ graaf, -graf/ n a machine that uses electrodes placed on the scalp to monitor the electrical activity of different parts of the brain, recording these as complex tracings. Irregularities recorded in the tracings may help in the diagnosis of organic brain disorders and in establishing clinical death. —**electroencephalography** /-in sefə lóggrəfi/ n

electroform /i léktrə fawrm/ (-forms, -forming, -formed) vt to form something, e.g. a medal, by using electrolysis to coat the surface of the mould or matrix with a metal

electro-funk n MUSIC same as **electro** (sense 2)

electrograph /i léktrō graaf, -graf/ n 1. ELECTRICAL ENGRAVING DEVICE an electrical device for engraving a design on a metal plate. Use: printing patterns on fabrics or wallpaper. 2. ELECTRICAL PICTURE TRANSMISSION DEVICE an apparatus used to transmit pictures by electrical means, e.g. by fax 3. TRANSMITTED PICTURE a picture transmitted and printed by an electrograph 4. PHYS ELECTROMETER an electrometer that produces a graphical record of the measurements it makes 5. PHYS GRAPH FROM ELECTROMETER the visual record produced by an electrometer

electrohydraulic /i léktrō hī dróllik/ adj using, or relating to the use of, electrical and hydraulic components —**electrohydraulically** adv

electrokinetics /i lék trōki néttiks, -kī-/ n a branch of physics that deals with the motion of electrically charged particles (takes a singular verb) —**electrokinetic** adj

electroluminescence /i léktrō loomi néss'nss/ n the emission of light by the application of an electric field to a substance —**electroluminescent** adj

electrolyse /i léktrə līz/ (-lyses, -lysing, -lysed) vt to use electrolysis to decompose a chemical compound [Mid-19C. Blend of ELECTROLYSIS + ANALYSE]

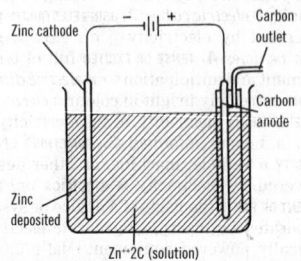

electrolysis: separation of zinc carbonate by electrolysis

electrolysis /i lek trólləssiss, éllek-/ n 1. the use of an electric current applied though a needle to remove body hair for cosmetic purposes, or to destroy warts, moles, or tumours for medical reasons 2. the conduction of electricity through something melted or dissolved in order to induce decomposition of the melted or dissolved chemical into its components

electrolyte /i léktrō līt/ n 1. CHEM COMPOUND SEPARABLE INTO IONS IN SOLUTION a chemical compound that separates into ions in a solution or when molten, and is able to conduct electricity 2. CHEM ION IN ELECTROLYTE an ion in an electrolyte 3. PHYSIOL ION IN CELL any ion in cells, blood, or other organic material. Electrolytes help to control fluid levels in the body, maintain normal pH levels, and ensure the correct electric potential between nerve cells that enables the transmission of nerve signals.

electrolytic /i léktrō líttik/ adj 1. involved in or relating to electrolysis 2. relating to, containing, or consisting of electrolytes —**electrolytically** adv

electrolyze vt CHEM US spelling of **electrolyse**

electromagnet /i léktrō mágnit/ n a magnet consisting of a core, often made of soft iron, that is temporarily magnetized by an electric current flowing through a coil that surrounds it

electromagnetic /i léktrō mag néttik/ adj created by or relating to electromagnetism —**electromagnetically** adv

electromagnetic field n a field of force associated with a moving electric charge and consisting of electric and magnetic fields that are generated at right angles to each other

electromagnetic force n the force resulting from the interaction of charged particles and their electric and magnetic fields

electromagnetic interference n interference in a circuit caused by the radiation of an electric or magnetic field or the operation of a nearby electric motor, e.g. disturbance on a television set

electromagnetic radiation n radiation in the form of electromagnetic waves such as gamma rays, X-rays, ultraviolet light, visible light, infrared rays, microwaves, and radio waves. The radiation has magnetic and electric fields that are perpendicular to each other and to the direction of propagation, and travels without a supporting medium.

electromagnetic spectrum n the complete range of electromagnetic radiation from the shortest waves (**gamma rays**) to the longest (**radio waves**)

electromagnetic unit n any unit in the centimetre-gram-second system of units for measuring electricity and magnetism that gives a value of 1 to the magnetic constant, e.g. the abampere or the abvolt

electromagnetic wave n a wave of energy with a frequency within the electromagnetic spectrum, generated by the periodic fluctuation of an electromagnetic field resulting from the acceleration or oscillation of an electric charge. Electromagnetic waves can be reflected, refracted, and polarized, and exhibit interference and diffraction effects.

electromagnetism /i léktrō mágnə tizəm/ n 1. magnetism produced by an electric current 2. the branch of physics concerned with the interaction of electric and magnetic fields

electromechanical /i léktrō mi kánnik'l/ adj describes a mechanical device that is powered or controlled by electricity —**electromechanically** adv

electrometallurgy /i léktrō mi tállərji, -métt'l urji/ n the range of metallurgical processes in which electricity has a key role, e.g. electroplating and the use of arc furnaces

electrometer /i lek trómmitər, éllek-/ n a sensitive device for measuring extremely low voltages by means of the forces of attraction and repulsion between charged bodies on plates or wires

electromotive /i léktrō mőtiv/ adj relating to or producing an electric current

electromotive force n a force that causes the flow of electricity from one point to another

electromyogram /i léktrō mī ə gram/ n a graphical tracing of the electrical activity in a muscle at rest or during contraction, used to diagnose nerve and muscle disorders

electromyograph /i léktrō mī ə graaf, -graf/ n a machine for producing a graphical tracing of the electrical activity picked up via electrodes inserted into muscle tissue. It consists of an amplifier, an electrically activated trace-drawing pen, and a moving strip of paper.

electron /i lék tron/ n a stable negatively charged elementary particle with a small mass that is a fundamental constituent of matter and orbits the nucleus of an atom [Late 19C. < electric]

electron affinity n the amount of energy needed to remove an electron from a negatively charged ion

electron beam n PHYS same as **e-beam**

electronegative /i léktrō néggətiv/ adj 1. with negative electric charge, and so tending to move towards a positive electric pole 2. tending to gain electrons to form a bond in a chemical reaction

electronegativity /i léktrō negə tívvəti/ n a measure of the tendency of an atom in a molecule to attract the electrons in a chemical bond

electron gun n a device that directs a steady stream of electrons in a desired direction, e.g. in a cathode-ray tube

electronic /i lek trónnik, éllek-/ adj 1. USING VALVES, TRANSISTORS, OR SILICON CHIPS relating to devices, systems, or circuits that employ components such as valves, integrated circuits, or transistors in their design ○ an electronic sensor 2. BY COMPUTER relating to, using, or accessed through a computer or computer network, e.g. the Internet ○ electronic banking 3. PHYS OF ELECTRONS relating to electrons ○ the electronic spectrum 4. PHYS OF CONTROLLED FLOW OF ELECTRONS relating to, or produced or operated by, the controlled flow of electrons through a semiconductor, a gas, or free space —**electronically** adv

electronica /íllek trónnikə, éllek-/ n synthesized dance music that is written for home listening rather than purely for dancing to

electronic configuration n the three-dimensional arrangement within an atom or molecule of the atoms in their orbitals

electronic data processing n computer-based tasks involving the input and manipulation of data, usually using database programs

electronic depository transfer n the transfer of funds between bank accounts using the automated clearing house system

electronic flash n a flash device used in high-speed photography that produces a very bright light by passing an electric charge through a gas-filled tube

electronic funds transfer at point of sale *n* a system of paying for goods at the point of sale by the direct computerized transfer of money from the buyer's bank or building society account to the seller's

electronic journalism *n* news coverage that is transmitted electronically, e.g. by television or over the Internet

electronic magazine *n* a magazine that is distributed online over a computer network rather than being printed on paper

electronic mail *n* ONLINE full form of **e-mail**

electronic mall *n* a website that offers for sale the products and services of different vendors and handles all sales transactions for the vendors

electronic music *n* music produced or modified by electronic means, often with the aid of a computer

electronic newsgathering *n* television news coverage made at the time and place of the event or incident by means of video equipment

electronic organ *n* MUSIC same as **electric organ**

electronic point of sale *n* a computerized checkout system in shops that records sales by scanning bar codes, automatically updates the retailer's stock lists, and provides a printout of the customer's purchases

electronic publishing *n* the production of documents in computer-readable form for distribution over a computer network or in other formats such as CD-ROMs

electronic purse *n* a method of prepayment used in e-commerce, in which cash is stored electronically on a microchip

electronics /i lek trónniks, éllek-/ *n* the branch of technology concerned with the design, manufacture, and maintenance of electronic devices (*takes a singular verb*) ■ *npl* the electronic parts of a piece of equipment, or electronic devices and equipment generally (*takes a plural verb*)

electronic shopping *n* the ordering and purchase of goods and services over a computer network, especially over the Internet

electronic signature *n* an encoded attachment to an e-mail, verifying the identity of its sender

electronic smog *n* nonionizing radiation produced in the atmosphere by sources such as radar and radio and television broadcasting, considered by some people to pose a general health risk

electronic storefront *n* ONLINE same as **storefront** *n* (sense 1)

electronic superhighway *n* ONLINE same as **information superhighway**

electronic surveillance *n* the gathering of information using electronic devices such as video cameras and wiretaps, especially in crime detection and prevention or in espionage

electronic tagging *n* the supervision of an offender by means of an electronic tracking device such as a bracelet, used as an alternative to prison confinement

electronic transfer of funds *n* the transfer of money from one account to another by computer

electron lens *n* a device that creates an electric or magnetic field around the path of an electron beam so that the beam may be focused

electron micrograph *n* a photograph of a specimen taken using an electron microscope

electron microscope *n* a high-powered microscope that uses beams of electrons focused by an electron lens to create a magnified image on a fluorescent screen or photographic plate —**electron microscopy** *n*

electron multiplier *n* a device for amplifying a very small current using the effects of secondary emission. Electrons from the original current strike an anode, producing secondary electrons that are directed to the next anode in a multistage process until the desired level of current is obtained.

electron optics *n* the science that deals with the direction, deflection, or focusing of beams of elec-

trons by electric and magnetic fields, e.g. in electron lenses (*takes a singular verb*)

electron sea *n* a model for the electron state in metals in which a regular array of cations is surrounded by a group of loosely bound electrons

electron shell *n* PHYS same as **shell** *n* (sense 19)

electron transport *n* a process in which electrons are transferred from one compound to another with a release of energy occurring in the production of ATP

electron tube *n* a device that consists of a sealed glass vessel containing a gas or a vacuum, within which electrons flow between electrodes

electron volt *n* **1.** a unit of energy equal to the energy gained by an electron accelerated through a potential difference of one volt and equal to 1.602 x 10^{-19} joule. Symbol **eV 2.** the unit of mass of elementary particles, measured as a function of energy and usually expressed in terms of mega electron volts (**MeV**)

electro-osmosis *n* the movement of a liquid through a membrane under the effect of an electric field

electrophile /i léktrō fīl/ *n* an atom, molecule, or chemical group that is attracted to electrons or accepts them —**electrophilic** /i léktrō fíllik/ *adj*

electrophonic /i léktrə fónnik/ *adj* producing sound by means of electronic equipment

electrophoresis /i léktrō fə reéssiss/ *n* the movement of charged particles in a colloid or suspension when an electric field is applied to them [Early 20C. < ELECTRO- + Greek *phorēsis* 'being carried' (see -PHORESIS)] —**electrophoretic** /-réttik/ *adj*

electrophorus /i lek tróffərəss, éllek-/ (*plural* **-ri** /-rī/) *n* a device that produces electric charges from the friction between a disc and a metal plate [Late 18C. < ELECTRO- + *-phorus*, Latinization of -PHORE]

electrophotography /i léktrōfə tóggrəfi/ *n* any form of photography that uses electricity to transfer an image onto paper, as in laser printing and photocopying —**electrophotographic** /i léktrō fōtə gráffik/ *adj*

electrophysiology /i léktrō fizi ólləji/ *n* the branch of medicine or biology dealing with the study of electrical activity in human or animal bodies —**electrophysiological** /-lójjik'l/ *adj* —**electrophysiologically** *adv* —**electrophysiologist** *n*

electroplate /i léktrō playt/ *vt* (**-plates, -plating, -plated**) to use electrolysis to coat the surface of an object with metal ■ *n* objects coated with metal by means of electrolysis

electroporation /i léktrō pō ráysh'n/ *n* a method of introducing DNA from one organism into a protoplast of another using an electric pulse [< ELECTRO- + PORE¹]

electropositive /i léktrō pózzitiv/ *adj* **1.** with positive electric charge, and so tending to move towards a negative electric pole **2.** tending to release electrons to form a bond in a chemical reaction ▶ ◊ **electronegative**

electroreceptor /i léktrōri septər/ *n* an organ in fish such as sharks, electric eels, and catfish that detects electrical charges

electroscope /i léktrō skōp/ *n* a device that detects and measures an electric charge, usually consisting of a rod holding two strips of gold foil that separate when the same charge is applied to each —**electroscopic** /i léktrō skóppik/ *adj*

electrosensitivity /i léktrō senssə tívvəti/ *n* the ability in an animal to detect naturally occurring electrical currents and use them to navigate or locate objects

electroshock /i léktrō shok/ *N Am n* also **electroshock therapy** PSYCHIAT same as **electroconvulsive therapy** ■ *vt* (**-shocks, -shocking, -shocked**) to administer electroconvulsive therapy to a patient

electrostatic /i léktrō státtik/ *adj* **1.** produced by or relating to static electricity **2.** relating to electrostatics —**electrostatically** *adv*

electrostatic generator *n* PHYS same as **van de Graaff generator**

electrostatic precipitator *n* a device that removes small particles of smoke, dust, or oil from air by electrostatically charging them and then attracting

them to an oppositely charged collector plate or surface —**electrostatic precipitation** *n*

electrostatic printing *n* a photocopying or printing process in which images are reproduced on a surface using electrostatic charges

electrostatics /i léktrō státtiks/ *n* a branch of physics dealing with electric charges at rest (**static electricity**) (*takes a singular verb*)

electrostatic unit *n* a unit for measuring the magnitude of forces of repulsion between static electrical charges in the centimetre-gram-second system, e.g. the statampere and the statvolt

electrosurgery /i léktrō súrjəri/ *n* the use of an electrical device or current during surgery, e.g. to cut or cauterize tissue —**electrosurgical** *adj* —**electrosurgically** *adv*

electrotherapy /i léktrō thérrəpi/ *n* any form of medical treatment that uses electricity as a cure or relief, e.g. to stimulate nerves and the muscles they are connected to —**electrotherapeutic** /-therə pyóotik/ *adj*

electrothermal /i léktrō thúrm'l/ *adj* relating to electricity and heat, especially to the production of heat by electricity ◊ *electrothermal energy conversion*

electrotype /i léktrō tīp/ *n* **1.** DUPLICATE PRINTING PLATE MADE BY ELECTROPLATING a duplicate of a block of type or engraving made by electroplating a wax, lead, or plastic mould of the original **2.** SOMETHING PRINTED FROM ELECTROTYPE an item that has been printed from an electrotype ■ *vt* (**-types, -typing, -typed**) PRINT SOMETHING USING ELECTROTYPE to print something by a process that uses an electrotype —**electrotyper** *n*

electrovalency /i léktrō váylənssi/ (*plural* **-cies**), **electrovalence** /-váylənss/ *n* the combining power of an element, measured by the number of electrons one atom of it acquires from or transfers to another atom during the formation of a chemical compound —**electrovalent** *adj*

electrovalent bond *n* a chemical bond that is created during the formation of a compound by transfer of one or more electrons from one atom to another, the resulting oppositely charged ions being held together by attraction

electroweak /i léktrō week/ *adj* describes a type of fundamental interaction uniting electromagnetic forces with the weak interaction

electrum /i léktrəm/ *n* a pale-coloured alloy of silver and gold. Use: jewellery and ornaments. [14C. < Latin (see ELECTRIC)]

electuary /i léktyoō əri/ (*plural* **-ies**) *n* a sweet-tasting paste made by mixing a drug with syrup or honey, administered by being applied to the teeth, tongue, or gums (*archaic*) [14C. < late Latin *electuarium*, probably < Greek *eleikton* < *eleikhein* 'lick up']

eleemosynary /élli ee móssinəri, -mózzinəri, éllee-/ *adj* relating to, given as, or depending on charitable gifts (*formal*) [Late 16C. < medieval Latin *eleemosynarius* < *eleemosyna* 'alms' < Greek *eleos* 'mercy']

elegance /élligənss/ *n* **1.** a combination of graceful stylishness, distinction, and good taste in appearance, behaviour, or movement **2.** a satisfying or admirable neatness, ingenious simplicity, or precision in something ◊ *the elegance of the solution* [Early 16C. Via French < Latin *elegantia* < *elegant-* (see ELEGANT)]

elegant /élligənt/ *adj* **1.** stylishly graceful, and showing sophistication and good taste in appearance and behaviour **2.** pleasingly and often ingeniously neat, simple, or concise ◊ *an equation elegant in its simplicity* [15C. Via French < Latin *elegant-* 'choice, tasteful' < *eligire* (see ELECT)] —**elegantly** *adv*

elegiac /élli jī ək/, **elegiacal** /-jī ək'l/ *adj* **1.** expressing sorrow or regret (*literary*) ◊ *'The same elegiac and lonely tone continues to haunt the later poetry.'* (Northrop Frye, *The Bush Garden*; 1971) **2.** resembling or characteristic of a poetic elegy in form or content [Late 16C. Via French or late Latin < Greek *elegeiakos* < *elegos* 'song'] —**elegiacally** *adv*

elegiac couplet *n* a two-line unit of classical Greek and Latin poetry in which the first line contains six dactylic feet and the second line five

elegiac stanza *n* a four-line unit of poetry in which

each line contains five iambic feet and alternate lines rhyme

~~**elegible**~~ incorrect spelling of **eligible**

elegise *vti* another spelling of **elegize**

elegist /éllijist/ *n* a writer or speaker of an elegy

elegit /i léejit/ *n* a writ against a debtor's property that permits a creditor to keep it until the debt is paid [Early 16C. < medieval Latin, 'he or she has chosen' (occurring in the writ), form of Latin *eligire* (see ELECT)]

elegize /élli jīz/ (**-gizes, -gizing, -gized**), **elegise (-gises, -gising, -gised)** *v* **1.** *vti* to write or speak about somebody or something in a mournful sorrowful way ○ *He elegized his lost comrade.* **2.** *vi* to write, read, or recite an elegy

elegy /élləji/ (*plural* **-gies**) *n* **1.** a mournful or reflective poem **2.** a poem written in elegiac couplets or stanzas [Early 16C. Directly or via French < Latin *elegia* < Greek *elegos* 'song']

CULTURAL NOTE ***Elegy Written in a Country Churchyard***, a poem (1750) by Thomas Gray. Inspired by a churchyard at Stoke Poges, Buckinghamshire, England, it is a reflection on rural life, human ambitions, friendship, and mortality. It is considered the masterpiece of the 'graveyard' school of literature, which was popular in the 1740s and 1750s.

element /éllimənt/ *n* **1. SEPARATE PART OR GROUP** a separate identifiable part of something, or a distinct group within a larger group ○ *criminal elements in society* **2. SMALL QUANTITY** a small but significant trace of a quality or feeling ○ *There was an element of revenge in what she did.* **3. FACTOR** a cause or factor leading to something ○ *Surprise was the key element in ensuring the success of the operation.* **4. HABITAT** a habitat or environment suited to an individual person ○ *She's in her element in the garden.* ○ *Parties are not their natural element.* **5. HEATING PART OF APPLIANCE** a part of an electric heater, cooker, or other appliance that heats up when an electric current is passed through it **6.** CHEM **CHEMICALLY INDIVISIBLE SUBSTANCE** any substance that cannot be broken down into a simpler one by a chemical reaction. Elements consist of atoms with the same number of protons in their nuclei, and 92 occur naturally on Earth. See table on next page **7.** CHEM **SUPPOSED BASIC UNIT OF MATTER** any of the four primary substances, earth, air, fire, and water, that were formerly thought to be the materials from which all matter is constructed **8.** MATHS **CONSTITUENT OF GEOMETRIC FIGURE** a point, line, plane, or other part of which a geometric figure is composed **9.** MATHS **PART OF MATHEMATICAL QUANTITY** a part of a mathematical or geometric quantity, e.g. a number in an array or an angle in a triangle **10.** LOGIC, MATHS **SET MEMBER** in mathematics and logic, a member of a set **11.** ELEC **COMPONENT OF ELECTRIC CIRCUIT** any component of an electrical circuit **12.** OPTICS **COMPONENT OF OPTICAL SYSTEM** any lens or other component of an optical system **13.** ASTRON **PARAMETER-DEFINING ORBIT** any one of the parameters required to define the nature of an orbit and to determine the position of a planetary body within it **14.** GRAM **GRAMMATICAL UNIT** a word, part of a word, or sequence of words that retains the same meaning in various contexts [14C. Via French < Latin *elementum* 'rudiment']

elemental /élli mént'l/ *adj* **1. FUNDAMENTAL** basic and essential **2. RELATING TO NATURAL FORCES** relating to or caused by powerful natural forces ○ *elemental passions* **3. SIMPLIFIED OR SIMPLIFYING** reduced to, or reducing something to, a stark simplicity ○ *classic elemental sculptures* **4.** CHEM **OF CHEMICAL OR ANCIENT ELEMENTS** relating to the chemical elements, or to the elements of earth, air, fire, and water that were once thought to be the basic units of matter

elementary /élli méntəri/ *adj* **1. RUDIMENTARY** involving or encompassing only the most simple and basic facts or principles ○ *an elementary knowledge of computing* **2. SIMPLE TO DO OR UNDERSTAND** requiring little skill or knowledge **3.** *N Am* **OF ELEMENTARY SCHOOL** relating to an elementary school or the education provided there —**elementarily** *adv* —**elementariness** *n*

elementary particle *n* any one of the subatomic constituents of which matter and energy are composed, e.g. electrons, leptons, photons, or hadrons

elementary school *n* **1.** in the United States and Canada, a school that provides the first four to eight years of basic education **2.** formerly in the United Kingdom, a school of a type that was attended by children from the age of 5 until they left at 14

elements /éllimənts/ *npl* **1. FORCES OF WEATHER** the forces of the weather, e.g. wind, cold, rain, or sunshine, especially when thought of as harsh and damaging ○ *We're rather exposed to the elements up here on the hilltop.* **2. BASIC PRINCIPLES** the basic and most important things to be learned when studying a subject ○ *She was endeavouring to teach us the elements of a good prose style.* **3.** CHR **BREAD AND WINE IN COMMUNION** the bread and wine used in celebrating the Christian sacrament of Communion

elemi /éllimi/ *n* a fragrant resin obtained from various tropical trees. Use: varnishes, inks, ointments, perfumes. [Mid-16C. Via modern Latin < Arabic *al-lāmī*]

elenchus /i léngkəss/ (*plural* **-chi** /-kī/) *n* an argument that refutes a proposition by proving the opposite of its conclusions [Mid-17C. Via Latin < Greek *elegkhos* 'refutation'] —**elenctic** *adj*

elephant

elephant /éllifənt/ *n* **1.** (*plural* **elephants** or *same*) **LARGE ANIMAL WITH LONG TRUNK** a very large grey or greyish-brown animal with a long flexible trunk, prominent ears, thick legs, and pointed tusks. Native to: Africa, South Asia. Latin name: *Loxodonta africana* or *Loxodonta cyclotis* or *Elephas maximus.* **2.** (*plural* **elephants**) **SOMETHING VERY LARGE** somebody or something that is extremely large or much larger than average **3.** PAPER **LARGE SIZE OF SHEET OF PAPER** a size of drawing or writing paper, 584 ± 711 mm/23 ± 28 in [13C. Via French < Latin *elephantus* < Greek *elephās* 'elephant, ivory']

Elephanta Island /élli fántə-/ island in Mumbai harbour, western India, approximately 10 km/6 mi. east of Mumbai. Area: 5 sq. km/2 sq. mi.

elephantbird /éllifənt burd/ *n* BIRDS same as **aepyornis**

elephant folio *n* a book size from 61 to 63.5 cm/24 to 25 in in height

elephant garlic *n* a mild-flavoured variety of garlic with very large bulbs, often roasted as a vegetable. Latin name: *Allium ampeloprasum.*

elephant grass *n* tall coarse grass or a similar plant. Native to: tropical Africa, South Asia. Genera: *Typha* or *Pennisetum.*

elephant gun *n* a large-calibre gun, typically .410 or more, used in hunting big game.

elephantiasis /éllifən tī əssiss/ *n* a chronic disease in which parasitic worms obstruct the lymphatic system, causing enlargement of parts of the body, e.g. the legs and scrotum, and hardening of the surrounding skin. It is transmitted by mosquitoes. [Mid-16C. Via Latin < Greek < *elephās* 'elephant']

elephantine /élli fán tīn/ *adj* **1. SLOW AND HEAVY** moving in a slow, heavy, and often clumsy or awkward way ○ *the heavy elephantine tread of his feet* **2. ENORMOUS** very large or very great **3. SIMILAR TO ELEPHANT** resembling an elephant [Early 16C. Via Latin < Greek *elephantinos* < *elephās* 'elephant']

elephant seal *n* a large earless seal, the male of which has a long inflatable snout resembling an elephant's trunk. Native to: western North American coast, Antarctic islands. Latin name: *Mirounga angustirostris* or *Mirounga leonina.*

elephant's ear *n* **1.** any bergenia with large showy leaves **2.** PLANTS same as **taro**

elephant's foot (*plural* **elephant's foots**) *n* an ornamental climbing or trailing plant of the yam family with a large above-ground tuber that is sometimes used for food. Native to: southern Africa. Latin name: *Dioscorea elephantipes.*

Eleusinian /éllyoō sínni ən/ *adj* relating to Eleusis, a village near Athens where the Eleusinian mysteries were celebrated, or to the Eleusinian mysteries themselves ■ *n* somebody who was born in or was a citizen of Eleusis [Mid-17C. < Latin *Eleusinius* < Greek *Eleusinios* < *Eleusis*]

Eleusinian mysteries *npl* in ancient Greece, the secret religious rites celebrated annually at Eleusis and Athens that honoured Persephone, Demeter, and Dionysus

elev. *abbr* elevation

elevate /élli vayt/ (**-vates, -vating, -vated**) *vt* **1. RAISE SOMETHING UP** to raise something to a higher level or position **2. RAISE SOMEBODY TO HIGHER RANK** to raise or promote somebody or something to a high or higher status, rank, or office **3. INCREASE SOMETHING** to increase the amount or intensity of something ○ *This was one factor that elevated interest rates.* **4. RAISE SOMEBODY'S MIND OR SPIRIT** to lift somebody's mind or spirit to a more enlightened or exalted level (*formal*) **5.** ARMS **MAKE GUN BARREL POINT HIGHER** to make the barrel of a field gun point at a higher angle **6.** CHR **LIFT UP HOST OR CHALICE** to lift up the Host or the chalice in front of the congregation during a Mass [14C. < Latin *elevat-*, past participle of *elevare* < *levare* 'lighten']

SYNONYMS See ***raise.***

elevated /élli vaytid/ *adj* **1. AT HIGH LEVEL OR POSITION** raised above ground level or situated at a higher level than something else ○ *elevated track* **2. HIGH OR HIGHER IN RANK** high or higher in rank or status **3. INCREASED** increased in amount ○ *elevated levels of cholesterol* **4. AT HIGH MORAL OR INTELLECTUAL LEVEL** set at a high moral or intellectual level ○ *Milton's elevated conception of the role of the poet*

elevated railway *n* a rail system operating on a raised structure, usually above a street

elevation /élli váysh'n/ *n* **1. HEIGHT ABOVE LOCATION** the height above a specific reference point, especially sea level ○ *at an elevation of 1,000 metres above sea level* **2. RAISING SOMETHING, OR BEING RAISED** the act of raising somebody or something in height or status, or the process of being raised in height or status ○ *They congratulated him on his elevation to the cardinalship.* **3. ABILITY TO JUMP, OR HEIGHT REACHED** especially in ballet or figure skating, the ability of somebody to jump high and hold the position briefly, or the height somebody can reach in jumping **4. INCREASE** an increase in something (*technical*) ○ *Among the effects was an elevation in the level of dopamine.* **5.** ARCHIT **ARCHITECTURAL DRAWING OF SIDE OF BUILDING** a scale drawing of any side of a building or other structure ○ *the front elevation of the proposed new wing* **6.** CIV ENG **ANGLE IN SURVEYING** the angle between a horizontal line and the line from a surveying instrument to a point above the horizontal, e.g. between eye level and a line to a nearby rooftop **7.** ARMS **ANGLE OF GUN BARREL ABOVE HORIZONTAL** the angle to which the barrel of a large gun is raised above the horizontal **8.** CHR **RAISING OF HOST AND CHALICE** the raising up and showing to the people of the Host or chalice by a priest immediately after their consecration during a Mass **9.** ASTRON same as **altitude** (sense 4) —**elevational** *adj*

elevator /élli vaytər/ *n* **1.** *ANZ, N Am* **PLATFORM FOR TAKING UP OR DOWN** a platform, cage, or enclosed compartment that is raised or lowered mechanically and used to take people or things to a higher or lower level in a building. UK term **lift 2. HOISTING MACHINE** a machine with scoops or similar devices for hoisting something to a higher level **3. AIRCRAFT DEVICE CONTROLLING CLIMB AND DESCENT** a hinged flap, either of a pair on the rear portion of the horizontal stabilizing surface or tailplane of an aircraft, used to control the aircraft's up-and-down movement **4. AIRCRAFT PLATFORM ON CARRIER** on an aircraft carrier, a mechanized platform that transports aircraft from a below-the-deck hangar up to the flight deck and vice versa **5.** ANAT **MUSCLE THAT LIFTS PART OF BODY** a muscle that contracts to lift a part of the body **6.** *N Am* **GRAIN STOREHOUSE** a storehouse for grain, equipped with a mechanism for taking in, lifting, and discharging the grain

CHEMICAL ELEMENTS

element	symbol	at.no.	at.wt.
actinium	Ac	89	[226]
aluminum	Al	13	26.98
americium	Am	95	[243]
antimony	Sb	51	121.75
argon	Ar	18	39.95
arsenic	As	33	74.92
astatine	At	85	[210]
barium	Ba	56	137.34
berkelium	Bk	97	[247]
beryllium	Be	4	9.01
bismuth	Bi	83	208.98
bohrium	Bh	107	[264]
boron	B	5	10.81
bromine	Br	35	79.9
cadmium	Cd	48	112.4
calcium	Ca	20	40.08
californium	Cf	98	[251]
carbon	C	6	12.01
cerium	Ce	58	140.12
cesium	Cs	55	132.91
chlorine	Cl	17	35.45
chromium	Cr	24	52
cobalt	Co	27	58.93
copper	Cu	29	63.55
curium	Cm	96	[247]
darmstadtium	Ds	110	[271]
dubnium	Db	105	[262]
dysprosium	Dy	66	162.5
einsteinium	Es	99	[254]
erbium	Er	68	167.26
europium	Eu	63	151.96
fermium	Fm	100	[257]
fluorine	F	9	19
francium	Fr	87	[223]
gadolinium	Gd	64	157.25
gallium	Ga	31	69.72
germanium	Ge	32	72.59
gold	Au	79	196.97
hafnium	Hf	72	178.49
hassium	Hs	108	[269]
helium	He	2	4
holmium	Ho	67	164.93
hydrogen	H	1	1.01
indium	In	49	114.82
iodine	I	53	126.9
iridium	Ir	77	192.22
iron	Fe	26	55.85
krypton	Kr	36	83.8
lanthanum	La	57	138.91
lawrencium	Lr	103	[256]
lead	Pb	82	207.2
lithium	Li	3	6.94
lutetium	Lu	71	174.97
magnesium	Mg	12	24.31
manganese	Mn	25	54.94
meitnerium	Mt	109	[268]
mendelevium	Md	101	[258]
mercury	Hg	80	200.59
molybdenum	Mo	42	95.94
neodymium	Nd	60	144.24
neon	Ne	10	20.18
neptunium	Np	93	237.05
nickel	Ni	28	58.71
niobium	Nb	41	92.91
nitrogen	N	7	14.01
nobelium	No	102	[255]
osmium	Os	76	190.2
oxygen	O	8	16
palladium	Pd	46	106.4
phosphorus	P	15	30.97
platinum	Pt	78	195.09
plutonium	Pu	94	[244]
polonium	Po	84	209
potassium	K	19	39.1
praseodymium	Pr	59	140.91
promethium	Pm	61	[145]
protactinium	Pa	91	231.04
radium	Ra	88	[226]
radon	Rn	86	[222]
rhenium	Re	75	186.2
rhodium	Rh	45	102.91
rubidium	Rb	37	85.47
ruthenium	Ru	44	101.07
rutherfordium	Rf	104	[261]
samarium	Sm	62	150.4
scandium	Sc	21	44.96
seaborgium	Sg	106	[266]
selenium	Se	34	78.96
silicon	Si	14	28.09
silver	Ag	47	107.87
sodium	Na	11	22.99
strontium	Sr	38	87.62
sulfur	S	16	32.06
tantalum	Ta	73	180.95
technetium	Tc	43	98.91
tellurium	Te	52	127.6
terbium	Tb	65	158.93
thallium	Tl	81	204.37
thorium	Th	90	232.04
thulium	Tm	69	168.93
tin	Sn	50	118.69
titanium	Ti	22	47.9
tungsten (wolfram)	W	74	183.85
ununbium	Uub	112	277
ununhexium	Uuh	116	289
ununquadium	Uuq	114	285
unununium	Uuu	111	272.15
ununtrium	Uut	113	284
ununpentium	Uup	115	288
uranium	U	92	283.04
vanadium	V	23	50.94
xenon	Xe	54	131.3
ytterbium	Yb	70	173.04
yttrium	Y	39	88.91
zinc	Zn	30	65.38
zirconium	Zr	40	91.22

Elements are listed with their symbol, atomic number (at.no.), and atomic weight (at.wt.). Atomic weights shown in square brackets are for the longest lived isotopes; those for neptunium, protactinium, and technetium are for the most technologically important isotopes.

elevator music *n N Am* bland instrumental background music played over loudspeakers in lifts, shops, and other public places (*informal*)

eleven /i lévv'n/ *n* **1.** 11 the number 11 **2.** SOMETHING WITH VALUE OF 11 something in a numbered series with a value of 11 **3.** GROUP OF 11 a group of 11 objects or people **4.** TEAM OF 11 a team of 11 players, e.g. a football team, a hockey team, or a cricket team [Old English *endleofan* 'one over (ten)' < Germanic] —**eleven** *adj, pron*

eleven-plus *n* in the United Kingdom, an examination taken by some children in their last year of primary school to determine what sort of secondary education they will receive

elevenses /i lévv'nziz/ *n* a mid-morning snack (*takes a singular or plural verb*)

eleventh /i lévv'nth/ *n* one of 11 equal parts of something —**eleventh** *adj, adv*

eleventh hour *n* the last moment before something happens ○*Time after time you'll find solutions are* reached at the 59th minute of the eleventh hour.' (John Major, *Guardian Weekly*; 3 April 1994) — **eleventh-hour** *adj*

elevon /élli von/ *n* a hinged flap on an aircraft, especially one with a delta wing or no tail, that functions both as an elevator and an aileron [Mid-20C. Blend of ELEVATOR + AILERON]

elf /elf/ (*plural* **elves** /elvz/) *n* **1.** in folklore, a small lively imaginary being resembling a human with pointed ears, often considered to have a mischievous nature and magical powers **2.** any small person, especially a child, who plays pranks or tricks [Old English < Germanic] —**elflike** *adj*

ELF *abbr* **1.** LANGUAGE English as a Lingua Franca **2.** MEDIA extremely low frequency

elfin /élfin/ *adj* **1.** OF OR LIKE ELVES like, characteristic of, or associated with elves **2.** BY ELVES supposedly caused or made by elves **3.** SMALL AND LIVELY small, delicate, and charmingly sprightly, lively, or mischievous ○ *elfin features* **4.** MAGICAL having a magical charm or appeal

elfish /élfish/, **elvish** /élvish/ *adj* **1.** resembling or relating to an elf **2.** full of lively mischief —**elfishly** *adv*

elflock /élf lok/ *n* a tangled coil of hair (*often used in the plural*)

Elgar /él gaar/, **Sir Edward** (1857–1934) British composer. He was a major figure of late romanticism in music, writing both choral and orchestral works. His *Enigma Variations* (1899) and the patriotic *Pomp and Circumstance* marches (1901–07, 1930) are among his most popular pieces. See illustration on next page.

'There is music in the air, music all round us: the world is full of it, and you simply take as much as you require.'
[Sir Edward Elgar. Quoted in *Sir Edward Elgar*, R. J. Buckley; 1905]

AKG London

Sir Edward Elgar

Elgin /élgin/ **1.** city in northeastern Scotland and administrative centre of Moray district. Population: 87,507 (1998). **2.** city in northeastern Illinois, on the Fox River, north of Aurora and west of Chicago. Population: 96,539 (2002 estimate).

Elgin Marbles npl Greek sculptures from the Parthenon in Athens, brought to Britain in 1806 by Thomas Bruce, seventh earl of Elgin, and now in the British Museum in London. The Greek government has requested their return.

El Greco ♦ Greco, El

Elia /eéli ə/ ♦ Lamb, Charles

elicit /i líssit/ (-its, -iting, -ited) vt **1.** to cause or produce something as a reaction or response to a stimulus of some kind ○ His jokes failed to elicit even the faintest of smiles from her. **2.** to bring something to light or cause something to be disclosed, especially by a process of questioning or research ○ What were their chances of eliciting any worthwhile information from such an obstinately uncooperative witness? [Mid-17C. < Latin elicit-, past participle of elicere 'draw out (by trickery)' < lacere 'deceive'] —**elicitation** /i líssi táysh'n/ n —**elicitor** n

---

SPELLCHECK elicit or **illicit**? Do not confuse the spelling of **elicit** and **illicit**, which sound similar. **Elicit** is a verb meaning 'produce as a response' or 'bring to light', as in to elicit information. **Illicit** is an adjective meaning 'illegal' or 'socially unacceptable', as in engaging in illicit activities.

---

elide /i líd/ (elides, eliding, elided) vt **1.** to omit a vowel, consonant, or syllable of a word, or leave out part of a sentence or phrase **2.** to omit, delete, or ignore something (formal) [Late 16C. < Latin elidere 'strike out' < laedere 'strike']

eligible /éllijəb'l/ adj **1.** QUALIFIED entitled or qualified to do, be, or get something ○ She is eligible to run for office. **2.** MARRIAGEABLE considered a good candidate for marriage ○ the most eligible bachelor in town **3.** US ALLOWED BY RULES TO CATCH FOOTBALL in American football, permitted by the rules to catch a forward pass during a play ■ n SOMEBODY OR SOMETHING THAT MEETS REQUIREMENTS somebody or something that matches up to a set of requirements ○ We've separated the eligibles from the nonstarters. [15C. Via French, 'fit to be chosen' < late Latin eligibilis 'that may be chosen' < Latin eligere (see ELECT)] —**eligibility** /éllijə bílləti/ n —**eligibly** adv

Elijah /i líjə/ n in the Bible, a Hebrew prophet of the 9th century BC who fought against idolatry and paganism and maintained the worship of Jehovah

eliminate /i límmi nayt/ (-nates, -nating, -nated) vt **1.** GET RID OF SOMETHING to put an end to something, usually something undesirable ○ They are pledged to eliminate poverty by the end of the century. **2.** REJECT SOMEBODY OR SOMETHING to decide to exclude somebody or something from further consideration ○ The police eliminated him from the list of suspects. **3.** SPORTS DEFEAT SOMEBODY IN COMPETITION to defeat a player or team and put them out of a competition (usually passive) ○ The local team was eliminated in the first round. **4.** MURDER SOMEBODY to kill an opponent **5.** PHYSIOL GET RID OF BODILY WASTE to expel waste from the body (technical) **6.** MATHS REMOVE MATHEMATICAL VARIABLE to remove variables from two or more simultaneous mathematical equations by combining the equations [Mid-16C. < Latin eliminat-, past participle of eliminare 'turn out of doors' < limen 'threshold'] —**elim-**

---

ination /i límmi náysh'n/ n —**eliminative** /-ətiv/ adj —**eliminatory** /-ətəri/ adj

eliminator /i límmi naytər/ n a round in a competition or a question in a quiz after which competitors who are defeated are removed

ELINT /éllint/, **elint** n the gathering of information by electronic means, e.g. from aircraft or ships, or the section of the military intelligence service involved in this [Mid-20C. < shortenings of ELECTRONIC + IN-TELLIGENCE]

Elion /élli ən/, **Gertrude Belle** (1918–99) US chemist. She and fellow researcher George Hitchings pioneered research into drugs that kill harmful invading cells without damaging healthy body cells, which led to the development of AZT. They shared the 1988 Nobel Prize in physiology or medicine with James Black.

Barnaby's

George Eliot

Eliot /élli ət/, **George** (1819–80) British novelist. Her naturalistic and humanistic books include Adam Bede (1859) and Middlemarch (1871–72). Pseudonym of **Evans, Mary Ann**. See Cultural note at **mill**[1]

'A woman dictates before marriage in order that she may have an appetite for submission afterwards.'
[George Eliot, Middlemarch; 1871–72]

Eliot, Sir John (1592–1632) English politician. He was active in the early stages of Parliament's struggle against King Charles I, who imprisoned him in the Tower of London in 1629, where he died.

US Office of War Information

T. S. Eliot

Eliot, T. S. (1888–1965) US-born British poet, critic, and dramatist. His poem The Waste Land (1922) represents a landmark in modern English poetry. He won the Nobel Prize in literature (1948). Later works include Four Quartets (1935–43) and the verse drama Murder in the Cathedral (1935). Full name **Eliot, Thomas Stearns**. See Cultural note at **hollow, wasteland**

'Footfalls echo in the memory / Down the passage which we did not take / Towards the door we never opened / Into the rose garden. My words echo / Thus, in your mind.'
[T. S. Eliot, 'Burnt Norton', Four Quartets; 1943]

'Poetry is not a turning loose of emotion, but an escape from emotion; it is not the expression of personality, but an escape from personality.'
[T. S. Eliot, 'Tradition and the Individual Talent'; 1920]

ELISA /i lízə/ n a widely used technique for determining the presence or amount of protein in a biological sample, using an enzyme that bonds to an antibody or antigen and causes a colour change. Full form **enzyme-linked immunosorbent assay**

Elisha /i líshə/ n in the Bible, a Hebrew prophet of the 9th century BC who enjoyed political influence throughout the reigns of four kings of Israel. He was the disciple and successor of Elijah.

elision /i lízh'n/ (plural **-sions** or same) n **1.** the omission of a vowel, consonant, or syllable while pronouncing or writing something, sometimes as a natural shortening, as in 'he's', sometimes for literary or poetic effect, as in ''tis' **2.** the suppression, omission, or deletion of something, or what has been suppressed, omitted, or deleted (formal) [Late 16C. < Latin elision- < elidere 'strike out' (see ELIDE)]

elite /i leét, ay-/ n **1.** PRIVILEGED MINORITY a small group of people within a larger group who have more power, social standing, wealth, or talent than the rest of the group (takes a singular or plural verb) **2.** PRINTING SIZE OF PRINTING TYPE a 10-point type that has about 12 characters to the inch or just under 5 characters to the centimetre ■ adj **1.** RICHEST, BEST, OR MOST POWERFUL more talented, privileged, or highly trained than others ○ elite troops **2.** FOR RICH OR PRIVILEGED PEOPLE restricted to the rich or privileged ○ an elite school [Late 18C. < French < Latin eligere 'pick out' (see ELECT)]

elitism /i leétizəm, ay-/ n **1.** BELIEF IN CONCEPT OF SUPERIORITY the belief that some people or things are inherently superior to others and deserve pre-eminence, preferential treatment, or higher rewards because of their superiority **2.** BELIEF IN CONTROL BY SMALL GROUP the belief that government or control should be in the hands of a small group of privileged, wealthy, or intelligent people, or the active promotion of such a system **3.** CONTROL BY SMALL GROUP government or control by a small, specially qualified, or privileged group —**elitist** n, adj

elixir /i líksər/ n **1.** CURE-ALL a panacea or a quick or magical cure **2.** SWEETENED DRUG a sweetened solution of a drug in alcohol and water **3.** also **elixir of life** MIRACULOUS SUBSTANCE a substance once believed to prolong life indefinitely, or to transform base metals into gold [14C. Via medieval Latin < Arabic al-iksir < Greek xērion 'dry powder for treating wounds' < xēros 'dry']

Elizabeth /i lízzəbəth/ (1900–2002) queen consort of the United Kingdom. She married the second son of George V, who came to the throne as George VI in 1936, and was the mother of Queen Elizabeth II. Born **Bowes-Lyon, Lady Elizabeth**. Also known as **Queen Elizabeth, the Queen Mother**

'Now we can look the East End in the face.'
[Elizabeth. Surveying the damage caused to Buckingham Palace by a bomb during the Blitz in World War II; 1940]

Elizabeth I (1533–1603) queen of England and Ireland. The daughter of Henry VIII and Anne Boleyn, she established the Protestant Church in England and presided over a period of domestic political stability and global exploration.

'I know I have the body of a weak and feeble woman, but I have the heart and stomach of a king, and of a king of England too.'
[Elizabeth I, Speech to the troops at Tilbury on the approach of the Armada; 1588]

Elizabeth II (b. 1926) queen of the United Kingdom. Daughter of George VI and queen since 1952, she married Prince Philip in 1947 and has four children, Prince Charles, Princess Anne, Prince Andrew, and Prince Edward.

'1992 is not a year I shall look back on with undiluted pleasure. In the words of one of my more sympathetic correspondents, it has turned out to be an "annus horribilis".'
[Elizabeth II, Speech; 25 December 1992]

Elizabethan /i lízzə beéth'n/ adj **1.** relating to or characteristic of the life and times of Elizabeth I, queen of England and Ireland, who reigned from 1558 to 1603 **2.** suggesting or embodying a style of English Renaissance building from the reign of

Elizabeth I that emphasized symmetrical layouts and moulded or sculptured decoration with a German or Flemish influence

Elizabethan sonnet *n* LITERAT same as **Shakespearean sonnet**

Elizabethville /i lízzəbəth vil/ former name for **Lubumbashi**

elk /elk/ (*plural same* or **elks**) *n* **1.** a large thin-legged heavy-bodied deer with a long head and a bulbous pliable muzzle, the male of which has huge antlers. Native to: northern Europe, Asia, North America. Latin name: *Alces alces*. N Am term **moose 2.** *N Am* ZOOL same as **wapiti** [Old English *eolh*]

Elk *n* a member of a North American men's social and charitable organization, the Benevolent and Protective Order of Elks

elkhound /élk hownd/ *n UK, ANZ, Can* a medium-sized sturdy dog with pointed ears, a broad head, and a thick grey coat, belonging to a breed developed in Norway to hunt elk and other game. US term **Norwegian elkhound**

ell /el/ *n* **1.** something L-shaped or with a right-angled bend **2.** *US* an extension of a building, usually at right angles to the main part [Late 18C. Spelling of the letter *L*]

Ella /éllə/, **Mark Gordon** (*b.* 1959) Australian rugby player. He was the first Aboriginal captain of the Australian rugby team (1982).

ellagic acid /i lájjik-/ *n* a yellow crystalline compound. Source: oak galls, tannins. Use: reduction of bleeding. Formula: $C_{14}H_6O_8$. [Early 19C. < French *ellagique* < anagram of *galle* 'gallnut']

Ellef Ringnes Island /éllef ríng ness-/ uninhabited island of the Canadian Sverdrup Island group, located in the Arctic Ocean, in the Northwest Territories. Area: 11,295 sq. km/4,361 sq. mi.

Ellesmere Island /élz meer-/ uninhabited island in Nunavut Territory, northern Canada, in the Arctic Ocean close to the northwestern coast of Greenland. Area: 196,236 sq. km/75,767 sq. mi.

Ellesmere Island National Park Reserve former name for **Quttinirpaaq National Park**

Ellesmere Port town in Cheshire, northwestern England, situated on the River Mersey. Population: 64,504 (1991).

Ellice Islands /élliss-/ former name for **Tuvalu** (until 1975)

Barnaby's

Duke Ellington

Ellington /éllingtən/, **Duke** (1899–1974) US jazz pianist, composer, and bandleader. He came to fame in the early 1930s and is known for compositions such as 'Sophisticated Lady' (1933). Born **Ellington, Edward Kennedy**

'Music to me is a sound sensation, assimilation, anticipation, adulation, and reputation.'
[Duke Ellington, *Music is My Mistress*; 1973]

Elliott /élli ət/, **Herb** (*b.* 1938) Australian athlete. He was the winner of the gold medal for the 1,500 metres at the 1960 Olympics. Between 1957 and 1961 he was never defeated over this distance. Full name **Elliott, Herbert James**

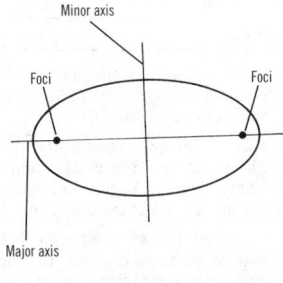

Minor axis

Foci Foci

Major axis

ellipse

ellipse /i líps/ *n* **1.** a two-dimensional shape like a stretched circle with slightly longer flatter sides **2.** the shape formed by the intersection of a right circular cone and an oblique plane that does not intersect the base of the cone [Mid-18C. Via French < Latin *ellipsis* < Greek *elleipsis* 'defect, omission' < *elleipein* 'leave out, fall short']

ellipsis /i lípsiss/ (*plural* **-lipses** /-líp seez/) *n* **1.** the omission of one or more words from a sentence, especially when what is omitted can be understood from the context. The omission of 'go' at the end of 'I went but my wife didn't' is an example of ellipsis. **2.** a printed mark, usually three dots (...), or, less often, asterisks (***), used to indicate that something has been omitted from a text [Early 17C. < Latin (see ELLIPSE)]

USAGE The *ellipsis* in the form of three dots is used when text is omitted from the beginning, middle, or end of a quotation: *Shakespeare wrote, 'When sorrows come, they come...in battalions'*. (The full quotation is *'When sorrows come, they come not single spies,/But in battalions'*.) Any punctuation that precedes or follows the omitted text may or may not be shown before or after the ellipsis: *You can fool all the people some of the time...but you cannot fool all the people all of the time*. When the ellipsis comes at the end of a sentence, it is usually followed by a full stop. Dots are also used in direct speech to show that the speaker is hesitating or has left something unsaid: *'I don't know... I'll try... I can't promise anything.'* In some styles of writing, asterisks are used when part of a word is omitted, usually part of a swearword.

ellipsoid /i líp soyd/ *n* a geometric surface or a solid figure shaped like a rugby ball. Any section through an ellipsoid is either an ellipse or a circle. ■ *adj* in the shape of an ellipsoid —**ellipsoidal** /íllip sóyd'l, éllip-/ *adj*

elliptical /i líptik'l/, **elliptic** /i líptik/ *adj* **1.** MATHS LIKE ELLIPSE in the shape or pattern of a geometric ellipse **2.** GRAM RELATING TO ELLIPSIS relating to ellipsis or containing an example of ellipsis **3.** HIGHLY ECONOMICAL IN SPEECH OR WRITING extremely concise in speech or writing, sometimes so concise as to be difficult or impossible to understand [Mid-17C. < Greek *elleiptikos* 'defective' < *elleipein* 'leave out, fall short'] —**elliptically** *adv*

elliptical galaxy *n* a galaxy with an overall elliptical or spherical shape and no arms or internal structure

ellipticity /íllip tíssəti, éllip-/ (*plural* **-ties**) *n* the deviation or degree of deviation of an ellipse or ellipsoid from a perfect circle or sphere. Ellipticity is measured as the ratio of the major axis to the minor axis of the ellipse or ellipsoid.

Ellis /élliss/, **Havelock** (1859–1939) British psychologist. His *Studies in the Psychology of Sex* (1897–1928) was a landmark in the analysis of sexual behaviour. Full name **Ellis, Henry Havelock**

'Pain and death are a part of life. To reject them is to reject life itself.'
[Havelock Ellis, *On Life and Sex: Essays of Love and Virtue*; 1922]

Ellis Island complex of one natural and two artificial islands in upper New York Bay, eastern New Jersey, and southeastern New York State, near Manhattan. From 1892 to 1954 it served as a chief entry point for immigrants to the United States. Area: 0.11 sq. km/0.04 sq. mi.

Ellsworth Land /élz wurth-/ high plateau in western Antarctica, south of the Antarctic Peninsula. It rises at the Vinson Massif, the highest point in Antarctica, to 5,140 m/16,863 ft.

elm

elm /elm/ *n* **1.** a deciduous tree with serrated leaves and winged fruits. Native to: northern temperate regions. Genus: *Ulmus*. **2.** the hard dense wood of an elm tree. Use: furniture, boats, construction. [Old English < Indo-European]

El-Mahallah el-Kubra /el mə haálə al kō braá/ industrial city in the central Nile delta, northern Egypt. Population: 408,000 (1992).

elm bark beetle *n* the beetle that spreads the fungus causing Dutch elm disease. Family: Scolytidae.

El Misti ♦ **Misti**

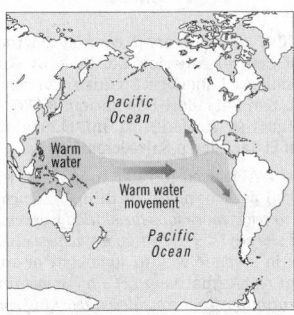

Pacific Ocean

Warm water

Warm water movement

Pacific Ocean

El Niño: map showing movement of warm water currents across the Pacific Ocean

El Niño /el neényō/ *n* a periodic change in the currents of the Pacific Ocean that occurs every five to eight years and brings unusually warm water to the coast of northern South America. It often leads to severe climate disruption to countries in and beside the Pacific. [< Spanish, shortening of *El Niño de Navidad* 'the Christmas Child'; from the time of year when the currents change]

elocution /éllə kyoósh'n/ *n* the art of speaking clearly and well, with correct enunciation [15C. < Latin *elocution-* < *eloqui* (see ELOQUENT)] —**elocutionary** *adj* —**elocutionist** *n*

elodea /ə lōdi ə/ *n* a plant that grows submerged in ponds and ditches. Use: oxygenating aquariums. Genus: *Elodea*. [Late 19C. < modern Latin < Greek *helōdēs* 'marshy']

Elohim /e lō him, éllō heém/ *n* in the Bible, a Hebrew word for God [Late 16C. < Hebrew *elōhīm*, plural of *elōah* 'God']

elongate /eé long gayt/ *vti* (**-gates, -gating, -gated**) LENGTHEN to make something longer, or become longer ■ *adj* **1.** LONG long and narrow or slender (*technical*) **2.** MADE LONGER lengthened or stretched out (*formal*) [Mid-16C. < late Latin *elongat-*, past participle of *elongare* 'lengthen' < Latin *longus* 'long'] —**elongated** *adj*

elongation /eé long gáysh'n/ *n* **1.** LENGTHENING the act of lengthening something, or the condition of being lengthened **2.** SOMETHING LENGTHENED something that has become or been made longer **3.** ASTRON ANGLE BETWEEN SUN AND ASTRONOMICAL OBJECT the angle between the Sun and either the Moon or a planet, as seen from Earth or a point in space

elope /i lṓp/ (**elopes, eloping, eloped**) vi to go away suddenly without telling anyone, especially in order to marry or cohabit with a lover without the knowledge or consent of parents or guardians [Late 16C. < Anglo-Norman *aloper* 'run away'] —**elopement** n —**eloper** n

eloquence /éllǝkwǝnss/ n **1.** the ability to speak forcefully, expressively, and persuasively **2.** forceful, expressive, and persuasive language

eloquent /éllǝkwǝnt/ adj **1.** said or saying something in a forceful, expressive, and persuasive way **2.** expressing a feeling or thought clearly, memorably, or movingly [14C. Via French < Latin *eloquent-*, present participle of *eloqui* 'speak out' < *loqui* 'speak'] —**eloquently** adv

El Paso /el pássō/ city in western Texas on the Rio Grande, a port of entry from Mexico. Population: 577,415 (2002 estimate).

Elphege, St ♦ **Alphege**

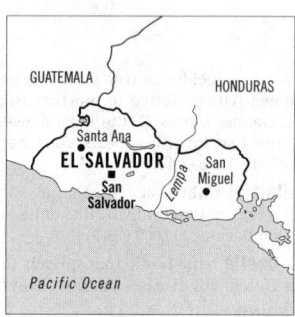

El Salvador

El Salvador /el sálvǝ dawr/ country on the Pacific coast of Central America, bordered by Guatemala and Honduras. Language: Spanish. Currency: colón. Capital: San Salvador. Population: 6,470,379 (2003). Area: 21,041 sq. km/8,124 sq. mi. Official name **Republic of El Salvador**. ◊ **Salvadoran**

else /elss/ adv **1.** used to refer in a vague way to an additional person, place, or thing ○ *Something else I'd like to see is more jobs for skilled workers.* ○ *What else did she say?* ○ *I didn't go anywhere else.* **2.** used to refer in a vague way to somebody or something different or alternative ○ *Let's try something else.* ○ *He was unhappy and considered working somewhere else.* **3.** same as **or else** [Old English *elles* < Indo-European] ◇ **or else 1.** otherwise ○ *Go away, or else I'll call the police.* **2.** used to make a threat ○ *Have it ready by tomorrow, or else!*

elsewhere /élss wáir/ adv at, in, or to another place ○ *If you're calling from elsewhere, please press 2 to contact reception.* ○ *They stock books that may be hard to find elsewhere.*

ELT n the teaching of English to non-native speakers of English. Full form **English Language Teaching**

eluant n CHEM another spelling of **eluent**

Éluard /élloo aar/, **Paul** (1895–1952) French poet. He is one of France's greatest 20th-century lyric poets and coauthor of the 1925 surrealist manifesto. He fought in the Communist Resistance in World War II. Pseudonym of **Grindel, Eugène**

'The earth is blue like an orange.'
[Paul Éluard, *L'Amour, la poésie* (*Love and Poetry*); 1929]

eluate /élloo ayt/ n the liquid left after the process of elution, consisting of dissolved matter and the solvent used [Mid-20C. < Latin *eluere* (see ELUTE)]

elucidate /i loóssi dayt/ (**-dates, -dating, -dated**) vti to explain or clarify something [Mid-16C. < late Latin *elucidat-*, past participle of *elucidare* 'make clear' < Latin *lucidus* 'clear'] —**elucidation** /i loóssi dáysh'n/ n —**elucidative** /-di ǝ/ adj —**elucidator** n —**elucidatory** /i loóssi dáytǝri/ adj

elude /i loód/ (**eludes, eluding, eluded**) vt **1.** to escape from or avoid somebody or something by cunning, skill, or resourcefulness **2.** to be beyond somebody's understanding or ability to be remembered ○ *Her name eludes me.* [Mid-16C. < Latin *eludere* 'deceive, escape from, win from somebody at play' < *ludere* 'play']

SPELLCHECK See *allude*.

USAGE See *avoid*.

eluent /éllyoo ǝnt/, **eluant** n a solvent used to remove something from a substance [Mid-20C. < Latin *eluent-*, present participle of *eluere* (see ELUTE)]

Elul /e loól/ n in the Jewish calendar, the sixth month of the religious year, lasting 29 days and falling at about the same time as August to September. See table at **calendar** [Mid-16C. < Hebrew *elūl*]

elusive /i loóssiv/ adj **1.** HARD TO FIND difficult to find or catch **2.** HARD TO PIN DOWN difficult to understand, define, or identify **3.** HARD TO REMEMBER not easily called to mind or memory —**elusively** adv —**elusiveness** n

SPELLCHECK elusive, illusive, or allusive? Do not confuse the spelling of *elusive*, *illusive*, and *allusive*, which sound similar. *Elusive*, the most frequent of the three adjectives, means 'difficult to catch, find, understand, or remember', as in *an elusive thief*. *Illusive* is another word for *illusory*, meaning 'consisting of an illusion'. *Allusive* means 'making an allusion' or 'characterized by allusions', as in *an allusive remark*.

elusory /i loóssǝri/ adj **1.** HARD TO FIND difficult to find or catch (*formal*) **2.** EVASIVE avoiding the issue in an evasive or deceitful way **3.** HARD TO GRASP not easy to understand

elute /i loót/ (**elutes, eluting, eluted**) vt to remove one substance from another, usually after adsorbed material from an adsorbent surface, by washing it out with a solvent (*technical*) [Mid-18C. < Latin *elut-*, past participle of *eluere* 'wash out' < *luere* 'wash'] —**elution** n

elutriate /i loótri ayt/ (**-ates, -ating, -ated**) vt to purify or separate something from a mixture by washing, decanting, or straining it (*technical*) [Mid-18C. < Latin *elutriat-*, past participle of *elutriare* 'wash out' < *lutriare* 'wash'] —**elutriation** /i loótri áysh'n/ n

eluvia GEOL plural of **eluvium**

eluvial /i loóvi ǝl/ adj of or relating to eluvium or eluviation

eluvial deposit n a concentration of an ore deposit formed as a result of the removal of less dense host material

eluviation /i loóvi áysh'n/ n a process by which material dissolved or suspended in water within soil moves down or sideways as rainwater moves through the soil

eluvium /i loóvi ǝm/ (*plural* **-via** /-vi ǝ/) n an accumulated mass of soil, sand, silt, or rock debris resulting from weathering or drifting [Late 19C. < Latin *eluere* (see ELUTE), after ALLUVIUM]

ELV n a used car that has no commercial value and is suitable only for scrapping. Full form **end-of-life vehicle**

elver /élvǝr/ n a young freshwater eel, especially one that migrates from salt water [Mid-17C. < dialect *ellfare*, literally 'eel-journey']

elves plural of **elf**

elvish adj another spelling of **elfish**

Ely /éeli/ cathedral city in Cambridgeshire, eastern England, situated on the River Ouse. It stands on a low hill in the fenland, known as the Isle of Ely. Population: 11,760 (1994).

Elysian /i lízzi ǝn/ adj **1.** relating to or typical of Elysium **2.** full of or giving great pleasure and delight (*literary*) [Mid-16C. < ELYSIUM [1]]

Elysian Fields npl MYTHOL same as **Elysium** [1] (sense 1)

Elysium [1] /i lízzi ǝm/ n **1.** in Greek mythology, the home of the blessed after death **2.** any ideally delightful or blissful place or condition

Elysium [2] /i lízzi ǝm/ extensive low bulge on the surface of Mars in the northern hemisphere gently rising to a height of approximately 5 km/3 mi., supporting the volcanoes Hecates Tholus and Elysium Mons

elytron /élli tron/ (*plural* **-tra** /-trǝ/), **elytrum** /-trǝm/ (*plural* **-tra**) n a tough front wing, occurring in pairs on beetles and some other insects, that acts as a protective covering for the rear wings [Mid-18C. < Greek *elutron* 'sheath']

em /em/ n **1.** a unit of measurement of print size, equal to the point size of the typeface being used **2.** PRINTING same as **pica** [1] [Late 18C. Representing pronunciation of M [1]; because the letter is about this width]

'em /ǝm/ contr them (*informal*) [14C. Originally variant of Old English *hem* 'them'; now regarded as a contraction]

EM abbr **1.** electromagnetic **2.** electron microscope

em- prefix same as **en-** (*used before m, b, or p*) ○ **embark**

emaciate /i máyssi ayt/ (**-ates, -ating, -ated**) vti to become, or make somebody or something become, extremely thin [Early 17C. < Latin *emaciat-*, past participle of *emaciare* 'make lean, waste away' < *macer* 'lean'] —**emaciation** /i máyssi áysh'n/ n

emaciated /i máyssi aytid/ adj extremely thin, especially because of starvation or illness

SYNONYMS See *thin*.

e-mail, **email** /ée mayl/ n **1.** COMPUTER-TO-COMPUTER COMMUNICATION SYSTEM a system that allows text-based messages to be exchanged electronically, e.g. between computers or mobile phones. Full form **electronic mail 2.** E-MAIL MESSAGE a communication sent by e-mail ■ vt (**e-mails, e-mailing, e-mailed**) COMMUNICATE SOMETHING BY E-MAIL to send a message to somebody by e-mail

e-mail address n a URL that gives the origin or destination of an electronic message

e-mail shorthand n the set of acronyms and abbreviations for common phrases originally used in e-mail and subsequently in chat rooms, instant messaging, and newsgroup postings

emalangeni MONEY plural of **lilangeni**

emanate /émmǝ nayt/ (**-nates, -nating, -nated**) v **1.** vi to come from or come out of somebody, something, or somewhere **2.** vt to emit, send out, or give out something such as rays or information (*formal*) [Mid-18C. < Latin *emanat-*, past participle of *emanare* 'flow out, arise' < *manare* 'flow'] —**emanative** adj

emanation /émmǝ náysh'n/ n **1.** ACT OF SENDING SOMETHING OUT the act of emitting, sending out, or giving out something **2.** SOMETHING SENT OUT something that issues or is sent out or given out from somebody, something, or somewhere **3.** PHYS RADIOACTIVE GAS any gas produced by radioactive decay, e.g. radon —**emanational** adj

emancipate /i mánssi payt/ (**-pates, -pating, -pated**) vt **1.** to free somebody from slavery, serfdom, or other such forms of bondage **2.** to free somebody from restrictions or conventions (*often passive*) [Early 17C. < Latin *emancipat-*, past participle of *emancipare* 'to free from parental power' < *mancipium* 'ownership'] —**emancipative** adj —**emancipator** n —**emancipatory** /-pǝtǝri/ adj

emancipation /i mánssi páysh'n/ n **1.** the act or process of setting somebody free or of freeing somebody from restrictions **2.** the condition or fact of being set free or freed from some restriction

emarginate /i maárji nayt/ adj describes leaves or petals with a notch at the tip [Late 18C. < Latin *emarginatus*, past participle of *emarginare* 'remove the edges of'] —**emargination** /i maárji náysh'n/ n

EMAS /ée mass/ n a voluntary scheme of the European Union in which commercial and other organizations are encouraged to assess their approach to environmental matters against a given set of criteria. Full form **Eco-Management and Audit Scheme**

emasculate /i máskyoō layt/ (**-lates, -lating, -lated**) vt **1.** CASTRATE SOMEBODY to remove the testicles of a male human being or animal (*literary*) **2.** WEAKEN SOMEBODY OR SOMETHING to deprive somebody or something of effectiveness, spirit, or force (*formal*; *sometimes considered offensive*) **3.** REMOVE STAMENS FROM FLOWER to remove the male reproductive organs (**stamens**) from a flower, e.g. to prevent self-pollination [Early 17C. < Latin *emasculat-*, past participle of *emasculare* 'remove the male glands of, castrate' < *masculus* 'male'] —**emasculation** /i máskyoō láysh'n/ n —**emasculative** /-lǝtiv/ adj —**emasculator** n —**emasculatory** /-lǝtǝri, -laytǝri/ adj

embalm /im baám, em-/ (**-balms, -balming, -balmed**) vt **1.** PRESERVE DEAD BODY to treat a dead body with a preservative substance in order to stop it decaying

2. KEEP SOMETHING INTACT to protect something from change (*formal*) **3. PERFUME SOMETHING** to give a sweet scent to something (*literary*) [14C. < French *embaumer* < *baume* 'balm'] —**embalmer** *n* —**embalmment** *n*

embank /im bángk/ (**-banks, -banking, -banked**) *vt* to surround or line a road, canal, or other area with an embankment

embankment /im bángkmənt/ *n* a ridge or raised platform built of earth or stone to confine a waterway or support a road or railway line

~~**embarass**~~ incorrect spelling of **embarrass**

embargo /em baárgō/ *n* (*plural* **-goes**) **1. RESTRICTION ON TRADE** a government order restricting or prohibiting commerce, especially trade in a given commodity or with a particular nation **2. OFFICIAL BAN** any official restraint or prohibition **3. ORDER HALTING MOVEMENT OF SHIPS** in the past, a government order that prohibited commercial ships from entering or leaving its ports, often as a measure during war ■ *vt* (**-goes, -going, -goed**) **1. SEIZE SOMETHING** to confiscate or seize something for government use **2. PROHIBIT OR FORBID SOMETHING** in the past, to place an embargo on something [Late 16C. < Spanish < *embargar* 'restrain, seize']

embark /em baárk/ (**-barks, -barking, -barked**) *vti* to go on board, or put or take somebody or something on board a ship or aircraft [Mid-16C. < French *embarquer* < *barque* 'ship'] —**embarkation** /ém baar káysh'n/ *n* —**embarkment** *n*
embark on, embark upon *vti* to start or engage in an undertaking

~~**embarras**~~ incorrect spelling of **embarrass**

embarras de richesses /ómba raá də ree shéss/ *n* an overabundance of desirable things that makes choice among them difficult [< French, 'embarrassment of wealth']

embarrass /im bárrəss, em-/ (**-rasses, -rassing, -rassed**) *v* **1.** *vti* to become or cause somebody to become painfully self-conscious, ill at ease, ashamed, or humiliated ○ *He's easily embarrassed.* **2.** *vt* to hinder or impede somebody or something (*archaic; often passive*) [Late 17C. Via French *embarrasser* 'impede, disconcert' < Portuguese *embaraçar* < *baraço* 'halter']

USAGE Note the spelling of *embarrass* with *-rr-* and *-ass*. *Harass* has only one *r*.

embarrassed /im bárrəst, em-/ *adj* **1.** painfully self-conscious, ill at ease, ashamed, or humiliated **2.** in financial difficulties because of a lack of money — **embarrassedly** *adv*

embarrassing /im bárrəssing, em-/ *adj* causing painful self-consciousness, uncomfortableness, shame, or humiliation —**embarrassingly** *adv*

embarrassment /im bárrəssmənt, em-/ *n* **1. ACUTE SELF-CONSCIOUSNESS** a feeling of painful self-consciousness, uncomfortableness, shame, or humiliation ○ *blushed and fell silent in embarrassment* **2. SOMETHING THAT CAUSES SELF-CONSCIOUSNESS** something that causes a feeling of painful self-consciousness, uncomfortableness, shame, or humiliation **3. LACK OF MONEY** a state of financial difficulty ○ *financial embarrassment*

embassy /émbəssi/ (*plural* **-sies**) *n* **1. AMBASSADOR'S HEADQUARTERS** the residence and place of business of an ambassador **2. EMBASSY STAFF** an ambassador with his or her ambassadorial staff **3. AMBASSADOR'S POSITION AND RESPONSIBILITIES** the mission, rank, or function of an ambassador [Late 16C. < Old French *ambassé* < assumed Vulgar Latin *ambactiare* 'go on a mission']

embattle /im bátt'l/ (**-tles, -tling, -tled**) *vt* **1.** to arrange forces in readiness for battle **2.** to fortify something such as a building, village, or position in battle (*archaic; usually passive*) [14C. < Old French *embataillier* < *bataille* 'battle']

embattled /im bátt'ld/ *adj* **1. UNDER ASSAULT** under attack or subject to controversy **2. MIL FIGHTING OR READY TO FIGHT** ready for or engaged in battle **3. CONSTR WITH BATTLEMENTS** provided with battlements (*archaic*) **4.** HERALDRY **LIKE BATTLEMENTS** in heraldry, used to describe a design with an edge resembling battlements

embayment /im báymənt/ *n* **1.** a bay in a coastline **2.** the process by which a bay is formed in a coastline

Embden-Meyerhof pathway /émdən mí ər hof-/ *n*

BIOCHEM same as **glycolysis** [After Gustav Georg *Embden* (1874–1933), German physiologist, and Otto Fritz *Meyerhof* (1884–1951), German-born US biochemist]

embed, imbed *v* /im béd/ (**-beds, -bedding, -bedded**) **1.** *vti* **PLACE SOMETHING OR BE PLACED SOLIDLY** to fix something or become fixed in a surrounding mass **2.** *vti* **FIX SOMETHING IN MIND** to fix something deeply in the mind or memory (*often passive*) **3.** *vi* **BECOME LODGED** to become deeply and solidly lodged in something **4.** *vt* MEDIA **ASSIGN REPORTER TO MILITARY UNIT** to officially assign a reporter to travel with a military unit during a war and report freely any information that does not jeopardize national security (*usually passive*) ○ *has been embedded with the 3rd Infantry Division since the war began* **5.** *vt* **SURROUND SOMETHING** to surround or cover something closely (*usually passive*) ■ *n* /ém bed/ MEDIA **REPORTER TRAVELLING WITH MILITARY UNIT** a reporter who has been officially assigned to travel with a military unit during a war and report freely any information that does not jeopardize national security ○ *Embeds bring credibility to the war as independent truth-tellers.*

embellish /im béllish/ (**-lishes, -lishing, -lished**) *vt* **1. BEAUTIFY SOMETHING** to increase the beauty of something by adding ornaments or decorations **2. ADD FALSE DETAILS TO SOMETHING** to make an account or description more interesting by inventing or exaggerating details **3.** MUSIC **ADD ORNAMENTATION TO MELODY** to add extra notes, accents, or trills to a melody to make it more beautiful or interesting [14C. < Old French *embelliss-*, stem of *embellir* 'make beautiful' < *bel* 'beautiful' < Latin *bellus*] —**embellishment** *n*

ember /émbər/ *n* **BURNING FRAGMENT** a small piece of glowing or smouldering material from a dying fire ■ **embers** *npl* **1. REMAINS OF FIRE** the glowing or smouldering remains of a dying fire **2. REMAINS OF PASSION** the dying but not yet extinguished remains of a great emotion, especially love (*literary*) [Old English *æmyrge* < Indo-European, 'to burn']

Ember Days /émbər-/ *npl* days of prayer and fasting in Roman Catholic and Anglican Churches. Date: the Wednesday, Friday, and Saturday following Pentecost, the first Sunday after Lent, 14 September, and 13 December. [< Old English *ymbryne* 'circuit' < *ryne* 'course, running'; because they 'come round' four times a year]

embezzle /im bézz'l/ (**-zles, -zling, -zled**) *vti* to take for personal use money or property that has been given on trust by others, without their knowledge or permission [15C. < Anglo-Norman *embesiler* 'steal' < Old French *besillier* 'gouge, destroy'] —**embezzlement** *n* —**embezzler** *n*

SYNONYMS See **steal**.

embitter /im bíttər/ (**-ters, -tering, -tered**) *vt* **1.** to make somebody feel bitter or aggrieved **2.** to make something more bitter or acrimonious —**embittered** *adj* —**embitterment** *n*

emblazon /im bláyz'n/ (**-zons, -zoning, -zoned**) *vt* **1. ADD DESIGN TO SOMETHING** to decorate or adorn something such as clothing with bright colours or a symbol or picture **2.** HERALDRY **DECORATE SHIELD OR FLAG** in heraldry, to decorate or adorn a shield or flag by depicting something, especially a coat of arms **3. MAKE SOMEBODY OR SOMETHING FAMOUS** to celebrate somebody or something, or make somebody or something famous (*literary; often passive*) —**emblazonment** *n*

emblazonry /im bláyz'nri/ (*plural* **-ries**) *n* **1.** the act or process of putting heraldic decorations on something such as a shield or flag **2.** heraldic decorations on such things as shields or flags

emblem /émbləm/ *n* **1. SYMBOL** something that visually symbolizes an object, idea, group, or quality **2. BADGE** a badge or sign that represents a person, group, or organization **3.** ART **ALLEGORICAL IMAGE** an allegorical picture, often with a motto, used to illustrate a moral lesson [15C. Via Latin, 'inlaid design' < Greek *emblēma* 'insertion' < *emballein* 'to insert' < *ballein* 'to throw']

emblematic /émblə máttik/, **emblematical** /-máttik'l/ *adj* relating to, consisting of, or acting as an emblem —**emblematically** *adv*

emblematize /em blémmə tīz/ (**-tizes, -tizing, -tized**), **emblematise** (**-tises, -tising, -tised**) *vt* to serve as a symbol of something (*formal*)

embodiment /im bóddimənt/ *n* **1.** a tangible or visible expression of an idea or quality **2.** the act or process by which something is made tangible or visible

embody /im bóddi/ (**-ies, -ying, -ied**) *vt* **1. MAKE SOMETHING TANGIBLE** to give a tangible or visible form to something abstract **2. INCORPORATE THINGS INTO ORGANIZED WHOLE** to gather and organize a number of things into a whole **3. PERSONIFY SOMETHING** to express or exemplify something abstract in bodily form

embolden /im bōld'n/ (**-ens, -ening, -ened**) *vt* to make somebody bold

embolectomy /émbə léktəmi/ (*plural* **-mies**) *n* the surgical removal of an embolus, usually a blood clot or other obstruction, in a blood vessel

emboli MED plural of **embolus**

embolic /em bóllik/ *adj* relating to or caused by an embolus or embolism

embolisation *n* MED another spelling of **embolization**

embolism /émbəlizəm/ *n* **1.** MED **BLOCKAGE OF ARTERY** a condition in which an artery is blocked by an embolus, usually a blood clot formed at one place in the circulation and then lodging in another **2.** MED same as **embolus** (*informal*) **3.** CALENDAR **INSERTION OF DAYS INTO CALENDAR** the insertion of a day or days into a calendar **4.** CHR **PRAYER DURING ROMAN CATHOLIC MASS** in the Roman Catholic Church, a prayer for deliverance from evil inserted in a Mass after the Lord's Prayer [14C. Via late Latin < Greek *embolismos* < *emballein* 'to insert' (see EMBLEM)]

embolization /émbə lī záysh'n/, **embolisation** *n* the process or condition in which a blood vessel is blocked by a blood clot or other obstruction (**embolus**)

embolus /émbələss/ (*plural* **-li** /-lī/) *n* a mass, most commonly a blood clot, that becomes lodged in a blood vessel and obstructs it [Mid-17C. Via Latin < Greek *embolos* 'peg, stopper, wedge' < *emballein* 'to insert' (see EMBLEM)]

embonpoint /om boN pwaáN/ *n* **1.** roundness of body shape caused by excess weight (*humorous*) ○ *'She was slightly inclined to embonpoint.'* (J. M. Barrie, *Peter Pan*; 1904) **2.** a woman's breasts or chest [Late 17C. < French *en bon point* 'in good condition']

embosom /im bóozəm/ (**-oms, -oming, -omed**) *vt* (*archaic*) **1.** to surround or envelop somebody or something, especially in a protective way **2.** to take somebody into your arms and hold him or her closely

emboss /im bóss/ (**-bosses, -bossing, -bossed**) *vt* **1.** to decorate or mark a surface with a slightly raised design or lettering **2.** to give something the form of a raised pattern on a surface ○ *The title was embossed in gold lettering on the cover.* [14C. < Old French *embocer* < *boce* 'protuberance'] —**embosser** *n* —**embossment** *n*

embouchure /ómboo shoor/ *n* **1.** MUSIC **POSITION OF LIPS AND TONGUE** the adjustment of the lips and tongue in playing a wind instrument **2.** MUSIC **MOUTHPIECE** the mouthpiece of a wind instrument **3.** GEOG **RIVER MOUTH** the mouth of a river **4.** GEOG **VALLEY MOUTH** the mouth of a valley where it becomes a plain [Mid-18C. < French < *emboucher* 'put to your mouth' < *bouche* 'mouth']

embourgeoisement /om boor zhwaaz maáN/ *n* the process by which a social group becomes middle-class in manners and attitudes [Mid-20C. < French, < *bourgeois* (see BOURGEOIS)]

embowed /im bōd, em-/ *adj* shaped like a vault or arch

embowel /im bów əl/ (**-els, -elling, -elled**) *vt* same as **disembowel** (*archaic*)

embower /im bów ər/ (**-ers, -ering, -ered**) *vt* to shelter or enclose somebody or something in a bower or a place or structure resembling a bower (*literary*)

embrace /im bráyss/ *v* (**-braces, -bracing, -braced**) **1.** *vti* **HUG SOMEBODY** to hug somebody in your arms affectionately or passionately, or hug each other affectionately or passionately **2.** *vt* **MAKE USE OF SOMETHING** to welcome and take advantage of something eagerly or willingly ○ *embrace an opportunity* **3.** *vt* **ADOPT SOMETHING** to adopt or take up something, especially a belief or way of life ○ *embraced free-market economics* **4.** *vt* **COMPRISE SOMETHING** to include something as part of a whole ○

a new electoral district embracing both suburban and urban areas **5.** *vt* SURROUND SOMETHING to surround or enclose something (*literary; often passive*) ■ *n* WARM HUG an affectionate or passionate hug [14C. < Old French *embracer* 'take into your arms' < Latin *bracchium* 'arm'] —**embraceable** *adj* —**embracement** *n* —**embracer** *n*

embracery /im bráyssəri/ *n* the offence of trying to influence a judge or jury, e.g. by bribery, threats, or promises

embranchment /im braánchmənt/ *n* **1.** a branching out of a feature of the natural landscape, e.g. a river or mountain range **2.** a branch of something such as a river or mountain range [Mid-19C. < French *embranchement* < *branche* (see BRANCH)]

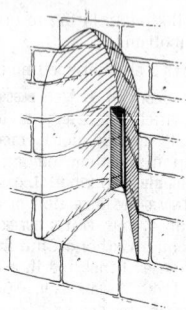

embrasure (sense 2)

embrasure /im bráyzhər/ *n* **1.** an opening in the wall of a building for a door or window, tapered so as to be wider on the inside than on the outside **2.** a slanted opening in the wall or parapet of a fortification, designed so that a defender can fire through it on attackers [Early 17C. < French, < obsolete *embraser* 'widen (a door or window)']

embrittle /im brítt'l/ (**-tles, -tling, -tled**) *vti* to become brittle, or make something become brittle

embrocate /émbrə kayt/ (**-cates, -cating, -cated**) *vt* to rub lotion or liniment onto a part of the body [Early 17C. < Latin *embrocat-*, past participle of *embrocare* 'treat with healing liquid' < late Latin *embroc(h)a* < Greek *embrokhē* 'lotion']

embrocation /émbrə káysh'n/ *n* a lotion or liniment that relieves muscle or joint pain

embroider /im bróydər/ (**-ders, -dering, -dered**) *v* **1.** *vti* DO DECORATIVE NEEDLEWORK to do decorative needlework, or decorate fabric with needlework ○ *embroidering a tablecloth by hand* **2.** *vt* SEW DECORATION ONTO FABRIC to sew a particular pattern onto fabric ○ *embroidered their initials on the towels* **3.** *vti* EMBELLISH STORY to add exaggerated or fictitious details to an account of something to make it more interesting [14C. < Anglo-Norman *enbrouder* < Old French *brouder* 'embroider' < Germanic] —**embroiderer** *n*

embroidery

embroidery /im bróydəri/ (*plural* **-ies**) *n* **1.** ACT OF MAKING DECORATIVE NEEDLEWORK the craft of using needlework to make decorative designs **2.** SOMETHING WITH DECORATIVE NEEDLEWORK something produced by or ornamented with decorative needlework **3.** EMBELLISHMENT OF STORY elaboration or embellishment added to make an account of something more interesting

embroil /im bróyl/ (**-broils, -broiling, -broiled**) *vt* **1.** to involve somebody or yourself in trouble, disagreement, or conflict **2.** to make something

confused or over-complicated [Early 17C. < French *embrouiller* 'confuse, confound' < *brouiller* 'mix confusedly' < Germanic]

embrue *vt* same as **imbrue**

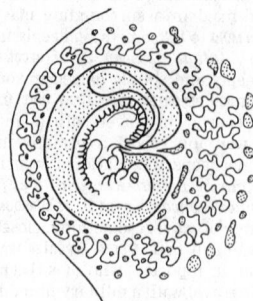

embryo: human embryo

embryo /émbri ō/ (*plural* **-os**) *n* **1.** HUMAN OFFSPRING IN INITIAL DEVELOPMENTAL STAGE a human offspring in the early stages following conception up to the end of the eighth week, after which it is classified as a foetus **2.** ANIMAL IN INITIAL DEVELOPMENTAL STAGE the developing young of an animal from the earliest stages after conception up to birth or hatching **3.** PLANT IN INITIAL DEVELOPMENTAL STAGE a plant in its earliest stages of development. In seed-bearing plants, the embryo is contained within the seed. **4.** EARLY FORM OF SOMETHING an early form or rudimentary stage of something ○ *the embryo of an exciting new invention* [14C. Via Latin < Greek *embruon* < *bruein* 'swell, grow']

embryogenesis /émbri ō jénnəssiss/, **embryogeny** /-ójjini/ *n* the formation and growth of an embryo — **embryogenetic** /-jə néttik/ *adj* —**embryogenic** *adj*

embryology /émbri ólləji/ *n* **1.** the scientific study of embryos and their development **2.** the study of the growth and development of the human embryo and foetus from conception to birth —**embryologic** /-lójjik/ *adj* —**embryological** *adj* —**embryologically** *adv* —**embryologist** *n*

embryonic /émbri ónnik/ *adj* **1.** in an initial or rudimentary stage of development ○ *our embryonic city planning effort* **2.** relating to or characteristic of an embryo —**embryonal** /émbri ən'l/ *adj* —**embryonically** *adv* —**embryotic** /émbri óttik/ *adj*

embryonic membrane *n* a membranous structure, e.g. the amnion, chorion, or yolk sac, that comes from a fertilized ovum but does not become part of the embryo

embryo sac *n* a large oval cell found inside a female reproductive organ (**ovule**) of a flowering plant that contains the egg cell, which gives rise to the embryo and the endosperm nuclei

embryotic *adj* BIOL same as **embryonic** (sense 2)

embryo transfer *n* the transplanting of an embryo from one female animal into the womb of a surrogate mother

embus /im búss/ (**-busses** or **-buses, -bussing** or **-busing, -bussed** or **-bused**) *vti* to put somebody, especially troops, on a bus, or get on a bus

emcee /ém seé/ (*informal*) *n* a person in charge of the proceedings at an event or entertainment. Same as **master of ceremonies** ■ *vti* (**-cees, -ceeing, -ceed**) to act as a master of ceremonies for an event [Mid-20C.< MC² 'master of ceremonies']

em dash *n* in printing, a dash that is one em long

-eme *suffix* a distinctive unit of linguistic structure ○ *lexeme* [< French *-ème* < *phonème* (see PHONEME)]

emend /i ménd/ (**emends, emending, emended**), **emendate** /eé men dayt/ (**-ates, -ating, -ated**) *vt* to correct or alter a text in order to improve it [15C. < Latin *emendare* 'take out a fault' < *menda* 'fault, blemish'] —**emendation** /eé men dáysh'n/ *n* —**emender** *n*

USAGE See *amend*.

emerald /émmərəld/ *n* a precious stone that is a form of beryl coloured green by chromium. Use: gems. ■ *adj, n* COLOURS same as **emerald green** [13C. Directly or via French *émeraude* < medieval Latin *esmeraldus*, alteration

of Latin *smaragdus*, via Greek *smaragdos* 'green gem' < Semitic, 'to shine']

Emerald /émmərəld/ town in southeastern Queensland, Australia. It is an agricultural and mining centre. Population: 13,251 (2002 estimate).

emerald cut *n* a rectangular multifaceted cut for gemstones, especially emeralds and diamonds

emerald green *n* a bright green colour, like that of an emerald —**emerald-green** *adj*

Emerald Isle *n* Ireland, so called because of its vividly green countryside and because the wearing of green was associated with the struggle for national sovereignty

emerge /i múrj/ (**emerges, emerging, emerged**) *v* **1.** *vi* COME OUT to appear out of or from behind something ○ *The butterfly emerges from the chrysalis.* **2.** *vi* SURVIVE to come out of an experience, condition, or situation, especially a difficult one ○ *emerged unscathed from the accident* **3.** *vti* BECOME KNOWN to become known or apparent ○ *It emerged that several officials had accepted bribes.* **4.** *vi* APPEAR OR HAPPEN to arise, appear, or occur ○ *They waited for a new leader to emerge.* [Late 16C. < Latin *emergere* 'rise out or up' < *mergere* 'dive, plunge'] —**emergence** *n*

emergency /i múrjənssi/ *n* (*plural* **-cies**) **1.** SUDDEN CRISIS REQUIRING ACTION an unexpected and sudden event that must be dealt with urgently **2.** *Aus* FOOTBALL RESERVE PLAYER in Australian Rules football, a reserve player who replaces a member of a team who is injured or who has to pull out at the last minute ■ *adj* **1.** USED IN EMERGENCY used or suitable for use in an emergency ○ *emergency funds* **2.** MED FOR IMMEDIATE TREATMENT requiring, providing, or given immediate medical attention ○ *emergency admissions*

emergency brake *n* N Am TRANSP same as **handbrake** (sense 1)

emergency cord *n* N Am same as **communication cord**

emergency department *n* ANZ a hospital department that treats emergency patients who have had accidents or been injured. Same as **accident and emergency**

emergency exit *n* an exit from a building or vehicle that is designed and designated as an escape route in an emergency such as a fire

emergency medicine *n* the branch of medicine dealing with the treatment of patients whose condition requires immediate action

emergency powers *npl* special powers given to a government or other authority to take extraordinary actions in order to cope with a crisis

emergency room *n* N Am HEALTH SERVICES same as **accident and emergency, emergency department**

emergency services *npl* the fire brigade, the police, and the ambulance service collectively, especially when mobilized to deal with emergencies

emergency vehicle *n* an ambulance, fire engine, police car, or other vehicle used by the emergency services

emergent /i múrjənt/ *adj* **1.** UK POL NEWLY INDEPENDENT newly or recently independent as a nation. ANZ, N Am term **emerging 2.** NEW appearing, arising, occurring, or developing, especially for the first time ■ *n* **1.** PLANT WITH UPPER PARTS ABOVE WATER a plant that has its roots under water but its upper part above the surface **2.** TALL TREE a forest tree that stands taller than surrounding trees

emergent evolution *n* a theory of evolution that states that new organisms and characteristics appear at critical turning points and cannot be predicted from those already in existence

emerging /i múrjing/ *adj* **1.** starting to appear, arise, occur, or develop **2.** ANZ, N Am same as **emergent** *adj* (sense 1)

emerging target *n* a target that is selected by military personnel during the course of combat, as opposed to one that has been selected prior to the start of fighting

emerita /i mérritə/ *adj* retired but retaining a professional title, especially as a woman professor (*used of women*) ○ *She's a professor emerita of biology.* ■ *n* (*plural* **-tae** /-teé/) a woman who has retired from a post but retains her former

professional title, especially as a professor [Early 20C. < Latin, form of *emeritus* (see EMERITUS)]

emeritus /i mérritəss/ *adj* retired but retaining a professional title, especially as a professor (*used of men*) ○ *He's a professor emeritus of chemistry.* ■ *n* (*plural* **-ti** /-tī/) a man who has retired from a post but retains his former professional title, especially as a professor [Early 17C. < Latin, past participle of *emerere* 'serve out, earn, deserve' < *merere* 'serve, earn']

emersed /i múrst/ *adj* describes the stems, leaves, or other parts of a water plant that stand above the water surface [Late 17C. < Latin *emersus*, past participle of *emergere* (see EMERGE)]

emersion /i múrsh'n/ *n* 1. the act or process of emerging 2. the reappearance of an astronomical object after it has been eclipsed or occulted

Library of Congress

Ralph Waldo Emerson

Emerson /émmərss'n/, **Ralph Waldo** (1803–82) US essayist, lecturer, and poet. He was a major figure in the philosophical movement known as transcendentalism. His landmark works include *Nature* (1836). —**Emersonian** /émmər sṓni ən/ *adj*

'Whoso would be a man must be a nonconformist.'
[Ralph Waldo Emerson, 'Self-Reliance', *Essays*; 1841]

'History is the action and reaction of these two, nature and thought—two boys pushing each other on the curbstone of the pavement.'
[Ralph Waldo Emerson, 'Fate', *The Conduct of Life*; 1860]

Emerson, Roy (*b.* 1936) Australian tennis player. He holds the record for the most grand slam titles won by a male tennis player, with 12 singles titles and 16 doubles titles (1961–67). Full name **Emerson, Roy Stanley**

emery /émməri/ *n* a variety of the mineral corundum. Use: abrasives. [15C. Via French *émeri* < Italian *smeriglio* < Greek *smuris* 'abrasive powder']

emery board *n* a small strip of card or thin wood coated with powdered emery. Use: filing fingernails.

emery paper *n* a strong paper coated with powdered emery. Use: abrasive for polishing.

emery wheel *n* a wheel coated with powdered emery. Use: abrasive for polishing.

emesis /émmississ/ *n* vomiting (*technical*) [Late 19C. < Greek, < *emein* 'to vomit']

emetic /i méttik/ *adj* causing a person or animal to vomit [Mid-17C. < Greek *emetikos* < *emein* 'to vomit'] —**emetic** *n* —**emetically** *adv*

emetine

emetine /émmə teen, -tin/ *n* a chemical compound extracted from a South American plant (**ipecacuanha**). Use: formerly, to induce vomiting. Formula: $C_{29}H_{40}O_4N_2$.

emf *abbr* PHYS electromotive force

EMF *abbr* 1. PHYS electromotive force 2. ECON European Monetary Fund

EMG *abbr* MED 1. electromyogram 2. electromyograph

-emia *suffix* another spelling of **-aemia**

emic /éemik/ *adj* 1. relating to the analysis of structural and functional elements of language or behaviour 2. relating to the organization and interpretation of data that makes use of the categories of the people being studied. ◊ **etic** [Mid-20C. Shortening of PHONEMIC]

emigrant /émmigrənt/ *n* somebody who leaves a place, especially his or her native country, to go and live elsewhere —**emigrant** *adj*

emigrate /émmi grayt/ (**-grates, -grating, -grated**) *vi* to leave a place, especially a native country, to go and live elsewhere [Late 18C. < Latin *emigrat-*, past participle of *emigrare* 'move away from a place' < *migrare* 'move from place to place'] —**emigration** /émmi gráysh'n/ *n*

émigré /émmi gray, áymi-/ *n* somebody who has moved from their own to another country to live, usually for political reasons [Late 18C. < French, past participle of *émigrer* < Latin *emigrare* (see EMIGRATE)]

Emilia-Romagna /i meéli ə rō máanyə/ region in Northern Italy, on the Adriatic Sea. Capital: Bologna. Population: 3,981,146 (2000). Area: 22,123 sq. km/8,542 sq. mi.

Emin /émmin/, **Tracey** (*b.* 1963) British artist. She uses her personal experience to make highly confessional multimedia works, e.g. *My Bed* (1998).

eminence /émminənss/, **eminency** /-nənssi/ (*plural* **-cies**) *n* 1. HIGH POSITION a position or rank of distinction or superiority 2. HILL a high or raised area of ground (*formal*) 3. ANAT BODY PROJECTION a projecting area of the body, especially a bone

Eminence, Eminency (*plural* **-cies**) *n* in the Roman Catholic Church, a title and form of address for a cardinal

éminence grise /áymi noNss greéz/ (*plural* **éminences grises** /*pronunc. same*/) *n* somebody who exerts great power or influence secretly or unofficially [< French, 'grey eminence', originally nickname of Père Joseph, secretary to Cardinal RICHELIEU]

eminency *n* same as **eminence**

Eminency *n* same as **Eminence**

eminent /émminənt/ *adj* 1. OF HIGH STANDING superior in position, fame, or achievement 2. NOTICEABLE easy to see or notice 3. HIGH in a high or raised position [15C. < Latin *eminent-*, present participle of *eminere* 'stand out, project' < *minere* 'stand, project']

eminent domain *n* the power of a government to take private property for public use, usually with compensation paid to the owner

eminently /émminəntli/ *adv* to a great degree ○ *He is eminently qualified to be a corporate officer.*

emir /e meér, ə meér/, **amir** /ə meér/ *n* 1. in some Islamic countries, an independent ruler, commander, or governor 2. a title for a descendant of the prophet Muhammad [Early 17C. Via French < Arabic *amīr* 'commander']

emirate /émmirət, e meérət/ *n* 1. an area ruled by an emir 2. the rank or office of an emir

emissary /émmissəri/ (*plural* **-ies**) *n* 1. an agent or representative sent on a particular mission 2. a secret agent or spy (*dated*) [Early 17C. < Latin *emissarius* 'somebody sent out' < *emiss-*, past participle of *emittere* (see EMIT)]

emission /i mísh'n/ *n* 1. LETTING SOMETHING OUT the act or process of letting something out or giving something out ○ *the emission of radiation* 2. SOMETHING GIVEN OUT something that is produced or given out ○ *harmful exhaust emissions* 3. PHYS RELEASED ENERGY energy released from a source, usually in the form of electromagnetic radiation 4. PHYSIOL SOMETHING RELEASED FROM BODY a bodily discharge, especially of semen [15C. < Latin *emission-* < *emiss-*, past participle of *emittere* (see EMIT)]

emission nebula *n* a cloud of interstellar gas and dust that emits light when electrons recombine with protons to form hydrogen atoms

emissivity /ímmi sívvəti, émmi-/ (*plural* **-ties**) *n* the ability of a surface to emit radiation, measured as the ratio of the energy radiated by a surface to that radiated by a black body at the same temperature. Symbol v

emit /i mít/ (**emits, emitting, emitted**) *vt* 1. PRODUCE SOMETHING to send or give out something ○ *an oil heater that emits smoke* 2. UTTER SOMETHING to utter a sound ○ *emitted a giggle* 3. PUT MONEY INTO CIRCULATION to put currency into circulation [Early 17C. < Latin *emittere* 'send out' < *mittere* 'send']

emitter /i míttər/ *n* 1. a person or thing that emits something 2. in a transistor, a layer of semiconductor material from which charge carriers such as electrons originate and control the flow of current

Emmanuel *n* BIBLE another spelling of **Immanuel**

Emmental /émmən taal/, **Emmenthal, Emmentaler** /émmən táalər/, **Emmenthaler** *n* a hard cheese of Swiss origin with large holes and a mild nutty flavour [Early 20C. After a region in Switzerland]

emmer /émmər/ *n* a wheat with awns and two grains in each spikelet, cultivated since ancient times. Use: fodder. Native to: Europe, Asia. Latin name: *Triticum dicoccum*. [Early 20C. < German]

emmet /émmit/ *n regional* same as **ant** (*archaic*) [Old English *æmete*, variant of *æmette* (see ANT)]

REGIONAL NOTE See **ant**.

Emmet /émmit/, **Robert** (1778–1803) Irish patriot. He was a member of the nationalist United Irishmen. With French encouragement, he launched an abortive uprising in Ireland in 1803, and was tried and hanged.

'Let no man write my epitaph…When my country takes her place among the nations of the earth, then and not till then let my epitaph be written.'
[Robert Emmet. Quoted in *This Most Distressful Country*, Robert Kee; 1972]

emmetropia /émmi trópi ə/ *n* the condition of the eye in which vision is accurate [Mid-19C. < Greek *emmetros* 'in measure' + *ōps* 'eye'] —**emmetropic** /-tróppik/ *adj*

Emmy /émmi/ (*plural* **-mys**) *n* a statuette awarded annually by the American Academy of Television Arts and Sciences for excellence in television programming, production, or performance [Mid-20C. Origin ?]

emollient /i mólli ənt/ *adj* 1. SOOTHING TO SKIN softening or soothing, especially to the skin 2. CALMING trying to avoid anger and argument by using a calming manner (*formal*) ■ *n* SOOTHING SUBSTANCE a substance that softens or soothes something, especially the skin [Mid-17C. < Latin *emollient-*, present participle of *emollire* 'soften' < *mollis* 'soft']

emolument /i móllyoōmənt/ *n* a payment for work done (*formal*) [15C. < Latin *emolumentum* 'profit, gain', literally 'fee paid for grinding grain' < *emolere* 'grind out']

SYNONYMS See **wage**.

emote /i mṓt/ (**emotes, emoting, emoted**) *vi* to make an exaggerated show of emotions, e.g. in the playing of a dramatic part [Early 20C. Back-formation < EMOTION]

:-)	:-(	I-I	;-)
Happy	Sad	Asleep	Winking
:-))	:-~)	:-*	:-&
Very happy	User has a cold	Blowing a kiss	Tongue tied
(:+(	(-D	:-()	:-O
Scared	Laughing	Talking	Shocked

emoticon

emoticon /i mṓti kon/ *n* an arrangement of keyboard characters intended to convey an emotion, usually viewed sideways [Late 20C. Blend of EMOTION + ICON]

emotion /i mṓsh'n/ *n* **1.** a strong feeling about somebody or something **2.** agitation or disturbance caused by strong feelings [Late 16C. < French, < *émouvoir* 'stir up the feelings of' < Latin *emovere* 'move out, remove' < *movere* 'to move']

emotional /i mṓsh'nəl/ *adj* **1.** EXPRESSING EMOTION relating to or expressing emotion **2.** EASILY AFFECTED BY EMOTIONS being by nature easily affected by or quick to express emotions **3.** AFFECTED BY EMOTION affected or characterized by emotion, especially sadness ○ *an emotional tribute* **4.** STIRRING EMOTIONS arousing or affecting the emotions ○ *that emotional moment when the flag is raised* **5.** INSPIRED BY EMOTION inspired or governed by emotion, and not by reason or willpower ○ *made a hasty and emotional decision* —**emotionality** /i mṓshə nállәti/ *n* —**emotionally** *adv*

emotional blackmail *n* the stirring up of uncomfortable feelings in somebody, especially sympathy or guilt, in order to persuade that person to do something

emotional cripple *n* an insulting term for somebody who has an emotional problem that prevents him or her from expressing feelings and having normal relationships with people (*offensive*)

emotional intelligence *n* personal attributes that enable people to succeed in life, including self-awareness, empathy, self-confidence, and self-control

emotionalise *vt* another spelling of **emotionalize**

emotionalism /i mṓsh'nəlizəm/ *n* **1.** a tendency to be easily swayed by the emotions **2.** an exaggerated or undue display of strong feelings

emotionalist /i mṓsh'nəlist/ *n* **1.** somebody whose thoughts or actions are greatly influenced by the emotions **2.** somebody who is unduly demonstrative

emotionalize /i mṓsh'nə līz/ (**-izes, -izing, -ized**), **emotionalise** (**-ises, -ising, -ised**) *vt* to present or treat something emotionally

emotionless /i mṓsh'n ləss/ *adj* not having or showing emotions —**emotionlessly** *adv* —**emotionlessness** *n*

emotive /i mṓtiv/ *adj* **1.** causing or intended to cause emotion ○ *a highly emotive issue* **2.** showing or characterized by emotion ○ *an emotive plea* [Mid-18C. < Latin *emotus*, past participle of *emovere* (see EMOTION)] —**emotively** *adv* —**emotiveness** *n*

emotivism /i mṓtivizəm/ *n* the philosophical theory that ethical statements are not statements of fact but instead reflect the feelings of the speaker

Emp. *abbr* **1.** Emperor **2.** Empire **3.** Empress

empale *vt* HERALDRY another spelling of **impale**

empanel *vt* LAW same as **impanel**

empathize /émpə thīz/ (**-thizes, -thizing, -thized**), **empathise** (**-thises, -thising, -thised**) *vi* to identify with and understand somebody else's feelings or difficulties ○ *empathized with them in their grief*

empathy /émpəthi/ *n* **1.** the ability to identify with and understand somebody else's feelings or difficulties **2.** the transfer of somebody's own feelings and emotions to an object such as a painting [Early 20C. < Greek *empatheia* 'affection, passion'] —**empathetic** /émpə théttik/ *adj* —**empathetically** *adv* —**empathic** /em páthik/ *adj* —**empathically** *adv*

Empedocles /em péddə kleez/ (490?–430 BC) Sicilian-born Greek philosopher and poet. He believed that matter was composed of the elements of earth, air, fire, and water. Known as **Empedocles of Akragas**

empennage /em pénnij, ómpə naázh/ *n* the tail portion of an aircraft, including the stabilizer, elevator, vertical fin, and rudder [Early 20C. < French, literally 'feathering (of an arrow)' < *empenner* 'to feather' < *penne* 'feather']

~~**emperer**~~ incorrect spelling of **emperor**

emperor /émpərər/ *n* **1.** *also* **Emperor** a man who rules an empire **2.** INSECTS same as **emperor butterfly 3.** INSECTS same as **emperor moth** [12C. Via French < Latin *imperator* 'commander' < *imperare* 'to command' < *parare* 'prepare']

emperor butterfly *n* a brightly coloured butterfly that typically has mottled purple and brownish markings. Family: Nymphalidae. [< imperial associations of purple]

emperor moth *n* a large brightly coloured moth with distinctive markings resembling eyes on its wings. Native to: Europe, Asia. Latin name: *Saturnia pyri*. [< its large size]

emperor penguin *n* the largest of the penguins, with bluish-grey and black feathers, a white chest, and yellowish-orange neck markings. It nurtures its young between its feet and a pouch-shaped fold in its abdomen. Native to: Antarctica. Latin name: *Aptenodytes forsteri*. [< its large size]

emphasis /émfəssiss/ (*plural* **-phases** /-fə seez/) *n* **1.** IMPORTANCE special importance, significance, or stress ○ *puts emphasis on exercise* **2.** FORCEFULNESS OF EXPRESSION forcefulness of expression to indicate the importance of something ○ *Your opening paragraph needs greater emphasis to grab the reader's attention.* **3.** EXTRA SPOKEN STRESS ON IMPORTANT WORD extra stress of voice put on a syllable, word, or phrase, usually to show its significance [Late 16C. Via Latin < Greek, 'significance, appearance' < *emphainein* 'to show, indicate' < *phainein* 'to show']

emphasize /émfə sīz/ (**-sizes, -sizing, -sized**), **emphasise** (**-sises, -sising, -sised**) *vt* to stress or give importance to something

emphatic /im fáttik/ *adj* **1.** WITH EMPHASIS expressed, thought, or done with emphasis **2.** DEFINITE forcible and definite ○ *an emphatic refusal* **3.** GRAM SHOWING EMPHASIS GRAMMATICALLY describes a grammatical form that shows emphasis, e.g. the auxiliary 'do' in the statement 'I do like apples' [Early 18C. Via late Latin < Greek *emphatikos* < *emphasis* (see EMPHASIS)]

emphatically /im fáttikli, em-/ *adv* **1.** with great force or definiteness **2.** used to reinforce the accuracy or appropriateness of a description ○ *It might be entertainment, but it is emphatically not education.*

emphysema /émfə seémə, -zeémə/ *n* **1.** a chronic medical disorder of the lungs in which the air sacs are dilated or enlarged and lack flexibility, so that breathing is impaired and infection sometimes occurs **2.** an unusual enlargement of an organ or body tissue caused by retention of air or other gas [Mid-17C. Via late Latin < Greek *emphusēma* 'swelling' < *emphusan* 'inflate' < *phusan* 'blow'] —**emphysematous** /émfə sémmətəss, -seém-, -zémm-, -zeém-/ *adj* —**emphysemic** *adj*

empire /ém pīr/ *n* **1.** LANDS RULED BY SINGLE AUTHORITY a group of nations, territories, or peoples ruled by a single authority, especially an emperor or empress **2.** MONARCHY HEADED BY EMPEROR OR EMPRESS a monarchy that has an emperor or empress as its ruler **3.** PERIOD OF EMPIRE'S EXISTENCE the period during which an empire exists **4.** LARGE FAR-FLUNG BUSINESS a very large, powerful, and extensive industrial or commercial organization **5.** PART OF ORGANIZATION SOMEBODY PERSONALLY CONTROLS a part of an organization controlled by a single person, especially somebody who is keenly protective of personal power **6.** ABSOLUTE POWER supreme or absolute power (*formal or literary*) [13C. Via French < Latin *imperium* 'command' < *imperare* (see EMPEROR)]

Empire /ém pīr/ *adj* relating to a style of architecture, furniture, and clothing popular during the French First Empire (1804–15) during the reign of Napoleon I

empire-building *n* the practice of attempting to acquire greater power and authority within an organization, especially by adding extra staff or subordinates —**empire-builder** *n*

Empire Day *n* CALENDAR former name for **Commonwealth Day** (until 1958)

Empire gown *n* a woman's dress popular during the French First Empire, characterized by a low-cut neckline and a high waist from which the skirt hangs straight and loose

Empire State Building *n* a skyscraper on Fifth Avenue in New York City built between 1930 and 1931. It has 102 storeys and was the tallest building in the world for 40 years.

empiric /em pírrik, im-/ *n* **1.** somebody who exclusively relies upon observation and experiment to determine the truth about something **2.** a charlatan or quack, especially in medicine (*archaic*) [Mid-16C. < Latin *empiricus* < Greek *empeirikos* 'experienced' < *empeiros* 'skilled' < *peira* 'trial']

empirical /em pírrik'l/ *adj* **1.** BASED ON OBSERVATION AND EXPERIMENT based on or characterized by observation and experiment instead of theory **2.** PHILOSOPHY DERIVED SOLELY FROM EXPERIENCE derived as knowledge from experience, particularly from sensory observation, and not derived from the application of logic **3.** MED BASED ON PRACTICAL MEDICAL EXPERIENCE based on practical experience in the medical treatment of real cases, and not on applied theory or scientific proof —**empirically** *adv*

empirical formula *n* a chemical formula showing the relative proportion of elements in a compound instead of their structural arrangement or molecular weights, e.g. the formula H_2O

empiricism /em pírrissízəm/ *n* **1.** APPLICATION OF OBSERVATION AND EXPERIMENT the application of observation and experiment, and not theory, in determining something **2.** PHILOSOPHY PHILOSOPHICAL BELIEF REGARDING SENSE-DERIVED KNOWLEDGE the philosophical belief that all knowledge is derived from the experience of the senses **3.** MED MEDICINE BASED SOLELY ON EXPERIENCE medicine that is based on practical experience, and not on theory or scientific proof —**empiricist** *n*

emplace /im pláyss/ (**-places, -placing, -placed**) *vt* to put something into place or position [Mid-19C. Back-formation < EMPLACEMENT]

emplacement /im pláyssmənt/ *n* **1.** a position that is specially prepared for a large gun or group of guns **2.** the act of putting something into place or position, or the condition of being in place or position [Early 19C. < French, literally 'placing in' < *place* 'place']

emplane /im pláyn/ (**-planes, -planing, -planed**) *vti UK, Can* TRANSP to board or allow somebody to board an aircraft. ANZ, US term **enplane**

employ /im plóy/ *vt* (**-ploys, -ploying, -ployed**) **1.** GIVE PAID WORK TO SOMEBODY to hire somebody to work in exchange for money **2.** KEEP SOMEBODY BUSY to keep somebody occupied doing something **3.** USE SOMETHING to make use of something ■ *n* **1.** EMPLOYED STATE the condition of working for pay (*formal*) ○ *I was in his employ for several years.* **2.** JOB a job or occupation (*archaic*) [15C. Via French *emploier* 'apply' < Latin *implicare* 'involve, enfold' < *plicare* 'to fold'] —**employability** /im plóy ə bíllәti/ *n* —**employable** *adj*

SYNONYMS See *use*.

employee /im plóy ee, ém ploy eé/ *n* a paid worker

employee association *n* a social or professional organization of employees who have the same employer

employer /im plóy ər/ *n* **1.** a person, business, or organization that engages and pays one or more workers **2.** somebody who uses something

employers' association *n* an organization of employers, usually working in a similar area, that provides support for its members and negotiates in industrial disputes

employment /im plóymənt/ *n* **1.** WORKING FOR PAY the condition of working for pay **2.** WORK OR JOB DONE BY SOMEBODY the work, especially paid work, that somebody does **3.** NUMBER OF PAID WORKERS IN POPULATION the total number of people who work for pay in a particular population ○ *falling employment in manufacturing* **4.** USE OF SOMETHING the use of, or practice of doing, something ○ *their employment of ritual to promote a group identity* ○ *engaged in her usual employment of playing solitaire*

employment agency *n* a commercial organization that finds jobs for people or people for jobs

emporium /em páwri əm/ (*plural* **-riums** or **-ria** /-ri ə/) *n* a shop, usually a large one, that offers a wide selection of goods [Late 16C. Via Latin < Greek *emporion* < *emporos* 'merchant, traveller' < *poros* 'journey']

empower /im pów ər/ (**-ers, -ering, -ered**) *vt* **1.** to give somebody power or authority (*often passive*) **2.** to give somebody a greater sense of confidence or self-esteem —**empowerment** *n*

empress /émprəss/, **Empress** *n* **1.** a woman who rules an empire **2.** the wife or widow of an emperor [12C. < Old French *empresse* < *emperor* (see EMPEROR)]

empressement /oN préss moN/ *n* great attentiveness or cordiality (*literary*) [Early 18C. < French, < *empresser* 'urge, be eager' < *presser* (see PRESS [1])]

emprise /em príz/ n (formal) **1.** a chivalrous, brave, or daring undertaking **2.** chivalrous skill or daring [13C. < Old French, < French emprendre, literally 'seize into' < Latin prendere 'seize']

empty /émpti/ adj (-tier, -tiest) **1.** CONTAINING NOTHING not containing or holding anything ○ a heap of empty packets **2.** UNFED hungry or lacking food ○ can't work on an empty stomach **3.** UNOCCUPIED unoccupied or uninhabited ○ There's an empty office next door. **4.** WITH NO PASSENGERS OR LOAD without passengers, a load, or cargo ○ The bus goes back to the depot empty. **5.** INSINCERE lacking sincerity or truthfulness ○ another empty promise **6.** MEANINGLESS without value, meaning, or purpose ○ contemplating his empty existence **7.** DULL devoid of vitality ○ an empty look **8.** MATHS, LOGIC WITHOUT SET MEMBERS describes a set that has no elements or members ■ v (-ties, -tying, -tied) **1.** vt REMOVE THE CONTENTS OF SOMETHING to remove or pour out the contents of something ○ emptied his pockets **2.** vti DISCHARGE OR TRANSFER to discharge or transfer something, or be discharged and transferred ○ The stream empties into the lake. **3.** empty yourself vr UNBURDEN YOURSELF to unburden or free yourself of something ○ empty yourself of feeling ■ n (plural -ties) CONTAINER WITHOUT CONTENTS a bottle or other container that has nothing in it [Old English æmtig 'unoccupied, at leisure' < æmetta 'rest, leisure'. Origin ?] —**emptily** adv —**emptiness** n

SYNONYMS See vacant.

empty-handed adj **1.** with nothing gained or achieved ○ came back from the negotiations empty-handed **2.** holding nothing in the hands

empty-headed adj regarded as lacking in intelligence or seriousness

empty nester n a parent whose children have grown up and moved away from home (informal)

empty-nest syndrome n distress, especially a lack of energy or an emotional letdown, experienced by a parent whose grown children have moved away from home

empyema /ém pī éemǝ/ n an accumulation of pus in a body cavity such as the chest [Early 17C. Via late Latin < Greek empuēma < empuein 'put pus in' < puon 'pus'] —**empyemic** adj

empyreal /ém pī rée ǝl, em pírri ǝl/ adj **1.** relating to the sky, the celestial sphere, or heaven **2.** glorious and sublime (literary) [15C. < medieval Latin empyreus (see EMPYREAN)]

empyrean /ém pī rée ǝn, em pírri ǝn/ n **1.** the sky or celestial sphere (literary) **2.** the highest part of heaven, believed in ancient Greek and Roman times to contain pure fire or light and believed by some Christians to be the dwelling place of God (archaic) ■ adj same as **empyreal** (sense 1) [15C. < medieval Latin empyreus < Greek empurios 'in fire' < pur 'fire']

EMS abbr **1.** E-COMMERCE electronics manufacturing services **2.** HEALTH SERVICES emergency medical services **3.** FIN European Monetary System

emu

emu /ée myoo/ n (plural **emus** or **same**) n a large flightless bird that is related to the ostrich and has three-toed feet and loose shaggy feathers. Native to: Australia. Latin name: Dromaius novaehollandiae. [Early 17C. < Portuguese ema]

EMU abbr **1.** also **emu** or **e.m.u.** PHYS electromagnetic unit **2.** /ée em yoo, ée myoo/ ECON European Monetary Union

emu bush n a plant whose small fruits are sometimes eaten by emus. Native to: Australia. Genus: Eremophila.

emulate /émyoo layt/ (-lates, -lating, -lated) vt **1.** TRY TO EQUAL SOMEBODY OR SOMETHING to try to equal or surpass somebody or something that is successful or admired **2.** COMPETE SUCCESSFULLY WITH SOMEBODY OR SOMETHING to be successful in comparison with somebody or something else ○ emulates the achievement of better-funded ventures **3.** COMPUT MODIFY TO IMITATE ANOTHER COMPUTER SYSTEM to modify a computer system so that it appears to behave like another computer system, and can thereby accept data and run programs that are designed for the system being emulated [Late 16C. < Latin aemulat-, past participle of aemulari 'to rival' < aemulus 'rival'] —**emulation** /émyoo láysh'n/ n —**emulative** adj

SYNONYMS See imitate.

emulator /émyoo laytǝr/ n **1.** somebody or something that emulates another person or thing **2.** a piece of hardware or software that permits a computer system to run programs and process data designed for a different type of computer system. ◊ **simulator** (sense 1)

emulous /émyoolǝss/ adj **1.** seeking to match or rival another's achievement or performance **2.** motivated or characterized by rivalry or imitation [14C. < Latin aemulus 'rival'] —**emulously** adv —**emulousness** n

emulsifier /i múlssi fī ǝr/ n a chemical agent that maintains or creates an emulsion. It is used especially as a food additive.

emulsify /i múlssi fī/ (-fies, -fying, -fied) vti to convert two or more liquids into an emulsion, or become an emulsion —**emulsifiable** /i múlssi fī ǝb'l, i múlssi fī ǝb'l/ adj —**emulsification** /i múlssifi káysh'n/ n

emulsion /i múlsh'n/ n **1.** SUSPENSION OF LIQUID WITHIN ANOTHER LIQUID a suspension of one liquid in another, e.g. oil in water or fat in milk **2.** WATER-BASED PAINT WITH MATT FINISH a water-based paint that usually has a matt finish. Use: interior decorating. **3.** PHOTOGRAPHY LIGHT-SENSITIVE PHOTOGRAPHIC COATING a thin light-sensitive coating of silver bromide or silver halide in a medium such as gelatin on a photographic plate, paper, or film [Early 17C. < Latin emuls-, past participle of emulgere 'milk out' < mulgere 'to milk'] —**emulsive** adj

emunctory /i múngktǝri/ (plural -ries) n a body part or organ that removes waste products from the body, e.g. the kidneys, lungs, or skin [14C. < medieval Latin emunctorius < Latin emungere 'blow the nose thoroughly' < mungere 'blow the nose']

en /en/ n a measure of printing width, half that of an em [Late 18C. Representing pronunciation of N [1]; because the letter is about this width]

EN abbr HEALTH SERVICES enrolled nurse

en- prefix **1.** to put or go into, or cover with ○ entomb ○ encamp ○ enfold **2.** to provide with ○ enlighten **3.** to cause to be ○ enlarge **4.** thoroughly ○ enmesh **5.** in, within, into ○ enzootic [Via French < Latin in 'in']

-en suffix **1.** to cause to be or have ○ brighten ○ strengthen **2.** to come to be or have ○ tauten ○ lengthen **3.** made of or resembling ○ wooden [Old English < Germanic]

enable /in áyb'l/ (-bles, -bling, -bled) vt **1.** PROVIDE SOMEBODY WITH MEANS to provide somebody with the resources, authority, or opportunity to do something **2.** MAKE SOMETHING POSSIBLE to make something possible or feasible ○ enabling legislation **3.** GIVE SOMEBODY OR SOMETHING LEGAL AUTHORITY to confer legal power or authority on somebody or something **4.** CAUSE SOMETHING TO START TO OPERATE to make a piece of equipment or computer system functional —**enablement** n —**enabler** n

enabling /in áybling/ adj conferring new legal powers

enact /in ákt/ (-acts, -acting, -acted) vt **1.** to make proposed legislation into law **2.** to perform or relate something using acting —**enactable** adj —**enactive** adj —**enactor** n

enactment /in áktmǝnt/ n **1.** the act or process of enacting something **2.** something that is enacted, especially a law

enalapril /i nállǝ pril/ n an ACE inhibitor drug. Use: temporary management of high blood pressure.

enamal incorrect spelling of **enamel**

enamel /i námm'l/ n **1.** GLASSY DECORATIVE OR PROTECTIVE COATING a glassy decorative or protective coating, usually coloured and opaque, that is fused onto metal, glass, or ceramics **2.** SOMETHING WITH ENAMEL COATING something that is coated with enamel **3.** PAINT WITH SHINY FINISH a paint that gives a shiny smooth finish when dry ○ nail enamel **5.** DENT HARD LAYER ON TOOTH a hard thin calcium-containing layer that covers and protects the crown of a tooth ■ vt (-els, -elling, -elled) **1.** COAT SOMETHING WITH ENAMEL to decorate or coat all or part of an object with enamel **2.** APPLY BRIGHT SHINY SURFACE TO SOMETHING to apply a shiny brightly coloured surface to something [14C. < Anglo-Norman enamailler 'to enamel in' < Old French esmail 'enamel' < Germanic, 'melting'] —**enameller** n

enamelling /i námm'ling/ n **1.** the process of applying enamel to something **2.** the surface of something coated with enamel

enamelware /i námm'l wair/ n household utensils coated with enamel

enamelwork /i námm'l wurk/ n HANDICRAFT same as **enamelling** (sense 2)

enamor vt US spelling of **enamour**

enamour /in ámmǝr/ (-ours, -ouring, -oured) vt (formal or literary) **1.** to inspire somebody with love or passion **2.** to charm, fascinate, or captivate somebody [13C. < Old French enamourer < en- 'cause to' + amour 'love']

enamoured /in ámmǝrd/ adj **1.** inspired with love or passion for somebody **2.** charmed, fascinated, or captivated by somebody or something ○ I wasn't greatly enamoured of her playing.

USAGE The right preposition: Although **enamoured** is quite similar in meaning to in love and smitten, it takes a different preposition. Compare: He is enamoured of her with She is in love with him and They are smitten with [or by] each other.

enantiomorph /i nánti ǝ mawrf/, **enantiomer** /-ǝmǝr/ n either of a pair of molecules that are mirror images of each other in structure but cannot be superimposed [Late 19C. < Greek enantios 'opposite'] —**enantiomorphic** /i nánti ǝ máwrfik/ adj —**enantiomorphism** n —**enantiomorphous** /i nánti ǝ máwrfǝss/ adj

enantioselective /i nánti ō si léktiv/ adj CHEM same as **stereoselective** [Late 20C. < Greek enantios 'opposite']

enarch vt BOT same as **inarch**

enate /ée nayt/ adj also **enatic** /ee náttik/ related through the mother ■ n somebody related on the mother's side [Mid-17C. < Latin enatus, past participle of enasci 'issue out, be born']

enation /ee náysh'n/ n a small outgrowth on an organ, especially on a leaf, caused by a virus infection [Mid-19C. < Latin enation- < enasci 'issue out, be born']

enc abbr **1.** enclosed **2.** enclosure

encaenia /en séeni ǝ/ n an event commemorating or dedicating an institution or community, e.g. a university, church, or city (formal) [14C. Via Latin < Greek egkainia 'dedication festival' < en 'in' + kainos 'new']

encage /in káyj/ (-cages, -caging, -caged) vt to confine somebody or something in a cage or in something resembling a cage (literary)

encamp /in kámp/ (-camps, -camping, -camped) v **1.** vi to lodge in a camp **2.** vt to provide somebody with lodging in a camp

encampment /in kámpmǝnt/ n **1.** CAMPSITE a place occupied by a camp **2.** STAYING IN CAMP residence in a camp **3.** MAKING CAMP the setting up of a camp

encapsulate /in kápsyoo layt/ (-lates, -lating, -lated), **incapsulate** v **1.** vt to express something in concise form **2.** vti to enclose something completely, or be enclosed completely —**encapsulation** /in kápsyoo láysh'n/ n —**encapsulator** n

encapsulated /in kápsyoo laytid/ adj describes an organ or tumour covered by a thin protective membrane

encase /in káyss/ (-cases, -casing, -cased) vt to

surround something completely with a case or cover —**encasement** n

encash /in kásh/ (-cashes, -cashing, -cashed) vt to convert a cheque or bond into cash —**encashable** adj —**encashment** n

encaustic /in káwstik, -kóstik/ adj having pigments mixed with wax applied to a surface by heat ■ n an object or work of art whose colours are fused to a surface by the application of heat, especially an earthenware tile decorated with an inlaid design in the style of medieval floor tiles [Late 16C. Via Latin < Greek egkaustikos < egkaiein 'burn in']

enceinte[1] /on sánt/ adj having a child developing in the womb (used euphemistically) [Early 17C. Via French < medieval Latin incincta 'not girded' < Latin cincta 'girded']

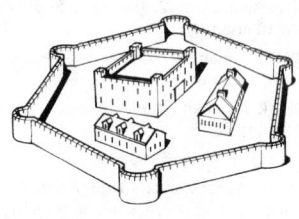

enceinte

enceinte[2] /on sánt/ n 1. a defensive wall or enclosure 2. a place protected by a defensive wall or enclosure [Early 18C. Via French < Latin incincta, past participle of incingere 'gird in']

Enceladus /en séllədəss/ n a small natural satellite of Saturn, discovered in 1789. It is 498 km/309 mi. in diameter and occupies an intermediate orbit.

encephal- prefix same as **encephalo-** (used before vowels)

encephalic /én si fállik, -ki-/ adj related to the brain or its location within the cranium [Mid-19C. < Greek egkephalos 'brain' (see ENCEPHALO-)]

encephalin n BIOCHEM another spelling of **enkephalin**

encephalitis /en séffə lítiss, -kéffə-/ n inflammation of the brain, usually caused by a viral infection —**encephalitic** /-líttik/ adj

encephalitis lethargica /-li thaárjikə/ n MED same as **sleeping sickness** (sense 2) (technical) [< modern Latin, 'sleepy encephalitis']

encephalo- prefix brain ○ encephalogram [Via modern Latin < Greek egkephalos 'brain' < en 'in' + kephalē 'head']

encephalogram /en séffələ gram, -kéffələ-/ n 1. an X-ray photograph of the brain 2. MED same as **electroencephalogram**

encephalograph /en séffələ graaf, -graf, -kéffələ-/ n MED 1. same as **encephalogram** (sense 1) 2. same as **electroencephalograph** —**encephalography** /en séffə lóggrəfi, -kéffə-/ n

encephalomyelitis /en séffələ mī ə lítiss, -kéffə-/ n inflammation of the brain and spinal cord —**encephalomyelitic** /-mī ə líttik/ adj

encephalon /en séffə lon, -kéffə-/ (plural -la /-lə/) n the brain of a vertebrate [Mid-18C. < Greek egkephalon 'what is inside the head' < kephalē 'head'] —**encephalous** adj

encephalopathy /en séffə lóppəthi, -kéffə-/ n a disease of the brain —**encephalopathic** /en séffələ páthik, -kéffələ-/ adj

enchain /in cháyn, en-/ (-chains, -chaining, -chained) vt 1. to bind somebody or something with chains (formal or literary) 2. to dominate somebody's attention or thoughts (literary) [14C. < French enchaîner < Latin catenare 'to chain'] —**enchainment** n

enchant /in cháant/ (-chants, -chanting, -chanted) vt 1. to charm, delight, or captivate somebody 2. to cast a spell on somebody or something [14C. Via French < Latin incantare 'chant a magic formula upon' < cantare 'sing'] —**enchanted** adj —**enchanter** n

enchanter's nightshade n a woodland plant with bristly fruits. Native to: northern hemisphere.

Flowers: small, white. Latin name: Circaea lutetiana.

enchanting /in cháanting/ adj captivating or delightful —**enchantingly** adv

enchantment /in cháantmənt/ n 1. STATE OF BEING ENCHANTED the act or condition of being enchanted 2. CHARM something that delights or captivates 3. SPELL a magic spell

enchantress /in cháantrəss/ n 1. a woman who is charming or delightful 2. a woman who casts spells

enchase /in cháyss/ (-chases, -chasing, -chased) vt 1. to set jewellery or other decorative objects with gems 2. to emboss, engrave, or carve designs on metal [15C. < French enchasser 'set (gems), encase' < chasse 'case, box']

enchilada /én chi laádə/ n a fried tortilla rolled around a savoury filling and served hot with a usually spicy sauce [Late 19C. < Mexican Spanish < past participle of enchilar 'season with chilli']

enchiridion /én kī ríddi ən/ (plural -ons or -a /-di ə/) n a manual or handbook (archaic) [Mid-16C. Via late Latin < Greek egkheiridion 'small thing in the hand' < kheir 'hand']

-enchyma suffix cellular tissue ○ aerenchyma [< PARENCHYMA]

encipher /in sífər/ (-phers, -phering, -phered) vt to convert a text into code or cipher —**encipherer** n —**encipherment** n

encircle /in súrk'l/ (-cles, -cling, -cled) vt 1. to form a circle around somebody or something 2. to move in a circle around somebody or something —**encirclement** n —**encircling** adj

Encke /éngkə/, Johann Franz (1791–1865) German astronomer. His significant research into the orbits of comets was rewarded posthumously when a comet was given his name.

encl. abbr 1. enclosed 2. enclosure

enclasp /in klaásp/ (-clasps, -clasping, -clasped) vt to embrace or hold somebody or something tightly (formal)

enclave /én klayv, ón-/ n 1. a small country or territory that is culturally or ethnically different from a surrounding larger and distinct political unit. ◊ **exclave** 2. a distinct group that lives or operates together within a larger community [Mid-19C. < French < Old French enclaver 'enclose' < Latin in 'in' + clavis 'key']

enclitic /in klíttik/ adj describes a word that depends on a preceding word for its formation or pronunciation [Mid-17C. Via late Latin < Greek egklitikos < egklinein 'lean on'] —**enclitic** n

enclose /in klóz/ (-closes, -closing, -closed), **inclose** vt 1. SURROUND SOMETHING to surround or shut in something 2. INSERT SOMETHING IN ENVELOPE OR PACKAGE to add something to the contents of an envelope or package 3. FENCE IN LAND OR BUILDING to surround land or a building with a fence, wall, or other boundary [14C. < Old French enclos, past participle of enclore < Latin includere 'shut in' (see INCLUDE)] —**enclosable** adj —**enclosed** adj

enclosed order n a Christian religious community whose members remain physically within it

enclosure /in klózhər/, **inclosure** n 1. LAND SURROUNDED BY BOUNDARY an area of land surrounded by a fence, wall, or other boundary 2. BOUNDARY FENCE a fence, wall, or other boundary surrounding something 3. SOMETHING INSIDE LETTER something extra enclosed in a letter or package 4. RESERVED AREA AT SPORTS EVENT an area of ground at a sports event set aside for specific spectators or competitors 5. ACT OF ENCLOSING LAND the act or process of enclosing land to prevent general use 6. HIST COMMON LAND TAKEN AS PRIVATE PROPERTY between the 12th and 19th centuries, the appropriation of land in England and Scotland, especially common land, so that it could be fenced or hedged as private property 7. CHR RESTRICTED PART OF CONVENT OR MONASTERY the part of a convent or monastery, especially the living quarters, that is restricted to members

encode /in kṓd/ (-codes, -coding, -coded) vt 1. CONVERT TEXT TO CODE to convert a message from plain text into code 2. COMPUT CONVERT COMPUTER CHARACTERS INTO DIGITAL FORM to convert input data such as analogue signals, characters, and commands into a digital form recognizable by a computer 3. GENETICS PROVIDE GENETIC

INFORMATION to carry the genetic information that enables a polypeptide, RNA molecule, or one of their constituent groups to be produced —**encodement** n

encomia plural of **encomium**

encomiast /en kṓmi ast/ n a speaker or writer of an encomium (formal) [Early 17C. < Greek egkōmiastēs < egkōmiazein 'to praise' < egkōmion (see ENCOMIUM)]

encomium /en kṓmi əm/ (plural -miums or -mia /-mi ə/) n (formal) 1. a formal text that expresses high praise for somebody 2. an expression of high praise [Mid-16C. Via Latin < Greek egkōmion 'eulogy' < kōmos 'revel']

encompass /in kúmpəss/ (-passes, -passing, -passed) vt 1. INCLUDE MUCH to include a wide or comprehensive range ○ The ceremony will encompass contributions from many parts of the world. 2. ENCIRCLE SOMETHING to surround, envelop, or encircle something 3. CAUSE SOMETHING TO OCCUR to cause or bring about something (formal) —**encompassment** n

encore /óng kawr/ n EXTRA OR REPEATED PERFORMANCE an additional or repeated performance of something in response to a demand from an audience ■ interj USED TO DEMAND REPEAT PERFORMANCE used to demand an additional or repeated performance of something ■ vt (-cores, -coring, -cored) ADD TO OR REPEAT PERFORMANCE to give an additional or repeated performance of something [Early 18C. < French, 'still, again']

encounter /in kówntər/ vt (-ters, -tering, -tered) 1. COME UP AGAINST SOMETHING to be faced with something difficult to deal with ○ We don't expect to encounter any major problems. 2. MEET SOMEBODY UNEXPECTEDLY to meet somebody or something, usually unexpectedly and briefly ○ I encountered the girl for the first time in 1993. 3. MEET SOMEBODY IN CONFLICT to confront somebody with hostility or aggression ■ n 1. UNEXPECTED MEETING a meeting with somebody or something, usually unexpected and brief 2. CONFRONTATION a hostile confrontation or difficult struggle [13C. < Old French encontrer 'confront' < late Latin incontra 'in front of' < Latin in- 'in' + contra 'against']

encounter group n a small group of people, often guided by a leader, who meet in order to achieve personal growth, self-awareness, and social skills by means of emotional expression and interaction

encourage /in kúrrij/ (-ages, -aging, -aged) vt 1. GIVE SOMEBODY HOPE OR CONFIDENCE to give somebody hope, confidence, or courage 2. URGE SOMEBODY TO DO SOMETHING to motivate somebody to take a course of action or continue doing something ○ encouraged me to finish the course 3. FOSTER SOMETHING to assist something to occur or increase ○ encourage new solutions to traffic problems [15C. < French encoragier < en- 'cause' + corage 'courage'] —**encouraging** adj —**encouragingly** adv

encouragement /in kúrrijmənt/ n 1. support of a kind that inspires confidence and a will to continue or develop 2. somebody who or something that gives somebody hope, confidence, or courage

encroach /in króch/ (-croaches, -croaching, -croached) vi 1. to intrude gradually or stealthily, often taking away somebody's authority, rights, or property ○ is encroaching on civil liberties 2. to exceed the proper limits of something [14C. < Old French encrochier 'seize' < croc 'hook' < Old Norse krókr] —**encroacher** n —**encroachingly** adv —**encroachment** n

en croute /oN króot/ adj, adv enclosed in a pastry crust ○ salmon en croute [Late 20C. < French en croûte 'in a crust']

encrust /in krúst/ (-crusts, -crusting, -crusted), **incrust** vt (often passive) 1. to cover something with a hard thick coating 2. to embellish something richly, especially with jewels [Early 17C. Via French < Latin incrustare < in- 'upon' + crusta 'crust']

encrustation /ín krust áysh'n/, **incrustation** n 1. the act of encrusting something, or the state of being encrusted 2. a hard thick coating or covering

encrypt /in krípt/ (-crypts, -crypting, -crypted) vt 1. to convert a text into code or cipher 2. to convert computer data and messages into something incomprehensible using a key, so that only a holder of the matching key can reconvert them —**encryption** /-krípsh'n/ n

enculturation /en kúlchə ráysh'n/ n the gradual acceptance by a person or group of the standards and practices of another person or culture —**enculturative** /en kúlchərətiv/ adj

encumber /in kúmbər/ (**-bers, -bering, -bered**), **incumber** *vt* **1.** to hamper or impede somebody or something **2.** to burden or weigh down somebody or something (*often passive*) [14C. < Old French *encombrer* 'obstruct' < *combre* 'barrier']

encumbrance /in kúmbrənss/ *n* **1.** a hindrance or burden to somebody **2.** a charge or claim on property, especially a mortgage

encumbrancer /in kúmbrənssər/ *n* somebody who has a legal claim on property, especially a mortgage

encyclical /en síklik'l/ *n* in the Roman Catholic Church, a formal statement issued by the pope to bishops, often on matters of doctrine [Mid-17C. < Greek *egkuklios* 'circular, general' < *kuklos* 'circle']

encyclopaedia, etc. another spelling of **encyclopedia, etc.**

encyclopedia /in sîklə peédi ə/, **encyclopaedia** *n* a reference work offering comprehensive information on all or specialized areas of knowledge [Mid-16C. < Greek *egkuklopaideia* 'general education' < *egkuklios* (see ENCYCLICAL) + *paideia* 'education' < *pais* 'boy, child']

encyclopedic /in sîklə peédik/, **encyclopaedic** *adj* covering or including a broad range of detailed knowledge such as is found in an encyclopedia —**encyclopedically** *adv*

encyclopedism /in sîklə peédizəm/, **encyclopaedism** *n* comprehensive learning or knowledge

encyclopedist /in sîklə peédist/, **encyclopaedist** *n* a compiler of or contributor to an encyclopedia

Encyclopedist *n* a writer or editor of the *Encyclopédie* (1751–72), a French reference work in which the advanced secular, technical, and political ideas of the period were articulated

encyst /en síst/ (**-cysts, -cysting, -cysted**) *vti* to enclose or be enclosed in a cyst —**encystation** /énsiss táysh'n/ *n* —**encysted** *adj* —**encystment** *n*

end[1] /end/ *n* **1.** EXTREMITY OF OBJECT the tip or extremity of a long narrow object ○ *I'm surprised he knows which end to hold the mike.* **2.** EXTREMITY OR LIMIT the limit, extent, or boundary of something ○ *They walked the valley from end to end.* ○ *at both ends of the political spectrum* **3.** FINAL PART the final part or finishing point of a period of time, of an event, or of a book, film, or other work ○ *His address is at the end of the article.* ○ *the end of the lesson* **4.** TERMINATION the act or result of stopping something ○ *a scandal that brought his career to an abrupt end* **5.** GOAL a goal, object, or purpose ○ *for purely political ends* **6.** PART OF COMMUNICATIONS LINK either of the places connected by a communications link ○ *Pick up the phone and find out who's on the other end.* **7.** DEATH the experience of death ○ *met an untimely end* **8.** LEFTOVER PIECE a piece or part of something that is left over **9.** SHARE OF JOINT RESPONSIBILITY a part or portion of shared responsibility ○ *Are you sure they'll honour their end of the deal?* **10.** SPORTS AREA ON PLAYING FIELD the area at each end of a playing field **11.** AMERICAN FOOTBALL PLAYER POSITIONED AT END OF LINE in American football, a player positioned at each end of the offensive or defensive line ■ *v* (**ends, ending, ended**) **1.** *vti* STOP to reach, or bring something to, a close or a final point ○ *She abruptly ended the meeting.* ○ *The meeting ended without an agreement being made.* **2.** *vi* STOP AT A PLACE to reach a particular place and stop there ○ *The road ends at a little village called Monkton.* [Old English *ende* < Indo-European, 'front'] ◇ **an end in itself** something that is worth having or doing although it may not lead to anything ○ *A friendship should be satisfying; it is an end in itself and not a means to an end.* ◇ **at a loose end** having no purpose or occupation ○ *With all her work done, she found herself at a loose end.* ◇ **at loose ends** *N Am* at a loose end ◇ **at the end of the day** after everything has been taken into consideration ○ *You can give them as much advice as you like, but at the end of the day they'll have to decide for themselves.* ◇ **come to** *or* **meet a sticky** *or* **bad end** to have an unpleasant or unfortunate outcome, especially a violent death (*informal*) ◇ **end for end** *US* reversed or inverted ○ *They turned the boxes end for end.* ◇ **end it all** to commit suicide ◇ **end on 1.** in such a way that an object's end piece or section is flush with a flat surface ○ *Set the desk end on to the wall.* **2.** *US* with the end facing or next to something ○ *The plane crash-landed, its tail section end on to the runway.* ◇ **end to end** in a row with the ends adjacent ○ *The beds of flowers were arranged end to end.* ◇ **get (hold of) the wrong end of the stick** to misunderstand what somebody is saying ◇ **in the end** when something has come to an end ○ *In the end, I had to admit he was right.* ◇ **look like the back end of a bus** an offensive term meaning to lack appealing physical features (*informal*) ◇ **make ends meet** to be able to afford to pay for the expenses of daily living ◇ **no end** very much indeed ◇ **no end of something** a great deal of something ○ *The old photocopier gave us no end of trouble.* ◇ **on end 1.** for an uninterrupted period ○ *The rain continued for weeks on end.* **2.** in a vertical position ○ *We left the table standing on end against the wall.* ◇ **the big end of town** *Aus* the companies with the most power and influence (*informal*) ◇ **the end of the line** *or* **road** the point beyond which somebody or something can no longer continue or survive ○ *The coming of the supermarkets was the end of the line for many small independent grocers.* ◇ **the thin end of the wedge** something bad or disadvantageous that seems quite minor but may well lead to something worse ◇ **the...to end all...** something that is so impressive or important that nothing else of the same kind will ever rival it ○ *the war to end all wars* ◇ **to no end** without success, or without achieving useful results (*formal*) ◇ **to the very end** for as long as is possible, however unpleasant the situation becomes ○ *The company's policy was to fight to the very end all consequent damage suits.* ◇ **until the end of time** forever

---

USAGE Avoid using the expression *to no end* (meaning 'without success') when *no end* (meaning 'very much indeed') is called for. Use *He annoyed her no end* [not *to no end*].

---

end in *vi* **1.** to have a particular kind of tip or extremity ○ *The dog's tail ends in a tuft of hair.* **2.** to have a particular outcome ○ *The relationship ended in an acrimonious split.*

end up *vi* **1.** to become something eventually **2.** to arrive at a destination at long last

end[2] /end/ (**ends, ending, ended**) *vt regional* to put hay or grain in a stack or barn [Early 17C. Origin ?]

end- *prefix* same as **endo-** (*used before vowels*)

-end *suffix* a person or thing to be treated in a particular way ○ *reverend* [< Latin *-endus, -endum*]

endamoeba /éndə meébə/ (*plural* **-bae** /-bee/ *or* **-bas**) *n* a parasitic protozoan found in the digestive tracts of some invertebrates, especially cockroaches and termites. Genus: *Endamoeba*.

endanger /in dáynjər/ (**-gers, -gering, -gered**) *vt* to expose somebody or something to danger —**endangered** *adj* —**endangerment** *n*

endangered species *n* a species whose numbers are so few, or are declining so quickly, that the animal, plant, or other organism may soon become extinct. Endangered species are sometimes protected under national or international law.

endarterectomy /én daartə réktəmi/ (*plural* **-mies**) *n* the surgical removal of material that is wholly or partially obstructing blood flow in an artery [Mid-20C. < END- + ARTERY]

en dash *n* in printing, a dash that is one en in length

endear /in deér/ (**-dears, -dearing, -deared**) *vt* to make somebody or something affectionately loved or greatly liked ○ *didn't endear herself to us*

endearing /in deéring/ *adj* producing feelings of affection or fondness —**endearingly** *adv*

endearment /in deérmənt/ *n* **1.** an expression of affection, especially a spoken one ○ *murmuring endearments* **2.** the showing of affection ○ *terms of endearment*

endeavor *vt, n* US spelling of **endeavour**

endeavour /in dévvər/ *vt* (**-ours, -ouring, -oured**) TRY HARD TO DO SOMETHING to make a serious and sincere effort to achieve something ■ *n* **1.** EFFORT an earnest attempt to achieve something **2.** ENTERPRISE an enterprise or directed activity ○ *offered help with my latest endeavour* [15C. < obsolete *put in dever*, partial translation of French *mettre en devoir* 'put in duty'] —**endeavourer** *n*

SYNONYMS See *try*.

---

endemic /en démmik/ *adj* **1.** MED RESTRICTED TO ONE PLACE describes a disease occurring within a particular area **2.** ECOL LIVING IN DEFINED GEOGRAPHICAL AREA describes a species of organism that is confined to a particular geographical region such as an island or river basin **3.** CHARACTERISTIC OF AREA characteristic of a particular place, or among a particular group, or area of interest or activity ■ *n* BIOL ORGANISM WITH LIMITED GEOGRAPHICAL RANGE a species of organism that is confined to a particular geographical region [Mid-17C. < Greek *endēmos* 'native' < *dēmos* 'people'] —**endemically** *adv* —**endemicity** /én de míssəti, éndə-/ *n* —**endemism** /éndəmizəm/ *n*

USAGE endemic or **epidemic**? The word ***endemic*** refers to something that is found throughout a particular area or group. Originally used of diseases, it is now often used in other contexts: *Corruption is endemic in the industry.* ***Endemic*** is sometimes misused in the sense of 'universal' or 'found everywhere', as in *Swearing these days is endemic*, meaning 'Everybody swears these days'. It is quite acceptable, however, to say *Swearing is endemic among young people* or *Swearing is endemic on the factory floor*, where group and area are specified. Do not confuse ***endemic*** with ***epidemic***, in its literal or figurative senses: an ***epidemic*** spreads rapidly and usually lasts for a limited period.

---

endergonic /éndər gónnik/ *adj* describes a chemical or biochemical reaction that requires energy [Mid-20C. < END- + Greek *ergon* 'work']

~~**endevour**~~ incorrect spelling of **endeavour**

endgame /énd gaym/ *n* **1.** the final stage of a process or contest ○ *As the trial neared its close, reporters watched closely to see what the prosecutor's endgame would be.* **2.** in chess, the final stage of a game in which only a few pieces are left on the board

ending /énding/ *n* **1.** FINAL PART the final or concluding part of something ○ *nerve endings* ○ *a sad ending* **2.** WAY SOMETHING IS FINISHED the manner in which something is ended **3.** GRAM END PART OF WORD the terminating part of a word, e.g. an inflection or derivational suffix **4.** CHESS same as **endgame** (sense 2) **5.** PSYCHOANAL PROCESS OF CONCLUDING RELATIONSHIP the process of concluding a relationship with another person, especially a therapist. An ending may offer somebody an opportunity to explore feelings about separation and loss.

endive /én dīv, éndiv, óN deev/ *n* **1.** a plant grown for its tightly packed curly leaves. Use: in salads, as a garnish. Latin name: *Cichorium endivia*. **2.** *US* same as **chicory** (sense 1) [14C. Via French < Latin *endivia* < medieval Greek *entubia*]

endless /éndləss/ *adj* **1.** having no apparent end or limit ○ *endless patience* **2.** made continuous by joining the ends ○ *an endless belt* —**endlessly** *adv* —**endlessness** *n*

end line *n* in sports, a line at the end of a court or field that marks the boundary of a playing area

end matter *n* PUBL same as **back matter**

end moraine *n* a ridge of rock, gravel, and soil at the terminal end of a glacier or ice field

endmost /énd mōst/ *adj* **1.** nearest or at the end **2.** last or most distant

endnote /énd nōt/ *n* a note of comment or reference placed at the end of a chapter, book, or essay

endo- *prefix* in, within, inside ○ *endotracheal* [< Greek *endo* < Indo-European, 'in']

endoblast /éndō blast/ *n* BIOL same as **endoderm** —**endoblastic** /éndō blástik/ *adj*

endocannabinoid /éndō kə nábbi noyd/ *n* a chemical substance in the body belonging to a group resembling organic chemicals found in cannabis

endocardia ANAT plural of **endocardium**

endocardial /éndō kaárdi əl/ *adj* **1.** located within the heart **2.** concerned with the thin membranous lining (**endocardium**) of the heart's cavities

endocarditis /éndō kaar dītiss/ *n* inflammation of the thin membranous lining (**endocardium**) of the heart's cavities —**endocarditic** /-dĭttik/ *adj*

endocardium /éndō kaárdi əm/ (*plural* **-dia** /-di ə/) *n*

the thin membranous lining of the heart's cavities

endocarp /éndə kaarp/ *n* the innermost of the three layers of the wall **(pericarp)** of a fruit. It may be toughened or hardened, as in a cherry stone or peach stone. (*technical*) —**endocarpal** /éndə ka̋arp'l/ *adj*

endocranium /éndō kráyni əm/ (*plural* **-nia** /-ni ə/) *n* ANAT same as **dura mater** —**endocranial** *adj*

endocrine /éndō krīn, -krin/ *adj* relating to the endocrine glands or their secretions. ◊ **exocrine** [Early 20C. < ENDO- + Greek *krinein* 'to separate']

endocrine disrupter *n* a substance that interferes with the endocrine system, sometimes causing reproductive or developmental problems, e.g. by mimicking a natural hormone

endocrine gland *n* any gland of the body that secretes hormones directly into the blood or lymph, e.g. the thyroid, pituitary, pineal, and adrenal glands

endocrinology /éndō kri nóləji, -krī-/ *n* a branch of medicine that deals with disorders of the endocrine glands —**endocrinologic** /éndō krinə lójjik/ *adj* —**endocrinological** *adj* —**endocrinologist** *n*

endocytosis /éndō sī tőssiss/ *n* the process by which a cell membrane folds inwards to take in substances bound to its surface

endoderm /éndō durm/ *n* in an animal embryo, the innermost layer that develops into the lining of the respiratory and digestive tracts [Mid-19C. < ENDO- + Greek *derma* 'skin'] —**endodermal** /éndō dúrm'l/ *adj*

endodermis /éndō dúrmiss/ *n* a layer of cells that marks the boundary between the inner core **(stele)** and outer surrounding tissue **(cortex)** of a plant root. It is also evident in the stems of some plants, notably ferns. [Late 19C. < ENDODERM, after *epidermis*]

endodontics /éndō dóntiks/, **endodontia** /-dónti ə/ *n* the branch of dentistry that deals with diseases of the dental pulp (*takes a singular verb*) [Mid-20C. < ENDO- + ORTHODONTICS] —**endodontic** *adj* —**endodontist** *n*

endoenzyme /éndō én zīm/ *n* an enzyme that is produced and functions inside cells

endoergic /éndō úrjik/ *adj* describes a chemical or nuclear reaction in which energy is absorbed. ◊ **exoergic** [Mid-20C. < ENDO- + Greek *ergon* 'work']

end-of-life *adj* relating to the needs of people who are dying or nearing the end of their lives ○ *a policy that provides end-of-life home care*

endogamy /en dóggəmi/ *n* **1.** the social practice of marrying another member of the same clan, people, or other kinship group **2.** pollination between the flowers of the same plant —**endogamous** *adj*

endogenous /en dójjənəss/ *adj* **1.** having no apparent external cause ○ *endogenous depression* **2.** originating or growing within an organism or tissue ○ *endogenous secretions* ◊ **exogenous** —**endogenously** *adv* —**endogeny** *n*

endolymph /éndō limf/ *n* the fluid inside the membranous labyrinth of the ear —**endolymphatic** /éndō lim fáttik/ *adj*

endometria ANAT plural of **endometrium**

endometriosis /éndō meetri őssiss/ *n* a medical condition in which the mucous membrane **(endometrium)** that normally lines only the womb is present and functioning in the ovaries or elsewhere in the body

endometrium /éndō me̋etri əm/ (*plural* **-tria** /-tri ə/) *n* the mucous membrane that lines the womb and increases in thickness in the later part of the menstrual cycle [Late 19C. < ENDO- + Greek *mētra* 'womb'] —**endometrial** *adj*

endomitosis /éndō mī tőssiss/ *n* a process by which chromosomes divide within a cell but the nucleus does not, resulting in an increase in chromosome number —**endomitotic** /-mī tóttik/ *adj*

endomorph /éndō mawrf/ *n* **1.** somebody whose body has a stocky build and a prominent abdomen. ◊ **ectomorph, mesomorph 2.** a mineral surrounded by another. An example is tourmaline, often found enclosed in quartz. ◊ **perimorph** —**endomorphic** /éndō máwrfik/ *adj* —**endomorphy** *n*

endonuclease /éndō nyo͝okli ayz/ *n* an enzyme that splits DNA or RNA

endoparasite /éndō párrə sīt/ *n* a parasite that lives inside its host, e.g. a tapeworm —**endoparasitic** /éndō parə síttik/ *adj* —**endoparasitism** *n*

endopeptidase /éndō pépti dayz/ *n* an enzyme that splits proteins into peptides

endophyte /éndō fīt/ *n* a plant or fungus that lives inside another plant. It may or may not be a parasite of its host plant. —**endophytic** /éndō fíttik/ *adj*

endoplasm /éndō plazəm/ *n* the inner, more fluid layer of cytoplasm in a cell —**endoplasmic** /éndō plázmik/ *adj*

endoplasmic reticulum *n* an intricate system of tubular membranes in the cytoplasm of a cell. It is responsible for the synthesis and transport of materials to and from cells.

end organ *n* the specialized end of a sensory or motor nerve

endorphin /en dáwrfin/ *n* a substance in the brain that attaches to the same cell receptors that morphine does. Endorphins are released when severe injury occurs, often abolishing all sensation of pain. [Late 20C. Blend of ENDOGENOUS + MORPHINE]

endorse /in dáwrss/ (**-dorses, -dorsing, -dorsed**), **indorse** *vt* **1. APPROVE SOMETHING FORMALLY** to give formal approval or permission for something ○ *This practice is not endorsed by head office.* **2. SUPPORT SOMEBODY OR SOMETHING** to give public support to somebody or something, especially during an election ○ *decided to endorse the mayor as a candidate for higher office* **3. PROMOTE PRODUCT** to give public approval of a product for advertising purposes ○ *a brand endorsed by a popular TV star* **4. SIGN BACK OF CHEQUE** to sign the back of a cheque, postal order, or negotiable document in order to cash it or to make it payable to a specific payee **5. SIGN RECEIPT** to sign a document to acknowledge receipt of a payment **6. WRITE ON DOCUMENT** to write a comment on the back of a document ○ *a fitness report that had been endorsed on the back by its recipient* **7. RECORD CONVICTIONS ON LICENCE** to record details of convictions for motoring offences on a driving licence ○ *You will pay a fine and have your licence endorsed with three penalty points.* [15C. < medieval Latin *indorsare* < Latin *dorsum* 'back'] —**endorsable** *adj* —**endorsee** /in dáwr se̋e/ *n* —**endorser** *n*

endorsement /in dáwrssmənt/, **indorsement** *n* **1. PUBLIC SUPPORT** public support for somebody or something **2. ADVERTISING TESTIMONIAL** an instance of public approval of a product for advertising purposes **3. OFFICIAL APPROVAL OR PERMISSION** official approval of or permission for something **4. SIGNATURE OR WRITTEN COMMENT** something, especially a signature, written on the back of a document to make it payable, to approve it, or to comment on it **5. ACT OF ENDORSING CHEQUE** an act or instance of endorsing a cheque or other financial document **6. RECORD OF OFFENCE** a record of a conviction for a motoring offence detailed on a driving licence **7.** INSUR **POLICY ALTERATION** a clause added to an insurance policy that changes the cover

endoscope /éndə skōp/ *n* a medical instrument consisting of a long tube inserted into the body, used for diagnostic examination and surgical procedures —**endoscopic** /éndə skóppik/ *adj* —**endoscopically** *adv* —**endoscopy** /en dóskəpi/ *n*

endoskeleton /éndō skéllitən/ *n* the internal skeleton of an animal, especially of a vertebrate —**endoskeletal** *adj*

endosmosis /énd oz mőssiss/ *n* osmosis in which fluid is absorbed into a cell from a surrounding fluid —**endosmotic** /énd oz móttik/ *adj* —**endosmotically** *adv*

endosperm /éndō spurm/ *n* the tissue that surrounds the embryo inside a plant seed and provides nourishment for it —**endospermic** /éndō spúrmik/ *adj*

endospore /éndō spawr/ *n* **1.** an asexual spore that is formed inside the cells of some bacteria and algae **2.** the inner layer of the wall of a spore —**endosporous** /en dóspərəss/ *adj*

endosteum /en dósti əm/ (*plural* **-a** /-ti ə/) *n* a layer of vascular tissue lining the inside of some bones, e.g. the femur [Late 19C. < END- + Greek *osteon* 'bone'] —**endosteal** *adj*

endosulfan /éndō súlfən/ *n* a toxic organochlorine compound. Use: control of insects, mites, and ticks. Formula: $C_9H_6Cl_6O_3S$. [Mid-20C. < ENDO- + *sulfur*, US spelling of SULPHUR]

endosymbiosis /éndō sím bi őssiss/ *n* **1.** symbiosis in which one organism lives inside the body of another and both function as a single organism **2.** a hypothetical evolutionary process by which some cellular structures may have developed as a result of the incorporation of free-living prokaryotes into the cytoplasm of eukaryotes —**endosymbiotic** /-óttik/ *adj*

endosymbiotic hypothesis *n* a theory that the mitochondria and chloroplasts found within eukaryotic cells originated as free-living prokaryotic organisms

endothecium /éndō the̋eshi əm, -the̋essi əm/ (*plural* **-cia** /-shi ə, -si ə/) *n* **1.** the inner tissue of the spore-producing capsule of a moss **2.** the tissue of the inner wall of an anther in a flower [Mid-19C. < ENDO- + Greek *thēkion* 'little case' < *thēkē* 'chest']

endothelia ANAT plural of **endothelium**

endothelioma /éndō theeli őmə/ (*plural* **-mas** or **-mata** /-mətə/) *n* a tumour of the cells that line internal body surfaces

endothelium /éndō the̋eli əm/ (*plural* **-lia** /-li ə/) *n* a layer of cells that lines the inside of some body cavities, e.g. blood vessels [Late 19C. < modern Latin < Greek *endon* 'within' + *thēlē* 'nipple'] —**endothelial** *adj*

endotherm /éndō thurm/ *n* an animal that is able to maintain a constant body temperature despite changes in the temperature of its environment [Mid-20C. < ENDO- + Greek *thermē* 'heat']

endothermic /éndō thúrmik/, **endothermal** /-thúrm'l/ *adj* **1.** maintaining a constant body temperature despite changes in the temperature of the environment **2.** describes a chemical reaction in which heat is absorbed. ◊ **exothermic** —**endothermy** /éndō thurmi/ *n*

endotoxin /éndō tóksin/ *n* a toxin produced within some bacteria that is released only when the bacteria disintegrate —**endotoxic** *adj*

endotracheal /éndō trə ke̋e əl/ *adj* located in or passed through the windpipe ○ *an endotracheal tube*

endotrophic /éndō trőffik, -tróffik/ *adj* describes an association **(mycorrhiza)** between a fungus and a plant in which the fungus obtains its nourishment from inside its plant host. ◊ **ectotrophic**

endow /in dów/ (**-dows, -dowing, -dowed**) *vt* **1.** to provide a person or institution with income or property **2.** to provide somebody or something with desirable qualities, abilities, or characteristics (*usually passive*) ○ *The area is endowed with a perfect climate.* [14C. < Anglo-Norman *endouer* < Latin *dotare* 'provide with a dowry' < *dot-* 'dowry']

endowment /in dówmənt/ *n* **1. NATURAL QUALITY** a natural ability or quality ○ *A sharp mind was only one of her many endowments.* **2. FUNDS OR PROPERTY** an amount of income or property that has been provided to a person or institution, especially an educational institution **3. GIVING OF ENDOWMENT** the giving of an endowment, or an instance of this

endowment assurance, **endowment insurance** *n* life assurance that pays a set amount to the policyholder when the policy matures or to a beneficiary if the policyholder dies before maturity

endowment mortgage *n* a mortgage in which the borrower pays interest to the lender and the capital to a life assurance policy that repays the loan at maturity or when the borrower dies

endozoic /éndō ző ik/ *adj* **1.** describes organisms that live inside an animal **2.** describes a method of seed dispersal in which the seeds are eaten by an animal and then passed out in the animal's faeces

endpaper /énd paypər/ *n* a sturdy sheet of paper pasted to the inside of a book's front or back cover and to the spine edge of the first or last page

end pin *n* the adjustable spike-shaped leg at the bottom of a cello or double bass that the instrument rests on while being played

endplay /énd play/ *n* in bridge, a play in which an opponent is forced to lead near the end of the hand and loses a trick that would otherwise have been won —**endplay** *vt*

end point *n* 1. the point at which something is complete or comes to an end ○ *We'll try to reach a convenient end point by 4.30.* 2. the point, marked by a colour change or other indicator, at which a titration is complete

endpoint /énd poynt/ *n* 1. the point located at each end of a line segment or at the end of a ray 2. any computer on a network that can transmit or receive data

end product *n* the final result of a process or series of events or operations

end rhyme *n* the use of rhyme at the ends of lines of poetry, or an example of this

endrin /éndrin/ *n* a white crystalline chlorinated hydrocarbon. Use: insecticide. Formula: $C_{12}H_8Cl_6O$. [Mid-20C. < END- + DIELDRIN]

end-stopped *adj* describes poetry containing a pause in meaning at the end of a line or couplet, as opposed to continuing into the next line or couplet

endue /in dyoó/ (**-dues, -duing, -dued**), **indue** *vt* to endow somebody or something with an ability or quality (*literary*) ○ *His successes have endued him with an aura of invincibility.* [14C. < French *enduire* < Latin *ducere* 'to lead']

endurance /in dyoórənss/ *n* 1. ABILITY TO BEAR PROLONGED HARDSHIP the ability or power to bear prolonged exertion, pain, or hardship ○ *an endurance test* ○ *legendary powers of endurance* 2. TOLERATION OF HARDSHIP toleration of prolonged suffering or hardship ○ *Their quiet endurance of the situation earned them many friends.* 3. PERSISTENCE OVER TIME the survival or persistence of something despite the ravages of time ○ *the endurance of ancient traditions* [15C. < French < *endurer* (see ENDURE)]

endure /in dyoór/ (**-dures, -during, -dured**) *v* 1. *vti* BEAR HARDSHIP to experience exertion, pain, or hardship without giving up ○ *The nation endured years of war to create a lasting peace.* 2. *vt* TOLERATE DISAGREEABLE THINGS to tolerate or accept somebody or something that is extremely disagreeable (*formal*) ○ *I cannot endure that song.* 3. *vi* SURVIVE to last or survive over a period of time, especially when faced with difficulties ○ *The philosophical ideas of the ancient Greeks endure to this day.* [14C. Via French *endurer* < Latin *indurare* 'harden' < *durus* 'hard'] —**endurable** *adj*

enduring /in dyoóring/ *adj* 1. persisting or surviving in the face of difficulties 2. patient or tolerant despite many difficulties —**enduringly** *adv*

enduro /in dyoórō/ (*plural* **-os**) *n* a long race, especially one involving motorcycles or cars, in which the emphasis is on endurance rather than speed [Mid-20C. Alteration of ENDURANCE]

end user *n* a person or group that is one of the ultimate consumers or users that a product has been designed for ○ *a survey that is designed to assess what the end user really needs*

endways /énd wayz/, **endwise** /-wīz/ *adv* 1. WITH END UP with an end up or forwards 2. TOWARDS ENDS towards the ends 3. WITH ENDS TOUCHING with one end next to another end

Endymion /en dímmi ən/ *n* in Greek mythology, a handsome man loved by the moon goddess Selene

end zone *n* either of the two areas at the ends of an American football field between the goal line and the end line where a touchdown is scored

ENE *abbr* east-northeast

-ene *suffix* an unsaturated organic compound ○ *butene* [< Greek *-ēnē*, form of *-ēnos*, adjective suffix]

enema /énnəmə/ (*plural* **-mas** or **-mata** /-mətə/) *n* 1. the insertion of a liquid into the bowels via the rectum as a treatment, especially for constipation, or as an aid to diagnosis 2. the liquid used when giving somebody an enema ○ *a barium enema* [Late 17C. Via late Latin < Greek < *enienai* 'send or put in' < *hienai* 'send']

enemy /énnəmi/ (*plural* **-mies**) *n* 1. UNFRIENDLY OPPONENT somebody who hates or seeks to harm somebody or something 2. MILITARY OPPONENT a person or group, especially a military force, that fights against another in combat or battle 3. HOSTILE POWER a hostile nation or power 4. SOMETHING HARMFUL OR OBSTRUCTIVE something that harms or opposes something else ○ *In a case like this, time is the enemy.* [13C. Via French < Latin *inimicus* 'enemy, unfriendly' < *amicus* 'friend']

energetic /énnər jéttik/ *adj* 1. displaying great vigour or force 2. requiring great vigour or stamina [Mid-17C. < Greek *energētikos* 'active' < *ergon* 'work'] —**energetically** *adv*

energetics /énnər jéttiks/ *n* the branch of physics that studies energy and its transformations (*takes a singular verb*)

energize /énnər jīz/ (**-gizes, -gizing, -gized**), **energise** (**-gises, -gising, -gised**) *v* 1. *vt* GIVE SOMEBODY OR SOMETHING ENERGY to supply somebody or something with strength or power ○ *He felt energized by his nap.* 2. *vti* MAKE OR BECOME ACTIVE to become, or cause something to become, vigorously active 3. *vt* ELEC SUPPLY WITH ELECTRICAL POWER to supply something with a source of electrical power —**energization** /énnər jī záysh'n/ *n* —**energizer** *n*

energy /énnərji/ (*plural* **-gies**) *n* 1. ABILITY TO DO THINGS the ability or power to work or make an effort ○ *His illness left him feeling drained of energy.* 2. VIGOUR liveliness and forcefulness ○ *She gave a performance that was full of energy.* 3. FORCEFUL EFFORT a vigorous effort or action ○ *We must concentrate our energies on the task in hand.* 4. POWER SUPPLY OR SOURCE a supply or source of electrical, mechanical, or other form of power 5. PHYS CAPACITY TO DO WORK the capacity of a body or system to do work. Symbol ***E*** [Mid-16C. Via French < Greek *energeia* < *ergon* 'work'. < Indo-European]

ORIGIN The Indo-European word from which ***energy*** is ultimately derived is also the ancestor of English *liturgy, organ, orgy, surgery*, and *work*, and perhaps also of *irk*.

energy audit *n* a survey of the use of energy in a building or organization, undertaken in order to make energy use as efficient as possible

energy balance *n* a mathematical relationship, using the principle of the conservation of energy, that shows the energy inputs and outputs of a process or system

energy band *n* PHYS same as **band**[2] *n* (sense 9)

energy-band theory *n* PHYS same as **band theory**

energy bar *n* a bar-shaped snack made of ingredients intended to boost somebody's physical energy

energy crisis *n* a situation in which available sources of energy are not sufficient to meet the demand

energy efficient *adj* using electrical or other energy in an economical way (*hyphenated when used before a noun*)

energy level *n* one of the discrete stable energy values that can be assumed by a physical system such as the electrons in an atom or an atomic nucleus

energy recovery *n* the extraction of energy from synthetic materials, e.g. by using the heat from incineration of solid waste to generate electricity

energy tax *n* a tax on an energy source intended to discourage environmentally damaging sources and encourage energy conservation or use of alternative sources

energy therapy *n* a holistic method of healing using energy supposedly contained in and surrounding the human body, mind, and spirit

enervate /énnər vayt/ (**-vates, -vating, -vated**) *vt* to weaken somebody's physical, mental, or moral vitality ○ *I was feeling quite enervated by the strain of moving house.* [Early 17C. < Latin *enervat-*, past participle of *enervare* 'extract the sinews of, weaken' < *nervus* 'sinew'] —**enervation** /énnər váysh'n/ *n*

enervated /énnər vaytid/ *adj* weakened or exhausted physically, mentally, or morally ○ *an enervated, dissolute age*

SYNONYMS See ***weak***.

enervating /énnər vayting/ *adj* causing the physical, mental, or moral vitality to weaken

e-network *n* an Internet forum, usually of a professional nature and requiring a subscription to participate

Enewetak /énnə weé tok, ə neéwi tok/ circular atoll in the northwestern Marshall Islands in the Northern Pacific Ocean, a former testing ground for nuclear weapons. Population: 715 (1988). Area: 5 sq. km/2 sq. mi.

enface /in fáyss/ (**-faces, -facing, -faced**) *vt* to mark something on the face of a document by writing, stamping, or printing —**enfacement** *n*

en famille /oN fa meé/ *adv* 1. with family members, especially at home 2. in an informal, relaxed, or casual way [Early 18C. < French, 'in the family']

enfant terrible /óN foN te reéblə/ (*plural* **enfants terribles** /*pronunc. same*/) *n* 1. somebody whose unconventional behaviour, attitudes, or remarks are shocking to others 2. a young person, especially in the arts, who has become successful because of work that is radically innovative or extremely avant-garde [< French, 'terrible child']

enfeeble /in feéb'l/ (**-bles, -bling, -bled**) *vt* to reduce the strength of somebody or something to the point of weakness [14C. < Old French *enfiblir* < *feble* (see FEEBLE)] —**enfeeblement** *n*

enfeoff /in feéf/ (**-feoffs, -feoffing, -feoffed**) *vt* formerly, to invest somebody with the freehold possession of a piece of land [14C. < Anglo-Norman *enfeoffer* < Old French *fief* (see FIEF)] —**enfeoffment** *n*

Enfield /én feeld/ *n* ARMS same as **Enfield rifle** [After a town in SE England]

Enfield musket /én feeld-/ *n* a muzzle-loading rifled musket used by British forces in the 19th century and by American troops in the American Civil War [See ENFIELD]

Enfield rifle *n* 1. a .303-calibre bolt-action breech-loading rifle, used by British forces in World War I and until the 1930s 2. a .30-calibre bolt-action breech-loading rifle used by US forces in World War I. 3. ARMS same as **Enfield musket** [See ENFIELD]

enfilade *n* /énfi layd/ 1. VULNERABLE POSITION a position in which troops are exposed to gunfire along the length of their formation. ◊ **defilade** 2. RAKING FIRE gunfire that strikes a body of troops along its whole length ■ *vt* /énfi láyd/ (**-lades, -lading, -laded**) 1. FIRE AT SOMETHING ALONG ITS LENGTH to attack a position or body of troops with gunfire along its whole length 2. PLACE TROOPS OR GUNS FOR FIRING to place guns or troops in a position from which they can fire on the whole length of an enemy position or body of troops [Early 18C. < French < *fil* 'thread' < Latin *filum*]

enfleurage /óN flur ráazh/ *n* a process used in making perfume in which oils acquire fragrance by being exposed to the scent of flowers [Mid-19C. < French < *enfleurer* 'saturate with the scent of flowers' < *fleur* 'flower']

~~enflict~~ incorrect spelling of **inflict**

enfold /in fṓld/ (**-folds, -folding, -folded**), **infold** *vt* 1. to surround or enclose somebody or something completely 2. to hold somebody or something in an embrace —**enfolder** *n*

~~enforcable~~ incorrect spelling of **enforceable**

enforce /in fáwrss/ (**-forces, -forcing, -forced**) *vt* 1. MAKE PEOPLE OBEY SOMETHING to compel obedience to a law, regulation, or command 2. IMPOSE SOMETHING to impose something by force 3. STRENGTHEN SOMETHING to give strength or emphasis to something ○ *enforce an argument* [13C. < French *enforcir* < Latin *fortis* 'strong'] —**enforceability** /in fáwrssə bílləti/ *n* —**enforceable** *adj* —**enforcement** *n*

enforcer /in fáwrssər/ *n* 1. somebody who enforces a rule, law, or order 2. *N Am* a member of a criminal gang who uses physical violence to intimidate and enforce compliance (*slang*)

enfranchise /in frán chīz/ (**-chises, -chising, -chised**) *vt* 1. GIVE SOMEBODY RIGHT TO VOTE to give somebody the right to vote in an election 2. SET SOMEBODY FREE to set somebody free, especially from slavery 3. GIVE TOWN RIGHT OF REPRESENTATION formerly, to grant political representation to a town or city [Early 16C. < Old French *enfranchir* < *franc* 'free' < Latin *francus*] —**enfranchisement** /-chizmənt/ *n*

ENG *abbr* electronic newsgathering

eng. *abbr* 1. engine 2. engineer 3. engineering

Eng. *abbr* 1. England 2. English

engage /in gáyj/ (**-gages, -gaging, -gaged**) *v* 1. *vti* INVOLVE SOMEBODY, OR BECOME INVOLVED to involve somebody in an activity, or become involved or take part in an activity ○ *engaged her in conversation for an hour*

2. *vt* REQUIRE USE OF SOMETHING to require the use or devotion of something ○ *Her writing engages most of her time.* **3.** *vt* ATTRACT SOMEBODY to hold the attention of, or win the affection of somebody ○ *He was engaged by the child's open manner.* **4.** *vti* PROMISE to commit yourself or something to an obligation ○ *She engaged to meet them tomorrow.* **5.** *vt* HIRE SOMEBODY to hire somebody for a job or to do some work **6.** *vt* RESERVE SOMETHING to reserve or rent something for personal use (*dated*) **7.** *vti* MIL FIGHT SOMEBODY to fight or begin a battle with an enemy **8.** *vti* MECH ENG INTERLOCK to become interlocked, or bring something together and cause something to interlock ○ *engaged the gears* [Early 16C. < French *engager* < *gage* 'pledge'] —**engager** *n*

engagé /óng ga zháy/ *adj* committed to a political cause or ideology, usually a left-wing one [Mid-20C. < French, past participle of *engager* (see ENGAGE)]

engaged /in gáyjd/ *adj* **1.** HAVING AGREED TO MARRY having agreed to be married ○ *the newly engaged couple* **2.** OCCUPIED busy doing something ○ *The Minister is otherwise engaged this afternoon.* **3.** TELECOM CURRENTLY BEING USED FOR TELEPHONE CALL describes a telephone line that is currently being used to make a telephone call. N Am term **busy 4.** MECH ENG WITH PARTS INTERLOCKED having teeth or other mechanical parts interlocked and often in operation **5.** CONSTR BUILT INTO OR ATTACHED TO WALL describes a part of a building that is built into or attached to a wall

engaged tone *n* a series of repeated short tones heard through a telephone when the line belonging to the number dialled is already being used. N Am term **busy signal**

engagée /óng ga zháy/ *adj* describes a woman who is committed to a political cause or ideology, usually a left-wing one [Mid-20C. < French, form of past participle of *engager* (see ENGAGE)]

engagement /in gáyjmənt/ *n* **1.** AGREEMENT TO MARRY an agreement to get married ○ *announce our engagement* **2.** COMMITMENT TO ATTEND an arrangement to be present at an event, especially a business or social appointment **3.** SHORT JOB a job that lasts for a short period of time, especially one for an entertainer in a club or theatre ○ *a week-long engagement in Las Vegas* **4.** BATTLE a hostile encounter involving military forces ○ *a minor engagement on the frontier* **5.** MECH ENG ACTIVE OR OPERATIONAL STATE an act or condition of being activated or becoming operational

SYNONYMS See *fight*.

engagement ring *n* a ring given by a man to his fiancée to mark their engagement to marry. It is worn on the ring finger of the left hand.

engaging /in gáyjing/ *adj* charming or pleasing in a way that attracts and holds the attention —**engagingly** *adv*

en garde /oN gaárd/ *interj* used to warn a fencer to assume the prescribed stance for the start of a match [< French, 'on guard']

Popperfoto
Friedrich Engels

Engels /éng g'lz/, **Friedrich** (1820–95) German political thinker and revolutionary. He cowrote the *Communist Manifesto* (1848) with Karl Marx and supported Marx financially. He lived mainly in England.

'The political authority of the state dies out. Man, at last the master of his own form of social organization, becomes at the same time the lord over Nature, his own master—free.'
[Friedrich Engels, *Socialism: Utopian and Scientific*; 1892]

engender /in jéndər/ (**-ders, -dering, -dered**) *v* **1.** *vti* to arise or come into existence, or cause something to do so ○ *Secrecy engenders suspicion.* **2.** *vt* to cause offspring to be conceived or born (*formal*) [14C. Via French < Latin *ingenerare* < *generare* 'produce'] —**engenderer** *n*

engine /énjin/ *n* **1.** MACHINE FOR POWERING EQUIPMENT a machine that converts an energy source into mechanical power or motion ○ *an oil-fired engine* **2.** RAIL RAILWAY LOCOMOTIVE a railway locomotive **3.** DRIVING FORCE OR ENERGY SOURCE something that supplies the driving force or energy to a movement, system, or trend ○ *a political movement that was seen as a great engine of social change* **4.** COMPUT COMPUTER SOFTWARE a computer program that performs a core or coordinating function for other programs, or has a special-purpose function **5.** MIL, HIST BATTLEFIELD MACHINE a battering ram, catapult, or other device used in warfare ○ *a siege engine* [14C. Via French < Latin *ingenium* 'talent, clever device'] —**engined** *adj* —**engineless** *adj*

engine block *n* N Am same as **cylinder block**

engine driver *n* somebody who operates a railway locomotive. N Am term **engineer**

engineer /énji neér/ *n* **1.** ENG ENGINEERING PROFESSIONAL somebody who is trained as a professional engineer **2.** MECH ENG MECHANIC somebody who operates or services machines **3.** NAUT, NAVY SHIP'S OFFICER an officer on a ship who is in charge of the engines **4.** MIL CONSTRUCTION SOLDIER a member of a unit of the armed forces that specializes in building and sometimes destroying bridges, fortifications, and other large structures **5.** PLANNER a planner, initiator, or supervisor of something, especially something that is achieved with ingenuity or secretiveness ○ *the engineer of the overthrow of the government* **6.** N Am RAIL same as **engine driver** ■ *vt* (**-neers, -neering, -neered**) **1.** CONTRIVE SOMETHING to plan something or bring it about, especially in an ingenious or secretive manner **2.** USE ENGINEERING SKILL TO DESIGN SOMETHING to use professional engineering skill to design or create something ○ *This car was engineered in Italy.* **3.** GENETICS DEVELOP SOMETHING BY GENETIC MODIFICATION to use the techniques of genetic modification to develop an organism or product [14C. < Old French *engineor* 'contriver' < Latin *ingenium* 'talent, clever device']

engineering /énji neéring/ *n* **1.** APPLICATION OF SCIENCE TO DESIGNING THINGS the application of science in the design, planning, construction, and maintenance of buildings, machines, and other manufactured things ○ *leading the world in engineering* **2.** PROFESSION INVOLVING TECHNICAL DESIGNING a branch of engineering pursued as a profession, e.g. civil engineering or electronic engineering **3.** CONTRIVANCE the planning or bringing about of something, especially when done with ingenuity or secretiveness

engine room *n* the place on board a ship where the engines are housed

enginery /énjinri/ (*plural* **-ries**) *n* a group of engines

engirdle /in gúrd'l/ (**-dles, -dling, -dled**) *vt* to surround or encircle something (*literary*)

englacial /in gláysh'l/ *adj* describes material or processes occurring within a glacier

England /íng glənd/ country forming the southern and largest part of the United Kingdom. Capital: London. Population: 49,138,831 (2001). Area: 130,410 sq. km/50,352 sq. mi.

Englified /íng gli fīd/ *adj* Scotland anglicized (*informal disapproving*)

English /íng glish/ *n* **1.** LANG LANGUAGE OF UK, US, AND CANADA an official language of the United Kingdom of Great Britain and Northern Ireland, the Republic of Ireland, the United States, Canada, Australia, New Zealand, South Africa, and several other countries. Native speakers: 350 million. Other speakers: 375 million. See panel on next page **2.** EDUC STUDY OF ENGLISH the English language, together with literature written in it, as a subject of study **3.** EASILY UNDERSTOOD ENGLISH clear, understandable spoken or written English, as distinct from technical jargon, dialect, or nonstandard or incomprehensible speech or writing **4.** *also* **english** N Am CUE GAMES same as **side** *n* (sense 20) ■ *npl* PEOPLE FROM ENGLAND people who come from England ■ *adj* **1.** OF ENGLISH relating to the language of English **2.** OF THE ENGLISH relating to the English or England [Old English *Englisc* < *Engle* 'the Angles'] —**Englishness** *n*

English bond *n* an arrangement of bricks in a wall in which layers (**courses**) of bricks laid end to end (**stretchers**) alternate with layers of bricks laid side to side (**headers**). The stretchers of all layers are aligned vertically, and the headers are centred on the stretchers and the mortar joints between them.

English breakfast *n* a breakfast usually consisting of cereal or fruit, followed by cooked bacon, eggs, sausages, and tomatoes, and then toast and marmalade or jam ○ *a choice of continental or full English breakfast*

English Canadian *n* Can a Canadian whose first language is English or who is of English ancestry —**English-Canadian** *adj*

English Channel /íng glish-/ area of water linking the North Sea with the Atlantic Ocean. It lies between England and France. Length: 565 km/351 mi. French name **La Manche**

English disease *n* recurring industrial unrest marked by many strikes, formerly regarded by non-British commentators as endemic in and damaging to British industry

English Heritage *n* a body partly funded by government that is responsible for maintaining buildings and monuments of historical interest in England. Official name **Historic Buildings and Monuments Commission for England**

English horn *n* US MUSIC same as **cor anglais**

Englishman /íng glishmən/ (*plural* **-men** /-mən/) *n* a man who comes from England

English muffin *n* N Am FOOD same as **muffin** (sense 1)

English Nature *n* the English division of the Nature Conservancy Council, a government agency responsible for various nature-conservation functions including national nature reserves, and for advising central government

English rose *n* an attractive girl or woman whose prettiness is considered to be quintessentially English

English setter *n* a hunting dog with a silky white coat with brown or black markings, belonging to a medium-sized breed of setter

English springer spaniel *n* a dog with a silky coat that may be a mixture of white, black, liver, or tan, belonging to a medium-sized breed of spaniel that was developed in England as a hunting dog

Englishwoman /íng glish wŏŏmən/ (*plural* **-women** /-wimin/) *n* a woman who comes from England

engobe /én gōb/ *n* liquid clay used to decorate a ceramic piece before it has been fired and usually applied before the piece has dried [Mid-19C. < French]

engorge /in gáwrj/ (**-gorges, -gorging, -gorged**) *v* **1.** *vti* FILL WITH BLOOD *vt* to fill something with blood until it is congested, or become filled with blood **2.** *vt* DEVOUR SOMETHING to eat something greedily **3.** **engorge yourself** GORGE YOURSELF *vr* to gorge or fill yourself with food [15C. < French *engorger* < Old French *gorge* 'throat' (see GORGE)] —**engorgement** *n*

engr. *abbr* **1.** engraved **2.** engraver **3.** engraving

engraft /in graáft/ (**-grafts, -grafting, -grafted**), **ingraft** *vt* **1.** ATTACH SOMETHING PERMANENTLY to attach something permanently to something else by a process resembling grafting **2.** IMPLANT SOMETHING PERMANENTLY to implant something permanently or deeply in something else **3.** GRAFT PLANT PART to graft a bud or other plant part from one plant onto another (*technical*) **4.** GRAFT ANIMAL TISSUE to graft animal tissue from one part of the body onto another part or onto another animal (*technical*) —**engraftment** *n*

engrailed /in gráyld/ *adj* **1.** edged with a series of concave indentations **2.** edged with a row of raised dots ○ *an engrailed gold coin* [14C. < Old French *engresler* 'make thin' < *gresle* 'thin' < Latin *gracilis*]

WORLD ENGLISH ***English***, a language originating in northwestern Europe, is the most widely used member of the Germanic language family. Anglo-Saxon settlers whose dialects were collectively known as 'Englisc' arrived in Britain in the 5th century and in due course their language became identified as the main one of the kingdom of England. This early English was a homogeneous tongue, and the characteristic hybrid vocabulary of the present-day language is the result, successively, of Scandinavian, Norman-French, and Greco-Latin influence. For convenience, English is usually divided into four historical phases: Old English (around 500–1150), Middle English (around 1150–around 1450), Early Modern English (around 1450–1700), and Modern English (around 1700 onwards). However, the distance and difference between Old and Modern English is as great as that between Latin and its descendant, French. After 1707, English became the primary language of first the United Kingdom and Ireland, then the British Empire at large, from which the United States broke away in the 1770s. The world's primary English-speaking countries today are the United States, the United Kingdom, Canada, Australia, Ireland, South Africa, New Zealand, and Singapore, and the many other nations and territories using English include Bangladesh, Ghana, Guyana, India, Hong Kong, Kenya, Jamaica, Malta, Malaysia, Nigeria, Pakistan, and the Philippines. All territories using the language tend to have distinctive pronunciations, grammatical features, and items of vocabulary, and, increasingly, varieties of the standard international language. English is a primary working language of the United Nations and the European Union and the sole working language of the Commonwealth, NATO, CARICOM, and ASEAN. It is also learned as a second language for purposes of education, employment, entertainment, electronic communication, and travel by a rapidly increasing number of people worldwide, approaching between one and two billion people. Since the 1960s the already immense literature of the language, primarily in the United States and United Kingdom, has been markedly extended throughout the English-speaking world, with English becoming overwhelmingly the primary language of global communication and the media. See also introductory essay on ***World English***.

engrain *vt* TEXTILES another spelling of **ingrain**

engram /én gram/ *n* a hypothetical physical impression made in neural tissue by a mental stimulus, once regarded as an explanation of the persistence of memory [Early 20C. < German *Engramm* < Greek *gramma* 'something written']

engrave /in gráyv/ (**-graves, -graving, -graved**) *vt* **1. CARVE OR ETCH MATERIAL** to carve or etch a hard surface with a design or lettering for decoration or printing ○ *engraved a silver cup* **2. CARVE OR ETCH DESIGN** to carve or etch a design or lettering into a hard surface for decoration or printing ○ *engraving a dedication on a watch* **3. PRINT IMAGE** to print an image, especially a raised image, from an engraved printing plate **4. IMPRESS SOMETHING** to impress something deeply, e.g. a memory on the mind —**engraver** *n*

engraving /in gráyving/ *n* **1.** PRINTING **ENGRAVED PRINT** a print of an image that was made using an engraved plate or block **2.** ART **ENGRAVED DESIGN** a design or lettering engraved into a hard surface for decoration or printing **3.** ART **CUTTING OR ETCHING OF IMAGES** the art or process of cutting or etching images into a hard surface **4.** PRINTING **ENGRAVED SURFACE** a plate, block, or other hard surface on which an image has been engraved for printing

engross[1] /in gróss/ (**-grosses, -grossing, -grossed**) *vt* **1.** to take up somebody's whole attention ○ *The children were engrossed by the story.* **2.** to buy all of a commodity or enough of it to control its market [14C. < Old French *en gros*, medieval Latin *in grosso* 'in bulk, wholesale' < late Latin *grossus* 'bulky, coarse'] —**engrosser** *n*

engross[2] /in gróss/ (**-grosses, -grossing, -grossed**) *vt* **1.** to write or print the final version of a legal document **2.** to copy a document in large clear handwriting (*dated*) [14C. < Anglo-Norman *engrosser*, medieval Latin *ingrossare* < late Latin *grossus* 'bulky, coarse'] —**engrosser** *n*

engrossing /in gróssing/ *adj* engaging somebody's whole attention —**engrossingly** *adv*

engrossment /in gróssmənt/ *n* **1. COMPLETELY ABSORBED STATE** the complete absorption of somebody's attention with something **2.** FIN **CORNERING OF COMMODITY MARKET** the purchasing of enough of a commodity to control the market in it **3.** LAW **FINAL LEGAL COPY** a formally prepared copy of a deed or other document for legal use **4.** LAW **PREPARATION OF DOCUMENT** the preparation of the final legal copy or a clean copy of a document (*dated*)

engulf /in gúlf/ (**-gulfs, -gulfing, -gulfed**), **ingulf** *vt* **1.** to surround, cover over, and swallow up somebody or something, as floodwaters do **2.** to overwhelm somebody or something with a great amount or number of something (*often passive*) ○ *A deep grief engulfed the country after his death.* —**engulfment** *n*

enhance /in haánss/ (**-hances, -hancing, -hanced**) *vt* **1.** to improve or add to the strength, worth, beauty, or other desirable quality of something **2.** to increase the clarity, degree of detail, or another quality of an electronic image by using a computer program [13C. < Anglo-Norman *enhauncer* 'raise up' < Latin *altus* 'high'] —**enhancement** *n* —**enhancer** *n*

enharmonic /én haar mónnik/ *adj* describes musical notes, e.g. A♯ and B♭, that appear differently in a score but have the same pitch in a tempered scale, e.g. on the piano. In other scales or on other instruments, enharmonic notes may actually have different pitches. —**enharmonically** *adv*

enigma /i nígmə/ *n* somebody or something that is not easily explained or understood [Mid-16C. Via Latin < Greek *ainigma* < *ainos* 'fable']

CULTURAL NOTE ***The Enigma Variations***, an orchestral work (1899) by British composer Edward Elgar. Elgar's most popular and widely performed work, it was originally entitled *Variations on an Original Theme*. Each of the variations is a musical portrait of a friend of Elgar, identified in the score only by his or her initials or nickname. The title of Elgar's piece influenced the Berlin engineer who built the now-famed German military cipher machine known as *Enigma*, a typewriter-like device capable of producing an infinite number of ciphers.

SYNONYMS See ***problem***.

enigmatic /énnig máttik/, **enigmatical** /-máttik'l/ *adj* having a quality of mystery and ambiguity and so difficult to understand or interpret —**enigmatically** *adv*

SYNONYMS See ***obscure***.

enisle /in íl/ (**-isles, -isling, -isled**) *vt* (*literary*) **1.** to isolate somebody or something from other people or things **2.** to make something into an island

enjambment /in jám mənt/, **enjambement** *n* the continuation of meaning, without pause or break, from one line of poetry to the next [Mid-19C. < French *enjambement* < *jambe* 'leg' (see JAMB)] —**enjambed** *adj*

enjoin /in jóyn/ (**-joins, -joining, -joined**) *vt* **1. COMMAND SOMEBODY** to command somebody to do something or behave in a particular way (*formal*) ○ *were enjoined to be silent* **2. IMPOSE SOMETHING** to impose a condition or course of action on others ○ *enjoined secrecy upon us* **3.** LAW **FORBID OR COMMAND LEGALLY** to forbid or command somebody to do something by means of a legal injunction —**enjoiner** *n* —**enjoinment** *n*

enjoy /in jóy/ (**-joys, -joying, -joyed**) *v* **1.** *vt* **FIND SOMETHING PLEASING** to take pleasure in something ○ *really enjoying the ballet* **2.** *vt* **HAVE USE OF SOMETHING** to have the full and satisfying use or benefit of something ○ *He will enjoy sole possession of the estate.* **3.** *vt* **BENEFIT FROM CIRCUMSTANCES** to benefit from a desirable condition or situation ○ *The resort enjoys months of uninterrupted sunshine.* **4. enjoy yourself** *vr* **HAVE GOOD EXPERIENCE** to have a pleasurable experience ○ *enjoyed themselves at the party* [14C. < Old French *enjoïr* < Latin *gaudere* 'rejoice'] —**enjoyer** *n*

enjoyable /in jóy əb'l/ *adj* providing or capable of providing pleasure ○ *The food is always enjoyable.* —**enjoyableness** *n* —**enjoyably** *adv*

enjoyment /in jóymənt/ *n* **1. PLEASURE** pleasure that results from using or experiencing something ○ *eating with great enjoyment* **2. EXPERIENCING OF SOMETHING PLEASURABLE** the experiencing of something that provides pleasure ○ *his obvious enjoyment of the concert* **3. SOURCE OF PLEASURE** something that gives pleasure ○ *Fishing is one of her chief enjoyments.* **4. USE OR BENEFIT** the use or benefit of something, especially as a legal right ○ *the enjoyment of his rights as a landowner*

enkephalin /en kéffəlin/, **encephalin** /en kéffəlin, -séffə-/ *n* either of two chemicals with opiate qualities that are secreted in the brain and spinal cord and act to relieve pain [Mid-20C. < Greek *egkephalos* 'brain' (see ENCEPHALO-)]

enkindle /in kínd'l/ (**-dles, -dling, -dled**) *v* **1.** *vt* to spark an emotional or intellectual response in somebody **2.** *vti* to set something on fire, or start burning —**enkindler** *n*

enl. *abbr* **1.** enlarged **2.** enlisted

enlace /in láyss/ (**-laces, -lacing, -laced**), **inlace** *v* **1.** *vt* to wrap something round with laces or something similar **2.** *vti* to intertwine with something, or become intertwined —**enlacement** *n*

enlarge /in laárj/ (**-larges, -larging, -larged**) *v* **1.** *vti* **MAKE OR BECOME LARGER** to increase the size, amount, or extent of something, or become larger **2.** *vti* **BROADEN IN SCOPE** to broaden the scope of something, or become broader in scope ○ *the need for the investigation to be enlarged* **3.** *vi* **GIVE MORE DETAIL** to speak or write at greater length or in more detail about something **4.** *vt* PHOTOGRAPHY **MAKE LARGER VERSION OF PHOTOGRAPH** to make a photographic print or image that is larger than the original negative, print, or slide —**enlarger** *n*

SYNONYMS See ***increase***.

enlargement /in laárjmənt/ *n* **1. PROCESS OF ENLARGING** the process of increasing, broadening, or enlarging something, or of being increased, broadened, or enlarged **2. ADDITION TO SOMETHING** something added to something else to make it larger ○ *an enlargement to a house* **3. ENLARGED CONDITION** the increased, broadened, or enlarged state of something **4.** PHOTOGRAPHY **ENLARGED PHOTOGRAPH** a photographic print or image that is larger than the negative, print, or slide from which it was made

enlighten /in lít'n/ (**-ens, -ening, -ened**) *vt* **1. GIVE INFORMATION TO SOMEBODY** to give clarifying information to somebody ○ *Let me enlighten you about our problems.* **2. FREE SOMEBODY FROM IGNORANCE** to free somebody from ignorance, prejudice, or superstition ○ *an article written to enlighten his critics* **3. TEACH SOMEBODY RELIGION** to teach religious beliefs to an unbeliever —**enlightener** *n* —**enlightening** *adj*

enlightened /in lít'nd/ *adj* **1. RATIONAL** free of ignorance, prejudice, or superstition ○ *an enlightened age* **2. WELL-INFORMED** having a sound and open-minded understanding of all the facts, or based on such an understanding ○ *an enlightened piece of legislation* **3. HAVING ACHIEVED GREAT SPIRITUALITY** having achieved the realization of a spiritual or religious understanding

enlightenment /in lít'nmənt/ *n* **1. ENLIGHTENING OF SOMEBODY** the enlightening of somebody, or something that enlightens somebody **2. ENLIGHTENED STATE** the condition of somebody who has been enlightened **3. ACHIEVEMENT OF SPIRITUAL STATE** the realization of spiritual or religious understanding, or, especially in Buddhism, the state attained when the cycle of reincarnation ends and human desire and suffering are transcended

Enlightenment *n* an 18th-century intellectual movement in Western Europe that emphasized reason and science in philosophy and in the study of human culture and the natural world

enlist /in líst/ (**-lists, -listing, -listed**) *vti* **1.** to enrol somebody in a branch of the armed forces, or join the armed forces **2.** to gain the cooperation or support of somebody or something, or become actively involved in an effort ○ *May I enlist your help in this?* —**enlistment** *n*

enlisted person *n US* a non-officer member of the US armed forces, especially of a rank below non-commissioned officer

enliven /in lív'n/ (**-ens, -ening, -ened**) *vt* **1.** to make

somebody or something more lively or interesting ○ *We felt enlivened after our walk in the fresh air.* **2.** to make something brighter or more cheerful ○ *A few more pictures on the wall would enliven this room.* —**enlivener** *n* —**enlivenment** *n*

en masse /óN máss/ *adv* as a body, or in a group ○ *people arriving en masse to vote* [Late 18C. < French, 'in a mass']

enmesh /in mésh/ (**-meshes, -meshing, -meshed**), **inmesh, immesh** /i mésh/ *vt* **1.** to entangle somebody or something in something from which it is difficult to be extricated or separated ○ *a government enmeshed in scandal* **2.** to catch somebody or something in the mesh of a net —**enmeshment** *n*

enmity /énmiti/ (*plural* **-ties**) *n* the extreme ill will or hatred that exists between enemies ○ *trying to resolve age-old enmities* [13C < Old French *enemistie* < Latin *inimicus* (see ENEMY)]

ennage /énnij/ *n* in printing, the number of ens calculated as being in a piece of text for typesetting

~~**ennemy**~~ incorrect spelling of **enemy**

Ennerdale Water /énnər dayl-/ lake in western Cumbria, northwestern England. Area: 5 sq. km/2 sq. mi.

Enniskillen /énniss kíllən/ town in Fermanagh, Northern Ireland. It stands on an island in the River Erne. Population: 11,436 (1991).

Ennius /énni əss/, **Quintus** (239–169? BC) Roman poet and dramatist, called the founding father of Roman poetry. He introduced the hexameter into Roman verse, invented the literary miscellany, and wrote an epic of Roman history, of which only fragments survive.

> 'How like us is that ugly brute, the ape!'
> [Quintus Ennius. Quoted in *De Divinatione (On Divination)*, Cicero; 1942 (tr. H. Rackham)]

ennoble /i nṓb'l/ (**-bles, -bling, -bled**) *vt* **1.** to confer a noble title on somebody ○ *ennobled for his services to his country* **2.** to make somebody or something noble or more dignified (*formal*) —**ennoblement** *n* —**ennobler** *n*

ennui /ón wee/ *n* weariness and dissatisfaction with life that results from a loss of interest or sense of excitement [Mid-18C. < French < Latin *in odio (est)* '(it is) hateful']

ENO *abbr* MUSIC English National Opera

enoki /e nṓki/, **enoki mushroom** *n* a white edible mushroom with a small cap and long thin stem. Native to: eastern Asia, North America. Latin name: *Flammulina velutipes*. [Late 20C. < Japanese]

enol /ée nol/ *n* an organic compound that has a hydroxyl group bonded to a carbon atom that is attached to another carbon atom by a double bond [Mid-20C. < -ENE + -OL [1]] —**enolic** /ee nóllik/ *adj*

enolase /éenō layz, -layss/ *n* an enzyme involved in the metabolism of carbohydrates

enology *n* WINE US spelling of **oenology**

enormity /i náwrməti/ (*plural* **-ties**) *n* **1.** WICKEDNESS extreme wickedness or moral offensiveness ○ *the enormity of his crimes against humanity* **2.** EXTREMELY WICKED DEED an extremely wicked or morally offensive deed **3.** ⚠ IMMENSITY an extreme greatness of size, amount, or degree that is overwhelming ○ *the enormity of the budget deficit* **4.** ⚠ GREAT SIGNIFICANCE great importance and consequence ○ *the enormity of the social change wrought by the Industrial Revolution* [15C. Via French < Latin *enormitas* < *enormis* 'irregular' (see ENORMOUS)]

USAGE enormity or **enormousness**? ***Enormity*** is the older word, and after several changes in usage over several centuries it settled down in the 19th century in the meanings associated with wickedness or moral offensiveness. It is used in this way both as a concept or attribute and as a specific instance with a plural form: *We were shocked by the enormity of the crime. The regime committed many enormities to suppress opposition.* ***Enormousness*** has the more neutral meaning in relation to size, so that *the enormousness of the task* implies only a great or difficult task. Although ***enormity*** is commonly used informally in this neutral sense, and to mean 'great significance', in formal writing a better course may be to find alternatives such as *vastness* or *immensity*.

enormous /i náwrməss/ *adj* unusually large or great in size, amount, or degree [Mid-16C. < Latin *enormis* 'irregular' < *norma* 'rule'] —**enormously** *adv*

enormousness *n* the quality of being huge in size, scope, or significance

USAGE See ***enormity***.

enough /i núf/ *adj* **1.** ADEQUATE as much as is needed ○ *enough time to go shopping* **2.** AS MUCH AS IS BEARABLE as much or as many as can be tolerated ○ *in enough trouble already* ■ *adv* **1.** TO THE NECESSARY EXTENT to an extent that is as much as is needed ○ *I couldn't run fast enough to catch the cat.* **2.** ADDS EMPHASIS used to give emphasis to adverbs ○ *Oddly enough, we'd met before.* **3.** TO A TOLERABLE DEGREE to an extent that is as much as can be tolerated ○ *She was arrogant enough before her promotion.* **4.** PASSABLY to a moderate or satisfactory extent ○ *speaks the language well enough* ■ *pron* NEEDED OR TOLERATED AMOUNT the amount that is needed or that can be tolerated ○ *Bring more money; we never have enough.* ■ *interj* STOP THAT! used to tell somebody firmly to stop doing something (*informal*) ○ *Enough! There will be no more teasing in the car.* [Old English *genōg* < Germanic] ◇ **enough is enough** used by a speaker to indicate that he or she will tolerate no more of something

enounce /i nównss/ (**enounces, enouncing, enounced**) *vt* **1.** to pronounce a word clearly and definitely **2.** to state something in an official way (*formal*) [Early 19C. Via French *énoncer* < Latin *enuntiare* 'tell' (see ENUNCIATE)] —**enouncement** *n*

en papillote ➧ **papillote**

en passant /ón páss ont, óN pa sóN/ *adv* **1.** in passing rather than as the full focus of somebody's attention (*formal*) ○ *He mentioned it en passant.* **2.** in chess, used when a pawn that has moved two squares is captured by an enemy pawn as if it had only moved one square ○ *capture a pawn en passant* [Mid-17C. < French, 'in passing']

enplane /in pláyn/ *vti ANZ, US* same as **emplane**

enprint /én print/ *n* a photographic print in standard size, usually 15 cm x 10 cm/6 in x 4 in, enlarged from a negative [Mid-20C. < *enlarged print*]

en prise /oN préez/ *adj* describes a chess piece positioned in such a way that it could be captured if it is not moved [Early 19C. < French, 'in (position for) capture']

enquire /in kwír/ (**-quires, -quiring, -quired**), **inquire** *v* **1.** *vti* to ask a question ○ *enquire about a job* ○ *The secretary enquired whether I intended to stay on another year.* **2.** *vi* to try to discover the facts of a case [13C. Via French < Latin *inquirere* 'enquire into' < *quaerere* 'seek'] —**enquirer** *n* ◇ **enquire after** to ask for news about somebody's health or welfare

USAGE enquire or **inquire**? For many users, the two spellings are interchangeable, as with *enquiry* and *inquiry*. A useful distinction that some people maintain, however, is to use ***enquire*** and *enquiry* in contexts of casual requests for information, and to reserve ***inquire*** and *inquiry* for contexts of formal, official, or academic investigation: *He enquired after her health. Try directory enquiries. The police are inquiring into the circumstances that led up to his disappearance. There will have to be a public inquiry into the allegations.*

enquiring /in kwíring/ *adj* **1.** eager to learn new things **2.** appearing to want to know or learn something —**enquiringly** *adv*

enquiry /in kwíri, en-/ (*plural* **-ies**), **inquiry** /in-/ *n* **1.** a formal investigation to determine the facts of a case **2.** a request for information

enrage /in ráyj/ (**-rages, -raging, -raged**) *vt* to make somebody furiously angry

enrapt /in rápt/ *adj* in a state of delight or ecstasy (*formal*)

enrapture /in rápchər/ (**-tures, -turing, -tured**) *vt* to fill somebody with delight

enrich /in rích/ (**-riches, -riching, -riched**) *vt* **1.** ENHANCE QUALITY OF SOMETHING to improve the quality of something, usually by adding something else to it ○ *enriching the curriculum with multimedia resources* **2.** FOOD INDUST IMPROVE NUTRITIONAL CONTENT OF FOOD to add substances such as vitamins or minerals to a food to improve its nutritional value ○ *calcium-enriched orange juice* **3.** MAKE SOMEBODY OR SOMETHING WEALTHIER to increase the amount of wealth that somebody or something has **4.** PHYS ADD MORE OF CONSTITUENT TO SUBSTANCE to boost the amount of an active substance in a mixture, e.g. in a fuel **5.** AGRIC IMPROVE SOIL to improve the nutrient value of soil by adding natural or artificial fertilizers **6.** ADORN SOMETHING to add to the beauty of something with decoration (*literary*) —**enricher** *n* —**enrichment** *n*

Enright /én rīt/, **D. J.** (1920–2002) British poet, author, and critic. He came to prominence as part of the so-called 'Movement' group of poets in the 1950s. Full name **Enright, Dennis Joseph**

enrobe /in rṓb/ (**-robes, -robing, -robed**) *v* **1.** *vti* to put ceremonial robes on somebody (*formal*) **2.** *vt* to invest somebody with a grand or noble quality (*literary*)

enrol /in rṓl/ (**-rols, -rolling, -rolled**) *v* **1.** *vti* ADD NAME TO REGISTER to enter your own or somebody else's name on an official register or list of members ○ *enrol the children in school* **2.** *vt* ENSURE AVAILABILITY OF RESOURCE to make sure that something, especially somebody's help, will definitely be available **3.** *vt* ROLL SOMETHING UP to form something into a roll **4.** *vt* WRITE OFFICIAL COPY OF SOMETHING to produce the final version of something, usually a formal document or record [14C. < Old French *enroller* 'put on a roll' < *rolle* (see ROLL)] —**enrollee** /in rṓ lée/ *n*

enrolment /in rṓlmənt/ *n* **1.** SIGNING UP FORMALLY the official act or process of entering your own or somebody else's name on a register or membership list **2.** NUMBER OF PEOPLE REGISTERED the number of people registered for something, e.g. a class ○ *a sharp increase in student enrolments* **3.** LIST OF PEOPLE REGISTERED a list of people registered for or enrolled in something

en route /ón róot, oN-/ *adv* during the journey to a destination [Late 18C. < French, 'on (the) way']

ens /enz/ (*plural* **entia** /énshi ə, énti ə/) *n* an actual entity, as distinct from a quality or characteristic [Mid-16C. < late Latin, present participle (after Latin *absens* 'absent') of Latin *esse* 'be']

Ens. *abbr* NAVY ensign

ENSA /énssə/ *n* a British organization formed to provide entertainment for Allied forces during World War II. Full form **Entertainments National Service Association**

ensconce /in skónss/ (**-sconces, -sconcing, -sconced**) *vt* to make somebody or yourself comfortably established, as though ready to stay a long while (*often passive*) ○ *were ensconced on the sofa*

ensemble /on sómb'l/ *n* **1.** GROUP OF PERFORMERS a group of musicians, dancers, or actors who perform together with roughly equal contributions from all members (*takes a singular or plural verb*) **2.** OUTFIT OF CLOTHES a number of different items of clothing and accessories, put together to create an outfit **3.** SOMETHING FORMED BY SEVERAL ITEMS something created from a number of individual parts put together deliberately **4.** MUSIC MUSICAL SECTION INVOLVING ALL PERFORMERS a section of a larger musical work, e.g. a ballet or opera, that all the cast perform together ■ *adj* PERFORMED AS GROUP performed collaboratively, with no performer given prominence [Mid-18C. < French, 'together' < Latin *insimul* 'in at the same time' < *simul* 'at the same time']

enshrine /in shrín/ (**-shrines, -shrining, -shrined**), **inshrine** *vt* **1.** to protect something from change, e.g. in a formal constitution ○ *principles enshrined in law* **2.** to keep or cherish something in a shrine or other special place —**enshrinement** *n*

enshroud /in shrówd/ (**-shrouds, -shrouding, -shrouded**) *vt* **1.** to cover or obscure something (*usually passive*) ○ *towers enshrouded in mist* **2.** to cover somebody in a shroud

ensiform /énssi fawrm/ *adj* describes leaves that are long and narrow with a pointed tip [Mid-16C. Via French < modern Latin *ensiformis* < Latin *ensi-* 'sword' + *forma* 'form, shape']

ensign /én sīn, énss'n/ *n* **1.** FLAG INDICATING NATIONALITY a flag that shows the nationality of the ship or aircraft

flying it or what military unit it belongs to **2. FLAG WITH UNION FLAG IN CORNER** a naval flag bearing a small Union Flag in the upper corner next to the staff **(canton) 3.** NAVY **US NAVY RANK** an officer in the US Navy or Coast Guard of the lowest rank **4. BADGE OF OFFICE** an emblem or sign that indicates authority or command **5. FLAG-BEARER** a bearer of a national emblem or a standard (*dated*) **6. FORMER RANK IN BRITISH ARMY** before 1871, a commissioned officer in the British infantry of the lowest rank [14C. < Old French *enseigne* < Latin *insignia* (plural) 'badges' < *signum* 'mark']

ensilage /énsilij/ *n* **1.** the harvesting and preservation of green fodder crops for future use by fermentation in a silo **2.** AGRIC same as **silage**

ensile /en sī́l/ **(-siles, -siling, -siled)** *vt* to preserve green fodder, e.g. grass, as silage by allowing it to ferment and become acidified in a silo [Late 19C. Via French < Spanish *ensilar* < *en* 'in' + *silo* (see SILO)]

enslave /in sláyv/ **(-slaves, -slaving, -slaved)** *vt* **1.** to take somebody prisoner and claim legal ownership of that person and his or her labour **2.** to subject somebody to a dominating influence that takes away his or her freedom —**enslaver** *n*

enslavement /in sláyvmənt/ *n* the state or condition of being enslaved or otherwise bound into servitude

ensnare /in snáir/ **(-snares, -snaring, -snared)**, **insnare** *vt* **1.** to lure somebody into a bad situation from which it is difficult to escape **2.** to catch an animal in a trap —**ensnarement** *n* —**ensnarer** *n*

ensnarl /in snaárl/ **(-snarls, -snarling, -snarled)** *vt* to involve somebody or something in a situation that causes delay (*often passive*)

Ensor /én sawr, óN-/, **James Sydney, Baron** (1860–1949) Belgian painter and engraver. He was a forerunner of expressionism. His works, notably *Christ's Entry into Brussels in 1889* (1888), often incorporated masked figures and macabre medieval imagery.

ensoul /in sṓl/ **(-souls, -souling, -souled)**, **insoul** *vt* (*literary*) **1.** to endow somebody with a soul **2.** to cherish deeply something such as a feeling or memory

ensphere /in sféer/ **(-spheres, -sphering, -sphered)**, **insphere** *vt* **1.** to make something sphere-shaped (*formal*) **2.** to enclose something in a sphere or in something like a sphere (*literary*)

enstatite /énstə tīt/ *n* a brown, grey, or yellowish magnesium iron silicate mineral of the pyroxene group. Source: igneous rocks, meteorites. [Mid-19C. < German *Enstatit* < Greek *enstat-* 'adversary'; from its refractoriness]

ensue /in syoó/ **(-sues, -suing, -sued)** *vi* **1.** to follow closely after something **2.** to be a consequence of something [14C. < Old French *ensu-*, stem of *ensuivre* < assumed Vulgar Latin *insequere* 'follow in' < Latin *sequi* 'follow']

ensuing /in syoó ing/ *adj* happening next or as a result

en suite /ón sweét, oN-/ *adj, adv* **AS ONE OF SET OF ROOMS** forming part of a larger unit or set of rooms ○ *an en suite bathroom* ■ *n* (*informal*) **1. ADJOINING BATHROOM** a bathroom leading off the bedroom **2. HOTEL ROOM WITH OWN BATHROOM** a hotel bedroom with an en suite bathroom [Late 18C. < French, 'in succession']

ensure /in shoór, in sháwr/ **(-sures, -suring, -sured)** *vt* to make sure that something will happen or be available ○ *ensure a supply of fresh food* ○ *We must ensure that the environment remains a central concern.* ○ *He thought his donation might ensure him an invitation.* [14C. < Anglo-Norman *enseurer*, alteration of Old French *asseurer, assurer* (see ASSURE)]

USAGE See ***assure***.

enswathe /in swáyth/ **(-swathes, -swathing, -swathed)** *vt* to wrap somebody or something in bandages or cloth (*literary*)

ENT *abbr* MED ear, nose, and throat

-ent *suffix* **1.** performing a particular action ○ *acquiescent* **2.** one that performs a particular action ○ *respondent* [< Latin *-ent-*, present participle ending] —**-ence** *suffix* —**-ency** *suffix*

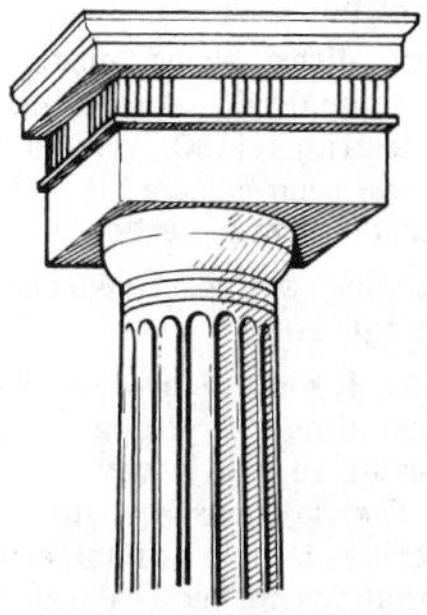

entablature

entablature /en tábblәchər/ *n* in classical architecture, the section of a structure that lies between the columns and the roof. It comprises, from bottom to top, the architrave, frieze, and cornice. [Early 17C. Via obsolete French < Italian *intavolatura* 'boarding' < *intavolare* 'board up, put on a table' < *tavola* 'table']

entablement /in táyb'lmənt/ *n* ARCHIT, SCULPTURE same as **plinth** (*technical*) [Mid-17C. < French < *table* 'table']

entail /in táyl/ *vt* **(-tails, -tailing, -tailed) 1. HAVE SOMETHING AS CONSEQUENCE** to involve or result in something inevitably **2. RESTRICT OWNERSHIP OF BEQUEST** to restrict the future ownership of property to particular descendants, through instructions written into a will ■ *n* LAW **1. RESTRICTION OF FUTURE OWNERSHIP** the limiting of the future ownership of bequeathed property to particular descendants **2. ENTAILED PROPERTY** a property that has been entailed **3. FUTURE OWNERS OF ENTAILED PROPERTY** the line of descendants who own an entailed property [14C. < EN- + Old French *taille* 'limitation' < *taillier* 'to cut' (see TAILOR)] —**entailment** *n*

entangle /in táng g'l/ **(-gles, -gling, -gled)** *vt* **1. TANGLE SOMETHING UP** to make something become twisted up in a mass of strands, e.g. netting or hair (*usually passive*) **2. PUT SOMEBODY IN DIFFICULT SITUATION** to involve somebody or something in a muddle that will be difficult to escape from (*usually passive*) ○ *were entangled in corporate politics* **3. COMPLICATE SOMETHING** to make something more complicated or confusing ○ *The story entangles the facts with value judgments.* —**entanglement** *n*

entasis /éntəssiss/ *n* in architecture, a slight bulge in the shaft of a column, designed to counter the visual impression of concavity that a perfectly straight column would give [Mid-18C. < Greek, 'straining' < *teinein* 'to stretch']

Entebbe /en tébbi/ city on the northwestern shore of Lake Victoria near Kampala, southern Uganda. Its airport, one of the largest in East Africa, was the scene of a successful Israeli raid on a hijacked commercial aircraft in 1976 leading to the release of over 100 hostages. Population: 41,638 (1991 estimate).

entelechy /in télləki/ *n* **1.** the real existence of a thing, not merely its theoretical existence **2.** in some philosophies, a life-giving force believed to be responsible for the development of all living things [Early 17C. Via late Latin < Greek *entelekheia* 'having completeness' < *entelēs* 'complete' < *telos* 'end']

entente /on tónt/ *n* **1.** a state of friendly agreement or understanding that exists or is declared between two or more countries **2.** the parties involved in an entente [Mid-19C. < French, 'understanding' < *entendre* (see INTEND)]

entente cordiale /on tónt kawrdi aál/ (*plural* **ententes cordiales** /pronunc. same/) *n* amicable relations between countries or states, especially the agreement formed between France and Britain in 1904 [< French, 'friendly understanding']

enter /éntər/ *v* **(-ters, -tering, -tered) 1.** *vti* **GO IN** to go or come into a place **2.** *vt* COMPUT **WRITE OR TYPE SOMETHING** to write or type something in a book or on a computer ○ *The names and addresses are entered into a database.* **3.** *vt* **SUBMIT SOMETHING FOR CONSIDERATION** to submit something officially, e.g. a proposal, complaint, or bid, for formal consideration **4.** *vti* **REGISTER AS COMPETITOR** to register to take part in a competition ○ *enter the race for president* **5.** *vt* **JOIN OR BECOME INVOLVED IN SOMETHING** to join or become officially involved in something, especially a body such as a college or company ○ *more women entering the profession* **6.** *vi* THEATRE **WALK ON** to come on stage during a play ○ *She enters stage right.* **7.** *vti* **MAKE HOLE IN SOMETHING** to force a way into something, or be pushed or inserted into something, especially the human body ○ *The bullet entered through the anterior abdominal wall.* **8.** *vt* LAW **TAKE LEGAL OWNERSHIP OF LAND** to go onto land and take legal possession of it ■ *n* COMPUT same as **return key** [13C. Via French < Latin *intrare* 'go in, enter' < *intra* 'inside, within']

enter into *vt* **1. TAKE PART IN SOMETHING ENTHUSIASTICALLY** to get actively involved in something ○ *Enter into the spirit of things.* **2. BE RELEVANT TO SOMETHING** to be one of the factors that are relevant to something ○ *Money doesn't enter into it.* **3. SIGN UP TO SOMETHING** to become one of the parties bound by a contract **4. CONSIDER SOMETHING FORMALLY** to go into a discussion or investigation about something ○ *I do not propose to enter into the issue of who is responsible.*

enter on, enter upon *vt* to start out on something such as an important task or a significant period

enter- *prefix* same as **entero-** (*used before vowels*)

enteral feeding /éntərəl-/ *n* direct infusion into the intestines of nutrients in liquid form [Partly < ENTERIC, partly back-formation < PARENTERAL]

enteric /en térrik/ *adj* relating to or situated in the intestine [Mid-19C. < Greek *enterikos* < *enteron* 'intestine']

enteric fever *n* MED same as **typhoid**

enteritis /éntə rī́tiss/ *n* inflammation of the intestine, most commonly of the small intestine

enter key *n* **1.** a key on a numeric keypad for entering calculations **2.** COMPUT same as **return key**

entero- *prefix* intestine ○ *enterotomy* [< Greek *enteron* < Indo-European, 'in, inside']

enterobiasis /éntərō bī́ əssiss/ *n* infestation of the large intestine with pinworms, especially in children

enterocoele /éntərō seel/ *n* a body cavity **(coelom)** formed from an outgrowth in the wall of an embryonic intestine, especially in invertebrate marine organisms such as starfish and sea urchins

enterocolitis /éntərō kə lī́tiss/ *n* inflammation of the small and large intestine as a result of infection

enterokinase /éntərō kī́ nayz/ *n* a duodenal enzyme that converts trypsinogen to trypsin

enteron /éntə ron/ *n* **1.** the alimentary canal, especially of an embryo **2.** the intestine of invertebrate sea animals, e.g. sea anemones and jellyfish, that has one opening that serves as both mouth and anus [Mid-19C. < Greek, 'intestine']

enteropathy /éntə róppəthi/ (*plural* **-thies**) *n* any disease of the intestines

enterostomy /éntə róstəmi/ (*plural* **-mies**) *n* the surgical creation of a permanent opening into the intestine through the abdominal wall —**enterostomal** *adj*

enterotomy /éntə róttəmi/ (*plural* **-mies**) *n* a surgical incision into the intestine

enterotoxin /éntərō tóksin/ *n* any toxin produced by bacteria that causes the vomiting and diarrhoea associated with food poisoning

enterovirus /éntərō vī́rəss/ (*plural* **-ruses**) *n* a virus that lives in the gastrointestinal tract but may multiply there and invade other parts of the body. Poliomyelitis is an enterovirus.

enterprise /éntər prīz/ *n* **1. COMMERCIAL BUSINESS** a commercial company **2. BUSINESS ACTIVITIES DIRECTED AT PROFIT** organized business activities aimed specifically at growth and profit **3. DARING NEW PROJECT** a new, often risky, venture that involves confidence and initiative **4. READINESS TO UNDERTAKE NEW VENTURES** readiness to put effort into new, often risky, ventures or activities [15C. < Old French *entreprise* < past participle of *entreprendre* 'undertake' < *prendre* 'take' (see PRIZE [2])]

Enterprise, Transport, and Lifelong Learning Department *n* a department of the Scottish Executive, responsible for industrial development, transport and communications, and further education

Enterprise Allowance Scheme *n* formerly, a gov-

ernment scheme to help unemployed people set up in business by providing an allowance

enterprise culture *n* a way of life that focuses on the importance of individual people creating their own businesses and wealth

enterprise software *n* computer software designed to integrate and automate all of a company's functions

enterprise zone *n* an economically depressed urban area where the government encourages new business ventures by offering financial incentives

enterprising /éntər prìzing/ *adj* showing initiative and a willingness to undertake new, often risky, projects —**enterprisingly** *adv*

entertain /éntər táyn/ (**-tains, -taining, -tained**) *v* **1.** *vti* AMUSE OR INTEREST AUDIENCE to engage a person or audience by providing amusing or interesting material **2.** *vti* OFFER HOSPITALITY to offer hospitality, especially by providing food and drink for guests at home **3.** *vt* CONSIDER SOMETHING to turn something over in the mind, looking at it from various points of view ○ *He would never entertain such an idea!* [15C. < Old French *entretenir* 'hold together, support' < assumed Vulgar Latin *intertenere* 'hold between' < Latin *tenere* 'hold']

entertainer /éntər táynər/ *n* a provider of entertainment, especially a professional one

entertaining /éntər táyning/ *adj* enjoyable to watch, read, or listen to —**entertainingly** *adv*

entertainment /éntər táynmənt/ *n* **1.** ART OF KEEPING PEOPLE ENTERTAINED the various ways of amusing people, especially by performing for them **2.** ENJOYMENT the amount of pleasure or amusement somebody gets from something **3.** PERFORMANCE OR EXHIBITION something that is produced or performed for an audience ○ *chief among the evening's entertainments*

enthalpy /én thəlpi, en thálpi/ *n* a thermodynamic property equal to the sum of the internal energy of a system and the product of its pressure and volume. Symbol **H** [Early 20C. < Greek *enthalpein* 'to warm within' < *thalpein* 'to heat']

enthral /in thráwl/ (**-thrals, -thralling, -thralled**), **inthrall** (**-thralls, -thralling, -thralled**) *vt* **1.** to delight or fascinate somebody thoroughly, engaging that person's attention completely **2.** to make somebody a prisoner and claim legal ownership of that person (*literary*) [Late 16C. < EN- + THRALL] —**enthralment** *n*

enthrall *vt* US spelling of **enthral**

enthralled /in thráwld/ *adj* fascinated and giving total attention to something

enthralling /in thráwling/ *adj* so interesting, delightful, or beautiful as to hold the attention completely

enthrone /in thrṓn/ (**-thrones, -throning, -throned**), **inthrone** *vt* **1.** to install a monarch or bishop, especially in a ceremony that involves seating the person on a throne (*formal*) **2.** to regard somebody as being worthy of adoration (*literary*) —**enthronement** *n*

enthuse /in thyóoz/ (**-thuses, -thusing, -thused**) *vti* **1.** to have, or make somebody feel, great excitement or interest **2.** to express enthusiasm about something or say something enthusiastically ○ *enthusing about the new restaurant* [Early 19C. Back-formation < ENTHUSIASM]

enthusiasm /in thyóozi azəm/ *n* **1.** passionate interest in or eagerness to do something **2.** something that arouses a consuming interest [Late 16C. Via late Latin < Greek *enthousiasmos* 'possession by (a) god' < *enthous* 'inspired' < *theos* 'god']

enthusiast /in thyóozi ast/ *n* somebody who is enthusiastic about something, especially a hobby [Early 17C. < Greek *enthousiastēs* 'somebody inspired (by a god)' < *enthous* (see ENTHUSIASM)]

enthusiastic /in thyóozi ástik/ *adj* showing passionate interest in something or eagerness about something —**enthusiastically** *adv*

enthymeme /énthə meem/ *n* an argument that assumes the truth of one or more premises and therefore omits them from the logical sequence [Late 16C. Via Latin < Greek *enthumēma* '(something) in mind' < *thumos* 'mind']

entia PHILOSOPHY plural of **ens**

entice /in tíss/ (**-tices, -ticing, -ticed**) *vt* to make a person or animal do something by offering something desirable [13C. Via Old French *enticier* < assumed Vulgar Latin *intitiare* 'set on fire' < Latin *titio* 'firebrand'] —**enticement** *n* —**enticer** *n*

enticing /in tíssing/ *adj* very desirable and hard to resist —**enticingly** *adv*

entire /in tír/ *adj* **1.** WHOLE as a whole, from beginning to end, or including everything ○ *rained the entire night* **2.** ABSOLUTE in every way, without doubt or question ○ *The day was an entire fiasco.* **3.** VET UNGELDED describes a male animal, especially a stallion or dog, that has not been castrated **4.** BOT SMOOTH-EDGED describes leaves with smooth edges that are not lobed or indented **5.** IN ONE PIECE not damaged or broken up (*literary*) ○ *'with strength entire, and free Will arm'd'* (John Milton, *Paradise Lost*; 1667) ■ *n* VET same as **stallion** (sense 1) [14C. Via Old French *entier* < Latin *integrum*, form of *integer* 'whole, intact']

entirely /in tírli/ *adv* **1.** in every sense ○ *an entirely different question* **2.** exclusively or individually ○ *I'm entirely at fault.*

entirety /in tírəti/ *n* the whole extent of something

~~**entirly**~~ incorrect spelling of **entirely**

entitle /in tít'l/ (**-tles, -tling, -tled**) *vt* **1.** GRANT SOMEBODY RIGHT to give somebody the right to have or to do something (*often passive*) **2.** GIVE TITLE TO SOMETHING to assign a title to something such as a book (*usually passive*) **3.** AWARD SOMEBODY HONOUR to confer an official position or honour on somebody that brings a particular title with it [14C. Via French < late Latin *intitulare* < Latin *titulus* 'inscription'] —**entitlement** *n*

entitlement card *n* a national identity card proposed by the UK government in the form of a smart card that could include personal information such as health and tax records as well as enable the bearer to claim state benefits

entitlement programme *n* in the United States, a government programme that targets a particular section of the population to receive specific social benefits

entity /éntəti/ (*plural* **-ties**) *n* **1.** OBJECT something that exists as or is perceived as a single separate object **2.** PHILOSOPHY EXISTENCE the state of having existence **3.** PHILOSOPHY ESSENTIAL NATURE the essence or character of something [Late 16C. < medieval Latin *entitas* < late Latin *ent-*, stem of *ens* (see ENS)]

entomb /in tóom/ (**-tombs, -tombing, -tombed**) *vt* **1.** PUT CORPSE IN TOMB to put a corpse into a tomb **2.** PUT SOMETHING IN DEEP PLACE to put something in a place that is hidden or very deep ○ *the secret vaults where the treasures were entombed* **3.** BURY SOMEBODY OR SOMETHING to serve as a tomb for somebody or something ○ *the collapsed mine that entombed them* —**entombment** *n*

entomo- *prefix* insect ○ *entomophilous* [Via French < Greek *entomon* < *entomos* 'cut in two' < *temnein* 'to cut'; because of insects' distinctly segmented bodies]

entomology /éntə mólləji/ *n* the branch of zoology that deals with the study of insects [Mid-18C. < French *entomologie* or modern Latin *entomologia* 'science of insects' < Greek *entomon* (see ENTOMO-)] —**entomological** /éntəmə lójjik'l/ *adj* —**entomologically** *adv* —**entomologist** *n*

entomophagous /éntə móffəgəss/ *adj* feeding on insects

entomophilous /éntə móffiləss/ *adj* describes flowering plants that are pollinated by insects —**entomophily** *n*

entourage /ón too raazh/ *n* **1.** a group of special employees who go with a high-ranking or famous person on visits and engagements **2.** the surroundings or environment (*literary*) [Mid-19C. < French < *entourer* 'surround' < *tour* 'circuit']

entr'acte /ón trakt/ (*plural* **-tr'actes**) *n* **1.** an interval between the acts of a play or opera **2.** an additional piece of entertainment during the break between the acts of a play or opera [Mid-18C. < obsolete French, 'between the act(s)' < *acte* 'act']

entrails /én traylz/ *npl* **1.** INTERNAL ORGANS an animal's or person's internal organs **2.** INNER WORKINGS the various working parts inside something, especially something complex **3.** ANIMAL ORGANS USED FOR DIVINATION the internal organs of a sacrificial animal, used by the ancient Romans to try to determine the will of the gods [13C. Via Old French *entrailles* < medieval Latin *intralia*, alteration of Latin *interanea* 'intestines' < *inter* 'between']

entrain[1] /in tráyn/ (**-trains, -training, -trained**) *vti* to board or to put somebody or something aboard a train [Late 19C. < EN-] —**entrainer** *n* —**entrainment** *n*

entrain[2] /in tráyn/ (**-trains, -training, -trained**) *vt* **1.** to cause something to happen as a consequence of an action **2.** to draw solid particles, air bubbles, or liquid drops into a moving fluid and carry them along in the flow [Mid-16C. < Old French *entraîner* 'drag away' < *traîner* 'drag'] —**entrainment** *n*

entrance[1] /éntrənss/ *n* **1.** WAY IN a door or gate through which people enter **2.** ENTERING OF SITE the act or an instance of entering a place ○ *a highly theatrical entrance* **3.** RIGHT OF ENTRY the right to go into a place or to enter an institution [15C. < Old French < *entrer* (see ENTER)]

entrance[2] /in tráanss/ (**-trances, -trancing, -tranced**) *vt* **1.** to hold somebody's attention and produce a sense of wonder in that person **2.** to make somebody go into a trance [Late 16C. < EN-] —**entrancing** *adj* —**entrancingly** *adv*

entrant /éntrənt/ *n* somebody who enters a competition or examination [Mid-17C. < French, present participle of *entrer* (see ENTER)]

SYNONYMS See ***candidate***.

entrap /in tráp/ (**-traps, -trapping, -trapped**) *vt* **1.** to be restrained or restricted by circumstances ○ *entrapped by poverty* **2.** to deceive somebody, especially to trick somebody into committing or admitting to a crime —**entrapment** *n*

entreat /in tréet/ (**-treats, -treating, -treated**) *vti* to beg somebody for something, often repeatedly [14C. < Old French *entraitier* 'treat in (a certain way)' < *traitier* (see TREAT)] —**entreatingly** *adv*

entreaty /in tréeti/ (*plural* **-ies**) *n* a serious and passionate request

entrechat /óntrə shaa/ *n* in ballet, a leap in which the dancer's legs are crossed rapidly in the air and the heels are beaten together [Late 18C. Via French < Italian *(capriola) intrecciata* 'intricate (caper)']

entrecôte /óntrə kōt/, **entrecôte steak** *n* a piece of beef without any bone, cut from between the ribs [Mid-19C. < French, 'between (the) rib(s)']

entrée /ón tray/ *n* **1.** MAIN COURSE a dish served as the main part of a meal **2.** DISH BEFORE MAIN COURSE in a formal dinner, a light dish served before the main course **3.** RIGHT OF ENTRY something that permits entry into something, especially to an exclusive group or place [Late 18C. < French (see ENTRY)]

entremets /óntrə may/ (*plural same*) *n* **1.** in a formal dinner, a light dish served between the main course and the dessert **2.** a sweet dish, especially one served after cheese in a dinner of several courses [15C. < Old French, 'between the course(s)' < *mes* 'course']

entrench /in trénch/ (**-trenches, -trenching, -trenched**), **intrench** *v* **1.** *vt* DIG DEFENSIVE DITCH ROUND SOMETHING to defend something by surrounding it with trenches **2.** *vt* PROTECT SOMETHING to take action to protect an argument or position **3.** *vi* TRESPASS to encroach upon or trespass on somebody else's property or things (*archaic*) —**entrenchment** *n*

entrenched /in trénçht/ *adj* **1.** firmly held and hard to change ○ *deeply entrenched political views* **2.** firmly established and unlikely to change

entre nous /óntrə nóo/ *adv* in confidence [Late 17C. < French, 'between ourselves']

entrepôt /óntrə pō/ *n* **1.** COMM same as **free port** (sense 2) **2.** a bonded warehouse [Early 18C. < French < *entreposer* 'place in, store' < *poser* 'to place']

entrepreneur /óntrəprə núr/ *n* somebody who initiates or finances new commercial enterprises [Late 19C. < French, 'somebody who undertakes' < *entreprendre* (see ENTERPRISE)] —**entrepreneurial** *adj* —**entrepreneurialism** *n* —**entrepreneurism** *n* —**entrepreneurship** *n*

entresol /óntrə sol/ *n* BUILDINGS same as **mezzanine** *n* (sense 1) [Early 18C. Via French < Spanish *entresuelo* 'between-level' < *suelo* 'level' < Latin *solea* 'sole, sandal']

entropy /éntrəpi/ n **1.** MEASURE OF DISORDER a measure of the disorder that exists in a system **2.** PHYS MEASURE OF UNAVAILABLE ENERGY a measure of the energy in a system or process that is unavailable to do work. In a reversible thermodynamic process, entropy is expressed as the heat absorbed or emitted divided by the absolute temperature. Symbol S **3.** COMMUNICATION MEASURE OF EFFICIENCY a measure of the random errors (noise) occurring in the transmission of signals, and from this a measure of the efficiency of transmission systems [Mid-19C. < Greek *en-* 'in' + *tropē* 'change', after ENERGY] —**entropic** /en tróppik/ adj —**entropically** adv

entrust /in trúst/ (-trusts, -trusting, -trusted), **intrust** vt to give something to another person to be responsible for —**entrustment** n

entry /éntri/ (plural **-tries**) n **1.** GOING IN an act or instance of somebody entering **2.** same as **entrance**¹ (sense 3) **3.** PIECE OF WRITTEN INFORMATION an item or piece of data included in a list or a book **4.** INCLUDING OF ITEM ON LIST the process of recording something in writing or on a computer ○ *data entry* **5.** WAY IN a way into a place **6.** ENTRANT a person, animal, or item entered in a contest, or the total number entered ○ *the winning entry* **7.** MUSIC START OF PERFORMANCE the point in a musical performance at which an individual performer starts to play or sing **8.** CARDS WINNING CARD in some games, a card that can win a trick and thus gain the lead for a player **9.** regional PASSAGE BETWEEN HOUSES a passage between the backs of two rows of houses, or leading into a block of flats, or to the backs of houses in a terrace [13C. Via French *entrée* < Latin *intrata* < past participle of *intrare* (see ENTER)]

entryism /éntri izəm/ n the tactic of joining an existing political party in large numbers with the purpose of changing its policies and direction —**entryist** n

entry-level adj at the lowest level and suitable for somebody who is new to a job, field, or subject

Entryphone /éntri fōn/ tdmk a trademark for an intercom system that links each flat in a building with the main door and allows the occupant to open the door remotely

entryway /éntri way/ n N Am a way into a place, e.g. a doorway or passageway

entwine /in twín/ (-twines, -twining, -twined), **intwine** vti to twist things together or to twist something round something else (often passive) —**entwinement** n

entwist /in twíst/ (-twists, -twisting, -twisted), **intwist** vti same as **entwine**

enucleate /i nyóokli ayt, -kli ət/ vt (-ates, -ating, -ated) **1.** BIOL TAKE OUT NUCLEUS to remove the nucleus of a cell **2.** SURG SURGICALLY REMOVE SOMETHING WHOLE to remove something surgically, e.g. a tumour, from its capsule while keeping it intact ■ adj BIOL LACKING NUCLEUS describes a cell without a nucleus [Mid-16C. < Latin *enucleat-*, past participle of *enucleare* 'remove the pit from (olives, fruit)' < *nucleus* 'kernel' (see NUCLEUS)] —**enucleation** /i nyóokli áysh'n/ n

enuff /i núf/ adj, pron another spelling of **enough** (informal)

E number n **1.** a code by which a given additive is identified on food labels, consisting of the letter E followed by a number **2.** a food additive (informal) [Abbreviation of EUROPEAN]

enumerate /i nyóomə rayt/ (-ates, -ating, -ated) vt **1.** to name a number of things on a list one by one **2.** to count how many things there are in something [Mid-17C. < Latin *enumerat-*, past participle of *enumerare* 'count out' < *numerus* 'number'] —**enumerable** adj —**enumeration** /i nyóomə ráysh'n/ n —**enumerative** adj —**enumerator** n

enunciate /i núnssi ayt/ (-ates, -ating, -ated) v **1.** vti to pronounce something distinctly **2.** vt to give a speech or statement that explains something clearly [Early 17C. < Latin *enuntiat-*, past participle of *enuntiare* 'announce' < *nuntius* 'message, messenger'] —**enunciation** /i núnssi áysh'n/ n —**enunciative** adj —**enunciatively** adv —**enunciator** n

enure vt LAW another spelling of **inure**

enuresis /énnyoō reéssiss/ n involuntary discharge of urine, especially while asleep (technical) [Late 18C. < modern Latin < Greek *enourein* 'urinate in' < *ouron* 'urine'] —**enuretic** /-réttik/ adj

envelop /in vélləp/ (-ops, -oping, -oped) vt **1.** WRAP SOMETHING UP to enclose somebody or something completely (often passive) **2.** HIDE SOMETHING OR SOMEBODY to conceal something or somebody (often passive) **3.** MIL SURROUND ENEMY to surround an enemy completely [14C. < Old French *envoluper* 'wrap in'] —**enveloper** n —**envelopment** n

---

SPELLCHECK **envelope** or **envelop**? Do not confuse the spelling of **envelope** and **envelop**, which are spelt similarly but have different pronunciations. The verb **envelop**, meaning 'wrap', 'hide', or 'surround', is stressed on the middle syllable. The noun **envelope** has an 'e' at each end and is stressed on the first and last syllables.

---

envelope /énvə lōp, ónvə-/ n **1.** PAPER COVER FOR LETTER a flat pocket of paper with a sealable flap for holding a letter **2.** ENCLOSING CASE something that surrounds or encloses something else ○ *seafood sauce in filo pastry envelopes* **3.** ZOOL ENCLOSING STRUCTURE a covering that encloses and protects an animal's body or a biological structure, e.g. a shell or membrane **4.** MATHS CURVE FORMING TANGENT a curve or surface that forms a tangent to each of the members of a set of curves or surfaces, e.g. circles with a common centre but different radii **5.** AVIAT BALLOON the bag of an airship or balloon that contains the gas **6.** AVIAT PERFORMANCE LIMITS OF AIRCRAFT the performance limits of a piece of equipment, particularly of an aircraft [Early 18C. < French *enveloppe* < *envelopper* 'wrap in'] ◇ **push the envelope** to try to accomplish more than is theoretically possible (informal)

SPELLCHECK See **envelop**.

---

envenom /in vénnəm/ (-oms, -oming, -omed) vt **1.** to cause somebody to become malicious or hostile (formal) **2.** to make something poisonous (technical)

Enver Pasha /énvər páshə/, **General** (1881–1922) Turkish soldier and politician. He was elected leader of the revolutionary Young Turks in 1908 and became Turkey's minister of war in 1914. After World War I he fled to Russia, where he died in an anti-Bolshevik uprising.

enviable /énvi əb'l/ adj likely to evoke feelings of envy ○ *in the enviable position of having two job offers to choose from* —**enviably** adv

envious /énvi əss/ adj wanting to have somebody else's success, good fortune, qualities, or possessions —**enviously** adv —**enviousness** n

~~enviroment~~ incorrect spelling of **environment**

environ /in vírən/ (-rons, -roning, -roned) vt same as **surround** v (sense 1) (formal) [14C. < Old French *environer* 'make a circle around' < *viron* 'circle' < *virer* 'to turn']

environment /in vírənmənt/ n **1.** SURROUNDING INFLUENCES all the external factors influencing the life and activities of people, plants, and animals **2.** NATURAL WORLD the natural world, especially when it is regarded as being at risk from the harmful influences of human activities **3.** SET OF CONDITIONS a set of external conditions, especially those affecting a particular activity (usually in combination) ○ *the home environment* ○ *a stimulating learning environment* **4.** COMPUT COMPUTING FRAMEWORK a framework within which a computer, program, or user operates

Environment Agency n the government agency responsible for environmental protection in England and Wales

environmental /in vírən mént'l/ adj **1.** relating to the natural world, especially to its conservation ○ *environmental groups* **2.** relating to, or caused by, a person's or animal's surroundings ○ *environmental hazards*

environmental accounting n the practice of including the indirect costs and benefits of a product or activity, e.g. its environmental effects on health and the economy, along with its direct costs when making business decisions

environmental art n creative art, usually on a grand scale, that is meant to invite the viewer to participate by interacting with the artwork

environmental assessment n the identification of the likely environmental effects of a proposed de-

velopment. ◊ **environmental impact statement**. Aus, N Am term **environmental impact study**

environmental audit n an assessment of the effectiveness of an organization's environmental policies or of its behaviour in relation to environmental issues

environmental equity n the equal distribution of environmental risk among population groups regardless of race, income, gender, or age

environmental health n the local government functions concerned with minimizing risks to public health and the local environment, including the monitoring of water and air quality, hygiene in restaurants and shops, and pest control

Environmental Health Officer n somebody employed in the Environmental Health Service who deals with matters that affect public health and the environment

Environmental Health Service n the British local government body responsible for making sure that the environment is safe and that acceptable standards of hygiene are maintained for the general public. Its responsibilities include checking that waste is properly disposed of, water supplies are uncontaminated, and restaurants and shops are hygienic.

environmental impact n the indirect and direct consequences of human actions on the natural environment

environmental impact statement n a written statement of the likely environmental effects of a proposed development based on a scientific assessment or study ○ *'After the public comment period, the NRC will issue a final environmental impact statement by November.'* (Washington Post; April 1999)

environmental impact study n Aus, N Am an analysis carried out to determine the impact of a specific project, often a building project, on the environment. UK term **environmental assessment**

environmentalism /in vírən mént'lizəm/ n **1.** the movement, especially in politics and consumer affairs, that works towards protecting the natural world from harmful human activities **2.** a theory stating that somebody's environment is more influential than heredity in determining his or her development

environmentalist /in vírən mént'list/ n **1.** somebody involved in issues relating to the protection of the natural world, especially a member of a political group campaigning against the perceived harmful effects of industrialized societies **2.** a supporter of the theory that somebody's environment is more influential than heredity in determining his or her development. ◊ **hereditarian**

environmental labelling n ENVIRON same as **ecolabelling** —**environmental label** n

environmentally /in vírən mént'li/ adv with regard to the natural world and its vulnerability to destructive influences ○ *the environmentally aware consumer*

environmentally friendly, **environment-friendly** adj designed to minimize harm to the natural world, e.g. by using biodegradable ingredients

Environmentally Sensitive Area n a rural area designated by the government as in need of protection from some modern farming practices. Farmers are compensated for adopting less damaging but less profitable methods.

environmental studies n a course of academic study including a range of disciplines that relate to the environment (takes a singular or plural verb)

environment-friendly adj ENVIRON same as **environmentally friendly**

environs /in vírənz/ npl the land or area surrounding a place [Mid-17C. < French, plural of *environ* 'surroundings' < *viron* (see ENVIRON)]

envisage /in vízzij/ (-ages, -aging, -aged) vt **1.** FORESEE SOMETHING to conceive of and contemplate a future possibility ○ *Do you envisage being able to avert a crisis?* **2.** VISUALIZE SOMETHING to form a mental picture of something or somebody **3.** CONSIDER SOMETHING to regard something in a particular way [Early 19C. < French *envisager* < *visage* 'face' (see VISAGE)]

USAGE envisage or **envision**? In the sense of 'form a mental picture', **envisage** is more common in British English, and **envision** in US English.

envision /in vízh'n/ (**-sions, -sioning, -sioned**) *vt* to form a mental picture of something, typically something that may occur or be possible in the future

USAGE See **envisage**.

envoi /én voy/ *n* LITERAT another spelling of **envoy** (sense 3)

envoy /én voy/ *n* **1.** OFFICIAL REPRESENTATIVE somebody acting as a diplomat on behalf of a national government or sent as its official messenger **2.** *also* **envoy extraordinary** (*plural* **envoys extraordinary**) DIPLOMATIC MINISTER a minister in the Diplomatic Service of a rank above chargé d'affaires **3.** *also* **envoi** LITERAT CONCLUSION OF LITERARY WORK the final section of a book or play, or a short stanza at the end of a poem, used for summing up or as a dedication [Mid-17C. < French *envoyé*, past participle of *envoyer* 'send' < assumed Vulgar Latin *inviare* 'put on the way' < Latin *via* 'way']

envy /énvi/ *n* the resentful or unhappy feeling of wanting somebody else's success, good fortune, qualities, or possessions ■ *vt* (**-vies, -vying, -vied**) to desire something possessed by somebody else ○ *envy them their success* [13C. Via French *envie* < Latin *invidia* < *invidere* 'look askance at' < *videre* 'see'] —**envyingly** *adv* ◇ **be the envy of** to be the object of somebody's envy

enwind /in wɪ́nd/ (**-winds, -winding, -wound** /-wównd/, **-wound**) *vt* to wind or coil something around somebody or something (*literary*)

enwomb /in woóm/ (**-wombs, -wombing, -wombed**) *vt* to hold something or somebody in a warm safe place (*literary*)

enwound past participle, past tense of **enwind**

enwrap /in ráp/ (**-wraps, -wrapping, -wrapped**), **inwrap** *vt* **1.** to wrap something or somebody up **2.** to involve or engross somebody or something thoroughly (*formal; often passive*)

enwreathe /in reéth/ (**-wreathes, -wreathing, -wreathed**), **inwreathe** *vt* to encircle something, especially with decorations (*literary*)

Enzed /en zéd/ *n* ANZ New Zealand (*informal*) [Early 20C. Representing the initial letters]

Enzedder /en zéddər/ *n* ANZ somebody from New Zealand (*informal*)

enzootic /én zō óttik/ *adj* describes an animal disease that occurs only within a specific geographical area ■ *n* a disease that affects animals in a specific area, locale, or region

enzyme /én zīm/ *n* any complex chemical produced by living cells that is a biochemical catalyst [Late 19C. < German *Enzym* < modern Greek *enzumos* 'leavened' < Greek *zumē* 'leaven'] —**enzymatic** /én zī máttik, énzi-/ *adj* —**enzymic** /en zīmik, -zímmik/ *adj* —**enzymically** *adv*

enzymology /énzi mólləji/ *n* the study of enzymes

eo- *prefix* oldest, earliest ○ *eolithic* [< Greek *ēōs* 'dawn' < Indo-European]

EOC *abbr* POL, HR Equal Opportunities Commission

Eocene /eé ō seen/ *n* the epoch of geological time, 55 million to 38 million years ago, during which the ancestors of many modern animals appeared. See table at **geological time** —**Eocene** *adj*

EOF *abbr* COMPUT end of file

eohippus /eé ō híppəss/ (*plural* **-puses**) *n* a small prehistoric horse that lived in North America. It was dog-sized and had four toes on the front feet and three on the back feet. [Late 19C. < modern Latin < Greek *ēōs* 'dawn' + *hippos* 'horse']

eolian *adj* METEOROL US spelling of **aeolian**

Eolian, etc. PEOPLES, LANG another spelling of **Aeolian, etc.**

eolith /eé ō lith/ *n* one of the oldest stone tools used by humans, believed by some scientists to have formed naturally

eolithic /eé ō líthik/ *adj* relating to the earliest part of the Stone Age, during which time simple stone tools began to be used

e.o.m. *abbr* **1.** end of message (*used in e-mails or text messages*) **2.** COMM end of the month

eon *n* GEOL, TIME another spelling of **aeon**

Eos /eé oss/ *n* in Greek mythology, the goddess of the dawn. Roman equivalent **Aurora** [1]

eosin /eé ōssin/ *n* a red crystalline solid. Use: biological stain, dye in cosmetics. Formula: $C_{20}H_8Br_4O_5K_2$. [Mid-19C. < Greek *ēōs* 'dawn'; because of its colour]

eosinophil /eé ō sínnōfil/ *n* a granular white blood cell that stains with the dye eosin and is thought to play a part in allergic reactions and the body's response to parasitic diseases —**eosinophilic** /-sinə fíllik/ *adj* —**eosinophilous** /-si nóffiləss/ *adj*

eosinophilia /eé ō sinə fílli ə/ *n* an increase in the number of granular white blood cells that stain with the dye eosin, occurring in some allergies and parasitic diseases

-eous *suffix* same as **-ous** [< Latin *-eus*]

EP *n* a gramophone record that is the size of a single but contains a longer recording and is designed to be played at 33⅓ revolutions per minute rather than 45 [Mid-20C. Abbreviation of *extended play*]

Ep. *abbr* BIBLE Epistle

e.p. *abbr* CHESS en passant

ep- *prefix* same as **epi-** (*used before vowels or h*)

EPA *n* a polyunsaturated essential fatty acid found in cold-water fish that has been linked to the reduction of cardiovascular disease and other health benefits. Full form **eicosapentaenoic acid**

EPAC /eé pak/ *n* an independent organization made up of leading politicians and business figures that advises the Australian federal government on economic policy. Full form **Economic Planning and Advisory Committee**

epact /eé pakt/ *n* a period of about 11 days that represents the difference between the lunar year and the solar year [Mid-16C. Via French < late Latin *epacta* < Greek *epaktē (hēmera)* 'added (day)' < *agein* 'to lead']

epanalepsis /i pánnə lépsiss/ (*plural* **-lepses** /-lép seez/) *n* a phrase or set of words repeated later on in a speech or text as a rhetorical device [Late 16C. < Greek, 'repetition' < *epana-* 'again' + *lēpsis* 'taking'] —**epanaleptic** *adj*

epanorthosis /i pán awr thóssiss/ (*plural* **-thoses** /-thó seez/) *n* the immediate rephrasing of something said or written in order to emphasize or correct it [Late 16C. < Greek, 'correction' < *epana-* 'again' + *orthōsis* 'making straight' < *orthos* 'straight'] —**epanorthotic** /-thóttik/ *adj*

e-paper *n* a thin flexible sheet on which electronic information can be downloaded and read

eparch /éppaark/ *n* **1.** a bishop in the Greek Orthodox Church **2.** in modern Greece, the governor of a subdivision of a province [Mid-17C. < Greek *eparkhos*, literally 'ruler over' < *arkhos* (see -ARCH)]

eparchy /éppaarki/ (*plural* **-chies**) *n* **1.** a bishop's diocese in the Greek Orthodox Church **2.** in modern Greece, a subdivision of a province [Late 18C. < Greek *eparkhia* 'prefecture, province' < *eparkhos* (see EPARCH)]

epaulet *n* CLOTHING US spelling of **epaulette**

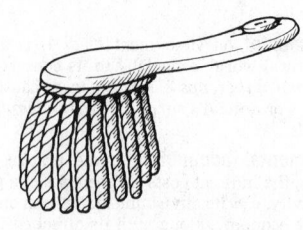

epaulette

epaulette /éppə lét/ *n* UK, Can a decoration on the shoulder of a jacket or coat, especially on a military uniform. In officers' dress, epaulettes are usually

made of gold or silver braid. [Late 18C. < French *épaulette* < *épaule* 'shoulder' < Latin *spatula* 'broad piece, shoulder blade' (see SPATULA)]

épée /éppay/ (*plural* **épées**) *n* **1.** a fencing sword that has a narrow triangular blade with a blunted end and a large guard for the hand, heavier than a foil. It derives from the type of sword formerly used in duelling. **2.** the sport of fencing using épées [Late 19C. < French, 'sword' < Latin *spatha* 'broad double-edged sword' (see SPATHE)] —**épéeist** *n*

epeirogeny /é pī rójjəni/, **epeirogenesis** /e pírō jénnəssiss/ *n* the slow movements of the Earth's crust leading to the formation of features such as continents [Late 19C. < Greek *ēpeiros* 'mainland, continent'] —**epeirogenic** /e pírō jénnik/ *adj* —**epeirogenically** *adv*

epenthesis /i pénthəssiss/ *n* insertion of an extra sound into a word, as happens in some dialect pronunciations or in a word's development over time. The 'b' in 'crumble' is an example of epenthesis. [Mid-17C. Via late Latin < Greek < *epentithenai* 'insert' < *tithenai* 'to place'] —**epenthetic** /éppen théttik/ *adj*

epergne /i púrn/ *n* a large elaborate centrepiece for a table with containers for fruit or confectionery [Mid-18C. Probably < French *épergne* 'savings, treasury' < Old French *espargnier* < Germanic]

epexegesis /e péksi jéessiss/ (*plural* **-geses** /-jée seez/) *n* **1.** the addition of words or phrases to a text to clarify its meaning **2.** a word or phrase added to help explain the sense of a text [Early 17C. < Greek *epexēgēsis* < *epi* 'in addition' + *exēgēsis* (see EXEGESIS)] —**epexegetic** /-jéttik/ *adj* —**epexegetical** *adj* —**epexegetically** *adv*

Eph. *abbr* BIBLE Ephesians

ephah /eéfə/, **epha** *n* an ancient Hebrew unit of dry measure, roughly equivalent to a bushel or 33 litres [14C. < Hebrew *ēpāh*]

ephebe /i feéb, éffeeb/, **ephebus** /i feébəss/ (*plural* **-bi** /-bī/), **ephebos** *n* in ancient Greece, a young man aged between 18 and 20 who had just reached manhood or full citizenship and was undergoing military training [Mid-19C. Via Latin < Greek *ephēbos* 'somebody approaching manhood' < *hēbē* 'early manhood'] —**ephebic** *adj*

ephedra /i féddrə/ (*plural* **-dras** or *same*) *n* a bush with slender green jointed stems and whorls of small scaly leaves. Some species are a source of the drug ephedrine. Native to: warm temperate regions. Genus: *Ephedra*. [Early 20C. < modern Latin (see EPHEDRINE)]

ephedrine /éffi dreen/, **ephedrin** /-drin/ *n* an alkaloid that dilates the air passages. Use: treatment of asthma and nasal congestion. [Late 19C. < modern Latin *Ephedra* < Latin *ephedra* 'horsetail' < Greek, plant of a genus including some that contain this substance]

ephemera [1] /i fémmərə, i feé-/ plural of **ephemeron**

ephemera [2] /i fémmərə, i feé-/ (*plural* **-ae** /-ee/ or **-as**) *n* **1.** something that is transitory and without lasting significance **2.** INSECTS same as **mayfly** (sense 1) [14C. < medieval Latin < late Latin *ephemerus* 'lasting only a day' < Greek *ephēmeros* < *hēmera* 'day']

ephemeral /i fémmərəl, i feé-/ *adj* lasting for only a short period of time and leaving no permanent trace ○ *the ephemeral nature of slang* ■ *n* a plant or insect that lives for only a short period of time. Groundsel and mayflies are ephemerals. —**ephemerality** /fémmə rálləti, i feé-/ *n* —**ephemerally** *adv* —**ephemeralness** *n*

SYNONYMS See ***temporary***.

ephemerid /i fémmərid, i feé-/ *n* an insect of the mayfly family that emerges in the summer from a long larval stage under water and lives only a matter of hours as an adult. Family: Ephemeridae. [Late 19C. < modern Latin *Ephemeridae* < Greek *ephēmeros* (see EPHEMERA [2])]

ephemeris /i fémməriss, i feé-/ (*plural* **ephemerides** /éffi mérrideez/) *n* a table listing the future positions of the Sun, Moon, and planets over a given period of time [Early 16C. Via Latin < Greek < *ephēmeros* (see EPHEMERA [2])]

ephemeris time *n* a system of time measurement

based on the Earth's orbit round the Sun and therefore independent of the irregularities of the Earth's rotation

ephemeron /i fémmərən, i fée-/ *n* (*plural* **-a** /-mərə/ or **-ons**) a short-lived thing (*usually used in the plural*) ■ **ephemera** *npl* collectable items that were originally designed to be short-lived ○ *He's a collector of ticket stubs, theatre programmes, and other ephemera.* [Late 16C. < Greek *ephēmeron*, form of *ephēmeros* (see EPHEMERA 2)]

Ephesians /i féezh'nz/ *n* a book of the Bible, originally a letter to the church in Ephesus and traditionally attributed to St Paul (*takes a singular verb*) See table at **Bible** [15C. < Latin *ephesius* 'of Ephesus' < Greek *ephesios* < *Ephesos* 'Ephesus']

Ephesus /éffəssəss/ ancient Greek city on the western coast of Asia Minor, in present-day Turkey. An important centre for early Christianity, it was also the site of the temple of Artemis, one of the Seven Wonders of the World.

ephod /ée fod, éffod/ *n* an embroidered garment, believed to be like an apron with shoulder straps, worn by Hebrew priests in ancient Israel [14C. < Hebrew *ēpōd*]

ephor /ée fawr, éffawr/ (*plural* **-ors** or **-ori** /éefə rī/) *n* in ancient Greece, each of five magistrates elected in some Dorian states, especially Sparta, to supervise the king [Late 16C. Directly or via Latin < Greek *ephoros* 'overseer' < *horan* 'to see'] —**ephoral** *adj* —**ephorate** *n*

Ephraimite /éefrayim īt/ *n* **1.** a member of the Hebrew tribe of Ephraim **2.** somebody who was born in the northern kingdom of Israel

epi- *prefix* **1.** on, over, above ○ *epiphyte* ○ *epipelagic* **2.** around, near ○ *epicalyx* **3.** after, in addition ○ *epiphenomenon* [< Greek *epi* 'upon']

epiblast /éppi blast/ *n* the outer layer of cells in an early embryo (**blastula**). It develops into ectoderm. —**epiblastic** /éppi blástik/ *adj*

epiboly /i píbbəli/ *n* the growth of a layer of rapidly dividing cells over a layer of more slowly dividing cells during embryo development in the eggs of birds and reptiles [Late 19C. < Greek *epibolē* 'throwing on' < *epiballein* < *ballein* 'to throw'] —**epibolic** /éppi bóllik/ *adj*

epic /éppik/ *n* **1.** LONG NARRATIVE POEM a lengthy narrative poem in elevated language celebrating the adventures and achievements of a legendary or traditional hero, e.g. Homer's *Odyssey* **2.** ELEVATED NARRATIVE POETRY the genre of poetic epics ○ *This term we'll cover epic, romance, and allegory.* **3.** LARGE-SCALE PRODUCTION a work of literature, cinema, television, or theatre that is large-scale and expensively produced and often deals with a historical theme **4.** LONG SERIES OF EVENTS a long series of events characterized by adventures or struggle ○ *Our trek across town turned out to be an epic.* ■ *adj* **1.** OF EPIC POETRY celebrating the adventures and achievements of a legendary or traditional hero, in elevated language ○ *Milton's 'Paradise Lost' is an epic poem.* **2.** IN STYLE OF EPIC POETRY having some of the characteristics of an epic ○ *an epic story of true love and adventure* **3.** VERY LARGE OR HEROIC impressive by virtue of greatness of size, scope, or heroism ○ *a scandal of epic proportions* [Late 16C. Via Latin < Greek *epikos* < *epos* 'word, song', from *ep-*, stem of *eipein* 'to say'] —**epical** *adj* —**epically** *adv*

epicalyx /éppi káyliks, -kálliks/ (*plural* **-lyxes** or **-lyces** /-li seez/) *n* a ring of modified leaves (**bracts**) that looks like an extra calyx at the base of a flower, e.g. in strawberries

epicanthic fold /éppi kánthik-/, **epicanthus** /-kánthəss/ (*plural* **-thi** /-thī/) *n* a fold of skin from the eyelid that partially covers the part of the eye nearest the nose

epicarp /éppi kaarp/ *n* BOT same as **exocarp**

epicene /éppi seen/ *adj* **1.** HAVING CHARACTERISTICS OF BOTH GENDERS having both male and female characteristics **2.** NEITHER MALE NOR FEMALE of neither male nor female gender **3.** WEAK lacking vigour and strength **4.** WITH FEMALE CHARACTERISTICS describes a male having typically female characteristics (*literary*) **5.** GRAM SAME FOR MASCULINE AND FEMININE having only one grammatical form for both masculine and feminine in languages where nouns have genders ■ *n* **1.** SOMEBODY OF UNCLEAR GENDER a person of indeterminate gender (*literary*) **2.** GRAM EPICENE NOUN a noun with the same grammatical form for both masculine and feminine in languages where nouns have genders [15C. Via late Latin < Greek *epikoinos* 'in common' < *koinos* 'common'] —**epicenism** /éppi séenizəm/ *n*

epicenter *n* SEISMOL US spelling of **epicentre**

epicentre /éppi sentər/ *n* **1.** the exact location on the Earth's surface directly above the focus of an earthquake or underground nuclear explosion **2.** the very centre or focal point ○ *Paris is the epicentre of the fashion world.* [Mid-19C. < Greek *epikentron* < *epikentros* 'situated on a centre' < *kentros* 'centre'] —**epicentral** /éppi séntrəl/ *adj*

epicotyl /éppi kóttil/ *n* the tip of a plant embryo above the embryonic leaves (**cotyledons**) that gives rise to the stem of the new plant [Late 19C. < EPI- + Greek *kotulē* 'cup, socket']

epic simile *n* a lengthy simile developed over a number of lines of verse in narrative poetry

Epictetus /éppik téetəss/ (AD 55–135) Greek philosopher. An advocate of Stoicism, he taught philosophy in Rome, preaching a doctrine of tolerance and calm acceptance of fate.

epicure /éppi kyoor/ *n* **1.** somebody who has developed a refined taste for food **2.** somebody who loves sensual pleasure and luxury [14C. < medieval Latin *epicurus*, after *Epicurus* 'Epicurus'] —**epicurism** *n*

epicurean /éppi kyŏŏ rée ən/ *adj* **1.** devoted to sensual pleasures and luxury, especially good food **2.** suitable for or pleasing to an epicure ○ *epicurean delicacies* ■ *n* same as **epicure** (sense 2) [14C. < French *épicurien* or Latin *epicureus*, after *Epicurus* 'Epicurus']

Epicurean *adj* relating to the philosophy of Epicureanism ■ *n* a follower of Epicureanism

Epicureanism /éppi kyŏŏrée ənizəm/ *n* the school of philosophy founded by Epicurus, or its teachings

Epicurus /éppi kyŏŏrəss/ (341–270 BC) Greek philosopher. His philosophy, Epicureanism, taught that the greatest good is freedom from pain and emotional disturbance.

> 'If you fight against all your sensations, you will have no standard to which to refer, and thus no means of judging even those judgments which you pronounce false.'
> [Epicurus, *The Principal Doctrines*; 4th century BC]

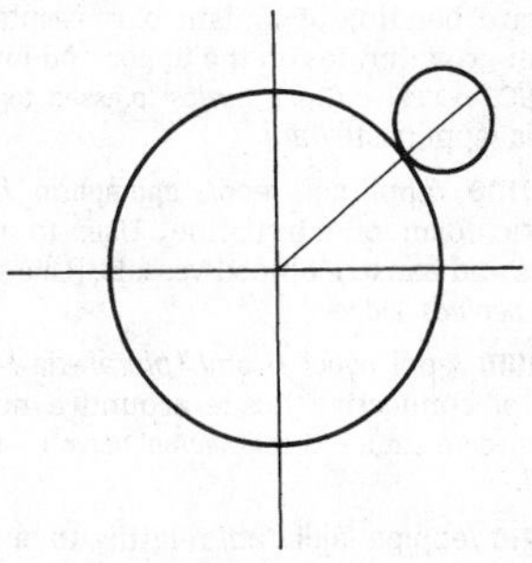

epicycle (sense 2)

epicycle /éppi sīk'l/ *n* **1.** in the Ptolemaic theory of the solar system, a circle that is followed by a planet, the circle itself being centred on a larger circle within which is the Earth. The epicycle accounts for irregularities of planetary motion in geocentric astronomy. **2.** a circle that rolls around the circumference of another circle, either inside or outside [14C. Via French or late Latin < Greek *epikuklos* < *kuklos* 'circle'] —**epicyclic** /éppi síklik, -síklik/ *adj* —**epicyclical** *adj*

epicyclic train *n* a system of gears arranged such that one or more gears engage with and revolve around a fixed or moving part

epicycloid /éppi sí kloyd/ *n* a mathematical curve traced by a point on the circumference of a circle that rolls around the outside of the circumference of another circle —**epicycloidal** /-sī klóyd'l/ *adj*

epidemic /éppi démmik/ *n* **1.** FAST-SPREADING DISEASE an outbreak of a disease that spreads more quickly and more extensively among a group of people than would normally be expected **2.** RAPID DEVELOPMENT a rapid and extensive development or growth, usually of something unpleasant ○ *an epidemic of civil unrest and rioting* ■ *adj* SPREADING UNUSUALLY QUICKLY AND EXTENSIVELY spreading more quickly and more extensively than would usually be expected ○ *Credit card crime is reaching epidemic proportions.* [Early 17C. < French *épidémique* < *épidémie* 'an epidemic' < Greek *epidēmia* 'disease prevalent among the people' < *dēmos* 'people'] —**epidemically** *adv* —**epidemicity** /éppidə míssəti/ *n*

USAGE See *endemic*.

SYNONYMS See *widespread*.

---

epidemiology /éppi deemi óllәji/ *n* **1.** the scientific and medical study of the causes and transmission of disease within a population **2.** the origin and development characteristics of a specific disease [Late 19C. < Greek *epidēmia* (see EPIDEMIC)] —**epidemiological** /-deemi ə lójjik'l/ *adj* —**epidemiologically** *adv* —**epidemiologist** *n*

epidermis /éppi dúrmiss/ *n* **1.** OUTER LAYER OF SKIN the thin outermost layer of the skin, itself made up of several layers, that covers and protects the underlying dermis **2.** ZOOL OUTER LAYER OF INVERTEBRATES' CELLS the outer layer of cells of invertebrates that secretes the protective waxy cuticle **3.** BOT OUTER CELL LAYER OF PLANT the outermost layer of cells of a plant. In woody plants the epidermis is usually replaced by corky protective tissue (**periderm**). [Early 17C. Via late Latin < Greek, 'outer skin' < *derma* 'skin'] —**epidermal** *adj* —**epidermic** *adj* —**epidermoid** *adj*

epidiascope /éppi dí ə skōp/ *n* a device for projecting an enlarged image of an opaque or transparent object onto a screen

epididymis /éppi díddimiss/ (*plural* **-mides** /éppidi dímmədeez/) *n* a coiled tube attached to the back and upper side of the testicle that stores sperm and is connected to the vas deferens [Early 17C. < Greek *epididumis* < *didumis* 'testicle, twin' < *duo* 'two'] —**epididymal** *adj*

epidote /éppi dōt/ *n* a shiny green, yellow, or black hydrous aluminosilicate mineral containing calcium and iron. Source: metamorphic rocks. [Early 19C. < French *épidote* < Greek *epididonai* 'give in addition' < *didonai* 'give'; from its very long crystals] —**epidotic** /éppi dóttik/ *adj*

epidural /éppi dyŏŏrəl/ *n* a local anaesthetic injected into the space between the outer membrane covering the spinal cord and the overlying bones of the spine. It is often used in childbirth. ■ *adj* located on or outside the outermost membrane covering the brain and spinal cord (**dura mater**) [Late 19C. < EPI- + *dura* < DURA MATER]

epifauna /éppi fawnə/ *npl* animals that live on the sea floor or attached to other animals or objects under water —**epifaunal** /éppi fáwn'l/ *adj*

epifocal /éppi fōk'l/ *adj* located or occurring at the point on the Earth's surface directly above the focus (**epicentre**) of an earthquake or underground nuclear explosion

epigamic /éppi gámmik/ *adj* describes a trait or behaviour that attracts a mate, e.g. large antlers or bright colours [Late 19C. < EPI- + Greek *gamos* 'marriage']

epigastrium /éppi gástri əm/ (*plural* **-tria** /-tri ə/) *n* the upper middle part of the abdomen [Late 17C. Via late Latin < Greek *epigastrion* < *epigastrios* 'over the stomach' < *gaster* 'stomach']

epigeal /éppi jée əl/ *adj* **1.** living or growing on, or right above the surface of the ground. ◊ **hypogeal** (sense 2) **2.** describes seed germination in which the embryo elongates so that the seed leaves (**cotyledons**) are carried above the soil to form the first leaves of the new plant [Mid-19C. < Greek *epigeios* 'on the earth' < *gē* 'earth']

epigene /éppi jeen/ *adj* formed or occurring at the Earth's surface, especially with reference to weathering, erosion, and deposition [Early 19C. Via French < Greek *epigenēs* 'born on or after' < *-genēs* 'born']

epigenesis /éppi jénnəssiss/ *n* **1.** the theory that the development of tissues and organs during embryonic development proceeds by successive gradual change **2.** change in the mineral content or

structure of a rock through external influences, e.g. the injection of a vein of ore into existing rock — **epigenesist** *n* —**epigenist** /i píjjənist/ *n*

epigenetic /éppi jə néttik/ *adj* **1.** BIOL OF EXTERNAL ORIGIN having an external rather than a genetic origin **2.** BIOL DEVELOPING BY GRADUAL CHANGE relating to embryo development by gradual change **3.** GENETICS OF GENE CONTROL UNASSOCIATED WITH DNA relating to the control of changes in gene function that do not involve changes in DNA sequences **4.** GEOL CHANGING AFTER FORMATION relating to changes in rock formations — **epigenetically** *adv*

epigenetics /éppi jə néttiks/ *n* control of changes in gene function that do not involve changes in DNA sequences (*takes a singular verb*)

epigenome /éppi jeénōm/ *n* a subset of genes whose function is controlled by specific biochemical factors as well as by their DNA sequence —**epigenomic** /éppi ji nómik/ *adj*

epigenomics /éppi ji nómiks/ *n* the study of the biochemical networks and linkages that control the function of genes within the epigenome (*takes a singular verb*)

epigenous /i píjjənəss/ *adj* on or growing on the upper surface of something such as a leaf. ◊ **hypogenous**

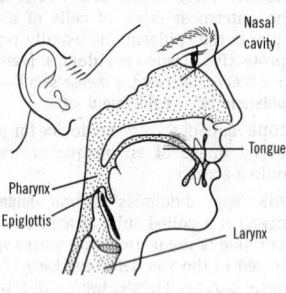

Nasal cavity

Tongue

Pharynx

Epiglottis

Larynx

epiglottis

epiglottis /éppi glóttiss/ (*plural* **-tises** or **-tides** /-tideez/) *n* a flap of cartilage situated at the base of the tongue that covers the opening to the air passages when swallowing, preventing food or liquids from entering the windpipe (**trachea**) [15C. < Greek *epiglōttis*, literally 'on the tongue' < *glōtta* (see GLOTTIS)] — **epiglottal** *adj* —**epiglottic** *adj*

epigone /éppi gōn/, **epigon** /-gon/ *n* a mediocre imitator of somebody else, especially of an important artist or philosopher (*literary*) [Mid-18C. Via French < Greek *epigonos* 'offspring' < *gignesthai* 'be born'] —**epigonic** /éppi gónnik/ *adj* —**epigonism** /i píggənizəm/ *n* —**epigonous** /e píggənəss/ *adj*

epigram /éppi gram/ *n* **1.** WITTY SAYING a concise, witty, and often paradoxical remark or saying **2.** LITERAT SHORT POEM a short poem, often expressing a single idea, that is usually satirical and has a witty ending **3.** WITTY FORM OF EXPRESSION a witty or concise mode of expression, either written or spoken [15C. Directly or via French < Latin *epigramma* < Greek < *graphein* 'write'] — **epigrammatism** /éppi grámmətizəm/ *n* —**epigrammatist** /éppi grámmətist/ *n*

epigrammatic /éppigrə máttik/, **epigrammatical** /-máttik'l/ *adj* **1.** containing or in the form of an epigram **2.** tending to use epigrams —**epigrammatically** *adv*

epigrammatize /éppi grámmə tīz/ (**-tizes, -tizing, -tized**), **epigrammatise** (**-tises, -tising, -tised**) *vti* to create a short and witty poem or saying about something

epigraph /éppi graaf, -graf/ *n* **1.** a quotation at the beginning of a book, chapter, or section of a book, usually related to its theme **2.** an inscription on something such as a statue or building [Late 16C. < Greek *epigraphē* < *epigraphein* 'write on' < *graphein* 'write'] —**epigraphic** /éppi gráffik/ *adj* —**epigraphical** *adj* —**epigraphically** *adv*

epigraphy /e píggrəfi/ *n* **1.** the study and deciphering of ancient inscriptions **2.** inscriptions or introductory quotations as a whole —**epigrapher** *n* —**epigraphist** *n*

epigynous /e píjjənəss/ *adj* describes a flower in which the sepals, petals, and stamens arise from the enlarged tip of the flower axis (**receptacle**) above the ovary [Mid-19C. < modern Latin *epigynus* < Greek *gunē* 'woman, pistil'] —**epigyny** *n*

epilation /éppi láysh'n/ *n* COSMETICS same as **depilation** [Late 19C. < French *épilation* < *épiler* 'remove hair' < Latin *pilus* 'hair']

epilepsy /éppi lepsi/ (*plural* **-sies**) *n* a medical disorder involving episodes of irregular electrical discharge in the brain and characterized by the periodic sudden loss or impairment of consciousness, often accompanied by convulsions [Mid-16C. Via French < Greek *epilēpsia* 'seizure' < *epilambanein* 'seize' < *lambanein* 'grasp']

epileptic /éppi léptik/ *adj* relating to or affected by epilepsy ■ *n* an offensive term for somebody who has epilepsy [Early 17C. Via French < Greek *epilēptikos* < *epilēpsia* (see EPILEPSY)] —**epileptically** *adv*

epileptiform /éppi lépti fawrm/ *adj* resembling epilepsy ◊ *epileptiform convulsions*

epileptogenic /éppi leptə jénnik/ *adj* causing or able to cause an epileptic episode

epileptoid /éppi lép toyd/ *adj* **1.** MED same as **epileptiform 2.** showing symptoms similar to those of epilepsy

epilimnion /éppi límni ən/ (*plural* **-nions** or **-nia** /-ni ə/) *n* the uppermost circulating layer of warm water in a lake with different temperatures at different levels in summer [Early 20C. < EPI- + Greek *limnion* 'small lake' < *limnē* 'lake']

epilogue /éppi log/ *n* **1.** LITERAT SHORT SECTION AT END OF BOOK a short chapter or section at the end of a literary work, sometimes detailing the fate of its characters **2.** THEATRE CONCLUDING SPEECH a short speech, usually in verse, that an actor addresses directly to the audience at the end of a play **3.** THEATRE ACTOR GIVING SHORT SPEECH the actor who addresses a short speech, usually in verse, directly to the audience at the end of a play **4.** FINAL PROGRAMME a short programme, usually of religious content, that used to be broadcast at the end of the day [15C. Via French < Greek *epilogos* 'additional speech' < *logos* 'speech'] —**epilogist** /e píllǝjist/ *n*

epimysium /éppi mízzi əm/ (*plural* **-ia** /-i ə/) *n* the covering of connective tissue surrounding a muscle [Early 20C. < modern Latin < Greek *mus* (see MUSCLE)]

epinasty /éppi nasti/ (*plural* **-ties**) *n* the outward and downward bending of a plant part resulting from different growth rates on the upper and lower sides [Late 19C. < EPI- + Greek *nastos* 'pressed together'] — **epinastic** /éppi nástik/ *adj*

epinephrine /éppi néf reen/, **epinephrin** /-rin/ *n* a synthetic form of adrenaline. Use: to relax the airways and constrict blood vessels. [Late 19C. < EPI- + Greek *nephros* 'kidney']

epineurium /éppi nyoòr ri əm/ (*plural* **-ria** /-ri ə/) *n* a sheath of connective tissue around a nerve [Late 19C. < modern Latin < Greek *neuron* 'nerve'] —**epineurial** /-əl/ *adj*

epipelagic /éppipə lájjik/ *adj* relating to or living in the upper zone of the ocean, from the surface to a depth of about 200 m/656 ft

EpiPen /éppi pen/ *tdmk* a trademark for a portable disposable hypodermic syringe that has a spring-activated needle and contains adrenaline (epinephrine), for use in an emergency by somebody with severe allergic reactions or asthma

epiphany /i píffəni/ (*plural* **-nies**) *n* **1.** a sudden intuitive leap of understanding, especially through an ordinary but striking occurrence ◊ *It came to him in an epiphany what his life's work was to be.* **2.** the supposed manifestation of a divine being [Early 17C. See EPIPHANY] —**epiphanic** /eppi fánnik/ *adj*

Epiphany /i píffəni/ *n* a Christian festival marking the visit of the Magi to celebrate Jesus Christ's birth or, in the Eastern Orthodox Church, the baptism of Jesus Christ. Date: 6 January. [14C. Via French < Greek *epiphaneia* 'manifestation' < *epiphainein* 'to manifest' < *phanein* 'to show']

epiphenomenalism /éppifi nómminəlizəm/ *n* the view that consciousness is merely an aftereffect of phys-

ical processes in the brain and nervous system — **epiphenomenalist** *n*

epiphenomenon /éppifi nómminən/ (*plural* **-na** /-ə/) *n* **1.** a secondary phenomenon resulting from another **2.** a secondary incidental condition or symptom that appears during the course of an illness — **epiphenomenal** *adj* —**epiphenomenally** *adv*

epiphysis /e píffəssiss/ (*plural* **-yses** /-ə seez/) *n* **1.** the end of a long bone that fuses with the shaft of the bone at the point where it was previously separated by cartilage to allow bone growth. Once the epiphyses fuse no further growth of long bones is possible. ◊ **diaphysis 2.** same as **pineal gland** (*archaic*) [Mid-17C. Via modern Latin < Greek *epiphusis* 'growing on' < *phusis* 'growth'] —**epiphyseal** /éppi fízzi əl/ *adj*

epiphyte /éppi fīt/ *n* a plant that grows on top of or is supported by another plant but does not depend on it for nutrition. Mosses, tropical orchids, and many ferns are epiphytes. —**epiphytic** /-fíttik/ *adj* — **epiphytically** *adv*

epiphytotic /éppi fī tóttik/ *adj* describes an outbreak of disease that rapidly affects many plants in a specific area ■ *n* an outbreak of a plant disease that suddenly and rapidly affects many plants in a specific area

Epis. *abbr* **1.** *also* **Episc.** CHR Episcopal **2.** *also* **Episc.** CHR Episcopalian **3.** BIBLE Epistle

episcopacy /i pískəpəssi/ *n* **1.** church government by bishops, as in the Roman Catholic, Eastern, and Anglican Churches **2.** CHR same as **episcopate** (sense 3) [Mid-17C. < ecclesiastical Latin *episcopatus* (see EPISCOPATE)]

episcopal /i pískəp'l/ *adj* **1.** relating to a bishop or bishops **2.** involving or recognizing church government by bishops [15C. < French *épiscopal* or ecclesiastical Latin *episcopalis* < *episcopus* (see BISHOP)] — **episcopally** *adv*

Episcopal *adj* relating to the Episcopal Church of Scotland or North America

Episcopal Church *n* an independent branch of the Anglican Church in North America and Scotland

episcopalian /i pískə páyli ən/ *adj* adhering to or practising church government by bishops ■ *n* a supporter of church government by bishops —**episcopalianism** *n*

Episcopalian *adj* relating to or belonging to the Episcopal Church of Scotland or North America ■ *n* a member of the Episcopal Church —**Episcopalianism** *n*

episcopalism /i pískəpəlizəm/ *n* the belief that authority in a church government should lie in a group of bishops

episcopate /i pískəpət/ *n* **1.** OFFICE OR POSITION OF BISHOP the office, position, or term of office of a bishop **2.** DIOCESE a bishop's diocese or jurisdiction **3.** BISHOPS bishops as a group [Mid-17C. < ecclesiastical Latin *episcopatus* < *episcopus* (see BISHOP)]

episcope /éppi skōp/ *n* a device for projecting an enlarged image of an opaque object such as a printed page or a photograph onto a screen using reflected light. N Am term **opaque projector**

episiotomy /i pízzi óttəmi/ (*plural* **-mies**) *n* an incision sometimes made to enlarge the vaginal opening in the late stages of labour to prevent tearing and facilitate the birth [Late 19C. < Greek *epision* 'pubic region']

episode /éppi sōd/ *n* **1.** SIGNIFICANT INCIDENT an event that is a part of but distinct from a greater whole and that often has specific significance ◊ *Let's try to put this unfortunate episode behind us, shall we?* **2.** LITERAT, MEDIA PART OF SERIALIZED WORK a part of a serialized story or programme that is published or broadcast separately **3.** LITERAT EVENT IN NARRATIVE an incident, description, or series of events in a narrative that is part of the whole but may digress from the main plot ◊ *The episode in the library reveals a lot about the main character.* **4.** MED OCCURRENCE OF ILLNESS an occurrence of a particular illness or symptom of an illness, usually one of a connected series, often repeated over a period of time ◊ *episodes of breathlessness and chest pain* **5.** THEATRE SECTION OF GREEK TRAGEDY a section of an ancient Greek tragedy between two choruses **6.** MUSIC DI-

GRESSIVE MUSICAL PASSAGE a digressive passage between two musical themes, e.g. in a rondo or fugue [Late 17C. < Greek *epeisodion* 'addition', form of *epeisodios* 'coming in besides' < *eisodos* 'coming in' < *hodos* 'road']

episodic /éppi sóddik/, **episodical** /-sóddik'l/ *adj* **1.** OF EPISODE relating to or resembling an episode **2.** DIVIDED INTO EPISODES divided into or composed of closely connected but independent sections **3.** SPORADIC happening at irregular intervals ○ *episodic pain in the lower back* **4.** TEMPORARY of a limited duration ○ *episodic wind squalls* —**episodically** *adv*

episome /éppi sōm/ *n* a genetic unit that can multiply independently in host cells or when integrated with a chromosome. Bacterial plasmids are examples of episomes. [Mid-20C. < EPI- + Greek *sōma* 'body'] —**episomal** /éppi sṓm'l/ *adj* —**episomally** *adv*

Epist. *abbr* BIBLE Epistle

epistasis /i pístəssiss/ (*plural* **-tases** /-tə seez/) *n* the nonappearance of a characteristic determined by one gene because it has been suppressed or masked by the activity of another gene [Early 19C. < Greek, 'stoppage' < *ephistanai* 'to stop' < *histanai* 'put'] —**epistatic** /éppi státtik/ *adj*

epistaxis /éppi stáksiss/ (*plural* **-staxes** /-sták seez/) *n* MED same as **nosebleed** (*technical*) [Late 18C. Via modern Latin < Greek < *epistazein* 'to drip at (the nose)' < *stazein* 'to drip']

epistemic /éppi stéemik, -stémmik/ *adj* relating to knowledge [Early 20C. < Greek *epistēmē* 'knowledge' < *epistasthai* 'know' < *histasthai* 'to stand'] —**epistemically** *adv*

epistemics /éppi stéemiks/ *n* the use of logic, philosophy, psychology, and linguistics to study knowledge and the way it is processed by humans (*takes a singular verb*)

epistemology /i písti mólləji/ *n* the branch of philosophy that studies the nature of knowledge, in particular its foundations, scope, and validity [Mid-19C. < Greek *epistēmē* (see EPISTEMIC)] —**epistemological** /i pístimə lójjik'l/ *adj* —**epistemologically** *adv* —**epistemologist** *n*

epistle /i píss'l/ *n* **1.** a long formal letter, often intended to provide instruction (*formal*) **2.** a literary work in the form of a letter [12C. Directly or via French < Latin *epistola* < Greek *epistolē* 'something sent' < *stellein* 'send']

Epistle *n* **1.** a letter written by the apostle Paul or other early Christian writers and included as a book of the Bible **2.** an excerpt from one of the Epistles read as part of a service in a Christian church

epistle side, **Epistle Side** *n* the right-hand side of a Christian church as somebody faces the altar [Because an excerpt from one of the Epistles is traditionally read from there as part of the Communion service]

epistolary /i pístələri/, **epistolatory** /-lətəri, -láytəri/ *adj* **1.** associated with, conducted by, or suitable for letters (*formal*) **2.** taking the form of a letter or a series of letters ○ *an epistolary novel* [Mid-17C. Directly or via French < Latin *epistolaris* < *epistola* (see EPISTLE)]

epistrophe /i pístrəfi/ *n* repetition of a word or phrase at the end of consecutive clauses or sentences for rhetorical effect [Late 16C. < Greek < *epistrephein* 'turn about' < *strephein* 'to turn']

epistyle /éppi stīl/ *n* ARCHIT same as **architrave** (sense 1) [Mid-16C. Directly or via French < Latin *epistylium* < Greek *epistulion* 'on a column' < *stulos* 'column']

epitaph /éppi taaf, -taf/ *n* **1.** an inscription on a tombstone or monument commemorating the person buried there **2.** a short speech or piece of writing celebrating the life of a recently deceased person [14C. Via French < Greek *epitaphion* 'something above a tomb or burial' < *taphos* 'funeral ceremonies, tomb'] —**epitaphic** /eppi táaffik, -táffik/ *adj*

epitasis /i píttəssiss/ (*plural* **-ases** /-ə seez/) *n* in classical drama, the middle part of a play that develops the main action [Late 16C. Via modern Latin < Greek < *epiteinein* 'intensify, stretch upon' < *teinein* 'to stretch']

epitaxy /éppi taksi/, **epitaxis** /éppi táksiss/ *n* growth of a layer of crystal on a single crystal of another substance [Mid-20C. < French *épitaxie* 'growth on' < Greek *taxis* 'growth'] —**epitaxial** /éppi táksi əl/ *adj*

epithalamium /éppithə láymi əm/ (*plural* **-mia** /-mi ə/), **epithalamion** /-mi ən/ *n* a poem or song written or performed in celebration of a wedding [Late 16C. < Greek *epithalamion* '(song sung) at the bridal chamber' < *thalamos* 'bridal chamber'] —**epithalamic** /-lámmik/ *adj*

epithelia ANAT plural of **epithelium**

epithelial /éppi théeli əl/ *adj* describes tissue that forms a thin protective layer on exposed bodily surfaces and forms the lining of internal cavities, ducts, and organs

epithelialize /éppi théeli ə līz/ (**-izes, -izing, -ized**), **epithelialise** (**-ises, -ising, -ised**), **epithelize** /-théelīz/, **epithelise** *vti* to become, or cause a part of the body to become, covered with epithelial tissue, as in the healing of a wound

epithelium /éppi théeli əm/ (*plural* **-lia** /-li ə/ or **-liums**) *n* a thin layer of tightly packed cells lining internal cavities, ducts, and organs of animals and covering exposed bodily surfaces, especially in wounds that are healing [Mid-18C. < modern Latin < Greek *thēlē* 'teat, nipple']

epithelize *vti* MED same as **epithelialize**

epithermal /éppi thúrm'l/ *adj* describes veins of gold or silver originally formed deep within the Earth's crust from ascending hot solutions

epithet /éppi thet/ *n* **1.** DESCRIPTIVE WORD ADDED TO NAME a descriptive word or phrase added to or substituted for the name of somebody or something, highlighting a feature or quality ○ *easy to see how she earned herself the epithet 'The All-Knowing'* **2.** INSULT an abusive insulting word or phrase **3.** BIOL PART OF TAXONOMIC NAME in biological classification, the species name that follows the genus name [Late 16C. Directly or via French *épithète* < Latin *epitheton* 'something added' < Greek *epitheto*, past participle of *epitithenai* 'put on' < *tithenai* 'to place'] —**epithetic** /éppi théttik/ *adj* —**epithetical** *adj*

epitome /i píttəmi/ *n* **1.** a highly representative example of a type, class, or characteristic ○ *Isn't she just the epitome of elegance?* **2.** a brief summary of a piece of writing (*formal*) [Early 16C. Via Latin < Greek < *epitemnein* 'to cut short' < *temnein* 'to cut']

epitomize /i píttə mīz/ (**-mizes, -mizing, -mized**), **epitomise** (**-mises, -mising, -mised**) *vt* **1.** to be a highly representative example of a type, class, or characteristic ○ *This incident epitomizes all that is wrong with modern society.* **2.** to write a brief summary of a piece of writing (*formal*) —**epitomist** *n* —**epitomization** /i píttə mī záysh'n/ *n*

~~epitomy~~ incorrect spelling of **epitome**

epizoic /éppi zṓ ik/ *adj* **1.** describes a nonparasitic animal or plant that lives on the external surface of a living animal **2.** describes plants whose seeds or spores are dispersed by being attached to the coats of animals —**epizoism** *n*

epizoon /éppi zṓ on/ (*plural* **-a** /-zṓ ə/), **epizoite** /-īt/ *n* an organism that lives on the external surface of a living animal [Mid-19C. < modern Latin, 'on an animal' < Greek *zōion* 'animal'] —**epizoan** *adj*

epizootic /éppi zō óttik/ *adj* describes an outbreak of disease that rapidly affects many animals in a specific area at the same time ■ *n* a disease that rapidly affects many animals in a specific area at the same time [Late 18C. < French *épizootique* 'at animals' < Greek *zōion* 'animal'] —**epizootically** *adv*

e pluribus unum /áy plóor ribəss óonəm, -yóonəm/ one out of many (*used as the motto of the United States*) [Latin]

EPNS *abbr* electroplated nickel silver

epoch /ée pok/ *n* **1.** SIGNIFICANT PERIOD a significant period in history or in somebody's life **2.** START OF HISTORICALLY SIGNIFICANT PERIOD the beginning of a long period of history considered particularly significant ○ *The invention of the telephone marked an epoch in the development of international communication.* **3.** GEOL UNIT OF GEOLOGICAL TIME a unit of geological time that is a division of a period and is characterized by rock formation ○ *the Holocene and Pleistocene epochs of the Quaternary period* **4.** ASTRON MOMENT IN TIME AS REFERENCE POINT a precise moment in time arbitrarily chosen as a reference point for defining the position of astronomical objects [Early 17C. Via modern Latin *epocha* < Greek *epokhē* 'pause (in time)' < *ekhein* 'to hold'] —**epochal** /éppok'l, ée pok'l/ *adj*

epoch-making *adj* having great historical importance or momentous significance ○ *Galileo's epoch-making discoveries*

epode /éppōd/ *n* **1.** in classical Greek drama, the part of a lyric ode that follows the strophe and the antistrophe **2.** a lyric ode characterized by couplets made up of a long line followed by a shorter one [Early 17C. Directly or via French < Latin *epodos* < Greek *epōidos* 'sung after' < *ōidē* 'song']

eponym /éppə nim/ *n* **1.** PERSON AFTER WHOM SOMETHING IS NAMED a person or mythical character from whom something such as an invention, activity, or place takes its name **2.** NAME DERIVED FROM PERSON a name derived from the name of a person or mythical character. For example, 'Rome' is an eponym coming from 'Romulus'. **3.** MED MEDICAL NAME FROM PERSON a medical name, e.g. that of a disease, derived from the name of a person [Mid-19C. < Greek *epōnumos* 'given as a name' < *onuma* 'name'] —**eponymic** /éppə nímmik/ *adj*

eponymous /i pónniməss/ *adj* having the name that is used as the title or name of something else, especially the title of a book, play, or film ○ *the eponymous hero of the play* —**eponymously** *adv*

EPOS /ée poss/ *abbr* electronic point of sale

epoxide /i póksīd/ *n* a chemical compound containing a three-membered ring consisting of an oxygen atom bonded to each of two carbon atoms

epoxide resin *n* CHEM same as **epoxy resin**

epoxy /i póksi/ *adj* relating to an epoxide or epoxy resin ■ *n* (*plural* **-ies**) CHEM same as **epoxy resin** ■ *vt* (**-ies, -ying, -ied**) to stick one thing to another using epoxy resin

epoxy resin *n* a tough synthetic resin, containing epoxy groups, that sets after the application of heat or pressure. Use: adhesives, surface coatings.

Epping Forest /épping-/ region of ancient woodland in Essex, southeastern England

EPROM /ée prom/ *n* an integrated circuit that can be reprogrammed by a user to correct an error in the program or to add a function. Full form **erasable-programmable read-only memory**

eps *abbr* FIN earnings per share

epsilon /ep sīlən, épsilon/ *n* the fifth letter of the Greek alphabet, represented in the English alphabet as 'e'. See table at **alphabet** [Early 18C. < Greek *e psilon* 'short e' (literally 'bare e')]

Epsom /épsəm/ town in Surrey, southeastern England. There is a racecourse on Epsom Downs, where the Derby horse race is run. Population: 90,437 (1991).

Epsom salts *n* a bitter-tasting preparation of hydrated magnesium sulphate. Use: formerly, as a laxative and to reduce swelling. (*takes a singular verb*) [Because originally obtained from a mineral spring at EPSOM]

Epstein /ép stīn/, **Sir Jacob** (1880–1959) US-born British sculptor. His massively powerful, usually nude figures, including *Genesis* (1931), caused an uproar. His later portrait bronzes and monumental works were more immediately popular and less controversial.

Epstein-Barr virus /ép stīn báar-/ *n* a virus believed to cause glandular fever and associated with Burkitt's lymphoma and some carcinomas [Mid-20C. After M. A. *Epstein* (b. 1921) and Y. M. *Barr* (b. 1932), British virologists]

EQ *n* the ratio of educational attainment to chronological age. Full form **educational quotient**

eq. *abbr* **1.** equal **2.** equation **3.** equivalent

equable /ékwəb'l/ *adj* **1.** calm and not easily disturbed ○ *She maintained the most equable of temperaments despite her financial problems.* **2.** free from variation and marked extremes [Mid-16C. < Latin *aequabilis* < *aequare* (see EQUATE)] —**equability** /ékwə bílləti/ *n* —**equably** *adv*

equal /éekwəl/ *adj* **1.** IDENTICAL identical in size, quantity, value, or standard ○ *equal quantities of flour and sugar* **2.** WITH THE SAME RIGHTS having the same

privileges, rights, status, and opportunities as others **3. WITH EVEN BALANCE** evenly balanced between opposing sides ○ *hoping for a more equal match in the second game* **4. EQUIPPED WITH NECESSARY QUALITIES** equipped with the necessary qualities or means to accomplish something ○ *didn't think he would be equal to the task* **5. EQUIVALENT** having the same effect, application, or meaning as somebody or something else ■ *n* **SOMEBODY OR SOMETHING EQUAL** somebody or something equal in quality to another ○ *As a defender he has no equal in the Premiership.* ■ *v* (**equals, equalling, equalled**) **1.** *vt* **DO SOMETHING EQUAL TO SOMETHING ELSE** to do, produce, or achieve something to the same standard or of the same value as something else ○ *And with that jump, she has equalled the world record.* **2.** *vi* **BECOME EQUAL** to become identical ○ *It will all equal out in the end.* **3.** *vt* MATHS **HAVE SAME VALUE AS SOMETHING ELSE** to be equal to something else, usually in value ○ *Two plus two equals four.* [14C. < Latin *aequalis* < *aequus* 'equal, even'] ◇ **first among equals** the most powerful or influential person in a group whose members are supposed to have equal status

equal-area *adj* on a map projection, accurately representing the relative sizes of regions that are of equal area, although distorting shape and direction

equalise, etc. another spelling of **equalize, etc.**

equalitarian /i kwólli táiri ən/ *n, adj* POL same as **egalitarian** —**equalitarianism** *n*

equality /i kwólləti/ (*plural* **-ties**) *n* **1.** rights, treatment, quantity, or value equal to all others in a specific group ○ *full equality under the law* **2.** an equation in which the quantities on each side of an equals sign are the same

equalize /éekwə līz/ (**-izes, -izing, -ized**), **equalise** (**-ises, -ising, -ised**) *v* **1.** *vt* to make things uniform or equal ○ *You must equalize the liquid levels in each bottle.* **2.** *vi* to score a point or goal that brings a score level with that of an opponent ○ *They equalized just before half-time.* —**equalization** /éekwə lī záysh'n/ *n*

equalizer /éekwə līzər/, **equaliser** *n* **1. SOMEBODY OR SOMETHING THAT EQUALIZES THINGS** somebody or something that makes things uniform or equal **2.** ELECTRONICS **ELECTRONIC SOUND ADJUSTER** an electronic device used to reduce distortion in a sound system by internally adjusting the system's response to different audio frequencies **3.** SPORTS **GOAL OR POINT THAT LEVELS SCORES** a goal or point that brings a person's or team's score level with that of an opponent

equally /éekwəli/ *adv* **1. IN SAME WAY** in an identical or uniform way ○ *treat people equally* **2. TO SAME EXTENT** to the same degree or extent ○ *This issue is equally important.* **3. IN SAME-SIZED AMOUNTS** in parts or amounts of the same size ○ *Divide it equally between four people.* **4. AT SAME TIME** used to introduce a second statement that is of equal importance to the first but may contrast or balance it ○ *I want the business to succeed, but, equally, I don't want to be working all the time.*

USAGE ***Equally*** and ***as*** cannot be used together. You can say *She is a brilliant pianist, and her brother is equally talented* or *She is a brilliant pianist, and her brother is as talented*, but not *She is a brilliant pianist, and her brother is equally as talented*.

equal opportunity *n* the availability of the same rights, position, and status to all people, regardless of gender, sexual preference, age, race, ethnicity, or religion (*often used in the plural; hyphenated before a noun*) ○ *a company providing equal opportunities* ○ *an equal-opportunities policy*

equal pay *n* the right of two people performing the same job to be paid the same amount of money regardless of differences of sex or race

equals sign, equal sign *n* a mathematical symbol (=) used to indicate that two or more numbers, symbols, or terms have the same value as each other

equal temperament *n* the division of a musical octave into 12 equal semitones in the tuning of an instrument

equanimity /ékwə nímməti, éekwə-/ *n* evenness of temper even under stress ○ *faced his critical constituents with equanimity* [Early 17C. < Latin *aequanimitas* < *aequus* 'equal, even' + *animus* 'mind'] —**equanimous** /i kwánniməss, i kwónni-/ *adj*

equate /i kwáyt, ee-/ (**equates, equating, equated**) *v* **1.** *vt* **CONSIDER AS EQUIVALENT TO SOMETHING** to treat something as equivalent to something else, or show or consider something to be equivalent to something else ○ *equating money with happiness* **2.** *vt* MATHS **FORM SOMETHING INTO EQUATION** to put something into the form of an equation involving an equality **3.** *vi* **APPEAR TO BE EQUAL** to be or appear to be the same (*formal*) ○ *Their two accounts of the incident seem to equate.* [15C. < Latin *aequat-*, past participle of *aequare* 'make equal' < *aequus* 'equal, even'] —**equatability** /i kwáytə bílləti, ee-/ *n* —**equatable** *adj*

equation /i kwáyzh'n/ *n* **1.** MATHS **STATEMENT OF EQUALITY** a mathematical statement that two expressions, usually divided by an equals sign, are of the same value **2. SITUATION INVOLVING MANY VARIABLE FACTORS** a situation that has two or more variable aspects to be considered ○ *The selling option just does not enter into the equation.* **3. ACT OF REGARDING AS EQUAL** the act or process of making things equal or considering them to be equal **4. STATE OF BEING EQUAL** the state of being the same or equivalent ○ *bring the balance of power into equation* **5.** CHEM **REPRESENTATION OF CHEMICAL REACTION** a written representation of the reactants and products in a chemical reaction —**equational** *adj* —**equationally** *adv*

equation of state *n* an equation that states the relationship between the pressure, temperature, and volume of a gas or liquid

equation of time *n* the difference between apparent solar time and mean solar time, usually expressed as a correction to the apparent time. It varies in a complex annual pattern between maxima of about 15 minutes in February and November.

equator /i kwáytər/ *n* **1.** GEOG **IMAGINARY CIRCLE AROUND EARTH** the imaginary great circle around Earth that is the same distance from the North and South Poles and divides Earth into the northern and southern hemispheres **2.** ASTRON **IMAGINARY CIRCLE AROUND ASTRONOMICAL OBJECT** the imaginary great circle around an astronomical object that is everywhere the same distance from the Poles **3.** ASTRON same as **celestial equator** **4.** MATHS **CIRCLE DIVIDING SPHERE INTO TWO** a circle that divides a sphere or other surface into two equal parts [14C. Directly or via French < medieval Latin *aequator*, in *aequator diei et noctis* 'equalizer of day and night' < Latin *aequare* (see EQUATE)]

equatorial /ékwə táwri əl, éekwə-/ *adj* **1.** relating to or present near the equator **2.** situated in the plane of an equator —**equatorially** *adv*

equatorial current *n* a current that moves in a westerly direction near the surface of an ocean at the equator

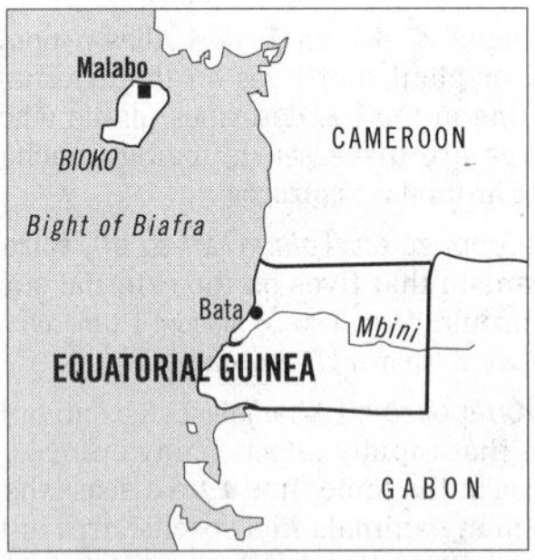

Equatorial Guinea

Equatorial Guinea /ékwə táwri əl-/ country in West Africa bordered by Cameroon, Gabon, and the Atlantic Ocean, and comprising a mainland section, Río Muni, and several islands. Language: Spanish. Currency: CFA franc. Capital: Malabo. Population: 510,473 (2003). Area: 28,051 sq. km/10,831 sq. mi. Official name **Republic of Equatorial Guinea**

equatorial plate *n* the area midway between the poles of the spindle of a dividing cell, where chromosomes are aligned

equatorial telescope *n* an astronomical telescope mounted so that it allows an astronomical object to be kept in view without adjustment as Earth rotates. This is accomplished by mounting it on two axes at right angles to each other, the one about which it rotates being parallel to Earth's axis.

equerry /i kwérri, ékwəri/ (*plural* **-ries**) *n* **1.** an officer who is the personal attendant of the British monarch or a member of the royal family **2.** formerly, an officer in an aristocratic or royal household who was responsible for the supervision of the horses [Early 16C. Via obsolete French *escurie* < Old French *escuierie* 'company of squires, prince's stables' < *escuier* (see ESQUIRE)]

equestrian /i kwéstri ən/ *adj* **1. OF HORSES** relating to horses or riding **2. DEPICTING SOMEBODY ON HORSEBACK** depicting somebody mounted on a horse ○ *an equestrian statue* **3. OF MOUNTED SOLDIERS** composed of soldiers on horseback ■ *n* **SKILLED RIDER** somebody who is skilled at riding horses or performing on horseback [Mid-17C. < Latin *equester* 'of a horse-rider' < *eques* 'horse-rider, knight' < *equus* 'horse'] —**equestrianism** *n*

equestrienne /i kwéstri én/ *n* a woman who is skilled at riding horses or performing on horseback [Mid-19C. < EQUESTRIAN after French nouns ending in *-enne*]

equi- *prefix* equal ○ *equimolar* [< Latin *aequus*]

equiangular /éekwi áng gyŏŏlər, ékwi-/ *adj* describes a geometric figure in which all the angles are equal [Mid-17C. < late Latin *equiangulus* < Latin *angulus* 'corner']

equidistant /éekwi dístənt, ékwi-/ *adj* situated at the same distance from two or more places or points ○ *Birmingham is equidistant from Leeds and London.* [Late 16C. < French *équidistant* or medieval Latin *equidistant-* < Latin *distant-* (see DISTANT)] —**equidistance** *n* —**equidistantly** *adv*

equilateral /éekwi láttərəl, ékwi-/ *adj* **WITH EQUAL SIDES** describes a geometric figure in which all the sides are of equal length ■ *n* **1. EQUAL-SIDED GEOMETRIC SHAPE** a geometric figure with all its sides of equal length **2. ANY SIDE OF EQUAL-SIDED GEOMETRIC SHAPE** any side of a geometric figure that is the same length as the other sides [Late 16C. Directly or via French *équilatéral* < late Latin *aequilateralis* < Latin *lateralis* (see LATERAL)] —**equilaterally** *adv*

equilibrant /i kwíllibrənt/ *n* a force able to balance out another force and produce an equilibrium [Late 19C. < French *équilibrant* < *équilibre* 'balance' < Latin *aequilibrium* (see EQUILIBRIUM)]

equilibrate /éekwi lī brayt, i kwílli-/ (**-brates, -brating, -brated**) *v* (*technical*) **1.** *vt* to counterbalance something, or bring something into a state of balance **2.** *vi* to be evenly balanced [Mid-17C. < late Latin *aequilibrat-*, past participle of *aequilibrare* < Latin *libra* 'balance'] —**equilibration** /éekwi lī bráysh'n, i kwílli-/ *n* —**equilibrator** *n* —**equilibratory** /i kwílli bráytəri/ *adj*

equilibrist /i kwíllibrist/ *n* a performer skilled in the art of balancing, especially tightrope walking (*archaic*)

equilibrium /éekwi líbbri əm, ékwi-/ (*plural* **-riums** or **-ria** /-ri ə/) *n* **1. EMOTIONAL STABILITY** a mental state of calmness and composure **2. SITUATION OF BALANCE** a state or situation in which opposing forces or factors balance each other out and stability is attained **3. BODILY BALANCE** a physical state or sense of being able to maintain bodily balance **4.** PHYS **BALANCE BETWEEN FORCES** a static or dynamic state in which all forces or processes are in balance and there is no resultant change **5.** CHEM **STATE OF BALANCE IN CHEMICAL REACTION** the state in a reversible chemical reaction in which the reaction and its reverse reaction proceed at the same rate and balance each other so there is no further change [Early 17C. < Latin *aequilibrium* 'equal balance' < *libra* 'balance']

equilibrium constant *n* the constant value that expresses the relationship between the concentration of products and starting substances in a reversible chemical reaction at equilibrium. The equilibrium constant is strongly temperature dependent.

equimolar /éekwi mṓlər, ékwi-/ *adj* having an equal concentration of moles in one litre of solution

equimolecular /éekwimə lékyŏŏlər, ékwi-/ *adj* describes a substance or mixture that has the same number of molecules as another

equine /é kwīn, ee-/ *adj* **1. OF HORSES** relating to, belonging to, or affecting horses **2. RESEMBLING HORSE** characteristic of or similar to a horse in appearance or behaviour **3.** ZOOL **BELONGING TO HORSE FAMILY** belonging to or characteristic of the family of mammals that includes horses, zebras, and donkeys ■ *n* ZOOL **HORSE**

OR HORSE'S RELATIVE a horse or other member of the horse family [Late 18C. < Latin *equinus* < *equus* 'horse']

equinoctial /eékwi nóksh'l, ékwi-/ *adj* **1.** TIME OCCURRING AT EQUINOX happening at or near either of the two equinoxes **2.** BOT WITH FLOWERS OPEN AT DEFINITE TIMES describes a plant whose flowers open and close at specific times of day **3.** ASTRON OF CELESTIAL EQUATOR relating to the celestial equator ■ *n* **1.** METEOROL STORM AT EQUINOX a storm or strong wind that occurs at an equinox **2.** ASTRON same as **celestial equator** [14C. < French *équinoctial* < Latin *aequinoctium* (see EQUINOX)]

equinoctial circle *n* ASTRON same as **celestial equator**

equinoctial point *n* either of the two points on the celestial sphere where the Sun crosses the celestial equator. The points are called respectively the First Point of Aries and the First Point of Libra.

equinoctial year *n* ASTRON same as **solar year**

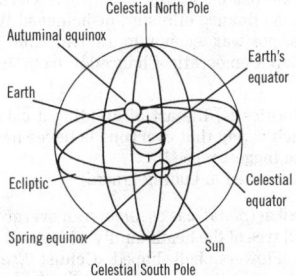

equinox: diagram showing the positions of the Sun and Earth at the spring and autumnal equinoxes

equinox /eékwi noks, ékwi-/ *n* **1.** either of the two annual crossings of the equator by the Sun, once in each direction, when the length of day and night are approximately equal everywhere on Earth. The equinoxes occur around 21 March and 23 September. **2.** ASTRON same as **equinoctial point** [14C. Directly or via French < Latin *aequinoctium* 'equal night' < *nox* 'night']

equip /i kwíp/ (**equips, equipping, equipped**) *vt* **1.** to provide somebody or something with what is needed for a particular activity or purpose, e.g. with the appropriate tools, supplies, parts, or clothing ○ *a computer equipped with a modem and a CD-ROM drive* ○ *They equipped themselves with the most up-to-date camping gear.* **2.** to prepare somebody with the necessary education, training, or experience to succeed at a task or role in life (*often passive*) ○ *I'm sorry, but I don't feel equipped to answer that question.* [Early 16C. < French *équiper*, probably < Old Norse *skipa* 'fit out a ship' < *skip* 'ship'] —**equipper** *n*

equipage /ékwipij/ *n* **1.** a horse-drawn carriage, especially a luxurious one, or a carriage together with its horses and attendants **2.** the equipment and supplies needed for an undertaking, especially a military expedition or ship's journey

equipartition /eékwi paar tísh'n, ékwi-/ *n* the equal distribution of energy among the components of motion, e.g. linear movement and rotation, of the gas molecules in a system

equiped incorrect spelling of **equipped**

equipment /i kwípmənt/ *n* **1.** NECESSARY ITEMS the tools, clothing, or other items needed for a particular activity or purpose ○ *camping equipment* **2.** PERSONAL RESOURCES FOR SUCCESS the intellectual and emotional resources that enable somebody to succeed at a task or role in life **3.** PROVIDING SOMEBODY WITH EQUIPMENT the equipping of somebody or something with what is necessary for a particular activity or purpose

equipoise /ékwi poyz, eékwi-/ (*formal*) *n* **1.** a condition in which weights are in balance or there is a balance between different social, emotional, or intellectual influences **2.** something that creates a balanced state, usually by counterbalancing some other force or thing ■ *vt* (**-poises, -poising, -poised**) same as **counterbalance**

equipollent /eékwi póllənt, ékwi-/ *adj* having the same weight, influence, validity, or effect as something else, or as each other (*formal*) [14C. < Old French

equipolent < Latin *pollere* 'be strong'] —**equipollence** *n* —**equipollency** *n* —**equipollently** *adv*

equipotential /eékwipə ténsh'l, ékwi-/ *adj* describes a surface that has the same electric or gravitational potential at all points —**equipotentiality** /-pə ténshi álləti/ *n*

equiprobable /eékwi próbbəb'l, ékwi-/ *adj* equally likely to be true or to occur according to logic or mathematics

equitable /ékwitəb'l/ *adj* **1.** characterized by justice or fairness and impartiality towards those involved (*formal*) **2.** applicable under the law of equity as distinguished from common or statute law [Mid-16C. < French *équitable* < *équité* (see EQUITY)] —**equitableness** *n* —**equitably** *adv*

equitation /ékwi táysh'n/ *n* the skill and theory of riding horses (*formal*) [Mid-16C. Directly or via French < Latin *equitation-* < *equitare* 'to ride on horseback' < *equus* 'horse']

equites /ékwi teez/ *npl* **1.** the cavalry of ancient Rome **2.** a privileged class of ancient Romans of a rank above the common people, whose members served as cavalry [Early 17C. < Latin, plural of *eques* (see EQUESTRIAN)]

equity /ékwiti/ *n* (*plural* **-ties**) **1.** FAIRNESS actions, treatment of others, or a general condition characterized by justice, fairness, and impartiality (*formal*) **2.** LAW MODIFICATION OF COMMON LAW the system of jurisprudence that supplements common and statutory law, when those bodies of law are inadequate in the attainment of justice **3.** LAW JUSTICE TEMPERED BY ETHICS justice applied in conformity with the law, but influenced at the same time by principles of ethics and fair play **4.** LAW FAIR CLAIM a claim that is judged to be just and fair **5.** FIN PART OF VALUE PAID the value of a piece of property over and above any mortgage or other liabilities relating to it ■ **equities** *npl* FIN SHARES ENTITLING HOLDER TO PROFITS shares of stock in a company that pays the holder some of its profits [14C. Via French *équité* < Latin *aequitas* < Latin *aequus* 'equal, even']

Equity *n* THEATRE the trade union for actors

equity capital *n* funds for a business raised by selling shares or by retaining earnings

equity of redemption *n* the right of a mortgagor to redeem mortgaged property by paying the sum owed within a reasonable time after the date on which payment was due

equiv. *abbr* equivalent

equivalence /i kwívvələnss/, **equivalency** /-lənssi/ *n* **1.** the fact of being the same, effectively the same, or interchangeable with something else **2.** the relationship between two statements, both of which are either true or false, and each of which can be proved from the other

equivalence relation *n* the relation between members of a set that is reflexive, symmetrical, and transitive, e.g. if 'a' equals 'b' and 'b' equals 'c', then 'a' equals 'c'

equivalency *n* same as **equivalence**

equivalent /i kwívvələnt/ *adj* **1.** EQUAL being the same, or effectively the same, in effect, value, or meaning as something and usually interchangeable with it ○ *That's equivalent to the amount of energy needed to power a single light bulb.* **2.** MATHS OF SAME SIZE BUT DIFFERENT SHAPE describes geometric figures that have different shapes but equal areas, e.g. a circle and a square, or equal volumes, e.g. a cylinder and a cube **3.** MATHS, LOGIC IN EQUIVALENCE RELATION describes members of a set that are in a reflexive, symmetrical, and transitive relation with each other **4.** MATHS WITH SAME SOLUTION describes equations that share a common solution or solutions, e.g. for both $2x-3 = x+2$ and $x-5 = 0$ the solution is $x = 5$ ■ *n* **1.** SOMETHING CONSIDERED THE SAME something that is considered to be equal to or have the same effect, value, or meaning as something else ○ *He's the Italian equivalent of the Chancellor of the Exchequer.* **2.** CHEM same as **equivalent weight** [15C. < French *équivalent* < late Latin *aequivalere* 'be of equal value' < Latin *valere* 'to be strong'] —**equivalently** *adv*

equivalent weight *n* the mass of a substance that will combine with or replace 8 parts by weight of oxygen or 1.008 parts of hydrogen

equivelent incorrect spelling of **equivalent**

equivocal /i kwívvək'l/ *adj* **1.** AMBIGUOUS open to more than one interpretation, especially in being deliberately expressed in an ambiguous way in an attempt to mislead somebody ○ *an equivocal reply to a tough question* **2.** DIFFICULT TO INTERPRET difficult to interpret, understand, or respond to ○ *Their stance on this issue is equivocal and nobody knows how they are likely to react.* **3.** RAISING DOUBTS arousing doubts and suspicions, especially about somebody's honesty or sincerity ○ *To arrive at the peace talks with an armed guard was an equivocal gesture.* [Mid-16C. < late Latin *aequivocus* (see EQUIVOCATE)] —**equivocality** /i kwívvə kálləti/ *n* —**equivocally** *adv* —**equivocalness** *n*

equivocate /i kwívvə kayt/ (**-cates, -cating, -cated**) *vi* to speak vaguely or ambiguously, especially in order to mislead ○ *When pressed for a firm answer, she equivocated.* [15C. < late Latin *aequivocat-*, past participle of *aequivocare* < *aequivocus* 'ambiguous' < Latin *vox* 'voice'] —**equivocatingly** *adv* —**equivocator** *n* —**equivocatory** *adj*

equivocation /i kwívvə káysh'n/ *n* **1.** USE OF AMBIGUITY the use of vague or ambiguous and sometimes misleading language ○ *What we ask for is facts: what we get is equivocation or downright lies.* **2.** AMBIGUOUS STATEMENT an expression or statement that is vague or ambiguous and often deliberately misleading ○ *Their equivocations could not disguise the fact that corruption was rife in the committee.* **3.** LOGIC WRONG LOGICAL CONCLUSION an invalid conclusion based on statements in which one term has two different meanings

equivoque /ékwi vōk, eékwi-/, **equivoke** *n* (*formal*) **1.** PLAY ON WORDS an amusing use of an ambiguous word **2.** AMBIGUOUS WORD OR PHRASE a word or phrase with a double meaning **3.** AMBIGUITY ambiguity, double meaning, or misleading words and expressions [Early 17C. Directly or via French *équivoque* < late Latin *aequivocus* (see EQUIVOCATE)]

Equuleus /e kwoóli əss/ *n* a constellation of the northern hemisphere, the second-smallest of the constellations. See illustration at **constellation**

er[1] /ur/ *interj* used to express hesitation [Mid-19C. Natural sound]

er[2] *abbr* Eritrea (*used in Internet addresses*) See table at **domain name**

Er *symbol* CHEM ELEM erbium

ER *abbr* **1.** Eduardus Rex **2.** Elizabetha Regina **3.** N Am HEALTH SERVICES emergency room

-er[1] *suffix* **1.** somebody or something that performs or undergoes a particular action ○ *adjuster* ○ *fryer* **2.** somebody connected with, often as an occupation ○ *trucker* **3.** somebody or something that has a particular characteristic, quality, or form ○ *fore-and-after* **4.** somebody from a particular place ○ *Londoner* ○ *foreigner* [Partly Old English *-ere* < Germanic; partly via Anglo-Norman < Latin *-arius*; partly < Old French *-eor* (see -OR[1])]

-er[2] *suffix* more ○ *greener* ○ *slower* [Old English *-re, -ra* < Germanic]

era /eérə/ *n* **1.** TIME DISTINCTIVE PERIOD OF HISTORY a period of time made distinctive by a significant development, feature, event, or personality ○ *during the postwar era* **2.** TIME PERIOD WITH ITS OWN CHRONOLOGICAL SYSTEM a time period within which years are consecutively numbered from a particular significant event that provides its starting point ○ *the Christian era* **3.** TIME DATE THAT BEGINS PERIOD a significant date or event that is regarded as the beginning of a new period of time ○ *The agreement marked an era in US-Soviet relations.* **4.** GEOL DIVISION OF EARTH'S HISTORY a division of geological time comprising several periods ○ *the Precambrian era* [Mid-17C. < late Latin *aera* 'number used as a basis for counting']

ERA[1] *n* a law passed by Parliament in 1988, covering the publication of information on schools, open enrolment, and grant-maintained schools. Full form **Education Reform Act**

ERA[2] *abbr* US LAW Equal Rights Amendment

eradicate /i ráddi kayt/ (**-cates, -cating, -cated**) *vt* to destroy or get rid of something completely, so that it can never recur or return [15C. < Latin *eradicat-*, past participle of *eradicare* 'pull up by the roots' < *radix*

'root'] —**eradicable** *adj* —**eradicably** /-kəbli/ *adv* —**eradication** /i ráddi káysh'n/ *n* —**eradicative** *adj* —**eradicator** *n*

erase /i ráyz/ (**erases, erasing, erased**) *vt* **1. REMOVE WRITTEN MATERIAL** to remove written, typed, or printed material by rubbing it out, or obliterate it with something such as correction fluid **2. ELIMINATE SOMETHING** to remove or destroy something completely ○ *an ancient civilization, all traces of which had been erased over time* **3.** COMPUT **DELETE RECORDED DATA** to delete data or recorded material from a computer's memory, a magnetic tape, or other storage medium [Late 16C. < Latin *eras-*, past participle of *eradere* 'scrape out' < *radere* 'to scrape'] —**erasability** /i ráyzə bílləti/ *n* —**erasable** *adj*

eraser /i ráyzər/ *n N Am* same as **rubber**[1] (sense 3)

Erasmus /i rázməss/, **Desiderius** (1466?–1536) Dutch scholar and writer. His works, combining a Christian outlook with Renaissance humanism, influenced both sides during the Reformation. Among his many other works was a new edition of the Greek New Testament (1516).

> 'It is an unscrupulous intellect that does not pay to antiquity its due reverence...There are many kinds of genius; each age has its different gifts.'
> [Desiderius Erasmus, *Works of Hilary*; 1523]

Erastianism /i rásti ənizəm/ *n* the theory that the state, not a church, should have the ultimate authority in ecclesiastical matters [Late 17C. After Thomas *Erastus* (1524–83), Swiss-German theologian] —**Erastian** *n, adj*

erasure /i ráyzhər/ *n* **1.** the complete removal or destruction of something ○ *an erasure of data from a hard drive* **2.** the place where something has been rubbed out, or the mark left behind

Erato /érratō/ *n* in Greek mythology, the Muse of lyric poetry, one of the nine Muses believed to inspire and nurture the arts

Eratosthenes[1] /érrə tósthə neez/ prominent deep crater on the Moon with a distinctive central peak, located at the southern edge of Mare Imbrium, 58 km/36 mi. in diameter

Eratosthenes[2] (276?–196? BC) Greek astronomer and mathematician. He is best known for his calculation of the Earth's circumference, which remained the most accurate one available until the 17th century.

erbium /úrbi əm/ *n* a soft silvery metallic element of the rare-earth group. Source: monazite, bastnaesite. Use: alloys, pigment. Symbol **Er**. See table at **element** [Mid-19C. After *Ytterby*, town in Sweden]

Erdogan /úrdō gaán/, **Recep Tayyip** (*b.* 1954) Turkish prime minister. A former mayor of Istanbul, he was convicted of inciting religious hatred in 1998, and on his release founded the Islamist-based Justice and Development Party (AK). Winning a prime ministerial election in 2002, he was nevertheless unable to take up the post until a constitutional amendment allowed a person with a criminal conviction to become a member of parliament, a prerequisite for holding the prime minister's office. He won a by-election and became prime minister in 2003.

ere /air/ *prep, conj* before or earlier in time than (*literary or archaic*) [Old English *ǣr* < Germanic]

SPELLCHECK See *air*

Erebus, Mount /érribəss/ active volcano on the eastern coast of Ross Island, Antarctica. Height: 3,794 m/12,448 ft.

erect /i rékt/ *adj* **1. STRAIGHT AND VERTICAL** in an upright position ○ *an erect plant stem* **2.** PHYSIOL **FIRM AND RIGID** stiff and swollen as a result of being filled with blood, e.g. when sexually aroused **3.** OPTICS **RIGHT SIDE UP** describes an optically produced image that is the correct way up and not inverted ■ *v* (**erects, erecting, erected**) **1.** *vt* **CONSTRUCT SOMETHING** to build a structure from basic parts and materials ○ *The building was erected in 1885.* ○ *erected a climbing frame* **2.** *vt* **PUT SOMETHING TOGETHER** to fit something together and put it into position so that it is ready for use **3.** *vt* **SET SOMETHING UPRIGHT** to fix something in an upright position **4.** *vt* **ESTABLISH SYSTEM OR THEORY** to bring an organization, system, or theory into being ○ *The corporation erected a new legal department to deal with mergers and acquisitions.* **5.** *vt* MATHS **DRAW FIGURE ON BASE** to draw or construct a line or figure on a given base **6.** *vti* PHYSIOL **BECOME OR MAKE RIGID** to become, or cause an organ to become, stiff and swollen by being filled with blood [14C. < Latin *erect-*, past participle of *erigere* 'set up' < *regere* 'direct, rule'] —**erectable** *adj* —**erectly** *adv* —**erectness** *n*

erecter *n* ANAT, CONSTR another spelling of **erector**

erectile /i rék tīl/ *adj* capable of filling with blood under pressure, swelling, and becoming stiff —**erectility** /i rék tílləti/ *n*

erectile dysfunction *n* a medical condition that prevents a man from achieving an erection or maintaining one throughout sexual intercourse

erection /i réksh'n/ *n* **1. PUTTING SOMETHING UP** the construction or setting up of something **2. SWELLING OF TISSUE** the stiffened and swollen state of erectile tissue, especially that of the penis, usually as a result of sexual arousal **3. STRUCTURE** something that has been built or constructed (*formal*)

erector /i réktər/, **erecter** *n* **1.** a muscle that is capable of raising or holding up a body part **2.** somebody or something that erects things, generally things made elsewhere

E region *n* the middle part of the ionosphere, lying approximately 80 to 110 km/50 to 70 mi. above the Earth's surface, that reflects medium-length radio waves

erelong /air lóng/ *adv* soon or in a short time (*literary or archaic*)

eremite /érrə mīt/ *n* a hermit, especially one who lives alone for religious reasons (*literary*) [13C. Via French or late Latin < Greek *erēmitēs* (see HERMIT)] —**eremitic** /érrə míttik/ *adj* —**eremitical** *adj* —**eremitism** *n*

erethism /érrithizəm/ *n* excessive sensitivity of a body part to stimuli (*technical*) [Early 19C. < French *éréthisme* < Greek *erethizein* 'irritate'] —**erethismic** /érri thízmik/ *adj* —**erethistic** /érri thístik/ *adj* —**erethitic** /érri thíttik/ *adj*

erf /urf/ (*plural* **erfs** or **erven** /úrvən/) *n S Africa* a small plot of land on which to build, usually in an urban area [Late 17C. < Dutch, 'land, yard']

erg[1] /urg/ *n* the centimetre-gram-second unit of energy or work equal to the work done by a force of one dyne acting through a distance of one centimetre. 1 erg is equivalent to 10^{-7} joule. [Late 19C. < Greek *ergon* 'work']

erg[2] /urg/ (*plural* **ergs** or **areg** /ə rég/) *n* a large, relatively flat area of desert covered with shifting windswept sand, especially in the Sahara [Late 19C. Via French < Arabic *'irḳ, 'erg*]

ergative /úrgətiv/ GRAM *adj* **1. ALLOWING OBJECT TO BE SUBJECT** describes a class of verbs in which the object of the transitive form can be used as the subject of the intransitive form with an equivalent meaning. 'Open' is an example of an ergative verb in 'I opened the door' and 'The door opened'. **2. INDICATING DOER OF ACTION AS OBJECT** describes a case of nouns in languages such as Inuit and Basque indicating that the object of the verb acts, while the subject is affected by the action ■ *n* **ERGATIVE WORD** an ergative verb, or a noun in the ergative case [Mid-20C. < Greek *ergatēs* 'worker' < *ergon* 'work']

ergo /úrgō/ *adv, conj* therefore [14C. < Latin]

ergocalciferol /úrgō kal síffə rol/ *n* BIOCHEM same as **vitamin** D_2 [Mid-20C. < ERGOSTEROL]

ergometer /ur gómmitər/ *n* an instrument for measuring muscle power or work done by muscles, e.g. when exercising [Late 19C. < Greek *ergon* 'work'] —**ergometric** /úrgə méttrik/ *adj*

ergonomic /úrgə nómmik/ *adj* designed for maximum comfort, efficiency, safety, and ease of use, especially in the workplace —**ergonomically** *adv*

ergonomics /úrgə nómmiks/ *n* the study of how a workplace and the equipment used there can best be designed for comfort, efficiency, safety, and productivity (*takes a singular verb*) ■ *npl* those factors or qualities in the design of something, especially a workplace or equipment used by people at work, that contribute to comfort, efficiency, safety, and ease of use (*takes a plural verb*) [Mid-20C. < Greek *ergon* 'work' after ECONOMICS] —**ergonometric** /úrgənə méttrik/ *adj* —**ergonomist** /ur gónnəmist/ *n*

ergosterol /ur góstə rol/ *n* a sterol present in yeast and moulds that is converted to vitamin D_2 by ultraviolet light [Early 20C. < ERGOT]

ergot /úrgət, úrgot/ *n* **1.** a disease of cereals caused by the parasitic fungus *Claviceps purpurea* that grows in dense black masses (**sclerotia**) in the grains of the ear **2.** the dried sclerotia of an ergot fungus containing physiologically active substances. Use: treatment of migraine, initiation of labour in pregnancy. [Late 17C. < French, 'cock's spur'; from the appearance of the diseased grain] —**ergotic** /ur góttik/ *adj*

ergotamine /ur góttə meen/ *n* an alkaloid drug derived from ergot that causes constriction of blood vessels. Use: treatment of migraine. Formula: $C_{33}H_{35}N_5O_5$.

ergotism /úrgətizəm/ *n* a severe toxic reaction to food containing ergot-contaminated grain, or excessive amounts of drugs containing ergot derivatives. The toxin produces neurological and gastrointestinal symptoms and, if not properly treated, gangrene.

Erhard /áir haard/, **Ludwig** (1897–1977) German politician. As finance minister, he achieved West Germany's postwar economic revival and was the Christian Democratic Chancellor from 1963 until 1966.

> '[Politics is] the art of dividing a cake in such a way that everyone believes he has the biggest piece.'
> [Attributed to Ludwig Erhard]

erica /érrikə/ (*plural* **-cas** or *same*) *n* an evergreen bush or small tree of the heath family with small leathery leaves. Flowers: bell-shaped. Genus: *Erica*. [Early 17C. Via modern Latin < Greek *ereikē* 'heath']

ericaceous /érri káyshəss/ *adj* **1.** belonging or relating to the heath family, a group of evergreen bushes and small trees that includes the heath, heather, rhododendron, azalea, and arbutus **2.** describes potting compost that is suitable for ericaceous and other acid-loving or lime-hating plants

Ericson /érriks'n/, **Leif** (975–1020) Icelandic explorer. He is traditionally believed to have been the first European to reach the North American mainland.

Eric the Red /érrik-/ (950?–1000?) Norwegian explorer. He was the father of Leif Ericson. Banished from Scandinavia for manslaughter, he explored Greenland (982–86), where he established the first European settlement. Born **Thorvaldson, Eric**

Eridanus /e ríddənəss/ *n* a large faint constellation of the southern hemisphere. See illustration at **constellation**

Erie, Lake /éeri/ lake in the United States and Canada. It is one of the five Great Lakes of North America. Area: 25,700 sq. km/9,910 sq. mi.

Erie Canal artificial inland waterway between Buffalo, on Lake Erie, and Albany, New York, where it links with the River Hudson. Length: 547 km/340 mi.

Erigena /érri jéenə, -gáynə/, **Johannes Scotus** (815?–877?) Irish-born scholar. In his fusion of traditional Christianity with neo-Platonism, he was a pioneer of medieval scholasticism.

erigeron /i ríjjə ron/ (*plural* **-ons** or *same*) *n* a plant of the daisy family, many species of which are cultivated as ornamentals. Fleabane is a type of erigeron. Genus: *Erigeron*. [Early 17C. Via Latin < Greek, 'early old man'; from its former application to the groundsel, an early flowering plant with fluffy white seed heads]

Erikson /érrikss'n/, **Erik** (1902–94) German-born US psychoanalyst. He developed the concept of the identity crisis, as well as making major contributions to the area of child psychology. Full name **Erikson, Erik Homburger**

> 'The identity crisis...occurs in that period of the life cycle when each youth must forge for himself some central perspective and direction, some working unity, out of the effective remnants of his childhood and the hopes of his anticipated adulthood.'
> [Erik Erikson, *Young Man Luther*; 1958]

Erin /érrin/ *n* the country of Ireland (*literary*)

Erin go bragh /érrin gō bra'a/ *interj Ireland* an expression meaning 'Ireland forever' [< ERIN + Irish *go brách, go bráth* 'till doomsday']

Erinyes /i rínni eez/ *npl* MYTHOL same as **Furies**

eristic /e rístik/ (*formal*) *adj* also **eristical** /e rístik'l/ ARGUMENTATIVE fond of or characterized by argument or controversy ■ *n* **1.** ART OF DISPUTING the skill or practice of debating, especially in a manner involving subtle logic and specious argument **2.** DEBATER somebody who is an expert or delights in argument or controversy [Mid-17C. < Greek *eristikos* < *eris* 'strife'] **—eristically** *adv*

Eritrea

Eritrea /érri tráy ə/ country on the Red Sea coast in northeastern Africa, bordered by Sudan and Ethiopia. A former Italian colony, it became part of Ethiopia in 1952 and fully independent in 1993. Language: Tigrinya, Tigre, Arabic. Currency: nakfa. Capital: Asmara. Population: 4,362,254 (2003). Area: 121,144 sq. km/46,774 sq. mi. Official name **State of Eritrea —Eritrean** *n, adj*

erk /urk/ *n* **1.** AIR FORCE LOW-RANKING MEMBER OF RAF an aircraftman or -woman or other low-ranking member of the Royal Air Force (*slang*) **2.** NAVY SEAMAN an ordinary sailor in the Royal Navy (*slang*) **3.** OFFENSIVE TERM an offensive term for somebody who is disliked or despised (*dated slang insult*) [Early 20C. Origin ?]

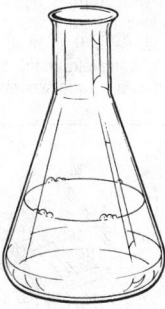
Erlenmeyer flask

Erlenmeyer flask /úrlən mī ər-/ *n* a cone-shaped laboratory flask with a narrow neck and broad flat bottom [Late 19C. After Emil *Erlenmeyer* (1825–1909), German chemist]

ERM *abbr* ECON Exchange Rate Mechanism

ermine

ermine /úrmin/ (*plural* **-mines** or *same*) *n* **1.** a stoat, especially in its white winter coat **2.** the white fur

of an ermine, once valued as a symbol of wealth, nobility, or high rank [12C. < Old French *(h)ermine*, probably < medieval Latin *(mus) Armenius* 'Armenian (mouse)']

erne /urn/ (*plural* **ernes** or *same*), **ern** (*plural* **erns** or *same*) *n* a long-winged sea eagle. Native to: Europe. Latin name: *Haliaeetus albicilla*. [Old English *earn* < Indo-European]

Erne /urn/ major river in Ireland, rising in County Cavan, Republic of Ireland, and flowing north into Northern Ireland and west through Donegal, before emptying into Donegal Bay. Along its route it broadens into two large lakes, Upper and Lower Lough Erne.

Ernie /úrni/, **ERNIE** *n* in the United Kingdom, the machine used for drawing winning premium bond numbers [Mid-20C. Acronym < *electronic random number indicating equipment*]

Max Ernst

Ernst /airnst, urnst/, **Max** (1891–1976) German-born French artist. A cofounder of Dada and surrealism, he is known for the startling and violent imagery of his works.

> 'The virtue of pride, which was once the beauty of mankind, has given place to that fount of all ugliness, Christian humility.'
> [Attributed to Max Ernst]

erode /i rṓd/ (**erodes, eroding, eroded**) *v* **1.** *vti* WEAR AWAY LAND to wear away outer layers of rock or soil, or be gradually worn away by the action of wind or water **2.** *vt* GEOL FORM LAND FEATURE BY WEATHERING to form a land feature such as a valley or gully by the action of wind or water **3.** *vti* DESTROY SOMETHING GRADUALLY to diminish or destroy something gradually over time, or be gradually diminished or destroyed ○ *Higher inflation will erode our savings.* **4.** *vti* CHEM EAT SUBSTANCE AWAY to eat into or destroy something by corrosion or chemical action, or be damaged or destroyed in this way **5.** *vt* MED WEAR TISSUE AWAY to cause surface tissue to wear away as a result of decay, ulceration, cancer, or the chemical processes associated with inflammation [Early 17C. Directly or via French < Latin *erodere* 'gnaw off' < *rodere* 'gnaw'] **—erodent** /i rṓd'nt/ *n, adj* **—erodibility** /i rṓdə bílləti/ *n* **—erodible** /i rṓdəb'l/ *adj*

erogenous /i rójjənəss/, **erogenic** /érrə jénnik/, **erotogenic** /i rṓttə jénnik/ *adj* **1.** sensitive and arousing sexual feelings when touched or stroked **2.** stimulating sexual desire [Late 19C. < EROS]

erogenous zone *n* an area of the body that is sensitive to sexual stimulation

Eros /éer oss/ *n* **1.** GREEK GOD OF LOVE in Greek mythology, the god of love. Roman equivalent **Cupid 2.** *also* **eros** SEXUAL LOVE sexual love or desire **3.** PSYCHOANAL INSTINCT FOR SELF-PRESERVATION in psychoanalytic theory, the instincts for self-preservation, pleasure, and procreation considered as a group [Late 17C. Via Latin < Greek, 'sexual love']

erosion /i rṓzh'n/ *n* **1.** GRADUAL BREAKING DOWN the gradual destruction or reduction and weakening of something ○ *The erosion of profits was due to careless management.* **2.** WEARING AWAY OF ROCK the gradual wearing away of rock or soil by physical breakdown, chemical solution, and transportation of material, as caused, e.g. by water, wind, or ice **3.** DENT LOSS OF TOOTH ENAMEL loss of tooth enamel caused by excessive intake of acidic citrus juices or through repeated contact with stomach acid, as in bulimia **4.** MED WEARING AWAY OF TISSUE the wearing away of

surface tissue by disease, ulceration, cancer, or the chemical processes associated with inflammation [Mid-16C. < French *érosion* < Latin *eros-*, past participle of *erodere* (see ERODE)] **—erosional** *adj* **—erosionally** *adv*

erosive /i rṓssiv/ *adj* causing the gradual breaking down or wearing away of something, especially rock or soil **—erosiveness** *n* **—erosivity** /irṓ sívvəti/ *n*

erotic /i róttik/ *adj* **1.** arousing, or designed to arouse, feelings of sexual desire **2.** characterized by or arising out of sexual desire [Mid-17C. Via French < Greek *erōtikos* < *erōs* 'sexual love'] **—erotically** *adv*

erotica /i róttikə/ *n* art or literature intended to arouse sexual desire by portraying sex in an explicit way. ◊ **pornography** [Mid-19C. < Greek *erōtika*, neuter plural of *erōtikos* (see EROTIC)]

eroticise *vt* another spelling of **eroticize**

eroticism /i rótti sizəm/, **erotism** /érrə tizəm/ *n* **1.** EROTIC QUALITY an erotic quality in something, especially an erotic style or subject in literature or art ○ *the eroticism of her poetry* **2.** SEXUAL DESIRE feelings of sexual desire **3.** EXCESSIVE SEXUAL EXCITEMENT unusually persistent or frequent sexual interest or desire **—eroticist** *n*

eroticize /i rótti sīz/ (**-cizes, -cizing, -cized**), **eroticise** (**-cises, -cising, -cised**), **erotize** /érrə tīz/ (**-tizes, -tizing, -tized**), **erotise** (**-tises, -tising, -tised**) *vt* to make something erotic, especially by giving a sexual quality to something not usually regarded in that way ○ *The paintings were thought to eroticize flowers.* **—eroticization** /i rótti sī záysh'n/ *n*

erotism *n* same as **eroticism**

erotize *vt* same as **eroticize**

eroto- *prefix* sexual desire ○ *erotogenic* [< Greek *erōt-*, stem of *erōs* 'sexual love']

erotogenic *adj* same as **erogenous**

erotology /érrə tólləji/ *n* the study of erotic material and the stimulation of sexual desire **—erotological** /érrətə lójjik'l/ *adj* **—erotologist** *n*

erotomania /i róttō máyni ə/ *n* **1.** excessive and insatiable feelings of sexual desire **2.** the delusion of being loved by and romantically involved in a relationship with a person, especially somebody famous or of high social position **—erotomaniac** *n*

err /ur, air/ (**errs, erring, erred**) *vi* (*formal*) **1.** to make a mistake or do an incorrect thing ○ *The committee erred in interpreting the contract.* **2.** to behave badly and do something that is morally wrong ○ *'To err is human, to forgive, divine.'* (Alexander Pope, *Essay On Criticism*; 1711) [13C. Via French < Latin *errare* 'to wander']

SPELLCHECK See *air.*

errancy /érrənssi/ *n* (*formal*) **1.** incorrect or morally wrong behaviour **2.** the propensity for making mistakes or acting improperly

errand /érrənd/ *n* **1.** a short trip somewhere to do something on behalf of somebody else, e.g. to buy something or deliver a message ○ *She sometimes runs errands for me if I'm not well enough to go out.* **2.** a task that somebody goes somewhere to carry out for somebody else [Old English *ærende* 'message, mission' < ?]

errant /érrənt/ *adj* **1.** BEHAVING BADLY behaving in an unacceptable manner **2.** TAKING WRONG ROUTE wandering from an intended course, or not reaching an intended destination **3.** MOVING IRREGULARLY with no regular or purposeful pattern of motion **4.** LOOKING FOR ADVENTURE wandering in search of adventure and romance (*literary*) [14C. < Latin *errant-*, present participle of *errare* 'to wander'] **—errantly** *adv*

errantry /érrəntri/ *n* the wandering, romantic, and adventurous life of a knight errant

errata PRINTING plural of **erratum**

erratic /i ráttik/ *adj* **1.** INCONSISTENT not predictable, regular, or consistent, especially in being likely to depart from expected standards at any time ○ *His driving tends to be rather erratic.* **2.** OFTEN CHANGING DIRECTION often changing direction and not following any definite course **3.** GEOL CARRIED AND DEPOSITED BY ICE describes a rock or boulder that was carried from its source by ice and deposited when the ice melted ■ *n* **1.** SOMEBODY BEHAVING UNPREDICTABLY somebody who

behaves unpredictably **2.** GEOL **ROCK MOVED BY ICE** a rock or boulder that was carried from its source by ice and deposited when the ice melted [14C. < Old French *erratique* < Latin *errare* 'to wander'] —**erratically** *adv* —**erraticism** /i ráttissizəm/ *n*

erratum /e ra͞atəm/ *n* (*plural* **-ta** /-tə/) a mistake in printing or writing, especially one noted on a list that is included with a printed book ■ **errata** *npl* a list of mistakes noticed after a book was printed, often included as a separate sheet in the book [Mid-16C. < Latin, form of past participle of *errare* 'to wander']

erroneous /i rōni əss/ *adj* incorrect, based on an incorrect assumption, or containing something that is incorrect [14C. < Old French *erroneus* < Latin *erron-* 'truant' < *errare* 'to wander'] —**erroneously** *adv* —**erroneousness** *n*

error /érrər/ *n* **1.** UNINTENTIONAL MISTAKE something unintentionally done wrong, e.g. as a result of poor judgment or lack of care ○ *The report blames the crash on human error.* ○ *errors in his addition* **2.** WRONG BELIEF a belief or opinion that is contrary to fact or to established doctrine ○ *a serious error of judgment* **3.** STATE OF BEING MISTAKEN the state of holding incorrect beliefs or opinions, or the fact of acting wrongly or misguidedly ○ *caused by human error* **4.** FACT OF BEING MISTAKE the state or fact of being a mistake, or of being inappropriate or unacceptable ○ *He's seen the error of his ways.* **5.** COMPUT PROBLEM IN COMPUTER PROGRAM the failure of a computer program, subroutine, or system to produce an anticipated result **6.** MATHS MATHEMATICAL DIFFERENCE a variation between the true value of a mathematical quantity and a calculated or measured value [13C. < Old French *err(o)ur* < Latin *errare* 'to wander'] —**errorless** *adj* ◇ **in error 1.** by mistake **2.** mistaken, or acting on the basis of a false assumption or belief

SYNONYMS See *mistake.*

error code *n* a unique combination of characters printed or displayed by a computer that identifies a specific error or problem in its operation

error message *n* a message indicating that a computer has encountered a problem, often suggesting alternative action. The message may take the form of a display on a monitor, text on a printer, a computer-generated voice, or a sequence of audio signals.

ersatz /áir zats/ *adj* imitating or presented as a substitute for something of superior quality (*disapproving*) [Late 19C. < German, 'replacement']

Erse /urss/ *n* the Gaelic language, especially Irish Gaelic [14C. Early Scots variant of IRISH] —**Erse** *adj*

Ershad /úrsh ad, ur shád/, **Hossain Mohammad** (*b.* 1930) Indian-born Bangladeshi soldier and politician. He seized power in Bangladesh in 1982, declared himself president in 1983, and retained office in a controversial election (1986). He resigned amid overwhelming popular opposition in 1990.

Erskine /úrskin/, **Ralph** (*b.* 1914) British architect. An appreciation of the needs of the community informs his large public housing projects, e.g. the Byker Wall estate (1969–82) in Newcastle upon Tyne.

Erskine, Thomas, 1st Baron Erskine (1750–1823) British advocate and politician. His forensic skill, often exercised in defending political radicals such as Thomas Paine, was considered matchless in his time. He was briefly lord chancellor (1806–07).

erst /urst/ *adv* in the past, or a long time ago (*archaic*) [Old English *ærest* 'first' < Germanic]

erstwhile /úrst wīl/ *adj* formerly holding a particular position or relationship ○ *Since leaving the bank, she has been ostracized by her erstwhile colleagues.* ■ *adv* at a time in the past (*archaic*)

ert /urt/ (**erts, erting, erted**) *vi S Africa* to lose consciousness and fall to the ground as a result of taking illegal drugs (*slang*)

erub *n* JUDAISM same as **eruv**

erucic acid /i ro͞ossik-/ *n* a soft colourless solid fatty acid. Source: rape seeds. Use: manufacture of plastics. [< Latin *eruca* 'rape plant']

eruct /i rúkt/ (**eructs, eructing, eructed**), **eructate** /i rúk tayt/ (**-tates, -tating, -tated**) *vti* to expel stomach gases through the mouth (*technical*) [Mid-17C. < Latin *eruct-*,

past participle of *eructare* 'to belch or vomit up' < *ructare* 'to belch'] —**eructation** /i rúk táysh'n, eé ruk-/ *n*

erudite /érro͞o dīt/ *adj* having or showing great knowledge gained from study and reading [15C. < Latin *erudit-*, past participle of *erudire* 'instruct' < *rudis* 'untrained'] —**eruditely** *adv*

erudition /érro͞o dísh'n/ *n* knowledge acquired through study and reading ○ *a work of great erudition*

SYNONYMS See *knowledge.*

erupt /i rúpt/ (**erupts, erupting, erupted**) *v* **1.** *vi* BURST OUT to burst out suddenly or violently ○ *suddenly erupted into shouting* **2.** *vti* VIOLENTLY RELEASE MATERIAL to eject material such as gas, steam, ash, or lava, usually violently, from within ○ *The volcano last erupted in 1935.* **3.** *vi* APPEAR ON SKIN to appear as a rash or blemish on the skin or a mucous membrane **4.** *vi* COME THROUGH GUM to break through and emerge from a gum (*technical*; *refers to growing teeth*) [Mid-17C. < Latin *erupt-*, past participle of *erumpere* 'to break out' < *rumpere* 'to break'] —**eruptible** *adj* —**eruptive** *adj* —**eruptively** *adv*

eruption /i rúpsh'n/ *n* **1.** OUTBURST a sudden outburst or occurrence of something **2.** VIOLENT RELEASE OF MATERIAL the violent ejection of material such as gas, steam, ash, or lava from a volcano **3.** MED RASH OR BLEMISH ON SKIN a rash or blemish, or the appearance of one, on the skin or a mucous membrane **4.** DENT EMERGENCE OF TOOTH an emergence of a growing tooth from a gum (*technical*)

eruv /érro͞ov/ (*plural* **-uvim** /-o͞ovim/ or **-uvs**), **erub** /érro͞ob/ (*plural* **-ubim** /-o͞obim/ or **-ubs**) *n* in some Jewish communities, a physical boundary within which some relaxations of the rules concerning the Jewish Sabbath are allowed. It may consist of the walls of a town, a natural barrier, or a special construction. [Early 18C. < Hebrew *'ērūbh* 'mixture']

erven *S Africa* plural of **erf**

Erving /úrving/, **Julius** (*b.* 1950) US basketball player. He is widely regarded as one of the greatest and most exciting scorers in basketball history. Full name **Erving II, Julius Winfield.** Known as **Dr J**

-ery *suffix* **1.** place for ○ *brewery* **2.** activity or behaviour ○ *trickery* **3.** collection of ○ *crockery* **4.** qualities or character of ○ *buffoonery* **5.** state or condition of ○ *drudgery* [< Old French *-erie* < *-er* '-er, -or' + *-ie* '-y']

erysipelas /érri síppələss/ *n* a severe skin rash accompanied by fever and vomiting and caused by a streptococcal bacterium. ◇ **St Anthony's fire** [14C. Via Latin < Greek *erusipelas* 'red skin'] —**erysipelatous** /érrissi péllətəss/ *adj*

erythema /érri theémə/ *n* redness of the skin as a result of a widening of the small blood vessels near its surface. It has various causes, including fever and inflammation. [Late 18C. < Greek *eruthēma* < *eruthros* 'red'] —**erythematous** /érri theémətəss, -thémmə-/ *adj* —**erythemic** *adj*

erythr- *prefix* same as **erythro-** (*used before vowels*)

erythrism /érri thrizəm, i ríth rizəm/ *n* unusual redness of plumage or hair, often with a ruddy complexion in humans [Late 19C. < Greek *eruthros* 'red'] —**erythrismal** /érri thrízm'l/ *adj*

erythrite /érri thrīt, i ríth rīt/ *n* a pale red cobalt arsenate mineral. Use: glass colourant. [Mid-19C. < Greek *eruthros* 'red']

erythro- *prefix* **1.** red ○ *erythrocyte* **2.** red blood cell ○ *erythroblast* [< Greek *eruthros* 'red' < Indo-European]

erythroblast /i ríthrə blast/ *n* an immature red blood cell that is found in bone marrow and eventually develops into a mature red blood cell. Unlike a mature red blood cell, an erythroblast has a nucleus. —**erythroblastic** /i ríthrə blástik/ *adj*

erythroblastosis /i ríthrō bla stóssiss/ *n* the presence of immature red blood cells in the bloodstream that occurs especially in erythroblastosis fetalis

erythroblastosis fetalis /-fi tálliss/ *n* a serious blood disease of foetuses and newborn babies, in which the antibodies produced by an RH negative mother destroy the red blood cells of an RH positive foetus [*Fetalis* < modern Latin, 'foetal']

erythrocyte /i ríthrō sīt/ *n* a red blood cell (*technical*) —**erythrocytic** /i ríthrō síttik/ *adj*

erythromycin /i ríthrō míssin/ *n* a broad-spectrum antibiotic derived from the bacterium *Streptomyces erythreus*

erythropoiesis /i ríthrō poy eéssiss/ *n* the formation of red blood cells, a process that begins with stem cells in the bone marrow and ends with the release of mature red blood cells (**erythrocytes**) into circulation [Early 20C. < ERYTHROCYTE] —**erythropoietic** /-éttik/ *adj*

erythropoietin /i ríthrō poy eétin, -éttin/ *n* a kidney hormone that stimulates the development of red blood cells in the bone marrow. The kidneys produce erythropoietin in response to lowered oxygen levels in body tissues. [Mid-20C. < ERYTHROPOIESIS]

es *abbr* Spain (*used in Internet addresses*) See table at **domain name** [Spanish *España*]

Es *symbol* CHEM ELEM einsteinium

ES *abbr* Eastern States

ESA *abbr* **1.** environmentally sensitive area **2.** European Space Agency

Esau /eé saw/ *n* in the Bible, the son of Isaac and Rebekah, who sold his birthright to his brother, Jacob

Esc *abbr* COMPUT escape (key)

escadrille /éskədril, éskə dríl/ *n* a squadron of usually six aircraft, especially a French air squadron of World War I [Early 20C. Via French < Spanish *escuadrilla* 'little squadron' < *escuadra* 'squadron']

escalade /éskə láyd/ *n* an attack involving the use of ladders to scale the walls of a fortified place ■ *vt* (**-lades, -lading, -laded**) to scale the walls of a fortification using ladders [Late 16C. Directly or via French < Spanish *escalada*] —**escalader** *n*

escalate /éskə layt/ (**-lates, -lating, -lated**) *vti* to become or cause something to become greater, more serious, or more intense [Early 20C. Back-formation < ESCALATOR] —**escalation** /éskə láysh'n/ *n* —**escalatory** /éskə láytəri/ *adj*

USAGE No one uses **escalate** now to mean 'travel on an escalator', and the figurative meaning has taken over completely. Its earliest and still most common uses are in connection with military activity and conflicts: *Tourists were advised not to travel to the country as terrorist attacks escalate.* It is used most effectively when it describes a development that proceeds in stages, rather than as a simple synonym for *increase* or *mount*.

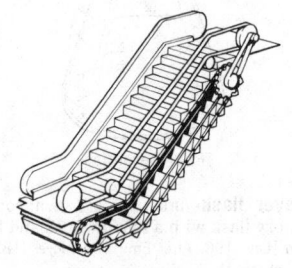

escalator

escalator /éskə laytər/ *n* **1.** a set of moving steps attached to a continuously circulating belt, that carries people up or down between levels in a building **2.** *also* **escalator clause** a stipulation in a contract that relates an increase or decrease in something to a change in something else, e.g. relating compensation to cost of living or prices to sales [Early 20C. < ESCALADE, after ELEVATOR]

escallop /éskə lop, e skólləp/ *n* HANDICRAFT same as **scallop** *n* (sense 5) [15C. < French *escalope* 'shell']

escalope /éskə lop, e skólləp/ *n UK, ANZ, Can* a slice of boneless lean meat, especially veal or poultry, that is beaten flat for cooking quickly or rolling around a stuffing. US term **scallop** [Early 19C. < French, 'shell'; probably because it curls into a shell shape in cooking]

escapade /éskə payd/ *n* something exciting or ad-

venturous that somebody does or is involved in, especially something showing recklessness or disregard for authority [Mid-17C. Via French < Spanish *escapada* 'an escape' < assumed Vulgar Latin *excappare* (see ESCAPE)]

escape /i skáyp/ v (-**capes**, -**caping**, -**caped**) **1.** *vti* BREAK FREE FROM CAPTIVITY to get free from captivity or confinement ○ *prisoners who attempted to escape* ○ *escaped their cage* **2.** *vt* AVOID BAD SITUATION to avoid danger, harm, or involvement in an unpleasant situation ○ *There's no escaping the fact that the house needs painting.* **3.** *vi* LEAK OUT to leak out from a container **4.** *vt* BE TEMPORARILY UNKNOWN TO SOMEBODY to fail to be noticed, remembered, or understood by somebody ○ *a little village whose name escapes me for the moment* **5.** *vti* BE UTTERED to be uttered by somebody unintentionally ○ *A muffled curse escaped his lips.* **6.** *vi* LEISURE TAKE SHORT HOLIDAY to get away from work or responsibilities and take a trip or short holiday **7.** *vi* COMPUT EXIT COMPUTER PROCEDURE to exit from a computer program or file, cancel a command or operation, or return from the currently active menu to a previous one **8.** *vi* BOT START GROWING IN WILD to spread from a garden or other cultivated area and become established in the wild (*refers to cultivated plants*) ■ *n* **1.** BREAKING FREE FROM CAPTIVITY an act of getting free from captivity or confinement ○ *He made his escape while the guard was asleep.* **2.** AVOIDANCE OF BAD SITUATION the avoidance of a dangerous, harmful, or unpleasant situation ○ *had a narrow escape* **3.** MEANS OF GETTING AWAY a method, means, or route by which somebody can escape from a place or situation **4.** DISTRACTION something that takes the mind off routine or serious matters ○ *an escape from daily routine* **5.** GAS OR LIQUID LEAK a leak of gas or liquid from a container **6.** LEISURE SHORT HOLIDAY a trip or short holiday taken to get away from work or responsibilities **7.** *also* **Escape** COMPUT COMPUTER KEY the key on a computer keyboard that allows a user to exit a program, cancel a command, or return to a previous menu ○ *Press escape to exit the program.* **8.** COMPUT same as **escape code 9.** BOT WILD PLANT FORMERLY CULTIVATED a plant that has spread from a garden or other cultivated area and is growing wild [13C. Via Old N French *escaper* < assumed Vulgar Latin *excappare* 'throw off your cloak' < *cappa* 'cloak'] —**escapable** *adj* —**escaper** *n*

escape artist *n* **1.** a performer who is skilled at escaping from restraints or confinement **2.** somebody who is skilled at escaping from difficulty or danger

escape clause *n* a clause in a contract that sets out the conditions under which a party to the contract can be released from his or her obligations under it

escape code *n* a character or sequence of characters in computer software that instructs an electronic device to read what follows as a command. For example, an escape code might instruct a printer to print in italic the text that follows the code.

escapee /i skáy pée, éskay-/ *n* somebody who has escaped

escape hatch *n* a small opening providing a way out of an enclosed space such as a submarine, through which people can escape in an emergency

escape key *n* COMPUT same as **escape** *n* (sense 7)

escapement /i skáypmənt/ *n* **1.** CLOCK MECHANISM in a

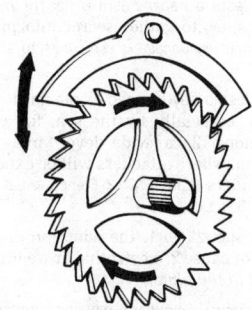

escapement: pallets on arm (top) engage teeth on wheel, driving gears in the movement

clock or watch, a mechanism that permits motion in only one direction, allowing power from a spring or falling weight to turn gears connected to the hands **2.** MUSIC PIANO MECHANISM in a piano, a mechanism that allows the hammer to rebound from a string after striking it **3.** TYPEWRITER MECHANISM in a typewriter or printer, a mechanism that regulates the relative movement between the paper carrier and the typing or printing position on a line [Late 18C. < its allowing a cogwheel to 'escape' or be released repeatedly]

escape road *n* a road branching off from a steep hill or sharp bend into which a vehicle can turn if it gets into difficulties

escape velocity *n* the minimum speed at which an object must travel to escape a planet's or moon's gravitational field in order to orbit around it or move off into space. At or near the Earth's surface, the escape velocity is about 40,000 kph/25,000 mph.

escape wheel *n* a toothed wheel in the mechanism of a clock or watch, designed to regulate the movement of the pendulum or balance wheel and so move the hands at regular intervals

escapism /i skáypizəm/ *n* **1.** something such as fantasy or entertainment that makes it possible to forget about the ordinary or unpleasant realities of life for a while **2.** the act of indulging in daydreams or fantasies to escape from everyday reality

escapist /i skáypist/ *adj* providing a means of forgetting about everyday or unpleasant realities for a while ■ *n* a daydreamer or fantasist who tries to avoid reality

escapologist /éskə pólləjist/ *n* same as **escape artist** (sense 1)

escapology /éskə pólləji/ *n* the skill of escaping from restraints or confinement as a form of entertainment

escargot /e skaárgō/ *n* a snail that is cooked and served as food, especially presented in its shell with melted garlic butter [Late 19C. Via French < Old Provençal *escaragol*]

escarole /éskərōl/ *n* N Am FOOD same as **endive** (sense 1) [Early 20C. Via French < Italian *scariola* < Latin *esca* 'food' (see ESCULENT)]

escarp /i skaárp/ *n* the inner side of a ditch dug as a fortification [Late 17C. Via French *escarpe* < Italian *scarpa* 'slope']

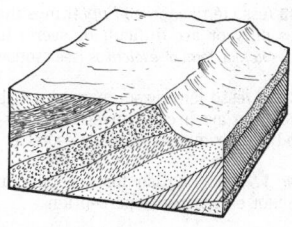

escarpment

escarpment /i skaárpmənt/ *n* **1.** a steep slope or cliff that marks the boundary of a flat or gently sloping upland area such as a plateau, often formed by faulting or erosion **2.** a steep slope constructed in front of a fortification

-escent *suffix* **1.** beginning or inclined to be, becoming, slightly ○ *acquiescent* ○ *alkalescent* **2.** having a particular kind of lustre ○ *iridescent* **3.** resembling, having ○ *arborescent* [Via French < Latin *-escent-*, present participle ending of verbs in *-escere*, expressing the beginning of action] —**-escence** *suffix*

eschar /és kaar/ *n* a dry scab formed on skin that has been burnt or cauterized [15C. Directly or via Old French *eschar(r)e* < late Latin *eschara* (see SCAR[1])]

eschatology /éskə tólləji/ *n* the body of religious doctrines concerning the human soul in its relation to death, judgment, heaven, and hell [Mid-19C. < Greek *eskhatos* 'last'] —**eschatological** /éskətə lójjik'l/ *adj* —**eschatologically** *adv* —**eschatologist** *n*

escheat /iss cheét/ *n* **1.** LAW REVERSION OF PROPERTY TO STATE the reversion of the property of a deceased person to the state in the United States, or to the Crown in England before 1926, when there are no legal heirs **2.** HIST REVERSION OF PROPERTY TO FEUDAL LORD in medieval England, the reversion to a feudal overlord of the property of a deceased person when there was no legal heir or when a tenant was outlawed **3.** LAW, HIST PROPERTY AFFECTED BY ESCHEAT property that reverts by escheat [13C. < Old French *eschete* and Anglo-Latin *escheta* < assumed Vulgar Latin *excadere* 'fall away' < Latin *cadere* 'fall'] —**escheatable** *adj*

Escher /éshər/, **M. C.** (1898–1972) Dutch graphic artist. He is known for his distinctive prints depicting intricate interlocking patterns and optical illusions based on mathematical concepts. Full name **Escher, Maurits Cornelius**

eschew /iss chóo/ (-**chews**, -**chewing**, -**chewed**) *vt* to avoid doing or using something on principle or as a matter of course [14C. < Old French *eschiver*] —**eschewal** *n*

eschscholzia /i shóltsi ə, ish-/, **eschscholtzia** *n* PLANTS same as **California poppy** [Late 19C. < modern Latin, after J. F. *Eschscholtz* (1793–1831), Russian naturalist]

Escoffier /i skóffi ay/, **Auguste** (1846–1935) French chef and cookery author. Master of the haute cuisine style of French cookery, he gained an international reputation while working in London at the Savoy (1890–98) and Carlton (1899–1919) hotels. Full name **Escoffier, Georges Auguste**

escolar /éskə laár/ *n* a fish with a slim bony body, jutting lower jaw, and sharp teeth. Native to: tropical and temperate deep seas. Family: Gempylidae. [Late 19C. Via Spanish, 'student' (because of the rings around its eyes resembling spectacles) < late Latin *scholaris* (see SCHOLAR)]

Escondido /éss kon deédō/ city in southwestern California, north of San Diego and east of Carlsbad. Population: 135,908 (2002 estimate).

escort *n* /éss kawrt/ **1.** PROTECTOR ON JOURNEY one or more persons accompanying somebody or something as a guard or guide, or as a mark of honour **2.** MALE SOCIAL PARTNER a man accompanying a woman on a social occasion **3.** HIRED SOCIAL PARTNER a man or woman who is hired to accompany another person as a companion, especially to a social event or entertainment **4.** MIL ACCOMPANYING MILITARY VESSEL OR AIRCRAFT one or more warships or fighter aircraft accompanying a larger, more vulnerable ship or aircraft as protection **5.** PROTECTION ON JOURNEY protection or restraint provided by an escort ○ *proceed under escort* ■ *vt* /i skáwrt/ (-**corts**, -**corting**, -**corted**) GO WITH SOMEBODY AS ESCORT to accompany somebody or something as an escort ○ *The butler will escort you to the door.* [Late 16C. Via French *escorte* < Italian *scorta* < *scorgere* 'to guide', via assumed Vulgar Latin *excorrigere* < Latin *corrigere* (see CORRECT)]

escritoire

escritoire /éskri twaár/ *n* a writing desk, often with a hinged flap that conceals drawers and pigeonholes [Late 16C. Via Old French, 'writing box' < medieval Latin *scriptorium* (see SCRIPTORIUM)]

escrow /éskrō, e skrṓ/ *n* an amount of money or property granted to somebody but held by a third party and only released after a specific condition has been met ■ *vt* (-**crows**, -**crowing**, -**crowed**) to place something in escrow [Mid-17C. < Anglo-Norman *escrowe* 'scroll', variant of Old French *escroe* (see SCROLL)] ◇ **in escrow** kept for somebody until a specific condition has been met

escudo /i skoͅo'dōͅ/ (*plural* **-dos**) *n* **1.** CURRENCY UNIT OF CAPE VERDE the main unit of currency of Cape Verde. See table at **currency 2.** FORMER PORTUGUESE CURRENCY the main unit of the former currency of Portugal **3.** FORMER SPANISH AND S AMERICAN CURRENCY a former unit of currency in Spain and several South American countries [Early 19C. Via Spanish and Portuguese < Latin *scutum* 'shield'; because early coins resembled heraldic shields]

esculent /éskyoͅoͅlənt/ (*formal*) *adj* fit to be eaten ■ *n* something edible, especially a plant [Early 17C. < Latin *esculentus* < *esca* 'food' < *edere* 'eat']

escutcheon (sense 2)

escutcheon /i skúchən/ *n* **1.** HERALDIC SHIELD a shield, especially one used in heraldry to display a coat of arms **2.** PROTECTIVE SHIELD a plate or shield fixed around something such as a light switch or keyhole, as an ornament or to protect the surrounding surface **3.** NAUT NAMEPLATE ON VESSEL a panel on the stern of a vessel on which the vessel's name is shown [15C. Via Anglo-Norman *escuchon* < Latin *scutum* 'shield'] — **escutcheoned** *adj*

Esd. *abbr* BIBLE Esdras

Esdraelon, Plain of /éss dray ée lon/ plain in northern Israel between the River Jordan on the east and the Mediterranean Sea on the west. It is approximately 60 km/35 mi. long and has an average width of 24 km/15 mi.

Esdras /éz drass/ *n* **1.** either of two books of the Apocrypha **2.** either of two books of the Roman Catholic version of the Bible (**Douay Bible**), equivalent to the books of Ezra and Nehemiah in the Authorized Version

ESE *abbr* COMPASS east-southeast

-ese *suffix* **1.** from, of, native to, or inhabiting a particular place ○ *Taiwanese* **2.** the language of a particular place ○ *Chinese* **3.** the style of language of a particular group (*disapproving*) ○ *officialese* [Via Old French *-eis*, Italian *-ese* < Latin *-ensis* 'originating in']

SYNONYMS See *language* and *jargon*[1].

~~esential~~ incorrect spelling of **essential**

eserine /éssə reen, -rin/ *n* PHARM former name for **physostigmine** [Mid-19C. < French *ésérine* < Efik *esere* 'Calabar bean']

Esfahan /ésfə haʾan/, **Isfahan** /ísfə-/ city in central Iran, capital of Esfahan Province. A former capital of Iran, it is renowned for its architecture. Population: 1,266,072 (1996).

Eshkol /ésh kol/, **Levi** (1895–1969) Russian-born Israeli politician. He was prime minister of Israel from 1963 until his death in 1969. Born **Shkolnik, Levi**

esker /éskər/, **eskar** /és kaar, éskər/ *n* a long narrow winding ridge of sand or gravel, deposited by a stream flowing under a glacier [Mid-19C. < Irish *eiscir*]

Eskimo /éskimō/ (*plural* **-mos** or **same**) *n* **1.** a member of a people indigenous to northern Canada, Alaska, Greenland, and Siberia, comprising the Inuit and Yupik people (*sometimes considered offensive*) **2.** the language group comprising Inuit and Yupik [Late 16C. < French *Esquimaux* < Algonquian] —**Eskimo** *adj*

USAGE See *Inuit*.

Eskimo-Aleut *n* a family of languages spoken in Greenland, Alaska, northern Canada, Siberia, and the Aleutian Islands

Eskimo dog

Eskimo dog *n* a large powerful dog with a thick coat and erect ears that is used to pull sledges in Arctic regions

Eskimo roll *n* a process or procedure by which a capsized kayak is rolled over underwater in order to come up righted

Eskişehir /ess keé she heer/ city in western Turkey, west of Ankara. Population: 470,981 (1997).

Esky /éski/ *tdmk Aus* a trademark for an insulated portable container for keeping food and beverages cool

ESL *abbr* EDUC English as a second language

ESOL /ee sol/ *abbr* EDUC English for speakers of other languages

ESOP /ee sop/ *n* an investment scheme in which employees acquire shares in the company they work for by making tax-deductible contributions. Full form **employee share ownership plan**

esophagus *n* ANAT US spelling of **oesophagus**

esoteric /éssō térrik, eéssō-/ *adj* **1.** RESTRICTED TO INITIATES intended for or understood by only an initiated few **2.** ABSTRUSE difficult to understand **3.** SECRET secret or highly confidential [Mid-17C. < Greek *esōterikos* 'belonging to an inner circle' < *esōterō* 'inner' < *esō* 'within'] —**esoterically** *adv*

SYNONYMS See *obscure*.

esoterica /éssō térrikə, eéssō-/ *npl* things that are for initiates only or are difficult or secret [Early 20C. < Greek *esōterika*, form of *esōterikos* (see ESOTERIC)]

esotericism /éssō térrissizəm, eéssō-/ *n* **1.** beliefs or practices that are arcane, mysterious, or secret **2.** the condition or quality of being esoteric

ESP *abbr* **1.** EDUC English for special purposes **2.** PARAPSYCHOL extrasensory perception

esp. *abbr* especially

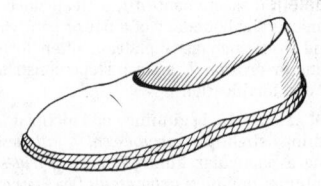

espadrille

espadrille /éspə dríl, éspədril/ *n* a light shoe with a fabric upper and a sole made of twisted cord [Late 19C. Via French < Provençal *espardilho* < *espart* 'esparto (grass)' (from which originally made) < Latin *spartum* (see ESPARTO)]

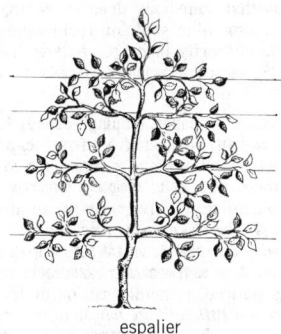

espalier

espalier /i spálli ay, -li ər/ *n* a plant, especially a fruit tree, trained to grow flat against a wall or other upright support [Mid-17C. Via French < Italian *spalliera* 'shoulder support' < *spalla* 'shoulder' < Latin *spatula* (see SPATULA)]

esparto /e spaártō/ (*plural* **-tos**), **esparto grass** *n* a coarse grass. Use: paper, ropes, mats. Native to: southern Europe, northern Africa. Latin name: *Stipa tenacissima*. [Mid-19C. Via Spanish < Latin *spartum* < Greek *sparton* 'rope']

especial /i spésh'l/ *adj* (*formal*) **1.** unusual or exceptional ○ *You'll need to take especial care.* **2.** mainly for somebody or something specific ○ *marked for my especial attention* [13C. Via Old French < Latin *specialis* 'of a specific kind' < *species* (see SPECIES)]

especially /i spésh'li/ *adv* **1.** EXCEPTIONALLY to an unusual or exceptional degree **2.** PARTICULARLY used to single out one among a range ○ *They're a helpful group, especially Mark.* **3.** CHIEFLY in most cases **4.** ⚠ SPECIALLY for a particular or specific purpose

USAGE **especially** or **specially**? Although traditionally there is a clear difference in meaning, the two words are often used interchangeably: *The hotel has specially designed ramps for people with disabilities.* (**Specially** is better here because the ramps are designed 'for a special purpose'.) *The buildings are not especially large.* (**Especially** is better here because the buildings are not 'exceptionally' large.) In rapid conversation, the first syllable of **especially** tends to be slurred or omitted, which may be why the words are not always distinguished when written.

~~especialy~~ incorrect spelling of **especially**

Esperance /éspərənss/ port on the southwestern coast of Western Australia, located in a farming region. Population: 13,329 (2002 estimate).

Esperanto /éspə rántō/ *n* an artificial language invented in 1887, based on the root forms of some words common to the major European languages. In general, the word order is similar to that of English, although the grammar is more highly inflected. [Late 19C. After Doctor *Esperanto* 'somebody who hopes', Esperanto pseudonym of Ludwik Zamenhof (1859–1917), Polish inventor of the language] —**Esperantist** *n*

espial /i spíʾ əl/ *n* (*archaic*) **1.** SIGHTING SOMETHING the act of sighting or discovering something **2.** NOTICING SOMETHING the act of noticing or detecting something **3.** SPYING ON SOMEBODY OR SOMETHING the act of secretly watching somebody or something [14C. < Old French *espialle* < *espier* (see SPY)]

espionage /éspi ə naazh, éspi ə naʾazh/ *n* the use of spying or spies to gather secret information [Late 18C. < French *espionnage* < *espionner* 'to spy' < *espion* 'spy']

esplanade /ésplə náyd, -naad, ésplə nayd/ *n* **1.** a long level area, especially by the sea, for walking or driving along **2.** a wide level area outside a fortification, where attackers will be exposed to fire from defenders [Late 17C. < French < Latin *explanare* 'flatten out' (see EXPLAIN)]

espousal /i spówz'l/ *n* **1.** the adoption of something as a belief or cause **2.** a betrothal or wedding (*formal; often used in the plural*)

espouse /i spówz/ (**-pouses, -pousing, -poused**) *vt* **1.** to adopt or support something as a belief or cause **2.** to marry somebody, or give somebody in marriage

(*archaic*) [15C. Via Old French *espouser* < Latin *sponsare* < *spons-* (see SPONSOR)] —**espouser** *n*

espressivo /éspre séevō/ *adv* played in an expressive way (*used as a musical direction*) [Late 19C. < Italian]

espresso /es préssō/, **expresso** /ik-/ *n* **1.** **STRONG DARK COFFEE** dark strong-tasting coffee made by using a special machine to pass steam under pressure or boiling water through finely ground coffee beans **2.** **CUP OF ESPRESSO** a serving of espresso coffee, usually in a small cup ○ *Two espressos and a cappuccino.* **3.** **ESPRESSO MACHINE** a machine for making espresso coffee ○ *the hiss of the espresso* [Mid-20C. < Italian *(caffè) espresso* 'pressed-out (coffee)' < past participle of *esprimere* 'press out' < Latin *exprimere* (see EXPRESS)]

esprit /e sprée/ *n* lively intelligence or wit [Late 16C. Via French < Latin *spiritus* (see SPIRIT)]

esprit de corps /e sprée də káwr/ *n* a feeling of pride in belonging to a group and a sense of identification with it [< French, 'group spirit']

espy /i spī/ (**-pies, -pying, -pied**) *vt* to catch sight of or detect something (*literary*) [14C. < Old French *espier* (see SPY)]

Esq. *abbr* Esquire (*used in correspondence*)

-esque *suffix* in the style or manner of ○ *Kafkaesque* ○ *statuesque* [Via French < assumed Vulgar Latin *-iscus* < Germanic]

Esquimalt /éski mawlt/ seaport and naval station on southeastern Vancouver Island, British Columbia, Canada. It is a suburb of the city of Victoria. Population: 16,192 (1991).

esquire /i skwīr/ *n* a youth serving as an attendant or shield bearer to a medieval knight, especially as a stage in his own training for knighthood [14C. Via Old French *escuier* < late Latin *scutarius* 'shield bearer' < Latin *scutum* 'shield']

Esquire *n* a courtesy title placed after a man's full name, in correspondence (*usually abbreviated*)

ESR *abbr* **1.** PHYS electron spin resonance **2.** MED erythrocyte sedimentation rate

ESRC *abbr* SOC SCI Economic and Social Research Council

ess /ess/ *n* **1.** the letter s or S **2.** something shaped like an S [Mid-16C. < Latin *es*]

-ess *suffix* woman or girl ○ *heiress* [Via Old French and Latin < Greek *-issa*]

USAGE The suffix **-ess** is gradually disappearing from the language, with the trend towards avoiding any unnecessary reference to gender. The suffixes *-er* and *-or* are not gender-specific in modern English: an *author* or *manager*, like a doctor or writer, may be male or female, so the words *authoress* and *manageress* are redundant. Some **-ess** words remain in use, for example *heiress* and *actress*, although *actor* is increasingly used of both men and women. See also ***gender-neutral***.

essay /éssay/ *n* **1.** **SHORT NONFICTION PROSE PIECE** a short analytical, descriptive, or interpretive piece of literary or journalistic prose dealing with a specific topic, especially from a personal and unsystematic viewpoint **2.** **SET WRITTEN PIECE** a short piece of written work set as an assignment for a student **3.** **WORK RESEMBLING WRITTEN ESSAY** an artistic or journalistic work resembling a written essay but in another medium ○ *not so much a short film as a cinematographic essay* **4.** **ATTEMPT AT SOMETHING** an attempt to accomplish something (*formal*) **5.** **TEST OF SOMETHING** a test or trial of something (*formal*) ■ *vt* (**-says, -saying, -sayed**) **ATTEMPT TO DO SOMETHING** to try out or attempt something (*formal*) ○ *Shall we essay a walk on the promenade?* [15C. < Old French *essaier* 'to try' < assumed Vulgar Latin *exagiare* 'weigh out' < Latin *agere* 'do']

essayist /éssay ist/ *n* a writer of literary or journalistic essays

essayistic /éssay ístik/ *adj* resembling or styled like a literary or journalistic essay

essay question *n* a question in an examination that must be answered in a prose piece of a specific length

Essen /éss'n/ industrial city in the Ruhr valley, North Rhine-Westphalia State, west-central Germany. Population: 617,955 (1997).

essence /éss'nss/ *n* **1.** **IDENTIFYING NATURE** the quality or nature of something that identifies it or makes it what it is ○ *You've described the city, but you haven't communicated its essence.* **2.** **MOST IMPORTANT FEATURE** the most important element or feature of something ○ *The essence of leadership is said to be the willingness of other people to follow.* **3.** **PERFECT FORM** the perfect or idealized form of something, especially when embodied in a person ○ *She's the essence of tact.* **4.** BIOCHEM **CHEMICAL CONSTITUENT OF PLANT** a purified plant extract **5.** COOK, COSMETICS **CONCENTRATED PLANT EXTRACT** a concentrated plant extract containing its unique flavour and fragrance ○ *vanilla essence* **6.** RELIG **SPIRITUAL ENTITY** a spiritual entity [14C. Via French < Latin *essentia* < *essent-*, present participle of *esse* 'be'] ◇ **in essence** fundamentally or intrinsically ◇ **of the essence** of the highest importance for achieving something

essential /i sénsh'l/ *adj* **1.** **NECESSARY** of the highest importance for achieving something ○ *It's essential that we arrive on time.* ○ *an essential ingredient* **2.** **BASIC** being the most basic element or feature of something or somebody ○ *reinforcing the essential organizational framework* **3.** **DEFINING** constituting the property or characteristic of something that makes it what it is **4.** **PERFECT** being the pure or perfect form or embodiment of something **5.** BIOCHEM **REQUIRED IN DIET** describes a nutrient that is not made by the body and is required in the diet for normal function ○ *essential vitamins and minerals* **6.** MED **WITHOUT KNOWN CAUSE** describes a disease that has no known cause ■ *n* (*usually used in the plural*) **1.** **SOMETHING NECESSARY** something that is absolutely necessary ○ *the essentials for survival* ○ *an essential for this kind of work* **2.** **FUNDAMENTAL ASPECT** a basic aspect of a particular subject ○ *You know the essentials of the case.* [14C. < late Latin *essentialis* < Latin *essentia* (see ESSENCE)] —**essentiality** /i sénshi állәti/ *n* —**essentially** *adv* —**essentialness** *n*

SYNONYMS See ***necessary***.

essential amino acid *n* any amino acid that the body cannot make and that must be obtained from food to maintain growth

essential element *n* a chemical element that is necessary to the healthy growth of an organism

essential fatty acid *n* a natural fat or oil found in whole grains, seeds, nuts, and oily fish, required in the diet to make prostaglandins

essentialism /i sénsh'lizәm/ *n* the doctrine that things have an essence or ideal nature that is independent of and prior to their existence —**essentialist** *n*

essential oil *n* an oil extracted from plant material

Essex /éssiks/ county in eastern England. The administrative centre is Chelmsford. Area: 3,674 sq. km/1,419 sq. mi.

Essex, Robert Devereux, 2nd Earl of (1566–1601) English soldier and courtier. His military successes in Europe against Spain were offset by diplomatic errors as lord lieutenant of Ireland (1599). Although he had been a favourite of Elizabeth I, he led an abortive insurrection in London and was beheaded.

Essex girl *n* an offensive term stereotyping a young woman from the Essex area as brash, lower-class, unintelligent, materialistic, and sexually promiscuous (*informal insult*)

Essex man *n* an offensive term stereotyping a man from the Essex area as vulgar in appearance and habits, with disposable income but no taste (*informal insult*)

essonite /éssә nīt/ *n* a yellow to brown garnet [Early 19C. < Greek *hēssōn* 'inferior' (because less hard than other garnets)]

EST *abbr* TIME Eastern Standard Time

-est[1], **-st** *suffix* second person singular of verbs (*archaic*) ○ *speakest* ○ *goest* [Old English < Germanic]

-est[2] *suffix* most ○ *hardest* ○ *sloppiest* [Old English < Germanic]

establish /i stábblish/ (**-lishes, -lishing, -lished**) *v* **1.** *vt* **START OR SET UP SOMETHING** to start or set up something that is intended to continue or be permanent ○ *The firm was established in 1954.* **2.** *vt* **PLACE SOMETHING PERMANENTLY** to place something securely and permanently in a position, situation, or condition ○ *A settlement was established here two hundred years ago.* **3.** *vt* **CONFIRM TRUTH OF SOMETHING** to investigate something and prove or confirm its truth or validity ○ *We need to establish the cause of the accident.* **4.** *vt* **CAUSE SOMETHING TO BE RECOGNIZED** to cause something or somebody to become generally accepted or recognized ○ *established her reputation as a lead vocalist* **5.** *vt* **MAKE CHURCH NATIONAL AND OFFICIAL** to make a church an official national institution **6.** *vti* **CAUSE PLANT TO GROW SUCCESSFULLY** to grow, or cause a plant to grow, successfully in a new place [14C. < Old French *establiss-*, stem of *establir* < Latin *stabilire* 'make stable' < *stabilis* 'stable'] —**establisher** *n*

established /i stábblisht/ *adj* **1.** **THRIVING** started or set up long enough ago and sufficiently successful to suggest likely continuation or permanence ○ *an established business* **2.** **ACCEPTED AS TRUE** generally recognized as being true or valid ○ *an established fact* **3.** **SUCCESSFUL** having gained public recognition in a sphere of activity ○ *an established author* **4.** **GROWING SUCCESSFULLY** growing strongly ○ *an established garden* **5.** **LEGALLY RECOGNIZED** legally recognized and sometimes financially supported as an official national institution ○ *an established church*

establishing shot /i stábblishing-/ *n* a shot in a film that introduces a new scene

establishment /i stábblishmәnt/ *n* **1.** **ESTABLISHING SOMETHING** the act of establishing something, or the condition of being established ○ *the establishment of new guidelines for users* **2.** **SOMETHING ESTABLISHED** something that is established as a business, institution, organization, or undertaking ○ *The establishment hired several new managers.* **3.** *also* **Establishment** **PEOPLE IN POWER** a group of people who hold power and control the institutions in a society or a professional group ○ *One period's avant-garde becomes the next's artistic establishment.* **4.** **BUSINESS PREMISES** a place of business ○ *barred them from the establishment* **5.** **HOUSEHOLD** a place of residence, or the household that occupies it **6.** **STAFF COMPLEMENT** the staff of an organization, institution, or department, especially with regard to its size and deployment —**establishmentarian** /i stábblishmәn táiri әn/ *n*

estaminet /e stámmi náy/ *n* a small and simple café, bar, or bistro, especially in France [Early 19C. < French]

estancia /e stánssi ә/ *n* a large landed estate, especially a cattle ranch, in South America [Mid-17C. Via Spanish, 'station' < medieval Latin *stantia* < Latin *stant-*, present participle of *stare* 'stand']

estate /i stáyt/ *n* **1.** **RURAL PROPERTY WITH RESIDENCE** an area of rural, privately owned property that includes a large residence **2.** **COMMERCIAL OR INDUSTRIAL AREA** a large area set aside for industrial or commercial use **3.** **ALL OF SOMEBODY'S PROPERTY** the whole of somebody's property, possessions, and capital **4.** **PROPERTY OF DEAD OR BANKRUPT PERSON** the assets and liabilities of somebody who is dead or bankrupt **5.** **SOMEBODY'S OVERALL SITUATION** the circumstances, period, or condition in which somebody lives **6.** CARS same as **estate car** **7.** POL, HIST **SECTOR OF SOCIETY** especially formerly in Europe, any of three traditional ranks or sectors of society with some political power, broadly, the clergy, the nobility, and the middle class **8.** POL, HIST **DIVISION OF PARLIAMENT** any of three divisions of parliament or constitutional government, either the Lords Temporal, Lords Spiritual, and the Commons, or the Crown, the House of Lords, and the House of Commons. The Scottish parliament before the Union was composed of the three estates of the high-ranking clergy, the barons, and the representatives of the royal burghs. **9.** AGRIC same as **plantation** (sense 1) [13C. < Old French *estat* (see STATE)]

estate agent *n* **1.** a person or business that sells or leases houses and other buildings and land on behalf of the owners. ◊ **real-estate agent** **2.** somebody who manages a landed property on behalf of its owner —**estate agency** *n*

estate-bottled *adj* describes wine bottled by the same vineyard at which it was made

estate car *n* UK a car with extra carrying space behind the seats, a rear seat that folds down, and a hinged rear door. ANZ, N Am term **station wagon** [< its ability to hold the owner's possessions]

estate duty *n* FIN same as **death duty**

estd, **est'd** *abbr* established

esteem /i steém/ *vt* (-teems, -teeming, -teemed) 1. VALUE SOMEBODY OR SOMETHING HIGHLY to have a high regard for somebody or something 2. REGARD SOMETHING IN PARTICULAR WAY to consider something or somebody as having a particular quality (*formal*) ○ *esteem it a privilege* ■ *n* 1. HIGH REGARD a high opinion and appreciation of somebody or something ○ *a relationship based on mutual esteem* 2. VALUATION judgment or estimation of the worth of somebody or something [Early 16C. Via French *estimer* 'to value' < Latin *aestimare* 'estimate, assess']

SYNONYMS See *regard*.

ester /éstər/ *n* an organic, often fragrant compound formed in a reaction between an acid and an alcohol with the elimination of water [Mid-19C. < German, contraction of *Essigäther* 'acetic ether']

esterase /éstə rayz, -rayss/ *n* any enzyme that catalyses the hydrolysis of an ester

esterify /e stérri fī/ (-fies, -fying, -fied) *vti* to change or make a substance change into an ester —**esterification** /ə stérrifi káysh'n/ *n*

Esth. *abbr* BIBLE Esther

Esther /éstər/ *n* 1. in the Bible, the Jewish queen of Persia who is described as having rescued her Jewish subjects from massacre 2. a book of the Bible that tells the story of Esther. See table at **Bible**

esthesia *n* MED US spelling of **aesthesia**

esthete, etc. N Am another spelling of **aesthete, etc.**

estimable /éstiməb'l/ *adj* deserving respect or admiration [15C. < French < Latin *aestimare* 'estimate, assess'] —**estimably** *adv*

estimate *v* /ésti mayt/ (-mates, -mating, -mated) 1. *vt* CALCULATE SOMETHING ROUGHLY to make an approximate calculation or assessment of something ○ *Can you estimate the time it will take?* 2. *vi* SUGGEST PRICE to assess something such as an item to be bought or a job to be done, and to state a likely price for it ○ *Ask at least two firms to estimate for the work.* ■ *n* /ésti mət/ 1. ROUGH CALCULATION an approximate calculation ○ *At least a thousand people attended, at my estimate.* ○ *Here are the estimates for next month's sales figures.* 2. APPROXIMATE PRICE an assessment of the likely price of something such as an item to be bought or a job to be done ○ *Their estimate is the lowest.* [Late 16C. < Latin *aestimare* 'estimate, assess'] —**estimative** *adj* —**estimator** *n*

USAGE estimate or estimation? Broadly speaking, *estimation* refers to a thinking or valuing process and *estimate* to the result of such a process. *An estimate of the time needed* is the figure produced by working out how long something will take, whereas *an estimation of the time needed* is the calculation process that produces that figure. *Estimation* also has the special meaning 'judgment or opinion', which *estimate* does not have: *What, in your estimation, is the cause of the problem? She went down in their estimation when the truth came out.*

estimation /ésti máysh'n/ *n* 1. a judgment or opinion about somebody or something ○ *Her behaviour bore out his estimation of her.* 2. the act of estimating something, or the result of this

USAGE See *estimate*.

estival, etc. BIOL US spelling of **aestival, etc.**

Estonia /e stóni ə/ country on the Gulf of Finland in northeastern Europe, north of Latvia and west of Russia. The smallest of the Baltic States, it gained its independence from the former Soviet Union in 1991 and became a member of the European Union in 2004. Language: Estonian. Currency: kroon. Capital: Tallinn. Population: 1,408,556 (2003). Area: 45,227 sq. km/17,462 sq. mi. Official name **Republic of Estonia**

Estonian /e stóni ən/ *n* 1. somebody who comes from Estonia 2. the official language of Estonia, belonging to the Finnic group of the Finno-Ugric branch of Uralic languages. Native speakers: 1.7 million. —**Estonian** *adj*

estop /i stóp/ (-tops, -topping, -topped) *vt* to use the legal rule of estoppel to prevent something [15C. < Anglo-Norman, Old French *estopper* 'plug up' < Latin *stuppa* 'tow, broken flax' (used for plugging gaps)] —**estoppage** *n*

estoppel /i stópp'l/ *n* a legal rule that prevents somebody from stating a position inconsistent with one previously stated, especially when the earlier representation has been relied upon by others [Mid-16C. < Old French *estouppail* 'stopper' < *estopper* (see ESTOP)]

estradiol /éstrə dí ol, eéstrə-l/ *n* an oestrogenic hormone present in the ovaries. Use: produced synthetically as a component of oral contraceptive products and for treatment of oestrogen deficiency and breast cancer. Formula: $C_{18}H_{24}O_2$. [Mid-20C. < *estrus*, US spelling of OESTRUS + DI-[1]]

estrane /és tràyn/, **oestrane** *n* a steroid hormone derived from testosterone. Use: hormone replacement therapy.

estrange /i stráynj/ (-tranges, -tranging, -tranged) *vt* to cause somebody to stop feeling friendly or affectionate towards somebody else or sympathetic towards a tradition or belief (*usually passive*) ○ *He managed to become estranged from all of his friends.* [15C. Via Old French *estrangier* 'alienate' < Latin *extraneare* 'treat as a stranger' < *extraneus* (see STRANGE)] —**estrangement** *n* —**estranger** *n*

estranged /i stráynjd/ *adj* no longer living with a husband or wife

e-strategy *n* a strategy for conducting business on the Internet

estreat /i street/ *n* a true extract from or copy of a legal record ■ *vt* (-treats, -treating, -treated) to make a copy from a legal record in order to prosecute somebody [15C. < Anglo-Norman *estrete*, past participle of *estraire* 'extract' < Latin *extrahere* (see EXTRACT)]

estriol *n* BIOCHEM US spelling of **oestriol**

estrogen *n* BIOCHEM US spelling of **oestrogen**

estrone *n* BIOCHEM US spelling of **oestrone**

estrous, etc. *adj* ZOOL US spelling of **oestrous, etc.**

estuarine /éstyoŏ rīn, -rin/ *adj* relating to, formed in, or found in an estuary

estuary /éstyoŏri/ (*plural* -ies) *n* the wide lower course of a river where the tide flows in, causing fresh and salt water to mix [Mid-16C. < Latin *aestuarium* < *aestus* 'heat, surge, tide'] —**estuarial** /éstyoŏ áiri əl/ *adj*

Estuary English, **Estuary** *n* a variety of standard English influenced by Cockney, spoken by people in London and southeastern England along the Thames Estuary (*informal*)

esu, **ESU** *abbr* PHYS electrostatic unit

esurient /i syoŏri ənt/ *adj* very hungry or greedy (*archaic or formal*) [Late 17C. < Latin *esurient-*, present participle of *esurire* 'be hungry' < *edere* 'eat'] —**esurience** *n* —**esuriency** *n*

Estonia

et *abbr* Ethiopia (*used in Internet addresses*) See table at **domain name**

ET *abbr* PARANORMAL extraterrestrial

-et *suffix* 1. small one ○ *falconet* 2. something worn on ○ *anklet* [< Old French]

eta[1] /eétə/ *n* the seventh letter of the Greek alphabet, represented in the English alphabet as 'e' or 'ē'. See table at **alphabet** [15C. < Greek *ēta*]

eta[2] /áytə/ (*plural* **etas** or *same*) *n* in former times, a member of a Japanese class that was restricted to doing menial tasks [Late 19C. < Japanese]

ETA[1] *abbr* TIME estimated time of arrival

ETA[2] /éttə/, **Eta** *n* a Basque nationalist guerrilla group that seeks separation and independence from Spain for the Basque region [Mid-20C. < Basque, acronym < *Euzkadi ta Askatsuna* 'Basque Nation and Liberty']

étagère /áy taa zháir/ *n* 1. a piece of furniture made up of open shelves, used to hold small objects 2. a free-standing set of shelves, one set back above the other, used to display objects such as pots of plants [Mid-19C. < French, later form of Old French *estagiere* 'scaffold' < *estage* (see STAGE)]

e-tail /eé tayl/ *n* online retail operations, especially those conducted on the Internet [Late 20C. Contraction of *electronic retail*] —**e-tailer** *n* —**e-tailing** *n*

et al.[1] /et ál/ *adv* and others (*used of joint authors of a book or article*) [Shortening of Latin *et alii*]

USAGE etc. or et al.? The abbreviation *etc.* (from the full form *et cetera*) came into English from the Latin expression *et cetera* ('and the rest'). Do not use *etc.* as a substitute for the adverb *et al.*, which came into English from another Latin expression, *et alii* ('and others'). Use *etc.* when you list some, or a few, of many items, as in *We will discuss the Plymouth Colony, the Puritans, the witchcraft trials, etc., in our early American literature seminar.* (Never write 'and etc.' or '& etc.', as these are redundant.) Use *et al.* when you mention one person or a few people out of several or many, as in bibliographies, footnotes, or textual references: *In the October issue of the Medical Journal, Smith, Jones, Roe, Doe, et al. [not etc.] discuss correct insertion of artificial airways.*

et al.[2] /et ál/ *adv* and elsewhere [Shortening of Latin *et alibi*]

etalon /éttə lon/ *n* a spectroscopic device that has two flat parallel reflecting surfaces. Use: measuring wavelengths. [Early 20C. < French *étalon* 'standard' < Old French *estal* 'standing place']

etamine /éttə meen/ *n* a light, loosely woven cotton or worsted fabric [Early 18C. < French < Latin *stamineus* 'made of threads' < *stamen* 'thread in the warp of a loom']

etc. *abbr* et cetera

USAGE See *et al.*[1].

et cetera /et séttərə, -séttrə, it-/, **etcetera** *adv* used to indicate that a list contains other unspecified items ■ *n* one of several or many unspecified things or people [< Latin, 'and the rest']

PRONUNCIATION The correct pronunciations of *et cetera* are /et séttərə/, /et séttrə/ (or /it-/), not /ek séttərə/ (or /ik-/).

etch /ech/ (etches, etching, etched) *v* 1. *vti* DESIGN CUT DESIGN INTO SOMETHING WITH ACID to create a design or drawing on the surface of something, especially a printing plate, by the action of an acid 2. *vti* MARK WITH SOMETHING SHARP to cut a design or mark into the surface of something using a sharp point or laser beam 3. *vt* MAKE SOMETHING CLEARLY VISIBLE to leave a clear and distinct impression of something

(*usually passive*) ○ *His sorrow was etched on his face.* [Mid-17C. Via Dutch *etsen* < Old High German *ezzen* 'eat away'] —**etcher** *n*

etching /éching/ *n* **1.** PRINT FROM ETCHED PLATE a print made from an etched plate **2.** CREATION OF CUT DESIGNS the art or process of creating etched designs or making prints from etched surfaces **3.** PLATE FOR PRINTING ETCHED DESIGN a printing plate with an etched design

ETD *abbr* TIME estimated time of departure

eternal /i túrn'l/ *adj* **1.** EXISTING THROUGH ALL TIME lasting for all time without beginning or end ○ *eternal life* **2.** UNCHANGING unaffected by the passage of time ○ *eternal truths* **3.** SEEMINGLY EVERLASTING seeming to go on forever or recur incessantly ○ *an eternal student* ■ *n* SOMETHING EVERLASTING something that lasts for all time without beginning or end [14C. Via French < late Latin *aeternal-* < Latin *aeternus* < *aevum* 'age'] —**eternality** /éétar nálləti/ *n* —**eternally** *adv*

Eternal *n* God as a universal spirit

Eternal City *n* Rome, the capital of Italy

eternalize /i túrn'l īz/ (**-izes**, **-izing**, **-ized**), **eternalise** (**-ises**, **-ising**, **-ised**) *vt* **1.** to make something eternal **2.** to make something everlastingly famous

eternal triangle *n* a sexual or romantic relationship among three people that involves jealousy or other emotional conflicts [Because known throughout history]

eternise *vt* another spelling of **eternize**

eternity /i túrnəti/ *n* **1.** INFINITE TIME time without beginning or end ○ *lost for all eternity* **2.** TIMELESSNESS the condition, quality, or fact of being without beginning or end **3.** RELIG TIMELESSNESS AFTER DEATH a timeless state conceived as being experienced after death **4.** VERY LONG TIME a very long or seemingly very long period of time ○ *It will take an eternity to put it together again.* ■ **eternities** *npl* TRUTHS SAID TO BE ETERNAL beliefs or ideas about life that are conceived as being timeless [14C. Via French < Latin *aeternitas* < *aeternus* (see ETERNAL)]

CULTURAL NOTE *From Here to Eternity*, a film (1953) by US director Fred Zinnemann. Based on James Jones's 1951 novel of the same name, it depicts the lives of US military personnel in Hawaii immediately prior to the attack on Pearl Harbor. It is perhaps best remembered for a scene in which Burt Lancaster and Deborah Kerr embrace in the surf.

eternity ring *n* a ring with gemstones set round its whole circumference, intended to symbolize everlasting love

eternize /i túr nīz/ (**-nizes**, **-nizing**, **-nized**), **eternise** (**-nises**, **-nising**, **-nised**) *vt* same as **eternalize** (sense 1) [Mid-16C. < French *éterniser* < Latin *aeternus* (see ETERNAL)]

etesian wind /i téezhi ən-/ *n* an annual summer wind that blows from the northwest in the Aegean Sea and other parts of the eastern Mediterranean [Early 17C. < Latin *etesius* 'annual' < Greek *etēsios* < *etos* 'year']

ETF *abbr* BANKING electronic transfer of funds

eth *n* LING another spelling of **edh**

-eth[1], **-th** *suffix* third person singular of verbs (*archaic*) ○ *goeth* ○ *speaketh* [Old English]

-eth[2] *suffix* another spelling of **-th**

ethambutol /e thámbyōo tol/ *n* a synthetically produced substance that acts against fungi and bacteria. Use: treatment of tuberculosis and other infections. [Mid-20C. < ETHYL + AMINE + BUTANOL]

ethanal /éethə nal, éthə-/ *n* CHEM same as **acetaldehyde**

ethanamide /i thánnə mīd/ *n* CHEM same as **acetamide**

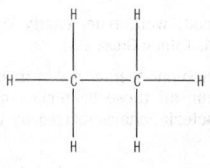

ethane

ethane /ée thayn, é thayn/ *n* a colourless odourless gas that is highly flammable. Source: petroleum, natural gas. Use: fuel, refrigeration. Formula: C_2H_6. [Late 19C. < ETHYL]

ethanedioic acid /ée thayn dī ṓ ik-, é thayn-/ *n* CHEM same as **oxalic acid**

ethanoate /éthə nṓ ət/ *n* CHEM same as **acetate**

ethanoic acid /éethənō ik-, éthə-/ *n* CHEM same as **acetic acid**

ethanoic anhydride /éethənō ik, éthə-/ *n* CHEM same as **acetic anhydride**

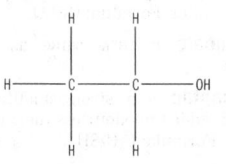

ethanol

ethanol /éthənol/ *n* a colourless liquid with a pleasant smell. Source: fermentation by yeasts and other microorganisms. Use: in alcoholic beverages, as solvent, in the manufacture of other chemicals. Formula: C_2H_5OH.

ethanolamine /éethə nóllə meen, éthə-/ *n* a colourless viscous liquid. Use: manufacture of antibiotics, cosmetics, detergents, herbicides. Formula: C_2H_7NO.

Ethelbert /éth'l burt/ (552?–616) king of Kent. He dominated southern England during his reign (560–616) and was the first Christian Anglo-Saxon monarch, being baptized in 597 by St Augustine of Canterbury.

Ethelred I /éth'l red/ (830?–871) king of Wessex and Kent. His reign (866–71) saw continual struggle with Danish invaders, whom he defeated at Ashdown in 871.

Ethelred II (968–1016) king of the English. His reign was marked by bitter military struggles. Known as **Ethelred the Unready**

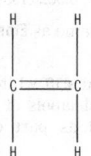

ethene

ethene /é theen/ *n* CHEM same as **ethylene** (*technical*) [Mid-19C. < ETHYL]

ether /éethər/ *n* **1.** CHEM LIQUID SOLVENT a volatile colourless liquid with a pleasant smell. Use: solvent, formerly as an anaesthetic. Formula: $C_2H_5OC_2H_5$. **2.** CHEM ORGANIC COMPOUND WITH LINKED HYDROCARBON GROUPS any organic compound containing two hydrocarbon groups linked by an oxygen atom **3.** *also* **aether** SKY the sky, or the upper reaches of the atmosphere (*literary*) **4.** *also* **aether** AIR Earth's atmosphere (*literary*) **5.** *also* **aether** PHYS HYPOTHETICAL ELECTROMAGNETIC MEDIUM a medium formerly believed to fill the atmosphere and outer space and to carry electromagnetic waves ○ *send a message across the ether* [14C. Via Latin < Greek *aithēr* 'upper air' < Indo-European, 'to burn'] —**etheric** /ee thérrik, i-/ *adj*

ethereal /i théeri əl/ *adj* **1.** EXQUISITE very delicate or highly refined ○ *ethereal beauty* **2.** AIRY very light,

airy, or insubstantial ○ *Her fragrance lingered in the room, an ethereal reminder of her presence.* **3.** HEAVENLY belonging to the sky or the celestial sphere **4.** CHEM OF ETHER consisting of, containing, or relating to ether [Early 16C. < Latin *aetherius* < Greek *aithēr* (see ETHER)] —**ethereality** /i théeri álləti/ *n* —**ethereally** *adv*

etherealize /i théeri ə līz/ (**-izes**, **-izing**, **-ized**), **etherealise** (**-ises**, **-ising**, **-ised**) *vt* to make something very delicate or highly refined —**etherealization** /i théeri ə lī záysh'n/ *n*

Etherege /éthərij/, **Sir George** (1635?–91) English playwright. His witty and mildly risqué plays such as *The Man of Mode* (1676), established the style for what is now called Restoration comedy.

etherify /éethəri fī, i thérri fī/ (**-fies**, **-fying**, **-fied**) *vt* to convert a substance, especially an alcohol, into ether —**etherification** /i thérrifi káysh'n/ *n*

etherize /éethə rīz/ (**-izes**, **-izing**, **-ized**), **etherise** (**-ises**, **-ising**, **-ised**) *vt* **1.** CHEM same as **etherify 2.** formerly, to anaesthetize a patient with ether —**etherization** /éethə rī záysh'n/ *n* —**etherizer** *n*

Ethernet /éethər net/ *tdmk* a trademark for a system for exchanging messages between computers on a local area network using coaxial, fibre-optic, or twisted-pair cables

ethic /éthik/ *n* a system of moral standards or principles ○ *the Protestant work ethic* ■ *adj* same as **ethical** (sense 2) [Late 19C. Via French *éthique* < Greek *ēthikos* 'ethical' < *ēthos* (see ETHOS)]

ethical /éthik'l/ *adj* **1.** CONFORMING TO ACCEPTED STANDARDS consistent with agreed principles of correct moral conduct ○ *While such activities are not strictly illegal, they are certainly not ethical.* **2.** OF ETHICS relating to or involving ethics **3.** PHARM AVAILABLE BY PRESCRIPTION ONLY describes a prescription drug —**ethicality** /éthi kálləti/ *n* —**ethically** *adv* —**ethicalness** *n*

ethicist /éthissist/ *n* a student of ethics, or a devotee of ethical ideals

ethics /éthiks/ *n* the study of moral standards and how they affect conduct (*takes a singular verb*) ■ *npl* a system of moral principles governing the appropriate conduct for a person or group (*takes a plural verb*) [15C. Via Old French *ethiques* < Greek *ēthika* < *ēthikos* (see ETHIC)]

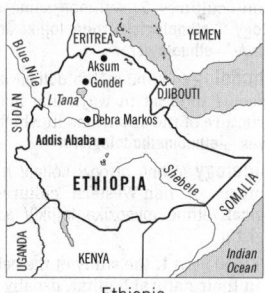

Ethiopia

Ethiopia /éethi ṓpi ə/ landlocked country in northeastern Africa, separated from the Red Sea by Eritrea and Djibouti, and from the Gulf of Aden by Somalia. It is the oldest independent country in Africa. Language: Amharic. Currency: birr. Capital: Addis Ababa. Population: 66,557,553 (2003). Area: 1,133,380 sq. km/437,600 sq. mi. Official name **Federal Democratic Republic of Ethiopia**. Former name **Abyssinia** —**Ethiopian** *n, adj*

Ethiopic /éethi óppik, -ṓpik/ *n* LANG same as **Ge'ez** [Mid-17C. Via Latin < Greek *aithiopikos* < *Aithiop-* 'Ethiopian' < *aithein* 'to burn' + *ōps* 'face']

ethmoid bone /éth moyd-/ *n* a perforated bone in the skull whose outer surfaces form part of the outer wall of the nasal cavity and the inner wall of the eye socket [Mid-18C. < Greek *ēthmoeidēs* 'like a sieve' < *ēthmos* 'sieve'] —**ethmoidal** /eth móyd'l/ *adj*

ethnic /éthnik/ *adj* **1.** SHARING CULTURAL CHARACTERISTICS sharing distinctive cultural traits as a group in society ○ *ethnic minorities* **2.** OF GROUP SHARING CULTURAL CHARACTERISTICS relating to a group or groups in society with distinctive cultural traits ○ *ethnic origins* **3.** OF PARTICULAR ORIGIN OR CULTURE relating to a person or to a large group of people who share a

national, racial, linguistic, or religious heritage, whether or not they reside in their countries of origin ○ *ethnic Albanians* **4.** CULTURALLY TRADITIONAL belonging to or associated with the traditional culture of a social group, especially a non-Western one ○ *ethnic clothing* ■ *n* N *Am* MEMBER OF ETHNIC GROUP a member of an ethnic group within a society [14C. Via late Latin, 'heathen' < Greek *ethnikos* < *ethnos* 'people, nation' < Indo-European, 'self'] —**ethnically** *adv*

ethnic cleansing *n* the violent elimination or removal of people from a country or area because of their ethnic backgrounds, by means of genocide or forced expulsion

ethnicity /eth níssəti/ (*plural* -**ties**) *n* ethnic affiliation or distinctiveness

ethnic minority *n* an ethnic group that is a minority within a nation or society

ethno- *prefix* people, culture ○ *ethnohistory* [< Greek *ethnos* (see ETHNIC)]

ethnobotany /éthnō bóttəni/ *n* the scientific study of the traditional classification and uses of plants in different human societies —**ethnobotanical** /éthnōbə tánnik'l/ *adj* —**ethnobotanically** *adv* —**ethnobotanist** *n*

ethnocentrism /éthnō séntrizəm/ *n* a belief in or assumption of the superiority of the social or cultural group that a person belongs to (*disapproving*) —**ethnocentric** *adj* —**ethnocentrically** *adv* —**ethnocentricity** /-sen tríssəti/ *n*

ethnogenesis /éthnō jénnəssiss/ *n* the creation of a new ethnic group identity

ethnography /eth nóggrəfi/ *n* a branch of anthropology concerned with the description of ethnic groups —**ethnographer** *n* —**ethnographic** /éthnə gráffik/ *adj* —**ethnographically** *adv*

ethnohistory /éthnō hístəri/ *n* the scientific study of how cultures have developed through history —**ethnohistorian** /éthnō hi stáwri ən/ *n* —**ethnohistoric** /-hi stórrik/ *adj*

ethnolinguistics /éthnō ling gwístiks/ *n* the scientific study of the relationship between language and culture (*takes a singular verb*) —**ethnolinguist** /éthnō líng gwist/ *n* —**ethnolinguistic** *adj* —**ethnolinguistically** *adv*

ethnology /eth nólləji/ *n* **1.** the scientific comparison of different cultures **2.** ANTHROP same as **cultural anthropology** —**ethnologic** /éthnə lójjik/ *adj* —**ethnologically** *adv* —**ethnologist** *n*

ethnomethodology /éthnō méthə dólləji/ *n* the study of how people interact in ways that maintain the social structure of the situations in which they find themselves —**ethnomethodologist** *n*

ethnomusicology /éthnō myoozi kólləji/ *n* the study of the music of non-Western cultures —**ethnomusicological** /éthnō myoozikə lójjik'l/ *adj* —**ethnomusicologist** *n*

ethology /i thólləji/ *n* **1.** the study of the behaviour of animals in their natural habitat, usually proposing evolutionary explanations **2.** PSYCHOL same as **human ethology** [Mid-17C. < Latin *ethologia* < Greek *ēthos* (see ETHOS)] —**ethological** /éethə lójjik'l/ *adj* —**ethologist** *n*

ethos /ée thoss/ *n* the fundamental and distinctive character of a group, social context, or period of time, typically expressed in attitudes, habits, and beliefs [Mid-19C. < Greek *ēthos* 'custom, disposition' < Indo-European, 'self']

ethoxy /ee thóksi/, **ethoxyl** /ee thóksil/ *adj* forming or containing a chemical group composed of ethyl and oxygen. Formula: CH_3CH_2O. [Late 19C. < ETHYL + OXY-]

ethoxyethane /ee thóksi ée thayn/ *n* CHEM same as **ether** (sense 1) (*technical*)

ethoxyl *adj* CHEM same as **ethoxy**

ethyl /ée thīl, éth'l/ *n* relating to the group of atoms derived from ethane after the loss of a hydrogen atom. Formula: $-C_2H_5$. [Mid-19C. < ETHER]

ethyl acetate *n* a volatile colourless liquid with a pleasant fruity smell. Use: manufacture of perfumes, solvent. Formula: $C_4H_8O_2$.

ethyl alcohol *n* CHEM same as **ethanol**

ethylamine /éthilə meén/ *n* a colourless volatile liquid. Use: oil refining, detergents. Formula: $C_2H_5NH_2$.

ethylate /éthi layt/ (-**ates**, -**ating**, -**ated**) *vt* to attach an ethyl group to a molecule or to one of the molecules of a compound —**ethylation** /éthi láysh'n/ *n*

ethyl carbamate *n* CHEM same as **urethane** (sense 1)

ethylene /éthi leen/ *n* a colourless flammable gas. Source: petroleum, natural gas, ripening fruit. Use: manufacture of polymers and other chemicals, in metallurgy, to ripen and colour harvested fruit. Formula: C_2H_4. —**ethylenic** /éthi leénik/ *adj*

ethylene glycol *n* a viscous colourless liquid with a sweet taste. Use: antifreeze, manufacture of polyester. Formula: $C_2H_6O_2$.

ethylene oxide *n* a soluble colourless gas. Use: synthesis of ethylene glycol and other chemicals, fumigant, sterilant. Formula: C_2H_4O.

ethyl ethanoate *n* CHEM same as **ethyl acetate** (*technical*)

ethyl mercaptan *n* a strong-smelling colourless liquid. Use: added to odourless fuels to make leaks detectable. Formula: C_2H_5SH.

ethyne /ée thīn, éth īn/ *n* CHEM same as **acetylene**

etic /éttik/ *adj* making use of pre-established categories for organizing and interpreting anthropological data, rather than categories recognized within the culture being studied. ◊ **emic** (sense 2) [Mid-20C. < PHONETIC]

-etic *suffix* used to form adjectives from nouns ending in -*esis* ○ *geodetic* [Via Latin < Greek -*ētikos* < -*etos*]

etiolated /ééti ə laytid/ *adj* **1.** describes a plant that is unusually tall and spindly and deficient in green pigment owing to lack of light **2.** feeble and without vigour or spirit [Late 18C. < French *étioler*] —**etiolation** /ééti ə láysh'n/ *n*

etiology *n* PHILOSOPHY, MED another spelling of **aetiology**

etiquette /étti ket/ *n* the rules and conventions governing correct or polite behaviour in society in general or in a specific social or professional group or situation ○ *Etiquette dictates that wedding invitations should be acknowledged in writing.* [Mid-18C. < French, literally 'ticket']

ETLLD *abbr* GOV Enterprise, Transport, and Lifelong Learning Department

Etna, Mount /étnə/ volcano in eastern Sicily. It is the highest active volcano in Europe and has had over 90 recorded eruptions. Height: 3,323 m/10,902 ft.

Eton[1] /eét'n/ town in Buckinghamshire, England, on the River Thames opposite Windsor, site of Eton College. Population: 5,962 (1991).

Eton[2] /eét'n/ *n* EDUC same as **Eton College** —**Etonian** /ee tóni ən/ *n, adj*

Eton collar *n* a broad stiff white collar turned down over the collar and lapels of a coat or jacket, especially one worn as part of the Eton College uniform

Eton College *n* a public school in the town of Eton, in southeastern England. It was founded in 1440 by Henry VI.

Eton crop *n* a hairstyle in which the hair is cut short and lies flat, fashionable among women in the 1920s [From its resemblance to a schoolboy's haircut]

Eton jacket *n* a short black jacket with wide lapels and an open front, formerly worn by the pupils of Eton College

Etosha National Park /e tóshə-/ national park in Namibia, southwestern Africa. Established in 1958, it contains the Etosha Pan, a salt desert that was once a lake. Area: 22,270 sq. km/8,598 sq. mi.

étrier /áytri ay/ *n* a short rope ladder using in mountain climbing [Mid-20C. < French, 'stirrup, rope ladder']

Etruria /e troóri ə/ ancient region on the Northwestern coast of peninsular Italy, where the Etruscan civilization flourished between about 800 and 300 BC. The region occupied roughly the same area as present-day Tuscany and part of Umbria, and at its greatest extent stretched from the Alps to the River Tiber. —**Etrurian** *n, adj*

Etruscan: gable end from Villa Giulia, Rome, Italy (4th century BC)

Etruscan /i trúskən/ *n* **1.** a member of an ancient people who lived in Etruria and were overcome by the Romans during the 2nd century BC. Their civilization flourished between about 800 and 300 BC. **2.** an extinct language spoken in ancient Etruria that has no relation to Indo-European languages [Early 18C. < Latin *Etruscus* 'of Etruria'] —**Etruscan** *adj*

et seq., et seqq. *adv* and the others following, especially the next page or pages in a book ○ *p.20 et seq.* [Shortening of Latin *et sequens, et sequentia* 'and the following one(s)']

-ette *suffix* **1.** small ○ *diskette* **2.** female ○ *suffragette* ○ *usherette* **3.** imitation ○ *leatherette* [< Old French, form of -*et*]

étude /áy tyood/ *n* a short musical composition for a solo instrument intended to develop a point of technique or to display the performer's skill, but often played for its artistic merit [Mid-19C. < French, 'study' < Latin *studium*]

étui /ay tweé/ *n* a small ornamental case for needles or other small items [Early 17C. < French, later form of Old French *estui* 'prison' < *estuier* 'to keep']

ety., etym. *abbr* **1.** etymological **2.** etymology

etyma LING *plural* of **etymon**

etymol. *abbr* LING **1.** etymological **2.** etymology

etymologize /étti móllə jīz/ (-**gizes**, -**gizing**, -**gized**), **etymologise** (-**gises**, -**gising**, -**gised**) *vti* to study, trace, or describe the origin and development of a word, or make a suggestion as to a word's possible origin and development

etymology /étti mólləji/ (*plural* -**gies**) *n* **1.** the study of the origins of words or parts of words and how they have arrived at their current form and meaning **2.** the origin of a word or part of a word, or a statement of this, and how it has arrived at its current form and meaning. An etymology often shows the different forms the word has taken in passing from one language to another, and sometimes shows related words in other languages. ○ *The words have the same spelling but different etymologies.* [14C. Via Old French < Greek *etumologia* < *etumon* (see ETYMON)] —**etymological** /éttimə lójjik'l/ *adj* —**etymologically** *adv* —**etymologist** *n*

etymon /étti mon/ (*plural* -**mons** or -**ma** /-mə/) *n* **1.** an earlier form of a word or part of a word, especially the first recorded form in any language **2.** a word or part of a word from which another word is derived [Late 16C. Via Latin < Greek *etumon* 'true sense of a word' < *etumos* 'true, original']

Eu *symbol* CHEM ELEM europium

EU *abbr* POL European Union

eu- *prefix* good, well, true, easily ○ *euphonious* ○ *euplastic* [Via Latin < Greek *eus*]

eubacteria /yoo bak teéri ə/ *npl* in modern biological classification, all those bacteria considered to be the true bacteria, characterized by their rigid cell walls

eucalypt *n* TREES same as **eucalyptus**

eucalyptol /yoókə líp tol/, **eucalyptole** /-tōl/ *n* a colourless oily liquid. Source: eucalyptus oil. Use: in pharmaceuticals, perfumes, flavourings. Formula: $C_{10}H_{18}O$.

eucalyptus

eucalyptus /yoˈóokə líptəss/ (*plural* **-tuses** or **-ti** /-tī/), **eucalypt** /yoˈóokə lipt/ *n* an evergreen tree that has aromatic leaves and produces timber, resin, and a medicinal oil. Native to: Australia. Genus: *Eucalyptus*. [Early 19C. < modern Latin < Greek *eu-* 'well' + *kaluptos* 'covered'; from the covering on the tree's buds]

eucaryote *n* BIOL another spelling of **eukaryote**

Eucharist /yoˈóokərist/ *n* **1.** same as **Communion 2.** the symbolic or consecrated bread and wine eaten and drunk during the ceremony of Communion [14C. < Old French < Greek *eukharistia* 'giving of thanks' < *eukharistos* 'grateful' < *kharizesthai* 'show favour'] —**Eucharistic** /yoˈóokə rístik/ *adj*

euchre /yoˈóokər/ *n* **1.** CARD GAME OF WINNING TRICKS a card game played with the highest 32 cards in the pack in which each player receives five cards and must take at least three tricks to win. It is played mainly in North America. **2.** THWARTING OF OPPONENT AT EUCHRE an instance of preventing another player from taking the three tricks needed to win a game of euchre ■ *vt* (**-chres, -chring, -chred**) **1.** THWART OPPONENT AT EUCHRE to prevent another player from taking the three tricks needed to win a game of euchre **2.** ANZ, N Am TRICK SOMEBODY to cheat, trick, or deceive somebody [Early 19C. Origin ?]

euchromatin /yoo krˈómətin/ *n* an expanded form of the material of which chromosomes are composed, occurring when DNA is being actively copied. It stains lightly only with basic dyes. ⋄ **heterochromatin** —**euchromatic** /yoˈóokrə máttik/ *adj*

Euclid /yoˈóoklid/ (*fl* 300 BC) Greek mathematician. He taught in Alexandria and compiled the 13-volume *Elements* (300? BC), the standard text on geometry until the 19th century. —**Euclidean** /yoo klíddi ən/ *adj*

Euclidean geometry *n* geometry according to the principles of Euclid, as described in his *Elements*, in which only one line parallel to another given line may pass through a given point

eudemon /yoo deˈémən/, **eudaemon** *n* a supposed benevolent supernatural being [Early 17C. < Greek *eudaimōn* 'having a guardian spirit, fortunate, happy' < *eu-* 'good' + *daimōn* 'spiritual being, guardian']

eudemonism /yoo deˈémənizəm/, **eudaemonism** *n* an ethical doctrine that characterizes the value of life in terms of happiness —**eudemonist** *n* —**eudemonistic** /yoo deˈémə nístik/ *adj*

eudiometer /yoˈóodi ómmitər/ *n* an instrument used to measure the volume changes that take place in chemical gas reactions [Late 18C. < Greek *eudios* 'fine (weather)' < *eu-* 'good' + *dios* 'heavenly'] —**eudiometric** /yoˈóodi ə méttrik/ *adj* —**eudiometrically** *adv* —**eudiometry** *n*

Eudoxus of Cnidus /yoo dóksəss əv knˈídəss/ (408–355 BC) Greek astronomer and mathematician. He developed a mathematical model for predicting planetary motion. His geometrical discoveries are thought to be behind much of Euclid's *Elements*.

eugenicist /yoo jénnissist/, **eugenist** /yoˈóojənist/ *n* a proposer of ways to improve human beings, especially by selective breeding, or somebody who advocates eugenics

eugenics /yoo jénniks/ *n* the proposed improvement of the human species by encouraging or permitting reproduction of only those people with genetic characteristics judged desirable. It has been regarded with disfavour since the Nazi period. (*takes a singular verb*) —**eugenic** *adj* —**eugenically** *adv*

Eugénie /yoo jéeni, ð zhay née/ (1826–1920) Spanish-born empress of France (1853–71). After her marriage to Napoleon III (1853), she exerted considerable influence in political and military matters and served as regent in the emperor's absence. She and her husband fled to England after the fall of the Second Empire (1871). Born **Eugenia María de Montijo de Guzman**

eugenist *n* SOC SCI same as **eugenicist**

eugenol

eugenol /yoˈóoji nol/ *n* a colourless oily liquid. Source: cloves. Use: in dentistry to reduce pain, in perfumes. Formula: $C_{10}H_{12}O_2$. [Late 19C. < modern Latin *Eugenia*, former taxonomic name of the clove tree, after Prince *Eugène* of Savoy (1663–1736), Austrian general]

euglena /yoo gleˈénə/ *n* a single-celled freshwater organism that has appendages (**flagella**) for locomotion and produces its food by photosynthesis. Genus: *Euglena*. [Mid-19C. < modern Latin < Greek *eu-* 'well' + *glēnē* 'eyeball'] —**euglenoid** *adj*

euhemerism /yoo heˈémərizəm/ *n* the theory that mythology has its origins in history, the gods being deified heroes of the past [Mid-19C. < Latin *Euhemerus* < Greek *Euēmeros*, 4C BC Greek writer] —**euhemerist** *n* —**euhemeristic** /yoo heˈémə rístik/ *adj* —**euhemeristically** *adv*

eukaryote /yoo kárri ot/, **eucaryote** *n* any organism with one or more cells that have visible nuclei and organelles. The group contains all living and fossil cellular organisms except bacteria and cyanobacteria. [Mid-20C. < EU- + Greek *karuōtos* 'having nuts' < *karuon* 'nut'] —**eukaryotic** /yoo kárri óttik/ *adj*

eulachon /yoˈóolə kon/ (*plural* **-chons** or *same*) *n* FISH same as **candlefish** [Mid-19C. < Lower Chinook *úƚxan*]

Euler /óylər, yoˈólər/, **Leonhard** (1707–83) Swiss mathematician. He and Joseph Lagrange were the leading mathematicians of the 18th century. In some 800 publications he laid the foundations of modern analytical mathematics.

eulogia¹ /yoo lóji ə/ *n* bread blessed and given after the liturgy in the Eastern Orthodox Church to those not present at Communion [Mid-18C. Via late Latin, 'consecrated bread' < Greek (see EULOGIUM)]

eulogia² plural of **eulogium**

eulogise *vt* another spelling of **eulogize**

eulogistic /yoˈóolə jístik/ *adj* full of praise for somebody or something —**eulogistically** *adv*

eulogium /yoo lóji əm/ (*plural* **-gia** /-ji ə/ or **-giums**) *n* same as **eulogy** (sense 1) (*formal*) [Early 17C. < medieval Latin, probably blend of *eulogia* 'praise' (< Greek, < *eu-* 'well' + *-logia* 'speaking') + Latin *elogium* 'epitaph']

eulogize /yoˈóolə jīz/ (**-gizes, -gizing, -gized**), **eulogise** (**-gises, -gising, -gised**) *vti* to praise somebody or something very highly —**eulogizer** *n*

eulogy /yoˈóolə ji/ (*plural* **-gies**) *n* **1.** a speech or piece of writing that praises somebody or something very highly, especially a tribute to somebody who has recently died **2.** great praise (*formal*) [15C. < medieval Latin *eulogium* (see EULOGIUM)] —**eulogist** *n*

Eumenides /yoo ménni deez/ *npl* in Greek mythology, three sister goddesses originally fertility goddesses, but later identified with the Furies [Late 17C. Via Latin < Greek < *eumenēs* 'kindly, friendly' < *menos* 'spirit']

eunuch /yoˈóonək/ *n* **1.** a man or boy whose testicles have been removed or do not function. Formerly, eunuchs were sometimes employed to guard the women of a harem or as court officials. **2.** a man

who is regarded as lacking power or effectiveness (*informal insult*) [15C. Via Latin < Greek *eunoukhos* 'attendant of a bedroom or harem' < *eunē* 'bed' + *ekhein* 'to keep']

eunuchoid /yoˈóonə koyd/ *adj* lacking fully developed male sexual organs or characteristics

euonymus /yoo ónniməss/ *n* a tree or bush grown for its decorative evergreen foliage and clusters of orange or red fruits. Native to: northern temperate regions. Genus: *Euonymus*. [Mid-19C. Via modern Latin < Greek *euōnumos* 'of good name, lucky']

eupatrid /yoo páttrid/ (*plural* **-ridae** /-dee/ or **-rids**) *n* somebody belonging to the hereditary class of nobles and landowners in ancient Athens [Mid-19C. < Greek *eupatridēs* 'somebody of noble ancestry' < *patēr* 'father']

eupepsia /yoo pépsi ə/ *n* good or efficient digestion [Early 18C. < Greek, 'digestibility' < *eupeptos* (see EUPEPTIC)]

eupeptic /yoo péptik/ *adj* **1.** relating to or producing good digestion **2.** having a cheerful manner or disposition [Late 17C. < Greek *eupeptos* 'easy to digest, having good digestion' < *eu-* 'well' + *peptein* 'digest'] —**eupeptically** *adv*

euphemise *vti* another spelling of **euphemize**

euphemism /yoˈóofəmizəm/ *n* **1.** a word or phrase used in place of a term that might be considered too direct, harsh, unpleasant, or offensive **2.** the use of a word or phrase that is more neutral, vague, or indirect to replace a direct, harsh, unpleasant, or offensive term [Late 16C. < Greek *euphēmismos* < *euphēmizein* 'speak with pleasing words' < *phēmē* 'speech'] —**euphemist** *n* —**euphemistic** /yoˈóofə místik/ *adj* —**euphemistically** *adv*

USAGE *Euphemisms* make the unpalatable more palatable. People use *euphemisms* chiefly to conceal feared things, for example death; to conceal the reality of unthinkable crimes; to conceal references to sex, body parts and fluids, and excrement; and to elevate otherwise lowly sounding or derogatory occupational titles and institutional names. For instance, there are hundreds of euphemisms used every day for *to die*, a few of which are *pass on/away*, *go to one's final rest*, and *depart/depart this life*. Two of the most notorious euphemisms for genocide are, of course, *the Final Solution* and *ethnic cleansing*. Euphemistic references to sex and physiology are legion: *break wind* for *fart* and *social disease* for *sexually transmitted disease* are typical. Euphemisms that elevate the language of occupational titles include, for example, *sanitation engineer* for *dustman*, and those that elevate rather harsh-sounding institutional names include *place of confinement* for *prison*. The capacity of a euphemism to conceal tends to diminish over the years, as it becomes more and more closely associated with its referent, and if the taboo against talking about the referent remains in force, a fresh euphemism needs to be found for it. For instance, *sexual intercourse* was once a euphemism (for *copulation*), but it has long since become a plainly understood neutral term, and *have sexual intercourse with somebody* now needs its *own* euphemism, *to sleep with somebody*. Euphemisms tend to turn into *dysphemisms*, their opposite, because the inescapable fact is that if something is feared or despised, the vocabulary used to refer to it will become tainted by those feelings, even if originally it was intended to disguise them.

euphemize /yoˈóofə mīz/ (**-mizes, -mizing, -mized**), **euphemise** (**-mises, -mising, -mised**) *vti* to avoid saying or writing something direct, harsh, unpleasant, or offensive by using milder or more indirect language —**euphemizer** *n*

euphonious /yoo fóni əss/ *adj* **1.** having a pleasant sound **2.** made easier to pronounce by a change in speech sounds —**euphoniously** *adv* —**euphoniousness** *n*

euphonise *vt* PHON another spelling of **euphonize**

euphonium /yoo fóni əm/ *n* a brass instrument similar to, but smaller than, a tuba, used mainly in military and brass bands. See illustration on next page [Mid-19C. < Greek *euphōnos* (see EUPHONY)]

euphonize /yoˈóofə nīz/ (**-nizes, -nizing, -nized**), **euphonise** (**-nises, -nising, -nised**) *vt* **1.** to make something sound pleasant **2.** to change speech sounds to make something easier to pronounce

euphonium

euphony /yoófəni/ (*plural* **-nies**) *n* **1.** a pleasant sound, especially in speech or pronunciation **2.** changing of speech sounds to make something easier to pronounce [15C. < French *euphonie* < Greek *euphōnos* 'sweet-voiced' < *phōnē* 'sound'] —**euphonic** /yoo fónnik/ *adj* —**euphonically** *adv*

euphorbia /yoo fáwrbi ə/ *n* a plant such as spurge or poinsettia with milky juice. Flowers: green. Genus: *Euphorbia*. [12C. < Latin *euphorbea* < *Euphorbus* (1C BC), physician to Juba, king of Mauritania]

euphoria /yoo fáwri ə/ *n* a feeling of great joy, excitement, or wellbeing ○ *She was in a state of euphoria after her win.* [Late 17C. Via modern Latin < Greek < *euphoros* 'borne well, healthy']

euphoriant /yoo fáwri ənt/ *n* a drug or other substance that induces euphoria —**euphoriant** *adj*

euphoric /yoo fórrik/ *adj* extremely happy or excited ○ *She'll be euphoric when she hears these results.* —**euphorically** *adv*

euphotic /yoo fótik, -fóttik/ *adj* describes the upper layer of a body of water that allows the penetration of enough light to support photosynthetic, or green, plants

Euphrates /yoo fráy teez/ river in Southwest Asia, rising in Turkey and flowing through Syria and Iraq before joining the River Tigris near the Persian Gulf. Length: 2,700 km/1,700 mi.

Euphrosyne /yoo frózzi nee/ *n* in Greek mythology, one of the three Graces who lived on Mount Olympus and tended the goddess Aphrodite

euphuism /yoó fyoo izəm/ *n* **1.** a literary style of the 16th and 17th centuries characterized by excessive use of devices such as alliteration, antithesis, and simile **2.** an affected or pompous expression or use of language (*formal*) [Late 16C. After *Euphues*, fictional character in the works of John *Lyly* (c. 1554–1606), English writer] —**euphuist** *n* —**euphuistic** /yoó fyoo ístik/ *adj* —**euphuistically** *adv*

euplastic /yoo plástik/ *adj* healing readily

euploid /yoó ployd/ *adj* describes a cell or organism with a chromosome number that is an even multiple of the basic chromosome set for the species —**euploid** *n* —**euploidy** *n*

Eur. *abbr* **1.** Europe **2.** European

Eur- *prefix* same as **Euro-** (*used before vowels*)

Eurasia /yoor áyshə, -áyzhə/ *n* the land mass consisting of the continents of Europe and Asia

Eurasian /yoor áyzh'n, -áysh'n/ *n* SOMEBODY OF EUROPEAN AND ASIAN DESCENT somebody of both European and Asian descent ■ *adj* **1.** OF EUROPE AND ASIA relating to the land mass consisting of the continents of Europe and Asia **2.** OF EUROPEAN AND ASIAN DESCENT being of both European and Asian descent

Euratom /yoor áttəm/ *n* an organization formed in 1957 to coordinate the development and use of atomic energy in Europe, later incorporated into the European Community [Mid-20C. Contraction of European Atomic Energy Commission]

eureka /yoo reékə/ *interj, n* used to express delight on finding, discovering, or solving something, or on finally succeeding in doing something ○ *I rolled back the rug and eureka – there it was!* [Early 17C. < Greek *heurēka* 'I have found (it)' < *heuriskein* 'to find', supposedly exclaimed by Archimedes when he discovered the principle of water displacement]

Eureka Stockade *n* an armed rebellion by gold miners in Ballarat, Victoria, Australia, in 1854, protesting against excessive taxation, corruption, and lack of political representation. The rebellion was suppressed, but its widespread support gained the miners the right to vote and a reduction in taxes.

eurhythmic /yoo ríthmik/, **eurythmic**, **eurhythmical** /-ríthmik'l/, **eurythmical** *adj* **1.** having an aesthetically pleasing rhythm or structure **2.** relating to eurhythmics or eurhythmy

eurhythmics /yoo ríthmiks/, **eurythmics** *n* a system of physical exercise, therapy, and musical training in which the body moves rhythmically and gracefully in interpretation of a piece of music (*takes a singular or plural verb*)

eurhythmy /yoo ríthmi/, **eurythmy** *n* **1.** harmony of proportion or structure **2.** a system of rhythmic movement performed to verse or music for artistic or therapeutic purposes. It was invented by Rudolf Steiner. [Late 16C. Via Latin < Greek *euruthmia* 'good proportion' < *rhuthmos* 'proportion, rhythm']

Euripides /yoo ríppi deez/ (480?–406? BC) Greek dramatist. After Aeschylus and Sophocles, he was the third of the great dramatists of the classical period in Athens. His works have been revived through the centuries and have influenced many writers, from Milton and Racine to those of the present day.

'Bodies devoid of mind are as statues in the marketplace.'
[Euripides, *Electra*; 5th century BC]

euro[1] /yoórō/ (*plural* **-ros** or *same*) *n* the main currency unit of the European Union, used since 2002 as local currency in most member states. See table at **currency**. ◊ **ECU** [Late 20C. Shortening of EUROPEAN]

euro[2] /yoórō/ (*plural* **-ros** or *same*) *n* Aus ZOOL same as **wallaroo** [Mid-19C. < an Aboriginal language]

Euro- *prefix* Europe, European ○ *Eurocurrency* [< EUROPE]

euro-ad *n* an advertisement that is designed or suitable for use in all countries of the European Union

Eurobeach /yoórō beech/ *n* a bathing beach in any of the countries of the European Union that meets the EU regulations for safe levels of bacteria in the water

Eurobond /yoórō bond/ *n* a bond measured in dollars or other currency and sold to investors from a country other than that whose currency is specified in the bond

Eurocentric /yoórō séntrik/ *adj* focusing on Europe or its people, institutions, and cultures, often in a way that is arrogantly dismissive of others —**Eurocentrism** *n*

Eurocheque /yoórō chek/ *n* a cheque that can be written in any European currency and the currency of some other countries, drawing on the writer's personal bank account in any of the participating countries

Eurocrat /yoórə krat/, **eurocrat** *n* an administrative official of the European Union, especially one in a senior post [Mid-20C. Blend of EURO- + BUREAUCRAT]

Eurocurrency /yoórō kurənssi/ (*plural* **-cies**) *n* money deposited by companies and governments in banks outside the country in whose currency its value is stated [Mid-20C. Because originally US dollars held in Europe]

Eurodollar /yoórō dolər/ *n* a US dollar on deposit in a bank outside the United States, especially a European bank (*usually used in the plural*)

Euroland /yoórō land/, **euroland** *n* the countries in the European Union using the main currency unit of the European Union, the euro

Euromarket /yoórō maarkit/ *n* **1.** the European Union considered as a single market **2.** the European financial markets collectively, especially when considered as a source of financing for international trade

Euro-MP *n* a member of the European Parliament

Europa /yoo rópə/ *n* **1.** in Greek mythology, a Phoenician princess who was abducted by Zeus and taken to the island of Crete. She was the mother of Minos. **2.** a large natural satellite of Jupiter, discovered in 1610 by Galileo. It is 3,130 km/1,940 mi. in diameter and thought to have a thin icy crust.

Europe /yoórəp/ second smallest continent after Australia, lying west of Asia, north of Africa, and east of the Atlantic Ocean. Population: 725,962,762 (2000). Area: 10,355,000 sq. km/3,997,900 sq. mi.

European /yoórə peé ən/ *adj* **1.** OF EUROPE relating to Europe or its peoples, languages, or cultures **2.** OF EUROPEAN UNION relating to the European Union ■ *n* **1.** SOMEBODY FROM EUROPE somebody who comes from Europe or is of European descent **2.** ADVOCATE OF EUROPEAN UNION a supporter of the principles and ideals of the European Union

European Commission *n* the executive arm of the European Union, which formulates policy and drafts most community legislation

European Community *n* an economic and political union of 12 European countries that developed from the European Economic Community and was itself replaced in 1993 by the European Union

European Court of Justice, **European Court** *n* an institution that ensures that the legislation of the European Union is interpreted and applied in the same way in each member state. There is one judge per member state, but the Court can sit as a panel of 13 judges instead of requiring all judges to be present.

European Currency Unit *n* FIN full form of **ECU**

European Economic Area *n* an economic union formed in 1994 of the member states of the European Union and Iceland, Liechtenstein, and Norway that allows non-EU members to participate in the Single Market

European Economic Community *n* an alliance of six European countries begun in 1957 to promote free trade in Europe, and subsequently expanded in both membership and areas of interest, and called the European Community and then the European Union

European Free Trade Association *n* a union of Western European countries, established in 1960 to eliminate trade tariffs among member states. The original members were Austria, Denmark, the United Kingdom, Norway, Portugal, Sweden, and Switzerland.

Europeanise *vt* another spelling of **Europeanize**

Europeanism /yoórə peé ənizəm/ *n* support for the European Union and its further development

Europeanize /yoórə peé ə nīz/ (**-izes**, **-izing**, **-ized**), **Europeanise** (**-ises**, **-ising**, **-ised**) *vt* **1.** to make somebody or something part of European culture, or change somebody or something to fit in with European life, customs, or ideas **2.** to make a country part of the European Union, or make something conform to the regulations or specifications of the European Union —**Europeanization** /yoórə peé ə nī záysh'n/ *n*

European Monetary System *n* formerly, a system for stabilizing currency exchange rates within the European Union, using the Exchange Rate Mechanism

European Parliament *n* the primarily advisory legislature of the European Union. It consists of directly elected representatives from each member state.

European Union *n* an economic and political alliance of 25 European nations. Its goals include a single economic community and social and political cooperation. See map on next page

europium /yoo rópi əm/ *n* a soft silvery-white metallic element of the rare-earth group. Source: monazite, bastnaesite. Use: lasers. Symbol **Eu**. See table at **element** [Early 20C. < modern Latin < Latin *Europa* 'Europe']

Eurosceptic /yoórō skeptik/ *n* a British person, especially a politician, who is not in favour of closer links between Britain and the European Union —**Euroscepticism** /yoórō sképtisizəm/ *n*

Eurostar /yoórō staar/ *tdmk* a trademark for the high-speed passenger train and train service designed specifically to use the Channel Tunnel linking southern England with France. It can run on

European Union: map showing member states

railway systems in both Britain and continental Europe.

Eurovision song contest /yoŏrō vizh'n-/ *n* an annual competition, broadcast on television, in which singers from primarily European countries perform a specially composed song and the participating nations vote for their favourite. The contest has been criticized for the blandness of the winning entries and the political nature of the voting.

Eurozone /yoŏrō zōn/, **eurozone** *n* the geographical area comprising the European Union countries using the euro as a monetary unit

eury- *prefix* wide, broad ○ *euryphagous* [< Greek *eurus*]

eurybathic /yoŏri báthik/ *adj* describes water organisms that tolerate a wide range of depths [Early 20C. < EURY- + Greek *bathos* 'depth'] —**eurybath** /yoŏri baath/ *n*

Eurydice /yoŏ ríddissi/ *n* in Greek mythology, the wife of Orpheus. When she died, Orpheus pursued her to Hades. His lyre-playing won her release, but his failure to observe conditions imposed resulted in her irrevocable loss.

euryhaline /yoŏri háy leen, -līn/ *adj* describes water organisms that tolerate a wide range of salinity [Late 19C. < EURY- + Greek *halinos* 'of salt']

euryphagous /yoŏ ríffəgəss/ *adj* describes organisms that consume a variety of different foods

eurypterid /yoŏ ríptərid/ *n* an extinct invertebrate animal that was common in fresh or brackish water during the Palaeozoic era. Order: Eurypterida. [Late 19C. < modern Latin *Eurypterida* < Greek *eury-* 'wide' + *pteron* 'wing']

eurythermal /yoŏri thúrm'l/, **eurythermic** /-thúrmik/, **eurythermous** /-thúrməss/ *adj* describes organisms that tolerate a wide range of temperatures —**eurytherm** /yoŏri thurm/ *n*

eurythmic, etc. MUSIC, FITNESS another spelling of **eurhythmic, etc.**

eurytopic /yoŏri tóppik/ *adj* describes organisms that

tolerate a wide range of environmental conditions [Mid-20C. < EURY- + Greek *topos* 'place']

Eusebius (of Caesarea) /yoo seébi əss/ (260?–340?) bishop and Christian scholar, probably born in Palestine. He was bishop of Caesarea and worked on texts with his teacher, Pamphilus of Caesarea, as well as writing his *Ecclesiastical History*, a history of the Church until 324. Known as **Eusebius Pamphili**

Eusebius (of Nicomedia) (d. 342?) Syrian bishop and Christian theologian. He helped to spread Arianism, which denies Jesus Christ's divinity. He was patriarch of Constantinople (339–42).

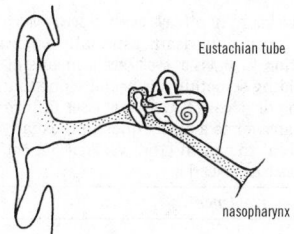

Eustachian tube

Eustachian tube /yoo stáysh'n-/ *n* a bony passage extending from the middle ear to the nasopharynx that has a role in equalizing air pressure on both sides of the eardrum [Mid-18C. After Bartolomeo Eustachio (1520–74), Italian anatomist]

eustasy /yoŏstássi/ (*plural* **-sies**) *n* a worldwide change in sea level caused, e.g. by melting glaciers [Mid-20C. < EUSTATIC]

eustatic /yoo státtik/ *adj* relating to a global change in sea level [Mid-20C. < Greek *eu* 'well' + *statikos* 'static']

eutectic /yoo téktik/ *adj* describes a mixture, es-

pecially an alloy, that has the lowest freezing point of all combinations or constituents, or the temperature at which this occurs [Late 19C. < Greek *eutēktos* 'easily melting' < *tēkein* 'melt'] —**eutectic** *n*

Euterpe /yoo túrpi/ *n* in Greek mythology, the Muse of lyric poetry and music, one of the nine Muses believed to inspire and nurture the arts

euthanasia /yoŏthə náyzi ə, -náyzhə/ *n* the act or practice of killing somebody who has an incurable illness or injury, or of assisting that person to die. Euthanasia is illegal in most countries. [Early 17C. < Greek, 'easy death' < *thanatos* 'death']

euthanize /yoŏthə nīz/ (**-nizes, -nizing, -nized**), **euthanise** (**-nises, -nising, -nised**), **euthanatize** /yoo thánnə tīz/ (**-tizes, -tizing, -tized**), **euthanatise** (**-tises, -tising, -tised**) *vt N Am* to kill an incurably ill or injured person or animal to relieve suffering

euthenics /yoo thénniks/ *n* the study of ways of enhancing people's environment and living standards in order to improve their health and wellbeing (*takes a singular verb*) [Early 20C. < Greek *euthenein* 'thrive') —**euthenist** /yoŏthənist/ *n*

eutherian /yoo theéri ən/ *n* a mammal whose young develop within the womb surrounded by a placenta. Subclass: Eutheria. [Late 19C. < modern Latin *Eutheria* < Greek *thērion* 'wild animal'] —**eutherian** *adj*

eutrophic /yoo trófik, -tróffik/ *adj* describes a body of water whose oxygen content is depleted by organic nutrients [Mid-20C. < Greek *eutrophia* 'good nutrition' < *trephein* 'nourish'] —**eutrophy** /yoŏtrəfi/ *n*

eutrophication /yoo trófi káysh'n, -tróffi-/ *n* the process by which a body of water becomes rich in dissolved nutrients from fertilizers or sewage, thereby encouraging the growth and decomposition of oxygen-depleting plant life and resulting in harm to other organisms

eV *symbol* ELEC electron volt

EVA *abbr* AEROSP extravehicular activity

evacuant /i vákyoo ənt/ *adj* describes a drug that empties the bowels —**evacuant** *n*

evacuate /i vákyoo ayt/ (**-ates, -ating, -ated**) *v* **1.** *vt* MAKE EVERYONE LEAVE PLACE to empty a dangerous or potentially dangerous place of people ○ *Towns near the nuclear plant were evacuated as a precautionary measure.* **2.** *vti* MOVE TO SAFETY to leave or cause people to leave a place of danger and go somewhere safer ○ *The government has evacuated all its embassy officials from the city.* **3.** *vt* EMPTY SOMETHING to empty something by removing all its contents (*formal*) **4.** *vti* PHYSIOL EMPTY BOWELS OR BLADDER to discharge faeces or urine from the body (*technical*) **5.** *vt* PHYS CREATE VACUUM IN SOMETHING to remove a gas from something, leaving a vacuum [14C. < Latin *evacuat-*, past participle of *evacuare* 'empty (the bowels)' < *vacuus* 'empty'] —**evacuative** *adj* —**evacuator** *n*

evacuation /i vákyoo áysh'n/ *n* **1.** CLEARING OF DANGEROUS PLACE an act or the process of emptying a dangerous or potentially dangerous place of people ○ *ordered the evacuation of the building* **2.** MOVING PEOPLE TO SAFETY a removal of people from a dangerous or potentially dangerous place to somewhere safe **3.** PHYSIOL DISCHARGE OF BODILY WASTE elimination of faeces or urine from the body (*technical*) **4.** PHYSIOL BODILY WASTE faeces or urine eliminated from the body (*technical*) **5.** PHYS CREATION OF VACUUM the process of creating a vacuum by the removal of a gas from something

evacuee /i vákyoo eé/ *n* somebody who is taken from a dangerous place and sent somewhere safer, especially during a war [Early 20C. < French *évacué*, past participle of *évacuer* 'cease to occupy' < Latin *evacuare* (see EVACUATE)]

evade /i váyd/ (**evades, evading, evaded**) *v* **1.** *vt* CLEVERLY ESCAPE SOMEBODY OR SOMETHING to escape or avoid somebody or something, usually by ingenuity or guile **2.** *vt* AVOID SOMETHING UNPLEASANT to avoid doing something unpleasant, especially something that is a moral or legal obligation **3.** *vti* GIVE INDIRECT RESPONSE to avoid dealing with or responding directly to something **4.** *vt* BE UNATTAINABLE TO SOMEBODY to be difficult or impossible for somebody to find, obtain, or achieve (*formal*) ○ *Success evaded him.* [Early 16C. Via French < Latin *evadere* 'to escape' < *vadere* 'go, walk'] —**evadable** *adj* —**evader** *n*

USAGE See *avoid.*

evaginate /i vájji nayt/ (**-nates, -nating, -nated**) *vt* to turn a hollow structure or bodily organ inside out [Mid-17C. < Latin *evaginat-*, past participle of *evaginare* 'unsheathe' < *vagina* 'sheath'] —**evagination** /i vájji náysh'n/ *n*

evaluate /i vállyoo ayt/ (**-ates, -ating, -ated**) *vt* **1. EXAMINE AND JUDGE SOMETHING** to consider or examine something in order to judge its value, quality, importance, extent, or condition ○ *We evaluated the situation carefully.* **2. PUT VALUE ON SOMETHING** to estimate the monetary value of something ○ *The appraiser evaluated the property at £100,000.* **3.** MATHS **FIND NUMERICAL VALUE OF SOMETHING** to calculate a numerical value for a mathematical expression [Mid-19C. Back-formation < EVALUATION] —**evaluator** *n*

evaluation /i vállyoo áysh'n/ *n* **1.** the act of considering or examining something in order to judge its value, quality, importance, extent, or condition **2.** a spoken or written statement of the value, quality, importance, extent, or condition of something [Mid-18C. < French *évaluation* < *évaluer* 'find the value of' < Old French *value* (see VALUE)]

evaluative /i vállyoo ətiv/ *adj* **1.** relating to or based on examination and judgment of the value, quality, or importance of something **2.** expressing a judgment about something, or assigning a value to it, as opposed to describing a fact

evan. *abbr* CHR **1.** evangelical **2.** evangelist

evanesce /évvə néss/ (**-nesces, -nescing, -nesced**) *vi* to grow less until completely gone (*literary*) ○ *His cares evanesced.* [Mid-19C. < Latin *evanescere* 'vanish' < *vanus* 'empty']

evanescent /évvə néss'nt/ *adj* disappearing after only a short time and soon forgotten —**evanescence** *n* —**evanescently** *adv*

SYNONYMS See *temporary.*

evang. *abbr* CHR **1.** evangelical **2.** evangelist

evangel /i vánjəl/ *n* CHR (*archaic*) **1.** same as **Gospel** (senses 1–2) **2.** *also* **Evangel** any of four Christian Gospels [14C. < Old French *evangile* < Greek *euaggelion* 'good news' < *euaggelos* 'bringing good news' < *eu* 'good' + *aggelein* 'announce']

evangelical /ée van jéllik'l/ *adj* **1.** *also* **Evangelical** *or* **evangelic** /-jéllik/ *or* **Evangelic OF PROTESTANT CHURCHES EMPHASIZING PERSONAL SALVATION** relating or belonging to any Protestant Christian church that emphasizes the authority of the Bible and salvation through the personal acceptance of Jesus Christ **2.** *also* **evangelic RELATING TO CHRISTIAN GOSPELS** relating to or based on the Gospels of the Christian Bible **3.** *also* **evangelic WITH STRONG BELIEFS** enthusiastic or zealous in support of a particular cause and very eager to make other people share its beliefs or ideals ■ *n* *also* **Evangelical HOLDER OF EVANGELICAL BELIEFS** somebody who has evangelical Christian beliefs —**evangelically** *adv*

evangelicalism /ée van jéllik'lizəm/, **Evangelicalism** *n* a Protestant movement of the Christian Church whose members believe in the authority of the Bible and salvation through the personal acceptance of Jesus Christ

evangelise *vti* CHR another spelling of **evangelize**

evangelism /i vánjəlizəm/ *n* **1.** the spreading of Christianity, especially through the activities of evangelists **2.** great enthusiasm, fervour, or zeal for a particular cause

evangelist /i vánjəlist/ *n* **1.** a Christian who tries to persuade other people to become Christian, especially at public gatherings or in broadcasts **2.** *also* **Evangelist** a writer of any of the four books of the Christian Bible known as a Gospel —**evangelistic** /i vánjə lístik/ *adj* —**evangelistically** *adv*

evangelize /i vánjə līz/ (**-izes, -izing, -ized**), **evangelise** (**-ises, -ising, -ised**) *vti* **1.** to convert somebody or the people of an area to Christianity, especially by preaching or missionary work **2.** to try to persuade other people to share enthusiasm for specific beliefs and ideals —**evangelization** /i vánjə lī záysh'n/ *n* —**evangelizer** *n*

Evans, Mount /évv'nz/ mountain in north-central Colorado, site of a high-altitude laboratory. Height: 4,348 m/14,264 ft.

Evans, Sir Arthur John (1851–1941) British archaeologist. His excavations on Crete (1899–1935), notably at Knossos, uncovered a Bronze Age culture he termed Minoan. His restoration techniques remain controversial.

Evans, Dame Edith (1888–1976) British actor. She is remembered for her Shakespearean roles and also for her performance as Lady Bracknell in the 1951 film of *The Importance of Being Earnest.* Full name **Evans, Dame Edith Mary**

Evans, Sir Geraint (1922–92) Welsh singer and teacher. He was an operatic baritone whose long career (1948–84) embraced some 70 roles, notably the title role in Giuseppe Verdi's *Falstaff.* Full name **Evans, Sir Geraint Llewellyn**

Evans-Pritchard /-príchərd/, **Sir E. E.** (1902–73) British anthropologist. Often living with the peoples he studied, he pioneered the view that sees culturally distinct beliefs as forming a coherent functional system. Full name **Evans-Pritchard, Sir Edward Evan**

Evansville /évv'nz vil/ city in southwestern Indiana, on the northern bank of the Ohio River, southwest of Bloomington. Population: 119,081 (2002 estimate).

evaporate /i váppə rayt/ (**-rates, -rating, -rated**) *v* **1.** *vti* **CHANGE LIQUID TO VAPOUR** to change a liquid into a vapour, usually by heating to below its boiling point, or change from a liquid to vapour in this way ○ *The water evaporates, increasing the moisture in the air.* **2.** *vt* **REMOVE LIQUID FROM SOMETHING** to remove liquid from something, usually by heating, to produce a more concentrated or solid substance **3.** *vi* **VANISH** to disappear gradually, or fade away to nothing **4.** *vt* PHYS **DEPOSIT FILM** to deposit something such as a metal film on a surface through the condensation of a vaporized substance [15C. < Latin *evaporat-*, past participle of *evaporare* 'go out in vapour' < *vapor* 'steam, heat'] —**evaporable** *adj* —**evaporative** *adj*

evaporated milk /i váppə raytid-/ *n* milk that has been thickened by removing some of the water by evaporation

evaporation /i váppə ráysh'n/ *n* a process in which something is changed from a liquid to a vapour without its temperature reaching boiling point

evaporator /i váppə raytər/ *n* **1.** the vaporization portion of a refrigeration system **2.** a vaporizing device that removes water or other solvents to obtain the dried or concentrated residue, e.g. in the preparation of powdered milk from milk

evaporite /i váppə rīt/ *n* a sedimentary rock or deposit that results from the evaporation of salt water in lagoons and saline lakes. Gypsum and rock salt are evaporites. [Early 20C. < EVAPORATION]

evapotranspiration /i váppō transpə ráysh'n/ *n* the return of moisture to the air through both evaporation from the soil and transpiration by plants [Mid-20C. < EVAPORATION]

evasion /i váyzh'n/ *n* **1. AVOIDANCE OF SOMETHING** avoidance of something unpleasant, especially a moral or legal obligation **2. MEANS OF AVOIDANCE** a means of escaping or avoiding something, especially one that involves cunning or deceit **3. AVOIDING OF ISSUE** failure to give a direct answer to a direct question, usually in order to conceal the truth [15C. Via French < Latin *evasion-* < *evadere* (see EVADE)]

USAGE See *avoidance.*

evasive /i váyssiv/ *adj* **1.** not giving a direct answer to a direct question, usually in order to conceal the truth **2.** intended to avoid something unpleasant, e.g. trouble or an attack ○ *took evasive action* —**evasively** *adv* —**evasiveness** *n*

Evatt /évvət/, **Herbert Vere** (1894–1965) Australian judge and politician. He was deputy prime minister of Australia (1946–49) and leader of the Australian Labor Party (1951–60). He was also first president of the general assembly of the United Nations (1948–49).

eve /eev/ *n* **1.** the day or days immediately before an important event or special occasion ○ *He died on the eve of his 100th birthday.* **2.** *also* **Eve** the day, evening, or night before a religious festival or public holiday **3.** same as **evening** *n* (senses 1–2) (*literary*) ○ *on a cold winter's eve* [12C. Variant of EVEN ²]

Eve /eev/ *n* in the Bible, the first woman created by God, and Adam's companion in the Garden of Eden

evection /i véksh'n/ *n* a periodic irregularity in the motion of the Moon caused by the variation in the gravitational attraction of the Sun as the Moon orbits Earth [Mid-17C. < Latin *evection-* < *evect-*, past participle of *evehere* 'carry out, elevate' < *vehere* 'carry'] —**evectional** *adj*

Evelyn /éevlin/, **John** (1620–1706) English writer and government official. His *Diary* (1640–1706), which gives a vivid picture of his contemporaries, was first published in 1818.

> 'This fatal night about ten, began that deplorable fire near Fish Street in London...all the sky were of a fiery aspect, like the top of a burning Oven, and the light seen above 40 miles round about for many nights.'
> [John Evelyn, *Diary*; 2–3 September 1666]

even¹ /éev'n/ *adj* **1. NOT SLOPING, ROUGH, OR IRREGULAR** having no slope, roughness, or irregularities **2. AT SAME HEIGHT** at the same distance above the ground or other point of reference **3. ALIGNED** lining up along the same horizontal or vertical line and usually with equal spaces between **4. NOT CHANGING OR FLUCTUATING** not changing or fluctuating in level or strength **5. SIMILAR THROUGHOUT** the same all over or throughout ○ *an even consistency* **6. EQUAL IN AMOUNT** equal in amount, number, or extent ○ *At the end of the first round, the score was even.* **7. WELL BALANCED** between competitors of equal strength or skill, and therefore fair or well balanced **8. EXACT IN AMOUNT** exact in amount, number, or extent ○ *an even dozen* **9. NOT OWING ANYTHING** not or no longer owing anything to each other (*informal*) ○ *Give me five pounds, and we'll call it even.* **10. CALM AND STEADY** calm and controlled **11.** MATHS **EXACTLY DIVISIBLE BY TWO** describes a number or quantity that can be exactly divided by two with nothing left over, e.g. 2, 6, 30, or 518. ◊ **odd** *adj* (sense 2) **12. WITH EVEN NUMBER** having a number that can be exactly divided by two ○ *on the even pages* ■ *vti* (**evens, evening** /éevəning/, **evened**) **LEVEL OR EQUALIZE** to make something more level or equal, or become more level or equal ○ *Atlanta scored three quick runs to even the score.* [Old English *efen* < Germanic] —**evener** *n* —**evenly** *adv* —**evenness** *n* ◇ **get even (with somebody)** to take revenge on somebody ○ *They took advantage of me, and I was determined to get even.*

even out *vti* **1.** to become or make something more flat, smooth, or level **2.** to make two or more different things more equal, or become more equal

even up *vti* to become or make something more equal, fair, or well balanced

even² /éev'n/ *n* same as **evening** *n* (senses 1–2) (*literary*) ○ *at even, when the sun was set* [Old English *æfen* (see EVENING)]

even³ /éev'n/ CORE MEANING: used for emphasis to indicate something surprising, unlikely, or extreme ○ *Even I know how to repair a puncture!*

adv **1. SO MUCH AS** used after a negative for emphasis to indicate something unexpected and usually annoying or disappointing ○ *She couldn't even remember my name.* **2. TO GREATER EXTENT** used for emphasis in comparisons to indicate the degree to which something exists ○ *His writing is even more untidy than hers, and hers is barely legible.* ○ *I never liked him much, but after today I like him even less.* **3. OR MORE EXACTLY** used to indicate that the description that follows applies in addition to and more strongly or precisely than the preceding one ○ *She is careful with her money, even miserly.* **4. TO UNEXPECTED EXTENT** used to emphasize that something is surprisingly true (*archaic*) ○ *I will follow thee even unto the ends of the earth.* [Old English *efne* < Germanic] ◇ **even so** regardless of anything else ○ *It sounds unlikely; even so, it could be true.*

even break *n* an equal opportunity for winning or losing

even chance *n* an equal likelihood that something will or will not happen

evenhanded /éev'n hándid/ *adj* treating everyone fairly, without favouritism or discrimination ○ *an evenhanded distribution of the profits* —**evenhandedly** *adv* —**evenhandedness** *n*

evening /eévning/ n **1.** LATE PART OF DAY the part of the day between afternoon and night, as daylight begins to fade **2.** TIME BEFORE BEDTIME the part of the day between sunset or the last main meal of the day and bedtime ○ *We went out for the evening.* **3.** ACTIVITY HELD DURING EVENING a social gathering, meeting, or entertainment held in the evening ○ *Thank you for an enjoyable evening.* **4.** PERIOD AT END the final part of a period of time, e.g. somebody's life or a historical era (*literary*) ○ *the evening of the British Empire* **5.** *regional* same as **afternoon** n (sense 1) ■ *interj* same as **good evening** (*informal*) [Old English æfnung < æfen < Indo-European, 'lateness']

evening class n a course or session of adult education held between approximately 7pm and 10pm, usually once a week throughout the school year

evening dress n **1.** clothing worn by men or women for formal social events held in the evening. A man in evening dress usually wears a dinner jacket and black tie, and a woman usually wears a full-length dress of elegant design. **2.** *UK* a woman's dress suitable for formal social events held in the evening, usually a full-length dress of elegant design. ANZ, N Am term **evening gown**

evening gown n ANZ, N Am same as **evening dress** (sense 2)

evening prayer, Evening Prayer n CHR same as **evensong**

evening primrose

evening primrose n a biennial plant with hairy leaves and seeds that yield an oil used especially in treatments for menstrual problems. Genus: *Oenothera*. [Because its yellow flowers open in the evening]

evenings /eévningz/ adv N Am in the evening, especially regularly

evening star n a bright planet that can be seen in the western sky around sunset, usually Venus but occasionally Mercury

Evenki /i véngki/ (*plural* same or **-kis**), **Ewenki** n **1.** a member of an ethnic group that lives mainly in eastern parts of Asia of the former Soviet Union and northwestern China **2.** a Tungusic language spoken in the eastern parts of Asia of the former Soviet Union and northwestern China. It belongs to the Mongolian branch of Altaic. Native speakers: 30,000. [Via Russian, 'Evenki people' < Evenki] —**Evenki** adj

even money n a betting situation in which the odds of winning or losing are equal and the winnings equal the stake ■ adj equally likely or unlikely ○ *It's even money she'll forget.*

evens /eév'nz/ adj, adv with equal odds of winning or losing a bet

evensong /eév'n song/ n the daily evening worship service of the Anglican Church

even-steven /-steévan/, **even Stevens** /-steévanz/ adj (*informal*) **1.** with all debts or grievances mutually settled **2.** with equal scores or chances of winning ○ *At the end of the first round the two teams were even-steven.* [Probably arbitrary]

event /i vént/ n **1.** IMPORTANT INCIDENT an occurrence, especially one that is particularly significant, interesting, exciting, or unusual ○ *the events leading up to the strike* **2.** ORGANIZED OCCASION an organized occasion such as a social function or sporting competition ○ *She has competed in many international events.* **3.** INDIVIDUAL SPORTING CONTEST a race or other competition that forms part of a larger sporting occasion such as the Olympic Games ○ *The 100 metres is his best event.* **4.** PHILOSOPHY SOMETHING THAT HAPPENS a hap-

pening or occurrence **5.** PHYS SINGLE POINT IN SPACE-TIME an occurrence defined in the theory of relativity as a single point in space-time **6.** COMPUT OCCURRENCE AFFECTING COMPUTER PROGRAM an occurrence or happening of significance to a computer program, e.g. the clicking of a mouse button or the completion of a write operation to a disk ■ *vi* (**events, eventing, evented**) RIDING COMPETE IN EVENTING to compete in equestrian competitions, especially eventing [Late 16C. < Latin *eventus* < past participle of *evenire* 'happen' < *venire* 'come'] ◇ **be wise after the event** to know with hindsight what should have been done or said in a situation ◇ **in the event** contrary to what was expected ◇ **in the event of something** if something should happen

event-driven adj describes a computer program with a main loop that waits for an event and then passes the details along

even-tempered adj not easily angered or upset

eventer /i véntər/ n a horse or rider that regularly competes at eventing

eventful /i véntf'l/ adj **1.** full of important, interesting, or exciting occurrences **2.** having a major effect on somebody's life —**eventfully** adv —**eventfulness** n

event horizon n the theoretical boundary surrounding a black hole, within which gravitational attraction is so great that nothing, not even radiation, can escape because the escape velocity is greater than the speed of light

eventide /eév'n tīd/ n same as **evening** n (senses 1–2) (*literary*)

eventide home n a home for senior citizens (*dated*)

eventing /i vénting/ n an equestrian competition that includes dressage, cross-country riding, and stadium jumping, usually over three days

eventless /i véntləss/ adj having no significant events

event marketing n promotional activities involving an event such as a sporting or social event, designed to bring a product to the attention of the public

eventual /i vénchoo əl/ adj happening in the course of time or events, usually much later ○ *her eventual fall from power* [Early 17C. < French *éventuel* < Latin *eventus* (see EVENT)]

eventuality /i vénchoo álləti/ (*plural* **-ties**) n a possible occurrence or result, especially something undesirable or unexpected ○ *We must be prepared for all eventualities.*

eventually /i vénchoo əli/ adv **1.** after a long time, especially after many problems or setbacks ○ *We eventually managed to open the door.* **2.** at some later time after a series of events ○ *She hopes eventually to study art.*

eventuate /i vénchoo ayt/ (**-ates, -ating, -ated**) vi to happen as a final result (*formal*)
eventuate in vt to cause or result in something, especially after an extended period of time (*formal*) ○ *The oil spill eventuated in the destruction of wildlife habitats along the coast.*

evenweave /eévan weev/ n a fabric with warp and weft threads that are equally thick and tense and in equal numbers in any square measurement

ever /évvər/ adv **1.** ⚠ AT ANY TIME used for emphasis in indicating any time in the past or future ○ *This is the most fascinating book I've ever read.* ○ *Will I ever see you again?* ○ *It's his biggest blunder ever.* **2.** USED TO INDICATE SURPRISE used for emphasis to indicate surprise, shock, or incomprehension at something ○ *Where ever can it be?* **3.** INCREASINGLY to an increasing degree (*formal*) ○ *The questions were becoming ever more technical.* **4.** USED AS INTENSIFIER used to emphasize a particular quality, especially to express enthusiasm (*informal*) ○ *It'll be ever such fun!* **5.** ALWAYS showing at all times a particular quality ○ *He is ever anxious to please.* [Old English æfre < Indo-European, 'eternity']

USAGE The best book **ever**: Some people object to this use of **ever** because they maintain that **ever** should include the future as well as the past. However, the future can rarely be accounted for, and the idiom is well established in conversational use, although it would not normally be used in more formal spoken or written English.

Mount Everest: western shoulder of the mountain

Everest, Mount /évvərist/ mountain in the Himalaya range on the border between Nepal and the Tibet Autonomous Region of China. It is the highest mountain in the world. Height: 8,850 m/29,035 ft.

everglade /évvər glayd/ n US a stretch of marshy grassland usually covered with water for at least part of the year

Everglades /évvər glaydz/ subtropical swamp covering much of southern Florida. Area: 12,950 sq. km/5,000 sq. mi.

Everglades National Park

Everglades National Park national park in southern Florida, established in 1947. It contains the largest subtropical wilderness in the United States. Area: 6,105 sq. km/2,357 sq. mi.

evergreen /évvər green/ adj **1.** WITH LEAVES THROUGHOUT YEAR describes a tree or bush that retains its foliage throughout the year **2.** REMAINING FRESH OR POPULAR describes people or things that always seem fresh, lively, or interesting, and that remain popular despite their age ■ n **1.** EVERGREEN TREE a tree or bush that retains its foliage throughout the year **2.** SOMEBODY OR SOMETHING STAYING LIVELY AND INTERESTING somebody or something that remains fresh, lively, interesting, or popular

everlasting /évvər laásting/ adj **1.** LASTING FOR EVER never failing or coming to an end **2.** LASTING LONG TIME continuing indefinitely or for a long time **3.** INCESSANT going on for too long and becoming tedious or annoying ○ *everlasting grumbling* ■ n **1.** INFINITY infinite time **2.** PLANTS FLOWER THAT LOOKS FRESH WHEN DRIED a plant with flowers that keep their shape and colour when dried, e.g. helichrysum —**everlastingly** adv —**everlastingness** n

Everlasting n same as **God**

everlasting flower n PLANTS same as **everlasting** n (sense 2)

evermore /évvər máwr/ adv from now until the end of time or the end of somebody's life (*literary*) ○ *I will be evermore in your debt.*

eversion /i vúrsh'n/ n **1.** the process or condition of being turned inside out ○ *eversion of the bladder* **2.** a condition of being turned outwards ○ *an eversion of the feet* [Mid-18C. Directly or via French < Latin *eversion-* < *evers-*, past participle of *evertere* (see EVERT)] —**eversible** adj

evert /i vúrt/ (**everts, everting, everted**) vt to turn an organ or other body part outwards or inside out [Mid-16C. < Latin *evertere* 'turn out' < *vertere* 'to turn']

Popperfoto
Chris Evert

Evert /évvərt/, **Chris** (*b.* 1954) US tennis player. She won 16 grand slam singles championships during her career (1972–89). Full name **Evert, Christine Marie**

> 'That's my whole game, playing steady and letting them make errors. I win more games that way than by hitting winners.'
> [Chris Evert, *Times*; 1 August 1972]

every /évvri/ CORE MEANING: used to indicate each member of a group without exception ○ *dangers to health with which every citizen is familiar* ○ *Every life has value.* ○ *The press have been scrutinizing his every decision.*
det **1. EACH EXCLUDING NONE** each member of a group, without exception ○ *Every life is precious.* **2. TO GREATEST EXTENT** used to emphasize that there is all there could be of a particular quality ○ *The government has every intention of exploring this issue.* **3. RECURRING AT PARTICULAR INTERVAL** used to indicate each occurrence in recurrent or intermittent groups of things, or to indicate a ratio ○ *We intend to meet every two weeks.* ○ *Take this medicine every three hours.* [13C. < Old English *ǣfre ǣlc* 'ever each'] ◇ **every other** each alternate thing, person, or occasion

USAGE See *each.*

everybody *pron* same as **everyone**

everyday /évvree day/ *adj* **1. ORDINARY AND UNREMARKABLE** having no remarkable feature to set it apart ○ *an everyday story of city life* **2. OCCURRING EACH DAY** happening or done each day ○ *an everyday occurrence* **3. USED ON ORDINARY OCCASIONS** suitable for use on ordinary days or for routine tasks, rather than on special occasions ■ *n* **ORDINARY OCCASIONS** routine or daily life

USAGE everyday or **every day**? When you intend using either of these words as an adjective or a noun meaning 'ordinary occasions', as in *everyday life* or *part of the everyday,* the one-word version is correct. Adverbial uses, as in *We should eat fruit every day,* and the noun use meaning 'each day', as in *Every day is different,* call for the two-word version. Thus *everyday in every way* means 'ordinary in all respects', whereas *every day in every way* means 'daily and completely'.

Everyman /évvri man/ *n* **1.** *also* **everyman** somebody, usually a man, considered to be typical or representative of all human beings **2.** the hero of a medieval morality play who represents the whole of the human race

every man jack, **every man Jack** *n* every single member of a group of people, without exception (*informal*) ○ *They ran away, every man jack of them.*

everyone /évvri wun/, **everybody** /-bodi/ *pron* every person, whether of a defined group or in general ○ *Everyone is going to come to the office party.* ○ *This is not just for one area; it will affect everyone around the country.*

everything /évvri thing/ *pron* **1.** all the items, actions, or facts in a given situation ○ *We used to sit in front of his mother's house and talk about everything.* ○ *Everything I do is for my family.* ○ *Is everything all right?* **2.** used to emphasize that somebody or something is the most important person or thing there is ○ *To them, family is everything.*

everywhere /évvri wair/ *adv* in or to all conceivable places ○ *Children everywhere play these games.* ○ *Her cat followed her everywhere she went.*

Everywoman /évvri wŏŏmən/, **everywoman** *n* a woman considered to be typical or representative of women generally

Eve's pudding *n* a baked pudding of apples topped with sponge [< the apple supposedly eaten by Eve in the Biblical account of the Garden of Eden]

eve-teasing *n S Asia* the harassment of young women —**eve-teaser** *n*

evict /i víkt/ (**evicts, evicting, evicted**) *vt* **1. EJECT SOMEBODY FROM PROPERTY** to force a tenant to leave a property, especially the tenant's residence, usually because he or she has failed to comply with the terms of the letting contract **2. THROW SOMEBODY OUT** to force somebody to leave a place, usually because of bad behaviour ○ *She was evicted from the game for insulting the referee.* **3. GET BACK PROPERTY** to recover property or title to property from somebody by legal means [15C. < Latin *evict-*, past participle of *evincere* (see EVINCE)] —**evictee** /i vík tée/ *n* —**eviction** *n* —**evictor** *n*

evidence /évvidənss/ *n* **1. SIGN OR PROOF** something that gives a sign or proof of the existence or truth of something, or that helps somebody to come to a particular conclusion ○ *There is no evidence that the disease is related to diet.* **2. PROOF OF GUILT** the objects or information used to prove or suggest the guilt of somebody accused of a crime ○ *The police have no evidence.* **3. STATEMENTS OF WITNESSES** the oral or written statements of witnesses and other people involved in a trial or official enquiry ■ *vt* (**-dences, -dencing, -denced**) **DEMONSTRATE OR PROVE** to demonstrate or prove something (*usually passive*) ○ *Their unwillingness to participate is evidenced by their failure to contact us.* ◇ **turn King's** *or* **Queen's evidence** to give evidence against a partner in crime so as to receive a less severe sentence

evidence-based medicine *n* the use of clinical methods and decision-making that have been thoroughly tested by properly controlled, peer-reviewed medical research

evident /évvidənt/ *adj* easy or clear to see or understand ○ *The full extent of her injuries did not become evident until they tried to move her.* [14C. Via Old French < Latin *evident-* 'clear' < *videre* 'see']

evidential /évvi dénsh'l/ *adj UK, ANZ, Can* relating to, consisting of, or based on evidence ○ *statements with no evidential value* US term **evidentiary** —**evidentially** *adv*

evidentiary /évvi dénshəri/ *adj US* same as **evidential**

evidently /évvidəntli/ *adv* **1.** used to indicate that something is undoubtedly true, often because it is there to be seen ○ *Evidently, you have not grasped all the ramifications of this proposal.* **2.** used to indicate that something may be true based on available evidence ○ *He then completely ignored her, evidently intent on hurting her feelings even more.*

evil /éev'l/ *adj* **1. MORALLY BAD** profoundly immoral or wrong **2. HARMFUL** deliberately causing great harm, pain, or upset ○ *This evil act is clearly the work of terrorists.* **3. CAUSING MISFORTUNE** characterized by, bringing, or signifying bad luck ○ *an evil omen* **4. MALICIOUS** characterized by a desire to cause hurt or harm ○ *an evil mood* **5. DEVILISH** connected with the devil or other powerful destructive forces ○ *evil spirits* **6. DISAGREEABLE** very unpleasant ○ *What an evil smell!* ■ *n* **1. WICKEDNESS** the quality of being profoundly immoral or wrong **2.** *also* **Evil FORCE CAUSING HARMFUL EFFECTS** the force believed to bring about harmful, painful, or unpleasant events ○ *a struggle between good and evil* **3. SOMETHING EVIL** a situation or thing that is very unpleasant, harmful, or morally wrong ○ *the social evil of alcoholism* [Old English *yfel* < Indo-European, 'exceeding due limits'] —**evilly** *adv* —**evilness** *n*

evildoer /éev'l doo ər, éev'l dŏŏ ər/ *n* somebody who does evil acts —**evildoing** *n*

evil eye *n* **1.** a piercing look that conveys strong feelings of hatred, disapproval, jealousy, or malice, or that supposedly can cause harm **2.** a supernatural or magical power that some people believe can bring harm or cause bad luck ○ *an amulet to protect children from the evil eye*

Evil One *n* RELIG same as **devil**

evince /i vínss/ (**evinces, evincing, evinced**) *vt* **1.** to show a feeling or a quality clearly ○ *She evinced her disapproval of the production by leaving the auditorium.* **2.** to indicate something by action or implication [Late 16C. < Latin *evincere* 'win out' < *vincere* 'conquer'] —**evincible** *adj* —**evincive** *adj*

eviscerate /i víssə rayt/ (**-ates, -ating, -ated**) *vt* **1. DISEMBOWEL SOMEBODY** to remove the internal organs or entrails of a person or an animal **2. REMOVE IMPORTANT PART OF SOMETHING** to remove an essential part of something and so weaken it **3.** SURG **REMOVE CONTENTS OF ORGAN** to remove the contents of the eyeball or another organ or body cavity [Late 16C. < Latin *eviscerat-*, past participle of *eviscerare* < *viscera* 'internal organs, entrails'] —**evisceration** /i víssə ráysh'n/ *n* —**eviscerator** *n*

Evita /i véetə/ ➧ **Perón, Eva**

evocation /éevō káysh'n, évvō-/ *n* **1.** a re-creation of something not present, especially an event or feeling from the past ○ *an accurate evocation of that period* **2.** the transfer of a case from a lower to a higher court for review

evocative /i vókətiv/ *adj* prompting vivid memories or images of things not present, especially things from the past ○ *an outfit evocative of the 1960s* —**evocatively** *adv* —**evocativeness** *n*

evoke /i vṓk/ (**evokes, evoking, evoked**) *vt* **1. STIMULATE MEMORIES FROM PAST** to bring to mind a memory or feeling, especially from the past ○ *evoke childhood memories* **2. CAUSE REACTION OR FEELING** to provoke a particular reaction or feeling ○ *Her question evoked a bitter retort.* **3. CAUSE SOMETHING TO APPEAR** to make beings appear who are normally invisible ○ *evoke a spirit* [Early 17C. < Latin *evocare* 'call out' < *vocare* 'to call'] —**evocable** /évvəkəb'l, i vṓkəb'l/ *adj* —**evocator** /évvə kaytər/ *n* —**evoker** *n*

evolute /éevə loot, évvə-/ *n* the curve formed by the set of points that are the centres of curvature of another geometric curve (**involute**) [Mid-18C. < Latin *evolut-*, past participle of *evolvere* (see EVOLVE)]

evolution /éevə lóosh'n, évvə-/ *n* **1.** BIOL **THEORY OF DEVELOPMENT FROM EARLIER FORMS** the theoretical process by which all species develop from earlier forms of life. According to this theory, natural variation in the genetic material of a population favours reproduction by some individuals more than others, so that over the generations all members of the population come to possess the favourable traits. **2.** BIOL **DEVELOPMENTAL PROCESS** the natural or artificially induced process by which new and different organisms develop as a result of changes in genetic material **3. GRADUAL DEVELOPMENT** the gradual development of something into a more complex or better form ○ *the evolution of democracy in Western Europe* **4. PATTERN CAUSED BY MOVEMENT** a pattern formed by a series of movements **5.** PHYS **GIVING OFF HEAT OR GAS** the emission of heat, gas, or vapour **6.** MATHS **FINDING ROOT OF NUMBER** an algebraic operation in which the root, e.g. the square root or cube root, of a number is found. ◊ **involution** (sense 6) **7.** MIL **MILITARY EXERCISE** a military exercise or manoeuvre carried out according to a plan [Early 17C. < Latin *evolut-*, past participle of *evolvere* (see EVOLVE)] —**evolutional** *adj* —**evolutionally** *adv*

evolutionary /éevə lóosh'nəri, évvə-/ *adj* **1. OF EVOLUTION** relating to the theory of biological evolution **2. FROM EVOLUTION** resulting from or conferred by evolution ○ *evolutionary advantage* **3. GRADUAL** developing in small increments that accumulate to bring about significant change ○ *an evolutionary process* —**evolutionarily** *adv*

evolutionism /éevə lóosh'nizəm, évvə-/ *n* **1.** the theory of biological evolution **2.** belief in the theory of biological evolution —**evolutionist** *n*

evolve /i vólv/ (**evolves, evolving, evolved**) *v* **1.** *vti* **DEVELOP GRADUALLY** to develop something gradually, often into something more complex or advanced, or undergo such development **2.** *vti* BIOL **DEVELOP VIA EVOLUTIONARY CHANGE** in evolutionary theory, to develop from an earlier biological form **3.** *vt* PHYS **EMIT HEAT OR GAS** to give off heat, gas, or vapour [Early 17C. < Latin *evolvere* 'roll out' < *volvere* 'to roll'] —**evolvable** *adj* —**evolvement** *n*

evry incorrect spelling of **every**

EW *abbr* MIL enlisted woman

ewe /yoo/ *n* a female sheep, especially when fully grown [Old English *ēowu* < Indo-European]

Ewe /é way, áy-/ (*plural same* or **Ewes**) *n* **1.** a member of a West African people living in coastal regions of Ghana, Togo, and Benin **2.** the language of the Ewe people, belonging to the Kwa branch of the Niger-Congo family. Native speakers: 3 million. [Mid-19C. < Ewe] —**Ewe** *adj*

ewe-neck *n* a thin concave neck in a horse or dog, considered to be a disadvantage —**ewe-necked** *adj*

Ewenki *n, adj* PEOPLES, LANG another spelling of **Evenki**

ewer

ewer /yoó ər/ *n* a large jug or pitcher with a wide spout [15C. < Anglo-Norman < Old French *aiguière* < Latin *aquarius* 'of water' < *aqua* 'water']

Ewing's sarcoma /yoó ingz-/, **Ewing's tumour** *n* a highly malignant cancerous tumour that develops in the long bones, pelvis, or ribs, usually in children and adolescents [Early 20C. After James *Ewing* (1866–1943), US pathologist]

EWO *abbr* EDUC Educational Welfare Officer

ewt /yoot/ *n S England* same as **newt** (*informal*) [14C. Variant of EFT]

REGIONAL NOTE See ***newt***.

ex[1] /eks/ *n* the letter X [Late 19C. < the pronunciation]

ex[2] /eks/ *n* a former spouse, boyfriend, or girlfriend (*informal*) [Early 19C. < EX-[1]]

ex[3] /eks/ *prep* **1.** not including or participating in ○ *ex dividend* **2.** sold directly from the place of production with no charge before collection ○ *ex works* [Mid-19C. < Latin (see EX-[1])]

Ex. *abbr* BIBLE Exodus

ex-[1] *prefix* **1.** out, outside, away ○ *exclave* ○ *explant* **2.** not, without **3.** former ○ *ex-convict* [< Latin, 'out of' < Indo-European, 'out']

ex-[2] *prefix* same as **exo-** (*used before vowels*)

exa- *prefix* one million million million (10^{18}). Symbol **E** [< HEXA-]

exacerbate /ig zássər bayt/ (**-bates, -bating, -bated**) *vt* to make an already bad or problematic situation worse ○ *Her silence merely exacerbated the problem.* [Mid-17C. < Latin *exacerbat-*, past participle of *exacerbare* 'make thoroughly harsh' < *acerbus* 'harsh, bitter'] —**exacerbation** /ig zássər báysh'n/ *n*

exact /ig zákt/ *adj* **1.** CORRECT accurate and correct in all important details ○ *an exact account* **2.** PRECISE precise and not allowing for any variation ○ *a cheque for the exact amount* **3.** THIS AND NO OTHER used to emphasize that what is being referred to is one precise and often significant thing and not any other ○ *on this exact spot* **4.** STRICT rigorous and thorough ○ *an exact argument* **5.** FUNCTIONING ACCURATELY characterized by precise measurements ○ *exact instruments* ■ *vt* (**-acts, -acting, -acted**) **1.** OBTAIN SOMETHING to demand and obtain something, especially payment ○ *exacted a heavy tribute from their defeated enemies* **2.** INFLICT SOMETHING AS SUFFERING to make somebody endure something unpleasant (*formal*) ○ *I was already thinking how I could exact revenge for what he had done.* **3.** REQUIRE SOMETHING to call for something as a matter of necessity or urgency [15C. < Latin *exact-*, past participle of *exigere* 'to demand' < *agere* 'to drive'] —**exactable** *adj* —**exactness** *n* —**exactor** *n*

exacta /ig záktə/ *n ANZ, US* a type of bet, especially on dogs or horses, that pays if the two entries chosen come in first and second in the order predicted. UK term **perfecta** [Mid-20C. < American Spanish *quiniela exacta* 'exact quinella', game of chance]

exacting /ig zákting/ *adj* **1.** requiring concentration and strict attention to detail ○ *an exacting job* **2.** demanding hard work and great effort ○ *an exacting boss* —**exactingly** *adv* —**exactingness** *n*

exaction /ig záksh'n/ *n* **1.** ACT OF DEMANDING AND OBTAINING SOMETHING the act of forcing somebody to give something, especially payment **2.** UNFAIR DEMAND an unfair or excessive demand for something, especially money (*formal*) **3.** PAYMENT OBTAINED BY FORCE a sum of money that has been forcibly demanded and obtained (*formal*)

exactitude /ig zákti tyood/ *n* the quality or state of being exact, precise, or accurate ○ *'The children were drilled in their parts with a military exactitude; obedience and punctuality became cardinal virtues.'* (Frank Norris, *McTeague – A Story of San Francisco*; 1899)

exactly /ig záktli/ *adv* **1.** PRECISELY used to emphasize that a particular quality or quantity is stated precisely ○ *One circuit of the park is exactly two miles.* **2.** FULLY used to emphasize that what is stated is true in all details or to the fullest extent ○ *He did exactly what I said he would.* **3.** SHOWING AGREEMENT used to indicate agreement that what has just been said is true or correct ○ *'We need to give this more thought'. 'Exactly'.* **4.** SHOWING DISAPPROVAL used in questions to ask for precise information, often implying suspicion or disapproval ○ *So exactly what are you doing?*

exact science *n* a science such as physics that deals with precise quantifiable measurements

~~exagerate~~ incorrect spelling of **exaggerate**

exaggerate /ig zájjə rayt/ (**-ates, -ating, -ated**) *v* **1.** *vti* to state that something is better, worse, larger, more common, or more important than is true or usual **2.** *vt* to make something appear more noticeable or prominent than is usual or desirable [Mid-16C. < Latin *exaggerat-*, past participle of *exaggerare* 'heap up' < *agger* 'heap' < *gerere* 'carry'] —**exaggeratingly** *adv* —**exaggeration** /ig zájjə ráysh'n/ *n* —**exaggerative** /ig zájjərətiv, -raytiv/ *adj* —**exaggerator** *n*

exaggerated /ig zájjə raytid/ *adj* made to seem better, worse, larger, or more important than is true or usual ○ *greatly exaggerated reports of widespread looting* —**exaggeratedly** *adv*

exalt /ig záwlt, -zólt/ (**-alts, -alting, -alted**) *vt* **1.** PRAISE SOMEBODY OR SOMETHING to praise or worship somebody or something (*formal*) **2.** PROMOTE SOMEBODY OR SOMETHING to raise somebody or something in rank, position, or esteem (*formal*) ○ *exalted to the rank of major* **3.** INTENSIFY SOMETHING to increase the intensity or effect of something (*formal*) **4.** STIMULATE SOMETHING to stimulate a mental quality or faculty (*archaic*) ○ *'Of Lorna, of my lifelong darling, of my more and more loved wife, I will not talk; for it is not seemly that a man should exalt his pride.'* (R. D. Blackmore, *Lorna Doone, A Romance of Exmoor*; 1869) [15C. < Latin *exaltare* 'put up high' < *altus* 'high'] —**exalter** *n*

exaltation /ég zawl táysh'n, ég zol-/ *n* **1.** FEELING OF EXTREME HAPPINESS a feeling of intense or excessive happiness or exhilaration (*formal*) ○ *the miseries and exaltations of romance* **2.** RAISING UP the act of raising or holding something up (*formal*) **3.** FLOCK a flock of larks (*literary*)

exalted /ig záwltid, -zóltid/ *adj* (*formal*) **1.** ELEVATED high in rank, position, or esteem **2.** NOBLE grand or noble in character **3.** HIGH-SPIRITED in very high spirits —**exaltedly** *adv* —**exaltedness** *n*

exam /ig zám/ *n* **1.** a test designed to assess somebody's ability or knowledge in a particular subject or field ○ *a chemistry exam* **2.** *US* same as **examination** (sense 3) [Mid-19C. Shortening of EXAMINATION]

examen /ig záymən/ *n* in the Roman Catholic Church, an examination of conscience [Early 17C. < Latin (see EXAMINE)]

examination /ig zámmi náysh'n/ *n* **1.** INSPECTION the process of looking at and considering something carefully with the aim of learning something ○ *Their applications are currently under examination.* **2.** EDUC full form of **exam** (sense 1) **3.** *UK, ANZ, Can* MED MEDICAL INSPECTION OF PATIENT a medical inspection carried out on a patient. US term **exam** **4.** LAW INTERROGATION IN LAW COURT an interrogation of a witness or other party to a case in a court of law

examination paper *n* EDUC same as **exam paper**

examine /ig zámmin/ (**-ines, -ining, -ined**) *vt* **1.** STUDY SOMETHING to inspect or study somebody or something in detail ○ *examine the scene for fingerprints* **2.** INVESTIGATE SOMETHING to analyse something in order to understand or expose it ○ *examine your conscience* **3.** EDUC TEST SOMEBODY to test the knowledge or ability of somebody by setting written, oral, or practical examinations **4.** MED INSPECT CONDITION OF PATIENT to inspect a patient in order to determine his or her condition or health ○ *examined by a doctor* **5.** LAW INTERROGATE WITNESS to ask questions of a witness or other party to a case in a court of law [14C. Via French < Latin *examinare* 'weigh' < *examen* 'weighing out' < *exigere* (see EXACT)] —**examinable** *adj* —**examinee** /ig zámmi neé/ *n* —**examiner** *n*

examine-in-chief (**examines-in-chief, examining-in-chief, examined-in-chief**) *vt* to ask questions of a witness or other person in a court of law who is giving primary evidence in support of the case being presented by the questioner. ◊ **cross-examine** —**examination-in-chief** *n*

exam paper *n* the printed set of questions used to test somebody's knowledge in an exam

example /ig zaámp'l/ *n* **1.** SAMPLE something that is representative by virtue of having typical features of the thing it represents ○ *a fine example of baroque carving* **2.** MODEL a person, action, or thing taken as a model to be copied or avoided by others ○ *Her achievement is an example to us all.* **3.** ILLUSTRATION SUPPORTING SOMETHING an illustration that supports or provides more information on an opinion, theory, or principle ○ *The prosecutor then listed several examples of the accused's mismanagement of funds.* **4.** LEARNING AID an exercise or description that illustrates a principle, method, or problem ○ *Each chapter contains easy-to-follow examples.* ■ *vt* (**-ples, -pling, -pled**) EXEMPLIFY SOMETHING to be an example of something (*archaic; usually passive*) [14C. < Old French < Latin *exemplum* < *eximere* 'take out' < *emere* 'take'] ◇ **for example** used to introduce a typical instance of somebody or something ◇ **make an example of somebody** to punish somebody as a warning to others who might be inclined to offend in the same way

exanthema /ék san theémə/ (*plural* **-mata** /-mətə/ or **-mas**), **exanthem** /ek sánthəm/ *n* **1.** a skin rash appearing as a sign of some infectious diseases such as measles **2.** a disease characterized by the appearance of a skin rash, e.g. measles or scarlet fever [Mid-17C. Via late Latin < Greek *exanthēma* 'eruption' < *anthein* 'to blossom' < *anthos* 'flower'] —**exanthematic** /ek sánthi máttik/ *adj* —**exanthematous** /ék san thémmətəss/ *adj*

exarch /éks aark/ *n* **1.** a bishop in the Eastern Orthodox Church of a rank above a metropolitan **2.** the ruler of a province in the Byzantine Empire [Late 16C. Via ecclesiastical Latin *exarchus* < Greek *exarkhos* 'leader' < *exarkhein* 'to lead' < *arkhein* 'to rule'] —**exarchal** /ek saárk'l/ *adj*

exarchate /éks aar kayt, ek saár-/, **exarchy** /-ki/ (*plural* **-chies**) *n* the office, domain, or term of an exarch

exasperate /ig záspə rayt, -zaáspə-/ (**-ates, -ating, -ated**) *vt* **1.** to make somebody very angry or frustrated, often by repeatedly doing something annoying (*usually passive*) ○ *Guests were exasperated by their hosts' constant bickering.* See Synonyms at **annoy** **2.** to make an unpleasant condition or feeling worse (*literary*) [Mid-16C. < Latin *exasperat-*, past participle of *exasperare* 'irritate, roughen' < *asper* 'rough'] —**exasperatedly** *adv* —**exasperating** *adj* —**exasperatingly** *adv* —**exasperation** /ig záspə ráysh'n, -zaáspə-/ *n*

SYNONYMS See ***annoy***.

~~exaust~~ incorrect spelling of **exhaust**

Excalibur /ek skállibər/ *n* in Arthurian legend, King Arthur's magic sword that was given to him by the mysterious Lady of the Lake [15C. Alteration of medieval Latin *Caliburnus* < Middle Welsh *Caletuwlch* or Middle Irish *Caladbolg*, sword of Irish legend]

ex cathedra /éks kə theédrə/ *adj, adv* with the authority of status or rank ○ *imposed the decisions ex cathedra* [< Latin, 'from the (teacher's) chair']

excavate /ékskə vayt/ (**-vates, -vating, -vated**) *v* **1.** *vti* REMOVE EARTH to remove earth or soil by digging or scooping out ○ *Several metres of soil were excavated from the building site.* **2.** *vti* HOLLOW SOMETHING OUT to make a hole or cavity in something by removing the material inside ○ *excavate a tooth* **3.** *vt* FORM SOMETHING BY HOLLOWING to form a shape or cavity by hollowing ○ *excavates a hollow in the sand as its nest* **4.** *vti* UNCOVER SOMETHING WITH DIFFICULTY to discover or uncover something valuable by effort **5.** *vti* ARCHAEOL DIG FOR ARTEFACTS to dig in a place carefully and methodically, taking notes about procedures, conditions, and finds, with a view to uncovering objects of archaeological interest [Late 16C. < Latin *excavat-*, past participle of *excavare* 'hollow out' < *cavus* 'hollow']

excavation /ékskə váysh'n/ *n* **1.** the act or process of digging out ○ *recent excavations in Sumatra* **2.** a hole that has been made by digging or hollowing something out, or part of an archaeological site that has been excavated

excavator /ékskə vaytər/ *n* **1.** a large machine with a hinged metal bucket attached to a hydraulic arm, used to move large quantities of earth or soil or for lifting **2.** a person or animal that digs or hollows something out, especially somebody engaged in archaeological excavation

~~**excede**~~ incorrect spelling of **exceed**

exceed /ik séed/ (**-ceeds, -ceeding, -ceeded**) *vt* **1.** BE GREATER THAN SOMETHING to be greater than something in quantity, degree, or scope ○ *The cost of the film is reported to have exceeded 20 million dollars.* **2.** GO BEYOND LIMITS to go beyond the limits of something in quantity, degree, or scope ○ *He was fined for exceeding the speed limit.* ○ *You've exceeded your authority.* **3.** OUTDO SOMETHING OR SOMEBODY to be better than something or somebody ○ *descriptions of nature that far exceed in merit anything else we've heard* [14C. Via Old French *excéder* < Latin *excedere* 'go beyond, depart' < *cedere* 'go']

SPELLCHECK See *accede.*

exceeding /ik séeding/ *adj* very great (*literary*) ○ *exceeding joy* ■ *adv* to an unusually high degree (*archaic*)

exceedingly /ik séedingli/ *adv* to an unusually high degree ○ *You've been exceedingly generous.*

excel /ik sél/ (**-cels, -celling, -celled**) *v* **1.** *vi* to be outstanding or have a particular talent in something ○ *excels in marketing* **2.** *vt* to do better than all others, than a given standard, or than previous personal achievement [15C. < Latin *excellere* 'rise above' < assumed *cellere* 'rise']

excellence /éksələnss/ *n* **1.** the quality or state of being outstanding and superior ○ *an award for excellence in photography* **2.** a feature or respect in which somebody or something is superior and outstanding

Excellency /éksələnssi/ (*plural* **-cies**), **Excellence** *n* a title and form of address for some high officials such as governors, ambassadors, and high-ranking Roman Catholic clergy

excellent /éksələnt/ *adj* of a very high quality or standard ■ *interj* used to show wholehearted approval or agreement [14C. Via French < Latin *excellent-* present participle of *excellere* (see EXCEL)] —**excellently** *adv*

excelsior /ek sélssi awr, ik-/ *n US* packing material made from wood shavings [Mid-19C. Originally proprietary name < Latin, 'higher']

except /ik sépt/ (**-cepts, -cepting, -cepted**) CORE MEANING: a grammatical word indicating the only person or thing that does not apply to a statement just made, or a fact that modifies the truth of that statement ○ (prep) *Every house in the street except ours is painted white.* ○ (prep) *I like all vegetables except cabbage.* ○ (conj) *The fires that annually sweep over the prairies prevent the growth of timber, except along the river courses.* ○ (conj) *He dislikes the game except when he wins.*

1. *prep* other than ○ *every house except ours* **2.** *conj* same as **unless** (*archaic*) **3.** *vt* to leave out or exclude somebody or something (*formal; usually passive*) [14C. < Latin *except-*, past participle of *excipere* 'take out' < *capere* 'take'] ◇ **except for** apart from ○ *He had always been healthy except for an irregular heartbeat.* ◇ **except that** with the exception of the fact that, or if it were not for the fact that ○ *The twins looked identical, except that one had dyed his hair.* ○ *I would come, except that I have another engagement.*

USAGE except, except for, or excepting: Often the question of whether to use ***except*** or ***except for*** is a matter of indifference: *We'd all seen the play except* [or *except for*] *Joe.* Where the exception is closely paired with what it is an exception to, ***except*** is more usual: *All of us except Joe had seen the play.* ***Except for*** is used where the connection to what is being excepted is indirect, and is also more common at the beginning of a sentence: *Except for that, we were in agreement.* ***Excepting*** is the correct choice after *not*: *She was the most important person in his life, not excepting his mother.*

USAGE See *accept.*

excepted /ik séptid/ *adj* with the exception of a particular person or thing ○ *present company excepted* ○ *'Hazel eyes excepted, two years more might make her all that he wished.'* (Jane Austen, *Emma*; 1816)

excepting /ik sépting/ *prep, conj* used to indicate the only person or thing excluded from a statement just made (*formal*)

USAGE See *except.*

exception /ik sépsh'n/ *n* **1.** SOMEBODY OR SOMETHING EXCLUDED somebody or something that is not included in or does not fit into a general rule, pattern, or judgment ○ *make an exception for family members* **2.** EXCLUSION the act or condition of being excluded **3.** CRITICISM a criticism, usually a negative one (*formal*) **4.** LAW LEGAL CLAUSE a clause in a legal document that limits the effect of a part or the whole of it ○ *has read through and approved all the exceptions* ◇ **take exception (to something)** to be annoyed or offended by something ◇ **the exception that proves the rule** something that, by being an exception, shows that a general rule exists

exceptionable /ik sépsh'nəb'l/ *adj* causing or liable to cause objection or offence (*formal*)

USAGE See *exceptional.*

exceptional /ik sépsh'nəl/ *adj* **1.** having or showing intelligence or ability well above average ○ *an exceptional talent* **2.** not conforming to a general rule or pattern ○ *exceptional circumstances* —**exceptionality** /ik sépshə nálləti/ *n* —**exceptionally** *adv*

USAGE exceptional or exceptionable? ***Exceptional*** is the more common word and refers, often favourably, to a person or thing unusual in some way: *She has exceptional powers of concentration.* However, ***exceptional*** is also used in a factual or neutral way: *Expenses can be reimbursed only in exceptional cases.* ***Exceptionable,*** despite its similar sound, has a very different meaning, referring to something that arouses disapproval or offence: *There was something in his manner that we found exceptionable.* More often, it is used in the negative form *unexceptionable,* meaning 'good enough to provide no reason for criticism or objection'.

exceptive /ik séptiv/ *adj* relating to or of the nature of an exception

excerpt *n* /éks urpt/ a section or passage taken from a longer work such as a book, film, musical composition, or document ■ *vt* /ek súrpt/ (**-cerpts, -cerpting, -cerpted**) to select a section or passage from a longer work (*usually passive*) [Mid-16C. < Latin *excerpt-*, past participle of *excerpere* 'pluck out' < *carpere* 'pluck'] —**excerptible** /ik súrptəb'l/ *adj* —**excerption** *n* —**excerptor** *n*

excess *n* /ik séss, éks ess/ **1.** SURPLUS an amount or quantity beyond what is considered proper, usual, or sufficient ○ *leaped up in an excess of enthusiasm* **2.** EXTRA the amount by which one quantity exceeds another **3.** UNRESTRAINED BEHAVIOUR behaviour or activity that goes beyond what is socially or morally acceptable, or beyond what is good for somebody's health or wellbeing ○ *led a life of excess* **4.** *UK, ANZ, Carib* INSUR MONEY PAID TOWARDS INSURANCE CLAIM a particular amount of money that a policy-holder must pay towards the cost of any insurance claim made ○ *an insurance policy with a £50 excess* N Am term **deductible** ■ *adj* /éks ess, ek séss/ **1.** MORE THAN ENOUGH more than is usual, required, or allowed ○ *excess capacity* **2.** REQUIRED IN ADDITION constituting or being required as an additional payment ○ *excess postage* ■ *vt* (**-cesses, -cessing, -cessed**) *US* DISMISS FROM EMPLOYMENT to dismiss an employee as part of a programme of redundancies ○ *was excessed in the most recent downsizing* [14C. Via French *excès* < Latin *excessus* < past participle of *excedere* (see EXCEED)] ◇ **to excess** beyond what is considered normal, sufficient, or healthy

SPELLCHECK See *access.*

excess baggage *n* luggage that is heavier than the amount a passenger is allowed to take on a flight without an extra charge

excess demand *n* demand for a product or service that outstrips the supply and so pushes the price up

excessive /ik séssiv/ *adj* beyond what is considered acceptable, proper, usual, or necessary ○ *excessive hilarity* —**excessively** *adv* —**excessiveness** *n*

excess luggage *n* TRAVEL same as **excess baggage**

excess supply *n* supply of a product or service that outstrips the demand and so pushes the price down

exch. *abbr* **1.** exchange **2.** POL exchequer

Exch. *abbr* POL Exchequer

exchange /iks cháynj/ *v* (**-changes, -changing, -changed**) **1.** *vt* GIVE SOMETHING AND GET SOMETHING to give something and receive something different in return ○ *exchange land for peace* ○ *exchange tokens for cash* **2.** *vti* SWAP to give something and receive another of the same or an equivalent in return ○ *exchange glances* **3.** *vt* REPLACE SOMETHING to hand something over and receive as a replacement something more suitable or more satisfactory ○ *exchanged her coat for one a size smaller* **4.** *vt* CHESS TAKE PIECE OF SIMILAR VALUE in chess, to take a piece in return for one, usually of similar value, that an opponent has just taken or will soon take ■ *n* **1.** GIVING AND RECEIVING the action or process or an instance of exchanging something for something else or for something the same ○ *an exchange of compliments* **2.** ARGUMENT a short conversation, often between two people or groups who are angry ○ *a bitter exchange* **3.** SOMETHING GIVEN OR RECEIVED something given or received in place of another **4.** EDUC ARRANGEMENT TO VISIT ANOTHER COUNTRY an arrangement between families, schools, or organizations in different countries for stays in each other's country **5.** FIN BUILDING USED FOR COMMERCIAL ACTIVITIES a building used as a centre for the trading of commodities, securities, or other assets **6.** FIN MONEY TRANSFER BETWEEN TWO CURRENCIES the transferring or a transfer of equal amounts of money between two currencies **7.** FIN SYSTEM OF PAYMENTS a system of payments in which commercial documents such as bills of exchange are used instead of money **8.** FIN FEE FOR PAYMENT the percentage or fee that is charged when paying in commercial documents instead of money **9.** TELECOM same as **telephone exchange** **10.** CHESS TAKING OF CHESS PIECES the taking of chess pieces of similar value by each player in consecutive or nearly consecutive moves **11.** PHYS TRANSFER OF PARTICLE the transfer of an elementary particle of one type between two others of a different type, creating a force [14C. < Old French < assumed Vulgar Latin *excambiare* < late Latin *cambiare* 'barter' (see CHANGE)] —**exchangeability** /iks cháynjə bílləti/ *n* —**exchangeable** *adj* —**exchanger** *n*

exchange force *n* a force existing between particles due to the transfer of another particle

exchange particle *n* a virtual particle that travels between elementary particles undergoing one of the four fundamental interactions, strong, weak, electromagnetic, and gravitational

exchange rate *n* the rate at which a unit of the currency of one country can be exchanged for a unit of the currency of another

Exchange Rate Mechanism *n* a system of controlling the exchange rate between some countries in the European Union that sets an agreed limit on the extent to which rates can fluctuate in relation to one another

exchange student *n* a student who studies in

another country as part of a programme in which students change places

exchequer /iks chékər/ *n* **1.** formerly in the United Kingdom and some other countries, the government department responsible for collecting taxes and managing public spending **2.** a national treasury or account, especially the UK government's account at the Bank of England, or the assets in it [13C. < Old French *eschequier* 'counting table, chessboard' < *eschec* 'check'; from the custom of counting royal revenue on a checked tablecloth]

Exchequer *n* **1.** POL, ECON another spelling of **exchequer 2.** LAW same as **Court of Exchequer**

excimer /ék sīmər/ *n* a stable atomic pair (**dimer**) in which one of the two bound atoms is in a higher energy state [Mid-20C. Contraction of *excited dimer*]

excipient /ik sípi ənt/ *n* an inert substance combined with a drug [Early 18C. < Latin *excipient-*, present participle of *excipere* 'take out' (see EXCEPT)]

excise[1] *n* /ék sīz/ **1.** TAX ON GOODS FOR HOME MARKET taxation of or a tax imposed on goods for a domestic market only **2.** LICENSING CHARGE a tax paid for a licence, such as one required to use a vehicle on public roads or to engage in some commercial activities ■ *vt* /ik sīz/ (**-cises, -cising, -cised**) TAX SOMEBODY OR SOMETHING to impose an excise on somebody or something [15C. Via Middle Dutch < Old French *acceis* 'tax, toll'] —**excisable** /ik sīzəb'l/ *adj*

excise[2] /ik sīz/ (**-cises, -cising, -cised**) *vt* **1.** to delete a part of something such as a text (*formal*) **2.** to remove something by cutting, especially in surgery [Late 16C. < Latin *excis-*, past participle of *excidere* 'to cut out' < *caedere* 'to cut'] —**excision** /ik sízh'n/ *n*

excised offshore places /ik sīzd-/ *npl Aus* outlying territories of Australia where, since September 2001, the automatic right of an arrival to apply for an Australian visa has been suspended

excise duty *n* tax imposed on goods intended for a domestic market only

exciseman /ék sīz man/ (*plural* **-men** /-men/) *n* formerly, somebody hired by the government to collect excise duty and prevent smuggling

excitable /ik sītəb'l/ *adj* **1.** nervous and liable to become quickly excited **2.** describes a nerve or tissue that is able to respond to a stimulus —**excitability** /ik sītə bílləti/ *n* —**excitableness** *n* —**excitably** *adv*

excitant /ik sītənt, éksitənt/ *n* a drug that stimulates or augments a response ■ *adj* tending to excite or stimulate something

excitation /éksi táysh'n, ék sī-/ *n* **1.** EXCITING the act or process of exciting something (*formal*) **2.** BEING EXCITED the state of being excited **3.** PHYSIOL ACTIVITY CAUSED BY STIMULATION the activity or altered condition produced in a cell, tissue, or organ as a result of stimulation **4.** ELEC ENG PRODUCTION OF MAGNETIC FIELD the production of a magnetic field in a generator or motor by passing electricity through the coil **5.** PHYS RAISING ENERGY OF ATOM the addition of sufficient energy to an electron, atom, atomic nucleus, or molecule to raise it from its lowest energy level (**ground state**) to a higher energy level **6.** ELECTRONICS APPLICATION OF SIGNAL MAKING TRANSISTOR OPERATE the application of an electrical signal to a device such as a transistor, causing it to operate —**excitatory** /ik sītətəri/ *adj*

excite /ik sīt/ (**-cites, -citing, -cited**) *v* **1.** *vti* STIMULATE FAVOURABLY to cause somebody to feel enjoyment or pleasurable anticipation ○ *a book with an opening that fails to excite* **2.** *vt* STIMULATE SOMEBODY UNFAVOURABLY to make a person or animal feel nervous apprehension or an unpleasant state of heightened emotion ○ *Don't excite the dog or he'll bite.* **3.** *vt* AROUSE EMOTION to cause somebody to feel a particular emotion or reaction ○ *excite suspicion* **4.** *vt* EVOKE SOMETHING IN MIND to cause a memory, thought, or other response to form in the mind ○ *an image that excited a memory* **5.** *vt* AROUSE SOMEBODY PHYSICALLY to cause somebody to feel physical desire **6.** *vt* PHYSIOL MAKE SOMETHING MORE ACTIVE to stimulate or increase the rate of activity of an organ, tissue, or other body part **7.** *vt* PHYS RAISE PARTICLE TO HIGHER ENERGY LEVEL to raise an electron, atom, atomic nucleus, or molecule above its lowest energy level (**ground state**) to a higher energy level **8.** *vt* ELEC ENG PRODUCE MAGNETIC FIELD IN ELECTRIC MACHINE to produce a magnetic field in a generator or motor by supplying electricity to the coil **9.** *vt* ELECTRONICS APPLY SIGNAL CAUSING DEVICE TO OPERATE to apply an electrical signal that will cause a device such as a transistor to operate [14C. Directly or via French < Latin *excitare* 'rouse' < *ciere* 'summon, set in motion'] —**excited** *adj* —**excitedly** *adv*

excited state *n* the condition of a physical system, especially of atoms and atomic nuclei, that has an energy level higher than the lowest possible level (**ground state**)

excitement /ik sītmənt/ *n* **1.** BEING EXCITED the feeling or condition of lively enjoyment or pleasant anticipation ○ *finding it difficult to contain her excitement* **2.** EXCITING SOMETHING the act or process of stimulating something ○ *excitement of electrons* **3.** EXCITING EVENT something that engages people's attention or emotions in a lively and compelling way ○ *Going in a helicopter was a great excitement for the children.*

exciter /ik sītər/ *n* **1.** CAUSE OF EXCITEMENT somebody or something that causes excitement **2.** ELEC ENG SMALL AUXILIARY GENERATOR a small generator or transmitter that provides the necessary energy to run a larger device or amplifier **3.** ELEC ENG ELECTRICAL OSCILLATOR an oscillator for supplying a radio transmitter with the basic wave that is modified to carry a radio signal

exciting /ik sīting/ *adj* causing feelings of happiness and enthusiasm or nervousness and tension —**excitingly** *adv*

exciton /éksi ton, ék sī ton/ *n* a mobile neutral combination of an electron in an excited state and a hole in a crystal. Exciton activity is important in semiconductors. [Mid-20C. < EXCITATION + -ON [1]]

excitotoxicity /éksitō tok síssəti/ *n* the degree to which a substance is believed to be toxic to nerve cells through excessive stimulation [Mid-20C. < EXCITER] —**excitotoxic** /éksitō tóksik/ *adj* —**excitotoxically** *adv*

excitotoxin /éksitō tóksin/ *n* a substance that is believed to kill or damage nerve cells through excessive stimulation [Late 20C. < EXCITER]

excl. *abbr* **1.** exclamation **2.** exclusive

exclaim /ik skláym/ (**-claims, -claiming, -claimed**) *vti* to speak or cry out loudly and suddenly, often through surprise, anger, or excitement [Late 16C. Directly or via French < Latin *exclamare* 'call out' < *clamare* 'call'] —**exclaimer** *n*

~~**exclaimation**~~ incorrect spelling of **exclamation**

exclamation /éksklə máysh'n/ *n* **1.** a word, phrase, or sentence that is shouted out suddenly, often through surprise, anger, or excitement ○ *an exclamation of horror* **2.** the act of crying out suddenly —**exclamational** *adj*

exclamation mark *n* **1.** a punctuation mark (!) used after an exclamation or interjection, and sometimes after a command **2.** a mark (!) used to indicate a road hazard or a mistake or point of note in a text, or as a mathematical or logical symbol ► N Am term **exclamation point**

USAGE The ***exclamation mark*** follows an expression of surprise, anger, admiration, pain, etc. which may or may not be a full sentence: *I couldn't believe my eyes! What a pity! Ouch!* It sometimes marks the end of a command or warning, especially in direct speech: *Come here! Look out!* The exclamation mark may be used for effect in creative writing or informal letters, but should not be overused. It is not normally used at all in formal writing. It should never be immediately preceded or followed by a full stop, but it may occasionally be used with a question mark in informal letters or e-mails to indicate exasperation or disbelief, especially in posing a rhetorical question: *How many times do I have to tell you?!*

---

exclamatory /ik sklámmətəri/ *adj* marked by or involving an exclamation or exclamations —**exclamatorily** *adv*

exclaustration /éks klaw stráysh'n/ *n* the return of a monk or nun to lay life after relinquishing vows [Mid-20C. < modern Latin *exclaustration-* 'putting out of the enclosed space' < Latin *claustrum* (see CLOISTER)]

exclave /éks klayv/ *n* a part of a country that is isolated from the main body of the country, being surrounded by foreign territory [Late 19C. < EX- [1] + ENCLAVE]

exclosure /eks klṓzhər/ *n* an area fenced in to keep out animals or intruders

exclude /ik sklóod/ (**-cludes, -cluding, -cluded**) *vt* **1.** KEEP SOMEBODY OR SOMETHING OUT to prevent somebody or something from entering or participating ○ *I felt excluded from the family celebrations.* **2.** REJECT SOMEBODY OR SOMETHING to prevent somebody or something from being considered or accepted ○ *cannot exclude the possibility of treason* **3.** OMIT SOMETHING OR SOMEBODY to fail to include something or somebody ○ *Three names were inadvertently excluded from the list.* **4.** EDUC BAN SCHOOLCHILD to ban a child from attending school on disciplinary grounds for a temporary, indefinite, or permanent period [14C. < Latin *excludere* 'to shut out' < *claudere* 'to shut'] —**excludability** /ik sklóodə bílləti/ *n* —**excludable** *adj* —**excluder** *n*

excluding /ik sklóoding/ *prep* used to mention items that are not being included or considered ○ *a annual income of £2 million, excluding the profits from overseas investments*

exclusion /ik sklóozh'n/ *n* **1.** EXCLUDING the act of excluding something or somebody **2.** BEING EXCLUDED the state of being excluded, especially from mainstream society and its advantages ○ *addressing the issue of social exclusion* **3.** EXCLUDED PERSON OR THING somebody or something that has been excluded [15C. < Latin *exclusion-* < *exclus-*, past participle of *excludere* (see EXCLUDE)] —**exclusionary** *adj*

exclusionary rule *n* a law that prevents illegally obtained evidence from being used in a criminal trial

exclusionist /ik sklóozh'nist/ *US adj* **1.** DISCRIMINATORY describes a policy that excludes individual people or groups from areas or rights and privileges **2.** PROTECTIONIST describes a policy that excludes specific imports or forms of commerce ■ *n* EXCLUSION ADVOCATE a supporter of exclusionist policies —**exclusionism** *n* —**exclusionistic** /ik sklóozh'n ístik/ *adj*

exclusion principle *n* QUANTUM PHYS same as **Pauli exclusion principle**

exclusion zone *n* **1.** an area where an authority has banned a particular activity **2.** an area that is out of bounds to people because a hazardous substance has been released ○ *the Chernobyl exclusion zone*

exclusive /ik sklóossiv/ *adj* **1.** HIGH-CLASS limited to a group of people, especially one considered fashionable or wealthy ○ *an exclusive club* **2.** SELECTIVE excluding or intending to exclude many from participation or consideration **3.** RESTRICTED IN USE only available to or used by one person, group, or organization ○ *Members have exclusive use of the pool.* **4.** APPEARING IN ONE PLACE published or broadcast in only one place ○ *exclusive coverage* **5.** SOLE being the only one **6.** EXCLUDING OTHER THINGS focused or targeted on one thing only ○ *exclusive attention* **7.** NOT INCLUDING STATED NUMBERS not including the numbers, dates, or other series members mentioned immediately before ○ *from 8 July to 17 July exclusive* ◊ **inclusive** (sense 1) **8.** COMM RESTRICTING TRADE restricting trade in some goods or services only to those who have signed the contract or agreement **9.** LOGIC WHERE BOTH CANNOT BE TRUE describes a proposition (**disjunction**) where one alternative rules out the other, e.g. being an odd number rules out the possibility of being an even number. ◊ **inclusive** (sense 6) ■ *n* REPORT IN ONE PUBLICATION OR PROGRAMME a news report or article that is printed in only one publication or broadcast on only one channel ○ *an exclusive on the wedding* [15C. < medieval Latin *exclusivus* < Latin *exclus-*, past participle of *excludere* (see EXCLUDE)] —**exclusively** *adv* —**exclusiveness** *n* —**exclusivity** /ék skloo sívvəti/ *n* ◇ **exclusive of** not including ○ *The price covers all your holiday costs, exclusive of travel insurance.*

exclusivism /ik sklóossivizəm/ *n* the practice or policy of being exclusive or excluding others —**exclusivist** *n, adj*

excogitate /eks kójji tayt/ (**-tates, -tating, -tated**) *vt* to consider or think about something carefully and thoroughly (*formal*) [Early 16C. < Latin *excogitat-*, past participle of *excogitare* 'think out' < *cogitare* 'think' (see COGITATE)] —**excogitable** *adj*

excommunicate vt /ékskə myoóni kayt/ (-cates, -cating, -cated) EXCLUDE SOMEBODY FROM CHRISTIAN COMMUNITY to exclude a baptized Christian from taking part in Communion because of doctrine or moral behaviour that is adjudged to offend against God or the Christian community ■ adj /ékskə myoónikət, -kayt/ EXCOMMUNICATED having been officially excluded from taking part in Communion ■ n /ékskə myoónikət, -kayt/ EXCOMMUNICATED PERSON somebody who has been formally excluded from taking part in Communion [15C. < late Latin *excommunicat-*, past participle of *excommunicare* 'put out of the community' < Latin *communis* 'common'] —**excommunicable** adj — **excommunication** /ékskə myoóni káysh'n/ n —**ex-communicative** adj —**excommunicator** n

ex-con /éks kón/ n same as **ex-convict** (informal) [Early 20C. Shortening]

ex-convict n somebody who has served time in prison

excoriate /ik skáwri ayt, -skórri-/ (-ates, -ating, -ated) vt 1. to severely criticize somebody or something (formal) ○ *The paper excoriated the government's conduct in this case.* 2. MED to remove skin from a person or animal [15C. < Latin *excoriat-*, past participle of *excoriare* 'strip off the hide' < *corium* 'hide, skin'] —**excoriation** /ik skáwri áysh'n, -skórri-/ n —**excoriator** n

excrement /ékskrimənt/ n waste material, particularly faeces, discharged from the body (technical) [Mid-16C. < Latin *excrementum* < *excretus*, past participle of *excernere* (see EXCRETE)] —**excremental** /ékskri mént'l/ adj

excrescence /ik skréss'nss/ n 1. a growth that sticks out from the body of a human, animal, or plant 2. an ugly addition or extension to something such as a building

excrescent /ik skréss'nt/ adj 1. SUPERFLUOUS added or growing out unnecessarily (formal) 2. BIOL RELATING TO OUTGROWTH relating to or like an outgrowth on an organism 3. LING ADDED IN SPEAKING describes a speech sound that occurs in a word to allow ease of pronunciation [15C. < Latin *excrescent-*, present participle of *excrescere* 'grow out' < *crescere* 'grow'] —**excrescently** adv

excreta /ik skreétə/ npl any waste matter discharged from the body, e.g. faeces or urine (technical) [Mid-19C. < Latin, 'things excreted' < form of past participle of *excernere* (see EXCRETE)] —**excretal** adj

excrete /ik skreét/ (-cretes, -creting, -creted) vt 1. to isolate and discharge waste matter generated during metabolism, e.g. through urinating or defecating (formal) 2. to eliminate waste matter from leaves and roots [Early 17C. < Latin *excret-*, past participle of *excernere* 'separate out, discharge' < *cernere* 'to separate'] —**excreter** n —**excretory** adj

excretion /ik skreésh'n/ n 1. the act or process of discharging waste matter from the tissues or organs 2. waste matter that has been discharged from an animal or a plant

excruciate /ik skroóshi ayt/ (-ates, -ating, -ated) vt (formal) 1. to inflict severe mental and emotional distress on somebody 2. to inflict physical pain on somebody [Late 16C. < Latin *excruciat-*, past participle of *excruciare* 'torture thoroughly' < *cruciare* 'torture, crucify' < *cruc-* 'cross'] —**excruciation** /ik skroóshi áysh'n/ n

excruciating /ik skroóshi ayting/ adj 1. extremely painful, physically or emotionally 2. intolerably embarrassing, tedious, or irritating ○ *The first act was bad enough, but the second was just excruciating.* —**excruciatingly** adv

exculpate /éks kul payt, iks kúl payt/ (-pates, -pating, -pated) vt to free somebody from blame or accusation of guilt (formal) [Mid-17C. < medieval Latin *exculpat-*, past participle of *exculpare* 'remove from blame' < Latin *culpa* 'blame'] —**exculpable** /iks kúlpəb'l/ adj —**exculpation** /éks kul páysh'n/ n

exculpatory /ik skúlpətəri/ adj tending to prove that somebody is free from guilt or blame (formal) ○ *exculpatory evidence*

excursion /ik skúrsh'n, -skúrzh'n/ n 1. SHORT TRIP a short trip to a place and back, for pleasure or a purpose 2. GROUP ON SHORT TRIP a group of people who are taking a short trip 3. DIGRESSION a temporary deviation from a regular course or pattern ○ *After an unsuccessful excursion into banking, he returned to public life.* 4.

PHYS ALTERNATING MOTION an oscillating or alternating motion away from a point of equilibrium and back 5. PHYS DISTANCE COVERED a distance that an oscillating body moves away from the point of equilibrium 6. PHYSIOL MOVEMENT OF BODY PART the movement of a part or organ of the body, e.g. the lungs, from the resting position to another position [Late 16C. < Latin *excursion-* < *excurs-*, past participle of *excurrere* 'run out' < *currere* 'to run']

CULTURAL NOTE *The Excursion*, a poem (1814) by the English poet William Wordsworth. Originally intended to be part of a philosophical work called *The Recluse*, it describes the poet's travels with a character called The Wanderer. On their way they meet Solitary, who has lost faith in human nature, and the Pastor, who describes the rewards of virtue.

excursionist /ik skúrsh'nist, -skúrzh'n-/ n somebody who goes on an excursion, especially for pleasure (dated)

excursive /ik skúrssiv/ adj tending to digress from the main topic, often in a rambling and wordy manner (formal) [Late 17C. < obsolete *excurse* 'digress' < Latin *excurs-* (see EXCURSION)] —**excursively** adv —**excursiveness** n

excursus /ek skúrssəss/ (plural -suses or same) n a lengthy digression from the main topic (formal) [Early 19C. < Latin, 'excursion' < *excurs-* (see EXCURSION)]

excusatory /ik skyoózətəri/ adj tending or serving to excuse somebody or something (formal)

excuse v /ik skyoóz/ (-cuses, -cusing, -cused) 1. vt FORGIVE SOMETHING to release somebody from blame or criticism for a mistake or wrongdoing ○ *excuse their tardiness* 2. vt OVERLOOK SOMETHING to make allowances for somebody or something ○ *Please excuse my spelling.* 3. vt RELEASE SOMEBODY FROM OBLIGATION to release somebody from an obligation or responsibility ○ *was excused from games because of a sprained ankle* 4. vt JUSTIFY SOMETHING to provide a reason or explanation for somebody's behaviour that makes it appear more acceptable or less offensive ○ *That doesn't excuse the way he acted last night.* 5. vt ALLOW SOMEBODY TO LEAVE to allow somebody to leave, or say politely that somebody should leave ○ *asked if he could be excused* 6. **excuse yourself** vr APOLOGIZE FOR LEAVING to leave with a polite apology or explanation ○ *excused herself and left the room* ■ n /ik skyoóss/ 1. JUSTIFICATION a reason or explanation, not necessarily true, given in order to make something appear more acceptable or less offensive ○ *There can be no excuse for laziness.* 2. FALSE REASON a false reason that enables somebody to do something he or she wants to do or avoid something he or she does not want to do ○ *the perfect excuse to do nothing* 3. BAD EXAMPLE an inept performer of a particular action or task (informal) ○ *a poor excuse for a cook* 4. N Am HR same as **sick note** [15C. Via French < Latin *excusare* 'remove from accusation' < *causa* 'accusation'] —**excusable** adj —**excusableness** n —**excusably** adv —**excuser** n ◇ **excuse me** 1. used to attract attention politely, e.g. when asking somebody to move aside or when interrupting somebody 2. used to apologize for doing something rude or embarrassing, e.g. belching 3. used to indicate politely that you disagree with something or think that it is incorrect 4. N Am used to ask somebody to repeat what he or she has just said because you did not hear it properly or did not understand it

excuse-me, **excuse-me dance** n a dance in which participants interrupt other pairs to invite a change of partner

ex-directory adj UK not included in a telephone directory available to the public. ANZ, N Am term **unlisted**

ex dividend adv, adj without the right to the current dividend on purchase

exe /éksi/ abbr a file extension for a program file. Full form **executable**

exeat /éksi at/ n 1. a short leave of absence from a boarding school or similar institution, usually lasting a day or a weekend 2. formal leave to move to a new diocese, granted by a bishop to a priest [Early 18C. < Latin, 'let him or her go out', form of *exire* (see EXIT)]

exec /ig zék/ n an executive or executive officer (informal) [Late 19C. Shortening]

execrable /éksikrəb'l/ adj 1. extremely bad, or of very low quality ○ *has execrable taste* 2. deserving to be detested ○ *execrable behaviour* [14C. Via French < Latin *execrabilis* < *execrari* (see EXECRATE)] —**execrably** adv

execrate /éksi krayt/ (-crates, -crating, -crated) v (literary or formal) 1. vt DETEST SOMEBODY OR SOMETHING to feel loathing for somebody or something 2. vt DENOUNCE SOMEBODY OR SOMETHING to declare somebody or something to be loathsome 3. vti CURSE SOMEBODY OR SOMETHING to curse or put a curse on somebody or something [Mid-16C. < Latin *execrari* 'undo consecration' < *sacrare* (see SACRED)] —**execrative** adj —**execrator** n

execration /éksi kráysh'n/ n (literary or formal) 1. CURSE a curse or swearword ○ *'With an execration the thoroughly terrified robber threw down the pocketbook, and the relieved owner hastened forward to pick it up.'* (Horatio Alger, Jr., *Struggling Upward*; 1868) 2. SOMETHING CURSED something that is cursed or detested 3. EXECRATING the act of execrating somebody or something, or the state of being execrated

executable /éksi kyootəb'l/ adj describes a computer file, often carrying the extension .exe, that can be run as a program —**executable** n

executant /ig zékyoótənt/ n a usually skilled performer of a musical, dance, or theatre piece (formal)

execute /éksi kyoot/ (-cutes, -cuting, -cuted) v 1. vt CARRY OUT INTENTION to put an instruction or plan into effect 2. vt PERFORM ACTION to complete an action or movement, especially one requiring skill 3. vt CREATE ART to produce or create something, usually a work of art, to a specific design ○ *execute a drawing* 4. vt PUT TO DEATH to kill somebody as part of a judicial or extrajudicial process 5. vti COMPUT RUN ON COMPUTER to run a computer file or program in response to a command or instruction 6. vt LAW CARRY OUT TERMS OF LEGAL DOCUMENT to carry out the terms laid out in a will, legal document, or legal decision ○ *execute a sentence* 7. vt LAW SIGN LEGAL DOCUMENT BEFORE WITNESSES to sign a will or other legal document in the presence of witnesses in order to make it binding [14C. < Latin *execut-*, past participle of *exsequi* 'follow out' < *sequi* 'follow']

SYNONYMS See **kill** and **perform**.

execution /éksi kyoósh'n/ n 1. KILLING the killing of somebody as part of a judicial or extrajudicial process 2. PERFORMING OF SOMETHING the carrying out of an action, instruction, command, or movement ○ *a plan that failed in execution* 3. MANNER OF PERFORMANCE the style or manner in which something is carried out or accomplished 4. LAW CARRYING OUT OF LEGAL PROVISIONS the carrying out of the provisions of a legal document such as a will or contract 5. LAW ENFORCEMENT OF COURT JUDGMENT the carrying out or enforcing of a judgment made in court 6. LAW WRIT a legal writ that orders the carrying out of a judgment or decision

executioner /éksi kyoósh'nər/ n 1. an official who puts to death somebody who has been sentenced to capital punishment 2. a hired assassin

execution time n the amount of time needed for a complete run of a computer program routine

executive /ig zékyoótiv/ n 1. SENIOR MANAGER a senior manager in a company or organization, whose job it is to make and implement major decisions 2. GOVERNMENT SECTION RESPONSIBLE FOR DECISIONS the section of a country's government that is responsible for implementing legislative decisions 3. COMMITTEE THAT MAKES DECISIONS a committee or group in a political organization that makes decisions and has the authority to implement them ○ *the executive of the Transport Union* ■ adj 1. OF POLICYMAKING responsible for or relating to the making and implementing of general decisions in a company, organization, or government ○ *a meeting of the executive committee* 2. FOR BUSINESSPEOPLE restricted to or designed to be used by businessmen and businesswomen ○ *the executive suite* 3. VERY EXPENSIVE very expensive and so only affordable by those who earn high salaries ○ *executive homes* [15C. < Old French *executif* < *executer* 'carry out' < Latin *execut-* (see EXECUTE)] —**executively** adv

executive agreement n an agreement between a US president and a foreign head of state that has not been given approval by the Senate

Executive Council *n* **1.** in Australia and New Zealand, a body made up of the Governor-General or Governor and government ministers. It meets in order to brief the Governor-General or Governor on policies and formally approve government appointments and legislation. **2.** in Canada, the cabinet of a provincial government

executive director *n* a director of a company who is employed by the company in a senior management position

executive jet *n* a small jet aircraft designed for private use, especially one used to transport corporate executives

executive lounge *n* a lounge in an airport or hotel for the use of people who are travelling first-class

Executive Mansion *n* POL same as **White House** (sense 1)

executive officer *n* **1.** somebody in a senior management position in an organization **2.** a military or naval officer who is second in command of a unit

executive privilege *n* the right of the US president and other government officials in the executive branch to refuse to reveal confidential material if this would interfere with the administration's ability to govern

executive producer *n* **1.** the head producer in charge of other producers at a film or television studio **2.** the producer who handles the finances for a film

executive secretary *n* **1.** a secretary who reports to a senior manager or executive in a company **2.** a senior official who handles an organization's business affairs

executive session *n* a meeting of the US Senate, closed to the public, to discuss confidential government business such as judicial appointments or the ratification of treaties

executive toy *n* a small but usually sophisticated and expensive toy marketed as suitable for an executive's desk and used to aid concentration or relieve stress

executor /ig zékyŏŏtər/ *n* **1.** somebody named in a will or appointed by a court to carry out the instructions contained in a will **2.** somebody who performs an action or task [13C. Via Anglo-Norman < Latin < *execut-* (see EXECUTE)] —**executorial** /ig zékyŏŏ táwri əl/ *adj* — **executorship** *n*

executory /ig zékyŏŏtəri/ *adj* **1.** coming into effect at a future time or in accordance with circumstances **2.** relating to the task or process of carrying out laws, policies, or instructions [15C. < late Latin *executorius* < Latin *executor* (see EXECUTOR)]

exedra /éksidrə, ek séedrə/ *n* **1.** FURNITURE **LONG CURVED OUTDOOR BENCH** a long curved or semicircular outdoor bench, usually with a high back **2.** ANCIENT HIST **CONVERSATION ROOM** in ancient Greece and Rome, a room for relaxation or conversation, especially a semicircular recess in a larger hall with a continuous bench along the wall **3.** ARCHIT **RECESS** a recess or niche (*technical*) [Early 18C. Via Latin < Greek, 'outside seat' < *hedra* 'seat']

exegesis /éksi jéessiss/ (*plural* -**geses** /-jée seez/) *n* **1.** the explanation or interpretation of texts, especially religious writings **2.** an explanation or interpretation of a specific text, especially a religious one [Early 17C. < Greek *exēgēsis* < *exēgeisthai* 'interpret' < *hēgeisthai* 'to guide']

exegete /éksi jeet/ *n* a student and interpreter of texts, especially religious writings [Mid-18C. < Greek *exēgētes* < *exēgeisthai* (see EXEGESIS)]

exegetic /éksi jéttik/, **exegetical** /-jéttik'l/ *adj* **1.** relating to the study and interpretation of texts, especially religious writings **2.** intended to explain or interpret something, especially a written text (*formal*) [Early 17C. < Greek *exēgetikos* < *exēgeisthai* (see EXEGESIS)] —**exegetically** *adv*

exegetics /éksi jéttiks/ *n* the branch of theology dealing with the study and interpretation of religious writings (*takes a singular verb*)

exegetist /éksi jéetist/ *n* RELIG same as **exegete**

~~exellent~~ incorrect spelling of **excellent**

exempla plural of **exemplum**

exemplar /ig zém plaar, -plər/ *n* **1.** IDEAL an ideal example of something, worthy of being copied or imitated (*literary*) ○ *Michelangelo's 'David' is an exemplar of Renaissance sculpture.* **2.** TYPICAL EXAMPLE a typical example or instance of something (*literary*) **3.** COPY OF BOOK a copy of a book or text, especially one from which further copies have originated [15C. Directly or via French < late Latin *exemplarium* < Latin *exemplum* (see EXAMPLE)]

exemplary /ig zémpləri/ *adj* **1.** SETTING EXAMPLE so good or admirable that others would do well to copy it ○ *the child's exemplary conduct* **2.** SERVING AS EXAMPLE designed to serve as a warning to others ○ *exemplary punishment* **3.** GIVING EXAMPLE serving as an illustration or example of something (*formal*) [Late 16C. < late Latin *exemplaris* < Latin *exemplum* (see EXAMPLE)] —**exemplarily** *adv* —**exemplariness** *n* —**exemplarity** /ég zem plárrəti/ *n*

exemplary damages *npl* legal damages well above the value of the loss suffered, awarded to punish the offender and deter others

exemplify /ig zémpli fī/ (-**fies**, -**fying**, -**fied**) *vt* **1.** BE EXAMPLE OF SOMETHING to show or illustrate something by being a typical or model example of it ○ *He exemplified all the qualities of a natural leader.* **2.** GIVE EXAMPLE OF SOMETHING to give an example or examples in order to make something clearer or more convincing ○ *Perhaps you could exemplify your point with a few statistics.* **3.** LAW MAKE COPY OF DOCUMENT to make an official copy of a legal document [15C. < medieval Latin *exemplificare* < Latin *exemplum* (see EXAMPLE)] —**exemplifiable** *adj* —**exemplification** /ig zémplifi káysh'n/ *n* —**exemplifier** *n*

exempli gratia /eg zém plī grááti aa/ *adv* full form of **e.g.** [Mid-17C. < Latin, 'for example's sake']

exemplum /ig zémpləm/ (*plural* -**pla** /-plə/) *n* **1.** a brief story told to illustrate a moral point or support an argument **2.** an example or illustration (*literary*) [Late 19C. < Latin (see EXAMPLE)]

exempt /ig zémpt/ *adj* NOT SUBJECT TO SOMETHING freed from or not subject to something such as a duty, tax, or military service that is required of others ○ *tax-exempt savings accounts* ○ *Students were exempt from service in the armed forces.* ■ *vt* (-**empts**, -**empting**, -**empted**) **1.** FREE SOMEBODY FROM OBLIGATION to allow or entitle somebody not to do something that others are obliged to do **2.** RELEASE SOMETHING FROM RULE to release something from a rule that applies to others ○ *a law that exempts certain capital gains from taxes* ■ *n* EXEMPTED PERSON OR THING somebody or something that is exempt from something [14C. Directly or via French < Latin *exempt-*, past participle of *eximere* (see EXAMPLE)] —**exemptible** *adj*

exemption /ig zémpsh'n/ *n* **1.** permission or entitlement not to do something that others are obliged to do **2.** somebody or something that is exempt, e.g. income that is not taxed ○ *a range of tax exemptions*

exenterate /ig zéntə rayt/ (-**ates**, -**ating**, -**ated**) *vt* to remove surgically all the organs and other contents of a body cavity, usually to minimize the spread of cancer [Early 17C. < Latin *exenterat-*, past participle of *exenterare*, alteration of Greek *exenterizein* 'remove the intestine' < *enteron* 'intestine'] —**exenteration** /ig zéntə ráysh'n/ *n*

~~exept~~ incorrect spelling of **except**

exequies /éksikwiz/ *npl* a funeral ceremony (*formal*) [14C. Via French < Latin *exsequias* 'funeral procession, obsequies' < *exsequi* 'accompany to the grave' (see EXECUTE)]

exercise /éksər sīz/ *n* **1.** PHYSICAL ACTIVITY physical activity and movement, especially when intended to keep a person or animal fit and healthy ○ *Regular exercise is important.* **2.** PHYSICAL MOVEMENT a physical movement or action, or a series of movements or actions, designed to make the body stronger and fitter or to show off gymnastic skill (*often used in the plural*) ○ *warm-up exercises* **3.** PRACTICE OF SKILL OR PROCEDURE a series of actions, movements, or tasks performed repeatedly or regularly as a way of practising and improving a skill or procedure (*often used in the plural*) ○ *voice exercises for singers* **4.** EDUC PIECE OF WORK a piece of work intended to test somebody's knowledge or skill ○ *Test yourself by doing the exercises at the back of the book.* **5.** MIL MILITARY TRAINING OPERATIONS OR MANOEUVRES a set of extensive operations or manoeuvres, usually under simulated combat conditions, intended to train military personnel, test their equipment, and assess their capabilities **6.** ACTIVITY INTENDED TO ACHIEVE PURPOSE an action, activity, or undertaking intended to achieve a specific purpose ○ *The object of the exercise is to make money fast.* **7.** CARRYING OUT OR USING SOMETHING the carrying out or making use of something such as a choice, duty, responsibility, or right (*formal*) ○ *We urge the exercise of patience and restraint.* ■ **exercises** *npl* N Am TRADITIONAL CEREMONIES ceremonies and speeches constituting a formal event ○ *graduation exercises* ■ *v* (-**cises**, -**cising**, -**cised**) **1.** *vi* TAKE EXERCISE to undertake physical exercise in order to keep fit and healthy **2.** *vt* SUBJECT BODY TO PHYSICAL EXERTION to subject the body, or part of it, to repetitive physical exertion or energetic movement in order to strengthen it or improve its condition ○ *a routine designed to exercise your back and thigh muscles* **3.** *vt* EXERT ANIMAL PHYSICALLY to make an animal exert itself physically in order to keep it healthy and fit **4.** *vt* PRACTISE AND DEVELOP SKILL to develop a particular faculty or skill by carrying out specific tasks or procedures repeatedly or systematically **5.** *vt* PUT SOMETHING TO PRACTICAL USE to make use of a right or responsibility ○ *They have the power to prevent the merger, if they choose to exercise it.* **6.** *vt* SHOW TYPE OF BEHAVIOUR to adopt a type of behaviour or a quality of character when dealing with a situation ○ *Exercise extreme care in your dealings with them.* **7.** *vt* OCCUPY OR WORRY SOMEBODY to be a cause for serious thought, worry, or anxiety (*formal*) ○ *It is not a question that has exercised me greatly in the past.* **8.** *vti* MIL TAKE PART IN MILITARY TRAINING OPERATIONS to take part in, or make troops take part in, large-scale operations or manoeuvres as part of combat training [14C. Via French < Latin *exercitium* < *exercere* 'keep busy' < *arcere* 'restrain'] —**exercisable** *adj*

exercise ball *n* a large inflated ball used in exercises to strengthen muscles and improve flexibility and balance

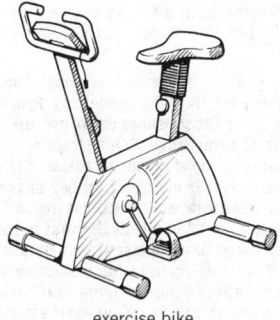

exercise bike

exercise bike, **exercise bicycle** *n* a fitness machine in the form of a stationary bicycle that is pedalled vigorously for exercise

exercise book *n* **1.** a book containing exercises in a subject for students to complete **2.** a book containing blank pages for school students to write or draw on

exercise price *n* the price at which the holder of stock options or warrants has the right to buy or sell

exerciser /éksər sīzər/ *n* **1.** a piece of equipment used to exercise all or part of the body **2.** somebody who performs physical exercises or who exercises something, especially somebody hired to exercise racehorses

~~exercize~~ incorrect spelling of **exercise**

exergonic /éksər gónnik/ *adj* describes a spontaneous biochemical reaction that releases energy [Mid-20C. < EX-[1] + Greek *ergon* 'work']

exergue /ek súrg, éks urg/ *n* the part of a coin or medal that carries secondary details such as the date and place of minting [Late 17C. Via French < medieval Latin *exergum* < Greek *ex-* 'outside' + *ergon* 'work']

~~exerpt~~ incorrect spelling of **excerpt**

exert /ig zúrt/ (-**erts**, -**erting**, -**erted**) *v* **1.** *vt* to apply influence, pressure, or authority in an attempt to

have a powerful effect on a situation **2. exert yourself** *vr* to make a strenuous physical or mental effort ○ *The doctor has told him not to exert himself in any way.* [Mid-17C. < Latin *ex(s)ert-*, past participle of *ex(s)erere* 'thrust out, put forth' < *serere* 'join, plait, entwine']

exertion /ig zúrsh'n/ *n* **1. STRENUOUS EFFORT** strenuous exercise or effort **2. STRENUOUS ACTION** an action that involves strenuous effort (*often used in the plural*) ○ *After his exertions in the garden, he felt he deserved a rest.* **3. BRINGING OF SOMETHING TO BEAR** the application of pressure or influence (*formal*) ○ *the exertion of pressure on unsuspecting clients*

Exeter /éksitər/ historic cathedral city on the River Exe in Devon, southwestern England. Population: 111,076 (2001).

exeunt /éksi unt, éks ay ənt/ *vi* used as a stage direction in a text in place of 'exit' when more than one actor is to leave the stage. ◊ **exit** *n* (sense 6), *v* (sense 4) [15C. < Latin, 'they go out', form of *exire* (see EXIT)]

exfoliant /eks fṓli ənt/ *n* a cosmetic cream or lotion designed to remove dead skin

exfoliate /eks fṓli ayt/ (**-ates, -ating, -ated**) *vti* **1.** to scrub skin with a gritty substance to remove the dead surface layer **2.** to remove or shed a thin outer layer from something such as a mineral or a bone during surgery [Mid-17C. < late Latin *exfoliat-*, past participle of *exfoliare* 'take leaves from' < Latin *folium* 'leaf'] —**exfoliation** /eks fṓli áysh'n/ *n* —**exfoliative** *adj* —**exfoliator** *n*

ex gratia /eks gráyshə/ *adj, adv* given as a gift, favour, or gesture of goodwill, rather than because it is owed ○ *an ex gratia payment* [Mid-18C. < Latin, 'out of kindness']

exhalation /éks hə láysh'n/ *n* **1. BREATH FROM LUNGS** a breath exhaled from the lungs **2. BREATHING OUT** the act of breathing out **3. SCENT OR VAPOUR GIVEN OFF** a scent, a vapour, or fumes given off by something (*literary*)

exhale /eks háyl, eg záyl/ (**-hales, -haling, -haled**) *v* **1.** *vti* to breathe out, or breathe something out **2.** *vt* to give off something such as a smell or a vapour (*literary*) [14C. Via French < Latin *exhalare* < *halare* 'breathe']

exhaust /ig záwst/ *v* (**-hausts, -hausting, -hausted**) **1.** *vt* **TIRE SOMEBODY OUT** to make somebody feel very tired or weak **2.** *vt* **USE SOMETHING UP** to use up all that is available of something ○ *Our supplies of fuel were now exhausted.* **3.** *vt* **TRY OUT ALL POSSIBILITIES** to try out or consider every one of a number of possibilities **4.** *vt* **SAY EVERYTHING ABOUT SOMETHING** to say or write everything about something, so that nothing is left to be discussed **5.** *vt* **DRAIN SOMETHING OF ITS RESOURCES** to draw off or use up all the resources contained within something ○ *over-grazing that has exhausted the pasture* **6.** *vti* INDUST **LET OUT WASTE GASES** to escape, or allow steam or waste gases to escape, at the end of an industrial process ○ *Waste gases are exhausted through the flue.* **7.** *vt* PHYS **REMOVE GAS TO CREATE VACUUM** to remove all of the air or gas from a container in order to create a vacuum inside it ■ *n* **1. DISCHARGE OF WASTE GASES** the discharge of waste gases, vapour, and fumes created by and released at the end of a process, especially from the working of an internal-combustion engine **2. ESCAPE SYSTEM FOR WASTE GASES** a pipe or other piece of apparatus through which waste gases escape [Mid-16C. < Latin *exhaust-*, past participle of *exhaurire* 'draw out' < *haurire* 'draw (water) out or up, drain'] —**exhausted** *adj* —**exhauster** *n* —**exhaustibility** /ig záwstə bílləti/ *n* —**exhaustible** *adj*

exhaustion /ig záwsch'n/ *n* **1.** a state of extreme physical or mental tiredness or collapse ○ *After five hours' walking in the heat, he was close to exhaustion.* **2.** the process of using up the entire stock or contents of something (*formal*) ○ *The aid agency fears the imminent exhaustion of food reserves.* [Early 17C. < Latin *exhaustion-* < *exhaust-* (see EXHAUST)]

exhaustive /ig záwstiv/ *adj* involving or dealing with everything relevant to the matter in hand ○ *an exhaustive account of the author's life* —**exhaustively** *adv* —**exhaustiveness** *n*

exhaust pipe *n* a pipe that allows waste gases to escape from a vehicle's engine. N Am term **tailpipe**

exhibit /ig zíbbit/ *v* (**-its, -iting, -ited**) **1.** *vti* **DISPLAY ART** to display something, especially a work of art, in a public place such as a museum or gallery **2.** *vt* **SHOW SOMETHING TO OTHERS** to show something off for others to look at or admire ○ *She decided it was a good time to exhibit her skills as a negotiator.* **3.** *vt* **REVEAL QUALITY** to show the outward signs of something, especially an emotion or a physical or mental condition (*formal*) ○ *The wings exhibited signs of metal fatigue.* **4.** *vt* LAW **GIVE SOMETHING AS EVIDENCE** to present something to be used as evidence in a court of law ■ *n* **1. OBJECT ON DISPLAY** an object displayed in public, especially in a museum or gallery or for a show or competition **2.** ARTS same as **exhibition** (sense 1) **3.** LAW **PIECE OF EVIDENCE** an object or document presented or identified as evidence in a court of law [15C. Partly < Latin *exhibere* 'hold out, display' < *habere* 'hold'; partly back-formation < EXHIBITION] —**exhibitory** *adj*

exhibition /éksi bísh'n/ *n* **1. PUBLIC DISPLAY OF WORKS OF ART** a public display, usually for a limited period, of a collection of works of art or objects of special interest **2. DISPLAYING OF SOMETHING** the displaying of something in public ○ *one or two of the works on exhibition* **3. DEMONSTRATION OF SKILL** a demonstration of a particular skill or craft ○ *a karate exhibition* **4. DISPLAY OF BEHAVIOUR** a display of a particular type of behaviour, usually bad behaviour ○ *an embarrassing exhibition of greed* **5.** EDUC **SCHOOL'S GRANT TO STUDENT** a sum of money, usually of lower value than a scholarship, that a school, college, or university awards a student to help with the cost of his or her studies [14C. Directly or via French < late Latin *exhibition-* 'handing over, display' < Latin *exhibere* (see EXHIBIT)] ◇ **make an exhibition of yourself** to behave embarrassingly in public and attract attention to yourself

CULTURAL NOTE ***Pictures at an Exhibition***, a suite (1874) of piano pieces by the Russian composer Modest Mussorgsky. The compositions were written in memory of the architect and painter Victor Alexandrovich Hartmann and inspired by paintings and drawings displayed at a memorial exhibition of the artist's work. They were later orchestrated by Maurice Ravel.

exhibitioner /éksi bísh'nər/ *n* a student who has been awarded a sum of money by a school or university to help with the cost of his or her studies

exhibition game *n* a sports contest played purely as a display of skill and an entertainment for spectators, with no prizes or competition points at stake

exhibitionism /éksi bísh'nizəm/ *n* **1.** loud, exaggerated, or boastful behaviour designed to attract attention **2.** a psychological disorder causing a compulsion to show the genitals in public —**exhibitionist** *n* —**exhibitionistic** /éksi bíshə nístik/ *adj*

exhibition match *n* SPORTS same as **exhibition game**

exhibitive /ig zíbbitiv/ *adj* displaying or demonstrating something (*formal*) ○ *an agreement exhibitive of the goodwill of both parties* —**exhibitively** *adv*

exhibitor /ig zíbbitər/, **exhibiter** *n* somebody who exhibits something, especially somebody whose artistic work is exhibited

exhilarate /ig zíllə rayt/ (**-rates, -rating, -rated**) *vt* to make somebody feel happy, excited, and more than usually vigorous and alive [Mid-16C. < Latin *exhilarat-*, past participle of *exhilarare* 'gladden thoroughly' < *hilarare* 'gladden' < Greek *hilaros* 'cheerful, glad'] —**exhilarating** *adj* —**exhilaratingly** *adv* —**exhilaration** /ig zíllə ráysh'n/ *n* —**exhilarative** /-rətiv/ *adj* —**exhilarator** *n*

~~**exhilerating**~~ incorrect spelling of **exhilarating**

~~**exhileration**~~ incorrect spelling of **exhilaration**

exhort /ig záwrt/ (**-horts, -horting, -horted**) *v* (*formal*) **1.** *vt* to urge somebody strongly and earnestly to do something **2.** *vi* to give somebody urgent or earnest advice [14C. Directly or via French < Latin *exhortari* 'encourage thoroughly' < *hortari* 'encourage, urge'] —**exhortative** /-tətiv/ *adj* —**exhorter** *n*

exhortation /égz awr táysh'n/ *n* (*formal*) **1.** something said or written in order to urge somebody strongly to do something **2.** the giving of earnest advice or encouragement

exhume /eks hyóom, ig zyóom/ (**-humes, -huming, -humed**) *vt* **1.** to dig up a corpse from a grave **2.** to reveal, re-establish, or refer again to something long forgotten or neglected ○ *Cultures are re-invented and dead traditions exhumed for the tourists.* [15C. < medieval Latin *exhumare* < *humare* 'bury' < Latin *humus* 'ground, earth'] —**exhumation** /éks hyoo máysh'n, ég zyoo-/ *n* —**exhumer** *n*

~~**exibition**~~ incorrect spelling of **exhibition**

exigency /éksijənssi, ig zíjjənssi/ (*plural* **-cies**), **exigence** /éksijənss/ *n* (*formal*) **1.** something that a situation demands or makes urgently necessary and that puts pressure on the people involved (*often used in the plural*) ○ *unable to cope with the exigencies of political life* **2.** a difficult situation requiring urgent action [Late 16C. < late Latin *exigentia* < Latin *exigent-*, present participle of *exigere* (see EXACT)]

exigent /éksijənt/ *adj* (*formal*) **1.** needing immediate action **2.** making heavy demands on somebody ○ *an exigent schoolteacher* [Early 17C. < Latin *exigent-* (see EXIGENCY)] —**exigently** *adv*

exiguous /ig zíggyoo əss, ik sígg-/ *adj* scanty or meagre (*formal*) ○ *eking out their exiguous supplies* [Mid-17C. < Latin *exiguus* < *exigere* 'weigh precisely, measure' (see EXACT)] —**exiguity** /éksi gyóo əti/ *n* —**exiguously** *adv* —**exiguousness** *n*

exile /égz īl, éks-/ *n* **1. ABSENCE FROM OWN COUNTRY** unwilling absence from a home country or place of residence, whether enforced by a government or court as a punishment, or self-imposed for political or religious reasons ○ *living in exile* **2. SOMEBODY LIVING OUTSIDE OWN COUNTRY** a citizen of one country who is forced or chooses to live in another **3. BANISHMENT** official expulsion from a home, country, or area, sometimes to a particular place, as a punishment ○ *exile to Siberia* ■ *vt* (**-iles, -iling, -iled**) **BANISH SOMEBODY FROM HOME OR COUNTRY** to order somebody to leave and stay away from his or her own country or home [14C. Via French < Latin *exilium* 'banishment' < *exul* 'banished person'] —**exilic** /eg zíllik, ek síllik/ *adj*

Exile *n* BIBLE same as **Babylonian captivity**

exine /éksin, -sīn/ *n* the outer layer of a pollen grain or other spore. The surface patterns vary among different plant groups, allowing the makeup of former plant populations to be deduced from preserved pollen samples. [Late 19C. Origin ?]

exist /ig zíst/ (**-ists, -isting, -isted**) *vi* **1. BE** to be, especially to be a real, actual, or current thing, not merely something imagined or written about ○ *Does life exist on other planets?* **2. LIVE** to be alive, or continue to live ○ *Humans need water and food to exist.* **3. OCCUR** to be present or found in a particular place or situation ○ *Shortages exist on products in high demand.* **4. SURVIVE** to manage to survive or stay alive ○ *The lost hikers existed for two days on berries.* **5. LIVE AN UNSATISFACTORY LIFE** to live an unsatisfactory, joyless, or humdrum life, as opposed to an exciting or meaningful one ○ *simply existing from day to day* [Early 17C. Probably back-formation < EXISTENCE]

~~**existance**~~ incorrect spelling of **existence**

existence /ig zístənss/ *n* **1. BEING REAL** the state of being real, actual, or current, rather than imagined, invented, or obsolete ○ *evidence for the existence of other worlds* **2. PRESENCE IN PLACE OR SITUATION** the presence or occurrence of something in a particular place or situation ○ *discovered the existence of the bacterium in sheep* **3. WAY OF LIVING** a way of living, especially a life of severe hardship ○ *scratch out a pitiable existence* **4. EVERYTHING** all living things ○ *hymns that celebrate the wonder of existence* **5. SINGLE LIVING THING** something that lives or exists (*literary or archaic*) [14C. Directly or via French < late Latin *existentia* < Latin *ex(s)istere* 'emerge, come into being' < *sistere* 'cause to stand firm']

existent /ig zístənt/ (*formal*) *adj* **1. REAL** real or actual, not imagined or invented **2. CURRENT** currently existing or in operation ■ *n* **REAL THING** a real or living thing

existential /égzi sténsh'l, éksi-/ *adj* **1. RELATING TO HUMAN EXISTENCE** concerned with or relating to existence, especially human existence **2.** PHILOSOPHY **CRUCIAL IN SHAPING INDIVIDUAL DESTINY** in the context of existentialism, involved in or vital to the shaping of a person's self-chosen mode of existence and moral stance with respect to the rest of the world **3.** LOGIC **ASSERTING EXISTENCE** governed by the existential quantifier and thus asserting the existence of something by saying that there is at least one object that possesses the properties specified ■ *n* LOGIC **EXISTENTIAL PROPOSITION** a proposition governed by the existential quantifier —**existentially** *adv*

existentialism /égzi sténsh'lizəm, éksi-/ *n* a philosophical movement begun in the 19th century that denies that the universe has any in-built meaning or purpose. It requires people to take responsibility for their own actions and shape their own destinies. [Mid-20C. < German *Existentialismus*, translation of Danish *existents-forhold* 'condition of existence'] —**existentialist** *n, adj*

existential quantifier *n* the logical constant, frequently symbolized as 'Ex', that is a prefix to another clause and that is read as saying 'there is at least one object such that'. ◊ **universal quantifier**

existing /ig zísting/ *adj* currently present, in operation, or available ○ *Existing legislation is inadequate to cover these cases.*

exit /éksit, égzit/ *n* **1.** MEANS OF LEAVING PLACE a door or other means of leaving a room or building **2.** DEPARTURE an act of leaving a room, building, or gathering **3.** PLACE FOR LEAVING MOTORWAY a slip road by which a vehicle can leave a motorway or other main road with limited access **4.** DEATH departure from life (*literary*) **5.** COMPUT TERMINATION OF COMPUTER OPERATION an act of terminating a computer operation **6.** THEATRE ACTOR'S LEAVING OF STAGE an actor's departure from the stage ■ *v* (**-its, -iting, -ited**) **1.** *vti* LEAVE to leave something such as a room, building, or gathering ○ *In the event of a fire, exit the building at the rear.* **2.** *vi* DIE to cease to live (*literary*) **3.** *vti* COMPUT TERMINATE COMPUTER PROGRAM to terminate the running of a computer operating system, program, or routine in a program **4.** *vi* THEATRE GO OFFSTAGE to leave the stage as part of a performance of a play (*refers to actors*) ◊ **exeunt** [Mid-16C. < Latin *exitus* 'departure' < past participle of *exire* 'go out' < *ire* 'go']

exit permit *n* in South Africa during apartheid rule, a permit granted to a banned person allowing him or her to leave the country without right of return

exit poll *n* a poll conducted by asking people how they voted as they leave the voting place, designed to give an early indication of the result of an election

exit visa *n* a visa that gives somebody official permission to leave a country, e.g. in time of war

ex libris /éks leébriss/ *adv* from the library of the person whose name follows (*used on bookplates*) [< Latin, 'from the books (of)']

Exmoor National Park /éks moor-, éks mawr-/ national park in a moorland region of Somerset and northern Devon. Area: 692 sq. km/267 sq. mi.

Exmoor pony *n* a small sturdy pony with a long thick mane and a light brown muzzle, belonging to a breed originating on Exmoor

Exmouth /éksməth/ **1.** port and seaside resort at the mouth of the River Exe, in Devon, southwestern England. Population: 28,414 (1991). **2.** town overlooking Exmouth Gulf on the coast of Western Australia, the site of the US-Australian Naval Communications Station. Population: 2,283 (2002 estimate).

Exmouth Gulf inlet of the sea in northwestern Western Australia. A major satellite communications station is situated nearby. Area: 3,000 sq. km/1,158 sq. mi.

ex nihilo /eks nīhilō/ *adv, adj* from or out of nothing (*formal*) [Late 16C. < Latin]

exo- *prefix* outside, external ○ *exothermic* [< Greek *exō* < *ex* 'out' < Indo-European]

exobiology /éksō bī ólləji/ *n* a branch of biology concerned with the possibility that life forms exist on other planets and with the problems of adapting the Earth's life forms to alien environments —**exobiological** /-bī ə lójjik'l/ *adj* —**exobiologist** *n*

exocarp /éksō kaarp/ *n* the outer layer of the fruit wall (**pericarp**), e.g. the skin of some fruits

Exocet /éksō set/ *tdmk* a trademark for a French-manufactured surface-to-surface guided missile with a high-explosive warhead, used by Argentinian forces against the British task force in the Falklands War of 1982

exocrine /éksō krīn, -krin/ *adj* relating to exocrine glands or their secretions. ◊ **endocrine** [Early 20C. < EXO- + Greek *krinein* 'to separate']

exocrine gland *n* a gland that releases a secretion through a duct to the surface of an organ, e.g. the sweat and salivary glands

exocyclic /éksō sīklik, -síklik/ *adj* situated outside a chemical ring structure ○ *an exocyclic bond*

exocytosis /éksō sī tṓssiss/ *n* the release to a cell surface of substances such as waste or secretions through vesicles. It occurs following the fusion of the membrane surrounding the vesicles with the membrane forming the outer wall of the cell. —**exocytotic** /-sī tóttik/ *adj*

exodontics /éksō dóntiks/, **exodontia** /éksō dónshə/ *n* the branch of dentistry concerned with extracting teeth (*takes a singular verb*) [Early 20C. < EXO- + Greek *odont-* 'tooth'] —**exodontist** *n*

exodus /éksədəss/ *n* a departure or going out or away from a place that involves large numbers of people [Pre-12C. Via ecclesiastical Latin, '(biblical Book of) Exodus' < Greek, 'way out' < *hodos* 'way, road']

Exodus *n* **1.** a book of the Bible which describes the flight of the Israelites from Egypt and Moses receiving the Ten Commandments on Mount Sinai. It is the second book of the Pentateuch. See table at **Bible 2.** in the Bible, the flight of Moses and the Israelites from Egypt

exoenzyme /éksō én zīm/ *n* an enzyme that acts outside the cell that secretes it

exoergic /éksō úrjik/ *adj* describes a nuclear or chemical reaction that produces energy. ◊ **endoergic** [Mid-20C. < EXO- + Greek *ergon* 'work']

ex officio /éks ə físhi ō/ *adv, adj* as a result of the official position somebody holds ○ *Heads of state are often ex officio heads of the armed forces.* [Mid-16C. < Latin, 'out of duty, on account of office']

exogamy /ek sóggəmi/ *n* **1.** the custom in some societies of marrying outside their people's own social group **2.** the fusion of sex cells (**gametes**) of organisms not closely related, as occurs in cross-pollination and outbreeding —**exogamous** *adj*

exogenous /ek sójjənəss/ *adj* originating outside an organism or system [Mid-19C. < modern Latin *exogena* 'growing on the outside' < Greek *genēs* 'born'] —**exogenously** *adv*

exon[1] /éks on/ *n* a discontinuous sequence of DNA that codes for protein synthesis and carries the genetic code for the final messenger RNA molecule. ◊ **intron** [Late 20C. < shortening of *expressed* + -ON [1]]

exon[2] /éks on/ *n* an officer belonging to a group of four who command the Yeomen of the Guard in London [Mid-18C. Representing pronunciation of French *exempt* 'exempt (from ordinary military duties)']

exonerate /ig zónnə rayt/ (**-ates, -ating, -ated**) *vt* **1.** to declare officially that somebody is not to blame or is not guilty of wrongdoing **2.** to relieve somebody from an obligation or responsibility [15C. < Latin *exonerat-*, past participle of *exonerare* 'take off a burden' < *onus* 'burden'] —**exoneration** /ig zónnə ráysh'n/ *n* —**exonerative** *adj*

exophthalmos /éks of thálməss/, **exophthalmus**, **exophthalmia** /-thálmi ə/ *n* unusual protrusion of the eyeball, sometimes resulting from an aneurysm [Early 17C. Directly or via modern Latin < Greek *exophthalmos* '(condition of) the eye being outside' < *ophthalmos* 'eye'] —**exophthalmic** *adj*

exor. *abbr* LAW executor

exorbitant /ig záwrbitənt/ *adj* **1.** far greater or higher than is reasonable ○ *exorbitant prices* **2.** going beyond what is usual, proper, or manageable [15C. < ecclesiastical Latin *exorbitant-*, present participle of *exorbitare* 'go out of the track' < Latin *orbita* 'track' < *orbis* 'circle'] —**exorbitance** *n* —**exorbitantly** *adv*

exorcise *vt* RELIG another spelling of **exorcize**

exorcism /éks awr sizəm/ *n* **1.** DRIVING OUT OF EVIL SPIRITS the use of prayers or religious rituals to drive out evil spirits believed to be possessing a person or place **2.** CEREMONY TO DRIVE OUT EVIL SPIRITS a religious ceremony in which somebody endeavours to drive out an evil spirit believed to be possessing a person or place **3.** THING DONE TO EXPEL EVIL a special ritual or spoken formula used with the intention of driving out evil spirits **4.** CLEARING MIND OF OPPRESSIVE FEELINGS the act of ridding the mind of oppressive feelings or memories [14C Via ecclesiastical Latin < ecclesiastical Greek *exorkismos* < *exorkizein* (see EXORCIZE)] —**exorcist** *n*

exorcize /éks awr sīz, éksər-/ (**-cizes, -cizing, -cized**), **exorcise** (**-cises, -cising, -cised**) *vt* **1.** FREE PERSON OR PLACE FROM EVIL to use prayers and religious rituals with the intention of ridding a person or place of the supposed presence or influence of evil spirits **2.** SEND EVIL AWAY to use prayers and religious rituals with the intention of driving away an evil spirit believed to be possessing a person or place **3.** GET RID OF OPPRESSIVE FEELING to clear the mind of a painful or oppressive feeling or memory [15C. Directly or via French < ecclesiastical Latin *exorcizare* < Greek *exorkizein* 'swear out (an evil spirit)' < *orkos* 'oath'] —**exorcizer** *n*

exordium /ek sáwrdi əm/ (*plural* **-diums** or **-dia** /-di ə/) *n* an opening section, especially of a lecture or a piece of scholarly writing (*formal*) [Late 16C. < Latin < *exordiri* 'begin'] —**exordial** *adj*

exoskeleton /éksō skéllitən/ *n* a hard covering on the outside of organisms such as crustaceans, insects, turtles, and armadillos that provides support and protection —**exoskeletal** *adj*

exosmosis /éks oz mṓssiss/ *n* movement of fluid towards a solution of lower concentration, as is the case when water percolates through a cell membrane into the medium surrounding the cell [Mid-19C. < French *exosmose* < Greek *ōsmos* 'act of pushing'] —**exosmotic** /-móttik/ *adj*

exosphere /éksō sfeer/ *n* the outermost region of the atmosphere of Earth or another planet —**exospheric** /éksō sférrik/ *adj*

exospore /éksō spawr/ *n* **1.** a spore that is formed outside a parent cell, or outside a spore-bearing organ, especially by extrusion **2.** the outermost layer of a spore

exostosis /éksō stṓssiss/ (*plural* **-toses** /-tṓseez/) *n* a benign bony growth on the surface of a bone or a tooth root, caused by inflammation or repeated trauma [Late 16C. < Greek, 'bony outgrowth' < *osteon* 'bone']

exoteric /éksō térrik/ *adj* capable of being understood by most people, not just an informed or select minority (*formal*) [Mid-17C. Via Latin < Greek *exōterikos* < *exōterō* 'outer' < *exō* 'outside'] —**exoterically** *adv*

exothermic /éksō thúrmik/, **exothermal** /-thúrm'l/ *adj* describes a chemical reaction that produces heat. ◊ **endothermic** [Late 19C. < French *exothermique* < Greek *thermē* 'heat'] —**exothermically** *adv*

exotic /ig zóttik/ *adj* **1.** STRIKINGLY DIFFERENT strikingly unusual and often very colourful and exciting or suggesting distant countries and unfamiliar cultures **2.** FROM DISTANT COUNTRY from or relating to distant, especially tropical, places ○ *exotic fruits* **3.** ECOL FROM ELSEWHERE introduced from another place or region ○ *an exotic species* ■ *n* SOMEBODY OR SOMETHING UNUSUAL AND STRIKING a person or thing that is foreign and unusual, especially a plant or animal [Late 16C. Via Latin *exoticus* < Greek *exōtikos* < *exō* 'out, outside'] —**exotically** *adv* —**exoticism** /ig zóttissizəm/ *n*

exotica /ig zóttikə/ *npl* exotic or extraordinary things, especially when forming a collection [Late 19C. < Latin, form of *exoticus* (see EXOTIC)]

exotic dancer *n* a striptease artist

exotoxin /éksō tóksin/ *n* a highly potent soluble toxin produced by a bacterium and released into its infected host, often affecting the central nervous system. Exotoxins are produced in diphtheria, botulism, and tetanus, and are among the most potent known toxins.

exp. *abbr* **1.** experiment **2.** experimental **3.** expired **4.** expires **5.** MATHS exponential function **6.** export **7.** exported **8.** express

expand /ik spánd/ (**-pands, -panding, -panded**) *v* **1.** *vti* MAKE OR BECOME LARGER to become or make something become larger in size, scope, or extent, or greater in number or amount ○ *We need to expand our client base.* **2.** *vti* DESCRIBE SOMETHING MORE FULLY to explain or describe something more fully, usually by giving more detail ○ *The film expands on themes familiar from her earlier work.* **3.** *vti* OPEN OUT to open out or open something out wider after being kept folded in **4.** *vt* GIVE FULL FORM OF SOMETHING to give the full form of something such as the abbreviation of a word **5.** *vi* RELAX to relax and become friendlier and more talkative (*formal*) **6.** *vti* PHYS INCREASE IN SIZE OR VOLUME to increase or cause something to increase in size or volume as a result of a rise in temperature or

decrease in pressure **7.** *vti* MATHS **REWRITE MATHEMATICAL EXPRESSION** to rewrite a mathematical expression as the sum or product of its terms, or be rewritten in this way. For example, $(x+1)(x-1)+2x$ expands to x^2+2x-1. [15C. Directly or via Anglo-Norman < Latin *expandere* 'spread out' < *pandere* 'spread'] —**expandability** /ik spándə bílləti/ *n* —**expandable** *adj* —**expander** *n* —**expansible** /ik spánssəb'l/ *adj*

SYNONYMS See *increase*.

expanded /ik spándid/ *adj* **1.** MADE LARGER extended, unfolded, or outstretched **2.** INDUST MADE INTO FOAM describes plastics made into a lightweight solid foam by the introduction of gas during the manufacturing process ○ *expanded polyurethane* **3.** PRINTING **WIDER THAN USUAL** describes typefaces or printed characters that are wider than usual in relation to their height

expanded metal *n* strong metal mesh made by cutting slits in sheet metal and stretching it out of shape. Use: reinforcing material in construction.

expanse /ik spánss/ *n* a wide area or surface, especially of sea, land, or sky [Mid-17C. < modern Latin *expansum* 'firmament' < Latin *expans-*, past participle of *expandere* (see EXPAND)]

expansile /ik spán sīl/ *adj* **1.** relating to expansion or the ability to expand **2.** able to expand or be expanded

expansion /ik spánsh'n/ *n* **1.** PROCESS OF ENLARGEMENT the process of increasing, or increasing something, in size, extent, scope, or number ○ *This site does not give us enough room for expansion.* **2.** INCREASE an increase, or the amount by which something increases, in size, extent, or scope ○ *Geologists measured the expansion of the volcanic island.* **3.** GROWTH BY LAND ACQUISITION the increase of a country's size by the acquisition of new territory ○ *westward expansion* **4.** FULLER TREATMENT a fuller or more detailed treatment or version of something ○ *The expansion of 'Dr' is 'Doctor'.* **5.** PHYS INCREASE IN DIMENSIONS an increase in the dimensions of something as a result of a rise in temperature or decrease in pressure **6.** MECH ENG **COMBUSTION STAGE IN ENGINE** a stage in an engine cycle during which the fuel and air mixture explodes, thereby increasing in volume and providing power **7.** MATHS **EXPANDED MATHEMATICAL EXPRESSION** the result of expanding a mathematical expression [Early 17C. < late Latin *expansion-* < Latin *expans-* (see EXPANSE)]

expansionary /ik spánsh'nəri/ *adj* bringing about expansion, especially economic or territorial expansion

expansion board *n* COMPUT same as **expansion card**

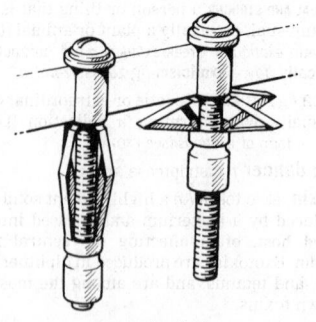

expansion bolt

expansion bolt *n* a bolt with an attachment on the screw end that expands as the bolt is tightened, thereby securing it

expansion card *n* a printed circuit board adding features or capability to a computer

expansionism /ik spánsh'nizəm/ *n* a policy of expanding a country's economy or territory —**expansionist** *n, adj* —**expansionistic** /ik spánshə nístik/ *adj*

expansion joint *n* a gap left between adjacent parts or surfaces, e.g. between the concrete sections that form the road surface of a bridge, to prevent buckling when they expand under heat

expansion slot *n* a receptacle for an expansion card that interfaces with a computer's internal circuitry

expansive /ik spánssiv/ *adj* **1.** COMMUNICATIVE willing to talk openly and at some length, usually in a relaxed and jovial way ○ *He gradually became more expansive once he got to know us.* **2.** LAVISH generous, lavish, or extravagant in scale ○ *an expansive lifestyle* **3.** EXPANDING capable of, having a tendency to, or typically undergoing expansion ○ *polymers with expansive capability* **4.** WITH OUTSTRETCHED ARMS with the arms stretched out and open wide ○ *an expansive gesture* **5.** EXTENSIVE covering a wide area or broad in scope (*formal*) ○ *a large house with expansive grounds* **6.** PSYCHIAT **HAVING EXAGGERATED FEELINGS OF SELF-WORTH** having or characterized by extreme feelings of euphoria and delusions of grandeur or self-importance —**expansively** *adv* —**expansiveness** *n*

ex parte /eks paárti/ *adj, adv* made or undertaken on behalf of only one of the parties involved in a court case [Early 17C. < Latin, 'from a (or the) side']

expat /éks pát/ *n* same as **expatriate** *n* (sense 1) (*informal*) [Mid-20C. Shortening]

expatiate /ek spáyshi ayt/ (**-ates, -ating, -ated**) *vi* to speak or write about something at length ○ *We had to listen to him expatiating on the shortcomings of our system.* [Mid-16C. < Latin *ex(s)patiat-*, past participle of *ex(s)patiari* 'walk out' < *spatiari* 'walk' < *spatium* 'space'] —**expatiation** /ek spáyshi áysh'n/ *n*

expatriate *n* /eks páttri ət, -páytri-, -ayt/ **1.** SOMEBODY WHO HAS MOVED ABROAD a citizen who has left his or her own country to live in another, usually for a prolonged period **2.** SOMEBODY WITHOUT CITIZENSHIP a citizen who has renounced his or her citizenship or whose citizenship has been repealed ■ *adj* /eks páttri ət, -páytri-, -ayt/ OF EXPATRIATES relating to people who live abroad ■ *v* /eks páttri ayt, -páytri-/ (**-ates, -ating, -ated**) **1.** *vi* SETTLE ABROAD to settle in another country **2.** *vti* TAKE AWAY SOMEBODY'S CITIZENSHIP to deprive somebody of native citizenship, or renounce native citizenship voluntarily **3.** *vt* EXILE SOMEBODY to send somebody away from his or her own country as a punishment [Mid-18C. < Latin *expatriat-*, past participle of *expatriare* 'leave your native land' < *patria* 'native land' < *pater* 'father'] —**expatriation** /eks páttri áysh'n, -páytri-/ *n*

~~**expatriot**~~ incorrect spelling of **expatriate**

expect /ik spékt/ (**-pects, -pecting, -pected**) *v* **1.** *vt* CONFIDENTLY BELIEVE SOMETHING to believe with confidence, or think it likely, that an event will happen in the future ○ *A few setbacks along the way were only to be expected.* **2.** *vt* WAIT FOR ANTICIPATED THING to wait for, or look forward to, something that is believed to be going to happen or arrive ○ *We'll expect you late morning, then.* ○ *I'm expecting a visit from them any day now.* **3.** *vt* DEMAND SOMETHING AS RIGHT OR DUTY to demand or anticipate receiving something because of a perceived right to it or because it is due or appropriate ○ *They expect you to abide by their rules.* **4.** *vti* BE GOING TO HAVE BABY to be pregnant with or look forward to the birth of a child (*informal*; used only in progressive tenses) ○ *She is expecting her third in July.* [Mid-16C. < Latin *ex(s)pectare* 'look out for' < *spectare* 'look at' < *specere* 'to look'] —**expectable** *adj* —**expectably** *adv* —**expectedly** *adv* —**expectedness** *n*

expectancy /ik spéktənssi/ (*plural* **-cies**), **expectance** /ik spéktənss/ *n* **1.** excited awareness that something is about to happen ○ *An air of expectancy hung over the crowd.* **2.** something expected, especially an amount or length of time expected on the basis of statistical calculations

expectant /ik spéktənt/ *adj* **1.** EXCITEDLY ANTICIPATING SOMETHING excitedly aware that something is about to happen **2.** EXPECTING BABY expecting the birth of a baby **3.** EXPECTING SOMETHING FAVOURABLE expecting something, especially something that will bring success or wealth (*formal*) [14C. Directly or via French < Latin *ex(s)pectant-*, present participle of *ex(s)pectare* (see EXPECT)]

expectantly /ik spéktəntli/ *adv* in the expectation that something interesting, exciting, or pleasurable will happen

expectation /ék spek táysh'n/ *n* **1.** ANTICIPATION OF SOMETHING HAPPENING a confident belief or strong hope that a particular event will happen **2.** NOTION OF SOMETHING a mental image of something expected, often compared to its reality (*often used in the plural*) ○ *All our expectations of a quiet evening at home were dashed by the arrival of guests.* **3.** EXPECTED STANDARD a standard of conduct or performance expected by or

of somebody (*often used in the plural*) ○ *Her work wasn't up to expectations.* **4.** same as **expectancy** (sense 1) ■ **expectations** *npl* PROSPECTS FOR FUTURE somebody's likely prospects of wealth or success in the future, especially of inheriting money under somebody's will

CULTURAL NOTE *Great Expectations*, a novel (1861) by Charles Dickens. It is the story of the orphan Pip, his early encounter with the convict Magwitch, and his love for the beautiful Estella, who lives with her eccentric guardian Miss Havisham. Pip subsequently receives a fortune from an unknown benefactor and moves to London, but is forced to return penniless to the humble blacksmith's home where he grew up. It is here that he ultimately reaches maturity and finds happiness.

expected value *n* the value of a random variable that is most likely to occur, calculated by multiplying the sum of every possible value by a factor representing the probability of its occurrence

expectorant /ik spéktərənt/ *adj* causing phlegm to be coughed up ■ *n* a medicine that stimulates the production of phlegm. Use: treatment of coughs.

expectorate /ik spéktə rayt/ (**-rates, -rating, -rated**) *vti* to cough up and spit out phlegm, thus clearing the bronchial passages [Early 17C. < Latin *expectorat-*, past participle of *expectorare* 'get out of the chest' < *pectus* 'chest, breast'] —**expectoration** /ik spéktə ráysh'n/ *n*

expediency /ik spéedi ənssi/ (*plural* **-cies**), **expedience** /-ənss/ *n* **1.** the use of methods that bring the most immediate benefits, based on practical rather than moral considerations **2.** the usefulness, appropriateness, or advisability of something, especially of a particular action or type of behaviour in a particular situation ○ *doubts about the expediency of such a course in the present crisis* **3.** same as **expedient**

expedient /ik spéedi ənt/ *adj* **1.** ADVANTAGEOUS advantageous for practical rather than moral reasons ○ *She changed her vote because it was expedient for her to do so.* **2.** APPROPRIATE appropriate, advisable, or useful in a situation that requires action ■ *n* SOMETHING ACHIEVING AIMS QUICKLY something done or a method used to achieve an aim quickly, regardless of whether it is fair, right, or wise in the long term [14C. Directly or via French < Latin *expedient-*, present participle of *expedire* (see EXPEDITE)] —**expediently** *adv*

expedite /ékspə dīt/ (**-dites, -diting, -dited**) *vt* (*formal*) **1.** to ensure that something takes place or is dealt with more quickly than usual **2.** to deal with something, especially a business transaction, swiftly and efficiently [15C. < Latin *expedit-*, past participle of *expedire* 'set free' < *pes* 'foot'] —**expediter** *n*

expedition /ékspə dísh'n/ *n* **1.** ORGANIZED JOURNEY BY GROUP a journey made by a group of people for a particular purpose, e.g. to explore unknown territory, to do scientific study, or to achieve a military objective ○ *a scientific expedition to the ocean floor* **2.** GROUP TAKING PART IN EXPEDITION a group of people who go on an expedition together ○ *The expedition returned at the end of the month.* **3.** OUTING a short journey, usually for a pleasurable purpose **4.** PROMPTNESS speed, promptness, or efficiency in doing something ○ *carried out our errand with expedition* [15C. Directly or via French < Latin *expedition-* < *expedire* (see EXPEDITE)]

expeditionary /ékspə dísh'nəri/ *adj* sent to fight or do military service in another country ○ *an expeditionary force*

expeditious /ékspə díshəss/ *adj* speedy, or carried out promptly and efficiently —**expeditiously** *adv* —**expeditiousness** *n*

expel /ik spél/ (**-pels, -pelling, -pelled**) *vt* **1.** to compel somebody to leave or give up membership of an institution such as a school, political party, or club ○ *expel a child from school* **2.** to push or drive something out with force ○ *Air is expelled under pressure from outlets under the hovercraft's apron.* [14C. < Latin *expellere* 'drive out' < *pellere* 'beat, drive'] —**expellable** *adj* —**expellee** /ik spél ée, éks pel-/ *n* —**expeller** *n*

expellant /ik spéllənt/, **expellent** *adj* capable of expelling something, especially from the body ■ *n* a medicine that causes the body to get rid of something undesirable, especially intestinal worms

~~**expence**~~ incorrect spelling of **expense**

expend /ik spénd/ (-pends, -pending, -pended) vt 1. to use up time, energy, effort, or some other resource 2. to spend money or an amount of money (formal) [15C. < Latin expendere 'weigh out (money in payment)' < pendere 'weigh'] —**expender** n

expendable /ik spéndəb'l/ adj 1. NOT WORTH PRESERVING not worth preserving or saving for reuse 2. DISPENSABLE easily sacrificed or dispensed with if the need arises or in order to achieve an aim ■ n EXPENDABLE ITEM an expendable person or thing —**expendability** /ik spéndə bílləti/ n

expenditure /ik spéndichər/ n 1. an amount of money spent, as a whole or on a particular thing ○ when income exceeds expenditure 2. the consuming or using up of something ○ the huge expenditure of time and human resources on this scheme [Mid-18C. After expenditor 'somebody in charge of expenditure']

expense /ik spénss/ n 1. MONEY SPENT ON SOMETHING the amount of money spent in order to buy or do something 2. SOMETHING EXPENSIVE TO BUY something that costs money, usually a lot of money, to buy, keep, or run 3. USING UP OF SOMETHING the using up or loss of something ○ preserved his integrity at the expense of his job 4. ACCT VALUE OF RESOURCE USED the value of a resource that has been used during the current accounting period and can be charged against revenues for that period ■ expenses npl BUSINESS EXPENDITURES an amount of money that somebody spends for business purposes that is reimbursable by an employer or deductible from income tax [14C. Via Anglo-Norman < late Latin expensa < Latin expendere (see EXPEND)]

expense account n 1. a facility given by an employer that entitles an employee to be repaid for some or all of the expenses incurred in the course of his or her employment 2. the amount of an employee's expenses during a particular period, or a record of this

~~expensiv~~ incorrect spelling of **expensive**

expensive /ik spénssiv/ adj 1. COSTING A LOT costing a large amount of money 2. CHARGING A LOT charging high prices 3. VERY DISADVANTAGEOUS involving serious losses or disadvantage to a particular person or group ○ an expensive first half for the home team —**expensively** adv —**expensiveness** n

~~experiance~~ incorrect spelling of **experience**

experience /ik speéri ənss/ n 1. INVOLVEMENT IN SOMETHING OVER TIME active involvement in an activity or exposure to events or people over a period of time that leads to an increase in knowledge or skill ○ Experience is the best teacher. 2. KNOWLEDGE OR SKILL ACQUIRED knowledge or skill gained through being involved in or exposed to something over a period of time ○ Paper qualifications are no substitute for real-life experience. 3. SUM TOTAL OF SOMEBODY'S EXPERIENCES the sum total of the things that have happened to a person and of his or her past thoughts and feelings ○ Nothing quite like this has ever been done before, at least not in my experience. 4. SOMETHING THAT HAPPENS TO SOMEBODY something that happens to somebody or an event that somebody is involved in ○ an experience that changed his life 5. DIRECT PERSONAL AWARENESS OF SOMETHING direct personal awareness of or contact with a particular thing ○ Very few of us remember our first experience of pain. 6. PHILOSOPHY KNOWLEDGE FROM OBSERVATION knowledge acquired through the senses, and not through abstract reasoning ■ vt (-ences, -encing, -enced) 1. HAVE PERSONAL KNOWLEDGE OF SOMETHING to be exposed to, involved in, or affected by something ○ the most thrilling ride I've ever experienced 2. FEEL SOMETHING to feel a particular sensation or emotion ○ experience a tingling sensation [14C. Via French < Latin experientia < experiri 'try out']

CULTURAL NOTE Songs of Experience, a collection of poems (1794) by William Blake. Blake's Songs of Innocence (1789) described the world from the optimistic viewpoint of an innocent child. In this, its adult counterpart, he portrays a world of disease, poverty, and irredeemable corruption. The collection includes perhaps his best-known poem, 'The Tyger'.

experienced /ik speéri ənst/ adj possessing knowledge and skill acquired through involvement in or exposure to something over a period of time ○ an experienced pilot

experiential /ik speéri énsh'l/ adj derived from or relating to experience as opposed to other methods of acquiring knowledge [Mid-17C. After a word such as inferential] —**experientially** adv

experiment n /ik spérrimənt/ 1. SCIENTIFIC TEST a test, especially a scientific one, carried out in order to discover whether a theory is correct or what the results of a particular course of action would be ○ a chemistry experiment 2. DOING SOMETHING NEW an attempt to do something new or to see what will happen ○ switching to decaffeinated coffee as an experiment 3. USE OF REPEATED TESTS AND TRIALS the use of tests and trials in order to make discoveries ○ developed the protocol by experiment ■ vi /ik spérri ment/ (-ments, -menting, -mented) 1. TRY NEW THINGS to try out new methods of doing or using things ○ a reluctance to experiment with new ingredients 2. SCI CARRY OUT SCIENTIFIC TEST to carry out a scientific test of a theory or process [14C. Directly or via Old French < Latin experimentum 'trial, test' < experiri 'try out'] —**experimentation** /ik spérri men táysh'n/ n —**experimenter** n

experimental /ik spérri mént'l/ adj 1. RELATING TO SOMETHING NEW AND UNTRIED employing ideas, methods, or materials that have not been tried before ○ a new, experimental form of treatment 2. SCI RELATING TO SCIENTIFIC EXPERIMENTS relating to, involving, or based on scientific experiments 3. BASED ON EXPERIENCE AND EVIDENCE based on experience and practical evidence, and not on ideas —**experimentally** adv

experimentalism /ik spérri mént'lizəm/ n the use of new techniques in artistic, literary, or musical works —**experimentalist** n

experimental psychology n the branch of psychology that studies the basic mechanisms of the mind, e.g. perception, thinking, learning, and memory, often using experiments with individuals in controlled situations

expert /éks purt/ n SOMEBODY SKILLED OR KNOWLEDGEABLE somebody with a great deal of knowledge about, or skill, training, or experience in, a particular field or activity ○ a medical expert ■ adj 1. SKILFUL OR KNOWLEDGEABLE having a great deal of knowledge about, or skill, training, or experience in, a particular field or activity ○ an expert pizza maker 2. DONE BY SOMEBODY WITH SPECIALIST KNOWLEDGE given or done by somebody who is skilled, trained, or experienced in the relevant subject area ○ expert advice [14C. Via French < Latin expert-, past participle of experiri 'try out'] —**expertly** adv —**expertness** n

expertise /éks pur teéz/ n the skill, knowledge, or opinion possessed by an expert [Mid-19C. < French < expert- (see EXPERT)]

expert system n a computer program that applies artificial-intelligence methods to problem-solving

expert witness n somebody called to answer questions in a court of law in order to provide specialized information relevant to the case being tried

expiate /ékspi ayt/ (-ates, -ating, -ated) vt to make amends, show remorse, or suffer punishment for wrongdoing [Late 16C. < Latin expiat-, past participle of expiare 'atone completely' < pius 'dutiful'] —**expiation** /ékspi áysh'n/ n —**expiator** n —**expiatory** /ékspi ətəri, ékspi áytəri/ adj

~~expidition~~ incorrect spelling of **expedition**

expiration date n N Am same as **expiry date**

expiratory /ik spírətəri/ adj relating to the process of breathing out, or used in breathing out

expire /ik spír/ (-pires, -piring, -pired) vi 1. to come to an end or be no longer valid or in operation ○ My visa has expired. 2. to die or release a last breath (formal or literary) 3. same as **exhale** (sense 1) (technical) [14C. Via French < Latin exspirare 'breathe out' < spirare 'breathe'] —**expiration** /ékspi ráysh'n/ n

expiry /ik spíri/ n 1. the fact of coming to an end and being no longer valid after a particular period of time ○ two weeks before the date of expiry 2. death, especially the death of a person (formal or literary)

expiry date n 1. a date printed on the packaging of food and medicines that indicates the time after which they should not be used 2. the date after which a credit card is no longer valid ▶ N Am term **expiration date**

explain /ik spláyn/ (-plains, -plaining, -plained) v 1.

vti GIVE DETAILS ABOUT SOMETHING to give an account of something with enough clarity and detail to be understood by somebody else ○ I explained to him that we had no option. 2. vt CLARIFY MEANING OF SOMETHING to make the meaning of something clear to somebody ○ Can you explain this sentence to me? 3. vti GIVE REASON FOR SOMETHING to give the reason for something that has happened, often as justification for it ○ Let me explain why I'm late. 4. explain yourself vr JUSTIFY BEHAVIOUR to give reasons to justify personal behaviour or actions ○ You'll have to explain yourself to the head teacher. 5. explain yourself vr MAKE SELF UNDERSTOOD to express ideas or thoughts in a way that is easily understood ○ I'm sorry, I'm not explaining myself very well. [Early 16C. < Latin explanare 'flatten out, unfold' < planus 'flat, clear'] —**explainable** adj —**explainer** n

explain away vt to give excuses, reasons, or explanations for something in an attempt to show that it is less serious, important, or problematic than it seems

~~explaination~~ incorrect spelling of **explanation**

explanation /éksplə náysh'n/ n 1. STATEMENT EXPLAINING SOMETHING a statement giving reasons for something or details of something ○ an explanation of how the machine works 2. GIVING DETAILS OR REASONS the act of giving details about something or reasons for something ○ The explanation of what had happened took some time. 3. DISCUSSION TO END MISUNDERSTANDING a discussion or clarification of something that removes misunderstandings or reconciles the parties [14C. < Latin explanation- < explanare (see EXPLAIN)]

explanatory /ik splánnətəri/ adj giving reasons or details that explain something ○ an explanatory leaflet [Early 17C. < late Latin explanatorius < Latin explanare (see EXPLAIN)] —**explanatorily** adv

explant /eks pláant/ vt (-plants, -planting, -planted) to remove living tissue from an organism and place it in a culture medium ■ n a piece of tissue removed from an organism and placed in a culture medium [Early 20C. After IMPLANT] —**explantation** /éks plaan táysh'n/ n

expletive /ik spleétiv/ n 1. LING SWEARWORD an exclamation, especially a swearword 2. GRAM WORD WITH NO MEANING a word that carries no meaning but has a grammatical function in a sentence. In the sentence 'There are three books on the table', 'there' is an expletive. 3. LITERAT MEANINGLESS WORD IN LINE OF POETRY a word added to a line of verse in order to fill it out, usually for the sake of the metre. In the line 'When and that I was a little tiny lad', the words 'and that' are expletives. ■ adj GRAM, LITERAT USED AS EXPLETIVE functioning as an expletive in a sentence or poem [Early 17C. < late Latin expletivus < explet-, past participle of explere 'fill up' < plere 'to fill']

expletory /ik spleétəri/ adj GRAM, LITERAT same as **expletive** [Late 17C. < Latin explet- (see EXPLETIVE)]

explicable /ik splíkəb'l, éksplik-/ adj able to be explained —**explicably** adv

explicate /ékspli kayt/ (-cates, -cating, -cated) vt 1. to explain something, especially a literary text, in a detailed and formal way 2. to explain and develop an idea or theory and show its implications [Early 16C. < Latin explicat-, past participle of explicare 'unfold' < plicare 'to fold'] —**explication** /ékspli káysh'n/ n —**explicative** /ik splíkətiv/ adj —**explicatively** adv —**explicator** n —**explicatory** /ik splíkətəri/ adj

explicit /ik splíssit/ adj 1. CLEAR AND OBVIOUS expressing all details in a clear and obvious way, leaving no doubt as to the intended meaning ○ Could you be more explicit about what the report needs to cover? 2. DEFINITE definite and unqualified, and not implied or guessed at ○ I didn't have explicit knowledge of what was going on, but I knew that something was happening. 3. SHOWING OR DESCRIBING SEX OPENLY portraying nudity or sexual activity in an open and direct way 4. MATHS WITH ONLY INDEPENDENT VARIABLES describes a mathematical function that contains only variables whose value is independent of the value of the other variables in the function [Early 17C. Directly or via French < Latin explicit-, irregular past participle of explicare (see EXPLICATE) —**explicitly** adv —**explicitness** n

USAGE explicit or implicit? Explicit means 'clear, obvious, and definite': explicit directions; had explicit knowledge of the plot because of being one of the

conspirators. ***Implicit*** means 'implied or unstated but understood', 'absolute', and 'present as a necessary component': *nodding and smiling that signified implicit agreement with our position; implicit faith; the implicit confidentiality between doctor and patient.*

---

explode /ik splṓd/ (**-plodes, -ploding, -ploded**) *v* **1.** *vti* **BLOW UP OR BURST** to blow up or burst with a sudden release of chemical or nuclear energy and a loud noise, or cause something to blow up or burst in this way **2.** *vti* **BURST OR SHATTER** to burst like a bomb or shatter into many pieces, or cause something to do this **3.** *vi* **EXPRESS EMOTION** to give vent to an emotion, suddenly or violently ○ *He exploded into roars of laughter.* **4.** *vi* **INCREASE DRAMATICALLY** to increase suddenly in extent or severity in an uncontrolled way ○ *The growth rate in home ownership exploded.* **5.** *vi* **PRODUCE VIVID DISPLAY** to produce a vivid, often sudden display of light or colour ○ *Her late paintings explode with intense reds and oranges.* **6.** *vi* **APPEAR SUDDENLY** to appear, start, or move suddenly and forcefully ○ *The band exploded onto the pop scene late last year.* **7.** *vt* **DISPROVE THEORY** to show that a belief or theory is completely wrong [Mid-16C. < Latin *explodere* 'drive off the stage by clapping' < *plaudere* 'to clap'] —**exploder** *n*

exploded /ik splṓdid/ *adj* showing the parts of something as separate items in a diagram, but with their relative positions maintained ○ *an exploded drawing*

exploit *vt* /ik splóyt/ (**-ploits, -ploiting, -ploited**) **1. TAKE ADVANTAGE OF SOMEBODY** to take selfish or unfair advantage of a person or situation, usually for personal gain **2. USE SOMETHING FOR BENEFIT** to use or develop something in order to gain a benefit ○ *fully exploit natural gas reserves* ■ *n* /éks ployt/ **EXCITING ACT** an interesting or daring action or achievement [Mid-16C. Via Old French, 'accomplishment' < Latin *explicit-*, past participle of *explicare* (see EXPLICATE)] —**exploitable** *adj* —**exploitative** *adj* —**exploitatively** *adv* —**exploiter** *n* —**exploitive** *adj*

exploitation /éks ploy táysh'n/ *n* **1.** the practice of taking selfish or unfair advantage of a person or situation, usually for personal gain **2.** the use or development of something in order to gain a benefit

exploration /éksplə ráysh'n/ *n* **1. TRAVEL FOR DISCOVERY** travel undertaken to discover what a place is like or where it is ○ *polar exploration* **2. INVESTIGATION OF SOMETHING** a careful investigation or study of something such as data, a particular subject, or possible courses of action **3. SEARCHING FOR NATURAL RESOURCES** the testing of a number of places for natural resources, e.g. drilling or boring for samples that will be examined for possible mineral deposits **4.** MED **EXAMINATION FOR DIAGNOSIS** the examination of a part of the body in order to make a diagnosis

exploratory /ik splórrətəri, -splάwrə-/ *adj* involving exploration ○ *an exploratory mission* ○ *exploratory surgery*

explore /ik splάwr/ (**-plores, -ploring, -plored**) *v* **1.** *vti* **TRAVEL FOR DISCOVERY** to travel to or in a place in order to discover what it is like or what is there **2.** *vti* **INVESTIGATE OR STUDY SOMETHING** to make a careful investigation or study of something ○ *exploring all possible avenues of research* **3.** *vti* **SEARCH PLACE FOR NATURAL RESOURCES** to make a search of an area for natural resources such as mineral deposits **4.** *vt* MED **EXAMINE SOMETHING TO MAKE DIAGNOSIS** to examine a part of the body in order to make a diagnosis [Mid-16C. Via French < Latin *explorare* 'search out' < *plorare* 'cry out']

explorer /ik splάwrər/ *n* somebody who travels to distant or unfamiliar places to find out more about them ○ *polar explorers of the early 20th century*

Explorer, Explorer Scout *n* a member of the branch of the Scout Association for young people aged between 14 and 18

explosion /ik splṓzh'n/ *n* **1. SUDDEN NOISY RELEASE OF ENERGY** the sudden loud release of energy and a rapidly expanding volume of gas that occurs when a bomb detonates or gas explodes **2. BURSTING OR SHATTERING OF SOMETHING** a bursting with a loud noise, or a shattering of something into many pieces **3. SUDDEN LOUD NOISE** a loud noise that occurs suddenly **4. SUDDEN BURST OF EMOTION** a sudden release of intense feeling such as anger ○ *an explosion of rage* **5. DRAMATIC INCREASE** a sudden and dramatic increase in something such as a population or an activity ○ *the explosion in e-mail subscriptions* **6. SUDDEN APPEARANCE** the sudden and forceful appearance or movement of somebody or something, or the sudden and forceful beginning of something **7. INTENSE DISPLAY** a vivid, often sudden display of light or colour **8.** PHON same as **plosion** [Early 17C. < Latin *explosion-* < *explos-*, past participle of *explodere* (see EXPLODE)]

explosive /ik splṓssiv, -splṓz-/ *adj* **1. LIKELY TO EXPLODE** able or serving to explode ○ *an explosive mixture of oxygen and methane* **2. OPERATED BY EXPLODING** designed to explode or operated by means of something that explodes ○ *an explosive device* **3. LIKELY TO GENERATE VIOLENT ANGER** likely to cause or erupt suddenly into angry disagreement or violence ○ *an explosive temperament* **4. SUDDEN AND DRAMATIC** happening or appearing suddenly and dramatically ○ *Tourism experienced explosive growth in the 1990s.* **5.** PHON same as **plosive** ■ *n* **1. SOMETHING THAT EXPLODES** a substance or device that suddenly produces a volume of rapidly expanding gas **2.** PHON same as **plosive** —**explosively** *adv* —**explosiveness** *n*

expo /ékspō/ *n* a large exhibition or trade fair [Mid-20C. Shortening of EXPOSITION]

exponent /ik spṓnənt/ *n* **1. ADVOCATE OF CAUSE** a supporter or promoter of a cause **2. EXPLAINER OF SOMETHING** somebody who explains or interprets something ○ *an exponent of Kant's philosophy* **3. PRACTITIONER OF ART OR SKILL** a performer or practitioner of an art or skill, especially somebody who is regarded as an excellent example of how something should be done ○ *an exponent of the rococo style* **4.** MATHS **NUMBER INDICATING MULTIPLICATION** a number or variable placed to the upper right of a number or mathematical expression that indicates the number of times the number or expression is to be multiplied by itself, as in 2^3, which equals 8 [Late 16C. < Latin *exponent-*, present participle of *exponere* (see EXPOUND)]

exponential /ékspə nénsh'l, ékspō-/ *adj* **1. RAPIDLY GROWING** rapidly becoming greater in size ○ *an exponential increase in sales* **2.** MATHS **INVOLVING MATHEMATICAL EXPONENT** describes a mathematical entity such as a curve, function, equation, or series that contains, is expressed as, or involves numbers or quantities raised to an exponent **3.** MATHS **USING BASE OF NATURAL LOGARITHMS** describes a mathematical entity that involves the transcendental number *e*, the base of natural logarithms, raised to an exponent —**exponentially** *adv*

exponential function *n* a mathematical expression with the formula e^x, in which *e* is the base of natural logarithms. Symbol **exp**

exponential notation *n* SCI same as **scientific notation**

exponentiation /ékspə nenshi áysh'n, ékspō-/ *n* the multiplication of a number or quantity by itself a given number of times, the number of times being the power to which the number or quantity is to be raised

export *v* /ik spάwrt, éks pawrt/ (**-ports, -porting, -ported**) **1.** *vti* COMM **SEND GOODS ABROAD** to send goods for sale or exchange to other countries **2.** *vt* SOC SCI **SPREAD ONE SOCIETY'S CULTURE TO ANOTHER** to cause the spread of ideas, values, or a way of life from one society, culture, or nation to another **3.** *vt* COMPUT **ALTER FORMAT OF COMPUTER DATA** to convert data from a computer program into a form suitable for a different program or environment ■ *n* /éks pawrt/ **1.** COMM **SELLING OF GOODS ABROAD** the selling of goods to other countries **2.** COMM **PRODUCT SOLD ABROAD** a product sold and transported to another country **3.** BEVERAGES **TYPE OF SCOTTISH BEER** a strong brown beer brewed in Scotland [15C. < Latin *exportare* 'carry away' < *portare* 'carry'] —**exportability** /ik spάwrtə bílləti, éks pawrtə-/ *n* —**exportable** *adj* —**exportation** /éks pawr táysh'n/ *n* —**exporter** *n*

expose /ik spṓz/ (**-poses, -posing, -posed**) *v* **1.** *vt* **PUT SOMEBODY IN UNPROTECTED SITUATION** to put somebody or something in a vulnerable or potentially dangerous situation ○ *financially exposed* **2.** *vt* **MAKE SOMEBODY EXPERIENCE SOMETHING** to cause somebody to have a personal and often enlightening experience of something ○ *exposing the children to theatre* **3.** *vt* **ALLOW SOMETHING TO BE SEEN** to uncover something or turn it over with the result that it can be seen ○ *expose the wound to the air* **4.** *vt* **REVEAL SOMEBODY'S WRONGDOINGS** to reveal that somebody has done something wrong, especially by publishing or broadcasting the information **5. expose yourself** *vr* **REVEAL PART OF BODY INDECENTLY** to uncover a part of the body, especially the genitals, in public in an indecent way **6.** *vt* PHOTOGRAPHY **ALLOW LIGHT ONTO FILM** to allow light to fall on light-sensitive material such as photographic film, usually by opening a camera shutter **7.** *vt* CULTL ANTHROP **LEAVE BABY TO DIE OUTSIDE** especially in earlier societies, to abandon a baby to die in the open air, e.g. because it was not healthy **8.** *vt* CHR **SHOW SOMETHING TO BE REVERED** to display something for religious veneration, e.g. the consecrated bread used in a Roman Catholic Communion service [15C. < French *exposer* < (after *poser* 'place') < Latin *exponere* 'set out' (see EXPOUND)] —**exposal** *n* —**exposer** *n*

exposé /ek spṓz ay/ (*plural* **-sés**) *n* **1.** a book or article that reveals details of a scandal or crime **2.** a formal and systematic statement giving facts about something [Early 19C. < French, past participle of *exposer* (see EXPOSE)]

exposed /ik spṓzd/ *adj* **1. VISIBLE OR UNPROTECTED** uncovered and therefore visible or without protection ○ *Cover any exposed areas of skin liberally with sunscreen.* **2. WITH NO SHELTER** unprotected from wind and weather by shelter from trees or higher ground **3. UNPROTECTED FROM HARM** vulnerable to danger or harm **4.** CLIMBING **CARRIED OUT ON ROCK FACE** describes a mountain ascent carried out on a high, sheer, and open rock face —**exposedness** /ik spṓzidnəss, -spṓzd-/ *n*

exposition /ékspə zísh'n/ *n* **1. DETAILED DESCRIPTION OR DISCUSSION** a detailed description of a theory, problem, or proposal discussing the issues involved, or a commentary on a written text discussing its meaning and implications **2. ACT OF DESCRIBING OR DISCUSSING SOMETHING** the act of describing and discussing a theory, problem, or proposal, or of commenting on a written text **3. EXHIBITION OR FAIR** a large exhibition, e.g. of industrial achievements, sometimes international in scope **4.** MUSIC **OPENING SECTION OF MUSICAL COMPOSITION** the opening section of a piece of music, especially of a sonata or fugue, in which the principal themes are introduced **5.** CHR **DISPLAYING SOMETHING TO PUBLIC** in Christianity, the act of showing or displaying something such as a relic or the Host for veneration **6.** LITERAT, THEATRE **FACTUAL BACKGROUND OF NOVEL OR PLAY** the basic facts of setting, period, character, or other relevant parts of a literary work, usually one that is fictional or meant for the theatre [14C. Directly or via French < Latin *exposition-* < *exposit-*, past participle of *exponere* (see EXPOUND)] —**expositive** /ik spózzitiv/ *adj* —**expositor** *n* —**expository** /-təri/ *adj*

ex post facto /éks pōst fáktō/ *adj, adv* applying to events that have already occurred as well as to subsequent events [Mid-17C. < Latin *ex postfacto*, literally 'from what is done afterwards']

expostulate /ik spóstyŏŏ layt/ (**-lates, -lating, -lated**) *vi* to express disagreement or disapproval, especially when attempting to dissuade somebody from doing something [Late 16C. < Latin *expostulat-*, past participle of *expostulare* 'demand from' < *postulare* 'to demand'] —**expostulation** /ik spóstyŏŏ láysh'n/ *n* —**expostulator** *n* —**expostulatory** *adj*

SYNONYMS See ***object***.

---

exposure /ik spṓzhər/ *n* **1. CONTACT WITH SOMETHING** the experience of coming into contact with an environmental condition or social influence that has a harmful or beneficial effect ○ *exposure to the classics* ○ *exposure to second-hand smoke* **2.** BROADCAST, MEDIA **PUBLICITY** the reporting of events by the broadcast or print media **3. REVELATION OF SCANDAL OR IDENTITY** the revelation of a scandal or of somebody's secrets or private information **4.** MED **HARMFUL EFFECTS OF WEATHER** the harmful effects of cold or other extreme weather conditions **5.** PHOTOGRAPHY **TIME THAT LIGHT FALLS ON FILM** an amount of light permitted to fall on light-sensitive material such as film or paper coated with emulsion **6.** PHOTOGRAPHY **TAKING OF PHOTOGRAPH** the act or process of taking a photograph **7.** PHOTOGRAPHY **FILM OR PLATE EXPOSED FOR PHOTOGRAPH** a section of film or a photographic plate exposed to light in taking a photograph **8.** ARCHIT **DIRECTION ROOM OR BUILDING FACES** the direction something faces or the way it is sited relative to sunlight or wind direction ○ *This room has a southern exposure.* **9.** FIN **RISK OF FINANCIAL LOSS** the state of being at risk of financial loss, or the amount of possible financial loss in-

volved **10.** CLIMBING **EXTENT TO WHICH ROCK IS EXPOSED** the extent to which a rock face is exposed to the weather **11.** CULTL ANTHROP **LEAVING BABY TO DIE** especially in earlier societies, the practice of abandoning a baby to die in the open air, e.g. because it was not healthy **12.** GEOL **ROCKY OUTCROPPING** the outcropping of bare rock in a landscape, enabling mapping of the underlying geology

exposure meter *n* a device for measuring the intensity of light for photography, often giving the value as a combination of shutter speed and lens aperture

expound /ik spównd/ (**-pounds, -pounding, -pounded**) *vti* to give a detailed description and explanation of a theory or viewpoint or an explanation of the meaning and implications of a written text [13C. Via Old French < Latin *exponere* 'explain, set out' < *ponere* 'to place'] —**expounder** *n*

express /ik spréss/ *v* (**-presses, -pressing, -pressed**) **1.** *vt* **SAY SOMETHING** to state thoughts or feelings in words ○ *I'd like to express my gratitude.* **2.** *vt* **SHOW MEANING SYMBOLICALLY** to convey meaning by gesture, behaviour, representation in art or drama, or in some other symbolic way ○ *Casual handholding can express profound love between two people.* **3. express yourself** *vr* **REVEAL YOUR THOUGHTS** to make your thoughts and feelings known to other people ○ *able to express herself through her music* **4.** *vt* **REPRESENT SOMETHING AS SYMBOL** to use a symbol, figure, or formula to represent something such as a quantity in a different way ○ *Express the fractions as decimal numbers.* **5.** *vt* **SQUEEZE SOMETHING OUT** to force a liquid out of something by squeezing or pressing (*formal*) **6.** *vt* MAIL **SEND SOMETHING BY SPECIAL FAST DELIVERY** to send a package or message using a special rapid-delivery service **7.** *vt* GENETICS **PRODUCE INHERITED CHARACTERISTIC** to produce an observable inherited characteristic ○ *Some genes are only expressed in adults.* ■ *adj* **1.** TRANSP, MAIL **DONE OR TRAVELLING VERY QUICKLY** travelling, moving, or delivered quickly and directly to the destination ○ *Take the express train.* **2.** COMM **FOR BRIEF TRANSACTIONS** relating to purchases or other transactions that can be completed quickly and easily, e.g. because only one or a few items are involved ○ *We can use the express checkout.* **3. STATED CLEARLY** stated in a clear unambiguous way ○ *his express wish* **4. SPECIFIC** definitely, and usually exclusively, intended or specified ○ *was formed for the express purpose of building affordable housing* ■ *adv* **BY RAPID TRANSFER OR TRANSPORT SYSTEM** by a special rapid-delivery service or an express train, bus, or similar mode of transport ■ *n* **1.** TRANSP **FAST TRAIN OR BUS** a fast train or bus that travels direct to its destination, making few or no stops on the way **2. FAST DELIVERY SERVICE** a special rapid delivery service, or the organization providing it [14C. < medieval Latin *expressare* 'press out' and Latin *expressus* 'clearly evident' < Latin *exprimere* 'press out' < *premere* 'press'] —**expresser** *n* —**expressible** *adj*

expression /ik sprésh'n/ *n* **1. LOOK ON SOMEBODY'S FACE** a look on somebody's face, conveying a thought or feeling ○ *listened with a puzzled expression* **2.** LANGUAGE **WORD OR PHRASE** a word or phrase that communicates an idea ○ *It's a common expression in this part of the country.* **3. CONVEYING OF THOUGHTS OR FEELINGS** the communication of thoughts or feelings, e.g. directly to another person ○ *a heart-rending expression of sorrow* **4. WAY OF COMMUNICATING SOMETHING** something done or given as a means of communicating a feeling or thought to somebody else ○ *As an expression of my gratitude, I'd like you to accept this vase.* **5. INFLECTION IN VOICE** somebody's intonation or tone of voice **6.** MUSIC **INTERPRETIVE ELEMENT OF MUSIC** the interpretive element of music, including tempo, dynamics, articulation, and phrasing, by which a player or singer evokes emotions **7.** MATHS **MATHEMATICAL REPRESENTATION** a combination of constants, operators, and variables representing numbers or quantities ○ *an algebraic expression* **8. EXTRACTION OF LIQUID** the pressing out of a liquid from a substance using pressure **9.** GENETICS **EFFECT OR ACTION OF GENE** the effect or action produced by a gene —**expressional** *adj*

expressionism /ik sprésh'nizəm/ *n* **1.** an artistic movement that flourished in Germany between 1905 and 1925 whose adherents sought to represent feelings and moods rather than objective reality, often distorting colour and form. The term is also used more loosely to apply to the work of Matisse and the Fauves. **2.** THEATRE, LITERAT a literary movement of the early 20th century, especially in the theatre, that represented external reality in a highly stylized and subjective manner, attempting to convey a psychological or spiritual reality rather than a record of actual events. The expressionists include the playwrights August Strindberg, Georg Wedekind, and Eugene O'Neill. —**expressionist** *n, adj* —**expressionistic** /ik spréshə nístik/ *adj* —**expressionistically** *adv*

expressionless /ik sprésh'nləss/ *adj* showing no emotion or interest by the tone of voice or facial movements —**expressionlessly** *adv* —**expressionlessness** *n*

expression mark *n* a symbol or written direction, often in Italian, that indicates the expression to be used in performing a piece of music

expressive /ik spréssiv/ *adj* **1. FULL OF EXPRESSION** expressing a great deal of feeling and meaning ○ *an expressive face* **2. CONVEYING SOMETHING** communicating a particular meaning ○ *a gesture expressive of the utmost contempt* **3.** MED **RELATING TO SPEAKING AND WRITING DISORDERS** relating to disorders involving the expression of ideas in speech and writing as opposed to the interpretation of what is heard or read —**expressively** *adv* —**expressiveness** *n*

expressivity /éks pre sívvəti/ (*plural* **-ties**) *n* **1.** the ability or the extent to which somebody has the ability to communicate emotion or meaning **2.** the extent to which a gene affects the observable characteristics (**phenotype**) of an organism

express lane *n US* ROADS same as **fast lane** (sense 1)

expressly /ik spréssli/ *adv* **1.** in a clear and unambiguous way ○ *He expressly rejected my offer.* **2.** in a way that shows a deliberate intention or choice ○ *He told me the present was meant expressly for me.*

expresso *n* BEVERAGES another spelling of **espresso**

expressway /ik spréss way/ *n Aus, N Am* a limited-access road with several lanes in each direction, designed for fast direct travel especially through or round a city

expropriate /ik sprṓpri ayt/ (**-ates, -ating, -ated**) *vt* to take property or money from somebody, either legally for the public good or illegally by theft or fraud [Late 16C. < medieval Latin *expropriat-*, past participle of *expropriare* 'take away and make your own' < Latin *proprius* 'your own'] —**expropriation** /ik sprṓpri áysh'n/ *n* —**expropriator** *n* —**expropriatory** *adj*

expulsion /ik spúlsh'n/ *n* **1.** the act of compelling somebody to leave or give up membership of an institution such as a school, political party, or club, usually as a punishment **2.** the forcing out of somebody or something from something ○ *expulsion of air from the lungs* [15C. < Latin *expulsion-* < *expuls-*, past participle of *expellere* (see EXPEL)] —**expulsive** *adj*

expunge /ik spúnj/ (**-punges, -punging, -punged**) *vt* **1.** to delete or blot out something unwanted **2.** to destroy or put an end to something [Early 17C. < Latin *expungere* 'prick out' < *pungere* 'mark with a point'; from the placing of points next to text to be deleted] —**expunction** /ik spúngksh'n/ *n* —**expunger** *n*

expurgate /ékspər gayt/ (**-gates, -gating, -gated**) *vt* to remove words or passages considered offensive or unsuitable from a book before publication [Late 17C. < Latin *expurgat-*, past participle of *expurgare* 'cleanse out' < *purgare* 'purify'] —**expurgation** /ékspər gáysh'n/ *n* —**expurgator** *n* —**expurgatorial** /ik spúrgə táwri əl/ *adj* —**expurgatory** /ek spúrgətəri/ *adj*

exquisite /ik skwízzit, ékskwizit/ *adj* **1. FINELY BEAUTIFUL** very beautiful and delicate or intricate ○ *exquisite workmanship* **2. EXCELLENT** perfect and delightful ○ *an exquisite translation of Ovid* **3. SENSITIVE AND DISCRIMINATING** sensitive and capable of detecting subtle differences ○ *exquisite taste in dress* **4. INTENSE** felt with a sharp intensity ○ *exquisite pain* [Mid-16C. < Latin *exquisit-*, past participle of *exquirere* 'seek out' < *quaerere* 'seek, ask'] —**exquisitely** *adv* —**exquisiteness** *n*

exsert /ek súrt/ *vt* (**-serts, -serting, -serted**) to thrust out or project something ○ *A bee exserts its sting.* ■ *adj also* **exserted** projecting beyond an enclosing or adjoining part ○ *an exsert stamen* [Early 19C. < Latin *ex(s)ert-*, past participle of *ex(s)erere* (see EXERT)] —**exsertion** *n*

ex-service *adj* **1.** formerly enlisted in the armed forces **2.** relating to or provided for people who formerly served in the armed forces

ex-serviceman *n* a man formerly in the armed forces

ex-serviceperson *n* somebody formerly in the armed forces

ex-servicewoman *n* a woman formerly in the armed forces

ex silentio /éks si lénshō/ *adv* LAW, LOGIC from or on the basis of a lack of evidence to the contrary [Early 20C. < Latin, 'from silence']

ext. *abbr* **1.** extension **2.** exterior **3.** external **4.** PHARM extract

extant /ek stánt, ékstənt/ *adj* still in existence ○ *Three copies of the document are extant.* [Mid-16C. < Latin *exstant-*, present participle of *exstare* 'exist' < *stare* 'to stand']

~~extasy~~ incorrect spelling of **ecstasy**

extemporaneous /ik stémpə ráyni əss/, **extemporary** /ik stémpərəri/, **extemporal** /ik stémpərəl/ *adj* **1. DONE UNREHEARSED** performed without any preparation **2. PREPARED BUT SAID WITHOUT NOTES** prepared in advance but delivered without notes **3. SKILLED AT SPEAKING UNREHEARSED** skilled at speaking without preparation or notes **4. MAKESHIFT** done as a temporary measure [Mid-17C. < late Latin *extemporaneus* < *ex tempore*, literally 'out of the moment'] —**extemporaneity** /ik stémpərə née əti, -náy-/ *n* —**extemporaneously** *adv* —**extemporaneousness** *n*

extempore /ik stémpəri/ *adj, adv* with little or no preparation [Mid-16C. < Latin *ex tempore*, literally 'out of the moment']

extemporize /ik stémpə rīz/ (**-rizes, -rizing, -rized**), **extemporise** (**-rises, -rising, -rised**) *vti* **1. PERFORM SOMETHING WITHOUT PREPARATION** to perform or say something without having made any preparation **2.** MUSIC **IMPROVISE MUSIC** to compose or perform a piece of music by improvising **3. HANDLE IN MAKESHIFT WAY** to do or devise something in a makeshift fashion [Mid-17C. < EXTEMPORE] —**extemporization** /ik stémpə rī záysh'n/ *n* —**extemporizer** *n*

extend /ik sténd/ (**-tends, -tending, -tended**) *v* **1.** *vti* **OPEN OUT INTO SPACE** to stretch out into space, or stretch something out into space ○ *fully extended the robot's arm* **2.** *vt* **INCREASE SIZE OF SOMETHING** to make something larger, longer, or broader in scope ○ *extend the driveway* ○ *extending the scope of the law* **3.** *vi* **OCCUPY DISTANCE OR SPACE** to continue for a distance or occupy a space, often within a particular range ○ *The city centre extends for another mile in both directions.* **4.** *vi* **CONTINUE FOR TIME** to last or continue for a period of time, usually a particular one ○ *talks extending over the weekend* **5.** *vt* **INCREASE TIME SPAN** to increase the length of time something lasts or the length of time before something applies or ceases to apply **6.** *vt* **INCREASE AMOUNT BY ADDING SOMETHING** to increase the amount of something by adding something else to it ○ *There's not much stew left, but we could always extend it by adding more potatoes and vegetables.* **7.** *vti* **BE APPLICABLE TO SOMEBODY OR SOMETHING** to affect or apply to somebody or something, or make something do this ○ *The offer extends to new readers too.* **8.** *vt* **OFFER OR GIVE SOMETHING** to offer or provide something to somebody ○ *extended the hand of friendship* **9.** *vt* **MAKE EXTRA EFFORT** to work, or make somebody or something work, as hard as possible to achieve the best possible result ○ *need to extend themselves to finish on time* **10.** *vt* ACCT **CALCULATE LINE TOTAL ON INVOICE** to calculate the total on the line of an invoice by multiplying quantity by price [14C. < Latin *extendere* 'stretch out' < *tendere* 'hold out, stretch'] —**extendability** /ik sténdə bílləti/ *n* —**extendable** *adj* —**extensible** /ik sténssəb'l/ *adj*

SYNONYMS See ***increase***.

extended /ik sténdid/ *adj* **1. LASTING LONGER THAN USUAL OR EXPECTED** lasting longer than expected or planned **2. MADE LONGER OR LARGER** stretched or pulled out, lengthened, enlarged, or expanded **3. HAVING WIDER RANGE** having wider influence, effect, or application **4.** PRINTING same as **expanded** (sense 3) —**extendedly** *adv*

Extended Binary Coded Decimal Interchange Code *n* COMPUT full form of **EBCDIC**

extended family *n* the family as a unit embracing parents and children together with grandparents,

aunts, uncles, cousins, and sometimes more distant relatives

extended-play *adj* (*not hyphenated when used after a verb*) **1.** describes a video tape format that can record four or six hours of material on a two-hour tape **2.** describes a vinyl record of the same size as a single but with two tracks on each side instead of one

extended school *n UK* a school that provides an education for children as well as a range of family and community services such as childcare, health care, and adult education

extender /ik sténdər/ *n* **1.** a substance that is added to a product to dilute it, add body to it, or modify it in other ways **2.** the part of a lowercase letter such as 'p' or 'h' that projects above or below the body of the letter

extensible /ik sténssəb'l/ *adj* having the capability of being extended [Early 17C. Directly or via French < medieval Latin *extensibilis* < Latin *extens-* (see EXTENSION)] —**extensibility** /ik sténssə bíllәti/ *n* —**extensibly** *adv*

Extensible Markup Language *n* COMPUT full form of **XML**

extensimeter *n* ENG same as **extensometer**

extension /ik sténsh'n/ *n* **1.** BUILDINGS **ADDITION TO BUILDING** a room or area added to an existing building ○ *We're having an extension built onto the kitchen.* **2.** **ADDITIONAL PIECE** a piece that has been or can be added, or that can be pulled out, to enlarge or lengthen something **3.** TELECOM **ADDITIONAL TELEPHONE LINE** an additional telephone line or telephone connected to the main line in a building or organization, often having its own number **4.** TELECOM **TELEPHONE NUMBER OF EXTENSION** the number used to contact a telephone extension within a building or organization **5.** ELEC same as **extension lead** **6.** **ADDITIONAL PERIOD OF TIME** an additional period of time allowed for completion of work or payment of a debt ○ *You'll never finish that essay on time: why don't you ask for an extension?* **7.** PUBLIC ADMIN **EXTENDED DRINKS LICENCE** permission to serve alcoholic drinks until a later time than usual **8.** **EXTENDING OR BEING EXTENDED** the act or process of increasing the size, scope, range, or application of something, or the fact of being increased in size, scope, range, or application ○ *the extension of parental leave to fathers* ○ *the extension of the waterway network* **9.** **RANGE** the range or sphere over which something extends **10.** **OFF-CAMPUS UNIVERSITY TEACHING PROGRAMME** courses or facilities provided by a college or university for people who are unable to attend classes on the campus or during scheduled class periods **11.** MED same as **traction** (sense 1) **12.** ANAT **STRAIGHTENING OF LIMB** the stretching out of a limb after it has been bent, or the position attained by a limb after stretching it **13.** LOGIC **BROADER SENSE OF EXPRESSION** the broad range of meaning of an expression, as opposed to its precise meaning. The extension of the term 'man' is the set comprising all men, whereas the meaning of the word 'man' is 'an adult male human being'. **14.** MATHS **SET INCLUDING TWO SIMILAR SETS** a mathematical set that includes as subsets all the members of a given set and of another similar set **15.** COMPUT same as **file extension** ■ **extensions** *npl* **EXTRA HAIR ATTACHED TO YOUR OWN** lengths of real or synthetic hair attached to the hair to create a longer hairstyle [Early 16C. < late Latin *extension-* < Latin *extens-*, past participle of *extendere* (see EXTEND)] —**extensional** *adj* —**extensionally** *adv*

extension cable *n* a cable that can be used to attach an extension lead to an electrical supply when the lead itself is too short to reach it

extension lead *n* a length of electrical lead with a plug at one end and a socket at the other, used to connect an appliance when the electrical supply is some distance away

extensive /ik sténssiv/ *adj* **1.** **VAST** covering a large area ○ *a hotel set in extensive grounds* **2.** **BROAD IN SCOPE** great in extent, range, or application ○ *extensive research into the origins of language* **3.** **LARGE IN AMOUNT** great in amount or number ○ *extensive water damage from the flooding* **4.** AGRIC **USING LOW TECHNOLOGICAL INPUT** relating to a farming practice in which a large area of land is cultivated using little labour and expense, resulting in a relatively small crop. ◊ **intensive** [Early 17C. Directly or via French < late Latin *extensivus* < Latin *extens-* (see EXTENSION)] —**extensively** *adv* —**extensiveness** *n*

extensometer /ék sten sómmitər/, **extensimeter** /-símmitər/ *n* a device for measuring small changes of length in a sample, especially those caused by stress or thermal expansion in a metal [Late 19C. < Latin *extens-* (see EXTENSION)]

extensor /ik sténssər, ik stén sawr/ *n* a muscle that straightens or extends a part of the body, e.g. an arm or leg [Early 18C. < modern Latin < Latin *extens-* (see EXTENSION)]

extent /ik stént/ *n* **1.** **RANGE OR SCOPE** the area or range covered or affected by something ○ *the location and extent of the damage* **2.** **DEGREE** the degree to which something applies ○ *To what extent should we allow newspaper reporters into people's private lives?* **3.** **REGION** an area of land or water **4.** LAW **WRIT ALLOWING SEIZURE OF PROPERTY** a writ that authorizes somebody to take possession of the property of a person who owes him or her money [Late 16C. Via Anglo-Norman, 'valuation of land' < medieval Latin *extenta* < Latin *extendere* (see EXTEND)]

extenuate /ik sténnyoo ayt/ (**-ates, -ating, -ated**) *vt* to make a mistake or wrongdoing seem less serious than it first appeared, e.g. by providing a mitigating excuse for it [Early 16C. < Latin *extenuat-*, past participle of *extenuare* 'thin out' < *tenuis* 'thin'] —**extenuating** *adj* —**extenuatingly** *adv* —**extenuation** /ik sténnyoo áysh'n/ *n* —**extenuative** /ik sténnyoo ətiv/ *adj* —**extenuator** *n* —**extenuatory** *adj*

extenuating circumstances *npl* factors that make somebody's actions excusable or less blameworthy

exterior /ik stéeri ər/ *adj* **1.** **ON OUTSIDE** on or for the outside of something ○ *the exterior walls of the building* **2.** **COMING FROM OUTSIDE** coming from outside or beyond somebody or something ○ *There must be some exterior cause for this.* **3.** ARTS **OUTDOOR** describes an image depicting an outdoor setting or a photograph or film scene taken out of doors ○ *an exterior shot* ■ *n* **1.** **OUTSIDE** the outside surface, appearance, or coating of something **2.** **OUTWARD APPEARANCE** somebody's outward appearance as distinct from his or her inner thoughts ○ *her calm exterior* **3.** ARTS **SCENE SET OUT OF DOORS** an outdoor scene, especially as represented in the visual arts [Early 16C. < Latin, 'more outward' < *exter* 'outward, on the outside'] —**exteriority** /ik stéeri órrəti, éks-/ *n*

exterior angle *n* **1.** an angle on the outside of a polygon, formed between a side and an extension of an adjacent side **2.** any of four angles formed on the outside of a pair of lines that are crossed by a third line

exteriorize /ik stéeri ə rīz/ (**-izes, -izing, -ized**), **exteriorise** (**-ises, -ising, -ised**) *vt* **1.** same as **externalize** **2.** to remove an internal organ from the body, e.g. in order to perform surgery on it —**exteriorization** /ik stéeri ə rī záysh'n/ *n*

exterminate /ik stúrmi nayt/ (**-nates, -nating, -nated**) *vt* to kill or destroy somebody or something completely ○ *a species nearly exterminated by hunting* [Late 16C. < Latin *exterminat-*, past participle of *exterminare* 'drive beyond the boundaries' < *termin-* 'boundary'] —**extermination** /ik stúrmi náysh'n/ *n* —**exterminatory** /-nətəri/ *adj*

exterminator /ik stúrmi naytər/ *n* **1.** somebody whose job is to kill unwanted insects and other animals **2.** somebody or something that kills or destroys somebody or something else completely

extern /ék sturn/, **externe** *n US* a nonresident doctor or other staff member attached to a hospital [Early 17C. Via French < Latin *externus* (see EXTERNAL)] —**externship** *n*

external /ik stúrn'l/ *adj* **1.** **OUTSIDE** situated on, happening on, or coming from the outside ○ *external forces* **2.** **FOR USE ON OUTSIDE** suitable or designed for use only on the outside or surface of something, especially the body ○ *This medication is for external use only.* **3.** **OUTSIDE SCOPE OF SOMETHING** existing outside the body or mind, or the limits of something ○ *the external world* **4.** **VISIBLE FROM OUTWARD APPEARANCE** conveyed by somebody's or something's outward appearance, as opposed to what is inside or underneath **5.** **OUTSIDE ORGANIZATION** relating to, forming, or from a separate or independent organization **6.** POL **RELATING TO FOREIGN COUNTRIES** dealing with or involving relations with foreign countries ■ *n* **1.** **EXTERIOR OF SOMETHING** the outer surface of something **2.** *Aus* EDUC **EXTRAMURAL STUDENT** a student studying at an educational institution on an extramural basis ■ **externals** *npl* **1.** **OUTWARD APPEARANCES** the outward appearance of somebody or something, especially when it is not considered to be a true indication of the person's or thing's real nature **2.** **SURROUNDINGS** somebody's or something's circumstances or environment [Late 16C. Partly < French *externe*, partly < Latin *externus* < *exter* 'outward, on the outside'] —**externally** *adv*

external-combustion engine *n* an engine that converts into power heat generated from fuel consumed outside the engine, e.g. a steam engine. ◊ **internal-combustion engine**

external degree *n* a degree for which the candidate does not follow a formal course of study within a university, but sits the required examinations to gain the qualification

external ear *n* the outside part of the ear, consisting of the auricle and auditory canal

external examination *n* an examination set and marked by an authority outside a candidate's own school, college, or university —**external examiner** *n*

externalism /ik stúrn'lizəm/ *n* **1.** excessive concern about outward forms and appearances, especially in religious matters **2.** the view that the content of thoughts depends at least partly on relationships with objects outside the mind —**externalist** *n*

externality /ékstur nálləti/ (*plural* **-ties**) *n* **1.** **QUALITY OF BEING EXTERNAL** the fact or quality of being external **2.** **SOMETHING OUTSIDE OR EXTERNAL** an outward form or appearance, or anything that is outside or external to somebody or something **3.** ECON **CONSEQUENCE OF PRODUCTION IGNORED IN PRICING** a factor such as environmental damage that results from the way something is produced but is not taken into account in establishing the market price of the goods or materials concerned **4.** PHILOSOPHY **EXISTENCE INDEPENDENT OF MIND** the quality something has of existing independently of the mind that perceives it

externalize /ik stúrnə līz/ (**-izes, -izing, -ized**), **externalise** (**-ises, -ising, -ised**) *vt* **1.** **GIVE OUTWARD EXPRESSION TO SOMETHING** to express ideas or feelings in some visible or perceptible way in order to communicate them to somebody else **2.** **PERCEIVE SOMETHING AS EXTERNAL** to attribute something to causes in the outside world **3.** PSYCHOL **ATTRIBUTE FEELINGS TO OUTSIDE CAUSES** to attribute emotions or inner conflicts to outside causes, sources, or surroundings —**externalization** /ik stúrnə lī záysh'n/ *n*

external respiration *n* the exchange of gases between an organism's respiratory system, e.g. the lungs in vertebrates, and the outside environment

externe /ék sturn/ *n US* HEALTH SERVICES another spelling of **extern**

exteroceptor /ékstərō séptər/ *n* a body part or sensory organ that is able to receive outside stimuli, e.g. the eye, ear, or any of the nerve endings in the skin [Early 20C. < Latin *exter* 'outward, on the outside' + RECEPTOR] —**exteroceptive** *adj*

exterritorial *adj* POL, LAW same as **extraterritorial**

extinct /ik stíngkt/ *adj* **1.** **HAVING NO LIVING MEMBERS** having no members of the species or family in existence, as is the case with many organisms known only from fossils **2.** **NO LONGER IN EXISTENCE** having died out or ceased to exist ○ *relics of extinct and forgotten civilizations* **3.** GEOL **NO LONGER ERUPTING** describes a volcano that is no longer active or likely to erupt **4.** SOC SCI, LAW **NOT NOW VALID** no longer valid or practised ○ *This custom has for many years been almost extinct.* **5.** **EXTINGUISHED** extinguished, quenched, or no longer burning [15C. < Latin *exstinct-*, past participle of *exstinguere* (see EXTINGUISH)]

SYNONYMS See ***dead***.

extinction /ik stíngksh'n/ *n* **1.** **FACT OF BECOMING EXTINCT** the gradual process by which a group of related organisms dies out **2.** **OBSOLESCENCE** the process or fact of disappearing completely from use ○ *'Dominant languages and dialects spread widely, and lead to the gradual extinction of other tongues.'* (Charles Darwin, *The Descent of Man*; 1871) **3.** GEOL **PROCESS OF BECOMING INACTIVE** the permanent ceasing of eruptions

in a volcano **4.** SOC SCI, LAW **STATE OF BEING NO LONGER VALID** the state of no longer being valid or practised, or the process of ceasing to be valid or practised **5.** **DESTRUCTION OF SOMEBODY OR SOMETHING** the destruction or killing off of somebody or something ○ *the extinction of self and ego through meditation* **6.** PHYS, ASTRON **LOWERING OF RADIATION INTENSITY** the reduction of radiation intensity because of absorption or scattering as it passes through matter. This effect is observed in the reduction in the intensity of electromagnetic radiation reaching Earth from astronomical objects because of the interference of interstellar gas and dust. **7.** PSYCHOL **REDUCTION IN RESPONSE** the decreasing or dying out of a behavioural response created by conditioning because of a lack of reinforcement —**extinctive** *adj*

extinguish /ik stíng gwish/ (**-guishes, -guishing, -guished**) *vt* **1. PUT OUT FIRE OR LIGHT** to put out something that is burning or giving off light ○ *The last of the oil-well fires was finally extinguished.* **2. END SOMETHING** to take away or bring to an end something such as a hope, feeling, custom, or practice ○ *As the days went by, hope for more survivors was extinguished.* **3. DESTROY SOMEBODY OR SOMETHING** to kill or destroy somebody or something completely (*literary*) ○ *They intended to extinguish the enemy by force of numbers.* **4. OUTSHINE** to outshine or eclipse somebody or something by having greater brilliance ○ *beauty that extinguishes all others by comparison* **5.** LAW **PAY DEBT** to pay off a debt **6.** LAW **MAKE SOMETHING INVALID** to make something no longer valid or applicable **7.** PSYCHOL **DECREASE RESPONSE** to cause a decrease in a behavioural response created by conditioning because of a lack of reinforcement [Early 16C. < Latin *exstinguere* 'quench completely' < *stinguere* 'quench, prick'] —**extinguishable** *adj* —**extinguishment** *n*

extinguisher /ik stíng gwishər/ *n* **1.** EMERGENCIES same as **fire extinguisher** **2.** somebody or something that puts an end to something else or eliminates its effects

extirpate /ék stur payt/ (**-pates, -pating, -pated**) *vt* **1.** to completely get rid of, kill off, or destroy somebody or something considered undesirable (*formal*) **2.** to remove something surgically [Mid-16C. < Latin *ex(s)tirpat-*, past participle of *ex(s)tirpare* 'root out' < *stirps* 'stem, root'] —**extirpation** /ék stur páysh'n/ *n* —**extirpative** /ék stur paytiv/ *adj* —**extirpator** *n*

extol /ik stṓl/ (**-tols, -tolling, -tolled**) *vt* to praise somebody or something with great enthusiasm and admiration (*literary*) [Early 16C. < Latin *extollere* 'raise up' < *tollere* 'raise'] —**extoller** *n* —**extolment** *n*

extort /ik stáwrt/ (**-torts, -torting, -torted**) *vt* to obtain something such as money or information from somebody by using force, threats, or other unacceptable methods [15C. < Latin *extort-*, past participle of *extorquere* 'twist out' < *torquere* 'to twist'] —**extorter** *n* —**extortive** *adj*

extortion /ik stáwrsh'n/ *n* **1.** LAW **OBTAINING SOMETHING BY ILLEGAL THREATS** the crime of obtaining something such as money or information from somebody by using force, threats, or other unacceptable methods **2.** **CHARGING OF UNFAIRLY HIGH PRICES** the charging of an excessive amount of money for something (*informal*) **3.** **GETTING SOMETHING BY FORCE** the acquisition of something through the use of force or threats —**extortionary** *adj* —**extortioner** *n* —**extortionist** *n*

extortionate /ik stáwrsh'nət/ *adj* **1.** highly excessive, especially in price **2.** involving or using extortion —**extortionately** *adv*

extra /ékstrə/ *adj* **1. MORE THAN USUAL** added to, or over and above, the usual, original, or necessary amount ○ *Take extra precautions when travelling in bad weather.* **2. MORE AND BETTER** greater in degree and of better quality than is normal **3. CHARGED FOR IN ADDITION** charged for in addition to the basic cost ○ *You get one free drink with the meal; further drinks are extra.* ■ *adv* **EXCEPTIONALLY** to a greater extent than is usual or expected ○ *Be extra careful at that crossing.* ■ *pron* **MORE** more than the usual amount or price ○ *The hotel charges extra for satellite television.* ■ *n* **1. SOMETHING ADDITIONAL** something additional or unexpected ○ *The remaining items are optional extras.* **2. SOMETHING CHARGED FOR IN ADDITION** something for which an additional charge is made, or the additional charge itself ○ *Make sure there are no hidden extras.* **3.** CINEMA **NONSPEAKING FILM ACTOR** somebody employed in a minor, usually nonspeaking, part in a film, e.g. in a crowd scene **4.** MEDIA **SPECIAL EDITION OF NEWSPAPER** a special edition of a newspaper or magazine, often reporting later news or concentrating on a particular subject ○ *a sports extra* **5. RUN SCORED WITHOUT HITTING BALL** in cricket, a run added to a team's score but not credited to an individual batsman, e.g. as a result of the bowler bowling a no-ball or a wide [Mid-17C. Probably shortening of EXTRAORDINARY]

extra-, **extro-** *prefix* beyond or outside something ○ *extraterrestrial* ○ *extracurricular* [< Latin *extra* 'outside, beyond' < *exter* 'outer']

extracellular /ékstrə séllyŏŏlər/ *adj* situated or happening outside a cell or cells —**extracellularly** *adv*

extrachromosomal /ékstrə krōmə sṓm'l/ *adj* describes an inheritance of characteristics that is controlled by factors not carried on chromosomes

extracorporeal /ékstrə kawr páwri əl/ *adj* situated or happening outside the body —**extracorporeally** *adv*

extra cover *n* **1.** in cricket, a fielding position that lies between cover and mid-off **2.** in cricket, a player fielding in the position of extra cover

extracranial /ékstrə kráyni əl/ *adj* situated or happening outside the skull

extract *vt* /ik strákt/ (**-tracts, -tracting, -tracted**) **1. PULL SOMETHING OUT** to pull something out, often using force ○ *have a tooth extracted* **2. OBTAIN SOMETHING FROM SOURCE** to obtain something from a source, usually by separating it out from other material ○ *a few snippets of information that I managed to extract from the conversation* **3. GET SOMETHING BY FORCE** to obtain something from somebody who is unwilling to give it, often by using force or threats ○ *extracted a confession from him* **4. COPY PASSAGE OF TEXT** to copy or remove a passage from a text ○ *This scene is extracted from the author's memoirs.* **5. DERIVE PLEASURE FROM SOMETHING** to obtain pleasure or enjoyment from something **6.** CHEM, INDUST **TAKE SOMETHING OUT OF COMPOUND** to obtain a substance from a compound, in solid, liquid, or gas form, by using an industrial or chemical process **7.** MATHS **FIND ROOT OF NUMBER** to calculate the value of the root, e.g. the square root or cube root, of a number ■ *n* /ék strakt/ **1. PASSAGE FROM TEXT OR FILM** a passage taken from a publication, film, or play ○ *an extract from her forthcoming book* **2. PURIFIED SUBSTANCE** a concentrated or purified substance obtained by first using a solvent to dissolve this substance when present in a mixture and then evaporating the solvent ○ *vanilla extract* **3.** CHEM, INDUST **SUBSTANCE SEPARATED FROM COMPOUND** a substance obtained from a compound by an industrial or chemical process ○ *mineral extracts* **4.** PHARM **CONCENTRATED SOLUTION** an alcohol solution of the pharmaceutically active agents in a natural product [15C. < Latin *extract-*, past participle of *extrahere* 'pull out' < *trahere* 'pull'] —**extractable** *adj*

extraction /ik stráksh'n/ *n* **1. TAKING OUT OF SOMETHING** the process of extracting something or of being extracted **2. SOMETHING EXTRACTED** something that has been extracted **3.** DENT **REMOVAL OF TOOTH** the removal of a tooth or teeth **4.** CHEM **SEPARATION OF SUBSTANCES** the separation of a substance from a mixture by dissolving one or more of the components in a solvent **5. ETHNIC ORIGIN** the original nationality of somebody's ancestors ○ *of Spanish extraction*

extractive /ik stráktiv/ *adj* **1. EXTRACTABLE** capable of being extracted **2. USED IN EXTRACTING** used in the process of extraction **3. OBTAINED BY EXTRACTION** obtained as a result of extraction ■ *n* **1. SOMETHING EXTRACTABLE** something that can be extracted **2.** CHEM **PART OF CHEMICAL EXTRACT** the insoluble part of a chemical extract —**extractively** *adv*

extractor /ik stráktər/ *n* **1.** a device that removes a liquid from a solid, e.g. the juice out of a fruit **2.** same as **extractor fan** **3.** the part of a firearm that removes spent cartridges from the chamber

extractor fan *n* an electric fan, often set into a window, used to remove steam, fumes, or stale air from a room or building

extracurricular /ékstrə kə ríkyŏŏlər/ *adj* **1.** EDUC **OUTSIDE NORMAL CURRICULUM** done or happening outside the normal curriculum of a school, college, or university **2. OUTSIDE SOMEBODY'S NORMAL DUTIES** not part of the normal duties of a job or profession **3. WITH SOMEBODY OTHER THAN PARTNER** involving somebody other than a spouse or partner (*informal*)

extraditable /ékstrə dītəb'l/ *adj* **1.** describes a crime for which somebody may be extradited **2.** liable to be extradited for a crime

extradite /ékstrə dīt/ (**-dites, -diting, -dited**) *vt* to return somebody accused of a crime by a different legal authority to that authority for trial or punishment [Mid-19C. Back-formation < EXTRADITION]

extradition /ékstrə dísh'n/ *n* the process of returning somebody accused of a crime by a different legal authority to that authority for trial or punishment [Mid-19C. < French < Latin *ex-* 'out' + *tradition-* 'deliverance' (see TRADITION)]

extrados /ek stráy doss/ (*plural same* or **-doses**) *n* the outer curve of an arch [Late 18C. < French < Latin *extra* 'outside' + French *dos* 'back']

extraembryonic membrane /ékstrə embri ónnik-/ *n* a membrane derived from embryonic tissue that lies outside the embryo, e.g. the yolk sac, amnion, and chorion

extragalactic /ékstrəgə láktik/ *adj* existing, originating, or happening outside the Milky Way, the galaxy that contains our solar system

extrajudicial /ékstrə joo dísh'l/ *adj* **1.** happening or originating outside the normal course of legal proceedings **2.** outside the jurisdiction of a court —**extrajudicially** *adv*

extralegal /ékstrə leeg'l/ *adj* not permitted by or subject to the law —**extralegally** *adv*

extralimital /ékstrə límmit'l/ *adj* describes a species or group of organisms found outside a given area, e.g. a population of lions outside a national park

extramarital /ékstrə márrit'l/ *adj* involving sexual relations with somebody other than a marriage partner

extramundane /ékstrə mun dáyn/ *adj* not belonging to the physical world [Mid-17C. < late Latin *extramundanus* < *extra mundum* 'outside the world or universe']

extramural /ékstrə myŏŏrəl/ *adj* **1.** outside or additional to the usual courses of study at a university, college, or other educational institution, though usually connected with them **2.** outside the walls or boundaries of something such as a castle, town, or organization [Mid-19C. < Latin *extra muros* 'outside the walls']

extraneous /ik stráyni əss/ *adj* **1. NOT RELEVANT** not relevant or applicable **2. NOT ESSENTIAL** not essential or important **3. COMING FROM OUTSIDE** existing or coming from outside [Mid-17C. < Latin *extraneus* 'foreign, strange' < *extra* (see EXTRA-)] —**extraneously** *adv* —**extraneousness** *n*

extranet /ékstrə net/ *n* an extension of the intranet of a company or organization, giving authorized outsiders controlled access to the intranet

extranuclear /ékstrə nyŏŏkli ər/ *adj* **1.** existing in or affecting parts of a cell outside the nucleus **2.** existing, happening, or originating outside the nucleus of an atom

extraordinaire /ik stráwdi náir/ *adj* excellent or outstanding (*used after nouns*) ○ *a piano player extraordinaire* [Mid-20C. Via French < Latin *extraordinarius* (see EXTRAORDINARY)]

extraordinary /ik stráwrd'nəri, ékstrə áwrd'nəri/ *adj* **1. UNUSUALLY EXCELLENT OR STRANGE** very unusual and deserving attention and comment because of being wonderful, excellent, strange, or shocking ○ *For a ten-year-old, her mathematical abilities are quite extraordinary.* **2. ADDITIONAL** additional and having a special purpose ○ *an extraordinary meeting* **3. EMPLOYED FOR SPECIAL PURPOSE** employed for a special purpose or to do additional work (*used after nouns*) ○ *ambassador extraordinary* **4. ADDITIONAL AND GREATER** additional to and going beyond the ordinary or established scope of something ○ *The president used his extraordinary powers to introduce major economic reform.* [15C. < Latin *extraordinarius* < *extra ordinem* 'out of order, exceptionally'] —**extraordinarily** *adv* —**extraordinariness** *n*

extraordinary general meeting *n* a meeting of a company or a formally constituted association, specially called by the board or a group of shareholders or members, to discuss a particular, and usually important, piece of business

extra point *n* in American football, a point scored by kicking the field goal awarded after a touchdown

extrapolate /ik stráppə layt/ (**-lates, -lating, -lated**) *v* **1.** *vti* to use known facts as the starting point from which to draw inferences or conclusions about something unknown ○ *We try to avoid extrapolating a flu epidemic from mere anecdotal evidence.* **2.** *vt* to estimate a value that falls outside a range of known values, e.g. by extending a curve on a graph [Mid-19C. < EXTRA- + INTERPOLATE] —**extrapolation** /ik stráppə láysh'n/ *n* —**extrapolative** /ik stráppələtiv/ *adj* —**extrapolator** *n*

extrasensory /ékstrə sénssəri/ *adj* relating to or involving powers of perception other than the normal five senses

extrasensory perception *n* the apparent ability of some people to become aware of things by means other than the normal senses, e.g. through clairvoyance or telepathy

extrasolar /ékstrə sṓlər/ *adj* existing in or relating to space outside our solar system

extraterrestrial /ékstrətə résstri əl/ *adj* existing or coming from somewhere outside Earth and its atmosphere ■ *n* a living being that comes from outside Earth, especially in science fiction

extraterritorial /ékstrə teri táwri əl/, **exterritorial** /éks teri-/ *adj* **1.** situated or coming from outside a country's territorial boundary **2.** LAW, POL relating to or involving exemption from the legal jurisdiction of a country of residence —**extraterritorially** *adv*

extraterritoriality /ékstrə teri tawri álləti/ *n* exemption from the legal jurisdiction of a country of residence, granted to people such as foreign diplomats

extra time *n* an additional fixed period played at the end of a match if the scores are equal at full time and a decisive result is needed. N Am term **overtime**

extrauterine /ékstrə yóotə rīn, -rin/ *adj* occurring or situated outside the womb ○ *an extrauterine pregnancy*

extravagance /ik strávvəgənss/, **extravagancy** /-gənssi/ (*plural* **-cies**) *n* **1.** IMMODERATE SPENDING excessive or wasteful spending of money ○ *was condemned to poverty by their father's extravagance* **2.** EXPENSIVE THING something that is expensive or wasteful ○ *A car like that is an extravagance in today's economic climate.* **3.** EXCESSIVENESS the exaggerated, excessive, or extremely flamboyant nature of something, e.g. a wild unreasonableness in somebody's speech or behaviour

extravagant /ik strávvəgənt/ *adj* **1.** SPENDING TOO MUCH characterized by excessive or wasteful spending ○ *was criticized for her extravagant lifestyle* **2.** UNREASONABLY HIGH IN PRICE unreasonably high in price or cost **3.** BEYOND WHAT IS REASONABLE exaggerated or unreasonable ○ *an extravagant claim* **4.** FLAMBOYANT profusely or exaggeratedly decorated, decorative, or showy **5.** ABUNDANT existing or produced in quantity ○ *extravagant praise* [14C. < medieval Latin < Latin *extra* 'outside' + *vagari* 'wander'] —**extravagantly** *adv*

extravaganza /ik strávvə gánzə/ *n* **1.** a lavish and spectacular entertainment **2.** any spectacular or elaborate display [Mid-18C. < Italian *estravaganza* 'peculiar behaviour' < *estravagante* 'extravagant']

~~**extravagent**~~ incorrect spelling of **extravagant**

extravasate /ik strávvə sayt/ (**-sates, -sating, -sated**) *vti* to leak, or cause blood or other fluid to leak, from a vessel into surrounding tissue as a result of injury, burns, or inflammation [Mid-17C. < EXTRA- + Latin *vas* 'vessel'] —**extravasation** /ik strávvə sáysh'n/ *n*

extravascular /ékstrə váskyóolər/ *adj* not contained in the body's blood or lymph vessels

extravehicular activity /ékstrə vi híkyóolər-/ *n* activity undertaken by an astronaut outside the spacecraft during a mission, e.g. a repair to the craft, or an experiment on the surface of the Moon

extraversion *n* PSYCHOL, MED same as **extroversion**

extravert *n, adj* PSYCHOL same as **extrovert**

extra-virgin olive oil *n* the highest quality of olive oil, made from the first cold pressing of ripe olives

extreme /ik stréem/ *adj* **1.** GREAT OR INTENSE highest in intensity or degree ○ *will withstand extreme pressure* **2.** NOT REASONABLE going far beyond what is reasonable, moderate, or normal ○ *an extreme reaction* ○ *the extreme right wing of the party* **3.** FARTHEST OUT farthest out, especially from the centre ○ *the extreme north of the country* **4.** SEVERE very strict or severe ○ *extreme and costly security measures* **5.** LEISURE, SPORTS SENSATION-SEEKING describes sports or leisure activities in which participants actively seek out dangerous or even life-threatening experiences ○ *extreme skiing* ■ *n* **1.** FURTHEST LIMIT the furthest limit or highest degree of something ○ *the extreme of bad taste* **2.** END OF SCALE something or somebody that represents each of the two ends of a scale or range, e.g. the highest or lowest degree of something, or a quality and its polar opposite ○ *alternated between the extremes of hope and despair* **3.** FIRST OR LAST TERM the first or last term in a mathematical proportion or series ■ **extremes** *npl* DRASTIC MEASURES drastic or unreasonable measures ○ *The authorities have been driven to extremes by the widespread popular unrest.* [15C. Via French < Latin *extremus* 'farthest, last' < *ex* 'out'] —**extremeness** *n*

extremely /ik stréemli/ *adv* to a very high degree ○ *She plays the violin extremely well.*

extremely high frequency *n* a radio frequency in the range between 30,000 and 300,000 megahertz

extremely low frequency *n* a radio frequency below 30 hertz

extremeophile /ik stréem ə fīl/ *n* an organism, especially a microorganism, that thrives in climatic or environmental extremes such as the intense heat of a boiling sulphur pool or the intense cold of Arctic permafrost

extreme unction *n* the Roman Catholic sacrament of anointing the sick (*dated*)

extremism /ik stréemizəm/ *n* the holding of extreme political or religious views or the taking of extreme actions on the basis of those views —**extremist** *n, adj*

extremity /ik strémməti/ *n* (*plural* **-ties**) **1.** HAND OR FOOT a limb of a person or animal, or the part of a limb that is farthest from the body, especially somebody's hand or foot (*often used in the plural*) **2.** FARTHEST POINT a point that is the farthest out, especially from the centre ○ *the southernmost extremity of the continent* **3.** HIGHEST DEGREE the highest degree or greatest intensity of something ○ *in the extremity of her grief* **4.** DANGER a situation or state of great danger or distress ○ *They prayed for help in their extremity.* ■ **extremities** *npl* DRASTIC MEASURES drastic or unreasonable measures (*formal*)

~~**extremly**~~ incorrect spelling of **extremely**

extricate /ékstri kayt/ (**-cates, -cating, -cated**) *vt* to release somebody or something with difficulty from a physical constraint or an unpleasant or complicated situation ○ *was unable to extricate himself from the contract* [Early 17C. < Latin *extricat-*, past participle of *extricare* 'remove from perplexities' < *tricae* 'perplexities'] —**extricable** /ik stríkəb'l, ékstrik-/ *adj* —**extrication** /ékstri káysh'n/ *n*

extrinsic /ek strínssik, -zik/ *adj* **1.** not an essential part of something ○ *It's a good point, but extrinsic to the argument.* **2.** coming or operating from outside something ○ *extrinsic influences* [Mid-16C. < late Latin *extrinsecus* 'outer' < Latin *exter* 'external' + adverb-forming ending *-im* + *secus* 'alongside of'] —**extrinsically** *adv*

extro- *prefix* same as **extra-** [Alteration, after INTRO-]

~~**extrordinary**~~ incorrect spelling of **extraordinary**

extrorse /ik stráwrss/, **extrorsal** /ik stráwrss'l/ *adj* used to describe a plant part that faces or turns outwards or away from a centre [Mid-19C. < late Latin *extrorsus* 'in an outward direction' < Latin *extra* 'outside' + *versus* 'towards', past participle of *vertere* 'to turn']

extroversion /ékstrə vúrsh'n/, **extraversion** *n* **1.** interest in and involvement with people and things outside the self **2.** the turning inside out of an organ or other body part, especially the womb [Mid-17C. < EXTRO- + Latin *version-* 'turning' < *vertere* 'to turn'] —**extroversive** *adj* —**extroversively** *adv*

extrovert /ékstrə vurt/, **extravert** *n* **1.** somebody who is sociable and self-confident **2.** somebody whose interests are directed outside the self [Early 20C. < EXTRO- + Latin *vertere* 'to turn'] —**extrovert** *adj* —**extroverted** *adj*

USAGE The original spelling is ***extravert***, which is still more common in American usage. In British English, however, the form ***extrovert***, influenced by *introvert*, is now standard.

extrude /ik stróod/ (**-trudes, -truding, -truded**) *vt* **1.** to force or squeeze something out **2.** to make something by forcing a semisoft material such as plastic or molten metal through a specially shaped mould or nozzle [Mid-16C. < Latin *extrudere* 'thrust out' < *trudere* 'to thrust'] —**extrudable** *adj*

extrusion /ik stróozh'n/ *n* **1.** INDUST SOMETHING FORMED BY BEING EXTRUDED something formed by forcing semisoft material through a specially shaped mould or nozzle **2.** INDUST PROCESS OF EXTRUDING the process or an instance of making something by forcing semisoft material through a specially shaped mould or nozzle **3.** GEOL IGNEOUS ROCK an igneous rock formed by the emission of molten material (**magma**) through cracks in the Earth's surface where it forms a lava flow **4.** GEOL MOVEMENT OF MOLTEN ROCK the movement of molten material (**magma**) from a volcano or through cracks in the Earth's surface to form solidified igneous rock [Mid-16C. < medieval Latin *extrusion-* < Latin *extrudere* (see EXTRUDE)]

extrusive /ik stróossiv/ *adj* describes rock formed from molten material (**magma**) that has flowed out of cracks in the Earth's surface

exuberant /ig zyóob'rənt/ *adj* **1.** FULL OF ENTHUSIASM full of happy high spirits and vitality **2.** ABUNDANT growing in great abundance or profusion **3.** LAVISH lavish or elaborate, often to the point of being excessive [15C. Via French < Latin *exuberant-*, present participle of *exuberare* 'be very fruitful' < *uberare* 'be fruitful' < *uber* 'fertile'] —**exuberance** *n* —**exuberantly** *adv*

exudate /éksyoo dayt, égz-/ *n* a substance such as sweat or a cellular waste product that is exuded from a cell or organ

exudation /éksyoo dáysh'n, égz-/ *n* **1.** the release of a substance through pores or a surface cut, e.g. the release of sweat from the body or resin from a tree **2.** BIOL same as **exudate** —**exudative** /éksyoo daytiv, égz-/ *adj*

exude /ig zyóod/ (**-udes, -uding, -uded**) *v* **1.** *vt* to communicate a particular quality or feeling in abundance and very clearly, usually through general behaviour and body language ○ *a voice that exuded confidence* **2.** *vti* to release something such as a liquid or an odour slowly from a gland, pore, membrane, or cut, or ooze out slowly [Late 16C. < Latin *ex(s)udare* 'ooze out like sweat' < *sudare* 'to sweat']

exult /ig zúlt/ (**-ults, -ulting, -ulted**) *vi* **1.** to be extremely happy or joyful about something ○ *exulted in his new-found freedom* **2.** to be very happy or triumphant about something unpleasant that happens to somebody else ○ *The victors exulted over their enemies' annihilation.* [Late 16C. Via French *exulter* < Latin *exsultare* 'keep leaping up' < *exsalire* 'leap out' < *salire* 'leap'] —**exultation** /ég zul táysh'n, ék sul-/ *n* —**exultingly** *adv*

exultant /ig zúltənt/ *adj* extremely happy, joyful, or triumphant ○ *an exultant roar from the crowd* —**exultantly** *adv*

exurb /éks urb/ *n US* a prosperous residential area outside a city, beyond the suburbs [Mid-20C. Back-formation < *exurban* (< Latin *ex* 'out of' + *urbs* 'city'), after SUBURB] —**exurban** /eks úrbən/ *adj* —**exurbanite** /eks úrbə nīt/ *n*

exurbia /eks úrbi ə/ *n US* the prosperous residential area beyond the suburbs of a city [Mid-20C. After SUBURBIA]

exuviae /ig zyóovi ee/ *npl* skins, shells, or other body coverings cast off by animals [Mid-17C. < Latin, 'things cast off' < *exuere* 'divest yourself of'] —**exuvial** *adj*

ex works *adv* excluding any costs incurred after an item leaves the factory, e.g. delivery charges and retailer's profit ○ *I know where I can buy one ex works.* —**ex-works** *adj*

-ey *suffix* same as **-y**[1] [Variant]

eyas /ī əss/ (*plural* **-ases** or **-asses**), **eyass** *n* a young hawk or falcon, especially one bred for falconry [15C. Alteration of obsolete *nias* < French *niais* 'bird taken from the nest' < Latin *nidus* 'nest']

Jan van Eyck: portrait engraving by Joachim von Sandrart

Eyck /īk/, **Jan van** (1390?–1441) Flemish painter. He painted in vivid oil colours in a naturalistic style and is regarded as the greatest Flemish artist of the 15th century.

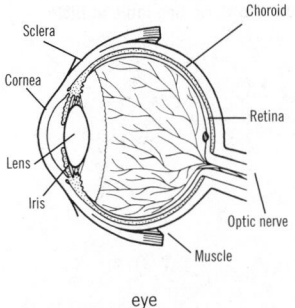

eye

eye /ī/ n 1. ORGAN OF VISION the organ of sight or light sensitivity in vertebrates, usually occurring in pairs. The eye is an approximately spherical organ with light-sensitive rod and cone cells in the retina, which is responsible for converting light into impulses that are transmitted to the brain for interpretation. 2. VISIBLE AREA OF EYE the externally visible part of the eye and the area of face around it, including the orbit, eyelid, and eyelashes 3. POWER OF SIGHT the ability to see (often used in the plural) ○ If my eyes get any worse I'll have to wear glasses. 4. ATTENTION somebody's attention or gaze ○ He took his eye off the prisoners at the wrong moment. 5. EXPRESSION a look, or the particular facial expression of somebody who is looking at something ○ She looked me over with a cold eye. 6. APPRECIATION OF SOMETHING an ability to recognize and appreciate something ○ He's got a good eye for talent. 7. OPINION a point of view or way of thinking ○ He can do no wrong in her eyes. 8. NEW SHOOT ON POTATO a dark round patch on a potato tuber, from which a new shoot grows 9. HOLE IN NEEDLE a hole in the top of a needle for passing a thread through 10. METEOROL CENTRE OF STORM a calm area at the centre of a storm 11. CLOTHING LOOP PART OF FASTENER a loop into which a small hook fits, used as a means of fastening two parts of a garment together 12. ZOOL same as **eyespot** (sense 2) ■ vt (**eyes, eyeing** or **eying, eyed**) 1. LOOK AT SOMETHING to look at something or somebody inquisitively ○ She quickly eyed the building up and down. 2. OGLE SOMEBODY to give somebody a look that signals sexual interest (informal) ○ A man was eyeing her from across the room. [Old English ēage < Indo-European] —**eyed** adj —**eyeless** adj ◇ **close** or **shut your eyes to something** to ignore or overlook something obvious ◇ **cry your eyes out** to cry bitterly ◇ **easy on the eye** pleasant to look at (informal) ◇ **eyes out on stalks** wide-eyed in extreme astonishment or shock (informal) ◇ **give somebody the (glad) eye** to look at somebody in a way that signals sexual interest ◇ **have eyes in the back of your head** to be aware of what is happening when unable to see it (informal; usually used in negative statements) ◇ **keep an eye on somebody** or **something 1.** to watch somebody or something closely **2.** to take care of somebody or something, especially for a short time ◇ **keep your eye on the ball** to pay close attention to the matter in hand ◇ **pick the eyes out of something** Aus to take the best pieces of something for yourself ◇ **see eye to eye**

(with somebody) to have a similar outlook or viewpoint to somebody else ◇ **turn a blind eye (to something)** to pretend not to be aware of something ◇ **with an eye to something** having something as a purpose or objective ◇ **with your eyes (wide) open** fully aware of the implications of what you are doing

eyeball /ī bawl/ n ROUND MASS OF EYE the round mass of the eye within its bony socket ■ **eyeballs** npl WEBSITE VISITORS users of the Internet who visit a particular website or use a particular product (slang) ○ sites competing for eyeballs ■ vt (-**balls, -balling, -balled**) N Am STARE AT SOMEBODY to stare at somebody or something intently (informal)

eye bank n a place where human corneas taken from people who have recently died are stored for use in corneal transplants

eyebath /ī baath/ n a small container that fits over the eye and is used to apply liquid medical treatment to it or to cleanse it. N Am term **eyecup**

eyebolt /ī bōlt/ n a bolt with an eye or ring at the end instead of the usual head, used for pulling, lifting, or fastening

eyebright /ī brīt/ n a plant of the snapdragon family. Flowers: white and purple, small. Genus: Euphrasia. [Because formerly used for treating eye diseases]

eyebrow /ī brow/ n 1. the arched line of hair above each eye socket 2. the upper bony ridge of the eye socket. Technical name **supraorbital ridge**

eyebrow pencil n a soft cosmetic pencil used to darken the eyebrows

eye candy n 1. something visually pleasing but intellectually undemanding (slang) 2. ONLINE, COMPUT ornamental visual features on a computer monitor or a webpage

eye-catching adj striking or unusual and so attracting people's attention easily —**eye-catcher** n —**eye-catchingly** adv

eye chart n a sheet printed with different sizes of letters, used to test eyesight

eye contact n the act of looking directly into the eyes of another person

eyecup /ī kup/ n N Am MED same as **eyebath**

eye dialect n the use of spellings that represent the sound of dialectal or nonstandard forms, e.g. 'enuff' or 'wimmin'

eye drops npl liquid medication for the eyes, usually applied with a dropper

eyeful /ī fool/ n 1. a long steady look at something or somebody (informal) ○ Get an eyeful of this! 2. an offensive term for somebody or something that is very beautiful, especially a woman who has a pleasing appearance (slang)

eyeglass /ī glaass/ n 1. a single framed lens for correcting defective vision, e.g. a monocle 2. OPTICS same as **eyepiece** ■ **eyeglasses** npl N Am a pair of glasses (formal)

eyehole /ī hōl/ n 1. HANDICRAFT, CLOTHING same as **eyelet** (sense 1) 2. BUILDINGS same as **peephole** (sense 2)

eyehook /ī hŏŏk/ n a hook that is fixed to a ring at the end of a rope or chain

eyelash /ī lash/ n a short stiff hair that grows in a row from the edge of the eyelid (often used in the plural)

eye lens n a lens in the eyepiece of an optical instrument such as a microscope or pair of binoculars

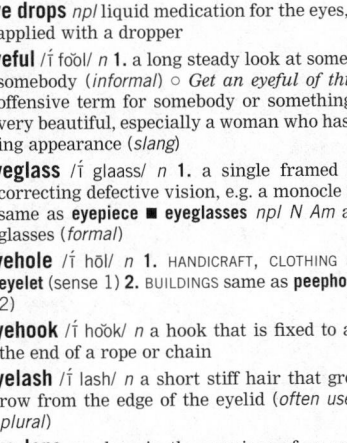

eyelet

eyelet /ī lət/ n 1. HOLE FOR CORD a small hole, especially one made in clothing, for a lace or cord to be passed through 2. METAL REINFORCEMENT FOR HOLE a small ring of metal or stiff fabric fixed to a hole, especially one made in clothing, to strengthen its edges 3. ORNAMENTED HOLE IN EMBROIDERY a small hole with ornamental stitched edges in embroidered fabric 4. BUILDINGS same as **peephole** (sense 2) [14C. Anglicization of Old French oillet 'little eye' < oil 'eye' < Latin oculus]

eyelevel /ī lev'l/ adj positioned approximately at the same height as somebody's eyes ○ a cooker with an eyelevel grill

eyelid /ī lid/ n a protective fold of skin and muscle that can be closed to cover the front of the eyeball ◇ **not bat an eyelid** to show no sign of emotion, especially of surprise

eyelift /ī lift/ n a surgical operation to improve the appearance of the area around the eyes, e.g. by removing wrinkles

eyeline /ī līn/ n the level of somebody's gaze when he or she is looking at something

eyeliner /ī līnər/ n a cosmetic worn along the edges of the eyelids to emphasize the eyes

eye-opener n a surprising or revealing experience or piece of information (informal) —**eye-opening** adj

eye patch n a covering worn over one eye to protect it or conceal it

eyepiece /ī peess/ n the part of an optical instrument that holds the lens on the side the user looks through

eye-popping adj so striking or unusual as to cause amazement (informal) ○ eye-popping entertainment —**eye-popper** n

eye rhyme n the use of words that, because they are similarly spelt, look as if they rhyme but are in fact pronounced differently, e.g. 'bough' and 'enough'

eyeshade /ī shayd/ n a tinted or opaque visor worn round the head to protect the eyes from glare

eye shadow n a coloured cosmetic for the area around the eyes, especially the eyelids

eyeshot /ī shot/ n the range over which the eye can see

eyesight /ī sīt/ n the power of sight

eye socket n either of the two bony recesses in the skull that contain the eyeballs

eyes-only adj intended to be seen only by the person to whom it is addressed ○ an eyes-only memo

eyesore /ī sawr/ n an offensively ugly building or place

eyespot /ī spot/ n 1. a small pigmented area or organelle that is sensitive to light, found in some algae and simple multicellular organisms, including some flatworms, and jellyfish 2. a marking shaped like an eye, e.g. on the wings of some butterflies or on a peacock's tail

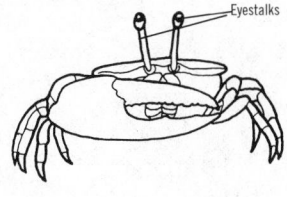

eyestalk

eyestalk /ī stawk/ n a flexible stalk with a compound eye at the tip, found in crustaceans and some molluscs

eyestrain /ī strayn/ n tiredness or irritation in the eyes caused, e.g., by an uncorrected visual defect or by prolonged close work. It is not recognized as a medical condition by ophthalmologists.

Eyetie /ī tī/ n a highly offensive term for an Italian

person (*taboo*) [Early 20C. < *Eyetalian*, representing a nonstandard pronunciation of ITALIAN] —**Eyetie** *adj*

eyetooth /ī tooth/ (*plural* -**teeth** /-teeth/) *n* a canine tooth found on each side of the upper jaw [Because directly below the eye] ◇ **give your eyeteeth for something** to be prepared to do anything to be able to do or have something

eyewash /ī wosh/ *n* **1.** a liquid used to cleanse or soothe the eyes **2.** pretentious nonsense that is intended to flatter or deceive (*informal*) ○ *The official version is just so much eyewash.*

eyewear /ī wair/ *n* something worn over the eyes to protect them or correct sight, e.g. glasses, goggles, or contact lenses

eyewitness /ī witnəss, ī witnəss/ *n* somebody who saw and can give evidence about an event

eyot /ayt, áyət/ *n regional* GEOG another spelling of **ait**

eyra /áirə/ *n* a jaguarundi in its reddish-brown seasonal colour phase [Early 17C. Via Spanish < Tupi-Guarani *(e)irára*]

Eyre, Lake /air/ largest salt lake in Australia, located in central South Australia. Area: 9,300 sq. km/3,600 sq. mi.

Eyre, Edward John (1815–1901) British explorer and colonial official. He completed the first overland trip from Sydney to Adelaide and led further expeditions into central and southwestern Australia.

Eyre Peninsula peninsula in southern South Australia that separates the Great Australian Bight from the Spencer Gulf. Area: 55,000 sq. km/21,236 sq. mi.

eyrie /éeri, áiri, īri/ *n* **1.** the nest of a bird of prey, especially an eagle, in a high and inaccessible place **2.** any high and inaccessible place, often a fortified one [15C. < medieval Latin *aeria*, probably via Old French *aire* < Latin *area* 'level ground, garden bed', later 'bird of prey's nest']

eyrir /áy reer/ (*plural* **aurar** /ō raar/) *n* a subunit of Icelandic currency. See table at **currency** [Early 20C. < Icelandic, probably < Latin *aureus* 'gold coin']

Eysenck /ī zengk/, **H. J.** (1916–97) German-born British psychologist. He was an authority on personality studies and contributed to the controversial area of the links between genetics and intelligence. Full name **Eysenck, Hans Jürgen**

Ez. *abbr* BIBLE Ezra

Ezek. *abbr* BIBLE Ezekiel

Ezekiel /i zéeki əl/ *n* **1.** in the Bible, a Hebrew priest and prophet who lived in the 6th century BC. As the Jews' spiritual leader during the Babylonian captivity, he foretold the creation of a Jewish nation. **2.** a book of the Bible that describes the Jews' exile in Babylon in the 6th century BC, traditionally attributed to Ezekiel. It contains prophecies of the destruction and subsequent rebuilding of Jerusalem and Judah. See table at **Bible**

e-zine /ée zeen/ *n* a website with contents and layout modelled on a print magazine [< *e(lectronic)* *(maga)zine*]

Ezr. *abbr* BIBLE Ezra

Ezra /ézzrə/ *n* **1.** in the Bible, a Hebrew high priest who lived in the 5th century BC. He led the Jews back to Jerusalem from their exile in Babylon and founded a Jewish nation. **2.** a book of the Bible that describes the rebuilding of the Jewish state in Judah after the Babylonian captivity, traditionally attributed to Ezra. See table at **Bible**

Ff

f[1] /ef/ (*plural* **f's**), **F** (*plural* **F's** or **Fs**) *n* **1.** the sixth letter of the English alphabet, representing a consonant sound **2.** a written representation of the letter 'f'

f[2] *symbol* **1.** MEASURE femto- **2.** OPTICS f-number **3.** PHYS focal length **4.** PHYS frequency (sense 4) **5.** MATHS function **6.** used to refer to the sixth vertical row of squares from the left on a chessboard

F[1] *symbol* **1.** MEASURE farad **2.** MEASURE faraday (*usually italicized*) **3.** CHEM ELEM fluorine **4.** PHYS force[1] (sense 9)

F[2] *abbr* **1.** MEASURE Fahrenheit **2.** false **3.** ELEC farad **4.** fathom **5.** COMMUNICATION fax (number) **6.** February **7.** EDUC Fellow **8.** female **9.** GRAM feminine **10.** METALL fine[1] *adj* (sense 12) **11.** PUBL folio **12.** following (page) **13.** MUSIC forte[2] *adv* (*used as a musical direction*) **14.** SPORTS foul **15.** Friday

F[3] /ef/ (*plural* **F's** or **Fs**) *n* **1.** 'F'-SHAPED OBJECT something shaped like a letter 'F' **2.** 4TH NOTE IN C MAJOR the fourth note of a scale in C major **3.** SOMETHING THAT PRODUCES F a string, key, or pipe tuned to produce the note F **4.** SCALE BEGINNING ON F a scale or key that starts on the note F **5.** WRITTEN SYMBOL FOR F a graphic representation of the tone of F **6.** EDUC LOWEST GRADE the sixth lowest grade in a series, also used to indicate a 'fail' in grading a student's work

f/ *symbol* PHOTOGRAPHY f-number

F2F *abbr* face-to-face (*used in e-mails or text messages*)

F2T *abbr* free to talk (*used in e-mails or text messages*)

fa *n* MUSIC another spelling of **fah**

FA *abbr* **1.** MIL field artillery **2.** FIN financial adviser **3.** ARTS fine art **4.** SOCCER Football Association **5.** SHIPPING freight agent

FAA *abbr* Fleet Air Arm

faas /faass/ *adj* too curious about other people's affairs (*slang; used in Black English*)

fab /fab/ *adj* same as **fabulous** (sense 3) (*informal*) ○ *It was a fab party!* [Mid-20C. Shortening]

FAB *abbr* COMM flavoured alcoholic beverage

Peter Carl Fabergé: decorative jewelled egg (1901)

Fabergé /fábbər zhay/, **Peter Carl** (1846–1920) Russian goldsmith and jeweller. He designed and produced highly decorative gifts, notably gold and enamel Easter eggs, for European royalty. Born **Fabergé, Karl Gustavovich**

Fabian /fáybi ən/ *adj* **1.** OF FABIAN SOCIETY relating to, belonging to, or associated with the Fabian Society **2.** CAUTIOUS using delaying tactics and avoiding direct confrontation ■ *n* MEMBER OF FABIAN SOCIETY a member

or supporter of the Fabian Society [Late 16C. < Latin *Fabianus* 'of Fabius' (see Quintus FABIUS MAXIMUS)]

Fabianism /fáybi ənizəm/ *n* the beliefs or tactics of the Fabian Society —**Fabianist** *n*

Fabian Society *n* a political organization founded in Britain in 1884 with the aim of bringing about socialism by gradual and lawful means rather than by revolution

Fabius Maximus /fáybi əss máksiməss/, **Quintus** (275?–203 BC) Roman general. As a result of his delaying tactics, Rome successfully countered the invasion of Hannibal during the Second Punic War. Full name **Fabius Maximus Verrucosus, Quintus**. Known as **Fabius Cunctator (the 'Delayer')**

fable /fáyb'l/ *n* **1.** STORY THAT TEACHES LESSON a short story with a moral, especially one in which the characters are animals **2.** LEGEND a story about supernatural, mythological, or legendary characters and events **3.** FALSE ACCOUNT a false or improbable account of something ○ *His version of events turned out to be a complete fable.* **4.** MYTHS AND LEGENDS myths and legends collectively ○ *a character out of fable* ■ *vt* (**-bles, -bling, -bled**) TELL STORY to tell a story or describe something in a fable (*archaic; usually passive*) [13C. Via Old French < Latin *fabula* 'story' < *fari* 'speak'] —**fabler** *n*

CULTURAL NOTE *Fables*, a collection of stories attributed to the Greek writer Aesop (620?–560? BC). Many of the tales feature animals as characters and each one illustrates a specific moral. Traditionally said to be the origin of the literary fable (although earlier examples have been found), they were used by the ancient Greeks for both educational and rhetorical purposes.

fabled /fáyb'ld/ *adj* **1.** famous because of being described or recounted in legends ○ *Eldorado, the fabled city of gold* **2.** made-up or fictitious

fabliau /fábbli ō/ (*plural* **-aux** /-ōz/) *n* a comic and often bawdy story in verse, especially of a kind popular in 12th- and 13th-century France [Early 19C. < French < plural of Old French *fablel* 'little story' < *fable* (see FABLE)]

Fablon /fáb lon/ *tdmk* a trademark for an adhesive-backed plastic material supplied in sheet form and used especially to cover shelves and other surfaces

Fabre /fábbrə/, **Jean Henri** (1823–1915) French entomologist. Renowned for his close observations, he highlighted the role of inherited instinct in insects.

    'History...records the names of royal bastards, but cannot tell us the origin of wheat.'
    [Attributed to Jean Henri Fabre]

Fabriano ♦ **Gentile da Fabriano**

fabric /fábbrik/ *n* **1.** CLOTH any type of cloth made from woven, knitted, or felted thread or fibres **2.** TEXTURE the particular texture or quality of a kind of cloth **3.** SUBSTANCE the fundamental structure or make-up of something ○ *the fabric of her being* **4.** INDUST STRUCTURAL MATERIAL the material from which something is constructed, especially a building, or the physical structure of something ○ *damage to the fabric of the church* [15C. Via Old French < Latin *fabrica* 'trade, manufactured object' < *faber* 'worker in metal or stone, artisan']

fabricate /fábbri kayt/ (**-cates, -cating, -cated**) *vt* **1.** INVENT FALSE STORY to make up something that is not

true ○ *accused police of fabricating evidence* **2.** CONSTRUCT SOMETHING to make or construct something from different parts **3.** FORGE SOMETHING to falsify something such as a signature or document [15C. < Latin *fabricat-*, past participle of *fabricare* 'make' < *fabrica* (see FABRIC)] —**fabricator** *n*

fabrication /fábbri káysh'n/ *n* **1.** DELIBERATELY UNTRUE ACCOUNT an invented statement, story, or account devised with intent to deceive ○ *The story is a complete fabrication.* **2.** CONCOCTING LIES the act of making up or falsifying something ○ *his fabrication of documents* **3.** ACT OF MAKING SOMETHING the construction of something, or something that has been constructed or made

SYNONYMS See **lie**[2].

fabric conditioner, **fabric softener** *n* liquid used in addition to detergent in a washing machine to keep fabric soft

fabulate /fábbyoo layt/ (**-lates, -lating, -lated**) *vt* to make a fictional account or representation of something [Early 17C. < Latin *fabulat-*, past participle of *fabulari* 'talk' < *fabula* (see FABLE)]

fabulism /fábbyoolizəm/ *n* a lie (*formal*)

fabulist /fábbyoolist/ *n* **1.** a writer or reciter of fables **2.** a teller of fanciful stories

fabulous /fábbyooləss/ *adj* **1.** AMAZING amazingly or almost unbelievably great or impressive ○ *paid out fabulous sums of money* **2.** TYPICAL OF FABLES described in or typical of myths and legends **3.** EXCELLENT extremely good, pleasant, or enjoyable (*informal*) ○ *You look fabulous in that outfit!* [15C. Directly or via French < Latin *fabulosus* 'celebrated in fable' < *fabula* (see FABLE)] —**fabulously** *adv* —**fabulousness** *n*

facade /fə saád/, **façade** *n* **1.** the face of a building, especially the principal or front face showing its most prominent architectural features **2.** the way something or somebody appears on the surface, especially when that appearance is false or meant to deceive ○ *Her geniality is just a facade.* [Mid-17C. < French < *face* (see FACE), after Italian *facciata*]

face /fayss/ *n* **1.** FRONT OF HEAD the front of the human head, where the eyes, nose, mouth, chin, cheeks, and forehead are **2.** PERSON somebody who is being looked at (*informal*) ○ *It's nice to see so many familiar faces here today.* **3.** COUNTENANCE a facial expression or look of a particular kind ○ *an unhappy face* **4.** UNPLEASANT FACIAL EXPRESSION an expression in which the face is distorted, e.g. to show distaste or as a way of being rude to somebody ○ *The children made faces behind his back.* **5.** WAY SOMETHING LOOKS the general or outward appearance of something ○ *The arrival of the motor car changed the face of the modern city.* **6.** FALSE APPEARANCE an outward appearance that does not show the true nature of somebody's feelings or is intended to deceive ○ *Even after a third defeat he was still putting on a brave face.* **7.** REPUTATION personal prestige or reputation ○ *a way of enabling her to back down without losing face* **8.** BOLDNESS impudence or self-assurance (*informal*) ○ *How can he have the face to come back here after what he said?* **9.** FACE MAKE-UP make-up applied to the face (*informal*) ○ *didn't even have time to put on my face* **10.** SURFACE OF OBJECT a plane surface or side of a three-dimensional object such as a geometric figure or gem ○ *A cube has six faces.* **11.** OUTSIDE OF BUILDING the exterior of the front or side of

AKG London

a large building ○ *the evening sun shining on the west face* **12.** SIDE OF CLIFF the steep exposed side of a cliff **13.** SIDE OF MOUNTAIN a steep mountainside, often named after the direction it faces ○ *the north face of the Eiger* **14.** WORKING AREA IN MINE an area in a mine from which a mineral such as coal is being extracted **15.** TYPEFACE a typeface, or the area of a printing character that actually prints **16.** DIAL ON CLOCK OR INSTRUMENT the surface of a timepiece or similar instrument that displays the time or other data **17.** SIDE OF CARD SHOWING VALUE the side of a playing card that is marked with numbers and symbols **18.** WORKING SURFACE OF IMPLEMENT the functional side of something such as a tool or golf club **19.** SIDE OF COIN either surface of a coin, especially one with somebody's head on it **20.** CELEBRITY somebody who is well-known or important (*informal*) ○ *We get a few faces in the club at the weekend.* ■ *v* (**faces, facing, faced**) **1.** *vti* TURN TOWARDS PARTICULAR DIRECTION to be positioned or turn so that the face or front side is directed a particular way or towards something or somebody ○ *The largest bedroom faces south.* **2.** *vt* BE OPPOSITE SOMEBODY OR SOMETHING to be in a position opposite somebody or something ○ *The boys faced each other.* **3.** *vt* COME UP AGAINST SOMEBODY OR SOMETHING to meet or confront somebody or something directly and bravely ○ *Their retreat was cut off and they had no choice but to stand and face the enemy.* **4.** *vt* ACCEPT FACTS to accept the reality of a difficult or unpleasant situation ○ *Let's face it, our chances of being on time are slim.* **5.** *vt* HAVE TO BE DEALT WITH to require to be dealt with by somebody ○ *She was faced with the task of breaking the news to her family.* ○ *the problems facing them* **6.** *vt* EXPECT SOMETHING BAD to have the prospect of experiencing something unpleasant, usually within a short period of time ○ *They face ruin if the bank calls in the loan.* ○ *could face a jail sentence* **7.** *vt* LINE OR DECORATE SOMETHING to line or trim the edge of something with a contrasting material ○ *The cuffs were faced with velvet.* **8.** *vt* SMOOTH STONE to put a smooth surface on a piece of stone [13C. Via French < Latin *facies* 'appearance, aspect, form, face'] —**faceable** *adj* ◇ **be staring somebody in the face** to be obvious but unnoticed ○ *Why call in a management consultant, when the cause of the problem is staring you in the face?* ◇ **be staring something in the face** to be facing something undesirable but inevitable ○ *We were staring bankruptcy in the face.* ◇ **face down** *or* **downwards** with the face or front placed downwards ◇ **face to face 1.** in the actual presence of another person **2.** in direct contact with, or having first-hand knowledge of, an unpleasant fact or situation ◇ **face up** *or* **upwards** with the face or front placed upwards ◇ **fly in the face of something** to defy something deliberately or recklessly ◇ **get in somebody's face** to annoy somebody (*informal*) ◇ **get out of my face** used for impolitely telling somebody to stop annoying you (*informal*) ◇ **have a long face** to look miserable or disappointed ◇ **in (the) face of something** when confronted by or in spite of something ○ *remained united in the face of strong opposition* ◇ **in your face, in yer face** so frank or direct as to be unnerving or intimidating (*informal; hyphenated when used before a noun*) ○ *an in-your-face style of documentary filmmaking* ◇ **not just a pretty face** having more to offer than an attractive appearance ◇ **on the face of it** judging by appearances only ◇ **set your face against something** to oppose something with determination ◇ **show your face (somewhere** *or* **at something)** to put in an appearance somewhere ○ *He won't dare show his face at her house again.* ◇ **written all over somebody's face** obvious from somebody's expression (*informal*) ○ *She was standing by the broken window with guilt written all over her face.*

ORIGIN The Latin word *facies* 'appearance, face' from which *face* is derived is also the source of English *facade, facet, superficial,* and *surface.*

face about *vti* to turn to face the other way, or turn somebody or something to face the other way

face down *vt* to prevail against somebody in a direct confrontation

face off *vi* **1.** in ice hockey, lacrosse, and other sports, to start or restart play by dropping the puck or ball between two opposing players **2.** to confront each other or somebody else (*informal*)

face out *vt* to endure something such as criticism or misfortune bravely

face up to *vt* **1.** to accept having to deal with something unpleasant **2.** to confront somebody or something bravely

faceache /fáyss ayk/ *n* an offensive term for somebody who is thought to be ugly or who looks unhappy (*slang insult*)

face angle *n* an angle between two flat surfaces on a polyhedron

face card *n N Am* same as **court card**

face-centred *adj* describes a crystal lattice with an atom in the centre of each unit cell face as well as at the corners

facecloth /fáyss kloth/ *n UK, NZ, Can* a small cloth used in washing the face and hands. Aus term **washer**. US term **washcloth**

-faced *suffix* **1.** having a particular number of faces **2.** having a face of a particular kind

facedown /fáyss down/ *n* a determined confrontation between two adversaries

face flannel *n* HOUSEHOLD same as **facecloth**

faceless /fáyssləss/ *adj* **1.** anonymous and impersonal ○ *infuriating replies from faceless officials* **2.** lacking character or distinctive features ○ *a faceless waiting room* —**facelessly** *adv* —**facelessness** *n*

facelift /fáyss lift/ *n* **1.** a surgical operation in which the skin of the face is pulled back and up to tighten it and remove wrinkles **2.** a renovation or refurbishment of something such as an area or a building ○ *The whole dockside area could do with a facelift.*

face mask *n* **1.** COSMETICS same as **face pack 2.** a covering for the whole head or the face alone, used either to protect or to disguise the face

face-off *n* **1.** in ice hockey, lacrosse, and other sports, a start or restart of play in which the referee drops the puck or ball between two opposing players **2.** a direct confrontation

face pack *n* a cosmetic preparation that cleanses the pores of the face and removes dead layers of skin

face paint *n* any of various paints used to decorate the face and be easily washed off ○ *She got a set of face paints for her birthday.*

face peel *n* COSMETICS same as **chemical peel**

faceplate /fáyss playt/ *n* **1.** PART OF LATHE a perforated metal disc at the end of the spindle or headstock of a lathe for holding a workpiece in place **2.** SEE-THROUGH PART OF HEADGEAR the transparent part of a piece of protective headgear that protects the face while allowing the wearer to see **3.** FRONT OF CATHODE-RAY TUBE the front of a cathode-ray tube, on which an image is seen

face powder *n* a flesh-coloured cosmetic powder applied to the face to make it look smoother or less shiny

facer /fáyssər/ *n* **1.** a lathe tool used to smooth a surface **2.** something that is astonishing or very difficult to deal with (*dated informal*) ○ *This latest development is a facer, and no mistake!*

face-saving *adj* intended to preserve somebody's reputation and dignity ○ *find a face-saving compromise* —**face-saver** *n*

facet /fássit/ *n* **1.** ASPECT OF SOMETHING a part or possible aspect of something ○ *an important facet of our work* **2.** FACE OF GEMSTONE any surface of a cut gemstone **3.** ZOOL PART OF INSECT EYE a lens segment in the compound eye of an insect or other arthropod **4.** ANAT FLAT AREA a smooth flat area on a hard surface such as a bone or a tooth ■ *vt* (**facets, faceting** *or* **facetting, faceted** *or* **facetted**) CUT FACETS IN SOMETHING to cut facets in something, especially a gemstone [Early 17C. < French *facette* 'little face' < *face* (see FACE)]

facetiae /fə seéshi ee/ *npl* (*archaic*) **1.** witty or humorous remarks **2.** coarsely humorous books [Early 16C. < Latin, 'jokes', plural of *facetia* (see FACETIOUS)]

face time *n* **1.** TIME SPENT ON TELEVISION the amount of time that somebody spends appearing on television ○ *We need more face time to sway public opinion on this issue.* **2.** EXTRA TIME AT PLACE OF EMPLOYMENT the amount of time somebody spends at his or her place of employment, especially beyond normal working hours ○ *What is she trying to prove with all this face time?* **3.** *US* TIME SPENT FACE-TO-FACE time spent dealing face to face with other people (*informal*) ○ *The schedule calls for weekly e-mail reports as well as some actual face time between team members.*

facetious /fə seéshəss/ *adj* intended to be humorous but often silly or inappropriate [Late 16C. < French *facétieux* < *facétie* 'joke' < Latin *facetia* < *facetus* 'graceful, witty'] —**facetiously** *adv* —**facetiousness** *n*

SYNONYMS See *funny.*

face-to-face *adj, adv* (*not hyphenated when used after a verb*) **1.** in the physical presence of somebody else ○ *a face-to-face encounter* **2.** in direct contact or confrontation ○ *We came face to face with the situation.*

facety /fáysti/, **facesty, faisty** *adj* considered cheeky or rude (*used in Black English*)

face value *n* **1.** the value that is shown on something, especially a note, coin, or stamp **2.** the apparent worth or meaning of something, which may be better than its true worth or meaning ○ *We'd be unwise to take his promises at face value.*

Facey /fáyssi/, **Albert Barnett** (1894–1982) Australian writer. He is the author of *A Fortunate Life* (1981), his autobiography.

facia *n* ARCHIT, BIOL another spelling of **fascia** (senses 1–3, 5)

facial /fáysh'l/ *adj* relating to the face ○ *an unhappy facial expression* ■ *n* a beauty treatment for the face, usually consisting of a facial massage followed by cleansing and makeup —**facially** *adv*

facialist *n* a beautician who specializes in beauty treatments for the face

facial nerve *n* a nerve of the seventh cranial pair that controls the muscles of the face and jaw, and the sensory abilities of the palate, front of the tongue, and nose

facial scrub *n* a slightly abrasive cream or lotion used on the face to remove a layer of dead skin and improve the complexion

-facient *suffix* causing, making ○ *febrifacient* [< Latin *facient-*, present participle of *facere* 'do, make']

facies /fáyshi eez, fáyshiz/ (*plural same*) *n* **1.** BIOL GENERAL APPEARANCE the general characteristic appearance of something such as a plant or animal species **2.** GEOL ROCK FEATURES INDICATING FORMATION the combined physical and chemical features of a rock that indicate the manner of its formation or deposition **3.** MED FACIAL APPEARANCE LINKED TO DISEASE the appearance of somebody's face as a characteristic of a particular disease or condition [Early 18C. < Latin (see FACE)]

facile /fáss īl/ *adj* **1.** FLUENT BUT INSINCERE produced, spoken, or speaking so fluently and easily as to seem insincere or superficial **2.** SUPERFICIAL made or arrived at without any serious thought or depth of feeling and therefore of little value or significance **3.** EASY TO DO requiring little effort **4.** WORKING EASILY working, acting, or done smoothly and easily [15C. Via French, 'easy' < Latin *facilis* 'easy to do, pliant, courteous' < *facere* 'do, make'] —**facilely** *adv* —**facileness** *n*

facilitate /fə síllə tayt/ (**-tates, -tating, -tated**) *vt* to make something easy or easier to do [Early 17C. Via French < Italian *facilitare* 'make easy' < *facile* 'easy' < Latin *facilis* (see FACILE)] —**facilitative** /-tətiv/ *adj*

facilitation /fə síllə táysh'n/ *n* **1.** the process of making something easy or easier **2.** a decrease in the resistance to a nerve impulse in a neural pathway, brought about by prior or repeated stimulation

facilitator /fə síllə taytər/ *n* **1.** somebody who enables a process to happen, especially somebody who encourages people to find their own solutions to problems or tasks **2.** an organizer and provider of services for a meeting, seminar, or other event

facility /fə sílləti/ *n* (*plural* **-ties**) **1.** SOMETHING WITH PARTICULAR FUNCTION something designed or created to provide a service or fulfil a need (*often used in the plural*) ○ *A wide range of facilities is available at the sports centre.* ○ *leisure facilities* ○ *a health-care*

facility **2.** SKILL an ability to do something easily **3.** EFFORTLESSNESS ease in doing something or in being done ■ **facilities** *npl* same as **toilet** (sense 2)

facing /fáyssing/ *n* **1.** LINING THAT FINISHES EDGE a lining sewn inside a garment to neaten the edges, or to decorate them when a part of it such as a collar is turned back **2.** CONSTR WALL SURFACE a layer of material that covers the outer surface of a wall to decorate or protect it ■ **facings** *npl* CUFFS AND COLLAR OF JACKET contrasting coverings on the cuffs and collar of a jacket, especially a military jacket

-facing *suffix* pointing in a particular direction

~~**facism**~~ incorrect spelling of **fascism**

façonné /fássə nay/, **faconne** *n* **1.** a fabric with a pattern or design woven into it **2.** the woven pattern on a façonné fabric [Late 19C. < French, 'fashioned']

facsimile /fak símməli/ *n* **1.** an exact copy or reproduction of something such as a document, a coin, or somebody's handwriting **2.** same as **fax** *n* (sense 1) (*dated*) ■ *vt* (**-les, -leing, -led**) to make an exact copy or reproduction of something [Late 16C. < modern Latin, < Latin *facere* 'do, make' + *simile* 'similar']

facsimile edition *n* a book or print that is reprinted in exactly the same style as an earlier edition, often being a photographic reproduction of the original

fact /fakt/ *n* **1.** SOMETHING KNOWN TO BE TRUE something that can be shown to be true, to exist, or to have happened **2.** TRUTH OR REALITY OF SOMETHING the truth or actual existence of something, as opposed to the supposition of something or a belief about something ○ *based on fact* **3.** PIECE OF INFORMATION a piece of information, e.g. a statistic or a statement of the truth **4.** LAW ACTUAL COURSE OF EVENTS the circumstances of an event or state of affairs, rather than an interpretation of its significance ○ *Matters of fact are issues for a jury, while matters of law are issues for the court.* **5.** LAW SOMETHING BASED ON EVIDENCE something that is based on or concerned with the evidence presented in a legal case [15C. < Latin *factum* 'deed' < *fact-*, past participle of *facere* 'do, make'] ◇ **after the fact** after something, especially a criminal act, has been done ◇ **before the fact** before something, especially a criminal act, has been done ◇ **in fact, in actual fact** used to correct a previous misunderstanding or to reinforce a previous statement

USAGE The phrase ***in fact***, as in *She is, in fact, correct*, is spelt as two words, never as *infact*.

ORIGIN The Latin word *facere* 'to do, make', from which **fact** is derived, is also the source of English *difficult, effect, facile, faction*[1], *factor, fashion, feasible, feat, feature*, and *fetish*.

fact-finding *adj* intended to find out information about something ○ *on a fact-finding mission* ■ *n* activity that is intended to find out information about something —**fact-finder** *n*

faction[1] /fáksh'n/ *n* **1.** a group that is a minority within a larger group and has interests or beliefs that are not always in harmony with the larger group **2.** conflict or dissension within a group [15C. Via French < Latin *faction-* 'act of making' < *fact-* (see FACT)] —**factional** *adj* —**factionally** *adv*

faction[2] /fáksh'n/ *n* **1.** writing or filmmaking that portrays real people or events by dramatizing the facts using the techniques of fiction **2.** a piece of writing, a film, or a television programme that portrays real people or events in a dramatized way [Mid-20C. Blend of FACT + FICTION] —**factional** *adj*

-faction *suffix* the making or production of something ○ *liquefaction* [Via French < Latin *-faction-* < *fact-* (see FACT)]

factionalise *vti* another spelling of **factionalize**[1], **factionalize**[2]

factionalism /fáksh'nəlizəm/ *n* the existence of or conflict between groups within a larger group —**factionalist** *n*

factionalize[1] /fáksh'nə līz/ (**-izes, -izing, -ized**), **factionalise** (**-ises, -ising, -ised**) *vti* to split into factions, or cause a group to split into factions [Late 20C. < FACTION[1]]

factionalize[2] /fáksh'nə līz/ (**-izes, -izing, -ized**), **factionalise** (**-ises, -ising, -ised**) *vt* to dramatize actual events [Late 20C. < FACTION[2]]

factious /fákshəss/ *adj* liable to cause, taking part in, or characteristic of conflict within a group [Mid-16C. Directly or via French < Latin *factiosus* < *factio, faction-* (see FACTION[1])] —**factiously** *adv* —**factiousness** *n*

factitious /fak tíshəss/ *adj* **1.** contrived and insincere rather than genuine **2.** not real or natural but artificial or invented (*formal*) [Mid-17C. < Latin *factitius* < *fact-* (see FACT)] —**factitiously** *adv* —**factitiousness** *n*

factitive /fáktətiv/ *adj* describes a verb that takes a direct object and a complement. An example is 'appoint' in 'They appointed her Head of Department' where 'her' is the direct object and 'Head of Department' is a noun complement. [Mid-19C. < modern Latin *factitivus* < Latin *factitare* 'do again' < *fact-* (see FACT)] —**factitively** *adv*

fact of life *n* an unavoidable truth, especially an unpleasant one ■ **facts of life** *npl* basic information on sexual matters and reproduction

factoid /fákt oyd/ *n* **1.** something that may not be true but is widely accepted as true because it is repeatedly quoted, especially in the media **2.** ⚠ a small and often unimportant bit of information

USAGE The popular meaning of ***factoid***, 'a small and often unimportant bit of information', is regarded by some people as incorrect.

factor /fáktər/ *n* **1.** INFLUENCE something that contributes to or has an influence on the outcome of something ○ *Access to emergency exits is an important factor when planning the layout of a public building.* **2.** LEVEL a quantity or level of something ○ *sunblock with a protection factor of 30* **3.** MATHS QUANTITY MULTIPLIED WITH OTHERS one of two or more numbers or quantities that can be multiplied together to give a particular number or quantity ○ *3 and 5 are factors of 15.* **4.** AMOUNT BY WHICH SOMETHING IS MULTIPLIED a particular amount by which something is multiplied ○ *The number of visitors to the museum has increased by a factor of three.* **5.** BUSINESS SOMEBODY TRADING FOR COMMISSION a person or organization that buys and sells goods for a commission **6.** BUSINESS BUSINESS AGENT an agent or transactor of business for somebody else **7.** *Scotland* BUSINESS MANAGER OF ESTATE a person who or firm that manages an estate or property on behalf of the owner **8.** BIOCHEM BIOLOGICAL SUBSTANCE a biological substance that has a physiological effect ■ *v* (**-tors, -toring, -tored**) **1.** *vi* BUSINESS ACT AS FACTOR to work as a factor **2.** *vt N Am* MATHS same as **factorize 3.** *vt Scotland* MANAGE ESTATE to manage an estate or property on behalf of the owner [15C. Via French < Latin, < *fact-* (see FACT)] —**factorability** /fáktərə bílləti/ *n* —**factorable** *adj*

factor in *vt* to include or consider something as contributing to or influencing something else, e.g. when making a decision

factorage /fáktərij/ *n* **1.** the fees or commission charged by a factor **2.** the business of working as a factor

factor analysis *n* a statistical technique used to determine the relative strength of various influences on an outcome

factorial /fak táwri əl/ *n* MATHS PRODUCT OF MULTIPLICATION the number resulting from multiplying a whole number by every whole number between itself and 1 inclusive. 6 factorial, or 6!, is 6 x 5 x 4 x 3 x 2 x 1 = 720. Symbol **!** ■ *adj* **1.** MATHS OF FACTORIAL relating to or involving a factorial **2.** BUSINESS INVOLVING FACTOR involving or characteristic of a commercial factor or the work of such a factor —**factorially** *adv*

factoring /fáktəring/ *n* **1.** the work of a commercial factor **2.** the business of buying debts at a discount so as to make a profit from collecting them

factorize /fáktə rīz/ (**-izes, -izing, -ized**), **factorise** (**-ises, -ising, -ised**) *vti* to find out or calculate the factors of an integer or equation, or be able to be resolved into factors. N Am term **factor** —**factorization** /fáktə rī záysh'n/ *n*

factorship /fáktərship/ *n* the position or business of being a factor for another person or business

factor VIII *n* a protein substance that promotes the clotting of blood. Its inherited absence causes haemophilia.

factory /fáktəri/ (*plural* **-ries**) *n* **1.** BUILDING WHERE GOODS ARE MANUFACTURED a building or complex of buildings where goods are manufactured on a large scale using machinery or automation (*often used before a noun*) ○ *a factory worker* **2.** PRODUCTIVE PLACE a place or organization that produces a particular thing regularly and in some quantity (*informal*) ○ *As far as popular music was concerned, it was a hit factory.* **3.** COMM PLACE ABROAD WHERE AGENTS DID BUSINESS formerly, a place where business was carried out abroad by commercial agents (**factors**), especially a trading station

factory farm *n* a farm where animals are reared on a large scale using intensive methods and modern equipment —**factory farming** *n*

factory floor *n* the area of a factory where the manufacturing process is carried out, as opposed to the administration areas

factory ship *n* a large fishing vessel equipped to process and freeze its own catch, or a whole fleet's catch, of fish or whales

factotum /fak tṓtəm/ *n* somebody employed to do a variety of jobs for somebody else [Mid-16C. < Latin, 'do everything!' < *fac*, imperative of *facere* 'do, make' + *totum* 'all']

fact sheet *n* a printed sheet or booklet giving information about something, especially a subject covered in a broadcast programme

factual /fákchoo əl/ *adj* **1.** involving, containing, or based on facts **2.** consisting of the truth or including only those things that are actual [Mid-19C. After ACTUAL] —**factuality** /fákchoo álləti/ *n* —**factually** *adv* —**factualness** *n*

factualism /fákchoo əlizəm/ *n* a strict devotion to or adherence to facts —**factualist** *n*

facula /fákyoo̅ lə/ (*plural* **-lae** /-lee/) *n* a large, bright, extremely hot region on the Sun's surface, usually occurring near a sunspot [Early 18C. < Latin, 'little torch'] —**facular** *adj*

facultative /fák'ltətiv/ *adj* **1.** NOT REQUIRED optional, not obligatory **2.** ALLOWING SOMETHING TO HAPPEN enabling or capable of permitting something to happen or be done, but not able to force its occurrence **3.** BIOL ASSOCIATED WITH VARIETY OF CONDITIONS able to live or take place under a range of external conditions ○ *a facultative parasite* —**facultatively** *adv*

faculty /fák'lti/ (*plural* **-ties**) *n* **1.** MENTAL POWER a mental power or ability such as reason or memory **2.** ABILITY a capacity or ability that somebody is born with or learns ○ *a great faculty for learning languages* **3.** EDUC DIVISION OF UNIVERSITY a department or group of departments dealing with a particular subject in a university or college **4.** EDUC TEACHING STAFF FOR PARTICULAR UNIVERSITY DIVISION the teaching staff of a particular faculty in a university or college **5.** *N Am* EDUC same as **staff**[1] *n* (sense 3) **6.** ALL MEMBERS OF PROFESSION all of the people who practise a particular profession, especially medicine **7.** POWER GRANTED BY AUTHORITY a power or right given by an authority [14C. Via French < Latin *facultas* < *facilis* 'easy']

Faculty of Advocates *n Scotland* the professional association for advocates in the Scottish legal system

FA Cup *n* **1.** a yearly competition in which teams are gradually eliminated, open to football teams that belong to the Football Association of England **2.** the trophy awarded to the winning team in the FA Cup

fad /fad/ *n* **1.** something that is very popular but only for a short time **2.** something that is important only to a particular person [Mid-19C. Origin ?]

Fadden /fádd'n/, **Sir Arthur William** (1895–1973) Australian politician. He was leader of the Country Party (1941–58) and was briefly prime minister of Australia in 1941. See table at **prime minister**

faddish /fáddish/ *adj ANZ, N Am* same as **faddy** (sense 2) —**faddishly** *adv* —**faddishness** *n*

faddism /fáddizəm/ *n* the existence of or participation in briefly popular fashions —**faddist** *n*

faddy /fáddi/ (**-dier, -diest**) *adj* **1.** tending to have strongly held likes and dislikes about food ○ *a faddy*

eater **2.** *UK* tending to have strongly held, but brief, enthusiasms. ANZ, N Am term **faddish** —**faddily** *adv* —**faddiness** *n*

fade /fayd/ *v* (**fades, fading, faded**) **1.** *vti* GRADUALLY BECOME LESS BRIGHT OR LOUD to lose brightness, colour, or loudness gradually, or make something do this ○ *The clothes had faded from months of washing.* **2.** *vi* BECOME TIRED to lose strength, freshness, and vigour ○ *His concentration faded after about an hour.* **3.** *vi* DISAPPEAR SLOWLY to die away or vanish gradually ○ *The film ends with a close-up that gradually fades to black.* **4.** *vi* LOSE EFFECTIVENESS to become less effective temporarily ○ *the engine faded* **5.** *vti* MAKE GOLF BALL CURVE in golf, to hit a ball so that, in a right-handed shot, it curves slightly from left to right, or be hit in this way ■ *n* **1.** GRADUAL LESSENING IN BRIGHTNESS OR LOUDNESS a gradual decrease in brightness, distinctness, or loudness **2.** GRADUAL DISAPPEARANCE OF IMAGE a gradual disappearance of an image in a film or television show **3.** *US* OFFENSIVE TERM an offensive term for a Black person who has adopted predominantly white friends and attitudes (*slang*) **4.** CURVING GOLF SHOT in golf, a shot in which the ball curves slightly from left to right in the air [14C. < French *fade* 'weak, pale'] —**fadable** *adj* —**fadedness** *n*

fade away *vi* **1.** to become gradually fainter or weaker and finally disappear **2.** to become thin and unhealthy

fade in *vti* to make a sound gradually audible or an image gradually visible, or become gradually audible or visible

fade out *vti* to make an image or sound gradually fainter until it disappears, or become gradually fainter before disappearing

fade up *vti* BROADCAST, CINEMA same as **fade in**

fade-in *n* the gradual introduction of a sound until it is audible or of an image until it is visible

fadeless /fáydləss/ *adj* not fading in sunlight or after washing —**fadelessly** *adv*

fade-out *n* **1.** a gradual decrease in brightness or loudness as an image or sound becomes fainter, until it disappears **2.** a gradual reduction in the strength of a television or radio broadcast signal, especially with temporary loss of reception, often because of transmission interference

fader /fáydər/ *n* a control on technical equipment that makes an image or sound fade in or out

fade-up *n* BROADCAST, CINEMA same as **fade-in**

fado /faá doo/ (*plural* **-dos**) *n* a sad Portuguese folk song with guitar accompaniment [Early 20C. < Portuguese, 'fate']

faeces /feésseez/ *npl* the body's solid waste matter, composed of undigested food, bacteria, water, and bile pigments and discharged from the bowel through the anus [14C. < Latin, plural of *faex* 'sediment, dregs'] —**faecal** /feék'l/ *adj*

faena /fa áynə/ *n* a series of manoeuvres in the final stages of a bullfight, leading up to the killing of the bull by the matador [Early 20C. < Spanish, 'task']

faerie /fáy əri, fáiri/, **faery** (*plural* **-ies**) *n* (*literary*) **1.** another spelling of **fairy** *n* (sense 1) **2.** the world of the fairies, or fairyland [Late 16C. Mock-medieval alteration of FAIRY]

Faeroe Islands /fáyrō īləndz/ another spelling of **Faroe Islands**

Faeroese *n, adj* LANG, PEOPLES another spelling of **Faroese**

faery *n* another spelling of **faerie** (*literary*)

faff /faf/ (**faffs, faffing, faffed**) [< *faff* 'blow as a light blustery wind', probably suggestive of the action]

faff about *or* **around** *vi* to waste time by being indecisive or fussing unnecessarily (*informal*)

fag[1] /fag/ *n* **1.** SOMETHING BORING something that is tedious or that makes somebody weary (*informal*) **2.** SCHOOLBOY'S HELPER at a public school, a schoolboy who has to do menial jobs and run errands for an older schoolboy (*dated*) ■ *v* (**fags, fagging, fagged**) **1.** *vi UK* ACT AS SCHOOLBOY'S HELPER at a public school, to do menial jobs and run errands for an older schoolboy (*dated*) **2.** *vti US* EXHAUST THROUGH WORK to exhaust somebody through drudgery or hard labour, or become exhausted in this way [Mid-16C. Origin ?]

fag[2] /fag/ *n* same as **cigarette** (*informal*) [Late 19C. Shortening of FAG END]

fag[3] /fag/ *n N Am* an offensive term for a gay man (*slang*) [Early 20C. Shortening of FAGGOT [2]] —**faggy** *adj*

fag end *n* **1.** CIGARETTE STUB the remaining part of a cigarette that has been smoked (*informal*) **2.** LAST AND WORST PART OF SOMETHING the last part of something after the best of it has been used ○ *the fag end of the day* **3.** REMNANT OF CLOTH the remaining part of a piece of cloth, most of which has been used

fagged /fagd/, **fagged out** *adj* feeling very tired or worn out (*informal*)

faggot[1] /fággət/ *n* **1.** BUNDLE OF STICKS FOR FIREWOOD a bundle of sticks or twigs, especially wood to be burnt as fuel **2.** BUNDLE OF PIECES OF METAL a bundle of pieces of metal, especially pieces of iron or steel for welding **3.** FOOD OFFAL MEATBALL a ball of chopped meat, usually pork offal, mixed with bread and herbs, that is baked in the oven ■ *vt* (**-gots, -goting, -goted, -goted**) **1.** COLLECT SOMETHING AND TIE INTO BUNDLE to collect things, especially sticks, and tie them into a bundle or bundles **2.** HANDICRAFT STITCH WITH FAGGOTING to sew something using faggoting [13C. Via Old French < Italian *faggotto* < Greek *phakelos* 'bundle']

faggot[2] /fággət/ *n N Am* an offensive term for a gay man (*slang*) [Early 20C. < FAGGOT [1] as an offensive term for a woman] —**faggoty** *adj*

faggoting /fággəting/ *n* **1.** a decorative way of sewing two hemmed pieces of fabric together, filling the gap between them with an insertion stitch **2.** an embroidery technique in which lengthways threads are pulled out and the cross threads tied into bundles, producing a decorative openwork effect

fag hag *n* an offensive term for a woman who enjoys socializing with gay men (*slang*)

fagot, etc. *n* INDUST, FOOD US spelling of **faggot, etc.**

fah /faa/, **fa** *n* a syllable that represents the fourth note in a scale when singing solfeggio. In fixed solfeggio it represents the note F.

Fahd /faad/ (*b.* 1923) king of Saudi Arabia (1982–). He held several ministerial posts from 1953 before succeeding his half-brother, Khalid, to the throne. Amid calls for democratic reform, he established the Consultative Council (1992) of 60 ministerial advisers.

fahlband /faál band/ *n* a thin bed of rock that contains metal sulphide minerals, although not in sufficient quantity to be used as an ore [Late 19C. < German, 'pale (ash-coloured) band']

Fahr. *abbr* Fahrenheit

Fahrenheit /fárrən hīt/ *adj* using or measured on a temperature scale on which water freezes at 32° and boils at 212° under normal atmospheric conditions. In scientific and technical contexts temperatures are now usually measured in degrees Celsius instead of Fahrenheit. ◊ **Celsius.** Symbol **F** [Mid-18C. After Gabriel *Fahrenheit* (1686–1736) German physicist]

faience /fī óNss, -aánss/, **faïence** *n* earthenware decorated with coloured opaque metallic glazes ○ *a faience bowl* [Late 17C. < French, after *Faïence* 'Faenza', town in N Italy]

fail /fayl/ *v* (**fails, failing, failed**) **1.** *vi* BE UNSUCCESSFUL to be unsuccessful in trying to do something ○ *This plan can't fail.* **2.** *vi* BE UNABLE TO DO SOMETHING to be incapable of doing something or unwilling to do it ○ *She failed to see what the problem was.* **3.** *vti* EDUC NOT PASS EXAM OR COURSE to fall short of the standard required to pass an examination, course, or piece of academic work ○ *He failed English.* **4.** *vt* EDUC JUDGE STUDENT NOT GOOD ENOUGH to judge a student not good enough to pass an examination, course, or piece of academic work **5.** *vi* STOP FUNCTIONING OR GROWING to stop working or not perform or grow as expected ○ *The brakes on the car failed.* **6.** *vi* COMM COLLAPSE FINANCIALLY to collapse financially, becoming insolvent or bankrupt ○ *The business failed after six years.* **7.** *vt* LET SOMEBODY DOWN to abandon, forsake, or let somebody down by not doing what is expected or needed ○ *My courage failed me.* **8.** *vi* BECOME WEAKER to lose strength, loudness, or brightness ○ *The light began to fail.* ■ *n* FAILURE an instance of falling short of the standard required to pass an examination, course, or piece of academic work, especially a grade given as an indication of this [13C. Via Old French *faillir* < Latin *fallere* 'deceive somebody's hopes, disappoint'] ◇ **without fail** without exception

failed /fayld/ *adj* unsuccessful, or not having done what is expected or needed ○ *a failed attempt to circumnavigate the world in a balloon*

failing /fáyling/ *n* a fault or weakness ■ *prep* if something does not happen ○ *Failing a resolution of the dispute by this afternoon, we will suspend negotiations.*

SYNONYMS See *flaw*[1].

failing school *n* in the United Kingdom, a school judged by the Secretary of State for Education, on the advice of inspectors, to be in need of special attention to bring it up to the required standard

faille /fayl/ *n* a closely woven, slightly ribbed silk, cotton, or rayon fabric [Mid-16C. < French]

fail-safe *adj* **1.** SWITCHING TO SAFE CONDITION designed to switch equipment or a system to a safe condition if there is a fault or failure **2.** SURE TO SUCCEED incapable of failing ■ *n* SOMETHING THAT SAFEGUARDS a fail-safe device or procedure

fail-soft *adj US* describes electronic equipment that can operate at a reduced level after the failure of a component or power supply

failure /fáylyər/ *n* **1.** LACK OF SUCCESS a lack of success in or at something **2.** SOMETHING LESS THAN THAT REQUIRED something that falls short of what is required or expected ○ *Failure will not be tolerated.* **3.** SOMEBODY OR SOMETHING THAT FAILS somebody or something that is unsuccessful ○ *She made him feel a failure.* **4.** BREAKDOWN OF SOMETHING a breakdown or decline in the performance of something, or an occasion when something stops working or stops working adequately ○ *engine failure* **5.** LACK OF DEVELOPMENT OR PRODUCTION inadequate growth, development, or production of something ○ *crop failure* **6.** BUSINESS BANKRUPTCY a financial collapse, usually leading to bankruptcy

failure to thrive *n* a pronounced lack of growth in a child because of inadequate absorption of nutrients or a serious heart or kidney condition, resulting in below-average height and weight

fain /fayn/ (*archaic*) *adv* HAPPILY with gladness or eagerness ■ *adj* **1.** EAGER willing or eager to do something **2.** COMPELLED forced by an obligation or circumstances to do something [Old English *fægen* 'glad' < Germanic]

fainéant /fáyni ənt/ (*literary*) *adj* unwilling to do anything ■ *n* somebody who is regarded as lazy [Early 17C. < French, alteration of *fait-nient* 'does nothing' < *faignant* 'shirker']

fainites /fáyn īts/ *interj regional* = **fains** (*archaic*) [Early 19C. Alteration of *fains I*]

fáinne /faán jə/ (*plural* **-nes**) *n* in Ireland, a ring worn on a pin to show willingness and the ability to speak Gaelic [< Irish, 'ring']

fains /faynz/ *interj* used to call for a truce or claim exemption from something (*archaic or regional*) [Early 19C. Origin ?]

faint /faynt/ *adj* **1.** DIM not bright, clear, or loud **2.** UNENTHUSIASTIC done feebly and without conviction ○ *damned the new book with faint praise* **3.** DIZZY dizzy or weak, as if about to become unconscious ○ *All of a sudden he felt faint.* **4.** SLIGHT remote or slight ○ *a faint chance* ■ *vi* (**faints, fainting, fainted**) **1.** LOSE CONSCIOUSNESS BRIEFLY to become unconscious, especially for a short time, because of a reduction in the flow of blood to the brain **2.** WEAKEN to become weak or lose courage (*archaic*) ■ *n* SUDDEN LOSS OF CONSCIOUSNESS a sudden, usually brief, loss of consciousness, caused by a reduction in the flow of blood to the brain. Technical name **syncope** (sense 1) [13C. < Old French < *faindre* 'pretend, shirk'] —**fainter** *n* —**faintish** *adj* —**faintly** *adv* —**faintness** *n*

SPELLCHECK faint or **feint**? Do not confuse the spelling of ***faint*** and ***feint***, which sound similar. ***Faint***, the more frequent of the two words, can be used as an adjective meaning 'dizzy', 'weak', or 'slight' (as in *to feel faint, a faint smell, a faint chance*), or as a noun or verb referring to a sudden loss of consciousness. ***Feint*** is a noun or

verb referring to a deceptive action in sport or combat; it is also an adjective used to describe lined paper.

faint-hearted *adj* lacking resolve, boldness, or enthusiasm —**faint-heartedly** *adv* —**faint-heartedness** *n*

SYNONYMS See *cowardly*.

fainting fit *n* an attack of dizziness, often leading to unconsciousness

fair[1] /fair/ *adj* **1.** REASONABLE OR UNBIASED not exhibiting any bias, and therefore reasonable or impartial ○ *a fair decision* **2.** DONE PROPERLY done according to the rules ○ *fair and free elections* **3.** LIGHT-COLOURED with light-coloured hair or skin **4.** SIZEABLE reasonably large in size or quantity ○ *They had a fair number of responses to the advertisement.* **5.** BETTER THAN ACCEPTABLE moderately good or reasonable ○ *a fair understanding* **6.** ACCEPTABLE no more than acceptable or average ○ *Your performance this year has only been fair.* **7.** NOT STORMY OR CLOUDY sunny or clear, and without much wind ○ *fair weather* **8.** NAUT GOOD FOR SAILING describes conditions that are favourable for sailing or travel by boat ○ *a fair wind* **9.** UNSULLIED not marred by any blemish or stain ○ *to preserve your fair name* **10.** FALSE DESPITE APPEARANCES seemingly good or true, but actually false or insincere ○ *fair words* **11.** PLEASING TO LOOK AT beautiful or pleasing to the eye (*literary*) ○ *a fair maiden* **12.** NOT BLOCKED clear and unobstructed ○ *a fair view of the enemy's forces* ■ *adv* **1.** PROPERLY in accordance with the rules or what is expected ○ *She's always played fair with me.* **2.** DIRECTLY in a direct or straight way, and squarely ○ *hit fair in the centre of the board* **3.** *regional* QUITE quite or rather (*informal*) ○ *I'm getting fair sick of this.* ■ *v* (**fairs, fairing, faired**) **1.** *vi Scotland* IMPROVE to become bright after cloud or rain (*refers to the weather or sky*) **2.** *vt* MAKE SMOOTH AND EVEN to smooth or streamline the surface of something such as an aircraft wing or tabletop [Old English *faeger* 'beautiful' < Germanic, 'suitable'] ◇ **fair and square** justly, fairly, or according to the rules ◇ **fair do's** used to call for fairness or justice, especially as a warning that an injustice may be occurring (*informal*) ◇ **fair enough 1.** used to say that you accept something, though you would have been happier with something better (*informal*) **2.** acceptable and understandable, but not ideal ◇ **fair's fair** used to urge or appeal for just or even treatment (*informal*) ◇ **fair to middling** reasonably good or reasonably well (*informal*; hyphenated when used before a noun) ◇ **no fair** *N Am* used to indicate that something is unfair or against the rules (*informal*)

SPELLCHECK **fair** or **fare**? Do not confuse the spelling of **fair** and **fare**, which sound similar. **Fair** is chiefly used as an adjective and has many meanings, including 'reasonable and just', 'light in colour', and 'moderately good', as in *fair treatment, fair hair, fair weather*. **Fair** is also used as a noun, denoting an outdoor entertainment or a commercial exhibition. The noun **fare**, on the other hand, means 'cost of travel', 'food', or 'entertainment', as in *fare-paying passengers, good wholesome fare, dull fare for viewers*. **Fare** is also used as a verb, meaning 'get on in a particular way': *How did she fare in the exam?*

fair[2] /fair/ *n* **1.** OUTDOOR EVENT WITH AMUSEMENTS a temporary outdoor entertainment with amusements such as machines to ride on, sideshows, and food stands, usually set up on open ground and moving from place to place. N Am term **carnival 2.** LIVESTOCK MARKET a large market selling a wide range of goods including livestock, sometimes with amusements and sideshows **3.** COMMERCIAL EXHIBITION an exhibition, often held annually, at which companies show their products to potential buyers ○ *a book fair* ○ *a trade fair* **4.** SALE TO RAISE MONEY a sale of goods to raise money for something, especially a charity **5.** *N Am* LEISURE, AGRIC same as **show** *n* (sense 3) **6.** *Scotland* TRADES HOLIDAY an annual two-week trades holiday observed in summer at different times in various towns, especially the Glasgow Fair, which occupies the last two weeks in July [13C. Via Old French < late Latin *feria* 'holiday' < Latin *feriae* (plural)]

Fairbanks /fáir bangks/ city in eastern Alaska, on the northern bank of the Tanana River, northeast of Anchorage. Population: 30,780 (2002 estimate).

Fairbanks, **Douglas** (1883–1939) US silent film actor. He is best known for his swashbuckling performances in films such as *The Mark of Zorro* (1920). Born **Ullman, Douglas Elton**

Fairburn /fáir burn/, **A. R. D.** (1904–57) New Zealand journalist and writer. His works include *Strange Rendezvous* (1952). Full name **Fairburn, Arthur Rex Dugard**

fair copy *n* an unmarked version of a document that has been corrected and retyped or printed out again

fair cow *n NZ* a person, thing, or situation that is disagreeable (*informal*)

fair dinkum (*informal*) *adj Aus* true or genuine ■ *adv Aus* used to emphasize or query the truthfulness or accuracy of what is being said ■ *n ANZ* same as **fair play** (sense 2)

Fairfax /fáir faks/, **John** (1804–77) British-born Australian newspaper proprietor. He was the owner of the *Sydney Morning Herald* and founder of the Fairfax media dynasty.

Fairfax, **Thomas, 3rd Baron Fairfax of Cameron** (1612–71) English general. He was commander of the Parliamentary army during the English Civil War.

fair game *n* a permissible object of pursuit, ridicule, or attack

fair go *ANZ* (*informal*) *n* a reasonable chance to attempt something ■ *interj* used to appeal for just treatment or acknowledge that something is just

fair green *n* GOLF same as **fairway** (sense 1)

fairground /fáir grownd/ *n* a large open outdoor space where fairs or exhibitions may be held

fair-haired *adj* with light-coloured hair

fair-haired boy *n N Am* same as **blue-eyed boy** (*informal*)

fairing[1] /fáiring/ *n* a streamlined structure added to an aircraft, car, or other vehicle to reduce drag

fairing[2] /fáiring/ *n* **1.** a sweet buttery biscuit **2.** a gift, especially one brought back from, or given at, a fair (*archaic*)

fairish /fáirish/ *adj* **1.** reasonably good or large ○ *a fairish amount* **2.** fairly light in colour

Fair Isle[1] /fáyr īl/ *n* **1.** a traditional Shetland Islands knitting design, used especially for sweaters, that incorporates bands of repeated multicoloured geometrical motifs **2.** a technique of knitting designs with two or more colours in which any colours not actually being knitted are woven into the back of the work [Mid-19C. After FAIR ISLE [2]]

Fair Isle[2] /fáir īl/ southernmost of the Shetland Islands, off the northern coast of Scotland. It is situated approximately midway between the main Shetland Islands and the Orkney Islands. Population: 70. Area: 15 sq. km/8 sq. mi.

fairlead /fáir leed/, **fairleader** /-leedər/ *n* a ring, hole, or other device through which a rope is guided in order to reduce friction and prevent chafing, or to keep it in place

fairly /fáirli/ *adv* **1.** HONESTLY in a just, honest, proper, or legitimate way **2.** MODERATELY to a reasonable or moderate degree ○ *a fairly easy decision* **3.** CONSIDERABLY to a considerable degree ○ *The ground fairly shook with the impact.*

fair-market value *n US* a price for something that both buyer and seller willingly agree to when neither party is under undue pressure to complete the transaction

fair-minded *adj* able to make impartial and just judgments, or resulting from such a judgment —**fair-mindedly** *adv* —**fair-mindedness** *n*

fairness /fáirnəss/ *n* **1.** the condition of being just or impartial **2.** the condition of being pleasing to look at ◇ **in (all) fairness** so as to be just and impartial ○ *In all fairness, I don't see how this is important.*

fair play *n* **1.** the playing of a game without cheating or breaking the rules **2.** conduct that is just and equitable ◇ **fair play to somebody** *Ireland* used to express general good wishes to somebody (*informal*)

fair sex *n* women and girls collectively (*literary; sometimes offensive*)

fair shake *n* (*informal*) **1.** just or reasonable treatment **2.** a reasonable chance to attempt something

fair-skinned *adj* having pale skin of a type that is easily burned by the sun

fair-spoken *adj* speaking in a pleasant and polite way (*archaic*) —**fair-spokenness** *n*

fair trade *n* development of a pricing structure for produce that does not put producers in developing countries at a disadvantage —**fair-trade** *adj*

fair-trade agreement *n US* an agreement between a manufacturer of a product and distributors or retailers that the product will not be sold for less than a price set by the manufacturer

fairway /fáir way/ *n* **1.** the closely mown area on a golf hole that forms the main avenue between a tee and a green **2.** a navigable channel or the usual course followed by boats in a river, harbour, or other body of water

Fairweather, **Mount** /fáir wethər/ mountain in the St Elias Mountains on the border between Alaska and British Columbia, Canada. Part of Glacier Bay National Park and Preserve, it is the highest peak in southern Alaska. Height: 4,663 m/15,299 ft.

Fairweather /fáir wethər/, **Ian** (1891–1974) Scottish-born Australian painter. His works show strong Asian and Aboriginal influences. Among his best-known paintings is *Monastery* (1960–61).

fair-weather *adj* **1.** able to be relied upon only when things are going well **2.** suitable, done, or taking part only when the weather is fine

Fairweather Cape cape on the southeastern coast of Alaska, approximately 55 km/35 mi. south of Mount Fairweather

fairy /fáiri/ *n* (*plural* -**ies**) **1.** SMALL SUPERNATURAL CREATURE an imaginary supernatural being, usually resembling a small person, with magic powers. In folklore, fairies may be kindly or malicious. **2.** OFFENSIVE TERM an offensive term for a gay man (*slang*) ■ *adj* OF FAIRIES relating to, belonging to, or characteristic of fairies ○ *a fairy princess* [14C. < Old French *faerie* 'enchantment' < *fae* 'fairy' < Latin *fata* 'the Fates', plural of *fatum* 'fate'] —**fairy-like** *adj*

fairy bread *n Aus* bread and butter sprinkled with tiny multicoloured sugar beads (**hundreds-and-thousands**) (*informal*)

fairy cycle *n* a small children's bicycle or tricycle

fairyfloss /fáiri floss/ *n Aus* cooked sugar syrup, coloured and spun from a machine onto a stick in fine strands, eaten traditionally at fairgrounds. UK, NZ term **candyfloss**. US term **cotton candy**

fairy godmother *n* **1.** in some fairy stories, a kind fairy in the form of a woman who gives vital help to somebody, especially to the hero or heroine. Perhaps the most famous fairy godmother is the one who appears to Cinderella and enables her to attend the prince's ball. **2.** somebody, especially a woman, who gives generous help, often anonymously

fairyland /fáiri land/ *n* **1.** the imaginary country where fairies live **2.** an enchanting place, e.g. a fantasy world existing in somebody's imagination

fairy lights *npl* a long string of small, often coloured, electric lights, used on Christmas trees and for other types of decoration

fairy penguin (*plural* **fairy penguins** or *same*) *n* a penguin with a bluish back that grows to only 40 cm/15.5 in tall. Native to: coastal waters of South Australia and the South Island, New Zealand. Latin name: *Eudyptula minor*.

fairy ring *n* a ring of grass darker than the surrounding grass, traditionally thought to be associated with dancing fairies but actually marking the outer edge of growth of various underground perennial fungi

fairy ring champignon *n* a buff-coloured edible fungus, often growing in a ring-shaped cluster. Latin name: *Marasmius oreades*.

fairy shrimp *n* a tiny soft-bodied crustacean found in fresh or brackish water that has an elongated body and eleven pairs of appendages. Order: Anostraca.

fairy tale, **fairy story** *n* **1.** a story for children about fairies or other imaginary beings and events, often containing a moral message **2.** an improbable invented account of something, often a false excuse

CULTURAL NOTE *Grimm's Fairy Tales*, a collection of folk tales (1812–15) compiled and edited by German scholars Jacob and Wilhelm Grimm. Based on written sources dating back to the 16th century and on German folk tales, it includes many stories now famous worldwide, including 'Cinderella', 'Hansel and Gretel', and 'Rumpelstiltskin'. With their universal themes the tales were seen by the Grimms as repositories of the hopes, passions, and fears of humankind.

fairy-tale *adj* **1.** derived from or typical of a fairy tale **2.** like something from a fairy tale, especially in being fortunate, happy, or extravagantly beautiful

fairy thorn *n N Ireland* a hawthorn bush left growing in the middle of a field through fear that misfortune would befall whoever chopped it down

fairy wren *n* a small songbird, the male of which has colourful feathers in the breeding season. Native to: Australia. Genus: *Malurus*.

Faisal /físs'l/ (1905–75) king of Saudi Arabia (1964–75). He was made foreign secretary of the newly formed Saudi Arabia in 1932 and became premier in 1953. After serving as regent, he forced his brother Saud to abdicate the throne and instituted extensive economic and social reforms during his reign. Full name **Faisal ibn Abdul Aziz**

> 'We feel that the Arabs and the Jews are cousins in race, having suffered similar oppression at the hands of powers stronger than ourselves.'
> [Faisal. Quoted in *Dawn of the Promised Land*, Ben Wicks; 1997]

Faisal I (1885–1933) king of Iraq (1921–33). An Arab nationalist leader, he was the first king of Iraq and the son of the founder of the Hashemite dynasty.

Faisal II (1935–58) king of Iraq (1939–58). A minor during most of his reign, he was assassinated during a military coup.

Faisalabad /físsələ bad/, **Faisalābād** city situated in the Punjab, northeastern Pakistan, 121 km/75 mi. west of Lahore. Population: 1,977,246 (1998).

faisty *adj* another spelling of **facety** (*slang; used in Black English*)

fait accompli /fáyt ə kóm plee/ (*plural* **faits accomplis** /*pronunc. same/*) *n* something that is already done or decided and seems unalterable [Mid-19C. < French, 'accomplished fact']

faites vos jeux /fáyt võ zhó/ *interj* used by a croupier in roulette and other gambling games to ask people to place their bets [< French]

faith /fayth/ *n* **1.** BELIEF OR TRUST belief in, devotion to, or trust in somebody or something, especially without logical proof ○ *I wouldn't put my faith in him to sort things out.* **2.** RELIGION OR RELIGIOUS GROUP a system of religious belief, or the group of people who adhere to it **3.** TRUST IN GOD belief in and devotion to God ○ *Her faith is unwavering.* **4.** SET OF BELIEFS a strongly held set of beliefs or principles ○ *people of different political faiths* **5.** LOYALTY allegiance or loyalty to somebody or something [13C. Via Old French *feid* < Latin *fides* 'trust, belief'] ◇ **keep faith with somebody** *or* **something** to be loyal or true to a person or promise ◇ **on faith** without demanding proof

faithful /fáythf'l/ *adj* **1.** CONSISTENTLY LOYAL consistently trustworthy and loyal, especially to a person, promise, or duty **2.** NOT ADULTEROUS OR PROMISCUOUS not having sexual relations with somebody other than a spouse or partner **3.** CONSCIENTIOUS displaying or resulting from a sense of responsibility or devotion to duty ○ *faithful performance of his duties* **4.** CORRECT accurate and true ○ *a faithful account of the events* **5.** UNWAVERING IN BELIEF believing firmly in something or somebody, especially a religion or a political doctrine ■ *n* SOMEBODY OR SOMETHING RELIABLE a person or thing that can be trusted and relied upon ■ *npl* **1.** *also* **Faithful** RELIGIOUS BELIEVERS the believers in a religion considered as a group, especially Muslims or Christians **2.** LOYAL SUPPORTERS people who are committed to something or somebody, especially the loyal members of a political party ○ *the party faithful* —**faithfulness** *n*

faithfully /fáythf'li/ *adv* in a loyal, true, or accurate way ◇ **yours faithfully** used immediately before the signature to end a letter that is not addressed to somebody by name

faith healer *n* a healer who attempts to treat illness or disorders through prayer, sometimes also by touching the affected person —**faith healing** *n*

faithless /fáythləss/ *adj* **1.** DISHONEST disloyal to somebody or something, e.g. in not keeping a promise or performing a duty **2.** UNTRUSTWORTHY not to be trusted or relied on **3.** NOT RELIGIOUS not believing in a religious faith —**faithlessly** *adv* —**faithlessness** *n*

faith school *n* a school that provides children with a general education, and was founded or is supported by a religious group

fajitas /fə heétəss/ *npl* a dish consisting of beef or other meat, especially chicken, that has been marinated, grilled, cut into strips, and served in a soft tortilla [Late 20C. < Mexican Spanish, literally 'little strips, belts']

fake[1] /fayk/ *n* SOMEBODY OR SOMETHING NOT GENUINE a person or thing that appears or is presented as being genuine but is not ■ *adj* NOT GENUINE not genuine, but meant to be taken for genuine ■ *v* (**fakes, faking, faked**) **1.** *vt* FALSELY PRESENT SOMETHING AS GENUINE to make or produce something and claim it is genuine when it is not **2.** *vti* PRETEND FEELING OR KNOWLEDGE to pretend to have, feel, or know something ○ *faked a knowledge of Italian* **3.** *vt* ARTS IMPROVISE WHILE PERFORMING to improvise or ad-lib a piece of music or lines in a play during a performance [Late 18C. < *feague*, 16C criminal slang for 'rob, tamper with', origin ?] —**faker** *n*

fake out *vt N Am* to deceive or surprise somebody, especially by bluffing (*informal*)

fake[2] /fayk/ *vt* NAUT (**fakes, faking, faked**) same as **flake**[3] ■ *n* (*plural* **fakes** or **flakes**) same as **flake**[3] [15C. Origin ?]

fakie /fáyki/ *adv* in skateboarding, moving backwards on the board (*slang*) —**fakie** *adj*

fakir /fáy keer, fə keer/, **fakeer**, **faqir** *n* **1.** a religious Muslim, especially a Sufi, who lives by begging **2.** a Hindu ascetic who lives by begging and whose religious practice often includes the performance of extraordinary feats of physical endurance [Early 17C. Directly or via French < Arabic, 'poor man']

fa-la /faa laa/, **fal la** *n* a refrain in 16th- and 17th-century English songs, using the meaningless syllables 'fa-la-la'

~~falacy~~ incorrect spelling of **fallacy**

falafel /fə laáf'l/, **felafel** *n* a deep-fried ball of ground chickpeas seasoned with onions and spices, originating in Southwest Asia [Mid-20C. Via Egyptian Arabic *falāfil* < Arabic *fulful* 'pepper']

Falange /fə lánj/ *n* a Spanish fascist movement founded in 1933 and dissolved in 1977. It was the official ruling party of Spain under General Francisco Franco. [Mid-20C. < Spanish, 'phalanx'] —**Falangist** *n*

Falasha /fə láshə/ (*plural* **-shas** or *same*) *n* a member of an Ethiopian Jewish religious group, most of whom now live in Israel (*often offensive*) [Early 18C. < Amharic, 'exile']

falbala /fálbələ/ *n* a gathered trimming or ruffle used as decoration [Early 18C. < French]

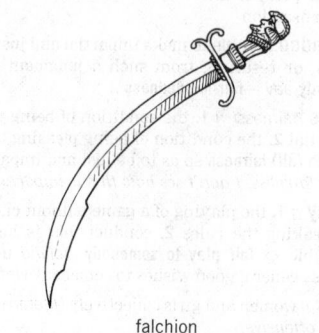
falchion

falchion /fáwlchən/ *n* a short sword with a broad, slightly curved blade, used in medieval times [14C. Via Old French *fauchon* < Latin *falc-*, 'sickle']

falcon /fáwlkən/ *n* **1.** a fast powerful bird of prey related to the hawk that often catches birds in flight. Family: Falconidae. **2.** a female hawk that is trained to hunt small birds and animals [13C. Via Old French < late Latin *falcon-*]

CULTURAL NOTE *The Maltese Falcon*, a film (1941) by US director John Huston. Based on Dashiell Hammett's 1930 detective novel, it is regarded as one of the finest examples of film noir. Private investigator Sam Spade's attempts to track down the murderer of his partner lead to a group of people who share a common interest in a priceless statuette of a falcon.

falconet /fáwlkə net/ *n* **1.** a small falcon found in forests. Native to: Asia. Genus: *Microhierax*. **2.** a small falcon found in open woodland. Native to: South America. Latin name: *Spiziapteryx*.

falconine /fáwlkə nīn/ *adj* relating to or typical of a falcon

falconry /fáwlkənri/ *n* the breeding, training, and use of falcons or other hawks to hunt small prey and return from flight at their handler's direction —**falconer** *n*

falderal /faáldə raal/, **folderol** /fóldə rol/ *n* **1.** TRINKET an attractive but valueless object or trinket **2.** NONSENSE silly nonsense (*dated*) **3.** SONG REFRAIN a meaningless chorus or refrain in a song (*archaic*) [Early 19C. < *fol de rol*, nonsense refrain in songs]

Faldo /fáldō/, **Nick** (*b.* 1957) British golfer. A British Ryder Cup team member, he has won the British Open three times (1987, 1990, and 1992) and is a three-time US Masters champion (1989, 1990, and 1996). Full name **Faldo, Nicholas Alexander**

> 'I didn't like team sports because it annoyed me that if you do your bit you could still go home a loser.'
> [Nick Faldo, *The Times*; 11 April 1989]

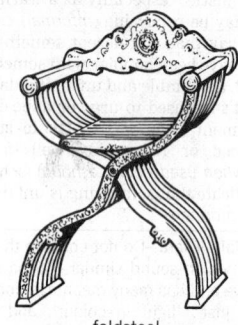
faldstool

faldstool /fáwld stool/ *n* **1.** FOLDING SEAT FOR BISHOP a folding seat, especially one used by a bishop when officiating away from the throne or at another church **2.** FOLDING STOOL FOR WORSHIPPER a small folding stool with a raised attachment like a desk at which a worshipper kneels to pray **3.** CORONATION STOOL FOR BRITISH SOVEREIGN a stool on which the British sovereign kneels at his or her coronation [Old English *fældstōl* < FOLD[1] + STOOL; partly < medieval Latin *faldistolium* < Germanic]

Faliscan /fə lískən/ *n* an ancient language spoken in Italy, related to the Latin language that replaced it [Late 17C. < Latin *Faliscus* 'of Falerii', important city of Etruria] —**Faliscan** *adj*

Falkirk /fáwl kurk/ **1.** industrial town in central Scotland situated between Edinburgh and Glasgow. Population: 141,145 (2001). **2.** council area in central Scotland, formerly part of the Central Region. Area: 299 sq. km/115 sq. mi.

Falkland Islands /fáwlklənd-/, **Falklands** /fáwlkləndz/ group of islands and British dependency in the South Atlantic Ocean, 483 km/300 mi. east of the Strait of Magellan. After a brief military conflict in 1982 with the United Kingdom, the government of Argentina maintains its claim to these islands. Population: 2,317 (1995). Area: 12,173 sq. km/4,700 sq. mi. Spanish name **Islas Malvinas**. See map on next page

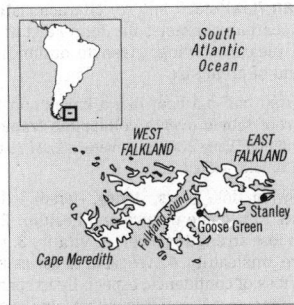

Falkland Islands

fall /fawl/ vi (**falls, falling, fell** /fel/, **fallen** /fáwlən/) **1.** MOVE DOWNWARDS to come down freely from a higher to a lower position, moved by the force of gravity ○ *The vase fell to the floor and shattered.* **2.** DROP OR BE LOWERED to drop or be dropped or lowered ○ *The curtain fell at the end of the performance.* **3.** COME DOWN SUDDENLY FROM UPRIGHT POSITION to drop or come down suddenly from an upright position, especially by accident ○ *The horse fell at the first fence.* **4.** BECOME LESS to become lower or be reduced in amount, value, or quality ○ *Prices have fallen in the last year.* **5.** ACOUSTICS BECOME LOWER IN PITCH to become lower in pitch or volume **6.** MIL BE TAKEN BY FORCE to be conquered or captured by a military force ○ *The city fell despite the best efforts of the army.* **7.** MIL DROP TO GROUND IN BATTLE to drop to the ground in battle after being wounded or having died ○ *He fell at the Battle of the Alamo.* **8.** POL COLLAPSE POLITICALLY to lose political power or be defeated ○ *The government fell after only six months in office.* **9.** BE DRAPED to hang down ○ *When her hair is down it falls across her shoulders.* **10.** TAKE PLACE to happen or occur as if falling on something and enveloping it ○ *Night fell suddenly.* **11.** DISPLAY DISAPPOINTMENT to show an expression of disappointment ○ *Their faces fell when they heard the result.* **12.** GROW SAD to become sad and gloomy or to lose hope ○ *Our hearts fell.* **13.** STOP TO LOOK to settle or come to rest ○ *His gaze fell on an open book.* **14.** BE AVERTED to look away or downwards ○ *Her eyes fell.* **15.** BEGIN TO BE IN PARTICULAR STATE to begin to be in, or enter into, a particular state or condition ○ *The class eventually fell silent.* ○ *fall to work* **16.** CHR SIN to sin or give in to temptation (archaic) **17.** GEOG SLOPE to slope downwards and away ○ *The land falls gradually to the lake.* **18.** BE DUE to become due ○ *When does the next payment fall?* **19.** CRICKET BE LOST to be lost to the bowling side in a cricket match ○ *The fourth wicket fell just after tea.* **20.** regional BECOME PREGNANT to become pregnant ○ *fell for a baby* ■ n **1.** ACT OF MOVING DOWN FREELY an act of falling or moving down freely or suddenly ○ *She broke her arm in a fall.* **2.** SOMETHING FALLEN something that falls or has fallen, or the amount that has fallen ○ *a heavy fall of snow* **3.** DISTANCE DOWN the distance that something drops or could fall ○ *a ten-foot fall* **4.** LOWERING OF SOMETHING a decrease in the amount, size, quantity, or quality of something ○ *Even a slight fall in prices is welcome.* **5.** N Am same as **autumn** (sense 1) **6.** GEOG SLOPE a slope that leads downwards and away **7.** GEOG WATERFALL a waterfall or steep rapids (often used in the plural, often used in placenames) ○ *Niagara Falls* **8.** MIL MILITARY LOSS a military defeat or the loss of something to an enemy ○ *the fall of Berlin in 1945* **9.** POL POLITICAL COLLAPSE a loss of political power or control ○ *the fall of the government* **10.** RELIG COMMISSION OF SIN a giving in to temptation or committing of a sin **11.** END OF HOISTING ROPE the end of a rope or chain to which power is applied when hoisting something **12.** WRESTLING MOVE FORCING OPPOSING WRESTLER TO FLOOR in wrestling, a scoring move in which a wrestler forces the opponent's shoulders to the floor for a specific period **13.** HAIRPIECE a hairpiece of long hair, usually attached to the top of the head with the join covered by the wearer's own hair **14.** BOT DOWNWARD FACING PART OF IRIS BLOSSOM the outer part of an iris flower, resembling a petal, that hangs down in front [Old English *feallan* < Germanic] ◇ **fall flat** to fail to have the intended effect ◇ **fall foul** or **afoul of 1.** to come into conflict with somebody or something **2.** NAUT to collide with something ◇ **fall short** to be less than is needed ◇ **fall short of something**

to fail to meet a desired standard ◇ **break a fall** *Carib* to fall, especially heavily

fall about vi to laugh noisily and uncontrollably (informal)

fall among vt to become associated unwittingly with a group of people

fall apart vi **1.** to collapse, fail, or break into pieces **2.** to be in a state of great emotional distress (informal)

fall away vi **1.** DECREASE to become smaller in number, quantity, or size ○ *Attendance fell away after the third week of the course.* **2.** SLOPE to slope downwards **3.** STOP ASSOCIATING WITH SOMEBODY to withdraw friendship, devotion, or support

fall back vi **1.** to retreat or move back, e.g. during a battle **2.** to be overtaken by others in a race or contest

fall back on, fall back upon vt to resort to something, especially something familiar, if other plans fail

fall behind v **1.** vti to fail to keep up with somebody or something **2.** vi to be late in doing something such as making a regular payment or completing a task ○ *He fell behind with the car payments.*

fall down vi **1.** to collapse or drop to the ground **2.** to be invalid or unsuccessful

fall down on vt to be unsuccessful or negligent in something

fall for vt **1.** to become infatuated or in love with somebody or something **2.** to be deceived by something (informal)

fall in vi **1.** to join or form an organized rank ○ *The whistle blew and the soldiers fell in.* **2.** to collapse inwards

fall in with vt **1.** to meet and start associating with somebody or a group **2.** to agree or comply with somebody or something

fall off v **1.** vi to decrease in size, number, or quality ○ *Share prices have fallen off in the last couple of days.* **2.** vti to deviate from a course to sail downwind, or make a boat sail downwind

fall on, fall upon vt **1.** ATTACK to attack somebody vigorously, especially by surprise (literary) **2.** BEGIN SOMETHING EAGERLY to begin eating or doing something eagerly **3.** BE RESPONSIBILITY OF to be born as a responsibility or liability ○ *It fell on the surgeon to tell the patient's family that the operation was unsuccessful.*

fall out v **1.** vi QUARREL WITH SOMEBODY to have a quarrel with somebody, especially one that leads to strained relations **2.** vi OCCUR to happen **3.** vti BREAK MILITARY RANKS to leave organized ranks or positions, or break up organized ranks or positions

fall over vti to drop accidentally to the ground, especially by tumbling from an upright position or tripping over something ○ *I fell over a pile of books that had been left on the floor.* ○ *Be careful you don't fall over!* ◇ **fall over yourself** to be very eager or enthusiastic in doing something ○ *He was falling over himself to make everybody feel at home.*

fall through vi to fail to happen in the expected way

fall to v **1.** vt BE DUTY OF SOMEBODY to be the responsibility, obligation, or duty of somebody or a group ○ *It falls to the council to decide the matter.* **2.** vti START to begin doing something **3.** vt BE GIVEN to be given by right or inheritance to somebody

fall upon vt same as **fall on**

Fall n in Judaism and Christianity, the lapse of humankind into a sinful state as a result of Adam and Eve's failure to obey God

fal la n MUSIC another spelling of **fa-la**

Falla /fíə/, **Manuel de** (1876–1946) Spanish composer and pianist. Among his compositions are ballets such as *Love, the Magician* (1915) and *The Three-Cornered Hat* (1919).

fallacious /fə láyshəss/ adj **1.** containing or involving a mistaken belief or idea **2.** deceptive or misleading [Early 16C. Via Old French < Latin *fallaciosus* < *fallacia* (see FALLACY)] —**fallaciously** adv —**fallaciousness** n

fallacy /fáləssi/ (plural -**cies**) n **1.** MISTAKEN BELIEF OR IDEA something that is believed to be true but is erroneous **2.** LOGIC INVALID ARGUMENT an argument or reasoning in which the conclusion does not follow from the premises **3.** LOGIC LOGICAL ERROR IN ARGUMENT a mistake made in a line of reasoning that invalidates it **4.** DECEPTIVENESS the condition of being misleading or deceptive [15C. Via Old French < Latin *fallacia* 'deception' < *fallere* 'deceive']

fallal /fal lál/ n a fancy ornament or piece of clothing [Early 18C. Origin ?] —**fallalery** /fal lálləri/ n

fallback /fáwl bak/ n **1.** something that can be used as a replacement or substitute if something else does not work **2.** a retreat or withdrawal

fallboard /fáwl bawrd/ n US the hinged cover that protects a piano keyboard when the instrument is not being played

fallen /fáwlen/ past participle of **fall** ■ adj **1.** KILLED killed in war or battle, especially while fighting **2.** ON GROUND on the ground after dropping down ○ *freshly fallen snow* ■ npl PEOPLE WHO DIED IN WAR those people killed in war or battle, especially while fighting

fallen angel n in Christian, Jewish, and Muslim tradition, a rebellious angel who was punished by God by being banished from heaven

fallen arch n a flattening of the arch of the foot (usually used in the plural)

fallen woman n a woman who is regarded as sinful or dishonoured because she has had sexual relations outside marriage (literary)

faller /fáwlər/ n **1.** a person, animal, or thing that falls **2.** N Am FORESTRY same as **feller**[1] (sense 1)

fallfish /fáwl fish/ (plural same or -**fishes**) n a large minnow that makes a substantial nest by piling up small pebbles. Native to: eastern North America. Latin name: *Semotilus corporalis*.

fall guy n (informal) **1.** somebody who takes the blame for somebody else's mistake or wrongdoing **2.** somebody who is easily tricked or deceived

fallible /fálləb'l/ adj **1.** liable to make mistakes **2.** liable to be wrong or misleading [15C. < medieval Latin *fallibilis* < Latin *fallere* 'deceive'] —**fallibility** /fállə bílləti/ n —**fallibleness** n —**fallibly** adv

falling band n a large collar, often trimmed with lace, turned down flat onto the shoulders, worn by men in the 17th century

falling-off n a decrease in size, number, or quality

falling-out (plural **fallings-out**) n a disagreement, especially one that leads to strained relations with somebody

falling sickness n MED same as **epilepsy** (archaic)

falling star n ASTRON same as **meteor** (sense 2)

fall line n **1.** GEOG IMAGINARY LINE ALONG TOP OF SLOPE an imaginary line along the edge of higher land, marked by rapids and waterfalls, that indicates where rivers begin to descend more steeply from a highland region to a lowland one **2.** SKIING NATURAL ROUTE OF DESCENT OF HILL the natural route of descent on a hill between two given points **3.** CLIMBING LINE CONNECTING HIGH AND LOW POINT vertical line connecting a high and low point on a mountain or cliff

falloff /fáwl of/ n a decrease or decline, especially in the price of or demand for something

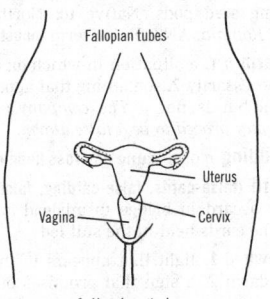

fallopian tube

fallopian tube /fə lópi ən-/, **Fallopian tube** n either of two narrow tubes through which a female mammal's eggs pass from either of the ovaries to the womb [Early 18C. After Gabriello *Fallopio* (1523–62), Italian anatomist]

fallout /fáwl owt/ n **1.** RADIOACTIVE PARTICLES a cloud of radioactive dust that is created by a nuclear explosion and settles back down to the ground **2.** DESCENT OF RADIOACTIVE DUST the descent from the at-

mosphere of particles from a cloud of radioactive dust **3.** INCIDENTAL CONSEQUENCES consequences, especially undesirable ones, that result incidentally from a situation or event

fallout shelter *n* a place of refuge built to protect people from the effects of a nuclear weapon

fallow[1] /fállō/ *adj* **1.** AGRIC LEFT UNSEEDED AFTER PLOUGHING left unseeded after ploughing for a period of time in order to recover natural fertility **2.** CURRENTLY INACTIVE currently inactive but with the possibility of activity or use in the future ■ *n* AGRIC LAND WITHOUT CROPS land that has not been planted or sown with crops [13C. < Old English *fealh* < *fealgian* 'break up land by ploughing'] —**fallowness** *n*

fallow[2] /fállō/ *adj* of a light yellowish-brown colour [Old English *fealu* < Indo-European] —**fallow** *n*

fallow deer

fallow deer *n* a deer, the male of which has broad flattened antlers and a brown coat spotted with white in summer. Native to: Europe, Asia. Latin name: *Dama dama*.

Falmouth /fálməth/ seaside resort on the estuary of the River Fal, Cornwall, southwestern England. Population: 31,431 (1998).

false /fawlss, folss/ *adj* (**falser, falsest**) **1.** INCORRECT not conforming to facts or truth ○ *was given false information* **2.** MISTAKEN resulting from a mistaken belief or a misunderstanding ○ *have a false impression of the situation* **3.** ARTIFICIAL imitating, copying, or having the same function as a particular thing and replacing or used alongside it ○ *false eyelashes* **4.** DELIBERATELY DECEPTIVE done with or having the intention of deceiving somebody ○ *false promises* **5.** NOT GENUINE intentionally made or adopted to deceive somebody ○ *false papers* **6.** TREACHEROUS disloyal and untrustworthy **7.** BIOL CONFUSABLE WITH PARTICULAR PLANT OR ANIMAL superficially resembling, and often mistaken for a particular plant or animal ○ *false acacia* ■ *adv* DISHONESTLY in a dishonest and disloyal way (*literary*) [Pre-12C. Directly or via Old French < Latin *falsus* < *fallere* 'deceive'] —**falsely** *adv* —**falseness** *n*

false acacia *n* UK a deciduous leguminous tree with spiny twigs, hanging clusters of fragrant flowers, and long seed pods. Native to: North America. Genus: *Robinia*. ANZ, N Am term **locust**

false alarm *n* **1.** a situation in which an alarm goes off unnecessarily **2.** something that appears to be a problem but is not ○ *The company's impending bankruptcy proved to be a false alarm.*

false bedding *n* GEOL same as **cross bedding**

false-card (**false-cards, false-carding, false-carded**) *vi* to play a card in bridge to mislead an opponent about the cards held in the suit led

false dawn *n* **1.** light that appears in the east just before dawn **2.** a sign that promises but does not deliver good results

false economy *n* an apparent short-term saving that eventually results in extra expense that could have been avoided

false friend *n* **1.** a word in a second language that closely resembles a word in somebody's first language but means something different **2.** a friend proved to be disloyal and untrustworthy

false fruit *n* BOT same as **pseudocarp**

falsehood /fáwlss hood, fólss-/ *n* **1.** LIE an intentionally untrue statement **2.** TELLING OF LIES the act of spreading lies ○ *a defendant noted for falsehood* **3.** SOMETHING NOT CONSISTENT WITH FACT something that does not correspond with the known or observable facts ○ *I can't answer for the truth or falsehood of his story as I've never been to China.*

SYNONYMS See *lie*[2].

false imprisonment *n* the unlawful confinement of somebody

false keel *n* an extension to a vessel's keel, added to protect the main keel or to increase stability

false memory syndrome *n* a situation in which examination, therapy, or hypnosis has elicited apparent memories, especially of childhood abuse, that are disputed by family members and often traumatic to the patient

false morel *n* a fungus with a lobed and folded cap of a rich to light brown, but without cavities like a true morel. It can cause poisoning, although some people eat it with no problems. Latin name: *Gyromitra esculenta*.

false move *n* an action showing an error of timing or judgment

false note *n* something that seems inappropriate, inconsistent, or badly timed

false position *n* a situation in which somebody is forced to act in an inconsistent or uncharacteristic way

false positive *n* **1.** MED, SCI the result of a medical, chemical, or biological test that appears to be positive but is in fact erroneous **2.** a situation in which data about a person produces an incorrect match against a checklist, e.g. when a passenger profile is matched against a list of suspected terrorists [Late 20C]

false pregnancy *n* N Am MED same as **phantom pregnancy**

false pretences *npl* deception or misrepresentation in order to gain something from somebody ○ *He gained her trust under false pretences.*

false rib *n* a rib connected to the lowest true rib rather than directly to the breastbone. In humans the three lower ribs on each side are false ribs.

false start *n* **1.** a situation in which a competitor in a race breaks a regulation governing the starting procedure and the race has to be restarted **2.** a failed attempt to begin something

false step *n* **1.** an action showing an error of judgment **2.** an act of stumbling

false topaz *n* CRYSTALS same as **citrine** *n* (sense 1)

falsetto /fawl séttō, fol-/ *n* (*plural* **-tos**) **1.** HIGH SINGING METHOD a method used by male singers to sing at a very high pitch by using more air and a combination of vocal chord vibration and head resonance. It is used by countertenors in classical music. **2.** FALSETTO SINGER a male singer who sings in a very high voice **3.** FALSETTO VOICE a very high voice used by a male singer ■ *adv* IN FALSETTO VOICE in an artificially or unusually high voice [Late 18C. < Italian, 'little false (one)' < *falso* 'false' < Latin *falsus* (see FALSE)]

falsework /fáwlss wurk, fólss-/ *n* a structure or frame that supports something that is being built

falsies /fáwlssiz, fólssiz/ *npl* two pads worn inside a bra to make the breasts look larger or more shapely (*informal*)

falsify /fáwlssi fī, fólss-/ (**-fies, -fying, -fied**) *vt* **1.** ALTER FRAUDULENTLY to alter something in order to deceive **2.** DISPROVE to prove that something is incorrect **3.** MISREPRESENT to misrepresent the facts in order to mislead ○ *They falsified every detail of their story.* [15C. Directly or via French *falsifier* < medieval Latin *falsificare* 'act dishonestly' < Latin *falsus* (see FALSE) + *facere* 'do, make'] —**falsifiability** /fáwlssi fī ə bílləti, fólss-/ *n* —**falsifiable** *adj* —**falsification** /fáwlssifi káysh'n, fólssi-/ *n* —**falsifier** *n*

falsity /fáwlssəti, fólss-/ (*plural* **-ties**) *n* **1.** the fact or condition of being untrue **2.** something that is untrue [13C. Directly or via French < Latin *falsitas* < *falsus* (see FALSE)]

Falstaffian /fawl staáfi ən/ *adj* characteristic of the Shakespearean character Sir John Falstaff in being bawdy, pleasure-loving, given to outlandish bragging, and of great size

faltboat /fált bōt/ *n* a boat like a kayak consisting of waterproof fabric over a collapsible frame. N Am term **foldboat** [Early 20C. < German *Faltboot* 'folding boat' < *falten* 'to fold' + *Boot* 'boat']

falter /fáwltər, fól-/ (**-ters, -tering, -tered**) *v* **1.** *vi* LOSE CONFIDENCE to become unsure and hesitant **2.** *vi* BEGIN TO FAIL to lose strength, power, or vitality **3.** *vi* STUMBLE to move unsteadily **4.** *vti* SPEAK OR ACT HESITANTLY to show a loss of confidence, especially to speak or act with hesitation ○ *Trembling with shame, she faltered an apology.* [14C. Origin ?] —**falterer** *n* —**falteringly** *adv*

SYNONYMS See *hesitate*.

Falun Gong /faá loon góng/ *n* a spiritual philosophy or movement, with roots in traditional Chinese belief, teaching cultivation of an orb of energy in the lower abdomen through breathing exercises. This is believed to lead to improved physical and spiritual health and even to the acquisition of supernatural powers. [Late 20C. < Chinese, 'law wheel']

fam. *abbr* **1.** familiar **2.** family

Famagusta /fámmə goóstə/ seaport and resort on the eastern coast of Cyprus, near Nicosia. It was a wealthy Venetian colony in the 15th and 16th centuries. Population: 20,516 (1989).

fame /faym/ *n* the condition of being very well known ○ *the fame that goes with being a recording star* ○ *His only claim to fame is being married to a socialite.* [12C. Via French < Latin *fama* 'talk, report, reputation']

USAGE **fame** or **notoriety**? In contemporary English **notoriety** is correctly used to mean only 'the condition of being well known for something disgraceful or otherwise undesirable', as in *a former politician whose notoriety stems from a society scandal*. A word with a similar meaning is *infamy*. **Fame** on the other hand is simply 'the condition of being very well known', as in *a pilot whose fame* [not *notoriety*] *stems from his extraordinary recovery from terrible injuries*. The same distinction holds with the adjectives ***notorious*** (and *infamous*) and ***famous*** ('widely known').

famed /faymd/ *adj* very well known ○ *The restaurant was famed for its steaks.*

familial /fə mílli əl/ *adj* relating to or involving a family

familiar /fə mílli ər/ *adj* **1.** OFTEN ENCOUNTERED well known, commonly seen or heard, and easily recognized **2.** ACQUAINTED WITH SOMETHING with a thorough knowledge and good understanding of something ○ *Are you familiar with the theory?* **3.** FRIENDLY in or characteristic of a close personal relationship with somebody **4.** IMPERTINENTLY INTIMATE unduly friendly or intimate in a way that is seen as presumptuous or impertinent (*dated*) ■ *n* **1.** INTIMATE FRIEND a close friend and companion (*formal*) **2.** PARANORMAL SPIRIT HELPING WITCH a supernatural being, often taking the form of a cat or other animal, that supposedly acts as a witch's assistant **3.** CHR LAY MEMBER OF MONASTERY a residential worker in a monastic community who has not taken a vow **4.** CHR HOUSEHOLD ATTENDANT OF POPE OR BISHOP a domestic servant in the household of a pope or Roman Catholic bishop [13C. Via French < Latin *familiaris* < *familia* (see FAMILY)] —**familiarly** *adv*

familiarise *vt* another spelling of **familiarize**

familiarity /fə mílli árrəti/ *n* **1.** GOOD KNOWLEDGE thorough knowledge and understanding of something ○ *Familiarity with database systems would be an advantage.* **2.** INTIMACY closeness and friendliness in a personal relationship **3.** FAMILIAR QUALITY the quality of being known ○ *The place had a strange familiarity about it.* **4.** (*plural* **familiarities**) UNWELCOME INTIMACY an intimacy that is improper and presumptuous (*dated*)

familiarize /fə mílli ə rīz/ (**-izes, -izing, -ized**), **familiarise** (**-ises, -ising, -ised**) *vt* to acquire or provide somebody with information or experience necessary for understanding or doing something ○ *You should familiarize yourself with the emergency procedure.* —**familiarization** /fə mílli ə rī záysh'n/ *n* —**familiarizer** *n*

familiar spirit *n* PARANORMAL same as **familiar** *n* (sense 2)

~~familier~~ incorrect spelling of **familiar**

family /fámmli/ *n* (*plural* **-lies**) **1.** GROUP OF RELATIVES a group of people who are closely related by birth, marriage, or adoption **2.** PEOPLE LIVING TOGETHER a group of people living together and functioning as a single household, usually consisting of parents and their children **3.** LINEAGE all the people who are descended from a common ancestor **4.** OFFSPRING a child or set of children born to somebody ○ *They're not ready to start a family.* **5.** GROUP WITH SOMETHING IN COMMON a group whose members are related in origin, characteristics, or occupation **6.** LING RELATED LANGUAGES a group of languages that have a common origin **7.** BIOL SET OF RELATED ORGANISMS in taxonomic classification, a category of related organisms, comprising one or more genera **8.** MATHS RELATED MATHEMATICAL SHAPES OR EXPRESSIONS a set of related mathematical curves, surfaces, or functions, usually expressed as a single equation containing one or more parameters or arbitrary constants ○ *a family of concentric circles* **9.** PHYS RELATED ISOTOPES a group of radioactive isotopes that collectively constitute a decay series or chain **10.** *US* CRIME BRANCH OF MAFIA a branch of the Mafia or of a similar large criminal group (*informal*). *S Asia* same as **wife** ■ *adj* **1.** USED BY FAMILY used, owned, or employed by a family, or suitable for one ○ *the family car* **2.** APPROPRIATE FOR CHILDREN suitable to be experienced by families with children ○ *family viewing* **3.** SERVING FAMILIES serving families and not just businesses or institutions ○ *a family butcher* [15C. < Latin *familia* 'servants of a household, household, family' < *famulus* 'servant'] ◇ **in the family way** pregnant (*informal dated*)

family allowance *n UK, Can* an allowance formerly paid by the government in the United Kingdom and Canada to parents or guardians of children below a specific age. Now called **child benefit**

family benefit *n* an allowance paid by a government to parents or guardians of dependent children, e.g. in New Zealand

family Bible *n* a large Bible handed down in a family from one generation to another, usually containing records of births, marriages, and deaths

family circle *n* the members of a family who are closely related and usually live together

family court *n* in the United States, Australia, and New Zealand, a court that rules on domestic disputes, especially those involving the care and custody of children

family credit *n* a regular payment formerly made by the UK government to families on a low income with at least one dependent child

Family Division *n* a branch of the High Court of Justice in England and Wales, handling divorce and cases concerning the custody of children

family doctor *n* a GP

family man *n* **1.** a married man who enjoys family life and spends a lot of time with his wife and children **2.** a married man with children

family name *n* same as **surname** *n* (sense 1)

family planning *n* the use of birth control methods to choose the number and timing of children born into a family

family room *n* **1.** a hotel room that can accommodate adults and their children **2.** a room reserved for the use of people with children, especially in a pub

family tree *n* a chart that shows the relationships of members of a family over time, including dates of marriages, births, and deaths

family woman *n* **1.** a married woman who enjoys family life and spends a lot of time with her husband and children **2.** a married woman with children

famine /fámmin/ *n* **1.** EXTREME FOOD SCARCITY a severe shortage of food resulting in widespread hunger **2.** DEFICIENCY OF SOMETHING a severe shortage of something **3.** EXTREME HUNGER extreme hunger and starvation [14C. < French < *faim* 'hunger' < Latin *fames*]

famish /fámmish/ (**-ishes**, **-ishing**, **-ished**) *vti* to be extremely hungry, or make somebody extremely

hungry (*often passive*) [14C. < obsolete *fame* < Old French *afamer* < Latin *fames* 'hunger'] —**famishment** *n*

famous /fáyməss/ *adj* **1.** known and recognized by many people **2.** excellent and satisfying (*dated*) [14C. Via Old French < Latin *famosus* < *fama* 'talk, report, reputation'] —**famously** *adv* —**famousness** *n*

USAGE See *fame*.

famulus /fámmyōōləss/ (*plural* **-li** /-lī/) *n* a personal secretary or attendant, especially to a scholar or magician (*literary*) [Mid-19C. < Latin, 'servant']

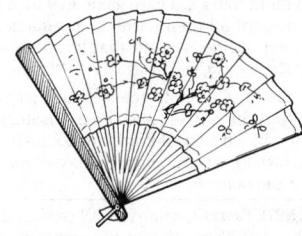

fan (sense 2)

fan[1] /fan/ *n* **1.** DEVICE FOR MOVING AIR a device to circulate currents of air, especially one with rotating blades **2.** PERSONAL COOLING DEVICE a flat disc on a handle or a folding semicircular device for waving to and fro in order to cool the face **3.** SOMETHING FAN-SHAPED something in the shape of an open hand-held fan, e.g. the tail of a peacock **4.** AGRIC WINNOWING MACHINE a machine with a series of revolving blades used to winnow or clean grain ■ *v* (**fans, fanning, fanned**) **1.** *vt* BLOW ON SOMETHING to blow a current of air steadily and lightly across or around something, either cooling or agitating it ○ *A cool breeze fanned the shore.* **2.** *vt* MOVE AIR USING FAN to move air about using a fan **3.** *vt* MAKE SITUATION TENSE to cause emotions to become more intense or a situation to become more volatile **4.** *vt* AGRIC SEPARATE GRAIN FROM CHAFF to winnow grain by blowing away the chaff **5.** *vt* ARMS FIRE GUN WITH REPEATED CHOPPING MOVEMENT to fire a gun repeatedly by holding the trigger back and chopping at the hammer with the open hand **6.** *vti* SPREAD ACROSS SOMETHING to spread out in the shape of an open hand-held fan, or spread something out in this way [Pre-12C. < Latin *vannus* 'device for winnowing grain'] —**fanner** *n*

fan out *vti* to spread out in the shape of an open hand-held fan, or spread something out in this way

fan[2] /fan/ *n* **1.** an enthusiastic admirer of a celebrity or public performer **2.** same as **fanatic** *n* (sense 2) [Late 19C. Shortening of FANATIC]

Fanakalo /fánnəkəlō/, **Fanagalo** /-gəlō/ *n* a pidgin spoken in parts of South Africa, based on Zulu and English and developed mainly in mining communities of Namibia and Zimbabwe, and near Johannesburg [Mid-20C. Probably < Zulu (*kuluma*) *fana ka lo* '(speak) like this'] —**Fanakalo** *adj*

fanatic /fə náttik/ *n* **1.** a holder of extreme or irrational enthusiasms or beliefs, especially in religion or politics **2.** somebody who is very enthusiastic about a pastime or hobby ■ *adj* same as **fanatical** [Mid-16C. Directly or via French < Latin *fanaticus* 'inspired by a god, frenzied' < *fanum* 'temple'] —**fanaticism** /fə náttisizəm/ *n*

fanatical /fə náttik'l/ *adj* excessively enthusiastic about a particular belief, cause, or activity —**fanatically** *adv*

fanaticise *vti* another spelling of **fanaticize**

fanaticize /fə nátti sīz/ (**-cizes**, **-cizing**, **-cized**), **fanaticise** (**-cises**, **-cising**, **-cised**) *vti* to make somebody fanatical about something, or become fanatical about something

fan belt *n* a continuous belt that turns a fan, especially one turning the cooling fan in the engine of a motor vehicle

fanciable /fánssi əb'l/ *adj* sexually desirable (*informal*)

fancier /fánssi ər/ *n* **1.** somebody who is especially interested in or enthusiastic about something **2.** somebody with a special interest in the breeding of a particular animal or plant ○ *a pigeon fancier*

fanciful /fánssif'l/ *adj* **1.** IMAGINARY based on imagination or dreams **2.** IMAGINATIVE AND IMPRACTICAL led by imagination rather than realism and practicality **3.** CURIOUSLY MADE strangely and imaginatively designed or made —**fancifully** *adv* —**fancifulness** *n*

fan club *n* an organization whose members are devoted to a celebrity or public performer, providing information and sometimes organizing special events

fancy /fánssi/ *adj* (**-cier, -ciest**) **1.** NOT PLAIN elaborately or ornately decorated **2.** INTRICATE intricately and skilfully performed ○ *fancy footwork* **3.** AIMING TO IMPRESS attempting or expected to impress ○ *bought a fancy car* **4.** EXPENSIVE expensively priced or highly valued ○ *fancy prices* ○ *fancy restaurants charging high prices* **5.** SELECTIVELY BRED describes animals that have been bred for specific features and qualities ■ *v* (**-cies, -cying, -cied**) **1.** *vt* WISH FOR SOMETHING to want to do or have something ○ *I fancy a walk this afternoon.* ○ *Do you fancy a coffee?* **2.** *vt* DESIRE SOMEBODY to find somebody sexually desirable (*informal*) ○ *I'm sure he fancies you!* **3.** *vr* FLATTER YOURSELF to have too high an opinion of yourself ○ *He rather fancies himself as a musician.* **4.** *vt* SUPPOSE SOMETHING to be inclined to think that something is the case ○ *I fancy that it will be bright and sunny tomorrow.* **5.** *vt* IMAGINE SOMETHING to form the idea of something in the imagination **6.** *vt* IDENTIFY SOMEBODY AS POTENTIAL WINNER to think that somebody will succeed ○ *Who do you fancy for the title?* ■ *interj* EXPRESSING SURPRISE used to express surprise or incredulity (*informal*) ○ *Fancy! All that money!* ○ *Fancy that! I would never have believed it!* ■ *n* (*plural* **-cies**) **1.** SUDDEN LIKING an impulsive liking for somebody or desire for something ○ *The hat caught my fancy.* ○ *She seems to have taken quite a fancy to him.* **2.** NOTION an unfounded belief about something **3.** SOMETHING IMAGINARY something created by the imagination, especially something of a playful or superficial nature **4.** LIKELY WINNER something or somebody thought likely to succeed or win **5.** PLAYFUL IMAGINATIVENESS the faculty of using the imagination playfully or inventively **6.** GOOD TASTE good critical taste and judgment (*formal*) **7.** BOXING ENTHUSIASTS enthusiasts of a sport or pastime, especially boxing (*archaic*) [15C. Contraction of FANTASY] —**fancily** *adv* —**fanciness** *n*

fancy dress *n* unusual clothing worn to a social gathering, often depicting a famous person, fictional character, or historical period [Because according to the wearer's fancy]

fancy-free *adj* free to go anywhere and do anything ○ *footloose and fancy-free*

fancy goods *npl* small items sold as gifts or novelties

fancy man *n* **1.** the lover or boyfriend of a woman, especially a married woman (*dated informal*) **2.** same as **pimp** (*archaic*)

fancy woman *n* **1.** the lover or girlfriend of a man, especially a married man (*dated informal*) **2.** a prostitute (*archaic*)

fancywork /fánssi wurk/ *n* embroidery and other decorative needlework

fan dance *n* an erotic dance in which large fans are used to mask and reveal parts of the dancer's nude body

fandangle /fan dáng g'l/ *n* a gaudy ornament or piece of jewellery of little value [Mid-19C. Origin ?]

fandango /fan dáng gō/ (*plural* **-gos**) *n* **1.** a vigorous Spanish or Latin American dance in triple time, traditionally performed by a man and woman as a courtship ritual **2.** the music for a fandango [Mid-18C. < Spanish]

fanfare /fán fair/ *n* **1.** a short dramatic series of notes played on trumpets or other brass instruments, especially to mark the arrival of somebody important **2.** any dramatic and ostentatious event, especially an announcement or publicity stunt [Mid-18C. < French]

fanfold /fán fōld/ *adj* folded into pleats by making alternate folds in opposite directions ○ *fanfold computer paper*

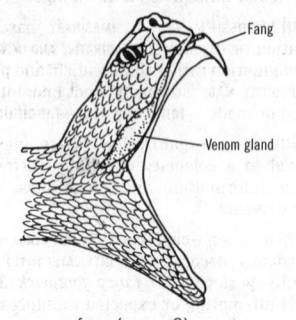

Fang

Venom gland

fang (sense 2)

fang /fang/ *n* 1. CANINE TOOTH a long pointed tooth of an animal on each side of the mouth towards the front 2. SNAKE'S TOOTH a tooth of a venomous snake, with a hollow or grooves through which venom is emitted 3. SPIDER'S MOUTHPART either of the pair of mouthparts of a spider, from which poison is emitted 4. *Aus* FAST DRIVE a high-speed drive in a motor vehicle (*slang*) ○ *Let's go for a fang down to the beach.* ■ **fangs** *npl* TEETH the teeth (*informal*) ■ *vti* (**fangs, fanging, fanged**) *Aus* DRIVE FAST to drive a motor vehicle at high speed (*slang*) [Pre-12C. < Old Norse, 'capture, grasp'] —**fanged** *adj*

Fang /fang/ (*plural same* or **Fangs**) *n* 1. a member of a people who live mainly in the rain forests of Gabon, Equatorial Guinea, and Cameroon 2. the Bantu language spoken by the Fang people, belonging to the Benue-Congo branch of the Niger-Congo family of languages. Native speakers: 2 million. [Mid-19C. < French *Fan*, probably < Fang *Pangwe*] —**Fang** *adj*

fangy /fángi/ (**-ier, -iest**) *adj Aus* able to move or function at high speed (*slang*)

fan heater *n* an electric heater that blows out a current of warm air using a fan

fanjet /fán jet/ *n US* AEROSP, AVIAT same as **turbofan**

Fan Kuan /fán kwán/ (*fl* 990–1030) Chinese artist. He is noted for his landscapes of mountains and streams, which he painted while living alone in the mountains.

fan letter *n* a letter written to a celebrity by a fan

fanlight /fán līt/ *n* 1. a semicircular window above a door or another window, often with struts forming the shape of an open hand-held fan 2. a small rectangular window above a door. US term **transom** 3. ARCHIT same as **skylight**

fan mail *n* letters sent to celebrities by their fans

fanny /fánni/ (*plural* **-nies**) *n* 1. a highly offensive term for the female genitals (*taboo slang*) 2. *N Am* the buttocks (*slang*) [Early 20C. Origin ?]

Fanny Adams /fánni áddəmz/ *n* tinned meat or stew, especially as fed to sailors (*archaic slang*) [Late 19C. After a young girl murdered and dismembered around 1867]

fanny pack *n N Am* CLOTHING same as **bum bag**

fan palm *n* a palm tree with divided fan-shaped leaves

fantabulous /fan tábbyōōləss/ *adj* extremely good (*humorous*) [Mid-20C. Blend of FANTASTIC + FABULOUS]

fantail (sense 4)

fantail /fán tayl/ *n* 1. FAN-SHAPED TAIL OR END a tail or the end of something shaped like an open hand-held fan 2. BIRDS PIGEON WITH FAN-SHAPED TAIL a breed of domestic pigeon with a broad fan-shaped tail 3. BIRDS BIRD WITH BROAD TAIL a small bird with a fan-shaped tail. Native to: Australia, New Zealand, Asia. Genus: *Rhipidura*. 4. FISH GOLDFISH WITH BROAD TAIL a goldfish with a broad double tail fin 5. WINDMILL SAIL a secondary sail on a windmill that keeps the main sails facing into the wind 6. *US* NAUT ROUNDED PART OF STERN a rounded overhanging part of a ship's stern

fan-tan /fán tan/ *n* 1. a Chinese gambling game in which players bet on how many items that have been concealed under a bowl remain after being counted off in fours 2. a card game in which players seek to discard all their cards in a sequence based on the same suit as a seven that has been led [Late 19C. < Chinese < *fān* 'turn, chance' + *tān* 'to spread out']

fantasia /fan táyzi ə, fántə zee ə/ *n* an instrumental composition in a free and improvisatory style, sometimes based on well-known melodies [Early 18C. < Italian, literally 'fantasy, imagination', via Latin < Greek *phantasia* (see FANTASY)]

CULTURAL NOTE *Fantasia*, a film (1940) produced by Walt Disney. This ambitious attempt to popularize classical music consists of cartoon animation matched to eight famous musical compositions. Its best-known sequences include hippos dancing to Ponchielli's 'Dance of the Hours' and Mickey Mouse as the protagonist of Dukas' 'The Sorcerer's Apprentice'.

fantasise *vti* another spelling of **fantasize**

fantasize /fántə sīz/ (**-sizes, -sizing, -sized**), **fantasise** (**-sises, -sising, -sised**) *vti* to indulge in fantasies of the imagination, or imagine something as a fantasy —**fantasist** *n*

fantast /fán tast/, **phantast** *n N Am* somebody who has impractical daydreams [Late 16C. Via medieval Latin *phantasta* and German *Phantast* < Greek *phantastēs* 'boaster' < *phantazein* (see FANTASY)]

fantastic /fan tástik/, **fantastical** /-ik'l/ *adj* 1. EXCELLENT extraordinarily good 2. BIZARRE extremely strange in appearance ○ *a rich fabric in a fantastic pattern of greens and blues* 3. INCREDIBLE apparently impossible but real or true ○ *the fantastic story of his journey home* 4. UNLIKELY unusual and unlikely to be successful ○ *a fantastic scheme to get rich quickly* 5. ENORMOUS much larger than is usual, expected, or desirable 6. IMAGINARY existing only in the imagination ■ *interj* EXPRESSING PLEASURE used to express surprise, pleasure, or approval (*informal*) ○ *You won the game? Fantastic!* [14C. Via French < Greek *phantastikos* < *phantazein* (see FANTASY)] —**fantasticality** /fan tásti kálləti/ *n* —**fantasticalness** *n*

fantastically /fan tástikli/ *adv* 1. VERY extremely 2. VERY WELL in a superb way 3. STRANGELY in a weird and strange way

fantasy /fántəssi/ *n* (*plural* **-sies**) 1. MENTAL IMAGE OR DREAM an image or dream created by the imagination 2. IMPRACTICAL IDEA an unrealistic and impractical idea ○ *She has this fantasy that someday she'll write a novel.* 3. IMAGINATIVE POWER the creative power of the imagination 4. PSYCHOL CREATION OF MENTAL IMAGES in psychology, the creation of exaggerated mental images in response to an ungratified need 5. LITERAT GENRE OF FICTION a type of fiction featuring imaginary worlds and magical or supernatural events 6. MUSIC same as **fantasia** ■ *vti* (**-sies, -sying, -sied**) same as **fantasize** [14C. Via Old French < Greek *phantasia* 'appearance, imagination' < *phantazein* 'make visible' < *phainein* 'to show']

fantasy football *n* a competition in which participants create an imaginary football team by choosing actual footballers from different teams. Points are scored according to the subsequent performance of the real footballers.

Fanti /fánti/ (*plural same* or **-tis**), **Fante** (*plural same* or **-tes**) *n* 1. a member of an African people living in the rainforests of Ghana and the Côte d'Ivoire 2. a dialect of Akan spoken in parts of Ghana and the Côte d'Ivoire [Early 19C. < Fanti] —**Fanti** *adj*

Fantin-Latour /fón taN la toór/, **Henri** (1836–1904) French painter and lithographer. He is famed for his group portraits and still lifes, especially those

of flowers. Full name **Fantin-Latour, Ignace Henri Jean Théodore**

fantod /fánt od/ *n* nervous anxiety (*informal*) ○ *He had a fit of the fantods.* [Mid-19C. Origin ?]

Fanu ♦ **Le Fanu, Sheridan**

fan vaulting *n* a form of vaulting in which ribs fan out from the four corners of a bay, like a fan

fanworm /fán wurm/ *n* a worm that lives in a tube or burrows in the seabed and has feathery tentacles resembling a fan, used for filtering food from the water. Families: Sabelidae or Serpulidae.

fanwort /fán wurt/ *n* a water plant of the lily family with fan-shaped submerged and floating leaves. Genus: *Cabomba*.

fanzine /fán zeen/ *n* an amateur magazine produced for fans of a pastime or celebrity [Mid-20C. < FAN [2] + MAGAZINE]

FAO *abbr* Food and Agriculture Organization (of the UN)

f.a.o. *abbr* for the attention of

FAQ /fak, éf ay kyoó/ *abbr* 1. SHIPPING free alongside quay 2. frequently asked questions

faqir *n* HINDUISM another spelling of **fakir**

FAQs /faks, éf ay kyoóz/ *abbr* frequently asked questions

far /faar/ (**farther** /fáarthər/ or **further** /fúrthər/, **farthest** /fáarthist/ or **furthest** /fúrthist/) CORE MEANING: an adverb and adjective indicating that something is a long way away in distance or time ○ *How far did you have to drive?* ○ (adj) *In the far distance were the lights of a settlement.*
1. *adv* NOT NEARBY at, to, or from a great distance ○ *We saw the first outline of the shore far ahead.* 2. *adv* NOT CLOSE IN TIME at or to a long time from the point of reference ○ *Sadly the time for completion falls far in the future.* 3. *adv* TO SPECIFIC EXTENT to the extent that is desirable or necessary ○ *How far will you take your complaint?* 4. *adv* MUCH OR MANY to or by a considerable degree ○ *Keeping a dog healthy is far more complicated than it seems.* ○ *There are far fewer factory jobs available these days.* 5. *adj* DISTANT remote in space or time ○ *He stood there, gazing out to the far horizon.* ○ *He had lived there once in the far past.* 6. *adj* MORE DISTANT more distant from somebody or something ○ *on the far side of the room* 7. *adj* EXTREME having an extreme position in a particular direction ○ *His politics are far left of centre.* [Old English *feor(r)*, via Germanic, 'farther beyond' < Indo-European] ◇ **as far as 1.** to the greatest distance possible ○ *moved away as far as he could without seeming rude* **2.** to the extent that ○ *She's happier as far as I can tell.* ◇ **far and away** without a doubt and by a large margin ○ *She is far and away the best player that we have.* ◇ **far and near** everywhere ○ *Doctors from far and near flocked to his bedside.* ◇ **far and wide** covering a great distance ○ *The church bells will be heard far and wide.* ◇ **far from** not at all ○ *I'm far from satisfied with the outcome.* ◇ **far from it** on the contrary ○ *He was not the tallest boy in the class – far from it.* ◇ **far gone 1.** in a state of deterioration and unable to function ○ *These shoes can't be repaired – they're too far gone.* **2.** very intoxicated (*informal*) ○ *She was too far gone to drive home.* ◇ **far out** used to express amazement and approval (*dated slang*) ◇ **go far 1.** to be very successful ○ *He is very talented and I am sure he will go far in his chosen career.* **2.** to last or be sufficient ○ *Three loaves of bread won't go far once my family gets going.* ◇ **go too far, take something too far** to do or say something that is unacceptable or that exceeds reasonable limits ○ *Harriet paused, and realized that she had gone too far.* ◇ **in so far as** to the extent that ◇ **so far 1.** up to this moment ○ *So far, 150 people have shown an interest in the product.* **2.** up to a certain point, extent, or degree ○ *Freedom of information can only go so far.* ◇ **so far so good** indicates satisfaction with progress made up to this point ○ *So far so good, but the last part of the climb is the hardest.*

Farabi /fə raábi/, **al-** (AD 873?–950?) Arabian philosopher. He influenced Islamic philosophy with his studies of Plato and Aristotle.

farad /fárrəd, fá rad/ *n* the SI unit of capacitance equal to that of a capacitor carrying one coulomb of charge when a potential difference of one volt is applied. Symbol **F** [Mid-19C. After Michael FARADAY]

faradaic *adj* ELEC same as **faradic**

faraday /fárrə day/ *n* a unit of electric charge equal to that needed to deposit a unit amount of singly charged substance during electrolysis, equivalent to 96,485 coulombs. Symbol **F** [Early 20C. After Michael FARADAY]

Michael Faraday

Faraday /fárrə day/, **Michael** (1791–1867) British physicist and chemist. He is best known for his discoveries of electromagnetic induction and of the laws of electrolysis. He also showed how electromagnetic induction could be used in generators and transformers.

'I express a wish that you may, in your generation, be fit to compare to a candle; that you may, like it, shine as lights to those about you; that, in all your actions, you may justify the beauty of the taper by making your deeds honourable and effectual in the discharge of your duty to your fellow men.'
[Michael Faraday, *A Course of Six Lectures on the Chemical History of a Candle*; 1861]

faradic /fə ráddik/, **faradaic** /fárrə dáy ik/ *adj* relating to an intermittent alternating current produced in the secondary winding of an induction coil [Late 19C. < French *faradique*, after Michael FARADAY]

faradise *vt* MED another spelling of **faradize**

faradism /fárrədizəm/ *n* the therapeutic application of an alternating electric current to stimulate nerve and muscle function [Late 19C. After Michael FARADAY]

faradize /fárrə dīz/ (-**dizes**, -**dizing**, -**dized**), **faradise** (-**dises**, -**dising**, -**dised**) *vt* to stimulate a nerve or muscle using an alternating current [Mid-19C. After Michael FARADAY] —**faradization** /fárrə dī záysh'n/ *n* —**faradizer** *n*

farandole /fárrəndōl/ *n* **1.** a lively dance from Provence in 6/8 or 4/4 time in which dancers link hands to form a weaving line following the leader **2.** the music for a farandole [Mid-19C. Via French < modern Provençal *farandoulo*]

faraway /fáərə wáy/ *adj* **1.** REMOTE a great distance away **2.** SOUNDING DISTANT heard from a distance **3.** DREAMY having a dreamy absent-minded expression or appearance —**farawayness** *n*

FARC /faark/ *abbr* Revolutionary Armed Forces of Colombia. Spanish name **Fuerzas Armadas Revolucionarias de Colombia**

farce /faarss/ *n* **1.** ABSURD SITUATION a ridiculous situation in which everything goes wrong or becomes a sham ○ *It was a complete farce – the bride changed her mind at the last minute and the two families had a public slanging match.* **2.** COMIC PLAY a comic play in which authority, order, and morality are at risk and ordinary people are caught up in extraordinary events **3.** STYLE OF COMIC DRAMA the style of comic drama in which authority, order, and morality are at risk and ordinary people are caught up in extraordinary events **4.** FOOD same as **forcemeat** [Early 16C. < French, 'stuffing' < Latin *farcire* 'to stuff']

farceur /faar súr/ *n* **1.** an actor in or writer of farces **2.** somebody who is intentionally comical (*literary*) [Late 17C. < French < *farce* (see FARCE)]

farcical /fáarssik'l/ *adj* **1.** resembling a farce in being ridiculous and confused **2.** performed or written in the style of a farce —**farcicality** /fáarssi kálləti/ *n* —**farcically** *adv*

far cry *n* a long way in distance or character

farcy /fáarssi/ *n* a form of the infectious horse disease glanders [14C. < French *farcin* < Latin *farcire* 'to stuff']

fardel /fáard'l/ *n* a bundle or pack of something tied up for carrying (*archaic*) [14C. < Old French, 'bundle, load' < *farde* 'bundle']

fare /fair/ *n* **1.** COST OF TRAVEL the amount charged for a journey **2.** PASSENGER a paying passenger in a taxi **3.** FOOD food that is provided, especially when simple and substantial **4.** ENTERTAINMENT the particular type of material provided by a magazine, television show, or other form of entertainment ○ *a channel offering the usual fare of makeover programmes and celebrity interviews* ■ *vi* (**fares, faring, fared**) **1.** MANAGE IN DOING SOMETHING to get on in a particular way in doing or experiencing something ○ *How did she fare in the exam?* **2.** HAPPEN to turn out in a particular way for somebody **3.** EAT to dine or be given food (*archaic*) **4.** TRAVEL to go on a journey (*literary*) [Old English *fær, faru* 'journey' < Germanic]

SPELLCHECK See **fair**[1].

Far East /faar éest/ a former term for the countries of East Asia, sometimes extended to include those of Southeast Asia (*dated*) —**Far-Eastern** *adj*

Fareham /fáirəm/ market town situated between Portsmouth and Southampton in Hampshire, southern England. Population: 107,977 (2001).

~~**Farenheit**~~ incorrect spelling of **Fahrenheit**

fare stage *n* **1.** one of the divisions of a bus route, used for calculating the fare **2.** a bus stop marking the boundary of a division in a bus route on which the fare is calculated

farewell /fair wél/ *n* **1.** EXPRESSION OF PARTING GOOD WISHES an act of leaving or an activity marking somebody's departure **2.** GOOD WISHES ON PARTING an expression of good wishes on parting ○ *came too late to bid her farewell* ■ *adj* SAYING GOODBYE marking an end, conclusion, or leave-taking ■ *interj* GOODBYE used to express good wishes at parting (*literary*) ○ *Farewell, my friend!* ■ *vt* Aus GIVE SOMEBODY SEND-OFF to give somebody a farewell party [14C. < *Fare well*, said to somebody setting out on a journey]

Farewell, Cape /fáir wel/ cape on the northern coast of the South Island, New Zealand. It is the northernmost point of the South Island.

farfalle /faar fáalay/ *npl* pasta made in the shape of bows [Early 17C. < Italian *farfalla* 'candle-fly, moth']

farfel /fáarf'l/, **farfal** *n* pasta in the shape of small grains [Late 19C. < Yiddish *farfl* < Middle High German *varveln* 'noodles, noodle soup']

far-fetched *adj* exaggerated and unconvincing

far-flung *adj* **1.** distributed over a wide area **2.** at a great distance

Fargo /fáargō/ city in southeastern North Dakota, on the Minnesota border, south of Grand Forks. Population: 91,204 (2002 estimate).

Faridabad /fə réedə bad/, **Farīdābād** industrial city in Haryana State, northern India. Population: 1,054,981 (2001).

farina /fə réenə/ *n* **1.** flour or meal made from wheat, nuts, or vegetables **2.** starch, especially that made from potatoes [14C. < Latin, 'ground corn, flour, meal' < *far* 'spelt, grain']

farinaceous /fárri náyshəss/ *adj* containing or consisting of starch [Mid-17C. < late Latin *farinaceus* < Latin *farina* (see FARINA)]

farinose /fárri nōss, -nōz/ *adj* **1.** consisting of or yielding food starch **2.** describes plant leaves or stems that have a powdery or floury appearance, especially because of a covering of fine whitish hairs [Early 18C. < late Latin *farinosus* < Latin *farina* (see FARINA)]

farkleberry /fáark'lbəri/ (*plural* -**ries**) *n* a bush of the heath family that has leathery leaves and hard black berries with stony seeds. Native to:

southeastern United States. Latin name: *Vaccinium arboreum*. [Mid-18C. Origin ?]

farl /faarl/ *n* Scotland a triangular oatcake, scone, or piece of shortbread, made by cutting a round cake into four sections [Late 17C. Contraction of *fardel* 'piece, quarter' < FOURTH + DEAL[1] (noun)]

farm /faarm/ *n* **1.** AGRICULTURAL LAND AND BUILDINGS an area of land where crops are grown or animals are reared for commercial purposes, together with appropriate buildings **2.** PLACE PRODUCING PARTICULAR ANIMALS OR CROPS an area of land or water where particular animals, birds, fish, or crops are raised for commercial purposes (*usually used in combination*) ○ *a trout farm* **3.** FARM BUILDINGS a farmhouse or group of farm buildings **4.** LAND USED BY INDUSTRY a piece of land on which something is stored, produced, or processed, especially on an industrial scale (*usually used in combination*) ○ *a sewage farm* **5.** Aus AUSTRALIAN ASSETS the national assets of Australia (*informal*) ■ *v* (**farms, farming, farmed**) **1.** *vti* USE LAND FOR AGRICULTURE to use land for growing crops and rearing animals for sale **2.** *vt* REAR SOMETHING COMMERCIALLY to rear animals, birds, or fish commercially **3.** *vt* same as **farm out** (sense 1) [14C. Via French, 'lease' < medieval Latin *firma* 'fixed payment' < Latin *firmare* 'fix, settle, confirm' < *firmus* 'firm'] —**farmable** *adj* —**farming** *n* ◇ **bet the farm** to take a considerable risk on a particular venture or outcome ◇ **buy the farm** US to die or be killed (*slang*)

CULTURAL NOTE *Animal Farm*, a novel (1945) by George Orwell. A satirical allegory of Stalinist Russia, it describes how a group of farm animals, led by pigs, overthrow their human owner and try to run the farm on egalitarian principles. Corrupted by power, the pigs distort their ideology to support their increasingly brutal tyranny, justifying their actions with slogans such as 'All animals are equal, but some are more equal than others'.

farm out *vt* **1.** to send work out to be done by somebody else **2.** to send children or animals to be looked after by somebody else

farm bike *n* NZ a motorcycle designed for use off the road

farmer /fáarmər/ *n* somebody who owns or operates a farm

farmer's lung *n* inflammation of the lungs marked by chronic shortness of breath and caused by an allergic reaction to fungal spores from mouldy hay

farmers' market *n* a market, usually held outdoors, where farmers sell fresh produce direct to the public

farmhand /fáarm hand/ *n* same as **farmworker**

farmhouse /fáarm howss/ *n* (*plural* -**houses** /-howziz/) **1.** a house on a farm, especially the main dwelling place of the farmer **2.** FOOD same as **farmhouse loaf** ■ *adj* produced on a farm or of a similar style or quality to that produced on a farm

farmhouse loaf *n* a large rectangular white loaf with a rounded top that is baked in a tin

farmland /fáarm land/ *n* land that is suitable for farming or used by farmers

farm school *n* S Africa a primary school in a rural area, often located on a farm

farmstay /fáarm stay/ *n* ANZ a stay on a farm as a paying guest, providing some experience of rural life

farmstead /fáarm sted/ *n* a farm and all its buildings, regarded as a unit

farmworker /fáarm wurkər/ *n* somebody whose job is to work on a farm

farmyard /fáarm yaard/ *n* an enclosed or surfaced area beside farm buildings

Farnborough /fáarnbərə/ town in Hampshire, southern England, the site of an annual air show. Population: 52,535 (1991).

Farnham /fáarnəm/, **John Peter** (*b*. 1949) British-born Australian recording artist. His *Whispering Jack* (1986) was the bestselling Australian album of the 1980s.

faro /fáirō/ *n* a card game in which players bet against the dealer on the order in which cards are turned up [Mid-18C. Probably alteration of PHARAOH, after Italian *faraone*]

Faro /faárō/ seaport on the southern coast of Portugal and capital of the Algarve District. It is the country's southernmost city. Population: 31,966 (1991).

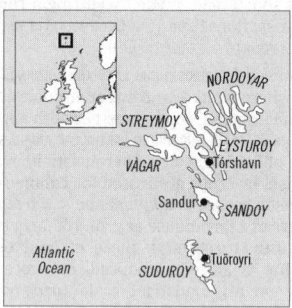

Faroe Islands

Faroe Islands /fáirō-/, **Faeroe Islands** group of islands in the North Atlantic Ocean, almost midway between Iceland and the Shetland Islands. The islands have been Danish territory since 1814. Capital: Tórshavn. Population: 45,661 (2001). Area: 1,399 sq. km/540 sq. mi.

Faroese /fáirō eez/ (plural same), **Faeroese** n 1. the North Germanic language spoken on the Faroe Islands. Native speakers: 45,000. 2. somebody who comes from the Faroe Islands —**Faroese** adj

far-off adj distant in location or time

farouche /fə roósh/ adj 1. unsociable and lacking grace because of fierceness, sullenness, or shyness 2. menacing in appearance or behaviour [Mid-18C. Via French < medieval Latin forasticus < Latin foras 'out of doors, outside']

Farouk I /fə roók/ (1920–65) king of Egypt. He was the last king of Egypt (1936–52), and after a coup lived in exile in Monaco.

> 'Soon there will be only five kings left—the Kings of England, Diamonds, Hearts, Spades, and Clubs.'
> [Farouk I, As I Recall, Lord Boyd-Orr; 1966]

far-out adj (dated slang) 1. strange and unconventional 2. extremely good or enjoyable —**far-outness** n

Farquhar /faárkər/, **George** (1678–1707) Irish dramatist. His best-known works are The Recruiting Officer (1706) and The Beaux' Stratagem (1707).

> 'There is no scandal like rags, nor any crime so shameful as poverty.'
> [George Farquhar, The Beaux' Stratagem; 1707]

farrago /fə raágō/ (plural -gos or -goes) n a confused mixture of things [Mid-17C. < Latin, 'mixed fodder for cattle, medley' < far 'spelt, grain']

Farrakhan /fárrə kaàn/, **Louis Abdul** (b. 1933) US religious leader. Having long been a member of the Nation of Islam, he led the organization after 1978 and broadened its base with calls for African American self-reliance. He organized the Million Man March in Washington, DC, in 1995. Born **Walcott, Louis Eugene**

far-reaching adj having widespread implications, influences, or effects

Farrelly /fárrəli/, **Midget** (b. 1944) Australian surfer. He was the winner of the first official surfing world championship, held in Sydney, Australia, in 1964. Born **Farrelly, Bernard**

Farrer /fárrər/, **William James** (1845–1906) British-born Australian agricultural scientist, who was a pioneer of wheat breeding in Australia. He developed domestic strains of wheat that produced greater yields than overseas strains.

farrier /fárri ər/ n a maker and fitter of horseshoes [Mid-16C. Via French < Latin ferrarius < ferrum 'horseshoe, iron'] —**farriery** n

farrow¹ /fárrō/ vi (-rows, -rowing, -rowed) to give birth to a litter of piglets ■ n a litter of young pigs [Old English fearh 'young pig' < Indo-European]

farrow² /fárrō/ adj not pregnant with a calf [15C.

Probably < Flemish verwe-, varwe-, in verwekoe, varwekoe 'cow that has become barren']

farruca /fə roókə/ n a flamenco dance [Early 20C. < Spanish, 'Galician or Asturian' < Farruco, pet form of Francisco 'Francis']

farseeing adj same as **farsighted** (senses 1, 3)

Farsi /faárssi/ n the official language of Iran, also spoken in Afghanistan, Bahrain, Tajikistan, and the United Arab Emirates, belonging to the Indo-Iranian branch of Indo-European. Native speakers: 30 million. Other speakers: 55 million. [Late 19C. Via Arabic, 'Persia', modern-day Iran < Persian Pars] —**Farsi** adj

farsighted /faár sítid/ adj 1. wise and able to anticipate the future 2. N Am OPHTHALMOL same as **long-sighted** (sense 1) 3. able to see a long way ○ farsighted birds of prey —**farsightedly** adv —**farsightedness** n

fart /faart/ vi (**farts, farting, farted**) an offensive term meaning to release intestinal gases through the anus, usually with an accompanying sound (slang) ■ n 1. an offensive term for a release of intestinal gases through the anus (slang) 2. an offensive term for somebody who is regarded as unpleasant, boring, or irritating (slang insult) [Old English feortan < Indo-European]

fart about vi an offensive term meaning to waste time by behaving foolishly (slang)

farther /faárthər/ adv 1. TO GREATER DISTANCE to or at a point that is more distant in space or time 2. TO GREATER EXTENT to a greater degree or extent ▶ ◇ **further** ■ adj 1. MORE DISTANT more distant in space or time 2. ADDITIONAL adding to the quantity or extent of something (archaic) [13C. Variant of FURTHER] —**farthermost** adj

USAGE See **further**.

farthest /faárthist/ adv 1. TO GREATEST DISTANCE to a more distant point in space or time than anything else 2. TO GREATEST EXTENT to a greater degree or extent than anything else ■ adj MOST DISTANT more distant in space or time than anything else

USAGE See **further**.

farthing /faárthing/ n 1. the lowest value or smallest amount 2. a former British coin worth a quarter of an old penny [Old English fēorthung 'quarter of a penny' < fēortha 'fourth' + -ing 'fractional part'] ◇ **not have a brass farthing** to have no money or assets (informal)

farthingale /faárthing gayl/ n a structure worn under the skirt by women in the late 16th and early 17th centuries to give it the shape of a cone, bell, or drum [Early 16C. Via Old French verdugale < Spanish verdugado < verdugo 'rod, stick']

fartlek /faárt lek/ n SPORTS same as **interval training** [Mid-20C. < Swedish < fart 'speed' + lek 'play']

Far West n US the area of the continental United States west of the Great Plains

FAS abbr 1. MED foetal alcohol syndrome 2. SHIPPING free alongside ship

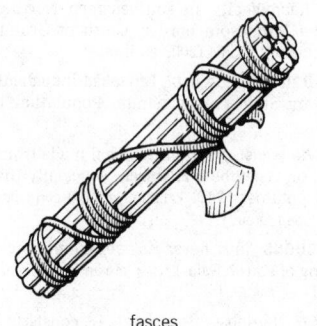

fasces

fasces /fáss eez/ npl in ancient Rome, a bundle of rods containing an axe with a projecting blade, carried in front of magistrates [Late 16C. < Latin, plural of fascis 'bundle']

fascia /fáyshə, fáyshi ə, fáshə, fáyssi ə/ (plural **-ciae** /-shi ee/ or **-cias**) n 1. also **facia** ARCHIT FLAT SURFACE ON BUILDING the flat horizontal surface immediately

below the edge of a roof 2. also **facia** NAMEPLATE OVER SHOP the flat surface that is above a shop window and usually carries the name of the shop 3. also **facia** AUTOMOT same as **dashboard** (sense 1) 4. ANAT CONNECTIVE TISSUE a sheet or band of connective tissue covering or binding together parts of the body such as muscles or organs 5. also **facia** BIOL BAND OF COLOUR a broad band of colour, e.g. on an insect [Mid-16C. < Latin, 'band, fillet, casing of a door'] —**fascial** /fáysh'l/ adj

fasciate /fáshi ayt/, **fasciated** /-aytid/ adj describes plant stems or branches that have grown together and become unusually flattened [Mid-17C. < Latin fasciare 'swathe' < fascia 'band, fillet'] —**fasciately** adv

fasciation /fáshi áysh'n/ n uncharacteristic fusion and flattening of several plant stems

fascicle /fássik'l/ n 1. BUNDLE a small bunch or bundle of something 2. BOT PLANT PARTS BUNCHED TOGETHER a cluster of plant parts such as branches, leaves, or stems 3. ANAT BUNDLE OF FIBRES a bundle of nerve, muscle, or tendon fibres 4. PUBL PART OF BOOK PUBLISHED AS INSTALMENT a section of a book published in instalments as a volume or pamphlet [15C. < Latin fasciculus 'small bundle' < fascis 'bundle'] —**fascicled** adj —**fascicular** /fə skíkyoölər/ adj —**fasciculate** /fə síkyoö layt, -lət/ adj

fascicule /fássi kyool/ n PUBL same as **fascicle** (sense 4) [Late 19C. < Latin fasciculus (see FASCICLE)]

fasciitis /fáshi ítiss/ n inflammation of the bands of connective tissue (**fascia**) between muscles or around organs, from infection or unknown causes [Late 19C. < FASCIA]

fascinate /fássi nayt/ (**-nates, -nating, -nated**) v 1. vti to hold somebody's attention completely or irresistibly 2. vt to make somebody or something unable to move, especially out of fear [Late 16C. < Latin fascinat-, past participle of fascinare 'bewitch' < fascinum 'spell, witchcraft'] —**fascinatedly** adv —**fascinator** n

fascinating /fássi nayting/ adj inspiring a great interest or attraction —**fascinatingly** adv

fascination /fássi náysh'n/ n 1. POWER TO CAPTURE ATTENTION the power to hold somebody's attention completely or irresistibly 2. SOMETHING FASCINATING something that inspires great interest 3. INTEREST IN SOMETHING complete absorption in something interesting ○ I can't understand his fascination with tarantulas.

fascine /fə seén/ n a long piece or bundle of wood used for engineering purposes to line or fill a trench [Late 17C. Via French < Latin fascina < fascis 'bundle']

fascioliasis /fə seé ə lí əssiss, fássi ə-/ n a disease caused by an infestation of parasitic liver flukes [Late 19C. < modern Latin Fasciola hepatica 'liver fluke' < Latin fasciola 'small bandage' < fascia 'band, fillet']

fascism /fáshizəm/, **Fascism** n any movement, ideology, or attitude that favours dictatorial government, centralized control of private enterprise, repression of all opposition, and extreme nationalism —**fascist** /fáshist/ n, adj —**fascistic** /fə shístik/ adj

fash¹ /fash/ (**fashes, fashing, fashed**) v N England, Scotland 1. vti to annoy somebody, or be annoyed 2. vi to take the trouble to do something [Mid-16C. < French fâcher 'annoy' < assumed Vulgar Latin fastidiare 'to disgust' < Latin fastidium 'disgust']

fash² /fash/ US (slang) n same as **fashion** n (senses 1–3) ■ adj same as **fashionable** [Late 19C. Shortening]

fashion /fásh'n/ n 1. CLOTHING STYLES style in clothing, hair, and personal appearance generally ○ the latest in men's fashions 2. BUSINESS OF STYLES the business of creating, promoting, or studying the latest styles in clothing and hair 3. CURRENT STYLE the style of dress, behaviour, way of living, or other expression that is popular at present ○ a way of speaking that is no longer in fashion 4. MANNER a particular way of behaving or doing something 5. SHAPE the form or shape of something 6. TYPE a type or variety ■ vt (**-ions, -ioning, -ioned**) 1. MAKE SOMETHING to give shape or form to something ○ fashion a chair from some leftover pieces of wood 2. INFLUENCE SOMETHING to change somebody's character or beliefs by influence or training ○ attitudes fashioned by his grandparents 3. ADAPT SOMETHING to adapt something or make

something suitable ○ *fashion it to fit over the bump in the middle* [14C. Via French *façon* 'shape' < Latin *faction-* (see FACTION [1])] —**fashioner** *n* ◇ **after a fashion** in some way but not very well

SYNONYMS See ***make.***

-fashion *suffix* in the manner of

fashionable /fásh'nəb'l/ *adj* **1.** following a style that is currently popular ○ *fashionable ideas* **2.** popular with rich, famous, or otherwise glamorous people ○ *a fashionable nightspot* —**fashionableness** *n* —**fashionably** *adv*

fashion house *n* a business that designs, makes, and sells fashionable clothes, typically associated with an important designer

fashionista /fásh'n ístə/ *n* somebody involved in the fashion industry (*informal*) [< FASHION + Spanish *-ista* < Latin *-ista* (see -IST)]

fashion model *n* somebody whose job is to model clothes

fashion photography *n* the art or practice of taking photographs of models wearing clothes or clothing accessories, especially for fashion magazines

fashion plate *n* **1.** a wearer of the latest fashions **2.** an illustration showing a style of clothing, especially a current or new fashion

fashion statement *n* an item of clothing or set of clothes that expresses something about the attitude, point of view, or lifestyle of the wearer

fashion victim *n* an overzealous or uncritical follower of fashion trends (*informal*)

~~fashon~~ incorrect spelling of **fashion**

~~fasinating~~ incorrect spelling of **fascinating**

Fassbinder /fáss bindər/, **Rainer Werner** (1946–82) German film director. He is renowned for politically controversial plays and films such as *The Marriage of Maria Braun* (1979) that often criticize social institutions.

> 'I hope to build a house with my films. Some of them are the cellar, some are the walls, and some are the windows. But I hope in time there will be a house.'
> [Rainer Werner Fassbinder. Quoted in *Halliwell's Filmgoer's Companion*, Leslie Halliwell; 1993]

fast[1] /faast/ *adj* **1.** ACTING OR MOVING RAPIDLY acting, functioning, or moving quickly, or capable of doing this ○ *a fast car* **2.** DONE QUICKLY lasting or taking a relatively short time ○ *a fast trip* **3.** RUNNING AHEAD OF TIME indicating a time that is later than the correct time ○ *My watch is ten minutes fast.* **4.** CONDUCIVE TO RAPID SPEED adapted to or allowing rapid movement ○ *driving in the fast lane* **5.** REQUIRING SPEEDY MOVEMENT requiring agility and quickness of movement and reaction **6.** PHOTOGRAPHY WITH SHORT EXPOSURE describes photographic equipment that requires or permits a relatively short exposure time **7.** DEBAUCHED energetically pursuing excitement and enjoyment (*informal*) ○ *in with a fast crowd* **8.** PROMISCUOUS wanting or tending to start sexual relationships with people very soon after meeting them (*informal*) **9.** TRICKY using quick-wittedness to trick or cheat people (*informal*) ○ *a fast bargainer* **10.** MADE EASILY acquired very easily and sometimes dishonestly (*informal*) ○ *fast money* **11.** UNFADING not liable to fade or change colour **12.** STRONG AND CLOSE strong, close, and steadfast, e.g. in a relationship (*literary*) ○ *fast friends* **13.** FASTENED firmly attached, fastened, or fixed **14.** SHUT firmly closed ■ *adv* **1.** RAPIDLY at great speed ○ *You drive too fast.* **2.** IMMEDIATELY in quick succession **3.** AT INCORRECT TIME ahead of the correct time ○ *The clock is running a little fast.* **4.** SOUNDLY in a deep and peaceful way ○ *fast asleep* **5.** FIRMLY allowing no movement or no chance of slipping or escaping ○ *held fast by ice* **6.** RECKLESSLY without regard to consequences (*informal*) ○ *live fast and die young* [Old English *fæst* 'firm' < Germanic] ◇ **pull a fast one** to trick or cheat somebody (*informal*)

fast[2] /faast/ *v* (**fasts, fasting, fasted**) **1.** *vi* ABSTAIN FROM FOOD to abstain from food, or some types of food, especially as an act of religious observance **2.** *vt* DEPRIVE SOMEBODY OF FOOD to deprive a person or animal of food ■ *n* PERIOD OF FASTING a period of time spent abstaining from food [Old English *fæstan* < Germanic] —**faster** *n*

fast-acting *adj* beginning to take effect soon after being used ○ *a fast-acting analgesic*

fastback /faást bak/ *n* **1.** a back of a car that forms a continuous curve downwards from the rear edge of the roof **2.** a car with a fastback

fastball /faast bawl/ *n* a baseball pitch at top speed

fast bowler *n* in cricket, a bowler who specializes in bowling the ball quickly —**fast bowling** *n*

fast break *n* in team sports, a swift counterattack made in an attempt to score before the opposing players have the chance to recover their defensive positions —**fast-break** *vi*

fast-breeder reactor *n* a nuclear reactor in which the chain reaction is maintained mainly by fast neutrons. It is capable of producing more fissionable material than it consumes.

fasten /faáss'n/ (**-tens, -tening, -tened**) *v* **1.** *vti* SECURE SOMETHING to attach something firmly, usually using parts or devices made to achieve this, or become firmly attached in this way ○ *These snaps won't fasten.* **2.** *vti* SHUT TIGHTLY to close something firmly or securely, or become firmly or securely closed ○ *fasten the door shut* **3.** *vt* HOLD SOMETHING FIRMLY to use a tool, device, or body part to hold somebody or something firmly **4.** *vti* CONCENTRATE ATTENTION to focus the mind or eyes concentratedly on something, or become focused in this way ○ *His suspicions fastened upon the woman sitting opposite him.* **5.** *vi* BECOME NUISANCE to single somebody out for attention in a persistent and usually unwelcome manner ○ *just some bloke who fastened onto me in the street* [Old English *fæstnian* < Germanic, 'firm']

fastener /faáss'nər/ *n* a device, e.g. a button, hook, or zip, used to close something, especially a piece of clothing

fastening /faáss'ning/ *n* a device that fastens something, e.g. a clasp, hook, or lock

fast food *n* highly processed restaurant foods that are prepared quickly or are available on demand (*hyphenated when used before a noun*) ○ *a fast-food diet of burgers and chips*

fast-forward *n* **1.** FUNCTION FOR WINDING TAPE FORWARDS a function on an electronic recording device such as a tape or video cassette recorder that causes the tape to wind forwards quickly **2.** BUTTON FOR FAST-FORWARD FUNCTION a mechanism used to control the fast-forward function on an electronic recording device, e.g. a button or switch ■ *vti* (**fast-forwards, fast-forwarding, fast-forwarded**) **1.** ADVANCE TAPE RAPIDLY to wind a tape forwards quickly on an electronic recording device **2.** ADVANCE QUICKLY to advance rapidly, or move something forwards rapidly, e.g. in time or in rate of progress (*informal*) ○ *decided to fast-forward negotiations so as to avoid a strike*

fastidious /fa stíddi əss/ *adj* **1.** concerned that even the smallest details should be just right ○ *fastidious about his appearance* **2.** easily disgusted by things that are not perfectly clean [15C. < Latin *fastidiosus* < *fastidium* 'disgust'] —**fastidiously** *adv* —**fastidiousness** *n*

fastigia MED plural of **fastigium**

fastigiate /fa stíjji ət, -ayt/, **fastigiated** /-aytid/ *adj* describes a tree or other plant with upright clustering branches that taper towards the top —**fastigiately** *adv*

fastigium /fa stíjji əm/ (*plural* **-iums** or **-ia** /-i ə/) *n* a period during which an illness, often a fever, is at its most severe [Late 17C. < Latin]

fasting /faásting/ *n* abstention from food, or some types of food, especially as an act of religious observance

fast lane *n* **1.** *UK, ANZ, Can* PASSING LANE OF MOTORWAY the lane of a motorway or dual carriageway that is used by vehicles travelling at high speed or overtaking slower traffic. US term **express lane 2.** HECTIC LIFESTYLE the kind of lifestyle that is busy, exciting, often highly stressful, and sometimes devoted to pleasure (*informal*) ○ *living life in the fast lane* **3.** ROUTE TO SUCCESS a rapid but extremely competitive route to progress, promotion, or success —**fast-lane** *adj*

fast motion *n* filmed action that is faster than is naturally possible, achieved by shooting the film at a rate slower than that projected. It is often used for comic effect. (*hyphenated when used before a noun*) ○ *a fast-motion sequence*

fastness /faástnəss/ *n* **1.** FIXEDNESS the state or quality of being firm, fixed, or secure ○ *deceived about the fastness of their friendship* **2.** UNFADING QUALITY the ability of a dye to retain its colour and not to fade **3.** FORTRESS a fortress, stronghold, or other secure place (*archaic or literary*)

fast neutron *n* a neutron that has energy in excess of 1.5 MeV, sufficient to produce fission in uranium 238

fast stream *n* a group of employees selected for rapid promotion within an organization

fast-talk *vt* to influence or deceive somebody with false but appealing arguments (*informal*) ○ *fast-talked them into parting with the car keys* —**fast-talker** *n* —**fast-talking** *adj*

fast track *n* **1.** a railway track for fast trains alongside one for slower trains **2.** a rapid and sometimes highly competitive route to progress or advancement that exists alongside the slower conventional one (*informal*) ○ *a fast track to promotion for the brightest recruits*

fast-track *v* **1.** *vti* GO QUICKLY to advance, develop, or process something rapidly, or be handled rapidly ○ *fast-tracking the best of the new recruits* **2.** *vt* DEAL WITH SOMETHING FIRST to give priority to somebody or something ○ *fast-track an application* ■ *adj* ADVANCING RAPIDLY progressing rapidly or encouraging rapid progress —**fast-tracker** *n*

fat /fat/ *n* **1.** NUTRITIONAL COMPONENT OF FOOD a water-soluble substance, solid at room temperature, that belongs to a group of chemicals that are main constituents of food derived from, e.g. animal tissue, nuts, and seeds. Fats are esters of glycerol and fatty acids. ○ *a diet that is lower in fat* **2.** ANAT TISSUE CONTAINING FAT animal or vegetable tissue made up of cells that contain fat, especially the layer of cells under the skin that in excess make somebody overweight **3.** COOK COOKING MEDIUM a solid or liquid substance that is derived from animals or plants and is used as a cooking medium or ingredient, e.g. butter or sunflower oil ○ *rub the fat into the flour* **4.** EXCESS amounts that are surplus to what is needed or wanted (*informal*) ○ *a budget with little fat* **5.** *Aus* OFFENSIVE TERM an offensive term for an erect penis (*slang*) ■ *adj* (**fatter, fattest**) **1.** OVERWEIGHT having a body weight greater than is considered desirable or advisable **2.** CONTAINING FAT containing a lot of fat or too much fat ○ *pork that was rather fat* **3.** THICK very wide or large ○ *a fat book* **4.** PROFITABLE bringing large profits or financial rewards ○ *a fat defence contract* **5.** REWARDING providing good opportunities or rewards ○ *offered a fat part in a film* **6.** RICH owning great wealth ○ *grown fat on the profits* **7.** PLENTIFUL with abundant contents, stocks, or supplies ○ *a fat savings account* **8.** CHEM RICH IN CONTENT with a high content of a particular material or substance, e.g. resin in wood or volatile hydrocarbons in coal **9.** MINIMAL very little (*informal*) ○ *A fat lot of help you are!* ■ *vti* (**fats, fatting, fatted**) AGRIC same as **fatten** (sense 1) (*archaic*) [Old English *fæt(t)* < Indo-European] —**fatly** *adv* —**fatness** *n* ◇ **chew the fat** to have a leisurely conversation (*slang*) ◇ **live off the fat of the land** to live easily by having essential things provided with little or no effort ◇ **the fat is in the fire** something irreversible has happened that will cause trouble

FAT /fat/ *n* in the MS-DOS disk-operating system, an internal store of information about the structure of files on a disk (*often used before a noun*) Full form **file allocation table**

Fatah, Al *n* POL ➧ **Al Fatah**

fatal /fáyt'l/ *adj* **1.** LEADING TO DEATH causing or capable of causing death ○ *a fatal car crash* **2.** RUINOUS causing destruction, disaster, or ruin ○ *a fatal mistake in calculations* **3.** DECISIVE marking an important or decisive stage in a process or series of events ○ *everything that's happened since that fatal day* **4.** PREDESTINED arranged or controlled by fate ■ *n US*

INSTANCE OF DEATH an instance of death, especially one caused by a car, plane, train, or bus crash (*informal*) ○ *a fatal on the turnpike during rush hour* [14C. Directly or via French < Latin *fatalis* < *fatum* (see FATE)] —**fatally** *adv*

CULTURAL NOTE ***The Fatal Shore***, a book (1987) by Australian writer Robert Hughes. A detailed history of the early years of Australia, focusing on the convict transportation system and the lives of those affected by it, it argues that the system was designed to rid Great Britain of an entire criminal underclass.

SYNONYMS See *deadly*.

fatalism /fáyt'lizəm/ *n* **1. DOCTRINE OF FATE** the philosophical doctrine according to which all events are fated to happen, so that human beings cannot change their destinies **2. BELIEF IN ALL-POWERFUL FATE** the belief that people are powerless against fate **3. FEELING OF POWERLESSNESS AGAINST FATE** an attitude of resignation and passivity that results from the belief that people are powerless against fate —**fatalist** *n* —**fatalistic** /fáyt'l ístik/ *adj* —**fatalistically** *adv*

fatality /fə tálləti, fay-/ (*plural* **-ties**) *n* **1. UNEXPECTED DEATH** a death resulting from accident or disaster ○ *The traffic accident resulted in three fatalities.* **2. DEADLINESS** the ability to cause death, disaster, or destruction ○ *fatality associated with toxic waste exposure* **3. PREDETERMINATION BY FATE** the quality or state of being predetermined by fate **4. EVENTS BELIEVED TO BE FATED** an event or train of events thought to be determined by fate

fatality rate *n* SOC SCI same as **death rate**

fata morgana /faátə mawr gaánə/, **Fata Morgana** *n* a mirage or an illusion [< Italian, 'Morgan le Fay'; from the belief that a fairy caused the mirage frequently seen near the Strait of Messina]

fatback /fát bak/ *n N Am* fatty meat from the upper part of a side of pork, usually dried and cured by salt

fat body *n* **1.** in the bodies of insects, especially larvae, a fatty tissue used as a source of energy during metamorphosis and hibernation **2.** in some amphibians and reptiles, a fatty tissue found near the genital glands

fat camp *n US* a residential camp that helps children to lose undesired weight (*slang*)

fat cat *n* somebody who is extremely wealthy and privileged, especially a businessperson whose wealth is regarded as undeserved (*informal; hyphenated when used before a noun*)

fat cell *n* a cell that synthesizes and stores fat

fate /fayt/ *n* **1. FORCE PREDETERMINING EVENTS** the force or principle believed to predetermine events ○ *little knew what fate had in store for him* **2. OUTCOME** a consequence or final result ○ *What was the fate of the mission?* **3. DESTINY** something with decisive or far-reaching consequences that inevitably happens to somebody or something ○ *felt it was her fate to marry him* **4. DISASTROUS CONSEQUENCE** a disastrous or ruinous outcome ■ *vt* (**fates, fating, fated**) **MAKE SOMETHING INEVITABLE** to predetermine something, usually with negative results (*usually passive*) [14C. < Latin *fatum* 'something spoken (by the gods)' < past participle of *fari* 'speak'] —**fated** *adj* ◇ **tempt fate** to do something risky that depends too much on luck for success and might end in misfortune or disaster

fateful /fáytf'l/ *adj* **1. WITH HIGHLY SIGNIFICANT CONSEQUENCES** certain to have very important, often dire consequences ○ *a fateful decision* **2. DECIDED BY FATE** predetermined or controlled by fate **3. OMINOUS** prefiguring what is to come, especially something disastrous ○ *a fateful sign* —**fatefully** *adv* —**fatefulness** *n*

Fates /fayts/ *npl* in Greek mythology, the three goddesses Clotho, Lachesis, and Atropos, often depicted as women of advanced years spinning a thread, who were believed to decree the events and duration of somebody's life. The Greeks believed that Clotho spun the thread that represented somebody's life, Lachesis decided the extent of it, and Atropos was responsible for cutting it. Greek equivalent **Moirai**. Roman equivalent **Parcae**

fat face *n* a typeface with wide main strokes and prominent serifs that produces a relatively heavy dark image when set as text

fat farm *n* a health farm dedicated to helping people lose weight (*slang*)

fat-free *adj* describes foods that contain no animal or vegetable fat

fathead /fát hed/ *n* an offensive term for somebody who is considered foolish or stupid (*slang insult*) —**fatheaded** /fát héddid/ *adj* —**fatheadedly** *adv* —**fatheadedness** *n*

fat hen *n* a common weed with a white covering over the whole plant. Latin name: *Chenopodium album.* US term **pigweed** [Origin ?]

father /faáthər/ *n* **1. MAN WHO IS PARENT** a man who is the parent of a human being, or a male animal that has produced offspring ○ *been like a father to me* **2. MAN ACTING AS PARENT** a man who brings up and looks after a child as if he were its father **3. MAN WHO IS ANCESTOR** a man who is an ancestor, especially the founder of a family or people ○ *the land of our fathers and mothers* **4. MAN WHO IS FOUNDER** a man who establishes, founds, or originates something ○ *the father of modern linguistics* **5. PROTOTYPE** something that is a prototype or original version of something else **6. MAN WHO IS LEADER** a man who is a community or civic leader ○ *the town fathers* **7. MAN WHO IS OLDEST MEMBER** the man who is the oldest or most senior member of an institution ■ *v* (**-thers, -thering, -thered**) **1.** *vt* **BECOME FATHER OF OFFSPRING** to cause a woman or female animal to produce offspring **2.** *vti* **BE LIKE FATHER TO SOMEBODY** to act as a father to somebody, especially by giving advice, comfort, and protection **3.** *vt* **FOUND SOMETHING** to establish, found, or originate something ○ *father a plan* [Old English *fæder* < Indo-European] —**fatherhood** *n*

CULTURAL NOTE ***Fathers and Sons***, a novel (1862) by Russian writer Ivan Turgenev. It deals with the conflicting attitudes towards social change (particularly the emancipation of serfs) among Russia's younger radical intelligentsia, represented by the novel's nihilistic protagonist, Bazarov, and the older liberal gentry, to which Turgenev himself belonged. The novel was seen as Turgenev's acknowledgment that Russia's future was now in the hands of a new generation.

Father *n* **1. GOD** in Christianity, God, especially when considered as the first person of the Trinity **2.** CHR same as **church father 3. TITLE FOR MEMBER OF CHRISTIAN CLERGY** a title and form of address used for a member of the Christian clergy, especially in the Roman Catholic, Orthodox, and Episcopal Churches **4. RESPECTFUL TITLE FOR MAN** a respectful term of address for a man who is past middle age **5. PERSONIFICATION** something personified as a man of advanced years

Father Christmas *n* the patron saint of children, commonly identified with Saint Nicholas, usually depicted as a jolly old man with a white beard who brings presents at Christmas.

father confessor *n* **1.** a Roman Catholic priest who hears confessions and gives advice **2.** a man in whom somebody confides and whose advice is sought

father figure *n* a man whom other people look up to for advice, inspiration, or protection

father-in-law (*plural* **fathers-in-law**) *n* the father of somebody's husband or wife

fatherland /faáthər land/ *n* **1.** somebody's native land or country **2.** the native land of somebody's ancestors

father-lasher *n* a large sea scorpion with short spines. Native to: European and North Atlantic coasts. Latin name: *Myoxocephalus scorpius* or *Myoxocephalus bubalis.*

fatherless /faáthərləss/ *adj* having no father or no one identified as a father —**fatherlessness** *n*

fatherly /faáthərli/ *adj* having or showing the qualities traditionally associated with a father such as love, support, and protection ○ *fatherly affection* —**fatherliness** *n*

father of the chapel *n* a shop steward representing members of a trade union in a printing office

Father's Day *n* a day observed as a celebration of fatherhood in the United Kingdom, the United States, Canada, Australia, and some other Commonwealth countries. Date: third Sunday in June, or, in Australia and New Zealand, first Sunday in September.

Father Time *n* the personification of time as a bearded man of advanced years, usually wearing a robe and carrying a scythe and an hourglass

fathom /fáthəm/ *n* **MEASURE OF WATER DEPTH** a unit of length equal to 1.83 m/6 ft, used mainly in nautical contexts for measuring the depth of water ■ *vt* (**-oms, -oming, -omed**) **1. COMPREHEND SOMETHING** to understand something, usually something profound or mystifying ○ *couldn't fathom why he came back* **2. MEASURE WATER DEPTH** to measure the depth of water, especially using a sounding line [Old English *fæþm*, origin ?] —**fathomable** *adj* —**fathomer** *n*

fathomless /fáthəmləss/ *adj* **1.** too deep to be measured **2.** impossible to understand —**fathomlessly** *adv* —**fathomlessness** *n*

fatigue /fə teég/ *n* **1. MENTAL OR PHYSICAL EXHAUSTION** extreme tiredness or weariness resulting from physical or mental activity ○ *weak with fatigue after the long march* **2. INABILITY TO RESPOND TO SITUATION** the temporary inability of somebody to respond to a situation as a result of overexposure or excessive activity (*often used in combination*) ○ *compassion fatigue* **3.** PHYSIOL **INABILITY TO RESPOND TO STIMULUS** the temporary inability of an organ or body part such as a muscle or nerve cell to respond to a stimulus and function normally after continuous activity or stimulation **4.** ENG **WEAKENING OF MATERIAL UNDER STRESS** the weakening or breakdown of a material subjected to prolonged or repeated stress ○ *metal fatigue* **5.** MIL **NONMILITARY WORK DONE BY SOLDIERS** manual or menial work done by soldiers, often as a punishment (*often used before a noun*) ■ **fatigues** *npl* MIL **INFORMAL MILITARY UNIFORMS** informal military uniforms worn every day and in battle, as distinct from formal uniforms ■ *vti* (**-tigues, -tiguing, -tigued**) **1. MAKE OR BECOME TIRED** to tire somebody out as a result of physical or mental activity, or become tired out in this way **2. WEAKEN UNDER STRESS** to weaken or break something, or become weakened or broken, when subjected to prolonged or repeated stress [Mid-17C. Via French, 'to tire' < Latin *fatigare*] —**fatigable** /fáttigəb'l/ *adj* —**fatigued** *adj*

Fatima /fáttimə/ AD (606?–632) Arabian religious figure. The youngest daughter of the prophet Muhammad, she is revered especially by Shiite Muslims.

Fátima /fáttimə/ village in west-central Portugal, northeast of Lisbon. It is a place of pilgrimage for Roman Catholics and has been a shrine since 1917. Population: 5,445 (1991).

Fatimid /fátti mid/, **Fatimite** /fátti mīt/ *n* **1.** a member of a Muslim dynasty, descended from Muhammad's daughter Fatima and her husband Ali, that ruled North Africa and parts of Egypt and Syria from AD 909 to 1171 **2.** a descendant of Muhammad's daughter Fatima and her husband Ali [Mid-19C. < Arabic *Fāṭima* 'Fatima']

fat lip *n* a lip swollen from having been hit in a fist fight (*informal*) ○ *gave him a fat lip*

fat mouse *n* a nocturnal short-tailed mouse eaten as a delicacy because of its high stored fat content. Native to: dry regions of Africa. Genus: *Steatomys.*

fatshedera /fáts héddərə/ *n* a hybrid ornamental plant with glossy leaves. Flowers: pale green. Latin name: *Fatsia japonica* ± *Hedera helix.* [Mid-20C. < modern Latin *Fatsia* (genus of shrubs) + *Hedera* (genus of climbing plants < Latin, 'ivy')]

fatsia /fátsi ə/ *n* a large plant with deeply divided, shiny green leaves, sometimes grown as a houseplant. Flowers: cream, in round clusters. Latin name: *Fatsia japonica.* [< modern Latin]

fatso /fátsō/ (*plural* **-sos** or **-soes**) *n* an offensive term for somebody who is overweight (*slang insult*) [Mid-20C. Probably < *fats*, offensive term for an overweight person]

fat stock *n* livestock that has been fattened and is ready for sale or slaughter

fat suit *n* a naturalistic costume designed to make an actor appear overweight

fatten /fátt'n/ (**-tens, -tening, -tened**) *v* **1.** *vti* FEED ANIMAL to make an animal fat by feeding it plentifully, usually for slaughter, or be made fat for this purpose **2.** *vti* MAKE OR BECOME FAT to become fat or fatter, or make somebody fat or fatter **3.** *vt* ENLARGE SOMETHING to make something larger, richer, or fuller ○ *fatten your wallet* **4.** *vt* FERTILIZE LAND to make land or soil more fertile —**fattenable** *adj* —**fattener** *n*

fattening /fátt'ning/ *adj* **1.** high in fat or calorie content, and so likely to make some people gain weight **2.** becoming fat and therefore suitable for slaughter —**fatteningly** *adv*

fatty /fátti/ *adj* (**-tier, -tiest**) **1.** CONTAINING FAT containing fat or grease, especially in large or distasteful amounts **2.** DERIVED FROM FAT derived from or chemically related to fat ○ *fatty alcohol* **3.** WITH ACCUMULATED FAT containing accumulated fat, sometimes in undesirable amounts ○ *fatty tissue* ■ *n* (*plural* **-ties**) OFFENSIVE TERM an offensive term for somebody who is overweight (*informal insult*) —**fattiness** *n*

fatty acid *n* an organic acid belonging to a group that may occur naturally as waxes, fats, and essential oils and consisting of a straight chain of carbon atoms linked by single bonds and ending in a carboxyl group. Source: animal and plant materials. Formula: $C_nH_{n+1}COOH$.

fatty degeneration *n* deterioration in the function of an organ such as the liver or heart, caused by the accumulation of unusually high levels of fats in its cells

fatty oil *n* CHEM same as **fixed oil**

fatuity /fə tyóo əti/ (*plural* **-ties**) *n* (*formal*) **1.** a lack of intelligence or thought combined with complacency **2.** an action or remark that shows a lack of intelligence or thought combined with complacency —**fatuitous** *adj*

fatuous /fáttyoo əss/ *adj* showing a lack of intelligence or thought combined with complacency ○ *a fatuous joke* [Early 17C. < Latin *fatuus*] —**fatuously** *adv* —**fatuousness** *n*

fatwa /fát waa/, **fatwah** *n* a formal legal opinion or religious decree issued by an Islamic leader [Early 17C. < Arabic *fatwā* < *aftā* 'decide a point of law']

fat wallet *n* a digital wallet where credit card and digital certificate information are stored on a user's computer

fatware /fát wair/ *n* COMPUT same as **bloatware**

faubourg /fố boorg/ *n* an inner suburb or quarter of a city, especially in France [15C. < French, alteration (after *faux* 'false') of Old French *forsborc* < Latin *foris* 'outside' + late Latin *burgus* 'fat' (< Germanic)]

fauces /fáw seez/ *npl* the passage between the back of the mouth and the pharynx [15C. < Latin, 'throat'] —**faucal** /fáwk'l/ *adj* —**faucial** /fáwsh'l/ *adj*

faucet /fáwssit/ *n* N Am same as **tap**² *n* (sense 1) [14C. Via Old French *fausset* or Provençal *falset* < *falser* 'bore in' < late Latin *falsare* 'to corrupt' < Latin *falsus* 'false']

Library of Congress

William Faulkner

Faulkner /fáwknər/, **William** (1897–1962) US writer. He is regarded as one of the greatest American novelists for his stream-of-consciousness works about Southern life, including *The Sound and the Fury* (1929). He won the Nobel Prize in literature (1949).

Full name **Faulkner, William Cuthbert**. See Cultural note at **fury** —**Faulknerian** /fawk néeri ən/ *adj*

'Time is dead as long as it is being clicked off little wheels; only when the clock stops does time come to life.'
[William Faulkner, 'June Second 1910', *The Sound and the Fury*; 1929]

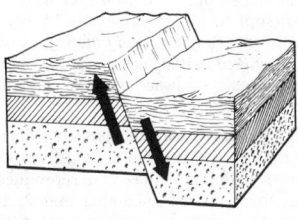

fault: displacement of rock layers in earth's crust

fault /fáwlt, fólt/ *n* **1.** RESPONSIBILITY FOR MISTAKE responsibility for a mistake, failure, or act of wrongdoing ○ *It's his fault we're late.* **2.** PERSONAL SHORTCOMING a failing or character weakness in somebody ○ *My main fault is laziness.* **3.** DEFECT something that detracts from the integrity, functioning, or perfection of something else ○ *an electrical fault* **4.** MISTAKE an error, especially in calculation **5.** MISDEMEANOUR a wrongful action **6.** GEOL DISPLACEMENT IN EARTH'S CRUST a displacement of rock layers in the Earth's crust in response to stress, accompanied by a break in the continuity of the rocks on each side of the fault line **7.** RACKET GAMES INVALID SERVE IN RACKET GAMES in racket games such as tennis, a serve that is invalid because it fails to land within a prescribed area **8.** SHOW JUMPING PENALTY MARK IN SHOWJUMPING a penalty mark awarded in showjumping for various errors such as a failure or refusal to clear a fence **9.** FIELD SPORTS LOSS OF SCENT OF ANIMAL an occasion on which the hounds in a hunt lose the scent of the animal they are chasing ■ *v* (**faults, faulting, faulted**) **1.** *vt* BLAME SOMEBODY OR SOMETHING to blame, criticize, or find a flaw in somebody or something ○ *You can't fault his results.* **2.** *vi* MAKE MISTAKE to commit a fault or make a mistake (*archaic*) **3.** *vi* GEOL DISPLACE to respond to stress by becoming displaced and developing as a geological fault (*refers to rock layers*) [13C. Via Old French *faut(e)* 'lack' < assumed Vulgar Latin *fallitum* 'failing' < Latin *fallere* 'fail'] ◇ **find fault with somebody** *or* **something** to criticize somebody or something, often unfairly ○ *She's always finding fault with the children's work.* ◇ **to a fault** excessively ○ *naive and generous to a fault*

SYNONYMS See *flaw*¹.

faultfinding /fáwlt fīnding, fólt-/ *n* **1.** constant and often petty complaining or criticism **2.** the process of locating and diagnosing faults within an electrical, electronic, or mechanical system (*often used before a noun*) ○ *faultfinding procedures* —**faultfinder** *n* —**faultfinding** *adj*

faultless /fáwltləss, fólt-/ *adj* having no faults or flaws ○ *a faultless performance* —**faultlessly** *adv* —**faultlessness** *n*

fault line *n* a linear feature on the Earth's surface, occurring where displaced rock layers have broken through the Earth's surface

fault plane *n* the surface along which displacement of rock layers has taken place in a geological fault

fault tolerance *n* the ability of a computer or network to preserve the integrity of data during a malfunction

faulty /fáwlti, fólti/ (**-ier, -iest**) *adj* containing flaws, especially ones that cause malfunctions ○ *faulty wiring* ○ *faulty logic* —**faultily** *adv* —**faultiness** *n*

faun /fáwn/ *n* in Roman mythology, a rural god, often depicted as a creature with the body of a man and the legs and horns of a goat. Greek equivalent **satyr** (sense 1) [14C. Directly or via French < Latin *Faunus* 'Faunus']

SPELLCHECK **faun** or **fawn**? Do not confuse the spelling of *faun* and *fawn*, which sound similar. A *faun* is a mythological being depicted as part man and part goat; a *fawn* is a young deer. **Fawn** is also an adjective and noun referring to a pale yellowish-brown colour, as in *a fawn jacket*, and a verb meaning 'try to win favour' or 'attempt to please somebody', as in *fawning over the celebrities he interviews*.

fauna /fáwnə/ (*plural* **-nas** or **-nae** /-nee/) *n* **1.** the animal life of a particular region or period, considered as a whole **2.** a catalogue or list describing the animals of a particular region or period [Late 18C. Via modern Latin < late Latin *Fauna* 'Fauna', an ancient Italian rural goddess, sister of FAUNUS] —**faunal** *adj* —**faunally** *adv* —**faunistic** /faw nístik/ *adv* —**faunistically** *adv*

Faunus /fáwnəss/ *n* in Roman mythology, the god of nature, farming, and fertility. He was the grandson of Saturn. Greek equivalent **Pan**

Fauré /fáwr ay/, **Gabriel** (1845–1924) French composer and organist. His best-known work is the *Requiem* (1887) for solo voices, choir, and orchestra. Full name **Fauré, Gabriel Urbain**

Faust /fowst/ (*b.* 1480?) German fortune teller and magician. Reputed to have sold his soul to the devil, he is most noted for the legends concerning him that formed the basis for numerous literary and musical works. —**Faustian** *adj*

faute de mieux /fốt də myố/ *adv* in the absence of something better ○ *the feeling that she had married him faute de mieux* [< French, 'lack of better']

fauteuil /fố tố i/ *n* an upholstered armchair, usually with open sides (*technical*) [Mid-18C. Via French < Old French *faudestuel* 'folding chair' < Germanic]

fauve /fốv/, **Fauve** *n* an artist belonging to an early 20th-century movement in French painting (**fauvism**) characterized by the use of simple forms and bright colours (*often used before a noun*) [Early 20C. < French, 'wild, wild animal', via Old French *falve* 'tawny' < Germanic]

fauvism /fốvizəm/, **Fauvism** *n* an early 20th-century movement in painting, begun in about 1905 by a group of French artists, including Matisse, and characterized by the use of simple forms and bright colours

fauvist /fốvist/ *n* ART same as **fauve** —**fauvist** *adj*

faux /fố/ *adj* made in imitation of a natural material such as leather or fur ○ *faux marble* [Late 20C. Via French < Latin *falsus* (see FALSE)]

faux ami /fố z a mee/ (*plural* **faux amis** /fố za mee/) *n* LING same as **false friend** (sense 1) [< French]

faux-naïf /fố nī eef/ *adj* pretending to be simple or without sophistication (*literary*) [< French, 'falsely naive'] —**faux-naïf** *n*

faux pas /fố paa/ (*plural* **faux pas** /fố paaz/) *n* an embarrassing mistake that breaks a social convention [< French, 'false step']

SYNONYMS See *mistake*.

fava bean /faávə-/ *n* N Am PLANTS, FOOD same as **broad bean** [Via Italian < Latin *faba*]

fave /fayv/ *n, adj* same as **favourite** (*slang*) [Mid-20C. Shortening]

favela /fə vélla, faa-/ *n* a shantytown or slum area, especially in Brazil [Mid-20C. < Brazilian Portuguese]

fave rave *n* a favourite person, thing, or experience (*slang*)

favism /faávizəm/ *n* acute anaemia caused by an allergic reaction to broad beans or the plant's pollen, usually as a result of a hereditary enzyme deficiency [Early 20C. < Italian *favismo* < *fava* 'broad bean' (see FAVA BEAN)]

favonian /fə vốni ən/ *adj* (*literary*) **1.** relating to the west or the west wind **2.** benign or kind [Mid-17C. < Latin *favonianus* < *Favonius* 'west wind']

favor *n, v* US spelling of **favour**

favorite *adj, n* US spelling of **favourite**

favour /fáyvər/ *n* **1.** KIND ACT an act of kindness performed or granted out of goodwill ○ *lent me the car as a favour* **2.** APPROVING ATTITUDE an approving,

friendly, or supportive attitude ○ *They seem to be out of favour with the judges.* **3. PREFERENCE** preferential treatment shown to somebody **4. TOKEN OF LOYALTY** something given or worn as a token of love, allegiance, or goodwill **5. SMALL GIFT** a small gift given to each guest at a party ■ **favours** *npl* **SEX** sexual intimacy, especially when consented to by a woman (*dated*) ■ *vt* **(-vours, -vouring, -voured) 1. PREFER SOMEBODY OR SOMETHING** to show a preference for somebody or something ○ *He favoured loud suits and colourful ties.* **2. TREAT SOMEBODY OR SOMETHING WITH KINDNESS** to treat somebody or something with particular approval or kindness **3. SUPPORT SOMEBODY OR SOMETHING** to express support for somebody or something ○ *voters who favoured reform* **4. ASSIST SOMEBODY OR SOMETHING** to be advantageous to somebody or something ○ *tax measures that favour the rich* **5. SHOW SOMEBODY PREFERENTIAL TREATMENT** to distinguish somebody by giving him or her something valuable ○ *favoured him with the best seat* **6. BE CAREFUL WITH SOMETHING** to treat or use something gently ○ *favouring a bad knee* **7. RESEMBLE SOMEBODY** to resemble somebody, usually a parent, in appearance ○ *favours her mother* [14C. Via Old French, 'friendly regard' < Latin *favor* < *favere* 'be well disposed towards'] —**favourer** *n* ◇ **curry favour with somebody** to try to gain favour with a superior by flattery and obsequiousness ○ *They put more energy into currying favour with the director than they ever put into their work.*

SYNONYMS See ***regard***.

favourable /fáyvərab'l/ *adj* **1. PROMISING** suggesting future improvement or good results ○ *a favourable outlook* **2. APPROVING** expressing approval or admiration ○ *a favourable reaction* **3. GAINING APPROVAL** winning approval or favour ○ *make a favourable impression* **4. CONSENTING** expressing agreement or consent ○ *a favourable response* **5. ADVANTAGEOUS** acting in a beneficial way ○ *favourable winds* —**favourableness** *n* —**favourably** *adv*

favoured /fáyvərd/ *adj* **1. CHOSEN** preferred to any other ○ *The favoured plan is unfortunately the costliest.* **2. DISTINGUISHED** enjoying the advantages of a particular thing ○ *a child favoured with his father's good nature* **3. PRIVILEGED** enjoying advantages or privileges denied to others —**favouredness** *n*

favourite /fáyvərit/ *adj* **MOST LIKED** preferred or most liked ■ *n* **1. PERSON OR THING LIKED MOST** somebody or something that is liked most of all or preferred to all others ○ *Which author is your favourite?* **2. SOMEBODY FAVOURED BY SUPERIOR** somebody who is treated with special favour by a superior **3. COMPETITOR MOST LIKELY TO WIN** a competitor considered to be the most likely to win, especially in a horse race [Late 16C. Via obsolete French *favorit* < Italian *favorito*, past participle of *favorire* 'to favour' < *favore* 'favour' < Latin *favor* (see FAVOUR)]

favouritism /fáyvərətizəm/ *n* **1.** the practice of giving special treatment or unfair advantages to a person or group ○ *accused of showing favouritism towards certain pupils* **2.** the state of being a favourite person or group

favus /fáyvəss/ *n* an infectious skin disease that affects people, especially on the scalp, and some domestic animals, causing the formation of dry yellowish encrustations. It is caused by a fungus, *Trichophyton schoenleinii*. [Mid-16C. < Latin, 'honeycomb']

Fawcett /fáwssit/, **Dame Millicent** (1847–1929) British suffragette. She headed the National Union of Women's Suffrage Societies (1897–1919). Born **Garrett, Millicent**

Fawkes /fawks/, **Guy** (1570–1606) English conspirator. He was executed for his role in the Gunpowder Plot against James I on 5 November, 1605.

> 'A desperate disease requires a dangerous remedy.'
> [Guy Fawkes. Quoted in *Dictionary of National Biography*; 1917]

Fawkner /fáwknər/, **John Pascoe** (1792–1869) British-born Australian pioneer. He was one of the first Europeans to explore and settle in the Port Phillip Bay region. He and John Batman are considered the cofounders of the city of Melbourne.

fawn[1] /fawn/ *n* **1. YOUNG DEER** a young deer, especially one that is unweaned or less than a year old **2. YELLOWISH-BROWN COLOUR** a pale yellowish-brown colour ■ *vi* **(fawns, fawning, fawned) PRODUCE FAWN** to give birth to a fawn [14C. Via French *faon* 'young animal' < assumed Vulgar Latin *feton-* < Latin *fetus* 'offspring'] —**fawn** *adj*

SPELLCHECK See *faun*.

fawn[2] /fawn/ **(fawns, fawning, fawned)** *vi* **1.** to seek attention or try to win favour by flattery and obsequious behaviour ○ *admirers fawning at his feet* **2.** to attempt to please somebody by showing enthusiastic affection ○ *started fawning all over me as soon as I walked in* [Old English *fagnian* 'rejoice' < *fægen* 'glad' < Germanic] —**fawner** *n* —**fawningly** *adv* —**fawningness** *n*

fax /faks/ *n* **1. MESSAGE SENT ELECTRONICALLY** a document or image that is transmitted in digitized electronic form over telephone lines and reproduced in its original form on the receiving end **2. SYSTEM FOR TRANSMITTING DOCUMENTS** a system of transmitting documents and images electronically over telephone lines (*often used before a noun*) ○ *sent by fax* **3.** *also* **fax machine TRANSMITTING MACHINE** a machine incorporating a telephone that sends and receives documents or images via fax ■ *vt* **(faxes, faxing, faxed) SEND BY FAX** to send a document or image electronically using a fax machine [Mid-20C. Shortening of FACSIMILE]

faxback /fáks bak/ *n* **1.** an automated system of responding by fax, used especially for requesting and receiving documents, e.g. by using a touch-tone phone, or by downloading a document from a website to a fax machine **2.** a document received in response to a request using a faxback system

fax-modem *n* a modem that enables a computer to send and receive faxes

fax-on-demand *n* technology that sends a fax automatically to somebody who telephones a particular number for information

fay[1] /fay/ *n* a fairy, elf, or other small supernatural being from folklore (*literary*) ○ *'You are, upon the whole, a sort of fay, or sprite – not a woman!'* (Thomas Hardy, *Jude the Obscure*; 1895) [14C. Via Old French *fa(i)e* 'fairy' < Latin *Fata*, goddess of fate < *fatum* (see FATE)]

fay[2] /fay/ **(fays, faying, fayed)** *vti* to join pieces of wood together tightly, or fit tightly inside another piece of wood [Old English *fēgan* < Indo-European, 'fasten']

Fayette ➧ **La Fayette, Marie Madeleine**

fayre /fair/ *n* a fair, especially one held to raise money for charity (*informal*) [Pseudo-archaic variant]

faze /fayz/ **(fazes, fazing, fazed)** *v* **1.** *vt* to disconcert or disturb somebody ○ *Bad news doesn't seem to faze her.* **2.** *vi Ireland* to have a visible effect on somebody ○ *The cold didn't faze on him.* [Mid-19C. Variant of dialectal *feeze* 'frighten' < Old English *fēsian* 'drive away' < Germanic]

SPELLCHECK faze or **phase**? Do not confuse the spelling of ***faze*** and ***phase***, which sound similar. ***Faze*** is a verb meaning 'disconcert': *Don't be fazed by the size of the instruction manual.* ***Phase***, the more common word, can be used as a noun meaning 'a stage of development', 'an aspect', or as a verb meaning 'do something in stages': *It's just a phase he's going through. The old system is being phased out.*

fazenda /fə zéndə/ *n* a large estate, farm, or plantation, especially in Brazil or Portugal [Early 19C. Via Portuguese, originally 'place with things to be done' < Latin *facienda* 'things to be done' < *facere* 'do, make']

FBA *abbr* Fellow of the British Academy

FBI *n* a bureau of the US Department of Justice that deals with matters of national security, interstate crime, and crimes against the government. Full form **Federal Bureau of Investigation**

FBU *abbr* Fire Brigades Union

FC *abbr* **1.** SOCCER Football Club **2.** TREES Forestry Commission

FCA *abbr* ACCT **1.** Fellow of the Institute of Chartered Accountants (in England and Wales) **2.** full cost accounting

FCCA *abbr* ACCT Fellow of the Chartered Association of Certified Accountants

FCII *abbr* INSUR Fellow of the Chartered Insurance Institute

F clef *n* MUSIC same as **bass clef**

FCO *abbr* GOV Foreign and Commonwealth Office

FCSD *abbr* GOV Financial and Central Services Department

FD *abbr* **1.** HIST, CHR Fidei Defensor **2.** BUSINESS free delivery

f/d, f.d. *abbr* BUSINESS free delivery

FDA *n* the federal agency that oversees trade in and the safety of food and drugs in the United States. Full form **Food and Drug Administration**

F distribution *n* a statistical measure of the spread or scattering of members of two observed random samples as a test of whether the samples have the same variability. The F distribution is obtained by taking the ratio of the chi-square distributions of the samples divided by the number of their degrees of freedom. [Mid-20C. After Sir Ronald *Fisher* (d. 1962), British statistician]

FDR *abbr* Franklin Delano Roosevelt

Fe *symbol* CHEM ELEM iron [< Latin *ferrum*]

FE *abbr* EDUC further education

fealty /fée əlti/ (*plural* **-ties**) *n* the loyalty sworn to a feudal lord by a vassal or tenant [13C. Via Old French *feau(l)te* < Latin *fidelitas* (see FIDELITY)]

fear /feer/ *n* **1. FEELING OF ANXIETY** an unpleasant feeling of anxiety or apprehension caused by the presence or anticipation of danger ○ *showed no signs of fear* **2. FRIGHTENING THOUGHT** an idea, thought, or other entity that causes feelings of fear ○ *irrational fears* **3. REVERENCE** respect or awe for somebody or something ○ *the fear of God* **4. WORRY** a concern about something that threatens to bring bad news or results (*often used in the plural*) ○ *fears for their safe return* **5. CHANCE** chance or likelihood of an undesirable thing happening ○ *There's no fear that he'll misunderstand.* ■ *v* **(fears, fearing, feared) 1.** *vti* **BE AFRAID** to be frightened of somebody or something or about taking action ○ *She fears going to the dentist.* **2.** *vt* **FEEL REVERENCE FOR SOMEBODY OR SOMETHING** to show respect for or be in awe of somebody or something ○ *fear God* **3.** *vt* **EXPRESS REGRETFULLY** to be sorry to say something (*formal*) ○ *I fear that you have not been successful on this occasion.* [Old English *fǣr* 'calamity, danger', *fǣran* 'frighten' < Indo-European, 'to try'] **fear for** *vt* to be worried or apprehensive about somebody or something that appears to be at risk or in danger

fearful /féerf'l/ *adj* **1. WORRIED** feeling anxiety or apprehension ○ *fearful for the safety of her investment* **2. FRIGHTENING** causing or likely to cause fear ○ *a fearful storm* **3. TIMID** nervous and easily frightened ○ *a fearful kitten* **4. SCARED** arising from or expressing fear ○ *a fearful expression* **5. FEELING REVERENCE** feeling respect or awe for somebody or something ○ *gazed in fearful wonder* **6. VERY BAD** extreme in degree, intensity, or badness (*informal*) ○ *had a fearful headache* —**fearfully** *adv* —**fearfulness** *n*

fearless /féerləss/ *adj* resolute in the face of dangers or challenges —**fearlessly** *adv* —**fearlessness** *n*

SYNONYMS See ***courage***.

fearsome /féerssəm/ *adj* **1. FRIGHTENING** inspiring fear ○ *a fearsome howling* **2. IMPRESSIVE** evoking awe and respect **3. TIMID** easily frightened —**fearsomely** *adv* —**fearsomeness** *n*

feart /feert/ *adj Scotland* feeling or showing fear [Variant of AFRAID]

~~**feasable**~~ incorrect spelling of **feasible**

feasibility /féezə bílləti/ (*plural* **-ties**) *n* **1.** the degree to which something can be achieved or put into effect (*often used before a noun*) ○ *examining the feasibility of the proposed merger* **2.** something that can be carried out or achieved ○ *That idea isn't even a remote feasibility.*

feasibility study *n* a preliminary study undertaken to assess whether a planned project is likely to be practical and successful and to estimate its cost

feasible /féezəb'l/ *adj* **1.** capable of being achieved or put into effect **2.** reasonable enough to be believed or accepted ○ *a feasible plan* [15C. < French *faisable* < *fais-*, stem of *faire* 'do' < Latin *facere* 'do, make'] —**feasibleness** *n* —**feasibly** *adv*

feast /feest/ *n* **1.** LARGE MEAL a large and elaborate meal **2.** CELEBRATORY MEAL an elaborate meal for many people that celebrates an occasion ○ *a wedding feast* **3.** SOMETHING VERY AGREEABLE something that provides a great deal of pleasure ○ *a feast for the eyes* **4.** RELIG RELIGIOUS CELEBRATION a periodic religious celebration, often marked by a special meal ■ *v* (**feasts, feasting, feasted**) **1.** *vi* ATTEND CELEBRATORY MEAL to be present at a celebratory meal **2.** *vi* ENJOY EATING to eat heartily or with enjoyment ○ *feasting on strawberries and cream* **3.** *vt* PROVIDE MEAL FOR SOMEBODY to entertain somebody with a feast **4.** *vi* TAKE DELIGHT to derive great or prolonged pleasure from something ○ *feast on the magnificent scenery* [12C. Via French < Latin *festa*, form of *festus* 'joyous'] —**feaster** *n*

feast day *n* **1.** a day on which a religious festival takes place **2.** a day on which an elaborate celebratory meal is enjoyed

Feast of Dedication, **Feast of Lights** *n* JUDAISM same as **Hanukkah**

Feast of Lots *n* JUDAISM same as **Purim**

Feast of St Michael and All Angels *n* CHR same as **Michaelmas**

Feast of Tabernacles *n* JUDAISM same as **Sukkoth**

Feast of the Assumption *n* CHR same as **Assumption** (sense 2)

Feast of the Holy Innocents *n* CHR same as **Holy Innocents' Day**

Feast of Weeks *n* JUDAISM same as **Shavuoth**

feat /feet/ *n* a remarkable act or achievement involving courage, skill, or strength ○ *achieved the impressive feat of winning three gold medals* [14C. Via Old French *fait* 'deed' < Latin *factum* (see FACT)]

feather /féthər/ *n* **1.** PART OF BIRD'S PLUMAGE a part of a bird's plumage, consisting of a hollow central shaft with numerous interlocking fine strands on either side **2.** SOMETHING RESEMBLING FEATHER something with light or wispy strands that give it a superficial resemblance to a bird's feather, e.g. the leaf of a plant **3.** SOMETHING UNIMPORTANT something small, trivial, or of minimal value **4.** MINERALS FLAW IN PRECIOUS STONE a feather-shaped flaw in a precious stone **5.** ARCHERY ARROW ATTACHMENT a piece of a feather attached to the end of an arrow or dart to make it fly straight **6.** ARCHERY BLUNT END OF ARROW the end of an arrow that has a feather fitted on it **7.** CONSTR PART OF WOOD JOINT a projecting strip of wood fitted into a groove in the edge of a board to form a joint **8.** NAVY, NAUT TRACK MADE BY PERISCOPE the track made on the surface of the sea by a submarine's periscope **9.** ROWING HORIZONTAL OAR POSITION the horizontal position in which an oar is held in order to reduce wind resistance when it is raised from the water between strokes ■ **feathers** *npl* **1.** ZOOL LONG HAIR ON ANIMALS fringes of hair on the legs or tails of some dogs and horses **2.** ATTIRE the clothes that somebody is wearing (*dated*) ■ *v* (**-ers, -ering, -ered**) **1.** *vt* FIT SOMETHING WITH FEATHERS to fit something such as an arrow with a feather or feathers **2.** *vt* COVER SOMETHING WITH FEATHERS to cover or decorate somebody or something with feathers **3.** *vti* FRAY to fray a surface or end by cutting it or wearing it away, or become frayed in this way **4.** *vi* SPREAD to grow or move out at an angle from a central line in a pattern resembling the structure of a feather **5.** *vti* ROWING TURN OAR BLADE HORIZONTAL to turn an oar so that the blade face is parallel to the water in order to reduce wind resistance when it is raised from the water between strokes **6.** *vt* AVIAT ALTER POSITION OF PROPELLER BLADES to change the angle of an aircraft's propeller so that the line of the blades is roughly parallel to the line of flight and air resistance is minimized **7.** *vt* CUT HAIR TO FORM LAYERS to style hair by cutting and thinning in order to give a layered texture **8.** *vt* CONSTR CONNECT BOARDS WITH TONGUE-AND-GROOVE JOINT to join two boards or pieces of wood by using a tongue-and-groove joint [Old English *feþer* < Indo-European, 'to fly'] —**feathered** *adj* —**featherlike** *adj* ◇ **a feather in somebody's cap** an act or achievement that gives somebody cause to be proud ○ *Getting the award is a real feather in my cap.*

featherbed /féthər bed/ (**-beds, -bedding, -bedded**) *v* **1.** *vt* to lavish attention or luxuries on somebody **2.** *vi* to overstaff or limit production, especially in compliance with a union contract, in order to save or create jobs

featherbedding /féthər bedding/ *n* the practice of overstaffing or limiting production, especially in compliance with a union contract, in order to save or create jobs

feather boa *n* a long thin scarf made of feathers

featherbone /féthər bōn/ *n* a substitute for whalebone, originally made from the quills of domestic fowl. Use: corset bones.

featherbrain /féthər brayn/ *n* somebody who is regarded as forgetful, thoughtless, or inattentive (*informal insult*) —**featherbrained** *adj*

feather duster *n* a brush used for dusting, made of long feathers attached to a stick

featheredge /féthər ej/ *n* **1.** TAPERED BOARD a board or plank with a thin tapering edge **2.** TAPERING EDGE OF BOARD the thinner tapering edge of a wedge-shaped board or plank **3.** PAPER same as **deckle edge** ■ *vt* (**-edges, -edging, -edged**) HONE TO EDGE to taper a side or end of a board or plank to a very thin edge

feather grass *n* a perennial grass plant that has feathery clusters of spikelets. Genus: *Stipa*.

featherhead /féthər hed/ *n* same as **featherbrain** (*informal insult*) —**featherheaded** /féthər héddid/ *adj*

feathering /fétharing/ *n* **1.** PLUMAGE the feathers on a bird **2.** FEATHERS ATTACHED TO ARROW the feathers attached to an arrow or dart, or their arrangement **3.** ZOOL LONG HAIR ON ANIMAL'S LEGS fringes of hair on the legs or tails of some dogs and horses **4.** PRINTING PATTERN OF INK SOAKING INTO PAPER the spreading of ink in lines like veins through printed paper that is too absorbent

feather star *n* a free-swimming invertebrate sea animal with between five and ten feathery arms radiating from a central disc. Order: Comatulida.

featherstitch /féthər stich/ *n* ornamental embroidery stitching with a zigzag pattern ■ *vt* (**-stitches, -stitching, -stitched**) to sew or decorate something with featherstitch

featherweight /féthər wayt/ *n* **1.** PROFESSIONAL WEIGHT CATEGORY in professional boxing, a weight category for competitors whose weight does not exceed 57.1 kg/126 pounds **2.** AMATEUR WEIGHT CATEGORY in amateur boxing, a weight category for competitors whose weight does not exceed 57 kg/125 pounds **3.** FEATHERWEIGHT BOXER a professional boxer who competes at featherweight level **4.** SPORTSPERSON in sports such as wrestling, a competitor at lightweight level **5.** SOMEBODY OR SOMETHING LIGHT OR INSIGNIFICANT somebody or something that is very light, small, or insignificant

feathery /féthəri/ *adj* **1.** similar to a feather or feathers, especially in lightness or softness **2.** made of or covered in feathers —**featheriness** *n*

feature /féechər/ *n* **1.** DISTINCTIVE PART a part of something that distinguishes it ○ *a geographical feature* **2.** PART OF FACE a part of a face that contributes to its distinct character, especially the eyes, nose, or mouth **3.** PUBL REGULAR ARTICLE a regular item in a newspaper or magazine **4.** PUBL MAIN STORY a story or article that is given particular prominence in a newspaper or magazine **5.** BROADCAST MAIN TELEVISION OR RADIO PROGRAMME a television or radio programme that is considered highly important or popular **6.** ATTRACTIVE ASPECT OF SOMETHING something offered as a special attraction, e.g. a particular aspect of something ○ *a refrigerator with several energy-saving features* **7.** CINEMA FULL-LENGTH FILM a full-length film for the cinema **8.** CINEMA MAIN FILM IN PROGRAMME formerly, the main film in a cinema programme **9.** LING PROPERTY OF A LINGUISTIC UNIT a distinctive property of a linguistic unit. Voicing is a feature of the consonants *b*, *d*, and *g*. ■ *v* (**-tures, -turing, -tured**) **1.** *vt* CONTAIN SOMETHING AS IMPORTANT ELEMENT to have or present somebody or something as an important element of something ○ *This week's activities will feature pony-trekking and golf.* **2.** *vti* GIVE OR HAVE PROMINENCE IN PERFORMANCE to give prominence to somebody taking part in a performance or to something performed or portrayed in a performance, or be given prominence in this way ○ *a film featuring two of today's most popular actors* **3.** *vi* FIGURE IN SOMETHING to figure in or be a part of something ○ *Marriage doesn't feature in their plans.* **4.** *vt regional* RESEMBLE SOMEBODY to resemble somebody physically, especially facially ○ *She features her mother.* [14C. Via Old French *faiture* 'form' < Latin *factura* 'something made' < *fact-* (see FACT)] —**featured** *adj*

feature creature *n* somebody who adds excessive features to a design, software program, or website, often at the expense of coherence or utility (*slang*)

feature film *n* a full-length film for the cinema

feature-length *adj* being as long as a feature film ○ *a feature-length episode*

featureless /féechərləss/ *adj* lacking any distinctive characteristics or properties

feature programme *n* a television or radio programme devoted to one issue or topic

Feb. *abbr* CALENDAR February

febrifacient /fébbri fáysh'nt/ *adj* causing, producing, or promoting fever [Early 19C. < Latin *febris* 'fever']

febrific /fi bríffik/, **febriferous** /fi bríffərəss/ *adj* **1.** capable of causing somebody to have a fever **2.** affected by a fever [Early 18C. < obsolete French *fébrifique* < Latin *febris* 'fever']

febrifuge /fébbri fyooj/ *n* a drug that reduces fever [Late 17C. < French *fébrifuge* < Latin *febris* 'fever'] —**febrifugal** /fi bríffyoog'l/ *adj* —**febrifuge** *adj*

febrile /féeb rīl/ *adj* relating to, involving, or typical of fever [Mid-17C. < French *fébrile* or medieval Latin *febrilis* < Latin *febris* 'fever']

February /fébbroo əri, fébbyoo ri/ (*plural* **-ies**) *n* in the Gregorian calendar, the second month of the year, lasting 28 days or, in leap years, 29 days. See table at **calendar** [14C. Via Old French *feverier* < Latin *februarius (mensis)* '(month) of purification'; from an annual Roman festival]

USAGE The generally preferred pronunciation of ***February*** is /fébbroo əri/, in which the first *r* is sounded. The variant pronunciation, to which some people object, is /fébbyoo əri/, in which the first *r* is dropped. This dropping of *r* is an example of a normal process that happens when some speakers are confronted with the repeated occurrence of the same sound within a word. Finding it difficult to articulate both sounds, especially when trying to say a word fast, some speakers will simply drop one of the two sounds. It is also possible that the variant pronunciation of ***February*** was influenced by the pronunciation /jánnyoo əri, jánnyoo ri/ for *January*.

~~**Febuary**~~ incorrect spelling of **February**

fec. *abbr* he or she made it [Latin *fecit*]

feces *npl* BIOL US spelling of **faeces**

feckless /fékləss/ *adj* **1.** unable or unwilling to do anything useful **2.** lacking the thought or organization necessary to succeed ○ *feckless attempts at starting a business* [Late 16C. < obsolete *feck* 'value, efficacy', shortening of EFFECT] —**fecklessly** *adv* —**fecklessness** *n*

fecula /fékyoolə/ (*plural* **-lae** /-lee/) *n* **1.** a starch extracted as sediment from a mixture of water and crushed plants **2.** a piece of excrement, especially an insect dropping [Late 17C. < Latin *faecula* 'crust of wine' < *faex* 'dregs, sediment']

feculent /fékyoolənt/ *adj* very dirty or foul, especially polluted by excrement (*formal*) [15C. Directly or via French < Latin *faeculentus* < *faeces* (see FAECES)] —**feculence** *n*

fecund /fékənd, féek-/ *adj* **1.** capable of producing much vegetation or many offspring **2.** able to produce many different and original ideas ○ *a fecund liar* [14C. Directly or via French < Latin *fecundus*]

fecundate /fékən dayt, féek-/ (**-dates, -dating, -dated**) *vt* **1.** MAKE SOMEBODY OR SOMETHING PRODUCTIVE to make somebody or something fruitful or productive (*literary*) **2.** FERTILIZE SOMETHING to fertilize a plant (*archaic*) **3.** IMPREGNATE WOMAN OR FEMALE ANIMAL to make a woman or female animal pregnant (*archaic*) —**fecundation** /fékən dáysh'n, féek-/ *n*

fecundity /fi kúndəti/ *n* **1.** the ability to produce offspring, especially in large numbers **2.** the ability to produce many different and original ideas (*formal*)

fed past participle, past tense of **feed**

Fed /fed/, **fed** *n US* a Federal agent or official, especially an agent of the FBI or the EPA (*informal*)

fed. *abbr* POL **1.** federal **2.** federated **3.** federation

Fed. *abbr* **1.** Federal **2.** Federated **3.** Federation

fedayee /fə da̋a yee/ (*plural* **-yeen** /-yeen/), **fidayee** *n* an Arab commando or guerrilla, especially one who fights against Israel [Mid-20C. < Arabic, Persian *fida'i* 'somebody who sacrifices himself or herself']

federal /féddərəl/ *adj* **1. MADE UP OF ALLIES** relating to a form of government in which several states or regions defer some powers, e.g. in foreign affairs, to a central government while retaining a limited measure of self-government **2. CENTRAL** relating to a political unit established on a federal basis, especially its central government **3. ASSOCIATED** relating to or characteristic of a unified body with constituent parts that retain a measure of autonomy ■ *n* **SUPPORTER OF ALLIANCE** a supporter of joining an alliance [Mid-17C. < Latin *foeder-*, stem of *foedus* 'treaty'] —**federally** *adv*

Federal Bureau of Investigation *n* full form of **FBI**

Federal Court *n* in Australia, a national court that has jurisdiction in matters relating to corruption, bankruptcy, industrial relations, corporation law, taxation, and trade. It can overrule decisions made by Supreme Courts of the Australian territories and some decisions made by state Supreme Courts.

federal district *n* an area in which the seat of the national government of a federation such as the United States is located

federal government *n* **1.** the central government of a federation **2.** in Australia, the national government based in Canberra

federalise *vt* POL another spelling of **federalize**

federalism /féddərəlizəm/ *n* **1. POLITICAL SYSTEM** a political system in which several states or regions defer some powers, e.g. in foreign affairs, to a central government while retaining a limited measure of self-government **2. PRINCIPLE OF FEDERAL POLITICAL SYSTEM** the principle of a federal system of government **3. SUPPORT FOR FEDERAL POLITICAL SYSTEM** support for a federal system of government

Federalism *n* the political doctrine of the former Federalist Party of the United States

federalist /féddərəlist/ *n* a supporter of a federal system of government

Federalist *n* a supporter of the former Federalist Party of the United States

Federalist Party *n* a former political party of the United States advocating a strong centralized government within the federal system. Founded in 1787, it declined in influence after 1800.

federalize /féddərə līz/ (**-izes, -izing, -ized**), **federalise** (**-ises, -ising, -ised**) *vt* **1.** to bring various states together in a federal union **2.** to place something under the control of a federal government —**federalization** /féddərə lī záysh'n/ *n*

Federal Republic of Germany /féddərəl-/ the former West Germany

Federal Republic of Yugoslavia HIST ♦ **Serbia and Montenegro**

Federal Reserve Bank *n* in the United States, one of the 12 reserve banks responsible for regulating the affiliated banks in its own district

federate /féddə rayt/ (**-ates, -ating, -ated**) *vti* to join together in a federation, or cause various bodies to join together in a federation [Late 17C. < Latin *foederat-*, past participle of *foederare* < *foedus* 'treaty']

Federated States of Micronesia ♦ **Micronesia** (sense 2)

federation /féddə ráysh'n/ *n* **1. POLITICAL UNIT** a political unit formed from smaller units on a federal basis **2. ALLIANCE** a group of various bodies or parties that have united to achieve a common goal **3. JOINING IN FEDERAL UNION** an act of joining in a federal union or a federal system of government [Early 18C. Via French < Latin *foederation-* < *foederat-* (see FEDERATE)]

Federation /féddə ráysh'n/ *n* **1.** the uniting of the Australian colonies on the first day of 1901 to form the Commonwealth of Australia, ruled by a single federal government **2.** an Australian architectural style, typical of the period during which Federation took place, that is characterized by redbrick walls, terracotta roof tiles, ornate window frames, and stained-glass windows

federative /féddərətiv/ *adj* relating to, characteristic of, or forming a federation [Late 17C. < Latin *foederat-* (see FEDERATE)]

fedora /fi dáwrə/ *n* a soft felt hat with a brim and a crease along the length of its crown [Late 19C. < *Fédora*, drama by Victorien Sardou (1831–1908), French playwright]

fed up *adj* having reached the limits of tolerance or patience with somebody or something (*informal*) ○ *got fed up with working all the time*

fee /fee/ *n* **1. PAYMENT FOR SERVICES** a payment for professional services **2. CHARGE MADE BY INSTITUTION** a charge made by an institution, e.g. for membership, entrance, or the administering of an examination **3. RIGHT TO OWNERSHIP OF LAND** a right to land that can be passed on by inheritance **4.** HIST same as **fief** (sense 1) [14C. Via Anglo-Norman variant of Old French *feu* < medieval Latin *feudum* (see FEUD [2])]

ORIGIN *Fee* and its close relatives *feudal* and *fief* take us back to the beginnings of European feudal society, when the ownership of cattle symbolized wealth. The Indo-European source of *fee*, denoting 'livestock', is also the source of the German word *Vieh* 'cattle'.

SYNONYMS See *wage*.

feeble /feéb'l/ (**-bler, -blest**) *adj* **1.** lacking physical or mental strength or health **2.** unlikely to convince ○ *a feeble excuse* [12C. Via Old French *fe(i)ble* < Latin *flebilis* 'lamentable, weak' < *flere* 'weep'] —**feebleness** *n* —**feebly** *adv*

SYNONYMS See *weak*.

feeble-minded *adj* **1. OFFENSIVE TERM** an offensive term meaning foolish or thoughtless **2. NOT WELL THOUGHT-OUT** done without forethought or planning ○ *a feeble-minded plan* **3. OFFENSIVE TERM** an offensive term meaning below average in intelligence (*dated*) —**feeble-mindedly** *adv* —**feeble-mindedness** *n*

feed /feed/ *v* (**feeds, feeding, fed** /fed/) **1.** *vt* **GIVE FOOD TO SOMEBODY** to give food to a person or an animal **2.** *vt* **GIVE SOMETHING AS FOOD** to give something as food to a person or an animal ○ *fed the horse carrots* **3.** *vt* **SERVE AS FOOD FOR SOMEBODY** to serve as or be enough food for a person or an animal ○ *This loaf won't feed us all.* **4.** *vi* **EAT** to eat food, or take regular nourishment ○ *Most whales feed on plankton.* **5.** *vt* **SUPPORT SOMETHING** to sustain or encourage a belief or behaviour ○ *Compliments merely feed vanity.* **6.** *vt* **PROVIDE SOMETHING WITH NECESSARY MATERIAL** to provide something with the necessary materials for operation **7.** *vti* **MOVE GRADUALLY** to move something gradually into, through, or out of something, or be moved in this way **8.** *vt* THEATRE **GIVE PERFORMER CUE** to deliver a line or cue to another performer **9.** *vti* **PASS BALL TO PLAYER** to pass a ball to a team-mate (*informal*) **10.** *vt* UTIL **SUPPLY WITH POWER** to supply power or an electrical signal to a system, component, or station **11.** *vt* RUGBY **PUT BALL IN SCRUMMAGE ILLEGALLY** in rugby, to put the ball into the scrummage illegally at the feet of team-mates ■ *n* **1. ACT OF FEEDING** an act or occasion of feeding **2. FOOD** food, especially for animals or babies **3. LARGE MEAL** a meal, especially a large and satisfying one (*informal*) **4. PROVIDER OF MATERIAL FOR MACHINE** a device that supplies material to a machine, e.g. the paper tray on a printer **5.** THEATRE **SOMEBODY WHO PROVIDES CUES** somebody who delivers a line or cue to a performer [Old English *fēdan* < Germanic]

feed into *vt* **1.** to add weight and impetus to something **2.** to connect with and contribute to something larger, e.g. a road or river

feed up *vt* to give a person or an animal plenty of food to eat in order to build up that person's or animal's weight

feedback /feéd bak/ *n* **1. RETURN OF OUTPUT** the return of part of the output of a machine, system, or circuit to the input in a way that affects its performance **2. NOISE IN LOUDSPEAKER** the high whistling or howling noise caused by feedback in a loudspeaker **3. RESPONSE** comments in the form of opinions about and reactions to something, intended to provide useful information for future decisions and development

feedback circuit *n* a circuit in which a portion of the output signal is returned to the input, often in order to control or stabilize the circuit

feedback control loop *n* the connection or path that forms an electrical loop from the output to the input of a feedback circuit

feedback factor *n* the fraction of an output signal that is returned to and combined with the input signal

feedback inhibition *n* an internal control on a hormone or enzyme that causes a reduction in activity once the end product reaches a specific concentration

feedback loop *n* a cycle of behaviour in which two people each act to reinforce the other's action

feedbag /feéd bag/ *n* **1.** a bag or sack containing food for livestock **2.** *N Am* same as **nosebag**

feeder /feédər/ *n* **1. EATER** a person or animal that eats, especially a particular food or in a particular way **2. CONTAINER FOR ANIMAL'S FOOD** a device that supplies food for birds or other animals ○ *a bird feeder in the garden* **3. SUPPLIER OF FOOD** somebody who provides food **4. MACHINE PART** a part of a machine that accepts or controls the input of material to be processed ○ *a document feeder* **5. BIB** a baby's bib or bottle (*dated*) **6.** GEOG **TRIBUTARY** a stream or river that joins the flow of a larger one **7.** TRANSP **CONNECTING CARRIER** a road, railway, or airline that carries traffic from a relatively small place to a city in order to connect with a larger carrier **8.** UTIL **POWER LINE** a power line that carries power from a generating station to a substation or network **9.** BROADCAST **CONNECTION** a line that connects an aerial to a receiver or transmitter **10.** EDUC **PRIMARY SCHOOL** a primary school from which a secondary school receives an annual intake of pupils **11.** GARDENING **PLANT REQUIRING FERTILIZER** a plant that requires a large amount of fertilizer to grow, and especially flower, well ○ *Fuchsias are gross feeders.*

feeder school *n* a school among several in an area whose pupils go on to study at a particular school or college at a higher level

feeding frenzy *n* **1.** an instance of frantic activity centred on a person or organization that occurs when other people, especially journalists, sense an opportunity they can exploit (*informal*) **2.** an intense violent period of eating that occurs when a large number of animals of the same or related species such as sharks or piranhas converge on a food source

feeding ground *n* an area where wildlife regularly comes to feed

feedlot /feéd lot/ *n N Am* an area or building in which livestock are kept while being fattened for slaughter

feedstock /feéd stok/ *n* a raw material used in the industrial manufacture of a product

feedstuff /feéd stuf/ *n* feed for livestock, especially consisting of processed and balanced ingredients

feedthrough /feéd throo/ *n* an electrical conductor that connects two sides of a circuit board

feel /feel/ *v* (**feels, feeling, felt** /felt/) **1.** *vi* **SEEM TO YOURSELF** to seem to yourself to be in a particular physical or emotional state ○ *Don't feel sad.* **2.** *vi* **CAUSE PARTICULAR SENSATION** to cause a particular physical or emotional sensation ○ *The water feels cold.* **3.** *vt* **EXPERIENCE SOMETHING** to experience an emotion or physical sensation ○ *felt no regret* **4.** *vt* **HAVE SENSATION IN BODY PART** to have physical sensation in a part of the body **5.** *vt* **BE AFFECTED BY SOMETHING** to be deeply affected emotionally by something painful **6.** *vt* **TOUCH SOMETHING** to perceive something using the sense of touch **7.** *vt* **EXAMINE SOMETHING** to test or examine something by touching it **8.** *vt* **ADVANCE HESITANTLY** to make your way forward slowly, guided by the sense of touch, or tentatively, because what is ahead is hard to see or uncertain **9.** *vi* **USE TOUCH IN SEARCHING** to use the sense of touch to try to find something ○ *feel around for my keys* **10.** *vt* **THINK SOMETHING IS TRUE** to be convinced about something by instinct or intuition rather than concrete evidence ○ *I feel you're lying to me.* **11.** *vt* **BE AWARE OF SOMETHING** to be instinctively aware of something, usually an emotion, that is not visible or apparent **12.** *vt* **BELIEVE SOMETHING** to have the opinion or belief that something is the case ○

She felt she could no longer carry on. ■ *n* **1. ACT OF TOUCHING** an act of touching something **2. IMPRESSION GAINED FROM TOUCH** an impression of something gained through touching or being touched by it ○ *the feel of wool against the skin* **3. SENSE OF TOUCH** the sensation felt on touching something ○ *hot to the feel* **4. IMPRESSION SENSED FROM SOMETHING** an impression, appearance, effect, or atmosphere sensed from something ○ *a hotel with a more traditional feel* **5. INSTINCT FOR SOMETHING** an instinctive understanding of, or talent for, something ○ *He has a feel for these things.* **6. GROPE** a sexual touch, usually uninvited (*informal*) [Old English *fēlan* < Indo-European] ◇ **feel like 1.** to have an inclination or desire for something ○ *I don't feel like eating at present.* **2.** to have or acknowledge a physical or emotional condition that is considered comparable to something else ○ *They made me feel like a criminal.*

feel *vt* to experience sympathy or compassion for somebody

feel out *vt* to try to establish, often in an indirect way, the nature of a situation or somebody's attitude or opinion about something

feel up *vt* to touch somebody sexually, especially without permission (*informal*)

feel up to *vt* to consider yourself ready for something or able to do something

feeler /féelər/ *n* **1. SOMEBODY WHO FEELS** somebody who or something that feels something **2. ATTEMPT TO TEST OTHERS' REACTION** something said or done to test the reaction of others to an idea, plan, or project **3. ZOOL TOUCHING ORGAN** an organ of touch in various animals, e.g. an insect's antenna

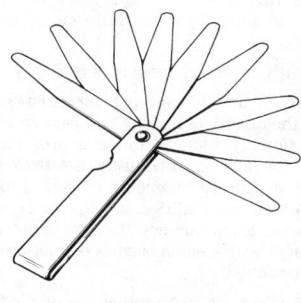

feeler gauge

feeler gauge *n* a thin strip of metal of a specific size used to measure or set a gap between parts of a mechanism

feel-good *adj* causing, involving, or typical of a sense of wellbeing or satisfaction

feel-good factor *n* something that causes or demonstrates a sense of wellbeing or satisfaction (*informal*) ○ *The government can show reduced unemployment figures and lower inflation but the all-important feel-good factor remains elusive in the public mind.*

feeling /féeling/ *n* **1. SENSE OF TOUCH** the sensation felt on touching something **2. ABILITY TO HAVE PHYSICAL SENSATION** the ability to perceive physical sensation in a part of the body ○ *Slowly the feeling returned to his fingers.* **3. SOMETHING EXPERIENCED PHYSICALLY OR MENTALLY** a perceived physical or mental sensation **4. SOMETHING FELT EMOTIONALLY** a perceived emotional state **5. AFFECTION** the emotional response of love, sympathy, or tenderness towards somebody **6. ABILITY TO EXPRESS EMOTION** the capacity to experience strong emotions **7. IMPRESSION SENSED** a particular impression, appearance, effect, or atmosphere sensed from something ○ *There was a feeling of abandonment about the old house.* **8. INSTINCTIVE AWARENESS** an instinctive awareness or presentiment of something ○ *I have a feeling you're going to be disappointed.* **9. INSTINCTIVE UNDERSTANDING OR TALENT** an instinctive understanding of or talent for something ○ *has a real feeling for this kind of work* **10. EXPRESSIVE ABILITY** the ability to express strong emotion, especially in performance ○ *Play the piece again with more feeling.* ■ **feelings** *npl* **SENSIBILITIES** somebody's emotional susceptibilities ○ *I didn't want to hurt their feelings.* ■ *adj* **1. SENSITIVE TO TOUCH** able to experience the sensation of touch **2. EXPRESSIVE** expressing or full of strong emotion **3.**

HAVING STRONG EMOTIONS easily or strongly affected by emotion —**feelingly** *adv*

fee-paying *adj* **1.** describes a school that charges parents directly for their children's education **2.** paying for a service ○ *Legal aid clients expect the same level of service as their fee-paying counterparts.*

fee simple (*plural* **fees simple**) *n* a form of property ownership in which the owner has outright and unconditional disposal rights

feet plural of **foot**

fee tail (*plural* **fees tail**) *n* a form of property ownership in which the property may be inherited only by a specific line of heirs

Fehling's solution /fáylingz-/ *n* a solution of copper sulphate, sodium potassium tartrate, and sodium hydroxide. Use: detection of aldehydes, including sugars. [Late 19C. After Hermann von *Fehling* (1812–85), German chemist]

Fehling's test, **Fehlings test** *n* the use of Fehling's solution to detect the presence of aldehydes and sugars [See FEHLING'S SOLUTION]

feign /fayn/ (**feigns, feigning, feigned**) *vt* **1. PRETEND SOMETHING** to make a show or pretence of something ○ *She feigned ignorance.* **2. INVENT SOMETHING** to make up or fabricate something **3. COPY SOMEBODY OR SOMETHING** to imitate or copy somebody or something [13C. < French *feign-*, present stem of *feindre* 'pretend, shirk' < Latin *fingere* 'fabricate, form']

feijoa /fay yṓ ə/ *n* **1.** a green fruit that tastes like pineapple and is eaten raw or cooked. Use: jams, preserves. **2.** a tree that produces feijoas. Native to: South America. Latin name: *Acca sellowiana*. [Late 19C. < modern Latin, after J. da Silva *Feijó* (1760–1824), Brazilian naturalist]

feijoada /fáy zhoo aád aa/ *n* a Brazilian party dish of meat with rice, black beans, green vegetables, and hot pepper sauce [Mid-20C. < Portuguese < *feijão* 'edible bean' < Latin *phaseolus*]

~~feind~~ incorrect spelling of **fiend**

feint[1] /faynt/ *n* **1. DECEPTIVE ACTION** a deceptive action made to disguise what is really intended **2. DECEPTIVE MOVE** a deceptive move in a competitive sport **3. MIL MOCK ATTACK** a mock attack by a military force, intended to draw the enemy's attention away from the true attack ■ *vti* (**feints, feinting, feinted**) **MAKE DECEPTIVE MOVE** to make a movement intended to deceive somebody [Late 17C. < French *feinte* 'sham, pretence' < past participle of *feindre* (see FEIGN)]

SPELLCHECK See *faint*.

feint[2] /faynt/ *adj* describes paper with faint horizontal lines across it as a guide for writing [Late 17C. < French *feinte* < form of *feindre* (see FEIGN)]

feisty /físti/ (**-ier, -iest**) *adj* (*informal*) **1.** characterized by spirited, sometimes aggressive, behaviour **2.** *N Am* likely to respond in an irritable or touchy way —**feistily** *adv* —**feistiness** *n*

felafel *n* **FOOD** another spelling of **falafel**

feldspar /féld spaar/, **felspar** /fél-/ *n* an extremely common aluminosilicate mineral containing varying proportions of calcium, sodium, potassium, and other elements. Feldspar minerals are subdivided into two groups, alkali feldspars and plagioclase feldspars. [Late 18C. Alteration of German *Feldspath*, literally 'field mineral']

feldspathic /feld spáthik/, **felspathic** /fel-/ *adj* consisting of, containing, or typical of feldspar [Mid-19C. < German *Feldspath* 'feldspar']

feldspathoid /féld spath oyd/ *n* a mineral of a group similar to the feldspars but lower in silica [Late 19C. < German *Feldspath* 'feldspar']

felicitate /fə líssi tayt/ (**-tates, -tating, -tated**) *vt* to congratulate somebody, or wish somebody happiness (*formal*) [Early 17C. < late Latin *felicitat-*, past participle of *felicitare* 'make happy' < Latin *felix* 'fruitful, happy'] —**felicitator** *n*

felicitation /fə lissi táysh'n/ (*formal*) *n* an act of congratulating somebody or wishing somebody happiness ■ **felicitations** *npl* used as a greeting or to wish somebody happiness

felicitous /fə líssitəss/ *adj* **1. APPROPRIATE** appropriate or highly suitable ○ *a felicitous choice of words* **2.**

PLEASANT pleasing or agreeable **3. FORTUNATE** happy or fortunate [Mid-16C. < FELICITY] —**felicitously** *adv* —**felicitousness** *n*

felicity /fə líssəti/ (*plural* **-ties**) *n* **1. HAPPINESS** happiness or contentment **2. SOMETHING PRODUCING HAPPINESS** something that creates happiness **3. APPROPRIATENESS** an appropriate or pleasing manner **4. SOMETHING APPROPRIATE** something appropriate or pleasing [14C. Via French < Latin *felicitas* < *felix* 'fruitful, happy']

felid /féelid/ (*plural* **-lids** or *same*) *n* ZOOL same as **feline** (*technical*) [Late 19C. < modern Latin *Felidae* < Latin *feles* 'cat']

feline /fée līn/ *adj* **1. OF CAT FAMILY** belonging to or typical of animals of the cat family, including lions, tigers, and domestic cats **2. RESEMBLING CAT** similar to a cat, especially in graceful movement or stealthiness ○ *feline suppleness* ■ *n* **MEMBER OF CAT FAMILY** an animal belonging to the cat family. Domestic cats, lions, and tigers are felines. Family: Felidae. [Late 17C. < Latin *felinus* < *feles* 'cat'] —**felinely** *adv* —**felineness** *n*

feline distemper *n* an infectious viral disease of cats that causes vomiting and diarrhoea and is often fatal

fell[1] /fel/ past tense of **fall**

fell[2] /fel/ *vt* (**fells, felling, felled**) **1. CHOP TREE DOWN** to cut down a tree **2. KNOCK SOMEBODY DOWN** to knock somebody down, or cause somebody to fall **3. HANDICRAFT SEW SEAM FLAT** to sew a seam by turning an edge over and sewing it down on the inside ■ *n* **1. NUMBER OF TREES CUT DOWN** an amount of timber cut down at one time or over one period **2. HANDICRAFT SEWN SEAM** a seam sewn by turning an edge over and sewing it down on the inside [Old English *fellan* 'cause to fall' < Germanic] —**fellable** *adj*

fell[3] /fel/ *adj* (*archaic or literary*) **1.** having an extremely cruel or vicious character **2.** capable of killing somebody or destroying something [13C. < Old French *fel*, form of *felon* (see FELON[1])]

fell[4] /fel/ *n* a hillside or mountainside without trees [13C. < Old Norse *fjall* 'hill' < Indo-European]

fell[5] /fel/ *n* **1.** the hide of an animal **2.** the thin membrane between an animal's hide and its flesh [Old English < Indo-European]

fella /féllə/ *n* a man or boy (*informal*) [Mid-19C. Representing nonstandard pronunciation of FELLOW]

fellah /féllə/ (*plural* **-lahin** /féllə heèn/ or **-laheen** or **-lahs**) *n* in an Arab country, a member of the labouring class who lives off the land [Mid-18C. < Arabic *fallah* 'tiller of the soil' < *falahah* 'split, till the soil']

fellate /fe láyt/ (**-lates, -lating, -lated**) *vti* to sexually stimulate a man's genitals using the tongue and lips [Late 19C. < Latin *fellat-* (see FELLATIO)] —**fellator** *n*

fellatio /fe láyshi ō/, **fellation** /fe láysh'n/ *n* the sexual stimulation of a man's genitals using the tongue and lips [Late 19C. < modern Latin < Latin *fellat-*, past participle of *fellare* 'suck']

feller[1] /féllər/ *n* **1.** somebody who fells trees **2.** a person who or a machine attachment that fells seams [14C. < FELL[2]]

feller[2] /féllər/ *n* a man or boy (*informal*) [Early 19C. Representing nonstandard pronunciation of FELLOW]

Federico Fellini: directing his *Satyricon* (1969)

Fellini /fe léeni/, **Federico** (1920–93) Italian film director. He was known for his use of fantasy and satire, and won Academy Awards for *La Strada*

(1954), *Nights of Cabiria* (1957), 8½ (1963), and *Amarcord* (1974).

> 'The visionary is the only true realist.'
> [Federico Fellini. Recalled on his death, *USA Today*; 1 November 1993]

felloe /félló/, **felly** /félli/ (*plural* **-lies**) *n* an outer rim of a wooden wheel, or a segment of this, with a metal tyre shrunk around it [Old English *felg* < Indo-European, 'turn']

fellow /félló/ *n* **1.** MALE a man or boy (*dated*) **2.** COMPANION a companion or colleague (*dated*) **3.** ONE OF PAIR either of a pair of objects (*dated*) **4.** EQUAL somebody or something of the same rank or quality (*dated*) **5.** BOYFRIEND somebody's boyfriend (*dated informal*) **6.** EDUC MEMBER OF UNIVERSITY STAFF somebody on the governing board of a university or college, usually also a member of the teaching staff ○ *a Cambridge fellow* **7.** EDUC GRADUATE STUDENT a graduate student who is supported by a university department to teach or do research ○ *a research fellow* ■ *adj* BEING IN SAME GROUP belonging to the same group, occupation, rank, or location [Pre-12C. < Old Norse *félagi* 'partner' < *fé* 'money']

CULTURAL NOTE *Poor Fellow My Country*, a novel (1975) by Australian writer Xavier Herbert. Set in northern Australia between 1936 and 1942, it depicts the disastrous effects of white settlement on Aboriginal peoples through the interwoven stories of pastoralists, government representatives, and local Aboriginals. Running to 850,000 words, it is the longest novel ever published in Australia.

Fellow *n* **1.** a member of a learned or scientific society ○ *Fellow of the Royal College of Surgeons* **2.** EDUC another spelling of **fellow** *n* (sense 6)

fellow feeling *n* an awareness of having interests in common with other people and feeling sympathy for them

fellowship /félló ship/ *n* **1.** SHARING OF EXPERIENCES a sharing of common interests, goals, experiences, or views **2.** GROUP OF LIKE-MINDED PEOPLE a group of people who share common interests, goals, experiences, or views **3.** COMPANIONSHIP companionship or friendly association **4.** SIMILARITY membership in a group, or the sharing of characteristics with others **5.** EDUC GRADUATE POST a university post awarded to a graduate student who is supported by a university department to teach or undertake research **6.** EDUC FINANCIAL ENDOWMENT a financial endowment set up to support graduate students **7.** EDUC MEMBERSHIP OF UNIVERSITY STAFF membership on the governing board of a university or college, usually also involving teaching duties

Fellowship *n* the fellows of a university or college considered as a body

fellow traveller *n* **1.** a sympathizer with the cause of an organized group, especially the Communist Party, without joining it **2.** somebody who takes the same journey as another at the same time

fell-running *n* the sport of competitive running over fells

fell-walking *n* the pastime of walking on fells

felly *n* same as **felloe**

felo de se /féeló di sée/ (*plural* **felones de se** /fee ló neez-/ or **felos de se**) *n* **1.** somebody who commits suicide **2.** an act of committing suicide [Early 17C. < Anglo-Latin, 'crime against yourself']

felon[1] /féllən/ *n* formerly in England and Wales, somebody guilty of a felony ■ *adj* characterized by evil or depravity (*archaic*) [13C. Via French < medieval Latin *fellon-* 'evildoer']

felon[2] /féllən/ *n* MED same as **whitlow** [14C. Origin ?]

felonious /fə lóni əss/ *adj* relating to felonies or a felony —**feloniously** *adv* —**feloniousness** *n*

felony /félləni/ (*plural* **-nies**) *n* formerly in England and Wales, and currently in the United States, a serious crime such as murder that is punished more severely than a misdemeanour [13C. < Old French *felonie* < *felon* (see FELON[1])]

felsic /félssik/ *adj* describes igneous rocks or minerals that are light in colour, indicating relatively high levels of quartz and feldspars [Early 20C. Blend of FELDSPAR + SILICA]

felsite /fél sīt/ *n* a light-coloured igneous rock that consists chiefly of feldspar and quartz and can only be precisely classified by microscopic examination [Late 18C. < FELDSPAR] —**felsitic** /fel síttik/ *adj*

felspar *n* MINERALS another spelling of **feldspar**

felspathic *adj* MINERALS another spelling of **feldspathic**

felt[1] /felt/ past participle, past tense of **feel**

felt[2] /felt/ *n* **1.** WOOL OR ANIMAL-HAIR FABRIC a fabric made from wool or animal hair by compressing, heating, or treating the fibres with chemicals **2.** SYNTHETIC FABRIC a synthetic fabric made by the process of matting, especially a heavy paper permeated with asphalt, used as a roof sealant ○ *roofing felt* ■ *v* (**felts, felting, felted**) **1.** *vt* MAKE FELT OUT OF SOMETHING to make wool or hair into felt fabric **2.** *vt* PUT FELT ON ROOF to cover a roof with roofing felt **3.** *vi* BECOME MATTED to become matted, or come to resemble felt [Old English < Indo-European, 'strike, beat, pound'] —**felty** *adj*

felting /félting/ *n* **1.** felt fabric **2.** the process of making felt

felt pen *n* same as **felt-tipped pen**

felt tip *n* **1.** a pen point made from felt or a similar compressed fibre **2.** same as **felt-tipped pen**

felt-tipped pen *n* a pen with a point made from felt or a similar compressed fibre

felucca

felucca /fə lúkə/ *n* a small sailing boat with curving triangular sails (**lateen-rigged**), used in the Mediterranean and on the Nile [Early 17C. Via Italian < Mediterranean Arabic *fluka*]

felwort /fél wurt/ *n* a plant of the gentian family. Flowers: purple. Native to: Europe, China. Latin name: *Gentianella amarella*. [Old English *feldwyrt* 'field plant']

fem *n*, *adj* another spelling of **femme** (*slang*)

fem. *abbr* **1.** BIOL female **2.** GRAM feminine

FEMA /féemə/ *abbr US* Federal Emergency Management Agency

female /fée mayl/ *adj* **1.** OF WOMEN relating or belonging to women or girls **2.** BIOL OF THE SEX THAT PRODUCES OFFSPRING relating or belonging to the sex that produces sex cells (**gametes**) that fuse with male sex cells during sexual reproduction **3.** BOT PRODUCING SEEDS describes the part of a plant that produces the female sex cells, e.g. a carpel **4.** BOT HAVING CARPELS describes flowers that have carpels but no stamens **5.** ENG MADE WITH RECESS describes a component or part of a component such as an electric socket that has a recess designed to receive a corresponding projecting part ■ *n* **1.** BIOL FEMALE ORGANISM a female person or animal **2.** OFFENSIVE TERM an offensive term for a girl or woman **3.** BOT PLANT WITH FEMALE FLOWERS a plant that has only female flowers [14C. Alteration (after MALE) of Old French *femelle* < Latin *femella* < *femina* (see FEMININE)] —**femaleness** *n*

female circumcision, **female genital mutilation** *n* the practice of circumcision of adolescent women in some cultures that generally involves the surgical removal of the clitoris or the sewing up of the vaginal opening

female impersonator *n* a man, often appearing as a solo theatrical performer, who dresses as and imitates a woman

feme /fem/ *n* a woman or wife [Mid-16C. Via Anglo-Norman < Latin *femina* (see FEMININE)]

feme covert /-kúvərt/ (*plural* **femes covert**) *n* a married woman [< Anglo-Norman, 'covered woman']

feme sole /-sól/ (*plural* **femes sole**) *n* a single woman, taken to include unmarried women, widows, divorcées, and married women living independently and separately from their husbands [< Anglo-Norman, 'single woman']

femineity /fémmə née əti/ *n* same as **femininity** (sense 1) [Early 19C. < Latin *femineus* 'womanish' < *femina* (see FEMININE)]

feminine /fémmənin/ *adj* **1.** CONVENTIONALLY ASSOCIATED WITH WOMEN conventionally thought to be appropriate for a woman or girl **2.** ATTRIBUTED TO WOMEN considered to be characteristic of women **3.** EFFEMINATE relating to qualities, actions, or types of behaviour in a man or boy that are conventionally associated with women or girls **4.** GRAM LINGUISTICALLY FEMALE IN GENDER describes a class of words or forms in various languages that includes the majority of words referring to females ■ *n* GRAM FEMININE WORD OR FORM a word or form that in a specific language is classified grammatically as feminine [14C. Via French < Latin *femininus* < *femina* 'woman' < Indo-European, 'suck'] —**femininely** *adv* —**feminineness** *n*

feminine caesura *n* a pause in a line of scanned verse that does not come immediately after a stressed syllable

feminine ending *n* **1.** an inflectional morpheme attached to the end of a word that marks it as belonging to the feminine gender **2.** an ending of a line of verse that finishes with an extra unstressed syllable

feminine rhyme *n* a rhyme scheme in which the lines containing rhyming words end in unstressed syllables

~~femininity~~ incorrect spelling of **femininity**

femininity /fémmə nínnəti/ *n* **1.** CONVENTIONALLY FEMININE QUALITY the quality of looking and behaving in ways conventionally thought to be appropriate for a woman or girl **2.** CONVENTIONAL IDEA ABOUT WOMEN a manner or feature commonly attributed to women **3.** EFFEMINACY the qualities, actions, or types of behaviour in a man or boy that are conventionally associated with women or girls **4.** WOMEN women as a group (*dated*)

feminise *vt* SOC SCI, MED another spelling of **feminize**

feminism /fémmənizəm/ *n* **1.** belief in the need to secure rights and opportunities for women equal to those of men, or a commitment to securing these **2.** the movement committed to securing and defending rights and opportunities for women that are equal to those of men [Mid-19C. < French *féminisme*] —**feminist** *n*, *adj*

feminize /fémmə nīz/ (**-nizes, -nizing, -nized**), **feminise** (**-nises, -nising, -nised**) *vt* **1.** MAKE SOMETHING SUITABLE FOR WOMEN to give somebody or something characteristics considered suitable for women ○ *seeking to feminize the profession* **2.** MAKE SOMEBODY CONVENTIONALLY LIKE WOMAN to make somebody behave in ways conventionally associated with women (*often passive*) **3.** MED MAKE MALE DEVELOP FEMALE SEXUAL CHARACTERISTICS to cause a man to develop secondary female sexual characteristics as a result of a hormone imbalance —**feminization** /fémmə nī záysh'n/ *n*

femme /fem/, **fem** (*slang*) *n* **1.** WOMAN a woman or girl **2.** SOMEBODY BEHAVING FEMININELY somebody who behaves in a conventionally feminine way ■ *adj* BEHAVING IN FEMININE WAY describes somebody, originally usually a lesbian, who behaves in a conventionally feminine way [Early 19C. < French < Latin *femina* (see FEMININE)]

femme fatale /fám fə taál/ (*plural* **femmes fatales** /*pronunc. same*/) *n* a woman who is considered to be highly attractive and to have a destructive effect on those who succumb to her charms (*disapproving*) [< French, 'deadly woman']

femora ANAT plural of **femur**

femoral /fémmərəl/ *adj* relating to, in, or involving the thigh or femur [Late 18C. < Latin *femor-*, stem of *femur* 'thigh']

femto- *prefix* a thousand million millionth (10^{-15}) ○

femtometre Symbol **f** [< Danish or Norwegian *femten* 'fifteen']

femur /féemər/ (*plural* **femurs** or **femora** /fémmərə/) *n* **1.** ANAT MAIN BONE IN HUMAN THIGH the main bone in the human thigh, the strongest bone in the body **2.** ZOOL LARGE BONE IN VERTEBRATE LEG a bone equivalent to the human thighbone in other vertebrates **3.** INSECTS INSECT LEG PART the third and largest segment of an insect's leg, between the trochanter and the tibia [Mid-16C. < Latin, 'thigh']

fen /fen/ *n* an inland area of low-lying marshy land, now often drained and cultivated because of its nutrient-rich soil [Old English *fen(n)* < Germanic]

fence /fenss/ *n* **1.** ENCLOSING STRUCTURE a structure erected to enclose an area and act as a barrier, especially one made of wood or with posts and wire **2.** OBSTACLE a specially constructed obstacle that horses must jump over in a race or as part of a showjumping circuit **3.** BUYER OF STOLEN GOODS somebody who buys stolen goods from thieves and then sells the goods (*slang*) ■ *v* (**fences, fencing, fenced**) **1.** *vt* ENCLOSE AREA WITH FENCE to enclose an area or bar a gap by erecting a fence **2.** *vti* DEAL IN STOLEN GOODS to buy or sell stolen goods (*slang*) **3.** *vi* FIGHT WITH SWORD to fight using a slender sword, formerly in combat, now as a competitive sport **4.** *vi* EVADE QUESTIONING to avoid answering a question ○ *a candidate fencing with the press* **5.** *vi* ARGUE to engage in repartee or witty argument with somebody [14C. Shortening of DEFENCE] —**fenceless** *adj* —**fencer** *n* ◇ **mend fences** to restore good relations with a friend or neighbour after a dispute or quarrel ◇ **sit** or **be on the fence** to refuse to make a choice between sides in a dispute or contest

fence in *vt* **1.** to enclose somebody or something inside a fence **2.** to prevent somebody from moving or acting freely

fence off *vt* to enclose or separate something with a fence

fence-sitter *n* somebody who is unwilling or unable to choose between sides (*informal*)

Popperfoto

fencing: as one fencer lunges forwards the other prepares to parry

fencing /fénssing/ *n* **1.** SWORD FIGHTING the art or practice of fighting with slender swords, formerly in combat, now as a competitive sport **2.** FENCE MATERIALS materials used in making fences, e.g. posts and wire **3.** FENCES fences considered collectively **4.** EVASIVENESS evasiveness in responding to questioning **5.** REPARTEE repartee or witty argument **6.** DEALING IN STOLEN GOODS the business of buying and selling stolen goods (*slang*)

fend /fend/ (**fends, fending, fended**) *v* **1.** *vt* to defend somebody or something from harm (*archaic*) **2.** *vi* *regional* to strive or make an effort [13C. Shortening of DEFEND] —**fend** *n*

fend for *vt* to support or provide for somebody, especially yourself ○ *He's used to fending for himself.*

fend off *vt* **1.** to push somebody or something away, or turn somebody or something aside **2.** to push against an approaching vessel or object in order to prevent a collision

fender /féndər/ *n* **1.** FIREGUARD a metal guard built onto the front of an open fire to prevent coals from falling out **2.** PROTECTIVE CUSHION an inflatable cylinder, rubber tyre, or something similar, hung over the side of a vessel to protect it from rubbing against a pier or another ship **3.** *N Am* AUTOMOT same as **wing** (sense 12) **4.** *N Am* CYCLING same as **mudguard 5.** *US* RAIL METAL GUARD AT FRONT OF LOCOMOTIVE a metal guard built

onto the front of a locomotive to push away any obstruction and lessen injury to people or animals struck by the locomotive

fender-bender *n* *N Am* a collision between vehicles in which only minor damage occurs (*informal*)

fender pile *n* a pile driven into the bottom of a body of water near a berth to protect the pier or wharf against damage by incoming vessels

Fenech /fénnək/, **Jeff** (*b.* 1964) Australian boxer. He was the winner of three world titles, including the IBC world bantamweight championship (1985), and the WBC super-bantamweight (1987) and featherweight (1988) championships. Full name **Fenech, Jeffrey**

fenestella /fénnə stéllə/ (*plural* **-lae** /-lee/) *n* **1.** PART OF ALTAR a small opening for holding relics at the south side of an altar in a Roman Catholic church **2.** NICHE IN CHANCEL WALL a niche in the wall of a chancel that houses the piscina and credence table **3.** ARCHIT WINDOW a small window or similar opening in a wall [Late 18C. < Latin, diminutive of *fenestra* 'window']

fenestra /fi néstrə/ (*plural* **-trae** /-tree/) *n* **1.** ANAT SMALL ANATOMICAL OPENING a small anatomical opening covered by a membrane, e.g. either of two cavities (**fenestra rotunda, fenestra ovalis**) inside the ear **2.** INSECTS TRANSPARENT MARKING a transparent marking on a moth's wing **3.** ARCHIT WINDOW a window or similar opening on the outer wall of a building [Early 19C. < Latin, 'window'] —**fenestral** *adj*

fenestrated /fénnə straytid, fə néss traytid/, **fenestrate** /fénnə strayt, fə néss trayt/ *adj* **1.** ARCHIT HAVING WINDOWS made with windows or similar openings **2.** BIOL WITH OPENINGS having openings or perforations **3.** INSECTS WITH TRANSPARENT MARKINGS describes a moth's wing that has transparent markings

fenestration /fénni stráysh'n/ *n* **1.** the design and placing of windows in a building **2.** the surgical cutting of an opening in the labyrinth of the inner ear to restore somebody's hearing

feng shui /fúng shwáy/ *n* a Chinese system that studies people's relationships to their environment, especially their home or workspace, in order to achieve maximum harmony with the spiritual forces believed to influence all places [Late 18C. < Chinese, 'wind water']

Fenian /féeni ən/ *n* **1.** IRISH REVOLUTIONARY a member of an Irish revolutionary republican organization founded in the United States in 1857 to fight for Irish independence **2.** LEGENDARY IRISH WARRIOR in Irish legend, a member of the warriors, the Fianna **3.** *regional* OFFENSIVE TERM an offensive term for an Irish Roman Catholic, especially one with nationalist sympathies [Early 19C. < Old Irish *féne*, the ancient population of Ireland] —**Fenianism** *n*

fenland /fén land/ *n* a wide inland area of low-lying marshy land, especially in East Anglia

fennec /fén ek/ *n* a small large-eared desert fox with light tan fur. Native to: North Africa. Latin name: *Vulpes zerda*. [Late 18C. Via Arabic *fanak* < Persian]

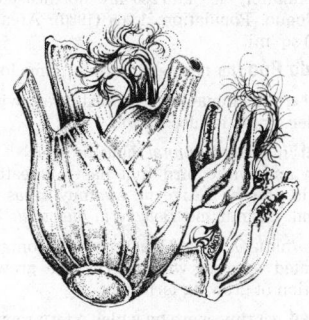

fennel

fennel /fénn'l/ *n* **1.** an aromatic plant, the seeds and feathery leaves of which have a light aniseed flavour. Use: cooking. Native to: Europe. Latin name: *Foeniculum vulgare* var. dulce. **2.** a plant that produces a clump of short edible stalks resembling celery but with an aniseed flavour. Latin name: *Foeniculum vulgare* var. azoricum. [Old English *finugle* < Latin *faeniculum*, diminutive of *faenum* 'hay']

Fens /fenz/ region of reclaimed marshland in eastern England surrounding the Wash and covering parts of Cambridgeshire, Lincolnshire, and Norfolk. Area: 1,800 sq. km/695 sq. mi.

fentanyl /féntənil/ *n* a narcotic drug. Use: painkiller. [Alteration of the drug's chemical name]

fenugreek

fenugreek /fénnyoo greek/ *n* **1.** the aromatic seeds of a leguminous plant. Use: in medicine, food flavouring. **2.** the leguminous plant whose seeds are fenugreek. Native to: Europe, Asia. Latin name: *Trigonella foenum-graecum*. [Old English *fenogrecum* and Old French *fenugrec* < Latin *faenugraecum* 'Greek hay', dried and used by the Romans for fodder]

fenuron /fénnyoo ron/ *n* a white crystalline compound. Use: herbicide. Formula: $C_9H_{12}N_2O$. [< alteration of PHEN- + UREA]

feoff /feef/ *n* HIST same as **fief** (sense 1) [13C. < Anglo-Norman *feoffer* < Old French *feu, fieu* 'fee' < medieval Latin *feudum* (see FEUD [2])] —**feoff** *vt* —**feoffment** /féfmənt, feéf-/ *n*

feoffee /fe feé/ *n* **1.** a vassal holding land granted by a feudal lord **2.** a trustee holding freehold property for a charitable purpose

feoffment /féfmənt, feéf-/ *n* a grant of freehold property by a feudal lord

FEP *abbr* COMPUT front-end processor

-fer *suffix* a person or thing that bears ○ *conifer* [< Latin < *ferre* 'carry']

feral /férrəl, feérəl/, **ferine** /fé rīn, feér īn/ *adj* **1.** GONE WILD describes animals or plants that live or grow in the wild after having been domestically reared or cultivated ○ *feral cats* **2.** SAVAGE similar to or typical of a wild animal, or living wild **3.** *Aus* HIPPIE unconventional in personal appearance or behaviour ■ *n Aus* ENVIRONMENTALIST a person who supports environmental causes and displays his or her rejection of materialism by dressing in an unconventional and often unkempt manner typified by dreadlocks, piercings etc. [Early 17C. < Latin *fera* 'wild animal']

fer-de-lance /fáir də laánss/ (*plural* same or **fer-de-lances** or **fers-de-lance** /*pronunc. same*/) *n* a large, highly venomous snake of the pit viper family. Native to: tropical America. Latin name: *Bothops atrox*. [Late 19C. < French, 'spearhead']

Ferdinand I /fúrdi nand/ (1005?–65) king of Castile (1035–65) and León (1037–65). He reconquered much of Portugal from the Moors. Known as **Ferdinand the Great**

Ferdinand I (1503–64) Holy Roman Emperor (1558–64), king of Bohemia (1526–64), and king of Germany (1531–64). He negotiated the treaties of Passau (1552) and Augsburg (1555), which ended the religious wars in Germany by allowing territorial princes to determine the religion of their subjects.

'Let justice be done, though the world perish.'
[Motto of Ferdinand I]

Ferdinand III (1608–57) king of Hungary. As king of Bohemia (1627–57) and Holy Roman Emperor (1637–57), he commanded the imperial armies fighting the Thirty Years' War.

Ferdinand V (1452–1516) king of Castile (1474–1504); as Ferdinand II, king of Sicily (1468–1516) and of Aragón (1479–1516); as Ferdinand III, king of Naples (1503–16). His marriage to Isabella I of Castile (1469)

united the two most powerful kingdoms of Spain. His reign saw the completion of the reconquest of Spain from the Moors (1492), the four voyages of Columbus to the Americas (1492–1504), and the establishment of the Spanish Inquisition (1478). Known as **Ferdinand the Catholic**

fe real /fə reèl/ *adv* really or honestly (*slang; used in Black English*)

feretory /férrətəri/ (*plural* **-ries**) *n* a container or an area in a church where relics are kept [14C. < Old French *fiertre* < Greek *pheretron* 'bier' < *pherein* 'carry']

Fergana /fər gaànə/ city in eastern Uzbekistan, about 420 km/260 mi. east of the capital, Tashkent. Population: 191,000 (1994). Former name **Skobelev** (1907–24)

Ferguson /fúrgəss'n/, **Sir Alex** (*b*. 1941) British footballer and manager. After successfully managing Aberdeen (1978–86) he moved to Manchester United, winning many competitions, including the unique treble of FA Cup, Premiership, and European Champions' league titles (1999).

feria /feéri ə/ (*plural* **-rias** or **-riae** /-ri ee/) *n* in the Roman Catholic Church, any weekday that is not a feast day [14C. < Latin, 'holiday'] —**ferial** *adj*

ferine *adj* ZOOL same as **feral** *adj* (sense 1)

Feringhee /fə ríng gi/, **Feringhi** *n* in South and Southwest Asia and parts of East Asia, an offensive term for a foreigner, especially one with white skin (*offensive*) [Early 17C. Via Urdu < Persian *firangi* 'Frankish, western']

ferly /fúrli/, **ferlie** *Scotland n* (*plural* **-lies**; *plural* **-lies**) a curious object or occurrence ■ *adj* (**-lier**, **-liest**) not usually seen or experienced [Old English *færlic* 'dangerous, alarming, awesome' < *fær* (see FEAR)]

Fermanagh /fər mánnə/ county in southwestern Northern Ireland. The main town is Enniskillen.

Fermat /fər mát, fúr maa/, **Pierre de** (1601–65) French mathematician. One of the greatest 17th-century mathematical theorists, he was a pioneer in the fields of probability theory, analytical geometry, and differential calculus.

'To divide a cube into two other cubes, a fourth power or in general any power whatever into two powers of the same denomination above the second is impossible, and I have assuredly found an admirable proof of this, but the margin is too narrow to contain it.'
[Attributed to Pierre de Fermat]

fermata /fər maàtə/ (*plural* **-matas** or **-mate** /-tay/) *n* **1.** an act of holding a musical note, chord, or pause longer than the indicated time value **2.** MUSIC same as **pause** *n* (sense 5) [Late 19C. < Italian]

Fermat's last theorem *n* hypothesis about whole numbers proven about 330 years after Fermat conjectured it in the mid-17th century. The theorem holds that of whole numbers raised to the same whole-numbered powers greater than two, no two of them add to a third; that is, $a^n + b^n = c^n$ has no solution in whole numbers if $n > 2$.

ferment *vti* /fər mént/ (**-ments**, **-menting**, **-mented**) **1.** SUBJECT TO OR UNDERGO FERMENTATION to subject something to fermentation, or be subjected to fermentation **2.** STIR OR BE STIRRED UP to stir up somebody or something, or be stirred up **3.** DEVELOP to cause, develop, or evolve something, or be developed or evolved ○ *Her brain was continually fermenting new schemes.* ■ *n* /fúr ment/ **1.** COMMOTION a state or situation of extreme agitation or commotion about something **2.** SUBSTANCE CAUSING FERMENTATION an agent, enzyme, or cell that causes fermentation [14C. < Old French *fermenter* < Latin *fermentum* 'yeast'] —**fermentability** /fər méntə bílləti/ *n* —**fermentable** *adj* —**fermentative** *adj*

SPELLCHECK Do not confuse the spelling of *ferment* and *foment* ('cause trouble'), which sound similar. The verb *ferment* means 'subject to the chemical process of fermentation', 'stir up', or 'develop', as in *ferment new ideas*. It is this last sense that perhaps most causes confusion with *foment*, which means 'stir up trouble or rebellion'.

fermentation /fúr men táysh'n/ *n* the breakdown of

carbohydrates by microorganisms. Many pharmaceuticals are produced by fermentation.

fermentation lock *n* a valve used in winemaking to seal a container of fermenting wine, allowing gas to escape but no air to enter

fermenter /fər méntər/ *n* **1.** BIOCHEM same as **ferment** *n* (sense 2) **2.** *also* **fermentor** an apparatus that maintains the ideal conditions for fermentation, e.g. the growing of microorganisms

fermi /fúrmi/ *n* a unit of length used mainly for nuclear distances, equivalent to 10^{-15} m [Early 20C. After Enrico FERMI]

Fermi /fúrmi/, **Enrico** (1901–54) Italian-born US physicist. He received the Nobel Prize in physics (1938) for his work on particle physics and nuclear fission. He constructed the first atomic pile at the University of Chicago (1942).

'Whatever Nature has in store for mankind, unpleasant as it may be, men must accept, for ignorance is never better than knowledge.'
[Enrico Fermi, *Atoms in the Family: My Life with Enrico Fermi*, Laura Fermi; 1955]

Fermi-Dirac statistics *n* statistical mechanics used to find the energy distribution of particles that obey the Pauli exclusion principle (*takes a singular or plural verb*) [After Enrico FERMI and Paul DIRAC]

fermion /fúrmi on/ *n* an elementary particle with a half-integral spin that obeys the Pauli exclusion principle. Electrons, protons, and neutrons are types of fermion. [After Enrico FERMI]

fermium /fúrmi əm/ *n* an artificially produced radioactive element. Source: bombardment of plutonium with neutrons. Use: tracer. Symbol **Fm**. See table at **element** [After Enrico FERMI]

fern

fern /furn/ (*plural* **ferns** or *same*) *n* a plant that has roots, stems, and fronds, but no flowers, and reproduces by means of spores. Order: Filicales. [Old English *fearn* < Indo-European] —**ferny** *adj*

Fernando de Noronha /fur nándō də no rónyə/ island group in the Atlantic Ocean off the coast of Brazil, approximately 400 km/250 mi. northeast of Cape São Roque. Population: 1,266 (1980). Area: 26 sq. km/10 sq. mi.

Fernando Póo /fər nándo pō/ former name for **Bioko**

fern bar *n* a fashionable bar or restaurant with ferns or other plants for decoration

fernbird /fúrn burd/ (*plural* **-birds** or *same*) *n* a small brown and white bird that has tail feathers resembling ferns. Native to: swampy areas of New Zealand. Latin name: *Bowdleria punctata*.

fernery /fúrnəri/ (*plural* **-ies**) *n* **1.** a container or cultivated area in which ferns are grown **2.** a collection of growing ferns

fern seed *n* a tiny spore by which a fern reproduces. Because their smallness makes them difficult to see, at one time it was believed that carrying fern seeds made somebody invisible. ○ *'We have the receipt of fern seed, we walk invisible'* (William Shakespeare, *Henry IV Pt I*; 1597)

ferntickles /fúrntik'lz/, **ferny-tickles** /fúrni-/ *npl regional* freckles [15C. Origin ?]

ferocious /fə rōshəss/ *adj* **1.** very fierce or savage **2.** very intense [Mid-17C. < Latin *feroc-* 'wild-looking']

—**ferociously** *adv* —**ferociousness** *n* —**ferocity** /fə róssəti/ *n*

-ferous *suffix* bearing, containing, producing ○ *diamondiferous* [< French *-fère* or Latin *-fer* 'carrying, bearing']

ferr- *prefix* same as **ferro-**

Ferrara /fə raàrə/ city on the River Po near Bologna in Emilia-Romagna Region, northern Italy. Population: 130,992 (2001).

Ferrari /fə raàri/, **Enzo** (1898–1988) Italian racing car driver and automobile manufacturer. From the 1950s, he designed and produced racing cars that achieved success in Grand Prix competitions.

ferredoxin /férrə dóksin/ *n* an iron-containing protein found in plants that is active in photosynthesis [Mid-20C. < Latin *ferrum* 'iron' + REDOX]

ferret[1] /férrit/ *n* (*plural* **-rets** or *same*) a typically albino polecat bred for use in hunting rabbits or rats and kept as a pet. Latin name: *Mustela eversmanni*. ■ *vti* (**-rets**, **-reting**, **-reted**) to hunt rabbits or rats using a ferret [14C. Via Old French *furet* < assumed Vulgar Latin *furittus* 'little thief' < Latin *fur* 'thief'] —**ferreter** *n* —**ferrety** *adj*

ferret about, **ferret around** *vi* to search in an area persistently ○ *ferreting about in a drawer*

ferret out *vt* **1.** to force somebody or something out of a hiding place by persistent searching **2.** to discover something hidden by persistent searching

ferret[2] /férrit/ *n* a narrow silk tape. Use: edging or binding fabric. [Mid-17C. Probably alteration of Italian *fioretti* 'floss silk' < *fiore* 'flower']

ferreting[1] /férriting/ *n* the practice of hunting rabbits or rats with ferrets

ferreting[2] /férriting/ *n* HANDICRAFT same as **ferret**[2]

ferri- *prefix* **1.** same as **ferro- 2.** ferric iron ○ *ferricyanide* [< Latin *ferrum* 'iron']

ferriage /férri ij/ *n* **1.** the action or business of transporting passengers or cargo by ferry **2.** the fee charged for carrying somebody or something by ferry

ferric /férrik/ *adj* containing iron, especially with a valency of three [Late 18C. < Latin *ferrum* 'iron']

ferric ammonium citrate *n* a nontoxic iron salt. Use: treatment of anaemia. Formula: $Fe(NH_4)_3(C_6H_5O_7)_2$.

ferric chloride *n* a dark red iron-containing salt. Use: in medicine as an astringent, in industry as a coagulating agent. Formula: $FeCl_3$.

ferric oxide *n* a reddish-brown solid containing iron and oxygen. Source: rust, haematite. Use: pigment, in jeweller's rouge for polishing, on magnetic recording tape. Formula: Fe_2O_3.

ferric sulphate *n* a pale yellow solid chemical containing iron, oxygen, and sulphur. Use: pigments, water purification, dyeing, medicine. Formula: $Fe_2(SO_4)_3$.

ferricyanide /férri sī́ ə nīd/ *n* any salt containing iron and six cyanide groups. Use: manufacture of pigments.

Ferrier /férri ər/, **Kathleen** (1912–53) British contralto. She studied music seriously from 1940 and is particularly famous for her performance in 1947 of Gustav Mahler's song cycle *Das Lied von der Erde*.

ferriferous /fe rífferəss/ *adj* describes a rock or mineral deposit that contains iron, often at a level high enough to make extraction economically worthwhile [Early 19C. < Latin *ferrum* 'iron']

ferrimagnetism /férri mágnətizəm/ *n* a property of some substances such as ferrites in which two different types of iron having unequal magnetic moments occur aligned in antiparallel, giving an appreciable bulk magnetization —**ferrimagnet** *n* —**ferrimagnetic** /férri mag néttik/ *adj* —**ferrimagnetically** *adv*

Ferris wheel /férriss-/, **ferris wheel** *n* a fairground ride consisting of a giant revolving wheel with seats that hang down from its rim and stay horizontal as the wheel rotates [Late 19C. After G. W. G. *Ferris* (1859–96), US engineer]

ferrite /férrīt/ *n* **1.** MAGNETIC IRON OXIDE a mixed oxide of iron and another metal such as cobalt or nickel. Use: in electronics, in magnets. **2.** FORM OF IRON OCCURRING IN

STEEL a form of iron occurring in steel, cast iron, and pig iron **3. IRON MINERAL** a mineral containing iron oxide, e.g. magnetite, occurring as small grains in various rocks [Mid-19C. < Latin *ferrum* 'iron']

ferritin /férritin/ *n* an iron-binding protein found in the liver, that stores iron in the body. When required, iron is released and used in the production of haemoglobin in red blood cells. [Mid-20C. < FERRI- + *-t-* + -IN]

ferro- *prefix* **1.** iron ○ *ferroalloy* **2.** ferrous iron ○ *ferrocyanide* [< Latin *ferrum* 'iron']

ferroalloy /férrō álloy/ *n* an iron alloy, containing a large proportion of one or more other elements, that is added to molten metal during iron and steel production to give the required composition

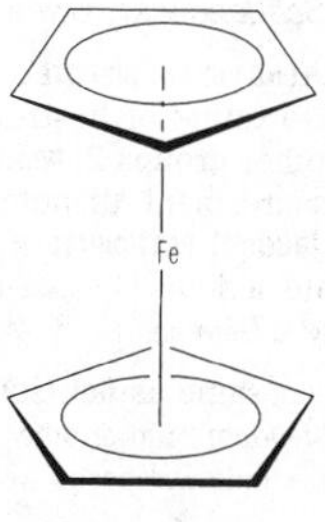

ferrocene

ferrocene /férrō seen/ *n* an orange-red crystalline solid in which an atom of iron is situated between two rings that are composed of five carbon and five hydrogen atoms. Formula: $Fe(C_5H_5)_2$. [Mid-20C. < FERRO- + contraction of *cyclopentadiene*, a hydrocarbon]

ferroconcrete /férrō kóng kreet/ *n* CONSTR same as **reinforced concrete**

ferrocyanide /férrō sí ə nīd/ *n* any salt containing iron and six cyanide groups. Use: in blue pigments.

ferroelectric /férrō i léktrik/ *adj* describes a crystalline compound that has a natural spontaneous electric polarization that can be reversed by the application of an electric field ■ *n* a substance that is ferroelectric —**ferroelectrically** *adv* —**ferroelectricity** /férrō i lek tríssəti, -éllek-/ *n*

ferromagnesian /férrō mag neézh'n/ *adj* describes silicate minerals that contain high levels of iron and magnesium, e.g. olivine

ferromagnetic /férrō mag néttik/ *adj* with the property of ferromagnetism. Iron, cobalt, and nickel are ferromagnetic metals. —**ferromagnetically** *adv*

ferromagnetism /férrō mágnətizəm/ *n* a property of some substances, including iron and some alloys, in which application of a weak magnetic field within a specific temperature range induces high magnetism. Small discrete regions within the substance (**domains**) align with the direction of an applied magnetic field and produce the bulk magnetization. —**ferromagnet** *n*

ferromanganese /férrō mang gə neéz, -máng gə neez/ *n* an alloy of iron and manganese used to add manganese during the making of steel and cast iron

ferronneries /fe rónnəriz/ *n* a variety of ceramics that copies forms from metalwork, e.g. candlesticks (*takes a singular verb*) [Early 20C. < French, 'iron work, wrought iron']

ferrosilicon /férrō síllikən/ *n* an alloy of iron and silicon. Use: production of steel and cast iron.

ferrotype /férrō tīp/ *n* a positive photograph made on a plate of sensitized iron

ferrous /férrəss/ *adj* containing iron with a valency of two [Mid-19C. < Latin *ferrum* 'iron']

ferrous oxide *n* a black solid containing iron and oxygen. Use: manufacture of steel and enamels. Formula: FeO.

ferrous sulphate *n* a white or pale green iron salt. Use: in inks, tanning, treatment of iron-deficient anaemia. Formula: $FeSO_4.7H_2O$.

ferrous sulphide *n* a black solid containing iron and sulphur. Source: pyrite, marcasite. Use: making hydrogen sulphide. Formula: FeS.

ferruginous /fe roójinəss/ *adj* **1.** containing or resembling iron **2.** of a reddish-brown colour, like rust [Mid-17C. < Latin *ferrugin-* 'iron rust' < *ferrum* 'iron']

ferrule /férrool, férrəl/, **ferule** *n* **1. PROTECTIVE CAP ON SHAFT** a usually metal cap or ring attached to the end of something long and thin such as a walking stick in order to strengthen it **2. CYLINDRICAL JOINT** a metal cylinder used to make a pipe joint **3. CONNECTION FOR FISHING ROD PIECES** a connection that joins the pieces of a fishing rod, consisting of male and female couplings that fit together ■ *vt* **FIT SOMETHING WITH FERRULE** to provide something with a ferrule [Early 17C. Alteration (after Latin *ferrum* 'iron') of *virolle* < Latin *viriae* 'bracelets']

ferry /férri/ *n* (*plural* **-ries**) **1. BOAT MAKING REGULAR SHORT CROSSINGS** a boat used to transport passengers, vehicles, or goods across water, especially one operating regularly across a river or narrow channel **2. COMMERCIAL TRANSPORT SERVICE** a commercial service transporting passengers, vehicles, or goods across water **3. PLACE WHERE FERRY BERTHS** a place where passengers, vehicles, or goods are transported across water by ferry **4. RIGHT TO OPERATE FERRY** a legal right to operate and charge for a ferry service ■ *v* (**-ries, -rying, -ried**) **1.** *vt* **TRANSPORT SOMEBODY OR SOMETHING BY FERRY** to transport somebody or something across water by ferry **2.** *vi* **GO BY FERRY** to travel by ferry **3.** *vt* **TRANSPORT PASSENGERS** to transport passengers or goods back and forth by any vehicle ○ *He had to ferry his children to school every morning.* **4.** *vt* **DELIVER AIRCRAFT** to deliver an aircraft by flying it to its operator [14C. < Old Norse *ferja*, or stem of *ferjuskip* 'ferryboat', *ferjukarl* 'ferryman' < Germanic]

ferryboat /férri bōt/ *n* same as **ferry** *n* (sense 1)

ferryman /férri man, -mən/ (*plural* **-men** /-mən/) *n* an owner, operator, or worker of a ferry

fertile /fúr tīl/ *adj* **1. ABLE TO PRODUCE OFFSPRING** capable of breeding or reproducing **2. ABLE TO DEVELOP** describes an egg or seed that has the capacity to grow and develop **3. REPRODUCING OFTEN** producing many offspring **4. PRODUCING GOOD CROPS** describes an area that produces many plants, fruit, or crops **5. RICH IN PLANT NUTRIENTS** describes soil or land that is rich in the nutrients needed to sustain the growth of healthy plants **6. CREATIVE** readily able to produce new ideas ○ *a fertile imagination* **7.** PHYS **CAPABLE OF BECOMING FISSILE** capable of being converted into fissile or fissionable material, typically in a nuclear reactor [15C. Directly or via French < Latin *fertilis* < *ferre* 'bear, carry'] —**fertilely** *adv* —**fertileness** *n*

Fertile Crescent /fúr tīl-/ area of fertile land in Southwest Asia reaching from Israel to the Persian Gulf and incorporating the Tigris and Euphrates rivers in Iraq. The ancient Babylonian, Sumerian, Assyrian, Phoenician, and Hebrew civilizations arose here.

fertilisation, etc. BIOL another spelling of **fertilization, etc.**

fertility /fur tílləti/ *n* **1.** the quality or condition of being fertile **2.** the birthrate of a population [15C. Via French < Latin *fertilitas* < *fertilis* (see FERTILE)]

fertility cult *n* a form of religion using ceremonies meant to ensure the fertility of the people and agriculture of a community

fertility drug *n* a drug that stimulates ovulation. Use: in in vitro fertilization.

fertility factor *n* GENETICS same as **sex factor**

fertilization /fúrti lī záysh'n/, **fertilisation** *n* **1. STARTING REPRODUCTION** the act or process of enabling reproduction by insemination or pollination **2. UNION OF MALE AND FEMALE CELLS** the union of male and female reproductive cells (**gametes**) to produce a fertilized reproductive cell (**zygote**). Fertilization can take place inside the female's body, as in humans, or outside the body, as in fish. **3. APPLICATION OF FERTILIZER** the act or process of applying fertilizer to soil or plants

fertilize /fúrti līz/ (**-lizes, -lizing, -lized**), **fertilise** (**-lises, -lising, -lised**) *vt* **1.** to cause a female gamete to develop a new individual by uniting it with a male gamete **2.** to apply fertilizer to soil or plants [Mid-17C. < FERTILE] —**fertilizable** *adj*

fertilizer /fúrti līzər/, **fertiliser** *n* an organic or synthetic substance usually added to or spread onto soil to increase its ability to support plant growth

ferula /férryŏŏlə, férrŏŏlə/ (*plural* **-las** or **-lae** /-lee/) *n* a tall plant with thick stems and finely divided leaves from which strong-smelling resinous gums are extracted that can be used medicinally. Native to: Mediterranean. Genus: *Ferula*. [14C. < Latin, 'fennel stalk, rod'] —**ferulaceous** /férroo láyshəss, férryoo-/ *adj*

ferule[1] /férrool, férrəl/ *n* a cane, rod, or flat piece of wood used to punish children by striking them, usually on the hand [15C. < Latin *ferula* 'fennel stalk, rod']

ferule[2] /férrool, férrəl/ *n*, *vt* CONSTR another spelling of **ferrule**

ferulic acid /fe roólik-/ *n* an aromatic chemical found in some plants that is similar to vanillin. Ferulic acid is a component of **asafoetida**, a bitter resin derived from a plant of the parsley family. Formula: $C_{10}H_{10}O_4$. [< Latin *ferula* 'fennel stalk, rod']

fervent /fúrvənt/ *adj* **1.** showing ardent or extremely passionate enthusiasm **2.** glowing as a result of intense heat (*archaic or literary*) [14C. Via Old French < Latin *fervent-*, present participle of *fervere* 'to boil'] —**fervency** *n* —**fervently** *adv*

fervid *adj* same as **fervent** [Late 16C. < Latin *fervidus* < *fervere* 'to boil'] —**fervidly** *adv* —**fervidness** *n*

fervor *n* US spelling of **fervour**

fervour /fúrvər/ *n* **1.** ardent or extremely passionate enthusiasm **2.** intense heat (*archaic or literary*) [14C. Via Old French < Latin *fervor* < *fervere* 'to boil']

Fès ♦ **Fez**

fescue /fés kyoo/, **fescue grass** *n* a perennial grass that has narrow spiky leaves. Use: lawns, pasture. Genus: *Festuca*. [14C. Alteration of *festu* < Old French, 'straw' < Latin *festuca*]

fess[1] /fess/, **fesse** *n* a broad horizontal band crossing the middle section of a heraldic shield [15C. Via Old French *fesse* < Latin *fascia* 'band, sash']

fess[2] /fess/ (**fesses, fessing, fessed**) [Early 19C. Shortening of CONFESS]

fess up *vi* to admit to something (*informal*) ○ *Come on, fess up! Was it you?*

fesse *n* another spelling of **fess**[1]

fess point *n* the central point of a heraldic shield

-fest *suffix* **1.** a gathering or festival of a particular type ○ *love-fest* ○ *talk-fest* **2.** a film filled with horrific gory detail ○ *'Night of the Living Dead' is a real gore-fest.* [Mid-19C. Via German *Fest* < Latin *festum* 'feast, festival']

festal /fést'l/ *adj* same as **festive** (*archaic*) [15C. Via Old French < Latin *festum* 'feast, festival'] —**festally** *adv*

fester /féstər/ *v* (**-ters, -tering, -tered**) **1.** *vi* **PRODUCE PUS** to produce pus because of an infection or ulceration, usually of the skin **2.** *vi* **BECOME ROTTEN** to decay **3.** *vi* **DETERIORATE** to be in or enter a state of decline ○ *neighbourhoods allowed to fester* **4. GET MORE INTENSE** to become increasingly intense or worse ○ *Hatred and tension continue to fester in the war-torn city.* ○ *festering discontent* ■ *n* MED **SORE DISCHARGING PUS** a small sore or ulcer containing or discharging pus [14C. Via Old French *festre* 'pipe-like ulcer' < Latin *fistula*]

festination /fésti náysh'n/ *n* a style of tottering walk that is characteristic of people with Parkinson's disease [Mid-16C. < Latin *festination-* < *festinare* 'to hurry']

festival /féstiv'l/ *n* **1. TIME OF CELEBRATION** a day or period of celebration, often one of religious significance **2. PROGRAMME OF CULTURAL EVENTS** a programme or series of performances or other cultural events, usually held at regular intervals, often in one place ■ *adj* **APPROPRIATE TO FESTIVAL** typical of or appropriate to a festival [14C. Via Old French < medieval Latin *festivalis* < Latin *festivus* (see FESTIVE)]

festivalgoer /féstiv'l gō ər/ *n* an attender of a festival

festive /féstiv/ *adj* **1.** relating to, suitable for, or typical of a feast, festival, or holiday **2.** marked by cheerfulness and joy ○ *in a festive mood* [Mid-17C. < Latin *festivus* 'festive' < *festum* 'feast, festival'] —**festively** *adv* —**festiveness** *n*

festive season *n* the period leading up to and including Christmas and the New Year

festivity /fe stívvəti/ *n* (*plural* **-ties**) **1.** ENJOYMENT the enjoyment or merrymaking typical of a celebration **2.** CELEBRATION a celebration, feast, or party ■ **festivities** *npl* CELEBRATIONS celebrations or merrymaking [14C. Directly or via French < Latin *festivitas* < *festivus* (see FESTIVE)]

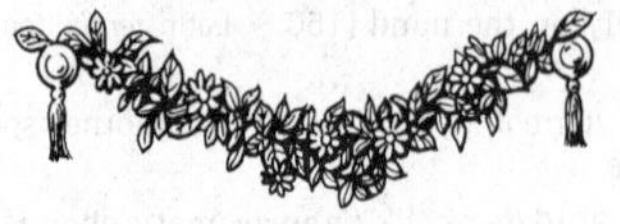

festoon

festoon /fe stoón/ *n* **1.** GARLAND an ornamental chain of flowers, leaves, or ribbons hanging in a loop or curve between two points **2.** ARTISTIC REPRESENTATION OF FESTOON a carved or painted representation of a festoon, e.g. on a building, in a painting, or on pottery ■ *vt* (**-toons, -tooning, -tooned**) **1.** HANG FESTOONS ON SOMETHING to decorate something with festoons **2.** JOIN WITH FESTOONS to join things together with festoons **3.** SHAPE INTO FESTOONS to make something into festoons [Mid-17C. Via French *feston* < Italian *festone* 'ornament for festivities' < assumed Vulgar Latin *festa* 'festivities' < Latin *festum* 'feast, festival'] —**festooned** *adj*

festoon blind *n* a blind for a window, made of cloth gathered into rows that can be drawn up to hang in curves

festschrift /fést shrift/, **Festschrift** (*plural* **-schrifts** or **-schriften** /-shriftən/) *n* a volume of writings by various people collected in honour of somebody such as a writer or scholar [Early 20C. < German, 'celebration-writing']

FET, F.E.T. *abbr* ELECTRONICS field-effect transistor

feta /féttə/ *n* a firm crumbly salty cheese made from sheep's or goat's milk and preserved in brine, originally from Greece. It is now produced in other countries, though still most often used as an ingredient in Greek dishes. [Mid-20C. < modern Greek *pheta*]

fetal *adj* another spelling of **foetal** (*technical*)

fetch[1] /fech/ *v* (**fetches, fetching, fetched**) **1.** *vt* GO AND GET SOMEBODY OR SOMETHING to go after and bring back somebody or something ○ *She went upstairs to fetch her car keys.* **2.** *vt* CAUSE SOMEBODY'S OR SOMETHING'S APPEARANCE to make somebody or something appear or come **3.** *vt* SELL SOMETHING AT PARTICULAR PRICE to sell something for a particular amount of money ○ *The painting fetched £600 at an auction.* **4.** *vti* RETRIEVE SOMETHING to retrieve animals that have been shot or something that has been thrown such as a stick or ball ○ *The boy threw the ball and told the dog to fetch it.* **5.** *vt* UTTER DEEP SIGH OR GROAN to utter a sigh or groan with a deep breath **6.** *vt* HIT SOMEBODY WITH BLOW to inflict a blow on somebody or on a part of somebody's body (*informal*) ○ *fetched his opponent a kick on the shins* **7.** *vt* DRAW IN BREATH to draw a breath or gasp of air into the lungs **8.** *vt* PLEASE SOMEBODY to attract or charm somebody (*often passive*) ○ *was fetched by the notion of going to London* **9.** *vt* ARRIVE SOMEWHERE BY BOAT to reach or arrive at a place by sailing ○ *fetched port at nightfall* **10.** *vt Malaysia* TAKE SOMEWHERE to take somebody somewhere ○ *My neighbour fetches me to the office every morning.* ■ *n* **1.** ACT OF FETCHING the act or an instance of fetching somebody or something **2.** STRATAGEM a dodge, trick, or stratagem ○ *They used cunning fetches to swindle money out of the gullible.* **3.** METEOROL DISTANCE WIND TRAVELS UNOBSTRUCTED the distance wind or waves can travel without obstruction [Old English *feccean*, origin ?] —**fetcher** *n* ◇ **fetch and carry (for somebody)** to do menial tasks for somebody

fetch up *v* **1.** *vi* ARRIVE to arrive or come to a halt somewhere (*informal*) ○ *After a week on the road, we fetched up at a small coastal town.* **2.** *vi* NAUT HALT SUDDENLY to come to a sudden halt ○ *The boat fetched up on a sandbar.* **3.** *vt* CAUSE SOMEBODY OR SOMETHING TO STOP to make somebody or something come to a stop ○ *His abrupt tone fetched me up short.* **4.** *vt* VOMIT to expel something from the stomach through the mouth (*informal*) **5.** *vt regional* BRING SOMEBODY UP to bring up children or rear animals (*dated*)

fetch[2] /fech/ *n* a vision, apparition, or ghost appearing as the doppelgänger of a living person [Late 17C. Origin ?]

fetching /féching/ *adj* **1.** pleasant, stylish, or becoming in appearance **2.** having a charming or captivating quality ○ *a fetching hat* —**fetchingly** *adv*

fête /fayt/, **fete** *n* **1.** BAZAAR a bazaar, sale, or other event organized to raise money for a cause or for charity, especially if held outdoors ○ *a school fête* **2.** PARTY a large elaborate party, often outdoors **3.** HOLIDAY a holiday or day of celebration **4.** RELIGIOUS FESTIVAL a religious festival, e.g. a saint's day ■ *vt* (**fêtes, fêting, fêted; fetes, feting, feted**) ARRANGE CELEBRATIONS FOR SOMEBODY to entertain or honour somebody with an elaborate party (*usually passive*) [Mid-18C. Via French, < Latin *festum* 'feast, festival']

fête champêtre /fáyt shaaN péttrə/ (*plural* **fêtes champêtres** /*pronunc. same*/) *n* an outdoor party or festival [< French, 'rural festival']

fetich *n* another spelling of **fetish** (*archaic*)

feticide *n* MED another spelling of **foeticide** (*technical*)

fetid /féttid, feétid/, **foetid** *adj* having a rotten or offensive smell ○ *fetid odour of rotten meat* [15C. < Latin *fetidus* < *fetere* 'to stink'] —**fetidly** *adv* —**fetidness** *n*

fetish /féttish/ *n* **1.** OBJECT OF OBSESSION an object, idea, or activity that somebody is irrationally obsessed with or attached to ○ *make a fetish of neatness* **2.** OBJECT AROUSING SEXUAL DESIRE something that arouses sexual excitement in somebody, e.g. an inanimate object or nonsexual part of the body **3.** MAGICAL OBJECT something, especially an inanimate object, that is revered or worshipped because it is believed to have magical powers or be animated by a spirit [Early 17C. Via French *fétiche* 'charm, sorcery' < Latin *factitius* 'made by art, artificial' (see FACTITIOUS)]

fetishise *vt* another spelling of **fetishize**

fetishism /féttishizəm/ *n* **1.** OBSESSION WITH SOMETHING an irrational obsession with or attachment to something **2.** SEXUAL AROUSAL WITH FETISH the use of a fetish to produce sexual arousal **3.** BELIEF IN FETISH the belief in, use of, or worship of a magical fetish —**fetishist** *n*

fetishize /féttishīz/ (**-izes, -izing, -ized**), **fetishise** (**-ises, -ising, -ised**) *vt* to make a fetish of something

fetlock /fét lok/ *n* **1.** PROJECTION ON HORSE'S LEG the part of the lower leg of a horse or related animal situated above and behind the hoof and projecting down from the associated joint **2.** HAIR ON FETLOCK the tuft of hair growing on a fetlock **3.** *also* **fetlock joint** LEG JOINT the joint at the fetlock [14C. Probably < form of FOOT + LOCK [2] 'hair']

fetor /feétər/, **foetor** *n* a strong offensive smell [15C. < Latin < *fetere* 'to stink']

fetoscope *n* MED another spelling of **foetoscope** (*technical*)

fe true /fə troó/ *adv* really or honestly (*slang; used in Black English*)

fetter /féttər/ *n* (*often used in the plural*) **1.** SHACKLE FOR ANKLES a chain or shackle fastened to somebody's ankles or feet **2.** RESTRAINT a means of confinement, restriction, or restraint ○ *These harsh rules keep us in fetters.* ■ *vt* (**-ters, -tering, -tered**) **1.** PUT FETTERS ON SOMEBODY to shackle somebody with fetters **2.** RESTRAIN SOMEBODY OR SOMETHING to confine, restrict, or restrain somebody or something ○ *fettered by her own inhibitions* [Old English *feter* < Germanic]

fettle /fétt'l/ *n* METALL same as **fettling** ■ *vt* (**-tles, -tling, -tled**) **1.** *regional* MAKE SOMETHING READY to put something in order or a state of readiness, especially by adding a finishing touch **2.** MANUF TRIM CASTING to remove moulding or excess material from a ceramic or metal casting **3.** METALL LINE FURNACE to line the hearth of a furnace with fettling **4.** METALL REPAIR FURNACE to repair the lining of a furnace [Old English *fetel* 'girdle, strap' < Germanic, 'hold'] —**fettler** *n* ◇ **in fine** *or* **good fettle** in good health, condition, or spirits

fettling /fétt'ling/ *n* loose material that is resistant to heat, typically sand or ore, used to line the hearths of some types of furnace before the molten metal is introduced

fettuccine /féttə cheéni/, **fettuccini** *n* **1.** pasta made in narrow flat strips, slightly narrower and thicker than tagliatelle (*takes a singular or plural verb*) **2.** a pasta dish made with fettuccine [Early 20C. < Italian, 'little ribbons']

fetus *n* another spelling of **foetus** (*technical*)

feu /fyoo/ *n* HIST, LAW **1.** RIGHT OF USE in Scotland, a right to use land or property in return for an annual payment (**feu duty**) **2.** LAND TENURE FOR RENT a form of land tenure in feudal times in Scotland, based on paying rent in money or grain and not on military service **3.** LAND FOR ANNUAL PAYMENT in Scotland, a piece of land held by feu [15C. < Old French (see FEE)]

feuar /fyoó ər/ *n Scotland* HIST, LAW a tenant of a feu

feud[1] /fyood/ *n* **1.** LONG VIOLENT DISPUTE a bitter prolonged violent quarrel or state of hostility between families, clans, or other groups **2.** PROLONGED DISAGREEMENT a prolonged disagreement, dispute, or quarrel ■ *vi* (**feuds, feuding, feuded**) PARTICIPATE IN FEUD to take part in or perpetuate a feud [13C. < Old French *fe(i)de* 'vendetta, hostility' < Germanic]

feud[2] /fyood/ *n* HIST same as **fief** (sense 1) [Early 17C. < medieval Latin *feudum* 'land or other property used as a reward for service' < Indo-European, 'wealth, cattle']

feudal /fyoód'l/ *adj* **1.** relating to, typical of, or resembling feudalism **2.** relating to a fief [Early 17C. < medieval Latin *feudalis* < *feudum* (see FEUD [2])] —**feudally** *adv*

feudalise *vt* POL another spelling of **feudalize**

feudalism /fyoód'lizəm/ *n* **1.** the legal and social system that existed in medieval Europe, in which vassals held land from lords in exchange for military service **2.** a system of economic, political, or social organization resembling European feudalism, e.g. in medieval Japan —**feudalist** *n* —**feudalistic** /fyoód'l ístik/ *adj*

feudality /fyoo dálləti/ (*plural* **-ties**) *n* **1.** the quality or condition of being feudal **2.** a feudal holding or system

feudalize /fyoód'l īz/ (**-izes, -izing, -ized**), **feudalise** (**-ises, -ising, -ised**) *vt* to make something feudal in nature —**feudalization** /fyoód'l ī záysh'n/ *n*

feudatory /fyoódə təri/ *n* (*plural* **-ries**) TENANT OF FEUDAL LAND somebody holding land by feudal tenure ■ *adj* **1.** INVOLVING FEUDAL RELATIONSHIP relating to or characteristic of the relationship between a feudal lord and a vassal **2.** SUBJECT TO OVERLORDSHIP owing feudal allegiance to an overlord or another state [Late 16C. < medieval Latin *feudatorius* < past participle of *feudare* 'invest with feudal property' < *feudum* (see FEUD [2])]

feu duty *n* an annual payment made by the owner of a building in Scotland to the nominal feudal superior for the right to use the land or property

feuilleton /fö́ i ton, fö́ i toN/ *n* **1.** a section of a European newspaper containing reviews, serial fiction, and articles of general interest **2.** an article, review, or other piece published in a feuilleton [Mid-19C. < French *feuillet* 'little leaf' < *feuille* 'leaf' < Latin *folium* 'leaf, page']

fever /feévər/ *n* **1.** UNUSUALLY HIGH BODY TEMPERATURE a body temperature that is unusually high, usually caused by bacterial or viral infections and commonly accompanied by shivering, headache, and an increased pulse rate. Technical name **pyrexia** **2.** DISEASE WITH FEVER a disease in which somebody typically has an unusually high body temperature, e.g. typhoid fever, yellow fever, or scarlet fever **3.** STATE OF EXCITEMENT a state of intense agitation, excitement, or emotion (*often used in combination*) ○ *On the morning of the wedding, everyone was in a fever of excitement.* **4.** CRAZE an intense and often brief enthusiasm or craze ■ *vt* (**-vers, -vering, -vered**) AGITATE SOMEBODY to throw somebody into a state of intense agitation, excitement, or emotion [Pre-12C < Latin *febris*]

fevered /feévərd/ *adj* **1.** affected by fever **2.** showing great agitation, excitement, or emotion

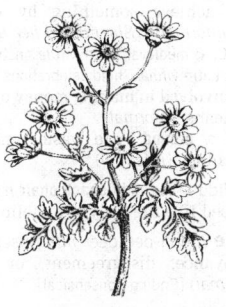

feverfew

feverfew /féevər fyoo/ *n* a perennial plant whose leaves are a popular remedy for headaches and migraine. Native to: Europe. Latin name: *Tanacetum parthenium*. [Pre-12C. < Latin *febris* 'fever' + -FUGE]

feverish /féevərish/ *adj* **1.** HAVING FEVER affected by a fever **2.** RELATING TO FEVER relating to, causing, or caused by a fever ○ *a feverish cold* **3.** AGITATED showing intense agitation, excitement, or emotion —**feverishly** *adv* —**feverishness** *n*

fever pitch *n* a state of intense agitation, excitement, or emotion

fever tree *n* a tree whose bark was used to treat malaria. Native to: southeastern United States. Latin name: *Pinckneya pubens*.

few /fyoo/ CORE MEANING: a grammatical word used to indicate that there are not many or hardly any people or things ○ (det) *There were few books on the shelves.* ○ (det) *spending her few free hours relaxing in front of the television* ○ (pron) *Many people have entered the contest, but few will be successful.* ○ (pron) *Few of the gardens had been cared for.* **1.** *npl, pron, det* a limited or exclusive number, e.g. an elite or minority of people ○ (npl) *the fortunate few who managed to escape sickness this winter* ○ (npl) *The needs of the many outweigh the needs of the few.* ○ (pron) *Few would have thought it so.* **2.** *det, pron* **a few** not very many people or things, but more than two, and sometimes more than might be expected ○ (det) *We had a few meetings before signing the contract.* ○ (pron) *Only a few ever achieve real artistic success.* ○ (pron) *A few of the kids wanted to watch a video.* [Old English *fēawa* < Indo-European] —**fewness** *n* ◇ **a good few** several, or a fairly large number (*informal*) ◇ **few and far between** scarce or infrequent (*informal*) ◇ **quite a few** a fairly large number (*informal*)

USAGE **fewer** or **less**? As a general rule, **fewer** is used with things you can count (*fewer meetings, fewer people*), whereas **less** is used with things you cannot count (*less time, less money*). The same difference applies to the use of **fewer than** and **less than**: *fewer than twenty people, less than an hour*. Designations of price, age, and measurement are normally regarded as singular, the idea being that, for example, *It cost less than ten pounds* has to do with an amount of money rather than a number of individual pounds. The use of **less** where the sense of countable number is strong (*You may use the express checkout if you have less than eight items*) is relatively common, though many object to it.

fey /fay/ *adj* **1.** OTHERWORLDLY having a manner or appearance that gives an impression of otherworldliness or unworldliness **2.** SUPERNATURAL relating to or typical of magic or the supernatural **3.** CLAIRVOYANT supposedly able to see into the future **4.** *Scotland* DOOMED TO DIE believed to be doomed or destined to die, especially as indicated by peculiar, usually elated behaviour [Old English *fǣge* 'fated to die' < Germanic] —**feyly** *adv* —**feyness** *n*

Feynman /fínmən/, Richard (1918–88) US physicist. He shared the Nobel Prize in physics (1965) for work on quantum electrodynamics. Full name **Feynman, Richard Phillips**

'For a successful technology, reality must take precedence over public relations, for nature cannot be fooled.'
[Richard Feynman, *Rogers Commission*

Report on the Space Shuttle Challenger Accident; 6 June 1986]

Feynman diagram /fínmən-/ *n* a diagrammatic representation of interactions between elementary particles [After Richard FEYNMAN]

fez /fez/ (*plural* **fezzes**) *n* a brimless felt hat shaped like a cone with a flat top, usually red with a black tassel, worn by men in eastern Mediterranean and North African countries. In the past it was the national headdress of Turkish men. [Early 19C. Via French < Turkish *fes*]

Fez /fez/, **Fès** /fess/ city in northern Morocco, northeast of Casablanca. The oldest of the country's four imperial cities, it is about 161 km/100 mi. east of Rabat. Population: 774,754 (1994).

Fezzan /fə zán/ desert region and former province in southwestern Libya. It was part of the Ottoman Empire between the 16th and 19th centuries.

ff *abbr* MUSIC fortissimo

ff. *abbr* **1.** PUBL folios **2.** following (*used of lines or pages*)

FH *abbr* fire hydrant

fhp *abbr* ENG friction horsepower

FHSA *abbr* SOC WELFARE, HEALTH SERVICES Family Health Services Authority

fiacre /fee áakrə/ *n* a small horse-drawn carriage with four wheels, formerly used for hire like a taxi [Late 17C. < French, after the Hôtel de St *Fiacre*]

fiancé /fi ón say/ *n* the man to whom a woman is engaged to be married [Mid-19C. < French, past participle of *fiancer* 'betroth' < Old French *fiance* 'a promise']

fiancée /fi ón say/ *n* the woman to whom a man is engaged to be married [Mid-19C. < French, form of *fiancé* (see FIANCÉ)]

fianchetto /fi ən chéttō, -kéttō/ *n* (*plural* **-tos** or **-ti** /-ti/) in chess, the initial movement (**development**) of a bishop from its original position to the second square of the adjacent knight's file ■ *vt* (**-tos, -toing, -toed**) to move a bishop using a fianchetto [Mid-19C. < Italian, 'little flank' < *fianco* 'flank']

Fianna /fée ənə/ *npl* in Irish legend, a band of warriors celebrated for feats of heroism [Late 18C. < Irish, 'band of warriors and hunters']

Fianna Fáil /fee ənə fóyl, -fáal/ *n* one of the two main Irish political parties, founded in 1926 [< Irish, 'warriors of Ireland']

fiasco /fi áskō/ (*plural* **-cos**) *n* a total failure, especially a humiliating or ludicrous one [Mid-19C. Via Italian, 'bottle' < medieval Latin *flasco* 'flask'; sense 'failure' from theatrical slang]

fiat /fée at, fí at/ *n* **1.** a formal or official authorization of something **2.** an authoritative and often arbitrary command [14C. < Latin, 'let it be done']

fiat money *n* paper money that a government declares to be legal tender although it is not based on or convertible into coins and therefore depends on government decree to determine its value

fib /fib/ (*informal*) *n* an insignificant or harmless lie ■ *vi* (**fibs, fibbing, fibbed**) to tell an insignificant or harmless lie [Early 17C. Origin ?] —**fibber** *n*

SYNONYMS See *lie*²·

fiber *n* US spelling of **fibre**

Fibonacci number /féebə náachi-/ *n* a number in an unending Fibonacci sequence [See FIBONACCI SEQUENCE]

Fibonacci sequence *n* an unending series of numbers in which each number except for the first two is the sum of the preceding two, e.g. 0,1,1,2,3,5,8.... Such sequences frequently have applications in botany, psychology, and astronomy. [After Leonardo *Fibonacci*, 13C Italian mathematician]

fibr- *prefix* same as **fibro-** (*used before vowels*)

fibre /fíbər/ *n* **1.** THIN THREAD a long slender thread or filament **2.** TEXTILES THREAD FOR YARN a fine thread of a natural or synthetic material that can be spun into yarn **3.** TEXTILES CLOTH cloth or material made of fibres **4.** TEXTILES FIBROUS STRUCTURE the texture or structure of a material made of fibres **5.** ESSENTIAL CHARACTER the fundamental character, quality, or makeup of something **6.** STRENGTH OF CHARACTER somebody's strength of

character or sense of right and wrong ○ *the moral fibre of this nation* **7.** HEALTH COARSE FIBROUS SUBSTANCES IN FOOD the coarse fibrous substances, largely composed of cellulose, that are found in grains, fruits, and vegetables, and aid digestion. This largely indigestible plant matter is considered to play a role in the prevention of many diseases of the digestive tract. **8.** BOT LONG THICK-WALLED PLANT CELL a long narrow plant cell with walls thickened with lignin that is a major component of the plant's supporting tissue. Fibre cells are frequently found in the outer walls of plant stems. **9.** BOT PLANT STRANDS FOR MAKING ROPE AND TEXTILES strands of fibre cells removed from the stems or leaves of plants such as flax or hemp, that can be separated and woven **10.** BOT THIN ROOT a thin narrow root of a plant **11.** ANAT THREAD-SHAPED BODY STRUCTURE a long thin structure of the body tissues, e.g. muscle cells and nerve cells [Mid-16C. Via French < Latin *fibra* 'filament'] —**fibred** *adj*

fibreboard /fíbər bawrd/ *n* building material made by compressing wood fibres into sheets

fibre bundle *n* a flexible group of parallel optical fibres held in a fixed arrangement with respect to one another

fibrefill /fíbər fil/ *n* synthetic stuffing or insulating material. Use: cushions, duvets, clothing.

fibreglass /fíbər glaass/ *n* **1.** compressed glass fibres. Use: insulation. **2.** a material made from fibreglass. Use: boat hulls, car bodies.

fibre optics *n* the technology of transferring information, e.g. in communications or computer technology, through thin flexible glass or plastic tubes (**optical fibres**) using modulated light waves. Information is transmitted in the form of coded pulses. (*takes a singular or plural verb*) —**fibre-optic** *adj*

fibrescope /fíbər skōp/ *n* an instrument that uses fibre optics to transmit images from inaccessible places such as the interior of the body. Use: microsurgery, diagnosis.

fibri- *prefix* same as **fibro-**

fibriform /fíbbri fawrm, fíbri-/ *adj* having the form of a fibre or fibres

fibril /fíbrəl/, **fibrilla** /fíbrələ/ (*plural* **-lae** /-lee/) *n* a small or delicate fibre or part of a fibre (*technical*) [Mid-17C. < modern Latin *fibrilla* 'little fibre' < Latin *fibra* 'fibre'] —**fibrillar** /fī bríllər, fi-/ *adj* —**fibrillary** *adj* —**fibrilliform** *adj* —**fibrillose** *adj* —**fibrillous** *adj*

fibrillate /fíbri layt, fíbbri-/ (**-lates, -lating, -lated**) *vti* to undergo rapid irregular beating or uncontrolled contraction, or make the heart or muscles undergo this [Mid-19C. < modern Latin *fibrilla* (see FIBRIL)] —**fibrillative** *adj*

fibrillation /fíbri láysh'n, fíbbri-/ *n* **1.** RAPID IRREGULAR HEARTBEAT rapid chaotic beating of the heart muscles in which the affected part of the heart may stop pumping blood **2.** RAPID CONTRACTION OF MUSCLE FIBRE rapid uncontrolled contraction of individual muscle fibres with little or no movement of the muscle as a whole **3.** FORMATION OF FIBRES the formation of fibres or fibrils

fibrin /fíbrin, fíbb-/ *n* an insoluble fibrous protein that is produced in the liver from the soluble protein fibrinogen and helps in blood clotting. It forms a network of fibres in which blood cells become trapped, thus producing a clot. [Early 19C. < FIBRE] —**fibrinoid** /fíbri noyd, fíbb-/ *adj* —**fibrinous** /fíbrinəss, fíbb-/ *adj*

fibrinogen /fi brínnəjən, fi-/ *n* a soluble protein present in the blood that is activated by thrombin to form fibrin. Fibrinogen is a clotting factor and is required to prevent major blood loss. —**fibrinogenic** /fíbrinō jénnik, fíbb-/ *adj* —**fibrinogenically** *adv* —**fibrinogenous** /fíbri nójjənəss, fíbb-/ *adj*

fibrinolysin /fíbrə nóllissin/ *n* an enzyme in blood that breaks down fibrin and disperses blood clots

fibrinolysis /fíbrə nóllississ/ *n* the destruction of fibrin and blood clots —**fibrinolytic** /fíbrinō líttik/ *adj*

fibro /fíbrō/ (*plural* **-bros**) *n* Aus **1.** fibrocement (*informal*) **2.** a house made of fibrocement [Mid-20C. Shortening] —**fibro** *adj*

fibro- *prefix* **1.** fibre ○ *fibroin* **2.** fibrous tissue ○ *fibroma* [< Latin *fibra* 'fibre']

fibroblast /fíbrō blast/ *n* a large flat cell in connective tissue that secretes collagen and elastic fibres

fibrocartilage /fíbrō kaártəlij, -kaár'tlij/ *n* strong, relatively inelastic cartilage containing bundles of collagen fibres

fibrocement /fíbrō si mént/ *n Aus* a building material made of cement bound with asbestos fibres into sheets

fibrocystic /fíbrō sístik/ *adj* describes an unusual growth of fibrous tissue that contains cystic spaces, occurring particularly in glandular tissue such as the breast. Fibrocystic disease of the pancreas is called cystic fibrosis.

fibroid /fí broyd/ *adj* resembling or consisting of fibres or fibrous tissue ■ *n* a benign growth composed of fibrous and muscle tissue, especially one that develops in the wall of the womb and is associated with painful and excessive menstrual flow. Fibroids can be removed surgically and are not life-threatening, but fibroids in the womb reduce the chance of pregnancy.

fibroin /fíbrō in/ *n* a tough white protein secreted by spiders and silkworms that quickly solidifies into the thread used to form webs and cocoons

fibroma /fí brṓmə/ (*plural* **-mas** or **-mata** /-mətə/) *n* a nonmalignant tumour of fibrous connective tissue such as cartilage —**fibromatous** *adj*

fibromyalgia /fíbrō mī áljee ə/ *n* a disorder causing aching muscles, sleep disorders, and fatigue, associated with raised levels of the brain chemicals that transmit nerve signals (**neurotransmitters**)

fibrose[1] /fíbrōss/ (**-broses, -brosing, -brosed**) *vi* to form tissue consisting of or resembling fibres [Late 19C. Back-formation < FIBROSIS]

fibrose[2] /fíbrōss/ *adj* containing or resembling fibres (*technical*) [Late 17C. < modern Latin *fibrosus* < Latin *fibra* 'filament']

fibrosis /fí brṓssiss/ *n* a thickening and scarring of connective tissue most often following injury, infection, lack of oxygen, or surgery [Late 19C. < Latin *fibra* 'fibre'] —**fibrotic** /fí bróttik/ *adj*

fibrositis /fíbrə sítiss/ *n* pain and stiffness, especially in the back muscles

fibrous /fíbrəss/ *adj* **1.** consisting of or resembling fibres **2.** describes a mineral that crystallizes in thin elongated threads, e.g. asbestos —**fibrously** *adv* —**fibrousness** *n*

fibrous root *n* a root system in some plants such as grasses that consists of numerous very fine branches of approximately the same length

fibrovascular /fíbrō váskyŏŏlər/ *adj* describes plant tissue that provides structural support and conducts sap

fibrovascular bundle *n* BOT same as **vascular bundle**

fibula /fíbbyŏŏlə/ (*plural* **-lae** /-lee/ or **-las**) *n* **1.** HUMAN LEG BONE the outer and narrower of the two bones in the human lower leg between the knee and ankle **2.** ANIMAL LEG BONE the thinner outer bone of the two bones in the lower leg or hind leg of terrestrial vertebrates between the knee and ankle **3.** BROOCH in ancient Greece and Rome, a brooch or clasp shaped like a modern safety pin used to fasten cloaks [Late 16C. < Latin, 'brooch, clasp'] —**fibular** *adj*

-fic *suffix* making, causing ○ *sudorific* [< Latin *-ficus* < *facere* 'make, do']

-fication *suffix* production, process ○ *versification* ○ *unification* [< Latin *-fication-* < *-ficatus*, past participle of verbs ending in *-ficare* 'make' < *facere* 'make, do']

fiche /feesh/ *n* (*informal*) **1.** same as **microfiche 2.** same as **ultrafiche** [Mid-20C. Shortening]

Fichte /fíktə, fíkhtə/, **Johann Gottlieb** (1762–1814) German philosopher. An important figure in the German philosophical school of idealism, he was a pupil of Kant, and his work, in particular *The Vocation of Man* (1800), was an important influence on Hegel and later philosophers.

fichu /feeshoo/ *n* a woman's triangular scarf made of a lightweight material such as muslin or lace, worn around the neck and shoulders, especially in the 18th and early 19th centuries [Mid-18C. < French, 'knotted', past participle of *ficher* 'stick in' < Latin *figere* 'to fix']

fickle /fík'l/ (**-ler, -lest**) *adj* likely to change, especially in affections, intentions, loyalties, or preferences [Old English *ficol* 'deceitful' < Indo-European, 'hostile'] —**fickleness** *n*

~~ficticious~~ incorrect spelling of **fictitious**

fictile /fík tīl/ *adj* **1.** MALLEABLE moulded or capable of being moulded, as clay can be for making pottery **2.** MADE OF CLAY moulded in earth or clay by a potter **3.** RELATING TO POTTERY-MAKING relating to the making of earthenware or pottery [Early 17C. < Latin *fictilis* < *fingere* 'to make, shape']

fiction /fíksh'n/ *n* **1.** LITERARY WORKS OF IMAGINATION novels and stories that describe imaginary people and events **2.** WORK OF FICTION a novel, story, or other work of fiction **3.** UNTRUE STATEMENT something that is untrue and has been made up to deceive people ○ *The account she gave was pure fiction.* **4.** PRETENSE the act of pretending or inventing something ○ *the fiction that their marriage had become* **5.** LAW SOMETHING ASSUMED TO BE TRUE something that is assumed in law to be true regardless of whether or not it is true [14C. Via Old French < Latin *fiction-* < *fingere* 'to make, shape'] —**fictional** *adj*

ORIGIN The Latin word *fingere* 'to make, shape', from which *fiction* is derived, is also the source of English *effigy, feign, figment,* and *figure.*

---

fictionalize /fíksh'nə līz/ (**-izes, -izing, -ized**), **fictionalise** (**-ises, -ising, -ised**) *vt* to make something into fiction, or make a fictional version of something ○ *a fictionalized life of Shakespeare* —**fictionalization** /fíksh'nə līzáysh'n/ *n*

fictitious /fik tíshəss/ *adj* **1.** FALSE not true or genuine, and intended to deceive ○ *He gave a fictitious name when confronted.* **2.** FICTIONAL invented by somebody's imagination, especially as part of a work of fiction **3.** LAW ASSUMED TO BE TRUE assumed to be true for legal purposes, regardless of whether or not it is true [Early 17C. < Latin *ficticius* < *fingere* 'to make, shape'] —**fictitiously** *adv* —**fictitiousness** *n*

fictive /fíktiv/ *adj* **1.** relating to fiction or imaginative invention **2.** not genuine or true [Late 15C. Directly or via French < medieval Latin *fictivus* < *fingere* 'to make, shape'] —**fictively** *adv*

ficus /feékəss/ (*plural* **-cuses**) *n* a tree, bush, or plant that belongs to the genus that includes the fig and many familiar garden or houseplants such as the rubber plant. Genus: *Ficus*. [15C. < Latin, 'fig tree, fig']

fid /fid/ *n* **1.** a bar used to support a topmast on a boat **2.** a tapered wooden implement used to separate the strands of a rope in splicing [Early 17C. Origin ?]

FID *abbr* Financial Institutions Duty

-fid *suffix* divided in parts ○ *multifid* [< Latin *-fidus* < *fid-*, stem of *findere* 'to split']

fidayee another spelling of **fedayee**

FID DEF, Fid. Def. *abbr* Fidei Defensor

fiddle /fídd'l/ *n* **1.** VIOLIN a musical instrument of the viol or violin family, especially the violin. Violins are often called fiddles in folk, bluegrass, or country music, but in classical music the term is sometimes disparaging. **2.** FRAUDULENT ACTIVITY a fraudulent or illegal way of getting money (*informal*) **3.** DELICATE OPERATION a difficult activity or operation requiring intricate work with the hands (*informal*) ○ *It can be a bit of a fiddle trying to change the battery in this watch.* **4.** TRIVIAL MATTERS nonsensical or trivial matters or behaviour **5.** NAUT GUARDRAIL ON SHIP'S TABLE a small guardrail on top of a table or stove on a ship, used to prevent things from sliding off ■ *v* (**-dles, -dling, -dled**) **1.** *vi* TINKER to tinker with something to try to make it work properly ○ *She fiddled with the controls on the video recorder.* **2.** *vi* MOVE HANDS NERVOUSLY to move the hands or fingers nervously or restlessly, or play with something in the hands in this way ○ *The schoolboy fiddled nervously with his tie.* **3.** *vti* WASTE TIME to waste time doing unimportant things ○ *fiddle the day away* **4.** *vi* PLAY VIOLIN to play the fiddle **5.** *vt* SWINDLE SOMEBODY to cheat a person or organization (*informal*) **6.** *vi* TAMPER to interfere, meddle, or tamper with something (*informal*) ○ *Who's been fiddling with my computer?* **7.** *vt* FALSIFY RECORDS to falsify something such as financial accounts, especially for dishonest personal gain (*informal*) **8.** *vt* GET SOMETHING BY CHEATING to get or achieve something by cheating or deceiving (*informal*) ○ *She fiddled her way into that job.* [Pre-12C. < medieval Latin *vitula* 'instrument played at festivals' < Latin *vitulari* 'hold celebrations'] ◇ **be on the fiddle** to be involved in making money by fraudulent or illegal means (*informal*)

fiddle about or **around** *vi* to waste time doing unimportant things (*informal*)

fiddleback /fídd'l bak/, **fiddleback chair** *n* a chair with a back shaped like the body of a violin

fiddle-de-dee /fídd'l dee deé/ *interj* used to express mild annoyance, disagreement, or impatience (*dated informal*) [Ending nonsensical]

fiddle-faddle /fídd'l fad'l/ *n* NONSENSE nonsense or trifling matters (*informal*) ■ *interj* NONSENSE used to express the view that something is nonsense (*dated informal*) ■ *vi* (**fiddle-faddles, fiddle-faddling, fiddle-faddled**) WASTE TIME to fuss over or waste time with unimportant matters (*informal*) [Late 16C. < FIDDLE + *faddle* 'nonsense'] —**fiddle-faddler** *n*

fiddlehead

fiddlehead /fídd'l hed/, **fiddleneck** /-nek/ *n* **1.** an ornamental carving on a ship's bow, shaped like the scroll at the end of the fingerboard of a violin **2.** *N Am* the coiled frond of a young fern, often cooked and eaten as a delicacy

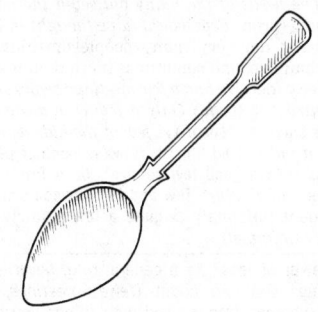

fiddle pattern

fiddle pattern *n* the design of a fork or spoon with a handle that has a tapering wide end —**fiddle-pattern** *adj*

fiddler /fídd'lər/ *n* **1.** VIOLIN PLAYER a player of the violin, especially in folk music **2.** SOMEBODY WHO TOYS WITH SOMETHING somebody who aimlessly plays or fiddles with something **3.** SWINDLER a cheat or swindler (*informal*) **4.** MARINE BIOL same as **fiddler crab**

fiddler crab *n* a small burrowing sea crab. Males

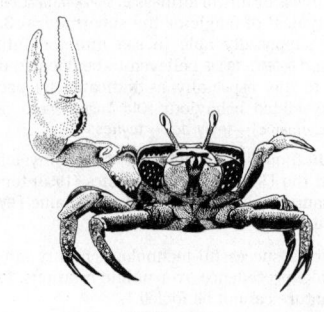

fiddler crab

have one enlarged claw that they move like a vio-linist's arm as a signal during courtship. Genus: *Uca*.

fiddlestick /fídd'l stik/ *n* (*informal*) **1.** a bow for playing a violin **2.** something that is unimportant or worthless ○ *I don't care a fiddlestick what you think.*

fiddlesticks /fídd'l stiks/ *interj* used to express mild annoyance, disagreement, or impatience (*dated informal*)

fiddlewood /fídd'l wŏŏd/ *n* **1.** the hard wood of a tropical American tree **2.** a tree that yields fid-dlewood. Native to: tropical America. Genus: *Citharexylum*.

fiddling /fídd'ling/ *adj* petty or unimportant

fiddly /fíddli/ (**-dlier, -dliest**) *adj* difficult to do, handle, or use, usually because intricate work with the hands or small objects are involved (*informal*) ○ *Changing the battery in this type of watch can be quite a fiddly job.*

FIDE *abbr* CHESS World Chess Federation [French acronym < *Fédération Internationale des Échecs*]

Fidei Defensor /fi dáy ee də fén sawr, fídi T-/ *n* HIST, CHR same as **Defender of the Faith** [< Latin]

fideism /feé day izəm, fídi-/ *n* the view that religious knowledge depends on faith and revelation [Late 19C. < Latin *fides* 'faith'] —**fideist** *n* —**fideistic** /feé day ístik, fídi-/ *adj*

Fidelism /fee déllizəm/ *n* the practice or policies of Castroism [Mid-20C. After Fidel CASTRO]

fidelity /fi délləti/ *n* **1.** LOYALTY loyalty to an allegiance, promise, or vow **2.** SEXUAL FAITHFULNESS faithfulness to a sexual partner, especially a husband or wife **3.** FACTUAL ACCURACY accuracy in reporting facts or details **4.** ELECTRONICS PRECISION OF REPRODUCTION the extent to which an electronic device such as a stereo system or television accurately reproduces sound or images [15C. Directly or via French < Latin *fidelitas* 'faithfulness' < *fides* 'faith']

fidelity card *n* US same as **loyalty card**

fidget /fíjjit/ *vi* (**-ets, -eting, -eted**) **1.** MOVE ABOUT NERVOUSLY to move about in a restless, absent-minded, or uneasy manner **2.** FIDDLE NERVOUSLY to fiddle or play with something in a restless, absent-minded, or uneasy manner ○ *He kept fidgeting with his glasses as he spoke to her.* ■ *n* SOMEBODY WHO FIDGETS somebody who behaves in a restless, absent-minded, or uneasy manner ■ **fidgets** *npl* UNEASINESS a state of restlessness, absent-mindedness, or unease expressed by con-tinual nervous movements [Late 17C. < *fidge* 'twitch, fidget', origin ?] —**fidgetingly** *adv*

fidgety /fíjjəti/ *adj* **1.** tending to fidget **2.** restless or ill at ease —**fidgetiness** *n*

fiducial /fi dyŏŏshi əl/ *adj* **1.** relating to or founded on trust or faith (*formal*) **2.** accepted or used as a standard of comparison, measurement, or reference **3.** LAW same as **fiduciary** *adj* (sense 2) [Late 16C. < late Latin *fiducialis* < Latin *fidere* 'to trust'] —**fiducially** *adv*

fiduciary /fi dyŏŏshi əri/ *adj* **1.** RELATING TO RELATIONSHIP INVOLVING TRUSTEE relating to the relationship between a trustee and the person or body for whom the trustee acts **2.** RELATING TO TRUST relating to or based on a trust ■ *n* (*plural* **-ies**) TRUSTEE a manager entrusted to control property or to act on behalf of and for the benefit of another [Late 16C. < Latin *fiduciarius* '(holding) in a trust' < *fidere* 'to trust'] —**fiduciarily** *adv*

fie /fi/ *interj* used to express disapproval of, or an-noyance or disgust with, somebody or something (*archaic*) [14C. Via French *fi* < Latin, expressing disgust at a stench]

fief /feef/ *n* **1.** a piece of land formerly granted by a feudal lord to somebody in return for service **2.** POL same as **fiefdom** [Early 17C. Via French < Old French *feu* < medieval Latin *feudum* (see FEUD 2)]

fiefdom /feéfdəm/ *n* **1.** something, e.g. territory or a sphere of activity, that is controlled or dominated by a particular person or group **2.** the lands con-trolled by a feudal lord

field /feeld/ *n* **1.** AGRIC AREA OF AGRICULTURAL LAND an area of open ground, especially one used to grow crops or graze livestock **2.** PLAYING AREA an open expanse of ground kept or marked out as a playing area for a particular sport **3.** GEOL AREA RICH IN RESOURCES an area of land or seabed that is rich in an ex-ploitable natural resource ○ *a gas field* **4.** GEOG BROAD AREA OF SOMETHING an expanse of something such as ice, snow, or lava ○ *an ice field* **5.** AREA OF ACTIVITY an activity or subject, especially one that is some-body's particular responsibility, speciality, or inter-est **6.** PLACE OUTSIDE INSTITUTION the environment outside a workplace, office, school, or laboratory in which somebody has direct contact with clients, the public, or the phenomena being studied ○ *out in the field* **7.** MIL AREA OF MILITARY OPERATIONS the location of military operations **8.** MIL same as **battlefield** (sense 1) **9.** MIL same as **battle** *n* (sense 1) (*literary or archaic*) **10.** GROUP OF CONTESTANTS all the participants in a race or other competitive event **11.** ALL PARTICIPANTS EXCEPT LEADER all the participants in a race or competitive event except the leader, winner, or favourite ○ *five lengths ahead of the field* **12.** CRICKET ARRANGEMENT OF FIELDERS a particular arrangement of cricket fielders around the wicket **13.** MATHS SET OF MATHEMATICAL EL-EMENTS a set of mathematical elements with two properties that are like addition and multiplication for ordinary numbers **14.** PHYS AREA OF FORCE an area or region within which a force exerts an influence at every point **15.** OPTICS same as **field of view** **16.** COMPUT STORAGE AREA FOR INFORMATION an area in a com-puter memory or program, or on a monitor screen, where information such as characters or numbers can be entered and manipulated **17.** HERALDRY BACK-GROUND FOR DESIGN the background surface or colour on which a design is displayed, e.g. on a flag, coin, or coat of arms ■ *v* (**fields, fielding, fielded**) **1.** *vt* SPORTS RETRIEVE BALL in cricket, rounders, or baseball, to retrieve, pick up, or catch a ball in play, usually after it has been struck by the person batting **2.** *vi* SPORTS BE FIELDER in cricket, rounders, or baseball, to act as a fielder **3.** *vt* SELECT SOMEBODY FOR COMPETITION to select a person, group, or team to participate in an event, especially a competitive event ○ *We did not have enough players to field a team.* **4.** *vt* DEPLOY GROUP to send out a large number of people or things to accomplish a task, especially to deploy military forces for action **5.** *vt* DEAL WITH QUESTION OR COMPLAINT to respond to something such as a question or com-plaint [Old English *feld* < Indo-European, 'flat'] ◇ **play the field** to be unwilling to commit to a sexual or romantic relationship with one person and prefer to have relationships with a number of people

field ambulance *n* a team of medical workers who give first aid to wounded soldiers in the front line of a battle

field artillery *n* large guns that are mobile enough to be brought close to the front line

field battery *n* a small unit of field guns

field bean *n* a broad bean with small seeds. Use: animal feed. Latin name: *Vicia faba*.

field boot *n* a close-fitting boot that comes up to the knee, worn by members of the armed forces

field coil *n* the coil of wire that, when carrying current, produces the magnetization inside an elec-trical motor or generator needed for it to operate

field cornet *n* S Africa formerly, a civilian invested with the authority of a military officer and em-powered to act as a magistrate. It was later a rank in the Boer commandos, and subsequently in the former South African army.

fieldcraft /feéld kraaft/ *n* knowledge and experience of nature combined with the skills necessary for living outdoors or in the wild

field day *n* **1.** TIME OF UNRESTRAINED ACTIVITY an opportunity for unrestrained activity ○ *If the slightest hint of this gets out, the press will have a field day.* ○ *had a field day shopping for new clothes* **2.** N Am DAY FOR AMATEUR COMPETITIONS a day devoted to amateur outdoor sports and competitions, especially at a school **3.** DAY FOR OUTDOOR ACTIVITIES a day spent in outdoor activities or study

field-effect transistor *n* a transistor, with three or more electrodes, in which the output current is controlled by a variable electric field

field emission *n* the liberation of electrons from the surface of a metallic conductor subjected to a strong electric field

fielder /feéldər/ *n* in cricket, rounders, or baseball, a player who is positioned on the field of play to catch or retrieve the ball when it is struck by the person batting

field event *n* an athletics event that takes place on an open area not on a track, e.g. the discus, javelin, long jump, or high jump

fieldfare /feéld fair/ (*plural* **-fares** or same) *n* a mi-gratory thrush with reddish-brown feathers, a grey head and rump, and a noisy call. Native to: Europe, Asia. Latin name: *Turdus pilaris*. [Assumed Old English *feldefare* 'field dweller']

field glasses *npl* same as **binoculars**

field goal *n* **1.** in American football, a score worth three points, made by kicking the ball over the crossbar from a point about ten yards behind the line of scrimmage **2.** in basketball, a goal made during normal play by throwing the ball through the basket. It is worth two points, or three points if scored from beyond a specific distance.

field-grade officer *n* MIL same as **field officer**

field guide *n* an illustrated manual that is used to identify plants, animals, or birds in their natural habitats

field hand *n* Can, US regional a labourer on a farm

field hockey *n* N Am same as **hockey** (sense 1)

field hospital *n* a centre for medical treatment on a battlefield or in an isolated place

Fielding /feélding/, **Henry** (1707–54) British novelist and dramatist. He is considered to be a founder of the English novel, with *Joseph Andrews* (1742) and *Tom Jones* (1749).

> 'It hath been often said, that it is not death, but dying, which is terrible.'
> [Henry Fielding, *Amelia*; 1751]

field lens *n* the lens that is farthest from the eye in the compound eyepiece of an optical instrument

field magnet *n* an electromagnet or permanent magnet that supplies the magnetic field in an elec-tric machine

field marshal *n* an officer in the British Army and in some other armies of the highest rank

fieldmouse

fieldmouse /feéld mowss/ *n* **1.** a small mouse with large eyes and ears and a long tail that lives in fields and gardens. Native to: Europe, Asia. Genus: *Apodemus*. **2.** N Am the most common North Ameri-can vole. Genus: *Microtus*.

field mushroom *n* a common edible mushroom. Latin name: *Agaricus campestris*. N Am term **meadow mushroom**

field officer *n* a military officer of middle rank, e.g. a major or colonel

field of fire *n* an area exposed to fire from a weapon or group of weapons

field of honour *n* a battlefield, or the site of a duel

field of view *n* the area in the eyepiece of an optical instrument in which the image is visible

field of vision *n* the whole area that can be seen by the eyes when they are kept fixed in one direction

W. C. Fields

Fields /feeldz/, **W. C.** (1880–1946) US actor and comedian. He is best known for his portrayal of irascible irresponsible characters struggling to keep one step ahead of the law. One of his most popular films is *My Little Chickadee* (1940). Born **Dukenfield, William Claude**

> 'It's a funny old world—a man's lucky to get out of it alive.'
> [W. C. Fields, *You're Telling Me*; 1934]

fieldsman /feeldzmən/ (*plural* -men /-mən/) *n* a fielder in cricket

field sports *npl* outdoor country sports that involve killing or capturing animals, especially hunting, shooting, and fishing

fieldstone /feeld stōn/ *n* a stone found in fields and used, often in unfinished form, for building

field study *n* a piece of research undertaken outside the laboratory or place of learning, usually in a natural environment or among the general public

field test *n* a test carried out on a product under normal conditions of use

field trial *n* 1. INDUST same as **field test** 2. a competition to determine how well hunting dogs perform

field trip *n* a trip made by students or researchers to study something firsthand

field umpire *n* in Australian Rules football, the official who monitors play, judges whether the rules are being followed, and penalizes fouls or infringements

field winding *n* ELEC same as **field coil**

fieldwork /feeld wurk/ *n* work undertaken outside the school, office, or laboratory in order to gain knowledge through direct contact and observation —**fieldworker** *n*

fiend /feend/ *n* 1. DEVIL an evil supernatural being, especially a devil from hell 2. SOMEBODY EVIL somebody regarded as wicked or cruel 3. SOMEBODY WITH STRONG INTEREST an ardent enthusiast of a subject or activity [Old English *fēond* 'hated person, enemy' (hence 'the enemy of everyone', the devil) < *fēogan* 'to hate' < Germanic]

fiendish /feendish/ *adj* 1. DIABOLICAL resembling a devil or demon 2. CUNNING AND MALICIOUS characterized by devilish cunning, ingenuity, and malice 3. PERPLEXING extremely difficult to solve or analyse 4. DISAGREEABLE extremely bad or unpleasant (*informal*) ○ *fiendish weather* —**fiendishly** *adv* —**fiendishness** *n*

~~fient~~ incorrect spelling of **feint**

fierce /feerss/ (**fiercer, fiercest**) *adj* 1. AGGRESSIVE characterized by or showing aggression or anger ○ *a fierce guard dog* 2. VIOLENT OR INTENSE characterized by the violence or intensity of the forces, activity, or participants involved ○ *It was a fierce battle.* ○ *a fierce storm* 3. PROFOUND deeply and intensely felt and often aggressively expressed ○ *He felt a fierce loyalty to his family.* [13C. Via Anglo-Norman *fers* 'brave, proud, hostile' < Latin *ferus* 'wild, untamed'] —**fiercely** *adv* —**fierceness** *n*

fieri facias /fī ə rī fáyshi əss/ *n* a legal document that authorizes a sheriff to sell enough of a debtor's property to settle the claim of a creditor [< Latin, 'you should cause to be done']

fiery /fíri/ (-ier, -iest) *adj* 1. GLOWING HOT burning or full of fire 2. RED bright red in colour 3. SHOWING INTENSE EMOTION full of or prone to sudden extremes of emotions 4. SPICY extremely hot or spicy to the taste —**fierily** *adv* —**fieriness** *n*

fiery cross *n* 1. formerly, in the Scottish Highlands, a burning wooden cross, carried by runners to call men to arms 2. in the United States, a burning wooden cross adopted as a symbol of the Ku Klux Klan

fiesta /fi éstə/ *n* 1. a celebration or festival linked to a religious holiday, especially in a Spanish-speaking country 2. an event in celebration of something [Mid-19C. Via Spanish < Latin *festum* 'feast, festival']

FIFA /feefə/ *n* the governing organization of international football [French acronym < *Fédération Internationale de Football Association*]

fife /fīf/ *n* a small high-pitched flute without keys, often used in military and marching bands [Mid-16C. Via German *Pfeife* or French *fifre* 'fife, fife player' < assumed Vulgar Latin *pipa* < Latin *pipare* 'to peep, chirp'] —**fifer** *n*

Fife /fīf/ council area in east-central Scotland. Area: 1,323 sq. km/511 sq. mi.

fife rail *n* a low rail round the lower part of the mast of a sailing ship, with belaying pins to which running rigging is attached [Origin ?]

FIFO /fífō/ *abbr* ACCT first in, first out

fifteen /fif teen/ *n* 1. 15 the number 15 2. SOMETHING WITH VALUE OF 15 something in a numbered series with a value of 15 3. GROUP OF 15 a group of 15 objects or people 4. TEAM OF 15 PLAYERS a team of 15 players, especially a rugby union team 5. 15 CINEMA, MEDIA UK FILM RATING in the United Kingdom, a rating given to films and videos considered unsuitable for those under the age of fifteen [Old English *fīftēne* < *fīf* 'five' + *-tēne* (< Germanic, 'ten')] —**fifteen** *adj, pron*

fifteenth /fif teenth/ *n* one of 15 equal parts of something —**fifteenth** *adj, adv*

fifth /fifth/ *n* 1. ONE OF 5 PARTS OF SOMETHING one of five equal parts of something 2. 5 IN SERIES item number five in a series 3. MUSIC 5-NOTE INTERVAL in a diatonic scale, an interval stretching from one note to another five notes higher, or the sound made when both these notes are played simultaneously 4. MUSIC same as **dominant** (sense 1) 5. AUTOMOT 5TH GEAR in some cars or motor vehicles, the fifth gear 6. BALLET same as **fifth position** [Old English *fīfta* < *fīf* (see FIVE)] —**fifth** *adj, adv*

Fifth *n* US same as **Fifth Amendment** (*informal*) ◇ **take the Fifth** to refuse to answer an awkward or self-incriminating question

Fifth Amendment *n* an amendment to the US Constitution stating, among other things, that defendants or witnesses in criminal trials need not testify against or incriminate themselves and may not be retried for an offence a second time

fifth column *n* a secret or subversive group that seeks to undermine the efforts of others and promote its own ends [Originally, a group of supporters that General Mola claimed to have inside Madrid during the Spanish Civil War, in addition to the four columns of his army besieging the city] —**fifth columnist** *n*

fifth-generation *adj* describes a highly advanced and as yet undeveloped level of computer technology, incorporating artificial intelligence

fifthly /fífthli/ *adv* used to introduce the fifth point in an argument or discussion

fifth position *n* in ballet, a position in which the feet are turned outwards with the heel of the front foot level with and touching the base of the big toe of the back foot

fifth wheel *n* N Am 1. somebody or something whose presence is superfluous or unwanted 2. same as **spare tyre** (sense 1) 3. a horizontal bearing that allows a vehicle's front axle to swivel left or right relative to its body, or that allows a trailer attached to a tractor vehicle to pivot

fiftieth /fíftii əth/ *n* 1. ONE OF 50 PARTS one of 50 equal parts of something 2. 50 IN SERIES item number 50 in a series 3. 50TH BIRTHDAY somebody's 50th birthday —**fiftieth** *adj, adv*

fifty /fífti/ *n* (*plural* -ties) 1. 50 the number 50 2. GROUP OF 50 a group of 50 objects or people 3. £50 NOTE a banknote worth 50 pounds ■ **fifties** *npl* 1. NUMBERS 50

TO 59 the numbers 50 to 59, particularly as a range of Fahrenheit temperatures ○ *in the low fifties* 2. YEARS FROM 50 TO 59 the years from 50 to 59 in a century 3. PERIOD FROM AGE 50 TO 59 the period of somebody's life from the age of 50 to 59 [Old English *fīftig* < FIVE + *-tig* 'ten'] —**fifty** *adj, pron*

fifty-fifty *adv* in two equally divided parts or shares ○ *We'll split the profits fifty-fifty.* ■ *adj* equally likely that either of two possibilities may come about ○ *a fifty-fifty chance*

fig

fig[1] /fig/ *n* 1. a pear-shaped fruit with sweet flesh and many seeds, often preserved or dried 2. a tree that produces figs. Native to: tropical and subtropical regions. Latin name: *Ficus carica*. [13C. Via Old French *figue* < Latin *ficus*] ◇ **not give** or **care a fig for somebody** or **something** not to care about somebody or something at all

fig[2] /fig/ *n* the way somebody is dressed, usually in particularly grand or formal clothing (*archaic*) [Mid-19C. < variant of archaic *feague* 'beat, work at briskly', origin ?]

fig. *abbr* 1. figurative 2. figure

fight /fīt/ *v* (**fights, fighting, fought** /fawt/, **fought**) 1. *vti* USE VIOLENCE to use violent physical means such as blows with fists or a weapon to try to overpower somebody 2. *vti* GO TO WAR to go to war, or engage in armed conflict with another country, force, or group 3. *vi* TAKE PART IN WAR to take part in a war or battle, e.g. as a member or unit of the armed forces involved in it 4. *vt* CARRY ON BATTLE OR CONTEST to enter into or carry on a battle or other contest such as an election or court case 5. *vi* STRUGGLE DETERMINEDLY to make a strenuous effort to do, obtain, achieve, or defend something 6. *vti* OPPOSE SOMETHING to make vigorous efforts to oppose, resist, or overcome something or somebody ○ *fight injustice* 7. *vi* ARGUE to quarrel with somebody or with each other 8. *vti* BOX AGAINST SOMEBODY to take part in a boxing match against somebody ■ *n* 1. VIOLENT ENCOUNTER a conflict between individual people or groups in which each tries to do physical harm to, or defeat, the other 2. MAJOR EFFORT a determined attempt to achieve something or resist something or somebody 3. VERBAL CONFRONTATION a verbal dispute or quarrel 4. PROPENSITY TO FIGHT the ability or willingness to continue a battle or struggle ○ *We've still got a lot of fight left in us.* 5. BOXING MATCH a boxing match or similar contest [Old English *feohtan* 'to fight' < W Germanic] —**fightable** *adj* ◇ **fight it out** to fight or argue until a decisive result is obtained ◇ **fight shy of something** to try to avoid something

SYNONYMS *fight, battle, war, conflict, engagement, skirmish, clash*

CORE MEANING: a struggle between opposing armed forces

fight a physical struggle between individual people or groups such as battalions or armies ○ *During the fight, the soldier overpowered the guard and captured his rifle.* ○ *The fight for the village was part of an operation against rebel resistance.* **battle** a large-scale fight between armed forces involving combat between armies, warships, or aircraft ○ *killed in the Battle of Waterloo* ○ *Her brother was one of the casualties of the land battle.* **war** a period of hostile relations between countries, states, or factions that leads to fighting between armed forces, especially in land, air, or sea battles ○ *at the outbreak of war* ○ *a long-running civil war* ○ *the war years* ○ *the post-war period* **conflict** warfare between opposing forces, especially a prolonged and bitter but sporadic struggle ○ *an end to*

bloody conflict in the region ○ a border conflict with sporadic troop clashes ○ armed conflict **engagement** a hostile encounter involving military forces ○ Planes attacked artillery and command sites in the largest military engagement of the war to date. **skirmish** an incident where fighting breaks out briefly between two small groups, sometimes as part of a larger battle ○ a skirmish with guerrillas in which several men were killed ○ The last skirmish in the three-day battle came just after midnight. **clash** a short fierce encounter with another person or group, often involving physical combat ○ tried to avoid a clash of arms ○ The meeting was marred by a clash between the demonstrators and security guards.

fight back v **1.** vi GET BACK AT SOMEBODY to resist or retaliate when attacked **2.** vi COUNTERATTACK to counterattack or make a determined effort to recover after initial defeat or difficulty **3.** vt RESTRAIN TEARS OR EMOTION to suppress something such as tears or the outward expression of an emotion or impulse

fight off vt **1.** to drive away or resist an attacker **2.** to make an effort not to succumb to something such as an illness or an unpleasant feeling

fighter /fítər/ n **1.** ATTACKING AIRCRAFT a fast armed military aircraft designed principally to attack enemy aircraft **2.** VERY DETERMINED PERSON a determined person who struggles to achieve or resist something **3.** SOLDIER somebody who fights, especially as a soldier **4.** BOXER a competitor in a boxing match

fighter-bomber n an aircraft designed to combine the roles of fighter and bomber

fighting chance /fíting-/ n a possibility of success, but only with sustained effort

fighting cock n a male domestic fowl kept for fighting. N Am term **gamecock**

fighting fish

fighting fish n a small brightly coloured, highly aggressive freshwater fish with long flowing fins, often kept in aquariums. Native to: Southeast Asia. Genus: Betta.

fight-or-flight reaction n a set of physiological changes, including an increase in heart rate, blood pressure, and the flow of epinephrine, that constitutes the body's instinctive response to impending danger or other stress

fig leaf n **1.** a stylized representation of a leaf of the fig tree, formerly used as a covering for the genitals in painting or sculpture **2.** an unconvincing or inadequate attempt to conceal something considered shameful or wrong

figment /fígmənt/ n something produced by or only existing in somebody's imagination [15C. < Latin figmentum 'formation, figure, creation' < fingere 'to form, shape']

figural /fíggərəl/ adj ARTS same as **figurative** (sense 2)

figurant /fíggyoōrənt/ n a male ballet dancer who does not perform solo [Late 18C. < French, present participle of figurer 'represent' < Latin figura (see FIGURE)]

figurante /fíggyoō rónt/ n a female ballet dancer who does not perform solo [Late 18C. < French, form of figurant (see FIGURANT)]

figuration /fíggə ráysh'n/ n **1.** FIGURATIVE REPRESENTATION OF SOMETHING a depiction of something in emblematic or allegorical form **2.** MUSIC USE OF MUSICAL FIGURES AS EMBELLISHMENT the use of musical figures or other ornaments to embellish or vary a theme **3.** ARTS GIVING SOMETHING FIGURATIVE FORM the process of giving allegorical or emblematic form to something ab-

stract, especially by representing it using human or animal figures

figurative /fíggərətiv, fíggyoō-/ adj **1.** NOT LITERAL using or containing a nonliteral sense of a word or words **2.** REPRESENTATIONAL relating to or representing form in art by means of human or animal figures **3.** REPRESENTING BY ALLEGORICAL FIGURES using an allegorical or emblematic human or animal figure to represent an abstract idea or quality —**figuratively** adv —**figurativeness** n

figure /fíggər/ n **1.** SYMBOL REPRESENTING NUMBER a symbol representing something other than a letter of the alphabet, especially a number **2.** AMOUNT EXPRESSED NUMERICALLY an amount or value expressed as a number **3.** SOMEBODY'S BODY SHAPE the shape of an individual human body, especially with regard to its slimness or attractiveness **4.** ARTS REPRESENTATION a representation of a human being in a picture or sculpture **5.** HUMAN SHAPE SEEN INDISTINCTLY a human shape seen in outline or indistinctly or that is unidentified **6.** SOMEBODY WITHIN PARTICULAR CONTEXT a person, especially with regard to status within a context, e.g. in history or in a community or profession ○ She was a prominent figure in her community. **7.** SOMEBODY SERVING AS EXAMPLE somebody regarded as having qualities that exemplify a particular role in life (usually used in combination) ○ a father figure **8.** WAY SOMEBODY APPEARS TO OTHERS the general impression somebody makes on other people **9.** PUBL ILLUSTRATIVE DRAWING OR DIAGRAM an illustrative drawing or diagram in a book or article **10.** SHAPE OR OUTLINE OF SOMETHING something represented by a shape or outline **11.** MATHS GEOMETRIC FORM any two- or three-dimensional geometric form consisting of points, lines, curves, or planes **12.** HANDICRAFT PATTERN OR DESIGN a pattern or design, especially on cloth or wood **13.** DANCE, ICE SKATING DANCE OR SKATING ROUTINE a sequence of movements performed by dancers or ice-skaters in a routine **14.** MUSIC GROUP OF MUSICAL NOTES a short progression of musical notes that produces a single distinct impression **15.** LOGIC FORM OF SYLLOGISM the form of a syllogism in Aristotelian logic as determined by the position of the middle term ■ **figures** npl MATHEMATICAL CALCULATIONS calculations involving numbers (informal) ■ v (-ures, -uring, -ured) **1.** vi BE INCLUDED IN SOMETHING to appear, take part, or be included in something ○ did not figure in the outcome **2.** vt IMAGINE SOMETHING to form an idea about or envision something **3.** vti US BE UNSURPRISING to be or happen as expected ○ It just figures they'd show up late. [13C. Via French < Latin figura 'form, shape, figure' < fingere 'make, shape'] ◇ **cut a fine** or **sorry figure** to look impressive or unimpressive ◇ **go figure** US used to indicate that you think a situation you have described is odd or hard to comprehend (slang)

figure on vt N Am to plan or assume that something should or will happen ○ We can figure on running at a loss this year.

figure out vt **1.** to find a solution or explanation for something **2.** to reach a decision or conclusion about something

SYNONYMS See deduce.

figured /fíggərd/ adj decorated with a design or pattern

figured bass n a bass part of a musical composition, typically baroque or classical, in which the notes have numbers written above them to indicate which chords to play

figure eight n N Am same as **figure of eight**

figurehead /fíggər hed/ n **1.** a carving, usually of a full- or half-length human figure, built into the bow of a sailing ship **2.** the apparent head of an organization or institution who has no real responsibility or authority

figure-hugging adj fitting closely around the body and revealing its shape

figure of eight n an outline of the number eight formed with two loops and one continuous line, e.g. in figure skating or aerobatics. N Am term **figure eight**

figure of merit n a parameter or characteristic of a machine, component, or instrument that is used as a measure of its performance

figure of speech n an expression or use of language in a nonliteral sense in order to achieve a particular effect. Metaphors, similes, and hyperbole are all common figures of speech.

figure skating n a form of competitive skating in which skaters trace patterns on the ice and perform spins, jumps, and other manoeuvres —**figure skater** n

figurine /fíggə reen/ n a small ornamental figure, often of ceramic or metal [Mid-19C. Via French < Italian figurina 'small figure' < Latin figura (see FIGURE)]

fig wasp n a wasp that breeds in caprifigs and pollinates the flowers of wild fig trees. Native to: Europe. Genus: Blastophaga.

figwort /fíg wurt/ (plural **-worts** or same) n a tall woodland plant of the snapdragon family. Flowers: small, greenish, in clusters. Genus: Scrophularia. [Mid-16C. < FIG¹ as dialect term for haemorrhoids, which it was used to treat]

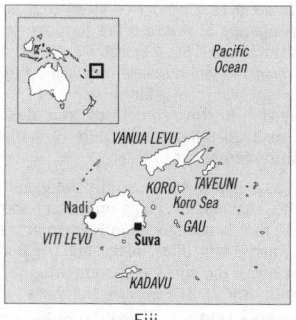

Fiji

Fiji /féeji/ island nation in the southern Pacific Ocean north of New Zealand and east of northern Australia. A British colony from 1874, it gained its independence in 1970. Having left the Commonwealth in 1987, it rejoined in 1997. Language: English. Currency: Fijian dollar. Capital: Suva. Population: 868,531 (2003). Area: 18,376 sq. km/7,095 sq. mi. Official name **Republic of Fiji**

Fijian /fee jée ən/ n **1.** a language spoken on the islands of Fiji, belonging to the eastern branch of the Austronesian family of languages. Native speakers: 400,000. **2.** somebody who comes from Fiji —**Fijian** adj

~~**filagree**~~ incorrect spelling of **filigree**

filament /fílləmənt/ n **1.** SLENDER STRAND OR FIBRE a slender strand or fibre of a material **2.** ELEC ENG WIRE CONDUCTOR IN LIGHT BULB a thin wire that produces light in an incandescent bulb or emits electrons in a valve when electricity passes through it **3.** BOT FLOWER PART the stalk that supports the pollen-bearing anther in the male reproductive organ (**stamen**) of a flower **4.** MICROBIOL LONG STRAND OF CELLS a long strand of similar cells joined end to end, as found in some bacteria and algae [Late 16C. < French, or modern Latin filamentum < Latin filum 'thread'] —**filamentary** /fíllə méntəri/ adj —**filamentous** /fíllə méntəss/ adj

filaria /fi láiri ə/ (plural **-ae** /fi láiri ee/ or same) n a parasitic worm that is carried as a larva by biting insects and lives as an adult in the blood or tissues of vertebrates, causing filariasis. Family: Filaridae. [Mid-19C. < modern Latin Filaria < Latin filum 'thread'] —**filarial** adj —**filarian** adj

filariasis /fíllə rí əssiss/ n a disease caused by parasitic worms (**filaria**) that inflames and obstructs the lymphatic glands, sometimes resulting in elephantiasis

filature /fílləchər/ n **1.** REELING OF SILK FROM COCOONS the process of reeling silk fibres from cocoons **2.** SILK REEL a spool used in filature **3.** SILK FACTORY a factory that reels silk fibres [Mid-18C. Via French < Italian filatura < Latin filum 'thread']

filbert /fílbərt/ (plural **-berts** or same) n **1.** FOOD same as **hazelnut 2.** TREES same as **hazel** (sense 2) [14C. < Anglo-Norman philbert, after St Philibert, whose feast day falls in August, when hazelnuts begin to ripen]

filch /filch/ (**filches, filching, filched**) vt to steal something opportunistically, usually a small item or

amount of little value (*informal*) [13C. Origin ?] —**filcher** *n*

SYNONYMS See *steal.*

file[1] /fīl/ *n* **1.** STORAGE FOR PAPERS a folder, cabinet, or other container that holds papers for convenient storage and reference **2.** ORDERED COLLECTION a collection of related documents or papers arranged so that they can be consulted easily **3.** COMPUT COMPUTER INFORMATION a uniquely named collection of program instructions or data stored on a hard drive, disk, or other storage medium and treated as a single entity **4.** LINE a line of people or things standing or moving one behind the other ■ *v* (**files, filing, filed**) **1.** *vt* STORE SOMETHING IN ORDER to arrange and store something in a file for future reference **2.** *vt* LAW SUBMIT SOMETHING to submit something such as a claim or complaint to the appropriate authority so that it can be put on record **3.** *vi* LAW BRING LAWSUIT to make a formal application for something such as a divorce ○ *filed for bankruptcy* **4.** *vt* MEDIA SEND IN NEWS REPORT to send in a report or story to a newspaper or news agency **5.** *vi* MOVE IN LINE to move in line one behind the other [15C. < French *filer* 'thread on a string' < Latin *filum* 'thread'; because documents were hung on string for easy reference] —**filer** *n*

file away *vt* **1.** to store something in a file for future reference **2.** to take careful note of something in order to remember it

file[2] /fīl/ *n* a metal tool, usually long and narrow and with sharpened ridges on one or more of its surfaces, that is used to smooth down or wear away wood or metal ■ *vti* (**files, filing, filed**) to smooth down or wear away the surface of something using a file [Old English *fēol* < Indo-European, 'cut, carve']

file allocation table *n* COMPUT full form of **FAT**

file cabinet *n N Am* COMM same as **filing cabinet**

file clerk *n N Am* same as **filing clerk**

file extension *n* a set of characters following the dot after the name of a DOS file, identifying the file type

filefish /fīl fish/ (*plural same* or **-fishes**) *n* a long bony fish with rough-edged scales, a tiny mouth, and a sharp dorsal spine over the eye. Native to: tropics. Family: Balistidae.

file format *n* the pattern and convention by which a computer program stores information in a file

file manager *n* a computer program that arranges and manipulates files and directories

filename /fīl naym/ *n* a set of characters, sometimes restricted in number, serving as an identifying title for a computer file and often including a file extension

file server *n* a computer in a network that stores application programs and data files accessed by other computers

filet FOOD *n* another spelling of **fillet** *n* (sense 1) ■ *vt* another spelling of **fillet** *v* (sense 1)

filet mignon /fíllay meen yon/ *n* a small round boneless piece of beef cut from the inside of the loin and usually grilled or fried [< French, 'dainty fillet']

filial /fílli əl/ *adj* **1.** relating or appropriate to a child's relationship with, or feelings towards, his or her parents ○ *filial duty* **2.** GENETICS describes the first generation that results from crossing two parental lines [15C. Directly or via Old French < late Latin *filialis* 'of a son or daughter' < Latin *filius* 'son', *filia* 'daughter'] —**filially** *adv* —**filialness** *n*

filiate /fílli ayt/ (**-ates, -ating, -ated**) *vt* **1.** to determine the paternity of a child in a court of law, especially an illegitimate child **2.** LAW same as **affiliate** (*formal*) [Late 18C. < medieval Latin *filiat-*, past participle of *filiare* 'acknowledge as your child' < Latin *filius* 'son', *filia* 'daughter']

filiation /fílli áysh'n/ *n* **1.** PROCESS OF ESTABLISHING PATERNITY the process of determining legally who is the father of a child whose paternity is in dispute **2.** BEING SOMEBODY'S CHILD the condition of being the child of particular parents (*formal*) **3.** AFFILIATION the act of affiliating, or the state of being affiliated (*formal*) [15C. Via Old French < medieval Latin *filiation-* 'relationship as a child' < Latin *filius* 'son', *filia* 'daughter']

filibeg /fílli beg/, **philibeg** *n Scotland* CLOTHING same as kilt (*literary*) [Mid-18C. < Scottish Gaelic *feileadh-beag* 'little kilt']

filibuster /fílli bustər/ *n* a tactic used to delay or prevent the passage of legislation, e.g. a long irrelevant speech ■ *vti* (**-ters, -tering, -tered**) to try to stop legislation being passed by making long speeches [Mid-19C. Via Spanish *filibustero* < Dutch *vrijbuiter* 'pirate'] —**filibusterer** *n* —**filibusterism** *n* —**filibusterous** *adj*

filicide /fílli sīd/ *n* (*formal*) **1.** the killing by a parent of a son or daughter **2.** a parent who kills his or her own son or daughter [Mid-17C. < Latin *filius* 'son', *filia* 'daughter'] —**filicidal** /fílli sīd'l/ *adj*

filiform /fílli fawrm/ *adj* long, thin, and fine like a thread [Mid-18C. < Latin *filum* 'thread']

AKG London

filigree: detail of decorative filigree and jewelled medieval book cover (1225–30)

filigree /fílli gree/ *n* **1.** LACY METAL ORNAMENTATION delicate decorative openwork made from thin twisted wire in silver, gold, or another metal **2.** DELICATE WORK a delicate ornamental tracery ■ *vt* (**-grees, -greeing, -greed**) FORM SOMETHING INTO DELICATE PATTERN to form something into a delicate ornamental openwork design [Late 17C. Alteration of French *filigrane* < Italian *filigrana* < Latin *filum* 'thread' + *granum* 'grain'] —**filigree** *adj*

filing[1] /fíling/ *n* the activity of storing files in their proper place

filing[2] /fíling/ *n* a tiny particle or shaving of metal, e.g. one removed with a file (*often used in the plural*) ○ *iron filings*

filing cabinet *n* a piece of office furniture containing drawers for storing files

filing clerk *n* an employee in an office who stores and retrieves documents and other records. N Am term **file clerk**

filing system *n* a method of organizing office files, especially one that identifies and organizes the major headings under which documents are to be filed

Filipino /fílli peénō/, **Pilipino** /pílla-/ *adj* OF THE PHILIPPINES relating to the Philippines, or their languages, peoples, or cultures ■ *n* (*plural* **-nos**) **1.** LANG OFFICIAL LANGUAGE OF THE PHILIPPINES the official language of the Philippines, an Austronesian language based on Tagalog. Native speakers: 15 million. **2.** PEOPLES SOMEBODY FROM THE PHILIPPINES somebody who comes from the Philippines [Late 19C. < Spanish < (*las islas*) *Filipinas* 'the Philippines']

fill /fil/ *v* (**fills, filling, filled**) **1.** *vti* MAKE SOMETHING FULL OR BECOME FULL to make a container full, or become full ○ *The bath filled rapidly.* **2.** *vt* TAKE UP ALL THE SPACE to take up the space inside or cover the surface area of something ○ *The room was filled with light.* **3.** *vt* COVER BLANK AREA to cover a page or a blank space on a page with writing or drawing **4.** *vt* BECOME ABUNDANT to become present and very noticeable throughout something ○ *The scent of spring filled the air.* **5.** *vti* MAKE SOMEBODY FEEL POWERFUL EMOTION to cause somebody to experience a strong emotion, usually to the exclusion of all others, or be taken over by a strong emotion ○ *The news filled me with dread.* **6.** *vt* CLOSE UP HOLE to plug a hole, crack, or cavity in something **7.** *vt* MEET NEED to satisfy a need or requirement ○ *The retreat filled her need for solitude.* **8.** *vt* OCCUPY FREE TIME to occupy a period of time with an activity ○ *They filled their days with DIY and gardening until she returned.* **9.** *vt* HOLD OFFICE to hold a job or office and carry out the duties associated with it **10.** *vt* CHOOSE SOMEBODY to elect or appoint somebody to a vacant job or position **11.** *vt* COOK PUT FILLING INTO SOMETHING to put a type of food into something such as a cake or sandwich as its filling **12.** *vt* CONSTR ADD SOMETHING TO RAISE SURFACE LEVEL to build up the surface of something with earth, stones, or other materials until it reaches a desired level **13.** *vti* POWER SAIL WITH WIND to stretch a sail and make it bulge, or bulge under the pressure of the wind ■ *n* **1.** PLENTY OF SOMETHING a sufficient or excessive quantity of something ○ *I've had my fill of his complaints.* **2.** ENOUGH TO MAKE CONTAINER FULL enough of something to fill a container, or the act of filling a container **3.** MATERIAL TO RAISE SURFACE material used to build up the surface of something to a desired level, e.g. earth or stones **4.** MUSIC IMPROVISED MUSIC music improvised to fill designated spaces in a jazz or other musical score [Old English *fyllan* < Germanic]

fill in *v* **1.** *vt* COMPLETE BLANK SPACES IN SOMETHING to write information into the blank spaces on a form or document **2.** *vt* COLOUR BLANK SPACE ON SOMETHING to cover a blank space on something with colouring or shading **3.** *vt* PLUG CAVITY AND MAKE SURFACE LEVEL to put material into a cavity in a surface to make the surface level **4.** *vt* OCCUPY TIME to spend a period of time that would otherwise be unoccupied in an activity **5.** *vi* BE SUBSTITUTE FOR SOMEBODY to act as a substitute for somebody **6.** *vt* GIVE SOMEBODY INFORMATION to supply somebody with new or necessary information about something **7.** *vt* BEAT SOMEBODY UP to subject somebody to a beating (*slang*)

fill out *v* **1.** *vt* to write information into the blank spaces on a form or document **2.** *vti* to become larger and more substantial, or make something larger and more substantial

fill up *v* **1.** *vti* BECOME OR MAKE SOMETHING FULL to become full, or make something full **2.** *vt* SATISFY SOMEBODY'S HUNGER to give somebody the feeling of having eaten enough **3.** *vi* AUTOMOT MAKE FUEL TANK FULL to fill a vehicle's tank with fuel

fille de joie /fée də zhwaá/ (*plural* **filles de joie** /*pronunc. same*/) *n* a female prostitute (*euphemistic*) [< French, 'girl of pleasure']

filled gold *n US* METALL same as **rolled gold**

filler /fíllər/ *n* **1.** SOMETHING THAT FILLS somebody who or something that fills something **2.** PLUGGING OR COATING SUBSTANCE a substance used to plug a crack or cavity or smooth a surface **3.** SUBSTANCE ADDED FOR BULK a substance that is used to fill spaces or add bulk or strength to a material, e.g. sizing **4.** MEDIA, BROADCAST LESS IMPORTANT MATERIAL something, often relatively unimportant, added to fill space or time, e.g. in a newspaper or broadcast **5.** TOBACCO FILLING the tobacco inside a cigar or cigarette **6.** INDUST PADDING a material that is used to stuff something such as a quilt or toy, e.g. cotton or down

fillér /féllair/ *n* a subunit of Hungarian currency. See table at **currency** [Early 20C. < Hungarian]

filler cap *n* AUTOMOT same as **petrol cap**

fillet /fíllit/ *n* **1.** *also* **filet** FOOD BONELESS PORTION OF FISH OR MEAT a boneless portion cut from a fish, a poultry breast, or the rib area of beef, lamb, or pork **2.** CLOTHING RIBBON WORN AROUND THE HEAD a ribbon worn across the forehead, as an ornament or to hold back the hair **3.** ARCHIT FLAT NARROW MOULDING a raised or sunken ornamental surface set between larger surfaces **4.** PRINTING DECORATIVE LINE ON THE COVER OF BOOK a thin decorative line impressed onto the cover of a book, or the tool used to make it ■ *vt* (**-lets, -leting, -leted**) **1.** *also* **filet** FOOD PREPARE BONELESS PORTION to cut and prepare boneless portions of fish, poultry, or meat **2.** USE BINDING OR DECORATION to bind hair or decorate a surface with a fillet [14C. < Old French *filet* < Latin *filum* 'thread']

fill-in *n* a temporary replacement or substitute for somebody

filling /fílling/ *n* **1.** SUBSTANCE USED TO FILL SOMETHING a substance used to fill the space inside something, pad it, or add bulk to it **2.** GETTING SOMETHING FILLED the process or an instance of having something such as a cavity in a tooth filled **3.** DENT PLUG FOR DECAYED TOOTH a plug made of metal or composite material used to fill a tooth cavity **4.** FOOD MIXTURE PUT INSIDE FOOD food, or a mixture of foods, that is put inside something else such as a pie, pastry case, or sandwich **5.**

TEXTILES **THREADS GOING ACROSS FABRIC** the horizontal threads or yarn in a woven fabric ■ *adj* **SATISFYING HUNGER** leaving somebody with the feeling of having eaten enough

filling station *n* TRANSP same as **petrol station**

fillip /fíllip/ *n* **1. FEELING OF ENCOURAGEMENT** something that provides a stimulus or encouragement to somebody or something **2. SNAPPING MOVEMENT OF FINGERS** a snapping of the tip of one of the fingers against the ball of the thumb in order to make a sound or to propel a small object ■ *vt* **(-lips, -liping, -liped) 1. PROPEL SOMETHING WITH FILLIP** to strike or propel something by snapping the fingertip against the ball of the thumb **2. GIVE SOMEBODY OR SOMETHING INCENTIVE** to provide a stimulus or encouragement to somebody or something [15C. An imitation of the sound of flicking or snapping the fingers]

fill light *n* in photography and film-making, a secondary source of light used to eliminate, reduce, or soften shadows

Fillmore /fíl mawr/, **Millard** (1800–74) 13th president of the United States. A member of the Whig Party, he served as vice president (1849–50) before assuming the presidency (1850–53) upon the death of Zachary Taylor. See table at **president**

> 'An honourable defeat is better than a dishonourable victory.'
> [Millard Fillmore, *Address*, 13 September 1844]

fill-up *n* a filling of something, especially a vehicle's fuel tank

filly /fílli/ (*plural* **-lies**) *n* **1.** a female horse under four years of age **2.** an offensive term for a young woman or girl (*dated informal*) [15C. < Old Norse *fylja*]

film /film/ *n* **1.** PHOTOGRAPHY **COATED STRIP FOR TAKING PICTURES** a thin translucent strip or sheet of cellulose coated with a light-sensitive emulsion, used in a camera to take still or moving pictures **2.** CINEMA **SERIES OF MOVING PICTURES ON SCREEN** a series of real or fictional events recorded by a camera and projected onto a screen as a sequence of moving pictures, usually with an accompanying soundtrack. N Am term **movie 3.** CINEMA **FILMS COLLECTIVELY** films collectively, considered as a medium for recording events, a form of entertainment, or an art form **4.** INDUST **VERY THIN SHEET OF SOMETHING** material, especially a plastic, in the form of a very thin, flexible, translucent, or transparent sheet. Use: wrapping. **5. THIN LAYER** a thin coating of a substance such as dust, liquid, or ice covering the surface of something **6. SOMETHING MAKING VIEW HAZY** a thin haze or mist or something similar that blurs somebody's view ■ **films** *npl* **FILM INDUSTRY** the industry of film-making (*informal*) ■ *v* **(films, filming, filmed) 1.** *vt* **TAKE PICTURES OF SOMETHING** to record somebody or something on film **2.** *vti* **MAKE FILM** to make or be involved in the making of a film **3.** *vt* **MAKE FILM OF SOMETHING** to make a film of a book, story, or event **4.** *vi* **BE GOOD FOR FILMING** to be a suitable subject for cinematic treatment ○ *a story that would film well* [Old English *filmen* 'membrane, skin' < Indo-European]

film over *vi* to become covered with a thin or misty layer of something

film badge *n* a piece of photographic film incorporated into a badge and used to register the wearer's exposure to nuclear radiation

filmgoer /film gō ər/ *n* somebody who goes to a cinema to see films, especially on a regular basis. N Am term **moviegoer**

filmi /fílmi/ *S Asia adj* **1. OF INDIAN FILM INDUSTRY** relating to the Indian film industry **2. SENSATIONAL** melodramatic or exaggerated ■ *n* (*plural* **-is**) **FILM STAR** a star of the Indian film industry [Late 20C. < FILM + Hindi *-i*, adjective suffix]

filmic /fílmik/ *adj* characteristic or reminiscent of a cinema film, especially in the techniques used to tell a story or describe a scene —**filmically** *adv*

film library *n* a large collection of cinema films or newsreels used as an archive or for hire

filmmaker /film maykər/ *n* a producer or director of cinema films —**filmmaking** *n*

film noir /film nwaár/ (*plural* **films noirs** /*pronunc. same*/) *n* a cinematic genre popular in the 1940s and 1950s, often filmed in urban settings with extensive use of shadows, cynical in outlook, and featuring antiheroes [Mid-20C. < French, 'black film']

filmography /film óggrəfi/ (*plural* **-phies**) *n* a list of the films made by an actor or director or on a topic [Mid-20C. Blend of FILM + BIBLIOGRAPHY]

filmsetting /film setting/ *n UK* a typesetting process that involves projecting the characters that are to be printed onto photographic film and then making printing plates from the film. ANZ, N Am term **photocomposition** —**filmset** *vt* —**filmsetter** *n*

film star *n* a well-known film actor or actress. N Am term **movie star**

filmstrip /film strip/ *n* a length of developed photographic film containing a series of still images to be projected onto a screen

filmy /fílmi/ (**-ier, -iest**) *adj* **1.** consisting or made of very thin translucent material **2.** covered or misted over with a thin layer of something —**filmily** *adv* —**filminess** *n*

filmy fern *n* a small fern that grows in humid regions, has translucent leaves, and forms sheets on moist rocks. Genus: *Hymenophyllum.*

filo /féelō/, **filo pastry** *n* very thin sheets of pastry dough used to make papery crisp small pastries or large dishes, used especially in Greek cooking. N Am term **phyllo** [Mid-20C. < Greek *phullo* 'leaf']

Filofax /fílō faks/ *tdmk* a trademark for a compact loose-leaf binder containing sheets of paper in different colours, used as a personal portable filing system and address book

fils[1] /filss/ (*plural* **filses** or *same*) *n* a subunit of currency in several Middle-Eastern countries. See table at **currency** [Late 19C. < Arabic *fals*, small copper coin]

fils[2] /feess/ *n* in France and French-speaking countries, a word used after a man's or boy's surname to distinguish him from his father of the same name ○ *Henri Dupont fils* [Late 19C. < French, 'son']

filter /fíltər/ *n* **1. STRAINING DEVICE** a device made of or containing a porous material used to collect particles from a liquid or gas passing through it **2. POROUS MATERIAL USED FOR STRAINING** any porous layer or material such as sand, paper, or cloth, used in or as a filter **3.** PHOTOGRAPHY **TINTED SCREEN** a tinted glass or dyed gelatin screen placed on a camera lens to control light or colour or distort an image **4.** COMPUT **DEVICE RESTRICTING THE PASSAGE OF FREQUENCIES** a device or computer program that allows the passage of some frequencies or digital elements and blocks others **5.** same as **filter tip** (sense 1) **6.** ROADS **DIRECTIONAL TRAFFIC SIGNAL** an additional traffic signal at a junction, in the form of a green arrow, to indicate that vehicles may turn left or right while traffic going straight ahead is halted ■ *v* **(-ters, -tering, -tered) 1.** *vti* **PASS SOMETHING THROUGH FILTER** to put something such as fluid, light, or electrical impulses through a filter to remove or recover something, or be passed through a filter to do this **2.** *vi* **PASS THROUGH SOMETHING** to seep or pass through a filter or something that is intended to act as a barrier ○ *The sunlight filtered in through the shutters.* **3.** *vi* **TRICKLE** to move or pass slowly and gradually ○ *People filtered into the auditorium.* **4.** *vti* ROADS **TURN WHILE TRAFFIC AHEAD HALTED** to turn right or left at a junction while the traffic going straight ahead is halted, or allow traffic to turn in this way [14C. Via Old French *filtre* 'felt' (used for filtering liquids) < medieval Latin *filtrum* < Germanic] —**filterable** *adj* —**filterer** *n* —**filterless** *adj* —**filtrable** *adj*

filter bed *n* a thick layer of gravel, clinker, or other filtering material in a tank, used to remove sewage or other impurities from liquids

filter cake *n* a deposit of semisolids or solids that are separated out and deposited between layers of filtering material after a fluid has been passed through them

filter coffee *n* **1.** coffee made by passing hot water through finely ground coffee held in a filter made of paper, cloth, or wire mesh. Aus, N Am term **drip coffee 2.** coffee beans ground to the right consistency for making filter coffee

filter-feeder *n* a sea animal that feeds on organic particles or small organisms that it filters from the water, e.g. a clam, sponge, or baleen whale —**filter-feeding** *adj*

filter paper *n* porous paper used as or in a filter

filter tip *n* **1.** a small cylindrical mouthpiece made of a dense porous material attached to the end of a cigarette to remove tar and other impurities from the smoke **2.** a cigarette with a filter tip —**filter-tipped** *adj*

filth /filth/ *n* **1. FOUL DIRT** dirt or refuse that is disgusting or excessive **2. MORALLY OBJECTIONABLE MATERIAL** something considered extremely morally objectionable or obscene, e.g. coarse language or explicit descriptions, or depictions of sexual activity **3. OFFENSIVE TERM** an offensive term for the police (*slang*) [Old English *fȳlð* < Germanic]

filthy /fílthi/ *adj* (**-ier, -iest**) **1. EXTREMELY DIRTY** extremely or disgustingly dirty ○ *Your hands are filthy!* **2. MORALLY OBJECTIONABLE** considered extremely morally objectionable or obscene **3. DESPICABLE** used to express contempt or strong disapproval (*informal*) ○ *a filthy liar* **4. UNPLEASANT** extremely unpleasant (*informal*) ■ *adv* **VERY** to an extreme degree (*informal*) ○ *filthy rich* —**filthily** *adv* —**filthiness** *n*

SYNONYMS See *dirty.*

filtrate /fíl trayt/ *n* the material that emerges from a filtering process, usually a liquid or gas from which impurities have been removed ■ *vti* **(-trates, -trating, -trated)** to pass through a filter, or put something through a filter [Early 17C. < modern Latin *filtrat-*, past participle of *filtrare* 'filter' < medieval Latin *filtrum* (see FILTER)]

filtration /fil tráysh'n/ *n* the process of passing or putting something through a filter

filum /fíləm/ (*plural* **-la** /-lə/) *n* a fine part or structure of a living organism that is long and thin like a thread [Mid-19C. < Latin, 'thread, filament, fibre']

FIMBRA /fímbrə/ *abbr* FIN Financial Intermediaries, Managers, and Brokers Regulatory Association

fimbria /fímbri ə/ (*plural* **-briae** /-bri ee/) *n* a fringed border or part in the body, e.g. that found at the entrance to the Fallopian tubes [Mid-18C. < Latin, 'border, fringe'] —**fimbrial** *adj*

fimbriate /fímbri ət/, **fimbriated** /-aytid/ *adj* describes parts of organisms that have a fringed border [15C. < Latin *fimbriatus* 'fringed' < *fimbria* 'border, fringe'] —**fimbriation** /fímbri áysh'n/ *n*

fin /fin/ *n* **1.** ZOOL **PART OF FISH USED FOR MOTION** a flexible organ, sometimes paddle-shaped or fan-shaped, extending from the body of a fish or other water animal and helping in balance and propulsion **2.** NAUT **PART ATTACHED TO HULL OF SUBMARINE** a wing-shaped often movable blade attached low on the hull of a vessel such as a submarine that helps to control and stabilize it **3.** AVIAT **UPRIGHT PART OF AIRCRAFT'S TAIL** a fixed vertical surface at the tail of an aircraft that gives stability and to which the rudder is attached **4.** AVIAT, AEROSP **STABILIZING STRUCTURE ON ROCKET OR MISSILE** any small flat fixed structure extending from the body of a rocket, missile, or aircraft that gives stability in flight **5. RIB ON HEATING DEVICE** a flat metal part projecting from a heating mechanism such as a radiator that helps to increase the transfer of heat to the surrounding air **6.** SWIMMING same as **flipper** (sense 2) **7.** AUTOMOT **DECORATIVE EXTENSION ON CAR BODY** an ornamental extension on the body of a motor vehicle, especially on the rear wing ■ *vi* **(fins, finning, finned) SWIM USING FINS** to swim or beat the water with fins, or show a fin above water [Old English *fin(n)* < Germanic] —**finned** *adj*

fin. *abbr* **1.** finance **2.** financial **3.** finish

Fin. *abbr* **1.** Finland **2.** Finnish

finagle /fi náyg'l/ (**-gles, -gling, -gled**) *vti* to trick, cheat, or manipulate somebody in order to obtain or achieve something (*informal*) ○ *He finagled his way out of the difficulty.* [Early 20C. Origin ?] —**finagler** *n*

final /fín'l/ *adj* **1. LAST** last of a number or series of similar things ○ *a final reminder* **2. ALLOWING NO CHANGE** conclusive and allowing no further discussion ○ *The editor's decision is final.* **3. ENDING** occurring at the end of something ○ *the final curtain* ■ *n* **END OF SERIES** the last and most important in a series of sporting or other contests that decides the winner of a tournament or competition ■ **finals** *npl* **1. LAST DECISIVE ROUNDS OF TOURNAMENT** the last decisive rounds of a knockout tournament or competition during

which the winners of previous rounds play each other **2.** LAST UNIVERSITY EXAMINATIONS the examinations that take place at the end of a course of study at university or studies for a professional qualification [14C. Directly or via French < Latin *finalis* 'last' < *finis* 'final moment, end']

final accounts *npl* the set of accounts produced by a business at the end of its accounting year

final approach *n* the last stage of an aircraft's descent before landing, from its turning into line with the runway to the procedures immediately preceding touchdown

final cause *n* in philosophy, the ultimate goal towards which a process is directed

final cut *n* the approved and edited version of a film prior to its being released for viewing by the public

finale /fi naáli/ *n* **1.** FINAL THEATRICAL SCENE a scene or musical number that brings a stage performance or an act of a performance to an end **2.** FINAL SECTION OF MUSIC a final movement or section of a musical composition **3.** FINAL EVENT IN SERIES an event that is the last or climactic event in a series [Mid-18C. Via Italian < Latin *finalis* (see FINAL)]

finalise *vt* another spelling of **finalize**

finalism /fín'lizəm/ *n* in philosophy, the belief or proposition that all events are determined by their final causes —**finalistic** /fín'l ístik/ *adj*

finalist /fín'list/ *n* a competitor who has qualified to take part in the finals of a contest

finality /fī nálləti/ (*plural* **-ties**) *n* **1.** the quality, state, or condition of being concluded or decided, permitting no further progress or development ○ *He spoke with an air of finality.* **2.** an act, belief, or statement that is final

finalize /fínə līz/ (**-izes, -izing, -ized**), **finalise** (**-ises, -ising, -ised**) *vt* **1.** to bring something to a point at which everything has been agreed upon and arranged **2.** to complete an agreement, sale, or other transaction —**finalization** /fínə lī záysh'n/ *n* —**finalizer** *n*

finally /fín'li/ *adv* **1.** AT LAST after a long period of time or a long delay and often after previous unsuccessful attempts ○ *So you've finally decided to ask her out, have you?* **2.** DEFINITIVELY in a way that rules out further continuance, change, or discussion ○ *The venue won't be finally decided until the next meeting.* **3.** AS LAST IN THE SERIES as the last in a series of things or actions ○ *We visited Belgium, Holland, Germany, and finally Switzerland.* **4.** AS THE LAST WORD used to introduce the last in a series of things said by somebody ○ *Finally, I'd like to thank all of you for coming here tonight.*

Final Solution, final solution *n* the plan to murder systematically all the Jews of Europe, conceived and put into action by the Nazis during World War II [Translation of German *Endlösung*]

~~**finaly**~~ incorrect spelling of **finally**

finance /fī nanss, fi nánss/ *n* **1.** CONTROL OF MONEY the business or art of managing the monetary resources of an organization, country, or person ○ *high finance* **2.** MONEY REQUIRED the money necessary to do something, especially to fund a project ■ **finances** *npl* THE MONEY SOMEBODY HAS the money at the disposal of an organization, country, or person ○ *It'll depend on the state of my finances at the end of the month.* ■ *vt* (**-nances, -nancing, -nanced**) PROVIDE MONEY FOR SOMETHING to raise or provide the money required for something or by somebody [14C. < French < *finer* 'to end, settle' < Latin *finis* 'end'] —**financeable** *adj*

finance bill *n* an act passed by a legislature to raise or provide money for public expenditure

finance company, finance house *n* a business enterprise that loans money to individual people or to companies against collateral, especially to buy items on hire purchase

financial /fī nánsh'l, fi-/ *adj* **1.** relating to or involving money or finance **2.** *ANZ* having enough or plenty of money to dispose of (*informal*) ○ *We're both working, so we're financial at the moment.* —**financially** *adv*

financial analyst *n* somebody working for a financial institution whose job involves studying the performance of particular companies and making recommendations to buy or sell their shares

Financial and Central Services Department *n* a department of the Scottish Executive, responsible for collecting taxes and managing public revenue

financial distress *n* the violation of loan covenants, the inability to pay current bills, or other difficulties relating to bankruptcy that a business may experience

financial institution *n* an organization, e.g. a bank or brokerage, or a building society, that offers financial services such as deposit taking, cheque accounts, loans, or various investment services

Financial Institutions Duty *n Aus* in all Australian states and territories except Queensland, a tax charged on all deposits made into financial institutions, usually paid by the customer

Financial Times Industrial Ordinary Share Index *n* an index of prices on the London Stock Exchange based on the average price of 30 shares. It is produced by the *Financial Times.*

Financial Times Stock Exchange 100 Index *n* FIN full form of **FTSE 100 Index**

financial year *n* a 12-month period at the end of which all accounts are completed in order to provide a statement of a company's, organization's, or government's financial condition. A financial year does not necessarily correspond to a calendar year, e.g. a tax year runs from 6 April to 5 April the following year. Same as **fiscal year**

financier /fī nánssi ər, fi-/ *n* a wealthy investor who is skilled in financial matters [Early 17C. < French < *finance* (see FINANCE)]

~~**finantial**~~ incorrect spelling of **financial**

finback /fín bak/ *n* a large baleen whale that has a prominent dorsal fin. Latin name: *Balaenoptera physalus.* ◊ **rorqual**

finch

finch /finch/ *n* a small songbird with a short broad beak for cracking seeds and colourful plumage, especially in males. Family: Fringillidae. [Old English *finc* < Germanic]

Finch /finch/, **Peter** (1916–77) British-born Australian actor. A stage and screen performer, he received a posthumous Academy Award for his role in *Network* (1976). Born **Mitchell, William**

find /fīnd/ *v* (**finds, finding, found** /fownd/) **1.** *vt* DISCOVER SOMETHING AFTER SEARCHING to discover something or somebody after a search ○ *He was found wandering a mile from his home.* **2.** *vt* GET SOMETHING BACK to recover something after losing it ○ *I can't find my car keys.* **3.** *vt* DISCOVER SOMETHING FOR FIRST TIME to realize, understand, or locate something for the first time, especially by studying or observing ○ *We have to find answers to the problem of global warming.* **4.** *vt* DISCOVER SOMETHING ACCIDENTALLY to notice or come across somebody or something by chance ○ *I found my glasses under the table.* **5.** *vt* EXPERIENCE SOMETHING to notice or experience something personally ○ *They found great comfort in their work.* ○ *I think you'll find them easy to get along with.* **6.** *vt* MANAGE TO GET SOMETHING to make a special effort to gather something together or summon something up ○ *I don't know where we'll find the money.* **7.** *vt* REACH GOAL to succeed in reaching something aimed for ○ *He has finally found his true form as a world-class tennis player.* **8.** *vt* SCI RECORD SOMETHING AS OCCURRING to observe something such as a natural species as existing or occurring (*often passive*) ○ *This species is found all across the continent.* **9.** *vti* LAW REACH VERDICT to decide about something or somebody at the end of a legal procedure, or announce the decision reached ○ *The jury found for the plaintiff.* **10.** *vt* SUPPLY NEED to bring or provide something that is necessary for a process to occur ○ *You will need to find your own transport and equipment for the job.* **11.** *vr* BECOME CONSCIOUS OF YOUR OWN CONDITION to become aware of being in a particular place or state ○ *He found himself in an empty street.* **12. find yourself** *vr* MAKE DECISIONS ABOUT YOUR OWN LIFE to become more self-aware and self-motivated (*informal*) ○ *She finally found herself and became a successful artist.* ■ *n* NEW DISCOVERY something noteworthy or valuable that has been found, or somebody who is talented and is brought to public attention ○ *a real find* [Old English *findan* < Indo-European, 'to tread, go'] —**findable** *adj*

find out *v* **1.** *vti* to get to know something, especially by asking somebody or searching in an appropriate source, or just by chance ○ *I don't know how they found out about the proposed merger.* **2.** *vt* to detect and expose an offence ○ *He was quickly found out and his lies exposed.*

finder /fíndər/ *n* **1.** a locator of things **2.** a small wide-angle telescope attached parallel to the optical axis of a larger telescope to help locate astronomical objects

fin de siècle /fáN də syéklə/ *n* the final years of the 19th century, characterized as being a time of decadence and self-doubt (*hyphenated before nouns*) [< French, 'end of the century']

finding /fínding/ *n* **1.** RESEARCH RESULT a piece of information obtained from an investigation, especially scientific research **2.** LAW VERDICT a conclusion that is reached and recorded at the end of a judicial or other formal enquiry ■ **findings** *npl US* MATERIALS FOR CRAFTWORK small articles or tools used in making craftwork, e.g. metal clips used on earrings

fine[1] /fīn/ *adj* (**finer, finest**) **1.** QUITE WELL OR SATISFACTORY in a good, acceptable, or comfortable condition (*informal*) ○ *Everything's fine, thank you.* **2.** NOT COARSE made up of tiny particles ○ *fine sand* **3.** SUNNY with sunny and clear skies ○ *a fine morning* **4.** THIN very thin, sharp, or delicate ○ *fine features* ○ *fine hair* **5.** GOOD-LOOKING very good to look at ○ *a fine view of the valley* **6.** OUTSTANDING far better than the average ○ *a fine wine* **7.** DELICATELY FORMED showing special skill, detail, or intricacy, especially in artistic work ○ *fine detail* **8.** SMALL AND DELICATE set very closely and carefully together ○ *fine stitching* **9.** UNPLEASANT extremely unsuitable or undesirable (*informal*; *used ironically*) ○ *This is a fine mess!* **10.** VERY SUBTLE so particular or small that it may hardly be noticeable ○ *a maze of fine legal detail* ○ *a fine distinction* **11.** SPURIOUSLY IMPRESSIVE sounding or looking good, but probably just for show (*used ironically*) ○ *nothing but fine gestures* **12.** EXTREMELY PURE with any or most impurities removed, especially in a precious metal ■ *adv* **1.** WELL very well (*informal*) ○ *It works just fine.* ○ *The patient is doing fine.* **2.** INTO SMALL PIECES into tiny or delicate bits ○ *Chop the onions very fine.* ■ *v* (**fines, fining, fined**) **1.** *vt* SHARPEN SOMETHING to make something thinner or sharper (*technical*) **2.** *vti* PURIFY to purify beer or wine, or be purified [13C. < French *fin* < Latin *finire* 'to finish' (see FINISH)] —**fineness** *n*

ORIGIN The Latin word *finire* 'to finish' from which ***fine*** is derived and the related nouns *finis* are also sources of English *affinity, confine, define, final, finance, finesse, finish, finite, paraffin,* and *refine.*

fine[2] /fīn/ *n* a sum of money that somebody is ordered to pay for breaking a law or rule ■ *vt* (**fines, fining, fined**) to take a fixed amount of money from somebody who has broken a law or a rule [13C. Via French *fin* < Latin *finis* 'end', in medieval Latin a sum to be paid on completion of legal proceedings] —**finable** *adj*

fine[3] /feen/ *n* WINE same as **fine champagne** [Shortening]

fine[4] /feé nay/ *n* the place on a music score that shows where the piece finishes after a repeated section, or the symbol that marks this place [Late 18C. < Italian < Latin *finis* 'end']

fine art *n* **1.** ARTS CREATION OF BEAUTIFUL OBJECTS artistic work that is meant to be appreciated for its own sake, rather than to serve some useful function **2.**

EDUC **COLLEGE COURSE IN ART** a course of study designed to teach students practical artistic skills as well as the theory and history of art **3.** ARTS **PURE ART** any art form that is considered to have purely aesthetic value, e.g. painting, sculpture, architecture, drawing, or engraving (*often used in the plural*) **4.** **IMPRESSIVELY DETAILED TECHNIQUE** something that requires great skill, talent, or precision (*informal*) ○ *the fine art of public speaking*

fine champagne /feén shaan pánya/ *n* a brandy made from grapes grown in the Grande and Petite Champagne areas of the Charente region of western France. At least half the grapes must come from the Grande Champagne area. [Mid-19C. < French < *fine* 'fine' + *champagne* 'open space' < late Latin *campania* 'level country' < Latin *Campania*, province in Italy]

fine chemical *n* a chemical product that is made in relatively small quantities and is typically high in cost, e.g. a flavouring or vitamin

Fine Gael /feéna gáyl/ *n* one of the major political parties in the Republic of Ireland, founded in 1933 [< Irish, literally 'tribe of Gaels']

fine-grained, **fine-grain** *adj* formed with a smooth, even, or closely patterned grain

fine leg *n* **1.** in cricket, a fielding position behind the batsman and close to the ball's line of flight, on the side opposite to the way the batsman's body is facing **2.** a fielder in cricket who has been positioned at fine leg

finely /fínli/ *adv* **1.** into small, thin, or delicate pieces **2.** in a careful, delicate, or sensitive way ○ *an actor finely tuned to her audience's reactions* ○ *finely wrought*

fine print *n* ANZ, N Am BUSINESS the detailed part of a document that is printed in small characters, often regarded with suspicion as containing unattractive conditions it is hoped the signer will not notice. UK term **small print**

finery[1] /fínəri/ *n* clothing, jewellery, or accessories that are especially dressy and smart, usually worn on special occasions [Late 17C. < FINE[1], after BRAVERY in the archaic sense 'ostentation, show']

finery[2] /fínəri/ (*plural* **-ies**) *n* a furnace that converts cast iron into wrought iron [Late 16C. < French *finerie* < Old French *finer* 'refine']

fines herbes /feénz áirb/ *npl* a mixture of finely chopped herbs used to flavour a dish [< French, 'fine herbs']

finespun /fín spún/ *adj* spun or stretched out thinly

finesse /fi néss/ *n* **1.** PHYSICAL SKILL elegant ability and dexterity ○ *using a combination of power and finesse* **2.** TACTFUL TREATMENT a delicate and skilful approach in dealing with a troublesome situation ○ *shows great tact and finesse* **3.** CARDS TACTIC IN BRIDGE in bridge, an attempt to win a trick with a lower-value card while holding a higher card not in sequence, hoping that an opponent cannot play an intervening card ■ *vti* (**-nesses, -nessing, -nessed**) **1.** CARDS TRY WINNING TRICK IN BRIDGE in bridge, to attempt to win a trick with a finesse **2.** BE TACTFUL to use, achieve, or handle something delicately and skilfully (*literary*) [Mid-16C. < French, 'fineness' < *fin* (see FINE[1])]

fine structure *n* the separation of light of particular wavelengths produced by atoms or molecules into two or more very similar wavelengths, caused by the interaction of particular quantum mechanical properties

fine-tooth comb, **fine-toothed comb** *n* **1.** a comb with very narrow tightly set teeth **2.** a thorough approach to an investigation or search, in which every detail is examined ○ *poring over the statements with a fine-tooth comb*

fine-tune (**fine-tunes, fine-tuning, fine-tuned**) *v* **1.** *vt* to adjust the engine of a motor vehicle in order to improve its performance **2.** *vti* to make tiny adjustments to something in order to achieve the best possible performance or appearance —**fine-tuning** *n*

fine up *vi* ANZ to become clear and sunny ○ *It should fine up later this afternoon in western parts of the state.*

finfish /fín fish/ *n* a sea fish, as opposed to a shellfish, jellyfish, or other so-called fish

finfoot /fín foŏt/ (*plural* **-foots** or *same*) *n* a diving bird that lives along rivers and lakes. Native to: Africa, Asia. Family: Heliornithidae.

Fingal's Cave

Fingal's Cave /fíng gəlz-/ cave on the island of Staffa in the Inner Hebrides, off the western coast of Scotland. Height: 18 m/60 ft. Length: 70 m/228 ft.

finger /fíng gər/ *n* **1.** ANAT DIGIT OF HAND a digit of the hand, sometimes excluding the thumb (*often used before a noun*) **2.** CLOTHING PART OF GLOVE a long narrow part of a glove that fits over a finger **3.** NARROW STRIP something that resembles a finger in shape ○ *a finger of sand* **4.** FOOD LONG NARROW PIECE OF FOOD a small portion of food about as long and thick as a finger **5.** BEVERAGES APPROXIMATE QUANTITY OF ALCOHOL an approximate measure of alcoholic beverage in a glass, equal in depth to the width of a finger **6.** MEASURE APPROXIMATE UNIT OF LENGTH an approximate unit of measurement, equal to the width or length of a finger ■ *v* (**-gers, -gering, -gered**) **1.** TOUCH SOMETHING to feel or move the fingers across something, often in a gentle, affectionate, or thoughtful way ○ *fingered the fabric lovingly* **2.** *vt* GIVE SOMEBODY UP TO THE POLICE to inform the police of the whereabouts or illegal activities of somebody (*slang*) **3.** *vti* MUSIC PLAY MUSICAL INSTRUMENT to handle the strings or keys of a musical instrument with the fingers **4.** *vt* MUSIC MARK MUSICAL SCORE FOR FINGERING to show on a musical score which fingers the musician should use **5.** *vt* ONLINE LOCATE COMPUTER USERS to obtain and display information about other users of the same computer or on other computers connected through a network or the Internet [Old English, < Indo-European, 'five'] —**fingerer** *n* —**fingerless** *adj* ◇ **cross your fingers** used to express a hope that things will turn out well ◇ **give (somebody) the finger** N Am to make an aggressively obscene gesture with the middle finger extended upwards and held towards somebody (*slang*) ◇ **have a finger in every pie** to be involved in many advantageous or lucrative projects ◇ **have a finger in the pie** to be involved in a particular project, especially in a way that other people find annoying ◇ **let something slip through your fingers** to fail to take advantage of something that would have been of benefit to you ◇ **put your finger on something** to identify something, especially something difficult or elusive ◇ **twist somebody round your little finger** to succeed in getting somebody to do exactly as you wish

fingerboard /fíng gər bawrd/ *n* **1.** a long strip of wood fixed on the neck of a stringed instrument against which strings are pressed in order to vary the pitch **2.** in skateboarding, a miniature board used to demonstrate or mimic stunts using the fingers

finger bowl *n* a small bowl of water put beside a place setting at a table so that fingers can be cleaned, e.g. after picking up food with the hands

finger buffet *n* a selection of food prepared for guests at a party to help themselves to and eat with their fingers, usually while standing

finger chip *n* S Asia a deep-fried potato chip

finger food *n* small items of food made to be eaten with the fingers

fingerfuck /fíng gər fuk/ (**-fucks, -fucking, -fucked**) *vt* a highly offensive term meaning to use the fingers to stimulate a woman's genitals (*taboo*)

finger hole *n* one of a series of holes on a woodwind instrument that a player covers with the fingers in order to register a pitch

fingering /fíng gəring/ *n* **1.** USE OF FINGERS ON MUSICAL INSTRUMENT the action or technique of using the fingers to play a musical instrument **2.** MARKINGS ON MUSICAL SCORE the markings on a musical score that show a musician which fingers to use **3.** USE OF FINGERS the use of the fingers to do something

Finger Lakes /fíng gər-/ group of eleven glacial lakes in western New York, the centre of the state's wine region

fingerling /fíng gərling/ *n* a small fish less than one year old, especially a salmon or trout

fingermark /fíng gər maark/ *n* a smear or greasy mark left after somebody has touched something with a finger

finger millet *n* a short-stemmed millet with an ear divided into five parts, cultivated widely in southern India, Sri Lanka, and parts of Africa. Latin name: *Eleusine coracana*. [Because its ears resemble the fingers of a hand]

fingernail /fíng gər nayl/ *n* a flat protective layer of keratin that covers the end part of a finger's upper surface

finger-paint *vti* to put paint directly onto a surface with the fingers —**finger-painting** *n*

fingerpick /fíng gər pik/ *n* a musician's plectrum with a curved part for attaching it to the finger —**fingerpick** *vti*

fingerplate *n* a metal plate fitted to a door near the handle to keep fingermarks off the door

finger post *n* a notice shaped like a pointing hand, indicating the direction, and usually the distance, to a particular place

fingerprint /fíng gər print/ *n* **1.** PATTERN ON FINGERTIP an impression of the curved lines of skin at the end of a finger that is left on a surface or made by pressing an inked finger onto paper **2.** DISTINGUISHING CHARACTERISTIC a unique characteristic, mark, or pattern that can be used to identify somebody or something ■ *vt* (**-prints, -printing, -printed**) RECORD FINGERPRINTS OF SOMEBODY to press each of somebody's fingertips in ink and then onto paper in order to make a set of marks that can be used to identify that person

finger puppet *n* a very small puppet that is put over and operated by one finger

finger roll *n* a small narrow soft bread roll

fingerspelling /fíng gər spelling/ *n* a form of sign language communication using the fingers to gesture the spelling of words

fingerstall /fíng gər stawl/ *n* a sheath-shaped protective covering worn over an injured finger

fingertip /fíng gər tip/ *n* the tip of a finger ■ *adj* involving the use of the fingertips and so very sensitive or delicate ○ *fingertip controls* ◇ **have something at your fingertips 1.** to know all the details of something thoroughly **2.** to have something available and nearby

finger wave *n* a wave in the hair made by shaping damp hair with the fingers and a comb

Fingo /fíng gō/ (*plural same* or **-gos**) *n* a member of an African people who live among the Xhosa in the Eastern Cape province of South Africa [Early 19C. < Xhosa *mfengu* 'destitute wanderer']

finial /fíni əl, fínni əl/ *n* **1.** ARCHIT ARCHITECTURAL DECORATION a carved decoration at the top of a gable, spire, or arched structure **2.** FURNITURE FURNITURE DECORATION an ornamental feature on the top or end of an object such as a piece of furniture, stair post, or curtain rail, e.g. a carved knob **3.** PRINTING CURVE IN TYPEFACE a curve that ends a main stroke in some italic typefaces [15C. < assumed Anglo-Norman or Anglo-Latin word, 'final' < Latin *finis* 'end'] —**finialled** *adj*

finicky /fínniki/ (**-ier, -iest**), **finicking** /-king/, **finical** /-k'l/ *adj* **1.** difficult to please, and tending to concentrate on small or unimportant details **2.** complicated by trivial details [Late 16C. Probably altered < FINE[1] + *-ical*] —**finickiness** *n*

SYNONYMS See *careful*.

fining /fíning/ *n* **1.** the process of clarifying a liquid, especially wine or beer **2.** the process of removing undissolved gas from molten glass

finis /fínniss/ *interj* used to indicate that something has or must come to an end completely [14C. < Latin, 'end']

finish /fínnish/ *v* (-ishes, -ishing, -ished) **1.** *vti* STOP to come to an end, or bring something to an end ○ *We've finished eating.* ○ *Can we finish work for tonight?* **2.** *vt* CONSUME to eat, drink, or use all of something ○ *Who finished the cake?* **3.** *vt* DESTROY SOMEBODY OR SOMETHING to kill, ruin, or exhaust somebody or something (*informal*) ○ *finished his career in business* **4.** *vt* COMPLETE SURFACE EFFECT OF SOMETHING to treat something, especially wood or metal, in order to achieve a desired surface effect **5.** *vt* GIVE SOMETHING OR SOMEBODY FINAL ENHANCEMENTS to give something or somebody the final touches, qualities, or skills that are required to create a desired effect ■ *n* **1.** END PART the terminating part of something **2.** SPECIAL TOP LAYER a surface texture or final coat applied to something, especially wood or metal ○ *a mirror with a gilt finish* **3.** SPORTS END OF RACE the final part of a race, especially a sprint, acceleration, or challenge, near the finishing line **4.** CONSTR, MANUF QUALITY OF WORKMANSHIP the degree of care with which a product has been manufactured or a job of work has been carried out, judged by its final appearance ○ *The finish on the woodwork is poor.* [14C. < Old French *feniss-*, stem of *fenir* < Latin *finire* < *finis* 'end'] —**finisher** *n*

finish off *vt* **1.** COMPLETE SOMETHING to bring something to an end, e.g. by making it as complete as is wished or needed **2.** USE SOMETHING UP to eat, drink, or use up all of something **3.** DESTROY SOMEBODY OR SOMETHING to kill, ruin, or exhaust somebody or something (*informal*)

finish up *v* **1.** *vt* same as **finish off** (sense 2) **2.** *vi* to be in a particular place or condition in the end, often not the planned one

finish up with *vt* to be left with something ○ *finished up with three identical pieces*

finish with *vt* **1.** to end a relationship or partnership with somebody (*informal*) **2.** to stop using, wanting, or being interested in something

finished /fínnisht/ *adj* **1.** produced and completed with skill and professionalism **2.** having no further prospect of success or development

finishing /fínnishing/ *n* the tasks that complete the production process of a garment, fabric, or material

finishing line *n* a real or imaginary line that marks the end of a race. N Am term **finish line**

finishing school *n* a fee-paying school for girls close to school-leaving age in which social skills, the arts, and academic courses are taught

finishing touch *n* a final small change or addition made to something

finish line *n* N Am same as **finishing line**

Finisterre, Cape /fínni stáir/ promontory in the autonomous region of Galicia, northwestern Spain, extending into the Atlantic Ocean and forming the westernmost part of the mainland

finite /fín īt/ *adj* **1.** LIMITED having an end or limit ○ *We have only a finite amount of resources.* **2.** MATHS COUNTABLE having a countable number of elements **3.** MEASURABLE subject to measurable limitations ○ *finite velocity* **4.** GRAM USING VERB THAT CREATES LIMITS appearing in a verb form that limits person, number, and tense [14C. < Latin *finitus*, past participle of *finire* (see FINISH)] —**finitely** *adv* —**finiteness** *n*

finitude /fínni tyood/ *n* the condition of being finite (*formal*)

fink /fingk/ N Am *n* **1.** SOMEBODY STRONGLY DISLIKED somebody regarded as contemptible (*dated slang insult*) **2.** INFORMER an informant who gives an authority such as the police information that incriminates somebody (*dated slang*) **3.** STRIKEBREAKER a worker who continues to work although colleagues are on strike (*dated slang disapproving*) ■ *vi* (finks, finking, finked) **1.** INFORM ON OTHERS to give an authority information about somebody's criminal or bad behaviour (*dated slang*) ○ *He finked on his buddies after the police questioned him.* **2.** BE STRIKEBREAKER to continue to work in defiance of a strike (*dated slang disapproving*) [Late 19C. Origin ?]

fink out *vi* N Am to fail to do something after previously agreeing or volunteering to do it (*slang*)

fin keel *n* a fin-shaped part that extends downwards

from the underside of a sailing boat to give extra stability

Finland

Finland /fínnlənd/ country in northern Europe on the Baltic Sea. Approximately a third of the country lies within the Arctic Circle. Language: Finnish, Swedish. Currency: markka. Capital: Helsinki. Population: 5,190,785 (2003). Area: 338,145 sq. km/130,559 sq. mi. Official name **Republic of Finland**. Finnish name **Suomi**

Finland, Gulf of arm of the Baltic Sea, extending about 400 km/250 mi. east between Finland and Estonia. Area: 30,044 sq. km/11,600 sq. mi.

Finlandize /fínnlən dīz/ (-izes, -izing, -ized), **Finlandise** (-ises, -ising, -ised) *vt* to make a small country or power act in an accommodating way towards a superpower [Mid-20C. From the behaviour of Finland towards the Soviet Union after World War II] —**Finlandization** /fínnlən dī záysh'n/ *n*

Finlay /fín lay/ river in north-central British Columbia, Canada, that flows southeast into Williston Lake. Length: 400 km/250 mi.

Finn /fin/ *n* **1.** somebody who comes from Finland **2.** somebody who speaks a Finnic language [Old English *Finnas* (plural)]

Finn /fin/, **Neil** (*b.* 1956) New Zealand singer and songwriter. A former member of the groups Split Enz and Crowded House, he began his solo career in 1998.

finnan haddock /fínnən-/, **finnan haddie** *Scotland informal* /-háddi/ *n* a haddock split and smoked on the bone over oak or peat so that the flesh takes on a pale yellow colour [< *Findon*, fishing village near Aberdeen]

Finnic /fínnik/ *n* a group of languages in northeastern Europe belonging to the Finno-Ugric branch of Uralic. Native speakers: 7 million. ■ *adj* **1.** relating to the Finnic group of languages or its speakers **2.** PEOPLES same as **Finnish**

~~finnish~~ incorrect spelling of **finish**

Finnish /fínnish/ *n* the Finnic official language of Finland, also spoken in Estonia and European Russia. Native speakers: 6 million. ■ *adj* relating to Finnish or the Finns

Finn MacCool /fín mə koól/ *n* in Irish legend, the chief of the band of warriors known as the Fianna

Finno-Ugric /fínnō yoógrik/, **Finno-Ugrian** /-yoógri ən/ *n* a group of northeastern European languages that is one of two major branches of Uralic. Native speakers: 22 million. —**Finno-Ugric** *adj*

fino /féenō/ *n* a very pale dry sherry [Mid-19C. < Spanish, 'fine' < Latin *finire* (see FINISH)]

finocchio /fi nóki ō/ (*plural same* or -os) *n* PLANTS same as **fennel** (sense 2) [Early 18C. Via Italian < Latin *faeniculum* (see FENNEL)]

fin whale *n* MARINE BIOL same as **finback**

FIO *abbr* for information only

f.i.o. *abbr* for information only

fiord *n* GEOG another spelling of **fjord**

Fiordland National Park /fyáwrdlənd-/ national park on the southwestern coast of the South Island, New Zealand, established in 1952. It was designated a World Heritage Site in 1986. Area: 12,116 sq. km/4,678 sq. mi.

Fiorentino /fyórrən teénō/, **Rosso** (1494–1540) Italian painter. His most famous work, *Descent from the Cross* (1521), features the bold use of colour and dramatic contrast that characterizes the mannerist school of painting. Born **di Guasparre, Giovanni Battista di Jacopo**

fioritura /fi áwri tyoórə/ (*plural* -re /-ray/) *n* an embellished vocal figure in opera of the 17th and 18th centuries, similar to a cadenza and often improvised. It was later applied to keyboard and violin music. [Mid-19C. < Italian < *fiorire* 'to flower' < Latin *florere* (see FLOURISH)]

fipple /fípp'l/ *n* a small wooden plug in a woodwind instrument or organ pipe that redirects air and creates vibrations [Early 17C. Origin ?]

fipple flute *n* an end-blown flute containing a fipple

fir

fir /fur/ (*plural* **firs** or *same*) *n* **1.** EVERGREEN TREE WITH NEEDLE-SHAPED LEAVES an evergreen tree with needle-shaped leaves and erect female cones. Genus: *Abies*. **2.** EVERGREEN LIKE FIR an evergreen tree that resembles a true fir, e.g. a Douglas fir **3.** WOOD OF FIR the wood of the fir or a related tree [14C. Origin ?]

Firbank /fúr bangk/, **Ronald** (1886–1926) British novelist. He was the author of humorous novels such as *Vainglory* (1915) and *Valmouth* (1919). Full name **Firbank, Arthur Annesley Ronald**

'The world is disgracefully managed, one hardly knows to whom to complain.'
[Ronald Firbank, *Vainglory*; 1915]

Firdawsi /feer dówssi/ (940?–1020?) Persian poet. He is best known for the epic *The Book of Kings* (1010), which traces the history of the Persian empire. Full name **Abdul Qasim Mansur**

fire /fīr/ *n* **1.** DESTRUCTIVE BURNING OF SOMETHING a situation in which something such as a building or an area of land is destroyed or damaged by burning (*often used before a noun*) ○ *destroyed by fire* ○ *fire damage* **2.** PILE OF BURNING FUEL a collection of material such as logs or coal that is set alight and used as fuel for heating, cooking, or burning something **3.** BLAZE the light, heat, and flames caused by something that is burning **4.** HEATING DEVICE an electric or gas-fuelled appliance that can be used to produce heat in a building **5.** PROCESS OF BURNING the rapid production of light, heat, and flames from something that is burning, e.g. in the combustion of wood, coal, or petroleum **6.** ARMS DISCHARGE FROM GUNS a discharge of ammunition from one or more guns ○ *The troops advanced under heavy fire.* **7.** ARMS LAUNCH OF PROJECTILE the process or timing of sending off a missile or rocket **8.** CONTINUOUS ATTACK a series of things that follow each other quickly and relentlessly, especially if hostile or intimidating ○ *She took heavy fire from her political opponents.* **9.** GEM'S BRILLIANCE the shine and sparkle of a gemstone **10.** PASSION energy, spirit, or intensity of feeling ○ *the composer's creative fire* **11.** PHILOSOPHY, ANCIENT HIST ONE OF ELEMENTS OF ANCIENTS in ancient and medieval philosophy, one of the four elements, the active principle of fire, also considered important in astrology ■ *v* (**fires, firing, fired**) **1.** *vti* ARMS DISCHARGE BULLET OR GUN to discharge ammunition or a projectile, or cause a weapon to do this **2.** *vi* ARMS BE DISCHARGED be activated and discharge ammunition or a projectile **3.** *vti* LAUNCH SOMETHING FORCEFULLY to launch something powerfully through the air, or be launched in this way **4.** *vt* DISMISS SOMEBODY FROM WORK to dismiss somebody from employment (*informal*) **5.** *vi* START UP

to begin to burn fuel and start working ○ *The engine fired and the racing car took off.* **6.** vt STOKE OR FILL WITH FUEL to keep supplying fuel to something such as a furnace, engine, or oven **7.** vt CERAMICS BAKE POTTERY IN KILN to put pottery into a kiln to be baked hard **8.** vt STRIKE SOMETHING WITH FORCE to hit or throw something forcefully **9.** vt EXCITE SOMEBODY to arouse strong emotion in somebody (*often passive*) ○ *She was fired with enthusiasm.* **10.** vt DESTROY SOMETHING WITH FIRE to cause something to burn, especially in order to destroy it (*formal or dated*) **11.** vt Malaysia, Singapore TELL SOMEBODY ABOUT to criticize or reprimand somebody (*informal*) ○ *The boss fired me twice last week.* ■ interj **1.** WARNING CRY used to tell others that a dangerous fire has started **2.** COMMAND TO SHOOT used to command the discharge of guns or other weapons, missiles, or projectiles ○ *Ready, aim, fire!* [Old English *fýr* < Indo-European]—**fired** adj—**firer** n ◇ **on fire 1.** in a condition of combustion in which flames, heat, and usually smoke are being produced **2.** full of eagerness or passion ◇ **open fire (on somebody or something)** to begin attacking somebody or something ◇ **play with fire** to do something dangerous or risky ◇ **set fire to something** to make something start burning ◇ **set the world on fire** to do something remarkable or very successful ◇ **under fire 1.** MIL shot at by weapons **2.** subject to severe criticism

CULTURAL NOTE *Pale Fire*, a novel (1962) by Russian-born US writer Vladimir Nabokov. Partly an attack on parasitic critics, it is presented as a long poem by John Shade, with introduction, notes, and index by Charles Kinbote. Kinbote's commentary gradually reveals him to be an unscrupulous critic, ready to use the work of others to further his own career.

SYNONYMS *fire, blaze, conflagration, inferno*
CORE MEANING: burning and flames

fire the light, heat, and flames caused by something burning, whether deliberately or accidentally produced ○ *the crackling fire in the hearth* ○ *a fire that gutted the building* **blaze** a brightly or intensely burning fire, or a large fire ○ *The blaze threatened to engulf a nearby house.* ○ *A 7,500-acre blaze closed the main road through the forest over the weekend.* **conflagration** a large fire that causes a great deal of damage ○ *The explosion of the fuel tanks consumed the plane in a terrifying conflagration.* **inferno** a very large fire burning fiercely and uncontrollably, or a place being consumed by a large uncontrollable fire ○ *The store rapidly became a roaring inferno of smoke and fire.*

fire away vi **1.** to begin or keep on shooting **2.** to begin doing something, especially asking questions (*informal*)

fire off vt **1.** to say or ask something quickly and aggressively, especially a question or demand ○ *firing off an angry e-mail* **2.** to discharge a bullet, missile or projectile

fire up v **1.** vti MAKE SOMEBODY ENTHUSIASTIC to cause somebody to become enthusiastic, or become enthusiastic **2.** vt GET SOMETHING GOING to initiate the operation of something **3.** vti START TO BURN to begin to burn, or set something burning

fire alarm n a bell or siren that is sounded if a fire starts

fire and brimstone n in the Christian religion, eternal punishment in hell [See Genesis 19:24, Revelation 19:20]

fire ant n a predatory ant that inflicts a painful sting. Native to: tropical and temperate regions. Genus: *Solenopsis.* [< the burning sensation its sting causes]

firearm /fír aarm/ n a portable weapon that fires ammunition, e.g. a pistol or rifle

fireback /fír bak/ n **1.** a metal lining placed behind a fireplace **2.** the area of wall where a fireback is placed

fireball /fír bawl/ n **1.** PHYS CENTRE OF NUCLEAR EXPLOSION the highly ionized spherical region of bright hot gas and dust at the centre of a nuclear explosion **2.** ASTRON BRIGHT METEOR an exceptionally bright meteor **3.** BALL LIGHTNING a discharge of ball lightning **4.** DYNAMIC PERSON an extremely energetic and dynamic person (*informal*) Same as **ball of fire**

firebird /fír burd/ n a songbird with bright red or orange feathers

fire blight n an infectious disease of apples, pears, and other fruit trees that blackens leaves and kills branches and is caused by the bacterium *Erwinia amylovora*

firebomb /fír bom/ n a bomb designed to start a fire —**firebomb** vti —**firebomber** n —**firebombing** n

firebox /fír boks/ n an enclosure for a fire in a stove, furnace, or the engine of a steam locomotive

firebrand /fír brand/ n **1.** somebody with a strong or aggressive personality who encourages unrest **2.** a burning stick carried by somebody as a torch or a weapon

firebrat /fír brat/ n a small wingless insect related to the silverfish, found in warm moist places. Latin name: *Thermobia domestica*.

firebreak /fír brayk/ n a strip of land that has been cleared of trees, bushes, and any other combustible material in order to prevent a fire from spreading

firebrick /fír brik/ n a brick that can withstand very high temperatures. Use: fireplaces, furnaces.

fire brigade n an organization of people trained to prevent, control, and extinguish fires and to rescue people from fires and other dangerous situations. N Am term **fire department**

firebug /fír bug/ n somebody who starts fires causing damage or destruction, especially repeatedly and for pleasure (*informal*)

fireclay /fír klay/ n a durable clay that can withstand great heat. Use: firebricks, crucibles, furnace linings.

fire control n the control of naval or artillery fire directed at a target

firecracker /fír krakər/ n a firework consisting of a small paper or cardboard cylinder filled with an explosive that makes one or several loud bangs when lit

firecrest /fír krest/ n a small bird of the warbler family. The top of its head is bright orange in the male and bright yellow in the female. Native to: Europe. Latin name: *Regulus ignicapillus*.

firedamp /fír damp/ n a mixture of methane and other hydrocarbon gases that forms in coalmines and is explosive when mixed with air [< DAMP 'noxious gas']

fire department n N Am EMERGENCIES same as **fire brigade**

firedog /fír dog/ n Southern US HOUSEHOLD same as **andiron**

fire door n **1.** a fireproof door that is normally kept closed or locked in order to ensure that any fire is confined to one area **2.** an emergency exit opened from inside

fire drill n a rehearsal for evacuating a building quickly and safely in the event of a fire or other emergency

fire-eater n **1.** an entertainer who appears to swallow flames from a burning stick **2.** an aggressive, angry, or argumentative person (*informal*) —**fire-eating** n

fire engine n a large road vehicle equipped with ladders, hoses, and other equipment for fighting fires and rescuing people

fire escape n a specially designed means of getting clear of a building if it catches fire, especially an exterior metal stairway attached to the building

fire extinguisher n a cylindrical metal container holding a substance such as foam or vaporizing liquid that can be sprayed onto a fire in order to put it out

firefight /fír fīt/ n a fierce battle involving a heavy exchange of gunfire

firefighter /fír fītər/ n somebody who attempts to control or extinguish fires, and to rescue people or animals from danger —**firefighting** n

firefly /fír flī/ (plural **-flies**) n a winged nocturnal beetle that, during courtship, produces an intermittent light from luminescent chemicals in its abdominal organs. Family: Lampyridae.

fireguard /fír gaard/ n a metal, usually meshed screen that is put around the front of an open fire, mainly to stop sparks from flying out and to prevent people from going too close **2.** same as **firebreak**

firehouse /fír howss/ n US EMERGENCIES same as **fire station**

fire hydrant n an upright pipe, usually in a street, connected to a water main with a valve to which a hose can be attached, e.g. by firefighters

fire insurance n insurance that offers cover against damage or loss caused by fire

fire irons npl a collection of implements used for tending a fire in a fireplace, especially a shovel, tongs, poker, and brush

firelight /fír līt/ n the flickering light given off by an open fire

firelighter /fír lītər/ n a small piece of an inflammable substance that helps fuel to catch fire quickly

firelock /fír lok/ n in early firearms, a mechanism that struck a spark from flint or steel and caused a charge to explode

fireman /fírmən/ (plural **-men** /-mən/) n **1.** MAN WHO IS FIREFIGHTER a man who is a firefighter, especially one who works for a fire brigade **2.** RAIL, BOATING STOKER a man who stokes a furnace, especially on a steam locomotive or steamboat **3.** DRIVER'S ASSISTANT an assistant to the driver of an electric or diesel train

fire marshal n N Am **1.** a state or local official whose job is to investigate suspicious fires and work in the areas of fire prevention and building inspection **2.** an employee of a plant or other industrial site who is responsible for firefighting equipment and fire safety procedures

Firenze /fi rént say/ ♦ **Florence**

fire opal n a translucent reddish opal

fireplace /fír playss/ n a recess, usually with a mantelpiece above it, built into the wall of a room as a place to light an open fire

firepower /fír pow ər/ n **1.** the capability of a military unit or weapon to direct effective fire at an enemy **2.** the capability or potential of a person, team, or organization for effective action

fire practice n EMERGENCIES same as **fire drill**

fireproof /fír proof/ adj treated or manufactured so as to be impossible or very difficult to burn and therefore destroy by fire —**fireproof** vt

fire raiser n a person who commits arson

fire-resistant adj treated or made so as to be very slow to catch fire and burn

fire-retardant adj tending not to catch fire easily and therefore checking the spread of fire

fire sale n a sale of goods or property damaged in a fire

fire screen n **1.** HOUSEHOLD same as **fireguard** (sense 1) **2.** a free-standing screen placed in front of a fireplace to act as a heat shield or as a decorative screen when a fire is not lit

fire service n the organization that firefighters work for

fire ship n formerly, a ship loaded with explosives or combustibles that was set on fire and allowed to drift as a weapon among enemy ships

fireside /fír sīd/ n the space around a fireplace or hearth ■ adj cosy, familiar, or homely ○ *a fireside chat*

fire sign n each of the three signs of the zodiac, Aries, Leo, and Sagittarius, traditionally associated with a fiery, assertive, and dynamic temperament

fire station n a building where professional firefighters are stationed and their vehicles and equipment are kept

firestone /fír stōn/ n a form of sandstone that can withstand great heat. Use: to line kilns and furnaces.

firestorm /fír stawrm/ n **1.** a large extremely intense fire sustained by strong inwardly rushing winds that feed a rising column of hot air **2.** US a strong, sometimes violent, upheaval or outburst ○ *a firestorm of protest*

firethorn /fír thawrn/ n ANZ, US PLANTS a thorny evergreen bush cultivated for its bright orange or red fruits. Native to: Europe, Asia. Genus: *Pyracantha*. UK, Can term **pyracantha**

fire trail n Aus a road through forest or bush land that enables firefighters to reach wildfires in remote areas

firetrap /fír trap/ n a building or structure regarded as a fire hazard, because it is either built of combustible materials or lacks adequate means of escape

fire tree n a New Zealand evergreen tree of the myrtle family with red flowers. Latin name: *Metrosideros tomentosa*.

firetruck /fír truk/ n N Am EMERGENCIES same as **fire engine**

firewalking /fír wawking/ n the rite or practice of walking barefoot over hot coals, ashes, or stones — **firewalker** n

firewall /fír wawl/ n 1. WALL PREVENTING THE SPREAD OF FIRE a fireproof wall put in place to ensure that if a fire occurs it is confined to one area 2. COMPUT SECURITY SOFTWARE a piece of computer software intended to prevent unauthorized access to system software or data 3. COMM BARRIER WITHIN COMPANY a legal barrier set up between sections of a company to prevent them from sharing inside information when this might lead to a conflict of interest

fire watcher n a lookout for fires, especially a member of an air-raid patrol during World War II

firewater /fír wawtər/ n strong and harsh-tasting alcoholic spirits (*dated slang*)

fireweed /fír weed/ n N Am PLANTS same as **rosebay willowherb** [Because often the first to grow on land that has been burnt]

firewoman /fír woomən/ (*plural* **-women** /-wimin/) n a woman who is a firefighter, especially one who works for a fire brigade

firewood /fír wood/ n wood that is burned as fuel

firework /fír wurk/ n BRIGHT EXPLODING OBJECT a package of manufactured chemicals designed to make a loud and brilliant explosion when lit ○ *a firework party* ■ **fireworks** npl 1. SHOW USING FIREWORKS a display of many brilliant fireworks 2. ANGRY OUTBURST a display of violent temper (*informal*) 3. SPECTACULAR DISPLAY an impressive display of talent (*informal*)

~~firey~~ incorrect spelling of **fiery**

firing /fíring/ n the application of great heat to a ceramic object in a kiln, in order to harden it or to fix an applied substance such as a glaze

firing line n 1. the forefront of a movement, operation, or activity, especially one that is controversial 2. an exposed position from which guns are fired at an enemy, or the troops who occupy it

firing order n the sequence of ignition of the cylinders in an internal-combustion engine

firing party n MIL same as **firing squad**

firing pin n the pin behind the barrel of a firearm that strikes the container of explosive (**primer**) to make the cartridge fire

firing squad n a group of soldiers who carry out an execution by gunfire or deliver a ceremonial volley over a grave

firkin /fúrkin/ n 1. a British unit of capacity used especially in the brewing industry, equal to nine gallons 2. a small wooden tub used, especially in the past, for storing food or liquids [14C. Probably < assumed Middle Dutch *verdelkijn* 'small fourth' < *veerde* 'fourth']

firm[1] /furm/ adj 1. NOT YIELDING TO TOUCH compact and solid when pressed ○ *a firm mattress* 2. SECURE fixed securely and unlikely to give way ○ *a firm hold* 3. DETERMINED showing certainty or determination ○ *You must be more firm with them.* 4. TRUSTWORTHY reliable and able to be trusted ○ *firm evidence* 5. STEADY showing no or few fluctuations ○ *a firm price* ■ adv UNYIELDINGLY in a determined and unshakable way ○ *standing firm despite a wave of criticism* ■ vti (**firms, firming, firmed**) MAKE OR BECOME FIRM to become firm or firmer, or make something firm or firmer [14C. Via Old French < Latin *firmus*] —**firmly** adv —**firmness** n

firm up v 1. vt to make something more definite, clear, or less liable to change ○ *Let's firm up the date of the meeting.* 2. vi to become less liable to fluctuation

firm[2] /furm/ n a group of people who form a commercial organization selling goods or services [14C. < Italian *firma* < late Latin *firmare* 'confirm by signing' < Latin, 'strengthen' < *firmus* 'strong']

firmament /fúrməmənt/ n 1. the sky, considered as an arch (*literary*) 2. the world occupied by all the celebrities in a particular field such as the theatre or sport ○ *a big name in the yachting firmament* [13C. Via French < Latin *firmamentum* < *firmus* 'strong']

firmware /fúrm wair/ n software stored on a memory chip in a computer or computer device instead of being part of a program [Because the instructions will not be lost when power is shut off]

firn /furn/ n GEOG same as **névé** (sense 1) [Mid-19C. Via German, 'of last year' < Old High German *firni* 'old']

firni /feérni/ n in South Asian cooking, a sweet made of noodles rice, or wheat simmered in milk, and nuts and raisins [Via Hindi *firnī* < Persian]

firn wind n a summer wind that blows downhill off a glacier during the day

first /furst/ adj 1. BEFORE REST IN ORDER preceding or ahead of any others in order 2. EARLIER THAN REST occurring before any others in a series 3. MOST IMPORTANT having a higher rank, significance, or authority than others in the same category 4. FUNDAMENTAL forming a basis or foundation for something 5. BEST best in quality or achievement 6. MUSIC PLAYING OR SINGING CHIEF PART playing or singing the most important or highest of two or more parts for instruments or voices of the same type ○ *the first violins* ○ *the first sopranos* ■ n 1. NEW THING something that has not been done before or has not occurred before 2. IN SERIES the ordinal number assigned to item number one in a series 3. ONE AHEAD OF ANY OTHER the one positioned before any other in achievement, rank, quality, or time 4. EDUC HIGHEST LEVEL OF UNDERGRADUATE DEGREE an undergraduate university degree awarded for the highest level of academic achievement 5. AUTOMOT FIRST GEAR the lowest forward gear in a motor vehicle 6. BALLET same as **first position** 7. MUSIC INSTRUMENT OR VOICE TAKING CHIEF PART the instrument or voice that plays or sings the most important or highest of two or more parts for instruments or voices of the same type ■ adv 1. BEFORE OTHERS IN TIME earlier than somebody or something else ○ *arriving first, as usual* 2. ORIGINALLY for the first time ○ *first tried it on a dare* 3. INITIALLY at the start ○ *seemed nervous at first* 4. MORE WILLINGLY used to indicate a preference [Old English *fyr(e)st* < Indo-European] ◇ **first come, first served** those who arrive or apply earliest will get what they want from a limited supply ○ *Tickets will be sold on a first come, first served basis.* ◇ **first in, best dressed** Aus the first person to do something will have the greatest chance of success

first aid n emergency medical treatment for somebody who is ill or injured, given before more thorough medical attention can be obtained

first aider n somebody trained in first aid, often a member of a workforce designated to deal with minor injuries

First Amendment n an amendment to the US Constitution that forbids Congress from interfering with a citizen's freedom of religion, speech, assembly, or petition

first base n 1. in baseball, the initial base that a player attempts to reach 2. in baseball, the position played by the infielder defending first base ◇ **get to first base** to succeed in the initial phase of an activity, especially in making advances to a prospective romantic or sexual partner (*informal*)

first-born n the first offspring to be born to a set of parents ■ adj born first of all

First Cause n in Christianity, God as the originator of everything

first class n 1. BEST ACCOMMODATION the best accommodation offered on an aeroplane, ship, or train 2. PRIORITY POSTAL SERVICE a postal service that guarantees priority in delivery in return for a higher charge 3. BEST CLASS the highest rank, standard, or quality

first-class adj 1. BEST of the highest standard of excellence 2. MOST LUXURIOUS most exclusive and expensive 3. MAIL GIVEN PRIORITY IN POSTAL SERVICE costing more to post and given priority in delivery —**first-class** adv

first course n a dish or selection of dishes served at the beginning of a meal

first cousin n same as **cousin** (sense 1)

first-day cover n an envelope, often specially designed, that bears a newly issued stamp and a postmark for the day on which it was first issued

first-degree burn n a burn marked by pain and reddening of the skin but without blistering or charring of tissue

first-degree murder n N Am murder that is carried out with the planned and deliberate intention of killing somebody

first edition n 1. ORIGINAL COPY OF BOOK a copy of a book in its original printed and published format 2. ORIGINAL PRINTING OF PUBLICATION the total number of copies of a book issued by the original publisher in the first instance 3. FIRST NEWSPAPER OF DAY the first batch or copy of a newspaper on a day of publication

first eleven n in football, cricket, and other team sports with eleven players per team, the best of several teams competing for the same club at different levels

first estate n in societies that date from feudal times, the social and political class that consists of senior members of the clergy

first fifteen n in rugby, the best of several teams competing for the same club at different levels

first finger n ANAT same as **index finger**

First Fleet n Aus the fleet of ships that transported the first group of convicts and immigrants to Australia in 1788

first floor n 1. the floor of a building immediately above the floor at ground level 2. N Am same as **ground floor**

first-foot Scotland n also **first-footer** the first person to visit a household in the New Year, especially one going first-footing ■ vti to be the first visitor to a household in the New Year, especially in the practice of first-footing

first-footing n Scotland the traditional practice of going to the house of a friend or neighbour soon after midnight on 31 December, with good wishes and gifts of food, drink, and fuel

first fruits npl 1. the first harvest of the season or year 2. the first results of an activity

first-generation adj 1. relating to or being the children of parents who have left one country to settle in another 2. describes the earliest computers, which were based on vacuum tubes

firsthand /fúrst hánd/ adj, adv obtained directly from an original source, and not via somebody else

first in, first out n COMPUT same as **push-up** (sense 2)

first lady n 1. also **First Lady** US US LEADER'S SPOUSE OR WOMAN PARTNER the wife of the president of the United States or of a US state governor, or the woman appointed by him to act as his official hostess 2. GOVERNMENT LEADER'S PARTNER the wife or woman partner of a high government official, especially of a country's leader 3. WOMAN NOTABLE IN HER PROFESSION the most important or respected woman member of a profession or field of activity

first language n 1. the language that somebody learned in infancy 2. the principal language in a neighbourhood, district, region, or country

first lieutenant n 1. a naval officer in charge of the upkeep and maintenance of a ship 2. US an officer in the US Army, Air Force, or Marine Corps of a rank above second lieutenant

first light n the earliest time of the day, when the sun begins to rise

firstling /fúrstling/ n the first offspring, product, or result (*archaic or literary*)

first love n 1. the first object of somebody's love or interest 2. the experience of being in love for the first time

firstly /fúrstli/ adv used to introduce the first point in an argument or discussion

first mate *n* an officer on a merchant ship or any non-naval vessel of a rank above second mate

first minister *n* the title of the leader of the National Assembly of Northern Ireland, Scotland, or Wales

first name *n* a personal name that accompanies a family name to identify somebody fully

first night *n* (*hyphenated when used before a noun*) **1.** FIRST PERFORMANCE OF A NEW SHOW the first public performance of a new production of a play or show ○ *first-night nerves* **2.** NIGHT OF THE FIRST PERFORMANCE the night on which the first performance of a new play or show takes place **3.** *also* **First Night** NEW YEAR'S EVE ENTERTAINMENT in the United States, a celebration when a city sponsors a public programme of cultural events and family-oriented entertainment. Date: New Year's Eve. —**first nighter** *n*

first offender *n* somebody with no previous criminal record who breaks the law and is convicted for the first time

first officer *n* **1.** NAUT same as **first mate 2.** the officer who is second-in-command on an aircraft after the captain

first-past-the-post *adj UK, Can* describes a voting system in which the winner needs to receive more votes than anyone else but does not need an absolute majority of the votes cast

first person *n* **1.** VERB OR PRONOUN FORM the form of a verb or pronoun used to refer to the speaker or writer. In English, the first-person singular pronoun is 'I', and the plural is 'we'. **2.** SET OF GRAMMATICAL FORMS the grammatical set containing the forms indicating the first person **3.** WRITING IN FIRST PERSON a style of writing using first-person forms ○ *Write your account in the first person.*

first-person shooter *n* a computer game, mainly involving the shooting of opponents, that uses first-person view

first-person view *n* in a computer game, a computer screen view corresponding to what the character being enacted by the player would see

first position *n* in ballet, a position in which the feet are turned outwards with the heels touching

first post *n* the first of two bugle calls at the end of the day, signalling to military personnel that it is time to retire to barracks before lights out

first principle *n* a fundamental rule underlying a theory, faith, or procedure

first principles *npl* the basic ideas that underpin something, or the basic rules that govern it

first quarter *n* one of four phases of the Moon, during which one half of the Moon's visible surface is illuminated by the Sun

first-rate *adj* of the best quality or the highest standard

first reading *n* the introduction of a bill in a legislature prior to debate and a vote

first refusal *n* the right to decide whether or not to buy something before it is offered to other potential buyers

first responder /-ri spóndər/ *n* the first person with official responsibility, e.g. a member of an ambulance crew or a police officer, who arrives at the scene of a disaster, accident, or life-threatening medical situation

first school *n* in some localities, a school for pupils from five to eight years of age

first strike *n* the use of nuclear weapons against an enemy state that is similarly armed, intended to destroy its military capacity and prevent it from attacking first (*hyphenated when used before a noun*) ○ *first-strike capability*

first thing *adv* **1.** very early in the morning **2.** before doing anything else

first-time buyer *n* somebody who is buying a house for the first time

first water *n* the highest grade in gemstones

First World *n* the principal industrialized countries of the world, including the United States, the United Kingdom, the nations of western Europe, Japan, Canada, Australia, and New Zealand

First World War *n* HIST same as **World War I**

firth /furth/ *n Scotland* (*often used in placenames*) **1.** a river estuary **2.** a wide inlet of the sea [14C. < Old Norse *fjörðr*]

fisc /fisk/ *n* **1.** *US* a public treasury **2.** royal funds, especially those belonging to a Roman emperor (*archaic*) [Late 16C. Directly or via French < Latin *fiscus* 'rush basket, purse, treasury']

fiscal /físk'l/ *adj* **1.** relating to public revenues, especially the revenue from taxation ○ *fiscal prudence* **2.** relating to financial matters in general ■ *n Scotland* LAW same as **procurator fiscal** [Mid-16C. Directly or via French < Latin *fiscalis* < *fiscus* 'rush basket, purse, treasury'] —**fiscally** *adv*

fiscal year *n N Am* same as **financial year**

Fischer /físhər/, **Bobby** (*b.* 1943) US chess player. In 1972, he became the first chess player from the United States to win the world championship, and he held the title until 1975. Full name **Fischer, Robert James**

'I like the moment when I break a man's ego.'
[Bobby Fischer, *Newsweek*; 31 July 1972]

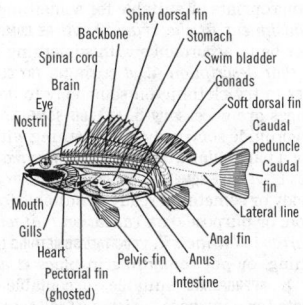

fish: anatomy of a fish

fish /fish/ *n* (*plural same* or *fishes*) **1.** WATER VERTEBRATE WITH GILLS a cold-blooded vertebrate animal that lives in water. It typically has jaws, fins, scales, a slender body, a two-chambered heart, and gills for providing oxygen to the blood. (*often used before a noun*) ○ *a fish tank* **2.** FISH CONSUMED AS FOOD the flesh of any edible fish eaten as food, either cooked or raw (*often used before a noun*) ○ *fish soup* **3.** SOMEBODY UNUSUAL an odd or unusual person (*informal*) ○ *an odd fish* ■ *v* (**fishes, fishing, fished**) **1.** *vi* CATCH FISH to use a rod, net, or other method to bring fish out of the water **2.** *vt* CATCH FISH IN PLACE to try to get fish from a particular river, lake, or stream **3.** *vi* SEARCH to feel around with the hands in order to find something (*informal*) [Old English *fisc* < Indo-European] ◇ **drink like a fish** to habitually drink a lot of alcohol (*informal*) ◇ **have other fish to fry** to have something else to do, usually something more interesting (*informal*) ◇ **like a fish out of water** ill at ease in a situation

fish for *vt* to try to obtain something, especially in an indirect way or in difficult circumstances ○ *fish for compliments*

fish out *vt* to find something or take something out, especially after searching with the hands (*informal*) ○ *fishing out a coin from his pocket*

Fish *n* ZODIAC same as **Pisces** (sense 2)

fish and chips *n* a fillet of fish deep-fried in batter, served with chips (*takes a singular or plural verb*)

fishbowl /fish bōl/ *n* **1.** a round clear open-topped container of water in which a pet goldfish is kept **2.** a place or condition of high public visibility and little or no personal privacy

fish cake *n* a round flat individual savoury cake made from cooked fish and potato, coated with breadcrumbs, and usually fried

fish duck *n* BIRDS same as **merganser**

fish eagle *n* an eagle, especially one with white feathers, that feeds on fish. Genus: *Haliaeetus.*

fisher /físhər/ *n* a species of marten with dense dark brown fur. Native to: northern North America. Latin name: *Martes pennanti.*

Fisher /físhər/, **Andrew** (1862–1928) Scottish-born politician. He was leader of the Australian Labor Party (1907–15) and prime minister (1908–09, 1910–13, and 1914–15). See table at **prime minister**

fisherman /físhərmən/ (*plural* **-men** /-mən/) *n* a man who catches fish as a sport or occupation

fisherman's bend *n* a knot used to tie the end of a line to a ring or spar

fisherman's knot *n* a knot for joining the ends of two ropes, consisting of one or two overhand knots that tighten with tension on the line

fisherperson /físhər purss'n/ (*plural* **-people** /-peep'l/ or **-persons**) *n* somebody who catches fish as a sport or occupation

fisherwoman /físhər wŏomən/ (*plural* **-women** /-wimin/) *n* a woman who catches fish as a sport or occupation

fishery /físhəri/ (*plural* **-ies**) *n* **1.** REGION OF WATER FOR FISHING a region of water where industrial fishing is practised **2.** FISHING INDUSTRY the catching, processing, or selling of fish, including the industries and occupations involved in these activities **3.** FISH BUSINESS a business that harvests, processes, or sells fish **4.** PLACE FOR REARING FISH a region of water or a tank in which fish are reared **5.** LAW RIGHT TO FISH the right to fish in an area

Fishes /físhiz/ *n* ZODIAC same as **Pisces** (sense 2)

Barnaby's

fisheye lens: view from a fisheye lens of Wall Street, New York City

fisheye lens /fish ī-/ *n* a wide-angle lens that gives an extremely wide field of view, up to 180 degrees. Straight lines are curved and distorted by this type of lens.

fish farm *n* a place with facilities for rearing fish commercially —**fish farmer** *n* —**fish farming** *n*

fish finger *n* a rectangular stick of filleted or minced fish covered in breadcrumbs or batter, usually bought frozen in packs. N Am term **fish stick**

fishgig /fish gig/ *n* a pole with barbs, used for spearing fish [Mid-16C. Alteration of FIZGIG, after FISH]

Fishguard /fish gaard/ port in Pembroke, southwestern Wales. It is the nearest port in Great Britain to the Republic of Ireland. Population: 2,903 (1991). Welsh name **Abergwaun**

fish hawk *n* BIRDS same as **osprey**

fishhook /fish hŏok/ *n* **1.** a sharp metal hook used for catching fish **2.** a symbol used in logic to represent a conditional such as 'if' or 'then'

fishing /físhing/ *n* the sport, industry, or occupation of catching fish

fishing expedition *n N Am* an investigation or line of questioning that strays from its ostensible purpose (*informal*)

fishing ground *n* an area of sea where a country has the right to fish

fishing rod *n* a long flexible pole to which a line and usually a reel are attached for catching fish

fish joint *n* a connection in which two rails or beams are joined together by one or more fishplates

fish kettle *n* an oblong pan, often with a rack inside, for cooking a whole fish

fish knife *n* a broad-bladed knife with blunt edges, used for eating fish

fish ladder *n* a series of pools on an incline, separated by short increments so as to enable fish to swim up past a dam or other obstruction

fish louse *n* a small flat rounded crustacean with sucking mouth parts that lives as a parasite on fish. Class: Branchiura.

fishmeal /fĭsh meel/ *n* a substance prepared from ground dried fish. Use: animal feed, fertilizer.

fishmonger /fĭsh mung gər/ *n* **1.** somebody whose job is to sell fish to people for food **2.** *also* **fishmonger's** (*plural same*) a shop where fish is sold

fishnet /fĭsh net/ *n* **1.** open mesh fabric. Use: stockings, tights. **2.** *N Am* a net used to catch fish

fish owl *n* a large owl that lives in wooded country near water and feeds mainly on fish. Native to: Asia, Africa. Genus: *Ketupa* or *Scotopelia*.

fishplate /fĭsh playt/ *n* a flat piece of metal bolted between two abutting rails or beams to join them, especially on a railway track [Mid-19C. Origin ?]

fishpond /fĭsh pond/ *n* a pond where fish are found or kept

fishskin disease /fĭshskin-/ *n* same as **ichthyosis** (*informal*)

fish slice *n* a kitchen utensil with a flat slotted blade, used for turning over food during cooking

fish stick *n* *N Am* same as **fish finger**

fishtail /fĭsh tayl/ *vi* (**-tails, -tailing, -tailed**) to move the tail of an aeroplane from side to side in order to reduce speed ■ *adj* describes the back of a skirt or dress that has a section that is closely gathered or pleated and then flares out

fishwife /fĭsh wīf/ *n* **1.** an offensive term for a woman who is regarded as loud-voiced and lacking in manners (*insult*) **2.** a woman selling fish (*archaic*)

fishy /fĭshi/ *adj* (**-ier, -iest**) *adj* **1.** LIKE FISH like fish, especially in taste, smell, or coldness or sliminess to the touch **2.** DUBIOUS arousing suspicion (*informal*) **3.** EXPRESSIONLESS cold and expressionless, like the eye of a fish —**fishily** *adv* —**fishiness** *n*

Fisk /fĭsk/, **Sir Ernest Thomas** (1886–1965) British-born Australian telecommunications engineer. In 1918 he received the first wireless transmission sent from the United Kingdom to Australia, and in 1924 established the first voice contact between the two countries.

fissi- *prefix* **1.** cleft, separated ○ *fissipedal* **2.** biological fission ○ *fissiparous* [< Latin *fiss-*, past participle of *findere* 'split' < Indo-European]

fissile /fĭssīl/ *adj* **1.** PHYS same as **fissionable 2.** describes a rock that can be split along a grain or a plane of cleavage, e.g. slate or schist [Mid-17C. < Latin *fiss-* (see FISSI-)] —**fissility** /fĭ sílləti/ *n*

fission /fĭsh'n/ *n* **1.** PHYS SPLITTING OF ATOMIC NUCLEUS RELEASING ENERGY the spontaneous or induced splitting of an atomic nucleus into smaller parts, usually accompanied by a significant release of energy **2.** BREAKING UP the act or process of separating into parts **3.** GENETICS DIVISION OF AN ORGANISM the division of a single-celled organism into two equal parts, each part growing into a complete organism [Early 17C. < Latin *fission-* < *fiss-* (see FISSI-)]

fissionable /fĭsh'nəb'l/ *adj* able to undergo nuclear fission —**fissionability** /fĭsh'nə bílləti/ *n*

fission bomb *n* same as **atom bomb** (*technical*)

fission-track dating *n* a way to determine the age of a mineral from the tracks made by fission products of the uranium it contains

fissiparous /fi síppərəss/ *adj* describes an organism that reproduces by dividing into two equal parts, each of which grows into a complete organism —**fissiparously** *adv*

fissiped /fĭssə ped/ *adj* describes animals that have toes separated from each other, e.g. dogs and cats ■ *n* an animal with separated toes. Suborder: Fissipedia. [Mid-17C. < late Latin *fissiped-* < Latin *fiss-* (see FISSI-) + *ped-* 'foot']

fissure /fĭshər/ *n* **1.** CRACK a long narrow crack or opening, especially in rock **2.** PROCESS OF SPLITTING the process of dividing along a line **3.** SCHISM IN GROUP a division into factions of a group or political party **4.** ANAT SPLIT IN BODY PART a natural or pathological division in a body part ■ *vti* (**-sures, -suring, -sured**) SPLIT, OR CAUSE TO SPLIT to split something along fairly regular lines, or undergo this process [14C. Directly or via French < Latin *fissura* < *fiss-* (see FISSI-)]

fist /fĭst/ *n* **1.** a hand with the fingers closed in the palm **2.** same as **hand** *n* (sense 2) (*informal*) **3.** same as **handful** (sense 1) (*informal*) **4.** PRINTING same as **index** *n* (sense 8) ■ *v* (**fists, fisting, fisted**) **1.** *vt* to hit somebody or something with a fist **2.** *vti* same as **fistfuck** (*taboo*) [Old English *fȳst* < Germanic] —**fistful** *n*

fistfight /fĭst fīt/ *n* a fight in which bare fists are used

fistfuck /fĭst fuk/ (**-fucks, -fucking, -fucked**) *vti* a highly offensive term meaning to insert a fist into somebody's vagina or anus for sexual pleasure (*taboo*)

fisticuffs /fĭsti kufs/ *npl* fighting using the fists (*archaic or humorous*) [Early 17C. Probably < *fisty* 'with the fists' + CUFF[2] 'blow']

fistula /fĭstyoolə/ (*plural* **-las** or **-lae** /-lee/) *n* an opening or passage between two organs or between an organ and the skin, caused by disease, injury, or congenital malformation [14C. Directly or via French < Latin *fistula* 'pipe, flute'] —**fistulous** *adj*

fit[1] /fĭt/ *v* (**fits, fitting, fitted**) **1.** *vti* BE THE RIGHT SIZE OR SHAPE to be of a suitable size or shape for something or somebody ○ *See if this jacket fits.* **2.** *vti* BE APPROPRIATE to be appropriate or suitable for something ○ *make the punishment fit the crime* **3.** *vti* BE COMPATIBLE to agree or be in accordance with something ○ *no one fitting that description* **4.** *vt* CLOTHING TRY CLOTHING ON SOMEBODY to try clothing on somebody to determine if changes are necessary **5.** *vt* EQUIP SOMEBODY OR SOMETHING to provide somebody or something with equipment of a particular kind ○ *fitted with extra security features* **6.** *vt* MAKE SOMEBODY OR SOMETHING READY to make somebody or something ready or suitable for a task, function, or purpose ○ *an education that will fit her for a career in business* **7.** *vt* INSTALL SOMETHING to install something, or put something in place ■ *adj* (**fitter, fittest**) **1.** APPROPRIATE suitable, acceptable, or appropriate for a purpose ○ *dishes fit for everyday use* **2.** WORTHY worthy or deserving of something ○ *not fit to serve as an officer* **3.** WELL IN HEALTH in good health **4.** STRONG AND HEALTHY physically strong and healthy, especially because of taking regular exercise ○ *getting fit* **5.** APPEARING LIKELY TO DO SOMETHING appearing likely to do something because of being in an extreme condition (*informal*) ○ *looked fit to drop* **6.** GOOD-LOOKING AND DESIRABLE good-looking and sexually desirable (*slang*) ■ *n* **1.** WAY THAT SOMETHING FITS the way in which something conforms to standards of proper length, tightness, and shape ○ *These shoes are a better fit than the other pair.* **2.** RELATIONSHIP FOR BEST FUNCTION a relationship between corresponding parts or related things that enables proper functioning ○ *check the replacement chassis for fit* **3.** MECH ENG CLOSENESS OF SURFACES the closeness of contact between adjacent surfaces in a mechanical assembly. Typical examples are shrink, sliding, or press fit. [14C. Origin ?] ◇ **fit to be tied** very angry and exasperated (*informal*)

fit in *v* **1.** *vi* to conform harmoniously to other members of a group or other things in a setting ○ *She's been able to fit in well at her new school.* **2.** *vt* to find a time or place for somebody or something that does not conflict with other arrangements ○ *The dentist can fit you in at three.* ○ *I love the theatre but can't fit it into my schedule.*

fit out *vt* to equip or provide something or somebody with required items such as supplies or clothes

fit up *vt* **1.** to provide or equip somebody or something with something **2.** to make somebody who is innocent appear guilty (*slang*)

fit[2] /fĭt/ *n* **1.** a sudden occurrence of a physical activity or an emotional mood ○ *a fit of laughing* ○ *a coughing fit* **2.** sudden violent convulsions, e.g. in a child with a high fever or somebody experiencing a seizure [Old English *fitt*, origin ?] ◇ **by fits and starts** starting and stopping repeatedly ◇ **throw a fit** to show strong emotion, especially anger (*informal*)

fitch /fĭch/, **fitchet** /fĭchit/ *n* ZOOL same as **polecat** [15C. < Middle Dutch *fisse*]

fitful /fĭtf'l/ *adj* starting and stopping irregularly ○ *a fitful sleep* —**fitfully** *adv* —**fitfulness** *n*

fitment /fĭtmənt/ *n* something that can be detached or taken down

fitness /fĭtnəss/ *n* **1.** BEING PHYSICALLY FIT the state of being physically fit **2.** SUITABILITY suitability of somebody or something for a particular purpose **3.** GENETICS ABILITY TO REPRODUCE SUCCESSFULLY the ability of an organism to produce offspring that survive and reproduce

fitness centre *n* a place with facilities and equipment for people to maintain or improve their physical fitness

fitted /fĭttid/ *adj* **1.** CLOSE-FITTING tailored to fit closely to the body ○ *a fitted jacket* **2.** MADE TO FIT SPACE built or fixed to fill or cover a specific space ○ *a fitted wardrobe* ○ *fitted carpets* **3.** WITH FITTED FURNITURE with fitted furniture ○ *a fitted kitchen*

fitted sheet *n* a sheet with elastic at the corners that makes it fit snugly over a mattress

fitter /fĭttər/ *n* **1.** a maintainer, repairer, or assembler of mechanical equipment **2.** somebody who alters clothes to make them fit

fitting /fĭtting/ *adj* SUITABLE appropriate for the circumstances ○ *a fitting end to her career* ■ *n* **1.** DETACHABLE PART a detachable part, especially for a device or machine **2.** TRYING ON OF CLOTHES the trying on of a piece of clothing to see if it requires alteration **3.** WORK OF FITTER the work performed by a fitter **4.** CLOTHES SIZE a size of clothes or shoes ■ **fittings** *npl* FURNITURE AND ACCESSORIES furniture and accessories that are not permanently fixed in place —**fittingly** *adv* —**fittingness** *n*

fitting room *n* a room for trying on or fitting clothes in a shop

fit-up *n* (*slang*) **1.** CRIME same as **frame-up** (sense 1) **2.** a set and its props that are easily erected

Fitzgerald /fĭts jérrəld/, **Edward** (1809–83) British poet and translator. He is best known for his translation (1859) into rhymed verse of the *Rubáiyát* by the Persian poet, Omar Khayyam.

AKG London
Ella Fitzgerald

Fitzgerald, Ella (1917–96) US jazz singer. She was known for her scat singing and extensive song repertoire.

> 'I always thought my music was pretty much hollering.'
> [Ella Fitzgerald, *Ella Fitzgerald*, Bud Kliment; 1988]

Library of Congress
F. Scott Fitzgerald

Fitzgerald, F. Scott (1896–1940) US writer. He wrote novels and short stories that chronicled the mood and manners of the 1920s. Among his works is *The Great Gatsby* (1925). Full name **Fitzgerald, Francis Scott Key.** See Cultural note at **great, tender**[1]

> 'Show me a hero and I will write you a tragedy.'

[F. Scott Fitzgerald, 'Notebooks E', *The Crack-Up: with Other Uncollected Pieces, Note-Books and Unpublished Letters*; 1945]

FitzGerald /fits jérrəld/, **G. F.** (1851–1901) Irish physicist. He suggested a way of producing electromagnetic waves that led to wireless telegraphy. He helped devise the Lorenz-FitzGerald contraction that was used by Einstein in his theory of relativity. Full name **FitzGerald, George Francis**

Fitzroy /fits roy/ river in northern Western Australia that rises in the Durack Range and empties into the Indian Ocean near Derby. Length: 620 km/385 mi.

Fitzsimmons /fits símmənz/, **Bob** (1862–1917) British-born New Zealand boxer. In 1897 he became the world heavyweight champion, a title he held until 1899. Full name **Fitzsimmons, Robert Prometheus**

'The bigger they come the harder they fall.' [Bob Fitzsimmons, *Brooklyn Daily Eagle*; 11 August 1900]

five /fīv/ *n* **1.** 5 the number 5 **2.** GROUP OF 5 a group of five objects or people **3.** SOMETHING WITH VALUE OF 5 something in a numbered series with a value of 5, e.g. a playing card ○ *the five of clubs* ○ *to throw a five* [Old English *fīf* < Indo-European] —**five** *adj, pron* ◇ **take five** to take a few minutes' break from work or other activity (*informal*)

five-and-dime *n N Am* a shop in the United States of a type, now obsolete, that sold household goods, toys, sweets, small pets, and other assorted items at reasonable prices

five-a-side *n* football with five players in each team, including the goalkeeper, usually played indoors

Five Civilized Nations, Five Civilized Tribes *npl* five Native North American peoples, the Choctaw, Cherokee, Chickasaw, Creek, and Seminole, who were briefly self-governing in the Indian Territory after being displaced from their land in the southeastern United States

five-eighth *n* **1.** *Aus* in rugby, a player positioned between the halfbacks and inside centre **2.** *NZ* in rugby union, either of two players positioned between the halfback and the centre

five-finger *n* PLANTS same as **cinquefoil**

fivefold /fīv fōld/ *adj* **1.** TIMES 5 with or equal to five times as much or as many **2.** WITH 5 PARTS composed of five parts or sections ■ *adv* BY FIVE TIMES AS MUCH by five times as much or as many

five hundred *n* euchre or rummy in which the winner is the first to reach 500 points

five Ks *npl* the five distinctive features of dress worn by members of a Sikh order (**Khalsa**) ◊ **kesh, kangha, kirpan, kuccha, kara**

Five Nations *n* the original Iroquois Confederacy of five Native North American peoples, the Mohawk, Onondaga, Cayuga, Oneida, and Seneca, founded in the 16th century and lasting until 1722

five nines *npl* a very high measure or degree of product reliability, used especially in information technology [< the figure 99.999% as a measure of near-completeness]

five o'clock shadow *n* beard growth noticeable later in the day on a man who shaved in the morning

five of a kind *n* a poker hand consisting of four cards of the same denomination plus a wild card

fivepenny /fīfpəni/ *adj* costing or worth five pence

Five Pillars of Islam *npl* the basic tenets of Islam, which are a belief in Allah and in Muhammad as his prophet, in prayer, in charity, in fasting, and in making a pilgrimage to Mecca

fivepins /fīvpinz/ *n* a bowling game played in Canada in which five skittles are used (*takes a singular verb*)

fiver /fīvər/ *n* (*informal*) **1.** a note worth five pounds **2.** *N Am* a banknote worth five dollars

fives /fīvz/ *n* a game that resembles squash but in which the ball is hit with the hand or a bat (*takes a singular verb*) [Mid-17C. Probably plural of FIVE]

five-spice powder *n* a Chinese mixed spice consisting of star anise, Sichuan pepper, cinnamon, fennel, and cloves

fivespot /fīv spot/ *n N Am* a banknote worth five dollars (*slang*)

five-star *adj* having the highest quality

five-star general *n* a general of the highest rank, with an insignia of five stars

five stones *n* the game of jacks when five small stones are used as the throwing pieces (*takes a singular verb*)

fix /fiks/ *v* (**fixes, fixing, fixed**) **1.** *vt* MEND OR CORRECT SOMETHING to repair, mend, or correct something **2.** *vt* FASTEN SOMETHING to fasten something in place **3.** *vt* AGREE SOMETHING to agree, arrange, or settle something, especially a time or a price **4.** *vt* ATTRIBUTE SOMETHING to attribute something, especially blame ○ *to fix the blame on other people* **5.** *vt* DIRECT SOMETHING to direct or concentrate the eyes, attention, or mind ○ *She fixed her eyes on the path ahead.* **6.** *vt* INFLUENCE SOMETHING DISHONESTLY to influence a person or outcome dishonestly (*informal*) ○ *The trial was fixed.* **7.** *vti* MAKE OR BECOME SECURE to make something stable, firm, or secure, or become so **8.** *vt* HOLD SOMEBODY'S ATTENTION to hold or capture the attention or interest of somebody ○ *fixed us with a baleful smile* **9.** *vt N Am* PREPARE SOMETHING AS FOOD to prepare something, especially a meal or a drink **10.** *vt* TAKE REVENGE ON SOMEBODY to take revenge on or punish somebody (*informal*) **11.** *vt N Am* ARRANGE OR ORDER SOMETHING to arrange or put something in order **12.** *vt N Am* VET STERILIZE ANIMAL to spay or castrate an animal (*informal*) **13.** *vt* BIOCHEM CONVERT NITROGEN TO A STABLE FORM to convert atmospheric nitrogen to a stable or biologically available form, as soil bacteria do **14.** *vti* CHEM MAKE OR BECOME STABLE to make a chemical or compound stable and nonvolatile, or undergo this process **15.** *vt* PHOTOGRAPHY, ART MAKE IMAGE PERMANENT to treat something such as a photographic film or plate with chemicals in order to make a permanent image **16.** *vt* BIOL PRESERVE SOMETHING FOR EXAMINATION to preserve a specimen in a chemical solution for study under a microscope **17.** *vi* DRUGS INJECT A DRUG to inject an illegal drug (*slang*) ■ *n* **1.** PREDICAMENT a predicament or difficult situation ○ *in a fix* **2.** SUPERFICIAL SOLUTION an immediate and often temporary solution (*informal*) ○ *a quick fix* **3.** NAVIG CALCULATION OF POSITION a calculation of the position of an object using radar or other forms of observation **4.** UNDERSTANDING an understanding or identification of something (*informal*) ○ *Do you have a fix on what the problem is?* **5.** INFLUENCING DISHONESTLY an instance of influencing an outcome or person dishonestly **6.** DRUGS ILLEGAL DRUG INJECTION an injection of an illegal drug (*slang*) **7.** STIMULATING DOSE a dose of or exposure to something pleasurable and stimulating (*humorous*) ○ *a chocolate fix* [15C. < Latin *fix-*, past participle of *figere* 'to fix'] —**fixable** *adj*

fix on *vt* to select something

fix up *vt* **1.** ARRANGE SOMETHING to arrange something such as a meeting or a date **2.** REPAIR SOMETHING to restore something to working order or proper order **3.** ARRANGE A CONTACT FOR SOMEBODY to arrange a business or social contact, or a romantic or sexual partner, for somebody

fixate /fiks áyt/ (**-ates, -ating, -ated**) *v* **1.** *vi* FOCUS ON SOMETHING to focus exclusively on something **2.** *vt* OBSESS SOMEBODY to obsess or preoccupy somebody or something totally **3.** *vti* PSYCHOL FORM A FIXATION to form or have a psychological fixation with a person or object **4.** *vti* BECOME OR MAKE FIXED to make something stable or secure, or become so [Late 19C. < Latin *fix-* (see FIX)]

fixation /fik sáysh'n/ *n* **1.** OBSESSION an obsession or preoccupation **2.** PSYCHOL, PSYCHOANAL IMMATURE PSYCHOSEXUAL BEHAVIOUR a theoretical strong libidinal attachment to a person or object, formed during early childhood, that results in neurotic or arrested psychosexual behaviour in adulthood **3.** BIOCHEM CONVERSION OF NITROGEN the conversion by soil bacteria of atmospheric nitrogen to a stable biologically available form **4.** CHEM STABILIZATION OF CHEMICAL the process of stabilizing a chemical or compound **5.** BIOL PRESERVING FOR EXAMINATION the preservation of biological specimens with chemicals

fixative /fíksətiv/ *n* (*plural same* or **-tives**) **1.** LIQUID SPRAYED FOR PROTECTION a liquid sprayed onto a drawing, photograph, or other surface to protect it **2.** GLUE a substance used to hold something in place **3.** COSMETICS PERFUME ADDITIVE a substance added to a perfume to make it evaporate less rapidly **4.** BIOL CHEMICAL PRESERVATIVE a chemical solution that preserves a biological specimen for microscopic study **5.** TEXTILES FABRIC ADDITIVE a substance applied to dyed fabrics to make the dye colourfast ■ *adj* TENDING TO FIX acting or tending to protect, preserve, or stabilize something

fixed /fikst/ *adj* **1.** SECURE immovable or securely in position **2.** NOT SUBJECT TO CHANGE not subject to change in amount or time **3.** NOT CHANGING unchanging in expression **4.** AGREED ON arranged or agreed upon **5.** HELD IN MIND firmly or dogmatically held in the mind **6.** PROVIDED WITH SOMETHING in the position of having something available for use ○ *How are you fixed for money?* **7.** DISHONESTLY ARRANGED unfairly or illegally arranged (*slang*) **8.** CHEM CHEMICALLY STABLE combined in stable form ○ *fixed nitrogen* **9.** ASTROL STABLE IN ZODIACAL TERMS describes Taurus, Leo, Scorpio, and Aquarius, signs of the zodiac associated with stability —**fixedly** /-idli/ *adv* —**fixedness** /-idnəss/ *n*

fixed action pattern *n* a pattern of behaviour in an organism that appears to be developed completely when first stimulated

fixed asset *n* an asset of a business that is central to its operation and is not traded (*usually used in the plural*)

fixed cost *n* a business expense that does not vary according to the amount of business (*usually used in the plural*)

fixed idea *n* PSYCHOL same as **idée fixe**

fixed income *n* income from securities such as bonds that are the same for each period

fixed line *adj* describes a telephone that is connected to a network via underground or overground lines

fixed oil *n* a nonvolatile oil composed of fatty acids, usually of animal or vegetable origin

fixed penalty *n* a fine of a specific amount given for an offence

fixed penalty notice *n* a ticket that the police can issue on the spot for minor motoring offences

fixed point *n* a temperature that has a fixed value under specific conditions and can be used to calibrate instruments, e.g. the boiling or freezing point

fixed-point *adj* describes numbers in which the decimal place is always in a fixed position

fixed-wing *adj* describes an aircraft that has stationary wings, especially as distinct from rotor blades

fixer /fíksər/ *n* **1.** SOMEBODY WHO ARRANGES SOMETHING DISHONEST somebody who arranges something, especially by dishonest or illegal means (*slang*) **2.** PHOTOGRAPHY CHEMICAL IN PHOTOGRAPHY a chemical that halts the development of a photographic image on film or paper **3.** SOMEBODY OR SOMETHING THAT FIXES a person who or an object that fixes something

fixing /fíksing/ *n* a means of holding an item in place ■ **fixings** *npl N Am* the ingredients required for a particular dish (*informal*)

fixity /fíksəti/ (*plural* **-ties**) *n* **1.** the quality or state of being fixed and unchanging **2.** something that is unchanging (*formal*)

fixture /fíkschər/ *n* **1.** OBJECT IN FIXED POSITION an object with a fixed position and function **2.** ESTABLISHED PERSON somebody considered to be permanently established in a place or position **3.** SPORTS EVENT a sports event or its date **4.** SOCIAL EVENT a select social event or its date [Late 16C. Probably alteration, after MIXTURE, of *fixure* < late Latin *fixura* < Latin *fix-* (see FIX)]

fizgig /fízgig/ *n* **1.** FISHING same as **fishgig 2.** a flippant or flirtatious girl (*dated*) **3.** a firework that fizzes when in motion (*dated*) [Early 16C. Probably < FIZZ + *gig* 'giddy girl']

fizz /fiz/ *vi* (**fizzes, fizzing, fizzed**) **1.** PRODUCE GAS BUBBLES to produce bubbles of gas **2.** HISS to make a hissing or continuous soft crackling sound ■ *n* **1.** EFFERVESCENCE the sparkling quality of a drink caused by bubbles of gas **2.** HISSING SOUND a hissing or continuous soft crackling sound **3.** LIVELINESS a quality of liveliness or excitement ○ *All the fizz has gone out of the election campaign.* **4.** SPARKLING DRINK a sparkling drink, especially champagne [Mid-17C. An imitation of the sound]

fizzer /fízzər/ *n Aus* an event that fails to live up to expectations (*informal*)

fizzle /fízz'l/ *vi* (**-zles, -zling, -zled**) **1. MAKE HISSING SOUND** to make a gentle hissing sound **2. FAIL AFTER GOOD START** to fail or peter out, especially after a good start (*informal*) ■ *n* **1. HISSING SOUND** a gentle hissing sound **2. FAILURE** a fiasco or total failure (*informal*) [Mid-16C. Probably < obsolete *fist* 'break wind' < Germanic]

fizzy /fízzi/ (**-ier, -iest**) *adj* producing or containing gas bubbles —**fizzily** *adv* —**fizziness** *n*

fj *abbr* Fiji (*used in Internet addresses*) See table at **domain name**

fjord: Geiranger fjord, Norway

fjord /fee awrd/, **fiord** *n* a long narrow coastal inlet with steep sides, often formed by glacial action, especially along the western coast of Norway [Late 17C. Via Norwegian < Old Norse *fjörðr*]

Fkr *abbr* MONEY krona²

FL *abbr* AIR FORCE Flight Lieutenant

fl, fl. *abbr* **1.** floor **2.** MONEY florin **3.** floruit **4.** MUSIC flute

Fl. *abbr* **1.** Flanders **2.** Flemish

flab /flab/ *n* excess or unwanted fat on somebody's body (*informal*) [Early 20C. Back-formation < FLABBY]

flabbergast /flábbər gaast/ (**-gasts, -gasting, -gasted**) *vt* to amaze or astonish somebody completely (*informal; usually passive*) [Late 18C. Origin ?]

flabby /flábbi/ (**-bier, -biest**) *adj* (*informal*) **1.** having excess body fat or sagging flesh **2.** done without vitality or force [Late 17C. Alteration of *flappy*] —**flabbily** *adv* —**flabbiness** *n*

flabella BIOL, CHR plural of **flabellum**

flabellate /flə béllit/, **flabelliform** /flə bélli fawrm/ *adj* describes an organism or body part that is shaped like an open hand-held fan [Late 18C. < Latin *flabellum* (see FLABELLUM)]

flabellum /flə béllem/ (*plural* **-la** /-lə/) *n* **1.** a fan-shaped organ or body part **2.** a fan with a long handle, formerly used in the Roman Catholic Church to keep away insects during the Mass [Mid-19C. < Latin, 'fan' < *flabrum* 'gust' < *flare* 'to blow']

flaccid /flássid, fláksid/ *adj* **1.** soft, limp, or lacking firmness **2.** lacking energy, enthusiasm, or competence [Early 17C. Directly or via French < Latin *flaccidus* < *flaccus* 'flabby'] —**flaccidity** /fla síddəti, flak síd-/ *n* —**flaccidly** *adv*

~~flacid~~ incorrect spelling of **flaccid**

flack¹ /flak/ *N Am* (*slang*) *n* a press agent or publicist ■ *vti* (**flacks, flacking, flacked**) to act as a press agent or publicity agent for somebody [Mid-20C. Origin ?] —**flacker** *n* —**flackery** *n*

flack² *n* ARMS another spelling of **flak**

flacon /flákən/ *n* a small, often decorated, stoppered bottle used especially for perfume [Early 19C. < French (see FLAGON)]

flag¹ /flag/ *n* **1. CLOTH FLOWN AS EMBLEM** a piece of cloth, often rectangular and flown from a pole, carrying a distinctive design and used as an emblem or for signalling **2. DECORATION** a small ornament, emblem, or badge showing the colours and design of a flag **3. IDENTITY SYMBOLIZED BY FLAG** a national or group identity symbolized by a flag **4. MARKING DEVICE** a marking device, e.g. a tab, that is attached to something to make it easier to identify or more conspicuous **5.** MEDIA same as **masthead** (sense 2) **6.** NAVY same as **flagship** (sense 2) **7.** VERTEB **HAIR FRINGE BENEATH DOG'S TAIL**

a fringe of hair that grows on the lower part of the tail in some dog breeds such as setters **8.** ZOOL **DEER'S TAIL** the tail of a deer **9.** AMERICAN FOOTBALL **PENALTY MARKER** a coloured cloth thrown to the ground by a football official in American football to indicate illegal play **10.** COMPUT **COMPUTER PROGRAM MARKER** an indicator generated by a computer program to denote a condition such as an error **11.** MUSIC **NOTE MARKER** an angled line on the stem of a musical note, indicating its value **12.** TRANSP **MARKER SHOWING A TAXI FOR HIRE** formerly, a small marker on a taximeter, raised to show a taxi's availability for hire ■ *vt* (**flags, flagging, flagged**) **1. MARK SOMETHING** to mark something such as a page or a place, in order to draw attention to it ○ *I've flagged the passages that need rewriting.* **2. INDICATE SOMETHING** to draw somebody's attention to something ○ *The report flagged up items for concern.* **3. SEND SOMEBODY MESSAGE BY FLAG** to signal somebody or send somebody information using a flag **4.** AMERICAN FOOTBALL **INDICATE PENALTY** in American football, to indicate a penalty by throwing down a flag **5. DECORATE SOMETHING WITH FLAGS** to decorate something with flags **6.** FIELD SPORTS **ATTRACT ANIMAL'S ATTENTION** to attract the attention or curiosity of wild game by waving something [Mid-16C. Origin ?] —**flagger** *n* ◇ **show the flag** to attend a gathering just to show loyalty or support towards a country, company, or family

CULTURAL NOTE *Flag*, a painting by US artist Jasper Johns (1945). The first of many such variations that Johns created on this theme, it consists of a US flag painted on canvas using encaustic. Its apparent banality infuriated many commentators; others responded positively to its playful ambiguity (is it a flag or a painting?) and saw it as Johns' reaction to the emotionalism of Abstract Expressionism.

flag down *vt* to stop a vehicle or its driver by making signs to the driver

flag² /flag/ (**flags, flagging, flagged**) *vi* **1.** to become weak, tired, or less attentive **2.** to hang down limply, or droop [Mid-16C. Origin ?]

flag³ /flag/ *n* CONSTR, GEOL same as **flagstone** (sense 1) ■ *vt* (**flags, flagging, flagged**) CONSTR, ROADS to pave a surface with flagstones [15C. Probably < N Germanic] —**flagged** *adj*

flag⁴ /flag/ *n* **1.** a plant of the iris family, usually one with large flowers and leaves **2.** a long narrow leaf of a plant such as an iris [14C. Origin ?]

flag captain *n* the captain of the flagship of a fleet

flag conservative *n US* a zealous neoconservative who believes that the United States is duty-bound to engage in global policing for the good of the civilized world and to engage in combat if necessary, in order to ensure the furtherance of the national interest, national security, and the security of US allies ○ *'Flag conservatives truly believe America is not only fit to run the world but that it must.'* (Norman Mailer, 'Only in America', *New York Review of Books*; 27 March 2003) [Early 21C]

flag day *n* a day on which people collect money for a charity, and those who contribute are given a small sticker. N Am term **tag day**

Flag Day *n* a holiday in the United States marking the official adoption of the design of the US flag in 1777. Date: 14 June.

flagella BIOL plural of **flagellum**

flagellant /flájjələnt/, **flagellator** /-laytər/ *n* **1.** a penitent who whips himself or herself as a means of repentance **2.** somebody who uses whipping to achieve pleasure [Late 16C. < Latin *flagellant-*, present participle of *flagellare* 'to whip' < *flagellum* (see FLAGELLUM)] —**flagellantism** *n*

flagellar /flə jéllər/ *adj* relating to a flagellum

flagellate¹ /flájjə layt/ (**-lates, -lating, -lated**) *vt* to whip somebody, especially for sexual or religious purposes [Early 17C. < Latin *flagellat-*, past participle of *flagellare* 'to whip' < *flagellum* (see FLAGELLUM)]

flagellate² /flájjələt, -layt/ *n* MICROORGANISM WITH FLAGELLA a microorganism with long thin cellular appendages (**flagella**). Some flagellates are pathogenic parasites that cause diseases such as giardiasis in humans. ■ *adj also* **flagellated** BIOL **1. RESEMBLING A THREAD** similar to a long thin cellular appendage (**flagellum**) **2. WITH APPENDAGES RESEMBLING THREADS** describes an organism

or cell that has long thin cellular appendages (**flagella**) [Mid-19C. < FLAGELLUM]

flagellation¹ /flájjə láysh'n/ *n* the act of whipping yourself or somebody else, especially for sexual or religious purposes

flagellation² /flájjə láysh'n/ *n* the formation or arrangement of flagella on an organism

flagellator /flájjə laytər/ *n* RELIG, PSYCHOL same as **flagellant**

flagelliform /flə jéllə fawrm/ *adj* describes an organism or body part that is long, tapering, and very narrow [Early 19C. < FLAGELLUM]

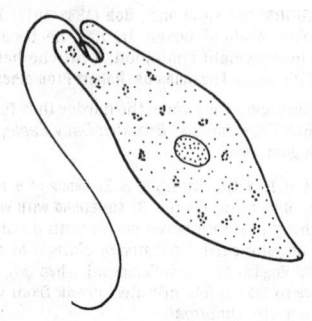

flagellum

flagellum /flə jéllem/ (*plural* **-la** /-lə/ or **-lums**) *n* **1.** a long thin tapering outgrowth of the cells of many microorganisms such as protozoans, that is a means of locomotion **2.** the very thin terminal part of an insect's antenna [Early 19C. < Latin, 'little scourge' < *flagrum* 'scourge']

flageolet¹ /flájjə lét/ *n* a slender-podded variety of French bean that can be eaten either fresh or dried [Late 19C. Via French < Latin *phaseolus* 'bean']

flageolet² /flájjə lét/ *n* a musical instrument of the 16th and 17th centuries resembling the flute [Mid-17C. < French, 'little flute' < Old French *flageol* 'flute']

flag fall *n* the minimum amount charged for the hire of a taxi

flagging¹ /flágging/ *adj* decreasing in strength, power, or ability —**flaggingly** *adv*

flagging² /flágging/ *n* an area paved with flagstones

flagitious /flə jíshəss/ *adj* (*formal*) **1.** extremely cruel, wicked, or vicious **2.** notorious or infamous [14C. < Latin *flagitiosus* < *flagitium* 'shameful crime' < *flagitare* 'demand vehemently'] —**flagitiously** *adv* —**flagitiousness** *n*

flagman /flágmən/ (*plural* **-men** /-mən/) *n* a man who holds a flag, usually to make signals, e.g. to control traffic

flag of convenience *n* a flag of a country under which a ship is registered because of its favourable regulations, not for any real connection with the ship's owners or business

flag officer *n* a naval officer of a rank at or above rear admiral

flag of truce *n* a white flag flown to indicate surrender, a request or offer of conference, or other peaceful intent

flagon /flággən/ *n* **1.** JUG a jug with a handle, narrow neck, spout, and sometimes a lid **2.** LARGE BOTTLE FOR ALCOHOLIC DRINK a large bottle with a short or narrow neck for an alcoholic drink, especially cider **3.** AMOUNT HELD IN FLAGON the amount that a flagon contains [14C. Via French *flacon* < late Latin *flascon-* 'flask']

flagperson /flág purss'n/ (*plural* **-persons** or **-people** /-peep'l/) *n* somebody who holds a flag, usually to make signals, e.g. to control traffic

flagpole /flág pōl/ *n* a pole on which a flag is flown ◇ **run something up the flagpole** to put forward an idea or suggestion in order to gauge general reaction to it (*informal*)

flag rank *n* a rank at admiral level that entitles the holder to fly a Royal Navy flag or pennant

flagrant /fláygrənt/ *adj* very obvious and contrary to standards of conduct or morality ○ *a flagrant violation of the suspect's civil rights* [15C. Directly or

via French < Latin *flagrant-*, present participle of *flagrare* 'to burn'] —**flagrance** *n* —**flagrancy** *n* —**flagrantly** *adv*

USAGE See *blatant*.

flagship /flág ship/ *n* **1. MOST IMPORTANT OF GROUP** the most important or prestigious among a group of similar and related things ○ *the flagship of the hotel chain* ○ *the company's flagship hotel* **2. NAVY COMMANDING SHIP** the ship from which the admiral or unit commander controls the operation of a fleet **3. SHIPPING MAIN COMMERCIAL SHIP** the main ship in a commercial fleet

flagstaff /flág staaf/ *n* same as **flagpole**

flagstick /flág stik/ *n* the flag pole that marks the position of the hole on a putting green

flagstone /flág stōn/ (*plural same* or **-stones** /flag/) *n* **1.** a slab of stone or concrete used for making floors or paving **2.** fine-textured rock that can be split into slabs suitable for use in paving

flag stop *n N Am* a station or place where a bus or train stops only when signalled by somebody waiting to board

flag-waving *n* an excessive and emotional display of patriotism —**flag-waver** *n*

flagwoman /flág woomən/ (*plural* **-women** /-wimin/) *n* a woman who holds a flag, usually to make signals, e.g. to control traffic

Flaherty /flaáhərti/, **Robert Joseph** (1884–1951) US documentary filmmaker. He is known for his ethnographic documentary about Inuit life, *Nanook of the North* (1922).

flail /flayl/ *v* (**flails, flailing, flailed**) **1. *vti* THRASH AROUND** to thrash or swing something around violently or uncontrollably, or move in this way **2. *vt* HIT SOMETHING** to strike or hit something ■ *n* **1. AGRIC MANUAL THRESHING IMPLEMENT** a manual threshing implement consisting of a wooden handle attached to a free-swinging wooden or metal bar **2. ARMS WEAPON LIKE FLAIL** a weapon shaped like a threshing flail, used especially in the Middle Ages [Pre-12C. Probably an assumed Old English word (influenced by Old French *flaiel*) < Latin *flagellum* (see FLAGELLUM)]

flair /flair/ *n* **1.** a natural ability to do something well, especially creative or artistic ability **2.** obvious elegance or stylishness [Late 19C. < French, 'sense of smell' < Old French *flairer* 'to smell' < late Latin *flagrare*, alteration of Latin *fragrare* 'emit an odour']

SPELLCHECK See *flare*.

SYNONYMS See *talent*.

flak /flak/, **flack** *n* **1.** anti-aircraft fire directed from the ground **2.** strong adverse criticism (*informal*) [Mid-20C. < German, acronym < *Flieger Abwehr Kanone* 'aeroplane defence canon']

flake[1] /flayk/ *n* **1. SMALL FLAT PIECE** a small flat piece or small part of a layer broken or detached from a larger object **2. SMALL MANUFACTURED ITEM** a small thin flat object that is manufactured, sold, and used or consumed in quantity **3. *N Am* OFFENSIVE TERM** an offensive term for somebody regarded as eccentric or irrational (*informal insult*) **4. *Aus* FISH AS FOOD** the flesh of various types of shark and similar fish, sold as food and often used for fish and chips ■ *v* (**flakes, flaking, flaked**) **1. *vi* FALL OFF IN FLAKES** to form into flakes and fall or peel off **2. *vt* BREAK SOMETHING INTO FLAKES** to break something into flakes, or break flakes from something **3. *vt* COVER SOMETHING WITH FLAKES** to cover or coat something with flakes [14C. Probably < N Germanic] —**flaker** *n*

flake out *vi* to collapse or fall asleep because of exhaustion

flake[2] /flayk/ *n* a platform or frame for drying fish or other food [14C. Origin ?]

flake[3] /flayk/ *vt* (**flakes, flaking, flaked**) to coil or loop a rope so that it will not tangle when used ■ *n* a single loop of a rope that has been neatly coiled [Early 17C. Origin ?]

flake white *n* a pigment made from flakes of white lead

flak jacket *n* a reinforced vest or jacket for protection against gunfire or shrapnel

flaky /flaýki/ (**-ier, -iest**) *adj* **1. MADE OF FLAKES** made of or separating easily into small pieces ○ *with a flaky*

texture **2. BREAKING INTO FLAKES** forming or tending to break off in flakes ○ *flaky skin* **3. *N Am* AN OFFENSIVE TERM** an offensive term describing somebody regarded as eccentric or irrational (*informal insult*) —**flakily** *adv* —**flakiness** *n*

flaky pastry *n* a pastry made from layers of pastry dough dotted with fat that puffs up and forms light layers when baked

flam[1] /flam/ *regional n* a lie or deception ■ *vt* (**flams, flamming, flammed**) to cheat or deceive somebody [Early 17C. Origin ?]

flam[2] /flam/ *n* a drumbeat of two nearly simultaneous strokes [Late 18C. Probably an imitation of the sound]

flambé /flóm bay/ *adj* served with an alcoholic spirit, usually brandy, that has been poured over the food and set alight ○ *bananas flambé* ■ *vt* (**-bés, -béing, -béed**) to pour an alcoholic spirit over food and light it in order to burn off the alcohol and impart the flavour of the spirit to the food [Late 19C. < French, past participle of *flamber* 'singe, pass through flame' < Latin *flamma* 'flame']

flambeau /flámbō/ (*plural* **-beaux** /-bō/ or **-beaus**) *n* **1. TORCH** a lighted torch made of wicks dipped in wax **2. CANDLESTICK** a large decorative candlestick **3. *Carib* TORCH LIT WITH KEROSENE** a torch made by stuffing cloth into a bottle or sometimes a bamboo joint containing kerosene [Mid-17C. < French, 'torch, flame' < *flambe* (see FLAMBOYANT)]

Flamborough Head /flámbərə-/ headland on the eastern coast of Yorkshire, northern England. It has steep limestone cliffs and a lighthouse.

flamboyant /flam bóy ənt/ *adj* **1. SHOWY** showy and dashing in a self-satisfied way **2. BRIGHTLY-COLOURED** brightly-coloured and striking **3. HIGHLY DECORATED** elaborate or richly decorated **4. AUDACIOUS** unrestrained by prevailing standards of propriety **5. ARCHIT OF FRENCH GOTHIC ARCHITECTURE** relating to or characteristic of 14th- to 16th-century French Gothic architecture, which is noted for its fine detailing and pointed decoration ■ *n* **TREES** same as **royal poinciana** [Mid-19C. < French, present participle of *flamboyer* 'blaze' < *flambe* 'flame' < Latin *flamma* 'flame'] —**flamboyance** *n* —**flamboyantly** *adv*

flame /flaym/ *n* **1. HOT GLOWING BODY OF BURNING GAS** a hot glowing mass of burning gas, often carrying fine incandescent particles **2. STRONG FEELING** an intense feeling or emotion **3. ANGRY E-MAIL MESSAGE** a rude, abusive, or threatening e-mail message or newsgroup posting **4. REDDISH-ORANGE COLOUR** a brilliant reddish-orange colour **5. LOVER** a sweetheart or lover (*informal*) ○ *an old flame* ■ *v* (**flames, flaming, flamed**) **1. *vi* PRODUCE FLAME** to burn producing flame **2. *vi* HAVE FIERY GLOW** to have or develop a fiery glow, especially suddenly ○ *Her cheeks flamed as she spoke.* **3. *vi* FEEL STRONG EMOTION** to display or feel intense emotion **4. *vt* SUBJECT SOMETHING TO FIRE** to treat something with or subject something to flames **5. *vti* SEND JUDGMENTAL E-MAIL** to criticize somebody with offensive and disparaging e-mail **6. *vt* MAKE SOMETHING BURN** to make something burn (*archaic*) [14C. Via Anglo-Norman and French < Latin *flamma* 'flame'] —**flame** *adj* —**flamer** *n* —**flamy** *adj* ◇ **fan the flames** to make a tense or difficult situation worse ◇ **shoot somebody** or **something down in flames** to reject or refute an idea or suggestion emphatically

flame-arc lamp *n* a lamp that uses an electric arc maintained between carbon electrodes that are infused with metallic salts to provide colour to the flame

flame bait *n* an inflammatory statement intentionally posted in an online discussion group to elicit a strong response or start a flame war (*informal*)

flame carbon *n* a carbon electrode containing metallic salts that, with other similar carbon electrodes, has the effect of colouring the arc produced between the electrodes

flame cell *n* in some invertebrates such as flatworms, a hollow excretory cell that has a tuft of projections (**cilia**) resembling hairs whose movement serves to force out waste products [Because the movement of the cilia suggests tongues of flame]

flame gun *n* a flame-thrower used to burn weeds

flamen /fláymən/ (*plural* **flamens** or **flamines** /flámmi neez/) *n* in ancient Roman religion, a priest be-

longing to a group of 15, each of whom oversaw the rituals connected with a particular deity [14C. < Latin]

flamenco

flamenco /flə méngkō/ (*plural* **-cos**) *n* **1.** a dance of Spanish origin with hand clapping and stamping of feet **2.** the strongly rhythmic music that accompanies flamenco dancing [Late 19C. Via Spanish, 'Flemish person' < Middle Dutch *Vlaming*]

flame of the forest *n* a tree that is cultivated as an ornamental for its large, bright red sepals. Native to: tropical West Africa. Latin name: *Mussaenda erythrophylla*.

flameout /fláym owt/ *n* the unintentional extinguishing of the flame of a jet engine in flight, e.g. through a failure of combustion or the fuel supply

flameproof /fláym proof/ *adj* **1. RESISTANT TO FIRE** resistant to catching fire (*often used of textiles and clothing*) **2. ELEC ENG NOT EXPLOSIVE** describes electrical apparatus designed so that an explosion of inflammable gas inside will not ignite inflammable gas outside **3. COOK FOR COOKING WITH DIRECT HEAT** describes containers that can be used when cooking on a hob or under a grill ■ *vt* (**-proofs, -proofing, -proofed**) **MAKE SOMETHING FLAME RESISTANT** to make something resistant to flames or combustion —**flameproofer** *n*

flame-retardant, **flame-resistant** *adj* made or chemically treated to resist catching fire

flame test *n* a test for the presence of various metals in a substance by noting the colours produced when a small amount is placed in a flame and vaporized

flame-thrower *n* a weapon that projects a stream of burning liquid

flame tree *n* **1.** a tropical tree cultivated for its bright orange, yellow, or red flowers, e.g. royal poinciana **2.** a tree with bright red flowers that bloom in spring before its leaves emerge. Native to: Australia. Latin name: *Brachychiton acerifolius*.

flame war *n* a period of repeated exchanges of abusive and insulting e-mail between people or groups

flamines RELIG plural of **flamen**

flaming /fláyming/ *adj* **1. PRODUCING FLAMES** burning and producing flames **2. INTENSE** very angry, intense, or passionate ○ *flaming indignation* **3. USED TO EXPRESS ANGER** used to emphasize the following word or phrase and especially to express anger or annoyance (*informal*) ○ *I wish they wouldn't play their flaming music so loud!* **4. GLOWING** brightly glowing ○ *flaming cheeks* **5. VIVID IN COLOUR** vivid in colour ■ *n* **ONLINE DELUGE OF CRITICAL E-MAIL** a large volume of abusive and insulting e-mail directed at somebody

flamingo /flə míng gō/ (*plural* **-gos** or **-goes** or *same*) *n* **1.** a large long-necked wading bird with a downward-curving beak, webbed feet, and pinkish-white plumage with black wing feathers. Native to: tropical brackish waters. Family: Phoenicopteridae. See illustration on next page **2.** a deep pink colour tinged with orange [Mid-16C. Via Portuguese < obsolete Spanish *flamengo*] —**flamingo** *adj*

ORIGIN Whether its ultimate source is Dutch or Latin, the motivation behind the bird's name is its bright appearance. The Latin derivation would make it the 'flame'-coloured bird; the Dutch derivation would depend on the reputation the people of Flanders had in the Middle Ages for bright flamboyant dress (whence the Spanish dance, the *flamenco*).

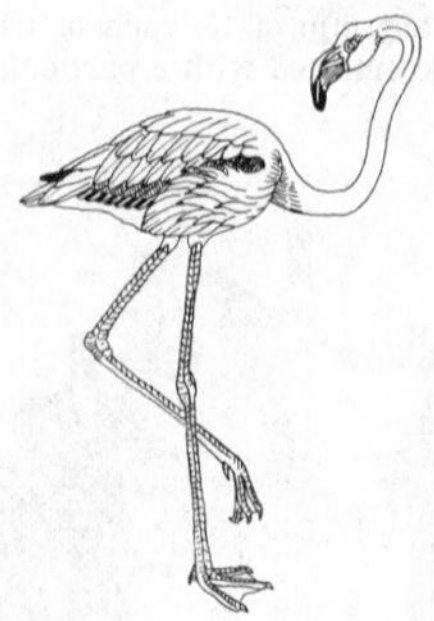

flamingo

flammable /flámməb'l/ *adj* readily capable of catching fire —**flammability** /flámmə bílləti/ *n*

USAGE flammable or **inflammable**? Although ***inflammable*** looks like the opposite of ***flammable***, the two words actually have the same meaning, both describing something that is easily set on fire. The *in-* prefix of ***inflammable*** means 'into', rather than 'not', and the adjective is ultimately derived from the same Latin word as the verb *inflame*. In view of the potentially disastrous consequences of such misinterpretation, ***flammable*** is usually considered to be the safer choice, especially in the labelling of commercial and industrial products. The word most frequently used to convey the opposite meaning is ***nonflammable***, but ***noninflammable*** also exists.

flan /flan/ *n* **1.** an open, usually round, pastry or sponge case with a savoury or fruit filling **2.** a circular metal blank ready to be stamped as a coin [Mid-19C. Via French < medieval Latin *fladon-* < Germanic]

Flanders /flaándərz/ region of Northwestern Europe that was a powerful independent state between the 11th and 14th centuries. It is equivalent to the present-day provinces of Flanders in Belgium, Nord Department in France, and part of Zeeland Province in the Netherlands.

Flanders poppy *n* a wild red poppy [Because the emblem of Allied soldiers who died on the battlefields of FLANDERS in World War I]

flâneur /flaa núr/ *n* an idler or loafer [Mid-19C. < French < *flâner* 'stroll, lounge about']

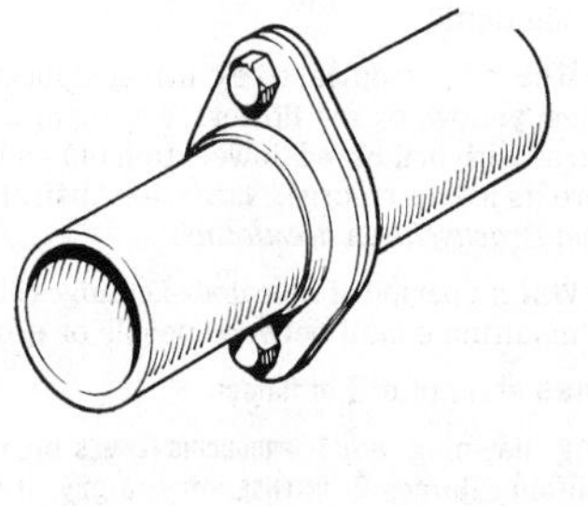

flange

flange /flanj/ *n* a projecting collar, rim, or rib on an object for fixing it to another object, holding it in place, or strengthening it. Flanges are often found on pipes and shafts. [Late 17C. Origin ?] —**flanged** /flanjd/ *adj*

flanged rail *n* an early form of rail with a raised edge (**flange**) on one side to stabilize wheels travelling on it. On modern trains the flange is on the wheel.

flank /flangk/ *n* **1.** ANAT **SIDE OF LOWER TORSO** each side of the body of a person or an animal between the last rib and the hip **2. CUT OF BEEF** a cut of meat, especially beef, from an animal's flank **3. SIDE OF SOMETHING** the side of any object **4.** MIL **SIDE OF MILITARY FORMATION** the left or right side of a military formation **5. SIDE OF SPORTS FIELD** either of the sides of a sports field inside the playing area ○ *not used to playing on the left flank* ■ *vt* (**flanks, flanking, flanked**) **BE BY SIDE OF SOMETHING** to be on or at the side of something or somebody ○ *He was flanked by secret service officers.* [Pre-12C. < French *flanc*]

flanker /flángkər/ *n* **1.** MIL **SOLDIER IN PROTECTIVE UNIT** a soldier in a unit that protects the flank of a military column on the march **2.** RUGBY **WING FORWARD** a wing forward who plays on either of the flanks **3.** AMERICAN FOOTBALL same as **flankerback 4.** AMERICAN FOOTBALL same as **split end** (sense 2) **5.** FOOTBALL **PLAYER PLAYING ON SIDE OF FIELD** in Australian Rules football, a player occupying a position on one side of the field, e.g. the right or left halfback or right or left half-forward

flankerback /flángkər bak/ *n* in American football, an offensive back positioned outside the play formation

flannel /flánn'l/ *n* **1. SOFT COTTON CLOTH** a soft cotton cloth with a nap on one side. Use: clothing, sleepwear, sheets. **2. SOFT WOOLLEN CLOTH** a soft closely woven woollen or wool-blend cloth. Use: clothing. **3.** HOUSEHOLD same as **facecloth 4. INSINCERE OR EVASIVE TALK** indirect, empty, deceptive, or flattering talk (*informal*) **5.** *regional* **VEST** a vest ■ **flannels** *npl* **1. TROUSERS MADE OF FLANNEL** clothing, especially trousers, made from flannel **2. WHITE TROUSERS WORN FOR CRICKET** white long trousers worn when playing particular sports, especially cricket ■ *v* (**flannels, flannelling, flanelled**) **1.** *vt* **WRAP SOMEBODY IN FLANNEL** to wrap or clothe somebody in flannel or flannels **2.** *vt* **CLEAN SOMETHING WITH FLANNEL** to wash, clean, or rub somebody or something with a flannel **3.** *vti* **TALK IN EVASIVE OR INSINCERE WAY** to talk in an evasive or flattering way, or talk to somebody in this way, especially to deceive [14C. Origin ?] —**flannelly** *adj*

REGIONAL NOTE See ***vest***.

flannelboard /flánn'l bawrd/ *n* a board covered with flannel to which pictures and cloth cutouts will stick that is used in primary education

flannelette /flánnə lét/ *n* a light cotton cloth with a soft brushed surface on one side

flannelflower /flánn'l flowər/ *n* a wild plant with leaves covered in soft white hairs. Flowers: creamy white. Native to: eastern Australia. Latin name: *Actinotus helianthi*.

Flannery /flánnəri/, **Tim** (*b.* 1956) Australian biologist. He is the author of *The Future Eaters* (1994) and *The Eternal Frontier* (2001). Full name **Flannery, Timothy**

flan ring *n* a round tin with a removable base, for cooking a flan or quiche

flap /flap/ *v* (**flaps, flapping, flapped**) **1.** *vti* **MOVE WINGS UP AND DOWN** to move something up and down, especially wings or arms during or as if in flight, or be moved up and down in this way **2.** *vi* **FLY BY MOVING WINGS** to fly by moving the wings repeatedly **3.** *vti* **MOVE OR SWAY REPEATEDLY** to cause something to move or sway in one direction and then another repeatedly and often noisily, or move in this way ○ *flags flapping in the breeze* **4.** *vt* **HIT WITH BROAD OBJECT** to hit somebody or something with a broad flat object ○ *He flapped his hand on the table.* **5.** *vt* **TOSS SOMETHING** to fling down or toss something (*informal*) ○ *flapped the report on the table* **6.** *vi* **BE PANICKY** to be flustered or panicky (*informal*) **7.** *vt* PHON **MAKE 'R' SOUND** to make an 'r' sound by briefly striking the roof of the mouth with the tongue, as in 'parrot' ■ *n* **1. FLAT THIN PIECE USED AS COVER** a flat thin piece attached along one edge, usually used as a cover for an opening ○ *the flap of an envelope* **2. DUST JACKET PART** either of the two parts of a dust jacket that fold inside a book's cover and are usually printed with information about the book or author **3. ACT OR SOUND OF FLAPPING** an act of or the sound made by flapping ○ *The bird disappeared with a flap of its wings.* **4. BLOW FROM BROAD OBJECT** a blow or slap from a broad object **5. PANICKED STATE** a state of panic or upset (*informal*) ○ *Don't get into a flap about it.* **6.** AVIAT **AIRCRAFT WING CONTROL SURFACE** a narrow movable surface attached to the rear edge of an aircraft wing that is used to create lift or drag **7.** SURG **MASS OF TISSUE FOR GRAFTING** a mass of tissue, used for surgical grafting, that remains partially attached and retains its blood supply **8.** PHON **'R' SOUND** an 'r' sound made by briefly striking the roof of the mouth with the tongue, as in 'parrot' [14C. Origin ?] —**flappy** *adj*

flapdoodle /fláp dood'l/ *n* silly talk or nonsense (*slang*) [Mid-19C. Origin ?]

flapjack /fláp jak/ *n* **1.** a cake made of oats, syrup, and butter and cut into squares before eating **2.** *N Am* FOOD same as **pancake** *n* (sense 1)

flapper /fláppər/ *n* **1. YOUNG UNCONVENTIONAL WOMAN OF 1920S** a young woman of the 1920s who disdained conventions of decorum and established fashion. Flappers were associated with the Charleston dance, bobbed hair, and very short dresses. **2. SOMETHING FLAPPING AROUND** an object that flaps around **3. BROAD FLAT OBJECT** a broad flat object used for striking something

flare /flair/ *v* (**flares, flaring, flared**) **1.** *vti* **BURN SUDDENLY AND BRIGHTLY** to burn suddenly and brightly, or cause something to burn in this way **2.** *vi* **START UP AGAIN** to recur, worsen, or intensify suddenly ○ *His gout flared up again.* **3.** *vi* **ANGER SUDDENLY** to become suddenly angry **4.** *vti* **WIDEN** to widen or spread outwards, or cause something to widen or spread outwards ○ *Her nostrils flared.* **5.** *vt* **SIGNAL SOMEBODY FOR HELP** to signal somebody for help by means of a device used to produce a light signal **6.** *vt* INDUST **BURN OFF GAS** to ignite and burn off unwanted waste gas in open air ■ *n* **1. SUDDEN BLAZE OF LIGHT** a sudden blaze of light or fire used to signal distress or location or for illumination ○ *the flare of naval signal lights* **2. DEVICE FOR PRODUCING FLARE** a device used to produce a light signal calling for help ○ *a distress flare* **3. FLAME** a sudden or unsteady flame ○ *the flare of distant oil wells* **4. WIDENING SHAPE** a shape that widens or spreads outwards ○ *a long skirt with a flare* **5. OUTBURST OF EMOTION** a sudden outburst, especially of a negative emotion ○ *a flare of anger* **6.** AMERICAN FOOTBALL **SHORT AND WIDE PASS** in American football, a pass to a back running laterally **7.** INDUST **FLAME FOR BURNING OFF WASTE GAS** a flame that burns off unwanted waste gas in the open air **8.** OPTICS, PHOTOGRAPHY **UNWANTED LIGHT IN OPTICAL DEVICE** unwanted light reaching a photographic image, especially when reflected from an internal lens **9.** MED **INFLAMMATION** an area of inflammation on the skin ■ **flares** *npl* **TROUSERS WITH WIDE LEGS BELOW KNEE** trousers with legs that widen significantly below the knee, first popular in the late 1960s [Mid-16C. Origin ?] —**flared** *adj*

SPELLCHECK flare or **flair**? Do not confuse the spelling of ***flare*** and ***flair***, which sound similar. ***Flare*** can be used as a noun or verb referring to a sudden blaze of light or fire, an outburst of emotion, or a widening out: *The petrol made the fire flare up. The crew set off distress flares. Tempers flared as the meeting progressed. She wore a flared skirt.* ***Flair*** is only used as a noun, meaning 'talent' or 'stylishness', as in *a flair for public speaking, to dress with flair.*

flareback /fláir bak/ *n* **1.** a flame inside a gun's breech caused by the ignition of gases remaining after the weapon has been fired **2.** a reaction or effect directed back towards a point of origin

flare stack *n* a large open-air burner used to dispose of excess flammable gas at an oil refinery, well, or platform

flare-up *n* **1. RECURRENCE OF SOMETHING** a recurrence of something, especially a disease **2. SUDDEN OCCURRENCE OF FIRE OR LIGHT** a sudden occurrence or increase of fire or light **3. SUDDEN OUTBURST OF AGGRESSION** a sudden occurrence of emotion or violence (*informal*)

flaring /fláiring/ *adj* **1. BURNING DIMLY** burning dimly or unsteadily **2. SHOWY** bright and showy **3. BECOMING WIDER** widening out —**flaringly** *adv*

flash /flash/ *v* (**flashes, flashing, flashed**) **1.** *vti* **EMIT LIGHT SUDDENLY** to cause light to appear suddenly or in brief bursts from something, or appear in this way ○ *We could see the lights of police cars flashing in the distance.* **2.** *vti* **REFLECT LIGHT FROM ANOTHER SOURCE** to reflect light suddenly or briefly, or make a source of light reflect from a surface ○ *sunlight flashing on the water* **3.** *vti* **CATCH FIRE SUDDENLY** to burst into flame suddenly, or cause something to burst into flame **4.** *vti* COMMUNICATION **SIGNAL TO SOMEBODY WITH LIGHTS** to signal to somebody or communicate something by quickly turning lights on and off **5.** *vi* **MOVE QUICKLY** to move or pass very quickly in a particular direction **6.** *vti* **APPEAR MOMENTARILY** to appear briefly, or cause something to appear briefly ○ *flash a message onto the screen* **7.** *vt* **DISPLAY SOMETHING OSTENTATIOUSLY** to show off or display something in order to impress people ○ *She's always flashing her money around.* **8.** *vt* **FILL SOMETHING WITH RUSH OF WATER** to fill something suddenly with a great flow of water **9.** *vt* **COAT SURFACE FOR**

PROTECTION to cover the surface of an object with a thin coating, usually for protection or as a stage in processing **10.** *vi* EXPOSE BODY INDECENTLY IN PUBLIC to expose the genitals briefly and intentionally in public (*informal*) **11.** *vt* CONSTR PROTECT ROOF FROM LEAKING to install pieces of sheet metal (**flashing**) on a roof joint or window joint to make it waterproof ■ *n* **1.** SUDDEN BURST OF LIGHT a sudden bright display of light, fire, or something bright ○ *flashes of lightning* **2.** SUDDEN BURST OF MOOD OR THOUGHT a sudden occurrence of an emotional mood or intellectual activity ○ *a flash of inspiration* **3.** LIGHT PATCH a patch of light or bright colour on a dark background, e.g. on an animal's coat **4.** BRIGHT LIGHTING USED IN PHOTOGRAPHY the brief illumination of a subject for photographic purposes **5.** DEVICE USED TO LIGHT PHOTOGRAPHIC SUBJECT a device used in flash photography to produce a short bright light **6.** RUSH OF WATER a sudden rush of water down a watercourse, or a device that produces this **7.** SHORT NEWS BROADCAST a sudden important news story requiring immediate broadcast **8.** MIL BADGE ON UNIFORM OR VEHICLE a badge or insignia on a uniform or vehicle **9.** CLOTHING COLOURED STRIP WORN ON SOCKS in Highland dress, a short strip of coloured material folded over the garter and protruding below the folded-over top of the socks (*usually used in the plural*) **10.** LANGUAGE USED IN UNDERWORLD the language used by criminals, thieves, and their associates (*archaic slang*) ■ *adj* **1.** UNEXPECTED sudden and brief ○ *flash thunderstorms* **2.** SHOWY expensive or expensive-looking, especially in a showy and vulgar way (*informal*) ○ *with his big car and his flash clothes* **3.** INSINCERE insincere, false, or counterfeit (*archaic*) ○ *an outpouring of flash sentiment* [13C. Probably an imitation of the sound of splashing] —**flashness** *n* ◇ **a flash in the pan** a sudden brief success that is not, or not likely to be, repeated ◇ **in a flash 1.** very rapidly **2.** suddenly

flash back *vi* **1.** to recall an intensely vivid memory of a traumatic experience **2.** to go back to a scene at an earlier point in a narrative, out of chronological order, to fill in information or explain something in the present

flash forward *vi* to jump forward in time to a scene at a later point in a narrative, out of chronological order, usually for dramatic effect or irony

flashback /flásh bak/ *n* **1.** PAINFUL MEMORY an intensely vivid memory of a traumatic experience that returns repeatedly **2.** EARLIER EVENT OR SCENE a scene or event from the past that appears in a narrative out of chronological order, to fill in information or explain something in the present ○ *Much of the film's exposition is handled through flashbacks.* **3.** DRUG AFTEREFFECT the later experiencing of the effects of a hallucinogenic drug such as LSD long after discontinuing use of the drug

flash blindness *n* temporary blindness after the flash of a gun discharge or other explosion, particularly at night

flashboard /flásh bawrd/ *n* a structure made of boards fitted at the top of a dam to add to its height and increase the amount of water that can be held back

flashbulb /flásh bulb/ *n* a small glass bulb filled with shredded metallic foil that produces a brief intense flash of light for taking photographs

flash burn *n* a burn caused by brief exposure to a source of intense heat

flashcard /flásh kaard/ *n* a card with words or numbers printed on it that is briefly displayed as a learning device

flash drive *n* a small plastic device functioning as a disk drive, containing memory chips that retain their contents without electrical power and that have a capacity of 16 megabytes and 2 gigabytes of data. On the end is a standard USB connector that fits into USB ports.

flasher /fláshər/ *n* **1.** FLASHING LIGHT a light that flashes as a signal, especially one on a road vehicle used to indicate the direction in which the driver intends to turn **2.** DEVICE MAKING LIGHT FLASH a device that switches a light on and off automatically to make it flash **3.** SOMEBODY WHO EXPOSES PRIVATE PARTS a person, especially a man, who gains pleasure from publicly exposing the genitals (*informal*)

flash flood *n* a sudden and often destructive surge of water down a narrow channel or sloping ground, usually caused by heavy rainfall

flash-forward *n* a scene or event from the future that appears in a narrative out of chronological order, usually for dramatic effect or irony

flashgun /flásh gun/ *n* a device that holds a flashtube or flashbulb and automatically discharges it as the attached camera's shutter opens

flashing /fláshing/ *n* pieces of sheet metal attached around the joints and angles of a roof to protect against leakage

flashlight /flásh līt/ *n* **1.** a brief intense flash of light produced by a photographic lamp **2.** any bright light that flashes, e.g. a beacon **3.** *N Am* same as **torch** *n* (sense 1)

flash memory *n* a programmable read-only computer memory chip that can be erased and reprogrammed in blocks rather than single bytes

flash-mobbing *n* the practice of people appearing in groups in public places after being mobilized by somebody on the Internet and performing harmless attention-seeking activities (*informal*) —**flash-mobber** *n*

flashover /flásh ōvər/ *n* an unintended electric arc around or over the surface of an insulator

flash photography *n* photography that illuminates its subject with a brief flash of artificial light

flash photolysis *n* a method of studying photochemical reactions in gases in which the gas is exposed to very brief intense flashes of light and the results are analysed with a spectroscope

flashpoint /flásh poynt/ *n* **1.** TROUBLE SPOT a place where violence is likely to break out suddenly, usually as a result of social or political tension **2.** CRITICAL STAGE the critical stage in some process, event, or situation at which action, change, or violence occurs **3.** CHEM TEMPERATURE OF VAPOUR IGNITION the lowest temperature at which a flammable liquid will give off enough vapour to ignite briefly when exposed to a flame

flashtube /flásh tyoob/ *n* a glass or quartz tube filled with xenon gas that emits a short intense burst of light for flash photography when electric current is passed through it

flash unit *n* a flashgun, or a unit comprising a flashgun and reflector

flashy /fláshi/ (-**ier, -iest**) *adj* **1.** smart and expensive-looking in an obvious or ostentatious way **2.** showing momentary or superficial brilliance —**flashily** *adv* —**flashiness** *n*

flask /flaask/ *n* **1.** SMALL BOTTLE a small glass bottle, often with a long neck, of the type used in laboratory work **2.** HOUSEHOLD same as **vacuum flask 3.** same as **hip flask 4.** ARMS, HIST same as **powder flask 5.** METALL MOULD USED IN FOUNDRY a frame packed full of sand, used in a foundry to make a mould **6.** INDUST CONTAINER FOR SPENT NUCLEAR FUEL a very strong container in which irradiated nuclear fuel is transported [14C. < medieval Latin *flasca*, late Latin *flascon-*]

flat[1] /flat/ *adj* (**flatter, flattest**) **1.** LEVEL AND HORIZONTAL level and horizontal, without any slope ○ *The flat plains stretch for miles.* **2.** EVEN AND SMOOTH even and smooth, without any bumps or hollows ○ *back on the flat road* **3.** NOT CURVED not curved inwards or outwards ○ *a boat with a flat bottom* **4.** WITH LITTLE CURVATURE with relatively little depth or curvature ○ *a vase with flat sides* **5.** LYING HORIZONTAL in a horizontal position, parallel with or stretched out on the ground ○ *plants lying flat after the heavy rain* **6.** TOUCHING SOMETHING ELSE with the whole extent touching another surface at all points ○ *Stand it flat against the wall.* **7.** NO LONGER FIZZY having lost effervescence ○ *flat champagne* **8.** WITHOUT ELECTRICAL CHARGE describes a battery that has lost its electrical charge **9.** NOT FULL OF AIR no longer full of air ○ *a flat tyre* **10.** BELOW CORRECT PITCH sounded or sounding a little lower than the intended pitch level ○ *Your E string is flat.* **11.** ONE SEMITONE BELOW NATURAL pitched one semitone below a particular note ○ *in the key of B flat* **12.** LACKING EXCITEMENT without any interest or excitement ○ *Some days life just seems flat.* **13.** WITHOUT FLAVOUR lacking flavour or seasoning ○ *This soup tastes rather flat.* **14.** MONOTONOUS IN SOUND with no variation in pitch or intonation ○ *expressed her displeasure in a flat voice* **15.** COMMERCIALLY INACTIVE not commercially active ○ *The market is fairly flat at the moment.* **16.** NOT VARYING not varying in amount or level ○ *They charge a flat fee of £50.* **17.** EMPHATICALLY ABSOLUTE categorical and without any qualification ○ *a flat denial of the charges* **18.** LOW-HEELED with low heels or no heels at all ○ *flat shoes* **19.** NOT SHINY not shiny or glossy ○ *a flat white paint* **20.** WITH LOW ARCHES describes feet with arches so low that all the sole makes contact with the ground **21.** MED INDICATING CESSATION OF PHYSIOLOGICAL ACTIVITY showing no variation on a monitoring machine, and thereby indicating that physiological activity has stopped ○ *a flat ECG* **22.** PHON RESEMBLING VOWEL SOUND IN 'FAT' describes the vowel 'a' as it is pronounced in 'fat' or 'badge' **23.** NAUT TAUT describes a sail that is stretched so as to be taut ■ *adv* (**flatter, flattest**) **1.** BELOW PITCH below the intended pitch ○ *She tends to sing flat.* **2.** EXACTLY no more and no less ○ *He ran the mile in four minutes flat.* **3.** VERY used to add emphasis (*informal*) ○ *flat broke* **4.** FIN WITHOUT INTEREST not accruing any interest ○ *The bonds were trading flat.* ■ *n* **1.** LEVEL SURFACE a flat part or surface ○ *the flat of a knife blade* **2.** DEFLATED TYRE a tyre that has become deflated (*informal*) **3.** MUSIC NOTE LOWERED BY SEMITONE a sign (♭) placed next to a note to show that it is to be lowered by a semitone, or a note that is lowered a semitone ○ *a key with four flats* **4.** GEOG LARGE STRETCH OF LEVEL GROUND a large stretch of level ground, e.g. of mud exposed at low tide or of salt deposits (*usually used in the plural*) ○ *the great salt flats* **5.** THEATRE MOVABLE SCENERY theatrical scenery mounted on a movable wooden frame **6.** NAUT same as **flatboat 7.** MAIL BIG FLAT ENVELOPE a large flat piece of mail **8.** HORSERACING RACING HORSES OVER LEVEL GROUND horseracing over level ground with no fences to be jumped, or the season in which this takes place ■ **flats** *npl* CLOTHING LOW-HEELED SHOES shoes with low heels ■ *vt* (**flats, flatting, flatted**) *ANZ, N Am* MUSIC same as **flatten** (senses 5–6) [14C. < Old Norse *flatr* < Indo-European] —**flatness** *n*

flat[2] /flat/ *n* **1.** SET OF ROOMS ON ONE FLOOR living quarters in part of a building, usually on one floor. N Am term **apartment 2.** *NZ* SHARED HOUSE a house that is shared as living quarters by a number of people ■ *vi ANZ* SHARE FLAT to share a flat with somebody (*informal*) ○ *We used to flat together at uni.* [Early 19C. Alteration, after FLAT[1], of Scots *flet* 'interior of a house' < Old English *flet(t)* 'house, floor' < Germanic]

flat back four *n* in football, a formation of four defenders deployed in a straight line across the pitch and generally maintaining this straight-line arrangement during play

flatbed /flát bed/ *n* TRANSP **1.** same as **flatbed trailer 2.** same as **flatbed truck**

flatbed lorry *n* TRANSP same as **flatbed truck**

flatbed press *n* PRINTING same as **cylinder press**

flatbed scanner *n* a device connected to a computer on which documents are laid flat and an optical sensor passes over them converting text and images into digital form for storage, retrieval, and transmission by the computer

flatbed trailer *n* a trailer consisting of a completely open platform with no sides or railings

flatbed truck, flatbed lorry *n* a truck that has a completely open platform at the rear with no sides or railings

flatboat /flát bōt/ *n* a large boat with a flat bottom used for transporting goods on shallow waterways

flatbread /flát bred/ *n* bread baked in round flat loaves and usually made with unleavened dough, e.g. pitta, nan, chapatis, and tortillas

flat cap *n* **1.** a cloth cap with a brim at the front and a flat soft top **2.** a hat with a low crown and a narrow brim worn in the 16th and 17th centuries by men, especially Londoners

flatcar /flát kaar/ *n N Am* a railway freight wagon that has no roof or sides

flat chat *Aus* (*informal*) *adv* at maximum speed or capacity ○ *We've got a deadline next week so we're all working flat chat.* ■ *adj* extremely busy ○ *Sorry, mate, I can't help you – I'm flat chat.*

flat-chested /flát chéstid/ *adj* having small breasts

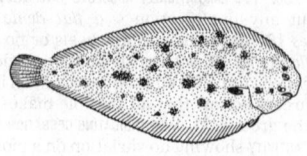

flatfish

flatfish /flát fish/ (*plural same* or **-fishes**) *n* any fish with a flat body and both eyes on the upper side, including the flounder, sole, and halibut. Order: Pleuronectiformes.

flatfoot /flát foot/ *n* **1.** a condition of the feet in which the arches are so low that all of the sole makes contact with the ground **2.** (*plural* **flatfoots** or **flatfeet** /-feet/) an offensive term for a police officer, typically one on foot patrol (*dated slang*)

flat-footed, flatfooted /flát foo'tid/ *adj* **1.** HAVING FLAT FEET having feet with arches so low that all the sole makes contact with the ground **2.** UNPREPARED unable to react or respond quickly ○ *Her question caught me flat-footed.* **3.** AWKWARD awkward or clumsy (*informal*) ■ *adv* UNEQUIVOCALLY in a firm and direct way (*informal*) ○'a *good many come out flat-footed and said it was scandalous'* (Mark Twain, *The Adventures of Huckleberry Finn*; 1884) —**flat-footedly** *adv* —**flat-footedness** *n*

flathead /flát hed/ (*plural* **-heads** or *same*) *n ANZ* a fish with a flat skull. Native to: Indian and Pacific oceans. Family: Platycephalidae.

Flathead (*plural same* or **-heads**) *n* a member of a Native North American people who originally lived in western Montana and northern Idaho

flatiron /flát ərn/ *n* an iron used to press clothes, especially one that has to be heated on a hearth or stove

flatland /flát land/ *n* an expanse of land that does not vary in height above sea level

flatlet /flátlət/ *n* a small flat that has only a few rooms

flatline /flát līn/ *n* a monitor read-out on an EEG or EKG indicating total cessation of brain or cardiac activity, respectively ■ *vi* (**-lines, -lining, -lined**) *N Am* to show none of the electrical currents associated with heart or brain activity on a monitor (*slang*) —**flatliner** *n*

flatly /flátli/ *adv* **1.** firmly and without qualification ○ *They flatly rejected our offer.* **2.** in a voice that shows no emotion

flatmate /flát mayt/ *n* somebody with whom a person shares a flat ○ *We're advertising for a new flatmate.*

flat out *adv* (*informal*) **1.** at top speed **2.** in a blunt manner ○ *told me flat out he didn't trust me*

flatpack /flát pak/ *n* an item of furniture that is sold as a set of pieces packed flat, for ease of storage and transportation, and assembled by the buyer

flat panel *n* a very thin computer screen with a flat viewing surface that employs liquid-crystal display technology, commonly used in portable personal computers —**flat-panel** *adj*

flatpick /flát pik/ *n* a flat thin piece of plastic or metal, usually triangular, used to pluck and strum a stringed instrument such as a guitar or banjo

flat race *n* **1.** a horse race that is run over level ground, without fences to be jumped **2.** in children's sports competitions, an ordinary race without obstacles or special features such as sacks or eggs and spoons (*dated*) —**flat racing** *n*

flat spin *n* **1.** a descent by an aircraft in tight circles and in a near- horizontal position **2.** ' in in-line skating, a trick by which an airborne skater turns the axis of the body until it is almost horizontal with the ramp, spins, and lands

flatten /flátt'n/ (**-tens, -tening, -tened**) *v* **1.** *vti* MAKE OR BECOME FLAT to make something flat or flatter, or become flat or flatter **2.** *vt* STAND FLAT AGAINST SOMETHING to press the body against a flat surface **3.** *vt* CRUSH OR HUMILIATE SOMEBODY to make somebody feel crushed or humiliated **4.** *vt* DEFEAT SOMEBODY to defeat somebody convincingly (*informal*) **5.** *vt UK* MUSIC TAKE NOTE DOWN ONE SEMITONE to lower a note one semitone. ANZ, N Am term **flat**[1] **6.** *vt UK* MUSIC SING OR PLAY SOMETHING FLAT to sing or play a note below the intended pitch. ANZ, N Am term **flat**[1] —**flattener** *n*

flatten out *v* **1.** *vi* to become lower and relatively stable ○ *Stock prices have flattened out over the year.* **2.** *vti* to spread out over an area, or spread something out

flatter[1] /flátter/ (**-ters, -tering, -tered**) *v* **1.** *vt* COMPLIMENT SOMEBODY TO WIN FAVOUR to compliment somebody too much, often without sincerity, especially in order to gain an advantage **2.** *vt* APPEAL TO SOMEBODY'S VANITY to please somebody by paying him or her particular attention, especially with a request to take some prominent role ○ *I was flattered to be asked to judge the competition.* **3.** *vt* MAKE SOMEBODY OR SOMETHING LOOK GOOD to show somebody or something to advantage, or make somebody or something seem better-looking in reality ○ *a studio portrait that really flatters her* **4.** **flatter yourself** *vr* CONGRATULATE YOURSELF EXCESSIVELY to feel satisfied with some aspect of yourself or with something you have done, especially when the perception is false ○ *He flatters himself on being a good judge of character.* [12C. Origin ?] —**flatterer** *n* —**flattering** *adj* —**flatteringly** *adv*

flatter[2] /flátter/ *n* any tool used to make something flat [< Old Norse *flatr* (see FLAT[1])]

flattery /flátteri/ *n* **1.** an act or instance of complimenting somebody, often excessively or insincerely, especially in order to gain an advantage **2.** complimentary remarks, especially when excessive or insincere [14C. < Old French *flaterie* < *flater* 'flatter']

flatties /fláttiz/ *npl* shoes with a low heel or no heel at all (*informal*)

flattish /fláttish/ *adj* somewhat or relatively flat ○ *a flattish hairdo*

flattop /flát top/ *n* a hairstyle in which the hair is brushed up and then cut short and flat across the top

flat tuning *n* the tuning of a musical instrument, or of instruments playing together, so that the pitch of the notes is lower than normal. This is sometimes done by early-music groups.

flatulent /fláttyoolənt/ *adj* **1.** FULL OF DIGESTIVE GAS having excessive gas (**flatus**)in the digestive system **2.** CAUSING WIND IN DIGESTIVE SYSTEM causing excessive gas (**flatus**) to be created in the stomach and intestines **3.** POMPOUS OR SELF-IMPORTANT having or showing excessive self-importance (*literary*) [Late 16C. Via French < modern Latin *flatulentus* < Latin *flatus* 'blowing, blast' < *flare* 'to blow'] —**flatulence** *n* —**flatulently** *adv*

flatus /fláytəss/ *n* gas produced in the digestive system by bacterial fermentation and containing high amounts of hydrogen sulphide and methane, usually expelled from the body through the anus (*technical*) [Mid-17C. < Latin (see FLATULENT)]

flatware /flát wair/ *n N Am* **1.** HOUSEHOLD same as **cutlery** (sense 1) **2.** dishes used for eating that are flat or relatively shallow, e.g. plates and saucers, as opposed to deeper pieces (**hollowware**)

flat-water *adj* done on a calm or slow-moving body of water

flatways /flát wayz/ *adv* with the flat side down or foremost

flatweave /flát weev/, **flat-woven** *adj* woven without a pile ○ *a flatweave carpet*

flat white *n ANZ* a cup of white coffee, usually made with espresso coffee and hot milk [Because it is not frothy]

flatwise /flát wīz/ *adv US* same as **flatways**

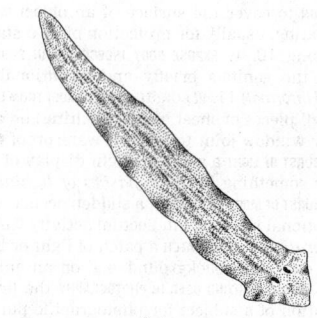

flatworm

flatworm /flát wurm/ *n* a worm with a soft, flattened body. Some flatworms, e.g. tapeworms, are parasites. Phylum: Platyhelminthes.

flat-woven *adj* TEXTILES same as **flatweave**

Flaubert /flō bair/, **Gustave** (1821–80) French novelist. A dominant figure in the realist school, he achieved fame with his first published novel, *Madame Bovary* (1857). See Cultural note at **Madame** —**Flaubertian** /flō báirti ən/ *adj*

'We shouldn't touch our idols: the gilt comes off on our hands.'
[Gustave Flaubert, *Madame Bovary*; 1857]

flaunching /fláwnching/ *n* a cement or mortar fillet that is designed to throw off water at the junction where a masonry chimney stack comes through a roof [Early 19C. < *flanch* 'to slope', origin ?]

flaunt /flawnt/ *v* (**flaunts, flaunting, flaunted**) **1.** *vt* SHOW SOMETHING OFF to display something ostentatiously ○ *She flaunts her wealth every chance she gets.* **2.** **flaunt yourself** *vr* PARADE YOURSELF to parade yourself without shame or modesty **3.** *vti* WAVE to wave or flutter in the wind, or make something wave or flutter by moving it around (*dated*) ■ *n* DISPLAY an ostentatious display [Mid-16C. Origin ?] —**flaunter** *n* —**flauntingly** *adv*

USAGE flaunt or **flout**? In terms of openly disobeying or defying a law or convention, *flout* is the correct choice: *The driver flouted the law when he double-parked.* When expressing the idea of shameless or ostentatious display, the correct choice is *flaunt*: *He flaunted his ill-gotten riches by purchasing a huge mansion and seven luxury cars.*

flautist /fláwtist/ *n* somebody who plays a flute [Mid-19C. < Italian *flautisto* < *flauto* 'flute' < Provençal *flaüt*]

flav- *prefix* same as **flavo-** (*used before vowels*)

flavanone /fláyvənōn/ *n* a substance derived from flavone [Mid-20C. < FLAVO- + -ANE + -ONE]

flavin /fláyvin/ *n* a yellowish pigment belonging to a group present in plants and animals [Mid-19C. < Latin *flavus* 'yellow']

flavo- *prefix* **1.** yellow ○ *flavone* **2.** flavin ○ *flavoprotein* [< Latin *flavus* 'yellow' < Indo-European]

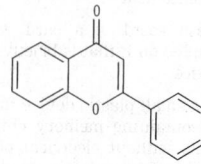

flavone

flavone /fláy vōn/ *n* a crystalline compound from which yellow pigments are derived. Formula: $C_{15}H_{10}O_2$.

flavonoid /fláyvə noyd/ *n* a naturally occurring phenolic compound belonging to a large group that includes many plant pigments. Flavonoids have beneficial effects in the human diet as antioxidants,

neutralizing free radicals which damage body tissue and lead to heart disease, strokes and cancer.

flavoprotein /fláyvō prṓ teen/ *n* an enzyme that is involved in cell respiration

flavor *n, vt* US spelling of **flavour**

flavour /fláyvər/ *n* **1. CHARACTERISTIC TASTE** an identifiable or distinctive quality of food or drink perceived with the combined senses of taste and smell ○ *The soup didn't have much flavour.* **2. SOMETHING ADDING FLAVOUR TO FOOD** a substance used to give food or drink an identifiable or distinctive taste **3. UNIQUE CHARACTERISTIC** the unique individual characteristic of an artistic work, especially a work of literature **4. TYPE** a type or kind of something (*informal*) ○ *Each flavour of the operating system provides its own unique commands or features.* **5. PHYS PROPERTY OF ELEMENTARY PARTICLES** a physical property that distinguishes types of quark and some types of lepton ■ *vt* (**-vours, -vouring, -voured**) **1. GIVE FLAVOUR TO FOOD** to give food or drink an identifiable or distinctive taste, usually by adding something ○ *Flavour the stew with rosemary.* **2. GIVE SOMETHING UNIQUENESS** to give a unique characteristic to an artistic work, especially a work of literature ○ *A certain terseness flavours her prose.* [14C. Alteration, after SAVOUR, of Old French *flaor* 'aroma' < blend of Latin *flatus* 'blowing' + *foetor* 'stench'] —**flavourer** *n* —**flavourful** *adj* —**flavourfully** *adv* —**flavourfulness** *n* —**flavourless** *adj* —**flavourlessly** *adv* —**flavourlessness** *n* —**flavoursome** *adj* —**flavoury** *adj*

flavoured alcoholic beverage *n* BEVERAGES same as **alcopop** (*technical*)

flavour enhancer *n* a substance, especially monosodium glutamate, added to processed food or drink to improve or intensify its flavour

flavouring /fláyvəring/ *n* a natural or artificial substance added to food or drink to give it an identifiable taste

flaw¹ /flaw/ *n* **1. PHYSICAL BLEMISH** a physical disfiguration that prevents something from being totally perfect and detracts from its value **2. DETRACTING FEATURE** a feature that is regarded as unfavourable ○ *There's a flaw in your argument.* **3. LAW INVALIDATING MISTAKE IN DOCUMENT** in a legal document, an error that can make it invalid [14C. Origin ?] —**flawed** *adj*

SYNONYMS *flaw, imperfection, fault, defect, blemish, failing, shortcoming, weakness*

CORE MEANING: something that detracts from perfection

flaw a physical disfigurement that prevents something from being totally perfect and detracts from its value, or a feature that is regarded as unfavourable ○ *a tiny flaw in the glass* ○ *a fatal flaw in their strategy*

imperfection something that makes somebody or something less than perfect ○ *a minor imperfection on the shiny surface* ○ *They accepted us, with all our imperfections, as co-workers.*

fault something that detracts from the integrity, functioning, or perfection of something, or a feature of somebody's character that is regarded as unfavourable ○ *a design fault* ○ *regarded it as a serious fault of the education system* ○ *His worst fault is his unreliability.*

defect a physical error in a machine or system, especially one that prevents it from functioning correctly, or a feature of something that is regarded as inadequate ○ *A house may show a hidden defect several years after construction.* ○ *a metabolic defect* ○ *regarded his disinclination to stand up for himself as a character defect*

failing a deficiency in the way that something takes place or operates, or a feature of somebody's character regarded with disapproval ○ *The management acknowledged this failing in the system.* ○ *At least unpunctuality isn't one of my failings.*

blemish a mark that detracts from the appearance of something, or a feature that detracts from somebody's personal reputation or good record ○ *a small blemish that only an expert would have noticed* ○ *the only blemish on an otherwise perfect record*

shortcoming a failure in a system or organization, or a feature of somebody's character regarded with disapproval ○ *The omission of this test is a serious shortcoming in the service offered.* ○ *The team's main shortcoming has been letting advantages slip away.*

weakness a weak point in the structure or arrangement of something, or a feature of somebody's character regarded with disapproval ○ *The intermittent supply of electricity is a definite*

---

weakness. ○ *They were asked to analyse their team's strengths and weaknesses.* ○ *Indecision was always one of his weaknesses.*

flaw² /flaw/ *n* **1.** a brief gust of wind **2.** a short storm or spell of bad weather [Early 16C. Probably < Middle Low German *vlāge*, or < N Germanic] —**flawy** *adj*

flawless /fláwləss/ *adj* without any blemish or imperfection ○ *a flawless performance* —**flawlessly** *adv* —**flawlessness** *n*

flax (sense 2)

flax /flaks/ *n* **1.** a fine light-coloured plant fibre. Use: linen textiles. **2.** a plant that yields oil from its seeds and flax from its stems. Latin name: *Linum usitatissimum*. [Old English *flæx* < Indo-European, 'plait'] —**flaxy** *adj*

flaxen /fláks'n/ *adj* **1.** of the pale greyish-yellow colour of flax **2.** made from flax fibres

Flaxman /fláksmən/, **John** (1755–1826) British sculptor and illustrator. He was appointed the first professor of sculpture at the Royal Academy in 1810. His simple illustrations of classical texts are characterized by clean neoclassical lines.

flaxseed /fláks seed/ *n* the seed of the flax plant, especially when used as the source of flaxseed oil. ◊ **linseed**

flaxseed oil *n* oil obtained from the seeds of the flax plant, especially as used in products to promote human and animal health

flay /flay/ (**flays, flaying, flayed**) *vt* **1. LASH OR FLOG SOMEBODY** to whip or beat a person or animal severely **2. STRIP SKIN OFF SOMEBODY** to remove the skin or outer covering from somebody or something **3. CRITICIZE SOMEBODY HARSHLY** to criticize somebody or something harshly and severely, and sometimes unfairly **4. STRIP SOMEBODY OF BELONGINGS** to take all the money or valuables from somebody, especially by the use of deceit, intimidation, or similar means (*dated*) [Old English *flēan* < Indo-European, 'to strike'] —**flayer** *n*

F layer *n* the transition zone between the solid inner core of Earth and its more fluid outer layer, at a depth of approximately 5,100 km/3,200 mi

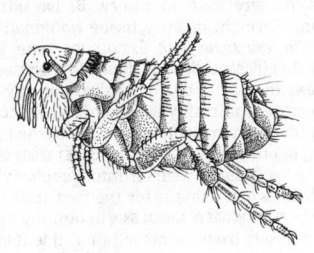

flea

flea /flee/ *n* **1.** a small wingless insect with legs adapted for jumping that sucks blood and lives as a parasite on warm-blooded animals. Order: Siphonaptera. **2.** a small beetle or crustacean that resembles or jumps like a flea, e.g. a water flea, flea beetle, or sand flea [Old English *flēa(h)* < Indo-European] ◊ **send somebody away** *or* **off with a flea in his** *or* **her ear** to sharply reprimand somebody for something that he or she has done

---

SPELLCHECK flea or **flee**? Do not confuse the spelling of **flea** and **flee**, which sound similar. **Flea** is a noun denoting a small parasitic insect: *The dog has fleas.* **Flee** is a verb meaning 'run away' or 'pass quickly': *We were forced to flee for our lives.*

fleabag /flee bag/ *n* (*informal*) **1.** a dirty or scruffy living being, especially one that is infested with fleas **2.** N Am a cheap shabby hotel or lodging house

fleabane /flee bayn/ *n* a wild plant of the daisy family with yellow flowers. Genus: *Erigeron*. [Because of its supposed ability to repel fleas]

flea beetle *n* a very small beetle with large hind legs adapted for jumping. The beetle and its larvae are pests of vegetable crops. Subfamily: Halticinae.

fleabite /flee bīt/ *n* **1.** the bite of a flea, or the small red mark caused by this **2.** a small loss or petty annoyance (*informal*)

flea-bitten *adj* **1. COVERED WITH FLEAS OR FLEABITES** covered with fleabites or infested with fleas **2. WITH PALE FLECKED COAT** describes a horse that has a pale coat with reddish-brown flecks **3. CHEAP AND SHABBY** cheap, shabby, or run-down (*informal*)

flea collar *n* a collar, usually for dogs or cats, containing a chemical that repels or kills fleas

flea-flicker *n* in American football, a play in which the ball is quickly passed laterally from one player to another to confuse the defence

fleam /fleem/ *n* **1.** a bevelled cutting edge on the teeth of a saw **2.** a surgical knife formerly used to open a vein in bloodletting [15C. Via Old French *flieme* < Greek *phlebotomon* 'vein-cutter' < *phlebos* 'vein']

flea market *n* a market, usually outdoors, with individual stalls selling various types of merchandise such as antiques, used household items, and cut-price goods

fleapit /flee pit/ *n* a cheap run-down cinema or theatre (*informal*)

fleawort /flee wurt/ (*plural same* or **-worts**) *n* a plant with furry leaves arranged in clusters. Flowers: yellow. Native to: Europe. Genus: *Senecio*. [Because of its supposed ability to repel fleas]

flèche

flèche /flaysh, flesh/, **fleche** *n* **1. ARCHIT SLENDER CHURCH SPIRE** a slender spire, especially one that emerges from the roof of a church at the point where the ridges intersect **2. ARCHIT BUTTRESS FEATURE** a joint at the top of a buttress, designed to add weight and assist in transferring load from roof to ground **3. MIL POINTED FORTIFICATION** a fortification with two faces that form a jutting angle [Early 18C. < French, 'arrow']

fléchette /flay shét/, **flechette** *n* a small arrow or dart used in various types of missile or projectile intended to kill or injure people [Early 20C. < French, 'little arrow' < *flèche* 'arrow']

fleck /flek/ *n* any one of a number of very small marks, streaks, or pieces scattered on a surface or throughout a block of something ○ *flecks of mica in granite* ■ *vt* (**flecks, flecking, flecked**) to mark something with small streaks or spots ○ *Sunlight flecked the path ahead.* [14C. Origin ?]

Flecker /flékər/, **James Elroy** (1884–1915) British poet. He was the author of the collection *The Golden Journey to Samarkand* (1913) and the verse drama *Hassan*, produced posthumously in 1922. Full name **Flecker, James Herman Elroy**

    'It was so old a ship—who knows, who

---

knows? / And yet so beautiful, I watched
in vain / To see the mast burst open with
a rose, / And the whole deck put on its
leaves again.'
[James Elroy Flecker, 'The Old Ships'; 1915]

flection *n* ANAT another spelling of **flexion**

fled past participle, past tense of **flee**

fledge /flej/ (**fledges, fledging, fledged**) *v* **1.** *vi* BECOME
CAPABLE OF FLIGHT to become capable of flight and leave
the nest (*refers to young birds*) **2.** *vt* RAISE YOUNG BIRD to
raise a young bird until it is capable of flight **3.** *vt*
ARCHERY EQUIP ARROW WITH FEATHERS to put feathers on
an arrow **4.** *vt* PROVIDE SOMETHING WITH FEATHERS to provide
or cover something with feathers or something
similar [Mid-16C. < obsolete *fledge* 'fledged, ready to fly'
< Germanic]

fledgling /fléjling/, **fledgeling** *n* **1.** YOUNG BIRD a young
bird that has recently become capable of flight
2. SOMEBODY INEXPERIENCED a young or inexperienced
person ■ *adj* INEXPERIENCED inexperienced because still
learning or just starting to do something ○ *a fledgling business*

flee /flee/ (**flees, fleeing, fled** /fled/) *v* **1.** *vti* to run away
from something ○ *fled the burning building* **2.** *vi* to
pass or disappear quickly (*literary*) [Old English *flēon*
< Indo-European] —**fleer** *n*

SPELLCHECK See **flea**.

fleece /fleess/ *n* **1.** WOOLLY COAT OF SHEEP the coat of wool
on a sheep or similar animal **2.** WOOL SHORN FROM SHEEP
the wool shorn at one time from a sheep or similar
animal **3.** SOFT COVERING a soft woolly covering or mass
○ *rocks with a fleece of moss* **4.** SOFT FABRIC WITH NAP OR
PILE a soft warm fabric with a brushed nap or woolly
pile. Use: outer garments, lining. **5.** WARM JACKET a
soft warm jacket ■ *vt* (**fleeces, fleecing, fleeced**) **1.**
SWINDLE SOMEBODY OUT OF MONEY to take too much money
from somebody by cheating or overcharging
(*informal*) ○ *They make their living by fleecing tourists.* **2.** GIVE SOFT WOOLLY COVER TO SOMETHING to cover something with something that is soft and woolly in
texture or appearance (*literary*) ○ *Clouds fleeced the
summer sky.* **3.** AGRIC SHEAR SHEEP to shear wool from
a sheep [Old English *flēos* < W Germanic] —**fleecer** *n*

fleecy /fleéssi/ (**-ier, -iest**) *adj* **1.** consisting of fleece or
something similar **2.** soft and woolly in appearance
or texture —**fleecily** *adv* —**fleeciness** *n*

fleet[1] /fleet/ *n* **1.** a number of warships functioning
as a single unit under one command, or all the
ships of a nation's navy **2.** a number of road vehicles, boats, or aircraft owned, working, or
managed as a unit, usually by a commercial enterprise ○ *The company has a large fleet of service
vehicles.* [Old English *flēot* 'ships' < *flēotan* 'to float, swim'
< Germanic]

fleet[2] /fleet/ *adj* (*literary*) **1.** moving quickly or nimbly
2. passing or fading quickly [Early 16C. Probably < Old
Norse *fljótr* < Germanic] —**fleetly** *adv* —**fleetness** *n*

fleet[3] /fleet/ *n* regional a creek or inlet [Old English *flēot*
< Germanic]

Fleet Admiral *n* an officer in the US Navy of the
highest rank, having an insignia of five stars, this
rank and title used only in wartime

Fleet Air Arm *n* the branch of the Royal Navy concerned with air operations

fleet chief petty officer *n* a noncommissioned officer
in the Royal Navy of a rank above petty officer

fleeting /fleéting/ *adj* passing or fading quickly [Old
English < *flēotan* (see FLEET[1])] —**fleetingly** *adv* —**fleet-
ingness** *n*

SYNONYMS See *temporary*.

Fleet Street *n* the people and practices involved in
the British newspaper industry [After a street in central
London where most British national newspapers were formerly produced]

fleishig /fláyshik, flî-/, **fleishik** *adj* under Jewish
dietary laws, relating to, containing, or used only
for meat or meat products. ◊ **pareve** [Mid-20C.
< Yiddish *fleyshik* < *fleysh* 'meat']

Fleming /flémming/ *n* **1.** somebody who comes from
Flanders **2.** a Belgian who speaks Flemish [Pre-12C.
Directly or via Old Norse < Middle Dutch *Vlaminc*]

Fleming /flémming/, **Sir Alexander** (1881–1955) British
microbiologist. He was the codeveloper of the
world's first antibiotic, penicillin. He shared the
Nobel Prize in physiology or medicine (1945) with
Howard Walter Florey and Ernst Boris Chain for
this discovery.

'It was astonishing that for some considerable distance around the mould
growth the staphococcal colonies were
undergoing lysis. What had formerly been
a well-grown colony was now a faint
shadow of its former self...I was sufficiently interested to pursue the subject.'
[Sir Alexander Fleming. Quoted in *Portraits
of Nobel Laureates in Medicine and Physiology*, Sarah R. Riedman and Elton T. Gus-
tafson; 1963]

Fleming, Ian (1908–64) British writer. His fictional
hero James Bond, secret agent 007, appeared in 12
novels and 7 short stories, beginning with *Casino
Royale* (1953).

'Most marriages don't add two people together. They subtract one from the other.'
[Ian Fleming, *Diamonds Are Forever*; 1956]

Flemish /flémmish/ *adj* OF FLANDERS relating to Flanders,
the Flemings, or their language or culture ■ *n*
LANGUAGE SPOKEN IN BELGIUM one of the official languages
of Belgium, belonging to the West Germanic group
of the Germanic branch of Indo-European and
closely related to Dutch. Native speakers: 5 million.
■ *npl* PEOPLE OF FLANDERS the people of Flanders, or
Flemish-speaking people [14C. < Middle Dutch *Vlā-
misch* < *Vlāmland* 'Flanders']

Flemish bond *n* a style of brickwork in which bricks
laid with the end facing out (**headers**) alternate
with those laid lengthways (**stretchers**), horizontally and vertically

Flemish school *n* art and artists of the 15th and 16th
centuries in the Netherlands. Artists of the Flemish
school, e.g. Van Eyck and Rogier van der Weyden,
combined carefully observed subjects with complex
religious iconography.

flense /flenss/ (**flenses, flensing, flensed**), **flench** /flench/
(**flenches, flenching, flenched**) *vt* to strip the skin or
blubber from a whale or seal [Early 19C. < Danish
flensa] —**flenser** *n*

flesh /flesh/ *n* **1.** SOFT TISSUE OF BODY the soft tissues,
primarily muscle and fat, that cover the bones of
people and other animals **2.** HUMAN SKIN AS OUTER SURFACE
the outer surface of the human body **3.** MEAT OF
ANIMALS the flesh of animals, including birds and
fish, regarded as food **4.** PULP OF FRUITS AND VEGETABLES
the soft pulpy edible parts of fruits and vegetables,
as opposed to the skin, core, stone, and other parts
that are not usually eaten **5.** PEOPLE people in general
(*literary*) ○ *the way of all flesh* **6.** PHYSICAL ASPECT OF
HUMANITY the physical body along with its needs and
limitations, as opposed to the soul, mind, or spirit
7. SUBSTANCE substance as distinct from form or style
○ *Actions give flesh to theory.* **8.** UNWANTED WEIGHT
unwanted weight or fatty tissue (*informal*) ○ *could
afford to lose some flesh* **9.** COLOURS same as **flesh-
colour** ■ *vt* (**fleshes, fleshing, fleshed**) **1.** INSTRUCT ANIMAL
BY FEEDING to teach a dog or bird to hunt by feeding
it the meat of a freshly killed animal **2.** ACCUSTOM TO
KILLING to accustom somebody to bloodshed and the
killing of other people (*literary*) **3.** GET BLOOD ON WEAPON
to thrust a pointed weapon into somebody's flesh,
especially when using it for the first time (*literary*)
4. MANUF CLEAN INSIDE OF ANIMAL SKIN in tanning, to scrape
away the soft tissue adhering to a hide [Old English
flǣsc 'soft tissue, meat' < Germanic] ◇ **in the flesh** in
person ◇ **press the flesh** to greet and shake the
hands of many people in public, as a political or
promotional exercise (*informal*)

flesh out *v* **1.** *vt* to add substance and detail to
something ○ *flesh out a business proposal* **2.** *vi* to
put on weight, or become overweight (*informal*)

flesh and blood *n* **1.** people, or a person, related to
somebody by birth **2.** RELIG same as **flesh** *n* (sense 6)

flesh-and-blood *adj* representing life, people, and
events in a way perceived as believable or realistic

flesh-colour *n* a pink colour with tinges of yellow or

grey, like that of a white person's skin —**flesh-
coloured** *adj*

flesher /flésher/ *n* **1.** in tanning, a person who or a
device that removes any flesh adhering to the inside
of an animal hide **2.** *Scotland* a dealer in meat
(*dated; still found on shop fronts*)

flesh fly *n* a fly whose larvae feed on the flesh of
living or dead animals. Family: Sarcophagidae.

fleshings /fléshingz/ *npl* flesh scraped from an animal's hide

fleshly /fléshli/ (**-lier, -liest**) *adj* **1.** BODILY relating to the
human body ○ *the fleshly concerns of daily living* **2.**
RELATING TO PHYSICAL PLEASURE enjoying or concerned
with the pleasures of the body **3.** NOT SPIRITUAL not
focused on spiritual matters —**fleshliness** *n*

fleshpot /flésh pot/ *n* a place known to provide sexual
or sensual entertainment (*usually used in the plural*)
○ *Police keep an eye on the local fleshpots.* [Mid-16C.
See Exodus 16:3]

flesh wound *n* a wound that penetrates the flesh but
does not damage bones or vital organs

fleshy /fléshi/ (**-ier, -iest**) *adj* **1.** PLUMP having a
noticeable amount of flesh on the body **2.** WITH MORE
FLESH with thicker or softer flesh than other parts of
the body ○ *the fleshy part of the hand at the base of
the thumb* **3.** SOFT AND JUICY with thick soft juicy pulp
○ *the fleshiest peaches of the season* —**fleshiness** *n*

fletch /flech/ (**fletches, fletching, fletched**) *vt* ARCHERY
same as **fledge** (sense 3) [Mid-17C. Alteration of FLEDGE,
influenced by FLETCHER]

fletcher /flécher/ *n* a maker of arrows [13C. < Old
French *flech(i)er* < *flèche* 'arrow']

Fletcher /flécher/, **John** (1579–1625) English dramatist.
A writer of Jacobean tragicomedies, he collaborated
with Francis Beaumont on many plays, including
The Maid's Tragedy (1610–11).

'Death hath so many doors to let out life.'
[John Fletcher, *The Custom of the Country*;
1647]

fletchings /fléchingz/ *npl* the feathered part of an
arrow

fleur-de-lis

fleur-de-lis /flúr də leé/ (*plural* **fleurs-de-lis** /flúr də
leéz/), **fleur-de-lys** (*plural* **fleurs-de-lys**) *n* **1.** a heraldic
symbol or design in the form of three tapering
petals tied by a surrounding band, formerly used
by the kings of France **2.** PLANTS same as **iris** (sense
2) [< Old French *flour de lys* 'flower of the lily']

fleuret /flur rét, floor-/, **fleurette** *n* a decorative motif in
the form of a small flower [Early 19C. < French, 'little
flower' < *fleur* 'flower' < Old French *flour* (see FLOWER)]

flew past tense of **fly**[1]

SPELLCHECK See *flu*.

flex[1] /fleks/ *v* (**flexes, flexing, flexed**) **1.** *vti* BEND to bend
something, or be able to be bent ○ *The board flexes as
you step on it.* **2.** *vt* BEND BODY PART to bend something,
especially a joint of the body **3.** *vti* PRODUCE MUSCULAR
CONTRACTION to move or tense a muscle, or become
tense or contracted ■ *n* BENDING ABILITY bending, or the
ability to bend [Early 16C. < Latin *flex-* (see FLEXIBLE)]

flex[2] /fleks/ *n* flexible insulated electric cable, especially a length of this attached to an electrical
appliance [Early 20C. Shortening of FLEXIBLE]

~~flexable~~ incorrect spelling of **flexible**

flexatone /fléksə tōn/ *n* a percussion instrument consisting of a handle with a narrow metal sheet attached that is struck to produce a tunable sound

flexible /fléksəb'l/ *adj* **1.** ABLE TO BEND WITHOUT BREAKING able to bend or be bent repeatedly without damage or injury **2.** ABLE TO ADAPT TO NEW SITUATION able to change or be changed according to circumstances **3.** SUBJECT TO INFLUENCE able to be persuaded or influenced [15C. Directly or via French < Latin *flexibilis* < *flex-*, past participle of *flectere* 'bend'] —**flexibility** /fléksə bíllәti/ *n* —**flexibly** *adv*

flexible benefits *n* a benefits programme for employees that offers them a range of types and levels of benefit from which to choose

flexile /fléksil, -sīl/ *adj* same as **flexible** (sense 1) [Mid-17C. < Latin *flexilis* < *flex-* (see FLEXIBLE)]

flexion /fléksh'n/, **flection** *n* **1.** BENDING OF LIMB the bending of a limb or joint **2.** POSITION OF BENT PART the position of a bent limb or joint **3.** BENDING OF SOMETHING the bending of something, or its bent state [Early 17C. < Latin *flexion-* < *flex-* (see FLEXIBLE)] —**flexional** *adj*

flexitime /fléksi tīm/ *n* a system that allows employees to set their own daily times of starting and finishing work, within specific limits [Late 20C. Blend of FLEXIBLE + TIME]

flexography /flek sóggrəfi/ *n* a relief printing technique that uses a rotary press, a flexible plate, and a water-based ink [Mid-20C. < Latin *flex-* (see FLEXIBLE)] —**flexographer** *n* —**flexographic** /fléksə gráffik/ *adj* —**flexographically** *adv*

flexor /fléksər/ *n* a muscle that bends a joint or limb when it is contracted [Early 17C. < modern Latin < Latin *flex-* (see FLEXIBLE)]

flextime /fléks tīm/ *n US* HR same as **flexitime**

flexuous /fléksyoo əss/, **flexuose** /-ōss/ *adj* curving, winding, or turning (*formal*) [Early 17C. < Latin *flexuosus* < *flex-* (see FLEXIBLE)] —**flexuosity** /fléksyŏo óssəti/ *n* —**flexuously** *adv*

flexure /flékshər/ *n* **1.** an act of bending or being flexed **2.** a bend or curve, e.g. in a body part or organ [Late 16C. < Latin *flexura* < *flex-* (see FLEXIBLE)] —**flexural** *adj*

flibbertigibbet /flíbbərti jíbbit, flíbbərti jibit/ *n* somebody who is regarded as silly, irresponsible, or scatterbrained, especially one who prattles or gossips (*dated*) [15C. Probably an imitation of the sound of meaningless prattle]

flic /flik/ *n* a member of the French police (*slang*) [Late 19C. < French]

flick[1] /flik/ *n* **1.** QUICK MOVEMENT a quick jerking movement **2.** QUICK BLOW a sharp light blow made with a quick jerking movement, usually of the finger **3.** SPLASH OF COLOUR a light splash or streak ○ *flicks of paint left on the floor* **4.** HOCKEY PENALTY SHOT in hockey, a penalty shot taken from the penalty spot ■ *v* (**flicks, flicking, flicked**) **1.** *vt* HIT SOMETHING WITH QUICK BLOW to hit something or somebody sharply or lightly with the end of something, usually with a quick jerking movement ○ *He flicked me with his towel.* **2.** *vti* MOVE JERKILY to move with a quick sharp jerk, or make something move with a quick sharp jerk ○ *The cow's tail flicked back and forth.* **3.** *vt* MOVE SOMETHING WITH QUICK BLOW to move, propel, or remove something with a sharp light blow or a quick movement of the finger or hand ○ *Would you flick that bug off me?* ○ *flick a switch* **4.** *vt* SOCCER GUIDE THE BALL GENTLY in football, to guide the ball gently and deftly with your foot or head into the goal or to a team-mate **5.** *vti* HOCKEY TAKE PENALTY SHOT in hockey, to take a penalty shot [15C. An imitation of the sound of a light blow]

flick through *vt* to turn the pages of a book or magazine quickly ○ *flicked through a couple of magazines while I waited*

flick[2] /flik/ (*dated informal*) *n* CINEMA same as **film** (sense 2) (*often used in combination*) ■ **flicks** *npl* the cinema [Early 20C. Shortening of FLICKER; from the flickering of early films]

flick[3] /flik/ *n* (*informal*) **1.** *S England, Wales* animal fat found around kidneys and other organs **2.** *N England* a side of bacon [Late 16C. Probably variant of FLITCH]

flicker /flíkər/ *vi* (**-ers, -ering, -ered**) **1.** SHINE UNSTEADILY to burn or shine unsteadily **2.** FLUTTER OR MOVE JERKILY to move with a fluttering or fast jerky motion **3.** APPEAR BRIEFLY to appear or exist only briefly ○ *A smile flickered across her face.* ■ *n* **1.** FLUCTUATING LIGHT an unsteady or wavering light ○ *the flicker of candles in the dark* **2.** QUICK MOVEMENT a quick fluttering movement **3.** TRANSIENT FEELING OR EXPRESSION a brief feeling that quickly passes, or an indication of this on somebody's face ○ *a flicker of anxiety* [Old English *flicorian* 'to flutter', suggestive of the movement] —**flickeringly** *adv*

flick knife *n* a pocketknife with a concealed blade that opens as soon as a button on the handle is pressed. N Am term **switchblade**

flick-on *n* in football and hockey, a light touch on a moving ball with the foot, head, or a stick intended to guide it towards a team-mate

flier /flī ər/, **flyer** *n* **1.** AVIAT AIRCRAFT PILOT the pilot of an aircraft **2.** AVIAT AIRCRAFT PASSENGER a passenger on an aircraft ○ *frequent fliers* **3.** MEDIA PRINTED SHEET WIDELY DISTRIBUTED a short piece of printed matter, usually an advertisement, that is widely distributed **4.** BUILDINGS STEP IN STRAIGHT STAIRCASE a rectangular step in a straight flight of stairs **5.** RISKY UNDERTAKING a daring or risky financial undertaking (*informal*) **6.** ATHLETICS, SWIMMING same as **flying start** (*informal*)

flight[1] /flīt/ *n* **1.** PROCESS OR ACT OF FLYING the process or act of moving through the air or through space **2.** AIR JOURNEY a journey through air or space in a form of transport ○ *daily flights of a thousand miles or more* **3.** TRAVEL SCHEDULED FLIGHT a scheduled flight with a commercial airline, usually designated by letters and numbers ○ *flight TC546 to Vancouver* **4.** ABILITY TO FLY the ability to travel through the air with wings ○ *an experimental ultralight tested for flight* ○ *an ancient bird incapable of flight* **5.** BUILDINGS SERIES OF STEPS BETWEEN FLOORS a group of stairs that go from one level of a building to another ○ *We live three flights up.* **6.** GROUP FLYING TOGETHER a group of aircraft or birds flying together, sometimes in a set pattern **7.** AIR FORCE GROUP OF AIRCRAFT a group of aircraft operating together as a separate unit ○ *the Queen's flight* **8.** RAPID MOVEMENT swift passage, progress, or motion, especially through the air **9.** EXTRAORDINARY MENTAL FEAT an act or the process of imagining extraordinary things ○ *a flight of the imagination* **10.** ARCHERY, DARTS TAIL OF ARROW OR DART the feathers on an arrow or dart **11.** HURDLES ON RACETRACK a line of hurdles across a racetrack ■ *v* (**flights, flighting, flighted**) **1.** *vi* FLY TOGETHER to fly or migrate together **2.** *vt* FIELD SPORTS SHOOT FLYING BIRD in hunting, to shoot a bird as it flies **3.** *vt* ARCHERY, DARTS PUT TAIL ON ARROW OR DART to put feathers on an arrow or dart **4.** *vt* LAUNCH OBJECT ON FLOATING COURSE to make a ball or dart seem to float inexorably towards its target [Old English *flyht* < Germanic]

flight[2] /flīt/ *n* the act of running away from something or somebody [12C. < assumed Old English, < Germanic]

flight arrow *n* a light arrow used for long-distance shooting

flight attendant *n* somebody employed by an airline to attend to the needs, comfort, and safety of passengers during flights

flight bag *n* a soft suitcase of a size that can be carried on an aircraft

flight coupon *n* a portion of an airline ticket that indicates the departure and arrival points of a passenger for a single journey or each leg of a journey

flight data recorder *n* same as **flight recorder**

flight deck *n* **1.** the upper deck of an aircraft carrier that is used as a runway **2.** the compartment at the front of an aeroplane where the pilot, copilot, and flight engineer sit

flight engineer *n* the crew member of an aeroplane who monitors the performance of its systems, including the engines

flight envelope *n* a set of limits to performance that exist in the design of an aircraft, e.g. altitude, range, payload, and manoeuvrability

flight feather *n* any feather in a bird's wing or tail that is necessary for flight, usually a large stiff one

flightless /flītləss/ *adj* describes birds that are incapable of flight. Ostriches, penguins, and kiwis are flightless birds.

flight level *n* the height at which a particular aircraft is allowed to fly at a particular time

flight lieutenant *n* an officer in the Royal Air Force of a rank above flying officer

flight line *n* the area of an airfield, especially a military airfield, where aeroplanes are parked, serviced, and loaded or unloaded

flight of fancy *n* an idea or thought that is very imaginative but completely impractical or even ridiculous

flight path *n* the course taken by an aircraft, spacecraft or projectile

flight plan *n* a record outlining the details of a proposed flight

flight recorder *n* an electronic instrument installed on an aircraft that records details of its performance in flight. The details recorded can be used to discover the cause of a crash.

flightseeing /flīt seeing/ *n* the practice or business of transporting tourists to otherwise inaccessible wilderness areas by helicopter, for viewing the areas by air or for organized hikes —**flightseer** *n*

flight sergeant *n* a noncommissioned officer in the Royal Air Force of a rank above sergeant

flight simulator *n* **1.** a computerized device that exactly reproduces the conditions that occur on the flight deck of an aircraft and that can be used to train pilots **2.** *also* **flight sim** a computer game that involves simulated flight control

flight surgeon *n* a medical officer in the US Air Force who practises aviation medicine and looks after the health of flight crews

flight-test (**flight-tests, flight-testing, flight-tested**) *vt* to test the performance of an aircraft, spacecraft, missile, or component in flight —**flight test** *n*

flighty /flīti/ (**-ier, -iest**) *adj* constantly changing plans, emotions, or opinions, especially in the choice of sexual partners —**flightily** *adv* —**flightiness** *n*

flimflam /flím flam/ (*slang*) *n* **1.** TRICK OR SWINDLE an attempt to cheat somebody **2.** DECEPTIVE TALK talk that confuses or deceives ■ *vt* (**-flams, -flamming, -flammed**) CHEAT SOMEBODY to cheat somebody [Mid-16C. Origin ?] —**flimflammer** *n* —**flimflammery** *n*

flimsy /flímzi/ *adj* (**-sier, -siest**) **1.** NOT STRONG weak and too easily broken ○ *flimsy furniture* **2.** EASILY TORN light, thin, and easily torn ○ *a flimsy cotton blouse* **3.** UNCONVINCING difficult to believe or accept ○ *The grounds for an appeal are flimsy at best.* ○ *a flimsy excuse* ■ *n* (*plural* **-sies**) COMM CARBON COPY a thin piece of carbon paper or a copy made with it [Early 18C. Probably < alteration of FILM after CLUMSY] —**flimsily** *adv* —**flimsiness** *n*

SYNONYMS See ***fragile***.

flinch[1] /flinch/ (**flinches, flinching, flinched**) *vi* **1.** to make an involuntary small backward movement in response to pain or something frightening or shocking **2.** to avoid thinking about something, confronting something, or doing something ○ *We will not flinch from danger.* [Mid-16C. < Old French *flenchir* 'turn aside' < Germanic, 'to bend'] —**flincher** *n* —**flinchingly** *adv*

SYNONYMS See ***recoil***.

flinch[2] /flinch/ (**flinches, flinching, flinched**) *vt* FISHERIES same as **flense** [Early 19C. Alteration]

flinders /flíndərz/ *npl* tiny fragments of something [15C. Origin ?]

Flinders /flíndərz/ river in northern Queensland, Australia that rises in the Great Dividing Range and flows northwest to the Gulf of Carpentaria. Length: 840 km/520 mi.

Flinders, Matthew (1774–1814) British explorer. He was the first sailor to circumnavigate Tasmania (1798) and Australia (1802–03).

Flinders bar *n* a bar of soft iron mounted under a compass to compensate for local magnetism and prevent it affecting the reading of the compass [After Matthew FLINDERS]

Flinders Island island off the coast of northeastern Tasmania, Australia. Local industries include fishing, farming, and tourism. Population: 868 (2002 estimate). Area: 2,089 sq. km/807 sq. mi.

Flinders Ranges mountain chain in eastern South Australia. More than 500 km/310 mi. long, its highest peak is St Mary's Peak, 1,166 m/3,825 ft.

fling /fling/ v (**flings, flinging, flung** /flung/) **1.** vt THROW SOMETHING VIOLENTLY to throw something or somebody carelessly or forcefully **2.** vr MOVE FORCEFULLY to move forcefully in a way that seems impressive or dramatic ○ *She flung herself onto the chair and began to sob.* **3.** vt MOVE YOUR HEAD OR ARMS to move your head or arms in a particular direction suddenly and dramatically **4.** vr WORK ENTHUSIASTICALLY AND ENERGETICALLY to start doing something with great enthusiasm and energy ○ *She flings herself into every project she undertakes.* ■ n (*informal*) **1.** SHORT AFFAIR a brief sexual relationship **2.** TIME FOR PLEASURE a short period of carefree enjoyment, especially before a time that is expected to be less exciting or enjoyable ○ *one last fling before settling down to a full-time job* [13C. < N Germanic < Indo-European, 'to strike'] —**flinger** n

SYNONYMS See *throw*.

fling off vt to take off a piece of clothing quickly, or remove forcefully something that is covering you

flint /flint/ (*plural same* or **flints**) n **1.** GEOL VERY HARD QUARTZ THAT MAKES SPARKS a very hard greyish-black fine-grained form of quartz that produces a spark when struck with steel. It occurs as nodules and bands in chalk. Flint was used in prehistoric times to make tools. **2.** PREHIST TOOL MADE OF FINE-GRAINED QUARTZ a piece of fine-grained quartz shaped into a tool by prehistoric people **3.** SPARK-MAKING ROCK a piece of flint used to make a spark **4.** PART OF CIGARETTE LIGHTER the part of a cigarette lighter, consisting of a small iron alloy cylinder, that makes a spark [Old English, < Germanic, 'to split']

Flint /flint/ city in southeastern Michigan, a major centre for assembling motor vehicles. Population: 121,763 (2002 estimate).

Flint, F. S. (1885–1960) British poet and translator. His *Cadences* (1915) features the sparse verse characteristic of the Imagist movement. His later work is written in a more romantic style. Full name **Flint, Frank Stewart**

flint corn n maize with kernels that contain hard starch, e.g. popcorn. Latin name: *Zea mays.*

flint glass n high-quality glass containing lead oxide that has a high refractive index. Use: lenses, cut glass, costume jewellery.

flint-knapping n the method, mainly used by prehistoric people, of chipping and splitting flint to make tools —**flint-knapper** n

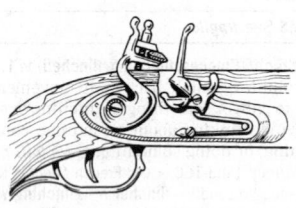

flintlock

flintlock /flint lok/ n **1.** a firearm with a firing mechanism (**gunlock**) where a flint embedded in the hammer ignites a gunpowder charge **2.** a firing mechanism (**gunlock**) that has a flint embedded in the hammer to produce the spark

Flintshire /flintshər/ county in northeastern Wales, on the border with England. Population: 148,594 (2001). Area: 437 sq. km/169 sq. mi.

flinty /flinti/ (**-ier, -iest**) adj **1.** hard, inflexible, and showing no emotion **2.** containing or related to flint —**flintily** adv —**flintiness** n

flip /flip/ v (**flips, flipping, flipped**) **1.** vti TURN SOMETHING OVER to turn something over from one side to the other with a quick movement of the wrist, hand, or fingers **2.** vt MOVE SOMETHING WITH QUICK LIGHT MOTION to move something with a small sharp quick motion

○ *She flipped the light on and walked in.* **3.** vt TOSS SOMETHING CARELESSLY to throw or toss something carelessly and lightly ○ *flip a pen across the table* **4.** vti TURN PAGES OF READING MATERIAL to turn the pages of a magazine or book quickly **5.** vti SPIN COIN to flick the edge of a coin with your thumb so that it spins in the air before landing **6.** vi GET SUDDENLY ANGRY to become very angry or upset suddenly (*slang*) ○ *When I told her I wouldn't help her, she just flipped.* **7.** vi GET EXCITED AT SOMETHING NICE to become excited over something that is pleasurable or attractive (*slang*) ■ adj (**flipper, flippest**) FLIPPANT showing a lack of seriousness that is considered inappropriate (*informal*) ○ *a flip remark* ■ n **1.** COIN'S SPIN the spin of a coin or other object as it is tossed or thrown **2.** SPORTS TURNING OF BODY a turning of the body through 360 degrees by springing from the ground or while diving **3.** BEVERAGES ALCOHOL AND EGG DRINK an alcoholic drink containing beaten egg [Mid-16C. Probably an imitation of the sound]

flipbook /flip book/ n a small book containing a series of images of the same thing in different positions that create the illusion of movement when the pages are turned quickly

flip chart n a visual aid consisting of a large pad of paper mounted on an easel, used to present information

flip-flop n **1.** CLOTHING BACKLESS SANDAL a backless foam-rubber sandal with a V-shaped strap secured between the toes and at the sides of the foot (*informal*) **2.** Aus, N Am CHANGE OF MIND a change of opinion, especially by a politician (*informal*) UK, NZ term **U-turn 3.** N Am GYMNASTICS BACKWARDS SOMERSAULT a backwards flip of the body **4.** ELECTRONICS CIRCUIT WITH TWO STABLE STATES an electronic circuit or mechanical device that has two stable states and can be switched between the two. Early computers used flip-flops as their memory storage units. ■ vi (**flip-flops, flip-flopping, flip-flopped**) N Am CHANGE OPINION to have a change of opinion, especially when this leads to a change of policy (*informal*) ○ *flip-flopped on the issue of employer responsibility*

flippant /flipənt/ adj showing a lack of seriousness that is thought inappropriate [Early 17C. < FLIP, after heraldic adjectives such as RAMPANT] —**flippancy** n —**flippantly** adv

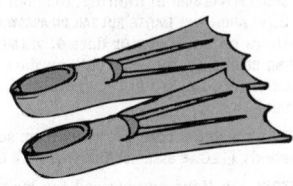

flipper (sense 2)

flipper /flipər/ n **1.** WATER ANIMAL'S LIMB a broad flat limb that an animal such as a penguin, seal, or whale uses for swimming **2.** DIVER'S FOOTWEAR a broad flat rubber extension worn on each of the feet to aid in swimming **3.** PINBALL FEATURE a small button-operated bat in a pinball machine that is used to keep the ball in play

flip phone n a mobile phone with one hinged section that opens up for use and folds up when not in use

flipping /fliping/ adj, adv used to emphasize annoyance or displeasure with something (*slang*) ○ *Will you turn that flipping music down?*

flip side n **1.** the disadvantages involved in doing something as opposed to the advantages that have previously been mentioned (*slang*) **2.** the song on a single record that the record company thinks will be less popular with record buyers, or the side of the record with that song on it (*dated*)

flip-top n a type of lid on a package that is hinged so that it moves up and down for opening and closing

flirt /flurt/ v (**flirts, flirting, flirted**) **1.** vi BEHAVE ALLURINGLY to behave in a playfully alluring way **2.** vt FLICK

SOMETHING to flick or jerk something ■ n SOMEBODY BEHAVING IN PLAYFULLY ALLURING WAY somebody who behaves in a playfully alluring way [Mid-16C. Origin ?] —**flirter** n —**flirtingly** adv

flirt with vt **1.** to consider an idea without doing anything serious about it or letting it have an effect ○ *flirted with the idea of going to college, but decided not to* **2.** to act in a way that may bring serious trouble or damage ○ *You're flirting with disaster when you drive that fast.*

flirtation /flur táysh'n/ n **1.** a short playful interaction based on lighthearted feeling, especially one that suggests sexual interest **2.** a period of considering or participating in something in a superficial way ○ *a flirtation with vegetarianism*

flirtatious /flur táyshəss/ adj behaving playfully and in a way that gives the impression of sexual interest —**flirtatiously** adv —**flirtatiousness** n

flirty /flúrti/ (**-ier, -iest**) adj **1.** same as **flirtatious** (*informal*) **2.** suitable for a flirtatious person or a person in a flirtatious mood —**flirtily** adv —**flirtiness** n

flit /flit/ (**flits, flitting, flitted**) vi **1.** MOVE FROM PLACE TO PLACE to move quickly from one place to another without stopping for long **2.** BE BRIEFLY PRESENT to be briefly present or visible **3.** N England, Scotland MOVE HOUSE to move to a different residence [12C. < Old Norse *flytja* 'carry about' < Germanic, 'to float'] —**flitter** n

flitch /flich/ n **1.** a log cut lengthways from a tree, ready for further processing at a mill **2.** a side of bacon or one side of a pork carcass without the leg or shoulder [Old English *flicce* < Germanic, 'to tear']

flite vi regional another spelling of **flyte**

flitter /flítter/ vi (**-ters, -tering, -tered**) to move about in a restless or nervous way ■ n a rapid, repetitive, or back-and-forth movement in something small [14C. < FLIT]

flittermouse /flítter mowss/ (*plural* **-mice** /-mīss/), **flitterbat** /flítter bat/ n regional ZOOL same as **bat** [3]

REGIONAL NOTE See **bat** [3].

flitting /flítting/ n N England, Scotland an act of moving house

float /flōt/ v (**floats, floating, floated**) **1.** vi REST ON SURFACE OF LIQUID to move or rest on the surface of a liquid without sinking **2.** vt PLACE OR MOVE SOMETHING ON LIQUID to place something or make something move on the surface of a liquid **3.** vi STAY UP IN AIR to move slowly and lightly through the air **4.** vi BE HEARD OR SMELT FAINTLY to carry across a distance, especially as a sound or smell ○ *The sound of laughter floated across the water.* **5.** vi LIVE AIMLESSLY to live without a fixed purpose or plan ○ *He floated from job to job.* **6.** vt PROPOSE PLAN to propose a plan for consideration in order to see what response it receives (*informal*) **7.** vi MOVE GRACEFULLY to move lightly and gracefully ○ *They floated across the dance floor.* **8.** vt FIN SELL SHARES IN COMPANY to finance a company by selling shares in it to the public on the stock exchange **9.** vt FIN SELL SHARES OR BONDS to offer shares or bonds for sale on a stock exchange **10.** vti ECON ALLOW CURRENCY VALUE TO CHANGE to allow the exchange rate value of a currency to fluctuate freely in an open market, or fluctuate in this way **11.** vt AGRIC IRRIGATE LAND to flood or irrigate land ■ n **1.** FLOATING OBJECT an object or device that floats or is used to keep another object buoyant **2.** UK SWIMMING SWIMMING AID a buoyant rectangular board that supports the arms and top of the body of a swimmer. ANZ, N Am term **kickboard 3.** COMM MONEY KEPT FOR CHANGE a small amount of money in coins and notes that shopkeepers keep in the till so that they can give customers change **4.** VEHICLE IN CARNIVAL PARADE a truck or other large vehicle that has been elaborately decorated for a carnival parade **5.** FISHING same as **bobber 6.** UK TRANSP DELIVERY VEHICLE a small, usually electrically-powered, delivery vehicle **7.** N Am BEVERAGES CARBONATED DRINK WITH ICE CREAM a carbonated drink with a scoop of ice cream floating in it **8.** NAUT PADDLE WHEEL BLADE a blade in a paddle wheel **9.** CONSTR PLASTERER'S TROWEL a tool with a handle and flat rectangular blade for applying plaster to a wall **10.** BANKING PERIOD BETWEEN DEPOSIT AND WITHDRAWAL the period between the deposit of funds by a customer and the availability of the funds for withdrawal **11.** MECH ENG BALL IN FLOW-REGULATING DEVICE

the hollow ball that rests on the water level in a tank as part of the device (**ballcock**) that regulates the flow of water into the tank **12.** BIOL same as **air bladder** [Old English *flotian* < Germanic] —**floatability** /flṓtə bíllәti/ *n* —**floatable** *adj*

float around *vi* to be the subject of frequent discussion or attention ○ *a rumour floating around about a pending engagement*

float chamber *n* a chamber in a carburettor that has a floating valve to control the entry and level of petrol

floater /flṓtәr/ *n* **1.** SOMETHING FLOATING somebody or something that is floating **2.** *N Am* CASUAL WORKER a casual labourer who goes from job to job (*informal*) **3.** *N Am* WORKER SHIFTING TO VARIOUS TASKS an employee who is switched from job to job as needed **4.** DEAD BODY a dead body found floating in water (*slang*) **5.** *Aus* FOOD MEAT PIE IN GRAVY a meat pie served in pea soup or gravy **6.** *US* INSURANCE POLICY an insurance policy that covers articles lost anywhere **7.** OPHTHALMOL SPOT INTERFERING WITH VISION a shadow of opaque debris in the vitreous humour of the eye seen as a moving dark spot, or as a group of them, by the person affected. Technical name **muscae volitantes**

float glass *n* flat polished transparent glass made by solidifying molten glass as it floats on liquid of higher density such as tin

floating /flṓting/ *adj* **1.** NOT FIXED INTO POSITION not fixed but moving around **2.** MED OUT OF NORMAL POSITION not in the normal place in the body, having moved out of position ○ *a floating kidney* **3.** FIN FLUCTUATING IN MONETARY VALUE free to fluctuate in exchange rate value in relation to other currencies ○ *the floating euro*

floating assets *npl* BUSINESS same as **current assets**

floating charge *n* an unsecured charge on the assets of a company that allows them to be commercially used until the company ceases operations or the creditor demands collateral

floating debt *n* short-term government borrowing

floating dock *n* **1.** a large structure that can be submerged to let a ship enter and then raised with the ship inside to be used as a dry dock **2.** a small dock supported by piles on which it can move up and down with any change in water level

floating island *n* a dessert consisting of custard on which are placed pieces of meringue that appear to float

floating-point *adj* describes numbers in which the digits and the location of the decimal place are treated separately

floating policy *n* an insurance policy that covers loss of or damage to goods being transported by sea, regardless of the ship carrying them

floating rib *n* a rib attached only to the spine and not to the breastbone. In humans the two lower ribs on each side are floating ribs.

floating voter *n UK* somebody who does not consistently vote for the same political party in elections. ANZ term **swinging voter**. N Am term **swing voter**

floatplane /flṓt playn/ *n* a seaplane that has one or more floats that enable it to land on water

float tank *n* ALTERN MED same as **flotation tank**

floaty /flṓti/ (**-ier, -iest**) *adj* **1.** seeming to move slowly through the air **2.** capable of floating easily

floc /flok/ *n* a woolly (**flocculent**) mass that forms in a liquid as a result of precipitation or the aggregation of suspended particles [Early 20C. Shortening of FLOCCULUS]

floccillation /flóksə láysh'n/ *n* aimless plucking at bedclothes, a sign that a person is approaching death [Mid-19C. < modern Latin *floccillus* 'little tuft of wool' < Latin *floccus* 'tuft of wool']

floccose /flókōss/ *adj* describes plant parts that are covered with tufts of soft hair [Mid-18C. < late Latin *floccosus* < Latin *floccus* 'tuft of wool']

flocculate /flókyoŏ layt/ (**-lates, -lating, -lated**) *vti* **1.** to cause particles suspended in water to aggregate into clumps or masses that then sink or can be removed by filtering, or aggregate in this way **2.** to form fluffy masses, or cause clouds to form fluffy masses —**flocculation** /flókyoŏ láysh'n/ *n*

floccule /flók yool/ *n* a small mass of woolly or cloudy particles [Mid-19C. < modern Latin *flocculus* (see FLOCCULUS)]

flocculent /flókyoŏlәnt/ *adj* **1.** WITH FLUFFY APPEARANCE having a fluffy or woolly appearance **2.** WITH WOOLLY MASSES describes the woolly mass of solids (**precipitate**) produced in a liquid by a chemical reaction **3.** INSECTS COVERED WITH TUFTS covered with soft waxy tufts or flakes [Early 19C. < Latin *floccus* 'tuft of wool'] —**flocculence** *n* —**flocculency** *n* —**flocculently** *adv*

flocculus /flókyoŏləss/ (*plural* **-li** /-lī/) *n* a mass of gas that appears as either a dark or a bright spot on the surface of the Sun, often near to a sunspot [Late 18C. < modern Latin, 'small tuft of wool' < Latin *floccus* 'tuft of wool']

floccus /flókəss/ (*plural* **-ci** /-sī/) *n* a tuft of woolly hair, or a fluffy or downy covering [Mid-19C. < Latin, 'tuft of wool']

flock /flok/ *n* **1.** GROUP OF ANIMALS a group of birds, sheep, or goats that travel, live, or feed together **2.** CROWD OF PEOPLE a large group of people of the same type **3.** CHR CONGREGATION the members of a church congregation under the leadership of a priest or minister ■ *vi* (**flocks, flocking, flocked**) GO IN LARGE NUMBERS to go to a place or event in large numbers [Old English *flocc*, origin ?]

flock paper *n* wallpaper with a raised pattern that is velvety to the touch [*Flock* 'powdered wool' (with which originally made) < Latin *floccus* 'tuft of wool']

Flodden Field /flódd'n-/ plain in Northumberland, northern England, near the Scottish border. It was the site of a battle in 1513 in which England beat Scotland, and in which King James IV of Scotland was killed.

floe /flō/ *n* GEOG same as **ice floe** [Early 19C. Probably < Norwegian *flo* 'layer']

SPELLCHECK floe or **flow**? Do not confuse the spelling of ***floe*** and ***flow***, which sound similar. ***Floe*** is only used as a noun, denoting a sheet of floating ice. The word ***flow*** is much more frequent in general usage and can be used as a verb or a noun, referring to free or smooth movement, for example of water or traffic: *Blood flows through the veins. There has been a steady flow of refugees across the border.*

---

flog /flog/ (**flogs, flogging, flogged**) *vt* **1.** to hit a person or animal very hard using something such as a whip, strap, or stick **2.** to criticize somebody very severely ○ *flogged in the press for his continual U-turns* **3.** COMM same as **sell** (*informal*) [Late 17C. Origin ?] —**flogging** *n*

flogger /flóggәr/ *n* **1.** somebody who approves of flogging as a punishment **2.** *Aus* a short stick with a bunch of crepe-paper streamers attached to one end, waved by sports fans and cheerleaders to express support for their team

flokati /flə kaáti/ (*plural* **-tis**) *n* a handwoven woollen Greek rug with a shaggy pile [Mid-20C. < modern Greek *phlokatē* < Latin *floccus* 'tuft of wool']

flong /flong/ *n* a sheet of papier-mâché used to make a mould for a metal plate for printing a page of newspaper [Late 19C. < French *flan* 'mould' (see FLAN)]

flood /flud/ *n* **1.** WATER COVERING PREVIOUSLY DRY AREA a very large amount of water that has overflowed from a source such as a river or a broken pipe onto a previously dry area **2.** HUGE NUMBER a very large number of people or things ○ *a flood of complaints* **3.** HIGH TIDE the flowing in to land of water, associated with a rising tide **4.** ELEC same as **floodlight** *n* (sense 1) ■ *v* (**floods, flooding, flooded**) **1.** *vti* COVER AREA WITH WATER to cover a previously dry area with large amounts of water, or be covered with large amounts of water **2.** *vi* OVERFLOW to undergo conditions in which water overflows banks or barriers **3.** *vi* ARRIVE IN LARGE NUMBERS to arrive somewhere in very large numbers ○ *Messages of support are still flooding in.* **4.** *vt* SEND SOMEBODY MANY CALLS OR LETTERS to send a very large number of calls, letters, or complaints to an organization (*usually used in the passive*) ○ *We have been flooded with offers of help.* **5.** *vi* FEEL EMOTION SUDDENLY AND INTENSELY to feel a particular emotion, sensation, or memory suddenly and intensely **6.** *vti* FILL WITH LIGHT to shine strongly so that a place becomes filled with a bright or glowing light (*literary*) **7.** *vt* ECON SUPPLY OR PRODUCE SOMETHING TO EXCESS to supply too much of a product to a market, pushing prices down and keeping them low **8.** *vti* AUTOMOT SUPPLY TOO MUCH PETROL TO CARBURETTOR to send too much petrol to a carburettor in a car engine, or be supplied with too much, so that the car fails to start **9.** *vi* MED BLEED COPIOUSLY FROM WOMB to bleed profusely from the womb, e.g. after childbirth (*technical*) **10.** *vi* MED BLEED COPIOUSLY IN MENSTRUATION to bleed profusely during a menstrual period (*technical*) [Old English *flōd* < Germanic] —**floodable** *adj* —**flooded** *adj* —**flooder** *n* ◇ **be in flood** to be so full of water that banks or barriers are overflowed ◇ **be in floods of tears** to cry a lot

flood out *vt* to force somebody to leave a place or stop using something because flooding makes it impossible to stay or continue

Flood *n* in the Bible (Genesis 7–8), a devastating flood, taken as a sign of God's anger at people's wickedness. The Flood was survived only by Noah, his family, and pairs of all the animal species that took refuge in the ship (**ark**) that Noah was told to build by God.

floodgate /flúd gayt/ *n* a gate in a sluice that is used to control the flow of water

flooding /flúdding/ *n* the situation that results when land that is usually dry is covered with water as a result of a river overflowing or heavy rain

floodlight /flúd līt/ *n* **1.** POWERFUL LAMP USED AT NIGHT a large powerful lamp that produces a strong broad beam of light and is used to illuminate the outside of public buildings or sports events at night **2.** POWERFUL BEAM OF LIGHT a broad powerful beam of intense bright light produced artificially ■ *vt* (**-lights, -lighting, -lit**) LIGHT SOMETHING WITH FLOODLIGHTS to illuminate something with floodlights

floodlit /flúd lit/ *adj* illuminated by floodlights ○ *a floodlit match*

floodmark /flúd maark/ *n* the highest level reached by a tide or flood water, or a mark that indicates this level

flood meadow *n Ireland, SW England, Wales* low-lying land likely to be waterlogged in wet weather

floodplain /flúd playn/, **flood plain** *n* an area of low-lying land across which a river flows that is covered with sediment as a result of frequent flooding

flood tide *n* **1.** the incoming tide, or the period of time between low water and the following high water **2.** an irresistible or overwhelming force of feeling such as strong public outrage or enthusiasm

floodwall /flúd wawl/ *n* a wall built along the seashore or the bank of a river to prevent flooding of adjacent land

floodwater /flúd wawtәr/ *n* the water of a flood that is carried over river and stream banks and inundates previously dry land

floor /flawr/ *n* **1.** PART OF ROOM TO WALK ON the flat horizontal part of a room on which people walk **2.** STOREY all the rooms on one level of a building ○ *an office on the fourth floor* **3.** LEVEL AREA a flat open space for an activity or for seating **4.** GEOG NATURAL GROUND LEVEL the ground at the bottom of an ocean, lake, cave, valley, or forest **5.** POL PART OF LEGISLATURE WHERE MEMBERS SIT the part of the building housing a legislative body where the members sit and where official debates and discussions take place **6.** FIN PLACE WHERE SECURITIES ARE TRADED the part of a stock exchange where securities, futures, or options contracts are traded **7.** MANUF WORKING AREA OF FACTORY the area of a factory where workers manufacture or assemble products **8.** COMM PART OF STORE FOR MERCHANDISE DISPLAY the part of a shop where merchandise is displayed and sold **9.** DANCE same as **dance floor** (*informal*) **10.** PEOPLE PRESENT AT MEETING all the people present in the audience at a meeting, as opposed to the main speakers ○ *I'll take questions from the floor later.* **11.** FIN LOWEST LIMIT a lower limit, e.g. on an interest rate or the value of an asset **12.** AUTOMOT PART OF CAR INTERIOR the flat lower part of a motor vehicle's interior where the accelerator, clutch, and brake pedals are found and where the driver and passengers put their feet. N Am term **floorboard** ■ *vt* (**floors, flooring, floored**) **1.**

ASTONISH SOMEBODY to make somebody feel astonished and unable to react ○ *He was floored by the announcement of the changes.* **2.** BOXING **KNOCK DOWN** to knock somebody down with a punch **3.** *N Am* AUTOMOT **PRESS ACCELERATOR DOWN HARD** to depress a motor vehicle's accelerator as far as it will go in order to increase speed to the maximum (*slang*) [Old English *flōr* < Indo-European, 'flat'] —**floorer** *n* ◇ **have the floor** to address a meeting, or have the right to address a meeting ◇ **take the floor 1.** to rise to speak to a group of people **2.** to begin to dance, e.g. in a ballroom or nightclub ◇ **wipe the floor with somebody** to defeat somebody completely and decisively (*informal*)

floorage /fláwrij/ *n* the floor area of a building

floorboard /fláwr bawrd/ *n* **1.** one of the strips of wood that are used to make a wood floor **2.** *N Am* same as **floor** *n* (sense 12)

floorcovering /fláwr kuvvəring/ *n* material for covering floor surfaces, e.g. carpeting, or a carpet or mat made from such a material

floor exercise *n* an event in a gymnastics competition that consists of a series of tumbling exercises in a timed routine performed on a mat

floor hockey *n N Am* a version of hockey played using hockey sticks and a plastic puck or ball in a gymnasium. It is occasionally played with sticks without blades and a rubber ring.

flooring /fláwring/ *n* the materials from which a floor is made

floor lamp *n N Am* same as **standard lamp**

floor leader *n* a member of an American legislative body chosen by fellow party members to organize their activities and strategy on the floor of the legislature

floor-length *adj* describes a garment such as a dress that extends to the floor or the ankles

floor manager *n* **1.** an employee of a department store or large shop who is in charge of one floor or department, supervising staff and dealing with customers' complaints **2.** the stage manager of a television programme

floor plan *n* a plan of a room or floor of a building drawn to scale as if viewed from above

floorshow /fláwr shō/ *n* a series of shows featuring dancers, singers, comedians, or magicians at a nightclub

floorwalker /fláwr wawkər/ *n N Am* COMM same as **shopwalker**

floozy /flóozi/, **floozie** (*plural* **-zies**) *n* an offensive term that deliberately insults a woman as being vulgar and promiscuous (*informal dated*) [Early 20C. Origin ?]

flop /flop/ *vi* (**flops, flopping, flopped**) **1.** **SIT OR LIE DOWN HEAVILY** to sit or lie down heavily by relaxing the muscles and letting the body fall **2.** **MOVE LIMPLY** to move limply or heavily **3.** **FAIL COMPLETELY** to be completely unsuccessful (*informal*) ■ *n* **1.** **TOTAL FAILURE** a complete failure (*informal*) **2.** **HEAVY DULL SOUND** the sound made by something falling heavily [Early 17C. Alteration of FLAP] —**flopper** *n*

flophouse /flóp howss/ (*plural* **-houses** /-howziz/) *n N Am* same as **dosshouse** (*informal*) [Early 20C. < FLOP 'lie down, sleep']

floppy /flóppi/ *adj* (**-pier, -piest**) soft and tending to hang down limply or loosely ■ *n* (*plural* **-pies**) COMPUT same as **floppy disk** (*informal*) —**floppily** *adv* —**floppiness** *n*

floppy baby syndrome *n* MED same as **floppy infant syndrome**

floppy disk *n* a small flexible magnetically coated disk in a rigid plastic case on which data can be stored or retrieved by a computer [Late 20C. < its flexibility, as opposed to a HARD DISK]

floppy infant syndrome *n* a condition of marked muscle relaxation in a baby so that when supported face down the baby droops over the hand like an inverted 'U'

flops /flops/, **FLOPS** *abbr* floating-point operations per second (*used to indicate the speed of a computer*)

floptical /flóptik'l/ *adj* relating to a system for storing computer data on a disk that combines magnetic and optical technology [Late 20C. Blend of FLOPPY + OPTICAL]

flor. *abbr* floruit

flora /fláwrə/ (*plural* **-ras** or **-rae** /-ree/) *n* **1.** **PLANTS** plant life, especially all the plants found in a particular country, region, or time regarded as a group (*formal*) ○ *the flora of Australia* **2.** **DESCRIPTION OF PLANTS** a systematic set of descriptions of all the plants of a particular place or time **3.** MICROBIOL **BACTERIA THAT INHABIT BODY ORGANS** all the usually harmless bacteria inhabiting a part of the body, regarded as a group or population [Early 16C. < Latin *Flora*, Roman goddess of flowers < *flor-* 'flower']

floral /fláwrəl/ *adj* relating to, containing, or suggestive of flowers [Mid-17C. < Latin *Floralis* 'of Flora' or *flor-* (see FLORA)] —**florally** *adv*

floral envelope *n* BOT same as **perianth**

Florence /flórrənss/ capital of Florence Province and Tuscany Region, central Italy. Situated on the River Arno, about 233 km/145 mi. northwest of Rome, it is one of the world's leading artistic and cultural centres. Population: 356,118 (2001). Italian name **Firenze**

Florence fennel *n* PLANTS same as **fennel** (sense 2)

Florentine /flórrən tīn/ *adj* **1.** **OF FLORENCE** relating to the Italian city of Florence, or its people or culture **2.** ARTS, ARCHIT **TYPICAL OF ART OF RENAISSANCE FLORENCE** relating to the style of art or architecture in Florence during the Renaissance **3.** COOK **WITH SPINACH** cooked or served with spinach ○ *eggs Florentine* ■ *n* **1.** PEOPLES **SOMEBODY FROM FLORENCE** somebody who comes from the Italian city of Florence **2.** FOOD **TYPE OF BISCUIT** a biscuit containing candied peel, fruit, and nuts and covered in a thick layer of chocolate [13C. < Latin *Florentinus* < *Florentia* 'Florence']

Florentine stitch *n* HANDICRAFT same as **bargello**

Flores /flórress/ **1.** mountainous island in southeastern Indonesia, one of the Lesser Sunda Islands. The chief towns are Ende and Ruteng. Population: 272,750 (1989). Area: 14,200 sq. km/5,480 sq. mi. **2.** island in the northwestern Azores, in the Atlantic Ocean. Santa Cruz is the chief town. Population: 39,098 (1998). Area: 150 sq. km/58 sq. mi.

florescence /flaw réss'nss/ *n* flowering [Late 18C. < modern Latin *florescentia* < Latin *florescent-*, present participle of *florescere* 'begin to flower' < *florere* (see FLOURISH)] —**florescent** *adj*

~~floresent~~ incorrect spelling of **fluorescent**

Flores Sea sea situated between the eastern end of Java and the western end of the Banda Sea in Indonesia

floret /flórrət/ *n* **1.** a small flower, especially one in a flower head consisting of many flowers **2.** a small part into which the edible flower head of cauliflower or broccoli can be separated [Late 17C. < Latin *flor-* 'flower']

Florey /fláwri/, **Sir Howard Walter, Baron Florey of Adelaide and Marston** (1898–1968) Australian scientist. He was the codeveloper of the world's first antibiotic, penicillin. He shared the Nobel Prize in physiology or medicine (1945) with Alexander Fleming and Ernst Boris Chain for this discovery.

Florianópolis /flórri ə nóppəliss/ city and capital of Santa Catarina State, southern Brazil, situated on Santa Catarina Island. Population: 271,281 (1996).

floriated /fláwri aytid/ *adj* decorated with designs based on flowers and leaves [Mid-19C. < Latin *flor-* 'flower']

floribunda /flórri búndə/ *n* a hybrid cultivated rose. Flowers: small, in large sprays. [Late 19C. < modern Latin, form of *floribundus* 'flowering profusely' < Latin *flor-* 'flower']

florican /fláwri kan/ (*plural* **-cans** or *same*) *n* a small bustard, the male of which is black with white wing feathers. Native to: South Asia. Family: Otididae. [Late 19C. Origin ?]

floricane /fláwri kayn/ *n* a plant stem that flowers and bears fruit in its second year, e.g. in raspberries [< Latin *flor-* 'flower']

floriculture /fláwri kulchər/ *n* the growing of flowers as a crop [Early 19C. < Latin *flor-* 'flower', after HORTICULTURE] —**floricultural** /fláwri kúlchərəl/ *adj* —**floriculturally** *adv* —**floriculturist** *n*

florid /flórrid/ *adj* **1.** having an unhealthily glowing pink or red complexion **2.** ornate and overly complicated in wording and general style [Mid-17C. Via French < Latin *floridus* 'flowery' < *flor-* 'flower'] —**floridity** /flo ríddəti/ *n* —**floridly** *adv* —**floridness** *n*

Florida /flórridə/ state in the southeastern United States bordered by Alabama, Georgia, the Atlantic Ocean, and the Gulf of Mexico. Capital: Tallahassee. Population: 16,713,149 (2002 estimate). Area: 155,213 sq. km/59,928 sq. mi. —**Floridian** /flə ríddi ən/ *adj, n*

Florida, Straits of channel between the southern tip of Florida and the island of Cuba, connecting the Gulf of Mexico to the Atlantic Ocean. Length: 485 km/300 mi. Width: 80 to 240 km/50 to 150 mi.

Florida Keys /-keez/ chain of islands and reefs in southern Florida, extending southwestwards in an arc from the southern end of Biscayne Bay into the Gulf of Mexico. The islands, which include Key Largo and Key West, are connected by bridges and causeways and are a popular vacation destination. Length: 309 km/192 mi.

floriferous /flaw ríffərəss/ *adj* bearing or able to bear many flowers [Mid-17C. < Latin *florifer* < *flor-* 'flower'] —**floriferously** *adv* —**floriferousness** *n*

florilegium /fláwri léeji əm/ (*plural* **-gia** /-ji ə/) *n* an anthology of literary extracts (*archaic*) [Early 17C. < modern Latin, 'gathering of flowers']

florin /flórrin/ *n* **1.** **OLD BRITISH COIN** a unit of currency used in Britain between 1849 and 1968, equivalent to two shillings **2.** **GOLD OR SILVER COIN** a gold or silver coin, especially a Dutch guilder **3.** **FLORENTINE COIN** a gold coin first minted in Florence in 1252, or any similar coin used elsewhere in Europe [14C. Via Old French < Italian *fiorino* < *fiore* 'flower' (because originally a coin bearing a lily) < Latin *flor-*]

Florio /fláwri ō/, **John** (1553?–1625) English lexicographer and translator. He published an Italian-English dictionary (1598) and an English translation of Montaigne's *Essays* (1603).

> 'England is the paradise of women, the purgatory of men, and the hell of horses.'
> [John Florio, *Second Frutes*; 1591]

florist /flórrist/ *n* **1.** a dealer in flowers and ornamental plants **2.** *also* **florist's** (*plural same*) a shop that sells flowers and other ornamental plants [Early 17C. < Latin *flor-* 'flower']

floristics /flo rístiks/ *n* a branch of botany dealing with the types, numbers, distribution, and relationships of plant species in a particular area or areas (*takes a singular verb*) [Late 19C. < FLORA]

-florous *suffix* bearing flowers ○ *multiflorous* [< Latin *flor-* 'flower']

floruit /flórroo it/ *v* used, especially abbreviated as 'fl'., before the name or numerical designator of the period in the past when a particular person or movement was most active. (*formal*) [Mid-19C. < Latin, 'flourished']

flory /fláwri/ *adj* containing a fleur-de-lis [14C. < Old French *flo(u)ré* < *flour* (see FLOWER)]

Flory /fláwri/, **Paul John** (1910–85) US chemist. He was awarded the Nobel Prize in chemistry (1974) for his work on polymers.

floss /floss/ *vti* (**flosses, flossing, flossed**) DENT **CLEAN BETWEEN TEETH** to clean between individual teeth using dental floss ■ *n* **1.** DENT same as **dental floss** **2.** TEXTILES **SILKWORM FIBRES** short or waste fibres prepared from the outside of a silkworm's cocoon **3.** PLANTS **PLANT FIBRES** the mass of fine silken fibres that covers the seeds of the silk-cotton tree or of a cotton plant **4.** HANDICRAFT **EMBROIDERY THREAD** an embroidery thread made up of six strands loosely twisted together that can be separated for fine work [Mid-18C. Origin ?] —**flosser** *n*

flossy /flóssi/ (**-ier, -iest**) *adj* **1.** consisting of or looking like floss **2.** *US* ornate or showy in a flashy, often almost vulgar way —**flossily** *adv* —**flossiness** *n*

flotage /flṓtij/ *n* **1.** same as **flotation** (senses 2–3) **2.** NAUT same as **flotsam** (sense 1)

flotation /flō táysh'n/ *n* **1.** FIN **SELLING OF SHARES IN COMPANY** the financing of a company by selling shares in it

or a new debt issue or the offering of shares and bonds for sale on the stock exchange **2. FLOATING** the act, process, or condition of floating **3. CAPABILITY OF FLOATING** the ability to float on a liquid or remain on top of a soft surface (*technical*) **4.** TRANSP **ADHERENCE OF TYRE TO SURFACE** the ability of a tyre tread to adhere to and remain on top of a soft surface such as wet ground or snow **5.** CHEM **SEPARATION PROCESS** a process for separating materials such as a mixture of minerals in an ore according to their different abilities to float in a given liquid [Early 19C. < FLOAT]

flotation bags *npl* large bags that inflate when a helicopter or spacecraft lands in the sea and keep it afloat and upright

flotation device *n N Am* something that enables somebody to stay afloat in the sea, e.g. a life jacket or seat cushion (*technical*)

flotation tank *n* a sealed tank filled with salt water and minerals that somebody can float in to relieve stress

flotation therapy *n* a method of relieving stress that involves floating in salt water in a sealed tank while listening to music

flotel /flṓ tél/ *n* a moored boat or an oil rig that provides accommodation for offshore workers [Late 20C. Contraction of *floating hotel*]

flotilla /flō tíllə/ *n* **1.** a fleet of usually small boats **2.** a group of things operating or moving together [Early 18C < Spanish, 'small fleet' < *flota* 'fleet', via Old French < Old Norse *floti*]

flotsam /flótsəm/ *n* **1.** wreckage, debris, or refuse from a ship, found floating in the water. In maritime law, flotsam is what is found floating after a ship has sunk and jetsam is what was thrown from a ship while it was in trouble. **2.** people who live on the margins of society, e.g. homeless people (*sometimes offensive*) [Early 17C. < Anglo-Norman *floteson* < *floter* 'float' < Germanic] ◇ **flotsam and jetsam** discarded objects or odds and ends

flounce[1] /flownss/ (**flounces, flouncing, flounced**) *vi* to move with exaggerated angry swaggering motions showing displeasure or indignation [Mid-16C. Origin ?] —**flounce** *n*

flounce[2] /flownss/ *n* a strip of cloth that has been gathered into pleats on one side and then stitched onto a garment or curtain as a decoration [Early 18C. Alteration of Old French *fronce* 'pleat' (probably after FLOUNCE[1]) < Germanic]

flouncing /flównssing/ *n* material used to make flounces

flounder[1] /flówndər/ (**-ders, -dering, -dered**) *vi* **1.** MAKE UNCONTROLLED MOVEMENTS to make clumsy uncontrolled movements while trying to regain balance or move forward **2.** HESITATE IN CONFUSION to act in a way that shows confusion or a lack of purpose **3.** BE IN SERIOUS DIFFICULTY to have serious problems and be close to failing [Late 16C. Origin ?]

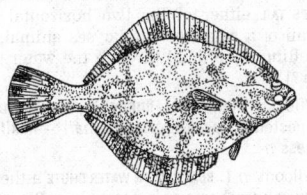

flounder

flounder[2] /flówndər/ (*plural same* or **-ders**) *n* **1.** EDIBLE FLATFISH an edible flatfish of shallow coastal waters. Families: Pleuronectidae or Bothidae. **2.** EDIBLE EUROPEAN FLATFISH an edible flatfish that has a greyish-brown mottled skin with orange spots and prickly scales. Native to: Europe. Latin name: *Platichthys flesus*. **3.** FLOUNDER AS FOOD the flesh of a flounder used as food [15C. Via Anglo-Norman *floundre* < N Germanic]

flour /flów ər/ *n* **1.** FINELY GROUND CEREAL GRAINS a powder made by grinding the edible parts of cereal grains.

Use: bread, cakes, pastry, sauce thickener. **2.** GROUND FOODSTUFF a finely ground powder made from any dried plant such as chickpea, banana, cassava, or potato ■ *vt* (**flours, flouring, floured**) COVER SOMETHING WITH FLOUR to cover or coat food, food preparation utensils, or a work surface with flour [13C. Variant of FLOWER 'the best (ground meal)']

SPELLCHECK flour or **flower**? Do not confuse the spelling of **flour** and **flower**, which sound similar. **Flour** is a powder used to make bread, pastry, etc.; the word is also used as a verb, meaning 'cover with flour'. The word **flower** is chiefly used as a noun, denoting the colourful part of a plant (as in *a bunch of flowers, roses coming into flower*); as a verb it means 'produce flowers' or 'develop to maturity'.

~~flourescent~~ incorrect spelling of **fluorescent**

~~flouride~~ incorrect spelling of **fluoride**

~~flourine~~ incorrect spelling of **fluorine**

flourish /flúrrish/ *v* (**-ishes, -ishing, -ished**) **1.** *vi* BE HEALTHY OR GROW WELL to be strong and healthy or grow well, especially because conditions are right **2.** *vi* DO WELL to sustain continuous steady strong growth ○ *The economy is flourishing.* **3.** *vt* BRANDISH SOMETHING to wave something in a dramatic way that draws attention to it ■ *n* **1.** HAND MOVEMENT a dramatic body movement that attracts attention, e.g. a sweep of the hand **2.** LOOP OR CURL an embellishment to something handwritten, e.g. a loop or curly line **3.** MUSIC ORNAMENTAL TRUMPET CALL a fanfare heralding the arrival of an important person **4.** MUSIC SHORT PRELUDE OR POSTLUDE a short, often improvised, passage at the beginning or end of a piece of music **5.** MUSIC SHOWY MUSICAL INTERLUDE a brief, often showy, technical passage within a piece of music [13C. < Old French *floriss-*, stem of *florir* 'to bloom' < Latin *florere* < *flor-* 'flower'] —**flourisher** *n*

floury /flów əri/ (**-ier, -iest**) *adj* **1.** covered or coated with flour, or tasting of flour **2.** easily crumbling when cooked ○ *floury potatoes*

flout /flowt/ (**flouts, flouting, flouted**) *vt* to show contempt for a law or convention by openly disobeying or defying it [Mid-16C. Origin ?] —**flouter** *n* —**floutingly** *adv*

USAGE See **flaunt**.

flow /flṓ/ *vi* (**flows, flowing, flowed**) **1.** MOVE FREELY FROM PLACE TO PLACE to move freely from one place to another in large numbers or amounts in a steady unbroken stream ○ *measures to allow traffic to flow freely* **2.** PHYS MOVE IN ONE MASS to move freely in one continuous mass (*refers to fluids*) **3.** PHYSIOL CIRCULATE IN BODY to move through the veins and arteries of the body (*refers especially to blood*) **4.** BE SAID FLUENTLY to be expressed uninhibitedly and eloquently ○ *The conversation began to flow.* **5.** BE AVAILABLE IN QUANTITY to be readily available and consumed in large amounts (*refers to alcoholic drinks*) **6.** BE EXPERIENCED INTENSELY to be experienced very intensely, often in a way that is visible to other people ○ *A wave of love flowed across her face.* **7.** EMANATE AS RESULT to derive from something as a result or series of results ○ *The consequences that flowed from the decision were worrying.* **8.** HANG LOOSELY to fall or hang loosely and gracefully (*refers to clothes or hair*) ○ *Her long hair flowed over her shoulders.* **9.** OCEANOG MOVE TOWARDS LAND to move towards the land as the tide rises (*refers to the sea or tidal water*) **10.** GEOL CHANGE SHAPE UNDER PRESSURE to change shape gradually in response to pressure without the development of cracks or

fissures ■ *n* **1.** UNHINDERED STEADY MOVEMENT a steady unbroken stream of people, goods, vehicles, money, or information from one place to another ○ *the unending flow of refugees* **2.** MASS OR QUANTITY FLOWING a mass or quantity of material that is flowing or has flowed ○ *a giant lava flow pouring down into the valley* **3.** MED MENSTRUAL BLOOD the quantity of blood during menstruation **4.** MOVEMENT OF FLUID OR ELECTRICAL CHARGE the movement of liquid, gas, or electrical charge **5.** OCEANOG TIDAL MOVEMENT TOWARDS LAND the movement of a rising tide towards the land **6.** COMMUNICATION ELOQUENT EXPRESSION OF THOUGHTS the continuous eloquent expression of thoughts or ideas in speech or writing **7.** *Scotland* GEOG BOGGY EXPANSE an expanse of wet peat bog ○ *the flow country* **8.** *US* PSYCHOL EXPERIENCE OF HEIGHTENED AWARENESS psychological and physical experience in which challenges presented are perfectly matched by the participants' skills, often resulting in heightened states of awareness, confidence, and performance [Old English *flōwan* < Indo-European] —**flowingly** *adv* ◇ **go with the flow 1.** to follow the lead of other people and react to their opinions or actions rather passively **2.** to adapt to the prevailing mood or situation in a relaxed way

SPELLCHECK See **floe**.

flowage /flṓ ij/ *n* **1.** FLOWING the act of flowing or overflowing **2.** OVERFLOWING WATER the water resulting from overflow **3.** PHYS GRADUAL DEFORMATION the gradual change in shape that occurs in solids such as asphalt that can flow without breaking when heat is applied

flow chart *n* a diagram that represents the sequence of operations in a process

flow-charting *n* the designing of a flow chart or charts

flow cytometry *n* a diagnostic test revealing the arrangement and amount of DNA in a cell, used to distinguish benign cells from malignant ones and to monitor the effect of anticancer treatment

flow diagram *n* MANAGEMT same as **flow chart**

flower /flów ər/ *n* **1.** COLOURED PART OF PLANT a coloured, sometimes scented, part of a plant that contains its reproductive organs. It consists of a leafy shoot with modified leaves, petals, and sepals surrounding male or female organs, stamens, and pistils. **2.** STEM WITH FLOWER a plant stem with one or more flowers that has been picked from the plant on which it grew **3.** PLANT WITH FLOWERS a small plant grown for the attractiveness of its flowers **4.** BOT FLOWERING STATE the state or period during which a plant has open blooms on it ○ *The roses are just coming into flower.* **5.** BEST the best part of or most perfect example of something ○ *the flower of the nation's youth* **6.** *N England* USED TO ADDRESS SOMEBODY AFFECTIONATELY used as a way of addressing somebody you like or love (*informal*) ■ *vi* (**-ers, -ering, -ered**) **1.** BOT PRODUCE BLOOMS to begin to produce blooms **2.** DEVELOP TO MATURITY to develop and reach maturity [12C. < Anglo-Norman *flur*, Old French *flour* < Latin *flor-* 'flower'] —**flowered** /flów ərd/ *adj* —**flowerless** *adj*

SPELLCHECK See **flour**.

flowerbed /flów ər bed/ *n* a clearly delineated area of a garden or park planted with flowering plants

flower child *n* a young person in the 1960s and 1970s who rejected materialism and war, especially the

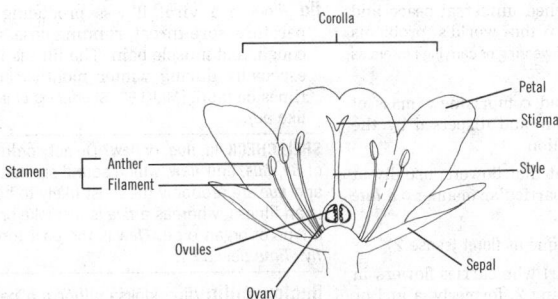

flower: cross section of a flower

Vietnam War, and preached universal peace and love as the solution to the world's problems (*informal*) [< their custom of wearing or carrying flowers as a symbol of peace]

flower clock *n* a seed head comprising a mass of seeds, each bearing a hair and dispersed by the wind, e.g. that of a dandelion

flowerer /flówərər/ *n* a plant that flowers, usually at a particular time or in a particular manner ○ *a late flowerer*

floweret /flówərət/ *n* FOOD same as **floret** (sense 2)

flower girl *n* **1.** a young girl who carries flowers in the procession at a wedding **2.** formerly, a girl or woman who sold flowers in the street

flower head *n* **1.** a cluster of small flowers on a single stem **2.** a dense arrangement of flower buds, e.g. in cauliflower or broccoli

flowering /flów əring/ *adj* capable of producing noticeable flowers ■ *n* the moment in the development of an idea, style, or movement when it gains recognition and becomes successful

flowering currant *n* a deciduous bush with dark green aromatic leaves. Flowers: small tubular red or pink. Latin name: *Ribes sanguineum.*

flowering dogwood *n* a deciduous tree with inconspicuous flowers surrounded by showy white or pink bracts, and leaves that turn red or purple in autumn. Latin name: *Cornus florida.*

flowering plant *n* any plant that is capable of producing noticeable flowers

flowerpecker *n* a small songbird with a long tongue that feeds on nectar, berries, and insects. Native to: Australia, Southeast Asia. Family: Dicaeidae.

flower people *npl* young 1960s-1970s peace activists, the flower children, regarded as a group (*informal*)

flowerpiercer /flówər peerssər/ *n* a small dull-coloured bird that feeds on nectar. Native to: tropics. Genus: *Diglossa.*

flowerpot /flów ər pot/ *n* a clay or plastic container in which plants are grown

flower power *n* the idea advocated by some young people in the 1960s and 1970s that universal peace and love should replace the materialism and militarism of Western society [< its adherents' custom of wearing or carrying flowers as a symbol of peace and love]

flower pressing *n* the process of preserving cut flowers by laying them on a flat surface and pressing them with a heavy object

flowers /flów ərz/ *n* a fine powder produced by sublimation or condensation (*takes a singular verb*)

flowery /flów əri/ (**-ier, -iest**) *adj* **1. POMPOUSLY LITERARY** full of ornate, overly elaborate expressions **2. ORNAMENTED WITH FLOWERS** decorated or patterned with flowers **3. LIKE FLOWERS** relating to flowers —**floweriness** *n*

flowmeter /flṓ meetər/ *n* an instrument for measuring the rate of flow of liquids or gases, especially in a pipe

flown past participle of **fly**[1]

flow-on *n ANZ* an increase in wages awarded to one union or group of workers as a result of a pay rise awarded to another union or group working in the same field, or the process by which this is done

flow sheet *n* **1.** MANAGEMT same as **flow chart 2.** a schematic diagram showing the equipment and connecting pipes that make up a process plant and sometimes showing flow rates and quantities of material

flowstone /flṓ stōn/ *n* a layered deposit of calcium carbonate (**calcite**) on rock where water has flowed or dripped, e.g. on the walls or floor of a cave

fl oz, fl. oz. *abbr* MEASURE fluid ounces

FLQ *n* a terrorist organization seeking the secession of Quebec from Canada. It was particularly active during the 1960s and 1970s. Full form **Front de Libération du Québec**

F. Lt *abbr* AIR FORCE Flight Lieutenant

F/Lt *abbr* AIR FORCE Flight Lieutenant

Flt Lt *abbr* AIR FORCE Flight Lieutenant

Flt Sgt *abbr* AIR FORCE Flight Sergeant

flu /floo/ *n* a viral illness producing a high temperature, sore throat, running nose, headache, dry cough, and muscle pain. The illness is widespread, especially during winter months, and can sometimes be fatal. [Mid-19C. Shortening of INFLUENZA] —**flu-like** *adj*

SPELLCHECK flu, flue, or **flew**? Do not confuse the spelling of ***flu, flue,*** and ***flew,*** which sound similar. The nouns ***flu*** and ***flue*** are probably the most likely to be confused: ***flu*** is an illness, whereas a ***flue*** is a smoke or heat outlet or a type of organ pipe. ***Flew*** is the past tense of the verb *fly: Time flew past.*

flucloxacillin /floo klóksə síllin/ *n* a penicillin drug. Use: treatment of streptococcal infections and pneumonia.

fluconazole /floo kónnə zṓl/ *n* an antifungal drug

fluctuate /flúkchoo ayt/ (**-ates, -ating, -ated**) *vi* to change often from high to low levels or from one thing to another in an unpredictable way [Mid-17C. < Latin *fluctuat-*, past participle of *fluctuare* < *fluere* 'to flow'] —**fluctuant** *adj*—**fluctuation** /flúkchoo áysh'n/ *n*

flue /floo/ *n* **1. SMOKE OR HEAT OUTLET** a shaft, tube, or pipe used as an outlet to carry smoke, gas, or heat, e.g. from a fireplace or furnace **2.** MUSIC **TYPE OF ORGAN PIPE** an organ pipe in which the sound is produced by passing air across an opening with a lip **3.** MUSIC **OPENING ON ORGAN PIPE** the lipped opening on an organ pipe that initiates vibrations and sound when air passes across it [15C. Origin ?]

SPELLCHECK See *flu.*

flue-cure (**flue-cures, flue-curing, flue-cured**) *vt* to cure tobacco with radiant heat supplied through flues from a furnace —**flue-cured** *adj*

flue gas *n* the smoke in the uptake of a boiler fire that consists mainly of carbon dioxide, carbon monoxide, and nitrogen

fluellin /floŏ éllən/, **fluellen** *n* an annual wild plant related to the toadflax, foxglove, and snapdragon. Genus: *Kickxia.* [Mid-16C. Alteration of Welsh *(llysiau) Llywelyn* 'Llewelyn's herbs', after LLYWELYN AP GRUFFUDD or LLYWELYN AP IORWERTH]

fluent /floŏ ənt/ *adj* **1. ABLE TO SPEAK WITH EASE** able to speak a language effortlessly and correctly **2. EFFORTLESSLY EXPRESSED** spoken or expressed effortlessly and correctly **3. SMOOTHLY FLOWING** flowing in a smooth graceful way (*literary*) [Late 16C. < Latin *fluent-*, present participle of *fluere* 'flow'] —**fluency** *n* —**fluently** *adv*

ORIGIN The Latin word *fluere* 'to flow', from which ***fluent*** is derived, is also the source of English *affluent, effluent, fluctuate, fluid, fluvial, flux, influence, mellifluous,* and *superfluous.*

flue pipe *n* MUSIC same as **flue** (sense 2)

flue stop *n* an organ stop that controls a set of flues

fluey /floŏ i/ (**-ier, -iest**) *adj* having the symptoms of flu (*informal*)

fluff /fluf/ *n* **1. LIGHT BALLS OF FIBRE** soft light balls of thread or fibre that collect together on material such as wool or cotton **2. DOWNY FUZZ** the soft downy fuzz found on young birds or some seeds **3. NONSENSE** something of no importance or consequence (*slang*) ■ *vt* (**fluffs, fluffing, fluffed**) **1. DO SOMETHING BADLY** to do something badly, especially because of loss of concentration or forgetfulness (*informal*) **2. SHAKE SOMETHING TO INSERT AIR** to shake, pat, or brush something in order to get air into it **3.** BIRDS **RAISE FEATHERS** to raise the feathers in a way that makes the body appear bigger [Late 18C. Origin ?]

fluffy /flúffi/ (**-ier, -iest**) *adj* **1. SOFT AND LIGHT** consisting of something soft and light to the touch such as wool or feathers **2. DOWNY OR FEATHERY** covered in something soft and light to the touch such as down or feathers **3.** COOK **SOFT AND LIGHT IN TEXTURE** soft and light in texture because air has been beaten or whisked in —**fluffily** *adv* —**fluffiness** *n*

flügelhorn /floŏg'l hawrn/, **flugelhorn** *n* a brass instrument with valves, similar to a cornet but with a larger bell [Mid-19C. < German *Flügelhorn* 'wing horn'; from its use to signal to beaters on the flanks in a shoot] —**flügelhornist** *n*

fluid /floŏ id/ *n* **1. LIQUID** a liquid substance (*not in technical use*) **2.** PHYS, CHEM **LIQUID OR GAS** a substance whose molecules flow freely, so that it has no fixed shape and little resistance to outside stress, e.g. a liquid or gas ■ *adj* **1.** PHYS **FLOWING** capable of flowing like a liquid or gas (*technical*) **2. MOVING OR SMOOTHLY CARRIED OUT** smooth and graceful in a way that seems relaxed ○ *a series of fluid arm movements* **3. UNSTABLE** likely to change ○ *The situation in the western sector is fluid.* [15C. Via Old French < Latin *fluidus* 'flowing' < *fluere* 'flow'] —**fluidal** *adj*—**fluidally** *adv*—**fluidity** /floo íddəti/ *n* —**fluidly** *adv*—**fluidness** *n*

fluid clutch *n* AUTOMOT same as **fluid drive**

fluid dram *n N Am* same as **drachm** (sense 1)

fluid drive *n* a device for transmitting rotation between two shafts by means of the acceleration and deceleration of a hydraulic fluid by turbines with blades, used in automatic transmissions in motor vehicles

fluid dynamics *n* the scientific study of the forces acting on liquids and gases and the resulting movements of these fluids (*takes a singular verb*)

fluidextract /floŏ id éks trakt/ *n* a concentrated solution in alcohol of a drug derived from a plant

fluidic /floŏ íddik/ *adj* **1.** relating to fluids **2.** relating to or operated by fluidics

fluidics /floŏ íddiks/ *n* the use of systems based on the movements and pressure of fluids to control operations, instruments, and industrial processes (*takes a singular verb*)

fluidize /floŏ i dīz/ (**-izes, -izing, -ized**), **fluidise** (**-ises, -ising, -ised**) *vt* **1.** to make something fluid **2.** to make a solid move as a fluid, e.g. by pulverizing it into fine powder and passing a gas through it in order to induce flow —**fluidization** /floŏ i dī záysh'n/ *n* —**fluidizer** *n*

fluidized bed *n* a powder or other solid particulate material suspended in an upward flow of air or other gas that behaves like a fluid. It is an effective way of transferring heat or moisture between a gas and a solid or of producing some chemical reactions.

fluid mechanics *n* the branch of mechanics that deals with the properties of gases and liquids and their application in practical engineering (*takes a singular verb*)

fluid ounce *n* **1.** a unit of liquid measurement in the imperial system equal to $\frac{1}{20}$ of an imperial pint or 28.41 ml **2.** a US unit of volume measurement equal to $\frac{1}{16}$ of a US pint or 29.57 ml

fluke[1] /flook/ *n* something surprising or unexpected that happens by accident (*informal*) ■ *vt* (**flukes, fluking, fluked**) to make a successful shot by accident, especially in pool, billiards, or snooker [Mid-19C. Origin ?]

fluke[2] /flook/ *n* **1.** ZOOL same as **trematode 2.** *regional* a flatfish, especially a flounder [Old English *flōc* < Indo-European, 'be flat']

fluke[3] /flook/ *n* **1. PART OF ANCHOR** either of the triangular blades at the end of each arm of an anchor **2. BARB ON HARPOON OR ARROW** a barb on the head of a harpoon or an arrow, or the barbed head itself **3. PART OF WHALE'S TAIL** either of the two horizontal lobes of the tail of a whale or similar sea animal, used in propelling the animal through the water [Mid-16C. Origin ?]

fluky /flooki/ (**-ier, -iest**), **flukey** *adj* accidentally and unexpectedly successful (*informal*) —**flukily** *adv* —**flukiness** *n*

flume /floom/ *n* **1. BOAT RIDE ON WATER CHUTE** a theme park ride involving boats on a water chute **2. NARROW GORGE** a narrow gorge with a stream running through it **3. ARTIFICIAL CHANNEL** an artificial water channel or chute used to transport logs, for studying water and sediment movement, or as part of a fairground ride [12C. Via Old French *flum* < Latin *flumen* 'river' < *fluere* 'flow']

flummery /flúmməri/ *n* **1.** meaningless words, statements, or language, especially when intended as flattery (*literary*) **2.** a cream, milk, or custard dessert set with gelatin and sometimes flavoured with Madeira and lemon [Early 17C. < Welsh *llymru*]

flummox /flúmməks/ (**-moxes, -moxing, -moxed**) *vt* to make somebody confused or perplexed and unable to react (*informal*) [Mid-19C. Origin ?]

flung past participle, past tense of **fling**

flunitrazepam /-trázzə-, floóonī tráyzə pam/ n a drug used to treat insomnia that is sometimes used illicitly as a date-rape drug because it causes semiconsciousness [Late 20C. < FLUORO- + NITRO- + -azepam, INN stem]

flunk /flungk/ (flunks, flunking, flunked) v (informal) 1. vti to fail an exam or course 2. vt N Am to give a student a failing grade [Early 19C. Origin ?] —**flunker** n

flunk out vi N Am to be expelled from a school, college, or course because of poor academic performance (informal)

flunky /flúngki/ (plural -kies), **flunkey** (plural -keys) n 1. an assistant who carries out unimportant jobs for somebody and who behaves obsequiously to that person (informal) 2. a man who is a servant in livery, e.g. a footman [Mid-18C. < Scots, Origin ?] —**flunkyism** n

fluor /floó awr/ n MINERALS same as **fluorite** [Early 17C. < modern Latin (see FLUORIC)]

fluor- prefix CHEM same as **fluoro-** (used before vowels)

fluorapatite /floór ráppə tīt/ n a common form of the mineral apatite, containing fluorine

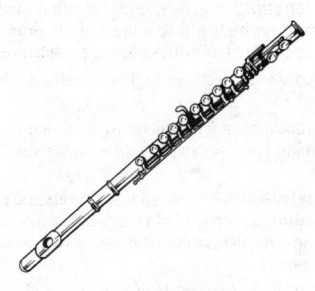

fluorene

fluorene /floór een/ n a white insoluble crystalline solid. Source: coal tar. Use: manufacture of dyes. Formula: $C_{13}H_{10}$. [Late 19C. < FLUORO- (because it fluoresces)]

fluoresce /floor réss/ (-resces, -rescing, -resced) vi to exhibit or undergo the phenomenon of fluorescence [Late 19C. Back-formation < FLUORESCENT] —**fluorescer** n

fluorescein

fluorescein /floor réssi in, floórə seen/ n an orange-red crystalline compound that fluoresces green in blue light. Use: to reveal features of the cornea. [Late 19C. < FLUORESCE + -EIN]

fluorescence /floor réss'nss/ n 1. the emission of electromagnetic radiation, especially light, by an object or substance exposed to radiation or bombarding particles 2. the radiation emitted as a result of fluorescence

fluorescent /floor réss'nt/ adj 1. PHYS CAPABLE OF FLUORESCING exhibiting or able to undergo fluorescence ○ a fluorescent dye 2. CONTAINING FLUORESCENT TUBES containing or produced by fluorescent tubes ○ fluorescent lighting 3. DAZZLING IN COLOUR very bright and dazzling in colour ○ fluorescent pink [Mid-19C. < FLUORSPAR (which has this property)]

fluorescent lamp, **fluorescent light** n an electric lamp containing a low pressure vapour, usually mercury, in a glass tube. Passing an electric current through

it produces ultraviolet radiation that is converted into visible light by a coating inside the tube.

fluorescent tube n the tube of a fluorescent lamp

fluoric /floó órrik/ adj relating to or produced from fluorine or fluorspar [Late 18C. < obsolete French fluorique < modern Latin fluor 'mineral used as a flux' < Latin fluere 'flow']

fluoridate /floóri dayt/ (-dates, -dating, -dated) vt to add small quantities of fluoride salts to a water supply —**fluoridation** /floóri dáysh'n/ n

fluoride /floór īd/ n a chemical compound consisting of fluorine and another element or group [Early 19C. < FLUORINE]

fluorimeter n PHYS same as **fluorometer**

fluorinate /floóri nayt/ (-nates, -nating, -nated) vt to treat something, or cause something to combine, with fluorine or a fluorine compound —**fluorination** /floóri náysh'n/ n

fluorine /floór een/ n a toxic pale yellow gaseous element of the halogen group that is the most reactive and oxidizing agent known. Source: fluorspar, cryolite. Use: water treatment, making fluorides and fluorocarbons. Symbol **F**. See table at **element** [Early 19C. < modern Latin fluor (see FLUORIC)]

fluorite /floór īt/ n a variously coloured crystalline mineral consisting of calcium fluoride. Use: flux. [Mid-19C. < modern Latin fluor (see FLUORIC)]

fluoro- prefix 1. fluorine ○ fluorocarbon 2. fluorescence ○ fluoroscope [< FLUORINE, FLUOR]

fluorocarbon /floóorō káarbən/ n a chemically inert compound containing carbon and fluorine. Use: nonstick coatings, lubricants, refrigerants, solvents.

fluorochemical /floóorō kémmik'l/ n a chemical compound containing fluorine

fluorochrome /floóorō krōm/ n a molecule or part of a molecule that exhibits fluorescence. Use: marker in biological specimens.

fluorography /floo róggrəfi/ n MED same as **photofluorography**

fluorometer /floor rómmitər/, **fluorimeter** /floor rímmitər/ n an instrument used to detect and measure fluorescence —**fluorometric** /floóorō méttrik/ adj —**fluorometry** n

fluoroscope /floóorə skōp/ n an instrument with which X-ray images of the body can be viewed directly on a screen —**fluoroscopic** /floóorə skóppik/ adj —**fluoroscopically** adv —**fluoroscopy** /floor róskəpi/ n

fluorosis /floor róssiss/ n a condition caused by excessive exposure to fluorine and marked by mottling of the teeth and damage to the bones —**fluorotic** /-róttik/ adj

fluorouracil /floóorō yoórassil/ n a fluorine-containing drug. Use: treatment of some cancers.

fluorspar /floór spaar/ n MINERALS same as **fluorite** [Late 18C. < modern Latin fluor (see FLUORIC)]

fluoxetine /floo óksə teen/ n a drug that raises serotonin levels. Use: treatment of anxiety and depression. [Late 20C. < FLUORINE + OXY- + -etine]

fluphenazine /floo fénnə zeen/ n a tranquillizing antipsychotic drug. Use: treatment of schizophrenia. [Mid-20C. Contraction of fluorophenothiazine, its chemical name]

flurry /flúrri/ n (plural -ries) 1. BURST OF ACTIVITY a short period when a lot of things happen 2. SHORT WEATHER PATTERN a sudden short period of snowfall or rainfall, or a gust of wind ■ v (-ries, -rying, -ried) 1. vt MAKE UNCERTAIN to make somebody feel agitated and confused 2. vi SNOW LIGHTLY to snow lightly and intermittently [Late 17C. Probably blend of obsolete flurr 'flutter' + HURRY]

flush[1] /flush/ v (flushes, flushing, flushed) 1. vti GO RED to become red in the face or on the skin, or make somebody become red 2. vti HAVE ROSY COLOUR to glow with a reddish colour, or make something glow in this way 3. vti MAKE WATER FLOW THROUGH TOILET to clean a toilet by making water flow through the bowl, or undergo this process 4. vt DISPOSE OF SOMETHING IN TOILET to put something into the toilet and flush it 5. vt CLEAN WITH WATER to clean or clear something by liberally pouring water or another liquid into, on, or through

it ■ n 1. REDDISHNESS a reddish colour or glow in the face or on the skin 2. SUDDEN FEELING a sudden intense feeling ○ a faint flush of hope 3. BEGINNING OF GOOD TIME the beginning of an exciting or pleasurable period ○ in the first flush of youth 4. SUDDEN RUSH OF THINGS a sudden increased number of things ○ a flush of new applications 5. SURGE OF WATER a liberal flow of water, e.g. to clean something such as a toilet 6. SURGE OF HEAT a sudden surge of heat 7. NEW GROWTH a burst of new growth appearing rapidly on a plant [13C. Origin ?] —**flushable** adj —**flusher** n

flush[2] /flush/ adj 1. LEVEL completely level so as to form an even surface 2. BESIDE OR AGAINST SOMETHING directly next to or closely against something ○ The chairs were flush against the wall. 3. TEMPORARILY RICH having plenty of money temporarily (informal) 4. ABUNDANT abundant or overflowing ○ a party flush with celebrities 5. PRINTING WITH EVEN MARGIN having an even margin on a printed page, without any indentations ■ adv 1. COMPLETELY LEVEL so as to be completely level and form an even surface without sticking out 2. DIRECTLY directly or squarely ○ was hit flush on the jaw ■ vt (flushes, flushing, flushed) FIT THINGS COMPLETELY LEVEL to fit two things so that they are completely level and form an even surface [Mid-16C. Probably < FLUSH[1]] —**flushness** n

flush[3] /flush/ vt (flushes, flushing, flushed) to force a person or animal out of hiding ■ n a bird or birds frightened out of hiding [13C. Origin ?] —**flusher** n

flush[4] /flush/ n in poker and other games, a hand consisting of cards all in the same suit [Early 16C. Via obsolete French flus < Latin fluxus (see FLUX)]

flushed /flusht/ adj 1. red in the face 2. feeling excited or happy

fluster /flústər/ vti (-ters, -tering, -tered) to become nervous or agitated, or make somebody become nervous or agitated ■ n a nervous or agitated state [Early 17C. Origin ?] —**flustered** adj

flute

flute /floot/ n 1. WIND INSTRUMENT WITH HIGH SOUND a woodwind instrument with a cylindrical narrow body, usually held out to the right of the player, who blows across a hole in the mouthpiece to generate a high-pitched sound. The flute family includes the piccolo, the alto flute, and the bass flute. 2. INSTRUMENT WITHOUT REED a wind instrument without a reed 3. ORGAN STOP an organ stop with a tone like a flute 4. ARCHIT GROOVE IN COLUMN a rounded groove running down an architectural column 5. DECORATIVE GROOVE a decorative groove or pleat 6. HOUSEHOLD TALL GLASS FOR SPARKLING WINE a tall narrow glass used for sparkling wines ■ v (flutes, fluting, fluted) 1. vi MAKE SOUND LIKE FLUTE to whistle, sing, or speak in a way that suggests the sound of a flute 2. vt MAKE FURROWS IN SOMETHING to make rounded grooves in something [14C. Via Old French flaute, Middle Dutch flute < Old Provençal flaut] —**fluted** adj

fluting /floóting/ n 1. DECORATIVE FURROWS decoration with parallel grooves. See illustration on next page 2. MAKING OF DECORATIVE FURROWS the forming of decorative grooves in something 3. MAKING OF FLUTE SOUND the act of playing a flute or of making sounds like those of a flute

flutist /floótist/ n N Am MUSIC same as **flautist**

flutter /flúttər/ v (-ters, -tering, -tered) 1. vi WAVE GENTLY to move gently but with quick changes in direction or with a wavy motion ○ A tissue fluttered to the ground. 2. vti MOVE SOMETHING LIGHT BACK AND FORTH to move something light or small in quick back-and-

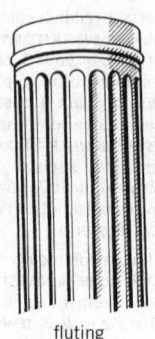

fluting

forth motions, or be moved in this way ○ *Her eyelids fluttered.* **3.** *vti* FLAP WINGS to flap the wings rapidly (*refers to birds*) **4.** *vi* FLY to move by flapping the wings rapidly (*refers to birds*) **5.** *vi* BEAT RAPIDLY to beat rapidly because of a medical disorder or because of nervousness or excitement (*refers to the heart*) **6.** *vi* QUIVER to have a quivering feeling because of nervousness or excitement **7.** *vt* MAKE NERVOUS to make somebody feel agitated or nervous (*usually used in the passive*) **8.** *vi* MOVE RESTLESSLY to move about in a restless or nervous way ■ *n* **1.** QUICK MOVEMENT a rapid, repetitive, or back-and-forth movement in something small **2.** AGITATION a state of nervous excitement or agitation **3.** MED RAPID HEARTBEAT a condition marked by rapid, but regular heartbeat **4.** RECORDING SOUND DISTORTION a high frequency distortion in the pitch of recorded sound **5.** GAMBLING SMALL BET a small bet on something (*informal*) [Old English *floterian* < Germanic] —**flutterer** *n* —**flutteringly** *adv* —**fluttery** *adj*

flutter kick *n* a swimming technique that consists of moving the legs rapidly up and down in short strokes

flutter-tonguing *n* a technique in wind-instrument playing in which a fluttering tone is produced by making a rolled 'r' while blowing —**flutter-tongue** *vti*

fluty /floóti/ (**-ier, -iest**) *adj* high-pitched and clear, like a flute

fluvial /floóvi əl/ *adj* produced by or found in a river or stream [14C. < Latin *fluvialis* < *fluvius* 'river' < *fluere* 'to flow']

fluviomarine /floóvi ō mə reén/ *adj* **1.** relating to water and sediment deposits of rivers in a sea or ocean **2.** BIOL same as **diadromous** [Mid-19C. < Latin *fluvius* 'river' (see FLUVIAL)]

flux /fluks/ *n* **1.** CONSTANT CHANGE constant change and instability **2.** METALL SOLDERING AID a substance that promotes the fusion of two substances or surfaces. Use: soldering, welding. **3.** PHYS RATE OF FLOW ACROSS AREA the rate of flow of something such as energy, particles, or fluid volume across or onto a given area **4.** PHYS STRENGTH OF FIELD IN PARTICULAR AREA the strength of a field such as a magnetic or electric field acting on a particular area, equal to the area size multiplied by the component of the field acting at right angles to the area **5.** MED EXCESSIVE BODILY DISCHARGE an excessive discharge or flow from the body, especially the bowels (*dated*) **6.** METALL SMELTING AID a substance added to molten ore that combines with impurities to form slag for extraction **7.** CERAMICS GLAZE COMPONENT a substance added to a ceramic glaze to make it flow more readily **8.** PHILOSOPHY THEORY OF CHANGE the notion that change is the fundamental nature of reality, as described by Heraclitus **9.** OCEANOG QUANTITY OF MOVEMENT the quantity of water or other material moved in a specific direction during a specific time period ■ *v* (**fluxes, fluxing, fluxed**) **1.** *vti* MAKE OR BECOME FLUID to make something fluid, or become fluid **2.** *vt* METALL PUT FLUX ON SOMETHING to apply flux to something, especially a joint being soldered [14C. Via Old French < Latin *fluxus*, < past participle of *fluere* 'flow']

flux density *n* the amount of flux per unit area

fluxion /flúksh'n/ *n* **1.** a flow or discharge of liquid **2.** MATHS a derivative representing the rate of change of a mathematical function in relation to an independent variable (*dated*) [Mid-16C. < French, or < Latin *flux-*, past participle of *fluere* 'flow'] —**fluxional** *adj* —**fluxionally** *adv* —**fluxionary** *adj*

fly[1] /flī/ *v* (**flies, flying, flew** /floo/, **flown** /flōn/) **1.** *vi* MOVE THROUGH AIR to travel through the air using wings or an engine **2.** *vi* TRAVEL IN AIRCRAFT to travel in an aircraft **3.** *vt* TAKE SOMEBODY OR SOMETHING BY AIR to take or send goods or passengers in an aircraft **4.** *vti* BE PILOT to pilot an aircraft or spacecraft **5.** *vt* TRAVEL OVER AREA BY AIR to travel over a particular area in an aircraft **6.** *vi* TRAVEL WITH AIRLINE OR IN CLASS to travel with a particular airline or in a particular class in an aircraft **7.** *vi* CARRY OUT MISSION BY AIR to carry out a mission or operation in an aircraft **8.** *vti* FLOAT THROUGH AIR to make something such as a kite move through the air, or move through the air **9.** *vti* DISPLAY FLAG ON POLE to display a flag by attaching it to a pole, building, or mast, or be displayed in this way **10.** *vt* SHIPPING SHOW COUNTRY OF REGISTRATION to display a flag that indicates a particular country of registration (*refers to a ship*) ○ *flying the Spanish flag* **11.** *vi* MOVE FREELY IN AIR to move freely because of the speed of the air ○ *She ran down the street, her hair flying.* **12.** *vi* GO VERY FAST to go to or from a place at top speed ○ *I must fly!* **13.** *vi* MOVE QUICKLY AND FORCEFULLY to move with speed through the air by force of impact ○ *sent debris flying everywhere* **14.** *vi* PASS QUICKLY to pass very fast ○ *The weekend had simply flown.* **15.** *vi* BE DISCUSSED INCREASINGLY to be passed on or gossiped about by a swiftly increasing number of people ○ *Bad news flies.* **16.** *vi* BE QUICK TO DO SOMETHING to rush to do something quickly ○ *He flew to our aid.* **17.** *vi* N Am BE ACCEPTABLE to be acceptable, successful, or useful (*informal*) ○ *come up with a proposal that will fly* **18.** *vi* DISAPPEAR to disappear or be used up quickly ○ *Money just flies out of her hands.* **19.** *vt* THEATRE HANG SOMETHING ABOVE STAGE to suspend lights or set components above a stage **20.** *vt* FIELD SPORTS MAKE HAWK CHASE PREY to cause a hawk to fly after prey ■ *n* (*plural* **flies**) **1.** CLOTHING FRONT OPENING OF TROUSERS a covered zip or row of buttons, especially one at the front of a pair of trousers (*usually pl*) **2.** ENTRANCE FLAP OF TENT a flap at the entrance of a tent **3.** ANZ, N Am CAMPING a light tarpaulin secured over the top of a tent. UK term **fly sheet 4.** WIDTH OF FLAG the distance between the outer edge of a flag and the staff it is attached to **5.** EDGE OF FLAG the outer edge of a flag **6.** TRANSP HORSE-DRAWN CARRIAGE in former times, a carriage for hire, drawn by one horse ■ **flies** *npl* THEATRE AREA ABOVE STAGE the space above a stage in a theatre, where lights and scenery are hung [Old English *flēogan* < Indo-European] —**flyable** *adj* ◇ **fly high** to enjoy a period of great success or happiness ◇ **let fly (at somebody) 1.** to speak angrily to somebody **2.** to throw something at somebody ◇ **on the fly** COMPUT while a computer program is running (*informal*)

fly at *vt* UK, ANZ, Can to attack somebody by rushing towards and hitting him or her, or by shouting angrily. US term **fly into**

fly in *vi* to arrive by aircraft

fly into *vt* **1.** to suddenly start feeling and expressing a strong emotion ○ *fly into a rage* **2.** US same as **fly at**

fly out *vi* to travel by plane to a particular destination or from a particular airport

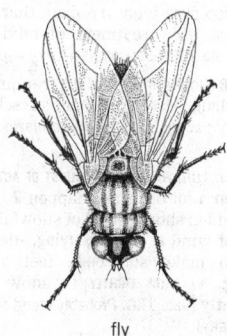

fly

fly[2] /flī/ (*plural* **flies**) *n* **1.** SMALL TWO-WINGED INSECT a two-winged insect, many of which are of an order that includes pests. Order: Diptera. **2.** FLYING INSECT a flying insect, e.g. a caddis fly or dragonfly (*usually used in combination*) **3.** FISHING FLY-FISHING LURE a fishhook with feathers or other attachments to make it resemble a flying insect. Use: fly-fishing. [Old English *flēoge* < Germanic] ◇ **a fly in the ointment** a problem that spoils a good situation ◇ **drink with the flies** *Aus* to

drink alcohol by yourself (*informal*) ◇ **there are no flies on somebody** used to say that somebody is intelligent and not easily tricked

fly[3] /flī/ *adj* **1.** smart and aware of everything that is happening (*informal*) **2.** N Am stylish and fashionable (*slang*) [Early 19C. Origin ?]

Fly /flī/ river in south-western Papua New Guinea, forming part of the border with Indonesia. Length: 1,050 km/650 mi.

fly agaric

fly agaric *n* a poisonous mushroom with a bright red or orange cap and white spots. Latin name: *Amanita muscaria*. [< its former use as an insecticide]

fly ash *n* fine particles of ash resulting from the combustion of a solid fuel

flyaway /flī ə way/ *adj* easily made airborne or affected by a breeze ○ *flyaway hair*

flyback /flī bak/ *n* in a television tube, the rapid return of the electron beam in the direction opposite to scanning

flyblow /flī blō/ *n* **1.** BLOWFLY EGG OR LARVA the egg or larva of a blowfly or flesh fly **2.** INFESTATION WITH BLOWFLY EGGS OR LARVAE an infestation with the eggs or larvae of a blowfly or flesh fly ■ *vt* (**-blows, -blowing, -blew** /-bloo/, **-blown** /-blōn/) CONTAMINATE to contaminate something with the eggs or larvae of a blowfly or flesh fly

flyblown /flī blōn/ *adj* **1.** DIRTY dirty and in bad condition **2.** CONTAMINATED WITH BLOWFLY EGGS OR LARVAE contaminated with the eggs or larvae of a blowfly or flesh fly and therefore not fit to eat **3.** TAINTED contaminated with something undesirable

flyboat /flī bōt/ *n* a small fast boat [Late 16C. < Dutch *vlieboot* < *Vlie*, channel off the N coast of the Netherlands]

fly bridge *n* NAUT same as **flying bridge**

flyby /flī bī/ *n* a flight close to a particular position or object, especially a flight by a space vehicle close to a planet, usually for observation purposes

fly-by-night *adj* **1.** UNSCRUPULOUS IN BUSINESS unscrupulous or not creditworthy in business or commerce **2.** EPHEMERAL not lasting long ■ *n also* **fly-by-nighter 1.** ABSCONDING DEBTOR somebody who leaves without paying debts **2.** DUBIOUS OR SHAKY BUSINESS a business with financial problems or a bad reputation

fly-by-wire *n* an aircraft flight control system that has electronic rather than mechanical controls

flycatcher

flycatcher /flī kachər/ *n* **1.** a songbird that has a slender beak and feeds on insects caught in flight. Families: Muscicapidae or Tyrannidae. **2.** any

similar bird of the same family. Native to: America. Family: Tyrannidae.

fly-drive *adj* describes a holiday or travel option that includes a flight and a hired car at the destination

flyer *n* another spelling of **flier**

fly-fish *vi* to fish using a rod, reel, and line, and a lure resembling a fly —**fly-fisher** *n* —**fly-fishing** *n*

flyfisherman /flī fishərmən/ (*plural* **-men** /-mən/) *n* a fisherman who uses a rod, reel, and line, and a lure resembling a fly

fly front *n* a covered zip or row of buttons at the front of a garment

fly gallery *n* a hidden platform above a stage from where objects suspended from the flies are controlled

fly half *n* RUGBY same as **stand-off half**

flying /flī ing/ *adj* **1.** CAPABLE OF OR IN FLIGHT capable of flight, or in flight **2.** MOVING FAST moving very quickly **3.** HAPPENING QUICKLY happening or passing very quickly **4.** SAILING NOT HELD AT EDGE describes a sail held at the corners only, not the edge ■ *n* **1.** AIR TRAVEL travel by aircraft **2.** PILOTING the piloting of aircraft

CULTURAL NOTE *The Flying Dutchman*, an opera (1843) by German composer Richard Wagner. The protagonist is a Dutch seaman who, as a result of an act of blasphemy, has been condemned to roam the seas until he is saved by the love of a woman. In Norway, he meets Senta, who commits a desperate act of faith that results in his redemption.

flying boat *n* a seaplane with a fuselage that acts like a boat's hull and provides buoyancy on water

flying bomb *n* an explosive robot plane, guided missile, or rocket bomb (*informal*)

flying bridge *n* an open deck of a ship with a secondary set of navigational devices

flying buttress

flying buttress *n* an exterior support for a wall (**buttress**) that sticks out from the wall and is typically arch-shaped, often used in Gothic cathedrals to withstand the outward thrust of the very high walls

flying doctor *n* in Australia, a doctor who visits patients in remote locations by aircraft

flying dragon *n* ZOOL same as **flying lizard**

flying field *n* a small airfield from which aircraft, usually light aircraft, can operate

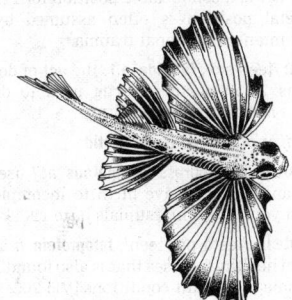

flying fish

flying fish *n* a fish with fins that can be held out like wings, enabling it to glide short distances above

the water. Native to: warm or tropical seas. Family: Exocoetidae.

flying fox

flying fox *n* a large fruit bat with a wingspan up to 152 cm/5 ft. Native to: Australasia. Genus: *Pteropus*.

flying frog *n* a frog with webbed feet that it uses to glide between the trees in which it lives. Native to: Asia. Latin name: *Racophorus reinwardii*.

flying gurnard *n* a sea fish that resembles the gurnard but has large fins enabling it to glide short distances above the water. Native to: tropics. Family: Dactylopteridae.

flying jib *n* on a ship with more than one sail at the front, the foremost triangular sail projecting from the vessel

flying leap *n* a jump or leap taken while running

flying lemur *n* a mammal with a flap of skin between its front and back limbs that it uses to glide between the trees in which it lives. Native to: Southeast Asia. Family: Dermoptera.

flying lizard *n* a small lizard with a flap of skin between its front and back limbs that it uses to glide through the air. Native to: tropics. Genus: *Draco*.

flying machine *n* an aircraft, especially a very early one

flying mare *n* a wrestling manoeuvre in which the attacker grasps the opponent's arm and then turns to throw the opponent over the shoulder

flying mouse *n* a computer mouse that can be lifted and used as a pointer in a three-dimensional environment

flying officer *n* an officer in the Royal Air Force of a rank above pilot officer

flying phalanger *n* a small marsupial with a flap of skin between its front and back limbs that it uses to glide between trees. Native to: Australasia. Family: Phalangeridae.

flying picket *n* a picketing striker who travels to various workplaces to support local strikes

flying saucer *n* a disc-shaped flying object believed to be an extraterrestrial spacecraft

flying squad *n* a group of police officers who can be quickly deployed

flying squirrel *n* a nocturnal squirrel with a flap of skin between its front and back limbs that it uses to glide between trees. Native to: northern Europe, North America, Asia. Family: Petauristinae.

flying start *n* a start of a race in which competitors cross the starting line at racing speed ◇ **off to a flying start** begun or beginning very successfully

flying tackle *n* a rugby tackle in which the tackling player is off the ground at the moment of impact

flying visit *n* a brief visit, sometimes unsatisfactorily or discourteously brief

fly-kick *n* in some martial arts, a kick executed in mid-air with one leg straight and the other flexed at the knee and hip

flyleaf /flī leef/ (*plural* **-leaves** /-leevz/) *n* the first page in a hardback book, which forms a continuous sheet with the page stuck inside the front cover [< FLY¹]

flyman /flīmən/ (*plural* **-men** /-mən/) *n* somebody, especially a man, whose job is to operate parts of the scenery from the flies in a theatre

Flymo /flīmō/ *tdmk* a trademark for a light lawn mower that rides on a cushion of air

Flynn [After Errol FLYNN] ◇ **in like Flynn** *Aus* prompt to seize an opportunity (*dated informal*)

Errol Flynn: as the Earl of Essex in *The Private Lives of Elizabeth and Essex* (1939)

Flynn /flin/, **Errol** (1909–59) Australian-born US actor. He played the swashbuckling hero in romantic costume drama films such as *Captain Blood* (1935) and *The Adventures of Robin Hood* (1938). Born **Flynn, Errol Leslie Thomas**

Flynn, John (1880–1951) Australian missionary. He was the founder of the Australian Inland Mission Aerial Medical Service (1928), which became the Royal Flying Doctor Service.

fly-on-the-wall *adj* describes a TV documentary showing people in their daily lives

fly orchid *n* an orchid in which the lower part of the flower resembles an insect. Native to: Europe. Latin name: *Ophrys insectifera*.

flyover /flī ōvər/ *n* **1.** *UK* a bridge with a main road on it crossing another main road. ANZ, N Am term **overpass 2.** *N Am* same as **fly-past**

flypaper /flī paypər/ *n* paper coated with a sticky poisonous substance that attracts and kills flies

fly-past *n* the flight of an aircraft or formation of aircraft over a place as a spectacle for people on the ground. N Am term **flyover**

flyperson /flī purss'n/ *n* somebody whose job is to operate parts of the scenery from the flies in a theatre

flyposting /flī pōsting/ *n* the practice of putting up posters in places where they are not legally permitted

fly rod *n* a long flexible fishing rod for use in fly-fishing

flysch /flish/, **Flysch** *n* a thick deposit of sedimentary rock formed in salt water by erosion of adjacent steep mountains [Early 19C. < Swiss German]

flyscreen /flī skreen/ *n* a screen made of wire mesh that fits over a window to exclude insects

fly sheet *n* *UK* a light tarpaulin secured over the top of a tent. ANZ, N Am term **fly¹**

flysheet /flī sheet/ *n* a sheet or pamphlet containing printed information or advertising

flyspeck /flī spek/ *n* **1.** FLY'S FAECES a tiny mark made by a fly's faeces **2.** TINY MARK a tiny mark or stain ■ *vt* (**-specks, -specking, -specked**) MARK WITH FLYSPECKS to mark something with the tiny spots of flies' faeces or similar stains (*usually used in the passive*)

fly spray *n* a poisonous liquid that kills insects, sprayed from an aerosol

fly swatter *n* a tool used to strike and kill insects, consisting of a long flexible handle with a flat piece of plastic net attached

Flytaal /flī taal/ *n* *S Africa* LANG same as **Tsotsitaal** [< Afrikaans < FLY³ + Afrikaans *taal* 'language']

flyte /flīt/ (**flytes, flyting, flyted**), **flite** (**flites, fliting, flited**) *vti Scotland* to give somebody a severe but eloquent scolding [Old English *flītan*]

flyting /flīting/ *n Scotland* an angry but eloquent scolding or verbal exchange

fly-tipping *n* the illegal deposit of rubbish in an unauthorized place —**fly-tipper** *n*

zh vision. In foreign words: kh German Bach; aN French vin; aaN French blanc; ö German schön, French feu; oN French bon; ôN French un; ü as in French rue. Stress marks: ´ as in secret /seékrət/, academic /ákə démmik/

flytrap /flī´ trap/ *n* 1. PLANTS same as **Venus flytrap** 2. a device for catching flies

fly-tying *n* the making of artificial flies that can be used to catch fish —**fly-tier** *n*

flyway /flī´ way/ *n* a traditional route taken by migrating birds

flyweight /flī´ wayt/ *n* 1. WEIGHT CATEGORY IN PROFESSIONAL BOXING in professional boxing, a weight category for competitors whose weight does not exceed 51 kg/112 lb 2. WEIGHT CATEGORY IN AMATEUR BOXING in amateur boxing, a weight category for competitors whose weight does not exceed 51 kg/112 lb 3. BOXER COMPETING AT FLYWEIGHT a professional or amateur boxer who competes at flyweight level

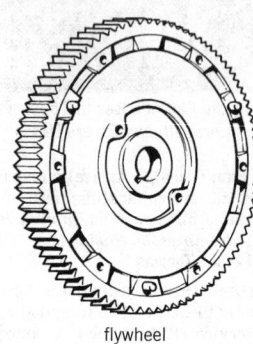

flywheel

flywheel /flī´ weel/ *n* a heavy wheel or disc that helps because of its inertia to maintain a constant speed of rotation in a machine or to store energy

flywhisk /flī´ wisk/ *n* a tool for brushing away flies, traditionally a bunch of horsehair attached to a handle

fm[1] *abbr* 1. MEASURE fathom 2. MEDIA frequency modulation

fm[2] *abbr* ONLINE Micronesia (*used in Internet addresses*) See table at **domain name**

Fm *symbol* CHEM ELEM fermium

FM *abbr* 1. (*plural* **FMs**) ARMY field manual 2. ENG figure of merit 3. MEDIA frequency modulation 4. Micronesia

FMCG *abbr* COMM fast-moving consumer goods

fml *abbr* formal

FMS *abbr* 1. PSYCHOL false memory syndrome 2. AVIAT flight management system

FNQ *abbr* Aus Far North Queensland

f-number *n* the ratio of the focal length to the effective diameter of a camera lens. Symbol **f** [Abbreviation of FOCAL]

fo *abbr* Faroe Islands (*used in Internet addresses*) See table at **domain name**

FO *abbr* 1. FIN finance officer 2. POL Foreign Office

fo. *abbr* PUBL folio

foal /fōl/ *n* an unweaned horse or related animal ▪ *vi* (**foals, foaling, foaled**) to give birth to a foal [Old English *fola* < Indo-European, 'small']

foam /fōm/ *n* 1. MASS OF BUBBLES a mass of bubbles of gas or air on the surface of a liquid 2. THICK FROTHY SUBSTANCE a thick but light mixture that contains a lot of tiny bubbles ○ *Beat the egg whites into a foam.* ○ *shaving foam* 3. FIRE-EXTINGUISHING SUBSTANCE a thick chemical froth used to extinguish flames 4. MATERIAL CONTAINING BUBBLES rubber, plastic, or other material filled with many small bubbles of air to make it soft or light 5. FROTHY SALIVA frothy saliva produced as a result of exertion or disease 6. same as **sea** (sense 1) (*literary*) ▪ *v* (**foams, foaming, foamed**) 1. *vi* PRODUCE BUBBLES to produce a mass of bubbles 2. *vi* PRODUCE FROTHY SALIVA to produce foam from the mouth 3. *vi* BE ANGRY to express great anger (*informal*) 4. *vt* FILL WITH BUBBLES to transform a material into foam by aerating it in liquid form and then solidifying it [Old English *fām* < Indo-European] —**foamy** *adj*

foamed slag *n* slag from a blast furnace that is aerated while it is still molten. Use: building or insulation material.

foamer /fō´mər/ *n* 1. a device used to make liquid

frothy by incorporating air 2. *US* somebody who is very devoted to a hobby, especially a model railway enthusiast

foam rubber *n* rubber that has been aerated to form a spongy material. Use: mattresses, padding, insulation.

fob[1] /fob/ *n* 1. CHAIN FOR POCKET WATCH a chain or ribbon used to attach a pocket watch to a waistcoat 2. ORNAMENT ON KEY RING an ornament attached to a key ring 3. ORNAMENT ON CHAIN a watch or ornament worn on the end of a chain or ribbon attached to clothing 4. POCKET FOR WATCH a small pocket on a waistcoat for a watch 5. ELECTRONIC DEVICE FOR OPENING DOORS a small portable electronic device that activates a door lock [Mid-17C. Origin ?]

fob[2] /fob/ (**fobs, fobbing, fobbed**) [Late 16C. Origin ?] **fob off** *vt* 1. STALL SOMEBODY WITH MISLEADING INFORMATION to give false or inadequate information to somebody in order to stop further questions 2. GIVE SOMETHING INFERIOR TO SOMEBODY to provide somebody with something different from and inferior to what he or she wanted 3. GIVE SOMETHING UNWANTED TO SOMEBODY to pass something unwanted to somebody else, using deceitful persuasion

FOB, F.O.B. *abbr* COMM free on board

f.o.b., fob *abbr* COMM free on board

fob watch *n* a round watch kept in a special pocket on a waistcoat

FoC *abbr* PRINTING father of the chapel

focaccia /fə káchə, fō-/ *n* flat Italian bread, often sprinkled with a topping before baking, and served hot or cold [Mid-20C. Via Italian < assumed Vulgar Latin *focacia* < Latin *focus* 'hearth, fireplace']

focal /fōk´l/ *adj* 1. PRINCIPAL main and most important 2. FOCUSING IMAGE relating to bringing an image into focus 3. AT OR FROM FOCAL POINT located at, passing through, or measured from a focal point —**focally** *adv*

focal distance *n* OPTICS same as **focal length**

focal infection *n* a bacterial infection in one part of the body that may cause symptoms elsewhere in the body

focalize /fōkə līz/ (**-izes, -izing, -ized**), **focalise** (**-ises, -ising, -ised**) *v* 1. *vti* to focus something, or be brought into focus 2. *vt* to limit something to a local area —**focalization** /fōkə lī záysh´n/ *n*

focal length *n* the distance from the centre of a lens or the surface of a mirror to the point at which light passing through the lens or reflected from the mirror is focused. Symbol **f**

focal-plane shutter *n* a camera shutter positioned just in front of the film, instead of being built into the lens

focal point *n* 1. the point at which parallel rays meeting a lens, curved mirror, or other optical system converge or appear to diverge 2. an object of concentrated or immediate attention

focal ratio *n* OPTICS same as **f-number**

Foch /fosh/, **Ferdinand** (1851–1929) French general. He was appointed supreme military commander of the Allied forces on the Western Front in the final year of World War I (1918).

'My centre is giving way, my right is retreating; situation excellent. I shall attack.'
[Ferdinand Foch, 'Ferdinand Foch', *Reputations Ten Years After*, B. H. Liddell Hart; 1928]

foci plural of **focus**

fo'c's'le *n* NAUT same as **forecastle**

focus /fōkəss/ *n* (*plural* **-cuses** or **-ci** /-sī/) 1. MAIN EMPHASIS concentrated effort or attention on a particular thing ○ *The committee's focus must be on finding solutions to the problem.* 2. AREA OF CONCERN an area of concern, responsibility, or investigation ○ *an enquiry with a narrow focus* 3. CONCENTRATED QUALITY a concentrated and unified quality ○ *to bring focus to the problem* 4. SHARPNESS OF IMAGE the quality that makes an image sharply defined with clear edges and contrast 5. SHARPNESS OF VISION the condition of seeing images sharply and clearly 6. (*plural* **foci**)

OPTICS same as **focal point** (sense 1) 7. PHOTOGRAPHY DEVICE FOR ADJUSTING CAMERA LENS a device on a camera for adjusting the lens 8. (*plural* **foci**) MED DISEASE ORIGIN the point from which a disease spreads or where it localizes 9. (*plural* **foci**) GEOG CENTRE OF EARTHQUAKE OR EXPLOSION the point of origin of an earthquake or underground nuclear explosion 10. (*plural* **foci**) MATHS POINT ON CONE a fixed point in a plane that in combination with a particular straight line specifies a conic section ▪ *vti* (**-cuses** or **-cusses, -cusing** or **-cussing, -cused** or **-cussed**) 1. CONCENTRATE MAINLY ON SOMETHING to concentrate effort or attention on a particular thing or a particular aspect of a thing 2. ADJUST VISION TO SEE CLEARLY to adjust your vision so that you see clearly and sharply, or become adjusted for clear vision 3. OPTICS ADJUST LENS to adjust a lens so that the image viewed is clear and sharp 4. OPTICS MEET AT SINGLE POINT to make rays of light meet at a single point, or meet at a single point [Mid-17C. < Latin, 'hearth, fireplace'] —**focusable** *adj* —**focuser** *n*

focused /fōkəst/, **focussed** *adj* 1. concentrated on a particular thing 2. single-minded and determined

focus group *n* a small group of representative people who are questioned about their opinions as part of political or market research

focussed *adj* another spelling of **focused**

fodder /fód´dər/ *n* 1. ANIMAL FOOD hay, straw, or similar food for livestock 2. MATERIAL FOR STIMULATING RESPONSE people, ideas, or images that are useful in stimulating a creative or critical response 3. EXPENDABLE PEOPLE OR THINGS people or things regarded as the necessary but expendable ingredient that makes a system or scheme work (*usually used in combination*) ○ *case studies seized upon as thesis fodder* ▪ *vt* (**-ders, -dering, -dered**) FEED LIVESTOCK to give food to livestock [Old English *fōdor* < Indo-European, 'to feed'] —**fodderer** *n*

foe /fō/ *n* an enemy or opponent of somebody or something (*formal*) [Old English *gefā* < Indo-European, 'hostile']

FOE, FoE *abbr* Friends of the Earth

foefie slide /fōoffi\ slīd/ *n* S Africa a means of crossing a river or ravine by being suspended by a pulley from a cable [Late 20C. Afrikaans *foefie*, 'stunt or trick']

foehn /fōn/, **föhn** *n* a warm dry wind that blows down the lee slope of a mountain range, originally and especially the Alps [Mid-19C. Via German < Latin *favonius* 'west wind' < *favere* 'favour, be well disposed towards']

foetal /feet´l/, **fetal** *adj* relating to or characteristic of a foetus [Early 19C. < FOETUS]

foetal alcohol syndrome *n* a condition affecting babies born to women who drank excessive amounts of alcohol during pregnancy, characterized by a range of effects including malformed facial features and learning difficulties

foetal haemoglobin *n* a haemoglobin common in the foetus and newborn, but normally present only in small amounts in adults, except in some forms of anaemia

foetal membrane *n* BIOL same as **extraembryonic membrane**

foetal position *n* a body position in which the body lies curled up on one side with the head bowed and the legs and arms drawn in towards the chest. As well as being a comfortable position for relaxation, the foetal position is often assumed by people during intense emotional trauma.

foeticide /feeti sīd/, **feticide** *n* 1. the act of destroying a foetus 2. an agent or drug used to destroy a foetus —**foeticidal** /feeti sīd´l/ *adj*

foetid *adj* another spelling of **fetid**

foetiparous /fi tippərəss/, **fetiparous** *adj* used to describe animals that give birth to incompletely developed young, e.g. marsupials [Late 19C. < FOETUS]

foetoprotein /feetō prō teen/, **fetoprotein** *n* a protein found in healthy foetuses that is also found in adults with some malignant conditions [Mid-20C. < FOETUS]

foetor *n* another spelling of **fetor**

foetoscope /feetō skōp/, **fetoscope** *n* a fibre-optic device for viewing a foetus in the uterus [Late 20C. < FOETUS + -*scope*] —**foetoscopy** /fee tóskəpi/ *n*

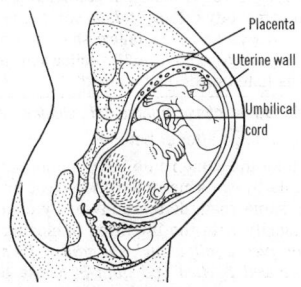

foetus: human foetus

foetus /féetəss/, **fetus** n an unborn vertebrate at a stage when all the structural features of the adult are recognizable, especially an unborn human offspring after eight weeks of development [14C. < Latin, 'offspring']

USAGE In technical contexts, the spelling with **fe-** is the agreed international standard for **fetus** and all related words.

fog /fog/ n **1.** THICK MIST condensed water vapour in the air at or near ground level **2.** CLOUD OF SOMETHING a cloud of something such as smoke in the air that reduces visibility **3.** HAZY MUDDLE a state of confusion or lack of clarity **4.** OBSCURING AGENT something that serves to obscure or conceal ○ *a fog of excuses* **5.** PHOTOGRAPHY **BLURRED AREA** an area on a photograph that is unclear or obscured by stray light **6.** CHEM **SUSPENDED PARTICLES** a cloud or suspension of liquid particles ■ v (**fogs, fogging, fogged**) **1.** vti MAKE OR BECOME OBSCURED to cause condensation to form on a transparent surface, or become covered with condensation **2.** vt MAKE SOMETHING UNCLEAR to make something unclear or confused **3.** vti PHOTOGRAPHY EXPOSE FILM TO LIGHT to contaminate film or a developing image with light, usually accidentally, or undergo this process [Mid-16C. Origin ?] —**fogged** adj

fog bank n a mass of thick fog, especially at sea

fogbound /fóg bownd/ adj **1.** unable to move or operate because visibility is diminished by fog **2.** enveloped in fog

fogbow /fóg bō/ n a faint arc of light seen opposite the sun in foggy conditions

fogdog /fóg dog/ n a bright white spot seen near the horizon in breaking fog

fogey n another spelling of **fogy**

Foggia /fójji ə/ capital of Foggia Province in Apulia Region, southeastern Italy. Population: 155,203 (2001).

foggy /fóggi/ (**-gier, -giest**) adj **1.** FILLED WITH FOG filled with or obscured by fog **2.** VAGUE very unclear or hazy ○ *only had a foggy idea of who he was* **3.** VISUALLY UNCLEAR obscured or translucent because of a covering of condensation or something similar — **foggily** adv —**fogginess** n

Foggy Bottom n US the US Department of State in Washington, DC, which is the US government department responsible for foreign policy and affairs (*informal*) [After a low-lying area near the Potomac River in Washington, DC]

foghorn /fóg hawrn/ n a horn sounded on a ship or boat when fog reduces visibility, as a warning to other vessels

fog light, **foglamp** /fóg lamp/ n a front or rear light on a car with a beam designed to penetrate fog

fogy /fógi/ (*plural* **-gies**), **fogey** (*plural* **-geys**) n an old-fashioned person who resists change or novelty [Late 18C. < Scots, origin ?] —**fogyish** adj —**fogyism** n

föhn n METEOROL another spelling of **foehn**

foible /fóyb'l/ n **1.** an idiosyncrasy or small weakness (*usually used in the plural*) **2.** the weakest part of a sword blade from the middle to the point [Mid-17C. Via obsolete French < Old French *feble* (see FEEBLE)]

foie gras /fwaá graá/ n goose liver swollen as a result of force-feeding the bird on maize, usually eaten as a pâté [Early 19C. < French, 'fatted liver']

foil[1] /foyl/ n **1.** METAL IN THIN SHEETS metal in a very thin flexible sheet **2.** GOOD CONTRAST TO SOMETHING a useful or interesting contrast to something **3.** METAL COATING ON MIRROR the thin reflective metal coating on the back of a mirror **4.** NAUT same as **hydrofoil** (sense 2) **5.** AVIAT same as **aerofoil 6.** ARCHIT ARC IN GOTHIC WINDOW an arc at the top of a Gothic window ■ vt (**foils, foiling, foiled**) COVER SOMETHING WITH FOIL to cover or coat something with metal foil [14C. Via Old French < Latin *folium* 'leaf', *folia* 'leaves']

foil[2] /foyl/ (**foils, foiling, foiled**) vt **1.** to prevent somebody from succeeding in something **2.** to obscure the trail in order to hinder pursuers (*refers to a hunted animal*) [14C. Origin ?]

foil[3] /foyl/ n a long thin sword with a small disc on the end, used in fencing [Late 16C. Origin ?]

foils /foylz/ n the art or sport of fencing with foils (*takes a singular verb*) —**foilsman** n

foist /foyst/ (**foists, foisting, foisted**) vt **1.** IMPOSE SOMETHING ON SOMEBODY to force somebody to accept something undesirable ○ *always foists the dirty jobs on me* **2.** GIVE SOMEBODY SOMETHING INFERIOR to give somebody something inferior on the pretence that it is genuine, valuable, or desirable ○ *tried to foist it off on us as an antique* **3.** INSERT SOMETHING SURREPTITIOUSLY to introduce or insert something surreptitiously [Mid-16C. Probably < Dutch dialect *vuisten* 'hold in your hand' (as when hiding dice) < Middle Dutch *vuist* 'fist']

Fokine /fo keén/, **Michel** (1880–1942) Russian-born US dancer and choreographer. His work revitalized traditional classical ballet by introducing increased expression into the predominantly technical dance form. Born **Fokine, Mikhail Mikhailovich**

FOL abbr ANZ POL Federation of Labour

folacin /fólləssin/ n BIOCHEM same as **folic acid** [Mid-20C. < FOLIC ACID]

folate /fó layt/ n **1.** BIOCHEM same as **folic acid 2.** a salt or ester of folic acid [Mid-20C. < FOLIC ACID]

fold[1] /fōld/ v (**folds, folding, folded**) **1.** vt BEND SOMETHING FLAT to bend something thin and flat over on itself **2.** vt MAKE SOMETHING SMALLER BY FOLDING to bend something over on itself more than once **3.** vti BEND SOMETHING TO MAKE IT COMPACT to bend part of something so as to make it more streamlined or more compact, or undergo this process ○ *This can be folded for easy storage.* **4.** vt DRAW LIMBS TOWARDS BODY to draw in the arms, legs, or hands towards the body, or place them together with the joints bent **5.** vt BRING WINGS TOGETHER to bring the wings together or next to the body **6.** vt COVER SOMETHING to wrap or cover something ○ *folded the note inside a magazine* **7.** vt PUT ARMS ROUND SOMEBODY to put your arms round somebody **8.** vi GO OUT OF BUSINESS to fail and stop operating as a business **9.** vi CARDS GIVE UP HAND in poker and other card games, to stop playing a hand in the belief that it cannot win **10.** vti GEOL DISTORT ROCK LAYER to cause a layer of rock to bend, or undergo this process **11.** vi BIOCHEM DEVELOP UNIQUE STRUCTURE to develop a specific three-dimensional structure that is unique to each different protein, in order to function properly (*refers to a protein chain*) ■ n **1.** BENT PART a part of something folded **2.** CREASE a line, crease, or raised part made when something has been folded **3.** HANGING FOLDED PART a part of something that hangs in a folded shape ○ *the heavy folds of the curtains* **4.** COIL a single coil in a rope, or a snake lying in coils **5.** GEOL DISTORTION IN ROCK LAYER a bend formed in a rock layer in response to forces in the rock **6.** SMALL VALLEY a small valley in a hilly area [Old English *fealdan* < Indo-European, 'to fold'] —**foldable** adj

fold in vt to add a food ingredient to a mixture carefully and lightly

fold up v **1.** vti to fold something completely, or become folded completely **2.** vi to collapse from laughter, pain, or strong emotion

fold[2] /fōld/ n **1.** ENCLOSED AREA FOR SHEEP an enclosed area where sheep or other livestock can be kept **2.** GROUP WITH THINGS IN COMMON a group to which something or somebody naturally belongs because of shared interests or traits **3.** ENCLOSED ANIMALS sheep or other livestock in a fold **4.** FLOCK a flock of sheep ■ vt (**folds, folding, folded**) ENCLOSE LIVESTOCK to put or keep livestock in an enclosed area [Old English *fald*, origin ?]

-fold suffix **1.** divided into parts ○ *manifold* **2.** times ○ *tenfold* [Old English *-feald*; related to *fealdan* (see FOLD[1])]

foldaway /fōld ə way/ adj designed to be folded for compact storage

foldboat /fōld bōt/ n N Am same as **faltboat** [See FALTBOAT]

folder /fōldər/ n **1.** FOLDED CARD TO HOLD PAPERS a piece of card folded to make a file in which papers can be held **2.** COMPUT FILE CONTAINER a conceptual container for computer files in some operating systems, corresponding to a directory or subdirectory **3.** FOLDED PAMPHLET a circular printed on folded paper

folderol n another spelling of **falderal**

folding /fōlding/ adj designed to be folded for compact storage

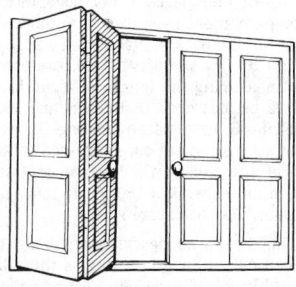

folding door

folding door n a door consisting of hinged panels that fold against each other

folding money n money in the form of notes rather than coins (*informal*)

folding press n a wrestling manoeuvre in which the opponent is pressed into a foetal position and held down

foldout /fōld owt/ n PUBL same as **gatefold** —**foldout** adj

foldup /fōld up/ adj designed to be folded for compact storage

foliaceous /fōli áyshəss/ adj **1.** BOT relating to or resembling a leaf **2.** GEOL consisting of thin sheets [Mid-17C. < Latin *foliaceus* < *folium* 'leaf']

foliage /fōli ij/ n **1.** the leaves of a plant or tree **2.** architectural ornamentation based on leaves and stems [Mid-15C. Alteration (after Latin *folium*) of Old French *foillage* < *foille* 'leaf' < Latin *folium*] —**foliaged** adj

foliage plant n a plant cultivated for its attractive leaves

foliar /fōli ər/ adj relating to, producing, or being the leaves of a plant [Late 19C. < modern Latin *foliaris* < Latin *folium* 'leaf']

foliate adj /fōli ət, -ayt/ **1.** RELATING TO LEAVES relating to or resembling leaves **2.** GEOL same as **foliated** (sense 1) **3.** LEAF-SHAPED in the shape of a leaf ■ v /fōli ayt/ (**-ates, -ating, -ated**) **1.** vt DECORATE SOMETHING WITH LEAVES to decorate something with leaves or very thin layers **2.** vt MAKE METAL INTO FOIL to form metal into a thin sheet or foil **3.** vt PUBL NUMBER PAGES OF BOOK to number the leaves of a book or manuscript **4.** vi DEVELOP LEAVES to develop foliage **5.** vti LAYER to separate something into very thin layers, or undergo this process [Early 17C. Adjective < Latin *foliatus* < *folium* 'leaf'; verb < Latin *folium*]

-foliate suffix having leaves ○ *bifoliate* [< Latin *foliatus* (see FOLIATE)]

foliated /fōli aytid/ adj **1.** GEOL formed in or composed of separable layers **2.** ARCHIT decorated with stylized architectural leaves or foliage

foliation /fōli áysh'n/ n **1.** LEAF FORMATION the formation of leaves **2.** BEARING OF LEAVES the state of being in leaf **3.** ARCHIT ORNAMENTATION architectural ornamentation consisting of stylized foliage **4.** ARCHIT GOTHIC WINDOW DECORATION architectural decoration consisting of carving between two arches (**cusps**) and arcs (**foils**) at the top of Gothic windows **5.** PUBL NUMBERING OF PAGES the numbering of consecutive pages in a book or manuscript **6.** GEOL LAYERED TEXTURE OF ROCK a characteristic of metamorphosed rocks in which min-

erals are aligned in one direction so that the rock can readily be split into thin layers

folic acid /fṓlik-, fóllik-/ *n* an important B complex vitamin, found in green vegetables and liver [< Latin *folium* 'leaf'; because found in leafy green vegetables]

folie à deux /fólli a dṓ/ (*plural* **folies à deux** /*pronunc. same*/) *n* a psychiatric disorder with symptoms common to two people who are very close. Often only one person actually has a disorder, the other choosing to share the symptoms or delusions of the first. [Late 19C. < French, 'dual delusion']

folio /fṓli ō/ *n* (*plural* **-os**) **1.** LARGE BOOK OR MANUSCRIPT a book or manuscript in the largest size usual for books, traditionally created by folding a single sheet of standard-sized printing paper once, giving two leaves or four pages **2.** LARGE SHEET FOR BOOK a standard-sized sheet of printing paper folded once to give two leaves or four pages **3.** PAGE NUMBERED ON FRONT a paper or parchment page that is numbered on the front but not the back **4.** PAGE NUMBER a page number (*technical*) **5.** LAW MEASUREMENT FOR LEGAL DOCUMENTS a unit for measuring the length of legal documents, usually 72 or 90 words in Britain and 100 in the United States **6.** ACCT LEDGER PAGE a page, or two facing pages, of a ledger ■ *vt* (**-os, -oing, -oed**) NUMBER PAGES to number the pages in a book ■ *adj* LARGE-FORMAT printed in folio size [Mid-15C. < late Latin *folio* 'at the page' < Latin *folium* 'leaf, page']

foliose /fṓli ōss, -ōz/ *adj* describes the body **(thallus)** of a lichen or similar plant that is thin, flattened, and lobed like a leaf [Early 18C. < Latin *foliosus* < *folium* 'leaf']

folk /fōk/ *npl* PEOPLE IN GENERAL people, especially people of the same type (*takes a plural verb*) ■ *n* MUSIC same as **folk music** (*takes a singular verb*) ■ *adj* **1.** TRADITIONAL IN COMMUNITY relating to the traditional culture passed down in a community or country ○ *folk customs* **2.** FROM IDEAS OF ORDINARY PEOPLE relating to the traditional beliefs or ideas of ordinary people [Old English *folc* < Indo-European, 'fill']

folk art *n* paintings and decorative objects made in a naive style

folk dance *n* **1.** a dance that is traditional to a culture, community, or country **2.** the music for a folk dance

Folkestone /fṓkstən/ port and resort in Kent, southeastern England. A major ferry port, it is the British terminal for the Channel Tunnel. Population: 45,587 (1991).

Folketing /fṓlkə ting/ *n* the parliament of Denmark [< Danish, 'people's assembly']

folk etymology *n* **1.** the replacement of an unfamiliar word or form by a more familiar one. An example is the replacement of *girasole* with *Jerusalem* in *Jerusalem artichoke*. **2.** an idea about the origin of a word that is generally believed but is incorrect. The idea that the origin of the word 'posh' is 'port out, starboard home', referring to the more expensive side of ships travelling between the UK and India, is a folk etymology.

folk hero *n* somebody who is renowned for activities that appeal to the public but which may be fictional or exaggerated

folkie /fṓki/ *n* (*informal*) **1.** a folk singer or musician **2.** a fan of folk music

folklore /fṓk lawr/ *n* **1.** TRADITIONAL LOCAL STORIES traditional stories and explanations passed down in a community or country **2.** LOCAL LEGENDS stories and gossip that become traditional within a group of people **3.** CULTL ANTHROP STUDY OF TRADITIONS the study of traditional stories, music, and customs —**folkloric** *adj*

folklorist /fṓk lawrist/ *n* a student of the traditional stories, music, and customs of a culture or community —**folkloristic** /fṓk law rístik/ *adj*

folk mass *n* a Christian mass in which folk music replaces some or all of the traditional music

folk medicine *n* medicine based on traditional customs and belief, often using herbal remedies

folk memory *n* a memory kept alive by a community and passed from one generation to the next

folk music *n* **1.** traditional songs and music, passed from one generation to the next **2.** modern music composed in imitation of traditional music

folk-rock *n* popular music that combines the melodies of folk music with the rhythms of rock music

folks /fōks/ *npl* **1.** same as **folk 2.** used to address a group of people (*informal*) ○ *Folks, we're ready to start now.* **3.** parents or close family

folk singer *n* a singer of folk songs —**folk singing** *n*

folk song *n* **1.** a traditional song that has been passed down orally **2.** a modern song composed in the style of traditional folk music, often performed by a solo singer —**folk singer** *n*

folksy /fṓksi/ (**-sier, -siest**) *adj* **1.** IN STYLE OF FOLK TRADITIONS simple and unsophisticated in the tradition of folk crafts or folklore **2.** AFFECTEDLY TRADITIONAL artificially or affectedly traditional and homy **3.** *US* FRIENDLY friendly and informal —**folksily** *adv* —**folksiness** *n*

folktale /fṓk tayl/, **folk tale** *n* a story or legend that is passed down orally from one generation to the next and becomes part of a community's tradition

follicle /fóllik'l/ *n* **1.** a small anatomical sac, cavity, or gland involved in secretion or excretion **2.** a dry case formed from a single fruit that splits along one side to release seeds [Early 15C. < Latin *folliculus* 'small sack' < *follis* 'bellows'] —**follicular** /fo líkyŏŏlər/ *adj*

follicle-stimulating hormone *n* a hormone that stimulates the growth of egg follicles in the ovaries and the making of sperm in the testes

folliculitis /fo líkyŏŏ lítiss/ *n* inflammation of one or more follicles, especially of the hair, producing small boils

follies /fólliz/, **Follies** *n* a theatrical revue with elaborate costumes, music, and dancing (*dated*; *takes a singular or plural verb*)

follow /fóllō/ *v* (**-lows, -lowing, -lowed**) **1.** *vti* COME AFTER SOMEBODY OR SOMETHING to come after somebody or something in position, time, or sequence ○ *the main course followed by dessert* **2.** *vt* ADD TO SOMETHING ALREADY DONE to add to something already done by doing something else, usually a related thing ○ *She'll follow her lecture with a demonstration.* **3.** *vti* GO AFTER SOMEBODY OR SOMETHING to take the same route behind another person, e.g. by walking down the street or driving along the same road, deliberately or by chance ○ *followed them home* **4.** *vt* KEEP SOMEBODY UNDER SURVEILLANCE to have somebody's movements under constant surveillance ○ *ordering the suspect to be followed* **5.** *vt* WATCH SOMEBODY OR SOMETHING CLOSELY to watch, observe, or pay close attention to somebody or something ○ *eyes seemed to follow me around the room* **6.** *vt* GO ALONG ROUTE to go along something such as a road or path ○ *following the path* **7.** *vt* TAKE SAME DIRECTION AS SOMETHING to take the same course or go in the same direction as something else ○ *The road follows the river along the valley.* **8.** *vt* GO AS DIRECTED BY SOMETHING to go in the direction indicated by something such as a signpost ○ *Follow that sign ahead.* **9.** *vt* OBEY SOMETHING to act in accordance with something, especially with instructions or directions given by somebody else ○ *only if you follow my instructions* **10.** *vt* DEVELOP IN ACCORDANCE WITH SOMETHING to be or develop in accordance with something, usually something already known about or established ○ *following the same pattern of behaviour* **11.** *vti* DO SAME AS SOMEBODY OR SOMETHING to imitate or do the same as somebody or something ○ *She followed her father into medicine.* **12.** *vti* UNDERSTAND SOMETHING to understand something such as an explanation or narrative ○ *can't follow her explanation* **13.** *vt* ENGAGE IN ACTIVITY to engage in or practise something such as a career, occupation, or lifestyle ○ *I decided to follow a career in law.* **14.** *vt* KEEP ABREAST OF SOMETHING to keep informed about or up to date with the progress of something ○ *Are you following the television series about twins?* **15.** *vt* BE ABOUT SOMETHING to be about somebody or something, especially to describe or depict what happens to somebody or something over a period of time ○ *The story follows a typical American family.* **16.** *vi* RESULT FROM SOMETHING to happen after and as a result of something else ○ *Issue too many instructions and confusion invariably follows.* **17.** *vti* BE LOGICAL RESULT to be a logical consequence of something ○ *follows from their loss of sponsorship* **18.** *vt* READ WORDS OR MUSIC to read the words or music of something while listening to it **19.** *vt Malaysia* ACCOMPANY SOMEBODY to go with somebody ○ *Can I follow you to the market?* ■ *n* CUE GAMES same as **follow shot** (sense 1) [Old English *folgian, fylgan*, origin ?] —**followable** *adj* ◇ as **follows** as listed or described next

SYNONYMS ***follow, chase, pursue, tail, shadow, stalk, trail***

CORE MEANING: to go after or behind

follow to take the same route behind another person, for example by walking down the street or driving along the same road, deliberately or by chance, and not necessarily with the intention of closing the gap ○ *'Will you please follow me', she said.* ○ *He's usually closely followed by two bodyguards.* **chase** to follow somebody quickly in order to catch him or her ○ *Once a pack of reporters had chased him to his car.* **pursue** to follow somebody, sometimes for a long time, in order to catch or capture him or her ○ *The group was pursued from the theatre by hordes of female fans.* **tail** (*informal*) to follow somebody secretly in order to keep watch on him or her ○ *The report claimed officers tailed him, tapped his phones, and screened his mail.* **shadow** to go everywhere that somebody else goes, especially secretly, in order to watch what he or she is doing. ○ *Until he saw the photographs, he had had no idea he was being shadowed.* **stalk** to follow or try to get close to a person or hunted animal unobtrusively, or harass a person criminally by following or contacting them obsessively. ○ *watched their cat patiently stalking a bird* ○ *an abusive man who stalked his former partner* **trail** to follow tracks or traces left by a person or animal that is no longer in sight ○ *The police trailed the missing couple all over Europe by their hotel registrations and bank withdrawals.* ○ *We could smell the pungent scent of fox as we trailed dog-like paw marks.*

follow on *vi* **1.** to continue or resume something such as a course of action or a narrative ○ *I'll follow on from where you left off.* **2.** to begin a second innings immediately after finishing the first because the score is a specific number of runs less than that of the other team. In test cricket, a first-innings deficit of 200 runs is required for a follow-on; in county cricket, one of 150 runs.

follow out *vt* to carry something out in full or to the end

follow through *v* **1.** *vti* to take further action as a consequence or extension of a previous action, especially to continue something through to completion **2.** *vi* in a sport, to continue the movement of an arm or leg past the point of contact or of release after hitting, throwing, or kicking a ball or other object

follow up *vt* **1.** to act or make further investigations on the basis of information received ○ *Police are following up a new lead.* **2.** to continue or add to something already done by doing some related thing ○ *I followed up my phone call with a letter of confirmation.*

follower /fóllō ər/ *n* **1.** SUPPORTER a supporter or admirer of a person, cause, or activity ○ *a follower of Martin Luther King* ○ *a follower of Manchester United* **2.** SOMEBODY COMING AFTER somebody who comes or travels after somebody or something else **3.** MEMBER OF ENTOURAGE a servant, attendant, or subordinate, usually one of a number of people accompanying an important person **4.** IMITATOR somebody or something that copies or imitates something else **5.** *regional* MOURNER a mourner ○ *The followers couldn't all get into the church.* **6.** *Aus* FOOTBALL same as **ruckman**

following /fóllō ing/ *adj* **1.** NEXT coming after in time or sequence **2.** ABOUT TO BE MENTIONED about to be mentioned or listed ○ *He has visited the following countries: Canada, France, and Australia.* **3.** MOVING SAME WAY blowing or flowing in the same direction as somebody or something, especially a boat or aircraft, is travelling ○ *a following wind* ■ *n* **1.** GROUP OF FOLLOWERS a group of people who admire or support somebody or something over a period of time ○ *The band has a large following in this country.* **2.** SOMETHING TO BE SPECIFIED the people or things about to be mentioned or listed (*takes a plural verb*) ○ *You will need the following: a piece of wood, a saw, a hammer, and some nails.* ■ *prep* AFTER after something, or after something and as a result of it ○ *Following the accident it was months before he felt safe in a car.*

follow-my-leader *n UK* a game in which the players, usually children, move along in a line, all copying the actions of the person at the front. ANZ, N Am term **follow-the-leader**

follow-on *adj* CONTINUING OR RESULTING coming after as a continuation or consequence ■ *n* **1.** CONTINUATION OR CONSEQUENCE OF PREVIOUS EVENT an action or event that is a continuation or consequence of a previous one **2.** CRICKET ACT OF FOLLOWING ON the immediate beginning of a second innings by a team that has been asked to follow on

follow shot *n* **1.** in billiards and similar games, a shot that makes the cue ball continue to move in the same direction as the target ball after striking it **2.** a camera shot in which the camera moves with the subject following alongside or behind

follow-the-leader *n ANZ, N Am* same as **follow-my-leader**

follow-through *n* **1.** further action continuing or completing something previously done or begun ○ *Your follow-through on the project was less than satisfactory.* **2.** in a sport, the continuation of the movement of an arm or leg past the point of contact or of release after hitting, throwing, or kicking a ball or other object

follow-up *n* **1.** further action or investigation or a subsequent event that results from and is intended to supplement something done before ○ *intended as a follow-up to the summit meeting in Vienna* **2.** a book, film, article, or report that continues a story or provides further information —**follow-up** *adj*

folly /fólli/ (*plural* **-lies**) *n* **1.** UNREASON thoughtlessness, recklessness, or thoughtless or reckless behaviour ○ *She realized, too late, the folly of her course of action.* ○ *It would be folly to continue.* **2.** IRRATIONAL THING a thoughtless or reckless act or idea (*often used in the plural*) **3.** ARCHIT ECCENTRIC BUILDING a building of eccentric or overelaborate design, usually built for decorative rather than practical purposes **4.** *US* MISGUIDED UNDERTAKING an undertaking that is excessively costly or extravagant, especially one that leads to financial loss or ruin [13C. < Old French *folie* < *fol* 'foolish' (see FOOL)]

Folsom /fólsəm/ *adj* relating to a prehistoric culture of the southern plains of North America that made leaf-shaped flint projectile points with a concave base [Early 20C. Village in NE New Mexico]

foment /fō mént, fə mént/ (**-ments, -menting, -mented**) *vt* to cause or stir up trouble or rebellion [14C. < late Latin *fomentare* < Latin *fomentum* 'warm soothing application' < *fovere* 'warm, keep warm'] —**fomentation** /fō men táysh'n, fōmən-/ *n*

SPELLCHECK See **ferment**.

fomites /fómi teez/ *npl* inanimate objects capable of carrying germs from an infected person to another person, e.g. clothes or bedding [Mid-19C. < Latin, plural of *fomes* 'kindling wood']

fond[1] /fond/ *adj* **1.** FEELING AFFECTION feeling love, affection, or preference for somebody or something ○ *I've grown fond of this old house.* **2.** EXPERIENCING PLEASURE liking or finding enjoyment in something ○ *fond of classical music* ○ *His dog is fond of chasing rabbits.* **3.** AFFECTIONATE showing or characterized by affection, love, or pleasant feelings ○ *fond memories of the time we spent there* **4.** OVERLY DOTING feeling or showing excessive affection, often to the point of being overindulgent with somebody ○ *Her fond parents could deny her nothing.* **5.** TOO OPTIMISTIC foolishly unrealistic ○ *fond hopes* [14C. Probably < past participle of obsolete *fon* 'be foolish' < *fon* 'fool', origin ?] —**fondly** *adv* —**fondness** *n*

SYNONYMS See **love**.

fond[2] /fond, foN/ *n* a background, especially of a piece of decorated lace [Mid-17C. Via French < Latin *fundus* 'bottom']

Fonda /fóndə/, **Henry** (1905–82) US film and stage actor. He is best known for films such as *The Grapes of Wrath* (1940) and *On Golden Pond* (1981), for which he won an Academy Award.

Fonda, **Jane** (*b.* 1937) US film actor and political activist. The daughter of Henry Fonda, she won Academy Awards for *Klute* (1971) and *Coming Home*

(1978). She has also written and produced popular exercise books and videotapes.

> 'A man has every season, while a woman has only the right to spring.'
> [Jane Fonda, *Daily Mail*; 13 September 1989]

Fonda, **Peter** (*b.* 1939) US film actor and director. The son of Henry Fonda, he is best known for the biker film *Easy Rider* (1969). Full name **Fonda, Peter Seymour**

fondant /fóndənt/ *n* **1.** a smooth paste made from boiled sugar syrup, often coloured or flavoured, used as a filling for chocolates or a coating for cakes, nuts, or fruit **2.** a sweet made from or filled with fondant [Late 19C. < French, present participle of *fondre* (see FONDUE)]

fondle /fónd'l/ (**-dles, -dling, -dled**) *v* **1.** *vt* to stroke, handle, or touch something or somebody in a loving or affectionate way ○ *idly fondling the cat's ears* **2.** to touch or caress somebody in an aggressive or unwelcome way [Late 17C. Back-formation < obsolete *fondling* 'foolish person' < FOND[1]] —**fondler** *n*

fondue /fón dyoo, -doo/ *n* a dish eaten by dipping small pieces of food into the contents of a pot, usually melted cheese, hot oil, or a sauce, placed on the table [Late 19C. < French, form of past participle of *fondre* 'melt' < Latin *fundere*]

Fonseca, **Gulf of** /fon sékə/ large inlet of the Pacific Ocean on the western coast of Central America, south of El Salvador, west of Honduras, and north of Nicaragua. Area: 1,940 sq. km/749 sq. mi.

font[1] /font/ *n* **1.** RECEPTACLE FOR BAPTISMAL WATER a large container in a Christian church that holds the water sprinkled in baptisms **2.** RECEPTACLE FOR HOLY WATER a container for holy water, usually found at the entrance to a Roman Catholic church **3.** HOLDER FOR LIQUID any holder for liquid, e.g. the part of an oil-burning lamp that contains the oil **4.** ABUNDANT SOURCE OF SOMETHING somebody or something seen as a source or inexhaustible supply of something (*literary*) **5.** FOUNTAIN a fountain, spring, or well (*literary*) [Pre-12C. < Latin *font-*, stem of *fons* 'spring'] —**fontal** *adj*

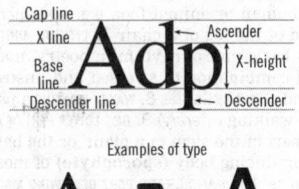

Examples of type

font

font[2] /font/, **fount** /fownt/ *n* a full set of printing type or of printed or screen characters of the same design and size [Late 16C. < Old French *fonte* 'casting' < *fondre* (see FONDUE)]

Fontaine /fon táyn/, **Pierre-François-Léonard** (1762–1853) French architect. With his partner Charles Percier, he introduced the Empire style of architecture, designing monumental projects such as the *Champs Elysées* (1806).

Fontainebleau /fóntinblō/ town in the Ile-de-France Region on the River Seine in France, about 64 km/40 mi. southeast of Paris, the site of a magnificent 16th-century chateau. Population: 15,942 (1999).

fontanel *n* ANAT US spelling of **fontanelle**

fontanelle /fóntə nél/ *n* a soft, membrane-covered space between the bones at the front and the back of a young baby's skull [15C. < Old French *fontenel* 'little spring' < *fontaine* (see FOUNTAIN)]

Fonteyn /fon táyn/, **Dame Margot** (1919–91) British ballet dancer. She was known for her role as Aurora in *The Sleeping Beauty* and her partnership with Rudolf Nureyev during the 1960s and 1970s. Born **Hookham, Margaret**

> 'I'm sure if everyone knew how physically cruel dancing really is, nobody would

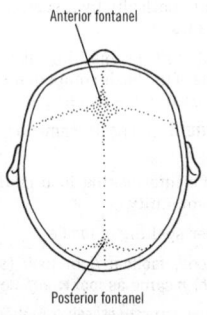

fontanelle

Dame Margot Fonteyn

watch—only those people who enjoy bull-fights!'
[Dame Margot Fonteyn. Quoted in *The Art of Margot Fonteyn*, Keith Money; 1965]

fontina /fon téenə/ *n* a semihard mild Italian cheese made from cows' milk [Mid-20C. < Italian dialect]

food /food/ *n* **1.** SOURCE OF NUTRIENTS material that provides living things with the nutrients they need for energy and growth **2.** SOLID NOURISHMENT substances, or a particular substance, providing nourishment for people or animals, especially in solid as opposed to liquid form ○ *gave them food and water* **3.** MENTAL STIMULUS something that sustains or stimulates the mind or soul ○ *food for thought* [Old English *fōda* < Indo-European] —**foodless** *adj*

food additive *n* a natural or artificial substance that is added to food during processing to make it look or taste better or last longer

Food and Drug Administration *n* full form of **FDA**

food bank *n N Am* a place where food is collected before being distributed to people without the money to buy food

food chain *n* a hierarchy of different living things, each of which feeds on the one below

food court *n* the part of a shopping centre where snacks and light meals can be bought from a number of different outlets, often with a communal eating area

food fish *n* any fish that people eat

food hall *n* the part of a department store where food is sold

foodie /fóodi/, **foody** (*plural* **-ies**) *n* an enthusiast of cooking, eating, or shopping for good food (*informal*)

food mile *n* a measure of the distance travelled by foodstuffs from producer to consumer, long distances being regarded as detrimental to quality, wasteful of energy, and prejudicial to local producers (*usually plural*)

food mixer *n* an electrical kitchen appliance used to beat eggs or cream or to mix together the ingredients for cakes and batters

food poisoning *n* acute inflammation of the mucous membrane of the stomach and intestines caused by eating food contaminated with toxic substances or with microorganisms that generate toxins

food processor *n* an electrical kitchen appliance consisting of a container in which food can be cut, sliced, shredded, grated, blended, beaten, or

liquidized automatically by a variety of removable revolving blades

foodstuff /fōod stuf/ *n* something that can be eaten, especially one of the basic components of the human diet (*usually used in the plural*)

food supplement *n* PHARM same as **supplement** *n* (sense 4)

food web *n* the interlocking food chains within an ecological community

foody *n* another spelling of **foodie**

foofool /fōo fool/, **foolfool** /fōol fool/ (*slang; used in Black English*) *n* same as **fool** ■ *adj* same as **foolish**

fool /fool/ *n* **1. UNINTELLIGENT PERSON** somebody considered to lack good sense or judgment ○ *Only a fool would invest in this scheme.* **2. RIDICULOUS PERSON** somebody considered to be or made to appear ridiculous ○ *I feel such a fool dressed like this.* **3.** FOOD **CREAMY FRUIT DESSERT** a cold dessert made from puréed fruit mixed with cream or custard **4. COURT ENTERTAINER** formerly, somebody employed to amuse a monarch or noble, usually by telling jokes, singing comical songs, or performing tricks **5.** *US* **ENTHUSIAST** somebody who is talented at, interested in, or fond of a particular thing ○ *an absolute fool for the finer things in life* ■ *adj N Am* **UNINTELLIGENT AND NOT SENSIBLE** showing a lack of good sense or judgment (*informal*) ○ *That fool salesman said it would fit.* ■ *v* (**fools, fooling, fooled**) **1.** *vt* **TRICK SOMEBODY** to trick or deceive somebody ○ *Don't be fooled by her promises.* **2.** *vi* **SPEAK IN JEST** to say something jokingly or not seriously, or pretend, jokingly, that something false is true ○ *I was only fooling – of course you can come.* **3.** *vi* **BEHAVE COMICALLY** to behave in a comical, playful, or silly way [13C. Via Old French *fol* 'fool, foolish' < Latin *follis* 'bellows, windbag'] ◇ **be nobody's fool** to be wise enough not to be easily deceived ◇ **make a fool (out) of somebody** to deceive or trick somebody, or make somebody look ridiculous ◇ **make a fool of yourself** to act in a foolish, ridiculous, or embarrassing way

fool around, fool about *vi* **1. BEHAVE IRRESPONSIBLY** to behave in a thoughtless or irresponsible way ○ *Don't fool around with those tools.* **2. CLOWN AROUND** to behave in a silly or comical way **3. WASTE TIME** to waste time by doing silly or unimportant things **4.** *N Am* **HAVE CASUAL SEX** to participate in casual or illicit sexual relationships

fool with *vt* to treat or handle somebody or something without due care or respect ○ *Who's been fooling with the TV?*

foolery /fōoləri/ (*plural* **-ies**) *n* (*dated*) **1.** irresponsible or playful behaviour **2.** an irresponsible or playful act

foolfool (*slang; used in Black English*) *n* same as **fool** ■ *adj* same as **foolish**

foolhardy /fōol haardi/ *adj* showing boldness or courage but not wisdom or good sense —**foolhardily** *adv* —**foolhardiness** *n*

foolish /fōolish/ *adj* **1. NOT SENSIBLE** showing, or resulting from, a lack of good sense or judgment ○ *foolish behaviour* **2. SEEMING RIDICULOUS** feeling or appearing ridiculous ○ *Wipe that foolish grin off your face!* **3. UNIMPORTANT** lacking importance or substance ○ *a foolish little worry* —**foolishly** *adv* —**foolishness** *n*

foolproof /fōol proof/ *adj* **1.** designed to continue working properly in the face of any kind of human error, incompetence, or misuse **2.** so well thought out that failure is thought to be impossible

fool's cap *n* a brightly coloured cap with points ending in bells or tassels, worn by court jesters

foolscap /fōol skap, fōolz kap/ *n* **1.** a large size of paper, approximately 34.3 cm/13.5 in by 43.2 cm/17 in, mostly used for writing and printing **2.** *US* CLOTHING same as **fool's cap** [Late 17C. In sense 1 < the watermark of a fool's cap originally on the paper]

fool's errand *n* a task that is performed for no good reason or that fails to accomplish anything useful

fool's gold *n* a sulphide mineral with a golden lustre, especially pyrite

fool's mate *n* in chess, the quickest checkmate, achieved on the second move by the player with the black pieces

fool's paradise *n* a state of happiness that is temporary and insubstantial because it is based on illusions or unrealistic hopes ○ *living in a fool's paradise*

fool's-parsley *n* a poisonous weed with finely divided leaves that resemble parsley and white flowers. Native to: Europe, naturalized in North America. Latin name: *Aethusa cynapium.*

foosball /fōoz bawl/ *n ANZ, N Am* a game based on football that is played on a table with rows of small model players. The models are attached to metal poles that pass through the sides of the table and are spun and moved from side to side in order to hit the ball. UK term **table football**

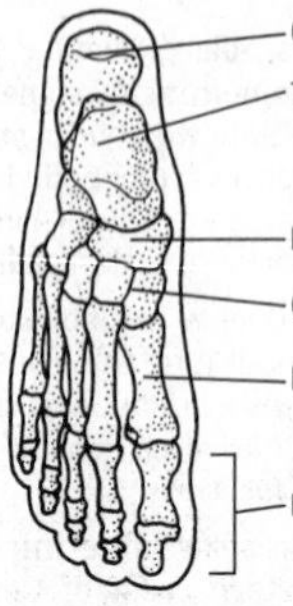

foot: bone structure of a human foot

foot /fo͝ot/ *n* (*plural* **feet** /feet/) **1. END OF LEG** the part of the leg of a vertebrate below the ankle joint that supports the rest of the body and maintains balance when standing and walking ○ *The wave knocked me off my feet.* **2. ORGAN OF ATTACHMENT** an organ or muscle surface that an invertebrate such as a mollusc uses to grip or move itself along **3. UNIT OF LENGTH** a unit of length in the imperial and US customary systems equal to 30.48 cm/12 in ○ *The aircraft is cruising at 30,000 feet.* Symbol **'** **4. LOWEST PART** the bottom or lowest part of something ○ *scribbled at the foot of the page* **5. PART OF SOCK OR BOOT** the part of a sock, stocking, or boot that is shaped to cover the foot **6. PART LIKE FOOT** something that is shaped like or acts like a human or animal foot, e.g. a shaped part at the end of the leg of a chair **7.** LITERAT **UNIT OF POETIC METRE** a basic unit of rhythm in poetry, made up of a fixed combination of stressed and unstressed or long and short syllables **8. WAY OF WALKING** a particular way of walking (*literary*) **9.** BOT **LOWER PART OF PLANT** the lower part of the stem of a plant, or the base of the spore-producing body (**sporophyte**) of mosses and liverworts **10.** HANDICRAFT **PART OF SEWING MACHINE** the part of a sewing machine, close to the needle, that is lowered onto the material to hold it in position. Most sewing machines have detachable and interchangeable feet for different functions. **11.** MIL **SOLDIERS WHO FIGHT ON FOOT** soldiers who fight principally on foot, rather than on horses or in vehicles (*takes a plural verb*) ○ *commanding a company of foot* ■ *npl* **1. foots** /fo͝ots/ FOOD INDUST **SEDIMENT** the solid material that gradually falls to the bottom of various liquids such as vegetable oil **2. foots** THEATRE same as **footlights** (sense 1) (*informal*) ■ *vt* (**foots, footing, footed**) **1. PAY FULL COST OF SOMETHING** to pay the full amount of something ○ *We had to foot the bill for the party.* **2. ADD UP NUMBERS** to add up the figures in a column ○ *footed the columns of the budget* **3. MAKE FOOT OF SOCK** in knitting or sewing, to add the part that will cover the foot to a sock or stocking [Old English *fōt* < Indo-European] —**footed** *adj* ◇ **a foot in the door** the first stage towards a goal, especially when this is difficult to achieve ◇ **drag your feet** to move or do something slowly and reluctantly on purpose (*informal*) ◇ **fall** *or* **land on your feet** to end up in a good position, especially after having been in a difficult situation ◇ **find your feet 1.** to become accustomed to a new situation and able to cope with it **2.** to manage to stand up, especially after having fallen ◇ **foot it 1.** to walk rather than ride in a vehicle or on a horse ○ *We had to foot it all the way home.* **2.** to dance (*dated*) ◇ **get off on the wrong foot** to begin something badly, e.g. a new relationship or job ◇ **get on** *or* **to your feet 1.** to rise from a reclining or sitting position **2.** to return to a healthy or financially stable condition after a period of illness or financial difficulty ◇ **have somebody** *or* **something at your feet** to be the object of enormous admiration and devotion from somebody or something ◇ **have feet of clay** to have a weakness or flaw that is not obvious at first ◇ **have** *or* **keep both** *or* **your feet on the ground** to act and think sensibly and realistically ◇ **land on your feet** same as **fall** *or* **land on your feet** ◇ **my foot!** used to say that something is ridiculous or untrue (*informal*) ○ *Too difficult, my foot!* ◇ **on foot** walking, as opposed to riding on horseback or in a vehicle ◇ **put your best foot forward** to try as hard as you can to impress or please somebody ◇ **put your feet up** to stop working and relax ◇ **put your foot down 1.** to be firm about something and make sure your wishes are obeyed or respected **2.** to make a motor vehicle travel faster by pressing the accelerator ◇ **put your foot in it** to make an embarrassing mistake, especially by being tactless (*informal*) ◇ **set foot in** *or* **on something** to go to or into a place ○ *I'll never set foot in that place again.* ◇ **shoot yourself in the foot** to do something that unexpectedly turns out to be disadvantageous or harmful to your own interests ◇ **sweep somebody off his** *or* **her feet** to charm somebody completely or make him or her fall in love with you in a very short time

ORIGIN The Indo-European word from which *foot* is ultimately derived is also the ancestor of English *antipodes, impede, octopus, pawn*[1], *pedal*[1], *pedestal, pedestrian, pedigree, pioneer, podium, tripod*, and *vamp*[2].

Foot /fo͝ot/, **Michael** (*b.* 1913) British politician and writer. A fiery orator and leader of the Labour Party (1980–83), his books include a biography of Aneurin Bevan (1962–73). He was the editor of *Tribune* and a political columnist on the *Daily Herald*.

> 'Men of power have not time to read; yet men who do not read are unfit for power.'
> [Michael Foot, *Debts Of Honour*; 1980]

footage /fo͝otij/ *n* **1. FILMED SEQUENCE SHOWING EVENT** a shot or sequence of shots on film or video tape, usually of a particular scene or event, or the length of film or videotape that contains these shots ○ *They had some good footage of the president's visit to the island.* **2. SIZE IN FEET** the size or amount of something measured in feet **3.** CINEMA **LENGTH OF PIECE OF FILM** the length of a piece of film in feet **4. PAYMENT BY SIZE** payment by the foot for work **5. AMOUNT PAID** the amount paid for work measured by the foot

foot-and-mouth disease *n* a highly contagious viral disease affecting animals with divided hooves, especially cattle, sheep, and pigs, in which the animal develops ulcers in the mouth and near the hooves

football /fo͝ot bawl/ *n* **1.** *UK* **GAME WITH ROUND BALL** a game in which 2 teams of 11 players try to kick or head a round ball into the goal defended by the opposing team. ANZ, N Am term **soccer** **2.** *US* same as **American football** **3.** *Can* **CANADIAN FOOTBALL** a game that is similar to American football but takes place on a larger field, has 12 players on each team, and uses 3 rather than 4 moves to advance at least 10 yards or score **4. BALL GAME** any game in which two teams kick or carry a ball into a goal or over a line, e.g. rugby, Australian Rules, or Gaelic football **5. BALL USED IN FOOTBALL** the large round ball used in the game of football **6. PROBLEM PASSED AROUND** a point or problem that is used as an excuse for argument by opposing groups, without any real attempt at finding a solution ○ *a political football* —**footballer** *n*

football pools *npl* **1.** GAMBLING same as **pools** **2.** an organized form of gambling, mainly by post, that involves predicting the outcome of football matches

footbath /fo͝ot baath/ (*plural* **-baths** /-baat͟hz/) *n* **1.** a bowl used when bathing the feet, or a shallow pool where people can disinfect their feet before entering a swimming pool **2.** the action of bathing the feet

footboard /fo͝ot bawrd/ *n* **1.** a vertical part across the bottom end of a bedstead **2.** a board or small platform used to support the feet in a vehicle

footboy /fo͝ot boy/ *n* a boy employed as a servant or page

foot brake *n* a brake operated by pressing a pedal with the foot, especially in a motor vehicle

footbridge /fo͝ot brij/ *n* a narrow bridge suitable for people walking and not for vehicles

foot-dragger *n* somebody who is slow or reluctant to do what is required (*informal*) —**foot-dragging** *n*

footer[1] /fo͝ottər/ *n* **1.** a piece of text, e.g. a title or date, below the main text on a page, especially one that is automatically inserted on each page by word-processing software **2.** somebody or something of a particular height or length in feet (*usually used in combination*) ○ *Both of her sons were six-footers.* **3.** ARCHIT, CONSTR same as **footing** (sense 5) [Early 17C. < FOOT]

footer[2] /fo͞otər/, **fouter** *Scotland vi* (**-ers, -ering, -ered**) **POTTER** to spend time doing trivial or useless things, or to play idly with something ○ *Can you not do something useful instead of footering about?* ■ *n* **1.** **SOMEBODY DOING TRIVIAL THINGS** somebody who does something trivial or useless, or who plays idly with something **2.** **AWKWARD JOB** a job that is awkward or involves working with small parts ○ *It was a bit of a footer putting it back together again.* [Late 16C. < Old French *foutre* 'have sex with' < Latin *futuere*]

footfall /fo͝ot fawl/ *n* **1.** the sound made by somebody's foot coming into contact with the ground as he or she walks **2.** the number of potential customers who visit a shop or business in a given period

foot fault *n* in tennis, a fault committed by a server whose foot touches any part of the baseline or court before the ball has been hit —**foot-fault** *vi*

footgear /fo͝ot geer/ *n* coverings worn on the feet, especially shoes and boots

foothill /fo͝ot hil/ *n* a hill at the bottom of a higher mountain or mountain range and forming part of the approaches to it (*often used in the plural*)

foothold /fo͝ot hōld/ *n* **1.** a secure starting position from which further advances can be made ○ *The company has gained a foothold in the multimedia industry.* **2.** a place or thing that will support the foot of a climber, especially a crack, hollow, or ledge in a rock face

footie /fo͝otti/ *n* (*informal*) **1.** same as **football** (sense 1) **2.** *Aus* same as **football** (sense 4)

footing /fo͝otting/ *n* **1.** **STABILITY OF FEET** a stable secure position for or placement of the feet when standing or walking ○ *He lost his footing on the icy slope.* **2.** **BASE FOR PROGRESS** a foundation or basis for further advancement or development ○ *gives the organization a firm footing* **3.** **STATUS** the status or condition of something, often in relation to something else ○ *The government moved swiftly to place the armed forces on a war footing.* ○ *put the discussion on a more scientific footing* **4.** **RELATIONSHIP** the position or status of people in relation to one another ○ *back on a friendly footing* **5.** ARCHIT, CONSTR **FOUNDATION** the foundation or base of a structure such as a wall or column

footle /fo͞ot'l/ *vi* (**-tles, -tling, -tled**) (*informal*) **1.** **ACT AIMLESSLY** to waste time doing unnecessary or unimportant things **2.** **ACT OR TALK POINTLESSLY** to talk nonsense, or behave in a pointless way ■ *n* **NONSENSE** silly nonsense [Late 19C. Origin ?] —**footler** *n*

footless /fo͝otləss/ *adj* lacking a foot or feet

footlights /fo͝ot līts/ *npl* **1.** a row of lights along the front of the stage in a theatre, directed away from the audience and towards the performers **2.** the theatre as a profession

footling /fo͞otling/ *adj* (*informal*) **1.** having no importance or serious usefulness **2.** lacking skill or competence

footloose /fo͝ot looss/ *adj* free to go anywhere and do anything because not limited by personal ties or responsibilities

footman /fo͝otmən/ (*plural* **-men** /-mən/) *n* **1.** **LIVERIED SERVANT** a man employed as a servant, especially a servant in uniform in a mansion or palace **2.** **FIRESIDE STAND** a low metal stand, usually with four legs, for utensils in a fireplace **3.** **INFANTRYMAN** a soldier who fights on foot (*archaic*)

footmark /fo͝ot maark/ *n* same as **footprint** (sense 1)

footnote /fo͝ot nōt/ *n* **1.** **INFORMATION AT FOOT OF PAGE** a note at the bottom of a page, giving further information about something mentioned in the text above. A reference number or symbol is usually printed after the relevant word in the text and before the corresponding footnote. **2.** **ADDITIONAL DETAIL** an extra comment or information added to what has just been said ○ *As a footnote, let me say that I only found this out yesterday.* **3.** **MINOR DETAIL** a relatively unimportant part of a larger issue or event ○ *His career is now but a footnote in history.* ■ *vt* (**-notes, -noting, -noted**) **SUPPLY TEXT WITH FOOTNOTES** to provide a text with footnotes, or provide a footnote for a particular reference within the text

footpad[1] /fo͝ot pad/ *n* a flat structure at the bottom of a leg of a spacecraft, designed to prevent the craft sinking into the surface it has landed on [< PAD [1]]

footpad[2] /fo͝ot pad/ *n* a robber or highwayman who operated on foot rather than on a horse (*archaic*) [Late 17C. < obsolete *pad* 'path, highwayman' < Dutch]

foot passenger *n* a passenger on a car ferry who is not travelling with a motor vehicle

footpath /fo͝ot paath/ (*plural* **-paths** /-paaths/) *n* a narrow path for people on foot ○ *Please keep to the footpath.*

footplate /fo͝ot playt/ *n* the part of a railway locomotive from which the driver operates the controls

foot-pound *n* in physics, a unit of work equal to the work done by lifting a mass of one pound vertically against gravity through a distance of one foot

foot-pound-second *adj* relating or belonging to a system of measurements based on the foot, pound, and second as base units of length, mass, and time

foot-pound-second units, **foot-pound-second system of units** *n* MEASURE, PHYS same as **fps units**

footprint /fo͝ot print/ *n* **1.** **OUTLINE OF FOOT** a mark made by the foot of a person or animal or a shoe, especially an indentation on something soft like snow or a dirty mark on a floor ○ *footprints in the ground below the window* **2.** **AREA OF SURFACE** an area of a surface, especially the amount of space a piece of computer hardware occupies on a desk, or a spacecraft's target landing area on the Moon or a planet **3.** **AREA WHERE SOMETHING IS EFFECTIVE** the area over which something occurs or is effective, e.g. the area where a signal from a communications satellite can be received **4.** **TROOP PRESENCE IN AREA** the presence, quantity, type, and defined mission of armed troops deployed to a region, nation, or area, e.g. for combat or peacekeeping duties ○ *The administration has not yet decided the size of the US Army's footprint in that region.*

footrace /fo͝ot rayss/, **foot race** *n* a race run by people on foot

footrest /fo͝ot rest/ *n* a support for both feet when sitting down, e.g. beneath a desk, or for one foot while standing, e.g. a low rail at a bar

footrope /fo͝ot rōp/ *n* **1.** a rope to which the lower edge of a sail is stitched **2.** a rope fixed beneath a ship's yard for sailors to stand on as they furl a sail

foot rot, **footrot** /fo͝ot rot/ *n* **1.** VET, AGRIC a bacterial infection of sheep and cattle that causes inflammation of the hooves **2.** a fungal disease that causes the roots and base of a plant to rot

foot rule *n* a strip of wood, metal, or plastic, used for measuring and drawing straight lines, that is one foot long or is marked in feet

footsie /fo͝otsi/ *n* a form of flirtation in which people use their feet to touch the feet and legs of somebody else, especially done secretly while sitting at a table (*informal*) ◇ **play footsie** (*informal*) **1.** to engage in footsie **2.** *US* to collaborate with another person or organization, often in an underhand way

Footsie /fo͝otsi/ *n* FIN same as **FTSE 100 Index** (*informal*) [Late 20C. Alteration of the acronym *FT-SE 100* 'Financial Times-Stock Exchange (100 share index)']

footslog /fo͝ot slog/ (**-slogs, -slogging, -slogged**) *vi* to march, tramp, or trudge on foot, especially over difficult ground such as thick mud —**footslogger** *n* —**footslogging** *n*

foot soldier *n* **1.** a soldier who fights principally on foot, not on horseback or in a vehicle **2.** somebody who does routine but essential work

footsore /fo͝ot sawr/ *adj* with feet that are painful or tired, usually from too much walking —**footsoreness** *n*

footstall /fo͝ot stawl/ *n* **1.** the pedestal or base of a structure, especially a pillar or statue **2.** a stirrup on a sidesaddle

footstep /fo͝ot step/ *n* **1.** **SOUND OF SOMEBODY WALKING** the sound made when somebody's foot hits the ground in walking ○ *I heard footsteps on the stairs.* **2.** **MOVEMENT OF FOOT WHEN WALKING** the action of raising a foot and putting it down somewhere else while walking **3.** **DISTANCE COVERED BY STEP** the distance covered by a single step in walking **4.** **MARK MADE BY FOOT** a mark left by the sole of a foot or shoe **5.** **STEP OR STAIR** a single step or stair on which to put a foot while moving up or down ◇ **follow in somebody's footsteps** to take the same course in life or work as another person in the past

footstone /fo͝ot stōn/ *n* a memorial stone at the foot of a grave

footstool /fo͝ot stool/ *n* a low stool, often with a padded top, on which to rest the feet while sitting down

footwall /fo͝ot wawl/ *n* the rock layer that lies immediately beneath a vein of ore or other mineral deposit or a fault plane

footway /fo͝ot way/ *n* a narrow path or walk for people on foot, e.g. beside a road or railway line

footwear /fo͝ot wair/ *n* coverings worn on the feet, especially shoes, boots, sandals, or slippers, but often including socks or stockings

footwell /fo͝ot wel/ *n* the hollow space below a motor vehicle's dashboard where people in the front seats can put their feet

footwork /fo͝ot wurk/ *n* **1.** **MOTION OF FEET** the movement of the feet in sport or dancing, especially when skilfully done **2.** **SKILFUL MANOEUVRING** skilful or devious manoeuvring in order to achieve or avoid something (*informal*) ○ *Their fancy footwork helped get them out of the problem.* **3.** *US* **WORK THAT INVOLVES WALKING** work that involves a lot of moving around, especially on foot

footworn /fo͝ot wawrn/ *adj* **1.** worn down or made thin by being walked on by many people for a long time **2.** same as **footsore**

footy /fo͝oti/, **footie** *n* same as **football** (sense 1) (*informal*) [Mid-20C. A humorous formation < FOOT]

foo yung /foo yúng, -yóng, -yo͝ong/, **foo young**, **fu yung** *n UK, ANZ, Can* a Chinese-style dish, similar to an omelette, in which the eggs are combined with bean sprouts, onions, and meat or seafood. US term **egg foo yung** [Mid-20C. < Cantonese *foō yung* 'hibiscus']

foozle /fo͞oz'l/ *vti* (**-zles, -zling, -zled**) to do something badly or clumsily, especially to bungle a shot in golf ■ *n* something done badly or clumsily, especially a bungled shot in golf [Mid-19C. Origin ?] —**foozler** *n*

fop /fop/ *n* a man who is so obsessed by fashion and vain about his own appearance that he becomes ridiculous [15C. Origin ?] —**foppery** *n* —**foppish** *adj* —**foppishly** *adv* —**foppishness** *n*

for *stressed* /fawr/; *unstressed* /fər/ CORE MEANING: a preposition indicating that something is directed at somebody, done to benefit somebody, or done on somebody's behalf ○ *Look – there's a letter for you.* ○ *I'd do anything for you.* ○ *The lawyer acted for some of the heirs.*

1. *prep* **AIMED AT** intended to be received or used by somebody, or aimed at somebody ○ *It's for you – it's a present.* ○ *advice for first-time buyers* **2.** *prep* **TO BENEFIT OF** intending or intended to benefit somebody or something ○ *She would make any sacrifice for the cause.* **3.** *prep* **ON BEHALF OF** on behalf of somebody or something ○ *Don't make excuses for him.* **4.** *prep* **INSTEAD OF** instead of or in place of somebody or something, sometimes mistakenly ○ *You'll have to find a stand-in for him while he's away.* ○ *I took her for the boss.* **5.** *prep* **IN SERVICE OF** in the service or employment of somebody or something ○ *She works for a large company.* **6.** *prep* **TOWARDS** in the direction of ○ *The following day, we headed for Paris.* **7.** *prep* **LASTING** indicating how long something lasts, continues, or extends ○ *The interview only lasted for a few minutes.* ○ *There was fog for the next mile or so.* **8.** *prep* **BECAUSE OF** indicating a reason why something happens or is done ○ *I did it for love.* **9.** *prep* **DESIGNED TO DO** indicating the purpose of an object, action, or activity ○ *That towel is for drying your hands on.* **10.** *prep* **LINKS CONCEPTS** used to link two

concepts, one of which is the object of the other ○ *a cause for concern* ○ *a passion for opera* **11.** *prep* **IN EXCHANGE FOR** at a cost of, or giving or receiving something in exchange ○ *got it for a few pounds* **12.** *prep* **AS TRIBUTE TO** in honour of ○ *gave a dinner for them* **13.** *prep* **GIVEN WHAT IS USUAL** with reference to the normal characteristics of something ○ *It's very warm for April.* **14.** *prep* **INDICATING OCCASION** at, or planned to be at, a particular time, or on a particular occasion ○ *The meeting was scheduled for four o'clock.* ○ *Will you be home for Christmas?* **15.** *prep* **INDICATES COMPARISON** indicating a comparison or equivalence between two things ○ *Pound for pound, the elephant's energy consumption is the lowest of all land animals.* **16.** *prep* **IN ORDER TO GET** in order to get, achieve, have, keep, or become something ○ *Lee's hoping for promotion.* ○ *He was searching for a place to sit.* **17.** *prep* **DESPITE** in spite of or notwithstanding something ○ *He enjoyed himself very much, for all his complaining.* **18.** *prep* **INDICATES RESPONSIBILITY** indicating that somebody has the right or responsibility to do something ○ *I can't help you – it's for you to decide.* **19.** *prep* **HAVING SAME MEANING AS** having the same meaning as another word or phrase ○ *The everyday term for rubella is German measles.* **20.** *prep* **INDICATES CROSS-REFERENCE** indicating that information can be found elsewhere ○ *For further details, consult the owner's manual.* **21.** *adv, prep* **IN SUPPORT OF SOMETHING** in favour of or in support of something ○ (prep) *Who's for the motion and who's against it?* ○ (adv) *Ten voted for, and eleven against.* **22.** *conj* **BECAUSE** for the reason or seeing that (*formal*) ○ *I left in haste, for I was already late for the appointment.* [Old English < Indo-European, 'forward'] ◇ **be (in) for it** to be likely to be punished (*informal*)

USAGE See *because*.

for. *abbr* **1.** foreign **2.** forestry

f.o.r. *abbr* COMM free on rail

for- *prefix* **1.** away, down, falsely ○ *forfend* ○ *forswear* **2.** completely, extremely ○ *forgather* [Old English; related to FOR]

fora plural of **forum**

forage /fórrij/ *n* **1. FOOD FOR ANIMALS** food for animals, especially crops grown to feed horses, cattle, and other livestock **2. SEARCH** a search or the process of searching for something, especially a search for food and supplies or a search among a varied collection of things **3. RAID BY SOLDIERS** a raid carried out by soldiers, especially to seize food or supplies ■ *v* (**-ages, -aging, -aged**) **1.** *vi* **WANDER AROUND SEARCHING** to go from place to place looking for food and supplies **2.** *vti* **RAID FOR FOOD** to raid a place, especially for food or supplies **3.** *vi* **SEARCH** to engage in a search ○ *He foraged around in the drawer and pulled out a faded photograph.* **4.** *vt* **FIND BY SEARCHING** to obtain something, especially food, from a place by searching or rummaging ○ *She foraged a half-eaten cake from the bin.* **5.** *vt* **FEED ANIMALS** to give forage to horses, cattle, or other animals [14C. < Old French *fourrage* < *fuerre* 'fodder, straw' < Germanic] —**forager** *n*

forage cap *n UK, ANZ, Can* MIL a peaked hat worn by some soldiers when they are not in dress uniform. US term **service cap**

foram /fáwrəm/ *n* MARINE BIOL same as **foraminifer** [Early 20C. Shortening]

foramen /fə ráy men, fo-/ (*plural* **-ramina** /-rámminə/ or **-ramens**) *n* a natural opening or cavity in a human or animal body, usually one through which blood vessels and nerves pass through bone [Late 17C. < Latin < *forare* 'bore a hole'] —**foraminal** /-rámmin'l/ *adj* —**foraminous** /-rámminəss/ *adj*

foramen magnum /-mágnəm/ *n* the opening at the base of the skull through which the spinal cord passes to become the medulla oblongata of the brain [Late 19C. < Latin, 'large opening']

foramen ovale /-ō vaáli/ *n* an opening in the wall between the two sides of the foetal heart that allows blood to pass from right to left. Sometimes it fails to close after birth and persists into adulthood. [Mid-19C. < Latin, 'oval opening']

foramina ANAT plural of **foramen**

foraminifer /fórrə mínnifər/ (*plural* **-fera** /-fərə/ or **-fers**) *n* a large protozoan found mainly in seawater that has a shell perforated with many small holes through which temporary cytoplasmic protrusions (**pseudopodia**) project. The calcium-containing shells of foraminifera are the main component of chalk and some limestone deposits. Order: Foraminfera. [Mid-19C. < modern Latin *Foraminifera* (plural) < Latin *foramen* (see FORAMEN) + *-fer* 'bearing'] —**foraminiferal** /fo rámmi níffərəl, fórrəmi-/ *adj* —**foraminiferous** /fo rámmi níffərəss, fórrəmi-/ *adj*

forasmuch as /fərəz múch əz/ *conj* since or in view of the fact that (*archaic*)

foray /fórray/ *n* **1. SUDDEN RAID** a sudden attack or raid by a military force **2. EXPLORATION OF SOMETHING UNFAMILIAR** an attempt at some new occupation or activity ○ *the ex-salesman's first foray into management* **3. BRIEF JOURNEY** a short trip or visit to a place, usually for a specific purpose ■ *v* (**-ays, -aying, -ayed**) **1.** *vi* **MAKE INCURSION** to make a sudden attack or raid **2.** *vt* **MAKE RAID ON** to raid or loot a place [14C. Back-formation < *forayer* < Old French *fourrier* < *fuerre* (see FORAGE)] —**forayer** *n*

forb /fawrb/ *n* any broad-leaved herbaceous plant that is not a grass, especially one that grows in a prairie or meadow [Early 20C. < Greek *phorbē* 'food' < *pherbein* 'to feed']

forbade, forbad past tense of **forbid**

forbear[1] /fawr báir/ (**-bears, -bearing, -bore** /-báwr/, **-borne** /-báwrn/) *v* (*formal*) **1.** *vi* to not do or say something that you could do or say, especially when this shows self-control or consideration for the feelings of others ○ *I forbore to criticize their efforts, though criticism was well deserved.* **2.** *vti* to tolerate something with patience or endurance ○ *willing to forbear their failures* [Old English *forberan*, literally 'bear against'] —**forbearer** *n* —**forbearing** *adj* —**forbearingly** *adv*

USAGE forbear or **forebear**? Either spelling may be used for the noun, meaning 'ancestor', but ***forebear*** is the more frequent of the two: *The walls were lined with portraits of his illustrious forebears* [or *forbears*]. ***Forbear*** is the only acceptable spelling for the verb, meaning 'hold back' or 'tolerate': *We must forbear* [not *forebear*] *from judging people on first impressions.*

forbear[2] *n* another spelling of **forebear**

forbearance /fawr báirənss/ *n* **1. PATIENCE** patience, tolerance, or self-control, especially in not responding to provocation (*formal*) **2. REFRAINING FROM ACTION** the fact of deliberately not doing or saying something when you could do or say it (*formal*) **3.** LAW **REFRAINING FROM LEGAL RIGHT** the fact of not exercising a legal right, especially of not insisting on payment of a debt at the due date and giving the debtor more time to pay

Forbes /fawrbz/ town and agricultural centre in central New South Wales, Australia. Population: 10,155 (2002 estimate).

Forbes, George William (1869–1947) prime minister of New Zealand (1930–35). A member of the Liberal party, he served as outright premier and minister of finance for his first year in office and then as head of a coalition government from 1931. See table at **prime minister**

Forbes 500 /fáwrbz fīv húndrəd/ *n* the top 500 companies in the United States, as listed by *Forbes* magazine

forbid /fər bíd/ (**-bids, -bidding, -bade** /-bád, -báyd/ or **-bad** /-bád/, **-bidden** /-bídd'n/ or **-bid**) *vt* **1. ORDER SOMEBODY NOT TO DO SOMETHING** to tell somebody, especially forcefully, not to do or have something ○ *I forbid you to mention his name.* **2. NOT ALLOW SOMETHING** to state authoritatively that something must not be done ○ *The rules of the game strictly forbid the use of a dictionary.* **3. MAKE SOMETHING IMPOSSIBLE** to make something impossible, or prevent something from happening (*formal*) ○ *Discretion forbids me to mention any names.* [Old English *forbēodan*, literally 'command against'] —**forbiddance** *n* —**forbidder** *n* ◇ **God** *or* **heaven forbid** used to express the hope that something will not happen or be done

forbidden /fər bídd'n/ *adj* **1. NOT PERMITTED** not allowed by order of somebody or by law ○ *That's a forbidden subject in this company.* **2. OUT OF BOUNDS** to which entry is not allowed, or allowed only to a specific person or group of people ○ *This part of the temple was forbidden to everybody except the high priest.* **3.** PHYS **IMPROBABLE OR DISALLOWED AS ENERGY LEVEL** describes an energy level or transition in a quantum mechanical system that is either highly improbable or disobeys selection rules and is therefore not allowed

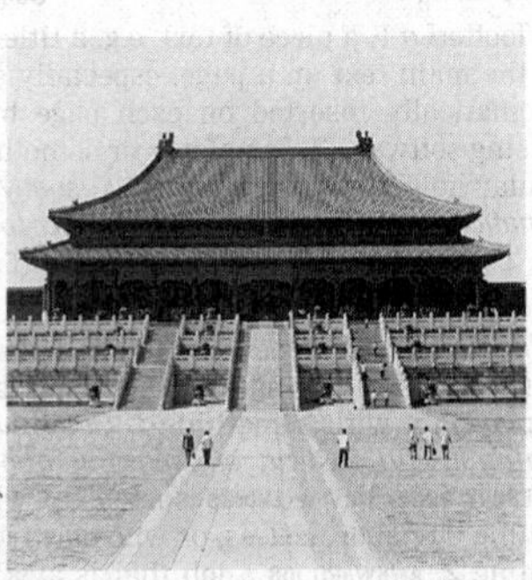

Forbidden City: Hall of Supreme Harmony

Forbidden City *n* a walled complex of buildings (1421–1911) in Beijing, China, that includes the former Imperial Palace. It was closed to ordinary citizens until 1912 and is now a museum.

forbidden fruit (*plural* **forbidden fruits** or *same*) *n* something desired or pleasurable that somebody is not allowed to have or do, especially some form of sexual indulgence that is illegal or considered immoral [< the fruit, forbidden to Adam and Eve, of the tree of knowledge of good and evil (Genesis 2:17)]

forbidding /fər bídding/ *adj* **1. HOSTILE** presenting an appearance that seems hostile or stern ○ *The mountains looked distant and forbidding.* **2. UNINVITING** appearing to involve a great deal of unpleasantness or difficulty ○ *the forbidding prospect of further difficulties ahead* **3. DANGEROUS OR THREATENING** appearing to present a danger or threat ○ *a rocky and forbidding shore* —**forbiddingly** *adv* —**forbiddingness** *n*

~~**forboding**~~ incorrect spelling of **foreboding**

forbore past tense of **forbear**[1]

forborne past participle of **forbear**[1]

force[1] /fawrss/ *n* **1. NATURAL STRENGTH** the power, strength, or energy that somebody or something possesses ○ *Trees were blown down by the force of the storm.* **2. PHYSICAL POWER** physical power, effort, or violence used against somebody or something that resists ○ *The use of force should be a last resort.* **3. EFFECTIVENESS** the condition of being effective, valid, or applicable ○ *The new regulations come into force next week.* **4. NONPHYSICAL POWER** power or strength that is intellectual or moral rather than physical ○ *swayed by the force of your argument* **5. SOMEBODY OR SOMETHING WITH GREAT INFLUENCE** somebody or something that has great power or influence, especially in a particular field ○ *She remained a force in local politics until her death.* **6. GROUP ORGANIZED TO FIGHT** a body of military personnel, ships, or aircraft brought together to fight in a battle or a war ○ *A naval task force has been sent to the area.* **7. POLICE OFFICERS** a professional body of police officers ○ *He left the force in 1985.* **8. PEOPLE WORKING TOGETHER** a group of people who work together for a particular purpose ○ *a sales force* **9.** PHYS **INFLUENCE THAT MOVES SOMETHING** a physical influence that tends to change the position of an object with mass, equal to the rate of change in momentum of the object. Symbol *F* **10.** METEOROL **WIND STRENGTH** the strength of the wind, especially as measured on the Beaufort scale, from 0 to 12 (*often used in combination*) ○ *a force nine gale* ■ **forces** *npl* **ORGANIZED MILITARY SERVICE** the professional military organizations belonging to a country ○ *Were you in the forces?* ■ *vt* (**forces, forcing, forced**) **1. COMPEL SOMEBODY** to use superior physical or mental power to make somebody or yourself do something that is not agreeable ○ *The weather forced us to turn back.* ○ *She forced herself to be polite to him.* **2. MOVE SOMETHING WITH STRENGTH** to use physical strength or violence to move something or somebody that puts up resistance ○ *If the key won't turn easily, don't force it.* ○ *I had to force the last bit of toothpaste out of the tube.* ○ *She forced the dog back into the house.* **3. CREATE PASSAGE BY STRENGTH** to create a way or passage through something using physical strength or another kind of power ○ *They forced a path through the jungle.* **4. OBTAIN SOMETHING BY PRESSURE** to obtain

something or make something happen by using physical or mental pressure ○ *She's been trying to force a confrontation all week.* **5.** BREAK SOMETHING OPEN to open something that is locked or jammed by using power or effort, often breaking or damaging it in the process ○ *This door has been forced.* **6.** STRAIN TO DO SOMETHING to produce or use something in a strained or unnatural way ○ *Just agree with whatever she says and try to force a smile.* **7.** MAKE PLANT MATURE to cause a plant to flower or mature before its normal time **8.** RAPE SOMEBODY to subject somebody to rape (*dated*) **9.** CARDS MAKE PLAYER PLAY SPECIFIC WAY in a card game, to give a player no choice but to play a specific card or make a specific bid or move [13C. < Old French < Latin *fortis* 'strong'] —**force-able** *adj* —**forceless** *adj* —**forcer** *n* ◇ **in force 1.** in a large or strong group **2.** effective or valid ◇ **join forces** to combine together, or combine with somebody else, for a joint effort

force down *vt* **1.** to eat or drink something very reluctantly, often because pressured to do so or to avoid offending somebody **2.** to compel an aircraft to land, usually because of lack of fuel, damage, or bad weather

force on, **force upon** *vt* to make somebody or a group of people accept something unwillingly ○ *This method was forced on us by headquarters.*

force[2] /fáwrss/ *n* N England GEOG same as **waterfall** [Early 17C. < Old Norse *fors*]

~~forceably~~ incorrect spelling of **forcibly**

forced /fawrst/ *adj* **1.** NOT NATURAL not natural or spontaneous, but produced by an act of will ○ *The courtiers greeted the king's witticism with forced laughter.* **2.** NECESSARY not done voluntarily but out of necessity ○ *a forced error* **3.** COMPELLED done because somebody who has power requires it —**forcedly** /-sidli/ *adv* —**forcedness** /-sidnəss/ *n*

forced labour *n* work that somebody is made to do against his or her will, often as a punishment or to repay a debt

forced landing *n* an unscheduled landing that a pilot of an aircraft is compelled to make, usually because of an emergency

forced march *n* a march of troops or prisoners made as quickly as possible and without the normal amounts of rest

force-feed *vt* **1.** to make people or animals swallow food against their will, e.g. by putting it directly down their throat through a funnel or tube. Animals may be force-fed to fatten them up, and people who refuse to eat may be force-fed to keep them alive. **2.** to make people learn or assimilate things, often without fully understanding them, that they might reject if given the choice

force field *n* in science fiction, an invisible protective barrier around something

forceful /fáwrssf'l/ *adj* **1.** possessing or characterized by strength and power **2.** tending to make a powerful impression on people or to persuade people ○ *a forceful argument for merging our businesses* —**forcefully** *adv* —**forcefulness** *n*

force-land *vti* to land an aircraft before it gets to its destination because of an emergency, or land in these circumstances ○ *The pilot had to force-land in a field.*

force majeure /fáwrss ma zhúr/ *n* **1.** an unexpected event that crucially affects somebody's ability to do something and can be used in law as an excuse for not having carried out the terms of an agreement (*formal*) **2.** a force that is superior in power or impossible to resist [Late 19C. < French, 'superior force']

force-march *vti* to make soldiers or prisoners march somewhere in the shortest possible time and without the normal amounts of rest, or march somewhere in this way ○ *The captured personnel were force-marched north.*

forcemeat /fáwrss meet/ *n* finely chopped meat, fish, or vegetables mixed with other ingredients and used as a stuffing or garnish [Late 17C. < variant of FARCE]

force of habit *n* the ability of a behaviour pattern that has become habitual to reassert itself automatically even in situations where it is no longer

appropriate ○ *Even after she retired, she woke at six every morning by force of habit.*

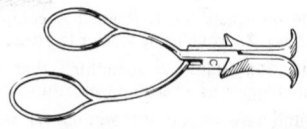

forceps

forceps /fáwr seps, -səps/ *npl* **1.** a specialized surgical instrument of different designs but always with two parts that move together to hold something such as dressings, tissues or organs **2.** a body part that is shaped or works like pincers, e.g. the grasping parts of some insects [Mid-16C. < Latin, 'pincers']

force pump *n* a pump that uses pressure to move a liquid

forcible /fáwrssəb'l/ *adj* **1.** using physical power against somebody or something that resists ○ *the forcible removal of the lock* **2.** having enough power or force to persuade people ○ *It was a forcible reminder that we must be on our guard.* —**forcibility** /fáwrssə bílləti/ *n* —**forcibleness** *n* —**forcibly** *adv*

forcing ground *n* a place where something develops rapidly, or where a lot of people are trained in something ○ *We move north to the Scottish Highlands, that great forcing ground for rock climbing.*

ford /fawrd/ *n* a shallow part of a river or stream where people, animals, or vehicles can cross it ■ *vt* (**fords, fording, forded**) to walk, ride, or drive across a river or stream at a place where the water is shallow [Old English < Germanic] —**fordable** *adj*

Ford /fawrd/, **Ford Madox** (1873–1939) British novelist. His masterpiece was *The Good Soldier* (1915). He founded the *English Review* (1908). Born **Hueffer, Ford Hermann**

> 'Only two classes of books are of universal appeal. The very best and the very worst.'
> [Ford Madox Ford, *Joseph Conrad*; 1924]

Gerald R. Ford

Ford, **Gerald R.** (*b*. 1913) 38th president of the United States. A Republican, he was the only president (1974–77) elected neither president nor vice president, having attained those posts following the resignations of Richard Nixon and Spiro Agnew, respectively. Full name **Ford, Gerald Rudolph**. See table at **president**

> 'Our long national nightmare is over. Our constitution works...'
> [Gerald R. Ford, *Gerald R. Ford*, J. G. Lankevich; 1977]

Ford, **Glenn** (*b*. 1916) Canadian-born US film actor. His films include *The Big Heat* (1953) and *Blackboard Jungle* (1955). Born **Newton Ford, Gwyllyn Samuel**

Ford, **Harrison** (*b*. 1942) US film actor. He is best known for his roles as Han Solo in the *Star Wars* trilogy (1977–83) and as Indiana Jones in the *Raiders of the Lost Ark* trilogy (1981–89).

> 'Los Angeles is where you've got to be an actor. You have no choice. You go there or New York. I flipped a coin...It came up New York. So I flipped it again.'
> [Harrison Ford, *Cinema*; 1981]

Henry Ford

Ford, **Henry** (1863–1947) US industrialist, best known for his pioneering achievements in the automobile industry. In 1903 he founded a major motor company, introducing assembly-line production on a massive scale.

> 'The whole secret of a successful life is to find out what it is one's destiny to do, and then do it.'
> [Henry Ford, 'Success', *Forum*; October 1928]

> 'History is more or less bunk.'
> [Henry Ford. Interview with Charles N. Wheeler, *Chicago Tribune*; 25 May 1916]

Ford, **John** (1895–1973) US film director. Winner of six Academy Awards, he is best known for his work on classic Westerns, including *Stagecoach* (1939). Born **O'Fearna, Sean Aloysius**

> 'It is easier to get an actor to be a cowboy than to get a cowboy to be an actor.'
> [Attributed to John Ford]

Forde /fawrd/, **Frank** (1890–1983) Australian politician. He was briefly a caretaker prime minister of Australia in July 1945 after the death of John Curtin. Full name **Forde, Francis Michael**. See table at **prime minister**

fore /fawr/ *adj* AT FRONT having a position at or near the front of something, especially of a ship, an aircraft, or an animal ■ *adv* TOWARDS FRONT at or towards the front, especially of a ship or aircraft ■ *n* FRONT the front of something, or something at the front (*literary*) ■ *interj* GOLF WARNING ABOUT GOLF BALL used to warn people that you are hitting a golf ball in their direction [Old English, 'before, previously' < Germanic] ◇ **to the fore** to a position of prominence or importance

fore- *prefix* **1.** before, earlier ○ *forejudge* **2.** front, in front ○ *forebrain* [Old English < *fore* (see FORE)]

fore-and-aft *adj* parallel to or running along the length of something, especially a ship

fore-and-after *n* a boat with a fore-and-aft rig

fore-and-aft rig *n* an arrangement of a ship's sails such that, when set, they are parallel to the length of the vessel

fore-and-aft sail *n* SAILING same as **gaffsail**

forearm[1] /fáwr aarm/ *n* the part of the human arm between the elbow and the wrist, or the corresponding part of an animal's foreleg

forearm[2] /fawr aárm/ (**-arms, -arming, -armed**) *vt* to prepare or arm somebody in advance

forearm smash *n* a blow struck with the forearm in wrestling

forebear /fáwr bair/, **forbear** *n* an ancestor, especially one who died a long time ago (*often used in the plural*) [15C. < FORE- + variant of obsolete *beer* 'somebody who is' < BE[1]]

USAGE See **forbear**[1].

forebode /fawr bód/ (**-bodes, -boding, -boded**) *vti* (*formal*) **1.** to be or give an advance warning of something that may happen, especially something

undesirable ○ *The gathering clouds foreboded a terrible storm.* **2.** to have a feeling that something bad is going to happen before it does —**foreboder** *n*

foreboding /fawr bṓding/ *n* **1.** PREMONITION a feeling that something bad is going to happen **2.** BAD OMEN a sign or warning that something bad is going to happen ■ *adj* OMINOUS indicating, warning, or suggesting that something undesirable is likely to happen —**forebodingly** *adv*

forebrain /fáwr brayn/ *n* the front section of the brain in adults, or the part furthest forward of the three parts of the brain in an embryo

forecaddie /fáwr kadi/ *n* in golf, a caddie who watches from the fairway to see where the balls land

forecast /fáwr kaast/ *vt* (**-casts, -casting, -casted, -cast** or **-casted**) **1.** SUGGEST WHAT WILL HAPPEN to predict or work out something that is likely to happen such as the weather conditions for the days ahead **2.** BE EARLY SIGN OF SOMETHING to be an advance indication of something that is likely or certain to happen ■ *n* **1.** WEATHER PREDICTION a prediction of weather conditions for the near future, usually broadcast on television or radio or printed in a newspaper ○ *Have you heard the forecast for tomorrow?* **2.** PREDICTION OF FUTURE DEVELOPMENTS an estimation or calculation of what is likely to happen in the future, especially in business or finance —**forecastable** *adj* —**forecaster** *n*

forecastle /fṓks'l/, **fo'c's'le** *n* **1.** the space at the front end of a ship below the main deck, traditionally where the crew's quarters were located **2.** a raised section of deck at the bow of a ship

forecheck /fáwr chek/ *vi* in ice hockey, to check a player of an opposing team in the opposition's defensive zone —**forechecker** *n*

foreclose /fawr klṓz/ (**-closes, -closing, -closed**) *v* **1.** *vti* END MORTGAGE to take away a mortgagee's right to redeem a mortgage, usually because payments have not been made ○ *The bank foreclosed on the property.* **2.** *vt* SHUT SOMEBODY OR SOMETHING OUT to bar or exclude somebody or something (*formal*) **3.** *vt* SETTLE SOMETHING BEFOREHAND to settle or resolve something in advance (*formal*) **4.** *vt* PREVENT SOMETHING to prevent or hinder something (*formal*) **5.** *vt* HOLD SOMETHING EXCLUSIVELY to have an exclusive right or claim to something (*formal*) [13C. < Old French *forclos,* past participle of *forclore* < Latin *foris* 'outside' + *claudere* 'shut, close'] —**foreclosable** *adj*

foreclosure /fawr klṓzhər/ *n* a legal process by which a mortgagee's right to redeem a mortgage is taken away, usually because of failing to make payments

forecourse /fáwr kawrss/ *n* a foresail, especially the lowest of a ship's foresails

forecourt /fáwr kawrt/ *n* **1.** an open area at the front of a building, especially one in front of a petrol station, hotel, or railway station **2.** the part of the court nearest the net or front wall in games such as tennis, badminton, and handball

foredeck /fáwr dek/ *n* the part of a ship's deck between the bridge and the forecastle

foredoom /fawr dóom/ (**-dooms, -dooming, -doomed**) *vt* to condemn something or somebody in advance to failure or destruction (*formal; usually passive*)

fore-edge *n* the outer edge of a printed page

forefather /fáwr faathər/ *n* (*often used in the plural*) **1.** a male ancestor, usually one who died long ago (*literary*) ○ *in the proud tradition of our forefathers* **2.** a member of an earlier generation from whom traditions, values, or ideas have been inherited

forefeet ZOOL, NAUT plural of **forefoot**

forefend *vt* another spelling of **forfend** (*archaic*)

forefinger /fáwr fing gər/ *n* ANAT same as **index finger**

forefoot /fáwr fòot/ (*plural* **-feet** /-feet/) *n* **1.** either of the front feet of a four-legged animal **2.** the front end of a ship's keel

forefront /fáwr frunt/ *n* **1.** the most prominent, important, active, or responsible position in something **2.** the part at or nearest the front of something

foregather *vi* another spelling of **forgather** (*formal*)

forego[1] /fawr gṓ/ (**-goes, -going, -went** /-wént/, **-gone** /-gón/) *vti* to go or come before something in position, time, or sequence (*archaic*) —**foregoer** *n*

forego[2] *vt* another spelling of **forgo**

foregoing /fawr gṓ ing, fáwr gō ing/ (*formal*) *adj* going or coming before something, especially in speech or writing ■ *n* in speech or writing, the thing or things just mentioned (*takes a singular or plural verb*) ○ *As is evident from the foregoing, much remains to be done.*

foregone /fáwr gon/ *adj* **1.** previously completed or determined **2.** previous or former (*archaic*)

foregone conclusion *n* something that will inevitably happen as a result of something else

foreground /fáwr grownd/ *n* **1.** PART THAT APPEARS NEAREST the part of a picture or scene that appears nearest the viewer **2.** same as **forefront** (sense 1) ■ *adj* COMPUT CURRENTLY RECEIVING COMMANDS currently receiving commands, usually through the keyboard, while other programs are operating independently ○ *foreground processing* ■ *vt* (**-grounds, -grounding, -grounded**) HIGHLIGHT SOMETHING to put something in an important position and so draw attention to it

foregut /fáwr gut/ *n* the front end of the embryonic gut in animals. In vertebrates it develops into the pharynx, oesophagus, stomach, and top part of the intestines.

forehand /fáwr hand/ *n* **1.** STROKE IN RACKET GAMES in racket games, a basic stroke played with the palm of the racket hand facing forwards **2.** RIDING FRONT PART OF HORSE the part of a horse in front of the rider and saddle ■ *adj* PLAYED AS FOREHAND in racket games, played with the palm of the racket hand facing forwards, or relating to a stroke played in this way ■ *adv* RACKET GAMES WITH FOREHAND STROKE in racket games, with a forehand stroke or action ■ *vt* (**-hands, -handing, -handed**) PLAY BALL WITH FOREHAND STROKE in racket games, to hit the ball with a forehand stroke —**forehanded** /fáwr hándid/ *adj, adv* —**forehandedly** *adv* —**forehandedness** *n*

forehead /fórrid, fáwr hed/ *n* the part of the face above the eyebrows, below the hairline and between the temples

forehock /fáwr hok/ *n* a cut of bacon taken from the front leg, including the hock and knuckle and the part up to the collar

forehoof /fáwr hoof/ (*plural* **-hooves** /-hoovz/ or **-hoofs**) *n* the hoof of either of the two front legs of a four-legged animal (**quadruped**)

foreign /fórrin/ *adj* **1.** OF ANOTHER COUNTRY relating to, from, or located in a country or countries other than your own ○ *She speaks three foreign languages.* **2.** DEALING WITH ANOTHER COUNTRY dealing with or involved with a country or countries other than your own ○ *foreign policy* **3.** COMING FROM OUTSIDE introduced from outside into a place where it does not belong, often in the human body **4.** UNCHARACTERISTIC not usually associated with a particular person or thing ○ *Such outbursts are quite foreign to her nature.* **5.** IRRELEVANT not related or relevant (*formal*) ○ *observations that are foreign to the matter in hand* **6.** LAW BEYOND JURISDICTION being beyond the jurisdiction of an area or a country ○ *foreign waters* [13C. < Old French *forein* < Latin *foras, foris* 'out of doors, abroad' < *fores* 'door'] —**foreignly** *adv* —**foreignness** *n*

Foreign and Commonwealth Office *n* the official name of the Foreign Office in the United Kingdom

foreign bill *n* a bill of exchange that is issued in one country but payable in another

foreign body *n* an unwanted substance or object that is in a place where it does not belong, especially in somebody's body, often introduced from an external location and causing irritation or contamination

foreign correspondent *n* a journalist who sends news reports from other countries for broadcast or publication in his or her own country

foreign draft *n* FIN same as **foreign bill**

foreigner /fórrinər/ *n* **1.** somebody who comes from a country other than your own **2.** somebody who does not feel, or is not deemed to be, part of a group

foreign exchange *n* **1.** the currencies of countries other than your own, or international currencies generally **2.** the conversion of one currency into another, or the buying and selling of different currencies

foreign legion *n* a section of an army consisting of foreign volunteers, especially that of the French army

foreign minister *n* a minister in a government who is responsible for relations with other countries

foreign ministry *n* in many countries, the department of government responsible for relations with other countries

foreign mission *n* **1.** diplomatic personnel sent to represent their country abroad **2.** missionaries who try to convert the inhabitants of another country to Christianity or another religion

Foreign Office *n* in the United Kingdom and some other countries, the department of the government that is responsible for relations with other countries

foreign-returned *adj S Asia* having lived abroad, especially for education or training, and now back living in South Asia

Foreign Secretary *n* the cabinet minister in the UK government who is responsible for relations with other countries and is head of the Foreign and Commonwealth Office

foreign service *n* a country's diplomatic and consular staff, especially that of the United States

forejudge /fawr júj/ (**-judges, -judging, -judged**) *vti* to judge a matter before knowing all the facts or evidence (*formal*) —**forejudgment** *n*

foreknowledge /fawr nóllij/ *n* knowledge or awareness that something is going to happen, either from information that has been acquired, or by paranormal means

forelady /fáwr laydi/ (*plural* **-dies**) *n US* HR same as **forewoman** (sense 1)

foreland /fáwrlənd/ *n* **1.** HEADLAND a stretch of land that juts out into the sea or an estuary **2.** LAND IN FRONT land described in relation to what lies behind it, especially a plain in front of mountains **3.** ROCK IN FRONT OF MOUNTAINS a stable mass of rock that juts out in front of a mountain belt

Foreland /fáwrlənd/ either of two headlands, North Foreland and South Foreland, both of which have lighthouses, on the eastern coast of Kent, south-eastern England

foreleg /fáwr leg/ *n* either of the two front legs of a four-legged animal (**quadruped**)

forelimb /fáwr lim/ *n* either of the two front limbs of a four-limbed vertebrate, e.g. a flipper, arm, wing, or fin

forelock[1] /fáwr lok/ *n* **1.** a lock of hair that grows or falls over the forehead **2.** the part of a horse's mane that falls forward between its ears ◇ **tug your forelock** to show too much respect or deference for somebody in authority (*dated*)

forelock[2] /fáwr lok/ *n* a pin or wedge inserted through the end of a bolt to stop it being removed

foreman /fáwrmən/ (*plural* **-men** /-mən/) *n* **1.** a man who is in charge of a group of other workers, e.g. on a building site or in a factory **2.** somebody, especially a man, chosen by the other members of a jury to be their leader —**foremanship** *n*

foremast /fáwr maast/; *nautical usage* /fáwrməst/ *n* the mast nearest the front or bow of a vessel with two or more masts

foremilk /fáwr milk/ *n* the relatively low-fat milk with a high sugar content that is produced by a woman's breast at the beginning of a breast feed

foremost /fáwr mōst/ *adj* **1.** CHIEF most important or notable **2.** FARTHEST FORWARD nearest to the front ○ *the foremost section of the aircraft* ■ *adv* **1.** IN FIRST POSITION most importantly, or in the most important position ○ *a partner who will put your interests foremost* **2.** TO FRONT at or towards the front [Old English *formest* < *forma* 'first' + -EST[2], later interpreted as < FORE + -MOST]

foremother /fáwr muthər/ *n* a female ancestor, usually one who died long ago

forename /fáwr naym/ *n* same as **first name**

forenoon /fáwr noon/ *n* the period of time between dawn and noon or immediately before noon

forensic /fə rénssik, -rénzik/ *adj* **1.** relating to the application of science to decide questions arising

from crime or litigation ○ *forensic evidence* **2.** relating to debate and formal argumentation ○ *forensic oratory* [Mid-17C. < Latin *forensis* 'of legal proceedings' < *forum* 'forum' (as a place for discussion)] —**forensicality** /fə rénssi kálləti, -rénzi-/ *n* —**forensically** *adv*

forensic medicine *n* the branch of medicine that has a specifically legal purpose, e.g. in establishing the cause of a death

forensics /fə rénssiks, -rénziks/ *n* the practice or study of formal debate (*takes a singular or plural verb*)

foreordain /fáwr awr dáyn/ (**-dains, -daining, -dained**) *vt* to arrange or determine an event in advance of its happening —**foreordination** /fáwr awrdi náysh'n/ *n*

forepart /fáwr paart/ *n* **1.** the front part of something, or the part of something in front **2.** the first or early part of a given period of time

forepaw /fáwr paw/ *n* either of the two front feet of a land mammal that does not have hooves

forepeak /fáwr peek/ *n* the interior part of a boat or ship nearest the bow

foreperson /fáwr purss'n/ (*plural* **-persons** or **-people** /-peep'l/) *n* **1.** a skilled worker who is in charge of a group of other workers, e.g. on a building site or in a factory **2.** somebody chosen by the other members of a jury to be their leader

fore plane *n* a plane used in carpentry or joinery for preliminary smoothing, intermediate in size between a jack plane and a jointer

foreplay /fáwr play/ *n* mutual sexual stimulation that takes place before intercourse

forequarter /fáwr kwawrtər/ *n* half of the front half of a pork, lamb, or beef carcass ■ **forequarters** *npl* the front legs, shoulders, and adjoining parts of a horse or similar animal

forereach /fawr reéch/ (**-reaches, -reaching, -reached**) *v* **1.** *vti* to gain on or pass another sailing vessel, especially when sailing into the wind **2.** *vi* to continue moving in a ship after the sails have been taken down or the engine switched off

forerun /fawr rún/ (**-runs, -running, -ran** /-rán/, **-run**) *vt* **1.** to serve as an indication of or anticipate something that is to happen (*formal*) **2.** to go before something (*archaic*)

forerunner /fáwr runər/ *n* **1.** PREDECESSOR an earlier person or thing that had a role or function similar to somebody or something coming later ○ *the forerunner of the modern food processor* **2.** SOMEBODY OR SOMETHING SHOWING FUTURE somebody or something that brings news of or is an indication of what is to happen ○ *a forerunner of unsettled weather* **3.** ONE AHEAD OF OTHERS somebody or something that goes ahead of others, e.g. a skier who skis down a course just before the beginning of a race

foresail /fáwr sayl/; *nautical usage* /fáwrss'l/ *n* **1.** the main square sail on the front mast of a square-rigged boat **2.** the main or lowest triangular sail on a fore-and-aft-rigged vessel

foresee /fawr seé/ (**-sees, -seeing, -saw** /-sáw/, **-seen** /-seén/) *vti* to know or expect that something is going to happen before it does ○ *He couldn't have foreseen the consequences of his actions.* —**foreseeable** *adj* —**foreseeably** *adv* —**foreseer** *n*

foreshadow /fawr sháddō/ (**-ows, -owing, -owed**) *vt* to indicate or suggest something, usually something unpleasant, that is going to happen —**foreshadower** *n*

foreshank /fáwr shangk/ *n* **1.** the upper part of either of the two front legs of a four-legged animal (**quadruped**) **2.** a cut of meat taken from the foreshank of a lamb or sheep

foresheet /fáwr sheet/ *n* a rope used to keep a corner of a foresail in place ■ **foresheets** *npl* the part of an open boat that lies forward of the structural member used as the foremost rower's seat

foreshock /fáwr shok/ *n* a slight tremor or minor earthquake, often one of many and usually preceding a larger earthquake or volcanic eruption

foreshore /fáwr shawr/ *n* **1.** the part of a shore that lies between the highest and lowest watermarks **2.** the part of a shore between the high watermark and cultivated or economically exploited land

foreshorten /fawr sháwrt'n/ (**-ens, -ening, -ened**) *vt* **1.** in visual arts, to make something appear shorter than it actually is in order to create a three-dimensional effect on the basis of the laws of perspective **2.** to make a text shorter (*formal*)

foresight /fáwr sīt/ *n* **1.** ABILITY TO THINK AHEAD the ability to envisage possible future problems or obstacles **2.** PREMONITION an act or instance of knowing something beforehand **3.** LOOKING FORWARDS the act of looking forwards **4.** READING TAKEN IN SURVEYING in surveying, an observation or measurement made looking forwards **5.** FRONT GUNSIGHT the front sight on a gun —**foresighted** /fawr sītid/ *adj*

foreskin /fáwr skin/ *n* a fold of skin that covers the end of the penis

forest /fórrist/ *n* **1.** LARGE DENSE GROWTH OF TREES a large area of land covered in trees and other plants growing close together, or the trees growing on it **2.** WOODLAND FOR HUNTING especially in former times, an area of woodland owned by a monarch and set aside for hunting **3.** LARGE NUMBER OF UPRIGHT OBJECTS a collection of often tall upright objects, densely packed and so resembling a forest of trees ○ *a forest of microphones* ■ *vt* (**-ests, -esting, -ested**) CREATE FOREST ON LAND to plant an area with a large number of trees [13C. Via French < late Latin *forestis (silva)* 'outside (woods)' < *foris* 'out of doors' (see FOREIGN)] —**forestal** *adj* —**forested** *adj* —**forestial** /fə résti əl/ *adj*

forestall /fawr stáwl/ (**-stalls, -stalling, -stalled**) *vt* **1.** to prevent or hinder somebody from doing something, or something from happening, by acting in advance **2.** to stop or slow down sales of a product in a market by buying that product in large quantities beforehand [14C. < Old English *foresteall* 'ambush' < *steall* 'standing place' < Germanic] —**forestaller** *n* —**forestalment** *n*

forestation /fórri stáysh'n/ *n* the planting or incidence of trees over a large area

forestay /fáwr stay/ *n* a rope or cable (**stay**) extending from the head of the foremast to the deck of a ship and used for supporting the mast

forester /fórristər/ *n* **1.** MANAGER OF FOREST somebody engaged in forest management and conservation **2.** FOREST DWELLER a person or animal living in a forest (*archaic*) **3.** INSECTS WOODLAND MOTH a woodland moth that flies by day. Family: Zyglaenidae.

forest floor *n* the layer of organic matter on the ground in a forest

forest green *adj* of a dark green colour, like the foliage on a pine tree ○ *forest-green uniforms* —**forest green** *n*

forestland /fórrist land/ *n* a piece of land covered with trees or set aside for the cultivation of trees

forest park *n* in New Zealand, a large forested area that is open to the public and has some recreational facilities

forestry /fórristri/ *n* **1.** PLANTING AND GROWING OF TREES the science or skill of planting and growing trees or managing forests **2.** FOREST MANAGEMENT the management of forests for profitable ends such as timber production **3.** COMMERCIAL FORESTLAND forestland, especially that planted and commercially managed rather than growing naturally

foretaste /fáwr tayst/ *n* a sample or indication of what is to come ■ *vt* (**-tastes, -tasting, -tasted**) to have a sample or indication of what is to come

foretell /fawr tél/ (**-tells, -telling, -told** /-tṓld/) *vt* to predict what is going to happen, especially by means of supposed magic or supernatural powers (*literary*) —**foreteller** *n*

forethought /fáwr thawt/ *n* careful thought in order to be prepared for the future —**forethoughtful** /fawr tháwtf'l/ *adj* —**forethoughtfully** *adv* —**forethoughtfulness** *n*

foretoken (*literary*) *n* /fáwr tṓk'n/ a warning sign of what is to come ■ *vt* /fawr tṓk'n/ (**-kens, -kening, -kened**) to be or give a warning sign of what is to come

foretold past participle, past tense of **foretell**

foretop /fáwr top/; *nautical usage* /fáwrtəp/ *n* a platform at the top of a ship's foremast

fore-topgallant *adj* relating to the section of a mast directly above the foremast

fore-topmast *n* the mast above the platform at the top of a ship's foremast

fore-topsail *n* a sail attached to the mast above the platform at the top of a ship's foremast

forever /fər évvər/ *adv* **1.** *also* **for ever** FOR ALL TIME for all future time **2.** *also* **for ever** FOR VERY LONG TIME for a very long or seemingly endless time (*informal*) ○ *It's going to take me forever to finish this.* **3.** CONSTANTLY regularly or constantly, and often annoyingly (*informal*) ○ *chattered forever* **4.** AT ALL TIMES at all times or on every occasion (*literary*) ○ *From that moment on, she was forever careful.*

forevermore /fər évvər máwr/, **for evermore** *adv* from now on and for all time (*literary*)

~~**foreward**~~ incorrect spelling of **forward**

forewarn /fawr wáwrn/ (**-warns, -warning, -warned**) *vt* to warn somebody about something that is going to happen (*often passive*) —**forewarner** *n* —**forewarningly** *adv*

forewent past tense of **forego**[1]

forewing /fáwr wing/ *n* either of the pair of front wings on a four-winged insect

forewoman /fáwr wŏŏmən/ (*plural* **-women** /-wimin/) *n* **1.** a woman who is in charge of a group of workers, e.g. on a building site or in a factory **2.** a woman chosen by the other members of a jury to be their leader

foreword /fáwr wurd/ *n* an introductory note, essay, or chapter in a book, often written by somebody other than the author

forex *abbr* FIN foreign exchange

foreyard /fáwr yaard/ *n* the lowest spar for supporting a sail on a foremast

Forfar /fáwrfər/ market town and administrative centre in Angus council area, eastern Scotland. Population: 12,961 (1991).

forfeit /fáwrfit/ *n* **1.** GIVING SOMETHING UP the act or an instance of giving something up or being deprived of something as a punishment **2.** PENALTY FOR WRONGDOING something that is taken away as a punishment or has to be given up to make up for a mistake or wrongdoing **3.** PENALTY FOR BREAKING LAW something that is taken away as a penalty for breaking a law or contract **4.** PENALTY IN GAME an object that a player must give up or a task that a player must perform as a penalty in a game ■ *adj* TAKEN AWAY AS PUNISHMENT taken away or given up as a punishment for a mistake or wrongdoing ■ *vt* (**-feits, -feiting, -feited**) **1.** BE DEPRIVED OF SOMETHING to lose something or have something taken away as punishment for a mistake or wrongdoing ○ *forfeit the right to your inheritance* **2.** GIVE SOMETHING UP to give something up willingly in order to pursue or obtain something else ○ *forfeited his peerage for a seat in the House of Commons* **3.** TAKE SOMETHING AWAY AS PENALTY to take something away as a penalty for breaking a law or contract [13C. < Old French *forfet*, past participle of *forfaire* 'commit a crime', literally 'do beyond' < *fors* 'beyond' < Latin *foris* (see FOREIGN)] —**forfeitable** *adj* —**forfeiter** *n*

forfeits /fáwrfits/ *n* a game in which a player must give something up or perform a task each time he or she commits a fault or loses a round (*takes a singular verb*)

forfeiture /fáwrfichər/ *n* **1.** something that has been taken away or has had to be given up as a penalty for breaking a law or contract **2.** the act of forfeiting something

forfend /fawr fénd/ (**-fends, -fending, -fended**), **forefend** *vti* to protect or secure against something happening (*archaic*) ○ *Heaven forfend that I should end up like that!*

~~**forfiet**~~ incorrect spelling of **forfeit**

forgather /fawr gáthər/ (**-ers, -ering, -ered**), **foregather** *vi* (*formal*) **1.** ASSEMBLE AS GROUP to come together as a group **2.** MEET BY CHANCE to meet, usually by chance **3.** ASSOCIATE to spend time socially with somebody [15C. < Dutch *vorgaderen* 'meet, assemble', altered after GATHER]

forgave past tense of **forgive**

forge[1] /fawrj/ *n* **1.** METAL WORKSHOP a workshop where metal is heated and shaped into objects by ham-

mering **2.** FURNACE FOR HEATING METAL a furnace used to heat metal to a very high temperature **3.** MACHINE FOR HAMMERING METAL a machine with two tool faces that are brought together to hammer pieces of metal into specific shapes ■ *v* (**forges, forging, forged**) **1.** *vti* MAKE ILLEGAL COPY OF SOMETHING to make or produce an illegal copy of something so that it looks genuine, usually for financial gain **2.** *vt* ESTABLISH SOMETHING WITH EFFORT to establish and strive to develop something with great effort ○ *forge a durable relationship with the community* **3.** *vt* SHAPE METAL to shape or form metal by heating and hammering it [13C. < French *forger* 'make' < Latin *fabricare* (see FABRICATE)] —**forgeability** /fáwrjə bílləti/ *n* —**forgeable** *adj* —**forger** *n*

forge[2] /fawrj/ (**forges, forging, forged**) *vi* **1.** to move forward with a sudden increase of speed ○ *forging past the runner on the inside* **2.** to move slowly and steadily ○ *'We were forging through a narrow passage, rock-lined, and tube-like.'* (Edgar Rice Burroughs, *The Gods of Mars*; 1913) [Mid-18C. Origin ?]

forge ahead *vi* to move forward rapidly or steadily and persistently

forgery /fáwrjəri/ (*plural* **-ies**) *n* **1.** the act of making or producing an illegal copy of something so that it looks genuine, usually for financial gain **2.** an illegal copy of something such as a document or painting that has been made to look genuine

forget /fər gét/ (**-gets, -getting, -got** /-gót/, **-gotten** /-gótt'n/) *v* **1.** *vti* NOT REMEMBER to fail or be unable to remember something, or to do something ○ *I'll never forget my first day at school.* ○ *Don't forget to call your mother.* **2.** *vt* LEAVE SOMETHING BEHIND to leave something behind accidentally ○ *I've forgotten my keys.* **3.** *vti* NEGLECT SOMEBODY OR SOMETHING to fail to give due attention to somebody or something ○ *Don't just disappear and forget us all.* **4.** *vt* STOP WORRYING ABOUT SOMETHING to stop thinking or worrying about somebody or something ○ *I'd just forget about it if I were you.* **5.** *vti* NOT MENTION SOMEBODY OR SOMETHING to fail to mention somebody or something **6. forget yourself** *vr* LOSE CONTROL to lose control of manners, emotions, or behaviour ○ *Oh dear, I'm forgetting myself! Let me take your coat.* [Old English *forgietan* 'miss your hold on' < Germanic] —**forgetter** *n* ◇ **forget it** (*informal*) **1.** used to let somebody know that something is not really very important and so not worth worrying about **2.** used to tell somebody that you are definitely not going to do something that has been suggested, proposed, or asked of you

SYNONYMS See ***overlook***.

forgetful /fər gétf'l/ *adj* **1.** tending to forget things **2.** not giving due attention to somebody or something (*formal*) ○ *forgetful of his contractual obligations* —**forgetfully** *adv* —**forgetfulness** *n*

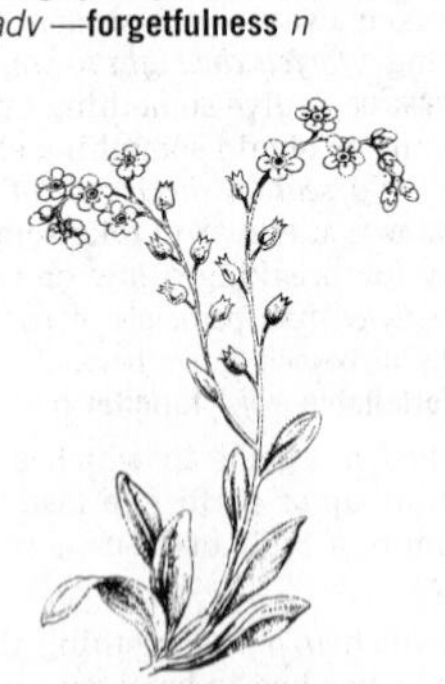

forget-me-not

forget-me-not *n* a small plant of the borage family. Flowers: small, delicate, pale blue. Genus: *Myosotis*. [Because worn by lovers]

forgettable /fər géttəb'l/ *adj* not easily remembered, or not worthy of being remembered

forgive /fər gív/ (**-gives, -giving, -gave** /-gáyv/, **-given** /-gívv'n/) *v* **1.** *vti* STOP BEING ANGRY ABOUT SOMETHING to stop being angry about or resenting somebody or somebody's behaviour **2.** *vt* PARDON SOMEBODY to excuse somebody for a mistake, misunderstanding, wrongdoing, or inappropriate behaviour **3.** *vt* CANCEL OBLIGATION to cancel an obligation such as a debt [Old English *forgiefan*, literally 'abstain from giving'] —**forgivable** *adj* —**forgivably** *adv* —**forgiver** *n*

forgiveness /fər gívnəss/ *n* **1.** the act of pardoning somebody for a mistake or wrongdoing **2.** the tendency to forgive offences readily and easily ○ *She had little forgiveness in her nature.* [Old English *forgiefenes*, literally 'forgiven-ness']

forgiving /fər gívving/ *adj* **1.** willing to forgive, especially in most circumstances **2.** allowing for or coping well with a degree of imprecision, lack of skill, or other imperfection —**forgivingly** *adv* —**forgivingness** *n*

forgo /fawr gṓ/ (**-goes, -going, -went** /-wént/, **-gone** /-gón/), **forego** *vt* to do without something, especially voluntarily ○ *forgo the comforts of home while travelling*

forgot past tense of **forget**

forgotten past participle of **forget**

~~**forhead**~~ incorrect spelling of **forehead**

~~**foriegn**~~ incorrect spelling of **foreign**

for instance *n* an example of something (*informal*) ○ *Give me a for instance.*

forint /fórrint/ *n* the main unit of Hungarian currency. See table at **currency** [Mid-20C. < Hungarian < Italian *fiorino* (see FLORIN)]

fork /fawrk/ *n* **1.** UTENSIL FOR EATING a small, usually metal utensil with a handle and two, three, or four prongs, used for eating or for preparing food **2.** GARDEN OR AGRICULTURAL TOOL a garden or agricultural tool with a handle and usually three or four prongs, used for digging, lifting, and turning over **3.** DIVIDING POINT IN ROAD OR RIVER the point where a road or river divides into two or more parts **4.** BRANCH OF ROAD OR RIVER one of the branches that a road or river divides into **5.** ENG PART OF MACHINE a part of a machine or device that has prongs or is fork-shaped **6.** CHESS CHESS POSITION a chess position in which two pieces are under attack from one of the opponent's pieces, usually the knight **7.** METEOROL FLASH OF LIGHTNING a branch or flash of the type of lightning that splits into two branches ■ *v* (**forks, forking, forked**) **1.** *vti* MOVE SOMETHING WITH FORK to carry, pick up, dig, or turn something over using a fork **2.** *vi* DIVIDE INTO TWO to split into two or more branches (*refers to roads and rivers*) **3.** *vi* GO ALONG FORK to take one of the branches that a road or river has divided into **4.** *vt* CAUSE SOMETHING TO BRANCH to make something into a shape that branches in two **5.** *vt* CHESS MOVE PIECE IN CHESS to position a chess piece so that it is threatening two of the opponent's pieces at the same time [Old English *forca*, via Germanic < Latin *furca* 'pitchfork'] —**forked** *adj* —**forker** *n* —**forkful** *n*

fork out, fork up *vti* to pay the money required for something, or spend a lot of money, often grudgingly (*informal*)

forkball /fáwrk bawl/ *n* in baseball, a pitch in which the ball is held between the spread index and middle finger. It usually dips sharply before reaching the batter. —**forkballer** *n*

forked lightning *n UK, ANZ, Can* lightning that appears as a jagged line of light splitting into two or more branches near the ground. US term **chain lightning**

forked tongue *n* a tongue that speaks lies or words that are insincere or misleading (*literary or humorous*)

forklift /fáwrk lift/ *n* **1.** a lifting device with two long rigid steel bars that can be raised and lowered, used especially to move pallets loaded with boxes or other goods **2.** VEHICLES same as **forklift truck** ■ *vt* (**-lifts, -lifting, -lifted**) to lift or move heavy loads using a forklift

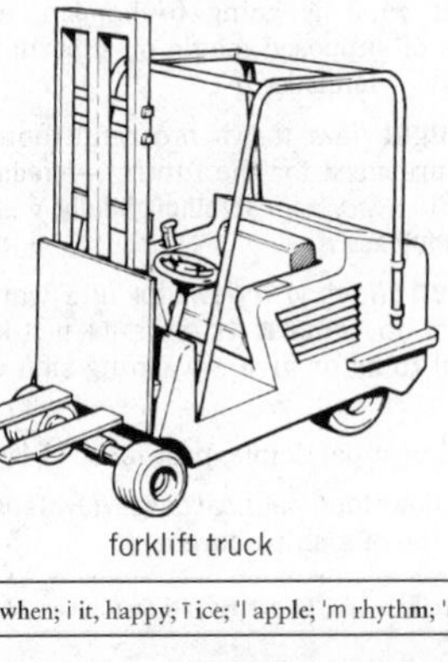

forklift truck

forklift truck *n* a small motor-driven vehicle equipped with a forklift, used especially in factories for moving goods on pallets

forklift upgrade *n* a major upgrade of a computer system or network necessitating a significant investment in new hardware and software

forlorn /fər láwrn, fawr-/ *adj* **1.** LONELY AND MISERABLE lonely and miserable, as though deserted or abandoned **2.** DESOLATE deserted or abandoned and showing signs of neglect **3.** HOPELESS desperate and doomed to failure (*literary*) [Old English *forloren*, past participle of *forlēosan* 'lose completely'] —**forlornly** *adv* —**forlornness** *n*

forlorn hope *n* **1.** a desperate or futile hope **2.** a desperate or doomed undertaking [By folk etymology < Dutch *forloren hoop* 'lost troop'; originally 'a group of soldiers sent on a hopeless mission']

form /fawrm/ *n* **1.** VARIETY OF SOMETHING a type of something that has various different types ○ *a rare form of cancer* **2.** MANIFESTATION the particular way that something is or appears to be ○ *bonuses in the form of extra days off* **3.** BASIC STRUCTURE the shape or structure of a thing that gives it its distinctive character, considered apart from its content, colour, texture, or composition **4.** SHAPE OF SOMETHING the shape or appearance of a thing that makes it identifiable ○ *a constellation in the form of a diamond* **5.** INDISTINCT SHAPE a shape like a person or other living thing that cannot be clearly made out ○ *a shadowy form in the distance* **6.** DOCUMENT a document, usually with blank spaces for answers or information to be supplied ○ *fill out the form* **7.** CONDITION OF SOMEBODY OR SOMETHING the condition of an organization, team, performer, athlete, or animal, with regard to fitness, health, and ability to perform well ○ *a violinist at the top of her form* **8.** TRACK RECORD the previous record of a horse, athlete, or team **9.** BEHAVIOUR behaviour or manners with reference to propriety ○ *It's considered bad form to cheat at games.* **10.** FORMULA a fixed set or order of words or procedures, e.g. in a religious ceremony or a legal document **11.** ARTS OUTLINE STRUCTURE the structure, design, or arrangement of a work of art or piece of writing, as opposed to its content **12.** ARTS MODE OF EXPRESSION a fixed mode of literary or musical expression ○ *a strict adherence to sonata form* **13.** ARTS, INDUST MOULD OR FRAME a mould, frame, or model within which or around which something can be shaped ○ *concrete forms* **14.** EDUC SCHOOL CLASS a class or year in a school **15.** CLOTHING HUMAN SHAPE a model of a human body or torso, used for fitting or displaying clothes **16.** FURNITURE BENCH a long low wooden seat or bench with no back rest **17.** *US* PRINTING same as **forme** **18.** ZOOL HARE'S LAIR the lair or nest in which a hare lives **19.** LING WORD IN RELATION TO ITS ROOT a word considered in relation to its root or the word it is derived from **20.** LING LOOK OR SOUND OF WORD the way a word is written or how it sounds, as opposed to its meaning **21.** BIOL SUBDIVISION OF SPECIES a subdivision of a species, ranking below variety, usually indicating a minor difference among members, e.g. in colour **22.** CRIMINAL RECORD recorded past criminal activity (*slang*) ■ *v* (**forms, forming, formed**) **1.** *vti* GIVE SHAPE TO SOMETHING to give a shape or arrangement to something, or take shape ○ *A circle of onlookers formed around the injured man.* **2.** *vti* START TO EXIST to cause something to develop or exist, or begin to develop or exist, especially as part of a natural process ○ *Crystals began to form at the bottom of the jar.* **3.** *vt* SET SOMETHING UP to establish or organize something ○ *form a task force to monitor the impact of deregulation* **4.** *vt* MAKE SOMETHING to make or construct something, often by arranging or combining component parts ○ *The plural is formed by adding an 's'.* **5.** *vt* CONCEIVE OF SOMETHING to develop an opinion, impression, or idea in the mind ○ *not enough information to form an opinion* **6.** *vt* CAUSE SOMETHING TO DEVELOP to influence somebody strongly through teaching, discipline, or example, and cause a particular personal development ○ *an early life in the country that formed his quiet nature* **7.** *vt* CREATE SOMETHING to acquire or establish and develop something intangible such as a habit or relationship ○ *considered forming an alliance* **8.** *vt* SERVE AS SOMETHING to constitute or be a basic element or characteristic of something ○ *a mountain range forming a natural boundary between the two countries* [13C. Via French < Latin *forma* 'mould, shape, beauty'] —**formable** *adj* ◇

take form to become visible, distinct, or discernible ○ *A plan started to take form in his mind.* ◇ **true to form** as could be expected judging from somebody's past behaviour ○ *True to form, they were exactly twenty minutes late.*

-form *suffix* having a particular form ○ *fibriform* [< Latin *forma* 'mould, shape, beauty']

formal /fáwrm'l/ *adj* **1.** OFFICIAL done or carried out in accordance with established or prescribed rules ○ *We made a formal protest.* **2.** CONVENTIONALLY CORRECT characterized by or organized in accordance with conventions governing ceremony, behaviour, or dress ○ *He's terribly formal and always calls me Mr Day.* **3.** METHODICAL done in an organized and precise manner ○ *formal research in artificial intelligence* **4.** NOT FAMILIAR IN STYLE used in serious, official, or public communication but not appropriate in everyday contexts ○ *a formal word* **5.** CLOTHING ELEGANT TO WEAR suitable for wearing for an important occasion, e.g. a jacket and tie for men and a full-length dress for women ○ *formal dress required* **6.** EDUC ACQUIRED IN SCHOOL OR COLLEGE undertaken or acquired by study in an educational institution ○ *no formal training as a journalist* **7.** ORDERED arranged or laid out in a regular, ordered, or symmetrical way ○ *a formal garden* **8.** OF FORM OR STRUCTURE relating to the form or structure of something **9.** OFFICIALLY CONSTITUTED officially constituted or organized as opposed to spontaneously developed ○ *a formal organization* **10.** LOGIC, MATHS SYMBOLIC relating to or using symbols and abstract structures rather than natural language **11.** PHILOSOPHY OF ESSENCE RATHER THAN CONTENT relating to the structure or essence of something rather than its content ■ *n N Am* SPECIAL CLOTHES an outfit of clothing for an important social occasion, especially a woman's full-length dress ○ *a new formal for the ball* [14C. < Latin *formalis* < *forma* 'mould, shape, beauty'] —**formally** *adv* —**formalness** *n*

formaldehyde /fawr máldi hīd/ *n* a colourless gas with a distinctive smell. Use: manufacture of resins and fertilizers, preservation of organic specimens. Formula: HCHO. [Late 19C. < FORMIC]

formalin /fáwrməlin/ *n* a solution of formaldehyde in water. Use: disinfectant, preservation of organic specimens. [Late 19C. < FORMALDEHYDE]

formalise *vti* another spelling of **formalize**

formalism /fáwrm'lizəm/ *n* **1.** EMPHASIS ON OUTWARD APPEARANCE a strong or excessive emphasis on outward appearance or form instead of content or meaning **2.** PHILOSOPHY, MATHS THEORY OF SYMBOLS the view that mathematical symbols are meaningless, though mathematical concepts and structures can be valuable **3.** THEATRE STYLIZATION stylization and emphasis on symbolism in theatrical productions —**formalist** *n* —**formalistic** /fáwrmə lístik/ *adj* —**formalistically** *adv*

formality /fawr mállәti/ (*plural* **-ties**) *n* **1.** FORMALNESS the quality or condition of being formal, or the degree to which something is formal ○ *dress to suit the formality of the occasion* **2.** OFFICIAL PROCEDURE an official procedure that must be followed as part of a longer procedure or event (*often used in the plural*) ○ *several formalities to complete at customs* **3.** NECESSARY BUT INSIGNIFICANT PROCEDURE a procedure that must be followed because it is a rule or custom, but has little significance or effect in itself ○ *just a formality* **4.** ATTENTION TO PROPRIETY strict or excessive attention to propriety or ceremony

formalize /fáwrmə līz/ (**-izes, -izing, -ized**), **formalise** (**-ises, -ising, -ised**) *vt* **1.** MAKE SOMETHING OFFICIAL to make something official or valid, e.g. by signing a document **2.** GIVE SHAPE TO SOMETHING to give a specific shape or form to something **3.** MAKE SOMETHING FORMAL to make something formal or more formal ○ *a formalized version of his earlier account* —**formalizable** *adj* —**formalization** /fáwrmə lī záysh'n/ *n* —**formalizer** *n*

formal logic *n* the branch of logic concerned with the formal methods of deducing conclusions from propositions

formal methods *npl* methods of specifying and evaluating computer systems using techniques from mathematics and logic

formant /fáwrmənt/ *n* a frequency range where vowel sounds are at their most distinctive and characteristic pitch [Early 20C. Via German < Latin *formant-*, present participle of *formare* < *forma* 'mould, shape, beauty']

format /fáwr mat/ *n* **1.** STRUCTURE the way in which something is presented, organized, or arranged ○ *change the format of the conference to accommodate more speakers* **2.** PUBL LAYOUT the layout and presentation of a publication, including its size and the paper and type used ○ *a small-format reference work* **3.** COMPUT DATA ORGANIZATION the structure or organization of digital data for storing, printing, or displaying ○ *files in ASCII format* ■ *vt* (**-mats, -matting, -matted**) **1.** ARRANGE LAYOUT OF SOMETHING to arrange the layout or organization of something **2.** COMPUT ORGANIZE DISK FOR DATA STORAGE to organize a disk in such a way that data can be stored on it [Mid-19C. Via French and German < Latin *formatus (liber)* '(book) shaped (in a special way)' < *formare* (see FORMANT)]

formate /fáwr mayt/ *n* any salt or ester of formic acid [Early 19C. < FORMIC]

formation /fawr máysh'n/ *n* **1.** DEVELOPMENT the process by which something develops or takes a particular shape ○ *a strong influence on the formation of her character* **2.** CREATION the process of creating something or coming into existence ○ *the formation of a bipartisan legislative committee* **3.** SHAPE OF SOMETHING the shape or structure that something develops into ○ *interesting cloud formations* **4.** FORMAL PATTERN the pattern into which a number of people or things are arranged ○ *Twelve planes flew past in formation.* **5.** GEOL ROCK UNIT a unit of rock consisting of a succession of strata or an igneous intrusion —**formational** *adj*

formation dance *n* a dance in which a line or circle of couples moves through a choreographed sequence of steps, often as a competition between teams —**formation dancing** *n*

formative /fáwrmətiv/ *adj* **1.** INFLUENTIAL important and influential, particularly in the shaping or development of character ○ *during their formative years* **2.** LING USED TO FORM WORDS relating to or used in the formation of derived words or inflected forms of words ■ *n* LING WORD-FORMING ELEMENT an element used in the formation of derived words or inflected forms of words, e.g. a suffix or prefix —**formatively** *adv*

formative assessment *n* the assessment at regular intervals of a student's progress with accompanying feedback in order to help to improve the student's performance

form class *n* **1.** GRAM same as **part of speech 2.** a group of words with one or more grammatical characteristics in common

form criticism *n* **1.** textual criticism that examines the literary conventions used in order to discover the origin and history of a text or its creators **2.** a method of analysing the Bible to determine the presumed original oral form of the written text by removing known historical conventions that emerged at a later period —**form critic** *n* —**form critical** *adj*

forme /fawrm/ *n* PRINTING a body of typographical elements assembled in a metal frame (**chase**) in preparation for printing [15C. Variant of FORM]

Formentera /fáwrmən táirə/ fourth largest of the Spanish Balearic Islands in the western Mediterranean Sea. Population: 5,435 (1998). Area: 81 sq. km/31 sq. mi.

former[1] /fáwrmər/ *adj* **1.** HAVING BEEN SOMETHING having had a particular name or status during an earlier period ○ *the former Soviet Union* **2.** PREVIOUS occurring at or existing in an earlier time or period ○ *met her on a former occasion* **3.** FIRST OF TWO being the first of two things or people mentioned **4.** PRECEDING earlier or near the beginning of a text or list ○ *a conclusion inconsistent with the argument in the former part of the paper* ■ *n* THE FIRST OF TWO the first of two things or people mentioned ○ *Smith and Brown both work here, the former is an accountant and the latter is an engineer.* [12C. < Old English *forma* 'first' < Germanic + ER]

former[2] /fáwrmər/ *n* **1.** SCHOOL STUDENT a member of a particular form or class in a school (*always used in combination*) ○ *a sixth former* **2.** SHAPER OF SOMETHING somebody or something that forms, creates, or shapes something (*usually in combination*) **3.** ELEC ENG SHAPING TOOL a tool used for giving the correct shape to an electrical coil or winding [14C. < FORM]

formerly /fáwrmərli/ *adv* during or at an earlier period, but no longer

Former Yugoslav Republic of Macedonia ➧ **Macedonia** (sense 1)

formestane /fawr méss tàyn/ *n* an oestrogen-blocking drug. Use: treatment of some breast cancers.

formfitting /fáwrm fitting/ *adj* fitting tightly around the contours of the body ○ *formfitting sportswear*

form genus *n* an artificial taxonomic category based on similarities that may be superficial. Imperfect fungi and fragmented plant fossils are grouped in form genera.

formic /fáwrmik/ *adj* **1.** relating to ants **2.** relating to or containing formic acid [Late 18C. < Latin *formica* 'ant']

Formica /fawr mīkə/ *tdmk* a trademark for a strong plastic laminate sheeting that is durable and easy to clean, and is often used to cover work surfaces

formic acid *n* a colourless corrosive liquid that occurs naturally in ants and some plants. Use: paper, textiles, insecticides, refrigerants. Formula: HCOOH.

formicary /fáwrmikəri/ (*plural* **-ies**), **formicarium** /fáwrmi káiri əm/ (*plural* **-ria** /-ri ə/) *n* an ant hill, including its subterranean passages (*technical*) [Early 19C. < medieval Latin *formicarium* < Latin *formica* 'ant']

formication /fáwrmi káysh'n/ *n* a neurologically based hallucination in which somebody feels as if insects are crawling on his or her skin. It is found in some cases of chemical toxicity and among drug and alcohol abusers. [Early 18C. < Latin *formication-* < *formicare* 'crawl like an ant' < *formica* 'ant']

formidable /fáwrmidəb'l, fər míddəb'l/ *adj* **1.** DIFFICULT TO DEAL WITH difficult to deal with or overcome ○ *a formidable task* **2.** AWE-INSPIRING inspiring respect or wonder because of size, strength, or ability ○ *a formidable display of skill* **3.** FRIGHTENING causing fear, dread, or alarm [14C. Directly or via French < Latin *formidabilis* < *formidare* 'to fear' < *formido* 'terror'] —**formidability** /fáwrmidə bílləti, fər míddə-/ *n* —**formidableness** *n* —**formidably** *adv*

USAGE The traditional pronunciation of ***formidable*** has the stress on the first syllable, but the alternative variant pronunciation, with the stress on the second syllable, is also heard.

formless /fáwrmləss/ *adj* **1.** SHAPELESS lacking a clear shape or structure ○ *a formless figure in the mist* **2.** DISORGANIZED lacking apparent organization or structure ○ *formless prose* **3.** NOT MATERIAL existing without a physical form ○ *formless beings* —**formlessly** *adv* —**formlessness** *n*

form letter *n* a printed letter that is sent out to a large number of people, e.g. one dealing with a frequently arising complaint, or one used in advertising

formula /fáwrmyŏŏlə/ (*plural* **-las** or **-lae** /-lee/) *n* **1.** PLAN a plan for or method of doing something ○ *agree on a peace formula to end fighting* **2.** METHOD OF DOING SOMETHING a prescribed and more or less invariable way of doing something to achieve a particular end **3.** ESTABLISHED FORM OF WORDS an established and recognized form of words, e.g. in a ceremony or legal document **4.** CHEM SET OF SYMBOLS REPRESENTING CHEMICAL COMPOSITION a representation of the composition of a chemical compound using symbols for the atoms of which it is composed **5.** MATHS, PHYS RULE EXPRESSED IN SYMBOLS a rule or principle represented in symbols, numbers, or letters, often in the form of an equation ○ *a formula for calculating the distance between planets* **6.** FOOD MILK FOR BABIES a preparation used as an alternative to human breast milk and intended to provide all the nutrients an infant requires **7. formula** (*plural* **-las**), **Formula** CATEGORY OF RACING CAR a category of racing car according to technical specifications such as engine capacity, size, and weight, used as a basis for professional competition (*usually used in combination*) ○ *formula one racing* [Early 17C. < Latin, 'little form' < *forma* 'mould, shape, beauty']

formulaic /fáwrmyŏŏ láy ik/ *adj* **1.** having the nature of or expressed in terms of a formula **2.** unoriginal

and reliant on previous models or ideas ○ *His writing is stilted and formulaic.* —**formulaically** *adv*

formularize /fáwrmyŏŏlə rīz/ (**-rizes, -rizing, -rized**), **formularise** (**-rises, -rising, -rised**) *vt* MATHS same as **formulate** (sense 3) —**formularization** /fáwrm yŏŏlə rī záysh'n/ *n* —**formularizer** *n*

formulary /fáwrmyŏŏləri/ *n* (*plural* **-ies**) **1.** PHARMACEUTICAL REFERENCE BOOK a reference book containing a list of pharmaceutical products with details of their use, preparation, properties, and formulas **2.** RELIGIOUS WRITINGS a book or collection of writings or procedures, especially ones connected with a church ■ *adj* OF FORMULA relating to or having the nature of a formula

formulate /fáwrmyŏŏ layt/ (**-lates, -lating, -lated**) *vt* **1.** DEVISE SOMETHING to draw something up carefully and in detail ○ *formulated his plan* **2.** EXPRESS SOMETHING WITH CARE to express or communicate something carefully or in specific words ○ *formulate an opinion* **3.** MATHS, PHYS EXPRESS SOMETHING IN FORMULA to express something by means of or as a formula —**formulation** /fáwrmyŏŏ láysh'n/ *n* —**formulator** *n*

formula weight *n* CHEM same as **molecular weight**

formulise *vt* another spelling of **formulize**

formulism /fáwrmyŏŏ lizəm/ *n* a belief in or reliance on formulas, especially inadequate or obsolete ones —**formulist** *n, adj* —**formulistic** /fáwrmyŏŏ lístik/ *adj*

formulize /fáwrmyŏŏ līz/ (**-lizes, -lizing, -lized**), **formulise** (**-lises, -lising, -lised**) *vt* MATHS same as **formulate** (sense 3) —**formulization** /fáwrmyŏŏ lī záysh'n, fáwrmyə-/ *n*

form word *n* GRAM same as **function word**

formwork /fáwrm wurk/ *n* a structure generally made of timber in which liquid concrete is placed, compacted, and allowed to harden

formyl /fáwr mīl/ *n* a chemical group containing carbon, hydrogen, and oxygen. Formula: HCO. [Mid-19C. < FORMIC]

Fornax /fáwr naks/ *n* a small constellation of the southern hemisphere. See illustration at **constellation**

fornicate[1] /fáwrni kayt/ (**-cates, -cating, -cated**) *vi* to have sexual intercourse outside marriage (*formal*) [Mid-16C. < ecclesiastical Latin *fornicat-*, past participle of *fornicari* < Latin *fornic-* 'arch, brothel' (because prostitutes in Rome solicited under building arches)] —**fornicator** *n*

fornicate[2] /fáwrnikət/, **fornicated** /-kaytid/ *adj* with an arched, vaulted, or bending form [Early 19C. < Latin *fornicatus* < *fornic-* 'arch, vault']

fornication /fáwrni káysh'n/ *n* **1.** sexual intercourse between two consenting adults who are not married to each other **2.** in the Bible, sexual intercourse between a man and woman who are not married, or any form of sexual behaviour considered to be immoral

fornix /fáwrniks/ (*plural* **-nices** /-ni seez/) *n* a structure or fold in the shape of an arch, especially either of two bands of white fibres in the brain [Late 17C. < Latin (stem *fornic-*), 'arch, vault']

Forrest /fórrist/, **Sir John, 1st Baron Forrest of Bunbury** (1847–1918) Australian explorer and politician. He was the leader of the first expedition to cross Australia from west to east. He subsequently became the first premier of Western Australia.

forsake /fər sáyk/ (**-sakes, -saking, -sook** /-sŏŏk/, **-saken** /-sáykən/) *vt* **1.** to withdraw companionship, protection, or support from somebody **2.** to give up, renounce, or sacrifice something that gives pleasure [Old English *forsacan* 'abstain from disputing'] —**forsaken** *adj* —**forsakenly** *adv* —**forsakenness** *n* —**forsaker** *n*

~~**forseeable**~~ incorrect spelling of **foreseeable**

forsooth /fər sŏŏth/ *adv* in truth (*archaic*) [Old English *forsoþ* 'for the truth']

Forster /fáwrstər/, **E. M.** (1879–1970) British novelist. He was the author of *A Room with a View* (1908), *Howards End* (1910), and *A Passage to India* (1924). Full name **Forster, Edward Morgan**. See Cultural note at **passage** [1], **view**

> 'The very poor are unthinkable and only to be approached by the statistician and the poet.'
> [E. M. Forster, *Howards End*; 1910]

forsterite /fáwrstə rīt/ *n* a magnesium silicate mineral of the olivine group [Early 19C. After J. R. *Forster* (1729–98), German naturalist]

Forster-Tuncurry /fáwrstər tun kúrri/ port and tourist centre on the northern coast of New South Wales, Australia, consisting of the twin towns of Forster and Tuncurry. Population: 15,943 (1996).

forswear /fawr swáir/ (**-swears, -swearing, -swore** /-swáwr/, **-sworn** /-swáwrn/) *v* (*archaic or literary*) **1.** *vt* to vow to stop doing, having, or using something ○ *forswear political violence* **2.** *vi* to be guilty of giving false evidence under oath [Old English *forswerian* 'renounce by swearing']

forsythia /fawr sīthi ə, fər-/ *n* a bush that flowers in early spring before its leaves emerge. Flowers: yellow. Genus: *Forsythia*. [Mid-19C. After William *Forsyth* (1737–1804), Scottish horticulturist]

fort /fawrt/ *n* **1.** a building or group of buildings with strong defences, usually strategically located and guarded by troops **2.** *N Am* a permanent military post consisting of several buildings ○ *Fort Bragg* [15C. Directly or via French < Italian *forte* 'strong (place)' < Latin *fortis* 'strong'] ◇ **hold the fort** to take charge of something in the absence of the person usually responsible (*informal*)

ORIGIN The Latin word *fortis* 'strong' from which **fort** is derived is also the source of English *forte*[1], *fortitude*, *fortress*, and *pianoforte*.

Fortaleza /fórtə létsə/ port and capital city of Ceará State, northeastern Brazil, situated at the mouth of the Paeju River on the Atlantic Ocean. Population: 1,965,513 (1996).

fortalice /fáwrtəliss/ *n* a small fort or part of the fortifications of a larger fort [15C. < medieval Latin *fortalitia* < Latin *fortis* 'strong']

forte[1] /fáwr tay, fawrt/ *n* **1.** something that somebody is particularly good at ○ *Cooking is not really my forte.* **2.** the strongest section of a sword's blade, between the middle and the hilt [Mid-17C. Via French *fort* 'strong' < Latin *fortis*; later influenced by FORTE [2]]

forte[2] /fáwr tay, fáwrti/ *adv* to be played or sung loudly (*used as a musical direction*) ■ *n* a note or passage of music played or sung, or to be played or sung, loudly [Early 18C. Via Italian, 'strong, loud' < Latin *fortis*] —**forte** *adj*

~~**forteen**~~ incorrect spelling of **fourteen**

fortepiano /fáwrti pi ánn ō/ (*plural* **-os**) *n* an early form of piano, especially a piano of the 18th century [Mid-18C. < Italian < *forte* 'loud' + *piano* 'soft']

forte-piano *adv* to be played or sung loudly and then suddenly softly (*used as a musical direction*) [Late 19C. < FORTE [2] + PIANO [2]] —**forte-piano** *adj*

forth /fawrth/ *adv* **1.** ONWARD forward in time, place, degree, or order (*formal*) ○ *from this day forth* **2.** INTO VIEW out into view (*formal*) ○ *brought forth the prisoner* **3.** ABROAD away from a particular place such as a country or region (*archaic*) [Old English *forþ* < Indo-European] ◇ **and so forth** used to indicate that there are more things of the kind just mentioned, without having to name them ○ *bottles, cans, jars, and so forth*

SPELLCHECK forth or **fourth**? Do not confuse the spelling of ***forth*** and ***fourth***, which sound similar. ***Forth*** is an adverb meaning 'forward', 'onwards', or 'out', as in *go forth, from that day forth, bring forth.* ***Fourth*** is a noun, adjective, and adverb referring to one of four parts or a position corresponding to the number four, as in *cut the pie into fourths, the fourth month of the year, come fourth in the race.*

Forth /fawrth/ river in southern Scotland that flows eastwards from Aberfoyle, Perth, and Kinross, to Alloa, where it widens to form the Firth of Forth. Length: 188 km/117 mi.

Forth, Firth of estuary of the River Forth in southeastern Scotland. It extends about 77 km/48 mi. eastwards from Alloa to the North Sea.

FORTH /fawrth/ *n* a high-level computer programming language used in scientific and industrial control applications [Late 20C. After the company that developed it]

forthcoming /fawrth kúmming/ *adj* **1.** FUTURE about to appear or happen ○ *plans for the forthcoming celebration* **2.** READY WHEN WANTED available when required or requested ○ *We were assured that the money would be forthcoming.* **3.** INFORMATIVE willing to talk or give information ○ *not very forthcoming about his personal life*

forthright /fáwrth rīt/ *adj* OUTSPOKEN direct in speech or manner and very honest ■ *adv* **1.** OUTSPOKENLY in a direct and very honest way ○ *answered the question forthright* **2.** IMMEDIATELY at once (*archaic*) —**forthrightly** *adv* —**forthrightness** *n*

forthwith /fáwrth wíth, -wí<u>th</u>/ *adv* without delay

fortieth /fáwrti əth/ *n* **1.** one of 40 equal parts of something **2.** somebody's 40th birthday —**fortieth** *adj, adv*

fortification /fáwrtifi káysh'n/ *n* **1.** STRUCTURE FOR DEFENCE a structure built in order to strengthen a place's defences, e.g. a wall, ditch, or rampart (*often used in the plural*) **2.** BUILDING OF DEFENCES the art or practice of strengthening or creating defences, e.g. by building walls or digging ditches **3.** PLACE THAT CAN BE DEFENDED a position or place that can be defended

fortified wine /fáwrti fīd-/ *n* a drink that is made from wine to which a strong alcohol such as grape brandy has been added, e.g. sherry, port, or Marsala. Fortified wines are usually drunk as aperitifs, digestifs, or liqueurs.

fortify /fáwrti fī/ (**-fies, -fying, -fied**) *vt* **1.** MAKE PLACE SAFER to make a place less susceptible to attack by building or creating defensive structures such as walls, ditches, or ramparts **2.** MAKE SOMETHING STRONGER to strengthen or reinforce the structure of something ○ *fortify a sea wall* **3.** ADD INGREDIENTS TO SOMETHING to add further ingredients to food or drink in order to improve its flavour or add nutrients (*usually passive*) ○ *breakfast cereal fortified with vitamins* **4.** ENCOURAGE SOMEBODY to give somebody physical, mental, or moral strength or encouragement **5.** MAKE SOMETHING MORE POWERFUL to make something more powerful or persuasive ○ *fortify an argument* [15C. Via French *fortifier* < late Latin *fortificare* 'make strong' < Latin *fortis* 'strong'] —**fortifiable** *adj* —**fortifier** *n* —**fortifyingly** *adv*

fortis /fáwrtiss/ *adj* describes a consonant that is produced with great muscular tension and pressure of breath, e.g. 'p' or 't' ■ *n* (*plural* **-tes**) a fortis consonant, e.g. 'p' or 't' [Early 20C. < Latin, 'strong']

fortissimo /fawr tíssimō/ *adv* extremely loudly (*used as a musical direction*) ■ *n* (*plural* **-mos** or **-mi** /-mee/) a passage of music, or an individual note or chord, played fortissimo [Early 18C. < Italian, 'loudest' < *forte* (see FORTE [2])] —**fortissimo** *adj*

fortitude /fáwrti tyood/ *n* strength and endurance in a difficult or painful situation [14C. Via French < Latin *fortitudo* 'strength, courage' < *fortis* 'strong'] —**fortitudinous** /fáwrti tyóodinəss/ *adj*

Fort Knox /fawrt nóks/ US military post and reservation in northern Hardin County, central Kentucky. It has been the location of the US Gold Depository since 1936. Area: 13350 sq. km/5155 sq. mi.

Fort Lauderdale /-láwdər dayl/ city and county seat of Broward County, southeastern Florida, situated on the Atlantic Ocean 40 km/25 mi. north of Miami. Population: 138,194 (2002 estimate).

fortnight /fáwrt nīt/ *n* a period of 14 days [Old English *feowertīne niht* 'fourteen nights']

fortnightly /fáwrt nītli/ *adj, adv* occurring once every 14 days ■ *n* (*plural* **-lies**) a publication that appears once every two weeks

FORTRAN /fáwr tran/ *n* the earliest high-level computer programming language [Mid-20C. Contraction of FORMULA + TRANSLATION]

fortress /fáwrtrəss/ *n* **1.** a fortified place with a long-term military presence, often including a town **2.** something that is impenetrable or acts as protection [14C. < Old French *forteresse* 'strong place' < Latin *fortis* 'strong']

fortuitous /fawr tyóo itəss/ *adj* **1.** happening by chance, especially giving rise to a fortunate outcome **2.** ⚠ bringing or indicating good fortune [Mid-17C. < Latin

fortuitus < *fors* 'chance, luck'] —**fortuitously** *adv* —**fortuitousness** *n*

USAGE fortuitous or **fortunate**? The word ***fortuitous*** means 'happening by chance', as in *a fortuitous encounter with my old roommate of 30 years ago, whom I hadn't seen since graduation.* Nowadays, it is frequently used in contexts where the chance event described has a fortunate outcome. An extended meaning, 'bringing or indicating good fortune', used in English at least since the 1920s, is controversial. Substitute ***fortunate*** for ***fortuitous*** when the meaning is 'lucky': *In a fortunate* [not *fortuitous*] *turn of events, the lost parcel was found and handed in by a passer-by.*

fortuity /fawr tyóo əti/ (*plural* **-ties**) *n* **1.** something that happens by chance or accident **2.** lucky chance or accident

fortunate /fáwrchənət/ *adj* **1. LUCKY** enjoying good luck **2. RESULTING FROM LUCK** happening as a result of good luck **3. BRINGING LUCK** bringing good luck [14C. < Latin *fortunatus* < *fortuna* 'fate, luck'] —**fortunateness** *n*

USAGE See *fortuitous*.

CULTURAL NOTE *A Fortunate Life*, an autobiography (1981) by Australian writer Albert Facey. This working man's account of his deprived childhood and subsequent involvement in many of the country's major events (World War I, the Depression, post-war unionism) is regarded as a classic story of an Australian Everyman.

fortunately /fáwrchənətli/ *adv* **1.** by lucky chance **2.** used to show that the speaker or writer is happy to be able to report something ○ *Fortunately, we've been given more time to finish the job.*

~~fortunatly~~ incorrect spelling of **fortunately**

fortune /fáwrchən/ *n* **1. GREAT WEALTH OR PROPERTY** a large amount of financial wealth or material possessions ○ *inherited the family fortune* **2. LARGE SUM OF MONEY** an extremely large amount of money (*informal*) ○ *That must have cost you a fortune.* **3.** also **Fortune FATE** chance, or the personification of chance, regarded as affecting human activities **4. LUCK** luck, especially good luck **5. DESTINY** somebody's personal destiny ○ *went to seek their fortune in other countries* ■ **fortunes** *npl* **LIFE'S UPS AND DOWNS** chance happenings throughout life that may turn out well or badly ○ *the fortunes of war* [13C. Via French < Latin *fortuna* 'fate, (good) luck']

fortune cookie *n* a Chinese biscuit folded and baked around a piece of paper on which a saying or a prediction of somebody's fortune is written. Fortune cookies are served in Chinese restaurants, especially in the United States.

fortune hunter *n* somebody who seeks riches, especially by attempting to marry a wealthy partner (*disapproving*) —**fortune hunting** *n* —**fortune-hunting** *adj*

fortune teller *n* somebody who predicts the future, e.g. by reading palms or using tarot cards —**fortune-telling** *n* —**fortune-telling** *adj*

Fort Wayne /-wáyn/ city in northeastern Indiana, southeast of Elkhart. The St Joseph, St Marys, and Maumee rivers run through the city. Population: 210,070 (2002 estimate).

Fort William /-wílyəm/ town at the foot of Ben Nevis, western Scotland. It is situated on the shore of Loch Eil, in the Great Glen. Population: 10,391 (1991).

Fort Worth /-wúrth/ city and county seat of Tarrant County in northeastern Texas, situated on the Trinity River, west of Dallas. Historically known for its stockyards, it is a major industrial centre. Population: 567,516 (2002 estimate).

forty /fáwrti/ *n* (*plural* **-ties**) **1. 40** the number 40 **2. GROUP OF 40** a group of forty objects or people **3. TENNIS POINT** in a game of tennis, the score awarded to a player with a score of thirty on winning a further point ■ **forties** *npl* **1. NUMBERS 40 TO 49** the numbers 40 to 49, particularly as a range of temperature **2. YEARS FROM 40 TO 49** the years from 40 to 49 in a century **3. PERIOD FROM AGE 40 TO 49** the period of somebody's life from the age of 40 to 49 [Old English *feowertig* < FOUR + -*tig* 'ten'] —**forty** *adj, pron*

forty-five *n* **1.** a record smaller than an LP that is played at 45 revolutions per minute **2.** also **.45** *N Am* a pistol with a .45 calibre

Forty-Five *n* the Jacobite Rebellion of 1745 to 1746

fortyish /fáwrti ish/ *adj* **1.** approximately 40 in number **2.** about the age of 40

forty-niner /-nínər/ *n* a prospector in the gold rush of 1849 in California

forty-ninth parallel *n* the border between the United States and Canada, that runs at 49° latitude along most of its length

fortysomething /fáwrti sumthing/ *n* somebody between 40 and 49 years of age (*informal*) ■ *adj* between 40 and 49 years of age

forty winks *n* a short sleep (*informal*; *takes a singular or plural verb*)

forum /fáwrəm/ (*plural* **-rums** or **-ra** /-rə/) *n* **1. PLACE TO EXPRESS YOURSELF** a medium in which the public may debate an issue or express opinions, e.g. a magazine or newspaper **2. MEETING FOR DISCUSSION** a meeting to discuss matters of general interest **3. INTERNET DISCUSSION GROUP** an Internet discussion group for participants with common interests **4. LAW COURT** a law court or tribunal **5. PUBLIC SQUARE IN ROMAN CITIES** in ancient Rome, a public square or marketplace in a city where business was conducted and the law courts were situated [15C. < Latin, 'enclosed space around a house, marketplace' < *foris* 'out of doors']

forward (**-wards, -warding, -warded**) CORE MEANING: to or towards a front position or direction ○ (adv) *Conover pushed his cup forward, but Johnny ignored it.* ○ (adj) *Most of the energy in petrol makes engines hot; less than half gets converted to forward motion.* **1.** *adv* also **forwards** /-wərdz/ **AHEAD** to or towards what is ahead in space or time ○ *He sprang forward and embraced his grandmother.* **2.** *adv* also **forwards PROGRESSING** towards a goal ○ *The company has taken a step forward in employee safety.* **3.** *adv* also **forwards INDICATES IMPROVEMENT** indicates that something progresses or improves ○ *The EU is moving forward on monetary union.* **4.** *adv* **forward** in UK nautical use also /fórrəd/, **forwards** in UK nautical use also /fórrədz/ **NAUT TO FRONT OF VESSEL** towards the front of a boat or ship ○ *I was ordered forward to swab the deck.* **5.** *adv* also **forwards TOWARDS FRONT** towards the front of something such as an aircraft or a building ○ *I'd like to be seated further forward.* **6.** *adv* also **forwards TO PUBLIC ATTENTION** from obscurity into public view ○ *The unknown actor came forward and accepted the lead role.* **7.** *adj* **AHEAD** directed towards what is ahead in space and time ○ *The magnetic field exerts a forward force on charged particles.* **8.** *adj* **RELATING TO FUTURE** directed towards a future goal ○ *forward planning* **9.** *adj* **NAUT AT FRONT OF VESSEL** situated at or near the front of a boat or ship ○ *the forward deck* **10.** *adj* **AT FRONT** situated at or near the front of something such as an aircraft or a building ○ *The forward seats are the most popular.* **11.** *adj* **UNRESTRAINED IN BEHAVIOUR** behaving boldly in defiance of moral or social restraints ○ *I'm not sure I approve of her behaviour – she's very forward.* **12.** *n* **SPORTS ATTACKING PLAYER** in some team sports such as football, rugby, hockey, or basketball, an attacking player **13.** *vt* **REDIRECT MAIL** to send on mail from the address to which it was originally sent ○ *She was anxious to know if any letters might have come that had not been forwarded to her.* **14.** *vt* **ADVANCE OR PROMOTE SOMETHING** to assist the progress of something ○ *I will do anything you like if it means we can forward your cause.* [Old English *foreweard* 'in the direction of the front' < *fore* (see FORE)] —**forwardly** *adv* —**forwardness** *n*

USAGE See *towards*.

forward bias *n* a voltage applied to a semiconductor or a junction in a semiconductor, in a direction to cause a higher current to flow. ◊ **reverse bias**

forwarder /fáwrwərdər/ *n* a person or company whose business is the collection, shipment, and delivery of goods

forwarding /fáwrwərding/ *n* the collection, shipment, and delivery of goods

forwarding address *n* a new address to which mail is to be redirected

forward-looking *adj* planning for or looking ahead to the future

forward market *n* a financial market in which contracts are entered for the purchase and sale of

commodities and stocks that are to be delivered at a future date

forward pass *n* **1.** in rugby, an illegal pass in which the ball goes forward **2.** in American football, a pass thrown from a position behind the line of scrimmage in the direction of the opposing team's goal

forward pocket *n* in Australian Rules football, either of two players occupying positions in the front line of attack, on either side of the full forward

forward roll *n* in gymnastics, a movement in which the body is rolled over in a forward direction, placing the head on the ground and bringing the feet over the head

forwards *adv* same as **forward**

forward slash *n* COMPUT, PRINTING same as **slash** *n* (sense 4)

USAGE See *slash*.

forward-stepped *adj* describes a mast positioned in the front of the boat

forward voltage *n* ELEC ENG same as **forward bias**

Fosbury flop /fózbəri-/ *n* in the high jump, a technique in which the contestant clears the bar with the back of the shoulders followed by the arched body [Mid-20C. After Richard (Dick) *Fosbury* (b. 1947), US athlete]

foscarnet /foss káarnət/ *n* an antiviral drug. Use: treatment of a type of herpes.

fossa[1] /fóssə/ (*plural* **-sae** /-see/) *n* a hollow, pit, or groove in a part of the body such as in a bone [Mid-17C. < Latin, 'ditch' (see FOSSE)]

fossa[2] /fóssə/ (*plural* **-sas** or **-sa** /-see/) *n* a slender reddish-brown carnivorous animal that resembles a cat, has sharp retractile claws, and feeds on small animals, birds, and insects. Native to: Madagascar. Latin name: *Cryptoprocta ferox*. [Mid-19C. < Malagasy *fosa*]

fosse /foss/ *n* a wide ditch, usually filled with water and used for defence [Pre-12C. Via French < Latin *fossa* < *fodere* 'dig']

Fosse /fóssi/, **Bob** (1927–87) US dancer, choreographer, and director. He won his first Tony Awards for his imaginative dance sequences in the Broadway musicals *Pajama Game* (1953) and *Damn Yankees* (1955), and he directed the Academy Award-winning films *Cabaret* (1972) and *All That Jazz* (1980). Full name **Fosse, Robert Louis**

> 'I've been accused of editing too much. But audiences get bored so quickly.'
> [Bob Fosse, *Cue*; 1 February 1980]

Fosse Way /fóss-/ Roman road in England that starts in Axminster, Devon, and runs northeastwards to Lincoln. Length: 300 km/200 mi.

fossick /fóssik/ (**-sicks, -sicking, -sicked**) *vi* ANZ **1.** to rummage or look for something ○ *She fossicked around in the drawer for the key.* **2.** to search for gold or gems in mines or streams that have already been worked [Mid-19C. < English dialect, 'ferret out, get by asking', origin ?] —**fossicker** *n*

fossil: trilobite

fossil /fóss'l/ *n* **1. PRESERVED REMAINS OF ANIMAL OR PLANT** the remains of an animal or plant preserved from an earlier era inside a rock or other geological deposit, often as an impression or in a petrified state **2. SOMEBODY WHO WILL NOT CHANGE** somebody regarded as old-fashioned and unwilling to change (*informal*

insult) **3. SOMETHING OUTDATED** something that has outlived its usefulness, e.g. a discredited theory **4. LING OLD WORD NOW USED SPECIFICALLY** a word or part of a word that was once used generally but now survives only in a few contexts, e.g. *couth* in *uncouth* [Mid-16C. Via French *fossile* < Latin *fossilis* 'dug up' < *fodere* 'dig']

fossil fuel *n* any carbon-containing fuel derived from the decomposed remains of prehistoric plants and animals, e.g. coal, peat, petroleum, and natural gas

fossiliferous /fóssi líffərəss/ *adj* describes a rock or other geological deposit that has fossils within it

fossilize /fóssə līz/ (-izes, -izing, -ized), **fossilise** (-ises, -ising, -ised) *vti* **1.** to convert something into a fossil, preserve something as a fossil, or become a fossil **2.** to become outdated, fixed, or unchanging, or make somebody or something incapable of change —**fossilizable** *adj* —**fossilization** /fóssə līzáysh'n/ *n* —**fossilized** *adj*

fossil water *n* water in underground strata that has accumulated over millions of years and is therefore not a renewable resource, unlike other ground water

fossorial /fo sáwri əl/ *adj* describes animals that have large forelimbs or other adaptations for digging and burrowing, or to describe the parts of the body used for this purpose [Mid-19C. < medieval Latin *fossorius* < Latin *fossor* 'digger' < *fodere* 'dig']

foster /fóstər/ *v* (-ters, -tering, -tered) **1.** *vti* **REAR CHILD WHO IS NOT YOURS** to look after or bring up somebody else's child when it cannot live with its own parents, often for a short period of time, in exchange for payment by a local authority **2.** *vt* **ARRANGE CARE FOR CHILD** to put a child temporarily in the care of adults who are not its parents **3.** *vt* **NURTURE CHILD** to provide a child with care and upbringing **4.** *vt* **DEVELOP SOMETHING** to encourage the development of something **5.** *vt* **KEEP ALIVE FEELING OR THOUGHT** to keep a feeling or thought alive ■ *adj* **PROVIDING OR RECEIVING PARENTAL CARE** giving or receiving a home and parental care and upbringing, usually on a short-term basis, although unrelated by blood or adoption. Foster care is provided for children whose natural parents are dead, absent, or unfit or unable to look after them. ○ *a foster child* [Old English *fostrian* 'nourish, raise a child' < *foster* 'food' < Germanic] —**fosterer** *n*

Foster /fóstər/, **David** (*b.* 1944) Australian novelist. His works include *Moonlite* (1981) and *The Glade Within the Grove* (1996).

Andrew Ward

Sir Norman Foster

Foster, Norman, Baron Foster of Thames Bank (*b.* 1935) British architect. His designs such as the terminal building (1991) for Stansted Airport, Essex combine elegant forms with complex engineering and technologically advanced materials. He won the Pritzker Architecture Prize in 1999. Full name **Foster, Norman Robert**

fosterage /fóstərij/ *n* **1. CARING FOR ANOTHER'S CHILD** the act of looking after or bringing up a child who is unrelated by blood or adoption, often on a short-term basis and in exchange for payment by a local authority **2. BEING FOSTER CHILD** the process of being looked after or brought up in a home by parents who are unrelated by blood or adoption **3. ENCOURAGING DEVELOPMENT** the process of encouraging the development of something beneficial

fosterling /fóstərling/ *n* a child who is fostered (*archaic or literary*)

~~fotograph~~ incorrect spelling of **photograph**

fou /foo/ *adj Scotland* extremely drunk (*informal*) [Mid-16C. Alteration of FULL [1]]

Foucault /fóokō/, **Jean-Bernard Léon** (1819–68) French physicist. He helped devise a way of calculating the speed of light and proved that it travelled more slowly through water than through air. He demonstrated the Earth's rotation by suspending a pendulum from the ceiling of the Panthéon dome, Paris (1851).

Foucault, Michel (1926–84) French philosopher. He showed how ideas of truth about human nature change in the course of history. His chief works were *Madness and Civilization* (1960), *The Order of Things* (1966), and *Discipline and Punish* (1975).

'Psychology can never tell the truth about madness because it is madness that holds the truth of psychology.'
[Michel Foucault, *Mental Illness and Psychology*; 1976]

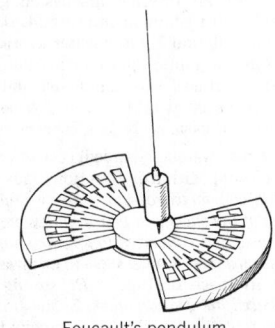
Foucault's pendulum

Foucault's pendulum /fóokōz-/ *n* a heavy free-swinging pendulum suspended by a long thin wire, whose plane of motion appears to change as Earth rotates [Mid-19C. After Jean-Bernard Léon FOUCAULT]

fouetté /fwéttay, foo ə tay/ *n* a ballet step in which the dancer stands on one foot and moves the other leg quickly out and in again, often while doing a pirouette [Mid-19C. < French, past participle of *fouetter* 'whip']

fought past participle, past tense of **fight**

foul /fowl/ *adj* **1. DISGUSTING** disgusting to the senses ○ *brackish, foul-tasting water* ○ *a foul smell* **2. FILLED WITH DIRT** clogged with dirt or so obstructed as to be unusable ○ *a foul pipe* **3. DIRTY** covered in dirt **4. CONTAMINATED** contaminated by impurities ○ *foul city air* **5. UNPLEASANT** extremely unpleasant or disagreeable in nature (*informal*) ○ *in a foul mood* **6. VULGAR** obscene or otherwise offensive in expression or behaviour ○ *foul language* **7. ILLEGAL IN SPORT** contrary to the rules of a sport **8. DISHONEST** behaving in an unfair and unacceptable way ○ *suspected of having got rich by foul means* **9. INCLEMENT** stormy or wet and unpleasant for outdoor activities **10. ROTTEN** decaying and rotten **11. EVIL** spiritually or morally vicious **12. ENSNARLED** entangled with something and unable to move ○ *a foul anchor line* ■ *n* **1. ILLEGAL ACTION IN SPORT** an illegal action against an opposing player, or an action that breaks the rules of a sport **2. ENTANGLEMENT PREVENTING MOVEMENT** an entanglement or collision that prevents movement ■ *v* (**fouls, fouling, fouled**) **1.** *vti* **ACT ILLEGALLY IN SPORT** to act illegally against an opposing player, or violate a rule of a sport **2.** *vti* **ENSNARL AND PREVENT MOVEMENT** to entangle or catch something so that it cannot move, or become entangled or caught and unable to move ○ *careful not to foul her fishing line* **3.** *vti* **OBSTRUCT OR BECOME OBSTRUCTED** to clog or block something, or become clogged or blocked **4.** *vt* **MAKE SOMETHING DIRTY** to make something dirty, especially by defecation **5.** *vt* **BRING SHAME ON SOMEBODY** to bring disgrace to a person or to somebody's reputation [Old English *ful* 'filthy, decaying' < Germanic] —**fouler** *n* —**foully** *adv* —**foulness** *n*

SPELLCHECK foul or fowl? Do not confuse the spelling of *foul* and *fowl*, which sound similar. *Foul* is used as an adjective meaning 'unpleasant' or 'vulgar' (as in *foul weather*, *foul language*) or as an adjective, verb, or noun referring to dirtiness, illegal action in sport, or entanglement preventing movement. *Fowl* is only used as a noun, denoting an edible bird or game bird.

foul up *vti* **1.** to do something badly or incompetently, or be bungled or mismanaged (*informal*) **2.** to clog or entangle something, or become clogged or entangled

foulard /fóo laar, -laard/ *n* **1.** a soft silk or rayon fabric, usually patterned **2.** something made of foulard, especially a scarf or handkerchief [Mid-19C. < French]

foul ball *n* in baseball, a struck ball that lands outside a foul line

foul line *n* **1. DESIGNATED LIMIT OF PLAY** in some sports, a boundary beyond which a ball or player is not permitted, e.g. the line in ten-pin bowling where the player must stop before releasing the ball **2. BASKETBALL LINE FOR FREE THROWS** in basketball, either of two lines on a court from which players get unobstructed chances to score a basket after they have been fouled **3. BASEBALL LINE SHOWING FAIR OR FOUL BALL** in baseball, either of the lines extending from home plate through first and third bases to the end of the playing field

foul-mouthed *adj* using obscene or otherwise offensive language, especially habitually

foul play *n* **1. UNFAIRNESS** unfair action or behaviour **2. CRIME** treachery or criminal violence **3. ACTION AGAINST RULES** action that is contrary to the rules of a sport

foul shot *n N Am* BASKETBALL same as **free throw**

foul-up *n* a blunder, or the confusion or failure that results from a blunder (*informal*)

found[1] /fownd/ (**founds, founding, founded**) *vt* **1.** to establish and organize something for the future such as an institution or business **2.** to support something such as a conclusion with evidence or reasoning [13C. Via French *fonder* < Latin *fundare* < *fundus* 'bottom, base']

found[2] /fownd/ (**founds, founding, founded**) *vt* **1.** to form something, especially metal or glass, by melting it and pouring it into a mould **2.** to produce objects such as machine parts by melting metal or glass and pouring it into moulds [14C. Via French *fondre* 'dissolve and blend' < Latin *fundere* 'pour, melt']

found[3] past participle, past tense of **find**

foundation /fown dáysh'n/ *n* **1. SUPPORT FOR BUILDING** a part of a building, usually below the ground, that transfers and distributes the weight of the building onto the ground (*often used in the plural*) **2. SUPPORT FOR IDEA** the basis of something such as a theory or an idea **3. COSMETICS BASE LAYER OF MAKE-UP** a cosmetic in liquid, cream, or cake form, usually coloured, that is applied as a base for make-up **4. ESTABLISHMENT OF INSTITUTION OR ORGANIZATION** the setting up of an institution or organization **5. CHARITABLE OR EDUCATIONAL ORGANIZATION** an institution that has been formally set up with an endowment fund, e.g. a school, research establishment, charitable trust, or hospital **6. FUND SUPPORTING INSTITUTION** an endowment fund that supports an institution **7. RULES OF INSTITUTION** the charter setting up an institution and the statutes and rules by which it is governed **8.** CLOTHING same as **foundation garment** —**foundational** *adj* —**foundationally** *adv*

foundation course *n* an introductory course of study, usually taken as a first level in more extended studies

foundation garment *n* a piece of women's underwear intended to control and shape her figure, e.g. a corset

foundation school *n* a state primary or secondary school that owns its own land and has responsibility for staffing and for admissions arrangements

foundation stone *n* **1.** a stone laid during a ceremony to mark the start of construction of a building or institution **2.** the basis on which something is founded

foundation stop *n* an organ stop with a strong fundamental tone

foundation subject *n* any of ten subjects specified in the 1988 National Curriculum that must be studied in schools in England and Wales, three of which have priority as core subjects

founder[1] /fówndər/ *n* somebody who establishes an institution, business, or organization [14C. < FOUND [1]]

founder[2] /fówndər/ *vi* (-ders, -dering, -dered) **1. BREAK DOWN** to fail (*refers to an undertaking*) ○ *Negotiations foundered on a single issue.* **2. SINK** to become filled

with water and sink (*refers to a ship*) **3. BE BOGGED DOWN** to become stuck in soft ground or snow **4. FALL** to stumble and fall (*refers to a horse and its rider*) **5. GO LAME** to be affected by laminitis (*refers especially to horses*) ■ *n* VET same as **laminitis** [14C. < Old French *fondrer* 'send or sink to the bottom, fall in ruins' < Latin *fundus* 'bottom']

founder member *n* a member of an organization who also helped to found it

founding father /fównding-/ *n* a founder of an institution, movement, or organization

Founding Father *n* one of the members of the convention that drafted the US Constitution

foundling /fówndling/ *n* an abandoned baby of unknown parentage (*dated*) [13C. < past participle of FIND]

found object *n* ARTS same as **objet trouvé**

foundry /fówndri/ (*plural* **-ries**) *n* **1.** a building equipped for the casting of metal or glass **2.** the skill or practice of casting metal or glass

fount[1] /fownt/ *n* (*literary*) **1.** a source of something **2.** a fountain or spring of water [16C. Shortening of FOUNTAIN]

fount[2] /fownt/ *n* another spelling of **font**[2]

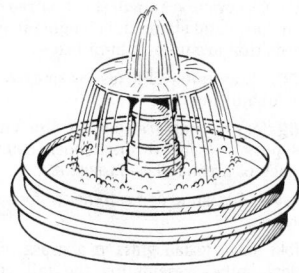

fountain

fountain /fówntin/ *n* **1. ORNAMENTAL WATER FEATURE** an ornamental structure featuring a jet or jets of water, often emerging from a statue into a pool **2. NATURAL SPRING** a natural source of water **3.** same as **drinking fountain 4. SPRAY OF LIQUID** a jet of water or some other liquid **5. SPRAY OF SUBSTANCE** a sudden discharge of something into the air such as sparks, lava, or steam **6. SOURCE** the source of something abstract **7. RESERVOIR OF LIQUID** a reservoir of liquid for use as needed, e.g. in an oil lamp or for printing ink [14C. < French *fontaine* < Latin *fontanus* 'of a spring' < *fons* 'spring']

fountainhead /fówntin hed/ *n* **1.** a spring that is the source of a stream **2.** the primary source of something abstract

fountain pen *n* a pen with a pointed metal tip (**nib**) that is supplied with ink from a refillable reservoir in the body of the pen or from an inserted cartridge

four /fawr/ *n* **1. 4** the number 4 **2. SOMETHING WITH VALUE OF 4** something in a numbered series with a value of four, e.g. a playing card ○ *the four of spades* ○ *throw a four* **3. GROUP OF 4** a group of four objects or people ○ *a four for bridge* **4. CRICKET SHOT SCORING 4 RUNS** in cricket, a shot that hits the ground and then bounces out of bounds. It scores four runs. **5.** ROWING **4-OARED RACING BOAT** a light narrow racing boat with four oars **6.** ROWING **4-MEMBER ROWING CREW** a rowing crew with four members **7.** BOWLS **BOWLING TEAM** a team of four bowls players ■ **fours** *npl* ROWING **BOAT RACES** races for boats with a crew of four ■ *prep* **4 FOR** the number 4 used to replace the word 'for' (*used in e-mails or text messages*) ○ *just 4 U* ■ *symbol* **4 FORE** the number 4 used to replace 'fore' within words (*used in e-mails or text messages*) ○ *B4 U go* [Old English *fēower* < Indo-European] —**four** *adj, pron*

four-ball *n* a match between two pairs of golfers in which the better score of each side at each hole is counted

four-by-four, **4x4** *n* a four-wheel-drive motor vehicle

four-by-two *n* a commonly used size of timber with a cross section measuring approximately 10 cm/4

in by approximately 5 cm/2 in. N Am term **two-by-four**

fourchette /foor shét/ *n* a small band that joins the folds of skin at the back of the opening to the vagina, sometimes torn in childbirth [Mid-18C. < French, 'small fork' < *fourche* < Latin *furca* 'pitchfork, forked stick']

four-colour *adj* describes the process of full-colour printing by superimposing images in cyan, magenta, yellow, and black

four-cycle *adj US* AUTOMOT same as **four-stroke**

four-dimensional *adj* having or determined by four dimensions, especially as in some formulations of relativity theory that use three spatial dimensions and a mathematically modified form of time as the fourth

Fourdrinier /foor drínni ər, -ni ay/ *n* a paper-making machine that produces a continuous web or roll of paper [Mid-19C. After Henry and Sealy *Fourdrinier*, British paper makers]

411 /fáwr wun wún/, **four-one-one** *n US* information, especially inside information or gossip, typically passed on orally (*informal*) ○ *They heard the 411 on a possible buyout and sold their stock.* [After a telephone number for directory enquiries]

four-eyes *n* an offensive term for somebody who wears spectacles (*informal insult*)

four flush *n* in poker, a bad hand containing four cards of the same suit and one odd card

four-flush (**four-flushes, four-flushing, four-flushed**) *vi* **1.** in poker, to bet coolly and boldly despite holding a bad hand such as a four flush **2.** *N Am* to try to mislead somebody in a bold way (*informal*) —**four-flusher** *n*

fourfold /fáwr fōld/ *adj, adv* MULTIPLIED BY 4 four times as great in size or amount ■ *adj* **1. WITH 4 ELEMENTS** with four parts or members **2. CONSISTING OF 4 PARTS** consisting of four parts or made up of four parts

404 /fáwr ō fáwr/ *n* an offensive term for somebody regarded as lacking in knowledge or intelligence (*slang insult*) ■ *adj* completely confused and unable to deal with a problem or situation (*slang*) [< an error message displayed on a web browser when the page requested cannot be located]

four-four-two *n* in soccer, one of the most common outfield team formations comprising four defenders, four midfielders, and two attackers

4GL *abbr* COMPUT fourth-generation language

four-handed /fáwr handid/ *adj* **1.** used to describe a game, especially a card game, played by four people **2.** composed or arranged for two people to play at the piano

Fourier /foori ay/, **Charles** (1772–1837) French social scientist. His *Theory of Four Movements and of General Destinies* (1808) advocated a socialist reorganization of society. Full name **Fourier, François Marie Charles**

'The extension of women's rights is the basic principle of all social progress.'
[Charles Fourier, *Theory of Four Movements and of General Destinies*; 1808]

Fourier, Jean-Baptiste Joseph, Baron (1768–1830) French mathematician. He used a trigonometric series, now called the Fourier series, to describe heat conduction in *The Analytical Theory of Heat* (1822). This method continues to be widely used in mathematical physics.

Fourier analysis /foóri ər-, foóri ay-/ *n* the analysis of a periodic function using the terms of a Fourier series as an approximation [Early 20C. See FOURIER SERIES]

Fourier series *n* an infinite trigonometric series of terms consisting of constants multiplied by sines or cosines, used in the approximation of periodic functions [Late 19C. After Jean-Baptiste Joseph FOURIER]

four-in-hand *n* **1.** a carriage drawn by four horses with one driver **2.** a team of four horses drawing a carriage

four-leaf clover, **four-leaved clover**, **four-leafed clover** *n* a clover leaf divided into four leaflets instead of the

usual three, believed to bring good luck to the person who finds it

four-letter word *n* a short English word relating to sex or excretion that is often used as a swearword and is generally regarded as offensive or taboo. They are sometimes written with some letters replaced by asterisks or a dash.

four-o'clock (*plural same* or **four-o'clocks**) *n* an ornamental plant. Flowers: tubular red, white, or yellow, opening in the late afternoon. Native to: tropical America. Latin name: *Mirabilis jalapa*.

fourpenny one /fáwrpəni-/ *n* a punch with the fist (*dated informal*) [Origin ?]

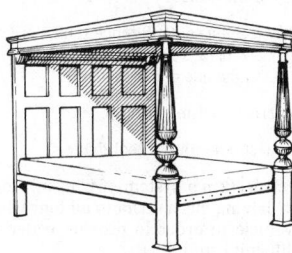

four-poster

four-poster, **four-poster bed** *n* a bed with a tall post at each corner, from which a canopy and curtains are sometimes hung

fourragère /foorə zhair/ *n* a braided cord awarded as a military decoration to a unit or person and usually worn on the left shoulder of a uniform [Early 20C. < French < *fourrage* (see FORAGE)]

fourscore /fawr skáwr/ *adj* the number 80, or a quantity of 80 (*archaic*) ○ *fourscore years and ten*

foursome /fáwrssəm/ *n* **1.** a group of four people, usually taking part in some activity together **2.** a game of golf between two pairs of players, especially when each pair has one ball that the partners hit alternately

foursquare /fawr skwáir/ *adv, adj* showing certainty and determination (*literary*) ■ *adj* solidly built and strong

four-star *adj* describes petrol that has a high octane number ■ *n* high-octane petrol, once the most commonly used in vehicles with petrol engines

four-stroke *adj UK, ANZ, Can* describes an internal-combustion engine in which the piston makes four strokes to complete a cycle. US term **four-cycle**

fourteen /fawr teén/ *n* **1. 14** the number 14 **2. SOMETHING WITH VALUE OF 14** something in a numbered series with a value of 14 **3. GROUP OF 14** a group of 14 objects or people —**fourteen** *adj, pron*

fourteenth /fawr teénth/ *n* one of 14 equal parts of something —**fourteenth** *adj*

fourth /fawrth/ *n* **1. ONE OF 4 PARTS OF SOMETHING** one of four equal parts of something **2. 4 IN SERIES** the ordinal number assigned to item number four in a series **3.** MUSIC **INTERVAL OF 4 NOTES** in a standard musical scale, the interval between one note and another that lies three notes above or below it. In the scale of C major, C and F form a fourth. **4.** MUSIC **NOTE 4TH AWAY FROM ANOTHER** in a standard musical scale, a note that is a fourth away from another note **5.** BALLET same as **fourth position** —**fourth** *adj, adv*

SPELLCHECK See **forth**.

fourth dimension *n* time in relativity theory modified mathematically and used in combination with the usual three spatial dimensions to specify the location in space and time of events —**fourth-dimensional** *adj*

fourth estate, **Fourth Estate** *n* journalists, the press, or the media in general [In addition to the three estates (the Lords Spiritual, the Lords Temporal, and the House of Commons)]

fourth-generation language *n* an advanced computer programming language that is more like

human language than are the standard high-level programming languages

fourthly /fáwrthli/ *adv* used to introduce the fourth point in an argument or discussion

Fourth of July *n US* same as **Independence Day**

fourth position *n* in ballet, a position in which the feet are turned outwards with the right leg extended so that the right foot is one step in front of the left foot

fourth-rate *adj* so bad that it is worse than second-rate and third-rate

Fourth World *n* the very poorest or least developed countries of the world

four-twenty *n S Asia* a confidence trickster (*informal*) [< the number of a section of the Indian Penal Code (popularized by the title of a Hindi film)]

~~fourty~~ incorrect spelling of **forty**

4WD *abbr* MECH ENG four-wheel drive

four-wheel drive *n* a system of transmitting power from the driving mechanism to all four wheels of a motor vehicle in order to provide better traction under difficult conditions

Fouta Djallon /fóőttə yaʼa lon/, **Futa Djallon** plateau region in north-central Guinea. Its highest point is the Massif du Tamgué, 1,537 m/5,043 ft. Area: 77,700 sq. km/30,000 sq. mi.

fouter *n, v Scotland* another spelling of **footer**[2]

fovea /fóvi ə/ (*plural* **-veae** /-vi eə/) *n* 1. a small hollow in the surface of a part of the body 2. ANAT same as **fovea centralis** [Late 17C. < Latin, 'small pit'] —**foveal** *adj* —**foveate** /-ayt/ *adj*

fovea centralis /-sen traʼaliss/ *n* a shallow pit in the centre of the retina that is free of blood vessels and has the highest concentration of cells sensitive to colour and bright light (**cones**). The fovea centralis is the area of most acute vision. [< Latin, 'central fovea']

Foveaux Strait /fóvō-/ stretch of the South Pacific Ocean between the South Island and Stewart Island, New Zealand. At its narrowest, it is 18 km/11 mi. wide.

foveola /fō vée ələ/ (*plural* **-lae** /-lee/) *n* a small fovea [Mid-19C. < Latin < *fovea* 'small pit'] —**foveolar** *adj* —**foveolated** *adj*

Fowey /foy/ small seaport and resort in Cornwall, southwestern England. Population: 1,939 (1991).

fowl /fowl/ (*plural* **fowls** or *same*) *n* 1. CHICKEN a bird kept for its meat and eggs, especially a chicken 2. EDIBLE OR GAME BIRD a bird that is used as food or hunted for sport, e.g. a goose or pheasant 3. BIRD'S FLESH the flesh of any edible bird 4. same as **bird** (sense 2) (*archaic*) [Old English *fugol* 'bird' < Germanic]

SPELLCHECK See *foul*.

fowler /fówlər/ *n* a shooter or trapper of wild birds

Fowles /fowlz/, **John** (*b.* 1926) British novelist. His works include *The Collector* (1963), *The Magus* (1965), and *The French Lieutenant's Woman* (1969). Full name **Fowles, John Robert**. See Cultural note at **magus**

'We all write poems; it is simply that poets are the ones who write in words.'
[John Fowles, *The French Lieutenant's Woman*; 1969]

fowling /fówling/ *n* the shooting or trapping of wild birds as a livelihood or for sport

fowling piece *n* a light gun that fires small shot, used in hunting game birds

fowl pest *n* a disease of domesticated poultry caused by an influenza virus that reduces the growth rate or egg production

fox

fox /foks/ *n* 1. WILD ANIMAL WITH BUSHY TAIL a carnivorous animal of the dog family that has a pointed muzzle, large ears, a long bushy tail, and usually reddish-brown or grey fur. Foxes are found throughout most of the world and hunt alone, mainly at night, relying on cunning and an acute sense of hearing and smell. Genus: *Vulpes*. 2. FOX FUR the fur of the fox 3. TRICKSTER a sly and cunning person (*informal*) 4. *N Am* GOOD-LOOKING PERSON a good-looking young person (*slang*) ■ *vt* (**foxes, foxing, foxed**) 1. BAFFLE SOMEBODY to confuse or baffle somebody (*often passive*) 2. DECEIVE OR OUTWIT SOMEBODY to deceive or outwit somebody by means of sly trickery [Old English, < Indo-European] —**fox-like** *adj*

Fox /foks/ (*plural same*) *n* 1. a member of a Native North American people who lived in Michigan, Wisconsin, Illinois, and Iowa, and now live mainly in Oklahoma and Iowa. Following US attempts under a spurious treaty to move the Fox from their lands in Illinois, they joined with the Sauk in the Black Hawk War of 1832. 2. a language spoken in parts of Iowa and Oklahoma, belonging to the Algonquian group of Algonquian-Wakashan. Native speakers: 2,000. [Translation of French *Renards*, translation of Iroquoian *Skenchiohronon* 'people of the red fox'] —**Fox** *adj*

Fox /foks/, **Charles James** (1749–1806) British politician. He was twice foreign secretary (1782, 1806) and one of the principal leaders of the Whig Party in the period of the French Revolution and the American War of Independence.

'Kings govern by means of popular assemblies only when they cannot do without them.'
[Charles James Fox, *Speech to Parliament*; 31 October 1776]

Fox, George (1624–91) British religious leader. The founder of the Quakers, he was frequently imprisoned for his beliefs. His celebrated journal was published posthumously (1694).

'I told them I lived in the virtue of that life and power that took away the occasion of all wars.'
[George Fox, *Journal*; 1694]

Fox, Vicente (*b.* 1942) Mexican politician. He was elected president of Mexico in 2000. Full name **Fox Quesada, Vicente**

Fox, Sir William (1812–93) British-born New Zealand explorer, politician, and painter. He was the premier of New Zealand four times (1856, 1861–62, 1869–72, 1873).

FOX /foks/ *abbr* FIN Futures and Options Exchange

foxed /fokst/ *adj* describes books or paper stained with yellowish-brown spots from having been kept in damp conditions

foxfire /fóks fīr/ *n* a luminescent glow produced by some fungi when in contact with rotting wood

Fox Glacier glacier in Westland National Park, on the southwestern coast of the South Island, New Zealand. Length: 14 km/9 mi.

foxglove

foxglove /fóks gluv/ (*plural same* or **-gloves**) *n* a tall plant that is the source of the drug digitalis. Flowers: purple or white, thimble-shaped. Latin name: *Digitalis purpurea*.

fox grape *n* a wild grape that has purplish fruit and is the source of many cultivated grape varieties. Native to: eastern United States. Latin name: *Vitis labrusca*.

foxhole /fóks hōl/ *n* a small hole dug in the ground to protect a sniper or other soldier from enemy fire

foxhound /fóks hownd/ *n* a small short-haired dog that has great speed and stamina, belonging to either of two breeds that are used to hunt foxes

fox hunter *n* 1. a hunter of foxes for sport 2. a horse used for foxhunting

foxhunting /fóks hunting/ *n* a sport in which mounted hunters pursue a fox through open countryside with a pack of foxhounds —**foxhunt** *n, vi*

foxie /fóksi/ *n Aus* same as **fox terrier** (*informal*) [Early 20C. Shortening]

foxtail /fóks tayl/, **foxtail grass** *n* a grass with soft cylindrical spikes resembling the tail of a fox. Genera: *Alopecurus* or *Setaria* or *Hordeum*.

fox terrier *n* a small dog that is either wire-haired or has a smooth coat, belonging to a breed that is white with dark markings

foxtrot /fóks trot/ *n* 1. DANCE BALLROOM DANCE a ballroom dance alternating longer slower walking steps and shorter quicker running steps, usually with four beats to the bar 2. MUSIC MUSIC the music for a foxtrot 3. RIDING HORSE'S SLOW TROTTING PACE a slow pace for a horse, between a trot and a walk, in which it takes short steps in a broken rhythm [Early 20C. < the short steps of the fox] —**foxtrot** *vi*

Foxtrot *n* a code word for the letter 'F', used in international radio communications

foxy /fóksi/ (**-ier, -iest**) *adj* 1. CRAFTY clever in a cunning or deceitful way 2. LIKE FOX like a fox, especially in appearance or through having a strong pungent smell 3. COLOURS REDDISH-BROWN of a reddish-brown colour, like fox fur 4. *N Am* ATTRACTIVE sensually alluring (*informal*) 5. PUBL same as **foxed** 6. WINE SHARP OR MUSKY having the rather sharp, pungent, or musky flavour of fox grapes —**foxiness** *n*

foyer /fóy ay, fwĭ ay/ *n* 1. the reception area in a public building such as a hotel or theatre 2. *US* the entrance hall or vestibule in a private house [Mid-19C. Via French < medieval Latin *focarius* < Latin *focus* 'fireplace, hearth']

fps *abbr* 1. MEASURE feet per second 2. *also* **f.p.s.** MEASURE foot-pound-second 3. PHOTOGRAPHY frames per second (*a measure of camera shutter speed*)

FPS[1] *n* a measure of the rate of screen refreshment in a real-time computer game. Full form **frames per second**

FPS[2] *abbr* COMPUT GAMES first-person shooter

fps units, **fps system of units** *n* a system of units based on the foot, second, and pound mass that is now almost wholly superseded by SI units

fr *abbr* France (*used in Internet addresses*) See table at **domain name**

Fr *symbol* CHEM ELEM francium

FR *abbr* BUILDINGS family room

fr. *abbr* 1. fragment 2. from

Fr. *abbr* 1. CHR Father 2. MONEY franc 3. France 4. Frau 5. French 6. CHR Friar 7. CALENDAR Friday

Fra /fraa/, **fra** *n* used as a title for an Italian monk or friar, the equivalent of the English title 'Brother' [Late 19C. < Italian, shortening of *frate* 'brother, friar' < Latin *frater*]

fracas /frák aa/ (*plural same*) *n* a noisy quarrel or fight [Early 18C. < French, 'crash, roar' < Italian *fracassare* 'cause an uproar']

fractal /frákt'l/ *n* an irregular or fragmented geometrical shape that can be repeatedly subdivided into parts, each of which is a smaller copy of the whole. Fractals are used in computer modelling of natural structures that do not have simple geometric shapes such as clouds, mountainous landscapes, and coastlines. [Late 20C. < French < Latin *fract-* (see FRACTION)] —**fractal** *adj*

fraction /fráksh'n/ *n* 1. MATHS **NUMBER THAT IS NOT WHOLE NUMBER** a number that is not a whole number, e.g. $\frac{1}{2}$ (**simple fraction**) or 0.5 (**decimal fraction**), formed by dividing one quantity into another 2. **SMALL AMOUNT** a small part, amount, or proportion of something ○ *a fraction of the cost* 3. **PART** a part or element of a larger whole or group ○ *spent a sizable fraction of his time working on this project* 4. CHEM **SEPARATED COMPONENT** an individual component or portion of a mixture, separated by differences in chemical or physical properties 5. CHR **BREAKING OF BREAD BY PRIEST** during Communion in the Roman Catholic tradition, the breaking off of a piece of bread by the priest who places it in the chalice [14C. Via Old French < late Latin *fraction-* < Latin *fract-*, past participle of *frangere* 'break'] ◇ **a fraction** by a very small amount or distance ○ *Move it just a fraction to the right.*

ORIGIN The Latin word *frangere* 'to break', from which ***fraction*** is derived, and forms related to it, are also sources of English *fracture, fragile, fragment, frail,* and *saxifrage.*

fractional /frákshənəl/ *adj* 1. **SLIGHT** very small or slight ○ *a fractional increase in temperature* 2. MATHS **OF FRACTIONS** relating to or involving fractions 3. CHEM **OF SEPARATION OF COMPONENTS** relating to the process of separating individual components from a mixture on the basis of the chemical or physical properties that make them different from other components

fractional distillation *n* the process of using a volatile liquid to separate components that have different boiling points, by first heating the liquid and then condensing and collecting the components as they vaporize

fractionalize /fráksh'nə līz/ (**-izes, -izing, -ized**), **fractionalise** (**-ises, -ising, -ised**) *vt* to divide something into parts or sections —**fractionalization** /fráksh'nə lī záysh'n/ *n*

fractionally /fráksh'nəli/ *adv* very slightly, or to a very slight degree

fractionate /frákshə nayt/ (**-ates, -ating, -ated**) *v* 1. *vti* to divide or break something into parts, or be divided or broken into parts (*formal*) 2. *vt* CHEM to separate a mixture into its components, e.g. by crystallization or distillation —**fractionation** /frákshə náysh'n/ *n* —**fractionator** *n*

fractious /frákshəss/ *adj* irritable and likely to complain or misbehave [Late 17C. < FRACTION] —**fractiously** *adv* —**fractiousness** *n*

fracture /frákchər/ *n* 1. **BONE BREAK** a break in a bone 2. **ACT OF BREAKING SOMETHING** the act of breaking something, especially a bone 3. **BREAK OR CRACK** a break, split, or crack in an object or a material 4. **SPLIT IN SYSTEM** a split or division in something such as a system, organization, or agreement ○ *the fractures that are already starting to appear in the peace treaty* 5. GEOL **ROCK BREAK** a break in a rock or mineral, across which there is a separation ■ *vti* (**-tures, -turing, -tured**) 1. **BREAK** to break or crack something, especially a particular bone or a bone in a particular part of the body, or be broken or cracked 2. **CAUSE OR UNDERGO DAMAGE** to cause damage or disruption to something or destroy it, or be damaged, disrupted, or destroyed [Mid-16C. Directly or via French < Latin *fractura* < *fract-* (see FRACTION)] —**fracturable** *adj*

frae /fray/ *prep Scotland* same as **from** (*nonstandard*) [13C. Variant of FRO]

frag /frag/ (**frags, fragging, fragged**) *vt* in a computer game, to kill an opponent [Mid-20C. Shortening of FRAGMENTATION] —**fragger** *n* —**fragging** *n*

fragfest /frág fest/ *n* a computer game that involves killing many opponents

fragile /frájj īl/ *adj* 1. **EASILY BROKEN** not having a strong structure or not made of robust materials, and therefore easily broken or damaged ○ *too fragile to be used as toys* 2. **NOT SECURE** unlikely to withstand any severe stresses and strains ○ *a fragile peace* 3. **PHYSICALLY WEAK** in a weak bodily condition, usually as a result of illness [15C. Directly or via French < Latin *fragilis* < source of *frangere* 'break'] —**fragilely** *adv* —**fragility** /frə jílləti/ *n*

SYNONYMS ***fragile, delicate, frail, flimsy***

CORE MEANING: easily broken or damaged

fragile not having a strong structure or not made of robust materials, and therefore easily broken or damaged ○ *protected by a fragile wooden structure* ○ *an ecologically fragile area* **delicate** having a fine, often beautiful, structure that is easily damaged or broken. ○ *a delicate lace fabric* ○ *delicate foliage* **frail** made of weak or delicate materials and easy to break or damage, or not secure, or physically weak and vulnerable to injury ○ *separated by a frail wooden barrier* ○ *a frail economy* ○ *a frail elderly relative* **flimsy** weak and too easily broken, or thin and easily torn ○ *huddled under flimsy shelters* ○ *a flimsy coat*

fragile-X syndrome *n* a genetic condition, caused by a damaged X chromosome with an apparently almost detached part near the end of the long arm, that causes learning difficulties in boys and men

fragment *n* /frágmənt/ 1. **BROKEN PIECE** a piece, usually a small piece, broken off something or left when something is shattered 2. **INCOMPLETE PIECE** an incomplete or isolated piece of something ○ *only heard fragments of the conversation* ■ *vti* /frag mént/ (**-ments, -menting, -mented**) 1. **BREAK INTO SMALL PIECES** to break something into small pieces, or be broken in this way ○ *The metal is designed to fragment on impact.* 2. **BREAK UP** to lose a sense of unity or cohesion, with the result that something splits into isolated and often conflicting elements, or cause something to do this ○ *Civil war had fragmented the nation and hindered development.* [Mid-16C. Directly or via French < Latin *fragmentum* < source of *frangere* 'break'] —**fragmented** /frag méntid/ *adj*

fragmental /frag ménť'l/ *adj* 1. same as **fragmentary** 2. describes rocks that are made up of fragments of preexisting rocks

fragmentary /frágməntəri/ *adj* consisting of the physical fragments or small disconnected items of something —**fragmentarily** *adv*

fragmentation /frágmən táysh'n, -men-/ *n* 1. **BREAKING UP OF SOMETHING** the process of shattering or breaking up into fragments 2. **LOSS OF UNITY AND COHESION** the loss of unity and cohesion and the splitting of something into isolated and often conflicting parts ○ *The result, inevitably, would be social fragmentation.* 3. **SHATTERING OF EXPLOSIVE DEVICE** the scattering of the shattered parts of a grenade or other explosive device 4. COMPUT **BREAKING UP OF DATA PACKET** the breaking up of computer data into smaller nonconsecutive pieces for more efficient storage and transmission. The danger inherent in this process is that the relationship between the pieces may be lost.

fragmentation bomb *n* a bomb or shell with a thick casing that is designed to shatter on detonation into many destructive fragments in order to cause maximum damage or injury

fragmentation grenade *n* a grenade with a thick casing that is designed to shatter on detonation into many destructive fragments in order to cause maximum damage or injury

fragmentize /frágmən tīz/ (**-tizes, -tizing, -tized**) *vti US* same as **fragment** *v*

Fragonard /frággə naar/, **Jean Honoré** (1732–1806) French painter and engraver. He is known for his rococo paintings such as *The Swing* (1766) and *The Progress of Love* (1771–73) that depict romantic scenes of contemporary life. His main source of income, commissions from the aristocracy, dried up at the start of the French Revolution.

fragrance /fráygrənss/ *n* 1. **SWEET SMELL** a pleasant sweet smell ○ *a plant with an exotic heady fragrance* 2. **SWEETNESS OF SMELL** the characteristic of being sweet-smelling 3. **PERFUME** something that has a distinctive smell, e.g. a perfume or cologne ○ *a great new fragrance for men* ○ *fragrance-free cosmetics* —**fragranced** *adj*

SYNONYMS See ***smell.***

fragrance strip *n* a sealed strip of card or paper included with something such as a magazine advertisement and impregnated with a fragrance that is released when the cover is peeled off

fragrancy /fráygrənssi/ *n* same as **fragrance** (sense 2)

fragrant /fráygrənt/ *adj* having a pleasant sweet smell [15C. Directly or via French < Latin *fragrant-*, present participle of *fragrare* 'emit a (good or bad) odour'] —**fragrantly** *adv*

fragrant orchid (*plural* **fragrant orchids** or *same*) *n* PLANTS same as **scented orchid**

fraidy-cat /fráydi-/ *n US* same as **scaredy-cat** (*informal*) [< shortening of AFRAID]

frail /frayl/ (**frailer, frailest**) *adj* 1. **PHYSICALLY WEAK** in a physically weakened state and vulnerable to injury ○ *a frail elderly relative* 2. **EASY TO BREAK OR DAMAGE** made of weak or delicate materials and easy to break or damage ○ *It didn't look as if such a frail chair would support her weight.* 3. **NOT SECURE** lacking any secure foundation in fact or reality and unlikely to be realized or be successful ○ *frail hopes of success* 4. **MORALLY WEAK** easily tempted and persuaded to do something morally bad or wrong [14C. Via Old French *fraile* < Latin *fragilis* (see FRAGILE)] —**frailly** *adv* —**frailness** *n*

SYNONYMS See ***fragile*** and ***weak.***

frailty /fráylti/ (*plural* **-ties**) *n* 1. **WEAKNESS** physical weakness, or weakness of materials and construction 2. **MORAL WEAKNESS** inherent moral weakness in humanity or in a person leading to difficulty in resisting temptation or avoiding wrongdoing 3. **CHARACTER FLAW** a character flaw arising out of moral weakness (*often used in the plural*) ○ *ordinary human frailties*

fraise /frayz/ *n* a cone-shaped grooved drill bit used for enlarging a previously drilled hole [Early 17C. < French, 'lining of a calf's abdomen'; from its numerous folds]

Fraktur /frak to͝or/, **fraktur** *n* a thick ornate style of printed letter, the standard typeface for all printing in German until the mid-20th century [Late 19C. Via German < Latin *fractura* (see FRACTURE)]

Fra Mauro /fraa máwrō/ eroded crater on the Moon north of Mare Nubium, approximately 95 km/59 mi. in diameter. Apollo 14 landed close to Fra Mauro in 1971.

framboesia /fram bēezi ə/ *n* MED same as **yaws** [Early 19C. < modern Latin < French *framboise* 'raspberry' (suggested by the sores produced by the disease)]

frame /fraym/ *n* 1. **SUPPORTING STRUCTURE** an underlying or supporting structure that consists of solid parts such as beams or struts with spaces between them and has something built around or on top of it ○ *a bike with a steel frame* 2. **SURROUNDING STRUCTURE** a structure that surrounds or encloses a particular space ○ *a picture frame* ○ *a door frame* 3. OPHTHALMOL **LENS-HOLDING PART OF SPECTACLES** the part of a pair of spectacles that holds the lenses and fits around the wearer's face 4. **PIECE OF EQUIPMENT** a piece of equipment made of bars fitted together with spaces between, e.g. for children to climb on or to help a person to walk ○ *a child's climbing frame* 5. **HOLLOW SHAPE FOR NEEDLECRAFT AND PAINTING** an open structure across which a piece of material can be stretched to be painted or embroidered, or across which threads can be stretched for weaving 6. **CONTEXT** the general background or context against or within which something takes place ○ *the story's historical frame* 7. **HUMAN BODY** somebody's body, especially with reference to its size and shape ○ *He eased his enormous*

frame into the chair. **8.** CINEMA, PHOTOGRAPHY **PICTURE ON STRIP OF FILM** one of the individual pictures that make up a strip of cinema film, or a single exposure on a strip of photographic negative or slide images **9.** MEDIA **TV PICTURE** the picture that appears on a television screen **10.** CINEMA, MEDIA **VISIBLE PART OF FILMED ACTION** in film, video, or TV, the particular area of action that is captured by the camera and forms the rectangular image that appears on the screen ○ *characters moving out of the frame to the left* **11.** PHOTOGRAPHY **IMAGE BORDER** the border or set of borders of a projected image **12.** PUBL **SINGLE PICTURE IN COMIC STRIP** one of the individual pictures that make up a comic strip **13.** GARDENING same as **cold frame 14.** N Am BOWLS **ROUND OF TEN-PIN BOWLING** one of the ten rounds in a ten-pin bowling game **15.** CUE GAMES **GAME IN SNOOKER** one of the individual games that make up a match in snooker, billiards, and pool. N Am term **rack**[1] **16.** CUE GAMES **TRIANGULAR TEMPLATE FOR SNOOKER BALLS** a wooden triangle used to arrange the target balls into their required positions at the beginning of a game of snooker or pool. N Am term **rack**[1] **17.** CUE GAMES **BALLS POSITIONED BY FRAME** the target balls when in position for the start of a game of snooker or pool. N Am term **rack**[1] **18.** COMPUT **SINGLE CYCLE OF PULSES** a single cycle of pulses in a string of repeated pulses **19.** CRIME same as **frame-up** (sense 1) (*slang*) **20.** ONLINE **AREA OF COMPUTER SCREEN** a rectangular area on a computer screen, containing all or a portion of a webpage. More than one frame can be displayed concurrently. **21.** COMPUT **DATA PACKET** a variable-length data packet preceded and followed by addressing and control information that is transmitted between network points as a unit. Some control frames contain no data. ■ **frames** *npl* **1.** OPHTHALMOL same as **frame** (sense 3) **2.** ONLINE **WEB BROWSER FEATURE** a web browser feature that segments the window being displayed, allowing the concurrent display of two or more pages on the same screen ■ *vt* (**frames, framing, framed**) **1.** PUT SOMETHING **IN FRAME** to mount a picture in a frame **2.** FORM SURROUNDING FRAMEWORK FOR SOMETHING to form a surrounding border or framework, especially a decorative or contrasting one, around something (*often passive*) ○ *a delicate face framed by abundant black hair* **3.** CONSTRUCT IDEA OR STATEMENT to construct or compose something that is to be written or spoken ○ *She framed her words carefully.* **4.** EXPRESS SOMETHING IN PARTICULAR WAY to express something in a particular type of language ○ *framed the argument in legal terms* **5.** MOUTH WORDS to mouth words silently **6.** CAUSE SOMEBODY TO APPEAR GUILTY to make an innocent person appear guilty, e.g. by forging incriminating evidence (*informal*) **7.** ARRANGE RESULT OF SOMETHING IN ADVANCE to use dishonest or illegal methods to arrange the result of a contest in advance, e.g. by paying a player to lose deliberately (*informal*) ■ *adj* CONSTR, ARCHIT **WITH WOODEN FRAMEWORK** constructed on a framework of wooden beams, then covered with boards or shingles ○ *a white frame house with black shutters* [Old English *framian* 'make progress, be helpful, prepare, shape' < *fram* (see FROM)] —**frameable** *adj* —**framer** *n* ◇ **in the frame** among those who are involved in something or under consideration for something (*informal*)

Janet Frame

Frame /fraym/, **Janet** (1924–2004) New Zealand writer. Her novels, short stories, and autobiographical works include *To the Island* (1982) and *An Angel at My Table* (1984). Born **Clutha, Janet Paterson Frame**. See Cultural note at **angel**

'Many patients confined in other wards of Seacliff had no name, only a nickname, no past no future, only an imprisoned Now, an eternal Island without its accompanying horizons, foot or handhold, or even without its everchanging sky.'
[Janet Frame, *An Angel at My Table*; 1984]

frame of mind *n* somebody's psychological state, attitude, or mood at a specific time

frame of reference *n* **1.** the set of norms, values, or ideas that affect the way somebody interacts with others, either in everyday life or in a particular situation **2.** MATHS a set of geometric axes used to determine the location of a point in space

frame rate *n* the refresh rate of what is shown on the screen in a real-time computer game

frame story *n* a narrative that provides the framework within which a number of different stories, which may or may not be connected, can be told. An example of a frame story is the pilgrims' ride to Canterbury that provides the starting point for Chaucer's *Canterbury Tales.*

frame-up *n* (*informal*) **1.** a conspiracy to make an innocent person appear guilty, e.g. by forging incriminating evidence **2.** a situation in which the result of a contest is dishonestly or illegally arranged in advance

framework /fráym wurk/ *n* **1.** UNDERLYING SET OF IDEAS a set of ideas, principles, agreements, or rules that provides the basis or outline for something intended to be more fully developed at a later stage ○ *providing a framework for next week's discussions* **2.** CONTEXT the general background to, or context for, a particular action or event ○ *within the framework of Jewish religious tradition* **3.** SYSTEM OF INTERCONNECTING BARS a structure of connected horizontal and vertical bars with spaces between them, especially one that forms the skeleton of another structure **4.** HANDICRAFT **ARTICLES WOVEN OR EMBROIDERED ON FRAME** articles produced by weaving or embroidering cloth on a frame

framing /fráyming/ *n* **1.** FRAMES frames or frameworks collectively **2.** WAY SOMETHING IS FRAMED the way that something is framed **3.** CINEMA **COMPOSITION OF FILM SCENE** the composition of a scene within the visual field of the camera for shooting in a film **4.** CINEMA **ADJUSTMENT OF FILM PROJECTOR SETTINGS** the adjustment of the settings on a film projector so that the image is in the correct position on the screen

franc /frangk/ *n* **1.** the main unit of currency in several French-speaking countries. See table at **currency 2.** the main unit of the former currency in France, Belgium, and Luxembourg [14C. < French]

France

France /fraanss/ largest country in western Europe. Its present constitution was established in 1958 with the proclamation of the Fifth Republic. Language: French. Currency: Euro. Capital: Paris. Population: 60,182,529 (2003). Area: 543,965 sq. km/210,026 sq. mi. Official name **French Republic**

France /fraaNss/, **Anatole** (1844–1924) French writer. He produced a large body of writings, including novels, drama, verse, critical and philosophical essays, and historical works. He won the Nobel Prize in literature (1921). Pseudonym of **Thibault, Jacques Anatole François**

'To die for an idea is to place a pretty high

price upon conjectures.'
[Anatole France, *The Revolt of the Angels*; 1933]

franchise /frán chīz/ *n* **1.** COMM **LICENCE TO SELL COMPANY'S PRODUCTS** an agreement or licence to sell a company's products exclusively in a particular area or to operate a business that carries that company's name **2.** BUSINESS OPERATED UNDER LICENCE a business licensed to sell a company's products exclusively in a particular area or to operate a business that carries that company's name **3.** COMM **AREA OF COMMERCIAL OPERATION** the area in which somebody has a commercial franchise **4.** PRIVILEGE GRANTED BY AUTHORITY a right or privilege, or an exemption from a duty or obligation, granted by a government or other authority **5.** RIGHT TO VOTE the right to vote, especially to elect representatives to a national legislature or a parliament **6.** N Am PROFESSIONAL SPORTS TEAM a professional sports team that is a member of an organized league (*informal*) **7.** US SPORTS **LICENCE FOR SPORTS TEAM** an agreement or licence to own a sports team **8.** *also* **franchise player** US VALUABLE SPORTS TEAM MEMBER a player who is valuable and important to a team (*informal*) [14C. < French < *franc* 'free' (see FRANK)] —**franchise** *vt* —**franchisee** /frán chī zeé/ *n* —**franchisement** /-chiz-/ *n* —**franchiser** *n*

Francis I /fráanssiss/ (1494–1547) king of France. His reign (1515–47) was dominated by conflict with Charles V, Holy Roman Emperor.

'Of all I had, only honour and life have been spared.'
[Francis I, *Letter to his mother, Louise of Savoy*; 24 February 1525]

Francis II (1768–1835) last Holy Roman Emperor (1792–1806) and, as Francis I, first emperor of Austria (1804–35). He dissolved the Holy Roman Empire in 1806 and united with Great Britain and Russia to defeat Napoleon (1815). In the subsequent Congress of Vienna (1815), he regained most of the territory Austria had lost in the Napoleonic wars.

Francis (of Assisi), St (1182–1226) Italian mystic and preacher. He founded the Franciscan and Poor Clare orders of the Roman Catholic Church. Born **Bernardone, Giovanni Francesco**

'Grant me the treasure of sublime poverty.'
[Francis (of Assisi). Quoted in *A History of Medieval Europe*, Maurice Keen; 1967]

Franciscan /fran sískən/ *n* a member of an order of friars and nuns, founded by St Francis of Assisi, that now has three separate branches and is largely devoted to missionary and charitable work [Late 16C. Via French < modern Latin *Franciscanus* < *Franciscus* 'Francis'] —**Franciscan** *adj*

Francis Ferdinand ♦ **Franz Ferdinand**

Francis Joseph I ♦ **Franz Josef**

Francis of Sales /-saál/, **St** (1567–1622) French priest and writer. A leader of the Counter-Reformation, he became bishop of Geneva (1602).

'Big fires flare up in a wind, but little ones are blown out unless they are carried in under cover.'
[Francis of Sales, *Introduction to The Devout Life*; 1609]

francium /fránss i əm/ *n* an unstable radioactive element of the alkali-metal group. Source: uranium ore, or made artificially from actinium and thorium. Symbol **Fr**. See table at **element** [Mid-20C. After FRANCE, home of its discoverer]

Franck /frangk, fraaNk/, **César Auguste** (1822–90) Belgian-born French composer and organist. He combined classical form with romantic content in his best-known work, the Symphony in D minor (1886–88), which has served as a model for subsequent French composers.

Franco /frángkō/, **Francisco** (1892–1975) Spanish general and national leader. He defeated the Republican army during the Spanish Civil War (1936–

Francisco Franco

39) and established a dictatorship in Spain in 1939, ruling until his death in 1975.

'If I didn't act with an iron hand, this would soon be chaos.'
[Francisco Franco, *Remark*; 1921]

Franco- *prefix* France, French ○ *Francophile* [< late Latin *Francus* 'Frank' < Germanic]

Franconian /frang kőni ən/ *n* a group of medieval dialects of German spoken in an area extending from present-day Bavaria and Alsace, and up the Rhine valley —**Franconian** *adj*

Francophile /fráŋkō fīl/, **Francophil** /-fil/ *n* somebody who likes France, the French people, or the French way of life ▪ *adj* liking or admiring France, the French people, or the French way of life —**Francophilia** /fráŋkə fílli ə/ *n*

Francophobe /fráŋkō fōb/ *n* somebody who intensely dislikes France, the French people, or the French way of life —**Francophobia** /fráŋkō fōbi ə/ *n*

Francophobic /fráŋkō fōbik/ *adj* having an intense dislike of France, the French people, or the French way of life

francophone /fráŋkō fōn/ *n* SPEAKER OF FRENCH somebody who speaks French, especially as a first language ▪ *adj* **1.** FRENCH-SPEAKING speaking French as a first or main language **2.** OF FRENCH-SPEAKING AREA relating to a place where French is used as the main language, the official language, or a lingua franca ○ *Francophone Africa* —**Francophonic** /fráŋkō fónnik/ *adj*

frangible /fránjəb'l/ *adj* brittle, or designed to be easily broken (*formal or technical*) ○ *glass and other frangible products* ○ *frangible aluminium masts* [15C. Directly or via Old French < medieval Latin *frangibilis* < *frangere* 'break'] —**frangibility** /fránjə bílləti/ *n*

frangipane /fránji payn/ *n* an almond-flavoured cream or paste used in pastries, cakes, and other sweet foods [Mid-19C. < French, 'frangipani' (perfume made with bitter almonds)]

frangipani /fránji pánni, -paání/ (*plural* **-is**) *n* **1.** TREES a deciduous tree with strongly perfumed, white, yellow, or pink flowers. Native to: tropical America. Genus: *Plumeria*. **2.** a perfume derived from frangipani flowers or imitating their scent **3.** FOOD same as **frangipane 4.** TREES same as **native frangipani** [Mid-19C. After Muzio *Frangipani*, 16C Italian creator of a perfume for gloves]

Franglais /fróng glay/, **franglais** *n* an informal form of French that includes many English loan words and phrases. For French traditionalists, it is seen as evidence of the extent to which British and American cultural imperialism has permeated French and French-Canadian life. [Mid-20C. < French, blend of *français* 'French' + *anglais* 'English'] —**Franglais** *adj*

frank /frangk/ *adj* **1.** EXPRESSING TRUE OPINION open, honest, and sometimes forceful in expressing true feelings and opinions ○ *Let me be frank with you.* **2.** SHOWING OPENNESS AND BLUNTNESS allowing people's true feelings and opinions to be openly and often bluntly stated ○ *a frank discussion of our differences* **3.** PLEASINGLY HONEST having or showing an appealingly open and honest nature ○ *has a frank manner that won her many friends* **4.** UNDISGUISED openly expressed, without concealment or disguise ○ *regarded him with frank loathing* ▪ *vt* (**franks, franking, franked**) MAIL **1.** PRINT MARK OVER STAMP to print an official mark over the stamp on a letter or parcel to show that

payment has been formally accepted **2.** PRINT MARK SHOWING POSTAGE PAID to print a mark on a letter or parcel, instead of using a postage stamp, to show that postage has been paid or that there is no postage charge ▪ *n* **1.** OFFICIAL MARK ON LETTER OR PARCEL an official mark printed on a letter or parcel to show that postage has been paid or that postage is free of charge **2.** MAIL RIGHT TO FREE POSTAL DELIVERY the right to have posted items delivered free of charge [14C. Via French, 'free, generous, candid' < medieval Latin *francus* 'Frank, free'; from the granting of full political freedom in Gaul only to the Franks] —**frankness** *n*

Frank /frangk/ *n* a member of a Germanic people who lived along the Rhine valley and spread westwards during the decline of the Roman Empire in the 4th century AD. They conquered vast areas of western Europe, taking over Gaul and becoming the dominant people in an area covering much of present-day western Germany. [Old English *Franca* < Germanic] —**Frankish** *adj*

Anne Frank

Frank /frangk/, **Anne** (1929–45) German-born Jewish writer. She kept a diary during her years in hiding during the German occupation of the Netherlands (1942–44). She and her family were captured in 1944, and she died in a concentration camp.

'I want to go on living even after death!'
[Anne Frank, *Diary*; 4 April 1944]

Frankenstein /fráŋkən stīn/ *n* **1.** CREATOR OF SOMETHING DESTRUCTIVE a creator of something that causes ruin or destruction, or brings about a personal downfall **2.** *also* **Frankenstein's monster** OUT-OF-CONTROL INVENTION a creation or invention that gets beyond its maker's control and threatens harm or destruction **3.** MONSTER a monster typically represented as a very large coarse-featured person, often with features such as bolts in the neck and a shambling walk [Early 19C. < novel by Mary Shelley (1818), in which the main character, Baron *Frankenstein*, creates a living man]

Frankenstein food *n* food or a food product produced using genetic engineering (*informal disapproving*)

Frankfort /fráŋkfurt/ capital of Kentucky, in the north-central part of the state, on the Kentucky River, northwest of Lexington and east of Louisville. Population: 27,660 (2002 estimate).

Frankfurt /fráŋk furt/ **1.** *also* **Frankfurt am Main** /-am mín/ city in west-central Germany, in the state of Hessen. Situated on the River Main, it is a major commercial and financial centre. Population: 652,412 (1997). **2.** *also* **Frankfurt an der Oder** /-an dur ṓdər/ city in northeastern Germany, in the state of Brandenburg. It is situated east of Berlin on the River Oder. Population: 87,863 (1989).

frankfurter /fráŋk furtər/, **frankfurt** /-furt/ *n* a thin-skinned sausage, originally from Germany, made of finely minced smoked pork or beef and grilled, fried, or boiled [Late 19C. < German *Frankfurter Wurst*, smoked sausage first produced in Frankfurt am Main]

Frankfurter /fráŋk furtər/, **Felix** (1882–1965) Austrian-born associate justice of the US Supreme Court (1939–62). He advocated judicial restraint.

'There is no inevitability in history except as men make it.'
[Attributed to Felix Frankfurter. Quoted in *Saturday Review*; 30 October 1954]

frankincense /fráŋkin senss/ *n* an aromatic gum or resin used as incense, especially in religious

ceremonies, and in perfumes. It is obtained from trees of the genus *Boswellia*, native to Africa. [14C. < Old French *franc encens* 'superior-quality incense']

franking machine *n* a machine that prints an official mark on items to be posted and records the cost of posting as an alternative to the use of postage stamps. Franking machines are issued by a postal authority to businesses and other organizations that handle large volumes of mail. N Am term **postage meter**

Frankish /fráŋkish/ *n* EXTINCT GERMANIC LANGUAGE an extinct Germanic language spoken by the Franks. The French vocabulary shows a heavy Frankish influence. ▪ *adj* **1.** OF FRANKS relating to the Franks **2.** OF FRANKISH relating to Frankish

Franklin /fráŋklin/ river in southwestern Tasmania, Australia. A popular white-water rafting river, it rises on Mount Huge near Lake St Clair and flows southwards into the Gordon River. Length: 120 km/75 mi.

Aretha Franklin

Franklin, Aretha (*b.* 1942) US soul singer. Known as 'The Queen of Soul', she began her recording career in 1960. Her most famous recordings include 'Respect' (1967) and 'I Never' (1967). Full name **Franklin, Aretha Louise**

'Now there's a plain bare fact...Soul came up from gospel and blues.'
[Aretha Franklin. Quoted in *Nowhere to Run*, Gerri Hirshey; 1984]

Franklin, Benjamin (1706–90) American diplomat, printer, author, and scientist. He helped draft, then signed, the Declaration of Independence (1776) and was a US diplomat to France (1776–85). His famous autobiography was published posthumously. Also renowned as a scientist, he invented the Franklin stove (1740s), lightning conductor (1752), and bifocal lens (1784).

'In this world nothing can be said to be certain but death and taxes.'
[Benjamin Franklin, *Letter to Jean-Baptiste Le Roy*; 13 November 1789]

Franklin, Sir John (1786–1847) British naval officer and explorer. He died on his fourth Arctic expedition, during which the Northwest Passage was discovered (1845).

Franklin, Miles (1879–1954) Australian writer and feminist. She is best known for her largely autobiographical first novel *My Brilliant Career* (1901). Full name **Franklin, Stella Maria Sarah Miles**. Pseudonym **Brent of Bin Bin**. See Cultural note at **career**

Franklin, Rosalind Elsie (1920–58) British biophysicist. Her research contributed to the discovery of the double-helix structure of DNA.

franklinite /fráŋkli nīt/ *n* a black weakly magnetic mineral of the spinel group, containing iron, manganese, and zinc [Early 19C. After *Franklin*, New Jersey]

frankly /fráŋkli/ *adv* **1.** used to indicate that you are expressing an honest personal opinion, often a negative one ○ *Most of what she said was, frankly, a pack of lies.* **2.** in an honest, sincere, and often blunt or forthright way ○ *was asked personal questions that he answered remarkably frankly*

frantic /frántik/ *adj* **1.** in a state in which it is impossible to keep feelings or behaviour under control, usually through fear, worry, or frustration **2.** characterized by great haste and excitement and

a great deal of usually disorganized activity [Early 16C. < French *frénétique* (see FRENETIC)] —**frantically** *adv* —**franticness** *n*

~~**franticly**~~ incorrect spelling of **frantically**

Franz Ferdinand /fránts fúrdi nand/ (1863–1914) Archduke of Austria. His assassination and that of his wife, the Duchess of Hohenburg, while on an official visit to Sarajevo in 1914, led to the outbreak of World War I.

Franz Josef /fránts yṓssəf/ (1830–1916) emperor of Austria (1848–1916) and king of Hungary (1867–1916). He divided his Austrian empire into the dual Austro-Hungarian monarchy in 1867, during a reign that was characterized by nationalist strife culminating in the outbreak of World War I (1914).

Franz-Josef Glacier /fránts jṓzəf-/ glacier in Westland National Park on the western coast of the South Island, New Zealand. Length: 11 km/7 mi.

Franz Josef Land archipelago of about 100 small ice-covered islands in the Arctic Ocean, northwestern Russia, including Alexandra Land, George Land, Wilczek Land, and Graham Bell Island. Area: 20,700 sq. km/7,990 sq. mi.

frap /frap/ (**fraps, frapping, frapped**) *vt* to tie something down, or tie things together, with ropes [Mid-16C. < Old French *fraper* 'hit']

frappé /fráppay/ *adj* BEVERAGES **CHILLED** chilled or poured over crushed ice ■ *n* **1.** BEVERAGES **ICED ALCOHOLIC DRINK** an alcoholic drink, especially a liqueur, served poured over crushed ice **2.** FOOD **COLD DESSERT** a dish consisting of fruit-flavoured water ice, served before a meal or as a dessert [Mid-19C. < French, past participle of *frapper* 'hit, chill']

Frappuccino /fráppo͝o cheénō/ *tdmk* a trademark for a drink made of coffee blended with milk, crushed ice, and flavourings

Fraser /fráyzər/ river in south-central British Columbia, Canada. It rises in the Rocky Mountains and empties into the Strait of Georgia, near Vancouver. Length: 1,370 km/850 mi.

Fraser, Dawn (*b.* 1937) Australian swimmer. She was the first woman to swim the 100 metres freestyle in under one minute and the first swimmer to win three consecutive Olympic gold medals in that event (1956, 1960, and 1964). Full name **Fraser, Dawn Lorraine**

Fraser, Malcolm (*b.* 1930) Australian politician. Elected as a member of parliament for the Liberal Party in 1955, he served as prime minister of Australia from 1975 to 1983. Full name **Fraser, John Malcolm**. See table at **prime minister**

Fraser, Neale (*b.* 1933) Australian tennis player. The winner of the 1960 Wimbledon men's singles title, he was the Australian Davis Cup team coach from 1970 to 1993. Full name **Fraser, Neale Andrew**

Fraser, Peter (1884–1950) Scottish-born New Zealand politician. A Labour Party politician, he served as prime minister of New Zealand from 1940 to 1949. See table at **prime minister**

Fraser Island island off the coast of southern Queensland, Australia. It is the largest sand island in the world. Population: 100. Area: 1,662 sq. km/642 sq. mi.

frass /frass/ *n* excrement or debris left behind by an insect or insect larva [Mid-19C. < German < *fressen* 'eat, devour']

frat /frat/ *n N Am* a fraternity at a college or university (*informal*) [Late 19C. Shortening]

fraternal /frə túrn'l/ *adj* **1. OF BROTHERS** existing between brothers or felt by one brother for another **2. SHOWING FRIENDSHIP AND MUTUAL SUPPORT** showing friendship and mutual support between people or groups with the same interests or aims ○ *fraternal greetings* **3. OF FRATERNITIES** relating to or organized as a fraternity **4.** BIOL **FROM TWO OVA** describes twins that have developed from two ova, instead of from a single ovum [15C. < medieval Latin *fraternalis* < Latin *frater* 'brother'] —**fraternalism** *n* —**fraternally** *adv*

fraternise *vi* SOCIOL, MIL another spelling of **fraternize**

fraternity /frə túrnəti/ (*plural* **-ties**) *n* **1. PEOPLE WITH SOMETHING IN COMMON** a group of people with something such as being in the same profession or sharing the same pastime in common ○ *the banking fraternity* **2. SOCIETY FORMED FOR COMMON PURPOSE** a group or society formed by people who share the same interests **3. BROTHERLY LOVE** feelings of friendship and mutual support between people ○ *liberty, equality, and fraternity* **4.** *N Am* **SOCIETY FOR COLLEGE MEN** a social society for men who are students at a North American college or university, with a name consisting of individually pronounced Greek letters [14C. Via French < Latin *fraternitas* < *frater* 'brother']

fraternize /fráttər nīz/ (**-nizes, -nizing, -nized**), **fraternise** (**-nises, -nising, -nised**) *vi* to spend time socially with other people, especially people with whom it is not regarded as acceptable to be friendly ○ *fraternizing with the enemy* [Early 17C. Via French < medieval Latin *fraternizare* < Latin *frater* 'brother'] —**fraternization** /fráttər nī záysh'n/ *n* —**fraternizer** *n*

fratricide /fráttri sīd, fráytri-/ *n* **1.** the crime of killing a brother **2.** somebody who kills a brother [15C. Via French < Latin *fratricida* 'brother-killer'] —**fratricidal** /fráttri sīd'l, fráytri-/ *adj*

Frau /frow/ (*plural* **Frauen** /frówən/ or **Fraus**) *n* in German-speaking countries, used as a title equivalent to English 'Mrs' or 'Ms' before the name or professional title of a married woman. It is also used as a courtesy title for some unmarried women, especially of senior status. ○ *Frau Koch* [Early 19C. < German, 'woman, wife']

fraud /frawd/ *n* **1. CRIME OF CHEATING SOMEBODY** the crime of obtaining money or some other benefit by deliberate deception **2. SOMEBODY WHO DECEIVES** somebody who deliberately deceives somebody else, usually for financial gain **3. SOMETHING INTENDED TO DECEIVE** something that is intended to deceive people ○ *a story that was subsequently exposed as a fraud* [14C. Via Old French < Latin *fraud-* 'cheating, fraud']

fraud squad *n* the section of the UK police force that deals with fraud

fraudster /fráwdstər/ *n* a criminal who obtains money or some other benefit by deliberate deception

fraudulent /fráwdyo͝olənt/ *adj* not honest, true, or fair, and intended to deceive people —**fraudulence** *n* —**fraudulently** *adv*

fraught /frawt/ *adj* **1.** full of or accompanied by problems, dangers, or difficulties ○ *an evening fraught with embarrassment* **2.** full of or expressing nervous tension and anxiety ○ *looking fraught and close to tears* [14C. < past participle of obsolete *fraught* 'load with cargo' < Middle Dutch or Middle Low German *vrachten*]

Fräulein /fróy līn, fròw-/ (*plural same* or **-leins**) *n* in German-speaking countries, used as a title equivalent to English 'Miss' before the name or professional title of a girl or unmarried woman. It is also used as a form of address. ○ *Fräulein Bauer* [Late 17C. < German, 'little woman' < *Frau* 'woman, wife']

Fraunhofer lines /frównhōfər-/ *npl* narrow dark lines in the Sun's spectrum, caused mainly by absorption in the cooler outer layers of the Sun's atmosphere [Mid-19C. After Joseph von *Fraunhofer* (1787–1826), German scientist]

fraxinella /fráksi néllə/ *n* PLANTS same as **gas plant** [Mid-17C. < modern Latin < Latin *fraxinus* 'ash tree'; from the shape of the leaves]

fray[1] /fray/ *vti* (**frays, fraying, frayed**) **1. WEAR AWAY AND HANG IN THREADS** to wear away the edge or surface of cloth or rope by friction, causing threads to hang loose, or be worn away in this way ○ *frayed at the cuffs* **2. MAKE OR BECOME STRAINED** to become strained, causing irritability or anger, or cause somebody's nerves, temper, or patience to become strained ○ *Soon tempers would start to fray.* ■ *n* **WORN PART WITH LOOSE THREADS** a worn area on cloth or rope, with loose threads showing [15C. Via French *frayer* < Latin *fricare* 'rub']

fray[2] /fray/ *n* **1.** an argument, quarrel, or rowdy fight ○ *Local newspapers were not slow to join the fray.* **2.** an exciting, energetic, or stressful activity or situation ○ *back to the fray* [14C. Shortening of AFFRAY]

Fray Bentos /fray bén toss/ port and capital of Río Negro Department, western Uruguay, situated on the River Uruguay, approximately 280 km/175 mi. northwest of Montevideo. Population: 20,135 (1985).

Frazer /fráyzə/, **Sir James George** (1854–1941) British anthropologist. In his most famous work, *The Golden Bough* (1890), he examines the relationship between myth and religion.

frazil /fráyzil, frázzil/ *n* ice that forms as small plates drifting in rapidly flowing water where it is too turbulent for pack ice to form [Late 19C. < Canadian French *frasil*]

frazzle /frázz'l/ *n* **1. EXHAUSTED STATE** a state of complete emotional and physical exhaustion **2.** *N Am* **FRAYED CONDITION** a frayed or tattered condition ■ *vt* (**-zles, -zling, -zled**) **EXHAUST SOMEBODY** to completely exhaust somebody emotionally and physically [Early 19C. Probably blend of FRAY[1] + FRIZZLE[1] or obsolete *fazle* 'ravel'] ◇ **to a frazzle 1.** into a state of complete emotional and physical exhaustion **2.** completely, especially until something is thoroughly scorched, blackened, or charred

frazzled /frázz'ld/ *adj* exhausted and in a very confused or irritable state (*informal*)

FRCS *abbr* Fellow of the Royal College of Surgeons

freak[1] /freek/ *n* **1. STRIKINGLY UNUSUAL PERSON, ANIMAL, OR PLANT** a person, animal, or plant that is strikingly unusual and appears to be unique or occurs very rarely (*sometimes considered offensive*) **2. UNUSUAL OCCURRENCE** a highly unusual or unlikely occurrence, often brought about by a unique or very rare combination of circumstances **3. OFFENSIVE TERM** an offensive term for somebody who is thought to behave unconventionally or have unusual tastes or habits (*informal insult*) **4. FANATIC** somebody who is fanatical about something (*informal*) ○ *a club for fitness freaks* **5. DRUG USER** an addict or user of a particular drug (*slang*) **6. IMPULSE** something somebody suddenly does or decides for no real reason ■ *adj* **HIGHLY UNUSUAL OR UNLIKELY** highly unusual or unlikely, and often brought about by a unique or very rare combination of circumstances ■ *vti* (**freaks, freaking, freaked**) **1. BECOME OR MAKE OVEREMOTIONAL** to become very nervous, upset, or angry, or make somebody become so (*informal*) ○ *a loud explosion that freaked the cattle* **2. BEHAVE STRANGELY** to behave wildly or irrationally, or make somebody behave wildly or irrationally, sometimes under the effects of hallucinations or feelings of paranoia, often as a result of taking drugs (*slang*) [Mid-16C. Origin ?]

freak out *vti* to become extremely upset or agitated, or make somebody become so (*slang*)

freak[2] /freek/ (**freaks, freaking, freaked**) *vt* to streak or spot something with colour (*archaic*) [Mid-17C. Origin ?]

freaking /freéking/ *adj N Am* an offensive term expressing strong feelings by its similarity in sound to other offensive terms (*slang*)

freakish /freékish/ *adj* **1.** extremely, disconcertingly, or ridiculously unusual (*offensive in some contexts*) ○ *a freakish accident* **2.** tending to change suddenly and unpredictably ○ *freakish weather* —**freakishly** *adv* —**freakishness** *n*

freak-out, **freakout** /freék owt/ *n* **1.** an outburst of emotion or agitated behaviour (*informal*) **2.** a drug-induced bout of hallucination or paranoia, especially a frightening one (*slang*)

freaky /freéki/ (**-ier, -iest**) *adj* unusual, strange, or bizarre (*slang*) —**freakily** *adv* —**freakiness** *n*

freckle /frék'l/ *n* a harmless small brownish patch on somebody's skin, usually one of a cluster, that becomes larger and deeper in colour when the skin is exposed to the sun. Freckles are caused by the presence of larger melanin-containing cells in the basal layer of the skin. ■ *vti* (**-les, -ling, -led**) to become marked with freckles, or mark something with freckles [15C. Alteration of obsolete *frecken* 'freckle' < Old Norse *freknur* 'freckles'] —**freckly** *adj*

Frederick I /fréddrik/ (1123?–90) Holy Roman Emperor and king of Germany (1152–90), and king of Italy (1155–90). His campaigns against the papacy and the allied northern Italian cities known as the Lombard League ended in defeat at the battle of Legnano (1176). He died while on campaign in the Third Crusade. Known as **Frederick Barbarossa**

Frederick II[1] (1194–1250) Holy Roman Emperor (1215–50) and, as Frederick I, king of Sicily (1198–1250). He

captured Jerusalem (1228) during the Fifth Crusade and established peace in Sicily. He struggled throughout his rule with the papacy and the allied northern Italian cities of the Lombard League, and was excommunicated three times (1227, 1239, and 1245).

Frederick II[2] (1712–86) king of Prussia. Under his political and military leadership (1740–86), Prussia doubled in size and became a major European power. He gathered a circle of writers and musicians about him at his palace of Sans Souci. Known as **Frederick the Great**

Fredericton /frédriktən/ capital of New Brunswick Province, eastern Canada, situated in the south-central part of the province, on the St John River. Population: 54,068 (2001).

free /free/ *adj* (**freer, freest**) **1. COSTING NOTHING** requiring no money to be paid ○ *Win a free meal for two.* **2. NOT KEPT PRISONER** not, or no longer, physically bound or restrained, e.g. as a prisoner or in slavery ○ *Once outside the prison walls he would be a free man.* ○ *They hoped to be set free within the week.* **3. NOT RESTRICTED IN RIGHTS** not subject to censorship or control by a ruler, government, or other authority, and enjoying civil liberties ○ *It's a free country.* **4. SELF-RULING** not ruled by a foreign country or power **5. NOT REGULATED** not controlled, restricted, or regulated by any external thing ○ *You are free to choose.* **6. NOT BUSY** not busy or occupied with work ○ *had virtually no free time* ○ *She'll be free in a moment.* **7. NOT BEING USED** not being used, reserved, or taken by somebody else ○ *no free seats left* **8. NOT ATTACHED** not tied or attached to something ○ *grabbed the free end of the rope* **9. NOT AFFECTED BY PARTICULAR THING** not subject to or affected by a particular thing, especially something undesirable (*often used in combination*) ○ *drinking water that is free of contamination* ○ *a trouble-free trip* **10. NOT CONTAINING SOMETHING** not containing a particular thing (*often used in combination*) ○ *a salt-free diet* **11. DISREGARDING TRADITIONAL LIMITATIONS** performed or written without being subjected to traditional conventions or restraints ○ *free verse* **12. NOT BLOCKED** not blocked or obstructed by anything ○ *allowing the free flow of electricity* **13. NOT PHYSICALLY RESTRICTED** not restricted by something such as tight clothing, stiffness, or lack of space ○ *interfering with its free movement* **14. GIVING SOMETHING READILY** giving or expending something generously or readily ○ *They're very free with their advice.* **15. NOT EXACT** not following the original version of something word for word or very precisely ○ *a free translation* **16. OPEN AND HONEST** spontaneous, open, and without awkwardness or reserve in speaking to or dealing with other people ○ *an appealingly free and open manner* **17.** CHEM **NOT CHEMICALLY COMBINED** not chemically combined with another substance **18.** PHYS **NOT INCORPORATED IN LARGER BODY** not permanently incorporated in a larger body such as an atom, molecule, or compound **19.** NAUT **FAVOURABLE** favourable to sailing ○ *a free wind* **20.** LING **ABLE TO BE USED ALONE** describes a unit of meaning (**morpheme**) that can be used on its own as a word, without needing to be part of another word ■ *adv* **1. WITHOUT COST** without paying any money ○ *They let you in free if you show your student card.* **2. OUT OF RESTRICTED POSITION** out of a position in which somebody or something is tied, fixed, restricted, or restrained ○ *managed to wriggle free from his grasp* ■ *vt* (**frees, freeing, freed**) **1. RELEASE SOMEBODY FROM CAPTIVITY** to release somebody from physical bonds or restrictions, captivity, or slavery ○ *The defendants were freed after their acquittal.* **2. RID SOMEBODY OR SOMETHING OF SOMETHING** to remove a restriction, a burden, or an unwanted or undesirable thing from somebody or something ○ *freed from the responsibilities of high public office* **3. MAKE SOMEBODY OR SOMETHING AVAILABLE** to make somebody or something available for use or able to do something ○ *This should free you to do more of your own research.* **4. UNCLOG SOMETHING OBSTRUCTED** to clear something of an obstruction [Old English *freo* < Indo-European, 'dear, beloved'] ◇ **for free** without paying ◇ **free and easy** relaxed, friendly, and informal ◇ **make free with somebody** to behave in too familiar and informal a way towards somebody ◇ **make free with something** to use something in an overfamiliar or overindulgent way, without showing respect or restraint

USAGE See *gift*.

free up *vt* **1.** to make available for use something that is currently occupied, otherwise employed, or subject to a restriction ○ *frees up some space on my hard disk* **2.** to enable something that is tightly fastened, jammed, or blocked to move freely (*informal*) ○ *freed up the clogged intersection*

free agent *n* **1.** somebody who does not depend on, or is not answerable to or for, somebody else **2.** *US* a professional athlete who is in a position to sign a contract to play for any team

free alongside ship *adj, adv* with the cost of delivery to the quayside included, but not the cost of loading onto a ship

free association *n* **1.** the spontaneous and uncensored expression of thoughts or ideas, in which each one is allowed to lead to or suggest the next **2.** in psychoanalysis, a technique for exploring a patient's unconscious by stimulating the spontaneous and uncensored expression of thoughts or feelings through the use of stimuli such as key words —**free-associate** *vi*

freebase /freé bayss/ *v* (**-basing, -based, -based**) **1.** *vt* **PREPARE COCAINE FOR SMOKING** to prepare cocaine for smoking by heating it with water and a volatile liquid such as ether in order to concentrate it **2.** *vti* **SMOKE COCAINE** to smoke or inhale freebased cocaine ■ *n* **CONCENTRATED COCAINE** cocaine that has been concentrated using water and a volatile liquid such as ether [< the 'freeing' of the concentrated cocaine base]

freebie /freébi/ *n* something given or obtained free of charge, especially a promotional gift (*informal*)

freeboard /freé bawrd/ *n* the distance between the deck of a ship and the level of the water

freebooter /freé bootər/ *n* a plunderer, especially a pirate [Late 16C. < Dutch *vrijbuiter* 'somebody who takes booty freely'] —**freeboot** *vi*

freeborn /freé bawrn/ *adj* **1.** born as a free citizen, and therefore not a slave or serf **2.** relating to or intended for people who are freeborn

freecarving *n* a style of snowboarding that focuses on carving deep tracks in the snow with tight cornering rather than on doing stunts

Free Church *n* a Protestant church free from state control in running its affairs and not part of the church established as the official church of the state

free climbing *n* mountain or rock climbing without aids such as spikes and ladders, though usually with ropes and other safety equipment

freediving /freé dīving/ *n* the extreme sport of submerging into deep water for as long as possible without the aid of oxygen tanks —**freediver** *n*

freedman /freédmən/ (*plural* **-men** /-men/) *n* a man who has been freed from slavery

freedom /freédəm/ *n* **1. ABILITY TO ACT FREELY** a state in which somebody is able to act and live as he or she chooses, without being subject to any undue restraints or restrictions ○ *live in freedom* ○ *religious freedom* **2. RELEASE FROM CAPTIVITY OR SLAVERY** release or rescue from being physically bound, or from being confined, enslaved, captured, or imprisoned **3. COUNTRY'S RIGHT TO SELF-RULE** a country's right to rule itself, without interference from, or domination by, another country or power **4. RIGHT TO ACT OR SPEAK FREELY** the right to speak or act without restriction, interference, or fear ○ *was given the freedom to take photographs and interview workers* **5. ABSENCE OF SOMETHING UNPLEASANT** the state of being unaffected by, or not subject to, something unpleasant or unwanted ○ *freedom from fear* **6. EASE OF MOVEMENT** the ability to move easily without being limited by something such as tight clothing or lack of space ○ *loose clothing allowing complete freedom of movement* **7. RIGHT TO OCCUPY PLACE** the right to use or occupy a place and treat it as your own ○ *In the closed season, we had the freedom of the whole house and the beach.* **8. HONORARY CITIZENSHIP** citizenship of a town or city, together with special privileges, formally awarded to somebody as an honour ○ *was given the freedom of the city* **9. FRANKNESS** openness and friendliness in speech or behaviour **10. EXCESSIVE CONFIDENCE OR FAMILIARITY** overconfidence, overfamiliarity, or a lack of proper restraint or decorum **11.** PHILOSOPHY **FREE WILL** the ability to exercise free will and make choices independently of any external determining force

Freedom Charter *n* a document setting out the basic rights of all South Africans, composed in 1955 in opposition to the Nationalist government and constituting the manifesto of the African National Congress

freedom fighter *n* a participant in an armed revolution against a government or political system regarded as unjust

freedom march *n* an organized march by people campaigning for civil rights, e.g. any of the marches that took place in the United States in the 1960s with the aim of ending racial segregation —**freedom marcher** *n*

freedom rider *n* a civil rights activist who, during the early 1960s, joined one of the interracial groups riding on buses through parts of the southern United States to protest against racial segregation

freedwoman /freéd wŏŏmən/ (*plural* **-women** /-wimin/) *n* a woman who has been freed from slavery

free electron *n* an electron that is not bonded to an atom or molecule and so is free to move under external electric or magnetic fields

free energy *n* a measure of the capacity of a system to do work, such as the likelihood of a particular chemical reaction to form products. Symbol *G*

free enterprise *n* the doctrine or practice of giving business the freedom to trade and make a profit without government control

free fall, free-fall *n* **1. RAPID DECLINE** a sudden sharp uncontrollable drop in something such as value, popularity, or credibility ○ *The value of the currency has gone into free fall.* **2. DESCENT WITH UNOPENED PARACHUTE** a descent through the air with an unopened parachute as the first part of a parachute jump **3.** PHYS **UNRESTRICTED MOVEMENT IN EARTH'S GRAVITATIONAL FIELD** an ideal state in which the only force to which something is subjected is the Earth's gravitational attraction. As an example, a craft in space is subject only to a diminished gravitational force and is not restricted by buoyancy or air resistance.

free-fall (**free-falls, free-falling, free-fell, free-fallen**) *vi* **1.** to descend through the air with an unopened parachute during the first part of a parachute jump **2.** to undergo a sudden sharp uncontrollable drop in something such as value, popularity, or credibility

free-fire zone *n* an area in a conflict zone where troops may fire on targets at will without requesting permission from a superior

free flight *n* the movement of a rocket or missile through the air after its engine has stopped

free-floating *adj* not committed or dedicated to one specific thing, especially a political party or cause

free-floating anxiety *n* a state of anxiety that is not associated with any specific event or external condition

Freefone /freé fōn/ *tdmk* a trademark for a phone system in which the holder of the phone number pays the cost of the call, not the caller

free-for-all *n* a disorganized argument, contest, or fight in which everyone present participates (*informal*)

free form *n* a shape, especially a piece of sculpture, that is asymmetrical and irregular, though usually with a flowing outline

freeform /freé fawrm/ *adj* **1.** unconventional in shape or design, especially in being asymmetrical and irregular, but with a flowing outline **2.** spontaneously or individually created, and not produced in accordance with accepted or prescribed standards

free hand *n* complete freedom to take action or make decisions ○ *gave him a free hand in designing the house*

freehand /freé hand/ *adj, adv* done by hand and without using drawing instruments such as rulers or compasses

freehanded /frée hándid/ *adj* giving generously, or always ready to give ○ *children of freehanded parents* —**freehandedly** *adv* —**freehandedness** *n*

free-heel skiing *n* the sport of downhill skiing in ski bindings similar to those used in cross-country that leave the heels free

freehold /frée hōld/ *n* **1.** legal ownership of a property giving the owner unconditional rights, including the right to grant leases and take out mortgages **2.** a property that has freehold status —**freeholder** *n*

free house *n* a pub that is not owned by a particular brewery and so is free to sell whatever beers and other products it chooses

free jazz *n* a style of jazz, developed in the 1960s, that has no set harmonies or melodic patterns

free kick *n* in football, a kick of a stationary ball awarded for an infringement by a member of the opposing team, who must stand at least ten yards from where the kick is taken. A goal can be scored by a player taking a direct free kick, whereas an indirect free kick requires that the ball touch another player before entering the goal.

free labour *n* workers who do not belong to any trade union

freelance /frée laanss/ *n* **1.** SOMEBODY WORKING FOR DIFFERENT COMPANIES a self-employed person working, or available to work, for a number of employers, and usually hired for a limited period **2.** MAVERICK somebody, especially a politician, who is not committed to any group and takes action or forms alliances independently **3.** *also* **free lance** HIST MEDIEVAL MERCENARY a mercenary soldier in medieval Europe ■ *adj* WORKING FREELANCE working or earning a living as a freelance ■ *adv* AS FREELANCE independently, as a freelance ○ *worked freelance as a journalist* ■ *vi* (**-lances, -lancing, -lanced**) WORK AS FREELANCE to work independently as a freelance [Early 19C. < the idea of a medieval knight with a lance offering his services to whoever was willing to pay]

freelancer /frée laanssər/ *n* HR same as **freelance** *n* (sense 1)

free-living *adj* able to live or move independently, and not parasitic, symbiotic, or sessile ○ *free-living organisms*

freeloader /frée lōdər/ *n* an exploiter of somebody else's generosity or hospitality (*informal*) —**freeload** /frée lōd, free lōd/ *vi*

free love *n* sexual relationships without marriage or commitment to a single partner, especially as practised by the 19th- and early-20th-century avant-garde and in the 1960s

free lunch *n* something given free and with nothing expected in return (*informal*)

freely /frée li/ *adv* **1.** WITHOUT RESTRICTIONS without restrictions, controls, or limits ○ *able to move freely from country to country* **2.** IN LARGE AMOUNTS in large or generous quantities ○ *gave freely to a number of well-known charities* **3.** OPENLY honestly and openly ○ *felt able to speak freely about his ordeal for the first time* **4.** WITHOUT TIGHTNESS OR STIFFNESS without being restricted by something such as tight clothing, stiffness, or lack of space ○ *clothes that allowed him to move more freely* **5.** USED TO EMPHASIZE HONESTY used to persuade somebody that you are being open and honest by accepting criticism ○ *I freely admit that mistakes were made.*

freeman /frée mən/ (*plural* **-men** /-mən/) *n* **1.** a man who has been formally given citizenship of a place, together with various special privileges, as an honour ○ *a freeman of the city* **2.** a man who is not a slave or serf

Freeman /frée mən/, **Cathy** (*b.* 1973) Australian sprinter. The first Aboriginal sprinter to win a gold medal at the Commonwealth Games (1994), she went on to win a gold medal in the 400 metres at the 2000 Olympic Games. Full name **Freeman, Catherine Astrid Salome**

free market *n* an economic system in which businesses operate without government control in matters such as pricing and wage levels —**free-market** *adj* —**free-marketeer** *n*

freemartin /frée maartin/ *n* a sterile female twin born with a male calf [Late 17C. Origin ?]

freemason /frée mayss'n/ *n* a member of an organization of skilled stonemasons travelling from place to place in medieval Europe [14C. Origin ?]

Freemason *n* a member of a worldwide society, the Free and Accepted Masons, that is known particularly for its charitable work and its secret rites

Freemasonry /frée mayss'nri/ *n* **1.** the institutions, beliefs, and practices of the Freemasons **2.** *also* **freemasonry** an instinctive understanding and comradeship among people with something in common

freeness /frée nəss/ *n* the quality or state of being free ◇ **love too much freeness** to live at the expense of others by imposing on their generosity and making no effort to live independently (*slang; used in Black English*)

freenet /frée net/ *n* an online computer information network that charges no access fees, often run by volunteers as a public service

free on board *adj, adv* with the cost of delivery to a port and loading onto a ship included

free on rail *adj, adv* with the cost of delivery to a railway station and loading onto a train included

free pardon *n* a legal statement declaring that somebody convicted of a crime has now had that conviction quashed

free port *n* **1.** a port open to commercial ships from all countries on equal terms **2.** a zone at a port or airport that allows the duty-free import of goods that are to be re-exported

freepost *n* in the UK, a system in which organizations pay the postal charges of customers who send them letters

free radical *n* a highly reactive atom or group of atoms with an unpaired electron

free-range *adj* **1.** free to move about and feed at will, and not confined in a battery or pen ○ *free-range chickens* **2.** produced by free-range poultry or livestock ○ *free-range eggs*

free rein *n* complete freedom to make decisions and take action without consulting anyone else

free ride *n* something obtained at no cost or with no effort (*slang*)

freeriding /frée rīding/ *n* a basic style of snowboarding that involves travelling over the snow without performing stunts —**freeride** *adj*

free selection *n* Aus in colonial Australia, the practice of taking up a plot of Crown land for agricultural use and then buying it by making a series of regular payments to the government

free settler *n* Aus a settler who emigrated to Australia through choice, rather than being transported as a convict

freesheet /frée sheet/ *n* a free newspaper or news sheet, especially one delivered to all the households in a particular area and funded by advertising

freesia

freesia /frée zhə, frée zi ə/ *n* a plant grown from a corm, popular as a cut flower. Flowers: fragrant, tubular, brightly coloured. Native to: southern Africa. Genus: *Freesia*. [Late 19C. After Friedrich H. T. Freese (1795–1896), German physician]

free skating *n* competitive ice skating in which the

skater makes up his or her own programme from a list of approved moves

freeskiing /frée skee ing/ *n* the sport of skiing on downhill skis that have curved tips front and back, permitting the skier to execute moves similar to those of snowboarders on slopes and in halfpipes [Late 20C.] —**freeskier** *n*

free-soloing *n* the sport of climbing boulders and rock faces without a safety line or a partner to catch or break a fall

free space *n* a region in which there is no matter and no gravitational or electromagnetic fields

free speech *n* the right to express any opinion publicly

free spirit *n* somebody who lives without regard to what convention dictates or what others expect —**free-spirited** *adj* —**free-spiritedness** *n*

free-spoken *adj* expressing opinions frankly, without worrying about embarrassing or offending others (*archaic or literary*)

freestanding /frée stánding/ *adj* **1.** standing alone, and not fixed to a wall, floor, or other structure for support **2.** GRAM grammatically independent and able to function as a main clause

Free State[1] *n* a US state in which slavery was not tolerated before the American Civil War

Free State[2] /frée stayt/ province in South Africa, in the central part of the country. Capital: Bloemfontein. Population: 2,706,754 (2001). Area: 129,480 sq. km/49,980 sq. mi.

freestone /frée stōn/ *n* **1.** a variety of masonry stone that has a uniform texture and can be chiselled without breaking or splitting, e.g. limestone or fine sandstone **2.** a stone to which the flesh of a fruit does not cling, or a fruit that has such a stone

freestyle /frée stīl/ *adj* **1.** WITH FREE CHOICE OF STYLE describes sporting events such as figure skating, surfing, and downhill skiing, in which any manoeuvre can be performed, with the contestants judged on their athleticism, technique, and artistry **2.** SWIMMING USING FRONT CRAWL describes a swimming contest in which the competitors can use any swimming stroke and usually use the front crawl **3.** WRESTLING NO-HOLDS-BARRED describes a wrestling style in which all legal holds and tactics are allowed ■ *n* **1.** SPORTS FREESTYLE CONTEST a freestyle race, event, or contest **2.** EXTREME SPORTS SNOWBOARDING STYLE FOCUSING ON STUNTS a style of snowboarding that focuses on performing stunts and special manoeuvres —**freestyler** *n*

freestyle skiing *n* the sport of downhill skiing, involving the performance of acrobatic moves such as high jumps and somersaults

freestyle wrestling *n* WRESTLING same as **all-in wrestling**

freestyling /frée stīling/ *n* EXTREME SPORTS same as **freestyle** *n* (sense 2)

free-swimming *adj* able to swim about freely, and not living attached to something or in one position ○ *free-swimming larvae*

freet /freet/ *n* Ireland same as **superstition** (sense 1) [Mid-16C. < Old Norse *frett* 'news, enquiry, augury']

freethinker /frée thíngkər/ *n* an independent thinker who refuses to accept established views or teachings, especially on religion —**freethinking** *adj, n*

free thought *n* thinking that refuses to accept established views or teachings, especially on religion

free throw *n* in basketball, an opportunity to shoot at the basket unhindered by the opposing players, awarded to a player who has been fouled

free-to-air *adj* describes television channels and programmes that are available free of charge to all customers

Freetown /frée town/ capital, largest city, and chief port of Sierra Leone, on the coast of West Africa. Founded in 1787 as a settlement for freed slaves, it became the capital when Sierra Leone gained independence in 1961. Population: 699,000 (1995).

free trade *n* international trade that is not subject to

protective regulations or tariffs intended to restrict foreign imports —**free-trader** *n*

free verse *n* verse without a fixed metrical pattern, usually having unrhymed lines of varying length

free vote *n* a vote in the British parliament or any similar body in which members may vote according to their consciences and personal opinions rather than as instructed by their party leaders

freeware /freé wair/ *n* any computer program or application that is available at no cost to the user

freeway /freé way/ *n* **1.** *Aus, N Am* a limited-access road usually consisting of three lanes for vehicles moving in both directions, intended for travelling relatively fast over long distances **2.** *N Am* a road that can be used without paying a toll

free-weight *n* a weight that is used for lifting exercises and is not attached to any other piece of apparatus, e.g. a dumbbell or barbell

freewheel /free weél/ *vi* (**-wheels, -wheeling, -wheeled**) **1.** TRAVEL WITHOUT USING POWER to continue moving on a bicycle or in a vehicle without using power to drive the wheels ○ *Once you get to the top, you can freewheel all the way down the other side.* **2.** LIVE IN CAREFREE WAY to live or act without conventional constraints, purpose, or regard for responsibilities ■ *n* **1.** DEVICE ON BICYCLE a mechanism in the hub of the rear wheel of a bicycle that enables the rear wheel to continue to rotate when the rider stops pedalling **2.** DEVICE IN MOTOR VEHICLE TRANSMISSION a mechanism in the transmission of a motor vehicle that disengages the drive shaft and allows it to rotate freely when revolving at a higher speed than the engine shaft

freewheeling /free weéling/ *adj* **1.** TRAVELLING WITHOUT POWER continuing to move without the use of power **2.** *N Am* CAREFREE without conventional constraints, purpose, or regard for responsibilities ○ *led a freewheeling life of travel and adventure* **3.** *N Am* UNSTRUCTURED not restricted by rules, formal structure, or established procedures ○ *a freewheeling discussion that touched on many topics* **4.** WITH FREEWHEEL relating to, having, or using a freewheel mechanism on a bicycle or in a motor vehicle

free will *n* the ability to act or make choices as a free and autonomous being and not solely as a result of compulsion or predestination ◇ **of your own free will** without being forced by somebody or something else

freewill /freé wil/ *adj* done willingly rather than by compulsion

freewoman /freé wŏŏmən/ (*plural* **-women** /-wimin/) *n* a woman who is not a slave or serf

free world *n* the countries of the world with democratic governments and capitalist or moderately socialist economic systems, as opposed to those with totalitarian or communist governments or economic systems

freeze /freez/ *v* (**freezes, freezing, froze** /frōz/, **frozen** /frṓz'n/) **1.** *vti* TURN LIQUID TO SOLID THROUGH COLD to change into a solid by the loss of heat, or cause liquid to do this, especially to change into ice ○ *Salt water freezes at a lower temperature than fresh water.* **2.** *vti* BECOME COVERED WITH ICE to become covered with ice, or cause the surface of something to be covered with ice ○ *The lake froze for only the second time in living memory.* **3.** *vti* BECOME BLOCKED WITH ICE to become blocked with ice, or cause something to become blocked with ice ○ *Do you think it's cold enough to freeze the pipes in the attic?* **4.** *vti* BECOME HARD THROUGH COLD to harden through the effects of cold or frost, or cause something to harden ○ *We couldn't play because the ground was frozen solid.* **5.** *vti* BECOME STUCK THROUGH COLD to become fixed or stuck to something else as a result of cold, or cause something to become fixed in this way ○ *The wipers were frozen to the windscreen.* **6.** *vt* PRESERVE SOMETHING WITH EXTREME COLD to preserve something, especially food, by subjecting it to and storing it at a temperature well below freezing point ○ *Store airtight up to two weeks or freeze.* **7.** *vti* FEEL VERY COLD to feel extremely cold, or cause somebody to feel extremely cold ○ *They left us to freeze outside, while they went into the house.* **8.** *vti* BE HARMED OR KILLED BY COLD to be harmed or killed, or harm or kill somebody or something, with cold or frost **9.** *vi* DROP TO FREEZING POINT to be at or fall to a temperature at or below freezing point ○ *The forecast says it's likely to freeze again tonight.* **10.** *vti* STOP MOVING to stop, or cause somebody to stop and remain still, e.g. as a result of fear or surprise or as part of a game ○ *A loose floorboard creaked in the passage; Jenny froze.* **11.** *vi* COME TO STANDSTILL THROUGH SHOCK to become unable to act, react, or speak in a normal way, usually through fear or shock ○ *I was OK in rehearsals, but in front of an audience, I simply froze.* **12.** *vi* STOP RESPONDING to stop responding to instructions (*refers to computers*) ○ *The screen freezes whenever I attempt to save a document.* **13.** *vt* TREAT SOMEBODY ICILY to discourage or intimidate somebody by behaving in an unfriendly or hostile way ○ *She froze him with an icy glare.* **14.** *vt* HALT SOMETHING BEFORE COMPLETION to halt or limit the development or production of something ○ *The talks remain frozen at the procedural stage.* **15.** *vt* KEEP SOMETHING AT PRESENT LEVEL to fix something such as prices, rents, or wages at a specific level, usually by government action to prevent an increase ○ *Interest rates were frozen at their 1996 level.* **16.** *vt* KEEP ASSET FROM DISAPPEARING to prevent a financial asset from being sold or liquidated ○ *They froze her bank account immediately.* **17.** *vt* PROHIBIT SOMETHING to stop the manufacture, sale, or use of something **18.** *vi* BECOME UNFRIENDLY to become suddenly unfriendly and uncommunicative ○ *When I asked him about campaign contributions, he simply froze up.* **19.** *vt* ANAESTHETIZE PART OF BODY to anaesthetize part of somebody's body with a local anaesthetic **20.** *vt* STOP FILM AT FRAME to stop a moving film at a specific frame and show that frame as a still image **21.** *vt* CAPTURE INSTANT OF MOVEMENT to produce a still photographic image of somebody or something in movement or action ○ *He pressed the Pause button, freezing her delighted expression.* ■ *n* **1.** VERY COLD WEATHER a period when the temperature drops and stays below freezing point, especially for a long time **2.** RESTRICTION ON SOMETHING a restrictive measure that prevents something such as prices, wages, or production from rising above a specific level ○ *a temporary freeze on imports* [Old English *frēosan* < Indo-European, 'freeze, burn']

SPELLCHECK freeze or **frieze**? Do not confuse the spelling of ***freeze*** and ***frieze***, which sound similar. ***Freeze*** is chiefly used as a verb, meaning 'make or become hard through cold', 'stop moving', or 'fix at a specific level'. It is sometimes used as a noun, as in *the big freeze of last winter, a price freeze.* ***Frieze*** is only used as a noun, denoting a decorative band on a wall.

freeze out *vt* to exclude somebody from participation in something by cold or unfriendly treatment (*informal*) ○ *We feel we are being frozen out of the negotiations.*

freeze-dry *vt* to preserve something, especially food, by first freezing it, then placing it in a vacuum to remove moisture before returning it to room temperature. The low processing temperature and absence of liquid water help to retain colour, flavour, and texture. —**freeze-dried** *adj* —**freeze-drying** *n*

freeze-etching *n* the preparation of a biological specimen for examination with an electron microscope by freezing and splitting it to reveal its internal structure and allow a replica to be made —**freeze-etch** *vt* —**freeze-etched** *adj*

freeze-frame *n* **1.** FRAME OF FILM VIEWED SINGLY a single frame of a film or video recording viewed as a static image **2.** DEVICE ALLOWING VIEWING OF SINGLE FRAME a device on a video recorder that enables a single static image to be viewed ■ *vt* PRESENT AS STATIC IMAGE to present something contained in a single frame from a film or video recording as a static image

freezer /freézər/ *n* a storage cabinet, compartment, or room where food or other perishable goods can be frozen and preserved at a very low temperature

freezer burn *n* the pale dry spots that form when moisture evaporates from frozen food that is inadequately wrapped

freeze-up *n* a period of extremely cold weather

freezing /freézing/ *adj* **1.** VERY COLD extremely cold (*informal*) **2.** FORMING ICE forming ice crystals on contact with a surface ○ *freezing fog* ■ *adv* VERY to an extreme degree (*informal*) ○ *freezing cold* ■ *n* FREEZING POINT the point at which water freezes

freezing mixture *n* a mixture of substances, usually ice and salt, used in laboratories to produce a temperature below the freezing point of water

freezing point *n* the temperature at which a liquid solidifies, e.g. the temperature at which water turns to ice

free zone *n* an area at a port or in a city where goods may be received or stored without payment of customs duties

Frege /fráygə/, **Gottlob** (1848–1925) German mathematician and logician. He devised the first complete system of symbolic logic in his 1879 work *Begriffsschrift* and is considered the founder of modern mathematical logic.

F region *n* the highest part of the ionosphere that reflects high-frequency radio waves. It is divided into two layers, the F_1, which extends upwards from 180 km/112 mi. and is present only during the day, and the F_2, extending upwards from 300 km/186 mi.

Freiburg /frī burg/ city in Baden-Württemberg State, southwestern Germany. It is the cultural and economic centre of the Black Forest. Population: 198,496 (1997).

Freidel-Crafts reaction /frīd'l kraáfts-/ *n* a chemical reaction using metallic halides such as aluminium chloride, or acids such as catalysts. Use: chemical manufacture. [After Charles *Friedel* (1832–99), French chemist, and James M. *Crafts* (1839–1917), US chemist]

freight /frayt/ *n* **1.** GOODS FOR TRANSPORT goods or cargo carried by a commercial means of transport **2.** COMMON CLASS OF TRANSPORT the ordinary method or class of commercial transport for goods, slower and cheaper than express **3.** CHARGE FOR CARRYING GOODS a charge paid for the transport of goods **4.** *US* RAIL same as **freight train** **5.** BURDEN a load or burden (*literary*) ■ *vt* (**freights, freighting, freighted**) **1.** TRANSPORT GOODS to send or transport goods or cargo by commercial carrier **2.** LOAD VEHICLE WITH CARGO to load a ship, train, aircraft, or vehicle with goods or cargo to be transported **3.** SHIPPING HIRE SHIP to hire or hire out a ship to transport goods and passengers **4.** BURDEN SOMETHING OR SOMEBODY to load something or somebody with something such as feeling, significance, or emotion (*literary; usually passive*) [15C. < Middle Low German or Middle Dutch *vrecht*]

freightage /fráytij/ *n* **1.** TRANSPORT CHARGE a charge paid for the transport of goods or cargo **2.** COMMERCIAL CARRIAGE OF GOODS the commercial transport of goods or cargo **3.** GOODS CARRIED the goods that are carried by a ship or vehicle

freight car *n* a railway wagon that carries freight, usually one that is enclosed

freighter /fráytər/ *n* **1.** a ship or aircraft designed to carry freight **2.** an employee who sends, forwards, or receives freight, or who charters something to carry freight

freight ton *n* a unit used in measuring and pricing freight in maritime shipping, varying according to the type of goods carried but usually corresponding to 1,000 kg or 40 cubic ft

freight train *n* a railway train that carries only freight

~~freind~~ incorrect spelling of **friend**

Frei Ruiz-Tagle /fráy roo eéss taá glay/, **Eduardo** (*b.* 1942) president of Chile. During his presidency (1994–2000), he attempted to curb military power by constitutional reform.

~~freize~~ incorrect spelling of **frieze**

Fremantle /freé mant'l/ city and port in southwestern Western Australia, now part of the metropolitan area of Perth. Population: 26,126 (2002 estimate).

fremitus /frémmitəss/ (*plural same*) *n* a vibration or tremor, resulting from a physical action such as speaking or coughing, felt by hand and used to assess whether the chest is affected by disease [Early 19C. < Latin, 'roaring' < *fremere* 'to roar']

Fremont /freé mont/ city on San Francisco Bay in

LANGUAGE HERITAGE *French* Much of English is made up of words from other languages, and it has such a long history and such deep assimilation of migrants from French that many words of French origin are unrecognized as such. Within a century of the Norman Conquest of England in 1066, Old English had adopted, for example, *castle, justice, place, service,* and *war.* During the medieval period French, while remaining the usual language of the court and the law, also penetrated all areas of English life, giving such diverse vocabulary as *language* itself, *adventure, cage, force, pain,* and *tavern,* and later also, for example, *agree, army, card, famine,* and *library.* Migration continued with words such as *passport, amuse,* and *aristocracy* (15th century), *bomb, career, favourite, improve,* and *society* (16th), *attitude, cosmetic, develop, group,* and *vest* (17th). From the 18th century words tend to be more identifiably of French origin: *amateur, bouquet, foyer, souvenir,* and *vaudeville* (18th); *cigarette, mirage,* and *questionnaire* (19th); *discotheque, saboteur,* and *voyeur* (20th).

In modern English particular mention might be made of the contribution of French in the areas of food and cooking, fashion, the arts (especially dance and music), automobiles, and aviation.

It has long been noted that words for the flesh of animals as food tend to derive from French while those for the animals themselves remain of English (Germanic) origin: thus *cow* (English) but *beef* (French); *sheep* (English) but *mutton* (French); *deer* (English) but *venison* (French). From the 18th century, however, such basic terms are supplemented by more sophisticated French émigrés: *cuisine* itself in the late 18th century, closely followed by *chef, gastronomy,* and *gourmet*; the 18th century also saw the arrival of terms ranging from *batterie de cuisine* ('a set of cooking utensils, pots, and pans') to *casserole, meringue,* and *terrine*; 19th-century culinary terms include *croissant, crouton, marmite,* and *sauté,* some of which could be encountered in a *restaurant* or *café*; the 20th century acquired *haute cuisine* at its beginning and *nouvelle cuisine* towards its end, as well as *coulis, gratinée,* and also a new sense ('long thin loaf') of *baguette.*

The world of *fashion* (itself a word adopted from French in the 14th century), clothing, and textiles is also inhabited by French migrants, from the basic *jacket* (15th century) and *beret* (early 19th) to *haute couture* (early 20th); the superficially modern *denim* dates from the late 17th century – the word derives from French *(serge) de Nîmes* ('serge') of Nîmes (a city in southwestern France). Fashionable migrants continue to be welcomed: the *bustier* and *faux* ('imitation', as in *faux fur*) both came into English towards the end of the 20th century.

The arts are also heavily indebted to French, which provides the language with many terms of music and dance, and practically all the standard terms of ballet (*ballerina,* from Italian, being the most notable exception): for example *arabesque, entrechat, pas de deux,* the *tutu* (from a baby-talk alteration of *cucu,* from *cul* 'buttocks'), and *ballet* itself. More general terms include *bass, clef, concert, harmony, lyric, octave,* and *tambourine*; a relatively recent and more exotic migrant is *zouk,* a style of dance music originating in Guadeloupe and Martinique. In the visual arts, French provided the *artist* and his or her *palette,* and especially the names of schools such as *impressionism* (with its *plein-air* painting) and *pointillism.* Other important 'isms' also came from French, including *chauvinism* and *feminism.*

Science and technology also have their fair share of French words, represented here by the *automobile* and the *aeroplane,* housed respectively in a *garage* and *hangar. Helicopter* also arrived from French, as did the less successful *ornithopter,* an early flying machine that operated using flapping wings, and the *limousine.* Other migrants into the vocabulary of *aviation* (formed in French from Latin *avis* 'bird') include *aeronautical, aileron, fuselage, monocoque,* and *parachute.*

Historically, Scotland has had a special relationship with France (the countries were formally allied between 1296 and 1560), and this is reflected in distinct items of vocabulary such as *vennel* ('alley'), *fash* ('annoy'), *Hogmanay,* and later *ashet* ('large shallow dish', mid-19th century from French *assiette*), a word taken by migrants to New Zealand.

A separate wave of migration of French words took place in North America, where French settlements in Canada introduced English to terms such as *coureur de bois* ('fur trapper', literally 'woods runner'), *mush* (a command to sledge dogs, originally in *mush on!* and probably from French *marchons* 'let us march'), *shanty* ('shack', thought to be from Canadian French *chantier* 'lumberjack's hut'), and *voyageur* ('transporter of furs and supplies'). The people of Quebec have been *Québécois* in English (late 19th century) almost as long as they have been *Quebecers* (mid-19th). Until 1803 parts of the United States (the 'Louisiana Purchase') were French territory: *Mardi Gras* (literally 'fat Tuesday'), the carnival around Shrove Tuesday, known especially from New Orleans, is one linguistic relic of this earlier time, as is the *bayou* ('area of slow-moving water'), via Louisiana French from Choctaw *bayuk* 'small river forming part of a delta'.

---

western California, southeast of San Francisco. Population: 206,856 (2002 estimate).

frena ANAT plural of **frenum**

French /french/ *n* **1.** the official language of France and some other countries, belonging to the Romance group of Indo-European that developed from Latin. Native speakers: 70 million. Other speakers: 220 million. **2.** BEVERAGES same as **French vermouth** ■ *npl* the people of France collectively [Old English *francisc* < Germanic] —**French** *adj*

CULTURAL NOTE *The French Connection,* a film (1971) by US director William Friedkin. Set in New York, it depicts the attempts of an uncompromising policeman, Popeye Doyle, to break up an international drug ring originating in Marseille, France. It is memorable for Gene Hackman's intense performance and a dramatic chase along elevated railway tracks.

French and Indian Wars *npl* a series of four North American wars (1689–1763) between French and British forces and their Native American allies

French bean *n* **1.** a long slim green bean pod eaten whole as a vegetable **2.** a small bushy or tall climbing bean plant with slim green pods. Flowers: white or purplish. Latin name: *Phaseolus vulgaris.* ► N Am term **string bean**

French bread *n* white bread in the form of a long slim cylindrical loaf with a crisp crust and soft inside

French Cameroons /-kámmə roōnz/ former region in west-central Africa, administered by France from 1919 to 1960, and now part of Cameroon

French Canada *n* the parts of Canada where French is spoken

French Canadian *n* **1.** somebody who comes from a French-speaking part of Canada **2.** the form of the French language spoken in Canada —**French-Canadian** *adj*

French chalk *n* a soft white variety of talc. Use: to make tailoring marks on cloth, to remove grease stains from clothes.

French Community *n* an association linking France and several former French colonies. It was created in 1958.

French Creole *n* somebody of European and African descent whose ancestors were French immigrants to Trinidad

French cricket *n* an informal form of cricket that is played with bats and a soft ball, with the batter's legs acting as the wicket

French cuff *n* a wide cuff, usually for a shirtsleeve, designed to be folded back upon itself and fastened with a cuff link

French curve *n* a thin piece of plastic or other material with curved edges and a number of curved shapes cut out of it, designed to help designers and engineers draw curves

French door *n N Am* ARCHIT same as **French window**

French dressing *n* **1.** a salad dressing made of oil and vinegar with seasoning, whisked or shaken until emulsified or mixed **2.** *N Am* a creamy salad dressing, usually made commercially, consisting of mayonnaise with tomato flavouring

French Equatorial Africa /-ekwə táwri əl-/ former French territory in west-central Africa between 1910 and 1958. It consisted of the present-day countries of the Central African Republic, Chad, the Republic of Congo, and Gabon.

French Foreign Legion *n* a section of the French army consisting of foreign volunteers

French fries, French fried potatoes *npl* thin strips of potato fried in deep fat

French Guiana /-gī ánnə, -gī aánə/ overseas region of France, situated on the northeastern coast of South America and bordered by Brazil, Suriname, and the Atlantic Ocean. It is France's oldest overseas territory and the only French territory on the American mainland. Capital: Cayenne. Population: 114,808 (1990). Area: 91,000 sq. km/35,135 sq. mi. —**French Guianan** *adj, n* —**French Guianese** /-gī ə neéz, -gi-/ *adj, n*

French Guinea former name for **Guinea**

French heel *n* a curved heel of medium height for women's shoes

French horn

French horn *n* a brass musical instrument with a long looped pipe ending in a wide round bell, with other pipes and valves attached to it within the loop. French horns have a mellow, brassy tone, and are usually played with one hand in the bell of the instrument to control its volume.

Frenchify /frénchi fī/ (-fies, -fying, -fied) *vt* to give a French appearance or character to something or somebody, especially in a way considered overrefined and decadent —**Frenchification** /frénchifi káysh'n/ *n*

French India former territory comprising four French colonies in southeastern India, including the city of Pondicherry. It was ceded to India in 1956.

French kiss *n* a kiss in which one partner's tongue is inserted in the other partner's mouth

French knickers *npl* women's wide-legged knickers

French knot *n* an embroidery stitch made by looping the thread around the needle before pushing it through the fabric

French leave *n* a quick departure or absence, without explanation or permission (*dated informal*) [< a supposed French custom of leaving a party without saying goodbye]

French letter *n* same as **condom** (*dated informal*) [Origin ?]

Frenchman /frénchmən/ (*plural* -men) *n* a man who comes from France

Frenchmans Cap /frénchmənz-/ mountain in southwestern Tasmania, Australia, at the heart of the Franklin-Lower Gordon Wild Rivers National Park. Height: 1,443 m/4,734 ft.

French marigold *n* a widely cultivated ornamental flower. Flowers: yellowish-orange heads with red petals. Latin name: *Tagetes patula.*

French mustard *n* a mild-tasting mustard made with wine or unripe grape juice

French pleat *n UK* a woman's hairstyle in which the

hair is formed into a vertical roll at the back of the head. ANZ, N Am term **French roll**

French polish *n* shellac dissolved in alcohol. Use: wood varnish. —**French-polish** *vt*

French Polynesia overseas territory of France, consisting of several groups of small islands in the eastern South Pacific Ocean. Language: French. Currency: CFP franc. Capital: Papeete. Population: 188,814 (1988). Area: 3,521 sq. km/1,359 sq. mi.

French press *n N Am* same as **cafetière**

French Republican Calendar, **French Revolutionary Calendar** *n* the calendar adopted by the French during and briefly after the French Revolution. It had 12 months of 30 days, each made up of three ten-day weeks. The months were given names alluding to nature and seasonal weather.

French roll *n ANZ, N Am* HAIR same as **French pleat**

French roof *n* ARCHIT same as **mansard roof**

French seam *n* a seam stitched twice, completely enclosing the raw edges of the fabric

French stick *n* a thin loaf of French bread

French Sudan former name for **Mali** (1898–1959)

French toast *n* **1.** sliced bread dipped in egg beaten with milk, lightly fried or grilled, and served dusted with sugar or as a savoury snack **2.** *regional* bread toasted on one side only and buttered on the other

French twist *n* HAIR same as **French pleat**

French vermouth *n* unsweetened vermouth

French West Africa former French colonial territory in western Africa between 1895 and 1958. It consisted of the present countries of Benin, Burkina Faso, Côte d'Ivoire, Guinea, Mali, Mauritania, Niger, and Senegal.

French window *n* either of a pair of doors in an outside wall made of glass panels and opening in the middle (*usually used in the plural*)

Frenchwoman /frénch wŏŏmən/ (*plural* **-women** /-wimin/) *n* a woman who comes from France

frenetic /frə néttik/ *adj* characterized by feverish activity, confusion, and hurry ○ *frenetic gestures* [14C. Via French and Latin < Greek *phrenētikos* < *phrenitis* 'delirium' < *phrēn* 'mind'] —**frenetically** *adv* —**freneticism** /-néttissizəm/ *n*

frenulum /frénnyŏŏləm/ (*plural* **-la** /-lə/) *n* **1.** a small stiff bristle on the hind wing of moths that keeps the forewings and hind wings together during flight **2.** a small fold of skin or membrane that limits the movement of an organ, typically smaller than a frenum [Early 18C. < modern Latin, 'small frenum' < Latin *frenum* (see FRENUM)]

frenum /freēnəm/ (*plural* **-nums** or **-na** /-nə/), **fraenum** (*plural* **-nums** or **-na**) *n* a small fold of skin or membrane that limits the movement of an organ, especially the band of tissue connecting the tongue to the floor of the mouth [Mid-18C. < Latin *frenum* 'bridle' < *frendere* 'grind']

frenzied /frénzid/ *adj* characterized by uncontrolled activity, agitation, or emotion —**frenziedly** *adv* —**frenziedness** *n*

frenzy /frénzi/ *n* **1.** a state of uncontrolled activity, agitation, or emotion **2.** a burst of energetic activity [14C. Via French < medieval Latin *phrenesia* < Greek *phrenitis* (see FRENETIC)]

freq. *abbr* **1.** PHYS, BROADCAST, STATS frequency **2.** GRAM frequentative **3.** frequently

frequency /freēkwənssi/ (*plural* **-cies**) *n* **1.** *also* **frequence** /freēkwənss/ **FREQUENT OCCURRENCE** the fact of happening often or regularly at short intervals ○ *quite good friends, judging by the frequency of his visits* **2. RATE OF OCCURRENCE** the number of times that something happens during a period of time ○ *We're trying to establish the frequency of his visits. Did he come once a month?* **3.** BROADCAST **WAVELENGTH FOR BROADCASTING** a wavelength on which a radio or television signal is broadcast and to which a receiving set can be tuned **4.** PHYS **RATE OF RECURRENCE** the number of times that something such as an oscillation, a waveform, or a cycle is repeated within a specific length of time, usually one second. Symbol *ν*, *f* **5.** STATS **NUMBER OF OCCURRENCES OF STATISTICAL RESULT** the number of times a particular result occurs in a statistical survey (**absolute frequency**), or the ratio of that number to the total results obtained in the survey (**relative frequency**)

frequency distribution *n* a way of classifying statistical data that allows comparisons of the results in each category

frequency modulation *n* a method of radio transmission in which the frequency of the wave carrying the signal is varied in accordance with the particularities of the sound being broadcast

frequent *adj* /freēkwənt/ **1. OCCURRING OFTEN** happening often or regularly at short intervals ○ *her frequent appearances on television* **2. HABITUAL** doing something often ○ *a frequent visitor to the museum* ■ *vt* /fri kwént/ (**-quents, -quenting, -quented**) **GO SOMEWHERE OFTEN** to go to or be in a place often [15C. Via French < Latin *frequent-* 'crowded, numerous'] —**frequentation** /freē kwen táysh'n/ *n* —**frequenter** /fri kwéntər/ *n*

frequentative /fri kwéntətiv/ *adj* describes a verb, verb form, or affix that expresses repeated action — **frequentative** *n*

frequent flier, **frequent flyer** *n* an air passenger who travels frequently, especially somebody registered to receive benefits for accumulated mileage ○ *a frequent-flier discount*

frequent guest *n* somebody who often stays at the same hotel or hotel chain, especially while travelling on business, and is therefore offered free overnight stays and other benefits

frequently /freēkwəntli/ *adv* on many occasions with little time between them ○ *They change their address so frequently, it's difficult to know where to send the letter.*

fresco: detail of 16th-century wall painting at Sigirya, Sri Lanka

fresco /fréskō/ *n* (*plural* **-coes** or **-cos**) **1. PAINTING DONE ON FRESH PLASTER** a painting on a wall or ceiling done by rapidly brushing watercolours onto fresh damp or partly dry plaster **2. TECHNIQUE OF PAINTING ON FRESH PLASTER** the technique or method of painting on fresh plaster ■ *vt* (**-coes, -coing, -coed**) **PAINT WALL OR CEILING WITH FRESCO** to paint a fresco on a wall or ceiling [Late 16C. < Italian, 'fresh' (referring to plaster)] —**frescoer** *n* — **frescoist** *n*

fresh /fresh/ *adj* **1. NOT STALE** recently harvested or made and showing no sign of staleness or decay ○ *peas fresh from the pod* **2. NOT PRESERVED** not having been preserved, matured, or processed, e.g. by canning or freezing ○ *fresh fruits and vegetables* **3. ADDITIONAL OR AS REPLACEMENT** additional to or replacing something that existed, was used before, or is past its best ○ *I took out the old ink cartridge and put in a fresh one.* **4. NEW** new or clean and showing no signs of previous use ○ *The hotel provides fresh towels.* **5. NOT AFFECTED BY TIME** not changed, diminished, or spoiled by the passage of time ○ *Write it down while it's still fresh in your memory.* **6. WHOLESOME** natural, pure, and wholesome, especially in smell ○ *the fresh smell of clean linen* **7. EXCITINGLY DIFFERENT** excitingly or refreshingly different from what somebody is used to or what has been done previously ○ *fresh ideas* **8. NOT TIRED** alert and full of energy ○ *I'd better get this done while my mind is still fresh.* **9. NOT SALTY** describes water that is not salty **10. BLOWING STRONGLY** describes a breeze or wind that is blowing quite strongly ○ *a fresh wind from the west* **11. COOL** cool or colder than usual ○ *It's rather fresh today.* **12. BRIGHT** pleasantly bright, light, and pure or clear **13. HEALTHY** healthy-looking and clear in appearance ○ *a fresh complexion* **14. RECENTLY ARRIVED** having recently come from a place, activity, or event ○ *Fresh from his trip to the Antarctic, Sir Ronald is in the studio to tell us about his experiences.* **15. WITHOUT EXPERIENCE** lacking experience **16. MAKING UNWANTED SEXUAL ADVANCES** making inappropriate sexual overtures to somebody (*informal*) **17. OVERFAMILIAR** bold and overfamiliar towards somebody, especially somebody considered a superior (*informal*) ○ *Don't you get fresh with me, young man.* **18.** AGRIC **HAVING RECENTLY CALVED** having recently calved and therefore able to give milk **19.** *Carib* **BAD SMELLING** especially of fish or meat, smelling slightly rotten ■ *adv* **RECENTLY** quite recently or newly ○ *fresh-cooked salmon* ■ *n* **COOL PERIOD** the cool early part of the day [Old English *fersc* 'pure, not salty', and partly < Old French *freis* 'new, recent' < Germanic] —**freshness** *n*

SYNONYMS See ***new***.

fresh air *n* the air outside a building or any other enclosed place, thought of as being healthy and reviving ○ *What you need is fresh air and exercise.*

fresh breeze *n* a wind of between 30 and 38 km/19 and 24 mi. per hour, classified as force five on the Beaufort scale

freshen /frésh'n/ (**-ens, -ening, -ened**) *v* **1.** *vti* **MAKE OR BECOME FRESH** to make something fresh or fresher, or become fresh or fresher **2.** *vi* **INCREASE IN STRENGTH** to blow more strongly (*refers to winds*) ○ *wind force three, freshening from the southwest* **3.** *vt* **REFILL DRINK** to refill somebody's glass or drink —**freshener** *n*

freshen up *v* **1.** *vi* to make yourself clean and neat by washing or changing clothes **2.** *vt* same as **freshen** (sense 3)

fresher /fréshər/ *n* a student in the first year at college or university. N Am term **freshman** [Late 19C. < shortening of FRESHMAN]

freshet /fréshət/ *n* **1.** a small sudden flood or rise in the level of a river, caused by heavy rainfall or a rapid thaw, especially after a period of dry weather **2.** a stream of fresh water emptying into a body of salt water [Late 16C. Probably < Old French *freschete* < *freis* (see FRESH)]

fresh-faced *adj* young and healthy-looking

fresh gale *n* a wind of between 62 and 74 km/39 and 46 mi. per hour, classified as force eight on the Beaufort scale

freshly /fréshli/ *adv* quite recently or newly

freshman /fréshmən/ (*plural* **-men** /-mən/) *n* **1.** *N Am* EDUC same as **fresher** (*dated*) **2.** *US* a beginner, or a newcomer to a post or position ○ *freshmen in the Senate*

freshwater /frésh wawtər/ *adj* **1.** relating to, consisting of, or living in fresh water **2.** used on or accustomed only to inland waters, not the sea

fresh-water Yankee *n Carib* an offensive term for somebody who returns to the Caribbean after a visit abroad, usually to the United States, behaving and speaking like somebody from the place visited (*slang*)

Fresnel lens /fráy nel-/ *n* a thin lens of short focal length with a surface consisting of concentric rings, each having a curvature corresponding to a similar ring of a plain convex lens [Mid-19C. After Augustin-Jean *Fresnel* (1788–1827), French physicist]

Fresno /fréznō/ city and county seat of Fresno County, central California, 249 km/155 mi. southeast of San Francisco. Population: 445,227 (2002 estimate).

fret[1] /fret/ *v* (**frets, fretting, fretted**) **1.** *vti* **WORRY** to be worried, irritated, or agitated about something, or cause somebody to be so **2.** *vti* **WEAR AWAY** to wear away or corrode the surface of something, or become worn away or corroded **3.** *vt* **MAKE HOLE BY CONSTANT RUBBING** to create a hole or groove in something by constant wear or rubbing **4.** *vti* **FLOW IN RIPPLES OR SMALL WAVES** to flow with a constant busy rippling motion or with small choppy waves, or cause water to flow in this way (*literary*) ○ *'I love the brooks that down their channels fret'* (Wordsworth, *Ode on Intimations of Immortality*; 1807) ■ *n* **1. FRETTING STATE** a restless complaining state brought on

by anxiety or irritation ○ *The baby's in a fret.* **2.** **HOLE MADE BY FRETTING** a hole, groove, or mark made by constant wear or rubbing [Old English *fretan* 'devour' < Germanic, 'eat up']

fret[2] /fret/ *n* a small ridge of a set placed across the fingerboard of a stringed instrument such as a guitar or sitar, indicating the position in which to place the fingers to produce a desired note [Early 16C. Origin ?] —**fretless** *adj* —**fretted** *adj*

fret[3] /fret/ *n* a pattern of repeated geometric figures, usually consisting of straight lines, used as an ornament or in an ornamental border [14C. < Old French *frete* 'trellis'] —**fret** *vt*

fretful /frétf'l/ *adj* easily worried, irritated, or agitated [Late 16C. < FRET[1]] —**fretfully** *adv* —**fretfulness** *n*

fretman /frétmən/ (*plural* **-men** /-mən/) *n* a musician who plays guitar, especially in jazz or pop music (*slang*) [Late 20C. < FRET[2]]

fretsaw /frét saw/ *n* a saw with a thin narrow fine-toothed blade usually mounted across a U-shaped frame. Use: cutting curved shapes in wood. [Mid-19C. < FRET[3]]

fretwork /frét wurk/ *n* **1.** ornamental woodwork made by cutting holes in a piece of wood with a fretsaw to create an intricate pattern of wood and spaces **2.** decorative designs consisting of frets [Early 17C. < FRET[3]]

Freud /froyd/, **Anna** (1895–1982) Austrian-born British psychoanalyst. The daughter of Sigmund Freud, she worked closely with her father in the development of psychoanalytical theory. She later specialized in child psychoanalysis, founding the Hampstead Child Therapy Course and Clinic in London in 1947 and establishing a journal, *Psychoanalytic Study of the Child*, in 1945.

Sigmund Freud

Freud, Sigmund (1856–1939) Austrian physician and founder of psychoanalysis. He developed many theories central to psychoanalysis, the psychology of human sexuality, and dream interpretation. His works include *The Interpretation of Dreams* (1900) and *Totem and Taboo* (1913).

'The conscious mind may be compared to a fountain playing in the sun and falling back into the great subterranean pool of subconscious from which it rises.'
[Sigmund Freud. Quoted in *Bartlett's Unfamiliar Quotations*, Leonard Louis Levinson (ed.); 1972]

Freudian /fróydi ən/ *adj* **1.** **RELATING TO FREUD** relating to Sigmund Freud, his writings, or his psychoanalytical theories and methods **2.** **CONCERNING ROLE OF SEXUALITY IN BEHAVIOUR** demonstrating or understandable in terms of Freud's theories, especially with regard to sexuality and its role in human relations ■ *n* **FOLLOWER OF FREUD** somebody who follows Freud or is influenced by Freud's theories or methods of psychoanalysis —**Freudianism** *n*

Freudian slip *n* an accidental mistake, usually the use of the wrong word in a sentence, thought to betray somebody's subconscious preoccupations

Freya /fráy ə/ *n* in Norse mythology, the goddess of love, fertility, and beauty

Freyberg /frí burg/, **Bernard Cyril, 1st Baron of Wellington and Munstead** (1889–1963) British-born New Zealand general and politician. He was winner of a Victoria Cross (1916), commander-in-chief of the New

Zealand forces in World War II, and governor general of New Zealand (1946–52).

Freycinet Peninsula /fráyssinət-/ peninsula in eastern Tasmania, Australia, part of which is in Freycinet National Park. Length: 30 km/19 mi.

FRG *abbr* Federal Republic of Germany

Fri. *abbr* CALENDAR Friday

friable /frí əb'l/ *adj* easily reduced to tiny particles ○ *sand incorporated to make the soil more friable* [Mid-16C. Directly or via French < Latin *friabilis* < *friare* 'crumble'] —**friability** /frí ə bílləti/ *n* —**friableness** *n*

SYNONYMS See *fragile*.

friand /frí ond/ *n Aus* a small moist cake made with ground almonds, egg whites, and sometimes with fruit, grated rind, or chocolate chips

friar /frí ər/ *n* a man belonging to a Roman Catholic religious order, especially a mendicant one. The four main orders of friars are the Augustinians, Carmelites, Dominicans, and Franciscans. [13C. Via French *frère* < Latin *frater* 'brother'] —**friarly** *adj*

friar's balsam *n* a mixture containing benzoin. Use: as an inhalant, for colds and sore throats.

friary /frí əri/ (*plural* **-ies**) *n* **1.** a community of friars **2.** a building housing a community of friars

fricassee /fríkə say, -see, fríkə sáy, -seé/ *n* meat, usually chicken or veal, cooked in its own stock, or a wine and stock mixture, then thickened with cream [Mid-16C. < French *fricassée*, form of past participle of *fricasser* 'cut up and cook in sauce'] —**fricassee** *vt*

fricative /fríkətiv/ *adj* describes a consonantal speech sound made by forcing the breath through a narrow opening [Mid-19C. < modern Latin *fricativus* < Latin *fricare* 'rub'] —**fricative** *n*

friction /fríksh'n/ *n* **1.** **RUBBING** the rubbing of two objects against each other when one or both are moving **2.** **DISAGREEMENT** disagreement or conflict, stopping short of violence, between people, groups, or nations with differing aims or views **3.** **MED THERAPEUTIC RUBBING** deliberate rubbing of a body part as a way of stimulating blood circulation, warming, or relieving pain **4.** **PHYS RESISTANCE ENCOUNTERED BY MOVING OBJECT** the resistance encountered by an object moving relative to another object with which it is in contact [Mid-16C. Via French < Latin *friction-* < *fricare* 'rub'] —**frictional** *adj*

friction clutch *n* a clutch in a vehicle or machine that transmits power through surface friction between two plates covered with a layer of a fibrous material such as asbestos

friction match *n* a match that lights when rubbed against an abrasive surface

friction tape *n US* same as **insulating tape**

Friday /frí day, -di/ *n* the fifth day of the traditional working week, coming after Thursday and before Saturday [Old English *Frīgedæg* 'day of the goddess Frigg']

Fridays /frídayz, -diz/ *adv* on every Friday

fridge /frij/ *n* HOUSEHOLD same as **refrigerator** (*informal*) [Early 20C. Shortening]

fridge-freezer *n* a refrigerator and a freezer contained as two separate cabinets in a single upright unit

fried /frīd/ *adj* **1.** **COOKED BY FRYING** having been cooked by frying **2.** *US* **INTOXICATED** incapacitated by alcohol or drugs (*informal*) **3.** *N Am* **EXHAUSTED** incoherent from fatigue (*slang*)

Betty Friedan

Friedan /free dán/, **Betty** (*b.* 1921) US feminist author and founder in 1966 of the National Organization for Women (NOW). Her landmark book *The Feminine Mystique* (1963) challenged the idealization of women's traditional roles. Born **Goldstein, Betty Naomi**

'Today the problem that has no name is how to juggle work, love, home, and children.'
[Betty Friedan, *The Second Stage*; 1987]

Friedman /freedmən/, **Milton** (*b.* 1912) US economist. He is considered a leading protagonist of the theory that a free market, rather than government intervention, can best produce a balanced rate of economic growth. He received the Nobel Prize in economics (1976).

'Inflation is a form of taxation that can be imposed without legislation.'
[Milton Friedman, *The Times*; 1981]

Friedrich /freedrik/, **Caspar David** (1774–1840) German painter. In his meticulously observed landscape paintings such as *Monk on the Seashore* (1809–10), the human figure is often depicted as solitary and insignificant.

Friedrichstrasse /freedreekh shtraasə/ *n* a fashionable street in Berlin, Germany, on which the border crossing Checkpoint Charlie was located during the Cold War

~~frieght~~ incorrect spelling of **freight**

friend /frend/ *n* **1.** **SOMEBODY EMOTIONALLY CLOSE** somebody who trusts and is fond of another ○ *I know her, in fact she's a friend of mine.* **2.** **ACQUAINTANCE** somebody who thinks well of or is on good terms with somebody else ○ *I've got a friend at the office who might be able to help out.* **3.** **ALLY** an ally, or somebody who is not an enemy ○ *You can say what you like about the government, you're among friends here.* **4.** **ADVOCATE OF CAUSE** a defender or supporter of a cause, group, or principle ○ *She's no friend of tax-and-spend policies.* **5.** **PATRON** a patron of a charity or institution. Friends of cultural institutions often receive privileges such as invitations to special events and the opportunity to make bookings before the general public. ○ *a friend of the Bournemouth Symphony Orchestra* ■ *v* (**friends, friending, friended**) **1.** *vt Malaysia, Singapore* **BE SOMEBODY'S FRIEND** to be friends with somebody (*informal*) ○ *I don't want to friend you any more!* **2.** *vi Carib* **BE LOVERS** to have a sexual relationship with somebody ○ *They friending long time.* [Old English *frēond* < Germanic, 'to love'] ◇ **be friends (with somebody)** to be a friend of or on friendly terms with somebody ◇ **make friends (with somebody)** to begin a friendship or become friendly with somebody

Friend *n* a member of the Religious Society of Friends, called Quakers

Friend /frend/, **Donald Stuart Leslie** (1915–89) Australian artist. He is noted for his decorative, sensual paintings and drawings, particularly those produced in Bali (1967–80).

friendless /fréndləss/ *adj* without a friend —**friendlessness** *n*

friendly /fréndli/ *adj* (**-lier, -liest**) **1.** **AFFECTIONATE AND TRUSTING** characteristic of or suitable to a relationship between friends ○ *She's been friendly to us since we moved in.* **2.** **HELPFUL** tending to be beneficial or favourable towards somebody or something (*sometimes used in combination*) ○ *She was only offering some friendly advice.* ○ *We support the campaign for wildlife-friendly farming.* **3.** **ON SAME SIDE** not antagonistic towards or in conflict with another ○ *encountered only friendly aircraft* **4.** **PLEASANT AND WELCOMING** having a pleasant welcoming atmosphere **5.** **NOT FIERCELY COMPETITIVE** not played or undertaken in a fiercely competitive mood **6.** **NOT PART OF COMPETITION** played mainly for practice or entertainment and not as a fixture in a competition or league **7.** **EASY TO USE** safe or easy to use or operate, or easy to understand (*usually used in combination*) ○ *made of child-friendly materials* **8.** **MAKING SEXUAL OVERTURES** behaving in a way that reveals a sexual desire for somebody or a desire to start a sexual relationship with somebody (*informal; used*

euphemistically) ■ n (plural **-lies**) GAME NOT FORMING PART OF COMPETITION a game that is played mainly for practice or entertainment and not as a fixture in a competition or league ○ *a series of friendlies* —**friendlily** adv —**friendliness** n ◇ **be friendly with somebody** to be a friend of or on friendly terms with somebody

friendly fire n gunfire or artillery fire coming from your own or your allies' forces, sometimes causing accidental death or injury

Friendly Islands /fréndli-/ ♦ Tonga[2]

friendly society n an association of people who contribute regularly to a fund in order to provide themselves with sickness benefits, life assurance, and retirement pensions when required

friendship /frénd ship/ n 1. RELATIONSHIP BETWEEN FRIENDS a relationship between two or more people who are friends ○ *a friendship that has lasted more than 40 years* 2. MUTUALLY FRIENDLY FEELINGS the mutual feelings of trust and affection and the behaviour that typify relationships between friends ○ *Any feeling of friendship towards him had long since disappeared.* 3. FRIENDLY RELATIONS a relationship between people, organizations, or countries that is characterized by mutual assistance, approval, and support ○ *Anglo-American friendship*

Friends of the Earth n an international organization that lobbies and campaigns on environmental matters (*takes a singular or plural verb*)

frier n COOK another spelling of **fryer**

fries /friz/ npl FOOD same as **French fries**

Friesian /freézh'n, freézi ən/ n UK a large black-and-white dairy cow belonging to a breed known for its abundant milk production. ANZ, N Am term **Holstein** ■ n, adj LANG, PEOPLES same as **Frisian** [Early 20C. Variant of FRISIAN]

Friesland /freézlənd/ coastal province in northern Netherlands, that includes four of the West Frisian Islands. Population: 624,435 (2000). Area: 3,361 sq. km/1,298 sq. mi.

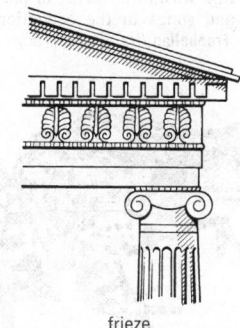

frieze

frieze[1] /freez/ n 1. a band of decoration running along the wall of a room, usually just below the ceiling 2. a horizontal band forming part of the entablature of a classical building, situated between the architrave and the cornice, and often decorated with sculpted ornaments or figures [Mid-16C. Via French < medieval Latin *frisium* < Latin *Phrygium (opus)* 'Phrygian (work)' (the Phrygians being famous for their crafts)]

SPELLCHECK See **freeze**.

frieze[2] /freez/ n coarse shaggy woollen cloth [15C. Via French *frise* < medieval Latin *frisia* 'Frisian (cloth)']

frig /frig/ (**frigs, frigging, frigged**) vti (taboo) 1. a highly offensive term meaning to have sexual intercourse with somebody 2. a highly offensive term meaning to masturbate, or masturbate somebody [Late 16C. Origin ?]

frig about, frig around vi an offensive term meaning to waste time or act in an aimless unproductive way (slang)

frigate

frigate /frígget/ n 1. WARSHIP SMALLER THAN DESTROYER a British warship next in size below a destroyer and with a similar armament and function 2. US MEDIUM-SIZED WARSHIP a US warship of medium size, larger than a destroyer but smaller than a cruiser, and used mainly for escort duty 3. SAILING SHIP EQUIPPED FOR WAR in the 18th and early 19th centuries, a fast square-rigged fighting ship next in size below a ship of the line [Late 16C. Via French *frégate* < Italian *fregata*]

frigatebird /frígget burd/ n a large black seabird with powerful wings, a forked tail, and a long hooked beak. Frigate birds often take food from other birds in flight. Native to: tropical waters. Family: Fregatidae. [Probably < its swift flight]

frigging /frígging/ adj, adv a highly offensive term expressing annoyance or disgust (taboo)

fright /frīt/ n 1. SUDDEN FEAR a sudden intense feeling of being threatened or in danger 2. EXPERIENCE OF BEING AFRAID an experience of sudden fear ○ *You gave me a terrible fright sneaking up that way.* 3. SOMETHING VERY UNPLEASANT LOOKING somebody or something that looks grotesque, ludicrous, or extremely unattractive (informal) ○ *My hair's a fright this morning.* ○ *What a fright Sam looked in that outfit.* [Old English *fryhto* < Germanic]

frighten /frīt'n/ (**-ens, -ening, -ened**) v 1. vti to make somebody feel fear, or be made to feel fear 2. vt to force or drive somebody or something away through fear ○ *had frightened off all the competition* —**frightened** adj

~~frightend~~ incorrect spelling of **frightened**

frightener /frít'nər/ n somebody or something that is frightening ◇ **put the frighteners on somebody** to frighten somebody into doing something or not doing something, especially for criminal purposes (slang)

frightening /frítning/ adj causing fear or alarm —**frighteningly** adv

frightful /frítf'l/ adj 1. VERY SERIOUS used to indicate the seriousness or severity of something ○ *now faced the frightful prospect of losing their farm* 2. FOUL extremely bad or unpleasant ○ *a frightful smell* 3. VERY GREAT used to indicate that somebody or something is an extreme example of a particular thing ○ *The speaker turned out to be a frightful bore.* 4. TERRIFYING capable of causing fear, shock, or dread ○ *looked down from a frightful height* —**frightfulness** n

frightfully /frítfəli/ adv extremely or excessively (dated or humorous) ○ *I'm frightfully sorry, but you'll have to go.*

fright wig n a wig that is intended to be amusing, with long hair sticking out in all directions

frigid /fríjjid/ adj 1. SEXUALLY UNRESPONSIVE unable or unwilling to respond sexually, to enjoy sexual intercourse, or to experience orgasm during intercourse 2. LACKING EMOTIONAL WARMTH lacking warmth, friendliness, or enthusiasm ○ *a frigid reply* 3. VERY COLD having a very cold temperature ○ *I was kept waiting in a frigid little room.* [15C. < Latin *frigidus* < *frigus* 'cold'] —**frigidity** /fri jíddəti/ n —**frigidly** adv —**frigidness** n

Frigid Zone n either of two areas of the Earth's surface, one lying between the Arctic Circle and the North Pole, the other lying between the Antarctic Circle and the South Pole

---

frijol /fri hól/ (plural **-joles** /-hóliz/), **frijole** /fri hóli, -hó lay/; or with Spanish pronunciation /fri khól ay/ n in the cooking of Mexico and the southwestern United States, a bean such as a pinto, kidney, or black bean [Late 16C. Via Spanish, Catalan *fesol*, and Latin *phaseolus* < Greek *phasēlos* 'legume']

frikkadel /fríkə dél/, **fricadel** n S Africa a fried ball of minced meat [Late 19C. Via Afrikaans < French *fricadelle* < *fricasser* 'cut up and cook in sauce']

frill /fril/ n 1. CLOTHING DECORATIVE BAND WITH MANY FOLDS a decorative strip of material gathered into many tight folds and sewn along one edge 2. COOK PAPER BAND WITH FRINGED EDGE a paper band with one edge cut into a fringe, placed on bone ends as decoration and to allow the meat to be picked up by the bone end 3. COOK DECORATIVE PAPER BAND ROUND CAKE a decorative paper band with both edges cut into a fringe, wrapped around the side of a cake 4. ZOOL RUFF OF FEATHERS, FUR, OR SKIN a ring of fur or feathers or a fold of skin around the neck of a bird or animal, looking like a frill 5. UNNECESSARY ADDITION an addition to something that is unnecessary, although it may enhance its appearance, interest, or value (usually used in the plural) ○ *No frills, thank you, just give me the basic model.* ■ vt (**frills, frilling, frilled**) 1. HANDICRAFT MAKE STRIP OF MATERIAL INTO FRILL to make a strip of fabric or paper into a frill 2. ADD FRILL TO SOMETHING to decorate something with a frill [Late 16C. Origin ?] —**frilled** adj —**frilliness** n —**frilly** adj

frilled lizard /fríld-/ n a large lizard with a broad membrane of skin around its neck that it can spread out like a ruff. Native to: Australia. Latin name: *Chlamydosaurus kingii*.

fringe /frinj/ n 1. HAIR HANGING OVER FOREHEAD a border of hair cut to fall over the forehead. N Am term **bangs**[1] (see **bang**) 2. DECORATIVE EDGING OF STRANDS a decorative border of short parallel strands or ravelled threads held closely together at one end by stitching and hanging loosely at the other end 3. ANY BORDER OR EDGING something that serves as or resembles a border ○ *a fringe of reeds circling the pond* 4. OUTER LIMIT the outer edge, or something considered to be on the outer edge and not central to an activity, interest, or issue (often used in the plural) ○ *outposts on the fringes of civilization* 5. LESS IMPORTANT AREA an area of action that is far away from the centre of activity or interest in a specific field (usually used in the plural) ○ *on the fringes of political life* 6. FACTION members of a group or organization who hold views not representative of the group and usually more extreme ○ *the radical fringe of a political party* 7. ARTS PART OF ARTS FESTIVAL part of an arts festival or similar event devoted to experimental or low-budget work 8. GOLF AREA BORDERING PUTTING GREEN the area surrounding a putting green on a golf course where the grass is allowed to grow slightly longer than on the green itself 9. OPTICS BAND PRODUCED BY DIFFRACTION OF LIGHT a light, dark, or coloured band of light produced by diffraction or interference 10. US FIN same as **fringe benefit** (informal) ■ adj 1. OUTLYING situated on the edge or away from the centre of something 2. MINOR playing a minor role in a play or story 3. UNCONVENTIONAL not part of the established or conventional mainstream of something such as the cinema, theatre, or medicine 4. NOT IN MAIN PART not in the main part of something such as a conference or organization, especially if putting forward or discussing radical or unconventional ideas ■ vt (**fringes, fringing, fringed**) 1. FORM FRINGE AROUND SOMETHING to form a fringe or border around something ○ *A thin moustache and beard fringed his lips.* 2. PUT DECORATIVE FRINGE ON SOMETHING to decorate something with a fringe or border [14C. Via French < Latin *fimbria* 'threads'] —**fringed** adj —**fringy** adj

CULTURAL NOTE *The Fringe Dwellers*, a novel (1961) by Australian writer Nene Gare. Set on the western coast of Australia, it tells the story of a mixed-race Aboriginal family, the Comeaways, who find themselves shunned and mistreated by white society and cut off from their Aboriginal traditions. It was made into a film by Bruce Beresford in 1986.

fringe area n an area at or just beyond the edge of a radio or television transmitter's range, where signals are likely to be weak or distorted

fringe benefit *n* **1.** an additional benefit provided to an employee, e.g. a company car or health insurance **2.** any additional or incidental advantage derived from an activity

fringed orchis /frínjd-/, **fringed orchid** *n* an orchid with a fringed lip. Flowers: yellow, white, purple, greenish. Native to: North America. Genus: *Habenaria*.

fringe dweller *n Aus* a resident on the edge of a town or city, usually in an impoverished area

fringing reef *n* a coral reef that borders or is directly attached to the shore of an island or a continent

frippery /fríppəri/ *n* (*plural* **-ies**) **1.** ARTICLE WORN FOR SHOW a showy item of clothing or an adornment worn for display or effect **2.** OSTENTATION pretentious display or showiness **3.** SOMETHING TRIFLING something of little value or importance ■ *adj* UNNECESSARY AND WITHOUT VALUE unnecessary, essentially valueless, and worn or used simply for display or effect [Mid-16C. < French *friperie* < Old French *frepe* 'rag, old clothes']

frippet /fríppit/ *n* a frivolous or extrovert young woman (*dated informal*) [Early 20C. Origin ?]

Frisbee /frízbi/ *tdmk* a trademark for a plastic disc thrown from person to person in a game

Frisch /frish/, **Max** (1911–91) Swiss dramatist and novelist. His plays include *The Fire Rasiers* (1958; tr. 1962) and *Andorra* (1961). Among his novels are *I'm Not Stiller* (1954), *Homo Faber* (1957), and *Man in the Holocene* (1979). Full name **Frisch, Max Rudolf**

> 'Joking is the third best method of hoodwinking people. The second best is sentimentality...But the best and safest method...is to tell the plain unvarnished truth.'
>
> [Max Frisch, *The Fire Raisers*; 1958; tr. 1962]

frisé /frée zay/ *n* a fabric with a long nap, usually of uncut loops. Use: upholstery, rugs. [Late 19C. < French < past participle of *friser* 'curl']

Frisian /frízh'n, frízzi ən/ *n* **1.** a West Germanic language spoken in the Netherlands and Germany. Native speakers: 350,000. **2.** somebody who comes from Friesland or the Frisian Islands [Late 16C. < Latin *Frisii* 'the Frisians' < Old Frisian *Frīsa*] —**Frisian** *adj*

Frisian Islands /frízh'n-, frízzi ən-/ group of islands in the North Sea off the coasts of the Netherlands, northwestern Germany, and southwestern Denmark. They include the Dutch West Frisian Islands, the German East Frisian Islands, and the North Frisian Islands, divided between Germany and Denmark.

frisk /frisk/ *v* (**frisks, frisking, frisked**) **1.** *vi* LEAP PLAYFULLY to leap, skip, or dance around in a carefree way **2.** *vt* SEARCH SOMEBODY QUICKLY to search somebody by quickly passing the hands over clothes and into pockets ■ *n* **1.** PLAYFUL LEAP a playful leap, skip, or dance **2.** QUICK SEARCH a quick search of somebody's clothes and pockets [Early 16C. < Old French *frisque* 'lively'] —**frisker** *n* —**frisking** *n*

frisket /frískit/ *n* a thin frame that keeps a sheet of paper in position and masks any portions not to be printed while the sheet is being printed on a hand-operated press [Late 17C. < French *frisquette* < Old French *frisque* 'lively']

frisky /fríski/ (**-ier, -iest**) *adj* behaving or tending to behave in a lively, playful way —**friskily** *adv* —**friskiness** *n*

frisson /frée-sson, frísson, free són/ *n* a brief intense reaction, usually a feeling of excitement, recognition, or terror, accompanied by a physical shudder or thrill [Late 18C. Via French, 'shiver' < assumed Vulgar Latin *friction-* < Latin *frigere* 'be cold']

frit[1] /frit/ *n* **1.** BASIC MATERIALS FOR GLASS the basic materials from which glass, pottery glazes, or enamels are made, when they are in a partially bonded state at the beginning of the manufacturing process **2.** GROUND FLUX a flux that is stabilized by melting it with silica and regrinding it into a fine powder ■ *vt* (**frits, fritting, fritted**) MAKE SOMETHING INTO FRIT to fuse or partially fuse materials in order to make frit [Mid-

17C. < Italian *fritta*, past participle of *friggere* 'fry' < Latin *frigere*]

frit[2] /frit/ *adj regional* frightened [Early 19C. Past participle of obsolete *fright* 'frighten' < Old English *fryhtan* < Germanic]

frit fly *n* a small black fly whose larvae are destructive to cereal crops. Latin name: *Oscinella frit*. [< Latin *frit* 'speck on an ear of corn']

fritillary /fri tíllari/ (*plural* **-ies**) *n* **1.** a plant of the lily family with long narrow leaves. Flowers: bell-shaped with spotted or chequered petals. Genus: *Fritillaria*. **2.** a brownish butterfly with black spots or narrow bands on its wings and usually silver spots on the underside of its hind wings. Family: Nymphalidae. [Mid-17C. < modern Latin *Fritillaria* < Latin *fritillus* 'dice box']

frittata /fri táətə/ *n* a firm thick Italian omelette that may contain any of a variety of chopped ingredients, including meat or vegetables [Mid-20C. < Italian < *fritto*, past participle of *friggere* (see FRIT[1])]

fritter[1] /fríttər/ *n* a piece of meat, fish, vegetable, or fruit dipped in batter and fried [14C. < French *friture* < Latin *frict-*, past participle of *frigere* 'fry']

fritter[2] /fríttər/ (**-ters, -tering, -tered**) *vt* to break, cut, or tear something into small pieces or shreds (*archaic*) [Early 18C. < obsolete *fritters* 'fragments, scraps', origin ?] **fritter away** *vt* to waste something by expending it in small quantities over a period of time on things that are not worthwhile

fritto misto /fríttō místō/ (*plural* **fritto mistos** or **fritti misti** /frítti místi/) *n* an Italian dish consisting of a mixture of bite-sized pieces of various foods such as seafood, meat, or vegetables, and sometimes sweet things such as cake, deep-fried in light batter [< Italian, 'mixed fry']

fritz /frits/ [Early 20C. Origin ?] ◇ **on the fritz** *N Am* out of order or not working properly (*informal*)

Friulan *n* LANG, PEOPLES same as **Friulian**

Friuli /free óoli/ historical region of southeastern Europe comprising parts of present-day northeastern Italy and Slovenia

Friulian /fri óoli ən/, **Friulan** /-óolən/ *n* **1.** a dialect of Rhaetian spoken in northwestern Italy **2.** somebody who comes from the region of Friuli or who speaks Friulian —**Friulian** *adj*

frivol /frívv'l/ (**-ols, -olling, -olled**) *v* **1.** *vi* to behave or spend time in a frivolous way **2.** *vt* to spend or waste something such as time or money foolishly or frivolously [Mid-19C. Back-formation < FRIVOLOUS] —**frivoller** *n*

frivolity /fri vólləti/ (*plural* **-ties**) *n* **1.** FRIVOLOUS BEHAVIOUR silly and trivial behaviour or activities **2.** SOMETHING FRIVOLOUS a frivolous action or thing **3.** TRIVIALITY the state of being trivial and unimportant [Late 18C. < French *frivolité* < Latin *frivolus* 'silly, unimportant']

frivolous /frívvələss/ *adj* **1.** lacking in intellectual substance and not worth serious consideration **2.** silly and trivial [15C. < Latin *frivolus* 'silly, unimportant'] —**frivolously** *adv* —**frivolousness** *n*

frizz /friz/ *vti* (**frizzes, frizzing, frizzed**) FORM INTO TIGHT CURLS to form a mass of tight curls or tufts, or be curled in this way (*refers to hair*) ■ *n* **1.** FRIZZED HAIR a mass of tightly curled or tufted hair **2.** FRIZZING the frizzing of hair [Late 16C. < French *friser* 'to curl']

frizzle[1] /frízz'l/ (**-zles, -zling, -zled**) *vti* **1.** to burn or shrivel, or cause something to burn or shrivel, especially while cooking **2.** to sizzle while frying or cooking, or fry or cook something so that it sizzles [Mid-18C. Probably blend of FRY[1] + FIZZLE or SIZZLE]

frizzle[2] /frízz'l/ *vti* (**-zles, -zling, -zled**) to frizz hair, or become frizzed ■ *n* a short tight curl [Mid-16C. Probably < FRIZZ]

frizzle fowl *n Carib* a chicken of a type that has very curly feathers, often considered to have magical qualities

frizzy /frízzi/ (**-zier, -ziest**), **frizzly** /frízzlee/ (**-zlier, -zliest**) *adj* forming or styled in tight curls —**frizzily** *adv* —**frizziness** *n* —**frizzliness** *n*

Frl. *abbr* Fräulein

fro /frō/ *adv* ♦ **to and fro** [13C. < Old Norse *frá* 'from']

Frobisher /frṓbishər/, **Sir Martin** (1535?–94) English navigator. He led an unsuccessful expedition in search of the Northwest Passage (1576), and played a prominent part in the defeat of the Spanish Armada (1588).

frock /frok/ *n* **1.** DRESS a woman's or girl's dress (*dated*) ○ *I'll put on my posh frock if the mayor's going to be there.* **2.** LOOSE OUTER GARMENT a loose baggy outer garment with sleeves that covers the top half of the body to below the waist, traditionally worn by artists and farm workers **3.** MONK'S GOWN a loose full-length gown with wide sleeves worn by the monks, friars, or clerics of some religious orders **4.** same as **frock coat** ■ *vt* (**frocks, frocking, frocked**) **1.** CHR INDUCT AS MEMBER OF CLERGY to invest somebody as a member of the clergy **2.** MIL ASSUME HIGHER RANK WITHOUT CORRESPONDING PAY to assume the title, uniform, and authority, but not the salary, of the next highest military rank before being officially promoted to it. This practice is more common in the Navy than in the other services. [14C. < French *froc* < Germanic]

frock coat

frock coat *n* in the 19th century, a man's knee-length coat for formal day wear

froe /frō/, **frow** *n* a cutting tool with one end of its blade fastened at right angles to a short handle. Use: to split wood along the grain to make shingles or barrel staves. [Late 16C. Origin ?]

Froebel /frṓb'l/, **Friedrich Wilhelm August** (1782–1852) German educator. He established the first kindergarten, and was an advocate of play, practical activities, and songs in the education of young children. —**Froebelian** /fra béeli ən/ *adj*

frog

frog[1] /frog/ *n* **1.** AMPHIB SMALL WEB-FOOTED WATER ANIMAL a small tailless amphibious animal with smooth moist skin, webbed feet, and long back legs used for jumping. Family: Ranidae. **2.** MUSIC NUT ON BOW a nut used to secure and tighten the strings of a violin bow and hold them away from the bow stick **3.** HANDICRAFT SUPPORT FOR FLOWERS IN ARRANGEMENT an object, usually with spikes or perforations, used to support the stems of flowers when making a flower arrangement **4.** another spelling of **Frog** (*slang offensive*) [Old English *frogga* < Germanic] ◇ **have a frog in your throat** to be hoarse and unable to speak clearly

frog[2] /frog/ *n* a decorative fastening for the front of a garment, consisting of a loop of braid or cord and a button, knot, or toggle that fits into the loop [Early 18C. Origin ?] —**frogged** *adj*

frog[3] /frog/ *n* a tough flexible pad in the middle of the sole of a horse's hoof [Early 17C. Origin ?]

frog[4] /frog/ *n* a steel plate used to guide the wheels of a train over a place where two rails cross [Mid-19C. Origin ?]

Frog /frog/ *n* an offensive term for a French person (*slang*) [Late 18C. < frogs' legs as a French dish]

frogeye /fróg ī/ *n* a fungal disease of plants that causes rounded spots to appear on the leaves

frogfish /fróg fish/ (*plural same* or **-fishes**) *n* a sea fish that lives near the seabed and has a globe-shaped warty or prickly body with fins adapted for catching prey. Family: Antennariidae.

frogging /frógging/ *n* ornamental braid fastenings on the front of a jacket [Late 19C. < FROG [2]]

froghopper /fróg hopər/ *n* **1.** a jumping plant-sucking insect with larvae that produce cuckoo spit. Family: Cercopidae. **2.** *Carib* an insect that sucks the juice from growing sugar cane, considered a major agricultural pest. Genus: *Aeneolamia*. [Early 18C. < their shape and leap]

frog kick *n* a kick used especially in swimming the breaststroke, in which the legs are first simultaneously bent, then straightened, to push the swimmer along

frogman /frógmən/ (*plural* **-men** /-mən/) *n* an underwater swimmer equipped with breathing apparatus, a wet suit, flippers, and other underwater gear, especially somebody engaged in military, police, or rescue work

frogmarch /fróg maarch/ *vt* (**-marches, -marching, -marched**) to force somebody to walk, feet off or almost off the ground and the arms twisted and pinned behind the back ■ *n* the act or process of frogmarching somebody

frogmouth /fróg mowth/ *n* a nocturnal bird with grey or brown plumage and a wide mouth with a powerful hooked beak. Native to: Australia, Asia. Family: Podargidae.

frogspawn /fróg spawn/ *n* a floating mass of fertilized frog's eggs in a transparent jelly

frog spit *n* **1.** a foamy green mass of small plants or algae floating on the surface of a pond **2.** INSECTS same as **cuckoo spit**

Froissart /frwass aar/, **Jean** (1333?–1410?) French historian and poet. His *Chronique de France, d'Angleterre, d'Ecosse et d'Espagne* (1372–1410?) is an important record of the major events of The Hundred Years' War (1337–1453) between England and France and of chivalric life in the late 14th century.

frolic /fróllik/ *vi* (**-ics, -icking, -icked**) **PLAY LIGHTHEARTEDLY** to frisk about, behave, or play in a carefree, uninhibited way ○ *children frolicking on the sands* ■ *n* **1. SOMETHING LIVELY AND CAREFREE** a lively carefree game, action, or amusement **2. CAREFREE PLAY** lively carefree play or behaviour ○ *'As a result, Anne had the golden summer of her life as far as freedom and frolic went.'* (Lucy Maud Montgomery, *Anne of Green Gables*; 1908) [Early 16C. < Dutch *vrolijk* 'glad, joyous' < *vro* 'happy'] —**frolicker** *n*

frolicsome /frólliksəm/ *adj* frisky and full of fun and high spirits

from *stressed* /from/; *unstressed* /frəm/ CORE MEANING: a preposition used to indicate the source or beginning of something, in terms of location, context, or time ○ *The condition can manifest itself anytime from adolescence onward.* ○ *Most funding comes from the government.* ○ *highlights from her latest novel* ○ *You can connect to our computer network from home.* *prep* **1. RANGE** used to indicate a range, either of time, amount, or things ○ *We are open from 2 to 4:30.* ○ *They sell everything, from washing machines to magazines.* **2. DISTANCE** used to indicate the distance between two things or places ○ *The nearest town is not far from here.* **3. USING** used to indicate the materials or substances something is made of ○ *built from native pine* **4. CAUSE** used to indicate the cause of or reason for something ○ *low morale resulting from staff cuts* **5. RESTRAINT** used to indicate that an action does not happen or should not happen ○ *prevented from seeing her* [Old English *fram, from* < Indo-European, 'forward, towards']

fromage frais /frómmaazh fráy/ *n* a fresh cheese with a light creamy taste, a texture like thick cream or yoghurt, and a variable fat content [< French, 'fresh cheese']

Frome, Lake /frōm/ usually dry salt lake in north-eastern South Australia. Area: 4700 sq. km/1800 sq. mi.

fromenty *n* BEVERAGES another spelling of **frumenty**

Fromm /from/, **Erich** (1900–80) German-born US psychoanalyst. He emphasized the link between human personalities and socioeconomic patterns. His books include *Fear of Freedom* (1942) and *The Sane Society* (1955).

> 'The deepest need of man is the need to overcome his separateness, to leave the prison of his aloneness.'
> [Erich Fromm, *The Art of Loving*; 1956]

frond /frond/ *n* **1.** a large leaf divided into many thin sections that is found on many flowerless plants, especially ferns and palms **2.** a growth that resembles the leaf of a fern or palm tree, especially a growth of seaweed that resembles leaves [Late 18C. < Latin *frond-*, stem of *frons* 'leaf'] —**fronded** *adj*

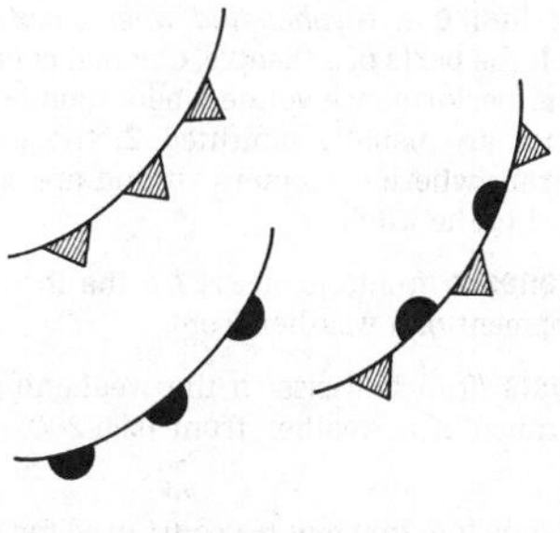

front: meteorological symbols indicating warm and cold weather fronts

front /frunt/ *n* **1. PART OR SURFACE FACING FORWARD** the part or surface that faces forward, is intended to be seen first, has the main entrance, or is facing the direction of motion or the direction people face ○ *You can only see the front of the house from here.* **2. FORWARD AREA** the area, section, or position just ahead of, close to, or at the forward part of something ○ *You sit in the front and I'll ride in the back.* **3. FRONT DOOR** the door at the front or the area beyond it ○ *I'll go out the front, and you go out the back.* **4. FIRST PAGES** the beginning or first pages of a book or magazine **5. FACADE OF BUILDING** a facade of a building, especially the one that faces the street, or a part of it ○ *Bring the car around to the front.* **6. SIDE OF PROPERTY ADJOINING SOMETHING** the side of a property that borders something else, e.g. a street, lake, or river **7. FORWARD DIRECTION** the direction straight ahead ○ *Face the front.* **8. POSITION AHEAD** a place or position approximately ahead of somebody ○ *To our front was a clump of trees.* **9. LEADING POSITION** a prominent or leading position in any field of activity ○ *companies at the front of genetic research* **10. NOTICEABLE POSITION** a conspicuous position ○ *a disturbing aspect that came to the front* **11. ASPECT** a way of viewing a situation ○ *Things looked desperate on all fronts.* **12. SEASIDE PROMENADE** a street, area of land, or promenade running alongside the beach or shore at a seaside or lakeside resort **13. DELIBERATELY ASSUMED BEHAVIOUR** a manner or type of behaviour adopted by somebody in order to deal with a situation or disguise the person's true feelings ○ *put on a brave front* **14. COVER FOR ILLEGAL ACTIVITIES** an apparently respectable person, organization, or business acting as a cover for illegal or secret activities ○ *The grocery store was a front for drug deals.* **15. FIGUREHEAD** a nominal leader or head who has no real authority **16.** MIL **BATTLE ZONE** an area where armies are facing one another, or where fighting between armies is taking place ○ *soldiers returning from the front* **17.** MIL **SPACE DEFENDED BY ARMY UNIT** the width of territory occupied or defended by an army or a military unit facing an enemy ○ *Each section was defending a front of some two miles.* **18.** MIL **DIRECTION IN WHICH TROOPS ARE FACING** the direction in which troops are facing when formed up in line **19. PARTICULAR AREA OF ACTIVITY** a particular area of activity or operations ○ *There have been a lot of changes on the domestic front.* **20.** METEOROL **INTERFACE BETWEEN AIR MASSES** a line along which one mass of air meets another that is different in temperature or density **21.** POL **GROUP WITH COMMON PURPOSE** a group of people or organizations with a common purpose, especially a broad political coalition ○ *a national liberation front* **22.** CLOTHING **PART OF GARMENT** the part of a garment or the clothing that covers the front part of the body, especially the chest ○ *You've got gravy all down your front.* **23.** CLOTHING **DETACHABLE FRONT FOR SHIRT** a detachable shirt front, especially part of a man's formal dress shirt **24. IMPERTINENCE** cheek or cockiness ○ *That took a bit of front!* **25. FACE** the face or forehead (*archaic*) ■ *adj* **1. AT FRONT** situated at, on, or near the front of something, or placed farther forward than others **2.** PHON **PRODUCED WITH TONGUE FORWARD** describes a vowel sound that is produced with the back of the tongue close to the forward part of the roof of the mouth ■ *v* (**fronts, fronting, fronted**) **1.** *vt* **FACE TOWARDS SOMETHING** to have a front that faces towards something ○ *a hotel fronting the ocean* **2.** *vt* **GIVE COVERING OR APPEARANCE TO SOMETHING** to give something a front or visible surface of a particular kind ○ *The building is fronted with red brick.* **3.** *vt* **BE HEAD OF GROUP** to be the head, leader, or spokesperson of a group or organization such as a band ○ *a group fronted by a young lawyer from London* **4.** *vt* **HOST PROGRAMME** to act as the presenter of a television or radio programme **5.** *vi* **ACT AS COVER FOR ILLEGAL ACTIVITY** to act as a respectable cover for something secret or illegal or for somebody doing something secret or illegal **6.** *vt* **CONFRONT SOMEBODY OR SOMETHING** to face up to somebody or something confidently (*archaic*) [13C. Via French < Latin *front-* 'forehead, front'] ◇ **in front 1.** leading or ahead of somebody or something else **2.** close to or in the front of something, or further forward than somebody else **3.** in the lead in a race or competition ○ *Polls show the current mayor far in front as the election nears.* ◇ **in front of 1.** ahead of somebody or in the direction in which somebody is facing **2.** close to the front of something **3.** in the presence, sight, or hearing of somebody ◇ **out front 1.** THEATRE in front of the curtain or in the auditorium, as opposed to on the stage **2.** at or to the front of a building ○ *I'll go out front and talk to them.* ◇ **up front 1.** close or closer to the front of something **2.** in advance, e.g. before any work is done or any goods are delivered

CULTURAL NOTE ***All Quiet on the Western Front***, a novel (1929) by German writer Erich Maria Remarque. This classic antiwar novel, which was based on the author's own experiences as an 18-year-old soldier in the German army during World War I, is a grimly realistic account of trench warfare. It was made into a film by Lewis Milestone in 1930.

front up *vi ANZ* to arrive or appear somewhere ○ *You can't just front up here and expect me to help you.*

frontage /fróntij/ *n* **1. FRONT OF BUILDING** the front side of a building or piece of property **2. LAND BETWEEN BUILDING AND STREET** the land between a building and a street or road **3. LENGTH OF FRONT** the length of the front of a building or piece of land next to a street, river, or lake **4. PIECE OF LAND ADJOINING SOMETHING** a piece of land situated next to a street, river, or lake **5. OUTLOOK** the direction in which a building faces

frontage road *n N Am* ROADS same as **service road**

frontal[1] /frúnt'l/ *adj* **1. AT OR IN FRONT** situated at or in the front of something **2. SHOWING FRONT OF SOMETHING** showing the front of somebody or of something, especially a naked body ○ *full frontal nudity* **3. DIRECT AND FORCEFUL** direct, forceful, and intended to be overwhelming ○ *made a frontal attack on her political opponent* **4.** ANAT **RELATING TO FOREHEAD** relating to the forehead or the front part of the skull **5.** METEOROL **RELATING TO WEATHER FRONTS** involving or relating to weather fronts **6.** MIL **TOWARDS ENEMY FRONT** directed against an enemy's front, usually across open ground ○ *a frontal attack* [Mid-17C. < modern Latin *frontalis* < Latin *front-* 'forehead, front'] —**frontally** *adv*

frontal[2] /frúnt'l/ *n* a cloth covering for the front of an altar in a Christian Church [14C. Via Old French *frontel* 'ornament for the forehead' < Latin *frontale* < *front-* (see FRONT)]

frontal bone *n* the bone forming the front part of the skull that shapes the forehead and part of the eye sockets and nasal cavity

frontal lobe *n* the front part of each hemisphere of the brain

frontal lobotomy *n* SURG same as **prefrontal lobotomy**

front bench *n* **1.** in Parliament, the bench on each side nearest the floor of the House, reserved for Government ministers on one side and their Opposition counterparts on the other **2.** the most important members of the Government or Opposition, who sit on the front bench in Parliament —**front-bencher** *n*

front burner *n* a position of importance or priority (*informal*) ○ *a scheme which seems to be no longer on the front burner*

frontcourt /frúnt kawrt/ *n* **1.** in basketball, the half of a court containing the basket in which a team attempts to score **2.** the forward and centre players of a basketball team

front desk *n* a reception desk or information desk near the main entrance of a building

front door *n* **1.** the main entrance to a house or other building, closed by a door **2.** the usual and unsuspicious way of achieving a position

front end *n* **1.** the user interface of a computer system **2.** COMPUT same as **front-end processor**

front-end *adj* **1.** relating to the start of a process or project, especially a commercial or financial one ○ *heavy front-end costs* **2.** relating to the user interface of a computer system

front-end load *n* an amount, making up a large part of the initial payments, paid by an investor in an insurance scheme or long-term investment, intended to cover commission and other expenses

front-end processor *n* a computer that carries out preliminary processing on data before passing it to another computer for further processing

frontier /frun teer/ *n* **1.** BORDERLAND a border between two countries, or the land immediately adjacent to this ○ *cross the frontier into Spain* **2.** EDGE OF SETTLEMENT the part of a country with expanding settlement that is being opened up by hunters, herders, and other pioneers in advance of full urban settlement **3.** LIMIT OF KNOWLEDGE the furthest limit of knowledge in a specific field ○ *pushing back the frontiers of science* [14C. < Anglo-Norman *frounter*, French *frontière* 'front part (of an army)' < *front* (see FRONT)]

frontiersman /frún teerzmən, frun téerzmən/ (*plural* **-men** /-mən/) *n* a man living in a frontier area, especially an area newly opened up for settlement

frontierswoman /frún teerz wõoman, frun téerz wõoman/ (*plural* **-women** /-wimin, -/) *n* a woman living in a frontier area, especially an area newly opened up for settlement

frontispiece /frúntiss peess/ *n* **1.** PUBL BOOK ILLUSTRATION an illustration at the beginning of a book, usually facing the title page **2.** ARCHIT BUILDING FACADE the principal facade of a building, treated as a separate element **3.** ARCHIT PEDIMENT a pediment, usually ornamental, above a window or door [Late 16C. Via French *frontispice* (altered after PIECE) < late Latin *frontispicium* 'facade' < Latin *frons* 'forehead' + *specere* 'look at']

frontlet /frúntlət/ *n* **1.** DECORATIVE BAND a decorative band worn on the forehead **2.** ZOOL ANIMAL'S FOREHEAD an animal's forehead, especially a bird's when it has a different colour from the rest of the head **3.** CHR ALTAR-CLOTH BORDER a decorated border on the frontal of an altar in a Christian Church [15C. < Old French *frontelet* 'little forehead band' < *frontel* (see FRONTAL²)]

front line *n* **1.** MIL the forward line of a battle, position, or formation (*hyphenated when used before a noun*) **2.** the most advanced, important, or conspicuous position in any situation ○ *on the front lines of the battle for equality* **3.** BASKETBALL same as **frontcourt** (sense 2)

frontline /frúnt līn/ *adj* **1.** AT LIMITS OF ATTAINMENT that is the most advanced or important of its kind ○ *a frontline technological development* **2.** BORDERING TROUBLE SPOT relating to countries that border another country in which an armed conflict is taking place

3. DEALING DIRECTLY WITH CUSTOMERS describes employees dealing directly with customers, or a job that requires them to do so

frontline state *n* a nation situated on the border of a war-torn or war-threatened area

front-load *vt* to assign the bulk of the costs of an insurance scheme or long-term investment to an early stage

front loader *n* a washing machine in which clothes are loaded through a door at the front rather than the top

frontman /frúntmən/ (*plural* **-men** /-mən/) *n* (*informal*) **1.** *also* **front man** an apparent leader of an organization or activity in which somebody else has the real power, secretly or illegally concealed **2.** a man who is lead singer of a band or other musical group

front matter *n* the material that appears in a book before the main text, e.g. the title page, copyright information, the table of contents, and the preface

front office *n* N Am the management or executives of an organization who decide on policy

front of house *n* (*hyphenated when used before a noun*) **1.** the parts of a theatre, cinema, concert hall, or other performance venue where members of the audience are usually admitted **2.** the parts of a restaurant where customers sit and are served, as opposed to the kitchen

frontogenesis /frúntō jénnississ/ *n* the formation or development of a weather front

frontolysis /frun tóllississ/ *n* the weakening or disappearance of a weather front [Mid-20C. < FRONT + -LYSIS]

fronton /frón ton, fron tón/ *n* a court used for the game of pelota or jai alai [Late 19C. < Spanish < *fronte* 'forehead' < Latin *front-* (see FRONT)]

front-page *adj* important or interesting enough to appear on the front page of a newspaper

front room *n* a sitting room in a house, often one reserved for more formal entertaining

frontrunner /frunt rúnnər, frúnt runər/ *n* somebody in a leading position in a race or contest (*informal*) ○ *the new frontrunner in the party leadership contest*

frontside 1080 /frúntsīd ten áyti/ *n* in snowboarding, three full revolutions 10 feet above a pipe, the most difficult move in the sport

frontwards /frúntwərdz/, **frontward** /-wərd/ *adv* towards or in the direction of the front

front-wheel drive *n* a system of powering motor vehicles that uses the engine to drive the front wheels only

frontwoman /frúnt wõoman/ (*plural* **-women** /-wimin/) *n* a woman who is lead singer of a band or other musical group (*informal*)

frost /frost/ *n* **1.** FROZEN WATER crystals of frozen water deposited on a cold surface **2.** FREEZING TEMPERATURE an outdoor temperature below freezing point, resulting in the deposit of ice crystals ○ *had a hard frost as late as May* **3.** CHILLY MANNER a coldness of manner **4.** FAILURE something that meets with an unenthusiastic reception, e.g. an artistic performance or a new book (*informal*) ○ *The opening night was a true frost.* **5.** FREEZING the act or process of freezing ■ *v* (**frosts, frosting, frosted**) **1.** *vti* METEOROL COVER OR BECOME COVERED WITH FROST to cover something with frost, especially hoar frost, or become covered with frost **2.** *vt* MAKE SURFACE OPAQUE to make something, especially glass or a window, unable to be seen through by giving its surface a rough or fine-grained texture **3.** *vt* N Am PUT ICING ON SOMETHING to cover a cake or other pastry with icing or frosting **4.** *vt* KILL PLANTS BY FREEZING to damage or kill crops or garden plants by freezing temperatures [Old English *forst, frost* < Germanic]

frost up *vi* to become covered in frost or ice, especially in a way that hinders a function ○ *The freezer has frosted up so much that the door won't close.*

Robert Frost
Library of Congress

Frost /frost/, **Robert** (1874–1963) US poet. He is best known for his spare poems about New England life, including 'Stopping by Woods on a Snowy Evening' and 'The Road Not Taken'. He was poetry consultant to the Library of Congress (1958–59) and he won the Pulitzer Prize four times (1924, 1931, 1937, and 1943). Full name **Frost, Robert Lee**. See Cultural note at **wood**

> 'The woods are lovely, dark and deep. /
> But I have promises to keep, / And miles
> to go before I sleep. / And miles to go
> before I sleep.'
> [Robert Frost, 'Stopping by Woods on a
> Snowy Evening'; 1923]

frostbite /fróst bīt/ *n* damage to body extremities caused by prolonged exposure to freezing conditions, characterized by numbness, tissue death, and gangrene ■ *vt* (**-bites, -biting, -bit** /-bit/, **-bitten** /-bitt'n/) to damage something by prolonged exposure to freezing conditions (*usually passive*)

frostbound /fróst bownd/ *adj* confined to one place because of frost ○ *We were frostbound in our cabin for three days.*

frost-free *adj* describes an appliance such as a refrigerator or freezer that does not need to be defrosted

frost heave, **frost heaving** *n* the cracking of the surface of a road or piece of ground by the freezing and upward expansion of subsurface water, or a damaged surface resulting from this

frosting /frósting/ *n* **1.** SOFT ICING a variety of soft icing for cakes made by whisking egg whites and sugar over hot water or incorporating hot syrup into whisked egg whites **2.** N Am RICH ICING icing that is typically thick and rich and made with sugar, milk, eggs, butter, or cream **3.** ROUGH SURFACE a roughened or dull surface produced on something, especially glass or metal

frost line *n* **1.** the point below the surface of the ground beyond which frost will not penetrate **2.** a line on a map joining places subject to the same number of frosts a year or to the same degree of frost

frost weathering *n* the shattering of rock caused by the freezing of water in surface cracks and hollows, and in the pore spaces

frostwork /fróst wurk/ *n* **1.** the patterns made by frost on various surfaces, especially windows, that often resemble tracery or the fronds of ferns **2.** decoration on metal or glass imitating the patterns made naturally by frost

frosty /frósti/ (**-ier, -iest**) *adj* **1.** VERY COLD cold enough for the formation of frost **2.** COVERED IN FROST covered in frost, especially hoar frost **3.** COLD IN MANNER cold and unwelcoming in manner **4.** WHITE LIKE FROST looking like hoar frost, especially in whiteness ○ *a shock of matted frosty hair* **5.** COLD TO TASTE cold to the touch or taste ○ *a frosty beer* —**frostily** *adv* —**frostiness** *n*

froth /froth/ *n* **1.** FOAM a mass of bubbles in or on the surface of a liquid **2.** FOAMY SALIVA a foamy mixture of saliva and air bubbles produced at the mouth in some diseases or by exhaustion **3.** TRIVIA anything seen as being insubstantial or trivial ○ *The conversation at the party was mostly froth and posturing.* ■ *v* (**froths, frothing, frothed**) **1.** *vt* CAUSE SOMETHING

TO FOAM to make something produce foam, or cover something with foam **2.** *vi* CREATE FOAM to produce foam or emerge as foam ○ *froth at the mouth* [14C. < Old Norse *froða* or *frauð*]

froth flotation *n* MIN EXTRACT same as **flotation** (sense 5)

frothy /fróthi/ (**-ier, -iest**) *adj* **1.** characterized by, covered in, or producing foam **2.** with no serious content or purpose ○ *a frothy sitcom* —**frothily** *adv* —**frothiness** *n*

frottage /fróttaazh, fro táazh/ *n* **1.** an artistic technique in which a rubbing is taken of a surface to create a design **2.** the obtaining of sexual pleasure by rubbing the clothed body against that of others, usually strangers in crowded places [Mid-20C. < French, 'rubbing, friction' < *frotter* 'rub']

Froude /frood/, **J. A.** (1818–94) British historian. Strongly influenced by Thomas Carlyle, he is best known for his 12-volume *History of England from the Fall of Wolsey to the Defeat of the Spanish Armada* (1856–70). Full name **Froude, James Anthony**

> 'Men are made by nature unequal. It is vain, therefore, to treat them as if they were equal.'
> [J. A. Froude, 'Party Politics'; 1877]

froufrou /froó froo/ *n* **1.** the sound made by the rustling of silk, especially women's dresses **2.** fancy trimmings or elaborate decoration, especially on women's clothes [Late 19C. < French, an imitation of the sound]

frow *n* another spelling of **froe**

froward /frṓ ərd/ *adj* stubbornly disobedient or contrary (*archaic*) [Old English *frāward* 'in a direction leading away from' < Old Norse *frá* 'from'] —**frowardly** *adv* —**frowardness** *n*

Froward, Cape /frṓ ərd/ cape in southern Chile, the southernmost tip of mainland South America. Spanish name **Cabo Froward**

frown /frown/ (**frowns, frowning, frowned**) *v* **1.** *vi* to show a facial expression of displeasure or concentration by wrinkling the brow **2.** *vt* to communicate something by frowning [14C. < Old French *froignier* 'to frown, snort' < *froigne* 'scowl'] —**frown** *n* —**frowner** *n* —**frowningly** *adv*

frown on, frown upon *vt* to dislike or disapprove of something

SYNONYMS See *disapprove*.

frowsty /frówsti/ (**-ier, -iest**) *adj UK* unpleasant to be in because of mustiness, staleness, or a bad smell ○ *a frowsty atmosphere in the room* ANZ, N Am term **frowzy** [Mid-19C. Origin ?] —**frowstiness** *n*

frowzy /frówzi/ (**-zier, -ziest**), **frowsy** (**-sier, -siest**) *adj* **1.** untidy or shabby in personal appearance or manner of dress ○ *a frowzy layabout* ○ *frowzy curtains at a tenement window* **2.** *ANZ, N Am* same as **frowsty** [Late 17C. Origin ?] —**frowziness** *n*

froze past tense of **freeze**

frozen /frṓz'n/ past participle of **freeze** ■ *adj* **1.** WITH ICE covered by or made into ice ○ *a frozen lake* **2.** AFFECTED BY ICE made inoperable, damaged, or obstructed by ice or freezing temperatures ○ *All trains are delayed because of frozen points.* ○ *no running water in the house because of frozen pipes* **3.** EXTREMELY COLD characterized by extreme cold ○ *the frozen north* **4.** PRESERVED BY FREEZING preserved by freezing for eating at a later time ○ *frozen pizza* **5.** IMMOBILE immobile or unable to move ○ *She stood there, frozen in terror.* **6.** FIN FIXED deliberately fixed at a given level to avoid undesirable economic or social consequences **7.** FIN NOT AVAILABLE TO BE SOLD describes assets that cannot be sold or otherwise liquidated —**frozenly** *adv* —**frozenness** *n*

frozen shoulder *n* a condition in which a shoulder joint becomes stiff and painful, especially after having been kept in one position for a time

frozen smoke *n* TECH same as **solid smoke**

FRS *abbr* Fellow of the Royal Society

fructan /frúktən/ *n* a natural polymer, composed of units of fructose arranged in a chain, that is an important source of stored energy for some plants [Mid-20C. < FRUCTOSE]

fructiferous /fruk tíffərəss, frŏok-/ *adj* describes a tree or other plant that bears fruit [Mid-17C. < Latin *fructifer* 'fruit-bearing' < *fructus* 'fruit' (see FRUIT)]

fructification /frúktifi káysh'n, frŏok-/ *n* **1.** PRODUCTION OF FRUIT the production of fruit or fruits by a tree or other plant **2.** FRUIT OF SEED-BEARING PLANT the fruit produced by a seed-bearing plant **3.** SEED-BEARING PART a seed-bearing or spore-bearing part of a plant, alga, or fungus

fructify /frúkti fī, frŏok-/ (**-fies, -fying, -fied**) *vti* to become productive or fruitful, or cause to become productive or fruitful (*formal or technical*) [14C. Via French *fructifier* < Latin *fructificare* < *fructus* 'fruit' (see FRUIT)]

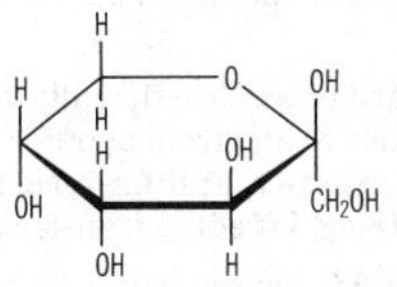

fructose

fructose /frúk tōz, -tōss, frŏok tōz/ *n* a simple sugar found in fruits and honey. Formula: $C_6H_{12}O_6$. [Mid-19C. < Latin *fructus* 'fruit' (see FRUIT)]

fructuous /frúk tyoo əss/ *adj* productive of much fruit, or full of fruit (*formal*) [14C. Directly or via Old French < Latin *fructuosus* < *fructus* 'fruit' (see FRUIT)]

frugal /froóg'l/ *adj* **1.** characterized by thriftiness and avoidance of waste **2.** involving very little expense [Early 16C. Directly or via French < Latin *frugalis* < *frugi* 'economical, useful' < *frug*, stem of *frux* 'fruit, value'] —**frugality** /froo gálləti/ *n* —**frugally** *adv* —**frugalness** *n*

frugivorous /froo jívvərəss/ *adj* describes an animal that eats mainly fruit [Early 18C. < Latin *frug-* 'fruit'] —**frugivore** /froóji vawr/ *n*

fruit /froot/ *n* **1.** EDIBLE PART OF PLANT an edible part of a plant, usually fleshy and containing seeds **2.** OVARY OF PLANT the ripened seed-bearing ovary of a plant. It is usually considered to be sweet and fleshy, as in plums, but may be dry, as in poppies, or be a simple edible supporting structure, as in strawberries. **3.** PRODUCE the produce of any plant grown or harvested by humans ○ *the fruits of the field* **4.** PRODUCT OF SOMETHING the product or consequence of something done ○ *We are now seeing the fruits of our efforts.* **5.** OFFSPRING the offspring of humans or animals (*dated*) **6.** SPORE-PRODUCING PART a spore-producing part of a plant **7.** WINE FRUITY TASTE a fruity taste in wine ○ *a big red with lots of fruit* **8.** *N Am* OFFENSIVE TERM an offensive term for a gay man (*slang*) ■ *vti* (**fruits, fruiting, fruited**) PRODUCE FRUIT to bear fruit, or cause a plant or tree to bear fruit ○ *This variety fruits in August.* [12C. Via French < Latin *fructus* 'enjoyment, produce, fruit' < past participle of *frui* 'enjoy, have the use of'] ◇ **bear fruit** to be successful in the end, typically after planning and effort have been expended

fruitage /froótij/ *n* **1.** FRUIT PRODUCTION the production of fruit, the condition of a plant or tree when bearing fruit, or the time when this happens **2.** FRUITS fruits as a group **3.** RESULT OR EFFECT the results or cumulative set of effects deriving from a usually long-term process (*formal*)

fruitarian /froo taíri ən/ *n* somebody who only eats fruit [Late 19C. After VEGETARIAN]

fruit bat *n* a large bat of a group including mostly fruit-eaters but some pollen- or nectar-eaters. Native to: Europe, Asia, Africa. Suborder: Megachiroptera.

fruitcake /froót kayk/ *n* **1.** a dense cake containing dried fruit such as raisins, currants, and sultanas **2.** an offensive term for somebody considered to be irrational or out of touch with reality (*insult*)

fruit cocktail *n* a fruit salad made up of small or diced fruits such as pears, peaches, and pineapple, typically sold canned in syrup and usually served as a dessert

fruit cup *n N Am* same as **fruit cocktail**

fruit drop *n* **1.** the falling from the tree of fruit that is not fully ripe **2.** a fruit-flavoured boiled sweet

fruiterer /froótərər/ *n* a dealer in fruit [15C. < obsolete *fruiter* 'dealer in or handler of fruit' < French *fruitier* < *fruit* (see FRUIT)]

fruit fly *n* **1.** a small insect that eats decaying fruit. Genus: *Drosophila*. **2.** a small insect that eats plant tissue. Order: Trypetidae.

fruitful /froótf'l/ *adj* **1.** BEARING MUCH FRUIT bearing fruit, especially in abundance **2.** PROLIFIC producing many offspring ○ *a fruitful marriage* **3.** CAUSING FERTILITY causing or promoting fertility or productivity ○ *fruitful soil* **4.** CREATIVE highly productive or creative ○ *a fruitful imagination* **5.** SUCCESSFUL OR BENEFICIAL producing useful results or benefits ○ *a fruitful investigation* —**fruitfully** *adv* —**fruitfulness** *n*

fruiting body *n* a part of some fungi from which spores are released

fruition /froo ísh'n/ *n* **1.** COMPLETION a state or point in which something has come to maturity or had a desired outcome ○ *Our plans have come to fruition.* **2.** ENJOYMENT OF INTENDED OUTCOME the enjoyment of a desired outcome when it happens ○ *a sense of fruition* **3.** BOT PLANT'S FRUIT PRODUCTION the production of fruit by a tree or other plant [15C. Via French < late Latin *fruition-* < Latin *frui* 'enjoy, have the use of']

fruitless /froótləss/ *adj* **1.** producing nothing, or nothing worthwhile ○ *a fruitless discussion* **2.** producing no fruit —**fruitlessly** *adv* —**fruitlessness** *n*

fruitlet /froótlət/ *n* **1.** a fruit of smaller than usual size **2.** a part of a multiple fruit

fruit machine *n UK* a coin-operated gambling machine played by pushing a button or pulling a lever that makes pictures of fruit or other objects spin briefly. It pays out if any of specific combinations of images appear. ANZ term **poker machine**. N Am term **slot machine**

fruit salad *n* a mixture of pieces of fresh or canned fruit, usually in fruit juice or syrup, served as a dessert

fruit sugar *n* BIOCHEM same as **fructose**

fruit tree *n* a tree cultivated for its fruit

fruitwood /froót wŏod/ *n* the wood of a fruit tree, especially when used in cabinet-making

fruity /froóti/ (**-ier, -iest**) *adj* **1.** OF FRUIT relating to, resembling, or reminiscent of fruit **2.** RICH IN TONE rich and resonant in voice tone **3.** SEXUALLY SUGGESTIVE salacious or indecent in content (*informal*) —**fruitily** *adv* —**fruitiness** *n*

frumentaceous /froómən táyshəss/ *adj* made from, containing, or like wheat or any similar grain [Mid-17C. < late Latin *frumentaceus* < *frumentum* 'corn, grain']

frumenty /froóménti/, **fromenty** /frṓ-/, **furmenty** /fúr-/, **furmety** /fúrməti/, **furmity** *n* an old-fashioned pudding of wheat cooked to a porridge with added flavouring [14C. < Old French *frumentee, fourmentee* < *frument, fourment* 'grain' < Latin *frumentum*]

frump /frump/ *n* (*informal insult*) **1.** an offensive term for a woman considered not to be good-looking or not to dress well **2.** *N Am* an offensive term for somebody considered to be drab, dull, or old-fashioned [Mid-16C. Probably shortening of *frumple* 'wrinkle' < Middle Dutch *verrompelen* 'rumple completely'] —**frumpish** *adj* —**frumpy** *adj*

frusemide /frússə mīd/ *n* PHARM same as **furosemide** (*dated*) [Mid-20C. < alteration of 1st syllable of *furyl* 'chemical derived from furan' + *-sem-*, origin ?]

frustrate /fru stráyt/ *vt* (**-trates, -trating, -trated**) **1.** THWART SOMEBODY OR SOMETHING to prevent somebody or something from succeeding or something from coming to fruition ○ *All attempts to put to sea were frustrated by high winds.* **2.** DISCOURAGE SOMEBODY to make somebody feel disappointed, exasperated, or weary because of thwarted aims or unsatisfied

desires ■ *adj* **THWARTED** thwarted or blocked (*archaic*) [15C. < Latin *frustrat-*, past participle of *frustrari* 'deceive, frustrate, render useless' < *frustra* 'in vain, without effect'] — **frustrater** *n* —**frustrating** *adj* —**frustratingly** *adv*

frustrated /frú stráytid/ *adj* feeling exasperated, discouraged, or unsatisfied

frustration /fru stráysh'n/ *n* **1. DISSATISFACTION** a feeling of disappointment, exasperation, or weariness caused by aims being thwarted or desires unsatisfied **2. FRUSTRATING OF SOMEBODY OR SOMETHING** an act or instance of causing somebody or something to be dissatisfied or unfulfilled **3. SOMETHING THAT THWARTS** something that blocks, thwarts, and upsets somebody all at the same time ○ *His lack of ambition was a frustration to his father.*

frustule /frúss tyool/ *n* the hard cell wall of a microscopic organism (**diatom**) [Mid-19C. < Latin *frustulum* 'small piece' < *frustum* 'bit (cut off), piece (of a whole)']

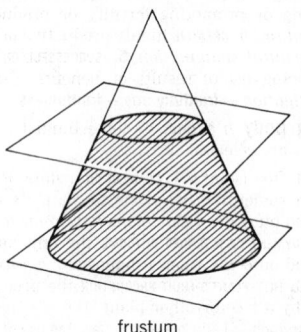

frustum

frustum /frústəm/ *n* the part of a solid between its base and a plane that cuts it parallel to the base [Mid-17C. < Latin, 'bit (cut off), piece (of a whole)']

frutescent /froo téss'nt/ *adj* looking or growing like a shrub [Early 18C. < Latin *frutex* 'shrub'] —**frutescence** *n*

fry[1] /frī/ *v* (**fries, frying, fried**) **1.** *vti* **COOK QUICKLY IN FAT** to cook something in fat over high heat, or be cooked in this way **2.** *vi* **BECOME HOT OR OVERHEATED** to become extremely hot as a result of the surrounding temperature (*informal*) ○ *We'll fry in this heat!* **3.** *vti* US **EXECUTE SOMEBODY, OR BE EXECUTED** to execute somebody in an electric chair, or be executed in this way (*slang*) ■ *n* (*plural* **fries**) **OFFAL** offal or a dish made from offal, especially as eaten fried [13C. Via French *frire* < Latin *frigere* 'roast, fry']

fry[2] /frī/ *npl* **1. YOUNG FISHES** the young of various fish **2. YOUNG ANIMALS** the young of various animals that breed or hatch in large numbers **3. CHILDREN** small offspring of human parents (*humorous*) [13C. Probably < Anglo-Norman *frei*, Old French *frai* 'spawn' < *froier* 'to spawn' < Latin *fricare* 'rub']

Fry /frī/, **Christopher** (*b.* 1907) British dramatist. His verse drama *The Lady's Not for Burning* (1948) brought him considerable popularity. Other plays include *Venus Observed* (1950) and *Curtmantle* (1962). Born **Harris, Christopher**

> 'Religion / Has made an honest woman of the supernatural, / And we won't have it kicking over the traces again.'
> [Christopher Fry, *The Lady's Not for Burning*; 1948]

Fry, Elizabeth (1780–1845) British prison reformer. A Quaker, she campaigned for improvements in prison conditions throughout Europe. Born **Gurney, Elizabeth**

FRY *abbr* HIST Federal Republic of Yugoslavia

Frye /frī/, **Northrop** (1912–91) Canadian literary critic. He is best known as a proponent of archetypal criticism. His most important work is his *Anatomy of Criticism* (1957). Full name **Frye, Herman Northrop**

> 'Value judgments are founded on the study of literature; the study of literature can never be founded on value judgments.'
> [Northrop Frye, *Anatomy of Criticism*; 1957]

fryer /frī ər/, **frier** *n* **1.** a container in which food is fried (*usually used in combination*) **2.** N Am a young chicken suitable for frying

frying pan *n* a shallow metal pan with a long handle, used for frying food ◇ **out of the frying pan (and) into the fire** from one difficult or dangerous situation to an even worse one

fry-up *n* (*informal*) **1.** an act or occasion of frying several types of food together for a meal **2.** a mixture of fried food

FSA[1] *abbr* ARTS Fellow of the Society of Antiquaries

FSA[2] *n* the regulatory body that oversees the financial services industry in the UK. Full form **Financial Services Authority**

FSH *abbr* **1.** BIOCHEM follicle-stimulating hormone **2.** AUTOMOT full service history

f-stop *n* a setting for a lens aperture that corresponds with an f-number

ft *abbr* **1.** MEASURE foot *or* feet **2.** MIL fort

FT *abbr* MEDIA Financial Times

fth., fthm. *abbr* MEASURE fathom

FT index *n* any share index compiled by the Financial Times

FTP *n* a standard procedure that allows one computer to transfer files to and from another over a network such as the Internet. Full form **file transfer protocol** ■ *vt* (**FTPs, FTPing, FTPed**) to transfer data using FTP

FTSE 100 Index /foŏtsee wun húndrəd-/, **FTSE** *n* an average of the London stock exchange prices of the stocks of the 100 largest British companies, published daily. Full form **Financial Times Stock Exchange 100 Index**

fubsy /fúbsi/ (**-sier, -siest**) *adj* an offensive term meaning of short stature and wide girth (*slang*) [Late 18C. < obsolete *fub(s)* 'small plump person', origin ?]

Fuchs /foŏks/, **Sir Vivian Ernest** (1908–99) British geologist and explorer. He led the first journey across Antarctica (1957–58).

fuchsia

fuchsia /fyoŏshə/ *n* **1.** a widely-cultivated tropical plant or bush. Flowers: purplish, reddish, or white, drooping. Genus: *Fuchsia*. **2.** a brilliant deep purplish-pink colour [Late 18C. < modern Latin, after Leonhard *Fuchs*] —**fuchsia** *adj*

fuchsin /foŏksin/, **fuchsine** /foŏk seen, -sin/ *n* a dark green crystalline solid that when dissolved in water makes a bluish-red solution. Use: textile dye, bacteria stain, disinfectant. Formula: $C_{20}H_{19}N_3.HCl$. [Mid-19C. < French *fuchsine*, or directly < German *Fuchs* 'fox' (translation of French *Renard*, the company that first produced the dye)]

fuci MARINE BIOL *plural of* **fucus**

fuck /fuk/ (*taboo*) *v* (**fucks, fucking, fucked**) **1.** *vti* a highly offensive term meaning to have sexual intercourse with somebody **2.** *vt* a highly offensive term used like a command, often followed by another word, to express anger, contempt, or rejection **3.** *vt* a highly offensive term meaning to ruin, botch, or destroy something ■ *n* **1.** a highly offensive term for an act of sexual intercourse **2.** a highly offensive term for somebody considered as a sexual partner of a particular quality **3.** a highly offensive term for something of little or no value ■ *interj* a highly offensive term used without a following word to express exasperation, fear, or surprise or to add emphasis [Early 16C. Origin ?]

fuck about, fuck around *vt* (*taboo*) **1.** a highly offensive term meaning to behave stupidly or carelessly **2.** a

highly offensive term meaning to treat somebody in a careless, insincere, or inconsiderate way

fuck off *vi* (*taboo*) **1.** a highly offensive term used as a command dismissing somebody in an angry or contemptuous way **2.** a highly offensive term meaning to go away

fuck over *vt* US a highly offensive term meaning to treat people unjustly or take advantage of them (*taboo*)

fuck up *v* (*taboo*) **1.** *vt* a highly offensive term meaning to damage or botch something **2.** *vt* a highly offensive term meaning to make somebody confused or inflict emotional or mental damage on somebody **3.** *vi* a highly offensive term meaning to make a bad mistake or bungle something

fuck with *vt* N Am a highly offensive term meaning to treat another person in a careless or disrespectful way (*taboo*)

fuck all (*taboo*) *pron* a highly offensive term meaning nothing at all ■ *det* a highly offensive term meaning not any

fucked *adj* (*taboo*) **1.** a highly offensive term meaning broken or destroyed **2.** a highly offensive term meaning in a situation in which trouble or failure is imminent

fucked up *adj* (*taboo*) **1.** a highly offensive term meaning affected by or displaying symptoms of psychological or emotional disorder **2.** a highly offensive term meaning mismanaged or very clumsily or badly done **3.** a highly offensive term meaning broken or destroyed **4.** a highly offensive term meaning completely intoxicated, especially as a result of taking drugs

fucker /fúkər/ *n* **1.** a highly offensive term expressing extreme dislike for somebody (*taboo insult*) **2.** a highly offensive term for any unnamed person (*taboo*)

fuckface /fúk fayss/ *n* a highly offensive term expressing extreme contempt for somebody (*taboo insult*)

fucking /fúking/ *adj* a highly offensive term intensifying or emphasizing a word or statement (*taboo*)

fuckup /fúk up/ *n* **1.** a highly offensive term meaning a bad mistake or something bungled (*taboo*) **2.** a highly offensive term meaning somebody regarded as incompetent (*taboo insult*)

fuckwit /fúk wit/ *n* a highly offensive term for somebody thought to be unintelligent (*taboo*)

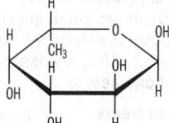

fucose

fucose /fyoŏ kōz, -köss/ *n* a six-carbon monosaccharide produced in plant polysaccharides [Early 20C. < FUCUS; from its presence in brown algae]

fucoxanthin /fyoŏkō zánthin/ *n* a brown carotenoid pigment found in some algae [Late 19C. < FUCUS; from its presence in brown algae]

fucus /fyoŏkəss/ (*plural* **-ci** /-sī/ *or* **-cuses**) *n* a greenish-brown seaweed. Genus: *Fucus*. [Early 17C. Via modern Latin < Latin, 'rock lichen, red or purple colour' < Greek *phukos* 'seaweed'] —**fucoid** /fyoŏ koyd/ *adj*

fuddle /fúdd'l/ *v* (**-dles, -dling, -dled**) **1.** *vt* **CONFUSE SOMEBODY AS IF WITH DRINK** to make a person or mental faculty confused, often through intoxication **2.** *vi* **DRINK TOO MUCH** to drink too much alcohol regularly (*archaic*) ■ *n* **FUDDLED STATE** a state of confusion or drunkenness [Late 16C. Origin ?]

fuddy-duddy /fúddi dudi/ (*plural* **fuddy-duddies**) *n* an old-fashioned or dull person, especially one past middle age (*informal; offensive in some contexts*) ○ *This is for kids, not fuddy-duddies like us.* [Early 20C. Origin ?]

FUD factor *n* a sales technique employed to cause a buyer to hesitate in purchasing a competing product. Asking the prospective customer if the competing item meets all applicable government or industry standards, warranties, and service contracts is an example. (*slang*) [Acronym < *fear, uncertainty, and doubt*]

fudge /fuj/ *n* **1.** SWEET a soft sweet made by boiling milk and sugar and then beating the liquid until it crystallizes and becomes slightly grainy in texture. Many flavourings and other ingredients can be added. **2.** *US* CHOCOLATE CAKE FILLING rich chocolate filling or topping, or squares of rich chocolate cake **3.** NONSENSE nonsensical talk (*informal*) ■ *vti* (**fudges, fudging, fudged**) ALTER SOMETHING TO DECEIVE to fiddle with or otherwise alter something in order to deceive or remain noncommittal (*informal*) ○ *fudged the figures to make the bottom line look better* [Early 17C. Origin ?]

Fuegian /fyoo ee′ji ən, fwáyji-/ *adj* relating to Tierra del Fuego, or its people or culture ■ *n* somebody, especially a Native South American, who comes from any of the islands of Tierra del Fuego

fuehrer *n* another spelling of **führer**

fuel /fyoó əl/ *n* **1.** SOURCE OF ENERGY something that is burned to provide power or heat **2.** SOURCE OF NUCLEAR ENERGY the fissionable material used to create power in a nuclear generator **3.** SOURCE OF STIMULATION something that stimulates or maintains something else, especially an emotion ○ *Her refusal to answer questions added fuel to his curiosity.* ■ *v* (**-els, -elling, -elled**) **1.** *vt* SUPPLY SOMETHING WITH FUEL to supply something with material to burn for power or heat **2.** *vt* STIMULATE SOMETHING to stimulate or maintain something, especially an emotion ○ *fuelled her passion* **3.** *vi* OBTAIN FUEL to take on supplies of fuel for running a vehicle [12C. Via Anglo-Norman *fuaille*, Old French *fouaille* < assumed Vulgar Latin *focalia* '(things) for the fire' < Latin *focus* 'fireplace, hearth'] —**fueller** *n*

fuel-air bomb *n* a thermobaric bomb

fuel cell *n* a device that generates electricity by converting the chemical energy of a fuel and an oxidant to electrical energy

fuel efficiency *n* the ability to make the best use of the fuel being used —**fuel-efficient** *adj*

fuel injection *n* a system for running an internal-combustion engine without using a carburettor, forcing vaporized fuel under pressure directly into the combustion chamber —**fuel-injected** *adj*

fuel oil *n* a product of liquid petroleum, burned chiefly to power ships and locomotives and to provide domestic heating

fuel rod *n* a metal tube containing nuclear fuel that is used in some types of nuclear reactor

Fuentes /fwént ayss/, **Carlos** (*b.* 1928) Mexican writer. He is known for his metaphysical novel *The Death of Artemio Cruz* (1962).

> 'Every storyteller is a child of Scheherazade, in a hurry to tell the tale so that death may be postponed one more time.'
> [Carlos Fuentes, 'The Storyteller', *The Picador Book of Latin American Stories*; 1998]

fufu /foó foo/ *n Carib, W Africa* a dish made from mashed plantain, yams, or cassava, eaten rolled into balls as the starchy accompaniment to soups or stews [Mid-18C. < Twi *fufuu*]

fug /fug/ *n* a stale or airless atmosphere (*informal*) [Late 19C. Probably alteration of FOG]

fugacious /fyoo gáyshəss/ *adj* **1.** fleeting or passing away quickly (*formal*) **2.** describes a plant or flower that lasts only briefly before withering or dropping [Early 17C. < Latin *fugac-* 'fleeing swiftly' < *fugere* 'flee'] —**fugaciously** *adv* —**fugaciousness** *n* —**fugacity** /-gássəti/ *n*

fugato /fyoo gaatō/ *adv, adj* in the style of a fugue ■ *n* (*plural* **-tos**) a piece of music in the style of a fugue

[Mid-19C. < Italian < past participle of *fugare* 'compose as a fugue' < *fuga* (see FUGUE)]

-fuge *suffix* something that drives out ○ *febrifuge* [Via French < Latin *fugere* 'flee', *fugare* 'drive out' < *fuga* 'flight']

fugitive /fyoójitiv/ *n* **1.** SOMEBODY WHO RUNS AWAY somebody who flees, e.g. from justice, enemies, or brutal treatment **2.** SOMETHING ELUSIVE an elusive or ephemeral thing ■ *adj* **1.** RUNNING AWAY fleeing, especially fleeing arrest or punishment **2.** BRIEF lasting only briefly ○ *the fugitive hours* **3.** ITINERANT moving around from place to place **4.** FOR SPECIFIC OCCASION written or composed for a specific occasion or on a subject of only passing interest (*literary*) ○ *a collection of essays, letters, and fugitive pieces* **5.** HARD TO UNDERSTAND difficult to understand or retain ○ *the fugitive nature of higher mathematics* [14C. Directly or via French < Latin *fugitivus* < *fugit-*, past participle of *fugere* 'flee'] —**fugitively** *adv* —**fugitiveness** *n*

fugle /fyoóg′l/ (**-gles, -gling, -gled**) *vi* to act as or like a fugleman in training or leading others [Mid-19C. Back-formation < FUGLEMAN]

fugleman /fyoóg′lmən/ *n* **1.** somebody acting as a leader or example to others **2.** formerly, a soldier used to teach drill movements by performing them in front of trainees [Early 19C. Alteration of German *Flügelmann* 'wing man, man on the flank']

fugu /fyoó goo/ *n* a poisonous pufferfish that is eaten, especially in Japan, after the poisonous parts are removed [Mid-20C. < Japanese]

fugue /fyoog/ *n* **1.** a musical form in which a theme is first stated, then repeated and varied with accompanying contrapuntal lines **2.** *also* **fugue state** a disordered state of mind in which somebody typically wanders from home and experiences a loss of memory relating only to the previous, rejected, environment [Late 16C. Directly or via French < Italian *fuga* < Latin, 'flight'] —**fugal** *adj*

führer /fyoórər/, **fuehrer** *n* a leader who is regarded as autocratic (*offensive in some contexts*) [Mid-20C. < German *Führer* 'leader', a title (in full *Führer und Reichskanzler* 'Leader and Chancellor of the Empire') adopted by Adolf Hitler, leader of the German National Socialist Party before and during World War II]

Mount Fuji

Fuji, Mount /foóji/, **Fujiyama** /foóji áamə/ highest mountain in Japan, on central Honshu Island, southwest of Tokyo. A dormant volcano in the shape of an almost perfect cone, it is considered to be sacred by many Japanese people. Height: 3,776 m/12,387 ft.

Fujian /foó jyén/, **Fukien** /foó kyén/ province in southeastern China, on the coast opposite the island of Taiwan. Capital: Fuzhou. Population: 32,610,000 (1997). Area: 120,000 sq. km/46,000 sq. mi.

Fujimori /foóji máwri/, **Alberto** (*b.* 1938) Peruvian politician. He served as president of Peru (1990–2000) becoming the first person of Japanese descent to lead a Latin American country.

Fujisawa /foóji saáwə/ city southwest of Yokohama in Kanagawa Prefecture, southeastern Honshu, Japan. Population: 382,038 (2002).

Fujita scale /foó jeétə-/ *n* a scale used to rank tornadoes by the amount of damage they do to man-made structures and natural objects. The scale runs from F-0 to F-5, with F-0 indicating light damage caused by winds of 64–116 kph/40–72 mph and F-5 indicating the devastation caused by winds of 415–

512 kph/261–318 mph. [Late 20C. After Tetsuya Theodore Fujita (1920–98), Japanese-born US chemist]

Fujiyama /foóji yaámə/ same as **Fuji, Mount**

Fukien another spelling of **Fujian**

Fukui /foo koó i/ capital city of Fukui Prefecture, west-central Honshu, Japan. Population: 249,656 (2002).

Fukuoka /foókoo ōkə/ port and capital city of Fukuoka Prefecture on northern Kyushu, southwestern Japan. Kyushu University was founded there in 1911. Population: 1,302,454 (2002).

Fukushima /foókoo sheémə/ capital city of Fukushima Prefecture, on the Abukuma River in north-central Honshu, Japan. Population: 288,926 (2002).

Fukuyama /foókoo yaámə/ city on the Inland Sea in Hiroshima Prefecture, Honshu Island, Japan. Population: 381,098 (2002).

-ful *suffix* **1.** full of ○ *hateful* **2.** having the nature of ○ *rightful* **3.** tending to ○ *forgetful* **4.** an amount that fills ○ *capful* **5.** full to ○ *brimful* [Old English, < *full* (see FULL[1])]

Fula /foólə/ (*plural same* or **-las**), **Fulah** (*plural same* or **-lahs**) *n* **1.** a member of an ethnically diverse nomadic people living in western and central Africa **2.** LANG same as **Fulani** (sense 1) [Late 18C. < Fulani *pulo* 'person'] —**Fula** *adj*

Fulani /foó laáni/ (*plural same* or **-nis**) *n* **1.** a Niger-Congo language spoken over a large area of West Africa, especially in Nigeria, Guinea-Bissau, Burkina-Faso, Gambia, Benin, Guinea, and Senegal. Native speakers: 15 million. **2.** PEOPLES same as **Fula** (sense 1) [Mid-19C. < Hausa] —**Fulani** *adj*

Fulbright /foól brīt/, **J. William** (1905–95) US educator and politician. While a US Democratic senator from Arkansas (1945–74) and chair of the influential Senate Foreign Relations Committee (1959–74), he was a leading critic of the Vietnam War. He sponsored the Fulbright Act (1946), which enacted a major US programme of international educational exchanges. Full name **Fulbright, James William**

> 'We must dare to think about "unthinkable things" because when things become unthinkable, thinking stops and action becomes mindless.'
> [J. William Fulbright, *Speech to the US Senate*; 27 March 1964]

fulcrum /foólkrəm/ (*plural* **-crums** or **-cra** /-krə/) *n* **1.** PIVOT the point or support about which a lever turns **2.** PROP something that supports something else revolving about it or depending on it ○ *The fulcrum of the building plan is the major retail tenant.* **3.** ZOOL SUPPORT IN ANIMAL part of an animal that acts as a hinge or support, especially scales on the fins of some fish [Late 17C. < Latin, 'post or foot of a couch, bedpost' < *fulcire* 'prop up, support']

fulfil /foól fíl/ (**-fils, -filling, -filled**) *v* **1.** *vt* ACHIEVE SOMETHING to do what is necessary to bring about or achieve something expected, desired, or promised ○ *went on to fulfil her early promise of greatness* **2.** *vt* CARRY OUT ORDER to do what is necessary to carry out a request or command ○ *The instructions have been fulfilled to the letter.* **3.** *vt* SATISFY SOMETHING to be good enough or of the type necessary to meet a standard or requirement **4.** *vt* COMPLETE SOMETHING to do what is necessary to complete or bring something to an end **5.** *vt* SUPPLY SOMETHING to supply the full amount of something ordered ○ *fulfil an order for new cars* **6.** **fulfil yourself** *vr* REALIZE AMBITIONS to feel satisfied with what you are doing or realize your expectations or ambitions [Old English *fullfyllan* 'fill up, make full' < FULL[1] + FILL] —**fulfiller** *n* —**fulfilment** *n*

SYNONYMS See *perform*.

fulfill *vt* US spelling of **fulfil**

fulfilled /foól fíld/ *adj* satisfied with what you are doing or that you have realized your expectations or ambitions ○ *a fulfilled person who had enjoyed a long successful career*

fulfilling /foól fílling/ *adj* giving satisfaction to somebody as an activity or goal in life ○ *a fulfilling job opportunity*

fulgent /fúljənt/ *adj* gleaming brilliantly (*literary*) [15C.

< Latin *fulgent-*, present participle of *fulgere* 'flash, shine'] —**fulgency** *n* —**fulgently** *adv*

fulgurate /fúlgyŏŏ rayt/ (**-rates, -rating, -rated**) *v* **1.** *vt* MED to destroy unwanted tissue such as a wart using a high-frequency electric current **2.** *vi* to flash with or like lightning (*formal*) [Mid-17C. < Latin *fulgurat-*, past participle of *fulgurare* 'lighten, flash' < *fulgere* 'flash, shine'] —**fulgurant** *adj* —**fulguration** /fúlgyŏŏ ráysh'n/ *n*

fulgurite /fúlgyŏŏ rīt/ *n* a tube of hard, glassy material formed by lightning striking sand [Mid-19C. < Latin *fulgur* 'lightning']

fuliginous /fyoo líjjinəss/ *adj* (*formal*) **1.** having the colour or consistency of soot or smoke **2.** like soot in cloudiness or obscurity [Late 16C. Directly or via French *fuligineux* < late Latin *fuliginosus* < Latin *fuligin-*, stem of *fuligo* 'soot'] —**fuliginously** *adv*

full[1] /fŏŏl/ *adj* **1.** FILLED TO CAPACITY holding as much or as many as is possible **2.** WITH MUCH OR MANY having a large amount or number of something ○ *full of mischief* **3.** GREATEST IN EXTENT being at the highest degree or largest extent ○ *at full speed* ○ *an engine running at full revolutions* ○ *I like my coffee full strength.* **4.** WITH NOTHING MISSING with nothing or nobody left out or missing, or with no part uncompleted or used ○ *the full complement of staff* **5.** COMPLETELY DEVELOPED at the end or peak of development ○ *roses in full bloom* **6.** COMPLETELY SO having reached or fulfilled all requirements for a position, rank, or description ○ *a full colonel* **7.** HAVING EATEN ENOUGH satisfied by an amount eaten or drunk **8.** BUSY filled with activity or achievement ○ *live a full life* **9.** PLUMP fleshy and with a rounded shape ○ *a full figure* **10.** WITH SAME PARENTS sharing both natural parents ○ *my full brother* **11.** CHARGED WITH EMOTION affected by strong deep emotion ○ *We left the place with full hearts and shining eyes.* **12.** PREOCCUPIED deeply preoccupied with something ○ *She's always full of her latest schemes.* **13.** SONOROUS with depth or power, e.g. of sound ○ *chanted in full voice* **14.** BEVERAGES RICHLY FLAVOURED with a rich strong flavour and substantial quality ○ *a full-flavoured coffee* **15.** CLOTHING WITH MUCH FABRIC made with a lot of fabric and not close-fitting **16.** same as **drunk** *adj* (sense 1) (*slang*) ■ *adv* **1.** COMPLETELY to the greatest or complete extent ○ *turned full round* **2.** EXACTLY in a precise or exact position ○ *He took a punch full on the mouth.* **3.** VERY to a high degree ○ *What happened next we know full well.* ■ *n* FULLEST STATE the greatest extent or highest degree ○ *We enjoyed ourselves to the full.* ■ *v* (**fulls, fulling, fulled**) **1.** *vt* HANDICRAFT SEW GATHERS AND TUCKS to make a garment full by sewing gathers in it **2.** *vi* BECOME FULL to wax and become full (*refers to the moon*) [Old English, < Indo-European] —**fullness** *n* —**fully** *adv* ◇ **be full of yourself** to be very conceited and arrogant ◇ **full up** completely full (*informal*) ◇ **in full** to the complete amount or extent, omitting nothing ○ *The opera has never been performed in full.*

full[2] /fŏŏl/ (**fulls, fulling, fulled**) *vti* to make cloth bulkier by dampening and beating it, or become bulkier by being dampened and beaten [14C. Probably back-formation < FULLER [1]]

fullback /fŏŏl bak/ *n* **1.** DEFENDER in sports such as football, rugby, or hockey, a player in a defensive position **2.** AMERICAN FOOTBALL ATTACKING PLAYER in American football, a player in the offensive backfield who lines up behind the quarterback and is used mainly for blocking **3.** FULLBACK POSITION the position played by a fullback **4.** CENTRAL DEFENDER in Australian Rules football, the central defender playing directly in front of his team's goal posts, between the two back pockets

full beam *n* the setting of a vehicle's headlights that sheds light far in front of the vehicle. N Am term **high beam**

full-blooded *adj* **1.** healthily vigorous or forceful **2.** of unmixed breed —**full-bloodedly** *adv* —**full-bloodedness** *n*

full-blown *adj* **1.** in its most complete, extreme, strongest, or developed form ○ *full-blown malaria* **2.** in bloom and fully open

full board *n* board at a hotel or guest house that includes accommodation and all meals. N Am term **American plan**

full-bodied *adj* **1.** with a rich strong flavour and substantial quality **2.** rich in tone and strong in volume

full-bottomed *adj* describes a wig that is long and full at the back

full circle *adv* back to the starting point, usually after passing through various stages

full cost accounting *n* the practice of including indirect costs and benefits of a product or activity, e.g. its social and environmental effects on health and the economy, along with its direct costs when making business decisions

full count *n* in baseball, the situation in which the batter has three balls and two strikes

full-court press *n* in basketball, the practice of putting pressure on opposing players in all parts of the court as opposed to merely defending the backcourt

full cousin *n* same as **cousin** (sense 1)

full-cream *adj* describes whole unskimmed milk or something made with this ○ *chocolate made with full-cream milk*

full dress *n* clothes suitable or prescribed for a ceremony or formal occasion (*hyphenated when used before a noun*)

full-dress *adj* of considerable importance and often exhaustively complete ○ *a full-dress investigation*

full duplex *n* a communications channel that supports the simultaneous transmission of data in two directions

full employment *n* the state of a country's economy in which everyone available for work has a job

fuller[1] /fŏŏllər/ *n* somebody who makes cloth bulkier by dampening and beating it [Pre-12C. < Latin *fullo*]

fuller[2] /fŏŏllər/ *n* a hammer used by a blacksmith for forging grooves and spreading hot iron [Early 19C. Origin ?]

Fuller /fŏŏllər/, **R. Buckminster** (1895–1983) US engineer, designer, architect, and writer. He used innovative technology to address the global problems facing humanity in the second half of the 20th century. He championed the geodesic dome as a versatile, sturdy, and cost-effective building structure. Full name **Fuller, Richard Buckminster**

> 'Now there is one outstandingly important fact regarding Spaceship Earth, and that is that no instruction book came with it.'
> [R. Buckminster Fuller, *Operating Manual for Spaceship Earth*; 10 June 1969]

Fuller, Roy (1912–92) British poet and novelist. He is noted for his *New and Collected Poems, 1934–84* (1985). He also wrote several novels, including *Image of a Society* (1956), and three volumes of memoirs.

Fuller, Thomas (1608–61) English clergyman, author, and historian. He was the author of the *History of the Worthies of England* (1662), a biographical dictionary.

> 'He that resolves to deal with none but honest men must leave off dealing.'
> [Thomas Fuller, *Gnomologia*; 1732]

fullerene /fŏŏllə reen/ *n* a form of carbon made up of up to 500 carbon atoms arranged in a sphere or tube [Late 20C. Shortening of BUCKMINSTERFULLERENE]

fuller's earth *n* an absorbent clay used in fulling cloth and in filtering liquids

fuller's teasel *n* a plant with large prickly flower heads, formerly used to raise the nap on cloth. Native to: Europe, Asia. Latin name: *Dipsacus sativus.*

full-faced *adj* with the whole of the face visible, facing the viewer ○ *a full-faced portrait*

full-fashioned *adj US* CLOTHING same as **fully-fashioned**

full-figured *adj* having a fleshy rounded body, or designed to be worn by somebody, especially a woman, with a fleshy rounded body

~~**fullfill**~~ incorrect spelling of **fulfil**

full-fledged *adj US* same as **fully-fledged**

full forward *n* in Australian Rules football, an attacking player playing at the centre of the forward line, directly in front of the opposing team's goal and between the two forward pockets

full-frontal *adj* **1.** showing the whole front of the body including the genitals **2.** whole-hearted and uninhibited (*informal*) ○ *She made a full-frontal attack on her opponents.*

full-grown *adj N Am* same as **fully-grown**

full house *n* a poker hand containing three cards of the same value and a pair of a different value

full-length *adj* **1.** REACHING TO ANKLES describes a garment such as a coat or skirt that extends to the ankles or floor **2.** SHOWING WHOLE BODY describes a mirror or portrait showing the whole length of the body **3.** NOT SHORTENED consisting of the whole or usual amount or duration of something

full marks *npl* **1.** a perfect score in an assessment or examination **2.** high praise or commendation (*informal*) ○ *Full marks to the driver for managing to find the place.*

full monty /-mónti/ *n* **1.** everything that is needed or appropriate or makes up a full set or the whole of something (*slang*) **2.** a striptease routine that ends with the performer completely naked [Origin ?]

ORIGIN There are various unsubstantiated theories about the origin of the ***full monty***. One refers it to Montague Burton, an early 20th-century British tailor and retailer of made-to-measure clothes: *the full Montague Burton* is said to have meant 'a three-piece suit for Sunday best'. Another explanation refers it to the full cooked English breakfast reputedly demanded by Field Marshal Bernard Montgomery. However the expression was not recorded until much later than the peak of fame of either of these men. The sense 'striptease routine' derives from a popular British film *The Full Monty* (1997), in which unemployed Sheffield steelworkers develop a striptease act to earn money and restore self-esteem.

---

full moon *n* **1.** the phase of the Moon when its surface as seen from Earth is fully illuminated by the Sun **2.** the period of time during which the Moon appears fully illuminated as a circle

full-motion video *n* a film sequence shown on a computer screen, e.g. within a computer game

full-mouthed *adj* **1.** having the complete set of adult teeth **2.** said loudly or vigorously

full nelson *n* a wrestling hold in which one wrestler puts both arms beneath an opponent's arms from behind and then exerts pressure by clasping the hands at the back of the opponent's neck

full-on *adj* **1.** ALL-OUT taken to the limits ○ *The wedding was a full-on display of pomp and ceremony.* **2.** OUT-AND-OUT possessing a particular quality to the fullest extent ○ *He's turned into a full-on computer nerd.* **3.** OVERPOWERING talkative and enthusiastic to an excessive degree ○ *She's a bit full-on, isn't she?*

full-page *adj* taking up the whole of the page on which it is printed ○ *a full-page illustration* ○ *a full-page story*

full point *n* GRAM same as **full stop**

full-rigged *adj* describes a sailing ship that has at least three square-rigged masts

full-scale *adj* **1.** having exactly the same dimensions and proportions as the original **2.** done with total commitment of effort and resources ○ *a full-scale manhunt*

full-size, **full-sized** *adj* being the normal size for its kind

full stop *n* **1.** the punctuation mark (.) that is used at the end of a sentence or in abbreviations. N Am term **period 2.** a complete halt or an end ○ *This delay has brought production to a full stop.*

USAGE A ***full stop*** is used at the end of a sentence that is not a question or exclamation: *It rained last Saturday.* It is also used after some abbreviations: *at 11 a.m. on 7 Aug. 2000.* The full stop is increasingly omitted in abbreviations, especially in contractions (e.g. *Dr, St, Ltd*) and after capital letters (e.g. *BBC, USA, VCR*). Shortened forms used as words in their own right (e.g. *gym, disco, pub*) and acronyms pronounced as words

(e.g. *Aids, laser, NATO*) should not be written with full stops. The same mark is used in decimal notation (*2.5 children*), where it is read as 'point'. It is also used in Internet addresses, where it is read as 'dot' (*.com*).

full time *adv* during all of the time considered standard or appropriate for the activity in question ○ *worked full time* ■ *n* in football and other sports, the end of a match

full-time *adj* **1.** involving or using all of the time considered standard or appropriate for an activity, especially work ○ *a full-time student* **2.** occurring at or indicating the end of a soccer or other match ○ *the full-time score* —**full-timer** *n*

full-wave rectifier *n* a circuit, used in the design of electronic equipment such as radios, computers, and televisions, that operates on both the positive and negative cycles of an alternating current

fully /fŏŏlli/ *adv* **1.** to the greatest extent possible or required ○ *The flight is fully booked.* **2.** to the full extent of a particular time, quantity, or number ○ *We waited fully 40 minutes.*

fully-fashioned *adj UK, ANZ, Can* shaped to fit the lines of the body ○ *fully-fashioned stockings* US term **full-fashioned**

fully-featured *adj* describes an electronic device or piece of software that has all the features that a user would hope for or expect

fully-fledged *adj* **1.** COMPLETELY DEVELOPED at a point of complete development or maturity ○ *a fully-fledged microelectronics industry* **2.** FULLY QUALIFIED with full status or rank ○ *a fully-fledged helicopter pilot* **3.** BIRDS ABLE TO FLY describes a young bird that is able to fly and leave the nest

fully-grown *adj* having developed to maturity or adulthood. N Am term **full-grown**

fulmar /fŏŏlmər/ *n* a seabird of the petrel family that resembles a gull in appearance and nesting habits. Native to: Arctic. Genus: *Fulmarus.* [Late 17C. < Old Norse *fúll* 'foul' (because it regurgitates its stomach's contents when disturbed) + *már* 'gull']

fulminant /fŏŏlminənt/ *adj* **1.** exploding violently **2.** describes illness coming on suddenly and with severe symptoms of short duration [Early 17C. Directly or via French < Latin *fulminant-*, present participle of *fulminare* (see FULMINATE)]

fulminate /fŏŏlmi nayt, fúl-/ *vti* (**-nates, -nating, -nated**) **1.** SPEAK SCATHINGLY to express forcible criticism of somebody or something ○ *an article fulminating against the arms trade* ○ *fulminated that it was unacceptable* **2.** EXPLODE to detonate or explode violently, or cause something to detonate or explode violently ■ *n* CHEM EXPLOSIVE SALT OR ESTER an explosive salt or ester of fulminic acid, especially fulminate of mercury [15C. < Latin *fulminat-*, past participle of *fulminare* 'lighten, strike with lightning' < *fulmen* 'lightning']—**fulmination** /fŏŏlmi náysh'n, fúl-/ *n* —**fulminator** *n* —**fulminatory** *adj*

fulminate of mercury *n* the mercury salt of fulminic acid. Use: in explosives and detonators. Formula: $HgC_2N_2O_2$.

fulminating /fŏŏlmi nayting, fúl-/ *adj* **1.** able or likely to explode or detonate **2.** MED same as **fulminant** (sense 2)

fulminic acid /fŏŏl minnik-, ful-/ *n* an unstable compound that smells of bitter almonds. Use: manufacture of explosives. Formula: HONC. [< Latin *fulmin-*, stem of *fulmen* 'lightning']

fulsome /fŏŏlssəm/ *adj* **1.** effusive or fawning to the point of being offensive ○ *embarrassed by their fulsome compliments* **2.** great in amount or intensity [13C. < FULL [1] + -SOME [1]] —**fulsomely** *adv* —**fulsomeness** *n*

fulvous /fŏŏlvəss, fúl-/ *adj* of an orange-brown colour (*literary*) [Mid-17C. < Latin *fulvus* 'reddish-yellow']

Fu Manchu moustache /fōō manchōō-/ *n* a moustache with long drooping ends [After a character in the novels of Sax Rohmer (British writer Arthur Sarsfield Ward (1886–1959))]

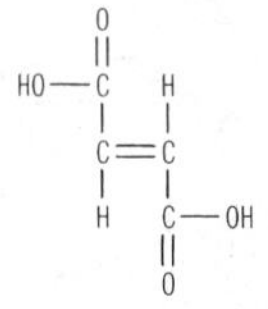

fumaric acid

fumaric acid /fyoo márrik-/ *n* a colourless crystalline solid. Source: some plants and moulds, or synthesized from benzene. Use: manufacture of resins. Formula: $C_4H_4O_4$. [< modern Latin *Fumaria* < late Latin *fumaria* 'fumatory' < Latin *fumus* 'smoke']

fumarole /fyōōmərōl/ *n* a vent in a volcanic area from which steam and hot gases such as sulphur dioxide are emitted [Early 19C. Via Italian *fumaruolo* < late Latin *fumariolum* 'vent, smoke-hole' < Latin *fumus* 'smoke'] —**fumarolic** /fyōōmə róllik/ *adj*

fumatory /fyōōmətəri/ *adj* relating to, involving, or typical of fumigation or smoking [Mid-19C. < Latin *fumat-*, past participle of *fumare* 'smoke']

fumble /fúmb'l/ *v* (**-bles, -bling, -bled**) **1.** *vti* GROPE CLUMSILY to grope clumsily in search of something ○ *fumbled in his pockets for his keys* ○ *fumbled her way along the passage* **2.** *vi* HESITATE to act clumsily, hesitantly, or unsuccessfully ○ *She fumbled through the introductions.* **3.** *vt* BUNGLE SOMETHING to do something clumsily or inefficiently ○ *This is your last chance, so don't fumble it.* **4.** *vti* DROP OR MISHANDLE BALL in sports, to drop or fail to catch a ball ■ *n* FUMBLED ACTION an act or instance of fumbling [Mid-16C. Origin ?] —**fumbler** *n* —**fumblingly** *adv*

fume /fyoom/ *v* (**fumes, fuming, fumed**) **1.** *vi* BE ANGRY to feel great anger, especially anger that is not fully expressed **2.** *vi* EMIT GAS to emit gas, smoke, or vapour, or be emitted in this form **3.** *vt* FUMIGATE to treat something with a gas, smoke, or other fumigant **4.** *vt* DARKEN WOOD to expose wood, especially oak, to vapour or gas given off by ammonia in order to darken it (*usually passive*) ■ *n* **1.** SMOKE smoke, gas, or vapour, especially when unpleasant or harmful (*often used in the plural*) ○ *a chemical that emits noxious fumes when exposed to air* **2.** ACRID SMELL an acrid or nauseating smell (*often used in the plural*) **3.** FIT OF ANGER a state of great anger [14C. Via French < Latin *fumus* 'smoke'] —**fumingly** *adv* —**fumy** *adj*

fume cupboard *n* an enclosed ventilated chamber in which to conduct chemistry experiments involving harmful vapours

fumet /fyoo mét/ *n* a strongly-flavoured stock obtained from cooking fish, meat, or vegetables [Early 18C. < French < *fumer* 'to smoke' < Latin *fumus* 'smoke']

fumigant /fyōōmigənt/ *n* a substance that gives off fumes, especially one used as a disinfectant or to kill pests [Late 19C. < Latin *fumigant-*, present participle of *fumigare* (see FUMIGATE)]

fumigate /fyōōmi gayt/ (**-gates, -gating, -gated**) *vti* to treat something with fumes, or be treated with fumes, especially to kill microorganisms or pests [Mid-16C. < Latin *fumigat-*, past participle of *fumigare* 'to smoke' < *fumus* 'smoke'] —**fumigation** /fyōōmi gáysh'n/ *n* —**fumigator** *n*

fuming sulphuric acid *n* a very concentrated solution of sulphuric acid that gives off fumes

fun /fun/ *n* **1.** AMUSEMENT a time or feeling of enjoyment or amusement ○ *Just for fun, we wore silly hats.* **2.** SOMETHING AMUSING something that provides enjoyment or amusement ○ *Skiing can be fun for the whole family.* **3.** MOCKERY playful joking, often at the expense of another ○ *What's said in fun can still hurt.* ■ *adj* (*informal*) **1.** AMUSING providing enjoyment or amusement ○ *We'll have a fun time tonight.* **2.** CHEAP AND FLAMBOYANT flamboyant in style and often made of cheap synthetic materials, designed to be used or worn for fun ○ *fun jewellery* ■ *vi* (**funs, funning, funned**) BEHAVE PLAYFULLY to behave in a playful or joking way (*informal*) ○ *Don't pay any attention to him; he's just funning.* [Late 17C. < obsolete *fon* 'fool', origin ?] ◇ **fun and games** difficulty or trouble (*informal; used ironically*) ○ *A broken sprinkler in the stockroom overnight gave us some fun and games in the morning.* ◇ **like fun** (*informal*) **1.** with great speed or effort ○ *We'll have to work like fun to finish this order on time.* **2.** *US* certainly not ○ *Like fun I am!* ◇ **make fun of somebody** *or* **something** to make somebody or something appear ridiculous ◇ **poke fun at somebody** *or* **something** to mock or ridicule somebody or something

Funabashi /fōōnə báshi/ city in Chiba Prefecture on the northeastern coast of Tokyo Bay, Honshu Island, Japan. Population: 551,916 (2002).

Funafuti /fōōnə fōōti/ atoll and capital of Tuvalu, located in the western Pacific Ocean. The atoll's main town is Fongafale. Population: 3,432 (1990). Area: 3 sq. km/1 sq. mi.

funambulist /fyoo námbyōōlist/ *n* an acrobat who walks while balancing on a suspended rope [Late 18C. < French *funambule* or Latin *funambulus* < *funis* 'rope' + *ambulare* 'to walk'] —**funambulate** *vi* —**funambulism** *n*

Funchal /fōōn shaál/ capital of the Madeira Islands, an autonomous region of Portugal, in the North Atlantic Ocean. Situated on the southern coast of Madeira, it is a major resort. Population: 115,950 (1995).

function /fúngksh'n/ *n* **1.** PURPOSE an action or use for which something is suited or designed ○ *Its function is to collect water.* ○ *a watch with an alarm function* **2.** ROLE an activity or role assigned to somebody or something **3.** EVENT a social gathering or ceremony, especially a formal or official occasion ○ *a black-tie function* **4.** UTILITY practical usefulness, as distinct from aesthetic appeal ○ *the relationship between form and function* **5.** DEPENDENT FACTOR a quality or characteristic that depends upon and varies with another ○ *Success is a function of determination and ability.* **6.** MATHS VARIABLE QUANTITY a variable quantity whose value depends upon the varying values of other quantities **7.** MATHS CORRESPONDENCE BETWEEN MEMBERS OF DIFFERENT SETS a relationship between two mathematical sets, in which each member of one set corresponds uniquely to a member of the other set. Symbol **f** **8.** COMPUT SINGLE COMPUTER OPERATION a named and stored basic operation of a computer yielding a single result when invoked **9.** COMPUT COMPUTER PROGRAM'S MAIN PURPOSE the purpose of a computer program or piece of computer equipment, e.g. database management or printing **10.** GRAM ROLE OF WORD OR PHRASE a grammatical role performed by a word or phrase in a specific construction ○ *Noun phrases can fulfil many functions.* ■ *vi* (**-tions, -tioning, -tioned**) **1.** SERVE PURPOSE to serve a particular purpose, or perform a particular role ○ *hats functioning both as fashion statements and as protection against the sun* **2.** BE IN WORKING ORDER to operate normally, fulfilling a purpose or role ○ *When the heart ceases to function, the patient is clinically dead.* [Mid-16C. < Latin *function-* < *funct-*, past participle of *fungi* 'perform'] —**functionless** *adj*

functional /fúngksh'nəl/ *adj* **1.** PRACTICAL having a practical application, or serving a useful purpose ○ *designs that are functional yet fun* **2.** OPERATIONAL in good working order, or working at the moment ○ *The lift will not be functional for several hours.* **3.** MED HAVING NO ORGANIC CAUSE without apparent organic or structural cause ○ *a functional disorder* **4.** LING RELATING TO LANGUAGE AS COMMUNICATION relating to the function of language as a communicating tool, rather than to its form ○ *functional linguistics* —**functionality** /fúngkshə nálləti/ *n* —**functionally** *adv*

functional food *n* food containing nutritional additives that is promoted as being beneficial to health and able to prevent or reduce diseases such as tooth decay and cancer ○ *'the first spread formulated to act against cholesterol in a market for so-called functional foods'* (*The Guardian*; April 1999)

functional genomics *n* the study of the relationships between gene structure and biological function in organisms (*takes a singular verb*)

functional group *n* a group of atoms that reacts as

a single unit and determines the properties and structure of a class of compounds, e.g. a hydroxyl group in alcohols

functional illiterate *n* somebody whose reading and writing abilities are inadequately developed to meet everyday needs —**functionally illiterate** *adj*

functionalism /fúngksh'nəlizəm/ *n* **1.** BELIEF IN FUNCTION OVER FORM belief that the intended function of something should determine its design, construction, and choice of materials, or a 20th-century design movement based on this belief **2.** PHILOSOPHY PHILOSOPHY EMPHASIZING PRACTICAL a philosophy or system that gives practical and utilitarian concerns priority over aesthetic concerns **3.** SOC SCI ASSESSMENT OF SOCIAL INSTITUTIONS BY ROLE the analysis and explanation of social institutions according to the function they perform in society, e.g. the family seen as an institution for social stability and cohesion —**functionalist** *n, adj*

functional literacy *n* the level of skill in reading and writing that a person needs to cope with everyday adult life

functional shift *n* a change in the grammatical function of a word, e.g. from noun to verb

---

USAGE **Functional shift** is a process in which a word shifts from one grammatical function to another. For example:

1. a noun can be used as a verb, e.g. *to access a computer file*
2. a verb as a noun, e.g. *having a laugh*
3. a noun as an adjective, e.g. *a prestige development*
4. an interjection as a verb, e.g. *Audiences were wowed by his new musical.*
5. an adverb as a noun, e.g. *the ins and outs*
6. an adverb as a verb, e.g. *upping the limit.*
Functional shift is sometimes controversial, but it has been a well-established phenomenon in English since the 16th century. Shakespeare used it enthusiastically: *'Be he ne'er so vile, this day shall gentle his condition'* (Henry V).

---

functionary /fúngksh'nəri/ (*plural* **-ies**) *n* an official, especially somebody with trivial duties

function change *n* GRAM same as **functional shift**

function key *n* a button on a computer keyboard or terminal that instructs the computer to perform a specific task. The same key may be programmed to perform different tasks in different programs.

function shift *n* GRAM same as **functional shift**

function word *n* a word that has little meaning on its own but serves a specific syntactic function in a phrase or sentence

functor /fúngktər/ *n* **1.** somebody or something that performs a function (*formal*) **2.** GRAM same as **function word** [Mid-20C. < FUNCTION]

fund /fund/ *n* **1.** SUPPLY a source or stock of something ○ *a vast fund of knowledge* **2.** RESERVE OF MONEY a sum of money saved or invested for a particular purpose **3.** ORGANIZATION ADMINISTERING RESERVE OF MONEY an organization that manages a sum of money for a particular purpose ■ **funds** *npl* **1.** MONEY money, especially money that is available to spend ○ *I'm a bit short of funds at the moment.* **2.** UK GOVERNMENT SECURITIES British government securities that finance the national debt and pay a fixed rate of interest ■ *vt* (**funds, funding, funded**) **1.** PROVIDE MONEY FOR SOMETHING to provide money needed to finance a project or keep it running (*often passive*) ○ *environmental projects that are funded by local government* **2.** FIN PROVIDE MONEY TO PAY DEBT to provide a sum of money to pay off a debt or its interest **3.** FIN MAKE DEBT LONG-TERM to convert a short-term debt into a long-term debt with a fixed rate of interest [Mid-17C. < Latin *fundus* 'bottom'] —**funder** *n*

fundament /fúndəmənt/ *n* **1.** the buttocks or the anus (*archaic or humorous*) **2.** an underlying principle or theory on which something is based (*formal; often used in the plural*) [13C. Via French < Latin *fundamentum* < *fundus* 'bottom']

fundamental /fúndə mént'l/ *adj* **1.** BASIC relating to or affecting the underlying principles or structure of something ○ *We need to make fundamental changes in our business.* **2.** CENTRAL serving as an essential part of something ○ *Privacy is of fundamental importance to her.* **3.** MUSIC OF CHORD'S LOWEST NOTE relating to the lowest note of a chord in root position, the note that gives the chord its basic harmony **4.** PHYS OF LOWEST FREQUENCY relating to or produced by the lowest frequency component in a complex vibration ■ *n* **1.** BASIC PRINCIPLE OR ELEMENT a basic and necessary component of something, especially an underlying rule or principle (*often used in the plural*) ○ *The class teaches the fundamentals of karate.* **2.** MUSIC PRINCIPAL TONE the principal tone in a chord, from which other harmonics are generated **3.** PHYS LOWEST FREQUENCY the lowest frequency in a vibration or periodic wave —**fundamentally** *adv*

fundamental interaction *n* PHYS same as **interaction** (sense 3)

fundamentalism /fúndə mént'lizəm/ *n* **1.** a religious or political movement based on a literal interpretation of and strict adherence to doctrine, especially as a return to former principles **2.** the belief that religious or political doctrine should be implemented literally, not interpreted or adapted —**fundamentalist** *n, adj* —**fundamentalistic** /fúndə ment'l ístik/ *adj*

fundamental law *n* the founding rules and principles or constitution on which a government is based, as distinct from its legislative acts

fundamental particle *n* PHYS same as **elementary particle**

fundamental unit *n* MEASURE same as **base unit**

-funded *suffix* with money provided by a particular institution or person ○ *government-funded*

funded debt /fúndid-/ *n* that part of the national debt that has no deadline for repayment

~~**fundemental**~~ incorrect spelling of **fundamental**

fundholder /fúnd hōldər/ *n* in the United Kingdom between 1991 and 1999, a general medical practice that opted to manage its own budget and contract directly with hospitals, rather than leave these administrative tasks to the local health authority —**fundholding** *adj*

fundi[1] /fúndi/ (*plural* **-dis**) *n* S Africa a learned person, or an expert on a topic ○ *The political fundis got together to work out a compromise.* [Mid-20C. Probably < Ndebele, Xhosa, or Zulu *umfundi* 'disciple, learner']

fundi[2] ANAT plural of **fundus** ■ *n* ENVIRON another spelling of **fundie**

fundie /fúndi/, **fundy** (*plural* **-ies**) *n* **1.** an offensive term for a member of a fundamentalist political or religious group (*informal; offensive*) **2.** a member of the radical wing of the Green movement [Late 20C. < German < *Fundamentalist* 'fundamentalist']

funding /fúnding/ *n* financial support

fundraiser /fúnd rayzər/ *n* **1.** somebody who generates money for a non-profit-making organization, especially an organizer of campaigns to raise money **2.** an activity or event that is intended to generate money to support a non-profit-making organization

fundraising /fúnd rayzing/ *n* the organized activity of soliciting and collecting money for a non-profit-making organization

fundus /fúndəss/ (*plural* **-di** /-dī/) *n* the part of a hollow organ of the body farthest from its opening, e.g. the part of the eye's retina opposite the pupil [Mid-18C. < Latin, 'bottom'] —**fundic** *adj*

fundy *n* RELIG another spelling of **fundie**

Fundy, Bay of /fúndi/ inlet of the Atlantic Ocean off Canada, separating New Brunswick and Nova Scotia, Canada. Its rapid tides are among the highest in the world, reaching 18 m/60 ft. Depth: 200 m/650 ft. Length: 275 km/171 mi.

funeral /fyóonərəl/ *n* **1.** CEREMONY FOR SOMEBODY WHO HAS DIED a rite held to mark the burial or cremation of a corpse, especially a ceremony held immediately before burial or cremation **2.** FUNERAL PROCESSION a procession of mourners following a body to its place of burial or cremation **3.** END an end to something's existence ○ *We have witnessed the funeral of the amateur game.* [14C. Via Old French *funerailles* 'funeral rites' < medieval Latin *funeralia* < late Latin *funeralis* 'of death rituals' < Latin *funer-*, stem of *funus* 'death ritual'] ◇ **be somebody's funeral** to be something disapproved of that somebody else chooses to do (*informal*) ○ *If he wants to work extra hours, that's his funeral.*

funeral director *n* US same as **undertaker** (sense 1)

funeral parlour, **funeral home** *n* a business establishment where corpses are prepared for burial or cremation and where a funeral service may also be performed and the body viewed by mourners. N Am term **funeral home**

funerary /fyóonərəri/ *adj* relating to or suitable for a burial or funeral [Late 17C. < late Latin *funerarius* < Latin *funer-* (see FUNERAL)]

funereal /fyoo neʹeri əl/ *adj* **1.** relating to or suitable for a funeral **2.** very slow, solemn, mournful, or dismal [Early 18C. < Latin *funereus* < *funer-* (see FUNERAL)] —**funereally** *adv*

funfair /fún fair/ *n* LEISURE same as **fair**[2] (sense 1)

funfest /fún fest/ *n* N Am a party, especially one at which amusing activities are organized (*informal*)

fun fur *n* synthetic fur fabric ○ *Orange fun fur was all the rage at the winter fashion shows that year.*

fungal /fúng g'l/, **fungous** /fúng gəss/ *adj* **1.** describes a condition caused by a fungus ○ *a fungal infection* **2.** relating to a fungus, or resembling a fungus in appearance or texture

fungi BIOL plural of **fungus**

fungible /fúnjib'l/ *adj* describes goods such as grain or wine that are perishable and traded or exchanged in measurable quantities or numbers ■ *n* a commodity that is fungible (*often used in the plural*) [Late 17C. < medieval Latin *fungibilis* < Latin *fungi* 'perform'] —**fungibility** /fúnjə bíllətee/ *n*

fungicide /fúnji sīd, fúng gi-/ *n* a substance used to destroy or inhibit the growth of fungi —**fungicidal** /fúnji sīd'l, fúng gi-/ *adj* —**fungicidally** *adv*

fungiform /fúnji fawrm, fúng gi-/ *adj* shaped like a mushroom

fungistat /fúnji stat, fúng gi-/ *n* a substance that inhibits the growth of fungi without killing them —**fungistatic** /fúnji státtik, fúng gi-/ *adj*

fungo /fúng gō/ (*plural* **-goes**) *n* in baseball, an act of hitting the ball high into the air using a special lightweight bat, usually to give fielders catching practice [Mid-19C. Origin ?]

fungoid /fúng goyd/ *adj* resembling, characteristic of, or caused by a fungus ○ *a fungoid growth* ■ *n* a fungus, or a growth resembling a fungus

fungous *adj* FUNGI same as **fungal**

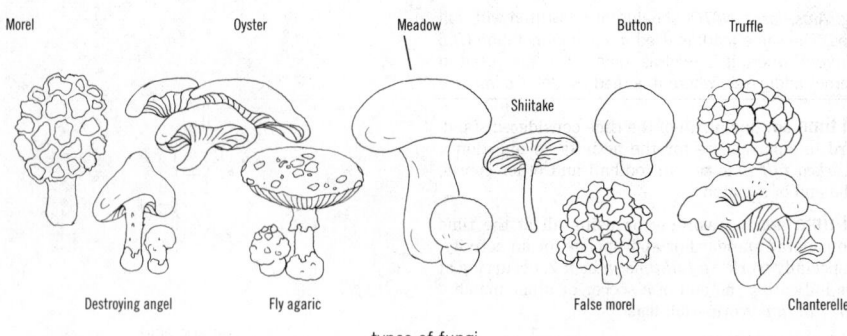

Morel   Oyster   Meadow   Button   Truffle   Shiitake   Destroying angel   Fly agaric   False morel   Chanterelle

types of fungi

fungus /fúng gəss/ (*plural* **-gi** /-gī/ *or* **-guses**) *n* a single-celled or multicellular organism without chlorophyll that reproduces by spores and lives by absorbing nutrients from organic matter. Fungi include mildews, moulds, mushrooms, rusts, smuts, and yeasts. See illustration on previous page [Early 16C. < Latin]

funicle /fyoōnik'l/ *n* ANAT, BOT same as **funiculus** [Mid-17C. Anglicization]

funicular /fyoō níkyoōlər/ *adj* **1.** OF ROPE'S TENSION relating to a rope, especially its tension **2.** MECH ENG ROPE-OPERATED operated by a rope or cable, especially one wound or pulled by a machine **3.** ANAT, BOT OF FUNICULUS relating to a funiculus ■ *n* RAIL **FUNICULAR RAILWAY** a funicular railway or railway car [Mid-17C. < Latin *funiculus* (see FUNICULUS)]

Barnaby's
funicular railway

funicular railway *n* a railway used on short steep inclines in which cars that counterbalance each other run on parallel tracks linked to a cable

funiculus /fyoō níkyoōləss/ (*plural* **-li** /-lī/) *n* **1.** a cord-shaped part of the body, e.g. the umbilical cord or a bundle of nerve fibres in the spinal cord **2.** a stalk of a plant ovule that connects it or a seed to the placenta [Mid-17C. < Latin, 'little rope' < *funis* 'rope']

funk[1] /fungk/ *n* **1.** popular music that derives from jazz, blues, and soul and is characterized by a heavy rhythmic bass and backbeat **2.** a rhythmic earthy quality in music (*slang*) [Mid-20C. Back-formation < FUNKY[1]]

funk[2] /fungk/ *n* **1.** FEAR a state of intense fear or panic (*informal*) ○ *in a funk about his exam tomorrow* **2.** COWARD an easily frightened or cowardly person (*dated informal*) ■ *vti* (**funks, funking, funked**) NOT DO SOMETHING OUT OF FEAR to fail to do something, in order to avoid doing it, because of fear (*informal*) ○ *I meant to tell her but funked at the last moment.* [Mid-18C. Origin ?]

funk[3] /fungk/ *n* N Am a strong unpleasant odour (*slang*) [Early 17C. Origin ?]

funked-up *adj* exhilarated by, fond of, or featuring funk music (*slang*)

funk hole *n* a place where somebody hides from danger (*informal*)

funky[1] /fúngki/ (**-ier, -iest**) *adj* **1.** MUSIC LIKE FUNK MUSIC with the backbeat and rhythmic bass typical of funk music (*slang*) **2.** MUSIC LIKE BLUES resembling blues music (*slang*) **3.** FASHION UNCONVENTIONAL offbeat, creative, and novel (*informal*) ○ *a return to the funky styles of the 1970s* **4.** N Am SMELLY with a strong unpleasant odour (*slang*) **5.** US UNCOMFORTABLE causing discomfort or unease (*slang*) ○ *Since we grounded him, any conversation has been pretty funky.* [Mid-20C. < FUNK[3]] —**funkily** *adv* —**funkiness** *n*

funky[2] /fúngki/ (**-ier, -iest**) *adj* in a state of fear or panic (*informal*) [Mid-19C. < FUNK[2]] —**funkily** *adv* —**funkiness** *n*

fun-loving *adj* relating to somebody who seeks and enjoys life's pleasures

funnel /fúnn'l/ *n* **1.** UTENSIL USED IN POURING LIQUIDS a cone-shaped utensil with a large opening at the top and a small opening or tube at the bottom. Use: to guide liquids and other substances into containers. **2.** CHIMNEY a vertical pipe from which smoke and exhaust gases escape, especially one on a steamship or steam train ■ *v* (**-nels, -nelling, -nelled**) **1.** *vti* MOVE INTO NARROW SPACE to move into and through a narrow space, or direct something into and through a narrow space ○ *an efficient system for funnelling crowds through the turnstiles* **2.** *vt* CONCENTRATE RESOURCES SOMEWHERE to direct or channel all of something from one place or use to another ○ *Funds were funnelled away from domestic projects.* **3.** *vt* MAKE FUNNEL-SHAPED to form something into the shape of a funnel [15C. Via Provençal *fonilh* < Latin *infundibulum* < *infundere* 'pour in' < *fundere* 'pour']

funnel cloud *n* a funnel-shaped cloud that projects from the base of a thundercloud and often develops into a tornado

funnelform /fúnn'l fawrm/ *adj* describes a flower or other plant part that is shaped like a funnel or cone

funnel neck *n* a straight high collar resembling a polo neck that has not been folded over, extending from the collarbone to the chin or jawline

funnel-web spider

funnel-web spider, **funnel-web** *n* a large black spider that is highly venomous and makes funnel-shaped webs. Native to: Australia. Family: Dipluridae.

funnily /fúnnili/ *adv* **1.** INTRODUCING COMMENT ON SOMETHING STRANGE used to introduce a comment on something considered strange or odd ○ *Funnily enough, nobody seemed to notice.* **2.** STRANGELY in a way that seems strange or odd ○ *The dog has been acting funnily ever since the operation.* **3.** COMICALLY in an amusing or humorous way

funny /fúnni/ *adj* (**-nier, -niest**) **1.** COMICAL causing amusement, especially enough to provoke laughter **2.** STRANGE odd or perplexing ○ *That's funny, I can't find my keys.* **3.** UNCONVENTIONAL out of the ordinary in a quaint or comical way ○ *a funny little doorway through an arch* **4.** UNWELL nauseated, faint, or otherwise slightly ill (*informal*) **5.** TRICKY slyly deceitful and dishonest (*informal*) ○ *Don't try anything funny, or I'll call the police.* ■ *n* (*plural* **-nies**) JOKE an amusing remark or joke (*informal*) [Mid-18C. < FUN] —**funniness** *n*

SYNONYMS *funny, amusing, comic, comical, droll, facetious, humorous, witty, hilarious*

CORE MEANING: causing or intended to cause amusement

funny causing amusement, especially enough to provoke laughter ○ *funny spontaneous banter* ○ *He realized the ad was trying to be funny, but it went beyond good taste.* **amusing** causing somebody to smile or laugh or be amused, often in a subdued way ○ *an amusing story about his early life* ○ *An amusing situation arose when she mistook me for my brother.* **comic** capable of inducing amusement, smiles, or laughter ○ *a company with a reputation for work which is moving and comic* ○ *a comic novel about the difficulties of being different* **comical** funny to the extent of being absurd, especially if unintentional ○ *Their dismay was almost comical.* ○ *a comical rolling walk* **droll** amusing in a wry or odd way ○ *a droll description of a new recruit who had arrived that day* **facetious** intended to be humorous but often silly or inappropriate. ○ *a facetious remark* **humorous** intended to be amusing and make people laugh ○ *He could keep people entertained with a seemingly endless fund of jokes and humorous anecdotes.* **witty** using words in an inventive, clever, and amusing way ○ *a witty parody of the Orpheus story* ○ *If the magazine's readers believe that they are buying it because it's witty or urbane, they are just kidding themselves.* **hilarious** extremely funny ○ *Just when you think you're in for a standard ending, the play surprises you with a hilarious twist.*

funny bone *n* (*informal*) **1.** the point at the outside of the elbow where a nerve is so close to the longer arm bone that a blow often causes a tingling sensation **2.** a person's sense of humour ○ *a story that tickled my funny bone* [< the tingling feeling when the nerve is hit]

funny business *n* dealings or goings-on that involve trickery, deceit, or dishonesty (*informal*)

funny farm *n* an offensive term for a psychiatric hospital (*dated slang*)

funny ha-ha *adj* funny in a humorous way, as distinct from funny in a strange way. ◊ **funny peculiar**

funny-looking *adj* having a strange or unexpected appearance

funny man *n* a man who is a comedian, clown, or humorist (*dated informal*)

funny money *n* (*informal*) **1.** COUNTERFEIT MONEY counterfeit or forged currency **2.** ILLICITLY GAINED MONEY money obtained from a legally or morally suspect source **3.** CURRENCY WITH LITTLE VALUE currency, especially an unfamiliar one, with an inflated value

funny peculiar *adj* funny in a strange way, as distinct from funny in a humorous way. ◊ **funny ha-ha**

fun park *n* an area with amusement facilities, especially water slides and rides

fun run *n* a noncompetitive run over a moderately long course, organized to promote health and fitness or to raise money for charity

funster /fúnstər/ *n* somebody who likes to have fun or who enjoys telling or playing jokes (*dated informal*)

fur /fur/ *n* **1.** MAMMAL'S COAT the soft dense coat of hair on a hairy animal **2.** ANIMAL HAIR hairs from an animal's coat **3.** DRESSED PELT a dressed pelt from an animal such as a mink or seal that includes the animal's soft coat of hair. Use: garments, decoration. **4.** FUR COAT a garment made from fur pelts, especially a coat, jacket, or stole **5.** SOMETHING HAIRY something with a fuzzy or hairy texture or appearance **6.** COATING ON TONGUE a whitish coating of dead cells on the tongue that sometimes accompanies an illness (*informal*) **7.** LIME DEPOSIT mineral deposits from hard water that cling to the insides of plumbing fixtures or of kettles and other water containers **8.** HERALDRY PELT ON COAT OF ARMS a representation of an animal skin on a coat of arms [14C. < obsolete *fur* 'to line' < Old French *forrer* < *forre* 'lining'] —**furred** *adj* ◊ **make the fur fly** to cause trouble or a disturbance (*informal*)
fur up *vti* to coat the insides of plumbing fixtures and water containers with mineral deposits from hard water, or become coated with these deposits

fur. *abbr* MEASURE furlong

furan /fyoō ran, fyoo rán/ *n* a colourless flammable liquid. Use: solvent, manufacture of polymers. [Late 19C. Contraction of FURFURAN]

furanose /fyoōrə nōz/ *n* a sugar made up of a ring of four carbon atoms and one oxygen atom

furbearer /fúr bairər/ *n* an animal with fur, especially fur with high commercial value, e.g. a fox or mink —**furbearing** *adj*

furbelow /fúrbelō/ *n* **1.** RUFFLE a gathered or pleated piece of material, especially as an ornament on a woman's garment **2.** FLAMBOYANT BEHAVIOUR a showy or pretentious way of behaving (*literary; often used in the plural*) ■ *vt* (**-lows, -lowing, -lowed**) DECORATE CLOTHING WITH RUFFLE to add a furbelow to a garment for ornamentation [Late 17C. Origin ?]

furbish /fúrbish/ (**-bishes, -bishing, -bished**) *vt* **1.** to brighten something by polishing ○ *stone steps were scrubbed and brasses were furbished* **2.** CONSTR same as **refurbish** (*literary*) [14C. < Old French *fourbiss-* < Germanic] —**furbisher** *n*

furcate /fúr kayt/ *vi* (**-cates, -cating, -cated**) to divide into two separate strands or branches ■ *adj* divided into separate strands or branches ○ *furcate leaves* [Early 19C. < late Latin *furcatus* 'forked' < Latin *furca* 'fork'] —**furcately** *adv* —**furcation** /fur káysh'n/ *n*

furcula /fúrkyoōlə/ (*plural* **-lae** /-lee/) *n* the V-shaped bone that is formed from two fused collarbones, found between the breasts of a bird (*technical*) [Mid-19C. < Latin, 'small fork' < *furca* 'fork'] —**furcular** *adj*

furfur /fúr fur/ (plural **-fures** /-fyoŏ reez/) n a tiny piece of scaly or flaky skin, e.g. a particle of dandruff (technical) [15C. < Latin, 'bran, scales']

furfuraceous /fúrfə ráyshəss/ adj 1. covered with or resembling particles of dandruff 2. relating to or resembling bran

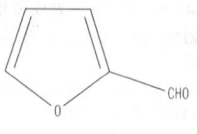

furfural

furfural /fúrfərəl/ n a colourless liquid with a distinctive smell. Source: plants. Use: manufacture of plastics, in oil refining, in agriculture. Formula: $C_5H_4O_2$.

furfuran /fúrfə ran/ n CHEM same as **furan**

Furies /fyoŏriz/ npl in Greek mythology, three terrifying snake-haired winged goddesses, named Alecto, Megaera, and Tisiphone, who mercilessly punished wrongdoing, especially when committed within families. They were later identified with the Eumenides.

furioso /fyoŏri óssō/ adv to be played with vigour and passion (used as a musical direction) [Mid-17C. Via Italian < Latin furiosus (see FURIOUS)] —**furioso** adj

furious /fyoŏri əss/ adj 1. extremely or violently angry ○ I was furious with him for spreading such lies. 2. involving a great deal of energy, violence, or speed ○ the pianist's furious assault on the keys [14C. Via French < Latin furiosus < furia 'rage' (see FURY)] —**furiously** adv —**furiousness** n

furl /furl/ vti (**furls, furling, furled**) to roll up and secure something made of fabric, or be rolled up and secured ■ n a rolled-up section of something such as a flag or sail [Late 16C. < French ferler < ferm 'firm, firmly' + lier 'to tie']

furlong /fúr long/ n a measure of distance equal to 220 yd (approximately 201 m), now used mainly on racecourses [Old English furlang < furh (see FURROW) + lang (see LONG[1])]

furlough /fúrlō/ n 1. LEAVE FROM DUTY leave of absence from duty, especially military duty 2. GRANT OF LEAVE an official paper authorizing leave of absence ■ vt (**-loughs, -loughing, -loughed**) GIVE LEAVE TO to grant leave of absence to somebody, especially a member of the armed forces [Early 17C. < Dutch verlo 'leave']

furmenty, **furmety**, **furmity** n FOOD same as **frumenty**

furn. abbr furnished

furnace /fúrniss/ n 1. ENCLOSURE PRODUCING GREAT HEAT a device in which heat is produced by burning fuel either to warm a building or to undertake an industrial process such as smelting metal ○ an oil furnace 2. SOMEWHERE HOT an extremely hot place (informal) ○ This kitchen is a furnace! 3. TERRIBLE EXPERIENCE a testing or demanding experience (literary) [13C. Via Old French fornais < Latin fornax]

Furneaux Group /fúrnō-/ group of islands situated off the coast of northeastern Tasmania, Australia. The largest islands are Flinders and Cape Barren Island. Population: 1,010. Area: 2,330 sq. km/900 sq. mi.

furnish /fúrnish/ (**-nishes, -nishing, -nished**) vt 1. to provide and install furniture and other fittings such as carpets and curtains in a place ○ The lobby is furnished in an Art Deco style. 2. to supply something, or provide somebody with something (formal) ○ Could you furnish us with the names and addresses of clients? [15C. < Old French furniss-, stem of furnir < Germanic] —**furnisher** n

furnished /fúrnishd/ adj containing or supplied with furniture ○ a furnished flat

furnishings /fúrnishingz/ npl articles of furniture and other useful or decorative items for a room, e.g. carpets and curtains

furniture /fúrnichər/ n 1. TABLES AND CHAIRS the movable items in a room or patio, e.g. chairs, desks, or cabinets, 2. FURNITURE, CONSTR FITTINGS ON WOODEN ARTICLES the metal or plastic accessories fitted to an item of joinery or cabinetwork, e.g. door hinges and drawer handles 3. PRINTING TYPE SEPARATORS in traditional hot-metal printing, strips of wood, metal, or plastic that are placed between type in order to make spaces and hold the type in place 4. EQUIPMENT the equipment or accessories used for an activity, e.g. a ship's tackle or a horse's saddle and harnesses (archaic) [Early 16C. < Old French fourniture < furnir (see FURNISH)]

furor /fyoŏr awr/ n US same as **furore** [15C. < Latin (see FURORE)]

furore /fyoŏ ráwri/ n 1. UPROAR an angry or indignant public reaction to something ○ The verdict of not guilty created a furore in the courtroom. 2. EXCITEMENT a state of intense excitement or activity ○ the furore surrounding the release of their latest album 3. CRAZE an enthusiastically embraced fad (archaic) [Late 18C. Via Italian < Latin furor < furere 'to rage']

furosemide /fyoŏrōssə mīd/ n N Am a drug that induces urination. Use: treatment of edema. [Mid-20C. < 1st syllable of furyl 'chemical derived from furan' + -sem-, origin ?]

furphy /fúrfi/ (plural **-phies**) n Aus a rumour or piece of gossip, especially one that is not true (slang) [Early 20C. After the Furphy family, manufacturers of water carts (where troops swapped gossip) in Australia during World War I]

Furphy /fúrfi/, **Joseph** (1843–1912) Australian writer. He is the author of Such is Life (1903), an account of Australian rural life in the 1880s.

furrier /fúrri ər/ n 1. a dealer in furs 2. a person or establishment that makes or sells clothes and accessories of animal fur [14C. Alteration (after CLOTHIER) of furrer < Old French forreor < forrer (see FUR)]

furriery /fúrri əri/ n 1. fur accessories and articles of clothing considered collectively 2. the business or craft of a furrier

furring /fúrring/ n 1. CLOTHING FUR PART OF CLOTHING fur trim or lining for a garment 2. MED WHITE COVERING a whitish coating of dead cells on the tongue of somebody who is ill 3. CONSTR MAKING OF SURFACE OF STRIPS the placing of strips of wood, metal, or brick across the studs or joists in a building to create a firm and level foundation for plaster, flooring, or another surface (often used before a noun) ○ furring strips 4. CONSTR STRIPS USED UNDER SURFACE strips used in a building for furring

furrow /fúrrō/ n 1. TRENCH IN PLOUGHED FIELD a narrow trench in soil made by a plough 2. GROOVE a rut or groove in a surface 3. WRINKLE ON FOREHEAD a wrinkle on the skin of the forehead, as a result of frowning or age 4. IRRIGATION TRENCH a narrow trench dug to deliver water to a field or garden ■ vti (**-rows, -rowing, -rowed**) MAKE FURROWS IN SOMETHING to make furrows in something, or become marked with furrows ○ He furrowed his brow. [Old English furh < Indo-European] —**furrowed** adj

furry /fúrri/ (**-rier, -riest**) adj 1. COVERED IN FUR covered in fur, or with a coat that is covered in fur ○ furry animals 2. LOOKING OR FEELING LIKE FUR resembling fur in texture or appearance 3. MED COVERED IN WHITISH COATING describes a tongue covered with a whitish coating of dead cells

fur seal n a seal with a double coat of fur, including a dense soft underfur that is highly valued for making garments. Many fur seal populations have been severely decreased by commercial hunting. Genera: Arctocephalus or Callorhinus.

Fur Seal Islands /fúr seel-/ ▸ **Pribilof Islands**

Fürth /fúrt/ city in the state of Bavaria, southern Germany, situated just northwest of Nuremberg. Population: 107,799 (1997).

further /fúrthər/ adj ADDITIONAL that is more than or adds to the quantity or extent of something ○ until further notice ○ Do you have anything further to add? ■ adv 1. TO GREATER DISTANCE to or at a point that is more distant in place or time ○ We pushed further into the woods. ○ further into the future 2. TO GREATER EXTENT to a greater degree or extent ○ Let's not pursue the matter any further. 3. IN ADDITION used to introduce an additional statement or point ○ She said further that she would not accept any excuses. ■ vt (**-thers, -thering, -thered**) ADVANCE SOMETHING to help or give a boost to the progress of something ○ All this media attention will further our cause. [Old English furþor, furþur 'more forward' < Germanic] —**furtherer** n —**furthermost** adj ◇ **further to** following on from something that has been written or discussed (formal) ○ Further to our phone conversation, I would like to confirm the order.

USAGE further or farther? Strictly speaking **farther** is the preferred spelling when referring to physical distance, as in Have we much farther to go? Now **further** is commonly used in this context, although its use is traditionally reserved for figurative contexts, as in I have nothing further to add, or It took a further two phone calls before I got through. **Furthest** and **farthest** behave similarly.

furtherance /fúrthərənss/ n advancement of an objective or interest ○ In the furtherance of equal opportunity, such discrimination is prohibited by law.

further education n education or training after the age of 16 that leads to a range of qualifications including degrees validated by a university

furthermore /fúrthər mawr, fúrthər máwr/ adv used to introduce an additional statement or point ○ She claimed furthermore that he did not own the shop but only worked there.

furthest /fúrthist/ adj MOST DISTANT more distant in place or time than anything else ○ the furthest planet from the Sun ■ adv 1. TO GREATEST EXTENT to a greater degree or extent than anything else ○ The dollar has fallen furthest against the pound for the last year. 2. TO GREATEST DISTANCE to or at a more distant point in space or time than anything else ○ Whoever gets the furthest wins the prize.

USAGE See **further**.

furtive /fúrtiv/ adj 1. done in a way that is intended to escape notice ○ conspirators exchanging furtive glances 2. presenting the appearance, or giving the impression, of somebody who has something to hide [Early 17C. Via French < Latin furtivus 'hidden, stolen' < furtum 'theft' < fur 'thief' < Indo-European, 'carry'] —**furtively** adv —**furtiveness** n

SYNONYMS See **secret**.

furuncle /fyoŏr ungk'l/ n a boil on the skin (technical) [Late 17C. < Latin furunculus 'knob on a vine' < fur 'thief' (because it 'steals' the sap)] —**furuncular** /fyoŏ rúngkyoŏlər/ adj —**furunculous** /fyoŏ rúngkyoŏləss/ adj

furunculosis /fyoŏ rúngkyoŏ lōssiss/ n 1. a medical condition in which large areas of the skin are covered in persistent boils 2. a virulent bacterial disease that affects salmon and trout and can be devastating in the densely populated waters of fish farms

fury /fyoŏri/ (plural **-ries**) n 1. RAGE violent anger ○ She could not contain her fury any longer. 2. BURST OF ANGER an outburst of violent anger ○ He stormed off in a fury. 3. WILD FORCE a state of excited or frenetic activity ○ debris scattered in the wake of the tornado's fury 4. OFFENSIVE TERM an offensive term for a woman who is regarded as malevolent and spiteful (dated) [14C. Via French < Latin furia < furere 'to rage'] ◇ **like fury** with great speed or energy

CULTURAL NOTE The Sound and the Fury, a novel (1929) by US writer William Faulkner. Set in the American South, it recounts the financial and moral decline of a wealthy family. The story, which centres on the daughter Caddy, is told in four parts, three of which are narrated by family members.

SYNONYMS See **anger**.

Fury n in Greek mythology, one of the Furies

furze /furz/ n PLANTS same as **gorse** [Old English fyrs, origin ?]

furze-pig n regional same as **hedgehog** [Because both the animal and gorse have spikes, and hedgehogs make a grunting noise]

REGIONAL NOTE See **hedgehog**.

fusain /fyoo záyn, fyoo zayn/ n **1.** ART **CHARCOAL STICK** a fine stick of charcoal for drawing, made from wood from the spindle tree **2.** ART **CHARCOAL DRAWING** a drawing or sketch done with fusain charcoal **3.** MINERALS **GREY COAL** dark grey bituminous carbon found in some kinds of coal [Late 19C. Via French, 'spindle tree, charcoal made from its wood' < Latin *fusus* 'spindle']

~~fuschia~~ incorrect spelling of **fuchsia**

fuscous /fúskəss/ adj of a dark greyish-brown colour (literary or technical) [Mid-17C. < Latin *fuscus* 'dusky']

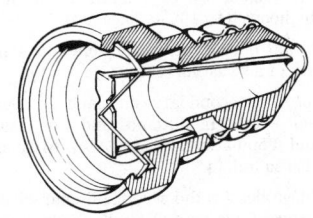

fuse

fuse[1] /fyooz/ n **ELECTRICAL CIRCUIT BREAKER** an electrical safety device containing a piece of a metal that melts if the current running through it exceeds a particular level, thereby breaking the circuit ■ vti (**fuses, fusing, fused**) **1.** **STOP WORKING BECAUSE OF DAMAGED FUSE** to stop functioning because of a damaged electrical fuse, or cause an electrical circuit or appliance to stop functioning ○ In trying to find the fault, he managed to fuse all the other lights too. **2.** **COMBINE** to unite or blend things, or become united or blended into a whole ○ sensations and ideas fusing intimately together **3.** **LIQUEFY** to melt something such as metal or plastic, or become melted at a very high temperature [Late 16C. < Latin *fus-*, past participle of *fundere* 'melt, pour']

fuse[2] /fyooz/ ARMS n **1.** **EXPLOSIVE LEAD** a cord or trail of a combustible substance that is ignited at one end to carry a flame to an explosive device farther away **2.** **DETONATOR** a mechanical or electrical detonator that triggers an exploding device such as a bomb or grenade ■ vt (**fuses, fusing, fused**) **EQUIP DEVICE WITH DETONATOR** to equip an exploding device such as a bomb or grenade with a mechanical or electrical detonator [Mid-17C. Via Italian *fuso* 'spindle' < Latin *fusus*]

fuse box n a box, often a cupboard fitted to a wall, that contains the fuses that protect all the electrical circuits in a building or part of a building

fused quartz, fused silica n GLASS same as **quartz glass**

fusee /fyoo zee/, **fuzee** n **1.** a large-headed match that is not easily extinguished in the wind **2.** a conical pulley with a spiral groove, used in clock and watch mechanisms [Late 16C. Via French *fusée* 'spindle, fuse, flare' < Latin *fusus* 'spindle']

fuselage /fyoozə laazh, -lij/ n the body of an aeroplane, containing the cockpit, passenger seating, and cargo hold but excluding the wings [Early 20C. < French < Latin *fusus* 'spindle']

Fuseli /fyooz'li/, **Henry** (1741–1825) Swiss painter and art critic. His imaginative paintings, emphasizing melodrama, fantasy, and horror, influenced key figures of the Romantic movement, notably William Blake. Born **Füssli, Johann Heinrich**

fusel oil /fyooz'l-/ n an oily liquid mixture. Source: insufficiently distilled alcoholic liquors. Use: solvent, in chemical manufacturing. [Mid-19C. < German *Fusel* 'bad liquor']

Fushun /foo shoon/ city and industrial centre in Liaoning Province, northeastern China. Population: 1,530,000 (1995).

fusible /fyoozəb'l/ adj describes metals and other materials that are easily melted or liquefied ○ *fusible alloys* —**fusibility** /fyoozə bílləti/ n

fusiform /fyoozi fawrm/ adj tapering at both ends, like a spindle ○ *fusiform bacteria* [Mid-18C. < Latin *fusus* 'spindle']

fusil /fyoozil/ n a lightweight musket with a flintlock firing mechanism [Late 16C. < French, 'steel in a flintlock, musket' < late Latin *focus* 'fire']

fusilier /fyoozi leer/, **fusileer** n formerly, a soldier in a British army regiment that was armed with lightweight muskets (**fusils**) [Late 17C. < French < *fusil* 'musket' (see FUSIL)]

fusillade /fyoozi layd, -laad/ n **1.** **BLAST OF GUNFIRE** the firing of several guns at once or in quick succession **2.** **ONSLAUGHT** a sustained attack or barrage, e.g. of missiles or words ■ vt (**-lades, -lading, -laded**) **FIRE AT ENEMY** to subject an enemy to a sustained burst of gunfire [Early 19C. < French < *fusiller* 'shoot' < *fusil* 'musket' (see FUSIL)]

fusilli /fyoo zílli/ npl pasta in the form of short spiral shapes [Late 20C. < Italian, 'little spindles' < Latin *fusus* 'spindle']

fusion /fyoozh'n/ n **1.** **BLENDING** the merger or a blending of two or more things such as materials or ideas ○ *a fusion of vegetarianism and pacifism* **2.** **HEATING AND LIQUEFYING SOMETHING** the molten state of a substance, or the change it undergoes to become molten **3.** PHYS same as **nuclear fusion 4.** MUSIC **COMBINATION OF MUSICAL STYLES** the merger, or the resulting blend, of musical styles or elements from more than one tradition, e.g. jazz and rock [Mid-16C. Directly or via French < Latin *fusion-* < *fundere* 'melt, pour']

SYNONYMS See **mixture**.

fusion bomb n a nuclear bomb, especially a hydrogen bomb, whose explosion is caused by the energy released by a nuclear fusion reaction

fusion food, fusion cuisine n a style of cooking that uses ingredients and techniques from around the world, especially one that combines Eastern and Western influences

fusion inhibitor n a drug that prevents a virus such as HIV from binding to and entering a human cell

fusionism /fyoozh'nizəm/ n the formation of political coalitions, support for their formation, or belief in their effectiveness —**fusionist** n, adj

fuss /fuss/ n **1.** **COMMOTION** activity that is needlessly or excessively busy or excited **2.** **NEEDLESS WORRY** excessive concern over details or trivial matters **3.** **PROTEST** a complaint or protestation, often over something insignificant ○ *The kids made a fuss about going to bed early.* **4.** **ARGUMENT** a noisy disagreement or dispute ○ *There'll be a fuss if he gets home late again.* **5.** **DISPLAY OF AFFECTION OR CONCERN** an excited or abundant display of affection or affectionate concern ○ *She was irritated by the fuss they made of her sprained ankle.* **6.** **EXCESSIVE DECORATION** decoration or ornamentation regarded as excessive ○ *I want a dress without so much fuss around the neckline.* ■ vi (**fusses, fussing, fussed**) **1.** **WORRY TOO MUCH** to be too concerned about details or trivial matters **2.** **FIDDLE WITH SOMETHING** to keep moving or touching something busily, nervously, or aimlessly ○ *He fussed with the dials, hoping he'd look like he knew what he was doing.* [Early 18C. Origin ?] —**fusser** n ◇ **not be fussed** to have no strong preference for something (informal) ○ *I'm not fussed where we sit.*

fussbudget /fúss bujit/ n N Am same as **fusspot** (informal) [Early 20C. < BUDGET 'bundle']

fussed ◇ **not fussed** not interested in or concerned about something, or having no firm opinion one way or the other (informal)

fusspot /fúss pot/ n somebody who worries a lot about unimportant things (informal) N Am term **fussbudget**

fussy /fússi/ (**-ier, -iest**) adj **1.** **CONCERNED WITH MINOR THINGS** tending to worry over details or trivial things **2.** **CHOOSY** very dogmatic about likes and dislikes ○ *a very fussy eater* **3.** **ELABORATE** made or decorated with excessive detail ○ *a dress with a fussy lace collar* —**fussily** adv —**fussiness** n

SYNONYMS See **careful**.

fustian /fústi ən/ n **1.** **COTTON-LINEN CLOTH** a coarse sturdy cloth that is a blend of cotton and linen **2.** **COTTON FABRIC WITH NAP** a hard-wearing cotton fabric, e.g. corduroy or moleskin **3.** **BOMBAST** pompous or pretentious speech or writing (formal) [13C. Via French < medieval Latin *fustaneum*]

fustic /fústik/ n **1.** **YELLOW DYE** a yellow dye obtained from the wood of some trees **2.** **WOOD YIELDING YELLOW DYE** the wood from which the dye fustic is obtained **3.** **DYE-YIELDING EUROPEAN TREE** a tree whose wood yields the dye fustic. Native to: Europe. Latin name: *Cotinus coggyria*. **4.** **DYE-YIELDING TROPICAL TREE** a tree whose wood yields the dye fustic. Native to: tropical America. Latin name: *Chlorophora tinctoria*. [15C. Via Old French *fustoc* < Arabic *fustuḳ* < Greek *pistakē* 'pistachio tree']

fusty /fústi/ (**-tier, -tiest**) adj **1.** smelling of damp, dust, mildew, or age **2.** old-fashioned and conservative in style, appearance, habits, or attitudes ○ *needed to transform a rather fusty image* [Late 15C. < obsolete *fust* 'wine cask', via French < Latin *fustis* 'wood, club'] —**fustily** adv —**fustiness** n

fut. abbr **1.** future **2.** FIN futures

Futa Djallon ♦ **Fouta Djallon**

futhark /foo thaark/, **futhorc** /-thawrk/, **futhork** n the runic alphabet of 24 letters, used in northwestern Europe between the 3rd and 17th centuries [Mid-19C < the first six letters: f, u, þ, a or o, r, and k]

futile /fyoo tíl/ adj **1.** having no practical effect or useful result **2.** lacking serious value, substance, or a sense of responsibility [Mid-16C. < Latin *futilis* 'leaky, worthless'] —**futilely** adv —**futileness** n

futilitarian /fyoo tílli táiri ən/ n a believer that human efforts are wasted and futile [Early 19C. < FUTILITY, after UTILITARIAN] —**futilitarian** adj —**futilitarianism** n

futility /fyoo tílləti/ (plural **-ties**) n **1.** lack of usefulness or effectiveness **2.** an action that has no use, purpose, or effect

futon /foo ton/ n **1.** a firm Japanese-style cotton-covered mattress used as a seat or bed, either on the floor or on a wooden frame **2.** a futon together with the wooden frame it sits on, especially a frame designed to convert from a sofa to a bed [Late 19C. < Japanese < *fu* 'quilt' (< Middle Chinese *phu*) + *ton* 'round' (< Middle Chinese *thuan*)]

futtock /fúttək/ n a curved middle timber forming the frame of a traditional wooden boat or ship [13C. Origin ?]

futtock plate n a circular metal plate fitted to the top of a ship's shorter masts. Ropes or rods supporting a taller mast are secured to futtock plates.

futtock shroud n a rope or rod stretching from the top of a taller mast to the top of a lower mast, to support the taller mast

future /fyoochər/ n **1.** **TIME TO COME** time that has yet to come ○ *saving money for the future* **2.** **HAPPENINGS TO COME** events that have not yet happened ○ *The future will be shaped by our advancing technology.* **3.** **EXPECTED FORTHCOMING CONDITION** an expected or projected state ○ *Her future is bleak.* **4.** GRAM **TENSE REFERRING TO THINGS TO COME** the tense or form of a verb used to refer to events that are going to happen or have not yet happened ■ **futures** npl FIN **COMMODITIES TRADED FOR LATER DELIVERY** goods or stocks sold for future delivery, or the contracts for them ■ adj **1.** **YET TO OCCUR** expected to be or happen at a time still to come ○ *my future sister-in-law* **2.** GRAM **OF TENSE EXPRESSING FUTURE** describes a verb form or tense that expresses actions or states that are going to happen or have not yet happened [14C. Via French < Latin *futurus* 'going to be']

futureless /fyoochərləss/ adj seeming to have no chance of developing or being successful ○ *ploughed money into futureless projects* —**futurelessness** n

future perfect n the form of a verb expressing a completed action in the future, as 'will have finished' does in the sentence 'They will have finished by tomorrow'

future shock n difficulty in, and stress from, coping

with rapid changes in society, especially technological changes

future tense *n* GRAM same as **future** (sense 4)

futurism /fyóochərizəm/ *n* **1.** *also* **Futurism** an early 20th-century artistic movement that attempted to express the dynamic nature of the modern age using technology as its subject **2.** belief in the need to look to the future rather than reflect on the past, coupled with an optimism that personal and social fulfilment lies in the future —**futurist** *n, adj*

futuristic /fyóochə rístik/ *adj* **1.** suggesting the future in design or technology **2.** depicting life in a future time —**futuristically** *adv*

futurity /fyoo tyóorəti, -chóorəti/ (*plural* **-ties**) *n* **1.** the future as a concept or state ○ *a grammatical construction expressing futurity* **2.** an event that is going to happen or has not happened yet (*formal*) ○ *We'll have to await those futurities before we can make a decision.*

futurology /fyóochə rólləji/ *n* the study and forecasting of the future, with predictions based on the likely outcomes of current trends —**futurological** /fyóochərə lójjik'l/ *adj* —**futurologist** *n*

Fuxin /foó shín/ city in Liaoning Province, northeastern China, west of Shenyang. Population: 879,477 (1991).

fu yung, **fu yong** *n* FOOD another spelling of **foo yung**

fuzee *n* MECH ENG another spelling of **fusee**

Fuzhou /foó zhṓ/ city and capital of Fujian Province, southeastern China, near the mouth of the Min River, northeast of Taiwan. Population: 1,590,000 (1995).

fuzz[1] /fuz/ *n* FLUFF a mass of short fine hairs or fibres ■ *vti* (**fuzzes**, **fuzzing**, **fuzzed**) **1.** COVER SOMETHING WITH FUZZ to become covered with fuzz, or cover something with fuzz ○ *sweaters that fuzz after the first wash* **2.** BLUR to make something such as an image or explanation blurred or unclear, or become blurred or unclear ○ *All this talk has fuzzed my brain.* [Late 16C. Probably < Dutch or Low German]

fuzz[2] /fuz/ *n* an offensive term for the police (*dated slang*) [Early 20C. Origin ?]

fuzzbox /fúz boks/ *n* an electrical device that distorts the sound that passes through it, especially a pedal-operated device wired to an electric guitar

fuzzy /fúzzi/ (**-ier, -iest**) *adj* **1.** COVERED WITH FUZZ covered with a mass of short fine hairs or fibres **2.** CONSISTING OF FUZZ in the form of a mass of short fine hairs or fibres **3.** FRIZZY describes hair growing in a very tight curly mass **4.** BLURRED not sharp enough to be seen or heard clearly ○ *a fuzzy picture* **5.** INCOHERENT not clearly thought out or set out ○ *The initial plan was fairly fuzzy.* **6.** COMPUT FOR FUZZY LOGIC using or designed to use fuzzy logic ○ *fuzzy computing* [Early 17C. Origin ?] —**fuzzily** *adv* —**fuzziness** *n*

fuzzyheaded /fúzzi héddid/ *adj* not thinking or communicating clearly (*informal*) ○ *a fuzzyheaded notion* —**fuzzyheadedness** *n*

fuzzy logic *n* logic that allows for imprecise or ambiguous answers to questions, forming the basis of computer programming designed to mimic human intelligence

fuzzy search *n* a computer search that returns not only exact matches to the search request, but also close matches that include possibilities and allow for such things as spelling errors

fuzzy-wuzzy /-wuzi/ (*plural* **fuzzy-wuzzies** or *same*) *n* **1.** a highly offensive name that British soldiers gave to their Sudanese enemies during the North African campaigns of the late 19th century (*taboo offensive*) **2.** a highly offensive term for a Black person (*dated taboo*)

fv *abbr* folio verso [Latin, 'on the reverse (left-hand) page']

fwd *abbr* forward

f.w.d. *abbr* AUTOMOT **1.** four-wheel drive **2.** front-wheel drive

f-word, **F-word** *n* a euphemism for the highly offensive word 'fuck'

fx *abbr* France, Metropolitan (*used in Internet addresses*) See table at **domain name**

FX *abbr* **1.** FIN foreign exchange **2.** CINEMA (special) effects

fy *abbr* fiscal year

-fy *suffix* (*usually used after* -i-) **1.** to make or produce ○ *satisfy* ○ *speechify* **2.** to cause to become or to resemble ○ *gasify* ○ *ladify* ○ *solidify* [Via Old French -*fier* < Latin *facere* 'do, make']

FYI *abbr* ONLINE for your information (*used in e-mails, text messages, or office memos*)

fyke /fīk/, **fyke-net** *n* a bag-shaped fishing net, held open by hoops [Mid-19C. < Dutch *fuik*]

fylfot /fíl fot/ *n* a decorative or religious symbol in the form of a swastika [15C. Origin ?]

Fyn /fün/ the second-largest island in Denmark, between southern Jutland and the island of Sjælland. Population: 470,528 (1996). Area: 2,978 sq. km/1,150 sq. mi.

fynbos /fáyn boss/ *n* the scrubland characteristic of the western Cape area of South Africa, consisting of bushes resembling heaths with hard leaves [Late 19C. < Afrikaans, literally 'fine bush']

FYROM *abbr* Former Yugoslav Republic of Macedonia

Fysh /fish/, **Sir Hudson** (1895–1974) Australian aviator and business executive. He co-founded a major airline in 1920. Full name **Fysh, Sir Wilmot Hudson**

fz. *abbr* MUSIC sforzando

g¹ /jee/ (*plural* **g's**), **G** (*plural* **G's** or **Gs**) *n* **1.** the seventh letter of the English alphabet, representing a consonant sound **2.** a written representation of the letter 'g'

g² *symbol* **1.** PHYS acceleration of free fall as a result of gravity **2.** used to refer to the seventh vertical row of squares from the left on a chessboard

g³ *abbr* **1.** gauge **2.** GRAM gender **3.** MEASURE gram **4.** MONEY guilder **5.** MONEY guinea

G¹ /jee/ (*plural* **G's** or **Gs**) *n* **1.** 'G'-SHAPED OBJECT something shaped like a letter 'G' **2.** MUSIC 5TH NOTE IN C MAJOR the fifth note of a scale in C major **3.** MUSIC SOMETHING THAT PRODUCES G a string, key, or pipe tuned to produce the note G **4.** MUSIC SCALE BEGINNING ON G a scale or key that starts on the note G **5.** MUSIC WRITTEN SYMBOL OF G a graphic representation of the tone of G **6.** CINEMA GENERAL-AUDIENCE FILM RATING in the United States, Canada, Australia, and New Zealand, a cinema censorship classification meaning that a film or video is suitable for anyone to watch **7.** *N Am* MONEY $1000 one thousand dollars (*slang*)

G² *symbol* **1.** ELEC conductance **2.** PHYS gravitational constant **3.** BIOCHEM guanine

G³ *abbr* **1.** SOC SCI gay (*in personal ads*) **2.** giga- **3.** EDUC good (*used in marking students' work*) **4.** MONEY guilder **5.** MONEY guinea **6.** Gulf (*used in placenames*)

G7 /jee sévv'n/ *n* the group of the seven most industrialized nations in the world that met to discuss and draw up global economic policies before they were joined by Russia to form G8. The seven were Canada, France, (West) Germany, Italy, Japan, the United Kingdom, and the United States. Full form **Group of Seven**

G8 /jee áyt/ *n* the group of the eight most industrialized nations in the world, comprising Canada, France, Germany, Italy, Japan, Russia, the United Kingdom, and the United States. Representatives from these countries meet regularly to discuss and draw up global economic policies. Full form **Group of Eight**

ga *abbr* Gabon (*used in Internet addresses*) See table at **domain name**

Ga *symbol* CHEM ELEM gallium

GA *abbr* **1.** LAW general agent **2.** General Assembly (of the United Nations) **3.** SHIPPING, INSUR general average **4.** ONLINE go ahead (*used in e-mails or text messages*)

gab /gab/ (**gabs, gabbing, gabbed**) *vi* to talk at length about trivial matters (*informal*) ○ *We just sat there gabbing all afternoon.* [Early 18C. Origin ?] —**gab** *n* — **gabber** *n*

GABA *abbr* BIOCHEM gamma-aminobutyric acid

gabardine /gábbər deén/ *n* **1.** a smooth hard-wearing cotton, wool, or synthetic fabric woven with a pattern of parallel diagonal ridges (**twill**) ○ *a gabardine jacket* **2.** a garment made of gabardine **3.** CLOTHING same as **gaberdine** (sense 1) [Early 20C. Alteration of GABERDINE]

Gabba /gábbə/ *n Aus* Woolloongabba Cricket Ground in Brisbane, a venue for international and state cricket matches and other sports fixtures, including Australian Rules football matches (*informal*)

gabble /gább'l/ (**-bles, -bling, -bled**) *v* **1.** *vti* to speak or say something rapidly and incoherently **2.** *vi* to make the high throaty sounds that geese and some other birds make [Late 16C. Origin ?] —**gabble** *n* — **gabbler** *n*

gabbro /gábbrō/ *n* a dark coarse-grained basic igneous rock containing calcium-rich plagioclase feldspar and pyroxene [Mid-19C. < Italian dialect, probably < Latin *glaber* 'smooth, bald'] —**gabbroic** /gə brō ik/ *adj*

gabby /gábbi/ (**-bier, -biest**) *adj* talking or inclined to talk to an excessive and irritating degree (*informal*)

gabelle /gə bél/ *n* **1.** a French tax on salt imposed until 1790 **2.** any tax, especially a tax imposed in a foreign country (*literary*) [15C. Via Old French *gabel* < Arabic *ḳabāla* 'tax, duty']

gaberdine /gábbər deén/ *n* **1.** a long loose coat or smock made of coarse cloth, worn by men, especially Jewish men, during the Middle Ages **2.** TEXTILES, CLOTHING same as **gabardine** (senses 1–2) [Early 16C. < Old French *gauvardine*]

Gabin /ga báN/, **Jean** (1904–76) French actor. His portrayal of a tragic hero in *Maria Chapdelaine* (1934) brought him instant fame. He is best known for his roles in Marcel Carné's film noir classics *Quai des brumes* (1938) and *Le Jour se lève* (1939). Born **Moncorgé, Jean-Alexis**

gabion /gáybi ən/ *n* **1.** a wickerwork basket filled with rocks, used as a temporary fortification **2.** a cylindrical metal container filled with earth and stones, used in the construction and rerouting of waterways and in flood control [Mid-16C. Via French < Italian *gabbione* 'large cage' < *gabbia* 'cage' < Latin *cavea*]

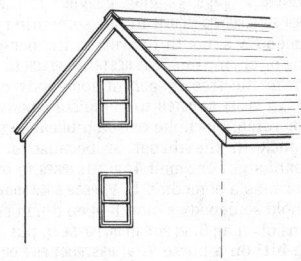

gable

gable /gáyb'l/ *n* **1.** the triangular top section of a side wall on a building with a pitched roof that fills the space beneath where the roof slopes meet **2.** ARCHIT same as **gable end 3.** a triangular structure added to a building for decoration, e.g. a canopy over a door or window [14C. Directly or via Old French < Old Norse *gafl*] —**gabled** *adj*

CULTURAL NOTE *Anne of Green Gables*, a children's story (1908) by Canadian writer Lucy Maud Montgomery. Set on Prince Edward Island in Canada, it is the story of a vivacious 11-year-old orphan, Anne Shirley, who is sent to live with farmers Matthew and Marilla Cuthbert. Having expected a boy, the Cuthberts cannot hide their disappointment, but Anne's courage, spirit, and vivid imagination soon win them over.

Gable /gáyb'l/, **Clark** (1901–60) US film actor. He won an Academy Award for his performance in the romantic comedy *It Happened One Night* (1934), but he is best known for his role as Rhett Butler in *Gone With the Wind* (1939). Full name **Gable, William Clark**

gable end *n* a side wall that comes to a peak where the slopes of a pitched roof meet

Clark Gable

gable roof *n* a roof with two slopes and a gable at each end

Gabo /gaábō/, **Naum** (1890–1977) Russian-born US sculptor, one of the founders of the constructivist school. His work drew on cubism, and he experimented with kinetic art. Born **Pevsner, Naum Neemia**

Gabon

Gabon /ga bón, gə bóN/ country in west-central Africa on the Atlantic coast. Formerly part of French Equatorial Africa, it became independent from France in 1960. Language: French. Currency: CFA franc. Capital: Libreville. Population: 1,321,560 (2003). Area: 267,667 sq. km/103,347 sq. mi. Official name **Gabonese Republic** —**Gabonese** /gábbə neéz/ *n, adj*

Gaborone /gábbə rōni/ capital of Botswana, situated in the southeast of the country, about 19 km/12 mi. from the border with South Africa. Population: 185,891 (2001).

Gabriel /gáybri əl/ *n* in Christian, Islamic, and Jewish tradition, an archangel who acts as God's messenger. In Christian and Jewish tradition, he appeared to Mary, Zacharias, and Daniel, and in Islamic tradition, he revealed the Koran to Muhammad.

gad¹ /gad/ *vi* (**gads, gadding, gadded**) to go around having fun in a carefree and aimless manner (*humorous*) ○ *gadding about* ■ *n* carefree or aimless wandering (*archaic*) [15C. Probably back-formation < obsolete *gadling* 'wanderer' < Old English *gædeling* 'companion' < Germanic] —**gadder** *n*

gad² /gad/ *n* **1.** MIN EXTRACT HEAVY TOOL in mining, a heavy steel or iron wedge with a pointed or chisel-shaped edge, used to break coal, rock, or ore from

the rock face **2.** AGRIC CATTLE PROD a sharp pointed tool used to drive cattle ■ *vt* (**gads, gadding, gadded**) MIN EXTRACT SEPARATE MINERALS FROM ROCK to break up coal or ore using a gad [13C. < Old Norse *gaddr* 'goad, spike' < Germanic, 'pointed stick']

gad[3] /gad/ *interj* used to express surprise or to add emphasis (*archaic*) [15C. Alteration of GOD]

gadabout /gáddə bowt/ *n* a restless and aimless seeker of pleasure (*humorous*)

Gadaffi another spelling of **Qaddafi**

gadarene /gáddə reén/ *adj* rushing headlong en masse (*literary*) [Early 19C. Via Latin < Greek *Gadarēnos* 'inhabitant of Gadara', town in the Bible where a herd of swine rushed into the sea (Matthew 8:28)]

Gaddafi another spelling of **Qaddafi**

gaddi /gáddi/ *n* S Asia an official office or a position of authority [Mid-19C. < Punjabi *gaddī*, Marathi *gādī*, or Bangla *gādi* 'cushion']

gadfly /gád flī/ (*plural* **-flies**) *n* **1.** a fly that irritates livestock by biting them and sucking their blood. Horseflies are a type of gadfly. Family: Tabanidae. **2.** somebody regarded as persistently annoying or irritating [< GAD[1]]

gadget /gájjit/ *n* **1.** a small device that performs or aids a simple task **2.** a small device that appears useful but is often unnecessary or superfluous [Late 19C. Origin ?] —**gadgety** *adj*

gadgeteer /gájji teér/ *n* an inventor or enthusiastic user of gadgets

gadgetry /gájjitri/ *n* gadgets collectively, especially when perceived as impressively complicated

gadid /gáydid/, **gadoid** /gáy doyd/ *n* a sea fish of the family that includes cod, haddock, and whiting. Family: Gadidae. ■ *adj* belonging to the family of sea fish that includes cod, haddock, and whiting [Mid-19C. < modern Latin *gadus* 'cod' < Greek *gados*]

gadolinite /gáddəlinīt/ *n* a black or brown silicate mineral containing beryllium, iron, and yttrium. Source: pegmatites. [Early 19C. After Johan *Gadolin* (1760–1852), Finnish mineralogist]

gadolinium /gáddə línni əm/ *n* a rare silvery-white metallic element. Source: monazite, bastnaesite. Use: high-temperature alloys, neutron absorber in nuclear reactors and fuels. Symbol **Gd**. See table at **element** [Late 19C. < GADOLINITE]

gadroon /gə drŏon/, **godroon** *n* an ornamental feature that consists of a series of convex curves or inverted fluting. It is often applied as an edging to a curved surface, especially on silver. [Late 17C. < French *godron* 'pucker, crease'] —**gadrooned** *adj* —**gadrooning** *n*

gadwall /gád wawl/ *n* a common freshwater duck with grey and brown feathers. Native to: Europe, North America. Latin name: *Anas strepera*. [Mid-17C. Origin ?]

gadzooks /gad zŏoks/ *interj* used to express surprise or as a mild oath (*archaic or humorous*) [Late 17C. < GAD[3] + *zooks*, origin ?]

Gaea /jée ə/ *n* MYTHOL same as **Gaia**

Gael /gayl/ *n* **1.** somebody from Scotland, Ireland, or the Isle of Man who speaks Gaelic **2.** somebody from the Scottish Highlands [Mid-18C. < Scottish Gaelic *Gael*, *Gàidheal* < Old Irish *Goídel*, plural of *Gáidil*]

Gaelic /gáylik, gállik/ *n* CELTIC LANGUAGE OF BRITISH ISLES any of the forms of the Celtic language used in Scotland, Ireland, or the Isle of Man ■ *adj* **1.** OF GAELIC relating to any of the forms of the Celtic language of Scotland, Ireland, or the Isle of Man **2.** OF GAELIC-SPEAKING PEOPLE relating to Gaelic-speaking people or their culture

LANGUAGE HERITAGE See *Celtic*.

Gaelic coffee *n* BEVERAGES same as **Irish coffee**

Gaelic football *n* a game played in Ireland with 15 players on each side, the aim of which is to punch or kick a ball into or over a goal

Gaeltacht /gáyl takht/ *n* the parts of Ireland or Scotland where Gaelic is spoken by a large proportion of the population [Early 20C. < Irish]

gaff[1] /gaf/ *n* **1.** HOOKED FISH POLE a pole with a large hook on the end that is used to hold and land a large fish **2.** POLE AT TOP OF SAIL a pole attached at the back of a mast and used to support the upper edge of a gaffsail **3.** HOOK FOR SOMEBODY MAINTAINING OVERHEAD LINE a climbing hook used by somebody erecting or repairing a

telephone or power line **4.** METAL SPUR ON FIGHTING COCK a metal spur that is fixed to the leg of a fighting cock ■ *vt* (**gaffs, gaffing, gaffed**) **1.** CATCH FISH WITH HOOKED POLE to catch and hold a fish with a gaff **2.** ARM SOMETHING WITH GAFF to provide or arm something such as a fighting cock with a gaff [14C. < Old French *gaffe* 'boat hook' (see GAFFE)]

gaff[2] /gaf/ *n* **1.** worthless nonsense (*informal*) **2.** *Carib* relaxed informal conversation [Early 19C. Origin ?] ◇ **blow the gaff** to reveal a secret (*slang*)

gaff[3] /gaf/ *n* **1.** the place where somebody lives (*slang*) ○ *Nice gaff you've got yourself here!* **2.** a music hall or theatre (*dated informal*) [Early 19C. Origin ?]

gaffe /gaf/ *n* a clumsy social mistake or breach of etiquette, e.g. an undiplomatic remark [Early 20C. < French, originally 'boat hook', via Old French < Old Provençal *gaf*]

gaffer /gáffər/ *n* **1.** *UK* BOSS the boss, owner, or supervisor of a workplace (*informal*) **2.** *UK* MAN a man of advanced years, especially a man from the country (*informal*) **3.** CHIEF LIGHTING ELECTRICIAN the chief electrician in charge of lighting on a film or television set (*informal*) **4.** *regional* HUSBAND somebody's husband [Late 16C. Probably contraction of GODFATHER]

gaff-rig *n* a sailing vessel rigged with a gaffsail — **gaff-rigged** *adj*

gaffsail /gáf sayl/ *n* a quadrilateral sail that extends behind the mast rather than across the boat. The upper edge is supported by a pole (**gaff**) attached to the mast.

gaff-topsail *n* a small, usually triangular, sail set above a gaffsail

gag /gag/ *n* **1.** SOMETHING PUT OVER MOUTH something such as a piece of cloth that is forcibly put over or into somebody's mouth to prevent the person from speaking or crying out **2.** RESTRAINT OF SPEECH a restraint on free speech ○ *put a gag on a newspaper* **3.** COMIC WORDS OR ACTION a comic story, action, or incident told or performed by an actor or comedian **4.** TRICK a trick, hoax, or practical joke (*informal*) **5.** CLOSURE OF PARLIAMENTARY DEBATE a procedure by which a parliamentary debate can be stopped and a vote taken immediately **6.** MOUTH PROP a device that is placed in a patient's mouth to keep it open during surgical work on the mouth or throat **7.** CHOKING an instance or the action of choking or retching (*informal*) ■ *v* (**gags, gagging, gagged**) **1.** *vt* PUT SOMETHING OVER SOMEBODY'S MOUTH to put something over or into somebody's mouth to prevent the person from speaking or crying out **2.** *vt* RESTRAIN SPEECH to prevent or restrain the free speech of somebody or something **3.** *vti* CHOKE OR RETCH to make somebody nearly choke or retch, or choke or retch because of something stuck in the throat or because of a very unpleasant sight or smell **4.** *vi* TELL JOKES to tell jokes or perform as a comedian **5.** *vt* PROP SOMEBODY'S MOUTH OPEN to hold somebody's mouth open during surgery by means of a gag **6.** *vt* PUT BIT ON HORSE to put a strong bit (**gag-bit**) on a horse **7.** *vt* OBSTRUCT PIPE OR VALVE to block or obstruct something such as a pipe or valve [15C. Probably an imitation of the sound of choking] ◇ **be gagging for it 1.** to want sex (*slang offensive; usually used by men when talking about a woman*) **2.** to want something very much (*slang*)

gaga /gáa gaa/ *adj* (*informal*) **1.** an offensive term that insults somebody's mental abilities, especially those of a person of advanced age **2.** completely infatuated or very enthusiastic ○ *totally gaga about that boyfriend of hers* [Early 20C. < French, an imitation of the sound of mumbling]

gagaku /gágga kŏo/ *n* an ancient form of Japanese classical music played at the imperial court and on ceremonial occasions [Early 20C. < Japanese]

Gagarin /gə gaárin/, **Yuri** (1934–68) Soviet cosmonaut. He became the first person to be launched into space when he orbited Earth in *Vostok I* on 12 April 1961. Full name **Gagarin, Yuri Alekseyevich**

'I don't see any God up here.'
[Yuri Gagarin, *Speaking from orbit*; 1961]

Gagauz /gə gáwz/ (*plural same* or **-gauzi** /-zi/) *n* **1.** a Turkic language spoken in an area north of the Black Sea, especially in southern Moldova, Ukraine, and Romania. Native speakers: 150,000. **2.** *also* **Gagauzian** /gə gáwzi ən/ a member of a Turkic people who live in southwestern Moldova —**Gagauz** *adj*

Yuri Gagarin

AKG London

gag-bit *n* a strong bit sometimes used to help control an unruly horse

gage[1] /gayj/ (*archaic*) *n* **1.** PLEDGE something that is given or left as security until a debt is paid or an obligation is fulfilled **2.** TOKEN OF CHALLENGE a glove or other object that is thrown down or offered as a challenge to fight **3.** CHALLENGE a challenge to fight ■ *vt* (**gages, gaging, gaged**) **1.** OFFER SOMETHING AS SECURITY to offer something as security against a debt or other obligation **2.** OFFER SOMETHING AS STAKE to offer something as a stake in a bet [13C. < Old French < Germanic]

gage[2] /gayj/ *n, vt* another spelling of **gauge**

gagger /gággər/ *n* a piece of metal used to wedge the core of a casting mould in position

gagging order /gágging-/ *n* a court order that forbids any public commentary or media reporting on a case that is currently being heard in court. N Am term **gag order**

gaggle /gágg'l/ *n* **1.** a flock of geese **2.** a group of people, especially a noisy or disorderly group ○ *a gaggle of children* [14C. Origin ?]

gagman /gág man/ (*plural* **-men** /-men/) *n* ARTS same as **gagster** (sense 1) (*informal*)

gag order *n* US LAW same as **gagging order**

gagster /gágstər/ *n* (*informal*) **1.** a writer or teller of jokes **2.** *N Am* a trickster or practical joker

gahnite /gáa nīt/ *n* a dark green mineral consisting of zinc aluminium oxide [Early 19C. After J. G. *Gahn* (1745–1818), Swedish chemist]

Gaia /gí ə/, **Gaea** /jée ə/ *n* in Greek mythology, the personification of the Earth

gaiety /gáy əti/ (*plural* **-ties**) *n* **1.** JOYFULNESS a lighthearted and lively feeling or way of behaving **2.** SPIRITED ACTIVITY joyful and lively activity or festivity **3.** BRIGHT APPEARANCE the showiness or bright colourful appearance of something such as clothing (*dated*) [Mid-17C. < Old French *gaieté* < *gai* 'happy']

gaijin /gí jin/ (*plural same*) *n* a foreigner in Japan or among Japanese people [Mid-20C. < Japanese]

gaily /gáyli/ *adv* **1.** JOYFULLY OR LIGHTHEARTEDLY in a happy, cheerful, or carefree manner **2.** SHOWING LACK OF CONCERN showing a lack of concern or awareness **3.** IN BRIGHT COLOURS brightly or colourfully (*dated*)

gain[1] /gayn/ *v* (**gains, gaining, gained**) **1.** *vt* ACQUIRE SOMETHING to obtain something or the benefit of something through effort, skill, or merit ○ *gain recognition as an actor* ○ *gained access to heads of state* **2.** *vti* BECOME GREATER to grow or increase or acquire more of something ○ *She was steadily gaining in confidence.* **3.** *vi* PROFIT to derive personal advantage from something ○ *No one stands to gain from the deal.* **4.** *vt* EARN SOMETHING to earn money or other compensation for work ○ *gain a living* ○ *apply for an internship to help gain credits towards a degree* **5.** *vi* GET CLOSER OR FARTHER AWAY to come closer to somebody or something pursued, or increase the distance from a pursuer ○ *They are behind but they're gaining on us.* **6.** *vt* WIN SOMETHING BY COMPETING to win something in competition or conflict ○ *gained second place in the dash* ○ *gain a decisive victory* **7.** *vti* INCREASE IN OR BY SOMETHING to come to have more of something, or increase by a particular amount ○ *The pound had gained two points.* ○ *gain weight* **8.** *vti* TIME RUN AHEAD OF CORRECT TIME to run fast, or run a particular amount of time ahead of the correct time (*refers to clocks or watches*) ○ *My watch gains at least ten minutes every day.* **9.** *vt* REACH PLACE to arrive

at a place that it was hoped to reach (*literary*) ○ *once we had finally gained the shore* ■ **1. ACHIEVEMENT** an advantage or improvement that has been earned or acquired through effort ○ *despite the political gains of recent years* **2. AMOUNT INCREASED** an increase or profit of a particular amount ○ *saw a 12 point gain in the market* **3. BENEFIT** financial profit or personal advantage ○ *abused power for personal gain* **4. ELEC ENG MEASURE OF INCREASE IN SIGNAL STRENGTH** a ratio of the output power to the input power of an amplifier that is more than one and indicates an increase in signal strength ■ **gains** *npl* **ACQUISITIONS** something acquired, earned, or won, especially money ○ *ill-gotten gains* [15C. < Old French *gaignier* < Germanic, 'graze, hunt'] —**gainable** *adj*

SYNONYMS See **get**[1].

gain[2] /gayn/ *n* **NOTCH** a notch or groove cut into a board so that another part can be fitted into it ■ *vt* (**gains, gaining, gained**) **1. CUT NOTCH** to cut a notch or groove into a board so that another part can be fitted into it **2. FIT PART IN NOTCH** to fit a part into a gain or connect parts using a gain [Mid-19C. Origin ?]

gainer /gáynər/ *n* **1.** somebody who or something that gains **2.** a dive in which the diver jumps forwards, does a back somersault in the air, and enters the water feet first, facing away from the board

gainful /gáynf'l/ *adj* bringing profit or advantage ○ *gainful employment* —**gainfully** *adv* —**gainfulness** *n*

gainsay /gáyn sáy/ (**gainsays, gainsaying, gainsaid** /-séd/) *vt* (*formal*) **1.** to say that something is false **2.** to oppose or contradict somebody ○ *I won't gainsay you.* [14C. < Old English *gegn* 'against' < Germanic] —**gainsayer** *n*

Gainsborough /gáynzbərə/, **Thomas** (1727–88) British painter. He painted society portraits and English landscapes including *The Watering Place* (1777).

'gainst /genst, gaynst/, **gainst** *prep* against (*literary*) [Late 16C. Shortening]

Gairdner, Lake /gáirdnər/ dry salt lake in south-central South Australia, about 385 km/240 mi. northwest of Adelaide. Area: 4,800 sq. km/1,900 sq. mi.

gait /gayt/ *n* **1.** a way of walking, running, or moving along on foot ○ *his familiar shambling gait* **2.** any of the four paces of a horse, namely walk, trot, canter, and gallop, each having a specific pattern of leg movements [15C. Variant of GATE 'way, street']

SPELLCHECK gait or **gate**? Do not confuse the spelling of **gait** and **gate**, which sound similar. **Gait** is only used as a noun, denoting a manner of moving on foot, as in *a horse's gait.* **Gate** is chiefly used as a noun, denoting a movable barrier (as in *shut the gate*), an arrival or departure point at an airport, etc., but it can also be a verb, meaning 'control with a gate', 'install a gate in', or 'confine to school or college grounds': *The students responsible for the prank were gated until the end of term.*

gaita /gíta/ *n* a Spanish woodwind instrument similar to bagpipes [Mid-19C. < Spanish and Portuguese]

-gaited *suffix* with a particular way of walking ○ *slow-gaited*

gaiter /gáytər/ *n* a strip of fabric, leather, or water-proof material covering the leg from the instep to either the ankle or the knee. Modern gaiters are usually made of waterproof fabric and are worn by climbers, walkers, and skiers. (*usually used in the plural*) [Early 18C. < French *guêtre*] —**gaitered** *adj*

Gaitskell /gáytskəl/, **Hugh** (1906–63) British politician. He was a member of parliament from 1945 and Labour Party leader (1955–63). Full name **Gaitskell, Hugh Todd Naylor**

> 'Surely the right course is to test the Russians, not the bombs.'
> [Hugh Gaitskell, *Observer*; 23 June 1957]

gal /gal/ *n* a girl or woman (*slang dated; sometimes considered offensive*) [Late 18C. Reproducing a pronunciation of GIRL]

GAL *abbr* **ONLINE** get a life (*used in e-mails or text messages*)

gal. *abbr* **MEASURE** gallon

Gal. *abbr* **BIBLE** Galatians

gala /gaʻalə/ *n* **1.** a special festive occasion that typically includes food and entertainment **2.** a sporting event, especially a swimming contest, with a variety of different races and competitions ○ *a swimming gala* [Early 17C. Via Old French *gale* 'merrymaking' < Arabic *khil'a* 'fine garment given as a present, festive attire, festive occasion']

galact- *prefix* same as **galacto-** (*used before vowels*)

galactagogue /gə láktə gog/ *adj* causing the pro-duction and secretion of milk ■ *n* an agent that stimulates the production and flow of breast milk [< GALACT- + Greek *agōgos* 'leading' < *agein* 'to lead']

galactic /gə láktik/ *adj* relating or belonging to a galaxy, especially the Milky Way [Mid-19C. < Greek *galakt-* (see GALAXY)] —**galactically** *adv*

galactic equator, galactic circle *n* the imaginary circle on the sky formed by the plane that passes through the centre of the Milky Way. It is inclined at approximately 62° to the celestial equator.

galactic halo *n* the large region of space surrounding the Milky Way, enclosing the main spiral arms, older fainter stars and globular clusters, and the outer regions of the galactic magnetic field

galacto- *prefix* milk ○ *galactosaemia* [< Greek *galakt-* (see GALAXY)]

galactopoiesis /gə láktō poy éssiss/ *n* the production of milk by the cells of the glandular structure of the breast

galactopoietic /gə láktō poy éttik/ *adj* stimulating lactation

galactorrhea *n* **MED** US spelling of **galactorrhoea**

galactorrhoea /gə láktō reé ə/ *n* excessive milk flow during lactation, or spontaneous milk flow in the absence of childbirth and nursing

galactosaemia /gə láktō seémi ə/ *n* a genetic disorder causing the absence of an enzyme necessary for the breakdown of galactose in milk to glucose

galactosamine /gə lák tóssə meen/ *n* an amino de-rivative of galactose, found in cartilage

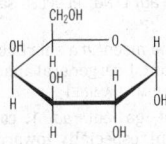

galactose

galactose /gə láktōss/ *n* a six-carbon sugar that is a constituent of lactose. Formula: $C_6H_{12}O_6$.

galactosemia *n* **MED** US spelling of **galactosaemia**

galactosidase /gə láktō síd ayss, -dayz/ *n* an enzyme that breaks down lactose

galactoside /gə láktō síd/ *n* a compound made up of galactose combined with another sugar or a nonsugar

galago /gə laʻagō/ (*plural* **-gos**) *n* **ZOOL** same as **bushbaby** [Mid-19C. < modern Latin]

galah /gə laʻa/ *n* **1.** a common cockatoo with a grey back and wings, a pink breast and head, and a pale pink crest. Native to: Australia. Latin name: *Eulophus roseicapillus*. **2.** *Aus* a silly or thoughtless person (*informal insult*) [Mid-19C. < an Aboriginal lan-guage]

Galahad /gállə had/ *n* **1.** in Arthurian legend, the noblest knight of the Round Table, who succeeded in his quest for the Holy Grail **2.** a man considered to be chivalrous, noble, or pure in actions or at-titudes

galangal /gə láng g'l/ *n* **1.** the pungent underground stem of a ginger plant, sold fresh or dried and ground. Use: cookery, medicine. **2.** a plant of the ginger family grown for its edible underground stem. Native to: eastern Asia. Latin name: *Alpinia officinarum*. **3.** **PLANTS** same as **galingale** [Pre-12C. Via Old French *galingal* < Arabic *kalanján*]

galantine /gállən teen/ *n* a dish of boned and cooked white meat, poultry, or fish, usually stuffed, moulded into shape, and served cold in its own jelly [14C. Via Old French < medieval Latin *galatina*]

galanty show /gə lánti-/ *n* a play performed by manipulating paper figures and casting their shadows on a screen [Origin ?]

Galapagos giant tortoise /gə láppəgəss-, -goss-/, **Gal-apagos tortoise** *n* a giant tortoise that is native to the Galápagos Islands. It grows up to 1.2 m/4 ft long and weighs up to 225 kg/500 lb. Latin name: *Geochelone elephantopus*.

Galapagos Islands

Galapagos Islands /gə láppəgəss-, -goss-/, **Galápagos Islands** group of islands in the Pacific Ocean ap-proximately 1,050 km/650 mi. west of Ecuador. They are known for harbouring unique species of wild-life, especially the giant tortoise. Population: 9,785 (1990). Area: 7,964 sq. km/3,075 sq. mi.

Galapagos tortoise *n* **REPT** same as **Galapagos giant tortoise**

galatea /gállə teé ə/ *n* a strong cotton fabric with a twill weave that is often striped. Use: clothes. [Late 19C. After HMS *Galatea*; originally used for children's sailor suits]

Galatea /gállə teé ə/ *n* a small inner natural satellite of Neptune, discovered in 1989 by the spacecraft Voyager 2. It is approximately 150 km/95 mi. in diameter.

Galaţi /ga látsi/ inland port in Romania, situated on the River Danube, northeast of Bucharest. Popu-lation: 641,647 (1997).

Galatians /gə láysh'nz/ *n* a book of the Bible, ori-ginally a letter addressed to the people of Galatia and traditionally attributed to St Paul (*takes a sin-gular verb*) See table at **Bible** [Early 17C. < *Galatia*, ancient country of central Asia Minor]

galaxy /gálləksi/ (*plural* **-ies**) *n* **1.** a group of billions of stars and their planets, gas, and dust that extends over many thousands of light-years and forms a unit within the universe. Held together by gravitational forces, most of the estimated 50 billion galaxies are shaped as spirals and ellipses, with the remainder being asymmetrical. **2.** a gathering of famous, brilliant, or distinguished people or things [14C. Via Old French < Greek *galaxias (kuklos)* 'milky (circle)' < *galakt-*, stem of *gala* 'milk']

Galaxy *n* **ASTRON** same as **Milky Way**

galbanum /gálbənəm/ *n* a yellowish to green or brown aromatic bitter gum resin derived from several related Asian plants. Use: incense, medicinally as a counterirritant. Genus: *Ferula*. [12C. Via Latin < Greek *khalbanē* < Semitic]

Galbraith /gal bráyth/, **John Kenneth** (*b.* 1908) Canadian-born US economist. Long a professor at Harvard, he published numerous scholarly and popular works such as *The Affluent Society* (1958) that examined the political ramifications of economics.

> 'Politics is not the art of the possible. It consists in choosing between the dis-astrous and the unpalatable.'
> [John Kenneth Galbraith, *Ambassador's Journal*; 1969]

> 'The salary of the chief executive of the large corporation is not a market reward for achievement. It is frequently in the nature of a warm personal gesture by the individual to himself.'
> [John Kenneth Galbraith, *Annals of an Abiding Liberal*; 1979]

gale /gayl/ *n* **1.** an extremely strong wind that measures 8 or 9 on the Beaufort scale and has a speed of between 63 km/39 mi. and 87 km/54 mi. per hour **2.** a very strong wind [Mid-16C. Origin ?]

galea /gáy li ə/ (*plural* **-ae** /-ee/) *n* a part or organ shaped like a helmet, e.g. the upper petal of some flowers or one of the mouthparts of an insect [Mid-19C. < Latin, 'helmet'] —**galeate** *adj*

gale-force *adj* describes air currents that measure between 7 and 10 on the Beaufort scale and have a speed of between 51 and 102 km/32 and 63 mi. per hour ○ *a gale-force wind*

Galen /gáylən/ (129–99?) Greek physician and scholar. His anatomical studies formed the basis of European medical practice for 1,400 years.

'That physician will hardly be thought very careful of the health of others who neglects his own.'
[Galen, *Of Protecting the Health*; 2nd century]

galena /gə leénə/ *n* a lustrous blue-grey crystalline mineral consisting of lead sulphide. Use: source of lead and silver. [Late 17C. < Latin, 'lead at a certain stage of smelting']

galenical /gay lénnik'l/ *n* any medicinal preparation made from plant or animal tissue ■ *adj* made from plant or animal tissue rather than synthesized [Mid-17C. < GALEN]

galenite /gáylə nīt/ *n* MINERALS same as **galena**

galère /ga láir/ *n* **1.** a group of people with a particular attribute or interest, especially something undesirable, in common **2.** an unpleasant predicament [Mid-18C. Via French, 'galley' < Catalan *galera* < Middle Greek *galea*]

gali /gúlli/ (*plural* **galis**) *n* S Asia a narrow passageway or lane, especially one running between or behind buildings [< Hindi]

Galibi /gaa leébi/ (*plural* same or **-bis** /-biz/) *n* **1.** a member of an indigenous South American people who live in French Guiana **2.** a Carib language spoken in French Guiana. Galibi is spoken by fewer than a thousand people. [Late 19C. < Carib, 'strong man'] —**Galibi** *adj*

Galicia /gə líshə/ **1.** autonomous region and former kingdom in northwestern Spain. It contains the provinces of La Coruña, Lugo, Orense, and Pontevedra. Capital: Santiago de Compostela. Population: 2,731,669 (1991). Area: 29,434 sq. km/9,464 sq. mi. **2.** historic region in eastern Europe. A former principality, it has belonged to Poland and Austria, and is now divided between southeastern Poland and western Ukraine. —**Galician** *adj*

Galilean[1] /gálli leé ən/ *n* **1.** somebody who comes from Galilee **2.** same as **Christian** (*archaic*) [Mid-16C. < Latin *Galilea* 'Galilee'] —**Galilean** *adj*

Galilean[2] /gálli leé ən/ *adj* relating to the Italian scientist Galileo, his theories, or his inventions [Early 18C. < GALILEO]

galilee /gálli lee/ *n* a small porch or chapel found at the western end of some medieval churches or cathedrals [15C. Via Old French < medieval Latin *galilea*, after Latin *Galilea* 'Galilee']

Galilee /gálli lee/ region of ancient Palestine, now part of northern Israel, situated between the River Jordan and the Sea of Galilee. It was the scene of Jesus Christ's ministry.

Galilee, Sea of freshwater lake on the River Jordan in northeastern Israel. It is 209 m/686 ft below sea level. Area: 166 sq. km/64 sq. mi.

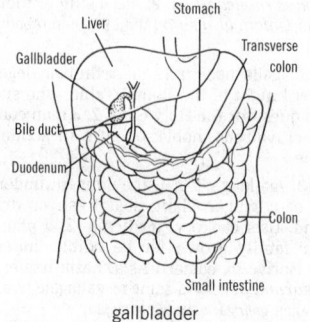
Galileo: portrait drawing by Guido Reni

Galileo /gálli láy ō/ (1564–1642) Italian physicist and astronomer. One of the founders of Europe's scientific revolution, his main contributions include the application of the telescope to astronomy and the discovery of the laws of falling bodies and the motions of projectiles. Born **Galilei, Galileo**

'In my studies of astronomy and philosophy I hold this opinion about the universe, that the Sun remains fixed in the centre of the circle of heavenly bodies, without changing its place; and the Earth, turning upon itself, moves round the Sun.'
[Galileo, *Letter to Cristina di Lorena, Grand-duchess of Tuscany*; 1615]

galingale /gálling gayl/ *n* a plant of the sedge family with aromatic roots. Flowers: reddish, growing in a cluster directly from the stem. Latin name: *Cyperus longus*. [Variant of GALANGAL]

galiot /gálli ət/, **galliot** *n* **1.** formerly, a light fast ship propelled by sails and oars used in the Mediterranean **2.** formerly, a light shallow single-masted Dutch merchant ship [15C. < Old French, 'little galley' < medieval Latin *galea* 'galley']

galipot /gálli pot/ *n* crude turpentine in resin form. Source: several southern European pine species. [Late 18C. Via French < Provençal *garapot* 'pine resin']

gall[1] /gawl/ *n* **1.** impudent boldness ○ *And then he had the gall to tell us to leave!* **2.** a feeling of bitterness or resentment (*literary*) **3.** BIOL same as **bile** (sense 1) (*archaic*) [12C. < Old Norse *gall* 'bile' < Germanic, 'yellow']

gall[2] /gawl/ *n* **1.** SORE CAUSED BY RUBBING a sore on the skin of an animal that is caused by friction **2.** CAUSE OF ANGER something that angers or irritates somebody (*dated*) **3.** ANGER a feeling of annoyance or anger (*dated*) ■ *vt* (**galls, galling, galled**) **1.** MAKE SOMEBODY ANGRY to make somebody extremely angry **2.** BREAK SURFACE DUE TO FRICTION to break or damage a surface, especially the skin, by friction or rubbing [14C. < Middle Low German *galle* 'sore']

gall[3] /gawl/ *n* a swelling on a tree or plant caused by insects, fungi, bacteria, or external damage [14C. Via Old French < Latin *galla* 'oak apple']

gall. *abbr* MEASURE gallon

Galla /gállə/ *n, adj* LANG, PEOPLES same as **Oromo** [Late 19C. Origin ?]

gallamine /gállə meen/ *n* a short-acting but powerful muscle relaxant. Use: general anaesthesia. [Late 19C. < Gallic (< GALLIUM) + AMINE]

gallant /gállənt, gə lánt/ *adj* **1.** COURTEOUS courteous and thoughtful, especially towards women **2.** BRAVE brave, spirited, and honourable (*literary*) **3.** MAJESTIC grand and majestic (*archaic*) ■ *n* **1.** MAN COURTEOUS TO WOMEN a man who is courteous and thoughtful in his behaviour towards women (*dated*) **2.** MALE LOVER a man who is a woman's lover (*archaic*) **3.** DANDY a fashionable young man (*archaic*) ■ *vti* (**-lants, -lanting, -lanted**) WOO to court a woman (*archaic*) [14C. < Old French, present participle of *galer* 'make merry'] —**gallantly** *adv*

Gallant /gə lánt/, **Mavis** (*b.* 1922) Canadian writer. She is known for her incisively written short stories, collected in volumes such as *Home Truths* (1981). Born **Young, Mavis**

gallantry /gálləntri/ (*plural* **-ries**) *n* **1.** COURAGE bravery, especially in war or in a situation of great danger **2.** COURTESY courteous and thoughtful behaviour, especially towards women **3.** SOMETHING GALLANT SAID OR DONE a courageous or chivalrous action or remark (*dated*)

gallbladder /gáwl bladər/ *n* a small muscular sac on the right underside of the liver, in which bile secreted by the liver is stored and concentrated until needed for the digestive process

Galle /gállə, gawl/ port on the southwestern coast of Sri Lanka. Population: 84,000 (1990 estimate).

galleass /gálli ass/, **galliass** *n* a large fast warship with three masts, used in the Mediterranean in the 16th and 17th centuries [Mid-16C. Via Old French < Old Italian *galeaza* 'large galley']

galleon

galleon /gálli ən/ *n* a large three-masted sailing ship used especially by the Spanish between the 15th and 18th centuries [Early 16C. Either via Middle Dutch *galjoen* < Old French *galion* 'large galley', or < Spanish *galeón*]

galleria /gállə reé ə/ *n* a roofed court with shops or businesses opening onto it, usually at several levels [Late 19C. < Italian]

gallery /gálləri/ (*plural* **-ies**) *n* **1.** PLACE FOR ART EXHIBITIONS a place where artwork is exhibited and sometimes sold **2.** STUDIO a photographer's studio **3.** BALCONY a balcony or passage running along the wall of a large building, often used for viewing an activity **4.** ENCLOSED WALKWAY a corridor, hall, or other enclosed passageway inside a building **5.** LONG NARROW ROOM a long narrow space or room used for a particular purpose **6.** COVERED WALKWAY a long covered passageway that is open on one or both sides **7.** UNDERGROUND PASSAGE an underground tunnel or passage, especially one made by an animal or one that is part of a mine or military site **8.** PART OF THEATRE a seating area projecting from the back and sides out over the main floor of a theatre, especially the highest section of this area containing the cheapest seats **9.** SEATS IN GALLERY the seats located in the gallery of a theatre **10.** AUDIENCE IN CHEAPEST SEATS the people who sit in the gallery of a theatre **11.** OFFENSIVE TERM an offensive term applied to the general public, viewed as having no discrimination or sophistication **12.** SPECTATORS a group of spectators, especially at a tennis or golf match **13.** STAGE RIG a narrow platform above a stage from which technicians can adjust lights, move props, or operate machinery **14.** ASSORTED COLLECTION a varied collection of people or things ○ *a gallery of famous names* **15.** SOUNDPROOF ROOM a soundproof room with a glass front in a television studio, from which the director or technical staff can oversee the studio floor **16.** SHIP'S BALCONY a platform or balcony at the rear of a ship **17.** DECORATIVE RAIL a decorative metal or wooden rail on a table top, shelf, or tray [15C. Via Old French *galerie* 'portico' < medieval Latin *galeria*] —**galleried** *adj* ◇ **play to the gallery** to do or say something that will appeal to those regarded as less educated, discriminating, or sophisticated

gallery forest *n* a strip of forest that grows along a river in an area where there are no other trees

galley /gálli/ (*plural* **-leys**) *n* **1.** LARGE SHIP a large ship propelled by oars or sails or both, that was used in ancient and medieval times, especially in the Mediterranean **2.** KITCHEN a kitchen on a boat, ship, train, or aircraft **3.** ROWING BOAT a long boat propelled by oars **4.** PRINT TRAY a long metal tray used for holding type that is ready for printing **5.** PRINTING same as **galley proof** [13C. Via Old French and medieval Latin < medieval Greek *galea*]

galley proof *n* a first test copy of printed material, usually not divided into pages, on which corrections are marked

Stomach
Liver
Transverse colon
Gallbladder
Bile duct
Duodenum
Colon
Small intestine
gallbladder

galley slave *n* **1.** formerly, one of a team of convicts or slaves forced to row a galley **2.** somebody who is given menial tasks to do (*dated humorous*)

gallfly /gáwl flī/ (*plural* **-flies**) *n* an insect that causes swellings (**galls**) on plants when it deposits its eggs on them, e.g. the gall midge or gall wasp

galliard /gálli aard/ *n* **1.** a lively European dance in triple time, popular in the 16th and 17th centuries **2.** the music for a galliard, written in triple time, part of the baroque dance suite [14C. < Old French]

galliass *n* another spelling of **galleass**

Gallic /gállik/ *adj* **1.** relating to France, or its language, people, or culture **2.** relating to ancient Gaul or the Gauls [Late 17C. < Latin *Gallia* 'Gaul']

gallic acid

gallic acid /gállik-/ *n* a colourless crystalline solid. Source: plants, tannin. Use: tanning agent, manufacture of inks and paper, in photography. Formula: $C_7H_6O_5$. [< Latin *galla* 'oak apple' (used in making the acid)]

Gallicanism /gállikənizəm/ *n* a French movement in favour of giving more autonomy to the Roman Catholic Church in individual countries and reducing the authority of the pope —**Gallican** *adj, n*

Gallicise *vt* LANG another spelling of **Gallicize**

Gallicism /gállissizəm/ *n* a word or phrase of French origin used in another language

Gallicize /gálli sīz/ (**-cizes, -cizing, -cized**), **Gallicise** (**-cises, -cising, -cised**) *vti* to become French or like something French, or make something such as a word, custom, or characteristic French —**Gallicization** /gálli sī záysh'n/ *n*

galligaskins /gálli gáskinz/ *npl* **1.** loose-fitting breeches or stockings that were worn by men in the 16th and 17th centuries **2.** leather leggings worn in the 19th century [Late 16C. Origin ?]

gallimaufry /gálli máwfri/ (*plural* **-fries**) *n* a jumble of various things or people [Mid-16C. < French *galimafrée*]

galling /gáwling/ *adj* having the effect of frustrating and annoying somebody —**gallingly** *adv*

gallinule /gálli nyool/ *n* a bird that both wades and swims and typically has dark feathers and a yellow-tipped red beak with a red shield above it. Native to: swampy regions. Family: Rallidae. [Late 18C. < modern Latin *gallinula* 'little hen']

galliot *n* another spelling of **galiot**

Gallipoli /gə líppəli/ peninsula in European Turkey, extending into the Dardanelles, and including an important seaport of the same name. It has historically been of great strategic importance to Istanbul. The peninsula was the site of a major World War I campaign in 1915, when Allied troops, including many from Australia and New Zealand, failed to take control of the Dardanelles.

gallipot /gálli pot/ *n* a small pot used by chemists as a container for medicaments [15C. Probably < GALLEY, because galleys brought such goods from the Mediterranean]

gallium /gálli əm/ *n* a rare metallic element, blue-grey when solid and silver when liquid. Source: coal, bauxite. Use: high-temperature thermometers, semiconductors, alloys. Symbol **Ga**. See table at **element** [Late 19C. < Latin *Gallia* 'France']

gallium arsenide *n* a dark-grey crystalline solid containing gallium and arsenic. Use: manufacture of semiconductors, solar cells, lasers. Formula: GaAs.

gallivant /gálli vant/ (**-vants, -vanting, -vanted**) *vi* (*informal*) **1.** to travel around with no purpose

except enjoyment **2.** to flirt or play romantically [Early 19C. Origin ?]

galliwasp /gálli wosp/ *n* a lizard with a long body that is related to the slowworm. Native to: marshes of Central America and the Caribbean. Family: Anguidae. [Late 17C. Origin ?]

gall midge *n* a small fly resembling a mosquito whose larvae cause swellings (**galls**) on plants. Family: Cecidomyidae.

gall mite *n* a mite that causes swellings (**galls**) on the fruits, leaves, or buds of plants. Family: Phytoptidae.

gallnut /gáwl nut/ *n* a small round swelling (**gall**) on a plant

galloglass /gállō glaass/, **gallowglass** *n* a medieval mercenary soldier or armed servant of a Celtic chieftain, especially in Ireland [15C. < Irish *gallóglach* 'young foreign servant, warrior']

gallon /gállən/ *n* **1.** UNIT OF VOLUME a unit of capacity in the imperial system equal to eight imperial pints (approximately 4.55 litres) **2.** US UNIT OF VOLUME a unit of capacity in the US customary system equal to eight US pints (approximately 3.79 litres) ■ *adj* HOLDING GALLON with a capacity of one gallon ○ *a gallon jar* [13C. < Anglo-Norman *galon* < medieval Latin *galleta* 'jug']

gallonage /gállənij/ *n* **1.** a capacity or amount measured in gallons **2.** the rate at which a liquid is used, pumped, or transmitted, measured in gallons per second, minute, or hour

galloon /gə loón/ *n* a narrow band of embroidery, lace, braid, or silver or gold thread, used as a trimming on clothes or upholstery [Early 17C. < French *galon* < *galonner* 'trim with braid'] —**gallooned** *adj*

galloot *n* another spelling of **galoot** (*slang insult*)

gallop /gálləp/ *n* **1.** FASTEST PACE OF HORSE the fastest pace of a horse, in which all four feet are off the ground at the same time **2.** FAST PACE OF FOUR-LEGGED ANIMAL a fast movement similar to a horse's gallop made by any four-legged animal **3.** FAST RIDE ON HORSE a ride on a horse at a gallop ■ *v* (**-lops, -loping, -loped**) **1.** *vti* RIDE HORSE FAST to ride a horse at a gallop **2.** *vi* DO SOMETHING VERY FAST to do something in a great hurry ○ *gallop through lunch* **3.** *vt* MOVE SOMETHING QUICKLY to move or transport something at a gallop or at a very fast pace [Early 16C. < Old French *galoper*, variant of *waloper* < Germanic] —**galloper** *n*

gallopade /gállə payd, -paad, gállə paád/ *n* DANCE, MUSIC same as **galop** [Mid-18C. < French *galopade* < *galoper* (see GALLOP)]

galloping /gálləping/ *adj* **1.** proceeding or developing at a very fast rate ○ *galloping pneumonia* **2.** resembling a gallop in speed or rhythm

Gallo-Romance /gállō-/, **Gallo-Roman** *n* a group of dialects spoken in France between the 7th and the 10th centuries. It constitutes an intermediate developmental stage between the end of Vulgar Latin and the appearance of Old French. —**Gallo-Romance** *adj*

Galloway[1] /gállə way/ region on the Solway Firth in southwestern Scotland, part of Dumfries and Galloway council area —**Gallovidian** /gállə víddi ən/ *adj, n*

Galloway[2] /gállə way/ *n* a cow belonging to a breed of hornless black beef cattle [After GALLOWAY[1]]

gallowglass *n* HIST another spelling of **galloglass**

gallows /gállōz/ (*plural* **same**) *n* **1.** FRAME FOR HANGING CRIMINALS a wooden frame, usually made of two upright posts and a crossbeam with a noose attached, used to execute people by hanging **2.** STRUCTURE LIKE GALLOWS a structure that resembles a gallows, e.g. one used to suspend slaughtered animals **3.** EXECUTION BY HANGING death by hanging as capital punishment for a criminal offence [13C. < Old Norse *gálgi* < Germanic, 'pole']

gallows bird *n* somebody who is regarded as deserving to be hanged (*archaic informal*)

gallows humour *n* macabre humour that finds irony or comedy in serious matters such as death

gallows tree *n* CRIME same as **gallows** (sense 1)

gallstone /gáwl stōn/ *n* a small hard mass that forms in the gallbladder, sometimes as a result of infection

or blockage. Gallstones consist mainly of cholesterol, bile pigments, and calcium salts.

Gallup /gálləp/, **George** (1901–84) US public opinion analyst and statistician. A pioneer in the use of statistical methods for determining public opinion on social, economic, and political issues, he is best known for founding the Gallup Poll (1935). Full name **Gallup, George Horace**

'I could prove God statistically.'
[Attributed to George Gallup]

Gallup poll *n* a survey in which a sample of people taken as a representative cross section of society are asked their opinions on a specific subject

gallus /gálləss/ *adj* Scotland daring in a cocky or foolhardy way (*informal*) [Late 16C. Alteration of GALLOWS; originally 'fit to be hanged']

galluses /gálləssiz/ *npl* Scotland, N Am braces for trousers [Mid-19C. Plural of *gallus*, alteration of GALLOWS; from the two supports]

gall wasp *n* a wasp that lays its eggs in plant tissue, causing swellings (**galls**). Family: Cynipidae.

galoot /gə loót/, **galloot** *n* somebody regarded as clumsy or thoughtless (*slang insult*) [Early 19C. Origin ?]

galop /gálləp, gə lóp/ *n* **1.** a lively dance in double time that was popular in the 19th century **2.** the music for a galop, in double time [Mid-19C. < French]

galore /gə láwr/ *adj* in large quantities or numbers (*used after a noun*) ○ *There'll be food galore at the party.* [Early 17C. < Irish *go leor* 'sufficiency']

galoshes /gə lóshiz/ *npl* a pair of waterproof shoes, often made of rubber, worn over other shoes as protection against rain or snow [14C. Via Old French *galoche* 'little sandal' < Latin *gallicula* < *Gallica (solea)* 'sandal (from Gaul)']

Galsworthy /gáwlz wurthi/, **John** (1867–1933) British novelist and playwright. His most famous work, a collection of five novels about the Edwardian and Victorian upper-middle classes entitled *The Forsyte Saga* (1922), was made into a television series in 1967 and again in 2002. See Cultural note at **saga**

'There is just one rule for politicians all over the world. Don't say in Power what you say in Opposition: if you do you only have to carry out what the other fellows have found impossible.'
[John Galsworthy, *Maid in Waiting*; 1931]

Galtieri /gálti áiri/, **Leopoldo** (1926–2003) Argentinian general and national leader. As president of Argentina's military junta (1981–82), he ordered the invasion of the Falkland Islands that provoked a war with the United Kingdom (1982). Full name **Galtieri, Leopoldo Fortunato**

galumph /gə lúmf/ (**-lumphs, -lumphing, -lumphed**) *vi* (*informal*) **1.** to walk or run in a boisterous or clumsy way **2.** to stride or march in a prancing triumphant way [Late 19C. Blend of GALLOP + TRIUMPH]

galuth /ga loóth/ *n* the Jewish Diaspora [Late 20C. < Hebrew *gālūth* 'exile']

galv. *abbr* **1.** galvanic **2.** galvanized

Galvani /gal vaáni/, **Luigi** (1737–98) Italian physiologist. A professor of anatomy, he studied the effects of electricity on animal nerves and muscles.

galvanic /gal vánnik/ *adj* **1.** relating to or involving the direct-current electricity that is chemically generated between dissimilar metals, e.g. in a battery **2.** sudden, startling, or convulsive, like an electric shock or its effects [Late 18C. < French *galvanique*, after Luigi GALVANI] —**galvanically** *adv*

galvanic cell *n* ELEC ENG same as **primary cell**

galvanic skin response *n* a change in the electrical conductivity of the skin caused by sweating and increased blood flow and linked to a strong emotion such as fear. Lie detector tests use this change as a way of measuring whether somebody is telling the truth.

galvanise *vt* MANUF, MED another spelling of **galvanize**

galvanism /gálvənizəm/ *n* **1.** the production of direct-current electricity from a chemical reaction, e.g. between dissimilar metals in a battery **2.** the application of electricity to the human body to stimulate nerves and muscles as part of a medical

treatment [Late 18C. < French *galvanisme*, after Luigi GALVANI]

galvanize /gálvə nīz/ (**-nizes, -nizing, -nized**), **galvanise** (**-nises, -nising, -nised**) *vt* **1. STIMULATE SOMEBODY TO ACT** to stimulate somebody or something into great activity **2. COAT METAL WITH ZINC** to coat a metal, usually iron or steel, with zinc to prevent corrosion **3. STIMULATE BODY ELECTRICALLY** to stimulate the nerves or muscles of somebody's body using an electric current [Early 19C. < French *galvaniser*, after Luigi GALVANI] —**galvanization** /gálvə nī záysh'n/ *n* —**galvanizer** *n*

galvanometer /gálvə nómmitər/ *n* an instrument used to detect or measure the strength and direction of small electric currents by means of a coil in a magnetic field that moves a pointer or light —**galvanometric** /gálvənə méttrik/ *adj* —**galvanometry** *n*

Galway /gáwl way/ **1.** seaport on Galway Bay and capital of County Galway, on the western coast of the Republic of Ireland. Population: 57,241 (2002). **2.** county in Connacht Province, western Republic of Ireland. Area: 5,939 sq. km/2,293 sq. mi. —**Galwegian** /gal wéejən/ *adj, n*

Galway Bay inlet of the Atlantic Ocean on the western coast of the Republic of Ireland

gam[1] /gam/ *n* **1. MIGRATING WHALES** a group of migrating whales **2. SOCIAL VISIT BETWEEN WHALERS** a social visit between whalers or other sailors, especially while at sea (*informal*) **3.** *NZ* **SEA BIRDS** a flock of sea birds ■ *vi* (**gams, gamming, gammed**) **MEET UP** to meet socially, especially at sea (*informal*) [Mid-19C. Origin ?]

gam[2] /gam/ *n* somebody's leg, especially a woman's (*old slang or considered offensive*) [Late 18C. Probably alteration of *gamb* 'heraldic device resembling an animal's leg' < northern form of Old French *jambe* 'leg']

Gama /gaámə/, **Vasco da** (1469?–1524) Portuguese navigator and explorer. He led the first European expedition to reach India by sailing round Africa (1497–99).

gama grass /gaámə-/ *n* a tall coarse grass that is grown for fodder. Native to: North America. Latin name: ***Tripsacum dactyloides***. [Mid-19C. Origin ?]

Gamay /gámmay/ *n* **1.** a fruity red wine made from a variety of black grape grown mainly in Burgundy, east-central France **2.** the black grape variety used to make Gamay [Mid-19C. After *Gamay*, village in Burgundy, France]

gamba /gámbə/ *n* MUSIC same as **viola da gamba**

gambade /gam báyd, -baád/ *n* RIDING same as **gambado**[2] [Early 16C. < French, probably < Italian *gambata* < *gamba* 'leg']

gambado[1] /gam báydō/ (*plural* **-dos** or **-does**) *n* **1.** either of a pair of protective leather holders for a rider's feet, attached to a horse's saddle **2.** either of a pair of rider's leggings [Mid-17C. < Italian *gamba* 'leg' + *-ado*]

gambado[2] /gam báy dō/ (*plural* **-dos** or **-does**) *n* **1. LOW JUMP BY HORSE** in dressage, a low leap in which the horse has all four feet off the ground **2. LEAP** a leap or caper **3. PRANK** a prank or escapade [Early 19C. < Spanish *gambada* < *gamba* 'leg']

gambeer *n* INDUST another spelling of **gambier**

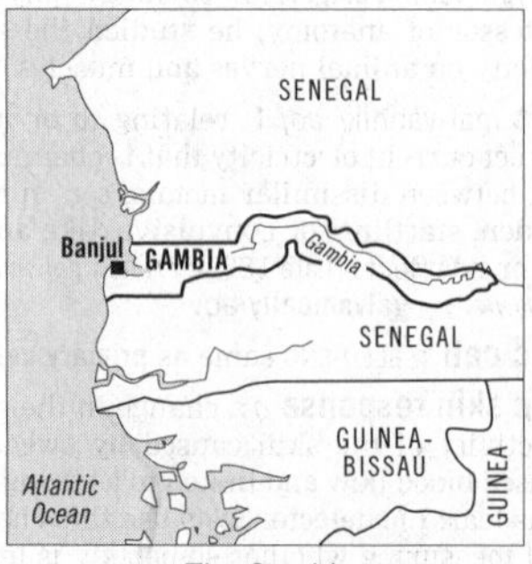

The Gambia

Gambia /gámbi ə/ **1.** *also* **the Gambia** country on the coast of West Africa, bordered on the north, east, and south by Senegal. It became an independent member of the Commonwealth in 1965. Language: English. Currency: dalasi. Capital: Banjul. Population: 1,501,050 (2003). Area: 11,295 sq. km/4,361 sq. mi. Official name **Republic of the Gambia 2.** river in western Africa that rises in Guinea, flows westwards through the Gambia, and empties into the Atlantic Ocean near Banjul. Length: 1,100 km/700 mi. —**Gambian** *n, adj*

gambier /gám beer/, **gambir**, **gambeer** *n* a resinous astringent substance. Source: leaves of a tropical Asian woody vine. Use: medicinally as an astringent or tonic, in tanning and dyeing. [Early 19C. < Malay *gambir*, the plant]

gambit /gámbit/ *n* **1. STRATAGEM** a manoeuvre or stratagem used to secure an advantage **2. CONVERSATIONAL OPENER** a remark used to open a conversation **3.** CHESS **OPENING MOVE IN CHESS** in chess, an opening move in which a player sacrifices a pawn or other minor piece in order to gain a strategic advantage [Mid-17C. < Italian *gambetto* 'act of tripping somebody up (in wrestling)' (after French *gambit*) < *gamba* 'leg']

gamble /gámb'l/ *v* (**-bles, -bling, -bled**) **1.** *vi* **PLAY GAMES OF CHANCE** to play games such as poker or roulette that involve risking money, or bet on horse races or other events, in the hope of winning money **2.** *vt* **BET MONEY** to bet a sum of money on the outcome of an event or competition **3.** *vi* **TAKE CHANCE ON SOMETHING** to take a risk in the hope and expectation of a desired result ○ *gambling on nice weather* **4.** *vi* **ENDANGER SOMETHING** to behave in a way that risks harming somebody or something ○ *gambled with the success of the show* **5.** *vt* **LOSE OR RISK LOSING SOMETHING** to lose or risk losing something, especially money, by betting or doing something dangerous or rash ○ *She gambled her inheritance away.* ■ *n* **1. BET** a bet made in the hope of winning money **2. RISKY ACTION** an action whose outcome is uncertain and very possibly undesirable ○ *I took a gamble on them being away from home.* [Early 18C. < GAME[1] + *-le*, literally 'keep on playing'] —**gambler** *n*

gambling /gámbling/ *n* the practice of playing games of chance or betting in the hope of winning money

gambling den *n* a place such as a club where people used to meet to take part in illegal games that involved gambling for money (*archaic informal*)

gamboge /gam bōj, -bōzh/ *n* **1. RESIN** a gum resin obtained from various Asian trees that produces a yellow pigment **2. YELLOW PIGMENT** a yellow pigment made from gamboge resin **3. YELLOW COLOUR** a strong yellow colour [Mid-17C. < modern Latin *gambaugium* < *Cambodia*]

gambol /gámb'l/ *vi* (**-bols, -bolling, -bolled**) to leap or skip about playfully ■ *n* an instance of leaping about playfully [Mid-16C. Alteration of GAMBADE]

gambrel /gámbrəl/ *n* **1.** the joint of a leg of an animal, especially a horse, that corresponds to the human ankle **2.** a frame in the shape of a horse's hind leg used by butchers for hanging animal carcasses **3.** ARCHIT same as **gambrel roof** [Mid-16C. < Old N French *gamberel* < *gambier* 'forked stick' < *gambe*, variant of *jambe* 'leg']

gambrel roof *n* **1.** a roof with sloping ends and sides and a small gable at both ends **2.** a two-sided roof that has two slopes on each side, the lower slope being steeper than the upper

game[1] /gaym/ *n* **1. SOMETHING PLAYED FOR FUN** an activity that people participate in, together or on their own, for fun ○ *It's only a game!* **2. COMPETITIVE ACTIVITY WITH RULES** a sporting or other activity in which players compete against each other by following a fixed set of rules ○ *How many people do you need to play this game?* **3. MATCH** an occasion when a competitive game is played ○ *Saturday's game has been cancelled.* **4. ASPECT OF GAME** an aspect of a competitive activity ○ *Their defensive game was terrible.* **5. STYLE OF PLAYING** the style or level of skill with which somebody plays a sport ○ *raise your game* **6. PART OF MATCH** in sports such as tennis, a subsection of play that goes towards making up a set or match **7. NUMBER NEEDED TO WIN** the total number of points needed to win a contest ○ *In table tennis, game is 21 points.* **8. RULES GOVERNING SPORT** the rules governing a particular competition or sport **9. EQUIPMENT** an item or set of items that is needed to play a particular game, e.g. a board, dice, counters, a pack of cards, or a piece of computer software ○ *a compendium of games* **10. ACTIVITY LIKE GAME** an activity that resembles a game, e.g. one that involves intense interest and competitiveness and is carried out by its own specific and often unspoken rules **11. STRATAGEM** a way of behaving that is aimed at manipulating people or trying to deceive them ○ *So that's your game?* **12. ILLEGAL ACTIVITY** a strategy, activity, or behaviour that is questionable, and often illegal (*informal*) **13. OCCUPATION** a business or occupation (*informal*) ○ *the advertising game* **14. SOMETHING NOT TAKEN SERIOUSLY** an activity or situation that somebody does not treat seriously ○ *Life's a game as far as he's concerned.* **15.** FIELD SPORTS **ANIMALS FOR HUNTING** wild animals, birds, or fish that are hunted for sport **16. MEAT OF HUNTED ANIMALS** the meat of wild animals, birds, or fish that have been killed for sport **17. RIDICULE** the act of ridiculing, criticizing, or tricking somebody for fun, or the target of such ridicule, criticism, or trickery ○ *She's easy game for a trickster like him.* **18.** MATHS **MATHEMATICAL MODEL** a mathematical model describing a contest played under specific rules in which each participant has only partial control ■ *adj* **1. READY AND WILLING** ready and willing to do something, especially something new or unusual **2. BRAVE** brave in spirit or character ■ *v* (**games, gaming, gamed**) **1.** *vi* **GAMBLE** to play games of chance for money **2.** *vi* COMPUT GAMES **PLAY COMPUTER GAMES** to play computer or video games **3.** *vt* **MANIPULATE SOMETHING CUNNINGLY** to manipulate something cunningly in order to advance yourself or attain your goals in an underhand manner (*slang*) ○ *gaming his way to the top of his profession* [Old English *gamen* < Germanic, 'people participating together'] —**gamely** *adv* —**gameness** *n* ◇ **a game of two halves** a game that might change later in the match, with the current loser starting to win ◇ **ahead of the game** anticipating and reacting more promptly than others to new developments ◇ **give the game away** to reveal a secret, usually without intending to ◇ **on the game** working as a prostitute (*informal*) ◇ **play the game** to follow the rules of a given situation, even if they are unspoken ◇ **the game's up** the plan or trick has failed or been discovered (*informal*)

game[2] /gaym/ *adj* an offensive term meaning injured or with impaired mobility (*dated*) [Late 18C. Origin ?]

game bird *n* a bird that is hunted for sport, e.g. a pheasant or grouse

game chips *npl* thin round slices of fried potato served with game

gamecock /gáym kok/ *n* *N Am* BIRDS same as **fighting cock**

game controller *n* a hand-held control mechanism for a computer game

game fish *n* **1.** a freshwater fish that is highly prized for angling and eating, e.g. a trout or salmon **2.** a fish, particularly a sea fish, that is caught for sport. Sharks are popular game fish. —**game fishing** *n*

game fowl *n* a domestic fowl bred and trained for fighting

gamekeeper /gáym keepər/ *n* somebody employed to look after birds or animals hunted for sport, especially on an estate or game reserve —**gamekeeping** *n*

gamelan /gámmə lan/ *n* an Indonesian orchestra that consists mainly of percussion instruments such as chimes, gongs, and wooden xylophones [Early 19C. < Javanese]

game law *n* a law that controls the catching and killing of fish, birds, or other animals for sport, e.g. one that specifies the extent of a hunting or shooting season

game of chance *n* a game, usually played for money, in which the outcome depends to some degree on chance, e.g. on the throw of dice

game of skill *n* a game in which the outcome depends entirely or principally on the skill of the players, e.g. chess or bridge

gamepad /gáym pad/ *n* a hand-held control mechanism for a computer game

game plan *n* **1.** a strategy that somebody devises to achieve a goal **2.** the strategy that a team or player devises for use during a game

gameplay /gáym play/ *n* the entertainment value of a computer game, including aspects such as user interface and game design

game-playing *n* manipulative or deceitful behaviour ○ *I've had enough of this endless game-playing.*

game point *n* **1.** in sports such as tennis and badminton, a situation in which one player or side has

only to win the next point to win the game **2.** in sports such as tennis and badminton, the point that will decide the final outcome of a game

gamer /gáymər/ n somebody who regularly plays computer or video games or role-play games

game reserve n a large area of land where birds or animals are kept in protected conditions in the wild, either for conservation purposes or to be hunted for sport. N Am term **game preserve**

game room n US LEISURE same as **games room**

games /gaymz/ npl an event that consists of many different sporting activities and usually lasts for several days ■ n gymnastics, athletics, team sports, and other forms of physical exercise taught to children at school (takes a singular verb)

games console n COMPUT GAMES same as **console**[2] (sense 6)

game show n a television programme in which people compete for money or prizes

gamesmanship /gáymzmənship/ n **1.** the use of tactics or stratagems to gain an advantage in business, politics, or life ○ political gamesmanship **2.** the use of unconventional but not strictly illegal tactics to gain an advantage in a competitive game —**gamesman** n

games room n a room in a house or public building that is set aside and equipped for games such as billiards or table tennis

gamester /gáymstər/ n somebody who plays gambling games (archaic)

gamet- prefix same as **gameto-**

gametangium /gámmi tánji əm/ (plural **-gia** /-ji ə/) n the part of a plant, especially an organ or cell in algae and fungi, where gametes are produced [Late 19C. < modern Latin gameta (see GAMETE) + Greek aggeion 'vessel'] —**gametangial** adj

gamete /gámmeet/ n a specialized male or female cell with half the normal number of chromosomes that unites with a cell of the opposite sex in the process of sexual reproduction. Ova and spermatozoa are gametes that unite to produce a cell (**zygote**) that may develop into an embryo. [Late 19C. < modern Latin gameta < Greek gamos 'marriage'] —**gametic** /gə méttik/ adj —**gametically** adv

game theory n a mathematical theory primarily concerned with determining an optimal strategy for situations in which there is competition or conflict, e.g. in business activities or military operations —**game theoretic** adj —**game theorist** n

gameto- prefix relating to a gamete ○ gametophore [< GAMETE]

gametocyte /gə méetō sīt/ n **1.** a cell that divides to produce two specialized male or female cells (**gametes**) **2.** the malaria organism in the stage in its life cycle during which it reproduces in the blood of a mosquito

gametogenesis /gə méetō jénnəssis/ n the production of gametes from gametocytes by cell division (**meiosis**) —**gametogenic** adj —**gametogenous** /gámmi tójjənəss/ adj

gametophore /gə méetō fawr/ n an upright branch in plants such as mosses that bears the reproductive organs —**gametophoric** /gə méetō fórrik/ adj

gametophyte /gə méetō fīt/ n in the life cycle of organisms such as mosses, fungi, and algae which have two distinct alternating forms, the form in which sex organs and gametes are produced —**gametophytic** /gə méetō fíttik/ adj

game warden n somebody who looks after wild animals, fish, or birds, e.g. on a game reserve

gamey adj another spelling of **gamy**

gamin /gámm in/ n a young child, usually a boy, often homeless, who roams the streets (archaic) [Mid-19C. < French]

gamine /gámmeen/ n **1.** BOYISH GIRL a girl or young woman who is boyish in appearance **2.** GIRL STREET URCHIN a young girl, often homeless, who roams the streets ■ adj APPEALINGLY BOYISH describes girls or young women who are charmingly boyish in appearance [Late 19C. < French, form of gamin 'child on the streets']

gaming /gáyming/ n **1.** the practice of playing games such as poker or roulette for money **2.** the practice

of playing computer games or role-play games —**gaming** adj

gamma /gámmə/ n **1.** 3RD LETTER OF GREEK ALPHABET the third letter of the Greek alphabet, represented in the English alphabet as 'g'. See table at **alphabet 2.** EDUC SCHOOL MARK the Greek letter gamma given as a mark to a student for a piece of academic work **3.** THIRD ITEM the third item in a list or classification system **4.** PHOTOGRAPHY MEASURE OF CONTRAST OF IMAGE a measure of the degree of contrast in a developed photograph or a television image **5.** CHEM 3RD POSITION IN CARBON CHAIN the third position in a carbon chain or ring, starting from a specific group or atom. Symbol γ ■ adj CHEM 3RD NEAREST TO DESIGNATED ATOM describes the third nearest atom to a particular atom or group of atoms in an organic molecule [15C. Via Latin < Greek]

Gamma n the third brightest star in a constellation (followed by the Latin genitive)

gamma-amino butyric acid n an amino acid that prevents onward transmission of nerve impulses in cells

gamma camera n a diagnostic instrument used in medicine to produce images of internal organs after the injection of a radioactive drug that releases gamma rays into the body

gamma decay n a radioactive decay process between two energy levels within a nucleus in which a gamma ray is emitted

gammadion /ga máydi ən/ n a pattern consisting of four capital Greek gammas, especially when joined at the centre to form a swastika [Mid-19C. < late Greek, < Greek gamma 'gamma']

gamma globulin n a protein component of blood serum that contains the antibodies, the body's main defence against infection. It is also produced commercially from human plasma and used in the treatment and prevention of diseases such as measles, hepatitis, and poliomyelitis.

gammahydroxybutyrate /gámmə hī droksi byóoti rayt/ n a colourless chemical compound with anaesthetic properties that occurs naturally in animals. Use: treating anxiety, as an anaesthetic. Formula: $C_4H_8O_3$.

gamma radiation n electromagnetic waves of higher frequency and shorter wavelength than X-rays that are emitted by some radioactive isotopes and in some nuclear reactions

gamma ray n a high-energy photon emitted after nuclear reactions or spontaneously from the nucleus of a radioactive atom that lowers the energy level of the nucleus. Gamma rays do not carry any electric charge or mass and share the high-frequency end of the electromagnetic spectrum with X-rays, which have similar properties.

gammon[1] /gámmən/ n **1.** the lower part of a side of bacon, cooked whole or cut into slices **2.** cured or smoked ham [15C. < Old N French gambon 'ham' < gambe 'leg']

gammon[2] /gámmən/ n a win in backgammon when the losing player has not succeeded in removing any pieces from the board [Mid-18C. < early form of GAME[1]] —**gammon** vt

gammon[3] /gámmən/ (dated informal) n false or meaningless talk that is intended to deceive somebody ■ vti (-mons, -moning, -moned) to trick or deceive somebody, especially by talking nonsense [Early 18C. Origin ?]

gammon[4] /gámmən/ (-mons, -moning, -moned) vt to fasten a bowsprit to the front of a ship [Late 17C. < GAMMON[1], probably with reference to the tying up of a ham]

gammy /gámmi/ (-mier, -miest) adj stiff or painful and unable to move as before, because of injury or some medical disorder (informal) ○ a gammy leg [Mid-19C. Variant of GAME[2]]

gamo- prefix **1.** joined together ○ gamosepalous **2.** sexual ○ gamogenesis [< Greek gamos 'marriage']

gamogenesis /gámmō jénnəssis/ n sexual reproduction (technical) —**gamogenetic** /-jə néttik/ adj —**gamogenetically** adv

gamosepalous /gámmō séppələss/ adj describes plants with sepals that are joined or partially joined together

Gamow /gám ov/, **George** (1904–68) Russian-born US theoretical physicist. He made important contributions in a variety of fields, including molecular biology and radioactivity. A proponent of the big bang theory that the universe was created in a gigantic explosion, he was also a prolific author of science books for the general public.

gamp /gamp/ n an umbrella, especially a large old one (archaic informal) [Mid-19C. After Sarah Gamp, character in Dickens's novel Martin Chuzzlewit, who carries an umbrella]

gamut /gámmət/ n **1.** FULL RANGE the entire range of something **2.** COMPLETE RANGE OF MUSICAL NOTES the whole series of recognized musical notes, from lowest to highest **3.** LOWEST MEDIEVAL MUSICAL NOTE the lowest note of medieval musical theory, two Gs below middle C **4.** MEDIEVAL MUSICAL SCALE SYSTEM the medieval scale system based around a repeated series of six notes (**hexachord**) [15C. Contraction of medieval Latin gamma ut < Greek gamma, letter representing the musical note one below the top note in the medieval scale, + ut, the lowest note]

gamy /gáymi/ (-ier, -iest), **gamey** (-ier, -iest) adj **1.** TASTING OF OR LIKE GAME having a strong flavour like that of a wild bird or animal that is hunted for food **2.** RANK-SMELLING having a strong bad smell **3.** LEWD sexually suggestive or obscene —**gamily** adv —**gaminess** n

-gamy suffix **1.** marriage ○ polygamy **2.** reproductive union ○ syngamy **3.** reproductive organs, method of fertilization ○ karyogamy [< Greek gamos 'marriage'] —**-gamic** suffix —**-gamous** suffix

ganache /ga násh, gə-/ n a sweet creamy chocolate filling or icing for cakes and pastries, made from cream and melted chocolate [Late 20C. Via French, 'jaw', and Italian ganascia < Greek gnathos]

Ganapati /gánnə pátti/ n HINDUISM same as **Ganesh**

Ganda /gándə/ n a Bantu language spoken in Uganda. Native speakers: 4 million. [Mid-20C. < Bantu] —**Ganda** adj

gander /gándər/ n **1.** MALE GOOSE an adult male goose **2.** LOOK a look or glance at somebody or something (informal) **3.** OFFENSIVE TERM an offensive term for somebody who is thought to be unserious and frivolous (informal insult) [Old English gandra < Indo-European, 'goose']

Gander /gándər/ town in northeastern Newfoundland, Canada that is home to the region's air traffic control centre. Population: 9,391 (2001).

Gandhi /gándi/, **Indira** (1917–84) prime minister of India. The daughter of Jawaharlal Nehru, she was twice prime minister (1966–77, 1980–84), and was assassinated by members of her Sikh bodyguard. Born Nehru, Indira Priyadarshini

> 'I don't mind if my life goes in the service of the nation. If I die today every drop of my blood will invigorate the nation.'
> [Indira Gandhi. Quoted in Sunday Times; 3 December 1989]

Mohandas Karamchand Gandhi

Gandhi, **Mohandas Karamchand** (1869–1948) Indian nationalist leader. His campaign of nonviolent civil resistance to British rule led to India's independence (1947). He was assassinated by a Hindu extremist as a protest against his pluralistic policies. Known as **Gandhi, Mahatma**

> 'Complete independence through truth and nonviolence means the independence of every unit, be it the humblest of the nation, without distinction of race, colour or creed.'

[Mohandas Karamchand Gandhi. Quoted in *Questions in the Philosophy of Restraint*, Indira Rothermund; 1963]

Gandhi, Sonia (1946–) Italian-born Indian politician. The widow of Indira Gandhi's son Rajiv, she became leader of the Congress Party in 1998 and was elected to Parliament in 1999. In 2004 her party won the general election, but she declined to be prime minister. Born **Maino, Sonia**

Gandhinagar /gándee núggər/ capital city of Gujarat State in western India, on the outskirts of Ahmedabad. It is India's second planned city, designed and built in the 1960s. Population: 225,000 (1995).

G & T, **g and t** *abbr* gin and tonic

gandy dancer /gándi-/ *n US* a labourer who lays or maintains railway tracks (*slang*) [Origin ?]

ganef /gaːanəf/, **ganev** /gaːanəv/, **ganof** /gaːannəf/, **gonif** /gónnəf/, **gonof** /gaːannəf/ *n* somebody regarded as unscrupulous, thieving, or cheating (*informal insult*) [Early 20C. Via Yiddish < Hebrew *gannāb*]

Ganesh /gə nésh/, **Ganesha** /-néesha/, **Ganesa** /-néessə/ *n* in Hinduism, the god of wisdom and problem-solving who is the son of Shiva and Parvati and is represented as a pot-bellied man with an elephant's head

Ganesh Chaturthi /-chə toorthi/ *n* a Hindu festival honouring the god Ganesh. Date: early Bhadrapada.

ganev *n* CRIME same as **ganef**

gang[1] /gang/ *n* **1.** GROUP OF TROUBLE-MAKING YOUNG PEOPLE a group of young people who spend time together for social reasons and may engage in delinquent behaviour **2.** GROUP OF CRIMINALS a group of people who work together for some criminal or antisocial purpose **3.** PEOPLE WHO ENJOY EACH OTHER'S COMPANY a group of people with similar interests who like to spend time together **4.** GROUP OF WORKERS a group of people working together, especially a group of labourers **5.** SET OF TOOLS a set of tools or devices arranged to be used or operated together ■ *vt* (**gangs, ganging, ganged**) **1.** PUT OBJECTS IN GROUP to group similar objects in a set **2.** ELECTRONICS COMBINE SWITCHES to combine several switches or devices on a single shaft so as to switch multiple connections at one time [12C. < Old Norse *gangr* 'journey']

gang up *vi* to join together in a group, especially for the purpose of attack, intimidation, or opposition

gang up on *vt* to join together in a group in order to attack, intimidate, or oppose somebody

gang[2] /gang/ (**gangs, ganging, ganged**) *vi Scotland* to go (*nonstandard*) [Old English *gangan* < Germanic]

gang[3] /gang/ *n* MIN EXTRACT another spelling of **gangue**

Ganga /gáng gə/ *n S Asia* Hindi name for **Ganges**

gangbang /gáng bang/ (*slang; considered offensive by some people*) *n* **1.** SERIAL INTERCOURSE WITH ONE PERSON sexual intercourse between one consenting person and several others in succession **2.** ORGY a group sex session in which participants have sex with a succession of partners **3.** GANG RAPE a multiple rape by a gang of people ■ *v* (**-bangs, -banging, -banged**) **1.** *vti* HAVE MULTIPLE INTERCOURSE WITH ONE PERSON to have sexual intercourse with somebody on the same occasion as others do **2.** *vti* GANG-RAPE to gang-rape somebody **3.** *vi US* BE MEMBER OF VIOLENT GANG to participate in the activities of a criminal or violent gang —**gangbanger** *n*

gangbuster /gáng bustər/ *n N Am* a law-enforcement officer charged with breaking up criminal gangs (*dated slang*) ■ *adj US* unusually successful or effective (*slang*) ○ *a gangbuster sale* ◇ **like gangbusters** *US* with a lot of energy or enthusiasm or to great effect (*slang*) ○ *The movie takes off like gangbusters and never lets up.*

ganger /gángər/ *n* the foreman of a group of workers

Ganges /gán jeez/ river in northern India, regarded as sacred by Hindus. It rises in the Himalaya range, flows southeastwards through Bangladesh, and empties into the Bay of Bengal, forming one of the world's largest deltas. Length: 2,510 km/1,560 mi. Hindi name **Ganga**

gangland /gáng land, -lənd/ *n* the world of organized crime —**gangland** *adj*

ganglia ANAT plural of **ganglion**

gangling /gáng gling/, **gangly** /-glee/ (**-glier, -gliest**) *adj*

Ganges

tall and thin, with a loose awkward gait [Early 19C. Origin ?]

ganglion /gáng gli ən/ (*plural* -**glia** /-gli ə/ *or* -**glions**) *n* **1.** a structure that contains a dense cluster of nerve cells **2.** a harmless swelling similar to a cyst that forms on a joint or tendon [Late 17C. < Greek *gagglion* 'tumour, nerve bundle'] —**ganglial** *adj* —**ganglionated** /gáng gli ə naytid/ *adj* —**ganglionic** /gáng gli ónnik/ *adj*

gangly *adj* same as **gangling**

gangmaster /gáng maastər/ *n* a person who gathers together and organizes or leads a group of casual and often travelling workers, especially in the agricultural or other seasonal industries

gangplank /gáng plangk/ *n* a movable walkway such as a bridge or plank, used when boarding or disembarking from a ship

gang rape *n* the rape of one person by several people in succession —**gang-rape** *vti*

gangrene /gáng green/ *n* local death and decay of soft tissues of the body as a result of lack of blood to the area ■ *vti* (**-grenes, -grening, -grened**) to affect body tissue with gangrene, or become affected with gangrene [Mid-16C. Via French < Greek *gaggraina*] —**gangrenous** /gáng grinəss/ *adj*

gangsta /gángstə/ *n* **1.** GANG MEMBER a member of an urban street gang **2.** MUSIC RAP PERFORMER somebody who performs gangsta rap ■ *adj* OF GANGS AND GANGSTA RAP relating to or characteristic of urban street gangs, their activities, or gangsta rap

gangsta rap /gángstə-/ *n* rap music in which the lyrics tend to deal with gangs and killings [Alteration of GANGSTER]

gangster /gángstər/ *n* a member of an organized gang of criminals, especially a racketeer —**gangsterish** *adj* —**gangsterism** *n*

Gangtok /gang tók/ capital city of Sikkim State in northeastern India. Population: 25,024 (1991).

gangue /gang/, **gang** *n* worthless rock or other matter occurring in a vein or deposit within or alongside a valuable mineral. ◊ **matrix** (sense 6) [Early 19C. Via French < German *Gang* 'way, lode']

gangway /gáng way/ *n* **1.** NARROW WALKWAY a narrow passageway, especially a temporary walkway **2.** ENTRANCE IN SHIP'S SIDE an opening in the side of a ship through which it is boarded by means of a gangplank **3.** NAUT same as **gangplank 4.** AISLE BETWEEN SEATS an aisle between seating, especially the one separating two blocks of seating in the House of Commons ■ *interj* MAKE WAY used to indicate to people in a crowd that they should make way because somebody is coming through

ganister /gánnistər/ *n* a hard rock containing silica that can endure high temperatures and is used to line furnaces [Early 19C. Origin ?]

ganja /gánjə, gaːan-/ *n* a potent form of marijuana used for smoking [Early 19C. < Hindi *gājā*]

gannet /gánnit/ *n* **1.** a large fish-eating seabird, usually white with black-tipped wings, that lives in offshore colonies. Genera: *Sula* or *Morus*. **2.** a gluttonous person (*informal*) [Old English *ganot* < Indo-European, 'goose']

ganof *n* CRIME another spelling of **ganef**

ganoid /gánnoyd/ *adj* describes a type of scale found on gar and other primitive fish, consisting of dentine-covered bone with a thick outer layer of a substance (**ganoine**) similar to enamel ■ *n* a primitive fish that has ganoid scales [Mid-19C. < French *ganoide* < Greek *ganos* 'brightness']

gannet

gansey /gánzi/ (*plural* -**seys**) *n regional* a heavy jumper, especially one worn by a fisherman [Late 19C. Alteration of GUERNSEY]

Gansu /gán soo/ agricultural province in northern China dominated by semiarid plateaus and basins. Capital: Lanzhou. Population: 24,670,000 (1997). Area: 454,000 sq. km/175,290 sq. mi.

gantline /gánt līn, -lin/ *n* a rope run through a pulley on a mast and used to hoist people or things [Mid-18C. Origin ?]

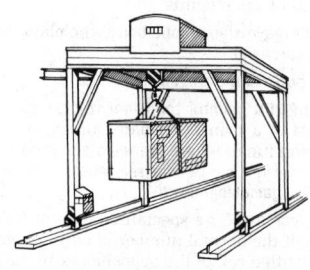

gantry (sense 2)

gantry /gántri/ (*plural* -**tries**) *n* **1.** a frame spanning railway tracks or one side of a motorway and used to display signals **2.** a spanning framework used to support machinery, e.g. the platform that supports a crane or the structure used to erect and service rockets [Late 16C. Origin ?]

Ganymede /gánni meed/ *n* **1.** in Greek mythology, a beautiful young Trojan prince whom Zeus carried off to Mount Olympus to be cupbearer to the gods. In later times he symbolized homosexual love or the spirit's ascent to heaven. **2.** the largest of Jupiter's moons

Gao /gaːa ō, gow/ town and ancient trading centre in eastern Mali, on the southern edge of the Sahara. It is situated on the River Niger. Population: 63,000 (1998).

Gao Kegong /gów kə góng/ (1248–1310?) Chinese artist. He is noted for his paintings of the mountain landscapes of southern China.

gaol *n*, *vt* CRIME another spelling of **jail**

CULTURAL NOTE *The Ballad of Reading Gaol*, a poem (1898) by Oscar Wilde. Wilde's last work, written while he was imprisoned for 'homosexual activities', it is the story of the trial and execution of murderer Charles Thomas Wooldridge, a fellow inmate at the jail. It deals with the harshness of prison conditions and the idea of forgiveness.

gaoler *n* CRIME another spelling of **jailer**

gap /gap/ *n* **1.** BREAK IN STRUCTURE a break or opening in a structure or arrangement such as a fence or military defence line **2.** SOMETHING MISSING an area where there is a complete or partial absence of something such as data ○ *gaps in his employment record* **3.** INTERVAL OF TIME an interval of time during which an action or event stops occurring ○ *after a gap of three years* **4.** DISPARITY a significant difference between two situations, attitudes, or perceptions ○ *the gap between rich and poor* **5.** PROBLEM CAUSED BY DISPARITY a problem caused by a difference between two situations, attitudes, or perceptions ○ *technology gap* ○ *generation gap* **6.** GEOG OPENING BETWEEN

MOUNTAINS a ravine or pass in a mountain range 7. ELEC ENG same as **spark gap** ■ *v* (**gaps, gapping, gapped**) 1. *vti* PRODUCE OR DEVELOP GAP to create a gap or opening in a barrier, or become open or separated by a gap 2. *vt* ELEC ENG ADJUST SPARK PLUG GAP to adjust the gap between the electrodes of a spark plug 3. *vt N England* AGRIC THIN OUT PLANTS to thin out plants to allow others more room to grow (*informal*) ○ *I hate having to gap the carrots.* [14C. < Old Norse, 'chasm'] —**gappy** *adj*

gape /gayp/ *vi* (**gapes, gaping, gaped**) 1. STARE WITH MOUTH OPEN to look at somebody or something in surprise or wonder, usually with an open mouth ○ *He stood gaping at us in disbelief.* 2. OPEN MOUTH to open the mouth wide 3. OPEN INTO GAP to open or split apart with a gap ○ *His wound was gaping open and he was losing blood.* ■ *n* 1. OPEN-MOUTHED STARE a stare of surprise or wonder in which the mouth is wide open 2. OPENING OF MOUTH an opening of the mouth wide, e.g. in surprise or wonder 3. YAWN an opening of the mouth to yawn 4. BIG GAP a wide opening in something 5. ZOOL WIDTH OF OPEN MOUTH the width of the open mouth of an animal [13C. < Old Norse *gapa* 'open the mouth']

SYNONYMS See ***gaze***.

gaping /gáyping/ *adj* wide open and deep ○ *gaping holes in the roof* —**gapingly** *adv*

gap-toothed *adj* having wide spaces between the teeth

gap year *n* a period of time taken off by a student after the completion of secondary education and before starting higher or further education

gar[1] /gaar/ (*plural same* or **gars**) *n* a large primitive freshwater fish with a heavy armour of bony scales and a long toothy jaw. Native to: North and Central America. Family: Lepisosteidae. [Mid-18C. Shortening of GARFISH]

gar[2] /gaar/ (**gars, garring, garred**) *vt Scotland* to make somebody do something (*nonstandard*) [13C. < Old Norse *gera* 'make']

garage /gárraazh, -rij/ *n* 1. BUILDING FOR MOTOR VEHICLES a building for parking or storing one or more motor vehicles 2. ESTABLISHMENT REPAIRING MOTOR VEHICLES an establishment that repairs and often sells motor vehicles, and sometimes sells petrol, diesel, and oil 3. *also* **garage music** MUSIC SOULFUL DANCE MUSIC a style of dance music inspired by disco and combining 4/4 rhythms with vocals, associated with soul music of the 1990s ■ *vt* (**-rages, -raging, -raged**) PUT VEHICLE IN GARAGE to park or store a motor vehicle in a garage [Early 20C. < French < *garer* 'to shelter']

garage sale *n ANZ, N Am* a sale of used or unwanted household items that is held in the garage or drive of the seller's home

Garagum Desert /gárrə gum-/ desert occupying a large proportion of Turkmenistan. Area: 350,000 sq. km/140,000 sq. mi.

garam masala /gaárəm mə saálə/ *n* a mixture of spices used in South Asian cooking to give a hot pungent flavour to a dish [Mid-20C. < Hindi *garam masālā* 'hot spices']

Garamond /gárrə mond/, **Garamond type** *n* a Roman typeface often used in books [Mid-19C. After Claude *Garamond* (1499–1561), French type founder]

~~garantee~~ incorrect spelling of **guarantee**

garb /gaarb/ *n* 1. TYPICAL OUTFIT a particular type of clothing, especially the uniform or typical outfit worn by members of a profession ○ *military garb* 2. APPEARANCE the outward appearance that somebody or something has ○ *The garb of compromise concealed their war plans.* ■ *vt* (**garbs, garbing, garbed**) DRESS SOMEBODY to clothe somebody or yourself in a particular type of clothing [Late 16C. Via obsolete French *garbe* 'elegance' < Italian *garbo*]

garbage /gaárbij/ *n* 1. NONSENSE talk or writing that is worthless nonsense or lies 2. SOMEBODY OR SOMETHING WORTHLESS somebody or something regarded as totally worthless 3. *N Am* DISCARDED WASTE discarded food waste or any other unwanted or useless material 4. COMPUT WORTHLESS DATA inaccurate, useless, or meaningless data in a computer [15C. < Anglo-Norman] —**garbagy** *adj*

garbage bin *n Aus* same as **dustbin**

garbage can *n N Am* HOUSEHOLD same as **dustbin**

garbage collector *n ANZ, N Am* OCCUPATIONS same as **dustman**

garbage disposal *n ANZ, N Am* HOUSEHOLD an electrical device, fitted in a kitchen sink, that grinds up food so that it can go into the waste pipe. UK term **waste disposal**

garbageman /gaárbij man/ (*plural* **-men** /-men/) *n ANZ, N Am* somebody employed to remove rubbish. UK term **dustman**

garbage truck *n ANZ, N Am* a large motor vehicle used to collect and compact waste materials left bagged or in containers outside buildings

garbanzo /gaar bánzō/ (*plural* **-zos**), **garbanzo bean** *n* FOOD same as **chickpea** (sense 1) [Mid-18C. < Spanish]

garble /gaárb'l/ *vt* (**-bles, -bling, -bled**) 1. JUMBLE MEANING OF SOMETHING to confuse a message or information so that it is misleading or unintelligible ○ *He garbled the details, but the outline of the story is clear.* 2. COMMUNICATION SCRAMBLE TRANSMISSION OF SOMETHING to cause the corruption of a transmitted message or signal ○ *The announcement was completely garbled.* ■ *n* COMMUNICATION 1. CONFUSED MESSAGE a confused or corrupted message, piece of information, or signal that is misleading or unintelligible 2. CONFUSING OF MESSAGE the act of confusing or corrupting a message, piece of information, or signal so that it is misleading or unintelligible [15C. Via Italian *garbellare* 'sift' and Arabic *ġarbala* < late Latin *cribellum* 'small sieve' < Latin *cribrum* 'sieve'] —**garbled** *adj*

garbo /gaárbō/ (*plural* **-bos**) *n Aus* a somebody employed to remove rubbish (*slang*) [Mid-20C. < GARBAGE]

Garbo /gaárbō/, **Greta** (1905–90) Swedish-born US film actor, noted for her beauty and reticence. Her films include *Anna Christie* (1930), *Grand Hotel* (1932), *Camille* (1937), and *Ninotchka* (1939). After her retirement in 1941, she lived as a recluse. Born **Gustaffson, Greta**

> 'I never said, "I want to be alone". I only said, "I want to be *left* alone". There is all the difference.'
> [Greta Garbo. Quoted in *Garbo*, John Bainbridge; 1955]

garboard /gaár bawrd/ *n* the continuous band of planking on a ship's hull next to its keel [Early 17C. < obsolete Dutch *gaarboord*]

garbology /gaar bólləji/ *n US* the study of a cultural group by an examination of what it discards [Late 20C. < GARBAGE] —**garbologist** *n*

García Lorca /gaar seé ə-/ ◆ **Lorca, Federico García**

García Márquez /gaar seé ə maár kez/, **Gabriel** (*b.* 1928) Colombian writer. In novels such as *100 Years of Solitude* (1967) and *Love in the Time of Cholera* (1985), he developed a distinctive style of fantasy blended with realism. He won the Nobel Prize in literature (1982). See Cultural note at **solitude**

garçon /gaár son, -soN/ *n* a waiter in a French restaurant or café [Early 17C. < French]

garda /gaárdə/ (*plural* **-daí** /-deé/) *n* a police officer in the Republic of Ireland [See GARDA]

Garda /gaárdə/ *n* the police force of the Republic of Ireland [Early 20C. < Irish, shortening of *Garda Síochána* 'civic guard']

Garda, Lake /gaárdə/ largest lake in Italy and the centre of a major resort region. It is situated in northern Italy, between Brescia and Verona. Area: 370 sq. km/143 sq. mi.

gardaí POLICE plural of **garda**

gardant *adj* HERALDRY another spelling of **guardant**

garden /gaárd'n/ *n* 1. CULTIVATED AREA AROUND HOUSE an area of cultivated land, often with a lawn, situated around, in front of, or behind a house (*often used in the plural in street names*) N Am term **yard**[2] 2. PLANTED AREA OF GROUND a plot of ground where plants such as fruits, vegetables, or flowers are grown 3. PARK a park or recreational area for the public, generally planted with flowers, bushes, and trees (*often used in the plural*) ○ *the botanical gardens* 4. FARMING REGION a fertile well-cultivated region 5. OUTDOOR EATING AND DRINKING ESTABLISHMENT an eating or drinking establishment that serves its patrons outdoors ○ *a beer garden* ■ *adj* 1. RELATING TO GARDEN relating to, produced in, frequenting, or used in a garden 2. ZOOL COMMON of the common or ordinary kind. N Am term **garden-variety** ■ *vi* (**-dens, -dening, -dened**) LOOK AFTER GARDEN to plan or tend a garden [14C. Via Old N French *gardin* < Vulgar Latin *(hortus) gardinus* 'enclosed (garden)'] —**gardener** *n*

CULTURAL NOTE ***The Secret Garden***, a children's story (1911) by Frances Hodgson Burnett. It is the tale of a lonely orphan, Mary Lennox, who is sent to live with her uncle Archibald, a widower whose wife died as a result of a fall from a tree in her beloved garden. In restoring the garden, Mary finds happiness and helps the family recover from its misfortune.

garden apartment *n N Am* 1. same as **garden flat** 2. a block of flats that has a garden or lawn

garden centre *n* a retail establishment that sells plants and gardening equipment

garden city *n* a planned town with landscaped gardens and parks

garden flat *n* a flat, situated on the ground floor or in the basement of a building, with access to a lawn or garden. N Am term **garden apartment**

garden gnome *n* a small statue representing a gnome, used as an ornament in gardens

gardenia /gaar deéni ə/ *n* an evergreen tree or bush with shiny leaves. Flowers: white, fragrant. Native to: Africa, Asia. Genus: *Gardenia*. [Mid-18C. < modern Latin, after Alexander *Garden* (1730–91), Scottish-American naturalist]

gardening /gaárd'ning/ *n* the activity of tending a garden, especially as a profession, task, or hobby

Garden of Eden *n* BIBLE same as **Eden**[1]

Garden of Gethsemane *n* same as **Gethsemane**

garden party *n* a large formal party held in a garden, especially in the grounds of a large house

garden suburb *n* a planned suburb with landscaped gardens and parks

garden-variety *adj N Am* same as **garden** *adj* (sense 2)

garderobe /gaárd rōb/ *n* 1. formerly, a wardrobe or room where clothes were kept 2. formerly, a small toilet consisting of a bench with holes made above a pit, usually built into a wall or projecting from it [14C. < Old French < *garder* 'keep' + *robe* 'robe']

~~gardian~~ incorrect spelling of **guardian**

Gardner /gaárdnər/, **Erle Stanley** (1889–1970) US writer and lawyer. A practising lawyer for about 20 years, he is best known for his fictional lawyer Perry Mason, who appeared in more than 80 of his detective novels.

Gardner, Wayne Michael (*b.* 1959) Australian motorcycle racer. He was the winner of the 1987 world road racing championship.

Gare /gaa/, **Nene** (1919–94) Australian novelist. Her works include the largely autobiographical *A House with Verandahs* (1980) and a collection of short stories entitled *Bend to the Wind* (1978). Her most famous work, *The Fringe Dwellers* (1961), was made into a film in 1986. See Cultural note at **fringe**

Garfield /gaár feeld/, **James A.** (1831–81) 20th president of the United States. A Republican member of the US House of Representatives (1863–80), he was president for only four months (1881) before he was assassinated. Full name **Garfield, James Abram**. See table at **president**

> 'The world's history is a divine poem, of which the history of every nation is a canto, and every man a word.'
> [Attributed to James A. Garfield, *The Meaning of History*, N. Gordon and Joyce Carper; 1991]

garfish /gaár fish/ (*plural* **-fishes** or *same*) *n* 1. a fish that is greenish to dark blue with silvery sides and has elongated jaws with sharp teeth. Native to: temperate European seas. Latin name: *Belone belone*. 2. FISH same as **gar**[1] [15C. < Old English *gār* 'spear'; from the shape of its jaw]

gargantuan /gaar gántyoo ən/ *adj* tremendously large in amount, number, or size [Late 16C. < *Gargantua*, giant hero of *Gargantua* (1534) by François Rabelais]

gargle /gaárg'l/ *v* (**-gles, -gling, -gled**) 1. *vti* CLEANSE MOUTH AND THROAT to rinse or disinfect the mouth and throat by holding liquid in the back of the mouth and stirring it up with air breathed out from the lungs

2. *vi* MAKE GUTTURAL SOUND to make a sound like that made when rinsing the mouth and throat with liquid ■ *n* **1.** MOUTHWASH a liquid used to rinse the mouth and throat **2.** GUTTURAL SOUND a sound like that made when rinsing the mouth and throat with liquid [Early 16C. < French *gargouiller* < Old French *gargouille* 'throat' < Latin *gurgulio* 'gullet']

gargoyle

gargoyle /ga´goyl/ *n* **1.** GROTESQUE DRAINAGE SPOUT a spout in the form of a grotesque animal or human figure that projects from the gutter of a building and is designed to cast rainwater clear of the building **2.** STATUE OF GROTESQUE FIGURE a grotesque carved figure **3.** SOMEBODY LIKE CARVED FIGURE somebody thought to resemble a carved gargoyle (*insult*) [15C. < Old French *gargouille* (see GARGLE)]

garib /ga´arib/ *adj S Asia* having a low income or lacking financial resources [Late 20C. < Hindi]

garibaldi /gárri báwldi/ *n* **1.** *also* **garibaldi biscuit** a flat square biscuit with a central layer of currants **2.** a woman's loose-fitting blouse that imitates the red shirt worn by Giuseppe Garibaldi [Mid-19C. After GARIBALDI]

Garibaldi /gárri báwldi/, **Giuseppe** (1807–82) French-born Italian patriot. He played a leading role in the unification of Italy (1859–61), defeating the rulers of Sicily and Naples at the head of his army, the so-called Red Shirts.

> 'Men, I am getting out of Rome. Anyone who wants to carry on the war against the outsiders, come with me. I can't offer you either honours or wages; I offer you hunger, thirst, forced marches, battles and death. Anyone who loves his country, follow me.'
> [Giuseppe Garibaldi, *Garibaldi*, G. Guerzoni; 1929]

garibaldi biscuit *n* FOOD same as **garibaldi** (sense 1)

Garifuna /gárri fóoná/ (*plural same* or **-nas**) *n* an Afro-Latino people of West African, Carib, and Arawak ancestry who now live on the Caribbean coasts of Guatemala, Belize, Honduras, and Nicaragua. They were passengers on a slave ship that wrecked off St. Vincent, but after being evicted by the British in 1797, resettled on the Central American coast. [Late 20C. < Arawakan] —**Garifuna** *adj*

garish /gáirish/ *adj* **1.** GAUDY crudely showy ○ *a garish outfit* **2.** TOO ORNATE excessively ornate or elaborate ○ *a garish balcony and staircase* **3.** DRESSED TOO BRIGHTLY wearing clothing or make-up that is extremely brightly coloured **4.** TOO BRIGHT excessively bright ○ *a hideous garish yellow* [Mid-16C. Origin ?] —**garishly** *adv* —**garishness** *n*

garland /ga´arlənd/ *n* **1.** FLOWER WREATH a wreath of intertwined flowers or leaves worn as an ornament or as a sign of honour **2.** HANGING FLOWER DECORATION a festoon of flowers or paper hung as decoration **3.** LITERAT LITERARY COLLECTION a collection of short pieces of literature ■ *vt* (-lands, -landing, -landed) PUT GARLAND ON SOMEBODY OR SOMETHING to decorate or adorn somebody or something with garlands [14C. < Old French *garlande*]

Garland /ga´arlənd/, **Judy** (1922–69) US film actor and singer. She starred in films including *The Wizard of Oz* (1939), *Meet Me in St Louis* (1944), and *A Star is Born* (1954), and from the 1950s performed primarily as a singer. Born **Gumm, Frances**

> 'We cast away priceless time in dreams, born of imagination, fed upon illusion, and put to death by reality.'

[Judy Garland. Quoted in *Judy Garland*, Anne Edwards; 1974]

garlic

garlic /ga´arlik/ (*plural same* or **-lics**) *n* **1.** BULB WITH STRONG ODOUR a bulb or clove with a pungent odour and flavour that is commonly used in cooking **2.** STRONG-TASTING PLANT a plant that is the source of garlic. Latin name: *Allium sativum*. **3.** PLANT LIKE GARLIC a plant related to or resembling true garlic [Old English *gārlēac* < *gār* 'spear' + LEEK] —**garlicky** *adj*

garlic bread *n* bread seasoned with butter and garlic and baked or toasted

garlic mustard *n* a hedgerow plant with heart-shaped leaves. Flowers: small, white, with a pungent garlicky smell. Native to: Europe, Asia. Latin name: *Alliaria petiolata*.

garlic press *n* a small kitchen tool, usually made of metal or plastic, that minces a clove of garlic by squeezing it through small holes

garlic salt *n* a preparation of salt and powdered garlic used as a food seasoning

garlic sausage *n* a salami flavoured with garlic

garment /ga´armənt/ *n* a piece of clothing ■ *vt* (-ments, -menting, -mented) to put clothing on somebody (*literary*; *often passive*) [14C. < French *garnement* 'equipment' < *garnir* (see GARNISH)]

garment bag *n* a piece of soft-sided luggage shaped for carrying dresses, suits, or other clothing on hangers

Garmo Peak /ga´armō-/ former name for **Ismail Samani Peak**

garner /ga´arnər/ *vt* (-ners, -nering, -nered) **1.** GATHER IN SOMETHING to gather something into storage or into a granary **2.** WIN OR GAIN SOMETHING to earn or acquire something by effort **3.** GATHER INFORMATION to collect or accumulate something such as information or facts ■ *n* GRANARY a storage place for grain (*archaic*) [12C. Via Anglo-Norman *gerner* 'storehouse' < Latin *granarium* (see GRANARY)]

Garner /ga´arnər/, **Helen** (*b.* 1942) Australian writer. Her works include the novel *Monkey Grip* (1977) and the nonfiction work *The First Stone* (1995).

garnet /ga´arnit/ *n* **1.** a variously coloured crystalline silicate mineral. Source: metamorphic and igneous rocks. Use: gems. **2.** a dark red colour [13C. Probably via Middle Dutch *garnate* < Old French *grenat* 'dark red' < *pome grenate* 'pomegranate', because of its colour] —**garnet** *adj*

garnierite /ga´arni ərīt/ *n* a soft green form of the mineral serpentine consisting of hydrated nickel magnesium silicate. Use: source of nickel. [Late 19C. After Jules *Garnier* (1839?–1904), French geologist]

garnish /ga´arnish/ *vt* (-nishes, -nishing, -nished) **1.** ENHANCE FOOD OR DRINK to add something as an accompaniment to food or drink that enhances its flavour or appearance **2.** EMBELLISH SOMETHING to decorate something with an ornament **3.** LAW same as **garnishee** ○ *garnish wages for child support* ■ *n* **1.** ENHANCEMENT FOR FOOD OR DRINK something added as an accompaniment to food or drink to enhance its flavour or appearance **2.** SOMETHING DECORATIVE an ornament or decoration for something [14C. < French *garniss-*, stem of *garnir* 'equip, adorn, warn' < Germanic] —**garnishing** *n*

garnishee /ga´arni shée/ *vt* (-ees, -eeing, -eed) **1.** CONFISCATE DEBTOR'S MONEY to take the money or property of a debtor by legal authority **2.** SUMMONS DEBTOR to serve somebody with a legal summons concerning the taking of wages or property to satisfy a debt ■

n SUMMONSED DEBTOR somebody who is served with a legal summons stating that wages or property may be taken to satisfy a debt

garnishment /ga´arnishmənt/ *n* **1.** a legal summons or warning concerning the taking of a debtor's property or wages to satisfy a debt **2.** an ornamentation or embellishment on or of something

garniture /ga´arnichər/ *n* something that decorates or embellishes something [15C. < French < *garnir* (see GARNISH)]

Garonne /ga rón/ river in southwestern France. Rising in the Spanish Pyrenees, it flows through Toulouse and Bordeaux before joining the Dordogne at the Gironde estuary. Length: 575 km/357 mi.

garpike /ga´ar pīk/ (*plural* **-pikes** or *same*) *n* FISH **1.** same as **gar**[1] **2.** same as **garfish** (sense 1)

garret /gárrət/ *n* a room at the top of a house, immediately below the roof [15C. < Old French *garite* 'watchtower' < *garir* 'defend' < Germanic, 'protect']

Garrett /gárrət/, **Peter** (*b.* 1953) Australian singer and political activist. He was a founding member of the rock group Midnight Oil (1977) and president of the Australian Conservation Foundation (1989–93, 1998–). Full name **Garrett, Peter Robert**

Garrick /gárrik/, **David** (1717–79) British actor, theatrical manager, and playwright. He brought a new naturalism to the stage in legendary performances, and managed London's Drury Lane Theatre (1747–76).

> 'Prologues precede the piece—in mournful verse; / As undertakers—walk before the hearse.'
> [David Garrick, *Apprentice*, Arthur Murphy; 1756]

garrison /gárriss'n/ *n* **1.** STATIONED TROOPS a body of troops stationed at a military post **2.** PLACE FOR STATIONING TROOPS a military post where troops are stationed ■ *vt* (-sons, -soning, -soned) **1.** SUPPLY PLACE WITH TROOPS to provide a fort or town with a military post and troops **2.** STATION TROOPS AT PLACE to station troops at a military post [13C. < Old French, 'fortification' < *garir* (see GARRET)]

garrotte /gə rót/, **garrote** *n* **1.** WEAPON FOR STRANGULATION a weapon consisting of a wire or cord with handles at each end, used in strangulation **2.** METAL BAND USED IN EXECUTIONS an iron band placed around the neck and tightened in order to execute somebody **3.** EXECUTION BY STRANGULATION a method of execution in which an iron band is tightened around somebody's neck until death occurs ■ *vt* (-rottes, -rotting, -rotted; -rotes, -roting, -roted) KILL SOMEBODY WITH GARROTTE to execute or kill somebody by means of a garrotte [Early 17C. < Spanish *garrote* 'cudgel, stick for tightening a cord']

garrulity /gə roóləti, ga-/ *n* excessive or pointless talkativeness

garrulous /gárrələss, gárryōō-/ *adj* **1.** excessively or pointlessly talkative **2.** using many or too many words [Early 17C. < Latin *garrulus* < *garrire* 'to chatter'] —**garrulously** *adv* —**garrulousness** *n*

SYNONYMS See *talkative*.

garter /ga´artər/ *n* **1.** an elastic band used to hold up a stocking, sock, or shirt sleeve **2.** *N Am* CLOTHING same as **suspender** (sense 1) [14C. < Old French *gartier* < *garet* 'bend of the knee' < Celtic] —**garter** *vt*

Garter *n* **1.** SOC SCI same as **Order of the Garter 2.** the badge that signifies membership of the Order of the Garter **3.** membership of the Order of the Garter

garter belt *n N Am* CLOTHING same as **suspender belt**

garter snake *n* a small nonpoisonous snake whose back is typically marked with yellow or red stripes running the length of the body. Native to: Central and North America. Genus: *Thamnophis*.

garter stitch *n* knitting done in the same stitch, whether knit or purl, for every row [< its use in making garters]

garth /gaarth/ *n* a small courtyard or enclosed space [14C. < Old Norse *garðr*]

Marcus Garvey

Garvey /gaárvi/, **Marcus** (1887–1940) Jamaican-born US civil rights advocate. He founded the Universal Negro Improvement Association (1914) and created a 'Back to Africa' movement in the United States. Full name **Garvey, Marcus Moziah**

'I asked, "Where is the black man's Government?" "Where is his King and his kingdom?" "Where is his President, his country, and his ambassador, his army, his navy, his men of big affairs?" I could not find them, and then I declared, "I will help to make them".'
[Marcus Garvey, 'The Negro's Greatest Enemy'; 1923]

Gary /gárri/ steel-producing city in northwestern Indiana, on the southern shore of Lake Michigan, west of Portage. Population: 100,945 (2002 estimate).

gas /gass/ n (plural **gases** or **gasses**) 1. CHEM SUBSTANCE SUCH AS AIR a substance that is neither a solid nor a liquid at ordinary temperatures and has the ability to expand infinitely, e.g. air 2. INDUST, GEOL FOSSIL FUEL a combustible gaseous substance used as a fuel, e.g. natural gas or coal gas 3. MIL, CRIME GAS FOR POISONING OR ASPHYXIATING a gaseous mixture used as a poison, irritant, or asphyxiating agent 4. PHARM ANAESTHETIC a gaseous substance used as an anaesthetic 5. N Am AUTOMOT PETROL petrol for internal-combustion engines 6. N Am AUTOMOT ACCELERATOR the pedal used for accelerating a motor vehicle (informal) ○ step on the gas 7. N Am PHYSIOL FLATULENCE the gaseous product of digestion (informal) 8. MIN EXTRACT METHANE AND AIR the highly explosive product of methane combined with air 9. SOMEBODY OR SOMETHING ENTERTAINING somebody or something that is very thrilling or entertaining (informal) 10. NONSENSE meaningless empty talk (informal) ■ v (**gases** or **gasses, gassing, gassed**) 1. vt HARM SOMEBODY WITH GAS to attack, injure, or kill a person or animal with a poisonous, irritating, or asphyxiating gas 2. vi RELEASE GAS to give off gas or a gas 3. vi TALK IDLY to talk too much, especially about unimportant matters (informal) [Mid-17C. < Dutch, alteration of Greek khaos 'empty space'] —**gassing** n

gasbag /gáss bag/ n somebody who talks too much, especially about trivial subjects (informal)

gas burner n a nozzle or opening from which gas issues and burns, e.g. on a cooker

gas chamber n a room in which people are killed by means of poisonous gas

gas chromatography n a method of separating the volatile constituents of a substance by means of gas for the purpose of analysis —**gas chromatograph** n

gascon /gásskən/ n a boastful person (archaic) [Late 18C. < Gascons' legendary boastfulness]

Gascon /gásskən/ n 1. somebody who lives in or was born or brought up in Gascony, formerly a province in southwestern France 2. a dialect of French spoken in Gascony [14C. Via French < Latin Vascon-] —**Gascon** adj

gas constant n the constant in an equation that describes the relation of the pressure and volume of a gas to its absolute temperature. It equals 8.314 joules per kelvin. Symbol **R**

gas-cooled reactor n a nuclear reactor that uses carbon dioxide or helium as a coolant

Gascoyne /gáss koyn/ river in northern Western Australia that rises between the Collier and Robinson

ranges and empties into the Indian Ocean at Shark Bay. Length: 760 km/470 mi.

Gascoyne-Cecil /gáss koyn séss'l/, **Robert Arthur Talbot ♦ Salisbury, Robert Arthur Talbot Gascoyne-Cecil**

gas-discharge tube n a tube containing gas from which light is emitted when an electric current is passed through the gas atoms and excites them

gaseous /gássi əss, gáyssi-/ adj 1. RESEMBLING GAS neither solid nor liquid and with a tendency to expand infinitely, as does air 2. CONTAINING GAS full of or containing gas 3. VERBOSE having or using too many words, especially in a meaningless way (informal) [Late 18C. After AQUEOUS] —**gaseousness** n

gas exchange n the transfer of gases between an organism and its environment, e.g. the process by which oxygen enters the body and carbon dioxide is expelled from it via the lungs

gas-fired adj fuelled by gas

gas fitter n a worker who fits and repairs gas pipes, gas fittings, and gas appliances

gas gangrene n a form of gangrene, caused by aerobic clostridia bacteria, in which gas forms in injured body tissue

gas-guzzler n N Am a motor vehicle that burns comparatively large amounts of fuel (informal)

gash /gash/ n a long deep narrow slash or cut [Mid-16C. Alteration of Old N French garser 'to cut', via late Latin charaxare 'sharpen' < Greek kharassein] —**gash** vt

gasholder /gáss hōldər/ n a very large tank used for storing gas that is used as combustible fuel

gasiform /gássi fawrm/ adj CHEM same as **gaseous** (sense 1)

gasify /gássi fī/ (-**fies, -fying, -fied**) vti to convert a solid or liquid into a gas, or become a gas —**gasification** /gássifi káysh'n/ n

gas jet n 1. UTIL same as **gas burner** 2. a flame of burning gas

Gaskell /gásk'l/, **Elizabeth** (1810–65) British novelist. Her novels document social conditions in newly industrialized Britain, and include Mary Barton (1848), Cranford (1853), and North and South (1855). Born **Stevenson, Elizabeth Cleghorn**. Known as **Gaskell, Mrs**

'I'll not listen to reason…Reason always means just what someone else has got to say.'
[Elizabeth Gaskell, Cranford; 1853]

gasket /gáskit/ n 1. a piece of material such as rubber, used to render a joint impermeable to gas or liquid 2. a light line for securing a furled sail [Early 17C. Origin ?]

gaskin /gáskin/ n the part of the back leg of a four-legged hoofed animal, especially a horse, that is equivalent to the lower thigh in humans [Late 16C. Origin ?]

gas law n a law governing the physical behaviour of gases, e.g. Boyle's law or Charles's law

gaslight /gáss līt/ n 1. light produced by burning coal gas or natural gas 2. a lamp or fixture that produces light by burning gas

gas-liquid chromatography n SCI same as **gas chromatography**

gaslit /gásslit/ adj illuminated by light from lamps or fixtures that burn gas

gasman /gáss man/ (plural -**men** /-men/) n a worker who checks gas meters in order to note the amount of gas used in a specific period

gas mark n a mark on the temperature regulator of the oven of a gas cooker, indicating a gradation of heat

gas mask

gas mask n a mask provided with a filter and worn to protect the wearer's face and lungs from harmful gases

gas meter n a device installed inside or outside a residential or commercial building to measure the amount of gas consumed in a specific period

gasohol /gássəhol/ n N Am a fuel used in motor vehicles that consists of 90 per cent petrol blended with 10 per cent alcohol. The alcohol is produced by the fermentation of an agricultural product high in sugar, e.g. corn. [Late 20C. Blend of GASOLINE + ALCOHOL]

gas oil n a light petroleum distillate with a viscosity and boiling point between that of paraffin and lubricating oil. Gas oils include diesel fuel, heating oil, and light fuel oils.

gasoline /gássəleen/ n N Am INDUST same as **petrol**

gasometer /ga sómmitər/ n 1. an apparatus for measuring and storing gas in a laboratory 2. UTIL same as **gasholder**

gasp /gaasp/ v (**gasps, gasping, gasped**) 1. vi BREATHE IN SHARPLY to draw in breath with a sudden short audible intake 2. vi LABOUR TO BREATHE to breathe with laborious effort 3. vt SAY SOMETHING WITH GASP to say something with a sudden short audible intake of breath ■ n 1. SUDDEN INTAKE OF BREATH a sudden short audible intake of breath, e.g. in surprise or pain 2. INSTANCE OF DIFFICULT BREATHING a laborious effort to breathe [14C. < Old Norse geispa 'yawn'] ◇ **be gasping (for something)** to feel a desperate need for a drink or cigarette (informal) ◇ **the last gasp** somebody's final attempt or action, or the final phase of something

Gaspé Peninsula /ga spáy-/ peninsula in southeastern Quebec Province, Canada, bordered by the St Lawrence River, Chaleur Bay, and New Brunswick. Area: 29,500 sq. km/11,400 sq. mi.

gasper /gáaspər/ n a cigarette, especially a cheap one (dated slang)

gas-permeable adj describes a type of contact lens that allows air to pass through it to the eye for added comfort

gas plant n a perennial plant of the rue family with strong-smelling leaves that give off a flammable gas. Flowers: white. Native to: Europe, Asia. Latin name: Dictamnus albus.

gasser /gássər/ n 1. a well that produces natural gas 2. same as **gasbag** (informal)

gas station n N Am COMM same as **petrol station**

gassy /gássi/ (-**sier, -siest**) adj 1. FULL OF GAS full of or containing gas such as carbon dioxide 2. LIKE GAS resembling gas in being neither a solid nor a liquid at ordinary temperatures and able to expand infinitely 3. VERBOSE having or using too many words, especially in a meaningless way (informal) —**gassily** adv —**gassiness** n

gastarbeiter /gást aar bītər/ (plural same or -**ters**), **Gastarbeiter** n an immigrant worker, especially one who came to the former West Germany in the 1960s and 1970s [Mid-20C. < German, 'guest worker']

gastight /gáss tīt/ adj preventing any gas from passing through

gastr- prefix same as **gastro-** (used before vowels)

gastrectomy /ga stréktəmi/ (plural -**mies**) n the surgical removal of all or part of the stomach. It is usually performed in the treatment of stomach cancer or severe stomach ulcers.

gastric /gástrik/ adj 1. OF STOMACH relating to, involving, or near the stomach 2. Aus HAVING UPSET STOMACH having a gastrointestinal illness, usually with diarrhoea and vomiting (informal) ○ Sorry I didn't make it last night. I was a bit gastric. ■ n Aus UPSET STOMACH a gastrointestinal illness, usually with diarrhoea and vomiting (informal) [Mid-17C. < modern Latin gastricus < Greek gastēr 'stomach']

gastric juice n the acidic digestive fluid secreted by glands in the stomach

gastric ulcer n an erosion in the stomach wall caused by gastric acid, digestive enzymes, or other factors that may include bacterial infection

gastrin /gástrin/ n a hormone produced in the stomach that increases the release of gastric juice

gastritis /ga strítiss/ *n* inflammation of the mucous membrane that lines the stomach

gastro- *prefix* stomach, belly ○ *gastrectomy* [< Greek *gastr-*, stem of *gastēr* 'stomach' (see GASTRIC)]

gastrocnemius /gásstrok neˈemi əss, -trək-/ (*plural* **-mii** /-mi ī/) *n* the largest muscle in the calf of the leg, extending from the thigh bone to the Achilles tendon. When it contracts, it causes the foot to point downwards. [Late 17C. Via modern Latin < Greek *gastroknēmia* 'calf of the leg' < *gastēr* 'stomach'; from its bulging form]

gastrodermis /gástrō dúrmiss/ *n* the inner lining of the body cavity of a cnidarian, forming a surface for the absorption of food

gastroduodenostomy /gástrō dyoō ō dee nóstəmi/ (*plural* **-mies**) *n* a surgical operation in which the duodenum is joined to an opening made in the stomach wall to bypass an obstruction or narrowing in the stomach outlet

gastroenteritis /gástrō entə rítiss/ *n* inflammation of the stomach and the intestines, with vomiting and diarrhoea, usually as a result of bacterial or viral infection

gastroenterology /gástrō entə rólləji/ *n* the branch of medicine concerned with the study and treatment of diseases of the stomach and intestines and their associated organs —**gastroenterologic** /-éntərə lójjik/ *adj* —**gastroenterologist** *n*

gastroesophageal reflux disease /gástrō i sóffə jeˈe əl-/ *n* the chronic reflux of stomach contents into the oesophagus, resulting in heartburn

gastrointestinal /gástrō in téstinəl/ *adj* relating to the stomach and intestines

gastrolith /gástrō lith/ *n* 1. a stone swallowed by an animal such as a bird or dinosaur as an aid to the digestion of food 2. a stone that has formed in the stomach

gastrology /ga strólləji/ *n* the study of the stomach and its diseases —**gastrologic** /gástrə lójjik/ *adj* —**gastrological** *adj* —**gastrologically** *adv* —**gastrologist** *n*

gastronome /gástrənōm/, **gastronomist** /ga strónnəmist/ *n* a connoisseur of good food [Early 19C. < French, back-formation < *gastronomie* (see GASTRONOMY)]

gastronomy /ga strónnəmi/ (*plural* **-mies**) *n* 1. the art and appreciation of preparing and eating good food 2. a particular style of cooking or dining, e.g. one that is characteristic of a particular country or region [Early 19C. Via French *gastronomie* < Greek *gastronomia*, alteration of *gastrologia* 'study of the stomach'] —**gastronomic** /gástrə nómmik/ *adj* —**gastronomically** *adv*

gastroplasty /ga stróppləsti/ (*plural* **-ties**) *n* a surgical operation to repair a malformation of the stomach

gastropod /gástrə pod/ *n* a mollusc that has a head with eyes, a large flattened foot, and often a single shell, e.g. a limpet, snail, or slug. Class: Gastropoda. [Early 19C. < modern Latin *Gastropoda* 'stomach-foot'] —**gastropod** *adj* —**gastropodan** /ga stróppədən/ *adj* —**gastropodous** /ga stróppədəss/ *adj*

gastropub /gástrō pub/ *n* a pub that serves good-quality food [Late 20C. < GASTRONOMY]

gastroscope /gástrə skōp/ *n* an instrument passed through the mouth and used to examine the stomach, consisting of a flexible tube that contains optical fibres coupled to an eyepiece and light source —**gastroscopic** /gástrə skóppik/ *adj* —**gastroscopy** /ga stróskəpi/ *n*

gastrostomy /ga stróstəmi/ (*plural* **-mies**) *n* a surgical operation in which an opening for a tube is made through the wall of the stomach and joined to an opening in the adjacent abdominal wall. It allows food and liquids to be placed directly into the stomach via a tube when the oesophagus is affected by disease or recovering from surgery.

gastrotomy /ga stróttəmi/ (*plural* **-mies**) *n* a surgical incision into the stomach for examination of the cavity or to remove a foreign object

gastrovascular /gástrō váskyoōlər/ *adj* describes a part of the body involved in both digestion and circulation, e.g. the central body cavity of some jellyfish

gastrula /gástroōlə/ (*plural* **-las** or **-lae** /-lee/) *n* the stage in embryonic development after the blastula during which the embryo develops two layers [Late 19C. < modern Latin, 'little stomach' < Greek *gastēr* 'stomach'] —**gastrular** *adj*

gastrulation /gástrōō láysh'n/ *n* the process of cell movements by which a developing embryo forms distinct layers that later grow into different organs —**gastrulate** *vi*

gas turbine *n* an internal-combustion engine in which a turbine is turned by hot gases consisting of compressed air and the products of the fuel's combustion

gasworks /gáss wurks/ (*plural same*) *n* a factory where gas for heating and illuminating is produced, especially from coal

gat¹ /gat/ *n* a passage or channel of water that extends inland from a shore [Late 16C. Probably < Old Norse *gat* 'hole']

gat² /gat/ *n* same as **handgun** (*dated slang*) [Early 20C. Shortening of GATLING GUN]

gat³ /gat/ past tense of **get**¹ (*archaic*)

gate /gayt/ *n* 1. BARRIER ACROSS GAP a movable barrier, usually on hinges, that closes a gap in a fence or wall 2. OPENING IN WALL an opening in a wall or fence 3. OPENING IN DEFENSIVE STRUCTURE an opening in a castle or city wall or other defensive structure 4. POINT OF ACCESS a means of access or entrance 5. ARRIVAL OR DEPARTURE POINT the area at an airport where passengers arrive and depart 6. BARRIER AT TOLLBOOTH a movable barrier restricting access, e.g. at a tollbooth 7. same as **starting gate** (sense 1) (*informal*) 8. BARRIER FOR FLUID a sliding barrier, valve, or other mechanism for regulating the passage of a fluid 9. SPECTATORS the total number of people who pay for admission to an entertainment or sporting event 10. MONEY FROM TICKETS the total amount of money paid for tickets for an entertainment or sporting event 11. SKIING PATH BETWEEN POLES the space between two markers through which a skier passes in a slalom race 12. COMPUT LOGIC CIRCUIT a logical device in a computer, with one output channel and one or more input channels, that emits a signal only when specific input conditions are met 13. ELECTRONICS REGULATING SWITCH an electronic switch that regulates the flow of current in a circuit 14. ROWING FASTENING FOR OAR a fastening with a hinge that serves to keep an oar in its rowlock 15. *N England, Scotland* WAY a path or road 16. *N England, Scotland* HABIT a habitual method or style of doing something ■ *vt* (**gates**, **gating**, **gated**) 1. CONFINE STUDENT TO SCHOOL GROUNDS to punish a student by confining him or her to the school or college grounds 2. CONTROL SOMETHING USING GATE to control or regulate somebody or something with a gate 3. PUT GATE IN SOMETHING to install a gate in something, e.g. in a fence [Old English *geat* < Germanic, 'opening in a wall'. Partly < Old Norse *gata* 'path']

SPELLCHECK See *gait*.

REGIONAL NOTE Gate can be used to mean 'a way, road, path', a fact illustrated by the many streets in the north of England with names such as *Broadgate*, *Cannongate*, *Stonegate*, and *Swinegate*. The /g/ pronunciation is due to Viking influence. The poet W. B. Yeats would have been called 'Gates' if his ancestors had been northerners.

-gate *suffix* political scandal [< WATERGATE]

gateau /gáttō/ (*plural* **-teaux** /-tōz/), **gâteau** (*plural* **-teaux** /gáttō/) *n* 1. a rich cake, usually consisting of several layers held together with a cream filling 2. savoury food baked and served in a form resembling a cake [Mid-19C. < French, 'cake']

gatecrasher /gáyt krashər/ *n* somebody who attends a party or other event without an invitation or ticket —**gatecrash** *vti*

gatefold /gáyt fōld/ *n* a page in a publication that is larger than the other pages and is folded to fit

gatehouse /gáyt howss/ (*plural* **-houses** /-howziz/) *n* a building or house above or beside a gate

gatekeeper /gáyt keepər/ *n* 1. a supervisor or guard who tends a gate 2. a person or group that controls access to somebody or something —**gatekeeping** *n*

gateleg table /gáyt leg-/ *n* a drop-leaf table with movable legs that swing out to support the leaves

gate money *n* LEISURE, SPORTS same as **gate** *n* (sense 10)

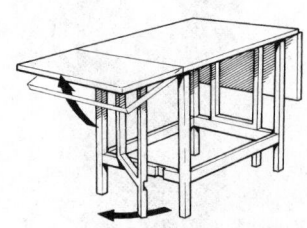

gateleg table

gatepost /gáyt pōst/ *n* one of the posts on each side of a gate. One post supports the gate and the gate closes against and is fastened to the other.

gater, 'gater *n* US REPT another spelling of **gator** (*informal*)

Gates /gayts/, **William Henry III** (*b.* 1955) US business executive. He is chief software architect and chairman of Microsoft Corporation, a leading software company, which he cofounded in 1975. He is also the author of *The Road Ahead* (1995) and *Business @ the Speed of Thought* (1999). Known as **Bill Gates**

> 'Technology is just a tool. In terms of getting the kids working together and motivating them, the teacher is the most important.'
> [William Henry Gates III, 'For the Record', *Independent on Sunday*; 12 October 1997]

Gateshead /gáyts hed/ industrial town in County Durham, northeastern England. Population: 191,151 (2001).

Gates of the Arctic National Park and Preserve national park consisting mainly of tundra in northern Alaska, north of the Arctic Circle. Area: 34,287 sq. km/13,238 sq. mi.

gateway /gáyt way/ *n* 1. OPENING WITH GATE an opening that may be closed by a gate 2. ACCESS POINT a means of access to something ○ *the gateway to educational success* 3. COMPUT COMPUTER-NETWORK CONNECTION software or hardware that links two computer networks 4. COMPUT NETWORK ENTRY POINT an entry point to a computer network

gateway drug *n* a drug that does not cause physical dependence but may lead to the use of addictive drugs

gateway page *n* the initial webpage that a visitor to a website sees and that contains key words and phrases that enable a search engine to find it

gather /gáthər/ *v* (**-ers**, **-ering**, **-ered**) 1. *vti* FORM INTO GROUP to bring people or things together to form a group, or come together to form a group 2. *vt* HARVEST SOMETHING to pick or harvest a crop 3. *vt* COLLECT DATA to compile something such as information or ideas from various sources 4. *vt* ATTRACT FOLLOWING to attract a group of people as supporters, followers, or an audience ○ *The street players have gathered quite a crowd.* 5. *vti* ACCUMULATE SOMETHING to accumulate a gradually increasing mass or quantity of something, or be accumulated gradually ○ *Clouds gathered on the horizon.* 6. *vt* FIND INNER STRENGTH to summon up energies, courage, or strength from within 7. *vt* SURMISE SOMETHING to conclude something from intuition or observation 8. *vt* BRING SOMEBODY OR SOMETHING CLOSE to draw somebody or something close 9. *vt* LIFT SOMEBODY OR SOMETHING UP to pick or scoop somebody or something up 10. *vti* WRINKLE BROW to draw the brow into wrinkles, or be drawn into wrinkles 11. *vt* PULL FABRIC TOGETHER to draw fabric together in a series of folds along a line of stitching 12. *vt* PRINTING PUT PAGES IN ORDER to assemble the printed sections of a book in the correct order for binding 13. *vt* GLASS PREPARE MOLTEN GLASS FOR BLOWING to collect molten glass at the end of a tube for blowing and shaping 14. *vi* MED FORM PUS-FILLED HEAD to form and fill with pus ■ *n* 1. FOLD IN FABRIC one in a series of folds in fabric 2. GLASS MOLTEN GLASS BALL a ball of molten glass collected on a tube for blowing and shaping [Old English *gaderian* < Indo-European, 'bring together'] —**gatherer** *n*

SYNONYMS See ***collect***[1].

gathering /gáthəring/ *n* **1. ASSEMBLY** a meeting or crowd of people **2. CLUSTER OF THINGS** a collection of objects **3. COLLECTING OF SOMETHING** the collecting of people or objects into a group **4. FOLDS IN CLOTH** a series of folds in fabric **5.** MED **BOIL** a pus-filled swelling

gathering stitch *n* a line of running stitches sewn with a single length of thread that can be pulled up to form gathers in the fabric

Gatling gun /gátling-/ *n* an early machine gun with multiple barrels firing in rotation [Mid-19C. After R. J. *Gatling* (1818–1903), US inventor]

gator /gáytər/, **'gator, gater, 'gater** *n US* same as **alligator** (sense 1) (*informal*) [Mid-19C. Shortening]

GATT /gat/, **Gatt** *abbr* General Agreement on Tariffs and Trade

Gatún, Lake /gə tóon/ artificial lake on the Chagres River in Panama. It is an important part of the Panama Canal system. Area: 430 sq. km/170 sq. mi.

gatvol /khát fawl/ *adj S Africa* extremely displeased or fed up (*slang*) [Late 20C < Afrikaans]

Gatwick /gátwik/ London's second largest international airport, located to the south of the city on the border between the counties of Surrey and Sussex

gauche /gōsh/ *adj* lacking grace or tact in social situations [Mid-18C. < French, 'left-handed'] —**gauchely** *adv* —**gaucheness** *n*

Gaucher disease /gōshay-/ *n* a genetic metabolic disorder in which a fatty substance accumulates in the body, especially the spleen, liver, lungs, and bone marrow. The disorder is characterized by bruising, fatigue, anaemia, low blood platelets, and enlargement of the liver and spleen. [Mid-20C. After P. C. E. *Gaucher* (1854–1918), French physician]

gaucherie /gōshəri, -rée/ *n* **1.** a lack of grace or tact in social situations **2.** an act that is graceless or tactless [Late 18C. < French, < *gauche* 'left-handed']

gaucho /gówchō/ (*plural* **-chos**) *n* a cowboy of the South American pampas or prairie [Early 19C. < American Spanish]

gaud /gawd/ *n* a showy trinket or ornament (*archaic*) [14C. Origin ?]

gaudery /gáwdəri/ (*plural* **-ies**) *n* showy and ostentatious clothing or jewellery, or its display

Gaudí /gow dée/, **Antoni** (1852–1926) Spanish architect. His individual and unconventional style of architecture is typified in the unfinished Church of the Sagrada Família (1883) in Barcelona. He was a leading exponent of the Catalan branch of art nouveau, 'modernisme'. Full name **Gaudí i Cornet, Antoni Plàcid**

gaudy[1] /gáwdi/ (**-ier, -iest**) *adj* brightly coloured or showily decorated to an unpleasant or vulgar degree [15C. < GAUD] —**gaudily** *adv* —**gaudiness** *n*

gaudy[2] /gáwdi/ (*plural* **-ies**) *n* an annual celebration or dinner held at some universities and university colleges [Mid-16C. < Latin *gaudium* 'joy' < *gaudere* 'rejoice']

gauffer *vt, n* HAIR another spelling of **goffer**

gauge /gayj/, **gage** *vt* (**gauges, gauging, gauged; gages, gaging, gaged**) **1. CALCULATE SOMETHING** to determine the amount, quantity, size, or extent of something ○ *It's quite difficult to gauge the distance accurately.* **2. EVALUATE SOMETHING** to form a judgment of something uncertain or variable, especially somebody's behaviour, feelings, or abilities ○ *Try to gauge his mood before launching the proposal.* **3. ENSURE CONFORMITY TO STANDARD** to ensure that something conforms to a standard of measurement ■ *n* **1. MEASURING DEVICE** a device or instrument for measuring an amount or quantity or for testing accuracy **2. MEASUREMENT** a standard measurement or scale of measurement **3. CRITERION** a standard or system of measurement for assessing somebody or something ○ *a gauge of the applicant's ability* **4. DISTANCE BETWEEN RAILS** the distance between the two rails of a railway track or tramway **5. DISTANCE BETWEEN WHEELS** the distance between two wheels on an axle of a vehicle **6. THICKNESS OF WIRE** the diameter of something, especially of wire or a needle **7. THICKNESS OF MATERIAL** the thickness of a thin material such as sheet metal or plastic film **8.** ARMS **DIAMETER INSIDE GUN BARREL** the diameter of the inside of a gun barrel, especially a shotgun barrel **9.** NAUT **RELATIVE POSITION** the position of a ship in relation to another vessel and the wind **10.** TEXTILES **FINENESS OF KNIT** the fineness of knitted fabric expressed in terms of the number of loops for each unit of width **11.** CONSTR **ADDED PROPORTION OF PLASTER OF PARIS** the proportion of plaster of Paris that is added to mortar to speed up the setting of the mixture [14C. < Old N French, variant of French *jauge*] —**gaugeable** *adj*

gauger /gáyjər/ *n* **1.** a customs officer whose job is to inspect bulk goods on which duty is supposed to be paid **2.** a person who or instrument that gauges something

gauge theory *n* a theory describing the interactions between elementary particles by considering particles to be quantized fields

Gauguin /gō gaN/, **Paul** (1848–1903) French painter. One of the most influential postimpressionist painters, he is known for his use of flat fields of deep colour. After 1891 he lived mostly in Polynesia, the inspiration for many of his most powerful works. Full name **Gauguin, Eugène Henri Paul**

Gauhati /gow haáti/ industrial city and port on the River Brahmaputra in Assam State, northeastern India. Population: 814,575 (2001).

Gaul /gawl/ *n* **1. ANCIENT FRANCE** an ancient region of western Europe that included large portions of France, Belgium, and neighbouring parts of Italy, the Netherlands, and Germany. It was invaded and conquered by the Romans before 100 BC and again in the Gallic Wars of 58–51 BC under Julius Caesar. **2. SOMEBODY FROM GAUL** somebody who came from ancient Gaul **3. FRENCH PERSON** somebody who is French [15C. < Latin *Gallus*]

gauleiter /gów lītər/, **Gauleiter** *n* **1.** a political head of a district in Nazi Germany **2.** a local official who behaves in a dictatorial manner (*informal insult*) [Mid-20C. < German < *Gau* 'administrative district' + *Leiter* 'leader']

Gaulish /gáwlish/ *n* an extinct Celtic language spoken in Gaul before the Roman conquest ■ *adj* relating to ancient Gaul, or its people, language, or culture

Gaulle ♦ **de Gaulle, Charles**

Gaullism /gōl izəm/ *n* **1.** the nationalist and conservative principles and policies of General Charles de Gaulle, leader of France after World War II, and his followers **2.** the political movement founded on the principles of Charles de Gaulle

Gaullist /gōlist/ *n* a supporter of Gaullism or de Gaulle ■ *adj* relating to, associated with, or supporting Gaullism or de Gaulle

gault /gawlt/ *n* a heavy dense clay or soil high in clay content, especially the material of a series of clay and marl beds in southern England [Late 16C. Origin ?]

gaunt /gawnt/ *adj* **1.** extremely thin and bony in appearance **2.** stark in outline or appearance [15C. Origin ?] —**gauntly** *adv* —**gauntness** *n*

gauntlet[1] /gáwntlət/ *n* a glove with a long wide cuff that covers and protects part of the forearm [15C. < French *gantelet* 'little glove' < *gant* 'glove' < Germanic] ◇ **throw down the gauntlet** to issue a challenge

gauntlet[2] /gáwntlət/ *n* a punishment formerly used in the military in which somebody was forced to run between two lines of men armed with weapons who beat him as he passed [Mid-17C. Alteration, influenced by GAUNTLET[1], of *gantlop* < Swedish *gatlopp* 'passageway'] ◇ **run the gauntlet** to endure attack or criticism from all sides

gaur /gów ər/ *n* a large wild ox with a dark coat. Native to: mountains of southeastern Asia. Latin name: *Bos gaurus.* [Early 19C. < Sanskrit *gaura* < Indo-European]

~~**gaurd**~~ incorrect spelling of **guard**

Gause's principle /gówziz-/, **Gause principle** /gáwz-/ *n* ECOL same as **competitive exclusion** [After G. F. *Gause* (1910–), Russian biologist]

gauss /gowss/ (*plural same*) *n* the cgs unit of magnetic flux density, equivalent to 10^{-4} tesla [Late 19C. After Karl Friedrich *Gauss* (1777–1855), German mathematician]

Gaussian /gówssi ən/ *adj* relating to or formulated by Karl Friedrich Gauss, especially statistically normal [Late 19C. After Karl Friedrich *Gauss* (see GAUSS)]

Gaussian curve *n* STATS same as **normal curve**

Gaussian distribution *n* STATS same as **normal distribution**

Gauteng /khow téng/ province in South Africa, in the north-central part of the country. Capital: Johannesburg. Population: 8,837,157 (2001). Area: 17,010 sq. km/6,568 sq. mi.

Gautier /gō tyay/, **Théophile** (1811–72) French writer. His works include the novel *Mademoiselle de Maupin* (1835) and the verse collection *Émaux et camées* (1852).

> 'Everything passes. Robust art alone is eternal, the bust survives the city.'
> [Théophile Gautier, 'L'Art'; 1857]

gauze /gawz/ *n* **1. FINELY WOVEN FABRIC** a thin, almost transparent, loosely woven cotton or silk cloth. Use: curtains, clothes. **2. SURGICAL DRESSING** a dressing for wounds made of loosely woven material such as cotton **3. WIRE MESH** a thin mesh made of wire or other material **4. PIECE OF WIRE MESH** a piece of wire gauze used as a screen or filter in something such as a smoker's pipe **5. HAZE** a fine haze or mist [Mid-16C. < French *gaze*] —**gauzily** *adv* —**gauzy** *adj*

gavage /gáv aazh/ *n* the feeding of an animal or a person through a tube passed into the stomach [Late 19C. < French < *gaver* 'stuff down the throat']

gave past tense of **give**

gavel /gávv'l/ *n* a small hammer used by an auctioneer, a judge, or chair of a meeting to draw people's attention or to mark the conclusion of a transaction ■ *vti* (**-els, -elling, -elled**) to use a gavel to bring an end to something or to stop discussion [Early 19C. Origin ?]

gavial /gáyvi əl/ *n Aus, US* a large reptile resembling a crocodile that has a very long narrow snout and feeds on fish and frogs. Native to: India, Borneo, Sumatra. Latin name: *Gavialis gangeticus.* UK, NZ, Can term **gharial** [Early 19C. Via French < Hindi *ghariyāl*]

Gävle /yévvlə/ port and capital of the county of Gävleborg, eastern Sweden, north of Stockholm. Population: 90,308 (1998).

gavotte /gə vót/ *n* **1.** a French country dance in 4/4 time, popular in the 18th century **2.** the music for a gavotte [Late 19C. Via French < Provençal *Gavot* 'inhabitant of the Alps']

Gawain /gaáwayn/ *n* in Arthurian legend, a knight who was the enemy of Sir Lancelot and who fought a mysterious green knight

Gawd /gawd/, **gawd** *interj, n* God, used to suggest irony in oaths (*slang*)

gawk /gawk/ *vi* (**gawks, gawking, gawked**) to stare stupidly or rudely (*informal*) ■ *n* somebody regarded as awkward or clumsy (*dated insult*) [Late 17C. Origin ?]

SYNONYMS See ***gaze.***

gawky /gáwki/ (**-ier, -iest**) *adj* awkward and clumsy, often because of being tall and not well coordinated (*informal*) —**gawkily** *adv* —**gawkiness** *n*

Gawler /gáwlər/ town in southern South Australia. It is an agricultural centre and a dormitory suburb of Adelaide. Population: 18,657 (2002 estimate).

gawp /gawp/ (**gawps, gawping, gawped**) *vi* to stare stupidly or rudely (*informal*) ○ *Don't just stand there gawping, help her!* [Late 17C. Origin ?]

SYNONYMS See ***gaze.***

gay /gay/ *adj* **1. ATTRACTED TO SAME SEX** relating to sexual attraction or activity among members of the same sex **2. MERRY** full of light-heartedness and merriment (*dated*) **3. BRIGHT IN COLOUR** brightly coloured (*dated*) **4. CAREFREE** having or showing a carefree spirit (*dated*) **5. DEBAUCHED** leading a debauched or dissolute life (*dated*) ■ *n* **GAY MAN OR LESBIAN** somebody, especially a man, who is attracted to other members of the same sex [13C. < Old French *gai* 'happy'] —**gayness** *n*

USAGE ***Gay*** is preferred to *homosexual*. The adjective ***gay*** encompasses both men and women, but when there is a need to specify both genders, as in *gay and lesbian alliances*, ***gay*** describes men. Avoid using ***gay*** as a noun, as in *He's a gay* and *Four gays walked in*, because it can be taken to be offensive. Preferred substitutes are *He is gay* and *Four gay people/men/women walked in.*

Gay /gay/, **John** (1685–1732) English poet and dramatist. He is best known for *The Beggar's Opera* (1728), a ballad opera combining burlesque and political satire.

> 'Tis a gross error, held in schools, / That Fortune always favours fools.'
> [John Gay, 'Pan and Fortune', *Fables*; 1727]

gayal /gə yál/ (*plural same* or **-yals**) *n* a wild or semidomesticated ox with a dark coat and white leg markings. Native to: South Asia, Myanmar. Latin name: *Bos frontalis*. [Late 18C. < Bengali]

gaydar /gáy daar/ *n* the supposed instinctive ability of gay people to identify others who are also gay (*informal*) [Blend of GAY + RADAR]

Marvin Gaye

Gaye /gay/, **Marvin** (1939–84) US singer and songwriter. He was one of the most successful soul singers from the 1960s and had an international bestselling hit with 'I Heard It Through the Grapevine' (1968).

Gay-Lussac's law /gay loóssaks-/ *n* the principle that when gases combine in a chemical reaction they do so in simple ratios of their volumes, and that any gaseous product is also produced in a simple ratio [Early 19C. After Joseph-Louis *Gay-Lussac* (1778–1850), French physicist]

gay pride *n* a movement that encourages gay people to be open and proud about their homosexuality (*informal*)

gay rights *npl* civil rights for gay people, particularly the right to be treated without discrimination both legally and socially (*informal*)

gaz. *abbr* **1.** MEDIA gazette **2.** PUBL gazetteer

Gaza /gáazə/ seaport and principal city of the Gaza Strip, on the Mediterranean coast. An important city in biblical times, it has both historical and current political significance. Population: 353,632 (1997).

gazar /gə záar/ *n* a stiff loosely woven silk [Mid-20C. Origin ?]

Gaza Strip region on the eastern Mediterranean coast bordered on the south by Egypt and on the east and north by Israel. Administered by Egypt from 1949 and Israel from 1967, it became an autonomous zone under the control of the Palestinian National Authority in 1994. The city of Gaza is the region's administrative centre. Population: 1,274,868 (2003). Area: 378 sq. km/146 sq. mi.

gaze /gayz/ *vi* (**gazes**, **gazing**, **gazed**) to look for a long time with unwavering attention ○ *He gazed longingly at the yacht.* ■ *n* a long steady look or stare [14C. Origin ?] —**gazer** *n*

SYNONYMS *gaze, gape, gawk, gawp, ogle, rubberneck, stare*

CORE MEANING: to look at somebody or something steadily or at length

gaze to look for a long time with unwavering attention ○ *He gazed into her eyes.* ○ *People stood around gazing up at the departure and arrival boards.* **gape** to look at somebody or something in surprise or wonder, usually with an open mouth ○ *The boys of sixteen and seventeen gaped at Lily as if she were a goddess.* ○ *Francis gaped – he just couldn't comprehend what he was seeing.* **gawk** or **gawp** (*informal*) to stare stupidly or rudely ○ *Hundreds of people crowded around, gawking at the sculpture.* ○ *He gawped at me as if I'd told him to swim the Atlantic.* **ogle** to look at somebody for sexual enjoyment or as a way of showing sexual interest ○ *lines of eyes, peeping and ogling* ○ *ogled the girls' legs* **rubberneck** (*informal*) to stare at somebody

---

or something in an excessively inquisitive or insensitive way ○ *One passer-by crashed his motorbike rubbernecking while driving by.* ○ *Rubbernecking motorists slowed to gape at the wreckage.* **stare** to look at somebody or something directly and intently without moving the eyes away, often as a result of curiosity or surprise, or to express rudeness or defiance ○ *He halted on the threshold and stared in astonishment at the collection of memorabilia that littered every surface.* ○ *He stared coldly at his father for a moment and then left the room.*

---

gazebo /gə zeéb ō/ (*plural* **-bos** or **-boes**) *n* **1.** a small, usually open-sided and slightly elevated building, situated in a spot that commands a good view **2.** a lightweight freestanding open-sided canopy for use in a garden, usually as a sunshade [Mid-18C. Origin ?]

gazelle

gazelle /gə zél/ (*plural* **-zelles** or *same*) *n* a small graceful swift antelope with long ringed horns and black face markings. Native to: plains of Africa and Asia. Genera: *Gazella* or *Procapra*. [Early 17C. < Old French *gazel*]

gazette /gə zét/ *n* **1.** NEWSPAPER a newspaper, especially a local newspaper or the official paper of an organization ○ *the South London Gazette* **2.** PUBLICATION WITH OFFICIAL NEWS an official publication in which government appointments, public notices, lists of bankruptcies, and other items appear ○ *the Court Gazette* ■ *vt* (**-zettes, -zetting, -zetted**) PUBLISH SOMETHING IN GAZETTE to publish or announce something or name somebody in a gazette (*often passive*) [Early 17C. Directly or via French < Italian *gazzetta* < Venetian dialect *gazeta de la novità* 'pennyworth of news']

gazetteer /gázzə teér/ *n* a dictionary or index of places, usually with descriptive or statistical information

gazillion /gə zíllyən/ *n* an extremely large number or quantity (*slang*) [Late 20C. < *Gaz-*, origin ? + MILLION or BILLION]

gazpacho /gəss páach ō/ *n* a chilled soup based on stock or tomato juice and containing chopped raw vegetables and seasoning [Early 19C. < Spanish]

gazump /gə zúmp/ (**-zumps, -zumping, -zumped**) *vt* (*informal*) **1.** to reject a previously agreed offer to buy a property after receiving a better offer from another buyer ○ *We've been gazumped!* **2.** to subject somebody to a swindle [Early 20C. Origin ?] —**gazump** *n* —**gazumper** *n*

gazunder /gə zúndər/ (**-ers, -ering, -ered**) *vt* to put pressure on a seller of property by lowering an offer that has already been agreed (*informal*) [Late 20C. Blend of GAZUMP + UNDER] —**gazunderer** *n*

GB *abbr* **1.** PHYS gilbert **2.** Great Britain

GBE *abbr* Knight or Dame Grand Cross of the Order of the British Empire

GBH *abbr* grievous bodily harm

GBLT *abbr* gay, bisexual, lesbian, transgender

Gbyte *abbr* COMPUT gigabyte

Gc *abbr* PHYS gigacycle

GC *abbr* George Cross

GCB *abbr* Knight or Dame Grand Cross of the Order of the Bath

GCE *n* an examination for secondary-school pupils in England and Wales at Advanced level (**A level**) and formerly at Ordinary level (**O level**), set and marked by various independent examination

---

boards. At Ordinary level it has been replaced by the GCSE. Full form **General Certificate of Education**

GCH *abbr* gas central heating

GCHQ *abbr* Government Communications Headquarters

G clef *n* MUSIC same as **treble clef**

GCMG *abbr* Grand Cross of the Order of St Michael and St George

GCS *abbr* MED Glasgow coma scale

GCSE *n* an examination for 16-year-olds in England and Wales that includes coursework assessment by individual schools as well as examination by independent boards. It was formed from a combination of the General Certificate of Education O level and the Certificate of Secondary Education. Full form **General Certificate of Secondary Education**

GCVO *abbr* Grand Cross of the Victorian Order

gd *abbr* Grenada (*used in Internet addresses*) See table at **domain name**

Gd *symbol* CHEM ELEM gadolinium

GD&WVVF *abbr* ONLINE grinning, ducking, and walking very very fast (*used in e-mails*)

Gdansk /gə dánsk/ city, seaport, and shipbuilding centre in northern Poland. It is situated at the mouth of the River Vistula, on the Baltic Sea. Population: 461,300 (1997). German name **Danzig**

g'day /gə dáy/ *interj* Aus hello or good day (*informal*) [Contraction]

GDI *abbr* COMPUT graphics device interface

Gdns *abbr* Gardens (*used in addresses*)

GDP *abbr* COMM gross domestic product

GDR *abbr* **1.** HIST German Democratic Republic **2.** ONLINE grinning, ducking, and running (*used in e-mails*)

Gdynia /gə dínnyə/ seaport and city on the Gulf of Gdansk, northern Poland. Population: 251,600 (1997).

ge *abbr* Georgia (*used in Internet addresses*) See table at **domain name**

Ge *symbol* CHEM ELEM germanium

ge- *prefix* same as **geo-** (*used before vowels*)

gean /geen/ *n* **1.** same as **sweet cherry 2.** Scotland same as **wild cherry** [Mid-16C. < Old French *guine*]

geanticline /jee ánti klīn/ *n* a large region of rock raised up from the Earth's surface [Late 19C. < Greek *gē* 'earth'] —**geanticlinal** /jee ánti klīn'l/ *adj*

gear /geer/ *n* **1.** FIXED TRANSMISSION SETTING one of several fixed transmission settings in a vehicle that determine power or direction **2.** TOOTHED PART THAT TRANSMITS MOTION a toothed mechanical part, e.g. a wheel or cylinder, that engages with a similar toothed part to transmit motion from one rotating body to another **3.** SET OF PARTS TO TRANSMIT MOTION a unit of a mechanism that transmits motion from one part to another part for performing a particular function ○ *steering gear* **4.** ENGAGED STATE the state of a vehicle when one of its gears is engaged ○ *The car won't start when it's in gear.* **5.** LEVEL OF EFFICIENCY the particular speed or efficiency with which somebody works (*informal*) ○ *I feel as if I'm still in first gear.* **6.** MACHINERY a piece or system of machinery with a particular function **7.** EQUIPMENT the equipment that is needed for a particular activity (*informal*) ○ *hiking gear* **8.** CLOTHES clothes and accessories of a particular kind (*informal*) ○ *You've got to have the right gear.* **9.** NAUT SAILING EQUIPMENT the equipment, rigging, and other objects that belong to a particular boat or sailor **10.** DRUGS illegal drugs (*slang*) **11.** RIDING HARNESS a horse's harness ■ *vt* (**gears, gearing, geared**) **1.** PUT GEARS IN SOMETHING to equip something with gears **2.** ENGAGE GEAR OF VEHICLE to put a vehicle into gear [13C < Old Norse *gervi* 'make ready']

gear to, gear towards *vt* to adapt or adjust something so that it fits in or works effectively with something else (*usually passive*) ○ *We've tried to gear ourselves to the younger market.*

gear up *vti* to prepare somebody or something to do something, take action in preparation for something (*usually passive or continuous*) ○ *We're all geared up for the next round of talks.*

gearbox /geér boks/ *n* a set of gears and the protective casing that covers it in a vehicle or engine ○ *A horrible clunking noise came from the gearbox.* N Am term **transmission**

---

a at; aa father; aw all; ay day; ai hair; ə about, item, edible, common, circus; e egg; ee eel; hw when; i it, happy; ī ice; 'l apple; 'm rhythm; 'n fashion; o odd; ō open; oö good; oo pool; ow owl; oy oil; th thin; th this; u up; ur urge;

gearing /géeri̅ng/ n **1.** SET OF GEARS a set of mechanical gears, or the power that it provides ○ *complaints about the gearing on the older model* **2.** PROVIDING SOMETHING WITH GEARS the process or act of providing a system with gears **3.** UK FIN PROPORTION OF CAPITAL AS DEBT the ratio of a company's debt capital to the value of its ordinary shares. ANZ, N Am term **leverage**

gear lever n a lever in a car or other vehicle or machine that is used to change or engage gears. N Am term **gearshift**

gearshift /géer shift/ n N Am MECH ENG same as **gear lever**

gear stick n MECH ENG same as **gear lever**

gear tooth n one of the many small projections on a gearwheel that fits in the space between two other projections on another gearwheel, thus engaging the gear

gear train n a collection of gears used to transmit power

gearwheel /géer weel/ n MECH ENG same as **gear** n (sense 2)

gebel n GEOG another spelling of **jebel**

gecko

gecko /gékō/ (plural **-os** or **-oes**) n a small tropical or subtropical nocturnal insect-eating lizard with hooked ridges on the pads of its feet that permit it to climb smooth vertical surfaces. Family: Gekkonidae. [Late 18C. < Malay dialect *geko(k)*]

gedanken experiment /gə dángkən-/ n a test of a hypothesis that can be performed only in the mind [Mid-20C. < German]

geddit /géddit/ interj do you understand? (slang) ○ *We're goin' now, geddit?* [Late 20C. Fast speech pronunciation of *get it*]

gee[1] /jee/ interj **1.** N Am EXPRESSING ENTHUSIASM used to express surprise or to register a reaction to something, especially enthusiasm or ironic enthusiasm **2.** HURRY UP! used to urge a horse, cow, or similar animal to move faster, to go straight ahead, or to turn right ■ vt (**gees, geeing, geed**) **1.** HURRY ANIMAL UP to urge a horse, cow, or similar animal to move faster, to go straight ahead, or to turn right **2.** ENCOURAGE SOMEBODY to encourage somebody to continue doing something or to do something faster (informal) [Mid-18C. Origin ?]

gee up interj used to urge a horse, cow, or similar animal to move faster, to go straight ahead, or to turn right ■ vt to urge a horse, cow, or similar animal to move faster, to go straight ahead, or to turn right

gee[2] /jee/ (plural **gees** or same) n US one thousand dollars (informal) [Mid-20C. Representing the pronunciation of G[1] (sense 7)]

Gee /jee/, **Maurice Gough** (b. 1931) New Zealand novelist. His novels include *Plumb* (1978).

geebung /jée bung/ n a flowering tree or bush with small edible fruit. Native to: Australia. Genus: *Persoonia*. [Early 19C. < an Aboriginal language]

gee-gee n same as **horse** (sense 1) (informal; usually used by children) [Mid-19C. Childish repetition of GEE[1]]

geek[1] /geek/ n **1.** AWKWARD PERSON somebody regarded as unattractive and socially awkward (insult) **2.** N Am COMPUT OBSESSIVE COMPUTER USER somebody who is a proud or enthusiastic user of computers or other technology, sometimes to an excessive degree (informal) **3.** US ARTS OUTRAGEOUS SIDESHOW PERFORMER a sideshow performer whose act consists of outrageous feats such as biting the heads off live animals [Late 19C. Probably variant of dialect *geck* 'fool' < Low Dutch] —**geeky** adj

geek[2] /geek/ n Aus same as **look** n (sense 1) (informal) [Early 20C. < Scottish and N English dialect *geck* 'toss the head scornfully, look proudly', probably < W Germanic]

Geelong /ji lóng/ industrial city and seaport in Victoria, southeastern Australia. Population: 153,100 (1997).

geese BIRDS plural of **goose**

gee whiz interj N Am same as **gee**[1] interj (sense 1)

gee-whiz adj N Am causing or characterized by wonderment (informal) ○ *a gee-whiz new electronic gadget*

Ge'ez /gée ez/ n an ancient language formerly spoken in Ethiopia and still the liturgical language in the Ethiopian Christian Church [Late 18C. < Ethiopic] —**Ge'ez** adj

geezer /géezər/ n same as **man** n (sense 1) (slang) [Late 19C. Representing dialect pronunciation of GUISER]

SPELLCHECK **geezer** or **geyser**? Do not confuse the spelling of **geezer** and **geyser**, which may sound similar. **Geezer** is a slang word for a man: *He's a likable geezer*. A **geyser**, on the other hand, is a hot spring or a household appliance for heating water.

gefilte fish /gə fílta-/ n a Jewish dish consisting of finely chopped fish mixed with crumbs, eggs, and seasoning and served as balls or cakes. Gefilte fish was originally a dish of finely chopped or minced fish stuffed in a fish's body cavity before boiling or poaching. [Late 19C. < Yiddish, 'stuffed fish']

gegenschein /gáygən shīn/ n a faint elliptical glow in the night sky opposite the setting sun, caused by the reflection of sunlight by dust in space [Late 19C. < German, 'opposite glow']

Geiger counter /gíger-/, **Geiger-Müller counter** /-mo̅o̅llər-/ n an instrument used to measure the intensity of ionizing radiation by detecting particles from a radioactive substance [Early 20C. After Hans Geiger (1882–1945), German physicist]

geisha /gáyshə/ (plural same or **-shas**), **geisha girl** n **1.** a Japanese woman educated to accompany men as a hostess, with skills such as dancing, conversation, and music **2.** a Japanese prostitute [Late 19C. < Japanese < *gei* 'art' (< Middle Chinese *nejh*) + *sha* 'person' (< Middle Chinese *tšiaʔ*)]

gel[1] /jel/ n **1.** HAIR STYLING PRODUCT a substance with the consistency of jelly that is used for styling hair **2.** CHEM SEMISOLID a semisolid mixture of small particles of a solid in a liquid (**colloid**) **3.** LIGHT FILTER a sheet of coloured acetate used in theatre, television, and film lighting to create different lighting effects ■ vi (**gels, gelling, gelled**) **1.** BECOME GEL to become semisolid, having been in a liquid state **2.** TAKE FORM to take on a definite form (informal) ○ *The idea didn't begin to gel until I got home.* **3.** GET ON to get on well together (informal) [Late 19C. Shortening of GELATIN] —**gelable** adj

gel[2] /jel/ n same as **girl** (dated; usually associated with the upper classes) ○ *She's a fine gel!* [Representing an English upper-class pronunciation of GIRL]

gelada /jéllədə/ (plural **-das** or same), **gelada baboon** n a large baboon with brown hair and a bare red patch on its chest. Native to: northeastern Africa. Latin name: *Theropithecus gelada*. [Mid-19C. < Amharic *čʼəllada*]

gelate /jé láyt/ (-ates, -ating, -ated) vi to become or form a gel [Early 20C. Back-formation < GELATION[2]]

gelati FOOD plural of **gelato**

gelatin /jélletin/, **gelatine** /-teen/ n **1.** a transparent protein material made from boiling animal hides, bone, and cartilage that forms a firm gel when mixed with water. Use: foods, medicine, glue, photography. **2.** THEATRE, CINEMA, MEDIA same as **gel**[1] n (sense 3) [Early 19C. Via French *gélatine* < Italian *gelatina* < Latin *gelata* 'frozen']

gelatinize /ji látti nīz/ (-nizes, -nizing, -nized), **gelatinise** (-nises, -nising, -nised) v **1.** vti to make something gelatinous, or become gelatinous **2.** vt to coat a photographic medium with gelatin —**gelatinization** /ji látti nī záysh'n/ n —**gelatinizer** n

gelatinous /ji láttinəss/ adj **1.** having a semisolid form resembling gelatin **2.** relating to or containing gelatin —**gelatinously** adv —**gelatinousness** n

gelation[1] /jə láysh'n/ n the solidification of a liquid by freezing (technical) [Mid-19C. < Latin *gelation-* < *gelare* 'freeze']

gelation[2] /jə láysh'n/ n the process of becoming a gel [Early 20C. < GEL[1]]

gelato /jə la̅a̅tō/ (plural **-ti** /-tee/) n an Italian ice cream made from milk, gelatin, sugar, and fruit [Early 20C. < Italian, 'frozen' < Latin *gelare* 'freeze']

geld[1] /geld/ (**gelds, gelding, gelded** or **gelt** /gelt/) vt **1.** to castrate an animal, especially a horse **2.** to take away the strength or virility of somebody or something [13C. < Old Norse *gelda* < *geldr* 'barren']

geld[2] /geld/ n a land tax paid by landholders to the crown in late Anglo-Saxon and Norman times [15C. Via medieval Latin *geldum* < Old English *gield* 'payment']

gelding /gélding/ n a castrated horse or other animal [14C. < GELD[1]]

Geldof /gél dof/, **Sir Bob** (b. 1954) Irish musician and philanthropist. He was the leader of the rock group the Boomtown Rats (1975–86), founded the charity Band Aid for famine relief (1984), and received an honorary knighthood (1986). Full name **Geldof, Robert Frederick Zenon**

'Most people get into bands for three very simple rock-and-roll reasons: to get laid, to get fame, and to get rich.'
[Sir Bob Geldof, *Melody Maker*; 27 August 1977]

gelid /jéllid/ adj exceedingly cold (literary) [Early 17C. < Latin *gelidus* < *gelu* 'frost, intense cold'] —**gelidity** /je líddəti/ n —**gelidly** adv

gelignite /jéllig nīt/ n dynamite consisting of gelled nitroglycerine, potassium nitrate, and wood pulp or guncotton. It is often used under water. [Late 19C. < GELATIN + Latin *ignis* 'fire']

Martha Gellhorn

Gellhorn /géll hawrn/, **Martha** (1908–98) US journalist and novelist. She became a war correspondent in 1937 and reported on the Spanish Civil War (1936–39) and World War II. Her novels include *A Stricken Field* (1940) and *Liana* (1948).

'Never believe governments, not any of them, not a word they say; keep an untrusting eye on all they do.'
[Martha Gellhorn, recalled on her death, *Daily Telegraph*; 17 February 1998]

gelt VET past participle, past tense of **geld**[1]

gem /jem/ n **1.** JEWEL a precious stone that has been cut and polished for use as jewellery or decoration **2.** SOMEBODY OR SOMETHING EXCELLENT somebody or something considered to be valuable, useful, or beautiful (informal) ○ *Our baby-sitter is such a gem!* ■ vt (**gems, gemming, gemmed**) DECORATE SOMETHING WITH GEMS to decorate something with gems or with something resembling gems (literary; usually passive) [Pre-12C. < Latin *gemma* 'bud, jewel']

Gemara /gə ma̅a̅rə/ n the second part of the Talmud, forming a set of commentaries on the first part of the Talmud, the Mishnah [Early 17C. < Aramaic *gəma̅ra̅* 'completion']

gemfish /jém fish/ (plural **-fishes** or same) n a food fish prized for its delicate flesh. Native to: southeastern Australia. Latin name: *Rexea solandri*.

geminate /jémmi nayt/ adj also **geminated** growing or arranged in pairs ○ *a geminate leaf* ■ vti (-nates, -nating, -nated) to make something paired, or become paired or doubled [Late 16C. < Latin *geminat-*, past

participle of *geminare* < *geminus* 'twin'] —**gemination** /jémmi náysh'n/ *n*

Gemini /jémmi nī/ *n* **1. CONSTELLATION IN NORTHERN HEMISPHERE** a zodiacal constellation of the northern hemisphere, also known as the Twins or Castor and Pollux, after its two brightest stars. See illustration at **constellation 2. 3RD ZODIAC SIGN** the third sign of the zodiac, represented by twins and lasting from approximately 21 May to 20 June. Gemini is classified as an air sign. **3.** *also* **Geminian SOMEBODY BORN UNDER GEMINI** somebody whose birthday falls between 21 May and 20 June [Pre-12C. < Latin, plural of *geminus* 'twin'] —**Gemini** *adj*

gemma /jémmə/ (*plural* **-mae** /-mee/) *n* an asexual bud-shaped structure that can detach from the parent and form a plant. Liverworts and mosses produce gemmae. [Late 18C. < Latin, 'bud, jewel'] —**gemmaceous** /je máyshəss/ *adj*

gemmate /jémmayt/ *adj* forming gemmae or reproducing by means of gemmae ■ *vi* (**-mates, -mating, -mated**) to form gemmae or reproduce by means of gemmae [Early 17C. < Latin *gemmat-*, past participle of *gemmare* 'produce buds' < *gemma* 'bud, jewel'] —**gemmation** /je máysh'n/ *n*

gemmiferous /je míffərəs/ *adj* **1.** producing precious stones **2.** producing gemmae

gemmiparous /je míppərəs/ *adj* BIOL same as **gemmate**

gemmology /je mólləji/, **gemology** *n* the study of gems and gemstones —**gemmological** /jémmə lójjik'l/ *adj*—**gemmologist** *n*

gemmule /jém yool/ *n* a reproductive structure produced by asexual reproduction in freshwater and sea sponges —**gemmulation** /jémmyoo láysh'n/ *n*

gemology *n* another spelling of **gemmology**

gemot /gi mōt/, **gemote** *n* an assembly for judicial or legislative purposes in pre-Norman England [Old English *gemōt* < *mōt* (see MOOT)]

gemsbok /gémz bok/ (*plural* **-boks** or *same*) *n* a large antelope with long straight horns and broad black markings on its head and upper legs. Native to: southwestern and eastern Africa. Latin name: *Oryx gazella*. [Late 18C. Via Afrikaans < Dutch, 'wild antelope buck']

gemstone /jém stōn/ *n* a mineral or stone suitable for use in jewellery after cutting and polishing

gemütlich /gə mṻtlikh/ *adj* warm and friendly [Mid-19C. < German < *Gemüt* 'heart, spirit']

gemütlichkeit /gə mṻtlikh kīt/ *n* warmth and friendliness [Mid-19C. < German < *gemütlich* (see GEMÜTLICH)]

gen /jen/ *n* same as **information** (*informal*) [Mid-20C. Origin ?]

gen up (**gens up, genning up, genned up**) *v* (*informal*) **1.** *vi* to find out all the information on a subject **2.** *vt* to give somebody all the information on a subject (*usually passive*)

gen. *abbr* **1.** BIOL, GRAM gender **2.** MIL general **3.** GRAM genitive **4.** BIOL genus

Gen. *abbr* **1.** MIL General **2.** BIBLE Genesis

-gen, **-gene** *suffix* **1.** something that produces ○ *hallucinogen* **2.** something that is produced ○ *phosgene* [Via French *-gène* < Greek *-genēs* 'born' < Indo-European, 'beget'] —**-genic** *suffix* —**-geny** *suffix*

gendarme /zhónd aarm, zhaaNd-/ *n* **1.** a police officer in France and French-speaking countries. In France, gendarmes are part of the armed forces, their responsibility being that of general law enforcement. **2.** a police officer (*slang*) [Mid-16C. < French, singular < *gens d'armes* 'men of arms']

gendarmerie /zhond aarməri, zhaaNd-/ *n* **1.** gendarmes considered as a body **2.** in France and French-speaking countries, a police station or police barracks [Mid-16C. < French < *gendarme* (see GENDARME)]

gender /jéndər/ *n* **1.** ⚠ **SOMEBODY'S SEX** the sex of a person or organism, or of a whole category of people or organisms (*often euphemistic to avoid the word 'sex'*) **2. FACT OF HAVING DIFFERENT GENDERS** the fact of people having or being aware of having different genders ○ *Gender is not an issue when we take on new staff.* **3.** GRAM **CATEGORIZATION OF NOUNS** the classification of nouns and pronouns in some languages according to the forms taken by adjectives, modifiers, and other grammatical items associated syntactically with them **4.** GRAM **CATEGORY OF NOUN** any one of the categories into which nouns and pronouns are divided in languages that have gender, e.g. masculine, feminine, neuter, or common [14C. < Old French *gendre* < Latin *gener-*, stem of *genus* 'birth, kind'] —**genderless** *adj*

USAGE gender or **sex**? Traditionally, ***gender*** has referred to grammatical classifications in languages, and ***sex*** has referred to the biological classifications to which gender is analogous. For some time, however, anthropologists have used ***gender*** to distinguish cultural categories from biological ones: *Gender roles are indistinct among the young of this society; the two sexes play together frequently.* Cultural and biological categories are interrelated, of course, and thus at times it can be difficult to decide which word is more appropriate. ***Gender*** has become the preferred form in the 21st century, as in *Gender is an important factor to consider when hiring new employees* and in idiomatic expressions such as *gender gap*.

gender awareness *n* sensitivity to the perceived differences between men and women or boys and girls in environments such as the workplace and the classroom

gender bender *n* an offensive term for somebody who dresses or acts in a way that is intended to blur the traditional distinctions between men and women (*slang*) —**gender bending** *n*

gender bias *n* unfair difference in the treatment of men or women because of their sex

gender dysphoria *n* PSYCHOL same as **gender identity disorder**

gendered /jéndərd/ *adj* relating to or appropriate to one gender rather than the other ○ *gendered clothing*

gender gap *n* a noticeable difference in behaviour or attitudes between men and women or boys and girls

gender identity disorder *n* a condition in which somebody identifies strongly with the opposite sex and experiences discomfort with his or her birth gender

gender-neutral *adj* avoiding references to masculinity and femininity and their cultural associations

USAGE It is increasingly regarded as good practice to avoid unnecessary reference to gender. Wherever possible, choose a gender-neutral alternative, for example *camera operator* or *police officer* for words like *cameraman* or *policewoman*. Do not use *he/him/his/etc.* or *she/her/etc.* to refer to people of unspecified gender, as in *A child of his age should be able to dress himself.* In this example, the best solution is to recast the sentence in the plural: *Children of that age should be able to dress themselves.* In other cases, *they/them/their* may be used as gender-neutral singular forms. A less controversial but more cumbersome option is *he or she/him or her/his or her.* See also ***-ess***, ***-person***, and ***they***.

gender reassignment *n* MED a surgical operation, usually with accompanying hormone treatment, that changes somebody's physical characteristics to approximate those of the opposite sex

gender-specific *adj* affecting or involving only men or only women, or only boys or only girls

gene /jeen/ *n* the basic unit capable of transmitting characteristics from one generation to the next. It consists of a specific sequence of DNA or RNA that occupies a fixed position (**locus**) on a chromosome. [Early 20C. Via German *Gen* < Greek *genos* 'birth, race']

ORIGIN The Indo-European word from which ***gene*** is ultimately derived is also the ancestor of English *gender, genealogy, general, generate, generous, genesis, genie, genital, genius, genocide, genre, gentle, genus, gonad, indigenous, ingenuous, innate, jaunty, kin, kind*[1], *nation*, and *nature*.

-gene *suffix* same as **-gen**

genealogy /jeeni álləji/ (*plural* **-gies**) *n* **1. STUDY OF HISTORY OF FAMILIES** the study of the history of families and the line of descent from their ancestors **2. FAMILY HISTORY** a pedigree or line of descent that can be traced directly from an ancestor or earlier form, especially that of a specific person or family **3. FAMILY TREE** a chart or table that shows the line of descent from an ancestor or earlier form, especially that of a specific person or family **4. STUDY OF PLANT OR ANIMAL DEVELOPMENT** the study of the line of development of a plant or animal from earlier forms [14C. Via French *généalogie* < Greek *genealogia* < *genea* 'race, generation'] —**genealogical** /jeeni ə lójjik'l/ *adj*—**genealogically** *adv*—**genealogist** *n*

gene amplification *n* GENETICS same as **amplification** (sense 6)

gene chip *n* a small piece of material (**substrate**) containing minute samples of DNA. Use: in genetic testing.

gene cloning *n* the process of producing any number of identical copies of a gene. Gene cloning is now carried out using a machine that automatically performs the polymerase chain reaction (**PCR**).

gene expression *n* the process by which a gene's coded information is converted into the structures operating in a cell

gene flow *n* the natural transfer of genes from one population into the genetic makeup of another population through hybridization and interbreeding

gene frequency *n* the ratio of a specific form of a gene (**allele**) to the total number of forms in a specific population

gene gun *n* a device for injecting tiny particles coated with DNA into cells or tissue as a method of genetic modification

gene mutation *n* GENETICS same as **point mutation**

~~geneology~~ incorrect spelling of **genealogy**

gene pool *n* the total of all genes carried by all individuals in an interbreeding population

gene probe *n* a fragment of DNA or RNA marked by a chemical or radioactive substance that will bind to a given gene, used as a tag in order to identify or isolate that gene

genera BIOL, LOGIC plural of **genus**

general /jénnərəl/ *adj* **1. OVERALL** relating to or including all or nearly all of the members of a category, group, or whole ○ *a general increase in demand* **2. USUAL** applying or happening in most cases ○ *as a general rule* **3. WIDESPREAD** shared or participated in by many ○ *a general sense that something ought to be done* **4. MISCELLANEOUS** having a varied content or wide scope ○ *a general store* **5. NOT SPECIALIZED** unspecialized or lacking specialized knowledge ○ *a book that was intended for the general reader* **6. NOT SPECIFIC** not specific, detailed, or clearly defined ○ *She spoke in the most general terms.* **7. HIGH-RANKING** with overall authority, or of superior rank ○ *a general manager* ■ *n* **1.** *also* **General HIGH RANKING OFFICER** British Army officer of a rank above lieutenant general **2.** MED same as **general anaesthetic** (*informal*) **3.** HEALTH SERVICES same as **general hospital** (*informal*) **4. THE PUBLIC** the public as a whole (*archaic*) [12C. Via French < Latin *generalis* 'of the whole class' < *genus* 'race, kind'] —**generalness** *n* ◇ **in general 1.** as a whole **2.** in most cases or circumstances

CULTURAL NOTE ***The General***, a film (1926) starring US actor Buster Keaton. Regarded as one of the greatest silent comedies, it is set during the American Civil War and is based on a historical incident: the hijack of a Confederate train by Union soldiers. Keaton plays railroad man Johnnie Gray, whose attempts to recapture the train involve superb visual gags, gripping drama, and brilliantly timed stunts.

general anaesthetic *n* an anaesthetic that produces loss of sensation in the whole body together with unconsciousness

general assembly, **General Assembly** *n* **1.** the assembly of the United Nations **2.** the highest governing body of various Presbyterian churches, especially the Church of Scotland, or the meeting of such a body

general average *n* liability for loss or damage to an insured ship or its cargo that is shared among all those with an interest in the venture

General Certificate of Education *n* EDUC full form of **GCE**

General Certificate of Secondary Education *n* EDUC full form of **GCSE**

generalcy /jénnərəlsi, jénnrəlsi/ *n* the office of general, or the period during which this office is held

general delivery *n N Am* MAIL same as **poste restante**

general election *n* an election in which the citizens of a country or state vote to elect representatives of all constituencies to a legislative body such as the Houses of Parliament

General Headquarters *n* MIL full form of **GHQ**

general hospital *n* a hospital that does not specialize in any one type of medical treatment

generalisation, etc. another spelling of **generalization, etc**

generalissimo /jénnərə líssimō/ (*plural* **-mos**) *n* in some countries, the supreme commander of a combined military force consisting of the army, navy, and air force [Early 17C. < Italian, 'great general' < Latin *generalis* (see GENERAL)]

generalist /jénnərəlist/ *n* somebody with knowledge, skills, or interests in many areas but with no speciality

generality /jénnə rálləti/ (*plural* **-ties**) *n* **1.** GENERAL STATEMENT a statement or remark that concerns the main aspects of something rather than the details **2.** STATE OF BEING GENERAL the quality or state of being general **3.** GENERAL PRINCIPLE a statement or principle that is true in most cases **4.** UNIMPORTANT REMARK a remark about something that is not important in itself but is useful to open or keep up a conversation **5.** same as **majority** (sense 1) (*archaic*)

generalization /jénnərə lī záysh'n/, **generalisation** *n* **1.** SWEEPING STATEMENT a statement presented as a general truth but based on limited or incomplete evidence **2.** GENERAL STATEMENT a statement or conclusion that is derived from and applies equally to a number of cases ○ *not enough data to permit a generalization* **3.** MAKING OF GENERALIZATIONS the making of general or sweeping statements **4.** LOGIC INFERENCE FROM INSTANCE the application of the rules of inference that go from an instance to a universal or to an existential statement **5.** PSYCHOL USE OF LEARNED RESPONSE the act of responding to a new stimulus in the same way as to a conditioned stimulus

generalize /jénnərə līz/ (**-izes, -izing, -ized**), **generalise** (**-ises, -ising, -ised**) *v* **1.** *vi* MAKE SWEEPING STATEMENT to state a supposed general truth about something on the basis of limited or incomplete evidence **2.** *vti* EXPRESS SOMETHING GENERAL to express something general on the basis of particulars **3.** *vti* GIVE WIDER USE TO SOMETHING to use something in a wider or different range of circumstances, or be used in this way **4.** *vt* MAKE SOMETHING GENERALLY KNOWN to bring something into general use or to general knowledge (*usually passive*) **5.** *vi* MED SPREAD to spread to other parts of the body **6.** *vti* LOGIC MAKE INFERENCE to infer a general conclusion from particulars or a universal statement from an instance —**generalizable** *adj*

general knowledge *n* knowledge of a broad range of facts or subjects

generally /jénnərəli/ *adv* **1.** USUALLY in most cases or circumstances **2.** AS WHOLE as a whole or without exception ○ *not meant for the public generally* **3.** VAGUELY without being specific, detailed, or clearly defined ○ *spoke generally about his life* **4.** WIDESPREAD so as to be widespread ○ *become generally known*

general meeting *n* a meeting to which all members of a group or organization are invited

General of the Air Force *n* an officer in the US Air Force of the highest rank, having an insignia of five stars, this rank and title used only in wartime

General of the Armies *n* formerly, an officer in the US Army of the highest rank, above a General of the Army

General of the Army *n* an officer in the US Army of the highest rank, having an insignia of five stars, this rank and title used only in wartime

general paralysis of the insane *n* MED full form of **GPI**

general practice *n* the work of a doctor who treats patients' general medical problems, referring them to specialists or hospitals for more specialized care

general practitioner *n* full form of **GP**[1]

general public *n* the people of a country considered as a whole ○ *Members of the general public are welcome to attend.*

general purpose *adj* useful for a wide variety of purposes

general relativity *n* PHYS same as **relativity** (sense 2)

generalship /jénnərəl ship/ *n* **1.** MILITARY COMMAND the art or practice of exercising military leadership in a war **2.** GENERAL'S RANK the rank or tenure of a general **3.** LEADERSHIP skilful leadership or management of people or an organization

general staff *n* a group of military officers whose job is to assist senior officers in the planning and coordination of military operations

general strike *n* a strike involving all or a majority of workers in a country

general studies *n* a course of study at school or university that covers a broad range of general topics rather than specializing in one specific area (*takes a singular verb*)

general theory of relativity *n* PHYS same as **relativity** (sense 2)

generate /jénnə rayt/ (**-ates, -ating, -ated**) *vt* **1.** CREATE SOMETHING to bring something into existence or effect ○ *measures to generate more income* **2.** PRODUCE ELECTRICITY to produce electricity from a power station or generator **3.** PRODUCE ENERGY to produce or originate a form of energy through a chemical or physical process **4.** MATHS, LING PRODUCE SET to produce a set or sequence by the application of defined rules or the performance of defined operations **5.** MATHS PRODUCE FORM to create a curve with a moving point or a surface with a moving curve [Early 16C. < Latin *generat-*, past participle of *generare* 'beget' < *genus* 'race, birth'] —**generable** *adj*

generation /jénnə ráysh'n/ *n* **1.** GROUP OF CONTEMPORARIES all of the people who were born at approximately the same time, considered as a group, and especially when considered as having shared interests and attitudes ○ *the younger generation* **2.** STAGE IN DESCENT a single stage in the descent of a family or a group of people, animals, or plants, or the individual members of that stage ○ *three generations down the line* **3.** TIME TAKEN TO PRODUCE NEW GENERATION the period of time that it takes for people, animals, or plants to grow up and produce their own offspring, in humans held to be between 30 and 35 years ○ *after three generations of war and conflict* **4.** PARTICULAR GENERATION IN SEQUENCE a particular numbered stage in the sequence of generations of a person being identified with a particular characteristic (*usually used in combination*) ○ *a first-generation immigrant* ○ *a third-generation graduate* **5.** NEW TYPE a particular stage in the development of a product or technology, especially one marking a significant advance ○ *one of the new generation of computers* **6.** PHASE IN LIFE CYCLE one of the successive phases that make up the life cycle of some organisms ○ *the gametophyte generation* **7.** PRODUCTION OF POWER the production of electricity, heat, or some other form of energy **8.** PRODUCTION OF YOUNG the act or process of bringing offspring into being **9.** MATHS GENERATING OF GROUP OR SHAPE the act or process of generating a set, sequence, curve, or surface **10.** PHYS NUCLEI IN CHAIN REACTION in a chain reaction, a group of nuclei that come from a previous group —**generational** *adj*

generation gap *n* the difference in attitudes, behaviour, and interests between people of different generations, especially between parents and their children

generation X, **Generation X** *n* the generation of people born roughly during the years 1965 to 1980 in Western countries, especially the United States, often regarded as disillusioned, cynical, or apathetic [< *Generation X: Tales for an Accelerated Culture*, novel by Douglas Coupland] —**generation Xer** *n*

generation Y, **Generation Y** *n* **1.** the generation of people born approximately in or after 1980 in Western countries, especially the United States (*informal*) **2.** SOCIOL same as **millennial** [After GENERATION X]

generative /jénnərətiv/ *adj* **1.** relating to the production of young **2.** involving the ability to produce or originate something ○ *generative linguistic theory* —**generatively** *adv* —**generativeness** *n*

generative cell *n* BIOL same as **gamete**

generative grammar *n* the rules from which all the grammatical sentences, and only the grammatical sentences, of a language can be generated

generator /jénnə raytər/ *n* **1.** DEVICE FOR PRODUCING ELECTRICITY a machine or device that is used to convert mechanical energy, such as that provided by the combustion of fuel or by wind or water, into electricity **2.** DEVICE FOR PRODUCING GAS a device in which a gas is formed **3.** ORIGINATOR somebody or something responsible for generating something such as an idea, plan, or strategy

generatrix /jénnə raytriks/ (*plural* **-trices** /-tri seez/) *n* an element such as a point or line that is used in the production of a geometric figure such as a curve or surface

generic /jə nérrik/ *adj* **1.** SUITABLE FOR BROAD RANGE usable or suitable in a variety of contexts ○ *generic software that can run on a variety of machines* **2.** BIOL OF GENUS relating to or characteristic of a genus **3.** PHARM WITH GENERAL NAME describes a pharmaceutical product that does not have a brand name or trademark [Late 17C. < French *générique* < Latin *genus* 'race, kind'] —**generically** *adv*

generosity /jénnə róssəti/ (*plural* **-ties**) *n* **1.** KINDNESS willingness to give money, help, or time freely **2.** NOBILITY nobility of character **3.** SUBSTANTIAL SIZE pleasingly large size or quantity ○ *He ate everything, despite the generosity of the portions.* **4.** GENEROUS ACT a generous, kind, or noble act [15C. < Latin *generositas* < *generosus* (see GENEROUS)]

generous /jénnərəss/ *adj* **1.** KIND willing to give money, help, or time freely ○ *a very generous offer* **2.** NOBLE having or showing nobility of character ○ *a generous gesture of forgiveness* **3.** SUBSTANTIAL pleasingly large in size or quantity ○ *a generous slice of cake* **4.** WINE FULL-FLAVOURED describes wine that is rich and full-flavoured [Late 16C. Via French *généreux* < Latin *generosus* 'of noble birth' < *genus* 'race, birth'] —**generously** *adv* —**generousness** *n*

SYNONYMS *generous, liberal, magnanimous, munificent, bountiful*

CORE MEANING: giving readily to others

generous willing to give money, help, or time freely ○ *I was deeply touched by her generous gift.* ○ *I've seen how generous he is with his time and what an inspiration he is to young writers.* **liberal** freely giving money, time, or other assets ○ *During her lifetime, she was a liberal benefactor to public institutions.* ○ *a liberal attitude towards government spending* **magnanimous** very generous, kind, or forgiving ○ *a magnanimous gesture of fair play* ○ *It is easy to be magnanimous, when you have been as fortunate in life as I have been.* **munificent** very generous in giving a lot of money ○ *received a munificent sum for books written and yet to be written* **bountiful** (*literary*) giving generously, particularly to less fortunate people ○ *Society has become more selfish and the rich are no longer so bountiful to the poor.*

gene sequence *n* the order of nucleotides in a gene

gene sequencing *n* the process of determining the individual arrangement of nucleotides that compose a specific gene

genesis /jénnəssiss/ (*plural* **-eses** /-əs seez/) *n* the time or circumstances of something's coming into being ○ *the genesis of this new project* [Early 17C. < GENESIS]

Genesis /jénnəssiss/ *n* a book of the Bible, in which the creation of the world is described. It is the first book of the Pentateuch. See table at **Bible** [Pre-12C. Via Latin < Greek, 'birth']

-genesis *suffix* production, origin ○ *sporogenesis* [Via Latin < Greek, 'birth']

gene splicing *n* a technique in which segments of DNA or RNA, often from different organisms, are combined, in order to be introduced into an organism

genet[1] /jénnit/ *n* **1.** a small carnivorous mammal related to the civet that has a ringed tail, spotted sides, and retractable claws. Native to: wooded regions of southern Europe and Africa. Genus: *Genetta*. **2.** the fur of the genet [14C. < Old French *genette*]

genet[2] /jénnit/ *n* ZOOL another spelling of **jennet**

Genet /zhə náy/, **Jean** (1910–86) French writer. He is best known for existentialist dramas such as *The Maids* (1947) and *The Balcony* (1957).

'To achieve harmony in bad taste is the height of elegance.'
[Jean Genet, *The Thief's Journal*; 1949]

gene therapy *n* the treatment of a genetic disease through the insertion of normal or genetically

altered genes into cells in order to replace or make up for the nonfunctional or missing genes

genetic /jə néttik/, **genetical** /-ik'l/ *adj* involving, resulting from, or relating to genes or genetics [Mid-19C. < GENESIS, after pairs such as *antithesis, antithetic*] —**genetically** *adv*

genetically modified *adj* describes an organism that has received genetic material from another, resulting in a permanent change in one or more of its characteristics

genetic code *n* the order of the nucleotide sequences in DNA or RNA that form the basis of heredity through their role in protein synthesis

genetic counselling *n* counselling that concerns the risks, treatments, and management of inherited genetic disorders for people with some likelihood of being affected by them, either personally or as parents —**genetic counsellor** *n*

genetic drift *n* the random changes that occur in the gene frequency of small isolated populations, resulting in the loss or preservation of genes over the generations

genetic engineering *n* GENETICS same as **genetic modification** —**genetic engineer** *n*

genetic fingerprinting *n* GENETICS same as **DNA fingerprinting** —**genetic fingerprint** *n*

geneticist /jə néttissist/ *n* a student of or specialist in genetics

genetic load *n* the average number of unfavourable recessive gene mutations per individual in a population

genetic manipulation *n* GENETICS same as **genetic modification**

genetic map *n* a graphic representation of the arrangement of genes on a chromosome

genetic mapping *n* the technique or process of identifying genes on a chromosome

genetic marker *n* a known, usually dominant, gene that is used to identify genes, chromosomes, and traits known to be associated with that gene

genetic modification *n* the alteration and recombination of genetic material by technological means, resulting in transgenic organisms

genetic probe *n* GENETICS same as **gene probe**

genetic profiling *n* GENETICS same as **DNA fingerprinting** —**genetic profile** *n*

genetics /jə néttiks/ *n* the branch of biology that deals with heredity and genetic variations (*takes a singular verb*) ■ *npl* the genetic makeup of an organism or group of organisms (*takes a plural verb*)

genetic screening *n* the analysis of DNA samples of a group of people, carried out in order to find out whether they carry the genes associated with specific inherited diseases or disorders

genetic sequencing *n* GENETICS same as **gene sequencing**

gene transfer *n* the insertion of genetic material from one organism into another in a laboratory procedure, to produce an effect such as resistance to disease

genetrix /jénnə triks/ (*plural* **-trices** /-tri seez/) *n* a biological mother (*technical*) [15C. Directly or via French < Latin < *gignere* 'beget']

geneva *n* BEVERAGES same as **genever**

Geneva /jə néevə/ city in western Switzerland, capital of Geneva Canton, situated at the western end of Lake Geneva. It is the headquarters of many international organizations, including the International Red Cross and the World Health Organization. Population: 175,800 (2001). French name **Genève** —**Genevan** *adj, n* —**Genevese** /jénnə véez/ *adj, n*

Geneva, Lake largest lake in central Europe. It straddles the border between Switzerland and the Haute-Savoie department in southeastern France. Area: 580 sq. km/224 sq. mi.

Geneva Convention *n* an international agreement that establishes standards for the treatment of those who are ill, wounded, or killed in battle and those who are prisoners of war

genever /jə néevər/, **geneva** *literary* /-və/ *n* Dutch gin [Early 18C. Via Dutch < Old French *genevre* < Latin *juniperus* 'juniper']

Genghis Khan /géng giss kaán, jéng-/ (1167?–1227) Mongol conqueror. His conquests extended the Mongolian empire throughout Asia from the Pacific to the Black Sea. Born **Temujin**

> 'It is forbidden ever to make peace with a monarch, a prince or a people who have not submitted.'
> [Genghis Khan, *Laws*; 1206?]

genial /jeéni əl/ *adj* **1.** having a kind and good-natured disposition or manner **2.** pleasantly mild and warm so as to be conducive to life and growth ○ *a genial climate* [Mid-16C. < Latin *genialis* 'nuptial' < *genius* (see GENIUS)] —**geniality** /jeéni álləti/ *n* —**genially** *adv* —**genialness** *n*

genic /jénnik/ *adj* relating to or produced by a gene or genes —**genically** *adv*

geniculate /jə níkyoolət/ *adj* **1.** bent at an angle like a knee ○ *geniculate antennae* **2.** with a joint or joints that can be bent like a knee [Early 17C. < Latin *geniculatus* 'knotted' < *genu* 'knee'] —**geniculately** *adv* —**geniculation** /jə níkyoo láysh'n/ *n*

genie /jeéni/ (*plural* **-nies** or **-nii** /-ni ī/) *n* in Arabian folklore, a magical spirit that has supernatural powers and will obey the commands of the person who summons it [Mid-17C. Via French *génie* < Latin *genius* (see GENIUS)]

genii[1] plural of **genius** (senses 4–6)

genii[2] plural of **genie**

genipap /jénni pap/ *n* **1.** a reddish-brown fruit resembling an orange. Use: preserves, drinks. **2.** an evergreen tree that produces genipaps. Native to: tropical America. Latin name: *Genipa americana.* [Early 17C. Via Portuguese *jenipapo* < Tupi *ianipaba*]

genistein /jə nístin/ *n* an isoflavone found in soya products that is a possible natural cancer preventive [Early 20C. < Latin *genista* 'broom (the plant)']

genital /jénnit'l/ *adj* relating to the external sexual organs or to reproduction [14C. Directly or via French < Latin *genitalis* < *gignere* 'beget'] —**genitally** *adv*

genital herpes *n* a sexually transmitted disease caused by the herpes simplex virus and affecting the genital and anal regions with painful blisters

genitals /jénnit'lz/, **genitalia** /jénni táyli ə/ *npl* the reproductive organs, especially the external sex organs

genital wart *n* a wart of the genital or anal area caused by a sexually transmitted virus

genitive /jénnətiv/ *n* **1.** a grammatical case that affects nouns, pronouns, and adjectives and that usually indicates possession **2.** a word or phrase in the genitive [14C. Directly or via French < Latin *genitivus* < *gignere* 'beget'] —**genitive** *adj*

genitor /jénnitər/ *n* a biological parent (*technical*) [15C. Directly or via French < Latin < *gignere* 'beget']

genitourinary /jénnitō yoórinəri/ *adj* relating to or affecting the genital and urinary organs [Mid-19C. < Latin *genitalis* (see GENITAL)]

geniture /jénnichər/ *n* somebody's birth (*archaic*) [Mid-16C. Directly or via French < Latin *genitura* < *gignere* 'beget']

genius /jeéni əss/ *n* **1.** SOMEBODY WITH OUTSTANDING TALENT somebody with exceptional ability, especially somebody whose intellectual or creative achievements gain worldwide recognition **2.** OUTSTANDING TALENT exceptional intellectual or creative ability **3.** SOMEBODY WITH SPECIFIC SKILL a person with great specialized skill ○ *a genius with computers* **4.** (*plural* **genii** /-ni ī/) QUALITY a special quality that characterizes a place, period, or people **5.** (*plural* **genii**) GUARDIAN SPIRIT in Roman mythology, a guardian spirit of a person, place, or institution **6.** (*plural* **genii**) DEMON a supposed demon or supernatural being **7.** INFLUENCE somebody who or something that exerts a strong influence ○ *an evil genius* [14C. < Latin, 'guardian spirit' < *gignere* 'beget']

SYNONYMS See ***talent***.

genius loci /-lṓ sī/ *n* **1.** the atmosphere that characterizes a place **2.** the supposed guardian spirit of a place [< Latin, 'spirit of the place']

genizah /ge neézə/ (*plural* **-zoth** /-zōt, -zōth/) *n* a repository for Hebrew documents and sacred books that are no longer in use, e.g. because they are old and worn, but must not be destroyed [Late 19C. < Hebrew, 'hiding place' < *gānaz* 'to hide']

genned-up /jénd-/ *adj* having acquired the necessary knowledge or information about somebody or something (*informal*)

genoa /jénnō ə, jə nṓ ə/, **genoa jib** *n* a very large triangular front sail on a sailing boat, especially a racing yacht [Mid-20C. After GENOA]

Genoa /jénnō ə/ seaport and industrial city on the Gulf of Genoa, northwestern Italy, the capital of Genoa Province, Liguria Region. Population: 610,307 (2001). —**Genoese** /jénnō eéz/ *n, adj*

genoa jib *n* SAILING same as **genoa**

genocide /jénnə sīd/ *n* the systematic killing of all the people from a national, ethnic, or religious group, or an attempt to do this [Mid-20C. < Greek *genos* 'race'] —**genocidal** /jénnə sīd'l/ *adj* —**genocidally** *adv*

genome /jeé nōm/ *n* the full complement of genetic information that an organism inherits from its parents, especially the set of chromosomes and the genes they carry [Mid-20C. < Greek *genos* 'offspring, race' + CHROMOSOME] —**genomic** /ji nṓmik/ *adj*

genomics /ji nṓmiks/ *n* the identification and study of gene sequences in the DNA of organisms (*takes a singular verb*)

genotoxicity /jénnō tok síssəti/ *n* the degree to which something causes damage to or mutation of DNA [Late 20C. < GENE] —**genotoxic** /-tóksik/ *adj* —**genotoxically** *adv*

genotoxin /jénnō tóksin/ *n* a substance that can cause damage to or mutation in DNA [Late 20C. < GENE]

genotype /jénnə tīp/ *n* **1.** the genetic makeup of an organism, as opposed to its physical characteristics (**phenotype**) **2.** a group of organisms that share a similar genetic makeup [Early 20C. < German *Genotypus* < Greek *genos* 'offspring, race' + Latin *typus* (see TYPE)] —**genotypic** /jénnə típpik/ *adj* —**genotypically** *adv*

-genous *suffix* used to form adjectives from nouns ending in '-gen' and '-geny' ○ *homogenous*

~~**genrally**~~ incorrect spelling of **generally**

~~**genration**~~ incorrect spelling of **generation**

genre /zhónrə, zhóNrə/ *n* **1.** one of the categories, based on form, style, or subject matter, into which artistic works of all kinds can be divided. For example, the detective novel is a genre of fiction. **2.** painting depicting household scenes [Early 19C. Via French, 'type' < Latin *genus* 'birth, kind']

SYNONYMS See ***type***.

genro /gén rṓ/ (*plural same*) *n* **1.** in Japan in the 19th and early 20th centuries, a group of elder statesmen who advised the emperor (*takes a singular or plural verb*) **2.** a member of the genro advising the Japanese emperor [Late 19C. < Japanese, 'first elders']

gens /jenz/ (*plural* **gentes** /jén teez/) *n* **1.** in ancient Rome, a group of aristocratic families with the same name, descended from a common ancestor on the male side (*takes a singular or plural verb*) **2.** a clan, especially one that traces its descent on the male side (*dated*) [Mid-19C. < Latin, 'race, clan']

gent /jent/ *n* same as **gentleman** (*dated informal*) [Mid-16C. Shortening]

gentamicin /jéntə mī́ssin/ *n* a broad-spectrum antibiotic, usually administered by injection. It can cause serious side effects. [Mid-20C. < *genta-*, origin ? + alteration of -MYCIN]

genteel /jen teél/ *adj* **1.** having or displaying refinement and good manners, especially manners that suggest an upper-class background **2.** overdoing the refinement, delicacy of behaviour, or snobbishness thought characteristic of the upper classes in order to create an impression of higher social status [Late 16C. < French *gentil* (see GENTLE)] —**genteelly** *adv* —**genteelness** *n*

genteelism /jen teélizəm/ *n* a word or phrase used in place of another one considered vulgar

gentes ANCIENT HIST, ANTHROP plural of **gens**

gentian /jénsh'n/ *n* **1.** SHOWY FLOWERING PLANT a plant belonging to a large family of annual or perennial species, several of which are cultivated as ornamental alpines. Flowers: typically bright blue or violet, trumpet-shaped. Native to: northern temperate regions and extending south to the Andes. Family: Gentianaceae. **2.** MEDICINAL ROOT the dried roots and rhizome of a European plant. Use: di-

gestive stimulant in herbal medicine. 3. **PLANT PRODUCING DIGESTIVE AID** the plant that produces the digestive stimulant gentian [14C. < Latin *gentiana*, after *Gentius*, 2C BC king of Illyria]

gentian blue *adj* of a purplish-blue colour —**gentian blue** *n*

gentian violet *n* a green dye derived from rosaniline that forms a violet solution in water. Use: biological stain, formerly, in antiseptic lotions.

gentile /jént īl/ *n* **1. NON-JEWISH PERSON** somebody who is not Jewish **2. SOMEBODY CHRISTIAN** a Christian, as distinguished from somebody who is Jewish **3. NON-MORMON** in the Church of Jesus Christ of Latter-Day Saints, somebody who is not a member of this Church **4. HEATHEN** a disbeliever in God (*disapproving*) ■ *adj* **1. NOT JEWISH** not belonging to the Jewish people or faith **2. CHRISTIAN** Christian, as distinguished from Jewish **3.** GRAM **DENOTING PLACE OR PEOPLE** describes a noun such as 'Welsh' or 'Texan' that gives the name of a place or a people [14C. < Latin *gentilis* 'of the same clan' (see GENTLE)]

Gentile da Fabriano /jen tée̍lay da fabri áanō/ (1370?–1427) Italian painter. Although much of his work has been lost, he is considered one of the greatest exponents of the International Gothic style. His most famous surviving work is the *Adoration of the Magi* (1423), an altarpiece painted in Florence. Born **di Massio, Gentile di Niccolò di Giovanni**

Gentileschi /jénti léski/, **Artemisia** (1593?–1651?) Italian painter. One of the first women to receive recognition as an artist, she used the technique of chiaroscuro to great effect, as seen in *Judith Slaying Holofernes* (1620?).

gentility /jen tíllәti/ *n* **1. REFINEMENT** courteous and well-mannered behaviour, especially when it suggests an upper-class background **2. UPPER-CLASS STATUS** the status or way of life of somebody from the upper classes **3. PRETENTIOUSNESS** exaggeratedly refined, delicate, or snobbish behaviour, affected in order to create an impression of higher social status **4. MEMBERS OF UPPER CLASS** people from the upper classes (*takes a singular or plural verb*) [14C. < French *gentilité* < *gentil* (see GENTLE)]

gentle /jént'l/ *adj* (**-tler, -tlest**) **1. KIND** having a mild and kind nature or manner **2. MILD** being moderate in force or degree so that the effects are not severe ○ *a gentle reprimand* **3. USING LITTLE FORCE** using little force or violence ○ *a gentle tap on the shoulder* **4. NOT STEEP** not rising very steeply ○ *a gentle slope* **5. UPPER-CLASS** relating to or having a high social status or class **6. CHIVALROUS** having a gracious and honourable manner (*archaic*) ■ *vt* (**-tles, -tling, -tled**) **1. SOOTHE SOMEBODY** to cause somebody to become less agitated by means of words or actions (*literary*) **2. TAME ANIMAL** to calm an animal and make it domesticated (*formal*) [Pre-12C. Via French *gentil* 'well-born' < Latin *gentilis* 'of the same clan' < *gens* 'race, clan'] —**gentleness** *n* —**gently** *adv*

gentle breeze *n* a wind of between 13 and 19 km/8 and 12 mi. per hour on the Beaufort scale

gentlefolk /jént'l fōk/, **gentlefolks** /-fōks/ *npl* people from a high social class, especially those with an independent income (*archaic*)

gentleman /jént'lmәn/ (*plural* **-men** /-mәn/) *n* **1. POLITE AND CULTURED MAN** a cultured man who behaves with courtesy and thoughtfulness **2. MAN** used as a polite term to refer to a man, regardless of his social position or behaviour ○ *Good morning, ladies and gentlemen.* **3. UPPER-CLASS MAN** a man from a high social class, especially a man with an independent income **4.** HIST **MAN WITH COAT OF ARMS** in English history, a man who was not strictly of noble birth but was entitled to a coat of arms. He ranked above a yeoman in the social order. —**gentlemanliness** *n* —**gentlemanly** *adj*

gentleman-at-arms *n* a member of a troop of forty men who act as a ceremonial guard for the British sovereign on state occasions

gentleman-farmer *n* **1.** a farmer with an independent source of income who farms for pleasure rather than for money **2.** a man who owns a farm but employs a manager and staff to work it

gentleman's agreement *n* an agreement based on trust, not written down, and not enforceable by law

gentleman's gentleman *n* the manservant of an upper-class man (*dated*)

gentlemen's agreement *n* same as **gentleman's agreement**

gentlewoman /jént'l wŏŏmәn/ (*plural* **-women** /-wimin/) *n* **1. POLITE AND CULTURED WOMAN** a cultured woman who behaves with courtesy and thoughtfulness **2. UPPER-CLASS WOMAN** a woman from a high social class, especially a woman with an independent income **3.** HIST **LADY'S PERSONAL ATTENDANT** a woman acting as a personal attendant to a lady of high social rank

gentrify /jéntri fī/ (**-fies, -fying, -fied**) *vt* to transform a traditionally working-class area into a middle-class neighbourhood, usually at the expense of local character and with the result that property becomes unaffordable for local people —**gentrification** /jéntrifi káysh'n/ *n*

gentry /jéntri/ *n* **1. UPPER CLASSES** the group of people who make up the upper social classes (*takes a singular or plural verb*) **2. ENGLISH SOCIAL CLASS** the English social class that ranks just below the aristocracy and consists of families who are not of noble birth but are entitled to have a coat of arms (*takes a singular or plural verb*) **3. PEOPLE** people of a particular kind ○ *the fur-clad gentry who live there* [14C. < Old French *genterie* 'nobility' < *gentil* (see GENTLE)]

gents /jents/ *n* a public toilet for men (*takes a singular or plural verb*) N Am term **men's room**

genuflect /jénnyŏŏ flekt/ (**-flects, -flecting, -flected**) *vi* **1.** to bend the right knee to the floor and rise again as a gesture of religious respect, especially in a Roman Catholic or Anglican church **2.** to show undeserved or unnecessarily deferential respect for somebody or something [Mid-19C. < ecclesiastical Latin *genuflectere* 'bend the knee' < Latin *genu* 'knee' + *flectere* 'bend'] —**genuflection** /jénnyŏŏ fléksh'n/ *n* —**genuflector** *n*

genuine /jénnyoo in/ *adj* **1. REAL** having the qualities or value claimed ○ *a genuine Cézanne* **2. SINCERELY FELT** not affected or pretended ○ *a look of genuine surprise* **3. CANDID** honest and open in relationships with others ○ *a very genuine person* **4. PURE BRED** being of unmixed breeding ○ *of genuine stock* [Late 16C. < Latin *genuinus*] —**genuinely** *adv* —**genuineness** *n*

genus /jéenәss, jénn-/ (*plural* **genera** /jénnәrә/) *n* **1.** BIOL **SET OF CLOSELY RELATED SPECIES** a category in the taxonomic classification of related organisms, comprising one or more species. Similar genera are grouped into families. **2.** LOGIC **BROADER TERM FOR SOMETHING** the more general class or kind in which something is included, e.g. the species 'dog' is included in the genus 'animal' **3. GROUP** a class or group of any kind [Mid-16C. < Latin, 'birth, race, kind']

geo- *prefix* **1.** earth, soil ○ *geomagnetic* ○ *geophyte* **2.** geography, global ○ *geostrategy* [< Greek *gē* 'Earth']

geoarchaeology /jée ō aarki óllәji/ *n* a branch of geology dealing with archaeological sites, especially their formation, including dating, mineral identification, and soil analysis —**geoarchaeologic** /jée ō aarki ә lójjik/ *adj* —**geoarchaeological** *adj* —**geoarchaeologist** *n*

geobotany /jée ō bóttәni/ *n* BOT same as **phytogeography** —**geobotanical** /jée ō bә tánnik'l/ *adj* —**geobotanist** *n*

geocentric /jée ō séntrik/ *adj* **1. HAVING EARTH AT ITS CENTRE** describes the solar system when it is regarded as having the Earth as its centre **2. CONSIDERED FROM EARTH'S CENTRE** measured from, or considered as if viewed from, the centre of the Earth **3. WITH EARTH AS CENTRE OF FOCUS** having the Earth and its inhabitants as the centre of a theory or belief —**geocentrically** *adv*

geochemistry /jée ō kémmistri/ *n* the study of the chemical composition of the Earth's solid matter, and of the solid matter of other planets, meteors, and asteroids —**geochemical** *adj* —**geochemically** *adv* —**geochemist** *n*

geochronology /jée ō krә nóllәji/ *n* the study of the ages and relative ages of geological events and rock formations —**geochronological** /jée ō krónnә lójjik'l/ *adj* —**geochronologically** *adv* —**geochronologist** *n*

geochronometry /jée ō krә nómmәtri/ *n* the measurement of the age of a rock, mineral, or sequence of rocks, or of an event such as a volcanic eruption —**geochronometric** /jée ō krónnә méttrik/ *adj*

geocorona /jée ō kә rṓnә/ *n* the outermost region of the Earth's atmosphere, reaching to a height approximately 15 times the radius of the Earth and consisting mainly of hydrogen

geode /jée ōd/ *n* **1.** a roughly spherical rock mass containing a cavity lined or filled with crystals that have grown unimpeded and so are frequently perfectly formed **2.** the crystal-lined cavity within a geode [Late 17C. Via Latin *geodes* < Greek *geōdēs* 'earthy' < *gē* 'Earth']

geodesic /jée ō dée̍ssik/ *adj* **1.** MATHS relating to the geometry of curved surfaces **2.** GEOG same as **geodetic** ■ *n* MATHS the shortest line between two points on a curved or flat surface

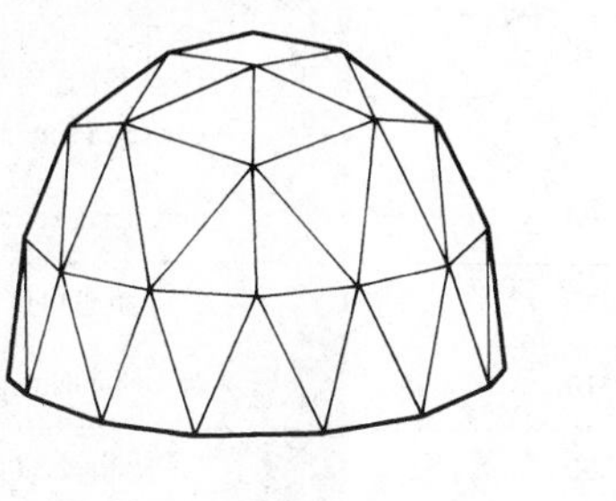

geodesic dome

geodesic dome *n* a dome that has many flat straight-sided faces formed by a framework of bars that intersect to form equilateral triangles or polygons

geodesic line *n* MATHS same as **geodesic**

geodesy /jee óddәssi/ *n* the branch of science that deals with the precise measurement of the size and shape of the Earth, the mapping of points on its surface, and the study of its gravitational field [Late 16C. Via modern Latin < Greek *geōdaisia* < *daiein* 'to divide'] —**geodesist** *n*

geodetic /jée ō déttik/, **geodetical** /-ik'l/ *adj* relating to the precise measurement of the Earth's surface or of points on its surface [Late 17C. < Greek *geōdaitēs* 'land surveyor' < *daiein* 'to divide'] —**geodetically** *adv*

geodetic survey *n* a survey of a very large area of land, with the curvature of the Earth's surface taken into account

geoduck /gŏŏ i duk/, **gweduc** *n* a very large clam. Native to: northwestern Pacific coast of North America. Latin name: *Panope generosa*. [Late 19C. < Salish *gʷídeq*]

geodynamics /jée ō dīnámmiks/ *n* a branch of geology concerned with the study of processes within the Earth's interior and their causative forces (*takes a singular verb*) —**geodynamic** *adj*

geodynamo /jée ō dīnәmō/ *n* the process whereby the rotational movement of the Earth's molten iron core sustains the planet's magnetic field

geoeconomics /jée ō eékә nómmiks, -ékә-/ *n* the study of how the economies of the world's nations relate to and affect each other (*takes a singular verb*) —**geoeconomic** *adj* —**geoeconomically** *adv* —**geoeconomist** /-i kónnәmist/ *n*

Geoffrey of Monmouth /jéffri әv mónmәth/ (1100?–54) English historian and cleric. His 12-volume *Historia Regum Britanniae* (*The History of the Kings of Britain*) (1139?) is a mixture of history and myth, parts of which later formed the basis of the legend of King Arthur.

geog. *abbr* **1.** geographic **2.** geographical **3.** geography

geographical /jée ә gráffik'l/, **geographic** /-gráffik/ *adj* relating to geography or to the geography of a specific region [Mid-16C. < French *géographique* or late Latin *geographicus* < Greek *geōgraphikos* < *geōgraphos* 'writer about the Earth'] —**geographically** *adv*

geographical mile *n* MEASURE same as **nautical mile**

geographic profiling *n* the science of predicting where a criminal lives, based on the locations and frequencies of the crimes committed and following the principle that most offenders carry out crimes relatively locally

geography /ji óggrәfi/ (*plural* **-phies**) *n* **1. STUDY OF EARTH'S PHYSICAL FEATURES** the study of all the physical features of the Earth's surface, including its climate and the

MAIN DIVISIONS OF GEOLOGICAL TIME

Million years ago	Division				Significant events
4,500+	pre-Archean Eon				formation of the Earth
4,000	Archean Eon				formation of land masses, oceans, atmosphere; first single-celled organisms, blue-green algae
2,500	Proterozoic Eon				formation of mountains, glaciers, ozone layer; first invertebrates
570	Phanerozoic Eon				
		Paleozoic Era			
			Cambrian Period		formation of S continent Gondwanaland; first shellfish, sponges
500			Ordovician Period		N America collides with Europe; primitive fish in shallow seas, first coral
435			Silurian Period		Europe separates from N America; first airbreathing animal (scorpion), land plants
410			Devonian Period		Eurasia, Gondwanaland, and America collide; first amphibians, insects
360			Carboniferous Period		
				Mississippian Period	first fern forests, swamps, winged insects, sharks
				Pennsylvanian Period	formation of coal, oil, gas deposits; first reptiles
290			Permian Period		continents combine to form Pangaea; first conifers, mass extinction of invertebrates
248		Mesozoic Era			
			Triassic Period		Pangaea breaks up; first dinosaurs, evergreen forests
206			Jurassic Period		N and S America move west; first mammals, birds
144			Cretaceous Period		Africa and India drift north; extinction of dinosaurs
65		Cenozoic Era			
			Tertiary Period		
				Paleocene Epoch	Antarctica and Australia split; first marsupials, hoofed mammals
55				Eocene Epoch	India joins Asia; first primates, bats, sea mammals
38				Oligocene Epoch	formation of Alps and Himalayas; first elephants, monkeys, great apes
24				Miocene Epoch	formation of Antarctic ice sheet, N prairies; first humanlike apes
5				Pliocene Epoch	formation of Sierra Nevada range; primate ancestors of *Homo sapiens*
1.6			Quaternary Period		
				Pleistocene Epoch	ice ages; mammoths, saber-toothed tigers, early humans
0.01				Holocene Epoch	melting ice sheets; extinctions caused by human activity, global warming

distribution of plant, animal, and human life **2. PHYSICAL FEATURES** the physical features of a place or region, e.g. mountains and rivers **3. LAYOUT OF PLACE** the arrangement of the different parts of a building, city, or other place **4. ARRANGEMENT** the way that something is arranged and the relationships between its different parts ○ *the geography of the criminal mind* [15C. Via Latin < Greek *geōgraphia* 'writing about the Earth'] —**geographer** *n*

geohydrology /jeˊe ō hī drólləji/ *n* GEOL same as **hydrogeology** —**geohydrologic** /jeˊe ō hīdrə lójjik/ *adj* —**geohydrologist** *n*

geoid /jeˊe oyd/ *n* **1.** the slightly flattened sphere that is the shape of the Earth, used in calculating the precise measurements of points on the Earth's surface **2.** a hypothetical surface of the Earth that would exist if a cross section were taken at sea level [Late 19C. < Greek *geoeidēs* (see GEODE)] —**geoidal** *adj*

geol. *abbr* **1.** geologic **2.** geological **3.** geology

geological time *n* the period of time that extends from the beginning of the world to the present day

geologize /ji ólla jīz/ (**-gizes, -gizing, -gized**), **geologise** (**-gises, -gising, -gised**) *vti* to study geology in general, or the geology of a specific place

geology /ji ólləji/ *n* **1.** the study of the structure of the Earth or another planet, especially its rocks, soil, and minerals, and its history and origins **2.** the rocks, minerals, and physical structure of a specific area [Mid-18C. < modern Latin *geologia* 'description of the Earth'] —**geologic** /jeˊe ə lójjik/ *adj* —**geological** *adj* —**geologically** *adv* —**geologist** *n*

geom. *abbr* **1.** geometric **2.** geometrical **3.** geometry

geomagnetic /jeˊe ō mag néttik/ *adj* relating to the magnetic properties of the Earth, or the study of them —**geomagnetically** *adv*

geomagnetic pole *n* GEOG same as **magnetic pole** (sense 2)

geomagnetic storm *n* METEOROL same as **magnetic storm**

geomagnetism /jeˊe ō mágnətizəm/ *n* **1.** the magnetic properties of Earth **2.** the study of the magnetic properties of Earth

geomancy /jeˊe ō manssi/ *n* the art or practice of making predictions based on patterns made by a handful of earth thrown on the ground or by lines connecting randomly placed dots [14C. Via medieval Latin < Greek *geōmanteia* 'divination from the Earth' < *manteia* 'divination'] —**geomancer** *n* —**geomantic** /jeˊe ō mántik/ *adj*

geometer /ji ómmitər/ *n* a student of or an expert in geometry [15C. Via late Latin < Greek *geōmetrēs* 'land measurer' < *gē* 'Earth' + *metrēs* 'measurer']

geometric /jeˊe ə méttrik/, **geometrical** /-ik'l/ *adj* **1. RELATING TO GEOMETRY** conforming to the laws and methods of geometry **2. USING SIMPLE LINES** using straight lines and simple shapes such as circles or squares **3. INCREASING FAST** increasing or decreasing

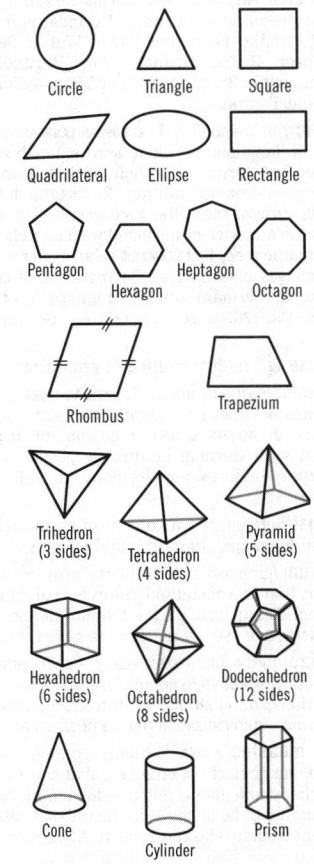

Circle · Triangle · Square

Quadrilateral · Ellipse · Rectangle

Pentagon · Hexagon · Heptagon · Octagon

Rhombus · Trapezium

Trihedron (3 sides) · Tetrahedron (4 sides) · Pyramid (5 sides)

Hexahedron (6 sides) · Octahedron (8 sides) · Dodecahedron (12 sides)

Cone · Cylinder · Prism

geometry: shapes and solids

very rapidly ○ *geometric growth* [Mid-17C. Via French *géométrique* < Greek *geōmetrikos* < *geōmetrēs* (see GEOMETER)] —**geometrically** *adv*

Geometric *adj* relating to a period of ancient Greek culture, between 900 and 700 BC, noted for its decorative use of simple lines and shapes, especially on pottery

geometrical *adj* same as **geometric**

geometric mean *n* the average of a set of *n* values, described mathematically as the *n*th root of their product

geometric progression *n* a series of numbers in which each number is separated by the same numerical step

geometrics /jeé ə métriks/ *npl* straight lines and simple shapes, e.g. circles or squares, used in design and decoration

geometric series *n* a series of numbers (**geometric progression**) separated by a constant numerical step expressed as a sum, e.g. 1+4+16+64

geometrid /ji ómmətrid/ *n* a moth with a slender body and broad wings and larvae that crawl with a characteristic looping movement. Family: Geometridae. [Late 19C. < modern Latin *Geometridae* 'land measurers'] —**geometrid** *adj*

geometrize /ji ómmə trīz/ (**-trizes, -trizing, -trized**), **geometrise** (**-trises, -trising, -trised**) *v* **1.** *vti* to represent something in geometric form **2.** *vti* to apply the principles of geometry to something —**geometrization** /ji ómmə trī záysh'n/ *n*

geometry /ji ómmətri/ *n* **1.** MATHEMATICS OF SHAPES the branch of mathematics that is concerned with the properties and relationships of points, lines, angles, curves, surfaces, and solids **2.** KIND OF GEOMETRY a particular system or class of geometry, e.g. a set of distinct theories or its application to a particular type of problem or object ○ *Euclidean geometry* ○ *solid geometry* **3.** ARRANGEMENT OF SOMETHING the way the different parts of something fit together in relation to each other [14C. Via French *géométrie* < Latin *geometria* 'measuring of the Earth' < *gē* 'Earth' + *metron* 'measure'] —**geometrician** /jeé ə me trísh'n, jee ómmə-/ *n*

geomorphic /jeé ō máwrfik/ *adj* relating to the surface features of the Earth or another planet

geomorphology /jeé ō mawr fólləji/ *n* the branch of geology that examines the formation and structure of the features of the surface of the Earth or of another planet —**geomorphologic** /jeé ō mawrfə lójjik/ *adj* —**geomorphological** *adj* —**geomorphologically** *adv* —**geomorphologist** *n*

geophagy /ji óffəji/ *n* the eating of soil, clay, or chalk

geophone /jeé ə fōn/ *n* an electronic instrument that picks up vibrations in the Earth

geophysics /jeé ō fízziks/ *n* the branch of earth science that deals with the physics and physical processes of the Earth, especially using noninvasive techniques such as acoustic surveys of the structure of rocks (*takes a singular verb*) —**geophysical** *adj* —**geophysically** *adv* —**geophysicist** *n*

geophyte /jeé ō fīt/ *n* a perennial plant that propagates from organs such as bulbs, tubers, or rhizomes that are below ground

geopolitics /jeé ō póllətiks/ *npl* **1.** the relationships that exist between a country's politics and its geography, or the influences that geography has on political relations between countries (*takes a plural verb*) ■ *n* the study of the interrelationship between politics, geography, and population distribution in or between countries (*takes a singular verb*) —**geopolitical** /jeé ō pə líttik'l/ *adj* —**geopolitically** *adv* —**geopolitician** /jeé ō póllə tísh'n/ *n*

geoponics /jeé ō pónniks/ *n* the scientific study of agriculture (*takes a singular verb*) [Early 17C. < Greek *geōponikos* 'of farming' < *geōponos* 'farmer'] —**geoponic** *adj*

geoprofiling /jeéō prófiling/ *n* CRIME same as **geographic profiling**

Geordie /jáwrdi/ *n* **1.** somebody who comes from Tyneside, especially somebody who speaks the local dialect of English **2.** the dialect of English spoken in Tyneside [Mid-19C. < local pronunciation of *Georgie*, diminutive of the name *George*] —**Geordie** *adj*

Geordieland /jáwrdi land/ *n* Tyneside (*informal*)

George /jawrj/, **St** (*d.* AD 303?) patron saint of England. According to legend, he killed a dragon that was terrorizing a village and then converted the inhabitants to Christianity. He was made patron saint of England in the 14th century.

George I (1660–1727) king of Great Britain and Ireland. German-born, he was the great-grandson of James I and the first of Britain's Hanoverian kings (1714–27).

George II (1683–1760) king of Great Britain and Ireland. German-born British monarch, who as king (1727–60) was a field commander in the War of the Austrian Succession (1740–48).

George III (1738–1820) king of Great Britain and Ireland. He was the first British-born Hanoverian king. His reign (1760–1820) was marked by the American War of Independence. In later years, he was increasingly affected by a psychiatric disorder that led finally to the establishment of a regency (1811) under his son, later George IV.

'Born and educated in this country I glory in the name of Briton.'
[George III, *Speech from the throne*; 1760]

George IV (1762–1830) king of Great Britain and Ireland. Notorious for his extravagant habits, he was regent for George III (1811–20) and king (1820–30).

George V (1865–1936) king of Great Britain and Ireland, king of Great Britain and Northern Ireland. His reign (1910–36) saw the partition of Ireland (1922). Notable for his naval career, he renounced the family's German titles during World War I.

'How is the Empire?'
[George V, *Attributed last words*; 21 January 1936]

George VI (1895–1952) He succeeded to the throne after the abdication of his brother Edward VIII (1936). He was greatly admired for his national leadership during World War II.

'It is not the walls that make the city, but the people who live within them. The walls of London may be battered, but the spirit of the Londoner stands resolute and undismayed.'
[George VI, *Radio broadcast*; 23 September 1940]

George Cross *n* a British medal awarded, especially to civilians, for gallantry [Because instituted in 1940 by GEORGE VI]

Georgetown /jáwrj town/ **1.** port and capital city of Guyana. It is on the Atlantic coast at the mouth of the Demerara River. Population: 275,000 (1999). **2.** affluent residential and commercial district of northwestern Washington, DC and the home of Georgetown University. Originally a separate port on the Potomac River, it was incorporated into the District of Columbia in 1871.

George Town 1. town and capital of the Cayman Islands, situated on Grand Cayman Island in the northwestern Caribbean. Population: 19,000 (1996). **2.** town in northern Tasmania, Australia. It is one of Australia's oldest settlements. Population: 6,483 (2002 estimate). **3.** seaport and capital city of Penang State, Malaysia. It was the site of the first British settlement in Malaysia. Population: 219,380 (1991).

georgette /jawr jét/ *n* a thin lightweight silk or cotton fabric with a matt finish (*often used before a noun*) [Early 20C. After Madame *Georgette* de la Plante, late 19C. Parisian dressmaker]

Georgia /jáwrjə/ **1.** country on the eastern coast of the Black Sea bordered on the north by Russia and on the south by Turkey, Armenia, and Azerbaijan. The country is dominated by the Greater Caucasus to the north and the Lesser Caucasus to the south. Language: Georgian. Currency: lari. Capital: Tbilisi. Population: 4,934,413 (2003). Area: 69,700 sq. km/26,900 sq. mi. Official name **Republic of Georgia 2.** state in the southeastern United States, bordered by South Carolina, the Atlantic Ocean, Florida, Alabama, North Carolina, and Tennessee. Capital: Atlanta. Population: 8,560,310 (2002 estimate). Area: 152,750 sq. km/58,977 sq. mi.

Georgian[1] /jáwrjən/ *adj* **1.** HIST OF 1714 TO 1830 IN BRITAIN relating to the time of the British kings George I, II, III, and IV, who reigned consecutively from 1714 to 1830 **2.** ARCHIT OF 18C ARCHITECTURAL STYLE built in or imitating a neoclassical style of architecture or furniture that flourished in Great Britain and the United States in the 18th and early 19th centuries **3.** LITERAT OF 20C LITERARY MOVEMENT relating to a movement in early 20th-century poetry that favoured traditional styles, especially pastoral ■ *n* **1.** HIST SOMEBODY FROM GEORGIAN TIMES somebody who lived during the Georgian period **2.** LITERAT GEORGIAN WRITER a writer whose works belong to the Georgian literary movement [Late 18C. < the man's name *George*]

Georgian[2] /jáwrjən/ *n* **1.** SOMEBODY FROM GEORGIA somebody who comes from the Republic of Georgia **2.** LANGUAGE OF GEORGIA the official language of the Republic of Georgia, belonging to the Kartvelian language family. Native speakers: 3.5 million. **3.** SOMEBODY FROM US STATE OF GEORGIA somebody who comes from the state of Georgia in the United States [15C. < GEORGIA] —**Georgian** *adj*

Georgian Bay /jáwrjən-/ northeastern arm of Lake Huron, in southeastern Ontario, Canada. Area: 15,000 sq. km/5,800 sq. mi.

georgic /jáwrjik/ *adj* relating to or depicting rural life (*literary*) ■ *n* a poem about rural life [Early 16C. Via Latin < Greek *geōrgikos* < *geōrgos* 'farmer' < *gē* 'Earth']

geoscience /jeé ō sí ənss/ n a science that deals with Earth, e.g. geology or geophysics —**geoscientist** n

geosphere /jeé ō sfeer/ n the solid matter of the Earth, as distinct from the seas, plants, animals, and surrounding atmosphere —**geospheric** /jeé ō sférrik/ adj

geostationary /jeé ō stáysh'nəri/ adj describes the orbit of a satellite that circles the Earth above the equator at a speed matching the Earth's rotation, thus appearing to remain stationary, or a satellite in such an orbit. Most communications satellites are in geostationary orbit.

geostrategy /jeé ō stráttəji/ (plural -gies) n 1. the study of strategy in relation to the geopolitical situation of a country or region 2. the policy of a nation based on a combination of geographical and political factors —**geostrategic** /-strə teéjik/ adj —**geostrategist** n

geostrophic /jeé ō stróffik/ adj arising from the rotation of the Earth —**geostrophically** adv

geosynchronous /jeé ō síng krənəss/ adj AEROSP same as **geostationary**

geosyncline /jeé ō síng klīn/ n a long broad depression in the Earth's crust where it has sunk over time as it has accumulated a thick layer of sedimentary deposits —**geosynclinal** /jeé ō sing klín'l/ adj

geotaxis /jeé ō táksiss/ n movement by an organism or cell in response to the force of gravity —**geotactic** adj —**geotactically** adv

geotectonic /jeé ō tek tónnik/ adj relating to the large-scale structure of the Earth's crust —**geotectonically** adv

geothermal /jeé ō thúrm'l/ adj relating to or produced by the heat in the interior of the Earth —**geothermally** adv

geothermal energy n energy in the form of heat obtained from hot circulating ground water

geothermal gradient n the change in temperature encountered with depth within the Earth

geotropism /jee óttrəpizəm/ n plant growth or movement in response to gravity. Upward growth of plant parts, against gravity, is called negative geotropism, and downward growth of roots is called positive geotropism. —**geotropic** /jeé ō tróppik/ adj —**geotropically** adv

gerah /geérə/ n an ancient Hebrew coin worth one twentieth of a shekel [Mid-16C. < Hebrew gērāh]

Geraldton /jérrəldtən/ port on Champion Bay, Western Australia, about 375 km/230 mi. north of Perth. Population: 19,728 (2002 estimate).

geraniol /ji ráyni ol/ n a pale yellow or colourless alcohol that smells like geraniums. Source: essential oils. Use: in perfumes, flavourings. Formula: $C_{10}H_{18}O$. [Late 19C. < GERANIUM]

geranium

geranium /jə ráyni əm/ n 1. PLANTS PLANT WITH BRIGHTLY COLOURED FLOWERS a popular garden plant with large rounded leaves. Flowers: bright red, pink, white, on tall stalks. Genus: Pelargonium. 2. PLANTS PLANT WITH SAUCER-SHAPED FLOWERS a plant with divided leaves, e.g. cranesbill and herb Robert. Flowers: pink, blue, white, red, saucer-shaped. Genus: Geranium. 3. COLOURS BRIGHT RED COLOUR a red colour tinged with orange, like that of a scarlet geranium [Mid-16C. Via Latin < Greek geranion < geranos 'crane'; from the resemblance of the spur on some species' fruit to a crane's bill] —**geranium** adj

gerbil

gerbil /júrb'l/ n a small rodent resembling a mouse with long back legs. Native to: hot dry parts of Africa, Asia. [Mid-19C. Via French gerbille < modern Latin gerbillus, diminutive of gerboa (see JERBOA)]

gerenuk /gérrinōōk/ (plural -nuks or same) n a slender antelope, the male of which has long horns that curve backwards. Native to: eastern Africa. Latin name: Litocranius walleri. [Late 19C. < Somali]

gerfalcon n BIRDS another spelling of **gyrfalcon**

geriatric /jérri áttrik/ adj 1. MED RELATING TO ELDERLY PEOPLE relating to the diagnosis, treatment, and prevention of illness in elderly people 2. OFFENSIVE TERM an offensive term meaning showing the effects of age ■ n MED ELDERLY PERSON an elderly person (technical; used in medical contexts) [Early 20C. < Greek gēras 'old age']

geriatrics /jérri áttriks/ n the branch of medicine that deals with the illnesses and medical care of elderly people (takes a singular verb) —**geriatrician** /jérri ə trísh'n/ n

Géricault /zháyri kó/, Théodore (1791–1824) French painter. The leading romantic painter of his time, he developed a colourful dramatic style exemplified in his best-known work Raft of the Medusa (1818–19).

germ /jurm/ n 1. MICROBIOL MICROORGANISM a microorganism, especially one that can cause disease 2. MICROBIOL CELL the smallest element in an organism such as a spore or a fertilized egg that is capable of growing into a complete adult or part 3. BEGINNING the first sign of something that will develop ○ the germ of an idea [Mid-15C. Via French germe < Latin germen 'seed, sprout' < gignere 'beget']

german /júrmən/ adj having the same parents, or closely related (formal) ○ brothers-german [Via French germain < Latin germanus 'having the same parents' < germen (see GERM)]

German /júrmən/ n 1. SOMEBODY FROM GERMANY somebody who comes from Germany 2. LANGUAGE OF GERMANY the official language of Germany, Austria, and Liechtenstein and one of the official languages of Switzerland, also spoken elsewhere in the world, belonging to the Germanic branch of Indo-European. Native speakers: 100 million. Other speakers: 100 million. See panel on next page 3. SOMEBODY WHO SPEAKS GERMAN somebody whose first language is German [14C. < Latin Germanus, applied to a group of related peoples of northern and central Europe] —**German** adj

germanate /júrmə nayt/ n a salt containing an anionic grouping of germanium and oxygen

German cockroach n a small brown cockroach that is a common pest throughout the world. Latin name: Blattella germanica.

German Democratic Republic /júrmən-/ former republic of central Europe, reunited with the rest of Germany in 1990. It was founded under the influence of the former Soviet Union in 1949 and recognized as an independent state in 1955. Area: 108,178 sq. km/41,768 sq. mi.

germander /jur mándər/ (plural -ders or same) n a plant of the mint family. Flowers: small, pink, white, or pale purple, with a small upper lip. Genus: Teucrium. [15C. Via medieval Latin germandr(e)a < Greek khamaidrus 'ground oak']

germane /jur máyn/ adj suitably related to something, especially something being discussed [Early 17C. Variant of GERMAN] —**germanely** adv —**germaneness** n

German East Africa former German territory comprising present-day Burundi, Rwanda, and mainland Tanzania. Following World War I, Belgium took over Ruanda-Urundi, Now Burundi and Rwanda, while Britain took over Tanganyika, Now mainland Tanzania.

Germanic /jur mánnik/ n 1. EUROPEAN LANGUAGE GROUP a group of languages spoken across northwestern Europe that forms a branch of Indo-European. Native speakers: 500 million. 2. ANCESTOR OF MODERN EUROPEAN LANGUAGE GROUP the reconstructed language that is the ancestor of modern languages classified as Germanic ■ adj 1. OF GERMANIC relating to the group of languages classified as Germanic 2. OF GERMANY relating to Germany, or its language, people, or culture [Mid-17C. < Latin Germanicus < Germanus (see GERMAN)]

germanise vti another spelling of **germanize**

Germanism /júrmənizəm/ n 1. GERMAN WORD a word or phrase borrowed or adapted from the German language 2. GERMAN QUALITY a custom or trait associated with German culture or people 3. LIKING FOR GERMANY fondness for Germany and all things German

Germanist /júrmənist/ n a student of or specialist in German language, literature, and culture

germanium /jur máyni əm/ n a brittle grey crystalline element that is a metalloid. Source: coal, zinc ore. Use: semiconductors, alloys. Symbol Ge. See table at **element** [Late 19C. < Latin Germanus (see GERMAN)]

germanize /júrmə nīz/ (-izes, -izing, -ized), **germanise** (-ises, -ising, -ised) vti to adopt German styles, tastes, institutions, or customs, or introduce them into something —**germanization** /júrmə nī záysh'n/ n

German measles n UK a highly contagious viral disease, particularly of children, that causes swelling of the lymph glands and a reddish-pink rash on the skin. It can be harmful to the unborn baby of a pregnant woman who contracts it. ANZ, N Am term **rubella**

Germanophile /jur mánnə fīl/ n an admirer of Germany and the German people

Germanophobe /jur mánnə fōb/ n a hater of Germany or the German people

German shepherd n Aus, N Am a large working dog with medium-length hair, pointed ears, and a muscular build, belonging to a breed originally developed in Germany that is often used as a guard dog or police dog. UK term **Alsatian**

German silver n METALL same as **nickel silver**

Germany /júrməni/ country in central Europe. Divided into East and West Germany following World War II, it became a unified country again in 1990. Language: German. Currency: euro. Capital: Berlin. Population: 82,398,326 (2003). Area: 356,970 sq. km/137,827 sq. mi. Official name **Federal Republic of Germany**. See map on next page

germ cell n MICROBIOL same as **germ** (sense 2)

germicide /júrmi sīd/ n a substance that kills germs —**germicidal** /júrmi síd'l/ adj

germinal /júrmin'l/ adj 1. relating to reproductive cells 2. relating or belonging to the earliest stage in the development of something (formal) [Early 19C. < Latin germen (see GERM)] —**germinally** adv

germinal disc n BIOL same as **blastodisc**

germinal vesicle n the enlarged nucleus of an egg before it develops into an ovum

germinate /júrmi nayt/ (-nates, -nating, -nated) v 1. vti to start to grow from a seed or spore into a new individual, or cause a seed or spore to do this 2. vi to be created and start to develop ○ seeds of doubt germinating in his mind [Late 16C. < Latin germinat-, past participle of germinare < germen (see GERM)] —**germination** /júrmi náysh'n/ n —**germinative** /-nətiv/ adj —**germinator** n

germ layer n any of the three distinct layers of cells formed during an embryo's early stages of development (**gastrulation**)

germ line n a group of cells in a developing embryo from which reproductive cells (**gametes**) develop, regarded as the line of descent from one generation to another

germplasm /júrm plazəm/ n the hereditary material that is transmitted from one generation to another

LANGUAGE HERITAGE *German* Much of English is made up of words from other languages, and German is an important contributor, especially to the vocabulary of medicine and other sciences. For example, *aspirin*, first recorded in English in the 19th century, comes directly from German: it is a contraction of *acetylierte Spirsäure* 'acetylated spiraeic acid', an old name for *salicylic acid*. Other such German émigrés are *cobalt* (late 17th century, from German *Kobalt*, a variant of *Kobold* 'harmful goblin', from miners' belief that cobalt ore was harmful to neighbouring silver ore), *heroin* (late 19th, from German *Heroin*, originally a trademark), and *peptide* (early 20th).

German scientific vocabulary has also used words whose ultimate ancestries lie in other lands and languages. Examples are *allergy*, which arrived in English in the early 20th century from German *Allergie* but is formed from Greek *allos* 'other'; *botulism*, which came from German *Botulismus* 'sausage poisoning', from Latin *botulus* 'sausage'; and *neuron*, which came from German *Neuron* from a Greek word meaning 'sinew, cord, nerve'. Occasionally German has combined with other languages to create what might be called 'international portmanteau words' combining the sound and meaning of two words. A good example is *lumpenproletariat*, a mix of German *Lumpen*, the plural of *Lump* 'ragamuffin', and French *prolétariat* 'the working class'.

Many direct borrowings from German are easily recognizable because they have gone through little or no structural alterations in transit. These words encompass many subject categories. A few examples are, by category: psychology *angst*, *gestalt*; politics *bund*, *realpolitik*; zoology *dachshund*, *schnauzer*; literature *festschrift*, *bildungsroman*; literature and sociology *Sturm und Drang*; music *leitmotif*; mythology *Götterdämmerung*; food *kaffeeklatsch*, *pretzel*, *sauerbraten*, *sauerkraut*, *stollen*, *strudel*, *zwieback*; education *kindergarten*; warfare *blitzkrieg* (from which we get *blitz*), *stalag* (a contraction of *Stammlager* 'main camp'); and general terms such as *ersatz*, *gesundheit*, *kitsch*, *schadenfreude*, *spiel*, *wunderkind*, and *zeitgeist*. Some English words come from German placenames. Among them are *frankfurter*, *hamburger*, *hock*, and *Rottweiler* from *Frankfurt am Main*, *Hamburg*, *Hocheim*, and *Rottweil*, respectively.

Some German borrowings into English have undergone structural alterations to such an extent that they no longer overtly resemble their ancestral roots. One is *poodle*, first recorded in English in the early 19th century, coming from German *Pudel*, a shortening of *Pudelhund*, from a Low German word *pudeln* 'to splash in water' plus *Hund* 'dog'. A few English words are direct loan translations from German. Among them are: *thing-in-itself*, a translation of *Ding an sich*, *Brownshirt*, a translation of *Braunhemd*, *superman*, from *Übermensch* (itself an 1883 coinage by Nietzsche and a direct borrowing into English as well), *world view*, a translation of *Weltanschauung* (also a direct borrowing into English), the expression *out of sight*, a translation of *ausgezeichnet*, and the infamous *Final Solution*, a translation of *Endlösung*. In another, rather quirky, migratory pattern, the English word *boxer* 'fighter' transited the English Channel to Germany, there to be applied to the dog because of its wide, flattened nose, and then returned to English in the early 20th century in this new sense.

Germany

germ theory *n* **1.** the theory that all infectious and contagious diseases are caused by microorganisms **2.** the theory that organisms develop from previous generations through the growth of germ cells

germ tube *n* a hollow tube that grows from a germinating spore

germ warfare *n* MIL same as **biological warfare**

germy /júrmi/ (**-ier**, **-iest**) *adj* full of harmful microorganisms (*informal*) —**germiness** *n*

gerodontics /jérrō dóntiks/ *n* the branch of dentistry focusing on the needs of elderly people (*takes a singular verb*) [Late 20C. < Greek *gēras* 'old age'] —**gerodontic** *adj*

Gerona /jə rốnə/, **Girona** city and capital of Gerona Province, Catalonia, northeastern Spain. It is situated about 90 km/55 mi. northeast of Barcelona. Population: 77,475 (2002).

Geronimo

Geronimo /jə rónnimō/ (1829–1909) Chiricahua Apache leader. A warrior of legendary courage, he began in 1876 to lead his people in raids on white settlers to oppose the forcible dispossession of Native Americans from their land in New Mexico. He was captured by government troops in 1886. He later became a farmer in Oklahoma. Born **Goyathlay**

> 'It [Arizona] is my land, my home, my father's land, to which I now ask to be allowed to return. I want to spend my last days there, and be buried among those mountains.'
> [Geronimo, *Letter to President Ulysses S. Grant*; 1877]

geront- *prefix* ageing, old age ○ *gerontology* [Via French < Greek *geront-*, stem of *gerōn* 'old man']

geronto- same as **geront-** [Via French < Greek *gerōn* 'old man']

gerontocracy /jérron tókrəssi/ (*plural* **-cies**) *n* **1.** a system of government in which the elders are chosen as rulers **2.** a group of elders who make up a government (*takes a singular or plural verb*) —**gerontocrat** /jə róntə krat/ *n* —**gerontocratic** /jə róntə kráttik/ *adj*

gerontology /jérron tólləji/ *n* the scientific study of ageing and its effects —**gerontologic** /jə róntə lójjik/ *adj* —**gerontological** *adj* —**gerontologist** *n*

Gerry /gérri/, **Elbridge** (1744–1814) vice president of the United States. He signed the Declaration of Independence and the Articles of Confederation, and as governor of Massachusetts (1810–12) reorganized electoral districts in a process that came to be called 'gerrymandering'. He was James Madison's vice president (1813–14).

gerrymander /jérri mandər/ *vti* (**-ders**, **-dering**, **-dered**) to manipulate an electoral area, usually by altering its boundaries, in order to gain an unfair political advantage in an election ■ *n* an unfair manipulation of an electoral area for political advantage [Early 19C. Blend of Elbridge GERRY + SALAMANDER, from the shape of an electoral district he created to favour his own party]

Gershwin /gúrshwin/, **George** (1898–1937) US composer. Jazz, classical, and popular influences combined in his outstandingly inventive works, many of which became American classics. He wrote *Rhapsody in Blue* (1924), and with his brother Ira Gershwin, the opera *Porgy and Bess* (1935), and songs including 'Someone to Watch Over Me'. Born **Gershwin, Jacob**

> 'It ain't necessarily so— / The things that you're liable / To read in the Bible— / It ain't necessarily so.'

George Gershwin

[George Gershwin, 'It Ain't Necessarily So', *Porgy and Bess*; 1935]

Gershwin, **Ira** (1896–1983) US lyricist and dramatist. A collaborator with his brother George Gershwin and other leading composers, he wrote lyrics for 20 Broadway musicals, and shared a Pulitzer Prize for *Of Thee I Sing* (1931). Born **Gershvin, Israel**

> 'I got rhythm, / I got music, / I got my man— / Who could ask for anything more?'
> [Ira Gershwin, 'I Got Rhythm', *Girl Crazy*; 1930]

gerund /jérrənd/ *n* a noun formed from a verb, describing an action, state, or process. In English, it is formed from the verb's *-ing* form, e.g. 'smoking' in 'No smoking'. In Latin it is a noun ending in '-ndum'. [Early 16C. < late Latin *gerundium* < Latin *gerere* 'carry on'] —**gerundial** /jə rúndi əl/ *adj*

gerundive /jə rúndiv/ *n* a Latin adjective ending in '-ndus', formed from a verb and meaning 'that must or ought to be done' [15C. < late Latin *gerundivus modus* 'gerundive mood' < *gerundium* (see GERUND)] —**gerundival** /jérrən dív'l/ *adj*

gesso /jéssō/ *n* **1.** a mixture of plaster and glue or size. Use: in sculpture, as a background for paintings. **2.** (*plural* **gessoes**) a painting done on gesso, or a sculpture made from it [Late 16C. Via Italian < Latin *gypsum* (see GYPSUM)] —**gessoed** *adj*

Gestalt /gə shtált/ (*plural* **-stalts** or **-stalten** /-shtáltən/), **gestalt** *n* a set of things such as a person's thoughts and experiences considered as a whole and regarded as amounting to more than the sum of its parts [Early 20C. < German, 'shape'] —**Gestaltist** *n*

Gestalt psychology *n* a branch of psychology that treats behaviour and perception as an integrated whole and not simply the sum of individual stimuli and responses

Gestalt therapy *n* a form of psychotherapy in which emphasis is placed on feelings and on the influence on personality development of unresolved personal issues from the past

Gestapo /ge staápō/ *n* the secret state police under the Nazi regime in Germany, noted for its brutality [Mid-20C. German acronym < *Geheime Staatspolizei* 'Secret State Police']

gestate /je stáyt/ (**-tates**, **-tating**, **-tated**) *vti* **1.** to carry offspring in the womb, or develop as offspring in the womb **2.** to develop in the mind, or allow an idea or plan to develop in the mind [Mid-19C. < Latin *gestat-* (see GESTATION)] —**gestatory** *adj*

gestation /je stáysh'n/ *n* **1.** BIOL CARRYING OF OFFSPRING IN WOMB the process of carrying offspring in the womb during pregnancy **2.** BIOL PERIOD OF DEVELOPMENT OF FOETUS the period of development of the offspring during pregnancy **3.** DEVELOPMENT the development of an idea or plan in the mind, or the time it takes to develop [Mid-16C. < Latin *gestation-* < *gestat-*, past participle of *gestare* 'carry in the womb' < *gerere* 'carry'] —**gestational** *adj*

gesticulate /je stíkyoŏ layt/ (**-lates**, **-lating**, **-lated**) *vti* to move the arms or hands when speaking, or express something with movements of the arms or hands [Early 17C. < Latin *gesticulat-*, past participle of *gesticulari* < *gestus* 'action, gesture' < *gerere* 'carry, act'] —**gesticulation** /je stíkyoŏ láysh'n/ *n* —**gesticulative** /-lətiv/ *adj* —**gesticulator** *n* —**gesticulatory** /-lətəri/ *adj*

gesture /jéschər/ *n* **1.** BODY MOVEMENT a movement made with a part of the body in order to express meaning

or emotion or to communicate an instruction **2.** ACTION COMMUNICATING SOMETHING an action intended to communicate feelings or intentions **3.** USE OF GESTURES the use of body movements to communicate ■ *vti* (**-tures, -turing, -tured**) MAKE BODY MOVEMENT to make a movement with a part of the body in order to express meaning or emotion or to communicate an instruction [15C. < medieval Latin *gestura* 'deportment' < Latin *gerere* 'carry, act'] —**gestural** *adj* —**gesturally** *adv*

ORIGIN The Latin word *gerere* 'to carry, act' from which ***gesture*** is derived, is also the source of English *congest, digest, gestation, gesticulate, ingest, jest,* and *suggestion.*

gesundheit /gə zo͝ont hīt/ *interj* used to wish good health to somebody who has just sneezed (*humorous*) [Early 20C. < German, 'health']

get[1] /get/ (**gets, getting, got** /got/) CORE MEANING: a verb indicating that somebody obtains, receives, earns, or is given something. It is often used instead of more formal terms such as 'obtain' or 'acquire'. ○ *We're trying to ensure that our child gets a good education.* ○ *Where will they get the money to buy the land?*

1. *vi* BECOME to become or begin to have a particular quality ○ *When I get nervous, I get scared.* **2.** *vt* CAUSE SOMETHING TO BE DONE to cause something to happen or be done ○ *I must get the car cleaned.* **3.** *vt* BRING SOMETHING to fetch or bring something ○ *I'm going back to my apartment to get my watch.* ○ *I'll get your coat for you.* **4.** *vt* CATCH ILLNESS to be affected by an illness or medical condition ○ *He got chicken pox last year.* **5.** *vi* BE IN PARTICULAR STATE to enter or leave a particular state or condition ○ *Get ready to leave in five minutes.* **6.** *vi* MOVE SOMEWHERE to succeed in moving or arriving somewhere ○ *It was already midnight when we got home.* **7.** *aux v* FORMS PASSIVES used instead of 'be' as an auxiliary verb to form passives ○ *If you play with matches you will get burned.* **8.** *vt* PREPARE FOOD to prepare a meal ○ *I'll get dinner tonight.* **9.** *vt* PERSUADE SOMEBODY to persuade somebody to do something ○ *Colleagues had tried to get her to take a vacation.* **10.** *vt* USE FORM OF TRANSPORTATION to take a particular form of transportation ○ *I don't want to drive – I'd rather get a plane.* **11.** *vt* OBTAIN RESULT to obtain a result, e.g. by experiment or calculation ○ *What's the answer? I get nine.* **12.** *vt* RECEIVE SIGNAL to receive a broadcast signal such as a radio or television broadcast ○ *I can't get Channel 5 with that aerial.* **13.** *vt* HAVE TIME to have the time or opportunity to do something ○ *I'll fix it as soon as I get the time.* **14.** *vt* HAVE IDEA to have or receive an idea, impression, feeling, or benefit ○ *You've got the wrong impression – I'm not like that at all.* ○ *I get a lot of pleasure from his stories.* **15.** *vt* MANAGE TO SEE SOMETHING to succeed in seeing something ○ *get a close-up look* **16.** *vt* BEGIN SOMETHING to begin doing something (*informal*) ○ *Let's get going – we have to be there by eight.* **17.** *vt* MANAGE SOMETHING to manage or contrive something (*informal*) ○ *How did she get to be so famous?* **18.** *vt* UNDERSTAND SOMETHING to hear or understand something, e.g. a joke or somebody's point (*informal*) ○ *What's that? I didn't get what you said.* **19.** *vt* IRRITATE SOMEBODY to annoy or irritate somebody (*informal*) ○ *That high whining noise really gets me.* **20.** *vt* ARREST SOMEBODY to arrest or capture somebody (*informal*) ○ *They got him just as he was running out of the bank.* **21.** *vt* HIT SOMEBODY to hit somebody on the body (*informal*) ○ *The blow got him in the face.* **22.** *vt* HAVE REVENGE ON SOMEBODY to have revenge on somebody, especially by killing the person (*informal*) ○ *The heroes get Dracula in the end.* **23.** *vi* GAIN ACCESS to gain access to somebody with intent to bribe him or her (*informal*) ○ *I thought he was incorruptible, but they finally got to him.* **24.** *vi* LEAVE to go away from a place or person (*informal; often used in commands*) ○ *Now get!* **25.** *vt* CONCEIVE SOMEBODY to beget or conceive somebody (*archaic*) [13C. < Old Norse *geta* < Indo-European, 'seize'] —**getable** *adj* ◇ **get with it** to become fashionable and responsive to new styles and ideas (*informal*)

USAGE The use of ***get*** instead of *be* to form the passive is more acceptable in some contexts than others: *The house is* [or *gets*] *cleaned once a fortnight. The fête was* [not *got*] *opened by the mayor.* ***Get*** is usually more informal than *be*: an interviewer might ask an interviewee *If you are offered the job, will you accept it?* whereas the interviewee might tell a friend, *If I get offered the job, I'll take it.* ***Get*** is probably most acceptable when it is used to imply that the subject of the sentence bears at least some responsibility for an event or action, as in *If you play with matches, you may get burned* as opposed to *The driver of the vehicle was badly burned in the crash.*

SYNONYMS ***get, acquire, obtain, gain, procure, secure***

CORE MEANING: to come into possession of something

get to obtain, receive, earn, or be given something ○ *He managed to get a job on a building site.* ○ *'The public will get a worse railway for more money', he claimed.* **acquire** to get possession of something, sometimes suggesting that time or effort was involved ○ *the knowledge, skills, and understanding that students are expected to acquire* ○ *He inherited some property and acquired more through marriage.* **obtain** to get something, especially by making an effort or having the necessary qualifications ○ *The best results are obtained from watercolours.* ○ *Schools and colleges can obtain the documents from the relevant agencies.* **gain** to get something through effort, skill, or merit ○ *The candidate was steadily gaining more support.* ○ *Students are encouraged to go on placement to gain experience of the world of work.* **procure** to get something, especially with effort or special care ○ *He procured a copy of the book from the local library.* **secure** to get something, especially after using considerable effort to persuade somebody to grant or allow it ○ *Having just secured world rights for her first book, she's leading a life of leisure.* ○ *The team has secured lucrative support from two local firms.*

get about *vi* **1.** MOVE ABOUT to be able to move about while affected by or recovering from a medical condition **2.** BECOME KNOWN to become known, especially contrary to somebody's wishes **3.** TRAVEL to travel, especially contrary to expectations **4.** same as **get around** (sense 1)

get across *v* **1.** *vti* to make something understood, or communicate clearly ○ *I don't seem to be getting across to you.* **2.** *vt* to annoy or irritate somebody ○ *She's really managed to get across him, somehow.*

get after *vt* to keep telling somebody to do something in an annoying way (*informal*) ○ *You'll have to get after him if you want it finished by the weekend.*

get ahead *vi* to become successful, especially when compared to others ○ *He's a good worker, but he hasn't got what it takes to get ahead in this line of business.*

get along *vi* **1.** BE FRIENDLY WITH SOMEBODY to be on good terms with somebody socially **2.** MANAGE to make progress in a situation ○ *How's he getting along in the new job?* **3.** LEAVE to leave a place (*often used in commands*)

get around *v* **1.** *vi* to be socially active and aware of what is happening ○ *I have the feeling you don't get around much.* **2.** *vti* same as **get round**

get at *vt* **1.** REACH SOMEBODY OR SOMETHING to succeed in reaching, finding, or making contact with somebody or something ○ *There's no way he'll get at the data without the password.* **2.** MEAN SOMETHING to imply, suggest, or be trying to say something ○ *What exactly are you getting at?* **3.** CRITICIZE SOMEBODY REPEATEDLY to criticize somebody continually and unreasonably ○ *You're always getting at me, and I'm sick of it.* **4.** BRIBE SOMEBODY to bribe or influence somebody ○ *It was obvious that some of the committee had been got at by our rivals.*

get away *vi* **1.** ESCAPE to escape from somebody or something ○ *They caught one man, but the rest got away.* **2.** LEAVE PLACE to succeed in leaving or spending time away from a place ○ *We hope to get away for a few days next month.* ■ *interj* EXPRESSING DISBELIEF used as an expression of disbelief ○ *Get away! He never said that – did he?*

get away with *vt* to manage to do something without being blamed or penalized or experiencing an expected bad result ○ *You could get away with a phone call, but it would be better to write.*

get back *vt* to recover something that has been given away, lent to somebody, or lost

get back at *vt* to take revenge on somebody

get back to *vt* **1.** to return to a place, topic, or activity ○ *Let's get back to what Steve was saying earlier.* **2.** to give somebody an answer or continue a discussion, especially by letter, e-mail, or telephone ○ *Leave it with me, and I'll get back to you as soon as possible.*

get by *vi* to manage to survive or just make ends meet ○ *It's hard to get by on £50 a week.*

get down *v* **1.** *vt* DEMORALIZE SOMEBODY to make somebody demoralized or discouraged ○ *This job is beginning to get me down.* **2.** *vt* WRITE SOMETHING to write something down, especially immediately **3.** *vt* SWALLOW SOMETHING to swallow something, especially unwillingly or with difficulty ○ *The medicine smelled so bad I just couldn't get it down.* **4.** *vi N Am* HAVE FUN to relax and enjoy yourself in an unrestrained way (*informal*) ○ *It's time to get down and party.* **5.** *vi Malaysia* LEAVE VEHICLE to get out of a vehicle ○ *Where do you have to get down?*

get down to *vt* to start concentrating seriously on something or on getting something done

get in *v* **1.** *vi* ARRIVE to arrive somewhere, especially home ○ *When does your plane get in?* **2.** *vi* BE CHOSEN to succeed in being admitted to a group or organization, e.g. by election or interview ○ *You know if they get in they'll change some of the old laws.* **3.** *vti* GET INVOLVED WITH SOMEBODY OR SOMETHING to become involved with a group or in an activity, or let somebody become involved ○ *got in with the wrong crowd* **4.** *vt* MANAGE TO DO SOMETHING to succeed in finding or making an opportunity to do something ○ *I don't think we can get four interviews in before lunch.*

get into *vt* **1.** to begin to experience difficulties, or make somebody experience difficulties ○ *You got us into this mess, you sort it out.* ○ *You'll get into all kinds of trouble if you do that.* **2.** to become involved or absorbed in something ○ *She's starting to get into programming.*

get off *v* **1.** *vi* LEAVE to set out from a place or position ○ *We have to get off at the crack of dawn tomorrow.* **2.** *vti* BE ABLE TO LEAVE WORK to be allowed to leave work, especially at the end of the working day ○ *What time do you get off this afternoon?* **3.** *vt* SEND COMMUNICATION OR PARCEL to send a written communication or parcel ○ *I need to get these letters off tonight.* **4.** *vi* HAVE LUCKY ESCAPE to experience only minor consequences of a mistake, misguided action, or accident ○ *Considering what might have happened, I think you got off very lightly.* **5.** *vti* GAIN ACQUITTAL to be acquitted in a court of law, or successfully defend somebody in a court of law (*informal*) ○ *A good lawyer could get him off with no trouble.* **6.** *vi US* BE SO BOLD to be bold enough to say or do something (*informal; usually disapproving*) ○ *Where does he get off thinking he can speak to me that way?* **7.** *vi* BE AROUSED OR EXCITED to experience excitement, physical arousal, or the effects of a drug (*slang*)

get off with *vt* to start a flirtation or sexual or romantic relationship with somebody (*informal*)

get on *vi* **1.** DEAL WITH SITUATION to deal with a situation and make reasonable progress of a particular kind ○ *How's Ben getting on at school?* **2.** BE FRIENDLY to have a reasonably friendly social relationship with somebody ○ *She gets on well with the neighbours.* **3.** KEEP GOING to continue doing something ○ *I'd better get on – I've got a lot more to do.* **4.** BECOME OLDER to become more advanced in years **5.** BE ALMOST SOMETHING to be approaching a particular age, time, number, or amount ○ *We collected getting on for 200 signatures.*

get out *v* **1.** *vti* LEAVE OR MAKE SOMEBODY LEAVE to leave a place or situation, or enable somebody to leave one **2.** *vi* BECOME KNOWN to become widely known, especially contrary to somebody's wishes ○ *If this ever gets out, I'll be so embarrassed!* **3.** *vt* PRODUCE OR PUBLISH SOMETHING to produce or publish something, especially a newspaper or magazine ■ *interj US* EXPRESSION OF DISBELIEF used as an expression of disbelief (*informal*) ○ *Get out! You actually said that?*

get out of *vt* to avoid doing or having to experience something, or enable somebody to avoid something ○ *He got out of paying for the meal.*

get over *vt* **1.** RECOVER FROM SOMETHING to recover from an illness or bad experience ○ *He's upset, but he'll get over it.* **2.** DEAL WITH DIFFICULTY to overcome or cope with a difficulty ○ *Once she'd got over her lack of confidence, she enjoyed the meeting.* **3.** MAKE PEOPLE UNDERSTAND OR ACCEPT SOMETHING to succeed in making something clear or persuasive ○ *He's very good at getting his ideas over to an audience.* **4.** GET SOMETHING FINISHED to finish dealing with something boring, annoying, or unpleasant ○ *I just want to get the whole thing over with as soon as possible.*

get round *v* **1.** *vt* DEAL SUCCESSFULLY WITH OBSTRUCTION to manage to operate in spite of a regulation, prohibition, or difficulty ○ *There must be some way of getting round the regulations.* **2.** *vt* PERSUADE SOMEBODY to talk or charm somebody into doing what you want ○ *could rely on Sheila to get round him* **3.** *vi* SAY OR DO SOMETHING AT LAST to say or do something after delay, hesitation, or being involved with other things ○ *She somehow never gets round to cleaning the house.* **4.** *vi* BECOME KNOWN to become widely known

get through v **1.** vt SURVIVE DIFFICULT TIME to endure to the end of a difficult time or situation ○ *How I got through those weeks I just don't know.* **2.** vt USE OR SPEND SOMETHING to use, eat, or spend something, especially a large amount in a short time ○ *We seem to be getting through the copier paper at an alarming rate.* **3.** vti MAKE SOMEBODY UNDERSTAND to make somebody understand something that is being communicated ○ *How can I get it through to you that this is our only hope?* **4.** vi SUCCEED IN CONTACTING SOMEBODY to contact somebody, especially by telephone ○ *I finally got through to her.*

get to vt to start to annoy somebody ○ *His whining was beginning to get to me.*

get together v **1.** vi MEET to meet for social or business purposes ○ *The project team needs to get together once a week or so.* **2.** vi FORM ALLIANCE to form an alliance or relationship ○ *They may be getting together to corner the market.* **3.** vt GATHER SOMETHING to bring together or accumulate something, especially money ○ *They managed to get together enough capital to start a business.* **4.** vt GET SOMETHING ORGANIZED to organize your personal affairs or focus your approach on an activity (*informal*) ○ *took some time off to get her life together* ◇ **get it together** to become organized and calm so as to perform efficiently (*slang*) ○ *had better get it together before his boss loses patience*

get up v **1.** vti GET OUT OF BED to get out of bed, or make somebody get out of bed **2.** vi STAND UP to rise to your feet from a seated position **3.** vt ROUSE ENERGY to rouse your energy, strength, courage, or similar qualities ○ *I'm trying to get up the enthusiasm to go back to work.* **4.** vt ORGANIZE SOMETHING to organize something by persuading other people to take part ○ *She got up a collection to help homeless people.* **5.** vt DRESS SOMEBODY to dress somebody in a particular way (*informal*) ○ *She was got up as Cleopatra.* **6.** vi GET STRONGER to become stronger or more turbulent (*refers to winds or the sea*)

get up to vt to do something bad or annoying (*informal*) ○ *I have no idea what they've been getting up to while we've been away.*

get² /get/ n **1.** RACKET GAMES DIFFICULT TENNIS RETURN in tennis and some other racket games, a shot that makes a return difficult **2.** AGRIC, HORSERACING MALE ANIMAL'S OFFSPRING the progeny sired by an animal, especially a racehorse **3.** N England, Scotland BRAT an unpleasant child (*often an insult, implying illegitimacy*) [14C. < GET¹]

geta /géttə/ (*plural* same or **-tas**) n a Japanese shoe with a wooden sole [Late 19C. < Japanese]

getaway /géttə way/ n **1.** an act of leaving a place, especially a quick exit made by somebody who has just committed a crime **2.** an act of starting to move, e.g. in a race

get-go, **getgo** /gétgō/ n N Am the very beginning of something (*informal*) ○ *I knew from the get-go this thing wasn't going to work.*

Gethsemane /geth sémməni/ n in the Bible, the olive grove just outside Jerusalem where Jesus Christ was betrayed after the Last Supper (Matthew 26:36)

get-out n a means of avoiding or escaping from something such as an obligation or commitment (*often used before a noun*) ○ *The contract had a get-out clause.* ◇ **as...as all get-out** N Am to the greatest possible extent (*slang*) ○ *The ground was as flat as all get-out.*

get-rich-quick adj bringing or desiring instant wealth, often at the expense of moral integrity (*informal*) ○ *lucrative schemes for get-rich-quick merchants*

getter /géttər/ n a substance added to absorb the unwanted product of a chemical process, e.g. the excess gas in a light bulb

get-together n a meeting or social gathering (*informal*)

get-tough adj taking a firm and decisive approach to social or political problems

Getty /gétti/, J. Paul (1892–1976) US oil executive. He became a multimillionaire at the head of his own oil company, and he founded the J. Paul Getty Museum in Malibu, California, to display his collection of art. Full name **Getty, Jean Paul**

'The meek shall inherit the earth but not the mineral rights.'

[J. Paul Getty. Quoted in *The Great Getty Crown*, Robert Lenzer; 1985]

Gettysburg /géttiz burg/ borough and county seat of Adams County in southern Pennsylvania, southwest of Harrisburg. It was the site of a decisive Northern victory during the American Civil War on 1–3 July 1863, when George Meade's troops halted the northward advance of Robert E. Lee. Abraham Lincoln's Gettysburg Address was delivered there on 19 November 1863, dedicating the Gettysburg National Cemetery. Population: 7,653 (2002 estimate).

getup /gét up/, **get-up** n the costume or clothes that somebody is wearing (*informal*)

get-up-and-go n energy and enthusiasm (*informal*)

get-well adj expressing the hope that somebody will soon recover from an illness ○ *a get-well card*

geullah /gə óollə/ n a Jewish prayer of thanks to God for the deliverance of the Jews from Egypt

GeV abbr MEASURE, PHYS giga-electron volt

gewgaw /gyóo gaw/ n a showy but inexpensive object, especially an ornament [12C. Origin ?]

Gewürztraminer /gə voörts trə meenər/ n **1.** a medium-dry, slightly spicy white wine made from a white grape grown mainly in Alsace and Germany **2.** a white grape variety. Use: to make Gewürztraminer. [Mid-20C. < German < *Gewürz* 'spice' + *Traminer*, type of grape < *Termeno* village in N Italy]

gey /gī/ adv Scotland **1.** same as **rather** adv (sense 4), interj **2.** extremely (*nonstandard*) [Early 18C. Variant of GAY]

geyser: Rotorua, New Zealand

geyser /geézə, gízə/ n **1.** a spring that throws a jet of hot water or steam into the air at intervals **2.** a gas-fired boiler that heats water for use in the home and is activated by turning on a tap [Late 18C. After *Geysir*, hot spring in Iceland < Old Norse *geysa* 'gush']

SPELLCHECK See *geezer*.

geyserite /gízə rīt/ n a grey or white mineral form of hydrated silica. Source: hot spring deposits.

gf abbr French Guiana (*used in Internet addresses*) See table at **domain name**

GF abbr ONLINE girlfriend (*used in e-mails or text messages*)

GFN abbr ONLINE gone for now (*used in e-mails or text messages*)

G-force n the force of gravity

gg abbr Guernsey (*used in Internet addresses*) See table at **domain name**

GG abbr **1.** Girl Guides **2.** ONLINE gotta go (*used in e-mails or text messages*) **3.** UK, Aus, Can, S Asia Governor General

gge abbr garage (*used in advertisements*)

gh abbr Ghana (*used in Internet addresses*) See table at **domain name**

GH abbr PHYSIOL growth hormone

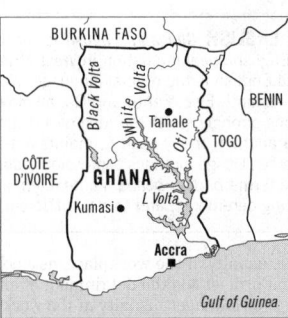

Ghana

Ghana /gaánə/ country on the northern coast of the Gulf of Guinea in West Africa, bordered by Burkina Faso, Togo, and Côte d'Ivoire. It became an independent member of the Commonwealth in 1957. Language: English. Currency: cedi. Capital: Accra. Population: 20,467,707 (2003). Area: 238,500 sq. km/92,090 sq. mi. Official name **Republic of Ghana**. Former name **Gold Coast** (sense 2) (1874–1957) — **Ghanaian** /gaa náy ən/ n, adj

Ghanaian English n a variety of English spoken in Ghana. See panel on next page

~~Ghandi~~ incorrect spelling of **Gandhi**

gharana /gə raánə/ n S Asia a distinctive performance style, school, or tradition in classical Indian music or dance [Mid-20C. < Hindi *gharānā* 'family']

gharara /gə raárə/ n loose trousers pleated below the knee, worn by women in or from South Asia, usually with a long tunic (**kameez**) [< Persian *garāra*]

gharial /gáiri əl, gárri-/ n UK, NZ, Can a large reptile resembling a crocodile that has a very long narrow snout and feeds on fish and frogs. Native to: India, Borneo, Sumatra. Latin name: *Gavialis gangeticus*. Aus, US term **gavial** [Early 19C < Hindi *ghariyāl*]

gharry /gárri/ (*plural* **-ries**) n S Asia a horse-drawn carriage, especially one for hire [Early 19C. < Hindi *gārī*]

ghastly /gaástli/ adj (**-lier, -liest**) **1.** HORRIFYING horrifying, shocking, or very upsetting ○ *She had a ghastly experience with the last dentist she went to.* **2.** TERRIBLE very bad or unpleasant ○ *There's a ghastly smell coming from somewhere in this room.* ○ *It was all a ghastly mistake.* **3.** NOT WELL feeling unwell (*informal*) **4.** VERY PALE very pale or white in a way that is reminiscent of a ghost or a corpse (*literary*) ■ adv EXTREMELY used to emphasize paleness or whiteness ○*'Her eyes grew large, her face ghastly pale.'* (Charlotte Gilman, *Herland*; 1915) [14C. < obsolete *gast* 'frighten' < Germanic] —**ghastliness** n

ghat /gaat/ n in South Asia, a place on a river bank with steps down to the water, especially one where people bathe as a sacred rite or one near which the dead are cremated [Early 17C. < Hindi *ghāt*]

Ghats ♦ Eastern Ghats, Western Ghats

ghazal /gaá zl/ n **1.** an Arabic, Persian, or Urdu lyric poem consisting of five or more couplets that may each have a different theme **2.** a lyric poem in Urdu, set to music and sung in a distinctive style. Ghazals are popular in Indian films. [Late 18C. Via Persian < Arabic *gazal*]

Ghazali /gə zaáli/, **al-** (1058–1111) Islamic theologian and philosopher. His *The Revival of the Religious Sciences* is a classic work of Islam. Full name **Ghazali, Abu Hamid Muhammad ibn Muhammad al-Tusi al-**

ghazi /gaázi/ n a warrior who has fought for Islam against non-Muslims [Mid-18C. < Arabic *al-gāzī*, form of *gazā* 'invade']

GHB abbr DRUGS gammahydroxybutyrate

ghee /gee/, **ghi** n clarified butter, especially as used in South Asian cooking [Mid-17C. Via Hindi *ghī* < Sanskrit *ghṛtam*]

Ghent /gent/ capital of East Flanders Province, northwestern Belgium. One of Belgium's oldest cities, it is situated about 56 km/35 mi. northwest of Brussels. Population: 224,074 (1999).

gherao /gə rów/ S Asia vt (**-raos, -raoing, -raoed**) to surround and detain an official, employer, or

WORLD ENGLISH ***Ghanaian English*** is the English language as used in Ghana (population 20 million), the largest English-speaking nation in West Africa after Nigeria. Local contact with the language dates from 1631. Standard English is the official language, West African Pidgin English is widespread, and indigenous languages include Ashanti, Ewe, Fanti, and Ga, all of which have an influence on English usage, especially in vocabulary. Ghanaians strongly resist the idea of a distinctive Ghanaian English, and although standard and pidgin shade into one another, many seek to maintain a sharp line between them. In local usage 'r' in such words as *art, door, worker*. Usage includes expressions adopted from local languages, often as the first element in compounds, as in the terms *bodom beads, kente cloth*, and in localisms such as an *airtight* 'a metal box', an *outdooring* 'a christening ceremony', and to *enskin* 'to enthrone a chief by draping him in an animal skin'.

manager, usually at the workplace, as a political or industrial protest ■ *n* the detainment of an official, employer, or manager, usually at the workplace, as a political or industrial protest [Mid-20C. < Hindi *ghernā* 'surround']

gherkin /gúrkin/ *n* **1.** SMALL CUCUMBER a small cucumber. Use: pickling. **2.** PRICKLY FRUIT a prickly hard-skinned fruit from a climbing plant. Use: pickling. **3.** TROPICAL CLIMBING PLANT a climbing plant of the cucumber family that produces gherkins. Native to: Caribbean. Latin name: *Cucumis anguria*. [Early 17C. < assumed obsolete Dutch *gurkkijn* 'small cucumber' < *gurk* 'cucumber']

ghetto /géttō/ (*plural* **-tos** or **-toes**) *n* **1.** AREA OF CITY INHABITED BY MINORITY an area of a city lived in by a minority group, especially a run-down and densely populated area lived in by a group that experiences discrimination **2.** JEWISH QUARTER in former times, an area in European towns in which the Jewish population was required to live **3.** STATE OF SOCIAL EXCLUSION the social situation of any group of people who are segregated in some way from the mainstream of a society or culture, resulting in discrimination or restriction of opportunity [Early 17C. < Italian]

ghetto blaster *n* a large radio and cassette or CD player with a built-in speaker at each end, carried by a handle at the top (*informal; often considered offensive*)

ghetto credibility *n* popularity and acceptability among Black people, especially young urban Black people (*slang; offensive in some contexts*)

ghettoize /géttō īz/ (**-izes, -izing, -ized**), **ghettoise** (**-ises, -ising, -ised**) *vt* **1.** to restrict a minority group to a specific area of a city **2.** to isolate, pigeonhole, or limit the scope or opportunities for somebody or something (*sometimes considered offensive*) — **ghettoization** /géttō ī záysh'n/ *n*

ghi *n* FOOD another spelling of **ghee**

Ghibelline /gíbbə līn/ *n* a member of a political party in medieval Italy that supported the claims of the Holy Roman Emperors to rule Italy and opposed the Guelphs, who supported the popes [Late 16C. < Italian *Ghibellino*, probably < Middle High German *Waiblingen*, estate belonging to family whose members included rulers of the Holy Roman Empire and kings of Germany and Sicily]

ghillie *n* CLOTHING, FIELD SPORTS another spelling of **gillie**

ghomasio *n* FOOD another spelling of **gomasio**

Ghose /gōsh/, **Aurobindo** (1872–1950) Indian nationalist, scholar, and philosopher. He participated in India's struggle for independence but abandoned politics in 1910 for yoga and Hindu philosophy. Also known as **Sri Aurobindo, Rishi Aurobindo**

ghost /gōst/ *n* **1.** SUPPOSED SPIRIT REMAINING AFTER DEATH the supposed spirit of somebody who has died, believed to appear as a shadowy form or to cause sounds, the movement of objects, or a frightening atmosphere in a place **2.** TRACE a faint, weak, or greatly reduced appearance, trace, or possibility of something ○ *the ghost of a smile* **3.** SECONDARY IMAGE a faint duplicate image of something seen on a screen or photograph or through a telescope, and caused by the reception of a double signal or by a mechanical defect **4.** NONEXISTENT PERSON OR THING an entity that seems to exist but does not, e.g. a name entered on a list by mistake **5.** LITERAT same as **ghostwriter** **6.** RELIG SOUL somebody's soul or spirit (*archaic*) ■ *vt* (**ghosts, ghosting, ghosted**) LITERAT WRITE SOMETHING UNDER ANOTHER'S NAME to be the ghostwriter of a work [Old English *gāst* < W Germanic] —**ghost-like** *adj* ◇ **give up the ghost 1.** to stop working or functioning for good (*informal*) **2.** to die (*literary*)

CULTURAL NOTE ***Ghosts***, a play (1881) by Norwegian dramatist Henrik Ibsen. Ibsen's penetrating study of hereditary determinism tells the story of Osvald Alving, who discovers that his recently deceased father led a debauched life and that the girl he loves is actually his illegitimate half-sister. These revelations also confirm Osvald's fears that he has inherited a degenerative sexually-transmitted disease from his father.

ghostbuster /gōst bustər/ *n* (*informal*) **1.** somebody supposedly able to drive away ghosts, poltergeists, and other apparitions **2.** an employee of the Inland Revenue whose job is to track down people who have not declared their income for tax purposes

ghost crab *n* a white burrowing crab. Native to: sandy shorelines in many parts of the world. Genus: *Ocypoda*.

ghost dance *n* **1.** a religious dance of Native North Americans, performed with the supposed participation of the spirits of all the Native North Americans murdered by the European immigrants **2.** *also* **Ghost Dance** a religious movement, widely spread among Plains Native American peoples in North America in the late 19th century, that promised the revival of traditional Native North American culture

ghost gum *n* a eucalyptus tree with pale grey-to-white bark. Native to: northern Australia. Latin name: *Eucalyptus papuana*. [< the pallid appearance of its trunk]

ghosting /gōsting/ *n* the appearance of faint duplicate images on a screen, monitor, or photograph, or through a telescope

ghostly /gōstli/ (**-lier, -liest**) *adj* **1.** like a ghost in being insubstantial, pale, or apparently not of this world **2.** having an atmosphere or quality that suggests ghosts or the presence of ghosts ○ *the ghostly music that opens the symphony* —**ghostliness** *n*

ghost moth *n* a large pale moth, the male of which is white and the female pale yellow with orange markings. Native to: Europe. Latin name: *Hepialis humuli*.

ghost site *n* a website that is obsolete and no longer updated, but still available for viewing

ghost story *n* a story about a ghost or ghosts, or a haunted place or person, intended to frighten the reader or hearer

ghost town *n* **1.** a town with few or no inhabitants, especially one that was formerly a busy prosperous place, e.g. an abandoned mining town in the western United States **2.** a formerly or usually inhabited place that is deserted (*informal*) ○ *The business district is a ghost town at the weekend.*

ghost train *n* a small open-topped train at a fairground that takes passengers through a dark space filled with amusingly frightening sights and sounds

ghost word *n* a word created through a mistake that may be copied afterwards into other texts and eventually enter a language

ghostwriter /gōst rītər/ *n* somebody who writes something for or with somebody else, the other person receiving sole credit as the author —**ghostwrite** *vti*

ghoul /gool/ *n* **1.** SOMEBODY MORBIDLY INTERESTED IN REPULSIVE THINGS somebody who is morbidly fascinated with death, disaster, or repulsive things **2.** PARANORMAL EVIL SPIRIT a supposed evil and terrifying spirit **3.** ISLAM BODY-SNATCHING DEMON in Islamic folklore, an evil demon that eats freshly buried bodies, and often abducts children or attacks unwary travellers [Late 18C. < Arabic *ğūl*]

ghoulish /goolish/ *adj* **1.** showing a morbid fascination with death, disaster, or repulsive things **2.** terrifyingly hideous or cruel —**ghoulishly** *adv* —**ghoulishness** *n*

GHQ *n* the headquarters of an organization, especially a military headquarters commanded by a general. Full form **General Headquarters**

ghyll *n* GEOG another spelling of **gill**[3]

GHz *symbol* MEASURE, ELEC gigahertz

gi[1] /gee/, **gie** *n* an outfit worn for karate or judo [< Japanese]

gi[2] *abbr* Gibraltar (*used in Internet addresses*) See table at **domain name**

GI[1] *n* US SOLDIER a soldier in the US armed forces ■ *adj US* **1.** FOR SOLDIERS provided or issued by the armed forces for the use of its members ○ *a GI hat* **2.** FOR VETERANS provided or intended for veterans of the armed forces ○ *GI benefits* [Mid-20C. Abbreviation of *government issue*, reinterpretation of *GI* 'galvanized iron' on various items of US Army equipment]

GI[2], **g.i.** *abbr* **1.** INDUST galvanized iron **2.** ANAT gastrointestinal

Giacometti /jákə métti/, **Alberto** (1901–66) Swiss sculptor and painter. He is best known for his bronze sculptures of elongated human figures such as *Stehende III* (1962).

giant /jī ənt/ *n* **1.** VERY TALL IMAGINARY CREATURE in fairy tales and legends, an imaginary being who resembles a human but is much taller, larger, and stronger **2.** SOMEBODY EXTRAORDINARILY ACCOMPLISHED somebody whose talents or achievements are particularly outstanding ○ *one of the giants of British cinema* **3.** SOMEBODY OR SOMETHING LARGER THAN USUAL a person, animal, plant, or organization that is much larger than is usual **4.** MYTHOLOGICAL BEING in Greek mythology, a being of immense size and strength who fought against Zeus and the other gods of Mount Olympus **5.** MIN EXTRACT same as **monitor** *n* (sense 10) **6.** ASTRON same as **giant star** ■ *adj* **1.** VERY BIG taller, larger, or more powerful than is usual ○ *a giant tidal wave* **2.** GREATER THAN USUAL greater than the usual number or amount ○ *a giant saving* [13C. Via Old French *geant* < Greek *gigant-*]

giant anteater *n* a large bushy-tailed anteater, now rare. Native to: pampas regions of South America. Latin name: *Myrmecophaga tridactyla*.

giant clam *n* an extremely large clam, weighing as much as 230kg/500 lb. Native to: Pacific and Indian oceans. Latin name: *Tridacna gigas*.

giantess /jī ən tess/ *n* in fairy tales and legends, an imaginary being similar to a woman in shape but much taller, larger, and stronger

giantism /jī əntizəm/ *n* MED same as **gigantism**

giant-killer *n* somebody or something that defeats a superior or better-known opponent, especially in sport, business, or politics —**giant-killing** *n*

giant panda *n* ZOOL same as **panda** (sense 1)

giant peacock moth *n* a mottled-brown moth with an oval like an eye on each wing and a wingspan that can reach 15 cm/6 in. Native to: Europe. Latin name: *Saturnia pyri*.

giant planet *n* one of the four largest planets in the solar system, Jupiter, Saturn, Uranus, and Neptune

giant redwood *n* TREES same as **giant sequoia**

Giant's Causeway /jī ənts-/ headland on the northern coast of Northern Ireland, consisting of thousands of polygonal columns of basalt, thought to be ancient lava formations

giant sequoia *n* a species of redwood tree that grows up to 80 m/260 ft high. Native to: California. Latin name: *Sequoiadendron giganteum*.

giant-sized *adj* much larger than others of the same type or class

giant slalom *n* a downhill ski race on a course that is longer and steeper than that used for a slalom

giant star *n* a low-density star with a diameter up to 100 times greater than that of the Sun

giant tortoise *n* a very large tortoise with a shell that can grow to be 1.2 m/4 ft long. Native to: Galápagos and Seychelles islands. Genus: *Geochelone*.

giardia /jee aárdi ə/ *n* **1.** a single-celled protozoan, some forms of which live as parasites in the gut of humans and other vertebrates, causing an infection (**giardiasis**). Genus: *Giardia*. **2.** MED same as **giardiasis** [Early 20C. < modern Latin, after A. *Giard* (1846–1908), French biologist]

giardiasis /jee aar dī əssiss/ *n* an infection of the gut with the water-borne microscopic protozoan giardia. It is usually caused by drinking contaminated water and results in severe diarrhoea and vomiting.

gib /gib/ *n* something that is made of metal and holds another piece of metal or a machine part in place, e.g. a wedge, pin, bolt, or plate ■ *vt* (**gibs, gibbing, gibbed**) to hold something in place with a gib [Late 18C. Origin ?]

Gib /jib/ *n* Gibraltar (*informal*) [Shortening]

gibber /jíbbər/ (**-bers, -bering, -bered**) *vi* to make sounds or speak words unintelligibly ○ *Stop gibbering and tell me what's gone wrong.* [Early 17C. Probably an imitation of the sound] —**gibber** *n*

gibberellic acid /jíbbə réllik-/ *n* a plant growth hormone involved in stem elongation. Formula: $C_{19}H_{22}O_6$.

gibberellin /jíbbə réllin/ *n* a plant hormone that promotes growth and seed germination [Mid-20C. < modern Latin *Gibbera*, genus of fungi < Latin *gibbus* 'hump']

gibbering /jíbbəring/ *adj* unable to make sounds or speak words intelligibly

gibberish /jíbbərish/ *n* spoken or written language perceived as unintelligible or devoid of sense [Early 16C Probably < GIBBER after SPANISH, POLISH, etc]

gibbet /jíbbit/ *n* **1.** HANGING POST an upright post with a beam projecting horizontally from its top, from which the bodies of executed criminals were hung on public display **2.** CRIME same as **gallows** (sense 1) ■ *vt* (**-bets, -beting, -beted**) **1.** DISPLAY BODY AFTER EXECUTION to display the body of a criminal on a gibbet after execution **2.** HANG SOMEBODY to execute somebody by hanging (*archaic*) **3.** ATTACK SOMEBODY'S REPUTATION to expose somebody to ridicule or contempt, especially in popular publications (*archaic*) [12C. < Old French *gibet* 'staff, gallows' < *gibe* 'staff']

gibbon

gibbon /gíbbən/ *n* a small tree-dwelling ape with a slender body and long arms that allow it to swing rapidly and agilely from branch to branch. Native to: Southeast Asia. Genus: *Hylobates*. [Late 18C. < French]

Gibbon /gíbbən/, **Edward** (1737–94) British historian. His major work, *The History of the Decline and Fall of the Roman Empire* (1776–88), is a classic of British historiography.

'Corruption, the most infallible symptom of constitutional liberty.'
[Edward Gibbon, *The History of the Decline and Fall of the Roman Empire*; 1776–88]

'History…is, indeed, little more than the register of the crimes, follies, and misfortunes of mankind.'
[Edward Gibbon, *The Decline and Fall of the Roman Empire*; 1776–88]

gibbous /gíbbəss/ *adj* **1.** describes the Moon or a planet before and after it is full, when it has more than half its disc illuminated **2.** bulging outwards or swollen [14C. < late Latin *gibbosus* 'hunchbacked' < Latin *gibbus* 'hump'] —**gibbosity** /gi bóssi ti/ *n* —**gibbously** *adv* —**gibbousness** *n*

Gibbs /gibz/, **J. Willard** (1839–1903) US mathematical physicist. He laid the foundations for the science of physical chemistry in *On the Equilibrium of Heterogeneous Substances* (1876–78). Full name **Gibbs, Josiah Willard**

Gibbs, May (1876–1969) British-born Australian writer and illustrator. She wrote children's books, including *Snugglepot and Cuddlepie* (1918).

Gibbs free energy *n* PHYS same as **free energy** [After J. Willard GIBBS]

gibbsite /gíbzīt/ *n* a grey-white mineral consisting of hydrated aluminium oxide. Source: laterite, bauxite. Use: source of aluminium. [Early 19C. After George *Gibbs* (1776–1833), US mineralogist]

gibe /jīb/, **jibe** *n* a comment that is intended to hurt or provoke somebody or to show derision or contempt ■ *vti* (**gibes, gibing, gibed; jibes, jibing, jibed**) to make a comment that is intended to hurt or provoke somebody or to show derision or contempt [Mid-16C. Origin ?] —**gibingly** *adv*

giblets /jíbbləts/ *n* the liver, heart, gizzard, and neck of a bird that has been prepared for cooking. Giblets are often boiled to make stock for gravy. [14C. < Old French *gibelet* 'game stew']

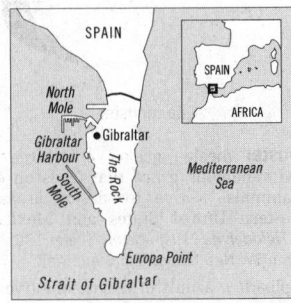
Gibraltar

Gibraltar /ji bráwltər, -brólt-/ British dependency on a narrow promontory that is near the southernmost point of the Iberian Peninsula. It occupies a strategic position at the western entrance to the Mediterranean Sea. Population: 27,000 (2001). Area: 6 sq. km/2 sq. mi. —**Gibraltarian** /jí brawl táiri ən, -brol-/ *n, adj*

Gibraltar, Rock of limestone and shale ridge near the southern tip of the Iberian Peninsula, overlooking the Strait of Gibraltar. Height: 426 m/1,398 ft.

Gibraltar, Strait of channel connecting the Mediterranean Sea to the Atlantic Ocean and separating North Africa from the Rock of Gibraltar. Length: 60 km/40 mi.

Gibran /ji braán/, **Khalil** (1883–1931) Lebanese-born US mystic, painter, and poet. His mystical works inspired a new school of Arab-American poetry, and *The Prophet* (1923) reached a wide popular audience.

'Everyone has experienced that truth: that love, like a running brook, is disregarded, taken for granted; but when the brook freezes over, then people begin to remember how it was when it ran, and they want it to run again.'
[Khalil Gibran. Quoted in *Beloved Prophet*, Virginia Hilu (ed.); 1972]

Gibson /gíbs'n/, **Mel** (*b.* 1956) US-born Australian actor. Best known for his action roles in *Mad Max* (1979) and the *Lethal Weapon* series (1987–98), he also directed and starred in the Academy Award-winning *Braveheart* (1995). Born **Gibson, Columcille Gerard**

Gibson Desert desert in central Western Australia, consisting mainly of sand ridges and plains. Area: 156,000 sq. km/60,200 sq. mi.

gid /gid/ *n* a disease affecting livestock, especially sheep, that makes them walk and stand unsteadily, caused by a tapeworm larva [Early 17C. Back-formation < GIDDY]

giddap /gi dáp, -dúp/ *interj* same as **giddyup**

giddy /gíddi/ (**-dier, -diest**) *adj* **1.** DIZZY feeling dizzy or unsteady and as if about to fall down **2.** CAUSING DIZZINESS causing dizziness or a feeling of unsteadiness ○ *climbed to a giddy height* **3.** NOT SENSIBLE not level-headed and sensible, but likely to act impulsively or behave foolishly (*dated*) [Old English *gidig* 'severely mentally ill' < Germanic] —**giddily** *adv* —**giddiness** *n*

giddyup /gíddi úp/ *interj* used to make a horse go faster [Early 20C. Alteration of GET UP]

Gide /zheed/, **André** (1869–1951) French writer. His many works of fiction and nonfiction frequently explore the theme of moral responsibility, and include his celebrated *Journal* (1939–51). He won the Nobel Prize in literature (1947). Full name **Gide, André Paul Guillaume**

'One does not discover new lands without consenting to lose sight of the shore for a very long time.'
[André Gide, *The Counterfeiters*; 1925]

gidgee /gíjjee/ *n* an acacia with leaves that can give off an unpleasant smell. Native to: inland Australia. Genus: *Acacia*. [Mid-19C. < Wiradhuri]

gie *n* MARTIAL ARTS another spelling of **gi** [1]

Gielgud /geel good/, **Sir John** (1904–2000) British actor. He was one of the leading Shakespearean interpreters of his generation. Full name **Gielgud, Sir Arthur John**

'Film people find it difficult to *place* me. The number of films that deal with crowned heads of Europe is rather limited.'
[Sir John Gielgud. Quoted in *Radio Times*; 4 November 1971]

gif /jif/ *abbr* a file extension for a GIF file. Full form **Graphic Interchange Format**

GIF /gif/ *n* a format for graphics files, widely used on the World Wide Web. Full form **Graphic Interchange Format**

gift /gift/ *n* **1.** SOMETHING GIVEN something that is given to somebody, usually on order to provide pleasure or to show gratitude ○ *a birthday gift* **2.** SPECIAL TALENT a natural ability that somebody appears to have been born with, especially an artistic ability or social skill ○ *a gift for making people feel at ease* **3.** ACT OF GIVING the act of giving something to somebody ○ *her gift of £500,000 to help to build a new school* **4.** SOMETHING EASILY GAINED something that is obtained or achieved easily (*informal*) ○ *The final goal was a gift from the Uruguay defence.* ■ *vt* (**gifts, gifting, gifted**) GIVE SOMETHING to give or concede something to somebody as a gift [13C. < Old Norse *gipt* < Germanic] ◇ **be in the gift of somebody** to be something that somebody has the right or power to give

USAGE Marketing people are fond of the expression *free gift*, but because any *gift* worthy of its name is free, the result of using the two words together is unnecessary and should be avoided.

SYNONYMS See *talent*.

GIFT /gift/ *n* a method designed to aid conception in which eggs are removed from a woman's ovary, mixed with sperm, and placed in one of her fallopian tubes. Full form **gamete intrafallopian transfer**

Gift Aid *n* a provision that allows charities to recover tax paid by donors on their charitable gifts —**Gift Aid** *vt*

gift certificate *n* N Am COMM same as **gift token**

gifted /gíftid/ *adj* **1.** TALENTED having great natural talent or intelligence **2.** SHOWING SOMEBODY'S TALENT showing that somebody has great natural talent or intelligence ○ *a gifted performance* **3.** EXCEPTIONAL requiring special education because of great natural talent or intelligence ○ *a gifted student* —**giftedly** *adv* —**giftedness** *n*

SYNONYMS See *intelligent*.

gift of the gab *n* a natural ability to talk fluently, eloquently, or persuasively (*informal*)

gift of tongues *n* the ability to produce utterances in a state of religious ecstasy or trance that are usually unintelligible and thought by some to manifest the influence of the Holy Spirit

gift shop *n* a shop selling small decorative or amusing items that are intended to be bought as gifts or souvenirs

gift token, gift voucher *n* a slip of paper issued by a shop that can be exchanged for goods worth its purchase price, usually given to somebody in an attractive card as a gift. N Am term **gift certificate**

giftware /gíft wair/ *n* goods that are marketed for

buying as gifts for other people, e.g. china and crystal

giftwrap /gíft rap/ *n* specially decorated paper used to wrap gifts ■ *vt* (**-wraps, -wrapping, -wrapped**) to wrap something in specially decorated paper

gift-wrapped *adj* 1. attractively packaged for offering as a gift 2. made, often unintentionally, very easy for somebody to obtain (*informal*) ○ *In the end, victory had come gift-wrapped.* —**gift-wrap** *vt* —**gift-wrapping** *n*

giftwrapping /gíft rapping/ *n* COMM same as **giftwrap**

Gifu /geé foo/ city and capital of Gifu Prefecture, central Honshu, Japan, 105 km/65 mi. northwest of Nagoya. Population: 401,269 (2002).

gig[1] /gig/ *n* 1. ONE-HORSE CARRIAGE a light open two-wheeled carriage pulled by a single horse. It was a popular form of private transport in 19th-century Europe and the United States. 2. ROWING BOAT a small light rowing boat carried on board a sailing ship 3. RACING BOAT a light rowing boat used for racing [Late 18C. Origin ?]

gig[2] /gig/ (*informal*) *n* a performance by a musician or group of musicians at a venue where they are booked to play but do not regularly perform ■ *vi* (**gigs, gigging, gigged**) to give a musical performance to an audience in exchange for payment [Early 20C. Origin ?]

gig[3] /gig/ *n* COMPUT same as **gigabyte** (*informal*) [Shortening]

giga- *prefix* 1. a thousand million (10^9) ○ *gigaton* Symbol **G** 2. in the binary system, a billion (2^{30}) ○ *gigabyte* [< Greek *gigas* 'giant']

gigabit /gíggəbit/ *n* a unit of capacity of a computer local area network, equal to one megabyte of computer information, or 1,073,741,824 bits

gigabyte /gíggə bīt/ *n* 1. a unit of computer data or storage space equivalent to 1,024 megabytes. Symbol **Gbyte** 2. one million bytes

gigacycle /gíggə sīk'l/ *n* a unit of electrical oscillation equal to 1000 million cycles

gigaflop /gíggə flop/ *n* a unit of computer processing speed equal to 1,000 million floating-point operations per second [Late 20C. < GIGA- + acronym < *floating-point operations per second*]

gigahertz /gíggə hurts/ (*plural same*) *n* a unit of frequency equal to 1000 million hertz, or cycles, per second. Symbol **GHz**

gigantic /jī gántik/ *adj* 1. very large, tall, or bulky ○ *a gigantic cargo plane* 2. very great ○ *a gigantic task* [Early 17C. < Latin *gigant-* 'giant' < Greek *gigas*] —**gigantically** *adv*

gigantism /jī gántizəm, jī gan-/ *n* excessive growth due to overproduction of growth hormone by the pituitary gland before the end of adolescence

gigantomachy /jígan tóməki/ (*plural* **-chies**) *n* in Greek mythology, the battle between the gods of Olympus and the rebellious giants who were children of the older gods (*literary*) [Late 16C. < Greek *gigantomachia* 'giant war']

gigaton /gíggə tun, jíggə-/ *n* a unit of explosive force equal to 1,000 million tons of TNT

gigawatt /gíggə wot, jíggə-/ *n* a unit of electrical power equal to 1,000 million watts. Symbol **GW**

giggle /gígg'l/ *vti* (**-gles, -gling, -gled**) LAUGH LIGHTLY to laugh audibly but not loudly, sometimes without meaning to, in a way that is characteristic of children ■ *n* 1. QUICK LAUGH a quiet laugh that is sometimes involuntary in a way that is characteristic of children 2. SOMETHING FUN something that is fun or that makes somebody laugh (*informal*) ■ **giggles** *npl* FIT OF LAUGHTER an uncontrollable and recurring urge to laugh (*informal*) [Early 16C. An imitation of the sound] —**giggler** *n* —**giggling** *adj* —**giggly** *adj*

GIGO /gígō/ *n* the principle that a computer program or process is only as good as the ideas or data put into it. Full form **garbage in, garbage out**

gigolo /jíggəlō/ (*plural* **-los**) *n* 1. a man who receives payments or gifts from a woman in exchange for being her sexual or social partner 2. a man whose job is to be a dancing partner or escort for a woman [Early 20C. < French < *gigole* 'professional dance partner who is a woman']

gigot /jíggət, zhígg-, zhiggō/ *n* 1. a French or Scottish cut of lamb or mutton taken from the leg 2. a leg of mutton [Early 16C. < French, 'small leg' < French dialect *gigue* 'leg' < *giguer* 'hop']

gigot sleeve *n* a sleeve that is close-fitting on the lower arm and full and loose on the upper arm [< its shape]

Gijón /gi hón/ seaport on the Bay of Biscay in Asturias Province, northwestern Spain. Population: 257,694 (2002).

Gila monster

Gila monster /heélə-, geélə-/ *n* a large brightly coloured venomous lizard that feeds on eggs and small animals. Native to: desert areas of the southwestern United States and Mexico. Latin name: *Heloderma suspectum*. [Late 19C. After the *Gila*River in SW New Mexico and S Arizona]

gilbert /gílbərt/ *n* a unit of magnetomotive force in the centimetre-gram-second system, equal to 0.7958 ampere-turns in the SI system [Late 19C. After William *Gilbert* (1544–1603), English physician and scientist]

Gilbert /gílbərt/, **Sir Humphrey** (1539?–83) English navigator. The half-brother of Sir Walter Raleigh, he claimed Newfoundland for England in 1583 and founded the first English colony in North America there, near present-day St John's.

> 'We are as near to heaven by sea as by land.'
> [Sir Humphrey Gilbert. Quoted in *Third and Last Voyages of the English Nation*, Richard Hakluyt; 1600]

Gilbert, Sir W. S. (1836–1911) British librettist and dramatist. He is best known for his long collaboration with Sir Arthur Sullivan, writing light operas including *The Pirates of Penzance* (1879). Full name **Gilbert, Sir William Schwenck**

Gilbert and Ellice Islands /-élliss-/ former British colony situated in the western Pacific Ocean. The group consisted of the Gilbert Islands, now part of Kiribati, and the Ellice Islands, now Tuvalu.

gild /gild/ (**gilds, gilding, gilded**) *vt* 1. COVER SOMETHING WITH GOLD to cover something with a thin layer of gold leaf or a substance that looks like gold 2. MAKE SOMETHING SEEM BETTER to make something seem better than it really is 3. COLOUR SOMETHING GOLD to give a golden colouring or tinge to something (*literary*) [Old English *gyldan* < Germanic] —**gilder** *n*

SPELLCHECK See **guild**.

gilded /gíldid/ *adj* 1. ARTS same as **gilt**[1] 2. wealthy and privileged ○ *gilded youth*

gilding /gílding/ *n* 1. the process of applying a thin layer of gold leaf or a substance that looks like gold to a surface 2. ARTS same as **gilt**[1] *n* (sense 1)

Gilead, Mount /gílli ad/ mountain in northwestern Jordan that also gives its name to an area east of the River Jordan, the Dead Sea, and the Sea of Galilee. Height: 1,096 m/3,597 ft.

Giles /jīlz/, **Ernest** (1835–97) British-born Australian explorer. He was the leader of five expeditions to central and western Australia between 1872 and 1876. Full name **Giles, William Ernest Powell**

gilet /zheé lay/ *n* 1. a bodice to a dress or a ballet-dancer's costume that is shaped like a waistcoat 2. a light sleeveless jacket, similar to a waistcoat but often longer, and sometimes made of padded or quilted material [Late 19C. < French]

gill[1] /gil/ *n* 1. the organ that fish and some other water animals use to breathe, consisting of a membrane

containing many blood vessels through which oxygen passes. They are internal in most fish and external in tadpoles and some molluscs. 2. a thin radiating plate on the underside of the cap of a mushroom or other fungus where its spores are produced [14C. < Old Norse] —**gilled** *adj* ◇ **green around the gills** looking on the point of being sick (*informal*) ◇ **to the gills** to the fullest possible extent

gill[2] /jil/ *n* a unit of liquid measure equal to a quarter of a pint (142 ml in the United Kingdom and 118 ml in the United States) [14C. Via Old French *gille* < late Latin *gillo* 'water pot']

gill[3] /gil/, **ghyll** *n* *regional* 1. a small fast-flowing stream, usually on a hill or mountain 2. a ravine with tree-covered sides [14C. < Old Norse *gil*]

gill[4] /jil/, **jill** *n* 1. *regional* a female ferret 2. a young woman (*archaic; sometimes considered offensive*) [15C. Shortening of the forename *Gillian*]

gill arch /gíl-/ *n* the bony or cartilaginous arch supporting the filaments that make up the gill of a fish

Gilles de la Tourette syndrome /jeél-/ *n* MED full form of **Tourette syndrome**

Gillespie /gi léspi/, **Dizzy** (1917–93) US jazz musician. A trumpeter with both large and small bands, he was a leading exponent of bebop and pioneered Afro-Cuban jazz in the United States. Full name **Gillespie, John Birks**

> 'It's taken me all my life to learn what not to play.'
> [Dizzy Gillespie. Quoted in *Jazz Is*, Nat Hentoff; 1976]

gill fungus /gíl-/ *n* a fungus that produces its spores from gills underneath a cap

gillie /gílli/, **ghillie** *n* 1. somebody whose job is to assist or guide people who go angling or deer-stalking in Scotland 2. a low-cut tongueless shoe that laces across the foot and sometimes up the ankle [Late 17C. < Gaelic *gille*]

Gillies /gílliss/, **Sir Harold** (1882–1960) New Zealand surgeon. He pioneered plastic surgery and wrote the standard text, *The Principles and Art of Plastic Surgery* (1957). Full name **Gillies, Sir Harold Delf**

Gillingham /jíllingəm/ town in southeastern England, on the River Medway. Population: 96,200 (1994).

gill net /gíl-/ *n* a net that is suspended vertically in the water like a curtain in order to catch fish by their gills —**gillnetter** *n*

gill slit /gíl-/ *n* one of the openings on either side of the head of a fish or amphibian that contain its gills

gillyflower /jílli flow ər/ *n* 1. a clove-scented pink or carnation 2. a scented stock or wallflower (*archaic*) [14C. < Alteration (after FLOWER) of French *girofle*, via medieval Latin *caryophyllum* 'clove' < Greek *karuophullon* 'nut leaf']

Gilmore /gíl mawr/, **Dame Mary Jean** (1865–1962) Australian poet and journalist. She campaigned for Aboriginal rights and radical social causes, and wrote nine collections of verse. Born **Cameron, Mary Jean**

gilt[1] /gilt/ *adj* COVERED WITH GILT covered with a thin layer of gold or a substance that looks like gold ■ *n* 1. THIN LAYER OF GOLD a thin layer of gold or a substance that looks like gold applied to a surface 2. GOVERNMENT BOND a bond issued by the British government (*often used in the plural*) [15C. < past participle of GILD] ◇ **take the gilt off the gingerbread** to spoil something that somebody was enjoying or looking forward to

SPELLCHECK See **guilt**.

gilt[2] /gilt/ *n* a young female pig, especially one that has not yet had a litter [14C. < Old Norse *gyltr*]

gilt-edged *adj* 1. VERY SAFE FINANCIALLY very safe as an investment ○ *gilt-edged securities* 2. WITH GOLD EDGE having a gilded edge 3. EXCELLENT very good, especially because of being free of risk and advantageous (*informal*) ○ *This is a gilt-edged opportunity to recoup our losses.*

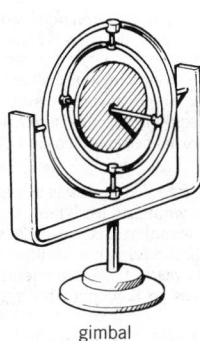

gimbal

gimbal /gímb'l, gí-/ n **1.** NAVIG RING FOR HOLDING COMPASS STEADY a pivoted ring mounted at right angles to one or two others to ensure that something such as a ship's compass always remains horizontal **2.** MECH ENG CONNECTION OF REVOLVING PARTS an interconnection that allows one part of a mechanism such as a clock's works to revolve independently of another revolving part that contains it ■ vt (**-bals, -balling, -balled**) PUT SOMETHING ON GIMBALS to support something on gimbals [Late 16C. Variant of GIMMAL]

gimcrack /jím krak/ adj showy or superficially appealing, but badly made and worthless [14C. Origin ?] —**gimcrack** n —**gimcrackery** n

gimel /gímm'l/ n the third letter of the Hebrew alphabet, represented in the English alphabet as 'g' or 'gh'. See table at **alphabet** [< Hebrew gīmel]

gimlet

gimlet /gímmlət/ n **1.** TOOL FOR BORING HOLES IN WOOD a small tool for boring holes in wood consisting of a slim metal rod with a sharp corkscrew end, fitted in a handle at a right angle **2.** COCKTAIL WITH LIME JUICE a cocktail made of vodka or gin with lime juice ■ adj PIERCING seeming to penetrate or pierce somebody or something ○'to meet anew the gimlet glances' (Thomas Hardy, *Jude the Obscure*; 1895) [14C. < Old French *guimbelet* 'small auger' < *guimble* 'auger' < Germanic]

gimlet-eyed adj having eyes that seem to penetrate or pierce, or to notice everything

gimmal /gímmǝl, jím-/ n MECH ENG, NAVIG same as **gimbal** [Late 16C. Alteration of obsolete *gemel* 'double ring', via Old French < Latin *gemellus* < *geminus* 'twin']

gimme /gímmi/ contr give me (*nonstandard*)

gimmick /gímmik/ n **1.** SOMETHING GRABBING ATTENTION something that attracts attention or publicity, e.g. a new technique or device **2.** DISHONEST TRICK a piece of trickery or manipulation intended to achieve a result dishonestly ○ *It's not a genuine offer, just a sales gimmick.* **3.** GADGET an ingenious device, mechanism, or ploy, especially one that works in a concealed way **4.** US HIDDEN DISADVANTAGE a piece of concealed information that, if known, would make an offer or opportunity less attractive ○ *It sounds great, but what's the gimmick?* [Early 20C. Origin ?] —**gimmicky** adj

gimmickry /gímmikri/ n **1.** gimmicks in general **2.** the use of a gimmick or gimmicks to deceive somebody or attract attention

gimp[1] /gimp/, **guimpe** /gamp/ n a silk or cotton trimming that has a wire or cord running through it [Mid-17C. < Dutch]

gimp[2] /gimp/ n **1.** US DIFFICULTY IN WALKING difficulty in

walking, caused by injury or stiffness (*informal*) **2.** N Am OFFENSIVE TERM an offensive term for somebody with a physical disability, especially somebody who has difficulty walking or who uses a wheelchair (*slang*) **3.** US CLUMSY PERSON somebody regarded as clumsy or ineffectual (*slang insult; often considered offensive*) [Early 20C. Origin ?] —**gimpy** adj

gin[1] /jin/ n **1.** a strong colourless alcoholic spirit distilled from grain and flavoured with juniper berries **2.** CARDS same as **gin rummy** (*informal*) [Early 18C. Shortening of GENEVER]

gin[2] /jin/ n **1.** MECH ENG HOIST a simple hoist operated by hand **2.** FIELD SPORTS TRAP a snare or trap, usually one consisting of a noose made of wire for catching small animals ■ vt (**gins, ginning, ginned**) **1.** FIELD SPORTS CATCH ANIMAL IN GIN to trap an animal with a gin **2.** INDUST CLEAN RAW COTTON to separate cotton from its seeds using a cotton gin [13C. Shortening of Old French *engin* 'engine']

gin and it n a drink consisting of gin and Italian vermouth (*informal*) [< shortening of ITALIAN]

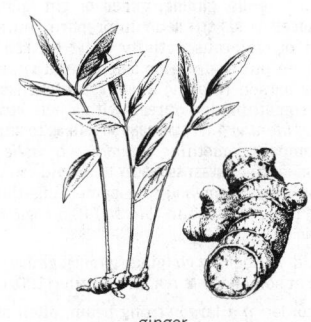

ginger

ginger /jínjər/ n **1.** HOT-TASTING SPICE the hot-tasting edible underground stem (**rhizome**) of an Asian plant, eaten fresh, pickled, candied, or in powdered form as a spice, especially in Asian cookery **2.** PLANT YIELDING GINGER a widely-cultivated plant that yields ginger. Native to: Asia. Latin name: *Zingiber officinale*. **3.** BROWNISH-YELLOW COLOUR a yellow colour with an orange or brownish tinge ■ vt (**-gers, -gering, -gered**) ADD GINGER TO SOMETHING to add ginger as a spice to something [Pre-12C. < Old French *gingi(m)bre*, via Latin and Greek < Pali *singivera*] —**ginger** adj —**gingery** adj

---

ORIGIN The source of the Pali word from which *ginger* derives was a Sanskrit compound meaning literally 'horn-body' – a reference to the shape of the edible ginger root. By the time it had passed through Greek *ziggiberis* into Latin, it had become *zinziberi*. After classical times this developed to *gingiber* or *gingiver*, which Old English borrowed as *gingifer*. English acquired the word again in the 13th century from Old French, and this combined with the descendant of the Old English form to produce Middle English *gingivere*, from which modern English ***ginger*** is derived.

---

ginger up vt to make something more lively, active, or interesting [< inserting a piece of ginger into the anus of a slothful horse]

ginger ale n an effervescent nonalcoholic drink flavoured with ginger

ginger beer n a mildly alcoholic cloudy effervescent drink made by fermenting a mixture of syrup and ginger

gingerbread /jínjər bred/ n **1.** GINGER-FLAVOURED CAKE a moist dark cake made with syrup or treacle and flavoured with ginger **2.** GINGER-FLAVOURED BISCUIT a ginger-flavoured biscuit, often cut into the stylized shape of a person, animal, or Christmas tree **3.** ARCHIT ELABORATE DECORATION showy and elaborate decoration, especially on the outside of a building (*often used before a noun*) ○ *a Victorian gingerbread style of cottage* [13C. By folk etymology (by association with BREAD) < Old French *gingembrat* 'preserved ginger' < medieval Latin *gingiber* 'ginger']

gingerbread man n a biscuit in the stylized shape of a person, made from gingerbread and often decorated with icing

ginger group n UK, Can a group, often within a party or association, whose aim is to stimulate debate

and press for more radical or decisive action on something

gingerly /jínjərli/ adv in a very cautious, wary, or tentative way ○ *He gingerly unscrewed the radiator cap.* ■ adj very cautious, wary, or tentative ○ *made a gingerly approach to the sick animal* [Early 16C. Origin ?] —**gingerliness** n

ginger nut, **ginger snap** n a small round crisp ginger-flavoured biscuit

ginger snap n a thin crisp biscuit flavoured with ginger

ginger wine n an alcoholic drink made by fermenting bruised ginger with sugar and water

gingham /gíngəm/ n a light plain-weave cotton fabric with checks in white and another colour (*often used before a noun*) ○ *a gingham dress* [Early 17C. Via Dutch *gingang* < Malay *genggang* 'striped']

gingili /jín jilli/ n S Asia in Indian cooking, sesame seeds or oil [Early 18C. < Hindi and Marathi *jiñjalī*]

gingiva /jin jíva, jínjiva/ (*plural* **-vae** /-vee/) n the gum around the roots of the teeth (*technical*) [Late 19C. < Latin] —**gingival** adj

gingivectomy /jínji véktəmi/ (*plural* **-mies**) n a surgical operation to remove tissue from the gums

gingivitis /jínji vítiss/ n inflammation of the gums around the roots of the teeth

gingko n TREES another spelling of **ginkgo**

ginglymus /jíng glíməss/ (*plural* **-mi** /-mī/) n a hinge joint of the human body (*technical*) [Late 16C. Via modern Latin < Greek *ginglumos* 'hinge']

gink /gingk/ n somebody, especially a man, who is considered strange, unintelligent, or clumsy (*informal insult*) [Early 20C. Origin ?]

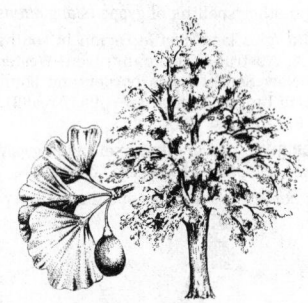

ginkgo

ginkgo /gíngkō/ (*plural* **-goes**), **gingko** (*plural* **-koes**) n a widely cultivated deciduous tree of primitive origin, with fan-shaped leaves. Native to: China. Latin name: *Ginkgo biloba*. [Late 18C. Via Japanese < Chinese *yínxíng* 'silver apricot']

ginkgo biloba /-bi lōbə/ n a herbal preparation made from the pulverized leaves of the ginkgo tree [< modern Latin genus name]

ginnal /jínal/, **jinnal** (*slang; used in Black English*) vti (**-nals, -nalling, -nalled; -nals, -naling, -naled**) to trick or cheat somebody ■ n somebody who cannot be trusted

ginnel /gínn'l/ n N England a narrow alley or passageway between two walls or buildings [Early 17C. Origin ?]

ginormous /jī náwrməss/ adj extraordinarily large in size (*informal*) [Mid-20C. Blend of GIGANTIC + ENORMOUS]

gin palace n a large bar or public house furnished or decorated in a gaudy and pretentious style (*dated*)

gin rummy n a card game similar to rummy in which two players collect sets and sequences of cards. A hand can be won if cards totalling ten or fewer points are uncombined. [< GIN[1]; pun on RUMMY[1], as if < RUM[1]]

Ginsberg /gínzbərg/, **Allen** (1926–97) US poet. His *Howl* (1956) launched the Beat movement.

> 'What if someone gave a war and Nobody
> came? Life would ring the bells of Ecstasy
> and Forever be Itself again.'
> [Allen Ginsberg, 'Graffiti'; 1972]

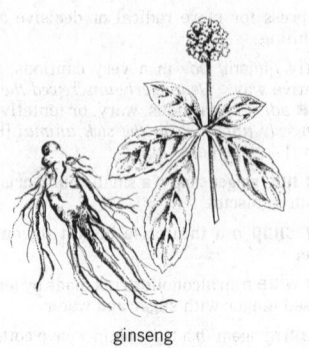

ginseng

ginseng /jín seng/ (*plural* **-sengs** or *same*) *n* **1.** a forked aromatic root used in traditional Chinese medicine and more widely as a tonic **2.** the plant that produces the ginseng root. Native to: South Asia, North America. Genus: *Panax*. [Mid-17C. < Chinese *rénshēn* < *rén* 'man' + *shēn*, type of herb]

gin sling *n* an iced drink consisting of gin, water, and lemon or lime juice [Origin ?]

Giorgione /jáwr jṓni/ (1478?–1510) Italian painter. Although none of his signed works has survived, the works that have been assigned to him, e.g. *The Tempest* (1507), give a new prominence to atmosphere at the expense of storytelling. Born **Barbarelli, Giorgio**

Giotto /jóttṓ/ (1267?–1337) Italian painter. One of the first European painters to portray human forms naturalistically, he exerted a profound influence on artists of the Renaissance. Full name **Giotto di Bondone**

gip *vt, n* another spelling of **gyp**²

gippo *n* another spelling of **gyppo** (*slang offensive*)

Gippsland /gíps land/ fertile region in southeastern Victoria, Australia, stretching from Western Port to the New South Wales border and bounded in the North by the Australian Alps. Area: 31,000 sq. km/11,970 sq. mi.

gippy tummy *n* MED another spelling of **gyppy tummy** (*informal; sometimes considered offensive*)

Gipsy *n, adj* PEOPLES another spelling of **Gypsy**

giraffe

giraffe /jə raáf/ (*plural* **-raffes** or *same*) *n* a large animal with an extremely long neck, long legs, and a yellowish coat mottled with brown patches. Giraffes are ruminants. Native to: open grassland in Africa. Latin name: *Giraffa camelopardalis*. [Late 16C. Via French *girafe* or Italian *giraffa* < Arabic *zarāfa*]

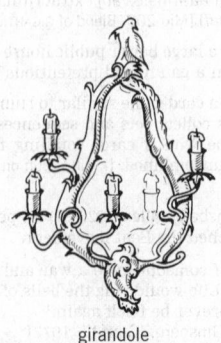

girandole

girandole /jírrəndōl/, **girandola** /ji rándələ/ *n* **1.** WALL-MOUNTED CANDLEHOLDER a wall-mounted branched candleholder that often incorporates a mirror between the candlestick branches **2.** STARBURST JEWELLERY an earring or pendant with a large central stone surrounded by several smaller ones **3.** ROTATING FIREWORK an elaborate rotating firework **4.** WATER JET a revolving water jet [Mid-17C. Via French < Italian *girandola* < late Latin *gyrare* 'gyrate']

girasol /jírrə sol/, **girasole** /-sol, -sōl/, **girosol** /-sol/ *n* MINERALS same as **fire opal** [Late 16C. < Italian *girasole* 'sunflower' < *girare* 'to turn' + *sole* 'sun']

Giraudoux /zheéerō doo/, **Jean** (1882–1944) French writer. He is remembered for witty novels and plays including *The Madwoman of Chaillot* produced posthumously in 1945. Full name **Giraudoux, Hyppolyte Jean**

> 'Human beings are like timid punctuation marks sprinkled among the incomprehensible sentences of life.'
> [Jean Giraudoux, *Siegfried*; 1922]

gird¹ /gurd/ (**girds, girding, girded** or **girt** /gurt/) *v* **1.** gird yourself *vr* GET SELF READY to prepare yourself for conflict or vigorous activity **2.** *vt* PUT BELT AROUND SOMEBODY to put a girdle or belt around yourself or another person (*literary*) **3.** *vt* FASTEN SOMETHING ON to secure something to yourself with a belt, straps, or a girdle (*literary*) **4.** *vt* SURROUND SOMETHING to surround or encompass something (*literary*) ○ *a castle girded with a moat* **5.** *vt* INVEST SOMEBODY to provide somebody with or dress somebody in something that is a sign of rank or honour (*literary*) [Old English *gyrdan* < Germanic]

gird² /gurd/ *N England vti* (**girds, girding, girded**) to jeer or gibe at somebody ■ *n* a jeer or gibe [12C. Origin ?]

girder /gúrdər/ *n* a large strong beam, often of steel, forming a main spanning and supporting part in a framework

girdle¹ /gúrd'l/ *n* **1.** WOMAN'S FOUNDATION GARMENT a woman's elasticated foundation garment or corset extending from the waist to the thigh **2.** NARROW BELT a cord worn round the waist to hold in a large loose-fitting garment such as a kaftan or a monk's habit **3.** SOMETHING THAT SURROUNDS something that surrounds or encircles something else (*literary*) **4.** ANAT RING OF BONE a ring-shaped structure of bone, especially the pelvic girdle or pectoral girdle, which support the upper and lower limbs respectively **5.** PART OF CUT GEMSTONE the outer edge of a gem, by which it is held in its setting **6.** FORESTRY RING ROUND TREE TRUNK a ring round a tree trunk made by removing the bark and underlying tissue in order to kill the tree ■ *vt* (**-dles, -dling, -dled**) **1.** SURROUND SOMETHING to surround or encircle something (*literary*) **2.** FORESTRY CUT RING OF BARK FROM TREE to remove a ring of bark and underlying tissue from a tree trunk in order to kill the tree [Old English *gyrdel* < Germanic]

girdle² /gúrd'l/ *n N England, Scotland* HOUSEHOLD same as **griddle** (*nonstandard*) [15C. Variant]

girdler /gúrdlər/ *n* an insect that makes a groove round a branch or twig in which to lay its eggs, thereby killing the branch

giri /gírri/ *n* a social obligation or debt (*informal*) [< Japanese]

girl /gurl/ *n* **1.** FEMALE CHILD a human female from birth until the age at which she is considered an adult **2.** ⚠ YOUNG WOMAN a young woman between childhood and adulthood (*often considered offensive*) **3.** ⚠ WOMAN OF ANY AGE a woman of any age, especially one who is a friend or contemporary, or who is younger than the speaker (*informal; often considered offensive*) ○ *a night out with the girls* **4.** DAUGHTER somebody's daughter, especially when a child (*informal*) **5.** GIRLFRIEND somebody's girlfriend **6.** WAY OF ADDRESSING WOMAN used as a friendly, intimate, or patronizing form of address to a woman (*sometimes considered offensive*) **7.** OFFENSIVE TERM an offensive term for a young woman servant or employee (*dated*) **8.** FEMALE ANIMAL a female animal, especially a young one (*informal; often used before a noun*) ○ *a girl kitten* [13C. Origin ?] —**girlhood** *n*

USAGE **girl** or **woman**? *Girl* is used more often as an alternative for **woman**, especially in reference to a young woman, than *boy* is for *man*. (*Boy* in reference to an adult is normally found only in the plural or in fixed compounds such as *boyfriend*.) However, the use of *girl*

for a teenager or an adult is often regarded as patronizing or disrespectful, especially when it comes from a man.

girl Friday *n* a young woman whose job is to be somebody's personal assistant and to do general office work (*sometimes considered offensive*) [After *Man Friday*, all-round helper in *Robinson Crusoe* (1719) by Daniel Defoe]

girlfriend /gurl frend/ *n* **1.** WOMAN OR GIRL SWEETHEART OR LOVER a girl or woman with whom somebody has a romantic or sexual relationship **2.** WOMAN FRIEND a woman who is the friend of another woman **3.** *US* WAY OF ADDRESSING WOMAN used as a friendly or intimate form of address to a woman by a woman friend (*informal*)

Girl Guide *n* a member of the Guide Association

girlie /gúrli/ *adj* (*informal*) **1.** SHOWING NUDE WOMEN showing or involving naked or scantily dressed women (*often considered offensive*) **2.** same as **girly** ■ *n* **1.** OFFENSIVE TERM an offensive term of address sometimes used by a man to a woman **2.** LITTLE GIRL a young girl (*dated informal*)

girliegirlie /gúrlee gurlee/ *adj* describes a man who has sexual relationships with numerous women (*slang; used in Black English*)

girlish /gúrlish/ *adj* **1.** characteristic of girls **2.** more suitable for a girl than for an adult woman — **girlishly** *adv* —**girlishness** *n*

girl next door *n* a woman or girl who is unaffected, approachable, and perceived as similar to yourself

girl power *n* the ability of or opportunity for teenage girls and young women to make decisions for themselves and shape their own lives

Girl Scout *n* a member of the girls' branch of the worldwide Scout movement in the United States

girly /gúrli/ (**-ier, -iest**) *adj* extremely or deliberately feminine (*informal*) ○ *a girly lace collar*

girn /gurn/ (**girns, girning, girned**), **gurn** (**gurns, gurning, gurned**) *vi* **1.** *N England, Scotland* COMPLAIN to complain, whine, or grumble **2.** *N England, Scotland* GRIMACE to make a bad-tempered or discontented face **3.** PULL WEIRD FACES to use the facial muscles to pull and twist the face into an absurdly grotesque expression, especially in a competition [14C. Alteration of GRIN]

giro /jírō/ *n* (*plural* **-ros**) **1.** BANK TRANSFER SYSTEM a system that enables money to be transferred quickly and cheaply between accounts or between the financial institutions of a country **2.** BENEFIT CHEQUE a cheque, cashable at a post office, for the payment of a state benefit such as unemployment benefit (*informal*) ■ *vt* (**-ros, -roing, -roed**) PAY MONEY BY GIRO to pay or transfer money by the giro system [Late 19C. Via German < Italian, 'circulation (of money)']

giron *n* HERALDRY another spelling of **gyron**

Girona another spelling of **Gerona**

Gironde /ji rónd, zhi róNd/ navigable river estuary in southwestern France, formed where the Dordogne and Garonne rivers meet. Length: 72 km/45 mi.

girosol *n* MINERALS another spelling of **girasol**

girt past participle, past tense of **gird**¹

girth /gurth/ *n* **1.** DISTANCE ROUND SOMETHING the distance round something thick and cylindrical such as a tree trunk or somebody's waist ○ *a man of ample girth* **2.** SADDLE BAND a broad band fastened around the belly of a horse to keep a saddle in place ■ *vt* (**girths, girthing, girthed**) **1.** FASTEN SADDLE ON HORSE to put or fasten a girth on a horse **2.** SURROUND SOMETHING to surround or encircle something (*literary*) [14C. < Old Norse *gjörð* 'girdle']

GISA *n* a strain of a common infection-causing bacterium that shows resistance to treatment by some of the commonly used glycopeptide antibiotics. Full form **glycopeptide intermediate Staphylococcus aureus**

gisarme /gi zaárm/ *n* a medieval foot soldier's weapon that had a long shaft and a head with an axe blade on one side and a sharp point on the other [13C. < Old French *guisarme*]

Gisborne /gízbərn/ administrative region and important wine area on the North Island, New Zealand, that includes the city of the same name. Population: 43,971 (2001). Area: 13,703 sq. km/5,291 sq. mi.

Giscard d'Estaing /zhís kaar destáN/, **Valéry** (*b.* 1926) French president (1974–81). He served as minister of finance twice (1962–66 and 1969–74) before succeeding Georges Pompidou to the presidency as an independent republican.

Gish /gish/, **Lillian** (1893–1993) US actor. Perhaps the greatest of all silent-film actors, she continued a long career on both stage and screen, appearing on film for the last time in 1987. Born **de Guiche, Lillian**

'You can't teach acting. You learn that from the human race.'
[Lillian Gish, *PBS TV*, 11 July 1988]

gismo *n* another spelling of **gizmo**

gist /jist/ *n* **1.** the essential point or meaning of something **2.** the essential grounds for a legal action [Early 18C. < Old French *cest action gist* 'this action lies']

git /git/ *n* an offensive term for somebody regarded as annoying, tiresome, unpleasant, or thoughtless (*informal insult*) [Mid-20C. Variant of GET [2]]

gite /zheet/ *n* a country cottage or small house in France offering fairly simple accommodation that can be rented for a self-catering holiday [Late 18C. < French *gîte* 'stopping place']

gittern /gíttərn/ *n* a medieval stringed instrument that was a forerunner of the guitar [14C. Via Old French *guiterne* < Latin *cithara* (see CITHARA)]

Giuliani /jòoli áanee/, **Rudolph W.** (*b.* 1944) US mayor of New York City (1993–2001) known for his tough stance against crime, and for his leadership after the terrorist attack on the World Trade Center (11 September 2001)

Giulio Romano /jòoli ō rō máanō/ (1499?–1546) Italian painter and architect in the mannerist style. He was the chief pupil of Raphael and assisted him in many of his works. His own paintings include the *Martyrdom of St Stephen.* He also designed the drainage system, cathedral, street plan, and several prominent buildings in Mantua.

~~**giutar**~~ incorrect spelling of **guitar**

give /giv/ (**gives, giving, gave** /gayv/, **given** /gívv'n/) CORE MEANING: a verb used to indicate that somebody presents or delivers something that he or she owns to another person to keep or use ○ *He gave Brian £800 with the understanding he would pay the rest at a later date.* ○ *The programme would give education grants to people who do community service.* ○ *My mother gave me this cardigan for Christmas.* ○ *What will you give me for the car?* ○ *When we arrived they gave us badges with our names on.*

1. *vt* PASS SOMETHING TO SOMEBODY to place something that you are holding in the temporary possession of another person ○ *Could you give me the phone?* ○ *He gave her the umbrella while he searched in his pockets for change.* **2.** *vt* GRANT SOMETHING TO SOMEBODY to allow somebody to have something such as power or a right ○ *Opponents of the bill claimed it gave too much power to the mine owners.* **3.** *vt* COMMUNICATE SOMETHING to impart or convey something such as information, advice, or opinions to somebody ○ *Give them my love.* **4.** *vt* CONVEY SOMETHING to cause somebody to have an idea or impression ○ *Whatever gave you that idea?* **5.** *vt* IMPART SOMETHING to make somebody experience a particular physical or emotional feeling ○ *She said the steady income gave her a sense of security.* **6.** *vt* PERFORM SOMETHING to carry out or perform something in public ○ *Not one of these actors gave a performance that was worthy of the prize.* **7.** *vt* MAKE OR DO SOMETHING used with nouns referring to physical actions to indicate that the action is being made or done ○ *She gave Paul a quick, accusing glance.* **8.** *vt* PROVIDE SERVICE to perform an action or service for somebody ○ *He gave her a foot massage to relax her.* ○ *The guide gave us a tour of the ruins.* **9.** *vt* DEVOTE SOMETHING to devote or sacrifice something such as time or effort ○ *He gave his whole life to helping children in need.* **10.** *vt* ORGANIZE SOMETHING to organize a social event ○ *They gave a party in her honour when she returned from the expedition.* **11.** *vt* CAUSE TO BELIEVE SOMETHING to lead somebody to have a particular understanding about something ○ *I was given to understand that they had left.* **12.** *vt* VALUE SOMETHING to estimate something at a particular amount or value ○ *What do you give for his chances of getting her back?* **13.** *vi* YIELD to collapse or break under pressure ○ *The wheel gave under the heavy load.* ○ *When people are under constant pressure from work and home, something has to give.* **14.** *vt* CONCEDE SOMETHING to yield to somebody's opinion, or admit that somebody has an advantage or a specific characteristic or ability ○ *You're not a coward, I'll give you that.* **15.** *vt* TOAST SOMEBODY to propose a toast to somebody ○ *I give you the bride and groom!* **16.** *vt* INTRODUCE SOMEBODY to present or introduce somebody such as a performer or speaker to an audience ○ *Ladies and gentlemen, I give you the Grand Panjandrum!* **17.** *n* RESILIENCE the ability or tendency to yield under pressure [Old English *giefan* < Indo-European] —**giver** *n* ◇ **give me...** I'd rather do or have... (*informal*) ○ *Give me a quiet evening with a book any time.* ◇ **give or take** used to indicate that a figure given is fairly accurate, within the stated range ○ *worth about half a million, give or take a few thousand pounds*

SYNONYMS ***give, present, confer, bestow, donate, grant***

CORE MEANING: to hand over something to somebody

give to place something that you are holding in the temporary possession of another person ○ *I gave her my key.* **present** to give something in a formal or ceremonial way ○ *He was presented with a consolation prize.* **confer** (*formal*) to give something such as a title, honour, or favour to somebody ○ *Several other honorary degrees were conferred at the ceremony.* **bestow** (*formal*) to present something, especially something valuable or undeserved, to somebody ○ *The award for lifetime achievement was bestowed on her not long before she died.* **donate** to give a contribution to a charitable organization or other good cause, or, in a medical context, to give blood for blood transfusions or organs for transplant ○ *The painting was donated to the gallery by the artist's widow.* **grant** to agree to allow a request, favour, or privilege, or formally or officially to give money or property ○ *We were granted the right to appeal.*

---

give away *vt* **1.** GIVE SOMETHING AS PRESENT to give or offer something without charging for it **2.** DISCLOSE SOMETHING BY MISTAKE to reveal information or a secret, often without meaning to **3.** BETRAY SOMEBODY to betray somebody by providing information **4.** PRESENT BRIDE TO HUSBAND AT WEDDING to accompany a bride to her future husband's side and formally present her to him just before the words of the wedding ceremony are spoken **5.** LET OPPONENT SCORE POINT to allow an opponent to get an advantage, especially inadvertently, through poor or illegal play **6.** *ANZ* ABANDON SOMETHING to abandon or give up on something

give back *vt* to return something, especially to its rightful or original owner

give in *v* **1.** *vi* LOSE to admit defeat **2.** *vi* ACCEPT CONDITIONS to accept demands or conditions **3.** *vt* HAND SOMETHING OVER to hand over or deliver something, especially a piece of school work, to somebody who is expecting it ○ *He gave his essay in a week late.* **4.** *vi N Am* BREAK to collapse or break under pressure

give of *vr* **give of yourself** to devote or dedicate your time or energy to something

give off *v* **1.** *vt* to send out or emit something **2.** *vi N Ireland* to speak one's mind angrily (*informal*)

give on to *vt* to overlook or lead to something ○ *The French windows give on to a small paved area.*

give out *v* **1.** *vt* HAND SOMETHING OVER to hand over or distribute something **2.** *vt* MAKE SOMETHING KNOWN to declare something or make something known, especially publicly ○ *She gave out the exam marks in reverse order.* **3.** *vt* EMIT SOMETHING to send out or emit something **4.** *vi* BE USED UP to run out or be finished ○ *My courage gave out, and I couldn't face her after all.* **5.** *vi* STOP WORKING to fail or stop working **6.** *vt* CRICKET DISMISS BATSMAN in cricket, to declare that a batsman is dismissed

give over *vi* to stop doing something, especially something that is annoying to others (*informal; usually as a command*)

give over to *v* **1.** *vt* to dedicate or assign something to a particular purpose or use ○ *This area will be given over to a children's playground.* **2. give yourself over to** *vr* to abandon yourself to an emotion or experience (*literary*) ○ *She gave herself over to despair.*

give up *v* **1.** *vi* SURRENDER to surrender or admit defeat **2.** *vt* HAND OVER SOMEBODY OR SOMETHING to hand over or part with somebody or something ○ *She gave up her seat to the man with a baby.* **3.** *vt* STOP USING OR DOING SOMETHING to stop or renounce using or doing something ○ *give up chocolate for a week* **4.** *vt* STOP TRYING to abandon a pursuit that has a goal ○ *Darkness fell, but they didn't give up looking for the missing children.* **5.** *vt* LOSE HOPE FOR SOMEBODY OR SOMETHING to stop hoping for a good outcome with regard to somebody or something ○ *Where have you been? We'd given you up as lost.* **6.** *vt* DEVOTE YOURSELF TO SOMETHING to devote or dedicate yourself to an emotion, experience, or activity, especially exclusively ○ *He gave himself up to working for the cause.* **7.** *vt* REVEAL INFORMATION to reveal information or a secret ◇ **give it up for somebody or something** to applaud somebody *or* something enthusiastically (*informal*)

give up on *vt* **1.** to abandon something, especially a plan **2.** to lose hope about somebody or something

give-and-take *n* (*informal*) **1.** mutual cooperation and understanding between people or groups, often involving concessions on all sides **2.** a useful exchange of ideas or information in which everyone involved benefits

giveaway /gív ə way/ *n* **1.** SOMETHING THAT REVEALS something that serves to reveal, betray, or expose something ○ *Her accent's a dead giveaway.* **2.** GIFT something that is offered free of charge or at very little cost, often as a publicity gimmick or incentive to buy (*informal*) **3.** MEDIA same as **freesheet 4.** *US* GAME SHOW a radio or TV game show that offers contestants the chance to win prizes, especially cash prizes (*informal*) ■ *adj* (*informal*) **1.** VERY INEXPENSIVE extremely low in price **2.** FREE free of charge ○ *a giveaway sample of a new shampoo*

giveback /gív bak/ *n* something that is or has been returned (*informal*)

given /gívv'n/ past participle of **give** ■ *adj* **1.** PARTICULAR relating to a particular person, thing, or concept ○ *from any given starting point* **2.** ARRANGED EARLIER previously arranged or specified ○ *If I can't make it at the given time, I'll phone you.* **3.** VALIDATED validated or executed on the date mentioned (*formal*) ○ *this last will and testament given by my hand this 13th day of February 1898* ■ *prep* **1.** GRANTED assuming that somebody has the opportunity or ability to do or have something ○ *Given time, I'm sure we can find a solution.* **2.** IN VIEW OF taking into consideration ○ *given the uncertainty of the situation* ■ *n* ACCEPTED FACT a fact or event that is accepted as true or definite at the outset and that affects subsequent reasoning ◇ **given to** inclined to something or likely to do or be something

given name *n* the name or names that somebody is given at birth or baptism in addition to the family name

Giza /geézə/ city in northern Egypt on the western bank of the River Nile, southwest of Cairo. It is the site of the Sphinx and Egypt's three most famous pyramids. Population: 4,779,000 (1998).

gizmo /gízmō/ (*plural* **-mos**), **gismo** *n* a gadget, especially a mechanical or electrical device considered to be more complicated than necessary or one whose name is not known or forgotten (*informal*) [Mid-20C. Origin ?]

gizzard /gízzərd/ *n* **1.** PART OF BIRD'S DIGESTIVE TRACT a thick-walled muscular sac in the alimentary tract of birds where food is broken down by muscular action and by small stones ingested for that purpose **2.** DIGESTIVE STRUCTURE a structure in invertebrates and fish where digestion takes place **3.** STOMACH the stomach or alimentary canal generally (*informal*) [14C. Via Old French *giser* < Latin *gigeria* 'cooked poultry entrails']

GLA *n* an essential fatty acid required to form prostaglandins, found in high concentrations in evening primrose oil and borage oil. It can be taken as a dietary supplement for menstrual disorders and for the pain of arthritis. Full form **gamma linolenic acid**

glabella /glə béllə/ (*plural* **-lae** /-lee/) *n* the part of the human forehead that lies just above the nose and between the eyebrows. It is one of the crucial points used in measuring and classifying skull types in physical anthropology and craniometry. [Early 19C. < modern Latin < Latin *glaber* 'hairless'] —**glabellar** *adj*

glabrate /gláybrayt, -brət/ *adj* BIOL same as **glabrous** [Mid-19C. < Latin *glabrare* 'make hairless' < *glaber* 'hairless']

glabrescent /glay bréssənt/ *adj* becoming hairless over time [Mid-19C. < Latin *glabescere* 'become smooth' < *glaber* 'hairless']

glabrous /gláybrəss/ *adj* smooth and lacking hairs or

bristles ○ *glabrous leaves* [Mid-17C. < Latin *glaber* 'hairless'] —**glabrousness** *n*

glacé /glássay/ *adj* **1.** GLAZED WITH SUGAR SOLUTION coated with a sugar solution that results in a glazed finish ○ *glacé cherries* **2.** MADE FROM ICING SUGAR AND LIQUID made by mixing icing sugar and a liquid, usually water **3.** SMOOTHLY GLOSSY having a smooth glossy finish [Mid-19C. < French, past participle of *glacer* 'glaze' < *glace* (see GLACIER)]

Glace Bay /gláyss-/ town on the Atlantic coast in Cape Breton County, northeastern Nova Scotia, Canada, situated on the Atlantic Ocean 19 km/12 mi. east of Sydney. Population: 21,187 (2001).

glacial /gláysh'l/ *adj* **1.** RELATING TO GLACIER relating to or caused by a glacier or glaciers ○ *glacial movements and deposits* **2.** CONTAINING EXPANSES OF ICE characterized by the presence of ice masses **3.** ICE-AGE describes any geological time when a large part of the Earth was covered in ice **4.** EXTREMELY COLD icily or bitingly cold ○ *a glacial wind* **5.** COLDLY HOSTILE unfriendly or hostile ○ *a glacial look* **6.** DETACHED characterized by detachment and an absence of emotion ○ *glacial determination* **7.** SLOW moving or advancing extremely slowly ○ *the glacial pace of the negotiations* ■ *n also* **Glacial** GEOL same as **glacial period** [Mid-17C. Via Old French < Latin *glacialis* 'icy' < *glacies* 'ice'] —**glacially** *adv*

glacial acetic acid *n* acetic acid that is 99.8% or more pure [Because it forms crystals resembling ice]

glacial period *n* any period of geological time when most of the Earth was covered in ice

glaciate /gláyssi ayt/ (**-ates, -ating, -ated**) *v* **1.** *vti* to cover something with a glacier, or become covered with a glacier **2.** *vt* to affect something by the action of a glacier, especially by erosion [Early 17C. < Latin *glaciat-*, past participle of *glaciare* 'freeze' < *glacies* 'ice'] —**glaciation** /gláyssi áysh'n/ *n*

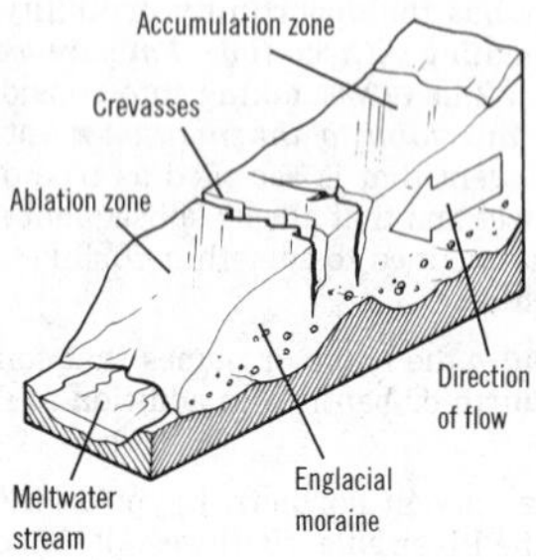
Accumulation zone
Crevasses
Ablation zone
Direction of flow
Meltwater stream
Englacial moraine

glacier: composition of a glacier

glacier /glássi ər, gláyssi-/ *n* a large body of continuously accumulating ice and compacted snow, formed in mountain valleys or at the poles, that deforms under its own weight and slowly moves [Mid-18C. < French < *glace* 'ice' < Latin *glacies*] —**glaciered** *adj*

glacier cream *n* a sunblock designed to combat the effects of ultraviolet radiation that climbers experience above the snow line, where the sun reflects strongly off the snow

glacier meal *n* GEOL same as **rock flour**

glacier milk *n* water cloudy with particles of rock that flows from a melting glacier

glaciology /gláyssi óllәji/ *n* the branch of scientific study concerned with the formation, movement, and effects of glaciers and ice in general —**glaciologic** /gláyssi ə lójjik/ *adj* —**glaciological** *adj* —**glaciologist** *n*

glacis /glássiss, glássi, gláyssis/ (*plural* **-cises** or **-cis** /glássiz, gláyssiz, -seez/) *n* **1.** GENTLE INCLINE a slope, especially one that is not very long or steep **2.** DEFENSIVE SLOPE a slope in front of a fortification designed to make it easier to fire on attacking forces **3.** NEUTRAL TERRITORY a stretch of neutral ground between two opposing or warring forces **4.** MIL same as **glacis plate** [Late 17C. < French < Old French *glacier* (see GLANCE)]

glacis plate *n* the armoured plate at the front of a military tank [< its slant]

glad[1] /glad/ *adj* (**gladder, gladdest**) **1.** DELIGHTED happy and pleased ○ *I'm so glad you came.* **2.** CHEERFULLY WILLING willing or ready to do something ○ *always glad to help* **3.** GRATEFUL appreciative of or grateful for something ○ *glad of the chance to relax* **4.** PLEASING giving pleasure, delight, or happiness ○ *on this glad occasion* **5.** BRIGHT bright and cheerful (*literary*) ○ *this glad June day* ■ *vti* (**glads, gladding, gladded**) GLADDEN to gladden somebody, or become glad (*archaic*) [Old English *glæd* < Germanic] —**gladly** *adv* —**gladness** *n*

glad[2] /glad/ *n* PLANTS same as **gladiolus** (*informal*) [Early 20C. Shortening]

gladden /gládd'n/ (**-dens, -dening, -dened**) *vti* to feel cheerful and hopeful, or cause somebody to feel cheerful and hopeful ○ *It gladdens my heart to hear that.*

glade /glayd/ *n* an area in a wood or forest without trees or bushes [Early 16C. Origin ?] —**glady** *adj*

glad hand *n* **1.** a hand extended in welcome or greeting, especially one that is offered insincerely or for motives of self-advancement **2.** a friendly welcome

glad-hand *vti* to offer somebody a friendly greeting or handshake, often insincerely or for motives of self-advancement —**glad-hander** *n*

gladiate /gláddi ət/ *adj* shaped like the blade of a sword ○ *the gladiate leaves of an iris* [Late 18C. < Latin *gladius* 'sword']

gladiator /gláddi aytər/ *n* **1.** FIGHTER IN ROMAN ARENA in ancient Rome, a professional fighter who fought another combatant or a wild animal in public entertainments set in an arena. Often gladiators were criminals or slaves who were equipped with nets, nooses, swords, or other weapons. **2.** KEEN SUPPORTER OR CAMPAIGNER a vigorous fighter or campaigner for or against a cause or person **3.** *US* BOXER a professional boxer (*informal*) [Mid-16C. < Latin < *gladius* 'sword'] —**gladiatorial** /gláddi ə táwri əl/ *adj*

gladiolus /gláddi ṓləss/ (*plural same* or **-li** /-lī/ or **-luses**), **gladiola** /-lə/ (*plural* **-las** or *same*) *n* **1.** a widely grown plant with long sword-shaped leaves. Flowers: large, funnel-shaped, arranged in tall spikes. Native to: tropics, southern Africa. Genus: *Gladiolus*. **2.** the large central part of the breastbone (**sternum**) [16C. < Latin, 'little sword' < *gladius* 'sword']

glad rags *npl* somebody's best clothes, reserved for special occasions (*informal*)

gladsome /gládssəm/ *adj* feeling, showing, or bringing happiness (*literary*) ○ *gladsome tidings* —**gladsomely** *adv* —**gladsomeness** *n*

Gladstone[1] /gládstən/ *n* a small four-wheeled horse-drawn carriage with a collapsible roof [Mid-19C. See GLADSTONE BAG]

Gladstone[2] /gládstən/ coastal city in southeastern Queensland, Australia, an industrial centre and tourist resort. It is the gateway to the southern Great Barrier Reef. Population: 27,099 (2002 estimate).

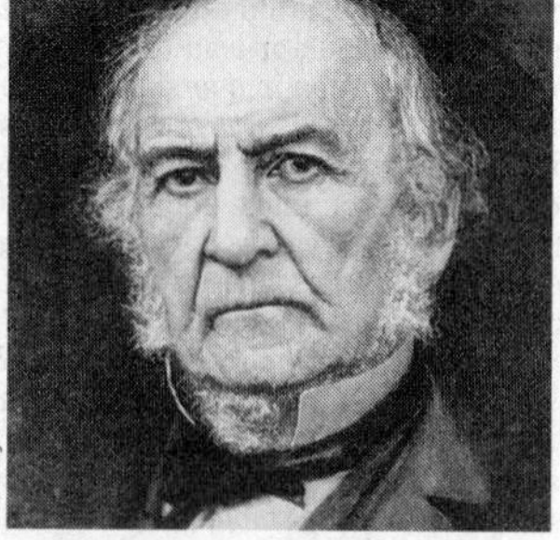
Barnaby's

W. E. Gladstone

Gladstone, W. E. (1809–98) British politician. The leader of the Liberal Party after 1867, he was four times prime minister between 1868 and 1894 (1868–74, 1880–85, 1886, and 1892–94). He introduced national education in Britain (1870). Full name **Gladstone, William Ewart**

> 'National injustice is the surest road to national downfall.'
> [W. E. Gladstone, *Speech at Plumstead, London*; 1878]

Gladstone bag *n* a small suitcase or portmanteau consisting of a rigid frame on which two compartments of the same size are hinged together [Late 19C. After W. E. GLADSTONE, noted for the amount of travelling he undertook in his public life]

Glagolitic /glággō líttik/ *adj* **1.** belonging or relating to an ancient Slavonic alphabet that was replaced by the Cyrillic alphabet **2.** belonging or relating to a Roman Catholic community of southwestern Croatia, whose liturgical books are still written in the Glagolitic alphabet [Early 19C. < modern Latin *glagoliticus* < Serbo-Croatian *glagŏljica* < Old Church Slavonic *glagolŭ* 'word']

glair /glair/, **glaire** *n* **1.** EGG WHITE a sizing, glazing, or adhesive substance made from egg white and used especially in bookbinding **2.** SUBSTANCE SIMILAR TO EGG-WHITE SIZING a substance that resembles glair in appearance or function ■ *vt* (**glairs, glairing, glaired; glaires, glairing, glaired**) PUT GLAIR ON SOMETHING to apply glair to something [14C. Via French < Latin *clarus* 'clear']

glam /glam/ *n* **1.** MUSIC same as **glam rock** (*informal*) **2.** EXTREME GLAMOUR glamour, especially when it is overstated or ironic (*slang*) ■ *adj* EXTREMELY GLAMOROUS glamorous, especially in an overstated or ironic way (*slang*) ○ *a really glam dress* ■ *vt* (**glams, glamming, glammed**) *also* **glam up** GLAMORIZE EXCESSIVELY to make somebody or something glamorous, especially in an overstated or ironic way (*slang*) [Mid-20C. Shortening]

Glamorgan /glə máwrgən/ former county in southern Wales that included the present-day counties of Cardiff and Swansea

glamorize /glámmə rīz/ (**-izes, -izing, -ized**), **glamorise** (**-ises, -ising, -ised**) *vt* **1.** to make somebody or something glamorous **2.** to make something seem more interesting, romantic, or glamorous than it really is —**glamorization** /glámmə rī záysh'n/ *n* —**glamorizer** *n*

glamorous /glámmərəss/, **glamourous** *adj* **1.** desirable, especially in an exciting, stylish, or opulent way ○ *a glamorous lifestyle* **2.** dressed or made up to be good-looking, especially in a high-fashion manner ○ *glamorous models strutting along the catwalk* —**glamorously** *adv* —**glamorousness** *n*

glamour /glámmər/ *n* **1.** EXCITING ALLURE an irresistible alluring quality that somebody or something possesses by virtue of seeming much more exciting, romantic, or fashionable than ordinary people or things ○ *the glamour of a career in the movies* **2.** EXPENSIVE GOOD LOOKS striking physical good looks or sexual impact, especially when it is enhanced with highly fashionable clothes or makeup **3.** SPELL a magical spell or charm (*archaic*) [Early 18C. Alteration of GRAMMAR 'enchantment, spell'] —**glamour** *adj*

glamourous *adj* another spelling of **glamorous**

glam rock *n* a style of pop music of the 1970s performed by singers and musicians wearing outrageous clothes, makeup, hairstyles, and platform-soled boots. Its most famous exponents were the singers Gary Glitter and Marc Bolan and the band Sweet.

glance /glaanss/ *v* (**glances, glancing, glanced**) **1.** *vi* LOOK QUICKLY to look at something quickly, especially for only a second or two ○ *He glanced in our direction.* **2.** *vi* MAKE CURSORY EXAMINATION to look over or through something without really studying it **3.** *vi* TOUCH ON SOMETHING BRIEFLY to make a brief or passing allusion to something ○ *an introductory course that merely glances at the wider historical issues* **4.** *vi* GLINT to reflect or shine, especially intermittently or for only a short time ○ *green feathers glancing in the sunlight* **5.** *vt* STRIKE SOMETHING AT ANGLE to strike something briefly or lightly at an angle ○ *The stone glanced his shoulder.* **6.** *vt* DEFLECT CRICKET BALL in cricket, to hit a bowled ball with the bat held at an angle so that the ball is deflected to the leg side ■ *n* **1.** QUICK LOOK a quick look at somebody or something ○ *a glance in our direction* **2.** PASSING MENTION a brief mention of something ○ *The book takes only a brief glance at contemporary music.* **3.** CURSORY EXAMINATION a cursory quick examination of something ○ *I haven't even had a glance at the report yet.* **4.** OBLIQUE STRIKE an act or instance of something striking another thing briefly or lightly at an angle **5.** GLINT OF LIGHT a sudden or quick flash or gleam of light ○ *glances of sunlight through the trees* **6.** DEFLECTION OF CRICKET BALL in cricket, a stroke in which the bat is held at an angle so that the ball is deflected to the leg side [15C. Alteration (influenced by *glent* 'to shine') of *glace* < Old French *glacier* 'to slide' < *glace* (see GLACIER)] ◇ **at a glance** im-

mediately and without having to make a close study ◇ **at first glance** initially or on first examination **glance off** *vt* to come into quick light contact with something and then deflect at an angle ○ *The stone glanced off the windscreen.*

glancing /glaánssing/ *adj* **1. STRIKING OBLIQUELY** coming into contact with another object and then deflecting at an angle ○ *a glancing blow* **2. FLICKERING OR FLASHING** giving off light in a flickering or flashing manner **3. TEMPORARY** lasting only a short time —**glancingly** *adv*

gland[1] /gland/ *n* **1. SECRETING CELL MASS** in animals, a cell or group of cells that secretes a specific substance. Endocrine glands secrete directly into the bloodstream, while exocrine glands secrete through ducts into a cavity or to the surface of the body. **2. ORGAN LIKE GLAND** an anatomical structure that resembles a gland, especially a lymph node (*not in technical usage*) **3. PLANT ORGAN** in plants, a cell or group of cells that secrete substances, e.g. a nectary gland [Late 17C. Via French < Latin *glandula* 'tonsil' < *glans* 'acorn'] —**glandless** *adj*

gland[2] /gland/ *n* a metal sleeve fitted round a rotating shaft or rod to prevent leakage, e.g. round a shaft emerging from a ship's hull [Early 19C. Probably < Old Norse *glam* 'noise']

glanders /glándərz/ *n* an infectious, often fatal, disease of horses, characterized by ulcers of the skin, lungs, or upper respiratory tract and heavy discharge of mucus from the nose. It is caused by the bacterium *Pseudomonas mallei*. (*takes a singular verb*) [15C. < Old French *glandres* 'swelling of the glands' < Latin *glandula* (see GLAND [1])] —**glandered** *adj* —**glanderous** *adj*

glandes ANAT plural of **glans**

glandular /glándyoōlər/ *adj* **1. RELATING TO GLANDS** relating to, functioning as, or affecting a gland or glands **2. RESULTING FROM GLAND DYSFUNCTION** describes a medical condition caused by a malfunctioning gland or glands **3. HAVING GLAND** characterized by the presence of a gland or glands **4. BODILY** natural to the body, especially hormonally or sexually (*informal*) [Mid-18C. Via French *glandulaire* < Latin *glandula* (see GLAND [1])]

glandular fever *n* an acute infectious disease caused by the Epstein-Barr virus and marked by fever, swelling of the lymph nodes, sore throat, and an increased amount of lymphocytes in the blood. Technical name **infectious mononucleosis**

glandule /glándyool/ *n* a small gland or a part resembling a small gland [14C. Directly or via French < Latin *glandula* (see GLAND [1])]

glandulous /glándyoōləss/ *adj* ANAT, MED same as **glandular** —**glandulously** *adv*

glans /glanz/ (*plural* **glandes** /glándeez/) *n* **1.** *also* **glans penis** the rounded tip of a penis **2.** *also* **glans clitoridis** /-kli tórri diss/ the erectile tissue at the tip of a clitoris [Mid-17C. < Latin, 'acorn']

glare[1] /glair/ *v* (**glares, glaring, glared**) **1.** *vi* **STARE STONILY** to stare intently and angrily **2.** *vt* **EXPRESS SOMETHING WITH STARE** to express or signal anger, disapproval, contempt, or another negative emotion by giving a steady stare ○ *He glared his disapproval at the youngsters.* **3.** *vi* **BE UNPLEASANTLY BRIGHT** to shine brightly and intensely, often dazzlingly **4.** *vi* **STAND OUT OBTRUSIVELY** to be very conspicuous, blatant, or obtrusive ○ *Mistakes glared from every page of the report.* **5.** *vi* **BE UNPLEASANTLY AND OVERLY ORNATE** to be excessively decorated or garish ■ *n* **1. ANGRY LOOK** a prolonged stare expressing anger, disapproval, contempt, or another negative emotion **2. EXCESSIVE BRIGHTNESS** dazzling or uncomfortable brightness ○ *a screen on the monitor to reduce glare* **3. MEDIA SPOTLIGHT** excessive attention from the media **4. GAUDY ORNAMENTATION** gaudy coloration or decoration [13C. < Middle Low German *glaren* 'gleam']

glare[2] /glair/ *N Am n* METEOROL same as **black ice** ■ *adj* having a smooth and slippery surface [Mid-16C. Origin ?]

glaring /gláiring/ *adj* **1. OBVIOUS** easily perceived or detected ○ *a report full of glaring mistakes* **2. ANGRY** expressing anger, disapproval, contempt, or another negative emotion ○ *a glaring look of sheer contempt* **3. UNPLEASANTLY BRIGHT** intensely or dazzlingly bright **4. GARISH** gaudy or brash, especially in a tasteless way ○ *painted in glaring oranges and greens* —**glaringly** *adv* —**glaringness** *n*

glary /gláiri/ (**-ier, -iest**) *adj* **1.** staring steadily and often angrily ○ *glary eyes* **2.** dazzlingly or uncomfortably bright ○ *a glary computer screen*

Glasgow /glaázgō, glázgō/ **1.** city on the River Clyde, southwestern Scotland. An industrial and commercial centre, it has a cathedral and three universities. Population: 606,651 (2001). **2.** *also* **City of Glasgow** council area in west-central Scotland. Area: 175 sq. km/68 sq. mi.

Glasgow coma scale *n* a system for assessing the severity of brain impairment in somebody with a brain injury that uses the sum of scores given for eye-opening, verbal, and motor responses. A high score of 15 indicates no impairment and a score of 8 or less indicates severe impairment.

glasnost /gláss nost/ *n* a policy that commits a government or organization to greater accountability, openness, discussion, and freer disclosure of information than previously, especially that of Mikhail Gorbachev in the former Soviet Union [Late 20C. < Russian, 'publicness']

glass /glaass/ *n* **1. TRANSPARENT SOLID SUBSTANCE** a hard, usually transparent substance that shatters easily. Source: sand melted in combination with other oxides such as lime or soda. Use: windows, bottles, lenses. **2. UNCRYSTALLIZED SUBSTANCE LIKE GLASS** a solid substance similar to glass formed by melting and cooling without crystallizing **3. GLASS CONTAINER** a container without a handle made from glass, for drinking from **4. QUANTITY IN GLASS** the amount a drinking glass holds **5.** GARDENING **PROTECTING COVER** a cloche, greenhouse window, or insulating material used to protect germinating plants ○ *Keep the seedlings under glass for the first four weeks.* **6.** HOUSEHOLD same as **glassware** **7.** HOUSEHOLD same as **looking glass** **8.** OPTICS same as **magnifying glass** **9.** GEOL same as **volcanic glass** **10.** DRUGS **ILLEGAL DRUG** a smokable form of methamphetamine used as an illegal drug **11.** METEOROL same as **barometer** (*dated*) ■ **glasses** *npl* **1. OUTER EYEWEAR** a pair of sight-correcting or protective lenses set in frames that fit over the ears and sit on the bridge of the nose **2.** same as **binoculars** ■ *vt* (**glasses, glassing, glassed**) **1. PUT GLASS OVER SOMETHING** to cover or fit something with glass ○ *glassed the porch* **2. INSERT INTO GLASS CONTAINER** to put something into a glass container or one made of a material resembling glass ○ *glassed the specimens in formalin* **3. CUT USING GLASS** to injure somebody with a drinking glass or a broken part of a drinking glass, usually in the face (*slang*) [Old English *glæs* < Germanic] —**glass** *adj* —**glassful** *n* —**glass-like** *adj*

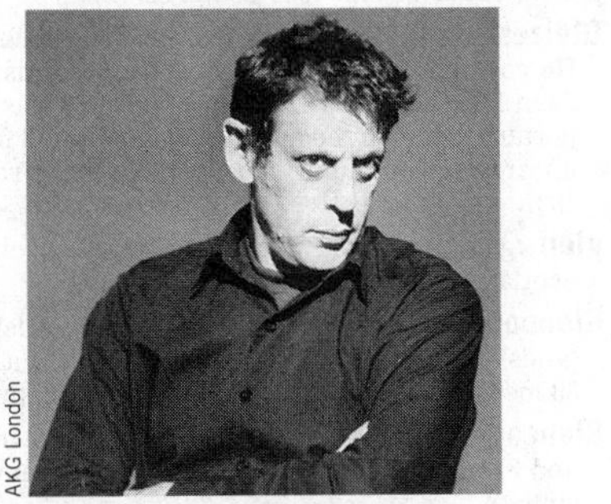
AKG London

Philip Glass

Glass /glaass/, **Philip** (*b.* 1937) US composer. He is known for his minimalist compositions, including the opera *Einstein on the Beach* (1976).

glass blowing *n* the forming or shaping of a glass object by blowing air through a tube into a mass of semimolten glass —**glass blower** *n*

glass case *n* a display cabinet made mainly of glass and used to exhibit objects of interest or value

glass ceiling *n* an unofficial but real impediment to somebody's advancement into upper-level management positions because of discrimination based on the person's gender, age, race, ethnicity, or sexual preference

glass chin *n* BOXING same as **glass jaw** (*informal*)

glass cloth *n* **1.** a cloth, usually made of closely woven linen, used for drying glasses and dishes **2.** a polishing cloth with fine particles of glass in it

glass cutter *n* **1.** a tool used to cut glass or to etch designs into glass **2.** somebody whose job is to cut glass or to make cut glass

glassed-in /glaást-/ *adj* made using glass panes ○ *a glassed-in conservatory*

glass eel *n* a larval form of the American or European eel with a flattened transparent body. Native to: Atlantic Ocean.

glass eye *n* an artificial eye made from glass, or material similar to glass, so as to resemble a natural eye

glass fibre *n* INDUST same as **fibreglass** (sense 2)

glassfish /glaáss fish/ (*plural same* or **-fishes**) *n* **1.** a small, almost transparent tropical fish often kept in aquariums. Genus: *Chanda*. **2.** a slender, almost transparent sea fish eaten as a delicacy in Japan. Native to: northwestern Pacific. Latin name: *Salangichthys microdon*.

glass harmonica *n* a set of drinking glasses or glass bowls, filled to graduated levels with water, that produce sounds of different pitches when their rims are rubbed with a moist finger. It was popular as a musical instrument in the 18th century, when various mechanical versions also existed.

glasshouse /glaáss howss/ (*plural* **-houses** /-howziz/) *n* **1.** GARDENING same as **greenhouse** **2.** a public position that brings somebody a high level of media attention and scrutiny **3.** a military prison or detention centre (*slang*)

glassine /gla seén/ *n* a transparent paper treated with a glaze to make it greaseproof and resistant to the passage of air. Use: book jackets, food packaging.

glass jaw *n* in boxing, a jaw that is highly vulnerable to an opponent's punches (*informal*)

glassmaker /glaáss maykər/ *n* somebody whose job is to make glass or glass objects —**glassmaking** *n*

glass snake *n* a limbless lizard, or one with vestigial limbs, that can snap off its tail as a defence mechanism to confuse predators. Native to: Europe, Asia, North America. Genus: *Ophisaurus*. [< its brittle tail]

glassware /glaáss wair/ *n* objects made of glass considered as a group

glass wool *n* fine-spun glass fibres formed into a woolly mass. Use: insulation, in air filters, in the manufacture of fibreglass.

glasswork /glaáss wurk/ *n* **1.** the technique or result of cutting and fitting glass, especially glass panes for windows, doors, and conservatories **2.** the production or manufacture of glass or glass objects **3.** HOUSEHOLD same as **glassware** —**glassworker** *n*

glassworks /glaáss wurks/ (*plural same*) *n* a factory for the manufacture of glass or glass objects

glasswort /glaáss wurt/ (*plural same* or **-worts**) *n* a plant with fleshy stems and small leaves that was formerly a source of the soda used in making glass. Native to: salt marshes. Genus: *Salicornia*.

glassy /glaássi/ (**-ier, -iest**) *adj* **1. SMOOTH AND SLIPPERY** having a highly smooth, slippery, and often reflective surface **2. LIKE GLASS** resembling glass in being smooth, reflective, or transparent **3. BLANKLY EXPRESSIONLESS** lacking expression or animation ○ *a blank glassy look* —**glassily** *adv* —**glassiness** *n*

glassy-eyed *adj* having a blank staring expression

Glastonbury /glástənbəri/ historic market town in Somerset, southwestern England. The site of a 10th-century abbey and an Iron Age lake village, it also hosts an annual music festival. Population: 8,100 (1993 estimate).

Glaswegian /glaaz weéjən/ *n* somebody who comes from Glasgow, Scotland [Early 19C. < GLASGOW, after NORWEGIAN] —**Glaswegian** *adj*

Glauber's salt /glówbərz-/, **Glauber salt** *n* a colourless crystalline sodium sulphate. Use: in solar energy systems, manufacture of dyes, glass, and paper, laxative. [Mid-18C. After Johann Rudolf *Glauber* (1604–68), German chemist]

glaucoma /glaw kṓmə/ *n* an eye disorder marked by unusually high pressure within the eyeball that leads to damage of the optic disc [Mid-17C. Directly or via Latin < Greek *glaukōma* < *glaukos* 'blue-grey, green'] —**glaucomatous** *adj*

glauconite /gláwkə nīt/ *n* a green clay mineral containing iron and potassium. Use: fertilizer. [Mid-19C.

< German *Glaukonit* < Greek *glaukos* 'blue-grey, green'] —**glauconitic** /gláwkə níttik/ *adj*

glaucous /gláwkəss/ *adj* **1.** describes plants or fruit that are covered in a greyish, whitish, or bluish waxy or powdery substance **2.** of a dull greyish-green or blue colour [Late 17C. < Latin *glaucus* 'blue-grey, green' < Greek *glaukos*]

glaur /glawr/ *n Scotland* soft or slimy mud [15C. Origin ?] —**glaury** *adj*

glaze /glayz/ *v* (**glazes, glazing, glazed**) **1.** *vt* CERAMICS **COVER POTTERY WITH FINISH LIKE GLASS** to put a clear or coloured coating on a ceramic object and fire it in a kiln, in order to fix the coloration, make it watertight, or give it a shiny appearance **2.** *vt* COOK **COAT FOOD WITH MILK OR EGG** to brush food with milk, egg, or sugar before baking in order to produce a shiny brown finish **3.** *vt* ART **COAT OIL PAINTING** to give something, especially an oil painting, a transparent or semitransparent coating in order to enhance or slightly alter the colour tones **4.** *vt* COVERINGS **GIVE PROTECTIVE COVERING TO SOMETHING** to place a protective or decorative coating on something, especially a natural material such as leather, cotton, or paper **5.** *vti* MAKE OR BECOME GLASSY to become unfocused and expressionless as a result of loss of interest, distraction, or tiredness, or cause the eyes to become like this **6.** *vt* METEOROL **COVER SOMETHING WITH ICE** to cause a thin layer of ice to form on something **7.** *vt* CONSTR **FIT SOMETHING WITH GLASS** to fit glass into or over something, especially a window, door, or picture ■ *n* **1.** CERAMICS **COVERING RESEMBLING GLASS** a shiny, smooth, transparent, or coloured glassy coating on a ceramic object, produced by firing the treated object in a kiln, or the substance or process employed to achieve this **2.** COOK **COATING FOR FOOD** a shiny brown finish on food or the substance used for achieving this effect **3.** ART **COATING FOR OIL PAINTING** a transparent or semitransparent coating on something, especially an oil painting, used to enhance or slightly alter the colour tones, or the substance used to achieve this effect **4.** COVERINGS **PROTECTIVE COVERING** a protective or decorative coating on something, especially a natural material such as leather, cotton, or paper, or the substance used for making this kind of coating **5.** *N Am* METEOROL same as **glaze ice** [14C. < GLASS, after GRAZE[1], GRASS] —**glazer** *n*
glaze over *vi* to become unfocused and expressionless as a result of loss of interest, distraction, or tiredness (*refers to eyes*) ○ *Her eyes glazed over as the sedative began to take effect.*

glazed /glayzd/ *adj* **1.** APPEARING UNINTERESTED OR DISTRACTED showing that you are not at all interested or that you are distracted or tired ○ *sat with a glazed expression trying to stay awake* **2.** WITH SHINY COATING covered with a clear shiny protective or decorative coating **3.** FITTED WITH GLASS fitted with or covered with glass

glaze ice, glazed frost *n* a thin coating of ice formed when rain or moisture in the air comes into contact with a surface that is cold enough to cause it to freeze. N Am term **glaze**

glazier /gláyzi ər/ *n* somebody whose job is to fit glass, especially in windows and doors

glazing /gláyzing/ *n* **1.** HARD SHINY COATING the glaze coating on an object **2.** COVERING OF SOMETHING WITH GLAZE an act or the process of putting a glaze on something **3.** GLASS FOR WINDOW glass in general, especially the type of glass used in doors or windows or glass that has been fitted in windows or doors **4.** FITTING OF SOMETHING WITH GLASS an act or the process of fitting glass into something

glazing bar *n* a wooden or metallic strip used to support or separate panes of glass in windows and doors

GLBT *abbr* gay, lesbian, bisexual, or transgender

GLC *abbr* **1.** CHEM gas-liquid chromatography **2.** HIST Greater London Council

gleam /gleem/ *vi* (**gleams, gleaming, gleamed**) **1.** SHINE BRIGHTLY to shine brightly and continuously **2.** FLASH FOR SHORT TIME to flash, flicker, or appear briefly or indistinctly ■ *n* **1.** BRIGHT SHINE a steady bright shine **2.** FLASH OF LIGHT a beam of light, especially one that is reflected, dim, or coming from an indistinct source **3.** BRIEF SHOW a slight or momentary indication of something ○ *a gleam of interest* [Old English *glǣm* < Germanic] —**gleamer** *n* ◇ **a gleam in somebody's eye**

something at the very earliest stage of planning or development

gleaming /gleeming/ *adj* shining, especially with health, cleanliness, or newness ○ *gleaming black hair* —**gleamingly** *adv*

glean /gleen/ (**gleans, gleaning, gleaned**) *v* **1.** *vt* to obtain information in small amounts over a period of time **2.** *vti* to go over a field or area that has just been harvested and gather by hand any usable parts of the crop that remain [14C. Via Old French *glener* < late Latin *glennare* < Celtic] —**gleaner** *n*

gleanings /gleeningz/ *npl* **1.** objects or ideas that have been gathered or amassed over a period of time, especially when they form a collection or comprehensive whole **2.** the usable parts of a crop that are left behind in a harvested field or area and can be gathered in by hand

gleba /gleebə/ (*plural* **-bae** /-bee/) *n* a mass of tissue in which spores are formed in the fruiting bodies of fungi such as truffles and puffballs [Mid-19C. < Latin, 'clod']

glebe /gleeb/ *n* **1.** a piece of land belonging to a church and given over temporarily to a member of the clergy to provide additional income **2.** land or soil, especially when considered as a source of abundant natural produce (*literary*) [14C. < Latin *gleba* 'clod']

glee /glee/ *n* **1.** GREAT DELIGHT joyful or animated delight **2.** GLOATINGLY JUBILANT FEELING jubilant and often smug pleasure, especially as a result of somebody else's bad luck or failure **3.** MUSIC SONG FOR UNACCOMPANIED VOICES a part song for three or more unaccompanied voices of a type that first became popular in England in the 18th century [Old English *glēo* < Germanic, 'merriment'] —**gleeful** *adj*

glee club *n N Am* a choral society that concentrates on singing short part songs

~~**gleeming**~~ incorrect spelling of **gleaming**

gleet /gleet/ *n* **1.** inflammation of the urethra, accompanied by a discharge of pus and mucus, and characteristic of a late stage in the development of gonorrhoea **2.** a discharge of pus and mucus in a late stage of gonorrhoea [14C. < Old French *glette* 'slime' < Latin *glittus* 'sticky']

glei *n* GEOL another spelling of **gley**

Gleichschaltung /glíkh shaltoong/ *n* the forced standardization and complete suppression of all opposition in the political, social, and economic life and institutions of a country by an oppressive government or regime [Mid-20C. < German]

Gleizes /glez/, **Albert Leon** (1881–1953) French artist. He cowrote an influential defence of cubism with Jean Metzinger, *Du Cubisme* (1912). He was an important figure in the cubist movement and founded an artists' community in southeastern France in 1927.

glen /glen/ *n* a long narrow valley, especially in Scotland [15C. < Scottish Gaelic *gleann*]

Glencoe /glén kó/ mountain pass in the Scottish Highlands where, in 1692, Campbell soldiers massacred 38 men of the MacDonald clan. Length: 8 km/5 mi.

Gleneagles /glen eeg'lz/ picturesque valley in Perth and Kinross, Scotland, the site of a well-known golf course

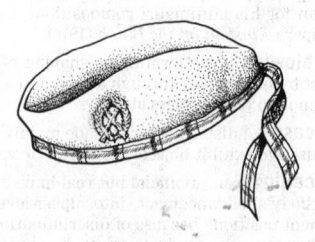

glengarry

glengarry /glen gárri/ (*plural* **-ries**) *n* a small brimless hat with a crown creased from front to back and usually a pair of ribbons hanging from the back, sometimes worn as part of Scottish highland dress.

It also forms part of the uniform of some Scottish regiments. [Mid-19C. After *Glengarry* in the Highlands of Scotland]

AKG London

John Glenn

Glenn /glen/, **John** (*b.* 1921) US astronaut and senator. He was the first US astronaut to orbit Earth (1962), and the oldest astronaut ever to go into space (1998). He was a Democratic US senator from Ohio (1974–99). Full name **Glenn, John Herschel, Jr.**

glenoid /gleen oyd/ *adj* **1.** shaped like a small shallow cup or socket **2.** relating to the cup-shaped socket in the shoulder that holds the head of the humerus [Early 18C. < French *glénoïde* < Greek *glēnē* 'eyeball, socket']

Glenrothes /glen róthiss/ town in Fife, Scotland, designated a new town in 1948. It is the administrative centre of Fife council area. Population: 38,650 (1991).

gley /glay/, **glei** *n* a sticky bluish-grey clay soil or soil layer that forms in heavily waterlogged areas [Early 20C < Ukrainian *glei*]

glia /glee ə/ *n UK, Can* the network of supporting tissue and fibres that nourishes nerve cells within the brain and spinal cord. It comprises several layers of cells and makes up about 40 per cent of the total volume of nerve tissue. ANZ, US term **neuroglia** [Late 19C. < Greek, 'glue'] —**glial** *adj*

gliadin /glí ədin/, **gliadine** /-deen/ *n* a simple cereal protein, e.g. from wheat or rye [Mid-19C. < French *gliadine* < Greek *glia* 'glue']

glib /glib/ *adj* **1.** SLICK fluent in a superficial or insincere way ○ *a glib talker* **2.** SUPERFICIAL shallow and lacking thought or preparation ○ *a glib generalization* **3.** CASUAL AND RELAXED easy, unconcerned, and informal in attitude ○ *a glib smile* [Late 16C. Origin ?] —**glibly** *adv* —**glibness** *n*

glibenclamide /gli bénklə mïd/ *n* a sulphonylurea drug. Use: treatment of non-insulin-dependent diabetes. N Am term **glyburide**

glide /glïd/ *v* (**glides, gliding, glided**) **1.** *vti* MOVE SMOOTHLY to move in a smooth, effortless, and often graceful way, or cause something to move in this way ○ *seals gliding through the water* **2.** *vi* CHANGE STATE SMOOTHLY to pass smoothly, slowly, or gradually into a particular state ○ *gliding in and out of consciousness* **3.** *vti* AVIAT LAND WITHOUT USING ENGINE to bring an aircraft in to land without using engine power, or land without using the engine **4.** *vi* MUSIC USE PORTAMENTO in music, to slide from one note to another **5.** *vi* PHON MAKE INTERMEDIATE SPEECH SOUND to produce an intrusive speech sound when moving from one point of articulation to the next **6.** *vt* CRICKET same as **glance** *v* (sense 6) ■ *n* **1.** SMOOTH MOVEMENT a smooth, effortless, and often graceful movement **2.** DANCE SMOOTH FLOWING DANCE a dance with a smooth flowing movement **3.** DANCE DANCE STEP a smoothly flowing dance step **4.** AVIAT LANDING WITHOUT USING ENGINE a controlled aircraft descent using no engine power **5.** GEOG SLOW-MOVING WATER a stretch of calm, slowly flowing water in a river or large stream **6.** MUSIC same as **portamento 7.** MUSIC EXTENSION FOR TROMBONE a piece of metal tubing used to extend the length of a trombone so that lower notes can be produced **8.** PHON INTERMEDIATE SPEECH SOUND an intrusive speech sound produced when a speaker is moving from one point of articulation to the next, e.g. the 'w' sound in the middle of 'going' **9.** PHON same as **semivowel 10.** CRICKET same as **glance** *n* (sense 6) **11.** FURNITURE METAL DISC ON FURNITURE a metal or plastic disc fixed to the bottom of the leg of a piece of furniture, to facilitate moving it across the floor **12.** FURNITURE TRACK FOR DRAWER a track along which a

drawer can be slid in or out easily [Old English *glīdan* < Germanic]

glide path *n* the prescribed descent of an aircraft coming in to land that is shown to the pilot by means of a radio beam and acts as an aid to navigation

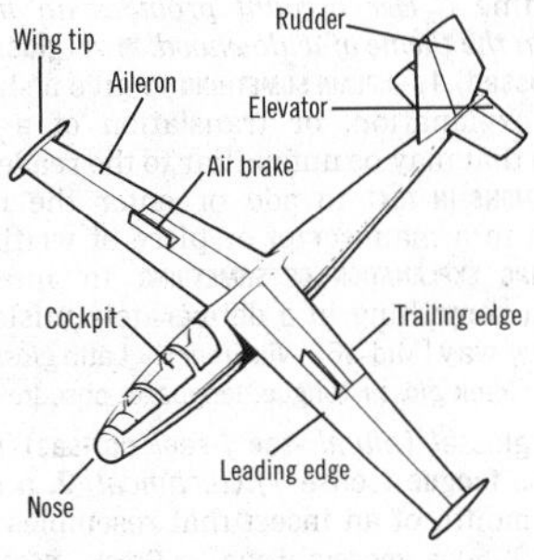

glider

glider /glídər/ *n* **1.** AVIAT an aircraft without an engine that flies by riding air currents. It becomes airborne by being towed up by an aeroplane or by being catapulted into the air from the ground. **2.** ZOOL same as **flying phalanger 3.** FURNITURE a type of rocking chair in which the rockers move on a stationary base beneath the chair

glide slope *n* AVIAT same as **glide path**

glide time *n NZ* a system of working with flexitime

gliding *n* the activity of flying a glider

glimmer /glímmər/ *vi* (**-mers, -mering, -mered**) **1.** EMIT DIM GLOW to emit a faint or intermittent light **2.** BE PRESENT TO SMALL EXTENT to be present faintly or in only a small amount ○ *Hope still glimmered in their hearts.* ■ *n* **1.** FAINT FLASHING LIGHT a faint or intermittent glowing light ○ *a glimmer of campfires in the distance* **2.** SMALL AMOUNT OF SOMETHING a faint sign or small amount of something ○ *a glimmer of interest* [15C. Probably < N Germanic]

glimmering /glímməring/ *n* same as **glimmer** *n* (sense 2) ■ *adj* emitting a faint or intermittent light

glimpse /glimps/ *n* **1.** BRIEF LOOK a quick or incomplete look or sighting of somebody or something ○ *I just caught a glimpse of her face in the crowd.* **2.** SMALL INDICATION a small, brief, or indistinct indication or appearance of something ■ *vt* (**glimpses, glimpsing, glimpsed**) SEE SOMETHING OR SOMEBODY BRIEFLY to catch sight of somebody or something briefly or incompletely [14C. Ultimately < Germanic]

glint /glint/ *vi* (**glints, glinting, glinted**) FLASH BRIEFLY to gleam or flash, especially brightly or momentarily ○ *Anger glinted in her eyes.* ■ *n* **1.** BRIEF FLASH a slight or momentary gleam or flash ○ *a glint of daylight through the curtains* **2.** SLIGHT INDICATION a slight indication of something ○ *a glint of humour in his eyes* **3.** SHININESS a shiny or glossy appearance [15C. Probably alteration of *glent* 'to gleam' < N Germanic]

glioma /glī ṓmə/ (*plural* **-mata** /-mətə/ or **-mas**) *n* a tumour composed of connective tissue (**glia**) of the nervous system and affecting the brain or spinal cord [Late 19C. < Greek *glia* 'glue'] —**gliomatous** *adj*

glissade /gli sáad/ *n* **1.** a gliding ballet step in which one foot slides forwards, backwards, or to one side **2.** a controlled slide down a snowy slope made without skis by somebody in a standing or crouching position [Mid-19C. < French < Old French *glisser* 'to slide' < Old Dutch *glissen*] —**glissade** *vi* —**glissader** *n*

glissando /gli sándō/ (*plural* **-di** /-dee/ or **-dos**) *n* **1.** an act of sliding a finger or thumb up or down a keyboard or harp strings from one note to another **2.** an act of sliding a finger along a stringed instrument's fingerboard or slowly moving a trombone's slide in and out to create a smooth change in pitch between two notes [Late 19C. < Italian < Old French *glisser* (see GLISSADE)]

glisten /glíss'n/ (**-tens, -tening, -tened**) *vi* **1.** to shine brightly or reflect light from a wet surface ○ *leaves glistening after the rain* **2.** to have a glossy sheen (*refers to hair or an animal's pelt*) [Old English *glisnian* < Germanic] —**glisten** *n*

glister /glístər/ (**-ters, -tering, -tered**) *vi* to glitter brightly (*archaic*) [14C. Probably < Middle Low German *glistern*]

glitch /glich/ *n* **1.** a minor hitch or technical problem ○ *glitches in the software* **2.** a sudden unwanted electronic signal, e.g. from a power surge or a temporary irregular supply of power [Mid-20C. Probably < Yiddish *glitsh* 'slip' < Old High German *glītan* 'to glide'] —**glitchy** *adj*

glitter /glíttər/ *vi* (**-ters, -tering, -tered**) **1.** SPARKLE to sparkle or shimmer brightly ○ *an evening gown glittering with sequins* **2.** SHINE WITH EMOTION to look bright or expressive with an emotion such as anger or love (*refers to eyes*) **3.** BE VIVACIOUS to exhibit liveliness and charm ○ *a radiant personality who glittered at every event she attended* **4.** BE FULL OF GLAMOUR to be characterized by the presence of somebody or something glamorous ○ *The event glittered with Hollywood stars.* ■ *n* **1.** SPARKLY DECORATION small pieces of reflective material, e.g. on a greetings card or in eye makeup **2.** SPARKLING LIGHT bright sparkling light **3.** GLAMOUR dazzling glamour ○ *the glitter of a command performance at the opera* [14C. < Old Norse *glitra*] —**glitteringly** *adj* —**glittery** *adj*

glitterati /glíttə ráati/ *npl* famous, rich, or fashionable people thought of as a group, especially those who are frequently photographed by the media (*informal*) [Mid-20C. Blend of GLITTER + LITERATI]

glittering *adj* **1.** SUCCESSFUL involving outstanding successes or achievements ○ *a glittering career* **2.** GLAMOROUS attended by many people who are glamorous or famous ○ *a glittering event* **3.** SPARKLING reflecting light in bright sparkling flashes ○ *glittering diamonds*

glittering prize *n* an object or position that is coveted by many people (*informal; often in the plural*) ○ *He was already being groomed for the glittering prizes of politics.*

glitz /glits/ *n* **1.** glamour, especially that associated with show business or celebrities **2.** extravagant and often tasteless display, especially of wealth [Late 20C. Back-formation < GLITZY]

glitzy /glítsi/ (**-ier, -iest**) *adj* **1.** glamorous, especially in relation to show business or celebrities **2.** extravagant and often tasteless, especially in the display of wealth [Mid-20C. Probably < German *glitzern* 'to glitter'] —**glitzily** *adv* —**glitziness** *n*

Gliwice /gli vítsə/ industrial city in Katowice Province, southern Poland, west of the city of Katowice. Population: 212,800 (1997).

gloaming /glṓming/ *n* the period of fading light after sunset but before dark (*literary*) [Old English *glōmung* < *glōm* 'twilight' < Germanic]

gloat /glōt/ (**gloats, gloating, gloated**) *vi* to feel or express smug self-satisfaction about something such as an achievement, a possession, or somebody else's misfortune [Late 16C. Origin ?] —**gloat** *n* —**gloater** *n* —**gloatingly** *adv*

glob /glob/ *n* a small amount of a soft or semiliquid substance (*informal*) [14C. Origin ?] —**globby** *adj*

global /glṓb'l/ *adj* **1.** WORLDWIDE relating to or happening throughout the whole world **2.** OVERALL taking all the different aspects of a situation into account **3.** SPHERICAL shaped like a globe or sphere **4.** COMPUT RELATING TO WHOLE OF SYSTEM covering or affecting the whole of a computer system, program, or file —**globally** *adv*

global economy *n* the interdependent economies of the world's nations, regarded as a single economic system ○ *Decisions taken at the meeting were significant not only for the region but for the global economy.*

globalise *vti* SOC SCI, BUSINESS another spelling of **globalize**

globalism /glṓb'lizəm/ *n* the belief or advocacy that political policies should take worldwide issues into account before focusing on national or state concerns —**globalist** *n*

globalize /glṓbə līz/ (**-izes, -izing, -ized**), **globalise** (**-ises, -ising, -ised**) *vti* **1.** to become adopted on a global scale, or cause something, especially social institutions, to become adopted on a global scale **2.** to become international or start operating at the international level, or cause something, especially a business or company, to become international —**globalization** /glṓbə lī záysh'n/ *n* —**globalizer** *n*

global village *n* the whole world considered as a single community served by electronic media and information technology

global warming *n* an increase in the world's temperatures, believed to be caused in part by the greenhouse effect

globe /glōb/ *n* **1.** MAP OF EARTH ON SPHERE a hollow sphere representing Earth and illustrated with the continents, seas, and islands, especially one showing and labelling the countries **2.** EARTH the planet Earth **3.** HOLLOW SPHERICAL OBJECT a rounded hollow object, especially one made of glass, e.g. a cover for a lamp, or a goldfish bowl **4.** PART OF MONARCH'S REGALIA a hollow sphere, usually made of gold or another precious metal, that forms part of a monarch's regalia and symbolizes the power or sovereignty of the ruler **5.** *ANZ, Can, S Africa* same as **light bulb** ■ *vti* (**globes, globing, globed**) FORM INTO GLOBE to form a globe, or cause something to form a globe [Mid-16C. Directly or via Old French < Latin *globus* 'ball, sphere'] —**globoid** *adj, n*

globe amaranth *n* an ornamental garden plant with colourful whorls of leaves and flower heads made up of several distinct blossoms. Latin name: *Gomphrena globosa.*

globe artichoke *n* PLANTS, FOOD same as **artichoke** (senses 1–2)

globefish /glṓb fish/ (*plural same* or **-fishes**) *n* FISH **1.** same as **puffer** (sense 2) **2.** same as **porcupine fish** [< its shape when inflated]

globeflower /glṓb flowər/ *n* a poisonous plant with ball-shaped flowers, consisting of large white, pale-yellow, or orange sepals that almost entirely enclose the smaller petals. Genus: *Trollius.*

globe thistle *n* a plant with jagged-edged leaves. Flowers: large white, bluish, ball-shaped. Native to: Asia, Mediterranean. Genus: *Echinops.*

globetrot /glṓb trot/ (**-trots, -trotting, -trotted**) *vi* to travel frequently and to a great variety of distant destinations —**globetrotter** *n*

globigerina /glṓbijə réenə/ (*plural* **-nas** or **-nae** /-nee/) *n* a marine protozoan with a spiny rounded spiral shell. Genus: *Globigerina.* [Mid-19C. < modern Latin < Latin *globus* 'ball, sphere' + *gerere* 'carry'] —**globigerinal** *adj*

globigerina ooze *n* a deposit on the ocean floor that consists of globigerina shells and is found almost worldwide

globin /glṓbin/ *n* the protein component of haemoglobin [Late 19C. Shortening of HAEMOGLOBIN]

globoid /glṓ boyd/ *adj* shaped like a ball ■ *n* a ball-shaped part, especially one found in plant granules

globose /glṓbōss/, **globous** /glṓbəss/ *adj* BIOL same as **globoid** [15C. < Latin *globosus* < *globus* 'ball, sphere'] —**globosely** *adv* —**globosity** /glō bóssəti/ *n*

globular /glóbyoolər/ *adj* **1.** having the shape of a ball **2.** containing or consisting of globules [Mid-17C. < Latin *globolus* (see GLOBULE)] —**globularity** /glóbbyoo lárrəti/ *n* —**globularly** *adv*

globular cluster *n* an approximately spherical cluster of densely packed stars, located within a spherical halo around the Milky Way galaxy

globule /glóbbyool/ *n* a small ball-shaped object, especially one that is liquid or semiliquid [Mid-17C. Via French < Latin *globulus* 'little globe' < *globus* 'ball, sphere']

globuliferous /glóbbyoo líffərəss/ *adj* composed of, containing, or producing globules

globulin /glóbbyoolin/ *n* a protein found in blood serum

glocalization /glōkə lī záysh'n/ *n* the process of adapting an internationally sold product or service to different local cultures and markets [Late 20C. Blend of GLOBAL and *localization* (see LOCALIZE)]

glochidium /glō kíddi əm/ (*plural* **-ia** /-i ə/) *n* **1.** *also* **glochid** /glṓkid/ a barbed hair or bristle that grows on plants such as the prickly pear or among the spores on ferns **2.** a parasitic larva of some mussels that has hooks or suckers used to attach itself to the fins or gills of fish. Family: Unionidae. [Late 19C. < modern Latin < Greek *glōkhis* 'arrowhead'] —**glochidial** *adj* —**glochidiate** /-ət/ *adj*

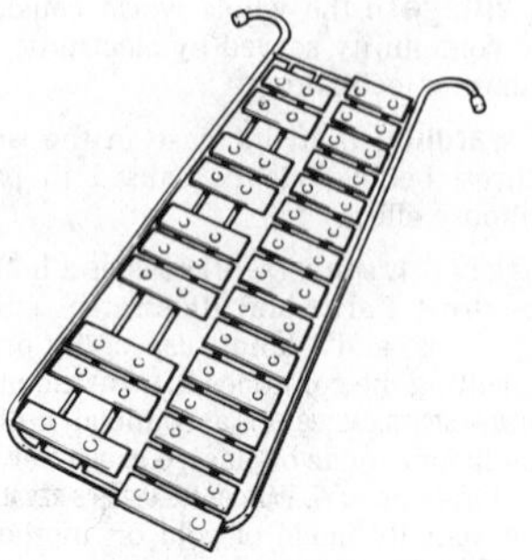
glockenspiel

glockenspiel /glókən shpeel/ *n* a percussion instrument consisting of a set of tuned metallic bars, played by striking the individual bars with small light hammers [Early 19C. < German, 'bell-play']

glogg /glog/ *n* a hot punch consisting of brandy, red wine, and sherry, and flavoured with sugar, spices, fruit pieces, and blanched almonds. It was originally served in Scandinavia at Christmas. [Early 20C. < Swedish *glögg*]

glomerate /glómmərət/ *adj* **1.** formed into a tight ball or cluster **2.** tightly wound together, like a ball of string [Late 18C. < Latin *glomerat-*, past participle of *glomerare* 'make into a ball' < *glomus* 'ball of thread']

glomerule /glómmə rool/ *n* **1.** a flat-topped flower head formed by a compact cluster of short-stalked flowers **2.** a cluster of spores formed into a ball shape [Late 18C. Via French < modern Latin *glomerulus* (see GLOMERULUS)] —**glomerulate** /glo mérrələt/ *adj*

glomeruli ANAT plural of **glomerulus**

glomerulonephritis /glō mérrəlō nə frítiss/ *n* an inflammatory disease affecting the clusters of capillaries (**glomeruli**) in the cortex of a kidney

glomerulus /glō mérrələss/ (*plural* **-li** /-lī/) *n* **1.** a tightly packed cluster of blood vessels, nerve fibres, or other cells **2.** a round cluster of interconnected capillaries found in the cortex of a kidney, which remove body waste to be excreted as urine [Mid-19C. < modern Latin, 'little ball' < Latin *glomus* 'ball of thread'] —**glomerular** *adj*

gloom /gloom/ *n* **1.** MURKY DARKNESS a state of darkness or partial darkness, especially one in which shadows or poor visibility create a cheerless or dispiriting atmosphere **2.** DESPONDENCY a feeling or atmosphere of despair, despondency, or misery ■ *v* (**glooms, glooming, gloomed**) **1.** *vi* BE DESPONDENT to feel or look despondent or miserable **2.** *vti* MAKE OR BECOME DARK to become dark, or cause something to become dark [13C. Origin ?] ◇ **gloom and doom** a feeling or expression of despondency and a belief that disaster is about to strike

gloomy /gloómi/ (**-ier, -iest**) *adj* **1.** MURKILY DARK dark in a way that creates a cheerless or dispiriting atmosphere **2.** OFFERING LITTLE HOPE causing a feeling of despair and hopelessness ○ *gloomy prospects* ○ *a gloomy scene of poverty* **3.** DESPONDENT having a feeling of sadness, often accompanied by a morbid or uninterested outlook on life —**gloomily** *adv* —**gloominess** *n*

gloop /gloop/ *n* semiliquid sticky or messy material (*informal*) N Am term **goop** [Late 20C. An imitation of the sound semi-liquid material makes when poured or handled] —**gloopy** *adj*

glop /glop/ *n* (*informal*) **1.** *N Am* a soft lump or mixture of something, especially unappetizing food ○ *a glop of cold mashed potatoes* **2.** *US* something that is considered to be oversentimental or of little value, e.g. a piece of music or writing [Early 20C. An imitation of the sound semiliquid material makes when poured or handled] —**gloppy** *adj*

Gloria /gláwri ə/ *n* **1.** a hymn or set of words in Latin that begins with the word 'Gloria' and is used in the Christian liturgy to praise God **2.** the words of the Gloria set to music [15C. < Latin, 'glory']

Gloria in Excelsis /-ek sélsiss, -eks chélsiss/ *n* **1.** a hymn or set of words in Latin that begins with the words 'Gloria in Excelsis' and is used in the Christian liturgy to praise God **2.** the words of Gloria in Excelsis set to music [< Latin, 'glory in the high places']

Gloria Patri /-paátree/ *n* **1.** a short hymn or set of words in Latin that begins with the words 'Gloria Patri' and is used in the Christian liturgy to praise God **2.** the words of Gloria Patri set to music [< Latin, 'glory to the father']

glorified /gláwri fīd/ *adj* described in much more grandiose or fanciful terms than are warranted ○ *They call it an antique auction, but it's really just a glorified car-boot sale.*

glorify /gláwri fī/ (**-fies, -fying, -fied**) *vt* **1.** MAKE SOMETHING APPEAR SUPERIOR to cause something to seem more pleasant, important, or desirable than is actually the case **2.** EXTOL SOMEBODY OR SOMETHING to praise somebody or something highly **3.** RELIG PRAISE DEITY to worship or offer praise to a deity —**glorification** /gláwrifi káysh'n/ *n* —**glorifier** *n*

gloriole /gláwri ōl/ *n* a halo around somebody's head [Mid-19C. Via French < Latin *gloriola* 'little glory' < *gloria* 'glory']

gloriosa /glawri ṓssə/ (*plural* **-sas** or *same*) *n* a tropical climbing plant of the lily family, popular as a greenhouse plant. Flowers: large, yellow, orange, red. Genus: *Gloriosa.* [< modern Latin < Latin *gloriosus* (see GLORIOUS)]

glorious /gláwri əss/ *adj* **1.** EXCEPTIONALLY LOVELY beautiful in a way that inspires wonder or joy ○ *glorious summer weather* **2.** OUTSTANDING so good or distinguished as to merit praise and lasting fame ○ *a glorious career* **3.** ENJOYABLE highly enjoyable **4.** INEBRIATED uproariously drunk (*archaic informal*) [14C. Via Anglo-Norman, Old French < Latin *gloriosus* < *gloria* 'glory'] —**gloriously** *adv* —**gloriousness** *n*

Glorious Revolution *n* the overthrow of King James II in 1688 that established the power of Parliament over the monarch

Glorious Twelfth *n* the first day of the grouse-shooting season. Date: 12 August.

glory /gláwri/ *n* (*plural* **-ries**) **1.** EXALTATION the fame, admiration, and honour that is given to somebody who does something important **2.** ACHIEVEMENT something that brings or confers admiration, praise, honour, or fame **3.** PRAISE OF DEITY praise and thanksgiving offered as an act of worship to a deity ○ *Glory to God in the highest.* **4.** AWESOME SPLENDOUR majesty or splendour **5.** ASTOUNDING BEAUTY beauty that inspires feelings of wonder or joy ○ *the glory of a bright spring morning* **6.** HEAVEN the idealized beauty and bliss of heaven **7.** HALO a halo around somebody's head ■ *interj* EXPRESSING SURPRISE used to express great surprise, shock, dismay, or pleasure (*dated*) [13C. Via Anglo-Norman, Old French < Latin *gloria*] ◇ **glory be** used to express great surprise, shock, dismay, or pleasure (*dated*) ◇ **go to glory** to die (*dated*) ◇ **in your glory** in a state of great happiness, satisfaction, or triumph

glory in *vt* to derive great pride, pleasure, amusement, or satisfaction from something

glory-box *n ANZ* a collection of household goods that a woman collects to use when she is married (*dated*)

glory days *npl* the period of somebody's greatest achievement or happiness

glory-hole *n* **1.** a cupboard or small room used for storage, especially of rarely used objects, where they are often kept in a messy or disorganized way (*dated*) ○ *There's a box of old photographs somewhere in the glory-hole.* **2.** a storage space below deck near the stern of a ship [Origin ?]

glory-of-the-snow (*plural same* or **glory-of-the-snows**) *n* a widely-cultivated, small bulbous plant of the lily family. Flowers: blue, early-blooming. Native to: eastern Mediterranean, western Asia. Latin name: *Chionodoxa luciliae.*

Glos. *abbr* Gloucestershire

gloss[1] /gloss/ *n* **1.** SHININESS a shiny quality, especially on a smooth surface **2.** DECEPTIVE AND SUPERFICIAL ATTRACTIVENESS an attractive appearance that often conceals something unattractive or inferior **3.** CONSTR same as **gloss paint** **4.** MAKEUP a makeup or cosmetic designed to impart a shine ○ *lip gloss* ■ *vt* (**glosses, glossing, glossed**) **1.** MAKE SOMETHING SHINY to apply a coating or gloss to a surface to make it shine **2.** USE GLOSS PAINT ON SOMETHING to apply gloss paint to something [Mid-16C. Origin ?]

gloss over *vt* to intentionally leave out negative information, or treat something superficially, in order to make it appear more attractive or acceptable

gloss[2] /gloss/ *n* **1.** EXPLANATORY PHRASE a short definition, explanation, or translation of a word or phrase that may be unfamiliar to the reader, often located in a margin or collected in an appendix or glossary **2.** INTERPRETATION an interpretation or explanation of something ○ *Her account provides an interesting gloss on the theme of widowhood.* ■ *vt* (**glosses, glossing, glossed**) **1.** EXPLAIN SOMETHING to give a short definition, explanation, or translation of a word or phrase that may be unfamiliar to the reader **2.** INSERT EXPLANATIONS IN TEXT to add or enter the necessary glosses in a manuscript or piece of writing **3.** GIVE MISLEADING EXPLANATION OF SOMETHING to interpret or explain something in a deliberately misleading or negative way [Mid-16C. Via French < Latin *glossa* 'obscure word' < Greek *glōssa* 'tongue, language, obscure word']

glossa /glóssə/ (*plural* **-sae** /-see/ or **-sas**) *n* **1.** ANAT same as **tongue** (sense 1) (*technical*) **2.** a structure in the mouth of an insect that resembles a tongue [Late 19C. Via modern Latin < Greek *glōssa* 'tongue, language, obscure word'] —**glossal** *adj*

glossary /glóssəri/ (*plural* **-ries**) *n* an alphabetical collection of specialist terms and their meanings, usually in the form of an appendix to a book [14C. < Latin *glossarium* < *glossa* (see GLOSS [2])] —**glossarial** /glo sáiri əl/ *adj* —**glossarially** *adv* —**glossarist** *n*

glossectomy /glo séktəmi/ (*plural* **-mies**) *n* partial or total removal of the tongue by surgery [< Greek *glōssa* 'tongue']

glosseme /gló seem/ *n* the smallest meaningful unit of a language [Early 20C. < Greek *glōssema* 'word requiring explanation' < *glōssa* 'tongue, language, obscure word']

glossitis /glo sítiss/ *n* inflammation of the tongue [Early 19C. < Greek *glōssa* 'tongue'] —**glossitic** /glo síttik/ *adj*

glossolalia /glóssō láyli ə/ *n* **1.** RELIG same as **speaking in tongues** **2.** nonsensical or invented speech, especially resulting from a trance or schizophrenia [Late 19C. < Greek *glōssa* 'tongue, language, obscure word']

glossopharyngeal /glóssō farin jée əl/ *adj* relating to the tongue and pharynx [Early 19C. < Greek *glōssa* 'tongue']

glossopharyngeal nerve *n* either of the ninth pair of cranial nerves, which activate the muscles of the tongue, pharynx, and parotid gland

gloss paint *n* a paint that produces a smooth shiny durable surface

glossy /glóssi/ *adj* (**-ier, -iest**) **1.** SHINY AND SMOOTH having a smooth shiny surface or texture ○ *A glossy coat is the sign of a healthy animal.* **2.** SUPERFICIALLY STYLISH creating a superficial impression of wealth, beauty, or fashionable elegance (*informal*) ○ *a glossy lifestyle that conceals years of financial struggle* ■ *n* (*plural* **-ies**) **1.** PHOTO WITH SHINY FINISH a photograph printed on shiny smooth paper ○ *Please provide an 8 x 10 glossy.* **2.** same as **glossy magazine** (*informal*) —**glossily** *adv* —**glossiness** *n*

glossy magazine *n* a magazine containing high-quality colour photographs, especially a fashion magazine. N Am term **slick**

glost firing /glóst-/ *n* the final high-temperature firing of ceramic ware once it has been coated with glaze, during which the glaze is melted and fused onto the pot [Probably < alteration of GLOSS [1]]

glottal /glótt'l/ *adj* **1.** relating to the glottis **2.** describes a speech sound that is produced by wholly or partially closing the glottis

glottal stop *n* a consonantal speech sound created by closing and then opening the glottis before a vowel, which produces a sudden audible release of air. In languages such as Arabic, glottal stops are part of the standard consonant system.

glottis /glóttiss/ (*plural* **-tises** or **-tides** /-ti deez/) *n* **1.** the long opening between the vocal cords at the upper part of a vertebrate's windpipe (**larynx**). The glottis is open during breathing but is closed by the epiglottis during swallowing. **2.** all of the anatomy of the larynx that is involved in producing the voice in a human or vertebrate animal [Late 16C. Via modern Latin < Greek < *glōtta*, variant of *glōssa* 'tongue']

Gloucester /glóstər/ cathedral city on the River Severn in Gloucestershire, west-central England. Population: 109,885 (2001).

Gloucestershire /glóstərshər/ largely rural county in west-central England, on the border with Wales. Area: 2,642 sq. km/1,024 sq. mi.

glove /gluv/ *n* 1. SHAPED COVERING FOR HAND a shaped covering for the hand that includes five separated sections for the thumb and fingers, and extends to the wrist or the elbow 2. SPORTS PROTECTION FOR HAND a padded protective covering for the hand worn in some sports 3. CLOTHING same as **gauntlet**[1] ■ *vt* (**gloves, gloving, gloved**) PUT GLOVE ON SOMETHING to cover the hand with a glove, or cover an object with something that is like a glove ○ *Gloved and hatted, the children ventured out into the snow.* [Old English *glōf* < Germanic, 'hand'] —**gloveless** *adj* ◇ **the gloves are off** used to indicate that a course of action is about to be pursued in a ruthless and uncompromisingly aggressive way ○ *The gloves are off in the political debate.*

glove box *n* 1. AUTOMOT same as **glove compartment** 2. a sealed container that allows radioactive or toxic substances to be handled safely using a pair of gloves attached to openings in its sides

glove compartment *n* a small enclosed storage space in the dashboard of a vehicle

glove puppet *n UK, ANZ, Can* a puppet that fits over the hand like a glove and is operated by the user's thumb and fingers. US term **hand puppet**

Glover /glúvər/, **Denis James Matthews** (1912–80) New Zealand writer. He is the author of prose and poetry including *Enter Without Knowing* (1964).

glow /glō/ *n* 1. LIGHT FROM SOMETHING HOT a light produced by something that has been heated to a high temperature but is not in flame ○ *the glow of the embers in the grate* 2. SOFT STEADY LIGHT a soft steady light, especially one without heat or flames ○ *the glow of the neon lights* 3. SOFT REFLECTED LIGHT a soft warm reflected light ○ *the golden glow of the tapestries on the far wall* 4. ROSINESS OF COMPLEXION a brightness or redness in somebody's complexion, e.g. because of exercise or good health ○ *the healthy glow that exercise gives you* 5. REDNESS OF EMBARRASSMENT a redness of the face or complexion, especially one caused by embarrassment ○ *face suffused with a glow of shame* 6. HAPPY FEELING a sense of happiness or wellbeing ○ *a warm glow of satisfaction* ■ *vi* (**glows, glowing, glowed**) 1. EMIT LIGHT AND HEAT to emit light as a result of being extremely hot ○ *The embers of the fire still glowed in the grate.* 2. EMIT SOFT STEADY LIGHT to emit a soft steady light without heat or flames ○ *the neon signs glowing red and blue* 3. REFLECT LIGHT SOFTLY to emit a soft warm reflected light ○ *the walls glowing orange and gold in the afternoon sun* 4. SHINE WITH HEALTH to show the bright eyes and smooth skin that are a sign of good health 5. BE FLUSHED WITH EMBARRASSMENT to have blood rush to the face, especially because of embarrassment 6. FEEL WARM AND CONTENTED to feel a pleasant warm sensation owing to happiness, satisfaction, or love ○ *The winners glowed with pride.* [Old English *glōwan* < Germanic]

glower /glów ər/ *vi* (**-ers, -ering, -ered**) to look at somebody or something with sullen anger or strong resentment ■ *n* a sullen or resentful stare [15C. Origin ?] —**glowering** *adj* —**gloweringly** *adv*

glowing /glō ing/ *adj* 1. SHINING SOFTLY AND STEADILY emitting a soft steady light 2. REDDISH-GOLD rich, strong, or bright in colour, especially when reddish or gold ○ *the glowing colours of autumn* 3. FULL OF PRAISE praising somebody or something in very warm appreciative terms ○ *glowing reports of the performance* 4. ROSY red or rosy as a result of excitement, wellbeing, or good health —**glowingly** *adv*

glow plug *n* a plug fitted to a diesel engine that makes it easier to start in cold weather by warming it up

glow stick /glō stik/ *n* LEISURE, SAFETY same as **lightstick**

glowworm /glō wurm/ *n* a larva of some types of firefly, or a beetle of a closely related family, that emits greenish light from organs in its abdomen. Families: Lampyridae or Phengodidae.

gloxinia /glok sínni ə/ *n* a popular house plant with large colourful bell-shaped flowers. Native to: tropical America. Genus: *Sinningia*. [Early 19C. After Benjamin *Gloxin*, 18C German botanist]

gloze /glōz/ (**glozes, glozing, glozed**) *vt* to attempt to underplay or minimize something unpleasant or embarrassing ○ *tried to gloze over the scandalous story* [13C. < French *gloser* < *glose* 'comment, gloss' < Latin *glossa* (see GLOSS[2])]

gluc- *prefix* same as **gluco-** (*used before vowels*)

glucagon /glóoka gon/ *n* a pancreatic hormone that raises blood sugar by promoting conversion of glycogen to glucose in the liver [Early 20C. < GLUCO- + Greek *agōn*, present participle of *agein* 'lead']

gluco- *prefix* glucose ○ *glucocorticoid* [< GLUCOSE]

glucocorticoid /glóokō cáwrti koyd/ *n* a steroid hormone (**corticoid**) that influences carbohydrate metabolism. Use: treatment of inflammatory conditions.

gluconeogenesis /glóokō nee ə jénnəssiss/ *n* the production of glucose, especially in the liver, from amino acids, fats, and other substances that are not carbohydrates —**gluconeogenetic** /-jə néttik/ *adj*

glucosamine /gloo kóssəmin/ *n* 1. an amino derivative of glucose that occurs naturally in supportive tissues and plant cell walls 2. ALTERN MED, BIOCHEM same as **glucosamine sulphate** [Late 19C. < GLUCOSE]

glucosamine sulphate *n* a substance derived from the chitin of shellfish. Use: as a food supplement, as a treatment for arthritis and other joint disorders.

glucose

glucose /glóo kōz, -kōss/ *n* 1. a six-carbon monosaccharide produced in plants by photosynthesis and in animals by the metabolism of carbohydrates. The commonest form, dextrose, is used by all living organisms. Formula: $C_6H_{12}O_6$. 2. a syrup containing dextrose, maltose, dextrin, and water that is obtained from starch. Use: food manufacture, alcoholic fermentation. [Mid-19C. Via French < Greek *gleukos* 'sweet wine']

glucosidase /gloo kóssi dayz/ *n* an enzyme that splits glucose off glucosides

glucoside /glóokō sīd/ *n* a glycoside that yields glucose on hydrolysis —**glucosidal** *adj* —**glucosidic** /glóokō síddik/ *adj* —**glucosidically** *adv*

glucosuria /glóo kō soóri ə/ *n* MED same as **glycosuria** —**glucosuric** *adj*

glucuronic acid /glóo kyoo ronik-/ *n* an acid derived from glucose that is present in cartilage and detoxifies poisons [Early 20C. < GLUCO- + Greek *ouron* 'urine']

glue /gloo/ *n* 1. ANIMAL-BASED ADHESIVE an adhesive substance obtained by boiling animal parts such as bones, hides, horns, and hooves 2. ADHESIVE a natural or synthetic substance used as an adhesive 3. SOMETHING THAT UNITES PEOPLE a unifying factor or influence ○ *Mutual love and understanding is the glue that holds this family together.* ■ *vt* (**glues, gluing, glued**) 1. STICK THINGS TOGETHER to stick things together or reconstitute something using an adhesive substance ○ *It took hours to glue the vase back together.* 2. KEEP SOMEBODY STILL to cause somebody to remain still, or cause somebody to give all his or her attention (*informal; usually passive*) ○ *eyes glued to the TV* [13C. Via French *glu* < Latin *gluten*] —**glue-like** *adj* —**gluey** *adj* —**gluily** *adv* —**gluiness** *n*

glue ear *n* a condition affecting young children that results from poor drainage of the middle ear. It is a common cause of impaired hearing during early years, sometimes leading to educational disadvantage if untreated.

glue-sniffing *n* the practice of inhaling the fumes from glues and volatile solvents in order to become intoxicated —**glue-sniffer** *n*

glug /glug/ *n* 1. a gurgling sound of a quantity of liquid being poured from a bottle or similar vessel 2. a quantity of liquid, especially of an alcoholic drink, drunk or poured from a bottle or similar vessel ○ *Here, have a glug of champagne.* [Late 17C. An imitation of the sound] —**glug** *vti* —**gluggable** *adj*

gluhwein /glóo vīn/ *n* warmed red wine flavoured with spices and added sugar [Late 19C. < German *Glühwein* < *glühen* 'to glow' + *Wein* 'wine']

glum /glum/ (**glummer, glummest**) *adj* quietly melancholic or miserable [Mid-16C. < variant of GLOOM 'feel or look despondent'] —**glumly** *adv* —**glumness** *n*

glume /gloom/ *n* either of a pair of dry leaves at the base of the spikelet in an ear of a grass or cereal plant [Late 18C. < Latin *gluma* 'husk'] —**glumaceous** /gloo máyshəss/ *adj*

gluon /glóo on/ *n* a theoretical elementary particle without mass, thought to be involved in binding the subatomic particles (**quarks**) together [Late 20C. < GLUE]

glut /glut/ *n* EXCESS SUPPLY a larger supply of something than is needed, especially of a crop or product ○ *There is usually a glut of fresh vegetables in August.* ■ *vt* (**gluts, glutting, glutted**) 1. SUPPLY MARKET WITH TOO MUCH to supply a market with an excess of something, especially a product, leading to a fall in price ○ *Cheaper products from abroad glutted the market, lowering profits.* 2. GIVE SOMEBODY ENOUGH OR TOO MUCH to feed or supply somebody with enough or more than enough of something [14C. Probably via Old French *gloutir* 'swallow' < Latin *gluttire* (see GLUTTON)]

glutaeus *n* ANAT another spelling of **gluteus**

glutamate /glóotə mayt/ *n* a salt or ester of glutamic acid, especially its sodium salt (**monosodium glutamate**)

glutamic acid

glutamic acid /gloo támmik-/ *n* an amino acid found in plant and animal proteins that triggers nerve impulses in cells. Formula: $C_5H_9NO_4$. [< GLUTEN + AMINE]

glutamine

glutamine /glóotə meen/ *n* an amino acid found in proteins and synthesized by humans and animals. Formula: $C_5H_{10}N_2O_3$. [Late 19C. Blend of *glutamic* (see GLUTAMIC ACID) + AMINE]

glutaminic acid /glóotə mínnik-/ *n* BIOCHEM same as **glutamic acid**

glutaraldehyde /glóotə ráldi hīd/ *n* an oily water-soluble liquid. Use: disinfectant, tanning agent, biological fixative. Formula: $C_5H_8O_2$. See illustration on next page [Mid-19C. < *glutaric* < GLUTEN]

glutathione /glóotə thíon/ *n* a peptide consisting of glutamic acid, cysteine, and glycine that is an im-

glutaraldehyde

portant antioxidant [Early 20C. < *glutamic* (see GLUTAMIC ACID)]

glutei ANAT plural of **gluteus**

gluten /glóot'n/ *n* a mixture of two proteins found in some cereal grains, especially wheat. People who have coeliac disease are allergic to gluten. [Late 16C. Via French < Latin, 'glue']

glutes /gloots/ *npl* the gluteus muscles (*informal*) [< GLUTEUS]

gluteus /glóoti əss/ (*plural* **-tei** /-ti ī/), **glutaeus** (*plural* **-taei** /-ti ī/) *n* a large muscle in the buttocks in a group of three that move the thigh in humans, especially the gluteus maximus [Late 17C. Via Modern Latin < Greek *gloutos* 'buttock'] —**gluteal** *adj*

gluteus maximus /-máksiməss/ (*plural* **glutei maximi** /-mī/) *n* the outermost of the three large gluteus muscles that form each buttock in humans [< modern Latin, 'largest gluteus']

glutinous /glóotinəss/ *adj* having a sticky consistency ○ *glutinous rice*

glutton /glútt'n/ *n* **1.** somebody who habitually eats or drinks too much **2.** ZOOL same as **wolverine** [13C. Via Old French < Latin *glutton-* < *gluttire* 'to swallow' < *gula* 'throat'] —**gluttonous** *adj* —**gluttonously** *adv* ◇ **a glutton for punishment** somebody who appears to need or enjoy difficulty, discomfort, or stress

gluttony /glútt'ni/ *n* the act or practice of eating and drinking to excess. Gluttony is one of the seven deadly sins in Christian tradition.

glyburide /glī byoór īd/ *n* N Am PHARM same as **glibenclamide**

glyc- *prefix* same as **glyco-** (*used before vowels*)

glyceride /glíssə rīd/ *n* an ester formed by the combination of glycerol with an acid. Source: animal and vegetable fats and oils. [Mid-19C. < GLYCERIN]

glycerin

glycerin /glíssərin/, **glycerine** *n* a thick, sweet, odourless, colourless, or pale yellow liquid. Source: fats and oils as a by-product of soap manufacture. Use: solvent, antifreeze, plasticizer, manufacture of soaps, cosmetics, lubricants, and dynamite. Formula: $C_3H_8O_3$. [Mid-19C. < French < Greek *glukeros*, alteration of *glukus* 'sweet']

glycerol /glíssə rol/ *n* CHEM same as **glycerin** (*technical*) [Late 19C. < GLYCERIN]

glyceryl /glíssəril/ *n* a chemical group derived from glycerol by removing or replacing hydroxide, especially a trivalent group CH_2CHCH_2 [Mid-19C. < GLYCERIN]

glyceryl trinitrate *n* CHEM same as **nitroglycerine**

glycine

glycine /glī'ss een/ *n* an amino acid found in most proteins that inhibits the transmission of nerve impulses in cells. Formula: $C_2H_5NO_2$. [Mid-19C. < Greek *glukus* 'sweet']

glycitein /glíssitin/ *n* an isoflavone derivative found in soya products that is a possible natural cancer preventative

glyco- *prefix* **1.** sugar ○ *glycosuria* **2.** glycogen ○ *glycolysis* [< Greek *glukus* 'sweet' < Indo-European]

glycogen /glíkəjən/ *n* a polysaccharide found in the liver and muscles that is easily converted to glucose for energy —**glycogenic** /glīkō jénnik/ *adj*

glycogenesis /glīkō jénnəsiss/ *n* the formation of glycogen from glucose —**glycogenetic** /-jə néttik/ *adj*

glycogenolysis /glī kōjə nóllississ/ *n* the breakdown of glycogen to glucose —**glycogenolytic** /-jénnə líttik/ *adj*

glycol /glī kol/ *n* CHEM **1.** same as **ethylene glycol 2.** same as **diol** [Mid-19C. < GLYCERIN] —**glycolic** /glī kóllik/ *adj*

glycolic acid *n* a compound found in unripe fruit. Use: tanning, pesticides, pharmaceuticals, adhesives, plasticizers.

glycolipid /glī kō líppid/ *n* a sugar-containing lipid present in cell membranes

glycolysis /glī kólləssiss/ *n* the breakdown of glucose to pyruvate, with the release of usable energy. This metabolic process takes place in nearly all living cells. —**glycolytic** /glíkō líttik/ *adj*

glycopeptide /glīkō pép tīd/ *n* a peptide that contains carbohydrate

glycopeptide intermediate Staphylococcus aureus /-áwri əss/ *n* MED, MICROBIOL full form of **GISA**

glycoprotein /glī kō prṓ teen/ *n* a protein that contains carbohydrate

glycoside /glíkō sīd/ *n* a compound belonging to a group that reacts with water to form a sugar and a nonsugar. Some glycosides are used medicinally. [Mid-20C. < *glycose*, variant of GLUCOSE] —**glycosidic** /glīko síddik/ *adj*

glycosuria /glíkōs syoóri ə/ *n* the presence of sugar in the urine, usually a sign of diabetes [Mid-19C. < *glycose*, variant of GLUCOSE] —**glycosuric** *adj*

glycosylation /glíkō sī láysh'n/ *n* the addition of a saccharide unit to a protein [Mid-20C. < *glycose*, variant of GLUCOSE]

Glyndebourne /glīnd bawrn/ site of an annual international opera festival held in the village of Glynde in East Sussex, southern England

glyph /glif/ *n* **1.** ARCHIT CARVED GROOVE IN ANCIENT GREEK ARCHITECTURE an ornamental carved channel or groove, especially a vertical one like those on a Doric frieze **2.** ANCIENT HIST CARVED SYMBOL OR CHARACTER a symbol or character, especially one that has been incised or carved out in a stone surface like the characters of the ancient Maya writing system **3.** COMPUT CHARACTER IN FONT the symbol or symbols that form a single character in a font [Late 18C. Via French *glyphe* < Greek *gluphē* 'carving' < *gluphein* 'carve'] —**glyphic** *adj*

glyphosate /glífə sayt/ *n* a herbicide that is taken into the system of a plant, affecting its growth. Use: control of perennial grasses and many weeds, especially in arable fields.

glyptic /glíptik/ *adj* relating to the art of engraving or carving, especially on precious stones [Early 19C.

Directly or via French *glyptique* < Greek *gluptikos* < *gluptēs* 'carver' < *gluphein* 'carve']

glyptography /glip tóggrəfi/, **glyptics** /glíptiks/ *n* the art or process of engraving or carving on precious stones —**glyptograph** /glíptə graaf, -graf/ *n* —**glyptographer** *n* —**glyptographic** /glíptō gráffik/ *adj* —**glyptographical** *adj*

gm[1] *abbr* gram[1]

gm[2] *abbr* Gambia (*used in Internet addresses*) See table at **domain name**

GM *abbr* **1.** BUSINESS general manager **2.** GENETICS genetic modification **3.** GENETICS genetically modified **4.** George Medal **5.** CHESS grand master **6.** EDUC grant-maintained **7.** ARMS guided missile

G-man *n* US an agent of the US Federal Bureau of Investigation (*dated slang*) [< abbreviation of GOVERNMENT]

GMO *abbr* GENETICS genetically modified organism

GMS *abbr* EDUC grant-maintained status

GMT *abbr* Greenwich Mean Time

GMTA *abbr* great minds think alike (*used in e-mails or text messages*)

GMW *abbr* CHEM gram-molecular weight

gn *abbr* Guinea (*used in Internet addresses*) See table at **domain name**

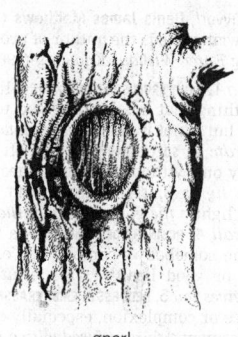

gnarl

gnarl /naarl/ *n* a hard lump, knot, or swelling on a tree trunk or branch [Early 19C. Back-formation < GNARLED]

gnarled /naarld/ *adj* **1.** twisted and full of knots ○ *an ancient gnarled tree* **2.** twisted, misshapen, or weather-beaten because of age, hard work, or illness ○ *gnarled hands* [Early 17C. Alteration of *knurled*]

gnarly /naʼarli/ (**-ier, -iest**) *adj* extremely difficult, risky, and challenging (*slang*) ○ *gnarly surf off Santa Monica beach* [< GNARL, perhaps from the way rough water appeared to surfers]

gnash /nash/ (**gnashes, gnashing, gnashed**) *vt* to grind your teeth together, especially in pain, anger, or frustration [15C. Origin ?]

gnashers /náshərz/ *npl* natural or artificial teeth (*informal*)

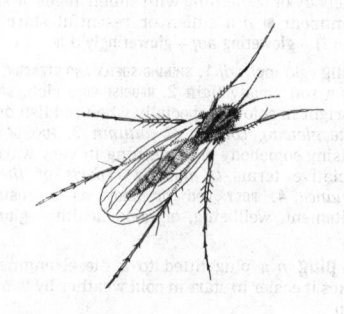

gnat

gnat /nat/ *n* a small two-winged biting fly, e.g. a black fly or a midge [Old English *gnætt* < Indo-European]

gnatcatcher /nát kachər/ *n* a small songbird with a long tail and slender beak that feeds on insects. Native to: North America. Genus: *Polioptila*.

gnathic /náthik/, **gnathal** /náth'l/ *adj* relating to the jaw [Late 19C. < Greek *gnathos* 'jaw']

gnathion /náythi on/ *n* the lowest point on the midline of the lower jaw [Late 19C. < Greek *gnathos* 'jaw']

gnathostome /náythə stōm/ *n* a vertebrate that has a mouth with jaws, as do all vertebrates except agnathans. Lampreys and hagfish are gnathostomes. Superclass: Gnathostomata. [Early 20C. < Greek *gnathos* 'jaw' + *stoma* 'mouth']

-gnathous *suffix* having a particular kind of jaw ○ *prognathous* [< Greek *gnathos* 'jaw' < Indo-European]

gnaw /naw/ (**gnaws, gnawing, gnawed, gnawed** or **gnawn** *archaic* /nawn/) *v* **1.** *vti* CHEW AT SOMETHING to chew or bite on something persistently, often reducing it gradually to a particular state ○ *a terrier gnawing away at a huge bone* **2.** *vt* MAKE SOMETHING BY CHEWING to make something by grinding with the teeth and chewing ○ *The hamster escaped by gnawing a hole in its cage.* **3.** *vi* CAUSE WORRY to cause somebody constant anxiety or distress ○ *That question still gnaws at me after all these years.* **4.** *vi* GRADUALLY REDUCE to reduce the effectiveness or influence of something bit by bit ○ *a profound sense of unease that gnaws away at our sense of wellbeing* **5.** *vt* ERODE SOMETHING to wear something away often until it reaches a particular shape or size ○ *The wind and waves had gnawed the rocks into fantastic shapes.* [Old English *gnagen* < Germanic] —**gnaw** *n* —**gnawable** *adj* —**gnawer** *n*

gnawing /náwing/ *adj* persistent and troubling or uncomfortable ○ *gnawing doubts* —**gnawingly** *adv*

gnawn past participle of **gnaw** (*archaic*)

gneiss /nīss/ *n* a coarse-grained high-grade metamorphic rock formed at high pressures and temperatures, in which light and dark mineral constituents are segregated into visible bands [Mid-18C. < German] —**gneissic** *adj* —**gneissose** *adj*

gnocchi /nóki/ *npl* in Italian cookery, dumplings made of potato, semolina, or flour, usually boiled and served with soup or a sauce [Late 19C. < Italian]

gnome[1] /nōm/ *n* **1.** in folklore and fairy tales, a small imaginary being usually portrayed as a hunchbacked man with a long white beard who lives underground guarding treasure **2.** same as **garden gnome 3.** an offensive term that deliberately insults somebody's relatively small size and appearance [Mid-17C. Via French < modern Latin *gnomus*] —**gnomelike** *adj* ◇ **the gnomes of Zurich** international bankers and financiers, especially those based in Switzerland (*dated humorous*)

gnome[2] /nōm/ *n* a short saying or proverb that expresses a general idea or principle [Late 16C. < Greek *gnōmē* 'opinion, judgment' < *gignōskein* 'know']

gnomic /nṓmik/ *adj* **1.** resembling or containing proverbs or other short pithy sayings that express basic truths ○ *His gnomic utterances were widely quoted by journalists.* **2.** opaque or difficult to understand [Early 19C. Directly or via French < Greek *gnōmikos* < *gnōmē* (see GNOME [2])] —**gnomically** *adv*

gnomon /nṓ mon/ *n* **1.** the arm of a sundial, used to show the time of day by the position of its shadow **2.** the part of a parallelogram that is left when a smaller similar parallelogram has been taken from its corner [Mid-16C. Directly or via French or Latin < Greek *gnōmōn* 'indicator' < *gignōskein* 'know'] —**gnomonic** /nō mónnik/ *adj* —**gnomonically** *adv*

gnosis /nṓssiss/ *n* knowledge of spiritual truths reputedly possessed by the ancient Gnostics, who believed them to be essential to salvation [Late 16C. < Greek *gnōsis* 'investigation, knowledge' < *gignōskein* 'know']

gnostic /nóstik/ *adj* relating to knowledge, especially knowledge of spiritual truths [Mid-17C. See GNOSTIC]

Gnostic /nóstik/ *n* somebody who believes in Gnosticism [Late 16C. Via ecclesiastical Latin < Greek *gnōstikos* < *gignōskein* 'know'] —**Gnostic** *adj*

Gnosticism /nóstissizəm/ *n* a pre-Christian and early Christian religious movement teaching that salvation comes by learning esoteric spiritual truths that free humanity from the material world, believed in this movement to be evil

gnotobiotics /nṓ tō bī óttiks/ *n* the scientific study of organisms living either in a germ-free or a controlled environment, as when a known contaminant has been introduced (*takes a singular verb*) [Mid-20C. < Greek *gnōtos* 'known'] —**gnotobiotic** *adj* —**gnotobiotically** *adv*

GNP *abbr* ECON gross national product

gnu

gnu /noo/ (*plural same* or **gnus**) *n* a large antelope with a head resembling that of an ox, a short mane, a beard, downward curving horns, and a tufted tail. Native to: Africa. Latin name: *Connochaetes gnou* or *Connochaetes taurinus*. [Late 18C. Probably via Dutch *gnoe* < Khoisan]

GNVQ *n* in the United Kingdom, a qualification designed to provide vocationally orientated skills and knowledge for progression from school to employment or university. They are available at three levels, foundation, intermediate, and advanced. Full form **General National Vocational Qualification**

go[1] /gō/ (**goes, going, went** /went/, **gone** /gon/, *plural* **gos**) CORE MEANING: a basic intransitive verb of motion expressing movement from an unspecified point of departure or from a place that is already known or assumed ○ *Have you any idea where he went?* ○ *She never went anywhere without her spectacles.* ○ *Johnny went back inside for another coffee.* ○ *I've always wanted to go to Paris.*

1. *vi* DEPART to leave a place ○ *Please don't go.* ○ *He's going tomorrow.* **2.** *vi* MOVE TO ACT to move towards a person or place with the intention of doing something specific ○ *We had to go and pick up our young son who was playing at a friend's house.* ○ *After the wedding they went to live in Spain.* **3.** *vi* PROCEED TO ACTIVITY to leave a place and proceed towards an activity, often a recreational activity ○ *They go for a jog every morning.* **4.** *vi* ATTEND to attend a place regularly ○ *She went to evening classes to get more qualifications.* **5.** *vi* TAKE PART to take part in a television or radio programme ○ *The President went on television to defend his government's decision.* **6.** *vi* LEAD to lead to, or begin or end at, a particular place (*refers to a route or travel service*) ○ *Take the road that goes into the city centre.* ○ *The new bus service will go from Edinburgh to London.* **7.** *vi* ELAPSE to elapse or pass (*refers to time*) ○ *The year went pleasantly.* **8.** *vi* BE ALLOTTED to be allotted to a particular recipient or used for a particular purpose (*refers to money or other resources*) ○ *The house will go to his surviving children.* ○ *Much of her income went on household bills.* **9.** *vi* BE GIVEN to be given to somebody as a quality or attribute ○ *The credit should go to the one who tries hardest.* **10.** *vi* BE DISCARDED to be eliminated, given up, or got rid of ○ *This old sweater has just got to go!* ○ *Thousands of jobs will have to go.* **11.** *vi* BE SPENT to be spent or used up ○ *By the end of the evening all the food had gone.* **12.** *vi* LEAVE JOB to leave a job or organization ○ *He was costing the company thousands and had to go.* **13.** *vi* BLEND IN to blend, harmonize, or be appropriate with something else ○ *They wanted to find a carpet that would go with the existing decor.* ○ *Those trousers just don't go.* **14.** *vi* FIT IN to fit in a place because of being the right shape or size ○ *I tried to push the package through the letter box but it wouldn't go.* **15.** *vi* BELONG to have somewhere as a usual or proper place ○ *The towels go in the cupboard in the bathroom.* **16.** *vi* BE PUT to be put into something as one of the parts that form it ○ *all the elements that go to make a successful musical* **17.** *vi* FUNCTION to function or operate ○ *Can you get my car going again?* ○ *Without capital to make it go, our business plan was merely hopes written out on paper.* **18.** *vi* FAIL to get weaker and begin to fail or give way ○ *My eyesight is starting to go.* **19.** *vi* BREAK DOWN to stop working properly and start to break down ○ *I think the battery may be going.* **20.** *vi* same as **die**[1] (sense 1) (*euphemistic*) ○ *I'm afraid she has gone.* **21.** *vi* BECOME to change so as to come to be in a particular state or condition ○ *Their pet's behaviour went out of control.* **22.** *vi* BE DRESSED OR EQUIPPED to be in a particular state with regard to dress or equipment ○ *They went barefoot on the beach.* **23.** *vi* PROCEED to proceed or happen in a particular way ○ *How did it go at work today?* ○ *We were trying to figure out what really went wrong.* ○ *The intruder went unchallenged.* **24.** *vi* MAKE NOISE AS SIGNAL to make a noise such as a ring or a knock to attract attention ○ *She had just closed the front door when the phone went.* **25.** *vi* MAKE NOISE to make a particular noise ○ *The horn went beep.* ○ *Cows go 'moo'.* **26.** *vi* REACH POINT to proceed to or reach a particular position or level ○ *'The freedom she experienced, the indulgence with which she was treated, went beyond her expectations.'* (Thomas Hardy, *The Mayor of Casterbridge*; 1886) **27.** *vi* SERVE to be of such a nature or quality as to do something ○ *It just goes to show how careful you have to be.* **28.** *vi* COMPARE to compare with other people or things of the same kind ○ *As holidays abroad go, it was probably the best we've ever had.* **29.** *vi* SOUND to proceed in terms of sound or words (*refers to a piece of music or writing*) ○ *How does that tune go again?* **30.** *vi* ACCOMPANY EACH OTHER to occur with or be present at the same time as something else ○ *It's not necessarily the case that intelligence and common sense go together.* **31.** *vi* CIRCULATE to circulate as information around a place or among people ○ *It soon went round the whole village that she had inherited a fortune.* **32.** *vi* HAVE RECOURSE to turn to a procedure as a result of unresolved problems ○ *They couldn't agree, so they went to arbitration.* **33.** *vi* BE AUTHORITY to be necessarily accepted as what will be the case in a given situation ○ *Whatever she says goes in our home.* **34.** *vi* ENDURE to continue surviving or succeeding in a difficult situation ○ *Human beings can go for much longer without food than without water.* **35.** *vt* BET SOMETHING IN CARDS to bet or bid a particular set of cards in a card game ○ *I go three clubs.* **36.** *vt* SAY SOMETHING to say something quoted (*nonstandard*) ○ *So she goes, 'If you want it done then do it yourself'.* **37.** *vi Carib* WILL will do something ○ *I go see you tomorrow.* **38.** *vi* EXPRESSING FUTURE ACTION used to express future action or intent (*used in progressive tenses*) ○ *What are we going to do?* **39.** *n* ATTEMPT MADE an attempt or chance to do something ○ *She passed the exam on the second go.* **40.** *n* TURN TAKEN a move or turn in a game ○ *It's your go.* **41.** *n* ENERGY energy and vibrancy (*informal*) ○ *I've had so much more go since changing my diet.* **42.** *adj* FUNCTIONING ready and operating properly (*informal*) ○ *All systems are go.* [Old English *gān* < Indo-European] ◇ **anything goes** used to indicate that anything is to be tolerated or accepted as the norm ○ *In this place almost anything goes!* ◇ **at one go** all at the same time ◇ **don't even go there** used to indicate that a topic is considered too unpleasant to be mentioned or explored (*informal*) ◇ **have a go (at something)** to make an attempt at something (*informal*) ○ *He said that he had never skied before but he was willing to have a go at it.* ◇ **have a go at somebody** to attack somebody verbally (*informal*) ◇ **here we go!** used as a chant by football supporters either when their team is winning or to encourage their team to win ◇ **here we go (again)!** used to express displeasure or resignation that something, usually something bad, that has happened before is now happening again ○ *Here we go again! This old car simply won't start.* ◇ **it is all go** used to indicate that there is a lot of activity and hard work happening (*informal*) ○ *It's all go around here!* ◇ **make a go of something** to make a success of something ○ *They couldn't make a go of the relationship.* ◇ **on the go** very active and busy ○ *a two-career couple, always on the go* ◇ **there you go** *N Am* used to express general encouragement or approval to somebody else (*informal*) ◇ **there you go again** used to complain that somebody has done something bad or wrong yet again ○ *There you go again, misinterpreting and twisting what I'm saying.* ◇ **to go** to be taken home rather than consumed on the premises ○ *one pizza to go*

go about *v* **1.** *vt* TACKLE SOMETHING to deal with a problem, assignment, or task **2.** *vt* CONSTANTLY BEHAVE IN PARTICULAR WAY to spend a lot of time behaving in a particular way ○ *She's been going about causing trouble in the office.* **3.** *vti* same as **go around** (senses 1–3) **4.** *vi* CHANGE TACK to change tack in a sailing boat

go after *vt* **1.** to make a deliberate effort to get or find something seen as desirable or advantageous ○ *I decided to go after a teaching job I saw in the*

paper. **2.** to try to catch somebody who is running away

go ahead *vi* **1.** to start or continue with something, especially after a period of uncertainty or delay ○ *Let's go ahead and start our meal without her.* **2.** used to indicate that somebody is welcome to do something (*informal*) ○ *'Would you mind if I used your phone?''Sure, go ahead'.*

go along *vi* **1.** to accompany somebody on a journey ○ *I went along just to keep her company.* **2.** to develop or progress in a particular manner, especially favourably (*informal*) ○ *Things were going along reasonably well until she lost her job again.*

go along with *vt* to accept something or obey somebody, especially reluctantly or to the surprise of others ○ *You can't go along with it – it's breaking the law.*

go around *v* **1.** *vi* KEEP COMPANY to spend a lot of time with a particular person or as a member of a particular group ○ *We went around together all the time.* **2.** *vi* TRAVEL FROM PLACE TO PLACE to travel from one place to another ○ *We tend to go around by taxi.* **3.** *vti* BE WIDELY KNOWN OR CURRENT to be experienced or known by a lot of people, often in a particular place **4.** *vti* BE ENOUGH FOR EVERYONE to be able to be distributed to everyone ○ *There aren't enough pens to go around, so you'll have to share.* ◇ **what goes around comes around** used to say that whatever happens now will have an effect in the future (*informal*)

go at *vt* to attempt something enthusiastically or energetically ○ *He went at the snow shovelling as if it were a race.*

go away *vi* **1.** to leave the place where you live, especially in order to take a holiday (*informal*) ○ *Are you going away this summer?* **2.** used to tell somebody to leave because he or she is annoying you ○ *Go away! I'm busy.*

go back *vi* **1.** ORIGINATE FROM TIME to originate from a particular date, period, or time ○ *a tradition that goes back hundreds of years to the time of Henry VIII* **2.** BE RESET HOUR EARLIER to be required to be reset an hour earlier, to Greenwich Mean Time from British Summer Time ○ *when the clocks go back an hour* **3.** RETURN TO WORK to return to work after being absent, e.g. because of holidays, illness, or industrial action (*informal*) **4.** *Malaysia* GO HOME to return to your home

go back on *vt* to have a change of mind about something previously agreed or promised ○ *You can't go back on your word – a deal's a deal.*

go by *v* **1.** *vi* PASS IN TIME to move onwards in terms of time ○ *As the years go by, he gets more and more mellow.* **2.** *vt* REGARD SOMETHING AS TRUE to treat advice or information as reliable or true **3.** *vt* USE PARTICULAR SOURCE OF INFORMATION to use a particular way of doing something or finding something out ○ *All we had to go by was a soggy map.*

go down *vi* **1.** SINK to sink beneath the surface of a body of water ○ *An oil tanker went down off the coast of Alaska.* **2.** CRASH to fall from the air and crash ○ *The plane went down somewhere in the mountains.* **3.** GO BELOW HORIZON to sink below the horizon ○ *The sun had already gone down by the time we got back.* **4.** BE RECEIVED to be received in a particular way ○ *an idea that didn't go down at all well with shareholders* **5.** BECOME ILL to become ill with a particular illness (*informal*) ○ *went down with flu* **6.** COMPUT MALFUNCTION to break down or stop working ○ *Since the airline's computers have gone down, we can't get flight information yet.* **7.** BE REMEMBERED to be remembered in a particular way ○ *She will surely go down as one of the greatest athletes of all time.* **8.** BE DEFEATED to be defeated in a vote or competition (*informal*) ○ *Manchester United went down 2–3 to Barnsley in the third round.* **9.** TAKE PLACE to happen or be happening (*slang*) ○ *Hey, what's going down?* ○ *When the robbery went down, the cops rushed to the scene.* **10.** SUFFER DISGRACE to be disgraced or ruined (*informal*) ○ *If he goes down, he'll take the whole department with him.* **11.** BE EATABLE OR DRINKABLE to be able to be eaten or drunk, especially easily or enjoyably (*informal*) ○ *With sick children, soup tends to go down more easily than solid foods.* **12.** BE RELEGATED in sports, to be relegated or demoted ○ *The local team only just managed to avoid going down this season.* **13.** BE SENT TO PRISON to be sent to prison, especially for a particular period or crime (*informal*) ○ *went down for burglary* **14.** EDUC LEAVE UNIVERSITY AT END OF TERM to leave college or university at the end of term or the end of the academic year **15.** CARDS FAIL TO ACHIEVE BRIDGE TRICKS in the game of bridge, to

fail to attain the number of tricks that has been contracted for

go down on *vt* a highly offensive term meaning to perform oral sex on somebody (*taboo*)

go for *vt* **1.** TRY TO OBTAIN SOMETHING YOU WANT to make an effort to obtain something because it is suitable for you or important to you (*informal*) ○ *I really think you should go for that sales job.* **2.** LIKE SOMEBODY OR SOMETHING LOT to prefer, like, or be interested in something or somebody (*informal*) ○ *I don't really go for science fiction.* **3.** CHOOSE SOMETHING to choose one thing rather than another (*informal*) ○ *I think I'll go for the chocolate cheesecake – how about you?* **4.** ATTACK SOMEBODY to attack somebody physically or verbally **5.** COMMAND PRICE to be worth or sold for a particular amount ○ *In the end the house went for far less than its market value.* **6.** BE RELEVANT TO SOMEBODY to apply or be relevant to somebody ○ *She needs to be more careful in her work – and that goes for you, too!* ◇ **go for it** not to stop or relax until you aggressively reach your goal (*slang; often used as a command*) ○ *The coach told the team to get out there and go for it.* ◇ **have something going for you** to be in a situation where something is useful or helpful to you to a particular extent (*informal*) ○ *She has a lot going for her in the tennis championship, given her season's record.*

go forward *vi* to be required to be reset an hour later, to British Summer Time from Greenwich Mean Time ○ *The clocks go forward tonight.*

go in *vi* **1.** BE OBSCURED to become hidden by clouds ○ *Once the sun went in, it got really cold.* **2.** BEGIN ATTACK to launch an attack, or begin another manoeuvre ○ *After the police went in, things rapidly got out of hand.* **3.** BE LEARNT to be learnt, remembered, or understood (*informal*) ○ *However many times I read it nothing seems to go in.* **4.** BEGIN INNINGS in cricket, to begin an innings (*refers to a player or a team*)

go in for *vt* **1.** ENTER COMPETITION to enter a competition or sporting event **2.** ENJOY DOING SOMETHING to enjoy a particular activity ○ *I don't really go in for team sports myself.* **3.** CHOOSE CAREER to choose a particular area of study or career ○ *decided to go in for the priesthood*

go into *vt* **1.** BEGIN CAREER to begin a job or career in a particular area of activity ○ *She went into advertising and made pots of money.* **2.** LOOK INTO SOMETHING to examine or look into something in detail and with thoroughness **3.** BE FACTOR OF NUMBER to be a factor of a number or amount ○ *15 won't go into 125.* **4.** CONTRIBUTE TOWARDS SOMETHING to contribute towards something, or be one of the parts that form something ○ *all the elements that go into making a successful musical* **5.** BE SPENT ON SOMETHING to be used or spent for a purpose ○ *Millions have gone into finding a cure.*

go in with *vt* to begin participating in a scheme or venture with other people ○ *I went in with four friends to start a restaurant.*

go off *v* **1.** *vi* BECOME BAD to become bad, stale, or rancid ○ *Milk goes off very quickly in this weather.* **2.** *vi* DETONATE to explode or be fired **3.** *vi* BEGIN SOUNDING to start to ring, sound, or vibrate ○ *The smoke alarm goes off whenever we make toast.* **4.** *vi* BE CARRIED OUT to be carried out or conducted in a particular manner ○ *I think the conference went off as well as could be expected.* **5.** *vi* DEPART to set out in a particular manner or for a particular place or purpose ○ *We decided to go off early.* ○ *endless TV images of soldiers going off to war* **6.** *vti* LEAVE PITCH OR STAGE to leave a sports pitch, stage, or other place ○ *The band went off early but came back to play three encores.* **7.** *vi* START BEHAVING IN PARTICULAR WAY to change behaviour and start behaving in a particular way ○ *When I suggested a few changes he went off into hysterics.* **8.** *vt* STOP LIKING SOMEBODY OR SOMETHING to stop liking somebody or something previously liked ○ *I soon went off him once he started telling jokes.* ○ *went off the idea once he found out how much it cost* **9.** *vi Aus* GO WELL to go exceptionally well (*slang*) **10.** *vi Aus* GET ANGRY to become very annoyed with somebody (*informal*)

go off at *vt Aus* to rebuke or upbraid somebody (*informal*) ○ *I knew he wouldn't be happy with my performance, but I didn't expect him to go off at me like that.*

go off with *vt* to begin a relationship with somebody, especially abandoning a spouse or partner in order to do this

go on *v* **1.** *vi* CARRY ON to continue in progress ○ *The dispute went on for another nine months before it*

was resolved. **2.** *vi* ELAPSE to elapse or move forwards, bringing change (*refers to time*) ○ *As time went on, I thought about it less.* **3.** *vi* OCCUR to happen or take place ○ *I asked him what was going on.* **4.** *vti* MAKE PUBLIC ENTRANCE to make an entrance onto a sports pitch, stage, or other public place ○ *She went on every night to rapturous applause.* ○ *The team went on the pitch feeling that they'd already won.* **5.** *vi* TALK TOO MUCH to talk too much and much too long ○ *She's always going on about her yacht.* **6.** *vi* CONTINUE SPEAKING to continue speaking, especially after a pause ○ *She then went on about the latest international incident.* **7.** *vi* DO SOMETHING AFTERWARDS to do something after the time or period you are referring to ○ *She finished fourth, but went on to win the championship the following year.* **8.** *vt* USE AS RELIABLE INFORMATION to use something as reliable information ○ *The police have very little to go on at this stage.* **9.** *vt* ENJOY SOMETHING to like or enjoy something (*informal*) ○ *I don't go much on his new haircut.* **10.** *vi* EXPRESSING ENCOURAGEMENT used to encourage somebody to do something, usually something the person is reluctant to do (*informal*) ○ *Go on, you'll have a great time!* ○ *Go on, lend me a fiver -just till the weekend.* **11.** *vi* EXPRESSING DISBELIEF used to expressing disbelief (*informal*) ○ *Oh, go on! I simply don't believe she could have done such a thing!* **12.** *vt* APPROXIMATE SOMETHING to be close to a particular age, time, or number (*used in progressive tenses*) ○ *He must be going on 50.*

go on at *vt* to criticize or nag another person persistently or at length (*informal*) ○ *He's always going on at me about how scruffy I look.*

go out *vi* **1.** SOCIALIZE to socialize and enjoy yourself away from home ○ *She loves going out, but he prefers to stay at home.* **2.** FLOW OUTWARDS FROM SHORE to flow away from the shoreline ○ *The tide had gone out.* **3.** BECOME UNFASHIONABLE to stop being fashionable ○ *Muttonchops went out in the late 1800s.* **4.** FINISH GAME to end your part in a game or competition by doing something you need to do ○ *You need to throw a six to go out.* **5.** BE FORCED OUT OF GAME to be forced to quit a game or competition ○ *The two lowest scoring teams in each round go out.* **6.** DATE SOMEBODY to go on a date with somebody ○ *They've been going out for six months.* **7.** BE BROADCAST to be broadcast on TV or the radio ○ *The programme went out last night.* **8.** BE EXTINGUISHED to stop burning or functioning ○ *The fire has gone out.*

go out to *vt* **1.** to be beaten by another team or contestant in a knock-out competition ○ *Liverpool went out to Newcastle in the semifinal.* **2.** to be offered or extended to a person or group ○ *Our thoughts go out tonight to the friends and relatives of the victims.*

go over *v* **1.** *vi* CHANGE TO NEW SYSTEM to change to a different system or way of doing things ○ *We went over from oil to gas when we got the central heating replaced.* **2.** *vi* CHANGE ALLEGIANCE to change allegiance and start supporting somebody or something else ○ *In a surprise move, the MP went over to Labour.* **3.** *vt* EXAMINE SOMETHING CAREFULLY to examine or check something carefully ○ *The police went over the car looking for fingerprints.* **4.** *vt* REHEARSE AND MEMORIZE SOMETHING to practise or repeat something in order to learn it ○ *The actors were all busy going over their lines.*

go round *v* **1.** *vti* same as **go around** **2.** *vi* to go and visit another person ○ *Let's go round and see Dave.*

go stern *vi Malaysia, Singapore* to move backwards in a vehicle (*informal*) ○ *You'll need to go stern a few more metres.*

go through *v* **1.** *vt* EXAMINE SOMETHING THOROUGHLY to examine or inspect something very carefully ○ *The police went through his luggage but found nothing suspicious.* **2.** *vi* GAIN OFFICIAL APPROVAL to be accepted or approved officially, after having gone through channels or set procedural stages **3.** *vt* UNDERGO UNPLEASANTNESS to undergo hardship or difficulties, usually in stages and over a period of time ○ *They're going through a series of business setbacks.* **4.** *vt* CONSUME SOMETHING IN QUANTITY to use, eat, or spend something, especially a large amount in a short time ○ *They go through hundreds of pounds of groceries a week.* **5.** *vi Aus* LEAVE to leave or depart (*informal*)

go through with *vt* to carry on with something until it has been completed or resolved, especially when this requires determination ○ *I'm determined to go through with this court case, come what may.*

go under *vi* **1.** SINK IN WATER to sink below the surface of the water ○ *I managed to grab him as he went*

under for the third time. **2.** FAIL to close down or fail **3.** LOSE CONSCIOUSNESS to lose consciousness, especially after being given an anaesthetic ○ *They began the operation as soon as she'd gone under.*

go up *vi* **1.** BE BUILT to be constructed ○ *A new super-market went up where the cinema used to be.* **2.** BE DISPLAYED to be put on display ○ *A notice has gone up saying how we can be contacted.* **3.** DETONATE OR IGNITE to explode or burst into flames ○ *The whole place went up in a matter of seconds.* **4.** GO TO UNIVERSITY to go to or return to a college or university at the beginning of a term or academic year

go with *vt* **1.** BE PART OF SOMETHING to be a normal or usual part of something ○ *The long hours go with the job.* **2.** ADOPT OR FOLLOW AN IDEA to adopt or follow a particular approach or point of view ○ *Just go with the plan as it stands for the time being and we'll see what happens.* **3.** DATE SOMEBODY to spend time romantically and socially with somebody (*informal*) ○ *Anna's been going with Alex for a month now.* **4.** HAVE SEX WITH SOMEBODY to have sexual intercourse with somebody (*informal*)

go without *vt* to be deprived of something such as money or food ○ *You'll have to go without breakfast if you want to catch the early train.* ○ *Children from rich families had new clothes, while poor children had to go without.*

go² /gō/ *n* a Japanese board game played with black and white stones on a surface marked with 19 lines intersecting each other to create 367 crossing points. The object of the game is to capture the larger part of the board and the opponent's stones. [Late 19C. < Japanese]

goa /gṓ ə/ *n* a gazelle with a brownish-grey coat, the male of which has backward curving horns. Native to: Tibet. Latin name: *Procapra picticaudata.* [Mid-19C. < Tibetan *dgoba*]

Goa /gṓ ə/ state on the western coast of India. Formerly a Portuguese territory, it was incorporated into India in 1961 and became a separate Indian state in 1987. Capital: Panaji. Population: 1,343,998 (2001). Area: 3,702 sq. km/1,429 sq. mi.

goad /gōd/ *vt* (**goads, goading, goaded**) **1.** CAUSE SOMEBODY TO ACT to provoke or incite somebody into action (*often passive*) **2.** PROD ANIMAL WITH STICK to prod an animal with a long pointed stick ■ *n* **1.** POINTED ANIMAL PROD a long pointed stick used for prodding cattle and other animals **2.** STIMULUS something that encourages an activity or process to begin, increase, or develop [Old English *gād* < Germanic]

SYNONYMS See *motive*.

go-ahead *n* permission or approval to proceed with something (*informal*) ○ *Once we get the go-ahead from the bank, we can get things moving.* ■ *adj* imaginative and ambitious ○ *a young go-ahead company at the forefront of information technology*

goal /gōl/ *n* **1.** TARGET AREA in a game such as football or hockey, the space or opening into which a ball or puck must go to score points, usually a pair of posts with a crossbar and often a net ○ *The kick landed just to the left of the goal.* **2.** SCORE the score gained by getting the ball or puck into the goal ○ *leading by three goals to two* **3.** SUCCESSFUL SHOT a successful attempt at hitting, kicking, or throwing a ball or hitting a puck into a goal ○ *one of the greatest goals of all time* **4.** AIM something that somebody wants to achieve ○ *One of my goals for this year is to learn Spanish.* **5.** RACE'S END the end of a race ○ *The runners are still several minutes from the goal.* **6.** FOOTBALL KICK SCORING POINTS in Australian Rules football, six points, scored by kicking the ball between the two goal posts [14C. Origin ?]

goal area *n* in football, the rectangular area marked out in front of the goal within which goalkeepers may handle the ball

goal difference *n* in football and other sports, the difference between the number of goals scored for and against a team in a specific competition. It is often used as a decider between teams with equal points.

goal-directed *adj* strongly motivated and highly organized in achieving tasks that are specified in advance

goalie /gṓli/ *n* same as **goalkeeper** (*informal*)

goalkeeper /gṓl keepər/ *n* in games such as football and hockey, a defensive player positioned in or near a goal whose main task is to keep the ball or puck from crossing the goal line into the goal

goal kick *n* **1.** in football, a free kick taken from the six-yard-line by a defensive player when the ball has been driven out of play over the end line (**goal line**) by an opposing player **2.** in rugby, a free kick by a member of the attacking team, aimed at clearing the defenders' crossbar and designed to convert a five-point try into a seven-point score

goalless /gṓl ləss/ *adj* **1.** without any goals being scored ○ *A goalless semifinal left everyone feeling cheated.* **2.** having no goals to aim for in life or work

goal line *n* in games such as football rugby, and hockey, the line where goalposts are positioned and over which the ball must pass or be carried to make a score. A try or touchdown can be scored anywhere along the line, but to score in soccer and hockey circumstances the ball also has to pass between the posts.

goalmouth /gṓl mowth/ (*plural* **-mouths** /-mowthz/) *n* in games such as football and hockey, the area directly in front of the goal

goal-oriented *adj* same as **goal-directed**

goalpost /gṓl pōst/ *n* in games such as football and hockey, either of two posts, usually supporting a crossbar between them, that together mark the boundary of the goal ◇ **move the goalposts** to change the rules or conditions after a project has started or a course of action has been embarked on ○ *We'll never finish the software if Marketing keeps moving the goalposts.*

goalscorer /gṓl skawrər/ *n* a player who scores or has just scored a goal

goal sneak *n* Aus in Australian Rules football, a player who plays near the opponent's goal and is adept at exploiting goal-scoring opportunities (*informal*)

goal square *n* in Australian Rules football, a square marked on the playing field, made up of the goal line, two lines projecting 9 m/29.25 ft out from the goal posts, and a fourth line that joins these two lines

goaltender /gṓl tendər/ *n* N Am SPORTS same as **goalkeeper**

goaltending /gṓl tending/ *n* **1.** in basketball, illegal interference with a ball that is in its downward arc towards the basket or that is in or on the rim of the basket **2.** N Am the act of trying to keep a puck or ball from entering a goal, especially in ice hockey

goal umpire *n* in Australian Rules football, either of two umpires positioned behind the goal posts who signal whether a goal or a behind has been scored by raising two or one flags, respectively

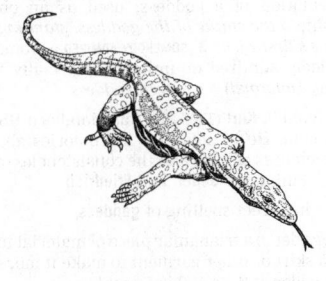

goanna

goanna /gō ánnə/ *n* a large monitor lizard of which there are several varieties. Native to: Australia. Genus: *Varanus.* [Mid-19C. Alteration of IGUANA]

goat /gōt/ *n* **1.** (*plural* **goats** or *same*) an agile animal that is related to sheep and has backward curving horns, straight hair, and a short tail. Goats are ruminants. Kept for: wool, meat, milk. Genus: *Capra.* **2.** a man who is regarded as lecherous (*insult*) **3.** same as **scapegoat** *n* (sense 1) [Old English *gāt* < Indo-European] —**goatish** *adj* ◇ **act** or **play the (giddy) goat** to behave in a silly way, often intentionally ◇ **get somebody's goat** to annoy or irritate somebody (*informal*) ○ *Their constant carping over trivia really gets my goat.*

Goat *n* ZODIAC same as **Capricorn** (sense 1)

goat antelope (*plural* **goat antelopes** or *same*) *n* a mammal related to goats that also has features characteristic of antelopes. Chamois, goral, and mountain goat are goat antelopes. Subfamily: Caprinae.

goat cheese *n* cheese made from goat's milk

Popperfoto

goatee: actor Tom Hanks wearing a goatee

goatee /gō tee/ *n* a short pointed beard on the chin but not the cheeks [< its resemblance to a goat's beard]

goatfish /gṓt fish/ (*plural same* or **-fishes**) *n* US same as **red mullet** [< barbels beneath its mouth]

goatherd /gṓt hurd/ *n* somebody who tends and herds goats

goat moth *n* a large pale-grey European moth with wood-boring larvae that give off an odour like that of goats. Latin name: *Cossus cossus.*

goatsbeard /gṓts beerd/ *n* **1.** a plant with woolly stems. Flowers: large, yellow, resembling the dandelion. Native to: Europe, Asia, now also growing in the United States. Latin name: *Tragopogon pratensis.* **2.** a tall perennial plant. Flowers: small, white, in long spikes. Native to: eastern North America. Latin name: *Aruncus dioicus.* [< the down on the seeds]

goat's cheese *n* FOOD same as **goat cheese**

goatskin /gṓt skin/ *n* **1.** LEATHER leather made from the skin of a goat **2.** LEATHER WINE FLASK a wine container made from the skin of a goat **3.** SKIN OF GOAT the skin or hide of a goat

goat's milk *n* milk from a goat, used for drinking and for making cheese

goat's rue *n* a leguminous plant used for feeding livestock. Flowers: white, purple, or pink. Native to: Europe, Asia. Latin name: *Galega officinalis.*

goatsucker /gṓt sukər/ *n* BIRDS same as **nightjar** [< a belief that it sucked milk from goats]

goat-water *n* Carib a lightly thickened stew made with goat meat and vegetables, often served at weddings and parties

go-away bird *n* S Africa a greyish-coloured touraco. Native to: Africa. Genus: *Corythaixoides.* [From its harsh cry which sounds like 'go away']

gob¹ /gob/ (*slang*) *n* a lump of a soft or wet substance ○ *a huge gob of whipped cream* ■ *vi* (**gobs, gobbing, gobbed**) to spit or eject phlegm from the throat [14C. < Old French *gobe* 'mouthful' < *gober* 'swallow']

gob² /gob/ *n* the human mouth (*slang disapproving*) [Mid-16C. Origin ?]

gob³ /gob/ *n* waste material from mining, e.g. clay or shale [Mid-19C. Origin ?]

gobbet /góbbit/ *n* **1.** QUANTITY OF LIQUID a quantity of liquid, often in a sticky blotch ○ *Gobbets of grease covered the top of the stove.* **2.** EXCERPT an extract from a text, especially one chosen for translation or comment in an examination **3.** HUNK OF FOOD a piece or chunk of something, especially raw meat (*archaic*) [13C. < Old French *gobet* 'small mouthful' < *gobe* (see GOB¹)]

gobble¹ /góbb'l/ (**-bles, -bling, -bled**) *vt* **1.** to eat something quickly and greedily ○ *He gobbled up all the pizza.* **2.** to use something up quickly or in large amounts (*informal humorous*) ○ *watching the payphone gobble her money* [Early 17C. Probably < GOB¹]

gobble² /góbb'l/ *vi* (**-bles, -bling, -bled**) to make the characteristic gurgling sound of a male turkey or a

sound resembling this ■ n, interj the gurgling sound made by a male turkey [Late 17C. An imitation of the sound]

gobbledegook /góbb'ldigook/, **gobbledygook** n language that is difficult or impossible to understand, especially nonsense or technical jargon (informal) ○ This manual is full of gobbledegook. [Mid-20C. An imitation of a turkey's gobble]

gobbler /góbblər/ n a male turkey (informal)

Gobelin /góbəlin/ n a tapestry produced by the Gobelin factory in Paris, characterized by vivid pictorial scenes

go-between n somebody who communicates or mediates between people during a negotiation, transaction, or secret operation

gobi /góbi/ n in Indian cooking, cauliflower or cabbage [< Punjabi]

Gobi Desert /góbi-/ desert in northern China and southern Mongolia, the coldest and one of the largest deserts in the world. Area: 1,300,000 sq. km/500,000 sq. mi.

goblet /góbblət/ n 1. a drinking vessel with a stem and base, especially one of metal or glass 2. a large bowl-shaped cup used formerly for drinking (archaic) [14C. < Old French gobelet 'small cup' < gobel 'cup']

goblet cell n a cell shaped like a goblet that secretes mucus. Goblet cells are found in the intestines and respiratory system of mammals and the epidermis of fish.

goblin /góbblin/ n an imaginary being resembling a small man of unpleasant appearance, usually evil or mischievous [14C. Probably via Anglo-Norman < medieval Latin gobelinus, a supposed spirit]

gobo[1] /góbō/ (plural **gobos** or **goboes**) n 1. a shield that is placed around a microphone to keep out unwanted sounds 2. a black screen placed around the lens of a camera or video camera to keep out unwanted light [Mid-20C. Origin ?]

gobo[2] /góbō/ n in Japanese and Hawaiian cuisine, the slender root of the burdock, having a sweet, earthy flavor. It is cooked thinly sliced or shredded and added to soup and stews. [< Japanese]

gobshite /gób shīt/ n UK regional, Ireland an offensive term for a person who is regarded as contemptible, especially for being unintelligent or incompetent (insult) [Mid-20C. < GOB[2] + variant of SHIT]

gobsmacked /gób smakt/ adj extremely surprised or shocked (slang) [< GOB[2]]

gobstopper /gób stopər/ n UK, ANZ, Can a large hard sweet that changes colour as it is sucked. US term **jawbreaker** [Early 20C. < GOB[2]]

gobstruck /gób struk/ adj same as **gobsmacked** (slang) [< GOB[2]]

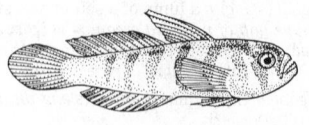

goby

goby /góbi/ (plural **-bies**) n a small long-bodied spiny-finned freshwater or sea fish whose pelvic fins form a sucker. Gobies are usually found in burrows or crevices. Family: Gobiidae. [Mid-18C. Via Latin gobius < Greek kōbios, a small fish]

go-by n a slight or snub (slang) ○ She tried to speak but he gave her the go-by.

go-cart, **go-kart** n 1. a light open-framed car large enough for a child or young teenager to sit in, containing a small engine and used for racing 2. MOTOR SPORTS same as **kart** [Late 17C. < GO[1] 'walk'; originally a device for helping a baby to walk]

god /god/ n 1. SUPERNATURAL BEING one of a group of supernatural male beings in some religions, each of which is worshipped as the personification or controller of some aspect of the universe ○ Thor, the Norse god of thunder 2. FIGURE OR IMAGE a representation of a god, used as an object of worship ○ the little bronze god standing in a niche above the altar 3. SOMETHING THAT DOMINATES something that is so important that it takes over somebody's life (informal) ○ worshipping the false god of fame 4. SOMEBODY ADMIRED a man who is widely admired or imitated (informal) ○ He was one of the rock music gods of the early Seventies. ■ **gods** npl 1. FATE the entire group of supernatural beings viewed as deciding human fate 2. THEATRE GALLERY the highest tier of seats in a theatre (informal) [Old English, < Indo-European, 'that which is invoked'] —**godlessly** adv —**godlessness** n

God n the being believed in monotheistic religions such as Judaism, Islam, and Christianity to be the all-powerful all-knowing creator of the universe, worshipped as the only god ■ interj used to express or emphasize feelings such as anger, helplessness, and frustration (sometimes considered offensive)

Godard /góddaar/, **Jean-Luc** (b. 1930) French film director. A director of the French new wave, he became influential in the 1960s with films such as Breathless (1960) and Weekend (1967).

> 'I like a film to have a beginning, a middle, and an end, but not necessarily in that order.'
> [Attributed to Jean-Luc Godard, Time; 14 September 1981]

Godavari /gō dáavəri/ river in central India that is sacred to Hindus. It rises in the Western Ghats and empties into the Bay of Bengal. Length: 1,400 km/900 mi.

god-awful, **God-awful** adj extremely bad or unpleasant (slang; sometimes considered offensive)

godchild /gód chīld/ (plural **-children** /-children/) n somebody whose spiritual upbringing is made the responsibility of one or more godparents. This arrangement is usually declared at the person's baptism or christening.

goddamn /góddam/ adj, adv also **goddam** or **goddamned** /góddamd/ N Am used to emphasize a word or idea, or to express anger, frustration, or some other strong emotion (slang; sometimes considered offensive)

goddaughter /gód dawtər/ n a girl or woman who is somebody's godchild

goddess /góddess/ n 1. SUPERNATURAL BEING one of the group of supernatural female beings in some religions, worshipped as the personification or controller of some aspect of the universe ○ Athena, the Greek goddess of wisdom 2. FIGURE OR IMAGE a representation of a goddess, used as an object of worship ○ the statue of the goddess, standing in the temple's first niche 3. SOMEBODY ADMIRED a woman who is widely admired or imitated, especially for her beauty (informal) ○ a screen goddess

Gödel /gúrd'l/, **Kurt** (1906–78) Austrian-born US mathematician. He is noted for his theories about the completeness of logic and the consistency of arithmetic. Full name **Gödel, Kurt Friedrich**

~~godess~~ incorrect spelling of **goddess**

godet /gō dét/ n a triangular piece of material inserted into a skirt or other garment to make it more flared or to widen it [Late 19C. < French]

godfather /gód faathər/ n 1. a man who is somebody's godparent 2. a man who heads a criminal organization, especially a Mafia leader (informal)

CULTURAL NOTE *The Godfather*, a film (1972) by US director Francis Ford Coppola. Based on the novel (1969) by Mario Puzo, it describes the attempts of the Sicilian Corleone family to maintain their control of the New York Mafia when a group of renegade families set up a drug-smuggling ring. Together with its two sequels, *The Godfather Part II* (1974) and *The Godfather Part III* (1990), it brought new meaning to terms such as 'godfather' and 'consigliere'.

God-fearing /-feering/ adj devout or deeply religious

godforsaken /gódfər sayk'n/ adj depressing, deserted,

or empty ○ The soldiers couldn't wait to get out of that godforsaken desert.

God-given adj existing or applying as part of the natural order of the universe rather than arranged by humanity ○ God-given abilities

godhead /gód hed/ n the nature or essence of being divine

Godhead n the Christian God, especially when considered as the Holy Trinity

godhood /gód hood/ n RELIG same as **godhead**

Godiva /gə dívə/, **Lady** (1040?–80?) English noblewoman. According to legend, she obtained a remission of heavy local taxes levied by her husband, Leofric, Earl of Chester, by riding naked through the marketplace in Coventry on a horse.

godless /gódləss/ adj 1. not believing in or worshipping God or any god (disapproving) 2. having an evil or immoral nature (formal) —**godlessly** adv —**godlessness** n

godlike /gód līk/ adj fit for God or a god, or having the qualities of God or a god, e.g. superhuman power, beauty, or imagination

godly /góddli/ (**-lier**, **-liest**) adj 1. devoted to or worshipping God (formal) 2. fit for or having the divine qualities of God or a god —**godliness** n

godmother /gód muthər/ n a woman who is somebody's godparent

godown /gó down/ n a warehouse, especially in South and Southeast Asia [Late 16C. Via Portuguese gudao < Tamil kitanku, Kannada gadangu 'store']

godparent /gód pairənt/ n a sponsor of a baptized child who promises to take a personal interest in him or her. Godparents often maintain close, almost familial relationships with a godchild.

godroon n HANDICRAFT another spelling of **gadroon**

God's Acre n a churchyard or cemetery (archaic) [< German Gottesacker]

God's country n a nation or piece of land that is dearly loved

godsend /gód send/ n 1. something good that happens unexpectedly 2. something received that proves extremely useful, or somebody who arrives and gives much-needed help [Early 19C. < God's send < SEND[1] 'thing sent']

God's gift n an extremely admirable, valued, or talented person (often used ironically) ○ He thought he was God's gift to the film industry.

god sim n a computer simulation game in which a player is managing a large imaginary territory such as a world or an ecosystem but does not represent a person

God slot n a scheduled time for religious programmes on radio or television (sometimes considered offensive)

godson /gód sun/ n a man or boy who is somebody's godchild

God's own /gód zōn/, **Godzone** n ANZ a country or area warmly regarded by its inhabitants as specially favoured, especially Australia or New Zealand (informal; often used ironically) [Shortening of God's own country]

God's own country n any country or piece of land seen as chosen and specially favoured

Godspeed /gód speed/ interj used to wish somebody a safe journey or successful endeavour (dated) [15C. < God speed you 'may God speed you']

God squad n 1. a Christian religious group, especially one that enthusiastically recruits new members (informal humorous or disapproving; sometimes considered offensive) 2. a medical ethics committee advising on life and death questions (slang)

Godthåb /gód hawb/ former name for **Nuuk**

Godunov /góddoo nof/, **Boris Fyodorovich** (1551?–1605) tsar of Russia (1598–1605). During his rule as regent to Tsar Fyodor I Ivanovich (1584–98) and as tsar, he strengthened the monarchy and the church, imposed a system of serfdom, and was the first Russian ruler to banish political exiles to Serbia.

Godwin Austen, Mount /góddwin óstin/ ♦ K2

godwit /gód wit/ n a large wading bird that has a long, slightly upturned beak and long legs and is related

to curlews and sandpipers. Native to: found worldwide. Genus: *Limosa*. [Mid-16C. Origin ?]

Godzone *n ANZ* same as **God's own** (*informal; often used ironically*)

Goebbels /góbl'z/, **Joseph** (1897–1945) German Nazi politician. He was Adolf Hitler's minister of propaganda (1933–45). Full name **Goebbels, Paul Joseph**

> 'Should the German people lay down arms, the Soviets…would occupy all eastern and south-eastern Europe together with the greater part of the Reich. Over all this territory, which with the Soviet Union included, would be of enormous extent, an iron curtain would at once descend.'
> [Joseph Goebbels, *Das Reich (The Reich)*; 23 February 1945]

goer /gó ər/ *n* **1.** REGULAR ATTENDER somebody who regularly attends something (*usually used in combination*) ○ *festival-goers* **2.** FAST MOVER a spirited or fast-moving person or animal (*informal*) **3.** PROMISCUOUS PERSON somebody regarded as promiscuous or sexually uninhibited (*slang; sometimes considered offensive*)

Goering /gúring, gö́ring/, **Göring, Hermann** (1893–1946) German Nazi leader. Adolf Hitler's second in command, he organized and commanded Nazi Germany's air force, directed its economy, and planned much of Germany's military strategy in World War II. Convicted of war crimes and sentenced to death at the Nuremberg trials (1946), he committed suicide before execution. Full name **Goering, Hermann Wilhelm**

Johann Wolfgang von Goethe: Portrait (1826) by Heinrich Christoph Kolbe

Goethe /gö́tə/, **Johann Wolfgang von** (1749–1832) German writer and scientist. A seminal figure of European literature, he was a prolific writer of poems, novels, plays, criticism, and letters. His masterwork is the dramatic poem *Faust* (published in two parts 1808, 1832). He was also author of the novel *The Sorrows of Young Werther* (1774).

> 'Besides, civilization, which now licks / Us all so smooth, has taught even the Devil tricks; / The northern fiend's becoming a lost cause— / Where are his horns these days, his tail, his claws?'
> [Johann Wolfgang von Goethe, *Faust*; 1808]

> 'Talent develops in quiet places, character in the full current of human life.'
> [Johann Wolfgang von Goethe, *Torquato Tasso*; 1790]

goethite /gó thīt/ *n* an earthy rust-coloured hydrated iron oxide mineral formed by the alteration of iron minerals [Early 19C. After GOETHE]

go-faster *adj* intended to make a motor vehicle look or sound sporty or fast (*informal*) ○ *a car with go-faster stripes*

gofer /gó́fər/ *n* somebody who runs errands or performs other menial tasks (*informal; sometimes offensive*) [Mid-20C. < reduced pronunciation of *go for*]

goffer /gó́ffər/, **gauffer** *vt* (*-fers, -fering, -fered*) **1.** CRIMP HAIR to make hair wavy or crimped using a heated iron or similar device **2.** PRESS FRILLS INTO FABRIC to press pleats into fabric to produce an ornamental frill using a heated iron or similar implement ■ *n* GOFFERING TOOL a tool used for goffering frills [Late 16C. < French *gaufrer* 'mark with a decorative tool' < *gaufre* 'honeycomb' < Middle Low German *wafel*]

Gog and Magog /góg ənd máy gog/ *npl* **1.** in parts of the Bible, the names given to the enemies of God's people. In the book of Ezekiel, Gog is named as the ruler of a land named Magog, while Revelations names Gog and Magog as nations that were under Satan's rule. **2.** in medieval times, legendary enemies of Alexander the Great said to live north of the Caucasus Mountains and used as emblems of ugliness

go-getter /gó gettər/ *n* an enterprising and forceful person (*informal*) —**go-getting** *adj, n*

gogga /khókhə/ *n S Africa* an insect or other small crawling or flying animal (*informal*) [Via Afrikaans < Khoikhoi *xo-xon* 'organisms that slither or creep']

goggle /gógg'l/ *v* (*-gles, -gling, -gled*) **1.** *vi* STARE WIDE-EYED to stare with eyes wide open, usually in astonishment **2.** *vti* ROLL EYES to roll the eyes about, or roll about in the eye socket ■ *adj* BULGING bulging from the eye socket ○ *goggle eyes* ■ *n* WIDE-EYED STARE a staring or leering look at somebody with eyes wide open [14C. Probably < a verb imitative of moving backwards and forwards] —**goggly** *adj*

goggle-box *n* a television set (*dated informal*)

goggle-eyed *adj* with staring eyes

goggles /gógg'lz/ *npl* protective glasses, usually made of plastic or glass and fitting tight to the face

Gogh ♦ **van Gogh, Vincent**

go-go *adj US* ENERGETIC characterized by energy and forcefulness ■ *n* STYLE OF MUSIC a style of US popular music from the 1980s, an amalgamation of disco, funk, and Latin sounds ■ *adj US* **1.** FIN SPECULATIVE bringing or expected to bring quick or high returns on any investment ○ *These go-go stocks carry risk and are not for the timid investor.* **2.** DISCO relating to or seen in discotheques or music clubs (*dated*) [Doubling of GO ¹, probably after French *à gogo* 'galore']

go-go dancer *n* an energetic, usually scantily dressed dancer, who entertains in a nightclub or pub (*dated*)

Gogol /gó́ gol, -gəl/, **Nikolay Vasilyevich** (1809–52) Russian writer. One of the greatest exponents of Russian literary realism, he is best known for his satirical play *The Government Inspector* (1836) and the novel *Dead Souls* (1842).

Goh Chok Tong /gó chok tóng/ (*b.* 1941) prime minister of Singapore (1990–). A member of the People's Action Party, he was elected to parliament in 1976 and held several ministerial portfolios before becoming deputy prime minister in 1985.

Goiânia /goy aʾani ə/ capital city of Goiás State in south-central Brazil. Population: 1,004,098 (1996).

Goidel /góyd'l/ *n* a Celt who speaks a Goidelic language [Late 19C. < Old Irish (see GAEL)]

Goidelic /goy déllik/ *n* the northern branch of the Celtic family of languages, comprising Irish Gaelic, Scottish Gaelic, and Manx. Native speakers: 300,000. —**Goidelic** *adj*

going /gó ing/ *n* **1.** ACT OF LEAVING an act of leaving somewhere **2.** CONDITIONS FOR PROGRESS conditions for making progress ○ *The going gets tough when you reach the rocky terrain.* **3.** CONDITIONS UNDER FOOT the state of the ground as it affects ease and speed of movement, especially for horses in a race ○ *The going is good on the track.* ■ *adj* **1.** SUCCESSFUL currently operating successfully ○ *a going business* **2.** ACCEPTED AS STANDARD currently accepted as standard or valid ○ *the going rate for platinum* **3.** EXISTING currently in existence or available ○ *the best thing going*

going-over (*plural* **goings-over**) *n* (*informal*) **1.** THOROUGH EXAMINATION a thorough examination or check ○ *They gave the results a thorough going-over before making their report.* **2.** ACT OF OVERHAULING an action by which something is thoroughly improved or restored to a previous condition, e.g. an act of cleaning, polishing, or dusting something ○ *The house got a complete going-over before the arrival of the in-laws.* **3.** SCOLDING OR BEATING a verbal scolding or physical beating

goings-on /gó ingz-/ *npl* events or activities, especially of a noteworthy or suspicious nature (*informal*)

goiter *n MED US* spelling of **goitre**

goitre /góytər/ *n* enlargement of the thyroid gland

appearing as a swelling of the front of the neck. Iodine deficiency is one of several causes. [Early 17C. Via French < Latin *guttur* 'throat'] —**goitrous** *adj*

go-kart *n* another spelling of **go-cart** (sense 1)

Golan Heights /gó lan-/ disputed upland region on the border between Israel and Syria, northeast of the Sea of Galilee. Administered by Syria until 1967, it was first occupied and then, in 1981, annexed by Israel. Area: 1,250 sq. km/483 sq. mi.

gold /gōld/ *n* **1.** YELLOW METALLIC ELEMENT a soft, heavy, corrosion-resistant, yellow metallic element that is highly valued, found in underground veins and alluvial deposits. Use: jewellery, alloys. Symbol **Au**. See table at **element 2.** RICH YELLOW HUE a deep rich yellow colour that resembles that of the metal gold **3.** THINGS MADE OF GOLD things made of gold, e.g. coins or pieces of jewellery **4.** WEALTH much money or wealth **5.** same as **gold medal** (*informal*) **6.** ARCHERY BULL'S EYE the bull's eye of a target, which is usually gilt [Old English < Indo-European] —**gold** *adj*

Whoopi Goldberg

Goldberg /gó́ldbərg/, **Whoopi** (*b.* 1949) US actor. Her films include *The Color Purple* (1985), and she won an Academy Award for her performance in *Ghost* (1990). Born **Johnson, Caryn**

gold brick *n* a brick or other thing that appears to be made of gold but is not actually valuable

gold card *n* a credit card issued to people with incomes higher than a specific amount, that allows the holder to have a special credit limit and other extra facilities

Gold Coast /gó́ld-/ **1.** city on the Pacific coast, southeastern Queensland, Australia. It straddles the border between Queensland and New South Wales. Population: 438,473 (2002 estimate). **2.** former name for **Ghana**

goldcrest

goldcrest /gó́ld krest/ *n* a very small, active, olive-green songbird with a yellow and black crown. Native to: Europe. Latin name: *Regulus regulus*.

gold digger *n* **1.** an offensive term for a person who is regarded as seeking intimate relationships for material gain (*insult*) **2.** a miner looking for gold deposits —**gold-digging** *n*

gold disc *n* **1.** *UK* a golden replica of a recording that has achieved a specific exceptionally high number of sales. ANZ, N Am term **gold record 2.** the master disc from which a CD-ROM is made

gold dust *n* **1.** small particles of gold occurring naturally **2.** PLANTS same as **alyssum** (sense 2)

golden /gốld'n/ adj **1. COLOURED LIKE GOLD** with the colour of gold ○ *golden hair* **2. MADE OF GOLD** made largely or wholly of gold ○ *a golden crown* **3. EXCELLENT** especially good **4. IDYLLIC** describes a period when there is general or individual success, happiness, or prosperity ○ *the golden years of their lives* **5. FAVOURED** popular or successful, or likely to become so ○ *the golden boys and girls of the downhill ski circuit* — **goldenly** adv —**goldenness** n

golden age n **1.** a period of great prosperity or achievement, especially in the arts **2.** in classical mythology, the first age of the world characterized by idyllic happiness and innocence

golden ager /-áygər/ n N Am somebody over retirement age

golden anniversary n a 50th anniversary, e.g. of a wedding, or its celebration

Golden Bay /gốld'n-/ bay on the northern coast of the South Island, New Zealand. It extends 40 km/25 mi. from Farewell Spit in the west to Separation Point in the east.

golden brown n a yellowish-brown colour —**golden-brown** adj

golden-brown alga n a freshwater or marine alga that is yellow to golden-brown in colour. Division: *Chrysophyta*. (*often used in the plural*)

golden calf n an unworthy object that is esteemed or worshipped, especially money [< that worshipped by the Israelites (Exodus 32)]

golden chain n TREES same as **laburnum**

Golden Delicious n a variety of eating apple with greenish or yellowish skin and a soft sweet flesh

golden eagle n a large dark-brown eagle with golden-brown feathers on its head and neck. Native to: mountainous regions of northern hemisphere. Latin name: *Aquila chrysaetos*.

goldeneye /gốld'n ī/ n **1.** a black-and-white diving duck with yellow eyes. Native to: northern regions. Latin name: *Bucephala clangula* or *Bucephala islandica*. **2.** an insect with yellow eyes and delicate lacy wings. Family: Chrysopidae.

Golden Fleece n in Greek mythology, the fleece of the winged ram Chrysomallus, kept in a sacred grove by King Aeëtes, from where it was stolen by Jason

Golden Gate Bridge

Golden Gate Bridge n a long suspension bridge across the entrance to San Francisco Bay, California, United States. It was opened in 1937 and links San Francisco with Marin County.

golden goal n formerly in some football competitions, the first goal scored in extra time after a drawn game, which decides the winning team

golden hamster n a small animal with tan fur, a short tail, and large cheek pouches for storing food, which is often kept as a pet or used as a laboratory animal. The widespread domestic population came from a single female and 12 young caught in Syria in 1930. Latin name: *Mesocricetus auratus*.

golden handcuffs npl generous benefits promised to an employee on joining a company to discourage him or her from leaving to work elsewhere (*informal*)

golden handshake n a large sum of money given to an employee to compensate for the loss of a job or compulsory early retirement (*informal*)

golden hello n a large sum of money given after an employment contract has been signed, offered as an inducement to somebody to take up the new job or join the hiring organization (*informal*)

Golden Horde n the Mongol army that invaded and dominated large parts of eastern Europe in the 13th century

Golden Horn inlet of the Bosporus in the European part of Turkey. It forms the harbour of Istanbul. Length: 8 km/5 mi.

golden jubilee n a 50th anniversary, especially of a public event, or its celebration

golden lion tamarin n a small monkey with brilliant golden fur and mane. Native to: coastal forests of Brazil. Latin name: *Leontopithecus rosalia*.

golden mean n **1.** the middle course that avoids extremes in either direction **2.** ARTS same as **golden section**

golden nematode n a small worm that can infest potato fields, causing severe damage to crops and loss of productive farm land. Latin name: *Heterodera rostochiensis*.

golden oldie n a song that was popular in the past and has remained popular or become popular again (*informal*)

golden opportunity n an especially good chance

golden parachute n an employment agreement that gives generous benefits to a senior executive who is forced to leave a company (*informal*)

golden retriever n a medium-sized dog belonging to a breed with cream to golden hair. Its companionable nature makes it a popular family pet.

goldenrod /gốld'n rod/ (*plural* **-rods** or *same*) n a tall-stemmed plant that blooms in late summer. Flowers: small, yellow, in clusters. Native to: Europe, North America. Genus: *Solidago*.

golden rule n **1.** a basic rule that must be followed **2.** the rule of conduct that advises people to treat others in the same manner as they wish to be treated themselves

goldenseal /gốld'n seel/ n a small perennial woodland plant of the buttercup family that has a thick yellow rootstock used in herbal medicine for its healing and antiseptic properties. Flowers: small, greenish. Native to: eastern North America. Latin name: *Hydrastis canadensis*.

golden section n the proportion arising from the division of a straight line into two so that the ratio of the whole line to the larger part is exactly the same as the ratio of the larger part to the smaller part [Because considered to be the most aesthetically pleasing proportion]

golden share n a controlling share retained by a government in a company that has been taken out of public ownership and privatized

golden syrup n a clear yellow syrup used in baking and for desserts. It is a traditional accompaniment for steamed sponge pudding and the main ingredient of the filling of treacle tart. It is made of three different types of sugar, with natural flavouring and colouring.

golden triangle n the part of Southeast Asia where Laos, Thailand, and Myanmar meet and where much opium is grown

golden wattle n a tree whose golden-yellow flowers are used as the floral emblem of Australia. Native to: Australia. Latin name: *Acacia pycantha*.

golden wedding, golden wedding anniversary n a 50th anniversary of a wedding, or its celebration

goldfield /gốld feeld/ n an area with gold mines

goldfinch /gốld finch/ n a small finch with yellow and black markings. Native to: North America, Europe, Asia. Genus: *Carduelis*.

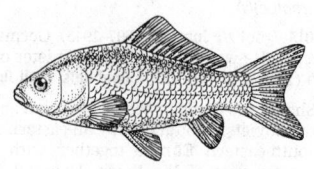

goldfish

goldfish /gốldfish/ (*plural same* or **-fishes**) n an orange-red freshwater aquarium and pond fish related to carps and minnows. Native to: East Asia. Latin name: *Carassius auratus*.

goldfish bowl n **1.** a clear glass or plastic bowl in which to raise and keep goldfish **2.** a situation or place that is always open to public view or scrutiny

gold leaf n gold that is beaten out into very thin sheets and used for gilding and lettering

Emma Goldman

Goldman /gốldmən/, **Emma** (1869–1940) Russian-born US anarchist. A fiery writer and lecturer, she was imprisoned and deported (1919) for her radical political activities in the United States, and wrote the autobiographical *Living My Life* (1931).

> 'If the production of any commodity necessitates the sacrifice of human life, society should do without that commodity, but it cannot do without that life.'
> [Emma Goldman, *Anarchism and Other Essays*; 1917]

gold medal n a medal that is made of gold or something representing gold, given as a first prize for excellence or winning a competition —**gold medallist** n

gold mine n **1.** a place where gold is mined **2.** a rich source of something valuable, especially easily obtained wealth ○ *Some of the smaller shops are little gold mines.* —**gold-miner** n —**gold-mining** n

gold plate n **1.** bowls, goblets, and other utensils made of gold **2.** a thin coating of gold on another metal, usually produced by electroplating

gold-plated adj having a thin coating of gold, usually produced by electroplating —**gold-plate** vt

gold record n ANZ, N Am MUSIC, RECORDING same as **gold disc** (sense 1)

gold reserve n a fund of gold in coins or bullion held by a central bank and regarded as providing a foundation for a paper currency and security for borrowing

gold-rimmed adj **1.** having a thin frame that is gold-coloured or made of gold ○ *gold-rimmed eye-glasses* **2.** decorated with a thin gold-coloured band at the edge ○ *a gold-rimmed mug*

gold rush n **1.** a sudden wave of migration to new territory because gold has been discovered there. One of the most famous gold rushes was to the Klondike in Yukon, Canada, from 1896. **2.** a sudden rush to make money from a new source or by a new means

CULTURAL NOTE *The Gold Rush*, a film (1925) by director and actor Charles Chaplin. Set during the California gold rush of 1849, it places Chaplin's gentle and sensitive Tramp character in the materialistic, amoral environment of a mining town to great comic effect. In one famous scene, Chaplin is reduced to eating his shoes, but eventually he strikes it rich and returns home a wealthy man.

goldsmith /gṓld smith/ *n* a maker of or dealer in gold objects

Goldsmith /gṓld smith/, **Sir James** (1933–97) French-born British business executive. He had extensive business interests, and used his fortune to fund conservative political causes such as the Referendum Party (1994). Full name **Goldsmith, Sir James Michael**

> 'Brussels is a madness. I will fight it from within.'
> [James Goldsmith. Referring to the European Union, *Times*; 10 June 1994]

Goldsmith, Oliver (1730–74) Irish-born British writer. He is best remembered for his novel *The Vicar of Wakefield* (1766) and his comedy *She Stoops to Conquer* (1773). See Cultural note at **stoop**[1]

> 'Such is the patriot's boast, where'er we roam, / His first, best country ever is, at home.'
> [Oliver Goldsmith, *The Traveller*; 1764]

> 'The true use of speech is not so much to express our wants as to conceal them.'
> [Oliver Goldsmith, 'On the Use of Language', *The Bee, no. 3*; 20 October 1759]

gold standard *n* **1.** a system of defining monetary units in terms of their value in gold, usually accompanied by the free circulation of gold and free exchange of currency into it **2.** the very best example of its kind

goldstone /gṓld stōn/ *n* MINERALS same as **aventurine** (sense 2)

goldthread /gṓld thred/ *n* a low-growing evergreen plant found in mossy woods or swamps. Native to: North America, northern Asia, and Europe. Latin name: *Coptis trifolia*.

Goldwyn /gṓldwin/, **Samuel** (1882–1974) Russian-born US film producer. He was one of Hollywood's most influential producers. His films include *The Best Years of Our Lives* (1946) and *Porgy and Bess* (1959). Born **Gelbfisz, Schmuel**

> 'A verbal contract isn't worth the paper it is written on.'
> [Samuel Goldwyn. Quoted in *The Great Goldwyn*, Alva Johnston; 1937]

golem /gṓləm, góy-/ *n* in Jewish legend, an imaginary being made of clay and brought to life by magical incantations. The most famous was made by Rabbi Loew in the 16th century to defend the Jews of Prague from a pogrom. [Late 19C. Via Yiddish < Hebrew *golem* 'shape, mass']

golf /golf/ *n* an outdoor game in which an array of special clubs with long shafts are used to hit a small ball from a prescribed starting point into a series of holes. The object of the game is to complete the course in as few strokes as possible. ■ *vi* (**golfs, golfing, golfed**) to play the game of golf [15C. Origin ?] —**golfer** *n*

Golf *n* a code word for the letter 'G', used in international radio communications

golf ball *n* a small hard ball used for playing golf

golf cart *n* a motorized vehicle used to drive around on a golf course during play

golf club *n* **1.** STICK FOR HITTING GOLF BALLS a specially designed club with a long shaft and a metal or wooden head, used in golf to strike the ball **2.** GOLFERS' ASSOCIATION an association of people who play golf, usually on the same course **3.** PREMISES OF GOLFERS' ASSOCIATION the premises or facilities used by a golf club

golf course *n* an area of land designed for playing golf on

golfing /gólfing/ *n* the activity of playing golf (*often used before a noun*) ○ *a golfing umbrella*

golf links *npl* a golf course situated beside the sea

golf widow *n* a woman whose husband or partner spends many hours playing golf (*informal; humorous*)

golgappa /gol gúppə/ *n* in Indian cooking, a ball of mashed potato with spices and tamarind juice, wrapped in puff pastry and fried [< Hindi]

Golgi apparatus /gólji-/, **Golgi body**, **Golgi complex** *n* a membranous structure in the cytoplasm of cells consisting of layers of flattened sacs and functioning in the processing and transporting of proteins [Early 20C. After Camillo *Golgi* (1844–1926), Italian histologist]

Golgotha /gólgəthə/ *n* same as **Calvary** [Via late Latin < Greek, alteration of Aramaic *gōgoltā* 'skull']

goliath /gə lī əth/ *n* a gigantic or overpowering opponent or competitor ○ *a corporation regarded as the goliath of the oil industry* [Late 16C. After GOLIATH]

Goliath /gə lī əth/ *n* **1.** in the Bible, a giant Philistine who was slain by David using a sling and a stone **2.** another spelling of **goliath**

Goliath beetle *n* a very large scarab beetle that can measure up to 15 cm/6 in in length and has bold black, white, and brown markings. Native to: tropical Africa. Latin name: *Goliathus giganteus*.

Goliath frog *n* a very large frog that can measure up to 30 cm/12 in. Native to: central Africa. Latin name: *Rana goliath*.

goliath grouper *n* a large dark spotted sea fish of the grouper family with rough scales. Native to: warm waters. Latin name: *Epinephelus itajara*.

golliwog /gólli wog/, **golliwogg** *n* an offensively grotesque cloth doll with a black face and hair and brightly coloured clothes. Now rarely made, the dolls are offensive to Black people, as is the term itself. (*offensive*) [Late 19C. After a character in books by US writer Bertha Upton (d. 1912)]

golly[1] /gólli/ *interj* used to express surprise, amazement, or anxiety, or for emphasis (*dated informal*) ○ *Golly, we're in real trouble now!* [Late 18C. Alteration of GOD]

golly[2] /gólli/ (*plural* -**lies**) *n* same as **golliwog** (*offensive*) [Mid-20C. Shortening]

gomasio /go mássi ō/, **ghomasio** *n* a seasoning mixture made of ground sesame seeds and salt, used especially in Japanese cookery [< Japanese]

gombeenism /góm beenizəm/, **gombeen** /góm been/ *n Ireland* money-lending at extortionate rates [Mid-19C. See GOMBEEN MAN]

gombeen man *n Ireland* **1.** a money-lender who charges exorbitant interest **2.** a small-time entrepreneur [< Irish *gaimbín* 'usury']

gombroon /góm broon/ *n* pottery made in Iran and elsewhere in imitation of white Chinese porcelain [Late 17C. After *Gombroon* (now Bandar Abbas), port in Iran]

Gomorrah /gə mórrə/ *n* a place or society marked by evil, depravity, and promiscuousness (*disapproving*) [Early 20C. After an ancient city destroyed by God because of its wickedness (Genesis 19)]

gon- *prefix* same as **gono-** (*used before vowels*)

-gon *suffix* a figure having a particular number of angles ○ *undecagon* ○ *polygon* [< Greek -*gōnon* < *gōnia* 'angle, corner' < Indo-European, 'knee, bend']

gonad /gṓ nad, gónnad/ *n* an organ that produces reproductive cells (**gametes**), e.g. a testis or an ovary [Late 19C. < modern Latin *gonas*, stem of *gonas* < Greek *gonos* 'seed, generation'] —**gonadal** /gṓ náyd'l, gō-/ *adj* —**gonadic** /gō náddik, gō-/ *adj*

gonadotrophic /gónnədə trṓfik/, **gonadotropic** /-tróppik/, *adj* stimulating or acting on the gonads

gonadotrophic-releasing hormone, **gonadotropic-releasing hormone** *n* a hormone released by the hypothalamus that causes the secretion of luteinizing hormone and follicle-stimulating hormone by the pituitary gland

gonadotrophin /gónnədə trṓfin/, **gonadotropin** /-trṓpin/ *n* a hormone secreted by the pituitary gland, and in some mammals by the placenta during pregnancy, that influences gonadal activity, including the onset of sexual maturity and regulation of reproductive activity

gonadotropic, etc. BIOCHEM another spelling of **gonadotrophic, etc.**

Gonaïves /gō nív/ town in western Haiti, situated northwest of Port-au-Prince. Population: 63,291 (1995).

Goncourt /góN koor/, **Edmond de** (1822–96) French novelist and diarist. He collaborated with his brother Jules de Goncourt (1830–70) on works including a 40-year journal of French social and literary life. Full name **Goncourt, Edmond Louis Antoine de**

> 'Antiquity was perhaps created to provide professors with their bread and butter.'
> [Edmond de Goncourt, *Le Journal des Goncourts* (*The Goncourt Journals*); 1887–96]

gondola

gondola /góndələ/ *n* **1.** VENETIAN CANAL BOAT a narrow flat-bottomed boat, used on the canals of Venice, that has a curved prow and stern and is moved along with a long pole **2.** CABLE CAR a car or cabin suspended from cables, especially one attached to a ski lift **3.** CAR BELOW BALLOON a basket or cabin suspended from a balloon or airship, for carrying people or equipment **4.** ISLAND OF SHELVES a free-standing shelving unit forming an island for displaying goods in a supermarket or other self-service shop [Mid-16C. Via Venetian Italian < Rhaeto-Romance *gondolà* 'to roll, rock']

gondolier /góndə leer/ *n* somebody who guides a gondola through water, especially on the canals of Venice

Gondwanaland /gon dwáənə land/ ancient landmass, consisting of the southern part of the supercontinent of Pangaea. Comprising South America, Africa, peninsular South Asia, Australia, and Antarctica, it began to break up approximately 200 million years ago.

gone /gon/ past participle of **go**[1] ■ *adj* **1.** ABSENT absent after leaving somewhere ○ *She has been gone for hours.* **2.** IRRECOVERABLE beyond hope of recovery ○ *All hopes for a truce are gone.* **3.** USED UP having been completely used up ○ *If the milk is all gone, we'll drink our coffee black.* **4.** ADVANCED IN TIME more advanced than a particular time or age ○ *It's gone six and we'll be late.* **5.** PREGNANT having been pregnant for a particular number of months ○ *She's eight months gone.* **6.** DEAD no longer living (*informal*) **7.** UNEASY giving a sensation of giddiness or sinking in the stomach **8.** EXHILARATED excited or exhilarated, e.g. while listening to music (*slang*) **9.** INFATUATED affected by a strong feeling of attraction towards somebody (*dated slang*) ○ *He's gone on your sister.*

goner /gónnər/ *n* somebody or something beyond hope of recovery, especially somebody who is dead or about to die (*slang*) ○ *It looks like he's a goner.*

gonfalon /gónfələn/ *n* a banner suspended from a crossbar, often with an edge cut like streamers, used as the standard of some medieval Italian republics or carried in church processions [Late 16C. Via Italian *gonfalone* < Old French *gonfanon* < Germanic, 'war banner']

gonfalonier /gónfələ neer/ *n* **1.** a bearer of a gonfalon **2.** the chief magistrate of some medieval Italian republics, who carried the republic's gonfalon

gong /gong/ *n* **1.** RESONANT BRONZE PLATE a circular bronze plate that makes a resonant sound when struck with a mallet, used as an orchestral percussion instrument or to summon people to meals **2.** WARNING BELL a round metal bell that is struck by a mechanically operated hammer, used as an alarm **3.** MEDAL a medal or decoration (*slang*) ■ *v* (**gongs, gonging, gonged**) **1.** *vi* SOUND LIKE GONG to sound res-

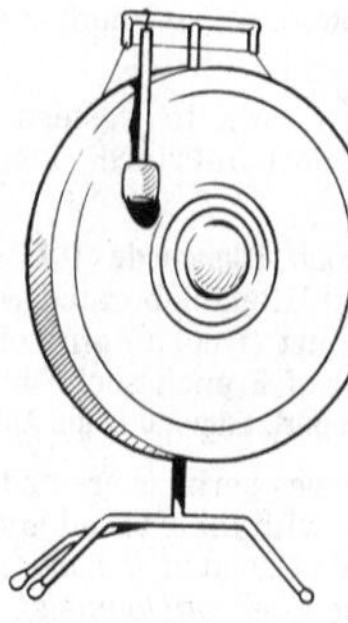

gong

onantly like a gong **2.** *vt* **SUMMON SOMEBODY** to summon somebody with a gong [Early 17C. < Malay, an imitation of the sound made]

Gongorism /góng gərizəm/ *n* a style in Spanish literature characterized by ornate devices, classical allusions, and deliberate obscurity [Early 19C. After *Góngora* y Argote (1561–1627), Spanish poet] —**Gongoristic** /góng gə rístik/ *adj*

gonidium /gō níddi əm/ (*plural* **-ia** /-i ə/) *n* **1.** an asexual reproductive cell in some algae, e.g. a zoospore **2.** a chlorophyll-containing algal cell in the body (**thallus**) of a lichen [Mid-19C. < modern Latin < Greek *gonos* 'offspring'] —**gonidial** *adj*

gonif *n* CRIME same as **ganef**

goniometer /gṓni ómmitər/ *n* **1.** an instrument for measuring angles, especially those between crystal faces **2.** a device for establishing the bearing of an incoming radio signal [Mid-18C. < French *goniomètre* < Greek *gonia* 'angle'] —**goniometric** /-ə méttrik/ *adj* —**goniometrical** *adj* —**goniometry** *n*

gonion /gṓni on/ *n* the point on either side of the lower jaw where it turns upwards [Late 19C. < French < Greek *gonia* 'angle']

goniotomy /gṓni óttəmi/ (*plural* **-mies**) *n* an operation to treat glaucoma by cutting into the narrow angle between the back of the cornea and the root of the iris to allow drainage of aqueous humour

gonk /gongk/ (**gonks, gonking, gonked**) *vti* to tell a lie to somebody about something or embellish the truth, especially in an online conversation in a chat room (*slang*) ○ *Are you gonking me?* [Mid-20C. Invention] —**gonk** *n*

gonna /gónnə, gúnnə/ *contr* going to (*nonstandard*)

gono- *prefix* sexual, generative, semen, seed ○ *gonopore* [< Greek *gonos* 'offspring, procreation' < Indo-European, 'beget']

gonococcus /gónnə kókəss/ (*plural* **-cocci** /-kóksī/) *n* a spherical bacterium that causes gonorrhoea. Latin name: *Neisseria gonorrhoeae*. [Late 19C. < GONORRHOEA] —**gonococcal** /-kók'l/ *adj* —**gonococcic** /-kóksik/ *adj*

gonof *n* CRIME same as **ganef**

gonopore /gónnə pawr/ *n* an external reproductive pore in some insects and worms through which reproductive cells are secreted

gonorrhoea /gónnə reé ə/, **gonorrhea** *n* a sexually transmitted bacterial disease that causes inflammation of the genital mucous membrane, burning pain when urinating, and a discharge. It is caused by a gonococcus bacterium. [16C. Via modern Latin < Greek *gonorrhoia* 'flowing of semen' < *gonos* 'semen'] —**gonorrhoeal** *adj*

-gony *suffix* **1.** origin ○ *cosmogony* **2.** method of reproduction ○ *schizogony* [< Greek *gonos* (see GONO-)]

Gonzales /gon zaáliz/, **Pancho** (1928–95) US tennis player. He dominated men's tennis in the 1950s, and in 1969 played the longest ever match at Wimbledon, defeating Charlie Pasarell after 112 games. Full name **Gonzales, Richard Alonzo**

gonzo /gónzō/ *adj* (*slang*) **1.** unusual or strange **2.** *N Am* characterized by subjective interpretation and exaggeration ○ *Gonzo journalism is unlike the work of the impartial observer.* [Late 20C. Origin ?]

goo /goo/ *n* (*informal*) **1.** a sticky substance, typically something unpleasant **2.** cloying emotionalism [Early 20C. Origin ?]

good /go͝od/ *adj* (**better** /béttər/, **best** /best/) **1.** **OF HIGH QUALITY** of a high quality or standard, either on an absolute scale or in relation to another or others ○ *The meal wasn't good.* ○ *He'll make a very good doctor.* ○ *I smashed one of my good plates.* **2.** **SUITABLE** having the appropriate qualities to be something or to fit a purpose ○ *Futons make good chairs as well as beds.* ○ *The bicycle is good for short trips.* **3.** **SKILLED** possessing the necessary skill or talent to do something ○ *I'm not a very good driver.* ○ *She's good at science.* **4.** **VIRTUOUS** having or showing an upright and virtuous character ○ *You're a good man, Joe.* **5.** **KIND** having or showing a kind and generous disposition ○ *She was always very good to me.* **6.** **AFFORDING PLEASURE** affording pleasure or comfort ○ *He's a man who insists on the finer things in life: good food, good books, and the theatre.* **7.** **UNDAMAGED** having undergone no deterioration or damage ○ *I smelled the meat and found it was still good.* **8.** **AMPLE** sufficiently large, or providing more than enough of something ○ *Between them they have a good income.* **9.** **HONOURABLE** worthy of honour or high esteem ○ *They come from a good family.* **10.** **VALID** acceptable as true or genuine and sufficient for the purpose ○ *There had better be a good explanation for this mess.* ○ *Don't travel unless your insurance is good.* **11.** **HELPFUL** helping somebody to organize thoughts or make decisions ○ *She gave me some good advice.* **12.** **PLEASANT** pleasant to look at ○ *Don't let her good looks distract you from her intelligence.* **13.** **BENEFICIAL** beneficial to health or wellbeing ○ *Eating lots of fruit is good for you.* ○ *It's good to talk.* **14.** **FAVOURABLE** suitable and likely to produce the right results or conditions ○ *a good time to have a holiday* **15.** **METICULOUS** careful and thorough ○ *Take a good look round.* **16.** **FINANCIALLY ADVANTAGEOUS** financially or commercially advantageous or reliable ○ *I made a few good investments last year.* **17.** **GENUINE** that is what it appears to be ○ *a good ten pound note* **18.** **OBEDIENT** well behaved and obedient ○ *The children are always good when we take them out.* **19.** **WELL MANNERED** socially correct ○ *very good behaviour* **20.** **ABLE TO DO MORE** remaining in operation or effect, or able to continue doing something ○ *The car will be good for another 6,000 miles.* **21.** **ABLE TO PAY** able to pay or contribute something or to allow a sum to be drawn ○ *He's good for at least £1,000.* **22.** **GUARANTEED TO BE PAID** describes a debt that will be paid in full ○ *a good debt* **23.** **PRODUCING RESULT** able to produce a particular result ○ *John is always good for a laugh.* **24.** **SIZABLE** considerable in extent or size ○ *a good selection of books on computers* **25.** **FULL** at least a particular time or length ○ *It's a good 30 years since we met.* **26.** **WITHIN BOUNDS** inside the required area for a shot, throw, or pass to be allowed ○ *The umpire said that the catch was good.* **27.** **USED IN EXCLAMATIONS** used in exclamations of surprise, dismay, or other strong feelings (*informal*) ○ *Good heavens! I've won first prize!* **28.** **HEALTHY** well in health (*informal*) ○ *'How are you?' 'I'm good, thanks'.* ■ *interj* **EXPRESSING SATISFACTION** used to express satisfaction or pleasure in something that has just been said or to confirm it ○ *'They've just arrived'. 'Good'.* ■ *n* **1.** **BENEFICIAL EFFECT** something resulting in a beneficial effect or state ○ *the common good* ○ *What good will complaining do?* **2.** **GOODNESS** the quality of being good **3.** **POSITIVE PART** the positive part or aspect of something ○ *You have to take the good with the bad in this agreement.* **4.** **SOMETHING WORTH HAVING** something worth having or achieving ○ *the future good of the nation* **5.** **ITEM OF MERCHANDISE** an item for sale or use, often one produced for later consumption ■ *npl* **VIRTUOUS PEOPLE** those who are virtuous and upright ○ *the great and the good* [Old English *gōd* < Germanic, 'unite'] ◇ **be (all) to the good** to be to somebody's benefit ◇ **be up to no good** to be in the process of doing or planning something wrong or illegal (*informal*) ◇ **for good** permanently from the time in question ○ *They've gone for good.* ◇ **give as good as you get** to contend as effectively as your opponent ◇ **good and** completely and entirely (*informal*) ○ *I'll get up in the morning when I'm good and ready, and not before.* ◇ **make good** to become successful, often after an unpromising start ◇ **make good something 1.** to perform something successfully ○ *We must make good our attempt to win the trophy.* **2.** to carry out something intended or promised ○ *She made good her promise to repay the money on time.* **3.** to compensate for something, especially for damage or loss **4.** to demonstrate the truth or correctness of something ○ *If you cannot make good these charges, the defendant will not stand trial.* ◇ **never had it so good** to have not possessed so many benefits before ◇ **to the good** richer by a particular amount of money ○ *By the end of the day, we were 50 pounds to the good.*

USAGE good or **well**? ***Good*** is the correct choice as an adjective after the linking verbs *be, appear,* and *seem,* and so-called sensory verbs such as *smell* and *taste*: *The jacket looks good. This steak tastes good.* ***Well*** is the correct choice as an adverb when it appears after other verbs that neither link nor designate sensory functions: *The jacket looks good and fits you well. Cook the steak well if you expect it to taste good.*

good afternoon *interj* used when people meet or part, or begin or end a telephone conversation, during the afternoon

Good Book *n* the Christian Bible (*informal*)

goodbye /go͝od bī́/ *interj* used when people part or end a telephone conversation ○ *Goodbye! I'll see you next year.* ■ *n* an act of making a farewell ○ *It's time to say our goodbyes and catch the plane.* [Late 16C. < *God be with you*]

good cause *n* **1.** something or somebody deserving help, especially a charity **2.** a sufficient legal standard or reason

good day *interj* used when people meet or part, or begin or end a telephone conversation, during daylight hours (*formal*)

good evening *interj* used when people meet or part, or begin or end a telephone conversation, during the evening

good faith *n* honesty of intention ○ *an effort to fulfil the contract in good faith*

good-for-nothing *n* an offensive term for a person who is regarded as lazy and irresponsible (*insult*) —**good-for-nothing** *adj*

Good Friday *n* a Christian holy day marking the death of Jesus Christ. Date: Friday before Easter Day.

Good Friday plant *n* PLANTS same as **moschatel**

good guy *n N Am* a worthy or law-abiding person, especially in a novel or film (*informal*)

goodhearted /go͝od haártid/ *adj* having or showing a kind and generous nature —**goodheartedly** *adv* —**goodheartedness** *n*

Good Hope, Cape of /go͝od hōp/ tip of the Cape Peninsula, South Africa. It is situated about 48 km/30 mi. south of Cape Town and was rounded by the Portuguese navigator Bartolomeu Dias in 1488.

good-humoured *adj* disposed to be cheerful and friendly, or reflecting such an attitude —**good-humouredly** *adv*

goodie *n* another spelling of **goody** *n* (sense 1)

goodies *npl* (*informal*) **1.** foods such as cakes and chocolates that are regarded as tasty treats **2.** objects that are nice to own or receive, especially small luxuries

goodish /go͝oddish/ *adj* **1.** moderately good in quality **2.** moderately large in quantity or extent ○ *a goodish helping*

Good King Henry *n* a weed of the goosefoot family with arrow-shaped leaves and small green flowers. Latin name: *Chenopodium bonus-henricus*.

good life *n* a life of carefree comfort and luxury ○ *living the good life in Palm Springs*

good-looking *adj* having a pleasant personal, especially facial, appearance —**good-looker** *n*

SYNONYMS ***good-looking, attractive, beautiful, handsome, lovely, pretty***

CORE MEANING: having a pleasing appearance

good-looking having a pleasant personal, especially facial, appearance ○ *She was strikingly good-looking, with dark hair and eyes.* ○ *a good-looking young man* **attractive** pleasing in appearance or manner, or sexually desirable ○ *an attractive young couple* ○ *an attractive smile and appealing manner* **beautiful** very pleasing and impressive to look at (more often used of women than of men) ○ *beautiful eyes* ○ *a beautiful child* **handsome** with good facial features or a pleasing general appearance (generally used of men, but also of women who have strong but pleasant features) ○ *They make a handsome couple.* **lovely** pleasing to look at (most often used of women) ○ *You are looking lovely*

tonight. **pretty** with a pleasant face that is appealing, rather than outstandingly beautiful (most often used of girls and women) ○ *a pretty young girl, aged eight*

good looks *npl* a pleasant personal appearance, especially facial appearance

goodly /góoddli/ (**-lier, -liest**) *adj* **1.** SOMEWHAT LARGE moderately large in quantity or extent **2.** ATTRACTIVE having a fine appearance (*archaic*) **3.** PLEASANT of a pleasing quality (*archaic*) —**goodliness** *n*

goodman /góodmən/ (*plural* **-men** /-mən/) *n* the man in charge of a household or family, especially a married man (*archaic*)

Goodman /góodmən/, **Benny** (1909–86) US jazz musician. A virtuoso clarinettist, he popularized swing music during the 1930s and 1940s leading his own band. Full name **Goodman, Benjamin David**. Known as the King of Swing

> 'Something happens when you find out that what you're doing is no longer music— that it's become entertainment. It's a subtle thing and affects what you're playing.'
> [Benny Goodman, *Interview, Hear Me Talkin' to Ya*; 1955]

good morning *interj* used when people meet or part, or begin or end a telephone conversation, during the morning

good name *n* **1.** somebody's reputation for honesty and integrity **2.** *S Asia* somebody's last name or family name [In sense 2 translation of Hindi *shubh naam*]

good nature *n* a pleasant and obliging disposition

good-natured *adj* having or showing a pleasant and obliging disposition —**good-naturedly** *adv* —**good-naturedness** *n*

goodness /góodnəss/ *n* **1.** GOOD QUALITY the quality of being good **2.** VIRTUOUSNESS personal virtue or kindness **3.** GOOD PART the nutrition or other benefit to be derived from something ○ *Vegetables lose a lot of their goodness if you overcook them.* ■ *interj* EXPRESSING SURPRISE used to express surprise or amazement, or for emphasis ○ *Goodness! What was that?* ◇ **for goodness sake** used to express surprise, exasperation, or extreme anxiety, or for emphasis ◇ **goodness knows** used to indicate bafflement or lack of knowledge about something ○ *Goodness knows what they're doing out there at midnight.*

goodnight /góod nít/ *interj* used to convey good wishes when people part or end a telephone conversation at night, especially at bedtime

good-o *interj* another spelling of **good-oh** (*informal*)

good offices *npl* help or support, especially help in resolving a dispute

good-oh, **good-o** *interj* UK, Aus, US used to express approval or agreement (*informal*)

good oil *n* Aus reliable information (*informal*) ○ *He gave me the good oil for Saturday's race.*

good old boy, **good ol' boy**, **good ole boy** *n* US a stereotype of a man who is part of a peer group and conforms to the behaviour characteristic of the group, especially a white man in parts of the rural southern United States (*often offensive*)

goods /góodz/ *n* (*takes a singular or plural verb*) **1.** MERCHANDISE articles for sale or use, often those produced for later consumption, as opposed to services **2.** GENUINE ARTICLE something that is genuinely what it should be (*slang*) ■ *npl* **1.** PORTABLE PROPERTY portable personal property (*takes a plural verb*) **2.** MERCHANDISE MOVED BY RAIL merchandise that is transported, especially by rail (*takes a plural verb; often used before a noun*) ○ *a goods train* **3.** SOMETHING PROMISED something promised or expected (*informal; takes a plural verb*) ○ *You can rely on her to come up with the goods.* **4.** INCRIMINATING EVIDENCE information or evidence that will incriminate somebody (*slang; takes a plural verb*)

Good Samaritan *n* a helper of those who are in trouble [< the parable of the Good Samaritan (Luke 10:30–37), who helps a stranger beaten by robbers]

goods and chattels *npl* items of movable property, as distinct from buildings and land (*formal; often humorous*)

goods and services tax *n* in Canada, Australia, and New Zealand, a value-added tax charged on all goods and services

good-sized *adj* rather large in size ○ *The recipe called for a good-sized piece of chocolate.*

good-tempered *adj* having or showing a placid disposition —**good-temperedly** *adv* —**good-temperedness** *n*

good-time girl *n* a young woman whose chief aim is thought to be the pursuit of pleasure (*informal; disapproving*)

good turn *n* a friendly act that helps or benefits somebody else ○ *One good turn deserves another.*

goodwife /góod wíf/ (*plural* **-wives** /-wīvz/) *n* the woman in charge of a household or family, especially a married woman (*archaic*)

goodwill /góod wíl/ *n* **1.** FRIENDLY DISPOSITION friendly disposition towards somebody or something (*often used before a noun*) ○ *a goodwill gesture* **2.** WILLINGNESS cheerful willingness to do something **3.** ACCT NONTANGIBLE VALUE OF BUSINESS the value of a business over and above its tangible assets **4.** CHARITY SHOP a shop that sells donated goods in order to raise money for charity

Goodwin Sands /góodwin-/ dangerous area of sandbanks at the entrance to the Strait of Dover, off the southern coast of Kent, southeastern England. Length: 16 km/10 mi.

Goodwood /góodwood/ country estate and racecourse in West Sussex, southern England, near Chichester

good word *n* a comment recommending somebody or made in favour or defence of somebody ○ *He promised to put in a good word for me.*

good works *npl* activities that are charitable or helpful to others

goody /góoddi/ *n* (*plural* **-ies**) **1.** also **goodie** SOMETHING SWEET something desirable, especially something sweet to eat (*often used in the plural*) **2.** SOMEBODY GOOD a good or law-abiding person, especially in a Western or a crime thriller (*informal*) ■ *interj* INDICATES DELIGHT used to express great pleasure (*informal*) ○ *Oh goody, ice cream!*

goody bag *n* **1.** a small bag of sweets and other treats given to each child at the end of a children's party **2.** a bag containing small, product-related gifts that a company gives to potential customers

Goodyear /góod yeer/, **Charles** (1800–60) US inventor. He discovered the vulcanization process for rubber (1839).

goody-goody (*informal*) *n* (*plural* **goody-goodies**) same as **goody two-shoes** ■ *adj* irritatingly well-behaved or smugly virtuous [Mid-19C. Reduplication of GOODY]

goody two-shoes *n* somebody smugly well-behaved, irritatingly virtuous, or sanctimonious (*informal*) [Mid-20C. < a character in a children's book]

gooey /góo i/ (**-ier, -iest**) *adj* **1.** sticky and soft ○ *gooey chocolate cake* **2.** cloyingly sentimental (*informal*) ○ *a gooey romantic novel* —**gooeyness** *n*

goof /goof/ *n* N Am **1.** MISTAKE a mistake or blunder (*informal*) **2.** OFFENSIVE TERM an offensive term for somebody regarded as unintelligent or incompetent (*informal insult*) ■ *v* (**goofs, goofing, goofed**) (*informal*) **1.** *vi* N Am MAKE MISTAKE to make a thoughtless or unintelligent mistake **2.** *vt* US BOTCH SOMETHING to spoil something through incompetence or lack of intelligence [Early 20C. Probably < dialect *goff* 'somebody considered unintelligent', via French and Italian < medieval Latin *gufus* 'awkward, unintelligent']

goof around *vi* N Am to behave in a playful or silly way (*informal*) ○ *Once the pressure of exams was off, the students just goofed around.*

goof off *v* N Am to waste time instead of working (*informal*) ○ *The crew goofed off when the boss left early.*

goofball /góof bawl/ *n* N Am **1.** an offensive term for somebody regarded as thoughtless or unintelligent (*slang insult*) **2.** a barbiturate or other drug in the form of a pill (*slang*)

goof-up *n* US a silly mistake (*informal*)

goofy /góofi/ (**-ier, -iest**) *adj* **1.** OFFENSIVE TERM an offensive term for somebody regarded as silly or unintelligent (*informal insult*) **2.** WITH TEETH THAT STICK OUT having or showing front teeth that protrude from the mouth (*informal*) ○ *a goofy grin* **3.** WITH RIGHT FOOT FORWARD in skateboarding and similar sports, used to describe

a stance on the board in which the rider's right foot is nearer the front end (*slang*) —**goofily** *adv* —**goofiness** *n* —**goofy** *adv*

goofy-footer *n* in skateboarding and similar sports, somebody who rides on the board with his or her right foot nearest to the front end —**goofy-foot** *adj* —**goofy-footed** *adj*

googly /góogli/ (*plural* **-glies**) *n* in cricket, a ball that looks like a leg break on delivery and then moves unexpectedly in the opposite direction after it pitches [Early 20C. Origin ?]

googol /góo gol/ *n* the number equal to the numeral 1 followed by 100 zeros or 10^{100} [Mid-20C. Invention]

googolplex /góo gol pleks/ *n* the number equal to the numeral 1 followed by 10^{100} zeros [Mid-20C. < GOOGOL + Latin *plexus* 'intricate, braided']

gook[1] /gook/ *n* N Am a highly offensive term for an East Asian or Southeast Asian person or somebody of East Asian or Southeast Asian descent (*slang; insult*) [Mid-20C. Origin ?]

gook[2] /gook/ *n* same as **guck**

gooly /góoli/ (*plural* **-lies**), **goolie** *n* an offensive term for a testicle (*slang*) [Mid-20C. Probably < Hindi *goli* 'ball, bullet']

goon /goon/ *n* **1.** CLUMSY PERSON somebody regarded as clumsy or uncouth (*informal insult*) **2.** SOMEBODY WHO ACTS SILLY somebody who behaves foolishly or bizarrely as a joke (*informal*) **3.** N Am THUG a professional gangster whose work is beating up or terrorizing people (*informal*) [Mid-19C. Origin ?]

goonda /goon daa/ *n* S Asia a ruffian or hooligan [Early 20C. < Hindi *gunḍā* 'rascal'] —**goondaism** *n*

gooney /góoni/ (*plural* **-neys**), **gooney bird** *n* an albatross, especially a black-footed albatross [Late 16C. Origin ?]

goop /goop/ *n* **1.** somebody regarded as unintelligent or thoughtless (*slang insult*) **2.** N Am same as **gloop** (*informal*) [Early 20C. Alteration] —**goopy** *adj*

goosander /goo sándər/ *n* a waterfowl with a narrow serrated beak, the male of which has a dark head and white body. Native to: Europe, North America. Latin name: *Mergus merganser*. [Early 17C. Probably < GOOSE + Old Norse *andar-*, stem of *ond* 'duck']

goose

goose /gooss/ *n* (*plural* **geese** /geess/) **1.** LONG-NECKED WATER BIRD a large waterfowl with a long neck and webbed feet, noted for its seasonal migrations and distinctive honking sound. Geese resemble swans but have shorter necks. Subfamily: Anserinae. **2.** FEMALE BIRD a female goose **3.** FLESH OF GOOSE the flesh of the goose, cooked and eaten as food **4.** OFFENSIVE TERM an offensive term for a person who is regarded as silly **5.** (*plural* **gooses**) TAILOR'S IRON an iron with a long curved handle, used by tailors for pressing and smoothing cloth **6.** (*plural* **gooses**) PROD IN BUTTOCKS a poke between or pinch on the buttocks (*slang*) ■ *vt* (**gooses, goosing, goosed**) (*slang*) **1.** PROD SOMEBODY IN BUTTOCKS to poke or pinch somebody on the buttocks **2.** US ENCOURAGE SOMEBODY to spur somebody on to action [Old English *gōs* < Indo-European] ◇ **kill the goose that lays the golden eggs** to destroy something that is or has been a regular, dependable source of profit or benefit

goose barnacle *n* a barnacle with a flattened shell, feathery appendages, and a fleshy stalk used to attach itself to surfaces, especially floating wood. Genus: *Lepas*.

gooseberry

gooseberry /gŏózbəri/ (*plural* **-ries**) *n* **1.** ACID FRUIT an acid-tasting green or sometimes red fruit of a spiny plant, usually eaten cooked and sweetened (*often used before a noun*) ○ *gooseberry pie* **2.** SPINY FRUIT BUSH a spiny fruit bush that produces gooseberries. Native to: Europe, Asia. Latin name: *Ribes uva-crispa.* **3.** UNWANTED EXTRA PERSON an unwanted single person with a couple or a group otherwise made up of couples (*informal*) ○ *I don't want to play gooseberry.* [Mid-16C. Origin ?]

gooseberry stone *n* MINERALS same as **grossularite**

goose bumps *npl* same as **goose pimples**

gooseflesh /gŏóss flesh/ *n* skin affected by goose pimples

goosefoot /gŏóss fŏŏt/ *n* a weed with small greenish flowers and berries and leaves that resemble a goose's foot. Genus: *Chenopodium.*

goosegog /gŏóz gog/ *n* same as **gooseberry** (*informal*) [Early 19C. < variant of GOB¹]

goosegrass /gŏóss graass/ *n* an annual plant with slender sprawling stems, narrow leaves, and spiny round fruits that cling to animals and clothing. Native to: Europe, Asia. Latin name: *Galium aparine.* N Am term **cleavers**

gooseneck /gŏóss nek/ *n* something curved like a goose's neck or U-shaped, e.g. a pipe joint or a flexible neck on a lamp (*often used before a noun*) ○ *a gooseneck lamp*

gooseneck barnacle *n* ZOOL same as **goose barnacle**

goose pimples *npl* temporary pimples on the skin brought on by cold or fear, or by sudden excitement, and caused by contraction of connective tissues (**papillae**) at the base of hairs —**goose-pimply** *adj*

goose step *n* a military marching step performed with straight legs swung high in a forward movement —**goose-step** *vi*

goosy /gŏóssi/ (**-ier**, **-iest**), **goosey** *adj* **1.** RESEMBLING GOOSE similar to a goose **2.** HAVING GOOSE PIMPLES affected by goose pimples or the nervousness or fear that can cause them (*informal*) **3.** SILLY behaving in what is regarded as a silly or scatterbrained way (*disapproving*)

gopher /gŏ́fər/ *n* **1.** a small short-tailed rodent that has fur-lined cheek pouches and short legs and digs sizable burrows. Native to: North and Central America. Family: Geomyidae. **2.** an Internet system that organizes files into menus containing links to text files, graphic images, databases, and additional menus (*often used before a noun*) ○ *a gopher site* [Late 18C. Origin ?]

gopherwood /gŏ́fər wŏŏd/ *n* in the Bible, the wood from which Noah's ark was supposed to have been made, or the tree from which it came [Early 17C. < Hebrew *gōpher*]

Gorakhpur /gáwrək poor/ industrial city in Uttar Pradesh State, northern India. It is a major railway junction and trading centre. Population: 505,566 (1991).

goral /gáwrəl/ *n* a small short-horned antelope. Native to: Himalaya region and adjacent Southeast Asia. Genus: *Nemorhaedus.* [Mid-19C. < a Himalayan language]

Gorazde /gə raáz dáy/ town in eastern Bosnia and Herzegovina. A predominantly Muslim town, it was one of six 'safe areas' designated by the UN Security Council during the Bosnian-Croatian-Serbian War. Population: 37,500 (1991).

gorb /gawrb/ *n Ireland* same as **glutton** (sense 1) [Early 19C. Origin ?]

Mikhail Gorbachev

Gorbachev /gáwrbə chof/, **Mikhail** (*b.* 1931) Soviet politician. As general secretary of the Soviet Communist Party (1985–91) and president (1988–91), he initiated democratic reforms that precipitated the disintegration of the Soviet Union and the end of the Cold War. He won the Nobel Peace Prize (1990). Full name **Gorbachev, Mikhail Sergeyevich**

'Democracy is the wholesome and pure air without which a socialist public organisation cannot live a full-blooded life.'
[Mikhail Gorbachev, *Report to the 27th Party Congress of the Communist Party of the USSR;* 25 February 1986]

Gorbals /gáwrb'lz/ district of Glasgow, Scotland, on the southern bank of the River Clyde

gorblimey *interj* same as **cor blimey**

GORD *abbr* MED gastro-oesophageal reflux disese

Gordian knot /gáwrdi ən-/ *n* a problem for which it is very difficult to find a solution [Late 16C. < the knot of *Gordius,* king of Gordium, which was to be loosed only by the future ruler of Asia: Alexander the Great sliced through it]

Nadine Gordimer

Gordimer /gáwrdimər/, **Nadine** (*b.* 1923) South African novelist. Her works examine the tensions of apartheid in South Africa. She won the Nobel Prize in literature (1991).

'When one says one writes for "anyone who reads me" one must be aware that "anyone" excludes a vast number of readers who cannot "read" you or me because of givens they do not share with us in unequal societies.'
[Nadine Gordimer, *Living in Hope and History;* 1999]

Gordon /gáwrd'n/, **Adam Lindsay** (1833–70) Azores-born Australian poet. He wrote about Australian rural life in such collections as *Bush Ballads and Galloping Rhymes* (1870).

'Life is mostly froth and bubble; / Two things stand like stone, / Kindness in another's trouble, / Courage in your own.'
[Adam Lindsay Gordon, *Ye Wearie Wayfarer;* 1866]

Gordon Bennett /gáwrd'n bénnit/ *interj* used to express surprise or annoyance (*informal*) [Late 20C. Alteration of GORBLIMEY, after James *Gordon* BENNETT]

Gordon River the longest river in Tasmania, Australia, rising in the centre of the island and flowing

west into the southern Indian Ocean. Length: 181 km/112 mi.

Gordon setter /gáwrd'n-/ *n* a gun dog with a long black-and-tan coat, belonging to a breed developed in Scotland [Mid-19C. After Alexander *Gordon,* 4th Duke of Gordon (1743–1827)]

gore¹ /gawr/ (**gores, goring, gored**) *vt* to pierce the flesh of a person or animal with horns or tusks [14C. Origin ?]

gore² /gawr/ *n* thick coagulating blood, especially blood shed as a result of violence [Old English *gor* 'dirt, dung' < Germanic]

gore³ /gawr/ *n* a triangular piece of cloth that is sewn to others to form loose skirt [Old English *gāra,* origin ?] —**gored** *adj*

Gore /gawr/ town on the River Mataura on the South Island, New Zealand. It is a centre of agriculture and light industry. Population: 9,927 (2001).

Gore, Al (*b.* 1948) vice president of the United States (1993–2001). A Democrat from Tennessee, he was a US representative (1977–85) and senator (1985–93) before becoming Bill Clinton's vice president. Full name **Gore, Albert Arnold, Jr.**

'If we allow the information superhighway to bypass the less fortunate sectors of our society—even for an interim period—we will find that the information rich will get richer while the information poor get poorer...'
[Al Gore, *Speech to the National Press Club;* 21 December 1993]

Górecki /gaw rétskee/, **Henryk Mikolaj** (*b.* 1933) Polish composer. A leading figure of musical postmodernism, he wrote avant-garde pieces in the 1950s and 1960s such as *Scontri* (1960) but his later works, including *Symphony No. 3* (1976), are influenced by Polish folk and religious music.

gorge /gawrj/ *n* **1.** NARROW VALLEY a deep narrow, usually rocky, valley **2.** CONTENTS OF STOMACH the contents of the stomach, especially when they are perceived as rising in the throat out of disgust or anger **3.** BIRDS HAWK'S FOOD POUCH a food storage pouch in the throat of a hawk **4.** OBSTRUCTION IN PASSAGE a mass of something obstructing a passage, especially a mass of ice obstructing a river **5.** MIL ENTRANCE TO OUTWORK a narrow entrance at the rear of an outwork in a fortification ■ *v* (**gorges, gorging, gorged**) **1.** *vti* EAT GREEDILY to eat something greedily and to excess ○ *They gorged on chocolates.* ○ *They sat at the counter gorging meat and potatoes.* **2.** *vt* PHYSIOL same as **engorge** (sense 1) [14C. Via French, 'throat' < Latin *gurge* 'abyss, whirlpool'] —**gorger** *n*

gorgeous /gáwrjəss/ *adj* **1.** outstandingly beautiful or richly coloured ○ *dressed in gorgeous silks* **2.** very pleasant (*informal*) ○ *a gorgeous spring morning* [15C. < Old French *gorgias* 'stylish, elegant'] —**gorgeously** *adv* —**gorgeousness** *n*

gorget /gáwrjit/ *n* **1.** MIL ARMOUR FOR THROAT a crescent-shaped piece of armour for protecting the throat **2.** CLOTHING PART OF NUN'S HEADDRESS the part of a nun's headdress that covers the neck and shoulders **3.** JEWELLERY NECKLACE a circular or crescent-shaped ornament worn round the neck **4.** ZOOL COLOURED BAND ON THROAT a band or patch of distinctive colour on the throat of a bird or other animal [15C. < Old French *gorgete* < *gorge* 'throat' (see GORGE)]

gorge-walking *n* the sport of canyoning

Gorgon /gáwrgən/ *n* **1.** in Greek mythology, a monstrous woman with snakes for hair who turned those who looked at her into stone **2.** *also* **gorgon** an offensive term for a woman regarded as very frightening or ugly (*insult*) [14C. < Latin *Gorgon-,* stem of *Gorgo* < Greek *Gorgō* < *gorgos* 'terrible'] —**Gorgonian** /gawr gŏ́ni ən/ *adj*

gorgonian /gawr gŏ́ni ən/ *n* a coral with a flexible horny branched skeleton. Family: Gorgonacea. [Mid-19C. < modern Latin *Gorgonia* < Latin *Gorgon-* (see GORGON)] —**gorgonian** *adj*

Gorgonzola /gáwrgən zŏ́lə/, **gorgonzola** *n* a moist Italian blue cheese with a strong flavour [Late 19C. After a Milanese village]

gorilla

gorilla /gə rílllə/ *n* **1.** the largest ape, with a relatively short but very powerful body and coarse dark hair. Native to: central Africa. Latin name: *Gorilla gorilla*. **2.** somebody who is regarded as large or brutal, especially a hired thug (*informal*) [Mid-19C. Via modern Latin < Greek *gorillas*]

SPELLCHECK Do not confuse the spelling of *gorilla* and *guerrilla* ('a paramilitary soldier'), which sound similar.

Göring another spelling of **Goering**

Gorki another spelling of **Gorky**

Gorky, **Gorki** former name for **Nizhniy Novgorod**

Gorky, **Arshile** (1904–48) Armenian-born US painter. His work helped introduce European surrealism into American art and influenced the abstract expressionists. Born **Adoian, Vosdanig Manoog**

Gorky, **Gorki, Maksim** (1868–1936) Russian writer. His works inaugurated socialist realism, and include the play *The Lower Depths* (1902) and an autobiographical trilogy (1913–23). Pseudonym of **Peshkov, Aleksei Maksimovich**

'When work is a pleasure, life is a joy! When work is a duty, life is slavery.'
[Maksim Gorky, *The Lower Depths*; 1902]

Görlitz /gúrlits, gőrlits/ industrial city in Saxony State, east-central Germany, on the border with Poland. Population: 67,755 (1997).

Gorlovka ♦ **Horlivka**

gormandize /gáwrmən dīz/ (**-izes, -izing, -ized**), **gormandise** (**-ises, -ising, -ised**) *vti* to eat food gluttonously [Mid-16C. < GOURMANDISE 'gluttony'] —**gormandizer** *n*

gormless /gáwrmləss/ *adj* lacking intelligence, common sense, or initiative (*informal*) [Mid-19C. Variant of *gaumless* < *gaum* 'understanding, heed' < Old Norse *gaumr*]

~~gorrilla~~ incorrect spelling of **gorilla**

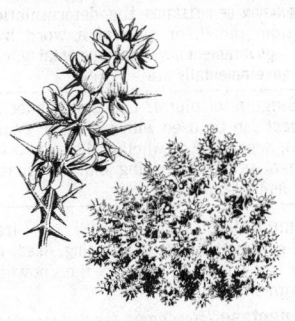

gorse

gorse /gawrss/ *n* a spiny bush with yellow flowers and black pods. Genus: *Ulex*. [Old English *gors* < Indo-European, 'be prickly or rough']

Gorton /gáwrt'n/, **Sir John Grey** (1911–2002) prime minister of Australia. A Liberal Party politician, he was prime minister from 1968 to 1971. See table at **prime minister**

gory /gáwri/ (**-rier, -riest**) *adj* **1.** BLOODY covered with blood or gore **2.** INVOLVING BLOODSHED involving much bloodshed **3.** HORRIBLE arousing horror or terror ○ *the gory details* —**gorily** *adv* —**goriness** *n*

Gosford /góssfərd/ coastal city in eastern New South Wales, Australia, situated 85 km/53 mi. north of Sydney. Population: 162,184 (2002 estimate).

gosh /gosh/ *interj* used to express surprise, amazement, or pleasure (*informal*) [Mid-18C. Substitution for GOD]

goshawk

goshawk /góss hawk/ *n* a large hawk with broad rounded wings and a long tail. Native to: Europe, North America. Latin name: *Accipiter gentilis*. [12C. < Old English *goshafoc* < forms of GOOSE + HAWK[1]]

gosht /gosht/ *n S Asia* red meat such as lamb or beef [< Hindi]

gosling /gózzling/ *n* a young goose [15C. < Old Norse *gøslingr* < *gas* 'goose']

go-slow *n* a protest by industrial workers in which they deliberately work slowly. N Am term **slowdown**

gospel /gósp'l/ *n* **1.** a set of beliefs held strongly by a group or person **2.** something believed to be absolutely and unquestionably true **3.** MUSIC same as **gospel music** [13C. < GOSPEL]

Gospel /gósp'l/ *n* **1.** TEACHINGS OF JESUS CHRIST the teachings of Jesus Christ and the story of his life **2.** BOOK OF BIBLE a book of the Bible belonging to a set of four, Matthew, Mark, Luke, and John, that tell the story of the life of Jesus Christ **3.** BIBLE EXTRACT an extract from one of the Gospels read as part of a Christian religious service [Old English *gōdspel* 'good news' < forms of GOOD + SPELL[2]]

gospeller /góspələr/ *n* **1.** a reader of the Gospel in a Christian religious service **2.** a preacher of the Gospel (*disapproving*)

gospel music *n* highly emotional evangelical vocal music that originated among African American Christians in the southern United States and was a strong influence in the development of soul music

gospel side *n* in a Christian church, the left side of the altar as faced by the congregation. ◊ **epistle side**

gospel truth *n* same as **gospel** (sense 2)

Gosport /góss pawrt/ town in Hampshire, southern England, on Portsmouth harbour. It is an English Channel port and the site of naval installations. Population: 76,415 (2001).

goss /goss/ *n* same as **gossip** *n* (sense 1) (*slang*) ○ *all the latest goss* [Shortening]

gossamer /góssəmər/ *n* **1.** FINE COBWEBS a fine film of cobwebs, often seen floating in the air or covered with dew on the ground **2.** DELICATE FABRIC a delicate, sheer fabric or gauze **3.** SOMETHING SHEER AND DELICATE something delicate, sheer, and filmy [14C. Probably < GOOSE + SUMMER[1], period of mild autumn weather when goose was in season and such webs were often seen in the air] —**gossamery** *adj*

gossan /góss'n, gózz'n/, **gozzan** /gózz'n/ *n* a yellow or red layer on the surface of minerals rich in iron oxide, produced by alteration and leaching of sulphide ores [Late 18C. Probably < Cornish < *gōs* 'blood']

Gosse /goss/, **Sir Edmund William** (1849–1928) British writer. Among his numerous works of literary criticism, biography, and poetry, he is best remembered for his autobiographical *Father and Son* (1907).

gossip /góssip/ *n* **1.** CONVERSATION ABOUT PERSONAL MATTERS conversation about the personal details of other people's lives, whether rumour or fact, especially when malicious **2.** CASUAL CONVERSATION informal conversation or writing about recent and often personal events ○ *They had a good gossip in the pub.* **3.** HABITUAL TALKER somebody who habitually discusses the personal details of others' lives ■ *vi* (**-sips,**

-siping, -siped) TALK ABOUT OTHER PEOPLE to spread rumours or tell people the personal details of others' lives, especially maliciously [Old English *godsibb* 'godparent, close friend' < GOD + SIB 'relative'] —**gossiper** *n* —**gossipry** *n* —**gossipy** *adj*

REGIONAL NOTE *Gossip* originally meant 'godmother' or 'sponsor in baptism', and illustrates a phenomenon called 'semantic degradation', where a word of high prestige loses some or all of its value. Many dialect words meaning 'to gossip' also mean 'to scold or nag'.

SYNONYMS See *talkative*.

gossip column *n* a regular feature in a magazine or newspaper in which rumours and personal or intimate facts about celebrities are exposed —**gossip columnist** *n*

gossipmonger /góssip mung gər/ *n* somebody who spreads gossip

gossoon /go sóon/ *n Ireland* a young boy (*informal*) [Late 17C. Via Irish < French *garçon* 'boy']

gossypol /góssi pol/ *n* a substance that inhibits sperm production. Source: cotton seeds. [Late 19C. < modern Latin *Gossypium* < Latin *gossypion* 'cotton tree']

got past participle, past tense of **get**[1]

Göta Canal /yőtə-/ waterway in southwestern Sweden, linking Gothenburg on the western coast with Stockholm on the Baltic coast. Length: 386 km/240 mi.

gotcha /góchə/ (*informal*) *interj* EXPRESSING TRIUMPH OVER ANOTHER used to indicate that somebody has been successfully tricked or caught out in some way or to indicate comprehension of something ■ *n* **1.** UNEXPECTED PROBLEM an unexpected problem or drawback **2.** UNFORESEEN SOFTWARE PROBLEM an unforeseen problem in the way a piece of software works [Mid-20C. < a pronunciation of *got you*]

Göteborg ♦ **Gothenburg**

goth /goth/ *n* **1.** SOMEBODY UNCIVILIZED an uncivilized or barbaric person **2.** MUSICAL STYLE a style of popular music that combines features of heavy metal with punk **3.** STYLE OF CLOTHES AND MAKE-UP a style of fashion, popular among men and women in the 1980s, characterized by black clothes, heavy silver jewellery, black eye makeup and lipstick, and often pale face makeup **4.** FOLLOWER OF GOTH MUSIC AND FASHION a fan of goth music and fashion [Mid-17C. < GOTH]

Goth /goth/ *n* **1.** a member of an ancient Germanic people who settled south of the Baltic and founded kingdoms in many parts of the Roman Empire between the 3rd and the 5th centuries **2.** MUSIC, FASHION another spelling of **goth** (senses 2–4) [Old English *gotan* 'Goths' < late Latin *Gothi* < Germanic]

Gotham /góthəm/ *n* a nickname for New York City [Originally used by Washington Irving, after *The Wise Men of Gotham*, folk tale; popularized by the Batman stories]

Gothenburg /góth'n burg/ seaport and industrial city on the River Göta estuary in southwestern Sweden. It is the second largest city and principal port of Sweden. Population: 459,593 (1998). Swedish name **Göteborg**

gothic /góthik/ *adj* **1.** UNCIVILIZED barbarous or uncivilized **2.** LITERAT another spelling of **Gothic** *adj* (sense 2–3) ■ *n* **1.** MUSIC, FASHION same as **goth** (senses 2–3) **2.** SIMPLE TYPEFACE a simple sans serif typeface with strokes of uniform width **3.** HEAVY ANGULAR TYPEFACE a heavy bold angular early typeface [Late 17C. < GOTHIC] —**gothically** *adv*

AKG London

Gothic: interior of Cologne Cathedral, Germany (begun 1248)

Gothic /góthik/ *adj* **1. OF MEDIEVAL ARCHITECTURAL STYLE** belonging to a style of architecture used in Western Europe between the 12th and 15th centuries, and characterized by pointed arches, flying buttresses, and high curved ceilings **2. OF MEDIEVAL ARTISTIC STYLE** belonging to a style of music, painting, or sculpture practised in parts of Europe between the 12th and 15th centuries **3. OF MIDDLE AGES** relating to or characteristic of the Middle Ages **4. OF EERIE FICTION STYLE** belonging to a genre of fiction characterized by gloom and darkness, often with a grotesque or supernatural plot unfolding in an eerie or lonely location such as a ruined castle **5. OF GOTHS** relating to the ancient Goths, or their language or culture ■ *n* **EXTINCT LANGUAGE OF ANCIENT GOTHS** an extinct language formerly spoken by the ancient Goths in parts of Scandinavia and around the Baltic Sea. It belongs to the East Germanic group of the Germanic branch of Indo-European languages. [Late 16C. Directly or via French < late Latin *Gothicus* < Gothik (see GOTH)] —**Gothically** *adv* —**Gothicizer** *n*

Gothic arch *n* a pointed arch, as found in Gothic churches

gothicism /góthi sizəm/ *n* crudeness of style or manner, or an example of such crudeness

Gothicism *n* use of the Gothic style of architecture, art, or literature —**Gothicist** *n*

Gothic Revival *n* a style of architecture based on a reintroduction of the Gothic style, popular in the 18th and 19th centuries

Gotland /góttlənd/, **Gottland** island and county of Sweden, situated in the Baltic Sea about 80 km/50 mi. from the mainland. Population: 58,120 (1995). Area: 3,140 sq. km/1,212 sq. mi.

go-to guy, **go-to person**, **go-to player** *n N Am* **1.** the member of a sports team who always gets the ball or puck and is counted on to score, especially in a close game (*slang*) **2.** somebody who can be trusted to provide a particular service or deal with a particular problem (*informal*) ○ *He's the go-to guy for cars when filmmakers come to town.*

gotta /góttə/ *vi* got to (*informal*) [Representing a pronunciation]

gotten *N Am* past participle of **get**[1]

Götterdämmerung /góttər dámmərŏong/, **götterdämmerung** *n* **1.** in Germanic mythology, the destruction of the gods after battle with the forces of doom **2.** the overthrow or violent ending of a regime or institution [Early 20C. < German, 'twilight of the gods']

Göttingen /gótingən/ university town in Lower Saxony, central Germany. It is situated about 89 km/55 mi. south of Hanover. Population: 127,519 (1997).

Gottland another spelling of **Gotland**

gouache /gŏo áash/ *n* **1. PAINTING TECHNIQUE** a method of painting in which opaque watercolours are mixed with gum **2. PAINT USED IN GOUACHE** the paint used in the gouache technique **3. GOUACHE PAINTING** a painting done with gouache [Late 19C. Via French < Italian *guazzo* 'puddle']

Gouda[1] /gówdə/ *n* a mild Dutch cheese, typically sold in a flat sphere covered in wax [Mid-19C. After GOUDA[2]]

Gouda[2] /gówdə/ city in South Holland Province, western Netherlands. Famous for its cheese, it is situated about 21 km/13 mi. northeast of Rotterdam. Population: 71,827 (2000).

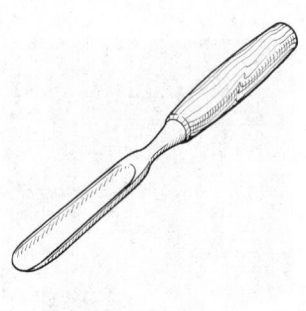

gouge

gouge /gowj/ *vt* (**gouges**, **gouging**, **gouged**) **1. CARVE OUT HOLE** to cut or scoop a hole or groove in something,

usually using a sharp tool **2. FORM ROUGHLY BY CUTTING** to form something by roughly cutting it out of surrounding material **3. INJURE SOMEBODY'S EYE** to attack somebody's eye with the thumb **4.** *N Am* **OVERCHARGE SOMEBODY** to cheat somebody or act dishonestly by demanding an unreasonably high price for goods or services (*informal*) ■ *n* **1. CHISEL WITH CONCAVE BLADE** a chisel with a concave blade. Use: cutting grooves and holes in wood. **2. SMALL HOLE** a mark, groove, or hole, usually made with a pointed tool **3.** *N Am* **OVERCHARGING** an instance of paying too much or being charged exorbitantly for goods or services (*informal*) **4.** GEOL **ROCK FRAGMENTS** clay material produced by the grinding together of rock surfaces in a fault or within a mineral vein [Late 15C. Via French < late Latin *gubia, gulbia* < Celtic] —**gouger** *n*

goujon /gŏojən/ *n* a long strip of fish or chicken coated in egg and breadcrumbs and deep-fried [Mid-20C. < French (see GUDGEON[1]); from their shape]

goulash /gŏol ash/ *n* **1.** a stew of Hungarian origin, made with beef, veal, lamb, or pork and seasoned with paprika **2.** a way of dealing cards that have already been arranged in a specific order, without shuffling them first [Mid-19C. < Hungarian *gulyás*, shortening of *gulyás hús* 'herdsman's meat']

Goulburn /gŏol burn/ city in eastern New South Wales, Australia. It is the commercial centre of a rural district. Population: 21,303 (2002 estimate).

Gould /goold/, **Shane** (*b.* 1956) Australian swimmer. She won five medals at the 1972 Olympics and retired from competitive swimming at age 16. Full name Gould, Shane Elizabeth

Gounod /gŏonō/, **Charles François** (1818–93) French composer. As well as sacred choral music, he wrote several operas including his best known work, *Faust* (1859), based on the poem by Goethe.

gourami /gŏo ráami/ (*plural same* or **-mis**) *n* a freshwater fish, many species of which are capable of breathing air and are often kept in aquariums. Native to: Southeast Asia. Family: Anabantidae. [Late 19C. Via Malay *gurami* 'freshwater carp' < Javanese *graméh*]

gourd

gourd /goord/ *n* **1.** a hard-skinned fleshy fruit produced by several different plants related to cucumbers and marrows. Use: dried decorations, hollowed out for bowls, cups. **2.** a plant that produces gourds. Native to: tropical regions, cultivated worldwide. Genera: *Curcurbita* or *Lagenaria*. [14C. Via Anglo-Norman *gurde* < Latin *cucurbita*] ◇ **off** or **out of your gourd** *N Am* not thinking clearly or rationally (*slang*)

gourde /goord/ *n* the main unit of currency in Haiti. See table at **currency** [Mid-19C. Via Haitian Creole < French *gourd* 'dull, heavy' < Latin *gurdus* 'unintelligent person']

gourmand /goormənd/ *n* a lover of food who often eats excessively or greedily [15C. < French, 'glutton']

gourmandise /gŏormən deez/ *n* an appreciation of good food and drink [15C. < French < *gourmand* 'glutton']

gourmet /goor may/ *n* somebody who enjoys and knows a lot about good food and drink ■ *adj* relating to high-quality food that is sophisticated, expensive, rare, or meticulously prepared [Early 19C. < French, alteration (influenced by *gourmand* 'glutton') of Middle French *groumet* 'servant, vintner's assistant' < English (**groom**)]

gout /gowt/ *n* **1.** a metabolic disorder mainly affecting men in which excess uric acid is produced and

deposited in the joints, causing painful swelling, especially in the toes and feet **2.** a large blob or clot of something, usually of blood [13C. Via French < Latin *gutta* 'drop of liquid'; from the belief that gout was caused by drops of a morbid fluid in the blood]

goutweed /gówt weed/ *n N Am* **PLANTS** same as **ground elder** [< its use in treating gout]

gouty /gówti/ (**-ier**, **-iest**) *adj* **1.** affected by or tending to contract gout **2.** resulting from or causing gout —**goutiness** *n*

gov *abbr* government organization (*used in Internet addresses*) See table at **domain name**

gov. /guv/ *abbr* **1.** government **2.** governor

~~govenor~~ incorrect spelling of **governor**

~~goverment~~ incorrect spelling of **government**

govern /gúvv'n/ (**-erns**, **-erning**, **-erned**) *v* **1.** *vti* **HAVE POLITICAL AUTHORITY** to be responsible officially for directing the affairs, policies, and economy of a state, country, or organization **2.** *vt* **CONTROL SOMETHING** to control, regulate, or direct something **3.** *vt* **HAVE INFLUENCE OVER SOMETHING** to have or exercise an influence over something ○ *issues that govern the final settlement* **4.** *vt* **RESTRAIN SOMETHING** to control something by restraint (*formal*) ○ *unable to govern her emotions* **5.** *vt* MECH ENG **CONTROL SPEED OF ENGINE** to maintain the speed of an engine or keep it from going above a specific level by controlling the fuel or steam supply **6.** *vt* LAW **BE LAW FOR SOMETHING** to be the defining rule for something **7.** *vt* GRAM **DETERMINE FORM OF WORD** to dictate the inflection, mood, or case of another word [13C. Via Old French *governer* and Latin *gubernare* < Greek *kubernan* 'steer'] —**governable** *adj*

governance /gúvv'nənss/ *n* **1. MANNER OF GOVERNMENT** the system or manner of government **2. STATE OF GOVERNING A PLACE** the act or state of governing a place **3. AUTHORITY** control or authority (*formal*)

governess /gúvvərnəss/ *n* especially formerly, a woman employed to teach children in their own homes, and sometimes also to care for the children [15C. < Old French *governeresse*, form of *governeour* 'governor']

governessy /gúvvərnəssi/ *adj* like a strict or prim governess

governing body /gúvv'ning-/ *n* a group of people appointed to supervise and regulate a field of activity or institution

government /gúvv'nmənt/ *n* **1. POLITICAL AUTHORITY** a group of people who have the power to make and enforce laws for a country or area **2. STYLE OF GOVERNMENT** a type of political system **3. THE STATE VIEWED AS RULER** the state and its administration viewed as the ruling political power **4. BRANCH OF GOVERNMENT** a branch or agency of a government, taken as the whole (*informal*) **5. CONTROL OF SOMETHING** the management or control of something **6.** EDUC **POLITICAL SCIENCE** political science as a subject of study **7.** GRAM **DETERMINATION OF INFLECTION** the determination of the inflection, mood, or case of a word by another word —**government** *adj* —**governmental** /gúvv'n mént'l/ *adj* —**governmentally** *adv*

USAGE Singular or plural? Like many collective nouns, *government* can be used with a singular or plural construction, depending on whether the emphasis is on the government as a body making joint decisions or on the individuals that constitute it.

governmentalize /gúvv'n mént'l īz/ (**-izes**, **-izing**, **-ized**), **governmentalise** (**-ises**, **-ising**, **-ised**) *vt* to put a sphere of activity under the power of the government

governmentese /gúvv'nmən teez/ *n* language that is full of difficult jargon, thought to be characteristic of language used by governments

Government House *n* in Australia, the official residence of the Governor-General

governor /gúvv'nər/ *n* **1. GOVERNING OFFICIAL** an appointed or elected official who governs a state, colony, or province for a specific term **2. GOVERNING BODY MEMBER** a member of a governing body of an institution **3. PRINCIPAL PRISON OFFICER** the principal officer in charge of a prison. N Am term **warden**[1] **4. REPRESENTATIVE OF BRITISH CROWN IN AUSTRALIA** the representative of the British crown in Australia at the level of state government. The governor must officially approve all legislation passed by the state parliament. **5.**

AUTHORITY FIGURE an authority figure, e.g. an employer or boss (*informal*) **6.** MECH ENG **REGULATING DEVICE** a device for regulating the speed of an engine — **governorship** *n*

governorate /gúvv'nərət/ *n* **1.** an administrative district of a country controlled by a governor ○ *Al Qayrawan Governorate* **2.** the condition of being a governor, or the term of office of a governor

governor general (*plural* **governors general** or **governor generals**) *n* **1.** the representative of the British Crown in some countries of the Commonwealth of Nations **2.** a governor who has authority over deputy governors —**governor-generalship** *n*

Governors Island /gúvv'nərz \ʻlʻlənd/ island in New York Bay, just south of the tip of Manhattan Island, that was used as a military post until the 19th century. Area: 70 hectares/173 acres.

govt *abbr* government

gowan /gów ən/ *n Scotland* any yellow or white field flower, especially a daisy [Late 16C. Probably alteration of *golland* 'buttercup' < N Germanic]

Gower Peninsula /gówər-/ rocky peninsula on the coast of Swansea district, southern Wales. Length: 24 km/15 mi.

gowk /gowk/ *n regional* an offensive term for somebody considered unintelligent or awkward (*insult*) [14C. < Old Norse *gaukr* 'cuckoo']

gown /gown/ *n* **1.** ELEGANT DRESS a woman's full-length elegant or formal dress for special occasions **2.** LONG ROBE a long robe, often dark in colour, worn on official occasions by people such as judges, professors, university graduates, and barristers **3.** LOOSE OUTER GARMENT a loose cloak or robe worn, e.g. by surgeons, to protect clothes **4.** EDUC MEMBERS OF A UNIVERSITY the members of a university, regarded as distinct from the rest of a town's population ■ *vt* (**gowns, gowning, gowned**) PUT GOWN ON SOMEBODY to dress somebody in a loose robe [14C. Via Old French *goune* < late Latin *gunna* 'fur or leather garment']

gownsman /gównzmən/ (*plural* **-men** /-mən/) *n* a man, e.g. an academic, who wears a gown for professional reasons (*dated*)

goy /goy/ (*plural* **goyim** /góy im/ or **goys**) *n* **1.** an offensive term for somebody who is not Jewish **2.** a Jewish name for an unintelligent man or boy (*insult*) [Mid-19C. Via Yiddish < Hebrew *gōy* '(non-Jewish) nation or people'] —**goyish** *adj*

Francisco de Goya: self-portrait

Barnaby's

Goya /góy ə/, **Francisco de** (1746–1828) Spanish painter. One of the greatest Spanish masters, he was known for his naturalistic tapestry designs, portraits, and several series of satirical etchings, including *The Caprices* (1797–99). Full name **Goya y Lucientes, Francisco José de**

goyim JUDAISM plural of **goy** (*offensive*)

gozzan *n* GEOL same as **gossan**

gp *abbr* Guadeloupe (*used in Internet addresses*) See table at **domain name**

GP[1] *n* a doctor who deals with patients' general medical problems, either at a surgery or, sometimes, at patients' homes. Full form **general practitioner**

GP[2] *abbr* **1.** MUSIC general pause **2.** HEALTH SERVICES general practice **3.** SPORTS Grand Prix

GPI *n* a condition that occurs in the late stages of syphilis and is characterized by dementia, speech difficulty, and inability to move. Full form **general paralysis of the insane**

GPMU *abbr* Graphical, Paper, and Media Union

GPO *abbr* HIST, MAIL General Post Office

GPRS *n* a system that provides immediate and continuous access to the Internet from wireless devices such as mobile phones. Full form **general packet radio service**

gps *abbr* MEASURE gallons per second

GPS[1] *n* a worldwide navigation system that uses information received from orbiting satellites. Full form **Global Positioning System**

GPS[2] *abbr Aus* EDUC Greater Public Schools

GPU *n* the Soviet secret police, from 1922 to 1923 [< Russian *Gosudarstvennoe politicheskoe upravlenie* 'State Political Directorate']

gq *abbr* Equatorial Guinea (*used in Internet addresses*) See table at **domain name**

gr *abbr* Greece (*used in Internet addresses*) See table at **domain name**

gr. *abbr* **1.** grade **2.** MEASURE grain **3.** MEASURE gram[1] **4.** MEASURE gross

Gr. *abbr* **1.** Greece **2.** PEOPLES, LANG Greek

GR8 *abbr* ONLINE great (*used in e-mails or text messages*)

Graafian follicle /gráafi ən-/ *n* a small fluid-filled sac (**vesicle**) containing a maturing ovum. Graafian follicles are found in the ovaries of mammals. [Mid-19C. After Regnier de *Graaf* (1641–73), Dutch anatomist]

grab /grab/ *v* (**grabs, grabbing, grabbed**) **1.** *vt* GRASP SOMETHING to take hold of something quickly, suddenly, or forcefully ○ *Grab a pen and sit down.* **2.** *vti* TRY TO GRASP to try to grasp something that is hard to reach or in short supply ○ *Stop grabbing or I won't give you any.* **3.** *vt* SEIZE SOMETHING to take something violently or dishonestly ○ *grab the money and run* **4.** *vt* HAVE EMOTIONAL IMPACT ON SOMEBODY to appeal to, attract, impress, or affect somebody emotionally (*informal*) ○ *The film didn't really grab me.* **5.** *vt* HURRIEDLY GET SOMETHING to obtain something quickly and without difficulty (*informal*) ○ *I'll just grab a bite to eat.* **6.** *vi N Am* TAKE HOLD SUDDENLY to take hold suddenly or intermittently ○ *The brakes grabbed and the car went into a skid.* ■ *n* **1.** GRABBING the act of grabbing something ○ *He made a grab at my arm.* **2.** SOMETHING GRABBED something that is grabbed **3.** DEVICE FOR GRABBING an apparatus or device used for grasping hold of something **4.** GRABBING ABILITY the ability or capacity to hold something fast [Late 16C. Probably < Middle Dutch or Middle Low German *grabben*] —**grabbable** *adj* — **grabber** *n* ◇ **up for grabs** available for the first comer to take or use (*informal*)

grab bag *n* **1.** something composed of miscellaneous or mismatched components (*informal*) **2.** *N Am* a box full of sealed bags containing unknown objects that can be purchased for a fixed price or are the prize in a party game

grab bar *n* a bar attached to a wall to provide a grip, e.g. near a bath or next to a toilet, for people who have difficulty in standing up

grabbing /grábbing/ *adj* with a character or way of behaving typified by constant attempts to obtain a large amount of something, especially money or something abstract like people's attention (*usually used in combination*)

grabble /grább'l/ (**-bles, -bling, -bled**) *vi* **1.** to scratch or search about with the hands **2.** to tumble or fall to the ground on all fours [Late 16C. Probably < Dutch *grabbelen* < *grabben* 'grab'] —**grabbler** *n*

grabby /grábbi/ (**-bier, -biest**) *adj* pushy and grasping (*informal disapproving*) —**grabbiness** *n*

graben /graabən/ *n* a broad valley, especially a rift valley [Late 19C. < German *Graben* 'ditch']

Grable /gráyb'l/, **Betty** (1916–73) US actor, dancer, and singer. She was a star of musical films in the 1940s. Full name **Grable, Elizabeth Ruth**

> 'There are two reasons why I am successful in show business and I am standing on both of them.'
> [Attributed to Betty Grable]

grab rail *n* SAFETY same as **grab bar**

Gracchus /grákəss/, **Gaius Sempronius** (153–121 BC) Roman politician and social reformer. During his two terms as tribune (123 and 122 BC), he sought to enforce the land reforms championed by his brother, Tiberius. He failed to get re-elected a third time and was found dead shortly afterwards.

Gracchus, Tiberius Sempronius (163–133 BC) Roman politician and social reformer. Popular with farmers and poorer members of society, he served as tribune (133 BC) and introduced a bill for land reform. He was murdered during a riot following the senate's opposition to his standing for a second term as tribune.

grace /grayss/ *n* **1.** ELEGANCE elegance, beauty, and smoothness of form or movement **2.** POLITENESS dignified, polite, and decent behaviour ○ *She fended off queries with her usual grace.* **3.** GENEROSITY OF SPIRIT a capacity to tolerate, accommodate, or forgive people **4.** PRAYER AT MEALTIMES a short prayer of thanks to God said before, or sometimes after, a meal **5.** FIN same as **grace period 6.** PLEASING QUALITY a pleasing and admirable quality or characteristic (*usually used in the plural*) **7.** GIFT OF GOD TO HUMANKIND in Christianity, the infinite love, mercy, favour, and goodwill shown to humankind by God **8.** FREEDOM FROM SIN in Christianity, the condition of being free of sin, e.g. through repentance to God **9.** MUSIC same as **grace note** ■ *vt* (**graces, gracing, graced**) **1.** CONTRIBUTE PLEASINGLY TO SOMETHING to make a pleasing contribution to an event, often by attending it (*often ironic*) ○ *So good of you to grace us with your presence.* **2.** ADD ELEGANCE TO SOMETHING to add elegance, beauty, or charm to something **3.** ORNAMENT MUSIC to add ornamental or decorative notes to a piece of music [12C. Via Old French *grace* < Latin *gratia* < *gratus* 'pleasing'] ◇ **fall from grace** to lose a favoured or privileged position ◇ **with (a) bad grace** in a rude and bad-tempered way ◇ **with (a) good grace** in a polite and willing way

Grace *n* used as a title when addressing a duke, duchess, or archbishop

Grace /grayss/, **Patricia** (b. 1937) New Zealand writer. Her fiction weaves traditional Maori motifs into modern narratives, and includes *Potiki* (1986).

Grace, W. G. (1848–1915) British cricketer. The dominant player of the Victorian era, he played for Gloucestershire, London County, and England in his 43-year career, and remains one of the legends of the game. Full name **Grace, William Gilbert**

> 'They came to see me bat, not to see you bowl.'
> [Attributed to W. G. Grace]

grace-and-favour *n UK* a property, e.g. a flat, owned by the British monarch who allows somebody to live in it rent-free as a mark of special favour or gratitude

grace cup *n* a cup of wine or liquor passed round at the end of a meal for a final toast

graceful /gráyssf'l/ *adj* **1.** showing elegance, beauty, and smoothness of form or movement **2.** marked by poise, dignity, and politeness —**gracefully** *adv* —**gracefulness** *n*

graceless /gráyssləss/ *adj* **1.** lacking elegance in form or movement **2.** bad-mannered and undignified —**gracelessly** *adv* —**gracelessness** *n*

grace note *n* a note added to a piece of music as an embellishment, usually played quickly before a principal note and written smaller than a normal note on the page

grace period *n* the extra time allowed before having to pay a debt or complete a transaction

Graces /gráyssiz/ *n* in Greek mythology, three sister goddesses, Aglaia, Euphrosyne, and Thalia, who had the power to grant charm, happiness, and beauty

gracile /grássīl/ *adj* gracefully slender and slight (*literary*) [Early 17C. < Latin *gracilis*] —**gracileness** *n* — **gracility** /gra sílləti/ *n*

gracilis /grássiliss/, **gracilis muscle** *n* a muscle in the thigh

gracious /gráyshəss/ *adj* **1.** KIND AND POLITE full of tact, kindness, and politeness ○ *a gracious refusal* **2.** CONDESCENDINGLY POLITE condescendingly indulgent and generous to perceived inferiors **3.** ELEGANT luxurious and elegant ○ *gracious living* **4.** HAVING DIVINE GRACE displaying divine grace, mercy, or compassion ■ *interj* EXPRESSES SURPRISE used to express surprise, dismay, or indignation [13C. Via French < Latin *gratiosus* 'agreeable' < *gratia* (see GRACE)] —**graciously** *adv* —**graciousness** *n*

grackle /grák'l/ *n* **1.** a starling with mostly black feathers. Native to: Europe, Asia. Genera: *Gracula* or *Onychognathus.* **2.** a noisy blackbird with metallic black feathers and a long keel-shaped tail. Native to: North America. Genus: *Quiscalus.* [Late 18C. Via modern Latin *Gracula* < Latin *graculus* 'jackdaw']

grad /grad/ *n* EDUC same as **graduate** *n* (sense 2) (*informal*) [Shortening of GRADUATE]

grad. *abbr* **1.** MATHS, BIOL, PHYS gradient **2.** EDUC graduated

gradable /gráydəb'l/ *adj* **1.** capable of being graded **2.** describes an adjective or adverb capable of having a comparative and superlative form —**gradability** /gráydə bílləti/ *n*

gradate /grə dáyt/ (**-dates, -dating, -dated**) *v* **1.** *vti* to pass imperceptibly from one shade or degree of intensity to another, or cause something to do this **2.** *vt* to arrange something in steps, grades, or ranks [Mid-18C. Back-formation < GRADATION]

gradation /grə dáysh'n/ *n* **1.** SERIES OF DEGREES a series of gradual and progressive degrees, steps, or stages **2.** SINGLE DEGREE a degree, step, or stage in a gradual progression **3.** DISCRETE ARRANGEMENT the arrangement of something according to size, rank, or quality **4.** COLOUR CHANGE the gradual and progressive change from one colour or tone to another **5.** PHON VOWEL CHANGE a change in the length or quality of a vowel within a word, signifying a change in function such as tense or number **6.** GEOG LEVELLING OF LAND the process of levelling land by erosion or deposition of sediment [Late 16C. Directly or via French < Latin *gradation-* 'making steps' < *gradus* 'step, stage'] —**gradational** *adj* —**gradationally** *adv*

grade /grayd/ *n* **1.** LEVEL IN SCALE OF PROGRESSION a level, step, or stage in a scale of progression, quality, or size (*often used in combination*) ○ *low-grade ore* **2.** MARK SHOWING A LEVEL a mark that indicates a level, step, or stage in a process **3.** MARK FOR QUALITY OF WORK a mark given for work in school or college, usually using the descending scale of A, B, C, D, E, and F ○ *She got a good grade for her essay.* **4.** YEAR IN SCHOOL a class or year in the US and Canadian school systems ○ *She'll be in the tenth grade this year.* **5.** RANK a rank or class **6.** PEOPLE IN RANK a group of people of the same rank **7.** FOOD CLASSIFICATION a category indicating the relative quality of food as determined by the US Department of Agriculture ○ *grade A eggs* **8.** *N Am* GRADIENT a gradient or slope, especially on a road or railroad **9.** MATHS UNIT OF ANGLE a unit of angle equal to 0.9° **10.** PHON VOWEL FORM a form of vowel morpheme when a vowel varies owing to gradation ■ *vt* (**grades, grading, graded**) **1.** ARRANGE THINGS BY DEGREES to arrange or classify things or people according to rank, quality, or level **2.** MAKE ROAD LEVEL to level a road or railway by adjusting its gradients **3.** *N Am* ASSIGN GRADE TO SOMETHING to assign a mark or rating to something such as a student's work [Early 16C. Via French < Latin *gradus* 'step, stage'] ◇ **make the grade** to meet the required standard

ORIGIN The Latin word *gradus* 'step', from which ***grade*** is derived, and its related verb *gradi* 'to walk, go', are also the sources of English *aggression, congress, degrade, degree, digress, gradient, gradual, ingredient, progress, retrograde,* and *transgress.*

grade crossing *n N Am* RAIL, ROADS same as **level crossing**

graded sediment /gráydid-/ *n* a sediment deposited on land or the seabed in which there is an upward gradation of the grains from coarse to fine

grade inflation *n N Am* the assignment of higher than deserved marks to students' work in order to compensate for diminishing expectations and falling educational standards

gradely /gráydli/ *regional adj* decent, fine, and respectable ■ *adv* promptly and properly [13C. < Old Norse *greiðligr* < *greiðr* 'ready, prompt']

grade point average *n Aus, N Am* the average of a student's marks over a fixed period, calculated by assigning a value of 4 to A, 3 to B, 2 to C, 1 to D, and 0 to F

grader /gráydər/ *n* **1.** EARTH LEVELLER a machine with a wide blade that levels earth, used in road construction **2.** *N Am* STUDENT a student in a particular grade in school ○ *first graders* **3.** SOMEBODY OR SOMETHING THAT GRADES a person who or machine that grades something

grade school *n N Am* an elementary or primary school

gradient /gráydi ənt/ *n* **1.** STEEPNESS the rate at which the steepness of a slope increases **2.** SLOPE an upward or downward slope, e.g. in a road or railway **3.** PHYS MEASURE OF CHANGE a measure of change in a physical quantity such as temperature or pressure over a particular distance **4.** BIOL RATE OF GROWTH a change in a series of alterations in the rate of growth or metabolism of an organism, cell, or organ **5.** MATHS SLOPE ON CURVE the slope of a line or a tangent at any point on a curve ■ *adj* SLOPING sloping evenly and uniformly [Mid-17C. Partly < Latin *gradient-*, present participle of *gradi* 'walk' (< *gradus* 'step'), partly < GRADE after QUOTIENT]

gradient post *n* a small post with arms to represent gradients that is used beside a railway line to indicate where the gradient changes

gradin /gráydin/, **gradine** *n* **1.** a raised step above or behind an altar in a church **2.** one of a set of steps arranged on a slope [Mid-19C. Via French < Italian *gradino* 'small step' < *grado* 'step' < Latin *gradus*]

gradual /grájjoo əl/ *adj* **1.** HAPPENING SLOWLY proceeding or developing slowly by steps or degrees ○ *a gradual improvement* **2.** CHANGING SLOWLY changing slowly ○ *a gradual incline* ■ *n* CHR **1.** SUNG VERSES in some Christian services, a set of scriptural verses sung after the epistle at Communion **2.** RELIGIOUS MUSIC BOOK a book of music for the sung parts of the Communion service [15C. < medieval Latin *gradualis* < Latin *gradus* 'step, stage'] —**gradually** *adv* —**gradualness** *n*

gradualism /grájjoo əlizəm/ *n* **1.** the principle, theory, or policy of allowing change, especially political change, to take place gradually rather than suddenly or drastically **2.** the theory that change in rocks and fossils happens by a gradual historical process —**gradualist** *n, adj* —**gradualistic** /grájjoo ə lístik/ *adj*

graduand /grájjoo and/ *n* a student who is about to graduate from university [Late 19C. < medieval Latin *graduandus* 'somebody on whom a degree is being conferred' < *graduare* (see GRADUATE)]

graduate *n* /grájjoo ət/ **1.** HOLDER OF DEGREE somebody who has obtained a first degree from a university or college **2.** *N Am* SOMEBODY WHO HAS COMPLETED STUDIES somebody who has obtained a diploma or degree, e.g. from a high school **3.** *US* SCI CONTAINER WITH MARKINGS a container, e.g. a flask or tube, with graduated markings that is used for measuring liquids ■ *v* /grájjoo ayt/ (**-ates, -ating, -ated**) **1.** *vi* RECEIVE DEGREE to receive a degree from a university or college **2.** *vi* MOVE UP to move upwards from one level or activity to another ○ *I've graduated from skiing to snowboarding.* **3.** *vt* MARK SOMETHING WITH DEGREES OR LEVELS to mark something with units of measurement **4.** *vt* SORT THINGS BY DIFFERENCES to sort things into groups according to quality, size, or type ■ *adj* /grájjoo ət/ *N Am* EDUC same as **postgraduate** [15C. < medieval Latin *graduat-*, past participle of *graduare* 'confer a degree on' < Latin *gradus* 'step, stage'] —**graduator** *n*

graduated /grájjoo aytid/ *adj* **1.** IN STAGES divided into regular steps or stages **2.** MARKED WITH LINES marked with lines to enable measurement **3.** FIN BASED ON INCOME describes a system of taxation under which those with the greatest income or assets pay the highest percentage of tax

graduate school *n N Am* a university or university department for students who have obtained a first degree

graduation /grájjoo áysh'n/ *n* **1.** COMPLETION OF STUDIES the completion of a degree ○ *the number of credits required for graduation* **2.** DEGREE CEREMONY a ceremony in which degrees are awarded to students who have successfully completed their studies ○ *attended her grandson's graduation* **3.** MARK ON INSTRUMENT a unit of measurement or division marked on an instrument **4.** DIVIDING PROCESS the process of marking or dividing something according to quantity or quality

gradus /gráydəss/ *n* **1.** a book of musical exercises arranged in order of difficulty **2.** a dictionary designed to aid in writing Greek or Latin verse [Mid-18C. Shortening of *Gradus ad Parnassum* 'Steps to Parnassus', manual of Latin composition]

Graecism /grées izəm/, **Grecism** *n* **1.** an idiom of the Greek language used in another language, often for stylistic effect **2.** Greek style, spirit, or characteristics as expressed in Greek culture, arts, architecture, and philosophy [Late 16C. < medieval Latin *Græcismus* < Latin *Græcus* (see GREEK)]

Graecize /grées īz/ (**-cizes, -cizing, -cized**), **Graecise** (**-cises, -cising, -cised**), **Grecize**, **Grecise** *vt* to make something Greek or Hellenic in style or form so that it becomes characteristic of the culture, civilization, or language of the ancient Greeks

Graeco-, **Greco-** *prefix* Greece, Greek ○ *Graeco-Roman* [< Latin *Graecus* (see GREEK)]

Graeco-Roman /gréekō-/ *adj* **1.** relating to, or characteristic of, both ancient Greece and ancient Rome or the influence of their civilizations **2.** describes a style of wrestling allowing no hold below the waist and no use of the legs to obtain a fall

Graf /graaf/, **Steffi** (*b.* 1969) German tennis player. She turned professional at the age of 13, and went on to win 22 grand slam titles, including seven Wimbledon trophies. She retired from tennis in 1999.

> 'It doesn't hurt to lose my crown, it hurts to lose.'
> [Steffi Graf, *Independent*; 22 June 1994]

graffiti /grə féeti/ *n* drawings or words that are scratched, painted, or sprayed on walls or other surfaces in public places (*takes a singular or plural verb*) [Mid-19C. < Italian, plural of *graffito* (see GRAFFITO)]

USAGE graffito or **graffiti**? ***Graffito*** is an Italian borrowing into English, and its plural in Italian is ***graffiti***. It is acceptable, however, to use ***graffiti*** as a singular when the meaning is 'inscriptions in general': *Graffiti has marred the walls on this block for far too long*, though *Graffiti have marred the walls...* is the more technically appropriate. ***Graffiti*** is also regularly used as a singular to mean 'an inscription': *It's just another gang-related graffiti*, though ***graffito*** is the more technically correct term.

graffito /grə féet ō/ (*plural* **-ti** /-ti/) *n* **1.** an instance of graffiti scratched, painted, or sprayed on a surface (*formal*) **2.** an ancient drawing or inscription on a wall or rock surface [Mid-19C. < Italian, 'scribbling' < *graffio* 'scratching', via Latin *graphium* 'stylus' < Greek *grapheion* < *graphein* 'write']

USAGE See ***graffiti***.

~~**grafitti**~~ incorrect spelling of **graffiti**

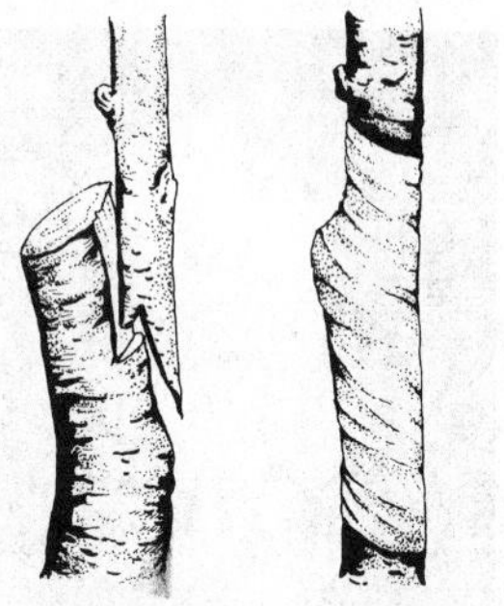

graft

graft[1] /graaft/ *n* **1.** TRANSPLANTED TISSUE a piece of living tissue or an organ that is transplanted to a patient's body, either from a donor or from another part of the patient's body. Grafts are used to replace damaged or diseased tissue or organs. **2.** PLANT TISSUE JOINED TO ANOTHER PLANT a piece of living tissue from the shoot of a plant that is joined to the stem and root system of another plant, resulting in the growth of a single plant **3.** GRAFT LOCATION the place where tissue is implanted by means of a graft **4.** GRAFTED PLANT a plant that is the product of a graft **5.** JOINING PROCESS the process of joining one thing to another ■ *vt* (**grafts, grafting, grafted**) **1.** TRANSPLANT TISSUE to transplant a piece of living tissue or an organ to a part of a patient's body. The tissue or organ may be either from a donor or from another part of the patient's body. **2.** UNITE PLANT TISSUE to join a piece of tissue from a part of one plant to the stem and root system of another plant to produce desirable characteristics such as vigour or resistance to disease in the new plant **3.** JOIN DISSIMILAR THINGS to join two things that do not share a natural relationship or affinity for each other [15C. Via Old

French *grafe* 'pencil' (from a similarity with the shoot of a plant) < late Latin *graphium* (see GRAFFITO)] —**grafter** *n*

graft[2] /graaft/ *n* **1.** WORK hard work (*informal*) **2.** CORRUPT ACTIONS OF OFFICIAL the use of dishonest or illegal means to gain money or property by somebody in a position of power or in elected office **3.** MONEY OBTAINED CORRUPTLY something obtained illegally by taking advantage of high position or office ■ *v* (**grafts, grafting, grafted**) (*informal*) **1.** *vi* TO WORK to work hard **2.** *vti* GET BY DECEIT to obtain money or property by deceit [Mid-19C. Origin ?] —**grafter** *n*

Grafton /graáftən/ city in northeastern New South Wales, Australia. It is an agricultural and regional service centre. Population: 17,341 (2002 estimate).

Graham /gráy əm/, **Billy** (*b.* 1918) US evangelist. A charismatic preacher, he has held large-scale evangelistic rallies throughout the United States and Europe since 1949. Full name **Graham, William Franklin**

'Heaven is full of answers to prayers for which no one ever bothered to ask.'
[Billy Graham, *Encounter Weekly*; 1996]

Katharine Graham

Graham, Katharine (1917–2001) US newspaper executive. She was publisher of *The Washington Post* (1969–79). Born **Meyer, Katharine**

'If we had failed to pursue the facts as far as they led, we would have denied the public any knowledge of an unprecedented scheme of political surveillance and sabotage.'
[Katharine Graham. On *The Washington Post*'s investigative reportage of the Watergate scandal, *The Washington Post*; 5 March 1973]

Martha Graham: performing in *Judith* (1957)

Graham, Martha (1893–1991) US dancer, choreographer, and teacher. The most influential figure in modern dance, she created a dance language using flexible movements intended to express emotional power.

'Every dance is a kind of fever chart of the heart…it makes visible the interior landscape.'
[Martha Graham, Recalled on her death; 1 April 1991]

graham cracker /gráy əm-/ *n N Am* a flat dry sweetened biscuit, light brown in colour and made from graham flour [see GRAHAM FLOUR]

Grahame /gráy əm/, **Kenneth** (1859–1932) British writer. He wrote the children's classic *The Wind in the Willows* (1908). See Cultural note at **willow**

'There is nothing—absolutely nothing—half so much worth doing as simply messing about in boats.'
[Kenneth Grahame, *The Wind in the Willows*; 1908]

graham flour *n N Am* unsifted whole-wheat flour [After Dr Sylvester *Graham* (1794–1851), American dietary reformer]

Graham Land northern section of the Antarctic Peninsula, part of the British Antarctic Territory

Graham's law *n* a law in chemistry relating the diffusion rate of a gas to the inverse square root of its density [After Thomas *Graham* (1805–69), Scottish chemist]

Grahamstown /gráy əmz town/ city in Eastern Cape Province, southern South Africa, situated about 100 km/60 mi. northeast of Port Elizabeth. Population: 19,783 (1991).

grail /grayl/ *n* something that is eagerly sought [Late 19C. < GRAIL]

Grail /grayl/ *n* according to medieval legend, the cup said to have been used by Jesus Christ at the Last Supper, and by Joseph of Arimathea to collect his blood and sweat at the Crucifixion. It was sought by medieval knights. [14C. Via Old French *grael* < medieval Latin *gradalis* 'dish']

grain /grayn/ *n* **1.** CEREALS cereal crops **2.** SMALL SEED a small hard seed **3.** TINY SINGLE PIECE a tiny individual piece of something such as sand or salt **4.** SMALL AMOUNT a tiny amount of something ○ *He doesn't have one grain of common sense!* **5.** PATTERN IN MATERIAL the arrangement, direction, or pattern of the fibres in wood, leather, stone, or paper, typically aligned along a single axis ○ *When painting, follow the grain of the wood.* **6.** PHOTOGRAPHIC PARTICLE a particle forming part of a photographic emulsion on whose size the extent of possible enlargement depends **7.** SIDE OF LEATHER the side of leather from which hair has been removed **8.** CHEM SMALL CRYSTAL a small crystal, especially one forming part of a crystalline solid **9.** BASIC QUALITY the basic quality or characteristic of something or somebody **10.** TEXTILES DIRECTION OF THREADS the line of the threads in a fabric **11.** MEASURE UNIT OF WEIGHT the smallest unit of weight in the avoirdupois (1/7000 pound) and apothecaries' systems (1/5760 pound), equal to approximately 0.065 grams **12.** INTERFERENCE AFFECTING TELEVISION IMAGE the granular effect on a television image caused by unwanted electrical signals **13.** PROPELLANT FOR ROCKET a mass of solid propellant for a rocket or missile **14.** DYE red or purple dye made from cochineal insects (*archaic*) ■ *v* (**grains, graining, grained**) **1.** *vti* GRANULATE to break down into small particles or grains, or make something break down into small particles **2.** *vt* MIMIC PATTERN OF WOOD to paint or stain a material with a pattern similar to wood or leather **3.** *vt* TREAT LEATHER to soften or raise the pattern of leather **4.** *vt* REMOVE HAIR FROM LEATHER to remove the hair from leather **5.** *vt* GIVE SOMETHING GRAINY APPEARANCE to give something a rough or granular appearance **6.** *vt* GIVE GRAIN TO ANIMAL to feed grain to an animal [13C. Via French < Latin *granum* 'seed'] —**grained** *adj* —**grainer** *n* —**grainless** *adj* ◇ **go against the grain** to be contrary to somebody's natural inclinations, wishes, or feelings

ORIGIN The Latin word *granum* 'seed', from which *grain* is derived, is also the source of English *filigree, garner, granary, grange, granite, gravy, ingrain,* and *pomegranate*. Its Indo-European ancestor in turn gave rise to English *corn*[1].

grain alcohol *n* alcohol made from a fermented cereal

grainfield /gráyn feeld/ *n* a field in which grain is grown

Grainger /gráynjər/, **Percy** (1882–1961) Australian-born US pianist and composer. His 400 compositions, many based on folk music, include *Green Bushes* (1905–21) and *Shepherds Hey* (1908–22). Born **Grainger, George Percy**. Full name **Grainger, Percy Aldridge**

grains of paradise *npl* the peppery brown seeds of a western African plant. Use: to add piquancy to mulled wine and other drinks, formerly, in veterinary medicine.

grain whisky *n* whisky that is made from any fermented cereal other than malted barley

grainy /gráyni/ (**-ier, -iest**) *adj* **1.** NOT CLEAR describes a photograph that is unclear and poorly defined because of a large grain size or overenlargement **2.** RESEMBLING GRAINS resembling or composed of grains **3.** NOT SMOOTH having a granular rather than a smooth texture **4.** LIKE WOOD GRAIN resembling the grain of wood, leather, stone, or paper —**graininess** *n*

grallatorial /grállə táwri əl/ *adj* describes a bird with long legs adapted for wading [Mid-19C. < modern Latin *grallatorius* < Latin *grallator* 'stilt-walker' < *grallae* 'stilts']

gram[1] /gram/, **gramme** *n* a metric unit of mass, equal to 0.001 kg or equivalent to approximately 0.035 oz. Symbol **g** [Late 18C. Via French *gramme* and late Latin *gramma* < Greek *gramma* 'small weight']

gram[2] /gram/ *n* an edible legume, e.g. chickpea, lentil, or mung bean [Early 18C. Via obsolete Portuguese < Latin *granum* 'seed']

gram. *abbr* GRAM **1.** grammar **2.** grammatical

-gram *suffix* **1.** something written, drawn, or recorded ○ *trigram* **2.** a message delivered by a third party ○ *telegram* ○ *kissagram* [< Greek *gramma* 'something written']

grama /graámə/, **gramma** /grámmə/, **grama grass, gramma grass** *n* a pasture grass that grows in western North America and South America. Genus: *Bouteloua*. [Mid-19C. Via American Spanish < Latin *gramen* 'grass']

gram atom *n* a quantity of a chemical element whose mass in grams is the same as its atomic weight

gram calorie *n* MEASURE same as **calorie** (sense 1)

gram equivalent *n* the quantity of a substance whose mass in grams is the same as its chemical equivalent weight

gram flour *n* a gluten-free flour, used in South Asian cookery, that is usually made from ground chickpeas and is pale yellow in colour [< GRAM[2]]

gramicidin /grámmi sídin/, **gramicidin D** *n* a toxic antibiotic applied externally in creams and drops [Mid-20C. < GRAM-POSITIVE + -CIDE]

gramineous /grə mínni əss/, **graminaceous** /grámmi náyshəss/ *adj* **1.** belonging to the grass family **2.** resembling grass (*technical*) [Mid-17C. < Latin *gramineus* < *gramin-*, stem of *gramen* 'grass'] —**gramineousness** *n*

graminivorous /grámmi nívvərəss/ *adj* feeding on grass (*technical*) [Mid-18C. < Latin *gramin-* (see GRAMINEOUS)]

gramma *n* PLANTS, BOT same as **grama**

grammar /grámmər/ *n* **1.** RULES FOR LANGUAGE the system of rules by which words are formed and put together to make sentences **2.** PARTICULAR SET OF LANGUAGE RULES the rules for speaking or writing a particular language, or an analysis of the rules of a particular aspect of language ○ *Spanish grammar* ○ *case grammar* **3.** QUALITY OF LANGUAGE the spoken or written form of language that somebody uses with regard to accepted standards of correctness ○ *bad grammar* **4.** GRAMMAR BOOK a book dealing with the grammar of a language **5.** ANALYTICAL SYSTEM a systematic treatment of the elementary principles of a subject and their interrelationships [14C. Via Old French *gramaire* and Latin *grammatica* < Greek *grammatikos* 'relating to letters' < *grammat-*, stem of *gramma* 'written character, letter']

grammarian /grə máiri ən/ *n* **1.** somebody who is skilled in grammar **2.** a writer on grammar, especially one who espouses prescriptive rules

grammar school *n* **1.** in the United Kingdom and some Commonwealth countries, a state secondary school teaching children who are traditionally selected for high academic ability **2.** *US* EDUC same as **elementary school**

grammatical /grə máttik'l/ *adj* **1.** relating to the rules of grammar **2.** conforming to the accepted rules of grammar [Early 16C. < late Latin *grammaticalis* < Greek *grammatikos* (see GRAMMAR)] —**grammaticality** /grə mátti kálləti/ *n* —**grammatically** *adv* —**grammaticalness** *n*

grammatology /grámmə tólləji/ *n* the study of writing systems [Mid-20C. < Greek *grammat-* 'written character' (see GRAMMAR)] —**grammatologic** /grámmətə lójjik/ *adj* —**grammatological** *adj* —**grammatologist** *n*

gramme *n* MEASURE another spelling of **gram**[1]

~~grammer~~ incorrect spelling of **grammar**

gram molecule *n* a quantity of a molecular chemical

compound whose mass in grams is the same as its molecular weight —**gram-molecular** *adj*

Grammy /grámmi/ *tdmk* a trademark for an award given annually for achievement in the recorded music industry

Gram-negative, **gram-negative** *adj* describes bacteria that lose the colour of a gentian violet stain when subjected to Gram's method of classifying bacteria

gramophone /grámmə fōn/ *n* RECORDING same as **record player** (*dated*) [Late 19C. Alteration of PHONOGRAM]

grampa /grám paa/ *n* same as **grandfather** (*informal*; *usually used by or to children*) [Contraction of GRANDPA]

Grampian Mountains /grámpi ən-/ mountain range in central Scotland that forms a natural division between the Highlands and Lowlands. The highest peak is Ben Nevis, 1,343 m/4,406 ft.

Grampian Region former region in northeastern Scotland that included the present-day council areas of Aberdeenshire and Moray

Grampians /grámpi ənz/ **1.** same as **Grampian Mountains 2.** group of rugged red sandstone mountains in western Victoria, Australia. The highest peak is Mount William, 1,168 m/3,832 ft.

Grampians National Park national park in western Victoria, Australia, established in 1984. It contains the Grampians. Area: 1,670 sq. km/645 sq. mi.

Gram-positive, **gram-positive** *adj* describes bacteria that retain the colour of a gentian violet stain when subjected to Gram's method of classifying bacteria

gramps /gramps/ *n* (*informal*) **1.** same as **grandfather** (*usually used by or to children*) **2.** a disrespectful term of address for a man of advanced years [< contraction of GRANDPA]

grampus /grámpəss/ (*plural same or* **-puses**) *n* a large grey dolphin with a blunt snout, short flippers, and a tall dark grey fin. Native to: warm seas. Latin name: *Grampus griseus*. [Early 16C. Alteration of Old French *graspeis* < medieval Latin *crassus piscis* 'fat fish']

Gram's method /grámz-/, **Gram's stain** *n* a technique used to classify bacteria according to their ability to lose or retain the colour of a gentian violet stain, applied within the framework of an established test procedure. The retention or loss of stain indicates a particular cell-wall structure and distinguishes two types of bacteria. [Late 19C. After H. C. J. *Gram* (1853–1938), Danish physician]

gran /gran/ *n* same as **grandmother** (*informal*; *usually used by or to children*) [Mid-19C. Shortening]

grana BIOL plural of **granum**

Granada /grə naádə/ city and capital of Granada Province in the autonomous region of Andalusia, southern Spain. It is the site of the Alhambra, a Moorish palace and citadel. Population: 240,522 (2002).

granadilla /gránnə díllə/ *n* **1.** a purple egg-shaped passion fruit **2.** a passionflower that produces granadillas. Native to: tropical regions. Latin name: *Passiflora quadrangularis*. [Early 17C. < Spanish, 'little pomegranate' < *granada* 'pomegranate']

granary /gránnəri/ (*plural* **-ries**) *n* **1.** a warehouse or storeroom for grain **2.** a region where grain is abundant [Late 16C. < Latin *granarium* < *granum* 'seed']

Granary /gránnəri/ *tdmk* trademark for bread that contains whole grains of wheat and has a nutty flavour

Gran Chaco /gran chákō/ thinly populated region in south-central South America, extending from southern Bolivia through Paraguay to northern Argentina. Area: 647,500 sq. km/250,000 sq. mi.

grand /grand/ *adj* **1.** OUTSTANDING outstanding and impressive in appearance, extent, or style ○ *making a grand entrance* **2.** IMPRESSIVE impressive, ambitious, and far-reaching ○ *a grand plan* **3.** WORTHY OF RESPECT worthy of great respect by virtue of exceptional ability or high rank ○ *among the grandest orchestras of our time* **4.** HAUGHTY self-important or haughty ○ *His friends always act a bit grand around her.* **5.** WONDERFUL wonderful, enjoyable, and memorable ○ *We had a grand time.* **6.** PRINCIPAL main or principal ○ *And now we move into the Grand Banqueting Hall.* **7.** TERRIFIC respected and admirable (*informal*) ○ *She's a grand lass.* ■ *n* (*informal*) **1.** (*plural same*) MONEY **1,000 POUNDS** a thousand pounds ○ *made ten grand on the deal* **2.** MUSIC same as **grand piano** [Early 16C. Via

Old French < Latin *grandis* 'great, full grown'] —**grandly** *adv* —**grandness** *n*

grand- *prefix* one generation further removed ○ *grandniece* ○ *grandfather* ■ *n US* one thousand (*informal*) [< GRAND]

granda /grán daa/ *n UK regional, Ireland, Scotland* same as **grandfather** (*informal*) [Variant of GRANDDAD]

grandad *n* another spelling of **granddad** (*informal*)

grandaddy *n* another spelling of **granddaddy** (*informal*)

grandam /grándəm/, **grandame** *n* a grandmother, or a woman who is no longer young (*archaic*) [13C. < Anglo-Norman *graund dame* 'grandmother']

~~grandaughter~~ incorrect spelling of **granddaughter**

grand-aunt *n* same as **great-aunt**

grandbaby /gránd baybi/ *n* a grandchild who is still a baby

Grand Bahama /gránd bə haámə/ island of the western Bahamas in the Atlantic Ocean off the eastern coast of Florida. Population: 40,898 (1990). Area: 1,114 sq. km/430 sq. mi.

Grand Banks shallow section of the Atlantic Ocean, off southeastern Newfoundland, Canada, that is an important fishing region. Area: 282,500 sq. km/109,100 sq. mi.

Grand Canal main thoroughfare of Venice, Italy. There are almost 200 palaces on the banks of the canal. Length: 3 km/2 mi.

Grand Canyon

Grand Canyon spectacular natural gorge carved by the Colorado River in northwestern Arizona. Its width varies from 8 to 29 km/5 to 18 mi., and its depth can exceed 1.6 km/1 mi. Length: 446 km/277 mi.

Grand Canyon National Park national park in northern Arizona, established in 1919. Its primary feature is the Grand Canyon of the Colorado River. Area: 4,927 sq. km/1,902 sq. mi.

grandchild /grán chīld/ (*plural* **-children** /-children/) *n* a child of a son or daughter

Grand Coulee Dam /-koóli-/ dam in Washington State on the Columbia River, 145 km/90 mi. west of Spokane. Completed in 1942, it is the world's largest concrete structure and a major source of hydroelectric power. Height: 168 m/550 ft.

granddad /grán dad/, **grandad** *n* (*informal*) **1.** same as **grandfather 2.** a disrespectful term of address for a man of advanced years

granddaddy /grán dadi/ (*plural* **-dies**), **grandaddy** *n* (*informal*) **1.** same as **grandfather 2.** something considered the oldest, first, or most important of its time

granddaughter /grán dawtər/ *n* a daughter of a son or daughter

grand duchess *n* **1.** GRAND DUKE'S SPOUSE the wife or widow of a grand duke **2.** NOBLEWOMAN OF HIGH RANK a woman who holds a rank above that of duchess **3.** RUSSIAN PRINCESS in tsarist Russia, a daughter of a tsar or of a tsar's descendants

grand duchy *n* a country, territory, or estate that has a grand duke or a grand duchess as its ruler

grand duke *n* **1.** a nobleman who holds a rank above that of a duke **2.** in tsarist Russia, a brother, son, uncle, or nephew of a tsar

grande dame /graaNd dám/ *n* a socially important, dignified woman, usually in later life [< French, 'great lady']

Grande Dixence Dam /gránd díks'nss-/ concrete dam on the River Dixence, southwestern Switzerland. Completed in 1962, it is one of the world's highest dams. Height: 284 m/932 ft.

grandee /gran deé/ *n* **1.** somebody highly influential and respected, especially a politician **2.** a high-ranking Spanish or Portuguese nobleman [Late 16C. Via Spanish and Portuguese *grande* < Latin *grandis* 'great']

grandeur /gránjər/ *n* the quality of being great or grand and very impressive [Early 16C. < French < *grand* (see GRAND)]

grandfather /gránd faathər/ *n* **1.** PARENT'S FATHER the father of a father or mother **2.** ANCESTOR a man who is an ancestor **3.** DISRESPECTFUL TERM OF ADDRESS a disrespectful term of address for a man of advanced years (*dated informal*) **4.** W Country same as **woodlouse** (*informal*) —**grandfatherly** *adj*

grandfather clause *n* **1.** a clause in prohibitive legislation that makes exceptions for those already engaged in the activity that it bans or regulates **2.** a clause in some Southern US states' constitutions, subsequently declared unconstitutional, that waived electoral literacy requirements for descendants of those allowed to vote before 1867. In effect it enabled illiterate white people to vote, while excluding illiterate Black people.

grandfather clock

grandfather clock *n* a large clock in a tall case that stands on the floor

grand final *n* the last round in a series of contests, competitions, or sports matches

grand finale *n* the closing spectacular scene or section of a performance or other show

Grand Guignol /gaáN gee nyōl/ *n* a sensational drama, often structured in short scenes with violent or horrific subject matter, that aims to horrify its audience [Early 20C. < *Le Grand Guignol*, theatre in Paris] —**grand guignol** *adj*

grandiloquence /gran dílləkwənss/ *n* a pompous or lofty manner of speaking or writing [Late 16C. < Latin *grandiloquus* 'speaking grandly' < *grandis* 'great' + *loqui* 'speak'] —**grandiloquent** *adj* —**grandiloquently** *adv*

grandiose /grándi ōss/ *adj* **1.** PRETENTIOUS AND POMPOUS pretentious, pompous, and imposing **2.** MAGNIFICENT impressive and magnificent **3.** TOO COMPLEX excessively complicated and unrealistic ○ *a grandiose plan* [Mid-19C. Via French < Italian *grandioso* 'imposing' < *grande* 'great' < Latin *grandis*] —**grandiosely** *adv* —**grandiosity** /grándi óssəti/ *n*

grandioso /grándi óss ō/ *adv* in a grand or imposing style (*used as a musical direction*) [Late 19C. < Italian, 'grandly'] —**grandioso** *adj*

grand jury *n* in US and Canadian law, a panel of 12 to 23 jurors called to decide whether there are grounds for a criminal prosecution in a case —**grand juror** *n*

grandkid /grán kid/ *n* same as **grandchild** (*informal*)

grand larceny *n* a robbery or theft of money or property with a value over the amount specified by law to constitute petty larceny

grandma /grán maa/ *n* (*informal*) **1.** same as **grandmother 2.** a disrespectful term of address for a woman of advanced years [Late 18C. Shortening]

grand mal /graán mál/ *n* a serious form of epilepsy in which there is loss of consciousness and severe convulsions [< French, 'great illness']

grandmama /gránmə maa/ *n* same as **grandmother** (*dated*)

Grand Manan Island /-mə nán-/ island at the entrance to the Bay of Fundy in southwestern New Brunswick, southeastern Canada. Population: 3,000. Area: 137 sq. km/53 sq. mi.

grand master, grandmaster /grán maastər/ *n* **1.** TOP CHESS PLAYER a champion chess player who plays at an international level **2.** SOMEBODY OUTSTANDING somebody at the top of a particular field in ability or achievement **3.** GROUP HEAD the head of a brotherhood of knights or of a fraternal organization such as the Masons

grandmother /grán muthər/ *n* **1.** PARENT'S MOTHER the mother of a father or mother **2.** ANCESTOR a woman who is an ancestor **3.** DISRESPECTFUL TERM OF ADDRESS a disrespectful term of address for a woman of advanced years (*dated informal*) —**grandmotherly** *adj*

grandmother clock *n* a clock in a tall case that stands on the floor, smaller than a grandfather clock

Grand National *n* a famous British steeplechase, held annually at Aintree in Liverpool since 1839. Competitors have to negotiate 31 fences around a 7.2 km/4 mi. 855 yd racecourse.

grandnephew /grán nef yoo/ *n* US same as **great-nephew**

grandniece /grán neess/ *n* US same as **great-niece**

grand old man *n* a man, usually past middle age, who is respected for his contribution to some field of activity such as politics, music, or sport ○ *the grand old man of British jazz*

grand opera *n* an opera on a serious dramatic theme in which all the words are sung and there is no spoken dialogue

grandpa /grán paa/ *n* (*informal*) **1.** same as **grandfather** **2.** a disrespectful term of address for a man of advanced years

grandpapa /gránpə paa/ *n* same as **grandfather** (*dated*)

grandparent /gránd pairənt/ *n* the mother or father of a mother or father —**grandparental** /gránd pə rént'l/ *adj* —**grandparenthood** *n*

grand piano

grand piano *n* a large piano in which the strings are fixed horizontally behind the keyboard in a long harp-shaped frame

Grand Pré /gron práy, graaN-/ village in central Nova Scotia, Canada, on Minas Basin, the site of Grand Pré National Historic Park

Grand Prix /grón prée/ (*plural same* or **Grands Prix** /*pronunc. same*/) *n* **1.** any of a number of important international annual races for racing cars, held to decide the world motor-racing championship **2.** any of various competitions in a variety of sports that have the same importance and prestige as a Grand Prix in motor-racing [< French, 'big prize']

Grand Rapids /-ráppidz/ city on the Grand River in west-central Michigan. An important furniture-manufacturing centre since the 19th century, it is also home to the Ford Presidential Museum. Population: 196,595 (1998).

Grand Remonstrance *n* a document issued by the Long Parliament in 1640 that listed problems with the King's government, abuses of power already rectified, and desired reforms

grandsire /grán sīr/ *n* **1.** same as **grandfather** (*archaic*) **2.** in bell-ringing, a method of change-ringing using an odd number of bells

grand slam *n* **1.** WINNING OF ALL MAJOR COMPETITIONS in sports such as tennis and golf, the winning of all of a series of major competitions by one player or team in one year **2.** MAJOR COMPETITION in sports such as tennis and golf, a major competition that is part of a series **3.** CARDS WINNING OF ALL TRICKS in bridge and similar card games, the winning of all 13 tricks in a game by one player or pair of players, or a contract to do so **4.** BASEBALL **4 RUNS** in baseball, a home run made when all the bases are loaded

grandson /grán sun/ *n* a son of a son or daughter

grandstand /gránd stand/ *n* **1.** STRUCTURE FOR SPECTATORS' SEATS an open structure or platform, usually with a roof, containing rows of seats for spectators at a sports stadium or racecourse **2.** SEATED SPECTATORS the spectators sitting in a grandstand ■ *adj* UNOBSTRUCTED clear, close, and unobstructed ○ *We had a grandstand view of the proceedings.* ■ *vi* (**-stands, -standing, -standed**) SEEK ATTENTION OR ADMIRATION to show off in order to impress people, especially spectators —**grandstander** *n*

grandstand finish *n* a finish to a race or competition that is exciting because the outcome is unclear until the very end [Because the finish line is typically in front of the grandstand]

grand total *n* a final and complete total of all amounts to be added

grand tour *n* **1.** a trip or tour that takes in visits to several places, or a visit that allows a complete inspection of all parts of one place **2.** formerly, a tour of the main European cities and cultural centres undertaken by young upper-class Englishmen as a way of completing their education

Grand Trunk Canal canal linking the rivers Mersey and Trent in England. Length: 150 km/93 mi.

grand-uncle *n* same as **great-uncle**

Grand Unified Theory *n* a mathematical representation linking the four fundamental forces, electromagnetic, gravitational, strong, and weak, that has been theorized but not yet achieved

Grand Union Canal canal in southern and central England connecting the River Thames in central London with the Midlands

~~**grandure**~~ incorrect spelling of **grandeur**

grange /graynj/ *n* **1.** a large farmhouse or country house with other buildings such as stables or barns attached to· it (*often in house names*) ○ *Norton Grange* **2.** a large farm building used for storing grain or hay (*archaic*) [13C. Via French < medieval Latin *granica villa* 'grain house' < Latin *granum* 'seed']

Grange *n* the Patrons of Husbandry, an association of US farmers founded in 1867 for their mutual support

grangerize /gráynjə rīz/ (**-izes, -izing, -ized**), **grangerise** (**-ises, -ising, -ised**) *vt* **1.** formerly, to illustrate a book with pictures cut out of another book or books **2.** formerly, to cut pictures out of a book or books in order to illustrate another one [Late 19C. After James Granger (1723–76), whose *Biographical History of England* had blank pages for illustrations] —**grangerizer** *n*

grani- *prefix* grain, seed ○ *granivorous* [< Latin *granum*]

granita /grə néetə/ *n* a sweetened flavoured water ice with a grainy texture [Mid-19C. < Italian, form of *granito* (see GRANITE)]

granite /gránnit/ *n* **1.** COARSE-GRAINED ROCK a coarse-grained igneous rock made up of feldspar, mica, and at least 20 per cent quartz. Use: building. **2.** TOUGHNESS determination or toughness of character **3.** STONE USED IN CURLING the rounded stone used in the sport of curling [Mid-17C. < Italian *granito* 'grainy' < Latin *granum* 'seed'] —**granitic** /grə níttik/ *adj* —**granitoid** *adj*

graniteware /gránnit wair/ *n* **1.** earthenware with a speckled glaze that gives it the appearance of granite **2.** iron articles, e.g. pots and bowls, coated with a glaze that gives a finish with the appearance of granite

granivorous /grə nívvərəss/ *adj* used to describe birds that feed on seeds and grain

granny /gránni/ (*plural* **-nies**), **grannie** *n* **1.** same as **grandmother** (*informal*) **2.** DISRESPECTFUL TERM OF ADDRESS a disrespectful term of address for a woman of advanced years (*informal*) **3.** FUSSY PERSON somebody who is regarded as annoyingly fastidious or fussy (*insult*) **4.** BUILDINGS CHIMNEY COVERING a revolving cap on a chimney pot **5.** same as **granny knot 6.** NZ same as **Granny Smith** (*informal*) [Mid-17C. Shortening of *grannam*, common pronunciation of GRANDAM]

granny-bashing *n* violence against or an assault on a woman of advanced years, especially for the purpose of robbery (*informal*)

granny bond *n* a savings bond that is index-linked to inflation, originally offered only to people over retirement age (*informal*)

granny-dumping *n* the abandonment in a public place of a senior citizen who is in deteriorating mental or physical health by a family member or members (*disapproving*)

granny flat *n* a self-contained flat in or attached to a family home in which an older parent could live independently. US term **in-law suite**

granny gear *n* the lowest gear on a bicycle that makes it possible to pedal up steep inclines (*informal*)

granny glasses *npl* spectacles consisting of small lenses set in gold or steel frames (*informal*)

granny knot *n* a reef knot incorrectly tied and therefore likely to come apart

Granny Smith *n* a cultivated variety of eating apple with green skin and crisp white flesh [Late 19C. After the nickname of Maria Ann Smith (1801–70), who first grew it in Sydney, Australia]

granny specs *npl* OPHTHALMOL same as **granny glasses** (*informal*)

grano- *prefix* granite ○ *granolith* [Via German < Italian *granito* (see GRANITE)]

granodiorite /gránnō dī ə rīt/ *n* a coarse-grained igneous rock containing plagioclase and orthoclase, whose composition is intermediate between granite and diorite —**granodioritic** /-dī ə ríttik/ *adj*

granola /grə nólə/ *n* N Am a breakfast cereal consisting of rolled oats mixed with other ingredients such as dried fruit and nuts [Early 20C. Originally a trade name]

granolith /gránnə lith/ *n* a paving material made from cement and granite chips —**granolithic** /gránnə líthik/ *adj*

granophyre /gránn ō fīr/ *n* a medium-grained light-coloured igneous rock consisting mainly of crystals of feldspar and quartz that have crystallized together [Late 19C. < German *Granophyr* < *Granit* 'granite' + *Porphyr* 'porphyry'] —**granophyric** /gránn ō fírrik/ *adj*

Gran Paradiso /gram párrə deézō/ mountain in the western Alps, northern Italy, situated within the Gran Paradiso National Park. Height: 4,061 m/13,323 ft.

grant /graant/ *vt* (**grants, granting, granted**) **1.** ALLOW SOMETHING AS FAVOUR to agree to allow a request, favour, or privilege ○ *She refused to grant any interviews.* **2.** ADMIT TRUTH OF SOMETHING to acknowledge, often reluctantly the truth or efficacy of something ○ *He's a hard worker, I grant you, but hardly managerial material.* **3.** LAW TRANSFER PROPERTY LEGALLY to transfer money, property or rights to somebody in a legal transaction ■ *n* **1.** MONEY GIVEN FOR SPECIFIC PURPOSE a sum of money given by the government, a local authority, or some other organization to fund such things as education, research, or home improvements **2.** GIFT something given to somebody as a favour or privilege, or the giving of it ○ *a land grant* **3.** LAW LEGAL TRANSACTION something transferred from one person to another in a legal transaction, or the making of such a transaction **4.** LAW DOCUMENT TRANSFERRING SOMETHING a legal document recording a transaction in which something is transferred from one person to another **5.** AREA OF LAND in the United States, a unit of territory in New Hampshire, Maine, or Vermont [13C. < Old French *granter*, variant of *creanter* 'guarantee', via assumed Vulgar Latin *credentare* < Latin *credere* 'believe'] —**grantable** *adj* —**granter** *n* ◇ **take somebody for granted** to fail to realize or appreciate the value of somebody ◇ **take something for granted 1.** to assume that something is true without checking **2.** to fail to appreciate or realize the value of something

SYNONYMS See *give*.

Grant /graant/, **Cary** (1904–86) British-born US film actor. He was a sophisticated leading man in films such as *The Philadelphia Story* (1940) and *North by Northwest* (1959). Born Leach, Alexander Archibald

'In the spring a young man's fancy lightly

turns to what he's been thinking about all winter.'
[Cary Grant, *The Awful Truth*; 1937]

Ulysses S. Grant

Grant, Ulysses S. (1822–85) 18th president of the United States. As the Union army's greatest general, he led his troops to victory in the American Civil War. His Republican administration (1869–77) is regarded as one of the most corrupt in US history. Full name **Grant, Hiram Ulysses Simpson.** See table at **president**

'The war is over—the rebels are our countrymen again.'
[Ulysses S. Grant, ordering his Union troops not to cheer after General Robert E. Lee's surrender at Appomattox, Virginia; 9 April 1865]

grant aid *n* financial help provided to a school or other educational establishment by central government

grant-aid *vt* to give grant aid to somebody or something

grant-aided school *n* a school in which independent managers control the appointment of the teachers and the religious instruction given, and are required to pay part of the upkeep costs

granted /graantid/ *adv, conj* used to acknowledge, often reluctantly, the truth of something

grantee /graan tee/ *n* somebody to whom something is transferred in a legal transaction

Granth /grunt/ *n* RELIG same as **Adi Granth** [Late 18C. Via Hindi < Sanskrit *granthaḥ* 'book, binding']

Grantham /gránthəm/ historic market town in Lincolnshire, eastern England. Population: 33,243 (1991).

Granth Sahib *n* RELIG same as **Adi Granth**

grant-in-aid (*plural* **grants-in-aid**) *n* a sum of money given as funding by a central government to a local government, or by central or local government to a department or institution

grant-maintained school *n* a self-governing school funded directly by central government instead of by a local education authority

grantor /graan táwr, graántər/ *n* somebody from whom something is transferred in a legal transaction

granular /gránnyoŏlər/ *adj* 1. consisting of small grains or particles 2. appearing to consist of or be covered in small grains or particles [Late 18C. < late Latin *granulum* (see GRANULE)] —**granularity** /gránnyoŏ lárrəti/ *n* —**granularly** *adv*

granulate /gránnyoŏ layt/ (-lates, -lating, -lated) *v* 1. *vti* MAKE INTO SMALL PARTICLES to form into small grains or particles, or make something do this 2. *vti* BECOME OR MAKE GRAINY IN TEXTURE to become rough and grainy in texture or appearance, or give something a rough and grainy texture or appearance 3. *vi* MED FORM HEALING TISSUE to form granulation tissue over a wound [Mid-17C. < late Latin *granulum* (see GRANULE)] —**granulative** *adj* —**granulator** *n*

granulated sugar /gránnyoŏ laytid-/ *n* white sugar in the form of a coarse powder with large particles

granulation /gránnyoŏ láysh'n/ *n* 1. MAKING OF SMALL PARTICLES the formation of small grains or particles 2. GRAINY TEXTURE a rough grainy texture or appearance 3. SMALL LUMP one of the individual small lumps that, together, give something a rough grainy texture or appearance 4. MED FORMATION OF HEALING TISSUE the formation of granulation tissue, or the tissue itself 5. ASTRON CELLULAR APPEARANCE OF SUN'S SURFACE the cel-

lular appearance of the Sun's disc when seen at high magnification [Early 17C. < late Latin *granulum* (see GRANULE)]

granulation tissue *n* connective tissue in the form of small grainy particles along with masses of tiny blood vessels that forms over healing wounds

granule /grán yool/ *n* 1. SMALL PARTICLE a small grain or particle 2. GEOL SMALL ROCK FRAGMENT a mineral or rock particle that is the size of a small grain 3. ASTRON TEMPORARY BRIGHT REGION ON SUN'S SURFACE a temporary bright region on the Sun's surface, usually with an approximate diameter of 1,000 km/320 mi [Mid-17C. < late Latin *granulum* 'small seed' < Latin *granum* 'seed']

granulite /gránnyoŏ līt/ *n* a coarse-grained metamorphic rock in which the minerals are of roughly equal size —**granulitic** /gránnyoŏ líttik/ *adj*

granulocyte /gránnyoŏlə sīt/ *n* a white blood cell that contains many granular particles in its cytoplasm —**granulocytic** /gránnyoŏlə síttik/ *adj*

granuloma /gránnyoŏ lōmə/ (*plural* **-mas** or **-mata** /-mətə/) *n* a small mass of granulation tissue caused by chronic infection —**granulomatous** *adj*

granulose /gránnyoŏ lõss/ *adj* 1. consisting of small grains or particles 2. appearing to consist of or be covered in small grains or particles

granum /gráynəm/ (*plural* **-na** /-nə/) *n* a stack of thin layers in a chloroplast in which the green pigment chlorophyll is contained [Late 19C. Via German < Latin, 'seed']

Granville-Barker /gránvil baárkər/, **Harley** (1877–1946) British actor, producer, and dramatist. He managed London theatres, wrote plays about social problems, and published a famous series of prefaces to William Shakespeare's plays (1927–46).

grape

grape /grayp/ *n* 1. EDIBLE FRUIT a green or purple berry with sweet juicy flesh that grows in bunches on a vine, eaten fresh or used to make wine or juice. Raisins, sultanas, and currants are dried grapes. 2. PLANTS same as **grapevine** (sense 1) 3. PLANT WITH FRUIT RESEMBLING GRAPES a plant that produces fruit resembling grapes ○ *Oregon grape* 4. BEVERAGES same as **wine** (*humorous*) 5. ARMS same as **grapeshot** 6. COLOURS DARK PURPLE a dark purple colour [13C. < Old French, 'bunch of grapes, hook (as used to harvest grapes)' < Germanic, 'hook'] —**grape** *adj*

CULTURAL NOTE *The Grapes of Wrath*, a novel (1939) by US writer John Steinbeck. A sympathetic portrayal of the plight of the rural poor during the Depression and an attack on capitalism, it tells of the tribulations suffered by the Joad family when they leave droughtstricken Oklahoma in search of work. It was made into a film by John Huston in 1940.

grape fern *n* a fern with fronds that bear spore capsules in clusters similar to those of grapes. Genus: *Botrychium*.

grapefruit /gráyp froot/ (*plural* **-fruits** or *same*) *n* 1. a large round yellow or pinkish citrus fruit with tart juicy flesh ○ *grapefruit juice* 2. an evergreen tree with large white flowers that produces grapefruits. Native to: tropical and subtropical regions. Latin name: *Citrus paradisi*. [Early 19C. Probably because the fruit grows in bunches, like grapes]

grape hyacinth *n* a perennial plant belonging to the lily family. Flowers: usually blue, dense, cup-shaped, in clusters. Genus: *Muscari*.

grape ivy *n* an evergreen climbing plant commonly kept as a house plant. Native to: South America. Latin name: *Rhoicissus rhomboidea*.

grapeseed /gráyp seed/ (*plural same* or **-seeds**) *n* a seed of a grape, from which an oil is extracted for use in cooking

grapeshot /gráyp shot/ *n* a number of small iron balls fired simultaneously from a cannon in order to kill enemy soldiers [< the resemblance to a bunch of grapes]

grape sugar *n* a fruit sugar obtained from grapes

grapevine /gráyp vīn/ *n* 1. a climbing plant on which grapes grow. Genus: *Vitis*. 2. the path of communication along which news, gossip, or rumour passes unofficially from person to person within a group, organization, or community (*informal*) ○ *I heard on the office grapevine that she was leaving.*

grapey /gráypi/ (-ier, -iest), **grapy** *adj* looking or tasting like a grape or grapes —**grapiness** *n*

graph[1] /graaf, graf/ *n* a diagram used to indicate relationships between two or more variable quantities. The quantities are usually measured along two axes set at right angles to each other. A graph may be in different forms, e.g. of a line joining points plotted between coordinates, or a series of parallel bars or boxes. ■ *vt* (**graphs, graphing, graphed**) to represent data by means of a graph, or add data to a graph [Late 19C. Shortening of *graphic formula*]

graph[2] /graaf, graf/ *n* a symbol, letter, or combination of letters used in writing to represent the smallest discrete unit of speech [Mid-20C. < Greek *graphē* 'writing' < *graphein* 'write']

graph- *prefix* same as **grapho-** (*used before vowels*)

-graph *suffix* 1. something written or drawn ○ *digraph* ○ *zincograph* 2. an instrument for writing, drawing, or recording ○ *pantograph* ○ *seismograph* [Via French or Latin < Greek *graphos* 'written, writing' < *graphein* 'write']

grapheme /grá feem/ *n* a written symbol, letter, or combination of letters that represents a single sound —**graphemic** /gra feemik/ *adj* —**graphemically** *adv*

graphemics /gra feemiks/ *n* LING same as **graphology** (sense 2)

-grapher *suffix* somebody who writes, draws, or records ○ *calligrapher* ○ *cinematographer* [< late Latin *-graphus* 'writer' < Greek *-graphos* < *graphein* 'write']

graphic /gráffik/ *adj* 1. VIVIDLY DETAILED including a number of vivid descriptive details, especially exciting or unpleasant ones ○ *her graphic description of the accident* 2. SHOWN IN WRITING representing something such as a sound by means of letters or other written symbols. 'Moo', 'woof', and 'miaow' are graphic representations of the sounds made by cows, dogs, and cats respectively. 3. SHOWN IN PICTURES representing something in the form of pictures or images 4. GRAPHS relating to or given in the form of a graph or diagram 5. OF GRAPHIC ARTS relating to the graphic arts 6. OF GRAPHICS relating to graphics 7. GEOL CONTAINING CRYSTALS LIKE LETTERS containing crystal structures that resemble letters ■ *n* (*often used in the plural*) 1. COMPUT PICTURE PRODUCED BY COMPUTER a picture, design, or visual display of data produced by a computer program 2. PUBL BOOK ILLUSTRATION an illustration or diagram in a book or magazine 3. CINEMA, MEDIA DISPLAYED TEXT IN FILM a part of a film that consists of illustration and text, e.g. titles, credits, or drawings [Mid-18C. Via Latin < Greek *graphikos* < *graphein* 'write'] —**graphically** *adv* —**graphicness** *n*

graphicacy /gráffikəssi/ *n* the ability to use and understand such things as symbols, diagrams, plans, and maps [Mid-20C. < GRAPHIC, after *literacy*]

graphical /gráffik'l/ *adj* MATHS same as **graphic** *adj* (sense 4)

graphical user interface *n* a user interface on a computer that relies on icons, menus, and a mouse, and not on typing in commands

graphic arts *npl* artistic processes based on the use of lines rather than colour, e.g. drawing, calligraphy, engraving, and printmaking —**graphic artist** *n*

graphic[2] **design** *n* the art of integrating text, typography, and illustrations in the production of books and magazines —**graphic designer** *n*

graphic equalizer *n* a device, e.g. on a radio or CD player, that allows adjustments to be made to the strength of sounds of different frequencies [Because the variable levels of the sounds are often displayed electronically in graphic format]

Graphic interface format *n* COMPUT full form of **GIF**

graphic novel *n* a fictional story for adults published in the form of a comic strip

graphics /gráffiks/ *n* (*takes a singular verb*) **1.** DIAGRAMS AND ILLUSTRATIONS the presentation of information in the form of diagrams and illustrations instead of as words or numbers **2.** COMPUT DISPLAY OF COMPUTER DATA AS SYMBOLS the art and science of storing, manipulating, and displaying computer data in the form of pictures, diagrams, graphs, or symbols **3.** ARCHIT, ENG MATHEMATICAL DRAWING the science of drawing something in accordance with mathematical principles, e.g. in architecture and engineering ■ *npl* ARTS same as **graphic arts** (*takes a plural verb*)

graphics adaptor *n* a circuit board in a computer that contains the necessary video memory to allow a bit-mapped display to be created

graphics card *n* a circuit board that enables a computer to display screen information

graphics device interface *n* a set of program instructions that allows the Windows™ operating system to output graphics to a computer screen or print device

graphics tablet *n* a device consisting of an electronic pen and an electronically sensitive surface, used to enter designs into a computer by drawing them

graphite /gráf īt/ *n* a soft dark carbon that conducts electricity, occurs naturally as a mineral, and is also produced industrially. Use: batteries, lubricants, polishes, electric motors, nuclear reactors, carbon fibres, pencil lead. [Late 18C. < German *Graphit* < Greek *graphein* 'write'] —**graphitic** /grə fíttik/ *adj*

graphitize /gráffi tīz/ (-tizes, -tizing, -tized), **graphitise** (-tises, -tising, -tised) *vt* **1.** to convert something into graphite **2.** to coat something with graphite, or mix graphite into it —**graphitizable** *adj* —**graphitization** /gráffi tī záysh'n/ *n*

grapho- *prefix* writing ○ *graphology* [< Greek *graphein* 'write']

graphology /gra fólləji/ *n* **1.** the study of handwriting, especially in order to assess somebody's personality from patterns or features of his or her writing **2.** the study of writing systems and their relationship to the sound systems of languages —**graphological** /gráffə lójjik'l/ *adj* —**graphologist** *n*

graph paper *n* paper on which a series of usually equally spaced vertical and horizontal intersecting lines has been imprinted to facilitate the drawing of graphs and diagrams

-graphy *suffix* **1.** a method of writing or making an image by means of a particular process or technique ○ *chirography* ○ *radiography* **2.** writing about or study of a particular subject ○ *biography* ○ *ethnography* [< Latin *-graphia* < Greek *graphein* 'write']

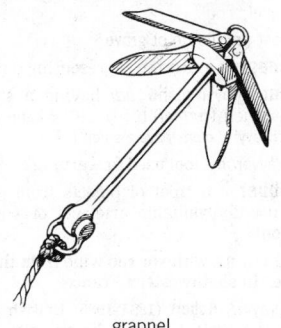
grapnel

grapnel /grápn'l/ *n* **1.** a device consisting of an iron shaft with several hooks at one end and a rope at the other by which it can be thrown to attach itself to something **2.** an anchor with three or more arms, especially one for anchoring a small boat [14C. < Anglo-Norman < Old French *grapon* < *grape* 'hook' (see GRAPE)]

grappa /gráppə/ *n* an Italian brandy distilled from what remains of grapes after they have been pressed for wine-making [Late 19C. < Italian, 'grape stalk, brandy']

Stéphane Grappelli

Grappelli /grə pélli/, **Stéphane** (1908–97) French musician. He is known for his playing of the violin in the jazz style.

grapple /grápp'l/ *v* (-ples, -pling, -pled) **1.** *vi* STRUGGLE WITH SOMEBODY to struggle with somebody in a close hand-to-hand fight **2.** *vi* STRUGGLE TO DEAL WITH SOMETHING to struggle to deal with or comprehend something ○ *The government continues to grapple with the economic crisis.* **3.** *vt* GRAB SOMEBODY to grab hold of somebody **4.** *vt* HOLD SOMETHING WITH HOOKED DEVICE to hook or hold something with a grapnel or other hooked device ■ *n* **1.** same as **grapnel** (sense 1) **2.** STRUGGLE a close struggle **3.** WRESTLING GRIP OR HOLD in wrestling, a grip or hold on an opponent [14C. < Old French *grapil* 'small hook' < *grape* 'hook' (see GRAPE)] —**grappler** *n*

grappling /grápling/, **grappling iron**, **grappling hook** *n* same as **grapnel** (sense 1)

graptolite /gráp tō līt/ *n* a small floating sea animal that lived in colonies between about 550 million and 325 million years ago and is now found as a fossil. Graptolite fossils are often used to date rocks. Orders: Graptoloidea or Dendroidea. [Mid-19C. < Greek *graptos*, past participle of *graphein* 'write']

grapy *adj* FOOD another spelling of **grapey**

Grasmere /gráass meer/ village in Cumbria, northwestern England, situated on the lake of the same name. It was once the home of William and Dorothy Wordsworth. Population: 1,100 (1981).

grasp /graasp/ *v* (grasps, grasping, grasped) **1.** *vt* TAKE HOLD OF SOMEBODY OR SOMETHING to take hold of somebody or something firmly, especially with the hand ○ *He grasped her arm and led her out into the garden.* **2.** *vi* TRY TO TAKE HOLD OF SOMETHING to attempt to take hold of somebody or something, especially with the hand ○ *He grasped at the rope.* **3.** *vt* HOLD SOMEBODY OR SOMETHING to hold somebody or something, especially in the hand ○ *She rushed into the room with a letter grasped in her hand.* **4.** *vt* TAKE OPPORTUNITY to take the opportunity to do something **5.** *vi* TRY TO TAKE OPPORTUNITY to attempt to take the opportunity to do something **6.** *vt* UNDERSTAND SOMETHING to manage to understand something ○ *I just can't grasp what you're getting at.* ■ *n* **1.** HOLD ON SOMETHING a hold or grip on something or somebody, especially with the hand ○ *A gust of wind snatched the umbrella from his grasp.* **2.** UNDERSTANDING an understanding of or ability to understand something ○ *a poor grasp of the facts* **3.** ABILITY TO DO SOMETHING the ability to do something ○ *Success was within her grasp.* **4.** CONTROL power or control ○ *in the tyrant's grasp* [14C. Origin ?] —**graspable** *adj*

grasper /gráaspər/ *n* **1.** somebody who is greedy for money **2.** somebody who grasps something

grasping /gráasping/ *adj* greedy for money —**graspingly** *adv* —**graspingness** *n*

grass /graass/ *n* (*plural same* or **grasses**) **1.** GREEN PLANT THAT FORMS LAWNS a low green narrow-leaved plant that grows in fields and gardens, is eaten by animals such as cows and sheep, and is used to make lawns and playing fields **2.** GRASS-COVERED AREA an area of grass such as a lawn or pasture **3.** HOLLOW-STEMMED GREEN PLANT a plant with hollow jointed stems and long narrow, usually green leaves and tiny flowers arranged in spikes. Grasses include important food plants such as wheat, oats, barley, rice, rye, maize, millet, and sorghum as well as sugar cane and bamboo. Family: Gramineae. **4.** PLANT LIKE GRASS a green plant not related to the true grasses, e.g.

grass: annual meadow grass

goosegrass or knotgrass **5.** DRUGS same as **marijuana** (*slang*) **6.** INFORMER somebody who informs on somebody else, especially to the police (*slang*) ■ *v* (**grasses, grassing, grassed**) **1.** *vti* COVER WITH GRASS to become covered with grass, or cause ground to become covered with grass **2.** *vi* BE INFORMER to inform on somebody, especially to the police (*slang*) **3.** *vt* AGRIC FEED ANIMAL ON GRASS to put an animal into a pasture to feed on grass **4.** *vt* BRING OPPONENT DOWN to make an opponent fall to the ground (*slang*) [Old English *græs*, *gærs* < Indo-European] ◇ **not let the grass grow under your feet** to act without delay or wasting time ◇ **put somebody out to grass** to impose retirement on somebody, usually on grounds of age (*informal*)

CULTURAL NOTE *Leaves of Grass*, a collection of verse (1855–92) by US poet Walt Whitman. Whitman constantly revised and expanded this collection to create a work that celebrates all aspects of human life from politics to the natural world and from procreation to mortality. Both its subject matter and its self-consciously modern style, based on long, loosely rhymed lines, were highly influential.

grass up *vt* to inform on somebody, especially to the police (*slang*)

Günter Grass

Grass /grass/, **Günter** (*b.* 1927) German writer and political activist. His novels such as *The Tin Drum* (1959) and *Dog Years* (1963) combine fantasy and symbolism with the theme of the materialism of modern life. He won the Nobel Prize in literature (1999).

> 'History offers no comfort. It hands out hard lessons. It makes absurd reading, mostly. Admittedly, it moves on, but progress is not the result of history. History is never-ending. We are always inside history, never outside it.'
> [Günter Grass, *Documents on the Workings of Politics*; 1971]

grass box *n* UK the container attached to a lawn mower that catches the grass cuttings. ANZ, N Am term **grass catcher**

grass carp *n* a plant-eating fish used for keeping water weeds under control. Native to: Russia, China. Latin name: *Ctenopharyngodon idella*.

grass catcher *n* ANZ, N Am GARDENING same as **grass box**

grass ceiling *n* a gender barrier preventing women golfers from participating in the sport at the highest level (*informal*) [Late 20C. Modelled on GLASS CEILING]

grass cloth *n* cloth made from loosely woven plant fibres

grass court *n* a grass-covered tennis court

grass-green *adj* having the colour of green grass —**grass green** *n*

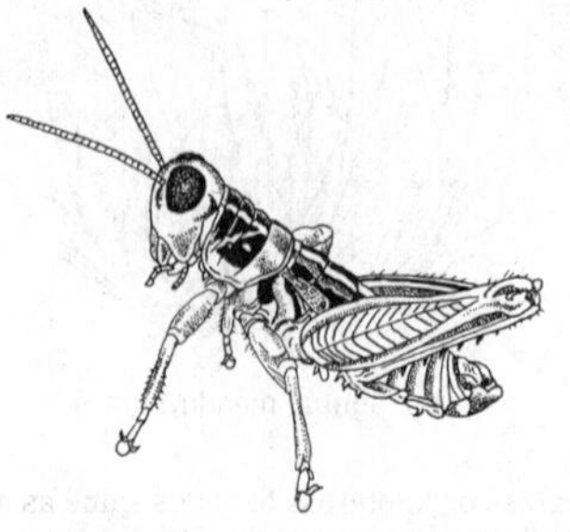
grasshopper

grasshopper /graáss hopər/ *n* **1. JUMPING INSECT** a slender plant-eating flying and jumping insect that produces a buzzing or whirring sound by rubbing its back legs against its forewings. Order: Orthoptera. **2. CREAMY COCKTAIL** a cocktail consisting of crème de menthe, crème de cacao, and cream ■ *adj* **NOT ABLE TO CONCENTRATE** unable to focus on one thing for very long ○ *has a grasshopper mind* [14C. < *grasshop* < Old English *gærshoppa*]

grassland /graáss land/ *n* **1.** land on which grass or low green plants are the main vegetation (*usually used in the plural*) **2.** land kept for pasture or for the production of forage crops

grass moth *n* a small straw-coloured night-flying moth that spends the daytime clinging to grass stems. Family: Pyralidae.

grass roots *npl* **1.** the ordinary people in a community or the ordinary members of an organization, as opposed to the leadership **2.** the origin, basis, fundamental aim, or basic meaning of something ○ *the grass roots of socialism*

grassroots /graáss roots/, **grass-roots** *adj* coming from, formed by, or involving the ordinary people in a community or the ordinary members of an organization, as opposed to the leadership

grass snake *n* a common nonpoisonous dark green snake. Native to: Europe, North Africa, Asia. Genus: *Natrix*.

grass tree *n* a tree with an unbranched trunk topped by a tuft of leaves resembling grass. Native to: eastern Australia. Genus: *Xanthorrhoea*.

grass widow *n* a woman whose husband or partner is frequently away from home or who has completely deserted her [Originally 'discarded mistress', thought of as having made love in a field]

grass widower *n* a man whose wife or partner is frequently away from home or who has completely deserted him

grassy /graássi/ (**-ier, -iest**) *adj* **1.** covered with grass **2.** looking, tasting, or feeling like grass —**grassiness** *n*

grate[1] /grayt/ *n* **1. BARS IN FRONT OF FIRE** a framework of metal bars used to keep solid fuel such as coal or wood within a fireplace, stove, or furnace **2. FIREPLACE** a fireplace, stove, or furnace **3. BARS OVER OPENING** a framework of bars covering and blocking an opening **4.** MIN EXTRACT **SIEVE FOR GRADING ORE** an iron plate with holes in it for grading crushed ore [14C. Via Old French < Latin *cratis* 'wickerwork']

grate[2] /grayt/ (**grates, grating, grated**) *v* **1.** *vti* **MAKE INTO SMALL PIECES** to shred something by rubbing it against a rough surface or a tool with sharp-edged holes in it, or be shredded in this way ○ *He chose a cheese that grates easily.* **2.** *vi* **MAKE NOISE OF RUBBING** to make a rough, vibrating, or creaking sound by being rubbed together, or cause things to make such a sound ○ *Grasshoppers make their characteristic sound by grating their back legs against their wings.* **3.** *vi* **IRRITATE** to be a source of irritation ○ *His constant sniggering really grates on me.* **4.** *vt* **SAY SOMETHING IN HARSH VOICE** to say something in a harsh rasping voice [14C. < Old French *grater* 'scrape' < Germanic] —**grated** *adj*

grateful /gráytf'l/ *adj* **1.** having or showing the desire or reason to thank somebody ○ *I'm very grateful to you for your help.* ○ *He received a grateful letter from them* **2.** giving pleasure or comfort (*archaic or literary*) [Mid-16C. < obsolete *grate* 'pleasing, thankful' < Latin *gratus*] —**gratefully** *adv* —**gratefulness** *n*

grater /gráytər/ *n* **1.** a device with many sharp-edged holes against which something such as cheese can be rubbed to reduce it to shreds or fine particles **2.** somebody who grates something

Gratian /gráysh'n/ (AD 359–383) Western Roman emperor (367–383). He served as coemperor until 375 with his father, Valentinian I, and from then with his half-brother, Valentinian II. He spent much of his rule fighting Germanic tribes in Gaul and was a strong supporter of the Christian Church. Full name **Flavius Gratianus**

graticule /grátti kyool/ *n* **1.** OPTICS same as **reticle 2.** the grid of latitudinal and longitudinal lines on a map [Late 19C. Via French < Latin *craticula* 'small grid' < *cratis* 'wickerwork']

gratification /gráttifi káysh'n/ *n* **1. SATISFACTION** a feeling of pleasure or satisfaction **2. ACT OF SATISFYING** the act of giving somebody pleasure or satisfaction **3. SOMETHING SATISFYING** something that gives pleasure or satisfaction

gratify /grátti fī/ (**-fies, -fying, -fied**) *vt* **1.** to make somebody feel pleased or satisfied (*often passive*) **2.** to satisfy a desire [15C. Directly or via French *gratifier* < Latin *gratificari* < *gratus* 'agreeable'] —**gratifier** *n* —**gratifying** *adj* —**gratifyingly** *adv*

gratin /grátt aN/ *n* **1.** a crust of browned breadcrumbs or melted grated cheese on top of food **2.** a cooked dish with a breadcrumb or melted grated cheese crust [Mid-17C. < French < Old French *grater* (see GRATE [2])]

gratin dish *n* a shallow ovenproof container used for cooking or serving a gratin

gratinee /grátti náy/ *adj* cooked or served with browned breadcrumbs or melted grated cheese on top [Early 20C. < French *gratinée*, past participle of *gratiner* 'cook au gratin']

grating[1] /gráyting/ *n* **1.** a framework of metal bars covering an opening **2.** OPTICS same as **diffraction grating** ■ **gratings** *npl* shreds or fine particles produced by grating something

grating[2] /gráyting/ *adj* **1.** unpleasantly rough, harsh, or vibrating **2.** irritating —**gratingly** *adv*

gratis /gráttiss, gráytiss, graá-/ *adj, adv* received or given without payment or obligation [15C. < Latin, 'out of kindness' < *gratia* (see GRACE)]

gratitude /grátti tyood/ *n* a feeling of being thankful to somebody for doing something ○ *I'd like to find some way of expressing my gratitude to her for all she did.* [15C. Directly or via French < Latin *gratitudo* < *gratus* 'pleasing']

gratuitous /grə tyóo itəss/ *adj* **1. UNNECESSARY** unnecessary and unjustifiable ○ *gratuitous remarks* **2. FREE** received or given without payment or obligation **3.** LAW **WITHOUT RETURN BENEFIT** not requiring any benefit or compensation in return [Mid-17C. Via French < Latin *gratuitus* 'freely given' < *gratus* 'pleasing'] —**gratuitously** *adv* —**gratuitousness** *n*

gratuity /grə tyóo əti/ (*plural* **-ties**) *n* **1.** a small gift, usually of money, given to somebody such as a waiter as thanks for service given **2.** a sum of money given to somebody, especially a member of the armed forces, when he or she retires [15C. Via French *gratuité* < medieval Latin *gratuitas* 'gift' < Latin *gratus* 'pleasing']

graupel /grówp'l/ *n* small soft white ice particles that fall as hail or snow [Late 19C. < German, 'small hulled corn' < Slavic]

grav /grav/ *n* a unit of acceleration that corresponds to the standard acceleration of free fall. Symbol **g** [Shortening of GRAVITY]

gravadlax *n* FOOD same as **gravlax**

gravamen /grə váy men/ (*plural* **-vamens** or **-vamina** /-vámminə/) *n* **1.** the most serious part of an accusation or charge made against an accused person **2.** a grievance against somebody (*formal*) [Early 17C. < medieval Latin, 'grievance' < Latin *gravare* 'weigh upon' < *gravis* 'heavy']

grave[1] /grayv/ *n* **1. BURIAL PLACE** a hole dug in the ground for a dead person's body, or another place of interment ○ *She goes every week to put fresh flowers on her husband's grave.* ○ *as silent as the grave* **2. LAST RESTING PLACE** a final resting place ○ *the sunken ship's watery grave* **3. DEATH** the end of life ○ *health care from the cradle to the grave* ○ *went to an early grave* **4. END OF SOMETHING** the end or destruction of something ○ *the grave of his ambition* [Old English *græf* < Indo-European, 'scratch, dig'] —**graveless** *adj* ◇ **turn in his** *or* **her grave** used to emphasize how displeased or upset somebody who is dead would be if he or she knew what was happening ○ *If she heard this version, she'd turn in her grave.*

grave[2] /grayv/ (**graver, gravest**) *adj* **1. SERIOUS IN MANNER** solemn and serious in manner **2. NEEDING SERIOUS THOUGHT** important and having serious consequences, and therefore requiring careful consideration **3. INVOLVING POSSIBLE HARM OR DANGER** causing, involving, or arising from a threat of serious consequences such as danger or harm ○ *Things are looking pretty grave here as the air raid sirens wail.* [15C. Via French < Latin *gravis* 'heavy'] —**gravely** *adv* —**graveness** *n*

grave[3] /graav/, **grave accent** *n* in some languages, a mark (`) placed above a letter to show that it is sounded in a specific way, as in ò and è. See table at **diacritic** [Early 17C. < French, 'heavy' (see GRAVE [2])]

grave[4] /grayv/ (**graves, graving, graved, graved** or **graven** /gráyv'n/) *vt* **1.** to fix something firmly in the mind (*literary*) ○ *graved it in her mind* **2.** to carve or engrave something (*archaic*) [Old English *grafan* 'dig, carve' < Germanic]

grave[5] /grayv/ (**graves, graving, graved**) *vt* to clean the bottom of a wooden ship and coat it with pitch [15C. Probably < French dialect *grave* 'sand, shore' < Old French (see GRAVEL), because the work was done while the ship was hauled up on a beach]

grave[6] /graáv ay/ *adv* to be played seriously or solemnly (*used as a musical direction*) [Late 16C. Via Italian < Latin *gravis* 'heavy'] —**grave** *adj*

grave accent /graáv-/ *n* LING same as **grave** [3]

graveclothes /gráyv klōthz/ *npl* the clothes or other wrappings that a dead body is buried in

gravedigger /gráyv digər/ *n* somebody employed to dig graves

gravel /grávv'l/ *n* **1. SMALL STONES** small stones used for paths or for making concrete **2.** GEOL **ROCK FRAGMENTS** a deposit or stratum of loose fragmentary sedimentary material **3.** MED **SMALL PARTICLES IN KIDNEY OR BLADDER** hard particles in the kidney or bladder that are much smaller than kidney stones and can pass through the urinary tract without causing a blockage, although they may cause severe pain ■ *vt* (**-els, -elling, -elled**) **1. LAY GRAVEL OVER SOMETHING** to cover a surface with gravel **2. BEWILDER SOMEBODY** to puzzle or confuse somebody [13C. < Old French < *grave* 'pebbles, shore' < Celtic]

gravel-blind *adj* almost totally sightless (*archaic; usually considered offensive*) [After SAND-BLIND]

gravelly /grávv'li/ *adj* **1. GRATING** sounding rough or harsh ○ *a gravelly voice* **2. LIKE GRAVEL** like or covered with gravel **3. WITH GRAVEL** made or manufactured with gravel

graven past participle of **grave** [4]

graven image *n* a carving representing a god

graveolent /gráyvi ələnt/ *adj* having a strong unpleasant smell (*formal*) [Early 17C. < Latin *graveolent-* < *gravis* 'heavy' + *olere* 'have a smell']

graver /gráyvər/ *n* a tool used for carving or engraving

grave robber *n* a thief of objects from graves or tombs, usually valuable artefacts or corpses for dissection

Graves /graav/ *n* a white or red wine from the district of Graves in southwestern France

Graves /grayvz/, **Robert** (1895–1985) British poet and novelist. A classical scholar, he was also a prolific writer of poetry and fiction. His works include *Goodbye to All That* (1929), *I, Claudius* (1934), and *The White Goddess* (1947). Full name **Graves, Robert Ranke**

> 'To be a poet is a condition rather than a profession.'
> [Robert Graves. Quoted in *Horizon*; September 1946]

Graves' disease /gráyvz-/ *n* an inflammatory disorder of the thyroid gland commonly associated with protrusion of the eyes [Mid-19C. After Robert J. *Graves* (1796–1853), Irish physician]

Gravesend /gráyvz énd/ port on the River Thames in Kent, southeastern England. Population: 51,435 (1991).

graveside /gráyv sīd/ *n* the area surrounding a grave (*often used before a noun*) ○ *a graveside service*

gravesite /gráyv sīt/ *n* the place where somebody's grave is located

gravestone /gráyv stōn/ *n* an ornamental piece of stone put at the head of a grave, on which are written the name, birth date, and death date of the person buried there

graveyard /gráyv yaard/ *n* **1.** a piece of ground, sometimes beside a church, set aside for people to be buried in **2.** a place where old, unwanted, useless objects, especially old cars, are left

graveyard poetry *n* sad reflective poems about death, often set in graveyards and usually by 18th-century British writers —**graveyard poet** *n*

graveyard shift *n* a shift of work running through the early hours of the morning, especially one running from midnight till eight o'clock the following morning, or the workers on such a shift

gravid /grávvid/ *adj* same as **pregnant** (*technical*) [Late 16C. < Latin *gravidus* < *gravis* 'heavy'] —**gravidity** /gra víddəti/ *n* —**gravidly** *adv* —**gravidness** *n*

gravida /grávvidə/ (*plural* **-das** or **-dae** /-dee/) *n* a pregnant woman (*technical*) [Mid-20C. < Latin, form of *gravidus* (see GRAVID)]

gravimeter /grə vímmitər/ *n* **1.** an instrument for measuring variations in the strength of the Earth's gravitational field from one place to another **2.** an instrument used to measure the relative density of a substance [Late 18C. < French *gravimètre* < Latin *gravis* (see GRAVE [2])]

gravimetric /grávvi métrik/ *adj* **1.** RELATING TO MEASUREMENT OF WEIGHT relating to or using the measurement of weight **2.** OF CHEMICAL ANALYSIS AND WEIGHT relating to chemical analysis involving the measurement of the weights of substances used in and produced by a chemical reaction **3.** MEASURING GRAVITATIONAL VARIATIONS relating to the measurement of variations in the strength of the Earth's gravitational field from one place to another —**gravimetrical** *adj* —**gravimetrically** *adv*

gravimetry /grə vímmətri/ *n* **1.** the measurement of density or weight **2.** the measurement of variations in the strength of the Earth's gravitational field from one place to another

graving dock /gráyving-/ *n* SHIPPING same as **dry dock** [< GRAVE [5]]

gravitas /grávvi tass, -taass/ *n* a serious and solemn attitude or way of behaving [Early 20C. < Latin (see GRAVITY)]

gravitate /grávvi tayt/ (**-tates, -tating, -tated**) *v* **1.** *vi* to move gradually and steadily towards somebody or something as if drawn by some force or attraction ○ *guests slowly gravitating to the kitchen* **2.** *vti* to move under the influence of the force of gravity, or cause something to do this [Mid-17C. < modern Latin *gravitat-*, past participle of *gravitare* < Latin *gravitas* (see GRAVITY)] —**gravitater** *n* —**gravitative** *adj*

gravitation /grávvi táysh'n/ *n* **1.** a gradual and steady movement towards somebody or something, as if drawn by some force or attraction **2.** the mutual force of attraction between all particles or bodies that have mass —**gravitational** *adj* —**gravitationally** *adv*

gravitational constant *n* the numerical factor relating force, mass, and distance in Newton's theory of gravitation. It has the value 6.673 ± 10^{-11} Nm^{2}kg^{-2}.

gravitational field *n* the region of space around an object that has mass, within which another object that has mass experiences the force of attraction

gravitational lens *n* a large astronomical object such as a galaxy whose gravitational field focuses or distorts the light from another object beyond it

gravitational redshift *n* the displacement of the spectrum of light emitted by an astronomical object towards longer wavelengths (**redshift**) because of the difference between the gravitational potential at the observer and source

gravitational wave *n* a hypothetical wave, predicted by relativity theory, that travels at the speed of light and propagates a gravitational field

graviton /grávvi ton/ *n* a hypothetical particle with zero charge and rest mass that is considered to be the quantum particle of the gravitational interaction [Mid-20C. < GRAVITATION]

gravity /grávvəti/ *n* **1.** GRAVITATIONAL FORCE the attraction due to gravitation that the Earth or another astronomical object exerts on an object on or near its surface **2.** PHYS same as **gravitation** (sense 2) **3.** SERIOUSNESS the seriousness of something considered in terms of its unfavourable consequences ○ *regarded it as a matter of the utmost gravity* **4.** SERIOUS BEHAVIOUR solemnity and seriousness in somebody's attitude or behaviour **5.** HEAVINESS the quality of being heavy **6.** WEIGHT the amount that something weighs (*formal*) [15C. Via French < Latin *gravitas* 'heaviness' < *gravis* 'heavy']

gravity feed *n* a mechanism or process for supplying something such as fuel to a boiler or materials to a manufacturing process by their downward movement under the influence of gravity —**gravity-fed** *adj*

gravity wave *n* PHYS same as **gravitational wave**

gravlax /gráv laks/, **gravadlax** /grávvəd-/ *n* a Scandinavian dish consisting of thin slices of dried salmon marinated in sugar, salt, pepper, and herbs, especially dill, and usually served as an appetizer [Mid-20C. < Swedish or Norwegian *gravlaks* 'buried salmon' (because originally marinated in a hole in the ground)]

gravure /grə vyóor, -vyáwr/ *n* **1.** PRINTING same as **intaglio** (sense 4) **2.** a plate used in or a print produced by intaglio printing **3.** PRINTING same as **photogravure** [Late 19C. < French < *graver* 'engrave']

gravy /gráyvi/ *n* the juices produced by meat while it is being roasted, fried, or grilled, or a sauce made with these juices or another liquid and poured over cooked meat and vegetables [14C. < Old French *grave*]

gravy boat *n* a small jug, usually long and narrow, in which gravy or other sauces are served

gravy ring *n Ireland* FOOD same as **doughnut**

gravy train *n* a way of getting a large amount of money or other benefits for very little effort (*informal*) ○ *scrambling to get on the gravy train*

gray[1] /gray/ *adj, n* COLOURS US spelling of **grey**

gray[2] /gray/ *n* the derived SI unit for the absorbed dose of ionizing radiation, equal to an absorption of 1 joule per kilogram. Symbol **Gy** [After L. H. *Gray* (1905–65), English radiobiologist]

Gray /gray/, **Thomas** (1716–71) British poet. His most famous work is his 'Elegy Written in a Country Churchyard' (1751). See Cultural note at **elegy**

> 'The boast of heraldry, the pomp of pow'r, / And all that beauty, all that wealth e'er gave, / Awaits alike th' inevitable hour: / The paths of glory lead but to the grave.' [Thomas Gray, 'Elegy Written in a Country Churchyard'; 1751]

grayling /gráyling/ (*plural* **-lings** or *same*) *n* **1.** a freshwater fish with silvery scales and a large dorsal fin, valued as a game fish. Native to: Russia, China. Genus: *Thymallus*. **2.** INSECTS a common grey butterfly. Native to: Europe. Latin name: *Eumenis semele*.

Graz /graats/ city and capital of Styria Province on the River Mur in southeastern Austria. Population: 240,513 (1999).

graze[1] /grayz/ (**grazes, grazing, grazed**) *v* **1.** *vti* EAT GRASS IN FIELDS to eat grass and other green plants in a field or fields **2.** *vt* PROVIDE GRASS FOR ANIMALS to allow animals such as cows and sheep to eat grass in fields ○ *Her ranch now grazes 100,000 head of cattle.* **3.** *vt* USE LAND FOR FEEDING ANIMALS to allow animals such as cows and sheep to eat the grass and green plants of a particular field or fields ○ *We usually graze those two fields over there.* **4.** *vi* EAT SNACKS to eat snacks throughout the day, instead of proper meals, especially while working (*slang*) **5.** *vi* EAT FOOD IN SUPERMARKET to eat food from the shelves of a supermarket while shopping, without subsequently paying for it at the checkout (*slang*) **6.** *vi* CHANGE TV CHANNELS to switch television channels frequently without watching much of any programme (*slang*) **7.** *vi* KEEP STOPPING AND STARTING to perform an activity in a desultory manner, e.g. by picking up and putting down magazines without reading much of any one (*slang*) [Old English *grasian* < *græs* (see GRASS)] —**grazeable** *adj* —**grazer** *n*

graze[2] /grayz/ *vt* (**grazes, grazing, grazed**) **1.** TOUCH SOMETHING LIGHTLY to touch against the surface of something lightly in passing **2.** BREAK SKIN SLIGHTLY to damage the surface of the skin of a part of the body slightly when it is rubbed against something rough and hard ■ *n* **1.** SLIGHT BREAK IN SKIN slight and shallow damage to the skin caused by rubbing against something rough and hard **2.** TOUCH OF SOMETHING the act of rubbing something or touching it lightly ○ *the graze of a bullet* [Late 16C. Origin ?]

grazier /gráyzi ər/ *n* **1.** an owner of cattle that are raised and fattened for market **2.** *Aus* a large-scale farmer who raises sheep or cattle

grazing /gráyzing/ *n* **1.** grass and green plants for animals such as cows and sheep to eat **2.** land with grass suitable for animals such as cows and sheep to feed on

grazioso /grátsi ṓssō, graá-/ *adv* in a graceful way (*used as a musical direction*) [Early 19C. Via Italian < Latin *gratiosus* (see GRACIOUS)] —**grazioso** *adj*

grease *n* /greess/ **1.** ANIMAL FAT thick soft animal fat, e.g. from cooked meat **2.** THICK LUBRICANT a thick oily substance, especially one used to make machinery run smoothly **3.** OIL FOR HAIR an oily substance used as a cosmetic for the hair **4.** OILY WOOL untreated wool from sheep that still contains its natural oils, or the natural oils in this wool **5.** BRIBERY bribes or bribery (*slang*) **6.** LONG-HAIRED MOTORCYCLISTS long-haired motorcyclists considered collectively (*dated slang insult*) ■ *vt* /greess, greez/ (**greases, greasing, greased**) **1.** PUT GREASE ON SOMETHING to put grease on something, e.g. in order to make it move smoothly or to stop something else sticking to it **2.** MAKE SOMETHING EASIER to make something such as progress or promotion easier or quicker (*informal*) ○ *His mother's money certainly greased his path to the boardroom.* [13C. Via Anglo-Norman *grece* < Latin *crassus* 'fat, thick'] ◇ **grease somebody's palm** *or* **hand** to bribe somebody to do something (*informal*)

greaseball /greéss bawl/ *n* **1.** *Aus, N Am* somebody who is habitually dirty or unkempt (*slang insult*) **2.** *Aus, US* a highly offensive term for somebody of Mediterranean or Latin American, especially Mexican, origin (*taboo; slang*)

grease gun *n* a hand-held device for forcing grease into machinery to lubricate it

grease monkey *n* an offensive term for a mechanic, especially one who works on motor vehicles or aircraft (*slang insult*)

greasepaint /greéss paynt/ *n* a thick greasy or waxy form of coloured makeup used by actors

grease pencil *n* a pencil containing a core of a waxy coloured substance that can write on glossy surfaces

greaseproof /greéss proof/ *adj* not allowing oil or grease to soak into it or pass through it

greaseproof paper *n* paper that does not allow oil or grease to soak into it or pass through it. Use: in cooking, preparing, or wrapping food. N Am term **wax paper**

greaser /greéssər, greézər/ *n* **1.** MECHANIC OR ENGINEER somebody whose job involves greasing machinery, especially a mechanic who works on motor vehicles or a ship's engineer (*slang*) **2.** LONG-HAIRED MOTORCYCLIST a usually young, long-haired, leather-jacketed motorcyclist, especially a member of a motorcycle gang (*slang insult*) **3.** SOMEBODY WHO TRIES TO GAIN FAVOUR a flatterer or groveller who tries to gain the favour or approval of a superior (*slang insult*)

greasewood /greéss wòod/ *n* **1.** a spiny desert bush that yields an oil used as fuel. Native to: western North America. Latin name: *Sarcobatus vermiculatus*. **2.** a bush that is similar to or related to the true greasewood, e.g. the creosote bush

greasy /greéssi, greézi/ (**-ier, -iest**) *adj* **1.** MADE OF GREASE consisting of grease or of something with the consistency of grease **2.** THICK WITH GREASE covered with or containing grease, often a lot or too much of it ○ *a greasy hamburger* **3.** HAVING EXCESSIVE NATURAL OILS producing or containing a lot of natural oils **4.** PRODUCED BY GREASE caused by grease or by something with the consistency of grease ○ *a greasy stain* **5.** SLIPPERY difficult to move, walk, or drive on because of wetness or iciness **6.** SMARMY unpleasantly and insincerely flattering, friendly, or grovelling —**greasily** *adv* —**greasiness** *n*

greasy spoon *n* a small, cheap, and often dirty café, especially one that serves fried food (*informal*)

great /grayt/ *adj* **1.** IMPRESSIVELY LARGE very large and impressive **2.** LARGE IN NUMBER large in number or with many parts ○ *a great crowd of well-wishers* **3.** BIGGER THAN OTHERS larger or more important than others of the same kind **4.** MUCH extreme or more than usual ○ *It gives me great pleasure to introduce our speaker tonight.* **5.** LASTING LONG TIME lasting a long time, or covering a long distance ○ *one of the world's great railway journeys* **6.** IMPORTANT very significant or important **7.** EXCEPTIONALLY TALENTED with exceptional talents or achievements **8.** POWERFUL powerful and influential ○ *striving to make our nation great again* **9.** EXPERT able to do something very well, or very skilful with something (*informal*) **10.** VERY GOOD very good or pleasing ○ *It was great to hear your news.* **11.** USEFUL very useful or suitable for a particular task (*informal*) ○ *This cast-iron pan is great for doing pancakes.* **12.** BEING GOOD EXAMPLE OF SOMETHING doing something often, enjoying something very much, or being a very good example of something ○ *Joe's a great one for the soaps – he never misses an episode.* **13.** USED FOR EMPHASIS used to emphasize how much of a quality somebody or something has (*informal*) ○ *Their new house is a great big place out in the country.* ○ *I can't wear this – there's a dirty great hole in the front!* **14.** same as **pregnant** (sense 1) (*archaic*) ■ *n* **1.** SOMEBODY GREAT somebody whose fame or influence has proved to be long-lasting ○ *one of the all-time greats of blues music* **2.** MUSIC PART OF PIPE ORGAN the principal division of a pipe organ ■ *adv* VERY WELL very well (*informal*) ○ *That's it; you're doing great.* ○ *Steve and I get along just great.* [Old English *grēat* 'thick, coarse' < Germanic] —**greatly** *adv*—**greatness** *n*

CULTURAL NOTE *The Great Gatsby*, a novel (1925) by US writer F. Scott Fitzgerald. Set on Long Island, New York, it is the story of enigmatic businessman Jay Gatsby, a symbol of the American obsession with wealth and status, whose attempts to revive a relationship with an old girlfriend lead to his downfall. It was made into films by Elliott Nugent in 1949 and by Jack Clayton in 1974.

great- *prefix* **1.** being a parent of somebody's grandparent ○ *great-grandmother* **2.** being a child of one of somebody's grandchildren ○ *great-grandson*

great ape *n* a large ape, e.g. a gorilla, chimpanzee, or orang-utan

Great Attractor *n* a large aggregation of galaxies, approximately 150 to 350 million light-years away, whose gravitational pull might account for the unexpected motions of many galaxies, including our own

great auk *n* a large flightless seabird that was hunted to extinction in the mid-19th century. Native to: formerly, North Atlantic coasts. Latin name: *Alca impennis*.

great-aunt *n* an aunt of somebody's father or mother

Great Australian Bight /grayt-/ wide inlet of the Indian Ocean off the southern coast of Australia. It stretches 1,100 km/685 mi. from Cape Pasley in Western Australia to Cape Carnot in South Australia.

Great Barrier Reef chain of coral reefs in the Coral Sea, located off the coast of Queensland, Australia. The largest deposit of coral in the world, the reef extends for 2,010 km/1,250 mi. Area: 348,600 sq. km/134,600 sq. mi.

Great Basin /-báyss'n/ desert covering most of Nevada and parts of Utah, Oregon, Idaho, and California. Area: 543,900 sq. km/210,000 sq. mi.

Great Bear *n* ASTRON same as **Ursa Major**

Great Bear Lake freshwater lake in Canada's Northwest Territories, lying astride the Arctic Circle. It is the world's seventh largest lake. Area: 31,790 sq. km/12,270 sq. mi.

Great Britain the largest island of the British Isles in northwestern Europe. It includes England, Scotland, and Wales.

great circle *n* a circle on the surface of a sphere such as the Earth that has a radius equal to the radius of the sphere, and whose centre is also the sphere's centre

greatcoat /gráyt kōt/ *n* a long thick heavy overcoat worn especially by soldiers

Great Dane

Great Dane *n* a very large dog with long legs, a square head, a deep muzzle, and short hair, belonging to a breed originating in Germany [Because Germans were formerly called Danes]

Great Depression *n* a drastic decline in the world economy resulting in mass unemployment and widespread poverty that lasted from 1929 until 1939

great divide *n* a major demarcation between two contrasting things, especially life and death

Great Divide *n* same as **Continental Divide**

Great Dividing Range /-di vǐding-/ system of mountain ranges and plateaus in Queensland, New South Wales, and Victoria, extending along the eastern border of Australia. The highest peak is Mount Kosciuszko, 2,228 m/7,310 ft.

Greater Antilles /gráytər an tílleez/ island group in the northern Caribbean, comprising Cuba, Jamaica, Hispaniola, and Puerto Rico

Greater Bairam *n* an Islamic festival marking the end of the Islamic year. Date: 70 days after the end of Ramadan.

greater celandine *n* a plant of the poppy family that yields an orange-coloured latex used to treat eye and skin disorders. Flowers: yellow. Latin name: *Chelidonium majus*.

greater omentum *n* the fold of the peritoneum that covers the intestines

Greater Public Schools *npl Aus* a group of Australian secondary schools, mainly private ones, with high reputations and prestige

Greater Sunda Islands ◗ **Sunda Islands**

greatest common divisor *n US* MATHS same as **highest common factor**

greatful incorrect spelling of **grateful**

Great Glen rift valley in Scotland that extends southwestwards from the Moray Firth to Loch Linnhe. It contains Loch Lochy and Loch Ness. Length: 156 km/97 mi.

great-grandchild *n* a son or daughter of somebody's grandchild

great-grandparent *n* the mother or father of somebody's grandmother or grandfather

great-hearted /-haártid/ *adj* **1.** with a generous and forgiving nature **2.** not easily frightened or dispirited —**great-heartedly** *adv*

Great Indian Desert ◗ **Thar Desert**

Great Karoo ◗ **Karoo**

Great Lake largest natural freshwater lake in Australia, located on Tasmania, near the Great Western Tiers. Area: 114 sq. km/44 sq. mi.

Great Lakes

Great Lakes group of five freshwater lakes in north-central North America, interconnected by natural and artificial channels. The largest group of lakes in the world, they are Lakes Superior, Michigan, Huron, Erie, and Ontario. Area: 244,100 sq. km/94,250 sq. mi.

Great Leap Forward *n* the attempt by the People's Republic of China from 1958 to 1960 to modernize agriculture by labour-intensive methods

great mountain buttercup *n* PLANTS same as **Mount Cook lily**

great-nephew *n UK, ANZ, Can* a son of somebody's nephew or niece

great-niece *n UK, ANZ, Can* a daughter of somebody's nephew or niece

great northern diver *n* a large black-and-white diving bird. Native to: especially North America. Latin name: *Gavia immer*. US term **loon**[1]

great organ *n* the main keyboard of an organ, and the pipes and mechanism relating to it

Great Plains vast high plateau region in central North America that stretches from northeastern Canada to southern Texas between the Canadian Shield and Central Lowlands on the east and the Rocky Mountains on the west. Area: 3,200,000 sq. km/1,200,000 sq. mi.

Great Power *n* a nation that has a far-reaching political, social, economic, and usually military influence internationally (*hyphenated when used before a noun*)

Great Rebellion *n* the Royalists' name for the English Civil War

Great Rift Valley depression extending more than 4,830 km/3,000 mi. from the valley of the River Jordan in Syria to Mozambique, forming the most extensive rift in the Earth's surface. The area is marked by a chain of seas and lakes and a series of volcanoes.

Great Russian *n* (*dated*) **1.** the Russian language **2.** a member of the main Russian-speaking ethnic group in Russia —**Great Russian** *adj*

Great St Bernard Pass /-sənt búrnərd-, -sáN bər naárd-/ mountain pass in western Europe, on the border between Valais, central Switzerland, and Aosta Province, Piedmont, northern Italy. Founded in the 11th century, it is named after the hospice founded at its summit by the French monk St Bernard. Height: 2,468 m/8,098 ft.

Great Salt Lake shallow body of salt water in northwestern Utah, near Salt Lake City. It is the largest salt lake in North America. Area: 5,200 sq. km/2,000 sq. mi.

Great Sandy Desert desert in northwestern Australia that contains large areas of sand dunes and salt marshes and some grassland. Area: 390,000 sq. km/150,000 sq. mi.

Great Schism *n* **1.** the period between 1378 and 1415 when there were rival popes, one reigning in Rome and the other in Avignon **2.** the separation of the Roman Catholic and Eastern Orthodox churches in 1054, as a result of theological disagreement

Great Seal *n* in the United Kingdom, the seal kept in the charge of the Lord Chancellor or, formerly, the Lord Keeper of the Seal, and used in sealing important state papers

Great Slave Lake freshwater lake in the Northwest Territories, northwestern Canada. It is the deepest lake in North America. Depth: 614 m/2,015 ft. Area: 28,570 sq. km/11,030 sq. mi.

Great Smoky Mountains /-smŏkee-/ mountain range in the southeastern United States, forming part of the Appalachian Mountain system, in western North Carolina and eastern Tennessee. Its highest point is Clingmans Dome (2,024 km/6,642 ft).

Great Smoky Mountains National Park national park in the southeastern United States, in western North Carolina and eastern Tennessee. Established in 1930, it contains some of the highest peaks in eastern North America. Area: 2,111 sq. km/815 sq. mi.

great tit *n* a large common tit with a short beak and yellow, black, and white markings. Native to: Europe, Asia. Latin name: *Parus major*.

Great Trek *n* a mass movement between 1836 and 1844 of Boer cattlemen in South Africa from the Cape to the north that eventually resulted in the establishment of the Transvaal and the Orange Free State

great-uncle *n* an uncle of somebody's father or mother

Great Victoria Desert desert in the states of Western Australia and South Australia, consisting of sand dunes, salt lakes, and low scrubland. Area: 390,000 sq. km/150,000 sq. mi.

Great Wall *n* **1.** a huge expanse of thousands of galaxies arranged in a supercluster that forms the largest system of astronomical objects observed in the universe **2.** HIST same as **Great Wall of China**

Great Wall of China
Barnaby's

Great Wall of China *n* a vast Chinese defensive fortification begun in the 3rd century BC and running along the northern border of the country for 2400 km/1500 mi

Great War *n* HIST same as **World War I**

great white shark *n* a large shark that is grey-brown with white underparts and preys on large fish, marine mammals, and carrion. Native to: warm and tropical waters. Latin name: *Carcharodon carcharias.*

Great Yarmouth /-yaármǝth/ port and coastal resort in Norfolk, eastern England. It is an important terminal for freight from continental Europe. Population: 90,810 (2001).

great year *n* a period of about 25,800 years, representing a complete cycle of the precession of the equinoxes

greave /greev/ *n* a piece of armour worn from the ankle to the knee (*usually used in the plural*) [14C. < Old French *greve* 'calf, shin']

grebe

grebe /greeb/ (*plural* **grebes** or *same*) *n* a mainly freshwater diving bird that has lobed toes and is a strong swimmer. Family: Podicipedidae. [Mid-18C. < French *grebe*]

Grecian /greésh'n/ *adj* **1.** relating to the ancient Greek style of architecture or sculpture **2.** PEOPLES same as **Greek** *n* (sense 1) (*dated*) ■ *n* (*dated*) **1.** a Hellenist **2.** LANG same as **Greek** *n* (sense 2) —**Grecianize** *vt*

Grecism *n* LANGUAGE, ANCIENT HIST another spelling of **Graecism**

Grecize *vt* ANCIENT HIST another spelling of **Graecize**

Greco /grékō/, **El** (1541–1614) Greek-born Spanish painter. His works combine the baroque style with exaggerated mannerism, and are characterized by lambent lighting and long figures. Born **Theotokopoulos, Domenikos**

Greco- *prefix* another spelling of **Graeco-**

Greece

Greece /greess/ country in southeastern Europe, comprising the southernmost part of the Balkan Peninsula and numerous islands in the eastern Mediterranean. Language: Greek. Currency: drachma. Capital: Athens. Population: 10,665,989 (2003). Area: 131,957 sq. km/50,949 sq. mi. Official name **Hellenic Republic**

greed /greed/ *n* **1.** the habit of eating to excess, or the desire to do so **2.** an overwhelming desire to have more of something such as money than is actually needed [Late 16C. Back-formation < GREEDY]

greedy /greédi/ (*-ier, -iest*) *adj* **1.** eating to excess, or wanting to do so **2.** having an overwhelming desire to have more of something such as money than is actually needed [Old English *grædig* < Germanic, 'hunger, greed'] —**greedily** *adv* —**greediness** *n*

greedyguts /greédi guts/ (*plural same*) *n* a greedy eater (*informal insult*)

greegree *n* ANTHROP another spelling of **grigri**

Greek /greek/ *n* **1.** SOMEBODY FROM GREECE somebody who comes from Greece **2.** LANGUAGE OF GREECE the official language of Greece and part of Cyprus. Native speakers: 12 million. **3.** LANG same as **Ancient Greek** ■ *adj* **1.** OF GREECE relating to Greece or its people, language, or culture **2.** OF GREEK relating to the ancient or modern Greek language **3.** OF ORTHODOX CHURCH relating to the Greek Orthodox Church ▶ See panel on next page [Old English *grecas*, via Latin *Graecus* < Greek *Graikos* 'the Hellenic people'] ◇ **beware of Greeks bearing gifts** be careful of possible treachery from somebody who appears to be kind (*sometimes offensive*) ◇ **it's (all) Greek to me** used to say that you cannot understand something

Greek Catholic *n* **1.** a member of the Eastern Orthodox Church **2.** a member of the Uniat Greek Church

Greek Church *n* CHR same as **Greek Orthodox Church**

Greek cross *n* a cross consisting of four arms of the same length

Greek key *n* an ornate pattern for a cornice or border consisting of lines that change direction at right angles to form a continuous band

Greek Orthodox Church *n* the national church of Greece, an independent branch of the Orthodox Church

Greek salad *n* a salad of tomatoes, lettuce, cucumber, olives, oregano, and feta cheese

green /green/ *adj* **1.** GRASS-COLOURED of a colour in the spectrum between yellow and blue, like the colour of grass **2.** HAVING EDIBLE GREEN LEAVES consisting of or containing green leaves of vegetables ○ *a green salad* **3.** GRASSY OR LEAFY consisting of or containing grass, plants, or foliage **4.** *also* **Green** POL ADVOCATING PROTECTION OF ENVIRONMENT supporting or promoting the protection of the environment **5.** MADE WITH LITTLE ENVIRONMENTAL HARM produced in an environmentally and ecologically friendly way, e.g. by using renewable resources **6.** NOT RIPE unripe or not mature ○ *green bananas* **7.** UNSMOKED still raw, not yet smoked **8.** JEALOUS envious or jealous **9.** SICKLY-LOOKING pale and sickly-looking, especially as a result of nausea **10.** INNOCENT naïve and lacking experience, especially because of being new to something **11.** NEW young, new, recent, or fresh **12.** WOODWORK UNSEASONED describes newly cut and unseasoned wood ○ *green wood* **13.** INDUST UNTANNED describes leather that is not yet tanned **14.** CERAMICS UNFIRED describes objects that are not yet fired ■ *n* **1.** COLOUR OF GRASS a primary colour between yellow and blue in the spectrum,

like the colour of grass **2.** GREEN COLOURING a green pigment or dye **3.** GREEN CLOTH green fabric or clothing **4.** GREEN THING a green object, especially the green ball in snooker **5.** GRASSY AREA an area of ground that is covered with grass, especially a public or communal area **6.** BOWLS GRASSY AREA FOR BOWLING an area of grass that is maintained for bowling and similar games **7.** GOLF GRASSY AREA SURROUNDING GOLF HOLE the closely mown area at the end of a fairway on a golf course on which the hole for the ball is located **8.** *Scotland* GRASSY AREA BELONGING TO HOUSE an area of grass belonging to a house or block of flats **9.** *also* **Green** POL ADVOCATE OF PROTECTION OF ENVIRONMENT a supporter or advocate of protecting the environment, especially a member of a political party concerned with environmental issues **10.** *UK* same as **greenery** (sense 2) **11.** *US* FIN MONEY cash or paper money (*slang*) ■ **greens** *npl* **1.** GREEN VEGETABLES vegetables with green leaves and stems, e.g. cabbage and spinach **2.** *ANZ, N Am* green foliage used for decoration. UK term **greenery 2.** *US* GREEN-COLOURED CLOTHING green clothing, e.g. US Army uniforms or operating room scrubs (*informal*) ■ *v* (**greens, greening, greened**) **1.** *vti* BECOME GREEN to become green, or make something green **2.** *vt* PLANT TREES IN AREA to plant trees and develop parks in urban areas **3.** *vti* ENVIRON BECOME ENVIRONMENTAL ADVOCATE to become aware of environmental issues, or make somebody aware of environmental issues [Old English *grene* < Germanic] —**greenish** *adj* —**greenly** *adv* —**greenness** *n* ◇ **go green** to become actively interested in environmental issues and support environmental causes

green accounting *n* BUSINESS, ENVIRON same as **environmental accounting**

green alga *n* an alga found mostly in fresh water. Division: *Chlorophyta.*

green audit *n* same as **environmental audit**

greenback /green bak/ *n* US a US bank note of any denomination (*slang*)

green bean *n* a bean that is eaten complete with its pod, e.g. a French bean or runner bean

green belt *n* **1.** a strip of undeveloped land around a city that cannot be built on because of government legislation preventing urban sprawl **2.** an irrigated area of land on the edge of a desert, designed to prevent any further encroachment by the desert

Green Beret *n* (*informal*) **1.** a British commando **2.** a US Special Forces soldier [< the regulation green beret worn by members]

greenbottle /green bot'l/, **greenbottle fly** *n* a fly that is metallic green in colour and lays its eggs in rotting vegetation or flesh. Genus: *Lucilia.*

green burial *n* a burial designed to have minimal environmental impact, typically with a corpse that has not been embalmed being placed in a biodegradable coffin or bag and buried in a grave marked with a sapling

green card *n* **1.** *US* IDENTITY CARD in the United States, an identity card and work permit issued to nationals of other countries **2.** DRIVING INSURANCE DOCUMENT an insurance document for motorists driving abroad **3.** BRITISH DISABLED PERSON'S IDENTITY CARD in the United Kingdom, an identity card issued by the government to a person with disabilities —**green-carder** *n*

green dragon *n* a tuberous plant that has divided leaves. Flowers: small, green, on a stalk enclosed in a tight green sheath. Native to: North America. Latin name: *Arisaema dracontium.*

Greene /green/, **Graham** (1904–91) British writer. His major novels, including *Brighton Rock* (1938) and *The Power and the Glory* (1940), incorporate themes of spiritual and moral struggle. He wrote the screenplay for the film *The Third Man* (1950). Full name **Greene, Henry Graham**. See illustration on next page

'There is always one moment in childhood when the door opens and lets the future in.'
[Graham Greene, *The Power and the Glory*; 1940]

green earth *n* ART same as **terre verte**

greenery /greénǝri/ *n* **1.** growing green foliage and plants **2.** *UK* green leaves and small branches from trees and bushes used for decoration. ANZ, N Am term **greens** (*see* **green**)

LANGUAGE HERITAGE *Greek* Much of English is made up of words from other languages, and a large proportion come from Greek, not usually directly, but indirectly via Latin and sometimes, again through Latin, immediately from French. The first words to migrate to English straight from Greek did not arrive until the late medieval and Renaissance periods, with the revival of classical learning, for example in the 15th century *aneurysm*, *epiglottis*, and some letters of the Greek alphabet that were not already known through Latin, *chi*, *eta*, *kappa*, and *psi*; in the early 16th century *sycamine* (a tree mentioned in the Bible) and the letter *omega*; in the mid-16th century *hegemony*; in the late 16th century, when the pace of migration picks up, *acme*, *anaglyph* ('decoration carved in low relief'), *apologize*, *epigraph*, *euphemism*, *nemesis*, *pathos*, *synchronism*, and geometrical shapes including the *hexahedron* and *parallelepiped* ('polyhedron consisting of six faces that are parallelograms'). These early migrants are typical of their successors: learned, literary, linguistic, medical, mathematical, generally scientific – not for the *hoi polloi* (mid-17th century). The 20th century followed up with, for example, (early 20th) *agnosia* ('loss of the ability to recognize familiar people or objects'), *bar* (a unit of pressure, from *baros* 'weight'), *clone* (from *klōn* 'twig'), *empathy*, and *kinesis*; (mid-20th) *deixis* ('use of words whose full meaning depends on context') and *topos* ('traditional theme in literature or rhetoric', in Greek 'place').

New words have continued to be formed from Greek elements combined with others, in the 20th century, for example, *autism* (from *autos* 'self'), *epistemic*, *holism*, *mastectomy* (from *mastos* 'breast'), *podiatry* (from *pod-* 'foot'), *Proterozoic* (from *proteros* 'former' + *zōē* 'life'), and various phobias such as *ailurophobia* (from *ailuros* 'cat') and *triskaidekaphobia* ('fear of the number thirteen'); among the more recent formations is the humorous *arctophile* ('collector of teddy bears', from *arktos* 'bear'). The prefix *tele-*, from Greek *tēle* 'far away', has become vigorously productive, with words from *television* to *teleconferencing* and *telemedicine*.

It may be noticed that many of these words, though directly from Greek, are spelt as if they came from Latin: the letter usually transliterated from the Greek alphabet as *k* is represented by *c*, Greek *kh* appears as *ch*, instances of *u* appear as *y*, and so on. So many Greek words passed through Latin in transit to English that the two languages readily hybridize. The process started early: *antithetical*, for example, a late 16th century formation, is based on Greek *antithetikos* but with a suffix derived from Latin *-alis*. Early Greek migrants through Latin include *acacia*, *idea*, and *tetanus* (14th century); *geography*, *iris*, and *magma* (15th); *asthmatic*, *basis*, *gymnastic*, *proboscis*, and *sympathy* (16th). The earliest arrival in English from Greek via Latin is not recognizably either, however: *bishop*, recorded in Old English and a common Germanic form with initial *b-* from a popular variant of Latin *episcopus* from Greek *episkopos*. Another Old English word with related forms in other Germanic languages is *church*, ultimately from Greek *kuriakon dōma* 'house of the lord'. Ecclesiastical words often took the road from Greek, including *ecclesiastic*, 15th century via French or ecclesiastical Latin from Greek *ekklēsiastikos*.

'Greek' alone usually refers to Ancient Greek, used from about 1500 BC to about AD 500: later periods are specified as 'late Greek', 'ecclesiastical Greek', etc. as appropriate. Modern Greek migrants are comparatively uncommon, but bring with them the pleasures of Greek food and drink: *feta* cheese, *filo* pastry (from *phullo* 'leaf'), *taramasalata* (from *taramas* 'preserved roe' + *salata* 'salad'), *ouzo*, and *retsina* (modern Greek from Greek *rētinē* 'pine resin').

AKG London

Graham Greene

green-eyed monster *n* jealousy or envy personified

greenfield /green feeld/ *adj* relating to or situated in a piece of open land that has not been built on

greenfinch /green finch/ (*plural* **-finches** or *same*) *n* a green-grey and yellow finch. Native to: Europe. Latin name: *Carduelis chloris*.

green fingers *npl* a natural ability to make plants grow well. N Am term **green thumb** —**green-fingered** *adj*

greenflag /green flág/ (**-flags**, **-flagging**, **-flagged**) *vt S Asia* to give approval or permission for something to proceed [< the use of a green flag in motor racing to start a race]

greenfly /green flī/ (*plural same* or **-flies**) *n* a green winged aphid that is a pest of garden plants, houseplants, and crops

greengage /green gayj/ *n* **1.** a sweet green plum **2.** a tree that produces greengages. Latin name: *Prunus domestica italica*. [Early 18C. After Sir William *Gage* (1657–1727), English botanist]

greengrocer /green gróssər/ *n* **1.** FRUIT AND VEGETABLE SELLER a dealer in fresh fruit and vegetables **2.** *also* **greengrocer's** (*plural same*) FRUIT AND VEGETABLE SHOP a shop that sells fresh fruits and vegetables **3.** AUSTRALIAN CICADA a large bright-green Australian cicada. Latin name: *Cyclochila australasiae*.

greengrocery /green gróssəri/ *n* (*plural* **-ies**) **1.** COMM same as **greengrocer** (sense 2) **2.** the trade or profession of a greengrocer ▪ **greengroceries** *npl* fresh fruit and vegetables sold by a greengrocer

greenhead /green hed/ *n* a male mallard duck

greenheart /green haart/ (*plural* **-hearts** or *same*) *n* **1.** TROPICAL WOOD a dark greenish wood from a tropical American laurel **2.** TROPICAL AMERICAN TREE an evergreen tree of the laurel family that yields greenheart. Native to: tropical America. Latin name: *Ocotea rodiaei*. **3.** TREE LIKE GREENHEART any tree similar to the tropical American greenheart

greenhorn /green hawrn/ *n* somebody who lacks experience and may be naive or gullible

SYNONYMS See *beginner*.

greenhouse /green howss/ (*plural* **-houses** /-howziz/) *n* a glass or transparent plastic structure, often on a metal or wooden frame, in which plants that need heat, light, and protection from the weather are grown

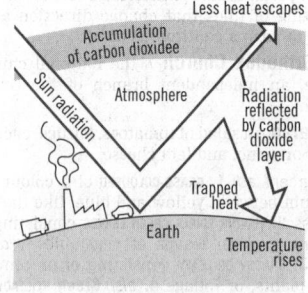

greenhouse effect

greenhouse effect *n* warming of the Earth's surface as a result of atmospheric pollution by gases. It is now feared that the warming effects are being undesirably increased, causing climate changes and melting polar icecaps.

greenhouse gas *n* a gas that contributes to the warming of the Earth's atmosphere by reflecting radiation from the Earth's surface, e.g. carbon dioxide, ozone, or water vapour

greenie /greeni/ *n Aus* a conservationist or environmentalist (*informal*; *often disapproving*)

greening /greening/ *n* **1.** GREEN APPLE an apple that is green when ripe **2.** PLANTING OF TREES the process of planting trees and other vegetation in an area **3.** INCREASING OF ENVIRONMENTAL AWARENESS the process of becoming more aware, or increasing others' awareness, of the environment and environmental issues

green keeper *n* somebody who manages and maintains a golf course or bowling green. N Am term **greenskeeper**

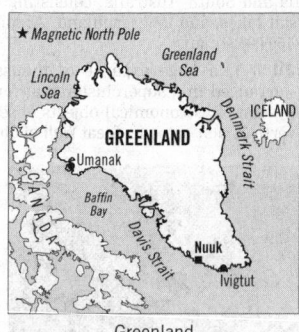

Greenland

Greenland /greenlənd/ island situated between the North Atlantic and Arctic oceans. The largest island in the world, it is a self-governing part of Denmark. Population: 56,385 (2003). Area: 2,175,600 sq. km/840,000 sq. mi. —**Greenlander** *n*

Greenlandic /green lándik/ *n* INUIT DIALECT a dialect of Inuit spoken in Greenland. Native speakers: 160,000. ▪ *adj* **1.** OF GREENLAND DIALECT relating to the dialect Greenlandic **2.** OF GREENLAND relating to Greenland or its language, people, or culture

Greenland right whale *n* ZOOL same as **bowhead**

Greenland Sea section of the Atlantic Ocean off the coast of northeastern Greenland that is covered by pack ice for most of the year

green light *n* **1.** a light that is green in colour and is used as a signal at intersections for vehicles or pedestrians to proceed **2.** permission to start work on something, especially a project or plan

greenlight /green līt/ (**-lights**, **-lighting**, **-lighted**) *vt US* to give approval or permission for something to proceed (*informal*) ○ *Are they going to greenlight the project?*

Green Line *n* in the state of Israel, the pre-1967 border along the West Bank and the Gaza Strip [Late 20C.]

greenling /greenling/ (*plural* **-lings** or *same*) *n* a fish with large pectoral fins, a large head, and a skin flap over each eye. Native to: northern Pacific coastal waters. Family: Hexagrammidae.

greenmail /green mayl/ *n* the purchase of enough of a company's shares to threaten it with takeover, thereby forcing the company to buy back the stock at a higher price to avoid the takeover ▪ *vt* (**-mails**, **-mailing**, **-mailed**) to subject a company to greenmail [Late 20C. < GREEN 'money' + BLACKMAIL] —**greenmailer** *n*

green man *n* an illuminated green symbol of a walking man at a pedestrian crossing that indicates that it is safe to cross

green manure *n* a growing crop that is ploughed directly back into the soil to act as a fertilizer

green monkey *n* a small olive green monkey that lives in large troops in woodlands or on the edge of savanna grasslands. Native to: Africa. Latin name: *Cercophithecus aethiops sabaeus*.

green monkey disease *n* MED same as **Marburg disease**

Green Mountains mountain range in the Appalachian system, extending from Canada into western Massachusetts. The highest peak is Mount Mansfield, 1,339 m/4,393 ft.

Greenock /greenək/ seaport on the Firth of Clyde, southwestern Scotland, the birthplace of James Watt. Population: 50,013 (1991).

greenockite /greenə kīt/ *n* a yellowish crystalline mineral consisting of cadmium sulphide [Mid-18C. After Charles Murray Cathcart, Lord *Greenock* (1783–1859)]

green onion *n* N Am same as **spring onion**

green paper *n* in the United Kingdom or Canada, a document that contains the government's policy proposals that are to be discussed in Parliament

Green Party *n* a political party whose primary policy is the protection of the environment

Greenpeace /green peess/ *n* an international organization that advocates the protection of the environment and takes nonviolent action to achieve its aims

green pepper *n* an unripe sweet pepper eaten raw or cooked. Latin name: *Capsicum annuum.*

green pound *n* the British pound as a unit of exchange in trading farm produce from the European Union under the Common Agricultural Policy

green revolution *n* the introduction of modern farming techniques and higher-yielding, more pest-resistant varieties of crops in order to significantly increase crop production

greenroom /green room, -room/ *n* a room in a studio, theatre, or concert hall where performers may relax before or after a performance or appearance

green salad *n* a salad made of lettuce or other green leaves of vegetables, sometimes including other raw green vegetables such as cucumber or green pepper. It is usually served with a vinaigrette dressing.

greensand /green sand/ *n* sandstone flecked with the dark-green clay mineral glauconite

Greensboro /greenzbərə/ city in northern North Carolina. It is the site of Guilford College. Population: 228,217 (2002 estimate).

greenshank /green shangk/ (*plural* **-shanks** or *same*) *n* a large sandpiper with long greenish legs. Native to: Europe, Asia. Latin name: *Tringa nebularia.*

greensickness /green siknəss/ *n* MED same as **chlorosis** (sense 2) —**greensick** *adj*

greenskeeper /greenz keepər/ *n* N Am GOLF same as **green keeper**

green snake *n* a slender nonpoisonous snake that is yellow-green in colour and feeds on insects, especially grasshoppers. Native to: North America. Genus: *Opheodryas.*

greenstick fracture *n* a bone fracture usually occurring in children, in which one side of the bone is broken and the other side is bent [< GREEN 'immature' + STICK[1] because it resembles one]

greenstone /green stōn/ *n* **1.** a green igneous rock containing the minerals feldspar and hornblende **2.** a dark New Zealand jade. Use: Maori weapons, jewellery.

greenstrip /green strip/ *n* US a firebreak on open grassland, planted with vegetation that does not burn easily

greensward /green swawrd/ *n* a grass-covered area (*archaic or literary*)

greentailing /green tayling/ *n* environmentally responsible retailing that involves the sale of products with the least impact on the environment or that increases the ecological awareness of the consumer (*informal*) [< GREEN + *retailing*]

green tariff electricity *n* electricity produced from renewable energy sources such as wind, water, and solar power

green tea *n* tea made from leaves that have been dried but not fermented. It is pale green in colour.

green thumb *n* N Am same as **green fingers**

green turtle *n* a large turtle that is sometimes killed for food. It comes to land only to bask, sleep, and lay eggs. Native to: warm seas. Latin name: *Chelonia mydas.* [< its green shell]

green vitriol *n* CHEM same as **ferrous sulphate**

greenware /green wair/ *n* clay objects that have dried but have not yet been fired

greenwash /green wosh/ *n* public relations' initiatives by a business or organization, e.g. advertising or public consultation, that purport to show concern for the environmental impact of its activities (*disapproving*) [Late 20C. < GREEN 'favourable to the environment', after WHITEWASH]

greenway /green way/ *n* N Am a stretch of undeveloped land close to an urban area that is kept for recreational use

Greenway /green way/, **Francis Howard** (1777–1837) British-born Australian architect. He was transported to Australia for forgery in 1814, and there designed numerous public buildings in New South Wales.

green-wellie *adj* relating to rich upper-class British people who enjoy country pursuits (*informal*) [< the stereotype of the green wellingtons worn by such people]

green welly brigade *n* members of the British upper middle class, especially those fond of rural pursuits (*informal*)

Greenwich /grénnich, -ij/ borough of London, on the southern bank of the River Thames. It is the site of the prime meridian, which passes through the Royal Greenwich Observatory. Population: 214,403 (2001).

Greenwich Mean Time *n* the time in a zone that includes the 0° meridian of Greenwich, London, used formerly as the main standard from which the time in other zones was calculated

Greenwich Village residential area in lower Manhattan, once popular with bohemians, artists, and writers and now a tourist attraction

greenwood /green wood/ *n* a forest or wood in the summer when the leaves are green (*archaic*)

green woodpecker *n* a large woodpecker with green feathers and a red crown that often feeds on the ground. Native to: Europe. Latin name: *Picus viridis.*

Germaine Greer

Greer /greer/, **Germaine** (*b.* 1939) Australian writer and feminist. She launched her career as a passionate advocate of women's empowerment with her first book, *The Female Eunuch* (1970).

'Human beings have an inalienable right to invent themselves; when that right is pre-empted, it is called brainwashing.'
[Germaine Greer, *Times*; 1 February 1986]

greet[1] /greet/ (**greets, greeting, greeted**) *vt* **1.** WELCOME SOMEBODY to welcome somebody in a cordial and usually conventional way **2.** ADDRESS SOMEBODY COURTEOUSLY to address somebody in a polite and usually conventional way on meeting **3.** ADDRESS SOMEBODY IN LETTER to address a person or group at the start of a letter using a set formula **4.** REPLY TO SOMETHING to receive or respond to something in a particular way ○ *The news was greeted with dismay.* **5.** BECOME NOTICEABLE TO SOMEBODY to become perceptible to somebody, especially by way of the senses such as vision, hearing, or smell ○ *The smell of a cake baking greeted them.* [Old English *gretan* < W Germanic, 'resound']

greet[2] /greet/ (**greets, greeting, greeted**) *vi* Scotland (*nonstandard*) **1.** to cry or weep **2.** to complain whiningly [Old English *grētan* and *grēotan* 'cry' < Germanic] —**greet** *n*

greeter /greetər/ *n* somebody employed to greet customers in a restaurant or similar business

greeting /greeting/ *n* **1.** FRIENDLY GESTURE a cordial and often conventional gesture or expression used when welcoming, meeting, or addressing somebody **2.** WELCOMING SOMEBODY an act of welcoming or addressing somebody with a greeting ■ **greetings** *npl* MESSAGE a friendly message or good wishes

greetings card *n* a folded piece of heavy paper with an image or design and a message to somebody to mark a special occasion

gregarine /gréggə reen/ *n* a protozoan that lives as a parasite in the digestive tracts of some insects, arthropods, annelids, and other invertebrates. Order: Gregarinida. ■ *adj also* **gregarinian** /gréggə rínni ən/ relating to or belonging to the order that comprises the gregarines [Mid-19C. < modern Latin *Gregarina* < Latin *gregarius* (see GREGARIOUS)]

gregarious /gri gáiri əss/ *adj* **1.** FRIENDLY very friendly and sociable **2.** LIVING COMMUNALLY describes organisms that live in groups **3.** GROWING TOGETHER describes plants that grow in clusters [Mid-17C. < Latin *gregarius* < *grex* 'flock'] —**gregariously** *adv* —**gregariousness** *n*

ORIGIN The Latin word *grex* 'flock', from which **gregarious** is derived, is also the source of English *aggregate*, *congregate*, and *egregious*.

Gregg /greg/, **Sir Norman McAlister** (1892–1966) Australian ophthalmologist. He discovered the danger posed to the developing foetus when a woman contracts rubella during pregnancy.

Gregorian calendar /gri gáwri ən-/ *n* the calendar introduced in 1582 by Pope Gregory XIII that is still in use and is a modification of the previous Roman calendar. It was not adopted by Britain and its colonies until 1752. ◊ **Hegira** (sense 2)

Gregorian chant *n* a liturgical chant of the Roman Catholic Church that is sung without accompaniment [< its supposed introduction by GREGORY I]

Gregorian telescope *n* an astronomical telescope that has a concave primary mirror with a central hole through which light is reflected from a smaller secondary concave mirror [After J. *Gregory* (1638–75), Scottish mathematician]

Gregory I /gréggəri/, **St** (540?–604) pope (590–604). He sent St Augustine to England to lead the country's conversion to Christianity. He is said to have introduced Gregorian chant into the Roman Catholic liturgy. Known as **Gregory the Great**

'Not Angles but angels.'
[Gregory I. Reported in *Ecclesiastical History of the English People*, Saint Bede the Venerable; 731]

Gregory VII, St (1020?–85) pope (1073–85). He sought to reassert papal authority within the Church and weaken secular influences. His reforms provoked the Holy Roman Emperor Henry IV to replace him with an antipope (1076).

Gregory XIII (1502–85) pope (1572–85). He built several universities and a papal palace in Rome, and devised the Gregorian calender (1582). Born **Ugo Buoncompagni**

greisen /gríz'n/ *n* a granite-derived rock consisting of mica and quartz [Late 19C. < German, probably < *greis* 'grey with age']

gremlin /grémmlin/ *n* **1.** a tiny mischievous imaginary being that is blamed for faults in tools, machinery, and electronic equipment (*informal*) **2.** Aus a young surfer (*slang*) [Early 20C. Probably after GOBLIN]

gremmie /grémmi/, **gremmy** (*plural* **-mies**) *n* Aus SURFING same as **gremlin** (sense 2) (*slang*)

Grenache /grə násh/ *n* a red grape variety. Use: to make red wine. [Mid-19C. < French]

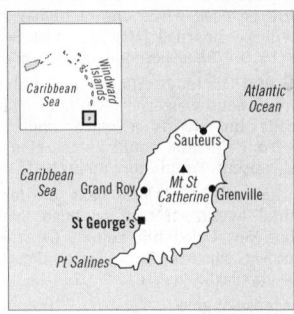
Grenada

Grenada /grə náydə/ independent state in the southeastern Caribbean Sea, comprising the island of Grenada and some of the southern Grenadines. It became an independent member of the Commonwealth in 1974. Language: English. Currency: East Caribbean dollar. Capital: St George's. Population: 89,258 (2003). Area: 344 sq. km/133 sq. mi. — **Grenadian** *n, adj*

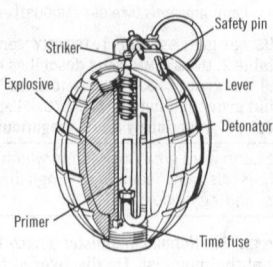

grenade

grenade /gri náyd/ *n* **1.** a small bomb that is thrown by hand or shot from a rifle or other weapon **2.** a sealed glass projectile that breaks on impact, releasing tear gas or chemicals to put out fires [Mid-16C. < French, alteration of *grenate* 'pomegranate' (shortening of *pome grenate*) after Spanish *granada*]

grenadier /grénnə deér/ (*plural* **-diers** or *same*) *n* **1.** GRENADE-CARRYING SOLDIER formerly, a soldier armed with grenades **2.** TALL STRONG SOLDIER formerly, a soldier assigned to a special company of a regiment on the basis of exceptional height and ability **3.** FISH a bottom-dwelling sea fish with a tapering body and no tail fin. Native to: deep waters worldwide. Family: Macrouridae. **4.** AFRICAN FINCH a finch with purple patches, a red beak, and a tapering tail. Native to: eastern Africa. Latin name: *Uraeginthus ianthinogaster*. [Late 17C. < French < *grenade* (see GRENADE)]

Grenadier, **Grenadier guard** *n* a British soldier belonging to the first regiment of the Guards Division, the troops of the Royal Household ■ **Grenadiers** *npl* in the British army, the first regiment of the Guards Division, the troops of the Royal Household

grenadine[1] /grénnə deen/ *n* **1.** a syrup made from pomegranates, used especially in cocktails **2.** a reddish-orange colour [Late 19C. < French (*sirop de*) *grenadine* < *grenade* (see GRENADE)] —**grenadine** *adj*

grenadine[2] /grénnə deen/ *n* a gauzy silk or woollen dress fabric [Mid-19C. < French, 'silk with a texture like grain' < *grain* (see GRAIN)]

Grenadines /grénnə deenz/, **Grenadine Islands** group of about 600 small islands, part of the Windward Islands, in the Caribbean Sea. The islands of the northern Grenadines are part of St Vincent and the Grenadines, some of the southern Grenadines belong to Grenada.

Grenoble /grə nốb'l/ industrial city and capital of Isère Department, in the Rhône-Alpes Region, southeastern France. Population: 153,317 (1999).

grenz rays /grénz-/ *npl* low-energy X-rays produced by electrons accelerated through less than 25 kilovolts [< German *Grenze* 'boundary']

Gresham's law /gréshəmz-/, **Gresham's theorem** *n* the theory that bad money drives good money out of circulation because a currency of lower intrinsic value will be used while one of higher intrinsic value will be hoarded [Mid-19C. After Sir Thomas Gresham (1519?–79), founder of the Royal Exchange]

Gretna Green /grétnə-/ village in Dumfries and Galloway, southwestern Scotland. It was historically notable as a place where eloping couples from England could be married without parental consent. Population: 3,149 (1991).

grevillia /grə vílli ə/ (*plural* **-leas** or **-lea**) *n* an ornamental evergreen tree or bush. Native to: Australia, New Caledonia. Genus: *Grevillea*. [Mid-19C. < modern Latin, after Charles Francis *Greville* (1749–1809), Scottish horticulturist]

grew past tense of **grow**

grey /gray/ *adj* **1.** OF COLOUR OF ASH of the colour of ash or lead ○ *a dull grey sky* ○ *city workers in grey suits* **2.** OF ELDERLY PEOPLE relating to, involving, or affecting people of advanced years ○ *grey marketing* ■ *n* **1.** COLOUR OF ASH the colour of ash or lead **2.** GREY COLOURING MATTER a pigment or dye formed from a combination of black and white that is like the colour of ash or lead ○ *Use greys and blues to emphasize the mood.* **3.** GREY CLOTHING fabric or clothing that is grey in colour **4.** *also* **Grey** CONFEDERATE SOLDIER a soldier of the

Confederacy in the American Civil War **5.** SOMETHING GREY a grey object ■ *vi* (**greys**, **greying**, **greyed**) TURN GREY to turn the colour grey ○ *His hair is greying*. [Old English *gr—æg* < Germanic] —**greyly** *adv* —**greyness** *n* —**greyish** *adj*

Grey /gray/, **Sir Edward, 1st Viscount Grey of Fallodon** (1862–1933) British politician. A member of the Liberal Party, he was Britain's secretary of state for foreign affairs (1905–16).

> 'The lamps are going out over all Europe; we shall not see them lit again in our lifetime.'
> [Sir Edward Grey, *Twenty-five Years, 1892–1916*; 1925]

Grey, **Sir George Edward** (1812–98) Portuguese-born British explorer and colonial administrator. He was governor of South Australia (1840–45), and governor (1845–53, 1861–68) and premier (1877–79) of New Zealand.

Grey, **Lady Jane** (1537–54) queen of England and Ireland. The great-granddaughter of Henry VII, she was named as the successor of Edward VI in 1553. She ruled for only nine days before being forced to abdicate, and was executed for treason.

Grey, **Zane** (1875–1939) US writer. His dozens of popular 'dime novels' helped define the Western as a literary genre, and included *Riders of the Purple Sage* (1912). Full name **Grey, Pearl Zane**

grey area *n* **1.** UNCLEAR SITUATION a situation, subject, or category of something that is unclear or hard to define or classify **2.** SOMETHING THAT CANNOT BE CLASSIFIED a part of something that does not belong to any specific category but contains features of more than one **3.** ECONOMICALLY DEPRESSED UK REGION in the United Kingdom, a part of the country suffering from high unemployment

greybar land /gráy baar-/ *n* the wait during a time-consuming computer operation while the graphic displaying a usually gray bar slowly moves across the screen (*informal*)

greybeard /gráy beerd/ *n* **1.** an elderly man (*dated*) **2.** an earthenware container for alcoholic drink — **greybearded** *adj*

grey eminence *n* same as **éminence grise**

Grey Friar *n* a member of the Franciscan order of friars [< the colour of the order's habit]

greyhen /gráy hen/ (*plural* **-hens** or *same*) *n* a female black grouse

greyhound

greyhound /gráy hownd/ *n* a tall slim fast-running dog with a smooth coat, narrow head, and long legs, widely used for racing [Old English *grīghund* < Germanic]

greying /gráy ing/ *n* same as **ageing** *n* (sense 1) ■ *adj* same as **ageing**

grey jay *n* a bird of the crow family that is grey with black markings on the head. Native to: coniferous forests, especially spruce forests, in North America. Latin name: *Perisoreus canadensis*.

greylag /gráy lag/, **greylag goose** *n* a common wild goose that is light brownish-grey with a large orange or pink beak and is the ancestor of the domestic farm goose. Native to: Europe, Asia. Latin name: *Anser anser*. [Early 18C. < GREY + dialect *lag* 'goose', origin ?]

grey literature *n* articles and information published, especially on the Internet, without a commercial purpose or the mediation of a commercial publisher

greymail /gráy mayl/ *n* a manoeuvre used by the defence in a spy trial whereby the government is threatened with the revelation of national secrets unless the case against the defendant is dropped [Late 20C. After BLACKMAIL]

grey market *n* **1.** trading in new shares before they have been officially issued on the stock exchange **2.** clandestine but legal trading in goods either at excessively high prices or at prices well below the manufacturer's recommended price

grey matter *n* **1.** intelligence or brains (*informal*) **2.** brownish-grey nerve tissue consisting mainly of nerve cell bodies within the brain and spinal cord

Greymouth /gráyməth/ town on the western coast of the South Island, New Zealand. A former gold-mining town, it is now the commercial centre of a mining and industrial region. Population: 9,528 (2001).

grey mullet *n UK* a thick-bodied fish with a blunt head. Native to: tropical and temperate coasts. Family: Mugilidae. ANZ, N Am term **mullet**

grey nomad *n Aus* a retired or semiretired person who travels around the country on extended holidays, usually in a caravan or camper van

grey pound *n* the consumer choices or spending power of older people

grey power *n* a movement of people and groups who act as advocates for issues that concern older people, e.g., health care, housing, and discrimination

grey scale *n* a series of shades from white to black used in displaying or printing text and graphics

grey squirrel *n* a large tree squirrel that has grey fur with a reddish tinge in the legs and head. Native to: North America, Great Britain, Ireland, South Africa. Latin name: *Sciurus carolinensis*.

grey vote *n* older people considered as a group that can be influenced to vote in a specific way ○ *the growing political importance of the grey vote*

greywacke /gráy wakə/ *n* a conglomerate rock composed of well-rounded pebbles cemented by a sandy infill [Late 18C. < German *Grauwacke* 'grey sandstone']

grey water *n* waste water from sinks, baths, and kitchen appliances

greywether /gráy wethər/ *n* GEOL same as **sarsen**

grey whale *n* a large baleen whale that has no dorsal fin but a line of bumps along part of its back. Native to: northern Pacific coastal waters. Latin name: *Eschrichtius gibbosus*.

grey wolf *n* a large intelligent highly social wild dog, varying in colour from white in the north of its range to black in the south. Native to: North America, Europe, Asia. Latin name: *Canis lupus*.

gribble /gríbb'l/ *n* a small marine crustacean of the woodlouse family that burrows into submerged wooden structures. Genus: *Limnoria*. [Late 18C. Origin ?]

gricer /gríssər/ *n* same as **trainspotter** (*informal*) [Mid-20C. Origin ?]

grid /grid/ *n* **1.** REFERENCE LINES ON MAP a network of evenly spaced horizontal and vertical lines on a map, used as a basis for finding specific points **2.** ADJACENT SQUARES a network of squares formed by horizontal and vertical lines **3.** GRATING MADE OF BARS a set of parallel or crisscrossing bars that form a grating **4.** UTIL NETWORK a network of cables, lines, or pipes for distributing electricity, gas, or water **5.** UTIL same as **national grid** (sense 1) **6.** ELECTRONICS CONTROL ELECTRODE the part of an electronic valve that controls the flow of current between the other electrodes, usually constructed as a metal screen or coil **7.** MOTOR SPORTS same as **starting grid 8.** AMERICAN FOOTBALL same as **gridiron** (sense 2) [Mid-19C. Shortening of GRIDIRON] —**gridded** *adj*

grid bias *n* a fixed voltage applied between the control electrode and the cathode in an electronic valve

gridder /gríddər/ *n US* an American football player (*informal*)

griddle /grídd'l/ *n* **1.** HEATED COOKING SURFACE a heavy flat metal plate heated and used for cooking food, especially batter mixtures **2.** SIEVE USED BY MINERS a sieve with a base formed from a wire mesh, used by miners ■ *vt* (**-dles**, **-dling**, **-dled**) COOK SOMETHING ON

GRIDDLE to cook something on a flat hot surface [Pre-12C. < Old French *gredil* 'gridiron' < Latin *cratis* 'crate']

griddlecake /grídd'l kayk/ *n* a cake similar to a scone, cooked on a griddle

gridiron /gríd ī ərn/ *n* **1. GRATING** a structure consisting of parallel bars **2. SPORTS AMERICAN FOOTBALL FIELD** a field marked with parallel white lines, on which American football is played **3. SPORTS AMERICAN FOOTBALL** the game of American football (*informal*) **4. HOUSEHOLD** same as **grill**[1] *n* (sense 2) **5. THEATRE STRUCTURE ABOVE STAGE** a structure of beams or bars above a theatre stage from which lighting and scenery are suspended [13C. Alteration of GRIDDLE, by association with IRON]

gridlock /gríd lok/ *n* **1.** a traffic jam in which congestion at one or two road junctions affects a wide area, so that traffic is unable to move in any direction **2.** a situation in which no progress can be made —**gridlocked** *adj*

grid reference *n* a reference, usually using numbers or letters, that specifies a position on a map or chart by referring to the superimposed grid

grief /greef/ *n* **1. INTENSE SORROW** great sadness, especially as a result of a death **2. CAUSE OF INTENSE SORROW** the cause of intense, deep, and profound sorrow, especially a specific event or situation **3. TROUBLE** annoyance or trouble (*informal*) ○ *His parents gave him grief for coming home so late.* ○ *I got grief for missing the appointment.* [Pre-12C. Via Anglo-Norman *gref* < Old French *grief* 'grieved' < *grever* (see GRIEVE[1])] ◇ **come to grief** to suffer misfortune or ruin ◇ **good grief** used to express surprise, exasperation, or dismay (*dated informal*)

grief-stricken *adj* deeply affected by grief

Edvard Grieg

Grieg /greeg/, **Edvard** (1843–1907) Norwegian composer. His work was permeated by the melodies and harmonies of Norwegian folk music. He was a noted composer of songs, and wrote the music to Henrik Ibsen's *Peer Gynt* (1875). Full name **Grieg, Edvard Hagerup**

grievance /gréevənss/ *n* **1. REASON FOR COMPLAINT** a cause for complaint or resentment that may or may not be well-founded **2. RESENTMENT** bitterness or anger at having received unfair treatment **3. FORMAL OBJECTION** a formal complaint made on the basis of something that somebody feels is unfair

grievance procedure *n* a formalized course of action that can be taken to settle a grievance in the workplace

grieve[1] /greev/ (**grieves, grieving, grieved**) *v* **1.** *vti* to experience great sadness over something such as a death **2.** *vt* to cause great sadness to somebody [Pre-12C. Via Old French *grever* 'to burden' < Latin *gravare* < *gravis* 'heavy, grave'] —**griever** *n*

grieve[2] /greev/ *n* Scotland a farm supervisor or manager [Old English *grǣfa*, variant of *gerēfa* (see REEVE[1])]

grievous /gréevəss/ *adj* **1.** extremely serious or significant ○ *a grievous mistake* **2.** very bad or severe ○ *a grievous wound* [13C. < French < *grever* (see GRIEVE[1])] —**grievously** *adv* —**grievousness** *n*

grievous bodily harm *n* serious physical injury intentionally done to another person

griffin

griffin /gríffin/, **gryphon** *n* a monster with the head and wings of an eagle and the body and tail of a lion [13C. Via Old French *grifoun* < Latin *gryphus* < Greek *grups*]

Griffin /gríffin/, **Walter Burley** (1876–1937) US-born Australian architect. In collaboration with his wife, Marion Griffin (1871–1961), he designed the new Australian capital city, Canberra (1914–35).

Griffith Joyner /gríffith jóynər/, **Florence** (1959–98) US athlete. A sprinter, she set world records in the 100– and 200-meter dashes in 1988 and won three gold medals at the 1988 Olympics (100 meters, 200 meters, 400-meter relay). Born **Griffith, Delorez Florence.** Known as **Flojo**

> 'I lift and reach out when I run, more like a guy than a girl.'
> [Florence Griffith Joyner, *The Independent*; 1 October 1988]

griffon /gríffən/ *n* **1.** a small dog like a terrier belonging to a breed with wiry hair and a short muzzle **2.** same as **griffin** [Late 18C. Via French < Old French *grifoun* (see GRIFFIN)]

griffon vulture *n* a large light-coloured vulture with dark wing and tail feathers. Native to: southern Europe, North Africa, southwestern Asia. Latin name: *Gyps fulvus.*

grift /grift/ *US* (*informal*) *n* **1. FRAUD** a swindle or confidence trick **2. PROCEEDS FROM FRAUD** money made from a swindle or confidence trick ■ *vti* (**grifts, grifting, grifted**) **SWINDLE SOMEBODY** to carry out a swindle, or obtain something by swindling [Early 20th. Probably alteration of GRAFT[2]] —**grifter** *n*

Grignard reagent /gréen yaar-/ *n* an organometallic compound belonging to a group whose molecules contain one magnesium and one halogen atom. Use: preparation of organic compounds. [Early 20C. After Victor *Grignard* (1871–1934), French chemist]

grigri /grée gree/ (*plural* **-gris**), **greegree** (*plural* **-grees**), **gris-gris** (*plural same*) *n* an African talisman or fetish [Late 18C. Via American Spanish < Carib *grugru* 'palm']

grike /grīk/, **gryke** *n* a deep cleft in a bare limestone rock surface [Late 18C. Origin ?]

Grikwa *n, adj* LANG, PEOPLES another spelling of **Griqua**

grill[1] /gril/ *v* (**grills, grilling, grilled**) **1.** *vti* **COOK FOOD UNDER HEAT** to cook food below direct heat, or be cooked in this way. Aus, N Am term **broil** *v* **2.** *vti* **COOK FOOD OVER HEAT** to cook food over direct heat without fat or oil, or be cooked in this way **3.** *vt* **INTERROGATE SOMEBODY** to question somebody in a persistent manner (*informal*) **4.** *vti* **SUBJECT OR BE SUBJECTED TO HEAT** to subject somebody or something to great heat, or be subjected to great heat, especially from the sun ■ *n* **1. PART OF COOKER RADIATING HEAT** a device on a cooker that radiates heat downwards. Aus, N Am term **broiler 2. GRATE FOR GRILLING** a flat surface of parallel metal bars, on which food is grilled **3. GRIDIRON PATTERN** a pattern made on a surface by a grill or gridiron **4. FOOD COOKED ON GRILL** a dish or portion of food cooked on a grill **5. RESTAURANT SERVING GRILLED FOOD** an establishment that serves food cooked on a grill [Mid-17C. < French *griller* < *grille* (see GRILLE)] —**griller** *n*

SPELLCHECK grill or grille? Do not confuse the spelling of **grill** and **grille**, which sound similar. *Grill*, the more frequent of the two words, is a verb meaning 'cook by direct heat' (as in *grill the sausages*) and a noun denoting a device used for this purpose or food cooked in this way (as in *browned under the grill, a mixed grill*). The verb *grill* also means 'interrogate': *We were grilled for several hours. Grille* is only used as a noun, denoting a

lattice of bars or a metal grating, as in *a radiator grille*, and an opening in a real tennis court. Although the spelling *grill* is sometimes used in the place of *grille*, the reverse should never be the case.

SYNONYMS See *question*.

grill[2] /gril/ *n* CONSTR, RACKET GAMES another spelling of **grille**

grillage /gríllij/ *n* a framework of beams and cross-beams built as a foundation for a building on soft ground

grille /gril/, **grill** *n* **1. CRISSCROSSED BARS** a pattern or lattice of bars, especially in front of a window **2. PART OF COOLING SYSTEM** a metal grating that allows cooling air into the radiator of a vehicle's engine **3. REAL TENNIS WALL OPENING** in real tennis, the opening in one corner of an end wall of the court [Mid-17C. < French, later form of Old French *graille* < Latin *cratis* 'grating, hurdle'] —**grilled** *adj*

SPELLCHECK See *grill*[1].

griller /gríllər/ *n* ANZ HOUSEHOLD same as **grill pan**

grilling /gríllij/ *n* an act or process of interrogating a person in an intimidating and persistent manner

grill pan *n* a metal tray used to put food on while cooking under a grill. Aus, N Am term **broiler pan**

grillroom /gríl room, -room/ *n* COMM same as **grill**[1] *n* (sense 5)

grillwork /gríl wurk/ *n* CONSTR same as **grille** (sense 1)

grilse /grilss/ (*plural* **grilses** or *same*) *n* a salmon when it returns from the sea for the first time [15C. Origin ?]

grim /grim/ (**grimmer, grimmest**) *adj* **1. DEPRESSING** depressingly gloomy ○ *a grim economic forecast* **2. FORBIDDING** forbidding and unattractive in appearance ○ *a grim mining town* **3. STERNLY SERIOUS** stern in a frightening and unnerving way ○ *a grim, set look on his face* **4. UNPLEASANT** extremely unpleasant, distressing, or sinister ○ *a grim accident scene* **5. UNYIELDING** refusing to give way or give up ○ *with grim determination* **6. IRONIC** disquietingly ironic ○ *a grim reminder of humankind's penchant for folly* **7. ILL** unwell, especially as a result of overindulgence in alcohol (*informal*) ○ *put in a pretty grim performance* [Old English, < Germanic] —**grimly** *adv* —**grimness** *n*

grimace /grímməss, gri máyss/ *n* a contorted twisting of the face that expresses disgust or pain [Mid-17C. Via French *grimache* < Spanish *grimazo* 'caricature' < *grima* 'fright'] —**grimace** *vi* —**grimacer** *n* —**grimacingly** *adv*

Grimaldi /gri máldi/ very large, dark-floored enclosure near the western edge of the Moon, approximately 220 km/135 mi. in diameter

grimalkin /gri máwlkin, -málkin/ *n* an old female cat [Late 16C. < GREY + obsolete *malkin* 'cat']

grime /grīm/ *n* dirt or soot, usually accumulated in a black layer or ingrained into a surface ■ *vt* (**grimes, griming, grimed**) to coat something with dirt or soot [13C. < Middle Low German *greme*]

Grimm /grim/, **Jacob** (1785–1863) German philologist and folklorist. He was the founder of comparative linguistics, and formulated grimm's law. In collaboration with his brother, Wilhelm Karl Grimm (1786–1859), he collected old German folk tales and published them in collections now known as *Grimm's Fairy Tales* (1812–15). Full name **Grimm, Jacob Ludwig Karl.** See Cultural note at **fairy tale**

Grimm's Law *n* a formula showing the systematic relationship between consonants in Germanic languages and consonants in other Indo-European languages, stating what phonetic changes took place [Mid-19C. After Jacob GRIMM]

Grim Reaper *n* a personification of death, shown as a cloaked man or skeleton holding a scythe

grimy /grími/ (**-ier, -iest**) *adj* heavily ingrained with accumulated dirt or soot —**grimily** *adv* —**griminess** *n*

SYNONYMS See *dirty*.

grin /grin/ *vi* (**grins, grinning, grinned**) to smile broadly, usually showing the teeth ■ *n* a broad smile that usually shows the teeth [Old English *grennian* 'bare your teeth' < Indo-European, 'be open'] —**grinner** *n* ◇ **grin and bear it** to tolerate something unpleasant without complaining (*informal*)

grind /grīnd/ *v* (**grinds, grinding, ground** /grownd/) **1.** *vti* PULVERIZE to crush something into very small pieces by rubbing it between two hard surfaces, or be crushed in this way **2.** *vti* MAKE RASPING NOISE to rub two surfaces together with a grating noise, or make a grating noise by rubbing things together ○ *grinding her teeth* **3.** *vt* PUSH SOMETHING DOWN WITH TWISTING MOTION to push something down firmly or crush something on a surface with a twisting or rotating motion ○ *grinding dirt into the carpet with every step* **4.** *vt N Am* COOK same as **mince** *v* (sense 1) **5.** *vt* SMOOTH OR SHARPEN SOMETHING to make something smooth or sharp by rubbing it against an abrasive surface ■ *n* EROTIC DANCE MOVEMENT an erotic circling and thrusting of the hips in dancing (*informal*) ■ *v* (**grinds, grinding, ground** /grownd/) *vi* MOVE NOISILY to move with a grating noise ■ *n US* HARD WORKER somebody who works or studies too hard (*informal*) ■ *v* (**grinds, grinding, ground** /grownd/) **1.** *vt* TURN HANDLE OF SOMETHING to operate something such as a barrel organ by turning its handle **2.** *vi* WORK HARD to study or work hard, especially too hard (*informal*) **3.** *vi* DANCE EROTICALLY to dance erotically with a circling and thrusting of the hips (*informal*) ■ *n* **1.** GRINDING an act of grinding **2.** GRINDING NOISE a grating noise like that of something grinding **3.** TEXTURE the texture of something that is ground ○ *a fine grind of coffee* **4.** SOMETHING BORING AND REPETITIVE something that is routine, dull, and tedious (*informal*) [Old English *grindan*, origin ?]

grind down *vt* to weaken somebody gradually by persistent oppression

grind on *vi* to continue in an unrelenting way

grind out *vt* **1.** DO SOMETHING BY ROTE to perform or produce something with little thought, care, or effort as a result of boredom or excessive familiarity with the process ○ *grinding out articles for the local paper* **2.** SAY SOMETHING WITH ROUGH VOICE to say something with a rough or grating voice **3.** PUT SOMETHING OUT BY CRUSHING to extinguish something by crushing it on a surface with a twisting motion

grinder /grīndər/ *n* **1.** somebody or something that grinds something ○ *a coffee grinder* **2.** a molar tooth

grinding /grīnding/ *adj* **1.** oppressive and relentless ○ *grinding poverty* **2.** characterized by a grating sound —**grindingly** *adv*

grindstone /grīnd stōn/ *n* **1.** an abrasive wheel that sharpens or polishes something **2.** a stone used for sharpening or polishing something **3.** INDUST same as **millstone** (sense 1)

gringo /gríng gō/ (*plural* **-gos**) *n* in Spain and Latin America, an offensive term for an English-speaking foreigner, especially a man (*offensive*) [Mid-19C. < Spanish, 'foreigner'] —**gringo** *adj*

griot /grée ō, gri ót/ *n* a member of a caste of professional oral historians in the Mali Empire [Early 19C. < French]

grip /grip/ *n* **1.** HOLDING ACTION an act or the action of taking or keeping a firm hold of something **2.** MANNER OF HOLDING the way that somebody holds something ○ *a firm grip* **3.** same as **handgrip** (senses 2–3) **4.** HOLDING DEVICE a device for holding something firmly **5.** ABILITY NOT TO SLIP the ability of something to adhere to a surface without slipping ○ *shoes with grip* **6.** CONTROL power over somebody or something ○ *in the grip of fear* **7.** COMPREHENSION a proper understanding of something **8.** HAIR same as **hairgrip** **9.** SMALL SUITCASE a bag or holdall used for carrying clothes and other personal items when travelling **10.** CINEMA, MEDIA MEMBER OF FILM CREW a member of a film or television crew who is responsible for moving equipment **11.** THEATRE STAGEHAND a worker who moves sets and props in a theatre ■ *v* (**grips, gripping, gripped**) **1.** *vt* GRASP SOMETHING FIRMLY to take or keep a firm hold of something **2.** *vti* STICK TO SURFACE to adhere to a surface without slipping **3.** *vt* AFFECT SOMEBODY OR SOMETHING GREATLY to overwhelm or take control of somebody or something ○ *gripped by fear* **4.** *vt* CAPTURE SOMEBODY'S INTEREST to capture somebody's interest, imagination, or attention ○ *a performance that gripped the audience* [Old English *gripe* 'grasp', *gripa* 'handful' < Germanic] —**gripper** *n* —**grippy** *adj* ◇ **get to grips with something** to begin to understand and deal with something ◇ **lose your grip** to stop being as effective or as much in control as formerly

gripe /grīp/ *v* (**gripes, griping, griped**) **1.** *vti* HAVE OR CAUSE STOMACH PAINS to experience severe stomach pains, or cause somebody to experience severe stomach pains **2.** *vi* GRUMBLE CONSTANTLY to complain continually and irritatingly (*informal*) **3.** *vi* SAIL INTO WIND to sail into the wind against the action of the helm ■ *n* MINOR COMPLAINT a minor but irritating grievance (*informal*) ■ **gripes** *npl* MOORING ROPES ropes that hold a boat to a dock [Old English *grīpan* 'seize' < Germanic] —**griper** *n*

SYNONYMS See ***complain***.

gripe water *n* a medicine given to babies to relieve colic

griping /grīping/ *adj* describes stomach pains that are sudden, sharp, and intense

grippe /grip/ *n* same as **influenza** (*dated*) [Late 18C. < French, literally 'seizure']

gripping /grípping/ *adj* holding the interest and attention completely —**grippingly** *adv*

Griqua /gréekwə/ (*plural same* or **-quas**), **Grikwa** (*plural same* or **-kwas**) *n* **1.** a member of a group of people of both African and European descent in South Africa **2.** the Khoisan language of the Griqua people, of which very few, if any, speakers remain [Mid-18C. < Nama] —**Griqua** *adj*

Gris /greess/, **Juan** (1887–1927) Spanish-born French artist. After 1906 he lived in Paris, where he was much influenced by cubism. In addition to paintings and collages, he designed sets for Diaghilev's ballets. Born **González, José Vittoriano**

AKG London

grisaille: *David and Goliath* by Andrea Mantegna

grisaille /gri záyl, -zī/ *n* **1.** a method of painting that uses only shades of grey **2.** a work of art produced by the grisaille method [Mid-19C. < French < *gris* 'grey']

griseofulvin /grízzi ō fóolvin, gríss-, -fúlvin/ *n* an antibiotic obtained from a fungus. Use: treatment of fungal skin conditions. [Mid-20C. < modern Latin *Griseofulvum* < medieval Latin *griseus* 'grey' + Latin *fulvus* 'reddish-yellow']

grisette /gri zét/ *n* **1.** formerly, a young working-class French woman **2.** a species of edible fungus with a grey, orange, or brown cap. Latin name: *Amanita fulva* or *Amanita vaginata*. [Early 18C. < French < *gris* 'grey']

gris-gris *n* ANTHROP another spelling of **grigri**

Grisham /gríshəm/, **John** (*b.* 1955) US writer and lawyer. His bestselling legal thrillers include *The Firm* (1991).

> 'I cannot write as well as some people; my talent is in coming up with good stories about lawyers. That is what I am good at.' [John Grisham, *Independent on Sunday*; 5 June 1994]

griskin /grískin/ *n* lean meat from a loin of pork [Late 17C. < obsolete *grice* 'pig' < Old Norse *gríss*]

grisly /grízzli/ (**-lier, -liest**) *adj* gruesomely unpleasant, or creating a sense of horror [12C. Ultimately < W Germanic, 'terror'] —**grisliness** *n*

SPELLCHECK Do not confuse the spelling of ***grisly*** and ***grizzly*** (a type of bear), which sound similar. ***Grisly*** is an adjective meaning 'gruesomely unpleasant', as in *the grisly remains of the corpse*, whereas ***grizzly*** is a noun, short for *grizzly bear*.

grison /grīss'n, gríz-/ (*plural* **-sons** or *same*) *n* a weasel that has striking grey, white, and black markings, and is sometimes used to hunt chinchillas. Native to: South America. Latin name: *Galictis vittata* or *Galictis cuja*. [Late 18C. < French < *gris* 'grey']

grist /grist/ *n* **1.** GRAIN GROUND INTO FLOUR grain that is ground into flour **2.** GRAIN PRODUCED AT ONE GRINDING the quantity of grain that is ground in one batch **3.** BREWING MALT malt grain that is used for brewing [Old English, < Germanic] ◇ **grist to the** *or* **somebody's mill** a potential source of advantage or profit to somebody

gristle /gríss'l/ *n* tough cartilage, especially in meat prepared for eating [Old English, origin ?] —**gristliness** *n* —**gristly** *adj*

gristmill /gríst mil/ *n* a mill where grain or corn is ground

grit /grit/ *n* **1.** SAND OR STONE GRAINS small pieces of sand or stone **2.** SANDSTONE sandstone, often used as a grindstone **3.** TEXTURE OF GRAINS the texture of stone or particles used for grinding **4.** PARTICLE SIZE a measure of the size of particles ○ *coarse grit* **5.** FIRMNESS OF CHARACTER determination or strength of character ■ *vt* (**grits, gritting, gritted**) **1.** CLENCH TEETH to clench the teeth, especially when under stress **2.** PUT GRIT ON SOMETHING to cover something with grit, especially an icy road [Old English *grēot* < Germanic]

grits /grits/ *n* (*takes a singular or plural verb*) **1.** grain that has had its husks removed or been coarsely ground **2.** *US* coarsely ground hulled maize that is boiled and eaten hot with butter, especially at breakfast in the southern United States [Late 16C. Plural of obsolete *grit* 'chaff' < Old English *grytta* 'coarse meal' < Germanic]

gritstone /grít stōn/ *n* GEOL, INDUST same as **grit** *n* (sense 2)

gritter /gríttər/ *n* a vehicle that spreads grit or salt on icy roads

gritty /grítti/ (**-tier, -tiest**) *adj* **1.** RESOLUTE courageous, resolute, or persistent **2.** REALISTIC having a stark realism ○ *a gritty detective novel* **3.** LIKE OR WITH GRIT resembling, containing, or covered with grit —**grittily** *adv* —**grittiness** *n*

grizzle[1] /grízz'l/ *vti* (**-zles, -zling, -zled**) BECOME OR MAKE GREY to make something grey, or become grey ■ *n* **1.** COLOURS GREY a grey colour **2.** GREY HAIR hair that is grey or streaked with grey **3.** GREY WIG a wig with grey hair [14C. < Old French *grisel* < *gris* 'grey']

grizzle[2] /grízz'l/ (**-zles, -zling, -zled**) *vi* (*informal*) **1.** to cry and whine quietly and persistently (*refers to young children*) **2.** to complain annoyingly and persistently [Mid-18C. Origin ?] —**grizzler** *n*

grizzled /grízz'ld/ *adj* **1.** streaked with grey, especially with grey hair ○ *his grizzled beard* **2.** with hair that is grey or streaked with grey

grizzly bear /grízzli-/, **grizzly** (*plural* **-zlies**) *n* a brown bear that has brown fur tipped with white. Native to: northwestern North America. Latin name: *Ursus arctos horribilis*.

SPELLCHECK See ***grisly***.

groan /grōn/ *n* **1.** MOURNFUL SOUND a long low cry expressing pain or misery **2.** LOUD CREAKING SOUND a loud creaking sound of something affected by pressure **3.** GRIEVANCE an aggrieved complaint (*informal*) ■ *v* (**groans, groaning, groaned**) **1.** *vi* MOAN to utter a moan **2.** *vt* SAY SOMETHING WITH GROAN to express something by means of a groan **3.** *vi* MAKE LOUD CREAKING SOUND to make a loud creaking sound as a result of pressure ○ *The floorboards groaned under their weight.* **4.** *vi* COMPLAIN to complain in an aggrieved way (*informal*) [Old English *grānian* < Indo-European, 'be open'] —**groaner** *n* —**groaningly** *adv*

groats /grōts/ *n* grain, especially oats, that has been crushed or has had the husks removed (*takes a singular or plural verb*) [14C. < Old English *grotan* < Germanic]

Gro-bag /grṓ bag/ *tdmk* a trademark for a plastic sack sold filled with compost and nutrients as a container for growing plants

grocer /grṓssər/ *n* **1.** an owner or manager of a shop selling food and other household goods **2.** *also* **grocer's** (*plural same*) *UK* a shop that sells food and other household goods. ANZ, N Am term **grocery store** [13C. Via Old French < medieval Latin *grossarius* 'wholesale dealer' < *grossus* 'large']

grocery /grṓssəri/ *n* (*plural* **-ies** /grṓssəriz/) **1.** COMM same as **grocer** (sense 2) **2.** the trade or profession of a grocer ■ **groceries** *npl* goods, especially food, sold in a grocer's shop

grocery store *n ANZ, N Am* same as **grocer** (sense 2)

grockle /grók'l/ *n regional* a tourist, especially one in

the holiday resorts of southwestern England (*insult*) [Mid-20C. Invention]

grody /gródi/ (**-dier, -diest**) *adj US* disgusting or extremely unpleasant (*slang*) [Mid-20C. Alteration of GROTESQUE]

Groening /gróning/, **Matt** (*b.* 1954) US cartoonist. He created the comic strips 'Life in Hell' (1980) and television's animated cartoon show 'The Simpsons' (1987).

grog /grog/ *n* 1. a mixture of alcohol, especially rum, and water 2. *ANZ* a beverage that contains alcohol (*informal*) [Mid-18C. Shortening of *Old Grogram*, nickname of Admiral Edward Vernon (from his grogram cloak)]

groggy /gróggi/ (**-gier, -giest**) *adj* feeling weak or dizzy, especially because of illness or overindulgence — **groggily** *adv* —**grogginess** *n*

grogram /grógrəm/ *n* a stiff fabric of silk and wool or mohair [Mid-16C. < French *gros grain* 'coarse grain']

grogshop /gróg shop/ *n Aus* a shop that sells alcoholic beverages (*informal*) UK term **off-licence**. US term **liquor store**

groin (sense 3)

groin[1] /groyn/ *n* 1. **AREA BETWEEN THIGHS AND ABDOMEN** the area between the tops of the thighs and the abdomen 2. **GENITALS** the genitals, especially the testicles 3. **ARCHIT EDGE BETWEEN VAULTS** a curved line forming the edge between two intersecting vaults [14C. Origin ?]

groin[2] *n GEOG* US spelling of **groyne**

groin vault *n* a ceiling created by the crossing of two or more simple arched vaults (**barrel vaults**)

grommet /grómmit, grúmm-/, **grummet** /grúmm-/ *n* 1. **PROTECTIVE EYELET** a protective eyelet in a material that prevents damage either to the material or to a rope passed through it 2. **REINFORCEMENT AROUND EYELET** a small ring of metal or plastic that reinforces an eyelet 3. **SAILING RING TO FASTEN SAIL** a ring used to fasten the edge of a sail to its stay 4. **MED TUBE FOR DRAINING EAR** a small tube for draining the ear canal of somebody who has glue ear 5. *Aus* **SURFER** a young, novice surfer (*slang*) [Early 17C. < obsolete French *gromette* 'curb of a bridle' < *gourmer* 'curb']

gromwell /grómmwəl, -wel/ *n* a hairy flowering plant of the borage family that produces hard smooth white seeds. Genus: *Lithospermum*. [13C. < Old French *gromil*]

Gromyko /grə meèkō/, **Andrey** (1909–89) president of the Soviet Union (1985–88). He was foreign minister (1957–85) and chairman of the Presidium of the Supreme Soviet (1985–88) of the Soviet Union during the Cold War. Full name **Gromyko, Andrey Andreyevich**

Groningen /gróningən, grónn-/ city and capital of Groningen Province, in the northeastern Netherlands, on the Hunze River. Population: 172,701 (2000).

groom /groom, groòm/ *n* 1. same as **bridegroom** 2. **SOMEBODY WHO CARES FOR HORSES** somebody whose job is to look after horses by cleaning them and their stables 3. **OFFICER IN ROYAL HOUSEHOLD** an officer in a royal household ■ *v* (**grooms, grooming, groomed**) 1. *vt* **CARE FOR ANIMAL'S APPEARANCE** to clean and brush or comb an animal 2. *vti* **CLEAN ANIMAL'S BODY** to clean the fur, skin, or feathers of another animal or of itself, often with the tongue 3. *vt* **CARE FOR YOUR PERSONAL APPEARANCE** to keep somebody else's or your own personal appearance neat ○ *a well-groomed young man* 4. *vt* **TRAIN SOMEBODY** to train and prepare somebody for a particular position ○ *being groomed for the presidency* 5. *vt* **ESTABLISH PREDATORY RELATIONSHIP** to develop the trust of a young person or his or her family in

order to engage in illegal sexual conduct 6. *vt* **SKIING MAKE PATH IN SNOW** to clear a path or track in snow by compacting the snow [12C. Origin ?] —**groomer** *n*

grooming /groòming/ *n* 1. the taking care of personal appearance, or the way in which somebody is groomed 2. the developing of the trust of a young person or his or her family in order to engage in illegal sexual conduct ○ *Internet grooming*

groomsman /groòmzmən, groòm-/ (*plural* **-men** /-mən/) *n* a man who is an attendant to a bridegroom

groom wear *n S Asia* clothing for the bridegroom at a wedding

Groote Eylandt /gróot īlənd/ island off the north-eastern Northern Territory, Australia, in the Gulf of Carpentaria. Population: 14,209 (1996). Area: 2,285 sq. km/882 sq. mi.

groove /groov/ *n* 1. **NARROW PASSAGE** a narrow channel or path in a surface 2. **TRACK CUT IN RECORD** a spiral track cut into a vinyl record along which the needle of the record player passes 3. **REGULARLY FOLLOWED PROCEDURE** a routine into which somebody has settled (*informal*) 4. **SUITABLE ACTIVITY** an activity or situation suited to somebody's talents or tastes (*slang*) 5. **CLIMBING, GEOG ROCK CLEFT** a cleft in rock 6. **MUSIC MUSICAL BEAT** a strong beat or rhythm in music (*slang*) ■ *v* (**grooves, grooving, grooved**) 1. *vt* **MAKE GROOVE IN SOMETHING** to cut a groove in a surface 2. *vi* **ENJOY YOURSELF** to enjoy yourself very much (*dated informal*) 3. *vi* **PLAY MUSIC RHYTHMICALLY** to play jazz or dance music with a strong beat (*slang*) [14C. < Dutch *groeve*] —**grooved** *adj* —**groover** *n* ◇ **groove it** same as **groove** *v* (sense 3) (*slang*) ◇ **in the groove** playing or performing in a highly accomplished manner (*dated slang*)

groovy /groòvi/ (**-ier, -iest**) *adj* 1. unfashionable or out of touch with modern youth culture (*slang; used ironically*) 2. used, often as an exclamation, to describe somebody or something that is fashionable, excellent, or pleasing (*dated slang*) [Mid-20C. < *in the groove*] —**groovily** *adv* —**grooviness** *n*

grope /grōp/ (**gropes, groping, groped**) *v* 1. *vi* **SEARCH BY FEELING** to search for something blindly or uncertainly by feeling with the hands ○ *groping for the light switch* 2. *vi* **BE WITHOUT GUIDANCE** to strive blindly or uncertainly for something ○ *groping for inspiration* 3. *vt* **FEEL YOUR WAY UNCERTAINLY** to feel your way forward slowly and hesitantly, e.g. in the dark ○ *They groped their way back out of the tunnel.* 4. *vt* **FONDLE SOMEBODY ROUGHLY** to caress or touch somebody's body for sexual pleasure, often roughly, awkwardly, or without the person's consent (*informal*) [Old English *grāpian* 'grasp at' < Germanic] —**grope** *n* —**gropingly** *adv*

groper[1] /grōpər/ *n* 1. somebody who gropes for something 2. somebody who touches or tries to touch another person's body for sexual pleasure, usually without that person's consent (*informal*) [Mid-16C. < GROPE]

groper[2] /grōpər/ *n ANZ* a heavy-bodied large-jawed sea fish. Native to: tropical and temperate waters. Family: Serranidae. [Late 19C. Variant of GROUPER]

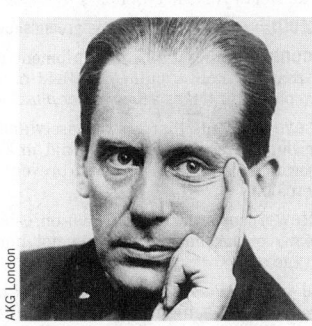

Walter Gropius

Gropius /grōpi əss/, **Walter** (1883–1969) German-born US architect and educator. A pioneer of the international style, he directed the Bauhaus design school in Weimar, Germany (1919–28). As head of Harvard University's architecture department (1938–52) he trained a generation of US architects in the modernist idiom. Full name **Gropius, Walter Adolph**

'Architecture begins where engineering ends.'
[Walter Gropius, *Speech, Harvard Department of Architecture, Architects on Architecture*; 1978]

grosbeak /gróss beek/ *n* a finch with a large beak for crushing seeds. Native to: Europe, North America. Family: Fringillidae or Emberizidae. [Late 17C. < French *grosbec* 'large beak']

groschen /grósh'n, grō-/ (*plural* same) *n* 1. **SUBUNIT OF FORMER AUSTRIAN CURRENCY** a subunit of the former Austrian currency 2. **FORMER COIN WORTH 10 PFENNIGS** a former German coin worth 10 pfennigs (*informal*) 3. **OLD GERMAN COIN** a former small German silver coin [Early 17C. Via German < medieval Latin (*denarius*) *grossus* 'thick (penny)']

grosgrain /grō grayn/ *n* a heavy corded silk or rayon fabric. Use: trimmings, ribbons. [Mid-19C. < French, 'coarse grain']

gros point /grō-/ *n UK, ANZ, Can* 1. an embroidery technique using large diagonal stitches 2. embroidery done with gros point ► US term **raised point** [< French *gros point (de Venise)* 'large stitch (from Venice)']

gross /grōss/ *adj, adv* 1. **WITHOUT DEDUCTIONS** before any usual deductions such as tax or expenses have been made ○ *gross salary* 2. **OVERALL** including all packaging and contents ○ *the gross weight of the shipment* ■ *adj* 1. **OBVIOUSLY WRONG** flagrantly wrong or unmitigated ○ *gross misconduct* 2. **VULGAR** vulgar or coarse 3. **WITHOUT GOOD TASTE** not sensitive to, or not able to appreciate, the finer things in life 4. **LUXURIANT** growing thickly or densely 5. **EXTREMELY OVERWEIGHT** overweight to an unhealthy or repellent degree (*informal*) 6. **DISGUSTING** disgusting or highly unpleasant (*informal*) ■ *n* 1. (*plural* same) **TWELVE DOZEN** a quantity of 144 or twelve dozen 2. (*plural* **grosses**) **SUM BEFORE DEDUCTIONS** a total, especially a total amount of money before any usual deductions are made ■ *vt* (**grosses, grossing, grossed**) **EARN MONEY** to earn or make an amount of money as profit before any usual deductions are made [14C. Via French < late Latin *grossus* 'bulky, coarse'] —**grossly** *adv* —**grossness** *n* **gross out** *vt N Am* to be disgusting or repellent to somebody (*slang*) ○ *language that really grossed me out*

gross anatomy *n* a branch of anatomy dealing with body parts that are visible to the naked eye

gross domestic product *n* the total value of all goods and services produced within a country in a year, minus net income from investments in other countries

Grossglockner /gróss glóknər/ mountain in southern Austria, in the Hohe Tauern range, part of the Eastern Alps. The highest peak in Austria, it rises to a height of 3,797 m/12,457 ft.

gross margin *n* gross profit divided by net sales revenue, expressed as a percentage

gross misconduct *n* behaviour in the workplace that may lead to a warning or to dismissal in extreme cases

Grossmith /grósmith/, **George** (1847–1912) British singer and journalist. A popular entertainer and comedian, he worked with Gilbert and Sullivan at the Opera Comique in London and wrote *Diary of a Nobody* (1892) with his brother Weedon (1852–1919). See Cultural note at **nobody**

'I left the room with silent dignity, but caught my foot in the mat.'
[George Grossmith, *The Diary of a Nobody*; 1892]

gross national product *n* the total value of all goods and services produced within a country in a year, including net income from investments in other countries

gross-out *n N Am* something considered disgusting or repellent (*slang*)

gross profit *n* the difference between sales revenue and the cost of goods sold

grossularite /gróssyoōlə rīt/, **grossular** /gróssyoōlər/ *n* a green variety of garnet. Use: gems. [Early 19C. < German *Grossularit* < modern Latin *grossularia* 'gooseberry' (because the gem is green) < French *groseille*]

grosz /grōsh/ (*plural* **groszy** /gróshi/ or **grosze**) *n* a subunit of Polish currency. See table at **currency**

[Mid-20C. Via Polish *grosz*, Czech *groš* < medieval Latin *(denarius) grossus* 'thick (penny)']

Grosz /grōss/, **George** (1893–1959) German-born US artist. He is known for his satirical caricatures of Berlin life during the 1920s and 1930s. Born **Grosz, Georg**

'To be a German means invariably to be crude, stupid, ugly, fat, and inflexible...to be a German means: to be a reactionary of the worst kind.'
[George Grosz, *Letter*, 1916]

groszy, **grosze** plural of **grosz**

grot /grot/ *n* dirt, mess, or rubbish (*informal*) [Mid-20C. Back-formation < GROTTY]

grotesque /grō tésk/ *adj* **1. DISTORTED** distorted, especially in a strange or disturbing way ○ *grotesque shadows* **2. INCONGRUOUS** seeming strange or ludicrous through being out of place or unexpected **3.** ARTS **BLENDING REALISTIC AND FANTASTIC** relating to or typical of a style of art that mixes the realistic and the fantastic ■ *n* **1. SOMETHING GROTESQUE** somebody or something considered to be grotesque **2.** ARTS **ART BLENDING REALISTIC AND FANTASTIC** a style of art, especially in 16th-century Europe, in which representations of real and fantastic figures are mixed **3.** ARTS **ARTISTIC PIECE** a piece of art in the grotesque style [Mid-16C. Via French < Italian *grottesca* 'like a grotto' < *grotta* (see GROTTO), from fanciful wall paintings found in excavated Roman ruins] —**grotesquely** *adv* —**grotesqueness** *n*

grotesquerie /grō téskəri/, **grotesquery** (*plural* **-ries**) *n* **1.** the grotesque quality of something **2.** something grotesque, especially a piece of art in the grotesque style

Grotius /grṓ ti əss/, **Hugo** (1583–1645) Dutch jurist. He is credited with writing the first works on international law, *Mare Liberum* (1609) (*The Free Sea*) and *De Jure Belli et Pacis* (1625) (*On the Law of War and Peace*).

Grotowski /grə tófskee/, **Jerzy** (1933–99) Polish theatre director. His emphasis on performance without elaborate staging, and his explorations of the relationship between performance and audience, greatly influenced late-20th-century theatre.

grotto /gróttō/ (*plural* **-toes** or **-tos**) *n* **1.** a cave, especially one with interesting natural features **2.** an imitation cave, especially as an ornamental shelter in a formal garden [Early 17C. Via Italian *grotta* < Latin *crypta* (see CRYPT)]

grotty /grótti/ (**-tier, -tiest**) *adj* (*informal*) **1. DIRTY OR SHABBY** distastefully dirty, shabby, or in poor condition **2. GENERALLY UNPLEASANT** generally unpleasant or despicable **3. UNWELL** physically unwell [Mid-20C. < GROTESQUE] —**grottily** *adv* —**grottiness** *n*

grouch /growch/ (*informal*) *vi* (**grouches, grouching, grouched**) **COMPLAIN** to complain or grumble ■ *n* **1. COMPLAINT** an instance of or cause for complaining **2. COMPLAINER** a habitually bad-tempered or complaining person **3. BAD MOOD** a mood characterized by complaining or sulking ○ *a day-long grouch* [Late 19C. Origin ?] —**grouchily** *adv* —**grouchiness** *n* —**grouchy** *adj*

ground[1] /grownd/ *n* **1. LAND SURFACE** the surface of the land **2. EARTH** the earth or soil that covers the land **3. LAND FOR PURPOSE** an area of land used for a particular purpose (*often used in the plural*) ○ *burial ground* **4. BATTLE AREA** the land held or fought over in battle ○ *prevent the enemy from gaining ground* **5. SEA BOTTOM** the bottom of the sea, a river, or a lake **6. SUBJECT** an area of knowledge or debate ○ *The lecture covered familiar ground.* **7. FOUNDATION** a reason or basis (*often used in the plural*) ○ *grounds for believing his story* **8. BACKGROUND** a background, e.g. the background colour of a flag **9.** ART **PAINTING SURFACE** an underlying surface or prepared area that paint is applied to **10.** ART **FIRST COAT OF PAINT** a first coat of paint applied to a surface being decorated **11.** CRICKET **AREA BEFORE STUMPS** in cricket, the area that a batsman must stand in, measuring from the popping crease to the stumps ○ *He was run out before he could regain his ground.* **12.** MUSIC same as **ground bass** **13.** *N Am* ELEC ENG same as **earth** *n* (sense 6) ■ **grounds** *npl* **1. SURROUNDING LAND** the land surrounding and belonging to a building **2. DREGS** the sediment or dregs of a drink, especially coffee ■ *adj* **ON GROUND** happening, living, working, or operating on the ground ○ *ground crews* ○ *a message from ground control* ■ *v* (**grounds, grounding, grounded**) **1.** *vt* **GIVE SOMEBODY BASIC INFORMATION** to teach somebody the basics about something ○ *was well grounded in machine operation* **2.** *vt* **SUPPORT SOMETHING** to base ideas, arguments, or beliefs on something ○ *a decision that was grounded in personal experience* **3.** *vi* **LAND ON GROUND** to land on the ground or hit the ground **4.** *vt* **PUT SOMETHING ON GROUND** to put something on the ground ○ *ground your rifles* **5.** *vt* **FIX SOMETHING** to fix something on or in something else as a foundation ○ *The fence posts are grounded in concrete.* **6.** *vt* **MAKE SOMEBODY STAY HOME** to restrict somebody to a place, especially a child to his or her home, as a punishment (*informal*) ○ *My dad grounded me for a week.* **7.** *vt* AVIAT **STOP PILOT OR PLANE FLYING** to prevent or forbid a pilot or aircraft from flying ○ *Bad weather grounded all outgoing flights.* **8.** *vti* NAUT **RUN AGROUND** to become stranded in a vessel, or cause a vessel to become stranded by running aground ○ *The ferry grounded on a reef.* **9.** *vi* ROADS **BECOME STRANDED ON ROAD HUMP** to become stranded on a hump or hump-backed bridge in the road (*refers to low-loading vehicles with a long wheelbase*) **10.** *vti* BASEBALL **HIT BALL TO GROUND** to strike a baseball so that it hits or rolls along the ground **11.** *vt N Am* ELEC ENG same as **earth** *n* (sense 7) **12.** *vt* ART **PREPARE PAINTING SURFACE** to apply a preparatory coat to a surface that is to be painted [Old English *grund* < Germanic] ◇ **break fresh** *or* **new ground** to do or discover something new ◇ **get (something) off the ground** to get something started or operating ◇ **hit the ground running** to begin to deal with a new situation with great energy and without delay, generally because of good prior preparation (*informal*) ◇ **hold** *or* **stand your ground** to stick resolutely to decisions, attitudes, or principles in the face of pressure to abandon them ◇ **run somebody** *or* **something to ground 1.** to find somebody or something finally, after a long and determined search **2.** to wear something out **3.** to manage something such as a business so badly that it fails ◇ **suit somebody down to the ground** to be perfectly suited to or suitable for somebody ◇ **the moral high ground** a position of moral superiority in relation to other people ◇ **thin on the ground** few in number or rare

ground out *vi* in baseball, to be put out after hitting a ground ball that is fielded and thrown to first base

ground[2] /grownd/ past participle, past tense of **grind**

groundbait /grównd bayt/ *n* bait thrown into water to attract fish

ground ball *n* in baseball, a ball that bounces on the ground or rolls along it after being hit

ground bass /-báyss/ *n* a short musical passage continually repeated by the bass as the basis for a changing melody

ground beetle *n* INSECTS same as **carabid**

groundbreaking /grównd brayking/ *adj* new and pioneering or innovative [Early 20C. < *break ground* 'turn the first spade of earth for a new building'] —**groundbreaker** *n*

groundburst /grównd burst/ *n* an explosion of a bomb or warhead on the ground rather than in the air

ground cherry *n* **1.** a small round fruit with a papery husk **2.** a plant that produces ground cherries. Native to: North America. Genus: *Physalis.*

ground cloth *n US* CAMPING same as **groundsheet**

ground control *n* the staff and equipment on the ground that monitor or guide the flight of an aircraft or spacecraft (*takes a singular or plural verb*)

ground cover *n* plants that grow densely and close to the ground, especially growing wild in a forest or deliberately planted in a garden to prevent weeds or soil erosion

ground crew *n* people working in aviation, especially technicians or mechanics, who do not normally work in the air

grounded /grówndid/ *adj* **1. IN TOUCH WITH REALITY** having a secure feeling of being in touch with reality and personal feelings **2. BASED ON EVIDENCE** based on reason, reliable evidence, or good sense **3. CONFINED AT HOME AS PUNISHMENT** not allowed out of the house as a punishment for bad behaviour **4.** CONSTR **CONNECTED TO GROUND** connected with a wire to the ground so that electrical current is carried safely away from a circuit in the event of a fault

ground elder *n* a perennial plant with leaves resembling those of elder and underground creeping stems, regarded as a weed. Native to: Europe, Asia. Latin name: *Aegopodium podagraria.* N Am term **goutweed**

grounder /grówndər/ *n* BASEBALL same as **ground ball**

ground floor *n* the floor of a building that is level with or nearest to street level ◇ **in** *or* **on the ground floor** involved in something, especially a business venture, at the earliest stage

ground fog *n* fog lying at or near ground level

ground forces *npl* military units that operate on land

ground frost *n* a temperature of 0°C or lower as registered on a thermometer touching the ground

ground game *n* hunted animals that cannot fly, e.g. hares and deer

ground glass *n* **1.** glass with a roughened non-transparent surface produced by abrading or etching **2.** glass that has been ground into fine particles, used as an abrasive

groundhog /grównd hog/ *n* ZOOL same as **woodchuck**

Groundhog Day *n* in the United States and Canada, the day when groundhogs are said to emerge from hibernation, prompting the popular forecast of an early spring if the weather is cloudy or six more weeks of winter if it is sunny. Date: 2 February.

grounding /grównding/ *n* training in or knowledge of the basics of something ○ *had a good grounding in maths*

ground ivy *n* an invasive evergreen ivy with scalloped leaves. Flowers: small, purple-blue. Native to: Europe, Asia, naturalized in North America. Latin name: *Glechoma hederacea.*

groundless /grówndləss/ *adj* not based on evidence or reason and not justified or true —**groundlessly** *adv* —**groundlessness** *n*

ground level *n* **1.** the level of the surface of the ground **2.** PHYS same as **ground state**

groundling /grówndling/ *n* **1. UNCULTURED PERSON** somebody disdained for having little or no appreciation of culture ○ *a movie pitched firmly at the groundlings* **2.** THEATRE **STANDING SPECTATOR** in Elizabethan England, an audience member standing in front of the stage in the cheapest part of the theatre **3.** BIOL **ANIMAL OR PLANT LIVING NEAR GROUND** an animal or plant that lives on or near the ground, or at the bottom of a river, lake, or the sea **4.** AVIAT **WORKER IN GROUND CREW** a member of the ground crew at an airport or air force base (*slang*)

ground loop *n* a sharp involuntary turn made by an aircraft that is taxiing, taking off, or landing, caused by unbalanced drag

groundmass /grównd mass/ *n* in some kinds of rock, the fine-grained base rock in which larger crystals are embedded

ground meristem *n* tissue in the stems and roots of plants consisting of actively dividing cells that become new tissue

groundnut /grównd nut/ *n* **1. EDIBLE TUBER** the edible tuber of a climbing vine **2.** (*plural* **groundnuts** or *same*) **CLIMBING PLANT** a climbing vine that produces groundnuts. Flowers: brownish, fragrant. Native to: North America. Latin name: *Apios americana.* **3. PLANT WITH EDIBLE TUBERS** a plant that produces underground pods or tubers containing edible nuts **4.** FOOD, PLANTS same as **peanut**

groundnut oil *n* a mild cooking oil extracted from peanuts

groundout /grównd owt/ *n* in baseball, the dismissal of a batter as a result of hitting a ground ball that is fielded and thrown to first base

ground pine *n* **1.** a variety of bugle plant. Flowers: two-lipped, yellow with red spots, pine-scented if crushed. Native to: Europe, North Africa. Latin name: *Ajuga chamaepitys.* **2.** a moss with spore-producing tissues grouped in cones. Native to: North America. Genus: *Lycopodium.*

ground plan *n* **1.** a scale drawing of a floor of a building, especially the ground floor **2.** a preliminary plan or general outline of something ○ *a ground plan for corporate expansion*

ground plum *n* **1.** an edible green fruit that resembles a plum shape and a pea in flavour **2.** a flowering plant that bears ground plums. Native to: central and western United States. Genus: *Astragalus.*

ground rent *n* rent paid, usually annually, by the owner of a building to the owner of the land on which it is built

ground rule *n* (*often used in the plural*) **1.** a basic rule of procedure ○ *Let's establish a few ground rules before we go any further.* **2.** a sports rule that is specific to a particular place of play

groundscraper /grównd skraypər, grówn-/ *n* a large low or medium-rise building, typically containing offices, that spreads horizontally and occupies a large amount of land [Late 20C. After SKYSCRAPER]

groundsel /grównds'l/ *n* a tall plant with deeply lobed leaves, toxic to livestock, and generally regarded as a weed. Flowers: yellow. Native to: Europe, Asia. Genus: *Senecio*. [Old English *grundeswylige*, alteration of *gundeswilgie* 'pus-swallower', because of its use in poultices]

groundsheet /grównd sheet/ *n UK, ANZ, Can* a sheet of waterproof material placed on the ground to protect a sleeping bag or the floor of a tent from ground dampness. US term **ground cloth**

groundsill /grównd sil/ *n* the joist in a timber structure that is nearest the ground

groundskeeper /grówndz keepər/ *n N Am* same as **groundsman** —**groundskeeping** *n*

ground sloth *n* an extinct ground-dwelling sloth that is believed to be the ancestor of modern tree sloths. Native to: Americas. Family: Megalonychoidea.

groundsman /grówndzmən/ *n* (*plural* **-men** /-mən/) somebody, especially a man, who maintains a playing field or the grounds of a property. N Am term **groundskeeper**

ground speed *n* the speed of a flying aircraft measured in relation to the ground it is travelling over and used for calculating flight times

groundsperson /grówndz purss'n/ *n* (*plural* **-persons** or **-people** /-peep'l/) *n* somebody who maintains a playing field or the grounds of a property. N Am term **groundskeeper**

ground squirrel *n* a ground-dwelling burrowing rodent related to the tree squirrels. Native to: North America, Europe, Africa, Asia. Family: Sciuridae.

ground staff *n* workers who maintain a playing field (+ *sing or pl verb*)

ground state *n* the state of lowest energy for a particle, atom, molecule, or system

ground stroke *n* in tennis, a shot played from any part of the court after the ball has bounced

ground substance *n* the solid, semisolid, or liquid material that exists between the cells in connective tissue, cartilage, or bone

groundswell /grównd swel/ *n* **1.** a strong growth of feeling or opinion that is evident but not always attributable to a specific source ○ *a groundswell of public opinion* **2.** a deep wide up-and-down movement of the sea, often caused by a far-off storm or an earthquake

ground water *n* water held underground in soil or permeable rock, often feeding springs and wells

ground wave *n* a radio wave transmitted directly from a transmitter to a receiver, without reflection from the ionosphere

groundwork /grównd wurk/ *n* basic preparatory tasks that form a foundation for something else

ground zero *n* **1.** POINT OF NUCLEAR EXPLOSION the point on the surface of land or water that is precisely the site of detonation of a nuclear weapon or the point immediately above or below it **2.** CENTRE OF ACTIVITY the focal point or centre of a particular activity or development ○ *The war-torn country has been ground zero for an international terrorist network.* **3.** BASIC LEVEL the most basic level or starting point for an activity ○ *to learn programming from ground zero*

Ground Zero *n* the huge debris field resulting from the terrorist attacks on the World Trade Center towers in New York City on 11 September 2001

group /groop/ *n* **1.** SET OF PEOPLE OR THINGS a number of people or things considered together or regarded as belonging together **2.** PEOPLE WITH SOMETHING IN COMMON a number of people sharing something in common such as an interest, belief, or political aim ○ *an unemployed workers' group* **3.** MUSIC BAND OF MUSICIANS a small number of musicians, especially in pop music, who play together as a unit **4.** COMM COMPANIES UNDER COMMON CONTROL a number of companies all controlled by a single company or common owner **5.** ARTS SET OF FIGURES IN ARTISTIC WORK a number of figures forming a distinct unit in a painting, sculpture, or other artistic composition **6.** MIL SET OF SEVERAL MILITARY UNITS a military formation made up of several complementary units **7.** AIR FORCE AIR FORMATION BETWEEN SQUADRON AND WING an air force formation made up of two or more squadrons, but smaller than a wing **8.** CHEM COLLECTION OF ATOMS a collection of atoms that is a distinct chemical unit, e.g. the hydroxy group **9.** CHEM COLLECTION OF SIMILAR ELEMENTS a set of chemical elements classified according to the vertical column they occupy in the periodic table. There are 18 such groups, and elements in the same group have similar properties. ○ *the alkaline earth group of elements* **10.** GEOL SET OF ROCK FORMATIONS a collection of rock formations that date from the same geological era and are considered as a stratigraphic unit **11.** MATHS MATHEMATICAL SET UNDER OPERATION a set of mathematical entities that are related by a particular operation. For example, consecutive numbers are a group under addition but not under multiplication. (*often used before a noun*) ■ *vti* (**groups, grouping, grouped**) FORM GROUP to come together as a unit, or bring people or things together to form a unit ○ *onlookers grouped in ones and twos* ■ *adj* OF GROUPS relating to groups, or forming a group ○ *group holidays* [Late 17C. Via French *groupe* < Italian *gruppo* 'group, knot'] —**groupable** *adj*

USAGE When *group* is used to refer to a collection of individuals regarded as a unit or a whole, a singular verb is used: *The group has decided not to go on the afternoon tour*, i.e. everybody in the group has decided unanimously to skip that tour. When the members of a group are regarded as separate individuals or factions, a plural verb is used: *The group have been arguing all morning about going or not going*, i.e. some members want to go and others do not.

group captain *n* an officer in the Royal Air Force senior to a wing commander and junior to an air commodore

group certificate *n* in Australia, a standard form issued by an employer at the end of the financial year which records an employee's income, tax payments and superannuation payments during the previous year

group dynamics *npl* the interpersonal processes, conscious and unconscious, that take place in the course of interactions among a group of people

grouper /groopər/ (*plural* **-pers** or *same*) *n* a heavy-bodied large-jawed sea fish. Native to: tropical and temperate waters. Family: Serranidae. [Early 17C. < Portuguese *garupa*]

groupie /groopi/ *n* (*informal*) **1.** an enthusiastic fan of a pop group, especially a female teenager seeking sexual intercourse with the object of her adulation **2.** an enthusiastic fan or supporter of something ○ *art groupies*

grouping /grooping/ *n* **1.** a set of people or things gathered into a group **2.** the act or process of forming a group or arranging people or things in groups

Group of Eight *n* INTERNAT REL full form of **G8**

Group of Seven *n* INTERNAT REL full form of **G7**

group practice *n* a medical, dental, or veterinary practice operated by several doctors, dentists, or vets working together

group theory *n* the study of the formation and properties of mathematical groups. It has applications in the study of the symmetry of molecules and crystal shapes.

group therapy *n* the treatment of psychological problems by placing patients in groups and, under the guidance of a trained therapist, encouraging them to discuss their problems with each other —**group therapist** *n*

groupthink /groop thingk/ *n* conformity in thought and behaviour among the members of a group, especially an unthinking acceptance of majority opinions

groupuscule /groopə skyool/ *n* a small political group, especially a splinter group of extremists or activists regarded as marginal (*disapproving*) [Mid-20C. < French, 'very small group' < *groupe* 'group' after *corpuscule* 'corpuscle']

groupware /groop wair/ *n* software designed to be shared collaboratively by a number of users on a computer network

grouse

grouse[1] /growss/ (*plural same*) *n* a large game bird that nests on the ground on moors and in forests and is usually reddish-brown with feathered feet and legs. Family: Tetraonidae. [Early 16C. Origin ?]

grouse[2] /growss/ (**grouses, grousing, groused**) *vi* to complain regularly and continually, often in a way that is not constructive (*informal*) [Early 19C. Origin ?] —**grouse** *n* —**grouser** *n*

SYNONYMS See *complain*.

grouse[3] /growss/ *adj ANZ* excellent or great (*slang*) [Early 20C. Origin ?]

grout /growt/ *n* **1.** MORTAR FOR FILLING GAPS thin mortar used to fill gaps, especially between tiles **2.** PLASTER fine plaster used to finish ceilings and walls ■ **grouts** *npl* DREGS the sediment that lies at the bottom of a liquid ■ *vt* (**grouts, grouting, grouted**) APPLY GROUT TO SOMETHING to use grout to fill gaps, especially between tiles, or to finish a ceiling or wall [Old English *grūt* < Germanic] —**grouter** *n*

grove /grōv/ *n* **1.** a small wood ○ *a hazel grove* **2.** a plantation of trees grown for their produce [Old English *grāf*, origin ?]

grovel /gróv'l/ (**-els, -elling, -elled**) *vi* **1.** BEHAVE IN SERVILE WAY to act in a servile way, showing exaggerated and false respect in order to please somebody or out of fear ○ *I've already apologized but now he wants me to grovel.* **2.** CRAWL to crawl or lie face down on the ground in humility or fear **3.** WALLOW to indulge in something unworthy (*literary*) [Late 19C. < obsolete *groof* 'with face downwards' < Old Norse *á grúfu* < *grúfa* 'proneness'] —**groveller** *n* —**grovellingly** *adv*

grow /grō/ (**grows, growing, grew** /groo/, **grown** /grōn/) *v* **1.** *vi* GET BIGGER to become larger in size through natural development **2.** *vi* BECOME LARGER OR GREATER to expand or become more developed or intense ○ *The number of members will grow rapidly.* **3.** *vi* INCREASE to increase in degree ○ *Excitement is growing.* **4.** *vi* DEVELOP NATURALLY to be capable of developing naturally and remaining in a naturally healthy state ○ *Plants won't grow in this soil.* **5.** *vi* BE PRODUCT OF SOMETHING to develop from something else ○ *Hatred grew out of mutual ignorance.* **6.** *vi* BECOME to move from one condition to another, especially gradually ○ *The night grew cold.* **7.** *vt* CAUSE SOMETHING TO GROW to make something, especially plants, grow and develop ○ *We grow tomatoes in the greenhouse.* **8.** *vt* DEVELOP SOMETHING NATURALLY to produce something or allow it to be produced as part of a natural process ○ *grow a moustache* **9.** ⚠ *vt* EXPAND SOMETHING to develop, expand, and stimulate something, especially a business, a line of business, or an economic market ○ *an attempt to grow the company's market share* [Old English *grōwan* < Indo-European] —**grower** *n*

USAGE Metaphorical uses of *grow* as a transitive verb are sometimes considered unacceptable: *grow the economy* and *grow a stock portfolio.* There are no grounds for objecting to literal physical senses of the transitive verb: *grow a beard; grow corn.* Nor are there grounds for objecting to metaphorical uses of the intransitive verb: *The economy grew rapidly.*

grow into *vt* to develop in size, maturity, or capability to suit something

grow on vt 1. to become gradually more acceptable or pleasing to somebody ○ *a song that grows on you* 2. to become gradually more apparent or powerful to somebody

grow out of vt to become too mature or too big in size for something

grow up vi 1. BECOME ADULT to develop into an adult 2. BEHAVE MORE MATURELY to behave in a more mature and sensible way 3. COME INTO EXISTENCE to come into existence and develop ○ *A town had grown up at the junction of the two rivers.*

growbag /grṓ bag/ n a plastic sack filled with compost and nutrients, sold as a container in which to grow plants

growing /grṓ ing/ adj 1. becoming greater in size or amount 2. becoming more intense or extreme ○ *growing anxiety*

growing pains npl 1. pains in the limbs that sometimes affect adolescents, thought to be caused by rapid bodily growth 2. problems associated with the early stages of something such as a developing project

growing point n the area in a plant where the cells are actively dividing to produce new tissue in the stems and roots

growing season n the time of year during which annual plants, especially farm crops, develop to maturity

growl /growl/ v (growls, growling, growled) 1. vti MAKE HOSTILE SOUND to make a low nonverbal sound in the throat that expresses hostility, or communicate something by means of this sound 2. vti SPEAK IN HOSTILE WAY to speak, or say something, in a deep voice that expresses impatience or hostility ○ *He was growling at the children.* 3. vi MAKE RUMBLING NOISE to make a low rumbling noise ■ n 1. ANIMAL'S HOSTILE NOISE the low throaty noise made by a hostile animal, especially a dog 2. HOSTILE UTTERANCE something said in a hostile throaty voice [Mid-17C. Probably < Old French *grouler* < Germanic, an imitation of the sound] —**growling** adj —**growlingly** adv —**growly** adj

growler /grṓwlər/ n 1. a small iceberg with very little showing above the water 2. a person or animal that growls

grown /grōn/ past participle of **grow** ■ adj having developed and matured

grown-up adj 1. FULLY MATURE fully developed and mature 2. FOR ADULTS relating to or for adults ■ n ADULT an adult person (*usually used by or to children*) ○ *Ask a grown-up to put it in the oven for you.*

growth /grōth/ n 1. GROWING PROCESS the process of becoming larger and more mature through natural development ○ *nutrients needed for healthy growth* 2. INCREASE an increase in numbers, size, power, or intensity 3. SOMETHING THAT GROWS something that grows or has grown ○ *three days' growth of beard* 4. MED TUMOUR a mass of cells with no physiological function, e.g. a tumour that forms in or on an organ ■ adj EXPANDING in the process of expanding or developing, especially rapidly ○ *a growth company*

growth factor n a substance produced by cells that stimulates them to multiply. When produced in excessive amounts, a growth factor may be associated with proliferating growth such as that seen in cancer.

growth fund n a unit trust that invests in stocks expected to appreciate significantly

growth hormone n a hormone, made and stored in the pituitary gland in the brain, that stimulates protein synthesis and the growth of the long bones of the limbs

growth industry n an industry that is expanding ○ *Microelectronics is one of the area's few growth industries.*

growth regulator n a natural or synthetic preparation that promotes or inhibits plant growth

growth ring n a concentric ring in the cross-section of a woody stem or trunk, representing the result of one year's growth

growth substance n a chemical produced by a plant that regulates its growth and development, and is usually made in the shoot tip and transported to other regions

groyne /groyn/ n a structure resembling a wall built out into a river or the sea to protect the shore from

erosion [Late 16C. < obsolete *groin* 'pig's snout', via Old French < late Latin *grunium* < Latin *grunnire* 'grunt']

grozer /grṓzər/ n N England same as **gooseberry** (senses 1–2) (*informal*) [Early 16C. < French *groseille*]

Grozny /grózni/, **Grozyy** capital of the Russian republic of Chechnya, at the foot of the Caucasus Mountains. Population: 372,742 (1995).

GRP abbr glass-reinforced plastic

grub /grub/ n 1. LARVA the larva of various insects, especially beetles 2. FOOD food, especially a meal (*informal*) ■ v (grubs, grubbing, grubbed) 1. vt DIG SOMETHING UP to dig or pull something out of the ground, especially without proper tools ○ *grubbing up potatoes* 2. vt CLEAR GROUND to remove roots and stumps from an area of ground 3. vi SEARCH ON GROUND to search on or in the ground for something 4. vi SEARCH LABORIOUSLY to search for something laboriously, usually by moving things and looking under things ○ *grubbing in the archives for evidence* 5. vi TOIL to work hard, especially at something dull or arduous [14C. < assumed Old English *grybban* < Indo-European, 'scratch, dig'] —**grubber** n

grubby /grúbbi/ (-bier, -biest) adj 1. DIRTY slightly dirty 2. HAVING GRUBS infested with grubs 3. CONTEMPTIBLE disliked or despised, especially for being sordid or dishonourable ○ *articles in his grubby little newsletter* —**grubbily** adv —**grubbiness** n

SYNONYMS See *dirty*.

grub-kick n a kick in rugby that makes the ball travel along the ground

grub screw n a small screw with no head, used to fix a movable part in position

grubstake /grúb stayk/ N Am n 1. BUSINESS ADVANCE FOR STARTING UP BUSINESS money or materials given to somebody starting a business in return for a share in any profits 2. MIN EXTRACT MONEY ADVANCED TO PROSPECTOR supplies or money given to a prospector in return for a share in any profits ■ vt (-stakes, -staking, -staked) ADVANCE MONEY TO to give money or supplies to somebody in business in return for a share of any profits [Mid-19C. < GRUB 'food' + STAKE[2]] —**grubstaker** n

Grub Street n the world of literary hackwork and those who work at it [After a former street in London]

grudge /gruj/ n RESENTMENT a feeling of resentment or ill will, especially one lasting for a long time ■ vt (grudges, grudging, grudged) 1. GIVE SOMETHING RELUCTANTLY to allow, give, or do something reluctantly ○ *He wouldn't grudge working late if he knew it was important.* 2. ENVY SOMETHING to be envious or resentful of somebody for something [14C. < Old French *grouchier* 'grumble'] —**grudger** n

grudge match n a match between players or teams who have a long-standing animosity between them or a specific past insult or injury to revenge

grudging /grújjing/ adj done or given reluctantly, or doing or giving something reluctantly —**grudgingly** adv

gruel /grṓo əl/ n a thin porridge made by boiling meal, especially oatmeal, in water [14C. < Old French < Germanic]

gruelling /grṓo əling/ adj extremely arduous or exhausting [< giving gruel as a punishment] —**gruellingly** adv

gruesome /grṓossəm/ adj involving or depicting death or injury in a disturbing or sickening way ○ *gruesome photographs of the accident* [Late 16C. < obsolete *grue* 'shudder' < N Germanic] —**gruesomely** adv —**gruesomeness** n

gruff /gruf/ adj 1. abrupt, angry, or impatient in manner or speech ○ *a gruff refusal* 2. harsh-sounding or throaty ○ *a gruff voice* [15C. < Flemish or Dutch *grof* 'rough, harsh'] —**gruffly** adv —**gruffness** n

grumble /grúmb'l/ v (-bles, -bling, -bled) 1. vi EXPRESS DISSATISFACTION to complain or mutter in a discontented way 2. vt SAY SOMETHING AS COMPLAINT to say something as a complaint ○ *Some entrants grumbled that there wasn't enough time.* 3. vi MAKE RUMBLING NOISES to make rumbling or growling noises ○ *thunder grumbling in the distance* ■ n 1. COMPLAINT a complaint or expression of discontent 2. RUMBLING NOISE a rumbling or growling noise [Late 16C. Probably < Middle Dutch *grommelen* 'mumble, grunt'] —**grumbler** n —**grumbly** adj

SYNONYMS See *complain*.

grumbling /grúmbling/ n a muted complaint or protest ○ *grumblings of discontent* ■ adj with a tendency to complain —**grumblingly** adv

grummet n same as **grommet**

grump /grump/ (*informal*) n SOMEBODY IN BAD MOOD somebody regarded as bad-tempered or sullen ■ **grumps** npl BAD-TEMPERED MOOD a bad-tempered or sullen mood ○ *a fit of the grumps* ■ vi (grumps, grumping, grumped) COMPLAIN to complain or be sullen [Early 18C. An imitation of somebody expressing displeasure]

grumpy /grúmpi/ (-ier, -iest) adj bad-tempered or sullen —**grumpily** adv —**grumpiness** n

Grundyism /grúndi izəm/ n a prudish narrow-minded attitude towards other people (*disapproving*) [Mid-19C. < Mrs *Grundy*, character in Thomas Moreton's play *Speed the Plough* (1798)]

grunge /grunj/ n 1. FILTH filth or rubbish (*informal*) 2. KIND OF ROCK MUSIC a variety of rock music that emerged in the 1980s in the United States and owes much to punk and heavy metal (*often used before a noun*) ○ *grunge rock* 3. UNKEMPT FASHION STYLE a style of dress, popularized by fans of grunge music, typified by second-hand clothes worn in layers, heavy footwear, unkempt hair, and an overall scruffy appearance ○ *designer grunge* 4. US UNAPPEALING PERSON somebody who looks dirty, unkempt, or otherwise unsavoury (*slang insult*) [Mid-20C. Back-formation < GRUNGY]

grungy /grúnji/ (-gier, -giest) adj 1. dirty, shabby, inferior, or otherwise undesirable (*informal*) 2. relating to or typical of grunge music or grunge fashions [Mid-20C. Origin ?] —**grunginess** n

grunion /grúnyən/ n a small fish that spawns on beaches. Native to: coastal waters of California, Mexico. Latin name: *Leuresthes tenuis*. [Early 20C. Probably < Spanish *gruñón* 'grunter' < Latin *grunnire* 'to grunt']

grunt[1] /grunt/ v (grunts, grunting, grunted) 1. vi MAKE NOISE OF PIG to make the half-nasal, half-throaty noise that a pig makes 2. vti SAY SOMETHING IN THROATY BURST to make a deep sound in the throat as an annoyed, half-hearted, or inattentive response to what somebody has said, or to indicate or say something in this way ○ *He grunted in acknowledgment of my greeting.* ■ n 1. NOISE OF PIG a half-nasal, half-throaty noise that a pig makes, or a vocal sound that resembles it 2. SEA FISH a bony fish that grunts when taken out of the water. Native to: warm and tropical seas. Family: Pomadasyidae. [Old English *grunettan* < Indo-European] —**grunter** n

grunt[2] /grunt/ n N Am an infantryman in the US Army or Marine Corps, especially one serving in Vietnam (*slang*) [Mid-20C. Alteration of *ground* < *ground man* 'low-ranking railway worker']

gruntled /grúnt'ld/ adj pleased or happy (*informal humorous*) [Early 20C. Back-formation < *disgruntled*]

gruntwork /grúnt wurk/ n N Am basic work that is necessary to the completion of a task but that is uninspiring or unrewarding (*informal*) UK term **donkeywork**

Grus /grṓoss/ n a small constellation of the southern hemisphere situated between Tucana and Piscis Austrinus. See illustration at **constellation** [Early 18C. < Latin *grus* 'crane (bird)']

Gruyère /grṓo yair/ n a hard Swiss cheese with occasional holes in it that has a mild nutty slightly sweet flavour. It is often used in cooking, e.g. in fondues. [Early 19C. After a town in Switzerland]

gr wt abbr COMM gross weight

gryke n GEOL another spelling of **grike**

gryphon n another spelling of **griffin**

gs abbr South Georgia (*used in Internet addresses*) See table at **domain name**

GS abbr 1. POL General Secretary 2. MIL general staff

GSM tdmk a trademark for an international wireless communications network for mobile phones. Full form **Global System for Mobile Communications**

gsoh abbr good sense of humour (*used in personal columns*)

G-spot n a highly sensitive small area in the vagina that, when stimulated, gives extreme sexual pleas-

ure (*informal*) [Late 20C. After Ernst *Gräfenberg* (1881–1957), German gynaecologist]

GSR *abbr* PHYSIOL galvanic skin response

GST *abbr* FIN goods and services tax

Gstaad /gə shtáat/ alpine ski resort in Bern Canton, western Switzerland. Population: 2,500 (1980 estimate).

G-string *n* a piece of material covering only the pubic area, supported by a narrow cord between the buttocks and around the waist [Late 19C. Origin ?]

G-suit *n* a close-fitting garment worn by pilots and astronauts that counters the blackout effects of high acceleration by applying pressure to the legs and lower body, thereby reducing blood supply loss to the head [Mid-20C. Shortening of *gravity-suit*]

gt *abbr* Guatemala (*used in Internet addresses*) See table at **domain name**

Gt *abbr* GEOG Great

GTG *abbr* got to go (*used in e-mails or text messages*)

GTi *abbr* Gran Turismo injection (*used as part of the name of a fast car*) [Italian, 'grand touring, injection']

gTLD *n* the portion of an Internet address that identifies it as belonging to a specific generic domain class, e.g. com, edu, or gov. Full form **generic top-level domain**

GTT *abbr* MED glucose tolerance test

gu *abbr* Guam (*used in Internet addresses*) See table at **domain name**

GU *abbr* MED, PHYSIOL genitourinary

guacamole /gwaáke móli/ *n* avocado mashed or puréed with tomato and lightly spiced with chilli, served as a dip or in salads [Early 20C. Via American Spanish < Nahuatl *ahuacamolli* 'avocado paste']

guacharo /gwaácha rōַ/ (*plural* **-ros**) *n* BIRDS same as **oilbird** [Early 19C. Via American Spanish *guácharo* < Quechua *wáhcha* 'orphan']

Guadalajara /gwaádəla háarə/ city in west-central Mexico, capital of Jalisco State, and the country's second largest city. Founded in 1530, it is a holiday resort and commercial centre. Population: 1,646,319 (2000).

Guadalcanal /gwaádəlkə nál/ mountainous island in the southwestern Pacific Ocean. It is the largest island of the Solomon Islands. In World War II, heavy fighting took place there between the United States and Japanese forces. Area: 6,475 sq. km/2,500 sq. mi.

Guadalquivir /gwaád'l kwi veér/ river in Andalusia, southern Spain. It rises in the Sierra de Segura and flows southwestwards through Córdoba and Seville before emptying into the Gulf of Cádiz. Length: 657 km/408 mi.

Guadalupe /gwaáde loõp/ **1.** island off the Baja California coast of Mexico in the Pacific Ocean. Area: 207 sq. km/80 sq. mi. **2.** city near Monterrey in Nuevo León State, northeastern Mexico. Population: 670,162 (2000).

Guadalupe Hidalgo /gwaáde loop hi dálgō/ former name for **Gustavo A. Madero**

Guadeloupe /gwaáde loõp/ overseas department of France consisting of a group of islands in the eastern Caribbean. Capital: Basse-Terre. Population: 431,170 (2001). Area: 1,780 sq. km/687 sq. mi.

Guadiana /gwa dyaánə/ river that rises south of Madrid, Spain, and flows westwards to Portugal. It forms part of the southern border between the two countries before emptying into the Gulf of Cádiz. Length: 829 km/515 mi.

~~guage~~ incorrect spelling of **gauge**

guaiac /gwí ak, -ək/ *n* PHARM same as **guaiacum** (sense 3) [Mid-16C. Anglicization]

guaiacol /gwí ə kol/ *n* a yellowish oily liquid. Source: guaiacum resin, wood creosote. Use: expectorant, antiseptic, local anaesthetic. [Mid-19C. < GUAIACUM]

guaiacum /gwí əkəm/ *n* **1.** TROPICAL AMERICAN TREE an evergreen tree that has dark dense oily wood and yields a medicinal resin. Native to: tropical America. Latin name: *Guaiacum officinale*. **2.** GUAIACUM WOOD the hard dense oily wood of the guaiacum tree **3.** GUAIACUM RESIN the brownish-green resin of the guaiacum tree. Use: in medicine, making varnishes.

[Mid-16C. Via modern Latin < American Spanish *guayacán* < Taino]

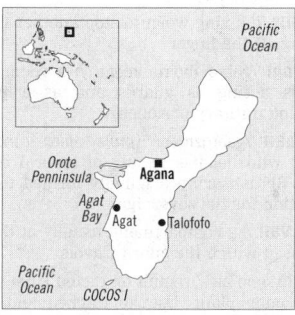

Guam

Guam /gwaam/ island and tourist resort in the northwestern Pacific Ocean. An unincorporated territory of the United States, it is the largest of the Mariana Islands. Capital: Agana. Population: 163,941 (2003). Area: 549 sq. km/212 sq. mi. —**Guamanian** /gwaa máyni ən/ *n, adj*

guan /gwaan/ *n* a large fruit-eating bird that lives in trees. Native to: Central and South America. Family: Cracidae. [Late 17C. Via American Spanish < Miskito *kwamu*]

guanaco /gwə naá kō/ (*plural* **-cos**) *n* an animal similar and related to the domesticated llama and alpaca. Native to: dry regions of the Andes. Latin name: *Lama guanaco*. [Early 17C. Via Spanish < Quechua *huanacu*]

Guanajuato /gwaáne hwaátō/ **1.** state in central Mexico. Capital: Guanajuato. Population: 4,663,032 (2000). Area: 30,770 sq. km/11,880 sq. mi. **2.** capital city of Guanajuato State in central Mexico. Population: 135,611 (2000).

Guangdong /gwáng dóong/ province of southern China, on the South China Sea. Capital: Guangzhou. Population: 69,610,000 (1997). Area: 197,100 sq. km/76,100 sq. mi.

Guangxi Zhuang /gwáng shee jwáng/ autonomous region in southeastern China, on the border with Vietnam. Capital: Nanning. Population: 42,245,765 (1990). Area: 220,400 sq. km/85,100 sq. mi.

Guangzhou /gwáng jo̅/ capital of Guangdong Province and chief port in southeastern China. It lies about 129 km/80 mi. northwest of Hong Kong. A major international trade fair is held there twice yearly. Population: 4,490,000 (1995).

guanidine /gwaáni deen/ *n* a strongly alkaline substance found in urine as a product of protein metabolism and in plant tissues. Use: manufacture of plastics and resins. Formula: CH_5N_3. [Mid-19C. < GUANO + -IDE + -INE]

guanine /gwaá neen/ *n* a purine derivative that is one of the four bases in DNA and RNA. Symbol **G** [Mid-19C. < GUANO]

guano /gwaánō/ *n* **1.** accumulated droppings of birds, bats, or seals, occurring where large established colonies of these animals are situated **2.** fertilizer consisting of dried bird or bat droppings that is rich in nutrients, including nitrates, oxalates, and phosphates, or a synthetic fertilizer with properties similar to those of natural guano [Early 17C. Via American Spanish < Quechua *huanu* 'dung']

guanosine /gwaánō seen/ *n* a compound containing guanine and ribose [Early 20C. < GUANINE + RIBOSE]

guanosine monophosphate *n* a constituent of the nucleic acids DNA and RNA that plays a part in various metabolic reactions and is composed of guanosine linked to a phosphate group

guanosine triphosphate *n* a nucleotide made of guanosine linked to three phosphate groups

Guantanamo Bay /gwan taánəmō-/ sheltered inlet of the Caribbean Sea, southeastern Cuba. It is the site of a major US naval base and a prison camp for suspected terrorists captured by the United States. Area: 36 sq. km/14 sq. mi.

Guanxiu /gwaán syoó/ (832–912) Chinese artist. He is noted for his paintings of Buddhist monks with exaggerated and grotesque features.

guanylic acid /gwaa níllik-/ *n* BIOCHEM same as **guanosine monophosphate** [Late 19C. < GUANOSINE]

Guaporé /gwáppō ráy, gwáppə-/ river in central South America that rises in western Brazil and flows northwest along the Brazil-Bolivia border before joining the River Mamoré. Length: 1,749 km/1,087 mi.

guar /goó aar/ *n* **1.** a plant of dry regions widely grown as fodder and for its seeds, which are used to make gum. Native to: South Asia. Latin name: *Cyamopsis tetragonolobus*. **2.** INDUST same as **guar gum** [Late 19C. < Hindi *guār*]

guaraní /gwaára neé/ (*plural same* or **-nís**) *n* **1.** the main unit of Paraguayan currency. See table at **currency 2.** a coin worth one guaraní [Mid-20C. < GUARANI]

Guarani /gwaára neé/ (*plural same* or **-nis**) *n* **1.** a member of a Native South American people who live in parts of Paraguay, Uruguay, Bolivia, and Brazil **2.** an official language of Paraguay, also spoken elsewhere in central South America, belonging to the Tupi-Guarani branch of Andean-Equatorial languages. Native speakers: 3 million. [Mid-18C. Via Spanish *Guaraní* < Guarini, a people of Paraguay] —**Guarani** *adj*

guarantee /gárrən teé/ *n* **1.** ASSURANCE something that assures a specific outcome ○ *There's no guarantee that the plan will work.* **2.** PROMISE OF QUALITY a formal promise that a product will be repaired free of charge if it breaks or fails within a particular period or that substandard work will be redone ○ *The television came with a five-year guarantee.* **3.** CERTIFICATE STATING PROMISE OF QUALITY a document setting out a promise of quality made by a manufacturer or the provider of a service **4.** LAW PROMISE TO BE RESPONSIBLE FOR ANOTHER a formal promise by one person to take responsibility for the debts or obligations of another person if that person fails to meet them **5.** LAW SOMEBODY RECEIVING FORMAL ASSURANCE a person or company given an assurance that somebody's debts or obligations will be dealt with **6.** LAW same as **guarantor** ■ *vt* (**-tees, -teeing, -teed**) **1.** GIVE ASSURANCE OF SOMETHING to promise something, or make something certain ○ *We can't guarantee availability of seats on tomorrow's flight.* **2.** PROMISE QUALITY OF GOODS OR SERVICES to give a formal, usually printed promise with regard to the quality of a product, saying that it will be repaired free of charge if it fails within a particular period, or that substandard work will be redone **3.** LAW ACCEPT RESPONSIBILITY FOR SOMEBODY to promise to fulfil another person's debts or obligations if that person fails to meet them [Late 17C. Probably alteration of GUARANTY]

guaranteed /gárrən teéd/ *adj* **1.** covered by a formal promise of quality and durability ○ *a guaranteed product* **2.** certain to happen or be done or provided ○ *a film guaranteed to have you in floods of tears*

guarantor /gárrən táwr/ *n* somebody who gives a guarantee, especially a formal promise to be responsible for somebody else's debts or obligations [Mid-19C. < GUARANTEE]

SYNONYMS See *backer*.

guaranty /gárrən tee/ *n* (*plural* **-ties**) **1.** something used as security for a formal promise **2.** the giving of something as security for a promise **3.** LAW same as **guarantor** (sense 4) ■ *vt* (**-ties, -tying, -tied**) LAW same as **guarantee** *v* (sense 3) [Early 16C. < Anglo-Norman *guarantie* < Old French *garantir* 'to warrant' < *garant* 'warrant']

SYNONYMS See *backer*.

guard /gaard/ *vt* (**guards, guarding, guarded**) **1.** PROTECT SOMEBODY OR SOMETHING to protect somebody or something against danger or loss by being vigilant and taking defensive measures **2.** PREVENT SOMEBODY FROM ESCAPING to watch over somebody held captive and prevent him or her from escaping ○ *Two police officers were guarding the prisoner.* **3.** CONTROL PASSAGE THROUGH PLACE to watch over and control passage through an entrance or across a boundary ○ *All of the mountain passes are guarded by troops.* **4.** PUT PROTECTIVE COVER ON SOMETHING to equip a machine or device with a protective cover **5.** CONTROL SOMETHING to control or restrain something such as speech or behaviour ○ *guard your tongue* **6.** *N Am* BASKETBALL HAMPER OPPONENT in basketball, to prevent an opponent from scoring or playing effectively ■ *n* **1.** PROTECTOR

a person or group that protects, watches over, restrains, or controls somebody or something ○ *The prisoner broke away from his guards.* **2. CEREMONIAL ESCORT** a usually mounted or motorized group forming a ceremonial escort **3. RAILWAY EMPLOYEE IN CHARGE OF PASSENGERS** a railway employee who is in charge of a train and whose job is to check tickets, announce stops, and attend to passengers' needs and safety. N Am term **conductor 4. ACT OF GUARDING** an act of guarding somebody or something, or the responsibility of guarding somebody or something **5. PROTECTIVE DEVICE** a device or part intended to protect the user against injury ○ *a guard on a lathe* **6. MEANS OF PROTECTION** any means of protection ○ *The pension is index-linked as a guard against inflation.* **7. DEFENCE** a defensive posture or state of mind ○ *Her guard was up.* **8. *also* Guard SOLDIER** in the British army and other armies, a soldier who belongs to any regiment originally formed to provide protection for the sovereign **9. *Ireland* GARDA** a member of the Garda (*informal*) **10. BODY PROTECTION** a piece of tough material worn to protect a part of the body from injury **11. DEFENSIVE POSITION IN BASKETBALL** in basketball, either of the two players who regularly defend the backcourt and initiate attacks **12. BATSMAN'S STANCE IN CRICKET** in cricket, a position taken by a batsman when ready to receive a bowled ball [15C. < French *garde* (noun), *garder* (verb) < Germanic] ◇ **mount** or **stand guard** to keep a watch or defensive posture ◇ **off (your) guard** having relaxed the usual precautions against attack ◇ **on (your) guard** prepared against attack

SYNONYMS See *safeguard*.

guard against *vt* to be wary of something or take precautions against it

guardant /gaárdənt/, **gardant** *adj* describes an animal on a coat of arms that has its face turned towards the observer ○ *a lion guardant* [Late 16C. < French *gardant*, present participle of *garder* 'guard']

guard cell *n* either of two specialized cells bordering pores in the epidermis of leaves that move to control the size of the aperture in response to changes in water levels. The guard cells and pore are called the stoma, and are situated on the underside, and sometimes the top side, of leaves and on young shoots.

guard dog *n* a dog used for guarding property or people

guarded /gaárdid/ *adj* reluctant to share information with others ○ *Officials reacted with guarded optimism to the proposal.* —**guardedly** *adv* —**guardedness** *n*

SYNONYMS See *cautious*.

guard hair *n* the long coarse outer hair on some animals that forms a protective layer over softer underfur

guardhouse /gaárd howss/ (*plural* **-houses** /-howziz/) *n* a building used to house soldiers acting as guards and as a place for detaining military prisoners

Guardi /gwaárdi/, **Francesco** (1712–93) Italian painter. He painted romantic landscapes of his native city, Venice, which are characterized by lively line and colour and a mood of fantasy.

guardian /gaárdi ən/ *n* **1. PROTECTOR** somebody who or something that guards, protects, or preserves somebody or something **2. LEGALLY RESPONSIBLE PERSON** somebody who is legally entrusted to manage somebody else's affairs, especially those of a minor **3. SUPERIOR FRANCISCAN** a superior in a Franciscan monastery [15C. < Anglo-Norman *gardein* < Old French *garder* 'to guard'] —**guardianship** *n*

guardian angel *n* **1.** somebody seen as the special protector of somebody's interests (*informal*) **2.** an angel believed to look after a particular person

Guardian Angel *n* a member of a vigilante group that patrols the streets of a city as a volunteer crime prevention squad. New York was the birthplace of the first such group.

guard of honour *n* **1.** a body of troops acting as a formal escort for somebody important during a ceremony **2.** two racks of lamb joints arranged for roasting with bone ends curved inwards and interleaved. For presenting at table, paper frills are often placed on the bone ends.

guardrail /gaárd rayl/ *n* **1.** a rail acting as a safety barrier at the side of a staircase, road, or deck of a

ship **2.** an additional rail laid close inside the main running rail on tight curves and at points to help a train's wheels stay on the track

guard ring *n* a ring worn to stop another ring from slipping off the finger

guardroom /gaárd room, -room/ *n* a room used by soldiers acting as guards and as a place for detaining military prisoners

guardsman /gaárdzmən/ (*plural* **-men** /-mən/) *n* a soldier who belongs to any of several regiments of the British army originally formed to provide protection for the sovereign

guard's van *n* a compartment, usually at the rear of a train, in which the guard travels

guar gum /goó aar-/ *n* gum extracted from the seeds of the guar plant. Use: to thicken and stabilize processed foods, in paper manufacture.

Guarneri /gwaa nérri/ family of Italian violin makers, including **Andrea** (1626–98) and his grandson **Giuseppe Antonio** (1687–1745)

~~**Guatamala**~~ incorrect spelling of **Guatemala**

Guatemala

Guatemala /gwaáte maálə/ the third largest country in Central America, bordered by Belize, Mexico, the Gulf of Honduras, Honduras, and El Salvador. About two thirds of the total land area of Guatemala is mountainous. Language: Spanish. Currency: quetzal. Capital: Guatemala City. Population: 13,909,384 (2003). Area: 108,889 sq. km/42,042 sq. mi. Official name **Republic of Guatemala** —**Guatemalan** *adj*, *n*

Guatemala City capital city of Guatemala, located in the south-central part of the country. It is the largest city in Central America and the nation's economic centre. It was the capital of the United Provinces of Central America between 1823 and 1834. Population: 1,015,303 (2000).

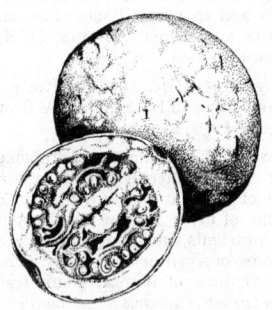

guava

guava /gwaávə/ *n* **1.** a pear-shaped fruit with red or yellow-green skin and cream or pink flesh. Use: eaten raw or made into jam. **2.** a tree that produces guavas. Native to: tropical America. Genus: *Psidium.* [Mid-16C. < Spanish *guayaba*, of Caribbean Native American origin]

Guayaquil /gwí ə keél/ largest city in Ecuador, situated in the west of the country. It is the capital of Guayas Province and Ecuador's main port. Population: 2,117,553 (2000). Full name **Santiago de Guayaquil**

guayule /gwə yoóli/ *n Southwest US* **1.** rubber made from the sap of an American bush **2.** the bush whose sap is a source of guayule. Native to: southwestern United States, Mexico. Latin name: *Parthenium ar-*

gentatum. [Early 20C. Via American Spanish < Nahuatl *cuauhuli* 'gum tree']

gubbins /gúbbinz/ (*informal*) *n* **1. WORTHLESS THING** a thing of no great value **2. NAMELESS GADGET** a gadget or device whose name somebody does not know or has forgotten (*takes a singular verb*) ■ *npl* **ODDMENTS** bits and pieces (*takes a singular verb*) [Mid-16C. < obsolete *gobbon* 'fragment' < Old French]

gubernatorial /goóbərnə táwri əl/ *adj* relating to, involving, or associated with a governor, especially a governor of a US state [Mid-18C. < Latin *gubernator* 'governor' < *gubernare* (see GOVERN)]

guck /guk/ *n* a slimy, oily, gooey, or otherwise unpleasant substance (*informal*) [Mid-20C. Origin ?]

guddle /gúdd'l/ *Scotland n* a state of untidiness or confusion, or an untidy place (*informal*) ■ *vi* (**-dles**, **-dling**, **-dled**) to use the hands to catch fish by groping under the water from the banks of a river ○ *guddling for trout* [Mid-17C. Origin ?]

gudgeon[1] /gújjən/ *n* **1. SMALL FISH** a small freshwater fish that is often used as bait. Native to: Europe. Latin name: *Gobio gobio.* **2. SILLY PERSON** somebody who is easily duped (*slang*) ■ *vt* (**-eons**, **-eoning**, **-eoned**) **CHEAT SOMEBODY** to dupe or cheat somebody (*slang*) [14C. Via Old French *goujon* < Latin *gobius* (see GOBY)]

gudgeon[2] /gújjən/ *n* a socket that a pin fits into, e.g. the pin of a hinge or the pivoting bolt of a ship's rudder [15C. < Old French *goujon* 'little gouge' < late Latin *gubia* (see GOUGE)]

gudgeon pin *n* a pin in a piston of an internal-combustion engine that is attached to the little end of a connecting rod. N Am term **wrist pin** [< GUDGEON[2]]

guelder rose /géldər-/ *n* a bushy deciduous bush with clusters of white flowers and red berries. Native to: Europe, Asia. Latin name: *Viburnum opulus.* [Late 16C. After *Gelderland*, Dutch province where it originated]

Guelph[1] /gwelf/, **Guelf** *n* a member of a political party in medieval Italy that supported the authority of the pope and opposed the Ghibellines, who supported the Holy Roman Emperor's claim to rule Italy [Late 16C. Via Italian *Guelfo* < Middle High German *Welf*, leading dynasty of the Holy Roman Empire] —**Guelphism** *n*

Guelph[2] /gwelf/ industrial city on the Speed River in southeastern Ontario, Canada, 96 km/60 mi. west of Toronto. Population: 106,920 (2001).

guenon /gwén nən, gə nón/ *n* a small long-tailed monkey that lives in trees. Native to: Africa. Genus: *Cercopithecus.* [Mid-19C. < French]

guerdon /gúrd'n/ *n* a reward or recompense (*literary*) [14C. Via Old French < medieval Latin *widerdonum* 're-payment', partial translation of Old High German *widarlōn* 'giving back']

gueridon /gérri doN/ *n* a small round ornate table or stand with a central pedestal [Mid-19C. After French, < a character in French farce]

guerilla *n MIL* another spelling of **guerrilla**

SPELLCHECK See *gorilla*.

Guernica /gúrnikə, gur neékə/ town near Bilbao in the Basque Country, northern Spain. An important centre of Basque culture, it was bombed in 1937 by German aircraft during the Spanish Civil War. Population: 15,485 (1998).

guernsey /gúrnzi/ (*plural* **-seys**) *n* **1.** *also* **Guernsey DAIRY COW** a light-brown and white dairy cow that produces rich milk, belonging to a breed originating on the island of Guernsey **2. SWEATER** a hand-knitted woollen sweater of a type that sailors and fishermen typically wear **3.** *Aus* **SPORTS JERSEY** a sleeveless woollen shirt or jumper worn by a football player [Early 19C. After GUERNSEY] ◇ **get** or **be given a guernsey** *Aus* to be congratulated for something, or have your efforts acknowledged in some way

Guernsey /gúrnzi/ island in the English Channel, the second largest of the Channel Islands. Dairy farming, tourism, and banking are the main trades. Capital: St Peter Port. Population: 64,818 (2003). Area: 65 sq. km/25 sq. mi.

guerrilla /gə ríllə, ge-/, **guerilla** *n* a member of an irregular paramilitary unit, usually with a political objective such as the overthrow of a government. Guerrillas usually operate in small groups to harass

and carry out sabotage. ○ *guerrilla warfare* [Early 19C. < Spanish, 'raiding party, skirmish' < *guerra* 'war']

SPELLCHECK See *gorilla*.

guess /gess/ *v* (**guesses, guessing, guessed**) **1.** *vti* PREDICT SOMETHING to form an opinion about something without enough evidence to make a definite judgment ○ *She guessed the number before he turned the card over.* ○ *Guess where I've been.* ○ *I could tell you what I think, but I'd only be guessing.* **2.** *vt* CONCLUDE SOMETHING CORRECTLY to arrive at a correct answer to or conjecture about something ○ *I guessed it would be you.* **3.** *vi* FIND CORRECT ANSWER to be correct in your thinking about what might be the case ○ *You'll never guess.* **4.** *vt* N Am SUPPOSE SOMETHING to think or suppose something ○ *I guess I'll have the steak.* ■ *n* **1.** OPINION an opinion or answer arrived at by guessing ○ *My guess is she'll head for home.* **2.** ACT OF GUESSING an act or the process of guessing ○ *Have another guess.* [13C. < N Germanic < Germanic, 'try to get'] —**guessable** *adj* —**guesser** *n* ◇ **anybody's guess** something that cannot be reliably predicted (*informal*)

guessing game *n* **1.** a game in which players must identify an unknown word, person, or object by asking a series of questions to gain information **2.** a situation of which the outcome is frustratingly unpredictable

guesstimate /géstimət/ (*informal*) *n* an estimate based largely on incomplete information or evidence ■ *vti* (**-mates, -mating, -mated**) to make an estimate of something based largely on incomplete evidence or information [Mid-20C. Blend of GUESS + ESTIMATE]

guesswork /géss wurk/ *n* the process of making guesses, or the conclusions arrived at by guessing

guest /gest/ *n* **1.** RECIPIENT OF HOSPITALITY somebody who receives hospitality from somebody else **2.** SOMEBODY ENTERTAINED AT ANOTHER'S EXPENSE a recipient of a meal or entertainment that is paid for by somebody else ○ *Club members are allowed to sign two people in as guests.* **3.** CUSTOMER somebody who pays to use the facilities of a hotel, restaurant, or other establishment **4.** SOMEBODY ASKED TO JOIN OTHERS somebody who is invited by an organization or institution to receive hospitality ○ *We have a distinguished guest at the meeting tonight.* **5.** SOMEBODY MAKING SPECIAL APPEARANCE somebody who appears by invitation in a radio or television programme ○ *our special guest for tonight's show* **6.** ZOOL ANIMAL USING ANOTHER'S NEST an organism, especially an insect, that shares the shelter of another or lives alongside the other as a parasite ■ *vi* (**guests, guesting, guested**) MAKE SPECIAL APPEARANCE to appear as a guest on a radio or television programme ■ *adj* **1.** APPEARING AS GUEST appearing or invited as a guest ○ *a guest star* **2.** FOR GUESTS for guests to use ○ *the guest bedroom* [13C. < Old Norse *gestr*] ◇ **be my guest** used to tell people that they are welcome to do as they please (*informal*)

guest beer *n* a beer kept on draught in a bar for a limited period only as an addition to the usual beers

guest book *n* a book or register that visitors or guests sign, e.g. at a bed-and-breakfast

guesthouse /gést howss/ (*plural* **-houses** /-howziz/) *n* **1.** a small hotel or private home that offers accommodation to paying guests **2.** N Am a small house used to accommodate visitors to a main house

guest night *n* an evening on which nonmembers are welcome to participate in the activities of a club or society

guest of honour *n* somebody invited to attend a gathering or event who is seen as highly important or the most important of the invited guests

guestroom /gést room, -room/ *n* a bedroom for visitors who stay for a short time

guest star *n* a well-known performer who makes a single or occasional appearance in a television or radio programme

guest-star *vti* to appear as a guest star, or feature somebody as a guest star

guest worker *n* a foreign national allowed to come and work, but not take up permanent residence, in another country

Che Guevara

Guevara /gə vaárə/, **Che** (1928–67) Argentine-born South American revolutionary leader. A radical political theorist and guerrilla fighter, he played a significant part in Fidel Castro's revolution (1956–59) and early administration in Cuba. He was executed while planning an uprising in Bolivia. Born **Guevara de la Serna, Ernesto**

'In the laborious work of revolutionaries, death is a frequent accident.'
[Che Guevara. Quoted in *We Say No*, Eduardo Galeano; 1992]

guff /guf/ *n* (*informal*) **1.** nonsense or empty talk **2.** Scotland a smell, especially a bad one [Early 19C. Probably suggesting a whiff of bad smelling air]

guffaw /gə fáw/ *vi* (**-faws, -fawing, -fawed**) to laugh loudly and raucously ■ *n* a loud and raucous laugh [Early 18C. An imitation of the sound]

Peggy Guggenheim

Guggenheim /gớoggən hīm/, **Peggy** (1898–1979) US art collector and philanthropist. She helped to promote the careers of such avant-garde artists as Jackson Pollock and her husband Max Ernst. She was one of the earliest collectors of surrealist and abstract art. Born **Guggenheim, Marguerite**

GUI /gớo i/ *abbr* COMPUT graphical user interface

Guiana /gi aánə, gī ánnə/ region of Northeastern South America, bordering the Atlantic Ocean and including Guyana, Suriname, French Guiana, and parts of Venezuela and Brazil. Area: 690,000 sq. mi./1,787,100 sq. km.

guidance /gíd'nss/ *n* **1.** LEADERSHIP leadership or direction **2.** ADVICE advice or counselling, especially counselling given to students on academic matters **3.** SYSTEMS THAT CONTROL FLIGHT the systems and devices that control the flight of an aircraft, missile, or spacecraft ○ *onboard guidance*

guidance counsellor *n* N Am in a US high school, somebody who gives students personal, academic, and career counselling

guide /gīd/ *v* (**guides, guiding, guided**) **1.** *vti* SHOW SOMEBODY THE WAY to lead somebody in the right direction **2.** *vt* ADVISE OR INFLUENCE SOMEBODY to advise or counsel somebody, or influence the way somebody behaves or acts ○ *Be guided by your conscience.* **3.** *vt* HELP SOMEBODY LEARN SOMETHING to teach somebody, or oversee training in something ○ *An instructor will be appointed to guide you through the course.* **4.** *vt* RUN ORGANIZATION to control the affairs of an organization or body **5.** *vt* STEER SOMETHING to steer a vehicle or animal ■ *n* **1.** SOMEBODY WHO SHOWS WAY somebody who leads and assists others in a place or towards a destination **2.** SOMEBODY WHO LEADS TOURISTS

somebody who supervises a tour **3.** INFLUENCE ON DECISION a strong influence on the decisions and behaviour of another ○ *Her grandmother's wisdom was her guide throughout life.* **4.** PUBL same as **guidebook 5.** SOURCE OF INFORMATION a publication or a section of a magazine or newspaper giving information on a subject ○ *a TV guide* **6.** CONTROLLING DEVICE a device that controls the movement or operation of a machine **7.** *also* **Guide** MEMBER OF GIRLS' SCOUTING ORGANIZATION a member of the Guide Association, a worldwide scouting organization for girls **8.** SOLDIER CONTROLLING MARCH a soldier stationed at the side of a column of marching soldiers to control alignment and lead the way [14C. < Old French *guider* < Germanic] —**guidable** *adj*

SYNONYMS *guide, conduct, direct, lead, steer, usher*
CORE MEANING: to show somebody the way to a place

guide to lead somebody in the right direction. ○ *Another rescue team, guided by a dog, located a woman alive under the rubble.* **conduct** to lead a person or group of people somewhere by going along with them ○ *He was conducted by an attendant through a maze of corridors to an enormous room.* **direct** to aim, point, or send something in a particular direction ○ *We didn't see a signpost that would have directed us to the Roman site.* **lead** to show other people the way, usually by going ahead of them ○ *He led us into the house and introduced us to his two nieces.* **steer** to encourage somebody to take a particular course or route by unobtrusively guiding them ○ *She steered them all forwards saying, 'Let's not stand about. The car's over there'.* **usher** to escort somebody to or from a place or a seat ○ *We were ushered to the front of the queue.* ○ *He ushered the young man into a comfortable chair on the far side of the room.*

Guide Association *n* a worldwide scouting organization for girls

guidebook /gíd book/ *n* a book containing information for tourists about a country, area, city, or institution

guided missile /gídid-/ *n* a self-propelled missile that can be steered in flight by remote control or by an onboard homing device

guide dog *n* a dog trained to lead a sightless person

guideline /gíd līn/ *n* **1.** an official recommendation indicating how something should be done or what sort of action should be taken in a particular circumstance **2.** a line that shows a correct position, route, or alignment, e.g. a fine line printed as an aid to lining up text or illustrations on a page

~~guidence~~ incorrect spelling of **guidance**

guidepost /gíd pōst/ *n* a direction sign at a roadside (*dated*)

guide price *n* the price that a seller can expect something, especially a house, to fetch

guider /gídər/ *n* N Ireland a vehicle made from planks and wheels to help children learn to walk

guiderail /gíd rayl/ *n* a rail designed to lead somebody in the right direction or help somebody move along, or to control the sideways movement of something

guide rope *n* a rope attached to an object or to another rope or cable and used to manoeuvre it into position or to steady a load

Guides /gídz/ *n* **1.** YOUTH ORG same as **Guide Association** (*takes a singular or plural verb*) **2.** a meeting of a group of Guides ○ *going to Guides*

guideway /gíd way/ *n* a groove or channel that controls the direction in which a moving object travels

guide word *n* US same as **catchword** (sense 2)

guiding /gíding/ *n* UK, Can the activities of the Guide Association

guiding light /gíding-/ *n* somebody or something that is a guide, example, or inspiration

Guido d'Arezzo /gweédō da rétsō/ (990?–1033?) Italian monk and music theorist. He introduced the four-line staff for musical notation and the system of using syllables to name the notes of the scale.

guidon /gíd'n/ *n* a regimental flag or pennant, or the soldier who carries it [Mid-16C. Via French < Italian *guidone* < *guida* 'guide']

guild /gild/, **gild** *n* **1.** ASSOCIATION OF PEOPLE WITH SIMILAR INTERESTS a club, society, or other organization of people with common interests or goals **2.** MEDIEVAL

TRADE ASSOCIATION an association of merchants or craftspersons in medieval Europe, formed to give help and advice to its members and to make regulations and set standards for a particular trade **3. GROUP OF ORGANISMS** a group of organisms that use the same environmental resources in a similar way [14C. Probably < Middle Low German, Middle Dutch *gilde* < Germanic] —**guildship** *n* —**guildsman** *n* —**guildswoman** *n*

SPELLCHECK guild or **gild**? Do not confuse the spelling of **guild** and **gild**, which sound similar. **Guild** is a noun denoting an association of people, as in *a guild of craftspeople, the Townswomen's Guild*. **Gild** is a verb meaning 'cover with gold' or 'tinge with a golden colour', as in *gild a picture frame, clouds gilded by the setting sun*. Note that the noun **guild** can also be spelt **gild**, but the verb **gild** cannot be spelt **guild**.

guilder /gíldər/, **gulden** /gooldən/ (*plural* **-dens** or *same*) *n* **1. FORMER CURRENCY UNIT OF NETHERLANDS** the main unit of the former currency of the Netherlands **2. CURRENCY UNIT OF SURINAME** the main unit of currency of Suriname. See table at **currency 3. OLD COIN** a gold or silver coin formerly used in Germany, Austria, and the Netherlands [15C. Alteration of Dutch *gulden* 'golden']

Guildford /gílfərd/ cathedral city on the River Wey in Surrey, southern England. It is the site of the University of Surrey. Population: 129,701 (2001).

guildhall /gíld hawl/ *n* **1.** the town hall in some towns **2.** the meeting place of a modern or medieval guild

guild socialism *n* a socialist movement in Great Britain in the early 20th century that advocated state ownership of industry but with each branch managed by guilds of workers —**guild socialist** *n*

guile /gíl/ *n* a cunning, deceitful, or treacherous quality [13C. Via French < Old Norse] —**guileful** *adj* —**guilefully** *adv* —**guilefulness** *n*

guileless /gíl ləss/ *adj* open and honest and not expecting others to behave differently —**guilelessly** *adv* —**guilelessness** *n*

Guilin /gwáy lín/ city in northeastern Guangxi Zhuangzu Province, southern China. It is located in a scenic limestone region made famous by Chinese classical painters and poets. Population: 376,362 (1991).

guillemot /gílli mot/ *n* a black-and-white narrow-beaked diving seabird of the auk family. Native to: northern Atlantic, northern Pacific. Genera: *Uria* or *Cepphus*. [Late 17C. < French, 'little William']

guilloche /gi lósh/ *n* in architecture, an ornamental border formed by two or more interlaced bands round a series of interlocking circles [19C. < French]

guillotine /gílla teen/ *n* **1. MACHINE FOR BEHEADING PEOPLE** a machine for executing people by beheading, consisting of a vertical wooden frame with grooves for a heavy sliding blade to be dropped from a height onto the person's neck. It became famous for its use during the French Revolution. **2. DEATH BY GUILLOTINE** execution by means of the guillotine **3. INSTRUMENT FOR CUTTING METAL OR PAPER** a cutting instrument, especially one for cutting sheet metal or paper, consisting of a platform with a blade attached to one side that is pulled down like a lever **4. TIME LIMIT ON LEGISLATIVE DEBATE** a limit on the time available for debate on a piece of legislation, designed to speed up parliamentary proceedings and prevent opponents of the legislation obstructing its progress [Late 18C. After Joseph-Ignace *Guillotin* (1738–1814), French physician] —**guillotine** *vt*

guilt /gilt/ *n* **1. AWARENESS OF WRONGDOING** an awareness of having done wrong or committed a crime, accompanied by feelings of shame and regret ○ *feelings of guilt* **2. FACT OF WRONGDOING** the fact of having committed a crime or done wrong ○ *an admission of guilt* **3. RESPONSIBILITY FOR WRONGDOING** the responsibility for committing a crime or doing wrong ○ *Some of the guilt must attach to the parents.* **4. LEGAL CULPABILITY** the responsibility, as determined by a court or other legal authority, for committing an offence that carries a legal penalty [Old English *gylt*, origin ?]

SPELLCHECK guilt or **gilt**? Do not confuse the spelling of **guilt** and **gilt**, which sound similar. **Guilt** is a noun denoting the fact or awareness of having done wrong: *Guilt was written all over her face*. **Gilt** is a noun or adjective referring to a thin layer of gold (as in *lettering*

in gilt, gilt picture frames) or a noun denoting a bond issued by the government (as in *trading in gilts*).

guiltless /gíltless/ *adj* not responsible for a crime or wrongdoing, or not deserving blame or criticism —**guiltlessly** *adv* —**guiltlessness** *n*

guilt trip *n* an exaggerated feeling or display of shame and regret, usually lasting some time (*informal*)

guilty /gílti/ (**-ier, -iest**) *adj* **1. RESPONSIBLE FOR WRONGDOING** responsible for a crime, wrong action, or error and deserving punishment, blame, or criticism ○ *He was guilty of a serious error of judgment.* **2. OFFICIALLY FOUND RESPONSIBLE FOR CRIME** found and declared responsible for committing an offence by a court or other legal authority **3. ASHAMED OF WRONGDOING** aware of having done wrong or committed a crime and regretful and ashamed about it ○ *I still feel guilty about having forgotten your birthday.* **4. SHOWING GUILT** indicating or suggesting that somebody feels guilt, has done wrong, or has something to hide ○ *a guilty look on his face* **5. CAUSING GUILT** causing or likely to cause emotions of shame and regret ○ *a guilty secret* —**guiltily** *adv* —**guiltiness** *n*

guilty conscience *n* a feeling of shame at having done wrong

Guimard /gímaa/, **Hector** (1867–1942) French architect. One of the most important figures of the art nouveau movement, he is best known for Castel Béranger (1898) in Paris and his designs for the entrances to several Paris Métro stations (1899–1905). Full name **Guimard, Hector Germain**

guimpe[1] /gimp, gamp/ *n* **1.** a short blouse designed to be worn under a dress or pinafore **2.** a starched cloth that covers the neck and shoulders, worn by some nuns as part of their habit [Mid-19C. < French < Old French *guimple* 'wimple']

guimpe[2] /gamp/ *n* CLOTHING another spelling of **gimp**[1]

Guin ▸ Le Guin, Ursula

guinea /gínni/ *n* **1.** a gold coin worth 21 shillings (£1.05p) that was a British unit of currency between 1663 and 1813 **2.** an amount equivalent to £1.05 or 21 shillings, the value of a guinea [Mid-16C. Because first made for trade with the *Guinea* coast of W Africa]

Guinea

Guinea /gínni/ country in West Africa, between Guinea-Bissau and Sierra Leone. It became independent from France in 1958. Language: French. Currency: Guinean franc. Capital: Conakry. Population: 9,030,220 (2003). Area: 245,857 sq. km/94,926 sq. mi. Official name **Republic of Guinea** —**Guinean** *adj, n*

Guinea, Gulf of arm of the Atlantic Ocean, West Africa, between Cape Palmas, at the southeastern tip of Liberia, and Cape Lopez, Gabon. The gulf forms two bays, the Bight of Benin and the Bight of Bonny (Biafra).

Guinea-Bissau

Guinea-Bissau /-bi sów/ country in West Africa, between Senegal and Guinea. It became independent from Portugal in 1974. Language: Portuguese. Currency: CFA franc. Capital: Bissau. Population: 1,360,827 (2003). Area: 36,125 sq. km/13,948 sq. mi. Official name **Republic of Guinea-Bissau**

guinea fowl /gínni fowl/ *n* a bird that is related to pheasants, is typically black with white speckles, and has a short tail and a bare head and neck. Kept for: food. Native to: Africa. Family: Numididae. [Late 18C. After the *Guinea* coast of W Africa]

guinea grass *n* a tall grass grown in Central and South America and parts of the United States. Use: animal fodder. Native to: Africa. Latin name: *Panicum maximum*. [Mid-18C. After the *Guinea* coast of W Africa]

guinea pig *n* **1.** a plump short-eared furry domesticated rodent that is similar to but larger than a hamster and is widely kept as a pet. Native to: South America. Latin name: *Cavia porcellus*. **2.** somebody or something used as the subject of an experiment, test, or trial [Mid-17C. After the *Guinea* coast of W Africa, probably from confusion with GUYANA]

guinea worm *n* a long thin worm that lives as a parasite under the skin of people and animals and can grow to more than a metre in length. Native to: Africa, Asia. Latin name: *Dracunculus medinensis*. [Late 17C. After the *Guinea* coast of W Africa]

guinep *n* **1.** *Carib* a small round fruit, with a hard green casing and slightly astringent edible yellowish pulp covering a large round seed **2.** a slow-growing tree that produces guineps. Native to: tropical America. Latin name: *Melicoccus bijugatus*.

Guinevere /gwínni veer/ *n* in Arthurian legend, the wife of King Arthur and the lover of the knight Sir Lancelot

Guinness /gínniss/, **Sir Alec** (1914–2000) British actor. He won an Academy Award for *The Bridge on the River Kwai* (1957). Among his numerous other film roles, he was identified closely with John Le Carré's fictional hero George Smiley.

Guinness, Arthur (1725–1803) Irish brewer. In the late 1700s, he developed a dark version of porter that still bears his name.

guipure /gi pyóoə/ *n* a heavy large-patterned lace that is not made on a mesh base but is joined together by threads [Mid-19C. < French *guiper* 'cover with cloth or yarn' < Germanic, 'wind round']

guiro /gweéró/ (*plural* **-ros**) *n* a musical instrument of Central and South America, made from a gourd with grooves cut so that a rasping sound is created when a stick is scraped across it [Late 19C. < Spanish, 'gourd']

guise /gíz/ *n* **1. DECEPTIVE OUTWARD APPEARANCE** a false outward appearance ○ *hiding her treacherous intentions under the guise of friendship* **2. FORM OR APPEARANCE** a shape or form, especially a changed one, in which something presents itself or is presented ○ *old ideas in a new guise* **3. COSTUME** a style of dress or personal appearance [14C. < French < Germanic]

guiser /gízər/ *n* Scotland any of a group of children who go around their neighbourhood at Halloween offering to perform something, usually a song, in return for money or food [15C. < *guise* 'dress up' < GUISE] —**guising** *n*

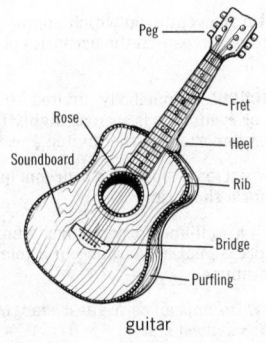
guitar

guitar /gi taár/ *n* a musical instrument with a long neck, a flat body shaped like a figure of eight, and usually six strings that are plucked or strummed

[Early 17C. Via Spanish *guitarra* < Greek *kithara* 'cithara'] —
guitarist *n*

guitarfish /gi taár fish/ (*plural* **-fishes** or *same*) *n* a ray
with large curving pectoral fins that give its body
a guitar shape. Native to: tropical and subtropical
waters. Family: Rhinobatidae.

Guitry /geé tree/, **Sacha** (1885–1957) Russian-born
French dramatist and actor. He wrote approximately 130 plays, in many of which he, his
wife, and his father played leading roles. Born
Guitry, Alexandre Georges

'The others were only my wives. But you,
my dear, will be my widow.'
[Attributed to Sacha Guitry]

Guiyang /gwáy yáng/ industrial city in southern China
and capital of Guizhou Province. Population:
1,930,000 (1995).

Guizhou /gwáy jṓ/ province in southwestern China,
dominated by a high plateau. Capital: Guiyang.
Population: 35,550,000 (1997). Area: 174,000 sq.
km/67,182 sq. mi.

Guizot /geézō/, **François Pierre Guillaume** (1787–1874)
French politician and historian. He served as minister of education (1832–37) and foreign minister
(1840–47) before becoming prime minister (1847–48).
The moderate liberal policies of his earlier years
gave way to a more conservative philosophy
towards the end of his career.

Gujarat /gōójja raát/ state in western India, bordered
in the Northwest by Pakistan and in the south and
southwest by the Arabian Sea. Language: Gujarati.
Capital: Gandhinagar. Population: 50,596,992 (2001).
Area: 196,024 sq. km/75,685 sq. mi.

Gujarati /gōójja raáti/ (*plural same*), **Gujerati** *n* **1.** an
Indic language spoken in the Indian states of
Gujarat and Maharashtra and in southern parts
of Pakistan, belonging to the Indo-Iranian branch of
Indo-European languages. Native speakers: 35
million. **2.** a member of a people living mainly in
the Indian state of Gujarat [Early 19C. < Hindi] —
Gujarati *adj*

Gujranwala /gōójran waálə/, **Gujrānwāla** city in northeastern Pakistan, in Punjab Province. Population:
1,124,799 (1998).

gul /gōōl/ *n* a large octagonal motif used in the patterns on Oriental rugs and resembling a rose with
straight-sided petals [Early 20C. < Persian, 'rose']

gulab jamun /gōō laáb yaámən/ *n* in Indian cooking,
deep-fried dough served in a sugar syrup flavoured
with rose water [< Hindi *gulāb* 'rose water' + *jāmun*
'fruit']

gulag /gōōl ag/ *n* **1.** POLITICAL PRISON IN FORMER USSR a prison
or labour camp in the former Soviet Union, to
which opponents of the government were sent **2.**
PRISON CAMP NETWORK IN FORMER USSR the network of political prisons and labour camps in the former Soviet
Union **3.** FORMER SOVIET PRISONS DEPARTMENT the department of the former Soviet security service that
was responsible for running the network of political
prisons **4.** PRISON FOR DISSENTERS any place that dissenters are sent to, or the isolating or imprisoning
of dissenters [Mid-20C. < Russian, acronym < *Glavnoe
upravlenie ispravitelno-trudovykh lagerei* 'Chief Administration for Corrective Labour Camps']

gulch /gulch/ *n N Am* a small rocky ravine, especially
one with a fast-flowing stream running through it
(*often used in placenames*) [Mid-19C. Origin ?]

gules /gyoolz/ *n* the colour red on a coat of arms [14C.
< Old French *go(u)les* 'red fur neckpiece' < plural of *go(u)le*
(see GULLET)]

gulf /gulf/ *n* **1.** INLET OF SEA a large inlet of a sea similar
to a bay but often longer and more enclosed by land
(*often used in placenames*) ○ *the Gulf of Mexico* **2.**
VAST DIFFERENCE a great difference, e.g. in points of
view, regarded as dividing or separating people or
groups **3.** WIDE HOLE a deep wide hole in the ground
[14C. Via French *golfe* < Greek *kolfos* 'bosom, bag, trough
between waves, abyss']

Gulf States *n* **1.** the countries that border the Persian
Gulf, considered as an economic or geopolitical
unit, especially in their role as oil producers. The
Gulf States are Iran, Iraq, Kuwait, Saudi Arabia,
Bahrain, Qatar, the United Arab Emirates, and
Oman. **2.** the states of the southern United States

that border the Gulf of Mexico, namely Florida,
Alabama, Mississippi, Louisiana, and Texas

Gulf Stream *n* a warm current that originates in the
Gulf of Mexico and flows northeastwards along the
coast of North America towards Newfoundland then
eastwards across the Atlantic Ocean to the coasts
of the British Isles

Gulf War *n* **1.** the war that took place in January and
February 1991 in the Persian Gulf between United
Nations forces and Iraq, following the invasion of
Kuwait by Iraq in August 1990. It resulted in the
withdrawal of Iraq from Kuwait. **2.** *also* **Gulf War II**
the war that took place in 2003 in Iraq between
the attacking forces of the United States, United
Kingdom, and Australia and troops loyal to Iraqi
president Saddam Hussein **3.** MIL, HIST same as **Iran-
Iraq War**

Gulf War syndrome *n* a group of medical symptoms,
including fatigue, skin disorders, and muscle pains,
experienced by some soldiers who fought in the
Gulf War of 1991. These conditions are believed by
some people to have been caused by exposure to
pesticides, vaccines, and chemical and biological
warfare agents.

gulfweed /gúlf weed/ *n* a brown seaweed that forms
thick floating masses. Native to: tropical Atlantic.
Genus: *Sargassum*.

gull

gull[1] /gul/ *n* a common, fairly large, web-footed white-
and-grey seabird usually with a yellow or red beak.
Native to: North American and European coasts.
Family: Laridae. [15C. < Celtic] —**gullery** *n*

gull[2] /gul/ (*archaic*) *vt* (**gulls, gulling, gulled**) to trick
or deceive somebody (*often passive*) ■ *n* somebody
regarded as easily deceived [Mid-16C. Origin ?]

Gullah /gúllə/ (*plural* **-lahs** or *same*) *n* **1.** a member of
a people of African descent who live along the
coasts of South Carolina, Georgia, and northern
Florida, and on the neighbouring Sea Islands **2.** the
creole language of the Gullah people, a form of
English that has been influenced by several West
African languages. Native speakers: 300,000. [Mid-
18C. Origin ?] —**Gullah** *adj*

gullet /gúllit/ *n* **1.** the oesophagus or throat **2.** a
groove or indentation in the protoplasm of some
protozoans that has a function in the intake of food
[14C. < Old French *goulet* 'little throat' < *go(u)le* 'throat'
< Latin *gula*]

gullible /gúlləb'l/ *adj* tending to trust and believe
people, and therefore easily tricked or deceived
[Early 19C. < GULL[2]] —**gullibility** /gúllə bílləti/ *n* —**gullibly** *adv*

gullwing /gúll wing/ *adj* describes a type of car door
that is hinged at the top and opens upwards ■ *n* an
aircraft wing in which the section attached to the
fuselage slants upwards and the outer section is
horizontal, or an aircraft with such a wing

gully /gúlli/ *n* (*plural* **-lies**) **1.** SMALL VALLEY a channel or
small valley, especially one carved out by persistent
heavy rainfall **2.** NARROW MOUNTAIN PASSAGE a narrow
passage between two rocky slopes on a mountain
3. CHANNEL MADE FOR WATER a gutter, open drain, or other
artificial channel for water, especially one at a
roadside **4.** FIELDING POSITION in cricket, a fielding
position between the last of the slips and point, or
a fielder in this position ○ *standing at gully* **5.**
CHANNEL BY BOWLING LANE the channel on either side of
a lane in ten-pin bowling **6.** *regional* NARROW PATH a
narrow path between buildings or fences ■ *vti* (**-lies,
-lying, -lied**) CUT OUT CHANNELS to wear away channels

in land or soil, or be worn into channels [Mid-17C.
< French *goulet* (see GULLET)]

gulp /gulp/ *v* (**gulps, gulping, gulped**) **1.** *vt* SWALLOW SOME-
THING FAST to swallow something greedily, hurriedly,
or frantically, taking in large amounts at a time ○
She gulped down her coffee and grabbed her coat. **2.**
vi GASP to gasp or choke **3.** *vi* MAKE SWALLOWING MOTION
to make a swallowing movement with the throat,
especially because of being frightened or nervous ○
He gulped and looked around nervously for the exit.
4. *vi* MAKE SWALLOWING SOUND to make a loud swallowing
sound with the throat, especially because of drinking too fast ■ *n* **1.** SWALLOWING MOTION OR SOUND a
swallowing movement or noise made with the
throat **2.** AMOUNT SWALLOWED a quantity of something,
especially drink, consumed in one large swallow
[15C. Probably < Middle Dutch *gulpen* 'swallow, guzzle'] —
gulper *n* —**gulpingly** *adv*

gulp back *vt* to attempt to stifle tears or sobs

gum[1] /gum/ *n* **1.** STICKY PLANT SUBSTANCE THAT HARDENS a
sticky substance found inside some plants, especially trees, that hardens when it is exposed to
air and dissolves when put in water **2.** ANY STICKY
PLANT SUBSTANCE any sticky substance found inside
plants, e.g. a resin **3.** SOMETHING STICKY any sticky
substance or deposit **4.** ADHESIVE glue made from a
sticky plant substance, or any soft synthetic glue
used for sticking paper or other lightweight materials **5.** TREE PRODUCING GUM any tree that produces
gum. Genera: *Eucalyptus* or *Liquidambar* or *Nyssa*.
6. same as **chewing gum** (*informal*) **7.** CHEWY SWEET a
chewy fruit-flavoured sweet ■ *vt* (**gums, gumming,
gummed**) STICK SOMETHING TO SOMETHING ELSE to stick something to something else, with or without gum or
glue [14C. Via Old French *gomme* < Greek *kommi*
< Egyptian *kemai*]

gum up *vt* to block or immobilize something with a
sticky substance that prevents parts from moving
○ *eyes all gummed up* ◇ **gum up the works** to bring
everything to a halt, usually by being obstructive
or incompetent (*informal*)

gum[2] /gum/ *n* the firm flesh that surrounds the roots
of the teeth (*often used in the plural*) [Old English
goma, origin ?]

GUM *abbr* genitourinary medicine

gum acacia *n* INDUST same as **gum arabic**

gum accroides /-ə króydeez/ *n* INDUST, MED same as
acaroid resin

gum ammoniac *n* INDUST same as **ammoniac**

gum arabic *n* a sticky substance taken from some
acacia trees. Use: in adhesives, confectionery, medicines. [Because the trees grow in the Middle East]

gumbo /gúmbō/ (*plural* **-bos**) *n* **1.** PLANTS same as **okra**
2. THICK STEW WITH OKRA a stew of fish, poultry, or meat
that has been thickened with okra **3.** *N Am* STICKY
SOIL silty soil that turns very sticky and muddy
when it becomes wet, found throughout the central
United States **4.** *US* MIXTURE a mixture or hotchpotch
(*informal*) ○ *The band played a gumbo of Cajun,
zydeco, and jazz music.* [Early 19C. < Louisiana French
gombo, probably < Bantu]

Gumbo *n* a French patois, incorporating aspects of
African languages, that is spoken in Louisiana and
the Caribbean —**Gumbo** *adj*

gumboil /gúm boyl/ *n* an abscess on the gum, especially near the root of a decayed tooth. Technical
name **parulis**

gum boot *n* a waterproof boot made of rubber or
plastic, especially one that comes to just below the
knee (*dated*)

gumdrop /gúm drop/ *n* a chewy fruit-flavoured sweet

gumma /gúmmə/ (*plural* **-mata** /-mətə/) *n* a rubbery
tumour that can occur in the tertiary stage of
syphilis [Early 18C. Via Modern Latin < Greek *kommi* (see
GUM[1])] —**gummatous** *adj*

gummosis /gə mṓssiss/ *n* the production of too much
gum by a tree, especially a fruit tree, as a result of
infection, a wound, or adverse weather

gummous /gúmməss/ *adj* **1.** sticky like the gum from
a tree **2.** containing gum

gummy[1] /gúmmi/ (**-mier, -miest**) *adj* **1.** like gum,
especially in being sticky or thick and slow-flowing
2. covered, clogged, or stuck together with a sticky
substance [14C. < GUM[1]] —**gumminess** *n*

gummy[2] /gúmmi/ (**-mier, -miest**) *adj* with only the gums showing, but no teeth, usually because the person concerned has no teeth [Late 19C. < GUM [2]] —**gummily** *adv*

gum nut *n Aus* the hard seed pod of a eucalyptus tree

gump /gump/ *vi* to muddle through difficult situations thanks to a series of lucky chances (*slang*) [Late 20C. < the 1994 film *Forrest Gump*]

CULTURAL NOTE ***Forrest Gump***, a film (1994) by US director Robert Zemeckis. It is the sentimental tale of a boy with mental disabilities who grows up to become a sports star, war hero, and successful business executive thanks to his uncomplicated world-view, traditional moral values, and uncanny ability to be in the right place at the right time.

gumption /gúmpsh'n/ *n* (*informal*) **1.** practical common sense and presence of mind ○ *Luckily, he had the gumption to call the police.* **2.** the courage to take what action is needed ○ *He wouldn't have the gumption to say so, even if he disagreed.* [Early 18C. Origin ?]

gum resin *n* a naturally occurring mixture of gum and resin taken from some plants and trees, e.g. the yellow pigment gamboge

gumshield /gúm sheeld/ *n* a hard plastic cover that fits inside somebody's mouth over the teeth and gums, worn as protection from injury by people involved in contact sports such as boxing and rugby. N Am term **mouth guard**

gumshoe /gúm shoo/ *n N Am* a detective, especially a private investigator (*informal*) [< moving with stealth in rubber overshoes]

gum tree *n* any tree that produces gum. Genera: *Eucalyptus* or *Liquidambar* or *Nyssa*. ◇ **up a gum tree** in a difficult or impossible situation (*informal*)

gum turpentine *n* INDUST same as **turpentine** *n* (sense 2)

gumwood /gúm wŏŏd/ *n* wood from any gum tree, especially a eucalyptus tree

gun /gun/ *n* **1.** WEAPON THAT FIRES BULLETS any weapon, from a small hand-held pistol to a large piece of artillery, that has a metal tube through which bullets or missiles are fired by an explosive charge **2.** DEVICE THAT FIRES SOMETHING any tool or instrument that forces something out under pressure ○ *a paint gun* **3.** SHOT FROM GUN a shot fired from a gun, e.g. as a military salute or a signal for a race to begin, or the sound of the shot ○ *Wait for the gun.* **4.** SOMEBODY WITH GUN somebody who is armed with a gun (*informal*) ○ *the fastest gun in the West* **5.** HUNTER a member of a party of hunters armed with shotguns **6.** *US* ACCELERATOR a vehicle's accelerator (*informal*) ○ *Give it the gun.* **7.** *Aus* SOMEBODY VERY GOOD AT SOMETHING an outstanding or expert performer in a particular activity (*informal*) ■ *vt* (**guns, gunning, gunned**) PRESS THROTTLE to rev up an engine (*informal*) ■ *adj Aus* VERY GOOD AT SOMETHING outstanding or expert in a particular activity (*informal*) ○ *She's been the gun player in the squad this year.* [14C. Probably < Scandinavian name *Gunnhildr* < *gunnr* 'battle' + *hildr* 'war', from the custom of giving women's names to weapons] ◇ **go great guns** to be working, operating, or doing something at great speed or very effectively and successfully ◇ **jump the gun 1.** to start a race before the starting gun goes off **2.** to act prematurely ◇ **stick to your guns** to refuse to change your plans or opinions even though you are under attack from other people ◇ **under the gun** *N Am* under great pressure ◇ **with (both) guns blazing** in a determined aggressive way

gun down *vt* to shoot and kill or severely injure somebody (*informal*)

gun for *vt* (*informal*) **1.** to set out to attack or criticize somebody or bring about somebody's downfall **2.** to plan or intend to get something for yourself ○ *She's gunning for a position in the Paris office.*

gunboat /gún bōt/ *n* a small fast ship with large guns mounted on it, used, e.g. by coastguards

gunboat diplomacy *n* negotiations between nations that involve threats to use military force

gun carriage *n* a platform with wheels on which a large military gun is mounted and transported or on which a coffin is laid during state funerals

gun control *n* legal measures to license, control, or restrict the ownership of firearms by members of the public

guncotton /gún kot'n/ *n* CHEM, INDUST same as **nitrocellulose**

gun court *n* a court that hears only cases that deal with gun-related crimes

gun deck *n* the deck of a sailing warship, below the main deck, where the cannons were situated

gun dog *n* **1.** a dog trained to find game and to bring back any game shot by a hunter or gamekeeper **2.** a dog of a breed that is traditionally regarded as suitable for training as a hunter's or gamekeeper's dog

gunfight /gún fīt/ *n* a fight between two or more people armed with handguns, especially in the days of the Wild West —**gunfighter** *n*

gunfire /gún fīr/ *n* shots fired from a gun or guns, or the sound of shots

gunflint /gún flint/ *n* a small piece of flint that ignites the gunpowder in an old-fashioned flintlock gun

gunge /gunj/ *n* an unpleasantly sticky, slimy, or messy semiliquid substance (*informal*) [Mid-20C. Origin ?] —**gungy** *adj*

gung ho /gúng hṓ/ *adj* (*informal*; *hyphenated when used before a noun*) **1.** eager to fight, especially in a military conflict **2.** extremely or excessively enthusiastic or eager [Mid-20C. < Chinese *honghé* 'work together' (shortening of *gongyèhézuòshè* 'Chinese Industrial Cooperative Society'), motto of US marines in Asia in World War II]

gunite /gúnn īt/ *n* a concrete building material that is sprayed from a high-pressure gun onto a mould or over reinforced concrete or steel in light construction

gunk /gungk/ *n* a greasy messy near-solid mass (*informal*) [Mid-20C. Probably invented to suggest lumpy grease] —**gunky** *adj*

gun lap *n* the last lap of an athletics race, signalled by the firing of a gun as the leading runner begins it

gun lobby *n* lobbyist groups who argue for the right of ordinary members of the public to buy and own guns. The gun lobby resists legislative attempts to put conditions on the ownership and availability of firearms and ammunition.

gunlock /gún lok/ *n* the mechanism by which the gunpowder charge was exploded in early types of gun, e.g. flintlock, matchlock, or wheel lock

gunman /gúnmən/ (*plural* **-men** /-mən/) *n* **1.** a man armed with a gun, especially a criminal or an assassin **2.** a man skilled in firing guns

gunmetal /gún met'l/ *n* **1.** GREY BRONZE FOR CANNONS a dark grey bronze. Use: formerly, to make cannons. **2.** DARK GREY METAL a dark grey alloy. Use: formerly, household and industrial items, children's toys. **3.** *also* **gunmetal grey** DARK GREY COLOUR a dark bluish-grey colour —**gunmetal** *adj* —**gunmetal-grey** *adj*

Gunn /gun/, **Mrs Aeneas** (1870–1961) Australian writer. She wrote *We of the Never Never* (1908), a bestselling account of life on a remote Australian farm. Born **Taylor, Jeannie**

Gunnar /gŏŏnaar, -ər/ *n* in Norse mythology, the husband of Brynhild, won for him by Sigurd who assumes Gunnar's form

Gunn effect *n* in a semiconductor, the microwave oscillation produced by a steady electric field that is larger than the normal threshold value [Mid-20C. After J. B. *Gunn*, (1928–), Egyptian-born British physicist]

gunnel[1] /gúnn'l/ *n* NAUT same as **gunwale**

gunnel[2] /gúnn'l/ (*plural* **-nels** or *same*) *n* a small fish that is similar to an eel. Native to: Atlantic and Pacific coastal waters. Family: Pholidae. [Late 17C. Origin ?]

Gunnell /gúnn'l/, **Sally** (*b.* 1966) British athlete. She dominated 400-metre hurdle running in the 1990s. Full name **Gunnell, Sally Janet**

gunner /gúnnər/ *n* **1.** SOLDIER WHO FIRES LARGE GUN a soldier who operates a large gun **2.** NCO WITH GUN-RELATED RESPONSIBILITIES a warrant officer in the British navy or the US Marines who is responsible for training gun operators and running the ammunition stores **3.** ARTILLERY SOLDIER a soldier in an artillery regiment, especially a private

gunnera /gúnnərə/ (*plural* **-as**) *n* a tropical plant with huge leaves. Native to: South America. Genus: *Gunnera*. [Late 18C. < modern Latin, after J. E. *Gunnerus* (1718–73), Norwegian botanist]

gunnery /gúnnəri/ *n* **1.** the knowledge and techniques involved in the effective use of guns or in their design and construction **2.** the use of guns, especially of large guns in battle

gunnery sergeant *n* a noncommissioned officer in the US Marine Corps of a rank above staff sergeant

gunny /gúnni/ (*plural* **-nies**) *n* **1.** coarse jute or hemp cloth **2.** a sack made from coarse jute or hemp cloth. N Am term **gunnysack** [Early 18C. < Hindi *gonī*]

gunplay /gún play/ *n* the shooting of guns, especially by armed criminals

gunpoint /gún poynt/ *n* the muzzle of a firearm ◇ **at gunpoint** under the threat of being shot and killed if orders are not obeyed

gunpowder /gún powdər/ *n* an explosive mixture of potassium nitrate, charcoal, and sulphur. Use: in fireworks and other explosives, e.g. in quarry blasting, and, formerly, as the charge in firearms.

Gunpowder Plot *n* a conspiracy by a group of Roman Catholics, including Guy Fawkes, to blow up Parliament in 1605

gunpowder tea *n* Chinese green tea with individual leaves rolled into small pellets

gunroom /gún room, -rŏŏm/ *n* **1.** a room in a house where guns are kept, especially shotguns **2.** the quarters of midshipmen and junior officers on a ship in the British navy

gunrunning /gún runing/ *n* the smuggling of illegal arms into a country, usually in order to supply terrorist or insurrectionist organizations —**gunrunner** *n*

gunship /gún ship/ *n* helicopter that is fitted with guns for use against ground targets

gunshot /gún shot/ *n* **1.** GUN'S NOISE the sound of a gun being fired **2.** BULLETS FIRED bullets or shot fired from a gun **3.** GUN'S RANGE the maximum distance that a bullet fired from a gun can travel

gun-shy *adj* **1.** extremely cautious, timid, or wary of taking risks **2.** afraid of guns or the noise they make when fired

gunsight /gún sīt/ *n* a device on a gun, often a projection on the barrel or a small telescope attached to the gun, used to assist somebody in aiming it

gunslinger /gún slingər/ *n* an armed fighter or criminal, especially in the frontier days of the Wild West (*informal*) —**gunslinging** *n*

gunsmith /gún smith/ *n* a maker, seller, or repairer of firearms

gunstock /gún stok/ *n* the shaped wooden or metal handle of a rifle that is pressed against the shoulder when the rifle is being fired

Gunther /gŏŏntər/ *n* in medieval Germanic mythology, the king of Burgundy and husband of Brunhild

Guntur /gŏŏn tŏŏr/ city in the River Krishna delta, in Andhra Pradesh State, southeastern India. Population: 471,051 (1991).

gunwale /gúnn'l/, **gunnel** *n* the top edge of a boat's sides that forms a ledge round the whole boat above the deck (*often used in the plural*) [15C. Because used in the past to support guns]

Gunwinggu /gun wing goo/, **Gunwinygu** *n* LANG same as **Kunwinjku**

gunwoman /gún wŏŏmən/ (*plural* **-women** /-wimin/) *n* a woman armed with a gun

Guo Xi /gwṓ shée/ (*fl* 1060–75) Chinese artist. He is noted for his large landscape murals and scrolls.

guppy /gúppi/ (*plural* **-pies**) *n* a small freshwater fish that has a brightly coloured tail, produces live young rather than eggs, and is popular in aquariums. Native to: Caribbean, South America. Latin name: *Poecilia reticulata*. [Early 20C. After the Reverend R. J. Lechmere *Guppy* (1836–1916), who sent the first specimen from Trinidad to the British Museum]

Gupta /gŏŏptə/ *n* an Indian dynasty of the 3rd to 6th centuries that established an empire in much of South Asia. Their rule, during which the arts, architecture, and literature flourished, is generally regarded as the Golden Age of India. [Late 19C. After *Chandragupta*, the dynasty's founder]

gur /gur/ *n S Asia* FOOD same as **jaggery** [< Hindi]

Gur /gŏŏ ər/ *n* a group of Niger-Congo languages spoken in western Central Africa. Native speakers: 10 million. —**Gur** *adj*

gurdwara /gúrd wäarə/ *n* a Sikh temple or other place of worship where Sikh scriptures are kept [Early 20C. < Punjabi *gurduārā*]

gurgle /gúrg'l/ (-**gles**, -**gling**, -**gled**) *v* 1. *vi* to make the deep bubbling noise that liquid makes when it is poured from a bottle 2. *vti* to make a bubbling sound in the throat, or say something with a bubbling sound in the throat [Mid-16C. < assumed Vulgar Latin *gurguliare* < Latin *gurgulio* 'gullet'] —**gurgle** *n* —**gurglingly** *adv*

Gurindji /gŏŏrinji/ (*plural same* or -**djis**) *n* 1. an Aboriginal people living in northern parts of Central Australia 2. the Aboriginal language of the Gurindji. Native speakers: 250. —**Gurindji** *adj*

Gurkha /gúrkə/ (*plural same* or -**khas**) *n* 1. a member of a Hindu people living mainly in Nepal, with small communities in Bhutan 2. a Gurkha serving in the British or Indian army [Early 19C. < Nepalese *Gurkha*, placename] —**Gurkha** *adj*

Gurkhali /gur kả·ali/ *n* the form of Nepali that is the lingua franca of Gurkha soldiers, especially those in the British army [Late 19C. < Nepalese *Gurkha*, placename] —**Gurkhali** *adj*

Gurmukhi /gŏŏr mŏŏki/ *n* the script in which Punjabi is written [Late 19C. < Punjabi]

gurnard /gúrnərd/ (*plural* -**nards** or *same*) *n* 1. a spiny-finned sea fish with an armoured head and sets of pectoral fins modified for crawling on the sea bottom, some species of which are used for food. Native to: Mediterranean, warmer waters of Atlantic, and some species in Pacific. Family: Triglidae. 2. FISH same as **flying gurnard** [14C. < Old French *gornart* < Latin *grunnire* 'grunt'; from the sound it makes when caught]

gurney /gúrni/ (*plural* -**neys**) *n* N Am HEALTH SERVICES same as **trolley** *n* (sense 2) [Late 19C. Origin ?]

guru /gŏŏ roo/ (*plural* -**rus**) *n* 1. HINDU OR SIKH RELIGIOUS TEACHER in Hinduism and Sikhism, a religious leader or teacher 2. LEADER OF RELIGIOUS GROUP a spiritual leader or intellectual guide for a religious group or movement, especially one considered not to be mainstream 3. INFLUENTIAL EXPERT somebody who has a reputation as an expert leader, teacher, or practitioner in a particular field ○ *a meeting of the world's software gurus* ○ *a style guru* 4. REVERED TEACHER AND COUNSELLOR a person's revered guide, mentor, or adviser in spiritual or intellectual matters [Early 17C. < Sanskrit, 'elder, teacher']

Guru Nanak /gŏŏ roo nả·anək/ ▸ **Nanak**

Guru Nanak Jananti /-jə nánti/ *n* a Sikh festival marking the birthday of Guru Nanak. Date: November.

gush /gush/ *vti* (**gushes**, **gushing**, **gushed**) 1. FLOW OUT FAST to flow out rapidly and in large quantities, or release large quantities of a liquid in a fast-flowing stream 2. SPEAK OR SAY SOMETHING EFFUSIVELY to express yourself, or say something, in an excessively enthusiastic, affectionate, or sentimental way ○ '*Your children are simply delightful!' she gushed.* ■ *n* 1. FLOW OF LIQUID a fast or copious flow of liquid from somewhere 2. EFFUSIVE OUTBURST an outburst of over-enthusiastic or overemotional speech or self-expression [14C. Probably an imitation of the sound of liquid gushing] —**gushing** *adj* —**gushingly** *adv*

gusher /gúshər/ *n* 1. an oil well from which oil flows freely and in large amounts, without having to be pumped 2. somebody who speaks or behaves in an exaggeratedly emotional or enthusiastic way

gushy /gúshi/ (-**ier**, -**iest**) *adj* characterized by overenthusiastic or overemotional speech or self-expression —**gushily** *adv* —**gushiness** *n*

Gusmão /gŏŏss maả ō, gŏŏss mów/, **Xanana** (*b.* 1946) president of Timor-Leste. A guerrilla leader in the fight for independence in Timor-Leste, he became its first president in 2002. Full name **Gusmão, José Alexandre Xanana**

gusset /gússit/ *n* 1. INSET PIECE OF FABRIC a piece of fabric inserted in a garment where added strength or freedom of movement is needed 2. FLAT PLATE REINFORCING JOINT a flat, often triangular plate, usually of steel or plywood, used to connect and reinforce a joint where several members meet at different

---

angles, e.g. in a pitched roof 3. CHAIN MAIL AT ARMOUR JOINT a section of chain mail protecting the unarmoured joints of a suit of armour [14C. < French *gousset* 'little pod' < *gousse* 'pod, shell']

gussy /gússi/ (-**sies**, -**sying**, -**sied**)
gussy up *vt* N Am to dress somebody in fancy clothes, or decorate something elaborately (*informal*; *often passive*) ○ *all gussied up in a frilly dress* ○ *The city was gussied up for the governor's visit.* [Mid-20C. Origin ?]

gust /gust/ *n* 1. BURST OF WIND a sudden powerful rush of wind 2. BURST OF EMOTION a sudden powerful experience or expression of an emotion ■ *vi* (**gusts**, **gusting**, **gusted**) BLOW IN BURSTS to blow, or be blown by the wind, in sudden powerful bursts [Late 16C. < Old Norse *gustr* < *gjósa* 'to gush']

gustation /gu stáysh'n/ *n* the action of tasting, or the sense of taste (*formal*) [Late 16C. Directly or via French < Latin *gustation-* < *gustare* 'to taste']

gustatory /gústətəri/, **gustatorial** /gústə táwri əl/ *adj* relating to the sense of taste or to the action or experience of tasting something (*formal*) [Late 17C. < Latin *gustare* 'to taste'] —**gustatorily** *adv*

Gustav V /gŏŏst aav/ (1858–1950) king of Sweden. His reign (1907–50) was characterized by progressive social reforms introduced by the ruling Social Democrat party and Sweden's neutrality in both World Wars.

Gustav II Adolph /gŏŏst aav áddolf/ (1594–1632) king of Sweden. Regarded as the founding father of modern Sweden for the domestic reforms instituted during his reign (1611–32), he also led the Protestant forces during the early part of Thirty Years' War (1618–48). Known as **the Lion of the North**

Gustav I Vasa /vaázə/ (1496–1560) king of Sweden. The founder of the Swedish royal house of Vasa, in the course of his reign (1523–60) he proclaimed Lutheranism as the state religion (1529) and achieved independence for Sweden from the Hanseatic League (1537).

Gustavo A. Madero /gŏŏ staávō aa mə dáirō/ city in south-central Mexico, near Mexico City. The Treaty of Guadalupe Hidalgo ending the Mexican War was signed there in 1848. Population: 1,309,211 (2000). Former name **Guadalupe Hidalgo** (until 1931)

Gustavus IV /gŏŏ staávəs/ (1778–1837) king of Sweden. His fierce opposition to Napoleon I and the French Republic during his reign (1792–1809) led to a loss of territory to France (1807) and Russia (1808) and to his abdication the following year.

Gustav VI Adolph /gŏŏst aav áddolf/ (1882–1973) king of Sweden. Known during his reign (1950–73) for his patronage of the arts, he had a reputation as a classical archaeologist and an authority on Chinese art.

gusto /gústō/ *n* lively enthusiasm or enjoyment [Early 17C Via Italian < Latin *gustus* 'taste']

gusty /gústi/ (-**ier**, -**iest**) *adj* 1. blowing in gusts, blown on gusts of wind, or characterized by recurring gusts ○ *a gusty day* 2. similar to a gust of wind, either in sound, or in occurring or being experienced in sudden powerful bursts ○ *gusty waves of emotion* —**gustily** *adv* —**gustiness** *n*

gut /gut/ *n* 1. ALIMENTARY CANAL the whole of the alimentary canal in people and animals, from the mouth to the anus, or the lower part of it (**intestine**), from the stomach to the anus 2. ABDOMEN somebody's belly, especially if it is noticeably large (*slang disapproving*) ○ *I've got to work off this gut.* 3. PLACE WHERE INSTINCTS ARE FELT the supposed location in the body of a person's deepest instinctively felt responses, as distinct from his or her rational or logical responses, or those instinctive responses themselves (*often used before a noun*) ○ *Let's just say, I feel in my gut something's wrong.* 4. INDUST same as **catgut** 5. FISHING CORD cord made of fibrous material taken from silkworms. Use: fishing lines. ■ *vt* (**guts**, **gutting**, **gutted**) 1. REMOVE ANIMAL'S INSIDES to remove the insides of a dead animal 2. DESTROY BUILDING'S INTERIOR to destroy the internal parts of a building, leaving only the outer walls standing ○ *The factory was completely gutted in the fire.* 3. REMOVE FIXTURES FROM ROOM OR BUILDING to remove all the internal fixtures and furnishings from a room or building 4. TAKE EXTRACTS FROM A TEXT to select extracts from a piece of writing for use elsewhere [Old English

---

guttas < Indo-European, 'pour'] ◇ **bust a gut** to struggle or work exceptionally hard to get something done (*slang*)

SYNONYMS See *courage*.

GUT /gut/ *abbr* PHYS Grand Unified Theory

gutbucket /gút bukit/ *n* 1. a home-made instrument played like a double bass, made by fixing a stick to an upturned basin and stretching a string along its length 2. a simple but highly emotional style of jazz or blues

gut course *n* US a college or university unit that is very easy to pass (*informal*)

Johannes Gutenberg: 15th-century engraving showing Gutenberg (left foreground) printing the Gutenberg Bible (1456?)

Gutenberg /gŏŏt'n burg/, **Johannes** (1400?–68) German printer. He is credited with the invention of moveable type, which he used in his Mainz printing press to print the 42-line Bible, known as the Gutenberg Bible. Full name **Gutenberg, Johannes Gensfleisch**

Guthrie /gúthri/, **Sir Tyrone** (1900–71) British stage director. He was closely identified with the Old Vic-Sadler's Wells Company in the 1940s and 1950s, and founded the Tyrone Guthrie Theatre in Minneapolis, Minnesota, in 1963. Full name **Guthrie, Sir William Tyrone**

Guthrie, **Woody** (1912–67) US folk singer and composer. Many of his hundreds of songs protested at the social injustice of the American Depression. He wrote 'This Land Is Your Land' (1940). Full name **Guthrie, Woodrow Wilson**

> 'You can't write a good song about a whorehouse unless you been in one.'
> [Woody Guthrie, recalled on his death; 4 October 1967]

gut job *n* N Am the restoration or repair of a building that includes the removal and rebuilding of the interior (*informal*)

gutless /gútləss/ *adj* seriously lacking in resolve and determination (*informal*) —**gutlessness** *n*

SYNONYMS See *cowardly*.

gut reaction *n* an immediate and instinctive reaction, rather than a well-thought-out response ○ *The boss's gut reaction is to be suspicious.*

gut rehabilitation, **gut renovation** *n* US CONSTR same as **gut job** (*informal*)

guts /guts/ *npl* (*takes a plural verb*) 1. INTESTINES the insides of a person or animal, especially the intestines 2. INNER OR CENTRAL PARTS the inner or central parts of something, e.g. the working parts of a machine or the basic principles that a theory is based on 3. COURAGE strength of character and boldness (*slang*) ■ *n* GLUTTON a very greedy person (*informal*; *takes a singular verb*) ◇ **hate somebody's guts** to dislike somebody very much (*informal*) ◇ **spill your guts** US to tell or confess everything (*informal*) ◇ **sweat your guts out** to work very hard (*informal*)

gutser /gútsər/ *n* ANZ an unfortunate event (*informal*) ◇ **come a gutser** ANZ (*informal*) 1. to have a fall 2. to fail or experience a misfortune

gutsy /gútsi/ (-**ier**, -**iest**) *adj* (*informal*) 1. COURAGEOUS showing courage, boldness, and determination 2. DONE WITH EMOTION done or performed with a great deal of vigour, passion, or emotion 3. GREEDY greedy or gluttonous —**gutsily** *adv* —**gutsiness** *n*

---

gutta /gúttə/ (*plural* **-tae** /-tee/) *n* **1.** one of a series of ornaments shaped like drops that are attached to the underside of a Doric entablature **2.** a drop of medicine (*dated; formerly, on prescriptions*) [14C. < Latin, 'drop']

gutta-percha /gúttə púrchə/ *n* **1.** a pliable substance made from a natural latex. Use: dental fillings, dressings, electrical insulation. **2.** a tree whose latex is a source of gutta-percha. Native to: Southeast Asia. Genera: *Palaquium* or *Payena*. [Mid-19C. Alteration (influenced by Latin *gutta* 'drop') of Malay *getah perca* 'gum strips of cloth']

guttate /gútt ayt/, **guttated** /-aytid/ *adj* having or resembling drops or spots [Early 19C. < Latin *guttatus* < *gutta* 'drop']

guttation /gu táysh'n/ *n* the oozing out of water droplets from the uninjured surface of a plant leaf

gutted /gúttid/ *adj* **1.** with the insides taken out, ready to be sold ○ *gutted haddock* **2.** desperately disappointed or upset (*informal*) ○ *They were absolutely gutted when they lost the match.*

gutter /gúttər/ *n* **1.** RAINWATER CHANNEL ON ROAD a channel at the edge of a road that carries water into a drain **2.** RAINWATER CHANNEL ON ROOF a metal or plastic channel fixed to the eaves of a roof for carrying away rainwater **3.** POOR OR DEGRADED STATE an impoverished and degraded existence or way of life ○ *She dragged me out of the gutter and made me respect myself.* **4.** BOWLING CHANNEL ON TEN-PIN BOWLING LANE the channel on either side of a ten-pin bowling lane **5.** PRINTING INNER MARGINS OF BOOK the blank space formed by the inner margins of two facing pages of a book **6.** STAMPS SPACE BETWEEN STAMPS ON SHEET the space between the printed design of one stamp and the next one on the sheet, where the perforations lie ■ *v* (**-ters, -tering, -tered**) **1.** *vi* MELT QUICKLY to burn down more quickly than usual because melting wax has formed a channel on one side (*refers to candles*) **2.** *vi* FLICKER to flicker when on the point of being extinguished **3.** *vt* FORM CHANNELS IN SOMETHING to wear away channels in the surface of something **4.** *vi* TRICKLE to run in a narrow stream or trickle ○ *The overflow was guttering down the wall.* ■ *adj* OF WORST KIND of the most vulgar, corrupt, or morally degraded kind (*disapproving*) [13C. < Anglo-Norman *gotere* < Latin *gutta* 'drop']

gutter out *vi* **1.** to go out after flickering for a while ○ *Most of the candles guttered out.* **2.** to come to an end finally, after gradually declining ○ *The peace process had all but guttered out.*

~~**gutteral**~~ incorrect spelling of **guttural**

gutter ball *n* in ten-pin bowling, a ball that, when bowled, rolls into the gutter and does not knock over any pins

guttering /gúttəring/ *n* **1.** the gutters on a roof **2.** metal or plastic channels for use as gutters

gutter press *n* low-quality newspapers and magazines that deal mostly with scandal and gossip rather than serious news

guttersnipe /gúttər snīp/ *n* **1.** somebody regarded as having a rough or vulgar manner, especially somebody with a lower-class background (*insult*) **2.** a child who wears dirty ragged clothes, has rough manners, and lives in the streets (*dated insult*) [Mid-19C. Via 'street cleaner' < 'common snipe' (a bird that likes wet muddy conditions)] —**guttersnipish** *adj*

guttural /gúttərəl/ *adj* **1.** characterized by harsh and grating speech sounds made in the throat or towards the back of the mouth **2.** PHON same as **velar** *adj* (sense 1) ■ *n* a speech sound produced in the throat or at the back of the mouth [Late 16C. Directly or via French < medieval Latin *gutturalis* < Latin *guttur* 'throat'] —**gutturalism** *n* —**gutturality** /gúttə rálləti/ *n* —**gutturally** *adv* —**gutturalness** *n*

gutturalize /gúttərə līz/ (**-izes, -izing, -ized**), **gutturalise** (**-ises, -ising, -ised**) *v* **1.** *vt* to pronounce a speech sound in the throat or towards the back of the mouth **2.** *vti* to speak or say something in a harsh rasping way —**gutturalization** /gúttərə lī záysh'n/ *n*

gutty /gútti/ (*plural* **-ties**) *n Scotland* same as **plimsoll** (*informal; usually used in the plural*) [Late 19C. < GUTTA-PERCHA]

gut-wrenching *adj* having a very powerful effect on the feelings, especially in stirring up pity or sympathy (*informal*)

guv /guv/ *n* (*informal*) **1.** used as a familiar term of address by one man to another, especially to one in a superior position **2.** used by men and women as a term of address for their boss [Mid-19C. Shortening of GUVNOR]

guvnor /gúvnər/ *n* **1.** same as **guv** (*informal*) **2.** used by upper-class young men to refer to or address their father (*dated informal*) ○ *The guvnor won't increase my allowance.* [Mid-19C. Representing a pronunciation of GOVERNOR]

guy[1] /gī/ *n* **1.** same as **man** *n* (sense 1) (*informal*) **2.** MODEL BURNT ON BONFIRE a homemade model of a man, like a scarecrow, originally intended as an effigy of Guy Fawkes, usually made by children and burnt on a fire on 5 November in Britain ○ *'Penny for the guy!'* **3.** *regional* same as **scarecrow** (*informal*) ■ **guys** *npl* USED TO ADDRESS PEOPLE used to address a group of people of either sex (*informal*) ○ *Hey, guys, where are you off to?* ■ *vt* (**guys, guying, guyed**) POKE FUN AT SOMEBODY to make fun of somebody or something, especially by a comical imitation [Early 19C. < *Guy Fawkes* (see GUY FAWKES NIGHT)]

REGIONAL NOTE See *man.*

CULTURAL NOTE ***Guys and Dolls***, a musical (1950) by US composer and lyricist Frank Loesser. It transforms a story by Damon Runyon into a classic American musical comedy. Nathan Detroit, a gambler in New York City, bets that gangster Sky Masterson can't persuade the next woman he sees to go to Havana with him. The woman in question turns out to be a prim reformer who runs a mission to save sinners. In the meantime, Detroit's own long-suffering fiancée is demanding a wedding. These small-time gangsters roister their way to an improbably happy ending. Frank Sinatra and Marlon Brando starred in a 1955 film version.

guy[2] /gī/ *n* same as **guyrope** ■ *vt* (**guys, guying, guyed**) to support or anchor something using ropes, cables, or chains [14C. Probably < Low German]

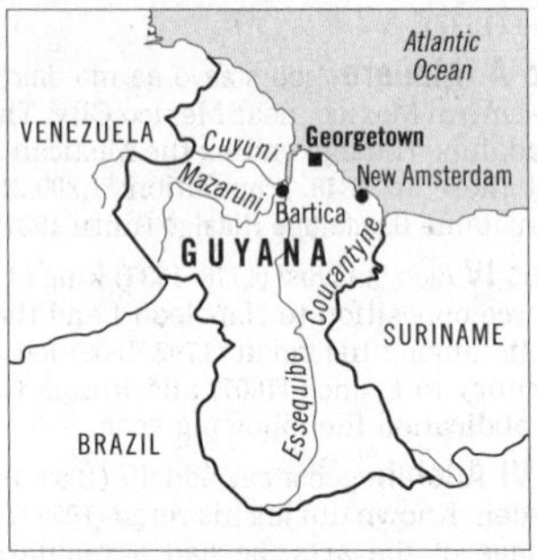

Guyana

Guyana /gī áanə/ country on the North Atlantic coast of South America bordered by Venezuela, Brazil, and Suriname. It became an independent member of the Commonwealth in 1966. Venezuela claims Guyana's territory west of the Essequibo river. Language: English. Currency: Guyana dollar. Capital: Georgetown. Population: 702,100 (2003). Area: 214,969 sq. km/83,000 sq. mi. Official name **Cooperative Republic of Guyana** —**Guyanese** /gī ə néez/ *adj, n*

Guy Fawkes Night /gī fáwks-/ *n* CALENDAR same as **Bonfire Night** [After *Guy Fawkes* (1570–1606), conspirator in the Gunpowder Plot]

guyline /gī līn/ *n* same as **guyrope**

guyot /gee ṓ/ *n* a flat-topped underwater mountain of a type commonly found in the Pacific Ocean and considered to be an extinct volcano [Mid-20C. After Arnold Henri *Guyot*, (1807–84), Swiss-born US geologist and geographer]

guyrope /gī rōp/ *n* a rope, wire, or chain tightened to hold something in position, e.g. any of the ropes pulled tight to keep a tent up

guywire /gī wīr/ *n US* same as **guyrope**

Guzmán Blanco /gŏŏss mán blánkō/, **Antonio** (1829–99) president of Venezuela (1870–77, 1879–84, 1886–88). During his presidency, he promoted public education and foreign investment.

guzzle /gúzz'l/ (**-zles, -zling, -zled**) *vti* to eat or drink something rapidly and in large quantities (*informal*) [Late 16C. Origin ?] —**guzzler** *n*

GVW *abbr* gross vehicle weight

gw *abbr* ONLINE Guinea-Bissau (*used in Internet addresses*) See table at **domain name**

GW *symbol* MEASURE gigawatt

GW 2 *abbr* MIL Gulf War II, fought in the spring of 2003 against Iraq [Early 21C.]

Gwadar /gwə daár/ port in southwestern Pakistan. Population: 17,000 (1981)

Gwalior /gwaáli awr/ city near Agra in Madhya Pradesh State, central India. Population: 690,765 (1991).

gweilo /gwī lṓ/ *n Hong Kong* a foreigner from the West (*informal*) [< Japanese]

Gwelo /gwéelō/ former name for **Gweru** (until 1982)

Gwent /gwent/ former county in southeastern Wales, approximately equivalent to present-day Monmouthshire

Gweru /gwáy roo/ city on the River Gweru in central Zimbabwe. It is a commercial, manufacturing, and transportation centre. Population: 128,027 (1992). Former name **Gwelo** (until 1982)

Gwyn /gwin/, **Gwynn, Nell** (1650–87) English actor. A leading performer in Restoration comedies, she became the mistress of Charles II and bore him two sons. Full name **Gwyn, Eleanor**

Gwynedd /gwínnəth/ mountainous county in northwestern Wales, dominated by Snowdonia National Park. Area: 3,867 sq. km/1,494 sq. mi. Population: 116,843 (2001).

gwyniad /gwínni ad/ (*plural* **-ads** or *same*) *n* a freshwater white fish. Native to: mainly Lake Bala, Wales. [Early 17C. < Welsh < *gwyn* 'white']

gy *abbr* ONLINE Guyana (*used in Internet addresses*) See table at **domain name**

Gy *symbol* PHYS gray[2]

Gyanendra /gya néndrə/ (*b.* 1947) king of Nepal (2001–). He was crowned king after his older brother, King Birendra, and several other members of the royal family were killed in a palace massacre. Full name **Gyanendra Bir Bikram Shah Dev**

Gyani /gyaáni/ *n S Asia* a title of respect for a Sikh scholar [< Hindi < Sanskrit *gyan* 'knowledge']

gybe /jīb/, **jibe** *vti* (**gybes, gybing, gybed; jibes, jibing, jibed**) **1.** SWING ACROSS BOAT to swing, or make a fore-and-aft sail swing, across from one side of the boat to the other when sailing before the wind **2.** CHANGE DIRECTION IN SAILING SHIP to change direction by turning away from the wind, as a result of a fore-and-aft-sail gybing, or cause a sailing ship to change direction in this way ■ *n* ACTION OF GYBING a sudden shift of a sail back and forth, or a sail's change in direction [Late 17C. < obsolete Dutch *gben*]

gym /jim/ *n* **1.** same as **gymnasium** (*informal*) **2.** physical education, especially as a school subject (*informal*) **3.** a sturdy metal or hard plastic frame designed for children's outdoor play and exercise (*often used in combination*) [Late 19C. Shortening]

gymkhana /jim kaánə/ *n* **1.** HORSE-RIDING EVENT a community-based outdoor event with various activities relating to horse-riding **2.** *US* SPORTING CONTEST a sporting event or contest **3.** SPORTS VENUE a place where a gymkhana or similar sporting event is held (*dated*) [Mid-19C. Alteration (influenced by words such as GYMNAST) of Urdu *gendkānah* 'ball house']

gymnasium /jim náyzi əm/ (*plural* **-siums** or **-sia** /-zi ə/) *n* a hall equipped for physical exercise or physical training of various kinds, e.g. in a school or a private club [Late 16C. Via Latin, 'school' < Greek *gumnasion* < *gumnazein* 'exercise naked, train' < *gumnos* 'naked']

gymnast /jím nast/ *n* an athlete who performs gymnastics, especially as a competitive sport [Late 16C. Directly or via French < Greek *gumnastēs* 'trainer of athletes' < *gumnazein* (see GYMNASIUM)]

gymnastic /jim nástik/ *adj* **1.** relating to or involving gymnastics ○ *gymnastic equipment* **2.** involving or demonstrating athleticism and agility ○ *a gymnastic dancing style* [Late 16C. Via Latin < Greek *gumnastikos* < *gumnazein* (see GYMNASIUM)] —**gymnastically** *adv*

gymnastics /jim nástiks/ *n* (*takes a singular verb*) **1.** PHYSICAL TRAINING USING GYMNASTIC EQUIPMENT physical training using equipment such as bars, rings, and vaulting horses, designed to develop agility and

muscular strength **2.** COMPETITIVE SPORT USING GYMNASTIC EQUIPMENT the competitive sport in which athletes perform a series of exercises on pieces of gymnastic equipment ■ npl (*takes a plural verb*) **1.** PHYSICAL EXERCISES movements, exercises, or activities that involve feats of physical strength and agility **2.** ACTIONS DEMONSTRATING AGILITY AND SKILL the performance of a series of complex mental or physical operations of a particular kind, usually rapidly and with great agility and skill ○ *verbal gymnastics*

gymnosperm /jímnə spurm/ *n* a woody vascular plant in which the ovules are carried naked on the scales of a cone, e.g. a conifer, cycad, or ginkgo [Mid-19C. Via modern Latin < Greek *gumnospermos* 'naked seed'] —**gymnospermous** /jímnə spúrməss/ *adj* —**gymnospermy** *n*

Gympie /gímpi/ town in southeastern Queensland, Australia, noted as an agricultural centre. Population: 10,784 (1991).

gym rat *n* somebody who spends a lot of time exercising or playing a sport at a gymnasium (*informal*)

gym shoe *n* same as **plimsoll**

gymslip /jím slip/ *n* a schoolgirl's sleeveless dress worn over a blouse as part of a school uniform

gyn- *prefix* same as **gyno-** (*used before vowels*)

gynae /gíni/ (*informal*) *adj* GYNAECOLOGICAL relating to gynaecology ■ *n* **1.** GYNAECOLOGIST a specialist in gynaecology **2.** GYNAECOLOGY gynaecology, or the gynaecology department of a hospital [Mid-20C. Shortening]

gynaec- *prefix* same as **gynaeco-** (*used before vowels*) [< Greek *gunaik-*, stem of *gunē* 'woman']

gynaeco- *prefix* woman ○ *gynaecology*

gynaecocracy /jínni kókrəssi, gíni-/ (*plural* **-cies**) *n* political dominance by women, or a political system that gives supreme power to women

gynaecoid /jínni koyd, gíni-/ *adj* physically resembling a woman, or physiologically typical of a woman ○ *a gynaecoid pelvis*

gynaecol. *abbr* MED **1.** gynaecological **2.** gynaecologist **3.** gynaecology

gynaecology /gíni kólləji/ *n* the branch of medicine that deals with women's health, especially with the health of women's reproductive organs —**gynaecological** /gínikə lójjik'l/ *adj* —**gynaecologist** *n*

gynaecomastia /jínni kō másti ə, gíni-/ *n* enlarged breasts on a man caused by hormonal imbalance or hormone therapy [Mid-19C. < GYNAECO- + Greek *mastos* 'breast']

gynaecopathy /jínni kóppəthi, gíni-/ (*plural* **-thies**) *n* a disease that affects only women

gynaephobia /jínnə fóbi ə, gínə-/ *n* an irrational and pathological fear of women

gynandromorph /ji nándrə mawrf/ *n* an organism, especially an insect, that has both male and female characteristics in a way that is atypical for its species [Late 19C. < GYNANDROUS] —**gynandromorphic** /ji nándrə máwrfik/ *adj* —**gynandromorphism** /-máwrfiz'm/ *n* —**gynandromorphous** /-máwrfəss/ *adj* —**gynandromorphy** *n*

gynandrous /ji nándrəss/ *adj* describes flowers such as orchids that have pistils and stamens united in a column [Early 19C. < Greek *gunandros* 'of doubtful sex' < *gunē* 'woman' + *andr-* 'man']

gynarchy /jí naarki, gí-/ (*plural* **-chies**) *n* POL same as **gynaecocracy** —**gynarchic** /jí naárkik, gí-/ *adj*

-gyne *suffix* **1.** female ○ *androgyne* **2.** female reproductive organ ○ *trichogyne* [< Greek *gunē* 'woman'] —**gynous** *suffix* —**gyny** *suffix*

gynec-, etc. US spelling of **gynaec-, etc.**

gyno- *prefix* **1.** female reproductive organ ○ *gynophore* **2.** woman ○ *gynocracy* [< Greek *gunē* 'woman']

gynocracy /jí nókrəssi, gí-/ (*plural* **-cies**) *n* POL same as **gynaecocracy**

gynodioecious /jínnō dī éeshəss, gínō-/ *adj* describes a plant species that has bisexual flowers on some plants and single-sex flowers on others —**gynodioecism** /-éessizəm/ *n*

gynoecium /jī néessi əm, gī-/ (*plural* **-cia** /-si ə/) *n* the carpels of a plant considered together [Mid-19C. Alteration (influenced by Greek *oikos* 'house') of modern Latin *gynaeceum* 'women's apartments' < Greek *gunaikeios* 'of women' < *gunē* 'woman']

gynogenesis /jīnə jénnəssiss, gīnə-/ *n* the development of an embryo without fusion of the egg and sperm nuclei, so that the embryo has only maternal chromosomes

gynophore /jīnə fawr, gīnə-/ *n* a pistil stalk that has its gynoecium raised above the rest of the flower —**gynophoric** /jīnə fórrik, gīnə-/ *adj*

Gyor /dyur, dyör/ port in northwestern Hungary, situated on the River Danube between Budapest and Vienna. Population: 127,275 (1999).

gyp¹ /jip/, **gip** (*sometimes considered offensive*) *vt* (**gyps, gypping, gypped; gips, gipping, gipped**) CHEAT SOMEBODY to cheat somebody, especially by overcharging (*informal*) ■ *n* **1.** CHEATER a cheater or swindler (*insult*) **2.** SCAM a scheme to trick or swindle people (*informal*) [Late 19C. Origin ? Sometimes taken to be a shortening of GYPSY and so offensive] —**gypper** *n*

gyp² /jip/, **gip** *n* pain, especially sharp or severe pain (*informal*) ○ *His arthritis was giving him gyp.* [Late 19C. Contraction of GEE UP]

gyppo /jíppō/ (*plural* **-pos**), **gippo** *n* **1.** an offensive term for a member of the Roma people (*slang*) **2.** an offensive term for an Egyptian, formerly used especially by British troops stationed in North Africa (*dated slang*) [Early 20C. Alteration of GYPSY and EGYPTIAN]

gyppy tummy /jíppi-/, **gippy tummy** *n* a stomach upset with a bout of diarrhoea, especially one happening to a Western visitor in a hot Eastern country (*informal; sometimes considered offensive*) [< alteration of EGYPTIAN, because it was common in the Middle East]

gypsiferous /jip sífferəss/ *adj* containing gypsum

gypsophila /jip sóffilə/ *n* a plant of the carnation family popular in bouquets. Flowers: tiny, white or pink, on long branching stalks. Native to: Mediterranean. Genus: *Gypsophila*. [Late 18C. < modern Latin, 'chalk-loving' < Greek *gupsos* 'chalk', because it grows in chalky soil]

gypsum /jípsəm/ *n* **1.** a white or colourless mineral consisting of hydrated calcium sulphate. Use: cement, plaster, fertilizers. **2.** CONSTR same as **plasterboard** (*informal*) [14C. Via Latin < Greek *gupsos* 'chalk, gypsum']

gypsy /jípsi/ (*plural* **-sies**), **gipsy** *n* somebody who has a nomadic or unconventional lifestyle (*informal*) [< GYPSY]

Gypsy /jípsi/ (*plural* **-sies**), **Gipsy** *n* an offensive term for a member of the Roma people [Mid-16C. Shortening of EGYPTIAN; because the Roma people were once thought to have come from Egypt] —**Gypsy** *adj*

gypsy moth

gypsy moth *n* a tussock moth with a spotted hairy caterpillar. Native to: Europe, but common in North America since the 19th century. Latin name: *Lymantria dispar*.

gypsy top *n* UK a women's top with an elasticated low neckline, usually worn off the shoulder, and long or short sleeves. ANZ, N Am term **peasant blouse**

gyral /jírəl/ *adj* moving in a path that is spiral or circular —**gyrally** *adv*

gyrate /jī ráyt/ *vi* (**-rates, -rating, -rated**) to move with a circular or spiral motion, especially around a fixed

central point ■ *adj* BIOL growing in a winding spiral or coil [Early 19C. < late Latin *gyrat-*, past participle of *gyrare* 'revolve' < Latin *gyrus* (see GYRUS)] —**gyrator** *n* —**gyratory** *adj*

gyration /jī ráysh'n/ *n* **1.** movement in a circle around a fixed centre ○ *the gyration of the rotor* **2.** a spiral or coil-shaped thing or part

gyre /jīr/ *n* a circle or spiral (*literary*) [Mid-16C. < Latin *gyrus* (see GYRUS)]

gyrene /jī reen, jī réen/ *n* a soldier in the US Marine Corps (*slang*) [Mid-20C. Origin ?]

gyrfalcon /júr fawlkən, -folkən/ *n* a large falcon varying in colour from white to dark brown. Native to: cold northern regions. Latin name: *Falco rusticolus*. [14C. Alteration (by association with Latin *gyrare* 'revolve') of Old French *gerfaucon*]

gyro /jírō/ (*plural* **-ros**) *n* N Am FOOD same as **doner kebab** [Late 20C. < modern Greek *guros* 'turning']

gyro- *prefix* **1.** spinning or rotating in a circle ○ *gyrostatics* **2.** gyroscope, gyroscopic ○ *gyrostabilizer* [< Greek *guros* 'ring, circle']

gyrocompass /jírō kumpəss/ *n* a navigational compass fitted with a gyroscope instead of a magnet

gyromagnetic /jírō mag néttik/ *adj* relating to or caused by the magnetism produced by the spinning motion of a charged particle ○ *gyromagnetic effect*

gyromagnetic ratio *n* the ratio of the magnetic moment to the angular momentum of a system

gyron /jírən/, **giron** *n* in heraldry, a triangular form made by two blinds drawn from the edge of an escutcheon to meet at the fesse-point and occupying half of the quarter [Late 16C. < French, 'gusset' < Germanic]

gyroplane /jírō playn/ *n* an aircraft fitted with an unpowered rotor for producing lift

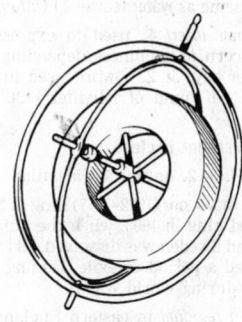
gyroscope

gyroscope /jírə skōp/ *n* a device consisting of a rotating heavy metal wheel pivoted inside a circular frame whose movement does not affect the wheel's orientation in space. Use: in compasses and other navigational aids, in stabilizing mechanisms on ships and aircraft. —**gyroscopic** /jírə skóppik/ *adj* —**gyroscopically** *adv*

gyrostabilizer /jírō stáybə līzər/ *n* a stabilizing system that uses gyroscopes to compensate and reduce the rolling or pitching motion of a ship or aircraft

gyrostat /jírō stat/ *n* a gyroscope or gyrostabilizer in which the rotating wheel is pivoted within a rigid case [Late 19C. < GYRO- + Greek *statos* 'standing']

gyrostatics /jírō státtiks/ *n* the branch of science that deals with rotating bodies (*takes a singular verb*) —**gyrostatic** *adj* —**gyrostatically** *adv*

gyrus /jírəss/ (*plural* **-ri** /-rī/) *n* a rounded ridge on the outer layer of the brain [Mid-19C. Via Latin, 'circle' < Greek *guros* 'ring, circle']

Gy Sgt *abbr* gunnery sergeant

Gyumri /gyoómri/ city in northwestern Armenia, the country's second most populated urban area. Population: 206,600 (1990). Former name **Leninakhan** (1924–90)

gyve /jīv/ (*archaic*) *n* a shackle or fetter, usually for the leg (*usually used in the plural*) ■ *vt* (**gyves, gyving, gyved**) to shackle or fetter somebody, especially by the leg [13C. Origin ?]

Hh

h¹ /aych/ (*plural* **h's**), **H** (*plural* **H's** or **Hs**) *n* **1.** the eighth letter of the English alphabet, representing a consonant sound **2.** a written representation of the letter 'h'

h² *symbol* **1.** hecto- **2.** PHYS Planck's constant **3.** used to refer to the eighth vertical row of squares from the left on a chessboard

h³ *abbr* **1.** harbour **2.** hard **3.** hardness **4.** height **5.** high **6.** BASEBALL hit **7.** horizontal **8.** MUSIC horn **9.** hospital **10.** hour **11.** MATHS hundred **12.** husband

H¹ *symbol* **1.** PHYS enthalpy **2.** MATHS, PHYS Hamiltonian function **3.** ELECTRONICS henry **4.** CHEM ELEM hydrogen

H² *abbr* **1.** harbour **2.** hard **3.** hardness **4.** height **5.** high

H³ /aych/ (*plural* **H's** or **Hs**) *n* something shaped like a letter 'H'

H2 *abbr* ONLINE how to (*used in e-mails or text messages*)

H₂0 *n* CHEM same as **water** (sense 1) (*informal*)

ha¹ /haa/, **hah** *interj* **1.** used to express surprise, triumph, scorn, or happiness, depending on the way the speaker says it **2.** a word used in writing to represent the sound of laughter [13C. Natural exclamation]

ha² *symbol* MEASURE hectare

Ha. *abbr* **1.** Haiti **2.** Haitian **3.** Hawaiian

Haakon VII /háwk on/ (1872–1957) king of Norway. He was elected king in 1905, when the union between Norway and Sweden was dissolved. His reign (1905–57) included a period in exile, leading Norwegian resistance during World War II.

haar /haar/ *n regional* in eastern England and Scotland, a cold mist or fog off the North Sea coast, or rolling in from the North Sea [Late 17C. Origin ?]

Haarlem /haárləm/, **Harlem** city in North Holland Province, western Netherlands, 20 km/12 mi. west of Amsterdam. Population: 148,772 (2000).

Hab. *abbr* Habakkuk

Habakkuk /hábbəkək/ *n* **1.** in the Bible, a Hebrew priest who lived in the 7th century BC **2.** a book of the Bible that contains the prophecies traditionally attributed to Habakkuk. See table at **Bible**

habanera /hábbə náirə/ *n* **1.** a slow dance of Cuban origin in 2/4 time **2.** the music for a habanera. There is a famous example in the opera 'Carmen', sung by Carmen herself. [Late 19C. < Spanish, 'of Havana']

habdabs /háb dabz/ *npl* a fit of extreme nervous anxiety or irritation (*informal*) [Mid-20C. Origin ?]

habdalah /hav daálə/, **havdalah** *n* a Jewish ceremony that marks the end of the Sabbath or another holy day, or a prayer said during the ceremony [Mid-18C. < Hebrew *habdālāh* 'separation, division']

habeas corpus /háybi əss káwrpəss/ *n* a writ issued in order to bring somebody who has been detained into court, usually for a decision on whether the detention is lawful [15C. < Latin, 'you may have the body']

Haber-Bosch process /haábər bósh-/ *n* CHEM same as **Haber process** [After Fritz *Haber* (1868–1934) and Karl *Bosch* (1874–1940), German chemists]

haberdasher /hábbər dashər/ *n* **1.** a dealer in small articles used in sewing, e.g. thread, ribbons, and buttons **2.** *N Am* a dealer in men's clothing and accessories [14C. Probably < Anglo-Norman *hapertas* 'small items of merchandise']

haberdashery /hábbər dashəri/ (*plural* **-ies**) *n* **1.** goods sold by a haberdasher **2.** a shop, or a department in a larger store, that sells haberdashery

habergeon /hábbərjən/ *n* a sleeveless chain mail jacket worn under armour [14C. < French *haubergeon* < Old French *hauberc* (SEE HAUBERK)]

Haber process /haábər-/ *n* a commercial process for catalytically producing ammonia from atmospheric nitrogen and hydrogen at high temperature and pressure [See HABER-BOSCH PROCESS]

~~**habeus corpus**~~ incorrect spelling of **habeas corpus**

habiliment /hə bíllimənt/ *n* GARMENT OR GARMENTS clothing, or an item of clothing (*archaic; usually used in the plural* ■ **habiliments** *npl* (*formal*) **1.** SPECIALIZED EQUIPMENT the equipment and gear needed for a task or activity **2.** SPECIAL CLOTHES items of clothing associated with somebody's work or position or an occasion [Early 17C. < Old French *habillement* < *habiller* 'fit out' < *habile*, easy to hold' < *habere* 'have, hold']

habilitate /hə bílli tayt/ (**-tates, -tating, -tated**) *v* **1.** *vi* PREPARE FOR POSITION to qualify for employment or an office (*formal*) **2.** *vt US* EQUIP MINING OPERATION to provide a mine with the equipment and money needed for operation **3.** *vt* CLOTHE SOMEBODY to clothe somebody in a particular way (*literary*) [Early 17C. < medieval Latin *habilitat-*, past participle of *habilitare* < Latin *habilitas* (SEE ABILITY)] —**habilitation** /hə bílli táysh'n/ *n* —**habilitator** *n*

habit /hábbit/ *n* **1.** REGULARLY REPEATED BEHAVIOUR PATTERN an action or pattern of behaviour that is repeated so often that it becomes typical of somebody, although he or she may be unaware of it ○ *I really need to get into the habit of writing down what I spend.* ○ *the annoying habit of finishing someone else's sentences* **2.** ATTITUDE somebody's attitude or general disposition **3.** ADDICTION an addiction to a drug (*slang*) **4.** CLOTHING OF RELIGIOUS ORDER a long loose gown, usually black, brown, grey, or white, traditionally worn by nuns, friars, and monks **5.** RIDING, CLOTHING same as **riding habit 6.** BOT, ZOOL GROWTH PATTERN the characteristic appearance, behaviour, or growth pattern of a plant or animal **7.** SHAPE OF CRYSTAL the characteristic growth pattern or shape of a crystal ■ *vt* (**-its, -iting, -ited**) CLOTHE SOMEBODY SPECIALLY to dress somebody in clothing distinctive to a particular position or office (*literary*) [12C Via French < Latin *habitus* < *habere* 'have, wear'] ◇ **kick the habit** to become free of an addiction, or stop doing something that has been a long-standing practice (*informal*)

ORIGIN The Latin word *habere* from which *habit* is derived was used reflexively to mean 'to be', and so its past participle *habitus* came to be used as a noun for 'how you are', that is, your 'state' or 'condition'. Subsequently this noun developed in two directions, coming to mean both 'outward condition or appearance', hence, eventually, 'clothing', and 'inner condition, quality, nature, character', and later 'usual way of behaving'. (The notion of adapting a verb meaning 'to have' to express 'how you are, how you act in particular situations' is duplicated in the English word 'behave'.)

SYNONYMS *habit, custom, tradition, practice, routine, wont*
CORE MEANING: established pattern of behaviour

habit an action or pattern of behaviour that is repeated so often that it becomes typical of somebody, although he or she may be unaware of it ○ *She had an irritating habit of phoning just as we were about to eat.* **custom** the way somebody usually or traditionally behaves in a situation ○ *It was his custom to walk three miles a day for health reasons.* ○ *The custom is for someone to give a short speech of thanks after the meal.* ○ *He wrote a book on local customs after he retired.* **tradition** a long-established action or pattern of behaviour in a community or group of people, often one that has been handed down from generation to generation ○ *They maintain the old local tradition of decorating the wells in spring.* **practice** an established way of doing something, especially one that has developed through experience and knowledge; **routine** the usual sequence for a set of activities, sometimes with the suggestion that this is monotonous and tedious ○ *The visit was clearly going to disrupt our daily routine.* ○ *Life settled into a routine of writing in the mornings and long walks in the afternoons.* **wont** (*formal*) something that somebody does regularly or habitually ○ *I went to the library on Thursday, as is my wont.*

---

habitable /hábbitəb'l/ *adj* considered fit to be lived in ○ *A lot of structural work will be needed before the house is habitable.* [14C. Via French < Latin *habitabilis* < *habitare* (SEE HABITAT)] —**habitability** /hábbitə bílləti/ *n* —**habitableness** *n* —**habitably** *adv*

habitant /hábbitənt/ *n* **1.** somebody living in a place (*literary*) **2.** *N Am* a farmer of French descent living in Canada or the United States [15C. < French < Old French *habiter* 'dwell' < Latin *habitare* (SEE HABITAT)]

habitat /hábbi tat/ *n* **1.** ECOL HOME ENVIRONMENT the natural conditions and environment in which a plant or animal lives, e.g. forest, desert, or wetlands **2.** TYPICAL LOCATION the place in which a person or group is usually found **3.** ARTIFICIALLY CREATED ENVIRONMENT a sealed controlled environment in which people can live in unusual conditions such as under the sea or in space [Late 18C. < 3rd person present singular of Latin *habitare* 'possess, inhabit' < *habere* 'have']

habitation /hábbi táysh'n/ *n* **1.** OCCUPANCY the state of being lived in by people or animals, or the act of living in a place ○ *unfit for human habitation* **2.** DWELLING PLACE a place in which to live ○ *The squirrels found a new habitation in a hollow tree.* **3.** DWELLINGS a group of dwellings and their inhabitants ○ *There is little evidence remaining of the ancient habitation.* [14C. Via French < Latin *habitation-* < *habitare* (SEE HABITAT)] —**habitational** *adj*

habit-forming *adj* capable of causing a physiological or psychological need in somebody ○ *habit-forming drugs*

habitual /hə bíchoo əl/ *adj* **1.** DONE AS HABIT done frequently and predictably **2.** PERSISTING IN BEHAVIOUR continuing in a particular practice as a result of an ingrained tendency ○ *a habitual criminal* **3.** CHARACTERISTIC characteristic of somebody's character or behaviour ○ *She tackled the problem with her habitual single-mindedness.* —**habitually** *adv* —**habitualness** *n*

SYNONYMS See *usual*.

habituate /hə bíchoo ayt/ (**-ates, -ating, -ated**) *v* **1.** *vt* MAKE SOMEBODY USED TO SOMETHING to accustom a person or animal to something through prolonged and regular exposure (*formal*) ○ *People living in cities become habituated to crowds.* **2.** *vti* PSYCHOL LEARN TO IGNORE STIMULUS to learn not to respond to a stimulus that is frequently repeated, or teach a person or animal to do this **3.** *vi* BECOME ACCUSTOMED TO DRUG to become dependent on or less affected by a medical or illegal drug through frequent use [16C. < late Latin

---

habituat-, past participle of *habituare* 'bring into a state' < Latin *habitus* (see HABIT)] —**habituation** /hə bíchoo áysh'n/ *n*

habitude /hábbi tyood/ *n* a tendency to act in a particular way (*formal*) —**habitudinal** /hábbi tyóod'n'l/ *adj*

habitué /hə bíchoo ay/ *n* a regular visitor of a place [Early 19C. < French < past participle of *habituer* < late Latin *habituare* (see HABITUATE)]

habitus /hábbitəss/ (*plural same*) *n* the general appearance, posture, or physical state of a patient, especially with regard to susceptibility to disease [Late 19C. < Latin (see HABIT)]

haboob /hə bóob/ *n* a violent sandstorm or dust storm that sweeps across the deserts of northern Africa and Arabia and the plains of South Asia [Late 19C. < Arabic *habub* 'violent storm']

Habsburg /hábz burg/, **Hapsburg** /háps-/ *n* a member of a German royal family, prominent between the 13th and 20th centuries in Europe, that included rulers of the Holy Roman Empire, Spain, and Austria-Hungary

habu /haá boo/ (*plural* **-bus**) *n* a large light brown poisonous snake with black markings. Native to: Okinawa and neighbouring Pacific islands. Latin name: *Trimeresurus flavoviridis*. [Late 19C. < Japanese]

háček /haá chek/ *n* in some Slavic and other languages, a mark (ˇ) placed over a letter to indicate a change in pronunciation. For example, in Czech it changes the sound of the letter 'c' to 'ch'. See table at **diacritic** [Mid-20C. < Czech, 'small hook' < *hak* 'hook']

hachure /ha shyóor/ *n* a short shading line, usually one of a group of such lines drawn in parallel, used on a map to indicate the direction and steepness of a slope [Mid-19C. < French < *hacher* 'mark with hatches, chop' (see HATCH [3])]

hacienda /hássi éndə/ *n* **1.** in Spain or Spanish-speaking parts of America, a large estate, farm, or ranch **2.** in Spain or Spanish-speaking parts of America, the main residence on a hacienda [Mid-18C. Via Spanish, 'domestic work, large estate' < Latin *facienda* 'things needing to be done' < *facere* 'do']

hack[1] /hak/ *v* (**hacks, hacking, hacked**) **1.** *vti* CUT SOMETHING USING REPEATED BLOWS to cut or chop something by striking it with short repeated blows using a sharp tool such as a knife or an axe **2.** *vt* CUT WAY THROUGH OBSTRUCTION to cut a path or way through an obstruction, e.g. undergrowth ○ *I had to hack my way through the bureaucracy to get the job done.* **3.** *vt* CHOP SOMETHING OFF OR INTO PARTS to cut, shape, or divide something roughly or carelessly (*informal*) ○ *He's hacked a whole chunk off that article I wrote for the magazine.* **4.** *vi* COMPUT GAIN UNAUTHORIZED ACCESS TO COMPUTER DATA to use a computer or other technological device or system in order to gain unauthorized access to data held by another person or organization **5.** *vt* COPE WITH SOMETHING to succeed at or endure something (*informal*) ○ *I wonder if he can hack getting up at five every day.* **6.** *vi* COUGH WITH RASPING NOISE to cough persistently in short dry bursts with a rasping noise **7.** *vt* SOCCER, RUGBY KICK FOOTBALL PLAYER'S SHINS in rugby or football, to commit a foul by kicking the shins of an opposing player **8.** *vt* BASKETBALL HIT BASKETBALL PLAYER'S ARM in basketball, to commit a foul by striking another player on the arm ■ *n* **1.** QUICK CHOP a short violent blow with a sharp tool **2.** CUT MADE BY HACKING SOMETHING a rough cut made by a quick blow with a sharp tool, e.g. a notch in a tree made with an axe **3.** TOOL FOR HACKING a tool used for chopping something or breaking up hard ground, e.g. a pickaxe **4.** COUGHING NOISE a short dry cough **5.** WOUND FROM KICK a wound from being kicked **6.** SOCCER, RUGBY DISABLING KICK IN FOOTBALL a kick on the shins in rugby or football, meant to disable a player temporarily **7.** COMPUT SUCCESSFUL EFFORT an extremely good, often very time-consuming, work effort that produces exactly what is needed (*informal*) [Old English *haccian* 'cut in pieces' < W Germanic] ◇ **not be able to hack it** to not be able to manage or cope (*informal*)

hack around *vi US* to spend time doing silly or unimportant things or doing nothing at all (*informal*)

hack[2] /hak/ *n* **1.** DRUDGE a mediocre and unimaginative person, especially somebody engaged in dull or uninspired work **2.** UNORIGINAL WRITER a writer who produces routine unoriginal writing, especially for newspapers, magazines, television, or films **3.** POL UNCRITICAL POLITICAL PARTY WORKER a political party member who serves the party uncritically and in a routine capacity **4.** HORSE FOR RIDING a horse for riding or driving **5.** OLD HORSE a horse that is in bad condition through age or overwork **6.** HORSE FOR HIRE a horse that is hired out **7.** HORSE RIDE a ride on a horse, usually through the countryside **8.** same as **journalist** (*informal*) **9.** *N Am* same as **taxi** (*informal*) ■ *v* (**hacks, hacking, hacked**) **1.** *vti* TAKE HORSE RIDE SOMEWHERE to ride a horse, or go on a horse ride, for pleasure, usually through the countryside **2.** *vi* RIDING GO RIDING to ride a horse for exercise at a normal pace **3.** *vi US* DRIVE TAXI to work as a taxi driver (*informal*) ■ *adj* TRITE lacking quality and originality ○ *The film had a really hack plot.* [Early 18C. Shortening of HACKNEY]

hack[3] /hak/ *n* **1.** FEEDING RACK a rack on which fodder for cattle is placed **2.** FEEDING POST FOR HAWKS in falconry, a board from which a hawk takes meat **3.** PILE OF BRICKS a pile or row of unfired bricks that have been laid out to dry [Late 16C. Variant of HATCH [1]]

hackamore /hákə mawr/ *n N Am* a bridle without a bit but with an adjustable band by which a rider can exert pressure on a horse's nose, used especially to break young horses [Mid-19C. Alteration (by association with HACK [2]) of Spanish *jaquima* < Arabic *shaqīmah* 'restraint, bit']

hack and slasher *n* a computer game that features a great deal of violence (*slang*)

hackberry /hákbəri/ (*plural* **-ries**) *n* a tree of the elm family with soft yellowish wood and fruit resembling cherries. Native to: North America. Latin name: *Celtis occidentalis*. [Mid-18C. < variant of *hag* < N Germanic]

hacked off *adj* annoyed or dissatisfied (*informal*)

hacker /hákər/ *n* **1.** SOMEBODY ACCESSING ANOTHER'S COMPUTER WITHOUT AUTHORIZATION a computer user who gains unauthorized access to a computer system or data belonging to somebody else **2.** COMPUTER ENTHUSIAST somebody who is interested or skilled in computer technology and programming **3.** SOMEBODY WHO CHOPS somebody who cuts or chops something **4.** *N Am* AMATEUR PLAYER somebody who enjoys a sport but lacks skill in it

hacker ethic *n* the belief that all technical information should be freely shared and that gaining unauthorized access to computer systems is acceptable if there is no injury or expense to others

hackie /háki/ *n US* a taxi driver (*informal*)

hacking coat /háking-/ *n* CLOTHING same as **hacking jacket**

hacking cough *n* a repeated cough that is short, dry, and rasping

hacking jacket *n* a tweed or woollen jacket with side or back vents and a full skirt, worn especially for horse riding

hackle[1] /hák'l/ *n* **1.** BIRDS BIRD'S NECK FEATHER a long slender feather on the neck or lower back of a male bird, especially a domestic fowl **2.** FISHING FEATHERS USED FOR FISHING FLY a tuft of feathers from the neck of a bird used in making an artificial fly for fishing **3.** FISHING FISHING FLY MADE FROM FEATHERS an artificial fly for fishing made from the neck feathers of a bird **4.** MIL FEATHERED ORNAMENT an ornament made of feathers worn in the headdress of some Highland regiments **5.** TEXTILES FLAX COMB a steel comb with long teeth used to comb out flax, hemp, or jute fibres ■ **hackles** *npl* HAIRS ON ANIMAL'S NECK the line of hairs on the back of the neck and along the spine of an animal, especially a dog or cat, that stand up when it is threatened or angry ■ *vt* (**-les, -ling, -led**) **1.** FISHING PUT FEATHERS ON FISHING FLY to trim an artificial fly with the neck feathers of a bird **2.** TEXTILES COMB FLAX BEFORE SPINNING to comb out flax, hemp, or jute fibres using a hackle [15C. Probably < assumed Old English *hacule* 'little hook' < Germanic] —**hackler** *n* ◇ **make somebody's hackles rise, raise somebody's hackles, get somebody's hackles up** to make somebody angry or hostile

hackle[2] /hák'l/ (**-les, -ling, -led**) *vti* to mangle something by cutting it roughly [Late 16C. < HACK [1]]

hackly /hákli/ (**-lier, -liest**) *adj* having a rough jagged surface

Hackman /hákmən/, **Gene** (*b.* 1930) US film actor. He won Academy Awards for *The French Connection* (1971) and *Unforgiven* (1992). Full name **Hackman, Eugene Alden**

hackmatack /hákmə tak/ *n* TREES, INDUST same as **tamarack** [Late 18C. < Algonquian *akemantek* 'snowshoe wood']

hackney /hákni/ (*plural* **-neys**) *n* **1.** a car, carriage, or similar vehicle providing a taxi service **2.** a horse for riding or driving [13C. Probably after *Hackney*, NE London]

hackneyed /háknid/ *adj* made commonplace and stale by overuse ○ *the same old hackneyed sales talk*

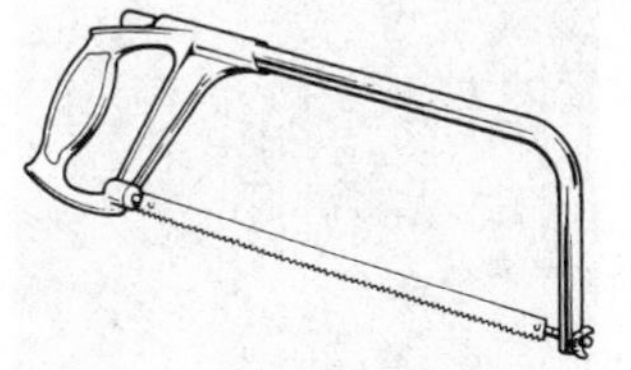

hacksaw

hacksaw /hák saw/ *n* a handsaw with a small-toothed steel blade stretched taut across a frame, used for cutting metal ■ *vt* (**-saws, -sawing, -sawed, -sawn** /-sawn/ or **-sawed**) to cut something using a hacksaw

hacktivism /háktivizəm/ *n* the activity of breaking into and sabotaging a computer system via the Internet as a political protest ○ *'The apparent increase in hacktivism may be due in part to the growing importance of the Internet as a means of communication.'* (*Wired website*; April 1999) [Late 20C. Blend of HACKER + ACTIVISM] —**hacktivist** *n, adj*

hackwork /hák wurk/ *n* ordinary literary, artistic, or professional work that somebody is hired to do (*disapproving*)

had past participle, past tense of **have**

hadaway /háddə wáy/ *interj N England* **1.** used to urge somebody to hurry **2.** used to express scepticism [Origin ?]

haddock /háddək/ (*plural same* or **-docks**) *n* **1.** a fish that is related to but smaller than the cod. Native to: northern Atlantic. Latin name: *Melanogrammus aeglefinus*. **2.** the flesh of a haddock used as food [14C. Via Anglo-Norman *hadoc* < Old French *(h)adot*]

hade /hayd/ *n* GEOL the angle between the vertical plane and a plane containing a vein, fault, or lode ■ *vi* (**hades, hading, haded**) to be at an angle to the vertical [Late 17C. Origin ?]

Hadean /háydi ən/ *adj* **1.** relating to Hades **2.** relating to the Hadean aeon

Hadean aeon *n* the period of geological time not confirmed by rock formation records, beginning approximately 4.6 billion years ago with the formation of the Earth

Hades /háy deez/ *n* **1.** in Greek mythology, the underworld kingdom inhabited by the souls of the dead. Roman equivalent **Dis 2.** in Greek mythology, the god of the underworld and husband of Persephone. Roman equivalent **Pluto** (sense 2) **3.** *also* **hades** same as **hell** (*informal*) [Late 16C. < Greek *Haidēs*, god of the dead]

Hadhramaut /haádrə máwt/, **Hadramaut** coastal region in the southern Arabian peninsula, shared between Yemen and Oman. The ancient civilization that flourished there is called 'Hazarmaveth' in the Bible. Area: 155,400 sq. km/60,000 sq. mi.

Hadith /háddith/, **hadith** *n* the collected traditions, teachings, and stories of the prophet Muhammad, accepted as a source of Islamic doctrine and law second only to the Koran [Early 18C. < Arabic *ḥadīṯ* 'tradition']

hadj, etc. ISLAM another spelling of **hajj, etc.**

Hadlee /háddli/, **Sir Richard** (*b.* 1951) New Zealand cricketer. He was an all-rounder who in 1990 set a world record of 431 Test wickets. Full name **Hadlee, Sir Richard John**

hadn't /hádd'nt/ *contr* had not

Hadramaut another spelling of **Hadhramaut**

Hadrian /háydri ən/ (76–138) Roman emperor. As emperor (117–138) he consolidated the Roman Empire by establishing a series of defense fortifications, including Hadrian's Wall, that marked the end of Roman territorial expansion.

'Little soul, wandering, gentle guest and companion of the body, into what places will you now go?'
[Hadrian, *Dying words*; 138]

Hadrian's Wall

Hadrian's Wall *n* a fortified wall built across northern England in the early 2nd century on the orders of the Roman emperor Hadrian, as a defence against the Picts. It marked the northern boundary of the Roman Empire.

hadron /háddron/ *n* an elementary particle that is made up of gluons or quarks or both and participates in the strong interaction [Mid-20C. < Greek *hadros* 'bulky'] —**hadronic** /ha drónnik, hə-/ *adj*

hadrosaur /háddrə sawr/, **hadrosaurus** /-sáwrəss/ (*plural* **-uses**) *n* an amphibious plant-eating dinosaur with a snout resembling a duck's bill and strong hind legs for walking in swamps. Hadrosaur fossils have been found in sediments from the Upper Cretaceous period. Genus: *Anatosaurus*. [Late 19C. < modern Latin *hadrosaurus* < Greek *hadros* 'bulky' + *sauros* 'lizard']

hadst /hadst/ *v* 2nd person singular past of **have** (*archaic*)

haecceity /hek seé əti, heek-, hīk-/ *n* the essential property that makes an individual uniquely that individual [Mid-17C. < medieval Latin *heicceitas* < Latin *haec* 'this']

Haeckel /hék'l/, **Ernst** (1834–1919) German zoologist and evolutionist. He was an early advocate of Charles Darwin's theories, and is chiefly remembered for producing genealogical trees of species development. Full name **Haeckel, Ernst Heinrich Philipp August**

Haeckel's law the theory proposing as a law that an embryo in each stage of development resembles an organism that its species descended from [After Ernst HAECKEL]

haem /heem/ *n* the deep red, nonprotein portion of haemoglobin that contains iron [Early 20C. Backformation < HAEMOGLOBIN]

haem- *prefix* same as **haemo-** (*used before vowels*)

haema- /héemə/ *prefix* blood ○ *haemangioma* [< Greek *haima*]

haemagglutinate /héemə glóoti nayt/ (**-nates**, **-nating**, **-nated**) *vti* to cause red blood cells to clump together, or become clumped together —**haemagglutination** /héemə glóoti náysh'n/ *n*

haemagglutinin /héemə glóotinin/ *n* an agent that causes red blood cells to clump together, e.g. a virus or an antibody

haemal /héem'l/ *adj* 1. found in or associated with the blood or blood vessels 2. located on or associated with the side of the body where the heart and major arteries and veins are found [Mid-19C. < Greek *haima* 'blood']

haemangioma /hi mánji ómə/ (*plural* **-mata** /-mətə/ or **-mas**) *n* a benign tumour or birthmark consisting of a dense, often raised cluster of blood vessels in the skin

haemat- *prefix* same as **haemato-** (*used before vowels*)

haematein /héemə teé in/ *n* a red-brown compound used to stain samples for microscope study

haematic /hee máttik/ *adj* relating to or acting on blood

haematin /héemətin/ *n* a breakdown product of haemoglobin

haematinic /héemə tínnik/ *adj* describes a drug or other agent that increases blood haemoglobin

haematite /héemə tīt/ *n* a black, brown, or red mineral consisting of iron oxide, often in very large deposits. Use: source of iron. [15C. Via Latin < Greek *haimatitēs* 'blood-like (stone)'] —**haematitic** /héemə títtik/ *adj*

haemato- *prefix* blood ○ *haematoblast* [< Greek *haimat-*, stem of *haima*]

haematoblast /hee máttō blast/ *n* an immature blood cell, especially a red blood cell

haematocrit /héemətō krit/ *n* 1. the percentage of a blood sample that consists of red blood cells, measured after the blood has been centrifuged and the cells compacted 2. a centrifuge used to compact the red blood cells in a blood sample in order to determine the percentage of the blood that consists of cells [Late 19C. < HAEMATO- + Greek *kritēs* 'judge' (see CRITIC)]

haematogenesis /héemətō jénnəssiss/ *n* PHYSIOL same as **haematopoiesis** —**haematogenic** /héemətō jénnik/ *adj*

haematogenous /héemə tójjinəss/ *adj* 1. MAKING BLOOD producing blood 2. OF BLOOD originating in or derived from blood 3. SPREAD BY BLOOD spread by means of blood

haematology /héemə tólləji/ *n* the branch of medicine devoted to the study of blood, blood-producing tissues, and diseases of the blood —**haematologic** /héemətə lójjik/ *adj* —**haematologically** *adv* —**haematologist** *n*

haematoma /héemə tómə/ (*plural* **-mas** or **-mata** /-mətə/) *n* a semisolid mass of blood in the tissues, caused by injury, disease, or a clotting disorder

haematophagous /héemə tóffəgəss/ *adj* feeding on blood [Mid-19C. < HAEMATO- + Greek *phagein* 'eat']

haematopoiesis /héemətō poy eéssiss/, **haemopoiesis** /héemō-/ *n* the formation of red blood cells in the blood-forming tissues of the body —**haematopoietic** /-poy éttik/ *adj*

haematoxylin /héemə tóksilin/ *n* a dye used to stain microscope slides for study [Mid-19C. < modern Latin *Haematoxylum* < Greek *haimat-* 'blood' + *xulon* 'wood']

haematozoon /héemətō zó on/ (*plural* **-zoa** /-zó ə/) *n* a parasitic protozoan or other microorganism that lives in blood —**haematozoal** *adj*

haematuria /héemə tyóori ə/ *n* the presence of blood in the urine, as a result of injury to or disease of the kidneys, ureters, bladder, or urethra —**haematuric** *adj*

-haemia *suffix* another spelling of **-aemia**

haemic /héemik/ *adj* relating to blood [Mid-19C. < Greek *haima* 'blood']

haemo- *prefix* blood ○ *haemolysis* [< Greek *haima*]

haemochromatosis /héemō krómə tóssiss/ *n* a genetic disorder in which there is excess accumulation of iron in the body leading to damage of many organs, especially the liver and pancreas [Late 19C. < HAEMO- + Greek *khromat-* 'colour']

haemocoel /héemə seel/ *n* a body cavity in spiders, crustaceans, and other arthropods through which the blood or haemolymph circulates [Mid-19C. < HAEMO- + Greek *koilos* 'hollow']

haemocyanin /héemō sī ənin/ *n* a bluish pigment found in the blood or haemolymph of some arthropods and molluscs that functions like haemoglobin, transporting oxygen to tissues [Late 19C. < HAEMO- + Greek *kuan(e)os* 'dark blue']

haemocyte /héemō sīt/ *n* a blood cell (*technical*)

haemodialysis /héemō dī álləsiss/ *n* dialysis of the blood (*technical*)

haemoflagellate /héemō flájjə layt/ *n* a flagellate protozoan that lives as a parasite in blood

haemoglobin /héemə glóbin/ *n* an iron-containing protein in red blood cells that transports oxygen around the body

haemoglobinuria /héemə glóbi nyoóri ə/ *n* the pres-

ence in the urine of haemoglobin that has been freed from red blood cells —**haemoglobinuric** *adj*

haemolymph /héemōlimf/ *n* a fluid in some invertebrates that functions like the blood in vertebrates [Late 19C. < HAEMO- + Latin *lympha* 'clear liquid'] —**haemolymphatic** /héemō lim fáttik/ *adj*

haemolyse /héemə līz/ (**-lyses**, **-lysing**, **-lysed**) *vti* to destroy red blood cells and release haemoglobin, or undergo destruction and release haemoglobin [Early 20C. < HAEMO- + variant of -LYZE]

haemolysin /héemō líssin, hi móllissin/ *n* a bacterial toxin, antibody, or other agent that destroys red blood cells, releasing free haemoglobin

haemolysis /hi móllississ/ *n* the destruction of red blood cells and the release of the haemoglobin they contain —**haemolytic** /héemə líttik/ *adj*

haemolytic anaemia *n* anaemia that results from the destruction of red blood cells and may be caused by bacteria, genetic disorders, or toxic chemicals

haemophilia /héemə fílli ə/ *n* a disorder linked to a recessive gene on the X-chromosome and occurring almost exclusively in men and boys, in which the blood clots much more slowly than normally, resulting in extensive bleeding from even minor injuries

haemophiliac /héemə fílliak/ *n* somebody who has haemophilia

haemophilic /héemə fíllik/ *adj* 1. relating to, resembling, or affected with haemophilia 2. describes bacteria that are adapted to thrive in blood or a medium rich in blood

haemopoiesis *n* PHYSIOL same as **haematopoiesis**

haemoptysis /hi móptississ/ *n* the coughing up of blood or mucus containing blood (*technical*) [Mid-17C. < HAEMO- + Greek *ptusis* 'act of spitting']

~~**haemorrage**~~ incorrect spelling of **haemorrhage**

haemorrhage /hémmərij/ *n* 1. EXCESSIVE BLEEDING the loss of blood from a ruptured blood vessel, either internally or externally ○ *a cerebral haemorrhage* 2. UNCONTROLLED LOSS a large uncontrolled loss of something valuable ○ *a haemorrhage of cash that threatened the firm* ○ *v* (**-rhages**, **-rhaging**, **-rhaged**) 1. *vi* BLEED HEAVILY to bleed profusely and uncontrollably ○ *The wound was haemorrhaging badly.* 2. *vti* LOSE SOMETHING VALUABLE to experience a sudden, uncontrolled, and massive loss of something valuable ○ *The failed business had been haemorrhaging money for months.* [15C. Via French or medieval Latin < Greek *haimorrhagia* < *haima* 'blood' + *rhēgnunai* 'break, burst'] —**haemorrhagic** /hémmə rájjik/ *adj*

haemorrhagic fever *n* a viral infection that results in fever, chills, and profuse internal bleeding from the capillaries, e.g. dengue or Ebola

haemorrhoidectomy /hémməroy déktəmi/ *n* a surgical procedure to remove haemorrhoids

haemorrhoids /hémmə roydz/ *npl* painful varicose veins in the canal of the anus —**haemorrhoidal** /hémmə róyd'l/ *adj*

haemosiderin /héemō síddərin/ *n* a protein that stores iron

haemostasis /héemō stáyssiss/, **haemostasia** /héemō stáyzi ə/ *n* 1. the stopping of bleeding or haemorrhaging in an organ or body part 2. the stopping of the blood flow through an organ or body part

haemostat /héemō stat/ *n* 1. a surgical instrument that stops bleeding by clamping a blood vessel 2. a chemical agent that stops bleeding

haemostatic /héemō státtik/ *adj* stopping or slowing down the flow of blood ■ *n* an agent that stops or slows down the flow of blood

haere mai /hīrə mī/ *interj* NZ used to welcome somebody [Mid-18C. < Maori, literally 'come here']

haere ra /hīrə ra/ *interj* NZ used to say goodbye [< Maori, literally 'go away' or home]

hafiz /haáfiz/ *n* the title used to address somebody who has committed the Koran to memory [Mid-17C. Via Persian < Arabic *ḥāfiẓ* 'guardian']

hafnium /háfni əm/ *n* a bright silvery metallic element. Source: zirconium ores. Use: absorption of neutrons in nuclear reactor rods, manufacture of tungsten filaments. Symbol **Hf**. See table at **element** [Early 20C. < modern Latin < *Hafnia*, Latin name for Copenhagen, Denmark]

haft /haaft/ *n* the handle of a knife, axe, or other weapon or tool (*literary*) [Old English *hæft(e)* < Germanic] —**haft** *vt* —**hafter** *n*

haftarah /haáftə raa/ (*plural* **-rahs** or **-roth** /-rōt/ or **-rot**), **haftorah** (*plural* **-rahs** or **-roth** or **-rot**), **haphtarah** *n* a reading from the Prophets following each lesson from the Torah in synagogue services on the Sabbath [Early 18C. < Hebrew *haphṭārāh* 'conclusion']

hag[1] /hag/ *n* **1.** an offensive term that deliberately insults a woman's appearance, temperament, and age (*slang*) **2.** a witch, especially an elderly one **3.** FISH same as **hagfish** [14C. Origin ?] —**haggish** *adj*

hag[2] /hag/ *n N England, Scotland* **1.** a relatively firm spot in a bog **2.** a boggy area on a moor [Mid-17C. < Old Norse *hǫgg* 'gap']

Hag. *abbr* BIBLE Haggai

Hagar /háy gaar, -gər/ *n* in the Bible, an Egyptian servant of Sarah who bore Sarah's husband, Abraham, a son named Ishmael (Genesis 16, 21:1–21) [< Hebrew *Haghar*]

hagbut /hág but/ *n* ARMS same as **harquebus** [Mid-16C. Variant of *hackbut* < French *haquebut(e)*, alteration of *haquebusche* < Middle Dutch *hakebus* (see HARQUEBUS)] —**hagbuteer** /hág bu teér/ *n* —**hagbutter** *n*

hagfish /hág fish/ (*plural same* or **-fishes**) *n* a primitive jawless fish with a long body and a sucking mouth that it uses for feeding off other fishes. Native to: seas worldwide. Family: Myxinidae.

Haggadah /ha gaádə/ (*plural* **-dahs** or **-doth** /-dōth/), **Haggada** (*plural* **-das** or **-doth**), **Aggadah** /agə daá/ (*plural* **Aggadoth** /-dáwt/) *n* **1.** RABBINIC LITERATURE ON BIBLICAL STORIES those sections of the Talmud and other rabbinic literature that deal with biblical narrative and stories and legends on biblical themes, rather than with religious law and regulations **2.** PASSOVER SERVICE, OR BOOK CONTAINING IT the service for the ritual meal (**Seder**) celebrated by Jews at Passover, or the book containing this service. It includes the story of the Exodus from Egypt. **3.** STORY OF ISRAELITES' EXODUS FROM EGYPT the account of the Exodus of the Israelites from Egypt that is central to the Jewish Passover ritual [Mid-19C. < Hebrew *haggāḏāh* 'tale' < *higgīḏ* 'tell'] —**haggadic** /ha gáddik/ *adj*

Haggai /hággī, hággay ī/ *n* **1.** in the Bible, a Hebrew prophet who urged the Israelites to rebuild their temple in Jerusalem in prophecies believed to have been made in 520 BC **2.** a book of the Bible that describes the rebuilding of the Israelites' temple after their return to Jerusalem from exile in Babylon and records the prophecies traditionally attributed to Haggai. See table at **Bible**

haggard /hággərd/ *adj* **1.** TIRED-LOOKING showing signs of tiredness, anxiety, or hunger on the face, e.g. dark rings around the eyes **2.** WILD wild and unruly in appearance **3.** BIRDS UNMANAGEABLE in falconry, used to describe a hawk that has reached maturity before being captured and is therefore wild and unmanageable ■ *n* HAWK in falconry, a captured wild adult hawk [Late 16C. < French *hagard* 'untamed' (used of hawks)] —**haggardly** *adv* —**haggardness** *n*

Haggard /hággərd/, **Sir H. Rider** (1856–1925) British novelist. He wrote *King Solomon's Mines* (1885) and *She* (1887). Full name **Haggard, Sir Henry Rider**

haggis /hággiss/ (*plural* **-gises**) *n* a Scottish dish made from offal mixed with suet, oats, onions, and seasonings, which is packed into a round sausage skin and usually boiled. Haggis is traditionally cooked in a cleaned sheep's stomach, but artificial casings are now frequently used. [15C. Origin ?]

ORIGIN One possible source of ***haggis*** is Middle English *haggen*, meaning 'to chop', a northern variant of *hack*. From this view, its name would refer to its chopped-up contents. An alternative possibility is Old French *agace*, meaning 'magpie'. This is supported by a parallel semantic development of English *pie*, which originally meant 'magpie' but was apparently applied to a 'pastry case with a filling' from the notion that the collection of edible odds and ends in a pie resembles the collection of trinkets assembled by the acquisitive magpie. The miscellaneous assortment of sheep's entrails and other ingredients in a haggis would therefore represent the magpie's hoard.

haggle /hágg'l/ (**-gles, -gling, -gled**) *vi* to argue over something such as a price or contract in order to reach an agreement [Late 16C. < variant of HACK[1]] —**haggle** *n* —**haggler** *n*

hagio- *prefix* saints, holy ○ *hagiolatry* ○ *hagioscope* [< Greek *hagios* 'holy']

hagiocracy /hággi ókrəssi/ (*plural* **-cies**) *n* **1.** government by saints, prophets, or other holy people **2.** a state or community governed by holy people

Hagiographa /hággi óggrəfə/ *n* the last of the three main parts into which the Hebrew Bible is divided [Late 16C. Via late Latin < Greek < *hagios* 'holy' + *grapha* 'writings']

hagiographer /hággi óggrəfər/, **hagiographist** /-fist/ *n* **1.** BIOGRAPHER OF SAINTS a writer of biographies of the saints **2.** REVERENTIAL BIOGRAPHER a writer of biographies that treat their subjects with undue reverence **3.** WRITER OF HEBREW BIBLE a writer of the Hagiographa

hagiography /hággi óggrəfi/ (*plural* **-phies**) *n* **1.** biography of a saint or the saints **2.** biography that treats its subject with undue reverence —**hagiographic** /hággi ə gráffik/ *adj*

hagiolatry /hággi óllətri/ *n* the worship or idolizing of saints

hagiology /hággi ólləji/ (*plural* **-gies**) *n* **1.** WRITINGS ABOUT SAINTS literature about the lives of the saints **2.** BIOGRAPHY OF SAINT a biography of a saint, or a collection of such biographies **3.** LIST OF SAINTS an authoritative list of saints **4.** SACRED WRITINGS a collection or history of sacred writings —**hagiological** /-ík'l/ *adj* —**hagiologist** *n*

hagioscope /hággi ə skōp/ *n* a narrow opening in an interior wall of a church that allows members of the congregation seated at the sides to see the altar —**hagioscopic** /hággi ə skóppik/ *adj*

hag-ridden *adj* **1.** plagued by fear or mental anguish **2.** an offensive term for a man thought to be troubled or dominated by women

Hague, The /hayg/ city in the western Netherlands, seat of the Dutch government and capital of South Holland Province. Population: 440,900 (2000). Dutch name **Den Haag**

hah *interj* another spelling of **ha**[1]

ha-ha[1] /haá haa/, **haw-haw** /háw haw/ *interj* **1.** in writing used to indicate the sound of somebody laughing **2.** used to tease or ridicule somebody (*informal*) ○ *'Where is it?' 'Ha-ha, wouldn't you like to know?'* [Old English. Natural exclamation]

ha-ha[2] /haá haa/, **haw-haw** /háw haw/ *n* a deep ditch or steep change in level, sometimes supported by a wall, that marks the boundary of a large garden but is not visible from within it [Early 18C. < French; probably < a cry of surprise when finding one]

hahnium /haáni əm/ *n* dubnium or hassium [Late 20C. After Otto *Hahn* (1879–1968), German chemist]

haick *n* CLOTHING another spelling of **haik**

Haida /hídə/ (*plural same* or **-das**) *n* **1.** a member of a Native North American people living along and off the coast of British Columbia and the adjoining Alaskan coast. The Haida are particularly noted for their intricately carved dugout canoes and miniature totems. **2.** the language of the Haida, now spoken by very few people [Early 20C. < Haida, 'people'] —**Haida** *adj* —**Haidan** *adj*

Haidar Ali /hídər aáli/ (1722–82) Indian soldier and ruler. The sultan of Mysore (1759–82), he waged war against the British in India and was defeated by Sir Eyre Coote (1781–82).

Haifa /hífə/ city and chief seaport of Israel, situated in the northern part of the country. Population: 265,700 (1999).

Haig /hayg/, **Douglas, 1st Earl Haig** (1861–1928) British field marshal. During World War I, he was made commander of the British Expeditionary Forces in France.

> 'Every position must be held to the last man: there must be no retirement. With our backs to the wall, and believing in the justice of our cause, each one of us must fight on to the end.'
> [Douglas Haig, *Order to the British troops*; 2 April 1918]

haik /hīk, hayk/, **haick** *n* a loose-fitting North African garment made from a rectangle of cloth, usually white, that is wrapped around the head and body. It is worn by men and women. [Early 18C. < Arabic *hā'ik*]

Haikou /hí kṓ/ capital of Hainan Province in China, on the northern side of the island of Hainan. Population: 280,153 (1991).

haiku /híkoo/ (*plural same*) *n* a form of Japanese poetry with 17 syllables in three unrhymed lines of five, seven, and five syllables, often describing nature or a season [Late 19C. < Japanese < *hai* 'amusement' (< Middle Chinese *bə ij*) + *ku* 'sentence' (< Middle Chinese *kuə h*)]

hail[1] /hayl/ *n* **1.** small balls of ice and hardened snow that fall like rain **2.** a barrage of something such as missiles or insults ○ *a hail of exploding flying glass* [Old English *hagol, hægl* < Indo-European] —**hail** *vi*

hail[2] /hayl/ *vt* (**hails, hailing, hailed**) **1.** ACCLAIM SOMEBODY OR SOMETHING to praise or approve a person, action, or accomplishment with enthusiasm ○ *The press hailed her as a child prodigy.* **2.** GET SOMEBODY'S ATTENTION BY SHOUTING to attract the attention of somebody or something such as a taxi or ship by calling or signalling ○ *hail a taxi* **3.** GREET SOMEBODY to welcome or greet somebody upon meeting ○ *We hailed each other like long-lost buddies.* ■ *interj* EXCLAMATION OF GREETING used to greet, welcome, or acclaim somebody (*archaic or literary*) [12C. Variant of HALE[1]] —**hail** *n* —**hailer** *n* ◇ **within hail** near enough to hear a shout or see a signal (*dated*)

hail from *vt* to live in or come from a particular place, especially as a birthplace or place of origin ○ *Her husband hails from Manchester.*

hail up *vt* to greet somebody upon meeting (*slang; used in Black English*)

Haile Selassie I /híli sə lássi/ (1892–1975) emperor of Ethiopia. He acceded to the Ethiopian throne in 1916 and was a modernizing emperor (1930–36, 1942–74). Born **Makonnen, Ras Tafari**

hail-fellow-well-met *adj* very friendly, especially in a way that presumes an intimacy that does not exist ■ *n* an exuberantly friendly person [< the greeting *Hail, fellow! Well met!*]

Hail Mary (*plural* **Hail Marys**) *n* a Roman Catholic prayer to the Virgin Mary based on Gabriel's and Elizabeth's greetings to her as recorded in the Gospel of Luke in the Bible. Churchgoers are often required to repeat the prayer as a penance, given in the sacrament of reconciliation. [Translation of medieval Latin *Ave, Maria*, opening words of the prayer]

Hailsham /háylshəm/, **Quintin Hogg, 2nd Viscount, Baron Hailsham of St Marylebone** (1907–2001) British politician. First elected to Parliament in 1938, he held many government posts, and was Lord Chancellor (1970–74, 1979–87). Full name **Hogg, Quintin McGarel**

hailstone /háyl stōn/ *n* a pellet of ice and hardened snow that falls like rain

hailstorm /háyl stawrm/ *n* a storm that includes a downpour of hail

Hainan /hí nán/ province in southeastern China comprising the island of Hainan in the South China Sea. Capital: Haikou. Population: 7,340,000 (1997). Area: 34,300 sq. km/13,200 sq. mi.

Haiphong /hí fóng/ city and seaport in northern Vietnam, on the Red River delta. Population: 783,133 (1992).

hair /hair/ *n* **1.** STRANDS GROWING ON HEAD OR BODY the mass of fine flexible protein strands that grow from follicles on the skin of a person or animal, especially those on somebody's head **2.** SINGLE STRAND a fine strand that grows out of the skin of a person or animal ○ *The rug was covered with dog hairs.* **3.** FINE GROWTH ON PLANT a thin flexible growth on a plant resembling a human or animal hair **4.** FABRIC fabric made from animal hair **5.** TINY AMOUNT a tiny amount or degree ○ *won by a hair* [Old English *hær* < Germanic] —**haired** /haird/ *adj* —**hairless** *adj* —**hairlessness** *n* ◇ **be tearing your hair out** to be very irritated or frustrated ◇ **have somebody by the short hairs** to have somebody in your control or power (*informal*) ◇ **let your hair down** to behave in a more relaxed way than usual (*informal*) ◇ **not turn a hair** to remain completely calm ◇ **split hairs** to argue about or give undue significance to fine distinctions and details ◇ **the hair of the dog (that bit you)** an alcoholic drink taken as a supposed cure for a hangover (*informal*)

zh vision. In foreign words: kh German Bach; aN French vin; aaN French blanc; ö German schön, French feu; öN French bon; öN French un; ü as in French rue. Stress marks: ´ as in secret /seékrət/, academic /ákə démmik/

hairball /háir bawl/ *n* a ball of hair that accumulates in the stomach of some animals such as cats and cows when they clean themselves. It often causes indigestion and retching.

hairband /háir band/ *n* a strip of fabric worn on the head to keep the hair in place or out of the eyes

~~hair-brained~~ incorrect spelling of **harebrained**

hairbreadth *n* same as **hair's-breadth** ■ *adj* exceedingly narrow

hairbrush /háir brush/ *n* a brush for smoothing and styling hair

hair cell *n* a sensory cell with fine projections resembling hairs, especially one in the inner ear that transmits information on sound or movement to the brain

hairclip /háir klip/ *n ANZ* HAIR same as **hairgrip**

haircloth /háir kloth/ *n* a thick coarse fabric made from horse's or camel's hair. Use: upholstery.

haircut /háir kut/ *n* **1.** a session in which somebody's hair is cut **2.** the shape or style in which somebody's hair is cut ○ *How do you like my new haircut?* —**haircutter** *n* —**haircutting** *n*, *adj*

hairdo /háir doo/ (*plural* **-dos**) *n* the way in which somebody's hair has been cut or styled (*informal*)

hairdresser /háir dresser/ *n* **1.** somebody whose job is to cut and style people's hair **2.** a shop or salon where a hairdresser works

hairdressing /háir dressing/ *n* **1.** CARE OF HAIR the cutting or styling of hair **2.** HAIRDRESSER'S PROFESSION the occupation of a hairdresser **3.** HAIR CARE PRODUCT a preparation used to style or care for the hair, especially an oil, cream, or gel

hairdryer /háir drī ər/, **hairdrier** *n* a device that uses heated air for drying hair, either hand-held or in the shape of a dome that fits over the head

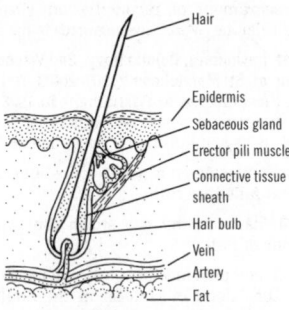

cross-section of hair follicle

hair follicle *n* a small tubular pit in the outer layer of skin (**epidermis**) enclosing the base of a growing hair

hairgrip /háir grip/ *n UK* a small metal or plastic pin bent double, used to grip the hair and keep it in place. ANZ, US term **bobby pin**

hairline /háir līn/ *n* **1.** WHERE HAIR BEGINS ON HEAD the line across the top of the forehead behind which the hair grows **2.** THIN LINE a very narrow line that is barely visible **3.** THIN STROKE a very thin line on a typeface, or a typeface containing thin lines **4.** FABRIC WITH FINE STRIPES a textile pattern of very thin stripes, or a fabric with such stripes

hairnet /háir net/ *n* a circular piece of fine netting with an elastic edge, worn to hold the hair in place, especially in bed

hairpiece /háir peess/ *n* a wig, toupee, or other piece of false hair, worn to conceal hair loss or to add bulk or length to somebody's natural hair

hairpin /háir pin/ *n* **1.** BENT WIRE FOR HOLDING HAIR a U-shaped piece of metal wire used to hold the hair in place **2.** U SHAPE something with a U shape, especially a sharp bend in a road **3.** SYMBOL FOR CRESCENDO OR DIMINUENDO a long V-shaped mark used in written music to indicate an increase or decrease in loudness (*informal*)

hairpin bend *n* a very sharp bend in a road or on a racing circuit that almost doubles back on itself. N Am term **hairpin curve**

hair-raising /háir rayzing/ *adj* causing intense fear or excitement —**hair-raiser** *n* —**hair-raisingly** *adv*

hair's-breadth *n* a very small margin or distance

hair shirt *n* **1.** a shirt made from a harsh scratchy haircloth that was once worn next to the skin by religious people as a form of self-imposed punishment **2.** a self-imposed punishment in the form of private suffering

hair slide *n* a decorative clip with a hinged back used to hold hair in place

hair space *n* the thinnest space used to separate words and letters in typesetting

hairsplitting /háir spliting/ *n* overattention to unimportant details and fine distinctions, especially in an argument —**hairsplitter** *n* —**hairsplitting** *adj*

hairspray /háir språy/ *n* a substance sprayed onto the hair to hold it in place

hairspring /háir spring/ *n* a very fine coiled spring that controls the movement of the balance wheel in a watch or clock

hairstreak /háir streek/ *n* a brown or greyish butterfly with delicate streaks on the underside of its wings and fine tails resembling hairs on its hind wings. Subfamily: Theclinae. Native to: tropical America.

hair stroke *n* a very fine line in writing or printing

hairstyle /háir stīl/ *n* the way in which somebody's hair is cut and arranged ○ *How do you like my new hairstyle?* —**hairstyling** *n* —**hairstylist** *n*

hair trigger *n* **1.** a gun trigger that needs very little pressure to activate it **2.** a response or mechanism that reacts to the slightest provocation or impulse (*hyphenated before a noun*) [< the thin spring that it activates]

hairweaving /háir weeving/ *n* the interweaving of a hairpiece with somebody's own hair, often done to disguise hair loss —**hairweave** *n*, *vt* —**hairweaver** *n*

hairworm /háir wurm/ *n* a long slender worm found in water or damp soil whose larvae live as parasites on arthropods. Phylum: Nematomorpha.

hairy /háiri/ (**-ier**, **-iest**) *adj* **1.** COVERED WITH HAIR covered with hair or filaments resembling hair **2.** MADE OF HAIR made of hair, or similar in texture to something made of hair **3.** FRIGHTENING filled with dangers or difficulties (*informal*) —**hairiness** *n*

hairy woodpecker *n* a large woodpecker with black-and-white markings and a long beak. Native to: North America. Latin name: *Picoides villosus.*

Haiti

Haiti /háyti/ country occupying the western third of the island of Hispaniola in the northern Caribbean. Language: French, Haitian Creole. Currency: gourde. Capital: Port-au-Prince. Population: 7,527,817 (2003). Area: 27,750 sq. km/10,714 sq. mi. Official name **Republic of Haiti** —**Haitian** /háysh'n, haa eesh'n/ *n*, *adj*

Haitian Creole *n* the French-based creole spoken in Haiti. Native speakers: 4 million. —**Haitian Creole** *adj*

Haitink /hītingk/, **Bernard** (*b.* 1929) Dutch conductor. One of the leading conductors of the later 20th century, he led the Concertgebouw Orchestra in Amsterdam (1961–88) and the London Philharmonic Orchestra in England (1967–79).

haj, etc. ISLAM another spelling of **hajj, etc.**

hajj /haj/, **hadj**, **haj** *n* the pilgrimage to Mecca, Saudi Arabia, that is a principal religious obligation of adult Muslims [Late 17C. < Arabic, 'pilgrimage']

hajja /hájjə/, **hadja**, **haja** *n* a Muslim woman who has made the pilgrimage to Mecca (*also used as a title*) [< form of Turkish, Persian *ḥājī* (see HAJJI)]

Hajjaj /ha jáj/ *n* the governor of the eastern provinces of India during the Arab Umayyad dynasty

hajji /hájji/ (*plural* **-jis**), **hadji**, **haji** (*plural* **-is**) *n* a Muslim who has made the pilgrimage to Mecca (*also used as a title*) [Early 17C. Directly or via Turkish < Persian *ḥājī* 'pilgrim' < Arabic *ḥajj* 'pilgrimage']

haka /háakə/ *n* **1.** NZ a traditional Maori war dance with vocal accompaniment by the dancers **2.** a version of the traditional haka performed by sports teams, especially the New Zealand rugby team [Mid-19C. < Maori]

hake /hayk/ (*plural same* or **hakes**) *n* **1.** a valuable food fish similar to cod that has two dorsal fins and an elongated body. Native to: seas worldwide. Genus: *Merluccius.* **2.** the flesh of a hake used as food [15C. Origin ?]

hakea /háaki ə, háy-/ *n* a bush or tree with hard woody fruit. Native to: Australia. Genus: *Hakea.* [Mid-19C. < modern Latin, after C. L. von Hake (1745–1818), German amateur botanist]

hakim[1] /ha keém/, **hakeem** *n* a Muslim doctor who uses traditional remedies [Mid-17C. < Arabic *ḥakīm* 'wise man']

hakim[2] /hə keém/ *n* a Muslim judge, ruler, or administrator [Early 17C. < Arabic *ḥakim* 'ruler']

Hakluyt /hák loot/, **Richard** (1552?–1616) English geographer. His works on English naval exploration include *Divers Voyages Touching the Discovery of America and the Islands Adjacent* (1582).

Hakodate /háakō daả tay/ seaport on Tsugaru Strait in southern Hokkaido, Japan, famous for its breweries. Population: 284,690 (2002).

haku /háakoo/ *n Hawaii* a crown made of fresh flowers

hal- *prefix* same as **halo-** (*used before vowels*)

Halab /há lab/ ♦ **Aleppo**

Halacha /hə laákə/, **Halakha**, **Halakhah** *n* the body of Jewish law beginning with the Pentateuch, developed by the rabbis [Mid-19C. < Hebrew *hă lākah* 'law']

halal /hə laál, hállal/ *adj* **1.** RITUALLY SLAUGHTERED describes meat from animals that have been slaughtered in the ritual way prescribed by Islamic law **2.** OF HALAL MEAT relating to halal meat ■ *n* MEAT FROM RITUALLY SLAUGHTERED ANIMALS meat from animals that have been slaughtered in the ritual way prescribed by Islamic law ■ *vt* (**-lals**, **-lalling**, **-lalled**) SLAUGHTER ANIMALS RITUALLY to slaughter animals for meat in the ritual way prescribed by Islamic law [Mid-19C. < Arabic *ḥalāl* 'lawful']

halala /hə laálə/ (*plural same* or **-las**) *n* a subunit of Saudi Arabian currency. See table at **currency** [Mid-20C. < Arabic]

halation /hə láysh'n/ *n* **1.** a blurred bright patch around a light source on a photographic image. It is caused by light being reflected off the film base and back onto the light-sensitive layer. **2.** a patch or ring of glowing light round a bright object on a television screen [Mid-19C. < HALO]

halberd

halberd /hálbərd/, **halbert** /-bərt/ *n* an axe blade and pick with a spearhead on top, mounted on a long handle and used as a weapon in the 15th and 16th centuries. See illustration on previous page [15C. Via French < Middle High German *helmbarde* < *helm* 'handle' + *barde* 'hatchet'] —**halberdier** /hálbər de̅e̅r/ *n*

halcyon /hálssi ən/ *adj* tranquil and free from disturbance or care (*literary*) ■ *n* **1.** in Greek mythology, a bird resembling the kingfisher, believed to have had the power to calm the waves at the time of the winter solstice when it nested at sea **2.** same as **kingfisher** (*literary*) [14C. Via Latin < Greek *(h)alkuōn*, mythical bird]

halcyon days *npl* **1.** a time of happiness and tranquillity (*literary*) **2.** two weeks of calm weather during the winter solstice

Haldane /háwl dayn/, **J. B. S.** (1892–1964) British geneticist. He specialized in the mathematics of natural selection and in haemophilia and colour blindness. He wrote for specialist and popular audiences and was a noted Marxist in the 1930s and 1940s. Full name **Haldane, John Burdon Sanderson**

> 'The layman finds such a law as dxdt = K(d–2xdy–2) much less simple than "it oozes", of which it is the mathematical statement.'
> [J. B. S. Haldane, *Possible Worlds*; 1927]

Haldane, Richard Burdon, Viscount Haldane of Cloan (1856–1928) British philosopher and politician. He is principally remembered for his term as secretary of state for war (1905–12), when he laid plans for troop mobilization prior to World War I.

haldi /húldi/ *n* turmeric used as a spice in Indian cuisine [Mid-19C. Via Hindi < Sanskrit *haridrā*]

hale[1] /hayl/ (**haler, halest**) *adj* in robust good health ○ *hale and hearty* [Old English *hāl* (see WHOLE)] —**haleness** *n*

hale[2] /hayl/ (**hales, haling, haled**) *vt* **1.** to compel somebody to go somewhere, especially to court (*formal*) **2.** to pull or drag somebody or something with great effort (*archaic*) [13C. Via French < Old Norse *hala*] —**haler** *n*

haler /haáلər/ (*plural* **halers** or **haleru** /-lə roo/), **heller** /héllər/ (*plural* **-lers** or **-leru**) *n* a minor unit of currency in the Czech Republic. See table at **currency** [Mid-20C. Via Czech < Middle High German *haller* 'silver coin', after *Hall*, town in SW Germany]

Haley /háyli/, **Alex** (1921–92) US writer. He is best known for his autobiographical novel *Roots* (1976), which won a Pulitzer citation and was made into an acclaimed TV miniseries. Full name **Haley, Alexander Murray Palmer**

> 'History is written by the winners.'
> [Alex Haley, *Interview, The David Frost Television Show*; 20 April 1972]

Haley, Bill (1925–81) US musician. He drew on his background in country and western and rhythm and blues in recording some of the first rock-and-roll hits, including 'Rock Around the Clock' (1955), with the Comets, the band he formed in 1952. Full name **Haley, William John Clifton**

> '*We* never sold no sex or sideburns. If we wanted to sell sex or sideburns, we'd have dressed differently.'
> [Bill Haley. Quoted in *All You Need is Love*, Tony Palmer; 1977]

half /haaf/ *n* (*plural* **halves** /haavz/), *det, pron* **ONE OF TWO EQUAL PARTS** either of two equal or nearly equal parts into which a whole can be divided ○ (n) *Arrange the apricot halves in a gratin dish.* ○ (n) *The recession began in the second half of 1990.* ○ (adj) *You don't have to pay for the first half hour.* ○ (det) *I'll pay half the bill.* ○ (pron) *I invited 20, but only half showed up.* ■ *n* **1.** SPORTS **PLAYING PERIOD** either of two periods of play into which some games are divided ○ *We started off well but failed to score in the second half.* **2. LOWER FARE** a fare costing more or less half the ordinary amount on public transport, usually for a child or senior citizen ○ *Two and two halves please.* **3. MEASURE OF BEER** a half pint of beer, lager, or cider **4.** *UK* **ONE OF TWO PARTS OF YEAR** either of the two parts into which an academic year may be divided ○ *We've got exams at the end of the half.* ANZ, N Am term **semester** ■ *adj, adv* **1. PARTIAL** to some extent but not complete or completely ○ (adj) *She gave me a half-smile* ○ (adv) *She was half laughing, half crying* **2. EQUALLY** in equal parts ○ (adj) *We each have half ownership in the building.* ○ (adv) *He's half French, half Spanish.* ■ *adj* **30 MINUTES AFTER** describes the time 30 minutes after a particular hour (*informal*) ○ *They're arriving for dinner at half six.* [Old English *healf* < Germanic] ◇ **by half** to a too great extent ○ *I don't trust him – he's too friendly by half.* ◇ **go halves (with somebody)** to share something equally with somebody ○ *If we go halves on the petrol the journey shouldn't be too expensive.* ◇ **half your luck** *Aus* used to express envy (*informal*) ◇ **not do things by halves** to do things thoroughly and often on a large scale ◇ **not half 1.** not at all ○ *Mmm! This cake's not half bad!* **2.** much less than half ○ *She's not half as busy as you are.* ○ *This isn't half the fun I thought it would be.* **3.** used as an understatement to indicate enthusiasm (*informal*) ○ *Just look at them – his new girlfriend can't half dance!*

USAGE Singular or plural? The pronoun ***half*** is singular in form, but the word is treated as plural when it is followed by a plural noun (with or without *of*) or when it refers back to a plural: *Half the people are late. The other half of them aren't coming at all. At least half are behaving inexcusably.* With many singular nouns, ***half*** can be used in the forms *half a share, half of a share,* and *a half share.*

---

half-a-crown *n* same as **half-crown**

half-and-half *adj* **WITH HALF OF EACH** containing half each of two things ■ *adv* **IN HALF** in two equal portions ■ *n* **1. TWO THINGS MIXED EQUALLY** a mixture of two things in equal parts **2. MIXTURE OF ALCOHOLIC BEVERAGES** an alcoholic drink made up of equal parts of stout and beer or bitter and mild

half-arsed /-aárst/ *adj* (*slang*) **1.** an offensive term meaning badly organized or carried out **2.** an offensive term meaning lacking forcefulness or effectiveness

halfback /haáf bak/ *n* **1.** SPORTS **PLAYER NEAR DEFENSIVE LINE** in a team sport, a player who is positioned just in front of the last defensive line **2.** SPORTS **POSITION OF HALFBACK** the position of somebody playing as a halfback **3.** FOOTBALL same as **midfielder** (*dated*) **4.** RUGBY **PLAYER BEHIND SCRUM** in rugby, either of the two players positioned immediately behind the scrum **5.** FOOTBALL **PLAYER IN FRONT OF BACKS** in Australian Rules, one of the three players playing in a line between the backs and the centre line

half-baked *adj* (*informal*) **1.** not well thought out and likely to fail **2.** lacking the ability to act with reason and common sense ○ *That's about what you'd expect from a department run by a load of half-baked idealists.*

halfbeak /haáf beek/ *n* a small fish with a short upper jaw and long lower jaw. Native to: warm seas, lakes, and rivers. Family: Hemiramphidae.

half binding *n* bookbinding in which the back and sometimes the corners of a book are bound in one material and the sides in another

half-blood *n* **1. HALF-BROTHER OR HALF-SISTER** somebody who is related to somebody else by having one parent in common **2. RELATIONSHIP SHARING ONE PARENT** the relationship between two people who have one parent in common **3.** *US* **OFFENSIVE TERM** an offensive term for somebody of racially mixed parentage, especially Native American and white

half-blooded *adj* **1.** having only one parent in common **2.** an offensive term meaning with racially different parents

half-blue *adj* at the universities of Oxford and Cambridge, a player who is a substitute for a blue or who plays for the university in a minor sport

half board *n* the price of a room in a hotel for a night with breakfast and one main meal included (*hyphenated before a noun*)

half boot *n* a boot that reaches anywhere from the top of the ankle to mid-calf

half-bound *adj* describes a book that is bound on the back and sometimes the corners in one material and on the sides in another

half-breed *n* **1. OFFSPRING OF ONLY ONE PUREBRED PARENT** a domestic animal with only one parent of known pedigree **2. HYBRID ANIMAL OR PLANT** an animal or plant that is a hybrid product of two distinct types **3. OFFENSIVE TERM** an offensive term for a person of mixed racial parentage, especially Native American and white (*insult*)

half-brother *n* a son of one of your parents by a different partner

half-caste *n* an offensive term for somebody of mixed racial parentage —**half-caste** *adj*

half cock *n* a position on a single-action firearm in which the hammer is half-raised and locked so that the trigger cannot be pulled ◇ **go off at half cock 1.** to fail because of poor planning, timing, or preparation **2.** to do or say something before thinking about it

half-cocked *adj* **1.** describes a single-action firearm with the hammer half-raised and locked so that the trigger cannot be pulled **2.** lacking adequate planning, thought, or preparation

half-crown *n* a former British coin worth two shillings and sixpence

half-cut *adj* rather drunk (*informal*)

half-day *n* either the morning or the afternoon of a normal working day, especially when taken as a holiday

half-dead *adj* tired and worn-out (*informal*)

half-dollar *n* a US coin worth 50 cents

half-forward *n* in Australian Rules football, any of the three players playing in a line between the centre line and the forwards

half gainer *n* a dive in which the diver jumps from the board facing forwards and then does a half backward somersault to enter the water headfirst, facing the board

half-hardy *adj* describes a plant that can survive outdoors in mild frosts

half-hearted *adj* with little enthusiasm and no real interest in the result —**half-heartedly** *adv* —**half-heartedness** *n*

half hitch *n* a knot made by looping a piece of rope round an object then passing the end of the rope round itself and through the loop

half-holiday *n* either the morning or afternoon of a normal working day or school day taken as a holiday

half-hour *n* **1.** a period of 30 minutes **2.** the point in time 30 minutes after the start of an hour ○ *Isn't that clock supposed to chime on the half-hour?* —**half-hourly** *adv, adj*

half-inch *n* a measurement of length equal to half an inch or roughly 13 mm ■ *vt Cockney* to steal something (*slang*) [As verb rhyming slang for 'pinch']

half-jack *n S Africa* a flat pocket-sized bottle of spirits (*informal*)

half-length *adj* **1. SHOWN ABOVE WAIST** describes a portrait depicting the subject from the waist up but including the hands **2. REACHING TO KNEE** coming down to the knee rather than the ankles ■ *n* **PORTRAIT FROM WAIST UP** a portrait depicting the subject from the waist up but including the hands

half-life *n* **1.** the time a radioactive substance takes to lose half its radioactivity through decay. Symbol $T_{\frac{1}{2}}$ **2.** the time it takes for half a given amount of a substance such as a drug to be removed from living tissue through natural biological activity

half-light *n* the soft dim light seen at dawn and dusk

half-line *n* MATHS same as **ray**[1] (sense 4)

half-marathon *n* a race on foot covering 21.243 km/13 mi. 352 yd

half-mast *n* the position, roughly halfway down a flagpole, to which a flag is lowered as a sign of respect when an important person dies —**half-mast** *vt*

half measure *n* an inadequate or ineffectual action

half-moon *n* **1. MOON VISIBLE AS SEMICIRCLE** the Moon when only half its face is illuminated during the first or last quarter **2. SOMETHING SEMICIRCULAR** anything with the shape of a semicircle or crescent **3. AREA OF FINGERNAIL** a pale semicircle at the base of the fingernail

half nelson *n* a hold in which a wrestler passes an arm under the opponent's arm from behind to the back of the neck and then levers the opponent's arm backwards [Because only one arm is held, whereas both are held in a full nelson]

half note *n N Am* MUSIC same as **minim** (sense 1)

halfpenny /háypni, -pəni/ (*plural same* or **-nies**) *n* a former British coin worth half an old or new penny, withdrawn in 1985

halfpennyworth /háypni wurth, háypərth/ *n* **1.** an amount of something that could be bought for half a penny (*dated*) **2.** a very small amount (*dated informal*)

half-pie *adj NZ* partly or poorly done (*informal*) [Origin ?]

half-pint *n* **1.** half of a pint **2.** an offensive term for a short person (*insult*)

halfpipe /háaf pīp/ *n* a structure in the shape of the bottom half of a pipe, built for freestyle snowboarding, in-line skating, and skateboarding

half-price *n* half the usual price ■ *adj, adv* at half the usual price

half relief *n* sculptural relief that projects roughly halfway from the background

half rest *n N Am* same as **minim rest**

half rhyme *n* an imperfect rhyme where there is a similarity in the sounds but not the identity of stressed vowels that is found in full rhymes

half seas over *adj* somewhat drunk (*dated informal*)

half-sister *n* a daughter of one of your parents by a different partner

half-size *n* a size that is halfway between two whole-numbered sizes ○ *Do you have half-sizes in this style?*

half-slip *n* a woman's undergarment that hangs from the waist and is worn as a lining for a skirt or dress

half sole *n* an additional layer on a piece of footwear that covers the wide part of the base

half-sole *vt* to put a new half sole on a shoe or boot

half step *n US* MUSIC same as **semitone**

half term *n* a short holiday for schools halfway through an academic term (*hyphenated when used before a noun*)

half tide *n* the time during which the tide is halfway between its high and low levels

half-timbered

half-timbered *adj* built with a visible frame of wooden beams as well as plaster, stone, or brick. Many Tudor buildings were half-timbered. —**half-timbering** *n*

half-time *n* a short break between the halves of a game, during which players rest

half title *n* **1.** the title of a book printed on the right-hand page before the main title page **2.** a title printed on a separate page at the beginning of a section of a book

halftone /háaf tōn/ *n* **1.** a shade or tone halfway between light and dark **2.** a photoengraving process by which shading is produced by photographing an image through a screen, then etching a plate so that the shading is reproduced as dots

half-track *n* a military vehicle with wheels on the front axles and continuous chain treads on the axles that supply motive power

half-truth *n* a statement that includes only some of the relevant facts or information and so is intended or likely to be misleading

half volley *n* a stroke or shot that makes contact with the ball immediately after it has bounced

half-volley *vti* to strike a ball immediately after it has bounced

halfway /háaf wáy/ *adv, adj* **1.** at or to the middle point between two things in space or time ○ *reach the halfway point* **2.** to only some extent, degree, or distance

halfway house *n* **1.** COMPROMISE a combination of the qualities of two things that may not be as good as either of them ○ *The style is a sort of halfway house between late romanticism and early modernism.* **2.** REHABILITATION CENTRE a hostel or centre designed to ease people back into society after their release from an institution such as prison or a psychiatric hospital **3.** HALFWAY TO END OF SOMETHING the halfway point in progress towards a goal **4.** STOPPING PLACE a resting place for travellers halfway through a long journey

halfwit /háaf wit/ *n* an offensive term for somebody who is regarded as behaving in a thoughtless or unintelligent way (*insult*) —**half-witted** /haaf wíttid/ *adj* —**half-wittedly** *adv* —**half-wittedness** *n*

half-yearly *adv, adj* done or happening every six months or in the middle of the calendar or financial year

halibut /hállibət/ (*plural* **-buts** or *same*) *n* **1.** a large flatfish. Native to: northern Atlantic, Pacific oceans. Genus: *Hippoglossus*. **2.** the flesh of a halibut used as food [15C. < form of HOLY + dialect *butt* 'flatfish' (< Middle Low German or Middle Dutch)]

Halicarnassus /hálli kaar nássəss/ ancient city near Bodrum in the southwestern part of present-day Turkey. It was the site of the Mausoleum, the tomb of King Mausolus, which was one of the Seven Wonders of the World.

halide /háylīd, hállid/, **halid** /hállīd, -lid/ *n* a chemical compound of a halogen with another element or group of atoms [Late 19C. < HALOGEN]

halier /hállyər/ *n* a subunit of Slovakian currency. See table at **currency** [Mid-20C. Via Czech < Middle High German *haller* (SEE HALER)]

Halifax /hálli faks/ **1.** manufacturing town in West Yorkshire, northern England, that grew up as a centre of textile making. Population: 91,069 (1991). **2.** Atlantic seaport and capital of Nova Scotia Province, Canada. Population: 276,221 (2001).

haliplankton /hálli plangktən/ *n* plankton found in the sea [< Greek *hals*'salt']

halite /háylīt, hállit/ *n* a colourless or white crystalline mineral consisting of sodium chloride. Source: dried up lake beds. Use: table salt, source of chlorine. [Mid-19C. < Greek *hals* 'salt']

halitosis /hálli tốssiss/ *n* MED same as **bad breath** [Late 19C. < Latin *halitus* 'health']

hall /hawl/ *n* **1.** ENTRANCE ROOM an entrance room in a house, flat, or building, with doors leading to other rooms **2.** CORRIDOR a connecting passage or corridor with doors leading to other rooms **3.** BUILDING WITH LARGE PUBLIC ROOM a building with a large room used for public events or activities such as meetings, entertainment, and exhibitions **4.** LARGE ROOM a large room in a building such as a school, university, or castle, used for such purposes as dining or receptions **5.** LARGE HOUSE the main house on a large estate **6.** DINING ROOM a large dining room in a university, college, or school **7.** EDUC same as **hall of residence** [Old English < Germanic, 'cover, conceal']

Hall, **Ben** (1837–65) Australian bushranger. He led several daring raids on mail coaches and banks in New South Wales, Australia. Full name **Hall, Benjamin**

Hall, **John** (1824–1907) British-born premier of New Zealand (1879–82). His government extended the right to vote to all men.

Hall, **Ken** (1901–94) Australian film director. He directed early Australian comedies, including *On Our Selection* (1932). Full name **Hall, Kenneth George**

Hall, Sir Peter (*b.* 1930) British theatre director. He led the Royal Shakespeare Company (1960–68), Covent Garden Opera (1969–71), and the National Theatre (1973–88) in London. Full name **Hall, Sir Peter Reginald Frederick**

'We do not necessarily improve with age: for better or worse we become more like ourselves.'
[Sir Peter Hall, *Observer*; 24 January 1988]

Hall, **Rodney** (*b.* 1935) Australian novelist and poet.

His works include *Captivity Captive* (1988) and *The Day We Had Hitler Home* (2000).

Hall, **Roger** (*b.* 1939) British-born New Zealand playwright. His plays include *Middle Age Spread* (1977). Full name **Hall, Roger Leighton**

hallah *n* JUDAISM another spelling of **challah**

Halle /hállə/ city in central Germany, situated on the River Saale, 50 km/31 mi. northwest of Leipzig. Population: 290,051 (1997).

Hallé /hállay/, **Sir Charles** (1819–95) German-born British conductor and pianist. He founded the Hallé Orchestra in Manchester in 1858. Born **Halle, Karl**

Hallel /háa layl, hállel/, **hallel** *n* Psalms 113 to 118, recited during the Jewish morning service at festivals as an expression of joy [Early 18C. < Hebrew, 'praise']

hallelujah /hálli loōyə/, **halleluiah**, **alleluia** /álli-/ *interj* **1.** USED TO EXPRESS PRAISE TO GOD used to express praise or thanks to God **2.** USED TO EXPRESS RELIEF used to express relief, welcome, or gratitude ○ *Hallelujah! The old car finally started.* ■ *n* **1.** CRY OF 'HALLELUJAH!' a thankful cry of 'hallelujah!' **2.** HYMN OF PRAISE a song or piece of religious music expressing praise to God [Pre-12C. Via Latin and Greek < Hebrew *hallělūyāh* 'praise ye the Lord']

Haller /hállər/, **Albrecht von** (1707–77) Swiss biologist. He wrote the great neurological and physiological treatise *Elements of the Physiology of the Human Body* (1757–66).

Halley /hálli, háwli/, **Edmond** (1656–1742) British astronomer. He is chiefly remembered for calculating the period of orbit (76 years) of the comet now named after him.

halliard *n* NAUT another spelling of **halyard**

Hall-Jones /háwl jốnz/, **William** (1851–1936) British-born prime minister of New Zealand (1906). A Liberal Party politician, he was briefly prime minister of New Zealand in 1906. He was the first premier to be officially called prime minister. See table at **prime minister**

hallmark (sense 3)

hallmark /háwl maark/ *n* **1.** MARK OF QUALITY a mark showing that something is of high quality **2.** DISTINGUISHING MARK a feature of something that distinguishes it from others ○ *Discreet service is the hallmark of a fine restaurant.* **3.** OFFICIAL MARK ON PRECIOUS METAL a mark stamped on articles made of gold, silver, or platinum to show that the metal used meets the proper standards of purity ■ *vt* (**-marks, -marking, -marked**) STAMP SOMETHING WITH MARK INDICATING QUALITY to stamp an object made of gold, silver, or platinum to show that the metal used meets the proper standards of purity [Early 18C. After *Goldsmiths' Hall* in London]

hallo¹ *interj*, *n* same as **hello**

hallo² *interj*, *n*, *vti* same as **halloo**

hall of fame *n* **1.** *N Am* a museum where portraits, memorabilia, or belongings of people who have excelled in a particular sphere of activity are displayed **2.** the group of people whose achievements in a particular field are at the highest level

hall of residence *n* a campus building where students live while attending a college or university. N Am term **dormitory**

halloo /hə loō/, **halloa** /hə lố/, **hallo** *interj* **1.** CALL TO ATTRACT ATTENTION used to try to attract somebody's attention **2.** CALL TO URGE ON HUNTING DOGS used to spur on dogs in a hunt ■ *v* (**-loos, -looing, -looed; -loas, -loaing, -loaed; -los, -loing, -loed**) **1.** *vi* CALL OUT 'HALLOO!'

to utter a call of 'halloo!' **2.** *vt* SPUR DOGS ON to spur hunting dogs on by shouting halloos **3.** *vt* SHOUT SOMETHING to shout out something to somebody [Late 17C. Alteration of *holla* < French *holà*] —**halloo** *n*

halloumi *n* FOOD another spelling of **haloumi**

hallow /hállō/ (**-lows, -lowing, -lowed**) *vt* **1.** to make somebody or something holy **2.** to have great respect or reverence for somebody or something [Old English *hālgian* < Indo-European] —**hallower** *n*

hallowed /hállōd/ *adj* **1.** holy or kept for religious use ○ *buried in hallowed ground* **2.** regarded with great respect or reverence ○ *the hallowed pages of our country's history* —**hallowedness** *n*

Halloween /hállō éen/, **Hallowe'en** *n* the eve of All Saints' Day, originally celebrated by Celtic peoples but now popular with children in the United Kingdom, the United States, and Canada. The children dress up, often as witches or ghosts, and play traditional games or go from door to door asking for sweets and saying 'trick or treat'. Date: the night of 31 October. [Late 18C. Shortening of *All Hallow Even*, the eve of All Saints' Day (see ALLHALLOWS, EVEN [2])]

Hallowmas /hállō mass/ *n* CALENDAR same as **All Saints' Day** (*archaic*) [14C. Shortening of *Allhallowmas* (see ALLHALLOWS, MASS)]

halls of ivy *npl US* institutions or an institution of higher learning, especially those regarded as particularly prestigious ○ *After four years in the halls of ivy, she had to adjust to a 9 to 5 job.* [< the traditional ivy-covered buildings]

hall stand *n* a piece of furniture, usually kept in the hall of a house, where people can hang their coats, hats, and umbrellas. N Am term **hall tree**

Hallstatt /hál stat/, **Hallstattian** /hal státti ən/ *adj* relating to or characteristic of a European culture of the late Bronze Age and early Iron Age [Mid-19C. After a town in Austria where a burial ground of this culture was found]

hall tree *n N Am* FURNITURE same as **hall stand**

halluces ANAT plural of **hallux**

hallucinate /hə lóossi nayt/ (**-nates, -nating, -nated**) *vti* to imagine seeing, hearing, or otherwise sensing people, things, or events that are not present or actually occurring at the time [Early 19C. < Latin *hallucinat-*, past participle of *hallucinari* 'dream, be distracted'] —**hallucinative** /-ətiv/ *adj* —**hallucinator** *n*

hallucination /hə lóossi náysh'n/ *n* **1.** the perception of somebody or something that is not really there, which is often a symptom of a psychiatric disorder or a response to some drugs **2.** something that somebody imagines seeing, hearing, or otherwise sensing when it is not present or actually occurring at the time (*often used in the plural*) —**hallucinational** *adj*

hallucinatory /hə lóossinətəri/ *adj* **1.** relating to or involving the belief that something is being seen, heard, or otherwise sensed when it is not present or actually occurring at the time **2.** causing somebody to believe that he or she is seeing, hearing, or otherwise sensing things that are not present or actually occurring at the time

hallucinogen /hə lóossinə jen/ *n* a substance, especially a drug such as LSD, that causes hallucinations —**hallucinogenic** /hə lóossinə jénnik/ *adj*

hallucinosis /hə lóossi nṓssiss/ *n* a psychiatric disorder that involves hallucinations

hallux /hálləks/ (*plural* **-luces** /hállyoo seez/) *n* the big toe on a human foot, or the first digit on the hind foot of some mammals, birds, reptiles, and amphibians (*technical*) [Mid-19C. Via modern Latin < Latin *hallus*]

hallux valgus /-válgəss/ *n* a medical condition affecting the big toe in which its tip points towards the little toe and its base sticks out on the inner edge of the foot [*Valgus* < Latin, 'bowlegged']

hallway /háwl way/ *n* BUILDINGS same as **hall** (senses 1–2)

halm *n* BOT another spelling of **haulm**

halma /hálmə/ *n* a board game similar to Chinese chequers [Late 19C. < Greek, 'leap']

Halmahera /hálmə héerə/ largest island of the Moluccas, Indonesia, situated on the equator. Area: 17,800 sq. km/6,873 sq. mi.

halo /háylō/ *n* (*plural* **-loes** or **-los**) **1.** CIRCLE OF LIGHT ROUND SAINT'S HEAD a ring or circle of light around the head of a saint in a religious painting **2.** IMAGINED AURA OF GLORY an aura of glory imagined to surround somebody or something famous or revered **3.** SOMETHING RESEMBLING RING OF LIGHT something that resembles or suggests a ring of light **4.** LIGHT CIRCLE AROUND MOON OR SUN a circle of light around the Moon or Sun, caused by light refracting from ice crystals in the atmosphere **5.** BODY OF STARS a thinly populated spherical region of stars and other luminous objects surrounding a galaxy ■ *vt* (**-los, -loing, -loed**) SURROUND SOMEBODY OR SOMETHING WITH HALO to surround somebody or something with a halo [Mid-16C. Via medieval Latin < Greek *halos* 'disc around the Sun or Moon']

halo- *prefix* **1.** salt ○ *halobiont* **2.** halogen ○ *halocarbon* [Via French < Greek *hals* < Indo-European]

halobiont /hállō bī ont/ *n* an organism that flourishes in a salty environment —**halobiontic** /hállō bī óntik/ *adj*

halocarbon /hállō kaárbən/ *n* a compound such as a fluorocarbon that contains carbon and a halogen

halocline /hállō klīn/ *n* a vertical gradient in the saltiness of the ocean

halo effect *n* the tendency to judge somebody as being totally good because one aspect of his or her character is good [< the haloes of angels]

halogen /hálləjən/ *n* any of the five electronegative elements, namely fluorine, chlorine, iodine, bromine, or astatine ■ *adj* describes lamps or heat sources that have a filament surrounded by halogen vapour ○ *a halogen bulb* [Mid-19C. < HALO-; because they readily form salts when combined with metals]

halogenate /hálləjə nayt/ (**-nates, -nating, -nated**) *vt* to treat or combine something with a halogen —**halogenation** /hálləjə náysh'n/ *n*

halon /háy lon/ *n* a stable halocarbon used to put out fires [Mid-20C. < HALOGEN]

haloperidol /hállō pérri dol/ *n* a tranquillizing drug. Use: treatment of schizophrenia, mania, and psychoses. [Mid-20C. < HALO- + PIPERIDINE]

halophile /hállō fīl/ *n* an organism that lives in salty conditions —**halophilic** /hállō fíllik/ *adj*

halophyte /hállō fīt/ *n* a plant capable of growing in salty soil —**halophytic** /hállō fíttik/ *adj* —**halophytism** *n*

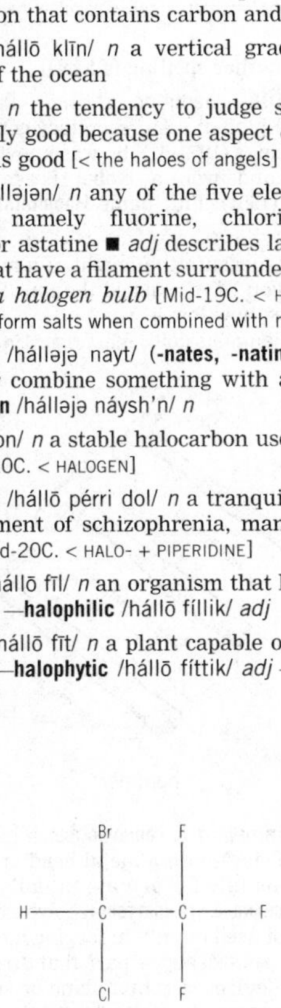

halothane

halothane /hállō thayn/ *n* a colourless liquid. Use: anaesthetic. Formula: $C_2HBrClF_3$. [Mid-20C. < HALO- + ETHANE]

haloumi /hə lóomi/ *n* a salty white Greek cheese with a rubbery texture that is usually grilled and eaten hot [< modern Greek]

Hals /halss/, **Frans** (1580?–1666) Flemish-born Dutch painter. He was known principally as a painter of lighthearted portraits. His work includes *The Laughing Cavalier* (1624).

halt[1] /hawlt, holt/ *n* **1.** TEMPORARY STOP an end or temporary stop ○ *The sudden rain brought the game to an abrupt halt.* **2.** SMALL RAILWAY STATION a small, often rural railway station, especially one that has no ticket office or public toilets ■ *interj* COMMAND USED TO MAKE SOMEBODY STOP used to command somebody to stop ○ *Halt! Identify yourself!* ■ *vti* (**halts, halting, halted**) STOP to stop, or make somebody or something stop [Late 16C. < German *halten* 'to stop, hold'] ◇ **grind to a halt** to come gradually to a complete stop

halt[2] /hawlt, holt/ *vi* (**halts, halting, halted**) **1.** ACT HESITANTLY to act or behave without certainty or confidence **2.** BE DEFECTIVE to have flaws or inconsistencies in logical development or in poetic rhythm **3.** OFFENSIVE TERM an offensive term meaning to have difficulty in walking (*archaic*) ■ *adj* OFFENSIVE TERM an offensive term meaning walking with difficulty (*archaic*) [Old English *healtian* 'walk with a limp' < Germanic]

halter[1] /háwltər, hólt-/ *n* **1.** BACKLESS GARMENT a woman's garment, worn between the shoulders and waist, that fastens or passes behind the neck and leaves the arms, shoulders, and back bare ○ *wore shorts and a halter on hot summer days* **2.** DEVICE FOR LEADING ANIMAL an arrangement of ropes or leather straps put over the head of an animal, especially a horse, and used to lead it **3.** ROPE FOR HANGING SOMEBODY a rope with a noose, used to hang somebody **4.** HANGING death by hanging ○ *destined for the halter* [< Old English *hælftre* < Germanic, 'hold on to'] —**halter** *vt*

halter[2] *n* INSECTS another spelling of **haltere**

haltere /hál teer/ (*plural* **-teres** /-téer eez/) *n* either of a pair of projecting parts in insects of the fly family that are rudimentary hind wings and are used to maintain balance in flight [Mid-16C. < Greek *haltēres* (plural) 'weights like dumbbells used in jumping' < *hallestai* 'to jump']

haltertop /háwltər top, hólt-/ *n* CLOTHING same as **halter**[1] (sense 1)

halting /háwlting, hólt-/ *adj* hesitant or done with frequent irregular pauses ○ *halting speech* —**haltingly** *adv* —**haltingness** *n*

halutz *n* JUDAISM another spelling of **chalutz**

halva /hálvə, hál vaa/, **halvah** *n* a confection made from crushed sesame seeds and honey with various flavourings, originally from Southwest Asia [Mid-17C. Via Turkish < Arabic *ḥalwā*]

halve /haav/ (**halves, halving, halved**) *v* **1.** *vt* DIVIDE SOMETHING IN TWO to divide something into two equal parts **2.** *vt* DISTRIBUTE SOMETHING EQUALLY to divide something equally between two people **3.** *vti* REDUCE SOMETHING BY HALF to reduce something by half, or be reduced by half **4.** *vt* GOLF DRAW HOLE OR MATCH in golf, to draw at a hole or match by playing the same number of strokes as an opponent [14C. < HALF]

halves plural of **half**

halwa /hál waa/ *n* in Indian cooking, a dish made of almonds, carrots, or semolina boiled with milk, sweetened with sugar and spiced with cardamom [< Arabic *ḥalwā* 'halva']

halyard /hállyərd/, **halliard** *n* a rope used to raise or lower something such as a sail or flag [14C. Alteration of *halier* < HALE [2]]

ham[1] /ham/ *n* **1.** MEAT FROM PIG'S THIGH meat cut from the thigh of the hind leg of a pig after curing by salting or smoking ○ *a slice of ham* ○ *a ham sandwich* **2.** PIG'S THIGH the thigh of the hind leg of a pig **3.** HOLLOW AREA BEHIND KNEE the hollow area behind somebody's knee ■ **hams** *npl* BUTTOCKS the back of somebody's thighs including the buttocks [Old English *hamm* 'back of the knee' < Germanic, 'be crooked']

ham[2] /ham/ *n* somebody, especially an actor, who performs in an exaggerated showy style ■ *vti* (**hams, hamming, hammed**) to behave, overact, or perform a role in an exaggerated showy style ○ *always hamming it up* [Late 19C. Origin ?] —**ham** *adj* —**hammy** *adj*

ham[3] /ham/ *n* a licensed amateur radio operator [Early 20C. Origin ?]

Ham /ham/ *n* in the Bible, the second son of Noah, formerly considered to be the ancestor of the Hamite people (Genesis 10:1)

Hama /haám aa/, **Hamāh** ancient city in west-central Syria, 121 km/75 mi. southwest of Aleppo. Population: 264,348 (1994).

hamadryad /hámmə drī əd, -ad/ *n* **1.** in Greek and Roman mythology, a minor deity who lives in a tree and dies when the tree dies **2.** ZOOL same as **king cobra** [14C. Via Latin *Hamadryad-*, *Hamadryas* < Greek *Hamadruad-* < *hama* 'together' + *Druad-* (see DRYAD)]

hamadryas baboon /hámmə drī əss-/ *n* a baboon, the adult male of which has a long silvery mane, that was sacred to the ancient Egyptians. Native to: northeastern Africa, Arabia. Latin name: *Papio hamadryas*. [Late 19C. Via modern Latin < Latin *Hamadryas* (see HAMADRYAD)]

Hamāh another spelling of **Hama**

hamal /hə máal/, **hammal**, **hamaul** *n* in an Islamic country, a porter or servant [Mid-18C. < Arabic *hammāl* < *hamala* 'carry']

Hamamatsu /háammə mát soo/ coastal manufacturing city in southern Honshu, Japan. Population: 573,504 (2002).

hamantasch /háamən tash/ (*plural* **-taschen** /-tash'n/) *n* a triangular pastry filled with spiced dried fruit or poppy seeds and eaten during the Jewish feast of Purim [< Yiddish < *Haman*, persecutor of the Jews in the Book of Esther + *tasch* < German *Tasche* 'bag, pocket']

hamartia /hə máarti ə/ *n* a flaw in the character of the protagonist of a literary tragedy that brings about his or her downfall [Late 18C. < Greek, 'error, sin' < *hamartanein* 'miss the mark, make a mistake']

Hamas /hámmass, ha máss/ *n* a fundamentalist Islamic Palestinian organization supporting and engaging in resistance to Israel in the Israeli-occupied territories [Late 20C. < Arabic *hamas* 'enthusiasm, zeal', identified with acronym < *harakat al-Muqawama al-Islamiyya* 'Islamic Resistance Movement']

hamate /háy mayt/ *adj* shaped like a hook ■ *n* a small hook-shaped bone in the wrist, at the base of the third and little fingers [Early 18C. < Latin *hamatus* < *hamus* 'hook']

hamaul *n* another spelling of **hamal**

Hamburg /hám burg/ city and major seaport in north-central Germany, situated on the rivers Elbe and Alster. Population: 1,705,872 (1997).

hamburger /hám burgər/ *n* **1.** CAKE OF MINCED MEAT a flat cake of minced meat, usually beef, that is grilled or fried and usually served in a bun **2.** MINCED-BEEF SANDWICH a sandwich containing a flat cake of grilled or fried minced beef or other meat in a bun, usually with other ingredients such as lettuce and condiments **3.** *N Am* MINCE minced beef [Late 19C. < *Hamburg steak*, after HAMBURG, Germany]

hame /haym/ *n* either of a pair of metal or wooden bars curved to fit over the neck of a draught animal and to which the traces are attached [14C. < Middle Dutch]

Hamersley Range /hámmərzli-/ range of mountains in northwestern Western Australia, containing large iron ore deposits

hametz *n* JUDAISM another spelling of **chametz**

ham-fisted *adj* clumsy with the hands (*informal*) N Am term **ham-handed** —**ham-fistedly** *adv* —**ham-fistedness** *n*

Hamhung /hám hŏŏng/, **Hamhŭng** industrial city in South Hamgyŏng Province, North Korea. Population: 709,730 (1993).

Hamilton /hámm'ltən/ **1.** industrial town in central Scotland, near Glasgow. Population: 49,991 (1991). **2.** seaport and capital of Bermuda, situated on Bermuda Island. Population: 1,000 (1990 estimate). **3.** city in southeastern Ontario, Canada, at the western end of Lake Ontario. Population: 618,820 (2001). **4.** city in the west of the North Island, New Zealand, situated on the Waikato River. Population: 138,792 (2001).

Hamilton, **Emma**, **Lady** (1765–1815) British courtier. She is remembered as the mistress of Horatio Nelson, with whom she had a child, Horatia Nelson (1801–81). Born **Lyon, Emma**

Hamilton, **James**, **3rd Marquis and 1st Duke of Hamilton** (1606–49) Scottish nobleman. He led an army into England in support of Charles I but was defeated at Preston by Oliver Cromwell (1648).

Hamilton, **Sir William** (1788–1856) Scottish philosopher. His *Lectures on Metaphysics and Logic* (1859–60) introduced Immanuel Kant to British readers.

'On earth there is nothing great but man; in man there is nothing great but mind.'
[Sir William Hamilton, *Lectures on Metaphysics and Logic*, Mamsel and Veitch (eds.); 1859–60]

Hamilton, **Sir William** (1805–65) Irish mathematician. He introduced the method of quaternions into algebra and helped to discover the wave theory of light. Full name **Hamilton, Sir William Rowan**

Hamiltonian function /hámmil tŏni ən-/ *n* a mathematical function used to describe the dynamics of a system such as particles in motion that uses momentum and spatial coordinates. Symbol *H* [Mid-19C. After Sir William Rowan HAMILTON] —**Hamiltonianism** *n*

Hamilton Island island and tourist destination off the east of Queensland, Australia, situated 1,160 km/719 mi. north of Brisbane. Population: 1,500 (1996).

Hamite /hámm īt/ *n* a member of a group of peoples who live in North Africa [Mid-19C. After HAM]

Hamitic /ha míttik, hə-/ *n* GROUP OF AFRICAN LANGUAGES a group of languages spoken in parts of northeastern Africa. Native speakers: 6 million. ■ *adj* **1.** OF HAMITES relating to the Hamites **2.** OF HAMITIC relating to Hamitic

Hamito-Semitic /hámmitō-/ *n, adj* LANG same as **Afro-Asiatic** (*not in technical use*)

hamlet /hámmlət/ *n* **1.** a small village or group of houses **2.** a group of homesteads or households [14C. < Old French *hamelet* 'small village' < *ham* 'village' < W Germanic]

hammal *n* another spelling of **hamal**

Hammarskjöld /hámmər shŏŏld/, **Dag** (1905–61) Swedish diplomat. As secretary-general of the United Nations (1953–61), he was known as a skilful mediator, and won a Nobel Peace Prize posthumously (1961). Full name **Hammarskjöld, Hjalmar Agne Carl**

'Never measure the height of a mountain, until you have reached the top. Then you will see how low it was.'
[Dag Hammarskjöld, *Markings*; 1964]

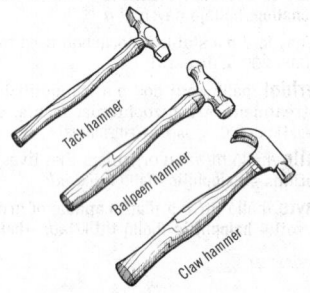

hammer

hammer /hámmər/ *n* **1.** POUNDING TOOL a hand tool consisting of a shaft with a metal head at right angles to it, used mainly for driving in nails and beating metal **2.** MECHANICAL STRIKING TOOL a powered mechanical striking tool used mainly in forging metal ○ *a steam hammer* **3.** STRIKING PART a part that strikes another in various devices, e.g. in a piano or striking clock **4.** ARMS PART OF GUN the part of the firing mechanism of a gun that delivers the impact that detonates the cartridge **5.** ATHLETICS OBJECT FOR THROWING a heavy metal ball attached to a handle of flexible wire, thrown in an athletics field event **6.** ATHLETICS same as **hammer throw 7.** AUCTIONEER'S GAVEL a gavel used by an auctioneer **8.** ANAT same as **malleus** ■ *v* (**-mers**, **-mering**, **-mered**) **1.** *vti* POUND SOMETHING IN to force something such as a nail into something else by pounding it with a hammer **2.** *vt* BEAT SOMETHING INTO SHAPE to beat something with a hammer, especially to shape it ○ *hammering tin into bowls* **3.** *vti* HIT SOMETHING HARD AND REPEATEDLY to hit or strike something hard and repeatedly ○ *hammering at the door* **4.** *vt* CAUSE SOMETHING TO BE REMEMBERED to cause something to be remembered, realized, or understood by repeating it forcefully and frequently ○ *They had caution hammered into them by the driving instructor.* **5.** *vi* MOVE WITH POWERFUL RHYTHM to produce fast powerful rhythmic movements or beats ○ *Their hearts were hammering.* **6.** *vt* DAMAGE SOMETHING SEVERELY to inflict serious damage on something **7.** *vt* BEAT SOMEBODY UP to beat somebody severely (*informal*) **8.** *vt* DEFEAT SOMEBODY BY LARGE MARGIN to inflict a convincing defeat on somebody, especially an opponent in a competitive sport (*informal*) ○ *Our team got hammered in last week's game.* **9.** *vt* CRITICIZE SOMEBODY OR SOMETHING HEAVILY to subject somebody or something to severe criticism (*informal*) ○ *The critics really hammered his last play.* **10.** *vt* FIN FORMALLY DECLARE

INSOLVENT to announce the insolvency of a member of the London Stock Exchange, who is then not allowed to trade **11.** *vt* FIN CAUSE STOCK MARKET TO DROP to cause a stock market to drop by suddenly selling a security or securities in large quantities [Old English *hamor* < Germanic, 'stone, stone tool'] —**hammerer** *n* ◇ **go at it hammer and tongs 1.** to do something with maximum energy and force **2.** to fight or argue violently ◇ **go** *or* **come under the hammer** to be up for auction or sale

hammer away at *vt* to work hard, determinedly, and steadily at something ○ *hammering away at the new novel*

hammer out *vt* **1.** SHAPE METAL WITH HAMMER to shape or reshape metal with a hammer **2.** AGREE ON OR ESTABLISH SOMETHING to agree on or establish something after prolonged discussion or argument ○ *hammer out a revised contract* **3.** PLAY MUSIC ENERGETICALLY to play a piece of music on a piano energetically and forcefully ○ *She can really hammer out a tune.*

Hammer /hámmər/, **Armand** (1898–1990) US industrialist, art collector, and philanthropist. He established trade links with the Soviet Union in the 1920s and increased his personal fortune in a long career in the oil industry. He made major gifts to US art and educational institutions.

'When I work 14 hours a day, seven days a week, I get lucky.'
[Armand Hammer, *Guardian*; 30 December 1990]

hammer and sickle

hammer and sickle *n* a symbol of Soviet Communism representing industrial and agricultural workers, used on the flag of the former Soviet Union

hammer blow *n* something that has a damaging or destructive effect ○ *This year's drought has been a hammer blow to farmers.*

hammer dulcimer *n* a large dulcimer played with light hammers and supported by a stand

Hammerfest /hámmər fest/ fishing port in northern Norway, the northernmost town in Europe. Population: 9,216 (1998).

hammerhead /hámmər hed/ (*plural* **-heads** or *same*) *n* **1.** FISH same as **hammerhead shark 2.** a large brown wading bird with a prominent crest on the back of its head. Native to: tropical African wetlands, ponds, and lakes. Latin name: *Scopus umbretta*. **3.** a fruit bat, the male of which has an enlarged square head and a muzzle shaped like the head of a hammer. Native to: Africa. Latin name: *Hypsignathus monstrosus*.

hammerheaded /hámmər héddid/ *adj* having a head that is wide and extends to each side of the body

hammerhead shark

hammerhead shark *n* a shark with a head that has a lateral extension on each side with an eye at the end. Genus: *Sphyrna*. See illustration on previous page

hammerkop /hámmər kop/ (*plural* **-kops** or *same*) *n* BIRDS same as **hammerhead** (sense 2) [Mid-19C. < Afrikaans *hamerkop* 'hammerhead']

hammerlock /hámmər lok/ *n* a wrestling hold in which an opponent's arm is twisted upwards behind the back [Origin ?]

Hammerstein /hámmər stīn/, **Oscar II** (1895–1960) US librettist. He collaborated with Richard Rodgers on some of the classics of the musical stage, including the Pulitzer Prize-winning *Oklahoma!* (1943) and *South Pacific* (1949).

hammer throw *n* a field event in which competing athletes try to throw a heavy metal ball attached to a handle of flexible wire as far as they can

hammertoe /hámmər tō/ *n* 1. a medical condition in which the joint between the two small bones of a toe is permanently bent downwards in a claw shape 2. a toe affected by hammertoe

Hammett /hámmət/, **Dashiell** (1894–1961) US writer. He helped to establish and define the detective genre with *The Maltese Falcon* (1930) and *The Thin Man* (1932). Full name **Hammett, Samuel Dashiell**

'Talking's something you can't do judiciously unless you keep in practice.'
[Dashiell Hammett, *The Maltese Falcon*; 1930]

hammock /hámmək/ *n* a hanging bed made of canvas or netting and suspended between two supports [Mid-16C. Via Spanish *hamaca* < Taino]

Hammond /hámmənd/, **Dame Joan** (1912–96) New Zealand-born Australian opera singer. She was a soprano who performed regularly at Covent Garden and with major opera companies around the world. She was also a championship golfer and swimmer. Full name **Hammond, Dame Joan Hood**

Hammurabic code /hámmoŏ ráabik-/ *n* the first known code of law, written down by Hammurabi, king of Babylonia (1792–50 BC)

Hampden /hámdən/, **John** (1594–1643) English political leader. He was the most notable of five MPs whose attempted imprisonment by Charles I in 1642 sparked the Civil War.

hamper[1] /hámpər/ *vt* (**-pers, -pering, -pered**) to restrict the free movement or progress of somebody or something ■ *n* equipment on board a ship that is essential but likely to get in the way [14C. Origin ?] —**hamperer** *n*

SYNONYMS See *hinder*[1].

hamper[2] /hámpər/ *n* 1. a large basket with a cover that is used for carrying food, especially for picnics 2. *N Am* a large basket with a cover that is used for holding soiled laundry [14C. < Anglo-Norman *hanaper* 'basket for holding goblets' < Old French *hanap* 'goblet' < Germanic]

Hampshire[1] /hámpshər/ (*plural* **-shires** or *same*) *n* 1. a black-and-white pig belonging to a breed developed in the United States from stock imported from Hampshire, England 2. a large sheep with a black face and no horns, belonging to an English breed [Mid-17C. After HAMPSHIRE[2]]

Hampshire[2] /hámpshər/ county in southern England, bordering the English Channel. Area: 3,769 sq. km/1,455 sq. mi.

Hampshire Down *n* BREED same as **Hampshire**[1] (sense 2)

Hampton /hámptən/ city and port in southeastern Virginia, situated on Hampton Roads opposite Norfolk. It is the home of Langley Air Force Base and Hampton University. Population: 145,921 (2002 estimate).

Hampton Court /hámptən-/ *n* a royal palace by the River Thames in southwestern London, mainly dating from the Tudor period

hamster

hamster /hámstər/ *n* 1. a small rodent with a short tail and large cheek pouches for storing food, often kept as a pet. Native to: Europe, Asia. Family: Muridae. 2. a cordless computer mouse that operates through an infrared connection [Early 17C. Via German < Old High German *hamustro*]

hamstring /hám string/ *n* 1. ANAT LEG TENDON either of the two prominent common tendons of the muscles (**hamstring muscle**) behind the knee 2. ANAT same as **hamstring muscle** 3. ZOOL TENDON IN ANIMAL'S LEG a large tendon at the back of the hock of an animal's hind leg ■ *vt* (**-strings, -stringing, -strung** /-strung/) 1. CUT HAMSTRING OF PERSON OR ANIMAL to cut the hamstring of a person or animal causing inability to use the leg normally 2. THWART SOMEBODY OR SOMETHING to make somebody or something powerless or ineffective ○ *hamstrung by lack of funds*

hamstring muscle *n* a muscle belonging to a group of three at the back of the thigh that control leg movements such as flexing the knee

hamstrung past participle, past tense of **hamstring**

Hamsun /hámsoŏn/, **Knut** (1859–1952) Norwegian author. His best-known work is *Growth of the Soil* (1917). He won a Nobel Prize in literature (1920). Pseudonym of **Pedersen, Knut**

hamulus /hámmyoŏləss/ (*plural* **-li** /-lī/) *n* a hook-shaped part at the end of a bone [Early 18C. < Latin, 'small hook' < *hamus* 'hook'] —**hamular** *adj* —**hamulate** *adj* —**hamulose** *adj* —**hamulous** *adj*

hamza /hámzə/, **hamzah** *n* a sign (ʾ) used in Arabic script to represent a glottal stop [Early 19C. < Arabic]

Han[1] /han/ (*plural* *same* or **Hans**) *n* 1. a member of a Chinese dynasty that ruled from 206 BC to AD 220 and was responsible for systematizing Chinese bureaucracy, promoting Confucianism, and consolidating Chinese government and territory 2. PEOPLES same as **Han Chinese** [Mid-18C. < Chinese *Hàn*] —**Han** *adj*

Han[2] /han/ ♦ **Han Jiang**

Hanabusa Itcho /hánnə boŏssə íchō/ (1652–1724) Japanese painter. He was noted for his caricatures and his depictions of city life. Born **Tage, Shinko**

Han Chinese *n* a member of the largest ethnic group in China, making up approximately 93% of the Chinese population —**Han Chinese** *adj*

Hancock /hán kok/, **Lang** (1909–92) Australian mineral prospector and industrialist. He is regarded as the founder of the Australian iron ore industry. Full name **Hancock, Langley George**

Hancock /hán kok/, **Tony** (1924–68) British comedian. Known for his lugubrious demeanour, he first came to stardom with the radio show *Hancock's Half Hour* (1954–59), later adapted for television (1956–61). Full name **Hancock, Anthony John**

hand /hand/ *n* 1. END OF HUMAN ARM the part of the human arm below the wrist, consisting of a thumb, four fingers, and a palm and capable of holding and manipulating things 2. ANIMAL PART CORRESPONDING TO HUMAN HAND the part of an animal's limb that corresponds to a human hand in shape or function 3. POINTER ON CLOCK a pointer on a clock, watch, dial, or gauge 4. PLAYER'S CARDS the cards dealt to a player in a card game ○ *a losing hand* 5. ROUND IN CARD GAME a round in a card game ○ *played one last hand of bridge* 6. CARD PLAYER somebody who plays a card game 7. INFLUENCE the influence or directing action of somebody or something 8. PART IN DOING SOMETHING a share in the performance of an action ○ *Who else*

had a hand in this? 9. HELP help to do something ○ *Give me a hand.* 10. OFFER OF AGREEMENT a sign of agreement or acceptance, especially of an offer of marriage ○ *Here's my hand on it.* 11. SIDE side or direction ○ *surrounded by enemies at every hand* 12. CLAP a round of applause ○ *a big hand for our next contestant* 13. POSSESSION OR POWER the possession, power, responsibility, or care of somebody (*usually used in the plural*) ○ *Your future is in your own hands.* 14. DEGREE OF CLOSENESS TO SOURCE a degree of closeness to actual involvement in something being talked about ○ *I heard about it at third hand.* 15. MEMBER OF SHIP'S CREW a member of the crew of a vessel ○ *Attention, all hands!* 16. SOMEBODY DOING OR MAKING SOMETHING a maker or doer of something, especially to a particular level of competence or experience ○ *I'm an old hand at this.* 17. WORKER a worker, especially one doing manual work ○ *a farm hand* 18. HANDWRITING somebody's handwriting ○ *an admirably clear hand* 19. SKILL ability or skill ○ *She has a good hand for gardening.* 20. APPROACH OR METHOD a distinctive way of doing something ○ *the bungling hand of an amateur* 21. SHOW JUMPING MEASURE OF HORSE'S HEIGHT a measure of the height of a horse, equal to 10.2 cm/4 in 22. PRINTING same as **index** *n* (sense 8) 23. FOOD INDUST BUNCH a bunch of something, especially bananas 24. FOOD INDUST CUT OF PORK a cut of pork from the front leg of the animal 25. *US* TEXTILES same as **handle** *n* (sense 4) ■ *v* (**hands, handing, handed**) 1. *vt* PASS SOMETHING BY HAND to pass something to somebody by hand ○ *She handed me a glass.* 2. *vt* LEAD SOMEBODY BY HAND to help or lead somebody by the hand ○ *She handed her aunt into the taxi.* 3. *vti* SAILING FURL to furl a sail [Old English < Germanic] —**handless** *adj* ◇ **all hands on deck** 1. used as a call or signal for all members of a ship's crew to assemble on deck, e.g. in an emergency 2. used to indicate that help is required from everybody available ○ *When the van arrives, it'll be all hands on deck to load it up.* ◇ **at hand** 1. nearby 2. about to happen ◇ **by hand** not using a machine ◇ **change hands** to pass to a different owner ◇ **force somebody's hand** to pressure somebody to do something against his or her will or earlier than planned ◇ **(from) hand to mouth** with barely enough to live on for your daily needs ◇ **hand in glove** in cooperation with somebody, usually for some secret or illegal purpose ◇ **hand in hand** 1. in close cooperation 2. inseparably closely 3. holding hands ◇ **hand over fist** in large quantities or amounts ○ *losing money hand over fist* ◇ **hold somebody's hand** to provide reassurance, guidance, and support to somebody ◇ **in hand** 1. under control 2. remaining or unused ◇ **not turn a hand** *N Am* to make no attempt to help somebody ◇ **off somebody's hands** no longer somebody's responsibility or problem ◇ **on hand** near and available ◇ **on the one hand...on the other hand...** used to present two conflicting aspects of a situation ○ *On the one hand we have plenty of time, but on the other hand our resources are limited.* ◇ **out of hand** 1. out of control ○ *The situation's getting out of hand.* 2. immediately and without consideration or explanation ○ *My suggestions were dismissed out of hand.* ◇ **out of somebody's hands** unable to be influenced by somebody ◇ **overplay your hand** to make overconfident use of an advantage and fail as a result ◇ **put your hand up to** 1. to volunteer to do something ○ *If you want to get into this type of work, put your hand up to do unpaid work experience.* 2. to acknowledge or accept something ○ *You have an ethical and professional obligation to put your hand up to this problem.* ◇ **show your hand** to reveal your plans or intentions ◇ **take somebody** or **something in hand** to begin to bring somebody or something under control ◇ **throw in your hand** 1. to admit defeat in a card game by laying your cards down 2. to admit or accept defeat ◇ **to hand** close by ◇ **try your hand at something** to make an attempt at something, usually for the first time ◇ **turn your hand to something** to do something for the first time and be competent at it ◇ **wait on somebody hand and foot** to attend to somebody's every need, often with bad grace ◇ **wash your hands of somebody** or **something** to refuse to continue being responsible for somebody or something

hand down *vt* 1. BEQUEATH SOMETHING to pass something on to a later generation or time 2. PASS CLOTHES ON to pass clothes on from an older to a younger child 3. *N Am* PRONOUNCE VERDICT OR SENTENCE to decide on a verdict or sentence and announce it in court

hand in *vt* 1. to give or submit something to some-

body ○ *handed in her notice* **2.** to return or surrender something, especially something lost or illegal
hand off *vt* in rugby, to push or hold an opponent away or deflect a tackle with an open hand
hand on *vt* to pass something to the next person or generation
hand out *vt* **1.** to distribute or give something by hand **2.** to administer or award something
hand over *v* **1.** *vt* to surrender somebody, or give something away to somebody else ○ *handed over the suspects* **2.** *vti* to transfer control of a commentary during a broadcast to somebody else ○ *I'll now hand you over to our match commentator.*

HAND *abbr* ONLINE have a nice day (*used in e-mails or text messages*)

hand axe *n* a chipped stone tool rounded at one end and pointed at the other, used for a variety of purposes during the Lower and Middle Palaeolithic periods

handbag /hánd bag/ *n* **1. WOMAN'S SMALL BAG** a small bag, with or without a strap or handle, used by women to carry personal items such as keys, money, and cosmetics. N Am term **purse 2. TRAVELLING BAG** a small light travelling bag that is easily carried by hand ■ *vt* (**-bags, -bagging, -bagged**) **ATTACK SOMEBODY OR SOMETHING VERBALLY** to make a strong verbal attack on somebody or something (*informal; refers to women*)

handball /hánd bawl/ *n* **1. PROHIBITED HANDLING OF FOOTBALL** in football, a rule infringement committed when a player other than a goalkeeper inside his or her penalty area uses a hand to control the ball **2. BALL GAME PLAYED AGAINST WALL** a game for two or four people in which players hit a small hard ball against a wall with their hands **3. BALL USED IN HANDBALL** the small hard rubber or synthetic ball used in the game of handball **4. GOAL-SCORING BALL GAME** a team game similar to basketball in which players dribble the ball and pass it, and goals are scored by hitting the ball into the goal with the hand **5.** FOOTBALL same as **handpass** ■ *vi* (**-balls, -balling, -balled**) FOOTBALL same as **handpass** —**handballer** *n*

handbarrow /hánd barrō/ *n* a flat rectangular board for transporting loads that has a pair of handles at each end and is carried by two people

handbasin /hánd bayss'n/ *n* same as **washbasin**

handbell /hánd bel/ *n* a small bell held in the hand to be rung, often one of a tuned set used to play a musical piece or to practise ring-changing

handbill /hánd bil/ *n* a small sheet of paper with a notice or advertisement printed on it, distributed by hand

handblown /hánd blōn/ *adj* describes glassware blown using a hand-held tube ○ *a handblown vase*

handbook /hánd bŏŏk/ *n* **1. REFERENCE BOOK** a reference book, especially one small enough to be carried in the hand, giving concise information on a particular subject ○ *a handbook of English–French expressions* **2. MANUAL** a concise manual explaining how something works or how to use it **3. SHORT TRAVEL GUIDE** a concise guide designed to help travellers and tourists find their way around a region, city, or other geographical location

handbrake /hánd brayk/ *n* **1.** a brake operated manually by a lever, used to prevent a vehicle from rolling when stationary. N Am term **emergency brake 2.** either of two manual brakes on the handlebars of a bicycle or motorcycle, used to slow or stop the vehicle

handbreadth /hánd bredth, -breth/, **hand's-breadth** *n* the width of a hand, used as an approximate measure of length

h & c *abbr* hot and cold (water)

handcart /hánd kaart/ *n* a small cart with two or four wheels, pulled or pushed by hand

handclap /hánd klap/ *n* a clapping of the hands, done to gain attention, applaud, or keep a rhythm

handclasp /hánd klaasp/ *n US* same as **handshake** (sense 1)

handcraft /hánd kraaft/ *n* ARTS same as **handicraft** (sense 3) ■ *vt* (**-crafts, -crafting, -crafted**) to make something using manual skill —**handcrafter** *n*

handcuff /hánd kuf/ *n* **WRIST RESTRAINTS** either of a pair of joined metal rings locked around somebody's wrists as a restraint (*usually used in the plural*) ■ *vt* (**-cuffs, -cuffing, -cuffed**) **1. PUT SOMEBODY IN HANDCUFFS** to restrain somebody by using handcuffs **2. GREATLY HAMPER SOMEBODY OR SOMETHING** to make somebody or something ineffective ○ *handcuffed by bureaucratic regulations*

-handed *suffix* **1.** using or involving a particular hand ○ *right-handed* **2.** involving a particular number of people ○ *four-handed chess*

handedness /hándidnəss/ *n* **1.** the tendency to prefer the use of one hand over the other **2.** the property of some objects whereby they cannot be superimposed on their mirror images

AKG London
George Frederick Handel

Handel /hánd'l/, **George Frederick** (1685–1759) German-born British composer. He is best known for his oratorio *Messiah* (1742) and the orchestral suites *Music for the Royal Fireworks* (1749) and *Water Music* (1717). Born **Händel Georg Friedrich**

hand-eye coordination *n* the ability to perform tasks that involve coordinating the movement of the hands and eyes, e.g. catching or hitting a ball

handfeed /hánd feed/ (**-feeds, -feeding, -fed** /-fed/) *vt* **1.** to feed a person or animal by hand **2.** to feed material into a machine by hand rather than by means of an automatic or machine feed

handful /hánd fŏŏl/ *n* **1. AMOUNT CONTAINED BY HAND** an amount that can be held in the hand **2. SMALL AMOUNT OR NUMBER** a small amount or number of people or things ○ *Only a handful of students turned up for the lecture.* **3. SOMEBODY OR SOMETHING DIFFICULT** somebody or something that is difficult to cope with or control (*informal*) ○ *Together those two are a real handful!*

CULTURAL NOTE ***A Handful of Dust***, a novel (1934) by Evelyn Waugh. One of Waugh's early satires, it tells the story of Tony Last, a haughty country gentleman whose wife leaves him for a young socialite. His response is to set off on an ill-advised expedition to South America, where he ends up the captive of an eccentric local with a penchant for Dickens.

hand glass *n* **1.** a magnifying glass with a handle for holding in the hand **2.** a small mirror for holding in the hand (*dated*) **3.** GARDENING same as **cold frame**

hand grenade *n* a small bomb designed to be thrown by hand and detonated by a time fuse

handgrip /hánd grip/ *n* **1.** same as **grip** *n* (sense 2) **2. HANDLE** a handle, or the part of something that can be held with the hand ○ *My motorbike needs a new handgrip.* **3. COVERING FOR HANDLE** a piece of material that covers a handle and makes it easier to keep hold of **4. TRAVELLING BAG** a small light travelling bag that is easily carried by hand

handgun /hánd gun/ *n* a gun that can be held and fired in one hand

hand-held *adj* **1. HELD IN HAND** made to be operated while held in the hand **2.** CINEMA, MEDIA **SHOT WITH PORTABLE CAMERA** filmed with a camera that is carried by the operator rather than mounted on a support ○ *black-and-white hand-held footage* ■ *n* COMPUT **SMALL COMPUTER** a pocket-sized computer or personal digital assistant that accepts handwritten or keyboard input

handhold /hánd hōld/ *n* **1.** something that somebody climbing can grasp for support, e.g. a projecting piece of rock or a fissure in a cliff face **2.** a firm grip with the hand or hands

handholding /hánd hōlding/ *n* the giving of reassurance and guidance to somebody

hand-hot *adj* describes hot water that is not too hot for putting the bare hands into

handicap /hándi kap/ *n* **1. HINDRANCE** something that hinders or is a disadvantage to somebody or something **2.** HORSERACING, SPORTS **BALANCED CONTEST** a contest, especially a horse race, in which individual competitors are given an advantage or disadvantage in an attempt to give every contestant an equal chance ○ *a handicap race* **3. ADDED ADVANTAGE OR DISADVANTAGE** an advantage or disadvantage given to a competitor in a handicap **4.** GOLF **GOLFER'S COMPENSATION IN STROKES** a compensation in strokes given to a golfer on the basis of skill in past performances **5.** MED **MEDICAL CONDITION** a physical or mental disability (*often considered offensive*) ■ *vt* (**-caps, -capping, -capped**) **1. HINDER SOMEBODY OR SOMETHING** to hinder or be a disadvantage to somebody or something **2.** HORSERACING, SPORTS **GIVE HANDICAP TO COMPETITOR** to give an advantage or disadvantage to a competitor in a contest, especially a horse race [Mid-17C. < *hand in cap* 'betting game in which contestants place their hands in a hat with their wagers']

ORIGIN In the original game of ***handicap***, one contestant put up an item of personal property against something belonging to the other contestant, offering to exchange the one for the other. An umpire adjudicated on the difference in value between the two articles. The contestants then placed their hands in a hat, along with some forfeit money, and the way in which they withdrew their hands – full or empty – signified whether they accepted the adjudication. If they both either accepted or rejected it, the umpire got the forfeit money; if they disagreed, the one who accepted it got the money. The application to horseracing arose in the 18th century from the notion of an umpire adjudicating on the weight disadvantage to be given to a specific horse.

handicapped /hándi kapt/ *adj* **1. DISABLED** having a physical or mental disability (*often considered offensive*) **2. FOR PEOPLE WITH DISABILITIES** for use by people with disabilities ○ *the handicapped entrance near the car park* ■ *npl* **OFFENSIVE TERM** an offensive term for people who have a physical or mental disability

USAGE Although ***handicapped*** has a long history of use by those so affected, *disabled* and *people with disabilities* are preferred over the adjective and noun uses of ***handicapped*** when referring to people.

handicapper /hándi kappər/ *n* **1.** somebody who assigns handicaps to competitors in a contest, especially to racehorses **2.** somebody who forecasts horse-race results, especially somebody who provides published advice to betters

handicraft /hándi kraaft/ *n* **1. CRAFT** a craft or occupation in which manual skill is needed, e.g. weaving **2. OBJECT MADE BY HAND** something made using manual skill **3. MANUAL SKILL** skill in making things with the hands [13C. Alteration of HANDCRAFT, after HANDIWORK] —**handicrafter** *n*

handily /hándili/ *adv* **1. CONVENIENTLY** in a convenient way ○ *handily close to the station* **2. SKILFULLY** in a skilful way **3.** *N Am* **EASILY** in an easy way ○ *She took the second set handily.*

handiwork /hándi wurk/ *n* **1. SOMEBODY'S DOING** the result of a particular person's action ○ *The broken window was the handiwork of local vandals.* **2. WORK DONE BY HAND** work done or produced by hand **3. SKILL WITH WHICH SOMETHING IS DONE** the skill with which something is done, especially something requiring manual skill [Old English *handgeweorc* < *hand* 'hand' + *geweorc* 'body of work' < *weorc* 'work']

hand-jam *n* an act of wedging the hand into a rock crack to aid in climbing

hand job *n* an offensive term for the act of masturbation

handkerchief /hángkər chif, -cheef/ (*plural* **-chiefs** or **-chieves** /-cheevz/) *n* a square of cloth or absorbent paper used mainly to wipe areas of the face, especially the nose

hand-knit *vti* to knit something by hand, not on a machine

handle /hánd'l/ *v* (**-dles, -dling, -dled**) **1.** *vt* **TOUCH SOMETHING** to touch, pick up, or move something with the hands ○ *Don't handle the merchandise.* **2.** *vt* **OPERATE SOMETHING** to operate or make use of something with the hands **3.** *vt* **TAKE CHARGE OF SOMETHING** to take care of or be responsible for something ○ *Who handles the import side of the business?* **4.** *vt* **DEAL WITH SOMEBODY OR SOMETHING** to deal with or cope with

somebody or something ○ *She's good at handling difficult customers.* **5.** *vt* **BE MANAGER OF SOMEBODY** to manage or supervise somebody ○ *He handles a string of professional boxers.* **6.** *vt* **BE ABOUT SOMETHING** to discuss or deal with a subject ○ *an article handling the subject of global warming* **7.** *vt* **TRADE IN SOMETHING** to deal in particular goods, sometimes illegally **8.** *vi* **RESPOND TO CONTROL** to respond to control or use, often in a particular way ○ *The little yacht handled like a dream.* ■ *n* **1. PART FOR HOLDING OR OPERATING SOMETHING** a part of a thing by which it is held, moved, or operated **2. MEANS** an opportunity, pretext, or means of doing something **3. NAME** somebody's name (*slang*) ○ *What's your handle?* **4.** *UK, ANZ, Can* TEXTILES **FEEL OF TEXTILE** the feel of a fabric, used to determine its quality. US term **hand 5.** *US* GAMBLING **TOTAL AMOUNT BET** the total sum of money bet on a race, series of races, or other event [Old English *handlian* (verb), *handle* (noun) < HAND] —**handleability** /hánd'lə bílləti/ *n* —**handleable** *adj* —**handleless** *adj* ◇ **fly off the handle** to lose your temper, especially without justification (*informal*) ◇ **get a handle on something** to understand or be able to control a situation fully ○ *It's a difficult problem to get a handle on.*

handlebar /hánd'l baar/ *n* a bar with handles at each end, used to steer a vehicle such as a bicycle or motorcycle

AKG London

handlebar moustache: William II, Emperor of Germany and King of Prussia (photographed in 1898)

handlebar moustache *n* a thick broad moustache that curls up at the ends

handler /hándlər/ *n* **1. ANIMAL TRAINER** somebody who trains or manages a working animal, e.g. a police dog or a show dog **2. BOXER'S TRAINER** a boxer's trainer or second **3. MANAGER** somebody who manages the career of somebody or the running of something **4. DEALER OR OPERATOR** somebody who works or deals with a particular thing ○ *a baggage handler* **5.** COMPUT **PART OF COMPUTER PROGRAM** a part of a computer program that handles a particular operation or problem

handling /hándling/ *n* **1. WAY SOMEBODY HANDLES SOMETHING** the way in which somebody handles or deals with something ○ *The report criticized his handling of the affair.* **2. TREATMENT** the way in which a subject is treated or dealt with in a written work or other work of art **3. SOMETHING'S RESPONSE** the way in which something responds to control or use ○ *the car's excellent handling* **4. USE OF HANDS TO DO SOMETHING** the act of touching, moving, or operating something with the hands ○ *baggage handling* **5. COPING WITH SOMEBODY OR SOMETHING** the act of dealing with something, or of managing or supervising somebody **6.** COMM **TRANSPORT AND PACKAGING** the transport and packaging of goods ○ *The cost includes a charge for handling.* **7. RECEIVING STOLEN GOODS** the receiving of goods known to be stolen

handling charge *n* a charge levied by a shop or other organization for obtaining, packaging, and sending a particular item

handmade /hánd máyd/ *adj* made by hand, not by machine ○ *handmade furniture*

handmaid /hánd mayd/, **handmaiden** /-mayd'n/ *n* **1.** something that provides help or support in a subsidiary role (*literary*) ○ *Hard work and focus are the handmaids of genius.* **2.** a woman or girl servant (*archaic*)

hand-me-down *n* **1.** an item of clothing, usually outgrown, passed down from a family member or friend to another **2.** something taken up or used by a person or group that has been used before and discarded

hand-off *n* in rugby, a pushing or holding away of an opponent or a deflection of a tackle with an open hand

handout /hánd owt/ *n* **1.** something given as charity to somebody in need, e.g. money or food **2.** a document that is distributed to a group, e.g. a press release, an advertisement, or material accompanying a meeting or lecture

handover /hándōvər/ *n* **1.** a surrendering of somebody or a giving away of something to somebody else ○ *the handover of power to the civilian authorities* **2.** a transfer of the control of the commentary during a broadcast to somebody else

handpainted /hand páyntid/ *adj* painted individually by hand

handpass /hánd paass/ *n* in Australian Rules, a pass made by striking the ball with the fist ■ *vi* (**-passes, -passing, -passed**) in Australian Rules, to pass the ball by striking it with the fist

handphone /hánd fōn/ *n Malaysia, Singapore* TELECOM same as **mobile phone**

hand-pick *vt* **1.** to choose somebody or something with care and personal attention, especially for a particular purpose ○ *need to hand-pick people we can trust* **2.** to pick or harvest something by hand, not by machine —**hand-picked** *adj*

hand plant *n* in skateboarding, a move in which the board is held to the feet with one hand while the skateboarder performs a handstand on a ramp or obstacle with the other

hand press *n* a printing press operated by hand

handprint /hánd print/ *n* a mark or impression made by the palm of the hand and fingers

hand puppet *n US* same as **glove puppet**

handrail /hánd rayl/ *n* a rail to hold with the hand for support, e.g. at the side of stairs or a ramp

handsaw /hánd saw/ *n* a saw for use with one hand

hand's-breadth *n* MEASURE same as **handbreadth**

hands down *adv* **1.** in a way that is not open to question ○ *They won hands down.* **2.** without encountering any problems, obstacles, or opposition ○ *whizzed through the exam hands down* [< a jockey not needing to ride hard to win] —**hands-down** *adj*

handsel /hánss'l/, **hansel** (*archaic*) *n* **1. GOOD-LUCK GIFT** a gift given for good luck at the beginning of something, especially a new year **2. FIRST PAYMENT** a first payment for something, or the first money taken in by a new business ■ *vt* (**-sels, -selling, -selled**) **1. GIVE GOOD-LUCK GIFT TO SOMEBODY** to give somebody a good-luck gift at the beginning of something, especially a new year **2. INAUGURATE SOMETHING** to begin or launch something with ceremony **3. USE SOMETHING FOR FIRST TIME** to use or do something for the first time [14C. Blend of Old English *handselen* 'a handing over' + Old Norse *handsal* 'giving the hand']

handset /hánd set/ *n* the part of a telephone that is held in the hand and contains the parts used for speaking into and listening to

hands-free *adj* describes devices that allow somebody to use portable communications equipment such as mobile phones or two-way radios without having to hold them —**handsfree** /handz frée/ *adv*

handshake /hánd shayk/ *n* **1.** a gesture of gripping and shaking another person's hand, used as a greeting or farewell and to seal an agreement **2.** an exchange of signals between a computer and another computer or external device indicating that a link is established and communication is possible —**handshaking** *n*

hands-off *adj* not wanting or needing to interfere in or control something ○ *a hands-off policy with respect to the running of the business*

handsome /hánssəm/ *adj* **1. GOOD-LOOKING** with good-looking facial features or a pleasing general appearance **2. SUBSTANTIAL** pleasingly large in extent or size ○ *won by a handsome margin* ○ *earning a handsome salary* **3. PLEASINGLY WELL MADE** of obvious high quality ○ *published in two handsome volumes* [15C. Originally 'easy to handle', then 'handy, suitable'] —**handsomeness** *n*

SYNONYMS See ***good-looking***.

handsomely /hánssəmli/ *adv* in an amount that is more than expected

hands-on *adj* **1. USING SOMETHING** involving the actual use or doing of something ○ *a hands-on carpentry course* **2. INVOLVING PHYSICAL TOUCHING** involving physical touching of something ○ *a museum with hands-on exhibits for children* **3. PERSONALLY INVOLVED** giving personal attention to or taking personal control of somebody or something ○ *a hands-on manager*

handspike /hánd spīk/ *n* a metal bar used as a lever [Early 16C. Alteration of Dutch *handspaak* < *hand* 'hand' + *spaak* 'spoke']

handspring /hánd spring/ *n* a gymnastic movement in which somebody flips the body forwards or backwards and lands briefly on the hands before continuing the flip so as to land on the feet again

handstand /hánd stand/ *n* an act of balancing the body on the hands with the legs straight up in the air

hand-to-hand *adj* taking place at close quarters and involving bodily contact ○ *hand-to-hand fighting* —**hand to hand** *adv*

hand-to-mouth *adj* having barely enough money or food for daily needs —**hand to mouth** *adv*

handwork /hánd wurk/ *n* work done by hand, not by a machine —**handworker** *n*

handwoven /hánd wōv'n/ *adj* **1.** woven on a hand-operated loom, not a mechanical one **2.** woven using the hands

handwringing /hánd ringing/ *n* **1.** the demonstration or expression of concern about something, often without any constructive action being taken **2.** the repeated clasping and squeezing of the hands together as a result of anxiety or grief

handwrite /hánd rīt/ (**-writes, -writing, -wrote** /-rōt/, **-written** /-ritt'n/) *vt* to write something by hand using a pen or pencil

handwriting /hánd rīting/ *n* **1.** writing done by hand using a pen or pencil **2.** somebody's individual way of writing by hand ○ *I recognized my father's handwriting on the envelope.* ◇ **see the handwriting on the wall** to foresee a future disaster or decline in somebody's fortunes

handwritten /hand rítt'n/ past participle of **handwrite** ■ *adj* written by hand rather than typed or printed ○ *a handwritten letter*

handwrote past tense of **handwrite**

handwrought /hánd ráwt/ *adj* shaped by hand, especially by hammering

handy /hándi/ (**-ier, -iest**) *adj* **1. CONVENIENT** located in a convenient place, especially nearby and easy to reach **2. USEFUL** useful or easy to use **3. SKILFUL** skilful at doing a number of different things —**handiness** *n*

handyman /hándi man/ (*plural* **-men** /-men/) *n* somebody who is skilled at doing, or paid to do, small jobs such as household repairs

handyperson /hándi purss'n/ (*plural* **-persons** or **-people** /-peep'l/) *n* **1.** somebody who earns pay by doing varied small maintenance and repair jobs **2.** somebody who has the experience and skill to perform a variety of small maintenance and repair jobs

handywoman /hándi wŏŏmən/ (*plural* **-women** /-wimin/) *n* **1.** a woman who has the experience and skill to perform a variety of small maintenance and repair jobs **2.** a woman who earns pay by doing varied small maintenance and repair jobs

hang /hang/ *v* (**hangs, hanging, hung** /hung/) **1.** *vti* **SUSPEND** to suspend or fasten something so that it is held up from above and not supported from below, or be suspended or fastened in this way **2.** *vt* **FIX SOMETHING ON HINGES** to fix something such as a door on hinges so that it can move freely **3.** *vti* **DISPLAY PAINTING** to put pictures or paintings on display, or be put on display **4.** *vt* **PUT DECORATIONS ON SOMETHING** to decorate or furnish a place or object with something ○ *trees hung with lights* **5.** *vt* **PUT UP WALLPAPER** to fix wallpaper onto walls, usually using a paste solution **6.** (*past tense and past participle* **hanged**) *vti* **KILL SOMEBODY WITH ROPE** to kill somebody or yourself by fastening a rope round the neck and removing any other support for the body, or die in this way, especially as a form of legal execution **7.** *vt* **LET SOMETHING DROOP** to let something, especially the head, droop ○ *hung their heads in shame* **8.** *vi* **BE UNRESOLVED** to be unresolved or in doubt ○ *His academic future hangs in the balance.* **9.** *vti* **FOLD OR DROOP** to fold or bend something

over or across something, or be folded or bent over or across something **10.** *vi* DRAPE to drape from a point of suspension in a particular way ○ *The jacket hung badly on her.* **11.** *vi* ELAPSE SLOWLY to pass by or elapse slowly ○ *Time hung heavily when she was away.* **12.** *vt* LAW PREVENT JURY FROM DECIDING to prevent a jury from reaching a verdict (*usually used in the passive*) **13.** *vti* BASEBALL PITCH BASEBALL THAT FAILS TO BREAK in baseball, to pitch the ball in such a way that it fails to break, or be pitched in this way **14.** *vi* COMPUT ALLOW NO INPUT OR OUTPUT to refuse additional input and be unable to generate output until rebooted (*refers to computers*) **15.** *vt* COOK SUSPEND GUTTED ANIMAL to suspend meat or a recently killed game animal until the flesh begins to decompose slightly and becomes more tender and highly flavoured **16.** *vt* N Am MAKE TURN to make a particular turn, especially when driving a car (*informal*) ○ *hang a left* **17.** (*past tense and past participle* hanged) *vt* EXCLAMATION INDICATING ANNOYANCE used to express annoyance at something (*dated informal*) ○ *Hang it all!* ○ *I'll be hanged if I'll let them get away with this!* ■ *n* **1.** WAY OF HANGING the way that something hangs **2.** SLOPE a downward slope **3.** EXHIBITION OF ARTWORK an exhibition of artwork, especially paintings [Old English *hangian* (intransitive) < W Germanic] ◇ **get the hang of something** to learn a skill or activity ◇ **hang somebody out to dry** US to leave somebody to struggle through a bad situation without support (*slang*) ◇ **hang your hat** US to live in a particular place (*informal*) ○ *So this is where you hang your hat!* ◇ **not give** *or* **care a hang** (for *or* about somebody *or* something) to be completely unconcerned or indifferent about somebody or something (*dated informal*)

hang about *vi* same as **hang around** ■ *interj* used to ask or command somebody to wait (*informal*)

hang around *vi* **1.** to loiter or waste time **2.** to spend time regularly with somebody ○ *He hangs around with the drama crowd.*

hang back *vi* to show reluctance to do something

hang in *vi* to endure or persevere in doing something (*informal*) ○ *She hung in as long as she could.*

hang on *v* **1.** *vi* HOLD ON TIGHTLY to hold on tightly to something **2.** *vi* KEEP GOING to persist in an endeavour in spite of obstacles or difficulties **3.** *vt* DEPEND ON SOMETHING to be dependent on something **4.** *vi* WAIT to wait or show patience for a short time ○ *Hang on a minute while I find out.* **5.** *vt* LISTEN CLOSELY TO SOMEBODY to listen attentively to what somebody says ○ *hanging on his every word*

hang on in *vi* same as **hang in** (*informal*)

hang out *v* **1.** *vti* SUSPEND OUTSIDE to suspend something in the open air so that it will dry or so that it can be seen, or be suspended in this way ○ *hang the washing out* **2.** *vi* BE AROUND SOMEWHERE to be regularly present somewhere (*informal*) ○ *usually hangs out in the cafeteria* **3.** *vi* ASSOCIATE to spend time regularly with somebody (*informal*) **4.** *vi* N Am SPEND TIME SOMEWHERE to spend time somewhere in a casual or relaxed way (*informal*)

hang over *v* **1.** *vi* to be imminent or threatening for somebody or something, or be unwelcomely associated with somebody or something **2.** *vi* to be put off to a later date ○ *Our holiday plans will hang over until next year.*

hang together *vi* to be consistent or cohesive ○ *Everything in his story hangs together.*

hang tough *vi* to remain resistant or unyielding (*slang*) ○ *He hung tough all through the negotiations.*

hang up *v* **1.** *vt* to put something on a peg, hook, or hanger **2.** *vi* to end a telephone call by returning the receiver to its original position

hang upon *vt* same as **hang on** (senses 3, 5)

hangar /háng-gər/ *n* a large building in which aircraft are kept or repaired [Late 17C. < French, 'shed']

hangdog /háng dog/ *adj* having an expression that indicates guilt or sadness [Late 17C. Originally referring to somebody who deserved to be hanged like a dog]

hanger /háng-gər/ *n* **1.** FRAME FOR HANGING GARMENT a triangular frame of metal, wood, or plastic over which clothes can be draped for storage or display **2.** PEG OR HOOK FOR HANGING SOMETHING a support from which

something can be hung, e.g. a peg or hook **3.** SOMEBODY WHO HANGS SOMETHING somebody who hangs or suspends something **4.** SMALL WOOD a small wood on the side of a hill **5.** SHORT SWORD a short sword worn on a belt

hanger-on (*plural* hangers-on) *n* somebody who latches on to a richer or more prominent person or group in the hope of gain

hang-glider

hang-glider *n* an aircraft without an engine that consists of a rigid frame in the shape of a wing, with the pilot usually suspended in a harness below the wing —**hang-glide** *vi* —**hang-gliding** *n*

hangi /húngi, hángi/ (*plural same*) *n NZ* **1.** a pit for cooking outdoors, in which wrapped food is placed on hot stones and then covered with earth **2.** a feast consisting of food cooked in a hangi [Mid-19C. < Maori]

hanging /hánging/ *n* **1.** METHOD OF KILLING the act of killing somebody by putting the neck in a noose and removing any other support for the body, especially as a form of legal execution **2.** FABRIC HUNG ON WALL a drapery, tapestry, or decorative fabric hung on a wall (*often used in the plural*) ■ *adj* **1.** PUNISHABLE BY DEATH punishable by death, or seen as deserving the death penalty ○ *a hanging offence* **2.** SEVERE OR UNMERCIFUL tending to impose severe punishments, especially the death penalty ○ *a hanging judge* **3.** AT TOP OF SLOPE positioned at the top of a steep slope or height

hanging basket *n* a container for plants, usually trailing plants, that is hung up outside

hanging indent, **hanging indentation** *n* an indenting of all the lines of a paragraph of text except the first

hanging participle *n* GRAM same as **dangling participle**

hanging wall *n* the rocks that hang over a seam of coal or other mineral vein

hangman /hángmən/ (*plural* -men /-mən/) *n* **1.** an official who carries out the death penalty of hanging **2.** a game in which one player has to guess the letters of a word before the other player has drawn a stylized gallows, with one line for every wrong guess

hangnail /háng nayl/ *n* a small piece of skin partly detached from the side or base of a fingernail [Late 17C. By folk etymology < *agnail* 'corn on the foot' < Old English *angnægl* < *ang-* (< Germanic, 'tight') + NAIL]

hangout /háng owt/ *n* a place frequented by a particular person or group of people, especially for relaxation (*informal*) ○ *The café is a favourite teen hangout.*

hangover /háng ōvər/ *n* **1.** a set symptoms including headache, nausea, thirst, and sickness that result from drinking too much alcohol **2.** something that remains from an earlier time

Hang Seng index /háng séng-/ *n* an index based on the relative prices of selected shares on the Hong Kong Stock Exchange [After the *Hang Seng Bank*, Hong Kong]

hang ten *v Aus* to ride a surfboard with your toes hanging over the front of the board (*slang*)

hang time *n* **1.** the time that elapses between the time a computer freezes, preventing the user from accomplishing any useful work, and restarts, allowing work to resume **2.** the amount of time spent viewing a website. Longer viewing times are considered commercially more valuable, on the as-

sumption that the message is holding the viewer's interest.

Hangul /háng gōōl/, **hangul** *n* the alphabet used for Korean writing [Mid-20C. < Korean *han kul* 'Korea alphabet']

hang-up *n* **1.** a psychological or emotional problem or fixation about something (*informal*) **2.** a persistent impediment or source of delay ○ *Bureaucratic inefficiency was the main hang-up.*

Hangzhou /háng jṓ/ *n* seaport and capital city of Zhejiang Province in southeastern China. Population: 4,210,000 (1995).

Han Jiang /hán jyáng/, **Han** *river* of central China, a tributary of the River Yangtze and major trade artery. Length: 1,532 km/952 mi.

hank /hangk/ *n* **1.** LOOSE COIL OF FIBRE a length of fibre such as rope or wool that has been wrapped round itself to form a loose coil **2.** SAILING ATTACHMENT FOR SAIL a ring-shaped fitting that can be opened to secure the leading edge of a sail **3.** MEASURE LENGTH OF YARN a length of yarn when reeled. A hank of cotton is 767 m/840 yd. [14C. < Old Norse *hönk* < Germanic]

hanker /hángkər/ (**-kers, -kering, -kered**) *vi* to want something very badly and persistently ○ *hankers after something she can't have* [Early 17C. Origin ?] —**hankerer** *n* —**hankering** *n*

~~**hankerchief**~~ incorrect spelling of **handkerchief**

hankie /hángki/, **hanky** (*plural* -kies) *n* same as **handkerchief** (*informal*) [Late 19C. Shortening]

Hanks /hangks/, **Tom** (*b.* 1956) US actor. He won Academy Awards for *Philadelphia* (1993) and *Forrest Gump* (1994). Full name **Hanks, Thomas J.**

hanky *n* another spelling of **hankie** (*informal*)

hanky-panky /hángki pángki/ *n* **1.** frivolous and slightly indecent sexual activity **2.** illicit or suspicious behaviour ○ *suspected financial hanky-panky* [Mid-19C. Alteration of HOCUS-POCUS]

Hannibal /hánnib'l/ (247–183 BC) Carthaginian general. At the beginning of the Second Punic War (218–202 BC), he marched across the Alps to northern Italy with elephants and a 40,000-strong army. It is one of the most famous military exploits in history. He was less successful in a subsequent African campaign against Scipio, and died in exile.

Hanoi /ha nóy/ *n* capital city of Vietnam, located in the northern part of the country. Population: 3,734,000 (2000).

Hanover[1] /hánnōvər/ *n* city in northwestern Germany, situated on the River Leine. Population: 525,763 (1997). ■ former state and province in northern Germany

Hanover[2] /hánnōvər, ha nṓfər/ *n* the royal house of Great Britain from 1714, when the elector of Hanover ascended the British throne as George I, until 1901, when Queen Victoria died

Hanoverian /hánnō véeri ən/ *adj* **1.** OF HOUSE OF HANOVER relating to the British rulers from 1714 to 1901, belonging to the house of Hanover **2.** OF HANOVER relating to Hanover, Germany ■ *n* HANOVERIAN MONARCH a supporter or monarch of the British Hanoverian line

Hansard /hán saard/ *n* the official published reports of proceedings in the British or Canadian parliaments or of similar legislative bodies in the Commonwealth [Late 19C. After Luke *Hansard* (1752–1828), British printer]

Hanse /hánssə, hánzə, hanss/ *n* **1.** HIST same as **Hanseatic League 2.** the fee paid by a new member of the Hanseatic League [12C. < Old High German *hansa* 'troop, company']

Hanseatic /hánssi áttik/ *adj* relating to the Hanseatic League or one of the towns in it [Early 17C. < medieval Latin *Hanseaticus* < *Hansa* 'the Hanseatic League']

Hanseatic League *n* an organized network of towns in northern Europe between the 15th and 17th centuries that protected each other and promoted trade with each other

hansel *n* another spelling of **handsel**

Hansen's disease /hánss'nz-/ *n* MED same as **leprosy** [Early 20C. After Gerhard *Hansen* (1841–1921), Norwegian physician]

hansom

hansom /hánssəm/, **hansom cab** n a covered two-wheeled vehicle drawn by one horse and carrying two passengers inside while the driver sits outside on a raised seat at the rear [Mid-19C. After Joseph Aloysius Hansom (1803–82), British architect]

hantavirus /hántə vīrəss/ n a virus belonging to a group that affects small rodents and can be passed to humans, causing fever, headache, nausea, and vomiting [Late 20C. < Hantaan, river in Korea]

Hants. /hants/ abbr Hampshire

Hanukkah /hánnəkə, haʹan-, khaʹan-/, **Hanukah**, **Chanukah** n a Jewish festival marking the rededication to Judaism of the Temple in Jerusalem in 165 BC and celebrated by the kindling of eight lights. Date: from 25th day of Kislev, in December, for eight days. [Late 19C. < Hebrew hanukkah 'consecration']

hanuman /húnnoŏ maʹan/ n a slender long-tailed langur monkey, considered sacred in South Asia. Native to: South Asia. Latin name: Presbytis entellus. [Mid-19C. < HANUMAN]

Hanuman /húnnoŏ maʹan/ n in Hinduism, a leader of monkeys who assists Rama [Early 19C. < Sanskrit, 'large-jawed']

hao /how/ (plural same) n a minor currency unit of Vietnam. See table at **currency** [Mid-20C. < Vietnamese]

haole /hówli/ n Hawaii somebody, especially a white person, who lives in Hawaii but is not of Polynesian descent [Mid-19C. < Hawaiian] —**haole** adj

Haora /hówrə/, **Howrah** industrial port in Bangla State, eastern India, on the Hugli River, opposite Kolkata. Population: 1,008,704 (2001).

hap[1] /hap/ (archaic) n a happening or occurrence ■ vi (**haps**, **happing**, **happed**) to happen or occur [13C. < Old Norse happ]

hap[2] /hap/ n Scotland something used to cover a person or bed, e.g. a cloak or quilt ■ vt (**haps**, **happing**, **happed**) Scotland, US regional to wrap somebody up in warm clothes [13C. Origin ?]

hapax legomenon /háppaks lə gómmi non, -nən/ (plural **hapax legomena** /-nə/) n a word of which there is only one recorded use [Mid-17C. < Greek, 'said only once']

hapen incorrect spelling of **happen**

ha'penny /háypni/ (plural **-nies**) n COINS same as **halfpenny** [Mid-16C. Contraction]

haphazard /hap házzərd/ adj happening or done in a way that has not been planned [Late 16C. < HAP[1] + HAZARD, literally 'hazard of chance'] —**haphazardly** adv —**haphazardness** n

haphtarah /JUDAISM another spelling of **haftarah**

hapl- prefix same as **haplo-** (used before vowels)

hapless /háppləss/ adj unlucky or unfortunate —**haplessly** adv —**haplessness** n

haplite /hápplīt/ n GEOL same as **aplite** [Variant] —**haplitic** /hap líttik/ adj

haplo- prefix 1. single ○ haplology 2. haploid ○ haplont [< Greek haplous 'single' < Indo-European]

haplography /hap lóggrəfi/ n the accidental omission of a letter or written syllable that should be repeated, e.g. in writing 'mispell' for 'misspell'

haploid /hápployd/ adj having a single set of unpaired chromosomes —**haploid** n

haplology /hap lólləji/ n the accidental omission of one or more repeated syllables or sounds when speaking —**haplologic** /hápplə lójjik/ adj

haplont /há plont/ n an organism, especially an algal plant, that is haploid at one stage of its life cycle [Early 20C. < HAPLO- + -ONT] —**haplontic** /ha plóntik/ adj

haplosis /ha plóssiss/ n the production of haploids during cell division (**meiosis**)

haplotype /hápplə tīp/ n a segment of DNA containing closely linked gene variations that are inherited as a unit [Mid-20C. < HAPLO- + TYPE]

ha'p'orth /háypərth/ (plural same) n same as **halfpennyworth** (dated) [Late 17C. Contraction]

happen /háppən/ v (**-pens**, **-pening**, **-pened**) 1. vi OCCUR to take place ○ How did it happen? ○ a go-getter who can really make things happen 2. vt DO SOMETHING BY CHANCE to do something by chance and without a previous plan ○ If you happen to see him, give him these keys. 3. vi AFFECT SOMEBODY OR SOMETHING to affect somebody or something, especially in an unpleasant way ○ If anything happens to him, you'll regret it. 4. vti OCCUR BY CHANCE to occur or exist by chance ○ It happened to be the last one in the shop. ■ adv N England PERHAPS used to suggest that something may occur or be the case ○ Happen we'll go for a walk. [14C. < HAP[1]]

happen along, **happen by** vi N Am to appear or pass by chance or unexpectedly (informal)

happen on, **happen upon** vt to discover or encounter somebody or something by chance

happenchance /háppən chaanss/ n same as **happenstance** [Mid-20C. Alteration]

happening /háppəning/ n 1. OCCURRENCE something that occurs 2. ARTISTIC PERFORMANCE an improvised or informal performance or demonstration, often dramatic in form and using audience participation (informal) ■ adj FASHIONABLE at the forefront of what is fashionable and exciting (informal)

happenstance /háppʹn stanss/ n a chance occurrence or event [Late 19C. Blend of HAPPENING + CIRCUMSTANCE]

happi coat /háppi-/ n an open Japanese jacket that has wide loose sleeves and is usually tied with a sash, or a fashion garment resembling this [Late 19C. < Japanese happi]

happily /háppili/ adv 1. FORTUNATELY used to indicate that something that could have been difficult or disastrous is luckily not so ○ Happily, no one was hurt. 2. WILLINGLY with willingness ○ I'd happily contribute. 3. IN HAPPY WAY in a pleased, contented, or joyful way

happy /háppi/ (**-pier**, **-piest**) adj 1. FEELING PLEASURE feeling or showing pleasure, contentment, or joy ○ happy smiling faces 2. CAUSING PLEASURE causing or characterized by pleasure, contentment, or joy ○ a happy childhood 3. SATISFIED feeling satisfied that something is right or has been done right ○ Are you happy with your performance? 4. WILLING willing to do something ○ I'd be only too happy to help. 5. FORTUNATE resulting unexpectedly in something pleasant or welcome ○ a happy coincidence 6. TIPSY slightly drunk (informal) 7. USED IN GREETINGS used in formulae to express a hope that somebody will enjoy a special day or holiday ○ Happy birthday! 8. TOO READY TO USE SOMETHING inclined to use a particular thing too readily or be too enthusiastic about a particular thing (used in combination) ○ trigger-happy [14C. < HAP[1]] —**happiness** n

happy-clappy /-kláppi/ adj describes a style of religious worship, especially Christian worship, marked by enthusiastic singing of modern hymns written in a pop or folk style (informal disapproving)

happy event n the birth of a baby (informal)

happy-go-lucky adj tending not to worry about the future

happy hard core n uplifting hard-core music, often achieving its emotional effect by the use of piano riffs over straightforward rhythms

happy hour n a period of time, usually in the late afternoon or early evening, during which a pub or bar serves alcoholic drinks at reduced prices

happy hunting ground n 1. among some Native American peoples, a place of peace and abundance to which people are believed to go after death 2. a place that provides plenty of something desired ○ The arcade was a happy hunting ground for somebody looking for gifts.

happy medium n a satisfying compromise

happyness incorrect spelling of **happiness**

happy release n a release from a sad or deplorable condition, especially through death

Hapsburg another spelling of **Habsburg**

hapten /háptən/, **haptene** /háp teen/ n an antigen that can only stimulate antibody production when combined with a specific protein [Early 20C. < Greek haptein 'fasten']

haptic /háptik/ adj relating to the sense of touch [Late 19C. < Greek haptikos < haptesthai 'grasp, touch' < haptein 'fasten']

haptoglobin /háptə glóbin/ n a plasma protein that combines with free haemoglobin in the bloodstream [Mid-20C. < Greek haptein 'fasten']

haptotropism /háptō trópizəm/ n BOT same as **thigmotropism** [Late 19C. < Greek haptein 'fasten']

hapu /haápoo/ n NZ a principal social unit of Maori society, consisting of a group of extended families holding land in common or larger groupings [Mid-19C. < Maori]

hara-kiri /hárrə kírri, -keʹeri/ n in Japan, a traditional form of suicide, sometimes ritually performed as a point of honour, involving disembowelment with a sword [Mid-19C. < Japanese, 'belly-cutting']

Harald I /hárrəld/ (850?–933?) king of Norway. He unified Norway in a long military campaign culminating in the Battle of Hafrsfjord (about 885). Known as **Harald the Fairhaired**

haram /haa raám/, **haraam** adj describes food forbidden by Islamic law [Early 17C. < Arabic harām 'forbidden']

harangue /hə ráng/ (**-rangues**, **-ranguing**, **-rangued**) vti to criticize or question somebody, or try to persuade somebody to do something in a forceful angry way [15C. Via French < medieval Latin harenga] —**harangue** n —**haranguer** n

Harar ♦ **Harer**

Harare /hə raári/ capital city of Zimbabwe, located in the northeastern part of the country. Population: 1,752,000 (2000).

harass /hárrəss, hə ráss/ (**-rasses**, **-rassing**, **-rassed**) vt 1. to persistently annoy, attack, or bother somebody 2. to exhaust an enemy by attacking repeatedly [Early 17C. < French harasser < harer 'set a dog on (by crying "hare")'] —**harasser** n

USAGE The traditional pronunciation of **harass** (and its derivatives **harassed** and **harassment**) has the stress on the first syllable, but the variant pronunciation, with the stress on the second syllable, is also heard.

USAGE See **embarrass**.

harassed /hárrəst, hə rást/ adj stressed and anxious because of having too much to do or worry about

harassment /hárrəssmənt, hə rássmənt/ n behaviour that threatens or torments somebody, especially persistently

Harbin /haar bín/ capital city of Heilongjiang Province in northeastern China. Population: 4,470,000 (1995).

harbinger /haárbinjər/ n somebody or something that foreshadows or anticipates a future event [12C. < Old French herberger < herbergier 'provide shelter for an army' < Germanic] —**harbinger** vt

harbor n, vti NAUT US spelling of **harbour**

harbour /haárbər/ n 1. PORT a part of a body of water near a coast in which ships can anchor safely (often used in placenames) 2. PLACE OF REFUGE a place that is safe and sheltered ■ v (**-bours**, **-bouring**, **-boured**) 1. vt SHELTER SOMEBODY to provide somebody with shelter or sanctuary ○ accused of harbouring a fugitive 2. vt KEEP SOMETHING IN MIND to privately have and continue to keep in mind an emotion or thought ○ had harboured a secret fear of the dark since childhood 3. vt BE HABITAT FOR SOMEBODY OR SOMETHING to be a place where somebody or something can live or be found ○ Many patients now harbour bacteria resistant to these antibiotics. 4. vti NAUT KEEP SHIP IN HARBOUR to take shelter in a harbour, or shelter a ship in a harbour [Old English hereboorg 'lodging' < Germanic, 'army shelter'] —**harbourer** n

harbourage /haárbərij/ n NAUT same as **harbour** n (sense 1)

harbour master n an official who supervises and administers the general activities of a harbour or port

harbour seal *n* a small seal that is greyish-black with paler spots. Native to: northern coasts of North America, Europe, and Asia. Latin name: *Phoca vitulina.*

hard /haard/ *adj* **1.** NOT EASILY BENT firm, stiff, or rigid, and not easily cut, pierced, or bent ○ *a hard mattress* ○ *Do not move the object until the glue has gone hard.* **2.** DIFFICULT OR AWKWARD difficult or awkward to do or achieve ○ *a hard decision* **3.** DIFFICULT TO UNDERSTAND difficult to understand or explain **4.** INVOLVING EFFORT involving a great deal of mental or physical effort or exertion ○ *a hard climb* **5.** PERFORMING ENERGETICALLY doing something with energy or industriousness ○ *a hard worker* **6.** MIGHTY using a lot of force or violence ○ *a hard tug on the rope* **7.** DEMANDING AND STRICT making inflexible and heavy demands ○ *a hard taskmaster* **8.** PROBLEMATIC difficult to endure and full of problems ○ *a hard life* **9.** UNSYMPATHETIC showing little or no sympathy, compassion, or gentleness ○ *She's as hard as nails.* **10.** RESENTFUL marked by resentment or bitterness ○ *no hard feelings* **11.** REAL OR TRUE demonstrably real, true, or certain ○ *cold hard facts* **12.** PENETRATING seeming to penetrate and discover intentions or thoughts ○ *a hard stare* **13.** TOUGH tough, violent, and ruthless ○ *a hard man* **14.** POL RADICAL politically radical or extreme ○ *the hard left* **15.** SEVERE marked by weather conditions such as extreme cold or severe storms ○ *a hard winter* **16.** TOUGHENED rough or leathery, and unyielding ○ *hard skin* **17.** CHEM CONTAINING MINERAL SALTS containing mineral salts and preventing soap from lathering well ○ *hard water* **18.** FIRM OR CRISP IN TEXTURE having a crisp, firm, or stale crust or texture **19.** ERECT stiff and erect (*informal*) **20.** SOC SCI same as **hard-core** (sense 2) **21.** PHYS EASILY ABLE TO PENETRATE SUBSTANCES describes radiation, especially high frequency X-rays, that has a high energy and is thus easily able to penetrate substances including metals, or relating to this type of radiation ○ *hard vacuum* **22.** BEVERAGES HIGH IN ALCOHOL describes beverages that have a high alcoholic content, especially alcohol produced by distillation ○ *hard liquor* **23.** DRUGS ADDICTIVE AND DANGEROUS TO HEALTH describes drugs that are highly addictive and particularly dangerous to the health ○ *hard drugs* **24.** PHON PRONOUNCED LIKE 'K' OR 'G' describes the consonants 'c' and 'g' when they are pronounced with a 'k' sound, as in 'come', and a 'g' sound, as in 'go' ■ *adv* **1.** FORCEFULLY with a lot of force ○ *hit the ball hard* **2.** ALL THE WAY to the greatest degree or extent ○ *pulled the truck over hard* **3.** ENERGETICALLY with vigour and energy or industriousness ○ *worked hard* **4.** WITH CONCENTRATION with great mental concentration ○ *studied hard* **5.** WITH DIFFICULTY with effort and great difficulty ○ *Her victory was hard won.* **6.** COMPACTLY into a solid or compact state ○ *set hard* **7.** SEVERELY in a way that causes anguish or hardship ○ *hit hard by the recession* **8.** SLOWLY slowly and with difficulty ○ *hatred that dies hard* ■ *n* **1.** BEACH WHERE BOAT CAN LAND a beach or slope that is convenient for hauling vessels out of water **2.** ROAD a road across a foreshore [Old English *heard* < Indo-European, 'strength'] ◇ **be hard on somebody 1.** to treat somebody severely **2.** to be unfortunate for somebody ◇ **be hard put to do something** to find it difficult to do something ◇ **go hard with somebody** to cause difficulty or distress to somebody (*dated*) ◇ **hard by** close by

USAGE See *hardly.*

CULTURAL NOTE ***Hard Times***, a novel (1854) by Charles Dickens. This story of the loveless upbringing of Tom and Louisa Gradgrind contrasts the soullessness of utilitarianism, as personified by their father Thomas Gradgrind, with the natural warmth and generosity of the human spirit, symbolized by their adopted sister Sissy Jupe, a member of a travelling circus.

SYNONYMS ***hard, difficult, strenuous, tough, arduous, laborious***

CORE MEANING: requiring effort or exertion

hard requiring mental or physical effort or exertion ○ *The work was always hard and sometimes dangerous.* ○ *It is hard to imagine Pauline being afraid of anything.* **difficult** requiring a lot of planning or effort to do, understand, or deal with ○ *Some of the questions on this paper are too difficult for the children.* ○ *Improvements in this area may turn out to be the most difficult to achieve.* **strenuous** requiring physical effort, energy, stamina, or strength ○ *strenuous physical activity* ○ *The fittest men are involved in the more strenuous tasks, while the less fit do other work.* **tough** physically or mentally challenging ○ *Tough decisions await the government, not least over public spending.* ○ *It will be tough for him, but I think he'll cope.* **arduous** requiring hard work or continuous physical effort ○ *a long and arduous task* ○ *He left the comforts of the capital to make the arduous journey north.* **laborious** requiring much unwelcome, often tedious effort. ○ *slow laborious manual methods* ○ *Producing charts and graphs on conventional printers is a very laborious process.*

hard-and-fast *adj* unable to be changed or adapted

Hardanger Fjord /haárd angər-/ large fjord on the southwestern coast of Norway. Length: 183 km/114 mi.

hard-ass *n US* an offensive term for somebody who is perceived as inflexible and uncompromising (*slang insult*) —**hard-assed** *adj*

hardback /haárd bak/ *n* a book with a rigid cover

hardbake /haárd bayk/ *n* almond toffee (*archaic*)

hardball /haárd bawl/ *n* **1.** tough or ruthless behaviour, especially in politics or business (*informal*) ○ *These guys play hardball.* **2.** *N Am* SPORTS same as **baseball** (sense 1)

hard-bitten *adj* tough and experienced

hardboard /haárd bawrd/ *n* thin stiff sheets of compressed sawdust and wood chips

hard-boiled *adj* **1.** describes an egg boiled until the yolk and white are firm **2.** tough, realistic, and unsentimental (*informal*) —**hard-boil** *vt*

hardboot /haárd boot/ (**-boots, -booting, -booted**) *vt* COMPUT same as **coldboot**

hardbound /haárd bownd/ *adj* bound as a book in a stiff cover

hard case *n* **1.** somebody who is rough, tough, and ruthless (*informal*) **2.** *Aus* somebody who is unconventional or amusing (*dated informal*)

hard cash *n* money in the form of coins or notes

hard cheese *interj* used to comment on and express a lack of sympathy for somebody's misfortune (*informal*)

hard cider *n N Am* BEVERAGES same as **cider** (sense 1)

hard coal *n* INDUST same as **anthracite**

hard copy *n* data from a computer printed out on paper

hard core *n* **1.** COMMITTED NUCLEUS OF GROUP the most committed, faithful, and active members of a group or organization **2.** MUSIC FAST ROCK MUSIC rock music with repetitive rhythmic synthesized sounds and a fast tempo **3.** ROADS FOUNDATION FOR ROADS OR PAVING stones and other rubble used to form a foundation under roads or paving

hard-core, hardcore /haárd kawr/ *adj* **1.** UNCOMPROMISING uncompromising and committed **2.** SHOWING EXPLICIT SEX depicting sexual acts in an explicit way **3.** MUSIC RELATING TO FAST ROCK MUSIC describes rock music with repetitive rhythmic synthesized sounds and a fast tempo

hardcover /haárd kuvər/ *n* PUBL same as **hardback**

hard disk, hard drive *n* a rigid disk inside a computer that holds a large quantity of data and programs

hardears /haárd eerz/ *adj Carib* stubborn and unwilling to take orders or advice

hard-edge *adj* describes a US style of abstract painting that developed in the 1960s, marked by sharply outlined coloured forms

hard-edged *adj* realistic, direct, and uncompromising

harden /haárd'n/ *v* (**-ens, -ening, -ened**) **1.** *vti* BECOME OR MAKE HARD to become hard, firm, or solid, or make something do this ○ *The glue hardened overnight.* **2.** *vti* MAKE OR BECOME LESS SYMPATHETIC to become more tough, callous, or unfeeling, or make somebody do this **3.** *vti* MAKE OR BECOME MORE DETERMINED to become more determined and resolute, or make somebody do this **4.** *vti* MAKE OR BECOME STRONGER to become stronger or more resistant, or make somebody or something do this **5.** *vi* COMM STABILIZE to become stable after fluctuation ○ *Prices are hardening.* ■ *adj Carib* STUBBORN stubborn and disobedient or intransigent

harden off *vti* to accustom a plant grown indoors to outdoor conditions by gradually exposing it to cold, wind, or sunlight before planting it out, or become accustomed to outdoor conditions in this way

hardened /haárd'nd/ *adj* **1.** STRENGTHENED made harder or stronger ○ *hardened steel* **2.** SECURED AGAINST NUCLEAR ATTACK strengthened in order to survive an attack by nuclear weapons **3.** TOUGHENED BY EXPERIENCE sufficiently experienced to have become blasé about something that most people would find unpleasant or difficult

hardener /haárd'nər/, **hardening** /haárd'ning/ *n* an ingredient or element that makes something hard, e.g. a substance added to paint to make it more durable

hardening of the arteries *n* MED same as **atherosclerosis** (*not in technical use*)

hard-fisted *adj* not generous with money

hardhack /haárd hak/ (*plural* **-hacks** or *same*) *n* a bush of the rose family with downy leaves. Flowers: pink or white, in clusters. Native to: North America. Latin name: *Spiraea tomentosa.* [Mid-19C. Origin ?]

hardhat /haárd hat/ *n* **1.** PROTECTIVE HELMET a helmet made of metal or plastic worn for protection by workers in a factory or on a construction site **2.** *US* CONSTRUCTION WORKER a worker in the construction industry (*informal*) **3.** *US* CONSERVATIVE a politically very conservative patriot (*informal*) —**hard-hat** *adj*

hardhead /haárd hed/ *n* a logical and unsentimental person

hardheaded /haárd héddid/ *adj* behaving in a logical and unsentimental way —**hardheadedly** *adv* —**hardheadedness** *n*

hardheads /haárd hedz/ (*plural same*) *n* a plant of the daisy family with lance-shaped. Flowers: reddish-purple, globular flower heads. Native to: Europe, Asia. Latin name: *Centaurea nigra.* N Am term **knapweed**

hardhearted /haárd haártid/ *adj* showing no sympathy for other people's feelings —**hardheartedly** *adv* —**hardheartedness** *n*

hard-hitting *adj* direct and uncompromising ○ *a hard-hitting documentary*

Hardie /haárdi/, **Keir** (1856–1915) British politician. He founded the Scottish Labour Party (1888), the first labour party in the United Kingdom. Full name **Hardie, James Keir**

> 'If a workman steals five shillings from the pocket of his employer, he gets sixty days in jail; if an employer steals a thousand a year from the wages of the workers, he is made an elder in the Kirk, created a Bailie, and invited to deliver lectures against Socialism.'
>
> [Keir Hardie, *Keir Hardie's Speeches and Writings*; 1928]

hardihood /haárdihòod/ *n* **1.** the quality of being tough and able to withstand difficulty or hard work **2.** bold audacity

Harding /haárding/, **Warren G.** (1865–1923) 29th president of the United States. A conservative Republican from Ohio elected on the promise of a 'return to normalcy' after World War I, he presided (1921–23) over a federal administration distinguished primarily by its flagrant corruption. Full name **Harding, Warren Gamaliel.** See table at **president**

> 'I wish for an America no less alert in guarding against dangers from within than it is watchful against enemies from without.'
>
> [Warren G. Harding, *New York Times*; 5 March 1921]

hard labour *n* a sentence of compulsory work imposed in addition to a term of imprisonment, not used as a sentence in the United Kingdom since 1948

hard landing *n* **1.** an uncontrolled landing by an aircraft or spacecraft that results in its being damaged or destroyed **2.** a downward trend in economic activity after a period of expansion

hardline /haárd līn/ *adj* inflexible and uncompromising —**hardliner** *n*

hard lines *interj* used to comment that somebody is or has been unfortunate (*dated; often ironic*)

hard-luck *adj* involving or suffering a lot of personal

misfortune ○ *She had a soft spot for other people's hard-luck stories.*

hardly /ha'ardli/ CORE MEANING: an adverb with negative meaning, used to indicate that something is true or exists to a very minimal extent ○ *She lived so privately, hardly anyone even spoke to her.* ○ *Though we hardly knew him, we could sense his good humour.* ○ *I looked out of the window; it was hardly raining.*

adv **1.** NOT indicates that something is almost entirely untrue or impossible ○ *We are hardly going to give up with success in view.* ○ *It's hardly likely that I would tell you.* **2.** ONLY WITH DIFFICULTY only with great awkwardness, difficulty, or embarrassment ○ *I was so shocked I could hardly speak.* **3.** SELDOM indicates that something seldom occurs (*used with a negative such as 'without'*) ○ *Hardly a day passes without acclaim for this exciting new invention.* **4.** AS SOON AS indicates that one event follows quickly after another ○ *Hardly had I rung the bell when the bolt was shot back.* **5.** USED TO DISAGREE used to indicate surprise, disagreement, or annoyance ○ *'I thought you were going at about sixty miles an hour.' 'Well, hardly. Maybe forty.'*

USAGE *Hardly*, like *barely* and *scarcely*, has a negative force, rendering unnecessary the use of another negative in the clause or sentence: *I can* [not *can't*] *hardly see you.* Note that *when* and not *than* is used in any continuation of the sentence: *Hardly* [or *barely* or *scarcely*] *had I begun to speak when* [not *than*] *she interrupted me.* (After *no sooner*, however, *than* is correct.) *Hardly* is limited to these special uses; the usual adverb from the adjective *hard* is also *hard*: *They are all working hard to get ready for their exams.*

hard man *n* a man who is perceived as vicious and ruthless, often with criminal tendencies

hard mouth *n* a horse's mouth that is insensitive to pressure from the bit, or a horse's ability to resist this pressure

hardmouthed /haard mówthd/ *adj* describes a horse that fails to respond when the rider pulls on the bit in its mouth

hardness /ha'ardnəss/ *n* **1.** FIRMNESS, SOLIDITY, AND COMPACTNESS the state or quality of being firm, solid, and compact **2.** UNYIELDING TOUGHNESS the state or quality of being tough and unyielding **3.** CHEM WATER QUALITY the degree to which water contains mineral salts **4.** METALL, MEASURE DEGREE TO WHICH METAL IS HARD the degree to which a metal may be scratched, abraded, indented, or machined, measured according to any of several scales

hard news *n* news that concerns specific events and is strictly factual —**hard-news** *adj*

hard-nosed *adj* tough, realistic, and unsentimental (*informal*)

hard nut *n* a physically tough person who is good at dealing with violent situations (*informal*)

hard of hearing *adj* MED same as **hearing-impaired** (*sometimes considered offensive*)

hard-on *n* a highly offensive term for an erect penis (*slang taboo*)

hard palate *n* the bony front portion of the roof of the mouth

hardpan /ha'ard pan/ *n* a layer of hard matter, especially clay, that lies under soft soil and that plant roots cannot penetrate

hard-pressed *adj* **1.** subject to a lot of pressure and lacking sufficient resources **2.** finding something very difficult

hard rock *n* a form of rock music that has simple lyrics and a strong insistent beat

hard rubber *n* rubber treated with sulphur to make it hard and stiff

hard sauce *n* ANZ, N Am butter creamed with sugar and often flavoured with brandy or whisky, usually served with plum pudding. UK term **brandy butter**

hard science *n* a science such as physics, chemistry, geology, or astronomy in which data can be precisely quantified and theories tested

hard sell *n* a direct, aggressive, and insistent way of selling or advertising

hard-shell, **hard-shelled** *adj* N Am rigid and uncompromising in attitude

hard-shell clam *n* ZOOL same as **quahog**

hard-shelled *adj* N Am same as **hard-shell**

hardship /ha'ard ship/ *n* **1.** difficulty or suffering caused by a lack of something, especially money **2.** something that causes difficulty or suffering

hard shoulder *n* UK an area at the side of a motorway where a vehicle can stop in an emergency. ANZ, N Am term **shoulder**

hardstand /ha'ard stand/ *n* N Am TRANSP same as **hard standing**

hard standing *n* a hard surface on which aircraft or motor vehicles may be parked. N Am term **hardstand**

hard stuff *n* something that is intoxicating, addictive, and potentially very dangerous to the health, especially strong alcohol (*informal*)

hardtack /ha'ard tak/ *n* a hard thin unsalted bread or biscuit formerly eaten aboard ships or as military rations

hard up *adj* short of money (*informal*)

hardware /ha'ard wair/ *n* **1.** COMPUT COMPUTER EQUIPMENT AND PERIPHERALS the equipment and devices that make up a computer system as opposed to the programs used on it **2.** TOOLS AND IMPLEMENTS tools and implements, usually made of metal, e.g. hinges, hammers, and cutlery **3.** ARMS MILITARY WEAPONS heavy military weapons and equipment **4.** ARMS GUN a gun or guns (*informal*)

hard-wearing *adj* not easily damaged or worn out despite frequent use

hard wheat *n* a wheat with hard kernels and a high gluten content. Use: flour for bread.

hardwire /ha'ard wīr/ (**-wires, -wiring, -wired**) *vt* to build a function into a computer with hardware rather than programming

hardwired /haard wírd/ *adj* directly wired into a computer or physically connected to a computer system or network ○ *a hardwired circuit*

hard-won *adj* achieved after much effort

hardwood /ha'ard woŏd/ *n* **1.** wood from a broad-leaved tree as opposed to from a conifer **2.** a tree that produces hardwood

hard word *n* Ireland (*informal*) **1.** dismissal from employment **2.** a reprimand or unfair criticism ◇ **put the hard word on somebody** ANZ to put pressure on somebody to do something (*informal*)

hard-working *adj* tending to work industriously

hardy /ha'ardi/ (**-dier, -diest**) *adj* **1.** ROBUST sufficiently robust to withstand fatigue, hardship, or adverse physical conditions **2.** BOT NOT SENSITIVE TO COLD describes plants that are able to live outdoors during the winter ○ *a hardy shrub* **3.** COURAGEOUS courageous and daring [13C. < French *hardi* < *hardir* 'become bold' < Germanic] —**hardily** *adv* —**hardiness** *n*

Hardy /ha'ardi/, **Oliver** (1892–1957) US comedian. He appeared with Stan Laurel in a series of classic comedy films in the 1920s and 1930s.

'Here's another fine mess you've gotten me into.'
[Oliver Hardy. Quoted in *Filmgoer's Book of Quotes*, Leslie Halliwell; 1973]

Hardy, **Thomas** (1769–1839) British sailor. He was flag captain of the *Victory* at the Battle of Trafalgar (1805), and attended Horatio Nelson as he was dying. Full name **Hardy, Thomas Masterman**

Hardy, **Thomas** (1840–1928) British novelist and poet. He wrote brooding novels of the West Country including *The Mayor of Casterbridge* (1886), and from the 1890s devoted himself to poetry. See Cultural note at **madding, mayor**

'It is hard for a woman to define her feelings in language which is chiefly made by men to express theirs.'
[Thomas Hardy, *Far from the Madding Crowd*; 1874]

'A novel is an impression, not an argument.'
[Thomas Hardy. Preface, *Tess of the D'Urbervilles*, 5th ed.; 1892]

hardy annual *n* an annual plant that is not readily damaged by frost

hard yards *npl* Aus hard work (*informal*) ○ *He had to do the hard yards drumming up support.*

hardy perennial *n* **1.** a perennial plant that needs no protection in winter **2.** something that people have continued to use, discuss, or enjoy for a number of years ○ *The controversy, apparently settled in Coleridge's 1817 article, remains a hardy perennial in studies of Wordsworth.*

Hardy-Weinberg law /-wĭn burg-/, **Hardy-Weinberg distribution** *n* a principle of genetics stating that gene frequencies remain constant from one generation to the next if mating is random and there are no outside influences such as mutation and immigration [Mid-20C. After G. H. *Hardy* (1877–1947), British mathematician, and Wilhelm *Weinberg* (1862–1937), German physician]

hare

hare /hair/ *n* (*plural same* or **hares**) a fast-running animal that resembles a rabbit but is larger, has longer ears and large hind legs, and does not burrow. Genus: *Lepus*. ■ *vi* (**hares, haring, hared**) to run or move very fast [Old English *hara* < Germanic]

SPELLCHECK See **hair**.

Hare /hair/, **Sir David** (*b.* 1947) British playwright. His plays explore political and moral themes in contemporary Britain and include the trilogy *Racing Demon* (1989), *Murmuring Judges* (1991), and *The Absence of War* (1993).

hare and hounds, **hare and hounds race** *n* an outdoor game in which one group of players, the hounds, follows a trail of scraps of paper left by another group, the hares, and tries to catch them up before they reach a designated point

harebell

harebell /hair bel/ *n* a low-growing delicate wild plant with slender stems. Flowers: blue, bell-shaped. Native to: northern temperate regions. Latin name: *Campanula rotundiflora*.

harebrained /hair braynd/ *adj* regarded as impractical and likely to fail

Hare Krishna /harri-/ *n* **1.** a religious group that bases its practice on worship of the god Krishna **2.** a member of Hare Krishna [Late 20C. < Sanskrit, 'O Lord Krishna', chant used by devotees]

harelip /hair lip/ *n* same as **cleft lip** (*offensive*) —**harelipped** *adj*

harem /haa reem, haa reem, hairəm/ *n* **1.** WOMEN'S PART OF HOUSE in a traditional Muslim home, the separate private quarters reserved for wives and concubines **2.** GROUP OF WOMEN the wives and concubines who live in a harem **3.** WOMEN FOLLOWERS a group of women admirers or followers (*humorous; sometimes considered offensive*) **4.** ZOOL GROUP OF ANIMALS a group of

female animals of the same species associated for breeding purposes with one male [Mid-17C. Via Turkish < Arabic *haram* 'prohibited (place), women's quarters']

harem pants *npl* women's trousers made of soft thin cloth, with wide legs that are gathered at the ankle

Harer /há͞arər/, **Hārer, Harar** city in eastern Ethiopia, the centre of a coffee-growing area. Population: 131,139 (1994).

hare's-foot (*plural same* or **hare's-foots**), **hare's-foot clover** *n* a clover that grows on sandy soil. Flowers: white or pink, almost hidden by their calyx. Latin name: *Trifolium arvense*. [< the appearance of the soft hair about the flowers]

harestail /háírz tayl/ *n* a variety of cotton grass that grows on moors and has a single flower head [< its similarity to a hare's tail]

harewood /háír woŏd/ *n* the greenish-coloured wood of the sycamore maple. Use: furniture. [Late 17C. < German dialect *Ehre* < Latin *acer* 'maple, sycamore']

Hargrave /há͞ar grayv/, **Lawrence** (1850–1915) British-born Australian aviator and explorer. He designed several early aircraft.

Hargreaves /há͞ar greevz/, **James** (1720–78) British inventor. His invention of the spinning jenny in 1764 heralded a new era in industrial history.

haricot /hárrikō/ *n* **1.** a small white oval dried bean, cooked and eaten as a vegetable **2.** a bean plant whose seeds are dried and stored as haricots. Latin name: *Phaseolus vulgaris*. **3.** FOOD same as **French bean** [Mid-17C. < French]

Harijan /húrrijən/ *n S Asia* same as **Dalit** [Mid-20C. < Sanskrit, 'God's people']

Haring /háíring/, **Keith** (1958–90) US painter. He is best known for his graffiti art works inspired by the urban culture of New York.

harissa /hə ríssə/ *n* a spicy oily paste made from chilli and tomatoes, used as an ingredient in North African cooking or as an accompaniment for dishes such as couscous

hark /haark/ (**harks, harking, harked**) *vi* to listen to somebody or something (*archaic*) [12C. Probably < assumed Old English *heorcnian*]

hark back *vi* **1.** to think or speak again about something from the past **2.** to be similar in some respects to something in the past

harken *vi* another spelling of **hearken**

harl /haarl/ *Scotland vt* (**harls, harling, harled**) to cover the exterior walls of a building with lime and gravel or sand ■ *n* a mixture of lime and gravel or sand used for covering a building's exterior walls [13C. Origin ?]

Harlech /há͞arlək/ village in northwestern Wales, dominated by the ruins of its castle. Population: 1,233 (1991).

Harlem /há͞arləm/ **1.** district of New York City, on Manhattan Island, originally named Nieuw Haarlem by Dutch settlers in 1658 **2.** another spelling of **Haarlem**

Harlem Globetrotters /-glŏb trottərz/ *npl* a US basketball team that tours widely to play exhibition matches during which the team displays skilled comic manoeuvres

harlequin /há͞arləkwin/ *n* a clown or buffoon ■ *adj* varied in colour and having a pattern of irregular shapes [Late 18C. < HARLEQUIN]

Harlequin /há͞arləkwin/ *n* a comic dramatic character featured in the Italian commedia dell'arte and the English harlequinade, usually shown wearing multicoloured diamond-patterned tights and a black mask [Late 16C. < obsolete French, variant of *Hellequin*, legendary leader of night-raiding demon horsemen]

harlequinade /há͞arləkwi náyd/ *n* **1.** a pantomime, play, or other performance featuring a harlequin as a character **2.** clowning or silly behaviour

harlequin duck *n* a small diving duck that has blue and red feathers with black and white markings. Native to: North America, Iceland, eastern Siberia. Latin name: *Histrionicus histrionicus*.

Harley Street /há͞arli-/ *n* a street in central London famous for the number of eminent doctors who have private practices there

harling /há͞arling/ *n Scotland* CONSTR same as **harl**

harlot /há͞arlət/ *n* same as **prostitute** (*archaic or literary*) [13C. < Old French, 'vagabond, rogue, beggar']

Harlow /há͞arlō/ town in Essex, southeastern England, designated a new town in 1947. Population: 78,768 (2001).

Harlow, Jean (1911–37) US actor. Her platinum-blond hair and frankly sexual screen presence characterized her films, including *Dinner at Eight* (1933). Born **Carpenter, Harlean**

harm /haarm/ *n* physical, mental, or moral impairment or deterioration ■ *vt* (**harms, harming, harmed**) to cause physical, mental, or moral impairment or deterioration [Old English *hearm* < Germanic]

SYNONYMS *harm, damage, hurt, injure, wound*

CORE MEANING: to weaken or impair somebody or something

harm to cause physical, mental, moral or social impairment or deterioration. ○ *Smoking while pregnant harms your baby.* ○ *decisions that will harm the economy* **damage** to cause physical injury that makes something less useful, valuable, or able to function, or to have a harmful effect on something ○ *The storm caused severe damage to the roof.* ○ *The bombings have damaged the prospects for a negotiated settlement.* **hurt** to cause somebody, yourself, or an animal physical injury or pain, or cause emotional distress ○ *Laura tripped and fell, but didn't hurt herself.* ○ *His words hurt.* **injure** to cause physical damage to a person, animal, or body part, or cause emotional distress ○ *Two other people were seriously injured in the accident.* ○ *The reviews were cruel and badly injured their pride.* **wound** to cause physical damage to a person, animal, or body part, or to upset or offend somebody ○ *wounded in battle* ○ *He feels wounded by the accusations.*

harmattan /haar mátt'n/ *n* an extremely dry dusty wind that blows from the Sahara towards the western coast of Africa, especially between November and March [Late 17C. < Twi *haramata*]

harmful /há͞armf'l/ *adj* causing damage or injury ○ *The plant is harmful to humans.* —**harmfully** *adv* —**harmfulness** *n*

harmless /há͞armləss/ *adj* **1.** not likely to cause damage or injury **2.** not likely to cause offence or upset ○ *Don't worry; he's harmless enough.* —**harmlessly** *adv* —**harmlessness** *n*

harmonic /haar mónnik/ *adj* **1.** PRODUCED BY HARMONY relating to, produced, or marked by harmony **2.** PHYS RELATING TO INTEGRAL MULTIPLE OF FREQUENCY describes a frequency that is an integral multiple of a fundamental frequency ■ *n* **1.** PHYS MULTIPLE OF FUNDAMENTAL FREQUENCY a single oscillation having a frequency that is an integral multiple of a fundamental frequency, e.g. 220 Hz and 330 Hz are both harmonics of 110 Hz **2.** OVERTONE ON STRINGED INSTRUMENT an overtone produced on an instrument, e.g. by lightly touching a vibrating string at a point where the string to either side will continue to vibrate [Late 16C. Via Latin *harmonicus* < Greek *harmonikos* < *harmonia* (see HARMONY)] —**harmonically** *adv*

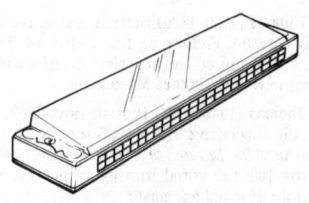

harmonica

harmonica /haar mónnikə/ *n* a small musical instrument whose narrow metal case houses a set of metal reeds that are made to sound by exhaling or inhaling air past them [Mid-18C. Via Italian *armonica* < Latin *harmonicus* (see HARMONIC)]

harmonic analysis *n* the representation of a periodic function by a series of sines and cosines, especially by a Fourier series

harmonic distortion *n* the unwanted presence of distorted frequencies at the output of an electronic device such as an audio amplifier

harmonic mean *n* the reciprocal of the arithmetic mean of the reciprocals of a finite set of numbers

harmonic minor scale *n* a version of the minor scale in which the seventh note is raised by a semitone, both ascending and descending

harmonic motion *n N Am* PHYS same as **simple harmonic motion**

harmonic progression *n* a sequence of numbers whose reciprocals form an arithmetic progression, e.g. 1/2, 1/5, 1/8, 1/11

harmonics /haar mónniks/ *n* the branch of science that deals with the physical properties of musical sound (*takes a singular verb*)

harmonic series *n* an infinite series of numbers constructed by adding the numbers in a harmonic progression to one another, e.g. 1/2+1/5+1/8+1/11

harmonious /haar mŏni əss/ *adj* **1.** SHOWING ACCORD characterized by friendly agreement or accord **2.** RELATING TO HARMONY relating to or sounding in musical harmony **3.** BLENDING PLEASANTLY having a pleasing combination of parts or colours —**harmoniously** *adv* —**harmoniousness** *n*

harmonise *vti* POL, MUSIC another spelling of **harmonize**

harmonist /há͞armənist/ *n* **1.** somebody who is skilled in creating harmony **2.** somebody who researches and tries to find similarities in parallel texts, especially the four Gospels —**harmonistic** /há͞armə nístik/ *adj* —**harmonistically** *adv*

harmonium /haar mŏni əm/ *n* an organ in which a pair of bellows operated by the player's feet blow air into the reeds to produce musical sound [Mid-19C. < French < Latin *harmonia* (see HARMONY) or Greek *harmonios* 'harmonious']

harmonize /há͞armə nīz/ (**-nizes, -nizing, -nized**), **harmonise** (**-nises, -nising, -nised**) *vti* BLEND PLEASINGLY to combine pleasingly, or make things combine pleasingly **2.** *vt* MAKE SYSTEMS AGREE to make rules, regulations, or systems similar or in accord with each other **3.** *vt* ADD HARMONY TO MELODY to provide a harmony for a melody **4.** *vi* PLAY IN HARMONY to sing or play musical instruments in harmony —**harmonizable** *adj* —**harmonization** /há͞armə nī záysh'n/ *n* —**harmonizer** *n*

harmonized sales tax /há͞armə nīzd-/ *n* in the provinces of Nova Scotia, New Brunswick, and Newfoundland, a tax combining the goods and services tax and the provincial sales tax

harmony /há͞arməni/ (*plural* **-nies**) *n* **1.** FRIENDLY AGREEMENT a situation in which there is friendly agreement or accord **2.** PLEASING COMBINATION OF SOUNDS a pleasing combination of musical sounds **3.** NOTES SUNG OR PLAYED TOGETHER a combination of notes that are sung or played at the same time. Changing harmony is one of the most characteristic features of Western music, providing momentum and richness to the melody. **4.** STUDY OF CHORDS IN MUSIC the study of the way in which musical chords are constructed and function in relation to one another **5.** PLEASANTNESS IN ARRANGEMENT a pleasing effect produced by an arrangement of things, parts, or colours **6.** STUDY OF TEXTS a study or collation of the similarities in parallel texts, especially the four Gospels **7.** PARALLEL TEXT a book or manuscript in which several versions of the same text, often a biblical text, are laid out in parallel columns ○ *a Gospel harmony* [14C. Via French and Latin < Greek *harmonia* 'agreement, concord' < *harmozein* 'fit together']

Harnack /há͞arn ak/, **Adolf von** (1851–1930) German theologian. One of the leading Protestant scholars of his day, he advocated a return to biblical Christianity. His major work was *History of Dogma* (1886–90).

harness /há͞arnəss/ *n* **1.** STRAPS FOR ANIMAL a set of leather straps fitted to an animal such as a horse so that it can be attached to a cart or carriage for pulling **2.** STRAPS FITTED TO PERSON a set of straps fitted to somebody to fasten him or her or to keep the him or her in position ■ *vt* (**-nesses, -nessing, -nessed**) **1.** GET CONTROL OF AND USE SOMETHING to gain control of something and use it for some purpose ○ *seek to harness the skills and resources of a number of agencies* **2.** FIT ANIMAL WITH HARNESS to put a harness on an animal [13C. Via Old French *harneis* < assumed Old

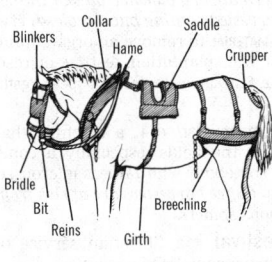

harness

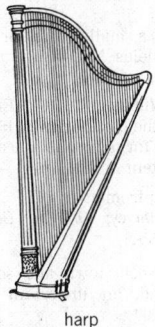

harp

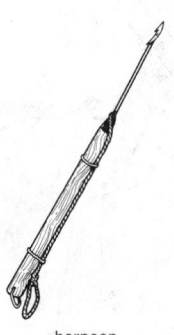

harpoon

harrier

Norse *hernest* 'provisions for an army' < *herr* 'army'] — **harnesser** *n* ◇ **in harness 1.** doing your usual work **2.** working cooperatively with a person or group

harness hitch *n* a knot with one loop and no free ends, used in tying harnesses

harness race *n* a horse race in which specially bred horses pull small carriages around a course wearing special harnesses to ensure that they move as required by the race rules —**harness racing** *n*

Harney Peak /haárni-/ mountain in the Black Hills, southwestern South Dakota, and the highest peak in the state. Height: 2,207 m/7,242 ft.

Harold I /hárrəld/ (*d.* 1040) Danish-born king of the English. He was the illegitimate son of Canute II and ruled England (1037–40) in constant strife with his half-brother, Hardecanute. Known as **Harold Harefoot**

Harold II (1020?–66) king of the English. The last Saxon king of England (1066), he was killed fighting William the Conqueror at the Battle of Hastings.

> 'He will give him seven feet of English ground, or as much more as he may be taller than other men.'
> [*King Harold's Saga*, Snorri Sturluson; 1260]

haroseth /hə róseth/, **haroset** /-róset/, **charoseth** /khə-/, **charoset** /khə-/ *n* a mixture of apples, nuts, spices, and wine, eaten as part of the Passover Seder meal. The mixture symbolizes the clay used by the Israelites to make bricks during their enslavement in Egypt. [Late 19C. < Hebrew *ḥarōset* < *ḥeres* 'earthenware']

harp /haarp/ *n* **1.** TRIANGULAR STRINGED INSTRUMENT a triangular-shaped instrument that has a curved neck and strings stretched between the neck and the body, at an angle to the sound box. The modern orchestral harp is large and played by a seated player. **2.** HARMONICA a reed harmonica (*informal*) ■ *vi* (**harps, harping, harped**) PLAY HARP to play the harp [Old English *hearpe* < Germanic] —**harper** *n* —**harpist** *n* **harp on** *vti* to repeat or stress something in a way that becomes tiresome

Harpers Ferry /haárpərz férri/ historic town and tourist resort in eastern West Virginia, situated at the confluence of the Potomac and Shenandoah rivers. Population: 304 (2002 estimate).

harpoon /haar póon/ *n* a long pointed piece of metal attached to a cord and thrown or fired from a gun in order to capture whales or other large sea animals ■ *vt* (**-poons, -pooning, -pooned**) to catch a whale or other large sea animal using a harpoon [Early 17C. < Old French *harpon* 'clamp' < *harpe* 'dog's

claw, clamp' < Greek *harpē* 'sickle'] —**harpooneer** /haár poo neér/ *n* —**harpooner** *n*

harp seal *n* a brownish-grey earless seal that is whitish when very young, formerly hunted for its fur. Native to: coastal regions and ice floes of the North Atlantic Ocean. Latin name: *Pagophilus groenlandicus.* [< the shape of its markings]

harpsichord /haárpsi kawrd/ *n* a keyboard instrument resembling a piano that has horizontal strings plucked by leather or quill points connected to the keys. It was superseded by the piano in the 19th century. [Early 17C. < French *harpechorde* < Latin *harpa* 'harp' + *chorda* 'string'] —**harpsichordist** *n*

Harpur /haárpər/, **Charles** (1813–68) Australian poet and playwright. Considered by many to be Australia's first major poet, he wrote *The Creek of the Four Graves* (1853).

harpy /haárpi/ (*plural* **-pies**) *n* **1.** an offensive term for a woman regarded as bad-tempered or nagging (*insult*) **2.** somebody who preys on others [< HARPY]

Harpy /haárpi/ (*plural* **-pies**) *n* in Greek mythology, a monster that was half woman and half bird of prey. The Harpies were thought to live on the Strophades Islands and carry out acts of vengeance on behalf of the gods. [14C. Directly or via French < Latin *harpyia* < Greek *harpuiai* (plural) 'snatchers' < *harpazein* 'seize']

harpy eagle *n* a huge eagle with a blackish back, white underparts, and a grey head with a double crest. Native to: lowland forests of southern Mexico to northern Argentina. Latin name: *Harpia harpyja.*

harquebus /haárkwibəss/, **arquebus** /aár-/ *n* an early portable gun with a long barrel, supported by a tripod by a hook or on a forked post [Mid-16C. Via French *(h)arquebuse* < Middle Dutch *hakebus* < *hake(n)* 'hook' + *bus(se)* 'gun'; from the hook supporting it] —**harquebusier** /haárkwibə seér/ *n*

~~**harrass**~~ incorrect spelling of **harass**

harridan /hárridən/ *n* an offensive term for a woman that deliberately insults her age as advanced and her temperament as assertive (*insult*) [Late 17C. Origin ?]

harried /hárrid/ *adj* looking or feeling tired and annoyed

harrier[1] /hárri ər/ (*plural* **-ers** or *same*) *n* a slender graceful hawk with long wings and a long tail that hunts by flying low over marshland and grassland to catch mice, snakes, frogs, and fish. Native to: all continents except Antarctica. Genus: *Circus.* [Mid-16C. < *harrow* 'rob', variant of HARRY[1]; later influenced by HARRIER[3]]

harrier[2] /hárri ər/ *n* **1.** a small hound resembling a foxhound used for hunting hares or rabbits **2.** a

cross-country runner (*often used in the name of athletics clubs*) [15C. Origin ?]

harrier[3] /hárri ər/ *n* **1.** somebody who repeatedly attacks another person or group physically or verbally **2.** somebody who raids or pillages a place [Early 16C. < HARRY[1]]

harrington jacket /hárringtən-/ *n* a short close-fitting lined jacket with a zipped front and usually a collar that can be folded down or buttoned up [Origin ?]

Harris /hárriss/ the southern part of the island of Lewis in the Outer Hebrides, Scotland. It is famous for its tweed. Area: 500 sq. km/193 sq. mi.

Harris, Sir Arthur Travers (1892–1984) British air marshal. Commander in chief of the RAF Bomber Command (1942–45), he supervised the British bombing of Germany's industrial heartland during World War II. Known as **Bomber Harris**

Harris, Frank (1856–1931) Irish-born US journalist and writer. He gained notoriety for his scandalous semi-fictional autobiography, *My Life and Loves*, published in three volumes (1922, 1925, 1927). Born **Harris, James Thomas**

> 'A history of humanity to the present time in which Shakespeare is not mentioned and Jesus is dismissed in a page carelessly, as if not worth contempt, shocks me.'
> [Frank Harris, *My Life and Loves*; 1925]

Harris, Max (1921–95) Australian writer and publisher. A founder of the avant-garde journal *Angry Penguins*, he wrote the verse collection *The Angry Eye* (1973). Full name **Harris, Maxwell Henley**

Harrisburg /hárriss burg/ city and capital of Pennsylvania, located in the southern part of the state. Population: 48,540 (2002 estimate).

Harrison /hárriss'n/, **Benjamin** (1726?–91) American patriot. A longtime member of the Virginia House of Burgesses (1749–75), he presided over the Continental Congress (1774–77) and signed the Declaration of Independence (1776). He was governor of Virginia (1781–84).

Harrison, Benjamin (1833–1901) 23rd president of the United States. The grandson of William Henry Harrison, he was a Republican senator (1881–87) before his election as president. His administration (1889–93) enacted protectionist tariffs and other pro-business legislation. See table at **president**

> 'Lincoln had faith in time, and time has justified his faith.'
> [Benjamin Harrison, *Lincoln Day Address*; 1898]

Harrison, George (1943–2001) British musician. The lead guitarist with the Beatles, he later turned to solo music projects and film production.

> 'All things must pass, all things must pass away.'
> [George Harrison, *All Things Must Pass*; 1971]

Harrison, Sir Rex (1908–90) British actor. He starred in comedies including *Blithe Spirit* (1945) and *My Fair Lady* (1964), for which he won an Academy Award. Full name **Harrison, Sir Reginald Carey**

Harrison, Tony (*b.* 1937) British poet. Known for his adaptations of Greek drama, his poetic works include 'Earthworks' (1964) and 'V' (1985).

> '*How you became a poet's a mystery! / Wherever did you get your talent from? / I say, I had two uncles, Joe and Harry— / one was a stammerer, the other dumb.*'
> [Tony Harrison, 'Heredity', *The School of Eloquence*; 1978]

Harrison, William Henry (1773–1841) 9th president of the United States. He was elected president in 1840 on the strength of his military successes against the Native North Americans and in the War of 1812, but died after one month in office. See table at **president**

> 'We admit of no government by divine right...the only legitimate right to govern is an express grant of power from the governed.'
> [William Henry Harrison, *Inaugural presidential address*; 4 March 1841]

Harris tweed *n* a thick woven woollen cloth traditionally made in Harris in the Outer Hebrides, Scotland

Harrogate /hárrəgət/ spa town in North Yorkshire, northern England, noted for its mineral springs. Population: 151,336 (2001).

harrow[1] /hárrō/ *n* a piece of farm equipment with sharp teeth or discs that is used to break up soil and clods of dirt and to even up a ploughed field ■ *vti* (**-rows, -rowing, -rowed**) to break up land by pulling a harrow over it, or be broken up with a harrow [12C. < Old Norse *herfi*] —**harrower** *n*

harrow[2] /hárrō/ (**-rows, -rowing, -rowed**) *vt* same as **harry**[1] (*archaic*) [14C. Variant]

harrowing /hárrō ing/ *adj* causing feelings of fear, horror, or distress ○ *harrowing scenes of hurricane devastation* [Early 19C. < HARROW[2] in archaic sense 'wound, distress'] —**harrowingly** *adv*

Harrow School /hárrō-/ *n* a public school for boys in northwestern London. It was founded in 1571. —**Harrovian** /hə rôvi ən/ *n*

harrumph /hə rúmf/ (**-rumphs, -rumphing, -rumphed**) *vti* **1.** to say something expressing criticism and displeasure, often muttering so that listeners are aware of the tone but cannot hear the exact words **2.** to clear the throat, or make a noise that resembles the sound of clearing the throat [Mid-20C. An imitation of the sound] —**harrumph** *n*

harry[1] /hárri/ (**-ries, -rying, -ried**) *vt* **1.** to cause somebody physical, mental, or emotional distress by repeated physical or verbal attacks ○ *harried parents* **2.** to raid or pillage a place, especially during a war [Old English *hergian* 'ravage' < Germanic, 'army']

harry[2] /hárri/ (*plural* **-ries**) *n regional* the smallest or weakest piglet in a litter [Probably < the man's name *Harry*]

REGIONAL NOTE See *underling*.

Harry /hári/, **Prince** (*b.* 1984) He is the younger son of Prince Charles and Diana, Princess of Wales. Full name **Henry Charles Albert David**

harry-wiggles (*plural same*) *n regional* INSECTS same as **earwig**

harsh /haársh/ *adj* **1.** DIFFICULT TO ENDURE bleak or inhospitable and therefore difficult to endure ○ *a rugged and harsh environment* ○ *a harsh winter* ○ *harsh prison conditions* **2.** SEVERELY CRITICAL severely scrutinizing, critical, and rigid in manner ○ *harsh criticism* **3.** PUNITIVE exacting to the point of being punitive ○ *Harsh penalties will be imposed.* **4.** JARRING jarring or unpleasant to the senses ○ *a harsh voice* ○ *a harsh light* [14C. Ultimately < Germanic] —**harshen** *vti* —**harshly** *adv* —**harshness** *n*

Harsha /haárshə/ *n* a descendant of the Guptas in India, who created a large empire in northern India between 616 and 654

harslet *n* COOK another spelling of **haslet**

hart /haart/ (*plural* **harts** or *same*) *n* a male deer, especially a male red deer over five years of age [Old English *heor(o)t* < Indo-European, 'horn, head']

Hart /haart/, **Lorenz** (1895–1943) US lyricist. He collaborated with Richard Rodgers for 20 years, producing a string of classic musicals including *On Your Toes* (1936) and *Pal Joey* (1940). Full name **Hart, Lorenz Milton**

    'Bewitched, bothered, and bewildered am I.'
    [Lorenz Hart, 'Bewitched', *Pal Joey*; 1940]

Hart, Pro (*b.* 1928) Australian painter. He is noted for his naive style and his depictions of life in and around the central Australian town of Broken Hill. Born **Hart, Kevin Charles**

hartal /haar taál, hur taál, haár taal/ *n S Asia* a general closing of shops and suspending of work, especially as an indication or means of political protest [Early 20C. < Hindi *hartāl* 'shop locking']

hartebeest

hartebeest /haárti beest/ (*plural* **-beests** or *same*) *n* a large antelope with humped shoulders, a long narrow face, and lyre-shaped horns. Native to: eastern and southern Africa. Genus: *Alcelaphus*. [Late 18C. < obsolete Afrikaans]

Hartford /haártfərd/ city and capital of Connecticut, situated on the Connecticut River 58 km/36 mi. northeast of New Haven. It is home to Trinity College. Population: 124,558 (2002 estimate).

Hartford Wits *npl* a group of writers, most of whom attended Yale College (later Yale University), who collaborated on works of political satire at the end of the 18th and beginning of the 19th centuries

Hartlepool /haártli pool/ industrial town and seaport in northeastern England. Population: 87,310 (1991).

Hartley /haártli/, **David** (1732–1813) British politician and inventor. He assisted Benjamin Franklin in drafting the Treaty of Paris (1783) and invented a house fireproofing system.

Hartnell /haártnəl/, **Sir Norman** (1901–79) British couturier. He was known for designing tailored women's suits, elaborate gowns, and, most notably, Elizabeth II's wedding dress. Full name **Hartnell, Sir Norman Bishop**

Hartog /haár tog/, **Dirk** (*fl* 16th-17th centuries) Dutch navigator. His Dutch East India Company expedition to Java in 1616 reached Australia instead, where he made the earliest recorded European exploration of the west coast.

hart's-tongue (*plural* **hart's-tongues** or *same*) *n* an evergreen fern that has narrow undivided fronds bearing rows of spore-producing organs. Native to: Europe, Asia. Latin name: *Phyllitis scolopendrium*. [< the shape of its fronds]

harum-scarum /háirəm skáirəm/ *adj* careless or irresponsible ○ *harum-scarum methods* [Late 17C. Probably rhyming alteration of HARE (verb) + SCARE] —**harum-scarum** *adv*

Harun ar-Rashid /ha roón al ra sheéd/ (766–809) Abbasid caliph of Baghdad. His splendid court, a centre of Islamic culture, is described in the *Arabian Nights*.

haruspex /hə rú speks/ (*plural* **-pices** /-pi seez/), **aruspex** /ə-/ *n* in ancient Rome, a priest who attempted to foretell the future, especially by examining the entrails of animals [15C. < Latin]

Harvard system /haárvərd-/ *n* a bibliographic reference system, used in academic publishing, in which the author and date are given in the text and the full reference is supplied in a general list of references [After *Harvard* University, Massachusetts]

harvest /haárvist/ *n* **1.** QUANTITY OF CROP the quantity of a crop that is gathered or ripens during a season ○ *a record harvest of wheat* ○ *Variations in the world harvest can be tracked to 0.1 per cent.* **2.** CROP THAT IS GATHERED the crop that is gathered or ripens during a season ○ *A few days of rain can destroy an entire harvest of strawberries.* **3.** SEASON IN WHICH CROPS ARE GATHERED the season during which crops ripen and are gathered **4.** CONSEQUENCES the consequences of previous actions or behaviour **5.** BIOL REMOVAL OF BIOLOGICAL MATERIAL the removal of an organ, fluid, cells, or tissue for transplantation, testing, or research ■ *v* (**-vests, -vesting, -vested**) **1.** *vti* GATHER CROP to gather a crop for use or sale ○ *Farmers expect to harvest a bumper crop this year.* **2.** *vt* KILL ANIMALS to kill animals for food, sport, or to control their population ○ *The deer are being harvested to control the spread of the disease.* **3.** *vt* REAP RESULTS OF SOMETHING to experience

the consequences of previous actions or behaviour ○ *In the aftermath of a violent civil war the beleaguered people harvested nothing but sorrow.* **4.** *vt* BIOL REMOVE BIOLOGICAL MATERIAL to remove an organ, fluid, cells, or tissue for transplantation, testing, or research [Old English *hærfest* 'autumn' < Indo-European, 'gather'] —**harvestable** *adj*

harvester /haárvistər/ *n* **1.** a machine that gathers crops from the fields, especially a combine harvester **2.** somebody who gathers in crops, especially by hand ○ *Coffee harvesters are at risk from the bites of poisonous spiders.*

harvest festival *n* a Christian service of thanksgiving after a completed harvest

harvest home *n* **1.** the gathering of the harvest, especially its safe completion **2.** a celebration of the completion of the harvest (*hyphenated before a noun*) ○ *a harvest-home dance*

harvestman /haárvist mən/ (*plural* **-men** /-mən/) *n* **1.** N Am INSECTS same as **daddy longlegs** (sense 2) **2.** an agricultural labourer, especially, before agriculture became mechanized, one who left home to find work at harvest time

harvest mite *n UK* the bright-red parasitic larva of a free-living mite that feeds on the skin and other tissues of mammals, including humans, causing irritation and swelling. Some species transmit diseases such as scrub typhus. Genus: *Trombicula* or *Neotrombicula*. ANZ, N Am term **chigger** [Because common at harvest time]

harvest moon *n* the full moon nearest to the autumnal equinox. It rises for several nights at nearly the same time at points successively further north on the eastern horizon.

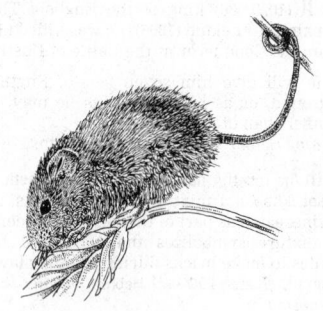

harvest mouse

harvest mouse *n* a small reddish-brown mouse often found in grain fields. Native to: Europe, Asia. Latin name: *Micromys minutus*.

Harvey /haárvi/, **William** (1578–1657) English physician. He discovered the circulation of blood and the role of the heart. He formally published his work on the circulatory system in 1628.

    'Everything from an egg.'
    [William Harvey, *On the Generation of Animals*; 1651]

Harwich /hárrij, -ich/ town and seaport in Essex, eastern England, an important ferry terminal. Population: 15,000

Harwood /haár wŏod/, **Gwen** (1920–95) Australian poet. Influenced by the philosophy of Ludwig Wittgenstein, her published works include *The Lion's Bride* (1981) and *Bone Scan* (1988). Born **Foster, Gwendoline Nessie**

Haryana /húrri aánə/ state in Northwestern India. The union territory of Delhi forms an enclave on its eastern boundary. Capital: Chandigarh. Population: 21,082,989 (2000). Area: 44,212 sq. km/17,070 sq. mi.

Harz Mountains /haárts-/ mountain range in central Germany, between the Elbe and Weser rivers south of Brunswick. The highest peak is the Brocken. Height: 1,141 m/3,743 ft.

has 3rd person singular present of **have**

Hasan /ha sán/ (AD 625?–669?) Arabian religious figure. The son of Fatima, grandson of Muhammad, and elder brother of Husain, he is revered as a martyr by Shiite Muslims.

has-been *n* somebody who formerly was successful, important, or popular, but is no longer (*informal*) ○

It's hard to be a hero one day and a has-been the next.

Hasegawa Tohaku /hássi gaáawə tō haákoo/ (1539–1610) Japanese artist. He was noted for his ink screen paintings, which often featured monkeys, and founded his own school of painting.

Hašek /hásh ek/, **Jaroslav** (1883–1923) Czech writer. He is best known for his four-volume unfinished satirical novel *The Good Soldier Schweik* (1921–23).

hash[1] /hash/ *n* **1.** *UK, ANZ, Can* SYMBOL # the symbol #, especially on a telephone keypad or a computer keyboard. US term **pound sign 2.** FRIED DISH OF POTATOES AND MEAT a dish of cooked potatoes or other vegetables, usually combined with chopped-up pieces of cooked meat, and reheated, usually by frying until golden brown ○ *corned-beef hash* ■ *vt* (**hashes, hashing, hashed**) **1.** COMPUT APPLY ALGORITHM TO CHARACTER STRING to apply an algorithm to a character string, especially in order to find an address of a record **2.** *US* CUT FOOD INTO TINY PIECES to chop meat or vegetables into tiny pieces [Late 16C. < French *hacher* 'hack, cut into small pieces' < *hache* (see HATCHET)] ◇ **make a hash of something** to do something very badly (*informal*) ○ *I made a real hash of the exam.* ◇ **settle somebody's hash** to assert yourself over somebody, especially somebody hostile or troublesome (*informal*) **hash out, hash over** *vt US* same as **thrash out** ○ *They hashed out their differences with an arbitrator.*

hash[2] /hash/ *n* same as **hashish** (*slang*) [Mid-20C. Shortening]

hash browns *npl* cooked potatoes chopped up, sometimes with onions, and fried until golden brown. Occasionally hash browns are formed into small cakes or patties.

hasheesh *n* DRUGS another spelling of **hashish**

HaShem /hásh em/ *n* in Judaism, a substitute word used when referring to God in contexts other than prayers or scriptural readings, because the name for God is considered too holy for such use [< Hebrew, 'the name']

Hashemite /háshə mīt/ *n* **1.** a member of an ancient Arabian dynasty that included the prophet Muhammad and claimed to be directly descended from his great-grandfather, Hashim. The Hashemites were traditionally the custodians of the Kaaba, the sacred Muslim shrine at Mecca. **2.** a member of a modern Arabian dynasty that traces its lineage, via the prophet Muhammad's daughter Fatima, directly to the prophet Muhammad. The dynasty has ruled Jordan since 1926. [Late 17C. After *Hashim*, Muhammad's great-grandfather] —**Hashemite** *adj*

hashish /háshish, há sheesh, ha sheesh/, **hasheesh** /há sheesh, ha sheesh/ *n* a purified resin, prepared from the flowering tops of the female cannabis plant, that is smoked or chewed for its narcotic and intoxicating properties and is widely illegal [Late 16C. < Arabic *ḥašīš* 'dry herb, powdered hemp']

hash mark *n* **1.** *UK, ANZ, Can* COMPUT same as **hash**[1] *n* (sense 1) **2.** *N Am* a stripe sewn on US Army uniforms, one for every two years of active duty **3.** in American football, a line indicating how close to a sideline a football may be at the start of a play

Hasid /hássid/ (*plural* **-dim**), **Hassid, Chasid** /khaássid/, **Chassid** *n* a member of a Jewish movement of popular mysticism founded in Eastern Europe in the 18th century. It emphasized a person's emotional relationship with God, and is now represented by a number of different religious groups. [Early 19C. < Hebrew *ḥāsîd* 'pious'] —**Hasidic** /ha síddik/ *adj* —**Hasidism** *n*

hask /hask/ *regional adj* describes a cough that is dry or hoarse ■ *n* a cough, especially that of an animal [14C. Variant of HARSH]

Haskalah /háskə laá/, **Haskala** *n* the Jewish enlightenment movement, which originated in 18th-century Germany and aimed to integrate Jews into Western European society, e.g. by the use of German instead of Yiddish. It also emphasized secular intellectualism rather than religious learning. [< Hebrew *haśkālāh* 'enlightenment']

hasky /háski/ *adj regional* (*informal*) **1.** without rain **2.** sarcastic or quick-tempered

haslet /házlət, hắyzlət/, **harslet** /haárzlət/ *n* a meat loaf, seasoned with herbs, made from the offal of pigs

[14C. < Old French *haslet* 'small piece of meat roasted on a spit' < *haste* 'spit']

hasn't /házz'nt/ *contr* has not

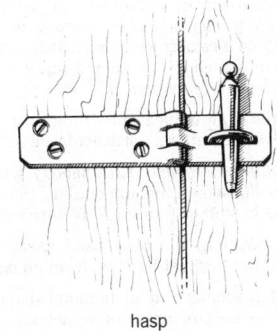

hasp

hasp /haasp/ *n* a hinged metal fastening that fits over a staple and is secured by a pin, bolt, or padlock [Old English *hæpse* 'fastening' < Germanic] —**hasp** *vt*

Hassan II /hə saán/ (1929–99) king of Morocco. Educated in France, he ruled Morocco from 1961 to 1999. Born **Moulay Hassan ben Mohammed Alaoui**

Hassan /ha sán/, **Abdiqasim Salad** (*b.* 1942) president of Somalia (2000–). A former deputy premier and interior minister, he was elected president by the transitional national government of clan elders established in 2000.

~~**hassel**~~ incorrect spelling of **hassle**

Hassid *n* JUDAISM another spelling of **Hasid**

hassium /hássi əm/ *n* an extremely rare unstable element. Source: high-energy atomic collisions. Symbol **Hs**. See table at **element** [Late 20C. < modern Latin < Latin *Hassias* 'Hesse', Germany]

hassle /háss'l/ (*informal*) *n* a source or the experience of aggravation or annoying difficulty ○ *It's just not worth the hassle.* ■ *vt* (**-sles, -sling, -sled**) to bother or annoy somebody, especially by continually asking that person to do something ○ *Stop hassling me about washing the car.* [Late 19C. Origin ?]

hassock /hássək/ *n* **1.** a thick firm cushion used for kneeling on, especially in a Christian church **2.** a thick clump of grass **3.** *N Am* FURNITURE same as **pouf**[1] (sense 1) [Old English *hassuc* 'clump of grass', origin ?]

hast /hast/ 2nd person singular present of **have** (*archaic*)

hastate /hás tayt/ *adj* describes a leaf that is shaped like an arrowhead, with a tip pointing forwards and two sideways-pointing lobes at the base [Late 18C. < Latin *hastatus* 'armed with a spear' < *hasta* 'spear']

haste /hayst/ *n* great speed, especially in situations where time is limited (*formal*) ○ *Make haste, or you will be very late!* ○ *The general proceeded with haste to his headquarters.* ■ *vti* (**hastes, hasting, hasted**) same as **hasten** (senses 2–3) (*literary or archaic*) [13C. < Old French < Germanic] ◇ **more haste less speed** a way of saying that it is not worth rushing something because too many mistakes will be made

hasten /háyss'n/ (**-tens, -tening, -tened**) *v* **1.** *vi* DO SOMETHING IMMEDIATELY to do or say something without delay, often in order to correct what might otherwise be a misleading impression ○ *'But she's perfectly right', he hastened to add.* **2.** *vt* SPEED SOMETHING UP to make something happen more quickly ○ *A holiday would hasten his recovery.* **3.** *vi* GO SOMEWHERE QUICKLY to go somewhere quickly or without delay (*literary*) ○ *hastened to her side*

Hastings /háystingz/ **1.** historic seaside town in East Sussex, southern England. The Battle of Hastings was fought nearby in 1066. Population: 85,029 (2001). **2.** city in the eastern part of the North Island, New Zealand. It is a major agricultural centre. Population: 59,139 (2001).

Hastings, Warren (1732–1818) British colonial administrator. As the first governor general of India (1773–85), he secured British rule and enacted legal and administrative reforms. He was impeached in Parliament for high crimes and misdemeanours (1788–95) and, although he was eventually acquitted, his career and fortune were destroyed.

hasty /háysti/ (**-ier, -iest**) *adj* done, taking place, or acting in a hurry because of impetuosity or lack of time ○ *a hasty marriage* —**hastily** *adv* —**hastiness** *n*

hasty pudding *n* a sweet milk pudding made with flour, semolina, or tapioca [Origin ?]

hat

Pillbox
Top hat
Fedora
Deerstalker
Boater
Bowler
Trilby
Skullcap
Stovepipe
Cloche
Beret

hat /hat/ *n* **1.** a covering for the head, worn for protection from the weather or as a fashion accessory ○ *The children hung their hats and coats up when they came in.* **2.** an area of interest or responsibility of somebody who has more than one interest or responsibility in a particular situation ○ *Which hat will you be wearing at the meeting – parent or teacher?* [Old English *hæt(t)*, via Germanic, 'hood, cowl' < Indo-European, 'to cover'] —**hatted** *adj* ◇ **hang up your hat 1.** to retire from work ○ *When this project's finished he's going to hang up his hat and retire to the country.* **2.** to settle down to a calmer, more stable lifestyle after an extended period of stress or activity ○ *Children of military personnel move so frequently that they'd like to find just one place in which to hang up their hats.* ◇ **hats off to somebody** a way of saying that somebody has gained your respect or admiration ◇ **keep something under your hat** to keep something secret ◇ **my hat** used to express disbelief or disagreement (*dated informal*) ◇ **pass the hat round** to collect contributions for

somebody or something ◇ **pull something out of the hat** to do something that seemed very difficult or impossible to achieve, as if by a magic trick (*informal*) ◇ **take your hat off to somebody** to acknowledge admiration or respect for somebody ○ *You have to take your hat off to her – she's stuck by him for 25 years.* ◇ **talk through your hat** to talk nonsense (*informal*) ○ *You're talking through your hat, and I don't take a word of it seriously.* ◇ **throw your hat into the ring** to volunteer to take part in a particular contest ○ *I didn't think I'd get the job, but I decided to throw my hat into the ring anyway.*

hatband /hát band/ *n* a thin strip of leather, cloth, ribbon, or other material that is fixed round a hat just above the brim

hatbox /hát boks/ *n* a large hard box with a removable or liftable lid, used for storing, carrying, or protecting a hat or hats

hatch[1] /hach/ *n* **1.** a door cut into the floor or ceiling of something, especially on a boat or an aircraft. It is lifted to provide access to the area below or above it. A hatch may also provide access to an attic or cellar in a building. **2.** a small connecting hole in a wall between two rooms, or the small doors that cover this hole ○ *an escape hatch* ○ *There's a serving hatch between the kitchen and the living room.* **3.** CARS same as **hatchback** [Old English *hæcc* 'lower half of a door, wicket' < Germanic]

hatch[2] /hach/ (**hatches, hatching, hatched**) v **1.** *vi* COME OUT OF EGG to emerge from an egg **2.** *vi* BREAK OPEN FOR RELEASE OF YOUNG to break open so that the young inside may be released (*refers to eggs*) **3.** *vt* CAUSE YOUNG TO EMERGE FROM EGG to cause a young organism such as a chick, fish, or insect, to emerge from its egg ○ *Birds hatch their chicks by sitting on the nests.* **4.** *vt* SECRETLY DEVISE PLOT to secretly devise a plot, plan, or scheme, usually an illicit or illegal one, or one that is ill-advised in some way [15C. Origin ?]
hatch out *vi* to emerge from an egg

hatch[3] /hach/ (**hatches, hatching, hatched**) *vti* in graphic art, to mark or cover something with parallel crossed lines to show shading, or be marked in this way [15C. < French *hacher* 'to chop' < *hache* (see HATCHET)] —**hatching** *n*

hatchback

hatchback /hách bak/ *n* a car with a rear door that is hinged from the roof to allow easy access to storage space behind the rear seats. The storage space usually has a removable shelf between the top of the seats and the rear window. ○ *a five-door hatchback*

hatchery /háchəri/ (*plural* -ies) *n* a place where fish or poultry eggs are hatched commercially under artificial conditions

hatchet

hatchet /háchit/ *n* a small axe that can be used with one hand ○ *wield a hatchet* [14C. < French *hachette* 'small axe' < *hache* 'axe' < medieval Latin *hapia* < Germanic] ◇ **bury the hatchet** to make peace with somebody after a disagreement ○ *They fell out years ago, but it looks as if they've finally decided to bury the hatchet.* ◇ **do a hatchet job on somebody** *or* **something** to criticize somebody or something severely, especially in print (*informal*)

hatchet face *n* an unpleasantly long thin face with sharp or gaunt features —**hatchet-faced** *adj*

hatchet man *n* (*informal*) **1.** somebody who is employed to do something unpopular, especially to make cuts in staff or funding **2.** *N Am* a hired killer

hatchling /háchling/ *n* a bird, fish, insect, or other organism that has just hatched from an egg

hatchment /háchmənt/ *n* a diamond-shaped panel bearing the coat of arms of somebody who has died [Early 16C. Probably < obsolete French *hachement*, alteration of Old French *acesmement* 'adornment' < *acesmer* 'adorn']

hatchway /hách way/ *n* BUILDINGS same as **hatch**[1] (sense 2)

hate /hayt/ v (**hates, hating, hated**). **1.** *vt* DISLIKE SOMEBODY OR SOMETHING INTENSELY to dislike somebody or something intensely, often in a way that evokes feelings of anger, hostility, or animosity ○ *Love her or hate her, you have to admit she's got a great singing voice.* ○ *Having come to hate her husband, the defendant admits that she attempted to poison him.* **2.** *vti* HAVE STRONG DISTASTE FOR SOMETHING to have strong distaste or aversion for something, somebody, or something that has to be done ○ *I hate this show; it's so boring.* ○ *I hate to say it, but I know we're going to lose.* ○ *Some people seem to have been born to hate.* ■ *n* **1.** FEELING OF INTENSE HOSTILITY a feeling of intense hostility towards somebody or something ○ *You could see the hate in his eyes.* **2.** SOMETHING HATED something that is hated [Old English *hete* (noun), *hatian* (verb) < Indo-European] —**hateable** *adj* —**hated** *adj* —**hater** *n*

SYNONYMS See *dislike*.

hate crime *n* a crime that is motivated by hate, prejudice, or intolerance of somebody's religion, ethnicity, or sexual orientation

hateful /háytf'l/ *adj* **1.** characterized by malevolence or spite **2.** eliciting feelings or reactions of hatred, detestation, or abhorrence —**hatefully** *adv* —**hatefulness** *n*

hate mail *n* mail that expresses the sender's anger about something, usually towards the recipient, in a threatening or offensive way

Hatfield /hát feeld/ town in Hertfordshire, southeastern England, designated a new town in 1948. Population: 31,104 (1991).

hatful /hát fool/ *n* a large quantity or number of something ○ *received a hatful of compliments on the performance*

hath /hath/ 3rd person singular present of **have** (*archaic*)

Hathaway /háthə way/, **Anne** (1556–1623) English wife of William Shakespeare. She was born into a farming family, and married William Shakespeare, eight years her junior, in 1582.

hatha yoga /háthə-, húttə-/ *n* a low-impact yoga that helps to regulate breathing by exercises consisting of postures and stretches intended to sustain healthy bodily functioning and induce emotional calmness [< Sanskrit, 'force yoga']

hatpin /hát pin/ *n* a long thin pin, often with a decoration at the end, that is pushed through a hat and into the hair to keep the hat securely on the head

hatred /háytrid/ *n* a feeling of intense hostility towards somebody or something [12C. < HATE + suffix < Old English *ræden* 'state, condition']

SYNONYMS See *dislike*.

Hatshepsut /hát shép soot/ (*fl* 15th century BC) queen of Egypt of the 18th Dynasty. She ruled from 1479–57 and crowned herself pharaoh in 1473 after years of ruling jointly with her husband, Thutmose II, and his son, Thutmose III.

hat stand

hat stand *n* a tall free-standing piece of furniture consisting of a base with a pole fixed into it with hooks round the top on which hats, coats, and umbrellas can be hung

hatter /háttər/ *n* a maker or seller of hats

Hatteras, Cape /háttərəss/ promontory projecting into the Atlantic Ocean in eastern North Carolina. It is renowned for treacherous weather conditions.

Hattersley /háttərzli/, **Roy, Lord** (b. 1932) British politician. Elected to Parliament in 1964, he was deputy leader of the Labour Party (1983–92), and was made a life peer in 1997. Full name **Hattersley, Roy Sydney George, Lord**

hat trick *n* in football, a series of three wins or successes, especially three goals scored by the same player [Probably < the former cricketing practice of awarding a hat to a bowler who took three wickets with three consecutive balls]

hauberk /háw burk/ *n* a long, often sleeveless, tunic made of chain mail. It was originally intended as protection just for the neck and shoulders but it developed into a longer tunic in the 12th and 13th centuries. [13C. < Old French *hau(s)berc* < Germanic, 'neck-protector']

haugh /haw, haakh/ *n Scotland* a low-lying stretch of land in a river valley, often unproductive because of frequent flooding [14C. Probably < Old English *healh* 'corner, nook, small hollow in a slope']

Haughey /háwhi/, **Charles** (b. 1925) Irish politician. He was leader of the Fianna Fáil Party (1979–92) and prime minister of Ireland (1979–81, 1982, and 1987–92).

'If you were to elect the head of the Orange Order as President of this Republic, the Unionists would still find we are doing something dishonest, deceitful, and totally unacceptable to them.'
[Charles Haughey, *Irish Times*; 30 June 1986]

haughty /háwti/ (-**tier**, -**tiest**) *adj* behaving in a superior, condescending, or arrogant way ○ *haughty self-assurance* [Mid-16C. < archaic *haught* < French *haut(e)* 'high'] —**haughtily** *adv* —**haughtiness** *n*

haul /hawl/ v (**hauls, hauling, hauled**) **1.** *vt* PULL OR DRAG SOMETHING to pull something with continuous and laborious movements **2.** *vt* MOVE SOMETHING WITH EFFORT to transport something that is heavy and bulky from one place to another **3.** *vt* SAILING CHANGE BOAT'S COURSE to change a vessel's course so as to sail closer to the wind **4.** *vi* NAUT BLOW CLOSER TO BOW to blow from a direction that is closer to a vessel's bow (*refers to winds*) **5.** *vt* NAUT HOIST VESSEL INTO DRY DOCK to hoist a vessel from the water into a dry dock, e.g. to make repairs ■ *n* **1.** STOLEN ITEMS goods that have been stolen, or the value of these stolen goods ○ *The haul was mainly silver and paintings.* **2.** CONFISCATED CONTRABAND illegal goods that are confiscated by the authorities **3.** FISHING SINGLE CATCH OF FISH the amount of fish caught in a single catch **4.** DISTANCE SOMETHING IS TRANSPORTED a distance over which something is transported or pulled, or which somebody travels with difficulty [13C. Variant of HALE[2]]

SYNONYMS See *pull*.

haul off *vi* to manoeuvre a vessel in order to avoid something

haul up *vt* to force somebody to appear before a court or another disciplinary body for judgment ○ *witnesses who were hauled up before a grand jury*

haulage /háwlij/ *n* **1.** the business or process of transporting goods, usually by road or rail **2.** the cost of transporting goods, or the rate charged for transporting goods

hauler /háwlər/ *n N Am* TRANSP same as **haulier**

haulier /háwli ər/ *n* a person or company whose business is transporting goods, especially by road. N Am term **hauler**

haulm /hawm/, **halm** *n* **1.** the stems or stalks of grain, beans, peas, potatoes, or grasses, especially after harvesting. Use: thatching, litter. **2.** a single stem of a grain, bean, pea, potato, or grass [Old English *h(e)alm* < Indo-European]

haunch /hawnch/ *n* **1.** **HIP, BUTTOCK, AND UPPER THIGH** the part of the body comprising the hip, buttock, and upper thigh ○ *She sat back on her haunches.* **2.** **ANIMAL LEG** one of the back legs of a four-legged animal, either when it is alive, or as a cut of meat **3.** ARCHIT **UPPER PART OF ARCH** the upper curving part of each side of an arch [12C. < French *hanche* < Germanic]

haunt /hawnt/ *vt* (**haunts, haunting, haunted**) **1.** **DISCOMFIT SOMEBODY BY UNPLEASANT REMINDERS** to cause somebody unease, worry, or regret by continual presence or recurrence in his or her life ○ *haunted by doubt* **2.** **VISIT SOMEWHERE CONTINUALLY** to go often to a place ○ *She no longer haunts the late-night bars* **3.** PARANORMAL **APPEAR TO SOMEBODY AS GHOST** to frequent a place or appear to somebody in the form of a ghost or other supposed supernatural being ■ *n* **PLACE SOMEBODY OFTEN VISITS** a place that somebody likes and often visits ○ *a holiday away from the usual tourist haunts* [12C. < French *hanter* 'frequent a place' < Germanic, 'home'] — **haunter** *n*

haunted /háwntid/ *adj* **1.** inhabited by or visited regularly by a ghost or other supposed supernatural being **2.** looking strangely frightened or worried

haunting /háwnting/ *adj* evoking strong emotion, especially a sense of sadness, that persists for a long time ○ *a haunting testament to war's destruction* — **hauntingly** *adv*

Hauraki Gulf /how ráaki-/ bay on the northeastern coast of the North Island, New Zealand. The city of Auckland is located on its southwestern shore. Area: 2,290 sq. km/884 sq. mi.

Hausa /hówssə/ (*plural same* or **-sas**) *n* **1.** PEOPLES **MEMBER OF W AFRICAN PEOPLE** a member of a people living mainly in northern Nigeria and southern Niger **2.** LANG **LANGUAGE OF W AFRICA** a language spoken in Nigeria, Niger, and other parts of eastern West Africa, belonging to the Chadic branch of Afro-Asiatic. Native speakers: 25 million. Other speakers: 40 million. **3.** RELIG **SPIRITUAL TRADITION OF NIGERIA** the tradition combining aspects of Islam and of local religious beliefs associated with the Hausa, after the collapse of the Songhay Empire [Early 19C. < Hausa] — **Hausa** *adj*

hausfrau /hówss frow/ (*plural* **-fraus**) *n* a traditional housewife, conventionally believed to be interested mostly in her home and family (*sometimes offensive*) ○ *She wanted a career, not a life as a hausfrau.* [Late 18C. < German < *Haus* 'house' + *Frau* 'wife, woman']

Hausmann /hówssmən/, **Raoul** (1886–1971) Austrian poet and artist. He was a founding member of the Dada movement in Berlin. His work includes photomontages and 'phonetic poems', several of which he recorded.

Haussmann /óss man/, **George-Eugène, Baron** (1809–91) French town planner. His redesign of Paris in the 1850s and 1860s, with its broad avenues and parks, influenced urban design around the world.

haustellum /haw stélləm/ (*plural* **-la** /-lə/) *n* the tip of the proboscis, or elongated mouthpart, that is adapted for sucking food in many insects such as flies [Early 19C. < modern Latin, 'small scoop' < Latin *haustrum* 'scoop' < *haurire* 'draw up']

haustorium /haw stáwri əm/ (*plural* **-ria** /-ri ə/) *n* a structure of a parasitic plant or fungus that penetrates host tissues to obtain food and water [Late 19C. < Latin *haustor* 'water-drawer, drinker' < *haurire* 'draw up']

hautboy /ṓ boy, hṓ-/ (*plural* **-boys**), **hautbois** (*plural same*) *n* **1.** a strawberry with large fruit. Native to: Europe, Asia. Latin name: *Fragaria moschata*. **2.** MUSIC same as **oboe** (*archaic*) [Mid-16C. < French *hautbois* 'oboe' < *haut* 'high' (from its high pitch) + *bois* 'wood' < Germanic]

haute couture /ṓt koo tyóor/ *n* exclusive and expensive clothing made for an individual customer by a fashion designer, or the industry that produces such clothing [Early 20C. < French, 'high dressmaking']

haute cuisine /ṓt kwi zéen/ *n* classic high-quality French cooking (*hyphenated when used before a noun*) [Early 20C. < French, 'high cooking']

haute école /ṓt ay kol/ *n* the skill and art of expert horsemanship [Mid-19C. < French, 'high school']

hauteur /ō túr/ *n* a haughty manner, feeling, or quality [Early 17C. < French < *haute* 'high' < Latin *altus*]

haut monde /ṓ mónd/ *n* the highest stratum of society, international or domestic, and those in it ○ *a denizen of the haut monde, invited to every international ball and gala* [Mid-19C. < French, 'high world']

havala /hə vaálə/, **hawala** *n S Asia* FIN a means of exchanging foreign currency unofficially and sometimes illegally without records [< Hindi]

Havana[1] /hə vánnə/ capital, port, and largest city of Cuba, on the northwestern coast of the country. Population: 2,189,716 (2000). —**Havanan** *adj, n*

Havana[2] /hə vánnə/, **Havana cigar** *n* a high-quality cigar made in Cuba [Early 19C. < HAVANA [1]]

Havant /hávvənt/ seaside town in Hampshire, southern England. Population: 116,849 (2001).

Havarti /hə vaárti/ *n* a pale, moist, semihard Danish cheese with tiny holes, a slightly rubbery texture, and a mild buttery flavour [Mid-20C. After the farm of a 19C Danish cheese maker]

havdalah *n* JUDAISM another spelling of **habdalah**

have *stressed* /hav/; *unstressed* /həv, əv/ (**has** *stressed* /haz/; *unstressed* /həz, əz/, **having, had** *stressed* /had/; *unstressed* /həd, əd/) CORE MEANING: a verb indicating that somebody possesses something, either materially or as a characteristic or attribute ○ *She has a small cottage in the country.* ○ *He has beautiful eyes.*

1. *vt* **OWN SOMETHING** to be the owner or possessor of something ○ *I don't have a lot of money.* **2.** *vt* **POSSESS CHARACTERISTIC** to be the possessor of a quality or characteristic ○ *She had long blonde hair.* **3.** *aux v* **FORMS PERFECT TENSES** used to form the following tenses or aspects: the present perfect, the past perfect, the future perfect, and the continuous forms of these (*used before the past participle of a verb or at the beginning of a question, or with 'got' to indicate possession*) ○ *I have finished my dinner, thank you.* ○ *Have you finished yet?* ○ *I have got a new car.* **4.** *modal v* **EXPRESSES COMPULSION** expresses compulsion, obligation, or necessity ○ *We have to go now.* ○ *said he'd do it if he had to* **5.** *modal v* **EXPRESSES CERTAINTY** expresses conviction or certainty ○ *There just has to be a solution to the problem.* **6.** *vt* **RECEIVE SOMETHING** to receive or obtain something ○ *I had a Christmas card from him.* **7.** *vt* **EAT SOMETHING** to eat or drink something ○ *We have breakfast at eight.* **8.** *vt* **THINK OF SOMETHING** to think of something, or hold something in the mind ○ *Listen! I have a good idea.* **9.** *vt* **EXPERIENCE SOMETHING** to experience or undergo something ○ *He went to the carnival to have a good time.* ○ *I had a shock.* **10.** *vt* **BE AFFECTED BY SOMETHING** to be affected by something, especially something of a medical nature ○ *I've had the flu for the last week.* **11.** *vt* **ENGAGE IN SOMETHING** to engage or participate in something ○ *They had a long talk about cars.* **12.** *vt* **ARRANGE SOMETHING** to organize or arrange something ○ *We had a party last week.* **13.** *vt* **ARRANGE FOR SOMETHING TO BE DONE** to arrange for somebody to do something for you or on your behalf ○ *I've just had my hair cut.* **14.** *vt* **TOLERATE SOMETHING** to tolerate or put up with something (*usually used in negative statements*) ○ *I won't have such behaviour any longer!* **15.** *vt* **RECEIVE SOMEBODY** to receive somebody as a guest ○ *We had Mother to stay over Christmas.* **16.** *vt* **BRING CHILD INTO EXISTENCE** to be the parent of a child, or conceive, carry, or give birth to a child ○ *She's had three children and now she's having another one.* **17.** *vt* **PUT SOMEBODY OR SOMETHING SOMEWHERE** to put or place somebody or something in a particular place ○ *I'll have you two in the front row, please.* **18.** *vt* **UNDERGO SOMETHING** to be the victim of an unpleasant action or experience ○ *I had my car stolen.* **19.** *vt* **MAKE SOMETHING HAPPEN** to direct or cause somebody to do something, or cause something to happen ○ *If you see him tomorrow, have him call me.* **20.** *vt* **CHEAT SOMEBODY** to cheat or outwit somebody (*slang; usually passive*) ○ *I think you've been had in this deal.* [Old English *habban* < Indo-European, 'grasp'] ◇ **have done with something** to finish with something ○ *Let's put everything else in this box and have done with it.* ◇ **have (got) it in for somebody** to dislike somebody and want to do that person harm ◇ **have had it 1.** to have no prospect of success ○ *We've had it now.* **2.** to be too worn out, damaged, or exhausted to function properly (*informal*) ○ *I'm afraid this printer has just about had it.* ○ *I've had it – you go on, I'm turning back.* ◇ **have had it with somebody** *or* **something** to have lost patience with somebody *or* something ○ *I've had it with delays.* ◇ **have it** to declare or assert something ○ *Rumour has it that they are planning to get engaged.* ◇ **have it out (with somebody)** to engage in a spirited, aggressive argument over an issue with somebody ○ *OK, let's have it out now and get this settled once and for all.* ◇ **have something on somebody** to have unfavourable information about somebody's activities ◇ **have to do with 1.** to be relevant to ○ *Does your question have anything to do with the topic under discussion?* **2.** to have a friendship or relationship with ○ *She will have nothing to do with him any more.* ◇ **have what it takes** to have the necessary skills, personality, or attitude to be successful at something ○ *He doesn't really have what it takes to be a professional actor.* ◇ **not having any (of something)** refusing to take part or become involved in something ○ *They tried to involve him in the conspiracy, but it soon became clear that he wasn't having any.*

USAGE See ***do***[1].

have on *vt* **1.** to have an item of clothing on your body **2.** to tell somebody something untrue as a joke or tease (*informal*)

have up *vt* to cause somebody to appear for trial (*informal*) ○ *He was had up for breaking and entering.*

Havel /haáv'l, hávv'l/, **Václav** (*b.* 1936) Czech dramatist and statesman. He was a dissident playwright who became a leader of the Charter 77 Czech democracy movement under Communist rule. After the democratic revolution in 1989 he became president of Czechoslovakia (1989) and then of the Czech Republic (1993–2003).

> 'Truth is not merely what we are thinking, but also why, to whom, and under what circumstances we say it.'
> [Václav Havel, *Temptation*; 1985]

haveli /húvvə lée/ (*plural* **-lis**) *n S Asia* a large stately house [Via Hindi < Arabic *havelī*]

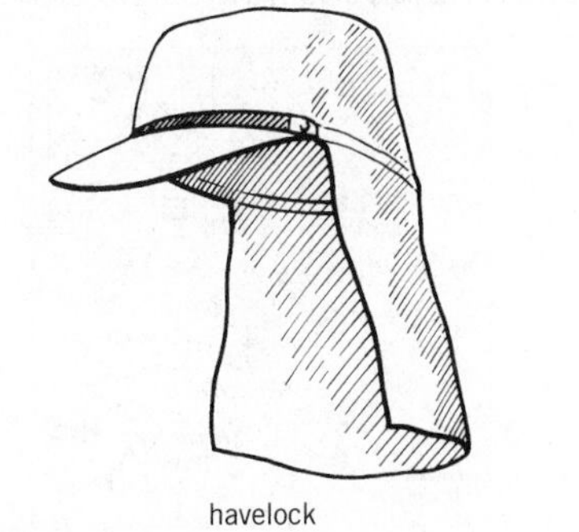

havelock

havelock /háv lok/ *n* a light-coloured cover for a soldier's cap, with a flap extending over the back of the neck to protect the head and neck from the sun [Mid-19C. After Sir Henry *Havelock* (1795–1857), British major-general]

haven /háyv'n/ *n* **1.** a place sought for rest, shelter, or protection ○ *a haven for wildlife* **2.** a harbour or port facility where ships and boats come in and tie up (*literary*) [Pre-12C. < Old Norse *hǫfn* 'place that holds (ships)']

have-nots *npl* people who are not rich or privileged, especially compared with those who are ○ *a country with the highest income inequality between the haves and have-nots*

haven't /hávv'nt/ *contr* have not

haver /háyvər/ *n, interj also* **havers** *N England, Scotland* same as **nonsense** *n* (sense 1), *interj* ■ *vi* (**-ers, -ering, -ered**) **1.** to be unable to make a choice or come to

a decision **2.** *N England, Scotland* to talk nonsense or speak inconsequentially [Early 18C. Origin ?]

Haverfordwest /hávvərfərd wést, haárfərd-/ market town in Pembrokeshire, southwestern Wales. It is the administrative centre of the county. Population: 13,454 (1991).

haversack /hávvər sak/ *n* a strong bag carried on the back or the shoulder, used especially by travellers or hikers [Mid-18C. Via French *havresac* < obsolete German *Habersack* < *Haber* 'oats' + *Sack* 'bag']

Haversian canal /hə vúrsh'n-, -vúrssi ən-/ *n* a tiny longitudinal channel in bone tissue. The canals form a network that contains blood vessels and nerve fibres. [Mid-19C. After Clopton *Havers* (1650?–1702), English physician and anatomist]

Haversian system *n* a Haversian canal along with the concentric layers of compact bone surrounding it [See HAVERSIAN CANAL]

haversine /hávvər sīn/ *n* in mathematics, half the value of the versed sine [Late 19C. Contraction of *half versed sine*]

haves /havz/ *npl* people who are rich and privileged, especially compared with those who are not [Mid-18C. < HAVE]

havildar /hávv'l daar/ *n S Asia* an army or police officer of a rank equivalent to sergeant [Late 17C. Via Urdu *hawildār* < Persian *hawāl(a)dār* 'charge holder']

Havilland ♦ **De Havilland, Sir Geoffrey**

Havilland ♦ **de Havilland, Olivia**

havoc /hávvək/ *n* **1.** DEVASTATION widespread damage, destruction, or devastation ○ *the havoc wreaked by the storm* **2.** CHAOS a condition or situation of disruptive chaos ■ *adj Malaysia, Singapore* DIFFICULT TO CONTROL difficult to control, manage, discipline, or govern (*informal*) ○ *Her kids look really havoc!* [15C. < Anglo-Norman (*crier*) *havok* '(to cry) havoc', signal to an army to seize plunder, alteration of Old French *havo(t)* 'pillage']

haw[1] /haw/ *n* **1.** PLANTS same as **hawthorn 2.** the round or oval fruit of the hawthorn, usually red or yellow and containing seeds [Old English *haga*, origin ?]

haw[2] /haw/ *n* a sound that people make when they are hesitating to speak ■ *vi* (**haws, hawing, hawed**) to make a sound indicative of hesitation while speaking [Mid-17C. An imitation of the sound]

haw[3] /haw/ *n* VET same as **nictitating membrane** [Early 16C. Origin ?]

haw[4] /haw/ *interj* used to command an animal or a team of animals to turn left [Late 17C. Origin ?]

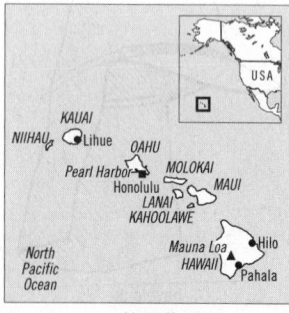

Hawaii

Hawaii /hə wí i/ **1.** state of the United States in the northern Pacific Ocean, consisting of eight main islands, Oahu, Hawaii, Kahoolawe, Kauai, Lanai, Maui, Molokai, and Niihau, and over 100 others. Capital: Honolulu. Population: 1,244,898 (2002 estimate). Area: 16,729 sq. km/6,459 sq. mi. **2.** the largest island in the state of Hawaii. Population: 154,794 (2002 estimate). Area: 10,432 sq. km/4,028 sq. mi.

Hawaii-Aleutian Standard Time *n* the standard time in the time zone centred on 150° west longitude, which includes Hawaii and the western Aleutian Islands. It is ten hours behind Universal Time.

Hawaiian /hə wí ən, -wí i ən/ *n* **1.** somebody who comes from Hawaii **2.** a language spoken in Hawaii and other neighbouring islands, belonging to the Polynesian branch of Austronesian. Native speakers: 70,000. —**Hawaiian** *adj*

Hawaiian appliqué *n* appliqué in which a large central motif, from a design cut from folded paper, is applied to a foundation fabric and made into a quilt. Traditional Hawaiian appliqué is made in two solid colours, typically red, green, orange, or blue on white.

Hawaiian English *n* a variety of English spoken in Hawaii

Hawaiian goose *n* BIRDS same as **nene**

Hawaiian guitar *n* a small steel-strung guitar with a sliding glass or metal bar that fits across the strings in order to change the pitch of the whole instrument. It is usually played horizontally on a stand, and the strings are plucked with a thimble.

Hawaiian Islands island group in the central North Pacific Ocean, consisting of eight main islands: Hawaii, Maui, Oahu, Kauai, Molokai, Lanai, Niihau, and Kahoolawe, and many islets, making up most of the US state of Hawaii

Hawaii Standard Time, Hawaii Time *n* TIME same as **Hawaii-Aleutian Standard Time**

haway /hə wáy/ *interj N England* used as a greeting (*informal*) [Origin ?]

Haweswater /háwz wawtər/ lake in Cumbria, northwestern England, now enlarged and used as a reservoir. Area: 4 sq. km/2 sq. mi.

hawfinch

hawfinch /háw finch/ (*plural* **-finches** or *same*) *n* a songbird with a thick conical silvery beak, brown feathers, black-and-white wings, and a white-tipped tail. Native to: Europe, Asia. Latin name: *Coccothraustes coccothraustes*. [< HAW[1]]

haw-haw[1] *interj* same as **ha-ha**[1]

haw-haw[2] *n* GARDENING same as **ha-ha**[2]

Hawick /hoyk/ historic town in the Scottish Borders district on the River Teviot. Population: 15,812 (1991).

hawk[1] /hawk/ *n* **1.** BIRD OF PREY a bird of prey that is active in the daytime, typically having broad wings, a short hooked beak, strong talons, and a long tail. Family: Accipitridae. **2.** SOMEBODY FAVOURING FORCE somebody who favours the use of military force in implementing foreign policy **3.** AGGRESSIVE COMPETITOR a fiercely competitive, aggressive, predatory, or combative person ○ *a marketing hawk who wanted to put the competition out of business* ■ *v* (**hawks, hawking, hawked**) **1.** *vi* FIELD SPORTS HUNT WITH HAWKS to hunt for prey on the wing, or hunt for prey using hawks and similar birds of prey **2.** *vti* BIRDS ATTACK ON WING to pursue or attack something while flying in a way similar to that of a hawk ○ *big brown bats hawking at small prey* ○ *tiny birds hawking insects in the morning sky* [Old English *h(e)afoc* < Indo-European, 'grasp'] —**hawker** *n* —**hawking** *n*

hawk[2] /hawk/ *vti* (**hawks, hawking, hawked**) CLEAR THROAT to clear the throat noisily of phlegm ■ *n* **1.** ATTEMPT AT CLEARING THROAT a noisy attempt to clear the throat of phlegm **2.** SALIVA OR PHLEGM saliva or phlegm, es-

pecially when somebody spits it out [Late 16C. Probably an imitation of the sound]

hawk[3] /hawk/ (**hawks, hawking, hawked**) *vti* to engage in selling merchandise on the street or from door to door [14C. Probably back-formation < *hawker*, probably < Middle Low German *hōker* < *hōken* 'peddle'] —**hawker** *n*

hawk[4] /hawk/ *n* a metal square with a wooden handle underneath, used by a plasterer to hold wet plaster or mortar before applying it to a surface [15C. Origin ?]

hawkbill *n* ZOOL same as **hawksbill**

hawkbit /háwk bit/ (*plural* **-bits** or *same*) *n* a perennial plant with lobed leaves. Flowers: yellow. Native to: grasslands. Genus: *Leontodon*. [Early 18C. Blend of HAWKWEED + *devil's bit*, wild plant with a short rootstock, popularly said to have been bitten off by the devil]

Bob Hawke

Hawke /hawk/, **Bob** (*b.* 1929) Australian politician. He was leader of the Australian Labor Party and prime minister of Australia (1983–91). Full name **Hawke, Robert James Lee**. See table at **prime minister**

'Obviously, any person who claims they didn't get anything wrong is an idiot. Of course, there were some things we got wrong.'
[Bob Hawke, *The Age*; 1 March 2003]

Hawke Bay bay on the eastern coast of the North Island, New Zealand. It extends from Mahia Peninsula in the north to Cape Kidnappers in the south.

Hawker /háwkər/, **Harry George** (1889–1921) Australian aviator. He was chief test pilot with the Sopwith Aviation Company (1913–20) and a designer of early aircraft.

Hawke's Bay /háwks-/ administrative region of New Zealand, located in the east of the North Island and bordering Hawke Bay. Population: 142,947 (2001). Area: 21,178 sq. km/8,177 sq. mi.

Hawkesbury /háwksbəri/ river in eastern New South Wales, Australia, which rises in the Great Dividing Range. Length: 480 km/298 mi.

hawk-eyed *adj* quick to see things that are not obvious, often as a result of having very keen eyesight ○ *The hawk-eyed appraiser spotted a tiny chip in the antique teapot.*

Stephen Hawking

Hawking /háwking/, **Stephen** (*b.* 1942) British physicist and mathematician. His research focused on space-time and unified field theory. His lectures, films, and books, including *A Brief History of Time* (1988) and *The Universe in a Nutshell* (2001), made difficult concepts in physics accessible to the public. Full name **Hawking, Stephen William**. See illustration on previous page and Cultural note at **time**

'Even if there is only one possible unified theory, it is just a set of rules and equations. What is it that breathes fire into the equations and makes a universe for them to describe?... Why does the universe go to all the bother of existing?'
[Stephen Hawking, *A Brief History of Time*; 1988]

Hawkins /háwkinz/, **Coleman** (1904–69) US musician. His technique and improvisational skills laid the foundations for the tenor saxophone in bebop jazz. His best-known album is *Body and Soul* (1939).

'I like most music unless it's wrong.'
[Coleman Hawkins. Quoted in *The World of Swing*, Stanley Dance; 1974]

hawkish /háwkish/ *adj* favouring the use of military force in implementing foreign policy rather than diplomatic solutions —**hawkishly** *adv* —**hawkishness** *n*

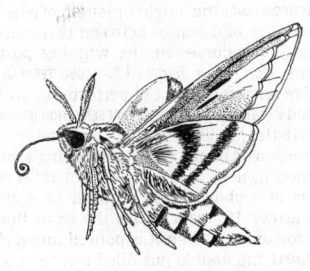

hawk moth

hawk moth *n* a moth with a thick body and long narrow wings that enable it to hover over flowers and feed on their nectar. Family: Sphingidae.

hawk owl

hawk owl *n* an owl with a long slender tail and brownish speckled feathers that resembles a hawk when in flight. Native to: North America, Europe, Asia. Latin name: *Surnia ulula*.

Hawks /hawks/, **Howard** (1896–1977) US film director. During his 45-year career, he directed many Hollywood classics, including *Bringing Up Baby* (1938) and *The Big Sleep* (1946). Full name **Hawks, Howard Winchester**

hawk's beard (*plural* **hawk's beards** or *same*) *n* a composite plant with milky juice. Flowers: small, yellow, resembling the dandelion. Genus: *Crepis*.

hawksbill /háwks bil/ (*plural* **-bills** or *same*), **hawksbill turtle**, **hawkbill** /háwk bil/ (*plural* **-bills** or *same*) *n* a sea turtle, reaching 61 cm/2 ft in length, that has a yellowish-brown shell of overlapping plates. Native to: tropics. Latin name: *Eretmochelys imbricata*. [< the shape of its mouth]

hawk's-eye *n* a dark blue semiprecious stone that is a variety of crocidolite. Use: gems.

Hawksmoor /háwks moŏr, -mawr/, **Nicholas** (1661–1736) English architect. He was a pupil of Sir Christopher Wren and assistant to Sir John Vanbrugh. His work includes several London churches, parts of Westminster Abbey, London, and All Souls, Oxford.

hawkweed

hawkweed /háwk weed/ (*plural same* or **-weeds**) *n* a plant typically with hairy leaves, sometimes found as a weed. Flowers: yellow or orange, resembling dandelions. Genus: *Hieracium*.

Haworth /hów erth/ historic village in West Yorkshire, northern England. It was once home to the Brontë family. Population: 4,956 (1991).

Haworth, Sir Norman (1883–1950) British biochemist. He was awarded the Nobel Prize in chemistry with Paul Karrer (1937) for his research into the structure of vitamin C. Full name **Haworth, Sir Walter Norman**

hawse /hawz/ *n* **1.** LOCATION OF SHIP'S HAWSEHOLES the area of a ship in which the hawseholes are to be found **2.** same as **hawsehole 3.** SPACE BETWEEN BOW AND ANCHOR the space between the bow and the anchors of a ship lying at anchor **4.** ANCHOR DEPLOYMENT the way in which a ship's anchor lines are deployed, starboard and port, when both are deployed together at the same time ■ *vi* (**hawses, hawsing, hawsed**) PITCH VIOLENTLY WHEN AT ANCHOR to pitch violently when lying at anchor [13C < Old Norse *hals*, Old English *h(e)als* 'neck, ship's prow' < Indo-European, 'revolve']

hawsehole /háwz hōl/ *n* an opening in the bow of a ship through which a large heavy line is passed for towing or mooring the ship

hawsepipe /háwz pīp/ *n* a pipe on each side of a ship's bow for use in deploying and weighing anchor, with the anchor lines running through each pipe

hawser /háwzər/ *n* a large heavy cable that is used when mooring or towing a ship [13C. < Anglo-Norman *haucer* < Old French *haucier* 'to hoist' < Latin *altus* 'high']

hawser-laid *adj* describes rope composed of three strands that are made by being twisted in a left-handed direction, then twisted together in a right-handed direction

hawthorn /háw thawrn/ *n* a thorny bush or tree of the rose family with white or pink flowers and reddish berries. Genus: *Crataegus*.

Nathaniel Hawthorne

Hawthorne /háw thawrn/, **Nathaniel** (1804–64) US writer. His novels and short stories frequently deal with Puritan sin and atonement, and include *The Scarlet Letter* (1850). Born **Hathorne, Nathaniel**

'No man, for any considerable period, can wear one face to himself, and another to the multitude, without finally getting bewildered as to which may be the true.'

[Nathaniel Hawthorne, *The Scarlet Letter*; 1850]

Hawthorne effect /háw thawrn-/ *n* an effect in social research in which findings are attributable to the attention of researchers to the subjects of their research rather than to factors significant to the research topic. An example is when variables of both a positive and a negative nature produce the same effect. [Mid-20C. After a plant of the Western Electric Company in Cicero (Chicago, Illinois)]

hay /hay/ *n* CUT AND DRIED GRASS grass or other plants that are cut, dried, and then often used as fodder ○ *a bale of hay* ■ *v* (**hays, haying, hayed**) **1.** *vi* CUT, BALE, AND STORE HAY to mow hay and bale or roll it, and then store it ○ *He's been haying all day.* **2.** *vt* GIVE HAY TO ANIMAL to feed an animal or animals with hay [Old English *hēg* 'something that can be cut down' < Indo-European, 'hew, strike'] ◇ **hit the hay** to go to bed (*slang*) ○ *We hit the hay at nine, completely exhausted.* ◇ **make hay while the sun shines** to take advantage of opportunities when they present themselves

CULTURAL NOTE *The Hay Wain*, a painting (1821) by artist John Constable. The most popular of Constable's many depictions of his native Suffolk, it shows a hay cart crossing a river. By combining a bold style with close observation of nature, Constable creates a realistic image of an idealistic world, in which humans and nature are in close harmony.

haybox /háy boks/ *n* an insulated box, originally filled with hay, used to allow food that has been boiled to finish cooking without more fuel

haycock /háy kok/ *n* a cone-shaped pile of hay that is left in a field until it is dry enough to be stored

Hayden /háyd'n/, **Bill** (*b.* 1933) Australian politician. The leader of the Australian Labor Party (1977–83), he served as governor general of Australia (1989–96). Full name **Hayden, William George**

Hay diet /háy-/ *n* a diet in which protein and carbohydrate foods are not eaten at the same time, claimed to be helpful for digestive complaints and weight loss [Mid-20C. After William Howard *Hay* (1866–1940), US physician]

Haydn /híd'n/, **Joseph** (1732–1809) Austrian composer. His hundreds of symphonies, concertos, string quartets, and operas helped define the classical style, and include the popular oratorio *The Creation* (1798). Full name **Haydn, Franz Joseph**

Hayek /hí ek/, **Friedrich A. von** (1899–1992) Austrian-born British economist. An influential advocate of an unfettered free market, he led a monetarist attack on Keynesian economics. He shared a Nobel Prize in economics (1974). Full name **Hayek, Friedrich August von**

Hayes /hayz/, **Rutherford B.** (1822–93) 19th president of the United States. A Republican, he reformed the civil service and withdrew the last federal troops from the Reconstruction South during his presidential term (1877–81). Full name **Hayes, Rutherford Birchard**. See table at **president**

'He serves his party best who serves his country best.'
[Rutherford B. Hayes, *Inaugural address*, Washington, DC; 5 March 1877]

hay fever *n* an allergic reaction to pollen that irritates the upper respiratory tract and the eyes, resulting in symptoms including a runny and itchy nose, itchy and watering eyes, and sneezing. Technical name **pollinosis**

hayfork /háy fawrk/ *n* **1.** AGRIC same as **pitchfork 2.** a machine-operated fork for moving hay

haylage /háy lij/ *n* silage made from partially dried grass [Mid-20C. Blend of HAY + SILAGE]

hayloft /háy loft/ *n* a loft for storing hay over a stable or a barn

haymaker /háy maykər/ *n* **1.** AGRIC WORKER PROCESSING HAY an agricultural worker whose job it is to cut, turn, toss, spread, or carry hay after it has been mown **2.** AGRIC MACHINE PROCESSING HAY a machine for breaking down stems of hay to improve the drying process **3.** CRICKET SWEEPING STROKE in cricket, a sweeping stroke with the bat **4.** BOXING POWERFUL SWINGING PUNCH a powerful swinging punch, especially in a boxing match (*slang*)

Library of Congress

haymow /háy mō/ *n* 1. AGRIC same as **hayloft** 2. a quantity of hay stored in a barn or loft

hayrack /háy rak/ *n* 1. **RACK HOLDING FEED** a rack that holds hay and from which livestock feed 2. **RACK ON CART** a rack attached to a cart to increase its capacity for carrying hay 3. **CART WITH HAYRACK** a cart fitted with a hayrack

hayrick /háy rik/ *n* AGRIC same as **haystack**

hayride /háy rīd/ *n N Am* a ride taken for pleasure by a group of people in a wagon or other vehicle that is full of hay or straw

hayseed /háy seed/ *n* 1. **GRASS SEED FROM HAY** grass seed that is shaken out of hay 2. **PIECES OF GRASS** pieces of grass or straw that fall from hay 3. *N Am* **OFFENSIVE TERM** an offensive term that deliberately insults somebody's rural base or background and his or her intelligence and level of sophistication (*informal insult*)

haystack /háy stak/ *n* a large pile of hay, especially one that is built in the open and covered with thatch for winter storage

Haywards Heath /háywərdz-/ market and dormitory town in West Sussex, southern England. Population: 28,923 (1991).

haywire /háy wīr/ *adj* functioning erratically, or not functioning at all (*informal*) ○ *A powerful magnet can make the television set go haywire.* [< the springy nature of wire used to tie up bundles of hay, and sometimes for makeshift repairs]

Hayworth /háywərth/, **Rita** (1918–87) US actor. A dancer from her childhood, she appeared in films including *Gilda* (1946). Born **Cansino, Margarita Carmen**

hazan *n* JUDAISM another spelling of **hazzan**

hazard /házzərd/ *n* 1. **POTENTIAL DANGER** something that is potentially very dangerous 2. ENG **DANGEROUS OUTCOME** a dangerous or otherwise unwanted outcome, especially one resulting from the failure of an engineered system 3. GOLF **OBSTACLE ON GOLF COURSE** a natural or constructed obstacle on a golf course, e.g. a bunker or a lake 4. GAMBLING **DICE GAME** a dice game resembling craps 5. CUE GAMES **SCORING STROKE IN BILLIARDS** in billiards, a scoring stroke made when a ball is pocketed, either a ball other than the striker's (**winning hazard**) or the striker's cue ball itself (**losing hazard**) 6. RACKET GAMES **RECEIVER'S SIDE IN REAL TENNIS** in real tennis, the receiver's side of the court ■ *vt* (**-ards, -arding, -arded**) 1. **SUGGEST SOMETHING TENTATIVELY** to offer a tentative explanation of something ○ *Would anyone like to hazard a guess as to what this could possibly mean?* 2. **RISK LOSS OF SOMETHING** to chance or risk something, especially in order to gain something else [13C. Via Old French *hasard* 'game of chance played with dice' < Arabic *az-zahr* 'the dice, the chance']

hazard light *n* either of a pair of car lights, usually the indicators, that flash on and off to warn other drivers of potential danger

hazardous /házzərdəss/ *adj* potentially very dangerous to living beings or the environment —**hazardously** *adv* —**hazardousness** *n*

hazardous waste *n* a by-product of manufacturing processes or nuclear processing that is toxic and presents a potential threat to people and the environment

hazard pay *n N Am* same as **danger money**

hazard warning light *n* AUTOMOT same as **hazard light**

haze[1] /hayz/ *n* 1. **PARTICLES IN ATMOSPHERE** mist, cloud, or smoke suspended in the atmosphere and obscuring or obstructing the view 2. **VAGUE OBSCURING FACTOR** something that is vague and serves to obscure something 3. **DISORIENTATED MENTAL OR PHYSICAL STATE** a mental or physical state or condition when feelings and perceptions are vague, disorientating, or obscured ■ *vi* (**hazes, hazing, hazed**) **BECOME FILLED WITH PARTICLES** to become saturated with suspended particles ○ *As the temperatures rose, the sky began to haze over.* [Early 18C. Probably back-formation < HAZY]

haze[2] /hayz/ (**hazes, hazing, hazed**) *vti N Am* to persecute or torture somebody in a subordinate position, especially a first-year military academy cadet or a potential fraternity recruit. Many institutions have now prohibited hazing. [Late 17C. Origin ?] —**hazer** *n*

hazel /háyz'l/ (*plural* **-zels** or *same*) *n* 1. FOOD same as **hazelnut** 2. TREES **SMALL TREE WITH EDIBLE NUTS** a bush or small tree of the birch family with edible brown nuts. Genus: *Corylus*. 3. INDUST **WOOD OF HAZEL** the wood of the hazel tree. Use: baskets, hurdles. 4. COLOURS **LIGHT-BROWN COLOUR** a light-brown colour with a tinge of green or gold, like a ripe hazelnut [Old English *hæsel* < Indo-European] —**hazel** *adj*

hazelnut /háyz'l nut/ *n* an edible nut from a hazel tree

Hazlitt /házlit/, **William** (1778–1830) British essayist. He is regarded as one of the most brilliant English prose stylists. His collections of essays include *Table Talk* (1821–22) and *The Spirit of the Age* (1825).

> 'The least pain in our little finger gives us more concern and uneasiness than the destruction of millions of our fellow beings.'
> [William Hazlitt, 'American Literature—Dr. Channing', *Edinburgh Review*; October 1829]

> 'There is not a more mean, stupid, dastardly, pitiful, selfish, spiteful, envious, ungrateful animal than the public. It is the greatest of cowards, for it is afraid of itself.'
> [William Hazlitt, 'On Living to One's Self', *Table Talk*; 1821–22]

HAZMAT /ház mat/, **haz/mat** *abbr* INDUST hazardous material

hazy /háyzi/ (**-ier, -iest**) *adj* 1. **VISUALLY OBSCURED** unclear, especially because partially obscured or obstructed by mist, cloud, or smoke 2. **IMPRECISE** not specific or clearly remembered 3. **NOT KNOWLEDGEABLE** showing a lack of understanding or knowledge [Early 17C. Origin ?] —**hazily** *adv* —**haziness** *n*

hazzan /haáz'n, khə zaán/ (*plural* **-zanim** /-zənim/ or **-zans**), **hazan**, **chazan** *n* a cantor in a synagogue [Mid-17C. < Hebrew *ḥazzān* 'cantor']

Hazzard /házzərd/, **Shirley** (*b.* 1931) Australian-born US writer. Her novels include *The Transit of Venus* (1980).

Hb *abbr* BIOCHEM haemoglobin

HB *abbr* hard black (*used of pencil lead*)

H-beam *n* a structural steel member shaped like an H in section. It is similar to an I-beam.

HBM *abbr* 1. Her Britannic Majesty 2. His Britannic Majesty

H-bomb *n* ARMS same as **hydrogen bomb**

HC *abbr* House of Commons

HCF, hcf *abbr* MATHS highest common factor

HCFC *n* a gas containing carbon, chlorine, fluorine, and hydrogen that has been identified as being less damaging to the ozone layer than CFCs. Full form **hydrochlorofluorocarbon**

HCI *abbr* human-computer interaction

hd *abbr* 1. hand 2. head

HD *abbr* 1. COMPUT hard disk 2. COMPUT hard drive 3. heavy-duty 4. BIOCHEM, ELECTRONICS high-density

HDL *abbr* high-density lipoprotein

HDSL *abbr* TELECOM, ONLINE 1. High-Bit-Rate Digital Subscriber Line 2. High-Data Rate Digital Subscriber Line

HDTV *abbr* high-definition television

he[1] *stressed* /hee/; *unstressed* /hi, i/ *pron* used to refer to a male person or animal that has been previously mentioned or whose identity is known (*used as the subject of a verb*) ■ *n* a male animal or boy, especially used of a new baby ○ *Is your puppy a he or a she?* [Old English < Indo-European, 'this (here)']

USAGE Formerly, *he* was often used to refer to somebody whose gender was not specified: *A child needs time to learn and can then move at his own pace.* More recently this usage has been avoided. Because English does not have a gender-neutral pronoun in the third person singular that can be used to refer to people, 'he or she' may need to be used, especially in formal contexts. In informal contexts *they* is often used instead. Another alternative is to use the plural: *Children need time to learn and can then move at their own pace.* See also **they**.

he[2] /hay/ *n* the fifth letter of the Hebrew alphabet, represented in the English alphabet as 'h'. See table at **alphabet** [Mid-17C. < Hebrew *hē*]

He *symbol* CHEM ELEM helium

HE *abbr* 1. His Eminence 2. His Excellency

head /hed/ *n* 1. **TOP PART OF BODY** the topmost part of a vertebrate body, where the brain, eyes, nose, ears, mouth, and jaws are situated 2. **MOST FORWARD SECTION OF BODY** the section of the body of an invertebrate that is forward of all other segments 3. **CENTRE OF INTELLECT** the centre of a human being's faculties of intellect, emotion, and reasoning ○ *She worked out a solution in her head.* ○ *Use your head, and don't panic!* ○ *a good head for figures* 4. **LEADER OF OTHERS** the chief leader, supervisor, or manager 5. EDUC same as **head teacher** 6. **TOP OF LONG THIN OBJECT** the wider top of a long thin object ○ *the head of a nail* ○ *a hammer head* 7. **HIGHEST PART** the highest, uppermost, or foremost part of something ○ *was invited to sit at the head of the table* ○ *standing by the head of the bed* ○ *Move to the head of the queue.* 8. **SECTION IN SPEECH OR TEXT** one of the main sections or topics of a written or spoken discourse ○ *listed under three main heads* 9. **CRISIS POINT** a critical juncture in a situation or series of events, at which time some action must be taken, however painful ○ *The dispute came to a head at the monthly meeting.* ○ *The looming deadline brought matters to a head.* 10. *Carib* **STATE OF MIND** somebody's state of mind at a specific time, especially as perceived by others ○ *Wha' head you pushing?* 11. (*plural same*) **COUNTABLE UNIT** a single unit in a number of people or animals, especially when they are being counted ○ *500 head of cattle* 12. **MEASURE OF DISTANCE** the height or length of a head, used as a measure of distance between two individuals, especially racehorses at the winning post ○ *The favourite won by a head.* 13. **TABOO TERM** a highly offensive term for an act of performing oral sex on somebody (*taboo*) 14. ARTS **REPRESENTATION OF HUMAN HEAD** an artistic, photographic, or televised representation or image of a human being's face, hair, eyes, mouth, nose, and ears 15. BOT **TOP OF PLANT** the top part of a plant where a flower or a cluster of leaves grows 16. **FROTH ON BEER** the froth that forms on the top of beer when it is poured into a glass 17. **TOP OF PIMPLE** the visible pus-filled centre of a spot or boil 18. COINS **OBVERSE OF COIN** the side of a coin that shows a leader's head or other main design 19. ELECTRONICS **ELECTROMAGNETIC RECORDING DEVICE** the part of a machine that records, reads, or erases sounds, images, or data, e.g. on a tape recorder or video recorder (*often used in the plural*) 20. **TITLE** a heading, e.g. a newspaper headline or a title before a section in a text 21. MED same as **headache** (sense 1) (*informal*) ○ *I've got a terrible head.* 22. **USER OF ILLICIT DRUGS** a habitual user of a drug (*slang; only in combination*) ○ *a cokehead* 23. GEOG **SOURCE OF RIVER** the source of a river or stream, or the point at which a river or stream enters a lake 24. GEOG **PROMONTORY** a headland that juts out into the sea or other stretch of water (*often used in placenames*) 25. GEOG **TOP OF VALLEY** the high end of a valley 26. MUSIC **PART OF DRUM** the stretched membrane of a drum or tambourine 27. PHYS **REQUIRED HEIGHT OF LIQUID SURFACE** the height that the surface of a liquid has to be above a specific level to produce a stated pressure at that level 28. PHYS **PRESSURE OF LIQUID** the pressure at the lower of two points in a column of liquid resulting from the difference in height 29. PHYS **PRESSURE** the pressure exerted by a liquid or gas ○ *a head of steam* 30. NAUT **SHIP'S TOILET** a lavatory on a ship 31. MIN EXTRACT **PART OF COAL MINE** a passage where coal is mined underground 32. TRANSP **TERMINAL** the destination point of a transport route 33. MECH ENG **DEVICE FOR HOLDING CUTTING TOOLS** a part of a boring or turning machine such as a lathe that holds cutting tools to the work in progress 34. MECH ENG same as **cylinder head** 35. **heads** COINS **POSITION OF COIN WITH HEAD UPWARDS** the head of a coin turned up after a toss ■ *adj* **CHIEF IN RANK** most important in rank ○ *the head gardener* ○ *I had a call from head office.* ■ *v* (**heads, heading, headed**) 1. *vt* **CONTROL OTHERS OR ORGANIZATION** to be in the first position of authority and exercise control over people or an organization 2. *vt* **BE AT FRONT OF GROUP** to be at the front or the top of something ○ *The mayor headed the procession as it entered the town.* ○ *The list was headed by some very well-known names.* 3. *vi* **GO IN PARTICULAR DIRECTION** to move or go in a particular direction or to a particular position ○ *He headed towards the station.* ○ *I think we're heading for trouble here.* 4. *vt* **CAUSE SOMETHING TO GO SOMEWHERE** to make something move in a particular direction or to a particular place ○ *The pilot headed the plane on*

a northeasterly course. **5.** *vt* **BE OR GIVE HEADING FOR TEXT** to act as or supply a heading on a written page ○ *A short quotation heads each chapter of this book.* ○ *Let's head the letter with our logo.* **6.** *vt* FOOTBALL **HIT BALL WITH HEAD** to use the head to hit a ball ○ *He headed the ball into the goal.* [Old English *hēafod* < Indo-European] —**headed** *adj* ◇ **be above** *or* **over somebody's head** to be too difficult for somebody to understand ◇ **be head and shoulders above somebody** to be notably superior to somebody ◇ **be off your head** to be mentally or emotionally challenged or highly upset ◇ **give somebody his** *or* **her head** to relax control or supervision of somebody ◇ **go off your head** to become completely irrational (*informal*) ◇ **go over somebody's head** to bypass the usual person and address a request or complaint to a more important person in order to get what you want ○ *If he refuses to cooperate, I'll go over his head and speak to his superiors.* ◇ **go to somebody's head 1.** to make somebody conceited or overconfident **2.** to make somebody dizzy or light-headed ○ *The high altitudes of the Rocky Mountains went right to my head.* ◇ **have your head in the clouds** to be completely unrealistic, overoptimistic, or engaged in daydreaming ◇ **head over heels 1.** rolling or turning so that the feet are in the air and the head below them so as to land on the back or the feet **2.** completely ○ *They fell head over heels in love.* ◇ **keep your head** to remain calm or unexcited ◇ **keep your head down** to avoid drawing attention to yourself at a time of danger or difficulty ◇ **knock something on the head** to put an end to something, or prevent it from developing any further (*informal*) ◇ **let somebody have his** *or* **her head** same as **give somebody his** *or* **her head** ◇ **lose your head** to panic or lose self-control ◇ **rear its ugly head** used to say that something unpleasant appears or happens

head off *v* **1.** *vt* **INTERCEPT PERSON OR ANIMAL** to stop a person or animal from proceeding in a particular direction by placing yourself between the person or animal and the goal sought ○ *Let's try and head the robbers off at the pass.* ○ *We took a short cut to head her off before she reached the station.* **2.** *vt* **FORESTALL SOMETHING** to try in advance to prevent something from taking place, or to prevent somebody from doing something, that might prove difficult or unpleasant ○ *We need to head off any attempt to have the matter raised again in committee.* **3.** *vi* **GO** to go off, or leave a place and go in a particular direction ○ *The others headed off down the hill while we stayed to enjoy the view a little longer.*

headache /héd ayk/ *n* **1.** a pain in the head lasting for some time caused by changes in pressure in the blood vessels leading to and from the brain **2.** something that causes worry or difficulty (*informal*) —**headachy** *adj*

headband /héd band/ *n* **1.** a band worn on or around the head to keep the hair in place or as decoration **2.** a band of usually absorbent material worn around the head across the forehead to absorb sweat and keep hair off the face

headbang /héd bang/ (**-bangs, -banging, -banged**) *vi* to dance to heavy metal music by moving the head violently backwards and forwards to the beat of the music (*slang*)

headbanger /héd bangər/ *n* **1.** an offensive term that deliberately insults somebody's intelligence or rationality (*informal insult*) **2.** somebody whose favourite music is heavy metal (*slang*)

head-bath *n S Asia* a bath that includes washing the hair

headboard /héd bawrd/ *n* an upright board, often padded or covered in fabric, used to form the head of a bed

head boy *n* a boy in the senior years at a secondary school who has been elected to represent the school and to act as a role model for younger pupils

head-butt *vt* to hit somebody a deliberate hard blow with the forehead or the top of the head ■ *n* a deliberate blow with the forehead or the top of the head

headcam /héd kam/ *n* a video camera mounted on a person's head or on headgear

headcase /héd kayss/ *n* an offensive term that deliberately shows contempt for or ridicules somebody's mental condition (*slang insult*)

headcheese /héd cheez/ (*plural* **-cheeses** or *same*) *n N Am* FOOD same as **brawn** (sense 3) [Because the ingredients are pressed together as in cheese-making]

head cold *n* a viral infection of the nose, throat, and bronchial tubes, characterized by sneezing, headaches, nasal congestion, and coughing

head collar *n* SHOW JUMPING same as **headpiece** (sense 3)

head count *n* the process of counting the people in a group one by one, or the number arrived at by this process ○ *After a head count, we found there were 265 people in the hall.*

headdress /héd dress/ *n* a decorative covering worn on the head, usually as a sign of rank, for ceremonial purposes, or as personal display

header /héddər/ *n* **1.** SOCCER **SHOT WITH HEAD** a deliberate use of the head to play, pass, or shoot the ball in football ○ *He scored with a flying header.* **2. HEADLONG FALL** a headlong plunge or fall **3.** COMPUT **HEADING FOR PAGE** a heading for each page of a word-processed or faxed document, usually automatically inserted and consisting of text or a page number **4.** COMPUT **PLACE FOR INFORMATION ABOUT MESSAGE** a place at the top of an e-mail for information about the message, including subject, sender, and receiver **5.** CONSTR **CROSSWISE BRICK** a brick or stone positioned crosswise in a wall and level with its outer surface **6.** ENG same as **header tank 7.** INDUST **MAKER, FITTER, OR REMOVER OF TOPS** a person or machine that makes, fits, or removes the tops of something

header tank *n* a raised tank that ensures a constant pressure or supply of fluid to a system, especially water to a central heating system

headfast /héd faast/ *n* a mooring rope at the bow of a ship

headfirst /héd fúrst/ *adv, adj* in a movement or position where the head is in front of the rest of the body and is the first thing that reaches, enters, or strikes something ○ *He insisted on going down the slide headfirst.* ○ *taking a headfirst dive into the pool* ■ *adv* abruptly and without taking time to think about or prepare for something ○ *They rush into things headfirst and think about the consequences afterwards.*

headful /hédfòol/ *n* **1.** a large amount of something that has been learned, thought, or imagined (*informal*) ○ *a headful of facts* **2.** a thick mass of hair ○ *a headful of curls*

head game *n* the psychological aspect of a competitive endeavour, especially a sport

head gate *n* **1.** the gate that controls the flow of water into the upstream end of a canal lock **2.** CIV ENG same as **floodgate**

headgear /héd geer/ *n* **1.** CLOTHING **SOMETHING COVERING HEAD** something worn on the head, especially a hat ○ *sporting some very natty headgear* **2.** MIN EXTRACT **HOISTING MECHANISM AT MINESHAFT** an apparatus at the top of a mineshaft for lifting things out of and lowering them into a mine **3.** RIDING **PART OF HARNESS** the part of a harness that fits over a horse's head

head girl *n* a girl in the senior years at a secondary school who has been elected to represent the school and to act as a role model for younger pupils

headhunt /héd hunt/ (**-hunts, -hunting, -hunted**) *v* **1.** *vt* to recruit, or attempt to recruit, an executive or highly valued employee from one company to fill a similar position in another enterprise ○ *The agency headhunted her to work for an American bank.* **2.** *vi* to seek, collect, and preserve the heads of enemies as trophies or ceremonial objects —**headhunter** *n* —**headhunting** *n*

heading /hédding/ *n* **1.** PRINTING **TITLE** something that forms the head, top, edge, or front of something, especially as a title for a paragraph, section, chapter, or page ○ *The chapter headings are to be set in 24-point bold.* **2. CATEGORY OF SUBJECT MATTER** a division into which the subject matter of a document, discourse, or discussion is divided ○ *That information definitely comes under the heading of matters not to be aired in public.* **3.** NAVIG **COURSE** the direction in which a ship or aircraft is travelling, often given as a compass bearing ○ *If we continue on our present heading we should sight land in one hour.* **4.** MIN EXTRACT **MINE TUNNEL** a horizontal tunnel in a mine, or the end of such a tunnel

headlamp /héd lamp/ *n* AUTOMOT same as **headlight**

headland /héddlənd/ *n* **1.** a narrow piece of land jutting out into water, usually with steep high cliffs **2.** a strip of land left unploughed at the edge of a field

headless /héddləss/ *adj* **1.** having no head on the body **2.** having no leader, guide, or director —**headlessness** *n*

headlight /héd līt/ *n* a powerful light attached to the front of a motor vehicle or a locomotive, or the beam of light cast by it ○ *He was driving without headlights.*

headline /héd līn/ *n* **1.** MEDIA **TITLE OF NEWSPAPER ARTICLE** a caption printed at the top of a page or article in a newspaper, usually in large heavy letters and often summarizing the content that follows it ○ *an article with the headline 'Sharp Fall in Share Prices'* **2.** PRINTING **LINE AT TOP OF PAGE** a line printed at the top of a page of a book or document giving the page number and sometimes other information such as the title or the author's name ■ **headlines** *npl* MEDIA, BROADCAST **MAIN NEWS ITEMS** the most important items of news covered by a newspaper or a news broadcast ○ *Her name has seldom been out of the headlines since she announced her intention to sue.* ○ *We bring you the headlines every hour on the hour.* ■ *v* (**-lines, -lining, -lined**) **1.** *vt* MEDIA **PROVIDE HEADING FOR TEXT** to give a prominent title or caption to something ○ *a story headlined 'POP STAR ENTERS HOSPITAL'* **2.** *vt US* **PUBLICIZE SOMEBODY AS STAR** to present somebody as the leading attraction of a show **3.** *vti US* **APPEAR AS STAR** to appear as the leading attraction of a show

headliner /héd līnər/ *n US* a performer who is advertised as a leading attraction in a show

head-load *n* something carried on somebody's head —**head-load** *vt*

headlock /héd lok/ *n* a hold in which a wrestler tightly grips an arm around an opponent's head

headlong /héd long/ *adv, adj* **1. WITH HEAD FOREMOST** with the head in front of the rest of the body, especially in a rapid uncontrolled movement **2. MOVING FAST AND OUT OF CONTROL** moving or travelling in a fast uncontrolled way **3. WITH TOO MUCH HASTE** acting, happening, or done in an impetuous way with little or no thought for the consequences ○ *She had thrown herself headlong into an even worse situation.* [14C. < HEAD + -LING [2], altered by association with *-long* 'foremost']

head louse *n* a louse that lives on a human head among the hair, feeding by sucking blood and gluing its eggs to the hair shafts near the skin surface. Latin name: *Pediculus humanus capitis.*

headman /hédmən, -man/ (*plural* **-men** /-mən, -men/) *n* **1.** in some small-scale societies, a man who is the leader of a community or village **2.** a leader or overseer, e.g. of a group of workers

headmaster /hed maástər/ *n* a man who is the head teacher of a school —**headmasterly** *adj* —**headmastership** *n*

headmistress /hed místrəss/ *n* a woman who is the head teacher of a school —**headmistressy** *adj*

head money *n* a reward paid for the capture or killing of a fugitive or outlaw

headmost /héd mōst/ *adj* forward to the greatest extent (*archaic*)

headnote /héd nōt/ *n* a brief note at the top of a chapter or a page that summarizes what follows, especially points of law or a legal decision

head office *n* **1.** the administrative centre from which the affairs of an organization are directed ○ *Have you discussed it with head office?* **2.** the senior employees who direct the affairs of an organization ○ *Have you discussed it with head office?*

head of government *n* the person in charge of a country's or state's government

head of programming *n UK* an executive who is responsible for the selection of television or radio programmes. ANZ, N Am term **program director**

head of state *n* the chief representative of a country or state, who may or may not also be the head of government

head of the river (*plural* **heads of the river**) *n* **1.** a regatta held on a river involving a series of races for rowing crews **2.** the winner of a regatta held on a river

head-on *adv, adj* **WITH FRONT FACING FORWARDS** with the front facing towards something ○ *We were sailing head-on into the teeth of the gale.* ○ *a head-on collision* ■ *adv* **WITHOUT EVASION OR COMPROMISE** making no attempt to avoid the dangers or difficulties involved in something ■ *adj* **UNCOMPROMISING** involving direct, fundamental, and uncompromising opposition ○ *He tried to avoid a head-on clash with his business partner.*

headperson /héd purss'n/ *n* in some small-scale societies, the leader of a community or village

headphones /héd fōnz/ *npl* a pair of listening devices joined by a band across the top of the head and worn in or over the ears

headpiece /héd peess/ *n* **1.** PRINTING **DESIGN AT TOP OF PAGE** an ornamental design printed at the beginning of a text **2.** CLOTHING **HEAD DECORATION OR PROTECTOR** an ornamental accessory for the head, or a protective head cover **3.** RIDING **BRIDLE PART** the part of a horse's bridle that fits around the head

head pin *n* BOWLS, LEISURE same as **kingpin** (sense 4)

headquarter /hed kwáwrtər/ (**-ters, -tering, -tered**) *v* **1.** *vt* to provide somebody with a centre of operations ○ *They headquartered their office in a former barracks.* **2.** *vi N Am* to set up a headquarters ○ *She headquartered in Paris.*

headquarters /hed kwáwrtərz, héd kwawrtərz/ *n* (*takes a singular or plural verb*) **1.** a military commander's central office, from which operations are controlled and orders issued ○ *Napoleon's headquarters were in a disused windmill.* ○ *Headquarters is on the radio, wanting to know our precise position.* **2.** the administrative centre from which the affairs of an organization are directed

headrace /héd rayss/ *n* a channel conveying water to a water wheel or turbine

headrail /héd rayl/ *n* **1.** the end of the table from which a game of billiards is started, nearest the baulk line **2.** a railing on a sailing vessel extending from the rear of the bow to the back of the figurehead

headreach /héd reech/ *n* the distance that a sailing boat makes to windward when tacking ■ *vt* (**-reaches, -reaching, -reached**) to make a better distance than another boat when tacking

head register *n* the higher register or falsetto of men's and boys' singing voices in which tone production is concentrated in the head and assisted by sympathetic vibration of the nasal and skull cavities

headrest /héd rest/ *n* an often padded support for the head, usually on the back of a seat, especially in a motor vehicle

head restraint *n* an adjustable headrest fitted to the back of a seat of a motor vehicle, designed to prevent neck injuries in an accident

head rhyme *n* LITERAT same as **alliteration**

headroom /héd room, -rŏŏm/ *n* the space or clearance overhead, e.g. in a room, doorway, the interior of a motor vehicle, or the underside of a bridge ○ *There's plenty of headroom in this car, even in the back seat.*

headsail /héd sayl/ *n* a sail attached to or set forward of the foremast of a vessel

headscarf /héd skaarf/ (*plural* **-scarves** /-skaarvz/) *n* a woman's scarf in the form of a square of fabric, for wearing on the head or round the neck

head sea *n* waves or a current running in a direction opposite to the course of a ship

headset /héd set/ *n* a pair of earphones, often with a small mouthpiece attached to enable two-way communication

headshaking /héd shayking/ *n* a series of side-to-side movements of the head, communicating or suggesting something such as disagreement, doubt, or refusal ○ *I noticed a lot of headshaking in the audience as you made that claim.*

headship /hédship/ *n* **1.** a position as the principal of a school **2.** somebody's position or authority as a leader

head shop *n* a shop that specializes in selling articles associated with the use of drugs such as hashish and marijuana (*slang*)

headshot /héd shot/ *n* **1.** a photograph or cinematic shot of a head, especially a person's head **2.** a gunshot aimed to hit the head of a person or animal

headshrinker /héd shringkər/ *n US* same as **psychiatrist** (*dated informal insult*)

headsman /hédzmən/ (*plural* **-men** /-mən/) *n* a public executioner who beheaded prisoners condemned to death

headsquare /héd skwair/ *n* CLOTHING same as **headscarf**

head staggers *n regional* a disease in cattle or horses characterized by loss of balance or staggering (*takes a singular or plural verb*)

headstall /héd stawl/ *n N Am* RIDING same as **headpiece** (sense 3) [< STALL[1] 'position, place']

headstand /héd stand/ *n* a position in gymnastics or yoga in which the body is balanced upside down on the head, usually using the hands for support

head start *n* an advantage in a competition or endeavour ○ *A good education gives you a head start when it comes to getting a job.*

headstock /héd stok/ *n* an assembly or part of a machine, especially in a lathe, that holds and supports a revolving part

headstone /héd stōn/ *n* **1.** a slab of stone placed at the head of a grave as a memorial to the person or people buried there **2.** ARCHIT same as **keystone** (sense 1)

headstream /héd streem/ *n* a stream that is the source, or one of the sources, of a river

headstrong /héd strong/ *adj* self-willed and determined not to follow orders or advice —**headstrongly** *adv* —**headstrongness** *n*

heads up *interj N Am* a command to watch out, especially for danger from overhead such as a falling object or a ball coming through the air

heads-up *n* **1.** *N Am* **WARNING** an early warning to somebody that something, typically something undesirable, is soon to happen ○ *gave the law firm a heads-up on the impending subpoena* **2.** *US* **SOMETHING REQUIRING ATTENTION** something that requires alert attention ■ *adj N Am* **ALERT AND RESOURCEFUL** showing quick resourcefulness and alertness in doing or observing something

heads-up display *n N Am* COMPUT GAMES same as **head-up display**

head teacher *n* a teacher who is in charge of a school, supervising teaching staff and overseeing day-to-day operations

head-tie *n Carib* a piece of cloth, usually square, that is wrapped and tied around the top of a woman's head, covering the hair

head-to-head *adv, adj* **WITH DIRECT ENCOUNTER** in or involving direct contact or confrontation ■ *adv* **WITH HEADS ADJACENT** placed or arranged with heads adjacent ○ *We put the beds head-to-head.* ■ *n* **DIRECT ENCOUNTER** a direct and immediate encounter

head trip *n US* (*dated slang*) **1.** an experience that stimulates or excites somebody mentally **2.** something done or a way of behaving that is intended mainly for personal gratification

head-up display *n* **1.** a display of instrument data projected onto a screen at eye level so that a pilot or driver does not have to look down to see it **2.** in computer games, a display of meters, dials, and other indicators around the margins of the screen ▶ N Am term **heads-up display**

head voice *n* MUSIC same as **head register**

head waiter *n* the person in charge of a group of servers at a restaurant, often also responsible for taking reservations and seating customers

head wall *n* a cliff forming one end of a valley

headwaters /héd wawtərz/ *npl* the streams that make up the beginnings of a river

headway /héd way/ *n* **1.** **PROGRESS** progress towards achieving something ○ *We're unable to make much headway with the project.* **2.** **FORWARD MOVEMENT** movement or rate of progress forwards **3.** CONSTR same as **headroom** **4.** TRANSP **DIFFERENCE IN TIME OR DISTANCE** the interval or distance between two vehicles, trains, or ships travelling in the same direction along the same route ◇ **make headway** to make progress in doing something or going somewhere

headwind /héd wind/ *n* a wind blowing against the direction of travel

headwoman /héd wŏŏmən/ (*plural* **-women** /-wimin/) *n* in some small-scale societies, a woman who is the leader of a community or village

headword /héd wurd/ *n* a word or phrase that forms a heading at the start of a text and is usually printed in distinctive type, especially a main entry word in a dictionary

headwork /héd wurk/ *n* **1.** mental activity or effort **2.** decoration on the keystone of an arch

heady /héddi/ (**-ier, -iest**) *adj* **1.** **EXHILARATING** causing or involving a feeling of energy, confidence, and elation **2.** **INTOXICATING** causing a feeling of light-headedness or intoxication **3.** **IMPETUOUS** impulsive and rash in behaviour —**headily** *adv* —**headiness** *n*

heal /heel/ (**heals, healing, healed**) *v* **1.** *vt* **CURE SOMEBODY OR SOMETHING FROM AILMENT** to restore a person, body part, or injury to health **2.** *vi* **BE REPAIRED NATURALLY** to be repaired and restored naturally, e.g. by the formation of scar tissue ○ *The broken bone seems to be healing quite nicely.* **3.** *vt* **PUT SOMETHING RIGHT** to repair or rectify something that causes discord and animosity ○ *Unless she can heal the rift within her party, she stands little chance in the election.* **4.** *vti* **BE MORALLY PURIFIED** to get rid of a wrong, evil, or spiritual affliction [Old English *hǣlan* < Germanic] —**healable** *adj*

SPELLCHECK heal or **heel**? Do not confuse the spelling of ***heal*** and ***heel***, which sound similar. ***Heal*** is only used as a verb, meaning 'restore or be restored to health' or 'put right': *His wounds have healed. Nothing could heal the rift between them.* ***Heel*** is chiefly used as a noun, denoting the back part of a foot, shoe, or sock (as in *her Achilles heel, head over heels in love, boots with high heels*) or the end part of something such as a loaf of bread or a violin bow. ***Heel*** is also used as a derogatory term, as a verb meaning 'repair or replace the heel of' or 'strike with the heel', and in the adjective compound *well-heeled.*

---

heal-all *n* PLANTS same as **selfheal**

healer /héelər/ *n* somebody who cures or treats illnesses or injuries

Healey /héeli/, **Denis, Baron Healey of Riddlesden** (*b.* 1917) British politician. A Labour MP from 1952, he was Chancellor of the Exchequer (1974–79) and deputy leader of the Labour Party (1980–83). Full name **Healey, Denis Winston**

healing /héeling/ *n* the process of curing somebody or something or of becoming well ○ *spiritual healing* ■ *adj* having the effect of curing or improving something ○ *healing lotions*

health /helth/ *n* **1.** **GENERAL PHYSICAL CONDITION** the general condition of the body or mind, especially in terms of the presence or absence of illnesses, injuries, or impairments **2.** **OVERALL CONDITION OF SOMETHING** the general condition of something in terms of soundness, vitality, and proper functioning ○ *There is concern about the financial health of the company.* **3.** **DRINKING TOAST** a toast drunk to wish for somebody's wellbeing and prosperity ○ *Here's a health to Her Majesty!* ■ *adj* **1.** **DEVOTED TO GENERAL WELLBEING** having the function of maintaining physical and mental wellbeing among the general public and the administration of medical and related services **2.** **GOOD FOR PEOPLE** promoting physical and mental wellbeing [Old English *hǣlþ* < Germanic] ◇ **drink somebody's health** to drink a toast to somebody

health camp *n NZ* a camp for children who need healthcare, usually located on the coast

healthcare /hélth kair/ *n* the provision of medical and related services aimed at maintaining good health, especially through the prevention and treatment of disease —**healthcare** *adj*

healthcare assistant *n* somebody with no specialized training employed in a hospital or other healthcare facility to perform basic nursing-support tasks such as bed-making or giving patients baths. Aus term **nursing assistant**. N Am term **nurse's aide**

health centre *n* a place, usually operated by a local authority, that houses a medical practice and other healthcare services

health club *n* a private club that offers fitness and leisure facilities such as a gym and a swimming pool

health farm *n* same as **health spa**

health food *n* food that is considered to be more beneficial to health than ordinary food, especially products that are organically grown or without chemical additives

healthful /hélthf'l/ *adj* beneficial to physical or mental health —**healthfully** *adv* —**healthfulness** *n*

health insurance *n* insurance to cover the costs or losses incurred if an insured person falls ill

health pack *n* **1.** a dietary supplement consisting of a combination of ingredients, with supposed benefits for a specific aspect of health **2.** in computer games, an object that restores a number of points lost, thus postponing the death of a character in the game

health salts *npl* mineral salts used as a mild laxative, e.g. magnesium sulphate

health service *n* a service that provides a population with medical care, especially one with a nationwide network of hospitals, clinics, and general practices

Health Service Commissioner *n* a senior British official who investigates complaints about services provided by healthcare authorities that have not been satisfactorily resolved at a lower level

health spa *n* **1.** a commercial establishment similar to a hotel, usually rural, that offers ways of improving health and fitness such as a controlled diet, exercise, and massage **2.** *US* a commercial establishment without accommodation that offers facilities for health and fitness

health tourism *n* the practice of visiting other countries specifically to benefit from the medical services available there, often because they are cheaper than at home —**health tourist** *n*

health visitor *n UK* a trained nurse who gives medical care and advice to people in their homes, especially to mothers of babies and young children, senior citizens, and physically disabled people

healthy /hélthi/ (**-ier, -iest**) *adj* **1.** IN GOOD CONDITION in good physical or mental condition **2.** BENEFICIAL TO HEALTH helping to maintain or bring about good health ○ *a healthy diet* **3.** SUGGESTIVE OF GOOD HEALTH showing that somebody is in good health **4.** PSYCHOLOGICALLY SOUND showing or encouraging moral or psychological soundness **5.** FUNCTIONING WELL in a prosperous and efficient condition ○ *a healthy economy* **6.** BIG large, usually satisfyingly large, in size or quantity (*informal*) —**healthily** *adv* —**healthiness** *n*

Heaney /héeni/, **Seamus** (*b.* 1939) Irish poet. His poems explore his native Northern Irish culture and language, although he has lived primarily in the Republic of Ireland since 1972. One of the leading English-language poets of his generation, he won a Nobel Prize in literature (1995). Full name **Heaney, Seamus Justin**

> 'Rained-on, flower-laden / Coffin after coffin / Seemed to float from the door / Of the packed cathedral / Like blossoms on slow water.'
> [Seamus Heaney, 'Casualty', *Field Work*; 1979]

heap /heep/ *n* **1.** ROUNDED PILE a large number of things lying on top of one another, or a large quantity of material, forming a roughly rounded shape ○ *They'd left all their dirty clothes in a heap on the floor.* ○ *All that was left of the building was a heap of rubble.* **2.** LARGE AMOUNT a large quantity or amount (*informal; often pl*) ○ *Don't worry, we've got heaps of time.* ○ *I've got a heap of things to see to before I can go home.* **3.** SOMETHING OLD OR RUNDOWN something that is old, rundown, or untidy-looking, especially an old building or car (*informal*) ■ *vt* (**heaps, heaping, heaped**) **1.** PUT THINGS IN PILE to collect or arrange something into a loose pile ○ *heaping the stuff all together in the middle of the yard* **2.** FILL SOMETHING UP to load or fill a shallow container, forming a roughly rounded mound **3.** GIVE SOMETHING IN ABUNDANCE to supply something in large quantities or amounts ○ *They heaped scorn on my suggestion.* [Old English *hēap* < Germanic] ◇ **all of a heap** into a state of shock, surprise, or confusion (*informal*) ○ *The news was totally unexpected and it knocked me all of a heap.*

heap up *v* **1.** *vti* to accumulate something, or be gathered, into a roughly rounded mound **2.** *vt* to collect or acquire something in large amounts

heaped /heept/ *adj* containing something in an amount large enough to rise up in a small heap ○ *a heaped teaspoonful of sugar* N Am term **heaping**

heaps /heeps/ (*informal*) *adv* very much or greatly ○ *I feel heaps better since I went to the doctor.* ■ *npl Aus* trouble, opposition, or adverse criticism ○ *I copped heaps for resigning from the team when I did.* ◇ **give it heaps** *Aus* to do something wholeheartedly and with special effort (*informal*) ◇ **give somebody heaps** *Aus* to reprimand somebody severely (*informal*)

hear /heer/ (**hears, hearing, heard** /hurd/) *v* **1.** *vti* PERCEIVE SOUNDS to perceive or be able to perceive sound **2.** *vti* GET TO KNOW SOMETHING to be informed of something, especially by being told about it **3.** *vt* LISTEN TO SOMETHING to listen to somebody or something ○ *I've heard him on the radio.* **4.** *vti* UNDERSTAND to understand fully by listening attentively ○ *Did you hear what I just said?* ○ *I won't stand for it, do you hear?* **5.** *vt* LAW PRESIDE OVER SOMETHING to consider something officially as a judge, commissioner, or member of a jury **6.** *vt* CHR ATTEND MASS to attend Mass in a Roman Catholic church [Old English *hīeran* < Germanic] —**hearable** *adj* —**hearer** *n* ◇ **hear, hear** used as an exclamation to show great approval

SPELLCHECK hear or **here**? Do not confuse the spelling of ***hear*** and ***here***, which sound similar. ***Hear*** is a verb meaning 'perceive a sound', 'listen', or 'be informed': *Did you hear that noise? She nodded in agreement and said, 'Hear, hear!' I hear they're getting married.* ***Here*** is an adverb meaning 'in this place': *Come here! Here you are!*

hear from *vt* to receive a communication such as a letter or telephone call from a person, place, or organization

hear of *vt* to consider something as a possibility ○ *She wouldn't hear of their paying the bill.*

hear out *vt* to continue listening until somebody or something has finished

heard past participle, past tense of **hear**

SPELLCHECK heard or **herd**? Do not confuse the spelling of ***heard*** and ***herd***, which sound similar. ***Heard*** is the past tense of the verb *hear*: *A scream was heard. I've never heard of him.* ***Herd*** is a noun or verb referring to a large group of animals or people: *The road was blocked by a herd of cattle. We were herded into the room.*

Heard and McDonald Islands /húrd ənd mək dónn'ld-/ dependency of Australia consisting of four small uninhabited islands in the southern Indian Ocean. Area: 412 sq. km/159 sq. mi. Official name **Territory of Heard Island and McDonald Islands**

hearing /héering/ *n* **1.** AWARENESS OF SOUND the perception of sound, made possible by vibratory changes in air pressure on the ear drums ○ *My hearing's going, so you'll have to speak louder.* **2.** EARSHOT the range within which something can be heard ○ *She moved out of hearing and I lost the end of the sentence.* **3.** CHANCE TO BE HEARD an opportunity to be heard, especially a chance to state an opinion or fact ○ *All I want is for my views to get a fair hearing.* **4.** LAW TRIAL the trial of a case in a court of law **5.** LAW PRELIMINARY EXAMINATION OF ACCUSED a preliminary judicial examination of an accused person to decide whether the case should proceed to trial **6.** LAW SESSION TO HEAR EVIDENCE a session of an investigative or legislative body at which witnesses are heard ◇ **hard of hearing** unable to hear well

hearing aid *n* a small amplifying device to enable somebody to hear better, usually worn in or behind the ear

hearing-and-speech-impaired *adj* unable to hear or speak

hearing dog *n* a dog trained to help a hearing-impaired person by indicating that it has heard a sound such as the ringing of a telephone or doorbell

hearing-impaired *adj* having a reduced or deficient ability to hear

hearing loss *n* a measurable reduction of the ability to hear or distinguish sounds, especially of a specific frequency

hearken /haárkən/ (**-kens, -kening, -kened**), **harken** *vi* to listen and pay attention (*archaic*) [Old English *he(o)rcnian* < HARK] —**hearkener** *n*

Hearne /hurn/, **Samuel** (1745–92) British explorer. Working for the Hudson's Bay Company, he was the first European to travel overland to the North American coast on the Arctic Ocean (1770–72).

hearsay /héer say/ *n* information that is heard from other people —**hearsay** *adj*

hearsay evidence *n* evidence consisting of testimony about other people that is not based on direct or personal knowledge. Hearsay evidence is not usually admissible in a court of law.

hearse /hurss/ *n* a vehicle in which a coffin is carried to a funeral or a dead body is taken away [13C. Via French *herse* < Latin *hirpex* 'rake, harrow']

ORIGIN Agricultural harrows in the Middle Ages were typically toothed triangular frames, so the word for a harrow came to be applied in French to a similar frame for holding candles, particularly those placed over a coffin at funeral services. This was the meaning of ***hearse*** when English acquired it, and its meaning gradually developed from 'canopy placed over a coffin' and 'coffin, bier' to the modern sense of 'funeral vehicle'.

Hearst /hurst/, **William Randolph** (1863–1951) US publisher and politician. He built up a vast national newspaper and media empire, and after 1927 lived in seclusion at his Californian castle, San Simeon. Orson Welles's film *Citizen Kane* (1941) is based on his career.

> 'A politician will do anything to keep his job—even become a patriot.'
> [William Randolph Hearst, *Syndicated editorial*; 28 August 1933]

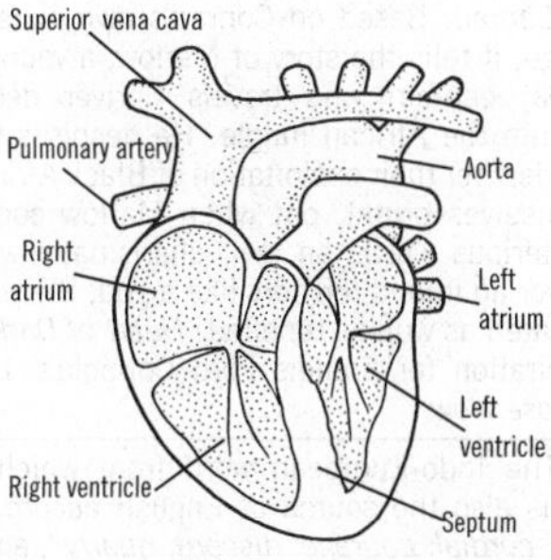
Superior vena cava
Pulmonary artery
Aorta
Right atrium
Left atrium
Left ventricle
Right ventricle
Septum

heart: human heart

heart /haart/ *n* **1.** BLOOD-PUMPING ORGAN a hollow muscular organ that pumps blood around the body, in humans situated in the centre of the chest with its apex directed to the left **2.** LEFT SIDE OF CHEST the area on the front of the human body that corresponds roughly to the position of the heart **3.** BASIS OF EMOTIONAL LIFE the source and centre of emotional life, where the deepest and sincerest feelings are located and a person is most vulnerable to pain **4.** CHARACTER somebody's essential character ○ *He can be bad-tempered at times, but he's got a very good heart.* **5.** COMPASSION the ability to feel humane and altruistic feelings ○ *If she had any heart she would forgive him.* **6.** AFFECTION affection, love, or warm admiration ○ *The chorus's singing won the hearts of the audience.* **7.** SPIRIT the capacity for courage and determination ○ *She put her whole heart into making a go of the business.* **8.** DISPOSITION a mood, mental state, or frame of mind ○ *took the remark in good heart* **9.** DEPICTION OF HEART a simplified and conventionalized picture of a heart as a rounded, roughly triangular shape, often used to signify love **10.** CENTRAL PART the distinctive, significant, and characteristic centre of something ○ *the heart of rural England* **11.** CENTRAL PART OF LEAFY VEGETABLE the compact central part of a vegetable such as lettuce, cabbage, or celery, where the leaves or stalks curl in tightly **12.** ANIMAL HEART USED AS FOOD the heart of an animal that is cleaned and trimmed, then cooked as food **13.** BELOVED PERSON somebody who is intensely loved ○ *Come to me, dear heart.* **14.** CARDS CARD WITH HEART-SHAPED SYMBOL a playing card of the suit of hearts [Old English *heorte* < Indo-European] —**-hearted** *adj* ◇ **a man** *or* **woman after your own heart** somebody with tastes, interests, or opinions that are similar to your own ◇ **at heart** in essence or reality, and despite contrary appearances ◇ **break somebody's heart** to cause somebody intense unhappiness and suffering ◇ **do somebody's heart good** to make somebody feel happy or satisfied ◇ **eat your heart out** (*informal*) **1.** to brood about something that makes you feel unhappy **2.** to

be consumed with envy ◇ **have somebody's welfare** *or* **interests at heart** to have somebody's wellbeing or interests in mind ◇ **heart and soul** completely, or with the greatest devotion ◇ **in your heart of hearts** in your deepest inner feelings ◇ **learn** *or* **know something by heart** to memorize *or* have memorized something ◇ **lose heart** to become discouraged ◇ **not have the heart to do something** to be unable to bring yourself to do something that is liable to hurt somebody else ◇ **set your heart on something, have your heart set on something** to have something as your ambition or greatest wish ◇ **somebody's heart is in his** *or* **her mouth** somebody is very afraid or apprehensive, usually at a moment of great danger or uncertainty ○ *My heart was in my mouth as I opened the envelope.* ◇ **somebody's heart is in the right place** somebody is kind or well-intentioned, often contrary to appearances ○ *Her brusque manner can be somewhat off-putting, but her heart is in the right place.* ◇ **take heart** to become encouraged and more confident ◇ **take something to heart 1.** to take something seriously **2.** to be upset by something ◇ **wear your heart on your sleeve** to reveal your feelings openly ◇ **with all your heart 1.** completely **2.** sincerely

CULTURAL NOTE ***Heart of Midlothian***, a novel (1818) by Scottish writer Sir Walter Scott. Widely regarded as Scott's best novel, it is set in the 1730s and tells the story of Effie Deans, who is wrongfully accused of the murder of a child. The title refers to the site of Effie's imprisonment: the Tolbooth jail in Edinburgh, in the county of Midlothian.

CULTURAL NOTE ***Heart of Darkness***, a novel (1902) by Joseph Conrad. Based on Conrad's own experience in the Congo, it tells the story of Marlow, a young English steamboat captain who travels upriver deeper and deeper into the African jungle. He despises the European traders for their exploitation of Black Africans, who are themselves brutal, but when Marlow comes upon the mysterious Kurtz, an evil, charismatic white man ruling over an inland territory like a god, the young man is fascinated as well as repelled. *Heart of Darkness* was the inspiration for Francis Ford Coppola's 1979 film *Apocalypse Now*.

ORIGIN The Indo-European word from which ***heart*** is derived is also the source of English *accord, cardiac, concord, cordial, courage, discord, quarry*², and *record*.

heartache /haʹart ayk/ *n* a powerful feeling of sorrow, anguish, or regret

heart attack *n* **1.** a sudden, serious, painful, and sometimes fatal interruption of the heart's normal functioning, especially due to a blockage in the coronary artery **2.** a sudden severe shock (*informal*) ○ *I had a heart attack when I looked in the drawer and saw that the money was gone.*

heartbeat /haʹart beet/ *n* **1.** CONTRACTION OF HEART MUSCLE a single contraction of the lower chambers of the heart that drives blood through the body **2.** CONTINUOUS PULSATION OF HEART the continuous pulsating movement and sound made by a beating heart **3.** DRIVING FORCE the driving force behind something

heart block *n* a condition in which the nerve impulses that control the heartbeat are irregular so that the ventricles and the atria no longer beat in time with one another

heartbreak /haʹart brayk/ *n* intense unhappiness or grief

heartbreaker /haʹart braykər/ *n* somebody or something that creates intense unhappiness, especially somebody with whom people fall in love and by whom they are later hurt

heartbreaking /haʹart brayking/ *adj* causing intense sadness or distress —**heartbreakingly** *adv*

heartbroken /haʹart brōkən/ *adj* intensely unhappy or disappointed because of something that has happened ○ *The children were heartbroken when we had to cancel the trip.* —**heartbrokenly** *adv* —**heartbrokenness** *n*

heartburn /haʹart burn/ *n* an uncomfortable burning sensation in the lower chest, usually caused by stomach acid flowing back into the lower end of the oesophagus [< HEART in the obsolete sense 'stomach']

heart disease *n* any medical condition of the heart or the blood vessels supplying it that impairs cardiac functioning

hearten /haʹart'n/ (**-ens, -ening, -ened**) *vt* to make somebody feel more cheerful and hopeful [< HEART in the obsolete sense 'encourage'] —**heartening** *adj*

heart failure *n* **1.** cessation of the normal functioning of the heart, leading to death **2.** a condition in which the heart cannot pump blood in sufficient volume to meet the needs of the body, causing breathlessness, enlargement of the liver, swollen ankles, and other symptoms

heartfelt /haʹart felt/ *adj* arising from strong and sincere emotion

Heartfield /haʹart feeld/, **John** (1891–1968) German painter and graphic artist. A leading member of the Dada movement after World War I, he pioneered the technique of photomontage. Many of his works such as *German Acorns* (1933) satirize Hitler, Nazism, or the Weimar Republic. Born **Herzfeld, Helmut**

hearth /haarth/ *n* **1.** FLOOR OF FIREPLACE the floor of a fireplace, especially when it extends into the room **2.** HOME LIFE the fireplace of a home, thought of as a symbol of the home and the life of the family who live in it **3.** METALL PART OF FOUNDRY FURNACE the lowest part of a foundry furnace where molten metal collects or ore is smelted [Old English *heorþ* < Germanic]

hearthrug /haʹarth rug/ *n* a rug for the floor in front of a fireplace

hearthside /haʹarth sīd/ *n* same as **fireside**

hearthstone /haʹarth stōn/ *n* **1.** a large stone used to form the hearth in a fireplace **2.** a soft variety of stone or a compound of pipeclay and stone used to clean and whiten fireplaces and doorsteps

heartily /haʹartili/ *adv* **1.** ENTHUSIASTICALLY in a sincere and enthusiastic way **2.** GOOD-NATUREDLY in a loud, vigorous, good-natured way **3.** COMPLETELY in a full and complete way **4.** HUNGRILY with a good appetite

heartland /haʹart land/ *n* a central area of a country or region that has special economic, political, military, or sentimental significance

heartless /haʹartləss/ *adj* having or showing no pity or kindness —**heartlessly** *adv* —**heartlessness** *n*

heart-lung machine *n* a machine that is used to take over the functions of the heart and lungs in pumping and oxygenating the blood, chiefly during heart surgery

heart massage *n* MED same as **cardiac compression**

heart murmur *n* an unusual sound coming from the heart that can be detected by a stethoscope and may indicate the presence of a heart disorder

heart of palm *n* the terminal bud of the cabbage palm, cooked and served as a vegetable or in salads

heart rate *n* the number of heartbeats occurring within a specific length of time

heartrending /haʹart rending/ *adj* causing intense sadness or distress, especially in sympathy with somebody else's unhappiness or hardship —**heartrendingly** *adv*

SYNONYMS See ***moving***.

hearts /haarts/ *n* **1.** one of the four suits used in cards, with a red heart shape as its symbol (*takes a singular or plural verb*) **2.** a card game in which players try either to avoid winning cards of the suit hearts and the queen of spades or to win all of these (*takes a singular verb*)

heart-searching *n* a thorough and often distressing self-examination of feelings and motives

heartsease /haʹarts eez/ (*plural* **-eases** or *same*) *n* a pansy, especially a wild pansy. Latin name: *Viola tricolor*.

heartsick /haʹart sik/ *adj* deeply disappointed or sad (*literary*) —**heartsickness** *n*

heart-smart *adj* describes food that is low in fat and cholesterol and therefore reduces the risk of heart disease (*informal*)

heartsore /haʹart sawr/ *adj* extremely sad or regretful (*archaic or literary*)

heart-stopping *adj* extremely frightening, unnerving, or exhilarating

heartstrings /haʹart stringz/ *npl* somebody's feelings, especially tender emotions ○ *a doleful expression that tugged at my heartstrings* [< STRING 'tendon', from the earlier belief that tendons brace the heart]

heartthrob /haʹart throb/ *n* an extraordinarily attractive person, especially a young film star or singer (*informal*)

heart-to-heart *n* a frank, intimate conversation ○ *had a heart-to-heart about their feelings for each other* —**heart-to-heart** *adj*

heartwarming /haʹart wawrming/ *adj* inspiring warm or kindly feelings, usually by showing life and human nature in a positive and reassuring light —**heartwarmingly** *adv*

SYNONYMS See ***moving***.

heartwood /haʹart wŏŏd/ *n* the wood at the centre of a tree trunk or branch that is older, darker, and harder than the wood surrounding it. Technical name **duramen**

heartworm /haʹart wurm/ (*plural* **-worms** or *same*) *n* **1.** a parasitic filarial worm that lives in the heart and associated blood vessels of members of the dog family, and occasionally in cats and seals **2.** an infection of the heart in members of the dog family, and occasionally in cats and seals, that is caused by parasitic worms

hearty /haʹarti/ *adj* (**-ier, -iest**) **1.** SINCERE AND ENTHUSIASTIC sincere and expressed in a cheerful, enthusiastic way **2.** LOUD AND ENTHUSIASTIC done in an unrestrainedly loud, vigorous, but usually good-humoured way **3.** HEALTHY showing physical health, strength, and vigour **4.** STRONGLY FELT sincerely and strongly felt **5.** SUBSTANTIAL AND NOURISHING substantial and giving considerable satisfaction and nourishment ○ *a hearty breakfast* **6.** EXCESSIVELY LOUD AND ENTHUSIASTIC annoyingly loud or boisterous, especially about sport or outdoor activities (*informal*) ■ *n* (*plural* **-ies**) BOISTEROUS SPORTING TYPE a loud boisterous person who is usually enthusiastic about sport or outdoor activities (*informal insult*) —**heartiness** *n*

heat /heet/ *n* **1.** ENERGY PERCEIVED AS TEMPERATURE a form of transferred energy that arises from the random motion of molecules and is felt as temperature, especially as warmth or hotness. Heat is transmitted by conduction, convection, or radiation. Symbol **Q** **2.** DEGREE OF HOTNESS the perceptible or measurable degree of hotness ○ *The heat in that kitchen is absolutely unbearable.* ○ *At what heat do I cook this?* **3.** SOURCE OF HIGHER TEMPERATURE a source of warmth, e.g. for cooking something or keeping a building warm ○ *Take the pan off the heat.* **4.** INTENSE EMOTION emotional intensity, especially in the form of anger or excitement ○ *I replied with some heat that my conscience was perfectly clear.* **5.** TIME OF MOST ACTIVITY the period or phase of something at which activity and excitement is at its most intense ○ *During the heat of the campaign, many rash promises were made.* **6.** MENTAL PRESSURE psychological pressure on a person or group, especially to produce or achieve something (*informal*) ○ *We're beginning to feel the heat as the deadline gets closer and closer.* **7.** *N Am* CRITICISM harsh criticism or reproach (*slang*) ○ *What's your problem? Can't you take the heat?* **8.** FOOD SPICY HOTNESS the hot or burning sensation produced in the mouth by spicy foods **9.** ZOOL SEXUALLY RECEPTIVE STAGE a time during a female mammal's reproductive cycle when she is fertile and ready to mate **10.** SPORTS PRELIMINARY ROUND one of several preliminary rounds before a race or contest, especially one in which competitors are eliminated, or one that determines players' starting order for the main event **11.** POLICE INTENSE POLICE ACTIVITY intensive police activity carried out in order to catch criminal suspects (*slang*) **12.** *US* POLICE POLICE the police (*slang*) ■ *vti* (**heats, heating, heated**) RAISE TEMPERATURE to become or make something warm or hot [Old English *hǣtu* < Germanic, 'hot'] —**heatless** *adj* ◇ **in the heat of the moment** during a brief period of anger, enthusiasm, or other strong emotion, and usually without thinking ○ *remarks made in the heat of the moment and later regretted* ◇ **turn on** *or* **up the heat (on somebody)** to apply increased pressure on somebody (*slang*)

heat up *vti* **1.** to make something hot or hotter, or become hot or hotter **2.** to become or make something more intense, exciting, or excited

heat balance *n* INDUST same as **energy balance**

heat barrier *n* SCI same as **thermal barrier**

heat capacity *n* the quantity of heat required to raise the temperature of one mole or gram of a substance by one degree Celsius. Symbol ***C***

heat death *n* a condition of a closed system in which energy is uniformly distributed throughout it, with none available for use. The universe might ultimately suffer heat death if it is a closed system.

heated /héetid/ *adj* **1.** made warm by artificially generated heat **2.** showing emotional intensity or anger ○ *a heated argument* —**heatedly** *adv* —**heatedness** *n*

heat engine *n* a machine that transforms heat into mechanical power, e.g. a steam or petrol engine

heater /héetər/ *n* **1.** HEATING DEVICE a device that uses fuel to produce heat in order to make something else warm or hot, especially a device to heat the air in a room or vehicle **2.** HEATING ELEMENT IN VALVE an element in a valve that carries the current for heating a cathode **3.** *N Am* HANDGUN a revolver or other handgun (*slang dated*)

heat exchanger *n* a device that transfers heat from one medium to another, usually by conduction through a solid barrier, e.g. a car radiator transferring heat from water to air

heat exhaustion *n* a condition of physical weakness or collapse often accompanied by nausea, muscle cramps, and dizziness, that is caused by exposure to intense heat

heath /heeth/ (*plural* **heaths** or *same*) *n* **1.** GEOG SHRUBBY UNCULTIVATED LAND a tract of uncultivated, open land with infertile, often sandy soil covered with rough grasses and small bushes or heather **2.** PLANTS LOW BUSH a plant of a family that includes heather and some other low-growing evergreen bushes, commonly found on heaths. Genera: *Erica* or *Calluna*. **3.** INSECTS BROWN BUTTERFLY a butterfly with coppery-brown wings. Genus: *Coenonympha*. [Old English *hǣþ* < Germanic, 'unploughed land']

Heath /heeth/, **Ted** (*b.* 1916) prime minister of Great Britain (1970–74). A Conservative MP from 1950, he was prime minister during a period of industrial unrest and Britain's accession to the European Economic Community. Full name **Heath, Sir Edward Richard George**. See table at **prime minister**

> 'We may be a small island, but we are not a small people.'
> [Ted Heath, *Observer*, 21 June 1970]

heathen /héeth'n/ (*plural* **-thens** or *same*) *n* **1.** an offensive term that deliberately insults somebody who does not acknowledge the God of the Bible, Torah, or Koran **2.** an offensive term that deliberately insults somebody's way of life, degree of knowledge, or nonbelief in religion [Old English *hǣþen* < Germanic, 'heath'] —**heathen** *adj* —**heathenish** *adj* —**heathenize** *vti*

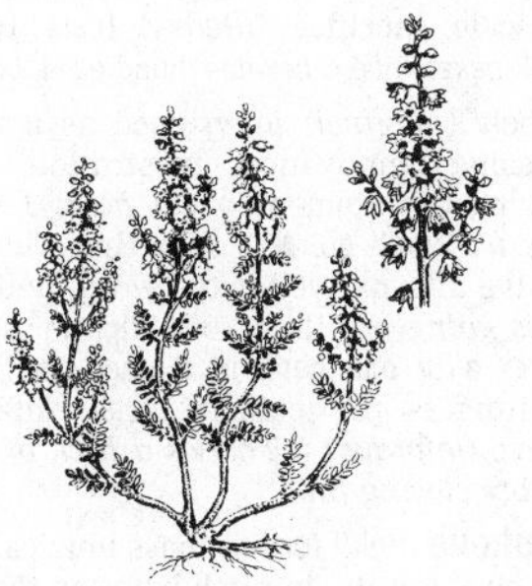

heather

heather /héthər/ *n* **1.** a low-growing evergreen plant with spiky leaves that grows in clusters. Flowers: small purple, pink, or white, bell-shaped. Native to: heaths and mountainsides in Europe and Asia. Latin name: *Calluna vulgaris*. **2.** a purple colour tinged with pink and blue [14C. Origin ?] —**heather** *adj* —**heathery** *adj*

heather grass *n* a perennial grass with flat hairless leaves. Native to: Europe. Latin name: *Sieglingia decumbens*. [Because it grows in the same places as heather]

heather mixture *n* a textile made of interwoven yarns of various colours, especially the colours of heather

Heath Robinson /heeth róbbinss'n/ *adj* constructed or improvised in a way that looks ramshackle and wildly implausible, especially through being overelaborate or overingenious (*humorous*) ○ *It's a bit Heath Robinson, but it ought to stop the sausages rolling off the barbecue.* N Am term **Rube Goldberg** [Early 20C. After W. *Heath Robinson* (1872–1944), British humorous artist]

Heathrow /héeth rō/ largest and busiest airport serving London, situated on the western outskirts of the capital

heating /héeting/ *n* **1.** the operation of warming something such as food, a room, or the interior of a building **2.** the equipment that produces heat to warm something, e.g. a central heating system ○ *The heating doesn't come on again until six o'clock in the evening.*

heating element *n* an insulated or covered wire whose high resistance to an electrical current causes its temperature to rise, providing heat to surrounding materials such as an electric blanket

heating pad *n* a fabric-covered pad that contains an electric heating element and is used to apply heat to various parts of the body

heat island *n* an urban area where the air temperature is consistently higher than in the surrounding region because of the generation and retention of heat created by human activity and human-made structures

heat lightning *n* lightning seen near the horizon, especially on hot evenings, without the sound of thunder, thought to be a reflection on clouds. The thunder accompanying the lightning is too distant to be heard.

heat of combustion *n* the amount of heat produced when one mole of a substance is burned in oxygen

heatproof /héet proof/ *adj* not damaged or affected when exposed to heat, e.g. in an oven or over a flame

heat prostration *n* MED same as **heat exhaustion**

heat pump *n* a mechanical or chemical device used to heat and air-condition buildings

heat rash *n* MED same as **prickly heat**

heat-resistant *adj* able to withstand the kind of damage normally caused by heat, but not completely flameproof or noninflammable

heat-seal *vt* to make packaging material, usually a thin clear plastic film, airtight around something by applying heat and pressure

heat-seeking *adj* able to detect and follow infrared radiation from heat ○ *The aircraft was brought down by a heat-seeking missile.*

heat shield *n* a coating or structure designed to protect against the effects of very high temperatures, especially the coating that protects spacecraft during re-entry into the Earth's atmosphere

heat-shock protein *n* a peptide that is released in response to adverse conditions, e.g. heart attacks, strokes, and breast cancer in humans or environmental stress in plants

heat sink *n* a device, often a metal plate, that conducts and dissipates unwanted heat generated by an electronic component or power supply

heatstroke /héet strōk/ *n* a condition caused by prolonged exposure to high temperatures, in which people experience high fever, headaches, hot dry skin, physical exhaustion, and sometimes physical collapse and coma

heat-treat *vt* to bring metal to the desired hardness by alternately heating and cooling it —**heat treatment** *n*

heat wave *n* a period of unusually hot weather

heaty /héeti/ *adj Malaysia, Singapore* used in some Asian medical systems to describe foods or food preparation methods that are believed to make the body hot and affect conditions such as fatigue or blood circulation. Mutton, ginger, and chocolate are examples of heaty foods.

heave /heev/ *v* (**heaves, heaving, heaved**) **1.** *vt* MOVE SOMETHING USING MUCH EFFORT to pull, push, lift, or throw something heavy by exerting great physical effort, especially in a concentrated or concerted burst ○ *We picked up the sack and heaved it into the truck.* **2.** *vi* EXERT PHYSICAL EFFORT IN RHYTHMIC BURST to exert great physical effort, especially in concentrated or concerted rhythmic bursts, when pulling on a rope or attempting to move something heavy ○ *All together now, heave!* ○ *heave on a rope* **3.** *vi* RISE AND FALL RHYTHMICALLY to rise and fall in a rhythmic or spasmodic way ○ *After the long run his chest was heaving.* **4.** *vt* LABORIOUSLY UTTER SOMETHING to utter a sound, especially a sigh, with a long outflow of breath or with effort and pain ○ *We can heave a sigh of relief now that the waiting is over.* **5.** *vi* MAKE SUDDEN INVOLUNTARY MOVEMENT to move suddenly in a violent involuntary motion, often associated with feelings of nausea ○ *The sight made my stomach heave.* **6.** *vti* VOMIT to vomit something up or try to vomit (*informal*) **7.** (*past* **hove** /hōv/) *vti* NAUT MOVE SHIP to move or make a ship move in a particular direction **8.** (*past* **hove**) *vi* APPEAR to become visible, like a ship appearing over the horizon ○ *Gradually, the end of summer hove into sight.* **9.** *vt* GEOL DISPLACE SOMETHING HORIZONTALLY to displace rock strata or a mineral lode in a horizontal direction, usually by the intersection of other strata or another lode ■ *n* **1.** EFFORTFUL BURST a burst of physical effort to pull on something or move something heavy ○ *We gave one final heave and the tree began to topple over.* **2.** THROW an act of throwing something fairly heavy, or the distance something is thrown **3.** UP-AND-DOWN MOVEMENT a rhythmic or spasmodic movement that rises and falls **4.** ACT OF VOMITING an act of or attempt at vomiting (*informal*) **5.** GEOL HORIZONTAL DISPLACEMENT rock strata or a lode that is displaced horizontally ■ *interj Carib* USED TO REPORT FIGHT in Trinidad, used to report that a fight has started (*informal*) [Old English *hebban* 'lift' < Germanic] —**heaver** *n*

heave down *vt* to turn a boat over for cleaning

heave to *vti* to bring a ship, especially a sailing vessel, to a stop

heave-ho /héev hṓ/ *interj* used to command or encourage sailors to pull together on a rope ■ *n* dismissal from something or rejection by somebody (*informal*) ○ *He's just been given the heave-ho from his job.*

heaven /hévv'n/ *n* **1.** *also* **Heaven** RELIG PERFECT DWELLING PLACE AFTER DEATH a place or condition of supreme happiness and peace where good people are believed to go after death, and, especially in Christianity, where God and the angels are believed to dwell **2.** BLISSFUL EXPERIENCE an experience of blissful happiness ○ *It's heaven not to have get up early in the morning.* **3.** SKY the sky as seen from Earth (*literary; often plural*) **4.** *also* **Heaven** RELIG GOD God, gods, or other divine agency ○ *Heaven protect us!* ○ *a gift from Heaven* ■ *interj also* **heavens** EXPRESSING ASTONISHMENT used to express great surprise, annoyance, or gratitude (*informal*) ○ *Heavens, is that the time?* [Old English *heofon*, origin ?] ◇ **for heaven's sake** used to express annoyance or exasperation ◇ **heaven knows** used to emphasize the truth of what somebody is saying ○ *Heaven knows, I've warned you about that already.* ◇ **heaven (only) knows** used to emphasize the fact that somebody is unable even to make a reasonable guess at something unknown or mysterious ○ *Heaven only knows what he's done with my keys.* ◇ **move heaven and earth** to do everything possible to make something happen

heavenly /hévv'nli/ (**-lier, -liest**) *adj* **1.** *also* **Heavenly** OF GOD AND HEAVEN belonging to the heaven and God of Christian belief ○ *A heavenly voice spoke to him out of the clouds.* **2.** IN THE SKY in the sky or space as seen from Earth **3.** LOVELY supremely delightful, delicious, or beautiful (*informal*) ○ *The chocolate mousse was heavenly.* —**heavenliness** *n*

heavenly body *n* ASTRON same as **celestial body**

heaven-sent *adj* happening or arriving at just the right time to help or benefit somebody greatly

heavenward /hévv'nwərd/ *adj* moving or directed upwards towards the sky or heaven ■ *adv* same as **heavenwards**

heavenwards /hévv'nwərdz/ *adv* upwards towards the sky or heaven ○ *He rolled his eyes heavenwards.*

heaves /heevz/ *n* a chronic lung disorder in horses marked by difficulty in breathing and believed to be caused by dust, moulds, or other air pollutants. The heaves resembles asthma in human beings. (*informal; takes a singular or plural verb*) ■ *npl* an attack of vomiting or retching (*slang; takes a plural verb*) ○ *The smell gave me the heaves.*

heavier-than-air *adj* unable to float in air because it weighs more than the air it displaces, and thus only able to fly under power using aerodynamic lift

heavily /hévvili/ *adv* **1.** WITH GREAT WEIGHT with a great weight **2.** LABORIOUSLY in a slow, clumsy, or laborious way **3.** SEVERELY in a severe, onerous, or comprehensive way ○ *heavily dependent on their parents* **4.** IN LARGE NUMBERS in large numbers or quantities **5.** SADLY in a sad and resigned way ○ *'It was my fault', he replied heavily.* ◇ **be heavily into** to be seriously or enthusiastically interested in something (*informal*) ○ *I didn't know you were heavily into astrology.*

heaving /héeving/ *adj* **1.** uncomfortably full of people (*informal*) **2.** gently rising and falling in regular alternation

Heaviside /hévvi sīd/, **Oliver** (1850–1925) British physicist. He predicted the existence of the ionosphere and contributed to the development of radio communications.

Heaviside layer *n* PHYS same as **E region**

heavy /hévvi/ *adj* (**-ier, -iest**) **1.** WEIGHING A LOT weighing a relatively large amount and thus difficult to lift, carry, or move ○ *We put heavy stones on the corners of the rug to stop it blowing away.* **2.** PRESENT IN LARGE AMOUNTS occurring or produced in large amounts or in greater amounts than normal ○ *heavy rain* **3.** FULL OR DENSE involving or using a larger amount of material, or having a thicker, denser texture than usual **4.** USING SOMETHING ABUNDANTLY using or consuming something a great deal ○ *heavy on petrol* **5.** NEEDING STRENGTH needing much strength and effort ○ *heavy road work* **6.** DEMANDING difficult to fulfil or cope with, and often burdensome or oppressive **7.** BUSY filled with a large or larger than normal amount of activity, business, or commitments ○ *a heavy day at work* **8.** POWERFUL struck or striking with a great deal of weight or force ○ *a heavy blow* **9.** BROAD AND DARK thick and dark-coloured or made with thick dark lines ○ *heavy underlining* **10.** EXPLICIT intended to give emphasis to something and to make the meaning or intention obvious **11.** UNSUBTLE lacking subtlety or delicacy ○ *heavy sarcasm* **12.** FLESHY large and solidly fleshy ○ *a man of heavy build* **13.** CLUMSY characteristic of somebody who is large and who moves slowly and deliberately or clumsily **14.** AFFECTED BY TIREDNESS tending to close or droop or feel weighed down by tiredness ○ *eyes heavy with sleep* **15.** SOUNDING LOUD AND DULL loud and dull in sound, as if produced by something large hitting or falling onto something ○ *a heavy thud* **16.** INDUSTRIAL-SCALE involved in large-scale industrial processes requiring large premises and a lot of equipment ○ *heavy industry* **17.** RUGGED AND STRONG specially adapted for rough work or for carrying large loads ○ *heavy excavating equipment* **18.** SAD sad or likely to make somebody feel sad ○ *a heavy heart* **19.** REQUIRING CONCENTRATION requiring concentrated attention to be understood or appreciated ○ *a heavy novel* **20.** STRICT strict or severe in behaviour **21.** POWERFUL AND LINGERING strong and lingering in smell ○ *a heavy odour of leeks* **22.** VIOLENT using or prepared to use violence (*informal*) ○ *the heavy mob* **23.** SERIOUS AND OPPRESSIVE significant, oppressively serious, or emotionally demanding (*slang*) ○ *I had a heavy scene with my friend tonight.* **24.** MIL LARGE-CALIBRE firing large-calibre ammunition **25.** MIL WITH LARGE WEAPONS carrying more or larger guns and armaments than is standard **26.** NAUT, OCEANOG ROUGH with large waves causing difficulties for boats ○ *heavy winds and seas* **27.** METEOROL DARK AND OVERCAST dark in colour and threatening rain or snow ○ *heavy skies* **28.** FOOD HARD TO DIGEST large in quantity and difficult to digest ○ *a heavy meal* **29.** MUSIC WITH POWERFUL BEAT describes rock music with a powerful, insistent beat **30.** CHEM WITH HIGH ATOMIC WEIGHT with a higher than normal atomic weight **31.** PHYS WITH HIGH SPECIFIC GRAVITY with a specific gravity that is higher than usual **32.** HORSERACING MUDDY wet, muddy, and not able to be travelled over at high speed ○ *Reports from the racecourse indicate that the going is heavy.* ■ *n* (*plural* **-ies**) **1.** VILLAIN a villain in a play, film, or other dramatic performance (*informal*) ○ *He played the heavy in a couple of westerns.* **2.** SOMEBODY WHO IS VIOLENT somebody hired to persuade people, by threats or violence, to do something (*slang; often used in the plural*) ○ *He sent in a bunch of heavies to do his dirty work.* **3.** MEDIA BROADSHEET a broadsheet newspaper (*informal; often used in the plural*) ○ *None of the heavies ran the story.* **4.** US IMPORTANT PERSON an important or influential person (*slang*) **5.** *Scotland* STRONG BITTER BEER a bitter brown beer [Old English *hefig* < Germanic, 'lift'] —**heaviness** /hévvinəss/ *n*

heavy breather *n* **1.** an anonymous telephone caller who breathes loudly into the mouthpiece as a means of suggesting sexual excitement or a physical threat **2.** somebody who breathes noisily or with difficulty, usually because of a medical condition —**heavy breathing** *n*

heavy chain *n* either of the larger polypeptide chains in an antibody

heavy cream *n N Am* cream with a high fat content that can be whipped to make it thicker

heavy-duty *adj* **1.** designed for hard wear or use in rough conditions **2.** more serious, substantial, or intensive than usual (*informal*)

heavy-footed *adj* slow, lumbering, or clumsy in walking

heavy goods vehicle *n* a road vehicle weighing more than 7.5 tonnes/16,500 lb, used for transporting goods

heavy-handed *adj* **1.** lacking skill or delicacy in handling objects or dealing with people **2.** relying on force or intimidation to exercise authority —**heavy-handedly** *adv* —**heavy-handedness** *n*

heavy-hearted *adj* feeling or showing sadness —**heavy-heartedly** *adv* —**heavy-heartedness** *n*

heavy hydrogen *n* an isotope of hydrogen with a mass number greater than one, especially deuterium

heavy metal *n* **1.** a style of loud rock music with a very strong beat (*hyphenated when used before a noun*) **2.** a metal, often toxic to organisms, that has a relative density of 5.0 or higher, e.g. lead, mercury, copper, and cadmium

heavy oil *n* a mixture of hydrocarbons distilled from coal tar that is heavier than water

heavy particle *n* CHEM same as **baryon**

heavyset /hévvi sét/ *adj* with a compact and powerful-looking build

heavy spar *n* the mineral form of barium sulphate

heavy water *n* water that has had its hydrogen atoms replaced with the hydrogen isotope deuterium. Use: nuclear reactors. Formula: D_2O.

heavy-water reactor *n* a nuclear reactor in which heavy water is used as a moderator

heavyweight /hévvi wayt/ *n* **1.** WEIGHT CATEGORY IN PROFESSIONAL BOXING in professional boxing, the heaviest weight category, for competitors whose weight does not exceed 79.5 kg/175 lb **2.** WEIGHT CATEGORY IN AMATEUR BOXING in amateur boxing, the heaviest weight category, for competitors whose weight does not exceed 91 kg/201 lb **3.** BOXER AT HEAVYWEIGHT LEVEL a professional or amateur boxer who competes at heavyweight level **4.** CONTESTANT IN HEAVIEST WEIGHT CLASS a contestant in the heaviest weight class of a sport **5.** HEAVY PERSON OR THING somebody or something whose weight is considerably above the average **6.** SOMEBODY OR SOMETHING POWERFUL OR INFLUENTIAL a person or organization with considerable power or influence, usually in a particular area

Heb. *abbr* **1.** Hebrew **2.** BIBLE Hebrews

hebdomad /hébdə mad/ *n* (*formal*) **1.** a group of seven people or things **2.** a period of seven days [Mid-16C. Via late Latin < Greek *hebdomad-* 'the number seven, period of seven days' < *hepta* 'seven']

hebdomadal /heb dómməd'l/ *adj* occurring on a weekly basis (*formal*)

Hebdomadal Council *n* the governing body of Oxford University

hebe /héebi/ *n* an evergreen bush widely cultivated for its blue, mauve, or white flowers. Native to: southern temperate regions. Genus: *Hebe*. [Mid-20C. After HEBE]

Hebe /héebi/ *n* in Greek mythology, the goddess of youth and the daughter of Zeus and Hera [Early 17C. < Greek *Hēbē*, literally 'youthful prime']

Hebei /hő báy/, **Hopeh** province in northern China. Its territories include the economic heartland of ancient Chinese civilization. Capital: Shijiazhuang. Population: 64,840,000 (1997). Area: 188,000 sq. km/72,600 sq. mi.

hebetude /hébbi tyood/ *n* mental lethargy (*literary*) [Early 17C. < late Latin *hebetudo* < Latin *hebet-* 'dull']

Hebr. *abbr* **1.** Hebrew **2.** BIBLE Hebrews

Hebraic /hi bráy ik/, **Hebraical** /-ik'l/ *adj* relating to the Israelites, or their language or culture [14C. Via late Latin < Greek *Hebraikos* < *Hebraios* (see HEBREW)] —**Hebraically** *adv*

Hebraicism *n* LANG same as **Hebraism**

Hebraise *vti* another spelling of **Hebraize**

Hebraism /hée brayizəm/, **Hebraicism** /hi bráyisizəm/ *n* a feature of the Hebrew language, especially one borrowed by another language, or something frequently found among Hebrews or their culture [Late 16C. Via French or modern Latin < late Greek *Hebraismos* < *Hebraios* (see HEBREW)]

Hebraist /hée bray ist/ *n* a specialist in the study of Hebrew

Hebraize /hée bray īz/ (**-izes, -izing, -ized**), **Hebraise** (**-ises, -ising, -ised**) *v* **1.** *vt* to give a language or culture Hebrew characteristics **2.** *vi* to adopt Hebrew idioms or customs [Mid-17C. < late Greek *Hebraizein* < *Hebraios* (see HEBREW)] —**Hebraization** /hée bray ī záysh'n/ *n* —**Hebraizer** *n*

Hebrew /héebroo/ *n* **1.** LANG a Semitic official language of Israel, also spoken elsewhere in the world. Native speakers: 5 million. See panel on next page **2.** PEOPLES, HIST same as **Israelite** (sense 1) ■ *adj* **1.** relating to Hebrew **2.** LANG, HIST same as **Hebraic** [13C. Via Old French *ebreu* < late Greek *Hebraios* < Aramaic *ibrāy*]

Hebrew calendar *n* CALENDAR same as **Jewish calendar**

Hebrews /hée brooz/ *n* a book of the Bible, originally a letter and thought to have been written towards the end of the 1st century AD (*takes a singular verb*) See table at **Bible**

Hebrew Scriptures *npl* the Bible of Judaism, consisting of the Pentateuch, the Prophets, and the Hagiographa

Hebrides /hébbrə deez/ collective name for the islands off the western coast of Scotland, comprising an outer chain of islands, the Outer Hebrides, separated by a sea channel from the Inner Hebrides nearer the mainland —**Hebridean** /hébbri dée ən/ *adj, n*

Hebron /hébbrən/ town in the West Bank territory, situated 32 km/20 mi. southwest of Jerusalem. Population: 119,401 (1997).

Hecate /hékəti/, **Hekate** *n* in Greek mythology, the goddess of darkness, witchcraft, and crossroads. She was the daughter of the Titans Perses and Asteria. [Late 16C. < Greek *Hekatē*, form of *hekatos* 'far-darting']

hecatomb /hékə tōm, hékə toom/ *n* **1.** in ancient Greece or Rome, a public sacrifice and feast, originally involving the slaughter of 100 oxen **2.** any large-scale sacrifice (*literary*) [Late 16C. Via Latin < Greek *hekatombē* < *hekaton* 'hundred' + *bous* 'ox']

heck /hek/ (*informal*) *interj* used as a mild way of expressing annoyance, frustration, or emphasizing a statement ○ *Oh heck, I suppose that means we can't go.* ■ *n* sometimes used as a less offensive alternative for the word 'hell' ○ *What the heck is going on?* [Late 19C. Euphemistic alteration of HELL] ◇ **a** *or* **one heck of a** used to indicate that something is particularly large, intense, or impressive (*informal*) ○ *There's a heck of a lot still to do before closing time.*

heckelphone /hék'l fōn/ *n* a bass musical instrument of the oboe family, in pitch between the cor anglais and the bassoon [Early 20C. < German *Heckelphon*, after Wilhelm *Heckel* (1856–1909), German instrument-maker]

heckle /hék'l/ *v* (**-les, -ling, -led**) **1.** *vti* INTERRUPT SOMEBODY WITH SHOUTING to shout remarks, insults, or questions in order to disconcert somebody who is making a speech or giving a performance **2.** *vt* DRESS FLAX OR HEMP to comb flax or hemp ■ *n* COMB FOR FLAX OR HEMP a comb used for dressing flax or hemp [14C. Variant of HACKLE [1]] —**heckler** *n*

HECS /heks/ *n* an Australian federal government scheme under which students contribute to the cost of their tertiary education. They either pay discounted fees when they are students or repay the full fees as an income tax after reaching a set level of income. Full form **Higher Education Contribution Scheme**

hect- *prefix* same as **hecto-** (*used before vowels*)

hectare /hék taar, -tair/ *n* a metric unit of area equal to 100 ares or 10,000 sq. m (2.471 acres) [Early 19C.

LANGUAGE HERITAGE ***Hebrew*** Much of English is made up of words from other languages, and Hebrew is an important contributor in this respect. To begin with, quite a few English first names, for example *Elizabeth, Emmanuel, Gabriel, Jonathan, Joan,* and *Josephine*, have internal elements derived from Hebrew. ***Jehovah*** and some other Judaeo-Christian terms for 'God' go back to Hebrew. ***Passover***, first recorded in the 16th century, is a translation of Hebrew *pesaḥ* 'to pass without affecting', an allusion to Exodus 12:11–27, in which it is said that God passes over the Israelites, while the first-born of other families are killed.

A good many Hebrew émigrés into English are, of course, integral to Judaism and Jewish life and culture, in the manner of ***Passover***. ***Bar mitzvah, bat mitzvah, chuppah, menorah, Seder, Torah, yeshiva,*** and ***Yom Kippur*** are but a few. Some of these have become generalized into the secular cultures of the English-speaking world: ***kosher, megillah***, and ***shekel*** are representative. Still others, for example ***amen, hallelujah, manna***, and ***Sabbath***, which are associated with both Judaism and Christianity, came into English via Latin and Greek but are ultimately of Hebrew origin.

Two English words of Hebrew origin that migrated into English in the 13th and 14th centuries respectively are ***cider*** and ***jubilee***. ***Cider*** came into English via French, Latin, and Greek, but goes back to Hebrew *šēkār* 'alcoholic drink'. ***Jubilee*** also entered English via French from Latin and Greek, and goes back to Hebrew *yōbēl* 'ram', from the ram's horn with which the year of restoration and restitution was proclaimed every 50 years. And some Hebrew émigrés into English entered Hebrew from other languages: ***cherub*** is probably of Akkadian origin, and ***hora*** is of Romanian origin. See also ***Yiddish***.

< French < Greek *hekaton* 'hundred' + French *are*, unit of area < Latin *area* 'open space']

hectic /héktik/ *adj* **1.** characterized by continual activity and haste, the lack of any time to rest or relax, and a sense of things barely under control ○ *Things have been a bit hectic at work this week.* **2.** MED symptomatic of or involving a recurrent afternoon fever, especially one accompanying tuberculosis ○ *a hectic flush* [14C. Via French < Greek *hektikos* 'habitual, consumptive' < *ekhein* 'have'] —**hectically** *adv*

hecto- *prefix* one hundred ○ *hectogram* Symbol **h** [Via French < Greek *hekaton* < Indo-European]

hectocotylus /héktō kóttiləss/ (*plural* **-li** /-lī/) *n* a tentacle with which male octopuses and related molluscs transfer sperm to the female during mating [Mid-19C. < modern Latin < French *hecto-* (see HECTO-) + Greek *kotulē* 'cup, something hollow']

hectogram /héktō gram/, **hectogramme** *n* a metric unit of mass equal to 100 grams [Late 18C. < French *hectogramme* < *hecto-* (see HECTO-) + *gramme* (see GRAM 1)]

hectolitre /hékto leetər/ *n* a metric unit of capacity equal to 100 litres [Early 19C. < French, < *hecto-* (see HECTO-) + *litre* (see LITRE)]

hectometre /héktō meetər/ *n* a metric unit of length equal to 100 metres [Early 19C. < French *hectomètre* < *hecto-* (see HECTO-) + *mètre* (see METRE 1)]

hector /héktər/ (**-tors, -toring, -tored**) *vti* to speak to somebody in a loud, threatening, or domineering tone intended to intimidate [Mid-17C. After HECTOR]

Hector /héktər/ *n* in Greek mythology, the main Trojan hero in the Trojan War and a son of King Priam and Queen Hecuba [14C. Via Latin < Greek *Hektōr* 'holding fast' < *ekhein* 'hold']

Hecuba /hékyoobə/ *n* in Greek mythology, the wife of King Priam of Troy and mother of 16 children, including Cassandra, Hector, and Paris [Via Latin < Greek *Hekabē*]

he'd *stressed* /heed/; *unstressed* /hid, id/ *contr* **1.** he had **2.** he would

heddle /hédd'l/ *n* one of the sets of vertical cords or wires in the frame on a loom that guides the warp threads [Early 16C. Origin ?]

hedge /hej/ *n* **1.** ROW OF BUSHES a close-set row of bushes, usually with their branches intermingled, forming a barrier or boundary in a garden, park, or field **2.** PROTECTIVE METHOD a means of protection against something, especially a means of guarding against financial loss ○ *a hedge against inflation* **3.** EVASIVE STATEMENT an evasive or noncommittal statement ■ *v* (**hedges, hedging, hedged**) **1.** *vt* PUT BUSHES AROUND SOMETHING to put a row of intermingled bushes around an area of ground **2.** *vi* WORK ON HEDGES to work at repairing, trimming, or planting a hedge, especially on a farm **3.** *vt* RESTRICT SOMETHING to restrict the scope or applicability of something by setting conditions ○ *It was a promise, but hedged in with so many ifs and buts that I wouldn't rely on it.* **4.** *vi* BE EVASIVE to avoid answering a question directly or definitely ○ *She could have given a straight answer, but instead she hedged.* **5.** *vi* FIN TRY TO OFFSET POSSIBLE LOSSES to take measures to offset any possible loss on a financial transaction, especially by investing in counterbalancing securities as a guard against price fluctuations [Old English *hegg* < Germanic, 'grasp'] —**hedger** *n* —**hedgy** *adj*

hedge-boar *n regional* same as **hedgehog** [See HEDGEHOG]

REGIONAL NOTE See ***hedgehog***.

hedge fund *n* **1.** a unit trust that invests in derivatives and other instruments that involve substantial risks and may yield extraordinary returns **2.** *US* an investment company that is organized as a limited partnership and uses high-risk techniques in the hope of making large profits

hedge garlic *n* PLANTS same as **garlic mustard**

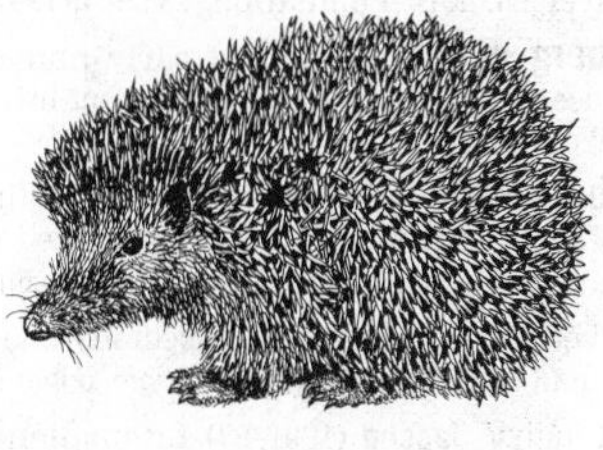

hedgehog

hedgehog /héj hog/, **hedge-hock** *n* **1.** a small animal that has a round body with stiff spines on the back and a small pointed snout. It can roll itself into a ball when attacked. Native to: Europe, Africa, Asia. Family: Erinaceidae. **2.** an underwater obstacle designed to keep landing craft from reaching a beach by ripping holes in the hulls [15C. Because the animal makes noises reminiscent of the squeals and grunts of pigs]

REGIONAL NOTE Modern traffic has drastically reduced the ***hedgehog*** population in Britain. Once, these little quadrupeds were found in all areas and names for them proliferated. They included *furze-pig, hedge-boar, hedge-hock, prickly-backed urchin*, and *urchin*.

hedgehop /héj hop/ (**-hops, -hopping, -hopped**) *vi* to fly very low above the ground, often so low that the aircraft must ascend to avoid obstacles on the ground (*refers to aircraft*) —**hedgehopper** *n*

hedgerow /héj rō/ *n* a row of bushes or small trees forming a hedge, especially round a field or along a country road or path

hedge-school *n* in 17th- and 18th-century Ireland, an unofficial school for Catholic children designed to evade legal restrictions on their education, often held out of doors

hedge sparrow *n* BIRDS same as **dunnock**

hedonic /hee dónnik/ *adj* **1.** concerned with pleasure **2.** characteristic of or relating to hedonism or hedonists [Mid-17C < Greek *hēdonikos* < *hēdonē* 'pleasure']

hedonism /heéd'nizəm, hédd'n-/ *n* **1.** a devotion, especially a self-indulgent one, to pleasure and happiness as a way of life **2.** a philosophical doctrine that holds that pleasure is the highest good or the source of moral values [Mid-19C. < Greek *hēdonē* 'pleasure'] —**hedonist** *n* —**hedonistic** /heédə nístik, héddə-/ *adj* —**hedonistically** *adv*

-hedron *suffix* a figure or crystal having a particular number or kind of surfaces ○ *pentahedron* [< modern Latin < Greek *hedra* 'seat, base'] —**-hedral** *suffix*

heebie-jeebies /heébi jeébiz/ *npl* uncomfortable nervous or anxious feelings (*slang*) ○ *There's something about thick fog that gives me the heebie-jeebies.* [Early 20C. Coined by Billy DeBeck (1890–1942), US cartoonist]

heed /heed/ *vti* (**heeds, heeding, heeded**) to give serious attention to a warning or advice and take it into account when acting ■ *n* serious attention paid to somebody or to something such as a warning, piece of advice, or request [Old English *hēdan* < Germanic] —**heeder** *n*

heedful /heédf'l/ *adj* paying attention to somebody or to something such as a warning, piece of advice, or danger —**heedfully** *adv* —**heedfulness** *n*

heedless /heédləss/ *adj* not paying attention to somebody or to something such as a warning, piece of advice, or danger —**heedlessly** *adv* —**heedlessness** *n*

heehaw /heé haw/ *n* **1.** the natural sound made by a donkey **2.** an unrefined noisy laugh (*informal*) [Early 19C. An imitation of the sound] —**heehaw** *vi*

heel[1] /heel/ *n* **1.** BACK OF FOOT the back part of a person's foot immediately below the ankle, or the same part of an animal's foot or paw **2.** BACK OF SHOE OR SOCK the part of a sock, stocking, shoe, or boot that covers the back part of somebody's foot **3.** BACK OF UNDERSIDE OF SHOE the back, usually thicker, portion of the underside of a shoe or other footwear that raises the foot off the ground ○ *I'll need to get new heels on these boots.* **4.** PHYSIOL THICKER PART OF PALM the thicker part of the palm of the hand, located next to the wrist **5.** CLOTHING PART OF GLOVE the part of a glove that covers the part of the palm located next to the wrist **6.** FOOD BREAD CRUST a crusty end of a loaf of bread **7.** FOOD CHEESE RIND the hard rind from a wedge of cheese **8.** GOLF PART OF GOLF CLUB the part of the head of a golf club where the shaft is attached **9.** MUSIC NECK SUPPORT a part that supports the neck of a stringed instrument at the point where it is attached to the body **10.** MUSIC END OF VIOLIN BOW the end of a violin bow that is held while playing the violin **11.** GARDENING PIECE ATTACHED TO CUTTING a small piece of a plant stem or tuber left attached to a cutting to promote the growth of new roots **12.** NAUT BOTTOM OF MAST the bottom end of a boat's mast **13.** NAUT STERN the stern end of a ship's keel **14.** OFFENSIVE TERM an offensive term that deliberately insults somebody's, especially a man's, behaviour (*insult*) ■ **heels** *npl* CLOTHING HIGH-HEELED SHOES shoes with high heels ■ *v* (**heels, heeling, heeled**) **1.** *vt* RENEW HEEL OF SHOE to fit, replace, or repair the heel of a shoe or boot **2.** *vi* FOLLOW BY SOMEBODY'S HEELS to follow closely at somebody's heels when commanded (*refers to dogs*) **3.** *vt* RIDING DIG HEELS INTO HORSE to hit or prod an animal being ridden with the heel **4.** *vi* DANCE MOVE HEELS to move the heels to music or touch a surface with the heels when dancing **5.** *vt* GOLF MISHIT GOLF BALL to mishit a golf ball with the heel of a club **6.** *vt* FOOTBALL USE HEEL TO KICK BALL to kick a ball with the heel, especially in rugby to pass the ball out of the scrummage using the heel [Old English *hēla* < Germanic] —**heeled** *adj* —**heelless** *adj* ◇ **cool** *or* **kick your heels** to wait or be kept waiting for a long time (*informal*) ◇ **dig in your heels** to hold stubbornly to a position or attitude ◇ **(hard) on the heels of somebody** *or* **something** **1.** close behind somebody or something **2.** soon after somebody or something ◇ **show (somebody) a clean pair of heels** to run away from somebody ◇ **take to your heels** to run off ◇ **to heel** **1.** directly behind the person with whom a dog is walking **2.** under control or discipline ◇ **turn on your heel** to turn round suddenly

SPELLCHECK See ***heal***.

heel[2] /heel/ *vti* (**heels, heeling, heeled**) to lean over to one side so far as to be in danger of capsizing, or cause a boat to lean in this way ○ *The ship heeled in the wind.* ■ *n* a leaning to one side, or the degree to which a boat is leaning [Late 16C. Alteration of *hield* (taken as past participle) < Old English *hieldan* 'lean, bend' < W Germanic]

heel[3]

heel in *vt* to place a plant in a hole and cover the roots with soil until it can be planted in its permanent place

heel-and-toe *adj* describes walking or racing that requires the heel of one foot to touch the ground

before the toe of the other is lifted from the ground ■ *vi* (**heel-and-toes, heel-and-toeing, heel-and-toed**) to operate the brake and accelerator pedals at the same time with one foot, usually to keep the engine revolutions high when shifting to a lower gear while racing

heelball /héel bawl/ *n* a black waxy substance used by shoemakers to blacken the edges of the heels and soles of shoes and boots or a similar substance used for making brass-rubbings

heelbar /héel baar/ *n* a small shop or a counter in a large shop where repairs are made to shoe soles and heels, often while the customer waits

heel bone *n* the quadrangular bone that forms the heel of the foot. Technical name **calcaneus**

heeler /héelər/ *n* **1.** a person or machine that fits, replaces, or repairs the heels of shoes or boots **2.** *Aus* an Australian sheep or cattle dog that herds by biting at the heels of the animals

heelpiece /héel peess/ *n* the part of a sock, stocking, shoe, or boot that fits round the heel of the foot

heelpost /héel pōst/ *n* a post to which the hinges of a gate or door are attached

heeltap /héel tap/ *n* **1.** a small quantity of an alcoholic drink remaining at the bottom of a glass after the rest has been swallowed **2.** a layer of leather or other material in the heel of a shoe or boot

Hefei /hő fáy/, **Hofei** /hő fáy/ capital city of Anhui Province, west of Nanjing, eastern China. Population: 1,320,000 (1995).

Hefner /héfnər/, **Hugh** (*b.* 1926) US publisher. He founded *Playboy* in 1953, and a string of related nightclubs. His own much publicized hedonistic lifestyle epitomized the sexual revolution of the 1960s and 1970s. Full name **Hefner, Hugh Marston**

heft /heft/ *vt* (**hefts, hefting, hefted**) **1.** LIFT SOMETHING to lift up something heavy, especially with a burst of effort **2.** ESTIMATE WEIGHT OF SOMETHING to lift something in order to estimate its weight ■ *n* GREAT WEIGHT substantial heaviness or bulk [15C. Probably < HEAVE, after pairs such as *cleave, cleft*] —**hefter** *n*

hefty /héfti/ (**-ier, -iest**) *adj* **1.** POWERFULLY BUILT big and strong in physique **2.** HEAVY large and heavy to lift **3.** EXPENSIVE involving a large sum of money **4.** FORCEFUL delivered with or characterized by great force and power **5.** STRENUOUS requiring a lot of effort to do **6.** LARGER THAN USUAL much larger than is usual or required ○ *a hefty sum* —**heftily** *adv* —**heftiness** *n*

Hegel /háyg'l/, **G. W. F.** (1770–1831) German philosopher. His idealist metaphysics exerted an enormous influence on 19th-century European thought. His works include *The Phenomenology of Mind* (1807) and the *Encyclopedia of the Philosophical Sciences in Outline* (1817). Full name **Hegel, Georg Wilhelm Friedrich** —**Hegelian** /hi gáyli ən/ *adj, n*

> 'The nature of Spirit may be understood by a glance at its direct opposite—Matter. As the essence of Matter is Gravity, so...we may affirm that the substance, the essence of Spirit is Freedom.'
> [G. W. F. Hegel, *Reason in History*; 1953 translation]

> 'What experience and history teach is this—that nations and governments have never learned anything from history, or acted upon any lessons they might have drawn from it.'
> [G. W. F. Hegel, *Lectures in the Philosophy of World History: Introduction*; 1830]

Hegelianism /hi gáyli ənizəm/ *n* the philosophy of G. W. F. Hegel, which proposes a unified solution to all philosophical problems through development of a reasoning process that ultimately interprets reality by way of the dialectic method.

hegemony /hi gémməni, -jémməni/ *n* control or dominating influence by one person or group, especially by one political group over society or one nation over others [Mid-16C. < Greek *hēgemonia* 'leadership' < *hēgisthai* 'lead'] —**hegemonic** /héggə mónnik, héjjə-/ *adj* —**hegemonism** *n* —**hegemonist** *n*

hegira /héjjirə, hi jírə/, **hejira** *n* a flight or withdrawal from somewhere, especially to escape from danger [Mid-18C. < HEGIRA]

Hegira /héjjirə, hi jírə/, **Hejira** *n* **1.** the withdrawal of the Prophet Muhammad from Mecca to Medina to escape persecution **2.** the Muslim era, dated from the first day of the lunar year in which Muhammad's withdrawal to Medina took place. This was 16 July, AD 622 in the Gregorian calendar. [Late 16C. Via medieval Latin < Arabic *hijra* 'the leaving of home and friends']

heh /hay/ *interj* used to express surprise or to attract attention [14C Natural exclamation]

Heian /háy ən/ *adj* characteristic of or relating to Japan from 794–1185, when Confucianism and other Chinese influences were at their height [Late 19C < Japanese *Heian-kyo*, now Kyoto, former capital of Japan]

heiau /háy ow/ *n Hawaii* an ancient temple or sacred place [Early 19C. < Hawaiian]

Heidegger /hī degər/, **Martin** (1889–1976) German philosopher. He greatly influenced the development of phenomenology and existentialism in the 20th century. His most important work is *Being and Time* (1927).

> 'We are too late for the gods / and too early for Being. Being's poem, / just begun, is man.'
> [Martin Heidegger, *Poetry, Language, Thought*; 1971]

> 'Thinking only begins at the point where we have come to know that Reason, glorified for centuries, is the most obstinate adversary of thinking.'
> [Martin Heidegger, *Being and Time*; 1927]

Heidelberg /hīd'l burg/ university city in Baden-Württemberg, southwestern Germany, situated on the River Neckar. Population: 138,964 (1997).

Heidelberg man *n* an extinct early human of the Pleistocene epoch that is known mainly from a fossilized jawbone

Heidelberg School /hīd'l burg-/ *n* a late 19th-century school of Australian artists who painted outdoors [After a suburb of Melbourne, Australia, near painting sites]

heifer /héffər/ *n* a young cow, especially one that has never had a calf [Old English *heahfore*, origin ?]

Heifetz /hīfits/, **Jascha** (1901–87) Lithuanian-born US violinist. Noted for his technical mastery, he was considered one of the greatest classical violinists of his time.

heigh-ho /hay-/ *interj* used to express boredom, disappointment, or weary resignation ○ *Heigh-ho. Here we go again.* [15C. < *heigh*, natural exclamation]

height /hīt/ *n* **1.** LENGTH UPWARDS the distance between the lowest and highest point of somebody or something ○ *a steep cliff about 70 metres in height* **2.** DISTANCE ABOVE POINT the distance that somebody or something is above the ground, sea, or another reference point **3.** NOTICEABLE TALLNESS the condition of being noticeably high or tall compared to others ○ *His height makes him stand out in a crowd.* **4.** HIGHEST POINT the top or highest point of something ○ *When you reach the height, you'll get a marvellous view.* **5.** HIGH POSITION a high place or position, especially one where somebody can see a view or how high up he or she is (*often used in the plural*) ○ *afraid of heights* **6.** MOST IMPORTANT OR ACTIVE LEVEL the level of greatest intensity, activity, importance, or success ○ *She was at the height of her powers.* **7.** MOST INTENSE LEVEL a high level of intensity or severity (*often used in the plural*) ○ *Their arrogance is reaching new heights.* **8.** EXTREME EXAMPLE the most extreme example of something ○ *It was the height of folly to have gone there on your own.* ■ **heights** *npl* HILLS OR MOUNTAINS an area of hilly or mountainous terrain, especially one that is noticeably elevated above the surrounding region (*often used in placenames*) [Old English *hēhþu* 'highest part' < Germanic]

CULTURAL NOTE ***Wuthering Heights***, a novel (1847) by Emily Brontë. Brontë's only novel, it is the story of a foundling, Heathcliff, whose mistreatment at the hands of his adoptive family leads him to seek revenge later in life. The novel is noted for its evocative descriptions of the Yorkshire moors, its complex morality, and its intensity of feeling.

heighten /hīt'n/ (**-ens, -ening, -ened**) *vti* **1.** INCREASE to make something such as a feeling or emotion greater or more intense, or become greater or more intense ○ *His attempts to reassure them served only to heighten their fears.* **2.** INTENSIFY IN BRIGHTNESS to make something such as a colour appear brighter or stronger, or appear to become brighter or stronger ○ *The sunlight heightened the flush on her cheeks.* **3.** EXTEND UPWARDS to make something higher, or become higher ○ *As protection, they heightened the city walls by a further three metres.* —**heightened** *adj* —**heightener** *n*

~~**heighth**~~ incorrect spelling of **height**

Heilongjiang /háy lŏong jī áng/ province in northeastern China, bordering Russia. Capital: Harbin. Population: 37,280,000 (1997). Area: 463,600 sq. km/179,000 sq. mi.

Heilong Jiang /háy lŏong jī áng/, **Heilung Chiang** Chinese name for **Amur**

Heimdall /háym daal/, **Heimdal, Heimdallr** /-daalər/ *n* in Norse mythology, a giant warrior who was the god of light and dawn [< Old Norse *Heimdallr* < *heimr* 'home, world']

Heimlich manoeuvre /hīmlik-/ *n* an emergency method for treating choking that uses an upward thrust immediately below the breastbone to expel food or another blockage from the windpipe [Late 20C. After Henry J. *Heimlich* (b. 1920), US surgeon]

Heine /hīnə/, **Heinrich** (1797–1856) German poet. One of Germany's greatest lyric poets, he spent his last 25 years in France. The poems in his *Book of Songs* (1827) inspired numerous musical settings by leading European composers.

> 'The arrow belongs not to the archer when it has once left the bow; the word no longer belongs to the speaker when it has once passed his lips.'
> [Heinrich Heine, *Religion and Philosophy*; 1840]

> 'Wherever books will be burned, men also, in the end, are burned.'
> [Heinrich Heine, *Almansor*; 1823]

Heinkel /hīngk'l/, **Ernst** (1888–1958) German engineer. He designed aircraft used by the German air force in both world wars, and built the first jet-propelled plane (1939). Full name **Heinkel, Ernst Heinrich**

Heinlein /hīn līn/, **Robert** (1907–88) US writer. His many works of science fiction, known for their technological sophistication, include *Stranger in a Strange Land* (1961). Full name **Heinlein, Robert Anson**

> 'The Earth is just too small and fragile a basket for the human race to keep all its eggs in.'
> [Robert Heinlein, *Speech*; Undated]

heinous /háynəss/ *adj* shockingly evil or wicked [14C. < Old French *haineus* < *hair* 'to hate' < Germanic] —**heinously** *adv* —**heinousness** *n*

heir /air/ *n* **1.** somebody who holds the right to receive a property, position, or title of somebody else when that person dies **2.** an inheritor of something such as a tradition, problem, or characteristic ○ *Our generation is the unfortunate heir to decades of pollution.* [14C. Via Old French *(h)eir* < Latin *heres*] —**heirless** *adj* —**heirship** *n*

SPELLCHECK See ***air***.

heir apparent (*plural* **heirs apparent**) *n* **1.** an heir whose entitlement to receive an inheritance cannot be altered by the birth of another heir **2.** the expected inheritor of somebody else's position, status, or influence

~~**heirarchy**~~ incorrect spelling of **hierarchy**

heir at law (*plural* **heirs at law**) *n* the heir of somebody's property under the law if that person dies without a valid will

heiress /áirəss/ *n* a woman or girl who receives or has by law the right to receive the property, position, or title of another when that person dies

heirloom /áir loom/ *n* **1.** something valuable that has been in the possession of a family for a long time and has been passed on from one generation to the next **2.** an item of personal property that is attached to the estate that a legal heir will inherit [< LOOM[2] in obsolete sense 'tool, utensil']

heir presumptive (*plural* **heirs presumptive**) *n* an heir whose entitlement to an inheritance will cease if another heir is born whose entitlement is greater

Heisenberg /híz'n burg/, **Werner** (1901–76) German physicist. He directed Germany's development of an atomic bomb during World War II. His most important research in theoretical physics included work on quantum theory and his discovery of the uncertainty principle. He won the Nobel Prize (1932).

> 'Natural science does not simply describe and explain nature, it is part of the inter-play between nature and ourselves.'
> [Werner Heisenberg, *Physics and Phil-osophy*; 1958]

Heisenberg uncertainty principle *n* PHYS same as **uncertainty principle**

heist /hīst/ *N Am* (*slang*) *n* a theft or robbery, especially of money or valuables, usually involving the use of weapons ∎ *vt* (**heists, heisting, heisted**) to steal or rob something, especially money or valuables, usually while carrying weapons [Mid-19C. Representing a local N American pronunciation of HOIST] — **heister** *n*

heita /háy taa/ *interj S Africa* used as a friendly greeting chiefly among young Black people (*informal*) [Mid-20C. Origin?]

heitiki /hay teéki/ *n NZ* a Maori fertility symbol (**tiki**) carved from greenstone in the shape of a foetus, worn as a neck ornament [Mid-19C. < Maori < *hei* 'wear round the neck' + *tiki* 'image']

Hejaz /hee jáz/ *n* province of western Saudi Arabia, bordering the Red Sea. Capital: Mecca. Area: 348,600 sq. km/134,600 sq. mi.

hejira, Hejira *n* another spelling of **hegira, Hegira**

Hekate *n* MYTHOL another spelling of **Hecate**

Heke Pokai /hékay pókī/, **Hone** (1810?–50) Maori leader. He was head of the Ngapuhi people and a strong opponent of British colonial government in New Zealand.

Hekla /héklə/ active volcano in southwestern Iceland. Height: 1,491 m/4,892 ft.

Hel /hel/, **Hela** /hé laa/ *n* **1.** in Norse mythology, the goddess of the dead and the underworld **2.** in Norse mythology, the underworld of the dead [< Old Norse]

HeLa cell /heélə-/, **Hela cell** *n* a cell from a strain of human cervical cancer cells that is used in medical and biological research [Mid-20C. Acronym < *Henrietta Lacks*, from whom the original cells were taken]

held past participle, past tense of **hold**[1]

Heldentenor /héldən tə nawr/ *n* a tenor or tenor voice with a robust dramatic quality that is suited especially for heroic roles in the operas of Richard Wagner [Early 20C. < German, 'hero tenor']

Helen /héllən/, **Helen of Troy** *n* in Greek mythology, the daughter of Zeus and Leda and the most beautiful woman in Greece. Her husband was Menelaus, the king of Sparta. Her abduction by Paris sparked the Trojan War.

Helena /héllənə/ city and capital of Montana, located in the western part of the state. Population: 26,353 (2002 estimate).

Helena, St (248?–328?) Roman empress. She was the mother of Constantine I. Among her religious pilgrimages, she visited Jerusalem in about 325, where she founded the Church of the Holy Sepulchre and is said to have discovered the True Cross, an important Christian relic.

Helene /hə leéni/ *n* a very small natural satellite of Saturn, discovered in 1980. It is irregular in shape, with a maximum dimension of 36 km/22 mi., and occupies an intermediate orbit.

helenium /hi leéni əm/ (*plural* **-ums** or *same*) *n* a plant of the daisy family. Flowers: yellow, dark reddish, or in some cultivated varieties bicolour. Native to: North and South America. Genus: *Helenium*. [Early 17C. Via modern Latin < Greek *helenion*]

Helen of Troy *n* MYTHOL same as **Helen**

Helensvale /héllənz vayl/ town in southeastern Queensland, Australia, a residential, tourist, and cattle-grazing centre. Population: 13,823 (1996).

heli /hélli/ (*plural* **-is**) *n* a rotary-wing aircraft (*informal*) [Shortening of HELICOPTER]

heli- *prefix* helicopter ○ *helipad* [< HELICOPTER]

heliacal /hi lí ək'l/ *adj* describes the rising or setting of a star that occurs at the same time as the rising or setting of the Sun, because of their near conjunction [Mid-16C. < late Latin *heliacus* < Greek *hēlios* 'sun'] — **heliacally** *adv*

helianthemum /heéli ánthəməm/ *n* an evergreen perennial that forms a low mound. Flowers: white, yellow, pink, orange. Native to: United States, Europe, Asia Minor. Genus: *Helianthemum*. [Early 19C. < modern Latin < Greek *hēlios* 'sun' + *anthemon* 'flower'; because the flower turns with the sun]

helianthus /heéli ánthəss/ (*plural* **-thuses** or *same*) *n* a tall perennial plant of the sunflower family. Flowers: yellow, like daisies. Genus: *Helianthus*. [Late 18C. < modern Latin < Greek *hēlios* 'sun' + *anthos* 'flower'; because the flower turns with the sun]

helibiking /hélli bīking/ *n* a sport in which mountain-bike riders are taken by helicopter to the top of a mountain and then ride down

heliborne /hélli bawrn/ *adj* transported by helicopter

helic- *prefix* same as **helico-** (*used before vowels*)

helical /héllik'l/ *adj* in the shape of a helix or spiral [Late 16C. < Latin *helix* (see HELIX)] — **helically** *adv*

helical gear *n* a gear whose teeth are formed to curve along a spiral path on the surface of the gear on an axis oblique to the axis of the gear itself

helices MATHS, ANAT plural of **helix**

helichrysum /hélli krízəm/ (*plural* **-sums** or *same*) *n* an annual or perennial plant of the daisy family with flowers that retain their colour when dried. Genus: *Helichrysum*. [Mid-16C. < Latin < Greek *helix* 'spiral' + *khrusos* 'gold']

helico- *prefix* helix, spiral ○ *helicograph* [< Greek *helik-*, stem of *helix*]

helicograph /héllikō graaf, -graf/ *n* an instrument for drawing spiral curves on a flat surface

helicoid /hélli koyd/ *adj* shaped or coiled like a spiral (*technical*) ○ *a helicoid shell* ∎ *n* a spiral geometric surface that resembles a thread on a screw [Late 17C. < Greek *helicoidēs* < *helix* 'spiral'] — **helicoidal** /hélli kóyd'l/ *adj* — **helicoidally** *adv*

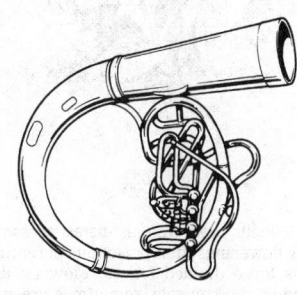

helicon

helicon /héllikən, -kon/ *n* a large bass tuba that encircles the player's body, used in marching bands [Late 19C. < Mount *Helicon* in Greece, reputed home of the Muses; influenced by HELIX]

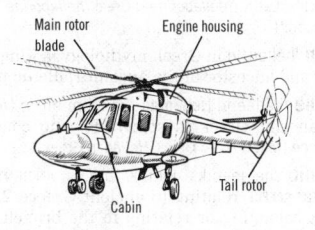

Main rotor blade — Engine housing — Tail rotor — Cabin

helicopter

helicopter /hélli koptər/ *n* an aircraft without wings that moves by means of large blades (**rotors**) that spin round above it. It can fly vertically and horizontally and can hover. ∎ *vti* (**-ters, -tering, -tered**) to travel or transport somebody or something in a helicopter ○ *The survivors were helicoptered to a hospital*. [Late 19C. < French *hélicoptère* < Greek *helix* 'spiral' + *pteron* 'wing']

helicopter gunship *n* a large heavily armed helicopter used to protect troops on the ground

helicopter view *n* a general outline or brief summary of a situation or subject ○ *a helicopter view of the state of the industry*

heliculture /hélli kulchər/ *n* the science or profession of raising snails for food [< modern Latin *Helix*, genus of spiral-shelled molluscs < Greek *helix* 'spiral'] — **helicultural** /hélli kúlchərəl/ *adj* — **heliculturalist** *n*

helideck /hélli dek/ *n* a deck on something such as a ship or offshore oil platform that is used as a landing site for helicopters

helio- *prefix* sun ○ *heliostat* [< Greek *hēlios* < Indo-European]

heliocentric /heéli ō séntrik/, **heliocentrical** /-séntrik'l/ *adj* **1.** with the Sun at the centre ○ *a heliocentric orbit* **2.** measured from or considered as if viewed from the centre of the Sun — **heliocentrically** *adv* — **heliocentricity** /-sen tríssəti/ *n*

Heliochrome /heéli ō krōm/ *tdmk* a trademark for a photograph that very accurately reproduces the colours of the subject photographed

heliodor /heéli ō dawr/ *n* a clear yellow variety of beryl from southwestern Africa. Use: gems. [Early 20C. < HELIO- + Greek *dōron* 'gift']

heliograph /heéli ə graaf, -graf/ *n* **1.** an apparatus that is used to send messages in Morse code by flashes of reflected sunlight **2.** an apparatus used to photograph the Sun — **heliographer** /heéli óggrəfər/ *n* — **heliographic** /heéli ə gráffik/ *adj*

heliolatry /heéli óllətri/ *n* worship of the Sun — **heliolater** *n* — **heliolatrous** *adj*

heliolithic /heéli ō líthik/ *adj* describes a culture or society characterized by worship of the Sun and the construction of monuments or temples using huge stones (**megaliths**)

heliometer /heéli ómmitər/ *n* a refracting telescope with a divided objective that is used to measure small angular distances between astronomical objects or points on the Moon — **heliometric** /heéli ə méttrik/ *adj* — **heliometrical** *adj* — **heliometrically** *adv* — **heliometry** *n*

heliopause /heéli ō pawz/ *n* the point marking the beginning of interstellar space and the endpoint boundary of our solar system, 10–15 billion miles from the Sun, where the pressure from solar winds is in balance with that of interstellar winds

heliophyte /heéli ō fīt/ *n* a plant that can survive and grow in direct sunlight or that grows best in direct sunlight

Heliopolis /heéli óppəliss/ city of ancient Egypt, northeast of present-day Cairo in the Nile delta. The great temple there was the centre of Sun worship, and reached the height of its influence in the 13th century BC.

Helios /heéli oss/ *n* in Greek mythology, the god of the sun. The son of Hyperion and Thea, he drove his golden chariot across the sky from east to west each day. Roman equivalent **Sol** (sense 2)

helioseismology /heéli ō sīz mólləji/ *n* the scientific study of the sound waves in the Sun's atmosphere

heliosphere /heéli ō sfeer/ *n* a spherical region round the Sun, approximately 100 astronomical units in radius, outside which interstellar space begins — **heliospheric** /heéli ō sférrik/ *adj*

heliostat /heéli ō stat/ *n* an instrument with an automatically rotated mirror that reflects the Sun's light in a constant direction, used to measure the Sun's radiation [Mid-18C. < modern Latin *heliostata* or French *héliostat*, both < Greek *hēlios* 'sun' + *statos* 'standing'] — **heliostatic** /heéli ō státtik/ *adj*

heliotaxis /heéli ō táksiss/ *n* movement towards or away from sunlight in an organism that is able to move about freely — **heliotactic** *adj*

heliotherapy /heéli ō thérrəpi/ *n* treatment of illness by exposure to direct sunlight

heliotrope /heéli ə trōp/ (*plural* **-tropes** or *same*) *n* **1.** PLANT WITH FRAGRANT FLOWERS a hairy plant of the borage family. Flowers: small, fragrant, white or purple, in clusters. Genus: *Heliotropium*. **2.** CULTIVATED PURPLE FLOWER a cultivated species of heliotrope. Flowers: small purple, very fragrant. Native to: South America. Latin name: *Heliotropium arborescens*. **3.** PLANTS, BOT FLOWER THAT TURNS TOWARDS SUN a plant with

flowers that turn towards the sun **4.** COLOURS **BLUISH COLOUR** a bluish-purple colour **5.** (*plural* **heliotropes**) MINERALS same as **bloodstone 6.** (*plural* **heliotropes**) CIV ENG **SURVEYING INSTRUMENT** an instrument used in geodesic surveying to reflect the Sun's rays over long distances [Pre-12C. Via Latin < Greek *heliotropion* < *helios* 'sun' + *tropos* 'turning'] —**heliotrope** *adj*

heliotropism /heeli óttrəpizəm/ *n* growth towards sunlight by a plant —**heliotropic** /heeli ə tróppik/ *adj* —**heliotropical** *adj* —**heliotropically** *adv*

heliozoan /heeli ō zṓ ən/ *n* a free-living, usually freshwater, protozoan that has a spherical shell and radiating projections (**pseudopodia**). Class: Heliozoa. [Late 19C. < modern Latin *Heliozoa* < Greek *hēlios* 'sun' + *zōion* 'animal'] —**heliozoic** *adj*

helipad /hélli pad/ *n* an area where helicopters take off and land

heliport /hélli pawrt/ *n* an airport designed for helicopters

heliskiing /hélli skee ing/ *n* skiing in which skiers are taken to a usually remote ski slope by helicopter

helistop /hélli stop/ *n* a place where helicopters can take off and land, usually without the support facilities found at a heliport

helium /heeli əm/ *n* a nonflammable inert gaseous element that is colourless and odourless. Source: natural gas. Use: inert atmospheres, cryogenic research, lasers, inflating balloons. Symbol **He**. See table at **element** [Late 19C. < Greek *hēlios* 'sun'; because its existence was deduced from its emission line in the solar spectrum]

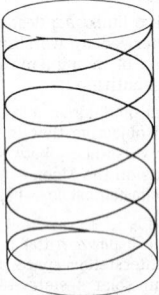

helix (sense 2)

helix /heeliks/ (*plural* **helices** /hélli seez/ or **helixes**) *n* **1.** SPIRAL OR COIL something in the form of a spiral or coil, e.g. a corkscrew or a coiled spring **2.** MATHS SPIRAL CURVE a mathematical curve that lies on a cylinder or cone and makes a constant angle with the straight lines lying in the cylinder or cone **3.** ANAT RIM OF EAR the rim of the external ear [Mid-16C. Via Latin < Greek]

CULTURAL NOTE *The Double Helix*, a memoir (1968) by US scientist James D. Watson. In this personal account of the landmark discovery of the structure of the DNA molecule in 1953, for which Watson later shared a Nobel Prize with Francis Crick and Maurice Wilkins, scientific research is shown to be a competitive race in which ego, politics, and luck play prominent roles. Watson's less than generous treatment of Maurice Wilkins' and Rosalind Franklin's contribution to his work caused much controversy when the book was published.

hell /hel/ *n* **1.** *also* **Hell** PLACE OF PUNISHMENT AFTER DEATH according to many religions, the place where the souls of people who are damned suffer eternal punishment after death **2.** *also* **Hell** DEVILISH POWER according to some religions, Satan or the powers of evil that live in hell **3.** UNDERWORLD according to some religions, the place where the spirits of all people go after death **4.** SUFFERING a state or place of extreme pain or misery, or something or somebody that causes extreme pain or misery ○ *Finals are absolute hell.* ○ *She went through hell until she heard they were safe.* ■ *interj* EXPRESSING ANNOYANCE used to express annoyance or surprise (*sometimes considered offensive*) ○ *Hell! I've lost the key.* [Old English *hel(l)* < Indo-European, 'conceal'] ◇ **a** *or* **one hell of a** used as an intensifier (*informal*) ◇ **come hell or high water** whatever difficulties there may be ◇ **from hell** of the worst sort imaginable (*informal*) ○ *The bus ride in the snowstorm was a trip from hell.* ◇ **give somebody hell** (*informal*) **1.** to scold somebody severely **2.** to

cause somebody trouble or pain ◇ **hell for leather** extremely rapidly and often recklessly (*informal*) ◇ **hell to pay** serious trouble or punishment that is sure to result from something (*informal*) ◇ **(just) for the hell of it** just for the sake of doing it and without any specific reason (*informal*) ◇ **like hell** (*informal*) **1.** very fast or very intensely **2.** used to emphasize disagreement or denial ◇ **play (merry) hell with something** to cause harm, disruption, or damage to something (*informal*) ◇ **raise hell** (*informal*) **1.** to object to something strongly and loudly **2.** to cause a noisy disturbance ◇ **the hell** (*informal*) **1.** used to emphasize annoyance ○ *Get the hell out of it. I'm trying to work.* **2.** used to emphasize disagreement or denial ○ *Did he offer to help? The hell he did.*

he'll *stressed* /heel/; *unstressed* /eel, il/ *contr* **1.** he shall **2.** he will

Helladic /he láddik/ *adj* associated with or characteristic of the Bronze Age civilization that flourished in Greece from 3000 to 1100 BC [Early 19C. < Greek *Helladikos* < *Hellas* 'Greece']

Hellas /héllass/ *n* **1.** the Greek name for Greece **2.** an extensive plain on the surface of Mars in the southern hemisphere, approximately 1800 km/1100 mi. across

hellbender /hél bendər/ *n* a large, dark grey salamander. Native to: rivers in eastern and central United States. Latin name: *Cryptobranchus alleganiensis*.

hell-bent *adj* absolutely determined to do something, regardless of the consequences (*informal*)

hellcat /hél kat/ *n* an offensive term for a woman regarded as being quick to lose her temper and likely to be violent (*informal*)

hellebore

hellebore /hélli bawr/ (*plural* **-bores** or *same*) *n* **1.** an early-flowering, often poisonous perennial plant that has large divided leaves. Flowers: drooping white, pink, dark purple, sometimes green. Native to: Europe, Asia. Genus: *Helleborus*. **2.** a poisonous plant of the buttercup family with large leaves. Flowers: greenish. Native to: North America. Genus: *Veratrum*. [Pre-12C. Via French < Greek *helleboros*]

helleborine /héllibə rīn, -reen/ *n* an orchid that grows in woodland. Native to: temperate regions. Genera: *Epipactis* or *Cephalanthera*. [Late 16C. Directly or via French < Latin *(h)elleborine* < Greek *helleborinē* 'plant like hellebore']

Hellen /héllən/ *n* in Greek mythology, a king of Thessaly and ancestor of the ancient Hellenic peoples

Hellene /hélleen/, **Hellenian** /he léeni ən/ *n* (*formal*) **1.** an ancient Greek **2.** somebody who comes from Greece [Mid-17C. < Greek *Hellēn* 'a Greek']

Hellenic /he léenik, -lénnik/ *adj* **1.** ANCIENT HIST OF ANCIENT GREECE relating to ancient Greece **2.** LANG OF GREEK belonging or relating to the branch of Indo-European consisting of the ancient and modern forms of Greek ■ *n* LANG GREEK LANGUAGE the Hellenic branch of Indo-European [Mid-17C. < Greek *Hellēnikos* < *Hellēn* 'a Greek'] —**Hellenically** *adv*

Hellenise *vti* ANCIENT HIST another spelling of **Hellenize**

Hellenism /héllənizəm/ *n* **1.** ANCIENT GREEK CULTURE the culture and civilization of ancient Greece, especially in the period after Alexander the Great when it spread to other parts of the Mediterranean, Southwest Asia, and North Africa **2.** ADMIRATION FOR ANCIENT GREEK CULTURE the enthusiasm for or adoption of ancient Greek culture or customs **3.** GREEK CHAR-

ACTERISTIC a Greek custom or idiom **4.** GREEK NATIONAL CHARACTER the supposed national character of the Greeks [Early 17C. < Greek *Hellēnismos* < *Hellēnizein* (see HELLENIZE)]

Hellenist /héllənist/ *n* **1.** a specialist in the study of Greek language, literature, culture, or history, or an admirer of the Greeks and their culture **2.** somebody, especially somebody Jewish, who adopted Greek customs, language, and culture during the 4th to 1st centuries BC [Early 17C. < Greek *Hellēnistēs* < *Hellēnizein* (see HELLENIZE)]

Hellenistic /héllə nístik/ *adj* **1.** OF ANCIENT GREEK CIVILIZATION characteristic of or relating to ancient Greek civilization during the late 4th to 1st centuries BC **2.** OF GREEKS characteristic of or associated with the Greeks **3.** PREFERRING GREEK CULTURE enthusiastic for or adopting ancient Greek culture or customs ○ *the Hellenistic Jews of Alexandria* —**Hellenistically** *adv*

Hellenize /héllə nīz/ (**-nizes, -nizing, -nized**), **Hellenise** (**-nises, -nising, -nised**) *vti* to adopt the language and culture of the ancient Greeks, or make something closer in character to the language and culture of the ancient Greeks [Early 17C. < Greek *Hellēnizein* 'speak Greek, make Greek' < *Hellēn* 'a Greek'] —**Hellenization** /héllə nī záysh'n/ *n* —**Hellenizer** *n*

heller /héllər/ (*plural same*) *n* **1.** a former German or Austrian coin **2.** MONEY, COINS another spelling of **haler** [Late 16C. < German, later form of *haller* (see HALER)]

Heller /héllər/, **Joseph** (1923–99) US writer. He is best known for his antiwar novel *Catch-22* (1961). See Cultural note at **catch-22**

'He was a self-made man who owed his lack of success to nobody.'
[Joseph Heller, *Catch-22*; 1961]

Hellespont /héllispont/ ♦ **Dardanelles**

hellfire /hél fīr/ *n* punishment in hell according to some religions, often described as eternal torment in the flames of hell's fires ■ *adj* detailing in a vigorous and emotional way the punishment sinners can expect in hell, according to some religions

hellgrammite /hélgrə mīt/ *n* N Am the large carnivorous larva of a dobsonfly, occurring in water and often used as fish bait [Mid-19C. Origin ?]

hellhole /hél hōl/ *n* a terrifying, unbearable, or evil place

hellhound /hél hownd/ *n* **1.** a supposed fiend, or a fiendish person **2.** especially in Greek mythology, a hound said to guard the gates of hell

hellion /héllyən/ *n* N Am a troublesome or rowdy person, especially a child (*informal*) [Mid-19C. Probably alteration, influenced by HELL, of Scots and N dialect *hallion* 'idler', origin ?]

hellish /héllish/ *adj* **1.** OF HELL like, from, or typical of hell ○ *a hellish scene of blazing homes and streets jammed with debris* **2.** DREADFUL extremely unpleasant or difficult (*informal*) ○ *The exam was absolutely hellish.* ■ *adv* EXTREMELY used as an intensifier (*informal*) ○ *hellish difficult* —**hellishly** *adv* —**hellishness** *n*

Lillian Hellman

Popperfoto

Hellman /hélmən/, **Lillian** (1905–84) US playwright. She was known for her powerful moral dramas such as *The Watch on the Rhine* (1941) and *Toys in the Attic* (1960). Full name **Hellman, Lillian Florence**

'Fashions in sin change.'
[Lillian Hellman, *The Watch on the Rhine*; 1941]

hello /hə lṓ, he-/, **hallo** /hə lṓ, ha-/, **hullo** /hə lṓ, hu-/ *interj, n* (*plural* **-los**) **1.** WORD USED AS GREETING a word used to greet somebody you meet, to answer a telephone call, or to begin a radio or television programme ○ *Hello. Nice to meet you.* ○ *After we had all said our hellos, we settled down to eat.* **2.** WORD TO ATTRACT ATTENTION a word used to attract attention ○ *Hello! Is there anyone in?* **3.** WORD EXPRESSING SURPRISE a word used to express surprise ○ *Hello! What's that doing here?* [Late 19C. Probably < French *holá* 'stop there!', used to attract attention]

hell-raiser *n* somebody whose idea of having a good time involves behaving in ways that other people consider drunken, rowdy, or disruptive

Hell's Angel *n* a member of a Californian gang of motorcyclists, mostly men, typically dressing in denim and leather and originally noted for violent antisocial behaviour, or a member of any similar gang elsewhere

helluva /héllәvә/ *adj* used as an intensifier (*informal*) ○ *a helluva party* [Early 20C. Representing *hell of a*]

helm[1] /helm/ *n* **1.** NAUT SHIP'S STEERING APPARATUS the apparatus used to steer a ship, especially the wheel or handle (**tiller**) by which the rudder is turned **2.** POSITION OF CONTROL a position of leadership or control within an organization, country, or enterprise ○ *The failing company needed a new chief at its helm.* ■ *vt* (**helms, helming, helmed**) **1.** NAUT STEER SHIP to be at the helm of a ship steering it **2.** DIRECT SOMETHING to be at the head of an organization, country, or enterprise directing it [Old English *helma* < Germanic, 'handle'] —**helmless** *adj*

helm[2] /helm/ *n* a military helmet, especially of an ancient or medieval type (*archaic or literary*) [Old English < Germanic, 'conceal, cover']

helmet /hélmit/ *n* **1.** HARD PROTECTIVE HEAD COVERING a hat or other head covering made of a hard material and worn to protect the head from injury, often part of a uniform, suit of armour, or protective clothing **2.** PROTECTIVE HAT any protective hat, e.g. against cold weather or the heat of the sun **3.** BIOL PART SHAPED LIKE HELMET a part of an organism resembling a helmet, e.g. a flower's sepal or corolla [15C. < Old French, diminutive of *helme* 'helmet' < Germanic] —**helmeted** *adj*

helminth /hélminth/ *n* a parasitic worm, e.g. a fluke, nematode, or tapeworm [Mid-19C. < Greek *helminth-* 'intestinal worm'] —**helminthoid** *adj*

helminthiasis /hélmin thī́ əssiss/ *n* infestation by parasitic worms, often causing disease

helminthic /hel mínthik/ *adj* **1.** caused by or relating to flukes, nematodes, or other parasitic worms (**helminths**) **2.** eradicating or expelling parasitic worms ■ *n* MED, VET same as **vermifuge**

helminthology /hélmin thólləji/ *n* the scientific study of parasitic worms —**helminthologist** *n*

Helmont /hél mont/, **Jan Baptista van** (1580–1644) Flemish chemist and physiologist. An early experimental chemist, he coined the term 'gas'.

helmsman /hélmzmən/ (*plural* **-men** /-mən/) *n* **1.** the steerer of a ship, especially a man **2.** somebody, especially a man, who is the director of an organization, country, or enterprise ○ *the country's helmsman in the crisis* —**helmsmanship** *n*

helmsperson /hélmz purss'n/ (*plural* **-persons** or **-people** /-peep'l/) *n* **1.** the steerer of a ship **2.** the director of an organization, country, or enterprise

helmswoman /hélmz wŏŏmən/ (*plural* **-women** /-wimin/) *n* **1.** a woman who is the steerer of a ship **2.** a woman who is the director of an organization, country, or enterprise

helo /héllō/ (*plural* **-os**) *n* (*informal*) **1.** a rotary-winged aircraft **2.** AVIAT same as **heliport** [Mid-20C. Shortening and alteration of HELICOPTER]

Héloïse /éllō eez/ (1098?–1164) French abbess. Her love affair with Peter Abelard, and their subsequent separation and correspondence, provided one of the world's great love stories.

helot /héllət/ *n* an enslaved person or serf [Early 19C. < HELOT] —**helotage** *n*

Helot /héllət/ *n* in ancient Sparta, a member of a class of serfs claimed as property by the state but assigned to individual Spartans to work on their land [Late 16C. Via Latin *Helotes* < Greek *Heilōtes*, probably after *Helos*, town in Laconia whose inhabitants were enslaved]

helotism /héllətizəm/ *n* **1.** a political or social system in which one group, class, or nation is systematically oppressed by another **2.** symbiosis found especially among ants, in which one species acts as workers for another, dominant species

help /help/ *v* (**helps, helping, helped**) **1.** *vti* ASSIST SOMEBODY to make it easier or possible for somebody to do something that one person cannot do alone by providing assistance ○ *Can you help me solve this problem?* ○ *Can I help with those bags?* **2.** *vti* ADVISE SOMEBODY to provide somebody with advice, directions, or other information ○ *Can you help me? I'm looking for Belmont Road.* **3.** *vti* BE USEFUL to make something easier or more likely ○ *It would help if you didn't keep shaking the ladder.* ○ *Would a degree help me get a better job?* **4.** *vti* MAKE THINGS BETTER to bring about an improvement in something unpleasant, unbearable, or unfortunate ○ *I took a couple of aspirins, but they didn't help my headache.* ○ *You look ridiculous in that dress, and the hat doesn't help.* **5.** *vti* PROVIDE FOR SOMEBODY'S NEEDS to provide somebody with something that he or she needs, especially money **6.** *vti* ADVANCE SOMETHING to promote the advancement or improvement of something ○ *Opening a new sports centre won't cut out teenage crime, but it might help.* **7.** *vt* SERVE SOMEBODY to serve somebody in a shop, restaurant, or other establishment ○ *Can I help you, sir?* **8.** *vt* BRING SOMEBODY FOOD to give somebody or yourself a serving of food ○ *He helped us all to some cake.* **9.** ⚠ *vt* KEEP SOMEBODY FROM DOING SOMETHING to keep somebody or yourself from doing something (*usually used in negative statements*) ○ *We couldn't help overhearing your conversation.* ○ *I didn't want to laugh, but I couldn't help myself.* **10.** *vt* PREVENT SOMETHING to prevent something from happening (*usually used in negative statements*) ○ *The child couldn't have helped the accident.* ■ *n* **1.** ASSISTANCE something that is done for or given to somebody in order to make something easier, possible, or better ○ *I could do with some help in the kitchen.* **2.** SOMEBODY OR SOMETHING THAT ASSISTS somebody who provides aid or assistance to somebody ○ *The headaches are pretty bad, but the aspirins are a help.* **3.** WAY OUT OF SOMETHING a way of avoiding doing something or of undoing something (*often used in negative statements*) ○ *Well, there's no help for it now but to start digging.* **4.** SOMEBODY PAID TO CLEAN somebody who is paid to help with the housework in somebody else's home **5.** SERVANTS COLLECTIVELY domestic servants as a group (*takes a singular or plural verb*) ○ *told us that the help have to eat in the kitchen* ■ *interj* CALLS FOR ASSISTANCE used to call for assistance when somebody is in danger or difficulty [Old English *helpan* < Germanic] ◇ **help yourself** to take something for your own use, usually without permission

---

USAGE can't help but: Traditionally, speakers and writers had a choice between, for example, *can't help doing* and *can't* [or *cannot*] *but do.* The latter is now uncommon. *Can't help but do* is often seen, but it is a redundant mixture of the two forms, and should be avoided in favour of *can't help doing.*

SYNONYMS See ***assistant***.

---

help out *vti* to give somebody some help, e.g. by doing some work or giving money

help desk *n* a service providing technical help and support for people using a computer package or network

helper /hélpər/ *n* somebody who helps with something, often in an informal or voluntary capacity

helper T cell, **helper cell** *n* a white blood cell that is part of the body's immune response, recognizing foreign antigens and stimulating the production of cells to control them

helpful /hélpf'l/ *adj* providing or willing to provide assistance, information, or other aid ○ *You might find this book helpful.* —**helpfully** *adv* —**helpfulness** *n*

helping /hélping/ *n* an amount of food served to somebody at one time

helping hand *n* something done to assist somebody else

helpless /hélpləss/ *adj* **1.** NEEDING HELP unable to manage without help **2.** DEFENCELESS unprotected and unable to provide an adequate defence against an attack **3.** UNABLE TO ACT EFFECTIVELY unable to do anything to protect somebody or prevent something from happening ○ *He was helpless to stop the assault.* **4.** UNRESTRAINED unable to exert control or restraint ○ *His jokes had us absolutely helpless.* —**helplessly** *adv* —**helplessness** *n*

helpline /hélp līn/ *n* a telephone service that provides advice or information to people who phone up with problems or enquiries

Helpmann /hélpmən/, **Sir Robert Murray** (1909–86) Australian ballet dancer and choreographer. He was principal dancer and choreographer at Sadler's Wells Ballet, London, in the 1930s and 1940s, and later joined the Australian Ballet (1964–76).

helpmate /hélp mayt/ *n* a helpful companion or partner, especially a spouse

helpmeet /hélp meet/ *n* a helpmate, especially a wife (*archaic; sometimes considered offensive*) [Late 17C. < 'an help meet for him' (Genesis 2:18, 20), with misinterpretation of MEET[2] 'suitable']

help screen *n* a pop-up screen in a computer program or website that contains advice on how to navigate the program or site

Helsingborg /hélssing bawrg/ city and seaport in Skåne province, southern Sweden, on the Øresund, opposite Denmark. Population: 116,337 (1998).

Helsingør /hélseng úr/ town and seaport in eastern Denmark on the island of Zealand, the setting of Shakespeare's play *Hamlet*, in which it is called Elsinore. Population: 44,860 (1998).

Helsinki /hel síngki/ capital city and chief seaport of Finland, situated on the Gulf of Finland in the south of the country. Population: 551,123 (2000).

helter-skelter /héltər skéltər/ *adv, adj* **1.** WITH HASTE with hurry and confusion ○ *The rabbits rushed helter-skelter down their burrows.* **2.** IN DISORDER without order or organization ○ *The winds had knocked the huge trees helter-skelter all over the park.* ■ *n* **1.** SPIRAL SLIDE a fairground amusement consisting of a high tower with a spiral slide round it **2.** CONFUSED STATE a hurried or disorganized situation or state [Late 16C. Probably formed to suggest hurried action]

~~**helth**~~ incorrect spelling of **health**

helve /helv/ *n* the handle of a tool such as an axe, pick, or hammer [Old English *helfe* < Germanic]

Helvellyn /hel véllin/ mountain in Cumbria, northwestern England. Height: 950 m/3,118 ft.

Helvetia /hel veéshə/ *n* the Latin name for Switzerland

Helvetian /hel veésh'n/ *n* **1.** somebody who comes from Switzerland **2.** a member of the Helvetii [Mid-16C. < Latin *Helvetia* 'Switzerland' < *Helvetius* 'of or with the Helvetii'] —**Helvetian** *adj*

Helvetic /hel véttik/ *adj* **1.** relating to Switzerland **2.** relating to the religious teachings of Ulrich Zwingli and other Swiss Protestant reformers [Early 18C. < Latin *Helvetia* (see HELVETIAN)] —**Helvetic** *n*

Helvetii /hel veéshi ī/ *npl* a Celtic people who came from southern Germany and migrated to the area that is now Switzerland, where they settled during the 2nd century BC [Late 19C. < Latin]

Helvétius /hel veéshi əss/, **Claude Adrien** (1715–71) French philosopher. His major work, *De l'esprit* (1758), was denounced and publicly burned for its insistence that self-interest alone drives human actions.

> 'Education made us what we are.'
> [Claude Adrien Helvétius, 'Discours 3', *De l'esprit*; 1758]

hem[1] /hem/ *n* **1.** FOLDED FABRIC EDGE a neat nonfraying edge made by folding fabric over and stitching it down **2.** HANDICRAFT same as **hemline** (sense 1) ■ *v* (**hems, hemming, hemmed**) **1.** *vti* MAKE HEM ON SOMETHING to fold over and stitch down fabric to make a hem on something ○ *hem curtains* **2.** *vt* ENCLOSE SOMEBODY OR SOMETHING to surround and enclose somebody or something ○ *The small yard was hemmed about by a tall hedge.* [Old English, related to Old Frisian *hemme* 'enclosed land']

hem in *vt* to confine and restrict somebody or something

hem[2] /hem/ *interj, n* a word used to represent the sound made by somebody clearing his or her throat or coughing quietly in order to attract attention,

warn somebody else, or hide embarrassment or uncertainty ■ vi (**hems, hemming, hemmed**) to make the sound 'hem', or otherwise hesitate in speech [15C. An imitation of the sound] ◇ **hem and haw** to hesitate while speaking or deciding something

hem-, etc. US spelling of **haem-,** etc.

he-man n a strong, muscular man (informal)

hemat-, etc. US spelling of **haemat-,** etc.

heme n BIOCHEM US spelling of **haem**

Hemel Hempstead /hémm'l hémpstid/ town in Hertfordshire, south-central England, designated a new town in 1947. Population: 79,235 (1991).

hemeralopia /hémmərə lópi ə/ n impaired vision in daylight (technical) [Early 18C. < modern Latin < Greek hēmeralōps 'day-blind eye'] —**hemeralopic** /-lóppik/ adj

hemerocallis /hémmə rō kálliss/ n PLANTS same as **day lily** [Mid-17C. < Greek hēmerokallis 'lily that flowers for a day' < hēmera 'day' + kallos 'beauty']

hemi- prefix half, partial ○ hemihydrate ○ hemimetabolous [< Greek hēmi- < Indo-European]

-hemia suffix same as **-aemia**

hemicellulose /hémmi séllyoō lōss, -lōz/ n any polysaccharide found in plant cell walls [Because less complex than cellulose]

hemichordate /hémmi káwr dayt/ n a sea animal resembling a worm that has a rudimentary cartilaginous skeleton (**notochord**) and numerous gill slits. Phylum: Hemichordata. [Late 19C. < modern Latin Hemichordata < Greek hēmi- 'half' + Latin chorda (see CORD)] —**hemichordate** adj

hemicycle /hémmi sīk'l/ n a structure or arrangement that has a semicircular shape [15C. Via French and Latin < Greek hēmikuklion 'semicircle'] —**hemicyclic** /hémmi sīklik, -síklik/ adj

hemidemisemiquaver /hémmi démmi sémmi kwáyvər/ n a musical note with the time value of half a demisemiquaver or one sixty-fourth of a semibreve. It is written as a filled note-head with a stem and four tails. N Am term **sixty-fourth note**

hemihedral /hémmi heédrəl/ adj describes crystals that have only half the number of faces needed for complete symmetry

hemihydrate /hémmi hī drayt/ n a hydrate that consists of two parts anhydrous compound to one part water, e.g. plaster of Paris

hemimetabolous /hémmi mə tábbələss/, **hemimetabolic** /hémmi metə bóllik/ adj describes winged insects that lack complete metamorphosis, e.g. grasshoppers, whose increasingly larger nymphs approach adult form without going through a pupal stage

hemimorphic /hémmi máwrfik/ adj describes crystals that do not have a horizontal axis of symmetry, so that the top and bottom of the crystal display different forms [Mid-19C. < HEMI- + Greek morphē 'form']

US Office of War Information

Ernest Hemingway

Hemingway /hémming way/, **Ernest** (1899–1961) US writer. He wrote fiction including *A Farewell to Arms* (1929) and *For Whom the Bell Tolls* (1940) in a distinctive terse style that complemented his own macho image and made him one of the century's leading novelists. He won the Nobel Prize in literature (1954). Full name **Hemingway, Ernest Miller**. See Cultural note at **bell**[1]

'The world breaks everyone and afterward many are strong at the broken places. But those that do not break it kills. It kills the

very good and the very gentle and the very brave impartially. If you are none of these you can be sure it will kill you too but there will be no special hurry.'
[Ernest Hemingway, *A Farewell to Arms*; 1929]

hemiola /hémmi ólə/ n a rhythmic alternation of two musical notes in the place of three, or of three notes in place of two [14C. Via medieval Latin < Greek hēmiolia 'in the ratio of one and a half to one' < holos 'whole']

hemiplegia /hémmi pleéji ə/ n total or partial inability to move experienced on one side of the body, caused by brain disease or injury [Early 17C. Via modern Latin < Greek hēmiplēgia < plēgē (see -PLEGIA)] —**hemiplegic** adj, n

hemipode /hémmi pōd/ n BIRDS same as **buttonquail** [Mid-19C. < HEMI + Greek podas 'foot']

hemipteran /hi míptərən/ n any insect that has mouthparts adapted for piercing and sucking and two pairs of wings, belonging to an order that includes stinkbugs, bedbugs, and other true bugs. Order: Hemiptera. [Late 19C. < modern Latin Hemiptera, literally 'with half a wing' < Greek pteron 'wing'; from the partly hardened forewings of bugs] —**hemipteran** adj —**hemipterous** adj

hemisphere /hémmi sfeer/ n **1.** HALF OF EARTH one half of the Earth, especially a half north or south of the equator or west or east of the prime meridian **2.** HALF OF SPHERE one half of a sphere or of anything spherical in shape **3.** ANAT same as **cerebral hemisphere 4.** ASTRON HALF OF CELESTIAL SPHERE one half of the celestial sphere, north or south of the celestial equator [14C. Via French or Latin < Greek hēmisphairion < sphaira 'ball'] —**hemispheric** /hémmi sférrik/ adj —**hemispherical** adj —**hemispherically** adv

hemistich /hémmi stik/ n one half of a line of poetry, usually separated from the rest by a caesura [Late 16C. Via late Latin < Greek hēmistikhion < stikhos 'line of verse']

hemizygous /hémmi zígəss/ adj having only one of a pair of genes, e.g. an unpaired X chromosome in males

hemline /hém līn/ n **1.** the bottom edge of a skirt, dress, or coat **2.** the height of the bottom edge of a woman's skirt, dress, or coat, especially the typical height on fashionable women's clothing during a specific period ○ *Hemlines are up again.*

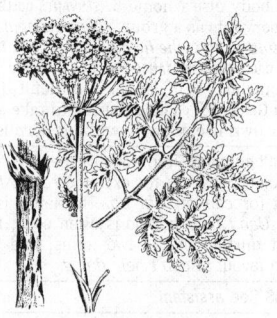

hemlock

hemlock /hém lok/ (plural **-locks** or same) n **1.** PLANTS POISONOUS PLANT a plant of the carrot family, with small white flowers and finely cut leaves, that is the source of a poison. Latin name: *Conium maculatum.* **2.** POISON a poison obtained from the fruit of hemlock plant. Hemlock was used in ancient Greece to execute people, and Socrates was forced to drink it when he was condemned to death. **3.** also **hemlock fir** or **hemlock spruce** TREES EVERGREEN TREE an evergreen tree of the pine family with short blunt needles and small cones. Genus: *Tsuga.* **4.** INDUST HEMLOCK WOOD the wood of the hemlock tree. Use: construction, paper pulp. [Old English hymlic(e), hemlic, origin ?]

hemmer /hémmər/ n **1.** somebody who sews hems in clothes or other items **2.** a sewing machine attachment for sewing hems

hemo-, etc. US spelling of **haemo-,** etc.

hemp /hemp/ n **1.** TEXTILES TOUGH FIBRE FROM ASIAN PLANT a tough fibre made from the stems of an Asian plant. Use: canvas, rope, paper, cloth. **2.** DRUGS NARCOTIC DRUG a narcotic drug made from an Asian plant that

is smoked, chewed, eaten, or drunk to produce a mildly euphoric reaction **3.** (plural same or **hemps**) PLANTS PLANT a plant that produces hemp. Native to: Asia. Latin name: *Cannabis sativa.* **4.** TEXTILES TOUGH FIBRE LIKE HEMP any strong fibre obtained from plant stems and used like hemp [Old English henep < Indo-European] —**hempen** adj

hemp agrimony n a tall composite plant with leaves like those of the hemp plant. Flowers: red, pink, or purple, in clusters. Native to: Europe, Asia, North Africa. Latin name: *Eupatorium cannabinum.*

hemp nettle n a bristly plant resembling a nettle with serrated leaves. Flowers: red, pink, purple, or white, two-lipped. Native to: Europe, Asia, naturalized in the United States. Latin name: *Galeopsis tetrahit.*

hemstitch /hém stich/ n **1.** STITCH USED FOR HEMMING a small overcast stitch used to secure a hem **2.** DECORATIVE STITCH a decorative stitch used to ornament the edge of a cloth, in which, after horizontal threads are removed, vertical threads are gathered in small regular bunches ■ vti (**-stitches, -stitching, -stitched**) EDGE SOMETHING WITH HEMSTITCH to hem or decorate an edge of cloth using hemstitch —**hemstitcher** n

hen /hen/ n **1.** DOMESTIC FOWL an adult female domestic fowl **2.** BIRDS FEMALE BIRD any adult female bird **3.** MARINE BIOL FEMALE SEA ANIMAL a female octopus, crab, or lobster **4.** OFFENSIVE TERM an offensive term that deliberately insults a woman's personality, activity, and age (dated) **5.** Scotland WAY OF ADDRESSING WOMAN OR GIRL an affectionate or familiar term of address used to a woman or girl (informal) [Old English henn < Indo-European, 'sing'] —**hennish** adj —**hennishly** adv —**hennishness** n ◇ **rare** or **scarce as hen's teeth** extremely valuable and hard to find

Henan /hő nán/ densely populated province in eastern China, including important sites of early Chinese civilization. Capital: Zhengzhou. Population: 91,720,000 (1997). Area: 167,000 sq. km/64,479 sq. mi.

hen-and-chickens (plural same or **hens-and-chickens**) n a plant, especially the houseleek, that produces new plants as offsets that grow at the end of horizontal shoots or runners from the main plant [< the resemblance to chicks surrounding the mother hen]

Henare /hénnəri/, **Sir James** (1911–89) New Zealand soldier. He commanded the Maori Battalion during World War II.

henbane /hén bayn/ n a poisonous plant of the nightshade family with hairy sticky leaves and a strong unpleasant smell. Use: source of the drugs hyoscyamine and scopolamine. Native to: Europe, Asia. Latin name: *Hyoscyamus niger.*

henbit /hénbit/ n a plant of the mint family. Flowers: small, white or reddish-purple, lipped. Native to: Europe, Asia, naturalized in the United States. Latin name: *Lamium amplexicaule.* [< BIT[1] in the obsolete sense 'morsel of food']

hence /henss/ adv **1.** BECAUSE OF THIS from this cause or for this reason (formal) ○ *I lent him money before, and he never paid it back; hence my reluctance to lend him more.* ○ *Her grandfather was Polish, hence her interest in Polish culture.* **2.** LATER THAN NOW later than the present time (formal) ○ *I'm sure the company will be in a much better financial position a year hence.* **3.** AWAY FROM HERE away from this place (archaic) ○ *Get you hence.* [13C. < Old English heonan 'hence' + adverb suffix -s (as in backwards, besides)]

henceforth /hénss fáwrth/, **henceforward** /-fáwrwərd/, **henceforwards** /-fáwrwərdz/ adv from this time forwards

Hench /hench/, **Philip Showalter** (1896–1965) US pathologist. He shared the Nobel Prize in physiology or medicine (1950) with biochemists Edward C. Kendall and Tadeus Reichstein for their research on hormones such as cortisone.

henchman /hénchmən/ (plural **-men** /-mən/) n **1.** SUPPORTER OF SOMEBODY DUBIOUS somebody, especially a man, who is a supporter or associate of somebody in a dubious cause, e.g. a member of a criminal's entourage, or somebody whose status comes from supporting a politician (disapproving) **2.** LOYAL FOLLOWER somebody, especially a man, who is a loyal supporter or follower, especially of somebody who holds a high office or position **3.** PAGE OR SQUIRE a page

or squire to somebody of high rank (*archaic*) [14C. < Old English *hengest* 'stallion']

henchwoman /hénch wŏŏmən/ (*plural* **-women** /-wimin/) *n* **1.** a woman who is a supporter or associate of somebody in a dubious cause, e.g. a member of a criminal's entourage, or somebody whose status comes from supporting a politician (*disapproving*) **2.** a woman who is a loyal supporter or follower, especially of somebody who holds a high office or position [Late 19C. After HENCHMAN]

hendeca- *prefix* eleven of such things as sides, facets, or units ○ *hendecasyllable* [< Greek *hendeka* 'eleven']

hendecasyllable /hén dekə silləb'l/ *n* a line of verse that consists of 11 syllables —**hendecasyllabic** /hén dekə si lábbik, hen déka-/ *adj*

hendiadys /hen dí ədiss/ *n* a literary device expressing an idea by means of two words linked by 'and', instead of a grammatically more complex form such as an adverb qualifying an adjective. Everyday examples of hendiadys are the expressions 'nice and soft', rather than 'nicely soft', and 'good and tight'. [Late 16C. < medieval Latin < Greek *hen dia duoin* 'one through two']

Jimi Hendrix

Popperfoto

Hendrix /héndriks/, **Jimi** (1942–70) US musician. A virtuoso blues-rock guitarist, he was known for songs like 'Wild Thing' and albums including *Are You Experienced?* (1967). His charismatic stage performance was captured in the film *Woodstock* (1970). Full name **Hendrix, James Marshall**

> 'A musician, if he's a messenger, is like a child who hasn't been handled too many times by man, hasn't had too many fingerprints across his brain.'
> [Jimi Hendrix, *Life*; 1969]

henequen /hénnikin/, **henequin** *n* **1.** a reddish fibre obtained from the leaves of a tropical American plant. Use: rope, twine, coarse fabric. **2.** a plant that has large thick fibrous leaves shaped like swords that yield henequen. Native to: tropical America, chiefly the Yucatán peninsula of Mexico. Latin name: *Agave fourcroydes*. [Early 17C. < Spanish]

henge /henj/ *n* a prehistoric oval or circular area, often bounded by a mound or ditch, that contains standing stones or wooden pillars that were erected during the Neolithic or Bronze Age [Mid-18C. Backformation < STONEHENGE]

Hengist /héng gist/ (d. 488) Saxon leader. With his brother Horsa (d. 455), he is said to have led a Saxon force to England in about 449, and to have ruled the Anglo-Saxons in Kent until his death.

henhouse /hén howss/ (*plural* **-houses** /-howziz/) *n* a shelter or small shed where hens or other domestic birds are housed

Henle's loop /hénliz-/ *n* ANAT same as **loop of Henle**

Henman /hénmən/, **Tim** (b. 1974) British tennis player. He has won nine singles titles and been a semifinalist at Wimbledon three times (1998, 1999, 2001). Full name **Henman, Timothy Henry**

henna /hénnə/ *n* **1.** COSMETICS, INDUST RED DYE a deep red dye made from plant leaves. Use: hair dye, cosmetics, fabric colourant. **2.** PLANTS SHRUB a bush with leaves that yield the red dye henna. Native to: Asia, North Africa. Latin name: *Lawsonia inermis*. **3.** COLOURS REDDISH-BROWN COLOUR a rich reddish-brown colour ■ *adj* COLOURS OF REDDISH-BROWN COLOUR of a rich reddish-brown colour ■ *vt* (**-nas, -naing, -naed**) COSMETICS, INDUST USE HENNA TO COLOUR SOMETHING or colour something with henna [Early 17C. < Arabic *ḥinnā*']

hen night *n* a party or evening out for a woman who is about to be married, attended only by her women friends (*sometimes considered offensive*)

henotheism /hénnə thi izəm/ *n* the worship of one god while acknowledging the existence of other gods [Mid-19C. < Greek *heno-* 'one' + *theos* 'god'] —**henotheist** *n* —**henotheistic** /hénnə thi ístik/ *adj*

hen party *n* a celebration or night out that is exclusively for women (*sometimes considered offensive*) N Am term **bachelorette party**

henpeck /hén pek/ (**-pecks, -pecking, -pecked**) *vt* an offensive term meaning to annoy or torment a husband or partner through continual nagging and fault-finding [< hens' practice of plucking the cock] —**henpecked** *adj*

Henrietta Maria /hénri éttə mə rée ə/ (1609–69) French-born queen consort of England. After her marriage to Charles I (1625), her involvement in English politics made her highly unpopular.

henry /hénri/ (*plural* **-ries**) *n* the SI unit of electrical inductance, equal to an electrical potential of one volt induced in a closed circuit by a current varying uniformly by one ampere per second. Symbol **H** [Late 19C. After Joseph *Henry* (1797–1878), US physicist]

Henry I /hénri/ (1068–1135) king of the English. He was the youngest son of William the Conqueror. His reign (1100–35) is notable for his conquest of Normandy (1106) and consolidation of his English and French realms.

> 'An illiterate king is a crowned ass.'
> [Attributed to Henry I. Described as a proverbial expression of Henry's in *De Gestis Regum Anglorum*, William of Malmesbury]

Henry II (1133–89) king of the English. The first Plantagenet English king (1154–89), he imposed a strong central administration and judicial reform and annexed Ireland (1171–72). His knights murdered Thomas à Becket (1170) after a long dispute over the power of the Church.

> 'Will no one rid me of this turbulent priest?'
> [Oral tradition, attributed to Henry II; 1170]

Henry III (1207–72) king of England. The son of King John, he began his long reign (1216–72) at the age of nine. His rule was marked by tensions with the nobility, which came to a head in 1264 with the short-lived rebellion of Simon de Montfort.

> 'All these things shall I keep faithfully and undiminished, as a man, as a Christian, as a soldier, and as a king, crowned and anointed.'
> [Henry III, *Oath*; 1258]

Henry IV (1367–1413) king of England. The son of John of Gaunt, he was the first Lancastrian English king. His reign (1399–1413) was marked by baronial revolts, Owen Glendower's Welsh rebellion (1400–09), and conflicts with Parliament over royal finance. Born **Bolingbroke, Henry**

> 'You have gold and I want gold. Where is it?'
> [Henry IV. To merchants from whom he wished to borrow money in 1407, *Eulogium Historiarum*]

Henry IV (1553–1610) king of France (1589–1610). The first Bourbon king of France, Henry was an effective military leader and brought stability to the country after years of religious warfare. He was assassinated by a Catholic extremist in 1610.

> 'I want there to be no peasant in my kingdom so poor that he is unable to have a chicken in his pot every Sunday.'
> [Henry IV. Quoted in *Histoire de Henri le Grand*, Hardouin de Péréfixe; 1681]

Henry V (1387–1422) king of England. He was the son of Henry IV. During his reign (1413–22) he invaded France, winning the Battle of Agincourt (1415) against superior forces, conquering Normandy (1417–20), and being declared heir to the French throne (1420).

> 'Do you not believe that the Almighty, with this small force of men on his side, can

conquer the hostile arrogance of the French, who pride themselves on their numbers and their own strength?'
> [Henry V; 25 October 1415]

Henry VI (1165–97) king of Germany and Holy Roman emperor. As German king (1190–97), he conquered and annexed Sicily (1194). He became Holy Roman emperor in 1191.

Henry VI (1421–71) king of England. The son of Henry V, he lost all of England's French possessions except Calais during his reign (1422–61, 1470–71). His ineffectual leadership at home sparked the Wars of the Roses (1455–85).

Henry VII (1457–1509) king of England. He ended the Wars of the Roses by defeating Richard III at Bosworth (1485), and founded the Tudor dynasty. His reign (1485–1509) was noted for national unity and efficient government administration. Born **Tudor, Henry**

Henry VIII (1491–1547) king of England and Ireland. He succeeded his father, Henry VII. During his reign (1509–47), he broke with the Roman Catholic Church (1534) and assumed control over the Church of England. He is notorious for his six marriages and execution of two of his wives.

> 'The kings of England in times past never had any superior but God. Wherefore know you that we will maintain the rights of the Crown…as any of our progenitors.'
> [Henry VIII, Remark; 1515]

Henry, Lenny (b. 1958) British comedian. A popular television performer, his appearances included *Tiswas* (1979–82) and *The Lenny Henry Show* (1984–95). Full name **Henry, Lehworth George**

Henry, O. (1862–1910) US writer. His short stories relied heavily on coincidence, dramatic irony, and surprise endings. Among the most famous is 'The Gift of the Magi' (1906). Born **Porter, William Sydney**

> 'Life is made up of sobs, sniffles and smiles, with sniffles predominating.'
> [O. Henry, 'The Gift of the Magi', *The Four Million*; 1906]

Henry's law *n* the principle that the amount of gas dissolved under equilibrium in a volume of liquid is in direct proportion to the pressure of the gas that contacts the liquid surface [Late 19C. After William *Henry* (1774–1836), British chemist]

Henson /hénss'n/, **Jim** (1936–90) US puppeteer. He invented the Muppets, which appeared on the television programmes *Sesame Street* and *The Muppet Show* (1976–81). Full name **Henson, James Maury**

hep[1] /hep/ (**hepper, heppest**) *adj* same as **hip**[3] (*dated slang*) [Early 20C. Origin ?]

hep[2] /hep/ *n* MED same as **hepatitis** (*informal*) [Shortening]

heparin /héppərin/ *n* an anticlotting agent present in the body. Use: produced synthetically to treat thrombosis. [Early 20C. < obsolete *hepar* 'sulphur compound', via late Latin < Greek *hēpar* 'liver (the organ)'] —**heparinoid** *adj*

hepat- *prefix* same as **hepato-** (*used before vowels*)

hepatectomy /héppə téktəmi/ (*plural* **-mies**) *n* surgical removal of all or part of the liver

hepatic /hi páttik/ *adj* **1.** ANAT OF LIVER relating to or affecting the liver **2.** COLOURS LIVER-COLOURED of a brownish-red colour like that of liver **3.** BOT OF LIVERWORT FAMILY relating to, belonging to, or resembling the members of the liverwort family of flowerless green plants ■ *n* **1.** DRUG FOR LIVER DISEASE a drug that treats liver disease **2.** PLANTS same as **liverwort** [14C. Via Latin < Greek *hēpatikos* < *hēpat-* 'liver (the organ)']

hepatica /hi páttikə/ *n* a woodland plant, related to the buttercup, that has three-lobed leaves. Flowers: white, lilac, purple. Native to: northern temperate regions. Genus: *Hepatica*. [15C. Via medieval Latin < Greek *hēpatikos* (see HEPATIC); from the shape of the leaves]

hepatitis /héppə títiss/ *n* inflammation of the liver, causing fever, jaundice, abdominal pain, and weakness

hepatitis A *n* a relatively mild form of hepatitis that is caused by a virus and transmitted through contaminated food and water

hepatitis B *n* a sometimes recurring or fatal form of hepatitis that is caused by a virus and transmitted through contact with infected blood, blood products, and bodily fluids

hepato- *prefix* person's or animal's liver ○ *hepatotoxic* [< Greek *hēpat-*, stem of *hēpar* < Indo-European]

hepatocellular /héppətō séllyoŏlər, hi pátta-/ *adj* relating to liver cells

hepatocyte /hi páttə sīt, héppətə-/ *n* a cell of the liver

hepatogenous /héppə tójjənəss/ *adj* originating in the liver

hepatoma /héppə tṓmə/ (*plural* **-mas** or **-mata** /-mətə/) *n* a tumour of the liver

hepatomegaly /héppətō méggəli, hi páttə-/ *n* enlargement of the liver

hepatopancreas /héppətō pángkri əss, hi páttə-/ *n* a glandular digestive organ of some invertebrates and fish that combines the digestive functions of the mammalian liver and pancreas

hepatotoxic /héppətō tóksik, hi páttə-/ *adj* describes a condition in which the liver is damaged

hepatotoxicity /héppətō tok síssəti, hi páttə-/ *n* **1.** a condition in which the liver is damaged **2.** the capacity or tendency of something to damage the liver

hepatotoxin /héppətō tóksin, hi páttə-/ *n* a substance that causes damage to the liver

Audrey Hepburn

Hepburn /hép burn/, **Audrey** (1929–93) Belgian-born US actor. She starred in numerous films, including *Funny Face* (1957) and *Breakfast at Tiffany's* (1961). During her last years she was a roving ambassador for UNICEF. Born **Heemstra Hepburn-Ruston, Edda van**

Katharine Hepburn

Hepburn, Katharine (1907?–2003) US actor. She is known for her roles as strong-willed heroines, and won Academy Awards for *Morning Glory* (1933), *Guess Who's Coming to Dinner* (1967), *The Lion in Winter* (1968), and *On Golden Pond* (1981). Full name **Hepburn, Katharine Houghton**

> 'First God made England, Ireland, and Scotland. That's when he corrected his mistakes and made Wales.'
> [Katharine Hepburn, *Time*; 7 August 1978]

> 'When a man says he likes a woman in a skirt, I tell him to try one.'
> [Katharine Hepburn, *WETA-TV, Washington, DC*; 27 June 1994]

hepcat /hép kat/ *n* a knowing and aware person, especially a jazz fan in the 1940s (*dated slang*) [Mid-20C. < HEP [1]]

Hephaestus /hi féestəss/, **Hephaistos** /hi fístəss/ *n* in Greek mythology, the god of fire and fire-based arts such as metalwork. He was the son of Hera and Zeus. Roman equivalent **Vulcan**

Hepplewhite: 18th-century chair

Hepplewhite /hépp'l wīt/ *adj* in or relating to the style of furniture designed by George Hepplewhite, characterized by graceful curving lines, delicate inlays, and often floral or ribbon designs. Open chair backs in the shape of a heart or shield are a feature of the style. ■ *n* furniture or a piece of furniture made by or in the style of Hepplewhite

Hepplewhite /hépp'l wīt/, **George** (*d.* 1786) British furniture designer. He produced over 300 designs in *The Cabinet-Maker and Upholsterer's Guide* (1788) that are characterized by a combination of simplicity and delicacy.

hept- *prefix* same as **hepta-** (*used before vowels*)

hepta- *prefix* seven ○ *heptahedron* [< Greek *hepta* < Indo-European]

heptachlor /héptə klawr/ *n* a chlorinated hydrocarbon. Use: pesticide. Formula: $C_{10}H_5Cl_7$.

heptad /hép tad/ *n* a set or series of seven [Mid-17C. < Greek *heptad-* 'the number seven' < *hepta* 'seven']

heptagon /héptəgən/ *n* a two-dimensional geometric figure formed of seven angles and seven sides [Late 16C. Directly or via French < medieval Latin *heptagonum* < Greek *heptagōnos* 'having seven angles'] —**heptagonal** /hep tággənəl/ *adj*

heptahedron /héptə heédrən/ (*plural* **-drons** or **-dra** /-drə/) *n* a three-dimensional geometric figure formed of seven plane faces —**heptahedral** *adj*

heptamerous /hep támmərəss/ *adj* describes plant parts such as petals or sepals that grow or are arranged in groups of seven

heptameter /hep támmitər/ *n* a line of poetry or verse composed of seven metric feet [Late 19C. Via late Latin < Greek *heptametron* < *hepta* 'seven' + *metron* 'metre'] —**heptametrical** /héptə méttrik'l/ *adj*

heptane /hép tayn/ *n* an isomeric form of an organic chemical, especially a colourless flammable liquid alkane hydrocarbon. Source: petroleum. Use: solvent, anaesthetic, determination of octane ratings. Formula: C_7H_{16}.

heptarch /hép taark/ *n* one of the seven rulers in a heptarchy

heptarchy /hép taarki/ (*plural* **-chies**) *n* **1.** government by seven rulers or leaders **2.** a state governed by seven rulers, or one divided into seven parts, each ruled by a different head —**heptarchic** /hep taárkik/ *adj* —**heptarchical** *adj*

Heptarchy *n* the association consisting of the seven English kingdoms of Kent, Sussex, Wessex, Essex, Northumbria, East Anglia, and Mercia during the period from the 5th to the 9th centuries AD

heptastich /héptəstik/ *n* a seven-line stanza or poem

Heptateuch /héptə tyook/ *n* the first seven books of the Bible, comprising Genesis, Exodus, Leviticus, Numbers, Deuteronomy, Joshua, and Judges [Late 17C. Via late Latin < Greek *heptateukhos* < *hepta* 'seven' + *teukhos* 'book']

heptathlon /hep táthlən, -lon/ *n* an athletics competition, usually for women, in which the contestants compete in seven different events and are awarded points for each to find the best all-round athlete. The events are the javelin, hurdles, high jump, long jump, shot put, sprint, and 800-metre race. [Late 20C. < HEPTA- + Greek *athlon* 'contest'] —**heptathlete** *n*

heptose /héptōss, -ōz/ *n* a sugar with seven carbon atoms in the molecule

Dame Barbara Hepworth: working on the plaster model for the bronze sculpture *Rock (Porthcurno)*

Hepworth /hép wurth/, **Dame Barbara** (1903–75) British sculptor. Many of her works, e.g. the Dag Hammarskjöld Memorial (1964) at the UN headquarters in New York, are massive abstract shapes in stone or wood, pierced by holes. Full name **Hepworth, Dame Jocelyn Barbara**

her *stressed* /hur/; *unstressed* /hər, ər/ *pron* (*as the object or complement of a verb or preposition*) **1. WOMAN OR GIRL NOT REFERRED TO BY NAME** used to refer to a woman, girl, or female animal who has been previously mentioned or whose identity is known ○ *Ask her to wait.* ○ *We left the report with her.* ○ *I know it's her.* **2. MACHINE** used to refer to a car, machine, or ship that has been previously mentioned or whose identity is known ○ *Fill her up, please.* **3. COUNTRY** used to refer to a country or nation when it has been mentioned or its identity is known (*formal*) ○ *Britain and those who trade with her* ■ *det* **RELATING TO HER** belonging to or associated with a woman, girl, female animal, car, machine, ship, country, or nation that has been mentioned earlier or whose identity is known ○ *That's her coat.* ○ *the Bismarck and her crew* [Old English *hire* < Indo-European, 'this']

her. *abbr* **1.** heraldic **2.** heraldry

Hera /heérə/ *n* in Greek mythology, the goddess of marriage and the wife of Zeus. She was often portrayed as jealous and resentful of infidelity. Roman equivalent **Juno** (sense 1)

Heracles /hérrə kleez/, **Herakles** *n* in Greek mythology, the son of Zeus and Alcmene, noted for his courage and great strength and the performing of 12 near-impossible labours. Roman equivalent **Hercules** (sense 1) —**Heraclean** /hérrə kleé ən/ *adj*

Heraclitus /hérrə klítəss/ (*fl* 500? BC) Greek philosopher. He was an early metaphysician. Only fragments remain of his major work, *On Nature*. —**Heraclitean** /hérrə klíshi ən/ *adj*

> 'The way up and the way down are one and the same.'
> [Heraclitus. Quoted in *The Presocratic Philosophers*, G. S. Kirk, J. E. Raven, and M. Schofield; 1983]

Heraclius /he rákli əss/ (575?–641) Byzantine emperor. He came to power in a coup (610) after deposing Phocas. He successfully repelled a Persian invasion (622–28), and reclaimed the True Cross, an important Christian relic (630).

Herakles *n* MYTHOL another spelling of **Heracles**

Heraklion /hi ráakli on/ seaport and the largest city on the Greek island of Crete. Population: 116,178 (1991). Greek name **Iráklion**

herald /hérrəld/ *n* **1. BRINGER OF NEWS** somebody who brings or announces important news **2. SIGN OF WHAT WILL HAPPEN** somebody or something that is a forerunner of something or gives an indication of something that is going to happen (*literary*) **3. HERALDRY HERALDIC OFFICIAL** an official who is concerned with heraldry and who is of a rank above the pursuivant **4. HIST OFFICIAL MESSENGER** an official messenger and representative of a king or leader in former times **5. HIST OFFICIAL AT MEDIEVAL TOURNAMENTS** at medieval tournaments and jousting contests, somebody who per-

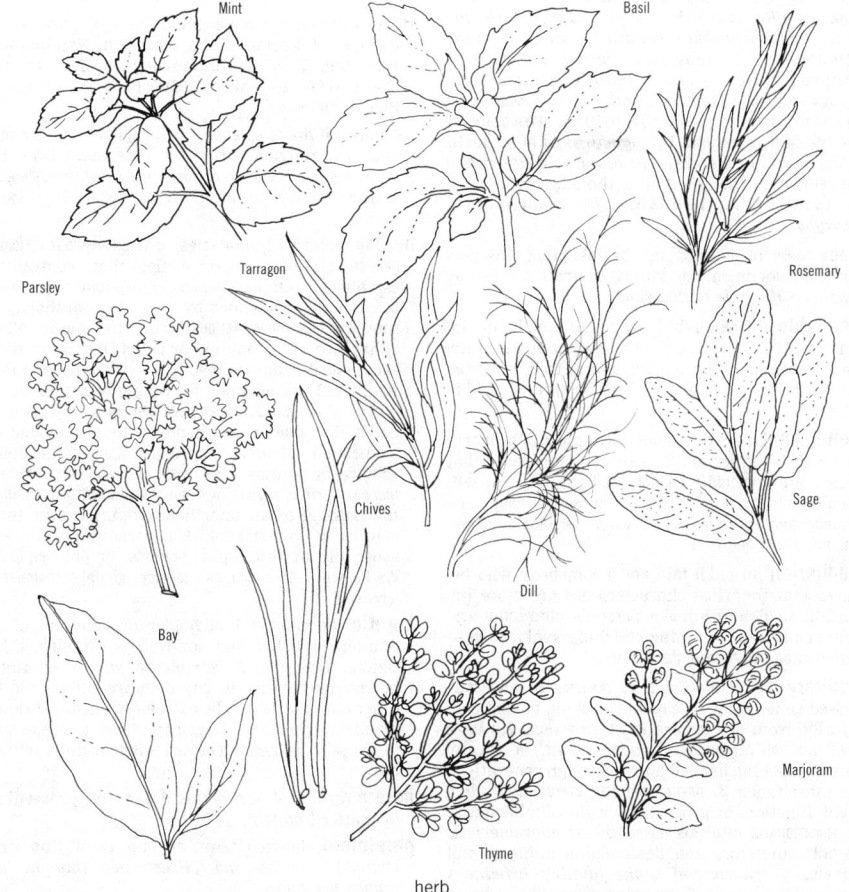

Mint   Basil   Parsley   Tarragon   Rosemary   Chives   Sage   Bay   Dill   Marjoram   Thyme

herb

formed official duties ■ *vt* (**-alds, -alding, -alded**) **1.** SIGNAL SOMETHING to give or be a sign that something is going to happen **2.** WELCOME SOMEBODY OR SOMETHING to welcome or announce somebody or something with enthusiasm [14C. < Old French *herault* < Germanic, 'commander of the army']

heraldic /hə ráldik, he-/ *adj* belonging or relating to heraldry or heralds —**heraldically** *adv*

herald moth *n* a nocturnal hibernating moth marked by mottled brown forewings and dull grey hind wings. Native to: northern Europe. Latin name: *Scoliopteryx libatrix*.

heraldry /hérrəldri/ *n* **1.** STUDY OF COATS OF ARMS the profession or study of the devising and granting of coats of arms and of determining who is entitled to bear them **2.** COATS OF ARMS coats of arms and the symbols and conventions connected with them **3.** POMP pomp and ceremony

heralds' college *n* HERALDRY same as **College of Arms**

Herat /hə rát/ city in northwestern Afghanistan, situated on the River Hari. Population: 177,300 (1988 estimate).

herb /hurb/ *n* **1.** a low-growing aromatic plant used fresh or dried for seasoning, for its medicinal properties, or in perfumes. Sage and rosemary are herbs. **2.** BOT a seed-producing flowering plant that does not produce woody stems and that forms new stems and leaves each season **3.** DRUGS same as **marijuana** (*slang*) [13C. Via French < Latin *herba* 'grass, herb']

herbaceous /hər báyshəss/ *adj* **1.** WITHOUT WOODY STEMS describes plants or plant parts that are fleshy and wither after each growing season, as opposed to plants such as trees that grow woody stems and are persistent **2.** RESEMBLING LEAVES similar to leaves in colour and general appearance **3.** OF AROMATIC PLANTS relating to aromatic herbs such as sage, dill, or thyme [Mid-17C. < Latin *herbaceus* < *herba* 'grass, herb'] —**herbaceously** *adv*

herbaceous border *n* a flower bed that is mainly planted with perennial plants rather than with annuals

herbage /húrbij/ *n* **1.** herbaceous plants, especially their leafy or succulent and edible parts **2.** grass and other vegetation growing in fields, pasture land, and meadows [14C. Via French < medieval Latin *herbagium* < Latin *herba* 'grass, herb']

herbal /húrb'l/ *adj* characteristic of, consisting of, or made with aromatic herbs ○ *a herbal remedy* ■ *n* a book that lists individual herbs and describes their properties and possible uses [Early 16C. < medieval Latin *herbalis* < Latin *herba* 'grass, herb']

herbalism /húrbə lizəm/ *n* **1.** same as **herbal medicine** (sense 1) **2.** the study of herbs and their medicinal uses **3.** the growth, collection, and sale or dispensing of aromatic herbs, especially those considered to have medicinal properties

herbalist /húrbəlist/ *n* **1.** SOMEBODY KNOWLEDGEABLE ABOUT HERBS a grower, collector, or seller of aromatic herbs, especially those considered to have medicinal properties **2.** *UK, ANZ, Can* ALTERN MED TRADITIONAL DOCTOR a traditional doctor who uses herbs and other medicines to remedy illness and discomfort **3.** BOTANIST a botanist, especially one concerned with the classification of plants (*archaic*)

herbal medicine *n* **1.** a system of medical treatment based on the properties of medicinal herbs **2.** a medication made from herbs

herbarium /hur báiri əm/ (*plural* **-iums** or **-ia** /-i ə/) *n* **1.** a collection of dried plants, especially one in which the plants have been mounted, systematically classified, and labelled for use in scientific studies **2.** a building, room, or other place where a herbarium is kept [Late 18C. < late Latin < Latin *herbarius* 'herbalist' < *herba* 'grass, herb'] —**herbarial** *adj*

herb bennet /-bénnit/ *n* a common wild plant that has long hairy stems and hooked seeds. Flowers: small, yellow. Native to: Europe, Asia, North Africa. Latin name: *Geum urbanum*.

herb Christopher (*plural* **herbs Christopher**) *n* PLANTS same as **baneberry** (sense 2) [After St CHRISTOPHER]

herbed /hurbd/ *adj* flavoured with herbs

Herbert /húrbərt/, **George** (1593–1633) English poet and cleric. A friend of Francis Bacon and John Donne,

he wrote poetry that was published posthumously in *The Temple* (1633).

'But as I rav'd and grew more fierce and wild / At every word, /Methought I heard one calling, "Child"; / And I replied, "My Lord".'
[George Herbert, 'The Collar', *The Temple: Sacred Poems and Private Ejaculations*; 1633]

Herbert, **Xavier** (1901–84) Australian novelist. His works include *Poor Fellow My Country* (1975), the longest novel ever published in Australia. Full name **Herbert, Alfred Francis Xavier**. See Cultural note at **fellow**

herb Gerard /-jérr aard/ (*plural* **herbs Gerard**) *n* PLANTS same as **ground elder** [After St *Gerard* of Toul (935?–94)]

herbicide /húrbi sīd/ *n* a chemical preparation designed to kill plants, especially weeds, or to inhibit their growth —**herbicidal** /húrbi sīd'l/ *adj* —**herbicidally** *adv*

herbivore /húrbi vawr/ *n* an animal that feeds only or mainly on grass and other plants [Mid-19C. < French, or back-formation < HERBIVOROUS]

herbivorous /hur bívvərəss/ *adj* eating only or mainly grass or other plants, or relating to the eating of such plants [Mid-17C. < modern Latin *herbivorus* 'eating grass' < Latin *herba* 'grass, herb']

herb Paris (*plural* **herbs Paris**) *n* a woodland plant having a whorl of four leaves at right angles to the stem and bearing a single black berry. Flowers: single, greenish-yellow. Native to: Europe. Latin name: *Paris quadrifolia*. [Partial translation of medieval Latin *herba paris* 'herb of a pair', assimilated to PARIS [2]]

herb Robert /-róbbərt/ (*plural* **herbs Robert**) *n* a common wild plant of the cranesbill family that has red-tinged leaves and stems with a strong unpleasant odour. Flowers: small, pink. Native to: temperate northern Europe, Asia. Latin name: *Geranium robertianum*. [Origin ?]

herby /húrbi/ (**-ier, -iest**) *adj* **1.** WITH HERBAL TASTE OR SMELL tasting or smelling of herbs **2.** OF AROMATIC HERBS relating to aromatic or medicinal herbs **3.** FULL OF GROWING HERBS having a lot of growing herbs or grass

Herculaneum /húrkyoŏ láyni əm/ ancient Roman town near modern Naples, destroyed with its neighbour Pompeii in the eruption of Vesuvius in AD 79

Herculean /húrkyoo leé ən, hur kyoóli ən/ *adj* **1.** relating to or associated with Hercules **2.** *also* **herculean** requiring a great deal of strength, effort, stamina, or resources

Hercules /húrkyoŏ leez/ *n* **1.** MYTHOL ROMAN MYTHOLOGICAL HERO in Roman mythology, the son of Jupiter and Alcmene, noted for his courage and great strength and the performing of 12 near-impossible labours. Greek equivalent **Heracles 2.** (*plural same* or **Herculeses**) VERY STRONG MAN a man with great or unusual strength **3.** ASTRON CONSTELLATION a constellation of the northern hemisphere. See illustration at **constellation**

Hercules' club *n* **1.** a small tree or bush of the ginseng family that has prickly leaves and bark that has medicinal properties. Native to: southeastern United States. Latin name: *Aralia spinosa*. **2.** a small spiny tree or bush related to the citrus family with bark and berries that have medicinal properties. Native to: southern United States. Latin name: *Zanthoxylum clava-herculis*.

Hercynian /hur sínni ən/ *n* the period of geological time during the late Palaeozoic era when some of the major European mountain ranges were being formed [Late 16C. < Latin *Hercynia (silva)* < Greek *Herkunios (drumos)*, forested mountain region between the Carpathian Mountains and the River Rhine] —**Hercynian** *adj*

herd /hurd/ *n* **1.** LARGE GROUP OF DOMESTIC ANIMALS a large number of domestic animals, especially cattle, often of the same breed, that are kept, driven, or reared together **2.** LARGE GROUP OF WILD ANIMALS a large number of wild animals of the same kind that live, feed, and travel as a group **3.** LARGE GROUP OF PEOPLE a large group of people, often with a common interest, purpose, or bond ○ *herds of eager shoppers* **4.** ORDINARY PEOPLE ACTING AS GROUP ordinary people considered as acting or thinking as a group and lacking the ability to think as individuals (*disapproving*) ○ *She was never one to follow the herd*. ■ *v* (**herds, herding, herded**) **1.**

vt CONTROL GROUP OF ANIMALS to drive, keep, or look after domestic animals as a group **2.** *vt* MOVE OR COLLECT GROUP to move people or animals somewhere as a group, or collect them into one ○ *We were herded onto buses.* **3.** *vi* FORM OR MOVE IN GROUP to gather together or go somewhere as a group [Old English *heord* < Indo-European, 'row, group'] ◇ **ride herd on somebody** *N Am* to supervise somebody strictly

SPELLCHECK See *heard*.

herd-book *n* a book that gives details of the pedigrees of domestic animals, especially cattle or pigs

herder /hérdər/ *n N Am* AGRIC same as **herdsman** (sense 2)

Herder /húrdər, háirdər/, **Johann Gottfried von** (1744–1803) German philosopher and critic. He is an important figure in the development of German romanticism, whose most important work is *Outline of a Philosophy of the History of Man* (1784–91).

herd instinct *n* the innate desire to belong to, be associated with, or imitate the behaviour of a group

herdsman /húrdzmən/ (*plural* **-men** /-mən/) *n* **1.** somebody, especially a man, who owns or breeds cattle or other livestock **2.** somebody, especially a man, who tends or drives domestic animals in groups, especially on open pasture or land. N Am term **herder** [Alteration of Old English *heordman* 'herdsman', after such words as *craftsman*]

herdsperson /húrdz purss'n/ (*plural* **-people** /-peep'l/ or **-persons**) *n* **1.** an owner or breeder of cattle or other livestock **2.** somebody who tends or drives domestic animals in groups, especially on open pasture or land

herdswoman /húrdz wŏŏmən/ (*plural* **-women** /-wimin/) *n* **1.** a woman who owns or breeds cattle or other livestock **2.** a woman who tends or drives domestic animals in groups, especially on open pasture or land

herd tester *n NZ* an official who inspects the health and hygiene of dairy cows and the production of milk —**herd testing** *n*

Herdwick /húrdwik/ *n* a hardy sheep with thick coarse wool belonging to a breed originating in the Lake District [Early 19C. < obsolete *herdwick* 'pasturage', literally 'herdsman's place']

here /heer/ CORE MEANING: an adverb used to refer to this place or to this time ○ *How long have you been waiting here?* ○ *Winter is here.*

adv **1.** IN THIS PLACE in, at, or to the place where you are, or at a place near you ○ *Have you been here before?* ○ *Come and sit here, beside me.* **2.** AT THIS POINT OR STAGE used to draw attention to a particular point or stage in a situation ○ *I want to say here, before I go further, that only part of the credit should be mine.* **3.** NOW indicates a situation or event that is happening at the present time ○ *The time for celebrations is here.* **4.** INDICATES OFFER indicates that somebody is offering something to somebody ○ *Here are some general guidelines.* ○ *Here's my card.* **5.** INTRODUCES SOMETHING used to introduce or draw attention to a topic ○ *Now, here is a question for everybody.* **6.** LIFE ON EARTH used to refer to people in general and their life on Earth ○ *Where did we come from? Why are we here?* [Old English *hēr* < Indo-European, 'this'] ◇ **(the) here and now** used to emphasize that you are talking about the present time ○ *I'm entitled to an explanation, and I want one here and now.* ○ *He outlined all sorts of schemes, but hadn't much practical advice about the here and now.* ◇ **here and there** in different places or at different points ○ *She'd picked up some general knowledge here and there.* ◇ **here goes** used to indicate that somebody is about to perform an action ○ *This is my first move on the chessboard – here goes!* ◇ **here we go again** used to indicate that an event or situation is, tiresomely or irritatingly, about to repeat itself ○ *Here we go again – making a mountain out of a molehill.* ◇ **neither here nor there** not relevant and therefore not important ○ *Why she wants this is neither here nor there, but we have to decide how we're going to reply.*

SPELLCHECK See *hear*.

hereabouts /heérə bówts/, **hereabout** /heérə bowt/ *adv* near here, or in this neighbourhood or area

hereafter /heer áaftər/ (*formal*) *adv* **1.** AFTER PRESENT TIME from now on or at a time in the future ○ *He believes this to be a universal law of nature; and we may hope hereafter to see the law proved true.* ○ *No one of us knows what may happen hereafter.* **2.** IN ANY FOLLOWING PART in a subsequent part of an article or document ○ *Here is established a Commerce Technology Advisory Board (hereafter in this section referred to as the "Advisory Board").* **3.** AFTER DEATH in the life that is thought by some to exist after death ○ *Mercy and forgiveness will be ours hereafter.* ■ *n* LIFE AFTER DEATH the life that is thought by some to exist after death ○ *Your deeds will be judged in the hereafter.*

hereby /heer bī́, heér bī/ *adv* by means of this declaration, document, or ruling (*formal*) ○ *I hereby renounce all claim to the estate.*

hereditable /hi rédditəb'l/ *adj* capable of being inherited [15C. < obsolete French *héréditable* or medieval Latin *hereditabilis*, both < ecclesiastical Latin *hereditare* 'inherit' (see HEREDITAMENT)] —**hereditability** /hi rédditə bíllәti/ *n*

hereditament /hérri díttəmənt/ *n* **1.** a piece of property that can be inherited **2.** a piece of property that passes automatically to a legal heir unless a will specifies otherwise [15C. < medieval Latin *hereditamentum* < ecclesiastical Latin *hereditare* 'inherit' < Latin *hered-* 'heir']

hereditarian /hi réddi táiri ən/ *n* somebody who believes that inherited characteristics are more important in determining a person's character and behaviour than environmental and social factors —**hereditarian** *adj* —**hereditarianism** *n*

hereditary /hi rédditəri/ *adj* **1.** TRANSMITTED GENETICALLY passed genetically, or capable of being passed genetically, from one generation to the next **2.** HANDED DOWN THROUGH GENERATIONS handed down, or legally capable of being handed down, through generations by inheritance **3.** HAVING INHERITED STATUS holding a right, function, or property by right of inheritance **4.** TRADITIONALLY HELD possessed by or characteristic of both ancestors and descendants although not physically transmitted ○ *the family's hereditary fondness for city life* **5.** RELATING TO INHERITANCE relating to inheritance or heredity **6.** MATHS, LOGIC SHARING RELATIONSHIP OR PROPERTY sharing or transmitting a relationship or property [15C. < Latin *hereditarius* < *hereditas* 'inheritance' (see HEREDITY)] —**hereditarily** *adv* —**hereditariness** *n*

heredity /hi rédditi/ *n* **1.** ANCESTRY ancestral background **2.** INHERITANCE the inherited right to something ○ *based on heredity* **3.** PASSING ON OF GENETIC FACTORS the transfer of genetically controlled characteristics such as hair colour or flower colour from one generation to the next in living organisms **4.** SET OF INHERITED CHARACTERISTICS in genetics, the complete set of inherited characteristics of an organism [Mid-16C. Directly or via French < Latin *hereditas* 'inheritance' < *hered-* 'heir']

Hereford[1] /hérrifərd/ *n* a hardy cow that has a distinctive red coat with white markings, belonging to a breed originating in England and bred for beef [Early 19C. After HEREFORDSHIRE]

Hereford[2] /hérrifərd/ historic cathedral city in Herefordshire, western England. Population: 50,539 (1994 estimate).

Hereford and Worcester former county in western England from 1974 to 1998, formed from the historic counties of Herefordshire and Worcestershire

Herefordshire /hérrifərdshər/ county in western England. It was disbanded in 1974 and reinstated as a unitary authority in 1998. Area: 2,181 sq. km/842 sq. mi.

herein /heer ín/ *adv* (*formal*) **1.** in this document, article, or proceeding ○ *Disclaimer: The views represented herein do not necessarily represent the views of the moderators.* **2.** introduces a clause in which somebody states an opinion about the nature or cause of something or goes on to give further detail ○ *People are not always conscious of the effect their behaviour is having on others, and herein lies the main problem.*

hereinafter /heérin áaftər/ *adv* later in this document, article, or proceeding (*formal*) ○ *the European Monetary Institute (hereinafter referred to as EMI)*

hereinbefore /heérinbi fáwr/ *adv* earlier in this document, article, or proceeding (*formal*)

hereof /heer óv/ *adv* of or concerning this (*formal*)

Herero /hə ráirō, háirərō/ (*plural same* or **-ros**) *n* **1.** a member of a people living mainly in Namibia and Botswana **2.** a Bantu language spoken by the Herero. Native speakers: 25,000. [Mid-19C. < Bantu] —**Herero** *adj*

heresiarch /hə reézi aark/ *n* a leader or founder of a heretical religious group or movement [Mid-16C. Via ecclesiastical Latin < ecclesiastical Greek *hairesiarkhēs* < Greek *hairesis* 'choice, group' (see HERESY) + *-arkhēs* 'ruler']

heresy /hérrəssi/ (*plural* **-sies**) *n* **1.** UNORTHODOX RELIGIOUS OPINION an opinion or belief that contradicts established religious teaching, especially one that is officially condemned by a religious authority **2.** HOLDING OF UNORTHODOX RELIGIOUS BELIEF the holding of, or adherence to, an opinion or belief that contradicts established religious teaching, especially one that is officially condemned by religious authorities ○ *guilty of heresy* **3.** UNORTHODOX OPINION an opinion or belief that does not coincide with established or traditional theory, especially in philosophy, science, or politics ○ *His views on child development were regarded as heresy.* **4.** HOLDING OF UNORTHODOX OPINION the holding of an unorthodox opinion that is in conflict with established or traditional theory, especially in philosophy, science, or politics [12C. Via French < Greek *hairesis* 'choice, group' < *haireisthai* 'choose']

heretic /hérrətik/ *n* **1.** a holder or adherent of an opinion or belief that contradicts established religious teaching **2.** somebody whose opinions, beliefs, or theories in any field are considered by others in that field to be extremely unconventional or unorthodox [14C. Via French < Greek *hairetikos* 'able to choose' < *haireisthai* 'choose'] —**heretical** /hə réttik'l/ *adj*

hereto /heer tŏŏ/ *adv* to this document, proceeding, or matter (*formal*)

heretofore /heértoo fáwr/ *adv* up until this time (*formal*) ○ *He had more liberty now than he had known heretofore.*

hereunder /heer úndər/ *adv* (*formal*) **1.** after this introduction, heading, or sentence **2.** by the terms of this instruction, agreement, or ruling

hereunto /heer ún too/ *adv* to this document, proceeding, or matter (*formal*)

hereupon /heérə pón/ *adv* (*formal*) **1.** immediately after or in response to this ○ *Hereupon the entire delegation left.* **2.** on this point, subject, or matter ○ *retired to deliberate before pronouncing hereupon*

Hereward the Wake /hérriwərd thə wáyk/ (*fl* 1060–71) Anglo-Saxon rebel. He attacked the Norman conquerors of England at Peterborough (1070), and defended his stronghold at the Isle of Ely (1071).

herewith /heer wíth, -wíth/ *adv* **1.** with this letter or other written, typed, or printed message ○ *Herewith the documents you requested.* **2.** by this statement, ruling, or document (*formal*) ○ *I herewith pronounce sentence of banishment.*

Herez /hə réz/, **Heriz** /hə ríz/ *n* a high quality Persian rug woven with a pattern of flowers or trees [After *Heris*, Iranian town]

heriot /hérri ət/ *n* in feudal England, a tribute or gift, often a prized animal or a treasured possession, given by a tenant's or villein's family to his lord at the tenant's death [Old English *heregeatwa* 'army trappings'; originally referring to the return of weapons]

heritable /hérritəb'l/ *adj* **1.** able to be passed on to an heir by the laws of inheritance **2.** having the legal right or qualification to inherit something [14C. < French < *hériter* 'inherit' < ecclesiastical Latin *hereditare* (see HEREDITAMENT)] —**heritability** /hérritə bílləti/ *n* —**heritably** *adv*

heritage /hérritij/ *n* **1.** SOMETHING SOMEBODY IS BORN TO the status, conditions, or character acquired by being born into a particular family or social class ○ *Respect for education was part of their Scottish heritage.* **2.** RICHES OF PAST a country's or area's history and historical buildings and sites that are considered to be of interest and value to present generations (*often used before a noun*) ○ *the town's heritage trail* **3.** SOMETHING PASSING FROM GENERATION TO GENERATION something that passes from one generation to the next in a social group, e.g. a way of life or traditional culture ○ *The celebration of Passover is part of the*

Jewish heritage. **4.** LEGAL INHERITANCE property or land that is or can be passed on to an heir [13C. < Old French < *hériter* (see HERITABLE)]

heritage coast *n* an area of coastline of special scenic and environmental value that is protected from undesirable development

heritage industry *n* a branch of the tourism industry responsible for preserving the art and artefacts of a place

heritage language *n* in English-speaking countries, a language other than English that is spoken at home or was spoken by somebody's ancestors

heritor /hérritər/ *n* an inheritor of property by law (*archaic or technical*) [15C. < Anglo-Norman < French *hériter* (see HERITABLE)]

Heriz *n* TEXTILES same as **Herez**

herl /hurl/ *n* **1.** the barb or barbs of a feather used for trimming an artificial fishing fly **2.** a fishing fly trimmed with a barb or barbs of a feather [14C. Probably < Middle Low German *herle* 'fibre of hemp or flax']

herm /hurm/, **herma** /húrmə/ (*plural* **-mae** /-mee/ or **-mai** /-mī/) *n* a square pillar topped with a bust, usually of the god Hermes, used as a marker in ancient Greece and Rome, and as an ornament in classical architecture [Late 16C. Via Latin < Greek *Hermēs* 'Hermes']

Herman /húrmən/, **Sali** (1898–1993) Swiss-born Australian painter. He is known for his depictions of Sydney slums. Full name **Herman, Sali Yakubowitsch**

hermaphrodite /hur máffrə dīt/ *n* **1.** ORGANISM THAT HAS BOTH SEXES a plant or animal that has both male and female reproductive organs and secondary sexual characteristics **2.** PERSON WHO HAS BOTH SEXES somebody who has both male and female sexual characteristics **3.** SOMEBODY OR SOMETHING COMBINING CONTRADICTORY ELEMENTS somebody or something that combines two very different features or qualities or seems to belong to two different classifications at once [15C. Via Latin < Greek *Hermaphroditos* 'Hermaphroditus'] —**hermaphrodism** *n* —**hermaphrodite** *adj* —**hermaphroditic** /hur máffrə díttik/ *adj* —**hermaphroditical** *adj* —**hermaphroditically** *adv* —**hermaphroditism** *n*

hermaphrodite brig *n* a two-masted sailing vessel with a square-rigged foremast and a square-rigged topsail above a fore-and-aft rig on the mainmast

Hermaphroditus /hur máffrə dítəss/ *n* in Greek mythology, the son of Hermes and Aphrodite, whose body was merged with the body of the nymph Salmacis to become half male and half female

hermeneutic /húrmə nyóotik/, **hermeneutical** /-nyóotik'l/ *adj* **1.** relating to or consisting in the interpretation of texts, especially the books of the Bible **2.** serving to interpret or explain something (*formal*) [Late 17C. < Greek *hermēneutikos* 'of interpreting' < *hermēneuein* 'interpret' < *hermēneus* 'interpreter'] —**hermeneutically** *adv* —**hermeneutist** *n*

hermeneutics /húrmə nyóotiks/ *n* (*takes a singular verb*) **1.** SCIENCE OF INTERPRETING TEXTS the science and methodology of interpreting texts, especially the books of the Bible **2.** THEOLOGY OF RELIGIOUS CONCEPTS the branch of theology that is concerned with explaining or interpreting religious concepts, theories, and principles **3.** PHILOSOPHY OF HUMAN BEHAVIOUR AND SOCIETY the branch of philosophy that is concerned with the study and interpretation of human behaviour, structures of society, and how people function within these structures **4.** DISCUSSION OF MEANING OF LIFE in existentialism, deliberation on the meaning and purpose of life

Hermes /húr meez/ *n* in Greek mythology, the messenger of the gods and a son of Zeus. He was the patron of athletes, thieves, and trade, and was usually depicted with wings on his cap and sandals. Roman equivalent **Mercury** (sense 1)

Hermes Trismegistus /-tríssmə jístəss, -gístəss/ *n* a name given to the Egyptian god Thoth by Greek neo-Platonists, who regarded him as a teacher of religion, magic, and alchemy

hermetic /hur méttik/, **hermetical** /-ik'l/ *adj* **1.** AIRTIGHT so tightly or perfectly fitting as to exclude the passage of air **2.** PROTECTED FROM OUTSIDE INFLUENCE protected from or preventing any outside interference or influence ○ *lead a solitary, hermetic existence* **3.** HARD TO UNDERSTAND obscure and difficult

for outsiders to understand **4.** *also* **Hermetic** INVOLVING ALCHEMY OR MAGIC associated with alchemy or magic [Mid-17C. < modern Latin *hermeticus* < HERMES TRISMEGISTUS] —**hermetically** *adv*

hermit /húrmit/ *n* **1.** somebody who chooses to live alone and to have little or no social contact **2.** somebody who, in early Christian times, chose to reject material things and to live apart from the rest of society, especially in order to be completely devoted to God [12C. Via Old French *hermite* or medieval Latin *heremita* < Greek *erēmitēs* < *erēmia* 'desert' < *erēmos* 'solitary'] —**hermitic** /hur míttik/ *adj* —**hermitical** *adj* —**hermitically** *adv*

hermitage /húrmitij/ *n* **1.** a building or shelter where a hermit lives or where a group of people live an isolated religious life **2.** a place of isolation or solitude where somebody can live apart from society [13C. < Old French < *hermite* (see HERMIT)]

Hermitage *n* a museum in St Petersburg, Russia, that contains one of the world's major collections of paintings. The nucleus of its collection was the art collection of Catherine the Great.

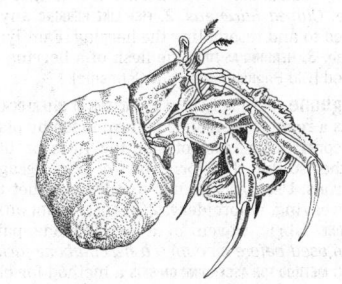

hermit crab

hermit crab *n* a soft-bodied crab that takes over an empty mollusc shell, usually a whelk shell, and carries it around on its back for protection and to hide in. It starts off with a small shell that, as it grows, is discarded for increasingly larger ones, so that it may change shells several times during its life span. Order: Decapoda.

hermit thrush *n* a brownish songbird with a speckled breast, reddish tail, and a distinctive spiralling song reminiscent of the sound of a flute. Native to: North America. Latin name: *Catharus guttatus.*

Hermon, Mount /húrmən/ highest peak in the Anti-Lebanon Mountains, on the Syria-Lebanon border. It has many associations with ancient Palestine. Height: 2,814 m /9,232 ft.

hernia /húrni ə/ (*plural* **-as** or **-ae** /-ee/) *n* a condition in which part of an internal organ projects through the wall of the cavity that contains it, especially the projection of the intestine from the abdominal cavity. It may be present at birth, especially in the region of the navel, be caused by muscular strain or injury, or result from a congenital weakness in the cavity wall. [14C. < Latin] —**hernial** *adj*

herniate /húrni ayt/ (**-ates, -ating, -ated**) *vi* to project through a rupture in the wall of a body cavity, or through a normal or potential opening that has become enlarged (*refers to organs or body parts*) —**herniated** *adj* —**herniation** /húrni áysh'n/ *n*

herniorrhaphy /húrni órrəfi/ (*plural* **-phies**) *n* the surgical repair of a rupture in the wall of a body cavity

hero /héerō/ (*plural* **-roes**) *n* **1.** REMARKABLY BRAVE PERSON somebody who commits an act of remarkable bravery or who has shown an admirable quality such as great courage or strength of character ○ *a war hero* **2.** SOMEBODY ADMIRED somebody who is admired for outstanding qualities or achievements ○ *heroes of the war against poverty* **3.** ARTS MAIN CHARACTER IN FICTIONAL PLOT the principal male character in a film, novel, or play, especially one who plays a vital role in plot development or around whom the plot is structured ○ '*Whether I shall turn out to be the hero of my own life, or whether that station will be held by anybody else, these pages must show.*' (Charles Dickens, *David Copperfield*; 1849–50) **4.** MYTHOL MAN WITH SUPERHUMAN POWERS in classical mythology, a man, especially the son of a god and a mortal, who is famous for possessing some

extraordinary gift such as superhuman strength ○ *the Greek heroes* **5.** *N Am* FOOD LONG SANDWICH a sandwich made from a long roll or loaf of bread with a filling of meat and cheese with lettuce and tomato [Mid-16C. Via Latin < Greek *hērōs* 'hero, warrior']

Hero /héerō/ *n* in Greek mythology, a priestess of Aphrodite whose lover Leander swam the Hellespont to visit her every night, and who drowned herself after he drowned in the strait

Hero (of Alexandria) /héer ō-/ (*b.* AD 20?) Greek mathematician and inventor. He designed numerous mechanical devices and devised a formula for calculating the area of a triangle.

Herod (the Great) /hérrəd-/ (73–4 BC) king of Judaea. Born in Palestine and supported by the Romans, he ruled Judaea from 37 BC to 4 BC in a period of relative prosperity. He is remembered in Jewish and Christian tradition as a tyrant and, according to the Bible, ordered the massacre of every male baby in Jerusalem (Matthew 2:16).

Herod Agrippa I /-ə gríppə/ (10? BC–AD 44) king of Judaea. He was the grandson of Herod the Great. As the Roman-appointed king of Judaea (41–44), he adopted policies favourable to the Jews. In the New Testament, he is said to have imprisoned St Peter and executed St James.

Herod Agrippa II (27–93?) Roman ruler in Palestine. The son of Herod Agrippa I, he was the Roman-appointed ruler in northern Palestine, where he supported Rome during the Jewish revolt (66–73).

Herod Antipas /-ánti pass/ (21 BC–AD 39) Galilean leader. The son of Herod the Great, he was tetrarch of Galilee and Perea (4 BC–AD 39) and ordered the execution of John the Baptist.

Herodotus /hə róddətəss/ (484?–425? BC) Greek historian. His anecdotal *History* includes a description of the war between the Greeks and Persians in the 5th century BC. He has been called 'the father of history'.

> '*Death is a delightful hiding place for weary men.*'
> [Herodotus, *The Histories*; 450? BC]

heroic /hi rṓ ik/, **heroical** /-rṓ ik'l/ *adj* **1.** COURAGEOUS showing great bravery, courage, or determination ○ *a heroic fight against a disease* **2.** SUITABLE FOR HERO characteristic of or suitable for a hero **3.** LARGE OR EXTREME large, extensive, or extreme, often daunting in aspect or done in response to a desperate situation ○ *heroic measures to save a person's life* **4.** MYTHOL RELATING TO MYTHICAL HERO characteristic of or involving the heroes of legend or mythology **5.** LITERAT OF HEROIC VERSE written in or characteristic of heroic verse **6.** SCULPTURE LARGER THAN LIFE-SIZE describes a piece of sculpture that is larger than life-size —**heroically** *adv*

heroic age *n* a time in a culture's mythology when heroes were believed to exist, especially the time in ancient Greek mythology up to and including the return from Troy

heroical *adj* same as **heroic**

heroic couplet *n* a two-line unit of verse consisting of rhyming iambic pentameters, usually part of a series of rhyming pairs

heroic drama *n* a play popular during the Restoration period, generally involving a warrior hero who must find a way to resolve a dilemma. This often involves finding a way of preserving both his honour and his love for a woman.

heroic metre *n* LITERAT same as **heroic verse**

heroic quatrain *n* a four-line unit of verse in which each line consists of five iambic feet and either alternate or adjacent lines rhyme

heroics /hi rṓ iks/ *npl* **1.** rash, inappropriate, or extravagantly courageous behaviour or talk ○ *There is no room for heroics on this expedition.* **2.** LITERAT same as **heroic verse**

heroic stanza *n* four lines of verse in which the first and third lines and the second and fourth lines rhyme

heroic tenor *n* MUSIC same as **Heldentenor**

heroic verse *n* a verse form used in epic poetry or other narrative poetry on heroic subjects, especially the ancient Greek and Latin hexameter, the iambic pentameter, or the alexandrine

heroin /hérrō in/ *n* a white powder derived from morphine that is a highly addictive narcotic drug. It is prohibited for medical use in most countries, but in the United Kingdom can be used in terminal cases where patients are in severe pain. (*often used before a noun*) ○ *a heroin addict* [Late 19C. < German]

SPELLCHECK heroin or **heroine**? Do not confuse the spelling of **heroin** and **heroine**, which sound similar. **Heroin** is an addictive drug, as in *heroin users, an overdose of heroin*. A **heroine** is a brave woman or girl or the main female character of a novel, play, or film.

heroine /hérrō in/ *n* **1.** REMARKABLY BRAVE WOMAN a woman who commits an act of remarkable bravery or who has shown great courage, strength of character, or another admirable quality **2.** ADMIRED WOMAN a woman who is admired or looked up to for her qualities or achievements ○ *heroines of the women's suffrage movement* **3.** ARTS MAIN FEMALE CHARACTER IN FICTIONAL PLOT the principal female character in a film, novel, or play, especially one who plays a vital role in plot development or around whom the plot is structured

SPELLCHECK See **heroin**.

heroism /hérrō izəm/ *n* remarkable physical or moral courage

heron

heron /hérrən/ *n* a freshwater wading bird with a long neck, tapered beak, and often a crested head, that feeds mainly on fish, frogs, and small mammals. Family: Ardeidae. [14C. < Old French < Germanic]

heronry /hérrənri/ (*plural* **-ries**) *n* a small area within which herons nest and raise their young

Herophilus /heer óffiləss/ (335?–280? BC) Greek anatomist. Considered the founder of scientific anatomy, he is known for his detailed description of the brain and nervous system.

> 'Medicines are nothing in themselves, if not properly used, but the very hands of the gods, if employed with reason and prudence.'
> [Attributed to Herophilus]

~~heros~~ incorrect spelling of **heroes**

hero worship *n* **1.** great admiration for somebody, especially if it borders on the excessive **2.** the ancient Greek or Roman practice of worshipping a mythological hero or heroes —**hero-worship** *vt* —**hero-worshipper** *n*

herpes /húr peez/ *n* a viral infection causing small painful blisters and inflammation, most commonly at the junction of skin and mucous membrane in the mouth or nose or in the genitals [14C. Via Latin < Greek < *herpein* 'creep']

herpes simplex /-sím pleks/ *n* either of two viral diseases marked by clusters of small watery blisters, one affecting the area of the mouth and lips and the other the genitals [< modern Latin, 'simple herpes']

herpesvirus /húr peez vīrəss/ *n* a DNA-containing virus that replicates in cell nuclei and causes diseases such as chickenpox, herpes, and shingles

herpes zoster /-zóstər/ *n* MED same as **shingles** (*technical*) [< modern Latin; *zoster* via Latin < Greek, 'girdle']

herpetic /-péttik/ *adj* relating to, affected by, or indicative of herpes ■ *n* somebody who has herpes (*technical*)

herpetology /húrpi tólləji/ *n* the scientific study of reptiles and amphibians [Early 19C. < Greek *herpeton* 'creeping thing, reptile' < *herpein* 'creep'] —**herpetologic** /húrpitə lójjik/ *adj* —**herpetological** *adj* —**herpetologically** *adv* —**herpetologist** *n*

Herr /hair, hur/ (*plural* **Herren** /hérrən/) *n* the German equivalent of 'Mister', used as a title before a surname or profession [Mid-17C. < German]

Herrenvolk /hérrən folk/ *n* in Nazi ideology, the German nation as a master race (*often offensive*) [Mid-20C. < German, 'master people']

Herrera-Estrella /hə ráyrə estréllə/, **Luis** (*b.* 1956) Mexican geneticist. While working at the University of Ghent in Belgium in 1983, he became the first person to create a genetically modified plant. Full name **Herrera-Estrella, Luis Rafael**

Herrick /hérrik/, **Robert** (1591–1674) English poet. Ordained in 1623, he wrote over 1,200 religious and secular poems published in *Hesperides* (1648).

> 'It is the end that crowns us, not the fight.'
> [Robert Herrick, 'The End'; 1648]

herring /hérring/ (*plural* **-rings** or *same*) *n* **1.** FISH OF N ATLANTIC a small commercially important fish with silvery scales. Native to: northern Atlantic. Latin name: *Clupea harengus*. **2.** FISH LIKE HERRING any fish related to and resembling the herring. Family: Clupeidae. **3.** HERRING AS FOOD the flesh of a herring used as food [Old English *hāring* < W Germanic]

herringbone /hérring bōn/ *n* **1.** PATTERN OF INTERLOCKING 'V' SHAPES a regular geometric pattern made by placing two contrasting rows of slanting lines or blocks together so that they form rows of 'V's, zigzags, or chevrons. Use: bricklaying, textiles, parquet flooring, weaving, embroidery. **2.** TEXTILES CLOTH WITH HERRINGBONE fabric woven in a herringbone pattern (*often used before a noun*) ○ *a herringbone jacket* **3.** SKIING METHOD FOR ASCENDING ON SKIS a method for climbing a slope on skis by facing the peak, with skis pointing out at an angle, and moving them upwards one step after the other ■ *v* (**-bones, -boning, -boned**) **1.** *vti* DECORATE SOMETHING WITH HERRINGBONE to decorate or make something such as cloth with a herringbone pattern **2.** *vi* SKIING GO UP SLOPE ON SKIS to ascend a slope on skis using the herringbone method ■ *n* HANDICRAFT same as **herringbone stitch**

herringbone bond *n* decorative bricklaying in which the bricks are placed at an angle to one another to form a herringbone pattern

herringbone gear *n* a gearwheel in which two sets of teeth interlock in a series of 'V' shapes

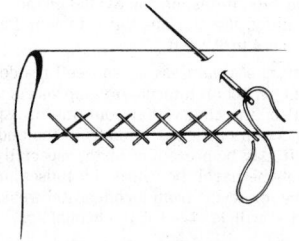

herringbone stitch

herringbone stitch *n* an embroidery or hemming stitch made with overlapping cross stitches that form a zigzag line

herring gull *n* a common gull with a body that is mainly white, a grey back, and grey wings with black tips. Native to: northern hemisphere. Latin name: *Larus argentatus*.

Herriot /érri ō/, **Édouard** (1872–1957) French prime minister (1924–25, 1926, 1932). He was imprisoned (1942–45) for resisting the Vichy government during World War II.

Herriot /hérri ət/, **James** (1916–95) British author of a popular series of books about his experiences as a vet in Yorkshire. Pseudonym of **James Alfred Wight**

hers /hurz/ *pron* **1.** SOMETHING BELONGING TO HER indicates that something belongs or relates to a woman, girl, or female animal who has been previously mentioned or whose identity is known ○ *She drew my face to hers and kissed me.* ○ *I knew an uncle of hers.* **2.** BELONGING TO COUNTRY indicates that something

belongs to or is associated with a country or nation when its identity is known (*formal*) **3.** BELONGING TO MACHINE indicates that something belongs to or is associated with a car, machine, or ship [14C. < HER + -'s]

Herschel /húrsh'l/, **Caroline** (1750–1848) German-born British astronomer. She worked with her brother William Herschel on numerous astronomical investigations. She discovered eight comets and three nebulae. Full name **Herschel, Caroline Lucretia**

Herschel, Sir John Frederick William (1792–1871) British astronomer. The son of William Herschel, he furthered his father's systematic studies of the skies, studied the stars of the southern hemisphere, and invented a photographic fixing agent.

Herschel, Sir William (1738–1822) German-born British astronomer. Assisted in his researches by his sister Caroline Herschel, he pioneered the study of stars. He catalogued double stars and nebulae and discovered the planet Uranus (1781). Born **Herschel, Friedrich Wilhelm**

herself *stressed* /hər sélf/; *unstressed* /ər sélf/ CORE MEANING: the form of 'her' used in reflexive and emphatic contexts ○ *She did it herself.*
pron **1.** REFERRING TO FEMALE SUBJECT OF VERB used to refer to the same woman, girl, or female animal as the subject of the verb ○ *She put her hand on the rail to support herself.* ○ *She decided to treat herself.* **2.** USED FOR EMPHASIS used to emphasize or clarify which woman, girl, or female animal is being referred to, often introducing a note of surprise or awe ○ *I received a letter from the author herself.* **3.** ALONE OR WITHOUT HELP used to show that a woman, girl, or female animal is alone or unaided ○ *sitting by herself in the garden* ○ *wrote the song herself* **4.** COUNTRY used to refer to a nation or country whose identity is known (*formal*) ○ *Britain is causing problems for herself with this policy.* **5.** MACHINE used to refer to a car, machine, or ship **6.** NORMAL SELF her normal self in terms of personality, health, or behaviour ○ *She's not herself today – I don't know what's the matter with her.*

herstory /húrstəri/ (*plural* **-ries**) *n* **1.** history as it affects women or looked at from the point of view of women, especially in contrast to conventional treatment of history, seen in feminist terms as having favoured men **2.** the study or recording of the life experiences, achievements, or expectations of a particular woman or group of women [Late 20C. < HISTORY, as if *his-* were 'of him']

Hertford /haártfərd/ historic market town in southeastern England, and the county town of Hertfordshire. Population: 21,665 (1991).

Hertfordshire /haártfərdshər/ county in southeastern England. Its administrative centre is Hertford. Area: 1,634 sq. km/632 sq. mi.

Herts. /haarts/ *abbr* Hertfordshire

hertz /hurts/ (*plural same*) *n* the SI unit of frequency equal to one cycle per second. Symbol **Hz** [Late 19C. After Heinrich HERTZ]

Hertz /hurts/, **Heinrich** (1857–94) German physicist. He was the first to produce electromagnetic waves under laboratory conditions, leading to the development of the telegraph and radio. The unit of frequency hertz is named after him. Full name **Hertz, Heinrich Rudolf** —**Hertzian** *adj*

Hertzian wave *n* a radio wave

Hertzog /húrts og/, **J. B. M.** (1866–1942) South African prime minister (1924–39). He founded the Nationalist Party (1914) and, as prime minister, secured the rights of Dutch-descended Afrikaners in South Africa while pursuing a policy of racial segregation. Full name **Hertzog, James Barry Munnik**

Hertzsprung-Russell diagram /húrts sprung-/ *n* a graph that plots the brightness of stars against their spectral type or colour. See illustration on next page [After Ejnar *Hertzsprung* (1873–1967), Danish astronomer, and Henry Norris *Russell* (1877–1957), US astronomer, who independently devised it]

Hervey Bay /haárvi-/ town located on a bay of the same name in southern Queensland, Australia. Population: 44,402 (2002 estimate).

Herzegovina /húrtsə gō véenə/ ◆ **Bosnia and Herzegovina**

Herzog /húrts og, háirs-/, **Chaim** (1918–97) British-born

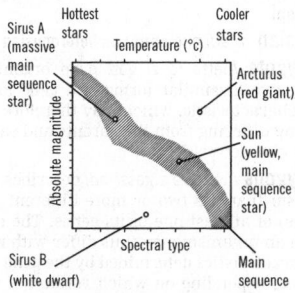

Hertzsprung-Russell diagram

Israeli president (1983–93). Before becoming president, he held several military and diplomatic posts, including Israeli ambassador to the United Nations (1975–78).

Herzog, Werner (b. 1942) German film director. He created powerful dramas about characters in the grip of anguish or obsession, including *Aguirre, the Wrath of God* (1972) and *Fitzcarraldo* (1982). Born Stipetic, Werner

he's *stressed* /heez/; *unstressed* /eez/ *contr* 1. he has ○ *He's finished his lunch.* 2. he is ○ *He's not the man I saw.*

Heshvan /héshvən/, **Cheshvan** /khésh vaan, -vən/ *n* in the Jewish calendar, the eighth month of the religious year, lasting 29 or 30 days and falling about the same time as October to November. See table at **calendar** [Mid-19C. < Hebrew *ḥeśwān*, shortening of *marḥeśwān* < Akkadian *araḥ samna* 'eighth month']

Hesione /hi sī́ əni/ *n* in Greek mythology, a princess whom Heracles rescued from a sea monster

hesitant /hézzitənt/ *adj* slow to do or say something because of indecision or lack of confidence —**hesitance** *n* —**hesitancy** *n* —**hesitantly** *adv*

SYNONYMS See *unwilling*.

hesitate /hézzi tayt/ (**-tates, -tating, -tated**) *vi* 1. to be slow in doing something, or pause while doing or saying something, often because of uncertainty or reluctance 2. to be reluctant to do or say something ○ *If you're puzzled by anything, don't hesitate to ask.* [Early 17C. < Latin *haesitat-*, past participle of *haesitare* 'stick fast' < *haerere* 'stick'] —**hesitater** *n* —**hesitatingly** *adv* —**hesitative** *adj*

SYNONYMS *hesitate, pause, falter, stumble, waver, vacillate*

CORE MEANING: to show uncertainty or indecision
hesitate to be slow in doing something, or pause while doing or saying something, as a result of uncertainty or reluctance ○ *He hesitated for a moment, then walked swiftly to the door.* ○ *Please do not hesitate to call me if you have any questions.* **pause** to stop doing something briefly before continuing, or to wait intentionally for a short period before doing something ○ *She paused for a moment to recover her self-possession.* ○ *Scarcely pausing for thought, she sat herself down at the keyboard and started to play.* **falter** to show a loss of confidence, especially to speak or act with hesitation ○ *new announcers who falter when they read the news* ○ *In such circumstances, our allies might falter in their commitment to the defence treaty.* **stumble** to speak or act in a halting, confused, or blundering way ○ *stumbling through polite replies as to her health* ○ *He stumbled over the words, not knowing how to express his sympathy.* **waver** to become unsure or begin to change from a previous opinion ○ *The defendant never wavered from his claim.* ○ *He saw the agony in her eyes and his resolve wavered.* **vacillate** to be indecisive or irresolute, changing between one opinion and another ○ *Her mind vacillated between laughing at her fears and suspecting something terrible.* ○ *The advantages the country once had have been squandered by vacillating political leadership.*

hesitation /hézzi táysh'n/ *n* 1. the act of hesitating or pausing 2. the state of being reluctant or undecided

~~hesitent~~ incorrect spelling of **hesitant**

Hesperian /he speéri ən/ *adj* 1. belonging to or connected with the west (*literary*) 2. relating to the Hesperides [Late 15C. < Latin *hesperius* 'western' < Greek *hesperios* < *hesperos* 'western, evening']

Hesperides /he spérri deez/ *npl* 1. in Greek mythology, the daughters of Atlas and Hesperus and the guards of a tree bearing golden apples from which Heracles was required to gather fruit as one of his 12 labours 2. in Greek mythology, islands far to the west in which a tree with golden apples grew [Late 16C. < Greek, plural of *hesperis* 'western' < *hesperos* 'western, evening'] —**Hesperidean** /héspə ríddi ən/ *adj*

hesperidin /he spérridin/ *n* a white or colourless crystalline glycoside. Source: citrus fruits. Use: treatment of capillary disease. [Mid-19C. < Greek *hesperid-*, stem of *hesperis* 'western' (see HESPERIDES)]

hesperidium /héspə ríddi əm/ *n* a fruit, e.g. a citrus fruit, consisting of a thick leathery rind and soft segmented pulp [Mid-19C. < HESPERIDES, with reference to the golden apples]

Hesperus /héspərəss/ *n* the planet Venus, especially just after sunset when it shines brightly (*literary*) [< Latin < Greek *hesperos* 'western, evening']

Hess /hess/, **Rudolf** (1894–1987) German Nazi deputy leader. Adolf Hitler's private secretary and deputy in the 1920s and 1930s, he was captured as a prisoner of war in Scotland (1941), convicted of war crimes at Nuremberg (1945–46), and imprisoned for life in Spandau Prison, West Berlin. Full name **Hess, Walter Richard Rudolf**

Hesse /hess, héssə/ state and historic duchy in west-central Germany. Largely an agricultural region, it is drained by the Rhine and Main rivers in the west and, in the northeast, by the River Weser. Capital: Wiesbaden. Population: 5,837,000 (1992). Area: 21,114 sq. km/8,152 sq. mi.

Hesse, Hermann (1877–1962) German novelist and poet. His spiritually probing novels include *Siddhartha* (1922) and *Steppenwolf* (1927). He was awarded the Nobel Prize in literature (1946).

'If you hate a person, you hate something in him that is part of yourself. What isn't part of ourselves doesn't disturb us.'
[Hermann Hesse, *Demian*; 1919]

hessian /héssi ən/ *n* a coarse strong jute or hemp fabric. Use: bags, upholstery. [Late 19C. < HESSIAN]

Hessian /héssi ən/ *n* somebody who comes from Hesse in Germany ■ *adj* relating to Hesse in Germany [Late 17C. < HESSE]

Hessian boot *n* a men's knee-high boot with a tasselled top, first worn by Hessian soldiers and fashionable at the beginning of the 19th century

Hessian fly *n* a small fly of the gallfly family that lays its eggs on grain plants, where the larvae bore into the stems and weaken them. It causes severe damage to crops, especially wheat, barley, and rye. Latin name: *Mayetiola destructor*. [Because inadvertently brought to N America by Hessian troops]

hessite /héss īt/ *n* a grey metallic mineral composed of silver telluride. Use: source of silver. [Mid-19C. After G. H. *Hess* (see HESS'S LAW)]

hessonite *n* MINERALS same as **essonite**

Hess's law /héssiz-/ *n* a law in chemistry stating that the heat absorbed or released during a reaction is the same whether the reaction occurs in one or several steps [After Germain Henri *Hess* (1802–50), Swiss-born Russian chemist]

Hester /héstər/, **Joy St Clair** (1920–60) Australian artist. She is noted for her expressionistic ink and gouache works.

Hestia /hésti ə/ *n* in Greek mythology, the goddess of the hearth. Roman equivalent **Vesta** (sense 1)

Heston /hést'n/, **Charlton** (b. 1924) US actor. He specialized in heroic roles that capitalized on his rugged good looks and powerful physique, and won an Academy Award for *Ben-Hur* (1959). In his later years he has frequently appeared on behalf of conservative political causes, notably as president of the National Rifle Association. Born **Carter, John Charlton**

Hesychast /héssi kast/ *n* a member of a school of meditative devotion developed by monks of the Greek Orthodox Church on Mount Athos in the 14th century and popular in 19th-century Russia [Mid-19C. < late Greek *hēsukhastēs* 'hermit' < *hēsukhazein* 'be still' < *hēsukhos* 'still, quiet'] —**Hesychastic** /héssi kástik/ *adj*

het /het/ (*slang disapproving*) *n* a heterosexual person ■ *adj* heterosexual [Shortening]

hetaera /hi teérə/ (*plural* **-rae** /-ree/ or **-ras**), **hetaira** /-tīrə/ (*plural* **-rai** /-rī/ or **-ras**) *n* in ancient Greece, one of a special class of women who were used as prostitutes and who were valued as highly cultured companions [Early 19C. < Greek, form of *hetairos* 'companion'] —**hetaeric** *adj*

hetaerism /hi teérizəm/, **hetairism** /-tīr-/ *n* 1. the social condition or institution of concubinage 2. the practice in some societies of sharing spouses or sexual partners —**hetaerist** *n* —**hetaeristic** /héttə rístik/ *adj*

hetaira, etc. ANCIENT HIST another spelling of **hetaera, etc.**

heter- *prefix* same as **hetero-** (*used before vowels*)

hetero /héttərō/ (*plural* **-os**) *n* a heterosexual person (*informal*) [Mid-20C. Shortening] —**hetero** *adj*

hetero- *prefix* 1. different, other ○ *heterochromatic* 2. containing atoms of different kinds ○ *heterocyclic* [< Greek *heteros* 'other' < Indo-European, 'one of two']

heteroatom /héttərō atəm/ *n* a noncarbon atom in a heterocyclic compound

heterocercal /héttərō súrk'l/ *adj* describes a fish's tail in which the vertebral column bends upwards and extends into the upper and larger lobe of the tail-fin, as in some sharks [Mid-19C. < HETERO- + Greek *kerkos* 'tail']

heterochromatic /héttərō krə máttik/ *adj* containing many different colours —**heterochromatism** /-krṓmətizəm/ *n*

heterochromatin /héttərō krṓmətin/ *n* chromatic material that contains few genes but stains readily with basic dyes and appears as nodules between chromosomes

heterochromosome /héttərō krṓməssōm/ *n* a chromosome consisting mainly of heterochromatin, especially a sex chromosome

heterochromous /héttərō krṓməss/ *adj* describes plant parts that exhibit different colours

heteroclite /héttərə klīt/, **heteroclitic** /-klíttik/ *adj* describes a word that is formed in an unusual or irregular way [Late 15C. Via late Latin < Greek *heteroklitos* < *heteros* 'the other' + *klīnein* 'to lean'] —**heteroclite** *n*

heterocyclic /héttərō sīklik, -síklik/ *adj* describes or relating to a ring system composed of atoms in which at least one is not a carbon atom

heterodactylous /héttərō dáktiləss/, **heterodactyl** /-dákt'l/ *adj* describes the feet of birds in which the first and second toes face backwards and the third and fourth toes face forwards. ◊ **zygodactyl**

heterodont /héttərə dont/ *adj* used to describe a mammal that has teeth of different types such as incisors, canines, premolars, and molars

heterodox /héttərə doks/ *adj* at variance with established or accepted beliefs or theories, especially in the field of religion [Early 17C. Via late Latin < Greek *heterodoxos* < *heteros* 'the other' + *doxa* 'opinion']

heterodoxy /héttərə doksi/ (*plural* **-ies**) *n* (*formal*) 1. the condition of being at variance with established or accepted beliefs or theories, especially in the field of religion 2. an opinion, belief, or theory that is at variance with those that are established or accepted

heterodyne /héttərə dīn/ *vt* (**-dynes, -dyning, -dyned**) to combine a received radio-frequency wave with a wave of a different frequency to produce frequencies equal to the sum of and the difference between the original two signals ■ *adj* consisting of, produced by, or operated by heterodyning signals

heteroecious /héttə rō eéshəss/ *adj* describes a parasite such as a tapeworm that lives in two or more hosts in the course of its life cycle [Late 19C. < HETERO- + Greek *oikia* 'house'] —**heteroecism** /-eéssizəm/ *n*

heterogamete /héttə rō gámmeet/ *n* 1. either of two reproductive cells (**gametes**) that differ in size, structure, and function, and that unite in the process of reproduction, e.g. the small sperm and large ova in humans 2. a reproductive cell produced by the sex that carries the chromosomes that determine the sex of the offspring

heterogametic /héttə rōgə méttik/ *adj* 1. describes the

sex that produces reproductive cells (**gametes**) of two different types, one type producing males and the other females **2.** relating to heterogametes

heterogamy /hétta róggəmi/ *n* **1.** BIOL **UNION OF DISSIMILAR REPRODUCTIVE CELLS** in sexual reproduction, the union of two types of sex cell (**heterogamete**) that are dissimilar in size, structure, and function **2.** BIOL **ALTERNATING OF FORMS OF REPRODUCTION** the alternation of sexual and asexual reproduction in some species such as aphids in which every other generation is produced from the female with no need for a male **3.** BOT **PRESENCE OF DIFFERENT FLOWERS ON PLANT** the production on the same plant of two kinds of flower, one bearing both male and female organs and the other bearing only female organs or being asexual —**heterogamic** /héttərō gámmik/ *adj* —**heterogamous** *adj*

heterogeneity /héttərō jə née əti, -náyəti/ *n* **1.** the diverse nature of something **2.** the state of being chemically heterogeneous

heterogeneous /héttərō jéeni əss/, **heterogenous** /hétta rójjenəss/ *adj* **1. CONSISTING OF DISSIMILAR PARTS** consisting of parts or aspects that are unrelated or unlike each other **2. UNRELATED** not related or similar **3.** CHEM **WITH TWO OR MORE PHASES** describes a chemical substance that has two or more phases **4.** MED **NOT FROM SAME BODY** originating outside the body, from another individual or species [Early 17C. < medieval Latin *heterogeneus* < Greek *heterogenēs* 'other kind' < *heteros* 'other' + *genos* 'kind'] —**heterogeneously** *adv* —**heterogeneousness** *n*

heterogenesis /héttərō jénnəssiss/ *n* the appearance of a mutation in a population

heterogenetic /héttərō jə néttik/ *adj* **1. OF HETEROGENESIS** relating to heterogenesis **2.** BIOL **FROM DISPARATE ANCESTORS** derived from ancestors not closely related **3. MUTATING** reproducing by heterogenesis —**heterogenetically** *adv*

heterogenic /héttərō jéenik/ *adj* describes a reproductive cell (**gamete**), individual, or population that has more than one variant (**allele**) of a specific gene

heterogenous *adj* same as **heterogeneous**

heterogony /hétta róggəni/ *n* a life cycle involving alternating parasitic and free-living generations —**heterogonous** *adj* —**heterogonously** *adv*

heterograft /hétta rō graaft/ *n* a graft of living tissue from one animal to another of a different species

heterography /hétta róggrəfi/ (*plural* **-phies**) *n* **1.** the use of different letters or groups of letters to represent the same sound or sounds **2.** a writing system that uses different combinations of letters to represent the same sound or sounds [Late 18C. < HETERO-, after ORTHOGRAPHY] —**heterographic** /héttərō gráffik/ *adj*

heterokaryon /héttərō kárri ən/ (*plural* **-ya** /-i ə/) *n* a cell that has two or more genetically different nuclei

heterokaryosis /héttərō kárri ṓssiss/ *n* the presence in a cell of two or more nuclei of different genetic origin. Heterokaryosis occurs naturally in some fungi when cells fuse but their nuclei do not, and can be induced artificially to study the interaction of cellular components of different species. —**heterokaryotic** /-óttik/ *adj*

heterologous /hétta rólləgəss/ *adj* **1.** MED **FROM DIFFERENT SPECIES** derived or taken from a different species **2.** IMMUNOL **NOT CORRESPONDING** describes an antigen and an antibody that do not correspond to each other **3.** BIOL **IN UNUSUAL LOCATION** not normally found in the part of the body in which it has been found **4.** BIOL **DIFFERING IN STRUCTURE AND ORIGIN** describes organisms or parts that differ from each other in structure or origin [Mid-19C. < HETERO- + Greek *logos* 'relation, ratio'] —**heterologously** *adv*

heterolysis /hétta rólləssiss/ *n* **1.** the breaking of a chemical bond in a compound, producing particles or ions of opposite charge, e.g. the formation of sodium and chloride ions in a salt solution **2.** the destruction of cells or proteins of one species by the action of enzymes or lysins from another, e.g. when the blood of one species causes the red blood cells of another species to rupture —**heterolytic** /héttərə líttik/ *adj*

heteromerous /hétta rómmərəss/ *adj* **1.** with parts of different types **2.** describes plants whose flowers do not have the same number of petals in each case or whose other parts are made up of different numbers of elements

heteromorphic /héttərō máwrfik/, **heteromorphous** /-máwrfəss/ *adj* **1.** BIOL **HAVING DIFFERENT APPEARANCE** differing in shape, size, or structure ○ *heteromorphic sex chromosomes* **2.** BIOL **TAKING DIFFERENT FORMS DURING LIFE CYCLE** taking different forms at different stages of its life cycle **3.** MED **INVOLVING ATYPICAL FORM** characterized by an atypical form or forms —**heteromorphism** *n* —**heteromorphy** /héttərō mawrfi/ *n*

heteronomous /hétta rónnəməss/ *adj* **1.** subject to other laws or rules or to laws and rules imposed by other people or institutions **2.** describes parts of an organism that have different modes of development and growth, and different functions [Early 19C. < HETERO- + Greek *nomos* 'law'] —**heteronomously** *adv* —**heteronomy** *n*

heteronym /héttərōnim/ *n* each of two or more words that are spelt the same, but differ in meaning and often in pronunciation, e.g. 'bow' (a ribbon) and 'bow' (of a ship) [Late 19C. < HETERO- + *-nym* as in SYNONYM] —**heteronymous** /hétta rónnəməss/ *adj* —**heteronymy** *n*

heteroousian /héttərō óozi ən/, **heterousian** /hétta róozi ən/ *n* in Christian theology, somebody who believes that God the Father and God the Son are not formed of the same substance [Late 17C. < Greek *heter(o)ousios* 'other substance' < *heteros* 'other' + *ousia* 'substance'] —**heteroousian** *adj*

heterophyllous /héttərō fílləss/ *adj* describes plants that have leaves of different shapes on the same plant. The sassafras tree is heterophyllous. —**heterophylly** /hétta róffili/ *n*

heteroplasty /héttərō plasti/ (*plural* **-ties**) *n* **1.** a surgical procedure to graft or transplant tissues or organs from one person or animal to another **2.** SURG same as **heterograft** —**heteroplastic** /héttərō plástik/ *adj*

heteroploid /héttərō ployd/ *adj* with a number of chromosomes that is, unusually, not an exact multiple of the basic chromosome number for that species ■ *n* a heteroploid cell or organism

heteropolar /héttərō pṓlər/ *adj* CHEM same as **polar** (sense 7) —**heteropolarity** /-pō lárrəti/ *n*

heteropolymer /héttərō póllimər/ *n* CHEM same as **copolymer** —**heteropolymeric** /-poli mérrik/ *adj*

heteropteran /hétta róptərən/ *n* an insect with mouthparts adapted for piercing and sucking, and partially hardened forewings with membranous tips. Bedbugs and other true bugs are heteropterans. Order: Heteroptera. [Mid-19C. < HETERO- + Greek *pteron* 'wing'] —**heteropteran** *adj*

heterosexism /héttərō séksizəm/ *n* discrimination against gays and lesbians by heterosexuals —**heterosexist** *n, adj*

heterosexual /héttərō sékshoo əl/ *n* **SOMEBODY SEXUALLY DESIRING OPPOSITE SEX** somebody who is sexually attracted to members of the opposite sex ■ *adj* **1. DESIRING OPPOSITE SEX** sexually attracted to members of the opposite sex **2. INVOLVING BOTH SEXES** relating to sexual desire or sexual relations between people of opposite sexes —**heterosexually** *adv*

heterosexuality /héttərō sékshoo álləti/ *n* sexual desire or sexual relations between people of opposite sexes

heterosis /hétta rṓssiss/ *n* BIOL same as **hybrid vigour** [Mid-19C. < Greek *heterōsis* 'making different' < *heteros* 'other']

heterosporous /héttərō spáwrəss, -róspərəss/ *adj* producing two types of spore, microspores and megaspores, on the same plant —**heterospory** /héttərō spáwri, -róspəri/ *n*

heterostyly /héttərō stīli/ *n* the possession of styles of different lengths on different plants of the same species, which is an aid to cross-pollination by insects —**heterostyled** *adj* —**heterostylous** /héttərō stīləss/ *adj*

heterotrophic /héttərō tróffik/ *adj* obtaining nourishment by digesting plant or animal matter, as animals do, as opposed to photosynthesizing food, as plants do —**heterotroph** /héttərō trōf/ *n* —**heterotrophy** /héttərō trōfi/ *n*

heterotropia /héttərō trṓpi ə/ *n* an alignment of the eyes that differs from the usual

heterotypic /hétta rō típpik/, **heterotypical** /-típpik'l/ *adj* differing from the standard or usual type in an organism

heterousian *n, adj* CHR same as **heteroousian**

heterozygote /hétta rō zī gōt/ *n* an organism possessing two dissimilar forms of a gene for a heritable characteristic, which may therefore produce offspring differing from the parents and each other in that characteristic

heterozygous /hétta rō zīgəss/ *adj* describes a cell or organism that has two or more different versions (**alleles**) of at least one of its genes. The offspring of such an organism may thus differ with regard to the characteristics determined by the gene or genes involved, depending on which version of the gene they inherit.

heth /het, heth, khet, kheth/, **cheth** *n* the eighth letter of the Hebrew alphabet, represented in the English alphabet as 'h'. See table at **alphabet** [Early 19C. < Hebrew *ḥēth*]

hetman /hétmən/ (*plural* **-mans**) *n* MIL same as **ataman** [Mid-18C. < Polish]

het up /het-/ *adj* extremely excited as a result of anticipation, anger, or anxiety (*informal*) [A past participle of HEAT]

heuchera /hyóokərə, hóy-/ *n* a cultivated plant with low-growing heart-shaped leaves. Flowers: small, usually red, in sprays. Native to: North America. Genus: *Heuchera*. [Late 19C. < modern Latin, after J. H. *Heucher* (1677–1747), German botanist]

heulandite /hyóolən dīt/ *n* a variously coloured crystalline mineral of the zeolite family, containing calcium and sodium [Early 19C. After H. *Heuland* (1777–1856), British mineralogist]

heuristic /hyoo rístik/ *adj* **1.** EDUC **ENCOURAGING DISCOVERY OF SOLUTIONS** relating to or using a method of teaching that encourages learners to discover solutions for themselves **2.** PHILOSOPHY, SCI **INVOLVING TRIAL AND ERROR** using or arrived at by a process of trial and error rather than set rules **3.** COMPUT **ABLE TO CHANGE** describes a computer program that modifies itself in response to the user, e.g. a spellchecker ■ *n* LOGIC **PROCEDURE FOR GETTING SOLUTION** a helpful procedure for arriving at a solution but not necessarily a proof [Early 19C. < alteration of Greek *heuriskein* 'find'] —**heuristically** *adv*

heuristics /hyoo rístiks/ *n* a method of solving a problem for which no formula exists, based on informal methods or experience, and employing a form of trial and error (**iteration**) (*takes a singular verb*)

hevea /héevi ə/ *n* a tree whose bark contains a milky sap that provides rubber. Native to: Amazon jungle. Genus: *Hevea*. [Late 19C. Via modern Latin < Quechua *hyeve*]

~~**heven**~~ incorrect spelling of **heaven**

Hevesy /hévvəshi/, **Georg von** (1885–1966) Hungarian chemist. He pioneered the use of radioactive trace elements to study the chemical processes of living organisms. He was awarded a Nobel Prize (1943). Full name **Hevesy, Georg Charles von**

hew /hyoo/ (**hews, hewing, hewed, hewn** /hyoon/ or **hewed**) *v* **1.** *vti* **CUT DOWN OR UP** to cut, break, or destroy something, especially wood or stone, with a cutting implement, especially an axe **2.** *vt* **MAKE SOMETHING BY CUTTING OR CARVING** to form or create something by cutting wood or stone ○ *hewed a path through the forest* **3.** *vt* **SEVER SOMETHING FROM SOMETHING ELSE** to cut something off from a larger block or mass **4.** *vti* **HIT WITH SWORD** to strike somebody with a sword or axe ○ *He hewed at his enemies with his claymore.* [Old English *hēawen* < Germanic] —**hewer** *n*

SPELLCHECK hew or **hue**? Do not confuse the spelling of ***hew*** and ***hue***, which sound similar. ***Hew*** is a verb meaning 'cut', as in *hew down a tree, roughly hewn wood, hew a path through the forest.* ***Hue*** is a noun denoting a shade of colour, a type, or the way something looks, as in *flowers of every hue, to put a different hue on the matter.* ***Hue*** is also the spelling used in the phrase *hue and cry.*

hew to *vt N Am* to conform closely to something such as a code or procedure

Hewett /hyóo it/, **Dorothy** (1923–2002) Australian writer. She has written plays, poems, autobiographical works and novels. Her controversial play *The Chapel Perilous* (1972) was banned for many years. Full name **Hewett, Dorothy Coade**

Hewish /hyoó ish/, **Antony** (*b.* 1924) British astronomer. He discovered the class of stars known as pulsars, and shared the Nobel Prize in physics (1974).

Hewitt /hyoó it/, **Lleyton** (*b.* 1981) Australian tennis player. He won the the US Open Men's Singles Championship in 2001 and the Wimbledon Men's Singles Championship in 2002.

hex /heks/ *n* 1. CURSE a curse or evil spell 2. BRINGER OF BAD LUCK somebody believed to bring bad luck or misfortune ■ *vt* (**hexes, hexing, hexed**) 1. CURSE OR BEWITCH SOMEBODY OR SOMETHING to put a curse or spell on somebody or something 2. HAVE BAD EFFECT ON SOMETHING to appear to have a bad effect on something, as if it were cursed or bewitched ○ *A string of accidents hexed their first attempt to climb the mountain.* [Mid-19C. Via Pennsylvanian German < German *Hexe* 'witch'] —**hexer** *n*

hex. *abbr* 1. hexagon 2. hexagonal

hex- *prefix* same as **hexa-** (*used before vowels*)

hexa- *prefix* six ○ *hexagon* [< Greek *hex* < Indo-European]

hexachlorophene /héksə kláwrə feen/ *n* a white odourless organic compound that has antibacterial and antiseptic properties. Use: soaps, toothpaste, deodorants. Formula: $(C_6HCl_3OH)_2CH_2$. [Late 20C. < HEXA- + CHLORO- + Greek *phaino-* 'shining']

hexachord /héksə kawrd/ *n* a series of six adjacent diatonic notes forming the basis of classical Greek and medieval music theory. There were three variants, the so-called natural, hard, and soft hexachords, which approximate to the modern C major, G major, and F major scales respectively.

hexadecanol /héksə dékə nol/ *n* CHEM, PHARM same as **cetyl alcohol**

hexadecimal /héksə déssim'l/ *adj* BASED ON NUMBER 16 using units of 16, in which the letters A to F are used as digits as well as the digits 0 to 9, as a basis for counting and ordering. Hexadecimal notation is used especially to represent binary code in computers. ■ *n* 1. NUMBER WITH BASE 16 a number used to count or order in units of 16 2. NOTATION FOR NUMBERS WITH BASE 16 the notation used to represent numbers with a base 16

hexagon /héksəgən/ *n* a two-dimensional geometric figure formed of six sides [Late 16C. Via late Latin < Greek *hexagōnon* 'six-angled' < *hexa-* 'six' + *gōnia* 'angle'] —**hexagonal** /hek sággən'l/ *adj*

hexagram /héksə gram/ *n* 1. a six-pointed star-shaped figure formed by extending the sides of a regular hexagon until they meet at six points 2. any of the 64 possible combinations of six broken or unbroken lines, used in divination, especially in the *I Ching*

hexahedron /héksə heédrən/ *n* a three-dimensional geometric figure formed of six plane faces, e.g. a cube [Late 16C. < Greek *hexaedron*, form of *hexaedros* 'six-sided' < *hexa-* 'six'] —**hexahedral** *adj*

hexahydrate /héksə hí drayt/ *n* a crystalline compound, each molecule of which contains six loosely bound water molecules (**water of crystallization**) from which the water escapes when the compound is heated, leaving the compound unchanged

hexamerous /hek sámmərəss/, **hexameral** /-sámmərəl/ *adj* with parts, especially petals or stamens, arranged in sets of six —**hexamerism** *n*

hexameter /hek sámmitər/ *n* a line of verse that has six metrical feet, usually all in the same or a related metre. The Greek and Latin poems the *Iliad*, *Odyssey*, and *Aeneid* are composed in hexameters. [14C. < Latin < Greek *hexametros* 'of six measures' < *hexa-* 'six' + *metron* 'measure'] —**hexametric** /héksə méttrik/ *adj*

hexamine /héksə meen/ *n* a solid camping fuel sold in blocks [Mid-20C. Contraction of *hexamethylene-tetramine*, an antibacterial agent]

hexane /hék sayn/ *n* a volatile hydrocarbon. Source: petroleum. Use: ingredient of petrol, solvent. Formula: C_6H_{14}.

Hexapla /héksəplə/ *n* an ancient version of the Hebrew Scriptures, compiled by the early Christian theologian Origen, that contains six parallel versions of the text [Early 17C. < Greek (*ta*) *hexapla*, its title, form of *hexaplous* 'sixfold' < *hexa-* 'six']

hexapody /hek sáppədi/ *n* (*plural* -**dies**) *n* a line of poetry consisting of six feet —**hexapodic** /héksə pódik/ *adj*

hexastich /héksə stik/, **hexastichon** /hek sásti kon/

(*plural* -**cha** /-kə/) *n* a unit of verse, e.g. a stanza or a short poem, that contains six lines [Late 16C. Via modern Latin < Greek *hexastikhon*, 'of six rows' < *hexa-* 'six' + *stikhos* 'row']

hexastyle /héksə stíl/ *adj* having six architectural columns or in the form of six columns ■ *n* a building, or a portico or other part, that has six columns

Hexateuch /héksə tyook/ *n* the first six books of the Bible, comprising Genesis, Exodus, Leviticus, Numbers, Deuteronomy, and Joshua [Late 19C. < HEXA- + Greek *teukhos* 'book', after PENTATEUCH]

hexavalent /héksə váylənt/ *adj* having a chemical valency of six

hexcentric /héks séntrik/ *n* a six-sided metal chock used in rock climbing

hexosan /hék sō san/ *n* a polysaccharide made of linked hexose units

hexose /héksōz, -sōss/ *n* a simple sugar containing six carbon atoms

hex sign *n* a stylized sign incorporating a circle and other elements, intended to ward off evil or bad luck

hexyl /héks'l/ *adj* relating to the group of atoms derived from hexane after the the loss of a hydrogen atom. Formula: C_6H_{13}.

hey /hay/ *interj* 1. DEMANDING ATTENTION used to get somebody's attention 2. EXPRESSING EMOTION used to express surprise, irritation, or dismay 3. GREETING used as a greeting (*informal*) [12C. Natural exclamation]

heyday /háy day/ *n* the time of somebody's or something's greatest success, popularity, or power [Late 16C. < obsolete *heyda* 'hurrah', origin ?, by association with DAY]

Heyerdahl /háy ər daal, hí-/, **Thor** (1914–2002) Norwegian anthropologist. He successfully crossed the Pacific in the balsa raft *Kon-Tiki* (1947) in an attempt to prove that Native South Americans could have migrated to Polynesia.

Heysen /híz'n/, **Sir Hans** (1877–1968) German-born Australian painter. A landscape artist, he is best known for his watercolour paintings of eucalyptus forests. Full name **Heysen, Sir Wilhelm Ernst Hans Franz**

Heywood /háywood/, **Thomas** (1574?–1641) English dramatist. He wrote more than 220 popular comedies and tragedies, notably *A Woman Killed with Kindness* (1603).

> 'Seven cities warr'd for Homer, being dead,
> / Who, living, had no roof to shroud his head.'
> [Thomas Heywood, 'The Hierarchy of the Blessed Angels'; 1635]

Hezekiah /hézzi kí ə/ (*fl* 715 BC) Judaean king. An important religious reformer, he ruled Judah from 715 BC to 687 BC.

Hf *symbol* CHEM ELEM hafnium

h.f. *abbr* MEDIA high frequency

HFC *abbr* CHEM hydrofluorocarbon

hg[1] *abbr* BIOCHEM haemoglobin

hg[2] *symbol* MEASURE hectogram

Hg *symbol* CHEM ELEM mercury

HG *abbr* 1. Her Grace 2. His Grace

HGH *abbr* BIOCHEM human growth hormone

HGV *abbr* heavy goods vehicle

hh *abbr* hands (*used as a measure of a horse's height*)

HH *abbr* 1. double hard (*used to indicate hardness of lead on pencils*) 2. Her Highness 3. LAW Her Honour 4. His Highness 5. RELIG His Holiness 6. LAW His Honour

H-Hour *n* the appointed time for a military event such as a planned attack to take place [*H* abbreviation of 'hour']

hi /hí/ *interj* 1. used as a greeting (*informal*) 2. used to attract somebody's attention (*archaic informal*) [12C. Natural exclamation]

HI *abbr* MED hearing-impaired

Hialeah /hí ə leé ə/ city in southeastern Florida, 8 km/5 mi. north and west of Miami. Population: 228,149 (2002 estimate).

hiatal /hí áyt'l/ *adj* relating to an opening, gap, or aperture in an organ of the body

hiatal hernia *n* N Am MED same as **hiatus hernia**

hiatus /hí áytəss, hi-/ (*plural* -**tuses** or *same*) *n* 1. UNEXPECTED GAP a break in something where there should be continuity 2. ANAT OPENING an opening or aperture in an organ, e.g. the opening in the diaphragm for the oesophagus 3. PHON SEPARATION BETWEEN VOWELS a break in pronunciation between two vowels that are next to each other in consecutive syllables without an intervening consonant, as in 're-examine' 4. PRINTING OMISSION a gap where something is missing, especially in manuscripts [Mid-16C. < Latin, 'gaping, opening' < *hiare* 'gape' < Indo-European]

hiatus hernia *n* a hernia in which the part of the stomach around the oesophagus entrance is forced up into the chest cavity through the normal opening in the diaphragm for the oesophagus. Hiatus hernia is associated with heartburn and can usually be corrected by surgery. N Am term **hiatal hernia**

Hiawatha /hí ə wóthə/ (*fl* 1550) Onondaga leader. He was instrumental in uniting the Iroquois League of Five Nations in about 1550. Known only through Iroquois legend, and as the hero of a narrative poem by Henry Wadsworth Longfellow, he is nevertheless believed by historians to have been a real person. Born **Heowenta**

hibachi /hi baáchi/ (*plural* -**chis**) *n* a portable barbecue of Japanese design, with a base for the fire with vents under it and one or more adjustable cooking racks [Mid-19C. < Japanese, 'fire bowl']

hibakusha /hi baáko͝osha, híbbə koosha/ (*plural same* or -**shas**) *n* a survivor of the atomic bombing of Hiroshima or Nagasaki in 1945 [Mid-20C. < Japanese, 'somebody who suffers an explosion']

hibernaculum /híbər nákyo͝oləm/ (*plural* -**la** /-lə/) *n* 1. the winter den of a hibernating animal or insect 2. the covering of a plant bud that protects it during its dormant phase [Late 17C. < Latin < *hibernare* (see HIBERNATE)]

hibernal /hí búrn'l/ *adj* relating to winter as one of the six divisions of the year used to describe ecological communities [Early 17C. < late Latin *hibernalis* < *hibernus* 'wintry']

hibernate /híbər nayt/ (-**nates**, -**nating**, -**nated**) *vi* 1. to be in a dormant state resembling sleep over the winter while living off reserves of body fat, with a decrease in body temperature and pulse rate and slower metabolism. Animals that hibernate include bears, bats, and many amphibians. 2. to become less active, especially by staying at home rather than going out to socialize (*informal humorous*) [Early 19C. < Latin *hibernat-*, past participle of *hibernare* < *hiberna* 'winter quarters' < *hibernus* 'wintry'] —**hibernation** /híbər náysh'n/ *n* —**hibernator** *n*

Hibernia /hí búrni ə/ *n* Ireland (*archaic or literary*) [< Latin, alteration of *Iverna*, via Greek *I(w)ernē* < Celtic] —**Hibernian** *adj*, *n*

Hibernicism /hí búrnissizəm/, **Hibernianism** /hí búrni ənizəm/ *n* an Irish word, expression, or idiom in the English language. N Am term **Irishism**

Hiberno- *prefix* Irish [< medieval Latin *Hibernus* < Latin *Hibernia* (see HIBERNIA)]

Hiberno-English /hí búr nō-/ *n* the variety of English spoken in Ireland that has features from Irish Gaelic, including intonation and some Gaelic words and phrases —**Hiberno-English** *adj*

hibiscus

hibiscus /hí bískəss, hi-/ *n* a bush or small tree of the mallow family. Flowers: large, brightly coloured, with prominent stamen tubes. Genus: *Hibiscus*. [Early 18C. Via Latin < Greek *hibiskos* 'marsh mallow']

HIB vaccine /híb-/ *n* a vaccine that protects against the bacterium that causes meningitis, usually given in the first year of life [Late 20C. < *Haemophilus influenzae*, type *B*]

hic /hik/ *interj* used to represent the sound of a hiccup [Late 19C. An imitation of the sound]

hiccup /híkup/, **hiccough** *n* **1.** SUDDEN CONTRACTION OF DIAPHRAGM an abrupt involuntary contraction of the diaphragm that causes an intake of breath and closes the vocal cords, resulting in a convulsive gasp **2.** GULPING SOUND the gulping sound that accompanies a hiccup or a sound like this **3.** HITCH IN ARRANGEMENTS a temporary setback to somebody's plans or arrangements (*informal*) ▪ **hiccups** *npl* GULPING INTAKES OF BREATH an attack of repeated involuntary spasms of the diaphragm, resulting in periodic noisy gulps of breath ▪ *v* (**-cups, -cuping** or **-cupping, -cuped** or **-cupped; -coughs, -coughing, -coughed**) **1.** *vi* PRODUCE HICCUP to have a spasm of the diaphragm resulting in a hiccup **2.** *vi* MAKE HICCUP NOISES to make the sound of, or a sound like, a hiccup **3.** *vt* UTTER SOMETHING WHILE HICCUPING to say something with a hiccup or hiccups [Late 16C. An imitation of the sound]

hic jacet /hik jáysət, -yákət/ an inscription often found on gravestones, meaning 'here lies' [< Latin]

hick /hik/ *n* an offensive term that deliberately insults somebody's rural base or background and his or her intelligence and level of sophistication (*informal insult*) ▪ *adj* remote from big cities and regarded as lacking in sophistication (*informal*) [Mid-16C. < *Hick*, old pet form of the first name *Richard*]

Hick /hik/, **Graeme** (*b.* 1966) Rhodesian-born British cricketer. He has batted for Worcestershire and England. He scored his hundredth first-class century in 1998, the second-youngest cricketer to do so.

hickey /híki/ (*plural* **-eys** or **-ies**) *n* **1.** *US* PRINTING ERROR a printing error or imperfection **2.** *N Am* same as **doohickey** (*informal*) **3.** *N Am* BRUISING ON SKIN a mark on the skin caused especially by kissing, biting, or sucking and associated with physical intimacy (*informal*) **4.** *N Am* PIMPLE a pimple on the skin (*informal*) [Early 20C. Origin ?]

US Signal Corps

Wild Bill Hickok

Hickok /híkok/, **Wild Bill** (1837–76) US lawman, gunfighter, and scout. He was a Union spy and scout during the US Civil War and later a Kansas marshal known for his marksmanship. He also toured with Buffalo Bill's Wild West Show (1872–73). Born Hickok, James Butler

hickory

hickory /híkəri/ (*plural* **-ies**) *n* **1.** WOOD the hard light-coloured wood of a North American walnut tree.

Use: tool handles, sports equipment, furniture. **2.** N AMERICAN NUT TREE a deciduous tree of the walnut family that has compound leaves and nuts that are edible in some species and whose wood is hickory. Native to: North America. Genus: *Carya*. ○ *a hickory nut* **3.** HICKORY STICK a walking stick or switch made of hickory wood [Late 17C. < Virginia Algonquian *pocohiquara*, 'food or drink made from pounded nuts']

Hicksville, **hicksville** *n US* a place regarded as rural and backward (*slang*)

hid past participle, past tense of **hide** [1]

hidalgo /hi dálgō/ (*plural* **-gos**) *n* a Spanish nobleman of the lowest rank [Late 16C. < Spanish, contraction of *hijo de algo* 'son of something']

Hidalgo /hi dálgō/ state in east-central Mexico. Capital: Pachuca. Population: 2,235,591 (2000). Area: 20,987 sq. km/8,103 sq. mi.

hidden past participle of **hide** [1] ▪ *adj* **1.** made difficult to find or see ○ *a hidden doorway* **2.** not immediately obvious ○ *The package included a number of hidden costs.* **—hiddenness** *n*

hidden agenda *n* a plan, motive, or aim underlying somebody's actions that is kept secret from others

hiddenite /hídd'n īt/ *n* a semiprecious stone that is a rare green variety of spodumene. Use: gems. [Late 19C. After William E. *Hidden* (1853–1918), US mineralogist]

hidden tax *n* FIN same as **indirect tax**

hide [1] /híd/ *v* (**hides, hiding, hid** /hid/, **hidden** /hídd'n/ or **hid**) **1.** *vti* MOVE OUT OF SIGHT to conceal yourself, or something or somebody else, from view **2.** *vt* KEEP SOMETHING SECRET to prevent something from becoming known **3.** *vt* BLOCK VIEW OF SOMETHING to obscure something by passing, or passing something, in front of it, or by being temporarily or permanently in front of it ○ *The clouds hid the sun for a while.* **4.** *vt* TURN FACE AWAY to turn away or cover the face or eyes with the hands, e.g. so that the expression cannot be seen or in order to avoid seeing something ▪ *n* WILDLIFE OBSERVATION POST a place, often constructed to look like part of the natural environment, where somebody can hide in order to observe, or sometimes shoot, wild animals. N Am term **blind** [Old English *hȳdan* < W Germanic]

hide out *vi* to be in hiding, or go into hiding

hide [2] /híd/ *n* **1.** the skin of some larger animals, e.g. deer, cattle, or buffalo (*often used in combination*) **2.** a person's skin (*informal*) ○ *'A vengeance on your crafty wither'd hide!'* (William Shakespeare, *The Taming of the Shrew*; 1593) [Old English *hȳd* < Indo-European] ◇ **neither hide nor hair of somebody** *or* **something** no trace of somebody or something (*informal*) ○ *We could see neither hide nor hair of the lost keys.* ◇ **tan somebody's hide** to beat or whip somebody (*informal*)

hide [3] /híd/ *n* in Old English law, a measure of land equal to 120 acres [Old English *hīd* 'measure of land for supporting a family' < Germanic]

hide-and-seek *n* a children's game in which one player lets the others hide, and then tries to find them

hideaway /hídə way/ *n* a secluded place of retreat or concealment [Late 19C. < HIDE [1]]

hidebound /híd bownd/ *adj* **1.** NARROW-MINDED AND CONSERVATIVE unwilling to countenance new ideas or new ways of doing things **2.** WITH DRY STIFF SKIN having skin that is dry, stiff, and closely attached to the flesh, as a result of poor feeding ○ *hidebound cattle* **3.** TREES WITH TOO STIFF BARK describes trees with bark too stiff for normal growth [Mid-19C. < HIDE [2]]

hideous /híddi əss/ *adj* **1.** HORRIBLE TO SEE extremely unpleasant to see **2.** HORRIBLE TO HEAR frighteningly horrible to hear ○ *a hideous shriek* **3.** MORALLY REPULSIVE morally repulsive or disgusting **4.** CAUSING SUFFERING causing a great deal of suffering [14C. < Anglo-Norman *hidous*, Old French *hidos* < *hi(s)de* 'fear'] **—hideously** *adv* **—hideousness** *n*

SYNONYMS See *unattractive*.

hideout /híd owt/ *n* a place where somebody is hiding, especially somebody wanted by the police [Late 19C. < HIDE [1]]

hidey-hole /hídi hōl/, **hidy-hole** *n* a place of concealment for somebody or something (*informal*) [< variant of HIDING [1]]

hiding [1] /híding/ *n* a place where somebody is hiding or can hide, or the state of being hidden [13C. < HIDE [1]]

hiding [2] /híding/ *n* the punishment of being beaten (*informal*) [Early 19C. < HIDE [2]] ◇ **on a hiding to nothing** in a situation in which there is no chance of success

hidrosis /hi drōssiss, hī-/ *n* **1.** the production or excretion of sweat (*technical*) **2.** a skin disease that affects the sweat glands [Mid-19C. < Greek *hidrōsis* < *hidrōs* 'sweat'] **—hidrotic** /-dróttik/ *adj*

hidy-hole *n* another spelling of **hidey-hole** (*informal*)

hie /hī/ (**hies, hieing** or **hying, hied**) *vi* to go somewhere in a hurry (*archaic*) [Old English, origin ?]

~~**hiefer**~~ incorrect spelling of **heifer**

~~**hieght**~~ incorrect spelling of **height**

hieland /héelənd/ *adj* Scotland **1.** regarded as unsophisticated **2.** not very sensible [Early 16C. Variant of HIGHLAND]

hier- *prefix* same as **hiero-** (*used before vowels*)

hierarch /hír aark/ *n* somebody of high rank in a hierarchy, especially a priestly hierarchy [15C. Via medieval Latin < Greek *hierarkhēs* 'ruling sacred person' < *hieros* 'sacred' + *arkhēs* 'ruling']

hierarchical /hír aárkik'l/, **hierarchic** /hír aárkik/ *adj* **1.** relating to or arranged in a formally ranked order **2.** administered by a hierarchy composed of members of the clergy **—hierarchically** *adv*

hierarchize /hír aar kīz/ (**-chizes, -chizing, -chized**), **hierarchise** (**-chises, -chising, -chised**) *vt* to arrange something such as an organization in graduated ranks **—hierarchization** /hír aar kī záysh'n/ *n*

hierarchy /hír aarki/ (*plural* **-chies**) *n* **1.** FORMALLY RANKED GROUP an organization or group whose members are arranged in ranks, e.g. in ranks of power and seniority **2.** FORMAL GRADING OF GROUP the categorization of members of a group according to importance **3.** ANIMAL GROUP ORGANIZATION a form of social organization in animals in which different members of a group possess different levels of status, affecting their feeding and mating behaviour **4.** RELIG RANKED GROUP OF CLERGY a body of clergy organized into ranks **5.** CONTROLLING GROUP IN FORMAL ORGANIZATION those who are in charge of a formally organized group, especially the priests in control of the Roman Catholic Church or a local part of it **6.** BIOL SUBSET WITHIN RANKED SYSTEM a subset within a classification system, e.g. that for plants or animals

hieratic /hír áttik/, **hieratical** /-áttik'l/ *adj* **1.** RELIG OF PRIESTS relating to priests **2.** LING OF ANCIENT WRITING SYSTEM relating to a cursive version of ancient Egyptian hieroglyphics **3.** ARTS IN STYLIZED FORM fixed, formal, and stylized in a traditional way, e.g. as ancient Egyptian art is ▪ *n* LING ANCIENT WRITING SYSTEM a cursive version of ancient Egyptian hieroglyphics [Mid-17C. Via Latin < Greek *hieratikos* 'priestly' < *hiereus* 'sacred person' < *hieros* 'sacred'] **—hieratically** *adv*

hiero- *prefix* holy, sacred ○ *hierocracy* [< Greek *hieros* < Indo-European]

hierocracy /hír ókrəssi/ (*plural* **-cies**) *n* **1.** government by clergy **2.** a body of clergy that rules a place or country **—hierocratic** /hír ō kráttik/ *adj*

hierodule /hír ə dyool/ *n* in ancient Greece, an enslaved person kept in or associated with a temple, especially as a prostitute [Mid-19C. Via late Latin < Greek *hierodoulos* 'temple slave' < *hieron* 'sacred place' < *hieros* 'sacred' + *doulos* 'slave'] **—hierodulic** /hírə dyoólik/ *adj*

Barnaby's

hieroglyph: detail of wall painting in the tomb of Inherkha, Thebes, Egypt (1279–1212 BC)

hieroglyph /hírəglif/ *n* a symbol or picture used in a writing system to denote an object, concept, sound, or sequence of sounds, originally and especially in the writing system of the ancient Egyptians. See illustration on previous page [Late 16C. Back-formation < HIEROGLYPHIC]

hieroglyphic /hírə glíffik/ *adj* **1.** *also* **hieroglyphical** /hírə glíffik'l/ relating to or written in hieroglyphs **2.** difficult to read (*informal*) ■ *n* same as **hieroglyph** [Late 16C. Directly or via French < late Latin *hieroglyphicus* < Greek *hierogluphikos* 'sacred carving' < *hieros* 'sacred' + *gluphē* 'carving'] —**hieroglyphically** *adv*

hieroglyphics /hírə glíffiks/ *n* a writing system that uses symbols or pictures to denote objects, concepts, or sounds, originally and especially in the writing system of ancient Egypt (*takes a singular verb*) ■ *npl* writing that is difficult to decipher, or other indecipherable symbols (*informal; takes a plural verb*)

hierogram /hírō gram/ *n* a symbol with religious significance

Hieronymian /hírə nímmi ən/, **Hieronymic** /-nímmik/ *adj* relating to St Jerome [Mid-17C. < Latin *Hieronymus* 'Jerome']

hierophant /hírō fant/ *n* **1.** EXPLAINER OF MYSTERIES somebody who interprets and explains obscure and mysterious matters, especially sacred doctrines or mysteries **2.** INTERPRETER OF EVENTS somebody who explains or comments on everyday matters (*formal*) **3.** ANCIENT GREEK PRIEST in ancient Greece, a priest who revealed the mysteries at the annual festival of Eleusis [Late 17C. Via late Latin < Greek *hierophantēs* 'sacred person who reveals something' < *hieros* 'sacred' + *phen-*, stem of *phainein* 'reveal'] —**hierophantic** /hírə fántik/ *adj* —**hierophantically** *adv*

hifalutin *adj* another spelling of **highfalutin** (*informal*)

hi-fi /hí fí/ (*plural* **hi-fis**) *n* **1.** a set of high-quality equipment for reproducing and usually recording sound, which may include a CD player, tape deck, turntable, tuner, amplifier, and speakers **2.** RECORDING same as **high fidelity** [Mid-20C. Shortening of HIGH FIDELITY]

higgledy-piggledy /hígg'ldi pígg'ldi/ *adj* disorganized and untidy ■ *adv* in a disorganized, untidy state [Late 16C. Probably < the idea of pigs being messy, or being huddled together when herded]

Higgs boson /hígz-/ *n* a hypothetical subatomic particle with zero spin predicted in some gauge theories and thought to be the source of the mass of all other particles [Late 20C. After Peter Ware *Higgs* (b. 1929), British physicist]

high /hí/ *adj* (**higher, highest**) **1.** OF GREAT HEIGHT extending a long way from bottom to top, especially when viewed from the bottom ○ *a high wall* **2.** ABOVE SOMEBODY OR SOMETHING situated in a position above the onlooker, or above somebody or something else referred to ○ *The window was too high for him to see in.* **3.** IN HEIGHT ABOVE SOMETHING above or stretching upwards from a known base level such as sea or ground level ○ *ten feet high* **4.** ABOVE AVERAGE greater than the normal or average, e.g. in quantity, number, quality, intensity, or cost, or well above a smaller or lower level or amount ○ *a high cost of living* **5.** MUSIC RAISED IN PITCH raised in pitch towards the upper end of a range of sound ○ *can hit the high notes* **6.** METEOROL BLOWING STRONGLY blowing with a great deal of force ○ *a high wind* **7.** DEVELOPMENTALLY ADVANCED advanced in development or complexity ○ *high finance* **8.** BETTER THAN OTHERS superior in quality, character, or morals ○ *sets a high example* ○ *high standards* **9.** OF ELEVATED RANK important in status or rank ○ *a high official* **10.** VERY FAVOURABLE considering somebody or something to be particularly good ○ *held in high esteem* **11.** AT PEAK at the busiest or most important stage ○ *high summer* **12.** HAPPY animated and cheerful ○ *in high spirits* **13.** OVEREXCITED overexcited or overstimulated **14.** DRUGS INTOXICATED under the influence of alcohol or drugs (*slang*) **15.** FOOD WITH STRONG SMELL OR TASTE with a very strong smell or taste, either because it is pleasantly mature or because it has overmatured and begun to go bad **16.** GEOG FAR FROM EQUATOR at a considerable distance either north or south of the equator ○ *high latitude* **17.** PHON WITH TONGUE RAISED IN MOUTH formed with the back of the tongue close, or relatively close, to the roof of the mouth ○ *high vowel sounds* **18.** *also* **High** CHR RITUALISTIC favouring or involving formal and elaborate ritual and ceremonial **19.** AUTOMOT PRODUCING TOP SPEEDS resulting in a relatively large number of revolutions of the driven part as compared with the driving part in a transmission gear, and giving the top speed of travel or rotation ■ *adv* UPWARDS at, in, or into an elevated position ○ *The balloon rose high in the sky.* ■ *n* **1.** TOP PLACE a greater than usual level or position ○ *an all-time high* **2.** METEOROL same as **anticyclone** **3.** METEOROL TOP TEMPERATURE the maximum temperature reached or expected to be reached in a particular period ○ *Today's high will be in the nineties.* **4.** ELATED STATE a state of euphoria (*informal*) **5.** INTOXICATED STATE a state of intoxication by drugs or alcohol **6.** *N Am* AUTOMOT same as **top gear** (*informal*) [Old English *hēah* < Germanic] ◇ **high and dry 1.** stranded and abandoned, and perhaps helpless **2.** beyond the reach of water ◇ **high and low** in every conceivable place ◇ **high and mighty** arrogant and self-important ◇ **run high** to be at a level of great intensity ○ *Emotions ran high during the moving commemoration.*

SPELLCHECK higher or **hire**? Do not confuse the spelling of ***higher*** and ***hire***, which sound similar. ***Higher*** is an adjective or adverb, the comparative of *high*, as in *a higher shelf, flying higher.* ***Hire*** is a verb or noun that refers to employing somebody or renting something, as in *hire extra staff, boats for hire.*

High *n* a particular high school (*informal*) ○ *She goes to Kinross High.*

highball /hí bawl/ *n N Am* a long drink consisting of spirits mixed with ice and water or a carbonated drink ■ *vti* (**-balls, -balling, -balled**) to travel at high speed, or drive a vehicle at high speed (*slang*) [Earlier 'type of poker played with balls and a tall glass receptacle']

high beam *n N Am* AUTOMOT same as **full beam**

high blood pressure *n* unusually high blood pressure in the arteries. It encompasses atypical elevation of either the peak blood pressure at each heartbeat (**systolic pressure**), or the running pressure between heart beats (**diastolic pressure**), or both.

highborn /hí bawrn/ *adj* born into an aristocratic family (*literary*)

highboy /hí boy/ *n N Am* FURNITURE same as **tallboy** (sense 1)

high brass *n* brass consisting of 65 per cent copper and 35 per cent zinc

highbred /hí bred/ *adj* born of or descended from superior breeding stock

highbrow /hí brow/ *adj* dealing with serious subjects, especially cultural subjects, in an intellectual way ○ *'Conceits which would be only highbrow wisecracks in inferior writing have fused into a form that can only be called inevitable, the way it should be.'* (Northrop Frye, *The Bush Garden*; 1972) ■ *n* somebody with highbrow interests or tastes [< the idea that a high forehead signifies greater brain power]

high cal, high calorie *adj* with many calories or more calories than usual

highchair /hí cháir/ *n* a small chair with long legs and often a detachable tray, for older babies and toddlers to use at mealtimes

High Church *n* a section of the Anglican Church that stresses the essential unity of Anglican Christianity with Roman Catholicism and Orthodoxy, holds traditional views about the sacraments, and favours ritual and ceremony

high-class *adj* **1.** appealing to the rich or sophisticated, and therefore usually expensive **2.** showing or having the kind of sophistication associated with wealth

high comedy *n* comedy with humour depending on witty dialogue and a clever plot rather than slapstick

high command *n* **1.** the senior officers in a country's armed forces, who jointly take decisions on strategy and tactics **2.** the main headquarters of a military force

High Commission *n* the embassy of one country of the Commonwealth of Nations in another Commonwealth country

High Commissioner *n* **1.** the chief representative of a country of the Commonwealth of Nations in another Commonwealth country **2.** the person leading an international commission

high-concept *adj* describes a film that contains features likely to attract a large audience, e.g. big stars, fast action, and glamour

high country *n* lands that are in a mountainous region, but not so high as to have no pastoral or agricultural use (*hyphenated before a noun*)

high court *n* in the United States, a superior court, or a state's supreme court

High Court *n* **1.** UK COURT the High Court of Justice in England and Wales, or the High Court of Justiciary in Scotland **2.** US SUPREME COURT the Supreme Court of the United States **3.** AUSTRALIAN COURT in Australia, the federal supreme court and final court of appeal **4.** NEW ZEALAND COURT in New Zealand, a civil and criminal court inferior to the Court of Appeal but superior to the District Courts **5.** INDIAN COURT in India, the highest court of a state

High Court of Justice *n* the principal court for civil cases in England and Wales

High Court of Justiciary *n* the principal criminal court in Scotland

high day *n* a day of religious celebration (*archaic*) ◇ **on high days and holidays** on special occasions

high-definition television *n* a television system with twice the scanning capacity of normal television systems, allowing for far greater definition and less flickering

high-density lipoprotein *n* an aggregate of fat and protein that transports cholesterol away from the arteries. High levels of high-density lipoproteins are associated with a decreased risk of heart disease.

high-end *adj* expensive and likely to appeal to sophisticated and discerning people ○ *high-end products*

high-energy *adj* **1.** describes chemical reactions that take place with the release of substantial amounts of energy **2.** used in marketing to describe foods such as glucose drinks or high-sugar items such as honey that can be broken down easily by the body to provide a rapid supply of energy

high-energy physics *n* PHYS same as **particle physics**

Higher /hí ər/ *n* **1.** in Scotland, an examination in a single subject, usually taken after five or six years of secondary education (*often used before a noun*) **2.** in Scotland, a pass in a Higher examination

higher criticism *n* the establishment of the sources of biblical texts, using the techniques of textual criticism —**higher critic** *n*

higher education *n* education generally begun after A-levels or Highers, usually carried out at a university or college, and involving study for a degree, diploma, or similar advanced qualification

higher law *n* a moral law or ethical principle that is believed to be of greater validity than earthly law

higher learning *n* education or study at university level

higher mathematics *n* mathematics at an abstract and sophisticated level, including number theory and topology (*takes a singular verb*)

higher-up *n* somebody in a position of authority or at a higher level in a hierarchy (*informal*)

highest common factor *n UK, ANZ, Can* the highest number that can be exactly divided into each member of a set of numbers. For example, the highest common factor of 12, 60, and 84 is 12. US term **greatest common divisor**

high explosive *n* a liquid or solid substance that detonates without burning to produce a large release of energy. Use: rock blasting, military applications.

highfalutin /hífə lóotin, -t'n/, **hifalutin, highfaluting** /-ting/ *adj* affecting a grand style in an unconvincing way (*informal*) [Mid-19C. Origin ?]

high fashion *n* FASHION same as **haute couture**

high fidelity *n* extremely high-quality sound reproduction with minimal distortion, achieved with electronic equipment (*hyphenated when used before a noun*)

high-five *n* an informal greeting or gesture of elation or victory in which somebody slaps a raised palm

against the raised palm of somebody else (*slang*) — **high-five** *vti*

high-flier, **high-flyer** *n* a highly successful person, or somebody who seems destined for great achievement

high-flown *adj* giving an unconvincing appearance of being elegant, refined, or exalted ○ *a high-flown prose style* ○*'a warning against high-flown pretensions'* (Henry James, *Roderick Hudson*; 1876)

high-flyer *n* another spelling of **high-flier**

high-flying *adj* **1.** highly successful, or having the potential for great achievement **2.** flying or located at a great height

high frequency *n* a radio frequency in the range 3–30 MHz or of wavelength 10–100 metres (*hyphenated when used before a noun*)

high gain antenna *n* an antenna that amplifies very weak signals, often used in satellite communications

high gear *n N Am* same as **top gear** (sense 1)

High German *n* the form of German spoken originally in the southern part of the country that has become standard German —**High-German** *adj*

high-grade *adj* of a high quality, especially because of purity or concentration of contents

high ground *n* **1.** an area of land higher than its surroundings **2.** a position of superiority or advantage over others

high-handed *adj* overbearing and inconsiderate of other people's views or sensibilities —**high-handedly** *adv* —**high-handedness** *n*

high-hat *adj* snobbish and arrogant (*archaic*) ■ *vti* (**high-hats**, **high-hatting**, **high-hatted**) *N Am* to treat somebody in a haughty, disdainful way (*dated*)

high-hat cymbals *npl* a pair of cymbals held horizontally on a stand, with the upper one made to rise and fall against the lower one by the drummer's foot

high heels *npl* women's shoes with tall, often slender, heels that raise the back of the foot off the ground

High Holidays, **High Holy Days** *npl* the period of Jewish festivals from Rosh Hashanah to Yom Kippur

high horse *n* an attitude of arrogance and haughty disregard for others (*informal*) ○ *told him to get off his high horse*

high hurdles *n* a track-and-field event for men, in which the athletes cover a distance of 110 m outdoors, jumping over hurdles 107 cm/42 in high (*takes a singular or plural verb*) —**high hurdler** *n*

highjack, etc. CRIME another spelling of **hijack, etc.**

high jinks, **hijinks** /hī jingks/ *n* good-humoured boisterousness, frequently including mischievousness and pranks (*informal; takes a singular or plural verb*)

high jump *n* an athletics event in which the contestants run forward to gain momentum and then jump over a horizontal pole. The pole is raised higher in each successive round until all competitors have failed to get over it. —**high jumper** *n* —**high jumping** *n* ◇ **be for the high jump** to be about to be scolded, punished severely, or dismissed from a job (*informal*)

highland /hī lənd/ *n* HILLY LAND hilly ground, higher than its surroundings ■ **highlands** *npl* HILLY AREA an area or region that is largely hilly or mountainous ■ *adj* RELATING TO HIGHLANDS relating to or coming from highlands, especially those in Scotland —**highlander** *n*

Highland[1] /hī lənd/ *adj* relating to, found in, or originating from the Scottish Highlands —**Highlander** *n*

Highland[2] /hī lənd/ council area of Northern Scotland. Area: 25,784 sq. km/9,955 sq. mi.

Highland cattle *npl* cattle belonging to a hardy breed with long shaggy reddish-brown hair and long curved horns, originally developed in the Scottish Highlands

Highland Clearances *npl* the forcible removal of tenants from their land by many 18th- and 19th-century landlords in the Scottish Highlands, usually to introduce sheep farming

Highland cow *n* a cow belonging to a hardy breed with long shaggy reddish-brown hair and long curved horns, originally developed in the Scottish Highlands

Highland dress *n* a modern version of the traditional clothing of men from the Scottish Highlands, comprising a tartan kilt, a sporran, knee-length socks, a tweed or plain wool jacket, and brogues. Highland dress is worn, e.g., by some Scottish regiments, by pipe bands, and by some Scotsmen or men of Scottish descent on special occasions.

Highland fling *n* an energetic Scottish solo dance originally danced by men in Highland dress, but now also by women and children, most frequently in competitions at Highland Games

Highland Games *n* an outdoor meeting at which there are competitions in various traditional Scottish sports such as tossing the caber, in Scottish dancing, and in piping (*takes a singular or plural verb*)

Highland Park town in southeastern Michigan. Surrounded by Detroit, it evolved as a community after Henry Ford located his mass-production Model T factory there in 1909. Population: 16,281 (2002 estimate).

Highlands /hī ləndz/ mountainous area of mainland Scotland, north and west of a line from Dumbarton in the west to Stonehaven in the east

high-level *adj* involving participation by people at a high level in their organization or country, e.g. politicians, civil servants, or company directors

high-level language *n* a computer programming language with syntax and grammar crudely approximating a natural language. The pioneering high-level languages, FORTRAN, COBOL, and ALGOL, have largely been supplanted by BASIC, FORTH, Pascal, and C, especially for educational and personal-computer applications.

high-level waste *n* radioactive waste material retaining sufficient activity to need to be continuously cooled

high life *n* the luxurious lifestyle of fashionable society (*informal; often ironic*)

highlife /hī līf/ *n* a style of music that blends West African features with American jazz forms and is popular in West Africa

highlight /hī līt/ *n* **1.** BEST PART the most memorable, important, or exciting part of an experience or event **2.** REPRESENTATIVE PART an exemplary extract from a larger work that, along with others, is meant to represent it ○ *gave us highlights of the president's speech* **3.** ART, PHOTOGRAPHY CONTRASTING PALE AREA an area in a very light tone in a painting or photograph that provides contrast, illumination, or the appearance of illumination **4.** PHOTOGRAPHY REFLECTION the reflection of a light source in a picture, e.g. the reflection of a studio light in shiny hair or the reflection of light in somebody's eye ■ **highlights** *npl* LIGHT STREAKS IN HAIR strands of hair that are deliberately made lighter than the rest of the hair ■ *vt* (**-lights**, **-lighting**, **-lighted**) **1.** EMPHASIZE SOMETHING to draw attention to something, or make something particularly prominent or noticeable ○ *The report highlights the problems caused by polluted waterways.* **2.** MARK SOMETHING WITH HIGHLIGHTER to mark something, e.g. part of a text, with a highlighter pen **3.** PUT LIGHT STREAKS IN HAIR to put highlights in somebody's hair **4.** ART ADD LIGHT AREAS IN PICTURE to add highlights to parts of a picture to provide contrast, illumination, or the appearance of illumination

highlighter /hī lītər/ *n* **1.** a broad-tipped felt pen, often with transparent, brightly coloured ink, for marking important passages of text **2.** a cosmetic for the face that is used to emphasize features such as the eyes or cheekbones

high-low *n* **1.** a variety of poker in which both high and low hands win **2.** in bridge, a signal to a partner to lead a particular suit

highly /hī li/ *adv* **1.** EXTREMELY to a great extent, or in many ways ○ *highly likely to succeed* ○ *highly recommended* ○ *highly improbable* **2.** FAVOURABLY very favourably ○ *highly regarded* **3.** IN HIGH PLACE in a high position or rank ○ *highly placed officials who denied the story*

highly-strung *adj* by nature tense, nervous, or easily upset. N Am term **high-strung**

high-maintenance *adj* requiring an excessive

amount of attention or effort to maintain ○ *a high-maintenance car* ○ *a high-maintenance relationship*

High Mass *n* an elaborate Roman Catholic Mass in which a choir sings much of the service. It is usually celebrated by more than one priest.

high-minded *adj* having or showing high moral principles —**high-mindedly** *adv* —**high-mindedness** *n*

high-muck-a-muck /hī múkə múk/, **high-muckety-muck** /-múkəti-/ *n* *N Am* somebody in a position of importance and authority who behaves in an overbearing way (*informal*) [Mid-19C. Probably < Chinook Jargon *hiyu muckamuck*, literally 'plenty to eat' < Nootka, by association with HIGH]

highness /hī nəss/ *n* the condition, state, or extent of being high

Highness *n* a title and style of address for members of a royal family other than a sovereign

high noon *n* **1.** NOON EXACTLY the exact moment of noon **2.** PEAK OF ACHIEVEMENT the high point or most creative part of somebody's career or achievements **3.** *also* **High Noon** CRUCIAL TIME a time of confronting a serious problem or making a hard decision

CULTURAL NOTE **High Noon**, a film (1952) by US director Fred Zinnemann. In this classic western, lawman Will Kane (Gary Cooper) valiantly awaits and then confronts a killer seeking revenge for his recent incarceration. Shot in real time, the film's suspense is heightened by close-ups of Kane's anxious expressions and of clocks ticking steadily towards the moment of truth.

high-octane *adj* **1.** describes fuel that has a high octane content **2.** showing or demanding a high degree of commitment and effort in a drive for success (*informal*) ○ *high-octane lawyers*

high-performance *adj* designed to operate at greater speed or with greater power than other things of the same kind ○ *a high-performance sports car*

high-pitched *adj* **1.** AT TOP OF SOUND RANGE towards the upper end of the range of audible sound **2.** EMOTIONAL extremely emotional and intense **3.** CONSTR WITH STEEP SLOPE having a very steep slope **4.** FORMAL AND ELABORATE in a formal and flowery style

high places *npl* positions of power, authority, or influence

high point *n* the most successful, enjoyable, or important part of a period of time, activity, or experience ○ *This new promotion marked the high point of his career.*

high-powered, **high-power** *adj* **1.** DYNAMIC possessing great energy and impressive ability, especially as displayed in a professional environment ○ *a high-powered sales pitch* **2.** INFLUENTIAL having much power or influence **3.** OPTICS GREATLY ENLARGING giving a high magnification **4.** TECH VERY POWERFUL operating much more powerfully, or able to handle material of greater complexity and more quickly, than other equipment of the same type

high-pressure *adj* **1.** STRESSFUL causing stress, e.g. from deadlines or excessive demands ○ *She's at her best in high-pressure situations.* **2.** PERSISTENT aggressively persistent in seeking to bring about a result ○ *a high-pressure sales pitch* **3.** OPERATING AT GREATER THAN NORMAL PRESSURE using, or designed to withstand, forces exerted by liquid or gas at pressures higher than normal atmospheric pressure

high priest *n* **1.** MAIN PROPONENT the leading figure propounding a doctrine or ideology **2.** JUDAISM JEWISH CHIEF PRIEST a Jewish chief priest, especially the head of the priestly caste at the time of the Temple in Jerusalem **3.** CHR MORMON PRIEST a man who is a priest in the Church of Jesus Christ of Latter-Day Saints, belonging to the order of Melchizedek

high priestess *n* **1.** a woman who leads a religion or a religious group **2.** the leading woman propounding a doctrine or ideology

high profile *n* a prominent position or presence in the public eye

high-profile *adj* in or intended to be in the public eye, e.g. to attract attention, support, or business

high-ranking *adj* of high status or holding great responsibility in a hierarchical organization

high relief *n* a version of relief sculpture in which the carving projects from the background to more

than half its natural depth (*hyphenated when used before a noun*)

High Renaissance *n* the period in European art between about 1490 and 1520, when the work of Leonardo da Vinci, Michelangelo, Raphael, and other great artists reached the highest point of Renaissance perfection

high-res *adj* COMPUT another spelling of **hi-res** (*informal*)

high-resolution *adj* using a large number of dots or lines to portray an image in great detail in a video display or printed image

high-rise *adj* 1. ARCHIT MULTISTOREY consisting of several storeys, but usually fewer than for a skyscraper 2. CYCLING WITH HIGH HANDLEBARS describes a child's bicycle that has small wheels, very high handlebars, and a long narrow seat ■ *n* 1. ARCHIT TALL BUILDING a multi-storey building 2. CYCLING HIGH-RISE BICYCLE a child's high-rise bicycle

high-risk recreation *n* a recreational activity that involves an element of danger, e.g. hang-gliding, skydiving, bungee jumping, and white-water rafting. Experiencing the sensation of risk is an important motive for participation.

high road *n* 1. DIRECT ROUTE the easiest or most direct way to a place 2. MAIN ROAD a main road, usually in a town or village 3. RIGHT MORAL COURSE the most ethical course of action ○ *was commended for taking the high road and resigning*

high roller *n N Am* (*slang*) 1. a person or organization that spends money freely and extravagantly 2. a gambler who plays for high stakes —**high-rolling** *adj*

high school *n* 1. a secondary school, for pupils aged 11 to 16, 17, or 18 2. in the United States, a school that includes grades 9 or 10 to 12

high seas *npl* the open ocean, not under any nation's jurisdiction

high season *n* the most popular time of year for holidays, when resorts are at their busiest. N Am term **peak season**

high sign *n N Am* a secret signal, often prearranged, given as a warning or to convey information

Highsmith /hī́smith/, **Patricia** (1921–95) US writer. She wrote literary crime novels such as *Strangers on a Train* (1950) and *The Talented Mr Ripley* (1955). Born **Plangman, Mary Patricia**

high society *n* the fashionable wealthy classes in society

high-sounding *adj* grandiose and pretentious but unlikely to come to anything

high-speed *adj* 1. TRANSP CAPABLE OF GREAT SPEED moving or functioning at high speed, or capable of moving or functioning at high speed 2. PHOTOGRAPHY NEEDING LITTLE EXPOSURE needing a very short exposure time ○ *high-speed film* 3. PHOTOGRAPHY OPERATING AT FAST SPEEDS operating, done, or capable of making exposures at a very fast rate, at between 50 and several million frames per second ○ *a high-speed shutter*

high-spirited *adj* lively and full of fun or mischief —**high-spiritedly** *adv* —**high-spiritedness** *n*

high spot *n* the most memorable, important, or exciting part of an experience or event

high-stakes *adj* describes a risky situation in which somebody is likely to win or lose a great deal ○*'Everyone is getting in the starting blocks for a high-stakes fight.'* (*Washington Post*; November 1998)

high-stick *vt* in ice hockey, to strike an opponent with the blade of the stick above the legally specified height —**high-sticking** *n*

high street, **High Street** *n* 1. MAIN STREET IN TOWN a principal street where the main shops of a town are located 2. RETAIL TRADE the ordinary retail sector of the national economy (*informal*) 3. CONSUMERS GENERALLY the public, when viewed as consumers (*informal*)

high-strung *adj N Am* same as **highly-strung**

high style *n* the most up-to-date and stylish fashion, especially in clothing (*hyphenated before a noun*)

~~high~~ incorrect spelling of **height**

high table *n* a table in a large dining hall in some schools and university colleges at which the staff, principal teachers, or fellows sit

hightail /hī́ tayl/ (**-tails, -tailing, -tailed**) *vi* to rush away from a place (*slang*) [< the erect tail of a fleeing animal]

high tea *n* a meal served in the late afternoon or early evening, consisting of a cooked dish, usually hot, with bread and butter, cakes, and tea

high tech, **hi-tech** *n* 1. advanced technology and state-of-the-art devices and methods, especially in electronic engineering 2. a style of architecture and interior design that makes use of metal, glass, and plastic in a simple utilitarian way

high-tech, **hi-tech** *adj* 1. using or relating to advanced technological devices and methods 2. using metal, glass, and plastic in a simple utilitarian way in architecture and interior design

high technology *n* TECH same as **high tech** (sense 1)

high-tension *adj* designed for or operating at high voltage

high-test *adj* same as **high-octane** (sense 1)

high tide *n* 1. HIGHEST POINT OF TIDE the tide at its highest level 2. MOMENT OF HIGHEST TIDE the time when the tide reaches its highest level 3. PEAK OF SOMETHING the culmination or high point of something

high-toned *adj* culturally, morally, or socially superior (*dated slang*)

high-top *n* 1. SHOE THAT PROTECTS ANKLES a sports shoe that extends above the ankle to give it protection and support 2. N Am HIGH-SIDED TRAINER a trainer that covers the foot up to the ankle, e.g. those worn by basketball players ■ *adj* WITH UPPERS COVERING ANKLES having uppers that rise above the ankles and protect them

high treason *n* treason perpetrated by somebody against his or her own sovereign or country

high-up *n* HR same as **higher-up** (*informal*)

high-value target *n* an enemy person or site regarded by military personnel as of the highest priority and therefore essential to the successful completion of a mission

highveld /hī́ velt/ *n* in South Africa, the high-altitude grassy plateau of Gauteng and neighbouring Northern provinces

high-voltage *adj* 1. involving a voltage higher than 650 volts 2. virtuosic in skill, delivery, style, and performance ○ *a high-voltage rendition of the piano concerto*

high water *n* 1. same as **high tide** (senses 1–2) 2. the highest level reached by any stretch of water, e.g. during a flood (*hyphenated before a noun*) 3. the time when the water level of a river or other stretch of water is at its highest

high-water mark *n* 1. HIGHEST WATER LEVEL the highest level reached by any natural stretch of water, especially by the sea at high tide, but also by inland water such as a river during a flood 2. MARK SHOWING HIGHEST LEVEL a mark drawn to indicate the highest level reached by any natural stretch of water 3. PEAK OF SOMETHING a high point in an enterprise ○ *Winning the book award was the high-water mark in her career.*

high-water pants *npl US* trousers that are too short, especially because the person wearing them has grown out of them (*slang*)

highway /hī́ way/ *n* 1. ROADS PUBLIC ROAD any public road (*formal*; *often used before a noun*) 2. N Am MAIN ROAD a principal road, especially one that connects towns or cities and is part of a numbered system (*often used before a noun*) 3. DIRECT WAY a direct route or course ○ *the highway to fame*

Highway Code *n* a government-published booklet containing rules and information relating to the use of public roads in the United Kingdom, or the body of conventions that govern road use

highwayman /hī́ waymən/ (*plural* **-men** /-mən/) *n* formerly, somebody who forced people travelling by road to stop, usually at gunpoint, and robbed them

highway patrol *n* the law enforcement agency that patrols the public highways in some states of the United States

highway robbery *n N Am* same as **daylight robbery** (*informal*)

High Weald /hī́ weeld/ region between the North and South Downs in southeastern England, lying in

parts of East and West Sussex, Kent, and Surrey. Area: 1,460 sq. km/569 sq. mi.

high wire *n* a tightrope stretched high above the ground on which circus performers balance and perform acrobatics

high-wire *adj* holding the possibility of great risk, e.g. to life or reputation

High Wycombe /-wíkəm/ furniture-making town in Buckinghamshire, south-central England. Population: 71,718 (1991).

HIH *abbr* 1. Her Imperial Highness 2. His Imperial Highness

hi-hat cymbals *npl* MUSIC another spelling of **high-hat cymbals**

hijab /hi jáab/ *n* 1. a head covering worn by some Muslim women to conceal their hair and neck 2. the Islamic practice of dressing modestly in clothing that covers most of the body [Via Persian < Arabic *ḥajaba* 'to veil']

hijack /hī́ jak/, **highjack** *vt* (**-jacks, -jacking, -jacked**) 1. SEIZE TRANSPORT VEHICLE to take forcible control of a public transport vehicle, e.g. a passenger aircraft while in transit, taking the people on board hostage, and often diverting it to another destination 2. STOP VEHICLE TO ROB IT to seize a motor vehicle, e.g. an armoured car carrying money, in order to rob it of its contents 3. STEAL SOMETHING FROM SEIZED VEHICLE to steal merchandise, money, or any other items from a hijacked motor vehicle 4. STEAL IDEA to take somebody else's idea and use it, especially to the exclusion or detriment of the person from whom it was taken (*informal*) ■ *n* TRANSP same as **hijacking** [Early 20C. Origin ?] —**hijacker** *n*

hijacking /hī́ jaking/, **highjacking** *n* the forcible seizure of a public transport vehicle, e.g. a passenger aircraft while in transit, taking those on board hostage, and often diverting it to another destination

hijiki /hi jíki/, **hiziki** /-zí-/ *n* a Japanese seaweed that turns black when dried and is sold shredded to be used in cooking [Late 20C. < Japanese]

hijinks *n* another spelling of **high jinks** (*informal*)

hijra /híjjrə/ *n* in South Asia, a member of a community of male transvestites or eunuchs, traditionally performing as singers or dancers at religious festivals or on social occasions such as baptisms or weddings [< Hindi]

hike /hīk/ *v* (**hikes, hiking, hiked**) 1. *vti* TAKE LONG WALK to go for a long walk in the countryside, usually for pleasure 2. *vi* MIL GO ON TRAINING MARCH to march in a training exercise 3. *vt* RAISE AMOUNT OF SOMETHING to increase taxes, prices, or the level or quantity of something suddenly and by a large amount ○ *rumours that they plan to hike oil prices* 4. *vt* PULL SOMETHING UPWARDS to pull or raise something with a sudden strong movement ■ *n* 1. PLEASURABLE LONG WALK a long walk, usually across country for pleasure 2. SUDDEN LARGE INCREASE a sudden large increase in prices, taxes, or the level or quantity of something ○ *an unexpected hike in gas prices* [Early 19C. Origin ?] —**hiker** *n* ◇ **take a hike** *N Am* to leave abruptly, or, more often, used to tell somebody who is unwelcome to leave (*informal*)

hike up *vti* to move something up from the proper position, or become moved up from the proper position ○ *Her coat had hiked up at the back.*

Hilarion /hi lérri ən/, **St** (290?–371) Palestinian monk. He was educated in Alexandria, Egypt, where he converted to Christianity. On his return to Palestine, he lived as a hermit in marshes near Gaza.

hilarious /hi láiri əss/ *adj* extremely funny [Early 19C. < Latin *hilaris* 'cheerful' < Greek *hilaros*] —**hilariously** *adv*

SYNONYMS See *funny*.

hilarity /hi lárrəti/ *n* amusement or merry laughter [15C. Via French < Latin *hilaritas* < *hilaris* (see HILARIOUS)]

Hilary term /hílləri-/ *n* the spring term at Oxford University and the Inns of Court [Late 16C. After *Hilarius* (300?–67), bishop of Poitiers, France]

Hilbert /hílbərt/, **David** (1862–1943) German mathematician. He is best known for reducing geometry to a series of abstract equations, thereby giving it a more mathematical foundation.

'The importance of a scientific work can

be measured by the number of previous publications it makes superfluous to read.' [David Hilbert. Quoted in *The Unnatural Nature of Science*, Lewis Wolpert; 1993]

Hildegard (of Bingen) /híldə gaard əv bíngən/, **St** (1098–1179) German writer and composer. A nun, she is remembered for her book of visions, *Scivias* (1141–52), and for her devotional music and poetry. She also developed the idea of universal gravitation.

hili ANAT plural of **hilus**

hill /hil/ *n* **1.** HIGH LAND an area of land, usually rounded in shape, that is higher than the surrounding land but not as high as a mountain ○ *the hills north of Tavistock* **2.** GRADIENT IN ROAD a slope or gradient in a road ○ *You'll need to drop into second gear for this hill.* **3.** PILE OF EARTH a pile of something such as earth ■ *vt* (**hills, hilling, hilled**) MAKE EARTH INTO PILE to pile up earth, especially around the base of plants [Old English *hyll* < Indo-European, 'be prominent'] —**hiller** *n* ◇ **over the hill** at an age considered too advanced in years for something, or supposedly past the prime of life (*informal*)

Hill *n* same as **Capitol Hill** (*informal*) ○ *has worked on the Hill for two years*

Hill /hil/, **Archibald** (1886–1977) British physiologist. He was joint winner of the Nobel Prize in physiology or medicine (1922) for his research into the production of heat in muscle contractions. Full name **Hill, Archibald Vivian**

Hill, Damon (*b.* 1960) British racing driver. The son of Graham Hill, he won the Formula One world championship in 1996. Full name **Hill, Damon Graham Devereux**

Hill, David (1802–70) British photographer and painter. He is remembered for his collaboration with Robert Adamson on the production of about 1,500 photographs. Full name **Hill, David Octavius**

Hill, Ernestine (1899–1972) Australian author. She wrote the novels *The Great Australian Loneliness* (1937) and *My Love Must Wait* (1941).

Hill, Graham (1929–75) British racing driver. The father of Damon Hill, he was winner of the Grand Prix world championship (1962, 1968) and the Indianapolis 500 (1966). Full name **Hill, Norman Graham**

Hillary /híləri/, **Sir Edmund** (*b.* 1919) New Zealand mountaineer and explorer. On 29 May 1953, he and Tenzing Norkay became the first climbers to reach the summit of Mount Everest. Full name **Hillary, Sir Edmund Percival**

'Well, we knocked the bastard off!'
[Edmund Hillary. On summiting Mount Everest (1953), *Nothing Venture, Nothing Win*; 1975]

hillbilly /híl bili/ (*plural* **-lies**) *n* N Am a term used by people from the country to describe themselves with pride, but used by others as an insult for people whom they regard as ignorant and unsophisticated (*informal*; *offensive in some contexts*) [Early 20C. < pet form of the name *William*]

hillbilly music *n* a variety of country music, especially the music of the Appalachian Mountains, that features fiddles, banjos, guitars, and hammer dulcimers

hill climb *n* a competition in which car or motorcycle drivers compete to set the fastest time in reaching the top of a steep slope

hill country *n* NZ, US hilly rural land, especially when used as pasture for sheep or cattle

hillcrest /híl krest/ *n* the summit or the highest ridge of a hill

Hillel (the Elder) /híl el-/ (70? BC–AD 10?) Jewish rabbi and teacher. He founded a liberal school of scriptural interpretation that influenced later Jewish religious leaders.

Hilliard /híli ərd/, **Nicholas** (1547–1619) English painter and goldsmith. He is regarded as the founder of the English school of painting miniatures, and his portraits include Mary, Queen of Scots, and Elizabeth I.

hill myna *n* a black bird of the starling family often kept as a cagebird because of its ability to mimic human words. Native to: South Asia. Latin name: *Gracula religiosa*.

hillock /híllək/ *n* a small hill or mound —**hillocked** *adj* —**hillocky** *adj*

Hills hoist /hílz-/ *n* Aus a metal structure consisting of a pole surmounted by a rotating metal frame that supports clothes lines [After Lancelot Leonard ('Lance') *Hill* (1902–86)]

hillside /híl sīd/ *n* the slope or side of a hill

hill station *n* in South Asia, a town in the hills established by the British as a place of respite from the summer heat for officials and their families

hilltop /híl top/ *n* the summit of a hill

hilly /híli/ (**-ier, -iest**) *adj* **1.** having many hills ○ *hilly countryside* **2.** having a steep incline —**hilliness** *n*

hilt /hilt/ *n* the handle of a sword, knife, or dagger [Old English *hilt(e)* < Germanic] ◇ **(up) to the hilt** to the maximum

Hilton /híltən/, **Conrad** (1887–1979) US hotel-chain owner and executive. He bought many hotels and founded the Hilton Hotel Corporation in 1946.

Hilton, James (1900–54) British novelist. He wrote *Lost Horizon* (1933) and *Good-bye, Mr. Chips* (1934).

hilum /híləm/ (*plural* **-la** /-lə/) *n* **1.** a scar on the seed of a plant indicating where it was attached to the ovule **2.** ANZ, N Am same as **hilus** [Mid-17C. < Latin, 'trifle']

hilus /híləss/ (*plural* **-li** /-lī/) *n* UK an opening through which blood vessels and nerves enter and leave an organ. ANZ, N Am term **hilum** [Mid-19C. < modern Latin, alteration of HILUM]

him *stressed* /him/; *unstressed* /im/ *pron* used to refer to a man, boy, or male animal who has been previously mentioned or whose identity is known (*used as the object or complement of a verb or preposition*) ○ *She handed him the phone without a word.* ○ *John closed the door behind him.* ○ *It's him, I know it's him.* [Old English < Germanic]

HIM *abbr* **1.** Her Imperial Majesty **2.** His Imperial Majesty

Himachal Pradesh /hi máachəl prə désh/ mountainous state in northern India. Capital: Simla. Population: 6,077,248 (2001). Area: 55,673 sq. km/21,495 sq. mi.

Himalaya

Himalaya /hímmə láy ə/, **Himalayas** /-láy əz/ mountain system in southern Asia. Its highest peak, and the highest mountain in the world, is Mount Everest, 8,848 m/29,028 ft. Length: 2,400 km/1,500 mi. —**Himalayan** *adj*

Himalayan cat *n* ANZ, N Am a long-haired cat with the markings of a Siamese cat, bred by crossing a Persian cat with a Siamese cat. UK term **colourpoint**

Himalia /hi máali ə/ *n* a small natural satellite of Jupiter, discovered in 1904. It is approximately 180 km/112 mi. in diameter. [Late 20C. Probably < Greek *himalis*, name for DEMETER < *himalios* 'abundant']

himation /hi mátti on/ *n* in ancient Greece, a loose outer garment worn by men and women, consisting of a large rectangular piece of cloth draped over one shoulder and under the opposite arm [Mid-19C. < Greek, 'small garment' < *hima* 'garment' < *hennunai* 'clothe']

Himmler /hímmlər/, **Heinrich** (1900–45) German Nazi official. The head of the Nazi police forces (1936–45), he committed suicide rather than face trial for his part in the Holocaust.

'Most of you know what it means when a hundred corpses are lying together, when five hundred are lying there, or when a

thousand are lying there...This is an unwritten and never-to-be-written page of glory in our history.'
[Heinrich Himmler, *Speech to the S.S. (Nazi security forces), Poznań, Poland*; October 1943]

himself *stressed* /him sélf/; *unstressed* /im sélf/ CORE MEANING: the form of 'him' used in reflexive and emphatic contexts ○ *After a final struggle with himself, he handed the papers over.* ○ *If he himself doesn't know what he's doing, I don't see how I can help him.* ○ *He did it himself.*
pron **1.** REFERRING TO MALE SUBJECT OF VERB used to refer to the same man, boy, or male animal as the subject of the verb ○ *He decided to treat himself.* ○ *his sense of pride in himself* **2.** USED FOR EMPHASIS used to emphasize or clarify which man, boy, or male animal is being referred to, often introducing a note of surprise or awe ○ *a visit from the Prince himself* **3.** ALONE OR WITHOUT HELP used to show that a man, boy, or male animal is alone or unaided ○ *sitting by himself in a corner* ○ *tied his shoelaces himself* **4.** NORMAL SELF his normal self in terms of personality, health, or behaviour ○ *not feeling himself* **5.** also **Himself** *Ireland, Scotland* IMPORTANT MALE PERSON an important, or often self-important, man or boy (*informal*; *often used ironically*) ○ *Himself is wanting a word.*

Himyarite /hímmyə rīt/ *n* (*plural* **-ites** or *same*) a member of an ancient people who lived in the southern Arabian Peninsula ■ *adj* relating to the Himyarites [Mid-19C. After *Himyar*, legendary king of Yemen]

Himyaritic /hímmyə ríttik/ *n* an extinct language spoken by the ancient Himyarites in southwestern Arabia. It belongs to the Semitic branch of the Afro-Asiatic family of African languages. —**Himyaritic** *adj*

Hinayana /héenə yáanə/ *n* a form of Buddhism characterized by adherence to the early Pali scriptures and the nontheistic pursuit of purification through Nirvana. It is found mainly in Sri Lanka and Southeast Asia. [Mid-19C. < Sanskrit, 'lesser vehicle'] —**Hinayanist** *n* —**Hinayanistic** /héenə yaa nístik/ *adj*

Hinchinbrook Island /hínchinbrŏŏk-/ island off the northeastern coast of Australia, near the town of Caldwell in northern Queensland. Area: 394 sq. km/152 sq. mi.

Hinckley /híngkli/ town in Leicestershire, central England. Population: 40,608 (1991).

Hincks /hingks/, **Sir Francis** (1807–85) Irish-born Canadian colonial administrator. He advocated a bicultural nation, and cofounded the Reform Party in 1841.

hind[1] /hīnd/ *adj* at or forming the back part of something, especially a bodily organ or an animal ○ *the hind legs of a donkey* [13C. Probably shortening of BEHIND]

hind[2] /hīnd/ *n* **1.** a female red deer **2.** a spotted sea fish that is a type of groper. Native to: Atlantic Ocean. Genus: *Epinephelus*. [Old English < Indo-European, 'hornless']

Hind. *abbr* **1.** Hindi **2.** Hindu **3.** Hindustan **4.** Hindustani

hindbrain /hínd brayn/ *n* the rearmost part of the brain in a vertebrate embryo, which develops into the cerebellum, pons, and medulla oblongata

Hindemith /híndə mit/, **Paul** (1895–1963) German composer and violinist. A pioneer of *Gebrauchsmusik*, a utilitarian approach to composition, he also wrote ballets, concertos, and operas, including *Mathis der Maler* (1935).

Hindenburg /híndən burg/, **Paul von** (1847–1934) Prussian-born president of the German Republic (1925–34). A general in World War I, he became second president of the German Republic in 1925, and appointed Adolf Hitler chancellor in 1933.

'That man for a Chancellor? I'll make him a postmaster and he can lick the stamps with my head on them.'
[Paul von Hindenburg. Referring to Hitler, 13 August 1932, *Hindenburg: The Wooden Titan*, J. W. Wheeler-Bennett; 1936]

Hindenburg line *n* a strong defensive line of fortifications built by the German army near the border between France and Belgium in 1916–17 and

LANGUAGE HERITAGE ***Hindi*** Much of English is made up of words from other languages, and Hindi is a contributor in this respect. Many Hindi terms are used in South Asian English; others that were once the preserve of traders and colonial settlers are familiar outside the subcontinent through emigrant communities; others are completely naturalized in English, often to the extent that any sense of their origins is lost.

In this last category are, for example, ***bandanna, bangle, bungalow, cushy, dinghy, loot,*** and ***shampoo,*** and from Hindi in transit from Sanskrit, ***cheetah, chit, jungle, pundit,*** and ***thug. Bandanna,*** for example, arrived in the mid-18th century, probably via Portuguese, from Hindi *bāndhnū,* a method of tie-dyeing; ***bungalow*** (late 17th) is from Hindi *banglā* 'of Bengal' (a former province of northeastern India); ***cushy*** (early 20th), from Hindi *khūsh* 'pleasant', is so much part of the English language that it has developed derivatives *cushily* and *cushiness;* ***shampoo*** (mid-18th) was adopted from Hindi *cāpō,* from *cāpnā* 'knead, massage'. Europeans trading and empire-building in South Asia not only received words from, but also gave words to, the contact languages, and in the case of ***veranda*** were given one back: Hindi-speakers took Portuguese *varanda* 'railing, balcony' as *varaṇḍā* and in the early 18th century passed it on to English.

Names of flora and fauna inevitably were adopted into English, for example ***chukar*** (a partridge), ***guar*** (a plant with seeds used for gum), ***krait*** (a poisonous snake), and ***mugger*** (a crocodile).

South Asian cuisine has had considerable impact on English: migrants include ***basmati*** rice (from Hindi *bāsmatī* 'fragrant'), ***bhaji*** (Hindi *bhājī* 'fried vegetables'), ***chapati*** (from Hindi *capātī,* from *capānā* 'flatten'), ***chutney, dhal, garam masala*** (literally 'hot spices'), ***jalebi, lassi, mung bean, paratha,*** and ***raita.*** Dishes have been adapted and created for Western tastes: ***kedgeree*** (from Hindi *khicṛī*), a dish consisting of rice with flaked smoked fish and hard-boiled eggs, is of British origin.

Numerous Hindi terms for cloth and clothing have also moved into English: *dungarees* are made of ***dungaree*** (from Hindi *dungrī* 'kind of coarse cloth', named after a village near Mumbai [Bombay]). Other migrants in this category include ***chappal, churidars, dhoti,*** and ***nainsook.***

Within South Asian English, Hindi and English freely interact. English suffixes combine with Hindi forms (***goondaism*** from ***goonda*** 'ruffian, hooligan'); Hindi suffixes combine with English (***filmi,*** with the Hindi adjective suffix *-i*); Hindi and English nouns make hybrid compounds (***cyber dhaba*** 'roadside stall where people can use computers or the Internet', with *dhaba* a Hindi word for a roadside food stall); and Hindi terms are translated into English (***good name*** 'somebody's last name or family name', a loan translation from Hindi *shubh naam*).

South Asian immigrants to the Caribbean also brought some Hindi words, for example ***aja*** 'the father of somebody's father' (from Hindi *daadaa*), ***aji*** 'the mother of somebody's father' (from Hindi *daadii*), and ***bhaigan*** 'aubergine'; shared South Asian and Caribbean cuisine is reflected in words such as ***achar*** and ***roti.*** And elsewhere in the world South Asian traders have left their mark on the names of currencies: in Oman the ***baiza*** (via Arabic from Hindi *paisā*) and in the Maldives the ***rufiyaa*** (via Divehi, a form of Sinhalese, from Hindi *rūpiyā* 'rupee'). See also ***Sanskrit***

breached by an Allied offensive in 1918 [Because Paul von Hindenburg directed retreat to it]

hinder[1] /híndər/ *vt* (**-ders, -dering, -dered**) to delay or prevent the development or progress of somebody or something ○ *A heavy snowfall has hindered rescuers' attempts to reach the stranded climbers.* ■ *n* in squash and handball, an opponent's accidental interference, preventing fair and unobstructed return of the ball [Old English *hindrian* < Germanic] —**hinderer** *n*

SYNONYMS hinder, block, hamper, hold back, restrain, impede, obstruct

CORE MEANING: to put difficulties in the way of progress

hinder to delay or prevent the development or progress of somebody or something ○ *Does migration help or hinder a country's development?* ○ *Nothing in the by-laws can hinder the party from pushing its proposed measures through.* **block** to prevent or restrict movement through, into, or out of something, or prevent something from taking place ○ *Guards stepped forward to block the vehicle trying to enter the air base.* ○ *The company's operations were totally blocked by the injunction.* **hamper** to restrict the free movement or progress of somebody or something ○ *The rescue effort, hampered by foul weather over the weekend, was again halted on Monday.* ○ *She claimed her injury did not hamper her in today's race.* **hold back** to keep something from happening, or keep somebody from doing something ○ *The expense of data is holding back development in this area.* ○ *He stopped suddenly and held the child back.* **restrain** to keep somebody or something under control or within limits ○ *There were crash barriers along the route to restrain the crowds.* **impede** to interfere with the movement, progress, or development of somebody or something ○ *We had no torches, but darkness did not impede our progress.* ○ *The two leaders agreed not to let their rival claims to offshore oil fields impede the development of trade.* **obstruct** to cause a serious delay in action or progress, or to cause a blockage in a road, course, or passage ○ *pleaded guilty to charges of conspiring to obstruct justice* ○ *Obstructing the doors causes delay and can be dangerous.*

hinder[2] /híndər/ *adj* at or towards the rear of something ○ *at the hinder end of the conference* [Old English, origin ?]

~~**hinderance**~~ incorrect spelling of **hindrance**

Hindi /híndi/ *n* an Indic official language of India that developed from a literary form of Hindustani and is widely used as a lingua franca in many parts of the world. Native speakers: 200 million. Other speakers: 700 million. [Early 19C. < Urdu *hindī* < *Hind* 'India'] —**Hindi** *adj*

hindmilk /hínd milk/ *n* the milk produced after foremilk during breast-feeding, which is rich in fat content and high in calories

hindmost /hínd mōst/ *adj* farthest back, or last (*literary*)

hindquarter /hínd kwawrtər/ *n* either of the two back quarters of a carcass of beef, lamb, veal, or mutton consisting of one leg and one or two ribs ■ **hindquarters** *npl* the hind legs and adjoining parts of a four-legged animal

hindrance /híndrənss/ *n* **1.** somebody or something that prevents or makes it difficult for somebody to do something **2.** the act of obstructing progress

hindsight /hínd sīt/ *n* the ability or opportunity to understand and judge an event or experience after it has occurred ○ *With hindsight we should have chosen a warmer colour for the dining room.* ○ *That's easy to say with the benefit of hindsight.*

Hindu /hin dóo, hín doo/ *n* **1.** FOLLOWER OF HINDUISM somebody whose religion is Hinduism **2.** SOMEBODY FROM HINDUSTAN somebody who comes from Hindustan ■ *adj* **1.** OF HINDUISM relating to Hinduism **2.** OF HINDUS relating to Hindus or their culture [Mid-17C. Via Urdu < Persian *Hindū* < *Hind* 'India']

Hinduism /híndoo izəm/ *n* a major religion and religious tradition of South Asia, the oldest worldwide religion, characterized by a belief in reincarnation and a large pantheon of gods and goddesses

Hindu Kush /híndoo kóosh/ mountain system in Central Asia mainly in Afghanistan but extending into Jammu and Kashmir. The highest peak is Tirich Mir, 7,690 m/25,230 ft. Length: 1,000 km/600 mi.

Hindustan /híndoo staán/ *n* the Hindi-speaking region of Northern India, stretching from the Himalayan range to the Deccan and from Assam to Punjab, or the wider Hindi-speaking area of South Asia. The term is sometimes used to indicate the Ganges Plain, or sometimes the whole of India or parts of South Asia.

Hindustani /híndoo staáni/ *n* GROUP OF S ASIAN LANGUAGES a group of South Asian languages and dialects that includes all forms of Urdu and Hindi ■ *adj* **1.** OF HINDUSTAN relating to Hindustan **2.** OF HINDUSTANI relating to Hindustani [Early 17C. Via Urdu < Persian *Hindūstānī* 'of the Indian country']

Hindustani music *n S Asia* the classical music of northern India

Hindutva /hin dóotvə/ *n S Asia* great enthusiasm for the Hindu way of life, especially when including the desire for a Hindu state [< Hindi]

Hines /hīnz/, **Earl** (1905–83) US musician. A jazz pianist, he formed his own band (1928) and collaborated with Charlie Parker, Dizzy Gillespie, and Louis Armstrong. Full name **Hines, Earl Kenneth.** Known as **Fatha Hines**

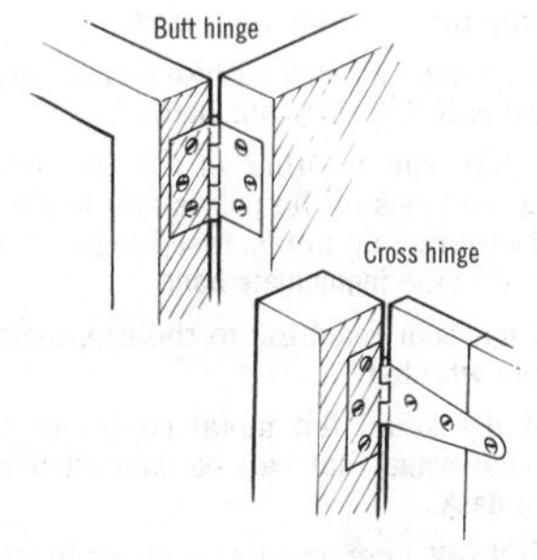

hinge

hinge /hinj/ *n* **1.** JOINT a movable joint of metal or plastic used to fasten two things, e.g. a box and its lid, together and allow one of them to pivot ○ *The hinges on the door need oiling.* **2.** ZOOL LIGAMENT a part in animals that operates like a hinge, e.g. the ligament that opens and closes the two halves of a clam or other bivalve mollusc **3.** ANAT same as **hinge joint 4.** SOMETHING VITAL something on which a subsequent action or an outcome depends **5.** STICKY PAPER STRIP a thin gummed paper strip that is folded in half to affix postage stamps to the pages of an album [13C. Probably ultimately < Germanic] —**hinged** *adj* —**hingeless** *adj*

hinge on (**hinges on, hinging on, hinged on**) *vt* to depend completely on something ○ *The success of the plan hinges on your full cooperation.*

hinge joint *n* a joint that allows movement in only one plane, e.g. a knee or elbow joint. Technical name **ginglymus**

Hinglish /híng glish/ *n* a language that combines features of Hindi and English, used in South Asia and elsewhere

Hinkler /híngklər/, **Bert** (1892–1933) Australian aviator. In 1928 he completed the first solo flight from London, England, to Darwin, Australia, in 16 days. Full name **Hinkler, Herbert John Louis**

hinny /hínni/ (*plural* **-nies**) *n* the offspring of a stallion and a female ass [Early 17C. Via Latin *hinnus* < Greek *(g)innos*]

Hinshelwood /hínsh'l wòod/, **Sir Cyril Norman** (1897–1967) British chemist. He was joint winner of the Nobel Prize in chemistry (1956) for his research into the kinetics of chemical chain reactions.

hint /hint/ *vti* (**hints, hinting, hinted**) SUGGEST SOMETHING INDIRECTLY to convey an idea or information in a roundabout way ○ *The President hinted that he might not seek a second term.* ■ *n* **1.** INDIRECT SUGGESTION an idea or information conveyed in a roundabout way ○ *Our daughter has been dropping hints that she'd like a guitar for her birthday.* **2.** PIECE OF ADVICE a useful piece of advice, or a practical suggestion ○ *The book had lots of useful hints on how to grow vegetables.* **3.** VERY SMALL AMOUNT an amount or trace of something that is so small that it can only just be noticed ○ *The walls need a hint of yellow.* [Early 17C. Probably alteration of obsolete *hent* 'grasp' < Germanic] —**hintingly** *adv* ◇ **take the hint** to understand what is being implied or suggested and to act accordingly

hinterland /híntər land/ *n* **1.** AREA SURROUNDING CITY a region, including communities and rural areas, that surrounds a city and depends on it economically and culturally ○ *an analysis of Milan and its hinterland* **2.** LAND ADJACENT TO WATER the land that lies next to coastline or a river **3.** REMOTE COUNTRY REGION a region that is remote from cities or their cultural influence [Late 19C. < German < *hinter* 'behind' + *Land* 'land']

hip[1] /hip/ *n* **1.** SIDE OF BODY BELOW WAIST the area on each side of the body between the waist and the thigh **2.** ANAT same as **hip joint 3.** ROOF ANGLE the angle formed where two adjacent sides of a sloping roof meet **4.** POINTED END OF OBSTACLE in skateboarding, the place where a ramp or obstacle comes to a point [Old English *hype* < Germanic] —**hipped** *adj*

hip[2] /hip/ *n* BOT same as **rosehip** [Old English *hēope* < Indo-European, 'thorn']

hip[3] /hip/ (**hipper, hippest**) *adj* aware of and influenced by the latest fashions in clothes, music, or ideas (*slang*) [Early 20C. Alteration of HEP[1]] —**hiply** *adv* —**hipness** *n* ◇ **be hip to something** *US* to be aware of something that is going on (*informal*)

hip bath *n* a bathtub shaped like a chair that you sit in to bathe. N Am term **sitz bath**

hipbone /híp bōn/ *n* either of the two large bones forming the sides of the pelvis and made up of the ilium, ischium, and pubis, fused together in adults. Technical name **innominate bone**

hip boot *n* a boot reaching to the hip, usually worn by people who fish

hip flask *n* a small flat metal container for an alcoholic beverage that can be carried in a pocket. US term **flask**

hip hip hooray *interj* used as a cheer to express joy or approval of somebody or something [*Hip*, origin ?]

hip-hop *n* a form of popular culture that started in African American inner-city areas, characterized by rap music, graffiti art, and breakdancing [< HIP[3]]

hip-huggers /-huggərz/ *npl N Am* CLOTHING same as **hipsters**

hip joint *n* the joint formed between the head of the thigh bone and the hipbone

~~hipocrisy~~ incorrect spelling of **hypocrisy**

Hipparchus /hi paárkəss/ (190?–120? BC) Greek astronomer and mathematician. The inventor of trigonometry, he also produced the earliest known star catalogue and discovered the precession of the equinoxes.

hippeastrum /híppi ástrəm/ *n* a cultivated plant belonging to the daffodil family. Flowers: huge, red or pink, funnel-shaped. Native to: Central and South America. Genus: *Hippeastrum*. [Early 19C. < modern Latin < Greek *hippeus* 'horseman' + *astron* 'star']

hipped /hipt/ *adj* preoccupied or obsessed with something (*informal*) ○ *She's just hipped on clothes.* [Early 20C. < HIP[3]]

hipped roof *n* ARCHIT same as **hip roof**

hippie /híppi/, **hippy** (*plural* **-pies**) *n* a young person, especially in the 1960s, who rejected accepted social and political values and proclaimed a belief in universal peace and love. Hippies often dressed unconventionally, lived communally, and used psychedelic drugs. (*informal*) [Mid-20C. < HIP[3]] —**hippiedom** —**hippiehood** *n* —**hippieness** *n*

hippo /híppō/ (*plural* **-pos**) *n* same as **hippopotamus** (*informal*) [Late 19C. Shortening]

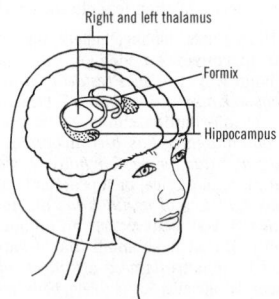

hippocampus (sense 2)

hippocampus /híppō kámpəss/ (*plural* **-pi** /-pī/) *n* **1.** a mythological sea creature with the head and forelegs of a horse and the tail of a fish **2.** a curved ridge of tissue in each cerebral hemisphere of the brain, concerned with basic drives, emotions, and short-term memory and forming part of the limbic system [Mid 16C. Via Latin < Greek *hippokampos* < *hippos* 'horse' + *kampos* 'sea monster'] —**hippocampal** *adj*

hip-pocket *n* a pocket at the back of a pair of trousers or a skirt [Late 19C]

hippocras /híppō krass/ *n* a medieval drink of spiced wine sweetened with honey [14C. Via Old French *hypocras* < medieval Latin (*vinum*) *Hippocraticum* 'wine of Hippocrates']

Hippocrates /hi pókrə teez/ (460?–377? BC) Greek phys-

---

ician. Known as 'the father of medicine', he gave his name to the Hippocratic oath. —**Hippocratic** /híppə kráttik/ *adj*

> 'Extreme remedies are most appropriate for extreme diseases.'
> [Hippocrates, *Aphorisms*; 415? BC]

Hippocratic oath *n* an oath traditionally taken by newly qualified doctors to observe the ethical standards of their profession, specifically to seek to preserve life [Because Hippocrates was the supposed author of such an oath]

hippodrome /híppə drōm/ *n* **1.** an open-air stadium in ancient Greece or Rome with an oval track that was used for horse or chariot racing **2.** a variety theatre or circus (*dated*) [Late 16C. Via French and Latin < Greek *hippodromos* < *hippos* 'horse' + *dromos* 'racecourse']

hippogriff /híppə grif/ *n* in Greek mythology, a monster with the body of a horse and the head, wings, and claws of a griffin [Mid-17C. Via French *hippogriffe* < Italian *ippogrifo* < Greek *hippos* 'horse' + Italian *grifo* 'griffin']

Hippolyta /hi póllitə/ *n* in Greek mythology, a queen of the Amazons. She was killed by Heracles because she refused to give up her girdle, which he had been sent to get as one of his labours.

Hippolytus /hi póllitəss/ *n* in Greek mythology, the son of Theseus. He was killed by Poseidon after rejecting the advances of his stepmother, Phaedra.

hippopotamus

hippopotamus /híppə póttəməss/ (*plural* **-muses** or **-mi** /-mī/) *n* a large amphibious animal that has a large head with a wide mouth, short legs, and a thick grey skin. Native to: rivers of eastern equatorial Africa. Latin name: *Hippopotamus amphibius*. [Mid-16C. Via Latin < Greek *hippopotamos* < *hippos* 'horse' + *potamos* 'river']

hippy[1] /híppi/ *n* another spelling of **hippie**

hippy[2] /híppi/ (**-pier, -piest**) *adj* having wide hips

hip roof *n* a roof with sloping ends as well as sides

hipster /hípstər/ *n* somebody conversant with fashions in music, clothes, and social attitudes, especially an enthusiast of modern jazz (*dated slang*) [< HIP[3]]

hipsters /hípstərz/ *npl* trousers that end at the hips instead of the waist. N Am term **hip-huggers** [< HIP[1]]

hiragana /heérə gaánə/ *n* a set of curly symbols, representing syllables and often conveying grammatical information when combined with pictorial symbols (**kanji**), used in writing Japanese. ◇ **kana** (sense 1), **katakana** [Early 19C. < Japanese, 'plain syllabary']

hire /hīr/ *v* (**hires, hiring, hired**) **1.** *vti* GIVE SOMEBODY WORK to employ somebody to work for you, or pay somebody to do a job for you **2.** *vt* PAY FOR USE OF SOMETHING to rent something from somebody for a period of time ○ *hired the village hall for the wedding reception* ◼ *n* ACT OF HIRING SOMETHING OR SOMEBODY the activity of renting something to somebody or of making the services of somebody available to another person for pay [Old English *hȳr* < Germanic] —**hirable** *adj* —**hirer** *n*

hire out *vt* to rent something to somebody or make the services of somebody available to another person for pay

hired gun /hírd-/ *n* (*slang*) **1.** *N Am* same as **hit man 2.** *ANZ, N Am* an expert brought in to solve a particularly complex or intractable problem ○ *The law firm brought in a hired gun from New York to*

---

handle the cross-examination of the prosecution's genetics expert at trial.

hired hand *n* a paid manual worker employed on a short-term basis, usually on a farm

hireling /hírling/ *n* somebody who works only for money, especially at menial or unpleasant tasks (*disapproving*)

hire purchase *n* a financing arrangement that enables somebody to take possession of an expensive item while making regular payments on it, with legal ownership transferred only after it is paid for. ◇ **installment plan**

hi-res /hí réz/, **high-res** *adj* COMPUT same as **high-resolution** (*informal*) [Shortening]

Hiri Motu /heéri mō too/ *n* a pidginized form of Motu that is an official language of Papua New Guinea. Native speakers: 150,000. —**Hiri Motu** *adj*

Hirohito, emperor of Japan

Hirohito /heérō heétō/ (1901–89) emperor of Japan. His reign (1926–89) was the longest in Japanese history. He renounced the belief that Japanese rulers are divine at the end of World War II (1945) and oversaw the transition to a constitutional monarchy.

> 'The war situation has developed not necessarily to Japan's advantage.'
> [Hirohito, announcing Japan's surrender, *Radio broadcast*; 15 August 1945]

Hiroshige /heérō sheé gay/ (1797–1858) Japanese artist. One of the most prolific and popular Japanese artists of the 19th century, he is known for his serene woodblock prints, particularly of landscapes. Full name **Hiroshige, Ando**

Hiroshima /hi róshimə, hírrə sheémə/ city in southwestern Honshu, Japan. It was devastated by the first atom bomb to be used in war, in August 1945. Population: 1,113,786 (2002).

hirple /húrp'l/ (**-les, -ling, -led**) *vi Scotland* to walk with a limp [15C. Probably < Old Norse *herpast* 'suffer from cramps']

Hirst /hurst/, **Damien** (*b.* 1965) British artist. He is known for his controversial experimental works, especially his series of animal carcasses preserved in formaldehyde. He won the Turner Prize in 1995.

hirsute /húr syoot/ *adj* **1.** having a large amount of hair ○ *a hirsute young man* **2.** describes a plant or plant part covered with long stiff hairs ○ *a hirsute leaf* [Early 17C. < Latin *hirsutus* 'shaggy'] —**hirsuteness** *n*

hirsutism /húr syootizəm/ *n* excessive growth of hair, e.g. on a woman's face or body

hirudin /hi roódin/ *n* a substance produced by the salivary glands of leeches that prevents blood from clotting [Early 20C. < Latin *hirudo* 'leech']

his *stressed* /hiz/; *unstressed* /iz/ *det, pron* indicates something belonging or relating to a man, boy, or male animal who has been previously mentioned or whose identity is known ○ *He stood at the sink washing his hands.* ○ *The fault was all his.* ○ *I went to school with a cousin of his.*

Hispanic /hi spánnik/ *adj* **1.** OF PEOPLE OF SPANISH DESCENT relating to people descended from Spanish or Latin-American people or their culture **2.** OF SPANISH-SPEAKING PEOPLE relating to Spanish-speaking people or their culture **3.** OF IBERIAN PENINSULA relating to Spain, Spain and Portugal, or Spain, Portugal, and Latin America **4.** OF ROMANCE LANGUAGES OF IBERIAN PENINSULA relating to the Romance languages of Spain, Portugal, or Latin America ◼ *n* PEOPLES same as **Hispanic American** [Late 16C. < Latin *Hispanicus* < *Hispania* 'Spain']

Hispanic American *n* somebody who comes from the United States and is of Spanish or Latin American descent —**Hispanic American** *adj*

Hispanicise *vt* another spelling of **Hispanicize**

Hispanicism /hi spánnisizəm/ *n* a Spanish word, expression, or other linguistic feature that has been adopted into another language [Mid-20C. < Latin *Hispania* 'Spain']

Hispanicist /hi spánnissist/ *n* a scholar of the languages and cultures of Spain and Spanish-speaking countries

Hispanicize /hi spánni sīz/ (**-cizes, -cizing, -cized**), **Hispanicise** (**-cises, -cising, -cised**) *vt* to make somebody or something Spanish in character, style, or culture —**Hispanicization** /hi spánni sī záysh'n/ *n*

Hispaniola /híspən yṓlə/ island in the Caribbean Sea, lying southeast of Cuba and west of Puerto Rico, and divided between Haiti and the Dominican Republic. Originally the home of an Arawak people, it was colonized by Spain after Christopher Columbus landed there in 1492 and named it Española. The western part, now Haiti, was ceded to France in 1697. Area: 78,460 sq. km/30,290 sq. mi.

Hispanism /híspənizəm/ *n* LING same as **Hispanicism**

Hispanist /híspənist/ *n* LING same as **Hispanicist**

Hispano /hi spánnō, hi spaán ō, híspə nṓ/ (*plural* **-nos**) *n* somebody of Spanish descent who lives in the southwestern United States. Many Hispanos are descended from people who lived in the region before its annexation by the United States. [Mid-20C. < Latin *Hispanus* 'Spanish']

Hispano-American *n* PEOPLES same as **Hispanic American** —**Hispano-American** *adj*

hispid /híspid/ *adj* rough, especially covered with stiff hairs or bristles ○ *a hispid leaf* [Mid-17C. < Latin *hispidus*] —**hispidity** /hi spíddəti/ *n*

hiss /hiss/ *v* (**hisses, hissing, hissed**) **1.** *vi* MAKE 'S' SOUND to make a sound like a loud continuous 's' ○ *the sound of car tyres hissing over a wet road* **2.** *vti* SHOW NEGATIVE OPINION OF SOMETHING to show disapproval or dislike of somebody or something, e.g. a performance, by making a hissing sound **3.** *vti* WHISPER LOUDLY to whisper loudly and angrily ○ *'Stop biting your nails', she hissed.* ■ *n* **1.** SOUND LIKE 'S' a sound like a loud continuous 's' ○ *the hiss of escaping air* **2.** SOUND EXPRESSING DISAPPROVAL a hissing sound used to express disapproval or dislike ○ *The news was greeted with a hiss.* [14C An imitation of the sound] —**hisser** *n*

Hiss /hiss/, **Alger** (1904–96) US lawyer and government official. A former senior State Department official, he was accused by the journalist Whittaker Chambers (1948) of spying for the Soviet Union, and imprisoned for perjury despite his protestations of innocence.

hisself *stressed* /hiz sélf/; *unstressed* /iz sélf/ *pron* same as **himself** (*nonstandard*)

hissy fit /híssi-/ *n* Can, Southern US a temper tantrum [Origin ?]

hist. *abbr* **1.** MED histology **2.** historic **3.** historical **4.** history

hist- *prefix* same as **histo-** (*used before vowels*)

histaminase /hi stámmi nayz, -nayss/ *n* an enzyme in the digestive system that inactivates histamine

histamine /hístə meen/ *n* an amine released by immune cells that produces allergic reactions [Early 20C. Blend of HISTIDINE + AMINE] —**histaminic** /hístə mínnik/ *adj*

histidine

histidine /hístə deen/ *n* an amino acid involved in the repair of tissues that is also the precursor of histamine. Formula: $C_6H_9N_3O_2$.

histiocyte /hísti ə sīt/ *n* a large immobile scavenging cell (**macrophage**) found in connective tissue —**histiocytic** /hísti ə síttik/ *adj*

histo- *prefix* living tissue ○ *histochemistry* [< Greek *histos* 'web']

histochemistry /híst ō kémmistri/ *n* the biochemistry of cells and tissues —**histochemical** *adj* —**histochemically** *adv*

histocompatibility /hístōkəm páttə bílləti/ *n* the degree of similarity between some antigens that determines the degree of success of a tissue graft or blood transfusion —**histocompatible** /hístōkəm páttəb'l/ *adj*

histocompatibility antigen *n* an antigen occurring on the surface of tissue cells that is used in self-identification and determines the acceptance of a tissue graft or blood transfusion

histodialysis /hístō dī álləssiss/ *n* MED same as **histolysis**

histogenesis /hístō jénnəssiss/ *n* the development of tissues —**histogenetic** /hístōjə néttik/ *adj* —**histogenetically** *adv* —**histogenic** /híst ō jénnik/ *adj* —**histogenically** *adv*

histogram /hístə gram/ *n* a statistical graph of a frequency distribution in which vertical rectangles of different heights are proportionate to corresponding frequencies

histology /hi stólləji/ *n* a branch of anatomy concerned with the study of the microscopic structures of animal and plant tissue —**histologic** /hístə lójjik/ *adj* —**histological** *adj* —**histologically** *adv* —**histologist** *n*

histolysis /hi stólləssiss/ *n* the breakdown and disintegration of bodily tissue —**histolytic** /hístə líttik/ *adj* —**histolytically** *adv*

histone /híst ōn/ *n* a simple protein bound to DNA, involved in the coiling of chromosomes. There are five types, together constituting about half the mass of chromosomes. [Late 19C. < German *Histon*]

histopathology /hístōpə thólləji/ *n* a branch of pathology concerned with the study of the microscopic changes in diseased tissues —**histopathologic** /hístō pàthə lójjik/ *adj* —**histopathological** *adj* —**histopathologically** *adv* —**histopathologist** *n*

histophysiology /hístō fízzi ólləji/ *n* a branch of physiology concerned with the structure and function of tissues —**histophysiologic** /-fízzi ə lójjik/ *adj* —**histophysiological** *adj*

histoplasmosis /hístō plaz móssiss/ *n* a severe disease of the lungs with symptoms resembling flu, caused by the fungus *Histoplasma capsulatum* [Early 20C. < modern Latin *Histoplasma*, genus name]

historian /hi stáwri ən/ *n* **1.** a student of or expert in history **2.** a writer of an account of historical events [15C. < French *historien* < Latin *historia* (see HISTORY)]

historiated /hi stáwri aytid/ *adj* describes decorative initials in books or maps and plans that are illustrated with symbolic flowers and animals or symbols in the form of flowers or animals [Late 19C. < French *historié* or directly < medieval Latin *historiare* 'adorn (with historical scenes), relate' < Latin *historia* (see HISTORY)]

historic /hi stórrik/ *adj* **1.** important in or affecting the course of history ○ *Yalta, scene of the historic meeting between Roosevelt, Stalin, and Churchill* ○ *a historic election victory* **2.** same as **historical** (sense 1)

USAGE historic or **historical**? Both these adjectives are derived from the noun *history*, but they are used in different ways. ***Historical*** means 'existing or happening in the past', 'describing events or people from the past', and 'relating to the past or to the study of history'; it may describe people or things, as in *a historical figure* or *a historical novel*. The principal meaning of ***historic***, on the other hand, is 'important in history': *the historic moment when the Berlin Wall came down*. ***Historic*** can sometimes be used in place of ***historical*** in the sense 'existing in, happening in, or relating to the past', but ***historical*** should never be used in place of ***historic***.

---

historical /hi stórrik'l/ *adj* **1.** FORMERLY EXISTING OR HAPPENING existing, happening, or relating to the past ○ *an*

important historical personage **2.** FORMERLY USED worn or used by people in the past ○ *historical uniforms of the 18th century* **3.** SUPPORTED BY FACTS FROM HISTORY based on the past, or describing people who lived in the past or events that happened in the past ○ *historical fiction* ○ *a historical film* **4.** RELATING TO STUDY OF HISTORY relating to or involving the study of history ○ *a series of historical monographs* **5.** RELATING TO EVOLUTION OF SOMETHING relating to the gradual change and development of phenomena such as languages or societies ○ *historical sociology*

USAGE See *historic*.

historical geology *n* a branch of geology that deals with the geological history of Earth

historical linguistics *n* the study of language as it changes and develops through time (*takes a singular verb*)

historically /hi stórrikli/ *adv* **1.** according to or with reference to history or its course ○ *The law will prove to be historically significant.* **2.** used to indicate that something has happened often in the past ○ *Historically, a rise in interest rates slows the rate of inflation.*

historical materialism *n* the part of Marx's theory of dialectical materialism that maintains that the development of social thought and institutions is based on material economic forces

historical novel *n* a novel set in the past that includes real events and people from that period

historical present *n* the present tense used to narrate actions that happened in the past to make them seem more vivid

historicise *vt* another spelling of **historicize**

historicism /hi stórrissizəm/ *n* **1.** the belief that natural laws beyond human control determine historical events **2.** the theory that each period of history has its own unique beliefs and values and can only be understood in its historical context —**historicist** *n*

historicity /hístə ríssəti/ *n* the state or fact of being historically authentic

historicize /hi stórri sīz/ (**-cizes, -cizing, -cized**), **historicise** (**-cises, -cising, -cised**) *vt* to give something the appearance of historical truth —**historicization** /hi stórri sī záysh'n/ *n*

Historic Places Trust *n* the statutory body in New Zealand whose duty it is to preserve historic sites, especially those of the Maori

historiography /hi stórri óggrəfi/ *n* **1.** METHODS OF HISTORICAL RESEARCH the principles, theories, or methods of historical research or writing **2.** WRITING OF HISTORY the writing of history based on scholarly disciplines such as the analysis and evaluation of source materials **3.** AVAILABLE DATA ON HISTORICAL TOPIC the existing findings and interpretations relating to a particular historical topic **4.** HISTORICAL LITERATURE a body of historical literature [Mid-16C. Via medieval Latin < Greek *historiographia* < *historia* (see HISTORY) + *graphia* 'writing'] —**historiographic** /hi stórri ə gráffik/ *n* —**historiographical** *adj* —**historiographically** *adv*

history /hístəri/ (*plural* **-ries**) *n* **1.** WHAT HAS HAPPENED the past events of a period in time or in the life or development of a people, an institution, or a place **2.** STUDY OF PAST EVENTS the branch of knowledge that records and analyses past events **3.** RECORD OF EVENTS a chronological account of past events of a period or in the life or development of a people, an institution, or a place ○ *a history of Byzantium* **4.** PERSONAL BACKGROUND the events and experiences of an individual's past ○ *We don't know very much about her personal history.* **5.** INTERESTING PAST an interesting or colourful past ○ *The car has a bit of a history attached to it.* **6.** HISTORICAL PLAY a play that deals with historical events [15C. Via Latin < Greek *historia* 'history, knowledge, narrative' < *histōr* 'learned man'] ◇ **be (ancient) history** to be something that happened a long time ago, or perhaps only recently in the past, and is no longer important or relevant ○ *The scandal is history, as far as I'm concerned.* ◇ **be history** used to indicate that somebody's life or influence, or something's importance, will be abruptly brought to an end ○ *If he's found guilty of bribery, he's history.*

history list *n* a record of the input of previous users of a computer

---

histrionic /hístri ónnik/, **histrionical** /-ik'l/ *adj* **1.** overdramatic in reaction or behaviour ○ *Paul gave a histrionic sigh and slumped in his chair.* **2.** relating to acting or actors (*formal*) [Mid-17C. < late Latin *histrionicus* < Latin *histrion-* 'actor'] —**histrionically** *adv*

histrionics /hístri ónniks/ *n* exaggerated emotional behaviour done for show or to get a reaction from somebody (*takes a singular or plural verb*) ○ *Let's hope there won't be any histrionics when you tell them.* ■ *npl* performances of dramatic works (*formal; takes a plural verb*)

hit /hit/ *v* (**hits, hitting, hit**) **1.** *vti* STRIKE DELIBERATELY to strike somebody or something deliberately with the hand or something held in it ○ *He hit me on the jaw with a good solid punch.* **2.** *vti* COME INTO CONTACT to come into violent contact with something ○ *His van skidded and hit a parked car.* **3.** *vt* MAKE BALL MOVE to make something such as a ball move by striking it with a bat or racket ○ *She kept hitting the ball over the fence into the next garden.* **4.** *vt* SCORE WITH BALL to score points in a sport by striking a ball well or delivering it successfully to a target ○ *You'll need to hit a home run to win.* **5.** *vt* STRIKE TARGET to reach an intended target with a ball or missile **6.** *vti* OCCUR TO SOMEBODY to be suddenly realized by somebody ○ *It suddenly hit him that he was unlikely to see her again.* **7.** *vt* AFFECT SOMEBODY OR SOMETHING BADLY to have an adverse effect on somebody or something ○ *The rise in interest rates is going to hit exporters hard.* **8.** *vt* ARRIVE AT PARTICULAR LEVEL to reach a particular level on a scale ○ *Unemployment has hit the 2 million mark.* **9.** *vt* PRODUCE SOMETHING ACCURATELY to render or represent something accurately ○ *hit a high C* **10.** *vt* CONFORM TO SOMETHING to conform to or agree with something ○ *Your comments hit a sympathetic note.* **11.** *vt* STRIKE BUTTON OR KEY to press or push a button or part of a machine (*informal*) ○ *Try to hit the keys smoothly.* **12.** *vi* HAPPEN to take place, usually with undesirable or adverse effects (*informal*) ○ *The storm hit before we could get home.* **13.** *vt* VIEW WEBPAGE to visit or view a particular webpage (*informal*) **14.** *vt* REACH PLACE to reach a particular place (*informal*) ○ *You'll hit a toll-free road about five miles farther on.* **15.** *vt* GIVE SOMEBODY INFORMATION to tell somebody something that may be of interest (*slang*) ○ *'Do you want to know what I think?' 'Okay, hit me.'* **16.** *vt* KILL SOMEBODY USING PROFESSIONAL KILLER to murder somebody, especially by employing a professional killer (*slang*) ○ *One of the croupiers got hit last night.* ■ *n* **1.** HARD BLOW a hard blow delivered with the hand or something held in it ○ *She gave it a good hit.* **2.** COLLISION a violent impact between things **3.** SOMETHING THAT HITS TARGET a ball or missile that successfully strikes the target ○ *We've taken a couple of hits, but nothing serious.* **4.** SUCCESS a person who or thing that is popular or successful ○ *The band had a big hit with their last CD.* ○ *The clown was a hit with the kids.* **5.** ACCESSING OF DATABASE OR INTERNET FILE an instance of a user retrieving an item from a database or contacting a file such as a home page through the Internet ○ *Her home page has received 3,000 hits since she opened it last month.* **6.** SOMETHING GIVEN a single item given or taken, e.g. a drink, or a card in the game of pontoon (*slang*) **7.** EFFECT OF DRUG a sense of a drug's effect (*slang*) **8.** PROFESSIONAL KILLING a murder, especially one committed by a professional killer (*slang*) **9.** BASEBALL same as **base hit** [Pre-12C. < Old Norse *hitta* 'find'] —**hittable** *adj* —**hitter** *n* ◇ **hit it off** to get on very well with somebody (*informal*)

hit back *vi* to retaliate against somebody or something for an attack

hit on, hit upon *vt* **1.** FIND ANSWER to think of a solution to a problem, especially by chance ○ *She then hit on the idea of painting the inside of the box black.* **2.** CHANCE ON SOMEBODY OR SOMETHING to find or encounter somebody or something unexpectedly **3.** *US* APPROACH SOMEBODY SEXUALLY to make sexual advances to somebody (*slang*)

hit out at *vi* **1.** to criticize somebody or something severely ○ *The bishop hit out at their human rights record.* **2.** to try to strike somebody repeatedly ○ *When the baby is in a tantrum, she hits out at people trying to comfort her.*

hit up *v* **1.** *vt NZ, US* to ask somebody for something, especially money (*slang*) ○ *How come you're suddenly hitting me up for the cab fare?* **2.** *vi Aus* in racket games, to hit the ball back and forth without scoring points, in order to warm up before a game

Hitachi /hi taáchi/ coastal industrial city in eastern Honshu, Japan. Population: 193,080 (2002).

hit-and-miss *adj* **1.** done in a careless haphazard way. N Am term **hit-or-miss** **2.** *N Am* same as **hit-or-miss** (sense 1)

hit-and-run *adj* **1.** NOT STOPPING AFTER CAUSING ACCIDENT describes a road accident in which the driver who has hit another person or motor vehicle leaves the scene without stopping ○ *a hit-and-run driver* **2.** FAST AND WITHOUT WARNING relying on surprise and speed to overcome an enemy ○ *Three fighter planes launched a hit-and-run attack at dawn.* ■ *n* HIT-AND-RUN ACCIDENT a hit-and-run road accident

hitch /hich/ *v* (**hitches, hitching, hitched**) **1.** *vt* JOIN SOMETHING TO SOMETHING ELSE to connect two things so that one can move the other, e.g. a horse to a wagon or a trailer to a car **2.** *vt* FASTEN SOMETHING TO STOP IT to fasten or tie something temporarily to keep it from moving away ○ *Hitch the boat to the dock before the current catches it.* **3.** *vti* HITCHHIKE to hitchhike a ride (*informal*) ○ *We hitched down through Italy in three days.* ■ *n* **1.** OBSTACLE an obstacle in the way of progress ○ *There's been a slight technical hitch.* **2.** *N Am* MEANS OF CONNECTING TWO THINGS a device used to connect two things, e.g. a ball on a vehicle for connecting a trailer **3.** KNOT THAT UNTIES EASILY a knot that can be easily untied, used for temporarily securing a line to something **4.** TUG a sudden pull on something [14C. Origin ?] —**hitcher** *n*

hitch up *vt* to pull up an item of clothing

Sir Alfred Hitchcock

Hitchcock /hích kok/, **Sir Alfred** (1899–1980) British film director. A prolific director and master of suspense, his films include *The 39 Steps* (1935), *Rebecca* (1940), and *Psycho* (1960). Full name **Hitchcock, Sir Alfred Joseph**

> 'A good film is when the price of the admission, the dinner, and the babysitter was well worth it.'
> [Sir Alfred Hitchcock. Quoted in *Halliwell's Filmgoer's Companion*, Leslie Halliwell; 1993]

hitched /hicht/ *adj* married (*informal*) ○ *They're getting hitched in a couple of weeks.*

hitchhike /hích hīk/ (**-hikes, -hiking, -hiked**) *vti* to get a ride from a passing vehicle, usually by standing at the side of the road and holding out the hand with the thumb raised —**hitchhiker** *n*

hitching post /híching-/ *n* a post or rail used to tie the reins of a horse to

Hitchings /híchingz/, **George Herbert** (1905–98) US biochemist. He and fellow researcher Gertrude Elion pioneered research into drugs that kill harmful invading cells without damaging healthy body cells, which led to the development of AZT. They shared the 1988 Nobel Prize in physiology or medicine with James Black.

hi-tech *n, adj* TECH another spelling of **high tech, high-tech**

hither /híthər/ *adv* to this place (*archaic or humorous*) ○ *Come hither, child.* ■ *adj* on the near side of something (*archaic*) [Old English *hider* < Indo-European, 'here, this'] ◇ **hither and thither** in many directions in a disorderly way

hitherto /híthər too, híthər too/ *adv* up to the present time or the time in question ○ *Hitherto most people had paid cash.*

hit in (*plural* **hit ins** or **hits in**) *n* in hockey, a hit from the sideline awarded to the opposition when the team in possession of the ball fails to keep it on the pitch

Hitler /híttlər/, **Adolf** (1889–1945) Austrian-born German Nazi leader. He cofounded the Nazi Party in Germany (1919) and became chancellor in 1933. His invasion of Poland in 1939 led to the outbreak of World War II. He implemented anti-Semitic policies that led to the Holocaust.

> 'All those who are not racially pure are mere chaff.'
> [Adolf Hitler, *Mein Kampf*; 1933]

Hitlerism /hítlərizəm/ *n* the extreme nationalistic ideology and fascistic policies developed by the Nazi Party under Adolf Hitler —**Hitlerist** *n* —**Hitlerite** *adj*

hit list *n* (*informal*) **1.** a list of things or people who are considered problems to be dealt with in the near future **2.** a list of potential murder victims

hit man *n* a hired killer, especially a man (*slang*)

hit-or-miss *adj* **1.** sometimes successful and sometimes not. N Am term **hit-and-miss** **2.** *N Am* same as **hit-and-miss** (sense 1)

hit out (*plural* **hit outs** or **hits out**) *n* **1.** in hockey, a hit taken from the 16-yard line that is awarded to the defence when the attacking team hit the ball over the goal line without scoring a goal **2.** in Australian Rules football, the act of pushing or punching the ball to a team-mate, at ball-up or throw-in

hit parade *n* a list of the best-selling pop records in the previous week (*dated*)

hitperson /hít purss'n/ (*plural* **-persons** or **-people** /-peep'l/) *n* a hired assassin (*slang*) N Am term **hired gun**

hit squad *n* (*slang*) **1.** a team of hired assassins or other killers **2.** a team of experts sent in to solve serious problems

Hittite /híttīt/ *n* **1.** a member of an ancient Anatolian people whose empire was based in Asia Minor during the second millennium BC **2.** an extinct Indo-European language spoken in Anatolia, parts of Syria, and surrounding areas during the second millennium BC. Despite evidence from ample cuneiform inscriptions, there is no consensus over which branch of Indo-European it belongs to. [Mid-16C. < Hebrew *Ḥittīm* < Hittite *Hatti*] —**Hittite** *adj*

hit-up *n Aus* RACKET GAMES same as **knock-up**

HIV *n* either of two strains of a retrovirus, HIV-1 or HIV-2, that destroys the immune system's helper T cells, the loss of which causes Aids. Full form **human immunodeficiency virus**

hive /hīv/ *n* **1.** HOME FOR BEES a shelter in which a colony of social bees, especially honeybees, builds its nest **2.** COLONY OF BEES a colony of honeybees ■ *v* (**hives, hiving, hived**) **1.** *vti* GATHER IN HIVE to gather in a hive, or cause bees to gather in a hive ○ *hive a swarm* **2.** *vt* KEEP HONEY IN HIVE to store honey in a hive **3.** *vt* KEEP SOMETHING TO USE LATER to store something for later use **4.** *vi* LIVE CLOSELY TOGETHER to live closely in a group [Old English *hȳf* < Indo-European, 'round container'] —**hiveless** *adj* ◇ **a hive of industry** *or* **activity** a very busy, active place

hive off *vt* **1.** to separate something from the whole or from a larger group, e.g. to divert work to a subsidiary company or to split a branch of knowledge into different areas **2.** to transfer an industry from governmental to private ownership

hives /hīvz/ *n* MED same as **urticaria** (*takes a singular or plural verb*) [Early 16C. Origin ?]

HIV-negative *adj* having taken a test that revealed no antibodies to HIV in the bloodstream

HIV-positive *adj* shown by a test for antibodies to HIV in the bloodstream to be infected with HIV

hiya /hī yaa/ *interj* a word used to say hello to somebody [Mid-20C. Apparently contraction of *how are you*, influenced by *hi* (interjection)]

hiziki *n* FOOD another spelling of **hijiki**

hk *abbr* Hong Kong (*used in Internet addresses*) See table at **domain name**

HK *abbr* House of Keys

hl *symbol* MEASURE hectolitre

HL *abbr* House of Lords

HLA *n* the major antigen compatibility complex in humans that is genetically determined and is involved in cell self-identification and histocompatibility. Full form **human lymphocyte antigen**

HLL *abbr* COMPUT high-level language

HLZ *abbr* MIL helicopter landing zone

hm *abbr* **1.** MEASURE hectometre **2.** Heard and McDonald Islands (*used in Internet addresses*) See table at **domain name**

h'm /m, hm/ *interj* used to represent a sound made while pausing during a conversation to consider something ○ *H'm, it'll take about two weeks.* [Mid-19C. Natural utterance]

HM *abbr* **1.** EDUC headmaster **2.** EDUC headmistress **3.** MUSIC heavy metal **4.** Her Majesty **5.** His Majesty

HMAS *abbr* **1.** Her Majesty's Australian ship **2.** His Majesty's Australian ship

HMCS *abbr* **1.** Her Majesty's Canadian Ship **2.** His Majesty's Canadian Ship

HMF *abbr* **1.** Her Majesty's Forces **2.** His Majesty's Forces

HMG *abbr* **1.** Her Majesty's Government **2.** His Majesty's Government

HMI *abbr* **1.** EDUC Her Majesty's Inspector (of Schools) **2.** His Majesty's Inspector (of Schools) **3.** COMPUT human-machine interface

HMO *n* a house in which two or more households share basic facilities. Full form **house in multiple occupation**

Hmong /máwng, hə máwng/ (*plural* **Hmongs** or *same*) *n* **1.** a member of a people living in southern China and mainly remote areas of northern Laos, Thailand, and Vietnam **2.** a language spoken in parts of southern China and in Laos, Thailand, Vietnam, and the United States, forming a main branch of the Miao-Yao language family. Native speakers: 5 million. —**Hmong** *adj*

hMPV *abbr* MICROBIOL human metapneumovirus

HMS *abbr* **1.** Her Majesty's Service **2.** Her Majesty's Ship **3.** His Majesty's Service **4.** His Majesty's Ship

HMSO *abbr* **1.** Her Majesty's Stationery Office **2.** His Majesty's Stationery Office

hn *abbr* Honduras (*used in Internet addresses*) See table at **domain name**

Hn *symbol* CHEM ELEM hahnium

HNC *n* in the United Kingdom, a qualification in a technical subject that is recognized by many professional and technical establishments. Full form **Higher National Certificate**

HND *n* in the United Kingdom, a vocational qualification that requires the equivalent of two years' full-time study after the age of 18 and is generally regarded as equivalent to a university pass degree. Full form **Higher National Diploma**

ho[1] /hō/ (*plural* **hos** or **hoes**) *n US* **1.** an offensive term for a prostitute (*slang*) **2.** an offensive term for a woman (*slang offensive insult*) [Late 20C. Pronunciation of WHORE]

ho[2] /hō/ *interj* **1. EXPRESSING VARIOUS EMOTIONS** used to express surprise, triumph, admiration, or derision, depending on the way the speaker says it **2. CALL FOR ATTENTION** used to attract somebody's attention **3. USED TO POINT OUT SOMETHING** used to draw somebody's attention to something (*used in combinations*) ○ *Land ho!* [13C. Natural exclamation]

Ho *symbol* CHEM ELEM holmium

Hoad /hōd/, **Lew** (1934–94) Australian tennis player. He won the Wimbledon singles championship in 1956 and 1957. Full name **Hoad, Lewis Alan**

hoar /hawr/ *adj* white or greyish white in colour, usually as a result of age or frost (*literary*) [Old English *hār* < Indo-European, 'shine']

hoard /hawrd/ (**hoards, hoarding, hoarded**) *vti* to collect and store, often secretly, large amounts of things such as food or money for future use [Old English *hord* < Indo-European] —**hoard** *n* —**hoarder** *n*

SPELLCHECK hoard or **horde**? Do not confuse the spelling of ***hoard*** and ***horde***, which sound similar. ***Hoard*** is used as a verb meaning 'collect and store for future use' (as in *to hoard money*) or as a noun denoting such a collection (as in *a hoard of valuables*). ***Horde*** is chiefly used as a noun, denoting a large group of people or animals (as in *hordes of visitors*); it is only occasionally used as a verb, meaning 'gather, move, or live in a large group'.

SYNONYMS See ***collect***[1].

hoarding /háwrding/ *n* **1.** MARKETING same as **billboard**[1] ○ *an advertising hoarding* **2.** a tall fence used to screen off a building site [Early 19C. < obsolete *hoard* 'hoarding', origin ?]

hoar frost /háwr-/ *n* the white frost that forms on grass or leaves in the morning when the dew freezes

hoarhound *n* PLANTS another spelling of **horehound**

hoarse /hawrss/ (**hoarser, hoarsest**) *adj* **1.** sounding rough and grating **2.** having a rough, harsh, grating voice [Old English *hās* < Germanic] —**hoarsely** *adv* —**hoarseness** *n*

SPELLCHECK hoarse or **horse**? Do not confuse the spelling of ***hoarse*** and ***horse***, which sound similar. The word ***hoarse*** is only used as an adjective, meaning 'rough or grating', as in *a hoarse voice*. The correct spelling of the noun, denoting an animal used for riding, is ***horse***.

hoarsen /háwrss'n/ (**-ens, -ening, -ened**) *vti* to become hoarse, or make the voice hoarse

hoary /háwri/ (**-ier, -iest**) *adj* **1. OVERUSED** old and stale from overuse ○ *Not that hoary old chestnut about the chicken crossing the road?* **2. WHITE WITH AGE** describes hair that has become white or grey with age **3. COVERED WITH PALE HAIRS** covered with grey or white hairs ○ *a plant with hoary leaves* —**hoarily** *adv* —**hoariness** *n*

hoatch *vi Scotland* another spelling of **hotch**

hoatching /hṓching/ *adj Scotland* full of people or things (*informal*) [Origin ?]

hoatzin /hō átsin, waát seén/ *n* a bird with brownish feathers, a very small crested head, and a specialized digestive system for leaves. Young birds have a digit resembling a claw on each wing, used for climbing and swimming. Native to: South America. Latin name: *Opisthocomus hoazin.* [Mid-17C. Via American Spanish < Nahuatl *uatzin*]

hoax /hōks/ *n* an act intended to trick people into believing something is real when it is not ■ *vt* (**hoaxes, hoaxing, hoaxed**) to trick people into believing something is real when it is not [Late 18C. Probably alteration of HOCUS] —**hoaxer** *n*

hob[1] /hob/ *n* **1.** a flat surface containing cooking rings, hot plates, or burners **2.** a small shelf or rack level with the top of the grate of a fireplace on which to set pans to keep them warm [Late 17C. Alteration of *hub*, origin ?]

hob[2] /hob/ *n* a hobgoblin or elf (*archaic*) [15C. < the name *Robert* or *Robin*]

Hobart /hṓ baart/ capital city of the island state of Tasmania in Australia, located on the River Derwent. Population: 195,000 (2002 estimate). —**Hobartian** *n, adj*

Hobbema /hóbbimə/, **Meindert** (1638–1709) Dutch painter. A specialist in detailed Dutch landscapes, his most famous work is *The Avenue, Middelharnis* (1689).

Hobbes /hobz/, **Thomas** (1588–1679) English philosopher and political theorist. In *Leviathan* (1651) he advocated absolute monarchy as the only means of controlling clashing human interests and desires and guaranteeing people's rights of self-preservation and happiness. —**Hobbesian** *adj, n* —**Hobbism** /hóbizm/ *n* —**Hobbist** *adj, n*

> 'Liberties...depend on the silence of the law.'
> [Thomas Hobbes, *Leviathan*; 1651]

hobbit /hóbbit/ *n* in the novels of J. R. R. Tolkien, a member of an imaginary good-natured little people who have brown furry legs and live underground. Tolkien's most famous hobbits are Bilbo Baggins, the hero of *The Hobbit*, and Frodo Baggins, the hero of *Lord of the Rings.* [Mid-20C. Coined by J. R. R. TOLKIEN]

hobble /hóbb'l/ *v* (**-bles, -bling, -bled**) **1.** *vi* **LIMP ALONG** to walk haltingly and unsteadily, taking short steps **2.** *vt* **LIMIT HORSE'S MOVEMENT** to tie the legs of a horse loosely together with a rope or strap to prevent it from moving away **3.** *vt* **RESTRICT SOMEBODY'S ACTIONS** to put restrictions on somebody or something to slow or prevent progress ■ *n* **1. UNSTEADY WALK** a halting unsteady walk **2. ROPE OR STRAP** something, e.g. a loop of rope or a strap, used to tie the legs of a horse [13C. Probably < Low German]

hobbledehoy /hóbb'ldi hóy/ *n* a clumsy or rude young man (*archaic*) [Mid-16C. Origin ?]

hobble skirt *n* a long skirt designed to be full at the hips but narrow at the ankles, first popular between 1910 and 1914

Hobbs /hobz/, **Jack** (1882–1963) British cricketer. With a career total of 61,237 runs, including 197 centuries, he was the first cricketer to be knighted (1953). Full name **Hobbs, Sir John Berry**

hobby[1] /hóbbi/ (*plural* **-bies**) *n* an activity engaged in for pleasure and relaxation during spare time ○ *Our oldest boy's hobby is flying kites.* [14C. Probably < *Hobin*, variant of the name *Robin*]

hobby[2] /hóbbi/ (*plural* **-bies**) *n* a small blackish falcon with a whitish chest and chestnut legs. Native to: Europe, Asia, migrating to Africa. Latin name: *Falco subbuteo.* [15C. < Old French *hobé, hobet*, diminutive of *hobe* 'falcon']

hobbyhorse /hóbbi hawrss/ *n* **1. TOY HORSE** a toy consisting of a long stick with the shape of a horse's head at one end **2. HORSE FIGURE IN FOLK DANCES** a representation of a horse that a Morris dancer or mummer wears around the waist so that it appears that the horse is being ridden **3. FAVOURITE TOPIC** a favourite subject about which somebody will talk given the slightest opportunity

hobbyist /hóbbi ist/ *n* somebody who pursues a hobby or leisure activity [Late 19C. < HOBBY[1]]

hobgoblin /hób góbblin, hób goblin/ *n* **1.** same as **goblin** **2.** a source of fear or worry [< HOB[2]]

hobnail /hób nayl/ *n* a short nail with a broad head that is used to protect the soles of boots —**hobnailed** *adj*

hobnob /hób nob/ (**-nobs, -nobbing, -nobbed**) *vi* to socialize in a familiar manner with somebody, especially somebody considered to be of a higher social class (*disapproving*) ○ *hobnobbing with the rich and famous* [Mid-18C. Probably < obsolete *hob or nob* 'have or not have']

hobo /hṓbō/ (*plural* **-boes**) *n* a poor and homeless person, especially somebody who travelled around the United States looking for work in the 1920s and 1930s [Late 19C. Origin ?]

hobson-jobson /hóbss'n jóbss'n/ *n* the assimilation of the sound of a word or words into the sound system of another language, as occurred when the French 'vin blanc' became the English 'plonk' [Late 19C. < title of an Anglo-Indian glossary by Yule and Burnell < Arabic *Yā Ḥasan! Yā Ḥusayn!* 'O Hasan! O Husain!', cry used at Muslim ceremonies]

Hobson's choice /hóbss'nz-/ *n* a choice between what is offered and nothing at all [Mid-17C. After Thomas *Hobson* (1554–1631), English liveryman who would only let his customers take the horse nearest the door]

Ho Chi Minh /hṓ cheé mín/ (1890–1969) Vietnamese politician. A founder member of the Communist Party (1918), he led Vietnamese resistance to French colonial rule (1946–54), and was prime minister (1954–55) and president of North Vietnam (1955–69). Born **Nguyen Tat Thanh**

> 'You will kill 10 of our men and we will kill 1 of yours and in the end it will be you who tire of it.'
> [Ho Chi Minh. Recalled on his death; 3 September 1969]

Ho Chi Minh City the largest city of Vietnam, in the southern part of the country. Population: 4,615,000 (2000). Former name **Saigon** (until 1975)

hock[1] /hok/ *n* **1.** the joint in the hind leg of a four-legged animal such as a horse or cow, corresponding to the human ankle **2.** a cut of cured meat, especially ham, taken from the lower joint of the leg immediately above the foot. It contains a comparatively small amount of meat but has a good flavour and jelly properties and is often used in stocks and soups. [Mid-16C. Shortening of obsolete *hock-shin* < Old English *hōhsinu* 'heel-sinew' < *hōh* 'heel']

hock[2] /hok/ *n* a German white wine, especially from the Rhineland [Early 17C. Shortening of obsolete *hock-amore*, Anglicization of German *Hochheimer* < *Hochheim*, German town]

hock[3] /hok/ (**hocks, hocking, hocked**) *vt* to deposit some-

thing as security against money borrowed, with the risk of losing it if the money is not paid back within a specific period (*slang*) [Mid-19C. < Dutch *hok* 'prison, debt'] ◇ **in hock 1.** left as security against money borrowed (*informal*) **2.** in debt (*informal*) **3.** in prison (*slang*)

hockey /hóki/ *n* **1.** an outdoor sport played on grass between two teams of eleven, using wooden sticks with curved ends. The aim is to hit a small hard ball into the opposing goal. N Am term **field hockey 2.** *N Am* same as **ice hockey** [Early 16C. Origin ?]

David Hockney

Hockney /hókni/, **David** (*b.* 1937) British painter. He was closely associated with the Pop Art movement. His fascination with water inspired 'swimming pool' paintings such as *A Bigger Splash* (1967).

'Art has to move you and design does not, unless it's a good design for a bus.'
[David Hockney, *Guardian*; 26 October 1988]

Hocktide /hók tīd/ *n* formerly, a festival during which money was raised for the church. Date: second Monday and Tuesday after Easter. [15C. < *Hock-* 'beginning of the second week after Easter', origin ?]

hocus /hókəss/ (**-cuses** or **-cusses**, **-cusing** or **-cussing**, **-cused** or **-cussed**) *vt* (*archaic*) **1.** DECEIVE SOMEBODY to deceive or trick somebody **2.** DOPE SOMEBODY to incapacitate a person or animal with drugs **3.** DRUG ALCOHOLIC DRINK to secretly add a drug to an alcoholic drink [Late 17C. Shortening of HOCUS-POCUS]

hocus-pocus /hókəss pókəss/ *n* (*plural* **hocus-pocuses** or **hocus-pocusses**) **1.** CONJURER'S INCANTATION a phrase or chant used by a magician or conjurer during a performance **2.** MAGIC TRICK a trick performed by a magician or conjurer **3.** TRICKERY a hoax or trickery ○ *The negotiations were ruined by the parties' hocus-pocus.* **4.** CONJURER a juggler or magician (*dated*) ■ *vti* (**hocus-pocuses** or **hocus-pocusses**, **hocus-pocusing** or **hocus-pocussing**, **hocus-pocused** or **hocus-pocussed**) DECEIVE to deceive or trick somebody [< pseudo-Latin *hax pax max Deus adimax*, used by conjurers]

hod /hod/ *n* **1.** a V-shaped tray on the end of a long pole, usually carried on the shoulder. Use: carrying bricks, mortar, and other building materials. **2.** HOUSEHOLD same as **coal scuttle** [Late 16C. < Old French *hotte* 'pannier, basket' < Germanic]

hod carrier *n* somebody hired to carry bricks and mortar in a hod

hodden /hódd'n/ *n Scotland* a coarse, undyed, homespun woollen fabric produced in Scotland [Late 16C. Origin ?]

Hoddle /hódd'l/, **Glenn** (*b.* 1957) British footballer and manager. He spent most of his playing career with Tottenham (1976–86). He won 53 international caps, and was England's manager (1996–99).

Hodge /hoj/ *n* a name for a typical agricultural labourer (*archaic*) [14C. Form of the first name *Roger*]

hodgepodge /hój poj/ *n N Am* same as **hotchpotch** (sense 1) [14C. Variant of HOTCHPOTCH]

Hodgkin /hójkin/, **Alan** (1914–98) British physiologist. He shared the Nobel Prize in physiology or medicine (1963) for his research into the chemical processes of nerve impulses. Full name **Hodgkin, Alan Lloyd**

Dorothy Mary Hodgkin

Hodgkin, **Dorothy Mary** (1910–94) Egyptian-born British chemist. She was awarded the Nobel Prize in chemistry (1964) for her work on X-rays, molecular science, and penicillin.

'I'm really an experimentalist. I used to say "I think with my hands". I just like manipulation.'
[Dorothy Mary Hodgkin. Quoted in *A Passion for Science*, Lewis Wolpert and Alison Richards; 1988]

Hodgkin, **Thomas** (1798–1866) British pathologist. He was the first person to detect the glandular disease of the lymph tissue later named 'Hodgkin's disease'.

Hodgkins /hójkinz/, **Frances Mary** (1869–1947) New Zealand painter. Noted for her watercolour still lifes and landscapes, she spent most of her working life in Europe.

Hodgkin's disease *n* a malignant form of lymphoma marked by progressive enlargement of the lymph nodes and spleen and sometimes of the liver [Mid-19C. After Thomas HODGKIN]

hodman /hódmən/ (*plural* **-men** /-mən/) *n* CONSTR same as **hod carrier**

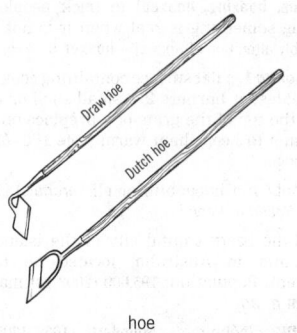

hoe

hoe /hō/ *n* a garden implement consisting of a long pole with a small flat metal blade set into one end at an angle. Use: weeding, turning over soil. [14C. < Old French *houe* < Germanic, 'cut down'] ■ *vti* (**hoes, hoeing, hoed**) to use a hoe to remove weeds or turn over the soil in a piece of ground —**hoer** *n*
hoe in *vi Aus* (*informal*) **1.** to begin eating with vigour or relish ○ *Come on, hoe in! Don't let a spread like this go to waste.* **2.** to begin an activity with vigour or enthusiasm ○ *We've got to get this done today, so hoe in everyone.*
hoe into *vt Aus* (*informal*) **1.** to eat something with vigour or relish ○ *When I arrived he was hoeing into the biggest plate of pasta you've ever seen.* **2.** to start doing something with vigour or enthusiasm ○ *He really hoed into the plastering.*

hoedown /hố down/ *n Can, Southern US* **1.** a noisy lively dance, especially a square dance, or a party for square dancing **2.** the music for a hoedown [< the idea of stopping work]

Hofei /hố fáy/ ♦ **Hefei**

Hoffman /hófmən/, **Dustin** (*b.* 1937) US actor. He starred in *The Graduate* (1967), and won Academy Awards for *Kramer vs. Kramer* (1979) and *Rain Man* (1988). Full name **Hoffman, Dustin Lee**

hog /hog/ *n* **1.** PIG a full-grown domestic pig, especially a castrated male pig **2.** *US* MEMBER OF PIG FAMILY any animal of the pig family, including both domesticated and wild species, e.g. the wild boar. Family: Suidae. **3.** *also* **hogg** *UK regional, ANZ* YOUNG SHEEP a young sheep that is older than a lamb and that has not yet been sheared **4.** SHIP'S BROOM a broom used to clean the bottom of a ship while it is in the water ■ *v* (**hogs, hogging, hogged**) **1.** *vt* TAKE EXCESS OF SOMETHING to take more of something or keep something for longer than is fair or polite (*informal*) ○ *He's been hogging the middle lane for the past two miles.* **2.** *vt* ARCH BACK to arch the back upwards **3.** *vt* TRIM HORSE'S MANE to trim the mane of a horse very short, causing it to stand up like the bristles of a hog's back **4.** *vti* WARP to cause the keel or plank of a ship to curve upwards in the middle, or curve in this way **5.** *vt* SCRUB SHIP'S BOTTOM to clean a ship's bottom with a broom while the ship is in the water [Pre-12C. Origin ?] —**hog-like** *adj* ◇ **go the whole hog** to do something wholeheartedly or completely and without restraint (*slang*)

hogan /hốgən/ *n* a traditional Navajo dwelling made of wood and mud, with a roof of earth [Late 19C. < Navajo]

Hogan /hốgən/, **Ben** (1912–97) US golfer. He won over 60 major golfing tournaments including four US Open championships (1948, 1950, 1951, 1953). Full name **Hogan, William Benjamin**

Hogan, **Paul** (*b.* 1939) Australian actor. Originally a television performer, he starred in the film *Crocodile Dundee* (1986) and cowrote and produced *Crocodile Dundee II* (1988).

Hogarth /hố gaarth/, **William** (1697–1764) British painter and engraver. He is best known for his series of satirical engravings, including *A Rake's Progress* (1733–35). —**Hogarthian** /hō gáarthi ən/ *adj*

'Comedy in painting, as well as in writing, ought to be allotted the first place.'
[William Hogarth. Quoted in *Hogarth Illustrated*, John Ireland; 1812]

hogback /hóg bak/ *n* a steep and narrow low ridge produced by the erosion of the softer surrounding rock strata

hog badger *n* a nocturnal badger with a long snout with which it roots for insects and grubs. Native to: Southeast Asia. Latin name: *Arctonyx collaris*. [< its cloven hooves]

hog cholera *n* VET same as **swine fever**

hogfish /hógfish/ (*plural same* or **-fishes**) *n* **1.** a brightly coloured fish of the wrasse family, especially one in which the first three spines of its dorsal fin are thicker and longer than the rest. Native to: tropical coral reefs. Latin name: *Lachnolaimus maximus*. **2.** FISH same as **pigfish** [< its grunting sound]

hogg *n UK regional, ANZ* ZOOL another spelling of **hog** *n* (sense 3)

Hogg /hog/, **James** (1770–1835) Scottish poet. A shepherd turned writer, he wrote ballads and the novel *The Private Memoirs and Confessions of a Justified Sinner* (1824).

'Where the pools are bright and deep, / Where the grey trout lies asleep, / Up the river and o'er the lea, / That's the way for Billy and me.'
[James Hogg, 'A Boy's Song', *A Poetic Mirror 1829–31*; 1831]

hogget /hóggit/ *n* **1.** *UK, ANZ, US regional* ZOOL same as **hog** *n* (sense 3) **2.** the wool from a sheep 12 to 14 months old

hoggish /hóggish/ *adj* greedy, selfish, or slovenly — **hoggishly** *adv* —**hoggishness** *n*

Hogmanay /hógmə nay, -náy/ *n Scotland* New Year's Eve as celebrated in Scotland and in parts of northern England [Early 17C. Probably < Norman dialect *hoguinané*, said when exchanging New Year's gifts < Old French *aguillanneuf*, contraction of *accueillis l'an neuf* 'welcome the new year']

hognose snake /hógnōz-/, **hognosed snake** /hógnōzd-/ *n* a nonvenomous snake with a thick body and an upturned snout resembling a hog's that is used for burrowing. Native to: North America. Genus: *Heterodon*. [< its upturned snout]

hog peanut *n* a vine of the legume family that has edible, fleshy, single-seeded pods that ripen on or beneath the ground. Flowers: white or pinkish, in

clusters. Native to: North America. Latin name: *Amphicarpaea bracteata.*

hog's back /hógz-/ *n* GEOG same as **hogback**

Hog's Back /hógz bak/ ridge in Surrey, southeastern England, running between the towns of Guildford and Farnham. Height: 154 m/505 ft.

hogshead /hógz hed/ *n* **1.** a unit of capacity for liquids or dry goods, used especially for alcohol, having various values but typically 54 imperial gallons or 63 US gallons **2.** a large cask or barrel, especially one having a capacity of one hogshead [14C. Origin ?]

hog-tie *vt N Am* **1.** to tie the legs of an animal or the feet and hands of a person together **2.** to hamper or impede somebody or something (*informal*)

hogwash /hóg wosh/ *n* **1.** rubbish or nonsense (*informal*) ○ *What a pile of hogwash!* **2.** leftovers of food that are given to pigs to eat

hogweed

hogweed /hóg weed/ *n* any coarse weed, e.g. sow thistle or knotweed

hog-wild *adj N Am* excited or enthusiastic to the point of losing any inhibitions (*slang*) ○ *He's gone hog-wild ever since he inherited the money.*

Hohhot /hṓ hót/ capital city of Nei Monggol Autonomous Region in northeastern China. Population: 1,090,000 (1995).

ho hum /hṓ húm/ *interj* used to express boredom, disappointment, or resignation (*informal*) ○ *Ho hum, off we go, I suppose.* [Probably formed to suggest a yawn]

hoick /hoyk/ (**hoicks, hoicking, hoicked**) *vti* to pull or lift something or somebody violently or suddenly (*informal*) [Late 19C. Origin ?]

hoicks /hoyks/ *n* a shout in hunting, used to urge hounds to move along faster [Early 17C. Origin ?]

hoi polloi /hóypə lóy, hóy pólloy/ *n* ordinary people, as opposed to the wealthy, well-educated, and cultivated elite (*disapproving*) [Mid-17C. < Greek, 'the many']

hoisin sauce /hóysin-/ *n* a dark sweet and spicy sauce of thick consistency made from fermented soya beans. Use: to flavour Chinese dishes, as a condiment. [< Chinese (Cantonese), 'delicacy of the sea']

hoist /hoyst/ *vt* (**hoists, hoisting, hoisted**) **LIFT SOMEBODY OR SOMETHING UP** to raise or lift somebody or something up, especially using a mechanical device such as a winch ■ *n* **1. DEVICE FOR LIFTING** a mechanical device or apparatus, e.g. a winch or elevator, designed for lifting people or heavy objects **2. LIFTING UP** an act of hoisting somebody or something **3. SIGNAL MADE WITH FLAGS** a message or signal conveyed from ship to ship by flags hoisted up the mast **4. SIZE OF SAIL** the height of a sail or flag [15C. Alteration of *hoise*, origin ?] —**hoister** *n*

SYNONYMS See ***raise***.

hoity-toity /hóyti tóyti/ *adj* arrogant and self-important (*informal*) [Alteration and repetition of obsolete *hoit* 'romp', origin ?]

Hokan /hṓkən/ *n* a group of Native American languages of the southwestern United States, including Chumash, Yuman, and other languages and linguistic groups [Early 20C. < Hokan *hok* 'two'] —**Hokan** *adj*

hoke /hōk/ (**hokes, hoking, hoked**) *vt* to introduce highly melodramatic or broadly comic features into a story, play, or speech, in order to captivate an audience [Early 20C. Back-formation < HOKUM]

hokey /hṓki/ (**-ier, -iest**) *adj N Am* (*informal*) **1.** obviously contrived or clearly not genuine **2.** corny, sentimental, or melodramatic [Mid-20C. < HOKE or HOKUM] —**hokeyness** *n* —**hokily** *adv*

hokey cokey /hṓki kṓki/ *n UK* a dance in which a circle of people, especially children, sing out instructions for movements that they perform at the same time. ANZ, N Am term **hokey-pokey** [Mid-20C. Origin ?]

hokey-pokey /hṓki pṓki/ *n* **1.** *ANZ, N Am* DANCE same as **hokey cokey 2.** *NZ* brittle porous butterscotch, sometimes also used as an ingredient in a type of ice cream [Mid-19C. Origin ?]

Hokkaido /ho kī́dō/ the second largest island of Japan, situated north of the main island of Honshu. Population: 5,643,647 (1990). Area: 78,460 sq. km/30,290 sq. mi.

Hokkien /hóki en/ *n* the form of the Chinese language that is most widely used in Singapore. Native speakers: 700,000. —**Hokkien** *adj*

hokku /hó koo/ (*plural same*) *n* LITERAT another spelling of **haiku** [Late 19C. < Japanese, 'opening verse (of a sequence of comic verses)']

hokum /hṓkəm/ *n N Am* **1.** something that on the surface appears to be true or credible but is in fact meaningless or untrue (*informal*) ○ *a load of hokum* **2.** highly melodramatic or broadly comic features introduced into a story, play, or speech, in order to captivate an audience [Early 20C. Origin ?]

Hokusai /hṓkoo sī/ (1760–1849) Japanese painter and book illustrator. The finest Japanese printmaker of his time, he was the leading member of the Ukiyo-e school. His best-known work is *Thirty-Six Views of Mount Fuji* (1826–33). Full name **Hokusai, Katsushika**

> 'If heaven had granted me five more years, I could have become a real painter.'
> [Hokusai. Quoted in *Famous Last Words*, Barnaby Conrad; 1962]

hol- *prefix* same as **holo-** (*used before vowels*)

holandric /hō lándrik, ho-/ *adj* describes genetic traits carried on the Y chromosome and therefore carried and inherited only by males [Mid-20C. < HOLO- + ANDRO-]

Holarctic /hō laárktik, ho-/ *adj* found in or characteristic of the regions of North America, Europe, and Asia combined, which share many faunal characteristics

Holbein (the Elder) /hól bīn-/, **Hans** (1460?–1524) German painter. The father and teacher of Hans Holbein the Younger, his most famous work is the St Sebastian Altar, Munich (1493).

Holbein (the Younger), Hans (1497–1543) German painter. The son of Hans Holbein the Elder, he is best remembered for his portraits of the court of Henry VIII.

hold[1] /hōld/ *v* (**holds, holding, held** /held/) **1.** *vt* **GRASP SOMETHING** to take something firmly and retain it in the hand or arms **2.** *vt* **LIFT AND SUPPORT SOMETHING** to carry, lift, or support temporarily an object or part of the body in a particular position ○ *Hold the rope a bit higher.* **3.** *vt* **FIX SOMETHING IN POSITION** to keep something fixed in a particular position ○ *The picture is held in place by two large hooks.* **4.** *vt* **EMBRACE SOMEBODY** to bring or have somebody within an embrace or supported by the arms **5.** *vt* **CONTAIN SOMETHING** to be the place where something is or can be kept ○ *a basket to hold all your sewing equipment* **6.** *vt* **KEEP SOMEBODY IN CUSTODY** to keep somebody in a particular place or condition, especially in custody **7.** *vt* **DELAY SOMEBODY** to cause delay to somebody ○ *What held you so long?* **8.** *vt* **RETAIN OR RESERVE SOMETHING** to retain or reserve something for later use or collection by somebody else ○ *Ask if they can hold the tickets for us at the box office.* **9.** *vt* **REFRAIN FROM SOMETHING** to refrain from doing or saying something ○ *Please hold your applause until the end.* **10.** *vt* **STOP SOMETHING FROM LEAVING OR OCCURRING** to stop something leaving or happening at the appointed time, usually for a particular purpose ○ *The guard held the train so that we could board.* **11.** *vt* MIL **KEEP SOMETHING BY FORCE** to keep possession of something by force, especially while under attack ○ *The insurgents held the town for some time before retreating.* **12.** *vt* **HAVE PARTICULAR CAPACITY** to contain or be able to contain a particular number or amount ○ *holds 20 passengers* **13.** *vt* **BE ABLE TO CONSUME SOMETHING** to consume something, especially alcohol, without ill effect **14.** *vt* **ARRANGE SOMETHING** to arrange, take part in, or observe an activity or event ○ *They hold a party every Friday night.* **15.** *vt* **POSSESS SOMETHING** to have the right to something as a possession or achievement ○ *The author holds the copyright to this book.* ○ *holds the property on a long lease* **16.** *vt* **HAVE PARTICULAR POSITION** to fulfil the duties of a particular title, office, or position ○ *held the office of treasurer* **17.** *vti* **KEEP PROMISE** to keep a promise or carry out an intention, or make sure that somebody does this ○ *held her to her agreement* **18.** *vt* **BELIEVE OR FEEL SOMETHING** to have a particular belief, opinion, or feeling ○ *We hold these truths to be self-evident.* **19.** *vt* **REGARD SOMEBODY IN PARTICULAR WAY** to regard somebody or something in a particular way ○ *She holds her professor in very high esteem.* **20.** *vt* **HAVE PARTICULAR BEARING** to keep or carry the body or a part of it in a particular attitude or position ○ *She holds herself well.* **21.** *vt* **ENGROSS SOMEBODY** to engage or captivate somebody or somebody's attention ○ *She held their attention with the dramatic tale of her solo crossing.* **22.** *vt* LAW **DECIDE SOMETHING LEGALLY** to decide or lay down something legally or authoritatively ○ *The appeal court held that the lower court acted properly.* **23.** *vt* MUSIC **SUSTAIN MUSICAL NOTE** to continue singing or playing a note or a chord for a particular length of time ○ *The trumpeter held the note for at least a full minute.* **24.** *vi* **PERSIST** to continue in a particular state or course **25.** *vi* **REMAIN FIRM** to remain fast or firm and not break or give way ○ *The dam held throughout the flooding.* **26.** *vi* **STAND FIRM** to maintain a position against attack or opposition ○ *Their defensive line held, despite heavy losses.* **27.** *vi* **REMAIN VALID** to remain in force or continue to be valid ○ *Many old sayings still hold true.* **28.** *vi* **STAY FINE** to continue to be fine and not become wet or cold (*refers to the weather*) ○ *We're meant to be going to a picnic on Saturday so I hope the weather holds.* **29.** *vti* COMMUNICATION **WAIT ON TELEPHONE** to maintain the connection on a telephone line while not talking, usually so that the person being called can speak to somebody else or transfer the call ○ *Could you hold, please, while I try to connect you?* ○ *Hold the line, please.* ■ *n* **1. GRASPING** the act or position of grasping or keeping possession of something ○ *She grabbed hold of the rope and pulled herself aboard.* ○ *has no hold on reality* **2. WRESTLING TECHNIQUE** in wrestling, a position or manner of grasping an opponent **3. SOMETHING GIVING SUPPORT** something that may be grasped or used as a support ○ *There were few holds on the sheer rock face.* **4. SOMETHING THAT RESTRAINS** a structure or receptacle used for keeping something in check, e.g. a lock on a canal **5. CONTROL OVER SOMEBODY OR SOMETHING** a controlling power or influence over somebody or something ○ *a firm hold on the public's imagination* **6. DELAYING OF SOMETHING** an act of delaying or restraining something, or an order to do this ○ *Put a hold on their dinner order.* **7.** MUSIC **MUSICAL NOTATION** a symbol appearing above or below a note or rest signalling that it can be prolonged beyond its prescribed time **8. PRISON** a prison cell or place of confinement **9. STRONGHOLD** a fortified place in a castle or other structure (*archaic*) [Old English *haldan, healdan* < Germanic, 'guard, watch'] ◇ **get hold of somebody** *or* **something** to succeed in finding somebody or obtaining something ◇ **hold good** to apply to something, or be true or valid ◇ **hold it** used to tell somebody to stop or wait ◇ **hold something against somebody** to resent something that somebody has done and to bear a grudge because of it ◇ **no holds barred** with no restrictions on what is allowed or included ◇ **on hold 1.** waiting to be connected or reconnected to somebody during a telephone call **2.** into or in a state of suspension or postponement ○ *put our holiday plans on hold*

hold back *v* **1.** *vti* to keep something from happening, or keep somebody from doing something ○ *His shyness holds him back from making friends.* **2.** *vt* to withhold something or retain something within your own control ○ *accused of holding back vital information* ○ *holding back tears*

SYNONYMS See *hinder*[1].

hold down *vt* to do enough in a job or position in order to keep it (*informal*) ○ *He can't even manage to hold down one job, let alone two!*

hold forth *vi* to speak at length and sometimes tediously on a subject ○ *holding forth for hours about their flash new car*

hold in *vt* **1.** to keep back or in check ○ *It was nearly*

impossible to hold in the hounds. **2.** to suppress something such as an emotion or feeling ○ *could barely hold in my anger*

hold off *v* **1.** *vti* REFRAIN to refrain from doing something ○ *We decided to hold off until after the election.* ○ *hold off making any decisions* **2.** *vt* RESIST SOMEBODY OR SOMETHING to keep somebody or something away or prevent somebody from approaching too close ○ *A handful of soldiers held off several enemy attacks.* **3.** *vi* NOT HAPPEN to not produce bad weather conditions after threatening to do so ○ *if the rain holds off*

hold on *vi* **1.** to wait for a short while ○ *Hold on, and let's see if we can sort out this problem.* **2.** to continue on a course of action or direction or maintain something such as a set of principles or a particular state of mind ○ *He held on until he knew all was lost.* ○ *The scientist held on to her theory and finally proved it correct.*

hold out *v* **1.** *vt* EXTEND SOMETHING to stretch out or extend a part of the body, or offer something to somebody by doing this ○ *She held out her hand.* **2.** *vi* LAST to keep up or continue to be in supply ○ *Is the food holding out?* **3.** *vi* ENDURE to continue to resist and not give in to something ○ *We managed to hold out for three days against the enemy.* **4.** *vi* RESIST to refuse to settle something or accept something until all demands or conditions are met ○ *holding out for a 6% pay rise*

hold over *vt* **1.** to postpone action on or consideration of something until a later date **2.** to use something, often information or photographs, to threaten or influence somebody (*informal*) ○ *You're not going to keep holding that over me, are you?*

hold together *vti* to remain united, or cause a group of people to remain united, often despite problems or disagreements ○ *He held the family together single-handed.* ○ *It was nothing more than a desire to earn money that held them together.*

hold up *v* **1.** *vt* CAUSE DELAY TO SOMEBODY OR SOMETHING to cause somebody or something to be late or take longer than intended ○ *Minor disagreements hold up any negotiation.* ○ *I was held up in traffic.* **2.** *vt* CRIME ROB SOMEBODY OR SOMETHING to rob a person or place using violence or threats, usually at gunpoint **3.** *vt* PRESENT SOMEBODY OR SOMETHING to show or display somebody or something for a particular reason ○ *The firefighter was held up as a hero.* **4.** *vi* ENDURE to continue to function or survive ○ *How's the bike holding up?* ○ *You've been holding up well under the strain.* **5.** *vi* REMAIN SAME to remain or be maintained at a particular level or in a particular state ○ *Prices have not held up well in this recession.* **6.** *vi* STAND UP TO SCRUTINY to remain persuasive or convincing even after closer examination ○ *I don't think these ideas will hold up.* **7.** *vi* CARDS NOT PLAY HIGH CARD to delay playing a high card in order to prevent a suit from being established

hold with *vt* to approve or agree with something ○ *She doesn't hold with that kind of thinking.*

hold[2] /hōld/ *n* the area below the deck of a ship or inside an aircraft in which cargo is carried [Late 16C. Alteration of HOLE, influenced by HOLD [1]]

holdall /hṓld awl/ *n* a capacious bag or case used for carrying miscellaneous items. N Am term **carryall**

holdback /hṓld bak/ *n* **1.** SOMETHING THAT HINDERS something that prevents somebody from doing or achieving something, or prevents an event or plan from going ahead **2.** DEVICE ON HORSE-DRAWN WAGON a device on the shaft of a horse-drawn wagon or carriage that attaches to the harness, allowing the horse to hold back or back up the vehicle **3.** SOMETHING HELD BACK something withheld, usually wages or money

hold button *n* a button on a telephone that allows somebody to put a caller on hold

Holden /hṓldən/, **William** (1918–81) US actor. He was a popular clean-cut hero in many 1940s and 1950s Hollywood films such as *Sunset Boulevard* (1950) and *Bridge on the River Kwai* (1957).

holder /hṓldər/ *n* **1.** CONTAINER something designed to hold another thing (*often used in combination*) ○ *a candle holder* **2.** OWNER somebody who owns, occupies, or is in possession of something such as property or a title ○ *the current holder of the world title* **3.** FIN SOMEBODY WITH PROMISE OF PAYMENT somebody in possession of and legally entitled to receive payment on or to negotiate a note, bill, or cheque

Hölderlin /húldərlin, hṓldər lin/, **Friedrich** (1770–1843) German poet. His works include a translation of Sophocles' *Antigone* and the novel *Hyperion* (1797–99). Full name **Hölderlin, Johann Christian Friedrich**

> 'Things divine are believed in / But by those who themselves are so.'
> [Friedrich Hölderlin, 'Applause of Men'; 1796–97]

holdfast /hṓld faast/ *n* **1.** CLAMP a device designed to hold something securely, e.g. a clamp or grip **2.** BOT PLANT'S MEANS OF ATTACHING ITSELF an organ at the base of a seaweed, water plant, or fungus that attaches the organism to a surface **3.** FIRM GRASP the action or fact of holding something fast or firmly

holding /hṓlding/ *n* **1.** LEASED LAND a piece of land that is leased from somebody else, especially when used for agricultural purposes **2.** PROPERTY legally owned property, especially stocks or bonds (*often used in the plural*) **3.** SPORTS HOLDING OR OBSTRUCTING OF OPPONENT in some sports such boxing, the illegal use of the arms to hold or obstruct an opponent **4.** PSYCHOL SENSE OF SECURITY the ability of a therapist or parent to make a client or child feel contained and secure during times of growth or change

holding company *n* a company that has a controlling interest in one or more other companies through ownership of their stocks or bonds

holding operation *n* a procedure or operation designed to maintain the present situation as it is

holding pattern *n* **1.** a usually circular pattern held by an aircraft while awaiting permission to land **2.** a state of suspended action or progress ○ *He's in a holding pattern until he knows whether he's been given the scholarship.*

holdout /hṓld owt/ *n* *N Am* a refusal to agree or compromise in order to obtain better terms in a settlement ○ *The holdout lasted three weeks.*

holdover /hṓld ōvər/ *n* **1.** ARTS a performer's engagement or a set of performances of a production that is allowed to continue beyond the term originally agreed **2.** *N Am* somebody who remains in a job or other position that has come under the control of a different organization ○ *keeping the personnel files of holdover employees* **3.** *N Am* same as **hangover** (sense 2)

holdup /hṓld up/ *n* **1.** ROBBERY an act of robbing a person or place using violence or threats, usually at gunpoint **2.** DELAY a situation in which somebody or something is delayed or takes longer than planned ○ *delayed by holdups on the M40* **3.** CARDS WITHHOLDING OF CARD the holding back of a card instead of playing it to take a trick early in the play of a hand

hole /hōl/ *n* **1.** CAVITY a hollow space in a solid object or area ○ *The hole had filled with water.* **2.** APERTURE a gap or opening in or through something ○ *a hole in my socks* ○ *a hole in the defensive line* **3.** BURROW a hollowed-out area in the earth where an animal such as a rabbit or mouse lives **4.** FLAW a fault or flaw in something such as logic, an argument, or a position ○ *But there are so many holes in her theory.* **5.** UNPLEASANT PLACE a dark or dirty place, especially a place where somebody lives (*informal*) **6.** AWKWARD SITUATION an awkward or embarrassing situation (*informal*) **7.** PRISONER'S CELL a prison cell or dungeon (*informal*) **8.** GOLF TARGET IN GOLF in golf, a small round cavity or cup on a green into which the ball is hit **9.** GOLF AREA OF GOLF COURSE a part of a golf course that consists of a tee, a fairway, and a green with a hole and is a basic element in scoring. A golf course usually has 18 holes. **10.** ELECTRONICS MOBILE SPACE IN SEMICONDUCTOR a space normally occupied by an electron in the lattice structure of a semiconductor material that is mobile and can act as a carrier of a positive charge ■ *v* (**holes, holing, holed**) **1.** *vt* PERFORATE SOMETHING to make a hole or holes in something ○ *This new device holes a ream of paper perfectly.* **2.** *vt* PUT BALL IN HOLE to hit or drive a ball into one of the holes of a golf course **3.** *vi* GO INTO HOLE to go or climb into a hole [Old English *hol* 'hollow', probably < Indo-European, 'hide, conceal'] —**holey** *adj* ◇ **make a hole in something** to use up a large part of something (*informal*) ○ *The monthly rent makes a considerable hole in my salary.* ◇ **pick holes in something** to look for and find minor mistakes in something, particularly in an argument

SPELLCHECK hole or **whole**? Do not confuse the spelling of ***hole*** and ***whole***, which sound similar. ***Hole*** is chiefly used as a noun, denoting a hollow space, a gap, an unpleasant place, or an awkward situation, as in *a hole in the ground*; it is also used as a verb, meaning 'make a hole in' or 'put in a hole'. ***Whole*** is an adjective, noun, or adverb referring to something in its entirety, as in *the whole world, the whole of the summer, a whole new ball game.*

SYNONYMS See ***criticize.***

hole out *vi* to hit a golf ball into a hole

hole up *vi* **1.** to hide away somewhere (*slang*) **2.** to go into a hole, cave, or other similar place to shelter or hibernate

hole-and-corner *adj* secret or secretive ○ *hole-and-corner activities*

hole card *n* in stud poker, a card dealt face down that only the holder can see

hole in one (*plural* **holes in one**) *n* a golf shot that enters the hole directly from the tee

hole-in-the-wall (*plural* **holes-in-the-wall**) *n* (*informal*) **1.** an automatic cash dispenser located in the outside wall of a bank or other building **2.** a small unpretentious out-of-the-way place such as a restaurant or other business

Holi /hṓli/ *n* a Hindu festival during which people celebrate the time when Krishna paid amorous attention to young women tending cows by spraying coloured water over each other. Date: early Phalguna. [Late 17C. < Hindi *holī*]

holiday /hólli day, -di/ *n* **1.** DAY OF LEISURE a day taken off or set aside for leisure and enjoyment as a break from work or usual activity **2.** PERIOD OF LEISURE a period of time free from work or usual activity and given over to leisure and enjoyment ○ *the summer holidays* ○ *on holiday in Spain* ○ *a holiday resort* N Am term **vacation** **3.** LEGAL DAY OFF a day set aside by law, statute, or custom as exempt from regular work or business activities, usually to celebrate or commemorate something that happened on or near that date ○ *a public holiday* **4.** HOLY DAY the day or days of a religious festival ■ *vi* (**-days, -daying, -dayed**) SPEND HOLIDAY to go on or spend a holiday. N Am term **vacation** [Old English *hāligdæg* 'holy day']

Holiday /hólli day/, **Billie** (1915–59) US jazz singer. Known for her emotionally charged renditions of popular songs, she collaborated with Count Basie and Artie Shaw. Her autobiography *Lady Sings the Blues* (1956) was later made into a film. Born **Holiday, Eleanora**. Known as **Lady Day**

> 'I can't stand to sing the same song the same way two nights in succession, let alone two years or ten years. If you can, then it ain't music, it's close-order drill, or exercise or yodeling or something, not music.'
> [Billie Holiday, *Lady Sings the Blues*; 1956]

holiday camp *n* a purpose-built site, often by the sea, that provides accommodation, organized leisure activities, and facilities for people who go there for a holiday

holidaymaker /hólli day maykər, -di-/ *n* somebody who is on holiday. N Am term **vacationer**

holier-than-thou /hṓli ər-/ (*disapproving*) *adj* aggressively or offensively pompous or self-righteous ○ *Her holier-than-thou attitude puts people off.* ■ *n* an aggressively or offensively pompous or self-righteous person or organization ○ *The chairman is regarded as one of the bigger holier-than-thous.*

holiness /hṓlinəss/ *n* the state or quality of being holy

Holiness *n* a title used in addressing or referring to the pope

holism /hṓlizəm/ *n* **1.** the view that a whole system of beliefs must be analysed rather than simply its individual components **2.** the theory of the importance of taking all of somebody's physical, mental, and social conditions into account in the treatment of illness [Early 20C. < Greek *holos* 'whole'] —**holist** *n*

holistic /hō lístik/ *adj* **1.** characterized by the view that a whole system of beliefs must be analysed rather than simply its individual components **2.** taking into account all of somebody's physical,

mental, and social conditions in the treatment of illness —**holistically** adv

holland /hóllənd/ n a strong smooth linen fabric. Use: upholstery. [14C. After HOLLAND]

Holland /hóllənd/ 1. ♦ Netherlands (informal) 2. former administrative division of Lincolnshire, England, known as the Parts of Holland. It was abolished in 1974.

Holland, **Sir Sidney George** (1893–1961) prime minister of New Zealand (1949–57). Elected to the New Zealand parliament in 1935, he became leader of the National Party in 1940. See table at **prime minister**

hollandaise sauce /hóllən dáyz-/, **hollandaise** n a rich creamy piquant sauce made from butter, egg yolks, and vinegar or lemon juice [< French, form of *Hollandais* 'Dutch']

Hollander /hólləndər/ n somebody who comes from the Netherlands (archaic)

Hollands /hóllǝndz/ n Dutch gin (archaic) [Late 18C. < obsolete Dutch *Hollandsch genever* 'Dutch gin']

holler /hóllər/ (informal) vti (-lers, -lering, -lered) N Am SHOUT to call out or shout something ○ *If you need me, just holler!* ■ n 1. N Am LOUD CRY a loud cry or shout 2. US WORK SONG a work song originally sung by enslaved African American people [Late 17C. Probably partly < Old French *halloer* 'pursue with shouting', an imitation of the sound, partly < French *holà* 'stop!' < *ho* 'ho' + *là* 'there']

hollow /hóllō/ adj 1. NOT SOLID having empty space inside ○ *a hollow tree trunk* 2. CONCAVE sunk deep into the surface of something 3. NOT FULL-TONED resonating or echoing as if in an empty space ○ *a hollow, booming sound* 4. INSINCERE not sincere or genuine ○ *a hollow laugh* 5. MEANINGLESS lacking meaning or substance ○ *a hollow victory* 6. HUNGRY having the feeling of an empty stomach ■ n 1. CAVITY a hollow or concave place or area ○ *held the chick in the hollow of his hand* 2. SMALL SHALLOW VALLEY a sunken or low-lying area of ground ■ v (-lows, -lowing, -lowed) 1. vt MAKE CAVITY IN SOMETHING to form a concave area or cavity in something by removing contents 2. vti MAKE OR BECOME HOLLOWED to make something hollow, or become hollow ○ *eyes hollowed from lack of sleep* ■ adv HOLLOWLY in a hollow way ○ *Their voices rang hollow in the emptied streets.* [Old English *holh* 'hollow place, hole, cave', related to HOLE] —**hollowly** adv —**hollowness** n

> CULTURAL NOTE *The Hollow Men*, a poem (1925) by US-born British writer T. S. Eliot. One of Eliot's most pessimistic works, it depicts a barren, ghostly land peopled by soulless beings. Its imagery and concern with the sterility of modern civilization link it to 'The Waste Land', but in 'The Hollow Men' the message, conveyed in short lines and repetitive phrases, is more direct and bereft of any hope of redemption. The oft-quoted words 'This is the way the world ends/ Not with a bang but a whimper' come from this poem.

Hollows /hóllōz/, **Fred** (1930–93) New Zealand-born Australian ophthalmologist. He was a pioneer of the treatment of trachoma among Aboriginal Australians and founder of eye health programmes in a number of developing countries. Full name **Hollows, Frederick Cossom**

hollowware /hóllō wair/ n N Am articles of tableware and kitchenware such as bowls, cups, and jugs that are hollow, as opposed to items such as plates and saucers

holly

holly /hólli/ (plural -lies) n 1. an evergreen tree or bush with glossy, prickly leaves and bright red berries. Genus: *Ilex*. 2. the leaves and berries of holly, used especially as a Christmas decoration [12C. Shortening of Old English *hole(g)n* < Germanic]

Holly /hólli/, **Buddy** (1938–59) US musician. His band, the Crickets, was one of the earliest rock-and-roll groups, and helped establish the standard lineup of two guitars, bass, and drums. His hit songs included 'That'll Be the Day' and 'Peggy Sue' (both 1957). He became a popular icon after his early death in a plane crash. Born **Holley, Charles Hardin**

hollyhock

hollyhock /hólli hok/ n a very tall flowering plant of the mallow family with hairy stems. Latin name: *Alcea rosea*. [13C. < alteration of HOLY + obsolete *hock* 'mallow', origin ?]

holly oak n TREES same as **holm oak** [Because its foliage resembles holly]

Hollywood[1] /hólliwood/ n the US film industry as a whole

Hollywood[2] /hólliwood/ district of Los Angeles, California, a centre of the US film and television industry

holm[1] /hōm/, **holme** n 1. a piece of low-lying flat land next to a river or stream 2. a small island in a river, lake, or estuary, or near the coastal mainland [Pre-12C. < Old Norse *holmr* 'islet in a bay, meadow' < Indo-European, 'be prominent']

holm[2] /hōm/ n 1. TREES same as **holm oak** 2. regional a holly tree or bush [14C. Alteration of obsolete *hollin* < Old English *hole(g)n* (see HOLLY)]

holme n GEOG another spelling of **holm**[1]

Holmes /hōmz/, **Oliver Wendell** (1809–94) US physician and writer. He is best known for his essays collected in volumes including *The Autocrat of the Breakfast-Table* (1858). His poems 'Old Ironsides' and 'Chambered Nautilus' are considered classics of American literature.

> 'Put not your trust in money, but put your money in trust.'
> [Oliver Wendell Holmes, *The Autocrat of the Breakfast-Table*; 1858]

> 'It is the province of knowledge to speak and it is the privilege of wisdom to listen.'
> [Oliver Wendell Holmes, *The Poet at the Breakfast-Table*; 1872]

Holmes, **Oliver Wendell, Jr.** (1841–1935) associate justice of the US Supreme Court (1902–32). He was known for his liberal interpretations of the US Constitution. Known as **the Great Dissenter**

> 'The life of the law has not been logic: it has been experience.'
> [Oliver Wendell Holmes, Jr., *Common Law*; 1881]

Holmes à Court /hōmz ə kawrt/, **Robert** (1937–90) South-African-born Australian business executive. He was the head of the Bell Group Ltd., one of Australia's largest companies during the 1980s. Full name **Holmes à Court, Michael Robert Hamilton**

> 'Big business is only small business with an extra nought on the end.'
> [Robert Holmes à Court, *Sydney Morning Herald*; 25 August 1985]

holmic /hólmik/ adj resembling or containing holmium

holmium /hólmi əm/ n a silvery-white malleable metallic element of the rare-earth group. Source: ga-

dolinite, monazite. Symbol Ho. See table at **element** [Late 19C. < *Holmia*, Latinized form of STOCKHOLM]

holm oak n a broad-leaved evergreen tree grown widely for ornament. Native to: southern Europe. Latin name: *Quercus ilex*. [< HOLM[2]]

holo- prefix whole, complete ○ *hologynic* [< Greek *holos* 'whole, entire' < Indo-European]

holocaust /hóllə kawst/ n 1. TOTAL DESTRUCTION wholesale or mass destruction, especially of human life ○ *a nuclear holocaust* 2. COMPLETE DESTRUCTION BY FIRE complete consumption by fire, especially of a large number of human beings or animals 3. BURNT OFFERING a religious sacrifice that is totally consumed by fire [13C. < Old French *holocauste* < Greek *holokaustos* 'burnt whole' < *kaiein* 'burn'] —**holocaustal** /hóllə káwst'l/ adj —**holocaustic** /-káwstik/ adj

> ORIGIN *Holocaust* was originally used in English for a 'burnt offering', a 'sacrifice completely consumed by fire' (Mark 12:33, 'more than all whole burnt offerings and sacrifices' in the Authorized Version of the Bible, was translated by William Tyndale in 1526 as 'a greater thing than all holocausts and sacrifices'). John Milton is the first English writer recorded as using it in the wider sense 'complete destruction by fire', in the late 17th century, and succeeding centuries its modern application to 'nuclear destruction' and 'mass murder' – Bishop Ken, for instance, wrote in 1711 'Should general Flame this World consume...An Holocaust for Fontal Sin', and Leitch Ritchie in 1833 refers to Louis VII making 'a holocaust of thirteen hundred persons in a church'. The specific application to the mass murder of the Jews by the Nazis during World War II was introduced by historians during the 1950s, probably as an equivalent to Hebrew *ḥurban* and *shoah* 'catastrophe' (used in the same sense).

Holocaust n the systematic extermination of millions of European Jews, as well as Roma, Slavs, intellectuals, gay people, and political dissidents, by the Nazis and their allies during World War II. In popular usage, Holocaust refers particularly to the extermination of European Jews.

Holocaust Day, **Holocaust Memorial Day** n an annual commemoration of the Holocaust. Date: 27th of Nisan in many countries, 27 January in the United Kingdom.

Holocene /hóllō seen/ n the present epoch of geological time, which began 10,000 years ago. See table at **geological time** [Late 19C. < French < Greek *holos* 'whole' + *kainos* 'new, recent'] —**Holocene** adj

holocrine /hóllō krin, -krīn/ adj relating to a gland whose secretions are derived from the substance of the gland itself, e.g. a sebaceous gland

holoenzyme /hóllō én zīm/ n an active enzyme composed of a protein and coenzyme

hologram /hóllə gram/ n 1. a three-dimensional image of an object that is a photographic record of light interference patterns produced using a photographic plate and light from a laser 2. the image produced by a hologram

holograph[1] /hóllə graaf, -graf/ n a document entirely handwritten by its author, especially a manuscript, letter, or unwitnessed will [Early 17C. Via late Latin < Greek *holographos* 'written whole'] —**holograph** adj

holograph[2] /hóllə graaf, -graf/ n OPTICS same as **hologram**

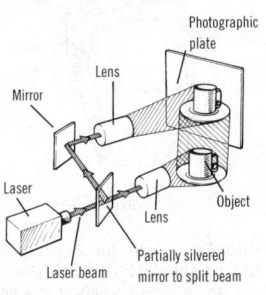

holography

holography /ho lóggrəfi/ n a method of recording and showing a three-dimensional image of an object

zh vision. In foreign words: kh German Bach; aN French vin; aaN French blanc; ŏ German schön, French feu; oN French bon; ōN French un; ū as in French rue. Stress marks: ´ as in secret /seékrət/, academic /ákə démmik/

using a photographic plate and light from a laser —
holographic /hólla gráffik/ adj —**holographically** adv

hologynic /hóllo jínnik, -gínik/ adj describes genetic
traits that are inherited and passed on only by
females [< HOLO- + Greek gunē 'woman']

holohedral /hóllo heédrəl/ adj describes crystals that
have all the faces required for complete symmetry

holoku /hólō koo/ (plural same) n a floor-length Hawaiian dress with a train, closely fitted and without
a waistline, worn on formal occasions and traditionally by brides [Late 19C. < Hawaiian]

holomorphic /hóllo máwrfik/ adj CRYSTALS same as
holohedral —**holomorphism** n

holomu'u /hóllo moò oo/ (plural same) n an ankle-
length Hawaiian dress, closely fitted and without
a waistline, often worn on formal occasions [<
Hawaiian]

holophrastic /hóllo frástik/ adj containing the idea of
a sentence or phrase in one word, e.g. 'goodbye'
[Mid-19C. < HOLO- + Greek phrastikos < phrazein 'tell']

holophyte /hóla fīt/ n an organism that synthesizes
complex organic molecules by photosynthesis

holophytic /hólla fíttik/ adj able to synthesize complex
organic molecules by photosynthesis

holoplankton /hóllo plángktən/ n organisms that
remain free-swimming plankton throughout their
life cycle

holothurian /hóllo thyoóri ən/ n an invertebrate sea
animal (**echinoderm**) of the class that includes the
sea cucumber. Holothurians have a mouth surrounded by tentacles at one end, an anus at the
other, and a body that contains calcitic material
but is not rigid. Class: Holothuroidea. [Mid-19C.
< modern Latin Holothuria < Latin holothurion, a sea crea-
ture] —**holothurian** adj

holotype /hóllo tīp/ n the individual organism used
in naming and describing a new species and usually
preserved afterwards —**holotypic** /hóllo típpik/ adj

holozoic /hóllo zó ik/ adj obtaining nutrition from
other organisms or organic matter, as most animals
do

hols /holz/ n holidays, especially school holidays or
somebody's main annual holiday (informal) ○ during
the hols [Early 20C. Contraction of holidays]

Holst /hōlst/, **Gustav** (1874–1934) British composer. He
is best remembered for his popular orchestral suite
The Planets (1914–16). Full name **Holst, Gustav Theodore**

'Never compose anything unless the not
composing of it becomes a positive nuisance to you.'
[Gustav Holst, Letter to W. G. Whittaker;
1921]

Holstein /hól stīn/, **Holstein-Friesian** n ANZ, N Am BREED
a large black-and-white dairy cow belonging to a
breed known for its abundant milk production. UK
term **Friesian** [Mid-19C. After a region, formerly of the
Netherlands, now of N Germany]

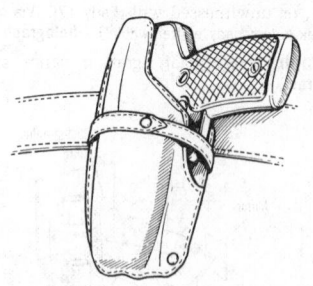
holster

holster /hólstər/ n a holder for a pistol, usually worn
on the hip or shoulder [Mid-17C. Probably < Dutch
< Indo-European, 'to cover'] —**holster** vt —**holstered** adj

holt[1] /hōlt/ n 1. a wood or copse (archaic) 2. regional
a wooded hill [Old English, < Germanic]

holt[2] /hōlt/ n the lair of an otter or another burrowing
animal [14C. Variant of HOLD[1] (noun)]

Holt /hōlt/, **Harold** (1908–67) prime minister of Aus-
tralia (1966–67). He entered the Australian House of
Representatives as a Liberal Party politician in
1935. In 1967 he disappeared while swimming off
Mornington Peninsula in Victoria. Full name **Holt,
Harold Edward**. See table at **prime minister**

holus-bolus /hóləss bóləss/ adv all at once or all
together (archaic) [Mid-19C. Origin ?]

holy /hóli/ adj (-lier, -liest) 1. SACRED relating to,
belonging to, or coming from a divine being or
power ○ holy relics 2. SAINTLY devoted to the service
of God, a god, or a goddess 3. PURE morally and
spiritually perfect and of a devoutly religious
character ○ a holy man 4. CONSECRATED dedicated or
set apart for religious purposes ○ these holy grounds
5. AWE-INSPIRING having a character that evokes
reverence ○ Arlington National Cemetery is a holy
place for many Americans. 6. USED IN EXPRESSIONS OF
SURPRISE used in various expressions to show
surprise (informal) ○ Holy mackerel! ■ n (plural -lies)
1. HOLY THING something sanctified or venerated 2.
HOLY PERSON a devoutly religious or saintly person
[Old English hālig < Germanic] —**holily** adv

Holy Alliance n an alliance between Russia, Prussia,
and Austria in 1815 advocating government according to Christian principles

Holy Ark n JUDAISM same as **ark** (sense 3)

Holy Bible n CHR same as **Bible** (sense 1)

Holy City n 1. Jerusalem as a city of great religious
significance 2. heaven in Christian tradition

Holy Communion n CHR same as **Communion** (senses
1, 3)

holy cow interj N Am used to express surprise or
annoyance

Holy Cross n in Christianity, the cross that Jesus
Christ died on

holy day n a day set aside for the celebration of a
religious festival

holy day of obligation n a Roman Catholic festival
during which Catholics are required to attend Mass
and abstain from some types of work

Holy Family n in Christianity, the young Jesus
Christ, his mother Mary, and Mary's husband, St
Joseph, especially as represented in art

Holy Father n in the Roman Catholic Church, the
pope

Holy Ghost n CHR same as **Holy Spirit**

holy grail n same as **grail**

Holy Grail n CHR same as **Grail**

Holyhead /hólli héd, hólli hed/ seaport and resort on
the northern coast of Holy Island, northwestern
Wales. Population: 11,796 (1991).

Holyhead Island ♦ **Holy Island** (sense 2)

Holy Innocents' Day n in the Christian Church, the
day that commemorates the order given by Herod
to massacre all baby boys in Bethlehem. Date: 28
December.

Holy Island /hóli-/ 1. ♦ **Lindisfarne** 2. island in
northwestern Wales, situated off the island of
Anglesey. Area: 39 sq. km/16 sq. mi.

Holy Joe /-jō/ n (dated slang) 1. a priest or other
member of the clergy 2. a sanctimonious or self-
righteous person

Holy Land region on the eastern shore of the Mediterranean Sea, comprising the historic region of
Palestine. It is regarded as holy by Christians, Jews,
and Muslims.

Holy Loch sea loch on the Firth of Clyde, Scotland

Holyoake /hóli ōk/, **Sir Keith** (1904–83) prime minister
of New Zealand (1957, 1960–72). A National Party
politician, he was the first politician to become
governor general (1977–80). Full name **Holyoake, Sir
Keith Jacka**. See table at **prime minister**

Holy Office n 1. a permanent committee of the Roman
Catholic College of Cardinals that deals with doctrine and morals 2. HIST same as **Inquisition**

holy of holies n 1. the innermost chamber in the
Jewish Temple in Jerusalem, where the Ark of the
Covenant was kept 2. a place considered to be
especially sacred

holy orders npl 1. RITE OF CHRISTIAN ORDINATION in the
Christian Church, the rite or sacrament of or-

dination as a minister or priest 2. CHRISTIAN MINISTER'S
OR PRIEST'S RANK the rank or position of a Christian
minister or priest 3. ROMAN CATHOLIC OR ANGLICAN RANKS
in the Roman Catholic Church, the ranks of priest,
deacon, and subdeacon, or in the Anglican Church,
the ranks of bishop, priest, and deacon

Holy Roller n an offensive term for a member of a
Christian group that worships in what is perceived
to be an ecstatic or frenzied way, with shouting,
bodily movements, and trances (slang) [< the movement of the body during worship]

Holy Roman Empire n an empire in Germany and
northern Italy from 800 to 1806, initially a revival
of the Western Roman Empire. It became confined
to Germany, and the emperor's authority was negligible after 1254. From 1438 the imperial crown was
held almost continuously by the Hapsburg
family. —**Holy Roman Emperor** n

Holyroodhouse /hóllirood hówss/ n an elaborately
decorated palace in Edinburgh, established in the
15th century as the principal residence of the
monarch of Scotland

Holy Saturday n in Christianity, the Saturday preceding Easter Sunday

Holy Scripture n all or part of the Christian Bible

Holy See n 1. in the Roman Catholic Church, the see
of the pope as Bishop of Rome 2. in the Roman
Catholic Church, the government departments, jurisdiction, and authority of the Vatican

Holy Sepulchre n in Christianity, the tomb in which
the body of Jesus Christ was laid after the Crucifixion

holy smoke interj N Am used to express surprise or
annoyance

Holy Spirit n in Christianity, the third person of the
Trinity, understood as the spiritual force of God

holystone /hóli stōn/ n a piece of soft sandstone used
for scouring the decks of ships [Origin ?] —**holystone**
vt

Holy Synod n the governing body of any of the
Eastern Orthodox Christian churches

holy terror n a difficult or frightening person
(informal) ○ That child is a holy terror.

Holy Thursday n 1. in the Anglican Church, As-
cension Day, the 40th day after Easter 2. in the
Roman Catholic Church, Maundy Thursday, the
Thursday before Easter, commemorating the Last
Supper and the day before Jesus Christ was cru-
cified

Holy Trinity n CHR same as **Trinity** (sense 1)

holy war n a war undertaken in the name of a religion

holy water n in Christianity, water that has been
blessed by a priest and is used in a church for
blessings, baptisms, and other holy rituals

Holy Week n in the Christian calendar, the final week
of Lent, beginning on Palm Sunday and including
Maundy Thursday, Good Friday, and Holy Saturday

Holy Writ n sacred Christian writings, especially the
Bible

Holy Year n in the Roman Catholic Church, a period
of remission from sin declared by the pope with
some conditions attached, usually at 25-year intervals

hom- prefix same as **homo-** (used before vowels)

homage /hómmij/ n 1. a show of reverence and respect
towards somebody 2. a formal public acknowledgment of allegiance on the part of a vassal
towards a feudal lord [13C. < Old French]

hombre /óm bray/ n N Am same as **man** n (sense 1)
(informal) [Mid-19C. Via Spanish < Latin homo 'human
being']

homburg /hóm burg/ n a man's felt hat with an upturned brim and a lengthways crease in the crown
[Late 19C. After Homburg, town in W Germany]

home /hōm/ n 1. ⚠ RESIDENCE the place where a person,
family, or household lives ○ invited them home 2.
FAMILY GROUP a family or any group that lives
together ○ Theirs was a happy home, full of love. 3.
BIRTHPLACE the place where somebody was born or
brought up or feels that he or she belongs ○ Home
is York. 4. NATIVE HABITAT the place where an animal
is most common or indigenous ○ home to the grizzly
bear 5. PLACE OF ORIGIN OF SOMETHING the place where

something originated or is based ○ *the home of football* ○ *home to the state university* **6. HEADQUARTERS** the headquarters or main place of operations of an organization, especially a sports team ○ *The team plays at home this weekend.* **7. SAFE PLACE** a place where a person or animal can find refuge and safety or live in security **8. PLACE OF ASSISTANCE** an establishment where somebody who is in need of care, rest, or medical attention can stay or find help ○ *My grandmother moved into a home.* **9.** COMPUT same as **homepage 10.** COMPUT **STARTING POINT OF CURSOR** the starting position of a cursor in an application or text **11. GRAVE** the place where somebody is imagined to dwell after death (*literary*) **12.** SPORTS **GOAL** in many games, the place or point that must be hit in order to score or reached in order to be safe from attack **13.** BASEBALL same as **home plate** ■ *adj* **1. DOMESTIC** relating to somebody's own home or country ○ *home cooking* **2. OF HOUSEHOLD** for, belonging to, or produced in a dwelling or household ○ *home life* **3. NATIVE** happening in or coming from somebody's native territory or permanent base, especially a sports team's own ground ○ *home news* ○ *a home game* **4. EFFECTIVE** to the point or central to achieving a goal ○ *She won the argument with that home thrust.* **5. PRINCIPAL** relating to or belonging to the headquarters of a business or enterprise ○ *She was promoted to the company's home office.* ■ *adv* **1. AT OR TO SOMEBODY'S HOME** at or to the house, household, or country where somebody lives ○ *He desperately wanted to get home.* **2. EFFECTIVELY** to the point or to a desired goal ○ *criticism that hit home* **3. TO CENTRE** to the centre or heart of something or as far as possible into a desired position ○ *drove the nail home* ■ *v* (**homes, homing, homed**) **1.** *vi* **GO HOME** to go back to the house, household, or country where you live **2.** *vi* **RETURN TO BASE** to return home, especially to fly home accurately (*refers to animals and birds*) **3.** *vi* **DWELL** to have a home and live in it (*dated*) **4.** *vt* **DIRECT SOMEBODY OR SOMETHING HOME** to take or send somebody or something home (*dated*) **5.** *vt* **PROVIDE SOMEBODY OR SOMETHING WITH HOME** to give a home to somebody or something [Old English *hām* < Germanic] —**home-like** *adj* ◇ **at home 1.** at ease or in a familiar and friendly place **2.** having knowledge of or familiarity with a subject or activity **3.** ready to receive visitors ◇ **come** *or* **be brought home to somebody** to be fully understood and appreciated by somebody ◇ **come home to roost** to result in undesirable or negative effects, usually after a fairly long period of time ◇ **home alone** left alone in a house or flat when supervision or companionship is required or desired (*informal*) ◇ **home and dry** *UK* with something successfully completed ◇ **home and hosed** *ANZ* same as **home and dry** ◇ **home free** *N Am* same as **home and dry** ◇ **play away from home** to be sexually unfaithful to a spouse or partner (*informal*) ◇ **take home something** to earn a particular amount of money after all deductions, e.g. for tax, have been made

USAGE home or **house**? Many consider ***home*** an affectation when used anywhere that ***house*** would be appropriate, as in *Beautiful homes now available.* ***Home*** is nonetheless useful to express the idea of dwelling places of various sorts, including flats and other dwellings that are not accurately described as houses. ***House***, in many contexts, suggests a single-family dwelling. For example, if *The tornado destroyed 17 homes* is meant to convey that 17 residential structures were demolished, the word should have been ***houses***. *Most homes in town lost electricity*, however, no doubt refers to households of all descriptions, so here ***homes*** is the better choice.

home in on *vt* **1.** to locate and proceed straight towards a particular target **2.** to direct all attention or energy towards something ○ *She instinctively homed in on the weakest aspects of the production.*

USAGE See *hone*[1].

Home (of the Hirsel) /hyoóm ō t͟hə húrss'l/, **Sir Alec Douglas-Home, Baron** ➧ **Douglas-Home, Sir Alec**

home banking *n* an electronic banking system that allows a customer to carry out transactions at home

home base *n* BASEBALL same as **home plate**

homebody /hṓm bodi/ (*plural* **-ies**) *n* somebody who prefers home to other places (*informal*)

homebound /hṓm bownd/ *adj* **1.** moving or travelling towards home **2.** *N Am* same as **housebound**

homeboy /hṓm boy/ *n N Am* a man or boy from somebody's home town, state, or neighbourhood, especially somebody who shares that person's own culture and customs (*informal*)

homebred /hṓm bréd/ *adj* **1.** bred or raised at home **2.** lacking worldly experience

home-brew *n* an alcoholic beverage, especially beer, that has been brewed at home for personal consumption —**home-brewed** *adj*

homebuyer /hṓm bī ər/ *n* somebody who is buying or is interested in buying a house or flat

home care *n* care provided at home by family members or professional carers to people who otherwise might require institutional care. US term **home healthcare**

homecoming /hṓm kuming/ *n* the arrival home of somebody who has been away ○ *a party to celebrate his homecoming*

Home Counties the counties nearest to London, England, usually taken to include Kent, Surrey, Essex, Buckinghamshire, Berkshire, Hertfordshire, and East and West Sussex. Middlesex, formerly included, is now part of London.

home economics *n* the science or study of diet, cookery, childcare, and other subjects related to the running of a home, as taught in schools (*takes a singular or plural verb*)

home equity loan *n* a loan in which the borrower's home is used as collateral, usually secondary to a first mortgage

home farm *n UK, S Africa* on an estate with a number of farms, the farm that produces food for the owner

home fries *npl N Am* boiled sliced potatoes fried in butter or oil, sometimes with onions and seasonings

home from home *n* a place in which somebody feels as comfortable and relaxed as at home

home front *n* **1.** the civilian effort and activity at home in support of a war waged abroad ○ *On the home front valiant efforts are being made to get the harvest in on time.* **2.** somebody's life at home

home furnishings *npl* articles that decorate a house and make it more comfortable, e.g. furniture, bedding, lighting, wallpaper, and carpets

homegirl /hṓm gurl/ *n N Am* a girl or woman from somebody's home town, state, or neighbourhood, especially one who shares that person's own culture and customs (*informal*)

home ground *n* **1.** surroundings that are familiar to somebody ○ *I'd prefer to meet them on my home ground.* **2.** an area of knowledge that somebody is familiar with and feels confident about ○ *I was on home ground then, and felt able to refute what he'd said quite forcefully.*

homegrown /hṓm grṓn/ *adj* **1.** grown in somebody's own garden or on somebody's own land **2.** produced by or coming from a specific area or region ○ *homegrown talent*

home guard *n* **1.** a local volunteer force formed to defend an area while the regular army is fighting elsewhere **2.** a member of a home guard

Home Guard *n* **1.** an army of volunteer civilians formed in the United Kingdom during World War II to help protect and police the country **2.** a member of a usually local or state military unit, especially an army unit (*dated*)

home health aide *n N Am* same as **carer** (sense 2)

home healthcare *n US* HEALTH SERVICES same as **home care**

home help *n* **1.** somebody who is paid to help with domestic tasks **2.** a service provided by a local authority to help people in need with domestic tasks they cannot perform

home improvement *n* **1.** a change or addition made to a house or flat that improves living conditions and increases its market value, or the making of such changes or additions **2.** the act of making home improvements

homeland /hṓm land/ *n* **1.** the country where somebody was born or where somebody lives and feels that he or she belongs **2.** in South Africa during the apartheid era, a partially self-governing region created and set aside for the Black population

home language *n* the language spoken regularly or most often in the home by the people living there

homeless /hṓmləss/ *adj* having no home of any kind ■ *npl* people without a home of any kind —**homelessness** *n*

home loan *n* a loan given by a bank to enable somebody to buy a house or flat

homely /hṓmli/ (**-lier, -liest**) *adj* **1. COSY** simple, comfortable, and unpretentious in a way that you feel resembles your own home **2. UNPRETENTIOUS IN MANNER** having a simple, unpretentious, and warm-hearted manner **3.** *N Am* **NOT GOOD-LOOKING** plain or less than pleasing in appearance ○ *a rather homely face* —**homeliness** *n*

SYNONYMS See ***unattractive.***

homemade /hṓm máyd/ *adj* **1.** made at home using traditional methods, instead of by a manufacturer ○ *Have you tried some of my homemade marmalade?* **2.** roughly or crudely constructed to perform a specific function or purpose

homemaker /hṓm maykər/ *n* somebody who stays at home to manage a household rather than working outside the home

home movie *n* an amateur film recording everyday events or a special occasion in somebody's life, e.g. a family holiday

homeo- *prefix* similar, alike ○ *homeotherm* [< Greek *homoios* 'similar' < *homos* (see HOMO-)]

homeobox /hṓmi ō boks/ *n* a short section of nucleotides with a base sequence that is almost identical in all genes that contain it

Home Office *n* in the United Kingdom, the department of the government that is responsible for domestic and internal affairs

homeopathy /hṓmi óppəthi/, **homoeopathy** *n* a complementary disease-treatment system in which a patient is given minute doses of natural substances that in larger doses would produce symptoms of the disease itself —**homeopath** /hṓmi ə path/ *n* —**homeopathic** /hṓmi ə páthik/ *adj* —**homeopathically** *adv* —**homeopathist** *n*

USAGE ***Homeopathic*** is sometimes used in a general way to refer to treatments for health when *herbal* or *natural* would be more appropriate.

homeostasis /hṓmi ō stáyssiss/, **homoeostasis** *n* a state of equilibrium or a tendency to reach equilibrium, either metabolically within a cell or organism or socially and psychologically within an individual or group —**homeostatic** /-státtik/ *adj*

homeotherm /hṓmi ō thurm/, **homoeotherm, homoiotherm** /hō móyə-/ *n* an organism whose stable body temperature is generally independent of the temperature of its surrounding environment [Late 19C. < HOMEO- + Greek *thermē* 'heat'] —**homeothermic** /hṓmi ō thúrmik/ *adj* —**homeothermy** *n*

homeotic /hṓmi óttik/, **homoeotic** *adj* describes mutation in which one part or organ is transformed into another part associated with a different segment of the organism [Late 19C. < Greek *homoiōtikos* 'becoming like' < *homoios* (see HOMEO-)]

homeowner /hṓm ōnər/ *n* somebody who owns a home

homepage /hṓm payj/ *n* **1.** the opening page of an Internet website **2.** somebody's personal website on the Internet, often containing personal data, photographs, or contact information

home plate *n* in baseball, a flat slab marking the area over which a pitcher must throw the ball for a strike and on which a base runner must land in order to score

home port *n* the place of registry or regular base of a ship

homer /hṓmər/ *n* **1.** BIRDS same as **homing pigeon** (*informal*) **2.** BASEBALL same as **home run** (*informal*) **3.** ELECTRONICS a device that provides signals for guiding missiles, ships, or aircraft to their destinations

Homer /hṓmər/ (*fl* 8th century BC) Greek poet. He is credited as the author of the *Iliad* and the *Odyssey*. See Cultural note at **odyssey**

'Hunger is insolent, and will be fed.'
[Homer, *Odyssey*; late 8th century BC]

home range *n* the geographical area to which an animal generally restricts its activities

Homeric /hō mérrik/ *adj* **1. OF HOMER** relating to Homer, his work, or his times ○ *'Thus vain and false are the mere human surmises and doubts which clash with Homeric writ!'* (Alexander William Kinglake, *Eothen*; 1844) **2. OF GREEK USED IN HOMER'S POETRY** relating to the early form of ancient Greek used in Homer's poetry **3. HEROIC** characteristic of a hero (*literary*) [Early 17C. Via Latin < Greek *Homērikos* < *Homēros* 'Homer'] —**Homerically** *adv*

Homeric laughter *n* loud continuous laughter, like that of the gods in Homer's epic poems (*literary*)

Homeric simile *n* LITERAT same as **epic simile**

home rule *n* **1.** the principle or practice of self-government by a part of a larger country or commonwealth such as a municipality, colony, territory, or principality **2.** in the United States, the partial autonomy granted to cities and some counties, under which they manage their own affairs, in accordance with the Constitution

Home Rule *n* the political aim of the Irish nationalists between 1870 and 1920 in their struggle to secure self-government for Ireland

home run *n* in baseball, a hit that allows a player to make a circuit of all four bases and score a run, usually by hitting the ball out of the playing area

homeschool /hōm skool/ *N Am vti* (**-schools, -schooling, -schooled**) to teach somebody at home, or be taught at home ■ *n* a school run usually by parents in the home for their children, using an approved curriculum

homeschooler /hōm skoolər/ *n N Am* **1.** a child who is undergoing or has undergone private education, typically by the parents at home **2.** a parent who educates his or her child or children at home

Home Secretary *n* in the United Kingdom, the head of the Home Office, in charge of internal and domestic affairs

home shopping *n* shopping done electronically from home either through an on-line retail service or a television shopping channel

homesick /hōm sik/ *adj* feeling sadness and longing to be at home with family and friends when away from them —**homesickness** *n*

homesite /hōm sīt/ *n ANZ, N Am* a plot of land on which a new home can be or is constructed

homespun /hōm spun/ *adj* **1. PLAIN AND SIMPLE** plain, simple, and unpretentious ○ *inspired us with his homespun wisdom* **2.** HANDICRAFT **MADE BY HAND AT HOME** spun or woven by hand at home ○ *homespun cotton* **3.** CLOTHING, HOUSEHOLD **MADE OF HOMESPUN FABRIC** made of fabric spun or woven by hand at home ○ *a homespun shirt* ■ *n* TEXTILES **1. CLOTH FROM HOMESPUN THREAD** a coarse plain cloth woven from homespun thread **2. ROUGH CLOTH WOVEN ON POWER LOOM** a cloth similar to homespun, but woven on an automatic or electric loom

homestay /hōm stay/ *n* **1.** *N Am* a visit to somebody's home in a foreign country, often a stay by an exchange student in a family's home (*informal*) **2.** *NZ* bed-and-breakfast accommodation in a private home as opposed to a guesthouse

homestead /hōm sted/ *n* **1. HOUSE, OUTBUILDINGS, AND LAND** a house, especially a farmhouse, with its dependent buildings and land, considered as a whole **2.** *N Am* LAW **RESIDENCE EXEMPT FROM FORCED SALE** in the United States, a house, adjoining land, and buildings declared as the owner's fixed residence and therefore exempt from seizure and forced sale for the recovery of debts **3.** *ANZ* **MANAGER'S HOUSE** in Australia and New Zealand, the home of the manager or owner of a large farm **4.** *N Am* HIST **LAND CLAIMED BY SETTLER** formerly, in the United States or Canada, a piece of land occupied by a settler or squatter under the terms of the US Homestead Act or the Canadian Dominion Lands Act —**homesteader** *n*

home straight *n* **1.** the part of a racecourse between the last turn and the finishing line **2.** the last part of a journey, task, or operation ○ *We're on the home straight now.* ► N Am term **home stretch**

home-style *adj N Am* made or presented as in somebody's home ○ *were served a home-style meal in the hotel* —**home-style** *adv*

home teacher *n UK* a teacher employed by the state system to teach in their own homes children with medical conditions that prevent them from going to school. US term **visiting teacher**

home time *n* the end of the school day

home town *n* the town or city where somebody was born, spent his or her childhood, or lives on a long-term basis

home truth *n* an unpleasant but true fact about somebody's character or behaviour that he or she is told by somebody else

home truths *npl* true statements that are unpleasant or upsetting to the person they concern

hometz *n* JUDAISM same as **chametz**

home unit *n ANZ* BUILDINGS same as **unit** (sense 6)

home video *n* a video recording produced at home, often a recording of family celebrations or events

homeward /hōmwərd/ *adj* going home or in the direction of home ■ *adv* same as **homewards**

homewards /hōmwərdz/ *adv* towards or in the direction of home ○ *homeward bound*

homework /hōm wurk/ *n* **1. SCHOOL WORK DONE AT HOME** school work that pupils do outside lesson times or at home **2. PREPARATORY WORK** facts that are found out about a particular subject, especially in preparation for writing or talking about it (*informal*) **3. PAID WORK DONE AT HOME** work done at home for money, especially piecework —**homeworker** *n* —**homeworking** *n* ◇ **do your homework** to do all the necessary research and preparation for something in a thorough manner

homey[1] /hōmi/ (**-ier, -iest**), **homy** *adj* feeling as comfortable and familiar as somebody's own home ○ *a homey little hotel* [Mid-19C. < HOME] —**homeyness** *n*

homey[2] /hōmi/, **homie** *n US* same as **homeboy, homegirl** (*slang*) [Late 20C. Shortening and alteration]

home zone *n* a residential street or group of streets where drivers do not have priority over pedestrians, cyclists, and children at play

homicidal /hómmi sīd'l/ *adj* capable of or intending to kill another human being unlawfully —**homicidally** *adv*

homicide /hómmi sīd/ *n* **1.** the act or an instance of unlawfully killing another human being **2.** somebody who kills another human being unlawfully [13C. Via French < Latin *homicidium, homicida* < *homo* 'human being' + *caedere* 'kill']

homicide bomber *n US* somebody, often a suicide bomber, who uses a bomb to attack others with the intention of killing them —**homicide bombing** *n*

homie /hōmi/ *adj* a friend or fellow gang member (*used in Black English*)

homiletic /hómmi léttik/, **homiletical** /-léttik'l/ *adj* **1.** relating to, or in the style of, a sermon or homily **2.** relating to the art of writing and preaching sermons [Mid-17C. Via late Latin < Greek *homilētikos* < *homilein* 'associate with, converse' < *homilos* 'crowd'] —**homiletically** *adv*

homiletics /hómmi léttiks/ *n* the art of writing and preaching sermons (*takes a singular verb*)

homily /hómmili/ (*plural* **-lies**) *n* **1. RELIGIOUS LECTURE** a sermon on a moral or religious topic **2. MORALIZING SPEECH** a speech or other piece of writing with a moralizing theme (*disapproving*) **3.** CHR **TALK BASED ON BIBLICAL PASSAGE** in the Roman Catholic Church, an address based on the scriptures of the day [14C. Via French < Greek *homilia* 'sermon' < *homilos* 'crowd'] —**homilist** *n*

homing /hōming/ *adj* **1.** relating to or possessing the ability to find the way home after travelling a long distance **2.** describes a missile or aircraft that has equipment that enables it to guide itself to its target

homing guidance *n* a system that enables a missile or aircraft to guide itself to its target

homing pigeon *n* a domestic pigeon that is trained to return to its roost, used for racing

hominid /hómminid/ *n* a primate belonging to a family of which the modern human being is the only species still in existence. Family: Hominidae. [Late 19C. < modern Latin *Hominidae* < Latin *homin-*, stem of Latin *homo* 'human being'] —**hominid** *adj*

hominization /hómmi nī záysh'n/, **hominisation** *n* the theorized evolutionary development of human characteristics that set hominids apart from other primates [Mid-20C. < French *hominisation* < Latin *homin-* (see HOMINID)]

hominoid /hómmi noyd/ *adj* **1.** resembling a human being **2.** relating to or belonging to the superfamily that includes human beings and apes. Superfamily: Hominoidea. [Early 20C. < Latin *homin-* (see HOMINID)]

hominy /hómmini/ *n US* dried and puffed whole grains of maize that are eaten boiled [Early 17C. Contraction of Virginia Algonquian *uskatahomen*, 'that which is ground']

hominy grits *n US* FOOD same as **grits**

homo /hōmō/ (*plural* **-mos**) *n* an offensive term for a gay man (*dated slang insult*) [Early 20C. Shortening]

homo- *prefix* alike, same ○ *homograph* [< Greek *homos* < Indo-European, 'one']

homocentric /hōmō séntrik, hómmō-/ *adj* describes circles and spheres that have the same centre

homocercal /hōmō súrk'l, hómmō-/ *adj* describes a fish that has a tail with two symmetrical lobes that extend beyond the end of the vertebral column, or a tail of this kind

homochromatic /hōmō krō máttik, hómmō-/ *adj* COLOURS same as **monochromatic** (sense 1)

homochromous /hōm ō krōməss, hómm ō-/ *adj* being of just one colour [Mid-19C. < HOMO- + Greek *khrōma* 'colour']

homocyclic /hōmō sīklik, hómmō-, -síklik/ *adj* describes a chemical compound in which molecules take the form of a ring in which all the atoms are the same

homocysteine /hōmō sís teen, hómmō-/ *n* an amino acid produced in the body during the metabolism of methionine. Raised levels of homocysteine are associated with atherosclerosis.

homodont /hōmə dont, hómmə-/ *adj* used to describe vertebrates that have teeth that are all similar in shape, as in most nonmammalian vertebrates [Late 19C. < HOMO- + Greek *odont-* 'tooth']

homoeo- *prefix* another spelling of **homeo-**

homoeopathy *n* ALTERN MED another spelling of **homeopathy**

homoeostasis *n* BIOL another spelling of **homeostasis**

homoeotherm *n* ZOOL another spelling of **homeotherm**

Homo erectus /hōmō i réktəss/ *n* an extinct ancestor of the modern human being (**Homo sapiens**) living approximately 1.5 million years ago and known by fossils to have had an upright stature, a smallish brain, and a low forehead [< modern Latin, 'upright man']

homoerotic /hōmō i róttik, hómmō-/ *adj* relating to or characterized by eroticism that is focused on or inspired by people of the same sex

homoeroticism /hōmō i róttisizəm/, **homoerotism** /hōmō érrətizəm/ *n* eroticism that is focused on or inspired by people of the same sex

homogametic /hōmogə méttik/ *adj* producing gametes that have the same type of sex chromosome

homogamy /ho móggəmi/ *n* the condition of a flower in which male and female organs mature at the same time —**homogamous** *adj*

homogenate /ho mójjənət, -nayt/ *n* a substance produced by homogenizing

homogeneity /hōmōjə neé əti, hómmō-, -náy-/ *n* **1.** the quality of being of the same or a similar nature **2.** the quality of having a uniform appearance or composition [Early 17C. < medieval Latin *homogeneitas* < *homogeneus* (see HOMOGENEOUS)]

homogeneous /hōmə jeéni əss, hómmə-/, **homogenous** /ho mójjənəss/ *adj* **1.** having the same kind of constituent elements, or being similar in nature ○ *a relatively small, culturally homogeneous community* **2.** having a uniform composition or structure [Mid-17C. < medieval Latin *homogeneus* < Greek *homogenēs* 'of the same kind'] —**homogeneously** *adv* —**homogeneousness** *n*

homogenize /ho mójjə nīz/ (**-nizes, -nizing, -nized**), **homogenise** (**-nises, -nising, -nised**) *v* **1.** *vt* to emulsify the fat particles in milk or cream in order to give it an even consistency **2.** *vti* to become homogeneous, or cause something to become homogeneous [Late 19C. < HOMOGENEOUS] —**homogenization** /ho mójjə nī záysh'n/ *n* —**homogenizer** *n*

homogenous *adj* another spelling of **homogeneous**

homogeny /ho mójjəni/ *n* a similarity in individuals, organs, or parts caused by a common ancestry

homograft /hómmə graaft/ *n* SURG same as **allograft**

homograph /hómmə graaf, -graf/ *n* a word that is spelt in the same way as one or more other words but is different in meaning, e.g. the verb 'project' and the noun 'project' —**homographic** /hómmə gráffik/ *adj*

Homo habilis /hṓmō hábbiliss/ *n* an extinct ancestor of the modern human being (**Homo sapiens**) living approximately 1.5 million years ago and characterized by its ability to make and use tools [< modern Latin, 'skilful man']

homoio- *prefix* another spelling of **homeo-**

homoiotherm *n* ZOOL another spelling of **homeotherm**

Homoiousian /hṓ moy oóssi ən/ *n* a Christian who believes that Jesus Christ is of a similar, but not identical, substance to God ■ *adj* relating to the doctrine of the Homoiousians [Late 17C. < Greek *homoiousios* 'of similar substance' < *homoios* 'similar' + *ousia* 'substance'] —**Homoiousianism** *n*

homologate /ho mólla gayt/ (**-gates, -gating, -gated**) *v* **1.** *vti* LAW to confirm or sanction the validity of something **2.** *vt* to give official recognition to a prototype car or car component, thus allowing it to be used in a motor race [Early 16C. < medieval Latin *homologat-*, past participle of *homologare* 'agree' < Greek *homologos* 'agreeing' (see HOMOLOGOUS)] —**homologation** /ho mólla gáysh'n/ *n*

homological /hómmə lójjik'l, hómmə-/ *adj* SCI same as **homologous** —**homologically** *adv*

homologize /ho mólla jīz/ (**-gizes, -gizing, -gized**), **homologise** (**-gises, -gising, -gised**) *vt* to make something have a similar or related structure, position, function, or value to something else —**homologizer** *n*

homologous /ho mólləgəss/ *adj* **1.** SIMILAR sharing a similar or related structure, position, function, or value **2.** BIOL HAVING SAME ORIGIN BUT DIFFERENT FUNCTION describes biological structures such as the wing of a bird and the fin of a fish that share the same origin but have a different function **3.** CHEM OF RELATED CHEMICAL COMPOUNDS relating to a series of organic chemical compounds such as a methylene group, each of which differs from the preceding by the addition of a constant component **4.** MED HAVING IDENTICAL TISSUE produced from identical tissue [Mid-17C. < medieval Latin *homologus* < Greek *homologos* 'agreeing' < *homos* 'same' + *legein* 'speak']

homolographic /ho mólla gráffik, hómmələ-/ *adj* MAPS same as **equal-area** [Mid-19C. Alteration (after HOMO-) of *homalographic* < Greek *homalos* 'even, level']

homologue /hómmə log/ *n* **1.** a part or organ that has the same evolutionary origin as another but differs in function, e.g. a bird's wing in relation to the fin of a fish **2.** a homologous chemical compound [Mid-19C. < French < Greek *homologos* 'agreeing' (see HOMOLOGOUS)]

homology /ho mólləji/ *n* **1.** BIOL similar characteristics in two animals that are a product of descent from a common ancestor rather than a product of a similar environment **2.** CHEM the correspondence between chemical compounds in a homologous series [Early 17C. Via late Latin < Greek *homologia* 'agreement' < *homologos* (see HOMOLOGOUS)]

homolosine projection /ho mólla sīn-, hō-/ *n* a map of the Earth's surface that distorts the oceans in order to represent the continents with a minimum of distortion [< HOMOLOGRAPHIC + SINE, because it is a homolographic projection based on sinusoidal curves]

homolysis /ho mólləssiss, hō-/ *n* the breakdown of a molecule into neutral atoms or radicals —**homolytic** /hómmə líttik, hṓmə-/ *adj*

homonym /hómmənim/ *n* **1.** WORD WITH SAME SPELLING OR SOUND a word that is spelt or pronounced in the same way as one or more other words but has a different meaning. Examples include the noun and adjective 'fleet', 'plane' and 'plain', pronounced the same but spelt differently, and the verb and noun 'sow', spelt the same but pronounced differently. **2.** SOMEBODY WITH SAME NAME somebody with the same name as somebody else **3.** BIOL DUPLICATE TAXONOMIC NAME a taxonomic name that is the same as one already designating a different species or genus and cannot therefore be used [Late 17C. < Latin *homonymum* < Greek *homōnumos* (see HOMONYMOUS)] —**homonymic** /hómmə

níммik/ *adj* —**homonymity** /hómmə nímməti/ *n* —**homonymy** /ho mónnimi/ *n*

homonymous /hə mónniməss/ *adj* **1.** having the same spelling or pronunciation but a different meaning, as do the words 'peace' and 'piece' **2.** having the same name as somebody or something else [Early 17C. Via Latin < Greek *homōnumos* 'having the same name' < *onuma* 'name'] —**homonymously** *adv*

Homoousian /hṓmō oóssi ən/ *n* a Christian who believes that Jesus Christ is of the same substance as God, in accordance with the Council of Nicaea's definition of the Trinity ■ *adj* relating to the doctrine of the Homoousians [Mid-16C. < Greek *homoousios* 'of the same substance' < *homos* 'same' + *ousia* 'substance'] —**Homoousianism** *n*

homophile /hṓmō fīl, hómmō-/ *adj* **1.** ADVOCATING GAY RIGHTS supporting the rights of gay and lesbian people and appreciating their culture **2.** GAY OR LESBIAN relating to or being gay or lesbian ■ *n* **1.** GAY OR LESBIAN a gay man or lesbian **2.** SUPPORTER OF GAY RIGHTS somebody who is sympathetic to gay and lesbian people and supports their rights

homophobia /hṓmō fṓbi ə, hómmō-/ *n* an irrational hatred, disapproval, or fear of homosexuality, gay and lesbian people, or their culture [Mid-20C. < HOMOSEXUAL]

homophobic /hṓmō fṓbik, hómmō-/ *adj* showing an irrational hatred, disapproval, or fear of homosexuality, gay and lesbian people, or their culture —**homophobe** /hṓmō fōb, hómmō-/ *n*

homophone /hómmə fōn/ *n* **1.** a word that is pronounced in the same way as one or more other words but is different in meaning and sometimes spelling, as are 'hair' and 'hare' **2.** a letter or diphthong that has the same sound as one or more other letters or diphthongs [Early 17C. < Greek *homophōnos* 'having the same sound']

homophonic /hómmə fónnik/ *adj* **1.** relating to part music in which the parts move together in simple harmonization **2.** LING same as **homophonous** (sense 1) —**homophonically** *adv*

homophonous /ho móffənəss/ *adj* **1.** having the same sound or pronunciation but a different meaning or spelling, as do the words 'pale' and 'pail' **2.** MUSIC same as **homophonic** (sense 1)

homophony /hə móffəni/ *n* **1.** LING the quality of having the same pronunciation as one or more other words with a different origin and meaning **2.** MUSIC music of a largely chordal style in which there is no independence of voice parts, but rather a simple harmonization of a melody [Mid-18C. < Greek *homophōnia* 'unison' < *homophōnos* 'having the same sound']

homoplastic /hṓmō plástik, hómmō-/ *adj* describes a tissue graft that is obtained from a member of the same species as the recipient —**homoplastically** *adv*

homopolar /hṓmō pṓlər, hómmō-/ *adj* having uniform polarity —**homopolarity** /-pō lárrəti/ *n*

homopteran /ho móptərən, hō-/ *n* an insect that has the ability to suck plant juices through its mouthparts, e.g. a cicada, scale insect, or aphid. Order: Homoptera. [Mid-19C. < modern Latin *Homoptera* < Greek *homos* 'same' + *pteron* 'wing'] —**homopteran** *adj*

Homo sapiens /hṓmō sáppi enz, -sáypi-/ *n* the species of modern human beings, the only extant species of the family that also included other species named Homo. Family: Hominidae. [< Latin, 'wise man']

homoscedastic /hṓmōski dástik, hómmō-/ *adj* characterized by equal statistical variances [Early 20C. < HOMO- + Greek *skedastos* 'able to be scattered' < *skedannunai* 'scatter'] —**homoscedasticity** /-ski dass tíssəti/ *n*

homosexual /hṓmō sékshoo əl, hómmə-/ *n* SOMEBODY ATTRACTED TO SAME SEX somebody who is sexually attracted to members of his or her own sex ■ *adj* **1.** ATTRACTED TO SAME SEX sexually attracted to members of the same sex **2.** OF HOMOSEXUALITY relating to sexual attraction or activity among members of the same sex

USAGE See **gay**.

homosexuality /hṓmō sék shoo álləti, hómmə-/ *n* sexual attraction to or sexual relations with somebody of the same sex

homosporous /ho móspərəss, hō-, hṓmə spáwrəss/ *adj* producing asexual spores of only one type

homotaxis /hṓmō táksiss, hómmō-/ *n* a similarity of composition, arrangement, or fossil content among rock strata of different ages or locations —**homotaxial** *adj* —**homotaxially** *adv* —**homotaxic** *adj*

homothallic /hṓmō thállik, hómmō-/ *adj* describes a plant that has both male and female reproductive organs on one thallus and is therefore able to fertilize itself —**homothallism** *n*

homozygote /hṓmō zígōt, hómmō-/ *n* an organism that has two identical genes at the same place on two corresponding chromosomes —**homozygotic** /-zī góttik/ *adj*

homozygous /hṓmō zígəss, hómmō-/ *adj* having two identical genes at the corresponding loci of homologous chromosomes —**homozygously** *adv*

Homs /homs, homz/ historic city in western Syria, situated on the River Orontes. Population: 540,133 (1994).

homunculus /ho múng kyoóləss/ (*plural* **-li** /-lī/), **homuncule** /-kyool/ *n* **1.** a diminutive human being **2.** in early biological theory, the fully formed human being that was thought to exist inside an egg or spermatozoon [Mid-17C. < Latin, 'little person' < *homo* 'human being'] —**homuncular** *adj*

homy *adj* another spelling of **homey**[1]

hon /hun/ *n* N Am used as an affectionate term of address (*informal*) [Early 20C. Shortening of HONEY]

hon. *abbr* **1.** honorary **2.** honourable

Hon. *abbr* Honourable

honan /hṓ nán/ *n* a rough-woven raw silk fabric, originally from China [Early 20C. After *Honan*, province of N China]

honcho /hónchō/ N Am (*slang*) *n* somebody who dominates a project, situation, or other people ■ *vt* (**-chos, -choing, -choed**) to manage or organize people or events ○ *He's the one who honchoed their election campaign.* [Mid-20C. < Japanese *hanchō* 'group leader']

Honda /hóndə/, **Soichiro** (1906–92) Japanese engineer and business executive. He founded the Honda Motor Company to manufacture motorcycles (1948) and cars (1963).

> 'To me success can only be achieved through repeated failure and introspection. In fact, success represents 1 per cent of your work which results from the 99 per cent that is called failure.'
> [Soichiro Honda. Quoted in *Thriving on Chaos*, Tom Peters; 1988]

hondle /hónd'l/ (**-dles, -dling, -dled**) *vti* US to haggle, bargain, or manoeuvre in order to get something desired (*informal*) [< Yiddish, probably < Polish *handel* 'trade']

Honduras

Honduras /hon dyoórəss/ country in Central America, with coastlines on the Caribbean Sea and the Pacific Ocean. Language: Spanish. Currency: lempira. Capital: Tegucigalpa. Population: 6,669,789 (2003). Area: 112,492 sq. km/43,433 sq. mi. Official name Republic of Honduras —**Honduran** *adj*

Honduras, Gulf of inlet of the Caribbean Sea, situated between southern Belize, eastern Guatemala, and northern Honduras

hone[1] /hōn/ *vt* (**hones, honing, honed**) **1.** IMPROVE SOMETHING WITH REFINEMENTS to bring something to a state of increased intensity, excellence, or completion, especially over a period of time ○ *honed the speech*

through rewrites **2. SHARPEN BLADE ON WHETSTONE** to sharpen a blade on a fine whetstone ■ *n* **1. WHETSTONE** a fine-grained sedimentary rock used as a whetstone for sharpening razors and other cutting tools. Emery and silicon carbide products are now largely used instead. **2. MACHINE TOOL** a tool with a rotating abrasive head, used to bore holes [Old English *hān* 'whetstone' < Indo-European, 'sharpen'] —**honer** *n*

USAGE hone in or **home in**? It is hard to imagine any context in which *hone in* could be correct. *Hone* is a transitive verb that means 'sharpen' (*hone a blade*) or, in a metaphorical extension of that idea, 'improve, refine' (*hone his ideas before speaking out*). It is the verb *home*, generally intransitive, whose meanings include 'return home accurately', that makes sense with the particle *in*: *home in on his enemy's weaknesses*.

hone² /hōn/ (**hones, honing, honed**) *vi regional* **1.** to long for somebody or something **2.** to complain about somebody or something, especially in a whining manner [Early 17C. < Old French *hognier* 'grumble']

Honecker /hónnəkər/, **Erich** (1912–94) secretary general of East Germany (1971–89). He served as East German head of state from 1971 until he was ousted in 1989, a year before the reunification of East and West Germany.

Honegger /hónnigər/, **Arthur** (1892–1955) French composer. He was a member of the Paris-based group of composers known as 'Les Six'. His works include *Pacific 231* (1923) and *King David* (1921).

> 'The first requirement for a composer is to be dead.'
>
> [Arthur Honegger, *Je suis compositeur (I am a Composer)*; 1951]

honest /ónnist/ *adj* **1. MORALLY UPRIGHT** never cheating, lying, or breaking the law **2. TRUTHFUL OR TRUE** expressing or embodying the truth **3. IMPARTIAL** presenting information in an impartial way **4. REASONABLE IN PARTICULAR SITUATION** reasonable and acceptable, given the circumstances ○ *an honest mistake* **5. UNPRETENTIOUS** having simple manners and no pretensions ○ *honest country folk* **6. RESPECTABLE** respectable and virtuous (*dated*) [13C. Via French < Latin *honestus* 'honourable' < *honos* 'honour'] —**honestness** *n* ◇ **honest to God** or **goodness 1.** used to express surprise or shock **2.** used to emphasize the truth of a statement

honest broker *n* a person, country, or organization that mediates in disputes [Translation of German *ehrlicher Makler*, describing Otto von BISMARCK]

honestly /ónnistli/ *adv* **1. IN FAIR WAY** in a way that is fair, truthful, and morally upright **2. GENUINELY** really and truly ○ *Can you honestly say that you care?* ■ *interj* **USED TO EXPRESS SURPRISE** used to express surprise, annoyance, or disapproval

honest-to-God, **honest-to-goodness** *adj* completely real or authentic (*informal*) ○ *You made a real, honest-to-God mess of that.*

honesty /ónnisti/ (*plural* **-ties**) *n* **1. MORAL UPRIGHTNESS** the quality, condition, or characteristic of being fair, truthful, and morally upright **2. TRUTHFULNESS** truthfulness, candour, or sincerity ○ *In all honesty, I really didn't know.* **3. PLANT** a hardy plant with flat silvery seed pods that are often used for indoor decoration. Flowers: purplish or white. Native to: Europe. Latin name: *Lunaria annua.*

honewort /hōn wurt/ *n* a perennial plant. Flowers: small, white, in clusters. Native to: Europe. Latin name: *Trinia glauca.* [Mid-17C. *Hone*, origin ?]

honey /húnni/ *n* **1. SWEET SUBSTANCE MADE BY BEES** a sweet sticky golden-brown fluid produced by bees from the nectar of flowers. Use: in cooking, spread on bread. **2. SWEET SUBSTANCE MADE BY OTHER INSECTS** a sweet sticky substance produced from nectar by insects other than bees **3. AFFECTIONATE TERM OF ADDRESS** used as an affectionate term of address (*informal*) **4. SOMEBODY VERY NICE** an attractive, endearing, or lovable person (*informal*) **5.** *US* **YELLOWISH COLOUR** a yellowish-brown colour **6.** *US* **SOMETHING EXTREMELY GOOD** an object, situation, or idea that is exceptionally good (*informal*) ○ *That's a honey of a motorboat.* ■ *vt* (**-eys, -eying, -eyed** *or* **-ied**) *US* **TALK FLATTERINGLY TO SOMEBODY** to talk to somebody in an affectionate and flattering way, especially insincerely and for selfish reasons (*informal*) [Old English *hunig* < Germanic] —**honey** *adj*

honey badger *n* ZOOL same as **ratel** [< its fondness for honey]

honey bear *n* ZOOL same as **kinkajou** [< its practice of sucking honey from the nests of bees]

honeybee /húnni bee/ *n* a honey-producing bee that lives in organized groups and has been domesticated for its honey and beeswax since ancient times. Latin name: *Apis mellifera.*

honeybun /húnni bun/, **honeybunch** /-bunch/ *n N Am* used as an affectionate term of address (*informal*)

honey-buzzard *n* a bird of prey that feeds on honey from bees' nests. Native to: Europe, Africa, Asia. Genus: *Pernis.*

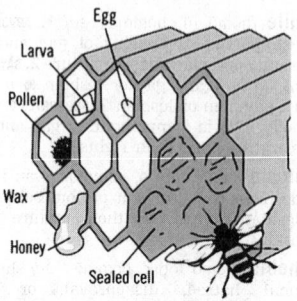

Egg
Larva
Pollen
Wax
Honey
Sealed cell

honeycomb

honeycomb /húnni kōm/ *n* **1. STRUCTURE OF SIX-SIDED CELLS** a collection of hexagonal cells constructed of wax by bees inside a hive or nest in which honey is stored, eggs are laid, and larvae develop **2. CELLS CONTAINING HONEY EATEN AS FOOD** a structure made up of waxy hexagonal cells containing honey that is extracted from a bees' hive or nest and eaten by animals and humans **3. SOMETHING LIKE HONEYCOMB** an object resembling a honeycomb in pattern or structure, especially by consisting of a network of hexagons **4. HONEYCOMB-PATTERNED FABRIC** a soft fabric woven in a pattern of ridges and hollows like those in a honeycomb. Use: towels, bedcovers. ■ *vt* (**-combs, -combing, -combed**) **1. PROVIDE SOMETHING WITH HOLES** to fill a wall, cliff, or structure with many cavities **2. INFILTRATE SOMETHING THOROUGHLY** to infiltrate a place or organization thoroughly ○ *an intelligence agency honeycombed by double agents* —**honeycombed** *adj*

honeycomb moth *n* INSECTS same as **wax moth**

honey creeper *n* **1.** a small bird with brightly coloured feathers and a long slender beak for sucking nectar from flowers. Native to: tropical America. Family: Coerebidae. **2.** a bird that resembles the honey creeper of tropical America. Native to: Hawaii. Family: Drepanididae.

honeydew /húnni dyoo/ *n* **1.** a sweet sticky substance deposited on leaves by aphids and some other insects as a by-product of the juices they suck from plants **2.** a sweet sticky substance produced by the leaves of some plants **3. FOOD** same as **honeydew melon** [< the belief that the substance was distilled from the air like dew] —**honeydewed** *adj*

honeydew melon *n* a melon with sweet pale green flesh and a smooth greenish-white rind. Latin name: *Cucumis melo.*

honeyeater /húnni eetər/ *n* a slender bird with a long beak and a long brush-tipped tongue for extracting nectar from flowers. Native to: Australia to Hawaii. Family: Meliphagidae.

honeyed /húnnid/, **honied** *adj* **1. INGRATIATING** intended to flatter or soothe **2. PLEASANT-SOUNDING** sweet and pleasant to hear **3. SWEETENED WITH HONEY** containing or sweetened with honey —**honeyedly** *adv*

honey fungus *n* a destructive fungus that grows in small tight clusters at the base of trees, with a golden or brown cap and black spreading filaments (**hyphae**). It is possibly the most serious fungal parasite affecting coniferous trees. Latin name: *Armillaria mellea.* [< its colour]

honey guide *n* **1.** a small bird that feeds on the wax and larvae remaining after people or animals have removed the honey from bees' nests. Native to: tropical forests of Africa and Asia. Family: Indicatoridae. **2.** a series of dots or lines on the perianth of a flower that guide insects towards the

nectar. They are sometimes only visible to the human eye in ultraviolet photographs.

honey locust *n* a thorny tree with compound leaves and pods containing a sweet pulp. Native to: eastern North America. Genus: *Gleditsia.*

honeymoon /húnni moon/ *n* **1.** a holiday taken by a newly married couple, usually immediately following the wedding or reception **2.** a short period of harmony or goodwill at the beginning of a relationship, especially in politics or business [Mid-16C. Originally 'waning affection', from the idea that although married love is at first as sweet as honey, it soon wanes like the moon] —**honeymoon** *vi* —**honeymooner** *n*

honey mouse *n* a small marsupial with a very long snout adapted for feeding on pollen and honey, a long tail, and light brown fur with dark stripes. Native to: Australia. Latin name: *Tarsipes spenserae.*

honey myrtle *n* a hardy bush with pink or purple flowers in hairy spikes. Native to: Australia. Genus: *Melaleuca.*

honeypot /húnni pot/ *n* **1.** anything that attracts or appeals to large numbers of people (*informal*) **2.** a server connected to the Internet that is used as a decoy to attract potential hackers in order to study their activities and techniques

honeypot site *n* a place that attracts a large number of tourists

honey-sucker *n* ZOOL same as **honey mouse**

honeysuckle

honeysuckle /húnni suk'l/ *n* **1. CLIMBING BUSH WITH FRAGRANT FLOWERS** a climbing bush with twining stems. Flowers: fragrant, tubular, with spreading twin-petal lobes. Genus: *Lonicera.* **2. AUSTRALIAN PLANT** a plant with large woody seed cones. Flowers: yellow, orange, red, grey, and green, in spike-shaped clusters. Native to: Australia. Genus: *Banksia.* **3. Ireland FUCHSIA** a fuchsia plant [< the belief that bees suck honey from it]

honeysuckle ornament *n* ARTS, ARCHIT same as **anthemion**

honey-sweet *adj* sounding or appearing sweet and attractive

honeytrap /húnni trap/ *n* a situation in which somebody is led to reveal information or do something wrong by a good-looking person, usually a young woman, selected for this purpose

hongi /hóngee/ *n* NZ a Maori greeting in which two people press or touch the side of each other's noses together, usually three times [Mid-19C. < Maori]

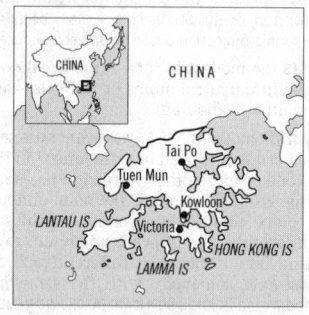

Hong Kong

Hong Kong /hóng kóng/ seaport and major commercial centre on the southeastern coast of China.

WORLD ENGLISH ***Hong Kong English*** is the variety of English used in Hong Kong, ranging from forms close to British, US, and Australian usage to those influenced by and mixed with Cantonese, the language of some 98% of the population. In Hong Kong English pronunciation 'r' is not pronounced in such words as *art, door,* and *worker.* It generally shares features with English as used in mainland China, Taiwan, and Singapore: e.g. glottal stops replacing the /p, t, k/ consonants at the ends of such words as *map, pat,* and *tack.* In grammar, there is a tendency to use the present tense when describing events in the past and future ('When I see him in school yesterday' and 'Tomorrow I ask him about it').

Hong Kong English has three sources of distinctive vocabulary. The first is represented by items taken directly from Chinese (especially Cantonese), e.g. *gweilo* (ghost man/person) for 'a European', and *feng shui* (wind-water), denoting a system of laws that govern spatial relationships with respect to the flow of energy, used in situating buildings advantageously. The second vocabulary source is represented by items that translate Chinese words and phrases, such as *dragon boat,* a long decorated boat configured as a dragon, used in racing at festivals, and *snakehead,* a smuggler of illegal immigrants from mainland China. A third vocabulary source is represented by items common to former British colonies, especially in Asia, e.g. *expat* (English), short for 'expatriate', *godown* (probably from Tamil), 'warehouse', and *shroff* (from Arabic through Indian languages), 'cashier'.

A former British colony, it is now a Chinese Special Administrative Region. Population: 7,210,505 (2001). Area: 1,092 sq. km/422 sq. mi.

Hong Kong English *n* a variety of English spoken in Hong Kong

Honiara /hōni aárə/ port and capital of the Solomon Islands, situated on the northern coast of Guadalcanal. Population: 35,288 (1990)

honied *adj* another spelling of **honeyed**

honi soit qui mal y pense /ónni swaá kee mál ee pónss/ the French motto of the Order of the Garter, meaning 'shame upon him who thinks evil of it' [< French]

Honiton lace /hónnitən-, húnni-/, **Honiton** *n* lace with a pattern of sprigs of flowers [After *Honiton* in Devon]

honk /hongk/ *n* 1. CRY OF GOOSE the raucous sound made by a goose 2. SOUND OF CAR HORN the sound made by a car horn 3. SOUND RESEMBLING GOOSE OR CAR HORN any sound, e.g. a laugh or a blowing of the nose, that resembles the sound made by a goose or a car horn ■ *v* (**honks, honking, honked**) 1. *vi* PRODUCE HONK to let out or give out a honk 2. *vti* SOUND CAR HORN to cause a car horn to make a honk [Mid-19C. An imitation of the sound]

honker /hóngkər/ *n* 1. a person, animal, or object that makes a honking sound, e.g. a goose or a car horn 2. a nose, especially a large one (*informal*)

honky /hóngki/ (*plural* **-kies**), **honkie, honkey** (*plural* **-keys**) *n N Am* a highly offensive term for a white person (*slang*) [Mid-20C. Origin ?]

honky-tonk /hóngki tongk/ *n* 1. RAGTIME PIANO-PLAYING a style of ragtime with a heavy beat, usually played on an upright piano with a tinny sound 2. COUNTRY MUSIC a style of country music associated with cheap, noisy, and often disreputable bars or nightclubs ○ *honky-tonk blues* 3. *N Am* CHEAP NIGHTCLUB a cheap, noisy, and often disreputable bar or nightclub (*slang*) ■ *vi* (**honky-tonks, honky-tonking, honky-tonked**) *US* VISIT HONKY-TONKS to frequent cheap noisy bars and nightclubs [Late 19C. Origin ?]

Honolulu /hónnə lóoloo/ urban area and capital of Hawaii, located on Oahu Island. Population: 378,155 (2002 estimate).

honor *n, vt* US spelling of **honour**

honorarium /ónnə ráiri əm/ (*plural* **-iums** or **-ia** /-i ə/) *n* an amount of money paid to somebody, especially a professional person, for providing a service [Mid-17C. < Latin, 'gift made on being admitted to a post of honour' < *honor-* (see HONOUR)]

SYNONYMS See *wage.*

honorary /ónnərəri/ *adj* 1. AWARDED AS HONOUR given, elected, or awarded for outstanding service or distinguished achievements, rather than for the completion of formal educational or legal requirements 2. SYMBOLIZING HONOUR CONFERRED representing the bestowal of an honour or distinction on somebody 3. UNPAID holding an office awarded as an honour and receiving no payment for services provided in that office 4. NOT LEGALLY ENFORCEABLE dependent on somebody's sense of honour and honesty for fulfilment, rather than on a legal agreement

honorary white *n* formerly in South Africa, a foreign visitor not considered white but granted the rights of whites under the apartheid regime

honorific /ónnə ríffik/ *adj* CONFERRING HONOUR given as a mark of distinction, esteem, or respect ■ *n* 1. TITLE OF RESPECT a title of respect, e.g. 'The Honourable', used in speech or writing 2. GRAMMATICAL FORM ACKNOWLEDGING INFERIORITY a phrase or word, e.g. a pronoun or a verb inflection, that is used to show respect to somebody of a higher status

honoris causa /ho náwriss kówzə/ *adv* as a mark of honour ○ *a doctorate in humane letters conferred honoris causa* [< Latin, 'for the sake of honour']

honour /ónnər/ *n* 1. PERSONAL INTEGRITY strong moral character or strength, and adherence to ethical principles ○ *It's a matter of honour.* 2. RESPECT great respect and admiration ○ *a mark of honour* 3. DIGNITY personal dignity that sometimes leads to recognition and glory ○ *Although defeated, he accepted the loss with honour.* 4. REPUTATION somebody's good name or good reputation ○ *My honour is at stake.* 5. SOURCE OF PRIDE somebody or something that brings respect or glory and is a source of pride to somebody or something else ○ *Your achievements are an honour to your parents and school.* 6. MARK OF DISTINCTION something, e.g. a gift, award, or gesture, that signifies high achievement or respect 7. GREAT PRIVILEGE a special privilege that is cherished, e.g. an opportunity to be introduced to somebody admired or respected or an opportunity to serve a worthy cause ○ *It is indeed an honour to have you here today.* 8. MEN'S CODE OF INTEGRITY a code of integrity in some societies, e.g. in feudal Europe and medieval Japan, that men upheld by force of arms 9. RIGHT TO TEE OFF FIRST in golf, the right to drive off first from the tee 10. WOMAN'S REPUTATION a woman's virginity or reputation for chastity (*dated*) ■ *npl* 1. **honours, Honours** ACADEMIC DISTINCTION official recognition of academic excellence given to students by colleges and universities at graduation 2. **honours** HIGHEST CARDS four or five of the highest cards, especially the ace, king, queen, jack, and ten of the trump suit ■ *vt* (**-ours, -ouring, -oured**) 1. ESTEEM SOMEBODY OR SOMETHING to have or show great respect and admiration for somebody or something 2. EXALT SOMEBODY to recognize somebody publicly or elevate somebody's status officially, usually by giving that person a title or an award 3. PAY TRIBUTE TO SOMEBODY to publicly praise somebody who has died and pay respects to him or her 4. DIGNIFY SOMEBODY OR SOMETHING to give prestige to somebody or something such as an occasion by choosing to appear, accompany, or take part 5. TREAT SOMETHING AS MONEY to accept a cheque or other financial instrument as money or as a substitute for money and pay it when it is due ○ *The bank won't honour a cheque without a signature.* 6. KEEP PROMISE to keep a promise, or fulfil the terms of an agreement or contract 7. BOW TO PARTNER to bow to another dancer in square dancing [12C. Via French < Latin *honor-*, stem of *honos*] —**honouree** /ónnə reé/ *n* —**honourer** *n* —**honourless** *adj* ◇ **do somebody the honour of doing something** to make somebody feel proud and pleased by agreeing to do something for that person (*formal*) ○ *Will you do me the honour of dancing the last waltz with me?* ◇ **do the honours** to act as host or hostess by doing something for a group of guests, e.g. pouring wine, carving meat, or cutting a cake (*informal*) ◇ **honour bound** obliged by a promise or ethical principles to do something ◇ **in honour of somebody** *or* **something** in recognition of or for the glorification of somebody or something ○ *I'd like to propose a toast in honour of the bride and groom.* ◇ **on your honour** 1. staking your reputation on something ○ *On my honour, I will tell the truth.* 2. being trusted to act in a particular way ○ *You are on your honour to behave well.*

Honour *n* used as a form of address to a judge ○ *Your Honour, may we approach the bench?*

honourable /ónnərəb'l/ *adj* 1. HAVING PERSONAL INTEGRITY guided by, or with a reputation for having, strong moral and ethical principles 2. DESERVING OR GAINING HONOUR worthy of or winning honour, respect, recognition, or glory 3. MORALLY UPRIGHT upright and moral in intent (*formal*) ○ *I hope his intentions are honourable.* —**honourability** /ónnərə bílləti/ *n* —**honourableness** *n* —**honourably** *adv*

Honourable *adj* 1. used as a title of respect before somebody's name to indicate entitlement to respect because of an official position held, or used to address a parliamentary colleague ○ *My Honourable friend has spoken on this matter before.* 2. used as a courtesy title in the United Kingdom for the children of some members of the aristocracy

honourable discharge *n* an official dismissal from the armed forces, signifying that all duties have been honourably fulfilled

honourable mention *n* an official or public commendation, usually granted to somebody who has done well in a competition but has not actually won an award

Honour Moderations *npl* at Oxford University, the first set of public examinations in some subjects according to which students are awarded first, second, or third class honours

Honours List *n* a list of the people who have been or are to be awarded honours such as a peerage or membership of a chivalric order by the British monarch

honours of war *npl* 1. the privileges that are accorded members of a defeated army 2. marks of respect paid by troops at the burial of another soldier

honour system *n* a system under which people are relied on to be honest without direct supervision

Hons *abbr* EDUC Honours

Hon. Sec. *abbr* Honorary Secretary

Honshu /hón shoo/ largest and most populous island of Japan. Area: 230,455 sq. km/88,979 sq. mi. Population: 99,254,194 (1990).

hooch[1] /hooch/, **hootch** *n N Am* cheap alcohol, especially illegally distilled spirits (*slang*) [Late 19C. Shortening of *hoochinoo*, after *Hoochinoo*, Tlingit village in Alaska where illegal liquor was thought to be distilled]

hooch[2] /hookh/ *interj Scotland* used to express exhilaration in traditional Scottish dancing [Natural exclamation]

Hooch /hooch, hōkh/, **Pieter de** (1629–84) Dutch painter. His works often depict domestic scenes of 17th-century Dutch life. His works include *The Pantry* (?1658).

hood[1] /hŏŏd/ *n* 1. COVERING FOR HEAD a loose covering for the head that is usually attached to the neck of a coat 2. COVER FOR DEVICE a cover for an appliance or machine, or for a part such as a camera lens 3. PART OF ACADEMIC ROBE an ornamental piece of cloth, often trimmed with fur or luxurious fabric, that hangs from the shoulders of an academic robe to indicate the status of the wearer 4. FOLDING ROOF the folding roof of a carriage, pram, or convertible car 5. COVER FOR CHIMNEY a fixed or revolving cover fitted to the top of a chimney to prevent downdraught 6. HEAD COVERING FOR FALCON a bag placed over the head of a falcon to keep it calm when it is not hunting 7. MARKING ON ANIMAL'S HEAD a crest, marking, or other conspicuous part on the head of an animal 8. *N Am* same as **bonnet** (sense 2) ■ *vt* (**hoods, hooding, hooded**) PUT HOOD ON HEAD to cover the head of a person, animal, or bird with a hood [Old English *hōd* < Indo-European, 'to cover'] —**hoodless** *adj* —**hood-like** *adj*

hood[2] /hŏŏd/ *n N Am* same as **hoodlum** (*slang*) [Late 19C. Shortening]

Hood /hŏŏd/, **Samuel, 1st Viscount** (1724–1816) British admiral. He was famed for his role in Britain's defeat of the French off St Kitts (1782) and Dominica (1784).

> 'Some people reach the age of 60 before others.'
>
> [Samuel Hood. Quoted in *Observer*, 23 February 1969]

-hood *suffix* 1. quality, state, condition ○ *knighthood*

2. a group of people ○ *brotherhood* 3. time, stage of life ○ *adulthood* [Old English *-hād* < Germanic]

hooded /ho͝oddid/ *adj* **1. COVERED BY HOOD** covered by or having a hood **2. PARTLY HIDDEN** partly concealed or covered ○ *dark, hooded eyes* **3. HAVING CREST** having a crest, markings, or a specialized structure on the head —**hoodedness** *n*

hooded crow *n* a crow that is a subspecies of the carrion crow with a black head, tail, and wings, and a grey body. Native to: Europe, Asia. Latin name: *Corvus corone cornix.*

hooded seal *n* a large grey-spotted seal, the mature male of which has an inflatable sac near its nose. Native to: the North Atlantic and Arctic oceans. Latin name: *Cystophora cristata.*

hoodia /ho͝odi ə/ *n* a cactus with short stems covered in white spikes. Flowers: saucer-shaped, deep red, brown, mottled yellow. Native to: southern Africa. Use: flesh of stems as appetite suppressant, with potential as weight-loss drug. Genus: *hoodia.*

hoodie /ho͝odi/ *n* **1.** *also* **hoodie crow** *Scotland* BIRDS same as **hooded crow 2.** CLOTHING same as **hoody**

hoodlum /ho͝odləm/ *n* **1.** a petty criminal or gangster, especially one prone to violence **2.** a young person who is violent or prone to committing crimes [Late 19C. Origin ?] —**hoodlumish** *adj* —**hoodlumism** *n*

hood mould *n* CONSTR same as **dripstone** (sense 1)

hoodoo /ho͞odoo/ *n* (*plural* **-doos**) **1.** RELIG same as **voodoo** *n* (sense 2) **2. BAD LUCK** bad luck or misfortune **3. BRINGER OF BAD LUCK** somebody or something believed to bring bad luck **4.** *N Am* **ODDLY SHAPED ROCK COLUMN** in the western United States and Canada, a column of rock that has been weathered into a strange shape ■ *vt* (**-doos, -dooing, -dooed**) **JINX SOMEBODY OR SOMETHING** to appear to bring bad luck or misfortune to somebody or something [Late 19C. Origin ?] —**hoodooism** *n*

hoodwink /ho͝od wingk/ (**-winks, -winking, -winked**) *vt* to deceive or dupe somebody, especially by being clever or cunning —**hoodwinker** *n*

hoody /ho͝odi/ (*plural* **-ies**), **hoodie** *n* a sweatshirt or fleece with a hood

hooey /ho͞o i/ *n* empty or nonsensical talk or ideas (*informal*) [Early 20C. Origin ?]

hoof /hoof, ho͝of/ *n* (*plural* **hooves** /hoovz, ho͝ovz/ or **hoofs**) **1. ANIMAL'S FOOT** the foot of a horse, deer, cow, or similar animal, covered with horny material **2. HORNY COVERING OF FOOT** the horny material covering the feet of animals such as horses, deer, and cattle **3. ANIMAL WITH HOOVES** an animal that has hooves, e.g. a horse, deer, or cow **4. HUMAN FOOT** the foot of a human being (*slang humorous*) ■ *v* (**hoofs, hoofing, hoofed**) **1.** *vt* **TRAVEL DISTANCE ON FOOT** to walk a particular distance (*slang*) **2.** *vt* **KICK SOMEBODY OR SOMETHING** to kick or trample a person or animal **3.** *vi* same as **dance** (*slang*) [Old English *hōf* < Indo-European] —**hoofless** *adj* ◇ **hoof it** (*slang*) **1.** same as **walk** *v* (sense 1) **2.** same as **dance** *v* (sense 1) ◇ **on the hoof 1.** used to describe an animal that is alive and has not yet been butchered **2.** without sufficient thought or attention (*informal*) **3.** while moving around or doing something else (*informal*) ○ *eating lunch on the hoof*

hoofed /hooft, ho͝oft/, **hooved** /hoovd, ho͝ovd/ *adj* having hooves, or with hooves of a particular size and type

hoofer /ho͞ofər, ho͝offər/ *n* a professional dancer, especially a tap dancer (*slang*)

hoofprint /ho͞of print, ho͝of-/ *n* an imprint of an animal's hoof

Hooghly another spelling of **Hugli**

hoo-hah /ho͞o haa/, **hoo-ha** *n* a loud noisy controversy or disturbance (*slang*) [Mid-20C. Probably < Yiddish *hu-ha,* an imitation of the sound of a disturbance]

hook /ho͝ok/ *n* **1. BENT PIECE OF METAL** a bent or curved piece of metal or other material, used to attach, suspend, fasten, or lift another object **2. SOMETHING LIKE HOOK** something resembling a curved piece of metal, especially a plant or animal part **3.** FISHING same as **fishhook 4. SNARE** a stratagem for trapping or snaring somebody **5. SOMETHING THAT ATTRACTS** a means of attracting or interesting somebody, especially a potential customer (*informal*) **6.** BOXING **SHORT SWINGING BLOW** in boxing, a short blow to an opponent delivered with a swing and a bent arm **7.** GOLF **SWERVING SHOT** a golf shot that swerves sharply from right to left in the case of a right-handed player **8. SHOT IN CRICKET** in cricket, a shot with the bat held parallel to the ground that sends the ball towards the leg side **9.** ICE HOCKEY **ACT OF RESTRAINING PLAYER** the act of using an ice hockey stick to prevent another player from moving freely **10.** MUSIC **CATCHY REFRAIN** a pleasing and easily remembered refrain in a pop song **11.** BASKETBALL same as **hook shot 12.** PRINTING **PART OF LETTER** in writing or printing, a short curve of a letter that extends above or below the line ○ *the hook of the 'g'* **13. CREST OF WAVE** the crest of a wave that is about to break **14.** AGRIC same as **sickle** *n* (sense 1) ■ *v* (**hooks, hooking, hooked**) **1.** *vti* **FASTEN WITH HOOK** to fasten something by means of hooks, or hooks and eyes, or be fastened in this way **2.** *vt* **ATTACH ONE THING TO ANOTHER** to attach one thing to another by means of a specially designed mechanical device ○ *hook the trailer to the car* **3.** *vti* **BEND LIKE HOOK** to curve in the shape of a hook, or cause something to curve in the shape of a hook ○ *The road hooks sharply to the left.* **4.** *vt* **ENSNARE SOMETHING** to catch or ensnare something using a hook **5.** *vt* **CATCH SOMEBODY'S ATTENTION** to attract and hold somebody's interest or attention **6.** *vt* BOXING **HIT SOMEBODY WITH CURVING BLOW** in boxing, to deliver a sharp curving blow to an opponent, using a curved or bent arm **7.** *vt* GOLF **STRIKE SWERVING BALL** in golf, to strike the ball so that it swerves sharply from right to left in the case of a right-handed player **8.** *vt* BASKETBALL **SHOOT BALL INTO BASKET** in basketball, to shoot the ball by sweeping the hand upwards and farther away from the basket while moving sideways towards the basket **9.** *vt* RUGBY **KICK BALL BACKWARDS** in rugby, to kick the ball backwards out of a scrum to the scrum half **10.** *vt* **STRIKE CRICKET BALL** in cricket, to strike the ball towards the leg side with the bat held parallel to the ground **11.** *vt* ICE HOCKEY **RESTRAIN PLAYER WITH STICK** to use an ice hockey stick to prevent another player from moving freely **12.** *vt* DRUGS **MAKE SOMEBODY ADDICTED** to cause somebody to become addicted or dependent on something, especially a drug (*slang*) **13.** *vt* **GORE SOMEBODY OR SOMETHING** to gore a person or animal with the horns or tusks **14.** *vt* AGRIC **CUT SOMETHING WITH SICKLE** to cut grass or similar plants with a sickle **15.** *vt* HANDICRAFT **MAKE RUG** to make a rug by pulling pieces of wool through holes in stiff canvas using a special hook **16.** *vt* **STEAL SOMETHING** to seize and steal something (*slang*) **17.** *vi* **BE PROSTITUTE** to work as a prostitute (*slang*) [Old English *hōc* < Indo-European, 'hook, tooth'] —**hookless** *adj* ◇ **by hook or by crook** by some means or other ◇ **get the hook** *N Am* to be removed unceremoniously from a place or position (*slang*) ◇ **give somebody the hook** *N Am* to remove somebody abruptly from a place or position (*informal*) ◇ **hook it** to run away (*slang dated*) ◇ **hook, line, and sinker** to the fullest possible extent (*informal*) ○ *They fell for the story hook, line, and sinker.* ◇ **off the hook 1.** free of a difficult situation (*informal*) **2.** with the receiver off its cradle so that no telephone calls can be received ◇ **on your own hook** *US* by your own efforts (*informal*) ◇ **sling your hook** to go away (*slang; usually used as a command*)

hook up *v* **1.** *vt* to connect two or more electronic devices ○ *Is the microphone hooked up?* **2.** *vti* to meet and become associated, or cause somebody to meet and become associated, with somebody else (*informal*)

hookah /ho͝okə/ *n* in Southwest and South Asia, a pipe for smoking tobacco or marijuana, consisting of a flexible tube with a mouthpiece attached to a container of water through which smoke is drawn and cooled [Mid-18C. Via Urdu < Arabic *ḥukka* 'jar']

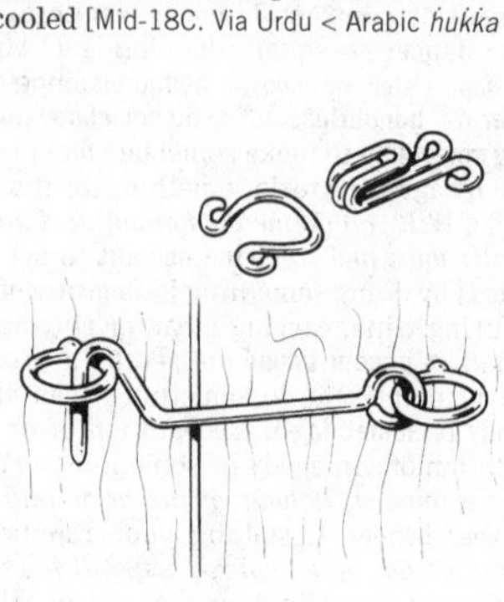

hook and eye: clothes fastener (top) and latch (bottom)

hook and eye (*plural* **hooks and eyes**) *n* **1.** a fastening for clothes consisting of a small hook inserted into a metal or thread loop **2.** *N Am* a latch for a gate or door consisting of a metal hook inserted into a screw eye

hookcheck /ho͝ok chek/ *n* ICE HOCKEY same as **hook** *n* (sense 9)

Hooke /ho͝ok/, **Robert** (1635–1703) British scientist and architect. He is best known for the formulation of Hooke's Law, the theory of elasticity.

hooked /ho͝okt/ *adj* **1. SHAPED LIKE HOOK** bent or shaped like a hook **2. WITH HOOK AT END** ending in a hook **3. ADDICTED** addicted to a drug (*slang*) **4. OBSESSED WITH SOMEBODY OR SOMETHING** in love with, compulsively attracted to, or obsessed with somebody or something (*slang*) **5. MADE USING YARN HOOK** made by hooking yarn through canvas

hooker[1] /ho͝okər/ *n* an offensive term for a prostitute (*slang*) [Mid-19C. Origin ?]

hooker[2] /ho͝okər/ *n* **1.** a person, animal, or object that catches something by hooking it **2.** in rugby, a front row forward who hooks the ball out of the scrum [Mid-16C. < HOOK]

hooker[3] /ho͝okər/ *n* **1.** a commercial fishing vessel that uses hooks and lines instead of nets **2.** a large cargo boat with several sails, formerly used off the western coast of Ireland and now used as a pleasure craft [Mid-17C. < Dutch *hoeker,* shortening of Middle Dutch *hoeckboot* 'fishing boat' < *hoec* 'fish-hook']

Hooker /ho͝okər/, **Joseph** (1814–79) US Union general. Known as an aggressive leader, he commanded the Army of the Potomac (1863). Known as **Fighting Joe**

Hooker, Sir William Jackson (1785–1865) British botanist. He wrote extensively on botany and became the first director of Kew Gardens, London (1841–65).

hookey *n* another spelling of **hooky** (*informal*)

hooknose /ho͝ok nōz/ *n* a nose with a noticeable curve, like an eagle's beak —**hooknosed** *adj*

Hook of Holland /ho͝ok-/ **1.** cape on the North Sea coast in the southwestern Netherlands. Dutch name **Hoek van Holland 2.** seaport on the Hook of Holland, situated approximately 10 km/6 mi. northwest of Rotterdam

hook shot *n* in basketball, a shot that is made by sweeping the hand upwards and farther away from the basket while moving sideways towards the basket

hook-tip *n* a moth that has forewings ending in a hooked point. Genus: *Daepana.*

hookup /ho͝ok up/ *n* **1. LINK BETWEEN SOURCE AND USER** a connection allowing a user access to a utility such as electricity, gas, or water ○ *a gas hookup* **2. ELECTRONIC SYSTEM** a number of items of electronic equipment designed to operate together (*informal*) **3. RELATIONSHIP** an alliance between people, groups, or things, especially an unlikely one (*informal*) ○ *a bizarre hookup between political enemies over an issue* **4.** FISHING **CATCH IN OFFSHORE FISHING** in offshore big game fishing, an act of catching a fish on the end of the line

hookworm /ho͝ok wurm/ *n* **1.** a blood-sucking, disease-causing nematode worm that bores through the skin, attaching itself to the intestinal walls with its hooked mouthparts. Family: Ancylostomatidae. **2.** MED same as **ancylostomiasis**

hooky /ho͝oki/, **hookey** *n* absence, especially from school, without permission (*informal*) [Mid-19C. Origin ?] ◇ **play hooky** to be absent without permission, especially from school

hooley /ho͞oli/ (*plural* **-leys**) *n Ireland, NZ* a noisy merry party (*informal*) [Late 19C. Origin ?]

hooligan /ho͞oligən/ *n* an aggressive young man, especially one acting as part of a group, who commits acts of vandalism and violence in public places (*informal*) [Late 19C. Origin ?]

hooliganism /ho͞oligənizəm/ *n* acts of vandalism and violence in public places, committed especially by youths

hoon /hoon/ *ANZ* (*informal*) *n* **1. LOUT** a lout or hooligan **2. SPEEDING DRIVER** somebody, especially a young man, who drives fast and recklessly **3. HIGH-SPEED DRIVE** an act of driving fast and recklessly ■ *vi* (**hoons, hooning, hooned**) **SPEED IN MOTOR VEHICLE** to drive fast and recklessly [Mid-20C. Origin ?] —**hooning** *n*

hoop /hoop/ n **1. RING HOLDING BARREL TOGETHER** the metal or wooden ring used to hold the staves of a barrel in place **2. LARGE RING-SHAPED TOY** a large light ring of wood, metal, or plastic used as a toy or exercise aid **3. PAPER-COVERED RING** a large light ring, often with paper stretched over it, through which circus animals or performers jump **4. EARRING** an earring formed from a continuous ring of metal **5. PART OF FINGER RING** the part of a ring that the finger fits through **6. RING HOLDING NET IN BASKETBALL** in basketball, the metal ring from which an open-bottomed net is suspended, through which the ball is thrown in order to score points **7.** HANDICRAFT **BAND FOR EMBROIDERY FABRIC** either of a pair of wooden or metal bands used to keep fabric taut when it is being embroidered **8. CROQUET HOOP** in croquet, a metal arch through which the ball is driven **9.** CLOTHING **SUPPORT FOR SKIRT** a lightweight cane, wire, or whalebone ring, or a structure made of several such rings, used, especially formerly, to stiffen a woman's skirt or petticoat **10.** CLOTHING **WIDE STIFF SKIRT** a petticoat or skirt stiffened by rings ■ vt (**hoops, hooping, hooped**) **PUT HOOP ROUND SOMETHING** to surround something with a hoop or band [Old English hōp < W Germanic] ◇ **jump or go through hoops (for somebody)** to go to extreme lengths to gain favour with somebody or to carry out somebody's wishes (informal)

hooper /hoopər/ n somebody who makes or repairs barrels

hoopla[1] /hoop laa/ n a fairground game in which a player tries to throw a small hoop over a prize in order to win it [Early 20C. < HOOP, influenced by HOOPLA[2]]

hoopla[2] /hoop laa/ n **1.** N Am **LOUD CELEBRATION** a noisy excited commotion or joyous celebrating (informal) **2.** N Am **GREAT PUBLIC UPROAR** a great amount of public fuss, commotion, or uproar with attendant publicity or media interest (slang) **3.** US **MISLEADING TALK** intentionally misleading talk or propaganda (informal) [Late 19C. Origin ?]

hoopoe

hoopoe /hoo poo/ (plural **-poes** or same) n a bird with a pinkish-brown head and back, a very prominent crest, a downward-curving beak, and a loud cry. Native to: Europe, Asia, Africa. Latin name: Upupa epops. [Mid-17C. Alteration of hoop, via Old French huppe < Latin upupa, an imitation of the bird's cry]

hoop pine n a timber tree with rough bark. Native to: Australia. Latin name: Araucaria cunninghamii.

hoop skirt n a long full skirt held out in the shape of a bell by a series of connected hoops, fashionable in the 18th and early 19th centuries

hoop snake n any harmless North American snake that was once believed to be able to take its tail in its mouth and roll along like a hoop, e.g. the mud snake

hooray /hoo ráy/, **hurray** /hə ráy, hoo ráy/ n **SHOUT OF JOY** a shout of happy excitement, victory, or jubilation ■ interj **1. USED AS SHOUT OF JOY** used as a shout of happy excitement, victory, or jubilation **2.** ANZ **GOODBYE** goodbye [Late 17C. Alteration of HURRAH]

Hooray Henry /hoo ray hénnri/ n a young upper-class man, generally educated at public school, who wears conservative clothes and behaves and speaks in a loud, extrovert manner (informal)

hooroo /hoo roo/ interj Aus same as **goodbye** (humorous) [Early 20C. Alteration of HURRAH]

hoosegow /hooss gow/ n N Am same as **jail** (slang) [Early 20C. Via Mexican Spanish jusgado < Spanish juzgado 'courtroom' < past participle of juzgar 'judge' < Latin judicare (see JUDICATURE)]

hoot /hoot/ n **1. OWL'S CRY** the long sad-sounding cry of some owls **2. SOUND LIKE OWL'S CRY** a sound similar to an owl's cry, e.g. the sound made by a train whistle or car horn **3. LAUGHING SOUND** a cry, especially of laughter, derision, or scorn **4. SOMEBODY OR SOMETHING HILARIOUS** a highly amusing person, object, or situation (slang) ■ vi **EMIT HOOT** to produce a hoot **2.** vi **MAKE LAUGHING SOUND** to utter a sound of laughter, derision, or scorn **3. SOUND CAR HORN** to cause a car horn to make a hoot **4.** vt **DRIVE PERFORMER OFF STAGE** to drive a public performer or speaker off a stage by jeering **5.** vt **EXPRESS FEELING WITH JEERS** to express a feeling such as contempt, derision, or scorn by jeering [12C. Probably an imitation of the sound] ◇ **not care** or **give a hoot** to show no interest or concern for something (informal)

hootch n BEVERAGES, DRUGS another spelling of **hooch**[1]

hootenanny /hoot'n anni/ (plural **-nies**) n (informal) **1.** N Am an informal or impromptu performance by folk singers, in which the audience participates **2.** US an object or gadget for which the name is not known [Early 20C. Origin ?]

hooter /hootər/ n **1. SOMEBODY OR SOMETHING THAT HOOTS** a person, animal, or object that hoots, especially a horn **2. LARGE NOSE** a nose, especially a large one (slang humorous) ■ **hooters** npl N Am **OFFENSIVE TERM** an offensive term for a woman's breasts, especially when large (slang)

hoots /hoots/ interj Scotland used to express impatience, disbelief, or annoyance (informal)

hooved adj ZOOL another spelling of **hoofed**

Hoover /hoovər/ tdmk a trademark for a vacuum cleaner

Herbert Hoover
Library of Congress

Hoover /hoovər/, **Herbert** (1874–1964) 31st president of the United States. A Republican president (1929–33), he opposed government assistance during the Depression. This made him unpopular, and he was defeated after one term by Franklin D. Roosevelt. Full name **Hoover, Herbert Clarke**. See table at **president**

'We are nearer today to the ideal of the abolition of poverty and fear from the lives of men and women than ever before in any land.'
[Herbert Hoover, Speech, New York; 22 October 1928]

Hoover, J. Edgar (1895–1972) US director of the FBI (1924–72). Under his long and controversial leadership, the FBI targeted gangsters in the 1930s, Communists in the 1940s and 1950s, and liberals and opponents of the Vietnam War in the 1960s. Full name **Hoover, John Edgar**

'You are honored by your friends …distinguished by your enemies. I have been very distinguished.'
[J. Edgar Hoover. Quoted in J. Edgar Hoover, Curt Gentry; 1991]

Hoover Dam n a dam on the Colorado River, on the Arizona-Nevada border, completed in 1936. It is 221 m/726 ft high.

hooves ZOOL plural of **hoof**

hop[1] /hop/ v (**hops, hopping, hopped**) **1.** vi **JUMP LIGHTLY ON ONE FOOT** to jump lightly or quickly, especially on one foot **2.** vi **JUMP LIGHTLY WITH ALL FEET** to move in a series of small jumps using both or all feet **3.** vt **LEAP OVER SOMETHING** to jump quickly or lightly over something **4.** vi **LIMP** to walk with a limp **5.** vi **GET ON OR OFF** to move quickly or lightly into, onto, out of, or off

something, especially a vehicle (informal) **6.** vt N Am **JUMP ABOARD VEHICLE** to get on a plane, train, bus, or other vehicle, usually quickly or after a sudden decision to do so (informal) ◇ hop a plane to California **7.** vt US **RIDE TRAIN WITHOUT TICKET** to ride on a train secretly without paying (informal) **8.** vi **JOURNEY BY PLANE** to make a journey by aeroplane across or over an area, especially a sea or ocean (informal) ■ n **1. SMALL QUICK JUMP** a small jump on one, both, or all feet **2.** N Am **BOUNCE** a bounce or rebound of a ball **3. FLIGHT** a flight or leg of a flight in an aeroplane (informal) ◇ a short hop from New York to Washington **4. DANCE** a social occasion at which people dance together, usually to popular music (dated informal) [Old English hoppian 'leap, limp' < Germanic] ◇ **catch somebody on the hop** to find somebody unprepared (informal) ◇ **keep somebody on the hop** to keep somebody busy and alert (informal)

hop[2] /hop/ n **1. CLIMBING VINE** a climbing vine of the mulberry family with lobed leaves. Flowers: green, arranged in spikes that look like pine cones. Latin name: Humulus lupulus. **2.** US **DRUG** a narcotic drug, e.g. opium (dated slang) ■ **hops** npl **DRIED HOP FLOWERS** the dried flowers of the hop plant. Use: in brewing, to add flavour to beer. [15C. < Middle Low German, Middle Dutch hoppe] —**hoppy** adj
hop up vt (slang) **1.** US to make somebody excited, or intoxicated, especially with drugs (often passive) **2.** N Am AUTOMOT same as **soup up**

hop, skip, and jump n a short distance (informal) ◇ It's just a hop, skip, and jump to the station.

hop, step, and jump n **1.** ATHLETICS same as **triple jump 2.** same as **hop, skip, and jump**

hope /hōp/ vti (**hopes, hoping, hoped**) **WANT OR EXPECT SOMETHING** to have a wish to have or do something or for something to happen or be true, especially something that seems possible or likely ■ n **1. CONFIDENT DESIRE** a feeling that something desirable is likely to happen ◇ The research offers hope to sufferers. **2. LIKELIHOOD OF SUCCESS** a chance that something desirable will happen or be possible ◇ There's not much hope that things will improve. **3. WISH OR DESIRE** something that somebody wants to have or do or wants to happen or be true ◇ My hope is that she will change her mind. **4. SOURCE OF SUCCESS** somebody or something that seems likely to bring success or relief ◇ We have to do this, it's our only hope. **5. TRUST** a feeling of trust (archaic) [Old English hopian (verb), hopa (noun), origin ?] —**hoper** n

Hope, A. D. (1907–2000) Australian poet and critic. An influential writer, his works include The wandering islands (1955) and Collected poems (1966). Full name **Hope, Alec Derwent**

Hope, Bob (1903–2003) British-born US comedian. Highlights of his long career in show business include his travelling revues entertaining US service personnel stationed abroad during World War II and his 'Road' films with Bing Crosby and Dorothy Lamour (1940–52), including The Road to Singapore (1940). Born **Hope, Leslie Townes**

'A bank is a place that will lend you money if you can prove that you don't need it.'
[Bob Hope, Life in the Crystal Palace, Alan Harrington; 1959]

hope chest n N Am same as **bottom drawer**

hoped-for adj awaited with longing

hopeful /hópf'l/ adj **1. HAVING HOPE** feeling fairly sure that something that is wanted will happen **2. GIVING HOPE** making somebody feel confident that something desirable will happen **3. SHOWING HOPE** showing a desire for something ■ n **SOMEBODY DESIRING SUCCESS** somebody who desires achievement, especially somebody who hopes to be successful in sport, the arts, or politics —**hopefulness** n

hopefully /hópfali/ adv **1.** in a way that shows somebody's hope of having or receiving something ◇ a hopefully worded apology **2.** △ used to indicate that somebody hopes something will happen or will be the case

USAGE Many adverbs that express a wish or comment, for example clearly, obviously, and thankfully, are routinely used to qualify a whole sentence: They clearly haven't understood the issue. Obviously, there is a problem. Thankfully, they didn't arrive too late. Many people object when **hopefully** is used in this way — in, for example, Hopefully, someone can resolve this — typically on the grounds that there is no one present in the

sentence who is meant to be doing the hoping. This argument would tell against a number of the well-established sentence adverbs as well. For example, in *They clearly haven't understood the issue*, 'they' are not finding anything clear. The grounds on which to object to *hopefully* as a sentence adverb may be illogical, therefore, but many people dislike it regardless. A recommendation often made is to replace the word with *it is to be hoped*. That, however, strikes many people as stilted and even worse than *hopefully*. Frequently the best choice is *let's hope*, or (in more formal contexts) *Let us hope that…*

Hopeh /hố páy/ ◆ **Hebei**

~~hopeing~~ incorrect spelling of **hoping**

hopeless /hốpləss/ *adj* **1. WITH NO HOPE OF SUCCESS** unable to succeed or improve, or unable to be resolved, helped, or cured **2. DESPAIRING** feeling or showing no hope **3. VERY BAD** showing a complete lack of ability, competence, or efficiency —**hopelessness** *n*

hopelessly /hốpləssli/ *adv* **1.** in a way that shows somebody has no hope of success, relief, or of getting what he or she wants **2.** actually or supposedly to too great a degree to be improved or to be of use

hophead /hóp hed/ *n* **1.** *N Am* somebody addicted to a narcotic drug such as heroin (*slang*) **2.** *Aus* same as **drunkard** (*informal*) **3.** *NZ* a habitual beer drinker (*informal*)

Hopi /hốpi/ (*plural same* or **-pis**) *n* **1.** a member of a Native North American people of northeastern Arizona **2.** a Shoshonean language spoken in northeastern Arizona. Native speakers: 5,000. [Late 19C. < Hopi, 'peaceable'] —**Hopi** *adj*

Hopkins /hốpkinz/, **Sir Anthony** (*b.* 1937) Welsh actor. His films include *Silence of the Lambs* (1991), *Remains of the Day* (1993), and *Shadowlands* (1993).

Hopkins, Sir Frederick (1861–1947) British biochemist. He was the joint winner of the Nobel Prize in physiology or medicine (1929) for research into the role of vitamins in diet. Full name **Hopkins, Sir Frederick Gowland**

Hopkins, Gerard Manley (1844–89) British poet. He was a technical innovator and is best remembered for his poem *The Wreck of the Deutschland* (1875).

> 'I have desired to go / Where springs not fail, / To fields where flies no sharp and sided hail / And a few lilies blow.'
> [Gerard Manley Hopkins, 'Heaven-Have'; 1864]

hoplite /hóp līt/ *n* in ancient Greece, a heavily armed foot soldier [Early 18C. < Greek *hoplitēs* < *hoplon* 'weapon' < *hepein* 'care for, work at'] —**hoplitic** /hop líttik/ *adj*

hoplology /hop lóllǝji/ *n* the study of weapons and armour [Late 19C. < Greek *hoplon* (see HOPLITE)] —**hoplologist** *n*

hopper[1] /hóppǝr/ *n* **1. FUNNEL-SHAPED DISPENSER** a large funnel-shaped container for storing and dispensing grain, fuel, or other materials **2. VEHICLE THAT DISCHARGES LOAD THROUGH FLOOR** a truck or railway goods wagon with sloping floors designed to carry dry bulk goods such as grain or cement that are discharged through an opening in the bottom **3. SOMEBODY OR SOMETHING THAT HOPS** somebody who or something that hops **4. JUMPING INSECT** a jumping insect, e.g. a leafhopper or treehopper. Order: Homoptera. [13C. < HOP[1]]

hopper[2] /hóppǝr/ *n* a machine used to harvest hops [Early 18C. < HOP[2]]

Edward Hopper

Hopper /hóppǝr/, **Edward** (1882–1967) US artist. His work, e.g. *Nighthawks* (1942), is known for its stark realism.

> 'A nation's art is greatest when it most reflects the character of its people.'
> [Edward Hopper. Quoted in *Aroused by Books*, Anatole Broyard; 1974]

hop-picker *n* a person or machine that harvests hops

hopping /hópping/ *n* going from one place of a particular kind to another of the same kind (*usually used in combination*) ○ *job-hopping*

hopping mad *adj* extremely angry (*informal*)

hopple /hópp'l/ HORSERACING *vt* same as **hobble** *v* (sense 2) ■ *n* same as **hobble** *n* (sense 2) [Late 16C. Probably < Low German] —**hoppler** *n*

hopsack /hóp sak/ *n* **1.** a coarsely woven cotton or woollen fabric. Use: clothes. **2.** a coarse hemp or jute fabric. Use: sacks, bags.

hopscotch

hopscotch /hóp skoch/ *n* a children's game in which players hop along squares marked in a pattern on the ground to pick up a small object thrown into one of the squares [Early 19C. < SCOTCH[1], 'scratched line']

hop trefoil *n* a plant related to peas, beans, and clover. Flowers: yellow, resembling hops. Native to: northern temperate grasslands. Latin name: *Trifolium campestre*. N Am term **hop clover**

hor. *abbr* **1.** horizon **2.** horizontal **3.** horology

hora /háwrǝ/, **horah** *n* **1.** a traditional circle dance of Israel and Romania **2.** the music for a hora [Late 19C. Directly or via modern Hebrew < Romanian *horă*]

Horace /hórrǝss/ (65–8 BC) Roman poet. The son of a freedman, he was educated in Rome and Athens, and became the pre-eminent lyric poet of his time. His most famous works are *Odes* (23 BC) and *Epistles* (20? BC). Full name **Flaccus, Quintus Horatius**

> 'Seize the day, and put as little trust as you can in the morrow.'
> [Horace, *Odes*; 23 BC]

Horae /háwr ee/ *npl* in Greek mythology, the goddesses of the seasons and the order of nature

horah *n* DANCE, MUSIC another spelling of **hora**

horal /háwrǝl/ *adj* same as **horary** (*formal*) [Early 18C. < late Latin *horalis* < Latin *hora* (see HOUR)]

horary /háwrǝri/ *adj* (*formal*) **1.** relating to an hour or hours **2.** same as **hourly** *adj* (sense 1) [Early 17C. < medieval Latin *horarius* < Latin *hora* (see HOUR)]

Horatian /hǝ ráysh'n/ *adj* written by or in the style of the ancient Roman poet Horace [Early 17C. < Latin *Horatianus* < Quintus *Horatius* Flaccus, Latin name of HORACE]

Horatian ode *n* an ode that has several stanzas, each of which has the same rhythmic pattern

horde /hawrd/ *n* **1. LARGE CROWD** a large group of people (*often used in the plural*) **2. NOMADIC GROUP** a group of nomads, especially of a people who live by hunting and foraging for food (**hunter-gatherers**) **3. SWARM OR PACK** a large group of insects or other animals moving in a mass ■ *vi* (**hordes, hording, horded**) **1. FORM OR LIVE IN CROWD** to gather together, move, or live in a large crowd or mass **2. LIVE IN GROUP** to live together in a nomadic group [Mid-16C. Directly or via French and German < Polish *horda* < Turkish *ordu* 'camp, army']

SPELLCHECK See *hoard*.

Hordern /háwrdǝrn/, **Sir Michael** (1911–95) British actor. An accomplished Shakespearean and film actor, his films include *The Spy Who Came in From the Cold* (1965).

horehound /háwr hownd/, **hoarhound** *n* **1.** a bitter perennial mint with downy leaves and square stems. Flowers: small white, yielding juice used as a flavouring and in cough remedies. Native to: Europe, Asia. Latin name: *Marrubium vulgare*. **2.** an extract of the horehound plant, or something flavoured with it, e.g. cough drops [Old English *hāre hūne* < *hār* 'hoar' + *hūne* 'horehound', origin ?]

~~horizen~~ incorrect spelling of **horizon**

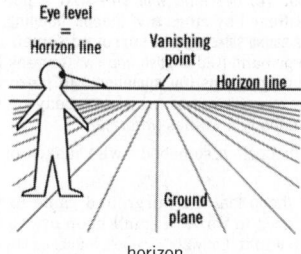
horizon

horizon /hǝ ríz'n/ *n* **1. PLACE WHERE EARTH MEETS SKY** the line in the furthest distance where the land or sea seems to meet the sky **2.** ASTRON **CIRCLE ON APPARENT SPHERE OF SKY** a circle formed on the celestial sphere by a plane tangent to a point on the Earth's surface **3.** ASTRON **CIRCLE ON CELESTIAL SPHERE** a circle formed on the celestial sphere by a plane through the centre of the Earth and parallel to the tangent of a point on Earth's surface **4.** GEOG **DISTINCT LAYER OF SOIL** a layer of soil having characteristics that distinguish it from other layers **5.** PALAEONT, GEOL **GEOLOGICAL LAYER** a distinct layer of rock or geological deposit within a stratum that can be dated, e.g. by its fossil content ■ **horizons** *npl* **RANGE OF EXPERIENCE** the range or limits of somebody's interests, knowledge, or experience [14C. Via French < late Latin < Greek *horizōn (kuklos)* 'limiting (circle)', present participle of *horizein* 'to limit' < *horos* 'limit'] —**horizonal** *adj*

horizontal /hórri zónt'l/ *adj* **1. LEVEL** parallel to the horizon **2. MEASURED PARALLEL TO HORIZON** measured or operating in a plane parallel to the horizon **3. HAVING SAME STATUS** at the same level within an organization ○ *a horizontal promotion* **4. APPLIED TO ALL** applied equally to all members, parts, or aspects of something ○ *a horizontal bonus* **5. OF HORIZON** relating to the horizon **6. LYING DOWN** lying down or in a reclining position (*informal*) **7.** GENETICS **OF TRANSFER OF GENETIC MATERIAL** relating to the transfer of genetic material from one individual to another of a different species ■ *n* **SOMETHING HORIZONTAL** a horizontal line, surface, or position [Mid-16C. < French, or modern Latin *horizontalis* < late Latin *horizont-*, stem of *horizon* (see HORIZON)] —**horizontality** /-zon tálləti/ *n* —**horizontally** *adv*

horizontal bar *n* **1.** a metal bar fixed in a horizontal position and used for gymnastic exercises **2.** a competitive gymnastics event involving feats of skill and strength on the horizontal bar

horizontal mobility *n* a change in social situation that does not involve a change in social status

Horlivka /háwr ljookǝ/ industrial city in eastern Ukraine. Population: 303,593 (1999).

hormogonium /háwrmǝ gốni ǝm/ (*plural* **-nia** /-ni ǝ/) *n* a section of a filament in some cyanobacteria that detaches and reproduces by cell division [Late 19C. < modern Latin < Greek *hormos* 'chain' + *gonos* 'generation, seed']

hormone /háwrmōn/ *n* **1. CHEMICAL IN BODY** a chemical secreted by an endocrine gland or some nerve cells that regulates the function of a specific tissue or organ **2. CHEMICAL IN PLANTS** a substance synthesized by plants that regulates their growth and development **3. REGULATING CHEMICAL IN INSECTS** a substance produced in the body of an insect that regulates various aspects of growth and development such as the change from larva to adult **4. REGULATING CHEMICAL**

a synthetic chemical that acts like a hormone [Early 20C. < Greek *hormōn*, present participle of *horman* 'set in motion' < *hormē* 'assault'] —**hormonal** /hawr mṓn'l/ *adj*—**hormonally** *adv*

hormone replacement therapy *n* treatment to maintain previous levels of oestrogen and other hormones in women during and after the menopause, to avoid bone fragility (**osteoporosis**) and protect against heart disease

Hormuz, Strait of /hawr mo͞oz, háwrmo͞oz/ narrow waterway between Iran and the Arabian Peninsula, linking the Persian Gulf with the Arabian Sea

horn /hawrn/ *n* **1.** AUTOMOT, EMERGENCIES **NOISE-MAKING WARNING DEVICE** a device, e.g. in a car, that produces a loud noise as a warning or signal **2.** ZOOL **PROJECTION ON ANIMAL'S HEAD** either of two permanent pointed projections on the head of some animals such as cattle, sheep, and antelope, consisting of a sheath of hardened protein over bone **3.** ZOOL **PROJECTION FROM NOSE OF RHINOCEROS** a solid outgrowth of keratin and fused hair from the nasal bone of a rhinoceros **4.** ZOOL **PROJECTION RESEMBLING HORN** a hard, pointed, or horn-shaped projection on a bird, reptile, fish, insect, or other animal **5.** INDUST **HARD SUBSTANCE OF HORNS** the hard substance that covers an animal's horns, consisting mainly of a tough protein (**keratin**) **6. SOMETHING MADE OF HORN** something made with a piece of horn or from a synthetic substance resembling it **7. PROJECTION ON DEVIL'S HEAD** either of a pair of parts resembling an animal's horns supposed to grow on the head of the devil or a cuckold **8. HORN-SHAPED THING** something shaped like a horn, e.g. either of the tips of a crescent moon, the pommel of a saddle, or the pointed end of an anvil **9.** GEOG **SHARP PEAK** a sharp pyramid-shaped mountain peak **10.** GEOG **HORN-SHAPED AREA** a horn-shaped body of water or land **11.** MUSIC **BRASS INSTRUMENT** a wind instrument, usually made of brass, with a long tube whose flared end produces a sound when the player's lips vibrate together into the mouthpiece **12.** MUSIC **WIND INSTRUMENT** any wind instrument used in a jazz band, especially a trumpet (*informal*) **13.** MUSIC **SIMPLE WIND INSTRUMENT** a simple or early musical instrument made from an animal's horn **14.** *N Am* TELECOM same as **telephone** (*slang*) **15. TABOO TERM** a highly offensive term for an erection of the penis (*taboo*) ■ *v* (**horns, horning, horned**) **1.** *vt* **PROVIDE SOMETHING WITH HORNS** to give something a horn or horns **2.** *vt* **ATTACK SOMEBODY WITH HORNS** to butt or gore somebody with the horns **3.** *vt US, Carib* **CUCKOLD SOMEBODY** to make a cuckold of somebody by having a sexual relationship with that person's spouse or partner (*informal*) **4.** *vi Malaysia, Singapore* **BLOW CAR HORN** to cause a car horn to make a warning sound ○ *Don't horn at other drivers except in an emergency.* [Old English, < Indo-European, 'horn, head'] —**hornless** *adj* ◇ **draw in your horns 1.** to spend or invest less money than usual or before **2.** to adopt a less active or less assertive position ◇ **lock horns (with somebody)** to engage in an argument or quarrel with somebody ◇ **on the horns of a dilemma** faced with making a decision between two things or two courses of action, each of which is problematic or unattractive

ORIGIN The Indo-European word from which ***horn*** is ultimately derived, is also the ancestor of English *carrot, corn*[2], *cornea, corner, cornet, cranium, ginger, hart, hornet, keratin, rhinoceros*, and *triceratops*.

horn in *vi* to intrude, interfere, or get involved in something without invitation (*informal*)

Horn, Cape /hawrn/ cape at the southern extremity of South America. Height: 424 m/1,391 ft. Spanish name **Cabo de Hornos**

hornbeam /háwrn beem/ *n* **1.** a tree with smooth greyish bark and hard white wood. Genus: *Carpinus.* **2.** the hard white wood of the hornbeam tree

hornbill /háwrn bil/ *n* a noisy tropical bird that has a large curved beak with a horny protuberance and is often found in large groups. Family: Bucerotidae.

hornblende /háwrn blend/ *n* a dark green to black mineral of the amphibole group, containing calcium, iron, magnesium, and sodium [Late 18C. < German] —**hornblendic** /hawrn bléndik/ *adj*

hornbook /háwrn bo͝ok/ *n* formerly, a page of text used as an aid in teaching reading, usually printed with the alphabet, letter combinations, and a religious passage, covered with a thin layer of horn

Horne /hawrn/, **Donald** (*b.* 1921) Australian writer and

hornbill

academic. His most famous work is *The Lucky Country* (1964). Full name **Horne, Donald Richmond**

horned /hawrnd/ *adj* having a horn or horns, or one or more projections that resemble horns

horned lizard *n* a small insect-eating lizard that has a flattened body, a short tail, and spikes like horns on its head. Native to: desert regions of the southwestern United States and Mexico. Genus: *Phrynosoma.*

horned melon *n* FOOD same as **Kiwano**

horned owl *n* a large owl with prominent ear tufts resembling horns. Latin name: *Bubo virginianus.*

horned pout *n* FISH same as **hornpout**

horned toad *n* REPT same as **horned lizard**

horned viper *n* a poisonous snake that has spines on its head that look like horns. Native to: dry regions of the Near East and Africa. Latin name: *Cerastes cornutus.*

hornet /háwrnit/ *n* a large stinging wasp that builds large group nests underground or hanging from a tree. Family: Vespidae. [Old English *hyrnet(u)* < Indo-European]

hornet's nest *n* a highly controversial issue or situation that is likely to lead to confrontation, opposition, or argument

hornfels /háwrn felz, -fels/ *n* a fine-grained metamorphic rock composed of silicate minerals and formed through the action of heat and pressure on shale [Mid-19C. < German, 'horn rock']

hornist /háwrnist/ *n* a musician who plays a horn

horn of plenty *n* **1.** ARTS same as **cornucopia** (sense 2) **2.** a funnel-shaped black and brown edible fungus found in deciduous woodland in autumn. Latin name: *Craterellus cornucopioides.*

hornpipe /háwrn pīp/ *n* **1.** DANCE **SAILORS' DANCE** a lively British dance traditionally performed by sailors **2.** MUSIC **MUSIC ACCOMPANYING HORNPIPE** the music for a hornpipe, or an orchestral piece based on this **3.** MUSIC **REED INSTRUMENT** a musical instrument with a single reed and a mouthpiece made of horn, traditionally used to play the music for a hornpipe

hornpout /háwrn powt/ *n* a small freshwater catfish with a large head and eight barbels. Native to: North America. Latin name: *Ictalurus nebulosus.*

horn-rims, horn-rimmed glasses *npl* spectacles with frames made from dark-coloured horn or a synthetic substance resembling this —**horn-rimmed** *adj*

hornstone /háwrn stōn/ *n* GEOL same as **hornfels** [Early 18C. Translation of German *Hornstein*]

hornswoggle /háwrn swogg'l/ (**-gles, -gling, -gled**) *vt N Am* to cheat, trick, or deceive somebody (*informal*) [Early 19C. Origin ?]

horntail /háwrn tayl/ *n* an insect that resembles a wasp and whose larvae burrow in wood. The female has a specialized egg-laying organ (**ovipositor**) used to lay eggs in wood. Family: Siricidae.

hornworm /háwrn wurm/ *n* the caterpillar of some hawk moths, with a projection on its tail that resembles a horn. Hornworms are often destructive agricultural pests.

hornwort /háwrn wurt/ *n* a rootless water plant that grows in branching submerged masses and has finely dissected leaves and tiny flowers. Genus: *Ceratophylum.* [< its branching stem]

horny /háwrni/ (**-ier, -iest**) *adj* **1. OF OR LIKE HORN** made of or resembling horn **2. AS TOUGH AS HORN** hard or rough like horn **3. FEELING SEXY** sexually excited, or easily aroused sexually (*informal*) **4. LOOKING SEXY** sexually attractive (*informal*) **5. WITH HORNS** having a horn or horns —**hornily** *adv* —**horniness** *n*

horol. *abbr* **1.** horological **2.** horology

Horologium /hórrə lṓji əm/ *n* a faint constellation of the southern hemisphere situated between Hydrus and Eridanus

horology /ho róllәji/ *n* **1.** the study or science of measuring time **2.** the art or skill of making clocks, watches, or other devices for telling the time [Early 19C. < Greek *hōra* 'time, hour'] —**horologic** /hórrə lójjik/ *adj*—**horological** *adj*—**horologically** *adv*—**horologist** *n*

horoscope /hórrə skōp/ *n* **1.** an astrologer's description of the personality and future of a person based on the position of the planets in relation to the sign of the zodiac under which the person was born **2.** the positions of the stars or planets relative to each another at a specific moment, especially the time of somebody's birth, or a diagram of these positions [Pre-12C. Via Latin < Greek *hōroskopos* 'time observer' < *hōra* 'time, hour' (of birth)] —**horoscopic** /hórrə skóppik/ *adj*

horoscopy /ho róskəpi/ *n* the making and interpretation of horoscopes

Horowitz /hórrə vits/, **Vladimir** (1904–89) Russian-born US pianist. He was known for his brilliant virtuosity. His interpretations of works by Liszt and Rachmaninov achieved popular and critical acclaim.

horrendous /ho réndəss, hə-/ *adj* **1.** sufficiently unpleasant, frightening, or shocking as to provoke horror **2.** very large, great, or high, often unreasonably or excessively so (*informal*) ○ *horrendous prices* [Mid-17C. < Latin *horrendus* 'to be shuddered at', form of *horrere* 'bristle, shudder with fear at'] —**horrendousness** *n*

horrendously /ho réndəssli, hə-/ *adv* to a very great and often unreasonable or excessive degree

horrible /hórrəb'l/ *adj* **1. VERY UNPLEASANT** very bad, unpleasant, or unsightly ○ *a horrible smell* **2. CAUSING HORROR** sufficiently frightening, distressing, or shocking as to provoke horror ○ *a horrible crime* **3. NASTY** unkind, rude, or badly behaved (*informal*) [13C. Via French < Latin *horribilis* < *horrere* 'bristle, shudder with fear at'] —**horribleness** *n*

horribly /hórrəbli/ *adv* **1.** in an unpleasant, frightening, distressing, or shocking way **2.** to a great or excessive extent ○ *horribly late*

horrid /hórrid/ *adj* **1. NASTY** callously unkind or nasty (*informal*) ○ *a horrid thing to say* **2. CAUSING DISGUST** provoking disgust or extreme displeasure ○ *a horrid taste* **3. CAUSING HORROR** dreadful, shocking, or frightening enough to cause horror ○ *a horrid accident* **4. BRISTLY** rough, shaggy, or bristly (*archaic*) [Late 16C. < Latin *horridus* 'bristly, rough, horrid' < *horrere* 'bristle, shudder with fear at'] —**horridly** *adv*—**horridness** *n*

horrific /ho ríffik, hə-/ *adj* frightening or disturbing enough to cause horror [Mid-17C. Directly or via French < Latin *horrificus* < *horrere* 'bristle, shudder with fear at'] —**horrifically** *adv*

horrify /hórri fī/ (**-fies, -fying, -fied**) *vt* **1.** to make somebody feel horror, disgust, or fright **2.** to make somebody shocked or dismayed [Late 18C. < Latin *horrificare* 'cause horror' < *horrere* 'bristle, shudder with fear at'] —**horrification** /hórrifi káysh'n/ *n* —**horrified** *adj* —**horrifying** *adj*—**horrifyingly** *adv*

horripilation /ho ríppi láysh'n/ *n* the standing on end of somebody's hair, e.g. because of fear or cold [Mid-17C. < late Latin *horripilation-* < Latin *horripilare* 'become hairy' < *horrere* 'to bristle' + *pilus* 'hair']

horror /hórrər/ *n* **1. INTENSE FEAR** a very strong feeling of fear, shock, or disgust **2. INTENSE DISLIKE** a feeling of distress or distaste ○ *He has a horror of spiders.* **3. SOMETHING CAUSING HORROR** something that causes a very strong feeling of fear, shock, or disgust ○ *the horrors of war* **4. SOMETHING UNPLEASANT** a very unpleasant or unsightly thing (*informal*) ○ *The new building is an absolute horror.* **5. SOMEBODY UNPLEASANT** a disagreeable or ill-mannered person, especially a badly behaved child (*informal*) ■ **horrors** *npl* (*informal*) **1. FEELING OF TERROR** a feeling of great fear, anxiety, or hopelessness **2.** MED same as **delirium tremens** ■ *adj* CINEMA, LITERAT **GROTESQUE AND TERRIFYING** describes a genre of motion picture or literature intended to thrill viewers or readers by provoking fear or revulsion through the portrayal of grotesque, violent, or

supernatural events [14C. Directly or via French < Latin < *horrere* 'bristle, shudder with fear at']

horror story *n* **1.** a story that is intended to frighten people, usually by describing gruesome or supernatural events **2.** a true account of something very unpleasant or shocking

horror-struck, horror-stricken *adj* suddenly shocked, frightened, or dismayed

hors concours /áwr koN koòr/ *adj* not participating in a competition or contest [< French, 'out of the competition']

hors de combat /áwr də kóm baa/ *adj* out of action and often in a seriously wounded condition [< French, 'out of the fight']

hors d'oeuvre /awr dúrv, -dúrvrə/ (*plural same* or **hors d'oeuvres** /-dúrv, -dúrvz, -dúrvrə/) *n* a small portion of food served cold or hot before a meal to stimulate the appetite [< French, 'outside the work']

horse /hawrss/ *n* **1.** FOUR-LEGGED ANIMAL a large four-legged animal with a mane, tail, hooves, and a long head. Kept for: riding, pulling vehicles, carrying loads. Latin name: *Equus caballus.* **2.** STALLION OR GELDING an adult male horse **3.** ANIMAL OF HORSE FAMILY an animal that belongs to the horse family, e.g. a donkey or zebra. Family: Equidae. **4.** GYMNASTICS same as **vaulting horse 5.** FRAME OR SUPPORT a frame or support, especially one mounted on four legs **6.** MIL MOUNTED SOLDIERS a unit of soldiers riding horses (*takes a singular or plural verb*) **7.** GEOL MASS OF ROCK IN ORE a mass of rock located in an ore vein **8.** DRUGS same as **heroin** (*dated slang*) **9.** AUTOMOT same as **horsepower** (*informal; usually used in the plural*) ■ **horses** *npl* HORSERACING horseracing, especially as a gambling activity (*informal*) ■ *v* (**horses, horsing, horsed**) **1.** *vt* GIVE SOMEBODY HORSE to provide somebody with a horse **2.** *vti* RIDING PUT OR GET ON HORSE to put a rider on a horse's back, or mount a horse **3.** *vi* ZOOL BE IN HEAT to be ready to mate with a male horse (*refers to mares*) [Old English *hors* < Germanic] ◊ **back the wrong horse** to make a bad choice ◊ **flog a dead horse** to pursue a topic or course of action that is likely to be totally unproductive ◊ **from the horse's mouth** from a well-informed and reliable source ◊ **look a gift horse in the mouth** to criticize something that has been given to you ◊ **wild horses would** or **could not...** no amount of force or persuasion could make somebody do a particular thing (*informal*) ○ *Wild horses wouldn't drag the secret out of me.*

SPELLCHECK See *hoarse*.

horse around, horse about *vi* to play or fool around in a boisterous manner

horse-and-buggy *adj* N Am adhering to things, fashions, or ideas that are old-fashioned and out of date (*informal*)

horseback /hawrss bak/ *adj, adv* sitting on or riding a horse ◊ **on horseback** sitting on or riding a horse

horse bean *n* a field bean used for feeding animals [< its use as fodder for horses]

horsebox /hawrss boks/ *n* UK a vehicle used to transport horses, e.g. a lorry with a special compartment. ANZ term **horse float.** N Am term **horsecar**

horse brass *n* a flat, usually circular, polished brass ornament originally attached to a horse's harness and now sometimes hung on walls or beams in houses or bars for decoration

horsecar /hawrss kaar/ *n* N Am RIDING, VEHICLES same as **horsebox**

horse chestnut *n* **1.** SEED a large shiny brown inedible

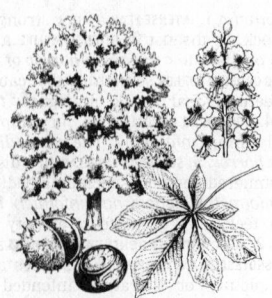

horse chestnut

seed with a fleshy, sometimes spiny husk **2.** TREE a large tree that has compound leaves, conical flower clusters, and sticky winter buds, and produces horse chestnuts. Native to: northern hemisphere. Genus: *Aesculus.* **3.** WOOD the soft wood of the horse chestnut tree

horsefeathers /hawrss fethərz/ *n, interj* N Am nonsense (*slang humorous; takes a singular verb*) [Early 20C. Alteration of HORSESHIT]

horseflesh /hawrss flesh/ *n* **1.** horses collectively **2.** the flesh of a horse, especially when sold or eaten as meat

horse float *n* ANZ same as **horsebox**

horsefly /hawrss flí/ (*plural* **-flies**) *n* a large two-winged fly, the female of which sucks the blood of horses and other animals. Genus: *Tabanus.*

Horse Guards *npl* a British cavalry regiment that, with the Life Guards, forms the Household Cavalry responsible for guarding the sovereign, especially during public ceremonies ■ *n* the headquarters of the Horse Guards in Whitehall, London

horsehair /hawrss hair/ *n* **1.** hair from a horse's mane and tail. Use: upholstery, mattress filling, cloth. **2.** fabric woven from the hair of a horse's mane and tail

horsehair worm *n* ZOOL same as **hairworm**

Horsehead nebula /hawrss hed-/ *n* a dark nebula in the constellation Orion, shaped like a horse's head

horsehide /hawrss híd/ *n* the tough thick skin of a horse, or leather made from a horse's skin

horse latitudes *npl* either of two regions at sea near the latitudes 30° S and 30° N marked by high atmospheric pressure and light variable winds or calms [Origin ?]

horselaugh /hawrss laaf/ *n* a loud, coarse, and often scornful laugh

horseleech /hawrss leech/ *n* a large freshwater leech. Genus: *Haemopis.* [*Horse* because large or coarse]

horseless carriage /hawrssləss-/ *n* a motor car, at a time when horse-drawn vehicles were still the usual form of transport (*archaic*)

horse mackerel *n* a swift torpedo-shaped fish. Native to: Atlantic Ocean, Mediterranean Sea, Black Sea. Latin name: *Trachurus trachurus.* [*Horse* because large or coarse]

horseman /hawrssmən/ (*plural* **-men** /-mən/) *n* a man who rides or is riding a horse, especially one who does so with skill —**horsemanship** *n*

horsemint /hawrss mint/ *n* **1.** a hairy wild mint. Flowers: small, pinkish-purple, in elongated clusters. Native to: Europe, Asia. Latin name: *Mentha longifolia.* **2.** a coarse mint. Flowers: showy, yellow with purple spots. Native to: North America. Latin name: *Monarda punctata.* [*Horse* because large or coarse]

horse mushroom *n* a large mushroom that smells of almonds. Latin name: *Agaricus arvensis.* [*Horse* because large or coarse]

horse opera *n* CINEMA same as **western** (*informal*)

horse pistol *n* a large pistol formerly used by horsemen and carried in a holster

horseplay /hawrss play/ *n* rough boisterous playful behaviour

horsepower /hawrss powər/ *n* a unit of power equal in the United Kingdom to 550 foot-pounds per second and in the United States to 745.7 watts [Supposedly equivalent to the work rate of a horse]

horse race *n* a race between horses ridden by jockeys on a flat circuit or over obstacles

horseracing /hawrss rayssing/ *n* a sport in which horses ridden by jockeys race against each other, usually with spectators and others betting on the result

horseradish

horseradish /hawrss radish/ *n* **1.** a long slim pungent root. Use: in cookery, especially peeled and grated to make a hot sharp-tasting sauce often served with beef. **2.** a tall coarse plant that yields horseradish. Flowers: white. Native to: North America. Latin name: *Armoracia lapathifolia.* [*Horse* because large or coarse]

horse riding *n* the practice of riding on horseback, especially as a recreation

horse sense *n* same as **common sense** (*informal*)

horseshit /hawrss shit/ *n* (*slang*) **1.** an offensive term for the excrement of a horse **2.** N Am an offensive term for nonsense

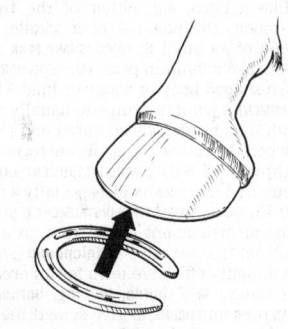

horseshoe

horseshoe /hawrss shoo/ *n* **1.** RIDING PROTECTION FOR HORSE'S HOOF a flat U-shaped piece of iron nailed to the bottom of a horse's hoof to protect it against hard surfaces. Horseshoes are regarded as symbols of good luck. **2.** GOOD-LUCK TOKEN a representation of a horseshoe regarded as a symbol of good luck **3.** SOMETHING HORSESHOE-SHAPED something that has the curved shape of a horseshoe ○ '... *every known superstition in the world is gathered into the horseshoe of the Carpathians ...*' (Bram Stoker, *Dracula*; 1897) ■ *vt* (**-shoes, -shoeing, -shoed**) RIDING same as **shoe** *v* (sense 1) —**horseshoer** *n*

horseshoe arch *n* an arch that narrows slightly below the upper rounded part. Horseshoe arches are characteristic of the Islamic architecture of southern Spain and North Africa.

horseshoe bat *n* a bat that has a horseshoe-shaped appendage that surrounds the nostrils. Native to: Europe, tropics. Family: Rhinolophidae.

horseshoe crab *n* an invertebrate sea animal that has a stiff pointed tail and rounded brown body resembling a horseshoe. Native to: eastern North America, Asia. Class: Merostomata.

Horseshoe Falls /hawrss shoo-/ crescent-shaped Canadian section of Niagara Falls on the US-Canadian border. Height: 49 m/161 ft.

horseshoes /hawrss shooz/ *n* N Am a game in which players throw horseshoes at a post and score points according to how close the horseshoes land to the post (*takes a singular verb*)

horse show *n* a sporting event in which horses and usually riders are judged on their skills in a variety of competitions such as riding or jumping

horsetail /hawrss tayl/ *n* **1.** a nonflowering plant that has a hollow jointed stem, tiny thin leaves, and spore-producing cones at the top of the stems. Genus: *Equisetum.* **2.** an object resembling a horse's tail, formerly used as a emblem of rank by Turkish pashas in the Ottoman Empire

a at; aa father; aw all; ay day; ai hair; ə about, item, edible, common, circus; e egg; ee eel; hw when; i it, happy; ī ice; ı̇ apple; 'm rhythm; 'n fashion; o odd; ō open; ŏŏ good; oo pool; ow owl; oy oil; th thin; th this; u up; ur urge;

horse-trading *n* negotiation that involves bargaining, compromise, and sometimes unscrupulous tactics such as secret or unofficial deals (*informal*) —**horse-trade** *vi* —**horse-trader** *n*

horsewhip /háwrss wip/ *n* **1.** WHIP FOR HORSE formerly, a whip used to keep a horse under control, e.g. when being driven, and usually made of a long strip of leather attached to a short handle **2.** *Carib* W INDIAN SNAKE a long thin common snake frequently found in bushes near homes. Native to: forests of Trinidad. ■ *vt* (**-whips, -whipping, -whipped**) BEAT PERSON OR ANIMAL SEVERELY to flog a person or animal with a horsewhip or with something similar, usually as a punishment

horsewoman /háwrss wŏŏmən/ (*plural* **-women** /-wimin/) *n* a woman who rides or is riding a horse, especially one who does so with skill

horsey /háwrssi/ (**-ier, -iest**), **horsy** *adj* **1.** RELATING TO HORSES relating to or characteristic of a horse **2.** LOOKING LIKE HORSE heavy, awkward, and unattractive in appearance **3.** INTERESTED IN HORSES very fond of horses and interested in activities involving horses such as riding, racing, showjumping, or hunting —**horsiness** *n*

Horsham /háwrshəm/ town in West Sussex, southern England, combining light industry, service industries, and agriculture. Population: 122,088 (2001).

horst /hawrst/ *n* an elevated block of the Earth's crust forced upwards between faults [Late 19C. < German, 'heap, mass']

horsy *adj* another spelling of **horsey**

hort. *abbr* **1.** horticultural **2.** horticulture

Horta /háwrtə/, **Baron Victor** (1861–1947) Belgian architect. He made extensive use of metal and glass, as in the *Maison du Peuple* (1899) in Brussels, and supervised the interior decoration of his buildings. Many of them feature the sinuous lines and organic forms characteristic of the art nouveau movement.

hortatory /háwrtətəri/, **hortative** /háwrtətiv/ *adj* urging, encouraging, or strongly advising a course of action to somebody (*formal*) [Late 16C. < late Latin *hortatorius* < Latin *hortari* 'exhort'] —**hortatorily** *adv*

horticulture /háwrti kulchər/ *n* **1.** the science, skill, or occupation of cultivating plants, especially flowers, fruit, and vegetables, in gardens or greenhouses **2.** a simple form of agriculture based on working small plots of land without using draught animals, ploughs, or irrigation [Late 17C. < Latin *hortus* 'garden'] —**horticultural** /háwrti kúlchərəl/ *adj* —**horticulturally** *adv* —**horticulturist** /háwrti kúlchərist/ *n*

Horus /háwrəss/ *n* in Egyptian mythology, the god of the Sun, the sky, and goodness, usually depicted as having a falcon's head. Horus was the son of Isis and Osiris.

Horvitz /háwr vits/, **H. Robert** (*b.* 1947) US molecular biologist. He worked on molecular genetics and the degeneration of cells, and shared the 2002 Nobel Prize in physiology or medicine with John Sulston and Sydney Brenner.

Hos. *abbr* BIBLE Hosea

hosanna /hō zánnə/, **hosannah** *n, interj* a cry of praise to God [Pre-12C. Via late Latin < Greek *hōsanna* < Rabbinic Hebrew *hōšaʿnā*, shortening of Hebrew *hōšīʿā-nnā* 'save, (we) pray' (Psalm 118:25)]

Hosay /hō sáy/ *n Carib* ISLAM same as **Muharram** (sense 2)

hose /hōz/ *n* FLEXIBLE TUBE a flexible tube or pipe, often made of rubber or plastic, through which fluids such as water or petrol can flow ■ *npl* **1.** CLOTHING LEG COVERINGS skintight leg coverings, e.g. stockings or socks (*formal*) **2.** CLOTHING, HIST TIGHT-FITTING TROUSERS close-fitting leg coverings that attached to a doublet, formerly worn by men ■ *vt* (**hoses, hosing, hosed**) **1.** DIRECT WATER ON SOMEBODY OR SOMETHING to spray, soak, wash, or rinse somebody or something with water from a hose **2.** *US* TRICK SOMEBODY to deceive or trick somebody (*slang*) [Old English *hosa* 'leg covering, husk' < Indo-European, 'to cover']

Hosea /hō zée ə/ *n* a book of the Bible that contains the prophecies traditionally attributed to the Hebrew prophet Hosea. See table at **Bible**

Hosein /hō sáyn/ *n Carib* ISLAM same as **Ashora** [Late 20C. Variant of HUSAIN]

hosel /hōz'l/ *n* the socket in the head of a golf club where the shaft is attached [Late 19C. < HOSE + *-el* 'small' < Latin *-ellus*]

hosepipe /hōz pīp/ *n* a long hose for domestic use, e.g. for watering gardens or washing cars

hoser /hōzər/ *n Can* an offensive term for somebody regarded as unintelligent and vulgar, especially a man whose main interests are ice hockey and drinking beer (*slang*)

hosier /hōzi ər/ *n* somebody who makes or sells hosiery (*archaic*)

hosiery /hōzi əri/ *n* socks, stockings, and tights, considered collectively

hospice /hóspiss/ *n* **1.** a usually small residential institution for terminally ill patients where treatment focuses on the patient's wellbeing rather than a cure and includes drugs for pain management, sometimes periods at home, and often spiritual counselling **2.** formerly, a place where pilgrims, travellers, and the homeless or destitute were offered lodging, usually by a religious order [Early 19C. Via French < Latin *hospitium* 'guesthouse, hospitality' < *hospit-* 'host, guest']

hospitable /ho spíttəb'l, hóspitəb'l/ *adj* **1.** friendly, welcoming, and generous to guests or strangers ○ *That's very hospitable of you.* **2.** pleasant, agreeable, and providing what somebody needs to live comfortably ○ *a hospitable climate* [Late 16C. < French < obsolete *hospiter* 'receive a guest' < Latin *hospit-* 'host, guest'] —**hospitability** /hóspitə bílləti/ *n* —**hospitably** *adv*

hospital /hóspit'l/ *n* **1.** BUILDING FOR MEDICAL CARE an institution where people receive medical, surgical, or psychiatric treatment and nursing care **2.** PLACE FOR REPAIRING THINGS a place where something is mended **3.** SOC WELFARE CHARITABLE HOME a charitable institution providing shelter, care, or education for orphaned children, elderly people, or the homeless or destitute (*archaic*) [13C. Via Old French, 'hostel' < medieval Latin *hospitale* 'guesthouse, inn' < Latin *hospit-* 'host, guest']

Hospital /hóspit'l/, **Janette Turner** (*b.* 1942) Australian novelist. She wrote *The Last Magician* (1992).

hospital-acquired infection *n* a disease caught by somebody while being treated in hospital for something else

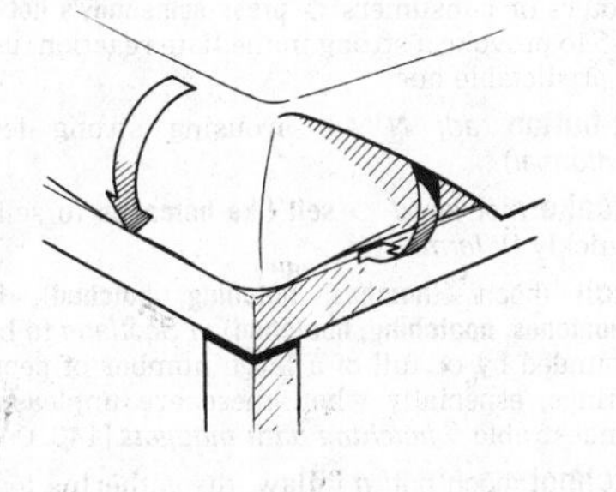

hospital corner

hospital corner *n* a neat overlapping fold of the bedding at each corner of a bed

Hospitaler *n* RELIG US spelling of **Hospitaller**

hospitalise *vt* MED another spelling of **hospitalize**

hospitality /hóspi tálləti/ *n* KINDNESS TO VISITORS friendly, welcoming, and generous treatment offered to guests or strangers ■ *adj* **1.** FOR GUESTS for the use of clients, guests, or visitors who are being entertained, especially by a company at a sports or arts event ○ *a hospitality box* ○ *a hospitality suite* **2.** BUSINESS OF CATERING AND ENTERTAINMENT describes the business of providing services such as catering and entertainment ○ *the hospitality industry*

hospitality box *n* a private room or enclosure in a sports stadium or arena with a view of the playing area that is hired by a person or organization for the use of guests

hospitality suite *n* a room or suite of rooms where invited guests or clients of a company, delegates to a conference, or other official visitors are welcomed and provided with free refreshments

hospitality tray *n* a set of items such as an electric kettle, cups, milk, and tea or coffee provided in a hotel room for making a hot drink

hospitalize /hóspitə līz/ (**-izes, -izing, -ized**), **hospitalise** (**-ises, -ising, -ised**) *vt* to admit somebody to hospital for treatment, diagnosis, or observation, usually as an inpatient —**hospitalization** /hóspitə lī záysh'n/ *n*

Hospitaller /hóspitələr/ *n* **1.** a member of a military religious order, the Knights of the Hospital of St John, founded in the late 11th century by European crusaders to care for sick pilgrims in Jerusalem **2.** *also* **hospitaller** a member of a religious order or charitable institution involved in the care of the sick, especially in hospital [14C. Via Old French *hospitalier* < medieval Latin *hospitalarius* < *hospitale* (see HOSPITAL)]

hospodar /hóspə daar/ *n* a prince or governor of Moldavia or Walachia during the time of Ottoman rule [Late 16C. Via Romanian < Ukrainian]

host[1] /hōst/ *n* **1.** SOMEBODY ENTERTAINING GUESTS somebody who invites and entertains guests **2.** BROADCAST SOMEBODY INTRODUCING GUESTS ON SHOW somebody who presents a television or radio programme such as a chat show or game show in which invited guests take part **3.** PLACE WHERE EVENT IS HELD a place or organization that provides the space and facilities for an event such as an international sporting competition **4.** BIOL ORGANISM INFECTED BY PARASITE a human, animal, plant, or other organism in or on which another organism, especially a parasite, lives **5.** MED GRAFT OR TRANSPLANT RECIPIENT the recipient of a transplanted or grafted embryo, tissue, or organ **6.** LEISURE LANDLORD OF INN the owner or manager of a pub or hotel (*dated*) **7.** *also* **host computer** COMPUT MAIN COMPUTER IN NETWORK the main computer that controls specific functions or files in a network **8.** *N Am* SOMEBODY GREETING CUSTOMERS IN RESTAURANT somebody employed in a restaurant to greet and seat customers ■ *vt* (**hosts, hosting, hosted**) **1.** ACCOMMODATE EVENT to provide the space and facilities for an event such as an international sporting competition **2.** BROADCAST INTRODUCE GUESTS ON SHOW to act as the host of a television or radio programme **3.** ENTERTAIN GUESTS to be the host of a social or official gathering **4.** ONLINE CREATE WEBSITE FOR SOMEBODY to create and maintain a website for somebody as a service [13C. Via Old French *(h)oste* 'host, guest' < Latin *hospit-*]

host[2] /hōst/ *n* **1.** a very large number of people or things **2.** MIL same as **army** (*archaic*) [14C. Via French < Latin *hostis* 'stranger, enemy' (in medieval Latin, 'army')]

Host /hōst/, **host** *n* the bread or wafer consecrated and eaten during the Christian ceremony of Communion [14C. Via French < Latin *hostia* 'sacrificial animal, victim']

hosta /hóstə/ *n UK, ANZ, Can* a perennial shade-loving plant with broad ribbed leaves. Flowers: white, blue, or lilac, tubular, in clusters. Genus: *Hosta*. US term **plantain lily** [Early 19C. < modern Latin, after Nicolaus T. *Host* (1761–1834), Austrian botanist]

hostage /hóstij/ *n* **1.** somebody held prisoner by a person or group such as a criminal or a terrorist organization until specific demands are met or money is handed over **2.** a person or group of people whose freedom of action is restricted or controlled by a more powerful organization by implied threats or other means [13C. < Old French *(h)ostage* < late Latin *obsidiatus* 'state of being a hostage' < *sedere* 'sit'] ◇ **a hostage to fortune** a remark or action that could potentially lead to trouble or difficulty and so is better avoided

host computer *n* COMPUT same as **host**[1] *n* (sense 7)

hostel /hóst'l/ *n* **1.** SUPERVISED LODGING FOR WORKERS OR EX-OFFENDERS a place where supervised lodging is provided for workers, juvenile offenders, or ex-offenders **2.** ACCOMMODATION FOR HOMELESS PEOPLE a place providing accommodation for people who are homeless **3.** TRAVEL same as **youth hostel** **4.** INN an inn or place of lodging (*archaic*) [13C. < Old French *(h)ostel* < medieval Latin *hospitale* (see HOSPITAL)]

hosteler, etc. TRAVEL US spelling of **hosteller, etc.**

hosteller /hóst'lər/ *n* somebody who stays at hostels while travelling for pleasure, especially a young person who stays at youth hostels

hostelling /hóst'ling/ *n* the practice of staying at hostels, especially youth hostels, while travelling for pleasure

hostelry /hóst'lri/ (*plural* **-ries**) *n* a hotel, pub, or inn (*humorous or archaic*)

hostess /hōstiss, hō stéss/ *n* **1.** WOMAN ENTERTAINING GUESTS a woman who invites, welcomes, and entertains guests, often providing them with food and drink **2.** BROADCAST WOMAN INTRODUCING GUESTS ON SHOW a woman

who presents a television or radio programme such as a chat show or game show in which invited guests take part **3.** PAID DANCE PARTNER a woman who is paid to be a dancing partner at a nightclub or dance hall **4.** *N Am* WOMAN GREETING RESTAURANT CUSTOMERS a woman who is employed in a restaurant to greet and seat customers **5.** *N Am* TRAVEL WOMAN ATTENDANT FOR PASSENGERS a woman who is employed to provide for the safety and comfort of passengers on an aircraft, ship, train, or bus (*dated*) [12C. < Old French *(h)ostesse* < *(h)oste* (see HOST [1])] —**hostess** *vti*

hostile /hóss tīl/ *adj* **1.** VERY UNFRIENDLY showing or feeling hatred, enmity, antagonism, or anger towards somebody **2.** AGAINST strongly opposed to somebody or something ○ *hostile to the idea* **3.** MIL RELATING TO ENEMY relating to, characteristic of, or belonging to an enemy, especially in warfare ○ *hostile fire* **4.** ADVERSE not favourable to life, health, development, or success ○ *a hostile environment* **5.** BUSINESS AGAINST MANAGEMENT'S WILL opposed by the owner or management of a company ○ *a hostile takeover* ■ *n* HOSTILE PERSON an enemy, especially in warfare [Late 16C. Directly or via French < Latin *hostilis* < *hostis* 'enemy, stranger'] —**hostilely** *adv*

hostile witness *n* a witness called by a party who gives evidence against that party

hostility /ho stíllәti/ *n* (*plural* **-ties**) **1.** INTENSE AGGRESSION OR ANGER a feeling or attitude of hatred, enmity, antagonism, or anger towards somebody **2.** STRONG OPPOSITION strong opposition to somebody or something **3.** HOSTILE ACT an act of hatred, enmity, antagonism, or anger against somebody ■ **hostilities** *npl* MIL ATTACKS open acts of warfare

hosting centre /hṓsting-/ *n* a business that provides Internet access and guarantees maintenance of Internet links to clients housing their own processors and software with it

hostler *n* HIST same as **ostler** (*archaic*)

hot /hot/ *adj* (**hotter, hottest**) **1.** VERY WARM at a high, relatively high, or very high temperature ○ *the hottest day of the year* **2.** TOO WARM FOR COMFORT feeling warmer than usual or desirable ○ *If you're hot, take your jumper off.* **3.** FOOD VERY SPICY spicy or peppery enough to cause a burning sensation in the mouth or throat **4.** CAUSING CONTROVERSY causing much discussion, disagreement, or controversy ○ *a hot topic* **5.** DANGEROUS unpleasant or uncomfortable because of antagonism, trouble, or danger (*informal*) ○ *It got too hot for him to handle.* **6.** QUICKLY ANGERED easily provoked or aroused ○ *a hot temper* **7.** INTENSE felt, done, or expressed with forceful intense energy ○ *hot competition* **8.** COLOURS BRIGHT bright and vivid ○ *hot pink* **9.** CLOSE following somebody or something very closely ○ *hot on the trail* **10.** PROMISING offering potential success or good fortune ○ *a hot tip* **11.** TOPICAL very recent or new and therefore of interest or importance ○ *hot off the press* **12.** EXCITING fresh and exciting (*informal*) ○ *a hot new talent* **13.** SUCCESSFUL very popular or successful (*informal*) ○ *one of the hottest items in the range* **14.** KNOWLEDGEABLE having, showing, or characterized by great skill or knowledge (*informal*) ○ *not very hot at maths* **15.** *N Am* LUCKY very lucky, e.g. in gambling (*informal*) **16.** WISE very good, wise, or sensible (*informal*) ○ *That idea's not so hot.* **17.** WELL well or good (*informal*) ○ *I don't feel too hot.* **18.** *N Am* ANGRY angry or agitated about something (*informal*) **19.** KEEN enthusiastically eager (*informal*) ○ *She's really hot on jazz.* **20.** STRICT very strict about something (*informal*) ○ *He's hot on getting the paperwork right.* **21.** PHYSICALLY ATTRACTED physically attracted or aroused (*slang*) **22.** PHYSICALLY ATTRACTIVE physically attractive or exciting (*slang*) **23.** STOLEN obtained illegally, especially by stealing (*slang*) ○ *hot jewels* **24.** ON RUN wanted by the police (*slang*) ○ *a hot suspect* **25.** *US* EAGER full of activity, energy, enthusiasm, or excitement **26.** MUSIC INVENTIVE AND EXCITING with strong rhythms or exciting improvisation (*informal*) **27.** AUTOMOT POWERFUL very fast and powerful (*slang*) ○ *a hot car* **28.** ELEC LIVE electrically charged ○ *a hot wire* **29.** PHYS RADIOACTIVE dangerously radioactive **30.** BIOL INFECTIOUS extremely infectious or lethal, or containing infectious viruses ○ *a hot zone* **31.** PHYS IN ELEVATED ENERGY STATE in an elevated energy state, usually caused by nuclear processes ○ *a hot atom* **32.** NEAR ANSWER very close to something to be found or discovered in a hunting or guessing game (*informal*) ○ *You're getting hotter.* **33.** *US* ABSURD funny, absurd, or unbelievable (*slang*) ○ *told a hot one about his hunting experiences* ■ **hots** *npl* DESIRE strong physical desire (*informal*) ■ *adv* INTENSELY in an eager, intense, or angry way ○ *They argued hot and long.* [Old English *hāt* < Germanic] —**hotness** *n* ◇ **blow** *or* **run hot and cold** to vacillate between emotions, opinions, or ideas, e.g. by being enthusiastic about somebody or something and then unenthusiastic ◇ **hot to trot** eager and willing (*slang*)

hot up *vti* **1.** to become more intense, active, or exciting, or make something do this (*informal*) **2.** to become faster or more powerful, or make something do this

hot air *n* impressive or boastful talk about achievements or intentions that has no substance (*informal*)

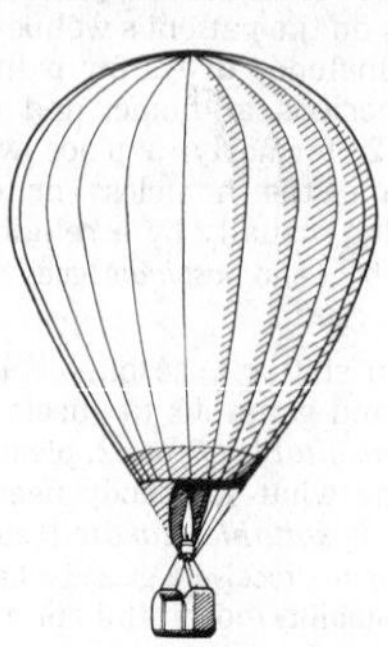

hot-air balloon

hot-air balloon *n* a lighter-than-air craft in which a compartment for pilot and passengers is suspended from a large nylon balloon that holds heated air or helium

hotbed /hót bed/ *n* **1.** an environment in which something flourishes or happens frequently, especially something undesirable **2.** a planting bed covered with glass and heated with electricity or by the action of fermenting manure to aid in quick germination of seeds and growth of plants

hot-blooded *adj* easily angered, excited, or physically aroused —**hot-bloodedness** *n*

hot button *n N Am* something that is known or likely to provoke a strong response, especially among voters or consumers ◇ **press somebody's hot button** *US* to provoke a strong immediate reaction, usually a predictable one

hot-button *adj N Am* arousing strong feelings (*informal*)

hotcake /hót kayk/ ◇ **sell like hotcakes** to sell very quickly (*informal*)

hotch /hoch/ (**hotches, hotching, hotched**), **hoatch** (**hoatches, hoatching, hoatched**) *vi Scotland* to be surrounded by or full of a large number of people or things, especially when these are unpleasant or undesirable ○ *hotching with maggots* [14C. Origin ?]

hotchpot /hóch pot/ *n* in law, the gathering together of property belonging to different people in order to divide it equally [14C. < Old French *hochepot* < *hocher* 'shake' + *pot* 'pot']

hotchpotch /hóch poch/ *n* **1.** a mixture of several unrelated things. N Am term **hodgepodge 2.** a stew consisting of a varied mixture of ingredients, usually mutton and vegetables [Late 16C. Rhyming alteration of HOTCHPOT]

hot comb *n* a comb that can be heated, usually electrically, and used to style or straighten the hair

hot cross bun *n* a sweet bun containing yeast, spices, and dried fruit, and marked with a cross on the top, traditionally eaten hot on Good Friday

hot-desking *n* the practice of using any available desk at work, instead of having a desk assigned to you —**hot-desk** *vi*

hot dish *n US* a dish of hot food cooked and served in a casserole, usually consisting of meat and vegetables, often with pasta

hot dog *n* a long sausage usually served hot on a bread roll with toppings such as fried onions, mustard, or ketchup ■ *interj N Am* used to express strong approval, delight, or surprise (*informal*)

hot-dog (**hot-dogs, hot-dogging, hot-dogged**) *vi N Am* to perform difficult, dangerous, or acrobatic stunts in a showy or impressive manner in skiing, surfing, or similar sports (*slang*) —**hot-dogger** *n* —**hot-dogging** *n*

hotel /hō tél/ *n* **1.** PLACE FOR OVERNIGHT STAY a building or commercial establishment where people pay for lodgings, meals, and sometimes other facilities or services **2.** *Aus* PUB an establishment that sells alcoholic beverages **3.** *S Asia* FOOD same as **restaurant 4.** CODE WORD FOR LETTER 'H' a code word for the letter 'H', used in international radio communications [Mid-17C. < French *hôtel*, modern form of Old French *(h)ostel* (see HOSTEL)]

hotelier /hōtélli әr, -télli ay/ *n* somebody who owns or runs a hotel [Early 20C. < French *hôtelier*, modern form of Old French *hostelier* 'hosteller' < *(h)ostel* (see HOSTEL)]

hotelkeeper /hō tél keepәr/ *n* TRAVEL same as **hotelier**

hotelling /hō télling/ *n* the practice of providing temporary desk space for an employee [Because a hotel is a temporary place to stay]

hot fence *n NZ* an electric fence round a farm

hot flash *n N Am* MED same as **hot flush**

hot flush *n* a sudden hot feeling, sometimes accompanied by sweating and redness of the face, experienced by some women during the menopause and caused by an endocrine imbalance. N Am term **hot flash**

hotfoot /hot fŏŏt, hót fŏŏt/ *adv* with great haste ◇ **hotfoot it** to go with great haste and eagerness, usually on foot (*informal*)

hot-gospeller *n* somebody who preaches religion or spreads propaganda in a very forceful or enthusiastic way (*informal; sometimes considered offensive*)

hothead /hót hed/ *n* somebody who is too easily angered or excited and who usually acts impetuously

hotheaded /hot héddid/ *adj* too easily angered or excited and usually acting impetuously —**hotheadedly** *adv* —**hotheadedness** *n*

hothouse /hót howss/ *n* (*plural* **-houses** /-howziz/) **1.** HEATED GREENHOUSE a heated building, usually with glass walls and a glass roof, in which tropical or delicate plants can grow at a stable warm temperature **2.** CENTRE OF ACTIVITY a place where a particular thing flourishes and develops, usually in an intensive way ○ *a hothouse of technological innovation* ■ *adj* SENSITIVE sensitive and delicate (*informal disapproving*) ○ *hothouse views on political strategy*

hothousing /hót howzing/ *n* a programme of providing children with intensive education

hot key *n* a computer key or combination of keys that provides a short cut for a specific function

hotline /hót līn/ *n* **1.** a telephone number that enables members of the public to make direct contact with a special service offering information, advice, or help, usually on a serious or urgent matter **2.** a telephone connection or similar link that allows direct communication between heads of government or other important people, especially in an emergency

hotlink /hót lingk/ *n* COMPUT same as **hyperlink**

hotlist /hót list/ *n* a browser configuration file of a computer user's most recent hypertext link selections

hotly /hóttli/ *adv* **1.** in an angry way **2.** in an intense and committed way ○ *hotly contested*

hot-melt *n* a fast-drying adhesive applied in a molten state

hot metal *n* **1.** printing type cast from molten metal in a crucible beside the printing machine **2.** a method of printing using hot metal type

hot money *n* funds transferred from one form of currency to another in order to take advantage of better exchange rates

hot pants *npl* **1.** very brief close-fitting shorts for women, first fashionable in the early 1970s **2.** very strong physical desire (*slang*)

hot plate *n* **1.** a flat heated surface, usually part of a cooker, on which food can be cooked **2.** a portable device with a flat heated surface on which cooked food can be heated or kept warm

hot plug *vt* COMPUT same as **hot-swap**

hot pot *n* a small heated pot of boiling water or broth used to cook pieces of food at the table, especially in Southeast Asian cookery

hotpot /hót pot/ n a stew of meat and vegetables cooked slowly in the oven in a covered container

hot potato n a sensitive or controversial issue that is awkward or difficult to deal with (informal)

hot press n a machine used to apply heat and pressure to a material such as paper or cloth —**hot-press** vt

hot rod n a car that has been modified to make it go very fast (slang)

hot-rod (hot-rods, hot-rodding, hot-rodded) v (slang) 1. vt to modify a car or its engine to make it very fast or powerful 2. vi to drive a hot rod —**hot-rodder** n

hot seat n N Am the electric chair (slang) ◇ **in the hot seat** facing or liable to face criticism or intense questioning (informal) ○ in the hot seat after the latest round of allegations

hot shoe n a camera accessory used to connect the camera and an electric flash

hotshot /hót shot/ n a successful, important, or highly skilled person, especially one who is showily confident (informal disapproving)

hot spot n 1. MIL PLACE OF POTENTIAL UNREST an area where fighting or trouble is likely to break out 2. LEISURE CENTRE OF ENTERTAINMENT a place that is a centre of entertainment and social activity, e.g. a lively nightclub (informal) 3. CENTRE FOR ACTIVITY a place where a lot of activity of a particular type takes place ○ a biodiversity hot spot 4. ENG SMALL AREA OF INTENSE HEAT a small area of something such as an engine that is at a much higher temperature than the rest 5. GEOG AREA OF GEOTHERMAL ACTIVITY a part of the Earth's surface subject to greater than usual geothermal activity 6. COMPUT SELECTABLE HYPERLINK a clickable image on a computer screen that acts as a hyperlink to another location 7. COMPUT WIRELESS INTERNET CONNECTION a building or locale in which wireless Internet users can access a high-speed Internet connection

hot spring n a spring of water heated by geothermal energy

hotspur /hót spur/ n a rash or impetuous person (archaic) [< Hotspur, nickname of Henry PERCY]

hot stuff n 1. VERY GOOD PERSON OR THING an impressive, attractive, exciting, or important person or thing (informal) 2. ATTRACTIVE PERSON a physically attractive person (informal) 3. SEXUALLY EXPLICIT THING something that is particularly erotic or sexually explicit

hot-swap vt to add or remove hardware devices to or from a computer while it is running and have the operating system automatically recognize the change

hot-tempered adj having or showing a short temper

Hottentot /hótt'n tot/ (plural same or -tots) n (dated) 1. an offensive term for a member of the Khoikhoi people 2. an offensive term for the languages of the Khoikhoi people [Late 17C. < Dutch, probably < a formula in a Nama song]

Hottentot fig n a cultivated low-growing succulent plant with edible fruit. Flowers: purplish or yellowish, resembling daisies. Native to: southern Africa. Latin name: Carpobrotus edulis.

hot ticket n a popular or fashionable person or thing (informal)

hottie /hótti/ n (informal) 1. also **hotty** (plural -ties) somebody who is sexually attractive 2. HOUSEHOLD same as **hot-water bottle**

hotting /hótting/ n the performing of difficult or dangerous high-speed stunts and manoeuvres in a stolen car (slang)

hottish /hóttish/ adj fairly, but not excessively hot

hot toddy n BEVERAGES same as **toddy** (sense 1)

hot tub n a large round bathtub filled with hot water for one or more people to relax, bathe, or socialize in —**hot-tubbing** n

hotty n another spelling of **hottie** (sense 1) (informal)

hot war n armed conflict between groups or nations, as opposed to political hostility

hot-water bottle n a container, usually made of rubber, filled with hot water and used to warm a bed or part of the body

hot-wire vt to start a car by bringing the ignition wires into contact with each other (informal)

houbara /hoo bárə/, **houbara bustard** n a bustard that has been reduced in numbers by hunting. Native

to: Canary Islands, Asia. Latin name: Chlamydotis undulata. [Early 19C.<Arabic]

Houdan /hoo dan/ n a domestic fowl belonging to a breed with black-and-white plumage and a characteristic full crest [Late 19C. After a village in the French department of Seine-et-Oise]

Houdini /hoo deeni/, **Harry** (1874–1926) Hungarian-born US magician. President of the Society of American Magicians, he was a master escapologist and specialized in escaping from various locked containers. Born **Weiss, Ehrich**

hough /hok/ n 1. ZOOL same as **hock**[1] (sense 1) 2. Scotland FOOD a cut of beef from the leg, used in stewing ■ vt (houghs, houghing, houghed) to hamstring an animal [Old English hōh 'heel' < Germanic]

hou high /hō-/ n Hong Kong a state of intoxication or excitement, e.g. from a drug (slang)

hou inch /hō-/ n Hong Kong an offensive term for somebody who is regarded as aloof or arrogant (insult)

hommos n FOOD another spelling of **hummus**

hound /hownd/ n 1. DOG BRED FOR HUNTING a dog with floppy ears, short hair, and a deep bark, belonging to a breed originally developed for hunting (often used in combination) 2. DOG a domestic dog, especially one viewed with disapproval (informal) 3. UNPLEASANT PERSON somebody regarded as contemptible or despicable (dated) 4. ENTHUSIAST somebody who pursues a particular activity with great enthusiasm or determination (informal) ○ a media hound ■ vt (hounds, hounding, hounded) 1. PURSUE DOGGEDLY to follow, chase, or pester somebody in a persistent or relentless manner 2. URGE OR NAG SOMEBODY to urge or force somebody to do something by nagging or harassment ○ hounded out of office by a hostile press [Old English hund 'dog' < Indo-European] —**hounder** n

ORIGIN The Indo-European word from which **hound** is ultimately derived, is also the ancestor of English canary, canine, chenille, corgi, cynic, dachshund, and kennel.

houndfish /hównd fish/ (plural same or -fishes) n a small shark or dogfish

hounds /howndz/ npl the part of a sailing ship's masthead that supports the topmast and the rigging [15C. Alteration of hune 'wooden projection below a masthead', origin ?]

hound's-tongue /hównd-/ n a coarse plant of the borage family with spiny clinging fruit. Flowers: small, reddish-purple. Native to: Europe, Asia. Genus: Cynoglossum. [< the shape and texture of its leaves]

houndstooth check /hównd tooth-/, **hound's-tooth check** n a fabric design of small jagged checks

hour /owr/ n 1. 60 MINUTES one of the 24 equal parts of a day, equivalent to 60 minutes or 3,600 seconds 2. 60-MINUTE INTERVAL SHOWN ON TIMEPIECE one of the intervals of 60 minutes shown on a clock or watch ○ There's a bus at 20 past the hour. 3. TIME OF DAY a time of day, with emphasis on the general portion of day or night being referred to ○ at this unearthly hour 4. REGULAR TIME FOR SOMETHING the time at which something usually takes place or is done ○ my lunch hour 5. SIGNIFICANT PERIOD a period during which something particularly significant happens 6. TIME OF SUCCESS a time when somebody is powerful, successful, or famous ○ their finest hour 7. TIME OF DEATH the time when somebody is going to die ○ As he started falling, he thought his hour had surely come. 8. WORK DONE IN 60 MINUTES the amount of work done in a period of sixty minutes ○ I have a couple of hours left to do on the report. 9. DISTANCE TRAVELLED IN 60 MINUTES the distance that can be travelled in sixty minutes ○ My office is only an hour away. 10. MEASURE, NAVIG MEASURE OF LONGITUDE a measure of longitude equal to 15 degrees or one twenty-fourth of a great circle ■ npl **hours** 1. LONG TIME a long but unspecified amount of time (informal) 2. TIMES FOR DOING PARTICULAR THINGS the times of day during which particular things are done ○ during school hours 3. TIME IN 24-HOUR CLOCK the time of day, when using a 24-hour clock ○ The flight leaves at 1300 hours. 4. CHR CANONICAL HOURS the canonical hours taken as a whole [12C. Via Old French houre < Latin hora < Greek hōra 'time, hour'] ◇ **at any hour** at any time, day or night ◇ **of the hour** enjoying the highest degree of relevance, importance, or popularity at the current moment or a particular time ○ The question of the hour is whether war is justified.

hour angle n the angle, measured positively westwards, between the plane containing the observer and the Earth's poles and the plane containing a specific astronomical object and the Earth's poles

hour circle n a great circle passing through the poles of the celestial sphere and intersecting the celestial equator at right angles, containing a point on the celestial sphere such as a star

hourglass

hourglass /ówr glaass/ n 1. a time-measurement device consisting of two transparent bulbs connected by a narrow tube and containing an amount of sand that takes a specific time to flow between the bulbs after inversion 2. an hourglass-shaped computer icon that shows that a task is being performed but is not yet completed

hourglass figure n a woman's body shape, curving out above and below a narrow waist like the shape of an hourglass

hour hand n the shorter wider hand on a nondigital clock or watch that indicates the hour

houri /hoori/ n 1. in Islamic belief, one of the beautiful young women who attend Muslim men in paradise 2. an attractive woman (dated; sometimes considered offensive) [Mid-18C. Via French < Arabic ḥawrā' 'woman with dark eyes']

hourly /ówrli/ adj 1. HAPPENING EACH HOUR happening at 60 minute intervals ○ hourly news 2. OCCURRING OFTEN happening frequently or continually ○ hourly changes 3. CALCULATED BY HOUR calculated as a particular amount for each hour worked ○ hourly wages 4. PAID BY HOUR working for pay that is calculated as a particular amount for each hour worked ○ an hourly employee ■ adv 1. ONCE AN HOUR happening once during an hour ○ The news is broadcast hourly. 2. OFTEN frequently or continually ○ The situation is changing hourly. 3. BY THE HOUR with a specific amount being paid for each hour worked ○ paid hourly 4. SOON at any time not long from now ○ Her arrival is expected hourly.

house n /howss/ (plural **houses** /hówziz/) 1. DWELLING a building made for people to live in, especially one built for a single group of occupants 2. OCCUPANTS OF HOUSE all of the people who are in a house at one time, particularly the people who usually live there 3. BUILDING FOR ANIMALS a building where animals are kept, especially in a zoo ○ the monkey house 4. PLACE OF ENTERTAINMENT a place where members of the public pay for food, drink, or other entertainment, e.g. a restaurant or club ○ the speciality of the house 5. THEATRE a theatre, especially the auditorium ○ played to a full house 6. THEATRE AUDIENCE the audience at a theatre ○ The dancers performed to an appreciative house. 7. BUSINESS OPERATION a company or a corporation creating or selling a particular product ○ a publishing house 8. DIVISION OF SCHOOL a group into which the pupils of some schools are divided. In residential schools this is based on the boarding houses where the pupils live. 9. also **House** LEGISLATIVE GROUP a legislative group in a government, or the place where it meets 10. also **House** FAMILY LINE a family line, including ancestors and descendants, especially a royal family ○ the House of Windsor 11. DIVISION OF ZODIAC in astrology, one of the 12 divisions of the zodiac 12. ZODIAC SIGN WHERE PLANET LIES in astrology, the sign of the zodiac in which a planet is

found at a specific time **13. CURLING TARGET** in curling, an area of concentric circles marked at each end of an ice rink, with the target in its centre **14. FAST DANCE MUSIC** a style of dance music first developed by adding electronic beats to disco records, and later characterized by the addition of repetitive vocals, extracts from other recordings, or synthesized sounds ■ *interj* **USED TO CLAIM WIN AT BINGO** shouted by people playing bingo to claim that they have the full set of numbers needed to win a game (*informal*) ■ *vt* /howz/ (**houses, housing, housed**) **1. GIVE SOMEBODY SOMEWHERE TO LIVE** to provide somebody with a place to live **2. CONTAIN SOMETHING** to contain, keep, or store something ○ *a shed that houses our lawn mowers* **3. PUT SOMETHING AWAY SAFELY ON BOAT** in sailing, to safely stow something such as oars or an anchor [Old English *hūs* < Germanic] ◇ **bring the house down** to provoke a great deal of laughter or applause ◇ **like a house on fire** very well, successfully, quickly, or strongly ○ *They got on like a house on fire.* ◇ **on the house** given free by somebody who would normally charge ◇ **play house** to take part in a children's game of pretending to be a family, with children playing the roles of both adults and children (*informal*) ◇ **put your house in order** to organize your life, work, or other enterprise properly

USAGE See *home*.

house agent *n* COMM same as **estate agent** (sense 1)

house arrest *n* a form of legal confinement in which people who have been arrested are not allowed to leave their own homes

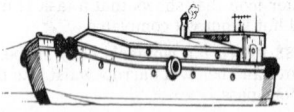

houseboat

houseboat /hówss bōt/ *n* a boat, especially a flat-bottomed river boat or barge, that is permanently moored and used as a house

housebound /hówss bownd/ *adj* unable to go out of doors because of illness or difficulty in travelling, or because of severe weather. N Am term **homebound**

houseboy /hówss boy/ *n* a man, especially in Africa or South Asia, employed to perform various household tasks (*often offensive*)

housebreak /hówss brayk/ *n* US CRIME same as **break-in** ■ *vt* (**-breaks, -breaking, -broke** /-brōk/, **-broken** /-brōkən/) N Am same as **housetrain**

housebreaking /hówss brayking/ *n* the action of illegally forcing entry into a house or other building in order to commit a crime —**housebreaker** *n*

house call *n* N Am a visit made by a doctor or other professional to a patient or client at home

housecarl /hówss kaarl/ *n* any one of the household warriors of an early English or Danish nobleman or king [Pre-12C. < Old Norse *húskarl* < *hús* 'house' + *karl* 'man']

house cat *n* a cat that lives with people as a pet

housecoat /hówss kōt/ *n* a woman's outer garment, often loose and comfortable, worn at home

house cricket *n* a dark-brown cricket that can become a nuisance indoors. Native to: North America, Europe. Latin name: *Acheta domesticus.*

housefather /hówss faathər/ *n* a man who is responsible for a group of young people living in an institution such as a hostel

house finch *n* a small common finch, the male of which has a red forehead, throat, breast, and rump. Native to: United States, Mexico. Latin name: *Carpodacus mexicanus.*

house fluffing *n* N Am the practice of changing the appearance of a house or room by rearranging existing items

housefly /hówss flī/ (*plural* **-flies**) *n* a common fly that lives in and around human dwellings in most parts of the world and is responsible for spreading numerous diseases. Latin name: *Musca domestica.*

houseful /hówss fool/ *n* the quantity of people or objects that a house can hold ○ *a houseful of antique furniture* ○ *We had a houseful last week when all our grandchildren were here.*

house guest *n* a guest in somebody's home

household /hówss hōld/ *n* **PEOPLE WHO LIVE TOGETHER** the people who live together in a single home ■ *adj* **1. OF HOUSEHOLD** relating to, belonging to, or used in a household **2. FAMILIAR TO ALL** very widely known ○ *a household word*

Household Cavalry *n* the cavalry regiments, the Horse Guards and the Life Guards, responsible for guarding the British sovereign, especially during public ceremonies

householder /hówss hōldər/ *n* an owner or renter of a house

household gods *npl* the deities believed to protect the home and its inhabitants, especially in the religion of ancient Rome

household goods *npl* things that people use in a house, especially kitchen utensils and small electrical appliances. N Am term **housewares**

household name *n* somebody or something that most people have heard of

household troops *npl* soldiers who accompany and guard a sovereign

household word *n* a popular saying, the name of a famous person, or an event that is very well known

house-hunt *v* to look for a residential property to buy or rent —**house-hunter** *n* —**house-hunting** *n*

househusband /hówss huzbənd/ *n* a man who does not go out to work but stays at home to manage a household [Mid-20C. After HOUSEWIFE]

housekeeper /hówss keepər/ *n* **1.** somebody employed to carry out or manage the work of looking after somebody else's house and the people who live there **2.** somebody who looks after his or her own house and its residents

housekeeping /hówss keeping/ *n* **1. HOUSEHOLD MAINTENANCE** the maintenance of a household, or the range of tasks involved in this **2. MONEY FOR RUNNING HOUSEHOLD** money used to pay for the things needed in maintaining a household ○ *Perhaps we could save a little extra from the housekeeping.* **3.** N Am **MANAGEMENT OF PROPERTY AND EQUIPMENT** the management and upkeep of equipment and property for a business or other organization **4. MAINTENANCE OF COMPUTER SYSTEM** the performance of routine tasks needed to keep a computer system working efficiently, e.g. deletion of unwanted files

houseleek /hówss leek/ *n* a flowering succulent plant with rosettes of leaves at the base of the stems. Native to: Europe. Genus: *Sempervivum.* [Because formerly planted on walls and roofs to protect the house from lightning]

house lights *npl* the lights inside a theatre or auditorium that illuminate the area where the audience sits

housemaid /hówss mayd/ *n* a woman employed to do housework (*dated*)

housemaid's knee *n* a swelling of the fluid-filled sac in front of the kneecap, caused by kneeling too much

houseman /hówss mən/ (*plural* **-men** /-mən/) *n* **1.** same as **househusband 2.** a hospital intern (*dated*)

house martin *n* a small swallow with blue-black feathers, a white rump, and a forked tail. Native to: Europe, China, Africa. Latin name: *Delichon urbica.* [< its habit of nesting under the eaves of houses]

housemaster /hówss maastər/ *n* a man who is in charge of the students living together in a house at a private boys' school

housemate /hówss mayt/ *n* somebody who shares a house with one or more other people who are not relatives

housemistress /hówss mistrəss/ *n* a woman who is in charge of the students living together at some prep schools and colleges

housemother /hówss muthər/ *n* a woman who is responsible for a group of young people living in an

institution such as a boarding house or a private school

house mouse *n* a grey or brownish-grey mouse that is common worldwide and is a household pest. Latin name: *Mus musculus.*

house music *n* MUSIC same as **house** *n* (sense 14) [Probably after the *Warehouse*, nightclub in Chicago]

House of Assembly *n* **1.** the law-making body or lower house of the legislature in some countries of the Commonwealth of Nations **2.** the lower house of the state parliament in South Australia and Tasmania

house of cards *n* something that is unstable and likely to fall down, like a structure built of playing cards

House of Commons *n* the lower house of Parliament in the United Kingdom and Canada

house of correction *n* formerly, an institution where people convicted of minor offences were imprisoned

house officer *n* UK a hospital doctor who is training to become a registrar, and eventually a GP or consultant

house of God *n* RELIG same as **house of worship**

house of ill fame *n* same as **brothel**

House of Keys *n* the lower house of the legislature of the Isle of Man

House of Lords *n* the nonelected upper house of Parliament in the United Kingdom, made up of life peers, some hereditary peers, and some bishops

House of Representatives *n* **1. LOWER HOUSE OF CONGRESS** the lower house of the US Congress and of most state legislatures in the United States **2. AUSTRALIAN FEDERAL PARLIAMENT** the lower house of the federal parliament of Australia **3. PARLIAMENT OF NEW ZEALAND** the sole chamber of the New Zealand parliament, formerly its lower chamber

House of the People *n* POL same as **Lok Sabha**

house of worship, house of God *n* a church, temple, synagogue, or other building used for religious services

house organ *n* a magazine published by a business or other organization for its employees or customers, containing information about the company, its products, and its employees

housepainter /hówss payntər/ *n* N Am a professional painter of houses

houseparent /hówss pairənt/ *n* an adult who, often together with his or her wife or husband, is responsible for a group of young people living in an institution such as a children's home or boarding school

house party *n* **1.** a party at somebody's home at which the guests stay overnight or for several days, especially at a wealthy person's country house **2.** the group of guests attending a house party

houseperson /hówss purss'n/ (*plural* **-persons** or **-people** /-peep'l/) *n* somebody who does not go out to work but stays at home to manage the household

houseplant /hówss plaant/ *n* a decorative plant grown indoors, especially one that would die if planted outdoors in a cold climate

house-proud *adj* taking pride in the appearance of the home and its state of cleanliness or repair, sometimes in an excessive or fussy way

house rule *n* a rule, usually not one of the regular rules in a game, that is observed in a casino or among a group of friends

house-sit *vi* to live in temporarily and take care of somebody else's house and property while that person is away —**housesitter** *n* —**housesitting** *n*

Houses of Parliament, London, designed by Sir Charles Barry (1840–60)

Barnaby's

Houses of Parliament *npl* **1.** the building in London in which the House of Commons and the House of Lords meet and work. See illustration on previous page **2.** the House of Commons and the House of Lords considered together ○ *The bill will go before the Houses of Parliament this year.*

house sparrow *n* a small hardy brown-and-grey bird with a black throat. Native to: Europe, Asia. Latin name: *Passer domesticus.* [< its living in or near human settlements]

house-to-house *adj* going or done from one house to the next ○ *a house-to-house search*

housetop /hówss top/ *n* the very top or roof of a house

housetrain /hówss trayn/ (**-trains, -training, -trained**) *vt* to teach a domestic animal to excrete outdoors or in a specific place. N Am term **housebreak** —**housetrained** *adj*

housewares /hówss wairz/ *npl* N Am same as **household goods**

housewarming /hówss wawrming/, **housewarming party** *n* a party that somebody gives to celebrate moving into a new house

housewife /hówss wīf/ (*plural* **-wives** /-wīvz/) *n* a woman who does not go out to work but stays at home to manage a household

housewifely /hówss wīfli/ *adj* **1.** relating to, done by, or thought appropriate for a housewife **2.** showing the qualities traditionally thought appropriate for a housewife, e.g. tidiness and careful management of money

housewoman /hówss woоmən/ (*plural* **-women** /-wimin/) *n* same as **housewife**

housework /hówss wurk/ *n* tasks that are regularly done in a house, e.g. dusting, vacuuming, washing clothes, and cooking

housey-housey /hówssi hówssi/ *n* the game of bingo (*dated*) [Alteration of HOUSE]

housing[1] /hówzing/ *n* **1.** ACCOMMODATION houses and other buildings where people live, considered collectively ○ *Decent housing is often hard to find.* **2.** PROVISION OF ACCOMMODATION the provision of places to live ○ *Housing of the homeless is our first priority.* **3.** MACHINE'S PROTECTIVE STRUCTURE a frame or structure that protects part of a machine ○ *a wheel housing* **4.** PLACE THAT PIECE FITS INTO a slot, groove, or hole in one piece of wood into which another piece is fitted **5.** NICHE FOR STATUE a small recess or hollow in which a statue can be placed [13C. < HOUSE]

housing[2] /hówzing/ *n* **1.** a piece of cloth that covers the back of a horse, used for protection or decoration **2.** the ornamental trappings for a horse (*often used in the plural*) [Mid-17C. < Old French *houce* < medieval Latin *hultia* 'protective covering' < Germanic]

housing association *n* a nonprofit-making-organization that provides houses and flats at fair rents

housing development *n* ANZ, N Am same as **housing estate**

housing estate *n* UK a planned area of houses or flats, usually built at the same time to a similar design, sometimes with a number of small shops. ANZ, N Am term **housing development**

housing project *n* N Am a group of houses or flats built with public money for low-income families

housing scheme *n* Scotland a housing estate built by a local authority, originally made up of homes to be rented by council tenants

Housman /hówssmən/, **A. E.** (1859–1936) British poet and scholar. His verse collections include *A Shropshire Lad* (1896) and *Last Poems* (1922). Full name **Housman, Alfred Edward.** See Cultural note at **lad**

> 'Clay lies still, but blood's a rover; /
> Breath's a ware that will not keep/Up, lad:
> when the journey's over / There'll be time
> enough to sleep.'
> [A. E. Housman, 'Reveillé', *A Shropshire Lad*; 1896]

Houston /hyoóstən/ *n* city in Texas, the fourth largest city in the United States. It is a major port and one of the world's chief oil centres. Population: 2,009,834 (2002 estimate).

houting /hówting/ (*plural* **-ings** or *same*) *n* a fish of the whitefish family that lives in salt water but produces its young in fresh water. Native to:

Europe. Latin name: *Coregonus oxyrhynchus.* [Late 19C. < Dutch]

HOV *abbr* high-occupancy vehicle

hove NAUT past tense of **heave** *v* (senses 7–8) (*formal*)

hovel /hóvv'l/ *n* a small, dirty, or poorly built house [14C. Origin ?]

hover /hóvvər/ (**-ers, -ering, -ered**) *v* **1.** *vi* FLOAT IN AIR to float or flutter in the air without moving very far from the same spot **2.** *vi* WAIT NEAR BY to wait near a person or place, usually in a nervous, inquisitive, or expectant way **3.** *vi* BE UNDECIDED to be unable to decide between alternatives **4.** *vi* BE UNSTABLE to be in a condition that is neither one of two alternatives nor the other ○ *hovering between life and death* **5.** *vi* STAY AROUND SAME LEVEL to stay near a particular point, changing only slightly ○ *temperatures hovering in the low teens* **6.** *vti* COMPUT PUT CURSOR OVER ICON to position the cursor over an icon on a computer screen to get pop-up information without clicking, or be positioned in this way [14C. < obsolete *hove* 'linger', origin ?] —**hover** *n* —**hoverer** *n* —**hoveringly** *adv*

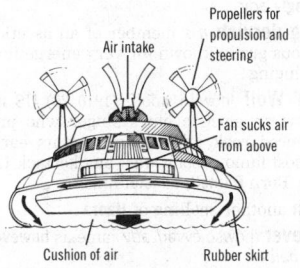

hovercraft

hovercraft /hóvvər kraaft/ (*plural* **-crafts** or *same*) *n* a vehicle that can travel over land and water supported by a cushion of air that it creates by blowing air downwards

hoverfly /hóvvər flī/ (*plural* **-flies**) *n* a fly that feeds on nectar and has a hovering style of flight. Many resemble wasps in colouring. Family: Syrphidae.

hover mower *n* a lawn mower with horizontally rotating blades that uses a cushion of downwards-directed air to lift itself slightly above the ground

hoverport /hóvvər pawrt/ *n* a place where hovercrafts load and unload [Mid-20C. Blend of HOVERCRAFT + AIRPORT]

how[1] /how/ *adv* **1.** IN WHAT WAY used to ask or report questions or to introduce statements about the manner in which something happens or is done ○ *How do I open the window?* ○ *I don't know how you manage to sew so neatly.* **2.** TO WHAT EXTENT used to ask or report questions or to introduce statements about the quantity or degree of something ○ *How high is the roof?* **3.** LIKE WHAT used to ask or report questions or to introduce statements about the quality or success of something ○ *How was the film?* ○ *We didn't realize how interesting the lecture would be.* **4.** USED IN EXCLAMATIONS used in exclamations to emphasize a word or statement ○ *How nice to see you!* ■ *rel adv* IN WHATEVER WAY used to indicate that it does not matter in what way somebody does something ○ *Do it how you want.* ■ *conj* THAT used to mention a fact or event ○ *Do you remember how we were ridiculed?* [Old English *hū* < Indo-European] ◇ **how about** (*informal*) **1.** used to make a suggestion ○ *How about some lunch?* **2.** used to change the subject of a conversation ○ *That's enough of my ideas. How about your own policies?* ◇ **how are you (doing)?** used to ask about somebody's health, or simply as a greeting when you meet somebody, especially somebody already known ◇ **how do you do?** used when meeting somebody for the first time

how[2] *n* GEOG another spelling of **howe**[2]

Howard /hów ərd/, **Catherine** (1520?–42) queen of England. She became the fifth wife of Henry VIII in 1540 and was beheaded when her premarital affairs were revealed.

Howard, Sir Ebenezer (1850–1928) British town planner. He introduced the garden city model of urban development, first applying his principles in Letchworth (1903) and Welwyn Garden City (1919).

Howard, John (1726–90) British penal reformer. He persuaded Parliament to pass two laws (1774) designed to improve prison conditions.

John Howard

Howard, John (*b.* 1939) Australian politician. Elected to the Australian parliament as a Liberal Party politician in 1974, he became prime minister in 1996. Full name **Howard, John Winston.** See table at **prime minister**

Howard, Leslie (1893–1943) British actor. He is best known for his roles as Henry Higgins in *Pygmalion* (1938) and Ashley Wilkes in *Gone With the Wind* (1939). Born **Steiner, Leslie Howard**

Howard, Michael (*b.* 1941) leader of the Conservative Party. Elected to the UK parliament in 1982, he served as Home Secretary from 1993 to 1997 and became leader of the Opposition in 2003.

Howard, Trevor (1916–88) British actor. An accomplished stage and screen performer, his films include *Brief Encounter* (1945) and *Mutiny on the Bounty* (1962). Full name **Howard, Trevor Wallace**

howbeit /how bee it/ *adv* however or nevertheless (*formal*)

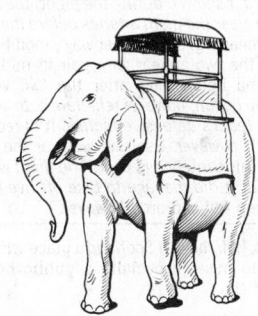

howdah

howdah /hówdə/ *n* a large seat for several people, often with a canopy, that rests on the back of an elephant [Late 18C. Via Urdu *haudah* < Arabic *hawdaj* 'litter carried by a camel']

how-do-you-do (*plural* **how-do-you-dos**) *n* **1.** a greeting or welcome ○ *got to business as soon as the how-do-you-dos were finished* **2.** a difficult or unsatisfactory situation (*informal*) ○ *a fine how-do-you-do* [< the greeting *How do you do?*]

howdy /hówdi/ *interj* N Am used as a greeting (*informal*) [Early 19C. < *How d'ye*, variant of *How do you do?*]

howe[1] /how/ *n* Scotland a hollow or valley (*often used in placenames*) ○ *We sat down, therefore, in a howe of the hillside* (Robert Louis Stevenson, *Kidnapped*; 1886) [Pre-12C. Variant of HOLE]

howe[2] /how/, **how** *n* regional a small prominent hill [14C. < Old Norse *haugr* 'mound' < Germanic]

Howe /how/, **Sir Geoffrey, Baron of Aberavon** (*b.* 1926) British politician. He served as Chancellor of the Exchequer (1979–83) and foreign secretary (1983–89) in Margaret Thatcher's government. Full name **Howe, Sir Richard Edward Geoffrey**

> 'Megaphone diplomacy leads to a dialogue of the deaf.'
> [Sir Geoffrey Howe, *Observer*; 29 September 1985]

Howe, William, 5th Viscount (1729–1814) British military commander. Second in command at the Battle

of Bunker Hill (1775), he became commander in chief of the British Army in North America (1776–78).

howe'er /how áir/ *contr* same as **however** (*literary*)

however /how évvər/ CORE MEANING: an adverb introducing some form of contrast ○ *I'm not sure how effective the campaign has been. I do, however, think that it has been distinctively different.*
adv 1. TO WHATEVER DEGREE used to indicate that no matter what happens, a situation remains the same ○ *However objective it may believe itself to be, it is still only an opinion.* **2.** IN WHATEVER WAY used to indicate that it does not matter in what way somebody does something ○ *Prepare the potatoes however you like.* **3.** HOW used as an emphatic form of 'how' ○ *What a surprise to see you! However did you find us?* **4.** NEVERTHELESS used to introduce a restricting or counterbalancing consideration ○ *I can come; however, I may have to leave early.*

USAGE See *although*.

USAGE When *however* appears within a sentence expressing ideas contrasting with what has been said in a previous sentence, put one comma before *however* and another after it: *The resort has closed for the season. Its staff members, however, are remaining on the property to service and repair the ski lifts. However* can also appear at the end of such a sentence, punctuated by a single comma just before it: *Its staff members are remaining on the property to service and repair the ski lifts, however.* Especially in American English, there is disagreement on whether *however* introducing a contrast should be used to start a sentence, but this is common in British English: *The chairman refused to resign. However, he soon changed his mind when further evidence came to light.*
However has other meanings, and those meanings dictate whether or not you punctuate the word and how. If you use *however* to mean 'to whatever degree', 'in whatever way', or 'how' at the outset of an introductory main clause, put a comma after the clause, as in *However hard it snowed during the night, the road crews were able to clear the main arteries before the rush hour.* If *however*, meaning 'in whatever way', modifies another adverb and the two appear as a pair in mid-sentence, put a comma before and after the two words: *The coaches have begun, however reluctantly, to admit major flaws in the team's defensive tactics.* It is redundant to pair *but* with *however*. Use one word or the other, not both. Thus, this sentence is poor: *The flight was initially cancelled but it did manage to take off five hours late, however.* Keep *but* and drop *however*.

howff /howf, hōf/, **howf** *n Scotland* a place where people often go to meet, especially a public house [Early 18C. Origin ?]

howitzer

howitzer /hówitsər/ *n* a cannon with a bore diameter greater than 30 mm and a maximum elevation of 60 degrees that fires projectiles in a curved trajectory [Late 17C. Via Dutch *houwitser* <Czech *haufnice* 'catapult' < *hauf* 'heap' (of stones) < Germanic]

howk /howk/ (**howks, howking, howked**) *vti Scotland* to dig, or dig something up or out (*informal*) [14C. Originally *holk*, related to HOLE, HOLLOW]

howl /howl/ *v* (**howls, howling, howled**) **1.** *vi* MAKE WHINING SOUND to make a long wavering or whining sound ○ *a coyote howling* **2.** *vi* CRY OUT to cry out in pain, anger, or distress **3.** *vi* ROAR WITH LAUGHTER to laugh loudly and unrestrainedly (*slang*) **4.** *vt* EXPRESS LOUDLY to express an emotion or opinion loudly and forcefully ○ *The crowd howled their disapproval.* ■ *n* **1.** MOANING CRY a long sad wavering cry **2.** LOUD CRY a cry

of pain, anger, or distress **3.** DRAWN-OUT WAVERING SOUND a long loud high wavering noise ○ *the howl of the wind* **4.** SOMETHING OR SOMEBODY HILARIOUS an extremely funny person or thing (*slang*) [13C. Probably an imitation of the sound]

howl down *vt* to prevent somebody or something from being heard by making loud cries of protest or mockery

howler /hówlər/ *n* **1.** a mistake that is so bad that it is funny (*informal*) **2.** somebody or something that makes a howling noise **3.** VERTEB same as **howler monkey**

howler monkey *n* any one of various mainly leaf-eating monkeys that live in trees and have a very loud booming call. Native to: tropical America. Genus: *Alouatta*.

howling /hówling/ *adj* **1.** LOUD AND WAVERING making a long loud high wavering noise ○ *a howling wind* **2.** VERY GREAT extreme or great in degree (*informal*) ○ *a howling success* **3.** DISMALLY DESOLATE desolate or drearily empty of human beings (*literary*) ■ *n* NOISE a succession of long high wavering noises such as animal cries or the sound of a strong wind — **howlingly** *adv*

howling dervish *n* a member of an ascetic Muslim religious group known for very energetic chanting and singing

Howlin' Wolf /hówlin wŏolf/ (1910–76) US musician. He was an electric blues singer who profoundly influenced rock and roll during its early years. His most famous song was 'Smokestack Lightnin'' (1956). Born **Burnett, Chester Arthur**

Howrah another spelling of **Haora**

howsoever /hówsō évvər/ *adv* same as **however** (*formal or archaic*)

how-to *adj* giving practical information and instructions on the way to do something (*informal*) ○ *another how-to guide on home decorating*

howtowdie /hów tówdi/ *n Scotland* a casserole made with a whole chicken, often served with spinach or poached eggs [Early 19C. Origin ?]

howzat /hów zát/ *interj* an exclamation shouted at a cricket umpire by players claiming that a batsman is out (*informal*) [Late 20C. Alteration of *How's that?*]

howzit /hówzit/ *interj S Africa* used as a greeting or to ask about another person's health or progress (*informal*) [Late 20C. Contraction of *How is it?*]

Hoxha /hójjə/, **Enver** (1908–85) Albanian politician. Founder of the Albanian Communist Party (1941), he served as Albania's prime minister (1944–54), foreign minister (1946–53), and first secretary of the Communist Party (1943–85).

hoy /hoy/ *n* a barge used to carry freight [15C. < Middle Dutch *hoei*]

hoya /hóyə/ *n* TREES same as **wax flower** [Mid-19C. < modern Latin, after Thomas *Hoy* (d. 1821), British gardener]

Hoy and West Mainland /hóy-/ National Scenic Area in Orkney, northeastern Scotland. The Old Man of Hoy is a pillar-shaped rock just off the coast of the island of Hoy. Area: 148 sq. km/57 sq. mi.

hoyden /hóyd'n/ *n* an offensive term that deliberately insults a young woman's self-control and thoughtfulness (*dated*) [Late 17C. Probably < Dutch *heiden* 'lout, heathen']

Hoyle /hoyl/, **Sir Fred** (1915–2001) British astronomer and writer. An expert in astrophysics, he wrote books on astronomy and works of science fiction. Although an advocate of the steady-state theory, he coined the term big bang to describe the theory that the universe originated from an explosion. Full name **Hoyle, Sir Frederick**

'Space isn't remote at all. It's only an hour's drive away if your car could go straight upwards.'
[Sir Fred Hoyle, *Observer*; 9 September 1979]

hp *abbr* MEASURE horsepower

HP *abbr* **1.** high pressure **2.** hire purchase **3.** Houses of Parliament

HPM *n* an e-bomb with capacitors that emit powerful electromagnetic impulses able to penetrate hardened targets such as underground bunkers via aerials, air vents, and plumbing pipes and cause massive power surges intended to destroy an

enemy's electrical and computer infrastructures [20C. Abbreviation of *high-power microwave*]

HPV *abbr* human papilloma virus

HQ *abbr* headquarters

hr *abbr* **1.** Croatia (*used in Internet addresses*) See table at **domain name 2.** hour

HR *abbr* **1.** Home Rule **2.** human resources **3.** GOV House of Representatives

HRE *abbr* **1.** Holy Roman Emperor **2.** Holy Roman Empire

HRH *abbr* **1.** Her Royal Highness **2.** His Royal Highness

hrs *abbr* hours

HRT *abbr* hormone replacement therapy

hryvnia /hrívni ə/ (*plural same* or **-as**) *n* the main unit of Ukrainian currency. See table at **currency** [< Ukrainian]

Hs *symbol* CHEM ELEM hassium

HS *abbr* **1.** EDUC high school **2.** Home Secretary

HSC *abbr* Higher School Certificate

HSE *abbr* Health and Safety Executive

HSH *abbr* **1.** Her Serene Highness **2.** His Serene Highness

Hsien Nien /syén nyén/ *n* CALENDAR same as **Chinese New Year**

HSRC *abbr* Human Sciences Research Council

HST *abbr* **1.** harmonized sales tax **2.** high-speed train **3.** hypersonic transport

ht *abbr* **1.** Haiti (*used in Internet addresses*) See table at **domain name 2.** heat **3.** height

HT *abbr* **1.** SPORTS half-time **2.** ELEC ENG high tension **3.** high tide

HTH *abbr* ONLINE (*used in e-mails or text messages*) **1.** happy to help **2.** hope this helps

HTLV *abbr* human T-cell lymphotropic virus

HTLV-I *n* a virus associated with cancers of the lymphatic system. Full form **human T-cell lymphotropic virus I**

HTLV-II *n* a virus associated with leukaemia. Full form **human T-cell lymphotropic virus II**

html, htm *abbr* a file extension for an HTML file. Full form **HyperText Markup Language**

HTML *n* the markup language used for creating documents on the World Wide Web. Full form **HyperText Markup Language**

Hts *abbr* GEOG Heights

HTTP, http *n* the client/server protocol that defines how messages are formatted and transmitted on the World Wide Web. Full form **HyperText Transfer Protocol**

hu *abbr* Hungary (*used in Internet addresses*) See table at **domain name**

huaca /waákə/ *n* one of the sacred spirits and powers whom Native South American peoples of the Andes believe to live in caves, rocks, and other natural formations [Early 17C. Via Spanish < Quechua *waca* 'god of the house']

Huainan /hwí nán/ industrial city in Anhui Province, eastern China. It is the centre of a large coalmining area. Population: 1,310,514 (1991).

Huang Hai /hwang hí/ ♦ **Yellow Sea**

Huang He /hwáng hǒ/ second longest river in China, flowing through the north-central part of the country. Length: 5,464 km/3,395 mi.

huarache /wə raá chee/ *n* a sandal of a type originally worn in Mexico, with the upper part made of woven leather straps and a rubber sole [Late 19C. < Mexican Spanish]

Huascarán /wáskə rán/ mountain in the Andes in west-central Peru. Snowcapped all year round, it is the highest peak in the country. Height: 6,768 m/22,205 ft.

hub /hub/ *n* **1.** CENTRAL PART the central part of a wheel or a similar rotating device such as a propeller **2.** CENTRE OF ACTIVITY a place that is a centre of activity or interest ○ *the region's financial hub* **3.** *also* **hub airport** CENTRAL AIRPORT a central airport that passengers can fly to from smaller local airports in order to catch an international or long-distance flight [Early 16C. Probably alteration of HOB[1]]

---

a at; aa father; aw all; ay day; ai hair; ə about, item, edible, common, circus; e egg; ee eel; hw when; i it, happy; ī ice; 'l apple; 'm rhythm; 'n fashion; o odd; ō open; oŏ good; oo pool; ow owl; oy oil; th thin; <u>th</u> this; u up; ur urge;

hubba-hubba /húbbə húbbə/ *interj N Am* used to express approval, enthusiasm, or pleasure (*dated slang*) [Mid-20C. Origin ?]

Hubble /húbb'l/, **Edwin** (1889–1953) US astronomer. Through his study of galaxies, he proved that the universe is larger than had previously been thought and is still expanding. Full name **Hubble, Edwin Powell**

hubble-bubble /húbb'l-/ *n* same as **hookah** [Early 17C. Alteration of BUBBLE]

Hubble constant, **Hubble's constant** *n* the ratio that expresses the rate of the universe's expansion, equal to the speed at which galaxies appear to be moving away from Earth divided by their distance [Mid-20C. After Edwin HUBBLE]

Hubble's law *n* the law holding that the speed at which distant galaxies are moving away from Earth is proportional to their distance from the observer [Mid-20C. After Edwin HUBBLE]

Popperfoto

Hubble Telescope: a space shuttle astronaut repairs the Hubble Telescope

Hubble Telescope, **Hubble Space Telescope** *n* a telescope mounted on a satellite that orbits the Earth, used to observe distant parts of the universe and photograph them. It was launched in 1990. [Late 20C. After Edwin HUBBLE]

hubbub /húbbub/ *n* **1.** a confused din, especially a number of voices speaking at once **2.** a fuss or period of excitement [Mid-16C. Probably < Celtic]

hubby /húbbi/ (*plural* **-bies**) *n* same as **husband** (*informal*) [Late 17C. Alteration of HUSBAND]

hubcap /húb kap/ *n* a round cover that protects the outside of the central part of a vehicle's wheel

Hubei /hoó báy/ province in central China comprising both mountainous territory and the lake-studded plain of the Yangtze River. Capital: Wuhan. Population: 58,250,000 (1997). Area: 187,500 sq. km/72,390 sq. mi.

hubris /hyoóbriss, hoó-/ *n* **1.** excessive pride or arrogance **2.** the excessive pride and ambition that usually leads to the downfall of a hero in classical tragedy [Late 19C. < Greek] —**hubristic** /hyoo brístik, hoo-/ *adj* —**hubristically** *adv*

huckaback /húkə bak/, **huck** /húk/ *n* a coarse absorbent cotton or linen fabric. Use: towels. [Late 17C. Origin ?]

huckleberry /húk'lbəri/ (*plural* **-ries**) *n* **1.** the edible dark-blue fruit of a bush related to the blueberry **2.** a bush that bears huckleberries. Native to: North America. Genus: *Gaylussacia*. [Late 16C. Probably alteration of *hurtleberry* 'whortleberry']

huckster /húkstər/ *n* **1.** AGGRESSIVE SALESPERSON an aggressive salesperson or promoter **2.** RETAILER somebody who sells small articles, especially a street pedlar ■ *v* (**-sters, -stering, -stered**) **1.** *vt* PEDDLE MERCHANDISE to sell or peddle something **2.** *vti* SELL SOMETHING AGGRESSIVELY to use aggressive methods to sell or promote something [12C. Origin ?]

HUD /hud/ *abbr* COMPUT head-up display

Huddersfield /húddərz feeld/ industrial town in West Yorkshire, northern England, that developed as a centre of the woollen textile industry. Population: 143,726 (1991).

huddle /húdd'l/ *v* (**-dles, -dling, -dled**) **1.** *vi* CROUCH to draw your arms and legs tightly into your body, or move in close to something, often for shelter or comfort ○ *He huddled in a doorway.* **2.** *vti* GATHER TIGHTLY TOGETHER to gather together in a tightly packed group, or make people or things do this ○ *huddled*

together for warmth **3.** *vi* TALK PRIVATELY to gather privately to confer, make plans, or gossip (*informal*) **4.** *vt* DO SOMETHING HASTILY to make or put together something carelessly or hastily ■ *n* **1.** TIGHT GROUP a group of people or things gathered closely together **2.** BRIEF TALK a quick private talk or gathering (*informal*) ○ *went into a huddle between meetings* [Late 16C. Origin ?]

Hudibrastic /hyoódi brástik/, **hudibrastic** *adj* mock-heroic, especially written in the style or metre used by Samuel Butler in his poem *Hudibras*

Hudson /húdss'n/ river in eastern New York State, and the longest in the state, emptying into Upper New York Bay at New York City. Length: 492 km/306 mi.

Hudson, Henry (1565?–1611?) English navigator. Attempting to find a northeastern passage to East Asia, he travelled the river, bay, and strait in North America that are now named after him.

Hudson, Rock (1925–85) US actor. He was a handsome romantic lead in films such as *Pillow Talk* (1959). Born **Scherer, Jr, Roy Harold**

Hudson Bay almost landlocked inland sea of east-central Canada, rich in wildlife. Native Americans and Inuit are the chief inhabitants of the region. Area: 1,230,000 sq. km/475,000 sq. mi. Depth: 258 m/846 ft.

Hudson's Bay Company /húdss'nz-/ *n* a fur-trading company chartered in England in 1670 to trade in North America and later much involved in fur trading, exploring, and claiming territory for the British crown [Because its original charter was to trade around Hudson Bay]

Hudson Strait body of water in northeastern Canada connecting Hudson Bay with the Atlantic Ocean and separating Baffin Island from northern Quebec. Depth: 880 m/2,890 ft. Length: 720 km/450 mi.

hue /hyoo/ *n* **1.** COLOUR a colour or shade of a colour ○ *flowers of every hue* **2.** SHADE OF COLOUR a particular shade of a colour ○ *a pleasing hue of green* **3.** PHYS PROPERTY OF COLOUR a property of a colour that enables it to be perceived, determined by its dominant wavelength **4.** TYPE a type or kind in a particular range ○ *all hues of political opinion* **5.** ASPECT the way that something looks ○ *This puts a completely different hue on the matter.* [Old English *hē(o)w* < Germanic]

SPELLCHECK See *hew*.

Hue /hway/ historic city in central Vietnam on the River Huong, near the South China Sea. It was the Nguyen royal capital from 1802 to 1945. Population: 219,149 (1992).

hue and cry *n* **1.** a great uproar or commotion about something **2.** formerly, a pursuit of somebody accused of a crime, with the pursuers calling on bystanders to join in the chase [< Anglo-Norman *hu e cri* 'outcry and cry']

-hued *suffix* of a particular colour or number of colours ○ *the many-hued rainbow* ○ *a rose-hued sunset*

huff /huf/ *n* FIT OF THE SULKS a brief mood of anger or resentment at something somebody has done ○ *walked out in a huff* ■ *v* (**huffs, huffing, huffed**) **1.** *vti* ANGER SOMEBODY, OR GET ANGRY to anger or offend somebody, or become angry or offended **2.** *vi* BLOW OR PANT to blow, pant, or breathe laboriously **3.** *vti* REMOVE OPPONENT'S PIECE IN DRAUGHTS to remove an opponent's draughtsman from the board as a penalty for failing to make an obligatory capture [Late 16C. An imitation of the sound of blowing] ◇ **huff and puff 1.** to blow or pant, or do this while moving with great difficulty **2.** to make noisy but empty threats or objections

huffy /húffi/ (**-ier, -iest**) *adj* easily offended or put into a huff —**huffily** *adv* —**huffiness** *n*

hug /hug/ *v* (**hugs, hugging, hugged**) **1.** *vti* EMBRACE AFFECTIONATELY to put your arms round somebody's body and hold the person tight to show affection or pleasure **2.** *vt* PUT YOUR ARMS ROUND SOMETHING to clasp your arms round a part of your own body ○ *hugging her knees to her chest* **3.** **hug yourself** *vr* CONGRATULATE YOURSELF to congratulate yourself or show great delight **4.** *vt* KEEP CLOSE TO SOMETHING to remain in close linear proximity to something while moving in a forward direction ○ *The boat hugged the coastline.* ■ *n* AN EMBRACE an affectionate embrace [Mid-16C. Probably < N Germanic] —**huggable** *adj* —**hugger** *n*

huge /hyooj/ (**huger, hugest**) *adj* **1.** ENORMOUS very big in size or amount **2.** LARGE IN SCOPE very large in scope or scale ○ *huge talent* **3.** SIGNIFICANTLY SUCCESSFUL very important or successful (*informal*) ○ *This band is going to be huge.* [12C. Shortening of Old French *ahuge*] —**hugeness** *n*

hugely /hyoójli/ *adv* to a great degree ○ *hugely successful*

huggermugger /húggər mugər/ *n* MUDDLED MESS a disorderly mess or muddle ■ *adj* **1.** DISORDERED confused or jumbled **2.** SECRETIVE clandestine or secret [Early 16C. Origin ?] —**huggermugger** *adv*

Huggins /húgginz/, **Sir William** (1824–1910) British astronomer. He revolutionized astronomy by using spectroscopy to study the chemical constituents, motions, and velocities of stars.

Hughes /hyooz/, **Howard** (1905–76) US industrialist. He became one of the richest people in the United States by expanding his family manufacturing business into a huge corporate conglomerate. A record-setting pilot during the 1930s, he became notorious for his reclusiveness and eccentricity in his later years. Full name **Hughes, Howard Robard**

> 'Never make a decision. Let someone else make it and then if it turns out to be the wrong one, you can disclaim it, and if it is the right one you can abide by it.'
> [Howard Hughes. Quoted in *The Hughes Legacy: Scramble for the Billion*; 1976]

Hughes, Langston (1902–67) US writer. A leader of the Harlem Renaissance, he incorporated the rhythms of jazz into his poems and stories about African American urban life. Full name **Hughes, James Mercer Langston**

> 'What happens to a dream deferred? / Does it dry up / like a raisin in the sun? / Or fester like a sore— / and then run?'
> [Langston Hughes, 'Harlem', *Montage of a Dream Deferred*; 1951]

Hughes, Richard (1900–76) British writer. He wrote *Danger* (1924), the BBC's first radio drama, and *A High Wind in Jamaica* (1929). Full name **Hughes, Richard Arthur Warren**

> 'Middle age snuffs out more talent than even wars or sudden deaths do.'
> [Richard Hughes, *The Fox in the Attic*; 1961]

Hughes, Robert (*b.* 1938) Australian art critic and writer. His best-known works include *The Shock of the New* (1981) and *The Fatal Shore* (1987). Full name **Hughes, Robert Studley Forrest**

> 'Never had a colony been founded so far from its parent state, or in such ignorance of the land it occupied.'
> [Robert Hughes, *The Fatal Shore*; 1987]

Hughes, Ted (1930–98) British poet. He was poet laureate (1984–98) and married the poet Sylvia Plath in 1956. His works include *Lupercal* (1960) and *Wodwo* (1967). Full name **Hughes, Edward James**

> 'He spins from the bars, but there's no cage to him / More than to the visionary his cell: / His stride is wildernesses of freedom: / The world rolls under the long thrust of his heel. / Over the cage floor the horizons come.'
> [Ted Hughes, 'The Jaguar', *The Hawk in the Rain*; 1957]

Hughes, Thomas (1822–96) British writer. His novel *Tom Brown's Schooldays* (1857) was based on his experiences at Rugby School in England.

> 'Life isn't all beer and skittles.'
> [Thomas Hughes, *Tom Brown's Schooldays*; 1857]

Hughes, William Morris (1862–1952) British-born prime minister of Australia (1915–23). He was expelled from the Labor Party (1916) but continued to serve as prime minister as a member of the Nationalist Party. See table at **prime minister**

Hughesian /hyoózi ən/ *adj* relating to or representative of the works of the 20th-century British poet Ted Hughes —**Hughesian** *n*

Hugli /hoógli/, **Hooghly** river in northeastern India. It is the most westerly of the channels by which the River Ganges reaches the Bay of Bengal. Length: 257 km/160 mi.

Hugo /hyóogō/, **Victor** (1802–85) French poet, novelist, and dramatist. A leading writer of the 19th century, he wrote *The Hunchback of Notre Dame* (1831) and *Les Misérables* (1862). Full name **Hugo, Victor Marie**

> 'The misery of a child is interesting to a mother, the misery of a young man is interesting to a young woman, the misery of an old man is interesting to nobody.'
> [Victor Hugo, 'Saint Denis', *Les Misérables*; 1862]

Huguenot /hyóogənō/ *n* a French Protestant, especially in the 16th and 17th centuries ■ *adj* relating to, belonging to, or characteristic of the French Protestant Church [Mid-16C. < French, alteration (based on the name of Besançon *Hugues*, leader of a Swiss political movement) of obsolete *eiguenot* < Swiss German *Eidgenosse* 'confederate', literally 'oath-companion'] —**Huguenotism** /hyóogə notizəm/ *n*

huh /hu/ *interj* **1.** used to show surprise, enquiry, disdain, or lack of interest **2.** used to invite comment, especially agreement, after an expressed opinion ○ *Great shot, huh?* [Early 17C. Natural exclamation]

hui /hóo ee/ (*plural same*) *n NZ* in a Maori community, a meeting for social, business, or religious purposes [Mid-19C. < Maori and Hawaiian]

huia /hóoyə/ (*plural same*) *n* an extinct bird that had feathers that were much prized by the Maori. Native to: formerly, New Zealand. Latin name: *Heteralocha acutirostris*. [Mid-19C. < Hawaiian; an imitation of its whistling cry]

Hu Jintao /hóo jin tów/ (*b.* 1942) Chinese president of the People's Republic of China (2003–). He was vice president of Jiang Zemin and was named in 2002 as the new leader of the Communist Party from March 2003.

hula /hóolə/ *n* a Polynesian or Hawaiian dance involving swaying the hips and miming gestures with the hands ■ *vi* (**-las, -laing, -laed**) to dance a hula [Early 19C. < Hawaiian]

Hula-Hoop *tdmk* a trademark for a plastic ring that people place around the waist and keep twirling by rhythmically moving the hips

hulk /hulk/ *n* **1.** SOMEBODY BIG a big, powerful, and often clumsy person **2.** EMPTY HULL the empty hull of a ship that has been wrecked or is too old to be sailed **3.** UNWIELDY SHIP a heavy ship that is difficult to steer **4.** SHELL OF STRUCTURE the shell of any old, abandoned, or burnt-out structure or vehicle **5.** OLD SHIP USED AS PRISON an old, permanently moored ship used in the 19th century as a prison (*often used in the plural*) ■ *vi* (**hulks, hulking, hulked**) MOVE CLUMSILY to move in a clumsy or awkward way [Pre-12C. Probably via Anglo-Latin *hulcus* < Greek *holkas* 'merchant barge, ship that is towed' < *helkein* 'pull']

hulking /húlking/, **hulky** /húlki/ (**-ier, -iest**) *adj* large, bulky, and often clumsy (*informal*)

hull /hul/ *n* **1.** BODY OF SHIP the body of a ship, excluding other parts such as the masts and engines **2.** BODY OF VEHICLE the main body of a large vehicle such as a tank or aeroplane **3.** ROCKET CASING the external casing of a rocket, missile, or spaceship **4.** OUTER COVERING the outer covering of a seed or fruit **5.** CALYX ON STRAWBERRY the calyx on a strawberry that stays attached to the fruit when it is picked but is not eaten ■ *vt* (**hulls, hulling, hulled**) **1.** REMOVE OUTER RIND to remove the outer rind or shell from a fruit or vegetable **2.** TAKE STRAWBERRY CALYX OFF to remove the calyx from a strawberry [Old English *hulu* < Indo-European, 'cover, conceal']

Hull /hul/ industrial and port city in northeastern England, situated on the Humber Estuary. Population: 243,595 (2001). Official name **Kingston-upon-Hull**

Hull, Cordell (1871–1955) US secretary of state (1933–44). During World War II, he planned the postwar United Nations and was awarded the Nobel Peace Prize (1945).

hullabaloo /húlləbə lóo/, **hullaballoo** *n* noisy excitement or fuss (*informal*) [Mid-18C. Alteration of *hollo-ballo* < *holla*, early variant of HELLO]

hullo *interj, n* another spelling of **hello**

Hulme /hulm/, **Denny** (1936–94) New Zealand motor-racing driver. He won the 1967 Formula One world championship. Full name **Hulme, Dennis Clive**

Hulme /hyoom/, **Keri** (*b.* 1947) New Zealand writer. She won the Booker Prize in 1985 for her first novel, *The Bone People* (1983).

Hulme /hyoom/, **T. E.** (1883–1917) British poet, critic, and philosopher. A founder member of the imagist movement, he championed modern abstract art and attacked liberalism as a spent political force. His extensive collection of notes were published posthumously as *Speculations* (1924) and *Further Speculations* (1955). Full name **Hulme, Thomas Ernest**

hum /hum/ *v* (**hums, humming, hummed**) **1.** *vti* SING WITH LIPS CLOSED to sing with lips closed and without words, or sing something in this way **2.** *vi* MAKE DRONING SOUND to make a steady prolonged droning sound ○ *bees humming* **3.** *vi* GIVE OFF LOW INDISTINCT NOISE to be filled with a low, continuous, indistinct noise ○ *a room that hummed with strange electronic equipment* **4.** *vi* BE EXTREMELY BUSY to be very busy or active (*informal*) ○ *This place is really humming.* **5.** *vi* STINK to smell unpleasantly (*informal*) ■ *n* **1.** DRONING NOISE a steady droning sound **2.** BAD SMELL an unpleasant smell (*informal*) ■ *interj* EXPRESSION OF DISPLEASURE OR INDECISION a low sound made to express displeasure, doubt, surprise, or indecision [14C. An imitation of the sound] —**hummable** *adj* ◇ **hum and haw** to hesitate while speaking or deciding about something

human /hyóomən/ *adj* **1.** OF PEOPLE relating to, involving, or characteristic of human beings ○ *human nature* ○ *human frailty* **2.** MADE UP OF PEOPLE composed of people ○ *the human race* ○ *a human chain* **3.** COMPASSIONATELY KIND showing kindness, compassion, or approachability **4.** IMPERFECT having the imperfections and weaknesses of a human being ○ *She's only human, so give her a break!* ■ *n* same as **human being** [14C. Via French < Latin *humanus*] —**humanness** *n*

USAGE human or **humane**? Do not confuse the spelling of ***human*** and ***humane***. Although the two words sound different, they share the meaning of 'compassionate', which is why they are sometimes confused. ***Human*** is chiefly used as an adjective or noun referring to a person or people (as in *a human being, human weaknesses, humans and other animals*), and it cannot be replaced by ***humane*** in such contexts. ***Humane*** also means 'involving minimal pain', as in *the humane killing of sick animals*, and it cannot be replaced by ***human*** in this sense.

CULTURAL NOTE *The Human Comedy*, a collection of novels and stories (1833–50) by French writer Honoré de Balzac. By linking his novels and stories through the use of common themes and characters, Balzac planned a work that would portray the human species in all stages of its development and all aspects of its behaviour. At the time of his death, the collection included a hundred novels and stories and about fifty incomplete works.

human being *n* **1.** a member of the species to which men and women belong. Latin name: *Homo sapiens*. **2.** a person, viewed especially as having imperfections and weaknesses ○ *I'm a human being, not a machine.*

humane /hyoo máyn/ *adj* **1.** COMPASSIONATE showing the better aspects of the human character, especially kindness and compassion **2.** INVOLVING MINIMAL PAIN done without inflicting any more pain than is necessary **3.** WITH EMPHASIS ON LIBERAL VALUES with an emphasis on respect for other people's views [15C. Variant of HUMAN] —**humanely** *adv* —**humaneness** *n*

USAGE See *human*.

human ecology *n* a branch of sociology that studies the relationships between human beings and their natural and social environments

human engineering *n* COMM same as **ergonomics**

human error *n* a mistake made by a person rather than being caused by a poorly designed process or the malfunctioning of a machine such as a computer ○ *Most of the accidents are attributable to human error.*

humane society *n* an organization that promotes the compassionate treatment of animals

human ethology *n* the study of human behaviour, especially aggressive and submissive behaviour in social contexts

human factors engineering *n* COMM same as **ergonomics**

Human Genome Project *n* a publicly funded international research initiative to sequence and identify human genes and record their positions on chromosomes

human immunodeficiency virus *n* MED full form of **HIV**

human interest *n* an element in something, especially a news report, that is about somebody's personal life or feelings and is expected to appeal to the public's sympathy or curiosity —**human-interest** *adj*

humanise *vt* another spelling of **humanize**

humanism /hyóomənizəm/ *n* **1.** BELIEF IN HUMAN-BASED MORALITY a system of thought that is based on the values, characteristics, and behaviour that are believed to be best in human beings, rather than on any supernatural authority **2.** CONCERN FOR PEOPLE a concern with the needs, wellbeing, and interests of people **3.** *also* **Humanism** RENAISSANCE CULTURAL MOVEMENT the secular cultural and intellectual movement of the Renaissance that spread throughout Europe as a result of the rediscovery of the arts and philosophy of the ancient Greeks and Romans —**humanist** *n, adj* —**humanistic** /hyóomə nístik/ *adj* —**humanistically** *adv*

humanitarian /hyoo mánní táiri ən/ *adj* **1.** CARING committed to improving the lives of other people ○ *a humanitarian organization* **2.** HUMAN involving and affecting human beings, especially in a harmful way (*informal*) ○ *a humanitarian disaster* ■ *n* **1.** CARING PERSON somebody who seeks to improve the lives of other people **2.** SOMEBODY BELIEVING IN HUMANITARIANISM somebody who believes in the philosophical theory of humanitarianism [Mid-19C. < HUMAN, after UNITARIAN and EGALITARIAN]

humanitarianism /hyoo mánni táiri ənizəm/ *n* **1.** a commitment to improving the lives of other people **2.** the philosophical doctrine holding that it is a human being's duty to improve the lives of other people

humanitarian space *n* a neutral and impartially administered zone occupied by international aid agencies in a region in which armed conflict is occurring

humanity /hyoo mánnəti/ *n* **1.** HUMAN RACE the human race considered as a whole **2.** QUALITIES OF HUMAN BEING the qualities or characteristics considered as a whole to be characteristic of human beings **3.** KINDNESS kindness or compassion for others ■ **humanities, Humanities** *npl* **1.** LIBERAL ARTS subjects such as history, languages, and philosophy that involve the study of culture and ideas, as distinct from the sciences **2.** CLASSICAL STUDIES the study of the language and literature of the ancient Greeks and Romans

humanize /hyóomə nīz/ (**-izes, -izing, -ized**), **humanise** (**-ises, -ising, -ised**) *vti* **1.** to make somebody or something humane in character, characteristics, or nature, or become humane **2.** to make something human or like humans, or become human or like humans —**humanization** /hyóomə nī záysh'n/ *n* —**humanizer** *n*

humankind /hyóomən kīnd/, **human kind** *n* all human beings considered as a whole ○ *'Human kind cannot bear very much reality.'* (T. S. Eliot, *Four Quartets, Burnt Norton*; 1935)

humanly /hyóomənli/ *adv* **1.** WITHIN LIMITS OF HUMAN ABILITY within the limits of human ability and knowledge ○ *if humanly possible* **2.** IN WAY CHARACTERISTIC OF HUMANS in a way generally considered to be characteristic of humans **3.** ACCORDING TO HUMAN EXPERIENCE as far as human knowledge or experience can judge

humanmade /hyóomən mayd/ *adj* made by human beings and not occurring naturally ○ *'Humanmade materials gradually deteriorate even when exposed to unpolluted rain, but acid rain accelerates this process.'* (*United States Environmental Protection Agency website*; April 1999)

human metapneumovirus /-metə nyóomō vīrəss/ *n* a single-stranded RNA virus discovered in 2001 that is a major cause of respiratory infections with symptoms similar to the common cold

human nature *n* the typical character that all human beings share, often seen as being imperfect

humanoid /hyóomə noyd/ *adj* describes a being from another planet that has the appearance or characteristics of a human —**humanoid** *n*

human papilloma virus *n* a virus that causes warts in the genital area of humans

human race *n* all people considered as a group

human relations *n* (*takes a singular verb*) **1.** the study of the ways in which people relate to each other in group situations, especially work, and how communication skills and sensitivity to other people's feelings can be improved **2.** the department of an organization or business that deals with employing staff and staffing issues generally

human resources *n* the field of business concerned with recruiting and managing employees (*takes a singular verb*) ○ *a career in human resources* ■ *npl* all the people who work in a business or organization, considered as a whole (*takes a plural verb*)

human rights *npl* the rights that are considered by most societies to belong automatically to everyone, e.g. the rights to freedom, justice, and equality

Humber Estuary /húmbər-/ navigable estuary in northeastern England. The rivers Trent, Yorkshire, Ouse, and Hull flow into it. Length: 60 km/40 mi.

Humberside /húmbər sīd/ former county of northeastern England from 1974 to 1996

humble /húmb'l/ *adj* (**-bler, -blest**) **1.** MODEST modest and unassuming in attitude and behaviour **2.** RESPECTFUL feeling or showing respect and deference towards other people **3.** LOWLY relatively low in rank and without pretensions ○ *of humble origins* ■ *vt* (**-bles, -bling, -bled**) **1.** MAKE SOMEBODY FEEL LESS IMPORTANT to make somebody feel less proud or convinced of his or her own importance **2.** DEGRADE SOMEBODY to lower somebody in rank or importance [13C. Via Old French (*h*)*umble* < Latin *humilis* 'lowly' < *humus* 'earth'] —**humbled** *adj* —**humbleness** *n* —**humbly** *adv*

humblebee /húmb'l bee/ *n* INSECTS same as **bumblebee** [15C. Probably alteration of Middle Low German *hummelbē* 'humming bee' < *hummel* 'hum, buzz' + *bē* 'bee']

humble pie *n* formerly, a pie made using the entrails of a newly killed animal, especially a deer (*archaic*) [Mid-17C. Alteration of *umble pie* < *umbles* 'edible animal entrails', via French dialect *nombles* < Latin *lumbulus* 'small loin'] ◊ **eat humble pie** to apologize or admit you have been wrong, especially in a way that makes you feel humiliated

humbling /húmbling/ *adj* making somebody lose confidence, self-importance, or pride —**humblingly** *adv*

Humboldt /húmbōlt/, **Alexander, Freiherr von** (1769–1859) German explorer and naturalist. He is best known for his encyclopedic account of the physical universe, *The Cosmos* (1845–62). Full name **Humboldt, Friedrich Wilhelm Heinrich Alexander**

Humboldt Current *n* a cold current of the South Pacific Ocean that flows north along the western coastline of South America, carrying nutrients that support rich fishing grounds

humbug /húm bug/ *n* **1.** NONSENSE something that is silly or makes no sense **2.** DECEPTION something that is meant to deceive or cheat people **3.** FRAUD somebody who deceives others by making false claims **4.** BOILED SWEET a boiled mint-flavoured sweet, usually decorated with stripes ■ *vt* (**-bugs, -bugging, -bugged**) **1.** DECEIVE to take part in a deception or deceive somebody **2.** *vt Carib* HINDER to hamper or prevent somebody from working ■ *interj* EXPRESSES DISAGREEMENT used to express the opinion that something is nonsense or deception (*archaic*) [Mid-18C. Origin ?]

humdinger /húmding gər/ *n* an exceptional or outstanding person or thing (*slang*) [Early 20C. Probably < HUM 'approving murmur' + *dinger* 'superlative thing']

humdrum /húm drum/ *adj* dull because of being too familiar and lacking variety [Mid-16C. Probably expressive alteration of HUM]

Hume /hyoom/, **Basil, Cardinal** (1923–99) British Roman Catholic cardinal. He became archbishop of Westminster in 1976, the first Benedictine monk to hold this office. Full name **Hume, George Basil**

'If you become holy, it is because God has made you so. You will not know it anyway.'
[Basil Hume, *Observer*; 10 January 1984]

Hume, David (1711–76) Scottish philosopher and historian. His major works are *A Treatise of Human Nature* (1739–40) and *An Enquiry Concerning Human Understanding* (1748).

'Good and ill, both natural and moral, are entirely relative to human sentiment and affection.'

[David Hume, 'The Sceptic', *Essays, Moral and Political*; 1741]

'Our reason must be consider'd as a kind of cause, of which truth is the natural effect.'
[David Hume, *A Treatise of Human Nature*; 1739–40]

Hume, John (*b.* 1937) Northern Irish politician. He was leader of the Social Democratic and Labour Party from 1979, and was joint winner of the Nobel Peace Prize (1998) for his contribution to the Northern Irish peace process.

'Every party in Ireland was founded on the gun.'
[Attributed to John Hume]

humectant /hyoo méktənt/ *n* a substance that absorbs or helps retain moisture, e.g. a skin lotion [Early 19C. < Latin (*h*)*umectant*-, present participle of (*h*)*umectare* 'moisten' < (*h*)*umectus* 'moist' < (*h*)*umere* 'be moist'] —**humectant** *adj*

humeral /hyoómərəl/ *adj* relating to, involving, or located in the humerus of the upper arm or forelimb ○ *a humeral injury*

humeral veil *n* a silk shawl covering the shoulders and hands, worn by a Roman Catholic priest while holding sacred vessels

humerus /hyoómərəss/ (*plural* **-meri** /-mə rī/) *n* the long bone of the human upper arm or of a forelimb in other animals [14C. < Latin, 'upper arm']

humic /hyoómik/ *adj* relating to, involving, containing, or typical of humus [Mid-19C. < HUMUS [1]]

humid /hyoómid/ *adj* with a relatively high level of moisture in the air [14C. < Latin (*h*)*umidus* < (*h*)*umere* 'be moist'] —**humidly** *adv*

SYNONYMS See *wet*.

humidifier /hyoo míddi fī ər/ *n* a device or machine that keeps the air moist inside an enclosed space

humidify /hyoo míddi fī/ (**-fies, -fying, -fied**) *vt* to make something, especially the air, more moist or damp —**humidification** /hyoo míddifi káysh'n/ *n*

humidistat /hyoo míddi stat/ *n* an instrument that measures or controls the relative humidity of the air [Early 20C. < HUMIDITY, after THERMOSTAT]

humidity /hyoo míddəti/ *n* **1.** the amount of moisture in the air **2.** the condition of having a high amount of moisture in the air **3.** METEOROL same as **relative humidity**

humidor /hyoómi dawr/ *n* a container, often a box or jar, in which tobacco products, especially cigars, can be stored to prevent them from drying out [Early 20C. < HUMID, after CUSPIDOR]

humify /hyoómi fī/ (**-fies, -fying, -fied**) *vti* to turn a substance into humus, or turn into humus

humiliate /hyoo mílli ayt/ (**-ates, -ating, -ated**) *vt* to damage somebody's dignity or pride, especially publicly [Mid-16C. < late Latin *humiliat*-, past participle of *humiliare* < Latin *humilis* (see HUMBLE)] —**humiliating** *adj* —**humiliatingly** *adv* —**humiliator** *n*

humiliation /hyoo mílli áysh'n/ *n* **1.** LOSS OF DIGNITY the feeling or condition of being lessened in dignity or pride **2.** LESSENING OF SOMEBODY'S DIGNITY the act of damaging somebody's dignity or pride **3.** SOMETHING THAT HUMILIATES something that damages somebody's pride or dignity

humility /hyoo mílləti/ *n* the quality of being modest or respectful [13C. Via French < Latin *humilitas* < *humilis* (see HUMBLE)]

~~**huminist**~~ incorrect spelling of **humanist**

humint /hyoómint/, **HUMINT** *n* intelligence information acquired from agents or others in enemy territory. Full form **human intelligence**

Hummel /hoómm'l/, **Johann** (1778–1837) German composer and pianist. He was a pupil of Wolfgang Amadeus Mozart and is best known for his work on piano fingering technique, *Klavierschule* (1828). Full name **Hummel, Johann Nepomuk**

hummingbird

hummingbird /húmming burd/ *n* a small brightly coloured nectar-eating bird that hovers, especially while feeding, by beating its wings rapidly, producing a humming sound. Native to: tropical America. Family: Trochilidae.

humming top *n* a child's spinning top that makes a humming sound as it spins

hummock /húmmək/ *n* **1.** a small hill or mound **2.** a ridge of ice in an ice field [Mid-16C. Origin ?] —**hummocky** *adj*

hummus /hoómmōoss/, **humus, hoommos** /hoómməss/ *n* a dish made with mashed chickpeas, tahini, oil, lemon juice, and garlic combined into a thick paste, originating in southwestern Asia [Mid-20C. < Arabic *ḥummuṣ* 'chickpea']

humongous /hyoo múng gəss/, **humungous** *adj* extremely large in size or amount (*informal*) [Mid-20C. Origin ?] —**humongously** *adv*

humor *n*, *vt* US spelling of **humour**

humoral /hyoómərəl/ *adj* relating to, involving, or typical of body fluids, especially blood serum

humoresque /hyoómə résk/ *n* a light or whimsical piece of music, especially 19th-century music [Late 19C. Alteration of German *Humoreske* < *Humor* 'humour' < English]

humorist /hyoómərist/ *n* **1.** somebody who writes or performs comic material **2.** somebody known to be amusing and to have a quick wit

humorous /hyoómərəss/ *adj* **1.** intended to be amusing and make people laugh **2.** witty or able to make people laugh —**humorously** *adv* —**humorousness** *n*

SYNONYMS See *funny*.

humour /hyoómər/ *n* **1.** FUNNY QUALITY the quality or content of something such as a story, performance, or joke that elicits amusement and laughter ○ *couldn't see the humour in it* **2.** ABILITY TO SEE SOMETHING IS FUNNY the ability to see that something is funny, or the enjoyment of things that are funny ○ *He has no sense of humour.* **3.** FUNNY THINGS AS GENRE writings and other material created to make people laugh **4.** SOMEBODY'S USUAL TEMPERAMENT somebody's character or usual attitude ○ *a writer of melancholy humour* **5.** MOOD a temporary mood or state of mind **6.** HIST BODY FLUID according to medieval science and medicine, any of the four main fluids of the human body, blood, yellow bile, black bile, or lymph, that determined somebody's mood and temperament ■ *vt* (**-mours, -mouring, -moured**) **1.** DO WHAT SOMEBODY WANTS to do what somebody wants in order to keep him or her happy **2.** COMPLY WITH SOMETHING to act in accordance with something (*archaic*) [14C. Via Anglo-Norman < Latin *humor* 'body fluid' < *humere* 'be moist']

humoured /hyoómərd/ *adj* having a particular character or frame of mind (*usually used in combination*) ○ *good-humoured*

humourless /hyoómərləss/ *adj* **1.** lacking a sense of humour **2.** having no amusing aspect —**humourlessly** *adv* —**humourlessness** *n*

~~**humourous**~~ incorrect spelling of **humorous**

hump /hump/ *n* **1.** ZOOL BUMP ON ANIMAL'S BACK a rounded protuberance on the back of some animals such as camels and some cattle **2.** MED CURVE OF BACK a pronounced convex curvature of somebody's upper spine resulting from injury or disease, a congenital condition, or an accumulation of fat **3.** BUMP IN SURFACE OF SOMETHING a rounded protruding mass, e.g. a mound of earth ■ *v* (**humps, humping, humped**) **1.** *vt* MOVE SOMETHING WITH EFFORT to carry something heavy with

difficulty (*informal*) **2.** *vti* OFFENSIVE TERM an offensive term meaning to have sexual intercourse with somebody (*slang*) **3.** *vt* MAKE SOMETHING INTO HUMP to form something into a hump [Mid-17C. Probably < Dutch *homp*, Low German *humpe*] ◇ **over the hump** past the worst or most difficult part of something ◇ **the hump** a mood of annoyance, resentment, or unhappiness (*informal*)

humpback /húmp bak/ *n* **1.** MED same as **hunchback 2.** MARINE BIOL same as **humpback whale 3.** CIV ENG same as **humpback bridge 4.** FISH same as **pink salmon** (sense 1) —**humpbacked** *adj*

humpback bridge, **hump-backed bridge** *n* a small narrow bridge with a steep approach and descent

humpback salmon *n* FISH same as **pink salmon** (sense 1) [Because the male develops a humped back during the breeding season]

humpback whale

humpback whale *n* a large dark-grey or black whale, up to 15.2 m/50 ft long, with a humped back and long white flippers, that feeds by sieving plankton and fish through baleen plates. Humpback whales communicate with each other using distinctive complex sounds that can travel over considerable distances. Latin name: *Megaptera novaengliae*.

Humperdinck /hoómpər dingk/, **Engelbert** (1854–1921) German composer. He wrote numerous operas, the most famous of which is *Hansel and Gretel* (1893).

humph /humf/ *interj* used to express annoyance, doubt, or dissatisfaction [Mid-16C. Natural exclamation]

Humphries /húmfriz/, **Barry** (*b.* 1934) Australian writer and performer. He is best known as the creator of the comic characters Dame Edna Everage and Sir Les Patterson. Full name **Humphries, John Barry**

humpty-dumpty /húmpti dúmpti/ (*plural* **humpty-dumpties**) *n* an offensive term for somebody perceived as being short and overweight (*informal*) [Late 18C. After *Humpty-Dumpty*, nursery-rhyme character]

humpy[1] /húmpi/ (**-ier, -iest**) *adj* **1.** having or full of humps **2.** feeling irritable and easily annoyed (*informal*) [Early 18C. < HUMP] —**humpiness** *n*

humpy[2] /húmpi/ (*plural* **-ies**) *n* Aus a small crudely constructed hut or shelter in the bush [Mid-19C. < Aboriginal *yumbi*, influenced by HUMP]

humungous *adj* another spelling of **humongous**

humus[1] /hyóoməss/ *n* a dark-brown organic component of soil that is derived from decomposed plant and animal remains and animal excrement. Humus improves the water-retaining properties of soil, adds nutrients, and makes it more workable. [Late 18C. < Latin, 'soil']

humus[2] /hoómmooss/ *n* FOOD another spelling of **hummus**

Hun /hun/ *n* **1.** MEMBER OF EARLY ASIAN NOMADIC PEOPLE a member of a nomadic people, probably originating in north-central Asia, who invaded China in the 3rd century BC and then spread westwards across Asia and into Europe. During the 4th century AD, under their leader Attila, they overran much of the Roman Empire. **2.** DESTRUCTIVE PERSON a barbaric and destructive person **3.** OFFENSIVE TERM an offensive term for a German person or the German people, used especially by their opponents during World Wars I and II (*dated slang*) [Old English *Hūne*, via Germanic < late Latin *Hunni* < Sogdian *xwn*]

Hunan /hoó nán/ province in central China, and an important agricultural and mineral producing region. Capital: Changsha. Population: 64,280,000 (1997). Area: 210,500 sq. km/81,270 sq. mi.

hunch /hunch/ *n* **1.** FEELING an intuitive feeling about something **2.** STOOP a curved posture of the body with the head down and shoulders forwards **3.** MED same as **hump** *n* (sense 2) **4.** PIECE a large lump or slice of something (*dated*) ■ *vti* (**hunches, hunching, hunched**) BEND UPPER BODY FORWARDS to bend the head down and the shoulders forwards, e.g. because of bad posture, illness, or the cold ○ *a typist hunching over the keyboard* ○ *hunched her shoulders against the wind* [15C. Origin ?]

hunchback /húnch bak/ *n* **1.** somebody with a hump on his or her back **2.** a back that shows a pronounced curvature of the spine —**hunchbacked** *adj*

CULTURAL NOTE *The Hunchback of Notre Dame*, a novel (1831) by French writer Victor Hugo. In this richly evocative medieval tragedy, Quasimodo, the hunchbacked bell-ringer at the Cathedral of Notre Dame in Paris, falls in love with a beautiful girl, Esmerelda. When corrupt priest Claude Frollo's harassment of Esmerelda results in her being executed for sorcery, Quasimodo murders Frollo by pushing him off the bell tower.

hundi /hoóndi/ *n S Asia* an informal banker's draft, especially used in transmitting currency from one country to another

hundred /húndrəd/ *n* **1.** 100 the number 100 **2.** GROUP OF 100 a group of a hundred people or objects **3.** LARGE NUMBER an unspecified large number ○ *attended by hundreds* **4.** THIRD DIGIT TO LEFT OF DECIMAL the number that is three places to the left of the decimal point in Arabic notation **5.** CRICKET 100 RUNS in cricket, a score of 100 runs by a batsman **6.** HIST COUNTY SUBDIVISION a historical subdivision of English, Irish, and some North American counties ■ **hundreds** *npl* **1.** 100 TO 999 the numbers 100 to 999 **2.** YEARS OF CENTURY the years of a particular century ○ *the seventeen-hundreds* **3.** TEMPERATURES OVER 100 numbers over 100, particularly as a range of Fahrenheit temperatures ○ *For three days the temperature was in the hundreds.* **4.** LARGE NUMBERS unspecified large numbers [Old English < Indo-European] —**hundredfold** *adj, adv*

hundred per cent ◇ **a** *or* **one hundred per cent** (*informal*) **1.** TOTALLY in a complete or full way ○ *She is a hundred per cent in charge.* **2.** COMPLETELY WELL completely fit and healthy ○ *I'm still not feeling a hundred per cent after the accident.*

hundreds-and-thousands *npl* tiny multicoloured sugar strands used for decorating cakes

hundredth /húndrədth/ *n* one of 100 equal parts of something

hundredweight /húndrəd wayt/ *n* **1.** a unit of mass in the British imperial system equal to 112 lb (50.80 kg) **2.** *N Am* MEASURE same as **cental 3.** MEASURE same as **metric hundredweight** [Probably originally 100 pounds]

Hundred Years' War *n* a series of wars fought between England and France from 1337 to 1453 that resulted in the final expulsion of the English from all French territories except Calais

hung /hung/ past participle, past tense of **hang** ■ *adj* **1.** unable to form a majority and therefore make decisions or reach a verdict ○ *a hung jury* ○ *a hung parliament* **2.** an offensive term meaning having male sexual organs of a particular size (*slang*)

Hung. *abbr* **1.** Hungarian **2.** Hungary

Hungarian /hung gáiri ən/ *n* **1.** somebody who comes from Hungary **2.** the official language of Hungary, also spoken in parts of neighbouring countries, belonging to one of the Ugric subgroups of Finno-Ugric. Native speakers: 14 million. —**Hungarian** *adj*

Hungarian goulash *n* FOOD same as **goulash** (sense 1)

Hungary

Hungary /húng gəri/ country in central Europe, first united as a country around AD 1000. It became a member of the European Union in 2004. Language: Hungarian. Currency: forint. Capital: Budapest. Population: 10,045,407 (2003). Area: 93,030 sq. km/35,919 sq. mi. Official name **Republic of Hungary**

hunger /húng gər/ *n* **1.** NEED TO EAT the need or desire for food **2.** STARVATION a lack of food leading to illness or death ○ *children dying of hunger* **3.** CRAVING a great need or desire for something ○ *a hunger for knowledge* ■ *vi* (**-gers, -gering, -gered**) CRAVE to feel a great need or desire for something [Old English *hungur* < Germanic]

hunger march *n* a march organized by unemployed people to draw attention to their plight

hunger strike *n* a refusal to eat over a period of time as a form of protest, especially by a prisoner —**hunger striker** *n*

hungover /hung óvər/, **hung over** *adj* suffering from the aftereffects of drinking too much alcohol

hungry /húng gri/ (**-grier, -griest**) *adj* **1.** WANTING TO EAT wanting or needing food **2.** CAUSING HUNGER using up a lot of energy and making somebody want or need food ○ *hungry work* **3.** AVID wanting or desiring something very much ○ *hungry for new experiences* **4.** AMBITIOUS having great ambition or a powerful desire to win (*informal*) ○ *They won because they were hungrier than we were.* [Old English *hungrig*, related to HUNGER] —**hungrily** *adv* —**hungriness** *n* ◇ **go hungry** to go without food

hung up *adj* (*informal*) **1.** in a state of worry or anxiety over something ○ *hung up over minor details* **2.** obsessed with somebody or something ○ *He's completely hung up on her.*

hunk /hungk/ *n* **1.** a large piece of something such as bread or cheese that is cut or torn off a larger portion **2.** a man who is well-built and very attractive physically (*informal*) [Early 19C. Origin ?]

hunker /húngkər/ (**-kers, -kering, -kered**) *vi* to squat down close to the ground [Early 18C. Origin ?] **hunker down** *vi* **1.** to settle down seriously to try to achieve something ○ *time to hunker down and start studying* **2.** US to hold stubbornly to an opinion (*informal*)

hunkers /húngkərz/ *npl* the hips, buttocks, and upper thighs of a person or animal (*dated informal*) [Mid-18C. Probably < HUNKER]

Hunkpapa /húngk paapə/ (*plural same or* **-pas**) *n* a member of a Native North American people, a branch of the Teton, who now live on both sides of the border between North and South Dakota. The Hunkpapa formerly lived in the border regions between Montana and North and South Dakota. [< Siouan, 'at the end of the circle' (of the Teton camp)]

hunky /húngki/ (**-ier, -iest**) *adj* masculine, well-built, and very attractive physically (*informal*) [Early 20C. < HUNK]

hunky-dory /-dáwri/ *adj* absolutely fine or satisfactory (*informal*) [Probably alteration of *hunky* 'all right' < obsolete *hunk* 'place where a game player is safe from capture' < Dutch *honk* 'home']

Hunnish /húnnish/ *adj* **1.** relating to the Huns **2.** *also* **hunnish** destructive and barbarous

hunt /hunt/ *v* (**hunts, hunting, hunted**) **1.** *vti* SEEK PREY to pursue an animal with the aim of capturing or killing it for sport or food ○ *Cats hunt mice and small birds.* ○ *They've been hunting together for years.* **2.** *vt* SEEK OUT SOMEBODY to search for and try to capture somebody **3.** *vi* SEARCH to search persistently for something difficult to find ○ *hunting for his missing keys* **4.** *vt* HOUND SOMEBODY to seek out and harass or persecute somebody **5.** *vi* FIELD SPORTS CHASE ANIMALS WITH HOUNDS to engage in a sport involving the pursuit of an animal, usually a fox, on horseback and with the aid of hounds **6.** *vt* FIELD SPORTS USE ANIMAL IN BLOOD SPORT to use a horse or hounds for the purpose of chasing and killing game, usually a fox **7.** *vt* FIELD SPORTS USE PARTICULAR PLACE FOR BLOOD SPORT to search a particular area for animals to capture or kill for sport or food **8.** *vi* ENG OSCILLATE ABOUT POSITION to oscillate about a fixed point ■ *n* **1.** ACT OF SEARCHING the act of looking for somebody or something carefully, thoroughly, and persistently [1.5.] **2.** FIELD SPORTS SEEKING OF PREY an attempt to capture or kill animals for sport or food **3.** HUNTING EXPEDITION an organized event in which riders and hounds pursue a fox or deer with the aim of killing it for sport **4.** *also* **Hunt**

ORGANIZED GROUP OF HUNTERS an organized group of people who hunt foxes or deer for sport ○ *She joined the local hunt.* [Old English *huntian* < Germanic] ◇ **hunt high and low** to search extremely thoroughly for somebody or something

Hunt /hunt/, **Geoff** (*b.* 1947) Australian squash player. He won the World Open title in 1976, 1977, 1979, and 1980. Full name **Hunt, Geoffrey Brian**

Hunt, Holman (1827–1910) British painter. He was a cofounder of the Pre-Raphaelite Brotherhood (1848) and his works include *The Scapegoat* (1854) and *May Morning on Magdalen Tower* (1888–91). Full name **Hunt, William Holman**

Hunt, James (1947–93) British racing driver. The Formula One world champion in 1976, he retired from racing in 1979 and took up motor racing commentary. Full name **Hunt, James Simon Wallis**

Hunt, Leigh (1784–1859) British poet. He was a friend of Keats, Byron, and Shelley. His works include two volumes of collected poems (1832, 1844) and his *Autobiography* (1850). Full name **Hunt, James Henry Leigh**

> 'Jenny kissed me when we met, / Jumping from the chair she sat in; / Time, you thief, who love to get / Sweets into your list, put that in: / Say I'm weary, say I'm sad, / Say that health and wealth have missed me, / Say I'm growing old, but add, / Jenny kissed me.'
> [Leigh Hunt, 'Rondeau'; 1838]

Hunt, Sam (*b.* 1946) New Zealand poet. A writer and performer of popular verse, his works include *South into Winter* (1973).

huntaway /húntə way/ *n* NZ a sheepdog that is trained to drive sheep without close supervision by a shepherd

hunted /húntid/ *adj* startled and panic-stricken, as if being pursued ○ *a hunted look*

hunter /húntər/ *n* **1.** **PREDATOR** a person or animal that hunts birds or animals for food or sport **2.** **HORSE** a powerful fast horse that is bred for and used in hunting **3.** **DOG** a dog that is bred for and used in hunting **4.** **SEEKER** somebody who seeks out a particular type of person or thing, especially as an occupation or hobby ○ *fossil hunters* **5.** **WATCH** a watch with a hinged metal cover to protect the watch face

Hunter /húntər/, **Bill** (*b.* 1941) Australian actor. His films include *Newsfront* (1978). Full name **Hunter, William**

Hunter, John (1728–93) Scottish anatomist and surgeon. Through his study of anatomy, biology, physiology, and pathology, he established surgery as a modern scientific discipline.

Hunter, William (1718–83) Scottish obstetrician. He introduced the dissection of cadavers as part of medical training. His advances in obstetrics led to its recognition as a branch of medicine.

hunter-gatherer *n* a member of a society in which people live by hunting game and gathering edible plants only, and grow no crops and raise no livestock

hunter-killer *adj* describes a naval vessel or force equipped with antisubmarine devices and designed to search for and destroy submarines

hunter's moon *n* the first full moon after the harvest moon

Hunter Valley /húntər-/ agricultural and industrial region in eastern New South Wales, Australia. Area: 22,000 sq. km/8,495 sq. mi.

hunting /húnting/ *n* **1.** the sport or practice of pursuing and killing or capturing wild animals **2.** the process of searching carefully for something, usually over a period of time ○ *job hunting*

hunting and gathering *n* the seeking of game and edible plants for subsistence, as practised by pre-agricultural and nomadic people, instead of raising livestock and growing crops for food

Huntingdon /húntingdən/ town in eastern England. Population: 18,000

Huntingdonshire /húntingdənshər/ historic former county in eastern England, now part of Cambridgeshire

hunting ground *n* **1.** a place where hunting is pursued or that is suitable for hunting **2.** a source of useful

or desired objects or information ○ *The town is a great hunting ground for antiques.*

hunting horn *n* a horn used to give signals during hunting, especially foxhunting

hunting knife *n* a broad knife used for killing or gutting game

hunting spider *n* ZOOL same as **wolf spider**

huntingtin /húntingtin/ *n* a protein that occurs naturally in nerve cells, but when mutated can cause Huntington's chorea [< HUNTINGTON'S CHOREA]

Huntington's chorea /húntingtənz ko ree ə/ *n* a hereditary disorder of the nervous system that manifests as jerky involuntary movements in early middle age, with behavioural changes and progressive dementia [Late 19C. After George *Huntington* (1851–1916), US neurologist]

hunting watch *n* JEWELLERY same as **hunter** (sense 5)

huntress /húntrəss/ *n* a woman or goddess who hunts (*literary*)

hunt saboteur *n* somebody who opposes foxhunting and travels to hunts in order to try to prevent or disrupt their occurrence

huntsman /húntsmən/ *n* (*plural* **-men** /-mən/) **1.** an official who is in charge of the hounds belonging to a hunt **2.** a man who hunts, either for a living or for sport **3.** ZOOL same as **huntsman spider**

huntsman spider *n* a large spider with a light brown or grey hairy body that lives in hot and tropical regions. Family: Sparassidae.

Huntsville /húntsvil/ city in northern Alabama, a major centre of aerospace research and manufacture, home to Redstone Arsenal. Population: 162,536 (2002 estimate).

huntswoman /húnts wŏomən/ *n* (*plural* **-women** /-wimin/) *n* a woman who hunts, either for a living or for sport

Huon pine /hyŏo on-/ *n* a large coniferous timber tree. Native to: South America, Australia, Southeast Asia. Latin name: *Dacrydium franklinii.* [Early 19C. After the River *Huon* in S Tasmania]

hup /hup/ *interj* used when lifting or raising something (*informal*) [Mid-20C. Origin ?]

huppah *n* JUDAISM another spelling of **chuppah**

Hurd /hurd/, **Sir Douglas** (*b.* 1930) British politician. He served in Conservative governments as Northern Ireland secretary (1984), home secretary (1985), and foreign secretary (1989–95) in the administrations of Margaret Thatcher and John Major. Full name **Hurd, Sir Douglas Richard**

hurdies /húrdiz/ *npl* Scotland the buttocks or haunches [Mid-16C. Origin ?]

hurdle /húrd'l/ *n* **1.** **DIFFICULTY OR OBSTACLE** a difficulty or obstacle that has to be overcome **2.** **BARRIER FOR RUNNER TO JUMP OVER** one of a number of light barriers over which runners have to jump in some athletics events **3.** **FENCE** a light framework made of intertwined branches or wattle that is used as a temporary fence **4.** **HORSERACING FENCE USED IN HORSE RACE** a fence of intertwined branches or wattle that horses jump over in a race, or a race over fences of this type **5.** HIST **FRAME FOR CONVICTS** a frame on which traitors were dragged and paraded before the public before being executed (*archaic*) ■ *v* (**-dles, -dling, -dled**) **1.** *vi* **RACE OVER HURDLES** to run in an athletics event in which hurdles must be jumped **2.** *vt* **CLEAR RACING BARRIER** to clear a barrier in a race **3.** *vt* **OVERCOME DIFFICULTY** to overcome a difficulty or obstacle **4.** *vt* **FENCE AREA** to fence off an area with hurdles [Old English *hyrdel* < Indo-European, 'to turn'] —**hurdler** *n*

hurdles /húrd'lz/ *n* an athletics event in which runners have to race to clear a series of light barriers (*takes a singular or plural verb*)

hurdy-gurdy /húrdi gúrdi, húrdi gurdi/ (*plural* **hurdy-gurdies**) *n* **1.** a mechanical musical instrument that is played by turning a handle, e.g. a barrel organ **2.** a medieval stringed instrument played by turning a crank attached to a rosined wheel that causes strings to vibrate while being controlled by a keyboard [Mid-18C. An imitation of the sound]

hurl /hurl/ *v* (**hurls, hurling, hurled**) **1.** *vt* **FLING SOMETHING** to throw something with great force **2.** *vt* **YELL SOMETHING** to utter something with great vehemence ○ *hurling abuse* **3.** *vti* BASEBALL **PITCH** to pitch a baseball **4.** *vi* **VOMIT** to vomit, especially with considerable force (*slang*) ■ *n* **1.** **STRONG THROW** a forceful throw, or

hurdy-gurdy (sense 2)

the act of throwing something with great force **2.** Scotland TRANSP **RIDE IN VEHICLE** a ride in a wheeled vehicle [12C. Probably suggesting the action] —**hurler** *n*

SYNONYMS See *throw*.

hurley /húrli/ *n* **1.** Ireland the game of hurling **2.** a long wooden stick with a curved end used in the game of hurling [Early 19C. < HURL]

hurling /húrling/ *n* an Irish field sport resembling hockey and lacrosse that is played with broad sticks and a leather ball that is passed from player to player through the air

hurly-burly /húrli burli/ *n* noisy and bustling activity [Alteration of *hurling and burling*, playful formation based on HURL]

Huron /hyŏorən, -on/ (*plural same* or **-rons**) *n* a member of a confederacy of Iroquoian peoples who lived around the Great Lakes and now live in Quebec, Ontario, and Oklahoma. During the 17th century, the population was greatly reduced by continual warring with the Iroquois and the arrival of smallpox and other European diseases. [Mid-17C. < French, 'boar' < Old French *hure* 'bristling hair'] —**Huron** *adj*

Huron, Lake /hyŏorən/ second largest of the Great Lakes, lying between the state of Michigan, United States, and the province of Ontario, Canada. Area: 59,600 sq. km/23,000 sq. mi. Depth: 229 m/751 ft.

hurrah /hŏo ráa, hə-/ *interj, n* same as **hooray** [Late 17C. Alteration of HUZZAH]

hurray *interj, n* another spelling of **hooray**

Hurrian /hŏori ən/ *n* **1.** a member of an ancient people who lived in Syria and Mesopotamia around 1500 BC **2.** the unaffiliated language of the Hurrian people [Early 20C. < Hittite, Assyrian *Harri, Hurri*] —**Hurrian** *adj*

hurricane /húrrikən, -kayn/ *n* **1.** **SEVERE STORM** a severe tropical storm with torrential rain and extremely strong winds. Hurricanes originate in areas of low pressure in equatorial regions of the Atlantic or Caribbean, and then strengthen, travelling northwest, north, or northeast. **2.** **HIGH WIND** a wind of above 119 km/74 mi. per hour, classified as force 12 or above on the Beaufort scale **3.** **FAST AND FORCEFUL PERSON OR THING** somebody or something resembling a violent storm in force, speed, or effect [Mid-16C. Via Spanish < Taino *hurakán* 'god of the storm']

hurricane deck *n* a deck on a ship with a cover from the sun

hurricane lamp *n* an oil or paraffin lamp with a glass cover to prevent the wick from being extinguished in wind or rain

hurried /húrrid/ *adj* done, made, or performed too quickly because of a real or perceived lack of time —**hurriedly** *adv* —**hurriedness** *n*

hurry /húrri/ *v* (**-ries, -rying, -ried**) **1.** *vi* **RUSH** to move or do something with great or excessive speed because of a real or perceived lack of time **2.** *vt* **SPEED SOMEBODY OR SOMETHING UP** to make or encourage somebody or something to act with greater speed ○ *Hurry up and put your coat on!* ■ *n* **1.** **HASTE** a state in which somebody is moving or doing something with great or excessive speed because of a real or perceived lack of time ○ *We were in such a hurry we left the tickets behind.* **2.** **URGENCY** the need to do something quickly ○ *What's the hurry?* [Early 17C. Origin ?] —**hurryingly** *adv* ◇ **in a hurry** readily or willingly (*informal*)

hurry-scurry *n* an undue rush to do something [Mid-18C. Repetition of HURRY]

hurry sickness *n* a compulsion to do everything quickly, or a chronic feeling of being short of time, attributed to the fast pace of modern life and causing symptoms such as anxiety and insomnia

hurst /hurst/ *n* a wooded area (*archaic*) [Old English *hyrst* < Germanic]

hurt /hurt/ *v* (**hurts, hurting, hurt**) **1.** *vti* **INJURE SOMEBODY OR SOMETHING** to cause somebody, yourself, or an animal physical injury or pain ○ *hurt his back when he fell down* ○ *Ouch! That hurts!* **2.** *vti* **CAUSE PAIN** to experience physical pain, or be a source of physical pain for a person or animal ○ *I hurt all over.* ○ *My arm's hurting me.* **3.** *vti* **UPSET** to feel emotional pain, or make somebody feel emotional pain ○ *was hurt by his unkind remarks* **4.** *vti* **IMPAIR** to have a negative effect on something ○ *This could hurt her chances of re-election.* **5.** *vi* **EXPERIENCE DIFFICULTIES** to undergo or experience difficulties or setbacks, e.g. in business or financial affairs (*informal*) ○ *The business is really hurting.* ■ *n* **1.** **PAIN** emotional or mental pain or suffering ○ *after all the hurt he's caused* **2.** **INJURY** an injury or wound, whether emotional, mental, or physical ○ *old hurts* [12C. < Old French *hurter* 'ram, collide', probably < Germanic] —**hurt** *adj* —**hurter** *n*

SYNONYMS See *harm.*

hurtful /húrtf'l/ *adj* causing emotional pain or suffering —**hurtfully** *adv* —**hurtfulness** *n*

hurtle /húrt'l/ (**-tles, -tling, -tled**) *vi* to move or travel at very high speed [13C. < HURT]

Husain /hoo sáyn/ (AD 626?–680) Arabian Muslim saint. The son of Fatima, grandson of Muhammad, and younger brother of Hasan, he was killed defending Islam and his death is commemorated in the festival of Ashora.

husband /húzbənd/ *n* the man to whom a woman is married ■ *vt* (**-bands, -banding, -banded**) to use and manage something economically and sensibly, e.g. resources or money [Pre-12C. < Old Norse *húsbóndi* 'man in charge of the house, farmer' < *hús* 'house' + *bóndi* 'dweller', present participle of *búa* 'dwell'] —**husbandage** *n* —**husbander** *n*

husbandman /húzbəndmən/ (*plural* **-men** /-mən/) *n* AGRIC, OCCUPATIONS same as **farmer** (*archaic*)

husbandry /húzbəndri/ *n* **1.** the science, skill, or art of farming **2.** the economical and sensible management of resources

Husein ♦ **Abdullah ibn Husein**

hush /hush/ *vti* (**hushes, hushing, hushed**) **MAKE SOMEBODY BE QUIET** to become silent, or make somebody do this ■ *interj* **BE QUIET** used to request or demand silence ■ *n* **SILENCE** a silence, especially after a period of noise or in expectation of something [Mid-16C. Probably back-formation < obsolete *husht* 'hush!', natural exclamation]

hush up *vt* to prevent something, especially something dishonourable or discreditable, from becoming publicly known (*informal*)

hushaby /húshə bī/ *interj* used to lull a child to sleep (*archaic*) [Mid-18C. < HUSH + *-aby* as in *lullaby*]

hushed *adj* made quiet, or quieter than usual ○ *speaking in hushed tones*

hush-hush *adj* secret or confidential (*informal*)

hush money *n* money paid as a bribe not to disclose information (*informal*)

Hush Puppies *tdmk* a trademark for a type of soft shoe

husk /husk/ *n* **1.** BOT **OUTER PLANT COVERING** the outer membranous covering of some fruits, nuts, and grains **2.** **USELESS OUTER SHELL** an empty outer shell or covering that no longer serves any useful purpose ■ *vt* (**husks, husking, husked**) **REMOVE HUSK FROM SOMETHING** to remove the husks from fruits, nuts, or grains [14C. Origin ?] —**husker** *n*

husky[1] /húski/ *adj* (**-ier, -iest**) **1.** **THROATY** hoarse and dry, either naturally or as a result of illness or emotion ○ *a husky voice* **2.** *N Am* **BURLY AND COMPACT IN PHYSIQUE** having a solid, burly, compact physique ○ *a husky boy* **3.** **RELATING TO HUSKS** relating to, containing, or resembling husks ■ *n* CLOTHING **PADDED WAISTCOAT** a short padded or quilted waistcoat [Mid-16C. < HUSK] —**huskily** *adv* —**huskiness** *n*

husky[2] /húski/ (*plural* **-kies**) *n* a large long-haired dog with a curled tail and pricked-up ears, belonging to a breed originally developed in Arctic regions and trained to pull sledges [Mid-19C. Probably alteration of ESKIMO in *Eskimo dog*]

huss /huss/ *n* the edible flesh of the European dogfish [15C. Origin ?]

Huss /huss/, **John** (1372?–1415) Bohemian religious reformer. He was burnt at the stake for supporting the teachings of the English reformer John Wycliffe. His execution led to the outbreak of the Hussite Wars (1419–36). Born **Hus, Jan**

> 'O holy simplicity!'
> [John Huss. While at the stake *Apophthegmata*, Zincgreff-Weidner; 1653]

hussar /hoo zaar/ *n* **1.** a soldier in any European light cavalry unit in the 18th and 19th centuries that adopted an ornate uniform similar to that of the Hungarian cavalry in the 15th century **2.** a member of the Hungarian cavalry in the 15th century [Mid-16C. Via Hungarian *huszár* 'light horseman' < Italian *corsaro* 'corsair']

Hussein I /hoo sáyn/ (1935–99) king of Jordan. Throughout his reign (1952–99), he was regarded by many as a moderating influence in the politics of Southwest Asia.

> 'We should face reality and our past mistakes in an honest, adult way. Boasting of glory does not make glory, and singing in the dark does not dispel fear.'
> [Hussein I, *Conference for Arab heads of state, Sudan*; 30 August 1967]

Hussein, Saddam (*b.* 1937) Iraqi national leader. As leader of the Baath Party, he became president of Iraq in 1979. Two years after the end of the Iran-Iraq War (1980–88), his invasion of Kuwait in August 1990 led to the Gulf War (1991). He was deposed and captured during the Iraq War of 2003.

> 'The mother of battles will be our battle of victory and martyrdom.'
> [Saddam Hussein, *Speech, Baghdad, Times*; 7 January 1991]

Hussite /hússīt/ *n* a follower of the teachings of John Huss —**Hussitism** /hússitizəm/ *n*

hussy /hússi/ (*plural* **-sies**) *n* an offensive term that deliberately insults a woman's manner or behaviour (*dated*) [Mid-16C. Contraction of HOUSEWIFE (the original sense)]

hustings /hústingz/ *npl* **1.** the political activities, e.g. speech-making and the organization of public rallies, that take place before an election **2.** in Great Britain before 1872, a platform from which parliamentary candidates were nominated and addressed electors [Pre-12C. < Old Norse *húsþing* 'king's council' < *hús* 'house' + *þing* 'meeting']

hustle /húss'l/ *v* (**-tles, -tling, -tled**) **1.** *vt* **HURRY SOMEBODY SOMEWHERE** to convey somebody roughly or hurriedly to or from a place ○ *hustled her into a waiting car* **2.** *vti* **HURRY** to go somewhere or deal with something fast or hurriedly ○ *We'd better hustle, or we'll be late.* ○ *They hustled the legislation through before the recess.* **3.** *vt N Am* **SELL SOMETHING AGGRESSIVELY** to sell goods or services using aggressive sales techniques **4.** *vti N Am* CRIME **SOLICIT CUSTOMERS IN SHADY DEALS** to solicit customers in shady or illegal deals, e.g. as a prostitute (*slang*) **5.** *vi N Am* CRIME **ENGAGE IN SMALL-TIME ILLEGAL DEALS** to engage in small-time illegal activity such as petty theft (*slang*) **6.** *vt* **PUSH SOMEBODY** to jostle or push somebody roughly ○ *One hustled me while the other stole my bag.* **7.** *vt* **COERCE SOMEBODY** to put pressure on somebody to do something without due thought ○ *hustled them into the purchase* ■ *n* **1.** **NOISY ACTIVITY** lively noisy continual activity ○ *enjoyed the hustle and bustle of the big city* **2.** *N Am* CRIME **RACKET OR SWINDLE** an act or scheme involving deceit, swindling, fraud, or petty theft (*slang*) [Late 17C. < Dutch *hutselen* 'shake (repeatedly), toss', < *hotsen* 'shake']

hustler /hússlər/ *n N Am* **1.** **AGGRESSIVELY DETERMINED PERSON** somebody who works aggressively and determinedly, especially to advance his or her career (*informal*) **2.** **PETTY CRIMINAL** somebody who engages in illegal activities such as petty theft or illegal gambling on a small scale (*informal*) **3.** **PROSTITUTE** a prostitute, especially a streetwalker or one who solicits in bars (*slang*)

Huston /hyoóstən/, **John** (1906–87) US film director and actor. The son of Walter Huston, he directed *The Maltese Falcon* (1941), *The African Queen* (1951), and won two Academy Awards for *The Treasure of the Sierra Madre* (1948).

> 'The directing of a picture involves coming out of your individual loneliness and taking a controlling part in putting together a small world.'
> [John Huston, *New York Journal*; 31 March 1960]

hut /hut/ *n* a small single-storey building, often made of wood, that is used as a simple house or shelter, or for storage, temporary accommodation, or leisure or community activities ○ *a scout hut* ■ *vt* (**huts, hutting, hutted**) to provide huts for a place, especially for accommodation [Mid-16C. Origin ?]

hutch /huch/ *n* **1.** a small shelter, usually constructed from wire and wood, for keeping small animals such as rabbits **2.** *N Am* a cupboard with drawers and usually open shelves on top, often used for storing and displaying dishes and kitchen utensils [12C. Via French *huche* < medieval Latin *hutica*]

Hutchinson-Gilford syndrome /húchins'n gílfərd-/ *n* MED same as **progeria** [After Sir Jonathan *Hutchinson* (1828–1913) and Hastings *Gilford* (1861–1941), British physicians]

hutment /hútmənt/ *n* a group of huts forming a military encampment

Hutterite /húttərīt/ *n* a member of an Anabaptist religious group who emigrated from Moravia mainly to Alberta and Manitoba in Canada, but also to areas of the northwestern United States where they formed farming communities [Late 19C. After Jacob *Hutter* (d. 1536), Moravian Anabaptist]

Hutton /hútt'n/, **James** (1726–97) Scottish geologist. He outlined the principles of uniformitarianism in *Theory of the Earth* (1795).

Hutt Valley /hút-/ urban area in the south of the North Island, New Zealand, near the city of Wellington. Population: 131,000 (2001).

Hutu /hoo too/ (*plural same* or **-tus**) *n* **1.** a member of a people who are the most populous in Rwanda and Burundi **2.** a Bantu language spoken in Rwanda and Burundi. Native speakers: 14 million. [Mid-20C. < Bantu] —**Hutu** *adj*

hutzpah *n* another spelling of **chutzpah**

Huxley /húksli/, **Aldous** (1894–1963) British novelist and essayist. His novels include *Point Counter Point* (1928), *Brave New World* (1932), and *Eyeless in Gaza* (1936). Full name **Huxley, Aldous Leonard**. See Cultural note at **brave new world**

> 'It takes two to make a murder. There are born victims, born to have their throats cut.'
> [Aldous Huxley, *Point Counter Point*; 1928]

> 'There can be no doubt that if tranquillizers could be bought as easily and cheaply as aspirin they would be consumed, not by the billions, as they are at present, but by the scores and hundreds of billions.'
> [Aldous Huxley, *Brave New World Revisited*; 1958]

Huxley, Andrew (*b.* 1917) British physiologist. He was joint winner of the Nobel Prize in physiology or medicine (1963) for his work on nerve impulses. Full name **Huxley, Andrew Fielding**

Huxley, Sir Julian (1887–1975) British biologist. He was the first director-general of UNESCO (1947–48) and the author of *Essays of a Biologist* (1923). Full name **Huxley, Sir Julian Sorell**

> 'The human race will be the cancer of the planet. Operationally, God is beginning to resemble not a ruler but the last fading smile of a cosmic Cheshire cat.'
> [Sir Julian Huxley, *Religion without Revelation*; 1957 ed.]

Huxley, T. H. (1825–95) British biologist. A supporter of Darwin, he wrote *Zoological Evidences as to Man's Place in Nature* (1863) and *Collected Essays* (1893–94). Full name **Huxley, Thomas Henry**

> 'The great tragedy of Science—the slaying of a beautiful hypothesis by an ugly fact.'
> [T. H. Huxley, 'Biogenesis and Abiogenesis', *Collected Essays*; 1893–94]

Huygens' eyepiece /hígənz-/ *n* an eyepiece consisting of two plano-convex lenses with their flat sides towards the eye, fitted mainly on optical instruments that are used for observation rather than measurement [Mid-19C. After Christiaan *Huygens* (1629–95), Dutch physicist and astronomer]

Huygens' principle *n* the proposition that every point on a wavefront acts as a source of secondary waves of light and that the wavefront at a later time is the envelope of these secondary waves [See HUYGENS' EYEPIECE]

huzzah /hoŏ zaá, hə-/ *interj, n* same as **hooray** (*archaic*) [Late 16C. Origin ?]

hv *abbr* PHYS high velocity

HV *abbr* 1. MED health visitor 2. PHYS high velocity 3. ELEC high voltage

HVAC *abbr* CIV ENG heating, ventilating, and air conditioning

HVT *abbr* MIL high-value target [Late 20C.]

HW *abbr* 1. ONLINE hardware 2. hazardous waste 3. high water 4. hit wicket 5. hot water

h.w. *abbr* CRICKET hit wicket

Hwange National Park /hwáng gi-/ largest national park in Zimbabwe, established in 1929. Area: 14,651 sq. km/5,657 sq. mi.

HWM *abbr* high-water mark

hwy *abbr* TRANSP highway

hwyl /hoŏ il/ *Wales* (*informal*) *n* good spirit or enthusiasm ■ *interj* used as a toast or to say goodbye [< Welsh]

hyacinth

hyacinth /hí ə sinth/ *n* a cultivated plant of the lily family. Flowers: fragrant pink, white, or blue, in spikes. Native to: northeastern Mediterranean. Latin name: *Hyacinthus orientalis.* [Mid-16C. Via French and Latin < Greek *huakinthos* 'plant sprung from the blood of Hyacinthus'] —**hyacinthine** /hí ə sín thīn/ *adj*

hyacinth bean *n* a deciduous woody-stemmed leguminous climbing plant. Flowers: pink, white. Latin name: *Dolichos lablab.*

hyacinth orchid *n* a leafless orchid that usually grows near eucalyptus trees. Flowers: dark pink with white spots. Native to: Australia. Latin name: *Dipodium punctatum.*

Hyacinthus /hí ə sínthəss/ *n* in Greek mythology, a young boy who was loved and accidentally killed by the god Apollo, who made a flower grow on the spot where the boy died

Hyades /hí ə deez/ *n* a cluster of over 200 stars in the constellation Taurus, whose five brightest members form a V-shaped group

hyaena *n* ZOOL another spelling of **hyena**

hyal- *prefix* same as **hyalo-** (*used before vowels*)

hyalin /hí ə lin/ *n* a clear glassy material found in hyaline cartilage or formed as a product of some skin diseases

hyaline /hí ə lin, -leen, -līn/ *adj* clear, translucent, and containing no fibres or granular material

hyaline cartilage *n* the most common type of cartilage, consisting of a bluish-white elastic material containing fine collagen fibres and providing flexibility and support at the joints. Hyaline cartilage is found at the ends of the long bones and in the nose and the larynx, and forms most of the foetal skeleton.

hyaline membrane disease *n* MED same as **respiratory distress syndrome**

hyalite /hí ə līt/ *n* a clear colourless variety of opal. Use: gems.

hyalitis /hí ə lítiss/ *n* inflammation of the transparent jelly (**vitreous humour**) that fills the chamber of the eye behind the lens

hyalo- *prefix* glass, glassy [< Greek *hualos* 'glass']

hyaloid /hí ə loyd/ *adj* clear and glassy in appearance

hyaloid membrane *n* a transparent insubstantial membrane surrounding the transparent jelly (**vitreous humour**) of the eye and separating it from the retina

hyaluronic acid /hí ə loŏ rónnik-/ *n* a complex viscous substance that lubricates joints and is present in connective tissue. It also plays a role in the healing of wounds. [< HYALOID (because first isolated in the vitreous humour) + *uronic* 'connected with urine']

hyaluronidase /hí ə loŏ rónnidayss, -dayz/ *n* an enzyme that breaks down hyaluronic acid, increasing the permeability of connective tissues

hybrid /híbrid/ *n* 1. BOT PLANT RESULTING FROM CROSSING a plant produced from a cross between two plants with different genetic constituents. Hybrids from crosses between crop varieties are often stronger and produce better yields than the original stock. 2. ZOOL ANIMAL RESULTING FROM CROSS-SPECIES MATING an animal that results from the mating of parents from two distinct species or subspecies 3. RESULT OF MIXING ELEMENTS something made up of a mixture of different aspects or components 4. LING WORD DERIVED FROM TWO LANGUAGES a word that has derived from two different languages, e.g. 'appendicitis', in which 'append' is from Latin and 'itis' is from Greek 5. AUTOMOT USING TWO FUELS a vehicle with an engine that runs on electricity and petrol, which it can alternate between ■ *adj* 1. BIOL CROSSBRED bred from two distinct species or subspecies 2. CONTAINING MIXED ELEMENTS made up of different aspects or components ○ *a hybrid literary form* 3. OF HYBRID being or relating to a hybrid 4. ELECTRONICS UNUSUAL AS ELECTRONIC CIRCUIT describes an electronic circuit that consists of two or more components not ordinarily combined with one another, e.g. a circuit that has integrated circuitry, transistors, and valves 5. ELECTRONICS WITH MULTIPLE INTEGRATED CIRCUITRY describes an electronic circuit containing more than one integrated circuit, all of which are attached to the same ceramic substrate [Early 17C. < Latin *hybrida*] —**hybridism** *n* —**hybridist** *n* —**hybridity** /hī bríddəti/ *n*

hybrid antibody *n* an artificial antibody synthesized to attach to two different antigens

hybrid bill *n* a parliamentary bill with some provisions affecting the public domain and others affecting private interests

hybrid computer *n* a computer employing both analogue and digital techniques

hybridize /híbri dīz/ (**-izes, -izing, -ized**), **hybridise** (**-ises, -ising, -ised**) *vti* to generate a new form of plant or animal, either by human intervention or naturally, by combining the genes of two different species or subspecies —**hybridizable** *adj* —**hybridization** /híbri dī záysh'n/ *n* —**hybridizer** *n*

hybridoma /híbri dṓmə/ *n* a hybrid cell produced by the fusion of a tumour cell with an antibody antibody-producing cell, which then proliferates and yields large amounts of a monoclonal antibody

hybrid rock *n* rock formed when molten magma incorporates solid material from the rock through which it flows, yielding a mixture of rock types

hybrid vigour *n* the increased growth, disease resistance, or fertility seen in hybrid species. For example mules, the offspring of mares and donkeys, are stronger and longer-lived than the parent animals.

hydathode /hídə thōd/ *n* a pore in the outer layer of a leaf that secretes water when the rate of transpiration is low, e.g. in humid conditions [Late 19C. < Greek *hudat-* 'water' + *hodos* 'way']

hydatid /hídətid/, **hydatid cyst** *n* a cyst formed in human tissue that contains the larvae of a tapeworm [Late 17C. < modern Latin < Greek *hudatis* 'drop of water, watery vesicle' < *hudat-* 'water']

hydatid disease *n* a condition resulting from the presence of hydatid cysts in the liver, lungs, or brain, which can cause malignancies, blindness, epilepsy, or fever

Hyderabad /hídərə bad/, **Hyderābād 1.** city and capital of Andhra Pradesh State, India, founded in 1589, situated on the River Musi. Population: 5,533,640 (2001). **2.** city in Sind Province, southeastern Pakistan, situated on the River Indus. Population: 1,151,274 (1998). **3.** former state in central India, now divided between the states of Andhra Pradesh, Karnataka, and Maharashtra

hydnocarpate /hídnō kaár payt/ *n* a salt of hydnocarpic acid

hydnocarpic acid /hídnō kaárpik-/ *n* a fatty acid containing a carbon ring in its structure. Source: glycerides in chaulmoogra oil. Formula: $C_{16}H_{28}O_2$. [< *hydnocarpus*, plant yielding an oil containing this acid < Greek *hudnon* 'truffle' + *karpos* 'fruit', from the fruit's appearance]

hydr- *prefix* same as **hydro-** (*used before vowels*)

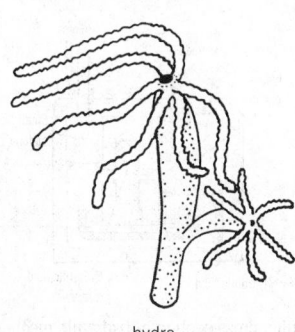

hydra

hydra /hídrə/ (*plural* **-dras** or **-drae** /-dree/) *n* a freshwater polyp with a cylindrical body at one end and a mouth surrounded by tentacles at the other. Genus: *Hydra.* [Late 18C. Via modern Latin < Greek *hudra* 'water snake']

Hydra *n* 1. a constellation near the celestial equator. See illustration at **constellation 2.** in Greek mythology, a monster that had nine heads and was killed by Heracles. When one head was cut off, another grew instantly in its place.

hydracid /hī drássid/ *n* an acid such as hydrochloric acid in which the hydrogen atoms are bound to an atom other than oxygen

hydragogue /hídrə gog/ *n* a laxative that acts by osmosis by drawing water into the intestinal canal from the blood, thereby softening the contents. Epsom salts, once the principal hydragogue, has now been superseded by complex sugars such as lactulose that work in the same way. [Mid-17C. Via late Latin < Greek *hudragōgos* 'conveying water' < *hudr-* 'water']

hydra-headed *adj* having many heads or parts like heads

hydralazine /hī drállə zeen/ *n* a drug that lowers blood pressure, usually given with drugs that cause increased urine output [Mid-20C. < HYDRO- + PHTHALIC ACID + AZINE]

hydrangea /hī dráynjə/ *n* an erect or climbing evergreen or deciduous bush. Flowers: white, pink, or blue, in large clusters in a variety of shapes. Native to: Asia. Genus: *Hydrangea.* [Mid-18C. < modern Latin, literally 'water pot'; from its cup-shaped seed pod]

hydrant /hídrənt/ *n* an upright pipe, usually in a street, connected to a water main with a valve to which a hose can be attached, e.g. by the fire service [Early 19C. < HYDRO-]

hydranth /hí dranth/ *n* the sedentary form in the life cycle of a cnidarian such as a sea anemone or a hydra [Late 19C. < HYDRA + Greek *anthos* 'flower']

hydrarch /hí draark/ *adj* describes the development of a sequence of ecological stages that begins in a freshwater habitat such as a pond [Early 20C. < HYDRO- + Greek *arkhē* 'beginning']

hydrase /hí drayss, -drayz/ *n* an enzyme that catalyses the addition or removal of water

hydrastine /hī drás teen, -tin/ *n* a poisonous white substance. Source: roots of the goldenseal plant. Use: formerly, to stop haemorrhaging, shrink the uterus, reduce inflammation of mucous membranes. Formula: $C_{21}H_{21}NO_6$. [Mid-19C. < modern Latin *Hydrastis*, plant genus name < HYDRO-]

hydrastinine /hī drásti neen, -nin/ *n* an organic compound forming colourless crystals, soluble in water and resembling hydrastine in its medicinal properties. Formula: $C_{11}H_{13}NO_3$.

hydrate /hī drayt, hī dráyt/ *vt* (**-drates, -drating, -drated**) **1.** GIVE WATER TO SOMEBODY OR SOMETHING to provide water for somebody or something in order to re-establish or maintain a correct fluid balance **2.** CHEM ADD WATER TO SOMETHING to add water to a chemical compound so that different crystals are formed ■ *n* CHEM COMPOUND CONTAINING WATER a chemical compound containing water molecules that can usually be expelled by heating, without decomposition of the compound [Early 19C. < French (noun) < Greek *hudr-* 'water'] —**hydration** /hīdráysh'n/ *n* —**hydrator** *n*

hydrated /hī draytid, hī dráytid/ *adj* describes a chemical compound that contains water

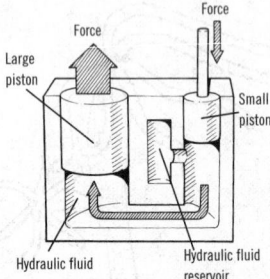

hydraulic: cross-section of hydraulic mechanism

hydraulic /hī dróllik/ *adj* relating to or operated by a device in which pressure applied to a piston is transmitted by a fluid to a larger piston, so as to give rise to a larger force [Early 17C. Via Latin < Greek *hudraulikos* < *hudōr* 'water' + *aulos* 'pipe'] —**hydraulically** *adv*

hydraulic brake *n* a brake in which force applied to a pedal is transmitted to the brake pads by an enclosed liquid, usually a glycol mixture

hydraulic coupling *n* an arrangement in which two pistons of different sizes are connected by an enclosed fluid that can transmit pressure from one piston to the other

hydraulic press *n* a device in which a relatively small force applied to a piston results in movement of a larger piston to which it is hydraulically coupled by an enclosed liquid. A hydraulic press is often the key part of machinery that forces materials to flow into a preformed shape.

hydraulic ram *n* **1.** the larger working piston of a hydraulic press **2.** a device that uses the kinetic energy of a flow of water to raise water to a reservoir that is higher than the water source itself

hydraulics /hī drólliks/ *n* the study of water or other fluids at rest or in motion, especially with respect to engineering applications (*takes a singular verb*)

hydrazide /hīdrə zīd/ *n* a compound formed by the reaction of hydrazine with a carboxylic acid [Late 19C. < HYDR- + AZO-]

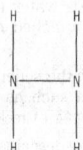

hydrazine

hydrazine /hīdrə zeen/ *n* a highly reactive colourless liquid or white crystalline solid made from sodium hypochlorite and ammonia. Use: in rocket fuel. Formula: $H_2N.NH_2$. [Late 19C. < HYDR- + AZO-]

hydrazoic acid /hīdrə zṓ ik-/ *n* a colourless liquid that is highly toxic and explosive in the presence of oxygen. Formula: HN_3. [< HYDR- + AZO-]

hydric /hídrik/ *adj* **1.** containing or using considerable amounts of water **2.** relating to an environment that is extremely wet

hydride /hī drīd/ *n* a chemical compound formed between hydrogen and a more electropositive atom, e.g. sodium hydride, or via a covalent bond, e.g. boron hydride. Hydrides can also be formed with transition metals such as platinum and palladium.

hydrilla /hī drílla/ (*plural* **-las** or *same*) *n* a plant that grows underwater in large masses and oxygenates the water. Genus: *Hydrilla*. [Early 19C. < modern Latin, 'little hydra' < Latin *hydra* (see HYDRA)]

hydriodic acid /hídri óddik-/ *n* a colourless or pale yellow strong acid. Source: dissolving of hydrogen iodide gas in water. [< HYDR- + IODINE]

hydro[1] /hídrō/ (*plural* **-dros**) *n* **1.** a power plant that generates electricity using water pressure **2.** power generated using water pressure [Early 20C. Shortening of HYDROELECTRIC]

hydro[2] /hídrō/ (*plural* **-dros**) *n* a hotel, resort, or clinic offering hydropathic treatment [Late 19C. Shortening of *hydropathic treatment*]

hydro- *prefix* **1.** water, liquid, moisture ○ *hydrobiology* **2.** hydrogen ○ *hydrocarbon* [< Greek *hudr-*, stem of *hudōr* 'water' < Indo-European]

hydroacoustics /hídrō ə koòstiks/ *n* the branch of acoustics that studies how sound travels in water (*takes a singular verb*)

hydrobiology /hídrō bī ólləji/ *n* the branch of biology that studies water animals and plants —**hydrobiological** /-bī ə lójjik'l/ *adj* —**hydrobiologist** *n*

hydrobromic acid /hídrō brómik-/ *n* a colourless or pale yellow strong acid. Source: dissolving hydrogen bromide gas in water. Formula: HBr.

hydrocarbon /hídrō kaárbən/ *n* an organic chemical compound containing only hydrogen and carbon atoms arranged in rows, rings, or both, and connected by single, double, or triple bonds. Hydrocarbons constitute a very large group including alkanes, alkenes, and alkynes. —**hydrocarbonaceous** /-kaarbə náyshəss/ *adj* —**hydrocarbonic** /-kaar bónnik/ *adj* —**hydrocarbonous** /-kaárbənəss/ *adj*

hydrocele /hídrō seel/ *n* an accumulation of watery liquid in a body cavity, especially in the sac round the testes. It is a painless condition that can be treated surgically by draining the fluid.

hydrocellulose /hídrō séllyoōlōss, -lōz/ *n* a gelatinous substance formed when cellulose is mixed with water, acids, or alkalis, e.g. in the manufacture of paper or rayon

hydrocephalus /hídrō séffələss, -kéffələss/, **hydrocephaly** /-séffəli, -kéffəli/ *n* an increase of cerebrospinal fluid round the brain, resulting in an enlargement of the head in infants, because the bones of the skull are still unfused. The fluid is blocked by a congenital condition or a disease, and can be drained into the abdominal cavity. [Late 17C. < modern Latin < Greek *hudōr* 'water' + *kephalē* 'head'] —**hydrocephalic** /-sə fállik, -kə-/ *adj* —**hydrocephaloid** /-séffə loyd, -kéffə-/ *adj* —**hydrocephalous** *adj*

hydrochloric acid /hídrə klórrik-/ *n* a strong colourless acid. Source: dissolving hydrogen chloride gas in water. Use: industrial and laboratory processes. Formula: HCl.

hydrochloride /hídrō kláwr īd/ *n* a salt formed when hydrochloric acid reacts with an organic base, e.g. aniline

hydrochlorofluorocarbon /hídrō klawrō floorō kaárbən/ *n* CHEM full form of HCFC [Late 20C. < HYDRO- CHLORIDE]

hydrochlorothiazide /hídrō kláwrō thī ə zīd/ *n* a drug used in the treatment of fluid retention and high blood pressure

hydrocolloid /hídrō kólloyd/ *n* a substance that forms a gel when mixed with water —**hydrocolloidal** /hídrōkə lóyd'l/ *adj*

hydrocolloid strip *n* a gelatinous waterproof dressing that seals a wound, retaining moisture and protecting from germs and dirt

hydrocoral /hídrə kórral/ *n* a multicellular organism that lives in the sea in colonies and builds calcareous skeletons within which the animals live. Order: Milleporina or Stylasterina.

hydrocortisone /hídrə káwrtizōn/ *n* **1.** a steroid hormone secreted by the adrenal cortex, involved in carbohydrate metabolism and the stress reaction **2.** a synthetic form of hydrocortisone. Use: treatment of allergies, inflammation, and adrenal failure.

hydrocracking /hídrō kraking/ *n* an industrial process in which the action of hydrogen under high pressure fragments long-chain hydrocarbons to produce more volatile compounds such as petrol and paraffin

hydrocyanic acid /hídrō sī ánnik-/ *n* a colourless weak acid that smells of almonds. Source: dissolving of hydrogen cyanide in water.

hydrodynamic /hídrō dī námmik/, **hydrodynamical** /-námmik'l/ *adj* **1.** relating to the mechanical properties of liquids **2.** operated by a moving liquid —**hydrodynamically** *adv*

hydrodynamics /hídrō dī námmiks/ *n* the area of fluid dynamics that is concerned with the study of liquids (*takes a singular verb*) —**hydrodynamicist** /-námmissist/ *n*

hydroelectric /hídrō i léktrik/ *adj* **1.** generated by converting the pressure of falling or running water to electricity by means of a turbine coupled to a generator **2.** relating to the generation of electricity by means of water pressure —**hydroelectrically** *adv* —**hydroelectricity** /hídrō i lek tríssəti/ *n*

hydrofluoric acid /hídrō floórrik-/ *n* an extremely poisonous corrosive colourless liquid. Source: dissolving of hydrogen fluoride in water. Use: etching glass, treatment of metal surfaces, cleaning masonry. Formula: HF.

hydrofluorocarbon /hídrō floorō kaárbən/ *n* a chemical compound composed of hydrogen, fluorine, and carbon. Use: preparation of plastics and pharmaceuticals.

hydrofoil

hydrofoil /hídrə foyl/ *n* **1.** a boat with wing-shaped blades fixed to struts under the hull that lift the boat out of the water as the speed increases **2.** a wing-shaped blade that lifts a hydrofoil out of the water

hydroforming /hídrō fawrming/ *n* **1.** a high-temperature process in which hydrogen, with other catalysts, causes some hydrocarbons to break down, lose hydrogen, and rearrange themselves into aromatic or cyclic forms. It is used in the petroleum industry to impart better antiknock properties to petrol. **2.** a process in which sheet metal is shaped by a punch forced against a flexible shaped block resting on a fluid-filled bag

hydrogel /hídrə jel/ *n* a thick fluid like a jelly, formed by the addition of a substance to water

hydrogen /hídrəjən/ *n* a highly reactive colourless gas, the lightest element and the most abundant in the universe. Source: water, most organic compounds. Use: industrial processes, production of ammonia, reduction of metal ores to metals. Symbol H. See table at **element** [Late 18C. < French *hydrogène* < Greek *hudōr* 'water' + French *-gène* (see -GEN)]

hydrogenase /hī drójjə nayss, -nayz/ *n* an enzyme that catalyses reduction reactions by hydrogen

hydrogenate /hī drójjə nayt/ (**-ates, -ating, -ated**) *vt* to add hydrogen to a compound in a chemical reaction —**hydrogenation** /hī drójjə náysh'n/ *n* —**hydrogenator** *n*

hydrogen bomb *n* an explosive weapon of mass destruction in which huge amounts of energy are released by the fusion of hydrogen nuclei

hydrogen bond *n* an electrostatic interaction between molecules of compounds in which hydrogen atoms are bound to electronegative atoms such as oxygen or nitrogen. The attraction between water molecules due to hydrogen bonds accounts for the relatively high boiling point of water.

hydrogen bromide *n* a colourless gas usually made by the combination of hydrogen and bromine in the presence of a catalyst such as platinum. It forms hydrobromic acid in water solution. Formula: HBr.

hydrogen carbonate *n* a salt of carbonic acid in which one hydrogen atom has been replaced, usually by a metal

hydrogen chloride *n* a colourless fuming corrosive gas. Source: by-product of organic chlorination reactions. Use: manufacture of PVC. Formula: HCl.

hydrogen cyanide *n* an extremely poisonous colourless liquid or gas with a characteristic smell of almonds. Source: reaction between an acid and a metal cyanide. Formula: HCN.

hydrogen embrittlement /-im brítt'lmənt/ *n* a process in which a metal is weakened by the incorporation of hydrogen in or below its surface, e.g. during plating or etching

hydrogen fluoride *n* a colourless corrosive liquid. Source: action of sulphuric acid on a metal fluoride. Formula: HF.

hydrogen iodide *n* a colourless poisonous gas. Source: reaction of hydrogen and iodine in the presence of a catalyst, usually platinum. Formula: HI.

hydrogen ion *n* a positively charged ion of hydrogen that is formed by the removal of an electron from a hydrogen atom and is present in solutions of acids in water. The degree to which a compound produces hydrogen ions in solution is measured on the pH scale, 1 being highly acidic, 7 being neutral, and 14 being highly alkaline.

hydrogenize /hī drójjə nīz/ (**-nizes, -nizing, -nized**), **hydrogenise** (**-nises, -nising, -nised**) *vt* CHEM same as **hydrogenate** —**hydrogenization** /hī drójjə nī záysh'n/ *n*

hydrogenolysis /hídrəjə nóllessiss/ *n* the breaking of a bond in a molecule of an organic compound by the action of hydrogen, accompanied by the addition of a hydrogen atom to each of the fragments

hydrogenous /hī drójjənəss/ *adj* containing hydrogen

hydrogen peroxide *n* a colourless viscous unstable liquid that readily decomposes in water and oxygen. Use: bleach, mild antiseptic, component in rocket fuel. Formula: H_2O_2.

hydrogen sulphate *n* a salt containing the ion HSO_4O^-, formed when one hydrogen atom is removed from sulphuric acid by reaction with a metal, metal salt, or organic group

hydrogen sulphide *n* a colourless flammable poisonous gas with a characteristic smell of rotten eggs. Source: action of a mineral acid such as hydrochloric acid on a metal sulphide. Formula: H_2S.

hydrogen sulphite *n* a salt containing the ion HSO_3^-

hydrogen tartrate *n* a salt or ester of tartaric acid, e.g. potassium hydrogen tartrate, that forms deposits in wine vats

hydrogeology /hídrō ji óllaji/ *n* the branch of geology that studies the movement of subsurface water through rocks and the effect of moving water on rocks, including their erosion —**hydrogeologic** /hídrō ji ə lójjik/ *adj* —**hydrogeological** *adj* —**hydrogeologist** *n*

hydrography /hī dróggrafi/ *n* the scientific study of seas, lakes, and rivers, especially the charting of tides and changes in coastal bathymetry or the measurement and recording of river flow —**hydrograph** /hídrə graaf, -graf/ *n* —**hydrographer** *n* —**hydrographic** /hídrə gráffik/ *adj* —**hydrographically** *adv*

hydroid /hī droyd/ *n* **1.** an invertebrate sea animal with an internal body cavity that lives in colonies, forming growths like tufts. Order: Hydroida. **2.** an asexual polyp that is part of the life cycle of hydrozoans [Mid-19C. < HYDRA]

hydrokinetics /hídrō ki néttiks, -kī-/ *n* the branch of physics concerned with the scientific study of the properties and behaviour of fluids in motion (*takes a singular verb*)

hydrolase /hídrə layz, -layss/ *n* an enzyme that controls hydrolysis, e.g. an esterase [Early 20C. < HYDROLYSIS]

~~**hydrolic**~~ incorrect spelling of **hydraulic**

hydrologic cycle /hídrə lójjik-/, **hydrological cycle** /-lójjik'l-/ *n* METEOROL same as **water cycle** (*technical*)

hydrology /hī drólləji/ *n* the scientific study of the properties, distribution, use, and circulation of the water on Earth and in the atmosphere in all of its forms —**hydrologist** *n*

hydrolysate /hī dróllə sayt/ *n* a substance produced by hydrolysis

hydrolyse /hídrə līz/ (**-lyses, -lysing, -lysed**) *vti* to undergo hydrolysis, or make a substance undergo hydrolysis [Late 19C. < HYDROLYSIS, after ANALYSIS, ANALYSE] —**hydrolysable** *adj* —**hydrolysation** /hídrə lī záysh'n/ *n*

hydrolysis /hī drólləssiss/ *n* a chemical reaction in which a compound reacts with water, causing decomposition and the production of two or more other compounds, e.g. in the conversion of starch to glucose —**hydrolytic** /hídrə líttik/ *adj* —**hydrolytically** *adv*

hydrolyze *vti* CHEM US spelling of **hydrolyse**

hydromagnetics /hídrō mag néttiks/ *n* MECH ENG same as **magnetohydrodynamics** (*takes a singular verb*) —**hydromagnetic** *adj*

hydromancy /hídrō manssi/ *n* the practice of attempting to foretell events or discover unknown knowledge by studying the appearance or movement of water —**hydromancer** *n* —**hydromantic** /hídrō mántik/ *adj*

hydromechanics /hídrō mi kánniks/ *n* MECH ENG same as **hydrodynamics** (*takes a singular verb*) —**hydromechanical** *adj*

hydromedusa /hídrōmi dyoóssə/ (*plural* **-sae** /-ssee/) *n* a free-swimming invertebrate sea animal, resembling a tiny jellyfish, that is the reproductive stage of a hydroid

hydromel /hídrō mel/ *n* a drink made of honey mixed in water. If allowed to ferment, it turns into mead. [15C. Via Latin < Greek *hudromeli* 'water honey' < *meli* 'honey']

hydrometallurgy /hídrō me tállərji/ *n* the extraction of metals from ores by treating them with aqueous chemical solutions, including extraction by electrolysis and ion exchange —**hydrometallurgical** /hídrō metə lúrjik'l/ *adj*

hydrometeor /hídrō méeti ər/ *n* a weather condition caused by condensation of water in the atmosphere, e.g. rain, snow, or fog —**hydrometeorological** /-méeti ərə lójjik'l/ *adj* —**hydrometeorologist** /-méeti ə rólləjist/ *n* —**hydrometeorology** *n*

hydrometer /hī drómmitər/ *n* a device, usually a sealed graduated tube containing a weighted bulb, used to determine the specific gravity or density of a liquid —**hydrometric** /hídrō méttrik/ *adj* —**hydrometrically** *adv* —**hydrometry** *n*

hydromorphic /hídrō máwrfik/ *adj* relating to or typical of a soil that has built up in the presence of excess water

hydronium ion /hī dróni əm-/ *n* CHEM same as **hydroxonium ion** [Contraction]

hydropathy /hī dróppəthi/ *n* the treatment of injuries or disease by applying water both internally and externally —**hydropath** /hídrə path/ *n* —**hydropathic** /hídrō páthik/ *adj* —**hydropathical** *adj* —**hydropathically** *adv*

hydroperoxide /hídrōpə rók sīd/ *n* an intermediate compound formed during the oxidation of unsaturated organic substances and containing the group -OOH

hydrophane /hídrə fayn/ *n* a translucent lustrous form of opal —**hydrophanous** /hī dróffənəss/ *adj*

hydrophilic /hídrō fíllik/ *adj* dissolving in, absorbing, or mixing easily with water —**hydrophile** /hídrə fīl/ *n* —**hydrophilicity** /hídrōfi líssəti/ *n*

hydrophobia /hídrō fóbi ə/ *n* **1.** MED same as **rabies 2.** an extremely intense aversion to water, especially the fear of drinking water or other liquids

hydrophobic /hídrō fóbik/ *adj* **1.** relating to or affected by an extreme fear of water **2.** CHEM not dissolving in, absorbing, or mixing easily with water —**hydrophobe** /hídrəfōb/ *n* —**hydrophobicity** /hídrōfō bíssəti/ *n*

hydrophone /hídrəfōn/ *n* an electronic receiver that can pick up sound travelling through water by

converting acoustic energy into electromagnetic waves. One use is tracking submarines.

hydrophyte /hídrə fīt/ *n* a plant that will only grow in water or in a very damp environment —**hydrophytic** /hídrə fíttik/ *adj*

hydroplane /hídrō playn/ *n* **1.** FAST BOAT a motorboat designed so that it rises up out of the water at high speed and skims along the surface **2.** VANE ON SUBMARINE a horizontal vane on a submarine, used to control its vertical movement **3.** *US* AEROSP same as **seaplane** ■ *vi* (**-planes, -planing, -planed**) **1.** SKIM SURFACE to skim along on the surface of the water **2.** *N Am* same as **aquaplane** *v* (sense 2)

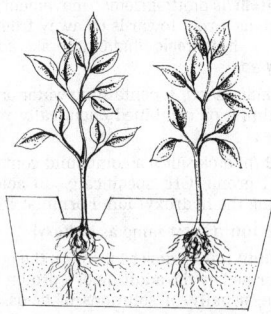
hydroponics

hydroponics /hídrō pónniks/ *n* the cultivation of plants in a nutrient liquid with or without gravel or another supporting medium (*takes a singular verb*) [Mid-20C. < HYDRO- + Greek *ponos* 'work'] —**hydroponic** *adj* —**hydroponically** *adv* —**hydroponicist** /hídrō pónnissist/ *n* —**hydroponist** /hī dróppənist/ *n*

hydropower /hídrō powər/ *n* electric power generated using water power

hydroquinone /hídrōkwi nón/, **hydroquinol** /-nól/ *n* a white crystalline compound. Use: photographic developer, in paints, in motor oils, in medicines. Formula: $C_6H_4(OH)_2$.

hydroscope /hídrə skōp/ *n* an optical instrument constructed from a series of mirrors encased in a tube, used for observing objects deep beneath the surface of a body of water —**hydroscopic** /hídrə skóppik/ *adj* —**hydroscopical** *adj* —**hydroscopically** *adv*

hydroski /hídrō skee/ *n* a hydrofoil on a seaplane, usually ski-shaped and retractable, used to give extra lift on takeoff

hydrosol /hídrə sol/ *n* a colloidal solution in which the particles are suspended in water [Mid-19C. < HYDRO- + SOLUTION] —**hydrosolic** /hídrə sóllik/ *adj*

hydrospace /hídrə spayss/ *n* the area beneath the surface of the seas

hydrosphere /hídrə sfeer/ *n* the portion of Earth's surface that is water, including the seas and water in the atmosphere —**hydrospheric** /hídrə sférrik/ *adj*

hydrostat /hídrō stat/ *n* a device designed to regulate the height of fluid in a column or container. Use: measurement and control of relative humidity or, in steam boilers, to detect a low water level

hydrostatic /hídrō státtik/, **hydrostatical** /-státtik'l/ *adj* **1.** relating to, involving, or typical of fluids that are at rest and the forces and pressures they exert **2.** relating to, involving, or typical of hydrostatics [Mid-17C. Probably < modern Latin *hydrostaticus* or < its source Greek *hudrostatēs* 'hydrostatic balance' < *statikos* 'causing to stand'] —**hydrostatically** *adv*

hydrostatics /hídrō státtiks/ *n* the scientific study of the equilibrium of liquids at rest and the forces and pressures exerted by them (*takes a singular verb*) —**hydrostatically** *adv*

hydrostatic skeleton *n* the most primitive form of skeletal structure, found in animals such as jellyfish and worms, that consists of layers of muscle around a fluid-filled body cavity

hydrotaxis /hídrō táksiss/ *n* the response of an organism or cell to the presence of water or moisture, usually detected as movement —**hydrotactic** /hídrō táktik/ *adj*

hydrotherapeutics /hídrō thérrə pyoótiks/ *n* the scientific study and theory of the external use of water for healing (*takes a singular verb*) —**hydrotherapeutic** *adj*

hydrotherapy /hídrō thérrəpi/ *n* the treatment of disease by the external use of water, e.g. by exercising weakened limbs in a pool —**hydrotherapist** *n*

hydrothermal /hídrō thúrm'l/ *adj* relating to, or produced by, the action of extremely hot water on the Earth's crust ○ *hydrothermal deposits* —**hydrothermally** *adv*

hydrothorax /hídrō tháw raks/ *n* a buildup of fluid in a pleural cavity, e.g. as a result of failing circulation caused by heart disease [Late 18C. < modern Latin < Greek *hudōr* 'water' + *thōrax* 'chest'] —**hydrothoracic** /hídrō thaw rássik/ *adj*

hydrotropism /hī dróttrəpizəm/ *n* movement by a plant part such as a root towards or away from a source of water —**hydrotropic** /hídrō tróppik/ *adj* —**hydrotropically** *adv*

hydrous /hídrəss/ *adj* 1. containing water or moisture 2. containing or combined chemically with water molecules

hydroxide /hī drók sīd/ *n* a compound containing the hydroxyl group -OH, specifically an acid or base containing the hydroxyl ion. Formula: OH⁻.

hydroxide ion *n* CHEM same as **hydroxyl**

hydroxonium ion /hī drok sóni əm-/ *n* the positive ion that is formed by the addition of a proton to a water molecule, usually in solutions of acids. Formula: H_3O^+. [Early 20C. < HYDRO- + *oxonium* < OXY-, after AMMONIUM]

hydroxy /hī dróksi/ *adj* containing one or more hydroxyl groups

hydroxyapatite /hī dróksi áppə tīt/ *n* a hydrated calcium phosphate mineral

hydroxyl /hī dróksil/ *n* the negative ion formed by the attachment of an oxygen atom and a hydrogen atom. Formula: OH⁻. [Mid-19C. < HYDRO- + OXY- + -YL] —**hydroxylic** /hī drok síllik/ *adj*

hydroxylamine /hī dróksilə meén, hī dróksil ámmin/ *n* a colourless crystalline compound that decomposes at room temperature and explodes on heating. Use: reducing agent, in the synthesis of organic molecules. Formula: NH_2OH.

hydroxylate /hī dróksi layt/ **(-ates, -ating, -ated)** *vt* to introduce hydroxyl into a compound —**hydroxylation** /hī dróksi láysh'n/ *n*

hydroxyl ion *n* CHEM same as **hydroxyl**

hydroxyproline /hī dróksi pró leen/ *n* an amino acid derived from proline that is a component of collagen

hydrozoan /hídrō zó ən/ *n* a sea or freshwater invertebrate animal, e.g. a polyp or jellyfish. Class: Hydrozoa. [Late 19C. < modern Latin *Hydrozoa* 'water animals' < Greek *hudōr* 'water' + *zōia*, plural of *zōion* 'animal']

Hydrus /hídrəss/ *n* a constellation of the southern hemisphere. See illustration at **constellation**

hyena

hyena /hī eénə/, **hyaena** *n* a carnivorous scavenging animal resembling a dog, with a sloping back and loping gait. Native to: Africa, South Asia. Family: Hyaenidae. [14C. Directly or via French < Latin *hyaena* < Greek *huaina*, form of *hus* 'pig'] —**hyenic** *adj*

hyetal /hī ət'l/ *adj* relating to rain or rainfall [Mid-19C. < Greek *huetos* 'rain' (see HYETO-)]

hyeto- *prefix* rain ○ *hyetograph* [< Greek *huetos* < *huein* 'to rain']

hyetograph /hī ətō graaf, -graf/ *n* 1. a chart or graph showing the pattern of rainfall in an area 2. an instrument that automatically collects rain and measures its amount —**hyetographically** /hī ətō gráffikli/ *adv* —**hyetography** /hī ə tóggrəfi/ *n*

Hygeia /hī jeé ə/ *n* in Greek mythology, the goddess of health. The daughter of Asclepius, she is often represented as a maiden feeding a snake.

~~hygeine~~ incorrect spelling of **hygiene**

Hygiea /hī jeé ə/ *n* the fourth-largest asteroid, discovered in 1849. It has a diameter of approximately 420 km.

hygiene /hī jeen/ *n* 1. the science dealing with the preservation of health 2. the practice or principles of cleanliness [Late 17C. Directly or via French *hygiène* < modern Latin *(ars) hygieina* 'healthful art' < Greek *hugiēs* 'healthy']

hygienic /hī jeénik/ *adj* 1. OF CLEANLINESS relating to the scientific study or principles of cleanliness 2. PROMOTING HEALTH promoting health or cleanliness 3. GERM-FREE clean or free from disease-causing microorganisms —**hygienically** *adv*

hygienics /hī jeéniks/ *n* HEALTH same as **hygiene** (sense 1) (*takes a singular verb*)

hygienist /hī jeenist/ *n* a student of or expert in the maintenance of hygiene

hygro- *prefix* moisture, humidity ○ *hygrometer* [< Greek *hugros* 'moist' < Indo-European]

hygrograph /hígrə graaf, -graf/ *n* an automatic hygrometer that records the humidity of the air

hygrometer /hī grómmitər/ *n* an instrument used to measure humidity —**hygrometric** /hígrə méttrik/ *adj* —**hygrometrically** *adv*

hygrophilous /hī gróffələss/ *adj* describes plants that are adapted to growing in damp places

hygrophyte /hígrə fīt/ *n* BOT same as **hydrophyte** —**hygrophytic** /hígrə fíttik/ *adj*

hygroscope /hígrə skōp/ *n* an instrument that shows changes in the humidity of the air but does not measure the changes

hygroscopic /hígrə skóppik/, **hygroscopical** /-skóppik'l/ *adj* capable of easily absorbing moisture, e.g. from the air —**hygroscopically** *adv* —**hygroscopicity** /hígrəskō píssəti/ *n*

hygrostat /hígrə stat/ *n* METEOROL same as **humidistat**

hying present participle of **hie**

Hyksos /híksoss/ (*plural same*) *n* a member of an ancient nomadic people from western Asia, probably of Semitic ancestry, who conquered and ruled Egypt between 1720 BC and 1560 BC [Early 17C. Via Greek *Huksōs* < Egyptian *heqa khoswe* 'foreign rulers'] —**Hyksos** *adj*

hyla /hílə/ *n* a tree frog of a genus found all over the world. Genus: *Hyla*. [Mid-19C. Via modern Latin < Greek *hulē* 'wood']

hylo- *prefix* matter ○ *hylotheism* [< Greek *hulē* 'wood, matter']

hylobate /hílə bayt/ *n* same as **gibbon** (*technical*) [Late 20C. < modern Latin *Hylobates*]

hylomorphism /hílə máwrfizəm/ *n* the belief that all material objects are made up of matter, which is only potential, and form, which makes the object an actuality

hylotheism /hílə theé izəm/ *n* the belief that God and the material world are the same

hylozoism /hílə zó izəm/ *n* the belief that all matter is living [Late 17C. < HYLO- + Greek *zōē* 'life'] —**hylozoic** *adj*

hymen /hī men/ *n* a thin mucous membrane that completely or partially covers the opening of the vagina [Mid-16C. Directly or via French < late Latin < Greek *humēn* 'membrane']

Hymen /hī men/ *n* in Greek mythology, the god of marriage, often represented as a youth holding a torch

hymeneal /hī me neé əl/ (*literary*) *adj* relating to, involving, or characteristic of marriage ■ *n* a song or poem celebrating a wedding [Early 17C. < Latin *hymenaeus* 'wedding song, wedding' < Greek *humenaios* < *Humēn* 'Hymen'] —**hymeneally** *adv*

hymenium /hī meéni əm/ (*plural* **-nia** /-ni ə/ *or* **-niums**) *n* a layer of spore-bearing structures within or on the surface of the fruiting body of a fungus [Early 19C. Via modern Latin < Greek *humenion* 'small membrane' < *humēn* 'membrane'] —**hymenial** *adj*

hymenopteran /hímə nóptərən/, **hymenopteron** *n* an insect that has two pairs of membranous wings and a very thin waist and that lives in socially complex colonies, e.g. the wasp, ant, and sawfly. Order: Hymenoptera. [Mid-19C. < modern Latin *Hymenoptera* < form of Greek *humenopteros* 'membrane-winged' < *humēn* 'membrane' + *pteron* 'wing'] —**hymenopteran** *adj* —**hymenopterous** *adj*

hymn /him/ *n* 1. RELIGIOUS SONG a song of praise to God, a god, or a saint 2. SONG OF PRAISE a song of praise to somebody or something other than a deity ■ *v* (**hymns, hymning, hymned**) 1. *vt* PRAISE SOMEBODY OR SOMETHING IN SONG to sing in praise of somebody or something 2. *vi* SING HYMNS to sing songs of praise [Pre-12C. Via Latin < Greek *humnos* 'song in praise of gods or heroes'] —**hymnic** /hímnik/ *adj*

hymnal /hímnəl/ *n* same as **hymn book** (*dated*)

hymn book *n* a book that contains the words and sometimes the music of hymns sung in church

hymnist /hímnist/ *n* a composer of hymns

hymnody /hímnədi/ (*plural* **-dies**) *n* 1. the composition or singing of hymns 2. hymns collectively, especially a group of hymns that share a characteristic such as time of composition or use in a particular church [Early 18C. Via medieval Latin < Greek *humnōidia* 'singing of hymns' < *humnos* 'song in praise of gods or heroes']

hymnology /him nólləji/ (*plural* **-gies**) *n* 1. the study of religious hymns 2. CHR same as **hymnody** —**hymnologic** /hímnə lójjik/ *adj* —**hymnological** *adj* —**hymnologist** *n*

hyoid /hí oyd/ *n* ANAT same as **hyoid bone** ■ *adj* relating to or involving the hyoid bone [Early 19C. Via French *hyoïde* < Greek *huoeidēs* 'shaped like the Greek letter upsilon' < *hu* 'upsilon']

hyoid bone *n* a U-shaped bone positioned at the base of the tongue and above the thyroid cartilage that supports the tongue and its muscles

hyoscine /hí ō seen/ *n* CHEM same as **scopolamine** [Late 19C. < modern Latin *Hyoscyamus* (see HYOSCYAMINE)]

hyoscyamine /hí ō sí ə meen/ *n* a poisonous alkaloid that resembles atropine. Source: henbane, belladonna. Use: dilates blood vessels, prevents or controls spasms. [Mid-19C. < modern Latin *Hyoscyamus*, genus name of the henbane < Greek *huoskuamos* 'pig's bean' < genitive of *hus* 'pig' + *kuamos* 'bean']

hyp. *abbr* 1. MATHS hypotenuse 2. hypothesis 3. hypothetical

hyp- *prefix* same as **hypo-** (*used before vowels*)

hypabyssal /híppə bíss'l/ *adj* describes igneous rocks, especially in the form of dykes or sills, created when molten magma rose to the surface of the Earth's crust but solidified before reaching it —**hypabyssally** *adv*

hypaesthesia /híp eess theézi ə/ *n* an unusually reduced sensitivity to touch [Late 19C. < modern Latin, 'condition of sensation being below normal' < Greek *hupo-* (see HYPO-) + *aisthēsis* 'sensation'] —**hypaesthetic** /híp eessthéttik/ *adj*

hypaethral /hi peéthrəl, hī-/ *adj* lacking a roof, or having a roof that is partly open to the sky, in the style of a classical temple [Late 18C. < Latin *hypaethrus* 'in the open air' < Greek *hupo-* (see HYPO-) + *hupaithros* < *aithēr* 'air']

hypallage /hī pálləji/ *n* a figure of speech in which the usual relations of words or phrases are interchanged, e.g. 'He nodded his agreeing head' [Late 16C. Via late Latin < Greek *hupallagē* 'interchange' < *hupo-* (see HYPO-) + *allag-*, stem of *allassein* 'to exchange' < *allos* 'other']

hypanthium /hī pánthi əm/ (*plural* **-thia** /-thi ə/) *n* the flat or cup-shaped area that bears the stamens, petals, and sepals of plants such as roses and cherries [Mid-19C. < modern Latin, 'structure under the flower' < Greek *hupo-* (see HYPO-) + *anthos* 'flower'] —**hypanthial** *adj*

Hypatia /hī páyshə/ (375–415) Greek philosopher. A follower of Plato, she taught in Alexandria, where she was renowned for her learning. Considered a pagan by many Christians, she was murdered by an Alexandrian mob.

'To rule by fettering the mind through fear of punishment in another world, is just as base as to use force.'
[Hypatia. Quoted in 'Hypatia', *Little Jour-*

neys to the Homes of Great Teachers*, Elbert Hubbard; 1908]

hype[1] /hīp/ (*informal*) *n* **1. PUBLICITY** greatly exaggerated publicity intended to excite public interest in something such as a film or theatrical production **2. SOMEBODY OR SOMETHING OVERPUBLICIZED** a widely publicized person or thing **3. DECEPTION** a deception or dishonest scheme ■ *vt* (**hypes, hyping, hyped**) **1. PUBLICIZE SOMEBODY OR SOMETHING** to promote somebody or something with intense publicity **2. ARTIFICIALLY BOOST SALES OF RECORDING** to boost sales of a pop recording artificially by employing people to buy quantities of it at numerous outlets [Early 20C. Partly back-formation < HYPERBOLE, partly < slang *hyper* 'somebody giving short change' (< HYPER-)]

hype[2] /hīp/ *n* (*slang*) **1.** a hypodermic needle or injection **2.** a drug addict [Early 20C shortening of HYPODERMIC]

hyped up *adj* highly stimulated or excited, especially by drugs (*slang*) [Early 20C. < shortening of HYPODERMIC]

hyper /hīpər/ *adj* (*informal*) **1.** behaving in an over-excited or hyperactive way **2.** easily excited, or having a highly strung temperament [Mid-20C. Shortening of HYPERACTIVE]

hyper- *prefix* **1.** over, above, beyond ○ *hyperextension* **2.** excessive, unusually high ○ *hypertension* [< Greek *huper* 'above, beyond' < Indo-European]

hyperacute *adj*	**hyperirritable** *adj*
hyperaggressive *adj*	**hypermasculine** *adj*
hyperalert *adj*	**hypermodern** *adj*
hyperarousal *n*	**hypernationalistic** *adj*
hyperaware *adj*	**hyperproduction** *n*
hyperawareness *n*	**hyperrational** *adj*
hypercautious *adj*	**hyperreactive** *adj*
hypercivilized *adj*	**hyperreactor** *n*
hypercompetitive *adj*	**hyperresponsive** *adj*
hyperconcentration *n*	**hypersalivation** *n*
hyperconscious *adj*	**hypersecretion** *n*
hyperconsciousness *n*	**hypersensitization** *n*
hyperefficient *adj*	**hypersensitize** *vt*
hyperemotional *adj*	**hypersomnolence** *n*
hyperenergetic *adj*	**hyperstimulate** *vt*
hyperexcitable *adj*	**hyperstimulation** *n*
hyperfastidious *adj*	**hypersusceptibility** *n*
hyperfeminine *adj*	**hypersusceptible** *adj*
hyperintellectual *adj*	**hypertense** *adj*
hyperintelligent *adj*	**hypervigilant** *adj*
hyperintense *adj*	**hypervirulent** *adj*
hyperirritability *n*	**hyperviscosity** *n*

hyperaccumulate /hīpərə kyoōmyoō layt/ (**-lates, -lating, -lated**) *vti* to take up and accumulate an unusually high concentration of metal from the environment (*refers to plant tissue*) —**hyperaccumulation** /hīpərə kyoōmyoō láysh'n/ *n* —**hyperaccumulator** *n*

hyperacidity /hīpərə síddəti/ *n* a condition in which excess stomach acid is produced, usually associated with the formation of a peptic or duodenal ulcer

hyperactive /hīpər áktiv/ *adj* unusually active, restless, and lacking the ability to concentrate for any length of time, especially as a result of attention deficit disorder —**hyperaction** *n* —**hyperactively** *adv* —**hyperactivity** /hīpər ak tívvəti/ *n*

hyperaemia /hīpər éemi ə/ *n* an unusually high level of blood in some part of the body —**hyperaemic** *adj*

hyperaesthesia /hīpər eess théezi ə/ *n* a heightened sensitivity of a part of the body such as the skin, or of any of the senses [Mid-19C. < modern Latin, 'condition of extreme sensation' < Greek *aisthēsis* 'sensation'] —**hyperaesthetic** /hīpər eess théttik/ *adj*

hyperbaric /hīpər bárrik/ *adj* relating to, involving, or occurring at pressures higher than normal [Mid-20C. < HYPER- + Greek *baros* 'weight'] —**hyperbarically** *adv*

hyperbaton /hī púrbə ton/ *n* a figure of speech in which the expected word order is inverted for emphasis, e.g. in 'you I hate' [Mid-16C. Via Latin < Greek *huperbaton* 'overstepping' < *huperbainein* 'step over' < *bainein* 'step, walk']

hyperbola /hī púrbələ/ (*plural* **-las** or **-lae** /-lee/) *n* a conic section formed by a point that moves in a plane so that the difference in its distance from two fixed points in the plane remains constant [Mid-17C. Via modern Latin < Greek *huperbolē* 'excess' (see HYPERBOLE)]

hyperbole /hī púrbəli/ *n* deliberate and obvious exaggeration used for effect, e.g. 'I could eat a million of these' [15C. Via Latin < Greek *huperbolē* 'excess', literally 'overthrow' < *ballein* 'to throw']

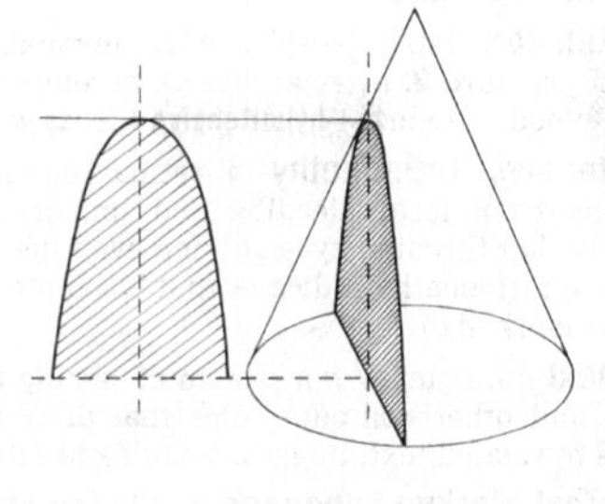

hyperbola

hyperbolic /hīpər bóllik/, **hyperbolical** /-bóllik'l/ *adj* **1. OF HYPERBOLA** relating to, involving, or typical of a hyperbola **2. OF GEOMETRIC SYSTEM** produced by or relating to a geometric system in which two lines can pass through any point in a plane without intersecting a specific line in the same plane **3. OF HYPERBOLIC FUNCTION** connected with or relating to a hyperbolic function **4. OF HYPERBOLE** relating to or constituting hyperbole —**hyperbolically** *adv*

hyperbolic function *n* any of six functions analogous to trigonometric functions but related to a hyperbola rather than a circle. Hyperbolic functions include the hyperbolic sine, hyperbolic cosine, hyperbolic tangent, hyperbolic cotangent, hyperbolic secant, and hyperbolic cosecant.

hyperbolize /hī púrbə līz/ (**-lizes, -lizing, -lized**), **hyperbolise** (**-lises, -lising, -lised**) *vti* to use deliberate and obvious exaggeration for effect, or describe something in obviously exaggerated terms

hyperboloid /hī púrbə loyd/ *n* a mathematical surface whose sections parallel to one coordinate plane form ellipses and those parallel to the other two coordinate planes form hyperbolas

hyperborean /hīpər báwri ən/ *adj* **1.** relating to the far northern regions of the world **2.** relating to peoples who live in the Arctic [Late 16C. < late Latin *hyperboreanus* < Latin *hyperboreus* < Greek *huperbore(i)os* < *boreios* 'northern' or *Boreas* 'north wind']

Hyperborean /hīpər báwri ən/ *n* in Greek mythology, a member of a people who lived beyond the north wind in a land that was always sunny and warm [15C. < late Latin *hyperboreanus* (see HYPERBOREAN)]

hypercalcaemia /hīpər kal séemi ə/ *n* an unusually high amount of calcium in the blood. US spelling **hypercalcemia** —**hypercalcaemic** *adj*

hypercapnia /hīpər káppni ə/ *n* an unusually high level of carbon dioxide in the blood [Early 20C. < modern Latin, 'condition of excessive smoke' < Greek *kapnos* 'smoke'] —**hypercapnic** *adj*

hypercharge /hīpər chaarj/ *n* a property of elementary particles that is calculated by adding together a particle's baryon number and its quantum property of strangeness [Mid-20C. Contraction of *hyperonic charge* (< HYPERON)]

hypercharged /hīpər chaárjd/ *adj* **1.** imbued with an atmosphere of exceptionally intense interest, excitement, or other strong emotion **2.** describes elementary particles with the property of hypercharge

hypercholesterolaemia /hīpərkə léstərə léemi ə/ *n* an unusually high level of cholesterol in the blood. US spelling **hypercholesterolemia** —**hypercholesterolaemic** *adj*

hypercorrect /hīpərkə rékt/ *adj* **1.** too greatly concerned about correctness **2.** showing or being the result of hypercorrection —**hypercorrectly** *adv* —**hypercorrectness** *n*

hypercorrection /hīpərkə réksh'n/ *n* a grammatical mistake or mispronunciation made by correcting something that is not actually wrong, e.g. saying 'between you and I' instead of 'between you and me'

hypercritical /hīpər kríttik'l/ *adj* criticizing somebody or something too severely or too much —**hypercritically** *adv* —**hypercriticism** *n*

hypercube /hīpər kyoob/ *n* a figure in four or more dimensions with sides that are all of the same length and angles that are all right angles

hyperemia *n* MED US spelling of **hyperaemia**

hyperesthesia *n* MED US spelling of **hyperaesthesia**

hypereutectic /hīpər yoo téktik/, **hypereutectoid** /-ték toyd/ *adj* describes a compound or alloy that contains a minor component in a higher proportion than in the mixture of the same elements that has the lowest melting point

hyperextension /hīpərik sténsh'n/ *n* the movement of a limb beyond its normal range —**hyperextend** *vt* —**hyperextended** *adj*

hyperfine structure /hīpər fīn-/ *n* the splitting of lines in a spectrum into two or more closely spaced fine lines, caused by magnetic interactions within atoms

hyperfocal distance /hīpərfōk'l-/ *n* the distance between a camera lens and the closest object that is in focus when the lens is focused at infinity

hyperfunction /hīpər fungksh'n/ *n* overactivity of a gland or other bodily organ

hypergamy /hī púrgəmi/ *n* a custom in some societies that requires a woman to marry a man of a higher social class than the one to which she belongs

hyperglycaemia /hīpər glī séemi ə/ *n* an unusually high level of sugar in the blood. US spelling **hyperglycemia** —**hyperglycaemic** *adj*

hypergolic /hīpər góllik/ *adj* describes a rocket propellant that ignites on contact with an oxidizer [Mid-20C. < German *Hypergol* 'hypergolic fuel' < *hyper-* 'hyper-' + *erg-* 'work' < Greek *ergon*] —**hypergol** /hīpər gol/ *n* —**hypergolically** *adv*

hyperhidrosis /hīpər hī drṓssiss/ *n* excessive sweating, either generalized or localized to a particular part of the body

hypericum /hī pérrikəm/ (*plural same* or **-cums**) *n* a herbaceous plant such as St John's wort that grows in temperate regions in many cultivated forms. Genus: *Hypericum*. [15C. Via Latin < Greek *hupereikon* < *huper-* (see HYPER-) + *ereikē* 'heath, heather']

hyperinflation /hīpərin fláysh'n/ *n* very high, rapid monetary inflation that is great enough to threaten a nation's economic stability —**hyperinflated** *adj* —**hyperinflationary** *adj*

hyperinsulinism /hīpər ínsyoōlinizəm/ *n* an unusually high level of insulin in the blood, causing hypoglycaemia

Hyperion /hī péeri ən/ *n* **1.** a large satellite of Saturn **2.** in Greek mythology, one of the Titans, son of Gaia and Uranus

hyperkeratosis /hīpər kérrə tṓssiss/ *n* an excessive thickening of the outer layer of the skin —**hyperkeratotic** /hīpər kérrə tóttik/ *adj*

hyperkinesia /hīpər ki néezi ə, -kī néezi ə/, **hyperkinesis** /-néessiss/ *n* **1.** unusually increased movement in a muscle, e.g. in a spasm **2.** excessive activity in children, e.g. in those affected by attention deficit disorder [Mid-19C. < HYPER- + Greek *kinēsis* (see KINESIS) + -IA] —**hyperkinetic** /hīpər ki néttik/ *adj*

hyperlink /hīpər lingk/ *n* a word, symbol, image, or other element in a hypertext document that links to another element in the same document or in another hypertext document

hyperlipaemia /hīpərli péemi ə/, **hyperlipidaemia** /hīpər líppi déemi ə/ *n* an excessive level of fats or lipids in the blood —**hyperlipaemic** *adj* —**hyperlipidaemic** *adj*

hypermarket /hīpər maarkit/ *n* a very large self-service store that sells products usually sold in department stores as well as those sold in supermarkets, e.g. clothes, hardware, electrical goods, and food [Late 20C. Translation of French *hypermarché*]

hypermedia /hīpər meedi ə/ *n* a hypertext system that supports the linking of graphics, audio and video elements, and text. The World Wide Web has many aspects of a complete hypermedia system.

hypermeter /hī púrmitər/ *n* a line of poetry or a metrical foot that has one or more syllables in addition to those usually occurring in a metrical foot or completed line of verse [Mid-17C. Via late Latin < Greek *hupermetros* (see HYPERMETROPIA)] —**hypermetric** /hīpər méttrik/ *adj* —**hypermetrical** *adj*

hypermetropia /hīpər mi trṓpi ə/, **hypermetropy** /-méttrəpi/ *n* MED same as **hyperopia** (*technical*) [Mid-19C. < modern Latin < Greek *hupermetros* 'beyond measure' < *metron* 'measure'] —**hypermetropic** /hīpərmi tróppik/ *adj* —**hypermetropical** *adj*

hypermnesia /hīpərm néezi ə/ *n* an unusually power-

ful ability to remember exactly, sometimes a symptom of a psychiatric disorder [Mid-19C. < modern Latin, 'condition of extreme memory' < Greek *mnēsis* 'memory'] —**hypermnesic** *adj*

hypermobile /hīpər mō bīl/ *adj* BIOL same as **double-jointed** —**hypermobility** /-mō bíllәti/ *n*

hypernova /hīpər nōvә/ (*plural* **-vae** /-nōvee/ or **-vas**) *n* a large, very energetic supernova that is believed to be a source of intense gamma-ray emissions

hypernym /hīpәrnim/ *n* LING same as **superordinate** (sense 1)

hyperon /hīpә ron/ *n* a comparatively massive baryon that may be unstable or partially stable and is short-lived [Mid-20C. < HYPER- + -ON [1]]

hyperopia /hīpər ōpi ә/ *n* long-sightedness —**hyperopic** /hīpər óppik/ *adj*

hyperostosis /hīpər o stóssiss/ *n* an unusual growth or thickening of bone [Mid-19C. < modern Latin, 'condition of excessive bone' < Greek *osteon* 'bone'] —**hyperostotic** /hīpər o stóttik/ *adj*

hyperparasite /hīpər párrә sīt/ *n* a parasite living on another parasite —**hyperparasitic** /hīpər parә síttik/ *adj* —**hyperparasitism** /hīpər párrәsitizәm/ *n*

hyperparathyroidism /hīpər parә thī roydizәm/ *n* an unusually high level of parathyroid hormone in the body, causing various disorders including kidney damage

hyperphagia /hīpər fáyji ә/ *n* a condition in which somebody compulsively overeats over a long period —**hyperphagic** /hīpər fájjik/ *adj*

hyperphysical /hīpər fízzik'l/ *adj* not governed by the natural laws of physics —**hyperphysically** *adv*

hyperpituitarism /hīpәrpi tyoó itәrizәm/ *n* excessively high activity of the pituitary gland, sometimes causing unusual bodily growth —**hyperpituitary** *adj*

hyperplane /hīpər playn/ *n* a figure in hyperspace that is the three-dimensional equivalent of a plane in ordinary space

hyperplasia /hīpər pláyzi ә/ *n* unusual growth in a part of the body, caused by an excessive multiplication of cells —**hyperplastic** /hīpər plástik/ *adj*

hyperploid /hīpər ployd/ *adj* having an extra chromosome or section of a chromosome. In Down's syndrome, there is an extra copy or segment of chromosome 21. —**hyperploidy** *n*

hyperpnoea /hīpәrp neé ә, hīpәr-/ *n* unusually deep or fast breathing, e.g. after physical exertion. US spelling **hyperpnea** [Mid-19C. < modern Latin, 'extreme breathing' < Greek *pnoē* 'breathing'] —**hyperpnoeic** *adj*

hyperpyrexia /hīpər pī réksi ә/ *n* a very high fever (*technical*) [Late 19C. < modern Latin, 'extreme fever' < *pyrexia* (see PYREXIA)] —**hyperpyretic** /hīpər pī réttik/ *adj* —**hyperpyrexial** *adj*

hyperreactivity /hīpər ree ak tívvәti/ *n* a condition of hypersensitivity resulting in an often severe reaction to a minimal stimulus, as happens, e.g., in asthma

hyperrealism /hīpər reé әlizәm/ *n* a style in the visual arts that uses realism to achieve a striking effect rather than photographic representation of real life —**hyperrealist** *adj, n* —**hyperrealistic** /hīpər ree ә lístik/ *adj*

hypersensitive /hīpər sénssәtiv/ *adj* **1.** very easily upset or offended **2.** showing a strong reaction to a drug, allergen, or other agent —**hypersensitiveness** *n* —**hypersensitivity** /hīpər senssә tívvәti/ *n*

hypersexual /hīpər sékshoo әl/ *adj* interested in or engaging in sexual activity to an unusual extent —**hypersexuality** /hīpər sekshoo állәti/ *n*

hypersonic /hīpər sónnik/ *adj* relating to or moving at a speed of at least five times the speed of sound —**hypersonically** *adv*

hyperspace /hīpər spayss/ *n* **1.** space with more than three dimensions **2.** in science fiction, a theoretical dimension in which things not physically possible in ordinary space such as intergalactic travel can happen —**hyperspatial** /hīpər spáysh'l/ *adj*

hypersthene /hīpәrs theen/ *n* a green, brown, or black pyroxene mineral containing iron and magnesium [Early 19C. < French *hypersthène* 'extremely strong (mineral)' < Greek *sthenos* 'strength'] —**hypersthenic** /hīpәrs thénnik/ *adj*

hypersurface /hīpər surfiss/ *n* a mathematical surface in hyperspace, analogous to a surface in three-dimensional space

hypertension /hīpər ténsh'n/ *n* **1.** unusually high blood pressure **2.** arterial disease accompanied by high blood pressure —**hypertensive** /-ténssiv/ *adj*

hypertensive retinopathy *n* retinal changes resulting from local bleeding and impaired blood supply that threaten eyesight and even life. Hypertensive retinopathy indicates that blood pressure is excessively high.

hypertext /hīpər tekst/ *n* a system of storing images, text, and other computer files that allows direct links to related text, images, sound, and other data

HyperText Markup Language *n* full form of **HTML**

HyperText Transfer Protocol *n* full form of **HTTP**

hyperthermia /hīpər thúrmi ә/ *n* unusually high body temperature, especially when induced for therapeutic reasons [Late 19C. < modern Latin, 'condition of extreme heat' < Greek *thermē* 'heat'] —**hyperthermal** *adj* —**hyperthermic** *adj*

hyperthyroidism /hīpər thī roy dizәm/ *n* **1.** the overproduction of thyroid hormones at dangerously high levels **2.** the condition in which basal metabolism increases as a result of overactivity of the thyroid gland —**hyperthyroid** *adj*

hypertonic /hīpər tónnik/ *adj* **1.** describes a fluid that has a higher osmotic pressure than another fluid **2.** describes a body part such as a muscle or artery that is under unusually high tension —**hypertonia** /hīpər tōni ә/ *n* —**hypertonicity** /hīpәrtō níssәti/ *n*

hypertrophy /hī púrtrәfi/ *n* (*plural* **-phies**) **1.** ENLARGEMENT BY CELL GROWTH a growth in size of an organ through an increase in the size, rather than the number, of its cells **2.** UNNECESSARY COMPLEXITY exaggerated or unnecessary growth or complexity ■ *vti* (**-phies, -phying, -phied**) GET BIGGER BY CELL GROWTH to grow larger through an increase in the size, rather than the number, of cells, or cause something to grow larger in this way —**hypertrophic** /hīpər tróffik/ *adj*

hyperventilate /hīpər vénti layt/ (**-lates, -lating, -lated**) *vi* to breathe unusually deeply or rapidly because of anxiety or organic disease and in excess of the body's requirements, causing too much loss of carbon dioxide —**hyperventilation** /hīpər venti láysh'n/ *n*

hypervitaminosis /hīpər víttәmi nóssiss/ *n* a condition in which adverse effects are caused by taking in too much of one or more vitamins

hypesthesia *n* MED US spelling of **hypaesthesia**

hypha /hīfә/ (*plural* **-phae** /-fee/) *n* a part of the vegetative portion of a fungus that resembles threads [Mid-19C. Via modern Latin < Greek *huphē* 'web'] —**hyphal** *adj*

hyphen /hīf'n/ *n* a punctuation mark (-) used at the end of a line when a word must be divided or to link the parts of a compound word or phrase ■ *vt* (**-phens, -phening, -phened**) GRAM same as **hyphenate** [Early 17C. Via late Latin < late Greek *huphen* 'sign joining two syllables or words' < *hupo* 'under' + *hen*, neuter of *heis* 'one']

USAGE Use of ***hyphen*** A number of compound words and phrases are joined by hyphens: *thirty-seven; well-wisher; old-fashioned; mother-in-law.* For some the hyphens are optional, or inserted only when the word or phrase is used before a noun: *a coffee-table book; a well-timed attack* (but *the book on the coffee table; if the attack is well timed*). Most words with prefixes do not have a hyphen, exceptions being those where a capital letter follows the prefix (e.g. *pre-Christian*) and those where the word could be confused with another (e.g. *re-form* meaning 'form again' as distinct from *reform*). A hyphen is sometimes inserted when a prefix ending in a vowel is added to a word beginning with a vowel (e.g. *co-opt, de-ice*). In writing and printing, a hyphen may also be used to show that a word has been broken at the end of a line. Note that the word must be divided between syllables (e.g. *stream-ing,* not *streaming*) and the hyphen is attached to the end of the first part, not the beginning of the second part. Ideally there should be at least two letters in each part of the divided word. See ***dash***.

---

hyphenate /hīfә nayt/ (**-ates, -ating, -ated**) *vt* to separate or join words or parts of words using a hyphen —**hyphenation** /hīfә náysh'n/ *n*

hyphenated /hīfә naytid/ *adj* **1.** WITH HYPHEN split or joined by a hyphen **2.** WITH HYPHEN IN SURNAME having a surname containing two or more family names connected by a hyphen **3.** *N Am* BELONGING TO TWO CATEGORIES belonging to a group of people identified in two ways that may be joined as one term e.g. 'Irish Americans' (*offensive in some contexts*)

hypn- *prefix* same as **hypno-** (*used before vowels*)

hypnagogic /hipnә gójjik/, **hypnogogic** *adj* in or relating to the state of drowsiness immediately before sleep [Late 19C. < French *hypnagogique* < Greek *hupno-* 'sleep' + *agōgos* 'leading' (see -AGOGUE)]

hypnagogic image *n* something of the nature of a hallucination seen or imagined by somebody just before falling asleep

hypno- *prefix* **1.** sleep ○ *hypnopompic* **2.** hypnosis ○ *hypnoanalysis* [< Greek *hupnos* 'sleep' < Indo-European]

hypnoanalysis /hipnō ә nállәssiss/ (*plural same* or **-yses** /-ә seez/) *n* psychoanalysis carried out on people who are in a state of hypnosis —**hypnoanalytic** /hipnō ánnә líttik/ *adj*

hypnogenesis /hipnō jénnәssiss/ *n* the process of inducing sleep or a state of hypnosis —**hypnogenetic** /hipnō jә néttik/ *adj* —**hypnogenetically** *adv*

hypnogogic *adj* same as **hypnagogic**

hypnoid /híp noyd/, **hypnoidal** /hip nóyd'l/ *adj* relating to, involving, or resembling sleep or hypnosis

hypnology /hip nóllәji/ *n* the scientific study of sleep or hypnosis —**hypnologic** /hippnә lójjik/ *adj* —**hypnologist** *n*

hypnopaedia /hipnә peédi ә/ *n* same as **sleep-learning** (*technical*) [Mid-20C. < HYPNO- + Greek *paideia* 'education']

hypnopompic /hipnә pómpik/ *adj* involving, typical of, or in the state between sleeping and waking [Early 20C. < HYPNO- + Greek *pompē* 'a sending away']

Hypnos /híp noss/ *n* in Greek mythology, the god of sleep [< Greek *Hupnos*, literally 'sleep']

hypnosis /hip nóssiss/ (*plural* **-noses** /-nō seez/) *n* **1.** a condition that can be artificially induced in people, in which they can respond to questions and are very susceptible to suggestions from the hypnotist **2.** the technique or practice of inducing a state of hypnosis in people

hypnotherapy /híppnō thérrәpi/ *n* the use of hypnosis in treating illness, e.g. in dealing with physical pain or psychological problems —**hypnotherapist** *n*

hypnotic /hip nóttik/ *adj* **1.** OF SLEEP OR HYPNOSIS producing sleep or hypnosis **2.** SUSCEPTIBLE TO HYPNOSIS susceptible to being hypnotized **3.** FASCINATING so fascinating that the attention of people watching or listening is absorbed completely (*informal*) ■ *n* **1.** SOMETHING CAUSING SLEEP a drug or other agent that causes sleep or drowsiness **2.** SOMEBODY EASILY HYPNOTIZED somebody who can be hypnotized easily [Early 17C. Via French *hypnotique* < Greek *hupnōtikos* 'putting to sleep' < *hupnoun* 'put to sleep' < *hupnos* 'sleep'] —**hypnotically** *adv*

hypnotise *vt* another spelling of **hypnotize**

hypnotism /hípnәtizәm/ *n* **1.** PSYCHOL same as **hypnosis** (sense 1) **2.** the theory and practice of hypnotizing people [Mid-19C. Shortening of *neuro-hypnotism* < HYPNOTIC]

hypnotist /hípnәtist/ *n* somebody who performs hypnosis

hypnotize /hípnә tīz/ (**-tizes, -tizing, -tized**), **hypnotise** (**-tises, -tising, -tised**) *vt* **1.** to put somebody into a state of hypnosis **2.** to fascinate or charm somebody utterly —**hypnotizability** /hípnә tīzә bíllәti/ *n* —**hypnotizable** *adj* —**hypnotization** /hípnә tī záysh'n/ *n* —**hypnotizer** *n*

hypo[1] /hīpō/ *n* (*plural* **-pos**) a hypodermic injection, needle, or syringe (*informal*) ■ *vt* (**-pos, -poing, -poed**) *US* to stimulate somebody or something to action in order to achieve some purpose or goal (*dated informal*) [Early 20C. Shortening of HYPODERMIC]

hypo[2] /hīpō/ *n* sodium thiosulphate, used in photographic processing as a fixing agent (*informal*) [Mid-20C. Shortening of *hyposulphite*, another name for thiosulphate]

hypo[3] /hīpō/ (*informal*) *n* a hypoglycaemic episode, as sometimes experienced by people being treated with insulin ■ *adj* experiencing hypoglycaemia [Shortening of *hypoglycaemic*]

hypo- *prefix* **1.** under, below ○ *hypodermis* **2.**

unusually low ○ *hypotonia* **3.** in a lower state of oxidation [< Greek *hupo* < Indo-European, 'under']

hypoacidity /hīpō ə síddəti/ *n* an unusually low level of acidity, especially in the stomach

hypoallergenic /hīpō állər jénnik/ *adj* not likely to cause an allergic reaction

hypoblast /hīpə blast/ *n* **1.** the inner germ layer of an embryo, which develops into the endoderm **2.** BIOL same as **endoderm** (*dated*) —**hypoblastic** /hīpə blástik/ *adj*

hypocalcaemia /hīpō kal seémi ə/ *n* an unusually low level of calcium in the blood. US spelling **hypocalcemia** —**hypocalcaemic** *adj*

hypocaust /hīpō kawst/ *n* in ancient Rome, a system of central heating in which hot air from an underground furnace circulated beneath floors and between double walls [Late 17C. Via Latin < Greek *hupokauston* 'place heated from below' < *kaiein* 'burn']

hypocentre /hīpō sentər/ *n* ARMS same as **ground zero** (sense 1)

hypochlorite /hīpə kláwrīt/ *n* a salt or ester of hypochlorous acid

hypochlorous acid /hīpə kláwrəss-/ *n* a weak unstable greenish-yellow acid that occurs only in solution or in its salts. Source: dissolving of chlorine in water. Use: in bleach, disinfectants. Formula: HOCl.

hypochondria /hīpə kóndri ə/ *n* **1.** an excessive, usually long-term preoccupation with health and bodily sensations, accompanied by a deluded conviction of having a serious disease without objective evidence **2.** ANAT plural of **hypochondrium** [Mid-16C. < late Latin (plural) 'upper abdomen' (formerly believed to be the seat of melancholy) < Greek *hupokhondrios* 'under the cartilage of the breastbone' < *khondros* 'cartilage']

hypochondriac /hīpə kóndri ak/ *n* **SOMEBODY WITH IMAGINARY ILLNESS** somebody who is unduly preoccupied with personal health and believes that illness is nearly always present or imminent ■ *adj* **1. BELIEVING IN NONEXISTENT ILLNESS** excessively preoccupied with health and persistently believing in a nonexistent illness, or relating to the attitudes or state of mind of somebody with this condition **2.** ANAT **OF HYPOCHONDRIUM** relating to, involving, or typical of the hypochondrium —**hypochondriacal** /hīpə kon drī ək'l/ *adj* —**hypochondriacally** *adv*

hypochondriasis /hīpə kon drī əssiss/ (*plural* **-ases** /-əseez/) *n* PSYCHOL same as **hypochondria** (sense 1)

hypochondrium /hīpə kóndri əm/ (*plural* **-dria** /-dri ə/) *n* the area of the upper abdomen on each side of the epigastrium below the lower ribs [Mid-17C. Back-formation < HYPOCHONDRIA (originally a plural form)]

hypocorism /hī pókərizəm/ *n* **1.** a pet name, especially a diminutive or abbreviated form of somebody's full name (*formal*) **2.** the use of a pet name to address somebody, instead of his or her full name [Early 16C. Via late Latin < Greek *hupokorisma* < *hupokorizesthai* 'play the child' < *korē* 'child'] —**hypocoristic** /hīpə kaw rístik/ *adj* —**hypocoristical** *adj* —**hypocoristically** *adv*

hypocotyl /hīpə kóttil/ *n* the part of an embryo plant lying between its cotyledons and its radicle [Late 19C. < HYPO- + COTYLEDON] —**hypocotylous** *adj*

~~**hypocrasy**, **hypocricy**~~ incorrect spelling of **hypocrisy**

hypocrisy /hi pókrəssi/ (*plural* **-sies**) *n* **1.** the false claim to or pretence of having admirable principles, beliefs, or feelings ○ *It would be sheer hypocrisy for them to turn round and do what they criticize in others.* **2.** an act or instance of hypocrisy ○ *the many hypocrisies of the party opposite* [12C. Via Old French *ypocrisie* < Greek *hupokrisis* 'acting a part' < *hupokrinesthai* 'act a part' < *krinein* 'to separate']

hypocrite /híppəkrit/ *n* somebody who pretends to have admirable principles, beliefs, or feelings but behaves otherwise [12C. Via Old French *ypocrite* < Greek *hupokritēs* 'actor, pretender' < *hupokrinesthai* (see HYPOCRISY)]

hypocritical /híppə kríttik'l/ *adj* showing, originating from, or of the nature of hypocrisy ○ *It would be hypocritical of me to congratulate you on defeating me.* —**hypocritically** *adv*

hypocycloid /hīpə sī kloyd/ *n* in geometry, a curve traced by a point on the circumference of a circle as it rolls along the inside circumference of another circle —**hypocycloidal** /hīpə sī klóyd'l/ *adj*

hypoderm *n* BOT, ANAT same as **hypodermis**

hypodermic /hīpə dúrmik/ *adj* relating to or involving the area of tissue lying beneath the skin ■ *n* a hypodermic injection, needle, or syringe [Mid-19C. < HYPO- + Greek *derma* 'skin'] —**hypodermically** *adv*

hypodermic injection *n* an injection into tissue under the skin

hypodermic needle *n* **1.** a thin hollow needle used with a syringe, suitable for administering hypodermic injections **2.** a hypodermic syringe to which a needle has been fitted (*informal*)

hypodermic syringe *n* a plastic or glass syringe to which a thin hollow needle is attached, used to inject medicine under the skin or to withdraw fluids, especially blood, from under the skin

hypodermis /hīpə dúrmiss/, **hypoderm** /hīpə durm/ *n* **1. TISSUE UNDER SKIN** the layer of fatty tissue beneath the skin **2. SKIN BENEATH ANIMAL'S SHELL** the epidermis of some animals such as arthropods that secretes a shell or other outer covering **3. CELLS UNDER PLANT SURFACE** the usually supportive and protective layer of cells immediately under the outer covering of a plant [Mid-19C. < HYPO-, after EPIDERMIS] —**hypodermal** *adj*

hypoesthesia /hīpō es theézi ə/ *n* US same as **hypaesthesia**

hypogastrium /hīpə gástri əm/ (*plural* **-tria** /-tri ə/) *n* the part of the front of the human abdomen that lies below the navel [Late 17C. Via modern Latin < Greek *hupogastrion* 'lower part of the belly' < *gastr-* 'belly'] —**hypogastric** *adj*

hypogea ANCIENT HIST plural of **hypogeum**

hypogeal /hīpə jeé əl/, **hypogean** /-jeé ən/, **hypogeous** /-jeé əss/ *adj* **1.** happening or living below ground **2.** describes a plant part that remains below ground while the stem of the plant grows [Late 17C. < late Latin *hypogeus* < Greek *hupogeios* 'underground' < *gē* 'ground, earth'] —**hypogeally** *adv*

hypogene /hīpə jeen/ *adj* describes rocks that are formed or lying beneath the Earth's surface —**hypogenic** /hīpə jénnik/ *adj*

hypogenous /hī pójjənəss/ *adj* on or growing on the underside of something such as a leaf. ◊ **epigenous**

hypogeous *adj* same as **hypogeal**

hypogeum /hīpə jeé əm/ (*plural* **-gea** /-jeé ə/) *n* an underground room or space in an ancient building, or an ancient underground burial chamber [Mid-17C. Via Latin < Greek *hupogeion*, form of *hupogeios* 'underground' (see HYPOGEAL)]

hypoglossal /hīpə glóss'l/ *adj* **1.** beneath or on the underside of the tongue **2.** relating to or involving the hypoglossal nerve [Mid-19C. < *hypoglossus* 'hypoglossal nerve' < HYPO- + Greek *glōssa* 'tongue']

hypoglossal nerve *n* either of the 12th pair of cranial nerves that serve the muscles of the tongue

hypoglycaemia /hīpō glī seémi ə/ *n* the medical condition of having an unusually low level of sugar in the blood. US spelling **hypoglycemia** —**hypoglycaemic** *adj*

hypoglycemia *n* US spelling of **hypoglycaemia**

hypogynous /hī pójjinəss/ *adj* describes a flower such as a buttercup that has its petals, sepals, or other parts situated below and apart from its ovary [Early 19C. < modern Latin *hypogynus* < *hypo-* 'below' + Greek *gunē* 'woman', used to mean 'pistil'] —**hypogyny** *n*

hypoid gear /hī poyd-/ *n* a gear often used in the transmission of motor vehicles, in which a hypocycloidal curve is used in arranging the meshing of the teeth [Early 20C. Origin ?]

hypolimnion /hīpō límni ən/ (*plural* **-nia** /-ni ə/) *n* the lower and colder layer of water in a lake, largely stagnant and remaining at a constant temperature (*technical*) [Early 20C. < HYPO- + Greek *limnion* 'small lake' < *limnē* 'lake']

hypomania /hīpō máyni ə/ *n* a condition of mild mania or overexcitement, especially when part of a bipolar manic-depressive cycle —**hypomanic** /hīpō mánnik/ *adj*

hyponasty /hīpə nasti/ *n* greater than normal growth on the underside of a plant part, causing the part to bend upwards [Late 19C. < HYPO- + Greek *nastos* 'pressed close, compact'] —**hyponastic** /hīpə nástik/ *adj* —**hyponastically** *adv*

hyponym /hīpənim/ *n* a word whose meaning is both narrower than and included in the meaning of a more general term. The words 'tulip' and 'rose' are hyponyms of 'flower'. —**hyponymy** /hī pónnimi/ *n*

hypophyge /hī póffiji/ *n* ARCHIT same as **apophyge** [< Greek *hupophugē* 'evasion, flight from under' < *phugē* 'flight']

hypophysectomy /hīpōfi séktəmi/ (*plural* **-mies**) *n* surgical removal of the pituitary gland

hypophysis /hī póffississ/ (*plural* **-yses** /-i seez/) *n* same as **pituitary gland** (*technical*) [Late 17C. Via modern Latin < Greek *hupophusis* 'offshoot' < *phusis* 'growth'] —**hypophyseal** /hīpə fízzi əl/ *adj*

hypopituitarism /hīpəpi tyoóitərizəm/ *n* failure of the pituitary gland to produce hormones, especially a deficiency in growth hormone, which can result in dwarfism —**hypopituitary** *adj*

hypoplasia /hīpō pláyzi ə/, **hypoplasty** /hīpō plasti/ *n* the failure of an organ or body part to grow or develop fully —**hypoplastic** /-plástik/ *adj*

hypoploid /hīpə ployd/ *adj* having a chromosome number slightly less than the diploid number —**hypoploidy** *n*

hypopnoea /hī pópni ə/ *n* breathing that is unusually shallow and slow [Via modern Latin < Greek *hupopnoia* < *pnoia* 'breathing'] —**hypopnoeic** /hīpō neé ik/ *adj*

hyposensitise *vt* another spelling of **hyposensitize**

hyposensitivity /hīpō sénssi tívvəti/ *n* an unusually low sensitivity to stimuli such as allergens —**hyposensitive** /hīpō sénssitiv/ *adj*

hyposensitize /hīpō sénsi tīz/ (**-tizes, -tizing, -tized**), **hyposensitise** (**-tises, -tising, -tised**) *vt* to lower somebody's sensitivity to something, e.g. in the treatment of allergies —**hyposensitization** /hīpō sénsi tī záysh'n/ *n*

hypostasis /hī póstəsiss/ (*plural* **-tases** /-tə seez/) *n* **1. ESSENCE** in philosophy, the essence or reality of something **2. ONE ELEMENT OF TRINITY** in Christian doctrine, one of the three parts of the Trinity **3. ESSENTIAL NATURE OF JESUS CHRIST** in Christian doctrine, the essential nature of Jesus Christ, in which the divine and the human are believed to be combined **4. SETTLING OF BODY FLUID** the settling of fluid in an organ or other part of the body, as a result of poor circulation, in patients kept in bed, and after death [Early 16C. Via late Latin < Greek *hupostasis* 'sediment, foundation, essence' < *huphistasthai* 'stand under, support' < *histasthai* 'stand'] —**hypostatic** /hīpə státtik/ *adj* —**hypostatical** *adj* —**hypostatically** *adv*

hypostatize /hī póstə tīz/ (**-tizes, -tizing, -tized**), **hypostatise** (**-tises, -tising, -tised**), **hypostasize** /hī póstə sīz/ (**-sizes, -sizing, -sized**), **hypostasise** (**-sises, -sising, -sised**) *vt* **1.** to treat something conceptual as if it were real **2.** to personify or embody something —**hypostasization** /hī póstə sī záysh'n/ *n* —**hypostatization** /hī póstə tī záysh'n/ *n*

hypostyle /hīpə stīl/ *adj* describes a classical building with a roof or ceiling that rests on many columns [Mid-19C. < Greek *hupostulos* 'resting upon pillars' < *stulos* 'pillar'] —**hypostyle** *n*

hypotaxis /hīpō táksiss/ *n* the subordinate status of one clause in relation to another separated from it by a subordinating conjunction. For example, in 'I will go when I am ready', the relationship between 'I am ready' and 'I will go' is one of hypotaxis. [Late 19C. < Greek *hupotaxis* 'subjection' < *hupotassein* 'arrange under' < *tassein* 'arrange'] —**hypotactic** *adj*

hypotension /hīpō ténsh'n/ *n* unusually low blood pressure —**hypotensive** *adj, n*

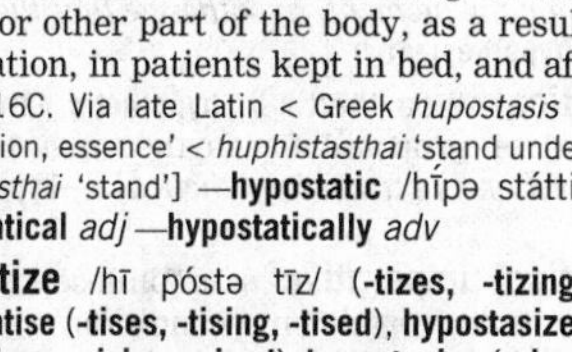

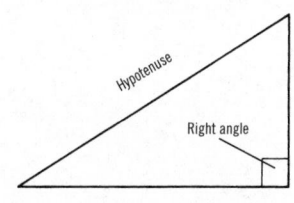

hypotenuse

hypotenuse /hī póttə nyooz/ *n* the longest side of a right-angled triangle, opposite the right angle [Late

16C. Via Latin *hypotenusa* < Greek *hupoteinousa* '(line) stretching under (the right angle)' < present participle of *hupoteinein* 'stretch under' < *teinein* 'stretch']

hypoth. *abbr* **1.** hypothesis **2.** hypothetical

hypothalamus /hīpō thálləməss/ (*plural* **-mi** /-mī/) *n* a central area on the underside of the brain, controlling involuntary functions such as body temperature and the release of hormones —**hypothalamic** /hīpōthə lámmik/ *adj*

hypothecate /hī pótha kayt/ (**-cates, -cating, -cated**) *vt* **1.** to designate money, especially public revenue, to be used for a specific purpose **2.** to pledge property or goods as security for a debt without surrendering ownership [Early 17C. < medieval Latin *hypothecat-*, past participle of *hypothecare* < late Latin *hypotheca* 'deposit' < Greek *hupothēkē* < *hupotithenai* 'deposit as a pledge'] —**hypothecation** /hī pótha káysh'n/ *n* —**hypothecator** *n*

hypothermal /hīpō thúrm'l/ *adj* **1.** relating to, involving, or typical of hypothermia **2.** describes rocks and minerals formed deep underground at high temperatures

hypothermia /hīpō thúrmi ə/ *n* **1.** dangerously low body temperature caused by prolonged exposure to cold **2.** lower-than-normal body temperature induced medically, e.g. to slow a patient's metabolism during heart surgery [Late 19C. < HYPO- + Greek *thermē* 'heat'] —**hypothermic** *adj*

hypothesis /hī pótha ssiss/ (*plural* **-eses** /-ə seez/) *n* **1.** THEORY NEEDING INVESTIGATION a tentative explanation for a phenomenon, used as a basis for further investigation ○ *The hypothesis of the big bang is one way to explain the beginning of the universe.* **2.** ASSUMPTION a statement that is assumed to be true for the sake of argument ○ *That is what would logically follow if you accepted the hypothesis.* **3.** ANTECEDENT CLAUSE in logic, the antecedent of a conditional statement [Late 16C. Via late Latin < Greek *hupothesis* 'foundation, base' < *thesis* 'placing'] —**hypothesist** *n*

hypothesize /hī pótha sīz/ (**-sizes, -sizing, -sized**), **hypothesise** (**-sises, -sising, -sised**) *vti* to offer something as a hypothesis, or form a hypothesis ○ *Let us, for the moment, hypothesize that the Earth is flat.* —**hypothesizer** *n*

hypothetical /hīpə théttik'l/, **hypothetic** /-théttik/ *adj* assumed or proposed for further investigation ○ *The question is purely hypothetical.* —**hypothetically** *adv*

hypothetical imperative *n* in philosophy, an imperative that depends on a condition, e.g. 'be kind to people if they are kind to you'

hypothyroidism /hīpō thī roydizəm/ *n* a deficiency in the production of thyroid hormones, or the slowing of the metabolic rate that results. A severe deficiency can result in sluggishness and weight gain (**myxoedema**). —**hypothyroid** *adj*

hypotonia /hīpə tōni ə/ *n* a condition in which the osmotic pressure in one fluid is lower than that in another, especially in the body [Late 19C. < HYPO- + Greek *tonos* 'tone']

hypotonic /hīpə tónnik/ *adj* **1.** with low or diminished muscle tone or tension **2.** with a lower osmotic pressure than another fluid —**hypotonicity** /hīpətə níssəti/ *n*

hypotrachelium /hīpō trə keeli əm/ *n* the lower part of the capital of an architectural column, or a groove between the capital and the main shaft [Mid-16C. Via Latin < Greek *hupotrakhēlion* < *trakhēlos* 'neck']

hypoventilate /hīpō vénti layt/ (**-lates, -lating, -lated**) *vi* to breathe in an unusually slow and shallow way leading to a dangerous build-up of carbon dioxide in the blood —**hypoventilation** /-vénti láysh'n/ *n*

hypoxaemia /hī pok seemi ə/ *n* inadequate oxygen in the blood. US spelling **hypoxemia** [Late 19C. < HYP- + OXYGEN] —**hypoxaemic** *adj*

hypoxemia *n* MED US spelling of **hypoxaemia**

hypoxia /hī póksi ə/ *n* an inadequacy in the oxygen reaching the body's tissues [Mid-20C. < HYP- + OXYGEN] —**hypoxic** *adj*

hypso- *prefix* height ○ *hypsometer* [< Greek *hupsos*]

hypsography /hip sóggrəfi/ *n* GEOG same as **hypsometry** —**hypsographic** /hípsə gráffik/ *adj* —**hypsographical** *adj*

hypsometer /hip sómmitər/ *n* **1.** an instrument that uses the boiling point of water at different altitudes to measure the elevation of a specific point on the Earth's surface **2.** an instrument for calculating the heights of trees by using the principles of geometric triangulation

hypsometry /hip sómmətri/ *n* the measurement of the elevation of land above sea level —**hypsometric** /hípsə méttrik/ *adj* —**hypsometrical** *adj* —**hypsometrically** *adv* —**hypsometrist** *n*

hyrax /hī raks/ (*plural* **-raxes** or **-races** /-rə seez/) *n* a small gregarious plant-eating mammal that resembles a rabbit with short ears and has toenails resembling hooves. Native to: Mediterranean, Southwest Asia. Family: Procaviidae. [Mid-19C. Via modern Latin < Greek *hurax* 'shrew-mouse']

hyson /hīss'n/ *n* a Chinese green tea [Mid-18C. < Chinese *xīchūn* 'bright spring']

hyssop /híssəp/ *n* **1.** AROMATIC HERB a fragrant plant similar to mint. Flowers: fragrant, pink, white, or blue, in spikes. Use: in aromatherapy and alternative medicine. Native to: Europe, Asia. Latin name: *Hyssopus officinalis.* **2.** PLANT LIKE HYSSOP a plant related to or similar to true hyssop **3.** BIBLICAL PLANT an unidentified plant whose twigs are described in the Bible as being used to sprinkle water during Hebrew religious ceremonies [Pre-12C. Via Latin < Greek *hussōpos*]

hyster- *prefix* same as **hystero-** (*used before vowels*)

hysterectomy /hístə réktəmi/ (*plural* **-mies**) *n* a surgical operation to remove a womb —**hysterectomize** *vt*

hysteresis /hístə reessiss/ *n* a delayed response by an object to changes in the forces acting on it, especially magnetic forces [Late 19C. < Greek *husterēsis* 'deficiency' < *husterein* 'be behind, come late' < *husteros* 'late'] —**hysteretic** /hístə réttik/ *adj*

hysteria /hi steeri ə/ *n* **1.** EMOTIONAL INSTABILITY CAUSED BY TRAUMA an emotionally unstable state brought about

hyssop

by a traumatic experience **2.** STATE OF EXTREME EMOTION a state of extreme or exaggerated emotion such as excitement or panic, especially among large numbers of people ○ *media hysteria about ministerial sleaze* **3.** LAUGHING OR CRYING uncontrollable laughter or crying **4.** PSYCHIAT same as **conversion disorder** (*dated*) [Early 19C. < Latin *hystericus* (see HYSTERIC)]

CULTURAL NOTE *Studies in Hysteria*, a book (1895) by Austrian psychologists Joseph Bauer and Sigmund Freud. A pioneering work in the field of psychoanalysis, it suggests that hysterical symptoms are the result of the memory's suppression of earlier traumatic events. The authors recommend that patients recall and confront these experiences in the hope of achieving catharsis.

hysteric /hi stérrik/ *adj* same as **hysterical** (senses 1–3) ■ *n* somebody affected by hysteria (*dated; sometimes considered offensive*) [Mid-17C. Via Latin *hystericus* < Greek *husterikos* 'affected in the womb' < *hustera* 'womb']

hysterical /hi stérrik'l/ *adj* **1.** AFFECTED BY HYSTERIA in a state of hysteria ○ *hysterical with grief* **2.** RELATING TO HYSTERIA relating to, caused by, or subject to hysteria **3.** UNCONTROLLABLE impossible to hold back or control ○ *hysterical sobbing coming from the next room* **4.** EXTREMELY FUNNY causing uncontrollable laughter (*informal*) ○ *one hysterical sketch after another*

hysterics /hi stérriks/ *n* (*takes a singular or plural verb*) **1.** a state of uncontrollable laughter (*informal*) ○ *had them in hysterics with her stories* **2.** a state of hysteria, or an episode of hysterical behaviour

hystero- *prefix* **1.** womb ○ *hysterotomy* **2.** hysteria ○ *hysterogenic* [< Greek *hustera* 'womb' < Indo-European]

hysterogenic /hístərə jénnik/ *adj* bringing about a state of emotional instability or hysteria

hysteron proteron /hístə ron próttə ron/ *n* a figure of speech in which the order of words or phrases is the reverse of what is usual, e.g. 'photographed in white and black' [Mid-16C. Via late Latin < Greek *husteron proteron* 'latter first']

hysterotomy /hístə róttəmi/ (*plural* **-mies**) *n* a surgical incision into a womb, carried out especially in order to perform a Caesarean

Hz *symbol* MEASURE, PHYS hertz

i¹ /ī/ (*plural* **i's**), **I** (*plural* **I's** or **Is**) *n* **1.** 9TH LETTER OF ENGLISH ALPHABET the ninth letter of the English alphabet, representing a vowel sound **2.** LETTER 'I' WRITTEN a written representation of the letter 'i' **3.** ROMAN NUMERAL the Roman numeral for 1 ◇ **dot the i's and cross the t's** to take care over the details of something ○ *We're in general agreement on the contract, but we still have to dot the i's and cross the t's.*

i² *symbol* **1.** one **2.** MATHS the imaginary number √‾-1

i³ *abbr* **1.** DENT incisor **2.** indicate **3.** BANKING interest **4.** GRAM intransitive **5.** island **6.** isle

I¹ /ī/ *n* a syllable of special significance in Rastafarian Theology. It combines the notions of self (I) and vision (**eye**). (*used in Black English*)

I² /ī/ *pron* a pronoun used by a speaker or writer to refer to himself or herself (*as the subject of a verb*) [Old English *ic* < Indo-European]

I³ /ī/ (*plural* **I's** or **Is**) *n* something shaped like a letter 'I'

I⁴ *symbol* **1.** ELEC electric current **2.** CHEM ELEM iodine **3.** CHEM ionization potential **4.** QUANTUM PHYS isospin **5.** PHYS moment of inertia **6.** one **7.** LOGIC a particular affirmative categorical statement **8.** MATHS unit matrix

I⁵ *abbr* **1.** Imperial **2.** (single column) inch (*in advertisements*) **3.** incumbent **4.** independence **5.** Independent **6.** Inspector **7.** Institute **8.** Instructor **9.** intelligence **10.** International **11.** interpreter **12.** Island **13.** Isle **14.** issue

I- *prefix* used in Rastafarian English to replace the first syllable of a word, especially one with positive connotations (*slang; used in Black English*) ○ *I-tal* ○ *I-ration*

-i- *infix* used as a connector to join word parts ○ *fossiliferous* [Via French < Latin]

-ia *suffix* **1.** placenames ○ *Australia* ○ *India* **2.** plurals ○ *genitalia* **3.** diseases or medical conditions ○ *dyslexia* **4.** classes or genera, or a specific example of a genus ○ *Mammalia* ○ *gardenia* **5.** things belonging to or associated with something ○ *regalia* [Directly or via modern Latin < Latin and Greek]

IAA *abbr* **1.** indoleacetic acid **2.** International Advertising Association

IAAF *abbr* **1.** International Amateur Athletic Federation **2.** International Association of Athletics Federations

IAB *abbr* **1.** Industrial Advisory Board **2.** Industrial Arbitration Board

Iacocca /ī ə kốkə/, **Lee** (*b.* 1924) US motor car executive. After a 32-year career at Ford, he became the president and chief executive officer of Chrysler Corporation (1978–92), which he helped rescue from failure. Full name **Iacocca, Lido Anthony**

> 'The cement in our whole democracy today is the worker who makes $15 an hour. He's the guy who will buy a house and a car and a refrigerator. He's the oil in the engine.' [Lee Iacocca, *Iacocca: An Autobiography*; 1985]

IAEA *abbr* International Atomic Energy Agency

IAF *abbr* Indian Air Force

-ial *suffix* connected with or belonging to something ○ *secretarial* ○ *imperial* [Directly or via French < Latin *-ialis, -iale*]

IAM *abbr* **1.** Institute of Administrative Management **2.** Institute of Advanced Motorists **3.** internal auditory meatus

iamb /ī am, ī amb/ *n* a metrical foot of one short or unstressed syllable followed by one long or stressed syllable. 'The ploughman homeward plods his weary way' consists of five iambs. [Mid-19C. Anglicization of IAMBUS]

iambi LITERAT plural of **iambus**

iambic /ī ámbik/ *adj* relating to or consisting of iambs ■ *n* **1.** LITERAT same as **iamb 2.** a poem or a line of poetry written in iambs (*often used in the plural*)

iambic pentameter *n* the most common rhythm in English poetry, consisting of five iambs in each line. 'The quality of mercy is not strained' is an iambic pentameter.

iambus /ī ámbəss/ (*plural* **-buses** or **-bi** /-bī/) *n* LITERAT same as **iamb** [Late 16C. Via Latin < Greek *iambos* 'iamb, lampoon' < *iaptein* 'attack in words']

-ian *suffix* belonging to, coming from, being involved in, or being like something ○ *Italian* ○ *Smithsonian* ○ *mathematician* [Directly or via French < Latin *-ianus*]

I-and-I *pron* same as **I** (*slang; used in Black English*)

IAP *abbr* ONLINE Internet access provider

Iapetus /ī áppitəss/ *n* a natural satellite of Saturn, discovered in 1671. It is 1,436 km in diameter and occupies an outer orbit.

IARC *abbr* International Agency for Research on Cancer

IAS¹ *abbr* **1.** COMPUT image analysis system **2.** COMPUT immediate access store **3.** Indian Administrative Service **4.** AVIAT indicated air speed

IAS² *n* a form issued by the Australian Taxation Office on which businesses report income and calculate related income tax payments. Full form **instalment activity statement**

Iaşi /yáshi/ city and capital of the county of the same name in eastern Romania, situated on a tributary of the River Prut. Population: 346,613 (1997).

-iasis *suffix* a disease characterized by or caused by a particular thing ○ *filariasis* [< -i- + Latin or Greek *-asis*, suffix of state or process]

IATA /ee aatə, ī-/ *abbr* International Air Transport Association

-iatric *suffix* of a particular field of medicine ○ *psychiatric* [< Greek *iatrikos* < *iatros* 'doctor' < *iasthai* 'heal']

-iatrics *suffix* a particular field of medicine ○ *paediatrics*

iatrogenic /ī áttrō jénnik/ *adj* describes a symptom or illness brought on unintentionally by something that a doctor does or says ○ *iatrogenic disorders* [Early 20C. < Greek *iatros* 'physician'] —**iatrogenically** *adv*

-iatry *suffix* a particular field of medicine or medical treatment ○ *psychiatry* [< Greek *-iatreia* 'art of healing' < *iatros* 'physician']

IAU *abbr* **1.** International Association of Universities **2.** International Astronomical Union

IB *abbr* **1.** COMM in bond **2.** ARMS incendiary bomb **3.** COMM industrial business **4.** EDUC International Baccalaureate **5.** COMM invoice book

ib. *abbr* ibidem

IBA *abbr* **1.** Independent Broadcasting Authority **2.** CHEM indolebutyric acid **3.** LAW International Bar Association **4.** BANKING Investment Bankers' Association

Ibadan /i báddən/ city and capital of Oyo State, southwestern Nigeria, situated 143 km/89 mi. northeast of Lagos. Population: 1,365,000 (1995).

Ibagué /ēéba gáy/ city and capital of Tolima department, central Columbia, situated on a high plain at an altitude of 1,311 m/4,300 ft. Population: 334,100 (1992).

IBD *abbr* **1.** inflammatory bowel disease **2.** ENG ion-beam deposition

I-beam *n* **1.** a metal beam or girder that is shaped like a capital 'I' in cross section **2.** *also* **I-beam cursor** a cursor shaped like a capital I that appears over text in Microsoft Windows applications

Iberia /ī beéri ə/ *n* **1.** the Iberian Peninsula **2.** ancient region in the Caucasus, roughly equivalent to present-day eastern Georgia

Iberian /ī beéri ən/ *n* **1.** a member of an ancient people who lived on the iberian peninsula or in the Caucasian state of Iberia **2.** somebody who comes from Spain or Portugal —**Iberian** *adj*

Iberian Peninsula /ī beéri ən-/ peninsula in southwestern Europe, divided into Spain and Portugal, together with Gibraltar

iberis /ī beériss/ *n* a cultivated low-growing plant. Flowers: white, pink, purple. Native to: Mediterranean. Genus: *Iberis*. [Mid-18C. < modern Latin]

ibex

ibex /ī beks/ (*plural* **ibexes** or *same*) *n* a wild mountain goat with long knobbly backward-curving horns. Native to: Europe, Asia, North Africa. Genus: *Capra*. [Early 17C. < Latin]

IBF *abbr* International Boxing Federation

Ibibio /i bíbbi ō/ (*plural same* or **-os**) *n* **1.** a member of a people living in southwestern Nigeria **2.** the Benue-Congo language of the Ibibio people. Native speakers: 2 million. [Early 19C. < Ibibio] —**Ibibio** *adj*

ibid. /íbbid/ *abbr* ibidem

ibidem /íbbi dem/ *adv* used to cite the same book, publication, chapter, or page previously cited [Mid-18C. < Latin, 'in the same place' < *ibi* 'there' + *-dem* 'that']

ibis /íbiss/ (*plural* **ibises** or *same*) *n* a gregarious wading bird with a downward-curving beak. Native to: warm climates. Family: Threskiornithidae. See illustration on next page [14C. Via Latin < Egyptian *hbj*]

Ibiza /i beéthə/ **1.** third largest island in the Balearic Islands, Spain, situated in the western Mediterranean Sea approximately 96 km/60 mi. from

ibis

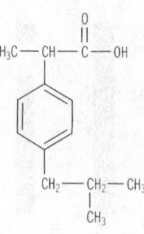

ibuprofen

the eastern coast of the mainland. Area: 570 sq. km/220 sq. mi. **2.** seaport and capital of the island of Ibiza, situated 129 km/80 mi. southwest of Palma. Population: 34,826 (2001). —**Ibizan** *adj*, *n*

Ibizan hound /i beéthən-/ *n* a smooth-haired dog like a small Alsatian, with a light brown or reddish coat that is sometimes spotted. It belongs to a breed originally developed in the Balearic Islands for hunting.

-ible *suffix* same as **-able** ○ *audible* [< Latin *-ibilis*] — **-ibility** *suffix*

Ibn Saud /íbbən sówd/, **Abdul Aziz** (1880?–1953) king of Saudi Arabia. As the first king of Saudi Arabia (1932–53), he helped to found the Arab League (1945) and opened up his country's oil reserves.

Ibo /eébō/ (*plural same* or **Ibos**), **Igbo** /ígbō/ (*plural same* or **-bos**) *n* **1.** a member of a people living in western Africa, especially in southeastern Nigeria. During the 1960s, the Ibo formed the breakaway state of Biafra. Fighting with Nigerian troops and severe famine led to enormous loss of life and the Ibo capitulated in 1970. **2.** a language spoken in southern parts of Nigeria and in some areas of Niger, belonging to the Kwa group of Niger-Congo languages. Native speakers: 17 million. [Mid-18C. < Ibo] —**Ibo** *adj*

Ibrahim /eé braa heem/ *n* BIBLE Arabic name for **Abraham**

IBRD *abbr* International Bank for Reconstruction and Development

IBS *abbr* irritable bowel syndrome

Henrik Ibsen

Ibsen /íbss'n/, **Henrik** (1828–1906) Norwegian playwright. The pioneering psychological realism of such works as *A Doll's House* (1879) and *Hedda Gabler* (1890) had a profound impact on 20th-century drama. Full name **Ibsen, Henrik Johan**. See Cultural note at **ghost, master builder**

> 'It's not just what we inherit from our mothers and fathers that haunts us. It's all kinds of old defunct theories, all sorts of old defunct beliefs, and things like that. It's not that they actually live on in us; they are simply lodged there, and we cannot get rid of them. I've only to pick up a newspaper and I seem to see ghosts gliding between the lines.'
> [Henrik Ibsen, *Ghosts*; 1881]

ibuprofen /í byoo pró fen/ *n* a nonsteroid anti-inflammatory drug. Use: relief of pain and swelling, especially in arthritis and rheumatism. [Mid-2OC. < ISO- + BUTYL + PROPIONIC + alteration of PHENYL]

-ic *suffix* **1.** of or relating to, having the nature of ○ *anarchic* ○ *Indic* **2.** with a valency that is higher than that of a related compound or ion ending in *-ous* ○ *cobaltic* [Directly or via French *-ique* < Latin *-icus* < Greek *-ikos*]

i/c *abbr* **1.** in charge (of) **2.** in command

ICA *abbr* **1.** Institute of Chartered Accountants **2.** Institute of Contemporary Arts **3.** International Coffee Agreement **4.** International Commodity Agreement **5.** International Cooperation Administration

ICAC /í kak, í see ay seé/ *n Aus* a New South Wales body set up to investigate corruption in the police force. Full form **Independent Commission Against Corruption**

ICAEW *abbr* Institute of Chartered Accountants in England and Wales

ICAO *abbr* **1.** International Civil Aeronautics Organization **2.** International Civil Aviation Organization

Icarus /íkərəss/ *n* **1.** in Greek mythology, the son of Daedalus, who drowned in the sea while attempting to escape from Crete after the sun melted his wings of wax and feathers **2.** an asteroid whose orbit is within 30 million km/19 million mi. of the Sun, closer than any other orbiting object —**Icarian** /i káiri ən/ *adj*

ICBM *abbr* intercontinental ballistic missile

ICC *abbr* **1.** International Chamber of Commerce **2.** International Criminal Court

ice /īss/ *n* **1.** FROZEN WATER water that has frozen into solid form ○ *puddles turning to ice* **2.** EXPANSE OF FROZEN WATER an area, layer, or body of frozen water ○ *a polar bear far out on the ice* **3.** SUBSTANCE LIKE ICE any substance resembling ice, e.g. the frozen form of carbon dioxide, known as dry ice **4.** PIECES OF FROZEN WATER ice, either crushed or in cubes, used to cool drinks or food **5.** ICE CREAM a serving of ice cream (*often on signs*) ○ *hot dogs, burgers, and ices* **6.** UNFRIENDLINESS animosity or excessive formality between people ○ *The atmosphere turned to ice when her ex-husband walked in.* **7.** ICE HOCKEY, ICE SKATING SKATING SURFACE a prepared frozen surface for ice skaters or ice-hockey players **8.** DIAMONDS diamonds, or jewellery, especially stolen merchandise or flashy diamond jewellery (*slang*) **9.** ILLEGAL DRUG a smokable form of methamphetamine used as an illegal drug (*slang*) ■ *v* (**ices, icing, iced**) **1.** *vi* FREEZE UP to freeze and develop a thin coating of ice on the surface ○ *The bridge iced, making it dangerous.* **2.** *vt* PUT ICING ON FOOD to cover something such as a cake with icing **3.** *vt* COOL DRINK to chill a drink with ice, or stir ice cubes into a drink [Old English *īs* < Germanic] —**iced** *adj* ◇ **break the ice** to ease the initial restraint or awkwardness of a meeting or social gathering ◇ **cut no ice** to fail to impress or make a difference ◇ **on ice 1.** in abeyance or in a state of being postponed ○ *We had so much work that we had to put the idea of a holiday on ice.* **2.** being chilled in a freezer, refrigerator, or among ice cubes ◇ **on thin ice** in an unsafe, difficult, or vulnerable situation (*informal*)

ice over *vi* to become covered with a layer of ice ○ *As soon as the loch iced over, people were out there with their skates.*

ice up *vi* to become coated with a layer of ice ○ *The windscreen will ice up if you don't put the car in the garage.*

ICE *abbr* **1.** ice, compress, elevation (*refers to first-aid treatment of injuries and bruises*) **2.** Institution of Civil Engineers **3.** internal-combustion engine **4.** International Cultural Exchange

ice age *n* a period in the Earth's history when temperatures fell worldwide and large areas of the Earth's surface were covered with glaciers

Ice Age *n* the most recent ice age during which most of the northern hemisphere was covered with glaciers, occurring during the Pleistocene epoch

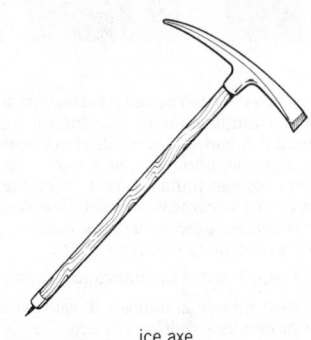

ice axe

ice axe *n* a lightweight tool resembling an axe, used by mountaineers to cut handholds and footholds in ice and provide additional balance during a slide down a snow-covered slope

ice bag *n* a waterproof bag filled with ice and held against an injured part of the body to ease pain or reduce swelling

ice beer *n* beer brewed by a process that freezes the beer and removes some of the ice, thus increasing the beer's alcohol content

iceberg /íss burg/ *n* **1.** a large mounded mass of ice that has broken away from a glacier and floats in the sea, with the greater part of its bulk under the water **2.** *N Am* somebody regarded as unemotional or unfriendly (*informal*) [Late 18C. < Dutch *ijsberg* 'ice mountain']

iceberg lettuce *n* a large round kind of lettuce with a tight head of pale crisp juicy leaves

iceblink /íss blingk/ *n* a yellowish glow in the sky, occurring when sunlight is reflected by a distant ice field

ice block *n ANZ* a sweet, cold confection consisting of flavoured water or ice cream frozen on a stick. UK term **ice lolly**

ice blue *adj* of a very pale blue colour —**ice blue** *n*

iceboat /íss bōt/ *n* NAUT same as **icebreaker** (sense 2)

icebound /íss bownd/ *adj* unable to move because of being covered with or surrounded by ice

icebox /íss boks/ *n* **1.** a small freezer compartment inside a refrigerator **2.** an insulated container or cabinet filled with ice and used to keep food and drinks cool and fresh **3.** *N Am* same as **refrigerator**

icebreaker /íss braykər/ *n* **1.** SOMETHING THAT RELAXES GROUP something used to ease the initial tension, restraint, or awkwardness of a meeting or social gathering, e.g. a joke or game **2.** SHIP FOR BREAKING ICE a ship with a reinforced bow used to break up ice and cut a passage through frozen navigable waters **3.** TOOL FOR BREAKING ICE any tool designed to break up ice, e.g. a small hammer with a sharpened head

ice bucket *n* **1.** a container, sometimes on a stand, filled with ice cubes or a mixture of ice and water and used to keep a bottle of wine cool **2.** a container in which ice cubes are kept cold, ready to be served in drinks

icecap /íss kap/ *n* a thick permanent covering of ice and snow such as at the North and South Poles or on a mountain top

ice-cold *adj* extremely cold ■ *n Aus* a cold beer (*informal*)

ice cream *n* **1.** a sweet frozen dessert or snack traditionally made with cream and egg yolks and flavoured with a variety of fruits or other extracts

2. a serving of ice cream, especially an ice-cream cone [Alteration of *iced cream*]

ice-cream cone, **ice-cream cornet** *n* 1. a hollow cone-shaped wafer designed to hold a serving of ice cream 2. an ice-cream cone containing a serving of ice cream

ice-cream soda *n* a refreshment consisting of ice cream in any kind of fizzy drink, sometimes with the addition of a flavoured syrup, served in a tall glass

ice dancing: Jayne Torvill and Christopher Dean

ice dancing *n* figure skating in which a pair of skaters perform routines based on ballroom dancing, and in which lifts and separation are restricted in competition. Competitive ice dancing also requires that the two skaters remain in close physical contact throughout their routine. —**ice-dance** *vi* —**ice dancer** *n*

ice fall *n* an avalanche or fall of isolated chunks of ice from a mountainside

icefall /íss fawl/ *n* 1. a waterfall that has frozen solid 2. a face of a glacier on which the gradient is so steep that the ice breaks up into a jumble of blocks [After WATERFALL]

ice field *n* a large flat expanse of ice formed where the land surface is level, therefore making it easy for ice to accumulate

ice fish *n* a spiny-finned fish that has a semi-transparent scaleless body and a low oxygen requirement, making it well suited to cold waters. Native to: Antarctic. Family: Chaenichthyidae.

ice floe *n* a sheet of floating ice smaller than an ice field

ice foot *n* a permanent band of ice along the coast of a polar region

ice hockey *n* SPORTS a game played on ice by two teams of six skaters. Points are scored by hitting a rubber disc (**puck**) into the opposing team's goal with a long flat-bladed stick. N Am term **hockey**

icehouse /íss howss/ (*plural* **-houses** /-howziz/) *n* a building where ice is made, stored, and sometimes sold

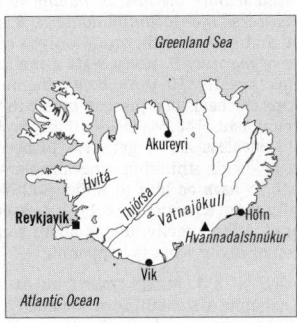

Iceland

Iceland /íssland/ island country in the North Atlantic Ocean, 300 km/185 mi. east of Greenland and 1,000 km/620 mi. west of Norway. Language: Icelandic. Currency: króna. Capital: Reykjavik. Population: 280,798 (2003). Area: 103,000 sq. km/39,800 sq. mi. Official name **Republic of Iceland** —**Icelander** *n*

Icelandic /íss lándik/ *adj* 1. OF ICELAND relating to Iceland, or its people 2. OF ICELANDIC LANGUAGE relating to the North Germanic language of modern Iceland

■ *n* LANGUAGE OF ICELAND the North Germanic language of modern Iceland. Native speakers: 250,000.

LANGUAGE HERITAGE See *Scandinavian*.

Iceland moss *n* a greyish-brown lichen grown as a food and also used medicinally. Native to: Arctic, northern Europe. Latin name: *Cetraria islandica*.

Iceland poppy *n* a poppy with leafless stems. Flowers: white, yellow. Native to: Arctic. Latin name: *Papaver nudicaule*.

Iceland spar *n* a transparent form of calcite. Use: optical instruments.

ice lolly *n* UK flavoured ice or ice cream frozen onto a stick

ice machine *n* a machine that produces ice cubes. N Am term **icemaker**

iceman /íss man/ (*plural* **-men** /-men/) *n* an explorer or mountaineer experienced in travelling on ice

ice milk *n* N Am a sweet frozen food like ice cream but made with skimmed milk

ice needle *n* a tiny needle-shaped ice crystal that forms in cold moist air and gathers with others into masses resembling clouds, often at high altitudes and in otherwise clear weather

Iceni /ī seé nī/ *npl* an ancient people of Britain who, under Queen Boudicca, attempted to overthrow the Romans in AD 61. The Romans fought off the Iceni and Boudicca committed suicide. [< Latin]

ice pack *n* 1. an ice-filled cloth or bag held against an injured part of the body to ease pain or reduce swelling 2. an area of pack ice

ice pick *n* a lightweight hand-held pick for chipping away or breaking up ice

ice plant *n* 1. a clump-forming plant with thick pale-green leaves. Flowers: dark pink, flat-topped. Native to: Mediterranean. Latin name: *Sedum spectabile*. 2. a low-growing plant with leaves that are covered with fine protruding sacs that glisten like ice crystals. Flowers: pink, white, resembling daisies. Native to: southern Africa. Latin name: *Mesembryanthemum crystallinum*.

ice point *n* the temperature, 0°C or 32°F, at which water freezes under a pressure of one atmosphere

ice rink *n* an area of frozen water used by ice-skaters, ice-hockey players, and curlers, especially an enclosed prepared surface

ice sheet *n* a thick covering of ice over a large area that remains for a long period of time

ice shelf *n* a thick mass of ice covering coastal land and extending out over the sea so that the extended portion floats

ice show *n* an entertainment performed by skaters on ice

ice skate *n* a boot with a metal blade fitted along the length of its sole, allowing the wearer to glide over an ice-covered surface

ice skating *n* the sport or pastime of using ice skates to glide over an ice-covered surface —**ice-skate** *vi* —**ice skater** *n*

ice storm *n* N Am a rainstorm in conditions so cold that the rain freezes as it hits the ground, forming sheets of ice

ice water *n* 1. water produced when ice melts 2. N Am very cold water or water chilled in a refrigerator or with ice cubes, served as a drink

ICFTU *abbr* International Confederation of Free Trade Unions

I.Chem.E. *abbr* Institution of Chemical Engineers

I Ching /eé chíng/ *n* 1. an ancient Chinese system of divination, based on a book of Taoist philosophy and expressed in hexagrams chosen at random and interpreted to answer questions and give advice 2. the book containing the symbols used in I Ching divination and an accompanying text that the reader may consult for help in interpreting the symbols [Late 19C. < Chinese, literally 'Book of Changes']

ichneumon fly /ik nyoómən-/, **ichneumon wasp**, **ichneumon** *n* a slender insect related to and resembling a wasp that is a parasite of many insect pests, laying its eggs in insect larvae. Family: Ichneumonidae. [Via Latin < Greek *ikhneumōn* 'mongoose',

literally 'tracker' < *ikhneuein* 'to track' < *ikhnos* 'track, footprint']

ichnite /ík nīt/, **ichnolite** /íknə līt/ *n* a fossilized footprint [Mid-19C. < Greek *ikhnos* 'track, footprint']

ichnography /ik nóggrəfi/ (*plural* **-phies**) *n* 1. the art or practice of drawing ground plans of the layout of buildings 2. a ground plan of the layout of a building [Late 16C. Directly or via French < Latin *ichnographia* < Greek *ikhnographia* 'track-drawing' < *ikhnos* 'track, footprint'] —**ichnographic** /íknə gráffik/ *adj* —**ichnographical** *adj* —**ichnographically** *adv*

ichnolite *n* PALAEONT same as **ichnite**

ichnology /ik nólləji/ *n* the scientific study of fossilized footprints [Mid-19C. < Greek *ikhnos* 'track, footprint'] —**ichnological** /íknə lójjik'l/ *adj*

ichor /í kawr/ *n* 1. a watery or slightly bloody discharge from a wound or an ulcer 2. in Greek mythology, the fluid said to run instead of body fluid through the veins of the gods [Mid-17C. < Greek *ikhōr*] —**ichorous** /íkərəss/ *adj*

ichthus /íkthəss/, **ichthys** /-thiss/ *n* a simple symbol that resembles a fish, consisting of two curves that bisect each other. It is a symbol of Christianity. [< Greek *ikhthus* 'fish']

ichthy- *prefix* same as **ichthyo-** (*used before vowels*)

ichthyo- *prefix* fish ○ *ichthyology* [Via Latin < Greek *ikhthus* 'fish']

ichthyoid /íkthi oyd/ *n* a fish, or a vertebrate that is similar to a fish, e.g. a lamprey or hagfish —**ichthyoid** *adj* —**ichthyoidal** /íkthi óyd'l/ *adj*

ichthyology /íkthi ólləji/ *n* the branch of zoology that deals with the scientific study of fish —**ichthyologic** /íkthi ə lójjik/ *adj* —**ichthyological** *adj* —**ichthyologically** *adv* —**ichthyologist** *n*

ichthyophagous /íkthi óffəgəss/ *adj* eating or feeding on fish

ichthyornis /íkthi áwrniss/ *n* an extinct toothed bird, similar to a gull, that lived during the Cretaceous period. Genus: *Ichthyornis*. [Late 19C. < modern Latin < Greek *ikhthus* 'fish' + *ornis* 'bird']

ichthyosaur /íkthi ə sawr/, **ichthyosaurus** /íkthi ə sáwrəss/ (*plural* **-ruses** or **-ri** /-rī/) *n* a prehistoric reptile with a long snout and paddle-shaped limbs that lived in the sea during the Mesozoic era. Order: Ichthyosauria. [Mid-19C. < modern Latin *Ichthyosauria* < Greek *ikhthus* 'fish' + *sauros* 'lizard'] —**ichthyosaurian** /íkthi ə sáwri ən/ *adj*

ichthyosis /íkthi óssiss/ *n* a disease that causes the skin to become dry, thick, and scaly

ichthys *n* CHR same as **ichthus**

-ician *suffix* somebody who practises or specializes in a particular thing ○ *musician* ○ *statistician* [< Old French *-icien* < *-ique* (see *-IC*)]

icicle /íssik'l/ *n* 1. a hanging tapered rod of ice, formed when dripping water freezes 2. somebody regarded as aloof or unemotional (*informal*) [14C. < ICE + obsolete *ickle* 'icicle' < Old English *gicel* < Germanic]

icily /íssili/ *adv* in a very aloof or unfriendly manner

icing /íssing/ *n* 1. GLAZING FOR CAKES a sugar-based decorative coating for cakes, either soft or hardened, made by mixing powdered sugar with water or another binding substance and often other ingredients or flavourings 2. FORMATION OF ICE the formation of ice on exposed surfaces ○ *Some roads will be liable to icing.* 3. SHOOTING PUCK INTO OPPOSING TERRITORY in ice hockey, the action of shooting the puck out of defensive territory and far into the opposing team's territory ◇ **the icing on the cake** something additional that makes something that was already good even better

icing sugar *n* UK, ANZ, Can powdered white sugar used to make icing, for sweetening, or for sprinkling. US term **confectioners' sugar**

ICJ *abbr* International Court of Justice

icky /íki/ (**-ier, -iest**) *adj* (*informal*) 1. NASTY generally nasty or unpleasant ○ *I had an icky feeling in their presence.* 2. STICKY disgustingly and messily sticky 3. SENTIMENTAL sentimental in a silly or childish way ○ *a script with some pretty icky lines* [Early 20C. Origin ?] —**ickiness** *n*

ICM *abbr* 1. Institute of Credit Management 2. Inter-

governmental Committee for Migrations (*part of the UN*)

icon: Eastern Orthodox icon of *Christus Acheiropoietus* in the Cathedral of the Assumption, Moscow

icon /ī kon/ *n* **1.** *also* **ikon** IMAGE OF HOLY PERSON a holy picture, carving, or statue of Jesus Christ, the Virgin Mary, or a saint, especially an oil painting on a wooden panel, of a type revered in the Eastern Orthodox churches **2.** SOMEBODY FAMOUS FOR SOMETHING somebody or something widely and uncritically admired, especially somebody or something symbolizing a movement or field of activity ○ *the all-time rock'n'roll icon* **3.** PICTURE ON COMPUTER SCREEN a small image on a computer screen that represents something such as a program or device that is activated by a mouse click ○ *Open the program by clicking on its icon.* **4.** RECOGNIZABLE SYMBOL a picture or symbol that is universally recognized to be representative of something [Mid-16C. Via Latin < Greek *eikōn* 'image']

icon- *prefix* same as **icono-** (*used before vowels*)

iconic /ī kónnik/ *adj* **1.** CHARACTERIZED BY FAME relating to or characteristic of somebody or something admired as an icon ○ *Their fame has grown to iconic proportions.* **2.** TYPICAL OF RELIGIOUS ICON relating to or characteristic of a religious icon ○ *iconic images* **3.** CONVENTIONAL made in a conventional style or pose, especially that of ancient Greek statues of athletes —**iconically** *adv*

iconic memory *n* a form of memory in which objects are retained briefly but clearly as a visual image after the stimulus has been removed. It develops between the ages of two and six when a child begins to use images to stand for objects.

icono- *prefix* icon, image ○ *iconolatry* ○ *iconoscope* [< Greek *eikōn*]

iconoclasm /ī kónnə klazəm/ *n* **1.** a challenge to or overturning of traditional beliefs, customs, and values **2.** the destruction of religious images used in worship, or opposition to their use in worship

iconoclast /ī kónnə klast/ *n* **1.** SOMEBODY CHALLENGING TRADITION somebody who challenges or overturns traditional beliefs, customs, and values **2.** DESTROYER OF RELIGIOUS IMAGES somebody who destroys religious images or opposes their use in worship **3.** HERETIC IN GREEK ORTHODOX CHURCH a member of an 8th-century movement in the Greek Orthodox Church that tried to end the use of icons [Mid-17C. Via medieval Latin < medieval Greek *eikonoklastēs* 'image-breaker' < Greek *eikōn* 'image'] —**iconoclastic** /ī kónnə klástik/ *adj* —**iconoclastically** *adv*

iconography /īkə nóggrəfi/ *n* **1.** SET OF RECOGNIZED IMAGES the set of symbols or images used in a particular field of activity such as music or cinema and recognized by people as having a particular meaning ○ *In the 1960s, peace signs and long hair were part of the iconography of rebellion.* **2.** SYMBOLS IN PAINTING the symbols and images used conventionally in a genre of painting, or the study and interpretation of these symbols and images ○ *the iconography used in Renaissance paintings of the Virgin and Child* **3.** IMAGES OF SOMEBODY OR SOMETHING SPECIFIC the collection, description, or study of images of somebody or something specific —**iconographer** *n* —**iconographic** /ī kónnə gráffik/ *adj* —**iconographical** *adj*

iconolatry /īkə nóllətri/ *n* the worshipping of religious images rather than of what they represent (*disapproving*) —**iconolater** *n*

iconology /īkə nólləji/ *n* **1.** the study of artistic images and their symbolism and interpretation **2.** the

images or symbols used in a specific field of activity —**iconological** /ī kónnə lójjik'l/ *adj* —**iconologist** *n*

iconomatic /ī kónnə máttik/ *adj* using images to represent the sounds of the names of things rather than the things themselves, e.g. in the transition from pictorial to phonetic representation, seen in the history of some languages [Late 19C. Contraction of *icononomatic* < Greek *eikōn* 'image' + *onomat-* 'name'] —**iconomaticism** /-máttisizəm/ *n*

iconoscope /ī kónnə skōp/ *n* an early form of television camera tube in which an image is converted into electrical impulses

iconostasis /īkə nóstəssiss/ (*plural* **-tases** /-tə seez/), **iconostas** /ī kónnə stass/ (*plural* **-tases** /-tassiz/) *n* a screen on which icons are mounted, used in Eastern Orthodox churches to separate the area around the altar from the main part of the church [Mid-19C. < modern Greek *eikonostasis* 'place where images stand']

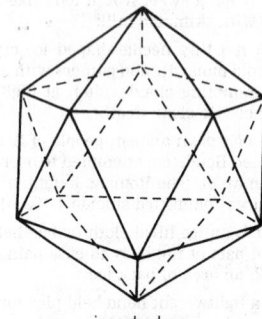

icosahedron

icosahedron /īkəssə heédrən/ (*plural* **-drons** or **-dra** /-drə/) *n* a three-dimensional geometric figure formed of 20 sides or faces [Late 16C. Via late Latin < Greek *eikosaedron* < *eikosi* 'twenty' + *hedra* 'base'] —**icosahedral** *adj*

icositetrahedron /īkəssi téttrə heédrən/ (*plural* **-drons** or **-dra** /-drə/) *n* a three-dimensional geometric figure formed of 24 sides or faces [Mid-19C. < Greek *eikosi* 'twenty' + *tetra-* 'four']

ICQ *n* a computer program that makes contact with a user who is chatting online [Late 20C. After *ICQ* Inc., name representing 'I seek you']

ICR *abbr* **1.** Institute for Cancer Research **2.** COMPUT intelligent character recognition

ICRC *abbr* International Committee of the Red Cross

ICS *abbr* **1.** instalment credit selling **2.** Institute of Chartered Shipbrokers **3.** International Chamber of Shipping **4.** investors' compensation scheme

-ics *suffix* **1.** a science, art, or knowledge ○ *physics* ○ *mathematics* **2.** an activity or action ○ *callisthenics* [< -IC + -S; translation of Greek *-ika* (plural)]

icterus /íktərəss/ *n* MED same as **jaundice** (*technical*) [Early 18C. Via Latin < Greek *ikteros*] —**icteric** /ik térrik/ *adj*

ictus /íktəss/ (*plural* **-tuses** or *same*) *n* **1.** MED same as **seizure** (sense 3) (*technical*) **2.** the stress that falls on syllables in poetic rhythm [Early 18C. < Latin, 'stroke' < past participle of *icere* 'strike'] —**ictal** *adj*

ICU *abbr* HEALTH SERVICES intensive care unit

ICVC *n* an investment scheme similar to that of a unit trust but differing in that it is organized as a company rather than a trust and has a single price rather than a bid offer spread. Full form **Investment Company with Variable Capital**

icy /íssi/ (**-ier**, **-iest**) *adj* **1.** ICE-COVERED covered in or involving ice **2.** VERY COLD extremely cold, like ice ○ *Your hands are icy.* **3.** UNFRIENDLY very aloof or unfriendly ○ *his reserved manner and icy voice* —**iciness** *n*

icy pole *n Aus* an ice lolly

id[1] /id/ *n* in Freudian psychoanalytic theory, the part of the psyche that is unconscious and is the source of primitive instinctive impulses and drives. The other parts of the psyche are the ego and the superego. [Early 20C. < Latin, 'it']

id[2] *abbr* ONLINE Indonesia (*used in Internet addresses*) See table at **domain name**

I'd /īd/ *contr* **1.** I had ○ *I'd forgotten you were coming.* **2.** I would or I should ○ *I'd leave now, if I were you.*

Id *n* ISLAM another spelling of **Eid**

ID[1] *abbr* **1.** MED infectious disease(s) **2.** *also* **i.d.** inner diameter **3.** *also* **i.d.** MEASURE inside diameter *or* internal diameter **4.** *also* **i.d.** MED intradermal

ID[2] *n* material or an official document that identifies somebody ■ *vt* (**IDs, IDing, IDed**) to identify somebody or check somebody's identity (*informal*) ○ *police to ID the suspect* [Abbreviation IDENTIFICATION]

id. *abbr* idem

-id *suffix* **1.** objects, especially meteors, that appear to come from a particular constellation ○ *Perseids* **2.** particular kinds of particle or body ○ *plastid* **3.** a member of a zoological family ○ *camelid* **4.** a member of a dynasty ○ *Abbasid* [Directly or via French *-ide* < Latin *-ides* < Greek *-idēs* 'offspring of']

IDA *abbr* International Development Association

Idaho /ídəhō/ state in the western United States bordered by Montana, Nevada, Oregon, Utah, Washington, and Wyoming, and British Columbia, Canada. Capital: Boise. Population: 1,341,131 (2002 estimate). Area: 216,456 sq. km/83,574 sq. mi. —**Idahoan** /īdə hō ən, īdə hō ən/ *adj, n*

Id al-Adha, etc. *n* ISLAM another spelling of **Eid al-Adha, etc.**

Ida Mountains /īdə-/ mountain range in northwestern Turkey, southeast of the ancient site of Troy. The highest peak is Mount Gargarus, 1,767 m/5,797 ft.

IDB *abbr* Industrial Development Bank

ID card *n* a card identifying its carrier, having on it information such as name, age, and often an address and a physical description or photograph (*informal*)

IDD *abbr* **1.** MED insulin-dependent diabetes **2.** TELECOM international direct dialling

-ide *suffix* **1.** a class of elements or compounds ○ *actinides* **2.** an organic compound derived from another compound ○ *anhydride* [< OXIDE]

idea /ī deé ə/ *n* **1.** OPINION a personal opinion or belief ○ *Do you have any ideas on how the problem should be tackled?* **2.** SUGGESTION a thought to be presented as a suggestion ○ *It was her idea to plant daisies.* **3.** IMPRESSION an impression or knowledge of something ○ *They saw us leaving together and got the wrong idea.* **4.** PLAN a realization of a possible way of doing something or of something to be done ○ *Watching the beaver building its dam gave me an idea.* **5.** AIM the aim or purpose of a project or plan ○ *The idea of the new scheme is to keep young people in school.* **6.** BRIEF OUTLINE a summary or the essential concept of something such as a book, report, project, or plan ○ *give you only a broad idea now, with a detailed outline to follow* **7.** THOUGHT a thought about or mental picture of something such as a future or possible event ○ *Sometimes the idea of having to speak in public is worse than actually doing it.* **8.** CONCEPT a concept that exists in the mind only ○ *discussing the idea of morality* **9.** MENTAL IMAGE a mental image that reflects reality **10.** MUSIC MOTIF a theme or motif that forms the basis of a piece of music throughout its development [14C. Via Latin < Greek, 'look' < *idein* 'to see'] —**idealess** *adj* ◇ **get ideas** to become ambitious or begin thinking undesirable thoughts (*informal*) ◇ **have no idea** to know nothing at all, especially about a particular subject ◇ **what's the big idea?** used, often angrily, to ask about somebody's intention or about what is happening

ideal /ī deé əl/ *n* **1.** PERFECT EXAMPLE an excellent or perfect example of something or somebody, or something that is considered a perfect example ○ *By her third film, she had become the world's ideal of beauty and grace.* **2.** PRINCIPLE a standard or principle to which people aspire ○ *political ideals* **3.** IMAGINARY OBJECT OR CONCEPT a concept that exists in the imagination only ■ *adj* **1.** BEST serving as the best or most perfect example **2.** PERFECT perfect but existing only in the imagination ○ *In an ideal world, such horrors wouldn't happen.* **3.** EXCELLENT excellent or perfectly suitable ○ *A later meeting would be ideal for me.* [15C. Directly or via French < late Latin *idealis* < Latin *idea* (see IDEA)] —**idealless** *adj* —**idealness** *n*

USAGE See *idyll.*

ideal gas *n* a hypothetical gas that obeys the gas laws perfectly at all temperatures and pressures

idealise *vt* another spelling of **idealize**

idealism /ī deé əlizəm/ *n* **1. BELIEF IN PERFECTION** belief in and pursuit of perfection as an attainable goal ○ *youthful idealism* **2. LIVING BY HIGH IDEALS** aspiring to or living in accordance with high standards or principles **3. BELIEF THAT MATERIAL THINGS ARE IMAGINARY** the philosophical belief that material things do not exist independently but only as constructions in the mind

idealist /ī deé əlist/ *n* **1. IMPRACTICAL PERSON** a perfectionist who rejects practical considerations ○ *too much of an idealist to compromise with her opponents* **2. SOMEBODY WITH HIGH IDEALS** somebody who aspires to or abides by high standards or principles **3.** PHILOSOPHY **BELIEVER IN IDEALISM** a believer in a philosophy holding that material objects do not exist independently of the mind —**idealistic** /ī deé ə lístik/ *adj* —**idealistically** *adv*

ideality /īdi álləti/ *n* **1.** the condition or quality of being ideal **2.** existence as an idea only, rather than as a concrete object

idealize /ī deé ə līz/ (**-izes, -izing, -ized**), **idealise** (**-ises, -ising, -ised**) *vt* to think of or represent somebody or something as being perfect, ignoring any imperfections that exist or may exist in reality ○ *paintings that idealize feminine beauty* —**idealization** /ī deé ə lī záysh'n/ *n* —**idealized** *adj* —**idealizer** *n*

ideally /ī deé əli/ *adv* **1. IN IDEAL SITUATION** if everything were perfect or as desired ○ *Ideally, I'd like to finish the job by next week.* **2. PERFECTLY** in a perfect manner ○ *She is ideally suited to the post.* **3. THEORETICALLY** in theory or in the imagination ○ *Ideally, there would be no prejudice or persecution in the world.*

~~**idealy**~~ incorrect spelling of **ideally**

ideate /īdi ayt/ (**-ates, -ating, -ated**) *vti* to form an idea of something, or form ideas [Early 17C. < medieval Latin *ideat-*, past participle of *ideare* 'form an idea' < Latin *idea* (see IDEA)] —**ideation** /īdi áysh'n/ *n* —**ideational** *adj* —**ideationally** *adv* —**ideative** /-ətiv, -aytiv/ *adj*

idée fixe /eé day feéks/ (*plural* **idées fixes** /*pronunc. same*/) *n* an idea that remains fixed and unchanging in the mind and often becomes an obsession [< French, 'fixed idea']

idée reçue /eé day rə syoō/ (*plural* **idées reçues** /*pronunc. same*/) *n* a conventional or commonplace idea [< French, 'received idea']

idem /íddem, ī-/ *pron* the same, especially a book, article, or chapter previously referred to [14C. < Latin (see IDENTITY)]

idempotent /ī dem pōt'nt, ī démpətənt/ *adj* describes a mathematical quantity that remains unchanged when multiplied by itself [Late 19C. < Latin *idem* (see IDENTITY) + *potent-* 'powerful']

ident /ī dent/ *n* a graphic that appears briefly to identify a television channel

identic /ī déntik/ *adj* describes diplomatic notes sent, or diplomatic action taken, by two or more governments in exactly the same form [Mid-17C. < medieval Latin *identicus* 'identical' < *ident-* (see IDENTITY)]

identical /ī déntik'l/ *adj* **1.** exactly the same as or equal to something else, or alike in every respect ○ *wearing identical dresses* ○ *His name was identical to mine.* **2.** describes twins of the same sex and with the same genetic makeup that have developed from a single fertilized egg —**identically** *adv* —**identicalness** *n*

identical rhyme *n* perfect rhyme of a whole syllable, including consonants and vowels, e.g. 'describe' and 'inscribe'

~~**identicle**~~ incorrect spelling of **identical**

identification /ī déntifi káysh'n/ *n* **1. NAMING SOMEBODY** the action of identifying somebody or something, or an act of recognizing and naming somebody or something **2. PROOF OF IDENTITY** something, especially a card or document, to prove that somebody is who he or she claims to be **3. STRONG FEELING OF AFFINITY** a powerful feeling of affinity with another person or group, which sometimes involves regarding somebody as a model and adopting his or her beliefs, values, or other characteristics

identification card *n N Am* same as **identity card**

identification parade *n* CRIME a group of people, including a suspect, shown by police to a witness to a crime in order to discover whether the witness can identify the person who committed it. N Am term **lineup**

identifier /ī dénti fī ər/ *n* a symbol that identifies, indicates, or names a body of data

identify /ī dénti fī/ (**-fies, -fying, -fied**) *vt* **1.** to recognize somebody or something and to be able to say who or what he, she, or it is **2.** to consider two or more things as being entirely or essentially the same [Mid-17C. Directly or via French *identifier* < medieval Latin *identificare* 'make the same' < *ident-* (see IDENTITY)] —**identifiability** /ī dénti fī ə bílləti/ *n* —**identifiable** *adj* —**identifiably** *adv*

identify with *vi* **1.** to feel a strong sympathetic or imaginative bond with somebody or something and a sense of understanding and sharing his, her, or its nature or concerns **2.** to consider somebody or something as closely linked with somebody or something such as a school of thought or political movement (*often passive*)

Identikit /ī déntikit/ *tdmk* a trademark for a set of pictures showing varied facial features that can be combined to produce a human likeness, e.g. of a missing person or of a criminal suspect

identity /ī déntəti/ (*plural* **-ties**) *n* **1. WHAT IDENTIFIES SOMEBODY OR SOMETHING** the name or essential character that identifies somebody or something **2. ESSENTIAL SELF** the set of characteristics that somebody recognizes as belonging uniquely to himself or herself and constituting his or her individual personality for life **3. SAMENESS** the fact or condition of being the same or exactly alike **4.** *ANZ* **CELEBRITY** somebody who is well known in a particular activity or place, e.g. racing (*informal*) **5.** MATHS **EQUATION TRUE FOR ALL ITS VARIABLES** a mathematical equation that remains valid whatever values are taken by its variables **6.** MATHS same as **identity element** [Late 16C. < late Latin *identitas* < *ident-*, combining form of Latin *idem* 'same' < *id* 'that']

identity card *n* a card carrying the holder's name, address, date of birth, and other particulars, together with a photograph, that serves as proof of his or her identity for official purposes. N Am term **identification card**

identity crisis *n* **1.** a period during which somebody feels great anxiety and uncertainty about his or her identity and role in life and society, typically experienced in adolescence or middle age **2.** a period of anxiety or confusion about the nature, aims, and role of a group, organization, or business

identity element *n* an element of a mathematical set that leaves other elements unchanged when combined with them

identity matrix *n* a square matrix that has the numeral 1 in each position on the principal diagonal and 0 in all other positions

identity parade *n UK* CRIME same as **identification parade**

identity theft *n* theft of personal information such as somebody's credit card details

ideo- *prefix* ideas ○ *ideomotor* [Via French < Greek *idea* (see IDEA)]

ideogram /íddi ə gram/, **ideograph** /íddi ə graaf, -graf/ *n* **1.** a symbol used in some writing systems, e.g. those of Japan and China, that directly but abstractly represents a thing or concept itself rather than the word for it **2.** a symbol or graphical character used to represent a word, e.g. '@' or '&' —**ideogrammatic** /íddi əgrə máttik/ *adj* —**ideogrammatically** *adv* —**ideographic** /íddi ə gráffik/ *adj* —**ideographically** *adv* —**ideography** /íddi óggrəfi/ *n*

ideologue /īdi ə log/ *n* a particularly zealous or doctrinaire supporter of an ideology

ideology /īdi ólləji/ (*plural* **-gies**) *n* **1.** a closely organized system of beliefs, values, and ideas forming the basis of a social, economic, or political philosophy or programme **2.** a set of beliefs, values, and opinions that shapes the way a person or a group such as a social class thinks, acts, and understands the world —**ideological** /īdi ə lójjik'l/ *adj* —**ideologist** *n*

ideomotor /īdi ə mōtər/ *adj* describes body movements triggered by thoughts rather than by external stimuli

ides /īdz/, **Ides** *n* in the ancient Roman calendar, the 15th day of March, May, July, and October, or the 13th day of any other month (*takes a singular or plural verb*) [12C. Directly or via French < Latin *idus* (plural)]

idgah /id gaa/ *n S Asia* a mosque or other place of prayer for Muslims [< Arabic *id* 'place' + Persian *gah* 'prayer']

-idine *suffix* a chemical compound related to another compound ○ *histidine* [< -IDE + -INE]

idio- *prefix* private, individual, proper, or distinctive ○ *idiolect* ○ *idiomorphic* [< Greek *idios* 'your own, private' < Indo-European, 'self']

idioblast /íddi ō blast/ *n* a specialized plant cell that differs from others in the same area of tissue. An idioblast is usually thick-walled and lacks chlorophyll. —**idioblastic** /íddi ō blástik/ *adj*

idiocy /íddi əssi/ *n* **1.** an offensive term meaning extreme lack of intelligence or foresight **2.** an offensive term for an extremely unintelligent or thoughtless act **3.** an offensive term in a now disused classification system for mental disability (*dated*) [Early 16C. < IDIOT]

idioglossia /íddi ō glóssi ə/ *n* **1.** a developmental speech difficulty in which a child substitutes different sounds for the correct ones, so that speech is intelligible only to parents or others familiar with it **2.** the invention and use by a child or closely involved siblings of language that is unintelligible to anyone else [Late 19C. < Greek *idioglōssos* < *idios* 'distinct' + *glōssa* 'tongue']

idiogram /íddi ō gram/ *n* a photograph or diagram showing the chromosomes of a cell or organism arranged in their homologous pairs according to the standard numbering system for that organism

idiographic /íddi ō gráffik/ *adj* concentrating on specific cases and the unique traits or functioning of individuals, rather than on broad generalizations about human behaviour. Idiographic research methods in psychology include the case study, which is characterized by the distinctiveness of each case.

idiolect /íddi ə lekt/ *n* an individual person's vocabulary and unique way of using language [Mid-20C. < IDIO- + DIALECT] —**idiolectal** /íddi ə lékt'l/ *adj*

SYNONYMS See *language.*

idiom /íddi əm/ *n* **1. FIXED EXPRESSION WITH NONLITERAL MEANING** a fixed distinctive expression whose meaning cannot be deduced from the combined meanings of its actual words **2. NATURAL WAY OF USING LANGUAGE** the way of using a language that comes naturally to its native speakers **3. STYLISTIC EXPRESSION** the style of expression of a specific person or group **4. DISTINGUISHING ARTISTIC STYLE** the characteristic style of an artist or artistic group [Late 16C. Directly or via French < late Latin *idioma* < Greek, 'property, peculiarity' < *idios* (see IDIO-)]

SYNONYMS See *jargon*[1].

idiomatic /íddi ə máttik/, **idiomatical** /-máttik'l/ *adj* **1. CHARACTERISTIC OF NATIVE-SPEAKER USE** characteristic of, or in keeping with, the way a language is ordinarily and naturally used by its native speakers **2. OF NATURE OF IDIOM** having a meaning not deducible from the combined meanings of the constituent words ○ *an idiomatic phrase* **3. CHARACTERISTIC OF STYLE** characteristic of a specific style, or using a distinctive style, especially in the arts —**idiomatically** *adv*

idiomorphic /íddi ō máwrfik/ *adj* describes minerals that occur naturally in the form of fully developed crystals —**idiomorphically** *adv* —**idiomorphism** *n*

idiopathic /íddi ō páthik/ *adj* describes a disease or disorder that has no known cause —**idiopathically** *adv* —**idiopathy** /íddi óppəthi/ *n*

idiophone /íddi ō fōn/ *n* a percussion instrument that is made from resonating material that does not

have to be tuned e.g. a gong or xylophone —**idiophonic** /íddi ō fónnik/ *adj*

~~**idiosyncracy**~~ incorrect spelling of **idiosyncrasy**

idiosyncrasy /íddi ō síngkrəssi/ (*plural* **-sies**) *n* **1.** a way of behaving, thinking, or feeling that is peculiar to an individual or group, especially an odd or unusual one **2.** an unusual or exaggerated reaction to a drug or food that is not caused by an allergy [Early 17C. Directly or via French *idiosyncrasie* < Greek *idiosugkrasia*, literally 'personal mixing together' < *krasis* 'mixing'] —**idiosyncratic** /íddi ō sing kráttik/ *adj*—**idiosyncratically** *adv*

idiot /íddi ət/ *n* **1.** an offensive term that deliberately insults somebody's intelligence (*insult*) **2.** an offensive term in a now disused classification system for somebody with an IQ of about 25 or under and a mental age of less than 3 years (*dated*) [14C. Via French and Latin < Greek *idiōtēs* 'private person, layperson' < *idios* (see IDIO-)]

idiot board *n* a placard, projector, or continuous roll of paper that prompts a television performer with lines to be spoken (*slang*)

idiot box *n* television, or a television set (*slang*) [< the belief that watching too much television causes stupidity]

idiot card *n* MEDIA same as **idiot board** (*slang*)

idiotic /íddi óttik/ *adj* an offensive term meaning showing a lack of good sense or intelligence —**idiotically** *adv*

idiot-proof *adj* constructed or designed so as not to fail or go wrong even if misused (*informal*)

idiot savant /éedi ō sa vóN, íddi ət sávvənt/ (*plural* **idiot savants** /*pronunc. same*/ or **idiots savants** /éedi ō sa vóN, íddi əts sávvənt/) *n* same as **autistic savant** (*dated offensive*) [< French, 'learned idiot']

idiot tape *n* a tape for a typesetting machine that contains text but no formatting except markers for new paragraphs

IDK *abbr* I don't know (*used in e-mails or text messages*)

idle /íd'l/ *adj* (**idler, idlest**) **1.** LAZY lazy and unwilling to work **2.** NOT WORKING OR IN USE not working, operating, producing, or in use **3.** FRIVOLOUS frivolous and a waste of time ○ *idle pleasures* **4.** UNFOUNDED having no basis in fact ○ *idle gossip* **5.** INEFFECTIVE unlikely to be carried out or impossible to put into effect ○ *idle threats* **6.** NOT EARNING MONEY not being used to yield a financial return ○ *idle funds* ■ *n* SPEED OF ENGINE WITH GEAR DISENGAGED the state in which a motor vehicle engine is running but is not in gear ■ *v* (**idles, idling, idled**) **1.** *vti* RUN WITHOUT APPLYING POWER to run gently while not in gear, or allow a motor vehicle engine to do this **2.** *vti* PASS TIME AIMLESSLY to be lazy and avoid work, or pass the time in this way ○ *He idled away the morning.* **3.** *vi* MOVE SLOWLY AND AIMLESSLY to move in a slow and lazy or aimless way **4.** *vt N Am* MAKE SOMEBODY UNEMPLOYED to make somebody unemployed or inactive [Old English *īdel* 'worthless, empty' < Germanic] —**idleness** *n* —**idly** *adv*

SPELLCHECK idle or **idol**? Do not confuse the spelling of ***idle*** and ***idol***, which sound similar. ***Idle*** is an adjective meaning 'lazy' or 'not in use', as in *machines lying idle*, or a verb meaning 'move slowly' or 'pass time lazily', as in *idle away the afternoon*. ***Idol*** is a noun denoting an object of adoration, as in *a pop idol, worshipping idols*.

idle gear (*plural* **idle gears** or **idler gears**) *n* a gear placed between two others to transmit motion, but not direction or speed

idle pulley *n* a freely rotating pulley wheel that guides or takes up slack from a drive belt by pressing against it

idler /ídlər/ *n* **1.** somebody who spends time in a lazy or relaxed way and habitually avoids work **2.** MECH ENG same as **idle wheel** (sense 1)

idler gear *n* MECH ENG same as **idle gear**

idler pulley *n* MECH ENG same as **idle pulley**

idler wheel *n* MECH ENG same as **idle wheel**

idle time *n* a period during which a device, machine, or employee is temporarily inactive

idle wheel *n* **1.** a gear wheel or roller placed between two others to transmit motion between them without changing their speed or direction or to provide support **2.** MECH ENG same as **idle pulley**

idli /íddli/ *npl S Asia* steamed rice cakes eaten for breakfast, especially in southern India [Mid-20C. < Malayalam and Kannada *iḍḍali*]

idocrase /ídə krayz, -krayss/ *n* MINERALS same as **vesuvianite** [Early 19C. < Greek *eidos* 'form' + *krasis* 'mixture']

idol /íd'l/ *n* **1.** OBJECT OF ADORATION somebody or something greatly admired or loved, often to excess **2.** OBJECT WORSHIPPED AS GOD something that is worshipped as a god, e.g. a statue or carved image **3.** FORBIDDEN OBJECT OF WORSHIP in monotheistic religions, an object of worship other than the one God [13C. Via French *idole* < Greek *eidōlon* 'image' < *eidos* 'form, shape']

SPELLCHECK See ***idle***.

idolater /ī dóllətər/ *n* (*disapproving*) **1.** a worshipper of idols **2.** somebody who shows excessive admiration or love for somebody or something [14C. < French *idolâtre* < Greek *eidōlolatrēs* 'image worshipper' < *eidōlon* (see IDOL)]

idolatry /ī dóllətri/ *n* (*disapproving*) **1.** the worship of idols or false gods **2.** excessive admiration or love shown for somebody or something [13C. Via French *idolâtrie* < Greek *eidōlolatreia* 'image-worship' < *eidōlon* (see IDOL)] —**idolatrous** *adj* —**idolatrously** *adv*

idolize /ídə līz/ (**-izes, -izing, -ized**), **idolise** (**-ises, -ising, -ised**) *vt* **1.** to feel great admiration or love for somebody or something, often to excess **2.** to worship something as an idol (*disapproving*) —**idolization** /ídə lī záysh'n/ *n* —**idolizer** *n*

IDP *abbr* integrated data processing

Idren /ídrən/ (*plural same*) *n* (*slang; used in Black English*) **1.** same as **brother 2.** a form of address for or way of referring to another Rastafarian man

Idriess /éedrəss/, **Ion** (1889–1979) Australian novelist. His novels include *Flynn of the Inland* (1932). Full name **Idriess, Ion Llewellyn**

IDTS *abbr* ONLINE I don't think so (*used in e-mails or text messages*)

Id ul-Adha, etc. *n* ISLAM another spelling of **Eid ul-Adha, etc.**

idyll /ídd'l, íd'l/ *n* **1.** EXPERIENCE OF SERENE HAPPINESS an experience or period of serene and carefree happiness, usually in beautiful surroundings and often idealized **2.** TRANQUIL CHARMING SCENE a scene or event characterized by tranquillity, simple beauty, and innocent charm, usually in a rural setting **3.** ARTS LITERARY PIECE ABOUT CHARMING RURAL LIFE a short work in verse or prose, a painting, or a piece of music depicting simple pastoral or rural scenes and the life of country folk, often in an idealized way [Late 16C. Via Latin *idyllium* 'pastoral poem' < Greek *eidullion* 'small picture' < *eidos* 'form']

USAGE idyll, idyllic, or **ideal**? Do not confuse ***idyll*** and ***idyllic*** with the noun and adjective ***ideal***. ***Idyll*** and ***idyllic*** are narrower in meaning, referring to carefree happiness, unspoiled beauty, and serenity, as in *a pastoral idyll* or *an idyllic way to spend a summer afternoon*. ***Ideal*** refers to perfection, or to being the best in every respect, as in *the ideal of beauty* or *the ideal way to tackle the problem*. An ***idyllic*** setting for a hotel, perhaps in the middle of the countryside, is not necessarily ***ideal***; an ***ideal*** setting for a hotel, perhaps near a major airport, may be far from ***idyllic***. Note that the title of Tennyson's *Idylls of the King*, a set of poems about Arthur, Guinevere, and Lancelot, does not refer to the ***ideals*** of the Knights of the Round Table.

idyllic /i díllik, ī-/ *adj* **1.** serenely beautiful, untroubled, and happy **2.** like an idyll, especially in having a simple, unspoiled, and especially rural charm —**idyllically** *adv*

idyllist /ídd'list, íd'list/ *n* a writer, composer, or painter of idylls

ie *abbr* Ireland (*used in Internet addresses*) See table at **domain name**

i.e. *abbr* that is to say [Latin *id est* 'that is']

USAGE See ***e.g.***

-ie *suffix* **1.** somebody or something that is small or dear ○ *doggie* ○ *auntie* **2.** somebody or something that has a particular character ○ *sweetie* **3.** somebody or something that has to do with ○ *townie* [Origin ?]

iechyd da /yáki dáa/ *interj Wales* used as a drinking toast to wish somebody good health [< Welsh, 'good health']

IEE *abbr* Institution of Electrical Engineers

IEEE /ī tripp'l ée/ *abbr* Institute of Electrical and Electronic Engineers

-ier *suffix* same as **er** [1]

~~**iether**~~ incorrect spelling of **either**

if /if/ CORE MEANING: a conjunction used to indicate the circumstances that would have to exist in order for an event to happen ○ *You can come with us if you want to.* ○ *Are you thinking of buying a new car? If so, talk to us first.*

1. *conj* USED IN INDIRECT QUESTIONS used in indirect speech to introduce a question that in direct speech requires the answer 'yes' or 'no' ○ *asked if I would stay* **2.** *conj* MODIFYING STATEMENT used to indicate a modification to a statement, usually to add something negative or to indicate that there is less of something than originally expected ○ *a gallant, if misguided, attempt* ○ *by Thursday, if not earlier* **3.** *conj* INTRODUCING EXCLAMATION used to introduce an exclamation expressing surprise or dismay ○ *If that isn't the last straw!* **4.** *n* DOUBT a doubt or uncertainty ○ *There is rather a large if about whether or not she'll finish her degree.* **5.** *n* CONDITION a condition or qualification ○ *I'm not very happy about the ifs that have been put into the contract.* [Old English *gif* < Germanic] ◇ **if only** used to introduce an expression of a hopeless wish or regret ○ *If only you had told me sooner!* ◇ **ifs and buts** excuses or protests

USAGE Ambiguous **if** construction: In *We have hundreds, if not thousands, of items in stock*, the *if not* fairly plainly means 'or even'. In *It's a clever idea, if not a practical one*, it fairly plainly means 'although not'. But in *He's good-looking, if not really handsome*, it is unclear which of those meanings is intended — at least out of context. Often it is clear what *if not* means only because the context shows what the phrase must mean. Where it will not be clear, another wording is preferable.

USAGE Substituting ***would have*** for *had* in an *if* clause (one stating a condition contrary to fact) is a grammatical error. Do not write: *If they would have done it properly to begin with, these problems would not exist.* Write instead: *If they had done it properly*... or, more formally, *Had they done it properly to begin with, these problems would not exist.* Avoid the incorrect form *they'd + have*, as in *If they'd have done it properly...*; here *they'd* is a contraction for *they had*. Write instead *If they'd done it properly*... or *If they had done it properly*....

USAGE When to use **if and when**: This expression is often used in cases where *if* or *when* alone would be enough, but there are occasions on which both are needed to convey a condition about both the likelihood and timing of an eventuality: in the sentence *Arrange repairs if and when necessary*, the omission of *if* could imply that repairs are always necessary at some point, and the omission of *when* could fail to make the point that repairs should be done promptly.

CULTURAL NOTE *If*, a poem (1910) by Rudyard Kipling. Although it does not rank among Kipling's greatest works, this poem is well known and loved by many for the message it contains, advocating such noble qualities as self-reliance, tolerance, modesty, and fortitude: 'If you can keep your head when all about you/ Are losing theirs and blaming it on you, ... you'll be a man, my son!'. The expression 'the common touch' comes from this poem: 'If you can talk with crowds and keep your virtue,/ Or walk with kings – nor lose the common touch'.

IF *abbr* ELECTRONICS intermediate frequency

IFA *abbr* independent financial adviser

IFC *abbr* International Finance Corporation (*of the United Nations*)

Ife /ée fay/ city in southwestern Nigeria, situated 87 km/54 mi. east of Ibadan. Population: 289,500 (1995).

iffy /íffi/ (**-fier, -fiest**) *adj* (*informal*) **1.** UNCERTAIN uncertain or unlikely to happen **2.** DUBIOUS dubious, suspicious, or unreliable ○ *My car is a bit iffy at the moment: will you drive?* **3.** UNDECIDED undecided or unsure about something ○ *feeling iffy about applying to university* —**iffiness** *n*

Ifni /éefni/ region of Morocco, situated on the southwestern coast of the country. Formerly an overseas

province of Spain, it was ceded to Morocco in 1969. Sidi Ifni is the only city. Area: 1,502 sq. km/580 sq. mi.

IFOR /í fawr/, **Ifor** n a NATO-led multinational force sent to maintain peace in the former Yugoslavia following the signing of the Dayton Accords. Full form **Implementation Force**

IFR abbr instrument flying regulations

IgA n a class of antibodies, found in respiratory and alimentary secretions as well as in saliva and tears, that help the body to neutralize harmful bacteria and viral antigens [Shortening of *immunoglobulin A*]

Igbo n, adj PEOPLES, LANG same as **Ibo**

IgD n a class of antibodies, present on most cell surfaces and predominant in B-cells, that help the body to resist antigens [Abbreviation of *immunoglobulin D*]

IgE n a class of antibodies, abundant in tissues, that help the body to expel intestinal parasites and cause allergic reactions in response to antigens [Abbreviation of *immunoglobulin E*]

IgG n a class of antibodies, predominant in serum, that pass through the placental wall into foetal circulation and help to prepare the immune system for the period of infancy [Abbreviation of *immunoglobulin G*]

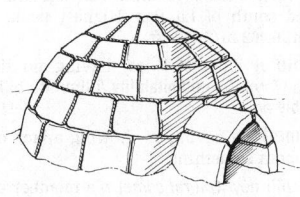
igloo

igloo /íggloo/ n 1. an Inuit dwelling, usually dome-shaped and built from blocks of packed snow 2. a small dome-shaped shelter or structure [Mid-19C. < Inuit *iglu* 'house']

IgM n a class of antibodies, circulating in the blood and secretions, that help the body to resist viruses [Abbreviation of *immunoglobulin M*]

IGM abbr CHESS International Grandmaster

ign.[1] abbr 1. ignites 2. ignition

ign.[2] abbr unknown [Latin *ignotus*]

Ignatius (of Antioch) /ig náyshəss-/, St (35?–107) bishop and martyr. He was one of the Apostolic Fathers of the Christian Church, and his seven epistles give important historical information about the early Church.

Ignatius Loyola /-loy ốlə, -lóy ələ/, St (1491–1556) Spanish priest who was cofounder of the Society of Jesus in 1534. He also produced a Jesuit training manual, *Spiritual Exercises* (1548).

igneous /ígni əss/ adj 1. describes rock formed under conditions of intense heat or produced by the solidification of volcanic magma on or below the Earth's surface 2. relating to or characteristic of fire (formal) [Mid-17C. < Latin *igneus* < *ignis* 'fire']

ignescent /ig néss'nt/ adj giving off sparks when struck, as a flint does [Early 19C. < Latin *ignescent-*, present participle of *ignescere* 'catch fire' < *ignis* 'fire']

ignimbrite /ígnim brīt/ n a volcanic rock consisting of droplets of lava and glass that were welded together by intense heat [Mid-20C. < Latin *ignis* 'fire' + *imbr-* 'rain']

ignis fatuus /ígniss fáttyoo əss/ (plural **ignes fatui** /íg neez fáttyoo ī/) n 1. SCI same as **will-o'-the-wisp** (sense 1) 2. something such as a hope or an aim that proves illusory or leads somebody astray (literary) [< Latin, 'foolish fire'; from its erratic movements]

ignite /ig nít/ (-nites, -niting, -nited) v 1. vti LIGHT OR CATCH FIRE to set fire to something, or catch fire 2. vti HEAT GAS UNTIL IT BURNS to heat a gas to the temperature at which it begins to burn, or be heated in this way 3.

vt AROUSE EMOTION to cause a strong emotion to arise or show itself in somebody [Mid-17C. < Latin *ignit-*, past participle of *ignire* 'set on fire' < *ignis* 'fire'] —**ignitability** /ig nítə bílləti/ n —**ignitable** adj —**igniter** n

ignition /ig nísh'n/ n 1. MEANS OF STARTING ENGINE a mechanism that determines when, where, and how a spark is delivered to an engine cylinder to ignite the fuel and start or run the engine 2. SPARK THAT IGNITES FUEL-AIR MIXTURE a spark in an internal-combustion engine that ignites and explodes a mixture of fuel and air 3. PROCESS OF IGNITING the process of setting something on fire

ignition point n the temperature at which a substance begins to burn and will remain alight

ignoble /ig nốbl/ adj 1. dishonourable and contrary to the high standards of conduct expected of somebody 2. not belonging to the nobility (formal) [15C. Directly or via French < Latin *ignobilis* 'not noble' < *(g)nobilis* (see NOBLE)] —**ignobility** /ígnō bílləti/ n —**ignobly** adv

SYNONYMS See *mean*[2].

ignominious /ígnə mínni əss/ adj 1. involving a total loss of dignity and self-respect, and making somebody or something appear shamefully weak and ineffective 2. deserving condemnation and contempt (formal) —**ignominiously** adv —**ignominiousness** n

ignominy /ígnəmini/ (plural **-ies**) n 1. a total loss of dignity and self-respect, or an incurring of public disgrace 2. a disgraceful act (formal) [Mid-16C. Directly or via French < Latin *ignominia* 'lacking name' < *nomin-* 'name, reputation']

ignoramus /ígnə ráyməss/ n an offensive term that deliberately insults somebody's level of intelligence or education (insult) [Late 16C. < modern Latin < Latin 'we do not know', form of *ignorare* (see IGNORE)]

ignorance /ígnərənss/ n 1. lack of knowledge or education 2. unawareness of something, often of something important ◇ **ignorance is bliss** it is often better not to know about something unpleasant

ignorant /ígnərənt/ adj 1. LACKING KNOWLEDGE lacking knowledge or education in general or in a specific subject 2. UNAWARE unaware of something ◇ *ignorant of the danger* 3. RESULTING FROM LACK OF KNOWLEDGE caused by a lack of knowledge, understanding, or experience ◇ *an ignorant mistake* 4. Carib QUARRELSOME quarrelsome and aggressive —**ignorantly** adv —**ignorantness** n

ignore /ig náwr/ (-nores, -noring, -nored) vt 1. to refuse to notice or pay attention to somebody or something 2. Aus to reject a bill of indictment on the grounds of insufficient evidence [15C. Directly or via French < Latin *ignorare* 'not know, ignore' < *(g)noscere* 'know'] ◇ **treat with ignore** to pay no attention to somebody or something ◇ *She treats me with complete ignore.*

~~ignorent~~ incorrect spelling of **ignorant**

Igorot /íggə rốt, éegə-/ (plural same or **-rots**) n a member of a people living in the mountainous northern part of Luzon in the Philippines [Early 19C. Via Spanish *Ygolote* < the local Philippine name] —**Igorot** adj

Iguaçu /í gwaa sóo/ river in southern Brazil and northeastern Argentina. Length: 1,200 km/745 mi.

Iguaçu Falls

Iguaçu Falls waterfalls on the Iguaçu River, in southern Brazil. In the wet season they form a single waterfall over 4 km/2.5 mi. wide and up to 80 m/260 ft high.

iguana

iguana /i gwáanə/ (plural **-nas** or same) n a large plant-eating lizard with a serrated fringe or crest running along its back from head to tail. Native to: tropical South and Central America. Family: Iguanidae. [Mid-16C. Via Spanish < Arawak *iwana*] —**iguanian** adj, n

iguanodon /i gwáanə don/ n a large long-tailed plant-eating dinosaur of the Jurassic and early Cretaceous periods. Genus: *Iguanodon*. [Early 19C. < IGUANA + Greek *odōn*, variant of *odous*, *odont-* 'tooth'; from the similarity of its teeth to those of an iguana]

Ihimaera /íhi mírə/, **Witi** (b. 1944) New Zealand novelist. His collection of short stories *Pounamu, Pounamu* (1972) was the first work by a Maori writer to be published in English in New Zealand. Full name **Ihimaera, Witi Tame**

ihp abbr AUTOMOT indicated horsepower

ihram /ee ráam/ n 1. a white cotton robe worn by Muslim men when they are pilgrims to Mecca, formed from pieces of cloth wound around the waist and over the shoulder 2. the state of holiness conferred on Muslims or symbolized by the wearing of the ihram [Early 18C. < Arabic *'iḥrām*]

IHS abbr CHR Jesus [< three letters of the capitalized form of the name of Jesus in Greek; later also taken as abbreviation of Latin *Iesus hominum salvator* 'Jesus saviour of humankind', *in hoc signo* 'in this sign (you shall conquer)', *in hac salus* 'in this (cross) is salvation', and other religious phrases]

iid abbr STATS independent identically distributed

IINM abbr ONLINE if I'm not mistaken (used in e-mails)

IIRC abbr ONLINE if I recall/remember correctly (used in e-mails)

IJsselmeer /íss'l meer/, **Ijsselmeer** shallow freshwater lake in the northern Netherlands that occupies part of what was formerly the Zuider Zee. The River IJssel flows into it.

ikat /ée kaat, i kát/ n a technique for making patterned fabric by using tie-dyed yarn [Mid-20C. < Malay, 'tie, fasten']

IKBS abbr INFO SCI intelligent knowledge-based system

ikebana /ík ay báanə, íki-/ n the Japanese art of arranging flowers in a formal balanced composition [Early 20C. < Japanese, 'living flowers']

Ike Taiga /í kay tígə/ (1723?–76) Japanese painter. His works, using ancient forms of calligraphy, are in the Bunjinga style. Also known as **Ikeno Taiga**

Ikhnaton another spelling of **Akhenaton**

Ikhwan /ík waan/ npl US in 20th-century Islam, a religious and military movement whose members practise Wahhabism. The Ikhwan played an important role in the unification of Saudi Arabia.

ikon n RELIG another spelling of **icon** (sense 1)

IKWUM abbr ONLINE I know what you mean (used in e-mails)

il abbr Israel (used in Internet addresses) See table at **domain name**

il- prefix same as **in-**[1], **in-**[2] (used before l)

-il suffix forming nouns and adjectives ◇ *utensil* ◇ *civil* [< Latin *-ilis*]

ilang-ilang n TREES another spelling of **ylang-ylang**

il Bronzino /il bron zeénō/ (1503–72) Italian painter. Known as a portraitist of the Medici family, Dante, and Boccaccio, he also painted religious pictures. Born **di Mariano, Agnolo di Cosimo**

-ile[1] *suffix* of, relating to, capable of ○ *volatile* [Via French < Latin *-ilis*]

-ile[2] *suffix* a portion of a particular size in a frequency distribution ○ *quartile* ○ *percentile* [Origin ?]

ilea ANAT plural of **ileum**

ileac /ílli ak/, **ileal** /-əl/ *adj* **1.** relating to the ileum **2.** relating to ileus [Early 19C. Alteration of ILIAC, after ILEUM, ILEUS]

~~ilegal~~ incorrect spelling of **illegal**

ileitis /ílli ítiss/ *n* inflammation of the ileum

ileostomy /ílli óstəmi/ (*plural* **-mies**) *n* **1.** a surgical operation in which an opening is made through the abdominal wall into the ileum, so that waste can be discharged out of the body without passing through the colon **2.** a surgical opening through the abdominal wall into the ileum

Ilesa /i láyshə/, **Ilesha** city in Kwara State, southwestern Nigeria, situated approximately 24 km/15 mi. southeast of Oshogbo. Population: 369,000 (1995).

ileum /ílli əm/ (*plural* **-ea** /-i ə/) *n* the third and lowest portion of the small intestine, extending from the jejunum to the pouch-shaped caecum at the beginning of the large intestine [Late 17C. < medieval Latin, variant of Latin *ilium* 'entrails']

ileus /ílli əss/ *n* a medical condition in which the contents of the intestines are unable to pass through owing to a physical obstruction or muscular inadequacy, often accompanied by extreme pain and vomiting [Late 17C. Via Latin < Greek *ileos* 'colic']

ilex /ī leks/ *n* **1.** a tree or bush belonging to a genus whose best-known member is the holly tree. Genus: *Ilex.* **2.** TREES same as **holm oak** [< Latin, 'holm oak']

Ilfracombe /ílfrə koom/ seaside resort in Devon, southwestern England. Population: 10,429 (1991).

ilia ANAT plural of **ilium**

iliac /ílli ak/ *adj* relating to the ilium and its surroundings [Early 16C. < late Latin *iliacus* 'relating to colic' < Latin *ilia* (plural) 'flanks']

Iliad /ílli əd/ *n* an ancient Greek epic poem, describing the siege and capture of Troy, ascribed to Homer and probably composed by oral tradition over several centuries before 700 BC [Early 17C. < Latin *Iliad-* < Greek *Ilias* 'of Troy' < *Ilion* 'Troy'] —**Iliadic** /ílli áddik/ *adj*

Iliamna /ílli ámnə/ volcanic peak in southwestern Alaska, situated on the western side of Cook Inlet. Height: 3,053 m/10,020 ft.

Iliamna, Lake largest lake in Alaska, in the southwest of the state, west of Cook Inlet. Area: 2,647 sq. km/1,022 sq. mi.

ilium /ílli əm/ (*plural* **-ia** /-i ə/) *n* the wide flat upper portion of the pelvis that is connected to the base of the vertebral column. The ilium is a separate bone at birth but later becomes fused with two other bones to form the hip bone (**innominate bone**). [14C. < late Latin, 'flank, groin' < Latin *ilia* (plural) 'flanks']

ilk[1] /ilk/ *n* a kind or sort of person or thing (*informal*) ○ *journalists and others of that ilk* ○ *'save forlorn hopes and their ilk'* (Stephen Crane, *The Red Badge of Courage*; 1895) [Old English *ilca* 'same', compound < Indo-European, 'same' + Germanic, 'form'] ◇ **of that ilk** *Scotland* coming from or owning the place of the same name as your own

ilk[2] /ilk/ *det Scotland* same as **ilka** [Old English *ylc*, northern variant of *ælc* (see EACH)]

ilka /ílkə/ *det Scotland* each or every [12C. < ILK[2] + A[4]]

Ilkeston /ílkstən/ town in Derbyshire, central England. Population: 35,134 (1991).

ill /il/ *adj* (**worse** /wurss/, **worst** /wurst/) **1.** UNWELL not in good health, having a disease, or feeling unwell or nauseous **2.** HARMFUL resulting in harm, pain, or trouble for somebody or something ○ *ill effects from the accident* **3.** UNKIND unkind and unfriendly ○ *ill feeling* **4.** UNFAVOURABLE predicting a bad future or outcome ○ *an ill wind* **5.** MORALLY BAD resulting from the actual or supposed moral badness of somebody or something ○ *of ill repute* **6.** BAD not up to the expected or required standard, e.g. of behaviour or competence ■ *adv* (**worse, worst**) **1.** BADLY badly, inadequately, or inappropriately ○ *treated them ill* **2.** UNFAVOURABLY in an adverse or unfavourable way, or so as to reflect badly on somebody or something ○ *bodes ill* **3.** WITH DIFFICULTY only with great difficulty and trouble ○ *can ill afford it* ■ *n* **1.** PROBLEM a serious problem or difficulty ○ *social ills* **2.** HARM evil or harm, especially as a fate wished on somebody ○ *wished them ill* [12C. < Old Norse *illr* 'evil, difficult', *illa* 'badly', *ilt* 'evil']

USAGE ill or **sick**? In general, somebody who feels *ill* is unwell in some way, often seriously, whereas somebody who feels *sick* may be less seriously ill or about to vomit. On the other hand, *ill* is less common in attributive position before a noun, and it is more natural to say *a sick child* than *an ill child.* So too there are set expressions in which *sick* is used but not *ill*, for example *sick leave, sick note, to go sick.*

- **ill-adjusted** *adj*
- **ill-behaved** *adj*
- **ill-boding** *adj*
- **ill-conceived** *adj*
- **ill-considered** *adj*
- **ill-defined** *adj*
- **ill-disguised** *adj*
- **ill-disposed** *adj*
- **ill-dressed** *adj*
- **ill-equipped** *adj*
- **ill-fitting** *adj*
- **ill-founded** *adj*
- **ill-nourished** *adj*
- **ill-prepared** *adj*
- **ill-suited** *adj*
- **ill-tempered** *adj*
- **ill-temperedly** *adv*
- **ill-timed** *adj*

I'll /īl/ *contr* I will or I shall

ill. *abbr* **1.** illustrated **2.** illustration **3.** illustrator

ill-advised *adj* not wise, prudent, or sensible —**ill-advisedly** *adv*

ill-affected *adj* hostile or unfriendly towards somebody or something (*formal*)

ill-assorted *adj* mismatched or incompatible

ill at ease *adj* uncomfortable and nervous

illation /i láysh'n/ *n* (*formal*) **1.** an inference drawn from something **2.** the act or process of drawing an inference from something [Mid-16C. < Latin *illation-* < *illat-* (see ILLATIVE)]

illative /i láytiv, íllə-/ *adj* **1.** INFERENTIAL relating to or involving the drawing of inferences (*formal*) **2.** LING STATING INFERENCE describes a word or phrase such as 'thus', 'therefore', or 'as a result' that marks or introduces an inference **3.** LING OF CASE OF FINNISH NOUN describes a case of nouns in Finnish and some other languages that indicates motion towards something. It is usually translated into English using the prepositions 'into' or 'towards'. ■ *n* LING **1.** SOMETHING THAT STATES INFERENCE a word, phrase, or morpheme that marks or introduces an inference **2.** CASE OF FINNISH NOUN the illative grammatical case in Finnish and some other languages [Late 16C. < Latin *illativus* < *illat-*, past participle of *inferre* (see INFER)] —**illatively** *adv*

Illawarra /íllə wórrə/ district in southeastern New South Wales, Australia, situated approximately 48 km/30 mi. south of Sydney. Population: 380,660 (1998).

ill-being *n* a feeling or condition of illness, unhappiness, or lack of prosperity [After WELLBEING]

ill-bred *adj* rude, impolite, or otherwise showing a lack of good manners or the results of a bad upbringing —**ill-breeding** *n*

illegal /i léeg'l/ *adj* **1.** AGAINST LAW contravening a specific law, especially a criminal law **2.** AGAINST RULES not allowed by the rules of something such as a game **3.** NOT PERMITTED BY COMPUTER not permitted in a computer program ■ *n* ILLEGAL IMMIGRANT somebody who has entered a country illegally —**illegally** *adv*

SYNONYMS See *unlawful.*

illegalise *vt* another spelling of **illegalize**

illegality /íllee gálləti/ (*plural* **-ties**) *n* **1.** the fact of being forbidden by law or by the rules of something **2.** an act that is against the law

illegalize /i léegə līz/ (**-izes, -izing, -ized**), **illegalise** (**-ises, -ising, -ised**) *vt* to declare officially and by law that something is illegal —**illegalization** /i léegə lī záysh'n/ *n*

illegible /i léjjəb'l/ *adj* impossible or very difficult to read —**illegibility** /i léjjə bílləti/ *n* —**illegibly** *adv*

illegitimate /íllə jíttəmət/ *adj* **1.** BORN OUT OF WEDLOCK born to parents who are not married to each other **2.** AGAINST LAW OR RULES not carried out, made, or constituted in accordance with the law, the rules governing a specific activity, or social norms and customs **3.** LOGIC NOT CORRECTLY REASONED not correctly inferred or reasoned —**illegitimacy** *n* —**illegitimately** *adv*

ill-fated *adj* ending in or doomed to disaster

ill-favoured *adj* **1.** unattractive in appearance, especially having an unattractive face **2.** offensively objectionable (*literary*) —**ill-favouredly** *adv* —**ill-favouredness** *n*

ill feeling *n* animosity or resentment towards somebody or something

ill-gotten *adj* acquired dishonestly or illegally ○ *ill-gotten gains*

ill health *n* the state of being in poor physical or mental condition

ill humour *n* a bad mood or bad temper —**ill-humoured** *adj*

illiberal /i líbbərəl/ *adj* **1.** narrow-minded and intolerant of ideas and behaviour that vary from a conservative standard **2.** not generous with something such as money or time (*formal*) —**illiberalism** *n* —**illiberality** /i líbbə rálləti/ *n* —**illiberally** *adv*

illicit /i líssit/ *adj* **1.** not allowed by the law **2.** considered wrong or unacceptable by prevailing social customs or standards —**illicitly** *adv* —**illicitness** *n*

SPELLCHECK See *elicit.*

SYNONYMS See *unlawful.*

Illimani /éelyi mánni/ mountain in western Bolivia, situated south of La Paz. Highest peak: Nevada Illimani 6,462 m/21,201 ft.

illimitable /i límmitəb'l/ *adj* having no limits or bounds (*formal*) —**illimitability** /i límmitə bílləti/ *n* —**illimitably** *adv*

ill-informed *adj* having or showing a lack of knowledge about something

Illinois[1] /ílli nóy/ (*plural same*) *n* a member of a confederacy of Algonquian peoples who lived in an area covering northern Illinois, eastern Iowa, and southern Wisconsin, and now live in northeastern Oklahoma [Early 18C. Via French < Algonquian] —**Illinois** *adj*

Illinois[2] /íllə nóy/ **1.** state in the north-central United States, bordered by Indiana, Iowa, Kentucky, Missouri, Wisconsin, and Lake Michigan. Capital: Springfield. Population: 12,600,620 (2002 estimate). Area: 150,007 sq. km/57,918 sq. mi. **2.** river in northern Illinois formed by the joining of the Des Plaines and Kankakee rivers. Length: 680 km/420 mi. —**Illinoisan** /-nóyən, -nóyz'n/ *adj, n*

illiquid /i líkwid/ *adj* **1.** not easily convertible into cash ○ *illiquid shares* **2.** lacking sufficient ready cash —**illiquidity** /ílli kwíddəti/ *n*

illite /íllīt/ *n* a clay mineral of the mica group containing potassium and aluminium. Source: shale, mudstone. [Mid-20C. After ILLINOIS[2]] —**illitic** /i líttik/ *adj*

illiterate /i líttərət/ *adj* **1.** OFFENSIVE TERM an offensive term meaning not able to read or write **2.** UNEDUCATED having or showing little or no knowledge of a particular subject ○ *artistically illiterate* **3.** MAKING MANY LANGUAGE MISTAKES full of or making many basic errors in the use of language ○ *illiterate prose* ■ *n* OFFENSIVE TERM an offensive term for somebody who lacks education and knowledge, especially somebody who cannot read or write —**illiteracy** *n* —**illiterately** *adv* —**illiterateness** *n*

ill-judged *adj* showing a lack of good judgment or an incorrect assessment of a situation

ill-mannered *adj* rude or impolite in behaviour —**ill-manneredly** *adv*

ill nature *n* a bad-tempered, unpleasant, or unkind disposition (*dated*)

ill-natured /-náychərd/ *adj* having a bad-tempered, unpleasant, or unkind disposition —**ill-naturedly** *adv* —**ill-naturedness** *n*

illness /ílnəss/ *n* **1.** a disease, sickness, or indisposition **2.** a state of bad health

illocution /íllə kyóosh'n/ *n* PHILOSOPHY, LING the intention of a speaker in saying a particular thing, e.g. naming, threatening, warning, or promising, as opposed to the literal meaning of the words spoken [Mid-20C. < IL- + LOCUTION] —**illocutionary** *adj*

illogic /i lójjik/ *n* the quality or condition of having no basis in logic

illogical /i lójjik'l/ *adj* **1.** apparently unreasonable or perverse, especially in not being or not giving the expected response **2.** not following the rules of logic, or not following logically from a previous premise, statement, or action —**illogicality** /i lójji kálləti/ *n* —**illogically** *adv*

ill-omened /-ṓmənd/ *adj* accompanied by signs suggesting disaster or failure

ill-sorted *adj* same as **ill-assorted**

ill-starred *adj* doomed to end in failure or disaster [< the belief that an unpropitious arrangement of the astronomical objects at the start of an undertaking predetermined an unhappy outcome]

ill-treat *vt* to behave cruelly or unkindly towards a person or animal —**ill-treated** *adj* —**ill-treatment** *n*

SYNONYMS See ***mistreat.***

illume /i lóom, i lyóom/ (**-lumes, -luming, -lumed**) *vt* to cast illumination on somebody or something (*literary or archaic*) [Early 17C. Contraction of ILLUMINE]

illuminance /i lóominənss/ *n* the amount of light, evaluated according to its capacity to produce visual stimulation, that reaches a unit of surface area during a unit of time. It is measured in lux. Symbol E_v

illuminant /i lóominənt/ *n* something that gives off or provides light [Mid-17C. < Latin *illuminant-*, present participle of *illuminare* (see ILLUMINATE)]

illuminate /i lóomi nayt/ (**-nates, -nating, -nated**) *v* **1.** *vti* **SHINE LIGHT ON SOMEBODY OR SOMETHING** to make somebody or something visible or bright with light, or be lit up **2.** *vt* **DECORATE SOMETHING WITH LIGHTS** to decorate something with lights for a celebration **3.** *vt* **CLARIFY SOMETHING** to make something easier to understand **4.** *vt* **CAUSE SOMEBODY TO LOOK HAPPY** to make something, especially somebody's face, look happy and animated **5.** *vti* **ENLIGHTEN SOMEBODY** to provide somebody with knowledge or with intellectual or spiritual enlightenment (*literary; often passive*) **6.** *vt* PRINTING **ADD COLOURED ELEMENTS TO PAGE** to add coloured letters, illustrations, or designs to a manuscript or the borders of a page [15C. < Latin *illuminat-*, past participle of *illuminare* 'light up' < *lumin-* 'light'] —**illuminated** *adj* —**illuminative** /i lúminətiv/ *adj* —**illuminator** *n*

illuminati /i lóomi naáti/, **Illuminati** *npl* a group claiming to have received special religious or spiritual enlightenment, especially an 18th-century German secret society with deist and republican ideas [Late 16C. Via Italian < Latin, plural of *illuminatus* < past participle of *illuminare* (see ILLUMINATE)]

illuminating /i lóomi nayting/ *adj* informative and enlightening, often by revealing or emphasizing facts that were previously obscure —**illuminatingly** *adv*

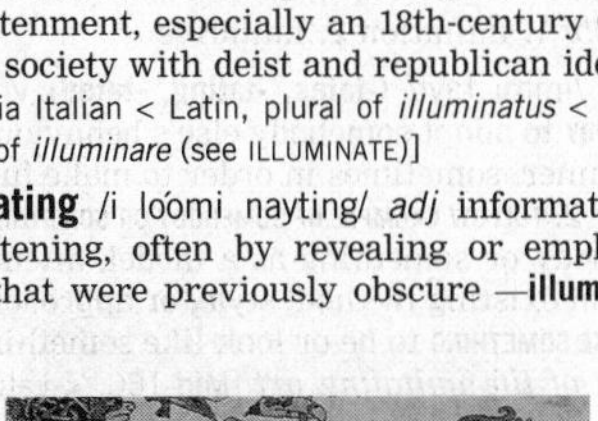

illumination: title page of the manuscript *Augustinus Questiones in Heptateuchon* (8th century)

illumination /i lóomi náysh'n/ *n* **1.** **ACT OF ILLUMINATING** the provision of light to make something visible or bright, or the fact of being lit up **2.** **USABLE LIGHT** the amount or strength of light available in a place or for a purpose **3.** **CLARIFICATION OF SOMETHING** the process of making something easier to understand **4.** **ENLIGHTENMENT** intellectual or spiritual enlightenment **5.** PRINTING **DECORATION ON PAGE** a coloured letter, design, or illustration decorating a manuscript or page, or the art or act of decorating written texts **6.** PHYS same as **illuminance** ■ **illuminations** *npl* **DECORATIVE STREET LIGHTS** a group of coloured lights used to decorate streets and public buildings, especially at Christmas or other festive occasions —**illuminational** *adj*

illumine /i lóomin/ (**-mines, -mining, -mined**) *vti* to illuminate somebody or something, or become illuminated (*formal*) [14C. Via French < Latin *illuminare* (see ILLUMINATE)] —**illuminable** *adj*

illuminism /i lóominizəm/ *n* the beliefs held by illuminati, especially their belief in or claim to special enlightenment

illus. *abbr* **1.** illustrated **2.** illustration **3.** illustrator

ill-use /-yóoz/ *vt* to treat somebody or something harshly or inappropriately —**ill-usage** *n* —**ill-use** /-yóoss/ *n* —**ill-used** *adj*

illusion /i lóozh'n/ *n* **1.** **SOMETHING WITH DECEPTIVE APPEARANCE** something that deceives the senses or mind, e.g. by appearing to exist when it does not or appearing to be one thing when it is in fact another **2.** **DECEPTIVE POWER OF APPEARANCES** the ability of appearances to deceive the mind and senses, or the capacity of the mind and senses to be deceived by appearances **3.** **FALSE IDEA** a false idea, conception, or belief about somebody or something **4.** PSYCHOL **MISTAKEN SENSORY PERCEPTION** a misinterpretation of an experience of sensory perception, especially a visual one, where the stimuli are objectively present and the mistaken perception is due to physical rather than psychological causes **5.** TEXTILES **GAUZE** a fine gauze. Use: trimming. [14C. Via French < Latin *illusion-* < *illus-*, past participle of *illudere* 'play at' < *ludus* 'play, sport'] —**illusionary** *adj* —**illusionless** *adj*

USAGE See ***allusion.***

illusionism /i lóozh'nizəm/ *n* the use of pictorial techniques to create illusions

illusionist /i lóozh'nist, i lyóo-/ *n* **1.** somebody who performs magical tricks **2.** an artist who creates pictorial illusions —**illusionistic** /i lóozh'n ístik, i lyóo-/ *adj* —**illusionistically** *adv*

illusive /i lóossiv, i lyóo-/ *adj* same as **illusory** [Early 17C. < medieval Latin *illusivus* 'deceptive' < Latin *illus-* (see ILLUSION)] —**illusively** *adv* —**illusiveness** *n*

SPELLCHECK See ***elusive.***

illusory /i lóozəri, i lóoss-/ *adj* produced by, based on, or consisting of an illusion [Late 16C. Directly or via French < ecclesiastical Latin *illusorius* 'ironic' < Latin *illus-* (see ILLUSION)] —**illusorily** *adv* —**illusoriness** *n*

illustrate /íllə strayt/ (**-trates, -trating, -trated**) *v* **1.** *vt* **ACCOMPANY SOMETHING WITH PICTURES** to provide explanatory or decorative pictures to accompany a printed, spoken, or electronic text ○ *The book was illustrated with diagrams.* **2.** *vti* **FULLY EXPLAIN SOMETHING** to clarify or explain something by giving examples or making comparisons **3.** *vt* **BE CHARACTERISTIC OF SOMETHING** to be a good example of something, or serve to demonstrate something and make it clear ○ *a case that illustrates the need for legislation* [Early 16C. < Latin *illustrat-*, past participle of *illustrare* 'light up' < *lustrare* (see LUSTRE)] —**illustratable** *adj* —**illustrator** *n*

illustration /íllə stráysh'n/ *n* **1.** **PICTURE THAT COMPLEMENTS TEXT** a drawing, picture, photograph, or diagram that accompanies and complements a printed, spoken, or electronic text **2.** **PROVISION OF PICTURES ACCOMPANYING TEXT** the art or process of producing or providing drawings, pictures, photographs, or diagrams to accompany a text **3.** **SOMETHING THAT HELPS TO EXPLAIN SOMETHING** an example or comparison that helps to clarify or explain something —**illustrational** *adj*

illustrative /íllәstrətiv, i lús-, íllə straytiv/ *adj* serving to illustrate or explain something —**illustratively** *adv*

illustrious /i lústri əss/ *adj* extremely distinguished and deservedly famous [Mid-16C. < Latin *illustris* 'bright, famous' < *illustrare* (see ILLUSTRATE)] —**illustriously** *adv* —**illustriousness** *n*

illuvia GEOL plural of **illuvium**

illuviation /i lóovi áysh'n/ *n* the process by which materials such as colloids and salts are washed from an upper layer of soil to a lower one [Early 20C. < IL- + ELUVIATION] —**illuviated** /i lóovi aytid/ *adj*

illuvium /i lóovi əm/ (*plural* **-viums** or **-via** /-vi ə/) *n* colloids, salts, or other material washed out from an upper to a lower layer of soil [Early 20C. < modern Latin < *-luvium* (as in ALLUVIUM)]

ill will *n* a feeling or attitude of hostility, unfriendliness, or dislike towards somebody ○ *They bore us no ill will.*

ill-wisher *n* somebody who wishes misfortune or evil to come to another person

Illyria /i lírri ə/ ancient region along the coast of the Adriatic Sea from Albania northwards

Illyrian /i lírri ən, i leéri ən/ *n* **1.** a member of a people who occupied Illyria from the late 3rd century BC until they were conquered by the Romans around 33 BC **2.** an extinct Indo-European language that was spoken in Illyria in ancient times, considered to be related to Albanian

ilmenite /ílmə nīt/ *n* a mixed oxide mineral containing iron and titanium. Source: igneous and metamorphic rocks. [Early 19C. After the *Ilmen* Mountains in the S Urals, Russia]

~~**ilness**~~ incorrect spelling of **illness**

Iloilo /eèlō eélō/ city and capital of Iloilo Province, on the southeastern coast of Panay, Philippines, on the Iloilo Strait. Population: 363,778 (1999).

Ilorin /i lórrən/ city and capital of Kwara State, southwestern Nigeria, situated approximately 274 km/170 mi. northeast of Lagos. Population: 464,000 (1995).

ILS *abbr* AEROSP instrument landing system

im *abbr* Isle of Man (*used in Internet addresses*) See table at **domain name**

I'm /īm/ *contr* I am

IM *abbr* **1.** ONLINE instant messaging **2.** CHESS International Master **3.** MED intramuscular

im-[1] *prefix* same as **in-**[1] (*used before b, m, and p*)

im-[2] *prefix* same as **in-**[2] (*used before b, m, and p*)

image /ímmij/ *n* **1.** **ACTUAL OR MENTAL PICTURE** a picture or likeness of somebody or something, produced either physically by a sculptor, painter, or photographer, or formed in the mind ○ *concerned about his public image* **2.** **LIKENESS SEEN OR PRODUCED** the likeness of somebody or something that appears in a mirror, through a lens, or on the retina of the eye, or is produced electronically on a screen **3.** **SOMEBODY CLOSELY RESEMBLING SOMEBODY ELSE** a person or thing bearing a close likeness to somebody or something else ○ *She's the image of her father.* **4.** **CONSPICUOUS EXAMPLE** a very typical or extreme example of something ○ *the very image of greed* **5.** **EXAMPLE OF FIGURATIVE LANGUAGE** a figure of speech, especially a metaphor or simile **6.** MATHS **SET OF FUNCTION'S VALUES** the value of a mathematical function corresponding to a specific value of the function's variable ■ *vt* (**-ages, -aging, -aged**) **1.** **CREATE IMAGE OF SOMEBODY OR SOMETHING** to produce a physical or mental image of somebody or something **2.** **MAKE VISUAL IMAGE OF BODY STRUCTURES** to produce a visual representation of bodily structures, using X-rays, ultrasound, radioactivity, heat, or magnetism and, usually, computerized scanning devices, as an aid to diagnosis and treatment **3.** **DESCRIBE SOMETHING IN VISUAL TERMS** to describe something vividly or in visual terms **4.** **TYPIFY SOMETHING** to embody or typify something [12C. Via French < Latin *imago* 'likeness'] —**imageable** *adj* —**imageless** *adj* —**imager** *n*

image compression *n* a technique for reducing the amount of digitized information needed to store a visual image electronically

image converter *n* an optical-electronic device that reproduces an image formed by invisible radiation such as ultraviolet or infrared on a photoemissive surface as a visible-light image on a luminescent surface

image intensifier *n* an optical-electronic device that amplifies an image formed by visible radiation on a photoemissive surface to present an enhanced image on a luminescent surface

image-maker *n* somebody employed to create a favourable public image of a business, organization, product, or public figure

image map *n* an electronic graphic image with variable areas that computer users can click on to activate hypertext links

imagery /ímmijəri/ *n* **1.** **METAPHORS AND SIMILES** the figurative language, especially metaphors and similes,

used in poetry, plays, and other literary works **2.** **MENTAL IMAGES** a set of mental pictures produced by the memory or imagination or conjured up by a stimulus ○ *dreams filled with surreal imagery* **3.** **IMAGES IN ARTISTIC WORK** the pictorial images found in works of art such as paintings and sculptures, or the art or process of making such images **4.** **IMAGES COLLECTIVELY** a group or set of images considered together ○ *studying the CAT-scan imagery*

image tube *n* an optical-electronic device that converts invisible radiation into a visible image, as in an image converter, or amplifies visible radiation into an enhanced image, as in an image intensifier

imaginable /i májjinəb'l/ *adj* capable of being imagined ○ *the worst meal imaginable* —**imaginability** /i májjinə bílləti/ *n* —**imaginably** *adv*

imaginary /i májjinəri/ *adj* **1.** existing only in the mind, not in reality **2.** relating to or containing imaginary numbers, or being the coefficient of the imaginary part in a complex number ■ *n* MATHS same as **imaginary number** [14C. < Latin *imaginarius* < *imagin-* 'likeness'] —**imaginarily** /i májji nárrili/ *adv*

imaginary number *n* a complex number in the form $a + ib$ where i is the square root of minus one, and b is not equal to zero

imaginary part *n* the real number, b, in the complex number $a + ib$, where i is the square root of minus one

imaginary unit *n* the positive square root of minus one

imagination /i májji náysh'n/ *n* **1.** **ABILITY TO VISUALIZE** the ability to form images and ideas in the mind, especially of things never seen or experienced directly **2.** **CREATIVE PART OF MIND** the part of the mind where ideas, thoughts, and images are formed **3.** **RESOURCEFULNESS** the ability to think of ways of dealing with difficulties or problems ○ *used real imagination in designing the experiment* —**imaginational** *adj*

imaginative /i májjinətiv/ *adj* **1.** **SKILLED AT VISUALIZING OR THINKING ORIGINALLY** good at thinking of new ideas or at visualizing things that have never been seen or experienced directly **2.** **ORIGINAL** new and original, or not likely to have been easily thought up by somebody else ○ *an imaginative solution to a long-standing problem* **3.** **UNLIKELY** seeming untrue, implausible, or unlikely (*often used ironically*) **4.** **OF IMAGINATION** relating to the ability to form images and ideas in the mind, or to think of new things —**imaginativeness** *n*

imaginatively /i májjinətivli/ *adv* in a new and original way that would not have occurred readily to most people

imagine /i májjin/ *v* (**-ines, -ining, -ined**) **1.** *vti* **FORM IMAGE OF SOMETHING IN MIND** to form an image or idea of somebody or something in the mind ○ *I can just imagine his reaction!* **2.** *vt* **SEE OR HEAR SOMETHING UNREAL** to see or hear something that is not there, or think something that is not true ○ *There's nothing there — you're imagining things!* **3.** *vt* **ASSUME SOMETHING** to suppose or assume something ■ *interj* **EXPRESSION OF SURPRISE** used to express surprise or indignation [14C. Via French < Latin *imaginare* 'make an image of', *imaginari* 'picture to yourself' < *imagin-* 'likeness'] —**imagined** *adj* —**imaginer** *n* —**imagining** *n* ◇ **imagine that!** used to express surprise or indignation

imagineer /i májji néer/ *n* somebody who has a creative imagination and is able to put it to practical use, e.g. in design or engineering projects ■ *vt* (**-neers, -neering, -neered**) to design or produce something by putting the imagination to practical use [Mid-20C. Blend of IMAGINE + ENGINEER] —**imagineering** *n*

~~imaginery~~ incorrect spelling of **imaginary**

imagines INSECTS, PSYCHOANAL plural of **imago**

imaging /ímmijing/ *n* **1.** a technique, often computerized, for obtaining images of bodies or body parts for diagnosis, emergency rescue, or surveillance **2.** the use of mental images to try to ease pain, alter the course of a disease, or help in achieving a goal

imagism /ímmijizəm/ *n* a literary movement of early 20th-century UK and US poets that sought to modernize poetic language by the use of ordinary language, free verse, and precise everyday imagery —**imagist** *n* —**imagistic** /ímmi jístik/ *adj* —**imagistically** *adv*

imago /i máygō, i maágō/ (*plural* **-goes** or **-gines** /-jə neez/) *n* **1.** an insect in its sexually mature adult state **2.** in psychoanalysis, an unconscious idealized mental picture, especially of a parent, that is formed early in life and retained in adulthood [Late 18C. < Latin, 'likeness']

imam /i maám, i mám/ *n* **1.** **LEADER OF MOSQUE PRAYERS** in Islam, a man who leads the prayers in a mosque **2.** *also* **Imam** **RELIGIOUS LEADER DESCENDED FROM MUHAMMAD** in the Shia branch of Islam, an Islamic religious leader regarded as a direct descendant of Muhammad or Ali and appointed by Allah **3.** **ISLAMIC COMMUNITY LEADER** in the Sunni branch of Islam, a leader of an Islamic community **4.** **ISLAMIC SCHOLAR** a respected Islamic scholar, especially a founder of a school of theology or law [Early 17C. < Arabic *'imām* 'leader']

imamate /i maá mayt/ *n* **1.** the title or position of an imam, or the period somebody spends as an imam **2.** the area of which an imam is in charge

I-man *pron* same as **I**[2] (*slang; used in Black English*)

IMarE *abbr* Institute of Marine Engineers

imaret /i maá ret/ *n* in Turkey, a place providing food and shelter for travellers and pilgrims [Early 17C. Via Turkish < Arabic *'imāra* 'building']

Imari /i maári/ *n* a Japanese porcelain that is brightly decorated, especially with a floral design [Late 19C. After a port in Kyushu, Japan]

IMAX /ī maks/ *tdmk* a trademark for a giant-screen, large-format film and motion-simulation entertainment complex, with a cinema screen that is ten times larger than a conventional screen and compatible with 3-D technology

imbalance /im bállənss/ *n* **1.** an unevenness, inequality, or bias existing between two or more people or things, especially in their degree of emphasis, proportions, or function **2.** a lack of harmony or an inability to function well or harmoniously, or something causing this state ○ *a hormonal imbalance* —**imbalanced** *adj*

imbecile /ímbə seel, -sīl/ *n* **1.** an offensive term that deliberately insults somebody's intellect (*insult*) **2.** in a former classification system, somebody with an IQ between 25 and 50 and a mental age of between three and seven years (*dated; now considered offensive*) [15C. Via French < Latin *imbecillus* 'without support' < *baculum* 'stick, staff'] —**imbecilic** /ímbə síllik/ *adj* —**imbecility** /ímbə sílləti/ *n*

imbed *vt* same as **embed**

imbibe /im bīb/ (**-bibes, -bibing, -bibed**) *v* **1.** *vti* **DRINK SOMETHING** to drink something, especially alcohol (*formal or humorous*) **2.** *vt* **TAKE IN SOMETHING MENTALLY** to take in and assimilate something such as an idea or experience (*literary*) **3.** *vti* **ABSORB SOMETHING** to absorb moisture, gas, light, or heat (*formal*) [14C. < Latin *imbibere* 'drink in' < *bibere* 'to drink'] —**imbiber** *n*

imbibition /ím bi bísh'n/ *n* the absorption or adsorption of something such as liquid or heat by a mixture (**colloid**) such as a gel [15C. < medieval Latin *imbibition-* 'absorption' < Latin *imbibere* (see IMBIBE)] —**imbibitional** *adj*

imbizo /im béezō/ *n S Africa* a meeting, originally one called by Zulu traditional leaders [Late 20C. < Zulu < *biza* 'summon']

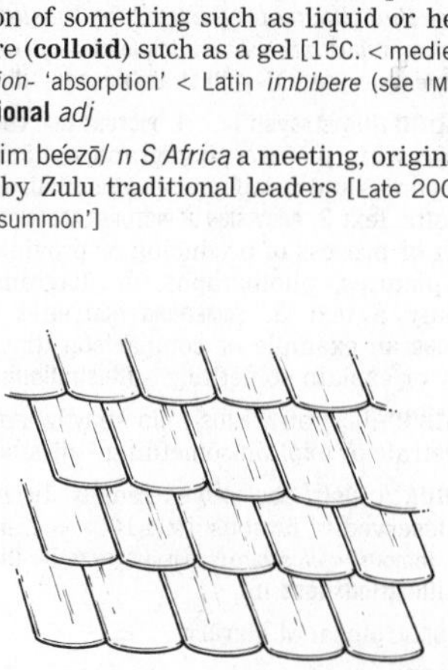

imbricate

imbricate *adj* /ímbrikət, -kayt/ **1.** ARCHIT **MADE OF OVERLAPPING TILES** consisting of overlapping tiles or slates **2.** BOT, ZOOL **OVERLAPPING LIKE ROOF TILES** describes plant or animal parts that overlap in a regular pattern ■ *vti* /ímbrikayt/ (**-cates, -cating, -cated**) **OVERLAP OR BE OVERLAPPING** to lay things so that they overlap in layers in a similar way to roof tiles, or be laid in this way [Mid-17C. < Latin *imbricat-*, past participle of *imbricare* 'cover with pantiles' < *imbric-* 'roof-tile' < *imber* 'rain'] —**imbricated** *adj* —**imbrication** /ímbri káysh'n/ *n*

imbroglio /im brṓli ō/ (*plural* **-glios**) *n* a confusing, messy, or complicated situation, especially one that involves disagreement or intrigue [Mid-18C. < Italian < *brogliare* 'mix up', probably < Old French *brōoillier*]

imbrue /im broó/ (**-brues, -bruing, -brued**) *vt* to stain something, especially with blood (*archaic or literary*) [Early 16C. < Old French *embruer* 'to soil, spatter'] —**imbruement** *n*

imbue /im byoó/ (**-bues, -buing, -bued**) *vt* **1.** to make somebody or something rich with a particular quality (*usually passive*) ○ *poetry imbued with melancholy* **2.** to saturate something with a substance, especially dye (*formal*) [Late 16C. < Latin *imbuere* 'moisten, stain']

IMCO *abbr* Intergovernmental Maritime Consultative Organization

IMechE *abbr* Institution of Mechanical Engineers

~~imediately~~ incorrect spelling of **immediately**

IMF *abbr* International Monetary Fund

~~imformation~~ incorrect spelling of **information**

IMHO *abbr* in my humble opinion (*used in e-mails or text messages*)

imidazole /ímmi dázzōl, i míddəzōl/ *n* an organic white crystalline base that inhibits the action of histamine. Formula: $C_3H_4N_2$. [Late 19C. < IMIDE + AZO- + -OLE]

imide /ímmīd/ *n* an organic compound containing an NH group combined with an acid group and derived from ammonia [Mid-19C. < French, alteration of *amide* (see AMIDE)] —**imidic** /i míddik/ *adj*

imine /ímmeen, i méen/ *n* an organic compound containing an NH group combined with a nonacid group and derived from ammonia [Late 19C. Alteration of AMINE]

IMinE *abbr* Institution of Mining Engineers

~~iminent~~ incorrect spelling of **imminent**

imipramine /i míppra meen/ *n* a tricyclic drug. Use: treatment of depression. [Mid-20C. Blend of IMINE + PROPYL + AMINE]

imit. *abbr* **1.** imitation **2.** imitative

imitate /ímmi tayt/ (**-tates, -tating, -tated**) *vt* **1.** **MIMIC SOMEBODY** to adopt somebody else's behaviour, voice, or manner, sometimes in order to make fun of him or her **2.** **FOLLOW EXAMPLE OF SOMEBODY OR SOMETHING** to use somebody or something as a model, attempting to copy an existing method, style, or approach **3.** **BE OR LOOK LIKE SOMETHING** to be or look like something else ○ *a case of life imitating art* [Mid-16C. < Latin *imitat-*, past participle of *imitari*] —**imitability** /ímmitə bílləti/ *n* —**imitable** *adj* —**imitator** *n*

SYNONYMS ***imitate, copy, emulate, mimic, take off, ape***

CORE MEANING: to adopt the behaviour of another person

imitate to adopt somebody else's behaviour, voice, or manner, often in order to make fun of him or her ○ *'What shall I do, Fiona?' Fiona sneered, imitating Fergus's voice.* ○ *Children learn many skills by imitating their parents.* **copy** to do exactly what somebody else does ○ *Lennie admired George and tried to copy him.* ○ *A puppy will often watch and copy an older dog's actions.* **emulate** to try to equal or surpass somebody who is successful or admired ○ *She has a tough act to follow in attempting to emulate the success of her predecessor.* ○ *He's a truly great president, and one that I would certainly try to emulate.* **mimic** to adopt somebody else's voice, gestures, or appearance, in a deliberate and exaggerated way, especially to amuse people ○ *mimicking the northern accent* ○ *She whined, mimicking a spoiled child.* **take off** (*informal*) to act like somebody to amuse other people ○ *He takes off John's way of speaking perfectly.* **ape** to act like somebody else in an absurd or grotesque way ○ *At home, the lifestyle of the nobles aped that of the royal household.*

imitation /ímmi táysh'n/ *n* **1.** **ACT OF IMITATING SOMETHING**

the act or an instance of imitating somebody or something, or of using something or somebody as a model **2.** COPY OR FAKE something made to be as much as possible like something else (*often used before a noun*) **3.** IMPRESSION OF SOMEBODY the act of mimicking somebody, or an impression of somebody **4.** MUSIC REPETITION OF MUSICAL MOTIF the repetition of a musical idea such as a melody or rhythmic figure in the part for another voice or instrument, often at another pitch and sometimes with variation ■ *adj* NOT GENUINE synthetic, intended as a copy of something, or not genuine ○ *imitation leather* —**imitational** *adj*

imitative /ímmitətiv/ *adj* **1.** designed to be like something else, but usually inferior to the original **2.** involving or practising imitation **3.** LANGUAGE same as **onomatopoeic** —**imitatively** *adv* —**imitativeness** *n*

imli /ímli/ *n* in South Asian cooking, tamarind used as a flavouring [Via Hindi < Sanskrit *amlikā*]

IMM *abbr* **1.** International Mercantile Marine **2.** International Monetary Market

immaculate /i mákyŏŏlət/ *adj* **1.** absolutely clean, tidy, and free from blemishes ○ *in immaculate condition* **2.** showing faultless perfection ○ *immaculate timing* [15C. < Latin *immaculatus* 'without stain' < *macula* 'blemish'] —**immaculacy** *n* —**immaculately** *adv* —**immaculateness** *n*

Immaculate Conception *n* **1.** in the Roman Catholic Church, the doctrine that the Virgin Mary's soul was free from the stain of original sin from the moment of her soul's conception. The term does not, contrary to popular belief, refer to the conception of Jesus Christ. **2.** in the Roman Catholic Church, the feast of the Immaculate Conception. Date: 8 December.

immanent /ímmənənt/ *adj* **1.** existing within or inherent in something (*formal*) **2.** describes God as existing in and extending into all parts of the created universe [Mid-16C. < late Latin *immanent-*, present participle of *immanere*, literally 'dwell within' < Latin *manere* 'remain, dwell'] —**immanence** *n* —**immanency** *n* —**immanently** *adv*

SPELLCHECK Do not confuse the spelling of ***immanent*** and ***imminent*** ('about to occur'), which sound similar.

immanentism /ímmənəntizəm/ *n* the belief that God exists in and extends into all parts of the created universe, including the individual —**immanentist** *adj, n* —**immanentistic** /ímmənən tístik/ *adj*

Immanuel /i mánnyoo əl/, **Emmanuel** *n* the Messiah referred to in Jewish and Christian scriptures, whom Christians believe to be Jesus Christ [15C. Via late Latin < Greek *Emmanouēl* < Hebrew *'immānū'ēl* 'with us is God']

immaterial /ímmə teéri əl/ *adj* **1.** lacking relevance or importance **2.** not made of matter, or not physically real —**immateriality** /ímmə teéri álləti/ *n* —**immaterially** *adv* —**immaterialness** *n*

immaterialise *vt* another spelling of **immaterialize**

immaterialism /ímmə teéri əlizzəm/ *n* the metaphysical doctrine that the material world does not exist except as ideas or perceptions in the mind, or that only spirits and nonphysical things exist

immaterialize /ímmə teéri ə līz/ (**-izes, -izing, -ized**), **immaterialise** (**-ising, -ising, -ised**) *vt* to take away the physical substance of something and make it spiritual or intangible —**immaterialization** /ímmə teéri ə lī záysh'n/ *n*

immature /ímmə tyóor, -chóor/ *adj* **1.** NOT FULLY DEVELOPED young, and not fully grown or developed **2.** CHILDISH lacking the wisdom or emotional development usually associated with adults **3.** STYLISTICALLY CRUDE AND IMPERFECT not yet having attained the perfection of a fully developed style ○ *an example of the artist's immature period* —**immaturely** *adv* —**immatureness** *n* —**immaturity** *n*

immeasurable /i mézhərəb'l/ *adj* too large or too much to be measured —**immeasurability** /i mézhərə bílləti/ *n* —**immeasurableness** *n* —**immeasurably** *adv*

immediate /i meédi ət/ *adj* **1.** WITHOUT PAUSE OR DELAY happening or done at first, at once, or without delay ○ *had no immediate comment* **2.** NEAREST nearest in time, space, or relationship ○ *his immediate family* ○ *the immediate future* **3.** CURRENT urgent or pressing, and so needing to be dealt with before anything else ○ *the immediate problem* **4.** HAVING DIRECT EFFECT affecting something directly, without anything intervening ○ *the immediate cause* **5.** PHILOSOPHY KNOWN FROM EXPERIENCE relating to something that is known about from personal experience or by intuition **6.** LOGIC DERIVED FROM SINGLE PREMISE describes an inference derived from a single premise, without any middle term, and often by conversion of a categorical statement. An example is 'some cows are brown, therefore some brown things are cows'. [14C. Directly or via French < late Latin *immediatus* 'not separated' < Latin *mediatus*, past participle of *mediare* (see MEDIATE)] —**immediacy** *n* —**immediateness** *n*

immediate annuity *n* an annuity whose payments begin less than one year after it is bought

immediate constituent *n* the first level into which a linguistic unit is analysed, e.g. the subject and predicate as parts of a sentence

immediately /i meédi ətli/ *adv* **1.** AT ONCE without delay or without pausing beforehand **2.** VERY CLOSELY very closely in space or time **3.** DIRECTLY directly, and without anyone or anything in between ■ *conj* AS SOON AS as soon as or at the moment that

immemorial /ímmi máwri əl/ *adj* so old that it seems always to have existed ○ *have known them since time immemorial* ○ *immemorial customs of the nation* —**immemorially** *adv*

immense /i ménss/ *adj* **1.** HUGE exceptionally great in extent or degree ○ *an immense desert* ○ *immense relief* **2.** UNABLE TO BE MEASURED too large to be measurable **3.** EXCELLENT very good or showing excellence (*slang*) [15C. Via French < Latin *immensus* 'not measured' < *mensus*, past participle of *metiri* 'measure'] —**immenseness** *n* —**immensity** *n*

immensely /i ménsli/ *adv* to very great extent or degree ○ *She was immensely rich.*

immerse /i múrss/ (**-merses, -mersing, -mersed**) *v* **1.** *vt* COVER SOMETHING COMPLETELY IN LIQUID to put something into a liquid so that it is entirely below the surface **2. immerse yourself** *vr* OCCUPY YOURSELF TOTALLY WITH SOMETHING to become completely occupied with something, giving all your time, energy, or concentration to it ○ *immersed herself in her work* **3.** *vt* CHR BAPTIZE SOMEBODY to baptize somebody, especially in the Baptist Church, by lowering the person's head and upper body, or sometimes the whole body, into water [Early 17C. < Latin *immers-*, past participle of *immergere* 'plunge into' < *mergere* 'plunge']

immersion /i múrsh'n/ *n* **1.** COMPLETE INVOLVEMENT involvement in something that completely occupies all the time, energy, or concentration available **2.** SUBMERSION the placement of something into a liquid so that it is completely covered **3.** EDUC INTENSIVE LANGUAGE TEACHING an intensive method of language teaching in which all teaching is carried out in the language that is being learned ○ *an immersion course in Gaelic* **4.** CHR BAPTISM BY DIPPING BODY IN WATER the practice, especially in the Baptist Church, of baptism by lowering somebody's head and upper body, or sometimes the whole body, into water **5.** UTIL same as **immersion heater** (*informal*) **6.** ASTRON PASSAGE OF ASTRONOMICAL OBJECT INTO ECLIPSE the movement of an astronomical object such as the Moon into the shadow of another object, causing an eclipse

immersion foot *n* MED same as **trench foot**

immersion heater *n* an electric water heater with the heating element completely submerged in the water, especially one that is part of a domestic hot-water tank

immersionism /i múrsh'nizəm/ *n* in some Christian denominations, the belief that immersion is the only true method of baptism

immersion suit *n* NAUT same as **survival suit**

immesh *vt* same as **enmesh**

immigrant /ímmigrənt/ *n* **1.** SOMEBODY SETTLING IN COUNTRY a newcomer to a country who has settled there **2.** PLANT OR ANIMAL IN NEW PLACE a plant or animal that establishes itself in a place where it was not found before ■ *adj* SETTLING IN ANOTHER COUNTRY relating to those who have come to settle in another country

immigrate /ímmi grayt/ (**-grates, -grating, -grated**) *vi* **1.** to enter a new country for the purpose of settling there **2.** to become established in a new environment (*refers to plants and animals*) —**immigrator** *n* —**immigratory** *adj*

immigration /ímmi gráysh'n/ *n* **1.** the act of entering a new country to settle permanently **2.** the control point at an airport, seaport, or border crossing where people entering a country must stop to have their passports officially checked —**immigrational** *adj*

imminent /ímminənt/ *adj* about to happen, or threatening to happen [Early 16C. < Latin *imminent-*, present participle of *imminere* 'hang over' < *minere* 'to project'] —**imminence** *n* —**imminently** *adv* —**imminentness** *n*

SPELLCHECK See ***immanent***.

immiscible /i míssəb'l/ *adj* describes two or more liquids that will not mix together to form a single homogeneous substance [Late 17C. < late Latin *immiscibilis* 'not subject to mixing' < Latin *miscere* 'to mix'] —**immiscibility** /i míssə bílləti/ *n* —**immiscibly** *adv*

immiserate /i mízzə rayt/ (**-ates, -ating, -ated**) *vt* to cause severe economic hardship to a person or a people (*literary*) —**immiseration** *n*

immitigable /i míttigəb'l/ *adj* incapable of being alleviated, weakened, or softened (*formal*) —**immitigability** /i míttigə bílləti/ *n* —**immitigably** *adv*

immittance /i mítt'nss/ *n* the joint concept of electrical admittance and impedance [Mid-20C. Blend of IMPEDANCE + ADMITTANCE]

immobile /i mō bīl/ *adj* **1.** without moving ○ *He stood perfectly immobile for a few seconds.* **2.** unable to move or be moved —**immobility** /ímmō bílləti/ *n*

immobilise *vt* another spelling of **immobilize**

immobiliser *n* AUTOMOT another spelling of **immobilizer**

immobilize /i mōbi līz/ (**-lizes, -lizing, -lized**), **immobilise** (**-lises, -lising, -lised**) *vt* **1.** RESTRICT MOVEMENT OF SOMEBODY OR SOMETHING to prevent somebody or something from moving (*often passive*) **2.** PUT MACHINE OUT OF ACTION to make a machine or device stop working, or adjust or damage it so that it cannot be made to work **3.** MED KEEP BROKEN LIMB STILL to rest a joint or keep the parts of a fractured limb fixed in place so that they are unable to move **4.** FIN TAKE MONEY OUT OF CIRCULATION to withdraw money or other capital from circulation to establish a reserve —**immobilization** /i mōbi lī záysh'n/ *n*

immobilizer /i mōbi līzər/, **immobiliser** *n* an electronic security device, fitted to a motor vehicle, that stops the engine from working and prevents the vehicle from being stolen

immoderate /i móddərət/ *adj* going beyond what is healthy, moral, appropriate, or socially acceptable —**immoderacy** *n* —**immoderately** *adv* —**immoderation** /i móddə ráysh'n/ *n*

immodest /i móddist/ *adj* **1.** boasting, or tending to boast a great deal **2.** likely to embarrass, offend, or shock people, especially because of open references to sexual matters or exposure of parts of the body that are normally covered —**immodestly** *adv* —**immodesty** *n*

immolate /ímmə layt/ (**-lates, -lating, -lated**) *vt* **1.** to kill a person or an animal, e.g. as a ritual sacrifice, or commit suicide as a protest, especially by burning (*formal*) **2.** to give up something that is highly valued (*literary*) [Mid-16C. < Latin *immolat-*, present participle of *immolare* 'sprinkle with meal' < *mola* 'meal, millstone'; from the custom of sprinkling sacrificial victims with meal] —**immolation** /ímmə láysh'n/ *n* —**immolator** *n*

immoral /i mórrəl/ *adj* contrary to accepted moral principles —**immorality** /ímmə rálləti/ *n* —**immorally** *adv*

immoral earnings *npl* money gained from sexual prostitution or similar activities

immoralist /i mórrəlist/ *n* somebody who behaves immorally or who urges others to behave so

immortal /i máwrt'l/ *adj* **1.** NEVER DYING able to have eternal life or existence **2.** FAMOUS very famous and likely to be remembered for a long time ■ *n* **1.** FAMOUS PERSON OR THING somebody or something so famous as to be remembered for a long time (*often used in the plural*) **2.** *also* **Immortal** DEITY a god who lives forever, especially a god of ancient Greece or Rome —**immortality** /ímmawr tálləti/ *n* —**immortally** *adv*

immortalize /i máwrt'l īz/ (**-izes, -izing, -ized**), **immortalise** (**-ises, -ising, -ised**) *vt* **1.** MAKE SOMEBODY'S MEMORY LIVE ON to make somebody or something famous for a very long time, especially as the

subject of a work of art such as a painting, novel, or film **2. GIVE ETERNAL LIFE TO SOMEBODY** to elevate a mortal person to the state of divinity or bestow eternal life on somebody **3.** BIOL **CAUSE SOMETHING TO REPRODUCE INDEFINITELY** to cause something such as human cells to reproduce indefinitely —**immortalization** /i máwrt'l ī záysh'n/ n

immortelle /ímmawr tél/ n PLANTS same as **everlasting** n (sense 2) [Mid-19C. < French, shortening of *fleur immortelle* 'undying flower']

immotile /i mó tīl/ adj describes a plant or animal part that cannot move —**immotility** /ímmō tílləti/ n

immovable /i moóvəb'l/, **immoveable** adj **1. UNABLE TO BE MOVED** fixed in a permanent position, or incapable of being moved **2. OF FIXED OPINION** sticking firmly to an opinion or decision **3. ALWAYS OCCURRING ON SAME DATE** describes a religious festival that always falls on the same date each year, as does Christmas but not Easter ■ n LAW **BUILDINGS OR LAND** property that consists of land or buildings (*often used in the plural*) —**immovability** /i moóvə bílləti/ n —**immovableness** n —**immovably** adv

immun. abbr **1.** immunity **2.** immunization **3.** immunology

immune /i moón/ adj **1. SAFE FROM DISEASE** protected from getting a disease because of natural resistance, resistance acquired after catching the disease, or resistance conferred by inoculation ○ *immune to smallpox* **2. RELATING TO DISEASE RESISTANCE** relating to or involved in a body's resistance to disease or the creation of this resistance **3. NOT SUBJECT TO SOMETHING** exempt from something that others are subject to or made to endure or perform ○ *immune from prosecution* **4. NOT AFFECTED BY SOMETHING** not sensitive or susceptible to something ○ *immune to flattery* [Late 19C. < Latin *immunis* 'exempt from public service' < *munis* 'ready for service']

immune complex n a combination of a disease-causing agent (**antigen**) and its corresponding antibody that plays a role in some types of immune response and may be associated with autoimmune disease

immune response n **1.** the overall activity of the body's immune system following the arrival of a disease-causing agent (**antigen**) **2.** the integrated defence mounted by an organism against a disease-causing agent (**antigen**), including the production of antibodies and white blood cells designed to destroy the antigen or render it harmless

immune system n the interacting combination of all the body's ways of recognizing cells, tissues, objects, and organisms that are not part of itself, and initiating the immune response to fight them

immunise vt another spelling of **immunize**

immunity /i moónəti/ (*plural* -**ties**) n **1.** a body's ability to resist a disease. Immunity may exist naturally or as a result of inoculation or previous infection. In active immunity, the body itself produces appropriate antibodies and lymphocytes, while in passive immunity, antibodies are introduced from another source, as from mother to foetus. ○ *immunity to smallpox* **2.** exemption or protection from something unpleasant, e.g. a duty or penalty, to which others are subject ○ *immunity from deportation*

immunize /ímmyōō nīz/ (-**nizes**, -**nizing**, -**nized**), **immunise** (-**nises**, -**nising**, -**nised**) vt **1.** to make somebody resistant to a disease, especially by inoculation ○ *people who were immunized against tuberculosis* **2.** give somebody exemption or protection from something to which others are subject, especially in a criminal matter under investigation —**immunization** /ímmyōō nī záysh'n/ n —**immunizer** n

immuno- prefix immune, immunity ○ *immunodeficiency* [< IMMUNE]

immunoassay /ímmyōōnō ássay/ n a technique for measuring the amount of antigens and antibodies in tissue —**immunoassayist** n

immunobiology /ímmyōōnō bī ólləji/ n a branch of biology dealing with the effects of the immune system on factors affecting the body, including disease, growth, and genetics —**immunobiologic** /ímmyōōnō bī ə lójjik/ adj —**immunobiological** adj

immunochemistry /ímmyōōnō kémmistri/ n the study of antibodies using chemical techniques —**immunochemical** adj

immunocompetence /ímmyōōnō kómpitənss/ n the ability of the body to develop an immune response in the presence of a disease-causing agent (**antigen**) —**immunocompetent** adj

immunocomplex /ímmyōōnō kómpleks/ n IMMUNOL same as **immune complex**

immunocompromised /ímmyōōnō kómprə mīzd/ adj lacking an adequate immune response as a result of disease, exposure to radiation, or treatment with immunosuppressive drugs

immunocytochemistry /ímmyōōnō sītō kémmistri/ n a branch of biochemistry that deals with the immunological reactions of cells —**immunocytochemical** n

immunodeficiency /ímmyōōnō di físh'nssi/ (*plural* -**cies**) n the inability, either inborn or acquired, of the body to produce an adequate immune response to fight disease —**immunodeficient** adj

immunodepression /ímmyōōnō di présh'n/ n MED same as **immunosuppression**

immunodiagnosis /ímmyōōnō dī əg nóssiss/ (*plural* -**noses** -seez/) n the diagnosis of disease by studying the antibodies in a sample of blood serum —**immunodiagnostic** /-nóstik/ adj

immunoelectrophoresis /ímmyōōnō i léktrō fə réessiss/ n a method of separating and identifying a mixture of antigens using electrophoresis to separate them and an antigen–antibody reaction to identify them —**immunoelectrophoretic** /-fə réttik/ adj —**immunoelectrophoretically** adv

immunofluorescence /ímmyōōnō floor réss'nss/ n the labelling of antibodies or disease-causing agents (**antigens**) with a fluorescent dye in order to identify or locate them in a tissue sample —**immunofluorescent** adj

immunogenetics /ímmyōōnō jə néttiks/ n the study of the genetic basis of the immune system. This study is especially important in organ transplantation, where a close genetic match of tissue lowers the likelihood of organ rejection. (*takes a singular verb*) —**immunogenetic** adj —**immunogeneticist** /-jə néttissist/ n

immunogenic /ímmyōōnō jénnik/ adj creating immunity or an immune response —**immunogenically** adv —**immunogenicity** /-jə níssəti/ n

immunoglobulin /ímmyōōnō glóbbyōōlin/ n an antibody belonging to a group formed by cells of the immune system and present in the blood. Immunoglobulins are found in blood serum, the respiratory and digestive tracts, and body secretions, and they are grouped into five classes on the basis of their structure and physiological activity.

immunohaematology /ímmyōōnō héemə tólləji/ n the discipline concerned with all aspects of immunology relating to the blood, including blood groups and blood disorders —**immunohaematologic** /-héemətə lójjik/ adj —**immunohaematological** adj

immunology /ímmyōō nólləji/ n the scientific study of the way the immune system works in the body, including allergies, resistance to disease, and acceptance or rejection of foreign tissue —**immunologic** /ímmyōōnō lójjik/ adj —**immunological** adj —**immunologically** adv —**immunologist** n

immunomodulation /ímmyōōnō moddyōō láysh'n/ n the modification of some aspect of the immune system as part of a treatment, especially the suppression of the immune system in order to encourage the body to accept a transplanted organ —**immunomodulatory** /-móddyōōlətəri, -moddyōō láytəri/ adj

immunopathology /ímmyōōnōpə thólləji/ n the study of disorders of the immune system and the resulting diseases or allergies —**immunopathologic** /-páthə lójjik/ adj —**immunopathological** adj —**immunopathologist** n

immunopharmacology /ímmyōōnō faarmə kólləji/ n the science or study of drugs used to treat allergic diseases and the immune system —**immunopharmacologic** /-faarməkə lójjik/ adj —**immunopharmacological** adj —**immunopharmacologist** n

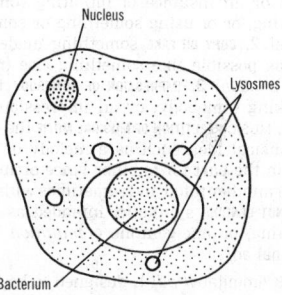
immunoreaction: section of immune cell ingesting and degrading disease-causing bacterium

immunoreaction /i myoónō ri áksh'n/ n the reaction between a disease-causing agent (**antigen**) and its specific antibody, either as the body's immune response or as part of a laboratory procedure —**immunoreactive** adj —**immunoreactivity** /i myoónō ri ak tívvəti/ n

immunosuppression /ímmyōōnō sə présh'n/ n the inhibition of the immune response, usually deliberately by administering drugs to prevent rejection of transplanted organs, but sometimes resulting from disease, as in the case of Aids —**immunosuppressant** adj, n —**immunosuppressive** adj, n

immunotherapy /ímmyōōnō thérrəpi/ n treatment of disease or other disorders by strengthening the body's immune system, e.g. by administering antibodies —**immunotherapeutic** /-thérrə pyoótik/ adj

immunotoxicity /ímmyōōnō tok sísseti/ n the degree to which something is toxic to the immune system —**immunotoxic** /ímmyōōnō tok sik/ adj —**immunotoxically** adv

immunotoxicology /ímmyōōnō toksi kólləji/ n a branch of medicine dealing with the effects of toxic substances on the immune system —**immunotoxicologic** /-toksikə lójjik/ adj —**immunotoxicological** adj —**immunotoxicologist** n

immure /i myoór/ (-**mures**, -**muring**, -**mured**) vt **1. IMPRISON SOMEBODY** to confine somebody in prison (*literary; usually passive*) **2. SHUT SOMEBODY AWAY** to shut away or seclude somebody (*formal; often passive*) **3. ENCLOSE SOMETHING** to enclose something in a wall or surround something with walls (*archaic*) [Late 16C. Directly or via French < Latin *immurare* 'wall in' < *murus* 'wall'] —**immurement** n

immutable /i myoótəb'l/ adj not changing or not able to be changed —**immutability** /i myoótə bílləti/ n —**immutableness** n —**immutably** adv

IMO abbr **1.** ONLINE in my opinion (*used in e-mails or text messages*) **2.** International Meteorological Organization **3.** International Miners' Organization

imp /imp/ n **1. NAUGHTY IMAGINARY BEING** a small, mischievous, imaginary being **2. MISCHIEVOUS CHILD** a high-spirited or mischievous child **3. DEMON** a small demon or devil ■ vt (**imps**, **imping**, **imped**) REPAIR HAWK'S FEATHERS in falconry, to repair the broken wing of a hawk or falcon by grafting on new feathers [Old English *impa* 'young shoot, scion', *impian* 'to graft' < Greek *emphuein* 'implant' < *phuein* 'grow']

IMP abbr **1.** imperial **2.** COMPUT interface message processor **3.** CARDS International Match Point

imp. abbr **1.** GRAM imperative **2.** GRAM imperfect **3.** imperial **4.** GRAM impersonal **5.** COMM import **6.** important **7.** COMM imported **8.** COMM importer **9.** PUBL imprimatur

Imp. abbr GOV **1.** Emperor **2.** Empress [Latin *Imperator* (masculine), *Imperatrix* (feminine)]

impact n /ím pakt/ **1. ACTION OF HITTING** the action of one object hitting another **2. FORCE OF COLLISION** the force with which one object hits another **3.** △ **STRONG EFFECT** the powerful or dramatic effect that something or somebody has ■ vti /im pákt/ (-**pacts**, -**pacting**, -**pacted**) **1. STRIKE SOMETHING** to strike something with force **2.** △ **HAVE EFFECT ON SOMETHING OR SOMEBODY** to have an immediate and strong effect on something or somebody [Early 17C. < Latin *impactus*, past participle of *impingere* (see IMPINGE)] —**impaction** /im páksh'n/ n

USAGE The noun ***impact***, in its figurative meaning, should normally convey some sense of powerful or dramatic consequence, and should not just be an alternative word for *effect* or *impression*. To use it in a context like *He had an impact on everyone in the room* – except in highly unusual circumstances – is to devalue the word. Many careful users of the language dislike the verb ***impact*** in any figurative sense, regardless of whether the verb is followed by *on*: *This impacts the company favourably* and *This impacts on the company*. The verb is undeniably common in business communication, but you can avoid it by using *affect*, *change*, or the like.

impact adhesive *n* a powerful glue that begins to form a bond as soon as the two coated surfaces are brought together

impacted /im páktid/ *adj* **1. WEDGED SIDEWAYS UNDER THE GUM** describes an unerupted tooth wedged sideways against a barrier, usually the root of another tooth, and thus unable to break through the gum **2. WITH BROKEN ENDS JAMMED TOGETHER** describes a bone fracture with the broken ends jammed tightly together by the initial trauma **3. DIFFICULT TO MOVE** unable to be moved, usually because of being jammed in a narrow space

impact printer *n* a printing device in which ink is pressed onto the paper by the printing element, as in a traditional typewriter

impact statement *n* a written statement outlining the effects of something on a specific person or place ○ *a consumer impact statement*

impact zone *n* in surfing, the best and also the most dangerous position on a wave, where the water is about to separate into droplets

impair /im páir/ (**-pairs, -pairing, -paired**) *vt* to lessen the quality, strength, or effectiveness of something [14C. < Old French *empeirier*, literally 'make worse' < Latin *pejor* 'worse'] —**impairable** *adj* —**impairer** *n* —**impairment** *n*

impaired /im páird/ *adj* with something absent or lessened, either temporarily or permanently (*usually used in combination*) ○ *hearing-impaired*

impala

impala /im paálə/ (*plural* **-las** or *same*) *n* a large reddish-brown antelope with long curved horns that makes spectacular leaps when alarmed. Native to: Africa. Latin name: *Aepyceros melampus*. [Late 19C. < Zulu]

impale /im páyl/ (**-pales, -paling, -paled**), **empale** *vt* **1.** to pierce somebody or something with a pointed object (*often passive*) **2.** to combine two coats of arms on a single shield, divided by a vertical stripe (**pale**) [Mid-16C. Directly or via French < medieval Latin *impalare* 'put on a stake' < Latin *palus* 'stake'] —**impalement** *n* —**impaler** *n*

impalpable /im pálpəb'l/ *adj* (*formal*) **1.** not capable of being perceived by the senses **2.** difficult to understand or grasp [Early 16C. Directly or via French < late Latin *impalpabilis* 'not touchable' < *palpare* 'touch gently'] —**impalpability** /im pálpə bílləti/ *n* —**impalpably** *adv*

impanation /ímpə náysh'n/ *n* according to some denominations of Christianity, the presence of the body and blood of Jesus Christ in bread and wine that has been consecrated for the service of Communion [Mid-16C. < medieval Latin *impanation-* < *impanare* 'embody in bread' < Latin *panis* 'bread']

impanel /im pánn'l/ (**-els, -elling, -elled**), **empanel** /em-/ *vt* **1.** to draw up a list of people to be selected for jury service **2.** to select a jury from a list of eligible persons [15C. < Anglo-Norman *empaneller* 'put on a list' < Old French *panel* 'list, jury list' (see PANEL)]

impart /im paárt/ (**-parts, -parting, -parted**) *vt* **1.** to communicate information or knowledge **2.** to give something a particular quality [Mid-16C. Via French < Latin *impartire* 'give a share in' < *pars* 'part'] —**impartation** /ím paar táysh'n/ *n*

impartial /im paársh'l/ *adj* having no direct involvement or interest and not favouring one person or side more than another —**impartiality** /im paárshi állәti/ *n* —**impartially** *adv*

impartible /im paártəb'l/ *adj* not able to be divided, or not to be divided up [Late 16C. < late Latin *impartibilis* 'not divisible' < *partire* (see PART)] —**impartibility** /im paártə bílləti/ *n* —**impartibly** *adv*

impassable /im paássəb'l/ *adj* **1.** impossible to travel on or through, e.g. because of being in bad condition or being blocked by snow, ice, or floodwaters **2.** impossible to solve or overcome ○ *impassable obstacles to peace* —**impassability** /im paássə bílləti/ *n* —**impassableness** *n* —**impassably** *adv*

impasse /am paáss, ám paass, im paáss, ím paass/ *n* a point at which no further progress can be made or agreement reached ○ *Talks have reached an impasse*. [Mid-19C. < French < *im-* 'not' + *passer* (see PASS)]

impassible /im pássəb'l/ *adj* **1.** not susceptible to or not capable of feeling physical pain or injury (*formal*) **2.** not capable of feeling or expressing emotion (*formal or literary*) [14C. Via French < ecclesiastical Latin *impassibilis* 'not feeling' < Latin *pass-*, past participle of *pati* 'suffer'] —**impassibility** /im pássə bílləti/ *n* —**impassibly** *adv*

impassion /im pásh'n/ (**-sions, -sioning, -sioned**) *vt* to arouse strong feelings in somebody (*usually passive*) ○ *a crowd that was impassioned by his oratory* [Late 16C. < Italian *impassionare* < *passione* 'passion' < late Latin *passion-* (see PASSION)]

impassioned /im pásh'nd/ *adj* expressing or revealing strong feelings —**impassionedly** *adv* —**impassionedness** *n*

impassive /im pássiv/ *adj* **1.** showing no outward sign of emotion, especially on the face **2.** feeling no emotions at all, either positive or negative [Early 17C. < IM-[1] + PASSIVE] —**impassively** *adv* —**impassiveness** *n* —**impassivity** /ímpə sívvəti/ *n*

SYNONYMS ***impassive, apathetic, phlegmatic, stolid, stoic, unmoved***

CORE MEANING: showing no emotional response or interest

impassive showing no outward sign of emotion, especially on the face ○ *the smile that transformed his usually impassive face* ○ *The defendant was impassive as the jury announced its verdict.* **apathetic** not taking any interest in anything, or not bothering to do anything ○ *The political turmoil of the last two years has left voters apathetic.* ○ *A recent report suggests that many people tend to be apathetic about the importance of health and fitness.* **phlegmatic** generally unemotional and difficult to arouse ○ *Although she was disappointed at the news, her response was phlegmatic.* **stolid** solemn, unemotional, and not easily excited or upset ○ *He was a stolid, dignified judge who spoke in slow, deliberate voice.* **stoic** showing admirable patience and endurance in the face of adversity without complaining or getting upset ○ *stoic acceptance of the lack of job security in the industry* **unmoved** having or showing no emotional reaction to something when it would usually be expected ○ *The country's head of state appeared unmoved by widespread international criticism of her policies.* ○ *The cities I had seen left me unmoved; they lacked the colour and variety I craved.*

impasto /im pástō/ *n* **1.** in art, the technique of applying paint so thickly that brush or knife strokes can be seen **2.** in art, paint applied so thickly that brush or knife strokes can be seen [Late 18C. < Italian, past participle of *impastare* 'paint thickly, encrust']

impatiens /im páyshi enz, -pátti-/ (*plural same*) *n* PLANTS same as **busy Lizzie** [Late 18C. Via modern Latin < Latin, stem *impatient-*; because its capsules tend to burst open when touched]

impatient /im páysh'nt/ *adj* **1. ANNOYED AT WAITING** annoyed or tending to be annoyed at being kept waiting or by being delayed **2. EAGER** eager to do something immediately, and unwilling to wait **3. EASILY ANNOYED** unable to tolerate a particular thing and easily annoyed by it ○ *He was impatient of formalities.* [14C. Via French < Latin *impatient-*, literally 'not enduring' < *pati* 'suffer'] —**impatience** *n* —**impatiently** *adv*

impeach /im peéch/ (**-peaches, -peaching, -peached**) *vt* **1. ACCUSE OFFICIAL OF OFFENCE** in the United States, to charge a serving government official with serious misconduct while in office **2. CAST SOMEBODY OUT OF PUBLIC OFFICE** in the United States, to remove somebody such as a president or a judge from public office because of having committed serious crimes and misdemeanours or because of other gross misconduct (*formal*) **3. DISPARAGE SOMEBODY** to question a person's good character (*formal*) **4.** LAW **ACCUSE SOMEBODY OF SERIOUS CRIME** to accuse somebody of a crime, especially treason or another crime against the state **5.** LAW **BRING CHARGES AGAINST SOMEBODY** to charge somebody with a crime or misdemeanour [14C. Via Old French *empecher* < late Latin *impedicare* 'entangle' < *pedica* 'snare'] —**impeachable** *adj* —**impeacher** *n* —**impeachment** *n*

impeccable /im pékəb'l/ *adj* **1.** so perfect or flawless as to be beyond criticism ○ *She had impeccable taste.* **2.** so perfect in character as to be incapable of sinning [Mid-16C. < Latin *impeccabilis* 'not liable to sin' < *peccare* 'to sin'] —**impeccability** /im pékə bílləti/ *n* —**impeccably** *adv*

impecunious /ímpi kyoóni əss/ *adj* having little or no money, and so unable to lead a comfortable life [Late 16C. < IM-[1] + obsolete *pecunious* 'wealthy' < Latin *pecunia* (see PECUNIARY)] —**impecuniosity** /-kyoóni óssəti/ *n* —**impecuniously** *adv* —**impecuniousness** *n*

impedance /im peéd'nss/ *n* **1. PREVENTION OF PROGRESS** something that delays or prevents progress, or the preventing of progress (*formal*) **2.** ELEC **OPPOSITION TO FLOW OF ALTERNATING CURRENT** the opposition in an electrical circuit to the flow of alternating current, consisting of resistance and reactance. Symbol *Z* **3.** ACOUSTICS **RATIO OF SOUND PRESSURE TO VELOCITY** the ratio of the sound pressure in a medium to the velocity of the particles in the medium

impede /im peéd/ (**-pedes, -peding, -peded**) *vt* to interfere with the movement, progress, or development of something or somebody [Late 16C. < Latin *impedire* 'shackle the feet' < *ped-* 'foot'] —**impeder** *n*

SYNONYMS See ***hinder***[1].

impediment /im péddimənt/ *n* **1. IMPAIRMENT** an impairment, especially one affecting speech **2. OBSTACLE** something that hinders progress **3.** (*plural* **impediments** or **impedimenta** /im péddi méntə/) LAW **LEGAL OBSTRUCTION** the reason a legal contract such as a marriage cannot be entered into [14C. < Latin *impedimentum* 'hindrance' < *impedire* (see IMPEDE)] —**impedimental** /im péddi mént'l/ *adj* —**impedimentary** /im péddi méntəri/ *adj*

impedimenta /im péddi méntə/ *npl* **1.** obstacles, hindrances, or obstructions to progress (*literary*) **2.** equipment and baggage carried by soldiers (*dated*) **3.** LAW plural of **impediment** (sense 3) [Early 17C. < Latin, plural of *impedimentum* (see IMPEDIMENT)]

impedor /im peédər/ *n* any electrical circuit component that has impedance [< IMPEDANCE]

impel /im pél/ (**-pels, -pelling, -pelled**) *vt* **1.** to force somebody to do something, or make somebody feel the need to do something ○ *Their behaviour impelled me to protest.* **2.** to start or keep something or somebody moving in a particular direction (*formal*) ○ *The boat was impelled towards the shore by the tide.* [15C. < Latin *impellere* 'drive towards' < *pellere* 'to beat']

impeller /im péllər/ *n* the rotating part that transmits motion in a device such as a centrifugal pump, turbine, or blower

impend /im pénd/ (**-pends, -pending, -pended**) *vi* **1.** to be threateningly close to happening (*formal*) **2.** to hover or hang above something, usually in a threatening way (*literary*) [Late 16C. < Latin *impendere* 'hang over' < *pendere* 'hang'] —**impendence** *n* —**impendency** *n* —**impendent** *adj*

impending /im pénding/ *adj* about to happen

impenetrable /im pénnitrəb'l/ *adj* **1.** IMPOSSIBLE TO GET IN OR THROUGH not able to be passed through or entered ○ *The woods formed an impenetrable barrier.* **2.** INCOMPREHENSIBLE impossible to understand or discern ○ *impenetrable legal jargon* **3.** CLOSED TO INFLUENCE not open to intellectual or moral influences, impressions, or ideas —**impenetrability** /im pénnitrə bílləti/ *n* —**impenetrably** *adv*

impenitent /im pénnit'nt/ *adj* having or showing no regret or sorrow for sin or misbehaviour ■ *n* an unrepentant person —**impenitence** *n* —**impenitency** *n* —**impenitently** *adv*

imperative /im pérrətiv/ *adj* **1.** NECESSARY absolutely necessary or unavoidable ○ *It is imperative that justice is seen to be done.* **2.** COMMANDING forceful and demanding the obedience and respect of others (*formal*) **3.** GRAM USED FOR GIVING ORDERS describes the mood or a form of a verb that expresses a command or request, e.g. the verb form 'come' in 'Come here!' ■ *n* **1.** PRIORITY something that must be done ○ *The general's imperative was to conquer or die.* **2.** GRAM WAY OF COMMANDING the mood of a verb used to give an order ○ *when the verb is used in the imperative* **3.** GRAM VERB EXPRESSING COMMAND OR REQUEST a verb in the imperative mood, e.g. 'close' in 'Please close the door' [15C. < late Latin *imperativus* 'specially ordered' < Latin *imperare* 'to command' < *parare* 'prepare'] —**imperatively** *adv* —**imperativeness** *n*

imperator /ímpə raá tawr/ *n* **1.** ROMAN GENERAL a victorious military commander during the time of the Roman Republic **2.** ROMAN EMPEROR the head of state of the Roman Empire **3.** ABSOLUTE RULER an absolute ruler or commander [Mid-16C. < Latin, 'commander' < *imperare* (see IMPERATIVE)] —**imperatorial** /im pérrə tàwri əl/ *adj*

imperceptible /ímpər séptəb'l/ *adj* very slight or gradual ○ *an imperceptible change in temperature* —**imperceptibility** /-septə bílləti/ *n* —**imperceptibly** *adv*

imperceptive /ímpər séptiv/ *adj* lacking the ability to notice things or to understand somebody or something —**imperceptively** *adv* —**imperceptivity** /-sep tívvəti/ *n*

impercipience /ímpər síppi ənss/ *n* a lack of perception (*formal*) ○ *the impercipience of the egotist* —**impercipient** *adj*

imperf. *abbr* **1.** GRAM, BOT imperfect **2.** ANAT, STAMPS imperforate

imperfect /im púrfikt/ *adj* **1.** FAULTY having a fault or defect **2.** NOT COMPLETE lacking a part **3.** BOT NOT ABLE TO REPRODUCE describes a flower that lacks either a stamen or a pistil and is therefore unable to reproduce **4.** MUSIC NOT PERFECT AS INTERVAL describes a musical interval other than the fourth, fifth, or octave **5.** MUSIC ENDING ON 5TH NOTE OF SCALE describes a cadence ending on the fifth note of the scale (**dominant**) rather than on the first note (**tonic**) **6.** GRAM EXPRESSING INCOMPLETE ACTION describes a verb form or tense that expresses past action going on but not completed **7.** LAW UNENFORCEABLE unable to be enforced ■ *n* GRAM **1.** VERB TENSE a grammatical tense that expresses incomplete or habitual action in the past **2.** VERB FORM a form of a verb used to express the imperfect tense —**imperfectly** *adv*

imperfect fungus *n* a fungus that forms only asexual spores (**conidia**). Order: Fungi Imperfecti.

imperfection /ímpər féksh'n/ *n* **1.** something that makes a person or thing less than perfect **2.** the possession of faults or defects

SYNONYMS See *flaw*[1].

imperfective /ímpər féktiv/ GRAM *adj* INDICATING INCOMPLETE ACTION describes a verb aspect expressing action that is not completed ■ *n* **1.** VERB ASPECT the imperfective aspect of the verb **2.** VERB FORM a verb form belonging to the imperfective aspect —**imperfectively** *adv*

imperforate /im púrfərit/ *adj* **1.** ANAT PARTIALLY OR COMPLETELY CLOSED describes a body part lacking an opening of the normal size, especially because of atypical development **2.** STAMPS WITH NO HOLES describes a sheet of postage stamps produced without the perforations that allow easy tearing or division ■ *n* STAMPS STAMP WITHOUT PERFORATIONS a stamp without perforations around it —**imperforation** /im púrfə ráysh'n/ *n*

imperia plural of **imperium**

imperial /im peéri əl/ *adj* **1.** OF EMPIRE OR EMPEROR involving or relating to an empire or its ruler **2.** INDICATING COUNTRY'S AUTHORITY involving or relating to the authority of a country over colonies or other countries **3.** SUPREMELY POWERFUL holding supreme power ○ *All are subject to the imperial power of the state.* **4.** GRAND very grand or majestic **5.** SUPERIOR OR LARGER better in quality or larger in size **6.** OF UK NONMETRIC MEASURES in the United Kingdom, belonging or conforming to the nonmetric system of weights and measures that includes the foot, pound, and gallon ■ *n* **1.** PAPER SIZE the largest of the traditional UK and US paper sizes. The UK imperial measures 559 x 762 mm/22 x 30 in. The US imperial measures 584 x 838 mm/23 x 33 in. **2.** SMALL BEARD a tuft or point of hair grown on the chin or below the lower lip. This style was made fashionable by the French emperor Napoleon III. **3.** RELATIVE OF EMPEROR OR EMPRESS somebody belonging to an imperial family (*formal*) **4.** TRANSP TRUNK FOR LUGGAGE especially in the past, a chest fitted onto the top of a coach to store travellers' bags, or the part of a coach's roof where this chest fits **5.** BEVERAGES LARGE WINE BOTTLE a wine bottle containing the equivalent of eight standard bottles, used for claret [14C. Via French < Latin *imperialis* < *imperium* (see EMPIRE)] —**imperially** *adv*

imperial gallon *n* MEASURE same as **gallon** *n* (sense 1)

imperialism /im peéri əlizəm/ *n* **1.** BELIEF IN EMPIRE-BUILDING the policy of extending the rule or influence of a country over other countries or colonies **2.** DOMINATION BY EMPIRE the political, military, or economic domination of one country over another **3.** TAKEOVER AND DOMINATION the extension of power or authority over others in the interests of domination ○ *cultural imperialism* —**imperialist** *n*, *adj* —**imperialistic** /im peéri ə lístik/ *adj* —**imperialistically** *adv*

imperil /im pérrəl/ (**-ils**, **-illing**, **-illed**) *vt* to put something or somebody in danger —**imperilment** *n*

imperious /im peéri əss/ *adj* haughty and domineering [Mid-16C. < Latin *imperiosus* < *imperium* (see EMPIRE)] —**imperiously** *adv* —**imperiousness** *n*

imperishable /im pérrishəb'l/ *adj* **1.** not liable to become spoilt, weak, or damaged through time and wear **2.** not forgotten or ignored over time (*literary*) ○ *The imperishable quality of great literature distinguishes it from humbler writing.* —**imperishability** /im pérrishə bílləti/ *n* —**imperishableness** *n* —**imperishably** *adv*

imperium /im peéri əm/ (*plural* **-ria** /-ri ə/) *n* **1.** SUPREME POWER supreme or imperial power (*formal*) **2.** EMPIRE an area controlled by a supreme power (*formal or literary*) **3.** LAW LEGAL RIGHT TO COMMAND the use of the power of the state to enforce the law [Mid-17C. < Latin (see EMPIRE)]

impermanent /im púrmənənt/ *adj* likely to change, go away, disappear, or fade —**impermanence** *n* —**impermanency** *n* —**impermanently** *adv*

impermeable /im púrmi əb'l/ *adj* not permitting the passage of liquid, gas, or other fluid —**impermeability** /im púrmi ə bílləti/ *n* —**impermeably** *adv*

impermissible /ímpər míssəb'l/ *adj* not allowed —**impermissibility** /ímpər míssə bílləti/ *n* —**impermissibly** *adv*

impersonal /im púrs'nəl/ *adj* **1.** NOT PERSONALIZED not referring to individual people or reflecting personalities but focusing on events and facts ○ *an impersonal style of reporting* **2.** ANONYMOUS not considering people as individuals ○ *an impersonal bureaucracy* **3.** COLD AND ALIENATING making somebody feel insignificant and ignored as a person ○ *The service in the restaurant was brisk and impersonal.* **4.** LACKING HUMAN TRAITS having no human characteristics or personality **5.** GRAM NOT SPECIFIC describes a clause or construction that includes a personal pronoun that does not refer to a specific person or thing, e.g. 'it is raining' or 'you shouldn't drink and drive' —**impersonality** /im púrssə nálləti/ *n* —**impersonally** *adv*

impersonalize /im púrs'nə līz/ (**-izes**, **-izing**, **-ized**), **impersonalise** (**-ises**, **-ising**, **-ised**) *vt* to make something neutral, lacking in human warmth, or without reference to individuals —**impersonalization** /im púrss'nə līzáysh'n/ *n*

impersonate /im púrssə nayt/ (**-ates**, **-ating**, **-ated**) *vt* **1.** to mimic the voice, appearance, and manners of

somebody else, especially in order to entertain **2.** to pretend to be somebody else, especially illegally in order to deceive [Early 17C. < IM + Latin *persona* 'mask worn by an actor, character', after INCORPORATE] —**impersonation** /im púrssə náysh'n/ *n* —**impersonator** *n*

impertinent /im púrtinənt/ *adj* **1.** showing a bold or rude lack of respect, especially to a superior **2.** not appropriate or relevant (*formal*) —**impertinence** *n* —**impertinently** *adv*

imperturbable /ímpər túrbəb'l/ *adj* not easily worried, distressed, or agitated —**imperturbability** /ímpər túrbə bílləti/ *n* —**imperturbableness** *n* —**imperturbably** *adv*

impervious /im púrvi əss/ *adj* **1.** remaining unmoved and unaffected by other people's opinions, arguments, or suggestions ○ *The directors were impervious to the growing resentment among the staff.* **2.** not allowing passage into or through something ○ *impervious to damp* [Mid-17C. < Latin *impervius* < *pervius* (see PERVIOUS)] —**imperviously** *adv* —**imperviousness** *n*

impetigo /impi tígō/ *n* a contagious infection of the skin caused by staphylococcal and streptococcal bacteria and characterized by blisters that form yellow-brown scabs [14C. < Latin < *impetere* (see IMPETUS)] —**impetiginous** /-tíjjinəss/ *adj*

impetuosity /im péttyoo óssəti/ (*plural* **-ties**) *n* (*formal*) **1.** a tendency to act rashly **2.** an act performed on the spur of the moment after little or no consideration

impetuous /im péttyoo əss/ *adj* **1.** ACTING IMPULSIVELY acting on the spur of the moment, without considering the consequences **2.** DONE ON IMPULSE done without thought as a reaction to an emotion or impulse **3.** VIOLENT moving with great force and energy (*literary*) [14C. Via French < late Latin *impetuosus* < *impetus* (see IMPETUS)] —**impetuously** *adv* —**impetuousness** *n*

impetus /ímpitəss/ *n* **1.** the energy or motivation to accomplish or undertake something **2.** PHYS a force that causes the motion of an object to overcome resistance and maintain its velocity [Mid-17C. < Latin, 'assault, force' < *impetere* 'assail' < *petere* 'seek']

Imphal /ímf'l, im faál/ capital city of Manipur State in northeastern India. Population: 198,535 (1991).

impi /ímpi/ (*plural same as* or **-ies**) *n* S Africa a band of armed Zulu warriors or soldiers [Mid-19C. < Zulu]

impiety /im pí əti/ (*plural* **-ties**) *n* **1.** LACK OF RELIGIOUS RESPECT a lack of due reverence for God or religion **2.** UNGODLY ACT an act that shows a lack of religious respect or devotion **3.** LACK OF RESPECT a lack of respect or dutifulness (*formal*)

imping /ímping/ *n* in falconry, a technique for repairing the broken wing of a hawk or falcon by grafting on new feathers [Old English *impa* 'young shoot, scion', *impian* 'to graft' < Greek *emphuein* 'implant' < *phuein* 'grow']

impinge /im pínj/ (**-pinges**, **-pingeing**, **-pinged**) *vi* **1.** to affect the limits of something, especially a right or law, often causing some kind of restriction (*formal*) ○ *Members claimed that cancelling the ballot impinged on their voting rights.* **2.** to strike or hit something ○ *Loud noise can impinge on the eardrum, causing temporary hearing damage.* [Mid-16C. < Latin *impingere* 'drive in forcibly' < *pangere* 'drive or fix in'] —**impingement** *n* —**impinger** *n*

impious /ímpi əss, im pí əss/ *adj* **1.** not showing due reverence for God or something holy **2.** showing a lack of respect for somebody or something (*formal*) —**impiously** *adv* —**impiousness** *n*

impish /ímpish/ *adj* wicked in a playful way, without causing serious harm —**impishly** *adv* —**impishness** *n*

implacable /im plákəb'l/ *adj* impossible to pacify or to reduce in strength or force ○ *an implacable foe* ○ *an implacable ice storm* [15C. < Latin *implacabilis* < *placabilis* 'easily appeased' < *placare* 'to calm'] —**implacability** /im plákə bílləti/ *n* —**implacableness** *n* —**implacably** *adv*

implant *v* /im plaánt/ (**-plants**, **-planting**, **-planted**) **1.** *vt* ESTABLISH HABITS OR NOTIONS to fix something deeply in somebody's mind or consciousness as a behaviour pattern, thought, or belief **2.** *vt* INSERT SOMETHING to fit or fix something small into something larger, which then encases it ○ *Gold fillings, implanted in his front teeth, flashed when he smiled.* **3.** *vt* BURY SOMETHING IN

GROUND to fix something in the ground, especially so that it grows **4.** *vt* SURG EMBED SOMETHING IN BODY to embed something such as a mechanical device in the body ○ *The hormone pellets are invisibly implanted just below the skin.* **5.** *vi* MED BECOME EMBEDDED IN WOMB to become embedded in the lining of the womb (*refers to embryos*) ■ *n* /ím plaant/ SURG SOMETHING INSERTED DURING SURGERY something inserted or embedded in the tissues or organs of the body during a surgical procedure, e.g. encapsulated drugs or fluid-filled sacs to replace or augment breast tissue —**implantable** *adj* —**implanter** *n*

implantation /ím plaan táysh'n/ *n* **1.** STATE OR PROCESS OF IMPLANTING the state of being fixed or embedded in something, or the process of becoming fixed or embedded in something **2.** SURG SURGICAL INSERTION OF SOMETHING the insertion or embedding of something into body tissues or organs during a surgical procedure **3.** MED ATTACHMENT OF EMBRYO the process by which or stage at which an embryo becomes embedded in the lining of the womb

implausible /im pláwzəb'l/ *adj* hardly likely to be true, acceptable, or possible —**implausibility** /im pláwzə bíllәti/ *n* —**implausibly** *adv*

implead /im pléed/ (**-pleads, -pleading, -pleaded**) *vti* to bring a lawsuit against a person or an organization in court —**impleadable** *adj* —**impleader** *n*

implement *n* /ímplimənt/ **1.** TOOL a useful piece of equipment, usually a specially shaped object designed to do a particular task ○ *writing implements* **2.** LAW REQUIREMENT something needed in order to achieve something else (*formal*) ■ *vt* /ímpli ment/ (**-ments, -menting, -mented**) **1.** CARRY OUT OR FULFIL SOMETHING to put something into effect or action ○ *The plan has yet to be fully implemented.* **2.** GIVE TOOLS TO SOMEBODY to provide or equip somebody with the tools or other means to do something (*formal*) [15C. < late Latin *implementum* 'filling' < Latin *implere* 'fill in' < *plere* 'to fill'] —**implemental** /ímpli mént'l/ *adj* —**implementation** /ímpli men táysh'n/ *n* —**implementer** *n*

implicate /ímpli kayt/ (**-cates, -cating, -cated**) *vt* **1.** SHOW CONNECTION OF SOMEBODY WITH SOMETHING to show that somebody or something played a part in or is connected to an activity such as a crime **2.** IMPLY SOMETHING to imply or involve something as a consequence (*formal*) ○ *Do you not see that his words implicate an error on my part?* **3.** ENTANGLE OR INTERWEAVE THINGS to wreathe, twist, or knit things together (*literary*) [15C. < Latin *implicat-*, past participle of *implicare* 'entangle' < *plicare* 'to fold'] —**implicative** /im plíkətiv, ímpli kaytiv/ *adj*

implication /ímpli káysh'n/ *n* **1.** INDIRECT SUGGESTION something that is implied or involved as a natural consequence of something else ○ *It is important to consider the wider implications of such a decision.* **2.** IMPLICIT UNDERSTANDING the state of implying or being implied, without being plainly expressed **3.** INVOLVEMENT the involvement or entanglement of somebody in something ○ *his implication in the crime* **4.** LOGIC LOGICAL RELATION in logic, a relationship between two propositions that holds when both propositions are true and fails when the first is true but the second is false —**implicational** *adj*

implicit /im plíssit/ *adj* **1.** IMPLIED not stated, but understood in what is expressed ○ *Asking us when we would like to start was an implicit acceptance of our terms.* **2.** ABSOLUTE not affected by any doubt or uncertainty ○ *implicit trust* **3.** CONTAINED present as a necessary part of something ○ *Confidentiality is implicit in the relationship between doctor and patient.* **4.** MATHS WITH ONLY DEPENDENT VARIABLES describes a mathematical function that contains only variables whose value is dependent on the value of the other variables in the function [Late 16C. Directly or via French < Latin *implicitus* 'entangled' < *implicare* (see IMPLICATE)] —**implicitly** *adv*

USAGE See *explicit*.

~~**impliment**~~ incorrect spelling of **implement**

implode /im plṓd/ (**-plodes, -ploding, -ploded**) *v* **1.** *vti* to collapse inwardly with force as a result of the external pressure being greater than the internal pressure, or cause something to collapse inwardly **2.** *vi* to suffer from total economic or political collapse e.g.as a result of poor management and financial insolvency. [Late 19C. < IM + Latin *plodere* 'to clap', after EXPLODE]

implore /im pláwr/ (**-plores, -ploring, -plored**) *vt* **1.** to plead with somebody to do something ○ *The tenants implored their landlord not to sell the building.* **2.** to beg or pray for something (*formal*) [Early 16C. Directly or via French < Latin *implorare* 'call upon with tears' < *plorare* 'weep'] —**imploration** /ímplə ráysh'n, ím plaw-/ *n* —**imploratory** *adj* —**implorer** *n*

imploring /im pláwring/ *adj* earnestly asking for something ○ *an imploring look* —**imploringly** *adv*

implosion /im plṓzh'n/ *n* **1.** the violent inward collapse of a vessel or structure resulting from the external pressure being greater than the internal pressure **2.** total economic or political collapse, e.g. as a result of poor management and financial insolvency ○ *the implosion of high-risk stocks* [Late 19C. < IMPLODE]

implosive /im plṓssiv, -plṓziv/ *adj* indicating or relating to violent inward collapse —**implosively** *adv*

imply /im plī́/ (**-plies, -plying, -plied**) *vt* **1.** to make something understood without expressing it directly **2.** to involve something as a necessary part or condition ○ *Such impressive exam results imply good teaching and study methods.* [14C. Via Old French *emplier* < Latin *implicare* (see IMPLICATE)] —**implied** *adj*

impolite /ímpə lī́t/ *adj* not showing proper manners or respect —**impolitely** *adv* —**impoliteness** *n*

impolitic /im póllətik/ *adj* likely to be disadvantageous and therefore not advisable ○ *It would be impolitic to refuse.* —**impoliticly** *adv*

imponderable /im póndərəb'l/ *adj* not quantifiable in terms of importance or effect ○ *Sheer inspiration remains an imponderable force in cultural and technological developments.* ■ *n* an event, factor, or other matter whose importance or effects cannot be calculated (*often used in the plural*) ○ *just another of life's imponderables* —**imponderability** /im póndərə bíllәti/ *n* —**imponderably** *adv*

import *vt* /im páwrt/ (**-ports, -porting, -ported**) **1.** BRING SOMETHING IN FROM ABROAD to bring something or cause something to be brought in from another country, usually for commercial or industrial purposes **2.** BRING IN SOMETHING FROM OUTSIDE to introduce something such as knowledge or expertise from an outside source **3.** IMPLY SOMETHING to mean something, often in addition to what is actually expressed (*formal*) **4.** COMPUT TRANSFER DATA to transfer data from one location to another in a computer or from one computer to another in a computer network, especially when a change of format is required ■ *n* /ím pawrt/ **1.** SOMETHING BROUGHT FROM ABROAD something that is brought into one country from another, usually for commercial or industrial purposes **2.** IDEA OR PERSON BROUGHT IN an idea, practice, or person introduced from the outside ○ *The new accounting system is an import from the private sector.* **3.** IMPORTATION the bringing in of something from abroad or an outside source ○ *Most governments forbid the import of such goods.* **4.** TRUE SIGNIFICANCE meaning or significance ○ *a foreign-policy decision of great import* [15C. < Latin *importare* 'carry in' (in medieval Latin, 'imply, be significant') < *portare* 'carry'] —**importability** /im páwrtə bíllәti/ *n* —**importable** *adj* —**importation** /ím pawr táysh'n/ *n* —**importer** *n*

importance /im páwrt'nss/ *n* **1.** value, relevance, or interest ○ *It is difficult to overestimate the importance of this breakthrough.* ○ *The age of the car is of no importance.* **2.** high position, rank, or reputation in society

important /im páwrt'nt/ *adj* **1.** HAVING VALUE OR SIGNIFICANCE worthy of note or consideration, especially for its interest, value, or relevance ○ *an important scientific discovery* ○ *an important author* **2.** HIGH-RANKING with high social position or influence among people **3.** POMPOUS seeming to assume more status, significance, or value than is actually due ○ *strode into the room with an important air* [15C. < medieval Latin *important-*, present participle of *importare* (see IMPORT)] —**importantly** *adv*

~~**importent**~~ incorrect spelling of **important**

importunate /im páwrtyoōnət/ *adj* (*formal*) **1.** continually asking for something, especially in a forceful, insistent, or troublesome manner ○ *importunate requests for a loan* **2.** requiring immediate attention and action ○ *importunate requests for medical aid* [Early 16C. < Latin *importunus* (see IMPORTUNE)] —**importunacy** *n* —**importunately** *adv*

importune /ím pawr tyoon, ím pawr tyoōn/ *vt* (**-tunes, -tuning, -tuned**) (*formal*) **1.** BOTHER SOMEBODY INSISTENTLY to ask somebody continually, repeatedly, or forcefully for something, especially in a troublesome way **2.** MAKE IMMORAL REQUEST OF SOMEBODY to ask somebody to have sexual relations in exchange for money ■ *adj* IMPORTUNATE persistent or pressing [Mid-16C. < French *importuner* or medieval Latin *importunari* < Latin *importunus* 'inconvenient, unseasonable' < *Portunus*, god of harbours] —**importunely** *adv* —**importuner** *n*

importunity /ím pawr tyoōnəti/ (*plural* **-ties**) *n* (*formal*) **1.** the fact of being troublesomely demanding or insistent **2.** a demand made repeatedly or insistently

impose /im pṓz/ (**-poses, -posing, -posed**) *v* **1.** *vt* LEVY OR ENFORCE SOMETHING to lay down something compulsory such as a tax or a punishment **2.** *vt* INSIST ON SOMETHING to make people agree to something or comply with something by having superior strength or authority ○ *We believe that one country should not try to impose its culture on another.* **3.** *vti* INCONVENIENCE SOMEBODY to demand somebody's attention or time in an unreasonable manner ○ *The guests' increasing demands imposed on the family's hospitality.* **4.** *vt* PASS OFF SOMETHING ON SOMEBODY to use deceit or fraud to give something to somebody or to persuade somebody to accept something **5.** *vt* PRINTING ARRANGE PAGES to order the pages of material such as a book or magazine for printing **6.** *vt* RELIG LAY ON HANDS to bless somebody, e.g. in confirmation or ordination, by laying hands on the person's head [15C. < French *imposer* (influenced by *poser* 'to put') < Latin *imponere* 'place into' < *ponere* 'to place'] —**imposable** *adj* —**imposer** *n*

imposing /im pṓzing/ *adj* large and stately, thus creating an impression of grandeur —**imposingly** *adv*

imposition /ímpə zísh'n/ *n* **1.** EXTRA TROUBLE a request or task, especially a time-consuming one, that is unreasonably expected of somebody **2.** ENFORCED DUTY a tax, fee, or penalty that is imposed on people **3.** ESTABLISHMENT OR ENFORCEMENT OF SOMETHING the official or legal process of laying down something compulsory such as a tax, fee, or penalty **4.** DECEPTION a deception or fraud (*literary*) **5.** PRINTING ARRANGEMENT OF PAGES the setting up and ordering of pages for printing **6.** RELIG BLESSING the laying of hands on somebody's head in a religious sacrament such as ordination or confirmation

impossibility /im póssə bíllәti/ (*plural* **-ties**) *n* **1.** something that cannot exist or cannot be done ○ *Living without water is a physical impossibility.* **2.** the likelihood that something will not happen or cannot be achieved ○ *the impossibility of finding another job close to home*

impossible /im póssəb'l/ *adj* **1.** NOT POSSIBLE not able to exist or be done ○ *an impossible task* **2.** TOO DIFFICULT very difficult to deal with and apparently without a solution ○ *The situation was impossible: I couldn't be honest without offending one of them.* **3.** NOT ENDURABLE unbearably difficult or not possible to endure **4.** NOT BELIEVABLE ridiculous or unreasonable, because not able to be true

impossibly /im póssəbli/ *adv* **1.** EXTREMELY to an extent that is almost unbelievable ○ *impossibly thin slices* **2.** NOT BY ANY MEANS in a way that could not be done or could not happen **3.** INFURIATINGLY to an infuriating or intolerable degree (*informal*)

impost[1] /ím pōst/ *n* **1.** a tax or other payment levied on goods brought into a country **2.** the weight a horse must carry, including that of the jockey, in a handicap race [15C. < Italian *imposta*, < past participle of *imporre* 'impose' < Latin *imponere* (see IMPOSE)]

impost[2] /ím pōst/ *n* the top part of a pillar, column, or wall, which may be decorated or moulded and on which a vault or arch rests [Mid-16C. < French < Latin *impostus impositus*, past participle of *imponere* (see IMPOSE)]

impostor /im póstər/, **imposter** *n* somebody who makes false claims of identity, often using somebody else's name or documents [Late 16C. Via French *imposteur* < Latin *impositor* < *imponere* (see IMPOSE)]

imposture /im póschər/ *n* the act of pretending to be somebody else in order to trick people, or an occasion on which this is done [Mid-16C. Via French

< late Latin *impostura* 'a putting on' < Latin *imponere* (see IMPOSE)]

impotent /ímpətənt/ *adj* **1.** unable to perform sexual intercourse, usually because erection of the penis cannot be achieved or sustained **2.** without the strength or power to do anything effective or helpful —**impotence** *n* —**impotently** *adv*

impound /im pównd/ (**-pounds, -pounding, -pounded**) *vt* **1. KEEP SOMETHING IN CONFINED PLACE** to lock something such as an illegally parked car in an enclosure or compound **2. TAKE SOMETHING INTO LEGAL CUSTODY** to take goods or possessions into official custody **3. WITHHOLD SOMETHING LEGALLY** to withhold something by legal means **4.** CIV ENG **HOLD WATER SUPPLY** to save and collect water in a dam or reservoir [15C. < IM-[2] + POUND[3]] —**impoundable** *adj* —**impoundage** *n* —**impounder** *n* —**impoundment** *n*

impoverish /im póvvərish/ (**-ishes, -ishing, -ished**) *vt* **1. MAKE SOMEBODY OR SOMETHING POOR** to cause somebody or something to be poor or poorer (*often passive*) **2. SPOIL OR REDUCE SOMETHING IN QUALITY** to take away some part or quality belonging to something, leaving it in a worse or weaker condition than before ○ *a vocabulary impoverished by technical jargon* **3. DEPRIVE SOMETHING OF NUTRIENTS** to take away the nutrients and richness from a substance such as soil [15C. < Old French *empoveriss-*, stem of *empov(e)rier* < *povre* (see POOR)] —**impoverisher** *n* —**impoverishment** *n*

impracticable /im práktikəb'l/ *adj* **1. NOT POSSIBLE** impossible to be carried out effectively **2. UNUSABLE** not in a fit condition for use **3. INTRACTABLE** impossible or almost impossible to deal with (*archaic*) —**impracticability** /im práktikə bílləti/ *n* —**impracticableness** *n* —**impracticably** *adv*

USAGE See ***practicable***.

impractical /im práktik'l/ *adj* **1.** not able to work effectively or be without problems when put into practice **2.** not able to perform practical tasks or deal easily with practical matters ○ *She is a brilliant academic, but completely impractical around the house.* —**impracticality** /im prákti kálləti/ *n* —**impractically** *adv*

USAGE See ***practicable***.

imprecate /ímpri kayt/ (**-cates, -cating, -cated**) *vti* to call down harm, especially a curse, on somebody (*formal*) [Early 17C. < Latin *imprecat-*, past participle of *imprecari* < *precari* (see PRAY)] —**imprecator** *n* —**imprecatory** *adj*

imprecation /ímpri káysh'n/ *n* (*formal*) **1. CURSE** an oath or curse **2. ACT OF CURSING SOMEBODY** the calling down of harm on somebody **3. ACT OF SWEARING** swearing or blasphemy

imprecise /ímpri sĭ́ss/ *adj* not exact or accurate —**imprecisely** *adv* —**impreciseness** *n* —**imprecision** /-sízh'n/ *n*

impregnable /im prégnəb'l/ *adj* **1.** too strong to be captured or entered by force ○ *an impregnable fortress* **2.** unable to be shaken or destroyed by any outside influence ○ *impregnable faith* —**impregnability** /im prégnə bílləti/ *n* —**impregnably** *adv*

impregnate *vt* /ím preg nayt/ (**-nates, -nating, -nated**) **1. SATURATE MATERIAL** to incorporate a chemical into a porous material such as wood or cloth, especially by soaking it thoroughly with a liquid (*usually passive*) **2. PERMEATE SOMETHING WITH QUALITY** to permeate something with a particular aura or tone, or make something contain a particular quality (*literary*) ○ *This was a major speech impregnated with references to the Crown in past centuries.* **3. MAKE FEMALE PREGNANT** to make a woman or female animal pregnant ■ *adj* /im prégnət/ **1. SATURATED** infused or saturated with something **2. PREGNANT** pregnant or fertilized [Early 17C. < late Latin *impregnat-*, past participle of *impregnare* < Latin *praegnas* (see PREGNANT)] —**impregnation** /ím preg náysh'n/ *n* —**impregnator** *n*

impresario /ímprə saári ō/ (*plural* **-os**) *n* **1.** a producer or promoter of commercial entertainment ventures, especially in musical theatre **2.** somebody in charge of an opera or ballet company who is responsible for business affairs, contracting artists, and commissioning new works [Mid-18C. < Italian, 'somebody who undertakes' < *impresa* 'undertaking' < *imprendere* 'undertake' < Latin *prendere* 'to take']

imprescriptible /ímpri skríptəb'l/ *adj* impossible to remove or violate ○ *the people's imprescriptible rights* [Late 16C. < medieval Latin *imprescriptibilis* < Latin *praescript-*, past participle of *praescribere* (see PRESCRIBE)] —**imprescriptibility** /ímpri skríptə bílləti/ *n* —**imprescriptibly** *adv*

impress[1] *v* /im préss/ (**-presses, -pressing, -pressed**) **1.** *vti* **AFFECT OR PLEASE SOMEBODY GREATLY** to have a strong, usually favourable effect on the mind or feelings of somebody (*often passive*) ○ *We were very impressed by the way we were treated.* **2.** *vt* **MAKE SOMETHING CLEARLY UNDERSTOOD** to make sure that somebody has a clear and lasting understanding, memory, or mental image of something ○ *She impressed on every child her expectation of complete honesty.* **3.** *vt* **PRESS SHAPE INTO SOMETHING** to make a pattern, design, or mark on something by pressing or stamping **4.** *vt* ELECTRONICS **APPLY VOLTAGE TO SOMETHING** to apply a voltage to an electronic circuit or device ■ *n* /ím press/ **STAMP** a characteristic mark (*literary*) [14C. < French *empresser* < Latin *impress-*, past participle of *imprimere* 'press in' < *premere* 'to press'] —**impresser** *n* —**impressibility** /im préssə bílləti/ *n* —**impressible** *adj*

impress[2] /im préss/ (**-presses, -pressing, -pressed**) *vt* **1.** to seize something by force for public use **2.** to compel people to serve in a navy or army, especially by arbitrary means [Late 16C. < IM-[2] + PRESS[2]] —**impressment** *n*

impression /im présh'n/ *n* **1. WHAT STAYS IN SOMEBODY'S MIND** a lasting effect, opinion, or mental image of somebody or something ○ *I made a bad impression by arriving late for the interview.* **2. GENERAL IDEA** a belief about or understanding of something ○ *I was under the impression that they were married.* **3. PRESSED-IN SHAPE** a pattern, design, or mark made by something hard being pressed onto something softer ○ *The intruder's boots had left an impression in the mud.* **4. IMITATING OF SOMEBODY** an entertainment in which a performer mimics the way a well-known person speaks and behaves, usually in a humorous or exaggerated way **5. MOULD TAKEN OF TEETH** a mould taken of the teeth and surrounding gums on which dentures, restorations, or dental appliances are constructed **6.** PRINTING, PUBL **COPIES OF BOOK** all the copies of a book printed at one time, or the printing of these **7.** PRINTING, PUBL **COPY OF BOOK** a printed copy of a book [14C. Via French < Latin *impression-* < past participle of *imprimere* 'press in' < *premere* 'press'] —**impressional** *adj* —**impressionally** *adv*

impressionable /im présh'nəb'l/ *adj* ready to accept or be impressed by the experiences, opinions, and personalities of other people —**impressionability** /im présh'nə bílləti/ *n* —**impressionably** *adv*

impressionism /im présh'nizəm/, **Impressionism** *n* **1.** a style of painting that concentrates on the general tone and effect produced by a subject, without elaboration of details. Monet and Renoir were practitioners of impressionism. **2.** a style of music, especially of late 19th-century France, characterized by the use of rich harmonies and tones rather than form to express scenes or emotions. Debussy and Ravel were practitioners of impressionism. [Late 19C. < French *impressionisme*]

impressionist /im présh'nist/ *n* **1.** a performer who mimics the way well-known people speak and behave, usually in a humorous exaggerated way **2.** *also* **Impressionist** an artist or composer whose work is in the style of impressionism, especially one active in France at the end of the 19th century

impressionistic /im préshə nístik/ *adj* **1.** giving a broad picture or general idea rather than an exact description **2.** relating to or in the style of impressionism or the impressionists in painting or music —**impressionistically** *adv*

impressive /im préssiv/ *adj* making a deep and usually favourable impression on the mind or senses —**impressively** *adv* —**impressiveness** *n*

imprest /ím prest/ *n* **1. ADVANCE OF MONEY** an advance payment of money, especially to somebody who is to carry out business for the state **2. LOAN TO DRAW ON** a loan, usually in the form of a petty cash account, that can be drawn on as needed **3. ADVANCE PAYMENT** a payment formerly made in advance to a British soldier or sailor on enlistment [Mid-16C. < IM-[2] + obsolete *prest* 'loan' < Old French < *prester* 'lend' < Latin *praesto* 'at hand']

imprimatur /ímpri maátər, -máytər/ *n* **1.** authority to do, say, or especially print something (*formal*) **2.** an authorization allowing a book or other work to be published, now usually confined to works sanctioned by the Roman Catholic Church [Mid-17C. < Latin, 'let it be printed']

imprint *n* /ímprint/ **1. PRESSED-IN SHAPE** a pattern, design, or mark that is made by pressing something down on or into something else ○ *saw the imprint of a foot on the soil* **2. LASTING EFFECT** an effect that remains and is recognizable for a long time ○ *The years of occupation left their imprint on all the inhabitants.* **3. SPECIAL MARK** a printed or stamped sign on an object, e.g. to indicate its origin **4.** PUBL **PRINTED PUBLICATION DETAILS** the name and address of the publisher and printer as shown at the front of a book ■ *v* /im prínt/ (**-prints, -printing, -printed**) **1.** *vt* **MARK SOMETHING BY PRESSING** to put a shape or design on something such as the surface of an object using a stamp or printing device **2.** *vt* **MAKE IDEA OR IMAGE PERMANENT** to fix an image, memory, opinion, or idea in a vivid or lasting way ○ *The scene was imprinted on her memory.* **3.** *vi* ZOOL **ESTABLISH SOCIAL ATTACHMENTS** to learn an attraction to members of the same species or substitutes very early in life —**imprinter** *n*

imprinting /im prínting/ *n* a form of rapid learning very early in an animal's social development that results in strong behavioural patterns of attraction to members of its own species, especially parents. Imprinting was first described by Konrad Lorenz in 1937 when he trained young ducks and geese to follow him and regard him as their mother.

imprison /im prízz'n/ (**-ons, -oning, -oned**) *vt* to lock somebody up in prison —**imprisonable** *adj* —**imprisoner** *n* —**imprisonment** *n*

improbable /im próbbəb'l/ *adj* not likely to happen or to be true —**improbability** /im próbbə bílləti/ *n* —**improbably** *adv*

improbity /im prṓbəti/ *n* lack of moral scruples or honesty (*formal*)

impromptu /im prómptyoo/ *adj* **DONE SPONTANEOUSLY** not prepared or planned in advance ○ *an impromptu speech* ■ *adv* **WITHOUT PRIOR PREPARATION** in an unrehearsed way ■ *n* **1. SHORT SOLO PIECE** a short piece of instrumental music whose style gives an impression of improvisation. Such pieces were a highly developed and popular form in the 19th century. **2. SPONTANEOUS OR UNREHEARSED ACT** something done or said without planning [Mid-17C. Via French < Latin *in promptu* 'at hand' < *promptus* (see PROMPT)]

improper /im próppər/ *adj* **1. UNSUITABLE** not appropriate to the context, the nature of the case, or the purpose in view (*formal*) **2. RUDE** not in accordance with accepted good manners or decorum **3. IRREGULAR** not in accordance with the accepted standards of something such as a profession ○ *the improper handling of funds* —**improperly** *adv* —**improperness** *n*

improper fraction *n* a fraction in which the numerator is equal to or greater than the denominator, e.g. $\frac{6}{4}$

impropriate *vt* /im prṓpri ayt/ (**-ates, -ating, -ated**) to put ecclesiastical property or tithes in lay hands ■ *adj* /im prṓpri ət/ describes ecclesiastical property that is under lay control [Early 16C. < Anglo-Latin *impropriat-*, past participle of *impropriare* 'to appropriate' < Latin *proprius* 'your own'] —**impropriation** /im prṓpri áysh'n/ *n* —**impropriator** *n*

impropriety /ímprə prī́ əti/ (*plural* **-ties**) *n* conduct that is not considered correct, moral, or appropriate in a given context

improve /im próov/ (**-proves, -proving, -proved**) *v* **1.** *vti* **MAKE OR BECOME BETTER** to make something better in quality or condition, or become better ○ *His health is improving daily.* **2.** *vt* **INCREASE VALUE OF PROPERTY** to make property such as land or buildings more valuable **3.** *vt* **USE SOMETHING WELL** to make good use of something or employ something to advantage (*formal*) [Early 16C. < Anglo-Norman *emprower* 'make a profit' < Old French *prou* 'profit' < late Latin *prode* 'profitable' < Latin *prodesse* (see PROUD)] —**improvability** /im proóvə bílləti/ *n* —**improvable** *adj* —**improvably** *adv* —**improver** *n* ◇ **on the improve** *Aus* getting better, e.g. healthier or more acceptable

improve on, improve upon *vt* to do better or be better than something, especially a previous standard or

record ○ *improved on her previous time by four seconds*

improved /im pro͞ovd/ *adj* in a better or more valuable condition

improvement /im pro͞ovmənt/ *n* 1. GETTING OR MAKING BETTER the process of making something better or of becoming better ○ *an improvement on her past performance* 2. CHANGE OR ADDITION a change or addition that makes something better 3. CHANGE THAT APPRECIATES VALUE a change or addition, especially to property or land, that increases value ○ *home improvements* 4. ADVANCE IN VALUE an increase in value, especially in the value of land or property

improvident /im prówvidənt/ *adj* 1. failing to put money aside or give any thought to forward planning 2. not sensible, cautious, or wise (*formal*) [15C. < IM-[1] + PROVIDENT, or < late Latin *improvident-*] —**improvidence** *n* —**improvidently** *adv*

improvise /ímprə vīz/ (**-vises, -vising, -vised**) *vti* 1. to perform or compose something, especially a sketch, play, song, or piece of music, without any preparation or set text to follow 2. to make a substitute for something out of the materials that happen to be available at the time ○ *If you haven't got a hammer, we'll have to improvise.* [Early 19C. Directly or via French < Italian *improvvisare* < Latin *improvisus* 'unforeseen' < *providere* (see PROVIDE)] —**improvisation** /ímprə vī záysh'n/ *n* —**improvisational** *adj* —**improvisationally** *adv* —**improvisatorial** /ímprə vīzə táwri əl/ *adj* —**improvisatory** /ímprə vī záytəri/ *adj* —**improviser** *n*

improvised explosive device *n* a device fabricated or placed in an improvised manner, incorporating lethal, noxious, pyrotechnic, or incendiary materials designed to destroy, incapacitate, harass, or distract. It may incorporate military parts, but is normally constructed from nonmilitary components. [Early 21C.]

imprudent /im pro͞od'nt/ *adj* showing no care, forethought, or judgment —**imprudence** *n* —**imprudently** *adv*

impudent /ímpyo͝odənt/ *adj* showing a lack of respect and excessive boldness [14C. < Latin *impudent-* < *pudent-* 'ashamed', present participle of *pudere* 'feel ashamed'] —**impudence** *n* —**impudently** *adv*

impudicity /ímpyo͞o díssəti/ *n* lack of modesty or shame (*formal*) [Early 16C. Directly or via French < Latin *impudicitas* < *pudere* 'feel ashamed']

impugn /im pyo͞on/ (**-pugns, -pugning, -pugned**) *vt* to suggest that something cannot be trusted, relied on, or respected ○ *Far be it from me to impugn his motives, but ...* [14C. < Latin *impugnare* 'fight against' < *pugnare* 'to fight' < *pugnus* 'fist'] —**impugnable** *adj* —**impugner** *n* —**impugnment** *n*

impulse /ím puls/ *n* 1. SUDDEN URGE a sudden desire, urge, or inclination (*often used before a noun*) ○ *She couldn't resist the impulse to ask him.* 2. INSTINCTIVE DRIVE an instinctive drive or natural tendency 3. MOTIVE a motivation or reason for a specific activity 4. FORCE DRIVING SOMETHING FORWARD a driving force producing a forward motion 5. FORWARD MOTION the motion produced by a driving force 6. PHYS FORCE ACTING OVER TIME a measure of momentum arrived at by multiplying the average force acting on a body by the length of time it acts 7. PHYSIOL NERVE OR MUSCLE SIGNAL a progressive wave of biochemically generated energy that travels along a nerve fibre or muscle and stimulates or inhibits activity [Mid-17C. < Latin *impulsus*, past participle of *impellere* (see IMPEL)]

impulse buying *n* the purchase of goods that may be unnecessary, caused by the sudden urge or desire to have them

impulsion /im púlsh'n/ *n* 1. ACT OR INSTANCE OF URGING the act of urging or forcing somebody into action, or an instance of this 2. MOVEMENT OR THRUSTING FORCE a movement that comes from being pushed or thrust, or the force that creates this movement 3. SUDDEN DESIRE a sudden desire, inclination, or urge

impulsive /im púlssiv/ *adj* 1. INCLINED TO ACT ON SUDDEN URGES having a tendency to act on sudden urges or desires 2. SPONTANEOUS based on or motivated by impulse 3. PHYS COMING IN BURSTS acting or coming in short bursts ○ *an impulsive sound* 4. ACOUSTICS SHORT AND PERCUSSIVE describes a sound that is of short duration and composed of a wide range of frequencies —**impulsively** *adv* —**impulsiveness** *n* —**impulsivity** /im pul sívvəti/ *n*

impunity /im pyo͞onəti/ *n* exemption from punishment, harm, or recrimination [Mid-16C. < Latin *impunitas* < *impunis* 'without punishment' < *poena* 'punishment']

impure /im pyo͝or/ *adj* 1. CONTAMINATED unclean because containing something harmful 2. ADULTERATED combined with something of inferior quality 3. SINFUL tainted with sin 4. HAVING MIXED STYLES combining a mixture of styles, or derived from more than one source 5. MIXED WITH OTHER COLOURS describes a colour mixed with others —**impurely** *adv* —**impureness** *n*

impurity /im pyo͝orəti/ (*plural* **-ties**) *n* 1. LACK OF PURITY the state or quality of being impure 2. CONTAMINANT a substance that adulterates or contaminates something ○ *drinking water that was found to contain impurities* 3. SOMETHING ADDED TO SEMICONDUCTOR a small amount of a substance added to a pure semiconductor to control its electrical conductivity

impute /im pyo͞ot/ (**-putes, -puting, -puted**) *vt* 1. ATTRIBUTE BAD ACTION TO SOMEBODY to attribute a usually undesirable action or event to somebody ○ *'He had married her with that bad past life hidden behind him, and she had no faith left to protest his innocence of the worst that was imputed to him.'* (George Eliot, *Middlemarch*; 1872) 2. ATTRIBUTE BAD QUALITY TO SOMEBODY to attribute a usually undesirable quality to a person, cause, or source ○ *'it was charity to impute some of her unbecoming indifference to the languor of ill-health'* (Jane Austen, *Emma*; 1816) 3. LAW CHARGE SOMEBODY RESPONSIBLE FOR ANOTHER'S CRIME to bring legal charges against somebody because a person that he or she is responsible for has committed an offence 4. EXTEND QUALITY TO SOMEBODY ELSE to regard a quality such as righteousness that applies to somebody as also applying to another person associated with him or her [14C. Via French < Latin *imputare* 'bring into the reckoning' < *putare* 'reckon'] —**imputable** *adj* —**imputation** /ímpyo͞o táysh'n/ *n* —**imputative** *adj* —**imputer** *n*

IMRT *abbr* MED intensity-modulated radiation therapy

IMS *abbr* 1. *S Asia* Indian Medical Service 2. INFO SCI information management systems 3. Institute of Management Services

in[1] /in/ CORE MEANING: a grammatical word indicating that something or somebody is within or inside something ○ (prep) *The dinner's in the oven.* ○ (adv) *I called by, but you weren't in.*

1. *prep* INDICATES PLACE indicates that something happens or is situated somewhere ○ *He spent a whole year in Russia.* 2. *prep* INDICATES STATE indicates a state or condition that something or somebody is experiencing ○ *The banking industry is in a state of flux.* 3. *prep* AFTER after a period of time that will pass before something happens ○ *She should be well enough to leave in a week or two.* 4. *prep* DURING indicates that something happens during a period of time ○ *He crossed the desert in 39 days.* 5. *prep* INDICATES HOW SOMETHING IS EXPRESSED indicates the means of communication used to express something ○ *I managed to write the whole speech in French.* 6. *prep* INDICATES SUBJECT AREA indicates a subject or field of activity ○ *She graduated with a degree in biology.* 7. *prep* AS CONSEQUENCE OF while doing something or as a consequence of something ○ *In reaching for a glass he knocked over the ashtray.* 8. *prep* COVERED BY indicates that something is wrapped or covered by something ○ *The floor was covered in balloons and toys.* 9. *prep* INDICATES HOW SOMEBODY IS DRESSED indicates that somebody is dressed in a particular way ○ *She was dressed in a smart suit.* 10. *prep* PREGNANT WITH pregnant with offspring ○ *The cows were in calf.* 11. *adj* FASHIONABLE fashionable or popular ○ *always knew which clubs were in* 12. *adj, adv* HOLDING POWER OR OFFICE indicates that a party or group has achieved or will achieve power or authority ○ *voted in overwhelmingly* 13. *adj* TAKING TURN TO BAT in sports such as cricket and rounders, used to indicate that a sports team or player is batting ○ *Any volunteers to go in first?* ○ *put the opposition in to bat* [Old English < Germanic] ◇ **in between** between ○ *Normal light consists of a wave that vibrates up and down, side to side, and every direction in between.* ◇ **in for** indicates that somebody will experience something such as a surprise or a shock ○ *Little did she know what she was in for.* ◇ **in on** having knowledge about or involvement in something ○ *The whole class was in on the plans for the surprise party.* ◇ **in that** introduces an explanation of a statement ○ *Action Park is unusual in that it fights lawsuits tenaciously and settles none.* ◇ **in with** associated with or friendly with ○ *a reporter perhaps too much in with the politicians to be objective* ○ *He's been getting in with a bad crowd.* ◇ **the ins and outs** all the detailed facts and points about something ○ *I don't know all the ins and outs of the matter, but she's leaving.*

USAGE See *into*.

in[2] *abbr* 1. MEASURE inch 2. MEASURE inches 3. ONLINE India (*used in Internet addresses*) See table at **domain name**

In *symbol* CHEM ELEM indium

IN *abbr* Indiana

in. *abbr* MEASURE inch, inches

in-[1] *prefix* not ○ *insensitive* ○ *incomplete* [< Latin]

in-[2] *prefix* in, into, towards, within ○ *infighting* ○ *inbound* [< IN [1]]

-in *suffix* an organic chemical or a pharmaceutical ○ *pectin* ○ *botulin* ○ *penicillin* [Alteration of -INE]

inability /ínnə bílləti/ *n* a lack of the ability, means, or power to do something ○ *his inability to face the truth*

~~**inable**~~ incorrect spelling of **enable**

in absentia /ín əb sénti ə/ *adv* in the absence of the person or persons concerned [< Latin, 'in absence']

inaccessible /ínnək séssəb'l/ *adj* 1. DIFFICULT TO GET TO difficult or impossible to gain access to or reach 2. DIFFICULT TO ACHIEVE difficult or impossible to afford or attain 3. HARD TO UNDERSTAND difficult or impossible to understand —**inaccessibility** /ínnək séssə bílləti/ *n* —**inaccessibly** *adv*

inaccuracy /in ákyo͝orəssi/ (*plural* **-cies**) *n* 1. lack of accuracy or correctness 2. something that is incorrect, especially something that has been measured, calculated, copied, or conveyed incorrectly

SYNONYMS See *mistake*.

inaccurate /in ákyo͝orət/ *adj* not accurate or correct —**inaccurately** *adv*

inaction /in áksh'n/ *n* 1. failure to take action when action is necessary ○ *'But in a nation that demands action, Congress has become the master of inaction.'* (National Public Telecomputing Network, *Bush speeches in campaign '92*) 2. lack of activity, especially laziness or idleness

inactivate /in ákti vayt/ (**-vates, -vating, -vated**) *vt* to make something inactive or unable to function —**inactivation** /in ákti váysh'n/ *n*

inactive /in áktiv/ *adj* 1. NOT TAKING ACTION taking no action, or taking no part in an action that others are involved in 2. NOT BEING USED OR OPERATED not in use, functioning, or operating 3. LAZY OR SEDENTARY not involving or taking part in physical activity 4. GEOG DORMANT describes a volcano that is not erupting but is not extinct 5. MIL NOT IN ACTIVE SERVICE not taking part in, or not being used for, active military service 6. CHEM INERT having little or no chemical reactivity 7. CHEM HAVING LOW RADIOACTIVITY having low or no measurable radioactivity 8. BIOL NOT AFFECTING LIVING THINGS having little if any discernible effect on living things as a result of the loss of some property such as the ability to infect or create antigens 9. MED NOT DEVELOPING OR SHOWING SYMPTOMS describes a disease that, though present in the body, is not developing or producing any symptoms —**inactively** *adv* —**inactiveness** *n* —**inactivity** /ín ak tívvəti/ *n*

inadequate /in áddikwət/ *adj* failing to reach an expected or required level or standard ○ *inadequate supplies of food* —**inadequacy** *n* —**inadequately** *adv*

inadmissible /ínnəd míssəb'l/ *adj* not admissible or allowable, especially in a court of law —**inadmissibility** /ínnəd missə bílləti/ *n* —**inadmissibly** *adv*

inadvertent /ínnəd vúrt'nt/ *adj* 1. done unintentionally or without thinking 2. failing to pay enough attention or take enough care [Mid-17C. < IN-[1] + Latin *advertent-*, present participle of *advertere* (see ADVERT [1])] —**inadvertence** *n*

inadvertently /ínəd vúrt'ntli/ *adv* without intending to or without realizing

inadvisable /ínnəd vízəb'l/ *adj* not to be advised or recommended —**inadvisability** /ínnəd vīzə bílləti/ *n* —**inadvisably** *adv*

in aeternum /in ee turnəm/ *adv* eternally or forever (*formal*) [< Latin, literally 'in eternal']

inalienable /in áyli ənəb'l/ *adj* not able to be transferred or taken away, e.g. because of being protected by law —**inalienability** /in áyli ənə bílləti/ *n* —**inalienably** *adv*

inalterable /in áwltərəb'l/ *adj* not able to be changed —**inalterability** /in áwltərə bílləti/ *n* —**inalterably** *adv*

inamorata /in ámmə raátə/ (*plural* **-tas**) *n* a woman whom somebody loves or with whom somebody has a romantic relationship (*literary*) [Late 16C. < Italian, form of *inamorato* (see INAMORATO)]

inamorato /in ámmə raátō/ (*plural* **-tos**) *n* a man whom somebody loves or with whom somebody has a romantic relationship [Late 16C. < Italian, past participle of *inamorare* 'fall in love' < *amore* 'love' < Latin *amor*]

inane /i náyn/ *adj* **1.** irritatingly silly or time-wasting **2.** empty, insubstantial, or void [Mid-16C. < Latin *inanis* 'empty'] —**inanely** *adv* —**inaneness** *n*

inanimate /in ánnimət/ *adj* **1.** DEAD OR INERT not in a physically live state **2.** NOT LIVELY not active, energetic, or lively ○ *'She had relapsed once more into the vacant inanimate creature who had opened the gate to us.'* (Wilkie Collins, *The Law and the Lady*; 1875) **3.** RELATING TO NOUNS FOR NONLIVING THINGS belonging to the category of nouns that refer to things and concepts considered to be without life [15C. < late Latin *inanimatus* 'lifeless' < Latin *animatus*, past participle of *animare* (see ANIMATE)] —**inanimately** *adv* —**inanimateness** *n*

inanition /ínnə nísh'n/ *n* **1.** exhaustion caused by lack of food or water or as a result of disease **2.** lethargy or lack of vitality (*literary*) [14C. < late Latin *inanition-* < Latin *inanis* 'empty']

inanity /i nánnəti/ (*plural* **-ties**) *n* **1.** MEANINGLESS QUALITY meaninglessness or senselessness that suggests a lack of understanding or intelligence **2.** SILLINESS silliness or foolishness **3.** SOMETHING INANE something that demonstrates or suggests inanity, e.g. a silly remark

inappetence /in áppitənss/, **inappetency** /-tənssi/ *n* lack of appetite (*formal*) —**inappetent** *adj*

inapplicable /ínnə plíkəb'l/ *adj* not applicable, suitable, or relevant —**inapplicability** /ínnə plikə bílləti/ *n* —**inapplicably** *adv*

inapposite /in áppəzit/ *adj* unsuitable or out of place —**inappositely** *adv* —**inappositeness** *n*

inappreciable /ínnə préeshəb'l/ *adj* too small to be noticed or significant —**inappreciably** *adv*

inappreciative /ínnə préeshətiv/ *adj* feeling or showing no appreciation —**inappreciatively** *adv* —**inappreciativeness** *n*

inapproachable /ínnə prṓchəb'l/ *adj* impossible to approach —**inapproachability** /ínnə prōchə bílləti/ *n* —**inapproachably** *adv*

inappropriate /ínnə prṓpri ət/ *adj* not fitting, timely, or suitable —**inappropriately** *adv* —**inappropriateness** *n*

inapt /in ápt/ *adj* **1.** not suitable or appropriate **2.** lacking aptitude, capability, or skill —**inaptitude** *n* —**inaptly** *adv* —**inaptness** *n*

inarch /in aárch/ (**-arches, -arching, -arched**), **enarch** *vt* to graft part of one plant onto another without separating it from its parent [Early 17C. < IN-[2] + ARCH[1], because the graft forms an arch between its parent and the new stock]

inarguable /in aár gyoo əb'l/ *adj* impossible to deny or take an opposing view about —**inarguably** *adv*

inarticulate /ín aar tíkyoolət/ *adj* **1.** EXPRESSING YOURSELF POORLY not good at choosing the right words or speaking fluently **2.** NOT EFFECTIVELY EXPRESSED not clearly or effectively expressed **3.** NOT UNDERSTANDABLE not understandable as speech or language **4.** NOT SPOKEN ABOUT not expressed, or not able to be expressed in words **5.** UNABLE TO SPEAK lacking the power to speak, especially because of feeling strong emotion **6.** NOT JOINTED describes body parts that have no joints or segments, e.g., the bones of the skull **7.** HAVING SHELL WITHOUT HINGE describes a class of brachiopods that have shells without a hinge and are held together only by muscles and the body wall —**inarticulacy** *n* —**inarticulately** *adv* —**inarticulateness** *n*

inartistic /ín aar tístik/ *adj* **1.** LACKING ARTISTIC SKILL possessing or demonstrating little or no artistic talent **2.** NOT CONFORMING TO RULES OF ART not in accordance with the principles of art **3.** NOT INTERESTED IN ARTS having no appreciation of or sensitivity to the arts —**inartistically** *adv*

inasmuch as /ínnəz múch əz/ *conj* **1.** used to introduce an explanation or reason ○ *'This was an idle and unpractical question, inasmuch as the answer was not forthcoming.'* (Henry James, *Confidence*) **2.** used to introduce a comment that limits the extent of something [< IN[1] + AS[1] + MUCH, after French *en tant* 'in so much']

inattention /ínnə ténsh'n/ *n* failure to take proper care or give enough attention to something

inattentive /ínnə téntiv/ *adj* not paying attention or taking proper care —**inattentively** *adv* —**inattentiveness** *n*

inaudible /in áwdəb'l/ *adj* not loud enough to be heard —**inaudibility** /in áwdə bílləti/ *n* —**inaudibly** *adv*

inaugural /i náwgyoorəl/ *adj* **1.** relating to or marking an official beginning, e.g. of a newly elected president's term **2.** being the first of a series ○ *an inaugural meeting* [Late 17C. < French < *inaugurer* 'inaugurate' < Latin *inaugurare* (see INAUGURATE)]

inaugurate /i náwgyoo rayt/ (**-rates, -rating, -rated**) *vt* **1.** SWEAR SOMEBODY FORMALLY INTO OFFICE to install somebody in office with a formal ceremony **2.** OPEN SOMETHING CEREMONIALLY to open or mark the beginning of something with a formal ceremony or dedication **3.** PUT SOMETHING INTO OPERATION to initiate something or put it into operation, especially in a formal or official manner [Late 16C. < Latin *inaugurat-*, past participle of *inaugurare* 'predict from birds' flight, install after observing the omens' < *augurari* 'predict from omens' < *augur* 'augur'] —**inaugurator** *n* —**inauguratory** /-rətəri/ *adj*

inauguration /i náwg yoo ráysh'n/ *n* **1.** INDUCTION INTO OFFICE the formal act of placing somebody in an official position, especially the President of the United States, or a ceremony held for this purpose **2.** CEREMONIAL OPENING OF SOMETHING a formal ceremony to open or mark the beginning of something such as a new building **3.** PUTTING SOMETHING INTO OPERATION the act of bringing something into service or putting it into operation, or an occasion on which this is done

inauspicious /ín aw spíshəss/ *adj* suggesting that the future is not very promising or that success is unlikely —**inauspiciously** *adv* —**inauspiciousness** *n*

inauthentic /ín aw théntik/ *adj* not authentic or genuine —**inauthenticity** /ín aw then tíssəti/ *n*

in-between *adj, adv* existing or occurring between two states, categories, or points ○ *one of his in-between moods when you don't know what he'll say* ■ *n* somebody or something that exists or happens in-between ○ *the oldest, the youngest, and the in-betweens*

inboard /ín bawrd/ *adj* **1.** LOCATED INSIDE BOAT'S HULL describes an engine that is located inside the hull of a boat, not fitted to the outside **2.** HAVING INBOARD ENGINE describes a boat that has an inboard engine ■ *n* BOAT WITH INBOARD MOTOR a boat that has an inboard motor ■ *adv* AWAY FROM SIDES more towards the centre of an aircraft or boat than towards the sides or edges

inborn /ín bawrn/ *adj* inherited from parents or possessed from birth

inbound[1] /ín bownd/ *adj* arriving, incoming, or heading towards an airport, port, or station [Late 19C. < IN-[2] + BOUND[3]]

inbound[2] /ín bownd/ (**-bounds, -bounding, -bounded**) *vti* in basketball, to put the ball back into play by passing it from out of bounds to a player on the court [Late 20C. Back-formation < INBOUNDS]

inbounds /ín bowndz/ *adj* in basketball, involving returning the ball into play ○ *on the ensuing inbounds play*

inbounds line *n* in American football, either of the two broken lines that run the length of the pitch

in-box *n N Am* same as **in-tray**

inbreathe /ín breeth/ (**-breathes, -breathing, -breathed**) *vt* **1.** to take something into the airways by breathing in (*technical or literary*) **2.** to inspire somebody or infuse somebody with something (*literary*)

inbred /ín bred/ *adj* **1.** INNATE existing naturally, through being possessed from birth or inherited from parents **2.** PRODUCED BY INBREEDING produced by the mating of closely related individuals of a species ■ *n* FORM RESULTING FROM INBREEDING a person or an animal whose health and intelligence are affected because his, her, or its ancestors were too closely related to each other

inbreed /ín bréed/ (**-breeds, -breeding, -bred** /-bréd/) *v* **1.** *vti* to mate closely related individuals of a species with each other, especially over many generations **2.** *vt* to cause something to develop in somebody —**inbreeder** *n*

inbreeding /ín breeding/ *n* the mating of closely related members of a species, especially over many generations. It may be used to enhance desired traits in animals or plants but is avoided in humans as it increases the risk of unwanted inherited characteristics.

in-built *adj* **1.** existing as part of somebody's character **2.** fitted inside something or existing as a part of it

in-by *adv, adj Scotland* **1.** further in, especially further inside a house **2.** to or towards a house, especially the main or only house on a piece of land such as a farm [Early 18C. < IN[1] + BY[1]]

inc. *abbr* **1.** included **2.** including **3.** inclusive **4.** income **5.** incomplete **6.** *also* **Inc.** *N Am* BUSINESS incorporated **7.** increase

Inca /íngkə/ (*plural same* or **-cas**) *n* **1.** a member of a Native South American people whose empire, based in Peru and covering the Andean region, lasted from the 12th century until the mid-16th century. The Incas were sophisticated engineers, architects, and artists who had a highly complex social structure. The descendants of the Incas form roughly half of today's population of Peru. **2.** a king, noble, or ruler of the Inca empire [Late 16C. < Quechua, 'royal person'] —**Inca** *adj* —**Incaic** /ing káyik/ *adj* —**Incan** *adj*

incalculable /in kálkyooləb'l/ *adj* **1.** too great or numerous to be measured **2.** too uncertain to assess or plan for in advance —**incalculability** /in kálkyoolə bílləti/ *n* —**incalculably** *adv*

incalescent /ínkə léss'nt/ *adj* becoming warmer or hotter than before (*technical*) [Mid-17C. < Latin *incalescent-*, present participle of *incalescere* 'get hotter' < *calere* 'be hot'] —**incalescence** *n*

in camera *adv, adj* **1.** IN PRIVATE in private or in secret **2.** IN CLOSED COURT in a court from which the public is barred **3.** IN JUDGE'S CHAMBERS in a judge's private chambers rather than in open court [< late Latin, 'in the chamber']

incandescence /ín kan déss'nss/ *n* **1.** EMISSION OF LIGHT BY HOT OBJECT the emission of light by an object as a result of its being heated to a high temperature **2.** LIGHT FROM HOT OBJECT the light produced by an object heated to a high temperature **3.** EMOTIONAL INTENSITY intensity of emotion such as anger or romantic passion —**incandesce** *vi*

incandescent /ín kan déss'nt/ *adj* **1.** GLOWING WITH HEAT emitting light as a consequence of being heated to a high temperature **2.** GLOWING BRIGHTLY shining or glowing brightly **3.** SHOWING INTENSE EMOTION feeling or displaying intense emotion such as anger or romantic passion [Late 18C. Directly or via French < Latin *incandescent-*, present participle of *incandescere* 'glow' < *candescere* 'become white' < *candidus* (see CANDID)] —**incandescently** *adv*

incandescent lamp *n* an electric lamp that produces light from an electrically heated filament

incantation /ín kan táysh'n/ *n* **1.** the ritual chanting or use of supposedly magic words **2.** a set of words spoken or chanted as a supposedly magic spell [14C. Via French < late Latin *incantation-* < Latin *incantare* 'to chant' < *cantare* 'sing'] —**incantational** *adj*

incapable /in káypəb'l/ *adj* **1.** LACKING NECESSARY ABILITY lacking the ability, character, or strength required to do something ○ *a woman incapable of admitting defeat* **2.** NOT GOOD ENOUGH unable to function or

perform adequately ○ *regarded as incapable by most of his colleagues* 3. UNABLE TO LOOK AFTER SELF not able to look after yourself ○ *exhausted and incapable* 4. IMPOSSIBLE too extreme for something to be possible ○ *damage incapable of repair* 5. LEGALLY INELIGIBLE legally disqualified or ineligible —**incapability** /in káypə bílləti/ *n* —**incapably** *adv*

incapacitant /ínkə pássitənt/ *n* a substance, e.g. tear gas, that can temporarily incapacitate somebody, used especially in riot control and biological warfare

incapacitate /ínkə pássi tayt/ (**-tates, -tating, -tated**) *vt* 1. to deprive somebody or something of power, force, or effectiveness 2. to disqualify somebody or make somebody legally ineligible —**incapacitation** /ínkə passi táysh'n/ *n*

incapacity /ínkə pássəti/ (*plural* **-ties**) *n* 1. INABILITY OR INEFFECTIVENESS lack of ability, force, or effectiveness 2. PHYSICAL OR MENTAL CHALLENGE a physical or mental challenge, making learning or performing basic tasks difficult 3. LEGAL DISQUALIFICATION a legal or official disqualification

incapsulate *vti* another spelling of **encapsulate**

in-car *adj* fitted or provided inside a car

incarcerate /in káarssə rayt/ (**-ates, -ating, -ated**) *vt* (*formal*) 1. to put somebody in prison 2. to place somebody in a place or situation of confinement [Early 16C. < medieval Latin *incarcerat-*, past participle of *incarcerare* < Latin *carcer* 'prison'] —**incarceration** /in káarssə ráysh'n/ *n* —**incarcerator** *n*

incardinate /in káardi nayt/ (**-nates, -nating, -nated**) *vt* 1. TRANSFER PRIEST to transfer a Roman Catholic priest to a new district under the authority of a different bishop 2. MAKE PRIEST CARDINAL to promote a member of the Roman Catholic clergy to the position of cardinal 3. MAKE PRIEST MOST SENIOR to promote a Roman Catholic priest to the position of most senior member of the clergy within an individual church or area [Early 17C. < late Latin *incardinat-*, past participle of *incardinare* 'ordain as chief priest' < Latin *cardinalis* (see CARDINAL)] —**incardination** /in káardi náysh'n/ *n*

incarnadine /in káarnə dīn/ (*literary*) *adj* CRIMSON of a crimson or blood-red colour ■ *n* CRIMSON COLOUR crimson or the colour of blood ■ *vt* (**-dines, -dining, -dined**) MAKE SOMETHING CRIMSON to tinge or stain something crimson or blood red [Late 16C. Via French < Italian *incarnatino* 'carnation', literally 'flesh-colour' < Latin *carn-* 'flesh']

incarnate *adj* /in káarnət/ 1. MADE HUMAN having a bodily form, especially a human form 2. PERSONIFIED being the epitome of something ○ *an adviser who is discretion incarnate* 3. PINK OR RED describes plant parts that are pink or crimson ■ *vt* /in káar nayt/ (**-nates, -nating, -nated**) 1. SHOW SOMETHING IN HUMAN FORM to give something a bodily form, especially a human form 2. PERSONIFY SOMETHING to be the epitome or personification of something 3. CAUSE SOMETHING TO HAPPEN to bring about something that exists as an idea or theory only [14C. < ecclesiastical Latin *incarnatus*, past participle of *incarnari* 'be made flesh' < Latin *carn-* 'flesh'] —**incarnator** /-naytər/ *n*

incarnation /in kaar náysh'n/ *n* 1. PERSONIFICATION OF SOMETHING somebody or something personifying, representing, or typifying a quality or idea 2. ONE LIFE IN SERIES OF LIVES one of a succession of lives or periods spent in the body of a particular animal or person 3. MANIFESTATION OF GOD a god's or spirit's appearance in human or animal form

Incarnation *n* in Christianity, God's taking human form as Jesus Christ

in case ➧ **case**[1]

incautious /in káwshəss/ *adj* careless, rash, or lacking in caution —**incaution** *n* —**incautiously** *adv* —**incautiousness** *n*

incendiarism /in séndi ərizəm/ *n* inflammatory talk or provocative behaviour designed or likely to cause civil unrest (*formal*)

incendiary /in séndi əri/ *adj* 1. CONTAINING CHEMICALS THAT CAUSE FIRE describes missiles containing highly flammable substances that will cause a fire on impact 2. LIKELY TO CATCH FIRE able to catch fire spontaneously or cause a fire easily 3. INCITING CIVIL UNREST designed or likely to cause civil unrest 4. RELATING TO ARSON relating to or involving the illegal burning of property ■ *n* (*plural* **-ies**) 1. BOMB DESIGNED TO CAUSE FIRE a bomb or missile containing a highly flammable substance such as napalm that is designed to cause a fire on impact 2. SOMEBODY INCITING TROUBLE an instigator of trouble or violence, especially for political motives (*formal*) 3. ARSONIST somebody who illegally sets fire to property [15C. < Latin *incendiarius* < *incendium* 'conflagration' < *incendere* (see INCENSE[1])]

incense[1] /ín senss/ *n* 1. SUBSTANCE BURNT FOR ITS SMELL a substance, usually fragrant gum or wood, that gives off a pleasant smell when burnt 2. SMOKE FROM INCENSE the smoke or fragrant smell produced when incense is burnt 3. FRAGRANCE a pleasant smell 4. PRAISE praise or adulation ■ *v* (**-censes, -censing, -censed**) 1. *vti* BURN INCENSE TO GOD to honour a god by burning incense 2. *vt* PERFUME SOMETHING WITH INCENSE to perfume something by burning incense [13C Via French *encens* < ecclesiastical Latin *incensum*, form of *incensus*, past participle of Latin *incendere* 'set fire to' < base of *candere* 'to glow'] —**incensation** /ín sen sáysh'n/ *n*

incense[2] /in sénss/ (**-censes, -censing, -censed**) *vt* to make somebody extremely angry [15C. Either < French *encenser* < *encens* 'incense', or < ecclesiastical Latin *incensare* < *incensum* (see INCENSE[1])] —**incensement** *n*

incense cedar /ín senss-/ *n* 1. a coniferous evergreen tree of the cypress family, with scaly leaves and aromatic wood. Native to: North America, Asia, New Zealand. Genera: *Austrocedrus* or *Calocedrus* or *Libocedrus*. 2. the scented durable wood of the incense cedar. Use: household fragrance, moth repellent, decking, fence posts, pencils.

incensory /in senssəri/ (*plural* **-ries**) *n* RELIG same as **censer** [Early 17C. < medieval Latin *incensorium* < ecclesiastical Latin *incensum* (see INCENSE[1])]

incentive /in séntiv/ *n* something that encourages or motivates somebody to do something ■ *adj* serving to encourage or motivate somebody [Early 17C. < Latin *incentivum* 'something that sets the tune' < *incinere* 'to sound' < *canere* 'sing'] —**incentively** *adv*

SYNONYMS See *motive*.

incentivize /in sénti vīz/ (**-izes, -izing, -ized**), **incentivise** (**-ises, -ising, -ised**) *vt* to motivate somebody by offering an incentive such as a higher rate of pay (*informal*)

inception /in sépsh'n/ *n* 1. the beginning of something (*formal*) 2. enrolment as a university student, especially one studying for a master's degree or doctorate (*dated formal*) [15C. Directly or via French < Latin *inception-* < *incipere* (see INCIPIENT)]

inceptive /in séptiv/ *adj* 1. INITIAL representing or coming at the beginning of something (*formal*) 2. GRAM EXPRESSING IDEA OF STARTING describes a verb or verb form that, in some languages, indicates the beginning of an action ■ *n* GRAM 1. INCEPTIVE ASPECT the inceptive aspect of verbs 2. INCEPTIVE VERB a verb in the inceptive aspect [Early 17C. < late Latin *inceptivus* < Latin *incipere* (see INCIPIENT)] —**inceptively** *adv*

incertitude /in súrtityood/ *n* 1. doubt or uncertainty 2. lack of self-confidence

incessant /in séss'nt/ *adj* continuing for a long time without stopping [15C. Directly or via French < late Latin *incessant-* < Latin *cessare* (see CEASE)] —**incessancy** *n* —**incessantly** *adv*

incest /ín sest/ *n* sexual activity between two people who are considered, for moral or genetic reasons, too closely related to have such a relationship. Incest is regarded as a serious taboo in almost every society, although cultures differ as to the extent to which marriages are allowed between relatives. [13C. < Latin *incestus* < *castus* 'pure']

incestuous /in séstyoo əss/ *adj* 1. RELATING TO OR INVOLVING INCEST relating to or involving a sexual relationship between two people who are considered, for moral or genetic reasons, too closely related to have such a relationship 2. GUILTY OF INCEST having had a sexual relationship with somebody considered to be too close a relative 3. UNHEALTHILY CLOSE unhealthily intimate or interconnected, especially so as to exclude the involvement or influence of others ○ *an incestuous friendship* —**incestuously** *adv* —**incestuousness** *n*

inch[1] /inch/ *n* 1. UNIT OF LENGTH a unit of length equal to 2.54 cm/$\frac{1}{12}$ of a foot. Symbol " 2. SMALL AMOUNT a very small amount, degree, or distance ○ *The committee won't budge an inch on this issue.* 3. AMOUNT OF RAIN OR SNOW a fall of enough rain or snow to cover a surface to a depth of one inch 4. UNIT OF ATMOSPHERIC PRESSURE a unit of atmospheric pressure equal to that needed to maintain a mercury column one inch high in a barometer ■ *vti* (**inches, inching, inched**) MOVE SLOWLY to move or cause somebody or something to move very slowly or by small degrees [Pre-12C. < Latin *uncia* 'one twelfth' < *unus* 'one']

inch[2] /inch/ *n* in Scotland and Ireland, a small island (*often used in placenames*) [15C. < Scottish Gaelic *innis* 'island']

inchoate /in kő ət/ *adj* (*formal*) 1. JUST BEGINNING just beginning to develop 2. IMPERFECTLY FORMED only partly formed 3. CHAOTIC lacking structure, order, or organization [Mid-16C. < Latin *inchoatus*, past participle of *inchoare* 'begin'] —**inchoately** *adv* —**inchoateness** *n* —**inchoation** /ín kō áysh'n/ *n*

inchoative /in kő ətiv/ *adj*, *n* GRAM same as **inceptive** *adj* (sense 2), *n*

Inchon /in chón/, **Inch'ŏn** city and major port at the mouth of the Han River in northwestern South Korea. In 1950, during the Korean War, it was the site of an amphibious landing by United Nations troops to liberate nearby Seoul. Population: 2,307,618 (1995). Former name **Chemulpo**

inchworm /ínch wurm/ *n* N Am same as **measuring worm**

incidence /ínssidənss/ *n* 1. RATE OF OCCURRENCE OF SOMETHING the frequency with which something occurs 2. INSTANCE OR MANNER OF SOMETHING HAPPENING an instance of something happening, or the manner in which it happens 3. IMPACT ON SURFACE the impact that something such as a ray of light or a projectile makes with a surface

USAGE **incidents** or **incidence**? Though pronounced similarly, these two words mean different things and so ought not to be confused. ***Incidents***, a plural noun, means 'events, occurrences', as in *Three incidents* [not *incidence*] *of speeding on campus have been reported. Five hundred incidents* [not *incidence*] *of Ebola virus were documented last year.* ***Incidence***, a singular noun, means variously 'the rate of occurrence of something happening' and 'an instance of something happening and how it happens', as in *studying the annual incidence* [not *incidents*] *of Ebola virus; increased incidence* [not *incidents*] *of poverty.*

incident /ínssidənt/ *n* 1. EVENT something that happens, especially a single event 2. VIOLENT OCCURRENCE a public occurrence, especially a violent one ○ *an incident outside a nightclub* 3. EVENT WITH POTENTIALLY SERIOUS CONSEQUENCES an event that may result in a crisis, especially one involving different countries ■ *adj* 1. RELATED TO SOMETHING accompanying something or occurring as a consequence of it (*formal*) 2. TOUCHING OR STRIKING coming into contact with a surface [15C. Directly or via French < Latin *incident-*, present participle of *incidere* 'fall upon' < *cadere* 'to fall']

USAGE See *incidence*.

incidental /ínssi dént'l/ *adj* 1. RELATED OR ACCOMPANYING related to or accompanying something more important 2. OCCURRING BY CHANCE occurring by chance or without intention 3. OCCASIONAL unimportant or occasional 4. RESULTING FROM SOMETHING occurring as a result of something (*formal*) ■ *n* MINOR ITEM something that is occasional or unimportant, e.g. a minor expense

incidentally /ínssi dént'li/ *adv* 1. used to introduce additional information such as something that the speaker has just thought of 2. by chance or by accident

incidental music *n* music that accompanies the action of a film, play, or television programme, as distinct from theme music or songs that feature in a musical

~~**incidently**~~ incorrect spelling of **incidentally**

incident room *n* a room in a police station where information about a specific crime is collected

incident tape *n* wide yellow and black tape used to cordon off an area and warn people of a crime scene. US term **crime scene tape**

incinerate /in sínnə rayt/ (**-ates, -ating, -ated**) *vti* to burn to ashes, or cause something to burn to ashes,

especially in an incinerator [15C. < medieval Latin *incinerat-*, past participle of *incinerare* < Latin *ciner-* 'ashes'] —**incineration** /in sínnə ráysh'n/ *n*

incinerator /in sínnə raytər/ *n* a furnace for destroying things by burning them, especially one used to burn rubbish

incipient /in síppi ənt/ *adj* beginning to appear or develop [Mid-17C. < Latin *incipient-*, present participle of *incipere* 'undertake' < *capere* 'to take'] —**incipience** *n* —**incipiently** *adv*

incipit /ínssipit, ínki-/ *n* the opening word or words of a medieval manuscript or an early printed book, by which it is often known in the absence of a title [Late 19C. < Latin, 'it begins', form of *incipere* (see INCIPIENT)]

incise /in síz/ (**-cises, -cising, -cised**) *vt* **1.** to cut into something, especially a body part during surgery **2.** to carve or engrave a pattern or design into something [Mid-16C. < French *inciser* < Latin *incis-*, past participle of *incidere* 'cut into' < *caedere* 'to cut']

incised /in sízd/ *adj* describes a leaf with edges that are deeply and sharply indented

incision /in sízh'n/ *n* **1.** CUT OR ACT OF CUTTING a cut or the act of cutting, especially when performed by a surgeon **2.** LEAF'S INDENTED EDGE a sharp indentation in the edge of a leaf **3.** FACT OF BEING INCISIVE the fact or quality of being quick to understand or able to express something clearly

incisive /in síssiv/ *adj* **1.** QUICK TO UNDERSTAND quick to understand, analyse, or act **2.** EXPRESSING OR EXPRESSED CLEARLY characterized by clear and direct expression **3.** CUTTING designed to be unkind or hurtful —**incisively** *adv* —**incisiveness** *n*

incisor /in sízər/ *n* one of the flat sharp-edged teeth in the front of the mouth, used for cutting and tearing food [Late 17C. < medieval Latin *dens incisor* 'cutter tooth' < Latin *incis-* (see INCISE)] —**incisal** *adj*

incite /in sít/ (**-cites, -citing, -cited**) *vt* to stir up feelings in or provoke action by somebody [15C. Via French < Latin *incitare* 'urge on' < *citare* (see CITE)] —**incitation** /in sī táysh'n/ *n* —**incitement** *n* —**inciter** *n*

incivility /ínssi vílləti/ (*plural* **-ties**) *n* **1.** rude or impolite behaviour or language **2.** a rude or impolite act or remark

incl. *abbr* **1.** including **2.** inclusive

inclement /in klémmənt/ *adj* **1.** unpleasant in being stormy, rainy, or snowy **2.** showing little or no mercy (*formal*) [Mid-16C. Directly or via French < Latin *inclement-* 'not clement' < *clement-* 'mild'] —**inclemency** *n* —**inclemently** *adv*

inclination /ínkli náysh'n/ *n* **1.** WAY SOMEBODY FEELS ABOUT SOMETHING a feeling that pushes somebody to make a particular choice or take a particular decision **2.** TENDENCY a tendency to do, prefer, or desire something **3.** DEVIATION FROM LINE OR PLANE the tilting of something away from a line or surface, or the degree to which it is tilted **4.** SLOPE a sloping surface **5.** BENDING OF SOMETHING a bending of something, e.g. a bowing of the head **6.** MATHS ANGLE ON GRAPH the angle between a line on a graph and the positive direction of the x-axis **7.** MATHS SMALLER ANGLE the smaller angle between two lines or planes **8.** ASTRON ANGLE OF ORBIT the angle between a planet's orbit and the apparent orbit of the Sun in relation to Earth **9.** GEOG same as **dip** *n* (sense 12) —**inclinational** *adj*

incline *vti* /in klín/ (**-clines, -clining, -clined**) **1.** BE OR MAKE LIKELY TO ACT to tend towards a particular belief or course of action, or make somebody tend towards a particular belief or course of action **2.** ANGLE OR BE ANGLED to lie at an angle, or put something at an angle **3.** BEND to bend something, especially the head or body when bowing or nodding, or be bent in this way ■ *n* /ín klīn/ **1.** SLOPE a slope or sloping surface **2.** RAIL same as **inclined railway** [14C. Via French < Latin *inclinare* 'lean towards' < *clinare* 'to lean'] —**inclinable** *adj* —**incliner** *n*

inclined /in klínd/ *adj* **1.** MOTIVATED TO DO SOMETHING moved or persuaded to do something ○ *I'm not inclined to listen to any more of this.* **2.** TALENTED IN PARTICULAR AREA naturally talented or interested in a particular field or area **3.** SLANTED OR FORMING ANGLE sloping or forming an angle with something else

inclined railway *n* a railway system, used on particularly steep slopes, that uses a cable to pull trains upwards

inclinometer /ínkli nómmitər/ *n* **1.** an instrument that measures angles or slopes such as the angle of an aircraft relative to the ground **2.** an instrument used to determine the angle made by the Earth's magnetic field relative to the horizontal plane [Mid-19C. < Latin *inclinare* (see INCLINE)]

inclose *vt* another spelling of **enclose**

inclosure *n* another spelling of **enclosure**

include /in klóod/ (**-cludes, -cluding, -cluded**) *vt* **1.** to have something as a constituent element **2.** to make somebody or something part of a group [15C. < Latin *includere* 'enclose' < *claudere* 'to shut'] —**includable** *adj*

USAGE See ***comprise***.

---

included /in klóodid/ *adj* **1.** CONTAINED WITHIN GROUP forming part of a group or whole **2.** BOT NOT PROTRUDING describes the stamens or carpels of a flower that do not protrude beyond the edges of the petals **3.** MATHS LOCATED BETWEEN INTERSECTING LINES formed by and contained in two intersecting lines

including /in klóoding/ *prep* used to introduce examples of people or things forming part of a particular group or whole ○ *It will cost you £39.95 including VAT.* ■ *conj* as well as ○ *Discussion of the market analysis – including whether it was skewed in favour of launching the project – went on for an hour.*

inclusion /in klóozh'n/ *n* **1.** PRESENCE IN GROUP the addition of somebody or something to, or the presence of somebody or something in, a group or mixture **2.** SOMEBODY OR SOMETHING INCLUDED somebody or something included in a group or mixture **3.** GEOL SUBSTANCE INSIDE MINERAL a solid, liquid, or gas contained within a mineral or rock **4.** METALL FOREIGN PARTICLE IN METAL a particle of foreign material within a piece of metal **5.** BIOL FOREIGN BODY IN CELL a nonliving mass in the cytoplasm or nucleus of a cell, e.g. a starch grain or droplet of fat **6.** MATHS RELATION BETWEEN SETS in mathematics, the relation between two classes or sets when the second is a subset of the first [Early 17C. < Latin *inclus-*, past participle of *includere* (see INCLUDE)] —**inclusionary** *adj*

inclusion body *n* a mass of virus particles inside a cell, formerly used in the diagnosis of some viral infections

inclusive /in klóossiv/ *adj* **1.** INCLUDING MANY THINGS including many things or everything **2.** WITHIN PARTICULAR LIMITS including the numbers, dates, or other series members mentioned immediately before ○ *the period from October 1 to July 31, inclusive* ◊ **exclusive** *adj* (sense 7) **3.** INCLUDING PEOPLE OF ALL KINDS not excluding any group or section of society **4.** NONDISCRIMINATORY describes language that avoids discrimination, limitation, or stereotypes based on gender **5.** GRAM INCLUDING SPEAKER AND PERSON ADDRESSED describes a pronoun such as 'we' that includes the speaker and the person or persons spoken to **6.** LOGIC CONTAINING AT LEAST ONE TRUE PROPOSITION describes a sentence in logic (**disjunction**) containing two propositions of which at least one and possibly both can be true [Late 16C. < medieval Latin *inclusivus* < Latin *inclus-* (see INCLUDE)] —**inclusively** *adv* —**inclusiveness** *n*

incoercible /ínkō úrssəb'l/ *adj* not giving in to force or pressure from others

incognita /in kog néetə/ *adj, adv* with the identity disguised or hidden, e.g. under an assumed name (*used to describe a woman or girl*) [Late 17C. < Italian, form of *incognito* 'incognito'] —**incognita** *n*

incognito /in kog néetō/ *adj, adv* IN DISGUISE with the identity disguised or hidden, e.g. under an assumed name ■ *n* (*plural* **-tos**) **1.** SOMEBODY IN DISGUISE somebody who acts or travels in disguise so as to be unrecognizable **2.** DISGUISE the character, disguise, or name assumed by somebody who is attempting to be unrecognizable [Mid-17C. Via Italian < Latin *incognitus* 'unknown' < *cognoscere* 'get to know' (see COGNITION)]

incoherent /in kō héerənt/ *adj* **1.** LACKING CLARITY OR ORGANIZATION not clearly expressed or well thought out, and consequently difficult to understand **2.** UNABLE TO EXPRESS THINGS CLEARLY unable to express thoughts or feelings clearly or logically **3.** NOT COHESIVE not sticking together as a mass **4.** PHYS OUT OF PHASE describes electromagnetic waves that have the same frequency but a random or changing phase —**incoherence** *n* —**incoherently** *adv*

incombustible /ínkəm bústəb'l/ *adj* not capable of being burnt —**incombustibility** /ínkəm bústə bílləti/ *n* —**incombustible** *n* —**incombustibly** *adv*

income /ín kum/ *n* **1.** the amount of money received over a period of time either as payment for work, goods, or services, or as profit on capital **2.** an act of coming in or flowing in [14C. < Old Norse *innkoma* 'arrival'; later < IN-[2] + COME]

income bond *n* a bond paying a rate of return in proportion to the issuer's income

income group *n* a section of the population grouped according to income, e.g. for the purpose of market research

incomer /ín kummər/ *n* somebody who settles in a place where he or she was not born

incomes policy *n* an economic policy that seeks to control inflation by controlling wage levels

income support *n* in the United Kingdom, a social security payment made to unemployed people and people on low incomes. It was introduced in 1986 to replace supplementary benefit.

income tax *n* a tax paid on money made from employment, business, or capital (*hyphenated when used before a noun*)

incoming /ín kumming/ *adj* **1.** ARRIVING arriving, coming in, or entering ○ *incoming flights* **2.** TAKING UP NEW JOB about to take up a new job or office ○ *the incoming president* **3.** BEING RECEIVED being received or taken in ○ *incoming signals* ■ *n* ARRIVAL an arrival or entrance (*formal*) ■ **incomings** *npl* INCOME sums of money earned or received

incommensurable /ínkə ménshərəb'l/ *adj* **1.** IMPOSSIBLE TO MEASURE not able to be compared or measured, especially because of lacking a common quality necessary for a comparison **2.** MATHS HAVING NO COMMON FACTOR having no common mathematical factor or measure other than 1 ■ *n* SOMETHING INCOMMENSURABLE something that cannot be compared or measured, especially a quality or a mathematical value —**incommensurability** /ínkə ménshərə bílləti/ *n* —**incommensurably** *adv*

incommensurate /ínkə ménshərət/ *adj* **1.** not proportionate to or up to the level of something **2.** same as **incommensurable** *adj* (sense 1) —**incommensurately** *adv* —**incommensurateness** *n*

incommode /ínkə mṓd/ (**-modes, -moding, -moded**) *vt* to cause inconvenience to somebody (*formal*) [Late 16C. Directly or via French < Latin *incommodare* < *commodus* 'convenient' (see COMMODE)]

incommodious /ínkə mṓdi əss/ *adj* (*formal*) **1.** uncomfortable because lacking in space **2.** causing inconvenience —**incommodiously** *adv* —**incommodiousness** *n*

incommunicable /ínkə myóonikəb'l/ *adj* **1.** not able to be expressed or conveyed to others **2.** not able to be transmitted or passed on to others —**incommunicability** /ínkə myóonikə bílləti/ *n* —**incommunicably** *adv*

incommunicado /ínkə myóoni kaádō/ *adj* prevented by circumstances or by force from communicating with others [Mid-19C. < Spanish *incomunicado* < *incomunicar* 'deprive of communication' < Latin *communicare* (see COMMUNICATE)] —**incommunicado** *adv*

incommunicative /ínkə myóonikətiv/ *adj* unwilling to communicate or provide information —**incommunicatively** *adv* —**incommunicativeness** *n*

incommutable /ínkə myóotəb'l/ *adj* not able to be changed, exchanged for something else, or reduced in severity —**incommutability** /ínkə myóotə bílləti/ *n* —**incommutably** *adv*

incomparable /in kómpərəb'l/ *adj* **1.** so excellent, outstanding, or unique as to have no equal **2.** impossible to compare with something else, because there is no basis for a comparison —**incomparability** /in kómpərə bílləti/ *n* —**incomparably** *adv*

incompatible /ínkəm páttəb'l/ *adj* **1.** UNABLE TO COOPERATE OR COEXIST unable to exist, cooperate, function, or get along with somebody or something else because of basic differences **2.** UNABLE TO BE HELD SIMULTANEOUSLY

unable to be held by one person simultaneously with another position or office **3.** IMMUNOL **LIKELY TO BE REJECTED BY DONOR** describes a tissue transplant or blood that is rejected by a recipient's immune system **4.** PHARM **NOT SUITABLE FOR USE IN COMBINATION** describes two or more drugs that should not be used together **5.** BOT **NOT ABLE TO BE POLLINATED** describes plants or varieties that cannot be successfully pollinated by or grafted onto each other **6.** LOGIC **CONTRADICTORY** describes two propositions that cannot both be true at the same time **7.** MATHS same as **inconsistent** (sense 4) —**incompatibility** /ínkəm páttə bílləti/ *n* —**incompatibly** *adv*

incompetent /in kómpitənt/ *adj* **1. BAD AT DOING SOMETHING** lacking the skills, qualities, or ability to do something properly **2.** LAW **LACKING NECESSARY STATUS** not having the necessary legal status, validity, or powers for the purpose in question ○ *The defendant was found incompetent to stand trial.* **3.** MED **DEFECTIVE** describes a body part such as a muscle that does not function properly ○ *an incompetent cervix* ■ *n* **SOMEBODY BAD AT DOING SOMETHING** somebody who lacks the skills, qualities, or ability to do something properly —**incompetence** *n* —**incompetently** *adv*

incomplete /ínkəm pléet/ *adj* **1.** lacking something such as a particular part that should be present or available **2.** not yet finished or fully developed —**incompletely** *adv* —**incompleteness** *n* —**incompletion** /-pléesh'n/ *n*

incomplete fracture *n* a fracture that does not go all the way through a bone

incompliant /ínkəm plí ənt/ *adj* unwilling to be flexible and accommodating, or to comply with something (*formal*) —**incompliance** *n* —**incompliantly** *adv*

incomprehensible /in kómpri hénssəb'l/ *adj* impossible or very difficult to understand —**incomprehensibility** /in kómpri hénssə bílləti/ *n* —**incomprehensibleness** *n* —**incomprehensibly** *adv*

incomprehension /in kómpri hénsh'n/ *n* an inability or failure to understand, or a state of bewilderment resulting from this

incompressible /ínkəm préssəb'l/ *adj* impossible or difficult to compress —**incompressibility** /ínkəm préssə bílləti/ *n* —**incompressibly** *adv*

inconceivable /ínkən séevəb'l/ *adj* **1.** impossible to imagine or to grasp mentally and understand **2.** so unlikely as to be beyond belief or thought impossible ○ *It's inconceivable that they should have made the same mistake twice.* —**inconceivability** /ínkən séevə bílləti/ *n* —**inconceivableness** *n* —**inconceivably** *adv*

inconclusive /ínkən klóossiv/ *adj* not producing a clear-cut result, firm conclusion, or decisive proof of something —**inconclusively** *adv* —**inconclusiveness** *n*

incongruent /in kóng groo ənt/ *adj* not corresponding in structure or content —**incongruence** *n* —**incongruently** *adv*

incongruity /ínkən gróo əti/ (*plural* **-ties**) *n* **1.** the fact of being incongruous **2.** something that does not seem to fit in with or be appropriate to its context

incongruous /in kóng groo əss/ *adj* **1.** unsuitable or out of place in a specific setting or context **2.** not in accord or consistent with something —**incongruously** *adv* —**incongruousness** *n*

inconsecutive /ínkən sékyòotiv/ *adj* not following in order one after another —**inconsecutively** *adv*

inconsequent /in kónsikwənt/ *adj* not following as a natural or logical result —**inconsequence** *n* —**inconsequently** *adv*

inconsequential /in kónssi kwénsh'l/ *adj* **1.** of little or no importance **2.** same as **inconsequent** —**inconsequentiality** /in kónssi kwénshi álləti/ *n* —**inconsequentially** *adv* —**inconsequentialness** *n*

inconsiderable /ínkən síddərəb'l/ *adj* **1.** small in size, amount, or value (*often used with 'not'*) ○ *It cost £1,500, a not inconsiderable sum.* **2.** so unimportant as to be not worth considering (*formal*) —**inconsiderably** *adv*

inconsiderate /ínkən síddərət/ *adj* lacking thought or consideration for other people and their feelings —**inconsiderately** *adv* —**inconsiderateness** *n* —**inconsideration** /ínkən síddə ráysh'n/ *n*

inconsistency /ínkən sístənssi/ (*plural* **-cies**), **inconsistence** /ínkən sístənss/ *n* **1.** the fact of being inconsistent **2.** something that contradicts something else or that is not in keeping with it

inconsistent /ínkən sístənt/ *adj* **1. CONTAINING CONFLICTING OR CONTRADICTORY ELEMENTS** containing aspects or parts that conflict with or contradict each other ○ *an inconsistent statement* **2. VARYING AND UNPREDICTABLE** unpredictable or unreliable by being likely to behave differently or achieve a different result if a particular situation is repeated ○ *inconsistent performance* **3. CONFLICTING OR INCOMPATIBLE WITH SOMETHING** conflicting with or not corresponding to something such as a rule, principle, or expectation ○ *behaviour inconsistent with company policy* **4.** MATHS **LACKING COMMON VALUES IN EQUATION** not having a common set of values for the unknowns in an equation —**inconsistently** *adv*

inconsolable /ínkən sṓləb'l/ *adj* so deeply distressed that nobody can offer any effective comfort —**inconsolability** /ínkən sṓlə bílləti/ *n* —**inconsolably** *adv*

inconspicuous /ínkən spíkyoo əss/ *adj* not easily seen or noticed —**inconspicuously** *adv*—**inconspicuousness** *n*

inconstant /in kónstənt/ *adj* **1.** unfaithful in relationships (*literary*) **2.** likely to change frequently and unpredictably ○ *an inconstant sea breeze* —**inconstancy** *n* —**inconstantly** *adv*

incontestable /ínkən téstəb'l/ *adj* impossible to question or dispute —**incontestability** /ínkən téstə bílləti/ *n* —**incontestably** *adv*

incontinent /in kóntinənt/ *adj* **1. UNABLE TO CONTROL BLADDER OR BOWELS** unable to control the bladder or bowels and liable to urinate or defecate involuntarily **2. LACKING SEXUAL CONTROL** lacking restraint in sexual matters, or engaging in premarital or extramarital sex **3. UNRESTRAINED** unrestrained and uncontrolled (*literary*) [14C. Directly or via French < Latin *incontinent-* 'not holding together' < *continere* (see CONTAIN)] —**incontinence** *n* —**incontinently** *adv*

incontrollable /ínkən trṓləb'l/ *adj* **1.** too strongly felt to be suppressed **2.** too unruly or wild to discipline or control —**incontrollability** /ínkən trṓlə bílləti/ *n* —**incontrollably** *adv*

incontrovertible /in kontrə vúrtəb'l/ *adj* certain, undeniable, and not open to question —**incontrovertibility** /in kontrə vúrtə bílləti/ *n* —**incontrovertibly** *adv*

inconvenience /ínkən véeni ənss/ *n* **1. LACK OF CONVENIENCE** the quality or fact of being inconvenient or causing discomfort, difficulty, or annoyance **2. ANNOYANCE** something that causes difficulties or annoyance ■ *vt* (**-iences, -iencing, -ienced**) **CAUSE DIFFICULTY TO SOMEBODY** to cause somebody difficulties, especially relatively minor or unnecessary ones, or ones involving unwanted extra effort, work, or trouble

inconvenient /ínkən véeni ənt/ *adj* causing or involving difficulties or unwanted extra effort, work, or trouble —**inconveniently** *adv*

inconvertible /ínkən vúrtəb'l/ *adj* **1.** not exchangeable for gold or silver **2.** not exchangeable for the currency of another country —**inconvertibility** /ínkən vúrtə bílləti/ *n* —**inconvertibly** *adv*

inconvincible /ínkən vínssəb'l/ *adj* impossible or very difficult to convince —**inconvincibility** /ínkən vínssə bílləti/ *n* —**inconvincibly** *adv*

incoordinate /ínkō áwrdinət/ *adj* lacking coordination —**incoordinately** *adv*

incoordination /ínkō áwrdi náysh'n/ *n* **1.** an inability to control voluntary muscular movements **2.** a lack of organization or of a consistent approach (*formal*)

incorporate *v* /in káwrpə rayt/ (**-rates, -rating, -rated**) **1.** *vti* **JOIN WITH SOMETHING THAT EXISTS** to combine something with, or include it within, something already formed, or be combined or included in this way **2.** *vti* **MERGE THINGS** to combine one thing with another, so as to form a united whole, or be combined in this way **3.** *vti* COMM **FORM OR BECOME CORPORATION** to form a corporation, or give something the legal form of a corporation **4.** *vt* **GIVE REAL FORM TO SOMETHING** to give material form to something (*formal*) ■ *adj* /in káwrpərət/ **1. UNITED** merged into a united whole (*formal*) **2.** LAW **LEGALLY FORMED AS CORPORATION** legally established as a corporation [14C. < late Latin *incorporat-*, past participle of *incorporare* 'make into a body' < Latin *corpus* 'body'] —**incorporable** *adj* —**incorporated** *adj* —**incorporation** /in káwrpə ráysh'n/ *n* —**incorporative** *adj* —**incorporator** *n*

incorporeal /ín kawr páwri əl/ *adj* **1.** lacking a physical body or existing solely as a spirit (*formal*) **2.** describes a legal entity that has no material existence of its own but is connected to an actual object such as a patent or copyright —**incorporeality** /-pawri álləti/ *n* —**incorporeally** *adv*

incorporeity /in káwrpə rée əti/ (*plural* **-ties**) *n* **1.** the condition or quality of being incorporeal **2.** something that is incorporeal

incorrect /ínkə rékt/ *adj* **1.** wrong, false, or inaccurate **2.** not appropriate, suitable, or proper —**incorrectly** *adv* —**incorrectness** *n*

incorrigible /in kórrijəb'l/ *adj* **1. IMPOSSIBLE TO CHANGE** impossible or very difficult to correct or reform ○ *incorrigible cynics* **2. UNRULY AND UNMANAGEABLE** impossible or very difficult to control or keep in order ■ *n* **SOMEBODY OR SOMETHING INCORRIGIBLE** somebody or something that is impossible or very difficult to correct or reform [14C. Directly or via French < Latin *incorrigibilis* 'not able to be corrected' < *corrigere* (see CORRECT)] —**incorrigibility** /in kórrijə bílləti/ *n* —**incorrigibly** *adv*

incorrupt /ínkə rúpt/ *adj* (*formal*) **1.** morally pure and uncorrupted **2.** containing no errors or alterations —**incorruption** *n* —**incorruptly** *adv*

incorruptible /ínkə rúptəb'l/ *adj* **1.** incapable of being morally corrupted, especially incapable of being bribed or motivated by selfish or base interests **2.** incapable of being affected by decay or decomposition —**incorruptibility** /ínkə rúptə bílləti/ *n* —**incorruptibly** *adv*

incr. *abbr* **1.** increase **2.** increased **3.** increasing **4.** increment

increase *vti* /in kréess, íng kreess/ (**-creases, -creasing, -creased**) **MAKE OR BECOME LARGER OR GREATER** to become, or make something become, larger in number, quantity, or degree ■ *n* /íng kreess, in kréess/ **1. ENLARGEMENT** a rise to a greater number, quantity, or degree, or the amount by which something is increased **2. INCREASING IN SIZE** the process of becoming or of making something larger in number, quantity, or degree [14C. Via French < Latin *increscere* < *crescere* 'grow'] —**increasable** *adj* —**increaser** /-ər/ *n*

SYNONYMS ***increase, expand, enlarge, extend, augment, intensify, amplify***

CORE MEANING: to make larger or greater

increase to become, or make something become, larger in number, quantity, or degree ○ *Admission prices are to be increased by ten per cent next season.* ○ *a world of ever increasing financial pressures* **expand** to become or cause to become larger or more extensive ○ *Wood expands and contracts with temperature and humidity changes.* ○ *The strong economy brought him an excellent opportunity to expand his business.* **enlarge** to increase the size, amount, or extent of something, or become larger ○ *Seating space was enlarged and access provided by vaulted passageways.* ○ *One effect of reading is to modify and enlarge the reader's experience.* **extend** to make larger in terms of length, area, period of time, or other existing limits ○ *Around the same time, both east and west breakwaters were extended.* ○ *The supermarket has extended its range of vegetables to include more exotic varieties.* **augment** (*formal*) to add to something in order to make it larger or more substantial ○ *augment the family income by doing some part-time work* ○ *The municipality needs new recruits to augment the existing police force.* **intensify** to become, or make something become, greater or stronger ○ *As fighting intensified, the capital was said to be without water and food supplies.* ○ *This episode only intensified Rachel's dislike of her sister's fiancé.* **amplify** to become, or make something become, greater in scope, stronger, or louder ○ *The house and shop walls amplify the noise.* ○ *attempting to amplify positive attitudes and reduce negative ones*

increased /in kréest, ing kréest/ *adj* larger in number, quantity, or degree —**increasedly** /in kréessidli/ *adv*

increasingly /in kréessingli/ *adv* in a way that increases over time ○ *As Election Day approaches, there is no front-runner, and the insults and accusations from both sides have been increasingly*

zh vision. In foreign words: kh German Bach; aN French vin; aaN French blanc; ö German schön, French feu; öN French bon; öN French un; ü as in French rue. Stress marks: ´ as in secret /séekrət/, academic /ákə démmik/

frequent and bellicose.' (Susan K. Livio, *Election '96: Senate Race*; 1996)

~~incredable~~ incorrect spelling of **incredible**

incredible /in kréddəb'l/ *adj* **1.** BEYOND BELIEF impossible or very difficult to believe ○ *I find it incredible that he wasn't nominated.* **2.** AMAZING very surprising ○ *It's incredible how many people have turned up.* **3.** MORE THAN THOUGHT POSSIBLE unexpectedly or astonishingly large or great (*informal*) ○ *an incredible amount of food* **4.** EXCELLENT extraordinarily good, talented, or enjoyable (*informal*) ○ *an incredible new band* —**incredibility** /in kréddə bílləti/ *n* —**incredibly** *adv*

incredulity /ínkrə dyoólǝti/ *n* a state or feeling of disbelief

incredulous /in kréddyoóləss/ *adj* **1.** unable or unwilling to believe something or completely unconvinced by it **2.** showing or characterized by disbelief —**incredulously** *adv* —**incredulousness** *n*

increment /íngkrimənt/ *n* **1.** INCREASE IN SOMETHING an addition to or increase in the amount or size of something, especially one of a series of small, often regular or planned increases to a salary **2.** ACT OF INCREASING the act or process of increasing **3.** MATHS SMALL CHANGE IN MATHEMATICAL VALUE a small positive or negative change in the value of a mathematical variable or function [15C. < Latin *incrementum* 'growth' < *increscere* (see INCREASE)] —**incremental** /íngkri mént'l/ *adj* —**incrementally** *adv*

incrementalism /íngkri mént'lizəm/ *n* SOC SCI same as **gradualism** (sense 1)

increscent /in kréss'nt/ *adj* describes an astronomical object, especially the Moon, that shows a lighted surface area that is increasing in size [Late 16C. < Latin *increscent-*, present participle of *increscere* (see INCREASE)]

incriminate /in krímmi nayt/ (**-nates, -nating, -nated**) *vt* **1.** to prove or make somebody appear to be guilty of a crime or mistake **2.** to accuse somebody of a crime or error (*formal*) [Mid-18C. < late Latin *incriminat-*, past participle of *incriminare* 'make criminal' < Latin *crimen* (see CRIME)] —**incriminating** *adj* —**incrimination** /in krímmi náysh'n/ *n* —**incriminator** *n* —**incriminatory** *adj*

incross /ín kross/ *n* an organism produced through inbreeding within the same strain or breed ■ *vti* (**-crosses, -crossing, -crossed**) to produce an organism by inbreeding within the same strain or breed, or be produced in this way

in-crowd *n* a small, fashionable, and exclusive or influential group, especially one that others want to be part of because of its prestige (*informal*)

incrust, etc. *v* another spelling of **encrust, etc.**

incubate /íngkyoó bayt/ (**-bates, -bating, -bated**) *vti* **1.** SIT ON EGGS to keep eggs warm by sitting on them so that the embryos inside can develop and hatch, or be kept warm in this way **2.** KEEP BABY IN INCUBATOR to keep a premature or unwell baby inside a controlled environment in order to keep it alive and assist its growth and development, or be kept in such an environment **3.** GROW MICROORGANISMS IN CONTROLLED ENVIRONMENT to keep cells or microorganisms at a controlled temperature in or on a medium so that they multiply, or be kept in or on such a medium **4.** BUILD UP DISEASE-PRODUCING GERMS to develop an infection, through the reproduction of germs, to the point at which the first signs of a disease appear, or be developed in this way **5.** GRADUALLY BRING SOMETHING INTO BEING to form or develop something such as a plan or an idea slowly and quietly over a period of time, or be formed or developed in this way [Mid-17C. < Latin *incubat-*, past participle of *incubare* 'lie down on' < *cubare* 'lie down'] —**incubative** *adj* —**incubatory** *adj*

incubation /íngkyoó báysh'n/ *n* **1.** PROCESS OF INCUBATING OR BEING INCUBATED the process of incubating something such as an egg or an idea, the process of being incubated, or the period of time taken by either process **2.** MAINTENANCE OF BABY IN CONTROLLED ENVIRONMENT the keeping of a premature or unwell baby in an environment in which the temperature, humidity, and oxygen levels can be easily controlled **3.** CONTROLLED GROWTH OF MICROORGANISMS the maintenance of cells or microorganisms under a controlled temperature in or on a medium so that they multiply **4.** GROWTH OF DISEASE-CAUSING MICROORGANISMS the

development of an infection inside the body to the point at which the first signs of disease become apparent **5.** GRADUAL DEVELOPMENT the slow development of something, especially through thought and planning **6.** MED same as **incubation period** —**incubational** *adj*

incubation period *n* the period between the time somebody is infected with a disease and the appearance of its first symptoms

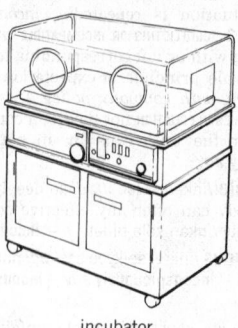

incubator

incubator /íngkyoó baytər/ *n* **1.** a hospital apparatus, usually a transparent box, in which a premature or unwell baby is kept in a controlled environment to protect it from infection and assist its growth and development **2.** an apparatus in which the temperature is kept at a constant level so that eggs can be artificially hatched, or cells and microorganisms can multiply in or on a growth medium

incubus /íngkyoóbəss/ (*plural* **-bi** /-bī/ *or* **-buses**) *n* **1.** something that causes somebody much worry or anxiety, especially a nightmare or obsession (*literary*) **2.** in medieval times, a male demon that was believed to have sexual intercourse with women while they were asleep [14C. < late Latin, 'nightmare' < Latin *incubare* (see INCUBATE)]

incudes ANAT plural of **incus**

inculcate /ín kul kayt/ (**-cates, -cating, -cated**) *vt* to fix something firmly in somebody's mind through frequent, forceful repetition [Mid-16C. < Latin *inculcat-*, past participle of *inculcare* 'stamp in' < *calcare* (see CAULK)] —**inculcation** /ín kul káysh'n/ *n* —**inculcator** *n*

inculpable /in kúlpəb'l/ *adj* free of guilt or blame (*formal*) [15C. < late Latin *inculpabilis* < Latin *culpabilis* (see CULPABLE)] —**inculpability** /in kúlpə bílləti/ *n* —**inculpableness** *n* —**inculpably** *adv*

inculpate /ín kul payt/ (**-pates, -pating, -pated**) *vt* to incriminate somebody, or put the blame for something on somebody (*formal*) [Late 18C. < late Latin *inculpat-*, past participle of *inculpare* 'put blame on' < Latin *culpa* 'blame, fault'] —**inculpation** /ín kul páysh'n/ *n* —**inculpative** /in kúlpətiv/ *adj* —**inculpatory** /in kúlpətəri/ *adj*

incumbency /in kúmbənssi/ *n* (*formal*) **1.** TENURE OF OFFICE the period of time during which somebody occupies an official post **2.** OFFICIAL POST an official post, especially in a church or political organization **3.** EXISTENCE AS DUTY the obligatory nature of something or the fact of its being a duty or obligation that must be performed **4.** OBLIGATION something that is necessary or obligatory, e.g. a duty

incumbent /in kúmbənt/ *n* SOMEBODY IN OFFICE somebody currently holding an official post, especially in a church or political organization ○ *He took comfort in the fact that incumbents are often offered the chance of serving a second term of office.* ■ *adj* **1.** OBLIGATORY necessary as a result of a duty, responsibility, or obligation (*formal*) ○ *It is incumbent on me to ensure that our generous hosts should not go unthanked.* **2.** IN OFFICE currently holding an official post [15C. < Latin *incumbent-*, present participle of *incumbere* 'lie in or on' < *-cumbere* 'lie down'] —**incumbently** *adv*

incumber *vt* another spelling of **encumber**

incunable *n* PRINTING same as **incunabulum**

incunabula /ínkyoó nábbyoólə/ *npl* the early stages or beginnings of something (*formal*) [Early 19C. < Latin, 'swaddling clothes, infancy' < *cunae* 'cradle']

incunabulum /ínkyoó nábbyoólǝm/ (*plural* **-la** /-lə/), **incunable** /in kyoónəb'l/ *n* a book printed from movable type before 1501 [Early 19C. < Latin, singular of *incunabula* (see INCUNABULA)]

incur /in kúr/ (**-curs, -curring, -curred**) *vt* **1.** to suffer something undesirable such as another person's anger or a financial loss as a result of an action ○ *incur their wrath* **2.** to become burdened with something such as a debt [15C. Via French < Latin *incurrere* 'run into' < *currere* 'run'] —**incurrable** *adj* —**incurrence** *n*

incurable /in kyoórəb'l/ *adj* **1.** IMPOSSIBLE TO CURE not possible to cure **2.** IMPOSSIBLE TO CHANGE not possible to change ■ *n* SOMEBODY OR SOMETHING IMPOSSIBLE TO CURE a person or animal with an illness or condition that cannot be cured —**incurability** /in kyoórə bílləti/ *n* —**incurableness** *n* —**incurably** *adv*

incurious /in kyoóri əss/ *adj* showing no curiosity about or interest in something —**incuriosity** /in kyoóri óssəti/ *n* —**incuriously** *adv* —**incuriousness** *n*

incurrent /in kúrrənt/ *adj* flowing or running inwards into something [Late 16C. < Latin *incurrent-*, present participle of *incurrere* (see INCUR)]

incursion /in kúrsh'n/ *n* **1.** a brief, hostile, and usually sudden invasion of somebody's territory **2.** the act of flowing, running, or intruding into something, usually with unpleasant or damaging effects (*formal*) [15C. Directly or via French < Latin *incursion-* 'a running in' < *incurrere* (see INCUR)] —**incursive** /in kúrssiv/ *adj*

incurvate *vti* /ínkur vayt/ (**-vates, -vating, -vated**) same as **incurve** *v* ■ *adj* /in kúr vayt/ curved or bending inwards [Late 16C. < Latin *incurvat-*, past participle of *incurvare* 'bend inwards' < *curvus* 'curved'] —**incurvation** /ínkur váysh'n/ *n* —**incurvature** /in kúrvachər/ *n*

incurve /in kúrv/ *vti* (**-curves, -curving, -curved**) to curve inwards, or make something do this ■ *n* a curve that bends inwards —**incurved** *adj*

incus /íngkəss/ (*plural* **-cudes** /-kyoód eez/) *n* a small anvil-shaped bone in the middle ear of mammals between the malleus and stapes bones [Mid-17C. < Latin, 'anvil' < *incudere* (see INCUSE)] —**incudal** /íngkyoód'l/ *adj* —**incudate** /íng kyoó dayt/ *adj*

incuse /in kyoóz/ *adj* STAMPED INTO COIN AS DESIGN hammered, stamped, or impressed on a coin as a design ■ *n* STAMPED-IN COIN DESIGN a design stamped, hammered, or impressed on a coin ■ *vt* (**-cuses, -cusing, -cused**) IMPRESS DESIGN ON COIN to hammer, stamp, or impress a design on a coin [Early 19C. < Latin *incus-*, past participle of *incudere* 'hammer on' < *cudere* 'to beat' < Indo-European]

incy, incy-wincy *adj* same as **eensy** (*informal*)

IND *abbr* in God's name [Latin *in nomine Dei*]

ind., ind *abbr* **1.** independence **2.** independent **3.** index **4.** GRAM indicative **5.** GRAM indirect **6.** industrial **7.** industry

Ind., Ind *abbr* **1.** Independent **2.** India[1] **3.** PEOPLES Indian **4.** Indies

indaba /in daábə/ *n* S Africa **1.** a political meeting, conference, or consultation, originally held with or among indigenous peoples of South Africa **2.** a problem or serious concern for somebody (*informal*) [Early 19C. < Zulu, 'discussion']

indamine /índə meen/ *n* an organic base that forms blue or green salts. Use: manufacture of dyes.

indebted /in déttid/ *adj* **1.** owing money to somebody **2.** obliged or grateful to somebody for something such as assistance or a favour received [13C. Alteration of Old French *endetté*, past participle of *endetter* 'put in debt' < *dette* (see DEBT)]

indebtedness /in déttidnəss/ *n* **1.** the condition of owing money to somebody or owing something thanks to them **2.** the total amount somebody owes

indecency /in déess'nsi/ (*plural* **-cies**) *n* **1.** offensiveness according to accepted standards, especially in sexual matters **2.** an act that offends against accepted standards of decency

indecent /in déess'nt/ *adj* **1.** unacceptable and offensive to accepted standards, especially in sexual matters **2.** inappropriate under the circumstances and disapproved of by others ○ *The funeral was arranged with indecent haste.* —**indecently** *adv*

indecent assault *n* a sexual assault on somebody that does not involve rape

indecent exposure *n* the criminal offence of deliberately displaying part of the body, usually the genitals, to somebody else in public

indeciduous /índi síddyoo əss/ *adj* BOT same as **evergreen** (*technical*)

indecipherable /índi sīfərəb'l/ *adj* impossible or very difficult to read or understand —**indecipherability** /índi sīfərə bílləti/ *n* —**indecipherably** *adv*

indecision /índi sízh'n/ *n* the inability to reach a decision, or uncertainty resulting from somebody's inability to reach a decision

indecisive /índi sīssiv/ *adj* **1.** unable or reluctant to make decisions generally or to come to a decision about something in particular **2.** not producing a clear result, especially a clear victory for somebody —**indecisively** *adv* —**indecisiveness** *n*

indeclinable /índi klīnəb'l/ *adj* used to describe a noun, adjective, or pronoun existing in one form only without grammatical inflections according to number, case, or gender [15C. Via French < Latin *indeclinabilis* 'not declinable' < *declinare* (see DECLINE)]

indecorous /in dékərəss/ *adj* rather rude or shocking because of being considered socially unacceptable —**indecorously** *adv* —**indecorousness** *n*

indecorum /índi káwrəm/ *n* **1.** behaviour that offends against what is socially acceptable **2.** an indecorous action

indeed /in deéd/ CORE MEANING: an adverb indicating agreement with or confirmation of something ○ *He is indeed an actor.* ○ *'Do you know that man?' 'Indeed I do'.*

adv **1.** WHAT IS MORE introduces a statement that strengthens or adds to a point just made ○ *I am willing, indeed eager, to speak on your behalf.* **2.** FOR EMPHASIS gives additional emphasis after a descriptive word or phrase ○ *The news, I learned, was grim indeed.* **3.** INDICATES RESPONSE expresses surprise, curiosity, or disbelief ○ *'He's applied for a job'. 'Has he indeed?'* [14C. < IN [1] + DEED]

indef. *abbr* GRAM indefinite

indefatigable /índi fáttigəb'l/ *adj* never showing any sign of getting tired or of relaxing an effort [Early 17C. Directly or via French < Latin *indefatigabilis* < *defatigare* 'tire out' < *fatigare* 'tire'] —**indefatigability** /índi fáttigə bílləti/ *n* —**indefatigably** *adv*

indefeasible /índi feézəb'l/ *adj* impossible to annul, make void, or forfeit —**indefeasibility** /índi feézə bílləti/ *n* —**indefeasibly** *adv*

indefectible /índi féktəb'l/ *adj* (*formal*) **1.** not affected by decay or failure **2.** having no fault or imperfection [Mid-17C. IN [1] < obsolete *defectible* 'liable to fail' < late Latin *defectibilis* < *defect-* (see DEFECT)] —**indefectibility** /índi féktə bílləti/ *n* —**indefectibly** *adv*

indefensible /índi fénssəb'l/ *adj* **1.** PERMITTING NO EXCUSE too bad or blameworthy to be in any way justified or excused ○ *indefensible conduct* **2.** UNABLE TO BE PROTECTED incapable of being defended from attack **3.** INVALID not based on fact, proof, or sound reasoning ○ *an indefensible argument* —**indefensibility** /índi fénssə bílləti/ *n* —**indefensibly** *adv*

indefinable /índi fīnəb'l/ *adj* impossible or very difficult to define, describe, or analyse —**indefinability** /índi fīnə bílləti/ *n* —**indefinably** *adv*

indefinite /in déffənət/ *adj* **1.** UNLIMITED not fixed or limited in length, size, duration, or quantity ○ *away for an indefinite period* **2.** NOT CLEAR not clear or not precisely defined or fixed ○ *indefinite plans* **3.** VAGUE AND UNCERTAIN unable or unwilling to give a clear indication of thoughts or plans **4.** BOT TOO MANY TO COUNT consisting of units that are too numerous to be counted precisely ○ *indefinite stamens* **5.** BOT same as **indeterminate** (sense 6) —**indefiniteness** *n*

indefinite article *n* a word that designates a noun referring to something that has not been mentioned before and is simply any one of its kind, e.g. 'a' or 'an' in English ○ *Choose a book and write a review of it.*

indefinite integral *n* an integral that when differentiated equals a given function

indefinitely /in déffənətli/ *adv* **1.** for a length of time that has no fixed or obvious end ○ *postponed indefinitely* **2.** in a general and unspecific or vague and imprecise way ○ *described indefinitely*

indefinite pronoun *n* a pronoun that does not refer to a specific person or thing, e.g. 'someone', 'nothing', or 'anything' in English

indehiscent /índi híss'nt/ *adj* describes a fruit that does not open up to release seeds when ripe —**indehiscence** *n*

indelible /in délləb'l/ *adj* **1.** IMPOSSIBLE TO REMOVE OR ALTER physically impossible to rub out, wash out, or alter **2.** CONTAINING INDELIBLE SUBSTANCE containing indelible ink or lead ○ *an indelible pencil* **3.** UNFORGETTABLE impossible to remove from the mind or memory and therefore remaining forever ○ *made an indelible impression on us* [15C. Directly or via French < Latin *indelebilis* 'not defaceable' < *delere* 'blot out'] —**indelibility** /in déllə bílləti/ *n* —**indelibly** *adv*

indelicate /in déllikət/ *adj* **1.** tactless, crude, or too frank, and therefore causing or likely to cause offence **2.** crude, rough, or coarse in texture or appearance —**indelicacy** *n* —**indelicately** *adv*

indemnify /in démni fī/ (**-fies, -fying, -fied**) *vt* **1.** to provide somebody with protection, especially financial protection, against possible loss, damage, or liability **2.** to pay compensation to somebody for loss, damage, or liability incurred [Early 17C. < Latin *indemnis* 'not injured' < *damnum* 'injury'] —**indemnification** /in démnifi káysh'n/ *n* —**indemnifier** *n*

indemnity /in démnəti/ (*plural* **-ties**) *n* **1.** INSURANCE protection or insurance against possible loss, damage, or liability **2.** COMPENSATION a compensation paid for loss, damage, or liability **3.** EXEMPTION FROM PENALTIES legal exemption from penalties or liabilities [15C. Via French < late Latin *indemnitas* 'security for damage' < Latin *indemnis* (see INDEMNIFY)]

indemonstrable /índi mónstrəb'l/ *adj* impossible to demonstrate or prove (*formal*) —**indemonstrability** /índi mónstrə bílləti/ *n* —**indemonstrably** *adv*

indene /ín deen/ *n* a colourless toxic liquid. Source: coal tar, petroleum. Use: manufacture of synthetic resins. Formula: C_9H_8. [Late 19C. < INDOLE + -ENE]

indent[1] *v* /in dént/ (**-dents, -denting, -dented**) **1.** *vti* BEGIN LINE IN FROM MARGIN to start a line or row of text some distance in from the margin **2.** *vt* FORM RECESS IN SOMETHING to form a deep recess in something (*often passive*) **3.** *vt* NOTCH SOMETHING to make jagged, notched, or serrated edges in something **4.** *vt* US FIT NOTCHED EDGES TOGETHER to join together two notched pieces of something **5.** *vt* TEAR COPIED DOCUMENT IN HALF to tear a document, especially one containing two copies of the same text, in half along an irregular line **6.** *vt* DRAW UP DOCUMENT IN DUPLICATE to draw up a document in two or more exact copies **7.** *vti* ORDER USING OFFICIAL FORM to place an order for supplies using an official form **8.** *vt* COMM ORDER FOREIGN GOODS to place an order for foreign goods, usually through an agent ■ *n* /ín dent, in dént/ **1.** SPACE SET IN FROM MARGIN a blank space left between the margin and the beginning of a line or row of text **2.** ORDER OF FOREIGN GOODS an order for foreign goods, usually placed through an agent **3.** OFFICIAL ORDER FOR SUPPLIES a requisition or official order for supplies **4.** LAW same as **indenture** (*archaic*) [14C. Directly or via Anglo-Norman < medieval Latin *indentare* < Latin *in-* 'in, into' + *dent-* 'tooth'] —**indented** *adj* —**indenter** *n*

ORIGIN Etymologically, English has two separate words *indent*, although they have converged to a considerable extent. The one meaning 'form a recess in' is simply a derivative of *dent*. ***Indent*** 'make a jagged edge on' owes its origin to Latin *dent* 'tooth'. This formed the basis of an Anglo-Latin verb *indentare* that denoted the drawing up of a contract between two parties on two identical documents that were cut along a matching line of notches or 'teeth' that could subsequently be rejoined to prove their authenticity. A specific use of such contracts was between master craftsmen and their trainees, who hence became known as *indentured* apprentices.

indent[2] *vt* /in dént/ (**-dents, -denting, -dented**) to press something inwards to form a dent ■ *n* /ín dent, in dént/ same as **dent** *n* (sense 1) [14C. < IN- [2] + DENT]

indentation /ín den táysh'n/ *n* **1.** NOTCH OR RECESS a notch, recess, or hollowed-out place in something such as an edge, boundary line, or coast **2.** JAGGED EDGE a series of notches or recesses, or the edge formed by this **3.** PRINTING LEAVING OF SPACE AT LINE BEGINNING the leaving of space between the margin and the beginning of a line or row, or the blank space left **4.** ACT OF INDENTING the act of indenting something, or the fact of being indented

indenture /in dénchər/ *n* **1.** CONTRACT WITH APPRENTICE a contract committing an apprentice or servant to serve a master for a specific period of time (*often plural*) **2.** WRITTEN AGREEMENT a written contract or agreement between two or more parties **3.** DUPLICATE DOCUMENT WITH TORN EDGE a document written in duplicate on a single sheet and torn in half so that the edges of the two resulting copies could be matched up to prove their authenticity **4.** AUTHORIZED LIST an official list or inventory that has been authenticated for use as a voucher ■ *vt* CONTRACT SOMEBODY FOR SERVICES to commit somebody to work as an apprentice or servant for a specific period of time by means of indentures —**indentured** *adj* —**indentureship** *n*

indentured servant *n* US an immigrant to North America between the 17th and 19th centuries who contracted to work for an employer for a number of years in exchange for passage and accommodation

~~**independant**~~ incorrect spelling of **independent**

independence /índi péndənss/ *n* freedom from dependence on or control by another person, organization, or state

Independence /índi péndənss/ city in western Missouri, a suburb of Kansas City. Population: 112,301 (2002 estimate).

Independence Day *n* US a national holiday in the United States marking the signing of the Declaration of Independence in 1776. Date: 4 July.

independency /índi péndənssi/ (*plural* **-cies**) *n* **1.** an independent state or territory **2.** same as **independence** (*archaic*)

Independency *n* the principle or policy that each local Christian church or congregation should be free of external ecclesiastical control

independent /índi péndənt/ *adj* **1.** NOT CONTROLLED BY ANOTHER in politics, free from the authority, control, or domination of somebody or something else, especially not controlled by another state or organization and able to self-govern **2.** ABLE TO FUNCTION BY SELF able to operate alone because not dependent on somebody or something else ○ *Each wheel has an independent suspension system.* **3.** SELF-SUPPORTING not forced to rely on another for money or support ○ *financially independent* **4.** SHOWING CONFIDENCE IN SELF capable of thinking or acting without consultation with or guidance from others ○ *an independent thinker* **5.** DONE WITHOUT OBSTRUCTION carried out or operating without interference or influence from interested parties ○ *an independent investigation* **6.** SUFFICIENT TO LIVE ON providing the means on which to live without having to work ○ *independent means* **7.** POL NOT AFFILIATED TO POLITICAL PARTY not belonging to, representing, or supporting any political party **8.** MATHS NOT SOLVABLE USING SOLUTION TO ANOTHER describes a system of equations in which no single equation is necessarily solved using a solution to the others **9.** STATS NOT AFFECTING OTHER VARIABLES in statistics, distributed in such a way that the value taken on by one variable leaves all others unaffected **10.** LOGIC NOT DEPENDENT ON AXIOM OR PROPOSITION not proved from another logical axiom or proposition ■ *n* **1.** SOMEBODY OR SOMETHING UNAFFECTED BY OTHERS somebody or something that is free from control, dependence, or interference **2.** POL NONPARTY POLITICIAN somebody, especially a politician, who is not a member, representative, or supporter of any political party —**independently** *adv*

Independent *n* **1.** somebody who believes that each Christian church or congregation should be free of external ecclesiastical control **2.** POL another spelling of **independent** *n* (sense 2) ■ *adj* another spelling of **independent** *adj* (sense 7)

independent assortment *n* in genetics, the principle that genes are inherited independently of one another, although genes close together on the same chromosome have a higher likelihood of being inherited together

independent clause *n* a clause that can stand on its own as a sentence, e.g. 'She'll go on holiday' in the sentence 'She'll go on holiday if she can raise the money'

independent invention *n* an invention arrived at independently, even though another group of people may have created the same invention in a different place at a different time

independent means *npl* money to live on that is gained from sources other than employment, e.g. from investments

independent school *n* a school that is not financed or run by a local authority or the government

independent variable *n* 1. the variable in a mathematical statement whose value, when specified, determines the value of another variable or other variables 2. a variable that is manipulated in an experiment in order to observe the effect on another variable

in-depth *adj* giving careful consideration to all details and aspects of a subject —**in depth** *adv*

indescribable /índi skríbəb'l/ *adj* 1. impossible or very difficult to describe ○ *an indescribable sensation* 2. so intense or extreme as to defy description ○ *indescribable joy* —**indescribability** /índi skríbə bíllati/ *n* —**indescribably** *adv*

~~indespensable~~ incorrect spelling of **indispensable**

~~indestructable~~ incorrect spelling of **indestructible**

indestructible /índi strúktəb'l/ *adj* impossible or very difficult to destroy —**indestructibility** /índi strúktə bíllati/ *n* —**indestructibly** *adv*

indeterminable /índi túrminəb'l/ *adj* 1. impossible to determine or ascertain exactly 2. impossible to resolve, answer, or settle —**indeterminably** *adv*

indeterminacy /índi túrminəssi/ *n* the condition or quality of being indeterminate

indeterminacy principle *n* QUANTUM PHYS same as **uncertainty principle**

indeterminate /índi túrminət/ *adj* 1. NOT KNOWN EXACTLY not known exactly, or impossible to work out 2. VAGUE not definite, precise, or clear 3. UNPREDICTABLE not having a predictable result or outcome 4. MATHS HAVING NO NUMERICAL MEANING having no numerical value or meaning, e.g. the expression '0/0' or '0⁰' 5. MATHS WITH UNKNOWN NUMBER OF SOLUTIONS having an infinite number of solutions 6. BOT GROWING AT TIP continuing to grow at the tip of the main stem instead of terminating in a flower bud —**indeterminately** *adv* —**indeterminateness** *n* —**indetermination** /índi túrmi náysh'n/ *n*

indeterminate sentence *n* a prison sentence with a date of release that can be varied according to the prisoner's conduct and other factors

indeterminate vowel *n* LING same as **schwa**

indeterminism /índi túrminizəm/ *n* the philosophical theory that human beings have free will and their actions are not always and completely determined by previous events —**indeterminist** *n* —**indeterministic** /índi túrmi nístik/ *adj*

index /ín deks/ *n* (*plural* **-dexes** or **-dices** /-di seez/) 1. ALPHABETICAL REFERENCE LIST an alphabetical list of topics, people, or titles, giving the location of where they are mentioned in a text 2. CATALOGUE a list of items in a set or collection such as the books in a library, usually including details of where to find them 3. PUBLICATION LISTING ARTICLES a periodical or book that lists published work alphabetically by subject, title, or author 4. PRINTING same as **thumb index** 5. NUMBER EXPRESSING RELATIONSHIP a scale, or a number on it, that expresses the price, value, or level of something in relation to something else or to a base number ○ *the consumer price index* 6. INDICATOR an indicator or sign of something ○ *One index of the gravity of the situation is the severance of diplomatic relations.* 7. POINTER a pointer or needle, especially on a piece of scientific equipment 8. PRINTING CHARACTER a character ☞ used by printers to draw attention to a paragraph, section, or note 9. MATHS same as **exponent** (sense 4) 10. MATHS NUMBER GIVEN AS SUPERSCRIPT a number or variable given as a superscript before a square-root sign showing which root is to be taken 11. MATHS SUBSCRIPT OR SUPERSCRIPT IDENTIFYING ELEMENT a subscript or superscript numeral that identifies an element or range in a set or sequence ■ *v* 1. *vti* MAKE INDEX FOR SOMETHING to compile an index for something such as a book or computer record 2. *vt* PUT SOMETHING IN INDEX to enter something such as a name, title, subject, or key word in an index 3. *vt* INDICATE

SOMETHING to be a sign or indicator of something (*formal*) 4. *vt* ECON MAKE SOMETHING INDEX-LINKED to make a variable such as wages index-linked [Late 16C. < Latin, 'forefinger', literally 'pointer' < Indo-European, 'to show'] —**indexer** *n*

Index *n* CHR same as **Index Librorum Prohibitorum**

indexation /ín dek sáysh'n/ *n* the linking of wages, pensions, or other remuneration to an index representing the cost of living, so that they are automatically adjusted up or down as that rises or falls

index case *n* the first documented case of an illness in an epidemiological study

index finger *n* the finger next to the thumb

index fossil *n* the fossil of an organism that is specific to a particular geological age and is used for dating or identifying rocks or rock layers in which it is found

index fund *n* a mutual fund that invests in companies listed in an important stock market index in order to match the market's overall performance

Index Librorum Prohibitorum /-lī bráwrəm prō híbbi táwrəm/ *n* a list formerly compiled by the Roman Catholic Church of books and publications that Church members were forbidden to read [< Latin, 'list of forbidden books'.]

index-linked *adj* adjusted up or down as the cost-of-living index rises or falls

index-linking *n* ECON same as **indexation**

index number *n* a number used to indicate the change in a value or quantity such as a price or unemployment, when compared with the level of that value or quantity at an earlier time. The base level is usually arbitrarily set at 100, and the increase or decrease in index numbers over time is often expressed as a percentage change.

Index of Industrial Production *n* a report produced by the Central Statistical Office showing the performance of the main UK industries

index of refraction *n* US same as **refractive index**

India

India¹ /índi ə/ country in South Asia, the second largest in the world by population and the seventh largest by area. It became an independent member of the Commonwealth in 1947. Language: Hindi, English. Currency: rupee. Capital: New Delhi. Population: 1,049,700,100 (2003). Area: 3,165,596 sq. km/1,222,243 sq. mi. Official name **Republic of India**

India² /índi ə/ *n* a code word for the letter 'I', used in international radio communications

India ink *n* N Am same as **Indian ink**

Indiaman /índi əmən/ *n* (*plural* **-men** /-mən/) *n* a large merchant sailing ship formerly used to transport goods to and from India [Early 18C. < INDIA¹ + MAN 'ship', as in *man of war*]

Indian /índi ən/ *n* 1. SOMEBODY FROM INDIA somebody who comes from India or is of Indian descent 2. ⚠ NATIVE AMERICAN a Native North, South, or Central American (*sometimes considered offensive*) 3. NATIVE AMERICAN LANGUAGE a language used by a Native North, South, or Central American people (*sometimes considered offensive*) ■ *adj* 1. RELATING TO INDIA relating to India, or its peoples, languages, or cultures 2. RELATING TO NATIVE AMERICANS relating to Native North, South, or Central Americans, or their languages or cultures (*sometimes considered offensive*)

USAGE Initially the term **Indian** was applied to the earliest inhabitants of the American continents because Columbus and other early European explorers, having arrived at North America's eastern coast, believed they had reached India by a new route. As a name thus applied in error by conquerors, **Indian** may well be regarded as insensitive or even offensive. Some of the people in question prefer to be called *American Indians* and some prefer the term *Native American*, this last choice being the one that is least likely to cause offence. The use of **Indian** to mean 'somebody from India' is perfectly acceptable.

Indiana /índi ánnə/ state in the north-central United States, bordered by Illinois, Kentucky, Michigan, Ohio, and Lake Michigan. Capital: Indianapolis. Population: 6,951,068 (2002 estimate). Area: 94,327 sq. km/36,420 sq. mi. —**Indianan** *n, adj*

Indian agent *n* an official in the United States or, formerly, in Canada, acting as a government representative to communities of Native North Americans

Indian American *n* an American of Indian descent

Indianapolis /índi ə náppəliss/ capital of Indiana, in the central part of the state, southwest of Fort Wayne on the White River. It is the largest city in the state. Population: 783,612 (2002 estimate).

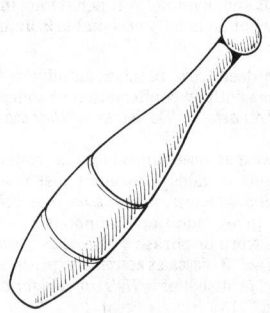

Indian club

Indian club *n* a club shaped like an elongated bottle, used in gymnastics and juggling

Indian English *n* a variety of English spoken in India

WORLD ENGLISH See *South Asian English*.

Indian file *n* an offensive term for single file (*dated*) [< a Native American custom of walking in single file]

Indian giver *n* N Am an offensive term for somebody who gives something and then asks for its return (*informal*)

Indian hemp *n* 1. PLANTS same as **hemp** (sense 3) 2. a perennial plant of the dogbane family whose roots can be used as a laxative and emetic. Native to: North America. Latin name: *Apocynum cannabinum*.

Indian ink *n* 1. a liquid black ink made from a pigment that is a mixture of lampblack and a binding agent 2. the black pigment, usually shaped into cakes or sticks, from which Indian ink is made ▶ N Am term **India ink** [Because originally brought to Europe from China and Japan via India]

Indian meal *n* US FOOD same as **cornmeal**

Indian Mutiny *n* a rebellion by Indian soldiers between 1857 and 1858 against British rule of India

Indian National Congress *n* an Indian political party that led the struggle for independence from the British Empire and dominated the post-independence government in the 20th century

Indian Ocean /índi ən-/ ocean situated east of Africa, south of Asia, west of Australia, and north of Antarctica. Its greatest known depth is 7,725 m/25,344 ft. Area: 73,440,000 sq. km/28,360,000 sq. mi.

Indian Pacific *n* the train service in Australia that runs between Perth, on the shore of the Indian Ocean, and Sydney, on the shore of the Pacific Ocean

Indian paintbrush *n* a wild plant of the figwort family with brightly coloured bracts that look like flowers.

Native to: North America. Latin name: *Castileja linariaefolia*.

Indian pipe *n* a perennial woodland plant whose single white stem and nodding flower resembles a tobacco pipe. Native to: North America, Asia. Latin name: *Monotropa uniflora*.

Indian red *n* **1.** a red pigment made of iron oxide. Use: paint, cosmetics, polish. **2.** a dark reddish-brown colour —**Indian red** *adj*

Indian rope-trick *n* the feat of appearing to climb an erect unsupported length of rope, performed by some magicians of South Asia

Indian Standard Time *n* the standard time in India, five-and-a-half hours later than Universal Coordinated Time

Indian subcontinent large region in South Asia, including the countries of Bangladesh, India, and Pakistan

Indian summer *n* **1.** a period of mild sunny weather occurring in autumn in the northern hemisphere **2.** a calm or productive and enjoyable period towards the end of somebody's life or the end of a process, period, or activity [Origin ?]

Indian tobacco *n* a very poisonous annual plant of the bluebell family that has oval toothed leaves and swollen seed capsules. Flowers: small, purplish. Native to: North America. Latin name: *Lobelia inflata*.

Indian wrestling *n* a form of wrestling in which one wrestler attempts to force down another's upraised arm or to throw a standing opponent off balance —**Indian-wrestle** *vti*

India paper *n* a thin fine paper originally made in South Asia, used for prints and illustrations

India rubber *n* INDUST same as **rubber**[1] (sense 1) (*dated*)

Indic /índik/ *n* a large group of languages of South Asia, forming a major division of Indo-Iranian. Native speakers: 700 million. [Mid-19C. Via Latin < Greek *Indikos* < *Indos* 'the Indus river'] —**Indic** *adj*

indic. *abbr* **1.** indicating **2.** GRAM indicative **3.** indicator

indican /índikən/ *n* **1.** a substance formed in the intestine by bacterial action and excreted in urine and sweat. Formula: $C_8H_6NO_4SK$. **2.** an off-white crystalline sugar derivative found in plants. Use: original source of indigo dye. [Mid-19C. < Latin *indicum* (see INDIGO)]

indicate /índi kayt/ (**-cates, -cating, -cated**) *v* **1.** *vt* **POINT TO SOMETHING** to point something out or point to something **2.** *vt* **SHOW EXISTENCE OR TRUTH OF SOMETHING** to be or provide a sign, signal, or symptom that something exists or is true **3.** *vt* **REGISTER MEASUREMENT** to register a measurement, e.g. of speed or temperature **4.** *vt* **SHOW WHAT SOMEBODY THINKS OR INTENDS** to state or show an opinion, feeling, instruction, or intention, especially briefly or indirectly **5.** *vt* **SHOW WHAT SHOULD BE DONE** to make somebody think that something should be done or used (*usually used in the passive*) ○ *In a case like this, a firm approach is indicated.* **6.** *vti* **GIVE SIGNALS AS DRIVER** to signal your intentions to other vehicles when driving, especially before turning or moving to the left or right **7.** *vt* MED **SHOW PRESENCE OF DISEASE** to point out the presence of, or remedy for, a disease or syndrome [Early 17C. < Latin *indicat-*, past participle of *indicare* 'point towards, show' < *dicare* 'proclaim'] —**indicant** *n* —**indicatable** *adj* —**indicatory** /in díkətəri/ *adj*

indicated horsepower /índi kaytid-/ *n* the theoretical power produced by a reciprocating engine such as a steam or internal-combustion engine, calculated as the power produced before reduction due to friction and mechanical movement

indication /índi káysh'n/ *n* **1.** **SIGN OF SOMETHING** a sign, signal, or symptom that something exists or is true **2.** **ACT OF INDICATING** an act of indicating or pointing to something **3.** **READING ON INSTRUMENT** a reading shown on a measuring instrument **4.** **SOMETHING NECESSARY OR DESIRABLE** something that is indicated as the right thing to do or use **5.** MED **MEDICAL SIGN** a medical sign or symptom that shows the presence of a disease or a remedy for it —**indicational** *adj*

indicative /in díkətiv/ *adj* **1.** **INDICATING EXISTENCE OR TRUTH** showing, suggesting, or pointing out that something exists or is true **2.** GRAM **RELATING TO BASIC MOOD OF VERBS** relating to the basic mood of verbs in ordinary objective statements in languages such as English ■ *n* GRAM **1.** **BASIC MOOD OF VERB** the basic mood of a verb in languages such as English, used for ordinary objective statements **2.** **VERB IN BASIC MOOD** a verb in the basic mood used for ordinary objective statements in languages such as English —**indicatively** *adv*

indicator /índi kaytər/ *n* **1.** **DRIVER'S SIGNAL** a device on a motor vehicle, usually a flashing light, that indicates that the driver is turning or moving to the left or right **2.** **SOMETHING THAT SHOWS WHAT CONDITIONS ARE** something observed or calculated that is used to show the presence or state of a condition or trend **3.** **MEASURING INSTRUMENT** an instrument or gauge that measures something and registers the measurement **4.** **SOMETHING GIVING INFORMATION** something such as a light, sign, or pointer that gives information, e.g. about which direction to follow **5.** CHEM **CHEMICAL SHOWING SOMETHING** a substance that shows the presence or concentration of a specific material or chemical, e.g. litmus **6.** ECOL same as **indicator organism**

indicator diagram *n* a graph showing the variation of pressure and volume in a cylinder of a reciprocating engine

indicator organism *n* an organism whose presence or absence in an environment indicates conditions such as its oxygen level or the presence of a contaminating substance

indices plural of **index**

indicium /in díssi əm/ (*plural* **-cia** /-si ə/) *n* a sign indicating the presence or nature of something such as a medical condition [Early 17C. < Latin < *indic-*, stem of *index* (see INDEX)]

indicolite /índikə līt/ *n* a blue-coloured variety of tourmaline. Use: gems. [Early 19C. < Latin *indicum* (see INDIGO)]

indict /in dít/ (**-dicts, -dicting, -dicted**) *vt* **1.** to charge somebody formally with commission of a crime **2.** to accuse somebody of wrongdoing [14C. < Anglo-Norman *enditer* < Latin *indict-*, past participle of *indicere* 'proclaim', literally 'say in' < *dicere* 'say'] —**indictee** /índī teé/ *n* —**indicter** *n* —**indictor** *n*

indictable /in dítəb'l/ *adj* **1.** liable to be charged with a criminal offence **2.** making somebody liable to be charged with commission of a crime ○ *an indictable offence*

indiction /in díksh'n/ *n* a cyclic period of 15 years begun during the reign of Constantine the Great in the later Roman Empire at the end of which property was evaluated for taxation [14C. < Latin *indiction-* 'declaration' < *indict-* (see INDICT); from the declaration setting the valuation on which tax was assessed] —**indictional** *adj*

indictment /in dítmənt/ *n* **1.** **STATEMENT OR FACT THAT ACCUSES** a statement or indication that something is wrong or somebody is to blame ○ *a stinging indictment of our prison system* **2.** **ACT OF INDICTING SOMEBODY** the act of indicting somebody or the condition of being indicted **3.** **CHARGE OF CRIMINAL WRONGDOING** a formal accusation of a serious crime **4.** **ACCUSATION BY LORD ADVOCATE IN SCOTLAND** in Scotland, an accusation of crime brought by the Lord Advocate

indie /índi/ (*slang*) *n* **INDEPENDENT COMPANY** a small independent business enterprise, especially one related to music ■ *adj* **1.** **ISSUED BY SMALL COMPANIES** issued by small independent record companies, or playing the sort of music recorded by such companies **2.** **FASHIONABLE** very stylish or in vogue [Early 20C. Shortening of INDEPENDENT]

Indiennes /índi én/ *n* a fabric with small brightly coloured French provincial patterns that are hand-printed using carved blocks. It was originally imported from India. [Late 19C. < French *(à l')indienne* '(in the) Indian (style)']

Indies ♦ **East Indies, West Indies**

indifference /in dífrənss/ *n* **1.** **LACK OF INTEREST IN SOMETHING** lack of interest, care, or concern **2.** **UNIMPORTANCE** lack of importance or significance ○ *It's a matter of complete indifference to me whether you go or stay.* **3.** **LOW QUALITY** ordinariness or lack of quality

indifferent /in dífrənt/ *adj* **1.** **WITHOUT CARE OR INTEREST** showing no care or concern for or interest in somebody or something ○ *She was indifferent to their criticism.* **2.** **FAVOURING NEITHER SIDE** without bias or preference for one person, group, or thing rather than another **3.** **ONLY AVERAGE** average or low in quality **4.** BIOL **UNDIFFERENTIATED** describes cells or tissues that are not specialized or differentiated **5.** SCI **NEUTRAL** having no properties that are affected by a process or reaction [14C. Directly or via French < Latin *indifferent-* 'making no difference' < *different-* (see DIFFERENT)]

indifferentism /in dífrəntizəm/ *n* the belief that variations in doctrine and practice within a religion are unimportant

indifferently /in díff rəntli/ *adv* **1.** **WITHOUT INTEREST** without showing interest or concern **2.** **NOT WELL** in a way that is only average or low in quality **3.** **EQUALLY** without differences or exceptions (*formal*)

indigen *n* same as **indigene** (*formal*)

indigence /índijənss/ *n* extreme poverty in which the basic necessities of life are lacking (*formal*)

indigene /índi jeen/, **indigen** /índijən/ *n* somebody or something that is native to a place (*formal*) [Late 16C. Via French < Latin *indigena* (see INDIGENOUS)]

indigenize /in díjji nīz/ (**-izes, -izing, -ized**), **indigenise** (**-ises, -ising, -ised**) *vti* to increase the use of local inhabitants for a task previously done by people from another country, usually the home country of an employing company —**indigenization** /in díjji nī záysh'n/ *n*

indigenous /in díjjinəss/ *adj* **1.** originating in and naturally living, growing, or occurring in a region or country **2.** natural or inborn (*formal*) [Mid-17C. < Latin *indigena*, literally 'born in' < *gignere* 'beget'] —**indigenity** /índi jénnəti/ *n* —**indigenously** *adv*

SYNONYMS See ***native***.

indigenous people *n* a people who occupy a region at the time of its contact with colonial powers or the outside world

indigent /índijənt/ (*formal*) *adj* lacking the necessities of life, e.g. food, clothing, and shelter ■ *n* an impoverished person [14C. Via French < Latin *indigent-*, present participle of *indigere*, literally 'lack in' < *egere* 'to need'] —**indigently** *adv*

indigestible /índi jéstəb'l/ *adj* **1.** difficult or impossible to digest **2.** hard to take in or understand (*informal*) —**indigestibility** /índi jéstə bílləti/ *n* —**indigestibly** *adv*

indigestion /índi jéschən/ *n* difficulty in digesting food, resulting in such symptoms as belching, heartburn, or stomach pains. Technical name **dyspepsia**

indigestive /índi jéstiv/ *adj* experiencing or resulting from indigestion

indignant /in dígnənt/ *adj* angry or annoyed at the apparent unfairness or unreasonableness of something [Late 16C. < Latin *indignant-*, present participle of *indignari* 'regard as unworthy' < *dignus* 'worthy'] —**indignantly** *adv*

indignation /índig náysh'n/ *n* anger because something seems unfair or unreasonable [14C. Directly or via French < Latin *indignation-* < *indignari* (see INDIGNANT)]

SYNONYMS See ***anger***.

indignity /in dígnəti/ (*plural* **-ties**) *n* a situation that results in a humiliating loss of dignity or self-esteem

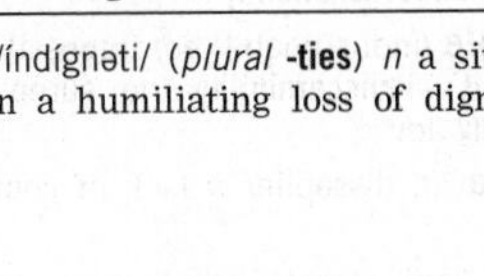

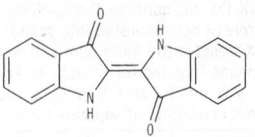

indigo: synthetic indigo

indigo /índigō/ (*plural* **-gos** or **-goes**) *n* **1.** **DEEP PURPLISH-BLUE COLOUR** a deep purplish-blue colour that lies between blue and violet on the visible spectrum **2.**

BLUE DYE a blue dye. Source: formerly from plants, but now usually made synthetically. **3.** PLANT YIELDING INDIGO DYE a tropical plant of the pea family with fronds of pointed leaves and flowers, a source of indigo dye. Flowers: red or purple, in spikes. Genus: *Indigofera*. [Mid-16C. Via Spanish and Portuguese < Latin *indicum* < Greek *indikon* 'the Indian substance', form of *Indikos* (see INDIC)] —**indigo** *adj*

indigo bird /índigō burd/ *n* a songbird, the male of which has deep purplish-black feathers. Native to: East Africa. Family: Viduidae.

indigo blue *n* same as **indigo** (senses 1–2) —**indigo-blue** *adj*

indigo snake *n* a large harmless deep-blue snake that preys on small animals. Native to: southern United States, Central and South America. Latin name: *Drymarchon corais*.

indigotin /in díggətin, índi gṓtin/ *n* same as **indigo** (sense 2) [Mid-19C. < INDIGO + *-t-* + -IN]

indirect /índi rékt, índī-/ *adj* **1.** NOT IN STRAIGHT LINE not in a direct line, course, or path **2.** NOT IMMEDIATE OR INTENDED not occurring as an immediate or intended effect or consequence **3.** DEVIOUS not obvious or straightforward in approach **4.** INVOLVING INTERMEDIATE STAGES not obtained or proceeding from an immediate or straightforward relationship —**indirectly** *adv* —**indirectness** *n*

indirect cost *n* a business expense that is not directly connected with a specific product or operation

indirect discourse *n* GRAM same as **indirect speech**

indirect free kick *n* in football, a free kick from which a goal cannot be scored unless the ball touches another player before it passes over the goal line

indirection /índə réksh'n, índī réksh'n/ *n* **1.** LACK OF DIRECTNESS lack of directness in a path, course, or procedure **2.** AIMLESSNESS lack of a goal or goals **3.** SOMETHING NOT HONEST an approach or action that is devious or deceitful

indirect labour *n* work that is not considered in determining costs per unit in producing or manufacturing something, e.g. work done by clerical or maintenance staff

indirect lighting *n* reflected or diffused light used to avoid glare or shadows

indirect object *n* the recipient of the action shown by a verb and its direct object, e.g. 'the cat' in 'She gave the cat a meal'

indirect proof *n* in logic, proof of a conclusion by showing that assuming its negation will lead to a contradiction

indirect question *n* a question reported in indirect speech, e.g. 'He asked why you were not there'

indirect speech *n* a report of something said or written that conveys what was said, but not the exact words in their original form, as in 'She said she would join us later'

indirect tax *n* a tax levied on goods or services, instead of directly on companies and individual people —**indirect taxation** *n*

indiscernible /índi súrnəb'l/ *adj* impossible to see or understand —**indiscernibility** /índi súrnə bíllәti/ *n* —**indiscernibly** *adv*

indiscipline /in díssəplin/ *n* lack of control or discipline

indiscreet /índi skréet/ *adj* lacking tact or discretion —**indiscreetly** *adv*

SPELLCHECK Do not confuse the spelling of ***indiscreet*** and ***indiscrete*** (= not separated into parts), which sound similar. ***Indiscreet*** is the more common word in general use and means 'not tactful or able to keep a secret'. ***Indiscrete*** is a much rarer formal or technical word meaning 'not consisting of separate parts'.

indiscrete /índi skréet/ *adj* not divided into parts, or appearing not to consist of separate parts —**indiscretely** *adv*

SPELLCHECK See *indiscreet*.

indiscretion /índi skrésh'n/ *n* **1.** lack of tact or good judgment **2.** something said or done that is tactless or unwise ○ *apologizing for past indiscretions* —**indiscretionary** *adj*

indiscriminate /índi skrímminət/ *adj* **1.** making no careful distinctions or choices **2.** random, haphazard, or confused —**indiscriminately** *adv* —**indiscriminateness** *n* —**indiscrimination** /índi skrímmi náysh'n/ *n* —**indiscriminative** *adj*

indiscriminating /índi skrímmi nayting/ *adj* lacking discrimination or judgment —**indiscriminatingly** *adv* —**indiscriminative** /índi skrímminətiv/ *adj*

indispensable /índi spénssəb'l/ *adj* **1.** NECESSARY extremely desirable or useful, or not to be done without **2.** HAVING TO BE FACED unavoidable, especially as a duty ■ *n* SOMETHING ESSENTIAL something that is essential and cannot be dispensed with —**indispensability** /índi spénssə bíllәti/ *n* —**indispensableness** *n* —**indispensably** *adv*

SYNONYMS See ***necessary***.

~~**indispensible**~~ incorrect spelling of **indispensable**

indispose /índi spṓz/ (**-poses, -posing, -posed**) *vt* **1.** MAKE SOMEBODY UNFIT to make somebody unfit for something (*formal*) **2.** MAKE SOMEBODY AVERSE TO SOMETHING to make somebody dislike the prospect of something or be unwilling to do something (*formal*) **3.** SICKEN SOMEBODY to make somebody ill (*archaic*)

indisposed /índi spṓzd/ *adj* (*formal*) **1.** too ill to do something **2.** unwilling to say or do something, especially because of a feeling of annoyance

indisposition /índispə zísh'n/ *n* (*formal*) **1.** an illness that is not serious **2.** reluctance or unwillingness to do something

indisputable /índi spyóotəb'l/ *adj* impossible to doubt, question, or deny —**indisputability** /índi spyóotə bíllәti/ *n* —**indisputably** *adv*

indissoluble /índi sóllyoob'l/ *adj* incapable of being dissolved, broken, or undone —**indissolubility** /índi sóllyoo bíllәti/ *n* —**indissolubly** *adv*

indistinct /índi stíngkt/ *adj* **1.** not seen or heard clearly **2.** not clearly remembered, understood, or thought out —**indistinctly** *adv* —**indistinctness** *n*

indistinctive /índi stíngktiv/ *adj* with no distinguishing qualities or features —**indistinctively** *adv*

indistinguishable /índi stíng gwishəb'l/ *adj* **1.** impossible to tell apart from somebody or something else ○ *His handwriting is indistinguishable from his father's.* **2.** very hard to see, hear, or understand —**indistinguishability** /índi stíng gwishə bíllәti/ *n* —**indistinguishably** *adv*

indite /in dī́t/ (**-dites, -diting, -dited**) *vt* to write or compose something such as a poem, letter, or speech (*archaic or literary*) [14C. < Old French *enditir*, literally 'compose in words in' < Latin *indict-* (see INDICT)]

indium /índi əm/ *n* a soft silvery rare metallic element. Source: zinc and tin ores. Use: alloys, transistors, electroplating. Symbol **In**. See table at **element**

indium phosphide *n* a brittle metallic solid. Use: manufacture of semiconductors, lasers, solar cells.

individual /índi víddyoo əl/ *n* **1.** SPECIFIC PERSON a specific person, distinct from others in a group ○ *belief in the individual's right to self-expression* **2.** ANY PERSON a human being, or a person of a specified type ○ *a panel consisting of four individuals* ○ *a very unfortunate individual* **3.** SEPARATE THING a separate entity or thing **4.** BIOL SEPARATE ORGANISM an independent organism separate from a group ○ *The plant part contains the embryo, which gives rise to a new individual.* ■ *adj* **1.** SEPARABLE FROM OTHERS singular and separable from others in a group or class ○ *Each individual bead is hand-sewn.* **2.** OF OR FOR ONE PERSON belonging to, relating to, or intended for one person only **3.** VERY DISTINCTIVE strikingly personal, unusual, or distinctive [15C. < medieval Latin *individualis* < Latin *individuus* 'not divisible' < *dividere* 'to divide']

individualise *vt* another spelling of **individualize**

individualism /índi víddyoo əlizəm/ *n* **1.** PURSUIT OF PERSONAL GOALS the pursuit of personal happiness and independence rather than collective goals or interests **2.** PERSONAL TRAIT a personal peculiarity or trait **3.** BELIEF IN IMPORTANCE OF INDIVIDUAL the belief that society exists for the benefit of individual people, who must not be constrained by government interventions or made subordinate to collective interests

individualist /índi víjjoo əlist/ *n* **1.** somebody of independent thought or behaviour **2.** a believer in the philosophy of individualism —**individualistic** /índi vidyoo ə lístik/ *adj* —**individualistically** *adv*

individuality /índi vidyoo állәti/ (*plural* **-ties**) *n* **1.** a specific personality, character, or characteristic that distinguishes one person or thing from another **2.** the state or condition of being separate from others

individualize /índi víddyoo ə līz/ (**-izes, -izing, -ized**), **individualise** (**-ises, -ising, -ised**) *vt* **1.** GIVE SOMEBODY OR SOMETHING INDIVIDUAL CHARACTER to give somebody or something a character that is separate and distinct from other people or things **2.** TREAT SOMEBODY OR SOMETHING INDIVIDUALLY to consider or treat somebody or something specifically, as distinct from other people or things **3.** ADAPT SOMETHING TO INDIVIDUAL REQUIREMENTS to make or modify something to suit a specific person —**individualization** /índi víddyoo ə lī záysh'n/ *n* —**individualizer** *n*

individually /índi víddyoo əli/ *adv* as a separate person or entity, not as part of a group or class

individual medley *n* a swimming race divided into three or four equal parts, in each of which the swimmers must use a particular stroke such as backstroke, crawl, breaststroke, or butterfly

individuate /índi víddyoo ayt/ (**-ates, -ating, -ated**) *vt* to make somebody or something separate and distinct from others [Early 17C. < medieval Latin *individuat-*, past participle of *individuare* < Latin *individuus* (see INDIVIDUAL)] —**individuator** *n*

individuation /índi vidyoo áysh'n/ *n* **1.** the act or process of making somebody or something separate and distinct from others **2.** in Jungian psychology, the development of the self, achieved by resolving the conflicts arising at life's transitional stages, in particular the transition from adolescence to adulthood. Jung believed this process could not be completed until middle age.

indivisible /índi vízzəb'l/ *adj* **1.** not capable of being separated into parts **2.** not capable of being divided by a given number without leaving a mathematical remainder —**indivisibility** /índi vizə bíllәti/ *n* —**indivisibly** *adv*

indo- *prefix* a chemical compound derived from indigo ○ *indoxyl* [< INDIGO]

Indo- *prefix* **1.** India ○ *Indo-European* **2.** Indic ○ *Indo-Iranian* [< INDIA [1], INDIC]

Indo-Canadian *n* a Canadian who came from India, or whose parents did —**Indo-Canadian** *adj*

Indochina

Indochina /índō chī́nə/ peninsula of Southeast Asia that includes Myanmar, Thailand, Cambodia, Vietnam, Laos, and the Malay Peninsula. In a narrower sense it refers only to Cambodia, Laos, and Vietnam. —**Indochinese** /índō chī néez/ *adj, n*

indocile /in dṓ sīl/ *adj* resisting discipline or instruction —**indocility** /índō síllәti/ *n*

indoctrinate /in dóktri nayt/ (**-nates, -nating, -nated**) *vt* to teach somebody a belief, doctrine, or ideology thoroughly and systematically, especially with the aim of discouraging independent thought or the acceptance of other opinions [Early 17C. < Old French *endoctriner*, literally 'teach in' < medieval Latin *doctrinare* 'teach' < Latin *doctrina* (see DOCTRINE)] —**indoctrination** /in dóktri náysh'n/ *n* —**indoctrinator** *n*

Indo-European /índō-/ *n* **1.** FAMILY OF EUROPEAN AND ASIAN LANGUAGES a large family of languages spoken from South Asia to Western Europe and the United States, comprising the Balto-Slavonic, Germanic, Italic, Indo-Iranian, Celtic, Greek, Albanian,

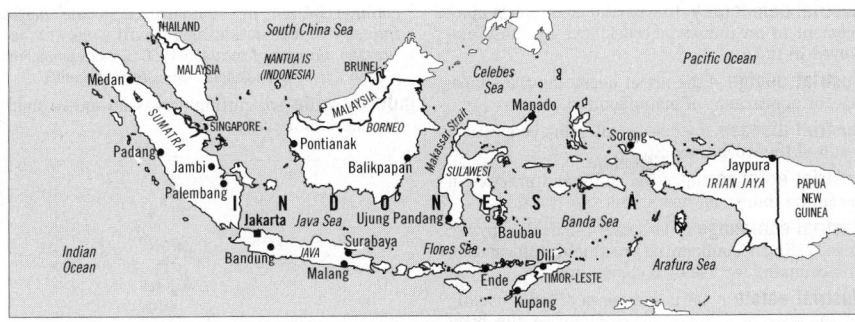

Indonesia

Armenian, Anatolian, and Tocharian branches. This language family includes many modern languages such as Bangla, English, French, German, Spanish, Russian, Hindi, and Urdu. **2. ANCESTOR OF MODERN INDO-EUROPEAN LANGUAGES** the reconstructed language that is the prehistoric ancestor of modern languages belonging to Indo-European **3. SPEAKER OF INDO-EUROPEAN LANGUAGE** a speaker of a language belonging to Indo-European, especially prehistoric Indo-European —**Indo-European** *adj*

Indo-Iranian *n* a group of languages spoken in northern South Asia and in parts of Southwest Asia, forming a branch of Indo-European and dividing into Indic and Iranian subgroups. Native speakers: 800 million. —**Indo-Iranian** *adj*

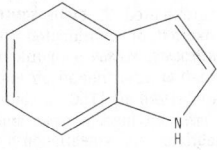

indole

indole /índōl/, **indol** /-dol/ *n* a crystalline compound. Source: plants, faeces, coal tar. Use: in perfumes, chemical reagent. Formula: C_8H_7N.

indoleacetic acid /índōlə seétik-, -ə séttik-/ *n* a plant hormone that stimulates growth and root formation in cuttings

indolebutyric acid /índōl byoo tírrik-/ *n* a synthetic plant hormone that stimulates growth in stems

indolent /índələnt/ *adj* **1.** lethargic and not showing any interest or making any effort **2.** describes a disease or condition that is slow to develop or be healed, and causes no pain [Mid-17C. < late Latin *indolent-* 'insensitive to pain' < Latin *dolere* 'suffer pain'] —**indolence** *n* —**indolently** *adv*

Indology /in dóllə ji/ *n* the study of the history, culture, or philosophy of the region comprising the countries of South Asia —**Indologist** *n*

indomethacin /índō méthəssin/ *n* a drug used to relieve pain, fever, and inflammation, especially from arthritis [Mid-20C. < INDOLE + METHYL + ACETIC + -IN]

indomitable /in dómmitəb'l/ *adj* brave, determined, and impossible to defeat or frighten [Mid-17C. < late Latin *indomitabilis* 'untamable' < Latin *domitare* 'to tame'] —**indomitability** /in dómmitə bílləti/ *n* —**indomitableness** *n* —**indomitably** *adv*

Indonesia /índə neézi ə, -neézhə/ country in Southeast Asia, the fourth most populous country in the world. It consists of more than 13,670 islands, 6,000 of which are inhabited. Language: Bahasa Indonesia. Currency: rupiah. Capital: Jakarta. Population: 234,893,450 (2003). Area: 1,904,443 sq. km/735,310 sq. mi. Official name **Republic of Indonesia**

Indonesian /índō neézi ən/ *n* **1.** somebody who comes from Indonesia **2.** LANG same as **Bahasa Indonesia** — **Indonesian** *adj*

indoor /ín dawr/ *adj* situated or done within a building

indoor air quality *n* the condition of the air inside buildings, including the extent of pollution caused by smoking, dust, mites, mould spores, radon, and gases and chemicals from materials and appliances

indoor-outdoor *adj* designed to be used inside or outside a building

indoors /in dáwrz/ *adv* into or inside a building

Indo-Pacific *n* a large group of languages spoken in New Guinea and the surrounding islands. Native speakers: 3 million. —**Indo-Pacific** *adj*

Indore /in dáwr/ **1.** former state, now part of Madhya Pradesh, central India **2.** city in western Madhya Pradesh, central India. It was the capital of the former state of Indore. Population: 1,639,044 (2001).

indorse *vt* another spelling of **endorse**

Indra /índrə/ *n* in Vedic mythology, a powerful warrior god and the ruler of the sky and weather. He became a subordinate god in later Hindu mythology.

indraught /ín draaft/ *n* an inward flow or current of air

indrawn /ín dráwn/ *adj* **1.** drawn in or pulled in **2.** unresponsive or extremely reserved

indri /índri/, **indris** /índriss/ (*plural same*) *n* a large rare black-and-white lemur with large eyes, silky fur, and a rudimentary tail. Native to: Madagascar. Latin name: *Indri indri*. [Mid-19C. < Malagasy *indry!* 'look!' or *indry izy!* 'there he is!']

indubitable /in dyoóbitəb'l/ *adj* obvious or definitely true, and not to be doubted [Early 17C. Directly or via French < Latin *indubitabilis* 'not doubtful' < *dubitare* 'to doubt'] —**indubitability** /in dyoóbitə bílləti/ *n* —**indubitably** *adv*

induce /in dyoóss/ (**-duces, -ducing, -duced**) *vt* **1. PERSUADE SOMEBODY TO DO SOMETHING** to persuade or influence somebody to do or think something **2. PRODUCE MENTAL OR PHYSICAL STATE** to bring about a thought, feeling, or physical condition **3. HASTEN BIRTH OF BABY** to make the process of labour or the birth of a baby start by a medical intervention, usually by administering a drug, before it happens naturally **4. REASON FROM OBSERVATION** to make a statement based on the observation of facts **5. PRODUCE SOMETHING BY INDUCTION** to produce an electric current or a magnetic field by induction [14C. < Latin *inducere* 'lead into, persuade' < *ducere* 'to lead']

induced drag /in dyoóst-/ *n* the drag force created by the lift of an aircraft

inducement /in dyoóss mənt/ *n* **1.** a prospect or reward that gives somebody a reason for acting in a specific way, especially something that is offered as an incentive **2.** the act of inducing something

SYNONYMS See **motive**.

inducer /in dyoóssər/ *n* in genetics, a substance that activates a structural gene within a cell

induct /in dúkt/ (**-ducts, -ducting, -ducted**) *vt* **1. FORMALLY GIVE SOMEBODY POSITION** to install somebody formally in a position or office **2. EXPOSE SOMEBODY TO NEW IDEAS** to introduce somebody to new beliefs, knowledge, or ideas **3.** *US* **ENLIST SOMEBODY FOR MILITARY SERVICE** to enlist somebody formally for service in the military **4.**

PHYS same as **induce** (sense 5) [14C. < Latin *induct-*, past participle of *inducere* (see INDUCE)] —**inductee** /ín duk teé/ *n*

inductance /in dúktənss/ *n* **1.** the property of an electric circuit or device whereby an electromotive force is created by a change of current in it or in a circuit near it. Symbol **L 2.** PHYS same as **inductor** (sense 2)

inductile /in dúktīl/ *adj* not pliable or yielding (*technical*) —**inductility** /ín duk tílləti/ *n*

induction /in dúksh'n/ *n* **1. ACT OF INDUCTING SOMEBODY** the act or process of inducting somebody into a position or an organization **2. PROCESS OF INDUCING SOMETHING** the process of inducing a state, feeling, or idea **3.** MED **PROCESS OF HASTENING BIRTH** the act or the process of medically hastening the birth of a baby **4.** LOGIC **CONCLUSION BASED ON EVIDENCE** a generalization based on observed instances, or the making of such generalizations, in the usual working method of scientists **5.** PHYS **CREATION OF ELECTRIC OR MAGNETIC FORCES** the process by which electric or magnetic forces are created in a circuit by being in proximity to an electric or magnetic field or a varying current without physical contact **6.** BIOL **PROCESS IN DEVELOPMENT OF EMBRYO** the process by which one part of an embryo affects the development of another, e.g. through the diffusion of hormones **7.** CHEM **SYNTHESIS OF ENZYME** the process by which the production of an enzyme is stimulated by the increased concentration of the substance it acts on **8.** MATHS **PROCESS OF MATHEMATICAL PROOF** a process for proving propositions with variables limited to positive integers by showing that the smallest instance is true and each following instance is derived from the one before **9.** *US* MIL **ACT OF ENLISTING SOMEBODY** the act of formally enlisting somebody into military service —**inductional** *adj*

induction coil *n* a transformer that produces an intermittent high-voltage current from a low-voltage direct current by means of several wire windings and, often, a soft iron core

induction cooking *n* a method of cooking food in metal pans using magnetic energy from induction coils beneath the ceramic hob on which the pans are placed

induction course *n* an introductory training course for people starting a new job, entering an educational institution, or joining an organization ○ *an induction course for Australian teachers coming to work in Britain*

induction hardening *n* a process by which the outer surface of a metal is hardened by rapid heating and cooling

induction heating *n* a process for raising the temperature of a metal by inducing an electric current within it

induction motor *n* an alternating-current motor in which current is induced into the rotor windings by stationary windings connected directly to the power source

inductive /in dúktiv/ *adj* **1.** PHYS **OF ELECTRIC OR MAGNETIC INDUCTION** involving, operating by, or caused by electric or magnetic induction **2.** PSYCHOL **PRODUCING MENTAL OR PHYSICAL STATE** relating to the process of inducing a feeling, idea, or state **3.** LOGIC **REACHING CONCLUSION BASED ON OBSERVATION** generalizing to produce a universal claim or principle from observed instances **3.** BIOL **AFFECTING ANOTHER EMBRYONIC PART** producing an effect on another embryonic part by induction —**inductively** *adv* —**inductiveness** *n*

inductor /in dúktər/ *n* **1. AGENT OF INDUCTION** somebody or something that inducts somebody or something else **2. PART OF CIRCUIT GENERATING FORCE** a part of an electric circuit, usually a coil, in which an electromotive force is generated by inductance **3. COMPONENT CAUSING INDUCTANCE** an electrical or electronic component designed to cause or work on inductance

indue *vt* another spelling of **endue**

indulge /in dúlj/ (**-dulges, -dulging, -dulged**) *v* **1.** *vti* **HAVE OR PERMIT TREAT** to allow yourself or somebody else to experience something enjoyable **2.** *vi* **DRINK ALCOHOL** to permit yourself to drink alcohol, especially to excess **3.** *vt* **GIVE DEBTOR TIME** to allow a debtor time to pay a bill [Early 17C. < Latin *indulgere* 'allow space for'] —**indulger** *n*

indulged /in dúljd/ *adj* pampered, spoiled, or catered to

indulgence /in dúljənss/ *n* **1.** YIELDING TO SOMEBODY'S WISH the act of gratifying or yielding to a wish **2.** SOMETHING ALLOWED AS LUXURY something that somebody lets himself or herself or another person have, especially a luxury **3.** TOLERANT ATTITUDE a kind or tolerant attitude towards somebody **4.** REMISSION OF PUNISHMENT FOR SIN in Roman Catholicism, a granting by the pope of partial remission of time to be spent in purgatory or of some other consequence of a sin. In the Middle Ages, a practice of selling indulgences grew up. **5.** BUSINESS PERIOD FOR REPAYMENT time given to a debtor to repay a bill

indulgent /in dúljənt/ *adj* tending to be tolerant and generally allowing people to have what they want —**indulgently** *adv*

induline /índyŏŏ lîn/, **indulin** /índyŏŏ lin/ *n* one of a large group of blue dyes resembling indigo

indult /in dúlt/ *n* a dispensation from the pope that allows a special exception to Roman Catholic Church law [15C. Via French < late Latin *indultum* 'grant, concession' < *indulgere* 'allow space for']

indumentum /índyŏŏ méntəm/ (*plural* **-ta** /-tə/ *or* **-tums**), **indument** /índyŏŏmənt/ *n* a covering of hairs on a plant, or of hair, fur, or feathers on an animal [Mid-19C. < Latin, 'garment' < *induere* 'put on']

induna /in dŏŏnə/ *n* S *Africa* a Black adviser or overseer, e.g. a counsellor of a tribal chief or a supervisor in a mine, factory, or farm [Mid-19C. < Zulu]

induplicate /in dyŏŏplikət, -kayt/ *adj* describes a bud or leaf that has its edges bent or folded inwards, so as to touch but not overlap —**induplication** /in dyŏŏpli káysh'n/ *n*

indurate *vti* /índyŏŏ rayt/ (**-rates, -rating, -rated**) to make something hard, or become hard (*literary or technical*) ■ *adj* /índyŏŏ rət/ unsympathetic or unfeeling (*literary*) [Mid-16C. < Latin *indurat-*, past participle of *indurare* 'make hard' < *durus* 'hard'] —**indurative** /in dyŏŏrətiv/ *adj*

induration /índyŏŏ ráysh'n/ *n* **1.** HARDENING the process of hardening something or of becoming hard (*literary or technical*) **2.** HARDENING OF SEDIMENT the process by which a soft geological sediment becomes hard **3.** MED HARDNESS IN BODY TISSUE a hardness in body tissue, especially a tumour

Indus[1] /índəss/ river in Asia. It rises in western Tibet and flows northwest across Jammu and Kashmir and then southwest through Pakistan to the Arabian Sea. Length: 2,900 km/1,800 mi.

Indus[2] /índəss/ *n* a faint constellation of the southern hemisphere. See illustration at **constellation**

indus. *abbr* **1.** industrial **2.** industry

indusium /in dyŏŏzi əm/ (*plural* **-sia** /-zi ə/) *n* **1.** a membrane on the underside of a fern leaf that protects developing spores **2.** an enveloping protective membrane [Early 18C. < Latin, 'tunic' < *induere* 'put on'] —**indusial** *adj*

industrial /in dústri əl/ *adj* **1.** OF INDUSTRY relating to, used in, or created by industry **2.** WITH MANY DEVELOPED INDUSTRIES having a large quantity of highly developed industries **3.** OF INDUSTRY'S WORKFORCE relating to or involving workers in industry ■ **industrials** *npl* SHARES IN INDUSTRIAL COMPANIES the shares and interest-bearing securities of industrial companies —**industrially** *adv*

industrial accident *n* an accident, often causing serious injury, that is job-related in that it usually happens on a work site such as a factory floor or a construction site

industrial action *n* a protest action such as a strike, undertaken by employees against working conditions, layoffs, or other grievances. N Am term **job action**

industrial archaeology *n* the study of sites, buildings, and equipment used by industries in the past

industrial award *n* Aus a judgment made by an industrial commission or a similar body in settlement of a dispute between employees and employers

industrial commission *n* in Australia, a state government body that rules on disputes between employees and management

industrial democracy *n* the partial or complete management of an industrial workplace by those employed in it

industrial design *n* the art of designing the shape, size, or appearance of manufactured objects

industrial disease *n* a disease affecting people as a result of the work they do

industrial engineering *n* the study and practice of designing industrial operations

industrial espionage *n* the secret removal, copying, or recording of confidential or valuable information in a company for use by a competitor

industrial estate *n* UK a large area of land, usually on the edge of a town, where factories and businesses are concentrated in accordance with local planning regulations

industrialise *vti* another spelling of **industrialize**

industrialism /in dústri əlizəm/ *n* the organization of an economy or a society around extensive manufacturing, rather than around agriculture, the production of handicrafts, or commerce

industrialist /in dústri əlist/ *n* an owner or controller of an industrial concern

industrialize /in dústri ə līz/ (**-izes, -izing, -ized**), **industrialise** (**-ises, -ising, -ised**) *vti* to adapt a country or group to industrial methods of production and manufacturing, with all the accompanying social changes, or to be adapted in this way —**industrialization** /in dústri ə lī záysh'n/ *n*

industrial medicine *n* a branch of medicine that specializes in the prevention or treatment of diseases, stresses, or hazards in the workplace

industrial melanism *n* the increase in the numbers of animals, especially moths, with dark coloration in places where industries create a lot of black smoke and predators more easily feed on lighter individuals

industrial misconduct *n* irregular or negligent conduct by an employee in a workplace, which may result in a penalty

industrial park *n* ANZ, N Am a large area of land where factories and businesses are concentrated in accordance with local zoning policy

industrial psychology *n* the study of human behaviour and attitudes in the workplace —**industrial psychologist** *n*

industrial relations *npl* **1.** the relationship between management and employees in an industrial company **2.** the relations and procedures between employers' organizations and trade unions that are institutionalized in an industrial society

Industrial Revolution *n* the social and economic changes in the United Kingdom, Europe, and the United States that began in the late 18th century and involved widespread adoption of industrial methods of production. The specialization of tasks, the concentration of capital, and the centralization of workforces were important aspects of these changes, which first affected the United Kingdom.

industrial sociology *n* the study of relationships and structures in industrial organizations

industrial-strength *adj* describes materials or chemicals that are strong or of a quality suitable for use in industry

industrial tribunal *n* a court that rules on disputes between employees and management

industrial union *n* a trade union made up of workers with different occupations who are all employed in one industry

Industrial Workers of the World *n* an international trade union with socialist aims that was founded in the United States in 1905 and lost influence after the 1920s

industrious /in dústri əss/ *adj* hard-working, conscientious, and energetic —**industriously** *adv* —**industriousness** *n*

industry /índəstri/ (*plural* **-tries**) *n* **1.** LARGE-SCALE PRODUCTION organized economic activity connected with the production, manufacture, or construction of a particular product or range of products **2.** WIDESPREAD ACTIVITY an activity that many people are involved in, especially one that has become commercialized or standardized ○ *the heritage industry* **3.** HARD WORK diligent hard work (*formal or literary*) ○ *a hive of industry* [15C. Directly or via French < Latin *industria* 'diligence' < *industrius* 'diligent']

industry-wide *adj* cutting across an entire field of commercial activity

Indus Valley Civilization: map of the Indus River Valley

Indus Valley Civilization *n* a Bronze-Age civilization that flourished in the lower Indus River Valley, mainly in present-day Pakistan and northern India, from about 2500 to 1700 BC. It was the earliest known civilization in South Asia and, with Mesopotamia and Egypt, one of the earliest anywhere in the world.

indwell /in dwél/ (**-dwells, -dwelling, -dwelled** *or* **-dwelt** /-dwélt/) *vti* to inhabit, infuse, or abide within a person, community, or place (*formal*) —**indweller** *n*

-ine *suffix* relating to, made of ○ *crystalline* ○ *murrhine* [Directly or via French < Latin *-inus*, Greek *-inos*]

inebriate *vt* /i neébri ayt/ (**-ates, -ating, -ated**) **1.** MAKE SOMEBODY INTOXICATED to cause somebody to become drunk or intoxicated **2.** EXCITE SOMEBODY to make somebody excited or exhilarated (*formal*) ■ *n* /i neébri ət/ INTOXICATED PERSON a drunk or intoxicated person (*formal*) ■ *adj* /i neébri ət/ INTOXICATED drunk or intoxicated (*formal*) [15C. < Latin *inebriat-*, past participle of *inebriare*, literally 'make drunk in' < *ebrius* 'drunk'] —**inebriated** *adj* —**inebriation** /i neébri áysh'n/ *n* —**inebriety** /ínni brî əti/ *n*

inedible /in éddəb'l/ *adj* unfit for consumption as food —**inedibility** /in éddə bílləti/ *n* —**inedibly** *adv*

inedited /in éddit id/ *adj* not having been edited or published

ineducable /in éddyŏŏkəb'l/ *adj* considered incapable of being educated (*archaic*) —**ineducability** /in éddyŏŏkə bílləti/ *n*

ineffable /in éffəb'l/ *adj* unable to be expressed in words [15C. Directly or via French < Latin *ineffabilis* 'unutterable' < *effari* 'speak out' < *fari* 'speak'] —**ineffability** /in éffə bílləti/ *n* —**ineffably** *adv*

ineffaceable /ínni fáyssəb'l/ *adj* incapable of being erased or removed (*formal*) —**ineffaceability** /ínni fáyssə bílləti/ *n* —**ineffaceably** *adv*

ineffective /ínni féktiv/ *adj* **1.** not producing the desired result or effect **2.** incompetent or inept —**ineffectively** *adv* —**ineffectiveness** *n*

ineffectual /ínni fékchoo əl/ *adj* **1.** not competent, decisive, or authoritative enough to achieve desired aims **2.** not able to produce a satisfactory outcome —**ineffectuality** /ínni fékchoo álləti/ *n* —**ineffectually** *adv* —**ineffectualness** *n*

inefficacious /in efi káyshəss/ *adj* not having a positive or useful effect (*formal*) —**inefficaciously** *adv* —**inefficacity** /-kássəti/ *n* —**inefficacy** /in éffikəssi/ *n*

inefficient /ínni físh'nt/ *adj* performing tasks in a way that is not organized or fails to make the best use of something, especially time —**inefficiency** *n* —**inefficiently** *adv*

inelastic /ínni lástik/ *adj* **1.** NOT STRETCHY unable to return quickly to its original shape and size after being bent, stretched, or squashed **2.** NOT EASILY CHANGED unable to incorporate changes or adapt to new circumstances easily **3.** PHYS NOT AFFECTING TRANSLATIONAL KINETIC ENERGY describes a collision that does not lead to an overall loss of translational kinetic energy **4.** ECON INSENSITIVE TO PRICE CHANGES describes supply or demand that is not affected by fluctuations in price —**inelasticity** /ínni lass tíssəti/ *n*

inelegant /in élligənt/ *adj* **1.** lacking grace, sophistication, and good taste in appearance or behaviour **2.** unnecessarily complicated or long —**inelegance** *n*

ineligible /in éllijəb'l/ *adj* not legally entitled or qualified to do, be, or get something —**ineligibility** *n*

ineluctable /ínni lúktəb'l/ *adj* same as **inescapable** (*formal*) ○ *the ineluctable casualties of warfare* [Early 17C. < Latin *ineluctabilis* < *eluctari* 'struggle out of'] —**ineluctability** /ínni lúktə bílləti/ *n* —**ineluctably** *adv*

inept /i népt/ *adj* **1.** lacking the competence or skill for a particular task **2.** not in keeping with what is right or proper for the circumstances [Mid-16C. < Latin *ineptus* 'not suitable' < *aptus* (see APT)] —**ineptitude** *n* —**ineptly** *adv* —**ineptness** *n*

inequable /in ékwəb'l/ *adj* not fair or uniform

inequality /ínni kwólləti/ (*plural* **-ties**) *n* **1.** DIFFERENCE IN STATUS social or economic disparity between people or groups **2.** LACK OF EQUAL TREATMENT unequal opportunity or treatment based on social, ethnic, racial, or economic disparity **3.** STATE OF BEING UNEQUAL the condition or an instance of not being equal **4.** MATHS STATEMENT INDICATING UNEQUAL QUANTITIES a mathematical statement indicating that two quantities are not equal, represented by the symbol <, >, or ≠, meaning less than, greater than, and not equal to. An unconditional inequality is one that is true for all values of a variable, while a conditional inequality is false for some values of a variable. **5.** UNEVENNESS ON SURFACE variability or unevenness on the surface of something

inequitable /in ékwitəb'l/ *adj* showing bias or favouritism (*formal*) —**inequitably** *adv*

inequity /in ékwəti/ (*plural* **-ties**) *n* **1.** lack of fairness or justice (*formal*) **2.** a situation or action that is not fair

inequivalve /in ékwi valv, -éekwi-/, **inequivalved** /-valvd/ *adj* describes a bivalve mollusc whose valves are unequal in size or form

ineradicable /ínni ráddikəb'l/ *adj* impossible to get rid of —**ineradicability** /ínni ráddikə bílləti/ *n* —**ineradicably** *adv*

inerrant /in érrənt/ *adj* **1.** incapable of making a mistake (*formal*) **2.** containing no mistakes —**inerrancy** *n*

inert /i núrt/ *adj* **1.** MOTIONLESS not moving or not able to move **2.** CHEM, BIOCHEM NONREACTIVE not readily changed by chemical or biological reaction **3.** SLUGGISH OR UNMOTIVATED lacking in energy or motivation [Mid-17C. < Latin *inert-* 'having no skill' < *art-* 'skill'] —**inertly** *adv* —**inertness** *n*

inert gas *n* CHEM same as **noble gas**

inertia /i núrshə/ *n* **1.** inability or unwillingness to move or act **2.** PHYS the property of a body by which it remains at rest or continues moving in a straight line unless acted upon by a directional force [Early 18C. < Latin, 'lack of skill, inactivity' < *inert-* (see INERT)] —**inertial** *adj* —**inertially** *adv*

inertial confinement fusion *n* nuclear fusion achieved by firing high-energy lasers or particle beams at small pellets, typically containing deuterium and sometimes also tritium

inertial force *n* a force as perceived by an observer in an accelerating or rotating frame of reference, that serves to confirm the validity of Newton's laws of motion, e.g. the perception of being forced backwards in an accelerating vehicle

inertial fusion *n* PHYS same as **inertial confinement fusion**

inertial guidance, **inertial navigation** *n* navigation by conversion of the accelerations experienced into distances and directions. It is used on aircraft, spacecraft, or missiles that use devices such as gyroscopes, accelerometers, and computers to calculate and adjust course.

inertia selling *n* the practice of sending unsolicited goods to people's homes and demanding payment if the goods are not returned

inescapable /ínni skáypəb'l/ *adj* impossible to avoid —**inescapability** /ínni skaypə bílləti/ *n* —**inescapably** *adv*

in esse /-éssi/ *adj* having actual existence as opposed to potential existence [< Latin, 'in existence']

inessential /ínni sénsh'l/ *adj* **1.** NOT ESSENTIAL not absolutely necessary **2.** WITHOUT ESSENCE without substance or being (*literary*) ■ *n* SOMETHING INESSENTIAL something that is unnecessary —**inessentiality** /ínni sénshi álləti/ *n* —**inessentially** *adv*

inessive /in éssiv/ *n* in the grammar of languages such as Finnish, a grammatical form (**case**) of nouns and pronouns that indicates the location of something [Late 19C. < Latin *inesse* 'be in or at' < *esse* 'be']

inestimable /in éstiməb'l/ *adj* **1.** too great to calculate **2.** having a worth that is so great that a value cannot be placed upon it —**inestimability** /in éstimə bílləti/ *n* —**inestimably** *adv*

inevitable /in évvitəb'l/ *adj* impossible to avoid or to prevent from happening ■ *n* something that is certain to happen ○ *deciding to accept the inevitable* [15C. < Latin *inevitabilis* 'not avoidable' < *evitare* 'shun'] —**inevitability** /in évvitə bílləti/ *n* —**inevitably** *adv*

~~**inevitible**~~ incorrect spelling of **inevitable**

inexact /ínnig zákt/ *adj* **1.** not entirely accurate **2.** not thorough or careful —**inexactitude** /ínnig zákti tyood/ *n* —**inexactly** *adv* —**inexactness** *n*

inexcusable /ínnik skyoózəb'l/ *adj* impossible to pardon or justify —**inexcusability** /ínnik skyoózə bílləti/ *n* —**inexcusableness** *n* —**inexcusably** *adv*

inexhaustible /ínnig záwstəb'l/ *adj* **1.** impossible to use up **2.** showing no sign of tiring —**inexhaustibility** /ínnig záwstə bílləti/ *n* —**inexhaustibly** *adv*

inexistent /ínnig zístənt/ *adj* not in existence

inexorable /in éksərəb'l/ *adj* **1.** impossible to stop **2.** not moved by anyone's attempts to plead or persuade (*formal*) [Mid-16C. Via French < Latin *inexorabilis* < *exorare* 'prevail upon' < *orare* 'pray'] —**inexorability** /in éksərə bílləti/ *n* —**inexorably** *adv*

inexpedient /ínnik speédi ənt/ *adj* not recommended or prudent (*formal*) —**inexpedience** *n* —**inexpediently** *adv*

inexpensive /ínnik spénssiv/ *adj* not costing much money —**inexpensively** *adv* —**inexpensiveness** *n*

inexperience /ínnik speéri ənss/ *n* **1.** lack of the experience that would lead to an increase in knowledge or skill **2.** lack of sophistication about worldly ways —**inexperienced** *adj*

inexpert /in ékspurt/ *adj* lacking in skill or experience —**inexpertly** *adv* —**inexpertness** *n*

inexpiable /in ékspi əb'l/ *adj* so bad that it cannot be atoned for (*formal*) [15C. < Latin *inexpiabilis* < *expiare* (see EXPIATE)] —**inexpiableness** *n* —**inexpiably** *adv*

inexplicable /ínnik splíkəb'l, in éksplikəb'l/, **inexplainable** /ínnik spláynəb'l/ *adj* unable to be explained or justified —**inexplicability** /ínnik splíkə bílləti, in éksplikə-/ *n* —**inexplicably** *adv*

inexplicit /ínnik splíssit/ *adj* not expressed or shown fully, openly, and unambiguously

inexpressible /ínnik spréssəb'l/ *adj* impossible to put into words —**inexpressibility** /ínnik spréssə bílləti/ *n* —**inexpressibly** *adv*

inexpressive /ínnik spréssiv/ *adj* conveying no feeling —**inexpressively** *adv* —**inexpressiveness** *n*

inexpugnable /ínnik spúgnəb'l/ *adj* (*formal*) **1.** impossible to take by force **2.** impossible to overcome [15C. Via French < Latin *inexpugnabilis* < *expugnare* 'fight off' < *pugnare* 'to fight'] —**inexpugnability** /ínnik spúgnə bílləti/ *n* —**inexpugnably** *adv*

inexpungible /ínnik spúnjəb'l/ *adj* impossible to remove or cancel out

inextensible /ínnik sténssəb'l/ *adj* impossible to stretch to a greater length —**inextensibility** /ínnik sténssə bílləti/ *n*

in extenso /ín ik sténssō/ *adv* at its full length ○ *quote a passage in extenso* [< Latin, 'at a stretch']

inextinguishable /ínnik stíng gwishəb'l/ *adj* impossible to extinguish or suppress —**inextinguishably** *adv*

inextirpable /ínnik stúrpəb'l/ *adj* impossible to remove or destroy (*formal*) [Early 17C. < Latin *inex(s)tirpabilis* < *ex(s)tirpare* (see EXTIRPATE)] —**inextirpableness** *n*

in extremis /in ik streémiss/ *adv* in desperate circumstances, especially at the point of death ■ *adj* on the point of death [< Latin, 'in the extremes']

inextricable /ínnik stríkəb'l, in ékstrikəb'l/ *adj* **1.** IMPOSSIBLE TO ESCAPE FROM impossible to get free from **2.** IMPOSSIBLE TO DISENTANGLE impossible to disentangle or undo **3.** EXTREMELY COMPLEX hopelessly involved or complex [Mid-16C. < Latin *inextricabilis* 'that cannot be disentangled' < *extricare* (see EXTRICATE)] —**inextricability** /ínnik stríkə bílləti, in ékstrikə-/ *n* —**inextricableness** *n* —**inextricably** *adv*

INF *abbr* intermediate-range nuclear forces

infallible /in fálləb'l/ *adj* **1.** NOT ERRING incapable of making a mistake **2.** INCAPABLE OF FAILING certain not to fail **3.** UNERRING IN DOCTRINE incapable of being mistaken in matters of doctrine and dogma [15C. < medieval Latin *infallibilis* < Latin *fallere* 'deceive, disappoint'] —**infallibility** /in fállə bílləti/ *n* —**infallibleness** *n* —**infallibly** *adv*

infamous /ínfəməss/ *adj* **1.** having an extremely bad reputation **2.** so bad as to earn somebody an extremely bad reputation —**infamously** *adv*

USAGE See *fame*.

infamy /ínfəmi/ (*plural* **-mies**) *n* **1.** NOTORIETY the disgrace to somebody's reputation caused by an infamous act or behaviour **2.** SHAMEFUL CONDUCT shameful or criminal conduct or character **3.** EVIL DEED a publicly known infamous act or event [15C. < French *infamie* < Latin *infamis* 'of ill repute', literally 'having no fame' < *fama* 'fame']

USAGE See *fame*.

infancy /ínfənssi/ *n* **1.** BABYHOOD the condition or time of childhood before a baby walks or talks **2.** BEGINNING an early stage of development for an idea, project, or enterprise **3.** TIME OF BEING MINOR the condition or time in which a young person is not legally considered an adult

infant /ínfənt/ *n* **1.** BABY a very young child that can neither walk nor talk **2.** YOUNG SCHOOLCHILD a schoolchild between the ages of five and seven **3.** LEGAL MINOR a young person legally considered a minor ■ **infants** *npl* INFANT SECTION OF SCHOOL the infant department of a primary school (*informal*) ■ *adj* JUST BEGINNING in an early stage of development [14C. Via French < Latin *infant-* 'not speaking' < *fari* 'speak'] —**infanthood** *n*

infanta /in fántə/ (*plural* **-tas**) *n* **1.** the daughter of a Spanish or Portuguese king **2.** the wife of an infante [Late 16C. < Spanish, Portuguese, form of *infante* (see INFANTE)]

infante /in fánti/ (*plural* **-tes**) *n* a son, other than the heir to the throne, of a Spanish or Portuguese king, especially the second son [Mid-16C. Via Spanish, Portuguese < Latin *infant-* (see INFANT)]

infanticide /in fánti sīd/ *n* **1.** MURDER OF INFANT the act of killing an infant **2.** KILLING OF BABIES the practice of killing newborn babies **3.** KILLER OF INFANT a killer of an infant —**infanticidal** /in fánti sīd'l/ *adj*

infantile /ínfən tīl/ *adj* **1.** showing a lack of maturity **2.** relating to infants or infancy —**infantility** /ínfən tílləti/ *n*

infantile paralysis *n* MED same as **poliomyelitis** (*dated*)

infantilise *vt* another spelling of **infantilize**

infantilism /in fántilizəm/ *n* childish or immature behaviour

infantilize /in fánti līz/ (**-izes, -izing, -ized**), **infantilise** (**-ises, -ising, -ised**) *vt* **1.** to make somebody infantile, or keep somebody in an infantile state **2.** to treat somebody as or consider somebody to be infantile —**infantilization** /in fánti lī záysh'n/ *n*

infant mortality rate *n* the number of infant deaths during the first year of life per thousand live births

infantry /ínfəntri/ (*plural* **-tries**) *n* **1.** soldiers who are trained to fight on foot, or a unit of such soldiers of infantry making up a regiment **2.** a unit or branch of an army [Late 16C. < French *infanterie* < Italian *infante* 'youth, foot soldier' < Latin *infant-* (see INFANT)]

infantryman /ínfəntrimən/ (*plural* **-men** /-mən/) *n* a soldier in an infantry

infant school *n* a school, or part of a school, for children between the ages of four or five and seven

infarct /in faárkt/ *n* an area of tissue that has recently died as a result of the sudden loss of its blood supply, e.g. following blockage of an artery by a

blood clot [Late 19C. < modern Latin *infarctus* < the past participle of Latin *infarcire* 'cram in' < *farcire* 'to stuff']

infarction /in faárksh'n/ *n* **1.** the formation of an infarct **2.** same as **infarct**

infatuate /in fáttyoo ayt/ (-ates, -ating, -ated) *vt* to make somebody behave irrationally as a result of a great, often temporary, passion (*usually passive*) [Mid-16C. < Latin *infatuat-*, past participle of *infatuare* 'make foolish' < *fatuus* 'foolish'] —**infatuated** *adj* —**infatuatedly** *adv*

infatuation /in fáttyoo áysh'n/ *n* **1.** an intense but short-lived and irrational passion for somebody or something **2.** the person or object that somebody is infatuated with

SYNONYMS See *love*.

infauna /in fáwnə/ *npl* organisms that live in tubes or burrows beneath the surface of the sea floor [Early 20C. < IN-² + FAUNA] —**infaunal** *adj*

infeasible /in feézəb'l/ *adj* not practical or easily achieved —**infeasibility** /in feézə bílləti/ *n* —**infeasibleness** *n* —**infeasibly** *adv*

infect /in fékt/ (-fects, -fecting, -fected) *vt* **1.** CAUSE INFECTION IN SOMEBODY to contaminate a person, animal, or organ with a disease-producing agent **2.** CAUSE SOMEBODY TO HAVE COMMUNICABLE DISEASE to give a person or animal a communicable disease **3.** ENTER PERSON OR ANIMAL to invade and live in the body of a person or animal (*refers to microorganisms or endoparasites*) **4.** AFFECT SOMEBODY OR SOMETHING ADVERSELY to corrupt or adversely affect somebody or something **5.** INFLUENCE SOMEBODY'S FEELINGS to communicate an emotion such as enthusiasm or fear to somebody **6.** COMPUT CONTAMINATE COMPUTER to copy to a computer system a computer virus that is capable of damaging the system's programs or data [14C. < Latin *infect-*, past participle of *inficere* 'stain', literally 'dip in' < *facere* 'do'] —**infected** *adj* —**infector** *n*

infection /in féksh'n/ *n* **1.** DISEASE a communicable disease **2.** INFECTING OF OTHERS the transmission of infectious microorganisms from one person to another **3.** INFECTING MICROORGANISM an infecting microorganism or agent **4.** STATE OF BEING INFECTED the reproduction and proliferation of microorganisms within the body **5.** TRANSMISSION OF FEELINGS the communication of emotions or attitudes between people **6.** MORAL CORRUPTION something that corrupts somebody morally

infectious /in fékshəss/ *adj* **1.** COMMUNICABLE describes a disease that is capable of being passed from one person to another **2.** CAUSED BY BACTERIA caused by bacteria, viruses, or other microorganisms **3.** CAUSING INFECTION bringing about infection **4.** AFFECTING FEELINGS OF OTHERS capable of affecting the emotions and attitudes of others —**infectiously** *adv* —**infectiousness** *n*

infectious hepatitis *n* MED same as **hepatitis A**

infectious mononucleosis *n* same as **glandular fever** (*technical*)

infective /in féktiv/ *adj* **1.** capable of producing an infection **2.** capable of affecting the emotions and attitudes of others —**infectiveness** *n* —**infectivity** /ín fek tívvəti/ *n*

infelicitous /ínfə líssitəss/ *adj* inappropriate to the situation or purpose (*formal*) —**infelicitously** *adv*

infelicity /ínfə líssəti/ (*plural* -ties) *n* (*formal*) **1.** the inappropriateness of something, especially an expression, to a particular situation **2.** something inappropriate to a situation or purpose, especially an expression [Early 17C. < Latin *infelicitas* 'unhappiness' < *felix* 'happy'] —**infelicitous** *adj*

infer /in fúr/ (-fers, -ferring, -ferred) *v* **1.** *vti* CONCLUDE SOMETHING FROM REASONING to come to a conclusion or form an opinion about something on the basis of evidence or reasoning ○ *I inferred from his behaviour that he was no longer interested in setting a good example.* **2.** *vt* INDICATE SOMETHING to lead you necessarily to suppose or conclude something (*formal*) ○ *The steepness of the cliffs would normally infer modern erosion.* **3.** *vt* IMPLY SOMETHING to imply or suggest something [Early 16C. < Latin *inferre* 'bring in' < *ferre* 'carry'] —**inferable** *adj* —**inferably** *adv* —**inferrer** *n*

SYNONYMS See *deduce*.

inference /ínfərənss/ *n* **1.** CONCLUSION a conclusion drawn from evidence or reasoning **2.** LOGIC REASONING PROCESS the process of reasoning from a premise to a conclusion **3.** IMPLICATION something that is implied [Late 16C. < medieval Latin *inferentia* < Latin *inferre* (see INFER)] —**inferential** /ínfə rénsh'l/ *adj* —**inferentially** *adv*

inferior /in feéri ər/ *adj* **1.** LOWER IN STANDING lower or low in rank, standing, or degree **2.** NOT AS GOOD lower in quality or value **3.** MEDIOCRE failing to meet a standard of quality, ability, or achievement **4.** ANAT LOWER IN BODY describes a body part or organ situated beneath another similar part **5.** BOT BELOW CALYX describes a plant ovary located below a calyx **6.** ASTRON BETWEEN EARTH AND SUN orbiting or taking place between Earth and the Sun. Mercury and Venus are designated as inferior planets. **7.** PRINTING PRINTED BELOW LINE written or printed at a slightly lower level than the rest of the characters in a line, e.g. the '2' in 'CO₂' ■ *n* **1.** LOWER RANKING PERSON somebody of lower status, rank, or quality **2.** PRINTING SUBSCRIPT CHARACTER a character printed or written below the line [15C. < Latin, 'lower' < *inferus* 'below'] —**inferiority** /in feéri órrəti/ *n* —**inferiorly** *adv*

inferiority complex *n* an overdeveloped sense of being inferior to other people. In extreme cases it can manifest itself in either withdrawn or aggressive social behaviour.

infernal /in fúrn'l/ *adj* **1.** VERY ANNOYING extremely annoying or unpleasant **2.** RELATING TO UNDERWORLD relating to hell or the underworld **3.** DIABOLICAL IN NATURE so extreme, wicked, or cruel as to be worthy of hell [14C. < Old French < late Latin *infernus* 'lower, the underworld' < Latin *inferus* 'below'] —**infernally** *adv*

inferno /in fúrnō/ (*plural* -nos) *n* **1.** a very large fire burning fiercely and uncontrollably, or a place being consumed by a large uncontrollable fire **2.** a place or situation that is reminiscent of hell, e.g. in being hot, fiery, or full of corruption [Mid-19C. Via Italian, 'hell' < late Latin *infernus* (see INFERNAL)]

CULTURAL NOTE See *fire*.

Inferno *n* RELIG same as **hell** *n* (sense 1)

CULTURAL NOTE *The Inferno*, a poem (1307?–20?) by Italian poet Dante Alighieri. The first part of the epic masterpiece *The Divine Comedy*, it describes the poet's journey through Hell with Virgil as his guide. Hell is depicted as funnel-shaped, with a different category of sinner on each of the circular steps, which decrease in size as they descend. The presence of certain historical figures among these sinners, and the punishments they receive, reflect Dante's personal opinions and judgments on past issues and events.

infertile /in fúr tīl/ *adj* **1.** STERILE physically incapable of conceiving offspring **2.** NOT PRODUCING CROPS incapable of producing crops **3.** NOT FERTILIZED describes an egg that has not been fertilized —**infertilely** *adv* —**infertility** /ínfər tílləti/ *n*

infest /in fést/ (-fests, -festing, -fested) *vt* **1.** to overrun a place or site in large numbers and become threatening, harmful, or unpleasant ○ *Their clothing was infested with lice.* **2.** to live as a parasite on or in something [Mid-16C. Directly or via French < Latin *infestare* 'to attack' < *infestus* 'hostile'] —**infestation** /ín fe stáysh'n/ *n* —**infested** *adj* —**infester** *n*

infibulate /in fíbbyoŏ layt/ (-lates, -lating, -lated) *vt* to close the vagina of a girl or woman partially by stitching it or closing it with a clasp. The clitoris is often removed at the same time. The practice is traditional in some northeastern African cultures, but disapproved of and even outlawed in some countries. [Early 17C. < Latin *infibulat-*, past participle of *infibulare* 'fasten with a pin' < *fibula* 'brooch'] —**infibulation** /in fíbbyoŏ láysh'n/ *n*

infidel /ínfid'l/ *n* (*disapproving*) **1.** somebody who does not believe in a major religion, especially Christianity or Islam **2.** somebody with no religious belief [15C. Directly or via French < Latin *infidelis* 'unbelieving' < *fidelis* 'faithful' < *fides* 'trust, belief']

infidelity /ínfi délləti/ (*plural* -ties) *n* **1.** UNFAITHFULNESS unfaithfulness or disloyalty, especially to a sexual partner **2.** UNFAITHFUL ACT an act of unfaithfulness or disloyalty, especially to a sexual partner **3.** DISBELIEF absence of religious belief (*disapproving*)

infield /ín feeld/ *n* **1.** CRICKET AREA NEAR WICKET IN CRICKET the area of the field of play that is close to the wickets **2.** BASEBALL DIAMOND the area of a baseball field bounded by home plate and the three bases **3.** BASEBALL PLAYERS IN INFIELD the defensive players in the infield considered together. They are the first, second, and third basemen and the shortstop. **4.** HORSERACING AREA WITHIN RACETRACK the area bounded by a racetrack **5.** FARMLAND CLOSE TO FARMHOUSE the farmland close to a farmhouse that is regularly manured and cropped

infielder /ín feeldər/ *n* **1.** a fielder stationed in the infield **2.** a defensive baseball player in the infield

infighting /ín fīting/ *n* **1.** conflict or rivalry between associates or members of the same organization **2.** boxing or fighting at close range —**infighter** *n*

infill /ín fil/ *n* the filling of gaps, especially of vacant areas between existing buildings ■ *vt* (-fills, -filling, -filled) to build new buildings in gaps between existing buildings —**infilling** *n*

infiltrate /ínfil trayt/ *vti* (-trates, -trating, -trated) **1.** ENTER ORGANIZATION TO SPY ON IT to become part of an organization, or enter a place, surreptitiously in order to gather information or influence events, or send agents to do this ○ *Activists were infiltrated into local party organizations.* **2.** MIL ENTER ENEMY TERRITORY SECRETLY to cross into enemy territory without the enemy's knowledge, or send somebody into enemy territory in this way ○ *infiltrate troops behind enemy lines* **3.** CHEM PERMEATE FLUID THROUGH SUBSTANCE to pass through a substance by filtration, or make a liquid or gas pass through a substance by filtration ■ *n* MED FATTY ACCUMULATION a substance that gradually accumulates in tissues and cells, e.g. fat —**infiltration** /ínfil tráysh'n/ *n* —**infiltrative** *adj* —**infiltrator** *n*

infimum /ínfiməm/ (*plural* -ma /-mə/) *n* a number less than or equal to all elements of a set, thus a lower bound, but greater than or equal to all other lower bounds of the set [Mid-20C. < Latin, 'lowest part']

infinite /ínfinət/ *adj* **1.** NOT MEASURABLE without any finite or measurable limits **2.** EXCEEDINGLY GREAT very great in size, number, degree, or extent ○ *He took infinite pains over it.* **3.** MATHS GREATER THAN ANY ASSIGNED VALUE greater in number, size, or scope than any arbitrarily assigned value **4.** MATHS WITH UNLIMITED SPATIAL EXTENT having unlimited spatial extent **5.** MATHS WITH INDEFINITE ELEMENTS having an indefinitely extendable number of terms or elements **6.** MATHS IN ONE-TO-ONE RELATIONSHIP describes a set able to be put into a one-to-one mathematical correspondence with a subset of itself ■ *n* SOMETHING INFINITE something that is infinite, e.g. space [14C. Via French < Latin *infinitus* 'not bounded' < *finitus* (see FINITE)] —**infinitely** *adv* —**infiniteness** *n*

Infinite *n* same as **God**

infinite loop *n* a series of instructions in a computer program containing errors that make it repeat endlessly

infinitesimal /ínfini téssim'l/ *adj* **1.** TINY very small in number, amount, or degree **2.** MATHS CLOSE TO ZERO able to assume values arbitrarily close to but greater than zero ■ *n* INFINITESIMAL NUMBER an infinitesimal number or function [Mid-17C. < modern Latin *infinitesimus* 'the number in a series corresponding to infinity' < Latin *infinitus* (see INFINITE)] —**infinitesimally** *adv*

infinitesimal calculus *n* MATHS same as **calculus** (sense 1)

infinitive /in fínnitiv/ *n* a form of a verb with no reference to a specific tense, person, or subject. In English, an infinitive is usually preceded by the word 'to', e.g., 'to see'. [15C. < late Latin *infinitivus* < Latin *infinitus* (see INFINITE)] —**infinitival** /in fínni tív'l/ *adj* —**infinitivally** *adv*

infinitude /in fínni tyood/ *n* **1.** the infinite nature of something **2.** a very great number, degree, or extent of something [Mid-17C. < Latin *infinitus* (see INFINITE)]

infinity /in fínnəti/ (*plural* -ties) *n* **1.** SOMETHING WITHOUT LIMITS limitless time, space, or distance ○ *Beyond the Earth lay infinity.* **2.** SOMETHING TOO GREAT TO COUNT an amount or number so great that it cannot be counted ○ *an infinity of stars* **3.** STATE OF BEING INFINITE the state or quality of being infinite **4.** MATHS CONCEPT OF BEING ALWAYS UNLIMITED the concept of being unlimited

by always being larger than any imposed value or boundary. For some purposes this may be considered as being the same as one divided by zero. **5.** MATHS **GEOMETRIC POINT AT INFINITE DISTANCE** a part of a geometric figure situated an infinite distance from the observer, e.g. the hypothetical point at which parallel lines meet in Euclidean geometry **6.** OPTICS **INFINITELY DISTANT POINT** a point sufficiently far from a lens or mirror that the light emitted from it falls in parallel rays on the surface [14C. < French *infinité* < Latin *infinitus* (see INFINITE)]

infirm /in fúrm/ *adj* **1.** NOT STRONG lacking strength and vitality because of sickness or age **2.** IRRESOLUTE lacking firmness of character or a strong will **3.** LAW LEGALLY UNSOUND describes a legal claim that is invalid or not supported ■ *npl* PEOPLE WHO ARE NOT STRONG people who lack strength and vitality, e.g. because of sickness or age (*sometimes considered offensive*) [14C. < Latin *infirmus* < *firmus* 'firm'] —**infirmly** *adv* —**infirmness** *n*

SYNONYMS See *weak*.

infirmary /in fúrməri/ (*plural* **-ries**) *n* a hospital or area within an institution where sick and injured people are cared for [15C. < medieval Latin *infirmaria* < Latin *infirmus* (see INFIRM)]

infirmity /in fúrməti/ (*plural* **-ties**) *n* **1.** LACK OF STRENGTH lack of strength and vitality **2.** CHARACTER FLAW a weakness or failing in somebody's character **3.** MINOR ILLNESS any medical condition that causes a lack of strength or vitality

infix /ín fiks/ *vt* (**-fixes, -fixing, -fixed**) **1.** FIX SOMETHING FIRMLY IN SOMETHING ELSE to insert something into another thing in order to secure it **2.** INSTIL SOMETHING IN MIND to secure something firmly in the mind **3.** GRAM PUT ELEMENT IN WORD to insert a linking element into a word. In the word 'acidophilus', the letter 'o' is an infix. ■ *n* GRAM AFFIX IN MIDDLE an affix inserted into the middle of a word —**infixation** /ínfik sáysh'n/ *n* —**infixion** *n*

infl. *abbr* **1.** inflammable **2.** BOT inflorescence **3.** influence **4.** influenced

in flagrante delicto /in flə gránti di líktō/, **in flagrante** *adv* **1.** in the act of having sexual relations, especially illicit sexual relations **2.** in the act of committing an offence [< Latin, 'in the heat of the crime']

inflame /in fláym/ (**-flames, -flaming, -flamed**) *v* **1.** *vt* PROVOKE POWERFUL RESPONSE IN SOMEBODY to excite an intense emotion, especially anger or jealousy, in somebody **2.** *vt* MAKE EMOTION STRONGER to make an emotion such as anger or jealousy become more intense **3.** *vti* MED MAKE TISSUE SWELL AND TURN RED to become, or make body tissue become, red and swollen, in response to injury or infection [14C. Via French < Latin *inflammare* < *flamma* 'flame'] —**inflamed** *adj* —**inflamer** *n*

inflammable /in flámməb'l/ *adj* **1.** EASILY SET ON FIRE quickly and easily set on fire and burned **2.** EASILY ROUSED easily made angry or passionate ■ *n* FLAMMABLE ITEM something that is quickly and easily set on fire and burned [Early 17C. < medieval Latin *inflammabilis* 'liable to inflammation' < Latin *inflammare* (see INFLAME)] —**inflammability** /in flámmə bílləti/ *n* —**inflammableness** *n* —**inflammably** *adv*

USAGE See *flammable*.

inflammation /ínflə máysh'n/ *n* **1.** swelling, redness, heat, and pain produced in an area of the body as a reaction to injury or infection **2.** a heightening or stirring up of emotion

inflammatory /in flámmətəri/ *adj* **1.** liable to arouse strong emotions, especially anger **2.** caused or characterized by inflammation —**inflammatorily** *adv*

inflammatory bowel disease *n* a disease causing inflammation of the bowel, typically Crohn's disease or ulcerative colitis

inflatable /in fláytəb'l/ *adj* made of expandable material that can be filled with air or gas ■ *n* something such as a boat, mattress, or plaything that has to be be filled with air or gas before use

inflate /in fláyt/ (**-flates, -flating, -flated**) *vti* **1.** EXPAND WITH AIR to fill something such as a ball, mattress, tyre, or boat with air or gas to bring it to the proper size, shape, and firmness for use, or to become filled with air or gas **2.** MAKE SOMETHING APPEAR GREATER to exaggerate

the size or importance of something, or become exaggerated in size or importance **3.** ECON INCREASE PRICES OR MONEY SUPPLY to cause inflation in prices or the money supply, or undergo inflation [15C. < Latin *inflat-*, past participle of *inflare* 'blow into' < *flare* 'to blow'] —**inflator** *n*

inflated /in fláytid/ *adj* **1.** UNDESERVEDLY GREAT greater than is justified or normal ○ *an inflated sense of her own importance* **2.** ECON EXCESSIVELY HIGH excessively or unusually high **3.** PRETENTIOUS exaggerated or pompous in expression **4.** BLOWN UP expanded with air or gas —**inflatedly** *adv* —**inflatedness** *n*

inflation /in fláysh'n/ *n* **1.** ECON HIGHER PRICES an increase in the supply of currency or credit relative to the availability of goods and services, resulting in higher prices and a decrease in the purchasing power of money **2.** BEING INFLATED the act of inflating something, or the condition of being inflated **3.** PROUD CONDITION the condition of being puffed up with pride **4.** ASTRON EARLY EXPANSION OF UNIVERSE a period of rapidly accelerating expansion of the early universe after the big bang

inflationary /in fláysh'nəri/ *adj* relating to or causing economic inflation ○ *inflationary policies*

inflationary spiral *n* a continuous economic cycle in which higher prices cause higher wages, which in turn cause even higher prices

inflationary theory *n* a theory in cosmology that there was a period of rapid acceleration during the expansion of the early universe after the big bang

inflationism /in fláysh'nizəm/ *n* the advocacy or policy of deliberately causing economic inflation through an increase in the supply of available currency and credit —**inflationist** *adj, n*

inflect /in flékt/ (**-flects, -flecting, -flected**) *v* **1.** *vt* VARY PITCH OF VOICE to change the pitch or tone of the voice **2.** *vti* GRAM CHANGE WORD FORM to change the form of a word, e.g. to show a change in tense, mood, gender, or number, or be changed in this way **3.** *vt* DIVERT COURSE OF SOMETHING to make something turn from a direct line or course [15C. < Latin *inflectere* 'bend in' < *flectere* 'to bend'] —**inflectable** *adj* —**inflected** *adj* —**inflective** *adj* —**inflector** *n*

inflection /in fléksh'n/, **inflexion** *n* **1.** CHANGE IN PITCH a change in the pitch or tone of the voice **2.** GRAM WORD CHANGE a change in the form of a word, often an addition at the end of it, that indicates a particular grammatical function, e.g. the 's' added to most English nouns when they are plural **3.** GRAM ALTERED FORM OF WORD an altered form of a word, e.g. one showing a change in tense, mood, gender, or number, or the part of the word that changes in this way **4.** BENDING a turning from a straight line or course, or a more general change in direction **5.** MATHS same as **point of inflection** —**inflectional** *adj* —**inflectionally** *adv* —**inflectionless** *adj*

inflection point *n* N Am same as **point of inflection**

inflexed /in flékst/ *adj* describes a plant part that is bent inwards or downwards towards the stem [Mid-17C. < Latin *inflex-*, past participle of *inflectere* (see INFLECT)]

inflexible /in fléksəb'l/ *adj* **1.** UNBENDING adhering firmly to a viewpoint or principle **2.** IMPOSSIBLE TO CHANGE firmly established and impossible to change ○ *an inflexible rule* **3.** RIGID stiff and bendable only with difficulty —**inflexibility** /in fléksə bílləti/ *n* —**inflexibly** *adv*

inflexion *n* GRAM, MATHS another spelling of **inflection**

inflict /in flíkt/ (**-flicts, -flicting, -flicted**) *vt* **1.** to be the cause of something harmful or unpleasant such as loss, injury, or damage to somebody or something ○ *Our artillery inflicted heavy casualties on the enemy forces.* **2.** to impose something burdensome or inconvenient on somebody ○ *In that case I won't inflict my company on you any longer.* [Mid-16C. < Latin *inflict-*, past participle of *infligere* 'strike upon' < *fligere* 'to hit'] —**inflictable** *adj* —**inflicter** *n* —**infliction** /in flíksh'n/ *n* —**inflictive** *adj*

USAGE See *afflict*.

in-flight *adj* taking place or provided for passengers during an aircraft journey ○ *in-flight entertainment*

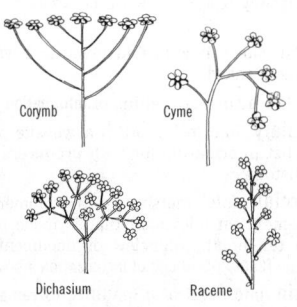

Corymb   Cyme

Dichasium   Raceme

inflorescence

inflorescence /ínflə réss'nss/ *n* BOT **1.** FLOWERING PART OF PLANT a flowering structure that consists of more than one flower and usually comprises distinct individual flowers **2.** WAY FLOWERS GROW the arrangement or manner in which flowers develop on a stalk **3.** FLOWERING the budding and flowering of a plant [Mid-18C. < modern Latin *inflorescentia* < Latin *inflorescere* 'come into flower' < *flor-* 'flower']

inflow /ín flō/ *n* **1.** SOMETHING THAT FLOWS IN something that flows into a place or container **2.** INFLUX an instance or the process of flowing in **3.** SITE OF INFLOW the point at which something flows in —**inflowing** *n*

influence /ín floo ənss/ *n* **1.** EFFECT ON SOMETHING the effect of something on a person, thing, or event ○ *Picasso's influence on the course of 20th-century art* **2.** POWER TO SWAY the power that somebody has to affect other people's thinking or actions by means of argument, example, or force of personality ○ *She came under the influence of one of her teachers.* **3.** SPECIAL ADVANTAGE the power or authority that comes from wealth, social status, or position **4.** SOMEBODY WHO CAN SWAY ANOTHER somebody or something able to affect the course of events or somebody's thinking or action ○ *He's a bad influence on you.* **5.** STARS' EFFECT ON PEOPLE in astrology, an emanation that is believed to come from the stars and planets and to affect human characteristics, personality, and actions ■ *vt* (**-ences, -encing, -enced**) **1.** SWAY SOMEBODY to have an effect on somebody that helps to determine that person's actions, behaviour, or way of thinking ○ *What influenced you in your choice of career?* **2.** AFFECT SOMETHING to have the power to affect something ○ *the factors that influence a nation's development* [14C. < medieval Latin *influentia* < Latin *influere* 'flow in' < *fluere* 'to flow'] —**influenceable** *adj* —**influencer** *n* ◇ **under the influence** intoxicated by having drunk alcohol (*informal*)

~~**influencial**~~ incorrect spelling of **influential**

influent /ín floo ənt/ *n* a stream flowing into a lake or larger river [15C. < Latin *influent-*, present participle of *influere* (see INFLUENCE)]

influential /ín floo énsh'l/ *adj* able to have a powerful effect on people and what they do, or on events —**influentially** *adv*

influenza /ín floo énzə/ *n* **1.** a viral illness producing a high temperature, sore throat, runny nose, headache, dry cough, and muscle pain. The illness is widespread, especially during winter months, and can sometimes be fatal. (*technical*) **2.** a viral disease of domestic animals, usually characterized by fever and respiratory problems [Mid-18C. Via Italian < medieval Latin *influentia* (see INFLUENCE); referring to the supposed influence of the stars] —**influenzal** *adj*

influx /ín fluks/ *n* **1.** a sudden arrival of a large number of people or things ○ *dealing with the influx of tourists into the city* **2.** a flowing in, especially of a stream or river [Late 16C. < late Latin *influxus* < past participle of Latin *influere* (see INFLUENCE)]

influx control *n* the control over the movement of Black people into urban areas exerted by the South African government in the apartheid era through its system of rigid pass laws

info[1] /ínfō/ *n* same as **information** (*informal*) [Early 20C. Shortening]

info[2] *abbr* ONLINE general use (*used in Internet addresses*) See table at **domain name**

infobahn /ínfō baan/ *n* ONLINE same as **information**

superhighway [Late 20C. Blend of INFORMATION + AUTOBAHN]

infold /in fṓld/ *v* **1.** *vi* to fold inwards **2.** *vt* another spelling of **enfold**

~~**infomation**~~ incorrect spelling of **information**

infomediary /ínfō meédi əri/ *n* a website providing specialist information for both producers of goods and customers

infomercial /ínfō múrsh'l/ *n* a commercial advertisement on television that is made to appear like a full-length interview or documentary programme [Late 20C. Blend of INFORMATION + COMMERCIAL]

infonesia /ínfō neési ə/ *n* inability to remember an item of information or its location, especially on the Internet (*informal*)

inform /in fáwrm/ (**-forms, -forming, -formed**) *v* **1.** *vt* **TELL SOMEBODY** to communicate information or knowledge to somebody ○ *The police informed us of the accident.* **2. inform yourself** *vr* **LEARN ABOUT SOMETHING** to familiarize yourself with a subject **3.** *vi* **GIVE INFORMATION TO POLICE** to give confidential or incriminating information about somebody else's activities, especially to the police **4.** *vt* ARTS **BE ESSENTIAL CHARACTERISTIC OF SOMETHING** to play an essential part in determining the nature, shape, or structure of something ○ *His religious beliefs inform his entire work.* **5.** *vt* **GIVE STRUCTURE TO SOMETHING** to give structure or substance to something (*formal*) ○ *the ethics that inform the profession* [14C. Via French < Latin *informare* 'give form to' < *forma* 'shape']

informal /in fáwrm'l/ *adj* **1. FREE OF CEREMONY** relaxed and casual rather than ceremonious and stiff **2. UNOFFICIAL** not officially prepared, organized, or sanctioned ○ *The two sides in the conflict held informal talks.* **3.** CLOTHING **CASUAL AND EVERYDAY** suitable for casual or everyday situations ○ *informal dress* **4.** LANGUAGE **COLLOQUIAL** more appropriate in spoken than written form —**informality** /ín fawr mállәti/ *n* —**informally** *adv*

informal economy *n* economic activities organized without government approval, outside mainstream industry and commerce

informal vote *n ANZ* a ballot paper which is not filled in or incorrectly filled in and is declared invalid

informant /in fáwrmәnt/ *n* **1.** somebody who gives information to somebody else **2.** somebody who gives confidential or incriminating information to the police about somebody else

informatics /ínfәr máttiks/ *n* INFO SCI same as **information science** (*takes a singular verb*) [Mid-20C. < INFORMATION, after Russian *informatika*]

information /ínfәr máysh'n/ *n* **1. KNOWLEDGE** definite knowledge acquired or supplied about something or somebody ○ *a bulletin giving the latest information on the trial* **2. GATHERED FACTS** the collected facts and data about a specific subject **3. MAKING FACTS KNOWN** the communication of facts and knowledge **4.** COMPUT **ORGANIZED COMPUTER DATA** the meaningful material derived from computer data by organizing it and interpreting it in a specific way **5.** LAW **FORMAL CRIMINAL ACCUSATION** a formal accusation of a crime brought before a court or magistrate **6.** TELECOM *N Am* same as **directory enquiries** —**informational** *adj* —**informationally** *adv*

SYNONYMS See ***knowledge***.

information age *n* a period characterized by widespread electronic access to information through the use of computer technology

information appliance *n* a small portable digital information-processing machine compatible with an electronic network

information processing *n* the organization, manipulation, analysis, and distribution of data, nowadays typically carried out by computers

information retrieval *n* the process of systematically searching for and retrieving stored computerized data

information science *n* the study of the collection, categorization, and distribution of data, particularly computer data

information superhighway *n* the worldwide computer network that includes the Internet, private networks, and proprietary online services. It permits the rapid sending of many different forms of data, including voice, video, and text.

information technology *n* the use of technologies from computing, electronics, and telecommunications to process and distribute information in digital and other forms

information theory *n* the mathematical study of the transmission, reception, storage, and retrieval of information based on the statistical analysis of communication between humans and machines

informative /in fáwrmәtiv/ *adj* providing useful information —**informatively** *adv* —**informativeness** *n*

informed /in fáwrmd/ *adj* **1.** having sufficient and sufficiently reliable information or knowledge to be able to understand a subject or situation and make appropriate judgments or decisions regarding it ○ *informed citizens* **2.** based on an accurate knowledge and understanding of the situation or subject in question ○ *an informed decision* —**informedly** /in fáwrmidli/ *adv*

informed consent *n* agreement by a patient to undergo an operation or medical treatment or take part in a clinical trial after being informed of and having understood the risks involved

informer /in fáwrmәr/ *n* **1.** somebody who gives the police or authorities information about criminal activities **2.** somebody or something that provides information about a subject or situation

infotainment /ínfō táynmәnt/ *n* television programmes that deal with serious issues or current affairs in an entertaining way [Late 20C. Blend of INFORMATION + ENTERTAINMENT] —**infotainer** *n*

infra /ínfrә/ *adv* used in an explanatory note to refer a reader to a point later in a text, especially in the phrase 'vide infra' (*formal*) [Late 19C. < Latin]

infra- *prefix* below, beneath, inferior ○ *infrasonic* ○ *infraclass* [< Latin *infra* 'below' < Indo-European]

infraclass /ínfrә klaass/ *n* a taxonomic category of organisms that is above an order and below a subclass

infracostal /ínfrә kóst'l/ *adj* lying below the ribs

infract /in frákt/ (**-fracts, -fracting, -fracted**) *vt* to fail to obey or fulfil a law, contract, or agreement [Late 18C. < Latin *infract-*, past participle of *infringere* (see INFRINGE)] —**infractor** *n*

infraction /in fráksh'n/ *n* failure to obey or fulfil a law, contract, or agreement, or an instance of this [15C. Directly and via French < Latin *infraction-* < *infractus* (see INFRACT)]

infra dig /ínfrә díg/ *adj* below the standard of social behaviour that somebody usually maintains (*informal*) [Early 19C. Shortening of Latin *infra dignitatem* 'beneath dignity']

infrahuman /ínfrә hyóomәn/ *adj* in the system of classifying living organisms, belonging to a lower order than human beings

infrangible /in fránjәb'l/ *adj* (*formal*) **1.** unable to be broken or separated into pieces **2.** unable to be disregarded or violated —**infrangibility** /in fránjә bíllәti/ *n* —**infrangibleness** *n* —**infrangibly** *adv*

infrared /ínfrә réd/ *n* the portion of the invisible electromagnetic spectrum consisting of radiation with wavelengths in the range 750 nm to 1 mm, between light and radio waves ○ *infrared radiation* ■ *adj* using, producing, or affected by infrared radiation [Late 19C. Because it lies below the red end of the visible spectrum]

infrared astronomy *n* the study of astronomical objects by examining the wavelengths they emit in the infrared range. Infrared sources within our galaxy include cool gas giants and the galactic centre.

infrared photography *n* photography with film that is sensitive to infrared radiation, used e.g. for taking pictures at night or in haze and in detecting camouflaged objects

infrasonic /ínfrә sónnik/ *adj* **1.** relating to sound at frequencies below 20 Hz, which cannot be heard by human beings but can be felt as vibration **2.** using or produced by infrasonic waves or vibrations —**infrasonically** *adv*

infrasound /ínfrә sownd/ *n* sound at frequencies below 20 Hz, which cannot be heard by humans but can be felt as vibration

infrastructure /ínfrә strukchәr/ *n* **1.** the most basic level of organizational structure in a complex body or system that serves as a foundation for the rest **2.** the large-scale public systems, services, and facilities of a country or region that are necessary for economic activity, including power and water supplies, public transport, telecommunications, roads, and schools

infrequent /in freékwәnt/ *adj* not appearing, happening, or encountered very often ○ *Her visits became more infrequent.* —**infrequence** *n* —**infrequency** *n* —**infrequently** *adv*

infringe /in frínj/ (**-fringes, -fringing, -fringed**) *v* **1.** *vt* to fail to obey a law or regulation or observe the terms of an agreement **2.** *vti* to take over land, rights, privileges, or activities that belong to somebody else, especially in a minor or gradual way ○ *infringing on our personal freedom* [Mid-16C. < Latin *infringere* 'to damage' < *frangere* 'to break'] —**infringement** *n* —**infringer** *n*

infundibula ANAT plural of **infundibulum**

infundibuliform /ín fun díbbyŏŏli fawrm/ *adj* describes a flower or other plant part that resembles a funnel in shape

infundibulum /ín fun díbbyŏŏlәm/ (*plural* **-la** /-lә/) *n* a funnel-shaped opening, passage, or structure in vertebrates, e.g. the stalk connecting the pituitary gland to the brain or the opening of a fallopian tube into the ovary [Mid-16C. < Latin, 'funnel' < *infundere* (see INFUSE)] —**infundibular** *adj* —**infundibulate** /ín fun díbbyŏŏ layt, -lәt/ *adj*

infuriate /in fyóori ayt/ (**-ates, -ating, -ated**) *vt* to make somebody extremely angry [Mid-17C. < medieval Latin *infuriat-*, past participle of *infuriare* < *furiare* 'to anger' < Latin *furia* (see FURY)] —**infuriated** *adj* —**infuriatedly** *adv* —**infuriating** *adj* —**infuriatingly** *adv* —**infuriation** /in fyóori áysh'n/ *n*

infuse /in fyóoz/ (**-fuses, -fusing, -fused**) *v* **1.** *vt* **FILL SOMEBODY WITH EMOTION** to fill somebody or something with a strong emotion such as hatred, enthusiasm, or desire (*often passive*) **2.** *vt* **INTRODUCE SOMETHING INTO SOMEBODY'S MIND** to fix an emotion, belief, or quality gradually but firmly in somebody else's mind **3.** *vti* **STEEP SOMETHING IN LIQUID** to soak tea or herbs in liquid to extract the flavour or another property, or be soaked in this way **4.** *vt* MED **GIVE LIQUID USING DRIP** to introduce a solution such as saline, sucrose, or glucose using a drip into a vein, body cavity, or the intestinal tract in order to treat or feed a patient [15C. < Old French *infuser* < past participle of Latin *infundere* 'pour in' < *fundere* 'pour'] —**infuser** *n* —**infusible** *adj*

infusion /in fyóozh'n/ *n* **1. ACT OF INFUSING SOMETHING** the act of soaking something in a liquid in order to extract soluble matter **2. LIQUID MADE BY INFUSING SOMETHING** a liquid that is made by infusing something, e.g. tea **3. INTRODUCTION OF SOMETHING NEEDED** the addition of a new or necessary quality or element to something ○ *an infusion of private capital into the project* **4.** MED **ADMINISTERING OF LIQUID THROUGH DRIP** the introduction of a solution such as saline, sucrose, or glucose through a drip in order to treat or feed a patient **5.** MED **LIQUID ADMINISTERED THROUGH DRIP** a solution introduced into the body by infusion [14C. Via French < Latin *infusion-* < past participle of *infundere* (see INFUSE)]

infusorial earth /ínfyŏŏ záwri әl-/ *n* MINERALS same as **diatomaceous earth** (sense 2)

-ing[1] *suffix* **1.** forming the present participle of verbs ○ *raining* **2.** forming adjectives from words other than verbs ○ *swashbuckling* [Alteration of *-ende* < Old English]

-ing[2] *suffix* **1.** action or process ○ *rowing* ○ *cooking* **2.** result of (*archaic*) [Old English *-ung, -ing*]

-ing[3] *suffix* somebody or something that has a particular character ○ *gelding* [Old English, 'belonging to']

ingather /in gáthәr/ (**-ers, -ering, -ered**) *v* **1.** *vt* to gather in a harvest of something **2.** *vi* to come together or assemble (*formal or literary*) —**ingatherer** *n*

ingenious /in jeéni әss/ *adj* **1.** possessing cleverness and imagination **2.** clever, original, and effective ○ *an ingenious solution* [15C. Via French < Latin *ingeniosus* < *ingenium* 'mind'] —**ingeniously** *adv* —**ingeniousness** *n*

USAGE ingenious or **ingenuous**? Though spelt similarly, these two words have different meanings and so should not be used interchangeably. ***Ingenious*** means 'inventive' and 'cleverly effective', as in *a famed researcher with an ingenious* [not *ingenuous*] *mind; an ingenious* [not *ingenuous*] *marketing strategy.* By contrast, ***ingenuous*** means 'innocently unworldly' and 'being or seeming to be honest, candid, and direct', as in *an ingenuous* [not *ingenious*] *young child; an ingenuous* [not *ingenious*] *answer to the reporter's hostile question.*

ingénue /ánzhə nyoo/ *n* a girl or young woman who is naive and lacks experience or understanding of life [Mid-19C. Via French < Latin *ingenuus* (see INGENUOUS)]

ingenuity /ìnjə nyoó əti/ *n* cleverness and originality [Late 16C. < Latin *ingenuitas* < *ingenuus* (see INGENUOUS)]

ingenuous /in jénnyoo əss/ *adj* **1.** showing innocence and a lack of worldly experience **2.** appearing honest and direct [Late 16C. < Latin *ingenuus* 'native, honest' < *gignere* 'beget'] —**ingenuously** *adv* —**ingenuousness** *n*

USAGE See ***ingenious.***

ingest /in jést/ (**-gests, -gesting, -gested**) *vt* to take food, liquid, or some other substance into the body by swallowing or absorbing it [Early 17C. < Latin *ingest-*, past participle of *ingerere* 'carry in' < *gerere* 'carry'] —**ingestion** *n* —**ingestive** *adj*

ingesta /in jéstə/ *npl* food or liquid taken into the body by swallowing or absorbing [Early 18C. < Latin < *ingest-* (see INGEST)]

Ingham /íngəm/ town in northeastern Queensland, Australia, a major centre of sugar production. Population: 5,075 (1991).

ingle /íng g'l/ *n* a fireplace, or an open fire burning in a fireplace (*archaic*) [Early 16C. Origin ?]

inglenook /íng g'l nòok/ *n* **1.** a recess for a seat or bench beside a large fireplace, sometimes covered by the chimney-breast **2.** a seat built in an inglenook, especially one of two benches facing each other

inglorious /in gláwri əss/ *adj* **1.** bringing shame or dishonour **2.** not having received recognition, and so unknown or obscure (*archaic or literary*) [Mid-16C. < Latin *inglorius* < *gloria* 'glory'] —**ingloriously** *adv* —**ingloriousness** *n*

ingoing /ín gō ing/ *adj* in the process of entering, arriving, being received, or taking office ■ *n* an amount paid by a new tenant for fixtures left by the previous tenant (*often used in the plural*)

ingot /íng gət/ *n* **1.** a metal casting that is shaped, typically in an oblong, for easy working or for recasting **2.** a mould used for the casting of ingots [14C. Probably < Old English *in* 'in' + *gotan*, past participle of *gēotan* 'pour']

ingot iron *n* very pure iron that is produced in the same way as steel but using methods that reduce the carbon, manganese, and silicon content

ingraft *vt* BIOL another spelling of **engraft**

ingrain /in gráyn/, **engrain** *vt* (**-grains, -graining, -grained**) **IMPRESS SOMETHING ON SOMEBODY'S MIND** to impress a feeling, belief, or experience firmly and indelibly on somebody's mind (*usually passive*) ○ *The sight is still ingrained on my memory.* ■ *adj* **1.** same as **ingrained** (sense 1) **2.** TEXTILES **PREDYED** dyed before being spun or woven ■ *n* TEXTILES **1. PREDYED YARN OR FIBRE** yarn or fibre that is dyed before being spun or woven **2. PREDYED RUG OR CARPET** a rug or carpet made of yarn or fibre that is dyed before being spun or woven [15C. < IN [1] + GRAIN in the archaic sense 'cochineal, dye']

ingrained /in gráynd/ *adj* **1. WORKED DEEP INTO SOMETHING** worked into the surface, pores, or fibres of something and very difficult to remove ○ *ingrained dirt* **2. IMPRESSED ON SOMEBODY'S MIND** firmly fixed in somebody's mind and only removed or challenged with difficulty ○ *ingrained attitudes* **3. HABITUAL** long-established or confirmed in a habit or practice ○ *ingrained liar* —**ingrainedly** /-idli/ *adv* —**ingrainedness** /-idnəss/ *n*

ingrate /in grayt, in gráyt/ (*formal or literary*) *n* somebody who shows or feels no gratitude ■ *adj* showing or feeling no gratitude [15C. Via French < Latin *ingratus* (see INGRATITUDE)]

ingratiate /in gráyshi ayt/ (**-ates, -ating, -ated**) *vr* **ingratiate yourself** to try to win somebody's favour by pleasing him or her, especially in order to gain an advantage ○ *She made blatant attempts to ingratiate herself with top management.* [Early 17C. < Italian *ingraziare* < *in grazia* 'into favour' < Latin *gratia* 'favour'] —**ingratiation** /in gráyshi áysh'n/ *n* —**ingratiatory** *adj*

ingratiating /in gráyshi ayting/ *adj* designed to win somebody's approval, especially in order to gain an advantage —**ingratiatingly** *adv*

ingratitude /in grátti tyood/ *n* failure to express or feel gratitude [14C. Directly or via French < Latin *ingratitudo* < *ingratus* 'ungrateful' < *gratus* 'grateful']

~~**ingrediant**~~ incorrect spelling of **ingredient**

ingredient /in greédi ənt/ *n* **1.** a component of a mixture, especially an item of food or flavouring included in the recipe for preparing a dish **2.** an element required for a situation, relationship, or plan ○ *What are the ingredients for a happy marriage?* [15C. < Latin *ingredient-*, present participle of *ingredi* 'enter' < *gradi* 'to step, walk']

Ingres /áng grə/, **Jean-Auguste-Dominique** (1780–1867) French artist. He was a leading exemplar of neoclassicism in paintings such as *Grande Odalisque* (1814).

'Drawing is the true test of art.'
[Jean-Auguste-Dominique Ingres, *Pensées d'Ingres*; 1922]

ingress /ín gress/ *n* (*formal*) **1. ENTRY** entry into a place **2. RIGHT OF ENTRY** the right to enter a place **3. ENTRANCE** a way of entering a place [15C. < Latin, 'entrance' < *ingredi* (see INGREDIENT)]

ingressive /in gréssiv/ *adj* **1. OF ENTRY** relating to entry into or the entrance to a place **2.** PHON **PRONOUNCED BY INHALING** describes a speech sound that is pronounced by inhaling rather than exhaling **3.** GRAM same as **inceptive** *adj* (sense 2) ■ *n* **1.** GRAM same as **inceptive 2.** PHON **INGRESSIVE SPEECH SOUND** a speech sound pronounced by inhaling

in-group *n* a group of people who show loyalty and preferential treatment to one another because they share common interests, beliefs, and attitudes

ingrowing /in grṓ ing/ *adj* growing or appearing to grow inwards. An ingrowing toenail does not actually grow inwards: inflamed tissue around the edge of the nail grows over it.

ingrown /in grṓn/ *adj* **1.** MED **GROWN INTO FLESH** appearing to grow into the flesh ○ *ingrown toenail* **2. NATURAL TO SOMEBODY** having become a natural part of somebody's character over a long period of time **3. INWARD-LOOKING** inward-looking and preoccupied with personal or local interests

ingrowth /in grōth/ *n* **1.** growth or apparent growth into the flesh **2.** something that grows inwards, e.g. a hair

ings /ingz/ *npl N England* land that lies close to or below sea level

inguinal /ing gwin'l/ *adj* located in or affecting the groin [15C. < Latin *inguinalis* < *inguen* 'groin']

ingulf *vt* another spelling of **engulf**

Ingush /ing goósh/ (*plural* **-gushes** or *same*) *n* a member of a people who live mainly in the Russian provinces of Ingushetia and Chechnya [Early 20C. < Russian *Ingúsh*, former autonomous area] —**Ingush** *adj*

inhabit /in hábbit/ (**-its, -iting, -ited**) *vt* **1.** to live in or occupy a particular place **2.** to be found in or pervade something ○ *the fears that inhabited each waking moment* [14C. Via French < Latin *inhabitare* < *habitare* 'possess, dwell' < *habere* 'have'] —**inhabitability** /in hábbitə bílləti/ *n* —**inhabitable** *adj* —**inhabitation** /in hàbbi táysh'n/ *n* —**inhabited** *adj* —**inhabiter** *n*

inhabitant /in hábbitənt/ *n* a person or animal that lives in a particular place or area —**inhabitancy** *n*

inhalant /in háylənt/ *adj* breathed in through the nose or mouth as a medicine or for its soothing effect ■ *n* a substance in the form of a vapour or gas that is inhaled, especially as a medicine or for its soothing effect

inhalation /ìnhə láysh'n/ *n* **1.** an intake of breath through the nose or mouth into the lungs **2.** a substance in the form of a vapour or gas that is inhaled, especially as a medicine or for its soothing effect [Early 17C. < medieval Latin *inhalation-* < Latin *inhalare* (see INHALE)] —**inhalational** *adj*

inhalation anthrax *n* a potentially fatal form of anthrax affecting the lungs

inhalator /ínhə laytər/ *n* MED **1.** same as **respirator** (sense 1) **2.** same as **inhaler** (sense 1)

inhale /in háyl/ (**-hales, -haling, -haled**) *vti* to breathe in, or draw a gas, liquid, or solid into the lungs through the nose or mouth [Early 18C. Either back-formation < INHALATION, or < Latin *inhalare* 'breathe upon' < *halare* 'breathe']

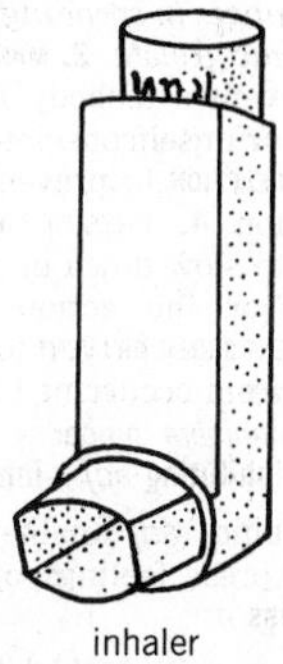

inhaler

inhaler /in háylər/ *n* **1.** a small device used for inhaling medicine in the form of a vapour or gas in order to ease a respiratory condition such as asthma or to relieve nasal congestion **2.** somebody who inhales something

inharmonious /ìn haar mṓni əss/ *adj* **1. DISCORDANT** lacking harmony, or sounding unpleasant **2. UNHAPPY** characterized by disagreement and conflict **3. CLASHING** not matching in colour or style —**inharmoniously** *adv*

inharmony /in haármәni/ *n* lack of harmony, accord, or agreement

inhaul /ín hawl/, **inhauler** /ín hawlər/ *n* a rope used to haul or hold in a sail

inhere /in heér/ (**-heres, -hering, -hered**) *vi* to be a natural and integral part of something (*formal*) [Mid-16C. < Latin *inhaerere* < *haerere* 'to stick']

inherent /in hérrənt, -heérənt/ *adj* part of the very nature of something, and therefore permanently characteristic of it or necessarily involved in it ○ *the risks inherent in investing in the stock market* [Late 16C. < Latin *inhaerent-*, present participle of *inhaerere* (see INHERE)] —**inherence** *n* —**inherency** *n* —**inherently** *adv*

inherit /in hérrit/ (**-its, -iting, -ited**) *v* **1.** *vti* **RECEIVE SOMETHING WHEN SOMEBODY DIES** to become the owner of something when somebody dies, in accordance with legal succession or the terms of a will, or as the result of a bequest or legacy **2.** *vt* **RECEIVE CHARACTERISTIC OR QUALITY FROM PARENT** to receive a characteristic or quality as a result of its being passed on genetically **3.** *vt* **GET SOMETHING FROM PREDECESSOR** to take something over from the person or group who previously lived in a place or did a job [14C. Via Old French *enheriter* 'make an heir' < late Latin *inhereditare* 'inherit' < Latin *heres* 'heir'] —**inheritor** *n*

inheritable /in hérritəb'l/ *adj* **1.** LAW same as **heritable** (sense 1) **2.** describes a characteristic or quality that can be transmitted genetically from parent to offspring —**inheritability** /in hérritə bílləti/ *n*

inheritance /in hérritənss/ *n* **1.** LAW **INHERITED WEALTH OR TITLE** money, property, or a title that has been inherited or is to be inherited **2.** LAW **OWNERSHIP OR SUCCESSION BY HEREDITY** hereditary ownership of wealth or a title, or the succession to wealth or a title **3.** LAW **RIGHT TO INHERIT** the right of an heir to inherit wealth or a title when an ancestor dies **4. HERITAGE** something that is inherited from the past **5.** GENETICS **TRANSMISSION OF GENETICALLY CONTROLLED CHARACTERISTICS** the transmission of genetically controlled characteristics or qualities from parent to offspring **6.** COMPUT **CREATION OF OBJECT WITH SAME VARIABLES** a feature of computer programming whereby a new object can be created from existing objects and, as a consequence of creation, possess the variables and methods of the parent object

inheritance tax *n* a tax levied on property received by inheritance or legal succession, calculated according to the value of the property received

inherited /in hérritid/ *adj* **1.** received by inheritance after the death of the previous owner **2.** controlled by a gene or genes passed on from parent to offspring

inhibin /in híbbin/ *n* a hormone secreted by the gonads that inhibits production of follicle-stimulating hormones [Mid-20C. < Latin *inhibere* (see INHIBIT)]

inhibit /in híbbit/ (**-its, -iting, -ited**) *vt* **1.** HOLD SOMETHING IN CHECK to stop something from continuing or developing ○ *Changes in spending patterns are likely to inhibit economic growth.* **2.** MAKE SOMEBODY FEEL SELF-CONSCIOUS to prevent somebody from behaving or speaking freely or unselfconsciously **3.** CHEM STOP OR RESTRICT CHEMICAL REACTION to prevent or slow down a chemical reaction **4.** PHYSIOL INTERFERE WITH BODILY PROCESS OR ORGAN to slow down or adversely affect a bodily process or the action of an organ **5.** ELECTRONICS PREVENT SIGNAL OR EVENT to prevent a specific signal or event from occurring [15C. < Latin *inhibit-*, past participle of *inhibere* 'hinder' < *habere* 'to hold'] —**inhibitable** *adj* —**inhibiting** *adj* —**inhibitive** *adj*

inhibited /in híbbitid/ *adj* unable to behave spontaneously or express feelings openly —**inhibitedly** *adv* —**inhibitedness** *n*

inhibiter *n* another spelling of **inhibitor**

inhibition /ín hi bísh'n/ *n* **1.** FEELING THAT INHIBITS SOMEBODY a feeling or belief that prevents somebody from behaving spontaneously or speaking freely **2.** SOMETHING THAT INHIBITS something that inhibits something, or the act of inhibiting something **3.** PSYCHOL INHIBITED MENTAL STATE a mental state in which somebody's activity or behaviour is stifled or obstructed **4.** PSYCHOL DIMINISHED RESPONSE TO STIMULUS in Pavlovian conditioning, the progressive weakening of a response to a stimulus after repeated presentations of the stimulus **5.** CHEM PREVENTION OF CHEMICAL REACTION the slowing down or prevention of a chemical reaction **6.** PHYSIOL OBSTRUCTION OF BODILY PROCESS OR ORGAN the suppression or blocking of a bodily process or the action of an organ **7.** SUSPENSION ORDER FROM BISHOP in the Church of England, an order from a bishop suspending a member of the clergy from his or her duties [14C. Via French < Latin *inhibition-* < *inhibere* (see INHIBIT)]

inhibitor /in híbbitər/, **inhibiter** *n* **1.** CHEM SUBSTANCE SLOWING CHEMICAL REACTION a substance that stops or slows a chemical reaction ○ *a rust inhibitor* **2.** BIOCHEM SUBSTANCE HALTING BIOLOGICAL PROCESS a substance that prevents the action of an enzyme **3.** SOMETHING THAT INHIBITS SOMETHING somebody or something that inhibits another person or thing —**inhibitory** *adj*

in-home *adj* available in somebody's home

inhospitable /ín ho spíttəb'l, in hóspit-/ *adj* **1.** not welcoming or friendly **2.** harsh and difficult to live or work in ○ *an inhospitable climate* —**inhospitableness** *n* —**inhospitably** *adv* —**inhospitality** /ín hóspi tálləti/ *n*

in-house *adj* working, carried out, or existing within a company or organization ■ *adv* within a company or organization

inhuman /in hyoómən/ *adj* **1.** VERY CRUEL showing great cruelty and a lack of humanity **2.** UNFEELING giving an impression of being cold and unfeeling **3.** NOT HUMAN not seeming to be human, or not characteristic of human beings —**inhumanly** *adv*

inhumane /ín hyoo máyn/ *adj* lacking compassion and causing excessive suffering —**inhumanely** *adv* —**inhumaneness** *n*

inhumanity /ín hyoo mánnəti/ (*plural* **-ties**) *n* **1.** great cruelty and lack of humanity **2.** an act of great cruelty

inhume /in hyoóm/ (**-humes, -huming, -humed**) *vt* to bury a dead body (*literary*) [Early 17C. < Latin *inhumare* < *humus* 'earth'] —**inhumation** /ín hyoo máysh'n/ *n* —**inhumer** *n*

inimical /i nímmik'l/ *adj* (*formal*) **1.** unfavourable to something ○ *activities inimical to the public good* **2.** showing hostility [Early 16C. < late Latin *inimicalis* < Latin *inimicus* 'unfriendly' < *amicus* 'friend'] —**inimicality** /i nímmi kálləti/ *n* —**inimically** *adv* —**inimicalness** *n*

inimitable /i nímmitəb'l/ *adj* impossible to imitate, especially because of being unique to a person or group ○ *She carried the speech off in her usual inimitable style.* —**inimitability** /i nímmitə bílləti/ *n* —**inimitableness** *n* —**inimitably** *adv*

inion /ínni ən/ *n* a projection of the occipital bone that forms a slight lump at the back of the skull just above the neck [Early 19C. < Greek, 'nape of the neck']

iniquitous /i níkwitəss/ *adj* immoral, especially in a way that results in great injustice or unfairness —**iniquitously** *adv* —**iniquitousness** *n*

iniquity /i níkwəti/ (*plural* **-ties**) *n* **1.** great injustice or extreme immorality **2.** a grossly immoral act [13C. Via French < Latin *iniquitas* < *iniquus* 'unjust' < *aequus* 'equal']

initial /i nísh'l/ *adj* **1.** COMING AT START coming first, or present at the beginning of an event or process ○ *My initial feeling was one of shock.* **2.** COMING FIRST IN WORD relating to or used as the first letter or letters of a word ■ *n* **1.** FIRST LETTER OF NAME the first letter of the name of a person, place, or organization **2.** PRINTING LARGE ORNATE FIRST LETTER the large and often highly decorative first letter of a verse, paragraph, or page, especially as seen in illuminated manuscripts **3.** BOT PLANT-TISSUE CELL a cell in the growing point (**meristem**) of a plant that gives rise to cells that will develop into different plant tissues ■ **initials** *npl* FIRST LETTERS OF SOMEBODY'S NAMES the first letter of each of the names of a person, place, or organization, used as an abbreviation or means of identification ■ *vt* (**-tials, -tialling, -tialled**) MARK SOMETHING WITH INITIALS to sign or mark a document with initials, especially in order to show approval or give authorization [Early 16C. < Latin *initialis* < *initium* 'beginning'] —**initialler** *n*

initialise *vti* COMPUT another spelling of **initialize**

initialism /i nísh'lizəm/ *n* an abbreviation made up of initial letters that are all pronounced separately, e.g. UN for United Nations

initialize /i níshə līz/ (**-izes, -izing, -ized**), **initialise** (**-ises, -ising, -ised**) *vti* to prepare a piece of computer hardware or software for use, often by resetting a memory location to its initial value —**initializer** *n*

initially /i nísh'li/ *adv* at first or to begin with

initial public offering *n* a first-time sale of company securities on a stock exchange to public investors

Initial Teaching Alphabet *n* an alphabet of 44 symbols, each representing a single sound in English, used to teach children to read

initiate *vt* /i níshi ayt/ (**-ates, -ating, -ated**) **1.** MAKE SOMETHING START to cause something, especially an important event or process, to begin ○ *to initiate talks* **2.** TEACH SOMEBODY ABOUT SOMETHING NEW to introduce somebody to a new activity, interest, or area ○ *She initiated me into the joys of snowboarding.* **3.** INTRODUCE SOMEBODY INTO GROUP to allow somebody to take part in a ritual or ceremony in order to become a member of a group, organization, or religion ■ *n* /i níshi ət/ **1.** SOMEBODY INITIATED INTO GROUP somebody who has been recently and ceremonially admitted to a group, organization, or religion **2.** SOMEBODY NEWLY INTRODUCED TO SOMETHING somebody recently introduced to a new activity, interest, or area ■ *adj* /i níshi ət/ **1.** RECENTLY INITIATED belonging or relating to those who have been recently introduced to a new activity, interest, or area **2.** HAVING SECRET OR SPECIAL KNOWLEDGE knowing the secrets of a group, organization, or religion [Mid-16C. < Latin *initiat-*, past participle of *initiare* 'begin' < *initium* 'beginning'] —**initiator** *n*

initiated /i níshi aytid/ *npl* those who know about something that seems difficult or complicated, or who know the secrets of a group, organization, or religion

initiation /i níshi áysh'n/ *n* **1.** ACTION THAT MAKES SOMETHING START action that causes something, especially an important process or event, to begin ○ *the initiation of legal proceedings* **2.** CEREMONY a usually secret or mysterious ceremony by which somebody is admitted to a group, organization, or religion (*sometimes used before nouns*) ○ *initiation rites* **3.** INTRODUCTION TO SOMETHING NEW the introduction of somebody to a new activity, interest, or area [Late 16C. < Latin *initiation-* < *initiat-* (see INITIATE)]

initiative /i níshətiv, i níshi ətiv/ *n* **1.** ABILITY TO ACT ON YOUR OWN the ability to act and make decisions without the help or advice of other people ○ *You'll just have to use your initiative.* **2.** INTRODUCTORY STEP the first step in a process that, once taken, determines subsequent events ○ *decided to take the initiative* **3.** PLAN a plan or strategy aimed at tackling a particular problem ○ *a peace initiative* **4.** ADVANTAGEOUS POSITION a favourable position that allows somebody to take pre-emptive action or control events ○ *lose the initiative* **5.** POL RIGHT TO INTRODUCE NEW LEGISLATION the right to bring a new law or measure before a legislative body **6.** POL PROPOSAL OF LEGISLATION BY CITIZENS a process valid in many US states and in Switzerland that allows citizens to propose legislation by petition ■ *adj* OF INITIATION used in or relating to initiation (*formal*) [Late 18C. < French < Latin *initiat-* (see INITIATE)]

initiatory /i níshi ətəri, i níshətəri/ *adj* **1.** occurring at or related to the beginning of something **2.** used in or characteristic of an initiation

inj. *abbr* MED **1.** injection **2.** injury

inject /in jékt/ (**-jects, -jecting, -jected**) *v* **1.** *vti* PUT FLUID INTO BODY WITH SYRINGE to introduce a drug, vaccine, or other fluid into part of the body using a syringe **2.** *vt* FORCE LIQUID OR GAS INTO SOMETHING to force a liquid or gas through a small opening into a confined space ○ *They injected an insulating foam into the cavity between the walls.* **3.** *vt* ADD SOMETHING TO SITUATION to introduce a particular quality or element into a situation ○ *an attempt to inject a little levity into the proceedings* **4.** *vt* AEROSP PUT ROCKET OR SATELLITE IN ORBIT to put a rocket or satellite into orbit or a spacecraft onto a trajectory to its destination [Late 16C. < Latin *inject-*, past participle of *inicere* 'throw in' < *iacere* 'to throw'] —**injectable** *adj*

injectant /in jéktənt/ *n* an injected substance

injecting room *n* Aus a medically supervised room or centre where drug addicts can inject drugs

injection /in jéksh'n/ *n* **1.** INJECTED DOSE OF DRUG a dose of a drug in liquid form that is injected into the body with a syringe **2.** INTRODUCTION OF FLUID WITH SYRINGE the introduction of a fluid into the body by means of a syringe **3.** AUTOMOT SPRAYING OF FUEL INTO ENGINE the process of spraying fuel through a pump into the inlet manifold or cylinder of an internal-combustion engine, eliminating the need for a carburettor **4.** ADDITION OF SOMETHING TO SITUATION the introduction of a particular quality or element into a situation ○ *His playing would benefit from an injection of muscle and soul.* **5.** PROVISION OF MONEY a provision of money for a country, organization, project, or person in financial need ○ *a cash injection* **6.** MATHS ONE-TO-ONE MAPPING OF SETS a one-to-one mapping of two algebraic sets such that each element of each set corresponds to only one element of the other set **7.** MANUF INTRODUCTION OF FLUID INTO CAVITY a process for introducing a fluid such as a plastic under pressure into a cavity **8.** AEROSP SENDING OF SATELLITE INTO ORBIT the placing of an artificial satellite into orbit or a space probe onto a trajectory **9.** AEROSP MOMENT OF SATELLITE INSERTION the moment or place at which a satellite or space probe is inserted into its intended orbit or trajectory —**injective** *adj*

injection moulding *n* a manufacturing process in which heated material (**thermoplastic**) is forced under pressure into a water-cooled mould —**injection-moulded** *adj*

in-joke *n* a joke that is shared and understood only by a small group of people

injudicious /ínjoŏ díshəss/ *adj* lacking in judgment or discretion —**injudiciously** *adv* —**injudiciousness** *n*

Injun /ínjən/ *n* an offensive term for a Native North American (*dated*) [Late 17C. < a pronunciation of INDIAN]

injunction /in júngksh'n/ *n* **1.** COURT ORDER a court order that requires somebody involved in a legal action to do something or refrain from doing something **2.** COMMAND a command or order, especially from somebody in a position of authority **3.** ACT OF ORDERING SOMEBODY the act of ordering somebody to do or not to do something [15C. < late Latin *injunction-* < Latin *injungere* 'enjoin' < *jungere* 'to join']

injure /ínjər/ (**-jures, -juring, -jured**) *vt* **1.** HURT SOMEBODY OR SOMETHING to cause physical damage to a person, animal, or body part **2.** OFFEND SOMEBODY to cause somebody distress by an unkind action or words **3.** DO LEGAL WRONG TO SOMEBODY to wrong somebody by word or deed in such a way that redress by legal means is available **4.** DAMAGE SOMEBODY'S REPUTATION to damage somebody's reputation, career, or chances of

success [15C. Via French < Latin *injuriare* < *injuria* (see INJURY)] —**injurable** *adj* —**injurer** *n*

SYNONYMS See ***harm***.

injurious /in jóori əss/ *adj* **1.** causing harm, hurt, damage, or distress **2.** damaging somebody's reputation, career, or chances of success [15C. Via French < Latin *injuriosus* < *injuria* (see INJURY)] —**injuriously** *adv* —**injuriousness** *n*

injury /ínjəri/ (*plural* **-ries**) *n* **1.** PHYSICAL DAMAGE physical damage to the body or a body part ○ *They escaped without injury.* **2.** WOUND an instance of physical damage to a body part ○ *a serious back injury* **3.** HARM TO REPUTATION harm caused to somebody's career or reputation by scandal, rumour, or defamation **4.** LAW INFRINGEMENT OF RIGHTS the violation of a person's or group's rights, against which legal action can be taken [14C. Via Anglo-Norman < Latin *injuria* 'a wrong' < *injurius* 'unjust' < *jus* 'justice']

injury benefit *n* a weekly payment made under the National Insurance system to somebody injured while at work, the amount of which is calculated according to the seriousness of the injury

injury time *n* extra time allowed at the end of some matches, especially football and rugby, to compensate for time spent attending to injured players during the game

~~**injust**~~ incorrect spelling of **unjust**

injustice /in jústiss/ *n* unfair or unjust treatment of somebody, or an instance of this [14C. Via French < Latin *injustitia* < *injustus* 'unjust' < + *justus* 'just']

ink /ingk/ *n* **1.** LIQUID FOR MAKING MARKS a coloured liquid or paste used for writing, printing, or drawing **2.** LIQUID EJECTED BY OCTOPUS OR SQUID a dark brown liquid (**sepia**) ejected from a gland (**ink sac**) near the anus by most cephalopods, including the octopus and the squid, to distract predators **3.** *US* PRINT PUBLICITY publicity, especially in the print media (*slang*) ○ *The stunt got him all kinds of ink.* ■ *vt* (**inks, inking, inked**) **1.** WRITE SOMETHING WITH INK to write or draw with ink on a piece of paper or other surface **2.** COVER SURFACE WITH INK to coat something with ink or apply ink to something, usually in preparation for printing **3.** *N Am* SIGN CONTRACT to put or obtain a signature on a contract or other document (*informal*) [13C. Via Old French *enque* < Greek *enkauston* 'purple ink' < *enkaiein* 'burn in'; from the process of encaustic painting] —**inker** *n*

ink in *vt* **1.** to go over the pencil lines of a drawing or design in ink **2.** to spread ink on a surface in preparation for printing

Inkatha /in kaátə/ *n* a Zulu political party that was founded in South Africa in 1975 [Late 20C. Shortening of Zulu *Inkatha Yenkululeko Yesizwe* 'Coil of the Freedom of the Nation']

inkberry /íngk berri/ (*plural* **-ries**) *n* **1.** a black berry from a North American evergreen bush **2.** an evergreen bush that has leathery dark-green leaves and produces black berries. Native to: eastern North America. Latin name: *Ilex glabra.* **3.** BOT same as **pokeweed** [Mid-18C. < the use of the berries for making ink]

inkblot /íngk blot/ *n* **1.** a stain or spot of spilt ink **2.** any of the ten abstract patterns resembling an inkblot used in the Rorschach test

inkblot test *n* PSYCHOL same as **Rorschach test**

ink-cap *n UK, ANZ, Can* a mushroom with a conical cap, on the underside of which are gills that dissolve into an inky black pulp after the spores mature. Genus: *Coprinus.* US term **inky cap**

inkhorn /íngk hawrn/ *n* a small portable ink container made from horn or a similar material and used in former times ■ *adj* excessively scholarly in style or language, especially in the use of terms derived from Latin and Greek

in-kind *adj N Am* **1.** in the form of goods or services rather than in cash **2.** giving something that is equivalent to what has been received

ink-jet printer *n* a printer that prints using particles or droplets of electrically charged ink from a matrix of tiny ink jets

inkle /íngk'l/ *n* a narrow linen tape. Use: trimmings. [Mid-16C. Origin ?]

inkling /íngkling/ *n* **1.** a vague idea or suspicion about a fact, event, or person ○ *I had no inkling that he was unhappy.* **2.** an indication of how to go about something ○ *Could you give me some inkling of where to look?* [Early 16C. < obsolete *inkle* 'utter in an undertone', origin ?]

ink sac *n* a large gland with an opening close to the anus of most cephalopods, including the octopus and squid, from which ink (**sepia**) is ejected to distract predators

inkstand /íngk stand/ *n* **1.** a rack or stand that is kept on a desk and contains pots of ink, pens, and other writing materials **2.** same as **inkwell**

inkwell /íngk wel/ *n* a small container for ink, especially one that fits into a hole in a desk

inky /íngki/ (**-ier, -iest**) *adj* **1.** consisting of or covered in ink **2.** black or dark blue in colour

inky cap *n US* FUNGI same as **ink-cap**

INLA *abbr Ireland* Irish National Liberation Army

inlace *vt* another spelling of **enlace**

inlaid /in láyd, ín layd/ *adj* **1.** set into the surface of wood or another material, usually to provide decoration **2.** decorated with an inlaid pattern

inland /ínlənd/ *adj* **1.** NOT NEAR COAST OR BORDER in or relating to the part of a country that is not near the coast or a border **2.** WITHIN COUNTRY occurring within a country, rather than between countries ■ *adv* IN OR INTO INLAND PART in or towards the interior of a country ■ *n* INLAND PART the interior of a country

inland bill *n* a bill that is both drawn and payable in the United Kingdom

Inland Revenue *n* in the United Kingdom, a government body responsible for the collection and administration of direct taxes such as income tax and corporation tax

Inland Revenue Department *n* in New Zealand, the government department responsible for the collection and administration of taxes

Inland Sea /ínlənd-/ arm of the Pacific Ocean in Japan, between the islands of Honshu, Shikoku, and Kyushu. Length: 430 km/270 mi.

in-law /ín law/ *n* a relative by marriage (*informal*)

inlay *vt* /in láy, ín lay/ (**inlays, inlaying, inlaid** /in láyd, -layd/) **1.** SET SOMETHING INTO SURFACE to set pieces of material such as wood, ivory, or stone into previously cut slots in a surface to form a decorative pattern **2.** DECORATE SOMETHING WITH INLAID DESIGN to decorate something such as a piece of furniture by setting pieces of wood, stone, ivory, or other material into its surface ■ *n* /ín lay/ **1.** PIECES OF MATERIAL SET INTO SURFACE pieces of material such as wood, ivory, or stone set into the surface of a piece of furniture to form a decorative pattern **2.** DECORATIVE PATTERN a decorative pattern formed by inlaying **3.** FILLING FOR TOOTH a filling made of gold or porcelain that is inserted into a cavity in a tooth and cemented in position —**inlayer** *n*

inlet /ín let/ *n* **1.** NARROW OPENING IN COASTLINE a narrow stretch of water reaching inland from a sea or lake **2.** STRETCH OF WATER BETWEEN TWO ISLANDS a narrow stretch of water between two islands **3.** PIECE OF EXTRA FABRIC a piece of fabric put into the seam of a garment to make it bigger or for decoration **4.** PASSAGE OR VALVE an opening through which liquid or gas enters a machine or other device ■ *vt* (**-lets, -letting, -let**) HANDICRAFT same as **inlay** [13C. < IN[1] + -LET]

inlier /ín lī ər/ *n* a rock formation in which older rocks are completely surrounded by younger rocks [Mid-19C. < IN-[2], after OUTLIER]

in-line *adj* describes a device or machine in which similar parts are located together and in a straight line

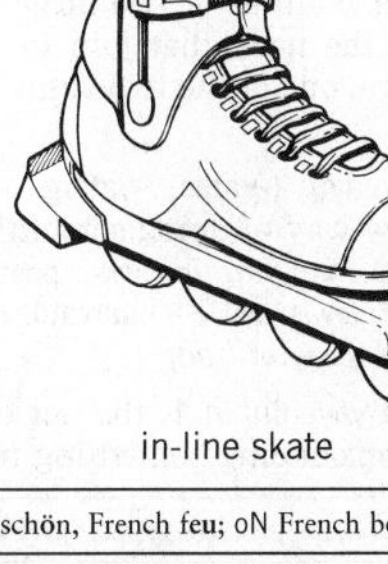

in-line skate

in-line skate *n* a roller skate with a boot that has three or four wheels mounted in a single line —**in-line skate** *vi* —**in-line skater** *n* —**in-line skating** *n*

~~**inlist**~~ incorrect spelling of **enlist**

in loc. cit. *adv* same as **loc. cit.** [Abbreviation of Latin *in loco citato* 'in the place cited']

in loco parentis /in lókō pə réntiss/ *adv* having or taking on the responsibilities of a parent when dealing with somebody else's child [< Latin, 'in the place of a parent']

inly /ínnli/ *adv* (*literary*) **1.** in an inwards way **2.** with deep or intimate understanding

inlying /ín lī ing/ *adj* situated within a country or region

inmate /ín mayt/ *n* somebody who is confined to a prison or a psychiatric hospital [Late 16C. < IN[1] + MATE[1] 'companion']

in medias res /in méedi ass ráyz/ *adv* straight in or into the middle of a sequence of events, especially in a literary narrative that has no introduction (*formal*) [< Latin, 'into the midst of things']

in memoriam /ín mi máwri əm/ *prep, adv* in memory of or in a person's memory (*used in epitaphs and obituaries*) [< Latin]

inmesh *vt* another spelling of **enmesh**

inmigrant /ín mīgrənt/ *adj* coming from a different part of the same country ■ *n* somebody who travels from a different part of the same country

inmigrate /ín mī grayt/ (**-grates, -grating, -grated**) *vi* to travel to a place from a different part of the same country —**inmigration** /ín mī gráysh'n/ *n*

inmost *adj* same as **innermost** [Old English *innemest* < *inne* 'in' + *mest* 'most']

inn /in/ *n* **1.** PUB a small hotel or pub offering food and sometimes accommodation (*often used in pub names*) ○ *a country inn* **2.** HOTEL formerly, a place that provided food and lodging for travellers **3.** RESIDENCE FOR STUDENTS formerly, a hall of residence for students, especially those studying law [Old English, < Indo-European, 'in']

INN *abbr* PHARM international nonproprietary name

inna /ínnə/ *prep* same as **in** (*slang; used in Black English*)

~~**innacurate**~~ incorrect spelling of **inaccurate**

innards /ínnərdz/ *npl* (*informal*) **1.** the internal organs of the body, especially the intestines **2.** the internal working parts of a machine or mechanical device [Early 19C. Alteration of INWARDS (plural noun)]

innate /i náyt/ *adj* **1.** PRESENT FROM BIRTH relating to qualities that a person or animal is born with **2.** INTEGRAL forming an integral part of something **3.** COMING FROM MIND coming directly from the mind rather than being acquired by experience or from external sources ○ *an innate sense of justice* **4.** BOT JOINED TO FILAMENT BY BASE describes an anther that is joined to the filament by its base only **5.** BIOL ORIGINATING WITHIN THALLUS forming an integral part of the thallus of an organism such as an alga or liverwort [15C. < Latin *innatus*, past participle of *innasci* 'be born in' < *nasci* 'be born'] —**innately** *adv* —**innateness** *n*

innate releasing mechanism *n* a process within the central nervous system of animals that, in response to specific stimuli, causes the animal to produce instinctive behaviour. An example is the way that chicks of some birds peck at the red dot on the adult's beak.

inner /ínnər/ *adj* **1.** NEAR OR CLOSER TO CENTRE located near or closer to the centre of something ○ *the inner suburbs* **2.** BEING OR OCCURRING INSIDE located or happening on the inside of something ○ *an inner door* **3.** OF THE MIND relating to somebody's private feelings or happening in somebody's mind ○ *a quiet exterior that hid an inner confidence* **4.** NOT OBVIOUS needing to be examined closely or thought about in order to be seen or understood ○ *searching for the inner meaning of the text* **5.** PRIVILEGED most privileged or influential ○ *the inner circle* ■ *n* **1.** PART OF TARGET the part of a target, especially of a dartboard, surrounding the bull's-eye **2.** HIT TARGET a hit on the inner of a target [Old English *innera* < Indo-European, 'in'] —**innerly** *adv* —**innerness** *n*

inner bar *n* in England and Wales, all the barristers that comprise the King's or Queen's Counsel

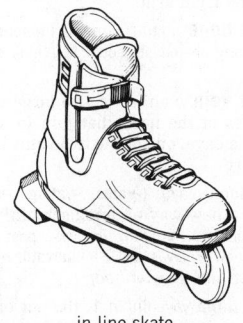

inner child *n* an adult's conception of himself or herself as a child, often used as a tool in therapeutic processes to explore feelings about the person's childhood

inner circle *n* a group of powerful or influential people within a larger group, often those closest to the leader

inner city *n* the central or innermost parts of a city, particularly when associated with social problems such as inadequate housing and high levels of crime and unemployment (*hyphenated when used before a noun*)

inner-directed *adj* guided by personal beliefs rather than by norms imposed by society

inner ear *n* the fluid-filled part of the ear, including the cochlea, which is responsible for hearing, and the semicircular canals, which control balance

Inner Light *n* in Quaker belief, the presence of God as a guiding force within the human soul

inner man *n* **1.** the soul or the spiritual or intellectual part of a man **2.** the appetite of a man (*humorous*)

Inner Mongolia /ínnər-/ ♦ **Nei Monggol**

innermost /ínnər mōst/ *adj* **1.** most important, private, or personal ○ *innermost thoughts* **2.** taking place or being situated farthest from the outside

inner planet *n* any of the four planets Mercury, Venus, Earth, or Mars whose orbits lie closest to the Sun and are within the asteroid belt

inner product *n* MATHS same as **scalar product**

inner sanctum *n* a very private place within a building or organization, to which only a few select or privileged people are admitted (*formal*)

inner sole *n* a foot-shaped piece of leather, sheepskin, or synthetic material worn inside a shoe or boot to provide a better fit or added warmth

inner space *n* **1.** the environment that exists beneath the surface of the sea **2.** somebody's inner spiritual or psychological depths

innerspring /ínnər spring/ *adj ANZ, N Am* FURNITURE describes a mattress that has many helical springs inside a thick padded cover. UK term **interior-sprung**

Inner Temple *n* a law society that, together with Gray's Inn, Lincoln's Inn, and the Middle Temple, forms the Inns of Court

inner tube *n* a hollow rubber ring filled with compressed air that fits inside a pneumatic tyre

innervate /ínnər vayt/ (**-vates, -vating, -vated**) *vt* **1.** to distribute nerves to an organ or body part **2.** to cause a muscle, organ, or other part of the body to act —**innervation** /ínnər váysh'n/ *n* —**innervational** *adj*

innerve /i núrv/ (**-nerves, -nerving, -nerved**) *vt* to provide a person or object with nervous energy or something resembling such energy

innerwear /ínnər wair/ *n* clothing that is worn next to the skin, e.g. a vest or a slip

inner woman *n* **1.** the soul or the spiritual or intellectual part of a woman **2.** the appetite of a woman (*humorous*)

inning /ínning/ *n* each of the divisions of a game of baseball or softball during which each team bats until it makes three outs. Nine innings are standard for baseball and seven for softball, but extra innings are played if the score remains tied. [Old English *innung* < *innian* 'put in' < IN [1]]

innings /ínningz/ (*plural same*) *n* **1.** PERIOD OF SUCCESS a period of opportunity or success, or a long active life or career ○ *He's had a good innings, and he's looking forward to retirement.* **2.** CRICKET TURN AT BATTING the turn of a cricket player or team at batting **3.** CRICKET RUNS SCORED DURING INNINGS the runs scored by a cricket player or team during a turn at batting

Innisfail /ínnəss fayl/ coastal town in northeastern Queensland, Australia, a fishing port and sugar-growing centre. Population: 8,487 (1991).

innit /ínnit/ *contr* **1.** isn't it (*nonstandard; used as a tag question at the end of a statement*) ○ *Nice weather, innit?* **2.** an all purpose, question-forming word, corresponding not only to 'isn't it?' but to more or less all the other similar phrases ○ *Spurs are playing Arsenal tomorrow, innit?*

innkeeper /ín keepər/ *n* an owner or manager of an inn

innocence /ínnəss'nss/ *n* **1.** ABSENCE OF GUILT the state of not being guilty of a crime or offence **2.** HARMLESSNESS harmlessness in intention **3.** FREEDOM FROM SIN freedom from sin or evil **4.** LACK OF WORLDLY EXPERIENCE a lack of experience of the world, especially when this results in a failure to recognize the harmful intentions of other people **5.** IGNORANCE ignorance of the serious consequences of something such as an act or remark **6.** CHASTITY sexual inexperience **7.** LAW LAWFULNESS the state of being permitted by law [14C. Via French < Latin *innocentia* < *innocent-* (see INNOCENT)] —**innocency** /ínnəss'nssi/ *n*

CULTURAL NOTE ***The Age of Innocence***, a novel (1920) by US writer Edith Wharton. It tells the story of a young man's failure to rise above the repressive social conventions of fashionable New York society in the late 19th century. Newland Archer, a sensitive and intelligent lawyer, falls in love with his wife's cousin, Ellen Olenska, a mysterious sophisticate who has returned from Europe bearing the social stigma of a marital separation. The novel reveals the subtle workings by which his elite tribe reaffirms its mores and thwarts his desire. Martin Scorsese directed a film adaptation in 1993.

innocent /ínnəss'nt/ *adj* **1.** NOT GUILTY not guilty of a crime or offence **2.** WITHIN THE LAW permitted by or acting within the law ○ *innocent pastimes* **3.** HARMLESS IN INTENTION not intended to cause harm ○ *an innocent remark* **4.** UNCORRUPTED pure and uncorrupted by evil, sin, or experience of the world ○ *an innocent mind* **5.** NAIVE more trusting or naive than most people through lack of experience of life or failure to recognize the motives of others ○ *an innocent young girl caught up in a terrible situation* **6.** IGNORANT OF SOMETHING having very little or no knowledge of something ○ *innocent of the finer points of etiquette* **7.** LACKING IN SOMETHING completely lacking in a particular quality ○ *innocent of any artistic skill* ■ *n* **1.** BLAMELESS PERSON a blameless vulnerable person, especially a very young child **2.** NAIVE PERSON a simple, naive, or inexperienced person [14C. Via French < Latin *innocent-* < *in-* 'not' + present participle of *nocere* 'harm'] —**innocently** *adv*

Innocent III /ínnəss'nt/ (1160?–1216) pope (1198–1216). He exercised considerable power over the European political rulers of the day, launched the Fourth Crusade (1204), and summoned the Fourth Lateran Council (1215).

> 'Nothing which happens in the world should escape the notice of the supreme pontiff.'
> [Innocent III, *Letter*, 1199]

~~**innoculation**~~ incorrect spelling of **inoculation**

innocuous /i nókyoo əss/ *adj* **1.** not intended to cause offence or provoke a strong reaction and unlikely to do so ○ *an innocuous comment* **2.** harmless in effect ○ *an innocuous-seeming white powder* [Late 16C. < Latin *innocuus* < *nocuus* 'hurtful' < *nocere* 'to harm'] —**innocuously** *adv* —**innocuousness** *n*

innominate /i nómminət/ *adj* **1.** without a name (*formal*) **2.** same as **anonymous** (senses 1–2) (*literary*) [Mid-17C. < late Latin *innominatus* < *nominatus* 'named' < *nominat-* (see NOMINATE)]

innominate artery *n* a short artery rising from the arch of the aorta towards the right upper part of the body. It divides to form the right common carotid artery, which supplies blood to the head, and the right subclavian artery, which supplies blood to the right arm.

innominate bone *n* ANAT same as **hipbone** (*technical*) [Because early anatomists could not think of anything it resembled]

innominate vein *n* either of two large veins on opposite sides of the neck that join to form the superior vena cava, one of the two veins taking blood to the heart

innovate /ínnə vayt/ (**-vates, -vating, -vated**) *vi* to introduce a new way of doing something or a new device [Mid-16C. < Latin *innovat-*, past participle of *innovare* 'renew' < *novus* 'new'] —**innovator** *n* —**innovatory** /ínnə váytəri, ínnə vaytəri/ *adj*

innovation /ínnə váysh'n/ *n* **1.** the act or process of inventing or introducing something new **2.** a new invention or way of doing something ○ *suspicious of fax machines and other technological innovations* —**innovational** *adj*

innovative /ínnə vaytiv, ínnəvətiv/ *adj* new and creative, especially in the way that something is done —**innovatively** *adv* —**innovativeness** *n*

Innsbruck /ínz brŏŏk/ city, tourist centre, and capital of the Tirol Province, western Austria, situated on the River Inn approximately 137 km/85 mi. southwest of Salzburg. Population: 113,826 (2001).

INN stem *n* one of the names selected by the World Health Organization that are the legally required generic names for product labelling for all EU countries and most other countries in the world. Most new generic drug names are formed by combining the most appropriate stem with a prefix that may or may not have some medical significance.

Innu /ínnoo/ *n* **1.** a member of an Algonquian people living in northern Quebec and Labrador **2.** the Algonquian language of the Innu people **3.** PEOPLES same as **Mushuau Innu** [< Montagnais, 'people'] —**Innu** *adj*

innuendo /ínnyoo éndō/ (*plural* **-does** or **-dos**) *n* **1.** HINT OF SOMETHING IMPROPER an indirect remark or gesture that usually carries a suggestion of impropriety ○ *'"I suppose Mary Garth admires Mr Lydgate," said Rosamund, not without a touch of innuendo.'* (George Eliot, *Middlemarch*; 1872) **2.** LAW INTERPRETATION OF POSSIBLY LIBELLOUS LANGUAGE in a legal action for libel or slander, an interpretation of words that are claimed to be libellous where the meaning is not obvious **3.** LAW GLOSS FOR TECHNICAL LEGAL WORD an explanation of a technical legal word, usually given in brackets [Mid-16C. < Latin, 'by intimation' < *innuere* 'nod to, signify']

Innuit *n, adj* PEOPLES, LANG another spelling of **Inuit**

innumerable /i nyŏŏmərəb'l/ *adj* too many to be counted [14C. < Latin *innumerabilis* < *numerus* 'number'] —**innumerability** /i nyŏŏmərə bílləti/ *n* —**innumerably** *adv*

innumerate /i nyŏŏmərət/ *adj* lacking a basic knowledge of mathematics and unable to use numbers in calculation

inobservance /ínnəb zúrvənss/ *n* **1.** failure to comply with something, especially a rule, law, or custom **2.** lack of heed or attention —**inobservant** *adj* —**inobservantly** *adv*

inobtrusive /ínnəb trŏŏssiv/ *adj* same as **unobtrusive**

~~**inocence**~~ incorrect spelling of **innocence**

inocula MED plural of **inoculum**

inoculant /i nókyŏŏlənt/ *n* MED same as **inoculum**

inoculate /i nókyŏŏ layt/ (**-lates, -lating, -lated**) *vt* **1.** to inject or introduce a serum, antigen, or a weakened form of a disease-producing pathogen into the body of a person or animal in order to create immunity to the disease ○ *inoculated every child against polio* **2.** to introduce microorganisms into a culture medium [15C. < Latin *inoculat-*, past participle of *inoculare* 'graft on a plant part' < *oculus* 'bud, eye'] —**inoculability** /i nókyŏŏlə bílləti/ *n* —**inoculable** *adj* —**inoculation** /i nókyŏŏ láysh'n/ *n* —**inoculative** *adj* —**inoculator** *n*

inoculum /i nókyŏŏləm/ (*plural* **-la** /-lə/) *n* material injected into a person or animal to create resistance to a disease [Early 20C. < Latin *inoculare* (see INOCULATE), after COAGULUM]

inodorous /in ṓdərəss/ *adj* having no smell

in-off *n* in snooker, a shot in which the ball hits another ball before falling into a pocket

inoffensive /ínnə fénssiv/ *adj* not causing harm, annoyance, or offence ○ *the remark was inoffensive enough* —**inoffensively** *adv* —**inoffensiveness** *n*

inofficious /ínnə físhəss/ *adj* violating standards of morality or natural affection, especially failing to give an heir a just share of an inheritance ○ *an inofficious will* —**inofficiously** *adv* —**inofficiousness** *n*

Inönü /éen ö nŏŏ/, **Ismet** (1884–1973) Turkish soldier and politician. He was the first premier of the Turkish Republic (1923–37) and its second president (1938–50).

inoperable /in óppərəb'l/ *adj* **1.** describes a medical condition that has advanced to a stage at which surgical intervention would serve no useful

purpose **2.** not practical or workable —**inoperability** /in óppərə bílləti/ n —**inoperableness** n —**inoperably** adv

inoperative /in óppərətiv/ adj **1.** not functioning properly or as usual **2.** not effective or no longer valid or able to be enforced —**inoperatively** adv —**inoperativeness** n

inopportune /in óppər tyoon/ adj happening at a bad moment or an inconvenient time —**inopportunely** adv —**inopportuneness** n —**inopportunity** /in óppər tyoonəti/ n

inordinate /in áwrdinət/ adj **1.** beyond reasonable limits in amount or degree ○ *capable of expressing an inordinate degree of unreason* (Henry James, *Roderick Hudson*; 1876) **2.** showing a lack of restraint or control (*archaic or literary*) [14C. < Latin *inordinatus* 'out of order' < *ordo* 'order'] —**inordinacy** n —**inordinately** adv

inorganic /ín awr gánnik/ adj **1.** composed of minerals rather than living material **2.** describes chemical compounds that contain no carbon, excluding the oxides of carbon, carbon disulphide, cyanides, and their associated acids and salts —**inorganically** adv

inorganic chemistry n the branch of chemistry relating to inorganic compounds

inosculate /in óskyoŏ layt/ (**-lates, -lating, -lated**) vti **1.** to join and blend with something else, or join or blend one thing with another **2.** ANAT to be united or joined through a series of continuous small openings, or unite or join things in this way [Late 17C. < IN-² + Latin *osculat-*, past participle of *osculare* 'provide with a mouth' < *osculum* 'little mouth' < *os* 'mouth'] —**inosculation** /in óskyoŏ láysh'n/ n

inosine /ínnə seen, ín ō-/ n an organic compound (**nucleoside**) involved in the formation of purines and energy metabolism. Use: sports supplement, transplant management.

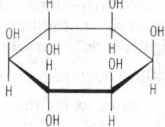

inositol

inositol /i nóssi tol/ n a cyclic alcohol that is a component of cell membranes and a precursor of various messenger molecules. Formula: $C_6H_{12}O_6$. [Late 19C. < Greek *in-* 'sinew' + -OSE² + -ITE¹ + -OL¹]

inotropic /ínnə tróppik, ínə-/ adj having an effect on the force of muscular contraction ○ *an inotropic drug* [Early 20C. < Greek *in-* 'sinew']

inpatient /ín paysh'nt/ n somebody receiving medical treatment that requires a hospital stay ■ adj relating to, designed for, or used by inpatients

in perpetuum /ín pur péttyoo əm/ adv LAW same as **forever** (sense 1) [< Latin]

in personam /ín pur sónəm/ adj, adv made about or directed at a person rather than at property [< Latin, 'against a person']

in petto /ín péttō/ adj not disclosing publicly the name of a cardinal appointed by the pope [Late 17C. < Italian, 'in the breast']

inphase /ín fayz/ adj of the same electrical phase

INPO abbr ONLINE in no particular order (*used in e-mails or text messages*)

in posse /ín póssi/ adj potentially rather than in reality (*formal*) [< Latin]

inpouring /ín pawring/ n a sudden flowing in of a large amount of something

in-process adj in the process of being manufactured

in propria persona /ín própri ə pur sónə/ adv in person, especially when unrepresented by a lawyer [< Latin, 'in your own person']

input /ín poŏt/ n **1.** CONTRIBUTION a contribution to something, especially comments or suggestions made to a group **2.** SOMETHING GOING IN something that enters a process or situation from the outside and is then acted upon or integrated ○ *sensory input* **3.** ELECTRONICS ELECTRICITY THAT DRIVES SOMETHING power, electrical energy, or an electrical signal that enters a device and is usually recovered in the form of work or some other output effect **4.** COMPUT COMPUTER TERMINAL a terminal or connection where data enters a computer ■ v (**-puts, -putting, -putted** or **-put**) **1.** vt CONTRIBUTE INFORMATION to provide information to help somebody make a decision (*informal*) **2.** ENTER DATA to enter data into a computer —**inputter** n

input/output n hardware or software that controls the passage of information into and out of a computer or computer component

input tax credit n in Australia, the amount of goods and services tax paid on an item or service purchased for business purposes that can be offset against the amount collected and owed to the Australian Taxation Office

inquest /ín kwest/ n **1.** an official enquiry held by a coroner into the facts of a case such as a sudden unexpected death or the discovery of something valuable that might be treasure trove **2.** an investigation of the facts of a situation, particularly one that had an undesired outcome (*literary*) [14C. Via French < Latin *inquesta* < *inquirere* 'enquire']

inquietude /in kwí ə tyood/ n a worried or restless state of mind (*literary*) [15C. < late Latin *inquietudo* < Latin *quietus* 'quiet']

inquiline /íngkwi līn/ n an animal that lives in the nest or home of another species [Mid-17C. < Latin *inquilinus* 'tenant, lodger' < *incolere* 'inhabit' < *colere* 'dwell']

inquire, etc. another spelling of **enquire, etc.**

inquisition /íngkwi zísh'n/ n **1.** a succession of detailed and relentless questions **2.** an enquiry or investigation that is harsh or unfair [14C. Via French < Latin *inquisition-* < *inquirere* (see ENQUIRE)] —**inquisitional** adj —**inquisitionist** n

Inquisition n a former organization in the Roman Catholic Church established to find, question, and sentence those who did not hold orthodox religious beliefs. The Spanish Inquisition lasted until the 19th century and was known for its harsh punishments and use of torture.

inquisitive /in kwízzətiv/ adj **1.** eager for knowledge **2.** too curious about other people's business [14C. Via French < late Latin *inquisitivus* < Latin *inquirere* (see ENQUIRE)] —**inquisitively** adv —**inquisitiveness** n

inquisitor /in kwízzitər/ n **1.** somebody who relentlessly asks searching or hostile questions **2.** *also* **Inquisitor** an official working for the Inquisition [Early 16C. Via French < Latin *inquirere* (see ENQUIRE)]

inquisitorial /in kwízzə táwri əl/ adj **1.** resembling a formal enquiry, especially in using rigorous or relentless questioning **2.** describes a trial in which one person is both judge and prosecutor —**inquisitorially** adv

inquorate /in kwáwrət, -rayt/ adj having too few people present to provide a quorum and therefore unable to make an official decision ○ *The meeting was declared inquorate.* [Late 20C. < IN-² + QUORATE]

in re /in reé, -ráy/ prep with regard to [< Latin, 'in the matter of']

in rem /-rém/ adj describes something such as a law or right made about or directed at property rather than a person [< Latin, 'against a thing']

in rerum natura /ín ráiroŏm na toŏrə/ adv in the nature of things (*formal*) [< Latin]

in-residence adj N Am officially connected with a university or other institution, often as a teacher or lecturer, but allowed time for original creative work (*used in combination*) ○ *She completed her book while serving as poet-in-residence at a small college.*

INRI abbr Jesus of Nazareth, king of the Jews (*used as an inscription over the head of the crucified Jesus Christ*) [Latin *Iesus Nazarenus Rex Iudaeorum*]

inro /ínrō/ (*plural same*) n a small ornamented box worn hanging from the sash of a kimono with compartments for holding cosmetics, perfumes, and

medicines [Early 17C. < Japanese *inrō* < *in* 'seal' + *rō* 'basket']

inroad /ín rōd/ n **1.** a gradual encroachment on something (*usually used in the plural*) ○ *Young companies using electronic sales methods have made inroads into traditional markets.* **2.** a sudden attack on an enemy camp (*archaic*) [Mid-16C. < IN¹ + ROAD in the obsolete sense 'a riding, raid']

inrush /ín rush/ n a sudden flooding or flowing in

ins. abbr **1.** inscription **2.** *also* **Ins.** inspector **3.** insulation **4.** insurance

insalivate /in sálli vayt/ (**-vates, -vating, -vated**) vt to mix food with saliva in the process of chewing —**insalivation** /in sálli váysh'n/ n

insalubrious /ínssə loŏ bri əss/ adj not pleasant, healthy, or wholesome —**insalubriously** adv —**insalubrity** n

insane /in sáyn/ adj **1.** LEGALLY CONSIDERED AS PSYCHIATRICALLY DISORDERED considered legally incompetent or irresponsible because of a psychiatric disorder **2.** LACKING REASONABLE THOUGHT showing a complete lack of reason or foresight (*informal*) **3.** Aus EXCELLENT extremely good (*slang*) ■ npl PEOPLE LEGALLY CONSIDERED AS PSYCHIATRICALLY DISORDERED people who are considered legally incompetent or irresponsible because of a psychiatric disorder (*dated*) [Mid-16C. < Latin *insanus* < *sanus* 'healthy, sane'] —**insanely** adv

insanitary /in sánnitəri/ adj dirty or unhygienic and thus likely to cause disease —**insanitation** /in sánni táysh'n/ n

insanity /in sánnəti/ (*plural* **-ties**) n **1.** extreme foolishness, or an act that demonstrates such foolishness **2.** legal incompetence or irresponsibility that results from a psychiatric disorder

insatiable /in sáyshəb'l/ adj always needing more and impossible to satisfy [15C. < Old French *insaciable* < Latin *satiare* (see SATIATE)] —**insatiability** /in sáyshə bílləti/ n —**insatiably** adv

insatiate /in sáyshi ət/ adj same as **insatiable** (*literary*) [15C. < Latin *insatiatus* < *satiatus*, past participle of *satiare* (see SATIATE)] —**insatiately** adv

inscape /ín skayp/ n the distinctive and essential inner quality of something, especially a natural object or a scene in nature [Mid-19C. Probably after LANDSCAPE]

inscribe /in skríb/ (**-scribes, -scribing, -scribed**) vt **1.** PUT WRITING ON SOMETHING to write, print, or engrave words or letters on a surface **2.** WRITE SOMETHING ON LIST to add a name to a list or book **3.** WRITE DEDICATION ON SOMETHING to write a signed message to somebody in a book or on a photograph, often when presenting it as a gift **4.** MATHS DRAW GEOMETRIC FIGURE WITHIN ANOTHER to draw a geometric figure within another so that all of the second figure lies within the first and touches it at as many points as possible ○ *inscribe a circle within a square* [15C. < Latin *inscribere* 'write on' < *scribere* 'write'] —**inscribable** adj —**inscriber** n

inscription /in skrípsh'n/ n **1.** a sequence of words or letters written, printed, or engraved on a surface **2.** a signed message written in a book or on a photograph, often when it is being presented as a gift [14C. < Latin *inscription-* past participle of *inscribere* (see INSCRIBE)] —**inscriptional** adj

inscriptive /in skríptiv/ adj relating to or constituting an inscription —**inscriptively** adv

inscrutable /in skroŏtəb'l/ adj not expressing anything clearly and thus hard to interpret ○ *his inscrutable expression* [15C. Via French < ecclesiastical Latin *inscrutabilis* < Latin *scrutari* 'investigate'] —**inscrutability** /in skroŏtə bílləti/ n —**inscrutably** adv

INSEAD /ínsi ad/, **Insead** n a leading European business school in Fontainebleau, France. Full form **Institut européen d'administration des affaires**

inseam /ín seem/ n N Am CLOTHING same as **inside leg**

insect /ín sekt/ n **1.** SMALL SIX-LEGGED ANIMAL an air-breathing invertebrate animal (**arthropod**) with a body that has well-defined segments, including a head, thorax, abdomen, two antennae, three pairs of legs, and usually two sets of wings. Class: Insecta. **2.** SOMETHING LIKE INSECT a small animal that resembles an insect, e.g. a spider or centipede (*not in technical use*) **3.** CONTEMPTIBLE PERSON somebody viewed with contempt, especially somebody regarded as un-

important (*insult*) [Early 17C. < Latin *insectum* < *insecare* 'cut up' < *secare* 'to cut'] —**insectan** /in séktən/ *adj*

insectarium /ínsek táiri əm/ (*plural* **-iums** or **-ia** /-i ə/), **insectary** /in séktəri/ (*plural* **-ries**) *n* a place for breeding or observing insects

insecticide /in sékti sīd/ *n* a chemical substance used to kill insects —**insecticidal** /in sékti sīd'l/ *adj* —**insecticidally** *adv*

insectivore /in sékti vawr/ *n* **1.** a small nocturnal mammal that feeds primarily on insects. Moles, shrews, and hedgehogs are all insectivores. **2.** any plant or animal that feeds primarily on insects [Mid-19C. < modern Latin *Insectivora* 'insect-eaters' < Latin *insectum* (see INSECT)] —**insectivorous** /ín sek tívvərəss/ *adj*

insecure /ínssi kyóor/ *adj* **1.** NOT CONFIDENT anxious and lacking in self-confidence **2.** NOT SAFE unsafe and unprotected ○ *insecure premises that are vulnerable to thieves* **3.** UNSTABLE not firm or steady ○ *an insecure walkway* ○ *an insecure grip on his hand* —**insecurely** *adv*

insecurity (*plural* **-ties**) *n* **1.** INSECURE CONDITION the state of being unsafe or insecure **2.** UNSAFE FEELING a state of mind characterized by self-doubt and vulnerability **3.** INSECURE PHENOMENON an instance or cause of being insecure

inselberg /ínz'l burg/ *n* an isolated hill or mountain, often heavily eroded on its lower slopes, rising abruptly from a plain [Early 20C. < German, 'island mountain']

inseminate /in sémmi nayt/ (**-nates, -nating, -nated**) *vt* to insert sperm into the reproductive tract of a female [Early 17C. < Latin *inseminat-*, past participle of *inseminare* 'implant' < *semen* 'seed'] —**insemination** /in sémmi náysh'n/ *n*

insensate /in sén sayt, -sət/ *adj* **1.** WITHOUT FEELING inanimate and thus unable to feel anything **2.** COLD AND HEARTLESS entirely lacking in sympathetic feeling or human kindness (*formal*) **3.** THOUGHTLESS lacking in common sense or reasonable thought (*formal*) [15C. < ecclesiastical Latin *insensatus* < late Latin *sensatus* 'equipped with senses' < Latin *sensus* (see SENSE)] —**insensately** *adv* —**insensateness** *n*

insensible /in sénssəb'l/ *adj* **1.** same as **insensate** (sense 1) **2.** NOT CONSCIOUS without feeling or consciousness **3.** NOT AWARE OR RESPONSIVE unaware of or unresponsive to something **4.** UNNOTICEABLE so small or gradual as to be almost imperceptible ○ *an insensible shift in emphasis* [14C. Via French < Latin *insensibilis* 'imperceptible' < *sensus* (see SENSE)] —**insensibility** /in sénssə bílləti/ *n* —**insensibly** *adv*

insensitive /in sénssətiv/ *adj* **1.** THOUGHTLESS insufficiently aware of other people's feelings and unable to respond to them appropriately **2.** NOT REACTING PHYSICALLY not responsive to a physical stimulus such as touch or sound **3.** INDIFFERENT AND UNRESPONSIVE indifferent to the importance of something and therefore not responding to it —**insensitively** *adv* —**insensitiveness** *n* —**insensitivity** /in sénssə tívvəti/ *n*

insentient /in sénshənt/ *adj* without life, consciousness, or perception —**insentience** *n*

inseparable /in séppərəb'l/ *adj* **1.** sharing a close friendship and always seen or found together ○ *The two girls became inseparable.* **2.** so closely linked as to be impossible to consider separately ○ *Reading and the ability to spell will seem inseparable.* —**inseparability** /in séppərə bílləti/ *n* —**inseparably** *adv*

insert *vt* /in súrt/ (**-serts, -serting, -serted**) **1.** PLACE SOMETHING INSIDE SOMETHING to put something inside or into something else ○ *Insert the screws in the holes already drilled.* **2.** ADD SOMETHING TO SOMETHING to add new material to the body of something, especially a text ■ *n* /ín surt/ **1.** ADVERTISING SUPPLEMENT IN MAGAZINE a supplement in the form of a single sheet or booklet placed inside a magazine or newspaper, usually as advertising **2.** ADDED PART a piece of fabric, usually contrasting, that is sewn into a main piece [15C. < Latin *insert-*, past participle of *inserere* < *serere* 'join'] —**insertable** *adj* —**inserter** *n*

insertion /in súrsh'n/ *n* **1.** ADDITION the act of putting something into something else **2.** SOMETHING ADDED material that is inserted into a text **3.** ATTACHMENT POINT the point of attachment of something, e.g. the point at which a leaf is joined to its stem or a muscle to a bone it moves **4.** GENETICS INSERTED GENETIC MATERIAL a segment of DNA that is inserted into a gene sequence **5.** AEROSP same as **injection** (senses 8–9) —**insertional** *adj*

insertion stitch *n* an embroidery stitch that joins two pieces of fabric together and decorates the gap between them

in-service *adj* **1.** taking place while somebody is employed full time ○ *in-service training* **2.** working as a full-time employee

insessorial /ín se sáwri əl/ *adj* used to describe birds that are adapted, or have feet that are adapted, for perching [Mid-19C. < modern Latin *Insessores*, former order name < past participle of Latin *insidere* (see INSIDIOUS)]

inset *vt* /in sét/ (**-sets, -setting, -set**) PLACE SMALLER THING IN LARGER THING to insert something into a larger thing, e.g. a gem in a crown, or a small map in the corner of a larger map ■ *n* /ín set/ **1.** THING PLACED IN SOMETHING LARGER something inserted into a larger thing ○ *a map of the state with city maps as insets* **2.** GEOG CHANNEL a place where something flows in, especially the tide

INSET /ín set/, **Inset** *abbr* EDUC in-service education of teachers

inshallah /in shállə/, **insh'allah** *interj* an expression meaning 'if God wills', used to suggest that something in the future is uncertain [Mid-19C. < Arabic *in šā 'Allāh*]

inshore /ín shawr/ *adj* near or towards the coast ○ *inshore waters* ■ *adv* towards the coast from the direction of the sea

inshrine *vt* another spelling of **enshrine**

inside /in sīd, ín sīd/ CORE MEANING: a grammatical word indicating the interior part of something, or the part that is enclosed by or surrounded with something ○ (adv) *I opened the door and looked inside.* ○ (adj) *his inside jacket pocket* ○ (n) *I looked round the room, gnawing the inside of my cheek nervously.* ○ (prep) *The jewels are kept inside a locked box.*

1. *adj, prep* WITHIN ORGANIZATION happening or coming from within an organization ○ *They had inside knowledge about the takeover bid.* ○ *things that were going on inside the committee* **2.** *adv, prep* RELATING TO INNER FEELINGS indicating emotions that are not expressed ○ *She doesn't like to look inside and face up to what she's really like.* ○ *Seeing her like that had snapped something inside him.* **3.** *prep* WITHIN PARTICULAR TIME done in a period of time less than the one stated (*informal*) ○ *We managed to completely redecorate the room inside seven hours.* **4.** *adj* AT EDGE OF ROAD farthest from the centre of a road **5.** *adj* SPORTS NEARER TO CENTRE OF PLAYING AREA in football, hockey, and other sports, describes a position nearer to the centre of the field than another of the same name ○ *inside right* ○ *inside centre* **6.** *adv* IN PRISON serving time in prison (*informal*) ○ *He was inside for three years.* **7.** *n* INNER EDGE the part of a road or path farthest from the centre ○ *was forced to overtake him on the inside* **8.** *n* PRIVILEGED ACCESS a position that gives access to privileged information ○ *information from someone on the inside* **9.** *npl* **insides** ANAT INTERNAL ORGANS the internal organs of the body, especially the stomach and bowels (*informal*) ◇ **inside of** within a particular period of time (*informal*) ◇ **inside out** with the part that is normally inside facing outwards ◇ **know something inside out** to know something extremely well

---

USAGE **inside**, **inside of**, or **within**? Though the idiomatic expressions ***inside*** and ***inside of*** in the sense 'within a given amount of time' are used in informal writing and conversation (*We'll be finished inside of a month*), the usage may be regarded as inappropriate to formal writing. Therefore, the safest choice is ***within***, as in *We'll be finished within a month.*

---

inside information *n* something secret or confidential known only to somebody who holds a position within a company or other organization

inside job *n* a crime carried out by or with the help of somebody who works for the person or organization affected (*informal*)

inside lane *n* the section of a multiple-lane road nearest to the left, used by vehicles being overtaken and those turning off the road

inside leg *n* **1.** the inner seam of a pair of trousers, from the crotch to the bottom of the trouser leg **2.** the measurement of a trouser leg's inner seam ▶ N Am term **inseam**

insider /in sīdər/ *n* a member of a group who knows all about its inner workings

insider dealing *n UK* profitable trading in securities that is done using access to privileged information. Such trading is usually illegal. ANZ, N Am term **insider trading**

insider trading *n ANZ, N Am* same as **insider dealing**

inside track *n* **1.** the lane of an oval racetrack nearest the centre and thus shorter than the outer lanes **2.** an advantageous position

insidious /in síddi əss/ *adj* slowly and subtly harmful or destructive ○ *an insidious evil* [Mid-16C. < Latin *insidiosus* < *insidiae* 'ambush' < *insidere* 'sit on, lie in wait' < *sedere* 'sit'] —**insidiously** *adv* —**insidiousness** *n*

USAGE **insidious** or **invidious**? Though these words are spelt similarly and both have negative meanings, they are not interchangeable. ***Insidious***, which comes from a Latin word meaning 'ambush', means 'slowly and subtly harmful': *the insidious effects of poverty*; *The candidate launched an insidious whispering campaign against his rival.* ***Invidious***, which comes from another Latin word meaning 'looking at with malice', means 'causing another person to feel resentment because of unfair treatment', 'feeling envious', and 'slighting and discriminatory to another person': *A judge should not hold membership of an organization that practices invidious discrimination on the basis of race, sex, religion, or national origin.*

---

insight /ín sīt/ *n* **1.** PERCEPTIVENESS the ability to see clearly and intuitively into the nature of a complex person, situation, or subject **2.** CLEAR PERCEPTION a clear perception of something ○ *thanked him for his remark and told him it was an interesting insight* **3.** SELF-AWARENESS the ability of somebody to understand and find solutions to his or her personal problems **4.** PERCEPTION THAT HALLUCINATIONS ARE NOT REAL the perception, lacking in some psychiatric disorders such as schizophrenia, that symptoms such as delusions and hallucinations are not objective —**insightful** /ín sītf'l/ *adj* —**insightfully** *adv* —**insightfulness** *n*

insight meditation *n* BUDDHISM same as **vipassana**

insigne /in sígni/ *n* same as **insignia** (*formal*; *only used in the singular*) [Late 18C. < Latin, singular of *insignia* (see INSIGNIA)]

insignia /in sígni ə/ (*plural same* or **-as**) *n* **1.** a badge of authority or membership of a group **2.** an identifying mark or sign [Mid-17C. < Latin (plural) < *insignis* 'marked' < *signum* 'sign']

insignificant /ínsig nífikənt/ *adj* **1.** WITHOUT IMPORTANCE too small and unimportant to be relevant ○ *statistically insignificant* **2.** WITHOUT MEANING having little or no meaning **3.** POWERLESS lacking in power or status —**insignificance** *n* —**insignificantly** *adv*

insincere /ín sin séer/ *adj* not genuine and not reflecting true feelings —**insincerely** *adv* —**insincerity** /ín sin sérrəti/ *n*

insinuate /in sínnyoo ayt/ (**-ates, -ating, -ated**) *v* **1.** *vti* to hint at something unpleasant or suggest it indirectly and gradually **2.** **insinuate yourself** *vr* to introduce yourself gradually and cunningly into a position, especially a place of confidence or favour [Early 16C. < Latin *insinuat-*, past participle of *insinuare* < *sinus* 'curve'] —**insinuatingly** *adv* —**insinuative** /in sínnyoo ətiv/ *adj* —**insinuator** *n*

insinuating /in sínnyoo ayting/ *adj* **1.** hinting at or implying something unpleasant **2.** trying gradually or cunningly to gain influence or favour

insinuation /in sínnyoo áysh'n/ *n* **1.** something unpleasant artfully and indirectly suggested to another person **2.** the act of hinting at something unpleasant or suggesting something indirectly and gradually

insipid /in síppid/ *adj* **1.** dull because lacking in character and lively qualities **2.** bland and without flavour [Early 17C. Directly or via French < late Latin *insipidus* 'tasteless' < *sapidus* 'having a flavour'] —**insipidity** /ínsi píddəti/ *n* —**insipidly** *adv* —**insipidness** *n*

insist /in síst/ (**-sists, -sisting, -sisted**) *vti* **1.** to state or demand something firmly in spite of disagreement

or resistance from others ○ *She insisted that he was wrong.* ○ *Please, you must take it, I insist!* **2.** to state or require something firmly and steadfastly ○ *They insist on punctuality.* ○ *He insisted there was nothing to worry about.* [Late 16C. < Latin *insistere* 'persist' < *sistere* 'to stand']

~~insistant~~ incorrect spelling of **insistent**

insistent /in sístənt/ *adj* **1.** persistent in maintaining or demanding something ○ *She was most insistent.* **2.** persistently calling for or compelling attention ○ *insistent pleas* —**insistence** *n* —**insistency** *n* —**insistently** *adv*

in situ /in síttyoo/ *adv, adj* in its natural or original place ○ *a useful tool for studying cell proliferation in situ under normal and pathological conditions* [< Latin]

insnare *vt* another spelling of **ensnare**

insobriety /ínssō brī´ əti/ *n* lack of moderation, especially in drinking alcohol

insofar as /ín sō faár əz/ *conj* used to introduce a statement that explains or qualifies a previous statement

insolate /ínsō layt/ (**-lates, -lating, -lated**) *vt* to expose something to sunlight (*technical*) [Early 17C. < Latin *insolat-*, past participle of *insolare* < *sol* 'sun']

insolation /ínssō láysh'n/ *n* **1.** exposure of something to sunlight **2.** ASTRON the rate of solar radiation received per unit area **3.** MED same as **sunstroke** (*technical*)

insole /ínsōl/ *n* **1.** the inner lining of a shoe **2.** a thin removable liner placed inside a shoe to make it warmer or more comfortable or to prevent the buildup of odour

insolent /ínssələnt/ *adj* showing an aggressive lack of respect in speech or behaviour [14C. < Latin *insolent-* 'unusual, arrogant' < *solere* 'be accustomed'] —**insolence** *n* —**insolently** *adv*

insolubilize /in sóllyōōbə līz/ (**-lizes, -lizing, -lized**), **insolubilise** (**-lises, -lising, -lised**) *vt* to make something incapable of being dissolved in a liquid —**insolubilization** /in sóllyōōbə lī záysh'n/ *n*

insoluble /in sóllyōōb'l/ *adj* **1.** incapable of being dissolved in a liquid **2.** not able to be solved —**insolubility** /in sóllyōō bíləti/ *n* —**insolubly** *adv*

insolvable /in sólvəb'l/ *adj* same as **insoluble** (sense 2) —**insolvability** /in sólvə bíləti/ *n*

insolvent /in sólvənt/ *adj* **1.** BANKRUPT unable to pay debts **2.** OF BANKRUPTCY relating to people or businesses that are bankrupt ■ *n* BANKRUPT PERSON somebody who is unable to pay any debts —**insolvency** *n*

insomnia /in sómni ə/ *n* inability to fall asleep or to remain asleep long enough to feel rested, especially when this is a problem that continues over time [Early 17C. < Latin < *insomnis* 'sleepless' < *somnus* 'sleep'] —**insomniac** *adj, n*

insomuch as /ínssō múch-/ *conj* used to introduce an explanation or reason

insomuch that *conj* used to indicate the extent to which something is true or is the case

insouciance /in soóssi ənss/ *n* cheerful lack of anxiety or concern [Early 19C. < French < *soucier* 'to care' < Latin *sollicitare* (see SOLICIT)] —**insouciant** *adj* —**insouciantly** *adv*

insoul *vt* another spelling of **ensoul**

insp. *abbr* **1.** inspected **2.** *also* **Insp.** inspector

inspan /in spán/ (**-spans, -spanning, -spanned**) *vt* S Africa to harness an animal to a vehicle [Early 19C. Via Afrikaans < Dutch *inspannen*]

inspect /in spékt/ (**-spects, -specting, -spected**) *vt* **1.** to examine something carefully in order to judge its quality or correctness ○ *She took the cheese out of the refrigerator and inspected it for mould.* **2.** to examine or review something officially ○ *The barracks is inspected every day.* [Early 17C. < Latin *inspect-*, past participle of *inspicere* < *specere* 'look at'] —**inspectable** *adj* —**inspective** *adj*

inspection /in spéksh'n/ *n* **1.** a critical examination of somebody or something aimed at forming a judgment or evaluation **2.** an official authoritative examination ○ *a motor vehicle inspection*

inspection arms *n* a position in which a rifle is held diagonally in front of the body with the muzzle pointing upwards to the left and the rifle chamber open for inspection

inspector /in spéktər/ *n* **1.** an official who examines something in order to judge its quality or compliance with rules or the law **2.** a British police officer of a rank above sergeant —**inspectoral** *adj* —**inspectorial** /ín spek táwri əl/ *adj* —**inspectorship** *n*

inspectorate /in spéktərət/ *n* **1.** GROUP OF INSPECTORS a group or department of inspectors **2.** INSPECTOR'S DISTRICT an area supervised by an inspector **3.** INSPECTOR'S DUTIES the office or duties of an inspector

inspector general (*plural* **inspectors general**) *n* **1.** an official who is the head of an inspectorate **2.** a military officer who investigates and reports on organizational matters

insphere *vt* another spelling of **ensphere**

inspiration /ínspi ráysh'n/ *n* **1.** STIMULATION TO DO CREATIVE WORK stimulation for the human mind to creative thought or to the making of art ○ *found inspiration in the landscape around her* **2.** SOMEBODY OR SOMETHING THAT INSPIRES somebody or something that inspires somebody to creative thought or to the making of art ○ *His book is an inspiration to all would-be travellers.* **3.** CREATIVENESS the quality of being stimulated to creative thought or activity, or the manifestation of this ○ *a moment of inspiration* **4.** GOOD IDEA a sudden brilliant idea **5.** DIVINE INFLUENCE divine guidance and influence on human beings **6.** PHYSIOL BREATHING IN the drawing of air into the lungs [14C. Via French < late Latin *inspiration-* < Latin *inspirare* (see INSPIRE)] —**inspirational** *adj*

inspirator /ínspi raytər/ *n* a device for drawing in a gas or vapour [Late 19C. < INSPIRE]

inspiratory /in spírətəri/ *adj* relating to the process of breathing in, or used in breathing in [Late 18C. < INSPIRE]

inspire /in spír/ (**-spires, -spiring, -spired**) *v* **1.** *vti* STIMULATE SOMEBODY TO DO SOMETHING to encourage somebody into greater effort, enthusiasm, or creativity ○ *a speech that inspired a generation* **2.** *vt* PROVOKE PARTICULAR FEELING to arouse a particular feeling in somebody ○ *inspires optimism* **3.** *vt* CAUSE CREATIVE ACTIVITY to stimulate somebody to do something, especially creative or artistic work ○ *inspired him to write a song* **4.** *vti* PHYSIOL BREATHE IN to inhale air or a gas into the lungs [14C. Via French < Latin *inspirare* < *spirare* 'breathe'] —**inspirable** *adj* —**inspirative** *adj* —**inspirer** *n*

inspired /in spírd/ *adj* **1.** brilliant and creative ○ *an inspired rendition of a classic song* ○ *She was an inspired teacher.* **2.** based on a particular motive or example (*usually used in combination*) ○ *a Jesuit-inspired curriculum*

inspiring /in spíring/ *adj* making somebody feel more enthusiastic, confident, or stimulated —**inspiringly** *adv*

inspirit /in spírrit/ (**-its, -iting, -ited**) *vt* to give energy or courage to somebody (*archaic or literary*) —**inspiriter** *n* —**inspiriting** *adj* —**inspiritingly** *adv*

inspissate /in spíss ayt/ (**-sates, -sating, -sated**) *vti* to become thicker in consistency, or cause something to thicken, especially by boiling or evaporation [Early 17C. < Latin *inspissat-*, past participle of *inspissare* 'thicken' < *spissus* 'thick'] —**inspissator** /ínspiss aytər/ *n*

inst. *abbr* **1.** instant **2.** instantaneous **3.** institute **4.** institution **5.** institutional

Inst. *abbr* **1.** Institute **2.** Institution

instability /ínstə bíləti/ *n* **1.** the quality of being unstable, erratic, or unpredictable **2.** a lack of steadiness or firmness

~~instalation~~ incorrect spelling of **installation**

install /in stáwl/, **instal** *v* (**-stalls, -stalling, -stalled; -stals, -stalling, -stalled**) **1.** *vt* FIT OR CONNECT SOMETHING to put machinery or equipment into place and make it ready for use **2.** *vt* COMPUT LOAD SOFTWARE to load software onto a computer **3.** *vt* PLACE SOMEBODY IN JOB to appoint somebody to a particular position or to induct somebody formally into office **4. install yourself** *vr* SETTLE IN to settle yourself comfortably somewhere ■ *n* COMPUT ACT OF LOADING SOFTWARE the act of loading software onto a computer ○ '*I opted for the full install, which can involve anything up to 72Mb of space.*' (*Internet Magazine*; November 1998) [15C.

Directly or via French < medieval Latin *installare* 'place in office' < *stallum* 'stall'] —**installer** *n*

installant /in stáwlənt/ *n* somebody who appoints somebody else to a particular position or formally inducts somebody else into office

installation /ínstə láysh'n/ *n* **1.** ACT OF INSTALLING EQUIPMENT the process of putting a piece of equipment or machinery in place and making it ready for use **2.** PLACE WITH EQUIPMENT a place housing equipment or machinery for a particular use ○ *a communications installation* **3.** SOMETHING THAT HAS BEEN INSTALLED a piece of equipment or system that has been put in place and made ready for use **4.** MIL MILITARY BASE a military base or camp ○ *The artillery installation on the island is marked in red on the map.* **5.** APPOINTING OF SOMEBODY TO POSITION the act of appointing somebody to a particular position or of inducting somebody formally into office **6.** ARTS ART EXHIBIT an artwork assembled by an artist that involves the arrangement of three-dimensional objects or the use of paint and other media directly on the walls or floors of the exhibition space ○ *an installation using video monitors and empty bottles*

installation program *n* a computer program used in installing applications or hardware

installment *n* US spelling of **instalment**

installment plan *n* N Am a system for buying merchandise involving a series of payments at regular intervals instead of a single lump sum

instalment /in stáwlmənt/ *n* **1.** one of a series of sums of money paid at regular intervals to settle a debt **2.** one of the parts of something that appears or is presented at intervals ○ *published in instalments* [Mid-18C. < Anglo-Norman *estalment* < Old French *estaler* 'to fix, place']

instalment activity statement *n* FIN full form of **IAS**

instance /ínstənss/ *n* **1.** ILLUSTRATION an example of a particular situation or event ○ *cited several instances of his being untruthful* **2.** EVENT an occurrence of something ○ *We can overlook it in this instance.* **3.** LAW LEGAL ACTION a legal proceeding or lawsuit ■ *vt* (**-stances, -stancing, -stanced**) GIVE SOMETHING AS EXAMPLE to offer something as an example [14C. Via French < Latin *instantia* < *instant-* (see INSTANT)] ◇ **for instance** as an example ◇ **in the first instance** used to indicate something that is or happens first, before other events or stages (*formal*)

instant /ínstənt/ *adj* **1.** IMMEDIATE happening immediately, without delay or effort ○ *an instant dislike* **2.** FOOD QUICK TO PREPARE describes food that is quickly and easily prepared, often premixed, precooked, or powdered ○ *instant coffee* **3.** URGENT AND PRESSING requiring immediate attention or an immediate response ○ *an instant need for help* **4.** CURRENT present or current (*archaic*) **5.** OF THIS MONTH happening in the current month (*archaic*) ○ *your letter of the 13th instant* ■ *n* **1.** SHORT TIME an extremely brief period of time ○ *for an instant* **2.** MOMENT IN TIME a particular moment in time ○ *The instant I saw his face I knew that something was wrong.* **3.** FOOD QUICKLY PREPARED PRODUCT a quickly prepared item of food or drink ■ *adv* INSTANTLY instantly (*literary*) [15C. Via French < Latin *instant-*, present participle of *instare* 'be present' < *stare* 'to stand'] —**instancy** *n*

instantaneous /ínstən táyni əss/ *adj* **1.** occurring immediately or almost immediately **2.** indicating the value of something at a given moment in time, expressed as the average value of a varying quantity over an infinitesimally small time interval ○ *instantaneous velocity* [Mid-17C. < medieval Latin *instantaneus* < Latin *instant-* (see INSTANT)] —**instantaneity** /in stánta náy əti, -neé əti/ *n* —**instantaneously** *adv* —**instantaneousness** *n*

instanter /in stántər/ *adv* without delay [Late 17C. Via medieval Latin < Latin *instant-* 'present' (see INSTANT)]

instantiate /in stánshi ayt/ (**-ates, -ating, -ated**) *vt* to provide an example to support or explain something [Mid-20C. < INSTANCE]

instantly /ínstəntli/ *adv* **1.** IMMEDIATELY immediately and without delay **2.** URGENTLY urgently or insistently (*archaic*) ■ *conj* AS SOON AS immediately after ○ *I phoned instantly I heard you were back.*

instant messaging *n* a system for real-time text messaging on the Internet

instanton /in stánton/ *n* in theoretical cosmology, a mathematical solution, one form of which implies that the universe began as a pea-sized structure of space, time, matter, and energy before the big bang

instant-on *adj* including a device or technology that allows for a rapid start-up, so eliminating the need for a warm-up period

instant replay *n ANZ, N Am* SPORTS, MEDIA a playing back of a videotape in slow motion, usually to show the movement of a ball or player in a sport shown on television. UK term **action replay**

instar /ín staar/ *n* in the life cycle of an arthropod such as an insect, a stage between two successive moults [Late 19C. < Latin, 'form, image']

instate /in stáyt/ (**-states, -stating, -stated**) *vt* to establish somebody in office —**instatement** *n*

in statu quo /in státtoo kwṓ/ *adv* in the same state (*formal*) [< Latin *in statu quo ante* 'in the (same) state as before']

instauration /ín staw ráysh'n/ *n* (*formal*) **1.** the restoration of something that has lapsed or fallen into decay **2.** the founding or establishment of something [Early 17C. < Latin *instauration-* < *instaurare* 'renew'] —**instaurator** /ín staw raytər/ *n*

instead /in stéd/ *adv* as a replacement or substitute for something [13C. < IN [1] + STEAD 'place'] ◇ **instead of** as an alternative to or substitute for something

instep /ín step/ *n* **1.** the arched middle portion of the human foot between the ankle and toes, especially its upper surface **2.** the part of a shoe that covers the middle portion of the foot [15C. Origin ?]

instigate /ínsti gayt/ (**-gates, -gating, -gated**) *vt* **1.** to cause a process to start **2.** to cause trouble, especially by urging somebody to do something destructive or wrong [Mid-16C. < Latin *instigat-*, past participle of *instigare* < *stigare* 'prick, incite'] —**instigation** /ínsti gáysh'n/ *n* —**instigative** *adj* —**instigator** *n*

instil /in stíl/ (**-stils, -stilling, -stilled**) *vt* **1.** to impress ideas, principles, or teachings gradually on somebody's mind ○ *tried to instil self-respect in my students* **2.** to pour medicine or another liquid into something drop by drop [15C. < Latin *instillare* < *stilla* 'drop'] —**instillation** /ínsti láysh'n/ *n* —**instiller** *n* —**instilment** *n*

instill *vt* US spelling of **instil**

instinct /ín stingkt/ *n* **1.** STRONG NATURAL IMPULSE a powerful impulse that feels natural rather than reasoned ○ *followed his instincts and took to his heels* **2.** BIOLOGICAL DRIVE an inborn pattern of behaviour characteristic of a species and shaped by biological necessities such as survival and reproduction ○ *the survival instinct* **3.** KNACK a natural gift or skill ○ *an instinct for putting people at ease* ■ *adj* FILLED completely filled or imbued with something (*formal*) ○ *a look instinct with compassion* [15C. < Latin *instinctus* 'impulse' < *instinguere* 'incite' < *stinguere* 'to sting'] —**instinctual** /in stíngktyoo əl/ *adj*

instinctive /in stíngktiv/ *adj* **1.** relating to, prompted by, or based on a strong natural impulse ○ *an instinctive fear of water* **2.** having a particular quality or skill spontaneously and without effort or instruction ○ *an instinctive feel for colour* ○ *an instinctive cook* —**instinctively** *adv* —**instinctiveness** *n*

institute /ínsti tyoot/ *n* **1.** ORGANIZATION WITH SPECIALIZED GOAL an organization for promoting something such as art, science, or the well-being of a group **2.** PLACE FOR ADVANCED STUDY an educational institution, especially one concerned with technical subjects **3.** PRINCIPLE an established principle or rule ■ **institutes** *npl* LAW LAW SUMMARY a summary of laws ■ *vt* (**-tutes, -tuting, -tuted**) **1.** START SOMETHING to start or initiate something in an official or formal way ○ *institute legal proceedings* **2.** SET SOMETHING UP to set up or establish something ○ *institute a literary prize* **3.** APPOINT SOMEBODY to appoint somebody to an office, especially a religious one [14C. < Latin *institut-*, past participle of *instituere* 'establish' < *statuere* 'set up' < *stare* 'to stand'] —**instituter** *n*

Institute of Advanced Motorists *n* an independent British motoring organization set up to improve driving standards and road safety, especially by administering an advanced driving test

institution /ínsti tyóosh'n/ *n* **1.** IMPORTANT ORGANIZATION a large organization that is influential in the community, e.g. a college, hospital, or bank **2.** ESTABLISHED PRACTICE an established law, custom, or practice ○ *the institution of marriage* **3.** STARTING OF SOMETHING the act of initiating or establishing something **4.** LONG-ESTABLISHED PERSON OR THING somebody or something that has been well known and established in a place for a long time (*informal*) **5.** PLACE OF CARE OR CONFINEMENT a place where people with mental or physical disabilities are cared for **6.** BUSINESS LARGE AND POWERFUL INVESTOR a large financial organization such as a pension fund that has considerable resources for making investments ○ *a mutual fund available only to institutions* —**institutional** *adj* —**institutionally** *adv* —**institutionary** *adj*

institutionalise *vt* SOC SCI another spelling of **institutionalize**

institutionalism /ínsti tyóosh'nəlizəm/ *n* a belief in the merits of established customs and systems —**institutionalist** *n*

institutionalize /ínsti tyóosh'nə līz/ (**-izes, -izing, -ized**), **institutionalise** (**-ises, -ising, -ised**) *vt* **1.** PUT SOMEBODY INTO INSTITUTION to put somebody into an institution such as a children's home, nursing home, or prison **2.** ESTABLISH SOMETHING AS USUAL to make something an established custom or an accepted part of the structure of a large organization or society **3.** MAKE SOMETHING INTO OR LIKE INSTITUTION to convert something into an institution, or make something resemble an institution —**institutionalization** /ínsti tyóosh'nə lī záysh'n/ *n*

institutionalized /ínsti tyóosh'nə līzd/ *adj* **1.** having become an established custom or an accepted part of the structure of a large organization or society because of having existed for so long **2.** lacking the will or ability to think and act independently because of having spent a long time in an institution such as a psychiatric hospital or prison

institutive /ínsti tyootiv/ *adj* serving to establish or being established —**institutively** *adv*

in-store *adj* happening, available, or situated within a large retail outlet such as a supermarket or department store ○ *an in-store bakery*

instr. *abbr* **1.** instruction **2.** EDUC instructor **3.** instrument **4.** GRAM, MUSIC instrumental

instruct /in strúkt/ (**-structs, -structing, -structed**) *vt* **1.** TRAIN SOMEBODY to teach somebody a subject or how to do something **2.** DIRECT SOMEBODY to tell somebody to do something, especially with authority or as an order **3.** GIVE SOMEBODY INFORMATION to inform somebody about something, especially in a formal or official manner ○ *We were instructed that the meeting had been postponed.* **4.** LAW BRIEF JURY AT END OF CASE to give information as a judge to a jury at the end of a case in order to explain the applicable points of law and summarize what has to be proved **5.** OBTAIN LEGAL REPRESENTATION to ask or authorize a lawyer to act on your behalf and supply him or her with relevant information [15C. < Latin *instruct-*, past participle of *instruere* 'prepare, equip' < *struere* 'build'] —**instructible** *adj*

SYNONYMS See ***teach***.

instruction /in strúksh'n/ *n* **1.** STATEMENT OF COMMAND a spoken or written statement of what must be done, especially delivered formally, with official authority, or as an order ○ *acting on instructions we received* **2.** TEACHING OR THINGS TAUGHT teaching in a particular subject or skill, or the facts or skills taught ○ *driving instruction* **3.** TEACHING PROCESS OR PROFESSION the act, process, or profession of teaching **4.** COMPUT COMPUTER COMMAND a code that tells a computer to perform a specific operation ■ **instructions** *npl* **1.** LIST OF THINGS TO DO printed information about how to do, make, assemble, use, or operate something ○ *The instructions are printed on the back of the packet.* **2.** LAW JUDGE'S SUMMARY the information given by a judge to a jury at the end of a case that explains the applicable points of law and summarizes what has to be proved **3.** LAW BRIEFING TO LAWYER the relevant information about a legal case given by a client to a solicitor or a solicitor to a barrister —**instructional** *adj* —**instructionally** *adv*

instructive /in strúktiv/ *adj* providing useful information or insight into something —**instructively** *adv* —**instructiveness** *n*

instructor /in strúktər/ *n* somebody who teaches something such as a sport or a practical skill ○ *a ski instructor* —**instructorship** *n*

instrument /ínstrōōmənt/ *n* **1.** TOOL a tool or mechanical device, especially one used for precision work in science, medicine, or technology **2.** MUSIC OBJECT THAT PRODUCES MUSIC an object used to produce music, e.g. a flute, guitar, or drum **3.** MEASURE MEASURING DEVICE a device that measures or controls something, e.g. a speedometer or voltmeter **4.** MEANS OF DOING SOMETHING somebody or something used as a means of achieving a desired result or accomplishing a particular purpose ○ *The secret police were the state's instrument for controlling the populace.* **5.** OBJECT USED FOR PURPOSE an object that has been or could be used for a purpose ○ *hit by a blunt instrument* **6.** LAW DOCUMENT a legal document (*formal*) ■ *vt* (**-ments, -menting, -mented**) **1.** MUSIC ARRANGE MUSIC to write or arrange a piece of music for performance on musical instruments **2.** MEASURE SUPPLY WITH MEASURING DEVICES to equip something with instruments for measurement or control [13C. Via French < Latin *instrumentum* < *instruere* 'prepare' (see INSTRUCT)]

instrumental /ínstrōō mént'l/ *adj* **1.** MAKING SOMETHING HAPPEN playing an important part in achieving a result or accomplishing a purpose ○ *She was instrumental in getting the legislation passed.* **2.** MUSIC FOR INSTRUMENTS, NOT VOICES performed on a musical instrument or instruments, not with the voice **3.** CONNECTED WITH INSTRUMENTS done with or produced by an instrument or instruments ○ *instrumental readings* **4.** GRAM INDICATING MEANS OF DOING SOMETHING used to describe a noun case that indicates that something is used for a purpose or is the means by which something is done **5.** PHILOSOPHY OF INSTRUMENTALISM relating to instrumentalism ■ *n* **1.** MUSIC MUSIC PLAYED BY INSTRUMENTS a piece of music that is performed on a musical instrument or instruments, not with the voice **2.** GRAM NOUN FORM INDICATING MEANS the instrumental case, or a noun in the instrumental case —**instrumentally** *adv*

instrumentalism /ínstrōō mént'lizəm/ *n* the belief that theories are useful tools for making predictions but cannot be literally true or false

instrumentalist /ínstrōō mént'list/ *n* **1.** MUSIC PLAYER OF INSTRUMENT somebody who plays a musical instrument **2.** PHILOSOPHY PROPONENT OF INSTRUMENTALISM a supporter or advocate of instrumentalism ■ *adj* PHILOSOPHY ADVOCATING INSTRUMENTALISM supporting or advocating instrumentalism

instrumentality /ínstrōō men tálləti/ (*plural* **-ties**) *n* (*formal*) **1.** QUALITY OF BEING INSTRUMENTAL the quality or state of being instrumental **2.** ACTION OR USE interventionist action ○ *'But for her instrumentality, the fatal knowledge would not have been imparted.'* (Elizabeth Gaskell, *Some Passages from the History of the Chomley Family*; 1865) **3.** *US* POL SECTION in the United States, a subsidiary branch of a department or agency

instrumental learning *n* a form of learning that takes place as a direct consequence of a reward or pleasant outcome for the learner

instrumentation /ínstrōō men táysh'n, ínstrəmən-/ *n* **1.** MUSIC ARRANGEMENT FOR MUSICAL INSTRUMENTS the composition or arrangement of music for performance, in which a combination of musical instruments is specified **2.** MUSIC MUSICAL INSTRUMENTS USED the instruments that are used to perform a piece of music **3.** EQUIPMENT FOR CONTROL OR OPERATION a set of instruments used for a specific purpose such as operating a machine or controlling an aircraft **4.** USE OF INSTRUMENTS the use of instruments as tools or for measurement or control **5.** MAKING OF INSTRUMENTS the design, development, or manufacture of instruments for use in science, medicine, technology, or industry **6.** MEANS the means or agency through which something is done (*formal*)

instrument board *n* TECH same as **instrument panel**

instrument flying *n* the flying of an aircraft using only information obtained from instruments rather than from what the pilot can see out of the window

instrument landing *n* the landing of an aircraft while relying on information obtained from instruments rather than from what the pilot can see out of the window

instrument panel *n* a set of instruments mounted at the front of a machine or in front of somebody driving or steering a motor vehicle, aircraft, or ship

insubordinate /ín sə báwrdinət/ *adj* refusing to obey orders or submit to authority ■ *n* somebody who refuses to obey orders or submit to authority —**insubordinately** *adv* —**insubordination** /ín sə báwrdə náysh'n/ *n*

insubstantial /ín səb stánsh'l/ *adj* **1.** not very large, solid, or strong **2.** not existing in reality ○ *an insubstantial apparition* —**insubstantiality** /ín ssəb stanshi állәti/ *n* —**insubstantially** *adv*

insufferable /in súffərəb'l/ *adj* so annoying, unpleasant, or uncomfortable as to be unbearable —**insufferableness** *n* —**insufferably** *adv*

insufficiency /ínsə físh'nssi/ (*plural* **-cies**) *n* **1. NOT ENOUGH** a smaller number or lesser amount than is needed ○ *an insufficiency of provisions for a long cruise* **2.** MED **UNFITNESS OR FAILURE** the inability or failure to perform competently, adequately, or as usual ○ *cardiac insufficiency* **3. FAILURE TO MEASURE UP** a failure to meet a standard or requirement ○ *the insufficiency of the causes presented to explain this phenomenon*

insufficient /ínsə físh'nt/ *adj* not enough in amount or quality to satisfy a purpose or standard ○ *We were given insufficient notice.* —**insufficiently** *adv*

insufflate /ínssə flayt, in súf layt/ (**-flates, -flating, -flated**) *vt* **1. BLOW INTO SOMETHING** to blow or breathe into something (*formal*) **2. BLOW SOMETHING INTO BODY CAVITY** to blow something such as air, powder, or gas into the lungs or another body cavity in the course of medical treatment **3. BLOW ON SOMEBODY OR SOMETHING** to blow or breathe on somebody or something as part of a Christian religious sacrament or ritual such as baptism or exorcism, in order to symbolize the Holy Spirit [Late 17C. < Latin *insufflat-*, past participle of *insufflare* < *sufflare* 'blow up'] —**insufflation** /ínssə fláysh'n/ *n* —**insufflator** *n*

insular /ínssyŏŏlər/ *adj* **1. LIMITED IN OUTLOOK** concerned only with local matters and not interested in new ideas or different cultures **2. NOT CLOSE TO OTHERS** physically or emotionally removed from others **3. OF ISLANDS** relating to or originating in an island **4.** ANAT **OF ISLANDS OF CELLS** relating to a collection of cells or tissue reminiscent of an island [Mid-16C. Via French < late Latin *insularis* < Latin *insula* 'island'] —**insularism** *n* —**insularity** /ínssyŏŏ lárrəti/ *n* —**insularly** *adv*

insulate /ínssyŏŏ layt/ (**-lates, -lating, -lated**) *vt* **1.** to prevent or reduce the passage of heat, electricity, or sound into, from, or through something, especially by surrounding it with some material **2.** to protect or isolate somebody from something, especially from something unpleasant or undesirable [Mid-16C < Latin *insula* 'island'] —**insulant** *n*

insulating tape *n UK, ANZ, Can* a thin strip of adhesive material that can be wrapped round bare wires or electrical connections to stop electricity from passing from them to somebody or something that touches them. US term **friction tape**

insulation /ínssyŏŏ láysh'n/ *n* **1. MATERIAL THAT INSULATES** material that prevents or reduces the passage of heat, electricity, or sound, e.g. a special fabric or a layer of air **2. PREVENTION OF CONDUCTION** the act of covering or surrounding something to prevent or reduce the passage of heat, electricity, or sound **3. PROTECTION** protection or isolation from something undesirable or unpleasant —**insulative** /ínssyŏŏlətiv, -laytiv/ *adj*

insulator /ínssyŏŏ laytər/ *n* a material or device that prevents or reduces the passage of heat, electricity, or sound

insulin /ínssyŏŏlin/ *n* a hormone produced in the pancreas that regulates the level of glucose in the blood [Early 20C. < Latin *insula* 'island', after the ISLETS OF LANGERHANS]

insulin shock, insulin reaction *n* a severe drop in blood sugar resulting from an excess of insulin and marked by sweating, dizziness, trembling, and eventual coma

insult *v* /in súlt/ (**-sults, -sulting, -sulted**) **1.** *vti* **BE OFFENSIVE TO SOMEBODY** to say or do something rude or insensitive that offends somebody **2.** *vt* **SHOW CONTEMPT FOR SOMEBODY OR SOMETHING** to say or do something that suggests a low opinion of somebody or something ○ *Don't insult me by offering me pity.* ■ *n* /ín sult/ **1. OFFENSIVE WORDS OR ACTION** a remark or action that offends somebody, usually because it is rude or insensitive **2. SOMETHING SHOWING CONTEMPT** a remark or action that suggests a low opinion of somebody or something ○ *The article is an insult to the intelligence of the reader.* ○ *The fee they offered was an insult.* **3.** MED **INJURY OR CAUSE OF INJURY** an injury or trauma to the body, or something that causes such harm [Mid-16C. Via French < Latin *insultare*, literally 'keep jumping on' < *salire* 'to jump'] —**insulter** *n*

USAGE Insults English has insult words for most races and cultures with which its speakers have come into extended contact, and for so-called minority groups within English-speaking society, even though such groups can and do constitute demographic majorities in many regions. When the people insulted are English-speakers, the insulting words can and often do become part of their own vocabulary. Those insulted will generally avoid using these terms in interaction with their insulters, since to do so would be to endorse the insulters' view of them. However, among themselves they may well deliberately adopt an insult in order to subvert it or rob it of its power. For instance, Australian Aboriginals reportedly are not averse to using terms like *Abo* and *blackfella* when talking to each other, even though they are highly offensive when applied to them by non-Aboriginals. The best-known example of this is *nigger*. It began (in the 16th century) as a neutral term for a Black person, but in the latter part of the 18th century it started to be used by white people as an abusive term. In spite of this, there is ample evidence that Black Americans continued to use it in relation to themselves throughout the 19th century, and in the 20th century it became a positive term of solidarity and pride among Blacks (often defiantly spelt *nigga* or *nigguh* in this context). It remains, of course, strictly taboo for a white speaker. Similarly, other groups may defy their detractors by adopting the insults directed at them: gay people may refer to themselves, polemically, as *queer*, as in *Queer Nation*; and some feminists have struck back against ageist put-downs by reclaiming *crone* and making it their own.

insulting /in súlting/ *adj* causing offence by being rude or insensitive or by suggesting a low opinion of somebody or something —**insultingly** *adv*

insuperable /in sóopərəb'l/ *adj* impossible to overcome, get rid of, or deal with successfully ○ *battling against insuperable odds* [14C. Directly or via French < Latin *insuperabilis* < *superare* 'to overcome' < *super* 'above'] —**insuperability** /in sóopərə bílləti/ *n* —**insuperably** *adv*

insupportable /ínsə páwrtəb'l/ *adj* **1.** too great, unpleasant, or difficult to bear ○ *insupportable heat* **2.** impossible to justify or defend ○ *an insupportable claim* —**insupportably** *adv*

insurable interest *n* a demonstrable interest in something covered by an insurance policy, the loss of which would cause deprivation or financial loss. Insurable interest must be shown whenever somebody takes out an insurance policy or makes a claim.

insurance /in shóoranss, -sháwr-/ *n* **1. FINANCIAL PROTECTION AGAINST LOSS OR HARM** an arrangement by which a company gives customers financial protection against loss or harm such as theft or illness in return for payment (**premium**) **2. MONEY PAID BY INSURANCE COMPANY** the sum of money that an insurance company pays or agrees to pay if a specific undesirable event occurs **3. PREMIUM** the payment made to obtain insurance ○ *My car insurance has gone up again.* **4. INSURANCE BUSINESS** the commercial business of providing insurance **5. MEANS OF PROTECTION** an act, measure, or provision that gives protection against an undesirable event or risk ○ *provided a map as insurance against getting lost* [15C. < Old French *enseürance* < *enseürer* (see ENSURE)]

USAGE See *assurance*.

insurance policy *n* a written contract between an insurance company and a person or organization requiring insurance against loss or harm

insure /in shóor, -sháwr/ (**-sures, -suring, -sured**) *v* **1.** *vti* to agree formally that, for a sum of money paid to a company, the company will pay compensation or costs if a particular harm or loss occurs to somebody or something ○ *insured the ring for £5,000* **2.** *vi* to get protection from something undesirable that might happen, usually by making contingency plans or taking precautionary or preventive measures **3.** *vt N Am* another spelling of **ensure** [15C. Variant of ENSURE] —**insurable** *adj* —**insured** *adj, n*

USAGE See *assure*.

~~insurence~~ incorrect spelling of **insurance**

insurer /in shóorər, -sháwr-/ *n* a person or company providing insurance

insurgent /in súrjənt/ *n* somebody who rebels against authority or leadership, especially somebody who belongs to a group involved in an uprising ■ *adj* rebelling against authority or leadership, especially against a government or ruler of a country [Mid-18C. < Latin *insurgent-*, present participle of *insurgere* 'rise up' < *surgere* 'to rise'] —**insurgence** *n* —**insurgency** *n* —**insurgently** *adv*

insurmountable /ín sər mówntəb'l/ *adj* impossible to overcome or deal with successfully —**insurmountability** /ín sər mówntə bílləti/ *n* —**insurmountably** *adv*

insurrection /ínssə réksh'n/ *n* a rebellion against the government or rulers of a country, often involving armed conflict [15C. < Latin *insurrection-* < past participle of *insurgere* 'rise up'] —**insurrectional** *adj* —**insurrectionary** *n, adj* —**insurrectionism** *n* —**insurrectionist** *n, adj*

insusceptible /ín sə séptəb'l/ *adj* **1.** not likely to be affected or influenced by something **2.** not able to undergo a particular process —**insusceptibility** /ín sə séptə bílləti/ *n* —**insusceptibly** *adv*

inswing /ín swing/ *n* in cricket, the curve of a bowled ball from the batter's off to leg side [Early 20C. Back-formation < INSWINGER]

inswinger /ín swingər/ *n* **1.** in cricket, a ball that curves through the air from the batter's off to leg side **2.** in football, a ball kicked, particularly from a corner, that curves through the air towards the goal

int *abbr* ONLINE international organization (*used in Internet addresses*) See table at **domain name**

int. *abbr* **1.** (military) intelligence **2.** intercept **3.** BANKING interest **4.** interim **5.** interior **6.** GRAM interjection **7.** intermediate **8.** internal **9.** international **10.** interpreter **11.** MATHS intersection **12.** interval **13.** interview **14.** GRAM intransitive

Int. *abbr* International

intact /in tákt/ *adj* **1. NOT DAMAGED** whole and undamaged ○ *found the ancient tomb intact* **2. COMPLETE** not having any missing parts ○ *kept the collection intact* **3.** ANAT **WITHOUT ANY REMOVED PARTS** having all body parts in place and undamaged [15C. < Latin *intactus* 'untouched' < *tangere* 'to touch'] —**intactly** *adv* —**intactness** *n*

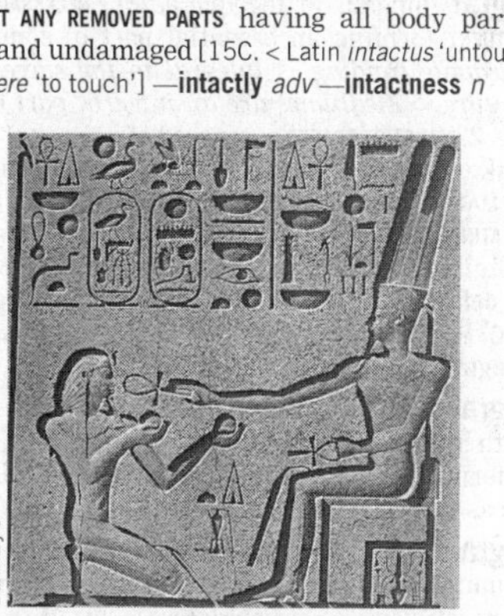

Barnaby's

intaglio: Ancient Egyptian granite carving

intaglio /in táali ō, -tálli ō/ (*plural* **-glios**) *n* **1. HOLLOWED-OUT DESIGN** a carving made by cutting a hollowed-out design in material such as stone **2. CARVING OF INTAGLIOS** the process or art of carving hollowed-out designs in material such as stone **3. CARVED GEM** a gem in which a hollowed-out design has been carved **4.** PRINTING **PRINTING WITH INCISED PLATES** a printing technique such as engraving or etching in which the design is cut into the plate instead of protruding from it **5.** PRINTING **INCISED PRINTING PLATE** a printing

plate into which a design is cut [Mid-17C. < Italian < *intagliare* 'engrave' < *tagliare* 'to cut']

intake /in tayk/ *n* **1. AMOUNT TAKEN IN** an amount taken in or consumed ○ *increase your intake of fluids* **2. PEOPLE ADMITTED** the number of people admitted to a place or organization at a particular time, or the people themselves, especially those entering an educational establishment at the beginning of an academic year ○ *The college has increased its intake of mature students.* **3. TAKING IN OF SOMETHING** the process of taking in a substance, especially by eating or drinking **4. OPENING THROUGH WHICH FLUID PASSES** an opening through which fluid enters a duct or contained area ○ *the fuel intake*

intangible /in tánjəb'l/ *adj* **1. NONMATERIAL** lacking material qualities, and so not able to be touched or seen ○ *intangible benefits* **2. HARD TO DESCRIBE** difficult to define or describe clearly, but nonetheless perceived ○ *an intangible quality of serenity in the music* ■ *n* **SOMETHING UNQUANTIFIABLE** an unquantifiable quality or asset ○ *such intangibles as duty* —**intangibility** /in tánjə bílləti/ *n* —**intangibly** *adv*

intangible asset *n* a business asset such as a firm's customer goodwill that is of value although it is not directly quantifiable in terms of goods produced or sold

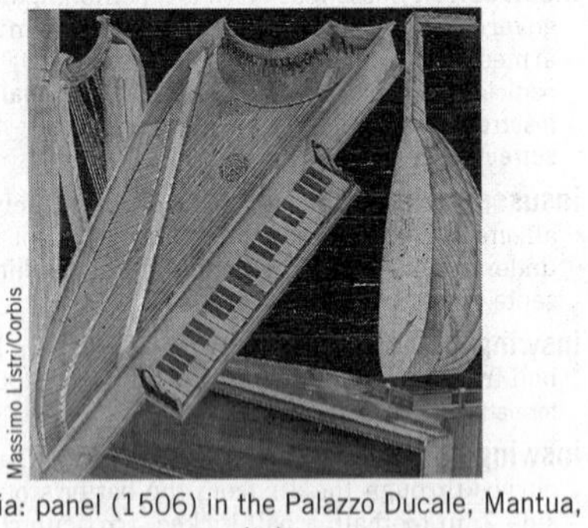
Massimo Listri/Corbis
intarsia: panel (1506) in the Palazzo Ducale, Mantua, Italy

intarsia /in taárssi ə/ *n* **1. WOOD INLAY** wood inlay using different colours of wood, commonly used in furniture in the Italian Renaissance **2.** HANDICRAFT **WAY OF KNITTING** a method of knitting with two or more coloured yarns in which the pattern can be seen from both sides of the finished piece **3.** HANDICRAFT **MAKING OF INTARSIAS** the art or process of making intarsias, e.g. for wall panels [Mid-19C. < German, alteration of Italian *intarsio* < Arabic *tarṣī'*]

integer /íntijər/ *n* **1.** a positive or negative whole number or zero **2.** a whole unit or entity (*technical*) [Early 16C. < Latin, 'whole']

integral /íntigrəl, in téggrəl/ *adj* **1. NECESSARY OR CONSTITUENT** forming an essential part of something ○ *Adequate funding is integral to the success of the venture.* ○ *Mealtimes are an integral part of family life.* **2. MADE UP OF PARTS** composed of parts that together make a whole **3. COMPLETE** having no missing parts **4.** MATHS **OF INTEGER** relating to an integer **5.** MATHS **RELATING TO INTEGRALS** relating to definite integrals, indefinite integrals, or integration ■ *n* MATHS **1.** same as **definite integral 2.** same as **indefinite integral** [Mid-16C. < late Latin *integralis* < Latin *integer* 'whole'] —**integrality** /ínti grálləti/ *n* —**integrally** *adv*

integral calculus *n* a branch of mathematics dealing with integrals and differential equations, used to determine areas, volumes, and lengths, and in many areas of applied mathematics

integrand /ínti grand/ *n* a mathematical function or equation to be integrated [Late 19C. < Latin *integrandus* 'to be integrated' < *integrare* (see INTEGRATE)]

integrant /íntigrənt/ (*formal*) *adj* part of a whole ■ *n* an integral part of something

integrate /ínti grayt/ (**-grates, -grating, -grated**) *v* **1.** *vti* **FIT IN WITH GROUP** to become an accepted member of a group and its activities, or help somebody do this ○ *integrating newcomers into the community* **2.** *vti* **MAKE INTO WHOLE** to join two or more objects or make something part of a larger whole, or be joined or made part of a larger whole ○ *integrating light rail into the regional transport plan* **3.** *vt* **MAKE SOMETHING OPEN TO ALL** to make a group, community, place, or organization and its opportunities available to everyone, regardless of race, ethnicity, religion, gender, or social class **4.** *vt* MATHS **FIND MATHEMATICAL INTEGRAL OF SOMETHING** to find the definite or indefinite integral of a function or equation [Mid-17C. < Latin *integrat-*, past participle of *integrare* 'make whole' < *integer* 'whole'] —**integrability** /íntigrə bílləti/ *n* —**integrable** *adj* —**integrative** *adj*

integrated /ínti graytid/ *adj* **1. COMBINED OR COMPOSITE** made up of aspects or parts that work well together ○ *an integrated communications system* **2. COMBINING DISSIMILAR THINGS** bringing together processes or functions that are normally separate **3. OPEN TO ALL PEOPLE** open to everyone, regardless of race, ethnicity, religion, gender, or social class

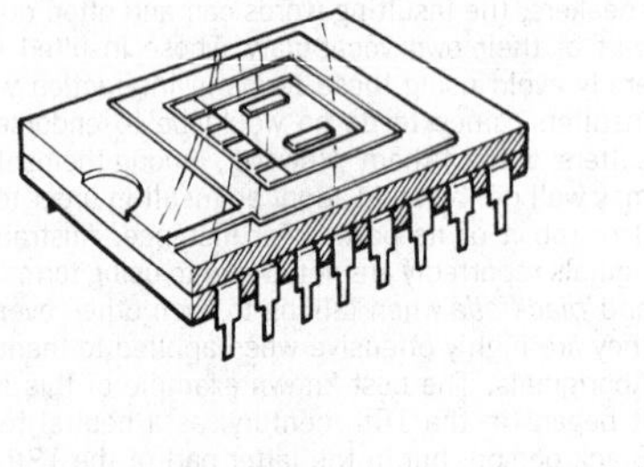
integrated circuit

integrated circuit *n* a tiny complex of electronic components contained on a thin chip or wafer of semiconducting material —**integrated circuitry** *n*

integration /ínti gráysh'n/ *n* **1. EQUAL ACCESS FOR ALL** the process of opening a group, community, place, or organization to all, regardless of race, ethnicity, religion, gender, or social class **2. ACCEPTANCE INTO COMMUNITY** the process of becoming an accepted member of a group or community **3. COMBINATION** a combination of parts or objects that work together well **4.** MATHS **MATHEMATICAL OPERATION** the mathematical process of finding the solution of a differential equation or a function whose differential equation is known **5.** PSYCHOL **ORGANIZATION OF PERSONALITY TRAITS** the process of coordinating separate personality elements into a balanced whole or producing behaviour compatible with somebody's environment

integrationist /ínti gráysh'nist/ *n* a supporter or activist who works to promote or maintain integration ■ *adj* supporting, promoting, or maintaining integration

integrator /ínti graytər/ *n* **1.** a computer component that performs numerical integration to solve differential equations **2.** somebody or something that brings about integration

integrin /in téggrin/ *n* a cell-surface receptor that is a glycoprotein involved in homeostasis, wound healing, and immune defence mechanisms [Late 20C. < INTEGRATE]

integrity /in téggrəti/ *n* **1. POSSESSION OF FIRM PRINCIPLES** the quality of possessing and steadfastly adhering to high moral principles or professional standards **2. COMPLETENESS** the state of being complete or undivided (*formal*) ○ *the territorial integrity of the nation* **3. WHOLENESS** the state of being sound or undamaged (*formal*) ○ *Their refusal to participate in the experiment will undermine its integrity.* [15C. Via French < Latin *integritas* < *integer* 'whole']

integument /in téggyoōmənt/ *n* an outer protective layer or part of an animal or plant, e.g. a shell, rind, husk, or skin [Early 17C. < Latin *integumentum* < *integere* 'cover up' < *tegere* 'to cover'] —**integumental** /in téggyoō mént'l/ *adj* —**integumentary** /in téggyoō méntəri/ *adj*

~~**intelectual**~~ incorrect spelling of **intellectual**

~~**inteligence**~~ incorrect spelling of **intelligence**

intellect /íntə lekt/ *n* **1.** somebody's ability to think, reason, and understand ○ *appeals to the intellect rather than the emotions* ○ *a highly developed intellect* **2.** a very intelligent and knowledgeable person ○ *some of the ablest intellects of the period* [14C. Via French < Latin *intellectus* < past participle of *intellegere* (see INTELLIGENT)]

intellection /íntə léksh'n/ *n* (*formal*) **1.** thinking, reasoning, or other mental activity **2.** a thought or an idea —**intellective** *adj* —**intellectively** *adv*

intellectual /íntə lékchoo əl/ *adj* **1. RELATING TO THOUGHT PROCESS** relating to or involving the mental processes of abstract thinking and reasoning rather than the emotions **2. INTELLIGENT AND KNOWLEDGEABLE** having a highly developed ability to think, reason, and understand, especially in combination with wide knowledge **3. FOR INTELLIGENT PEOPLE** intended for, appealing to, or done by intelligent people ○ *intellectual pursuits* ■ *n* **INTELLIGENT PERSON** somebody with a highly developed ability to reason and understand, especially if also well educated and interested in the arts or sciences or enjoying activities involving serious mental effort [15C. Via French < late Latin *intellectualis* < Latin *intellectus* (see INTELLECT)] —**intellectuality** /íntə lekchoo álləti/ *n* —**intellectually** *adv*

intellectualise *vti* another spelling of **intellectualize**

intellectualism /íntə lékchoo əlizəm/ *n* **1. DEVELOPMENT OF POWER TO THINK** the development and use of the ability to think, reason, and understand **2. TOO MUCH ATTENTION TO THINKING** overemphasis on intellectual processes or pursuits **3.** PHILOSOPHY **BELIEF THAT KNOWLEDGE COMES FROM REASONING** the doctrine that all that can truly be called knowledge is derived from reasoning —**intellectualist** *n* —**intellectualistic** /íntə lékchoo ə lístik/ *adj* —**intellectualistically** *adv*

intellectualize /íntə lékchoo ə līz/ (**-izes, -izing, -ized**), **intellectualise** (**-ises, -ising, -ised**) *v* **1.** *vti* **CONSIDER SOMETHING RATIONALLY** to analyse, deal with, or explain something exclusively by thinking or reasoning **2.** *vi* **THINK** to think or reason **3.** *vti* **MAKE OR BECOME INTELLECTUAL** to make somebody or something intellectual, or become intellectual ○ *intellectualized poetry* **4.** *vt* PSYCHOL **REASON AWAY PROBLEMS** to protect yourself unconsciously from the emotional stress that would come from dealing with fears or problems by reasoning them away —**intellectualization** /íntə lékchoo ə lī záysh'n/ *n* —**intellectualizer** *n*

intellectual property *n* original creative work manifested in a tangible form that can be legally protected, e.g. by a patent, trademark, or copyright

intelligence /in téllijənss/ *n* **1. ABILITY TO THINK AND LEARN** the ability to learn facts and skills and apply them, especially when this ability is highly developed **2. SECRET INFORMATION** information about secret plans or activities, especially those of foreign governments, the armed forces, business competitors, or criminals **3. GATHERING OF SECRET INFORMATION** the collection of secret military or political information **4. PEOPLE GATHERING SECRET INFORMATION** an organization that gathers information about the secret plans or activities of an adversary or potential adversary, or the people involved in gathering such information **5. INTELLIGENT SPIRIT** an entity capable of rational thought, especially one that does not have a physical form [14C. Via French < Latin *intelligentia* < *intelligent-* (see INTELLIGENT)] —**intelligential** /in télli jénsh'l/ *adj*

intelligence quotient *n* PSYCHOL, EDUC full form of **IQ**

intelligencer /in téllijənssər/ *n* somebody who supplies or gathers information, especially about secret plans or activities (*archaic*)

intelligent /in téllijənt/ *adj* **1. MENTALLY ABLE** having intelligence, especially to a highly developed degree **2. SENSIBLE OR RATIONAL** showing or resulting from an ability to think and understand things clearly and logically ○ *an intelligent solution* **3.** COMPUT **ABLE TO STORE AND PROCESS DATA** having a built-in electronic processing and data storage ability ○ *an intelligent terminal* **4.** COMPUT **SELF-REGULATING** programmed to be able to adjust to changes in the environment and make deductions from information being processed ○ *an intelligent building* [Early 16C. < Latin *intelligent-*, present participle of *intellegere* 'perceive, discern' < *inter-* 'between' + *legere* 'choose, read'] —**intelligently** *adv*

SYNONYMS ***intelligent, bright, quick, smart, clever, able, gifted***

CORE MEANING: having the ability to learn and understand easily

intelligent having a highly developed ability to learn facts and skills and apply them ○ *a highly intelligent group of engineers* ○ *We're looking for trainees who are intelligent, inquisitive, and passionate about their*

work. **bright** showing an ability to think, learn, or respond quickly, especially used of younger people ○ *He's a bright and unusually focused little boy.* ○ *lucky to work with some of the real comers and bright young people* **quick** alert, perceptive, and able to respond quickly ○ *She's quick: you'll only need to explain it to her once.* **smart** showing intelligence and mental alertness but sometimes suggesting insolent intelligence ○ *too smart to be taken in by the hype* ○ *He's smart, but it was a mistake for him not to take advice.* **clever** having sharp mental abilities, sometimes suggesting showy or superficial cleverness ○ *As a bridge player, he's very clever at anticipating his opponents' moves.* ○ *her clever exploitation of Hollywood's publicity machine* **able** capable or talented, also used in educational circles of children who are intelligent ○ *an exceptionally able manager who gets results from his team* ○ *accused of favouring the able children in the class* **gifted** talented, especially artistically or creatively, also used in educational circles of children who are exceptionally intelligent ○ *acclaimed as an exceptionally gifted pianist from the time of his first solo recital* ○ *took on the challenge of teaching the gifted students*

intelligentsia /in télli jéntsi ə/ *n* the most intelligent, intellectual, or highly educated members of a society or community, especially those who are interested in the arts, literature, philosophy, and politics [Early 20C. Via Russian *intelligentsiya* < Latin *intelligentia* (see INTELLIGENCE)]

intelligible /in téllijəb'l/ *adj* **1.** capable of being understood ○ *His speech was barely intelligible.* **2.** PHILOSOPHY perceptible only by the mind, not the senses [14C. Via French < Latin *intelligibilis* < *intellegere* (see INTELLIGENT)] —**intelligibility** /in téllijə bílləti/ *n* —**intelligibly** *adv*

Intelsat /ín tel sat/, **INTELSAT** *n* **1.** an international organization that owns the communications satellites that orbit Earth and whose members include the telecommunications agencies of most countries. Full form **International Telecommunications Satellite Organization 2.** a telecommunications satellite launched by Intelsat

intemperate /in témpərət/ *adj* **1.** LACKING SELF-CONTROL having or showing a lack of self-control, especially in expressing feelings or satisfying physical desires **2.** DRINKING TO EXCESS drinking too much alcohol, especially frequently **3.** METEOROL TOO HOT OR COLD extremely or unpleasantly hot or cold (*formal*) —**intemperance** *n* —**intemperately** *adv* —**intemperateness** *n*

intend /in ténd/ (**-tends, -tending, -tended**) *vt* **1.** MEAN TO DO SOMETHING to have something in mind as a plan ○ *I really intended to write, but I didn't have time.* **2.** DO OR SAY SOMETHING FOR PURPOSE to do, say, or produce something with a particular purpose, use, target, or group of people in mind ○ *a dictionary intended for schoolchildren* **3.** MEAN SOMETHING to signify or indicate something through speech or behaviour ○ *What impression did he intend to give us with such a remark?* [14C. Via French < Latin *intendere* < *in-* 'towards' + *tendere* 'to stretch']

intendant /in téndənt/ *n* an official or administrator in some countries, especially currently in parts of Latin America and formerly in France, Spain, and Portugal [Mid-17C. < French < Latin *intendent-*, present participle of *intendere* (see INTEND)] —**intendance** *n* —**intendancy** *n*

intended /in téndid/ *adj* **1.** ENVISAGED aimed at or designed for somebody or something ○ *our intended destination* **2.** PLANNED planned for the future ○ *an intended visit* **3.** DELIBERATE said or done deliberately ○ *an intended insult* ■ *n* FUTURE HUSBAND OR WIFE the person to whom somebody is engaged to be married (*dated or humorous*) ○ *He cherished the letter from his intended.* —**intendedly** *adv*

intending /in ténding/ *adj* planning to be or become something

intendment /in téndmənt/ *n* the meaning of something, especially a word or term, according to law

intens. *abbr* **1.** intensifier **2.** intensify **3.** intensive

intense /in ténss/ *adj* **1.** EXTREME great, strong, or extreme in a way that can be felt ○ *intense heat* **2.** EFFORTFUL OR ACTIVE involving great effort or much activity ○ *showed intense dedication to the task* **3.**

CONCENTRATED narrowly focused or concentrated ○ *an intense stare* **4.** PASSIONATE feeling or showing strong and deeply felt emotions in a serious way ○ *a very intense young student* **5.** *US* THRILLING extremely exciting or pleasing (*informal*) [15C. Via French < Latin *intensus*, past participle of *intendere* (see INTEND)] —**intenseness** *n*

intensely /in ténssli/ *adv* **1.** EXTREMELY very much **2.** STRONGLY strongly or brightly ○ *intensely pink curtains* **3.** PENETRATINGLY in a fixed and penetrating way **4.** PASSIONATELY with great passion or enthusiasm

intensifier /in ténssi fī ər/ *n* **1.** *UK, ANZ, Can* GRAM a word or phrase, e.g. 'definitely', 'quite', or 'hardly', that indicates the relative degree to which something applies, as in 'quite good' or 'hardly enough'. US term **intensive 2.** somebody or something that makes something larger, sharper, or stronger

intensify /in ténssi fī/ (**-fies, -fying, -fied**) *vti* **1.** to become, or make something become, greater or stronger ○ *media interest intensified as the week progressed* **2.** to do something with greater effort or more activity, or become more concentrated ○ *intensified the search* —**intensification** /in ténssifi káysh'n/ *n*

SYNONYMS See *increase*.

intension /in ténsh'n/ *n* **1.** LOGIC the meaning of an expression as opposed to what it refers to. The intension of the word 'human' is the property of being human, whereas it has as its reference, or extension, human beings as a group. **2.** same as **intensity** (sense 1) (*formal*) [Early 17C. < Latin *intension-* < *intensus* (see INTENSE)] —**intensional** *adj* —**intensionally** *adv*

intensional object *n* in logic, a concept, property, or proposition, as opposed to an individual, set, or truth value, which are the extensional counterparts of intensional objects

intensity /in ténssəti/ (*plural* **-ties**) *n* **1.** QUALITY OF BEING INTENSE the strength, power, force, or concentration of something ○ *The pain increased in intensity.* **2.** INTENSE MANNER a passionate and serious attitude or quality ○ *a rare emotional intensity in her work* **3.** PHYS MAGNITUDE OF ENERGY the strength of a source of energy such as light, electricity, or sound per unit area, mass, or time

intensive /in ténssiv/ *adj* **1.** CONCENTRATED involving concentrated effort, usually in order to achieve something in a comparatively short time ○ *an intensive course in German* **2.** AGRIC INCREASING AGRICULTURAL PRODUCTION relating to a form of agriculture in which scientific and technological methods such as the use of chemicals that boost growth or crop yields are used to increase productivity **3.** MAKING HEAVY USE OF SOMETHING requiring or using a great deal of a particular thing (*often used in combination*) ○ *capital-intensive* **4.** GRAM INDICATING HOW MUCH describes a word or phrase, e.g. 'extremely', that emphasizes or intensifies the word that it modifies ■ *n US* GRAM same as **intensifier** (sense 1) —**intensively** *adv* —**intensiveness** *n*

intensive care *n* **1.** HEALTH SERVICES same as **intensive care unit 2.** MED the monitoring, care, and treatment in hospital of patients who are seriously ill or injured, especially by the use of specialist equipment such as that aiding breathing. ◊ **critical care**

intensive care unit *n* the department of a hospital that is designed and equipped for the monitoring, care, and treatment of seriously ill or injured patients

intent /in tént/ *n* **1.** PLAN OR PURPOSE something planned, or the purpose that accompanies a plan ○*My intent is to use our attractive domestic market as the basis of a muscular free trade policy that will strengthen America's global economic reach...'* (*National Public Telecomputing Network, George H. W. Bush speeches in campaign '92; 1992*) **2.** LAW STATE OF MIND somebody's state of mind when deliberately committing or planning to commit an illegal act **3.** CONNOTATION the meaning or significance of something, especially when not explicitly expressed ■ *adj* **1.** WITH FIXED ATTENTION having full attention or effort concentrated or focused on one thing ○ *Intent on her work, she lost track of the time.* **2.** DETERMINED showing great determination to do something ○ *They are intent on catching the early train.* [13C. < Old French

entent < Latin *intendere* (see INTEND)] —**intently** *adv* —**intentness** *n* ◇ **to all intents and purposes** in effect, although not actually

intention /in ténsh'n/ *n* **1.** AIM OR OBJECTIVE something that somebody plans to do ○ *State your intentions.* **2.** QUALITY OF PURPOSEFULNESS the quality or state of having a purpose in mind ○ *She acted without intention.* ■ **intentions** *npl* SOMEBODY'S MARRIAGE PLANS somebody's plans with respect to marriage (*dated*) ○ *What are your intentions towards my daughter?* [14C. Via French < Latin *intention-* < *intendere* (see INTEND)]

intentional /in ténsh'nəl/ *adj* **1.** done on purpose, not by accident **2.** PHILOSOPHY involving thoughts such as beliefs or desires about different kinds of objects, including those that have no actual existence — **intentionality** /in ténshə nálləti/ *n* —**intentionally** *adv*

inter /in túr/ (**-ters, -terring, -terred**) *vt* to bury the remains of a corpse in a grave or tomb [15C. < Old French *enterer* < Latin *terra* 'earth']

inter- *prefix* **1.** between, among ○ *interlinear* ○ *interstate* ○ *intercut* **2.** mutual, reciprocal ○ *interchange* **3.** involving two or more groups ○ *international* [Directly or via French *entre* < Latin *inter* 'between, among' < Indo-European, 'more in']

inter-African *adj*	**interindustry** *adj*
interagency *adj*	**interinstitutional** *adj*
interallied *adj*	**interisland** *adj*
interatomic *adj*	**interjurisdictional** *adj*
interborough *adj*	**interlend** *vt*
interbranch *adj*	**interlobular** *adj*
intercaste *adj*	**intermigration** *n*
intercell *adj*	**intermolecular** *adj*
intercellular *adj*	**intermolecularly** *adv*
interchromosomal *adj*	**interoceanic** *adj*
interchurch *adj*	**interoffice** *adj*
intercity *adj*	**interorbital** *adj*
interclan *adj*	**interosculation** *n*
interclass *adj*	**interparish** *adj*
interclub *adj*	**interparticle** *adj*
intercoastal *adj*	**interparty** *adj*
intercollegiate *adj*	**interpenetrable** *adj*
intercommunal *adj*	**interpenetrate** *vti*
intercommunity *adj*	**interpenetration** *n*
intercompany *adj*	**interplanetary** *adj*
intercorporate *adj*	**interpopulation** *adj*
intercortical *adj*	**interprofessional** *adj*
intercountry *adj*	**interprovincial** *adj*
intercounty *adj*	**interracial** *adj*
intercultural *adj*	**interracially** *adv*
interculturally *adv*	**interregional** *adj*
interculture *adj*	**interreligious** *adj*
interdenominational *adj*	**interrenal** *adj*
interdepartmental *adj*	**interscholastic** *adj*
interdepartmentally *adv*	**interscholastically** *adv*
interdisciplinary *adj*	**interschool** *adj*
interdistrict *adj*	**intersegmental** *adj*
interdivisional *adj*	**intersensory** *adj*
interdominion *adj*	**intersocietal** *adj*
interethnic *adj*	**intersociety** *adj*
interfaculty *adj*	**interstratification** *n*
interfaith *adj*	**interstratify** *vt*
interfamilial *adj*	**intersystem** *adj*
interfamily *adj*	**interterritorial** *adj*
interfibre *adj*	**intertribal** *adj*
interfirm *adj*	**intertribally** *adv*
interfold *vt*	**interunion** *adj*
interfraternity *adj*	**interuniversity** *adj*
intergang *adj*	**interurban** *adj*
intergenerational *adj*	**intervarietal** *adj*
intergovernmental *adj*	**intervarsity** *adj*
intergovernmentally *adv*	**intervillage** *adj*
intergranular *adj*	**interwar** *adj*
intergroup *adj*	**interzonal** *adj*

interabang *n* PRINTING another spelling of **interrobang**

interact /íntər ákt/ (**-acts, -acting, -acted**) *vi* **1.** to be or become involved in communication, social activity, or work with somebody else or one another **2.** to have an effect on somebody or something else or on one another —**interactant** *n*

interaction /íntər áksh'n/ *n* **1.** COMMUNICATION OR COLLABORATION communication between or joint activity involving two or more people **2.** RECIPROCAL ACTION the combined or reciprocal action of two or more things that have an effect on each other and work together **3.** PHYS FORCE BETWEEN ELEMENTARY PARTICLES one of the four fundamental forces, gravitational, electromagnetic,

strong, and weak, that act between elementary particles —**interactional** *adj*

interactionism /íntər áksh'nizəm/ *n* in Western metaphysics, the theory that the mind and the body act on each other

interactive /íntər áktiv/ *adj* **1.** COMMUNICATING OR COLLABORATING involving the communication or collaboration of people or things **2.** COMPUT WITH USER-MACHINE COMMUNICATION allowing or involving the exchange of information or instructions between a person and a machine such as a computer or a television **3.** COMPUT OPERATOR-CONTROLLED operating on instructions entered by somebody at a keyboard or other input device —**interactively** *adv* —**interactivity** /íntər ak tívvətee/ *n*

inter alia /íntər áyli ə, -áali-, -álli-/ *adv* among other things ○ *budget funds for two new schools inter alia* [< Latin]

inter alios /íntər áyli ōss, -áali-, -álli-/ *adv* among other people [< Latin]

interauricular /íntər aw ríkyōōlər/ *adj* **1.** BETWEEN UPPER CHAMBERS OF HEART situated or occurring in the area lying between the right and left upper chambers (**auricles**) of the heart **2.** BETWEEN EARS situated or occurring in the area lying between the ears **3.** PHYSIOL INVOLVING TWO EARS involving a physiological or acoustic relationship between the two ears

interbank /íntər bángk/ *adj* between, connecting, or involving two or more banks

interbreed /íntər bréed/ (-**breeds, -breeding, -bred** /-bréd/) *vti* **1.** to produce offspring by mating with a member of a different breed or species, or mate an animal of one breed or species with one of another **2.** to breed within a closed population or narrow range of types, or make something breed in this way

interbroker dealer /íntər brṓkər-/ *n* a broker whose job is to make stock exchange dealings between other brokers easier

intercalary /in túrkələri/ *adj* **1.** INSERTED INTO CALENDAR added to the calendar year to keep calendar years concurrent with solar years. In the Gregorian calendar 29 February is an intercalary day in leap years. **2.** INDICATING YEAR WITH ADDITION describes a year to which an intercalary day or month has been added. A leap year is an intercalary year. **3.** INSERTED OR INTRODUCED inserted between other parts (*formal*) [Early 17C. < Latin *intercalarius* < *intercalare* (see INTERCALATE)]

intercalate /in túrkə layt/ (-**lates, -lating, -lated**) *v* **1.** *vt* to insert an extra day or month into a calendar year in order to keep it consistent with the solar year **2.** *vti* to place something into something else, inserting it between other parts, or be placed between other parts (*formal*) [Early 17C. < Latin *intercalat-*, past participle of *intercalare* < *calare* 'proclaim'] —**intercalation** /in túrkə láysh'n/ *n* —**intercalative** *adj*

intercede /íntər séed/ (-**cedes, -ceding, -ceded**) *vi* **1.** PLEAD FOR SOMEBODY to plead with somebody in authority on behalf of somebody else, especially somebody who is to be punished for something **2.** SPEAK FOR SOMEBODY to speak in support of somebody involved in a dispute **3.** MEDIATE IN DISPUTE to attempt to settle a dispute between other people [Late 16C. < Latin *intercedere* < *cedere* 'give way'] —**interceder** *n*

intercept /íntər sépt/ *v* (-**cepts, -cepting, -cepted**) **1.** *vti* INTERRUPT PROGRESS OF SOMEBODY OR SOMETHING to prevent people or objects from reaching their destination or target by stopping, diverting, or seizing them ○ *The contraband was intercepted by police at the dock.* **2.** *vt* GET BALL in sports, to gain possession of a ball intended for an opponent **3.** *vt* MATHS MARK EXTENT OF SOMETHING to include part of a curve, surface, or solid between two points or lines ■ *n* **1.** ACT OF INTERCEPTING the intercepting of something, especially a radio transmission, missile, or aircraft **2.** MATHS DISTANCE FROM ORIGIN TO AXIS CROSSING the distance from the origin of a coordinate system to the point where a curve or surface crosses an axis **3.** ASTRON DIFFERENCE BETWEEN CALCULATED AND OBSERVED ALTITUDE the difference between the calculated and observed altitude of an astronomical object [15C. < Latin *intercept-*, past participle of *intercipere* < *capere* 'seize'] —**interceptive** *adj*

intercepter *n* AIR FORCE, ARMS another spelling of **interceptor**

interception /íntər sépsh'n/ *n* **1.** the act or an instance of intercepting somebody or something **2.** something intercepted, especially a passed ball that is intercepted by an opponent while it is in the air

interceptor /íntər séptər/, **intercepter** *n* **1.** AIR FORCE FAST FIGHTER PLANE a fast, very manoeuvrable fighter plane designed to intercept enemy aircraft **2.** ARMS GUIDED MISSILE a guided missile designed to intercept enemy missiles or spacecraft **3.** INTERCEPTING PERSON OR THING somebody or something that intercepts

intercession /íntər sésh'n/ *n* **1.** INTERCEDING the action of pleading on somebody's behalf **2.** ATTEMPT TO RESOLVE CONFLICT the action of attempting to settle a dispute **3.** PRAYER OR PETITION a prayer to God, a god, or a saint on behalf of somebody or something [15C. Via French < Latin *intercession-* < *intercedere* (see INTERCEDE)] —**intercessional** *adj* —**intercessor** /íntər séssər, -sessər/ *n* —**intercessorial** /íntərssə sáwri əl/ *adj* —**intercessory** *adj*

interchange *v* /íntər cháynj/ (-**changes, -changing, -changed**) **1.** *vti* SWITCH OR SWAP PLACES to put each of two things in the place of the other, or change places with something else **2.** *vti* ALTERNATE OR FOLLOW EACH OTHER to arrange things alternately in a series, or be arranged in this way **3.** *vt* EXCHANGE THINGS to give something to somebody and receive a similar thing from them in return ■ *n* /íntər chaynj/ **1.** EXCHANGE OF THINGS an exchange of things, especially ideas, opinions, or information, among people **2.** ALTERNATION the action of alternating or changing places **3.** ROADS ROAD INTERSECTION a major road junction where vehicles can, by means of slip roads, bridges, and underpasses, change from one road to another without stopping or crossing other traffic **4.** *Aus* FOOTBALL SUBSTITUTE in Australian Rules football, each of four substitutes that a team can use during a game [14C. < Old French *entrechangier* < *entre* (see INTER-) + *changier* (see CHANGE)] —**interchanger** *n*

interchangeable /íntər cháynjəb'l/ *adj* capable of being switched, exchanged, or used in place of another or each other —**interchangeability** /íntər chaynjə bíllәti/ *n* —**interchangeably** *adv*

interchange bench *n* in Australian Rules football, the bench where the substitute players sit during the game

interchange fee *n* a fee paid by one bank to another to cover cardholder costs until payment is made

intercolumniation /íntərkə lúmni áysh'n/ *n* in architecture, a system used to space columns in a colonnade, based on the use of their diameters as a measurement

intercom /íntər kom/ *n* a system or device that allows people in different parts of a building, aircraft, or ship to speak to each other [Mid-20C. Shortening of *intercommunication system*]

intercommunicate /íntərkə myṓōni kayt/ (-**cates, -cating, -cated**) *vi* **1.** to communicate with each other **2.** to be connected to something else or each other, especially to another room by means of a door in the dividing wall ○ *intercommunicating hotel rooms* —**intercommunication** /-myooni káysh'n/ *n* —**intercommunicative** /-kətiv/ *adj* —**intercommunicator** *n*

intercommunion /íntərkə myṓōnyən/ *n* **1.** an arrangement between different Christian denominations enabling members to receive the Communion at each other's services **2.** a close relationship between people or groups, especially one that involves mutual participation or action

interconnect /íntərkə nékt/ (-**nects, -necting, -nected**) *vti* **1.** to be joined to something else or to a number of joined things, or make something part of such a network (*often passive*) ○ *The rooms are interconnected to form a suite.* **2.** to show a relationship between two or more things, or be related —**interconnection** *n*

interconnective /íntərkə néktiv/ *adj* connecting or capable of connecting with something else or with each other —**interconnectivity** /íntərkə nék tívvəti/ *n*

intercontinental /íntər konti nént'l/ *adj* **1.** involving or occurring between two or more continents **2.** going from one continent to another —**intercontinentally** *adv*

intercontinental ballistic missile *n* a ballistic missile with a range of 3,000 to 8,000 nautical miles

interconversion /íntərkən vúrsh'n/ *n* the mutual conversion of two or more things, e.g. heat into work, as in an engine, and work into heat —**interconvert** *vt* —**interconvertibility** /íntərkən vurtə bíllәti/ *n* —**interconvertible** *adj*

intercooler /íntər koolər/ *n* a heat exchanger that cools a fluid between successive stages of compression or chemical reaction

intercostal /íntər kóst'l/ *adj* situated or occurring between the ribs ○ *an intercostal nerve* [Late 16C. < INTER- + Latin *costa* 'side, rib']

intercourse /íntər kawrss/ *n* **1.** same as **sexual intercourse** **2.** exchanges between people or groups, especially conversation or social activity (*formal*) [15C. Via Old French *entrecours* 'commerce' < Latin *intercursus* 'running between' < *currere* 'to run']

intercrop /íntər króp, íntər krop/ (-**crops, -cropping, -cropped**) *vti* to grow different crops in the same field, usually in alternate rows, or plant a crop between the rows of another crop —**intercrop** /íntər krop/ *n*

intercropping /íntər kropping/ *n* the growing of two or more crops with different characteristics and requirements at the same time on the same plot of land

intercurrent /íntər kúrrənt/ *adj* **1.** occurring during and changing the course of an already existing disease ○ *treating an intercurrent infection* **2.** occurring at the same time as something else or during the period between two other events (*formal*) [Early 17C. < Latin *intercurrent-*, present participle of *intercurrere* 'run between' < *currere* 'to run'] —**intercurrence** *n* —**intercurrently** *adv*

intercut /íntər kút/ (-**cuts, -cutting, -cut**) *vt* to alternate scenes or shots of a film, usually to show different events taking place at the same time

interdental /íntər dént'l/ *adj* **1.** BETWEEN THE TEETH existing between or designed for use between the teeth **2.** WITH TONGUE BETWEEN TEETH describes a speech sound that is made by placing the tip of the tongue between the teeth ■ *n* SOUND MADE WITH TONGUE BETWEEN TEETH a sound made by putting the tip of the tongue between the teeth —**interdentally** *adv*

interdependent /íntərdi péndənt/ *adj* **1.** unable to exist or survive without each other ○ *interdependent organisms* **2.** relying on mutual assistance, support, cooperation, or interaction among constituent parts or members —**interdepend** *vi* —**interdependence** *n* —**interdependently** *adv*

interdict *n* /íntər dikt/ **1.** PROHIBITIVE ORDER a court order that prohibits something **2.** *Scotland* COURT ORDER BANNING SOMETHING TEMPORARILY a court order that bans some action that has been complained of as being against the law until the matter is tried in the proper court **3.** EXCLUSION FROM CHURCH SACRAMENTS a ban imposed by a pope, church council, or bishop that excludes a person, group, or nation from the sacraments of the Roman Catholic Church. In the past, the interdict was used to enforce obedience. ■ *vt* /íntər díkt/ (-**dicts, -dicting, -dicted**) **1.** BAN SOMEBODY OR SOMETHING BY LAW to prohibit something or forbid somebody from doing something, especially in accordance with civil or ecclesiastical law **2.** *US* PREVENT ILLEGAL ENTRY to prevent somebody or something entering a country illegally ○ *Patrols will be increased along the border to interdict smugglers.* **3.** KEEP ENEMY OUT OF AREA to keep an enemy from using an area by troop movements or other means [13C. Via French < Latin *interdictum* < *interdicere* 'prohibit' < *dicere* 'speak'] —**interdiction** *n* —**interdictor** *n* —**interdictory** *adj*

interdigital /íntər díjjit'l/ *adj* **1.** arranged in the form of two series of parallel strips that fit together like the fingers of clasped hands **2.** situated between the fingers or toes —**interdigitally** *adv*

interdigitate /íntər díjji tayt/ (-**tates, -tating, -tated**) *vti* to fit together like the fingers of clasped hands, or place or hold objects together in such a pattern —**interdigitation** /íntər díjji táysh'n/ *n*

interdine /íntər dīn/ (-**dines, -dining, -dined**) *vi* *S Asia* to eat a meal with somebody belonging to a different religion or caste

interest /íntrəst/ *n* **1.** CURIOSITY OR CONCERN a feeling of curiosity or concern about something that makes the attention turn towards it ○ *an interest in art* **2.**

QUALITY THAT ATTRACTS ATTENTION a power, quality, or aspect of something that attracts attention, concern, or curiosity ○ *It's of no interest to me.* **3. ENJOYABLE THING** something that somebody enjoys doing (*often used in the plural*) ○ *My leisure interests include sailing, music, reading, and walking.* **4. BENEFIT OR ADVANTAGE** the good, benefit, or advantage of somebody or something ○ *in the interests of peace* **5. INVOLVEMENT** somebody's involvement with something that makes its progress or success important to him or her ○ *took a personal interest in the progress of the project* **6. BORROWING CHARGE OR PAYMENT** a charge made for a loan or credit facility, or a payment made by a bank or other financial institution for the use of money deposited in an account **7. SHARE IN SOMETHING** a legal right to claim a share in something, especially in a business or property, or the business or property itself **8. CONNECTION** a personal or commercial connection with something or somebody, especially when this prevents somebody from being objective or impartial ○ *had to declare a conflict of interest* ■ **interests** *npl* **INFLUENTIAL GROUP** a group of people in business or society who have the same aims or support the same cause, especially a powerful or influential group ■ *vt* (**-ests, -esting, -ested**) **1. GET SOMEBODY'S ATTENTION** to attract or hold somebody's attention or arouse somebody's curiosity or concern ○ *It may interest you to know that the building used to be a mortuary.* **2. MAKE SOMEBODY WANT SOMETHING** to make somebody want to have or buy something, do something, or become involved with something ○ *I tried to interest him in helping with the preparations.* [15C. Alteration of Anglo-Norman *interesse* < medieval Latin, 'compensation for loss' < Latin, 'differ, be important', by association with Old French *interest* 'damage, loss' < Latin, 'it matters']

interested /íntrəstid/ *adj* **1. CURIOUS OR CONCERNED** paying attention to something or devoting time to something because of curiosity, concern, or enjoyment **2. WANTING SOMETHING** involved or wanting to be involved in something ○ *interested parties* **3. AFFECTED OR INVOLVED** having a legal right or share in something or a personal or commercial connection with something —**interestedly** *adv* —**interestedness** *n*

interest group *n* **1.** an occupational group that is concerned mainly with the economic interests of its members, e.g. a business organization, trade union, or professional association **2.** a group of people who share an interest in something such as a subject of study

interesting /íntrəsting/ *adj* **1.** arousing curiosity, attracting or holding attention, or provoking thought **2.** enjoyable because of being varied, challenging, stimulating, or exciting —**interestingly** *adv*

interface /íntər fayss/ *n* **1. COMMON BOUNDARY** the surface, place, or point where two things touch each other or meet **2. BOUNDARY BETWEEN THINGS** a common boundary between objects or different phases of a substance ○ *an oil-water interface* **3. POINT OF INTERACTION** the place, situation, or way in which two things or people act together or affect each other, or the point of connection between things **4.** COMPUT **BOUNDARY ACROSS WHICH DATA PASSES** a common boundary shared by two devices, or by a person and a device, across which data or information flows, e.g. the screen of a computer **5.** COMPUT **LINKING SOFTWARE** software that links a computer with another device, or the set of commands, messages, images, and other features allowing communication between computer and user **6.** ELECTRONICS **LINKING DEVICE** an electronic device or circuit or other point of physical contact between two pieces of equipment ■ *vti* (**-faces, -facing, -faced**) **1. HAVE OR GIVE COMMON BOUNDARY** to touch or meet at a surface, place, or point, or make things join in this way **2. INTERACT** to act together or affect each other, or make things or people interact **3. SERVE AS INTERFACE** to connect two or more pieces of equipment, or be connected —**interfacial** /íntər fáysh'l/ *adj* —**interfacially** *adv*

interfacing /íntər fayssing/ *n* a fabric that is used to stiffen or support collars, cuffs, or other parts of a garment

~~**interferance**~~ incorrect spelling of **interference**

interfere /íntər féer/ (**-feres, -fering, -fered**) *vi* **1. HAVE UNDESIRABLE EFFECT** to delay, hinder, or obstruct the natural or desired course of something ○ *The weather interfered with our plans.* **2. MEDDLE IN OTHER PEOPLE'S AFFAIRS** to participate in the affairs of others, especially by offering unwanted or unhelpful advice or by trying to resolve other people's disputes ○ *It's not advisable to interfere in a private quarrel.* **3. TOUCH ILLICITLY** to touch somebody sexually in a way contrary to law or moral standards (*used euphemistically*) **4.** PHYS **AFFECT DISPLACEMENT OR AMPLITUDE** to act together to increase, decrease, or cancel out displacement or amplitude **5.** COMMUNICATION, ELECTRONICS **CAUSE INTERFERENCE** to cause electronic interference **6. HIT HOOF AGAINST LEG** to hit one hoof against the opposite hoof or leg while walking (*refers to horses*) [15C. < Old French *s'entreferir* 'strike each other' < Latin *ferire* 'to strike'] —**interferer** *n*

interference /íntər féeranss/ *n* **1. HINDRANCE** hindrance or obstruction that prevents a natural or desired outcome **2. MEDDLING IN OTHER PEOPLE'S AFFAIRS** involvement in something without any invitation or justification ○ *He deeply resented any interference in his private life.* **3.** COMMUNICATION, ELECTRONICS **SIGNAL THAT INTERFERES** an unwanted signal that disrupts radio, telephone, or television reception **4.** PHYS **PROCESS OF WAVE INTERACTION** a process in light-wave transmission in which two or more waves are superimposed in such a way that they produce higher peaks, lower troughs, or a new wave pattern **5.** AMERICAN FOOTBALL **LEGAL BLOCKING** in American football, the legal blocking of defensive players to protect and make way for the player carrying the ball —**interferential** /íntərfə rénsh'l/ *adj* ◇ **run interference 1.** in American football, to carry out legal blocking of defensive players to protect and make way for the player carrying the ball **2.** *N Am* to contribute help or support to somebody or something, especially by preventing others from acting as a hindrance (*informal*)

interfering /íntər féering/ *adj* deliberately becoming involved in other people's affairs in a way that is neither needed nor welcome —**interferingly** *adv*

interferometer /íntərfə rómmitər/ *n* a device that uses an interference pattern to determine wave frequency, length, or velocity —**interferometric** /íntər feerə méttrik/ *adj* —**interferometrically** *adv* —**interferometry** *n*

interferon /íntər féer on/ *n* a protein produced by cells in response to virus infection that inhibits viral replication [Mid-20C. < INTERFERE]

interfertile /íntər fúr tīl/ *adj* able to interbreed with other species or subspecies and produce viable offspring —**interfertility** /íntərfər tílləti/ *n*

interfile /íntər fīl/ (**-files, -filing, -filed**) *vt* to put an item or items among similar items in a file

interflow /íntər flō/ (**-flows, -flowing, -flowed**) *vi* to merge into a single stream

interfluent /íntər flòo ənt/ *adj* **1.** merging into a single stream **2.** flowing between things or places [Mid-17C. < Latin *interfluent-*, present participle of *interfluere* 'flow together' < *fluere* 'to flow']

interfluve /íntər floov/ *n* **1.** the ridge line separating two river catchments **2.** a line joining points on one side of which water will flow to one river while on the other side water will flow to another river [Early 20C. Back-formation < *interfluvial*] —**interfluvial** /íntər flòovi əl/ *adj*

interfuse /íntər fyòoz/ (**-fuses, -fusing, -fused**) *vti* to mingle, blend, or fuse thoroughly, or mix two or more things in this way (*literary*) [Late 16C. < Latin *interfus-*, past participle of *interfundere* 'pour together' < *fundere* 'pour'] —**interfusion** *n*

intergalactic /íntərgə láktik/ *adj* situated, happening, or moving between galaxies, or involving two or more galaxies —**intergalactically** *adv*

interglacial /íntər gláysi əl, -gláysh'l/ *n* a period of warmer climate separating two periods of glaciation and displaying a characteristic sequence of changes in vegetation. The term is used especially for several such periods that occurred during the Pleistocene epoch, lasting from 1.8 million to 10,000 years ago. —**interglacial** *adj*

Intergovernmental Panel on Climate Change *n* an international body set up in 1988 to assess the scientific, technical, and socio-economic information relating to human-induced climate change

intergrade *vi* /íntər gráyd/ (**-grades, -grading, -graded**) **CHANGE BY STAGES** to be transformed from one form to another through a series of stages or forms that involve partial transitions ■ *n* /íntər grayd/ **1. TRANSITIONAL FORM** a transitional form or stage **2. TRANSITIONAL SOIL HORIZON** a transitional soil horizon between two distinctive soils —**intergradation** /íntər gray dáysh'n/ *n* —**intergradient** *adj*

intergrowth /íntər grōth/ *n* growth of one thing into or within another thing, or among other things, or the result of such growth

interim /íntərim/ *adj* **1. HAVING TEMPORARY EFFECT** serving as a temporary measure until something more complete and permanent can be established **2. HOLDING TEMPORARY OFFICE** serving temporarily until a permanent replacement can be elected or appointed ■ *n* **INTERVENING TIME** a period of time between two occurrences or periods ○ *in the interim* [Mid-16C. < Latin, 'meanwhile']

interim dividend *n* a dividend paid by a company before the end of its financial year

interionic /íntər ī ónnik/ *adj* situated between or involving two or more ions

interior /in téeri ər/ *n* **1. INSIDE PART** the inside of something ○ *The interior of the church was dark.* **2. INSIDE OF BUILDING OR ROOM** the inside of a building or room considered especially with regard to its decoration and furnishing **3. PART FARTHEST IN FROM EDGE** the part of something that is far or farthest from its edge, boundary, or surface, especially the part of a country or continent that is remote or farthest from the coast **4. PICTURE OF INSIDE OF ROOM** a painting or photograph of the inside of a room **5. INSIDE SET OR SCENE** a setting or actual location that represents the inside of a building, or a scene filmed inside a building **6.** POL another spelling of **Interior** ■ *adj* **1. LOCATED INSIDE** located in, suitable for, or occurring inside something **2. CENTRAL** remote or farthest from the edge, boundary, or surface of something, especially from the coast of a country or continent **3. OCCURRING IN MIND** taking place within somebody's mind and usually not expressed out loud **4.** POL another spelling of **Interior** [15C. Directly or via French < Latin, literally 'more in the midst of' < *inter* (see INTER-)] —**interiority** /in téeri órrəti/ *n* —**interiorly** *adv*

Interior *n* in the United States and some other countries, the internal affairs of the nation, especially as opposed to its foreign affairs ■ *adj* relating to the internal affairs of a country, especially as opposed to its foreign affairs

interior angle *n* **1.** the angle formed between two adjacent sides of a polygon and lying in its interior. The sum of the interior angles of any polygon is equal to the number of its sides minus two and multiplied by 180°. **2.** any of the four angles formed in the area between two lines by a third line that intersects them (**transversal**)

interior arranger *n* somebody whose business is to change the appearance of a house or room, using and rearranging furnishings and accessories that are already there

interior decoration *n* **1.** the way that a room or building is decorated and furnished **2.** *N Am* same as **interior design 3.** the skill or trade of somebody who specializes in wallpapering and painting interiors —**interior decorator** *n*

interior design *n* the art or process of planning the decoration and furnishings of a room or building. N Am term **interior decoration** —**interior designer** *n*

interiorize /in téeri ə rīz/ (**-izes, -izing, -ized**), **interiorise** (**-ises, -ising, -ised**) *vt* PSYCHOL same as **internalize** —**interiorization** /in téeri ə rī záysh'n/ *n*

interior monologue *n* an extended passage in a story or novel that expresses what a character is thinking and feeling

Interior Salish (*plural same*) *n* a member of a Native North American people who formerly lived in British Columbia, northern Washington, northern Idaho, and western Montana and now live on a reservation in Montana —**Interior Salish** *adj*

interior-sprung *adj UK* having many helical springs inside a thick padded cover. ANZ, N Am term **innerspring**

interj. *abbr* GRAM interjection

interjacent /íntər jáyss'nt/ *adj* occupying a position between one thing and another (*formal*) [Mid-16C. < Latin *interjacent-*, present participle of *interjacere* 'lie between' < *jacere* 'to lie']

interject /íntər jékt/ (**-jects, -jecting, -jected**) *vti* to say or insert something in a way that interrupts what is being said or discussed [Late 16C. < Latin *interject-*, past participle of *interjicere* 'interpose', literally 'throw between' < *jacere* 'to throw'] —**interjector** *n* —**interjectory** *adj*

interjection /íntər jéksh'n/ *n* **1.** a sound, word, or phrase that expresses a strong emotion such as pain or surprise but otherwise has no meaning **2.** something said loudly and abruptly, or something inserted in a text, especially something that interrupts what is being said or discussed —**interjectional** *adj* —**interjectionally** *adv*

interkinesis /íntərki neéssiss, -kī-/ *n* the period of rest between meiotic cell divisions, similar to the interphase stage in mitosis

interlace /íntər láyss/ (**-laces, -lacing, -laced**) *v* **1.** *vti* to join or interweave two or more things together, often in an intricate pattern, or be joined or interwoven in this way **2.** *vt* to break up the flow or relieve the monotony of something by occasionally inserting something different, e.g. jokes in a serious talk [14C. < Old French *entrelacier* 'lace together' < *lacier* 'to lace'] —**interlacement** *n*

interlaced scanning /íntər layst-/ *n* a technique used in television and computer monitors in which high vertical resolution is achieved by scanning all odd- and then all even-numbered lines

interlanguage /íntər láng widj/ *n* a form of language produced by learners of a second or foreign language, combining features of two or more languages

interlard /íntər laárd/ (**-lards, -larding, -larded**) *vt* to vary, punctuate, or interrupt speech or writing by interspersing contrasting material [Mid-16C. < French *entrelarder* 'mix with layers of fat' < *larde* 'lard']

interlay /íntər láy/ *vt* (**-lays, -laying, -laid** /-láyd/) to layer something with something else ■ *n* something laid between two surfaces

interleaf /íntər leef/ (*plural* **-leaves** /-leevz/) *n* an extra sheet or page, usually a blank one, inserted into a book

interleave /íntər leév/ (**-leaves, -leaving, -leaved**) *vt* to add extra sheets or pages, usually blank ones, between the pages of a book, e.g. to allow for notes or to protect illustrations [Mid-17C. < INTER- + LEAF]

interleaves plural of **interleaf**

interleukin /íntər lóokin/ *n* a chemical found in white blood cells that stimulates them to fight infection [Late 20C. < INTER- + LEUCOCYTE + -IN]

interleukin-1 *n* an interleukin that stimulates the production of other factors that activate the immune system

interleukin-2 *n* an interleukin that stimulates T-cells and is used in the treatment of cancer

interlibrary loan /íntər lībrəri-/ *n* **1.** BOOK-BORROWING SYSTEM a system by which libraries and library users can borrow books from other libraries **2.** BORROWING OF BOOK a borrowing of a book through an interlibrary loan system **3.** BOOK BORROWED a book borrowed through an interlibrary loan system

interline[1] /íntər lín/ (**-lines, -lining, -lined**) *vt* to write or print words between the lines of writing or printing in a text or document [15C. < medieval Latin *interlineare* < Latin *linea* (see LINE [1])] —**interlineation** /íntər línni áysh'n/ *n*

interline[2] /íntər lín/ (**-lines, -lining, -lined**) *vt* to put an extra lining between the fabric and the lining of a curtain or piece of clothing [15C. < INTER- + LINE [2]]

interlinear /íntər línni ər/, **interlineal** /-línni əl/ *adj* **1.** inserted between the lines of a text or document **2.** written or printed with different versions of the same text on alternate or succeeding lines [14C. < medieval Latin *interlinearis* < Latin *linea* (see LINE [1])] —**interlinearly** *adv*

Interlingua /íntər líng gwə/ *n* an artificial language designed to facilitate international communication, based on the common features of living Latinate languages [Early 20C. < INTER- + Latin *lingua* 'tongue, language']

interlining /íntər līning/ *n* an extra lining inserted between the fabric and lining of a curtain or piece of clothing to make it thicker or warmer, or the fabric used for this

interlink /íntər língk/ (**-links, -linking, -linked**) *vti* to connect something with something else in several ways, or be connected together in several ways

interlock *vti* /íntər lók/ (**-locks, -locking, -locked**) **1.** FIT TOGETHER CLOSELY to fit things together closely, especially by means of parts that mesh, hook, or dovetail, or be fitted together in this way **2.** OPERATE AS UNIT to connect parts in such a way that all move or operate if one does, or be connected in this way ■ *n* /íntər lok/ **1.** MECH ENG CONNECTING AND COORDINATING DEVICE a device that connects parts of something such as a machine in a way that coordinates their action **2.** CLOSE CONNECTION a close connection by means of parts that fit or fasten together closely and firmly **3.** TEXTILES TIGHTLY KNITTED FABRIC a fabric made with tightly knitted stitches **4.** HANDICRAFT CANVAS FOR NEEDLEPOINT canvas used for needlepoint that has the warp and weft threads knotted together to prevent movement **5.** COMPUT COMPUTER SECURITY DEVICE a security device designed to prevent unauthorized use of a computer, e.g. a password system ■ *adj* TIGHTLY KNITTED knitted with close, tight stitches

interlocking directorates /íntər loking-/ *npl* boards of directors that have enough members in common to place the companies that they oversee under the same control

interlocution /íntərlō kyóosh'n/ *n* a discussion or conversation involving two or more people (*formal*) [Mid-16C. < Latin *interlocution-* < *interlocut-*, past participle of *interloqui* 'interrupt', literally 'speak between' < *loqui* 'speak']

interlocutor /íntər lókyootər/ *n* **1.** a participant in a discussion or conversation (*formal*) **2.** a performer in a minstrel show who acted as the presenter and stood in the middle and bantered with the end men [Early 16C. < modern Latin < Latin *interlocut-* (see INTERLOCUTION)]

interlocutory /íntər lókyootəri/ *adj* **1.** issued provisionally during a lawsuit ○ *an interlocutory decree* **2.** involving or characteristic of conversation or discussion (*formal*)

interloper /íntər lōpər/ *n* **1.** an intruder into a place, gathering, or situation **2.** somebody who interferes in other people's affairs, especially for selfish reasons [Late 16C. After archaic *landloper* 'vagabond' < Middle Dutch *landlooper* 'land-runner' < *loopen* 'to run'] —**interlope** *vi*

interlude /íntər lood/ *n* **1.** a relatively short period of time between two longer periods, during which something happens that is different from what has happened before and what follows **2.** a short play, piece of music, or other entertainment performed during a break in the performance of a long work [14C. < medieval Latin *interludium* 'in-between-play' (because originally performed between the acts of a medieval mystery play) < Latin *ludus* 'play']

intermarriage /íntər márrij/ *n* **1.** marriage between members of different religious, social, or racial groups, or an instance of this **2.** marriage between members of the same people, clan, or other kinship group, or an instance of this

intermarry /íntər márri/ (**-ries, -rying, -ried**) *vi* **1.** to marry a member of a different religious, social, or racial group **2.** to marry a member of the same people, clan, or other kinship group

intermediary /íntər meédi əri/ *n* (*plural* **-ies**) **1.** GO-BETWEEN somebody who carries messages between people, or tries to help them reach an agreement **2.** MEANS OR MEDIUM something that functions as a means or medium for bringing something about ■ *adj* **1.** MEDIATING acting as a messenger or mediator between two or more people or groups **2.** LYING IN BETWEEN lying or occurring between two different forms, states, points, or extremes [Late 18C. < French *intermédiaire* < Latin *intermedius* (see INTERMEDIATE [1])]

intermediate[1] /íntər meédi ət/ *adj* **1.** BEING IN BETWEEN lying or occurring between two different forms, states, points, or extremes ○ *an intermediate course* **2.** GEOL CONTAINING BETWEEN 55% AND 66% SILICA describes an igneous rock with a silica content of between 55 per cent and 66 per cent ■ *n* **1.** SOMETHING BETWEEN TWO OTHER THINGS something that lies or occurs between two different forms, states, points, or extremes **2.** same as **intermediary** *n* (sense 1) **3.** CHEM CHEMICAL FOR FURTHER REACTIONS a chemical compound that is formed during a chemical reaction and is used in another reaction to obtain another compound **4.** CHEM SHORT-LIVED CHEMICAL COMPONENT a molecule, ion, or free radical that exists for a short time during a chemical reaction [15C. Directly or via French < medieval Latin *intermediatus* < Latin *intermedius* < *medius* 'middle'] —**intermediately** *adv* —**intermediateness** *n*

intermediate[2] /íntər meédi ayt/ (**-ates, -ating, -ated**) *vi* to act as a go-between or mediator between two or more people or groups [Early 16C. < INTER- + MEDIATE] —**intermediation** /íntər meédi áysh'n/ *n* —**intermediator** *n*

intermediate-acting *adj* having a period of therapeutic activity that is between that of long-acting and short-acting drugs

intermediate bulk container *n* a portable container for transporting liquids or solids that holds 500 to 1,000 litres/110 to 220 gallons or 500 to 1,500 kg/1,100 to 3,300 lb. It is intermediate in size between a drum and a tanker load.

intermediate court *n* a court at the middle level of the state court hierarchy in Australia, below the supreme courts but above the magistrates' courts. Intermediate courts include the county courts in Victoria, district courts in New South Wales, Western Australia, and Queensland, and local courts elsewhere.

intermediate frequency *n* the frequency that an incoming signal is changed to in a heterodyne receiver prior to amplification

intermediate host *n* an animal that is the host for an immature parasite, which then moves on to a different host before reproducing

intermediate-level waste *n* radioactive waste from reactors and processing plants that is solidified, mixed with concrete, and stored in drums. These drums are then placed for long-term storage in waste repositories.

intermediate-range ballistic missile *n* a ballistic missile that has a range of 1,200 to 1,600 km/750 to 1,000 mi

intermediate school *n* **1.** *US* EDUC same as **junior high, middle school** (sense 2) **2.** in New Zealand, a school that takes children between the ages of 11 and 13

intermediate technology *n* simple technology that is environmentally sensitive and based on local resources

intermediate treatment *n* care for children affected by emotional or personality disorders or psychiatric conditions that do not require hospitalization but do require close monitoring

intermediate vector boson *n* an elementary particle that transmits weak interactions between other elementary particles. The three postulated intermediate vector bosons, the W^+, W^-, and Z^0 particles, have all been observed.

intermedin /íntər meédin/ *n* PHYSIOL same as **melanocyte-stimulating hormone** [Mid-20C. < modern Latin *(pars) intermedia* 'intermediate (part) (of the pituitary)' < Latin *intermedius* (see INTERMEDIATE [1])]

interment /in túrmənt/ *n* the burial of a corpse, usually accompanied by a funeral ceremony

intermercial /íntər múrsh'l/ *n* ONLINE same as **interstitial** [Late 20C. < INTER- + COMMERCIAL]

intermesh /íntər mésh/ (**-meshes, -meshing, -meshed**) *vti* to engage or mesh with one another, or cause something such as the teeth of cogwheels to do so

intermetallic /íntərmi tállik/ *adj* consisting of two or more metals in specific proportions

intermezzo /íntər métsō, -médzō/ (*plural* **-zos** or **-zi** /-tsi, -dzi/) *n* **1.** a short piece of music that is performed between longer movements of an extended musical composition **2.** a short musical composition, usually for solo piano **3.** ARTS same as **interlude** (sense 2) [Late 18C. Via Italian < Latin *intermedius* (see INTERMEDIATE [1])]

interminable /in túrminəb'l/ *adj* so long and boring or frustrating as to seem endless ○ *interminable delays* [14C. Directly or via French < late Latin *interminabilis* 'unending' < Latin *terminare* (see TERMINATE)] —**interminability** /in túrminə bílləti/ *n* —**interminably** *adv*

intermingle /íntər míng g'l/ (-gles, -gling, -gled) vti to mix something together with something else, or become mixed together ○ *The scents of jasmine and honeysuckle intermingled.*

intermission /íntər mísh'n/ n 1. a pause in, or temporary discontinuation of, an activity 2. N Am same as **interval** (sense 3) [15C. Directly or via French < Latin *intermission-* < *intermiss-*, past participle of *intermittere* (see INTERMIT)]

intermit /íntər mít/ (-mits, -mitting, -mitted) vti (formal) 1. to discontinue doing something temporarily, or be discontinued temporarily 2. to stop for a short time or for short intervals, or cause something to stop in this way [Mid-16C. < Latin *intermittere* 'interrupt', literally 'send between' < *mittere* 'send'] —**intermittingly** adv—**intermittor** n

intermittent /íntər mítt'nt/ adj occurring at irregular intervals [Mid-16C. < Latin *intermittent-*, present participle of *intermittere* (see INTERMIT)] —**intermittence** n —**intermittently** adv

SYNONYMS See *periodic.*

intermittent claudication n a cramping pain, induced by exercise and relieved by rest, that is caused by inadequate blood supply to the affected muscles, usually the calves

intermittent current n a unidirectional current that is interrupted periodically

intermittent fever n a fever that rises and falls and then returns, occurring in diseases such as malaria

intermix /íntər míks/ (-mixes, -mixing, -mixed) vti same as **intermingle** —**intermixable** adj

intermodal /íntər mốd'l/ adj describes containers designed to be transferred from one mode of transport to another while in transit, e.g. from a train to a ship to a lorry ■ n a container for goods that can be transferred from one means of transport to another during shipment without being unpacked

intermodulation /íntər moddyoổ láysh'n/ n the undesired interaction of electronic signals of different frequencies transmitted within a nonlinear system, resulting in distortion

intermontane /íntər mon táyn/ adj describes basins that lie between two mountain ranges and often fill up with sediment washed down from them

intermural /íntər myoórəl/ adj involving participants from two or more educational institutions, athletic clubs, or other groups

intern v /in túrn/ (-terns, -terning, -terned) 1. vt DETAIN SOMEBODY to detain somebody in confinement as being a security threat 2. vi N Am WORK AS TRAINEE to work as a trainee gaining practical experience, e.g. as a junior doctor in a hospital ■ n /ín turn/ also **interne** 1. Aus, N Am JUNIOR DOCTOR IN HOSPITAL a doctor who has recently graduated from medical school and is receiving practical supervised training in a hospital 2. N Am TRAINEE an assistant or trainee working to gain practical experience in an occupation [Mid-19C. < French *interne* (noun), *interner* (verb) < Latin *internus* (see INTERNAL)] —**internment** /in túrnmənt/ n —**internship** /ín turn ship/ n

internal /in túrn'l/ adj 1. LOCATED INSIDE located within or affecting the inside of something, especially the inside of the body ○ *internal organs* 2. INTENDED FOR USE INSIDE effective when used or suitable for use inside something, especially inside the body 3. SELF-CONTAINED OR SELF-GENERATING existing, evident in, or arising from the nature, structure, or qualities that somebody or something has ○ *internal cohesion* 4. OCCURRING WITHIN COUNTRY originating, operating, or located within a country's borders ○ *internal affairs* 5. MENTAL involving or existing within the mind or spirit ○ *internal conflict* 6. OCCURRING WITHIN ORGANIZATION working at or carried out within an organization or institution such as a school, college, or university ○ *internal e-mail* [15C. Directly or via French < medieval Latin *internalis* < Latin *internus* 'inwards, within' < *inter* (see INTER-)] —**internality** /íntər nálləti/ n —**internally** adv—**internalness** n

internal clock n 1. a clock within a machine such as a computer, that may control some of the functions of the machine 2. BIOL same as **biological clock**

internal-combustion engine n an engine in which fuel is burnt in combustion chambers within the engine, instead of in an external furnace, and in which the energy released moves one or more pistons

internal ear n ANAT same as **inner ear**

internal energy n the total kinetic energy of the atoms and molecules of a system plus the potential energy of their mutual interaction. An increase in internal energy manifests as a rise in temperature or a change in phase. Symbol U

internalize /in túrnə līz/ (-izes, -izing, -ized), **internalise** (-ises, -ising, -ised) vt 1. to adopt the beliefs, values, and attitudes of others, either consciously or unconsciously 2. to deal with an emotion or conflict by thinking about it rather than expressing it openly —**internalization** /in túrnə līzáysh'n/ n

internal medicine n the branch of medicine concerned with the diagnosis and nonsurgical treatment of diseases affecting the internal organs, and with preventive medicine

internal resistance n the resistance within a source of electrical current such as a cell or generator

internal respiration n the metabolic use of oxygen by a cell to produce energy, resulting in the release of carbon dioxide

internal rhyme n a rhyme in which one of the rhyming words is within the line of poetry and the other is at the end of the same line or within the next line

internal secretion n a secretion, especially a hormone, that is absorbed into the blood directly after production

internal wave n a waveform that develops below the surface of a body of water where two water masses with different densities meet. An internal wave can develop in an estuary where salt water lies underneath less dense river water.

international /íntər násh'nəl/ adj 1. INVOLVING SEVERAL COUNTRIES involving two or more countries or their citizens 2. CROSSING NATIONAL BOUNDARIES extending beyond or across national boundaries 3. OF RELATIONS AMONG NATIONS dealing with or concerned with relations among nations ○ *the university's international studies department* ■ n 1. CONTEST BETWEEN TEAMS FROM DIFFERENT COUNTRIES a sports contest between teams or players from two or more countries 2. MEMBER OF INTERNATIONAL TEAM a member of a team representing his or her country in an international event —**internationality** /íntər násh'n álləti/ n —**internationally** adv

International /íntər násh'nəl/ n any of four international Socialist, Communist, or Anarchist organizations formed in 1864, 1889, 1919, and 1938 respectively

International Atomic Time n a precisely determined system of measuring time in which a second is defined in terms of atomic events that are known to a high degree of accuracy

international baccalaureate n a set of examinations in various subjects taken at the end of secondary education and accepted in many countries as a qualification for university entrance

International Bank for Reconstruction and Development n BANKING same as **World Bank**

International Brigade n a Communist and Socialist force of volunteers from different countries that fought on the Republican side during the Spanish Civil War

International Court of Justice n the chief judicial body of the United Nations, empowered to resolve international disputes between member nations who submit a case to the court

International Criminal Police Organization n full form of **Interpol**

International Date Line n an internationally agreed imaginary line running roughly along the 180° meridian of longitude, to the east of which the date is one day earlier than to the west

International Development Association n a specialized agency of the United Nations that provides credit to nations on easier terms than the World Bank

Internationale /íntər náshə náal/ n a revolutionary Socialist song written in France in 1871 and adopted as the anthem of the First, Second, and Third Inter-

nationals. A Russian version was the national anthem of the Soviet Union until 1944. [Early 20C. < French *(chanson) internationale* 'international (song)']

International Finance Corporation n a specialized agency of the United Nations that is affiliated with the World Bank and promotes private enterprise in developing nations by providing risk capital

International Gothic n a style of painting and other visual art that emerged in Europe with the increasing exchange of ideas and techniques among European artists towards the end of the 14th century

International Grandmaster n a chess player of the highest rank awarded to a participant in international competitions

internationalise vt another spelling of **internationalize**

internationalism /íntər násh'nəlizəm/ n 1. COOPERATION BETWEEN COUNTRIES a policy or spirit of cooperation and mutual understanding between countries 2. INTEREST IN OTHER COUNTRIES a willingness to understand and respect the concerns, attitudes, and ways of life of other countries 3. INTERNATIONAL CHARACTER OR QUALITY the international character or quality of somebody or something

internationalist /íntər násh'nəlist/ n 1. ADVOCATE OF INTERNATIONAL COOPERATION a supporter or advocate of greater cooperation and understanding between countries 2. SOMEBODY INTERESTED IN OTHER COUNTRIES somebody who is interested in other countries and understands and respects their peoples and cultures 3. Scotland SPORTS same as **international** n (sense 2) ■ adj FAVOURING INTERNATIONAL COOPERATION favouring greater cooperation and understanding between countries

internationalize /íntər násh'nə līz/ (-izes, -izing, -ized), **internationalise** (-ises, -ising, -ised) vt 1. to make something international in character, structure, or outlook 2. to place something under the protection or control of several countries instead of one country —**internationalization** /íntər násh'nə līzáysh'n/ n

international law n the accepted rules that govern countries in their relations with other countries

International Master n a chess player of a rank in international competitions that is below International Grandmaster

International Modernism n ARCHIT same as **International Style**

International Monetary Fund n a specialized agency of the United Nations that seeks to promote international monetary cooperation and the stabilization of national currencies and help nations resolve balance of payment problems

International Morse code n the form of Morse code used internationally

international nonproprietary name n each of 8,000 names selected by the World Health Organization that are the legally required generic names for pharmaceutical product labelling for most countries in the world, including all EU countries

International Organization for Standardization n SCI same as **ISO**[2]

International Phonetic Alphabet n a system of letters and marks, mostly based on the letters of the Roman alphabet, used internationally to represent speech sounds

International Practical Temperature Scale n a scientific temperature scale, expressed in degrees Celsius, that has eleven fixed temperature reference points, including the boiling point of oxygen and the freezing point of gold

international relations npl political and other dealings between two or more countries ■ n the branch of political science that studies the relations between countries (*takes a singular verb*)

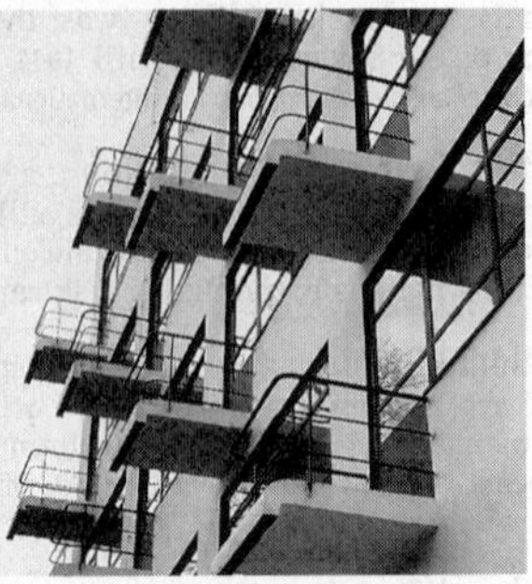
AKG London

International Style: studio building (1925) at the Bauhaus, Dessau, Germany

International Style *n* an early 20th-century architectural style in the United States and Europe that favoured the use of simple geometric lines, spacious interiors, and materials such as steel and reinforced concrete

International System (of Units) *n* an internationally accepted system of units of measurement used for scientific work. The basic units are the metre, kilogram, second, kelvin, mole, ampere, and candela, these being the basic quantities of length, mass, time, temperature, amount of substance, electric current, and luminous intensity.

International Telecommunication Union *n* a specialized agency of the United Nations that promotes international cooperation in telecommunications and allots radio frequencies for various purposes. It was founded in 1865 and affiliated with the United Nations in 1947.

international telegram *n* a message sent by telephone or telex from the United Kingdom to another country, where it is delivered in written or printed form

international unit *n* the amount of a hormone or vitamin required to produce a specific response

internaut *n* somebody who surfs the Internet [Late 20C. Blend of INTERNET + ASTRONAUT]

interne *n* another spelling of **intern**

internecine /intər neé sīn/ *adj* **1.** relating to or involving conflict within a group or organization ○ *an internecine feud* **2.** damaging or injuring participants on both sides of a conflict [Mid-17C. < Latin *internecinus* 'deadly' < *internecare* 'exterminate', literally 'kill completely' < *necare* 'kill' < *nex* 'death']

ORIGIN The original meaning of ***internecine*** is 'involving great slaughter'. Its modern meaning of 'involving conflict within a group', which can be traced back to the 18th century (Samuel Johnson in his *Dictionary* (1755) defined it as 'endeavouring mutual destruction'), arose from the standard interpretation of *inter-* as 'among, between', but in fact in the case of Latin *internecinus* it was being used simply to add emphasis.

internee /intər neé/ *n* an inmate of a prison, prisoner-of-war camp, or other similar place, especially during a war

internesia /intər neézhə/ *n US* an inability to remember either the location of or information contained in a website (*informal*) [Blend of INTERNET + AMNESIA]

Internet /intər net/, **internet** *n* a network that links computer networks all over the world by satellite and telephone, connecting users with service networks such as e-mail and the World Wide Web

Internet banking *n* a system of banking in which customers can view their account details, pay bills, and transfer money by means of the Internet

Internet café *n* ONLINE same as **cybercafé** (sense 1)

Internet hotel *n* a business that provides Internet and server facilities for other businesses

Internet protocol *n* the standard that controls the routing and structure of data transmitted over the Internet

Internet relay chat *n* ONLINE full form of **IRC**

Internet service provider *n* a business that provides access to the Internet, usually for a monthly fee. Some large providers offer users a wide range of news, information, and entertainment services.

Internet storefront *n* ONLINE, COMM same as **storefront** *n* (sense 1)

interneuron /intər nyoór on/ *n* a short nerve cell in the central nervous system that connects nerve cells such as sensory and motor nerve cells in a reflex arc —**interneuronal** /intər nyoórən'l/ *adj*

internist /in turnist/ *n* a doctor who specializes in the diagnosis, prevention, and nonsurgical treatment of diseases affecting the internal organs [Early 20C. < INTERNAL + -IST]

internode /intər nōd/ *n* **1.** the part of a plant stem between two nodes **2.** the part of the axon of a nerve cell that lies between the nodes of Ranvier and is covered by the myelin sheath [Mid-17C. < Latin *internodium* < *nodus* 'knot'] —**internodal** /intər nṓd'l/ *adj*

inter nos /intər nóss/ *adv* between or among ourselves (*formal or humorous*) [< Latin]

internuncial /intər núnsh'l/ *adj* **1.** describes nerve cells that connect one nerve cell to another **2.** acting as or connected with an internuncio of the Roman Catholic Church —**internuncially** *adv*

internuncio /intər núnshi ō/ (*plural* **-os**) *n* **1.** a diplomatic representative of the pope of a rank below a nuncio **2.** a messenger or go-between (*formal*) [Mid-17C. Via Italian *internunzio* < Latin *internuntius* 'intermediate messenger' < *nuntius* 'messenger']

interoperability /intər óppərəbílliti/ *n* the ability of the component parts of a system to operate successfully together —**interoperable** /-óppərəb'l/ *adj*

interpellate /in túrpə layt/ (**-lates, -lating, -lated**) *vt* in European legislatures, to interrupt a parliamentary debate by asking a question on an aspect of government policy [Late 19C. < Latin *interpellat-*, past participle of *interpellare* 'thrust yourself between' < variant of *pellere* 'beat'] —**interpellation** /in túrpə láysh'n/ *n* —**interpellator** *n*

interpersonal /intər púrss'nəl/ *adj* concerning or involving relationships between people —**interpersonally** *adv*

interphalangeal /intərfə lánji əl/ *adj* situated between the bones of the fingers or toes

interphase /intər fayz/ *n* the period during which a cell is not actively dividing, when other activities such as DNA synthesis take place

interplay /intər play/ *n* the way in which people or things repeatedly act on and react to each other

interplead /intər pleéd/ (**-pleads, -pleading, -pleaded** or **-pled** /-pléd/) *vi* to go to trial to resolve which of several claimants has the right to claim money or property held by a third party [Mid-16C. < Anglo-Norman *enterpleder* 'plead together' < *pleder* (see PLEAD)]

interpleader /intər pleédər/ *n* a trial to resolve which of several claimants can sue for money or property held by a third party, instituted by the third party to avoid several proceedings

Interpol /intər pol/ *n* an association of national police forces that promotes cooperation and mutual assistance in apprehending international criminals and criminals who flee abroad to avoid justice. The headquarters of Interpol is in Paris. Full form **International Criminal Police Organization**

interpolate /in túrpə layt/ (**-lates, -lating, -lated**) *v* **1.** *vt* INSERT SOMETHING INTO SOMETHING ELSE to add one thing, often an unnecessary item, between the existing parts of something else **2.** *vt* ALTER TEXT to alter or deliberately falsify a text by adding a comment or extra words to it **3.** *vti* INTERRUPT BY SAYING SOMETHING to say something that interrupts what somebody else is saying **4.** *vt* MATHS ESTIMATE VALUE OF MATHEMATICAL FUNCTION to estimate the value of a mathematical function that lies between known values, often by means of a graph [Early 17C. < Latin *interpolat-*, past participle of *interpolare* 'polish up'] —**interpolation** /in túrpə láysh'n/ *n* —**interpolative** /-ətiv/ *adj* —**interpolator** *n*

interpose /intər pṓz/ (**-poses, -posing, -posed**) *v* **1.** *vti* INTERRUPT BY SAYING SOMETHING to say something that interrupts what somebody else is saying **2.** *vt* PLACE SOMETHING BETWEEN PEOPLE OR THINGS to place yourself or something else between two people or things **3.** *vti* INTERVENE WITH SOMETHING to intervene or interfere in a situation such as a dispute [Late 16C. < French *interposer*, alteration (influenced by *poser* 'to place') of Latin *interponere* 'place between' < *ponere* 'to place'] —**interposable** *adj* —**interposal** *n* —**interposer** *n* —**interposition** /intərpə zísh'n/ *n*

~~**interpratation**~~ incorrect spelling of **interpretation**

interpret /in túrprit/ (**-prets, -preting, -preted**) *v* **1.** *vt* FIND MEANING OF SOMETHING to establish or explain the meaning or significance of something **2.** *vt* ASCRIBE MEANING TO SOMETHING to ascribe a particular meaning or significance to something ○ *I interpreted his gesture as an invitation.* **3.** *vt* PERFORM SOMETHING IN PARTICULAR WAY to perform something such as a play or piece of music in a way that conveys particular ideas or feelings about it **4.** *vti* TRANSLATE SOMETHING to translate what is said in one language into another so that speakers of different languages can communicate **5.** *vt* EXECUTE COMPUTER PROGRAM to convert instructions in a computer program written in a high-level language into machine language and execute them, one instruction at a time [14C. Directly or via French < Latin *interpretari* 'explain' < *interpret-*, stem of *interpres* 'broker'] —**interpretability** /in túrpritə bílləti/ *n* —**interpretable** *adj* —**interpretably** *adv*

interpretation /in túrpri táysh'n/ *n* **1.** ESTABLISHMENT OF MEANING an explanation or establishment of the meaning or significance of something **2.** ASCRIPTION OF PARTICULAR MEANING an ascription of a particular meaning or significance to something **3.** PERFORMANCE OF SOMETHING the way in which an artistic work such as a play or piece of music is performed in order to convey a specific understanding of the work **4.** TRANSLATION the oral translation of what is said in one language into another, so that speakers of different languages can communicate **5.** *Scotland* EDUC same as **comprehension** (sense 3) **6.** EXPLANATORY INFORMATION AT PLACE OF INTEREST explanatory information to help people understand what they are seeing or encountering at a place of interest —**interpretational** *adj*

interpretation centre *n* LEISURE same as **visitor centre**

interpretative /in túrpritətiv/ *adj* relating to, involving, or providing an interpretation or explanation of something —**interpretatively** *adv*

interpreter /in túrpritər/ *n* **1.** TRANSLATOR somebody who carries out oral translation from one language to another **2.** PERFORMER EXPRESSING PARTICULAR IDEAS somebody who performs something such as a play or piece of music in a way that expresses particular ideas or feelings about it **3.** PROGRAM EXECUTING INSTRUCTIONS a computer program that translates instructions in a program written in a high-level computer language into machine language and executes them —**interpretership** *n*

interpretive /in túrpritiv/ *adj* same as **interpretative** —**interpretively** *adv*

interpretive centre *n* LEISURE same as **visitor centre**

interpupillary /intər pyoópələri/ *adj* between the pupils of the eyes

interquartile range /intər kwáwr tīl-/ *n* a measure of the spread of a group of values equal to the difference between the upper limit for the lower quarter and the lower limit for the upper quarter

interregnum /intər régnəm/ (*plural* **-nums** or **-na** /-nə/) *n* **1.** TIME BETWEEN ONE REIGN AND NEXT the period of time between the end of one reign or regime and the beginning of the next **2.** TIME WITHOUT GOVERNMENT OR CONTROL a period of time during which there is no government, control, or authority **3.** INTERRUPTION a pause or gap in any continuous activity or series [Late 16C. < Latin, 'period between kingships' < *regnum* 'kingship'] —**interregnal** *adj*

interrelate /intər ri láyt/ (**-lates, -lating, -lated**) *vti* to have a relationship in which each person or thing depends on or is affected by the others, or cause people or things to have such a relationship —**interrelation** *n* —**interrelationship** *n*

interrelated /intərri láytid/ *adj* in a relationship in which each depends on or is affected by the other or others

interrobang /in térrə bang/, **interabang** *n* a punctuation mark in the form of a question mark over the top of an exclamation mark. It is used at the end of, or sometimes in place of, an utterance that is both question and exclamation, especially to indicate

disbelief. [Mid-20C. Blend of INTERROGATION MARK + BANG[1] (printers' slang for an exclamation mark)]

interrog. *abbr* 1. interrogate 2. interrogation 3. GRAM interrogative

interrogate /in térrə gayt/ (-gates, -gating, -gated) *vt* 1. to question somebody thoroughly, often in an aggressive or threatening manner and especially as part of a formal enquiry, e.g. in a police station or courtroom 2. to transmit a request to a program or device for information, e.g. to a printer for the status of a print job or to a database for specific data [15C. < Latin *interrogat*-, past participle of *interrogare*, literally 'ask in the presence of' < *rogare* 'ask'] —**interrogatee** /in térrəgə teé/ *n* —**interrogator** *n*

SYNONYMS See *question*.

interrogation /in térrə gáysh'n/ *n* 1. THOROUGH QUESTIONING the act or process of questioning somebody closely, often in an aggressive manner, especially as part of an official enquiry or trial 2. QUERY a question or query (*formal*) 3. COMPUT TRANSMISSION OF SIGNAL TO COMPUTER the transmission of a signal to a device or program that triggers a response —**interrogational** *adj*

interrogation mark *n* same as **question mark**

interrogative /íntə róggətiv/ *adj* 1. QUESTIONING questioning or seeming to question somebody or something 2. USED TO ASK QUESTION consisting of or used in asking a question ○ *an interrogative pronoun* ■ *n* 1. WORD USED TO ASK QUESTION a word or particle that is used to form a question, e.g. 'who', 'what', or 'where' 2. FORM OF QUESTION the form of a sentence that is used to ask a question —**interrogatively** *adv*

interrogatory /íntə róggətəri/ *adj* ASKING QUESTION asking a question, used to ask a question, or in the form of a question (*formal*) ■ *n* (*plural* -ries) 1. QUESTION a question or series of questions 2. FORMAL WRITTEN QUESTION a formal written question asked during a legal proceeding and usually answered under oath —**interrogatorily** *adv*

interrogee /in térrə geé/ *n* somebody who is interrogated [Mid-20C. < INTERROGATE]

interrupt /íntə rúpt/ *v* (-rupts, -rupting, -rupted) 1. *vti* HALT SPEAKER OR SPEAKER'S UTTERANCE to halt the flow of a speaker or of a speaker's utterance with a question or remark 2. *vti* DISTURB SOMEBODY OR SOMEBODY'S WORK to disturb somebody who is busy doing something, causing him or her to stop 3. *vt* CAUSE SOMETHING TO STOP to cause a break in the flow of something or put a temporary stop to something 4. *vt* TAKE A BREAK FROM SOMETHING to discontinue doing something temporarily 5. *vt* OBSTRUCT VIEW to block a view ■ *n* COMPUT 1. SIGNAL TO SUSPEND OPERATION a signal to a computer processor to suspend the currently running operation while it either performs the instruction specified by the signal or saves it in a queue to perform later 2. CIRCUIT SENDING SIGNAL INTERRUPTING COMPUTER PROCESS the circuit that conveys a signal to suspend a computer operation [14C. < Latin *interrupt*-, past participle of *interrumpere* 'break apart' < *rumpere* 'to break'] —**interrupter** *n* —**interruptible** *adj* —**interruptive** *adj* —**interruptively** *adv*

interrupted cadence /íntə ruptid-/ *n* in music, a cadence that does not end with the expected chord of the tonic but moves from the dominant to the submedient or subdominant

interrupted screw *n* a screw whose thread is broken in one or more places by a lengthways slot that enables a partial turn to lock or unlock the screw

interruption /íntə rúpsh'n/ *n* 1. the act of interrupting somebody, or something that interrupts somebody who is saying or doing something 2. a pause, break, or temporary halt in an ongoing activity or process

inter se /íntər sáy, íntər seé/ *adv*, *adj* between or among themselves [< Latin]

intersect /íntər sékt/ (-sects, -secting, -sected) *v* 1. *vti* CROSS to cross something, or cross each other 2. *vt* GO THROUGH SOMETHING to follow a path across or through something 3. *vti* OVERLAP to overlap or have things in common with something or each other 4. *vti* HAVE POINTS IN COMMON to overlap a figure or figures geometrically so as to have a point or set of points in common, or overlap each other in this way [Early 17C. < Latin *intersect*-, past participle of *intersecare* 'cut between' < *secare* 'to cut']

intersection /íntər séksh'n/ *n* 1. ACT OF INTERSECTING the act or fact of intersecting 2. CROSSROADS a place where two roads or paths cross each other 3. CROSSING POINT the place or point where two things cross each other 4. OVERLAPPING an overlapping between two things such as different personal interests or political positions 5. MATHS COMMON POINT a point or set of points common to two or more intersecting geometric figures 6. MATHS SET OF COMMON ELEMENTS a set that consists of all of the elements common to two or more other sets, thus being the largest set contained in all of the others —**intersectional** *adj*

interservice /íntər súrviss/ *adj* occurring among the various branches of the armed forces

intersex /íntər seks/ *n* an organism with characteristics of both sexes

intersexual /íntər sékshoo əl/ *adj* 1. occurring between males and females or affecting their relations 2. having characteristics of both sexes —**intersexualism** *n* —**intersexuality** /íntər sekshoo álləti/ *n* —**intersexually** *adv*

interspace *n* /íntər spayss/ SPACE OR INTERVAL a space or interval of time between two things ■ *vt* /íntər spáyss/ (-spaces, -spacing, -spaced) 1. PUT SOMETHING BETWEEN TWO THINGS to put something in the spaces or gaps between things 2. INSERT SPACES BETWEEN TWO THINGS to put spaces or breaks between things —**interspatial** /íntər spáysh'l/ *adj* —**interspatially** *adv*

interspecific /íntərspə síffik/ *adj* 1. created by crossing different species 2. occurring between or involving different species

intersperse /íntər spúrss/ (-sperses, -spersing, -spersed) *vt* 1. to break up the continuity or flow of something with something else 2. to put or insert something here and there among or in something else [Mid-16C. < Latin *interspers*-, past participle of *interspergere* 'scatter between' < *spargere* 'scatter'] —**interspersedly** /-idli/ *adv* —**interspersion** *n*

interstadial /íntər stáydi əl/ *adj* relating to a short period of relatively warmer climate within an ice age [Early 20C. < INTER- + Latin *stadium* 'stage']

interstate *adj* /íntər stáyt/ OCCURRING BETWEEN STATES occurring between, connecting, or involving two or more states ■ *n* /íntər stayt/ MAJOR MOTORWAY BETWEEN US CITIES a limited-access road that forms part of the federally funded system of motorways connecting the major cities of the United States ■ *adv* Aus TO OR IN ANOTHER STATE to or in another state or states

interstation /íntər stáysh'n/ *adj* occurring between or connecting stations

interstellar /íntər stéllər/ *adj* situated, happening, or moving between stars, or involving two or more stars

intersterile /íntər stérrīl/ *adj* not capable of interbreeding —**intersterility** /íntərstə rílləti/ *n*

interstice /in túrstiss/ *n* 1. SMALL SPACE a small opening, crack, or gap between two things 2. SPACE IN CRYSTAL LATTICE a space between neighbouring atoms in the lattice of a crystal 3. SPACE IN BODY TISSUE a small space in a tissue or between parts of the body [15C. Via French < Latin *interstitium* < *intersistere*, literally 'stand still in the middle' < *sistere* 'cause to stand' < *stare* 'to stand']

interstitial /íntər stísh'l/ *adj* 1. RELATING TO GAPS forming, situated in, or relating to one or more small openings, gaps, or cracks 2. GEOL OCCURRING BETWEEN OTHER MINERALS located in the pores or between the crystals of a rock 3. CHEM OF COMPOUND CONTAINING METALS AND NONMETALS relating to a compound, e.g. a carbide, in which ions or atoms of a nonmetal occupy positions in a metal lattice. Interstitial compounds generally have metallic characteristics. 4. PHYSIOL OCCURRING BETWEEN TISSUES lying between parts of an organ or between groups of cells or tissues. The interstitial cells between mammalian testicles are responsible for secreting male sex hormones. ■ *n* ONLINE UNSOLICITED ADVERTISEMENT ON INTERNET an unsolicited advertisement on the World Wide Web that briefly precedes a selected page —**interstitially** *adv*

interstitial-cell-stimulating hormone *n* BIOCHEM same as **luteinizing hormone**

intertestamental /íntər testə mént'l/ *adj* during, from, or relating to the period between the composition of the last books of the Hebrew Scriptures, called the Old Testament by Christians, and the first books of the New Testament of the Bible

intertextuality /íntər tekstyoo álləti/ *n* the relationship that exists between different texts, especially literary texts, or the reference in one text to others —**intertextual** /íntər tékstyoo əl/ *adj* —**intertextually** *adv*

intertexture /íntər tékschər/ *n* 1. an object or material that has been made by interweaving two or more things 2. an act of interweaving two or more things, or the fact of being interwoven

intertidal /íntər tíd'l/ *adj* occurring within, or forming, the area between the high and low tide levels in a coastal zone —**intertidally** *adv*

intertrigo /íntər trígo/ *n* the inflammation of two skin surfaces that are in constant contact, caused by friction or sweat [Early 18C. < Latin, 'chafing of the skin' < assumed *interterere* 'rub together' < *terere* 'to rub']

intertropical /íntər tróppik'l/ *adj* located or occurring between the Tropic of Capricorn and Tropic of Cancer

intertwine /íntər twín/ (-twines, -twining, -twined) *vti* 1. to twist two or more things closely together or around and through each other, or be or become twisted in this way 2. to become closely and intricately linked with each other, or link something closely and intricately with something else ○ *Their lives had intertwined.* —**intertwinement** *n*

intertwist /íntər twíst/ (-twists, -twisting, -twisted) *vti* same as **intertwine** (sense 1)

~~**interrupt**~~ incorrect spelling of **interrupt**

interval /íntərv'l/ *n* 1. INTERVENING PERIOD OF TIME a period of time between one event and the next 2. INTERVENING DISTANCE the distance between one thing and another 3. THEATRE BREAK IN PERFORMANCE a break between parts of a musical or theatrical performance or cinema showing. N Am term **intermission** 4. MUSIC DIFFERENCE IN MUSICAL PITCH the musical distance between the pitches of two notes 5. MATHS ALL NUMBERS BETWEEN TWO NUMBERS a set containing all the real numbers or points between two real numbers or points, which are called the endpoints. If the set includes the endpoints it is a closed interval, and if it excludes the endpoints it is an open interval. [14C. Via French < Latin *intervallum* 'space between ramparts' < *vallum* 'rampart'] —**intervallic** /íntər vállik/ *adj* ◇ **at intervals** 1. at different points in time 2. at various locations

intervalometer /íntərvə lómmitər/ *n* a device that is designed to activate a mechanism automatically at regular intervals, especially one that operates a camera shutter [Mid-20C. < INTERVAL]

interval signal *n* a piece of music or other sound that a radio station uses as its unique identifying signal, broadcasting it between and sometimes during programmes

interval training *n* a method of training, especially in athletics, that involves alternating between aerobic and nonaerobic exercise in the same session

intervene /íntər veén/ (-venes, -vening, -vened) *vi* 1. BECOME INVOLVED IN SITUATION to involve yourself deliberately in a situation, especially in a conflict or dispute, in order to influence what is happening and, most often, to prevent undesirable consequences ○ *The referee had to intervene to stop the fight.* 2. HAVE PREVENTIVE OR DELAYING EFFECT to occur or take effect in such a way as to stop or delay something ○ *The weather intervened before the contest could get under way.* 3. ELAPSE to elapse between one point in time and another 4. BREAK INTO CONVERSATION to break into a conversation or discussion 5. BE SITUATED IN BETWEEN to be located between two things 6. LAW ENTER LAWSUIT to enter a lawsuit as a third party in order to protect your own interests 7. ECON ACT TO MANIPULATE ECONOMIC MARKETS to take economic action that is designed to counter a trend in a market, especially in order to stabilize a country's currency [Late 16C. < Latin *intervenire* 'come between' < *venire* 'come']

intervener *n* another spelling of **intervenor**

intervening /íntər veéning/ *adj* occurring, coming, or standing between two things

intervenor /íntər veénər/, **intervener** *n* 1. somebody who intervenes in something 2. a party that enters

a lawsuit as a third party in order to protect its interests

intervention /íntər vénsh'n/ *n* **1. ACTION AFFECTING ANOTHER'S AFFAIRS** the act of intervening, especially a deliberate entry into a situation or dispute in order to influence events or prevent undesirable consequences **2. MARKET MANIPULATION** economic action that is designed to counter a trend in a market, especially in order to stabilize a country's currency **3. BUYING OF SURPLUS BY EU** the purchase of agricultural produce by the European Union when the market price falls below a specific level (**intervention price**) because there is a surplus —**interventional** *adj*

interventionism /íntər vénsh'nizəm/ *n* **1.** political interference or military involvement by one country in the affairs of another **2.** action by a government to influence and improve the country's economic situation or some aspect of it —**interventionist** *n, adj*

interventricular /íntər ven tríkyŏŏlər/ *adj* situated or occurring between the ventricles of the heart

intervertebral /íntər vúrtibrəl/ *adj* situated or occurring between the vertebrae of the backbone —**intervertebrally** *adv*

intervertebral disc *n* one of the flexible plates of cartilage connecting adjacent vertebrae of the backbone that impart flexibility and act as shock absorbers to protect the spinal cord from impact, e.g. when running

interview /íntər vyoo/ *n* **1. MEETING FOR ASKING QUESTIONS** a meeting during which somebody is asked questions, e.g. by a prospective employer, a journalist, or a researcher **2. RECORD OF INTERVIEW** a transcript, report on, or recording of an interview ■ *v* (**-views, -viewing, -viewed**) **1.** *vt* **ASK SOMEBODY QUESTIONS** to ask somebody a series of questions in an interview **2.** *vi* **PERFORM IN INTERVIEW** to speak and answer in a particular way in an interview ○ *She always interviews well.* [Early 16C. < obsolete French *entrevue* < *entrevoir* 'see each other' < *voir* 'see' < Latin *videre*] —**interviewable** *adj* —**interviewee** /íntər vyoo ée/ *n* —**interviewer** *n*

inter vivos /íntər vée voss/ *adv, adj* from one living person to another ○ *an inter vivos gift* [< Latin, 'between the living']

intervocalic /íntərvō kállik/ *adj* describes a speech sound occurring or inserted between vowels, e.g. between one word that ends with a vowel and another word that starts with a vowel —**intervocalically** *adv*

interweave /íntər wéev/ (**-weaves, -weaving, -wove** /-wṓv/, **-woven** /-wṓv'n/) *vti* **1.** to weave something into or with something else, or be woven together, into, or with something else **2.** to combine one thing with another, or be combined with something else —**interweavement** *n* —**interweaver** *n*

interzone /íntər zṓn/ *adj* between zones ■ *n* an intermediate zone

intestate /in tést ayt/ *adj* **1. LEAVING NO LEGALLY VALID WILL** not having made a legally valid will **2. NOT WILLED TO SOMEBODY** not having been assigned to somebody in a legally valid will ■ *n* **SOMEBODY LEAVING NO LEGALLY VALID WILL** somebody who has died without having made a legally valid will [14C. Directly or via French < Latin *intestatus* 'not having made a will' < *testari* 'make a will' < *testis* 'witness'] —**intestacy** /in téstəssi/ *n*

intestinal /in téstin'l/ *adj* **1.** found in or affecting the intestines **2.** characteristic of, forming part of, or relating to the intestines —**intestinally** *adv*

intestinal flora *npl* bacteria present in a healthy intestine that complete digestion, synthesize vitamin K, and create an acid environment that prevents infection by harmful bacteria

intestine /in téstin/ *n* the part of the digestive system between the stomach and the anus or cloaca that digests and absorbs food. In mammals, the small intestine digests and absorbs food from the stomach, and the large intestine then absorbs most of the remaining water in the food. (*often used in the plural*) [15C. Via French < Latin *intestinus* 'internal' < *intus* 'within']

intifada /ínti fáadə/ *n* the Palestinian uprising in the West Bank and Gaza Strip that started in 1987 in protest against the continued Israeli occupation [Late 20C. < Arabic *intifāḍa* 'a shaking off']

intimacy /íntiməssi/ (*plural* **-cies**) *n* **1. CLOSE RELATIONSHIP** a close personal relationship **2. QUIET ATMOSPHERE** a quiet and private atmosphere **3. DETAILED KNOWLEDGE** a detailed knowledge resulting from a close or long association or study **4. PRIVATE UTTERANCE OR ACTION** a private and personal utterance or action **5. SEXUAL ACT** a sexual act or sexual intercourse (*often used euphemistically*)

intimate[1] /íntimət/ *adj* **1. CLOSE** having, involving, or resulting from a close personal relationship **2. COSY** quiet and private or secluded, enabling people to feel relaxed with each other **3. PRIVATE AND PERSONAL** so private and personal as to be kept secret or discussed only with a close friend or relative **4. SEXUAL** involving or having a sexual relationship (*often used euphemistically*) **5. CLOSELY CONNECTED** very close because of the influence of one thing on another ○ *the intimate connection between power and corruption* **6. THOROUGH** very great and detailed as a result of extensive study or close experience ○ *an intimate knowledge of the workings of government* **7. WORN NEXT TO SKIN** intended to be worn next to the skin or in a private setting ○ *intimate apparel* **8. INNERMOST** relating to or involving the innermost nature of something ■ *n* **CLOSE FRIEND** a close personal friend [Early 17C. < late Latin *intimatus*, past participle of *intimare* (see INTIMATE [2])] —**intimately** *adv* —**intimateness** *n*

intimate[2] /ínti mayt/ (**-mates, -mating, -mated**) *vt* **1.** to hint at something or let something be known in a quiet, indirect, or subtle way **2.** to announce something formally [Early 16C. < late Latin *intimat-*, past participle of *intimare* 'make known' < *intimus* 'innermost'] —**intimater** *n* —**intimation** /ínti máysh'n/ *n*

intime /oN téem/ *adj* small, quiet, and private or secluded [Early 17C. Via French, 'intimate' < Latin *intimus* 'innermost']

intimidate /in tímmi dayt/ (**-dates, -dating, -dated**) *vt* **1.** to frighten somebody into doing or not doing something, e.g. by means of violence or blackmail **2.** to create a feeling of fear, awe, or inadequacy in another person [Mid-17C. < medieval Latin *intimidat-*, past participle of *intimidare* 'put in fear' < Latin *timidus* 'fearful'] —**intimidation** /in tímmi dáysh'n/ *n* —**intimidator** *n* —**intimidatory** /in tímmi dáytəri/ *adj*

intimidating /in tímmi dayting/ *adj* instilling fear, awe, or a sense of inadequacy —**intimidatingly** *adv*

intinction /in tíngksh'n/ *n* in a Christian religious service of Communion, the act of dipping the consecrated bread into the consecrated wine so that somebody taking Communion receives both [Late 19C. < late Latin *intinction-* < Latin *intingere* 'dip in' < *tingere* 'moisten']

intine /ín tin, ín teen/ *n* the inner wall of a pollen grain or spore [Mid-19C. Alteration of Latin *intimus* 'innermost']

intitule /in títtyool/ (**-ules, -uling, -uled**) *vt* to give a title to an act of parliament [15C. Via French < late Latin *intitulare* 'entitle' < Latin *titulus* 'inscription']

intl *abbr* international

into *stressed* /íntoo/; *unstressed* /íntə, íntŏŏ/ CORE MEANING: a preposition indicating that somebody or something moves inside something, either physically or figuratively ○ *I released the balloon into the air.* ○ *in case you get into difficulties* ○ *I decided to go into the army.* ○ *When did you go into partnership with them?*

prep **1. INDICATES MOVEMENT TO INSIDE** indicates that something or somebody moves or is moved from outside to inside or towards the inner part of something ○ *came into the house* **2. INDICATES MOVEMENT TO MIDST OF SOMETHING** indicates that something or somebody moves to the middle of something and becomes part of it or is surrounded by it ○ *leapt into the water* **3. INDICATES ENTRY** indicates entering a state, career, or period of time ○ *burst into action* ○ *went into marketing* **4. INDICATES ACCIDENTAL CONTACT** indicates coming up against something accidentally ○ *bumped into them* **5. INDICATES CHANGE** indicates becoming a new entity, shape, or form as a result of a change or transformation ○ *turned into a frog* **6. INDICATES RESULT** indicates a situation resulting from somebody's persuasion ○ *talked me into going* **7. INDICATES RESULT OF DIVIDING** indicates the number or nature of the smaller parts that are left when something is divided ○ *divided the cake into six* **8.** MATHS **INDICATES DIVISION** placed before a number being divided by another number to indicate the process of division ○ *9 into 63 equals 7.* **9. ENTHUSIASTIC ABOUT** indicates interest in or enthusiasm about something (*informal*) ○ *really into tennis* [Old English *in(n)tō* < IN [1] + TO [1]]

USAGE in, into, or **in to**? In formal written English, the preposition for inward movement is ***into***, not ***in***: *She came into* [not *in*] *the room. We welcomed him into* [not *in*] *the family.* It is sometimes acceptable to use either ***in*** or ***into***, but the latter is usually preferable in formal English: *He put it into* [or *in*] *his pocket.* Using ***in*** for ***into*** can be misleading, as in *She jumped in the pool.* (Did she jump into the pool, or was she already standing in the pool when she jumped?) Do not confuse ***into*** with ***in to*** – the preposition ***into*** is never written as two separate words; when the separate words ***in*** and ***to*** occur side by side, they should not be joined together: *I went into* [not *in to*] *the house. I went in to* [not *into*] *fetch my jacket.* See ***onto***.

intolerable /in tóllərəb'l/ *adj* **1.** so bad, difficult, or painful that it cannot be endured ○ *The pain was intolerable.* **2.** very unpleasant or annoying —**intolerability** /in tóllərə bílləti/ *n* —**intolerably** *adv*

intolerance /in tóllərənss/ *n* **1. REFUSAL TO ACCEPT DIFFERENCES** unwillingness or refusal to accept people who are different from you, or views, beliefs, or lifestyles that differ from your own ○ *racial intolerance* **2. STATE OF BEING INTOLERANT** the state of being easily annoyed ○ *her intolerance of noise* **3. ALLERGIC SENSITIVITY** the inability to eat or drink a particular food, ingredient, or substance, or to take a particular drug, without having an allergic reaction or becoming ill ○ *lactose intolerance* **4. UNFITNESS FOR SOMETHING** unable to thrive or survive in a particular environment

intolerant /in tóllərənt/ *adj* **1. REFUSING TO ACCEPT DIFFERENCES** showing an unwillingness or refusal to accept people who are different from you, or views, beliefs, or lifestyles that differ from your own ○ *an intolerant society* **2. EASILY ANNOYED** easily angered or annoyed ○ *He is rather intolerant of vague ideas and vague people.* **3. ALLERGIC TO SOMETHING** unable to eat or drink a particular food, ingredient, or substance, or to take a particular drug without having an allergic reaction or becoming ill **4. UNFITTED TO SOMETHING** unable to thrive or survive in a particular environment ○ *a plant intolerant of dry conditions* —**intolerantly** *adv*

~~**intolerent**~~ incorrect spelling of **intolerant**

intonate /íntō nayt/ (**-nates, -nating, -nated**) *v* **1.** *vt* **SAY SOMETHING IN PARTICULAR WAY** to say something in a particular tone of voice ○ *The way she intonated the word 'society' indicated her deep contempt for what it represented.* **2.** *vi* PHON **SPEAK WITH VARYING PITCH** to speak with the rising and falling pitch that is characteristic of ordinary speech **3.** *vt* PHON **PRONOUNCE CONSONANT WITH VOICING** to pronounce a consonant with a vibration of the vocal cords, as English speakers do when they pronounce the consonant 'v' as opposed to the consonant 'f' [Late 18C. < medieval Latin *intonat-*, past participle of *intonare* (see INTONE)]

intonation /íntə náysh'n/ *n* **1. PITCH OF VOICE** the rising or falling pitch of the voice when somebody says a word or syllable, or the rising and falling pattern of speech generally **2. INTONING** a saying or chanting of something in a solemn or serious way, or something said or chanted in this way **3.** MUSIC **ACCURACY OF PITCH** accuracy of pitch in performing music **4.** MUSIC **BEGINNING OF PLAINSONG** the opening phrase of a piece of plainsong, sung by a soloist or just a few members of the choir —**intonational** *adj*

intonation contour, **intonation pattern** *n* the pattern of rising and falling pitch in speech that helps to distinguish between questions, statements, and other types of speech

intone /in tṓn/ (**-tones, -toning, -toned**) *v* **1.** *vt* **SAY SOMETHING IN SOLEMN TONE** to say something, especially in a slow and serious or solemn way **2.** *vti* **CHANT PRAYER** to recite a prayer or other religious words in a chanting monotone **3.** *vt* **START PLAINSONG** to sing the opening phrase of a piece of plainsong [14C. Directly or via French < medieval Latin *intonare* '(sing) in tone' < Latin *tonus* 'tone' < Greek *tonos*] —**intonement** *n* —**intoner** *n*

in toto /in tṓtō/ *adv* in its entirety or as a whole ○ *considering his published works in toto* [< Latin]

intoxicant /in tóksikənt/ *n* something that causes physical or psychological intoxication, e.g. an alcoholic drink or great power ■ *adj* capable of making somebody intoxicated

intoxicate /in tóksi kayt/ (**-cates, -cating, -cated**) *v* **1.** *vt* to make somebody drunk with alcohol or stupefied with drugs or other substances **2.** *vt* to make somebody intensely excited or overjoyed, often so much so that the person becomes irrational **3.** *vti* MED same as **poison** *v* (sense 2) (*technical*) [15C. < medieval Latin *intoxicat-*, past participle of *intoxicare* 'to poison' < Latin *toxicum* 'poison' < Greek *toxikon*] —**intoxicable** *adj* —**intoxicated** *adj* —**intoxication** /in tóksi káysh'n/ *n* —**intoxicative** *adj* —**intoxicator** *n*

intoxicating /in tóksi kayting/ *adj* **1.** capable of making somebody intensely excited or overjoyed, often so much so that the person becomes irrational **2.** capable of making somebody drunk or stupefied (*formal*) —**intoxicatingly** *adv*

intra- *prefix* within or inside ○ *intranasal* [Directly or via modern Latin, 'on the inside' < Latin *intra* < Indo-European]

intra-arterial *adj* within or introduced into an artery or arteries —**intra-arterially** *adv*

intra-articular *adj* within or introduced into a joint of the body

intra-atomic *adj* existing or occurring within an atom or atoms, rather than between atoms

intracardiac /íntrə kaárdi ak/, **intracardial** /-kaárdi əl/ *adj* within or introduced into the heart —**intracardially** *adv*

intracellular /íntrə séllyŏŏlər/ *adj* within a cell or cells —**intracellularly** *adv*

intracerebral /íntrə sérrəbrəl/ *adj* existing or taking place inside the main part of the brain or cerebrum —**intracerebrally** *adv*

Intracoastal Waterway- /íntrə kṓst'l-/ system of protected waterways, including rivers, bays, coastal sounds, and canals, in the eastern and southeastern United States, made up of the Atlantic Intracoastal Waterway and the Gulf Intracoastal Waterway. Length: 4,000 km/2,485 mi.

intracompany /íntrə kúmpəni/ *adj* within the same company or between employees or divisions of the same company

intracranial /íntrə kráyni əl/ *adj* within or introduced into the skull —**intracranially** *adv*

intractable /in tráktəb'l/ *adj* **1.** DIFFICULT TO DEAL WITH difficult to deal with or solve ○ *an intractable problem* **2.** STRONG-WILLED AND RESISTANT TO OUTSIDE INFLUENCE stubbornly refusing to be controlled or submit to discipline ○ *Persuasion was tried, but she proved intractable.* **3.** DIFFICULT TO MANIPULATE difficult to shape or manipulate —**intractability** /in tráktə bílləti/ *n* —**intractably** *adv*

SYNONYMS See ***unruly***.

intracutaneous /íntrə kyoo táyni əss/ *adj* ANAT same as **intradermal** —**intracutaneously** *adv*

intradermal /íntrə dúrm'l/ *adj* within or introduced between the layers of the skin —**intradermally** *adv*

intradermal test *n* a test for immunity or allergic sensitivity involving the injection of small amounts of a test material into the skin through a fine needle

intradermic /íntrə dúrmik/ *adj* ANAT same as **intradermal**

intrados /in tráy doss/ (*plural same* or **-doses**) *n* the inner curve of an architectural arch [Late 18C. < French < Latin *intra* 'within' + French *dos* 'back' (< Latin *dorsum*)]

intragenic /íntrə jénnik/ *adj* located or occurring within the same gene

intralingual /íntrə líng gwəl/ *adj* occurring within a single language

intramolecular /íntrə mə lékyŏŏlər/ *adj* existing or occurring within a single molecule —**intramolecularly** *adv*

intramural /íntrə myóorəl/ *adj* **1.** occurring within, or involving members of, a single college, university, or similar institution **2.** within the tissue of the wall of a blood vessel or another hollow body part —**intramurally** *adv*

intramuscular /íntrə múskyŏŏlər/ *adj* within or into the substance of a muscle —**intramuscularly** *adv*

intranasal /íntrə náyz'l/ *adj* within or introduced into the nose —**intranasally** *adv*

intranational /íntrə násh'nəl/ *adj* existing or occurring within the boundaries of a single nation, rather than involving different nations

intranet /íntrə net/ *n* a network of computers, especially one using World Wide Web conventions, accessible only to authorized users such as those within a company

intransigent /in tránssijənt, -zijənt/, **intransigeant** *adj* stubbornly or unreasonably refusing even to consider changing a decision or attitude ■ *n* somebody who refuses to compromise or change an attitude or decision, especially in politics [Late 19C. < French < Spanish *los intransigentes*, a political party (literally 'the uncompromising ones') < *transigir* 'to compromise' < Latin *transigere* (see TRANSACTION)] —**intransigence** *n* —**intransigently** *adv*

intransitive /in tránssitiv/ *adj* describes a verb, or the use of a verb, without a direct object, e.g. the verb 'die' in the sentence 'He was slowly dying' ■ *n* a verb that does not take a direct object —**intransitively** *adv* —**intransitiveness** *n*

intranuclear /íntrə nyóokli ər/ *adj* **1.** existing or occurring within the nucleus of an atom **2.** existing or occurring within the nucleus of a cell

intraocular /íntrə ókyŏŏlər/ *adj* within or introduced into the inside of the eyeball —**intraocularly** *adv*

intraperitoneal /íntrə pérritō neé əl/ *adj* within or introduced into the peritoneal cavity —**intraperitoneally** *adv*

intrapersonal /íntrə púrss'nəl/ *adj* relating to the internal aspects of a person, especially emotions —**intrapersonally** *adv*

intrapreneur /íntrəprə núr/ *n* an employee with a flair for innovation and risk-taking who is given unusual freedom to develop products or subsidiary businesses within a company [Late 20C. < INTRA- + ENTREPRENEUR] —**intrapreneurial** *adj* —**intrapreneurialism** *n* —**intrapreneurially** *adv*

intrapsychic /íntrə sī́kik/ *adj* existing or occurring within the mind —**intrapsychically** *adv*

intraspecific /íntrəspə síffik/, **intraspecies** /-speésh eez, -speéss-/ *adj* existing within a single species or confined to members of one species

intrauterine /íntrə yóotə rīn/ *adj* existing, occurring, or designed to be used inside the womb

intrauterine device *n* a plastic or metal device that is inserted into the cavity of the womb in order to prevent pregnancy

intravascular /íntrə váskyŏŏlər/ *adj* situated or occurring within blood vessels or within a similar system of fluid-bearing vessels in plants —**intravascularly** *adv*

intravenous /íntrə veénəss/ *adj* **1.** existing or occurring inside a vein, or administered into a vein **2.** used in administering fluids or medicines into the veins —**intravenously** *adv*

intraventricular /íntrə ven tríkyŏŏlər/ *adj* within or introduced into a ventricle such as one in the heart or brain —**intraventricularly** *adv*

intravital /íntrə vī́t'l/, **intravitam** /-veé tam/ *adj* occurring in or used on a living cell or organism [Late 19C. < modern Latin *intra vitam* 'within life'] —**intravitally** *adv*

in-tray *n* a tray on somebody's desk for papers that have not yet been dealt with

intrazonal /íntrə zṓn'l/ *adj* describes a soil that has a well-developed and differentiated set of soil characteristics (**profile**), determined by the nature of the parent material and age of the soil

intrench *vti* CONSTR, POL another spelling of **entrench**

intrepid /in tréppid/ *adj* courageous and bold (*literary or humorous*) [Late 17C. Directly or via French < Latin *intrepidus* 'not agitated' < *trepidus* 'agitated'] —**intrepidity** /íntrə píddəti/ *n* —**intrepidly** *adv* —**intrepidness** *n*

~~**intrest**~~ incorrect spelling of **interest**

intricacy /íntrikəssi/ (*plural* **-cies**) *n* **1.** the character of something that has many aspects or parts arranged together in a particularly complex or artful way ○ *a carving of incredible intricacy* **2.** one of the parts or details making up a complex and often puzzling whole (*often used in the plural*) ○ *We had difficulty following the intricacies of the plot.*

intricate /íntrikət/ *adj* **1.** containing many details or small parts that are combined in a particularly complex or skilful way **2.** complex and difficult to understand or resolve, through having many interrelated elements, parts, or factors [15C. < Latin *intricatus*, past participle of *intricare* 'entangle' < *tricae* 'impediments, tricks'] —**intricately** *adv* —**intricateness** *n*

intrigant /íntrigənt/, **intriguant** *n* a deviser of secret plots or schemes (*archaic*)

intrigue *v* /in treég/ (**-trigues, -triguing, -trigued**) **1.** *vt* INTEREST SOMEBODY to make somebody greatly interested or curious **2.** *vi* SCHEME to scheme or use underhand methods to achieve something **3.** *vi* HAVE SECRET LOVER to carry on a secret love affair (*archaic*) ■ *n* /ín treeg, in treég/ **1.** SECRET PLOTTING secret scheming or plotting **2.** SECRET PLOT a secret scheme or plot [Early 17C. Via French < Italian *intrigo* < *intrigare* 'entangle' < Latin *intricare* (see INTRICATE)] —**intriguer** *n* —**intriguing** *adj* —**intriguingly** *adv*

intrinsic /in trínssik/, **intrinsical** /-trínssik'l/ *adj* **1.** BASIC AND ESSENTIAL belonging to something as one of the basic and essential features that make it what it is ○ *an intrinsic part of the plan* **2.** OF ITSELF by or in itself, rather than because of its associations or consequences ○ *has no intrinsic value* **3.** ANAT FOUND IN BODY PART occurring wholly within or belonging wholly to a part of the body such as an organ [15C. Via French < late Latin *intrinsecus* 'inward' < assumed Latin *intrim* 'within'] —**intrinsically** *adv*

intrinsic factor *n* a protein produced in the stomach that promotes the absorption of vitamin B_{12} in the small intestine. Insufficient intrinsic factor results in pernicious anaemia.

intrinsic semiconductor *n* a semiconductor of very high purity in which the density of charge carriers is that of the material itself and is not modified by the presence of impurities

intro /íntrō/ *n* an introduction, especially the opening few bars of a piece of pop music (*informal*) [Early 19C. Shortening]

intro. *abbr* **1.** introduction **2.** introductory

intro- *prefix* **1.** in, into ○ *intromission* **2.** inward ○ *introvert* [< Latin *intro* 'to the inside']

introd. *abbr* **1.** introduction **2.** introductory

introduce /íntrə dyóoss/ (**-duces, -ducing, -duced**) *v* **1.** *vt* PRESENT SOMEBODY TO SOMEBODY to make yourself or another person known to somebody else by saying who you are or who the other person is, as a way of beginning an acquaintance **2.** *vt* BRING IN SOMETHING NEW to bring something to a place, into existence, or into operation for the first time **3.** *vt* CAUSE SOMEBODY TO EXPERIENCE SOMETHING NEW to make somebody aware of something for the first time, or give somebody a first experience of something **4.** *vt* PREFACE SOMETHING WITH SOMETHING ELSE to begin an action with a preface of some sort, especially one designed to get people's attention **5.** *vt* TALK ABOUT SOMETHING NEW to mention a matter for the first time **6.** *vt* GIVE AUDIENCE FORETASTE to tell an audience a little about what or whom they are going to see or hear **7.** *vt* POL PRESENT LEGISLATION FORMALLY to present proposed legislation formally to an assembly, so that it can be debated and voted on **8.** *vt* INSERT SOMETHING INTO SOMETHING ELSE to insert one thing into another **9.** BOT, ZOOL BRING IN NEW SPECIES to place or establish an individual or species of plant or animal in a new habitat or environment [15C. Either < Latin *introducere* 'lead in' < *ducere* 'to lead', or back-formation < INTRODUCTION] —**introducer** *n* —**introducible** *adj*

introduction /íntrə dúksh'n/ *n* **1.** EXPLANATORY SECTION AT BEGINNING a section at the beginning of a book or other piece of writing that summarizes what it is about or sets the scene **2.** SOMETHING GIVING BASIC FACTS a book or course of study that gives somebody basic facts or skills in a field **3.** BEGINNING OF PIECE OF MUSIC the opening passage or movement of a piece of music **4.** PRESENTATION OF SOMEBODY TO SOMEBODY the act of formally presenting somebody or yourself to another person in order to make that person's ac-

quaintance **5.** PRESENTATION the act of presenting somebody or something to an audience, assembly, or other group **6.** FIRST EXPERIENCE somebody's first experience of something **7.** BRINGING IN SOMETHING NEW the act of bringing something to a place, into existence, or into operation for the first time **8.** SOMETHING BROUGHT IN something recently brought from elsewhere, into existence, or into operation **9.** INSERTION the insertion of something somewhere [14C. Directly or via French < Latin *introduction-* < *introduct-*, past participle of *introducere* (see INTRODUCE)]

introductory /íntrə dúktəri/ *adj* **1.** GIVING FORETASTE preparing for what is to be communicated or done later by means of a brief summary or by providing information necessary to understand it ○ *an introductory chapter* **2.** PROVIDING BASICS providing the basic facts or skills ○ *an introductory course* **3.** INITIAL made or used when something begins or is first introduced ○ *an introductory price* [14C. Directly or via French < late Latin *introductorius* < *introduct-* (see INTRODUCTION)] —**introductorily** *adv* —**introductoriness** *n*

introgression /íntrə grésh'n/ *n* the incorporation of genes from one species into the gene pool of another as a result of hybridization [Mid-17C. < INTRO- + *-gression* 'going', as in PROGRESSION] —**introgressant** *adj* —**introgressive** *adj*

introit /ín troyt/, **Introit** *n* **1.** the part of the Roman Catholic Mass consisting of psalm verses and the Gloria Patri, said or sung when the priest first approaches the altar **2.** a psalm or hymn sung as the minister enters the church at the beginning of the Anglican service of Communion [15C. Via French < medieval Latin *introitus* < Latin, 'entrance', past participle of *introire* 'go in' < *ire* 'go'] —**introital** /in tróyt'l/ *adj*

introjection /íntrə jéksh'n/ *n* the unconscious adoption by somebody of the values or attitudes of another person, whom he or she wants to impress or be accepted by [Mid-19C. < INTRO- + *-jection* as in PROJECTION] —**introject** /íntrə jékt/ *vt*

intromission /íntrə mísh'n/ *n* the insertion or admission of something into something else (*formal*) [Mid-16C. Directly or via French < medieval Latin *intromission-* < Latin *intromittere* 'send in' < *mittere* 'send'] —**intromissive** *adj*

intron /ín tron/ *n* a section of DNA that is not expressed in the gene product [Late 20C. < INTRAGENIC]

introrse /in tráwrss/ *adj* pointing and opening inwards, as the anthers of some flowers do, releasing pollen towards the centre of the flower [Mid-19C. < Latin *introrsus*, contraction of *introversus* < *versus*, past participle of *vertere* 'turn'] —**introrsely** *adv*

introspect /íntrə spékt/ (**-spects, -specting, -spected**) *vi* to undertake a detailed mental examination of your own feelings, thoughts, and motives [Late 17C. < Latin *introspectare* 'look into repeatedly' or its source Latin *introspect-*, past participle of *introspicere* 'look into' < *specere* 'to look']

introspection /íntrə spéksh'n/ *n* the detailed mental examination of your own feelings, thoughts, and motives —**introspectional** *adj*

introspectionism /íntrə spéksh'nizəm/ *n* a school of psychology concentrating on the study of immediate subjective experience. N Am term **introspective psychology** —**introspectionistic** /íntrə spékshə nístik/ *adj*

introspective /íntrə spéktiv/ *adj* involving, or frequently undertaking, a deep and candid examination of your own feelings, thoughts, and motives —**introspectively** *adv*

introspective psychology *n N Am* PSYCHOL same as **introspectionism**

introversion /íntrə vúrsh'n/ *n* **1.** the tendency to be self-absorbed and uninterested in other people and the world around **2.** a turning inwards of a hollow organ such as the womb into itself [Mid-17C. < INTRO-VERT]

introvert /íntrə vurt/ *n* **1.** a shy person who tends not to socialize much **2.** somebody whose feelings and thoughts are directed inwards ■ *adj* PSYCHOL, MED same as **introverted** [Mid-17C. < modern Latin *introvertere* 'turn in' < Latin *vertere* 'to turn']

introverted /íntrə vúrtid/ *adj* **1.** SHY tending to be shy and quiet or ill at ease in a group **2.** INTERESTED IN SELF self-absorbed and uninterested in other people and the world around **3.** MED TURNED INTO ITSELF turned into itself or pulled back inside a larger part

intrude /in tróod/ (**-trudes, -truding, -truded**) *v* **1.** *vi* INVADE SOMEBODY'S PRIVACY to disturb somebody's peace or privacy by going or being somewhere uninvited **2.** *vi* HAVE UNWELCOME EFFECT to be an unwelcome presence in, or make an unwelcome entry into, something ○ *The noise of large machinery intruded on the quiet afternoon.* **3.** *vt* INTRODUCE SOMETHING UNPLEASANT to introduce or mention something inappropriate or unwanted (*formal*) ○ *But let me not intrude my private grievances into this discussion.* **4.** *vti* GEOL MOVE INTO ROCK FORMATION to move in a molten state into a pre-existing rock formation, or force molten rock into a pre-existing rock formation [15C. Partly < Latin *intrudere* 'thrust in' < *trudere* 'to thrust'; partly < INTRUSION]

intruder /in tróodər/ *n* **1.** an illegal entrant into a building or property, usually in order to commit a crime **2.** somebody who is present where he or she is not welcome

intrusion /in tróozh'n/ *n* **1.** DISTURBANCE a disturbance of somebody's peace or privacy by an unwelcome arrival or presence **2.** SOMETHING UNWELCOME an unwelcome presence or effect that disturbs or upsets something **3.** CRIME UNLAWFUL ENTRY an illegal entry into a place, often by force, in order to commit a crime (*formal*) **4.** GEOL INTRUDED ROCK a body of igneous rock that has moved while molten into older solid rocks with subsequent alteration of those rocks. Dartmoor is a granite intrusion. **5.** GEOL MOVEMENT OF MOLTEN ROCK the movement of molten rock (**magma**) into pre-existing rock [14C. Directly or via French < medieval Latin *intrusion-* < Latin *intrus-*, past participle of *intrudere* (see INTRUDE)] —**intrusional** *adj*

intrusive /in tróossiv/ *adj* **1.** APPEARING WHERE UNWELCOME forcing itself or yourself into a situation or on people's attention in an unwelcome or inappropriate way **2.** CAUSING UNINVITED DISTURBANCE causing an uninvited and unwarranted disturbance of somebody's peace and privacy **3.** GEOL FORMED BY INTRUSION describes a rock formed by having moved while in a molten state into pre-existing rocks **4.** PHON OF CONNECTING SPEECH SOUND describes a speech sound that is introduced between two words only to facilitate more fluent pronunciation —**intrusively** *adv* —**intrusiveness** *n*

intrust *vt* another spelling of **entrust**

intubate /íntyoo bayt/ (**-bates, -bating, -bated**) *v* **1.** *vti* to insert a tube through the vocal cords and into the windpipe in order to provide a patient's lungs with oxygen, usually during surgery under anaesthesia **2.** *vt* to treat a patient by inserting a tube into the windpipe so that oxygen can be supplied to the lungs [Late 19C. < IN-[2] + Latin *tuba* 'tube'] —**intubation** /íntyoo báysh'n/ *n*

INTUC /ín tuk/ *abbr S Asia* Indian National Trade Union Congress

intuit /in tyóo it/ (**-its, -iting, -ited**) *vt* to be aware of or know something without having to think about it or learn it [Mid-19C. Back-formation < INTUITION] —**intuitable** *adj*

intuition /íntyoo ísh'n/ *n* **1.** INSTINCTIVE KNOWLEDGE the state of being aware of or knowing something without having to discover or perceive it, or the ability to do this **2.** INSTINCTIVE BELIEF something known or believed instinctively, without actual evidence for it **3.** PHILOSOPHY IMMEDIATE KNOWLEDGE immediate knowledge of something [15C. Directly or via French < late Latin *intuition-* 'consideration' < Latin *intueri* 'look upon' < *tueri* 'to look'] —**intuitional** *adj* —**intuitionally** *adv*

intuitionism /íntyoo ísh'nizəm/ *n* **1.** PHILOSOPHY DOCTRINE OF INTUITIVE PERCEPTION the doctrine that asserts that a perceived object is intuitively known to be real **2.** ETHICS ETHICAL PRINCIPLES UNDERSTOOD THROUGH INTUITION the doctrine that knowledge of goodness or obligation and the principles governing them can be discerned through intuition **3.** LOGIC, MATHS MATHEMATICAL THEORY a theory in the foundation of mathematics that holds that only proofs constrained by specific restrictions are permitted

intuitive /in tyóo itiv/ *adj* **1.** known directly and instinctively, without being discovered or consciously perceived **2.** knowing things instinctively —**intuitively** *adv* —**intuitiveness** *n*

intumesce /íntyoo méss/ (**-mesces, -mescing, -mesced**) *vi* to become enlarged or swollen as a result of increased flow of blood or other fluids [Late 18C. < Latin *intumescere* 'swell up' < *tumescere* (see TUMESCENT)] —**intumescence** *n*

intussuscept /íntəssə sépt/ (**-cepts, -cepting, -cepted**) *vti* to cause part of a tubular structure to slide partially into itself, e.g. as part of the intestine sometimes does [Early 19C. Back-formation < INTUSSUSCEPTION] —**intussusceptive** *adj*

intussusception /íntəssə sépsh'n/ *n* **1.** MED a sliding of a portion of a tubular organ into another portion, especially a condition of the bowel in which this happens, creating swelling that leads to obstruction **2.** BIOL the growth of the surface area of a cell wall by the incorporation of new particles into the wall [Early 18C. Directly or via French < modern Latin *intussusception-* < Latin *intus* 'within' + *susception-* 'undertaking' < *suscept-*, past participle of *suscipere* (see SUSCEPTIBLE)]

intwine *vti* another spelling of **entwine**

intwist *vt* another spelling of **entwist**

~~inuendo~~ incorrect spelling of **innuendo**

Inuit /ínnoo it, -yoo-/ (*plural same* or **-its**), **Innuit** *n* **1.** a member of an aboriginal people who live in the coastal Canadian Arctic, in Alaska, and in Greenland. The Inuit are related to the Yupik of Alaska and northeastern Siberia. **2.** a language of the Inuit, forming one branch of Eskimo-Aleut. Native speakers: 60,000. [Mid-18C. < Inuit, plural of *inuk* 'person'] —**Inuit** *adj*

USAGE The Inuit Circumpolar Conference, held in 1977 in Barrow, Alaska, chose officially to replace the term *Eskimo* with ***Inuit*** (which means 'the real people'). *Eskimo* nonetheless remains in common use, appearing even in academic contexts. Because some may find *Eskimo* offensive, care should be exercised in using this word.

Inuktitut /i nóoktətòot/ *n* a language of the Inuit people, especially those in the eastern Arctic [Late 20C. < Inuit, 'the Inuit way'] —**Inuktitut** *adj*

inulase /ínnyoo layz, -layss/ *n* an enzyme that brings about the breakdown of inulin [Late 19C. < INULIN]

inulin /ínnyoo lin/ *n* a fructose polysaccharide that is a food reserve found in the roots and tubers of various plants [Early 19C. < Latin *inula* 'elecampane']

inunction /in úngksh'n/ *n* **1.** the rubbing in of oil or ointment for medicinal purposes **2.** the anointing of somebody with oil as part of a religious ceremony (*formal*) [15C. < Latin *inunction-* < *inunguere* 'anoint' < *unguere* 'to smear']

inundate /ín un dayt, ínnən-/ (**-dates, -dating, -dated**) *vt* **1.** to overwhelm somebody with a huge quantity of things that must be dealt with **2.** to flood a place with water (*formal*) [Late 16C. Back-formation < INUNDATION] —**inundator** *n* —**inundatory** /in úndətəri/ *adj*

inundation /ín un dáysh'n, ínnən-/ *n* **1.** an accumulation of an overwhelming amount of things that somebody has to deal with **2.** a flood of water (*formal*) [15C. Directly or via French < Latin *inundation-* < *inundare* 'flow onto' < *unda* 'wave']

Inupiaq /i nóopi ak, i nyóo-/, **Inupik** /i nóo pik/ *n* a language of the Inuit people who live in northern Alaska [Mid-20C. < Inuit < *inuk* 'person' + *piaq* 'genuine'] —**Inupiaq** *adj*

Inupiat /i nóopi at, -nyóo-/ (*plural same*) *n* a member of an Inuit people who live along the Beaufort Sea and Chukchi coast of the Arctic Ocean [Late 20C. < Inuit (plural) < *inuk* 'person' + *piaq* 'genuine']

Inupik *n, adj* LANG another spelling of **Inupiaq**

inurbane /in ur báyn/ *adj* lacking good manners or sophistication —**inurbanely** *adv* —**inurbanity** /in ur bánnəti/ *n*

inure /i nyóor/ (**-ures, -uring, -ured**), **enure** *v* **1.** *vt* to make somebody used to something unpleasant over a period of time, so that he or she no longer is bothered or upset by it **2.** *vi* to come into legal operation or effect [15C. < assumed Anglo-Norman *eneurer* 'accustom by use' < assumed *eure* 'use' < Latin *opera* 'work'] —**inurement** *n*

inurn /in úrn/ (**-urns, -urning, -urned**) *vt* **1.** to place a cremated body's ashes in an urn **2.** to put a dead body in a grave (*formal*) —**inurnment** *n*

in utero /in yóotər ō/ *adv, adj* in, or while still inside, a woman's womb [< Latin]

inv. *abbr* 1. MATHS, GRAM invariable 2. invented 3. invention 4. inventor 5. COMM invoice

in vacuo /in vákyoo ō/ *adv* 1. in a vacuum 2. in isolation, without considering any legal evidence [< Latin]

invade /in váyd/ **(-vades, -vading, -vaded)** *v* **1.** *vti* **ENTER COUNTRY BY MILITARY FORCE** to enter a country by force with or as an army, especially in order to conquer it **2.** *vt* **ENTER AND SPREAD THROUGH SOMETHING** to enter and spread throughout something completely **3.** *vt* **GO SOMEWHERE IN NUMBERS** to enter or be present in a place in great numbers ○ *The town has been invaded by tourists.* **4.** *vt* **SPOIL SOMETHING** to spoil something by interfering with or in it, interrupting it, or reducing it ○ *invading our privacy* **5.** *vti* MED **CAUSE DISEASE** to enter and spread gradually throughout a part of the body, causing harm or damage **6.** *vti* BOT **GROW RAPIDLY AND HARMFULLY** to become established and spread rapidly in an area, crowding out the pre-existing plants [15C. Directly or via French < Latin *invadere* 'go in' < *vadere* 'to go'] —**invadable** *adj* —**invader** *n*

invaginate /in vájji nayt/ **(-nates, -nating, -nated)** *vti* to push the wall of a cavity or hollow organ into itself, or one section of a hollow organ into another, or be pushed in this way [Mid-17C. Back-formation < INVAGINATION]

invagination /in vájji náysh'n/ *n* **1.** MED **PUSHING SOMETHING INSIDE ITSELF** the pushing of something into itself or partially inside out, like a glove finger pushed into itself, or the condition of something that results from this **2.** MED **INVAGINATED ORGAN** a hollow organ or body part that has been pushed back inside itself **3.** BIOL **INFOLDING OF CELL STRUCTURE** the process of folding a portion of a cell structure inwards, e.g. when the cell membrane turns inwards during phagocytosis **4.** BIOL **FORMING OF HOLLOW GROWTH INSIDE** the pushing inwards of a layer of cells to produce a hollow ingrowth in something, e.g. when the wall of the blastula forms the gastrula [Mid-17C. < modern Latin *invagination-* < medieval Latin *invaginare* 'sheathe' < Latin *vagina* 'sheath']

invalid[1] /in vállid/ *adj* **1.** not acceptable or correct through being based on a mistake or employing flawed reasoning **2.** not legally binding or enforceable [Mid-16C. < Latin *invalidus* 'not strong' < *validus* (see VALID)] —**invalidly** *adv*

invalid[2] /ínvəlid, -leed/ *n* **1.** **SOMEBODY WITH PERSISTENT DISEASE** a patient who has been affected by a disease or medical disorder over a long period **2.** **OFFENSIVE TERM** an offensive term for somebody with disabilities (*dated*) ■ *adj* **1.** **AFFECTED BY PERSISTENT DISEASE** having a persistent disease or medical disorder **2.** **FOR SOMEBODY WITH PERSISTENT LONG-TERM DISEASE** intended for somebody who has a persistent long-term disease or medical disorder ■ *vt* **(-valids, -validing, -valided) 1.** **CAUSE SOMEBODY TO BE INVALID** to cause somebody to have a persistent long-term disease or medical disorder **2.** **SEND HOME BECAUSE OF ILLNESS** to send somebody away or home for good, especially from the armed forces, because of long-term illness or severe injury ○ *was invalided out of the army* [Mid-17C. < INVALID[1]]

invalidate /in válli dayt/ **(-dates, -dating, -dated)** *vt* **1.** to deprive something of its legal force or value, e.g. by failing to comply with some terms and conditions **2.** to prove that something is wrong or make something worthless —**invalidation** /in válli dáysh'n/ *n* —**invalidator** *n*

SYNONYMS See ***nullify.***

invalidism /ínvəlidizəm, -leed-/ *n* **1.** persistent illness or medical disorder **2.** an excessive preoccupation with the state of personal health that causes somebody to live like an invalid

invalidity /invə líddəti/ *n* **1.** **UNSOUNDNESS** a lack of soundness or accuracy that results from an error in reasoning **2.** LAW **LACK OF LEGALITY** the condition of not being legally binding or enforceable **3.** MED **STATE OF ILL-HEALTH** the state of having been affected by a disease or medical disorder over a long period

invalidity benefit *n* an allowance paid by the government to somebody whose long-term illness has prevented him or her from working for at least six months

invaluable /in vállyoo əb'l/ *adj* extremely useful or valuable —**invaluably** *adv*

invariable /in váiri əb'l/ *adj* never changing or varying ■ *n* a mathematical quantity that is a constant —**invariability** /in váiri ə bílləti/ *n* —**invariableness** *n*

invariably /in váiri əbli/ *adv* always or almost always

invariant /in váiri ənt/ *adj* **1.** same as **invariable 2.** MATHS describes a quantity or set of quantities that is not changed by a designated mathematical operation such as the transformation of coordinates ■ *n* MATHS a relationship that is not changed by a designated mathematical operation such as the transformation of coordinates —**invariance** *n* —**invariancy** *n*

invasion /in váyzh'n/ *n* **1.** **ATTEMPT TO CONQUER** a hostile entry by an armed force into a country's territory, especially with the intention of conquering it **2.** **ARRIVAL IN LARGE NUMBERS** the arrival of large numbers of people or things at one time ○ *an invasion of tourists* **3.** **SPOILING** a spoiling of something by interfering with it or taking some of it away **4.** **SPREAD OF SOMETHING HARMFUL** the arrival or spread of something that causes damage or harm **5.** MED **SPREAD OF DISEASE** the spread of disease-causing organisms or malignant cells in the body **6.** BOT **AGGRESSIVE SPREAD OF PLANT** the aggressive spread of a plant species in an area, stifling the growth of pre-existing species [15C. Directly or via French < late Latin *invasion-* < Latin *invas-*, past participle of *invadere* (see INVADE)]

invasive /in váyssiv/ *adj* **1.** MED **ATTACKING ADJACENT TISSUE** having or showing a tendency to spread from the point of origin to adjacent tissue, as some cancers do **2.** SURG **INTO PATIENT'S BODY** done by inserting something into or operating on the body through an incision or a natural orifice **3.** **INTRUDING** involving an intrusion or infringement, e.g. of somebody's privacy or rights **4.** BOT **GROWING AGGRESSIVELY** growing aggressively in an area and stifling the growth of pre-existing plants **5.** MIL **ATTACKING** involving or mounting a military attack on a territory, especially with a view to conquering it —**invasively** *adv* —**invasiveness** *n*

invective /in véktiv/ (*formal*) *n* abusive or violent language used to attack, blame, or denounce somebody ■ *adj* using abusive language [15C. Directly or via French < late Latin *invectivus* 'abusive' < Latin *invehere* 'carry in' < *vehere* 'carry'] —**invectively** *adv*

inveigh /in váy/ **(-veighs, -veighing, -veighed)** *vi* to speak angrily in criticism of or protest at something [15C. < Latin *invehere* (see INVECTIVE)] —**inveigher** *n*

inveigle /in váyg'l, -vée-/ **(-gles, -gling, -gled)** *vt* **1.** to charm or entice somebody into doing something that he or she would not otherwise have done ○ *They inveigled me into driving them to school.* **2.** to obtain something by persuading somebody to give it ○ *She inveigled an introduction to him.* [15C. < Anglo-Norman *envegler*, alteration of French *aveugler* 'deprive of sight' < assumed Vulgar Latin *aboculus* 'without an eye' < Latin *oculus* 'eye'] —**inveiglement** *n* —**inveigler** *n*

invent /in vént/ **(-vents, -venting, -vented)** *vt* **1.** to be the first to think of, make, or use something **2.** to make up something false such as a false excuse ○ *invented a reason for being late* [15C. < Latin *invent-*, past participle of *invenire* 'come upon' < *venire* 'come'] —**inventable** *adj*

invention /in vénsh'n/ *n* **1.** **CREATED THING** a thing that somebody has created, especially a device or process **2.** **ACT OF CREATING** the creation of something new **3.** **LIE** a lie, or the telling of lies (*often used euphemistically*) **4.** **CREATIVE ABILITY** the talent to create new things **5.** MUSIC **SHORT INSTRUMENTAL WORK** a short instrumental work, usually for keyboard, that has two or three parts and employs the technique of counterpoint —**inventional** *adj* —**inventionless** *adj*

inventive /in véntiv/ *adj* **1.** **SKILLED AT INVENTING** good at creating new things **2.** **DISPLAYING CREATIVITY** displaying creativity or imagination in its design ○ *an inventive solution to a long-standing problem* **3.** **INVOLVED IN INVENTION** involved in or concerned with invention —**inventively** *adv* —**inventiveness** *n*

inventor /in véntər/ *n* somebody who invents something

inventory /ínvəntəri/ *n* (*plural* **-ries**) **1.** **LIST OF ITEMS** a list of things, especially items of property **2.** ACCT **RECORD OF ASSETS** a record of a business's current assets, including property owned, merchandise on hand, and the value of work in progress and work completed but not sold **3.** BUSINESS **ASSETS** a company's assets as a whole, or the value of them **4.** COMM **STOCK OF GOODS** the merchandise or stock that a shop or company has on hand **5.** *N Am* BUSINESS same as **stocktaking** (sense 2) ■ *vt* **(-ries, -rying, -ried)** **MAKE INVENTORY OF SOMETHING** to make a list of items, or enter a specific item on an inventory [15C. < medieval Latin *inventorium*, alteration of late Latin *inventarium* 'list of what is found' < Latin *invenire* (see INVENT)] —**inventoriable** *adj* —**inventorial** /ínvən táwri əl/ *adj* —**inventorially** *adv*

inveracity /ínvə rássəti/ (*plural* **-ties**) *n* a lie, or the telling of lies (*humorous*)

Invercargill /ínvər kaárg'l/ city on the southern coast of the South Island, New Zealand. Situated on the River Waihopai, it is the commercial centre of a farming district. Population: 49,833 (2001).

Inverclyde /ínvər klíd/ council area near Glasgow, Scotland. Area: 162 sq. km/49 sq. mi.

inverness /ínvər néss/ *n* a long overcoat with a rounded collar and a detachable cape [Mid-19C. After INVERNESS]

Inverness /ínvər néss/ city in northern Scotland, at the northeastern end of the Caledonian Canal. Population: 63,850 (1993).

inverse /in vúrss, ín vurss/ *adj* **1.** **OPPOSITE OR REVERSING** opposite to or reversing something **2.** MATHS **INVOLVING OPPOSITELY AFFECTED VARIABLES** involving two variables that are in a mathematical relationship where, when one increases, the other decreases and vice versa ■ *n* **1.** **OPPOSITE** something that is a total opposite **2.** MATHS **ELEMENT OF SET** either of two elements of a set that when added together give 0, one being the negative of the other, e.g. 7 and –7 **3.** MATHS same as **inverse function 4.** LOGIC **OPPOSITE LOGICAL PROPOSITION** a logical proposition in which both the subject and the predicate are the opposite of another proposition [15C. < Latin *inversus*, past participle of *invertere* 'turn upside down', literally 'turn in' < *vertere* 'to turn'] —**inversely** *adv*

inverse function *n* a mathematical operation or function that exactly reverses another operation or function. Addition and subtraction are inverse functions.

inversely proportional *adj* **1.** opposite in size, degree, or rate of development **2.** involving a mathematical relationship in which an increase in one variable by a given factor brings about a decrease by the same factor in another

inverse square law *n* a law in physics stating that the magnitude of a physical quantity varies inversely with the square of its distance from its source

inversion /in vúrsh'n/ *n* **1.** **REVERSAL** a reversing of the order, arrangement, or position of something **2.** **REVERSED STATE OR THING** a state in which the order, arrangement, or position of something is reversed, or something in such a state **3.** METEOROL **TEMPERATURE INCREASE WITH ALTITUDE** a stable atmospheric condition in which air temperature increases vertically upwards through a layer **4.** MATHS **INVERTED RATIO** the transformation of a mathematical proportion by inverting the ratio and order of its terms **5.** MUSIC **CHANGING OF INTERVAL BY OCTAVE** a raising of the lower note of an interval, or a lowering of the upper note, by an octave **6.** MUSIC **MOVING OF CHORD TONE** a moving of the root tone of a chord to a position other than the lowest **7.** MUSIC **REVERSING OF MELODY INTERVALS** a converting of all the intervals in a melody from ascending to descending and vice versa **8.** GRAM same as **anastrophe 9.** CHEM **PRODUCTION OF OPPOSITE OPTICAL ACTIVITY** a chemical reaction in which an optically active compound gives a product with opposite optical configuration **10.** GENETICS **CHROMOSOMAL MUTATION** a chromosomal mutation in which a block of genes in a segment is in reverse order **11.** MED **INVERTING OF ORGAN** atypical positioning of an organ, especially the turning inwards or inside out of an organ —**inversive** *adj*

invert *vt* /in vúrt/ **(-verts, -verting, -verted) 1.** **REVERSE ARRANGEMENT OF SOMETHING** to reverse the order, position, or arrangement of something **2.** **CHANGE SOMETHING TO OPPOSITE** to change something to its opposite or contrary **3.** MUSIC **ALTER POSITION OF NOTES** to

change the position or arrangement of the musical notes in an interval, chord, or melody to produce inversion **4.** CHEM **CHANGE OPTICAL CONFIGURATION** to convert an optically active isomer into an isomer with the opposite configuration **5.** LOGIC **CONVERT LOGICAL PROPOSITION** to negate both the subject and predicate of a logical proposition ■ *n* /ín vurt/ CHEM **PRODUCT OF INVERSION** a substance obtained by optical inversion ■ *adj* /ín vurt/ CHEM **OPTICALLY INVERTED** subjected to optical inversion [Mid-16C. < Latin *invertere* (see INVERSE)] —**invertibility** /in vúrtə bíllәti/ *n* —**invertible** *adj*

invertase /in vúr tayz, -tayss/ *n* an enzyme that hydrolyses sucrose

invertebrate /in vúrtibrət/ *n* **ANIMAL WITHOUT BACKBONE** an animal that does not have a backbone, e.g. an insect or worm ■ *adj* **1. WITH NO BACKBONE** lacking a backbone or spinal column **2. OF INVERTEBRATES** relating to or consisting of animals that lack backbones ○ *invertebrate biology* **3. LACKING CHARACTER** lacking strength of character

inverted /in vúrtid/ *adj* **1. REVERSED** turned upside down, inside out, or back to front **2.** MUSIC **WITH FUNDAMENTAL NOTE REPOSITIONED** modified so that the fundamental note of the chord is not the lowest note of the chord **3.** MUSIC **WITH NOTES IN MIRROR IMAGE** with the musical notes so arranged that every ascending interval is made descending and vice versa

inverted comma *n* either of a pair of punctuation marks in double (" ") or single (' ') form, used around direct speech, quotations, and titles, or to give special emphasis to a word or phrase. N Am term **quotation mark**

USAGE ***Inverted commas*** are used to enclose direct speech and quotations: *'Where are you?' he called. Mae West said, 'A man in the house is worth two in the street'.* They are also used around some titles, e.g. those of poems, short stories, and articles: *Hilaire Belloc's poem 'On a Sundial'*, but titles of novels, plays, films, etc. are conventionally printed in italics instead. Inverted commas are often used to make a particular word or phrase stand out from the surrounding text, usually to draw attention to it or because the author is using it self-consciously or sceptically: *words such as 'toothbrush' and 'redcurrant'; in a more 'family-friendly' environment.* Either single (' ') or double (" ") inverted commas may be used in all these cases. Where one piece of direct speech occurs within another, or within a quotation, use inverted commas of the opposite type: *She said, 'I told him to leave and he asked "Why should I?"'*

inverted mordent *n* a musical ornament consisting of two notes of the same pitch separated by a third note one step above the others

inverted pleat *n* a flat symmetrical pleat formed by folding the fabric to the front on each side of the section being pleated

inverted snob *n* somebody who disapproves of his or her own or a higher social class —**inverted snobbery** *n*

inverter /in vúrtər/ *n* **1.** somebody or something that inverts or causes an inversion **2.** a device that changes direct current into alternating current and is commonly used on boats to operate devices such as radios from batteries

invert sugar *n* a mixture of glucose and fructose. Source: optical inversion of sucrose, fruits, honey. Use: in the food industry.

invest /in vést/ (**-vests, -vesting, -vested**) *v* **1.** *vti* **BUY SHARES OR BONDS** to use money to buy or participate in a business enterprise that offers the possibility of profit, especially by buying shares or bonds **2.** *vti* **DEPOSIT MONEY WITH BANK** to deposit money with a bank or other financial institution in an account that pays interest **3.** *vti* **SPEND MONEY ON PROJECT** to spend money on something in the hope of a future return or benefit **4.** *vt* **CONTRIBUTE EFFORT TO SOMETHING** to contribute time, energy, or effort to an activity, project, or undertaking in the expectation of a benefit ○ *investing all their energy into fund-raising* **5.** *vt* **GIVE SOMETHING PARTICULAR QUALITY** to provide somebody or something with a particular quality or characteristic (*often passive*) ○ *He endeavoured to ensure that the occasion was invested with a suitable grandeur.* **6.** *vt* **CONFER SOMETHING ON SOMEBODY** to confer something such as a power or right on a person or group ○ *invests the directors with unprecedented power* **7.** *vi* **MAKE PURCHASE** to use money to buy something, especially something that somebody should be able to use for a relatively long time (*informal*) ○ *It's time this family invested in a new car.* **8.** *vt* **INSTALL SOMEBODY IN OFFICIAL ROLE** to install somebody formally or ceremoniously in an official position (*formal*) ○ *was invested as queen of the carnival* **9.** *vt* **ADORN SOMEBODY OR SOMETHING** to dress, clothe, or cover somebody or something with a garment or other covering (*literary*) **10.** *vt* **BESIEGE SOMETHING** to lay siege to a place (*archaic*) [Mid-16C. Directly or via French < Latin *investire* 'clothe (in)' < *vestis* 'clothing'] —**investable** *adj*

investigate /in vésti gayt/ (**-gates, -gating, -gated**) *v* **1.** *vti* to carry out a detailed examination or enquiry, especially officially, in order to find out about something or somebody ○ *The local police are investigating a murder.* **2.** *vi* to have a look or go and see what has happened ○ *We heard noises downstairs, so Fred went down to investigate.* [Early 16C. < Latin *investigat-*, past participle of *investigare*, literally 'look into for traces' < *vestigium* 'footprint'] —**investigable** *adj*

investigation /in vésti gáysh'n/ *n* **1.** an examination or enquiry into something, especially a detailed one that is undertaken officially, or the act of undertaking an examination **2.** a look round a place or to see what has happened [15C. Directly or via French < Latin *investigat-*, past participle of *investigare* (see INVESTIGATE)] —**investigational** *adj*

investigative /in véstigətiv/ *adj* **1.** responsible for or specializing in investigating **2.** used in or relating to investigation ○ *investigative techniques*

investigator /in vésti gaytər/ *n* somebody who seeks facts about somebody or something on a professional basis, especially somebody who investigates crimes or prepares official or confidential reports

investigatory /in véstigətəri/ *adj* same as **investigative**

investiture /in véstichər/ *n* **1.** the formal installation of somebody in a position or role, especially an official one, or a ceremony held to mark this **2.** the appointment of bishops in the Roman Catholic Church by a civil ruler instead of by the Church [14C. < medieval Latin *investitura* < Latin *investire* 'clothe' (see INVEST); because the person is clothed in the insignia of the position]

investment /in véstmənt/ *n* **1. USE OF MONEY FOR FUTURE PROFIT** the outlay of money, e.g. by depositing it in a bank or by buying shares in a company, with the object of making a profit **2. MONEY INVESTED** an amount of money invested in something for the purpose of making a profit **3. SOMETHING IN WHICH MONEY IS INVESTED** something, e.g. a company, endeavour, or property, that money is invested in with the goal of making a profit **4. CONTRIBUTION TO ACTIVITY** a contribution of something such as time, energy, or effort to an activity, project, or undertaking, in the expectation of a benefit **5. PURCHASE** a purchase, especially something that somebody should be able to use for a relatively long time (*informal*) **6. INVESTITURE** the formal or ceremonial installation of somebody in a role or position, especially an official one (*formal*) **7.** MIL **SIEGE** a siege or besieging (*archaic*) **8.** ECON **MONEY IN COMPANY'S PROPERTY** the outlay of money that a company's existing buildings, equipment, and materials is equivalent to **9.** BIOL **OUTER LAYERS OF ORGANISM** the outer layers of an animal or organ

investment analyst *n* a researcher employed by a brokerage firm to research investments

investment bank *n* in the United States, a bank that offers financial services such as trading securities, raising capital, and managing corporate mergers and acquisitions

investment company *n N Am* a company that holds securities in other companies purely for investment

investment trust *n* a financial enterprise whose business is to invest the capital subscribed by its member shareholders in securities

investor /in véstər/ *n* a person, company, or other organization that has money invested in something, especially one that holds shares in publicly owned corporations ◇ **Investor in People** an award given to organizations that meet specific standards in providing training for employees

inveterate /in véttərət/ *adj* **1.** fixed in a habit or practice, especially a bad one **2.** firmly established and of long standing [14C. < Latin *inveteratus*, past participle of *inveterare* 'become old' < *veter-* 'old'] —**inveteracy** *n* —**inveterately** *adv* —**inveterateness** *n*

inviable /in vī əb'l/ *adj* unable to survive, especially financially or biologically —**inviability** /in vī ə bíllәti/ *n* —**inviableness** *n* —**inviably** *adv*

invidious /in víddi əss/ *adj* **1.** making or implying an unfair distinction ○ *an invidious comparison* **2.** unpleasant because producing or likely to produce jealousy, resentment, or hatred in other people ○ *placed in the invidious position of appearing to criticize from the sidelines* [Early 17C. < Latin *invidiosus* < *invidia* 'ill will', literally 'looking at' < *videre* 'to look'] —**invidiously** *adv* —**invidiousness** *n*

USAGE See ***insidious***.

invigilate /in víjji layt/ (**-lates, -lating, -lated**) *vti* to supervise an examination, especially in order to prevent cheating. N Am term **proctor** [Mid-16C. < Latin *invigilat-*, past participle of *invigilare* 'to watch' < *vigil* 'awake'] —**invigilation** /in vijji láysh'n/ *n*

invigilator /in víjji laytər/ *n* somebody who supervises students at an examination. N Am term **proctor**

invigorate /in víggə rayt/ (**-ates, -ating, -ated**) *vt* to fill somebody or something with energy or life [Mid-17C. Probably < *invigour* < Old French *envigourer* < Latin *vigor* 'vigour'] —**invigoration** /in viggə ráysh'n/ *n* —**invigorative** *adj* —**invigoratively** *adv* —**invigorator** *n*

invigorating /in víggə rayting/ *adj* filling somebody or something with energy or life —**invigoratingly** *adv*

invincible /in vínssəb'l/ *adj* **1. UNBEATABLE** too strong or skilful to ever be defeated **2. TOO DIFFICULT TO OVERCOME** so great or difficult as to be impossible to overcome **3. DEEP-ROOTED** too deep-rooted or ingrained to be altered [15C. Directly or via French < Latin *invincibilis* < *vincibilis* 'conquerable'] —**invincibility** /in vínssə bíllәti/ *n* —**invincibleness** *n* —**invincibly** *adv*

inviolable /in vī ələb'l/ *adj* **1.** secure from being infringed, breached, or broken ○ *The old traditions are no longer inviolable.* **2.** secure from violence or attack ○ *The monarch's person is inviolable.* [15C. Directly or via French < Latin *inviolabilis* < *violabilis* 'that may be injured'] —**inviolability** /in vī ələ bíllәti/ *n* —**inviolableness** *n* —**inviolably** *adv*

inviolate /in vī ələt/ *adj* **1.** not subject to change, damage, or destruction **2.** kept pure, untouched, or unblemished [15C. < Latin *inviolatus* < *violat-*, past participle of *violare* 'injure, treat violently'] —**inviolacy** *n* —**inviolately** *adv* —**inviolateness** *n*

invisible /in vízzəb'l/ *adj* **1. IMPOSSIBLE TO SEE** not able to be seen with the eyes **2. HIDDEN** hidden from view **3. MADE TRANSPARENT MAGICALLY** impossible to see as a result of magic or pseudo-scientific processes **4. NOT EASILY NOTICED** not readily noticed or detected **5. UNRECORDED STATISTICALLY** not reflected, recorded, or reported in economic statistics ○ *invisible earnings* ■ *n* **1. ITEM NOT IN FINANCIAL STATEMENT** an item not reported in a company's financial statement **2. INVISIBLE PERSON OR THING** somebody or something that is invisible ■ **invisibles** *npl* ECON **NONPHYSICAL EXPORTS AND IMPORTS** exports and imports such as financial and leisure services, as opposed to physical goods —**invisibility** /in vízzə bíllәti/ *n* —**invisibleness** *n* —**invisibly** *adv*

invisible ink *n* a liquid used to write something that cannot be seen until the paper is treated in some way, e.g. with heat

invitation /invi táysh'n/ *n* **1. OFFER** an offer to come or go somewhere, especially one promising pleasure or hospitality, or the making of such an offer **2. WRITTEN NOTE** a note or printed card that contains an invitation **3. ENCOURAGEMENT** encouragement to do something ■ *adj* **OPEN ONLY TO THOSE ASKED** open only to people who have been asked personally. N Am term **invitational**

invitational /ínvi táysh'nəl/ *adj* **1.** *N Am* same as **invitation 2.** *US* asked for or requested ■ *n N Am* an event, especially a sports tournament, that is open only to people who have been invited to participate

invitatory /in vītətəri/ *adj* inviting or encouraging something

invite *vt* /in vīt/ (**-vites, -viting, -vited**) **1. ASK SOMEBODY TO PARTICIPATE** to ask somebody politely to come or go somewhere, or ask somebody to do something **2.**

REQUEST SOMETHING to ask for something or say that something would be welcome ○ *She invited questions from the audience.* **3.** PROVOKE SOMETHING to encourage or provoke something that might not have happened otherwise ○ *an attitude that invites disaster* ■ *n* /ín vīt/ same as **invitation** (*informal*) [Mid-16C. Directly or via French < Latin *invitare*] —**invitee** /ín vī tée/ *n* —**inviter** *n*

inviting /in víting/ *adj* suggesting or offering pleasure or enjoyment ○ *Inviting smells were coming from the kitchen.* —**invitingly** *adv* —**invitingness** *n*

in vitro /in véetrō/ *adj, adv* in an artificial environment rather than inside a living organism, e.g. in a test tube [< Latin, 'in glass'.]

in vitro fertilization *n* fertilization of an ovum by sperm outside the body when normal conception is not achievable because of a woman's low fertility. After five days, this is followed by implantation in the womb.

in vivo /in véev ō/ *adj, adv* existing or carried out inside a living organism, e.g. in a test or experiment [< Latin, 'in the living'.]

invocation /ínvə káysh'n/ *n* **1.** CALLING UPON HIGHER POWER a calling upon a greater power such as God or a spirit for help **2.** PRAYER a short prayer forming part of a religious service **3.** QUOTING OF SOMETHING AS REASON the act of calling upon or quoting something such as a law as a reason or justification **4.** INCANTATION SUPPOSEDLY SUMMONING DEMON a casting of a spell in an attempt to make an evil spirit appear, or the spell itself —**invocational** *adj* —**invocatory** /in vókətəri/ *adj*

invoice /ín voyss/ *n* **1.** REQUEST FOR PAYMENT a written record of goods or services provided and the amount charged for them, sent to a customer or employer as a request for payment **2.** SHIPMENT OF GOODS a shipment of goods that is recorded on an invoice ■ *vt* (**-voices, -voicing, -voiced**) SEND INVOICE TO SOMEBODY to send somebody an invoice for payment [Mid-16C. Originally plural of obsolete *invoy* < obsolete French *envoy* < *envoyer* (see ENVOY)]

invoke /in vṓk/ (**-vokes, -voking, -voked**) *vt* **1.** CALL UPON GREATER POWER to call upon a greater power such as God or a spirit for help **2.** QUOTE SOMETHING IN SUPPORT to quote, rely on, or use something such as a law in support of an argument or case **3.** ASK FOR SOMETHING to ask or appeal for something **4.** ATTEMPT TO SUMMON DEMON to call upon an evil spirit to appear, e.g. by casting a spell **5.** AROUSE SOMETHING to create or arouse an idea, emotion, or image [15C. Via French < Latin *invocare* 'call upon' < *vocare* 'to call'] —**invoker** *n*

involucra PHYSIOL, BOT plural of **involucrum**

involucre /ínvə lookər, ínvə lóo-/ *n* a ring of modified leaves beneath a flower or flower cluster, e.g. in a dandelion or daisy flower [Late 16C. Directly or via French < Latin *involucrum* 'wrapper' < *involvere* 'roll into' < *volvere* 'to roll'] —**involucral** /ínvə lóokrəl/ *adj* —**involucrate** /ínvər lóokrət/ *adj*

involucrum /ínvə lóokrəm/ (*plural* **-cra** /-krə/) *n* **1.** a growth of new bone that forms around a mass of dead or infected bone **2.** BOT same as **involucre** [Late 17C. < Latin (see INVOLUCRE)]

involuntarily /in vóllәntərәli/ *adv* without wanting or intending to

involuntary /in vóllәntəri/ *adj* **1.** required or exacted against somebody's will or wishes **2.** spontaneous or automatic, and not controlled or controllable by the mind —**involuntariness** *n*

involuntary manslaughter *n* the unintentional and unlawful killing of one person by another in an act that the killer knew was dangerous or could be a threat to the lives of others

involuntary muscle *n* a muscle that acts independently of the will, especially in reflex functions

involute *adj* /ínvə loot/ **1.** *also* **involuted** /ínvə lóotid/ COMPLEX complicated or intricate **2.** *also* **involuted** ROLLING INWARDS having petals or leaves that roll inwards at the edges **3.** TIGHTLY WHORLED describes a shell whose axis is hidden by tight whorls ■ *n* /ínvə loot/ TYPE OF CURVE a curve traced by the end of a taut thread that cannot be extended as it is wound upon or unwound from another curve ■ *vi* /ínvə lóot/ (**-lutes, -luting, -luted**) BECOME INVOLUTE to become complex or inwardly rolled, whorled, or curved [Mid-17C. < Latin *involutus* 'intricate', past participle of *involvere* (see INVOLVE)] —**involutely** *adv*

involution /ínvə lóosh'n/ *n* **1.** COMPLICATION an act of making something complicated or intricate, or the condition of being complicated or intricate **2.** SOMETHING COMPLEX something complicated or intricate **3.** INVOLUTE PART an involute part or structure **4.** PHYSIOL DECLINE IN FUNCTION a decline or degeneration in the physiological function of an organ **5.** PHYSIOL DECREASE IN SIZE a return to normal size of a body or body part after expansion **6.** MATHS RAISING OF QUANTITY TO POWER the algebraic operation of raising a number, variable, or expression to a specified positive integral power, x^n **7.** GRAM COMPLEX GRAMMATICAL STRUCTURE a complicated grammatical construction **8.** BIOL DEVELOPMENTAL PROCESS FORMING TUBE the process by which some cells grow inwards over the edge of an organ or part until they rejoin the structure to form a tube. The bladder is formed by involution. —**involutional** *adj*

involve /in vólv/ (**-volves, -volving, -volved**) *vt* **1.** CONTAIN SOMETHING to contain or include something as a necessary element **2.** CONCERN SOMEBODY to be a matter that concerns or affects somebody **3.** CAUSE SOMEBODY TO PARTICIPATE to make somebody part of, or make somebody take part in, an event or ongoing process **4.** IMPLICATE SOMEBODY to connect a person with something, especially something disreputable **5.** ENGROSS SOMEBODY to take up somebody's whole attention **6.** COMPLICATE SOMETHING to make something complicated or difficult to follow (*often passive*) **7.** ENCLOSE SOMETHING to envelop something (*literary; often passive*) [Late 14C. < Latin *involvere* 'enfold' < *volvere* 'to roll'] —**involvement** *n* —**involver** *n* —**involving** *adj*

involved /in vólvd/ *adj* **1.** COMPLICATED complicated or difficult to follow **2.** CONNECTED connected with or participating in something **3.** IN RELATIONSHIP participating in a romantic or sexual relationship —**involvedly** /in vólvdli, -vidli/ *adv*

invulnerable /in vúlnərəb'l/ *adj* **1.** not able to be wounded, damaged, hurt, or affected ○ *invulnerable to criticism* **2.** not able to be successfully attacked —**invulnerability** /in vúlnərə bílləti/ *n* —**invulnerably** *adv*

inward /ínnwərd/ *adj* **1.** INSIDE situated within something **2.** OF MIND OR SPIRIT relating to or existing in the mind or spirit **3.** TOWARDS INSIDE moving towards the inside or centre of something ■ *adv* same as **inwards** ■ *n* THE INSIDE the inner part of something (*literary archaic*) ○ *'To kiss the tender inward of thy hand'* (William Shakespeare, *Sonnets*; 1609) —**inwardness** *n*

Inward Light *n* CHR same as **Inner Light**

inward-looking *adj* not concerned with other people or with what is happening in the wider world

inwardly /ínnwərdli/ *adv* **1.** to yourself, or without outward expression ○ *He raged inwardly at the injustice.* **2.** on or to the inside

inwards /ínnwərdz/ *adv* **1.** towards the inside or centre of something ○ *Several windows fell right inwards, through the weight of the snow against them.* **2.** in, into, or towards the mind or spirit ○ *with thoughts turning inwards*

inweave /in wéev/ (**-weaves, -weaving, -wove** /-wṓv/, **-woven** /-wṓv'n/) *vt* to weave something into a fabric or design

inwrap *vt* another spelling of **enwrap**

inwreathe *vt* another spelling of **enwreathe**

in-your-face *adj* (*informal*) **1.** expressing opinions in a forceful, sometimes aggressive, way ○ *Her approach is a little too in-your-face for me.* **2.** direct or provocative in a way that is designed to attract attention ○ *an in-your-face ad campaign*

io *abbr* ONLINE British Indian Ocean Territory (*used in Internet addresses*) See table at **domain name**

Io /ī ō/ *n* **1.** in Greek mythology, the daughter of the river god Inachus, turned into a heifer by the god Zeus to protect her from the jealousy of his wife Hera **2.** a large volcanically active satellite of Jupiter [Via Latin < Greek *Iō*]

I/O *abbr* COMPUT input/output

IOC *abbr* International Olympic Committee

iod- *prefix* same as **iodo-** (*used before vowels*)

iodate /ī ə dayt/ *n* a salt of iodic acid, e.g. sodium or potassium iodate. Use: in medicine. [Early 19C. < IODIC ACID]

iodic /ī óddik/ *adj* relating to, containing, or caused by iodine, especially with a valency of five

iodic acid *n* a colourless or white crystalline solid that is soluble in water. Use: in analytical chemistry, disinfectant, deodorant, antiseptic. Formula: HIO_3.

iodide /ī ə dīd/ *n* a salt of hydriodic acid that contains the univalent anion ion I^-. Metallic iodides such as silver, sodium, or potassium iodide are used in photography and in iodized table salt.

iodinate /ī ədi nayt/ (**-nates, -nating, -nated**) *vt* to treat something with iodine or an iodine compound, or add or substitute iodine atoms to or in an organic compound —**iodination** /ī ədi náysh'n/ *n*

iodine /ī ə deen/ *n* **1.** a poisonous, dark grey to purple-black, lustrous, nonmetallic crystalline element in the halogen family. Source: brine. Use: germicide, antiseptic, preparation of dyes, pharmaceuticals, tinctures, isotopes in medicine and industry. Symbol **I**. See table at **element** **2.** a mixture of iodine solution and potassium iodide in alcohol. Use: topical antiseptic. [Early 19C. < French *iode* < Greek *iōdēs* 'violet-coloured' < *ion* 'violet'] —**iodous** /ī óddəss/ *adj*

iodise *vt* CHEM another spelling of **iodize**

iodism /ī ədizəm/ *n* a form of poisoning caused by the ingestion of iodine or an iodine compound

iodize /ī ə dīz/ (**-dizes, -dizing, -dized**), **iodise** (**-dises, -dising, -dised**) *vt* to treat or combine something with iodine or an iodine compound —**iodization** /ī ə dī záysh'n/ *n* —**iodizer** *n*

iodo- *prefix* iodine ○ *iodophor* [< French *iode* (see IODINE)]

iodoform /ī óddə fawrm/ *n* a yellow volatile crystalline compound with a penetrating odour. Use: antiseptic, in ointments for minor skin diseases. Formula: CHI_3. [Mid-19C. < IODO- + FORMYL]

iodometry /ī ə dómmətri/ *n* an analytical process involving the liberation of or reaction with iodine by a substance in order to determine the quantity of the substance present in the sample being analysed [Late 19C. < IODO- + -METRY]

iodophor /ī óddə fawr/ *n* a substance consisting of iodine and a surface-active agent in solution that slowly releases elemental iodine. Use: disinfectant. [Mid-20C. < IODO- + *-phor*, variant of -PHORE]

iodopsin /ī ō dópsin/ *n* a photosensitive violet pigment in the retinal cones of the eye [Mid-20C. < Greek *iōdēs* (see IODINE) + OPSIN, after *rhodopsin*]

iolite /ī ō līt/ *n* MINERALS same as **cordierite** [Early 19C. < Greek *ion* 'violet']

IOM *abbr* Isle of Man

Io moth *n* a large yellow moth with a large spot resembling an eye on each of its hind wings. Native to: North America. Latin name: *Automeris io*. [After IO (sense 1)]

ion /ī ən, ī on/ *n* an atom or group of atoms that has acquired an electric charge by losing or gaining one or more electrons [Mid-19C. < Greek, 'moving thing' < present participle of *ienai* 'go'; because an ion moves towards the electrode of opposite charge]

-ion *suffix* **1.** action or process ○ *eruption* ○ *erosion* **2.** result of an action or process ○ *abrasion* **3.** condition, state ○ *elation* [Via French < Latin *-ion-*]

Iona /ī ṓnə/ low-lying island off the southwestern tip of Mull, in the Inner Hebrides, western Scotland. Population: 90. Area: 9 sq. km/3 sq. mi.

ion engine *n* a hypothetical rocket engine that derives its thrust from the electrostatic acceleration of a stream of positive ions. Because the engine does not provide enough thrust to escape the Earth's gravity, it could be used only in space.

Eugene Ionesco

Ionesco /ée ə nésk ố/, **Eugène** (1912–94) Romanian-born French dramatist. He was one of the chief exponents of the Theatre of the Absurd. His plays include *The Chairs* (1951) and *Rhinoceros* (1959).

'It's as we speak that we find our ideas, our words, ourselves too, in our words, and the city, the gardens, perhaps everything comes back and we're not orphans any more.'
[Eugène Ionesco, *The Chairs*; 1952]

ion exchange *n* the interchange of ions of the same charge between a solution and a solid in contact with it —**ion exchanger** *n*

Ionia /ī ốni ə/ region of ancient western Asia Minor on the Aegean coast that was colonized by the Greeks around 1000 BC —**Ionian** *adj, n*

Ionian Islands /ī ốni ən-/ group of seven Greek islands in the Ionian and Mediterranean seas. Corfu is the capital and largest city in the islands. Population: 191,003 (1991). Area: 2,250 sq. km/868 sq. mi.

Ionian mode *n* a medieval scale of notes that consists of the eight notes of the diatonic scale rising from G to G, corresponding to the modern C major scale

Ionian Sea part of the Mediterranean Sea, situated between the southeastern coast of Italy and western Greece

ionic /ī ốnnik/ *adj* relating to or containing matter in the form of charged atoms or groups of atoms [Late 19C. < ION]

Ionic /ī ốnnik/ *n* 1. IONIAN DIALECT an extinct dialect of Ancient Greek that was spoken mainly in Ionia 2. METRICAL FOOT in classical poetry, a metrical foot of two long syllables followed by two short ones (**greater Ionic**), or two short syllables followed by two long ones (**lesser Ionic**) ■ *adj* 1. OF ARCHITECTURAL ORDER relating to or typical of the order of architecture characterized by fluted columns and capitals with spiral scroll-shaped ornaments 2. IN IONIC METRE relating to, typical of, or expressed in Ionic metre [Early 17C. < Greek *lōnikos* 'of Ionia']

Ionic order *n* one of the five classical orders of architecture, characterized by fluted columns and capitals with spiral scroll-shaped ornaments

ionic propulsion *n* motion produced in reaction to the expulsion of a stream of accelerated ions

ionics /ī ốnniks/ *n* the study of the development and behaviour of solid electrolytes (*takes a singular verb*)

ion implantation *n* the use of a stream of electrically accelerated ions to implant impurities on or near the surface of the substrate during the manufacture of a semiconductor

ionise CHEM another spelling of **ionize**

ionization /ī ə nī záysh'n/, **ionisation** *n* a process in which an atom or molecule loses or gains electrons, acquiring an electric charge or changing an existing charge

ionization chamber *n* a device used to detect and measure ionizing radiation, consisting of a gas-filled tube with electrodes at each end between which a voltage is maintained. Radiation that ionizes gas molecules in the tube causes a current between the electrodes, the strength of which is a function of the radiation's intensity.

ionization potential *n* the energy needed to remove an electron from an atom or molecule and move it an infinite distance away

ionize /ī ə nīz/ (**-izes, -izing, -ized**), **ionise** (**-ises, -ising, -ised**) *vti* to undergo ionization, or cause something to undergo ionization —**ionizable** *adj*

ionone /ī ənōn/ *n* a yellow liquid smelling of violets. Source: plants. Use: manufacture of perfumes. Formula: $C_{13}H_{20}O$. [Late 19C. < Greek *ion* 'violet']

ionophore /ī ốnnə fawr/ *n* a molecule found in lipid membranes that helps transport ions across the membrane [Mid-20C. < ION]

ionosphere /ī ốnnə sfeer/ *n* four layers of the Earth's upper atmosphere in which incoming ionizing radiation from space creates ions and free electrons that can reflect radio signals, enabling their transmission around the world [Early 20C. < ION] —**ionospheric** /ī ốnnə sférrik/ *adj* —**ionospherically** *adv*

ionospheric wave *n* MEDIA same as **sky wave**

ion propulsion *n* AEROSP same as **ionic propulsion**

ion rocket *n* a rocket powered by an ion engine

iontophoresis /ī ốntəfə reéssiss/ *n* the movement of ions through biological material under the influence of an electric current [Early 20C. < Greek *iont-*, present participle of *ienai* 'go'] —**iontophoretic** /ī ốntəfə réttik/ *adj* —**iontophoretically** *adv*

ion trap *n* a technique for deflecting the ions in the electron beam in a cathode-ray tube to prevent damage to the phosphor caused by the ions bombarding the screen. Typically, a magnet is used to deflect the beam through a tiny opening in the electron gun while the heavier ions are deflected less and remain trapped in the gun.

iota /ī ốtə/ *n* 1. the ninth letter of the Greek alphabet, represented in the English alphabet as 'i'. See table at **alphabet** 2. a very small amount of something ○ *anyone with an iota of sense* [Early 17C. Via Latin < Greek *iōta* < Semitic]

iotacism /ī ốtəsizəm/ *n* the tendency in speakers of modern Greek to use the sound of iota in place of the sound of other vowel characters such as eta or upsilon [Mid-17C. Via Latin < Greek *iōtakismos* < *iōta* (see IOTA)]

IOU *n* a written acknowledgment of a debt between the writer and somebody else [Representation of *I owe you*]

IOW *abbr* 1. in other words (*used in e-mail messages or text messages*) 2. Isle of Wight

Iowa /ī ə́wə/ 1. state in the north-central United States bordered by Illinois, Minnesota, Missouri, Nebraska, South Dakota, and Wisconsin. Capital: Des Moines. Population: 2,936,760 (2002 estimate). Area: 145,754 sq. km/56,276 sq. mi. 2. river in Iowa that flows southeastwards and empties into the Mississippi River. Length: 530 km/330 mi. —**Iowan** *n, adj*

IP *abbr* ONLINE 1. image processing 2. Internet protocol

IPA *abbr* 1. Institute of Practitioners in Advertising 2. PHON International Phonetic Alphabet

IPCC *abbr* ENVIRON Intergovernmental Panel on Climate Change

ipecacuanha /íppi kakyoo ánnə/, **ipecac** /íppi kak/ *n* 1. an emetic made from dried roots 2. a bush, the roots of which are a source of ipecacuanha. Native to: South America. Latin name: *Cephaelis ipecacuanha*. [Early 17C. Via Portuguese < Tupi *ipe-kaã-guéne* 'low plant causing vomit']

Iphigenia /ífiji nī ə, i fíjji-/ *n* in Greek mythology, a daughter of Agamemnon, who was prepared to sacrifice her to Artemis in order to gain favourable winds for the Greek fleet to sail for Troy. Differing versions of the myth give different accounts of her fate.

IPL *abbr* COMPUT initial program load

IPO *abbr* FIN initial public offering

Ipoh /éepō/ city and capital of Perak State, western Malaysia. Population: 382,853 (1996).

ippon /i pón, íppon/ *n* a winning point awarded in judo or karate for perfect technique [Mid-20C. < Japanese]

IPR *abbr* LAW intellectual property rights

iproniazid /íprə nī əzid/ *n* a synthetic drug. Use: antidepressant and, formerly, to treat tuberculosis. [Mid-20C. Blend of ISOPROPYL + ISONIAZID]

ipsative /ípsətiv/ *adj* using yourself as the norm against which to measure something, e.g. your present performance against your past performance rather than the performance of others [Mid-20C. < Latin *ipse* 'self']

ipse dixit /ípsi díksit/ *n* something asserted dogmatically and without proof [Late 16C. < Latin, 'he himself said it']

ipsilateral /ípsi láttərəl/ *adj* being on or affecting the same side of the body [Early 20C. < Latin *ipse* 'same'] —**ipsilaterally** *adv*

ipsissima verba /ip síssimə vúrbə/ *npl* the precise words used in something that is quoted [< Latin, 'the very words']

ipso facto /ípsō fáktō/ *adv* as the result of a particular fact [< Latin, 'by the fact itself']

ipso jure /ípsō joóri/ *adv* by reason of a particular law [< Latin, 'by the law itself']

Ipswich /ípswich/ 1. town and administrative centre in Suffolk, England. Population: 117,069 (2001). 2. city in Queensland, eastern Australia, just outside Brisbane. Population: 128,967 (2002 estimate).

iq *abbr* Iraq (*used in Internet addresses*) See table at **domain name**

IQ *n* a measure of somebody's intelligence, obtained through a series of aptitude tests concentrating on different aspects of intellectual functioning. An IQ score of 100 represents 'average' intelligence. Full form **intelligence quotient**

Iqbal /ík bal/, **Sir Muhammad** (1875–1938) Indian philosopher, poet, and political leader. He became president of the Muslim League in 1930, and his separatist political philosophy underpinned the eventual formation of Pakistan.

Iquique /ee keé kay/ seaport, city, and capital of Tarapacá Region, northern Chile, situated 209 km/130 mi. south of the Peruvian border. Population: 177,892 (1998).

Iquitos /ee keé toss/ city and river port in northeastern Peru, situated on the upper River Amazon, 2,040 km/1,268 mi. overland northeast of Lima. Population: 334,013 (1998).

ir *abbr* Iran (*used in Internet addresses*) See table at **domain name**

Ir *symbol* CHEM ELEM iridium

IR *abbr* 1. COMPUT information retrieval 2. PHYS infrared (radiation) 3. Inland Revenue

Ir. *abbr* 1. Ireland 2. Irish

ir- *prefix* (*used before r*) 1. same as **in-**[1] 2. same as **in-**[2]

IRA[1] *n* an organization of Irish nationalists originally set up to strive for an independent Ireland by force of arms and still dedicated to achieving the unity of the island of Ireland. Full form **Irish Republican Army**

IRA[2] /íre/ *n US* a plan in the United States that permits working people to invest money for retirement and pay no tax on the amount invested either at the time of investment or after retirement. Full form **Individual Retirement Account**

irade /i raádi/ *n* a written decree of a Muslim ruler, especially, formerly, the sultan of Turkey [Late 19C. < Arabic *irādah* 'will, desire']

Iran

Iran /i ráan, i rán/ country in Southwest Asia, located south of the Caspian Sea, northeast of the Persian Gulf, and north of the Gulf of Oman. Language: Farsi. Currency: Iranian rial. Capital: Tehran. Population: 68,278,826 (2003). Area: 1,648,000 sq. km/636,300 sq. mi. Official name **Islamic Republic of Iran**. Former name **Persia**. See map on previous page

Iranian /i ráyni ən/ n **1.** somebody who comes from Iran **2.** a group of languages spoken in the region northeast of the Persian Gulf, a subgroup of the Indo-Iranian branch of Indo-European. Native speakers: 70 million. —**Iranian** adj

Iran-Iraq War n the war fought between Iran and Iraq that lasted from 1980 to 1988, following the invasion of border territory in Iran by Iraq

Iraq

Iraq /i ráak, i rák/ country in Southwest Asia, bordered by Turkey, Iran, Saudi Arabia, Kuwait, the Persian Gulf, Jordan, and Syria. Language: Arabic. Currency: Iraqi dinar. Capital: Baghdad. Population: 24,683,313 (2003). Area: 438,317 sq. km/169,235 sq. mi. Official name **Republic of Iraq**

Iraqi /i ráaki, i ráki/ n **1.** somebody who comes from Iraq **2.** the modern dialect of Arabic spoken in Iraq —**Iraqi** adj

Iraq War, **Iraqi War** n ▶ **Gulf War** (sense 2)

irascible /i rássəb'l/ adj **1.** easily provoked to anger or outbursts of temper **2.** showing or typical of anger ○ an irascible gesture [Mid-16C. Via French < Latin irascibilis 'quick to anger' < irasci 'grow angry' < ira 'anger'] —**irascibility** /i rássə bílləti/ n —**irascibleness** n —**irascibly** adv

irate /ī ráyt/ adj **1.** feeling great anger **2.** showing or typical of great anger ○ an irate phone call [Mid-19C. < Latin iratus, past participle of irasci 'grow angry'] —**irately** adv —**irateness** n

I-ration /ī ráysh'n/ n same as **Creation** (slang; used in Black English)

~~irrational~~ incorrect spelling of **irrational**

Irawadi GEOG another spelling of **Irrawaddy**

IRBM abbr intermediate-range ballistic missile

IRC n an Internet facility that enables two or more people to participate in real-time online discussions. Full form **Internet relay chat**

IRD abbr NZ Inland Revenue Department

IRD number n in New Zealand, a numerical code that identifies each member of the workforce for the purposes of paying income tax

ire /ī r/ n strong anger (literary) [13C. Via French < Latin ira 'anger'] —**ireful** adj

SYNONYMS See **anger**.

Ireland

Ireland /ī rlənd/ **1.** island in northwestern Europe, in the North Atlantic Ocean, west of Great Britain. It comprises the Republic of Ireland and the British province of Northern Ireland. Area: 84,429 sq. km/32,598 sq. mi. **2.** country occupying the southern, central, and northwestern parts of the island of Ireland. Language: English, Irish Gaelic. Currency: euro. Capital: Dublin. Population: 3,924,410 (2003). Area: 70,273 sq. km/27,133 sq. mi. Official name **Republic of Ireland**. Gaelic name **Éire**

Ireland, Northern ▶ **Northern Ireland**

Ireland /ī rlənd/, **David** (b. 1927) Australian novelist. His works include The Unknown Industrial Prisoner (1971).

irenic /ī réenik, ī rénnik/, **irenical** /-ik'l/ adj promoting or intended to promote peace (literary) [Mid-19C. < Greek eirēnikos 'peaceable' < eirēnē 'peace'] —**irenically** adv

irenicon n another spelling of **eirenicon** (formal)

irenics /ī réeniks, ī rénn-/ n a branch of theology that seeks to promote unity between different churches and religious groups (takes a singular verb)

irey adj another spelling of **irie** (slang; used in Black English)

Irian Jaya /írri ən jī ə/ province of Indonesia, consisting of the western half of the island of New Guinea and including islands off its northern and northwestern coasts. Capital: Jayapura. Population: 1,560,000 (1989). Area: 421,981 sq. km/162,928 sq. mi. Former name **West New Guinea** (1828–1962), **West Irian** (1963–72)

irid- prefix same as **irido-** (used before vowels)

iridaceous /írri dáyshəss/ adj relating or belonging to the family of flowering plants that includes the iris and crocus. Family: Iridaceae.

iridectomy /írri déktəmi/ (plural **-mies**) n the surgical removal of part of the iris of the eye

iridescent /írri déss'nt/ adj **1.** having rainbow colours that appear to move and change as the angle at which they are seen changes **2.** having a lustrous or brilliant appearance —**iridescence** n —**iridescently** adv

iridic¹ /i ríddik, ī-/ adj relating to, involving, or containing the element iridium [Mid-19C. < IRIDIUM]

iridic² /i ríddik, ī-/ adj relating to or typical of the iris of the eye [Late 19C. < Latin irid-, stem of iris 'iris (of the eye']

iridium /i ríddi əm, ī-/ n a brittle, corrosion-resistant, silver-white metallic element. Use: alloys for pen nibs, jewellery, watch and compass pivot bearings, surgical instruments, electrical contacts, chemical crucibles. Symbol **Ir**. See table at **element** [Early 19C. < Latin irid-, stem of iris 'rainbow']

irido- prefix **1.** iris ○ iridotomy ○ iridaceous **2.** rainbow ○ iridescent **3.** iridium ○ iridosmine [Via Latin < Greek irid-, stem of iris 'rainbow, iris (of the eye']

iridology /írri dólləji/ n a technique in alternative medicine by which diagnosis of various bodily disorders is claimed to be possible by examination of the fine structure of the iris of the eye —**iridologist** n

iridosmine /írri dóss mīn/, **iridosmium** /-dózmi əm/ n an ore and natural alloy of iridium and osmium in which the osmium content exceeds 35 per cent, with traces of platinum, rhodium, ruthenium, iron, and copper [Early 19C. Blend of IRIDIUM + OSMIUM]

iridotomy /írri dóttəmi/ (plural **-mies**) n a surgical operation in which the iris of the eye is cut into, nowadays using a laser

irie /īree/, **irey** adj good, pleasing, or enjoyable (slang; used in Black English) [Late 20C. Origin ?]

iris /īriss/ n **1.** PART OF EYE the coloured part of the eye that consists of a muscular diaphragm surrounding the pupil and regulates the light entering the eye by expanding and contracting the pupil **2.** FLOWERING PLANT a plant with long sword-shaped leaves. Flowers: many-coloured. Genus: Iris. **3.** same as **rainbow** n (sense 1) (literary) **4.** RAINBOW SHOW OF COLOURS a show of colours of various hues, like a rainbow **5.** PHOTOGRAPHY same as **iris diaphragm** [15C. Via Latin < Greek, 'rainbow, iris (of the eye']

iris in vi to open up the iris diaphragm of a camera gradually in order to expand the picture area

iris (sense 2)

iris out vi to close the iris diaphragm of a camera gradually in order to contract the picture area until the image darkens completely. Irising out was formerly a common way to end a film or sequence.

iris diaphragm n a diaphragm consisting of adjustable thin plates that control the size of an aperture, especially one used in a camera to control the amount of light allowed to enter

Irish /īrish/ adj **1.** OF IRELAND relating to the island or country of Ireland **2.** OF IRISH GAELIC relating to the Irish Gaelic language **3.** OF ENGLISH DIALECT OF IRELAND relating to the dialect of English spoken in Ireland ■ n LANG same as **Irish Gaelic** ■ npl PEOPLE FROM IRELAND people who come from Ireland [13C. < Old English Īr(as) 'inhabitants of Ireland', probably < Old Irish Ériu 'Ireland'] —**Irishness** n

LANGUAGE HERITAGE See **Celtic**.

Irish coffee n a hot drink of sweetened coffee containing Irish whiskey and topped with whipped cream

Irish elk n an extinct giant deer with large antlers that lived in the Pleistocene epoch. Native to: Europe, Asia. Genus: Megaloceros.

Irish English n the variety of English spoken in Ireland. See panel on next page —**Irish English** adj

Irish Gaelic n an official language of the Republic of Ireland, spoken mainly in the west of the country, belonging to the Celtic branch of Indo-European. Native speakers: 5,000. Other speakers: 1 million. —**Irish Gaelic** adj

Irish harp n a small diatonic harp constructed with a hollowed willow soundbox

Irishism /īrishizəm/ n N Am LANG same as **Hibernicism**

Irishman /īrishmən/ (plural **-men** /-mən/) n a man who comes from Ireland

Irish moss n an edible red seaweed from which a complex carbohydrate food additive (**carrageenan**) is obtained. Native to: coasts of Europe and North America. Latin name: Chondrus crispus.

Irish Republican Army n POL, MIL full form of **IRA**

Irish Sea /īrish-/ body of water situated between Great Britain and Ireland, connecting to the North Atlantic Ocean to the south through St George's Channel and to the north through the North Channel. Area: 100,000 sq. km/39,000 sq. mi.

Irish setter

Irish setter n a setter with a silky reddish coat, belonging to a breed originating in Ireland

Irish stew n a stew of lamb or mutton, potatoes, and onions

WORLD ENGLISH *Irish English* is the variety of English used in Ireland since at least the 16th century. For some observers, the terms *Irish English*, *Anglo-Irish*, and *Hiberno-English* mean much the same; for others, the term Irish English refers to English throughout Ireland, Anglo-Irish refers to a variety that originated among settlers from England (and has been especially associated with a Dublin elite), and Hiberno-English refers to usage markedly influenced by Irish Gaelic. All commentators agree, however, that it is difficult to draw a clear line between the various kinds of Irish English. Northern Irish English is generally regarded as a distinct variety of Irish English (but is not usually contrasted with a 'Southern Irish English'). Within Northern Ireland, the variety Ulster Scots derives from the settlement (or as it was called at the time, 'plantation') of Scottish Protestants in the North from the early 17th century onwards.

In Irish English *r* is generally pronounced in words such as *art*, *door*, and *worker*, with the tip of the tongue curled back and raised. The *wh* in words like *why* and *what* is pronounced as /hw/, so that *whales* and *Wales* are clearly distinguished. Words like *three* and *those* are commonly pronounced like 'tree' and 'dose', and words like *leave* and *tea* as 'lave' and 'tay'. There are distinctive grammatical forms influenced by Irish Gaelic. First, forms like these are used for emphasis and increased focus: *It's a fine man he is*, *It was to help her I went*, and *It's himself was the best player*. Second is the use of *after* and *-ing* to mark an action just completed: *She's after helping them this very morning*. The third is the omission of *yes* and *no* in answers: *Did you come yesterday? – I did*; *Can you see him now? – We can*. Vocabulary adapted from Gaelic includes the now internationally current *banshee* (from *bean sidhe* 'fairy woman'), *colleen* ('young woman', from *cailin*), *shillelagh* (a thick stick, from the town of the same name); and *whiskey* or *whisky* (both originally from Gaelic *uisge beatha* 'water of life').

Irish terrier *n* a terrier with a wiry reddish coat, belonging to a breed originating in Ireland

Irish Traveller, **Irish Traveler** *n* a descendant of nomadic Irish traders and craftspeople who immigrated to the United States in the mid-19th century and who maintain an itinerant lifestyle and speak a language derived from Gaelic

Irish whiskey *n* whisky made in Ireland, principally of barley

Irish wolfhound

Irish wolfhound *n* a large powerful dog with a rough shaggy coat, belonging to a breed developed in Ireland. The Irish wolfhound is the tallest breed of dog in the world.

Irishwoman /írish woomən/ (*plural* **-women** /-wimin/) *n* a woman who comes from Ireland

iritis /ī rítiss/ *n* inflammation of the iris of the eye [Early 19C. < IRIS] —**iritic** /ī ríttik/ *adj*

irk /urk/ (**irks**, **irking**, **irked**) *vt* to annoy somebody slightly, especially by being tedious [14C. Perhaps < Old Norse *yrkja* 'to work'; originally N English, 'grow weary or vexed']

SYNONYMS See *annoy* and *bother*.

irksome /úrksəm/ *adj* slightly annoying, especially because of being tedious —**irksomely** *adv* —**irksomeness** *n*

Irkutsk /ur koʻotsk, eer-/ city in southern Siberian Russia and capital of Irkutsk Oblast. It is situated on the River Angara, 72 km/45 mi. from the southwestern shore of Lake Baikal. Population: 668,449 (1995).

IRO *abbr* **1.** Inland Revenue Office **2.** INTERNAT REL, HIST International Refugee Organization **3.** international relief organization

iroko /ə rókō/ (*plural* **-kos**) *n* **1.** a hard brown African wood often used instead of teak **2.** a hardwood tree that produces iroko. Native to: tropical Africa. Genus: *Chlorophora*. [Late 19C. < Yoruba]

iron /ī ərn/ *n* **1.** METALLIC ELEMENT a heavy, magnetic, malleable, ductile, lustrous, silvery-white metallic element that is present in very small quantities in the blood and is the fourth most abundant element in the Earth's crust. Source: haematite, limonite, magnetite. Use: engineering and structural products. Symbol **Fe**. See table at **element 2.** HEATED TOOL a tool made of iron or steel, usually heated before and during use ○ *a soldering iron* **3.** CLOTHES PRESSER a small electrical appliance with a flat metal base that is heated and used to press clothes **4.** HARSH CHARACTER a strong, unyielding, or hard aspect of somebody's nature ○ *a will of iron* **5.** METAL-HEADED GOLF CLUB any golf club with a metal head, differentiated by numbers that indicate different angles of the face and lengths of the shaft **6.** US COMPUTER HARDWARE computer hardware, especially older and larger mainframes (*slang*) ○ *a company with some big iron* **7.** RIDING same as **stirrup** (sense 1) ■ **irons** *npl* RESTRAINTS FOR ARMS OR LEGS manacles or fetters for restraining the arms or legs ■ *adj* **1.** MADE OF IRON relating to or made of iron **2.** VERY STRONG very strong or hard **3.** TOUGH very robust or tough **4.** UNYIELDING very determined, unyielding, or cruel ■ *v* (**irons**, **ironing**, **ironed**) **1.** *vti* PRESS CLOTHES to press clothes or other fabrics with an iron to remove wrinkles **2.** *vt* COVER SOMETHING WITH IRON to cover or clad something with iron [Old English *īren* < Germanic] ◇ **have several irons in the fire** to be involved in several different activities at the same time ◇ **pump iron** to do weightlifting exercises for body building or fitness (*slang*) ◇ **strike while the iron is hot** to act while circumstances are favourable to a successful outcome

iron out *vt* **1.** to smooth away wrinkles in a garment or fabric using an iron **2.** to settle a dispute or resolve a problem by removing difficulties

iron age *n* in classical mythology, an era regarded as the third and last step in humankind's degeneration from the golden age

Iron Age *n* the period following the Bronze Age, beginning around 1500 BC in Southwest Asia, during which iron was increasingly used in making tools and weapons

ironbark /ī ərn baark/ *n* a eucalyptus tree with hard rough bark

iron blue *n* an insoluble compound. Use: in fertilizers, as a blue pigment in paint, ink, and paper dyeing. Formula: $Fe_7C_{18}N_{18} \cdot 10H_2O$.

ironbound /ī ərn bownd/ *adj* **1.** DECORATED WITH IRON wrapped or decorated with iron bands **2.** HARSH stern or unyielding **3.** RUGGED edged or enclosed with rocks (*literary*) ○ *an ironbound coast*

ironclad /ī ərn klad/ *adj* **1.** COVERED OR PROTECTED WITH IRON covered with iron, especially as a protection or armour **2.** STRONG strong, firm, or unyielding **3.** IRREFUTABLE not capable of being attacked or refuted ○ *an ironclad agreement* ■ *n* ARMOURED SHIP a 19th-century wooden warship armoured with metal plates

Iron Cross *n* the highest German military decoration, instituted in Prussia in 1813 and awarded during World Wars I and II

iron curtain *n* an impenetrable barrier to understanding, awareness, or agreement

Iron Curtain *n* **1.** the militarized border between the Communist bloc and Western Europe during the Cold War. The Iron Curtain existed from the end of World War II until the fall of Eastern European Communist governments between 1989 and 1991. ○ *'From Stettin in the Baltic to Trieste in the Adriatic, an iron curtain has descended across the continent.'*

(Sir Winston Churchill *Fulton, Missouri, Speech*; 1946) **2.** the policy of isolation that prevented freedom of travel and communication between Western and Eastern Europe during the Cold War

iron grey *adj* of a dark greenish-grey colour —**iron grey** *n*

iron hand *n* strict, harsh, or despotic control —**ironhanded** /ī ərn hándid/ *adj* —**ironhandedness** *n*

iron horse *n* a steam-powered railway locomotive (*archaic*)

ironic /ī rónnik/, **ironical** /ī rónnik'l/ *adj* **1.** deliberately stating the opposite of the truth, usually with the intention or result of being amusing **2.** △ involving a surprising or apparently contradictory fact

USAGE Is it really **irony** or is it merely coincidence? When you use *irony*, *ironic*, and *ironically*, be sure that you use them in contexts associated with stark incongruity, inconsistency, or even folly, and not in contexts associated with things merely coincidental or improbable. This use of *ironically* is inappropriate, and *coincidentally* is the better choice: *Ironically, both the defence counsel and the prosecutor went to public school.* Appropriate use of *ironically* requires an incongruity between what is expected and what has happened in fact: *Ironically, because they lacked sophisticated computers they developed efficient algorithms that can now add to the power of supercomputers.*

SYNONYMS See *sarcastic*.

ironically /ī rónnikli/ *adv* **1.** in a way that intends to create a humourous effect by using words to imply the opposite of their literal meaning **2.** △ used to indicate that the speaker finds a statement unexpected or incongruous

USAGE See *sentence adverb*.

ironing /ī ərning/ *n* **1.** the act of pressing clothes or other fabrics to remove wrinkles **2.** clothes that have been ironed or have to be ironed

ironing board *n* a covered, often padded board on legs on which clothes are ironed

ironize /ī ər nīz/ (**-izes**, **-izing**, **-ized**), **ironise** (**-ises**, **-ising**, **-ised**) *v* **1.** *vi* to use irony or be ironic **2.** *vt* to give something an ironic tone or make something ironic in nature

iron lung *n* an airtight metal cylinder encasing a patient up to the neck, formerly used to provide help in breathing by alternating air pressure within the cylinder

iron maiden *n* a medieval instrument of torture consisting of a hinged box shaped like a human body and lined with spikes that impale somebody placed inside as it is closed

ironman /ī ərn man/ (*plural* **-men** /-men/) *n* **1.** *also* **Ironman** a triathlon for men and women that includes competitions in, e.g. bicycling, swimming, and running **2.** ANZ, US a male athlete with great endurance who takes part in a triathlon or ironman competition

ironmonger /ī ərn mung gər/ *n* UK a dealer in tools and other articles made chiefly of metal —**ironmongery** *n*

iron oxide *n* any natural or synthetic compound of iron and oxygen

iron pan *n* a hard layer below the surface of sand or gravel in which iron salts from percolating water have precipitated, cementing the grains of the material together

ironperson /ī ərn purss'n/ (*plural* **-persons** or **-people** /-peep'l/) *n* ANZ, US an athlete with great endurance who takes part in a triathlon or ironman competition

iron pyrites *n* MINERALS same as **pyrite**

iron rations *npl* UK, ANZ, Can food designed to be used in an emergency, especially by military personnel. US term **iron ration**

ironside /ī ərn sīd/ *n* a man of great physical strength or endurance

Ironside *n* a nickname given to King Edmund II of England

ironsides /ī ərn sīdz/ (*plural* same) *n* same as **ironside**

Ironsides *npl* the cavalry regiment led by Oliver Cromwell in the English Civil War

ironstone /ī ərn stōn/ *n* **1.** any sedimentary rock that contains a large amount of iron ore **2.** a hard and durable variety of white pottery

ironware /ī ərn wair/ *n* goods, especially kitchen utensils, made of iron

iron-willed *adj* extremely strong-willed

ironwoman /ī ərn wŏŏmən/ (*plural* **-men** /-wimin/) *n ANZ, US* a female athlete with great endurance who takes part in a triathlon or ironman competition

ironwood /ī ərnwŏŏd/ (*plural* **-woods** or *same*) *n* **1.** a tree with very hard timber, e.g. a hornbeam **2.** the very hard wood of an ironwood tree

ironwork /ī ərn wurk/ *n* something made of iron, e.g. a gate, especially when it is decorative

ironworker /ī ərn wurkər/ *n* **1.** somebody employed in an ironworks **2.** a maker of ironwork

ironworks /ī ərn wurks/ (*plural same*) *n* a factory where iron is smelted or large metal goods are made

irony /īrəni/ (*plural* **-nies**) *n* **1.** HUMOUR BASED ON OPPOSITES humour based on using words to suggest the opposite of their literal meaning **2.** SOMETHING HUMOROUS BASED ON CONTRADICTION something said or written that uses humour based on words suggesting the opposite of their literal meaning **3.** INCONGRUITY incongruity between what actually happens and what might be expected to happen, especially when this disparity seems absurd or laughable **4.** INCONGRUOUS THING something that happens that is incongruous with what might be expected to happen, especially when this seems absurd or laughable **5.** THEATRE same as **dramatic irony** **6.** PHILOSOPHY same as **Socratic irony** [Early 16C. Via Latin *ironia* < Greek *eirōneia* 'pretended ignorance' < *eirōn* 'dissembler']

USAGE See *ironic*.

Iroquoian /írrə kwóy ən/ *n* **1.** a family of languages spoken by Iroquois peoples of eastern North America **2.** a member of a Native North American people who speaks an Iroquoian language —**Iroquoian** *adj*

Iroquois /írrə kwoy/ (*plural same*) *n* a member of a former confederacy of six Native North American peoples, the Mohawk, Oneida, Seneca, Onondaga, Cayuga, and Tuscarora. Originally settled along the Hudson River Valley, many Iroquois now live in urban areas. [Mid-17C. Via French < Algonquian] —**Iroquois** *adj*

irradiant /i ráydi ənt/ *adj* radiating light or shining brightly [Early 16C. < Latin *irradiant-*, present participle of *irradiare* (see IRRADIATE)]

irradiate /i ráydi ayt/ (**-ates, -ating, -ated**) *v* **1.** *vt* EXPOSE SOMEBODY OR SOMETHING TO RADIATION to expose somebody to or treat somebody or something with radiation or streams of particles **2.** *vt* PRESERVE FOOD to treat food with electromagnetic radiation to kill microorganisms and slow down the process of ripening and gradual deterioration or rotting **3.** *vt* LIGHT SOMETHING UP to make something brighter by shining light onto it **4.** *vt* MAKE SOMETHING INTELLIGIBLE to make something intellectually clear **5.** *vti* PHYS same as **radiate** *v* (sense 1) [Early 17C. < Latin *irradiat-*, past participle of *irradiare* 'illumine' < *radius* 'ray'] —**irradiative** *adj* —**irradiator** *n*

irradiation /i ráydi áysh'n/ *n* **1.** IRRADIATING the act of irradiating somebody or something, or the state of being irradiated **2.** LIGHTING EFFECT the visual effect by which a brightly lit thing appears larger against a dark background **3.** MEDICAL RADIATION the medical use of radiation, e.g. X-rays, gamma rays, or neutrons

irradicable /i ráddikəb'l/ *adj* incapable of being eradicated [Early 18C. < medieval Latin *irradicabilis* < Latin *radicare* 'take root', wrongly understood as 'root out'] —**irradicably** *adv*

irrational /i rásh'nəl/ *adj* **1.** LACKING IN REASON contrary to or lacking in reason or logic **2.** LACKING LOGICAL THOUGHT unable to think logically **3.** UNABLE TO THINK CLEARLY lacking the normal ability to think clearly, especially because of shock or injury to the brain **4.** MATHS CONTAINING IRRATIONAL NUMBER describes a mathematical expression that contains an irrational number **5.** LITERAT CONTAINING METRIC IRREGULARITY describes an irregularity in the metre of a classical poem, usually where there is a long foot instead of a short one ■ *n* **1.** IRRATIONAL PERSON an unclear or illogical thinker **2.** MATHS same as **irrational number** [15C. < Latin *irrationalis* < *rationalis* (see RATIONAL)] —**irrationality** /i rásh'n álləti/ *n* —**irrationally** *adv*

irrationalism /i rásh'nəlizəm/ *n* **1.** the state of lacking reason or logic **2.** the belief that feelings and intuition are more important than reason —**irrationalistic** /i rásh'nə lístik/ *adj*

irrational number *n* any real number that cannot be expressed as the exact ratio of two integers, e.g. $\sqrt{2}$; and π

Irrawaddy /írrə wóddi/, **Irawadi** principal river of Myanmar. Length: 2,100 km/1,300 mi.

irreal /i reéəl/ *adj* illusory or not actually existing (*literary*) —**irreality** /írri álləti/ *n*

irreclaimable /írri kláyməb'l/ *adj* not able to be reclaimed ○ *an irreclaimable desert* ○ *irreclaimable damages* —**irreclaimability** /írri kláymə bílləti/ *n* —**irreclaimably** *adv*

irreconcilable /i rékən sīləb'l/ *adj* **1.** INCOMPATIBLE not capable of being made to agree or coexist with something else **2.** UNRESOLVABLE incapable of being resolved **3.** IMPLACABLE determinedly hostile and unwilling to accept compromise —**irreconcilability** /i rékən sīlə bílləti/ *n* —**irreconcilably** *adv*

irrecoverable /írri kúvvərəb'l/ *adj* **1.** impossible to get back or regain **2.** impossible to repair or remedy —**irrecoverably** *adv*

irredeemable /írri deéməb'l/ *adj* **1.** WITHOUT HOPE OF IMPROVEMENT not able to be improved, corrected, or made good **2.** NOT REPAIRABLE impossible to repair **3.** CHR INCAPABLE OF REDEMPTION refusing to reform and unable to be saved **4.** FIN UNABLE TO BE PAID OFF not having a fixed date for repayment of the principal ○ *an irredeemable bond* **5.** FIN NOT CONVERTIBLE INTO COINS unable to be converted into coins —**irredeemability** /írri deémə bílləti/ *n* —**irredeemably** *adv*

irredenta /írri déntə/ *n* a territory that was once part of one country but is now ruled by another and is subject to claims that it should be returned to its former country [Early 20C. < Italian *(Italia) irredenta* (see IRREDENTIST)]

irredentist /írri déntist/ *n* a member of a group of people who support the return to their country of territories that used to belong to it but are now under foreign rule [Early 20C. < IRREDENTIST] —**irredentism** *n*

Irredentist /írri déntist/ *n* a member of a former Italian organization that advocated the adding to Italy of Italian-speaking territories that were under foreign control [Late 19C. < Italian *irredentista* < *(Italia) irredenta* 'unrecovered (Italy)' < *redento* 'redeemed' < Latin *redemptus*, past participle of *redimere* (see REDEEM)]

irreducible /írri dyóossəb'l/ *adj* **1.** INCAPABLE OF BEING DECREASED not able to be made smaller **2.** INCAPABLE OF SIMPLIFICATION not able to be simplified, or simplified further **3.** IMPOSSIBLE TO FACTOR INTO LESSER POLYNOMIALS in mathematics, used to describe a polynomial that cannot be factored into two polynomials of a lesser degree **4.** IMPOSSIBLE TO REDUCE TO RATIONAL EXPRESSION in mathematics, used to describe a radical that cannot be reduced to a rational expression —**irreducibility** /írri dyóossə bílləti/ *n* —**irreducibly** *adv*

irreflexive /írri fléksiv/ *adj* describes a relation in which, if a has the relation to b, then b does not have the relation to a

irreformable /írri fáwrməb'l/ *adj* **1.** incapable of being reformed **2.** impossible to revise or alter —**irreformability** /írri fáwrmə bílləti/ *n*

irrefrangible /írri fránjəb'l/ *adj* **1.** INCAPABLE OF BEING DISOBEYED impossible to disobey or violate (*formal*) **2.** INCAPABLE OF BEING BROKEN impossible to break or smash (*formal*) **3.** INCAPABLE OF BEING REFRACTED describes visible light or other radiation that cannot be refracted —**irrefrangibility** /írri fránjə bílləti/ *n* —**irrefrangibly** *adv*

irrefutable /írri fyóotəb'l, i réffyootəb'l/ *adj* impossible to refute or disprove [Early 17C. < late Latin *irrefutabilis* < Latin *refutare* 'refute'] —**irrefutability** /írri fyóotə bílləti, i réffyootə-/ *n* —**irrefutably** *adv*

irregardless /írri gaárdləss/ *adv* ⚠ (*nonstandard*) [Early 20C. Probably blend of IRRESPECTIVE + REGARDLESS]

USAGE Since the prefix *ir-* means 'not' (as it does in *irrespective*), and the suffix *-less* means 'without', ***irregardless*** is a double negative and regarded as nonstandard. As such, it is to be avoided, in favour of *irrespective* or *regardless*.

irregular /i réggyoolər/ *adj* **1.** NOT OF UNIFORM APPEARANCE not even, uniform, or symmetrical in appearance **2.** OCCURRING AT ODD INTERVALS not occurring at equally spaced intervals of time **3.** NONCONFORMING not conforming to common practices **4.** BEHAVING UNACCEPTABLY not conforming to accepted rules or standards of behaviour **5.** MIL UNOFFICIAL not forming part of an official military body **6.** GRAM NOT FORMED BY USUAL GRAMMATICAL RULES not following the usual rules of word formation ○ *an irregular verb* **7.** CONSTIPATED not having a regular daily bowel movement (*euphemistic*) **8.** BOT HAVING ASYMMETRICAL PARTS describes a plant that does not have symmetrical parts ■ *n* MIL SOLDIER NOT PART OF REGULAR FORCES a soldier who is not part of an official military body [15C. Via French < medieval Latin *irregularis* 'breaking a rule' < Latin *regularis* (see REGULAR)] —**irregularly** *adv*

irregularity /i réggyoo lárrəti/ (*plural* **-ties**) *n* **1.** BEING IRREGULAR the state of being irregular **2.** IRREGULAR THING something irregular, e.g. a bump in a road **3.** UNAUTHORIZED THING something unauthorized or unacceptable by usual standards

irrelative /i réllətiv/ *adj* **1.** not related or connected **2.** not relevant

irrelevant /i rélləvənt/ *adj* not relevant or important —**irrelevance** *n* —**irrelevancy** *n* —**irrelevantly** *adv*

~~**irrelevent**~~ incorrect spelling of **irrelevant**

irreligious /írri líjjəss/ *adj* **1.** lacking in any religious faith **2.** opposed to religion —**irreligiously** *adv* —**irreligiousness** *n*

irremediable /írri meédi əb'l/ *adj* impossible to remedy or put right [Mid-16C. < Latin *irremediabilis* < *remediare* 'to cure'] —**irremediably** *adv*

irremissible /írri míssəb'l/ *adj* **1.** not able to be pardoned or excused **2.** not able to be avoided or postponed [15C. Directly or via French < ecclesiastical Latin *irremissibilis* 'unpardonable' < Latin *remiss-*, past participle of *remittere* (see REMIT)] —**irremissibility** /írri míssə bílləti/ *n* —**irremissibly** *adv*

irremovable /írri moóvəb'l/ *adj* incapable of being removed —**irremovability** /írri moóvə bílləti/ *n* —**irremovably** *adv*

irreparable /i réppərəb'l/ *adj* not able to be repaired or put right ○ *did irreparable damage to the computer* [15C. Directly or via French < Latin *irreparabilis* 'not to be recovered' < *reparare* (see REPAIR [1])] —**irreparability** /i réppərə bílləti/ *n* —**irreparably** *adv*

irrepealable /írri peéləb'l/ *adj* not able to be repealed —**irrepealability** /írri peélə bílləti/ *n* —**irrepealably** *adv*

irreplaceable /írri pláyssəb'l/ *adj* not able to be replaced —**irreplaceability** /írri pláyssə bílləti/ *n* —**irreplaceably** *adv*

irreprehensible /i réppri hénssəb'l/ *adj* deserving no censure

irrepressible /írri préssəb'l/ *adj* not able to be controlled ○ *irrepressible high spirits* —**irrepressibility** /írri préssə bílləti/ *n* —**irrepressibly** *adv*

irreproachable /írri prṓchəb'l/ *adj* not incurring any reproach or criticism [Mid-17C. < French *irréprochable* < *réprochable* 'reproachable'] —**irreproachability** /írri prṓchə bílləti/ *n* —**irreproachably** *adv*

irreproducible /i reéprə dyóossəb'l/ *adj* impossible to reproduce —**irreproducibility** /i reéprə dyóossə bílləti/ *n*

~~**irresistable**~~ incorrect spelling of **irresistible**

irresistible /írri zístəb'l/ *adj* **1.** not able to be resisted or successfully opposed **2.** so desirable as to be very difficult to resist [Late 16C. < medieval Latin *irresistibilis* < Latin *resistere* 'resist'] —**irresistibility** /írri zístə bílləti/ *n* —**irresistibly** *adv*

irresoluble /írri zóllyoob'l/ *adj* incapable of being solved, reconciled, or explained [Mid-17C. < Latin *irresolubilis* 'indissoluble' < *resolvere* 'melt'] —**irresolubility** /írri zóllyoo bílləti/ *n* —**irresolubly** *adv*

irresolute /i rézzə loot/ *adj* unsure and unable to

take decisions —**irresolutely** adv —**irresoluteness** n —**irresolution** /i rézzə loŏsh'n/ n

irresolvable /írri zólvəb'l/ adj **1.** not able to be broken down into different parts **2.** not able to be solved —**irresolvability** /írri zólvə bílləti/ n —**irresolvably** adv

irrespective /írri spéktiv/ adv in spite of everything (informal) —**irrespectively** adv ◊ **irrespective of** without taking something into account ○ *We have to work together irrespective of our differences.*

USAGE See *irregardless.*

irresponsible /írri spónssəb'l/ adj **1.** not having or showing any care for the consequences of personal actions **2.** not legally capable of assuming responsibility for personal actions —**irresponsibility** /írri spónssə bílləti/ n —**irresponsibly** adv

irresponsive /írri spónssiv/ adj not responding quickly or favourably —**irresponsively** adv —**irresponsiveness** n

irretrievable /írri treévəb'l/ adj **1.** impossible to find or recover **2.** impossible to repair or put right —**irretrievability** /írri treévə bílləti/ n —**irretrievably** adv

~~**irrevelant**~~ incorrect spelling of **irrelevant**

~~**irreverant**~~ incorrect spelling of **irreverent**

irreverent /i révvərənt/ adj lacking in respect [Mid-16C. < Latin *irreverent-* < present participle of *revereri* (see REVERE)] —**irreverence** n —**irreverently** adv

irreversible /írri vúrssəb'l/ adj impossible to reverse or undo —**irreversibility** /írri vúrssə bílləti/ n —**irreversibly** adv

irrevocable /i révvəkəb'l/ adj impossible to revoke, undo, or change [14C. Directly or via French < Latin *irrevocabilis* 'that cannot be recalled' < *revocare* (see REVOKE)] —**irrevocability** /i révvəkə bílləti/ n —**irrevocably** adv

irrigate /írri gayt/ (-gates, -gating, -gated) vt **1.** AGRIC SUPPLY AREA WITH WATER to bring a supply of water to a dry area, especially in order to help crops to grow **2.** MED WASH OUT WOUND to make water or liquid medication flow through or over a body part or wound in order to cleanse it **3.** REFRESH SOMETHING to make something fresh [Early 17C. < Latin *irrigat-*, past participle of *irrigare*, literally 'to water in' < *rigare* 'to water'] —**irrigable** adj —**irrigation** /írri gáysh'n/ n —**irrigational** adj —**irrigative** adj —**irrigator** n

irritable /írritəb'l/ adj **1.** EASILY ANNOYED easily annoyed or exasperated **2.** MED SENSITIVE extremely sensitive, especially to inflammation **3.** BIOL RESPONSIVE TO STIMULI describes an organism that is able to respond to stimuli [Mid-17C. < Latin *irritabilis* 'easily enraged' < *irritare* 'provoke'] —**irritability** /írritə bílləti/ n —**irritably** adv

irritable bowel syndrome n a condition of the bowel in which there is recurrent pain with constipation or diarrhoea or alternating attacks of these

irritant /írritənt/ adj causing irritation, especially physical irritation [Early 17C. < Latin *irritant-*, present participle of *irritare* 'provoke'] —**irritancy** n —**irritant** n

irritate /írri tayt/ (-tates, -tating, -tated) v **1.** vti ANNOY SOMEBODY to cause somebody to feel annoyance or exasperation, or cause annoyance or exasperation **2.** vt MED INFLAME BODY PART to stimulate a body part excessively, causing a painful reaction such as inflammation **3.** vt BIOL STIMULATE ORGANISM to stimulate an organism in a way that provokes a response [Mid-16C. < Latin *irritat-*, past participle of *irritare* 'provoke'] —**irritating** adj —**irritatingly** adv —**irritative** adj —**irritator** n

SYNONYMS See *annoy.*

irritation /írri táysh'n/ n **1.** ANNOYANCE a feeling of impatience or exasperation **2.** ACT OF ANNOYING the act of causing annoyance or exasperation **3.** SOMEBODY OR SOMETHING ANNOYING somebody or something that causes annoyance or exasperation **4.** MED REACTION TO IRRITANT a painful reaction, especially an inflammation, caused by an irritant **5.** MED INFLAMING the act of causing a painful reaction, especially an inflammation

SYNONYMS See *anger.*

irrits /írrits/ npl Aus a feeling of annoyance (informal) [Late 20C. < shortening of IRRITATION]

irrupt /i rúpt/ (-rupts, -rupting, -rupted) vi **1.** to enter suddenly or violently **2.** to increase suddenly and rapidly, e.g. in number [Mid-19C. < Latin *irrupt-*, past participle of *irrumpere* 'break into a place' < *rumpere* 'to break']

irruption /i rúpsh'n/ n **1.** a sudden, often violent appearance of something ○ *the irruption of violence in everyday life* **2.** a very rapid and pervasive increase in the numbers of something, e.g. predators (technical)

irruptive /i rúptiv/ adj **1.** entering or likely to enter suddenly or violently **2.** describes igneous rock that is injected forcibly into pre-existing rock formations —**irruptively** adv

IRS abbr GOV Internal Revenue Service

Irtysh ♦ **Ob'-Irtysh**

Irving /úrving/, **Sir Henry** (1838–1905) British actor and theatrical manager. He was known for his Shakespearean roles, and for his 24-year acting partnership with Ellen Terry. Born **Brodribb, John Henry**

John Irving

Irving, John (b. 1942) US novelist. His works include *The World According to Garp* (1978) and *The Hotel New Hampshire* (1981).

Irving, Washington (1783–1859) US writer. The first US author to achieve international renown, he is best known for *The Sketch Book* (1819–20), which includes the stories 'Rip Van Winkle' and 'The Legend of Sleepy Hollow'.

'For what is history, but...huge libel on human nature, to which we industriously add page after page, volume after volume, as if we were holding up a monument to the honor, rather than the infamy of our species.'
[Washington Irving, *A History of New York*; 1809]

is[1] 3rd person singular present of **be**[1]

is[2] abbr ONLINE Iceland (used in Internet addresses) See table at **domain name**

IS abbr COMPUT information services

is. abbr GEOG **1.** island **2.** isle

Is. abbr **1.** BIBLE Isaiah **2.** GEOG Island (used in placenames) **3.** GEOG Isle (used in placenames)

is- prefix same as iso- (used before vowels)

ISA /íssə/ abbr **1.** FIN individual savings account **2.** AEROSP International Standard Atmosphere

Isa. abbr BIBLE Isaiah

Isaac /ízək/ n in the Bible, the son of Abraham and Sarah, who was offered by his father as a sacrifice to God, but was saved at the last moment by divine intervention. He was the father of Jacob and Esau. (Genesis 21–28)

Isabella I /ízzə béllə/ (1451–1504) queen of Castile and León. The heir to the crown of Castile and León, she married Ferdinand of Aragón (1469), bringing about the unification of Spain. As queen of Castile and León (1474–1504), she supported the Inquisition, expelled the Jews from Spain, and defeated Granada, the last Moorish kingdom in Spain. She sponsored Christopher Columbus's voyages. Known as **Isabella the Catholic**

Isabella II (1830–1904) queen of Spain. She ruled from 1833 until she was deposed in 1868. Her reign was marked by political turmoil and insurrection.

isagogics /íssə gójjiks/ n introductory studies, es-

pecially of the Bible in its literary and historical contexts (takes a singular verb) [Mid-19C. < *isagogic* 'introductory', via Latin < Greek *eisagōgikos* < *eisagōgē* 'introduction' < *eis* 'into' + *agein* 'to lead'] —**isagogic** adj

Isaiah /ī zī´ ə/ n **1.** in the Bible, a Hebrew prophet who lived in the latter half of the 8th century BC. He was the earliest of the major prophets. **2.** a book of the Bible that contains prophecies and apocalyptic material, traditionally attributed to Isaiah. See table at **Bible**

isalobar /ī sállə baar/ n a contour line on a weather chart joining places where equal changes in atmospheric pressure occur during a given time interval [Early 20C. < IS- + ALLO- + Greek *baros* 'weight', after ISOBAR]

isatin /íssətin/ n a water-soluble compound related to indigo and indole that crystallizes as orange needles. Use: manufacture of vat dyes. Formula: $C_6H_5NO_2$. [Mid-19C. < Greek *isatis* 'woad'] —**isatinic** /íssə tínnik/ adj

ISBN abbr PUBL International Standard Book Number

ischaemia /i skeémi ə/, **ischemia** n an inadequate supply of blood to a part of the body, caused by partial or total blockage of an artery [Late 19C. < modern Latin < Greek *iskhaimos* 'stopping blood' < *iskhein* 'to hold' + *haima* 'blood'] —**ischaemic** adj

Ischia /íski ə/ island in west-central Italy, situated in the Tyrrhenian Sea between the Gulf of Gaeta and the Bay of Naples. Its highest point is Mount Epomeo, 789 m/2,589 ft. Population: 18,253 (2001). Area: 47 sq. km/18 sq. mi.

ischium /íski əm/ (plural -chia /-ki ə/) n the lowest and rearmost of the three bones that make up each half of the pelvis [Early 17C. Via Latin < Greek *iskhion* 'hip joint'] —**ischial** adj

ISD abbr international subscriber dialling

ISDN n a digital telephone network that can transmit both voice and data messages ○ *an ISDN line* Full form **Integrated Services Digital Network**

ISE abbr FIN International Stock Exchange

-ise suffix another spelling of **-ize**

isentrope /íssentrōp/ n a line on a graph or chart linking points of equal entropy [Back-formation < ISENTROPIC]

isentropic /íssen tróppik/ adj **1.** describes a reaction or process that takes place without a change in entropy **2.** relating to an isentrope —**isentropically** adv

Iseult n ♦ **Tristan and Iseult**

Isfahan ♦ **Esfahan**

-ish suffix **1.** characteristic of, like, tending to ○ *churlish* ○ *babyish* ○ *bookish* **2.** of or relating to, from ○ *Gaulish* **3.** somewhat, approximately ○ *bluish* ○ *latish* [Old English *-isc* < Germanic]

Isherwood /íshərwoŏd/, **Christopher** (1904–86) British-born US writer. He described prewar Berlin in two volumes of short stories, *Mr Norris Changes Trains* (1935) and *Goodbye to Berlin* (1939). Full name **Isherwood, Christopher William Bradshaw**

'I am a camera with its shutter open, quite passive, recording, not thinking.'
[Christopher Isherwood, 'Berlin Diary', *Goodbye to Berlin*; 1939]

Ishiguro /íshi goŏrō/, **Kazuo** (b. 1954) Japanese-born British novelist. He won the Booker Prize for *The Remains of the Day* (1989).

Ishmael /ísh mayl/ n **1.** in the Bible, the son of Abraham, expelled into the desert after the birth of his brother Isaac, who was the forebear of twelve desert tribes. Muslims, who call him Ismail, regard themselves as his descendants. (Genesis 16–21) **2.** same as **outcast** (literary)

Ishmaelite /íshmi ə līt/ n **1.** in the Bible, a descendant of Abraham's son Ishmael **2.** same as **outcast** (literary) —**Ishmaelitish** adj —**Ishmaelitism** n

Ishtar /ísh taar/ n in Babylonian and Assyrian mythology, the queen of heaven and goddess of fertility. Tammuz was her consort. She was worshipped throughout Southwest Asia under various names, including the Phoenician Astarte.

Isicamtho n S Africa township slang, a more modern

version of Tsotsitaal [Late 20C. < Zulu *qamutha* or Xhosa *qamtha*, 'to speak volubly']

Isidore (of Seville) /ízzə dawr-/, **St** (560?–636) Spanish archbishop, theologian, and encyclopedist. He became archbishop of Seville in around 600, and is known for his encyclopedic reference work *Etymologiae*.

isinglass /íżing glaass/ *n* **1.** a transparent or translucent gelatin made from the air bladders of various fish, especially the sturgeon. Use: clarifying agent, in adhesives and jellies. **2.** MINERALS same as **mica** [Mid-16C. < obsolete early Dutch *huysenblas* 'sturgeon's bladder' < *huysen* 'sturgeon' + *blas* 'bladder']

Isis[1] /íssiss/ *n* in Egyptian mythology, the goddess of fertility, generally depicted wearing a cow's horns bearing a golden disc representing the sun. She was the wife of her brother Osiris and the mother of Horus.

Isis[2] /íssiss/ alternative name for the River Thames around Oxford, England

Iskenderun /iss kéndə roon/, **Iskenderon** /-ron/ city in southern Turkey, on the southeastern shore of the Gulf of Iskenderun, situated approximately 96 km/60 mi. southeast of Adana. Population: 154,807 (1990).

isl. *abbr* GEOG **1.** island **2.** isle

Isla de Culebra /éesslə day-/ ➧ **Culebra, Isla de**

Islam /íz laam, íss-/ *n* **1.** a monotheistic religion based on the word of God as revealed to Muhammad during the 7th century **2.** Muslim people, their culture, or their countries considered collectively [Early 17C. < Arabic *islām* 'submission (to God)' < base of *aslāma* 'he surrendered'] —**Islamic** /iz lámmik, iss-/ *adj*

Islamabad /iz lámmə bad/, **Islāmābād** city and capital of Pakistan, situated northeast of Rawalpindi. Population: 791,085 (1998).

Islamic Jihad *n* an Islamic fundamentalist organization committed to the introduction of an Islamic Palestinian state by armed opposition to Israel. It also opposes pro-Western Arab governments.

Islamise *vt* RELIG, LAW another spelling of **Islamize**

Islamism /ízz ləmizəm, íssla-/ *n* **1.** a conservative Islamic political movement **2.** the religion or principles of Islam —**Islamist** *adj, n*

Islamize /ízzlə mīz, íssla-/ (**-izes, -izing, -ized**), **Islamise** (**-ises, -ising, -ised**) *vt* **1.** to convert people or countries to Islam **2.** to cause people, institutions, or countries to follow Islamic law —**Islamization** /ízzlə mī záysh'n, íssla-/ *n*

island /íland/ *n* **1.** PIECE OF LAND SURROUNDED BY WATER an area of land, smaller than a continent, that is completely surrounded by water (*often used in placenames*) **2.** SOMETHING LIKE ISLAND something that is like an island because it is isolated or surrounded by something different ○ *'No man is an island, entire of itself.'* (John Donne, *Devotions upon Emergent Occasions*; 1624) **3.** ANAT ISOLATED BODY PART a body part or group of cells that is different in construction from its surroundings ■ *vt* (**-lands, -landing, -landed**) **1.** MAKE SOMETHING INTO ISLAND to form something into an island **2.** ISOLATE SOMEBODY to cause somebody to feel isolated, e.g. from contact with peers or colleagues **3.** FILL SEA WITH ISLANDS to provide a body of water with islands (*literary*) ○ *the many-islanded Aegean* **4.** UTIL ISOLATE ELECTRIC GRID SECTORS to isolate separate sectors of an electrical grid via widespread defensive blackouts to avoid permanent damage to utility equipment during periods of unusually heavy peak use and power failures ■ *n* ROADS same as **traffic island** [Old English *īegland* < *īeg* 'island' (< Indo-European, 'water') + LAND; spelling influenced by ISLE] —**islander** *n*

island arc *n* an arc-shaped chain of islands, usually found in an area of volcanic or seismic activity

island-hop *vi* to travel from island to island within the same chain, especially as part of a holiday (*informal*)

Islands, Bay of /í ləndz/ bay on the northeastern coast of the North Island, New Zealand. About 18 km/11 mi. wide, the bay contains about 150 islands and is a popular tourist destination.

islands of Langerhans *npl* ANAT same as **islets of Langerhans**

Islands of the Blessed *npl* MYTHOL same as **Hesperides** (sense 2)

Islay /ílə, í lay/ southernmost island of the Inner Hebrides, western Scotland. Population: 3,500. Area: 610 sq. km/236 sq. mi.

isle /íl/ *n* an island, often a small one (*literary*) [13C. Via Old French *ile, isle* < Latin *insula*]

SPELLCHECK See *aisle.*

Isle of Man /íl əv mán/ self-governing Crown dependency of the United Kingdom, lying in the Irish Sea midway between Northern Ireland and England. Language: English, Manx. Capital: Douglas. Population: 74,261 (2003). Area: 572 sq. km/221 sq. mi.

Isle of Wight /-wít/ largest offshore island of England, off the southern coast, in the English Channel. It is a separate county and Newport is the administrative centre. Population: 132,731 (2001). Area: 381 sq. km/147 sq. mi.

islet /ílət/ *n* a small isle or island

islets of Langerhans /-lángər hanss/ *npl* clusters of endocrine cells found in the pancreas that secrete insulin and glucagon

ism /ízzəm/ *n* a movement, doctrine, or system of belief (*informal*) [Late 17C. < -ISM]

-ism *suffix* **1.** action, process ○ *mesmerism* ○ *volcanism* **2.** characteristic behaviour or manner ○ *despotism* **3.** state, condition ○ *conservatism* ○ *gangsterism* **4.** unusual or unhealthy state ○ *caffeinism* **5.** doctrine, system of beliefs ○ *defeatism* ○ *Calvinism* **6.** prejudice ○ *sexism* **7.** distinctive feature or trait ○ *Southernism* ○ *vulgarism* [Via French < Latin *-ismus* < Greek *-ismos*]

Ismaili /íz maa éeli/ *n* a member of a branch of Shiite Muslims whose members believe that Ismail, son of the sixth imam, was the true seventh imam [Mid-19C. < Arabic < *'Ismā'īl*, proper name] —**Ismaili** *adj*

Ismailiyya /ízmə éeli ə/ city in northeastern Egypt, situated on Lake Timsah. It is the halfway station on the Suez Canal. Population: 255,000 (1992).

Ismail Samani Peak /iss mī éel sə maáni-/ mountain situated in central Tajikistan, and the highest peak in the country. Height: 7,495 m/24,590 ft. Former name **Garmo Peak** (until 1933), **Stalin Peak** (1933–62), **Communism Peak** (1962–98)

isn't /ízz'nt/ *contr* is not ○ *It isn't ready yet.*

ISO[1] *abbr* Imperial Service Order

ISO[2] *n* an international organization established in 1947 to standardize such things as units of measurement and the meanings of technical terms [< Greek *isos* 'equal' (not an abbreviation of *International Standards Organization*)]

iso- *prefix* **1.** equal, uniform ○ *isoelectric* ○ *isogloss* **2.** isomeric ○ *isooctane* **3.** of or for different members of the same species ○ *isoagglutination* [< Greek *isos* 'equal']

isoagglutination /íssō ə glooti náysh'n/ *n* the agglutination of red blood cells in one individual induced by antibodies in the serum of another individual of the same species —**isoagglutinative** /-ə glootinətiv/ *adj*

isoagglutinin /íssō ə glootinin/ *n* an antibody from one individual that causes the clumping together (agglutination) of red blood cells in another individual of the same species but of a different blood group

isobar /íssō baar/ *n* **1.** a line drawn on a weather map that connects places with equal atmospheric pressure. Isobars are often used collectively to indicate the movement or formation of weather systems. **2.** one of two or more atoms or elements that have the same mass number but different atomic numbers [Mid-19C. < Greek *isobaros* 'of equal weight'] —**isobarism** *n*

isobaric /íssō bárrik/ *adj* **1.** having constant or equal atmospheric pressure **2.** relating to isobars

isobaric spin *n* PHYS same as **isospin**

isobath /íssō bath/ *n* a line on a map of the sea that connects points that are at the same depth [Late 19C. < ISO- + Greek *bathos* 'depth'] —**isobathic** /íssō báthik/ *adj*

isobutane /íssō byoo tayn/ *n* a colourless gaseous hydrocarbon that is an isomer of butane. Use: fuel, refrigerant. Formula: C_4H_{10}.

isocarboxazid /íssō kaar bóksəzid/ *n* a drug that is a monoamine oxidase inhibitor. Use: antidepressant, treatment of agoraphobia. [Mid-20C. < ISO- + contraction of CARBONYL + OX- + HYDRAZIDE]

~~**isoceles**~~ incorrect spelling of **isosceles**

isocheim /íssō kīm/, **isochime** *n* a line on a weather map connecting places that have the same average temperature in winter [Mid-19C. < ISO- + Greek *kheima* 'winter weather'] —**isocheimal** /íssō kím'l/ *adj* —**isocheimenal** /íssō kímən'l/ *adj*

isochromatic /íssōkrō máttik/ *adj* **1.** OPTICS same as **orthochromatic** **2.** having the same colour or wavelength of light

isochronous /ī sókrənəss/, **isochronal** /-krən'l/ *adj* **1.** having the same frequency or periodicity **2.** measured or occurring at the same time, or lasting for the same length of time —**isochronously** *adv*

isochroous /ī sókrō əss/ *adj* having the same colour throughout [Mid-19C. < ISO- + Greek *khrōs* 'colour']

isoclinal /íssō klín'l/ *adj* **1.** having the same inclination or slope **2.** GEOL having the sides of a geological fold parallel to one another ■ *n* **1.** GEOL same as **isocline** (sense 1) **2.** MAPS same as **isoclinic line**

isocline /íssō klīn/ *n* **1.** a geological fold with rock beds that slope in the same direction **2.** MAPS same as **isoclinic line** [Late 19C. < Greek *isoklinēs* 'equally balanced', literally 'leaning equally' < *klinein* 'to lean']

isoclinic /íssō klínnik/ *adj* same as **isoclinal**

isoclinic line *n* a line on a map connecting points on the Earth's surface that have the same magnetic dip

isocyanate /íssō sí ə nayt/ *n* a chemical compound containing the chemical group -NCO. Use: in resins, adhesives.

isocyanide /íssō sí ə nīd/ *n* a colourless liquid with a pungent odour that contains the chemical group -NC

isodiametric /íssō dī ə méttrik/ *adj* having diameters or axes of equal length

isodose /íssōdōss/ *n* a dose of radiation of equal intensity applied to more than one part of the body as a medical treatment

isodynamic /íssō dī námmik/ *adj* **1.** having the same strength or intensity **2.** connecting points on a map of the Earth's surface that have the same magnetic intensity

isoelectric /íssō i léktrik/ *adj* having exactly the same electric potential

isoelectric point *n* the pH value at which the electric force on a molecule in a solution is zero

isoelectronic /íssō i lek trónnik, -éilek-/ *adj* having the same number of electrons or the same outer atomic structure —**isoelectronically** *adv*

isoenzyme /íssō én zīm/ *n* *ANZ, N Am* one of two or more enzymes that are different chemically but function in the same way. UK term **isozyme** —**isoenzymatic** /-en zī máttik/ *adj* —**isoenzymic** /-en zímmik/ *adj*

isoflavone /íssō fláyvōn/ *n* an isoflavonoid, e.g. genistein

isoflavonoid /íssō fláyvə noyd/ *n* a flavonoid belonging to a group that occurs in legumes, especially soya bean, and is converted by bacteria in the intestines into substances having activity similar to that of oestrogen

isogamete /íssō gámmeet/ *n* a gamete physically identical to another with which it unites to form a zygote —**isogametic** /-gə méttik/ *adj*

isogamy /ī sóggəmi/ *n* the fusion of isogametes in some algae and fungi during reproduction

isogeneic /íssōjə née ik/ *adj* IMMUNOL same as **syngeneic** [Mid-20C. Alteration of ISOGENIC]

isogenic /íssō jénnik/ *adj* having identical genes

isogenous /ī sójjənəss/ *adj* **1.** describes organs or parts of the body that have the same or a similar origin **2.** GENETICS same as **isogenic** —**isogeny** *n*

zh vision. In foreign words: kh German Bach; aN French vin; aaN French blanc; ö German schön, French feu; oN French bon; öN French un; ü as in French rue. Stress marks: ´ as in secret /séekrət/, academic /ákə démmik/

isogloss /íssō gloss/ n a line on a language map that surrounds an area within which a linguistic usage such as a dialectal word is found [Early 20C. < ISO- + Greek *glossa* 'language'] —**isoglossal** /íssō glóss'l/ adj —**isoglossic** /íssō glóssik/ adj —**isoglottal** /íssō glótt'l/ adj —**isoglottic** /íssō glóttik/ adj

isogon /íssō gon/ n a polygon whose angles are all equal [Late 17C. < Greek *isogōnios* 'equiangular']

isogonal /ī sóggən'l/ adj, n MATHS, PHYS same as **isogonic**

isogonal line n MAPS same as **isogonic line**

isogone /íssəgōn/ n MAPS same as **isogonic line** [Alteration of ISOGON]

isogonic /íssō gónnik/ adj MATHS having equal angles ■ n MAPS same as **isogonic line** [Mid-19C. < Greek *isogónios* 'equiangular']

isogonic line n a line on a map of the Earth's surface connecting points at which a compass would give the same deviation from true north

isograft /íssō graaft/ n a tissue graft taken from an individual genetically identical to the recipient of the graft, e.g. from an identical twin

isogram /íssō gram/ n MAPS, METEOROL same as **isopleth**

isohel /íssō hel/ n a line on a map connecting places that receive the same number of hours of sunshine in the course of a year [Early 20C. < ISO- + Greek *hēlios* 'sun']

isohyet /íssō hī ət/ n a line on a map connecting places that receive the same amount of rainfall in the course of a year [Late 19C. < ISO- + Greek *huetos* 'rain'] —**isohyetal** adj

isolate vt /íssə layt/ (-lates, -lating, -lated) **1.** SEPARATE SOMEBODY OR SOMETHING FROM OTHERS to separate somebody or something from others of the same type **2.** CUT PLACE OFF to make a place unreachable from the surrounding area ○ *Heavy snowfalls have temporarily isolated the town.* **3.** FIND CAUSE OF SOMETHING to discover which of a number of possible causes or factors is responsible for a specific phenomenon or problem ○ *He isolated a bug in the software as the cause of the failure.* **4.** MED QUARANTINE SOMEBODY to keep somebody who is infected away from other people in order to prevent the spread of a contagious disease **5.** BIOL SEPARATE OUT VIRUS to separate out a chemical or biological material such as a virus or bacterium in order to identify and study it **6.** ELECTRONICS INSULATE ELECTRONIC DEVICE to prevent a circuit or device from interacting with another or with an outside stimulus ■ n /íssələt/ **1.** LONE PERSON OR GROUP a person or group separated or cut off from others **2.** BIOL, CHEM MICROORGANISM GROWN IN LABORATORY a sample of biological material, especially a microorganism, that has been cultured for study **3.** FITNESS NUTRITIONAL PRODUCT cultured biological material prepared for use as a nutritional supplement ○ *whey protein isolate* **4.** LING ONLY LANGUAGE OF FAMILY a language that is the only known surviving member of its language family [Early 19C. Back-formation < ISOLATED < French *isolé* < late Latin *insulatus* 'made into an island' < Latin *insula* 'island'] —**isolable** adj —**isolatable** adj —**isolator** n

isolated /íssə laytid/ adj **1.** REMOTE far away from other inhabited areas or buildings **2.** ALONE OR LONELY not having enough social contact, friends, or support **3.** RARE happening rarely or only once and unlikely to prove a continuing problem ○ *an isolated incident* [Mid-18C. See ISOLATE]

isolated pawn n in chess, a pawn that is not supported by other pawns of the same colour round it

isolating /íssə layting/ adj LING same as **analytic** (sense 4)

isolation /íssō láysh'n/ n **1.** the process of separating somebody or something from others, or the fact of being alone and separated from others **2.** remoteness from other inhabited areas or buildings ◇ **in isolation 1.** separate from other related factors or things ○ *We have to look at the problem in isolation.* **2.** alone and physically separated from other people

isolationism /íssə láysh'nizəm/ n **1.** a government policy based on the belief that national interests are best served by avoiding economic and political alliances with other countries **2.** electronic ambient music that is generally produced without beats,

creating a soothing ambience with unusual sounds —**isolationist** n, adj

isolative /íssələtiv/ adj **1.** describes a sound change that occurs in all phonetic environments **2.** causing somebody or something to be separated or cut off

Isolde n ♦ **Tristan and Iseult**

isolecithal /íssō léssith'l/ adj describes the eggs of mammals and some other vertebrates in which the yolk is evenly distributed throughout the egg

$$H_3C-CH_2-\underset{\underset{CH_3}{|}}{CH}-\underset{\underset{NH_2}{|}}{CH}-\overset{\overset{O}{\|}}{C}-OH$$

isoleucine

isoleucine /íssō loŏ seen/ n an amino acid that is an isomer of leucine and is found in most proteins. Formula: $C_6H_{13}NO_2$.

isolex /íssō leks/ n a line on a language map that surrounds an area within which a particular word is used [Early 20C. < ISO- + Greek *lexis* 'word']

isoline /íssō līn/ n US MAPS, METEOROL same as **isopleth**

isologous /ī sóllagəss/ adj describes two organic compounds that have the same molecular structure but different atoms of the same valency [Mid-19C. < ISO- + Greek *logos* 'ratio']

isomagnetic /íssō mag néttik/ n a line on a map connecting points of the same magnetic force —**isomagnetic** adj

isomagnetic line n MAPS, PHYS same as **isomagnetic**

isomer /íssəmər/ n **1.** each of two or more molecules that have the same number of atoms but have different chemical structures and therefore different properties **2.** each of two or more nuclides that have the same mass number and atomic number but different energy states and half-lives [Mid-19C. < Greek *isomerēs* 'sharing equally'] —**isomeric** /íssō mérrik/ adj

isomerase /ī sómmə rayss, -rayz/ n an enzyme that converts one isomer into another

isomerise vti CHEM another spelling of **isomerize**

isomerism /ī sómmərizəm/ n **1.** the existence of two or more molecules that are isomers **2.** the existence of two or more nuclides that are isomers

isomerize /ī sómmə rīz/ (-izes, -izing, -ized), **isomerise** (-ises, -ising, -ised) vti to change something into an isomer, or become an isomer —**isomerization** /ī sómmə rī záysh'n/ n

isomerous /ī sómmərəss/ adj having physical parts that are similar in number, markings, or other characteristics

isometric /íssō méttrik/, **isometrical** /-méttrik'l/ adj **1.** PHYSIOL INVOLVING PUSHING MUSCLES AGAINST SOMETHING describes exercises in which muscles are put under tension but not allowed to contract **2.** EQUAL equal in dimension or measurement **3.** CRYSTALS WITH THREE EQUAL AXES describes a crystalline system that has three equal axes at right angles to one another **4.** LITERAT WITH LINES IN SAME METRE having the same number of metrical feet in each line of poetry **5.** ENG PROJECTED AT SAME ANGLE TO AXES projected so that the plane of projection of a three-dimensional drawing is at an equal angle to each of the three axes of the object drawn [Mid-19C. < Greek *isometria* 'equality of measure'] —**isometrically** adv

isometrics /íssō méttriks/ n a form of exercise in which the muscles are pushed against something fixed or against other muscles to strengthen them (*takes a singular or plural verb*)

isometropia /íssōmə trṓpi ə/ n the condition of equal refraction of light by both eyes [< Greek *isometros* 'of equal measure']

isometry /ī sómmətri/ (plural -tries) n **1.** equality of measure **2.** a geometric transformation in which the distance between any two points is preserved, e.g. the rotation of a plane

isomorph /íssō mawrf/ n a substance or organism that exhibits similarity in form or appearance to others (**isomorphism**)

isomorphic /íssō máwrfik/ adj **1.** having the same form or appearance as another organism or the same organism at a different stage in its life cycle **2.** describes mathematical sets with a one-to-one correspondence so that an operation such as addition or multiplication in one produces the same result as the analogous operation in the other **3.** CHEM same as **isomorphous** —**isomorphically** adv

isomorphism /íssō máwrfizəm/ n **1.** BIOL SIMILARITY IN ORGANISMS similarity in form or appearance between organisms of different ancestry or between different stages in the life cycle of the same organism **2.** MATHS CORRESPONDENCE BETWEEN SETS a one-to-one correspondence between sets so that an operation such as addition or multiplication in one produces the same result as the analogous operation in the other **3.** CHEM SIMILARITY BETWEEN CHEMICALS similarity in crystalline form between chemicals

isomorphous /íssō máwrfəss/ adj describes a chemical compound that is able to crystallize in a form similar to another chemical compound

isoniazid /íssō nī əzid/ n a colourless crystalline compound. Use: to treat tuberculosis. Formula: $C_6H_7N_3O$. [Mid-20C. < ISO- + contraction of *nicotinic* + HYDRAZIDE]

isooctane /íssō ók tayn/ n a flammable isomer of octane. Use: determination of the octane number of fuel. Formula: $(CH_3)_3CCH_2$.

isopach /íssō pak/, **isopachyte** /íssō pák īt/ n a line on a map of the Earth's surface connecting points where a rock stratum has equal thickness [Early 20C. < ISO- + Greek *pakhus* 'thick']

isophone /íssō fōn/ n a line on a language map surrounding an area within which a specific pronunciation is used

isopiestic /íssō pī éstik/ adj METEOROL, PHYS same as **isobaric** [< ISO- + Greek *piezein* 'to squeeze'] —**isopiestically** adv

isopleth /íssō pleth/ n UK, ANZ, Can a line on a map connecting points with the same value for variables such as temperature or air pressure. US term **isoline** [Early 20C. < Greek *isoplēthēs* 'equal in quantity'] —**isoplethic** /íssō pléthik/ adj

isopod /íssō pod/ n a small invertebrate animal with a flattened body and seven pairs of legs. Woodlice are isopods, but most isopods are sea animals. Order: Isopoda. [Mid-19C. < modern Latin *Isopoda*, literally 'equal foot' < Greek *pod-* 'foot'] —**isopodan** /ī sóppədən/ adj —**isopodous** /ī sóppədəss/ adj

isoprenaline /íssō prénnə leen/ n a drug that dilates the bronchial tubes. Use: treatment of asthma. N Am term **isoproterenol** [Mid-20C. Contraction of *N-isopropylnoradrenaline*]

$$H_2C=\underset{\underset{CH_3}{|}}{C}-CH=CH_2$$

isoprene

isoprene /íssō preen/ n a colourless flammable liquid hydrocarbon. Use: manufacture of synthetic rubber. Formula: C_5H_8. [Mid-19C. < ISO- + contraction of *prophylene*]

isopropanol /íssō prṓpə nol/ n CHEM same as **isopropyl alcohol**

isopropyl /íssō prṓpil/ n a chemical radical isomer of propyl. Formula: C_3H_7.

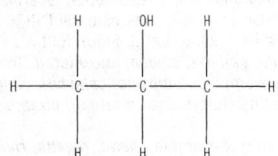

isopropyl alcohol

isopropyl alcohol n a colourless flammable alcohol. Use: antifreeze, rubbing alcohol, solvent. Formula: C_3H_8O.

isoproterenol /íssōprō térrə nol/ n N Am PHARM same as **isoprenaline** [Mid-20C. Contraction of *N-iso-propylarterenol*]

ISO rating n a measure of the sensitivity to light of a material such as photographic film or paper

isorhythm /íssō ríthəm/ n a technique of musical composition of the 14th and 15th centuries that uses a repeated rhythmic pattern —**isorhythmic** /íssō ríthmik/ adj

isosceles /ī sóssə leez/ adj 1. describes a triangle in which two of the three sides are of equal length 2. describes a trapezium in which the two nonparallel sides are of equal length [Mid-16C. Via late Latin < Greek *isokelēs* 'equally legged']

isoseismal /íssō sízm'l/, **isoseismic** /íssō sízmik/ adj relating to or showing equal strength of earthquake shock ■ n a line on a map connecting points of equal strength of earthquake shock

isosmotic /íss oz móttik/ adj US same as **isotonic** (sense 2) —**isosmotically** adv

isospin /íssō spin/ n a quantum characteristic of baryons and mesons that relates to the number of different values of electric charge they can have. Symbol I [Mid-20C. Contraction of ISOBARIC SPIN, ISOTOPIC SPIN]

isostasy /ī sóstəssi/ n a state of equilibrium between forces such as accumulated ice pushing down on a section of the Earth's surface and those pushing up from below [Late 19C. < ISO- + Greek *stasis* 'stoppage'] —**isostatic** /íssō státtik/ adj —**isostatically** adv

isostatic adjustment n a slow uplifting of the Earth's surface resulting from the removal of a load, as occurs after the melting of a glacier

isotach /íssō tak/ n a line on a weather map connecting points where the wind speed is equal [Mid-20C. < ISO- + Greek *takhos* 'speed']

isotactic /íssō táktik/ adj describes a polymer whose constituent molecules give it a repetitive spatial structure [Mid-20C. < ISO- + Greek *taktos* 'ordered']

isothere /íssō theer/ n a line on a weather map connecting places that have the same average temperature in summer [Mid-19C. < French *isothère* < Greek *isos* 'equal' + *theros* 'summer']

isotherm /íssō thurm/ n 1. a line drawn on a weather map that connects places with the same temperature 2. a line on a graph showing the relationship between variables, especially pressure and volume, at a constant temperature [Mid-19C. < French *isotherme*, literally 'equal heat' < Greek *thermē* 'heat' or *thermos* 'hot'] —**isothermal** adj —**isothermally** adv

isothiocyanate /íssō thī o sī ə nayt/ n a chemical compound containing the chemical group -NCS

isotone /íssətōn/ n each of two or more atoms with the same number of neutrons but different atomic numbers

isotonic /íssə tónnik/ adj 1. PHYSIOL OF MUSCLE TENSION AND CONTRACTION relating to the contraction and shortening of a muscle under relatively constant tension, e.g. in weightlifting 2. UK, ANZ, Can CHEM WITH EQUAL OSMOTIC PRESSURE relating to or exerting equal osmotic pressure. US term **isosmotic** 3. PHYSIOL WITH BALANCED CONCENTRATION OF SALTS AND MINERALS specially formulated to supply the body's chemical needs in situations in which minerals and fluids are used up by the body, e.g. during vigorous exercise ○ *isotonic drinks* —**isotonically** adv —**isotonicity** /íssə to níssəti/ n

isotope /íssətōp/ n each of two or more forms of a chemical element with the same atomic number but different numbers of neutrons [Early 20C. < ISO- + Greek *topos* 'place'; because isotopes of the same name occupy the same place in the periodic table] —**isotopic** /íssə tóppik/ adj

isotopic spin n PHYS same as **isospin**

isotropic /íssō tróppik/, **isotropous** /ī sóttrəpəss/ adj having physical properties that do not vary with direction [Mid-19C. < ISO- + Greek *tropos* 'turn'] —**isotropically** adv —**isotropism** /-tróppizəm/ n —**isotropy** /ī sóttrəpi/ n

isozyme /íssō zīm/ n UK each of two or more enzymes that are different chemically but function in the same way. ANZ, N Am term **isoenzyme** [Mid-20C. < ISO- + shortening of ENZYME]

ISP abbr ONLINE Internet service provider

I-spect /ī spékt/ interj same as **respect** (slang; used in Black English)

i-spin n QUANTUM PHYS same as **isospin**

I-spy n a children's guessing game in which players try to guess which thing in visual range another player has in mind, having been given the first letter of the word

Israel

Israel /íz rayl/ country in Southwest Asia formed in 1948 as a Jewish state in the historic region of Palestine, on the eastern shore of the Mediterranean Sea. Language: Hebrew, Arabic. Currency: shekel. Capital: Jerusalem. Population: 6,116,533 (2003). Area: 21,946 sq. km/8,473 sq. mi. Official name **State of Israel** —**Israeli** /iz ráyli/ n, adj

Israelite /ízzri ə līt, ízzrə-/ n 1. a member of the ancient Hebrew people descended from the patriarch Jacob 2. somebody who came from the ancient kingdom of Israel —**Israelitic** /ízzri ə líttik, ízzrə-/ adj

Israfil /ízzrə feel/, **Israfel** /-fel/, **Israfeel** /-feel/ n according to the Koran, the archangel who will herald the end of the world by sounding a trumpet on the Day of Judgment [< Hebrew, 'God heals']

~~Isreal~~ incorrect spelling of **Israel**

ISS abbr AEROSP International Space Station

Issachar /íssə kaar/ n 1. in the Bible, a son of Jacob and Leah 2. one of the twelve tribes of Israel, descended from Issachar [Via late Latin < Greek < Hebrew *Yiśśākhār*]

Issigonis /íssi góniss/, **Sir Alec** (1906–88) Palestinian-born British car designer. He is best known for designing the Morris Minor (1948) and the Mini (1959). Full name **Issigonis, Sir Alexander Arnold Constantine**

ISSN abbr PUBL International Standard Serial Number

issuant /íssyoo-, íshyoo-/ adj in heraldry, displaying an animal rising up from something with only its upper body showing

issue /íssyoo, íshoo/ n 1. SUBJECT OF CONCERN something for discussion or of general concern ○ *I want to raise several issues at the meeting.* 2. MAIN SUBJECT the central or most important topic in a discussion or debate ○ *The real issue is education.* 3. LAW LEGAL MATTER IN DISPUTE a legal matter in a dispute between two parties 4. ALLOTTING OF SOMETHING the distribution of something by an official body ○ *the issue of parking permits* 5. PUBL COPY OF PUBLICATION a copy of a magazine or newspaper published on a particular date 6. COMM OFFICIAL RELEASE OF SOMETHING a set of things such as new stamps or bonds that are made available for sale by an official body at a particular time 7. FIN STOCK MADE AVAILABLE a series of items such as shares in a company that becomes available at the same time 8. OFFICIAL ALLOTMENT something officially distributed or supplied, or an amount of something officially distributed or supplied ○ *government issue rations* 9. LAW PROGENY somebody's offspring ○ *died without issue* 10. △ PROBLEM OR DIFFICULTY a source of conflict, misgiving, or emotional distress (*informal*) ○ *had issues with some of her suggestions* 11. FINAL OUTCOME a final outcome or conclusion of a matter that is usually a solution to a problem or difficulty (*dated*) ○ *Let's bring our differences to an issue.* 12. SOURCE OF FLOW a place from which something flows 13. MED WOUND PRODUCING DISCHARGE an open wound or ulcer producing pus or blood 14. MED DISCHARGE FROM WOUND pus or blood coming from an open wound or ulcer 15. LAW PROFIT FROM PROPERTY profits made from owning land or buildings 16. LIBRARIES SYSTEM FOR TRACKING BOOK LOANS the system in a library used for keeping track of current loans 17. LIBRARIES ITEMS LOANED FROM LIBRARY the number of items such as books or CDs borrowed from a library at one time ■ v (-sues, -suing, -sued) 1. vt SUPPLY SOMETHING to supply or distribute something officially 2. vt ANNOUNCE SOMETHING PUBLICLY to make public something such as a bulletin, statement, or warning, or deliver it officially to somebody ○ *The mayor's office issued a press release.* 3. vt PUBL PUBLISH SOMETHING to publish something such as a newspaper, magazine, or book 4. vt COMM RELEASE SOMETHING FOR SALE to make a set of things such as new stamps or bonds available for sale at a particular time 5. vi ORIGINATE to emerge or come out from somewhere ○ *Smoke issued from the burning building.* 6. vi ARISE FROM CONDITION to result from or be produced by a particular thing or situation ○ *Our conclusions issue from analysis of the data.* 7. vi FIN ADD UP AS GAIN to accrue in the form of interest or profit [13C. < Old French < Latin *exitus*, past participle of *exire* (see EXIT)] —**issuable** adj —**issuance** n —**issueless** adj —**issuer** n ◇ **at issue** under discussion or to be decided ◇ **take issue with somebody** or **something** to disagree strongly with somebody about something

issue price n the price of new securities when they are first offered to the public

issuing house /íssyoo ing-, íshyoo-/ n a financial institution that issues shares on behalf of a company that wants to become public

Issyk-Kul /i sík kõõl/ lake in northeastern Kyrgyzstan. It has a maximum depth of 700 m/2,300 ft. Area: 6,100 sq. km/2,360 sq. mi.

-ist suffix 1. practising a particular skill or profession ○ *psychologist* ○ *etymologist* 2. following a particular belief or school of thought ○ *idealist* ○ *Socialist* 3. somebody who plays a particular instrument ○ *oboist* 4. somebody who is prejudiced against a particular social grouping ○ *racist* ○ *sexist* [Directly or via French < Latin *-ista* < Greek *-istēs*] —**-istic** suffix

Istanbul /iss tan bõõl/, **İstanbul** largest city in Turkey, situated in the northwest of the country on the Bosporus. Population: 9,451,000 (2000). Former name **Byzantium** (c.600 BC–AD 330), **Constantinople** (330–1930)

Isth., isth. abbr isthmus

isthmi GEOG plural of **isthmus**

isthmian /íssmi ən, ísth-/ adj 1. ANAT same as **isthmic** 2. relating to an isthmus of land ■ n somebody who lives on or comes from an isthmus

Isthmian *adj* relating to the Isthmus of Corinth or the Isthmus of Panama

Isthmian Games *npl* a sports festival held in ancient Greece on the Isthmus of Corinth that included horse racing and chariot racing

isthmic /íssmik, ísth-/ *adj* relating to an isthmus in the body ○ *an isthmic constriction*

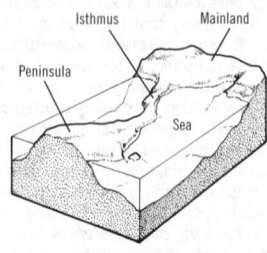

isthmus

isthmus /íssməss, ísth-/ (*plural* -**muses** or -**mi** /-mī/) *n*
1. a narrow strip of land that joins two larger areas of land ○ *The isthmus connects North and South America.* **2.** a narrow connection or passage between parts of the body [Mid-16C. Via Latin < Greek *isthmos* 'island'] —**isthmoid** *adj*

istle /ístli/, **ixtle** /íkstli/ *n* a strong fibre from some tropical plants such as agave or yucca. Use: rope, baskets, carpets. [Mid-19C. Via American Spanish *ixtle* < Nahuatl *ixtli*]

Istria /ístri ə/ peninsula in northwestern Croatia and southwestern Slovenia, projecting into the Adriatic Sea. Area: 3,885 sq. km/1,500 sq. mi.

it[1] /it/ CORE MEANING: a pronoun used to refer to an object or an animal, and sometimes a baby ○ *It's a lovely baby.* ○ *They've had the dog a week, and they still haven't thought of a name for it.*
1. *pron* INDICATING SPECIFIC SITUATION used to refer to a situation just described, or to an unspecified or implied situation ○ *He's very upset, but he won't talk about it.* **2.** *pron* INDICATING POINT OF VIEW used to indicate feelings or a viewpoint on a particular situation ○ *It's strange how things turn out.* **3.** *pron* INDICATING SOMETHING REPORTED used in the formation of passive sentences reporting a situation ○ *It was reported that several people had been arrested.* **4.** *pron* INDICATING WEATHER used as the subject of verbs such as 'be', 'get', 'seem', and 'feel' in order to describe something about the environment such as the temperature or the weather ○ *It's cold and rainy.* **5.** *pron* INDICATING TIME used to state the time, e.g. the time of day, the month, the year, or the season ○ *It's six o'clock.* **6.** *pron* INDICATING DESCRIPTION OF EXPERIENCE used to refer to life or a particular experience ○ *What's it like being famous?* **7.** *pron* EMPHASIZING FOLLOWING CLAUSE used to draw attention to the person, thing, or clause that immediately follows ○ *It's you who are always complaining!* ○ *It isn't that I don't care.* **8.** *pron* INDICATING CRISIS the crucial or ultimate point, the perfect situation, person, or thing, or the death or end of somebody or something ○ *When the car turned over I really thought that was it.* **9.** *pron* ATTRACTIVE OR SELLING QUALITY a quality considered by somebody to be the most important, e.g. talent, charm, sex appeal, or profitability (*informal*) ○ *You either have it or you don't.* **10.** *pron* SEX sexual intercourse (*slang*) **11.** *n* LEISURE PLAYER IN CHILDREN'S GAMES in children's informal games, the player who must do something to the others, e.g. run after and touch them in the game of tag ○ *You're it!* [Old English *hit* < Germanic]

it[2] *abbr* ONLINE Italy (*used in Internet addresses*). See table at **domain name**

IT *abbr* COMPUT information technology

ITA *abbr* **1.** MEDIA Independent Television Authority **2.** EDUC initial teaching alphabet

ital. *abbr* PUBL **1.** italic **2.** italics

Ital. *abbr* **1.** Italian **2.** Italy

I-tal, **ital** *adj* describes food that is organic, vegetarian, or cooked without added salt (*slang*; *used in Black English*)

Italian /i tállyən/ *n* **1.** somebody who comes from Italy **2.** the official language of Italy and an official language of Switzerland, a Romance language belonging to the Italic branch of Indo-European. Native speakers: 60 million. Other speakers: 60 million. [14C. < Italian *italiano* 'of Italy' < *Italia* 'Italy'] —**Italian** *adj*

Italianate /i tállyə nayt/ *adj* expressed, done, or made in an Italian style or character

Italian dressing *n* a salad dressing typically made with oil and vinegar, garlic, and oregano

Italianesque /i tállyə nésk/ *adj* same as **Italianate**

Italianise *vti* another spelling of **Italianize**

Italianism /i tállyənizəm/ *n* something that comes from or is characteristic of Italy, e.g. a word or phrase that is derived from Italian

Italianize /i tállyə nīz/ (-**izes**, -**izing**, -**ized**), **Italianise** (-**ises**, -**ising**, -**ised**) *vti* to make something Italian in character, or become Italian in character —**Italianization** /i tállyə nī záysh'n/ *n*

Italian sixth *n* a three-note chord consisting of an augmented sixth chord and a major third above the root of the chord, used for modulation and for providing colour

Italian sonnet *n* LITERAT same as **Petrarchan sonnet**

Italian vermouth *n* a dark-coloured sweet vermouth made in Italy

italic /i tállik/ *adj* **1.** WITH PRINTED LETTERS SLOPING TO RIGHT printed in or using letters that slope to the right. Italic letters are sometimes used in book titles or to show emphasis in text. **2.** WITH HANDWRITTEN LETTERS SLOPING TO RIGHT handwritten in letters that slope to the right ■ *n* ITALIC LETTER a printed letter that slopes to the right, or a font that uses such letters (*often used in the plural*) [Early 17C. < ITALIC; from its introduction by an Italian printer in 1501]

Italic /i tállik/ *n* BRANCH OF INDO-EUROPEAN LANGUAGE FAMILY a branch of the Indo-European language family that includes many former languages of Italy, including Latin and Umbrian ■ *adj* **1.** OF ITALIC relating to the language family Italic **2.** ANCIENT ITALIAN relating to ancient Italy [15C. Via Latin < Greek *Italikos* < *Italia* 'Italy']

italicise *vt* PRINTING another spelling of **italicize**

Italicism /i tállissizəm/ *n* a word or phrase that is borrowed from Italian

italicize /i tálli sīz/ (-**cizes**, -**cizing**, -**cized**), **italicise** (-**cises**, -**cising**, -**cised**) *vt* to print a word, letter, or document in italics, or change words to an italic font —**italicization** /i tálli sī záysh'n/ *n* —**italicized** *adj*

Italo- *prefix* Italy or Italian ○ *Italo-American* [< ITALIAN]

Italophile /i tállō fīl/ *n* somebody who loves Italy and

the Italian people, culture, or language —**Italophilia** /i tállō fílli ə/ *n*

Italy

Italy /íttəli/ country in southern Europe. Its mainland area projects as a peninsula into the Mediterranean Sea, and it includes, among others, the islands of Elba, Sicily, and Sardinia. Language: Italian. Currency: euro. Capital: Rome. Population: 57,998,353 (2003). Area: 301,323 sq. km/116,341 sq. mi. Official name **Italian Republic**

Itanagar /eétə núggər/ capital of Arunachal Pradesh State in northeastern India. Population: 17,300 (1991).

Itar Tass /eé taar-/, **ITAR-Tass** *n* a Russian news agency founded in 1992 to replace Tass, the news agency of the former Soviet Union [Late 20C. < Russian < acronym < *Informatsionnoe telegrafnoe agentsvo Rossii* 'Information Telegraph Agency of Russia' + TASS]

ITC *abbr* MEDIA Independent Television Commission

itch /ich/ *v* (**itches**, **itching**, **itched**) **1.** *vti* WANT TO SCRATCH to have an irritating sensation on the body that provokes a desire to scratch the skin, or produce or cause somebody to feel such a sensation **2.** *vi* BE ANXIOUS TO DO SOMETHING to be very eager or impatient to do something **3.** *vt* SCRATCH ITCHY SKIN to scratch the skin where it itches (*nonstandard*) ■ *n* **1.** FEELING OF WANTING TO SCRATCH an irritating sensation in the body that provokes a desire to scratch the skin **2.** LONGING FOR SOMETHING a restless or uneasy desire for something **3.** MED ITCHY SKIN DISORDER a skin disorder that causes the skin to itch, e.g. scabies [Old English *giccan* < Germanic] —**itchiness** *n* —**itching** *n* —**itchy** *adj*

itch mite *n* a tiny parasite that burrows into the skin and causes the disease scabies in humans. Latin name: *Sarcoptes scabiei*.

it'd /íttəd/ *contr* **1.** it had **2.** it would

-ite[1] *suffix* **1.** mineral, rock, ore, soil, fossil ○ *carnotite* ○ *nummulite* **2.** descendant or follower of ○ *Hamite*

○ *Hussite* **3.** native or resident of ○ *Israelite* ○ *urbanite* **4.** organ, body part, cell, protozoan ○ *sporozoite* **5.** commercial product, explosive ○ *cordite* **6.** product of a chemical process ○ *evaporite* [Via French and Latin < Greek *-itēs*]

-ite[2] *suffix* salt or ester of an acid with a name ending in *-ous* ○ *phosphite* [Alteration of -ATE]

item /ítəm/ *n* **1.** ONE IN COLLECTION a single thing in a group or collection of things **2.** ONE IN LIST a single thing in a list of things **3.** BROADCAST OR PUBLISHED REPORT a piece of information in a news report, e.g. in a newspaper or on television **4.** ACCT BOOK-KEEPING ENTRY an entry in a set of financial accounts **5.** COUPLE IN RELATIONSHIP a couple who are linked in a romantic or sexual relationship (*informal*) ■ *adv* INTRODUCING LISTED ITEM used to introduce an item in a list [Late 16C. < Latin, 'likewise' < *ita* 'thus, so']

itemize /ítə mīz/ (**-izes, -izing, -ized**), **itemise** (**-ises, -ising, -ised**) *vt* to list individually all the things that make up a set or whole ○ *an itemized bill* — **itemization** /ítə mī záysh'n/ *n* — **itemizer** *n*

iterance /íttərənss/ *n* same as **iteration** (sense 1) [Early 17C. < Latin *iterare* (see ITERATE)]

iterant /íttərənt/ *adj* marked by repetition or recurrence [Early 17C. < Latin *iterant-*, present participle of *iterare* (see ITERATE)]

iterate /íttə rayt/ (**-ates, -ating, -ated**) *vt* to say or do the same thing again [Mid-16C. < Latin *iterat-*, past participle of *iterare* 'repeat' < *iterum* 'again']

iteration /íttə ráysh'n/ *n* **1.** REPETITION an instance or the act of doing something again **2.** MATHS STEP-BY-STEP PROCESS a process of achieving a desired result by repeating a sequence of steps and successively getting closer to that result **3.** COMPUT REPETITION OF STEPS the repetition of a sequence of instructions in a computer program until a result is achieved **4.** NEW VERSION OF SOMETHING a different version of something, especially a new version of existing computer hardware or software

iterative /íttərətiv/ *adj* **1.** MATHS, LOGIC same as **recursive** (sense 2) **2.** COMPUT using repeated routines in a loop as part of a computer program **3.** GRAM, LING same as **frequentative 4.** repeating again and again — **iteratively** *adv*

It girl *n* a fashionable young woman who receives a lot of media attention and is widely admired, usually for a relatively short period of time

Ithaca /íthəkə/ **1.** island in western Greece, the traditional site of the legendary kingdom of Odysseus. Population: 1,715 (1991). Area: 96 sq. km/37 sq. mi. **2.** city in south-central New York State, south of Cayuga Lake and northwest of Binghamton. Population: 29,974 (2002 estimate).

ithyphallic /íthi fállik/ *adj* **1.** SHOWING ERECT PENIS IN ART in sculpture, painting, or other art, having or showing an erect penis **2.** IN METRE USED IN BACCHIC HYMNS relating to or composed in the metre used in hymns to the ancient Greek god Bacchus ■ *n* POEM a poem composed in ithyphallic metre [Early 17C. < late Latin *ithyphallicus* < Greek *ithuphallos* 'phallus carried in procession at festivals of Bacchus', literally 'straight phallus']

itinerant /ī tínnərənt/ *adj* travelling from place to place, especially to find work or as part of your work [Late 16C. < late Latin *itinerant-*, present participle of *itinerari* < Latin *itiner-* 'way, road, journey'] — **itinerancy** *n* — **itinerant** *n* — **itinerantly** *adv*

itinerary /ī tínnərəri/ *n* (*plural* **-ies**) **1.** LIST OF PLACES TO BE VISITED a plan for a journey listing different places in the order in which they are to be visited **2.** RECORD OF JOURNEY a written record of a journey to visit different places **3.** GUIDEBOOK a guidebook for travellers ■ *adj* INTENDED FOR TRAVELLING intended or used for the purpose of travelling [15C. < late Latin *itinerarius* < Latin *itiner-* 'way, road, journey']

itinerate /ī tínnə rayt/ (**-ates, -ating, -ated**) *vi* to move from place to place on a circuit (*refers to judges or preachers*) [Early 17C. < late Latin *itinerat-*, past participle of *itinerari* (see ITINERANT)] — **itineration** /ī tínnə ráysh'n/ *n*

-itis *suffix* **1.** inflammation, disease ○ *retinitis* **2.** excessive interest in ○ *spectatoritis* [< Greek]

it'll /ítt'l/ *contr* it will ○ *It'll be so good to see you.*

Ito Jakuchu /eétō ja koŏ choo/ (1716?–1800) Japanese artist. He is known for his meticulously detailed paintings of birds, flowers, and fish.

-itol *suffix* polyhydroxy alcohol ○ *inositol* [< -ITE[1] + -OL[1]]

its /its/ *det* used to indicate that something belongs or relates to something ○ *The government has changed its policy.* [Late 16C. < IT[1] + -'s (possessive)]

USAGE **its** or **it's**? The possessive form of the pronoun *it* is *its*, even though it does not have an apostrophe before the *s*. *The cat is licking its* [not *it's*] *paws.* **It's** is a contraction for *it is* or *it has*. *It's* [not *Its*] *going to rain tonight. It's* [not *Its*] *been rebuilt.*

it's /its/ *contr* **1.** it has ○ *It's begun to rain.* **2.** it is ○ *It's perfect.*

itself /it sélf/ CORE MEANING: a reflexive pronoun used to refer back to the subject of a verb or for emphasis *pron* **1.** USED TO REFER BACK TO SOMETHING used to refer back to the subject of a verb when it is an object, animal, or abstract thing ○ *His ignorance finally revealed itself.* **2.** USED TO EMPHASIZE SOMETHING used to emphasize the thing that is referred to ○ *The house itself was cheap compared to the land.* **3.** ITS NORMAL SELF the way it usually feels or behaves ○ *The dog's not itself since we moved to the city.*

itsy-bitsy /ítsi bítsi/ *adj* extremely small (*informal*) [Alteration of LITTLE + BIT[1]]

REGIONAL NOTE Dialects, like all varieties of English, use a number of reduplicated forms. Many of these are associated with baby talk, and the compound *itsy-bitsy* could have been popularized by the nursery rhyme 'Itsy-bitsy spider'. Other rhyming phrases associated with smallness are *teeny-weeny* and *teensy-weensy*. Dialect terms for 'little' include *dinky, titchy,* and *totty.*

itty-bitty /ítti-/ *adj N Am* same as **itsy-bitsy** (*informal*) [Alteration of LITTLE + BIT[1]]

ITU *abbr* **1.** MED intensive therapy unit **2.** International Telecommunication Union

ITV *abbr* Independent Television

IU *abbr* **1.** IMMUNOL immunizing unit **2.** PHARM international unit

IUCD *abbr* MED intrauterine contraceptive device

IUD *abbr* intrauterine device

-ium *suffix* chemical element, radical, or ion ○ *californium* [< modern Latin, alteration of Latin *-um*]

IV[1] *abbr* MED **1.** intravenous **2.** intravenously

IV[2] (*plural* **IVs** or **IV's**) *n* **1.** the injection of quantities of a therapeutic fluid such as blood, plasma, saline, or glucose directly into somebody's vein at an adjustable rate **2.** *N Am* the equipment used to administer an IV [Mid-20C. < INTRAVENOUS]

Ivan III /ívən/ (1440–1505) grand duke of Moscow. In the course of his reign (1462–1505), he declared himself sovereign of all Russia (1472) and greatly expanded his empire. He also ended Moscow's subjection to the Tatars (1480). Known as **Ivan the Great**

Ivan IV (1530–84) tsar of Russia. The grand duke of Moscow, he became the first tsar of Russia (1547–84). He expanded his empire into the Urals and Siberia and instigated major internal reforms, but is mainly remembered in history for the extreme despotism of his last 20 years. Known as **Ivan the Terrible**

'Did I ascend the throne by robbery or armed bloodshed? I was born to rule by the grace of God; and I do not even remember my father bequeathing the kingdom to me and blessing me—I grew up upon the throne.'
[Ivan IV, *Letter to Prince Kurbsky*; September 1577]

Ivanovo /i vaánəvə/ city in central Russia, situated approximately 233 km/145 mi. northeast of Moscow. Population: 504,005 (1995).

I've /īv/ *contr* I have

-ive *suffix* tending to or performing ○ *illustrative* [Via French < Latin *-ivus*]

Ives /īvz/, **Charles** (1874–1954) US composer. He was an early proponent of modernism in works such as *Three Places in New England* (1903–14), combining and distorting fragments of marches, hymns, and popular songs. Full name **Ives, Charles Edward**

'Music is one of the ways God has of beating in on man.'
[Charles Ives, 'Epitaph for David Twitchell'; 1924]

IVF *abbr* MED in vitro fertilization

ivied /ívid/ *adj* covered or overgrown with ivy

ivory /ívəri/ *n* (*plural* **-ries**) **1.** MATERIAL OF ELEPHANT'S TUSKS a hard cream-coloured substance (**dentine**) that forms the tusks of animals such as the elephant, walrus, and sperm whale and was formerly used to carve small decorative objects **2.** SOMETHING MADE OF IVORY an object made of ivory, e.g. a figurine of a person or animal **3.** COLOURS CREAMY WHITE a creamy-white colour, like that of an elephant's tusk ■ *ivories npl* **1.** PIANO KEYS the keys of a piano (*informal*) **2.** TEETH a person's teeth (*slang*) **3.** DICE dice for gambling or playing games (*slang*) [13C. Via Old French *ivurie* < Latin *ebur*] — **ivory** *adj*

ivory black *n* a black pigment made from burnt ivory

Ivory Coast /ívəri-/ English name for **Côte d'Ivoire**

ivory nut *n* the white nut of the ivory palm, whose kernel is used to make buttons or other small items

ivory palm, ivory-nut palm *n* a low-growing palm tree that yields ivory nuts. Native to: Brazil, Peru. Latin name: *Phytelephas macrocarpa*.

ivory tower *n* a state or situation in which somebody is sheltered from the practicalities or difficulties of ordinary life [Translation of French *tour d'ivoire*] — **ivory-towered** *adj*

ivy

ivy /ívi/ (*plural* **ivies** or *same*) *n* **1.** an evergreen climbing plant with woody stems and green, green-and-yellow, or green-and-white leaves that grows easily on walls or trees or along the ground. Genus: *Hedera*. **2.** a climbing plant that resembles the true ivy, e.g. Boston ivy, Japanese ivy, poison ivy, or ground ivy [Old English *īfig* < Germanic]

Ivy League *n* a group of prestigious and respected universities in the northeastern United States consisting of Brown, Columbia, Cornell, Dartmouth, Harvard, Princeton, the University of Pennsylvania, and Yale [< the presumption that the universities' buildings were ivy-clad on account of their great age] — **Ivy League** *adj* — **Ivy Leaguer** *n*

iwi /eéwi/ (*plural same*) *n NZ* a people or community with a common ancestor [< Maori]

Iwo /eéwō/ city in southwestern Nigeria, just north of Ibadan. Population: 353,000 (1995).

Iwo Jima /eéwō jeémə/ largest of the Volcano Islands of Japan, in the western Pacific Ocean, east of Taiwan. It was the scene of heavy fighting during World War II when US Marines invaded and captured the Japanese air base there in February and March 1945. Area: 36 sq. km/12 sq. mi.

IWW *abbr* Industrial Workers of the World

Ixion /ik sí ən/ *n* in Greek mythology, a king of Thessaly who was bound to a perpetually turning wheel by Zeus as punishment for making sexual advances to Hera

ixtle *n* TEXTILES another spelling of **istle**

Iyar /eé yaar/ *n* in the Jewish calendar, the second month of the religious year, lasting 29 days and falling about the same time as April to May. See table at **calendar** [Mid-18C. < Hebrew *iyyār*]

-ize *suffix* **1.** to cause to be, make ○ *formalize* **2.** to treat with or as ○ *oxidize* ○ *lionize* **3.** to become, become like ○ *crystallize* **4.** to engage in ○ *extemporize* [Via Old French *-iser* < Latin *-izare* < Greek *-izein*] —**ization** *suffix*

Izetbegovic /íz et béggəvich/, **Alija** (1925–2003) president of Bosnia and Herzegovina (1990–96), and Muslim representative in the three-member collective presidency of the republic of Bosnia and Herzegovina (1996–2000)

Izhevsk /i zhéfsk/ city and capital of Udmurtia, eastern Russia, located on the River Izh. Population: 787,340 (1995).

Izmir /íz meer/, **İzmir** city and seaport in western Turkey. Population: 2,130,359 (1997). Former name **Smyrna**

Izmit /ízmit/, **İzmit** city in northwestern Turkey, on the Gulf of Izmit. Population: 210,068 (1997).

izzard /ízzərd/ *n* the letter 'z' (*archaic*) [Mid-18C. Alteration of ZED]

izzat /ízzət/ *n S Asia* the honour or reputation of a person, organization, or institution [Mid-19C. < Persian and Urdu < Arabic *izza* 'glory']

j¹ /jay/ (*plural* **j's**), **J** (*plural* **J's** or **Js**) *n* **1.** the tenth letter of the English alphabet, representing a consonant sound **2.** a written representation of the letter 'J'

j² *symbol* **1.** ELEC electric current density **2.** MATHS the imaginary number √ -1

J¹ /jay/ (*plural* **J's** or **Js**) *n* something shaped like a letter 'J'

J² *symbol* PHYS joule

J³ *abbr* **1.** CARDS jack **2.** MEDIA journal **3.** LAW judge **4.** LAW justice

Ja. *abbr* Jamaica (*used in Black English*)

jab /jab/ *vti* (**jabs, jabbing, jabbed**) **1.** PUSH SHARPLY to make a short punching movement, or push something with a short punching movement **2.** MAKE SHORT FAST PUNCH to make a short fast punch at an opponent, e.g. in boxing ■ *n* **1.** PUNCHING MOVEMENT a short sharp punching movement **2.** SHORT SHARP PUNCH a short sharp punch, as used in boxing **3.** MED same as **injection** (sense 2) (*informal*) [Early 19C. Variant of *job* 'pierce, thrust', an imitation of the sound of a brief forcible action]

Jabalpur /júbb'l poór/ city in central India. It is a major commercial centre. Population: 1,117,200 (2001). Former name **Jubbulpore**

jabber /jábbər/ *vti* (**-bers, -bering, -bered**) to talk, or say something, rapidly and excitedly, so that what is said is often incomprehensible ■ *n* rapid speech that is incomprehensible [15C. Probably an imitation of the sound] —**jabberer** *n*

jabberwocky /jábbər woki/ *n* speech or writing that is meaningless or intended as humorous nonsense [Early 20C. < 'Jabberwocky', nonsense poem by Lewis Carroll]

jabiru

jabiru /jábbə roó/ (*plural* **-rus** or *same*) *n* **1.** a large tropical stork with white feathers and a naked head. Native to: Central and South America. Latin name: *Jabiru mycteria*. **2.** a large black-and-white stork. Native to: India to Australia. Latin name: *Ephippiorhynchus asiaticus*. [Late 18C. < Tupi-Guarani *jabirú* 'swollen-necked'; < the long neck of the tropical storks]

Jabiru /jábbə roó/ town in the Northern Territory, Australia, inside Kakadu National Park. It is a mining town and tourist resort. Population: 1,171 (2002 estimate).

jaborandi /jábbə rándi/ (*plural* **-dis** or *same*) *n* **1.** dried leaves that yield the drug pilocarpine **2.** a bush of the rue family whose leaves yield pilocarpine. Native to: tropical America. Genus: *Pilocarpus*. [Early 17C. Via Portuguese < Tupi-Guarani *jaburandi* 'some-

body who spits'; from the increased saliva of those who chew the leaves]

jabot /zhábbō/ (*plural* **-bots**) *n* **1.** an edging of ruffles at the upper front of a blouse or dress **2.** formerly, a set of ruffles attached to the neckband and falling in tiers down the front of a man's shirt [Early 19C. < French, 'bird's crop, shirt frill']

jacamar

jacamar /jákə maar/ (*plural* **-mars** or *same*) *n* a bird with a very long beak and iridescent blue or green feathers that lays its eggs in holes in earth banks. Native to: South and Central America. Family: Galbulidae. [Early 19C. < French]

jaçana

jaçana /jássə naá, jə kaánə/ (*plural* **-nas** or *same*) *n* a water bird with short rounded wings and tail and long toes that enable it to walk on floating plants. Male jaçanas incubate the eggs and raise the young birds. Native to: tropics, subtropics. Family: Jacanidae. [Mid-18C. Via Portuguese < Tupi-Guarani *jasanã*]

jacaranda /jákə rándə/ (*plural* **-das** or *same*) *n* **1.** a pleasant-smelling wood. Use: cabinetwork, veneers, carving. **2.** a widely cultivated tree or bush with ferny leaves and purple flowers that produces jacaranda. Native to: tropical America. Genus: *Jacaranda*. [Mid-18C. Via Portuguese < Tupi-Guarani *jakara'na*]

jacinth /jássinth, jáyss-/ *n* a reddish variety of zircon. Use: gems. [13C. < Old French *iacinte* or medieval Latin *iacintus*, alteration of Latin *hyacinthus* 'blue stone']

jack¹ /jak/ *n* **1.** LIFTING DEVICE a portable device that uses a mechanical or hydraulic lifting system to raise heavy objects, especially cars, a short distance **2.** PLAYING CARD a playing card ranking between a ten and a queen, with a picture of a young man on it **3.** ELECTRICAL SOCKET a female socket designed to receive a male plug in order to complete a circuit **4.** OBJECT

USED IN JACKS a small, usually metal object with six points that is used in the game of jacks **5.** TARGET BALL USED IN BOWLS in bowls, a small, usually white ball that players aim at **6.** MALE ANIMAL the male of various animals, especially the donkey **7.** *US* same as **jack rabbit 8.** TROPICAL FISH a warm-water sea fish that has a forked tail. Genus: *Caranx*. **9.** FLAG ON SHIP a small flag displayed to indicate the nationality of a ship **10.** BRACE ON MAST either one of a pair of wooden braces (**crosstrees**) at the head of a topgallant mast used to hold the mast stays away from the mast **11.** LABOURER a labourer or somebody who does odd jobs (*usually used in combination*) **12.** DEVICE THAT TURNS SPIT a device that mechanically turns a spit over an open fire **13.** *US* same as **applejack 14.** same as **money** (*slang*) **15.** *US* NOTHING AT ALL anything or nothing at all (*slang*) ○ *He doesn't know jack about plumbing.* ■ *vt* (**jacks, jacking, jacked**) **1.** RAISE SOMETHING WITH JACK to raise a heavy object a short distance using a jack **2.** *US* CRIME ROB SOMEBODY to steal something, especially a car, from somebody (*slang*) **3.** PRISE SOMETHING OPEN to open something by prising it apart (*slang*) ○ *Who jacked the door?* [14C. < the name *Jack*, nickname for *John*, often implying 'ordinary' or 'small'] ◇ **every man jack** every single person ◇ **jack shit** *US* an offensive term meaning anything or nothing at all (*slang*) ◇ **be jack of something** or **somebody** *ANZ* to be tired of or bored with something or somebody

jack around *v* **1.** *vi* to waste time, loaf, or act irresponsibly (*slang*) ○ *Stop jacking around and get to work!* **2.** *vt* to make things difficult for somebody, especially by teasing, bullying, or unfair treatment

jack in *vt* **1.** to stop doing an activity or job (*informal*) **2.** *also* **jack into** to connect somebody or something electronically to something (*slang*) ○ *We're jacked into the Internet.*

jack off *vti* *N Am* a highly offensive term meaning to masturbate, or masturbate somebody (*taboo*)

jack up *v* **1.** *vt* LIFT SOMETHING WITH JACK to use a jack to lift a heavy object, especially a motor vehicle, off the ground **2.** *vt* INCREASE AMOUNT OF SOMETHING to increase something, especially a price or salary, often to an unreasonably high level **3.** *vti* INJECT ILLEGAL DRUGS to inject a drug, especially heroin, intravenously (*slang*) **4.** *vi* *Aus* REFUSE TO OBEY to refuse to comply with instructions (*informal*)

jack² /jak/ *n* TREES another spelling of **jak**

jack³ /jak/ *n* a short sleeveless coat of armour used in the Middle Ages made of canvas covered with metal plates [14C. Via French < Spanish or Portuguese *jaco*]

Jack /jak/ *n* NAVY same as **sailor** (sense 1) (*dated informal*) [< the name *Jack*, nickname for *John*]

jackal /ják awl, ják'l/ (*plural* **-als** or *same*) *n* **1.** WILD ANIMAL RESEMBLING DOG a wild animal resembling a dog, with long legs, large ears, and a bushy tail, that often hunts in packs and feeds on small game, fruit, and the carcasses of dead animals. Native to: Africa, South Asia. Genus: *Canis*. See illustration on next page **2.** HELPER OR HENCHMAN somebody who carries out menial, unpleasant, or questionable tasks for somebody **3.** SWINDLER somebody who works with accomplices to deceive people, especially to swindle them [Early 17C. Via Turkish < Persian *šagāl*]

jackanapes /jákə nayps/ (*plural same*) *n* (*dated*) **1.** an impudent, self-centred person **2.** a child who behaves mischievously or impertinently [Early 16C. Originally *Jack Napes*, origin ?]

jackal

jackaroo /jákə roó/ (*plural* **-roos**), **jackeroo** *n Aus* a young male trainee worker on a sheep or cattle station (*informal*) [Late 19C. From the name *Jack* + shortening of KANGAROO]

jackass /ják ass/ *n* **1.** a male donkey or ass **2.** an offensive term that deliberately insults somebody's intelligence (*slang insult*) [Early 18C. < the name *Jack*] —**jackassery** *n*

jack bean *n* a climbing plant of the pea family with purple clustering flowers. Use: forage. Native to: tropical America, southern United States. Latin name: *Canavalia ensiformis*.

jackboot /ják boot/ *n* **1.** MILITARY BOOT a sturdy long black leather boot that comes up to, or over, the knee, worn especially by the military in Nazi Germany **2.** HARSH TREATMENT military or other rule that is characterized by cruelty, oppression, or arbitrary aggression **3.** RIDING BOOT a heavy boot of hard leather worn for riding [Late 17C. Origin ?]

jack-by-the-hedge (*plural* **jack-by-the-hedges**) *n* PLANTS same as **garlic mustard**

jack crevalle (*plural same* or **jack crevalles**) *n* a spiny-finned, game fish. Native to: western Florida coast. Latin name: *Caranx hippos*.

jackdaw /ják daw/ *n* a medium-sized noisy bird of the crow family known for stealing things, especially shiny objects. Native to: Europe, Asia. Latin name: *Corvus monedula*. [Mid-16C. < the name *Jack*]

Jackeen /ja keén/ *n Ireland* somebody from Dublin who is thought of as being well-read, confident, and particularly proud of his or her working- or lower-class origins, or sometimes, by non-Dubliners, as being smugly clever (*sometimes offensive*) [Mid-19C. Diminutive of the name *Jack*]

jackeroo *n Aus* another spelling of **jackaroo** (*informal*)

jacket /jákit/ *n* **1.** SHORT COAT a short, usually hip-length or waist-length coat, sometimes forming part of a suit **2.** PROTECTIVE CLOTHING something that is worn on the upper part of the body for protection or support ○ *a life jacket* **3.** POTATO SKIN the outer skin of an unpeeled cooked potato, especially a baked one **4.** same as **dust jacket 5.** FLOPPY DISK CASING the casing of a floppy disk **6.** BOILER COVER a cover or outer casing designed to insulate a boiler **7.** OUTER CASING OF PIPE an outer casing around a pipe that can be filled with steam or hot water to keep the contents of the pipe warm **8.** OUTER CASING OF BULLET an outer casing on some bullets and other types of ammunition **9.** COAT IDENTIFYING RACING DOG a distinctive coloured coat for an animal, especially a racing greyhound **10.** *N Am* same as **sleeve** (sense 2) **11.** *US* FOLDER a strong envelope or folder for holding papers or documents ■ *vt* (**-ets**, **-eting**, **-eted**) PUT JACKET ON SOMEBODY OR SOMETHING to put a jacket on somebody or something such as a book or record [15C. < French *jaquet*, diminutive of Old French *jacque* 'tunic' < *jacques* 'peasant' < the name *Jacques*]

jacket potato *n* same as **baked potato**

Jack Frost *n* a personification of frost, very cold wintry weather, or the effects that frost or cold weather can produce

jackfruit /ják froot/ *n* (*plural same* or **-fruits**) *n* **1.** FOOD same as **jak 2.** a tree that produces jaks and fine-grained yellowish wood. Native to: tropical Asia. Latin name: *Artocarpus heterophyllus*. [Mid-19C. < variant of JAK]

Jack-go-to-bed-at-noon *n* PLANTS same as **goatsbeard** (sense 1) [Because the flowers close up at about noon]

jackhammer /ják hammər/ *n* a hand-held power tool, usually powered by compressed air and used for splitting or drilling rock, or for breaking up paved areas [< JACK¹ implying 'small'] —**jackhammer** *vti*

Jackie-O /jáki ó/ *adj* describes a fashion style associated with Jacqueline Kennedy Onassis ○ *a neat little Jackie-O pillbox*

jack-in-office (*plural* **jacks-in-office**) *n* a self-important and inflexible petty official

jack-in-the-box (*plural* **jacks-in-the-box** or **jack-in-the-boxes**) *n* a child's toy consisting of a puppet on a spring inside a box. The puppet jumps out when a mechanism is triggered to open the lid.

jack-in-the-pulpit *n* **1.** a woodland plant with tiny flowers in a thick spike surrounded by a sheath. Native to: eastern North America. Latin name: *Arisaema triphyllum*. **2.** PLANTS same as **cuckoopint**

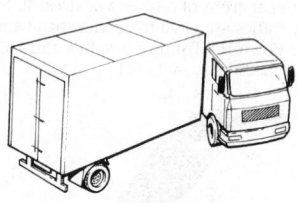

jackknife: a jackknifed lorry

jackknife /ják nīf/ *n* (*plural* **-knives**) **1.** FOLDING KNIFE a knife that has a pivoted blade that fits inside the handle when it is not in use **2.** DIVE a dive in which the diver jumps, bends the body at the waist while keeping the legs together and straight, then straightens out to enter the water headfirst ■ *v* (**-knifes** /-nīvz/, **-knifing**, **-knifed**) **1.** *vti* BEND DOUBLE to bend, or bend something, double or into an acute angle **2.** *vi* TRANSP LOSE CONTROL OF LORRY TRAILER to lose control of the trailer of an articulated lorry as a result of sudden braking or swerving at speed, or for the trailer to go out of control, so that it swings around violently and ends up at an acute angle to the cab ○ *The lorry struck a patch of ice and jackknifed.* **3.** *vi* SWIMMING DO JACKKNIFE DIVE to perform a jackknife dive [Early 18C. Origin ?]

jack ladder *n* NAUT same as **Jacob's ladder** (sense 1)

Jacklin /jáklin/, **Tony** (*b.* 1944) British golfer. The British Open champion (1969) and US Open champion (1970), he later captained Europe's Ryder Cup team (1983–89). Full name **Antony Jacklin**

jack-of-all-trades (*plural* **jacks-of-all-trades**) *n* somebody who can do many types of work

jack-o'-lantern *n* a lantern made from a hollowed-out pumpkin that has facial features cut out of it, used as a Halloween decoration

jack pine *n* a pine tree with short needles arranged in pairs and curving cones, whose timber is used for paper pulp. Native to: northern North America. Latin name: *Pinus banksiana*.

jack plane *n* a large joinery plane used for rough planing of wood and other surfaces [< JACK¹ implying 'instrument']

jackpot /ják pot/ *n* **1.** an amount of money won in a competition or lottery or as a payout from a fruit machine or other kind of gambling machine **2.** an accumulated stake in a poker game that can be competed for only by players holding a pair of jacks or a better hand [Late 19C. < a pair of jacks being the least required to compete for the pot in poker] ◇ **hit the jackpot** to achieve great success, especially financially

jack rabbit *n* a large hare with long hind legs and extremely long ears. Native to: prairies of western North America. Genus: *Lepus*. [< JACKASS, because of its long ears]

jack rafter *n* each of a set of sloping timber beams spanning the area between the eaves and the hip rafter of a roof. Each jack rafter is of a different

length to fit the changing dimension of the roof plane. [< JACK¹ implying 'small']

Jack Robinson [Origin ?] ◇ **before you can** or **could say Jack Robinson** without the slightest delay or hesitation (*informal*)

Jack Russell, **Jack Russell terrier** *n* a small terrier with short legs and a white coat with patchy markings in black, brown, or tan, or a combination of these colours [Early 20C. After John (*Jack*) Russell (1795–1883), British clergyman]

jacks /jaks/ *n* a game involving picking up small metal or plastic pieces in sequence between bouncing or throwing and catching a ball (*takes a singular verb*) [Early 19C. Shortening of JACKSTONES]

jackscrew /ják skroo/ *n* MECH ENG same as **screw jack**

jackshaft /ják shaaft/ *n* a short shaft that transmits power from a motor or engine to a machine

jacksie /jáksi/, **jacksy** (*plural* **-sies**), **jaxie**, **jaxy** (*plural* **-ies**) *n* an offensive term for the buttocks or anus [Late 19C. < JACK¹]

jacksmelt /ják smelt/ (*plural* **-smelts** or *same*) *n* a commercially important fish of the silverside family. Native to: northern American Pacific coast. Latin name: *Atherinopsis californiensis*.

Jackson /jáks'n/ city and capital of Mississippi, situated on the Pearl River in the central part of the state. An important telecommunications, transport, and commercial centre, it is home to Jackson State University. Population: 180,881 (2002 estimate).

Andrew Jackson

Jackson, **Andrew** (1767–1845) 7th president of the United States. His army defeated the British at New Orleans during the War of 1812. As Democratic president (1829–37), he opposed the Bank of America and greatly strengthened the presidency. Known as **Old Hickory**. See table at **president**

'There are no necessary evils in government. Its evils exist only in its abuses.'
[Andrew Jackson, *Veto of the Bank Bill*; 10 July 1832]

Jackson, **Glenda** (*b.* 1936) British actor and politician. She played in numerous Royal Shakespeare Company productions and in films, winning two Academy Awards, before becoming a Labour MP (1992).

'My mother polishes them to an inch of their lives until the metal shows. That sums up the Academy Awards—all glitter on the outside and base metal coming through. Nice presents for a day. But they don't make you any better.'
[Glenda Jackson, *People*; 18 March 1985]

Jackson, **Jesse** (*b.* 1941) US civil rights leader, minister, and politician. He was closely associated with civil rights leader Martin Luther King and the Southern Christian Leadership Conference in the 1960s, and later twice ran for the Democratic presidential nomination (1984, 1988) at the head of his own political organization, the Rainbow Coalition. Full name **Jackson, Jesse Louis**

'We are all precious in God's sight—the real rainbow coalition.'
[Jesse Jackson, *Speech to the Democratic National Convention*; 19 July 1988]

'The great temptation in these difficult days of racial polarization and economic injustice is to make political arguments

black and white and miss the moral imperative of wrong and right. Vanity asks, "Is it popular?" Politics asks "Will it win?" Morality and conscience ask, "Is it right?"'
[Jesse Jackson, *Speech to the Democratic National Convention*; 14 July 1992]

Jackson, Mahalia (1911–72) US singer. She helped to popularize gospel music during the 1940s and 1950s.

'Blues are the songs of despair, but gospel songs are the songs of hope.'
[Mahalia Jackson, *Movin' On Up*; 1966]

Library of Congress
Stonewall Jackson

Jackson, Stonewall (1824–63) US Confederate army general. He was one of the most successful Confederate commanders during the US Civil War (1861–65). Born **Jackson, Thomas Jonathan**

'Always mystify, mislead, and surprise the enemy, if possible.'
[Stonewall Jackson, *Motto*; 1860s]

'Let us cross over the river, and rest under the trees.'
[Stonewall Jackson, last words after having been shot accidentally by his own troops earlier in the month; 10 May 1863]

Jackson-Nelson /jáks'n néls'n/, Marjorie (b. 1931) Australian athlete and politician. She won two gold medals at the 1952 Olympic Games. She was appointed governor of the state of South Australia in 2001. Born **Jackson, Marjorie**

Jacksonville /jáks'n vil/ city in northeastern Florida. It is a major commercial and cultural centre. Population: 762,461 (2002 estimate).

jackstay /ják stay/ n **1.** a rod attached to a horizontal beam (**yard**) on a mast, used for securing a sail **2.** a support for the ring (**parrel**) that holds a boom to a mast

jackstone /ják stōn/ n a small piece of metal or plastic used in the game of jacks

jackstones /ják stōnz/ n LEISURE same as **jacks** (*takes a singular verb*) [Early 19C. < JACK¹ implying 'small']

jackstraw /ják straw/ n a small thin stick used in the game of jackstraws [Early 19C. < JACK¹ implying 'small']

jackstraws /ják strawz/ n a game that involves trying to remove small thin sticks from a pile one at a time without disturbing the rest of the pile (*takes a singular verb*)

jacksy n another spelling of **jacksie** (*offensive*)

Jack Tar n same as **sailor** (sense 1) (*dated informal*) [< the name *Jack* implying 'Everyman' + TAR² 'sailor']

Jack-the-lad n a cocky and flashy young man (*informal*) [< the nickname of *Jack* Sheppard, 18C thief]

Jack-the-rags (*plural same*) n *Wales* same as **Jack-the-lad** (*informal*)

Jack the Ripper /ják thə ríppər/ (*fl* 1880s) British murderer. He was the notorious unknown killer of at least five prostitutes in London's East End between August and November 1888.

jack-up, **jack-up rig** n an offshore oil rig with a floating hull and retractable legs that can be lowered to the seabed for support

Jacky Winter /jáki-/ n *Aus* a grey-brown flycatcher. Native to: Australia, New Guinea.

Jacob¹ /jáykəb/ n in the Bible, the second son of Isaac and Rebekah, and the grandson of Abraham. He tricked his older brother, Esau, out of his father's

blessing, and had a vision of ascent into heaven that came to be called 'Jacob's ladder' (Genesis 25–35).

Jacob² /jáykəb/, **Jacob sheep** n a sheep belonging to a breed originally found in the Scottish Hebrides, with two or four thick curved horns and a cream-coloured fleece with dark-brown patches on it. The fleece is popular with spinners and hand-loom weavers. [Mid-17C. After JACOB¹, who kept piebald sheep (Genesis 30:39)]

Jacobean /jákə bee ən/ adj **1.** OF JAMES I relating to King James I or to the period of his English reign, from 1603 to 1625 **2.** OF ARTISTIC STYLE in the style of furniture, architecture, or drama fashionable during the reign of King James I ■ n CONTEMPORARY OF JAMES I somebody, especially a prominent person, who lived during the reign of King James I of England [Late 18C. < ecclesiastical Latin *Jacobus* 'James']

Jacobean lily n a cultivated plant of the amaryllis family. Flowers: bright red. Native to: Mexico. Latin name: *Sprekelia formosissima*. [After St JAMES]

jacobin /jákəbin/ n a variety of pigeon with feathers over the neck and head that grow in the opposite direction to the others, giving it the appearance of having a hood [Late 17C. < French *jacobine*, form of *Jacobin* (see JACOBIN)]

Jacobin /jákəbin/ n **1.** HIST FRENCH REVOLUTIONARY EXTREMIST a member of a group of left-wing extremists founded during the French Revolution. In 1793, they overthrew the more moderate republicans, the Girondists, and this allowed Robespierre, the leader of the group, to adopt revolutionary measures and begin the Reign of Terror. **2.** POL LEFT-WING EXTREMIST a political radical, especially one who holds extreme left-wing views **3.** CHR FRIAR a French Dominican friar ■ adj HIST OF FRENCH JACOBINS relating to the Jacobins of the French Revolution or to their policies [14C. < Old French < ecclesiastical Latin *Jacobus*; because the Jacobin friars were established at the church of St Jacques in Paris] —**Jacobinic** /jákə bínnik/ adj —**Jacobinical** adj —**Jacobinically** adv —**Jacobinism** n

Jacobite /jákə bīt/ n **1.** a supporter of King James II of England and his descendants in the Stuart claim to the British throne **2.** a member of any of the Monophysite churches, especially of Syria [Late 17C. < ecclesiastical Latin *Jacobus* 'James'] —**Jacobite** adj —**Jacobitic** /jákə bíttik/ adj —**Jacobitical** adj —**Jacobitism** n

Jacob sheep n BREED same as **Jacob²**

Jacob's ladder n **1.** a ladder, used especially on ships, whose rungs are held together by ropes or chains, thus allowing it to be rolled up and stored in a small space **2.** a wild or garden plant with leaves divided into several leaflets in an arrangement similar to a ladder. Flowers: blue, white. Native to: North America. Genus: *Polemonium*. [< Jacob's vision of a ladder reaching to heaven in the Bible (Genesis 28:12)]

Jacob's staff n a medieval instrument for measuring distance [< the pilgrim's staff that is a symbol of St James (ecclesiastical Latin *Jacobus*), or the staff of Jacob in the Bible (Genesis 30:10)]

jaconet /jákənit/ n a cotton fabric that is like muslin but slightly heavier. Use: clothing, bandages. [Mid-18C. Anglicization of *Jagannāth(purī)* in India]

jacquard /ják aard/ n **1.** WEAVING TECHNIQUE a technique for producing intricate patterns in material by means of punched cards that give instructions to use or withhold various colours of thread **2.** LOOM ATTACHMENT a loom attachment with punched cards that makes jacquard patterns **3.** same as **jacquard loom 4.** PATTERNED MATERIAL a fabric that has been woven with a jacquard pattern [Mid-19C. After J. M. JACQUARD]

Jacquard /ják aard/, Joseph Marie (1752–1834) French inventor. His invention of the jacquard loom (1801–08), the first mechanical loom for weaving complex patterns, was an inspiration for modern computer programming.

jacquard loom n a loom with an attachment for making jacquard patterns

Jacques-Cartier /zhák kaárti ay/ river in southern Quebec, Canada that flows south into the St Lawrence River just south of Quebec City. Length: 113 km/70 mi.

jactitation /jákti táysh'n/ n **1.** MED UNCONTROLLED THRASHING AROUND violent and uncontrollable movements of the body and limbs, usually brought on by extremely high temperature, or occasionally by psychiatric disorders **2.** HARMFUL LIE in law, a false boast or claim, especially one that is intended to harm another **3.** BOASTING the act of boasting or exaggerating (*literary*) [Mid-17C. < medieval Latin *jactitation-* < Latin *jactitare* 'bring forward in public, boast' < *jacere* 'throw']

Jacuzzi /jə kóozi/ *tdmk* a trademark for a whirlpool bath with a system of underwater jets that deliver water under pressure in order to massage and invigorate the body

jade¹ /jayd/ n **1.** a semiprecious stone made of either nephrite or jadeite, varying in colour from a deep green to yellow and brown to white. Use: ornaments, jewellery. **2.** objects made of jade, collectively ○ *a collector of jade* **3.** COLOURS same as **jade green** [Late 16C. Via French *l'ejade* < Spanish *piedra de ijada* 'stone of the flanks' < Latin *ilia* 'flanks'] —**jade** adj

ORIGIN Despite the close association of *jade* with China and Japan, its name has no Asian connections. A derivative of Latin *ilia* 'flanks', the part of the body where the kidneys are situated, passed into Spanish as *ijada*. It was thought that jade could cure pain in the renal area, so the Spanish called it *piedra de ijada*, literally 'stone of the flanks', eventually reduced to *ijada*. In French it became *ejade*. Subsequently *l'ejade* 'the jade' became *le jade*, from which English *jade* is derived. (The alternative name for one of the types of *jade*, *nephrite*, is based on the same idea: it comes from Greek *nephros* 'kidney'.).

jade² /jayd/ n (*archaic*) **1.** an old horse, especially one that is worn out through overwork **2.** an offensive term for a woman that deliberately insults her temperament or morality [14C. Origin ?]

jaded /jáydid/ adj **1.** no longer interested in something, often because of having been overexposed to it **2.** exhausted, especially through overwork —**jadedly** adv —**jadedness** n

jade green n a pale milky green colour, like that of some types of jade —**jade-green** adj

jadeite /jáyd īt/ n a usually greenish pyroxene mineral consisting of sodium aluminium silicate. Source: metamorphic rocks. Use: ornaments, jewellery. —**jaditic** /jay díttik/ adj

j'adoube /zha dóob, zhə dóob/ interj an expression used by a chess player who is about to adjust a piece on the board, to ensure that this will not be counted as an official move [Early 19C. < French, 'I dub' (touch on the shoulder)]

jaeger /jáygər/ n **1.** N Am same as **skua 2.** a hunter, especially in Germany and Switzerland [Mid-19C. < German *Jäger* 'huntsman' < *jagen* 'hunt, pursue']

Jaén /haa én/ capital city of Jaén Province in southern Spain. It is an industrial centre. Population: 110,467 (2002).

Jaffa /jáffə/, **Jaffa orange** n a variety of large thick-skinned juicy orange [Late 19C. After Tel Aviv *-Jaffa*, variant of TEL AVIV-YAFO]

Jaffna /jáfnə/ port and capital city of Northern Province, in northern Sri Lanka. Population: 129,000 (1990 estimate).

jaffocking /jáffəking/ n *regional* an act of nagging at or scolding somebody

REGIONAL NOTE See *jawing*.

jag¹ /jag/ n **1.** a sharp projection, especially of rock **2.** *Scotland* MED same as **injection** (sense 2) (*informal*) ■ vt (**jags**, **jagging**, **jagged**) to cut notches in something, or cut something unevenly [14C. Origin ?]

jag² /jag/ n (*informal*) **1.** PERIOD OF INTOXICATION a period of intoxication by drugs or alcohol **2.** DRUNKEN STATE the state of being intoxicated from drugs or alcohol **3.** BINGE a period of time spent doing something in an uncontrolled or excessive way ○ *a crying jag* [Late 19C. Origin ?]

Jagan /yaágən/, Cheddi (1918–97) Guyanan politician. As the first prime minister of British Guiana (1961–69), he was instrumental in gaining Guyana's independence (1966), and later served as president (1992–97).

Jagannath /júggə naat, -nawt/, **Jaggannath**, **Jagannatha**

/júggə naathə/ *n* HINDUISM same as **Juggernaut** [Mid-17C. Earlier form of JUGGERNAUT]

Jagdeo /jágdi ǒ/, **Bharrat** (*b.* 1964) president of Guyana (1999–). A member of the Progressive People's Party, he also served as the country's finance minister (1995–99).

Jagganath *n* HINDUISM another spelling of **Jagannath**

jagged /jággid/ *adj* **1.** having sharp protruding parts or points ○ *jagged peaks of the distant mountains* **2.** having rough and uneven edges or surfaces ○ *a hastily drawn, jagged portrait* —**jaggedly** *adv* —**jaggedness** *n*

Mick Jagger

Jagger /jággər/, **Mick** (*b.* 1943) British rock musician and songwriter. He founded, with Keith Richards, the Rolling Stones, and wrote many of their hits, including 'Satisfaction' (1965). He was knighted in 2003. Full name **Jagger, Sir Michael Phillip**

'The only true performance is the one which attains madness.'
[Mick Jagger. Quoted in *The Wit and Wisdom of Rock and Roll*, Maxim Jabukowski (ed.); 1983]

jaggery /jággəri/ *n S Asia* in Southeast Asia, unrefined brown sugar, made from sugar cane or the sap of the date palm [Late 16C. Via Portuguese < Sanskrit *śarkarā* 'sugar']

jaggies /jággeez/ *npl* on a computer screen, the jagged or stepped edges of curves or diagonal lines caused by the image being formed of tiny rectangular pixels

jaggy /jággi/ (**-gier, -giest**) *adj* (*informal*) **1.** same as **jagged** (senses 1–2) **2.** *Scotland* prickly and irritating to the skin

jagir /jáˈa geer/ *n S Asia* a district where public revenues or payments-in-kind have been granted to a person or group [Early 17C. Via Urdu < Persian *jāgīr* < *jā* 'place' + *gīr* 'holding']

jaguar

jaguar /jággyoo ər/ *n* a large cat related to the leopard but with a shorter tail and black spots inside black rings on its tawny coat. Native to: southern North America, Central America, northern South America. Latin name: *Panthera onca.* [Early 17C. Via Portuguese < Tupi *jaguara*, Guarani *yaguará* 'carnivorous animal']

jaguarundi /jágwə rúndi/, **jaguarondi** /-róndi/ *n* a small slender cat that has a brownish, greyish, or reddish coat and small ears. Native to: Central and South America, occasionally southwestern United States. Latin name: *Felis yagouaroundi.* [Mid-19C. < Portuguese < *jaguar* (see JAGUAR) + Tupi-Guarani *undi* 'dark']

Jah /jaa/ *n* God, especially in Rastafarianism [Mid-16C. < Hebrew *Yāh*, shortening of *Yahweh* 'Jehovah']

Jahveh, Jahweh *n* RELIG another spelling of **Yahweh**

jai /jī/ *interj S Asia* victory to you! (*used as an expression of support*) [Mid-20C. < Hindi, 'long live!']

jai alai /hī ə līˈ/ *n* a version of the game pelota, for two or four players [Early 20C. < Spanish < Basque *jai* 'festival' + *alai* 'merry']

Jai Hind /jī hínd/ *interj S Asia* a slogan meaning 'victory to India', shouted especially at political rallies or used as a greeting [Mid-20C. < Hindi < *jai* 'long live!' + *Hind* 'India']

jail /jayl/, **gaol** *n* **1.** PLACE WHERE CRIMINALS ARE KEPT a secure place for keeping people found guilty of crimes or awaiting legal judgment **2.** LIFE AS PRISONER the state of being kept in a jail ○ *sentenced to three years' jail* ■ *vt* (**jails, jailing, jailed; gaols, gaoling, gaoled**) **1.** SEND SOMEBODY TO JAIL to sentence somebody to spend time in a jail ○ *The judge jailed her for three months.* **2.** LOCK SOMEBODY IN JAIL to keep somebody in a jail or other secure place ○ *prisoners who were jailed in a dungeon* [13C. Via Old French *jaiole*, Old N French *gaiole* < Latin *caveola*, diminutive of *cavea* 'cage']

jailbait /jáyl bayt/ *n* an offensive term for a minor under the age of consent who is sexually desirable to somebody older (*slang*)

jailbird /jáyl burd/ *n* a current or former prisoner, especially somebody with more than one experience of prison (*slang*)

jailbreak /jáyl brayk/ *n* a forceful escape from jail or prison

jailer /jáylər/, **jailor, gaoler** *n* a supervisor or employee who is in charge of prisoners in a jail

jail fever *n* same as **typhus** (*dated*)

jailhouse /jáyl howss/ *n N Am* same as **jail** *n* (sense 1) (*informal*)

jailor *n* another spelling of **jailer**

Jain /jīn, jayn/, **Jaina** /jīˈnə, jáynə/ *n* a believer in or follower of Jainism [Late 18C. < Hindi < Sanskrit *jaina* 'of a conqueror']

Jainism /jīˈnizəm, jáyn-/ *n* an ancient branch of Hinduism that rejects the notion of a supreme being and advocates a deep respect for all living things — **Jainist** *adj*

Jaipur /jī poórˈ/ capital city of Rajasthan State, northern India. It is a major commercial, manufacturing, and tourist centre. Population: 2,324,319 (2001).

jak /jak/, **jack** *n* a large greenish bulbous fruit produced by the jackfruit tree. It can weigh up to 27 kg/60 lb and has highly nutritious seeds. [Late 16C. Via Portuguese *jaca* < Malayalam *cakka*]

Jakarta /jə kaártə/ capital and largest city of Indonesia, located in the centre of the country, on the northwestern coast of the island of Java. Population: 8,389,443 (2000 estimate). Former name **Batavia**

jakes /jayks/ (*plural* **jakeses** or *same*) *n* **1.** a lavatory, especially an outside one or one without running water **2.** *W Country* human faeces, urine, or excrement generally (*informal*) [Mid-16C. Origin ?]

Jalalabad /jə laˈalə bad/, **Jalālābād** city in eastern Afghanistan, on the River Kabul. Population: 60,000 (1993).

Jalandhar ♦ Jullundur

jalap /jálləp/ *n* a twining plant of the convolvulus family, the dried tubers of which have a purgative effect. Native to: Mexico. Latin name: *Ipomoea purga.* [Mid-17C. Via French < abbreviation of Spanish *purga de Jalapa*, after *Jalapa*, Mexican city] —**jalapic** /jə láppik/ *adj*

jalapeño /hálə páy nyǒ/ (*plural* **-ños**), **jalapeño pepper** *n* a small hot pepper that is picked when green and is used extensively in Mexican cooking. Latin name: *Capsicum annuum.* [Mid-20C. < Mexican Spanish]

jalebi /jə láybi/ (*plural* **-bis**) *n* in Indian cooking, a dessert made of batter deep-fried in a coil shape and served in syrup [Mid-19C. < Hindi]

Jalisco /hə leéskǒ/ state in western Mexico. Capital: Guadalajara. Population: 6,322,002 (2000). Area: 78,390 sq. km/30,266 sq. mi.

jalopy /jə lóppi/ (*plural* **-ies**) *n* a rickety or battered old car (*dated informal*) [Early 20C. Origin ?]

jalouse /jə loóz/ (**-louses, -lousing, -loused**) *vt Scotland* to suspect that something is the case [Late 17C. < French *jalouser* 'envy, be jealous of']

jalousie

jalousie /zhállǒǒ zee/ *n* a shutter or window covering consisting of a set of angled parallel slats that can be opened to various degrees to control the amount of light or air passing through [Mid-18C. < French, literally 'jealousy']

jam¹ /jam/ *v* (**jams, jamming, jammed**) **1.** *vt* PUSH SOMETHING IN FORCIBLY to push something into a tight space with force ○ *jammed the clothes into the wardrobe* **2.** *vt* FILL SOMETHING UP to fill a place with people or things pressed closely together ○ *The fans jammed the streets to see their heroes.* ○ *jammed the fridge with delicacies* **3.** *vti* STOP SOMETHING WORKING to cause a piece of machinery or equipment to stick or stop working, or to become stuck or stop working ○ *The photocopier jammed.* **4.** *vt* BLOCK SOMETHING UP to block up something that functions as an exit, passage, or means of escape ○ *Leaves had jammed the drains.* **5.** *vt* PUT ON BRAKES HARD to apply the brakes of a vehicle suddenly and hard ○ *jammed on the brakes* **6.** *vt* CRUSH PART OF BODY to injure a part of the body, especially by squeezing or squashing it ○ *I jammed my finger in the door.* **7.** *vt* INTERFERE WITH BROADCASTING SIGNALS to block a radio or TV signal, usually by broadcasting other signals on the same frequency **8.** *vt* OVERWHELM SWITCHBOARD to overwhelm a switchboard with telephone calls **9.** *vt* RECORDING MAKE TAPE IMPOSSIBLE TO COPY to put a blocking device on something, especially a prerecorded video tape, in order to prevent it from being copied **10.** *vi* MUSIC IMPROVISE MUSIC TOGETHER to play music, especially jazz, rock, or pop, in an improvised way, often in a group ■ *n* **1.** same as **traffic jam 2.** DIFFICULT SITUATION a difficult, awkward, or embarrassing situation (*informal*) ○ *I can lend you some money if you're in a jam.* **3.** STOPPAGE an instance of something being blocked or prevented from functioning ○ *a paper jam in the printer* **4.** SIGNAL BLOCKAGE a blockage of radio or television signals **5.** RECORDING DEVICE TO PREVENT COPYING a device that prevents something, especially a prerecorded video tape, from being copied **6.** MUSIC same as **jam session** (*informal*) [Early 18C. Origin ?] —**jammable** *adj* —**jammer** *n*

jam² /jam/ *n* a spread made from fruit boiled with sugar ■ *vt* (**jams, jamming, jammed**) to make fruit into jam by boiling it with sugar [Mid-18C. Origin ?]

Jam. *abbr* **1.** Jamaica **2.** BIBLE James

jamadar /júmmə daar/, **jemadar** /jémmə daar/ *n S Asia* **1.** a junior officer in the Indian police force **2.** a minor official [Mid-18C. Via Urdu < Persian < Arabic *jamā'at* 'muster' + Persian *dār* 'holding, holder']

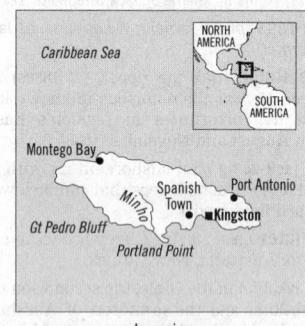
Jamaica

Jamaica /jə máykə/ island country situated south of Cuba in the northern Caribbean Sea. It is the third largest island of the Greater Antilles. It became an independent member of the Commonwealth in 1962. Language: English. Currency: Jamaican dollar. Capital: Kingston. Population: 2,695,867 (2003). Area: 10,991 sq. km/4,244 sq. mi. —**Jamaican** n, adj

Jamaica pepper n FOOD same as **allspice** (sense 1)

Jamaica rum n a slowly fermented rum that has a dark colour and a strong flavour

jamb /jam/, **jambe** n 1. either of the upright parts of a door or window frame or the sides of a fireplace 2. the inside vertical face of an opening [14C. Via Italian gamba or Old French jambe 'leg' < Greek kampē 'bend, joint']

jambalaya /jámbə líˈə, júmbə-/ n a Creole dish of rice with a mixture of fish and meat such as shrimps, chicken, ham, and spicy sausage [Late 19C. Via Louisiana French < Provençal jambalaia 'stewed mixture of rice and fowl']

jambe n CONSTR another spelling of **jamb**

Jambi /jámbi/ city and port in western Indonesia, on the island of Sumatra. It is the capital of Jambi Province. Population: 427,095 (1997).

jamboree /jámbə reé/ n 1. a large-scale planned celebration with various events and entertainments 2. a large gathering of members of the Scout or Guide movement, often on an international scale [Mid-19C. Origin ?]

Jam-dung /jám dung/, **Jam-down** n same as **Jamaica** (slang humorous; used in Black English) [Alteration after jam dung 'press down' <JAM [1], with reference to the oppressed state of many of the people]

James [1] /jaymz/ n a book of the Bible, originally a letter and traditionally attributed to James, a brother of Jesus Christ. See table at **Bible**

James [2] /jaymz/ river in western Virginia, formed at Iron Gate by the joining of the Cowpasture and Jackson rivers, that flows into the Chesapeake Bay. Length: 547 km/340 mi.

James [1], **St** (fl AD 1st century) One of the 12 apostles of Jesus Christ, he was a member of the inner circle of Jesus Christ's disciples. He was the son of Zebedee and Salome and the brother of St John. (Matthew 4:21). Known as **St James the Great**

James [2], **St** (fl AD 1st century) He was a relative of Jesus Christ, and is identified in the Bible as a leader of the early Christian Church in Jerusalem. (Mark 6:3). Known as **St James the Just**

James [3], **St** (d. AD 62?) One of the 12 apostles of Jesus Christ, he was the son of Alphaeus. (Matthew 10:3). Known as **St James the Less**

James I [1] (1208–76) king of Aragón. During his reign (1213–76), he captured the Balearic Islands (1229–35) and Valencia (1238) from the Moors. Known as **James the Conqueror**

James I [2] (1566–1625) king of England, Scotland, and Ireland. He was king of Scotland as James VI (1567–1625), and succeeded to the English throne in 1603. He authorized the King James Bible.

> 'The state of monarchy is the supremest thing upon earth: for kings are not only god's lieutenants upon earth, and sit upon God's throne, but even by God himself they are called gods.'
> [James I, Speech to Parliament; 21 March 1609]

James II (1633–1701) king of England, Scotland, and Ireland. His Roman Catholicism occasioned political conflict before and during his reign (1685–88), and he was deposed in the Revolution of 1688–89 by his nephew and son-in-law William III.

> 'I have often heretofore ventured my life in defence of this nation; and I shall go as far as any man in preserving it in all its just rights and liberties.'
> [James II, Address to the Privy Council; 1685]

James, Henry (1843–1916) US-born writer. He described the collision of American innocence and European worldliness in novels such as The Portrait of a Lady (1881) and The Golden Bowl (1904).

He was the brother of William James. See Cultural note at **ambassador**, **portrait**

> 'The Story is just the spoiled child of art.'
> [Henry James, The Ambassadors; 1903]

> 'Experience is never limited, and it is never complete; it is an immense sensibility, a kind of huge spider web of the finest silken threads suspended in the chamber of consciousness, and catching every air-borne particle in its tissue.'
> [Henry James, 'The Art of Fiction', Partial Portraits; 1888]

James, Jesse (1847–82) US outlaw. He robbed banks and trains between Missouri and Texas, and was killed in a shoot-out. Full name **James, Jesse Woodson**

P. D. James

James, P. D., Baroness James of Holland Park (b. 1920) British novelist. Her bestselling crime novels include The Black Tower (1975) and Original Sin (1994). Full name **James, Phyllis Dorothy**

> 'I had an interest in death from an early age. It fascinated me. When I heard "Humpty Dumpty sat on a wall", I thought, "Did he fall or was he pushed?"'
> [P. D. James, Paris Review; 1995]

> 'What the detective story is about is not murder but the restoration of order.'
> [P. D. James, Face; 12 December 1986]

James, William (1842–1910) US philosopher and psychologist. The brother of Henry James, he developed the philosophy of pragmatism, and encouraged an empirical approach to psychology.

> 'Man, biologically considered, and whatever else he may be into the bargain, is simply the most formidable of all the beasts of prey, and, indeed, the only one that preys systematically on its own species.'
> [William James, Atlantic Monthly; December 1904]

James Bay southern extension of Hudson Bay, between western Quebec and northeastern Ontario, Canada. Area: 32,000 sq. km/12,355 sq. mi.

Jamesian /jáymzi ən/ adj relating to or characteristic of Henry James or his literary style, e.g. in containing long complex sentences, or describing emotional states and relationships in minute detail

Jameson /jáyms'n/, **Sir Leander** (1853–1917) British-born South African politician. He led the Jameson Raid, an attempt to overthrow the Boer government in the Transvaal, South Africa (1895). Full name **Jameson, Sir Leander Starr**

Jamestown /jáymz town/ 1. city in southwestern New York State, east of Lake Chautauqua and southwest of Buffalo. Population: 31,033 (2002 estimate). 2. former village in southeastern Virginia, established on 14 May 1607 by the London Company as the first permanent English settlement in America

Jamestown Island island, once a peninsula, in eastern Virginia, on the James River. It was the site of Jamestown village, the first permanent settlement of English colonists in North America.

James VI /jaymz/ ♦ **James I**

jam jar n 1. a glass jar with a lid containing jam 2. same as **car** (sense 1) (slang)

jammies /jámmiz/ npl same as **pyjamas** (sense 1)

(informal; often used by or to children) [Late 20C. Shortening and alteration]

jammin' /jámmin/ adj excellent or first-rate (slang)

Jammu and Kashmir /júmmoo-/ state in northern India. It is the section of the disputed territory of Kashmir that is under Indian administration. Capital: Srinagar. Population: 10,069,917 (2001). Area: 101,387 sq. km/39,145 sq. mi.

jammy /jámmi/ (-mier, -miest) adj 1. STICKY WITH JAM covered in or filled with jam 2. LUCKY having or resulting from good luck (informal) 3. EXCELLENT excellent or profitable (slang) [Mid-19C. < JAM [2]]

jam-packed adj full to capacity or very crowded (informal) ○ The square was jam-packed with tourists.

jam session n a period of time spent making improvised music, especially jazz, rock, or pop music, as practice, for fun, or to experiment with new songs or techniques

Jamshedpur /júm shed poór/ city in eastern India, on the Subarnarekha River, in Bihar State. Population: 1,101,804 (2001).

Jan. abbr CALENDAR January

Janáček /yánnə chek/, **Leoš** (1854–1928) Czech composer. His music was influenced by traditional Czech folk songs, and includes the operas Jenufa (1904) and The Cunning Little Vixen (1924).

Janata /júnnə taa/ n S Asia the general public [< Hindi, 'the people']

Janata Dal /-daal/ n a political party founded in India in 1988 [Late 20C. < Hindi, 'people's party']

Jandal /jánd'l/ tdmk NZ a trademark for an open sandal that has a narrow strap between the big toe and the other toes

jandering /jándəring/ n regional an act of nagging at or scolding somebody

REGIONAL NOTE See **jawing**.

Jane Doe /jáyn dó/ n 1. US an average woman affected by everyday events 2. N Am a woman or girl, especially one who is involved in legal proceedings and whose identity is not known or is being protected [After JOHN DOE]

Janeite /jáyn īt/ n an expert on or admirer of the life and works of the English novelist Jane Austen [Late 19C. < the name Jane]

JANET /jánnit/ n an Internet-linked computer network used by academics and researchers, especially those affiliated to universities and institutes of higher education. Full form **Joint Academic Network**

jangle /jáng g'l/ vti (-gles, -gling, -gled) 1. MAKE METALLIC SOUND to make a harsh metallic noise, or cause something made of metal to make such a noise ○ heard his keys jangling 2. IRRITATE SOMEBODY'S NERVES to put somebody's nerves on edge, or be tense and on edge ○ The shock jangled her nerves. ■ n 1. METALLIC SOUND a harsh metallic noise 2. ARGUMENT a disagreement or quarrel (dated) [13C. < Old French jangler 'to chatter'] —**jangler** n —**jangly** adj

Janglish /jáng glish/ n LANG same as **Japlish** [Late 20C. Blend of JAPANESE + ENGLISH] —**Janglish** adj

janissary /jánnissəri/ (plural -ies), **janizary** /-zəri/ n 1. a member of the Turkish sultan's elite personal guard from the 14th century until 1826. Janissaries were recruited from Christians in the Balkans and disbanded as part of 19th-century reforms. 2. a loyal follower or supporter [Early 16C. Via French janissaire < Turkish yeniçeri 'new troops']

janitor /jánnitər/ n Scotland, N Am somebody whose job is to look after the cleaning and maintenance of a building, especially a school or an office block [Mid-16C. < Latin, 'door person' < janua 'door'] —**janitorial** /jánni táwri əl/ adj

janizary n same as **janissary**

jankers /jángkərz/ n punishment for a serviceman or servicewoman who has committed a military offence (slang) [Early 20C. Origin ?]

Jan Mayen /yan mí ən/ uninhabited island of Norway, lying between Iceland and Greenland in the Arctic Ocean. Area: 373 sq. km/144 sq. mi. Length: 63 km/39 mi.

Jansen /jánss'n/, **Cornelis** (1585–1638) Flemish theologian. He was the founder of the Roman Catholic

reform movement known as Jansenism. His post-humous work *Augustinus* (1640) was condemned as heretical.

Jansenism /jánss'nizəm/ *n* a Roman Catholic reform movement of the 17th and 18th centuries based on the theological views of Cornelis Jansen, who maintained that there can be no good act without divine will or the grace of God —**Jansenist** *n* —**Jansenistic** /jánssə nístik/ *adj* —**Jansenistical** *adj*

jansky /jánski/ (*plural* **-skys**) *n* a unit used to indicate the strength of radio sources in astronomy, equal to 10⁻²⁶ watts per square metre per hertz. Symbol **Jy** [Mid-20C. After Karl *Jansky*, US radio engineer]

January /jánnyŏŏ əri, jánnyŏŏri/ (*plural* **-ys**) *n* in the Gregorian calendar, the first month of the year, lasting 31 days. See table at **calendar** [Pre-12C. < Latin *Januarius* (*mensis*) 'month of Janus']

Janus /jáynəs/ *n* **1.** in Roman mythology, the god of beginnings, of the past and the future, of gates, doorways, and bridges, and of peace, traditionally depicted as having two faces. Unusually, he has no Greek counterpart. **2.** a small irregularly shaped satellite of Saturn, discovered in 1978

Jap /jap/ *n* a highly offensive term for a Japanese person (*taboo*) [Late 19C. shortening of JAPANESE]

japan /jə pán/ *n* **1.** BLACK VARNISH a lacquer that, when used to coat wood or metal, gives a glossy black finish **2.** VARNISHED OBJECTS decorative work that has been coated with japan or a similar kind of varnish ■ *vt* (**-pans, -panning, -panned**) APPLY JAPAN TO SOMETHING to varnish an object with japan [Late 17C. After JAPAN]

Japan

Japan /jə pán/ country in East Asia, comprising four large islands, Hokkaido, Honshu, Shikoku, and Kyushu, and more than 1,000 lesser adjacent islands. Language: Japanese. Currency: yen. Capital: Tokyo. Population: 127,214,500 (2003). Area: 377,837 sq. km/145,884 sq. mi.

Japan, Sea of sea between Korea and Japan that has been the subject of a dispute between the two countries. Area: 1,008,000 sq. km/389,200 sq. mi.

Japan clover *n* an annual plant grown as a forage crop. Native to: China, Japan, now widely grown in the southeastern United States. Latin name: *Lespedeza striata*.

Japan Current ♦ Kuroshio

Japanese /jáppə neéz/ (*plural same*) *n* **1.** somebody who comes from Japan **2.** the official language of Japan, also spoken in parts of Brazil and North America. Its linguistic affiliations are disputed. Native speakers: 126 million. —**Japanese** *adj*

Japanese beetle *n* a shiny green-and-brown scarab beetle that was accidentally introduced into the eastern United States where it is now a serious pest of cereal crops

Japanese cedar *n* ANZ, US an evergreen coniferous tree with a narrow conical crown, widely grown as an ornamental and for timber. Native to: China, Japan. Latin name: *Cryptomeria japonica*. UK, Can term **cryptomeria**

Japanese garden *n* a garden designed according to formal Japanese rules, distinguished by its use of foliage plants, rocks, sand, and wooden garden paths, bridges, and pavilions

Japanese iris *n* a cultivated ornamental plant. Flowers: reddish-purple, large-petalled. Native to: Asia. Latin name: *Iris ensata*.

Japanese knotweed *n* a tall fast-growing perennial plant with reddish-brown bamboo-like stems, originally an ornamental, but now considered an invasive weed in many countries. Flowers: creamy-white, in clusters. Native to: East Asia. Latin name: *Fallopia japonica*.

Japanese maple *n* a tree widely cultivated for its attractive deeply lobed leaves and purple flowers. Native to: Asia. Latin name: *Acer palmatum*.

Japanese millet *n* a coarse annual grass that has edible seeds and is grown for fodder. Native to: Asia. Latin name: *Echinochloa frumentacea*.

Japanese persimmon *n* **1.** a red or orange fruit that is bitter when unripe **2.** a tree that produces Japanese persimmons. Native to: Asia. Latin name: *Diospyros kaki*.

Japanese plum *n* **1.** a yellow or red fruit, often pickled or dried **2.** a tree that produces Japanese plums. Native to: Asia. Latin name: *Prunus salicina*.

Japanese quince *n* **1.** an aromatic round white, yellow, or green fruit that is hard and acidic when raw but is edible after processing **2.** an ornamental bush of the rose family that produces Japanese quinces and is cultivated for its bright red or pink flowers. Native to: Asia. Latin name: *Chaenomeles japonica*.

Japanese umbrella pine *n* a coniferous tree widely grown for ornament, with needles arranged in whorls like the ribs of an umbrella. Native to: central Japan. Latin name: *Sciadopitys verticillata*.

Japanize /jáppə nīz/ (**-nizes, -nizing, -nized**), **Japanise** (**-nises, -nising, -nised**) *v* **1.** *vti* SHOW JAPANESE INFLUENCE to become Japanese, or make something become Japanese, in appearance, nature, or style **2.** *vt* BUSINESS INTRODUCE JAPANESE METHODS TO SOMETHING to convert an area or industry to Japanese ways of working **3.** *vt* BUSINESS REPLACE BUSINESS WITH JAPANESE-BASED ONE to take a business over and replace it with a Japanese-based one —**Japanization** /jáppə nī záysh'n/ *n*

jape /jayp/ (*archaic or literary*) *n* a joke or an act of mischief ■ *vti* (**japes, japing, japed**) to joke, trick, or make fun of something [14C. < Old French *japer* 'yelp', influenced by *gaber* 'mock'] —**japer** *n* —**japery** *n*

Japheth /jáy feth/ *n* in the Bible, the third son of Noah and brother of Shem and Ham. He was traditionally regarded as the ancestor of a number of non-Semitic peoples of the Mediterranean (Genesis 10:1–5).

Japlish /jápplish/ *n* Japanese with many adoptions of English words, phrases, and idioms [Mid-20C. Blend of JAPANESE + ENGLISH] —**Japlish** *adj*

japonica /jə pónnikə/ *n* PLANTS **1.** same as **Japanese quince 2.** same as **camellia** (sense 1) [Early 19C. < modern Latin, form of *Japonicus* 'of Japan']

Jaques-Dalcroze /zhák dal krôz/, **Émile** (1865–1950) Swiss music teacher and composer. He was the originator of eurhythmics.

jar¹ /jaar/ *n* **1.** STORAGE CONTAINER a cylindrical container, usually one that has a wide mouth and a lid but no spout, typically made of glass, plastic, or earthenware ○ *pickle jars* **2.** JAR'S CONTENTS the amount a jar holds, or the contents of a jar **3.** ALCOHOLIC DRINK a glass of beer or other alcoholic drink (*informal*) ■ *vt* (**jars, jarring, jarred**) PUT SOMETHING IN JAR to put something into a jar, often sealing it in [Late 16C. Via French < Arabic *jarra*] —**jarful** *n*

jar² /jaar/ *v* (**jars, jarring, jarred**) **1.** *vt* SHAKE SOMETHING ABRUPTLY to give something an abrupt shake or shock especially so as to cause it to start vibrating ○ *When the furnace comes on it jars the table.* **2.** *vt* INJURE SOMETHING to cause injury to a body part by jolting it ○ *Sam jarred his neck in a car accident.* **3.** *vti* HAVE DISTURBING EFFECT ON SOMEBODY to have an irritating, unsettling, or unpleasantly disturbing effect on somebody or something ○ *That constant drilling really jars my nerves.* **4.** *vi* CLASH to look or seem bad or inappropriate in the context of something else ○ *The ultramodern dormitories jar with the older, Gothic classroom buildings.* **5.** *vti* GRATE to make a harsh grating noise, or cause something to make such a noise ■ *n* **1.** PHYSICAL JOLT an act of knocking against something with a sudden blow **2.** GRATING SOUND a harsh grating noise [15C. Probably an imitation of a discordant sound] —**jarring** *adj* —**jarringly** *adv*

jarbox /jaar boks/ *n Ireland* a kitchen sink (*informal*)

jardinière /zhaardini áir, -din yáir/ *n* a large, usually decorative flower pot or other holder for plants [Mid-19C. < French, 'female gardener']

jargon¹ /jaárgən/ *n* **1.** language that is used by a group, profession, or culture, especially when the words and phrases are not understood or used by other people ○ *typesetters' jargon* **2.** pretentious or meaningless language (*disapproving*) ○ *Cut the jargon and get to your point.* **3.** LING same as **pidgin** ■ *vi* same as **jargonize** (sense 2) [14C. < Old French *jargoun*] —**jargoneer** /jaárgə neér/ *n* —**jargonist** *n* —**jargonistic** /jaárgə nístik/ *adj*

USAGE The term **jargon** is applied chiefly to the words and phrases that are used and understood by people within a specific profession or field of study but not by others, as in *medical jargon*, *estate agents' jargon*, or *computer jargon*. (It is sometimes applied to the language of other groups of people, as in *football jargon* or *criminal jargon*, but such uses are less frequent.) Examples of Internet *jargon* include *secure server*, *netiquette*, *spamming*, and *viral marketing*. *Jargon* is an indispensable means of communication within its own sphere, but it is criticized when used unnecessarily in everyday contexts, or to impress, intimidate, or confuse outsiders.

SYNONYMS *jargon, vocabulary, terminology, slang, idiom, argot, parlance, lingo, -speak, -ese*

CORE MEANING: language used by a particular group of people

jargon language that is used by a group, profession, or culture, especially when the words and phrases are not understood or used by other people. ○ *technical jargon* ○ *The opportunity is staring us in the face to generate a billion-dollar 'tourism product' – to use that awful jargon.* **vocabulary** the set of words associated with a subject or area of activity, or used by an individual person ○ *the fashionable vocabulary of the times* ○ *Ongoing scientific, technological, and social changes generate a stream of new vocabulary.* **terminology** the expressions and words, or a set of expressions and words, used by people involved in a specialized activity or field of work ○ *commercial and financial terminology* ○ *Of the world's 53 subspecies of Asian hornbills, only nine, in the terminology of a recent conference on the status of these birds, are 'stable'.* **slang** words, expressions, and usages that are casual, vivid, racy, or playful replacements for standard ones, are often short-lived, and are usually considered unsuitable for formal contexts ○ *Scran is a slang word for food.* ○ *He used vulgar slang that is not appropriate for someone in his high position.* **idiom** the style of expression of a specific person or group ○ *This time the writer has failed to capture the American idiom.* ○ *I don't think there will be much difference in the central thrust of their politics; the idiom might change, but not the substance.* **argot** the special language used by a particular group of people ○ *teenage argot* ○ *the argot of the diplomatic community* **parlance** the style of speech or writing used by people in a specific context or profession ○ *Now accepted in common parlance, the computer term 'WYSIWYG' stands for What You See Is What You Get.* ○ *The West End is, in an estate agent's parlance, a 'desirable part of the town'.* **lingo** (*informal*) a foreign language, or a specialized set of terms requiring to be learned like a language ○ *My wife picked up the lingo as soon as we moved here.* ○ *An expert can help translate the complicated lingo of lawyers into plain English.* **-speak** (*disapproving*) a suffix added to nouns to describe the language used by a particular group of people or in a particular context ○ *I'm not put off by people using tech-speak.* ○ *The 40-page document is salted with politician-speak.* **-ese** (*disapproving*) a suffix added to nouns to describe the style of language associated with a particular group of people ○ *No matter what the government has to announce, it always seems to come out in a strangulated officialese.*

---

jargon² /jáar gon/, **jargoon** /jaar góon/ *n* a colourless, pale, or smoky zircon [Mid-18C. Via French < Italian *giargone* < Persian *zargūn* 'gold-coloured']

jargonize /jáargə nīz/ (**-izes, -izing, -ized**), **jargonise** (**-ises, -ising, -ised**) *v* 1. *vt* to convert ordinary language into jargon 2. *vi* to talk in jargon —**jargonization** /jáargə nī záysh'n/ *n*

jargoon *n* MINERALS same as **jargon²**

jarl /yaarl/ *n* formerly, a chieftain or nobleman in Scandinavia [Early 19C. < Old Norse *jarl* 'earl']—**jarldom** *n*

Jarlsberg /yaárlz burg/ *n* a type of mild pale-yellow Norwegian cheese that has large holes in it [After *Jarlesberg*, Norway]

Jarman /jaármən/, **Derek** (1942–94) British film director and painter. His experimental films, some with homoerotic themes, include *Sebastiane* (1976), *Jubilee* (1978), and *Caravaggio* (1986).

'Blue is the universal love in which man bathes – it is the terrestrial paradise…Blue transcends the solemn geography of human limits.'
[Derek Jarman, *Chroma*; 1994]

jarosite /járrə sīt/ *n* a yellow to brown mineral consisting of hydrous iron potassium sulphate [Mid-19C. After the *Jarosa* ravine, S Spain]

jarrah /járrə/ *n* 1. a dark reddish hard wood. Use: flooring, building. 2. a tree that yields jarrah. Native to: southwestern Australia. Latin name: *Eucalyptus marginata*. [Mid-19C. < Aboriginal *djarryl, jerrhyl*]

Jarrow /járrō/ industrial town and port on the River Tyne, northeastern England. During the 1930s, a

---

number of marches from there to London were held to protest against hunger and unemployment. Population: 29,325 (1991).

Jarry /zhárri/, **Alfred** (1873–1907) French dramatist and poet. The best known of his surrealist and absurdist works is the play *Ubu Roi* (written in 1888, first performed in 1896), a satire on bourgeois conventions.

'Death is only for the mediocre.'
[Alfred Jarry, *Gestes et Opinions du Docteur Faustroll, Pataphysicien*; 1911]

Jaruzelski /yárroō zélski/, **Wojciech** (b. 1923) Polish politician and general. As Communist head of state (1981–89) and president (1989–90) of Poland, he resisted liberal reforms, but in 1990 was defeated by Lech Wałesa in free elections. Full name **Jaruzelski, Wojciech Witold**

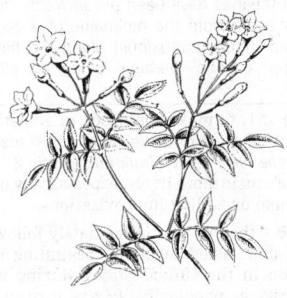

jasmine

jasmine /jázmin, jássmin/ (*plural* **-mines** or *same*), **jessamine** /jéssəmin/ *n* 1. a climbing plant often grown as a house or garden plant. Flowers: fragrant white, yellow, or red. Use: perfumes. Native to: tropics, subtropics. Genus: *Jasminum*. 2. a perfume made from the oil of a variety of jasmine [Mid-16C. Via French *jasmin, jessemin* < Persian *yāsaman*]

jasmine tea *n* a black tea flavoured with jasmine blossoms

Jason /jáyss'n/ *n* in Greek mythology, a prince who led a group of heroes on his ship, the *Argo*, on a quest to obtain the Golden Fleece and bring it back to Greece

jaspé /jás pay/ *adj* describes fabric that is streaked or veined with different colours like jasper [Mid-19C. < French, past participle of *jasper* 'to marble']

jasper /jáspər/ *n* 1. a red, iron-bearing chalcedony. Use: jewellery, ornaments. 2. CERAMICS same as **jasperware** [13C. Via Anglo-Norman *jaspre* < Latin *iaspid-* < Greek *iaspis* 'jasper' < Semitic]

jasperware /jáspər wair/ *n* an ornamental porcelain invented by Josiah Wedgwood in 1775. It usually has raised classical motifs in white on backgrounds of various colours that are created by staining the porcelain with metallic oxides.

Jat /jaat/ *n* a member of an Indo-European people living in the Punjab, northwestern India, and Pakistan [Early 17C. < Hindi *Jāt*]

jatha /jútta/ *n* S Asia a parade of people, especially Sikhs, carrying weapons [Early 20C. < Punjabi]

jati /jútti/ (*plural* **-is** or *same*) *n* S Asia a caste or subdivision of a caste [Late 19C. Via Hindi < Sanskrit 'birth']

jato /jáytō/, **JATO** *n* an auxiliary jet or rocket designed to aid the combined thrust of aircraft jet engines during take-off. Full form **jet-assisted take-off**

jaunce /jawnss/ (**jaunces, jauncing, jaunced**) *vi* same as **prance** (*archaic*) [Late 16C. Origin ?]

jaundice /jáwndiss/ *n* 1. ILLNESS CAUSING YELLOW SKIN a medical condition in which there is yellowing of the whites of the eyes, skin, and mucous membranes, caused by bile pigments in the blood. It is a symptom of liver diseases such as hepatitis and cirrhosis, or of a blocked bile duct, and sometimes occurs temporarily in new-born babies whose livers are slightly immature. Technical name **icterus** 2. CYNICAL STATE OF MIND an attitude that is characterized by cynical hostility, resentment, or suspicion ■ *vt* (**-dices, -dicing, -diced**) 1. MAKE SOMEBODY CYNICAL to alter somebody's attitude for the worse, especially when

---

it results in cynical hostility, resentment, or suspicion 2. AFFECT SOMEBODY WITH JAUNDICE to affect somebody with jaundice, as a symptom of liver disease [14C. < Old French *jaunice* < *jaune* 'yellow'] —**jaundiced** *adj*

jaunt /jawnt/ *n* a trip, especially a short one taken for fun or pleasure ■ *vi* (**jaunts, jaunting, jaunted**) to go on a short trip, especially for fun or pleasure [Late 16C. Origin ?]

jaunting car /jáwnting-/ *n* a lightweight two-wheeled open vehicle pulled by a single horse with lengthways seats positioned so that passengers either face each other or sit back-to-back. It was formerly widely used in Ireland.

jaunty /jáwnti/ (**-tier, -tiest**) *adj* 1. happy, carefree, and confident 2. fashionable and eye-catching in a casual way [Mid-17C. < French *gentil* 'polite, kind'] —**jauntily** *adv*—**jauntiness** *n*

Jaurès /zhō réss/, **Jean** (1859–1914) French politician and newspaper editor. Cofounder and editor of the newspaper *L'Humanité* (1904), he also helped to found the French Socialist Party (1905).

Jav. *abbr* 1. PEOPLES, LANG Javanese 2. *also* **jav.** ATHLETICS javelin

java /jaávə/ *n N Am* coffee, especially brewed coffee as opposed to instant coffee (*informal*) [Early 20C. < JAVA²]

Java¹ /jaávə/ island in Southeast Asia, the most populous island in Indonesia. Population: 101,742,117 (2000 estimate). Area: 134,045 sq. km/51,755 sq. mi.

Java² /jaávə/ *n* a variety of rich coffee grown on Java and the surrounding islands [Mid-19C. After JAVA¹]

Java³ /jaávə/ *tdmk* a trademark for a high-level computer programming language that allows small application programs to be downloaded from a server to a client along with the data that each program processes

Java man *n* a fossil human being found in Java and elsewhere in Indonesia, assumed to be from the Palaeolithic Age. The body and limbs of Java man are very similar to those of Homo sapiens, but the brain and skull are smaller. [< JAVA¹]

Javanese /jaávə néez/ (*plural same*) *n* 1. somebody who comes from Java 2. a language spoken on Java, belonging to the Western branch of Austronesian. Native speakers: 70 million. [Early 18C. < JAVA¹] —**Javanese** *adj*

Java Sea /jaávə-/ arm of the southern Pacific Ocean bordered by Borneo, Sulawesi, Java, and Sumatra. Area: 310,000 sq. km/120,000 sq. mi.

javelin /jávvəlin/ *n* 1. a long thin piece of wood, plastic, or metal with a pointed end, used as a weapon or thrown in field competitions 2. an athletics event in which the contestants compete to throw a javelin as far as possible [15C. < Middle French *javeline*, diminutive of Old French *javelot*]

javelina /hávvə léenə/ *n US* ZOOL same as **peccary** [Early 19C. < Spanish *jabalina*, form of *jabalí* 'wild boar' < Arabic *jabalīy*]

Javelle water /jávv'l-, jə vél-/, **Javel water** *n* a solution of sodium hypochlorite. Use: bleach, disinfectant. Formula: NaOCl. [Early 19C. After a village on the outskirts of Paris]

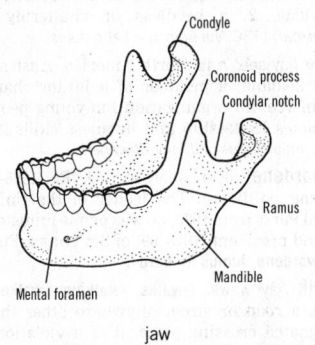

jaw

jaw /jaw/ *n* 1. BONE IN WHICH TEETH ARE SET either of the upper or lower bones that anchor the teeth and form the structural basis of the mouth in vertebrates. In humans and other higher vertebrates, the upper

jaw is known as the maxilla and the lower is the mandible. **2. INVERTEBRATE BITING PART** an invertebrate body part with a function or structure similar to a vertebrate jaw **3. GRIPPING PART** either of two hinged parts of a tool or machine used to grip objects securely **4. FACE PART** the lower, mobile part of the human face ○ *a strong square jaw* **5. IMPUDENCE** cheeky or impudent talk (*slang*) **6. LONG TALK** a long conversation or discussion (*slang*) **7. MORALIZING TALK** a moralizing talk or lecture (*slang*) ■ **jaws** *npl* **1.** GEOG **NATURAL ENTRANCE** a narrow opening in something such as a cave, gorge, canyon, or other natural feature **2. DANGEROUS PLACE** a situation that is dangerously close to something horrible or frightening ■ *vi* (**jaws, jawing, jawed**) (*slang*) **1. TALK AT LENGTH** to talk or gossip, usually at length **2. MORALIZE** to give a moralizing talk or lecture [14C. Origin ?] —**jawed** *adj* —**jawless** *adj*

jawan /jə waˈan/ *n S Asia* a private soldier or police constable [Mid-19C. < Urdu *jawān* 'young man']

Jawara /jaˈawərə/, **Sir Dawda** (*b.* 1924) Gambian politician. He was the first prime minister (1963–70) and president (1970–94) of the Gambia. Full name **Jawara, Sir Dawda Kairaba**

jawbone /jáw bōn/ *n* a bone in the jaw, especially the lower jaw ■ *vt* (**-bones, -boning, -boned**) *US* to coerce somebody to comply with something by using the authority of high office (*informal*) —**jawboner** *n*

jawbreaker /jáw braykər/ *n* **1.** a long word that is difficult to pronounce (*informal*) **2.** a machine that crushes rocks using powerful jaws **3.** *N Am* FOOD same as **gobstopper** (*informal*)

jawing /jáwing/ *n regional* an act of nagging at or scolding somebody

REGIONAL NOTE Dialects, like the standard language, have many synonyms for *scolding, nagging.* Among the most widespread alongside **jawing** are *blathering, cackling, cagmagging, calleting, canting, chackling, chamming, chittering, jaffocking, jandering,* and *mithering.* Many of these are also used for *gossip.*

jaw-jaw (*informal*) *n* talking or conversation, especially when long-winded or pointless ■ *vi* (**jaw-jaws, jaw-jawing, jaw-jawed**) to talk, especially in a long-winded or pointless way

jawline /jáw līn/ *n* the shape of somebody's lower jaw

jay

jay /jay/ *n* **1.** a noisy, often brightly coloured bird of the crow family, known for its intelligence. Family: Corvidae. **2.** a heedless or chattering person (*informal*) [13C. Via French < Latin *gaius*]

Jaycee /jáy seé/ *n* in North America, Australia, and New Zealand, a member of a junior chamber of commerce, an organization for young people that promotes leadership and business skills [Mid-20C. < the initial letters of *Junior Chamber*]

Jayewardene /jí ə waˈardənə/, **J. R.** (1906–96) Sri Lankan politician. The leader of the United National Party from 1970, he was prime minister (1977–78) and president (1978–89) of Sri Lanka. Full name **Jayawardene, Junius Richard**

jaywalk /jáy wawk/ (**-walks, -walking, -walked**) *vi* to cross a road or street anywhere other than at a designated crossing place. It is a violation of the law in some places, though prosecutions are rarely brought. [Early 20C. < JAY (sense 1)] —**jaywalker** *n* —**jaywalking** *n*

jazz /jaz/ *n* **1. SYNCOPATED POPULAR MUSIC** popular music that originated among Black people in New Orleans

in the late 19th century and is characterized by syncopated rhythms and improvisation. Jazz originally drew on ragtime, gospel, Black spiritual songs, West African rhythms, and European harmonies. **2. STUFF** unnamed related things or belongings (*slang*) ○ *Collect up the books and the rest of your jazz and lets get going.* **3. LIVELINESS** animated enthusiasm or vivacity (*slang*) **4.** *US* NONSENSE information or ideas regarded as untrue, misconceived, or misleading (*slang*) ○ *Don't be fooled if she starts giving you that jazz about being broke.* ■ *vi* (**jazzes, jazzing, jazzed**) LISTEN TO JAZZ to play or dance to jazz music [Early 20C. Origin ?] —**jazzer** *n*

ORIGIN The term *jazz* originated in the southern United States (it is first recorded in 1909, applied to a type of ragtime dance), and it is tempting to speculate that its ancestor crossed the Atlantic in the slave ships from Africa. In the absence of any certain origin, various colourful theories have been put forward – for example that *jazz* came from the nickname of a certain Jasbo Brown, an itinerant musician along the banks of the Mississippi ('Jasbo' perhaps being an alteration of 'Jasper').

jazz up *vt* **1.** to make somebody or something more interesting or decorative (*informal*) ○ *jazzed up his wardrobe with some Hawaiian shirts* **2.** to make a piece of music more lively, especially by quickening the tempo or adding improvisations

jazz age *n* the era that immediately followed World War I and lasted until the beginning of the Depression in the United States, during which jazz increased in popularity. It was a reaction to the austerity and hardship of the war and was characterized by extravagance and hedonism.

jazz band *n* a band that plays jazz, usually consisting of five or more instruments including one or more solo wind instruments and a rhythm section consisting of piano, double bass, and drums

jazzfest /jáz fest/ *n* a festival of jazz music

jazz-fusion *n* MUSIC same as **jazz-rock**

jazzman /jáz man/ (*plural* **-men** /-men/) *n* a man who plays or writes jazz music

jazzperson /jáz purss'n/ (*plural* **-people** /-peep'l/ or **-persons**) *n* somebody who plays or writes jazz music

jazz-rock *n* jazz music that incorporates aspects of rock music, especially its heavy repetitive beats and electronic amplification

jazzwoman /jáz woōmən/ (*plural* **-women** /-wimin/) *n* a woman who plays or writes jazz music

jazzy /jázzi/ (**-ier, -iest**) *adj* **1. SHOWY** showy, bright, and colourful (*informal*) **2. JAZZED UP TO APPEAL** made more lively or exaggerated for the sake of appeal (*informal*) **3. LIKE JAZZ** in the style of jazz music, especially with the syncopated rhythms of jazz — **jazzily** *adv* —**jazziness** *n*

JC *abbr* **1.** LAW jurisconsult **2.** Justice Clerk

J.C. *abbr* **1.** Jesus Christ **2.** Julius Caesar

JCB *tdmk* a trademark for a machine with a large shovel at the front and a digging arm at the back, used in excavating and in moving earth and rubble

JCL *n* a powerful computer language for writing a script used to control the execution of programs in batch processing systems. Full form **job control language**

J-cloth *tdmk* a trademark for a disposable cloth used for cleaning, dusting, washing dishes, and other domestic jobs

JCR *abbr* EDUC junior common room

JCS *abbr* MIL Joint Chiefs of Staff

JD *abbr* **1.** EDUC Diploma in Journalism **2.** EDUC, LAW Juris Doctor **3.** CRIME juvenile delinquent

je *abbr* ONLINE Jersey (*used in Internet addresses*) See table at **domain name**

jealous /jélləss/ *adj* **1. ENVIOUS** feeling bitter and unhappy because of another's advantages, possessions, or luck **2. SUSPICIOUS OF RIVALS** feeling suspicious about a rival's or competitor's influence, especially in regard to a loved one **3. WATCHFUL** possessively watchful of something ○ *keeps a jealous guard on his research* **4. DEMANDING LOYALTY** demanding exclusive loyalty or adherence (*archaic*) ○ *a jealous god.* [13C. Via Old French *gelos* < Latin *zelosus* < Greek

zēlos 'jealousy, enthusiasm'] —**jealously** *adv* —**jealousness** *n*

jealousy /jélləssi/ *n* **1.** jealous feelings or behaviour **2.** (*plural* **jealousies**) an instance of feeling jealous ○ *a man of many jealousies*

jean /jeen/ *n* a strong twill cotton. Use: work clothes, uniforms, overalls, jeans. [15C. Via Old French *Janne* < medieval Latin *Janua* 'Genoa']

jeans /jeenz/ *npl* casual trousers with raised seams, made from denim, jean, or another strong fabric

jebel /jébb'l/, **djebel, gebel** *n* in Southwest Asia or North Africa, a hill or mountain (*often used in placenames*) [Mid-19C. < Arabic *jabal* 'mountain']

Jedda ⧫ **Jiddah**

jeelie /jeéli/, **jeely** *n Scotland* jam or jelly [Variant of JELLY[1]]

jeep /jeep/ *n* a vehicle developed by the military in World War II with four-wheel drive, for use on poor roads or open terrain [Mid-20C. < GP, abbreviation of *general purpose*]

Jeep /jeep/ *tdmk* a trademark for a four-wheel-drive vehicle suitable for rough terrain

jeepers /jeépərz/, **jeepers creepers** *interj* used to express surprise (*dated informal*) [Early 20C. Alteration of *Jesus*]

jeepney /jeépni/ (*plural* **-neys**) *n* a jeep or similar vehicle that has been converted into a small bus, used in the Philippines as a form of public transport [Mid-20C. Blend of JEEP + JITNEY]

jeep safari *n* an organized group sightseeing tour or excursion in a Jeep or other four-wheel-drive vehicle

jeer /jeer/ *vti* (**jeers, jeering, jeered**) to shout or laugh at somebody or something in a mocking or scornful way ■ *n* a mocking or scornful shout or laugh [Mid-16C. Origin ?] —**jeerer** *n* —**jeeringly** *adv*

Jeeves /jeevz/ *n* a useful and reliable person who provides ready solutions to problems (*informal*) [Mid-20C. < a character in the novels of P. G. WODEHOUSE]

jeez /jeez/ *interj* used to express surprise, enthusiasm, or annoyance (*slang*) [Early 20C. Shortening of *Jesus*]

Thomas Jefferson

Jefferson /jéffərss'n/, **Thomas** (1743–1826) 3rd president of the United States. He was the author of the Declaration of Independence. As Democratic Republican president (1801–09), he strengthened the executive branch of government. See table at **president**

'We hold these truths to be self-evident: that all men are created equal; that they are endowed by their Creator with certain unalienable rights; that among these are life, liberty, and the pursuit of happiness.' [Thomas Jefferson, *Declaration of Independence*; 4 July 1776]

'Sometimes it is said that man cannot be trusted with the government of himself. Can he, then, be trusted with the government of others? Or have we found angels in the forms of kings to govern him? Let history answer this question.' [Thomas Jefferson, *First Inaugural Address*; 4 March 1801]

Jefferson City capital of Missouri and county seat of Cole County, situated in the central part of the state on the Missouri River, southeast of Columbia. Population: 39,079 (2002 estimate).

Jeffery /jéffri/, **Michael** (b. 1937) Australian soldier and politician. A former major general in the Australian army, he was governor of Western Australia (1993–2000) and became governor general of Australia in 2003.

Jeffrey /jéffri/, **Francis, Lord Jeffrey** (1773–1850) British critic and judge. He edited (1802–29) the influential *Edinburgh Review*, which he used as a platform to attack the romantic poets.

Jeffreys /jéffriz/, **Sir Alec J.** (b. 1950) British geneticist. While working at the University of Leicester in 1984, he developed the technique for establishing a person's genetic identification known as genetic fingerprinting. Full name **Jeffreys, Sir Alec John**

jehad *n* ISLAM another spelling of **jihad**

Jehoshaphat /ji hóshə fat/ in the Bible, a king of Judaea who succeeded Asa and formed an alliance with Ahab of Israel against Syria. (1, 2 Kings; 2 Chronicles).

Jehovah /ji hóvə/ *n* a translation of the Hebrew name of God used in the Bible [Mid-16C. < medieval Latin *Iehoua*, mistaken transliteration of *YHWH*, the name too sacred to pronounce, using the vowel points of Hebrew *ădōnāy* 'my lord']

Jehovah's Witness *n* a member of a religious group that believes in the imminence of Jesus Christ's personal reign on Earth and rejects secular law where it appears to conflict with the divine. Jehovah's Witnesses reject the doctrine of the Trinity.

Jehovist /ji hóvist/ *n* 1. BIBLE same as **Yahwist** 2. somebody who believes that the Hebrew word 'YHVH' in the Bible was pronounced 'Jehovah' —**Jehovism** *n* —**Jehovistic** /jeé hō vístik/ *adj*

Jehu /jeé hyoo/ *n* a fast or reckless driver (*dated informal*) [Early 17C. After the king of Israel who drove 'furiously' (2 Kings 9:20)]

jejune /ji jóon/ *adj* 1. BORING uninteresting and intellectually undemanding 2. CHILDISH lacking maturity or sophistication ○ *jejune chatter about concepts beyond their understanding* 3. WITHOUT PROPER NOURISHMENT lacking or not providing proper nourishment 4. BARREN not fertile [Early 17C. < Latin *jejunus* 'fasting, meagre'] —**jejunely** *adv* —**jejuneness** *n* —**jejunity** *n*

jejunostomy /ji joo nóstəmi/ (*plural* -**mies**) *n* 1. a surgical operation that creates access from the outside of the body into the middle part of the small intestine (**jejunum**) so that nourishment can be directly introduced 2. the opening formed in a jejunostomy

jejunum /ji jóonəm/ *n* the section of the small intestine situated between the duodenum and the ileum, whose main function is the absorption of nutrients from digested food [Mid-16C. < modern Latin < Latin *jejunus* 'fasting', because usually empty after death] —**jejunal** *adj*

Jekyll /jeék'l/, **Gertrude** (1843–1932) British landscape gardener and writer. Her garden designs, many made in collaboration with the architect Sir Edward Lutyens, and her writings were highly influential.

Jekyll and Hyde /jék'l ənd híd/ (*plural* **Jekyll and Hydes**) *n* somebody who has two distinct personalities, one good and the other evil [Late 19C. < *The Strange Case of Dr. Jekyll and Mr. Hyde* (1886), by R. L. Stevenson]

jell /jel/ (**jells, jelling, jelled**) *v* 1. *vti* SOLIDIFY to become set or firm, or cause a substance to become set or firm 2. *vti* TAKE SHAPE to become fixed or more definite in shape or form, or cause something to become fixed or more definite in shape or form 3. *vi* GET ON WELL TOGETHER to bond in a way that gives rise to mutual cooperation ○ *It's fun being with a bunch of guys who are fighting through adversity and jelling together.* (*The Philadelphia Inquirer*; 1997) [Mid-18C. Back-formation < JELLY [1]]

jellaba /jéllabə, jə láabə/, **djellaba** *n* a long, loose, sleeved garment with a hood, worn in Morocco and other parts of North Africa [Early 19C. < Moroccan Arabic *jellāb(a)*]

jellied gasoline /jéllid-/ *n* INDUST same as **napalm**

jellify /jélli fī/ (-**fies**, -**fying**, -**fied**) *vti* to turn into jelly, or cause a substance to turn into jelly —**jellification** /jéllifi káysh'n/ *n*

[1] /jélli/ *n* (*plural* -**lies**) 1. WOBBLY DESSERT a ...arent semisolid fruit-flavoured dessert made from gelatin 2. FRUIT PRESERVE a fruit preserve that is made by boiling fruit juice, sugar, and sometimes pectin until it has a semisolid consistency 3. THICKENED MEAT STOCK a savoury semisolid food made from gelatin boiled with meat stock ○ *calf's foot jelly* 4. SEMISOLID SUBSTANCE a substance that has the consistency of jelly, especially a pharmaceutical preparation ○ *petroleum jelly* 5. SANDAL a sandal, especially a child's sandal, made from transparent flexible plastic (*often used before a noun*) ○ *jelly shoes* ■ *vti* (-**lies**, -**lying**, -**lied**) THICKEN to set into a jelly, or cause something to set into a jelly [14C < Old French *gelee* 'frost, jelly' < Latin *gelare* 'freeze'] —**jelly-like** *adj* ◇ **turn to jelly** to feel shaky because of extreme fear, nervousness, or exhaustion (*informal*)

jelly[2] /jélli/ *n* same as **gelignite** (*informal*) [Mid-20C. Shortening and alteration]

jelly baby *n* a small fruit-flavoured jelly sweet in the shape of a baby

jelly bag *n* a bag used for straining the juice when making jelly or jam

jellybean /jélli been/ *n* a small bean-shaped fruit sweet with a hard coating and a soft jelly centre

jellyfish /jélli fish/ (*plural* -**fishes** or same) *n* 1. STINGING SEA ANIMAL an invertebrate sea animal that, in its reproductive stage, has a nearly transparent body shaped like an umbrella with trailing tentacles bearing stinging cells. Phylum: Coelenterata. 2. SEA ANIMAL LIKE JELLYFISH an invertebrate sea animal that looks similar to a true jellyfish 3. WEAK PERSON a weak or indecisive person (*informal*) ○ *I'm afraid I'm just a jellyfish when it comes to making decisions.*

jelly fungus *n* a fungus that grows on trees and has a gelatinous fruiting body. Order: Tremellales.

jelly mould *n* a shaped container for making jelly

jelly roll *n* N Am FOOD same as **swiss roll**

jelous incorrect spelling of **jealous**

jemadar *n* S Asia PUBLIC ADMIN another spelling of **jamadar**

jemmy /jémmi/ *n* (*plural* -**mies**) a short crowbar used as a lever, usually for prising things open ■ *vt* (-**mies**, -**mying**, -**mied**) to force something open with a jemmy ▶ N Am term (all senses) **jimmy** [Early 19C. < *Jemmy*, familiar form of the name *James*]

je ne sais quoi /zhə nə say kwáa/ *n* an indefinable quality that makes somebody or something more attractive or interesting (*literary or humorous*) [Mid-17C. < French, 'I do not know what']

Jenkins /jéngkinz/, **Roy, Baron Jenkins of Hillhead** (1920–2003) British politician. After serving as a minister in two Labour governments, he cofounded the Social Democratic Party (1981). He was the president of the European Commission (1977–81). Full name **Jenkins, Roy Harris**

> 'There are always great dangers in letting the best be the enemy of the good.'
> [Roy Jenkins, *Speech to Parliament*; 1975]

Jenner /jénnər/, **Edward** (1749–1823) British physician. He discovered the vaccine against smallpox.

> 'The deviation of man from the state in which he was originally placed by nature seems to have proved to him a prolific source of diseases.'
> [Attributed to Edward Jenner]

jennet /jénnit/, **genet** *n* 1. a female donkey 2. a small Spanish riding horse [15C. Via French *genet* < Spanish Arabic *Genēti* 'light horseman']

jenny /jénni/ (*plural* -**nies**) *n* 1. a female donkey 2. a female bird (*often used before a noun*) ○ *a jenny wren* 3. MANUF same as **spinning jenny** [Early 17C. < the name *Jenny*, diminutive of *Jane* and *Jennifer*]

jenny-longlegs /jénni lóng legz/ (*plural* same) *n* Scotland INSECTS same as **daddy longlegs** (*informal*)

Jenolan Caves /jə nólən-/ cave system in southeastern New South Wales, Australia. Located in the Blue Mountains National Park, the limestone cave system is a major tourist attraction.

jeopardize /jéppər dīz/ (-**izes**, -**izing**, -**ized**), **jeopardise** (-**ises**, -**ising**, -**ised**) *vt* to put somebody or something at risk of being lost, harmed, killed, or destroyed ○ *jeopardizing the entire mission through their indiscretion*

jeopardy /jéppərdi/ *n* 1. the risk of loss, harm, death, or destruction ○ *The entire project is in jeopardy.* 2. the risk of being convicted when put on trial for a crime [14C. < Old French *jeu* (< Latin *jocus* 'pastime') + *parti* (past participle of *partir* 'divide'), literally 'even or divided game']

jepardy incorrect spelling of **jeopardy**

Jer. *abbr* 1. BIBLE Jeremiah 2. Jersey 3. Jerusalem

jerboa

jerboa /jur bô ə/ *n* 1. a small nocturnal rodent that has large ears, a long tufted tail, and long hind legs adapted for leaping. Native to: dry regions of Asia and Africa. Family: Dipodidae. 2. a small marsupial with long hind legs and a long bushy tail. Native to: central desert areas of Australia. Genus: *Antechinomys*. [Mid-17C. Via modern Latin < Arabic *yarbū'(a)*, *jarbū*]

jeremiad /jérri mí əd/ *n* a long recitation of mournful complaints (*formal*) [Late 18C. < French *jérémiade* < *Jérémie* 'Jeremiah']

Jeremiah /jérri mí ə/ *n* 1. HEBREW PROPHET in the Bible, a Hebrew prophet who lived in Judah in the 7th and 6th centuries BC and was persecuted for prophesying the fall of Judah and Jerusalem and the Israelites' captivity in Babylon 2. BOOK OF BIBLE the book of the Bible that contains the prophecies traditionally attributed to Jeremiah. See table at **Bible** 3. NEGATIVE PERSON somebody with a gloomy attitude towards the present and future

Jerez de la Frontera /he réss də la fron táirə/ city in southwestern Spain, in Cádiz Province, Andalusia. It is the world's sherry capital. Population: 187,087 (2002).

Jericho /jérrikō/ town in the West Bank, in the Jordan Valley. It is regarded as the world's oldest town, with remains dating back to 8000 BC and, according to the Bible, was destroyed by Joshua after he led the Israelites back from captivity in Egypt (Joshua 3–8). Population: 14,744 (1997).

jerid /jə reéd/ *n* a javelin used by Persian, Turkish, and Arabian horsemen, especially during the time of the Ottoman Empire [Mid-17C. < Arabic *jarīd* 'palm branch stripped of its leaves, javelin']

jerk[1] /jurk/ *v* (**jerks, jerking, jerked**) 1. *vt* YANK SOMEBODY OR SOMETHING to pull somebody or something with a sudden strong movement ○ *He jerked her back from in front of the speeding car.* 2. *vti* MOVE JOLTINGLY to proceed with bumps and jolts, or cause somebody or something to do this ○ *The car jerked forwards.* 3. *vi* MOVE IN SPASM to move in response to muscular spasms (*refers to parts of the body*) 4. *vt* SAY SOMETHING ABRUPTLY to utter words or sounds suddenly and forcefully, e.g. from excitement ■ *n* 1. SUDDEN YANK a sudden strong pulling movement ○ *giving the door a jerk* 2. JOLTING MOTION a bumping or jolting motion ○ *moving in jerks* 3. TWITCH a spasmodic movement in a muscle 4. OFFENSIVE TERM an offensive term for somebody who is regarded as behaving foolishly (*slang insult*) 5. OVERHEAD LIFT IN WEIGHTLIFTING a lift in weightlifting in which a barbell is thrust from shoulder height to above the head ■ **jerks** *npl* 1. EXERCISES physical exercises, especially those such as press-ups that can be done without the use of special equipment (*dated informal*) 2. N Am SPASMODIC MOVEMENTS involuntary muscular movements often caused by nervousness or excitement [Mid-16C. Origin ?] —**jerker** *n*

jerk around *vt* N Am to encourage somebody to have unrealistic expectations by providing dishonest or

misleading information (*slang*) ◇ *You've jerked me around long enough.*

jerk off *vti* a highly offensive term meaning to masturbate, or masturbate somebody (*taboo*)

jerk[2] /jurk/ *vt* (**jerks, jerking, jerked**) PRESERVE MEAT IN STRIPS to preserve meat by cutting it into long thin strips and drying or smoking it ■ *adj* **1.** STRONGLY FLAVOURED AND SPICY made with strongly flavoured spices, including hot peppers and allspice, as a marinade or rub for grilled meats **2.** SPICY AND GRILLED marinated in a jerk sauce and grilled [Early 18C. Via American Spanish *charquear* < Quechua *echarquini* 'prepare dried meat']

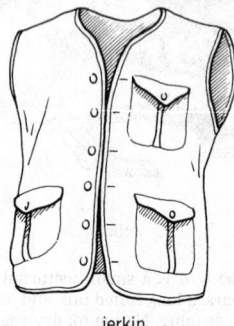

jerkin

jerkin /júrkin/ *n* **1.** a sleeveless coat or jacket worn by men or women **2.** a man's close-fitting sleeveless tunic, often made of leather, worn in the 16th and 17th centuries [Early 16C. Origin ?]

jerky[1] /júrki/ (**-ier, -iest**) *adj* moving irregularly with sudden stops and starts [Mid-19C. < JERK[1]] —**jerkily** *adv* —**jerkiness** *n*

jerky[2] /júrki/ *n* meat cut into thin strips and dried or smoked [Mid-19C. Alteration of *charqui*, via American Spanish < Quechua *cc'arki*]

jeroboam /jérrə bố əm/ *n* **1.** a large wine or champagne bottle holding the equivalent of four standard wine bottles, 3 litres/108 fl. oz **2.** a large Bordeaux wine bottle equivalent to six bottles, 4.5 litres/162 fl oz [Early 19C. After *Jeroboam* 'a mighty man of valour' (I Kings 11:28)]

Jeroboam I /jérrə bố əm/ (*fl* 10th century BC) king of Israel. According to the Bible (1, 2 Kings; 2 Chronicles), he was the first king of the ten northern tribes of Israel (922–901 BC).

Jeroboam II (*fl* 8th century BC) king of Israel. According to the Bible (2 Kings 13–15), he reigned from 786 to 746 BC.

Jerome /jə rốm/, St (347?–419?) Croatian-born monk and scholar. He translated the Vulgate, the first translation of the Bible from Hebrew into Latin. Born **Eusebius Hieronymus**

> 'I have revered always not crude verbosity, but holy simplicity.'
>
> [Jerome, 'Ad Pammachium', *Patrologia Latina*; 1864]

Jerome, Jerome K. (1859–1927) British novelist. He is best known for his humorous novel *Three Men in a Boat* (1889). Full name **Jerome, Jerome Klapka**

> 'Mere bald fabrication is useless; the veriest tyro can manage that. It is in the circumstantial detail, the embellishing touches of probability, the general air of scrupulous veracity, that the experienced angler is seen.'
>
> [Jerome K. Jerome, *Three Men in a Boat*; 1889]

> 'I like work; it fascinates me. I can sit and look at it for hours. I love to keep it by me; the idea of getting rid of it nearly breaks my heart.'
>
> [Jerome K. Jerome, *Three Men in a Boat*; 1889]

Jerry /jérri/ (*plural* **-ries**) *n* an offensive term for a German person, especially a German soldier in World War II (*dated slang insult*) [Early 20C. Alteration of GERMAN]

jerry-build *vt* to build something as quickly and cheaply as possible, with little regard for quality [Origin ?] —**jerry-builder** *n* —**jerry-building** *n* —**jerry-built** *adj*

jerry can *n* a flat-sided can with a capacity of approximately 20 litres/4.4 gal. of liquid, originally of German design and used in World War II [< alteration of GERMAN]

jersey /júrzi/ (*plural* **-seys**) *n* **1.** SWEATER a knitted woollen pullover **2.** SHIRT FOR SPORTS a long-sleeved shirt worn for playing sport, especially football and rugby **3.** CLOTHING MATERIAL a knitted fabric, usually made with a plain or stocking stitch. Use: clothing. [Late 16C. After JERSEY[1]]

Jersey[1] /júrzi/ largest and southernmost of the Channel Islands in the English Channel, a dependency of the British crown. Language: English, French. Capital: St Helier. Population: 89,361 (2001). Area: 116 sq. km/45 sq. mi.

Jersey[2] /júrzi/ (*plural* **-seys**) *n* a pale brown dairy cow that produces particularly creamy milk, belonging to a breed originating on the island of Jersey [Mid-19C. After JERSEY[1]]

Jerusalem /jə roossələm/ historic city lying at the intersection of Israel and the West Bank. The whole of the city is claimed by Israel as its capital, but this is disputed internationally. Population: 633,700 (1999).

Jerusalem artichoke *n* **1.** an edible tuber with reddish-brown knobbly skin and white flesh, eaten cooked as a vegetable **2.** a perennial plant that produces Jerusalem artichokes. Native to: North America. Latin name: *Helianthus tuberosus*. [< Italian *girasole* < *girare* 'turn' + *sole* 'sun']

Jerusalem cherry *n* a plant of the nightshade family with inedible orange or red berries, widely grown as a houseplant. Flowers: white. Native to: South America. Latin name: *Solanum pseudocapsicum*.

Jerusalem cross *n* a cross with equal arms each ending in a short bar at right angles and having a small cross in each of the four angles made by the main arms [Adopted by the Christian kings of Jerusalem (1099–1291)]

Jerusalem oak *n* a strong-smelling plant of the goosefoot family that grows as a weed. Flowers: white. Native to: northern United States, Canada. Latin name: *Chenopodium botrys*.

Jerusalem thorn *n* a thorny leguminous bush. Flowers: yellow, in long clusters. Native to: tropical America. Latin name: *Parkinsonia aculeata*.

Jerusalem Version *n* a modern version of the Bible produced from original language documents such as the Dead Sea Scrolls and containing the complete canon of biblical scripture, published in 1966

Jervis Bay /júrvəss-/ harbour in southeastern Australia, on the eastern coast of New South Wales. The headland on its southern side is part of the Australian Capital Territory. Area: 160 sq. km/60 sq. mi.

jess /jess/ *n* a short strap with a ring for attaching a leash, fastened round one of the legs of a falcon or other trained bird of prey ■ *vt* (**jesses, jessing, jessed**) to put a jess on a bird [14C. < Old French *ges*, form of *get* 'act of throwing' < Latin *jactus* < *jacere* 'to throw']

jessamine *n* PLANTS same as **jasmine**

Jesselton /jéss'ltən/ former name for **Kota Kinabalu**

Jesse window /jéssi-/ *n* a window in a church depicting Jesus Christ's lineage from Jesse, the father of King David

jest /jest/ *n* **1.** PLAYFUL JOKE something done or said in a playful joking manner (*literary*) ◇ *Forgive my little jest.* **2.** SOMETHING JOKED ABOUT an object of scorn or derision (*archaic*) ■ *vti* (**jests, jesting, jested**) JOKE PLAYFULLY to act, write, or speak in a playfully joking manner about something (*literary*) [13C. Via Old French *geste* 'romantic exploit' < Latin *gestus* < *gerere* 'behave, perform'] —**jestingly** *adv* ◇ **in jest** as a joke

jester /jéstər/ *n* **1.** an entertainer employed at a medieval court to amuse the monarch and guests **2.** somebody who likes fun or making jokes

Jesuit /jézzyoo it/ *n* **1.** MEMBER OF ROMAN CATHOLIC RELIGIOUS ORDER a member of the Society of Jesus, a Roman Catholic religious order engaged in missionary and educational work worldwide. The order was founded by Saint Ignatius Loyola in 1534 with the aim of defending Catholicism against the Reformation. **2.** *also* **jesuit** OFFENSIVE TERM an offensive term for somebody regarded as crafty or scheming, especially somebody who uses deliberately ambiguous or confusing words to deceive others (*insult*) ■ *adj* OF JESUITS relating to or belonging to the members of the Society of Jesus ◇ *a Jesuit priest* [Mid-16C. < French *jésuite* or modern Latin *Jesuita* 'follower of Jesus Christ' < *Jesus*] —**Jesuitic** /jézzyoo íttik/ *adj* —**Jesuitical** *adj* —**Jesuitically** *adv* —**Jesuitism** *n* —**Jesuitry** *n*

Jesus Christ /jeézəss-/, **Jesus** *n* **1.** FOUNDER OF CHRISTIANITY a Jewish religious teacher who lived from about 4 BC to AD 33. His life and teachings form the basis of Christianity. **2.** HUMAN EMBODIMENT OF DIVINE in Christian Science, the highest human embodiment of the divine idea ■ *interj* OFFENSIVE TERM an offensive term expressing frustration or dismay (*slang*)

Jesus freak *n* an offensive term for somebody who belongs to a youthful evangelical Christian group that is contemporary in tone (*slang*)

jet[1] /jet/ *n* **1.** PRESSURIZED STREAM OF FLUID a thin concentrated stream of liquid, air, or gas that is forced under pressure from a small nozzle or opening **2.** HOLE THROUGH WHICH FLUID IS FORCED a small nozzle or opening for letting out a stream of liquid, air, or gas **3.** AVIAT AIRCRAFT an aircraft powered by jet engines (*often used before a noun*) ◇ *a jet landing strip* **4.** AVIAT same as **jet engine** (*often used before a noun*) ◇ *using jet technology* ■ *v* (**jets, jetting, jetted**) **1.** *vi* AVIAT TRAVEL BY AIR to travel by air, especially by modern passenger aircraft ◇ *always jetting off to business meetings* **2.** *vti* FLOW FORCEFULLY IN THIN STREAM to be emitted forcefully in a thin concentrated stream, or emit something in this way ◇ *Water jetted from the broken pipe.* [Late 16C. Via Old French *jeter* 'to throw' < Latin *jacere*]

ORIGIN *Jet* was originally used in English to mean 'to protrude, stick out'. This sense is best preserved in the related *jetty* 'projecting pier', while the underlying meaning 'to throw' is still present in the related *jettison* 'throw something overboard'. *Jet* began to be used for 'to spurt out in a forceful stream' in the 17th century. The notion of using such a stream to create forward motion was first encapsulated in the term 'jet propulsion' in the mid-19th century, but it did not take concrete form for nearly a hundred years (the term *jet engine* is not recorded until 1943). Other English words descended from Latin *jacere* 'to throw', include *abject*, *dejected*, *ejaculate*, *eject*, *inject*, *interject*, *jettison*, *jetty*[1], *object*, *project*, *reject*, *subject*, and *trajectory*.

jet[2] /jet/ *n* **1.** a dense black variety of the mineral lignite. Use: jewellery, ornaments. **2.** COLOURS same as **jet black** [14C. Via Old French *jaiet* < Latin *gagates* < Greek *Gagatēs*, after *Gagai*, town in Asia Minor] —**jet** *adj*

JET /jet/ *abbr* **1.** Joint European Torus **2.** Joint European Transport

jet black *n* a very dark black colour —**jet-black** *adj*

jet boat *n* a boat powered by an engine that produces a pressurized stream of water directed backwards —**jet boating** *n*

jetbridge /jét brij/ *n* AVIAT same as **loading bridge**

jeté /zhə táy/ *n* a ballet leap from one leg to the other in which one leg is stretched forwards and the other backwards [Mid-19C. < French, past participle of *jeter* 'throw']

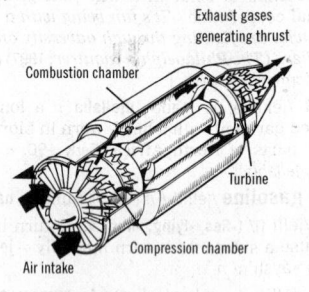

Exhaust gases generating thrust
Combustion chamber
Turbine
Compression chamber
Air intake

jet engine: cutaway view

jet engine *n* an engine, especially one used to propel an aircraft, that produces forward thrust by means of a rearward discharge of fluid, usually combustion gases. See illustration on previous page

jet fighter *n* a fighter plane that is powered by a jet engine or engines

jetfoil /jét foyl/ *n* a passenger-carrying jet-powered hydrofoil

jet lag *n* an internal physical disturbance experienced by air travellers on flights across different time zones. It affects the body's internal clock, disrupting sleeping patterns, eating schedules, and body temperature. —**jet-lagged** *adj*

jetliner /jét līnər/ *n* a large passenger aeroplane powered by jet engines [Mid-20C. Blend of JET¹ + AIRLINER]

jetpack /jét pak/ *n* a device fitted with pressurized metal containers that let out jets of gas, worn by astronauts on their backs to enable them to move around in space outside a spacecraft

jet plane *n* an aeroplane powered by jet engines

jet-propelled *adj* powered by means of engines that use jet propulsion

jet propulsion *n* forward thrust that results from the rearward discharge of a jet of fluid, especially a jet engine's combustion gases —**jet-propelled** *adj*

jetsam /jétsəm/ *n* **1.** cargo or equipment that either sinks or is washed ashore after being thrown overboard to lighten the load of a ship in distress **2.** things that have been discarded as useless or unwanted [Late 16C. Contraction of JETTISON]

jet set *n* wealthy people who travel internationally on a regular basis, especially in pursuit of pleasure (*informal*) —**jet-setter** *n* —**jet-setting** *n*

Jet Ski *tdmk* a trademark for a jet-propelled personal watercraft

jet stream *n* **1.** a strong permanent high-altitude wind current that moves east in a meandering pattern, affecting the development and movement of weather systems **2.** a flow of exhaust gases produced by a jet engine

jettison /jéttiss'n/ *vt* (**-sons, -soning, -soned**) **1.** REJECT SOMETHING to discard or abandon something such as an idea or project ○ *plans that had to be jettisoned* **2.** THROW SOMETHING OVERBOARD to throw something from a ship, aircraft, or vehicle ■ *n* **1.** REJECTION the discarding or abandoning of something **2.** SHIPPING SHIP'S DISCARDED CARGO the cargo and equipment thrown from a distressed ship to lighten it [15C. < Anglo-Norman *getteson* 'throwing cargo overboard' (to lighten a ship) < Latin *jectare* 'throw about'] —**jettisonable** *adj*

jetty¹ /jétti/ (*plural* **-ties**) *n* **1.** a landing pier **2.** a wall or other barrier built out into a body of water to shelter a harbour, protect a shoreline from erosion, or redirect water currents [15C. < Old French *jetee* 'something thrown (up as a breakwater)' < *jeter* (see JET¹)]

jetty² /jétti/ *adj* **1.** of a jet-black colour **2.** similar to or made of jet

jeu d'esprit /zhő de spreé/ (*plural* **jeux d'esprit** /zhő-/) *n* a witticism, especially one that appears in a work of literature [Early 18C. < French, 'game of spirit or wit']

jeunesse dorée /zhő ness dáwray/ *n* young people who enjoy wealth and privilege (*literary*) [Mid-19C. < French, 'gilded youth']

Jevons /jévv'nz/, **William** (1835–82) British economist and mathematician. He introduced the theory of marginal utility and pioneered the use of mathematics in economics. Full name **Jevons, William Stanley**

> 'It is clear that Economics, if it is to be a science at all, must be a mathematical science.'
> [William Jevons, *Theory of Political Economy*; 1871]

Jew /joo/ *n* **1.** BELIEVER IN JUDAISM somebody whose religion is Judaism **2.** MEMBER OF SEMITIC PEOPLE a member of a Semitic people descended from the ancient Hebrews, sharing cultural and religious ties based on Judaism **3.** SOMEBODY FROM ANCIENT JUDAEA somebody who lived or was born in ancient Judaea **4.** *also* **jew** OFFENSIVE TERM an offensive term for somebody who is regarded as miserly (*dated slang*) [Pre-12C. Via Old French *giu* < Latin *Judaeus*, Greek *Ioudaios* < Hebrew *yĕhūḏî*

< *yĕhūḏāh* 'Judah', son of the patriarch Jacob, and the tribe descended from him]

jewel /jóo əl/ *n* **1.** PERSONAL ORNAMENT an item, worn as an ornament, made of a gemstone placed in a setting of gold, silver, or other metal, e.g. a ring, necklace, or bracelet ○ *She wore her best jewels to the ball.* **2.** GEMSTONE a precious stone, e.g. a diamond or sapphire **3.** WATCH BEARING a small crystal or precious stone used as a bearing in a watch **4.** PRIZED EXAMPLE a fine example of a particular type of person or thing ○ *Her new teacher's such a jewel!* ■ *vt* (**-els, -elling, -elled**) ADORN SOMETHING WITH JEWELS to equip or decorate something with jewels [13C. < Anglo-Norman *juel < jeu* 'game' < Latin *jocus*] ◇ **the jewel in the crown** the best or most outstanding example of something

jewel beetle *n* a beetle with an iridescent body that gives it a superficial resemblance to a gemstone. Native to: Australia. Family: Buprestidae.

jewel box, jewel case *n* a hinged plastic case in which a CD is sold and stored

jeweled *adj* US spelling of **jewelled**

jeweler COMM US spelling of **jeweller**

~~**jewelery**~~ incorrect spelling of **jewelry**

jewelfish /jóo əl fish/ (*plural* **-fishes** or *same*) *n* a brightly coloured fish that is popular as an aquarium fish. Native to: Africa. Latin name: *Hemichromis bimaculatus*. [< its speckling of emerald green or sapphire]

jewelled *adj* decorated or equipped with jewels

jeweller /jóo ələr/ *n* somebody who makes, sells, or repairs jewellery

jeweller's rouge *n* UK, Can metal polish in the form of finely ground ferric oxide. ANZ, US term **crocus**

jewellery /jóo əlri/ *n* items worn as ornaments, e.g. necklaces, bracelets, earrings, or rings (*often used before a noun*) ○ *a jewellery box*

jewelry *n* US spelling of **jewellery**

Jewess /jóo iss/ *n* a highly offensive term for a Jewish woman or girl (*dated taboo*)

jewfish /jóo fish/ (*plural* **-fishes** or *same*) *n* an offensive term for a goliath grouper (*offensive*) [Probably because approved by Jewish dietary law]

Jewish /jóo ish/ *adj* **1.** relating to or practising Judaism **2.** relating to or belonging to a people descended from the ancient Hebrews —**Jewishly** *adv* —**Jewishness** *n*

Jewish calendar *n* the lunar calendar of the Jewish religious year. It has 12 months, with 13 in leap years, and dates from 3761 BC, considered the year of Creation.

Jewry /jóori/ *n* **1.** Jews in general **2.** JUDAISM same as **Judaism**

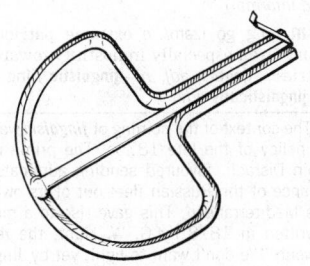

jew's harp

jew's harp *n* a small musical instrument held between the teeth and played by plucking a protruding metal tongue. It has a soft twanging sound. [Origin ?]

Jezebel /jézzə bel/ *n* **1.** in the Bible, a Phoenician princess and wife of King Ahab, who lived in the 9th century BC **2.** *also* **jezebel** an offensive term for a woman regarded as sexually immoral or manipulative (*insult*)

JFF *abbr* ONLINE just for fun (*used in e-mails or text messages*)

JFK *abbr* **1.** John Fitzgerald Kennedy **2.** TRAVEL John Fitzgerald Kennedy International Airport

Jhansi /jáanssi/, **Jhānsi** capital city of Jhansi District, central India, in Uttar Pradesh State. Population: 463,281 (2001).

Jharkhand /jáar kaánd/ state in northeastern India. Capital: Ranchi. Population: 26,909,428 (2000). Area: 79,714 sq. km/30,780 sq. mi.

Jhelum /jéeləm/ river in northwestern India and northeastern Pakistan. It runs through the Indian city of Srinagar. Length: 772 km/480 mi.

jhuggi /júggi/ *n* S Asia a shanty in an urban slum [Late 20C. < Hindi]

JHVH, JHWH *n* BIBLE another spelling of **YHWH**

-ji /jee/ *suffix* S Asia a respectful form of address added to a name or title ○ *doctorji* ○ *Janeji* [Via Hindi < Sanskrit *jaya* 'conquering']

Jiang Qing /jyáng chíng/, **Chiang Ch'ing** (1914–91) Chinese political activist. She was the third wife of Mao Zedong and was one of the prime movers in China's Cultural Revolution (1966–76). Born **Li Yunheshe**

Jiangsu /jyáng sóo/ province in eastern China, bordering on the Yellow Sea. Capital: Nanjing. Population: 71,100,000 (1997). Area: 102,600 sq. km/39,614 sq. mi.

Jiangxi /jyáng shée/ inland province in southeastern China. Capital: Nanchang. Population: 41,050,000 (1997). Area: 164,800 sq. km/63,630 sq. mi.

Jiang Zemin /jyáng tsay mín/ (*b.* 1926) president of the People's Republic of China (1993–2003). He introduced many economic reforms after succeeding Deng Xiaoping in 1993. He retired as Communist Party secretary in 2002, but remained influential as head of the Central Military Commission.

> 'History shows that anything conducive to our national stability is good.'
> [Jiang Zemin, *Times*; 14 May 1994]

jiao /jow/ (*plural same*) *n* a subunit of Chinese currency. See table at **currency** [Mid-20C. < Chinese *jiǎo*]

jib¹ /jib/ *n* a small triangular sail in front of the main or only mast on a sailing ship or sailing boat [Mid-17C. Origin ?]

jib² /jib/ *n* the projecting arm of a crane [Mid-18C. Origin ?]

jib³ /jib/ (**jibs, jibbing, jibbed**) *vi* **1.** to stop and refuse to move on (*refers to animals*) **2.** to be reluctant to do something [Early 19C. Origin ?] —**jibber** *n*

jib boom *n* an extension of the spar that sticks out from the front of a sailing ship (**bowsprit**) and supports the jib

jibe¹ *n*, *vti* another spelling of **gibe**

jibe² *vti*, *n* SAILING another spelling of **gybe**

jibe³ /jīb/ (**jibes, jibing, jibed**) *vi* N Am to conform or agree with somebody or something or with one another (*informal*) ○ *His story doesn't jibe with reality.* [Early 19C. Origin ?]

jibsheet /jíbsheet/ *n* the rope that controls the angle of the jib to the wind

JIC *abbr* ONLINE just in case (*used in e-mails or text messages*)

jicama /héekəmə/ *n* **1.** a starchy tuberous root eaten raw in salads or cooked as a vegetable **2.** the tropical plant of the pea family that produces the jicama root. Latin name: *Pachyrhizus erosus*. [Early 17C. Via Mexican Spanish < Nahuatl *xicama*]

JICRAR /jík raar/ *abbr* Joint Industry Committee for Radio Audience Research

JICTAR /jík taar/ *abbr* Joint Industry Committee for Television Advertising Research

Jiddah /jíddə/, **Jedda** /jéddə/ city and port in western Saudi Arabia, on the Red Sea, in Al Hijaz State. Population: 1,490,000 (1995).

jiffy /jíffi/, **jiff** /jif/ *n* the shortest possible length of time (*informal*) ○ *I'll be with you in a jiffy.* [Late 18C. Origin ?]

Jiffy /jíffi-/ *tdmk* a trademark for a padded mailing envelope

jig /jig/ *n* **1.** DANCE LIVELY DANCE a folk dance in triple time, especially one with kicking or jumping steps ○ *an Irish jig* **2.** MUSIC DANCING MUSIC the music for a jig **3.** WOODWORK, MANUF DEVICE FOR HOLDING PIECE OF WORK the part of a woodworking or metalworking

machine that holds the object to be worked on and guides the cutting or drilling tool **4.** FISHING **WIGGLY FISHING LURE** a fishing lure made to attract a fish's attention through its motion as it is jerked around in the water **5.** MIN EXTRACT **MINERAL-WASHING DEVICE** a device that cleans and separates coal or other excavated minerals from waste material by shaking and washing ■ *v* (**jigs, jigging, jigged**) **1.** *vti* **JERK AROUND QUICKLY** to move around in a quick jerky way, or cause somebody or something to do this **2.** *vi* **DANCE JIG** to engage in dancing a jig **3.** *vt* WOODWORK, MANUF **CUT WOOD GUIDED BY JIG** to cut or drill a piece of work using a jig as a guide **4.** *vti* FISHING **FISH WITH JIG** to fish, or catch a fish, using a jig **5.** *vt* MIN EXTRACT **CLEAN MINERALS WITH JIG** to wash and separate coal or other excavated minerals with a jig [Mid-16C. Origin ?] ◇ **the jig is up** it is all finished (*informal*)

jigger[1] /jíggər/ *n* **1.** MEASURE, BEVERAGES **MEASURE FOR ALCOHOLIC SPIRITS** a measure used for alcoholic spirits, equal to approximately 1.5 fl oz **2.** BEVERAGES **GLASS OF ALCOHOLIC SPIRITS** a small glass of alcoholic spirits containing approximately 1.5 fl oz **3.** MANUF **JIG OPERATOR** somebody who operates a mechanical jig **4.** *US* **SOMETHING OR OTHER** an object whose name is not known or cannot be recalled (*informal*) **5.** FISHING same as **jig** *n* (sense 4) **6.** SAILING **SAIL AT STERN** a small sail near the stern of a small sailing boat **7.** SAILING same as **jiggermast 8.** MECH ENG **DEVICE WITH JERKING MOTION** a mechanical device that operates with a jerking movement, e.g. a drill **9.** CUE GAMES **CUE REST** a cue rest in billiards (*informal*) [Early 18C. <JIG]

jigger[2] /jíggər/ *n* INSECTS same as **chigoe** (sense 1) [Late 18C. Alteration of CHIGGER]

jiggered /jíggərd/ *adj* (*informal*) **1.** damaged and no longer functioning properly **2.** *regional* tired out [Mid-19C. < JIGGER [1], the underlying idea being 'worn out by activity']

jiggermast /jíggər maast/ *n* **1.** the shorter mast near the stern of a small sailing boat **2.** the mast nearest the stern on a four-masted sailing ship

jiggery-pokery /jíggəri pṓkəri/ *n* devious, deceitful, or dishonest behaviour (*informal*) ○ *All this ridiculous jiggery-pokery going on behind my back!* [Late 19C. Origin ?]

jiggle /jígg'l/ *vti* (**-gles, -gling, -gled**) to move with small rapid movements in any direction, or cause something to do this ○ *He jiggled the ball before catching it.* ■ *n* a series of small rapid movements in any direction ○ *giving the key a quick jiggle in the lock* [Mid-19C. Blend of JIG + JOGGLE] —**jiggly** *adj*

jiggy /jíggi/ *n US* money or wealth (*slang*) ◇ **get jiggy with it** to become excited about or involved in something

jigsaw /jíg saw/ *n* **1.** HOBBIES same as **jigsaw puzzle 2.** WOODWORK **POWER SAW FOR CURVES** a machine saw with a narrow blade, used for cutting curves and shapes ■ *vt* (**-saws, -sawing, -sawed, -sawed** or **-sawn** /-sawn/) WOODWORK **CUT SOMETHING WITH JIGSAW** to cut or shape something using a jigsaw ■ *adj* **COMPLEX IN STRUCTURE** having many interrelating parts that form a complex whole ○ *the jigsaw nature of politics*

jigsaw puzzle *n* **1.** a puzzle in the form of interlocking irregularly shaped pieces that make a picture when fitted together **2.** something made up of many interconnecting parts whose relation to each other is difficult to understand ○ *help the police to piece together this jigsaw puzzle of motives*

jihad /ji hád/, **jehad** *n* **1.** a campaign waged by Muslims in defence of the Islamic faith against people, organizations, or countries regarded as hostile to Islam **2.** a relentless campaign against somebody or something [Mid-19C. < Arabic *jihād* 'effort'] —**jihadist** *n*

Jilin /jeé lín/ province in northeastern China. The southeast of the province borders Russia and North Korea. Capital: Changchun. Population: 1,420,000 (1995). Area: 187,000 sq. km/72,200 sq. mi.

jill *n* ZOOL another spelling of **gill** [4]

jillaroo /jíllə roó/ (*plural* **-roos**), **jilleroo** *n Aus* a woman who is a trainee worker on a sheep or cattle station (*informal*) [Mid-20C. After JACKAROO]

jillion /jíllyən/ *n* a number or amount too great to specify (*informal*) [Mid-20C. After BILLION]

jilt /jilt/ *vt* (**jilts, jilting, jilted**) to abruptly break off a romantic or sexual relationship with somebody ■ *n* somebody who abruptly breaks off a romantic or sexual relationship with somebody else [Mid-17C. Origin ?]

Jim Crow /jím krṓ/, **jim crow** *US n* **1.** *also* **jim crow** *or* **Jim Crowism** /jím krṓ izzəm/ *or* **jim crowism RACIAL DISCRIMINATION** the practice of discriminating against Black people, especially by operating systems of public segregation (*informal*) **2. TABOO TERM** a highly offensive term for a Black person (*taboo*) ■ *adj* **DISCRIMINATING AGAINST BLACK PEOPLE** discriminating against or intended to discriminate against Black people (*informal*) ○ *Jim Crow segregation laws* ○ *Jim Crow racial attitudes* [Mid-19C. After a Black character in a plantation song]

jimjams /jím jamz/ *npl* (*informal*) **1. PYJAMAS** a pair of pyjamas **2. DELIRIUM TREMENS** an attack of delirium tremens **3. NERVOUSNESS** an attack of nervous anxiety [Late 19C. Plural of obsolete *jimjam* 'trivial article, knick-knack']

jimmy /jímmi/ *N Am n* (*plural* **-mies**) same as **jemmy** ■ *vt* (**-mies, -mying, -mied**) same as **jemmy** [Mid-19C. Alteration of JEMMY]

Jimmy /jímmi/ *n Scotland* an informal way of addressing a man whose name is not known (*informal*) ○ *Hey, you, Jimmy!* [Mid-19C. Familiar form of the name *James*]

REGIONAL NOTE See *man*.

Jimmy Woodser /-wŏŏdzər/ *n ANZ* (*informal*) **1.** somebody, usually a man, who drinks alone **2.** a drink taken by somebody who is alone [Late 19C. < *Jimmy Wood* (1892) poem by Barcroft Boake, containing the line 'Who drinks alone, drinks toast to Jimmy Wood, sir']

jimsonweed /jímss'n weed/ *n N Am* PLANTS same as **thorn apple** [Late 17C. Alteration of JAMESTOWN, Virginia]

Jinan /jeé nán/, **Chi-nan** city and capital of Shandong Province on the Huang He, eastern China. Population: 3,470,000 (1995).

jingbang /jíng báng/ *n Scotland* a thing in its entirety (*informal*) ○ *the whole jingbang* [Mid-19C. Origin ?]

jingle /jíng g'l/ *n* **1. METALLIC TINKLE** a light musical noise like that of small bells or pieces of metal being shaken together **2. TUNE FOR ADVERTISING SOMETHING** a catchy tune or verse, usually one that is played repeatedly to advertise something ○ *the new jingle for the radio station* ■ *v* (**-gles, -gling, -gled**) **1.** *vti* **MAKE TINKLING SOUND** to make a light musical noise like that of small bells or pieces of metal being shaken together, or cause something to make this sound ○ *He jingled the coins in his pocket.* **2.** *vi* **HAVE EASILY REMEMBERED SOUND** to have a sound or rhyme that is catchy or repetitious [14C. An imitation of the sound] —**jingly** *adj*

jingo /jíng gō/ (*plural* **-goes**) *n* an extreme patriot, especially somebody who advocates hostility towards other countries [Late 17C. Origin ?] —**jingoish** *adj* ◇ **by jingo** used to express surprise or annoyance (*dated informal*)

jingoism /jíng gō izəm/ *n* extreme patriotism expressing itself especially in hostility towards other countries —**jingoist** *adj, n* —**jingoistic** /jíng gō ístik/ *adj* —**jingoistically** *adv*

ORIGIN The context of the coining of ***jingoism*** was British foreign policy of the late 1870s. The prime minister, Benjamin Disraeli, favoured sending gunboats to halt the advance of the Russian fleet out of its own waters into the Mediterranean. This gave rise to a music-hall song, written in 1878 by G. W. Hunt, the refrain of which went: 'We don't want to fight, yet by Jingo! if we do, We've got the ships, we've got the men, and got the money too'. Opponents of the policy picked up on the word *jingo* and used it as an icon of blind patriotism.

Jinja /jínjə/ city in southeastern Uganda, in the Eastern Region, on Lake Victoria. Population: 60,979 (1991).

jink /jingk/ *vi* (**jinks, jinking, jinked**) to make a quick sideways movement in order to evade somebody or something ■ *n* a quick evasive movement or manoeuvre [Late 17C. Origin ?]

Jinnah /jínnə/, **Muhammad Ali** (1876–1948) South Asian lawyer and politician. He became president of the Muslim League in India in 1935. His campaign for a separate Muslim state resulted in the creation of Pakistan in 1947, when he became the state's first president and governor-general.

> 'Muslims are a thousandfold more keen to get their independence than Hindus. But what do Hindus want? They want to remain the slave of the English but at the same time want us to become their slaves. They want the Muslims to be doubly enslaved.'
> [Muhammad Ali Jinnah, *Speech, Peshawar, Pakistan*; November 1945]

jinnal *vti, n* another spelling of **ginnal** (*slang*; *used in Black English*)

jinni /jínni/ (*plural* **jinn** /jin/), **djinni** (*plural* **djinn**) *n* in Islamic folklore, a spirit that can take on various human and animal forms and makes mischievous use of its supernatural powers [Early 19C. < Arabic *jinnī*]

Jin Nong /jín nóng/ (1687–1764?) Chinese artist. He frequently incorporated calligraphy into his paintings, which are often of fruit and plants.

jinriksha /jin ríkshə/, **jinricksha** *n* VEHICLES same as **rickshaw** (sense 1) [Late 19C. < Japanese, < *jin* 'man' + *riki* 'strength' + *sha* 'vehicle']

jinx /jingks/ *n* an unseen force, a person, or something such as a curse that is thought to bring bad luck ○ *There must be a jinx on this expedition.* ■ *vt* (**jinxes, jinxing, jinxed**) to make somebody or something likely to be unsuccessful or ineffective as a result of bad luck ○ *the feeling that they had been jinxed in some way* [Early 20C. Probably < *jynx* 'wryneck', from the bird's use in witchcraft] —**jinxed** *adj*

jipijapa /heépi haápə/ *n* a plant without a stem that resembles a palm and has large leaves that are used to make panama hats. Native to: Central and South America. Latin name: *Carludovica palmata*. [Mid-19C. After *Jipijapa*, town in Ecuador]

JIT *abbr* MANAGEMT just-in-time

jitney /jítni/ (*plural* **-neys**) *n N Am* a small bus that takes passengers on a regular route for a small fare [Early 20C. Origin ?]

jitter /jíttər/ *vi* (**-ters, -tering, -tered**) **BEHAVE NERVOUSLY** to behave in a nervous or restless way (*informal*) ■ *n* ELEC ENG **1. RAPID SIGNAL FLUCTUATION** an undesired rapid movement of electrical signals or images, e.g. on a television or oscilloscope screen, because of circuit instability or faulty components **2. DISTORTION IN DIGITIZED INFORMATION** a distortion in digitally transmitted or recorded sound or images, caused when two devices such as the recording and playback devices of audio recordings are not perfectly synchronized ■ **jitters** *npl* **NERVOUS ATTACK** feelings of nervousness or agitation (*informal*) ○ *He's got the jitters about his interview tomorrow.* [Early 20C. Origin ?]

jitterbug /jíttər bug/ *n* **1.** an energetic 1940s jazz dance for couples **2.** somebody who dances the jitterbug [Mid-20C. Origin ?] —**jitterbug** *vi*

jittery /jíttəri/ *adj* **1.** feeling nervous or agitated **2.** making rapid jumpy movements —**jitteriness** *n*

jiujitsu *n* MARTIAL ARTS another spelling of **jujitsu**

Jivaro /heévə rō/ (*plural same* or **-ros**) *n* **1.** a member of a Native South American people living in the tropical forests of Ecuador and northeastern Peru. Their ancestors were noted for their ritual of shrinking and preserving the heads of enemies they had killed. **2.** a language spoken by the Jivaro people, belonging to the Equatorial branch of Andean-Equatorial. Native speakers: 20,000. [Mid-19C. < Spanish *jíbaro*] —**Jivaro** *adj*

jive /jīv/ *n* **1.** DANCE **LIVELY DANCING STYLE** an uninhibited dance, often with a man swinging and throwing a woman, originally to jazz music and later to rock and roll **2. JAZZ MUSIC** jazz or swing music, especially that of the 1930s and 1940s **3.** LANGUAGE **JAZZ JARGON** the terminology and slang used by jazz musicians (*slang*) **4.** *N Am* **INSINCERE TALK** smooth talk that is often deceptive or insincere (*slang*) ■ *v* (**jives, jiving, jived**) **1.** *vi* **DANCE JIVE** to engage in dancing the jive **2.** *vi* LANGUAGE **TALK JIVE** to use the terminology and slang of jazz musicians (*slang*) **3.** *vti N Am* **FLATTER** to flatter or deceive somebody with smooth or insincere talk (*slang*) ○ *I know when you're jiving me.* ■ *adj US* **INSINCERE** lacking sincerity or honesty (*slang*) ○ *His comments are so jive!* [Early 20C. Origin ?] —**jiver** *n*

JJ, JJ. *abbr* **1.** BIBLE Judges **2.** LAW Justices

Jl *abbr* 1. BIBLE Joel 2. PUBL journal

Jl. *abbr* CALENDAR July

jm *abbr* ONLINE Jamaica (*used in Internet addresses*) See table at **domain name**

Jn *abbr* BIBLE John

jnd *abbr* PSYCHOL just noticeable difference

jnr, Jnr *abbr* junior

jo[1] /jō/ (*plural* **joes**) *n Scotland* somebody's boyfriend, girlfriend, or lover (*archaic or literary*) [Early 16C. Form of JOY]

jo[2] *abbr* ONLINE Jordan (*used in Internet addresses*) See table at **domain name**

Joan of Arc /jōn əv àark/, **St** (1412–31) French patriot and saint. She led the French to victory against the English, but was captured and burned at the stake as a heretic. She is the patron saint of France.

> 'If I said that God did not send me, I should condemn myself; truly God did send me.'
> [Attributed to Joan of Arc, *Remark at her trial*; February-May 1431]

João Pessoa /zhwów pe sō ə/ capital city of Paraíba State, in northeastern Brazil. It is an important trade centre. Population: 549,363 (1996). Former name **Parahyba**

job /job/ *n* 1. PAID OCCUPATION an activity such as a trade or profession that somebody does regularly for pay, or a paid position doing this ○ *She's got a new job.* 2. TASK something that remains to be done or dealt with ○ *I have a couple of jobs to do this afternoon.* ○ *several jobs around the house* 3. ASSIGNMENT an individual piece of work of a particular nature ○ *We managed to complete the job in under a week.* 4. FUNCTION the role that somebody or something fulfils ○ *It's her job to look after the finances.* 5. DIFFICULTY something that is difficult to accomplish ○ *I had quite a job getting it to start.* 6. QUALITY OF WORK DONE a completed piece of work of a particular quality ○ *They did a very good job on the exterior.* 7. PARTICULAR KIND OF OBJECT a particular kind of object, especially a manufactured item (*informal*) ○ *one of those big four-wheel-drive jobs* 8. AFFAIR something that happens or something that is done (*informal*) ○ *The party was one of those posh jobs.* 9. CRIME a criminal act, especially a robbery (*informal*) ○ *a bank job* 10. COMPUT PROGRAMMING TASK a computer programming task run as a single application or unit ■ *v* (**jobs, jobbing, jobbed**) 1. *vi* WORK OCCASIONALLY to take occasional or casual work ○ *He jobs as a gardener from time to time.* 2. *vti* DEAL IN WHOLESALE MERCHANDISE to buy and sell merchandise as a wholesaler or agent 3. *vt* DISTRIBUTE WORK TO OTHERS to subcontract portions of contract work to others ○ *job out the plumbing work on the house* 4. *vi* PROFIT FROM PUBLIC OFFICE to make a private gain from working in a public position 5. *vi* WORK AS STOCKJOBBER to deal in stocks as a stockjobber (*dated*) [Mid-16C. Origin ?] ◇ **be a good job** to be a fortunate circumstance (*informal*) ○ *It's a good job you decided to stay in tonight.* ◇ **give something up as a bad job** to abandon something that seems unlikely to be going to change for the better ◇ **good job** *US* used for telling somebody that they have done something correctly or well (*informal*) ◇ **just the job** exactly what is needed ◇ **make the best of a bad job** to get the best result possible from an unfavourable situation ◇ **on the job** 1. engaged in working 2. having sex (*slang*)

SYNONYMS ***job, assignment, task, chore, duty***

CORE MEANING: a piece of work to be done

job an activity that somebody regularly does for pay ○ *He had managed to get himself a job on a building site.* ○ *Omar said he would make himself useful doing odd jobs.* **assignment** a piece of work that somebody is given to do, or a post or position that somebody has been chosen for ○ *She rarely turned down a modelling assignment.* ○ *He had been sent on special assignment to assist the head of security at the port.* **task** a piece of work that somebody is given to do, usually quite short in duration or with a deadline ○ *R & D has the main task of carrying out the feasibility study and the development.* **chore** a routine task, especially an ordinary household task, that has to be done regularly ○ *ask for help with the household chores* ○ *Cleaning shoes was one of my regular chores.* **duty** something somebody is obliged to do for moral, legal, or religious reasons ○ *Fraud cannot be ruled out – we have a duty to explore all avenues.*

Job /jōb/ *n* 1. in the Bible, a righteous man whose faith withstood severe testing by God ○ *have the patience of Job* 2. a book of the Bible that describes Job's afflictions and eventual reward. See table at **Bible**

job action *n N Am* same as **industrial action**

jobber /jóbbər/ *n* 1. somebody who does odd jobs or casual work 2. FIN same as **stockjobber** (sense 1)

jobbery /jóbbəri/ *n* the corrupt practice of making private gains from public office, or an instance of this

jobbing /jóbbing/ *adj* working on a casual basis

Jobcentre /jób sentər/ *n* a local office, run by the government, where jobs are advertised and where people looking for work can receive help and advice

job club *n* a local association formed, under the auspices of a Jobcentre, to facilitate self-help in the search for work and to monitor progress in finding work

job description *n* an official written description of the responsibilities and requirements of a specific job, often one agreed between employer and employee

jobholder /jób hōldər/ *n US* a holder of a regular job

job-hunt *vi* to look for a job (*informal*) —**job hunter** *n*

jobless /jóbləss/ *adj* without a job ■ *npl* unemployed people considered collectively —**joblessness** *n*

job lot *n* a miscellaneous collection of articles, especially ones that are bought or sold together ○ *I bought it as a job lot.*

job-related illness *n* MED same as **industrial disease**

Jobs /jobz/, **Steve** (*b.* 1955) US entrepreneur. He co-founded Apple Computer Company (1976), which produced the first user-friendly home computer. Full name **Jobs, Steven Paul**

> 'Do you want to spend the rest of your life selling sugared water or do you want the chance to change the world?'
> [Steve Jobs, *Fortune*; 14 September 1987]

Job's comforter /jōbz-/ *n* somebody who, though appearing or intending to comfort a distressed person, only succeeds in worsening the situation [< the friends who came to 'comfort' Job in his affliction (Job 5:17)]

jobseeker /jób seekər/ *n* somebody who is actively looking for employment —**jobseeking** *n*

Jobseeker's Allowance *n* money that the government pays to unemployed people who are looking for jobs

job-sharing *n* the system of dividing up the responsibilities of a single full-time job between two or more part-time workers —**job-share** *n, vi* —**job-sharer** *n*

Job's tears /jōbz-/ *n* (*plural same*) a grass plant with sword-shaped leaves and hard white spherical seeds that are used as beads. Native to: tropical Asia. Latin name: *Coix lacryma-jobi.* ■ *npl* the hard white seeds of Job's tears, used as beads and, in East Asia, as a cereal [< its round shiny leaves]

jobsworth /jóbz wurth/ *n* a minor official who insists on following regulations to the letter, especially with the intention of being deliberately obstructive (*informal*) [Late 20C. < *It's more than my job's worth* (to do whatever is being requested)]

Jocasta /jə kástə/ *n* in Greek mythology, the wife of Laius, king of Thebes, and later of their son Oedipus

jock[1] /jok/ *n* same as **DJ**[1] (sense 1) (*informal*) [Late 18C. Shortening]

jock[2] /jok/ *n* (*informal*) 1. *N Am* an athlete, especially a male athlete in college 2. same as **jockstrap** [Mid-20C. Shortening of JOCKSTRAP]

Jock /jok/ *n* used to refer to or address a Scottish person, especially a man (*informal; offensive in some contexts*) [Scottish form of *John*]

jockey /jóki/ *n* (*plural* **-eys**) 1. RIDER OF RACEHORSE a rider of racehorses, especially professionally 2. *N Am* OPERATOR somebody whose work involves the use or operation of a particular device, vehicle, or object (*informal*) ○ *We desk jockeys need to get out and exercise more.* ■ *v* (**-eys, -eying, -eyed**) 1. *vti* RIDE RACEHORSE to ride a racehorse, especially as a professional jockey 2. *vi* TRY TO GAIN ADVANTAGE to manoeuvre in order to gain an advantage ○ *Watch them all jockeying for promotion.* 3. *vt* MANIPULATE SOMEBODY to trick somebody, usually for personal gain ○ *She has been jockeyed into doing work for which he gets the credit.* [Late 16C. < familiar form of JOCK]

jock itch *n ANZ, N Am* a fungal infection of the skin in the groin area, especially in men and boys. UK term **dhobi itch**

jockstrap /jók strap/ *n* an elasticated belt with a pouch at the front, worn by sportsmen to support their genitals or to keep a protective cup in place [Late 19C. < slang *jock* 'genitals', origin ?]

jocose /jə kōss, jō-/ *adj* (*literary*) 1. with a playful joking disposition 2. playfully humorous in style [Late 17C. < Latin *jocosus* 'full of joking' < *jocus* 'joke'] —**jocosely** *adv* —**jocoseness** *n* —**jocosity** /jə kóssə ti, jō-/ *n*

jocular /jókyōōlər/ *adj* 1. with a playful joking disposition 2. intended to be funny [Early 17C. < Latin *jocularis* 'of a little joke' < *jocus* 'joke'] —**jocularity** /jókyōō lárrəti/ *n* —**jocularly** *adv*

jocund /jókənd/ *adj* cheerful and full of good humour (*literary*) [14C. Via Old French *jocond* (influenced by Latin *jocus* 'joke') < Latin *jucundus* < *juvare* 'please, help'] —**jocundity** /jə kúndəti/ *n* —**jocundly** *adv*

Jodhpur /jódpoor/ city in northwestern India, in the state of Rajasthan. Population: 666,279 (1991).

jodhpurs /jódpərz/ *npl* riding breeches that are wide at the hip and narrow round the calves, often with reinforced patches at the knee and thigh where the rider's legs grip the horse [Late 19C. After JODHPUR]

Jodrell Bank Experimental Station /jóddrəl-/ observatory in Cheshire, northwestern England, with a giant radio telescope

Joe /jō/, **joe** *n* an ordinary man (*informal*) [Late 18C. Familiar form of the name *Joseph*]

Joe Bloggs /-blógz/ *n* the average man in the street (*informal*)

Joe Blow /-blō/ *n Aus, N Am* same as **Joe Bloggs** (*informal*)

joe job *n* (*informal*) 1. *Can* a boring or menial task 2. ONLINE same as **spoof** *n* (sense 3)

Joel /jō əl/ *n* 1. in the Bible, a Hebrew prophet who lived in the 6th century BC 2. a book of the Bible that contains the prophecies traditionally attributed to Joel, dating from the years following the Israelites' Babylonian exile. See table at **Bible**

Joe Public *n* the average member of the general public, or ordinary people considered collectively ○ *find out what Joe Public thinks about these issues*

joe-pye weed /jō pī-/ *n* a tall perennial plant with whorled leaves. Flowers: small, pink or purple, in clusters. Native to: North America. Latin name: *Eupatorium maculatum* or *Eupatorium purpureum*. [Early 19C. After *Joe Pye*, Native American turned into this plant according to a traditional story]

Joe Soap *n* used as a humorous way for somebody to refer to himself or herself, especially when feeling put upon (*informal*)

joey[1] /jō i/ *n Aus* a young animal, especially a kangaroo still young enough to be carried in its mother's pouch [Mid-19C. < Aboriginal *joè*]

joey[2] /jō i/ *n regional* the smallest or weakest piglet in a litter [Origin ?]

REGIONAL NOTE See ***underling.***

Joffre /zhóffrə/, **Joseph** (1852–1931) French general. He was commander in chief of the French army during the first two years of World War I. Full name **Joffre, Joseph Jacques Césaire**

> 'If the women working in the factories stopped for twenty minutes, France would lose the war.'
> [Joseph Joffre. Quoted in *La Grande Guerre 1914–18*, Marc Ferro; 1969]

jog /jog/ *v* (**jogs, jogging, jogged**) 1. *vi* TROT to run at a slow steady pace ○ *He jogged across the road to the*

shop. **2.** *vi* RUN FOR EXERCISE to run at a slow steady pace as a fitness exercise ○ *She jogs round the park every morning.* **3.** *vi* GO SLOWLY BUT STEADILY to move along at a slow steady pace ○ *The little steam train jogged along the track.* **4.** *vi* PLOD to progress at a slow dull pace ○ *How are things? – Oh, you know: jogging along.* **5.** *vt* NUDGE SOMETHING to give a light push or shake to something ○ *A hand jogged his elbow and he turned.* **6.** *vt* REMIND SOMEBODY to cause somebody to remember something ○ *thought the photo might have jogged your memory* ■ *n* **1.** SPELL OF RUNNING a spell of slow steady running for exercise ○ *I'm going for a quick jog.* **2.** SLOW SPEED a slow steady pace or motion ○ *moving along at a jog* **3.** NUDGE a light push or shake **4.** REMINDER something that reminds somebody ○ *a hint that might give your memory a jog* [Mid-16C. Origin ?]

jogger /jóggər/ *n* somebody who runs at a moderate pace, often over long distances, for exercise ■ **joggers** *npl* loose-fitting trousers with an elasticated waist and ankles, used for jogging

jogging /jógging/ *n* a fitness or recreational activity that involves running at a moderate pace, often over long distances

joggle /jóggʼl/ *n* **1.** SHAKING ACTION a gentle shaking motion or action **2.** MASONRY JOINT a joint between two pieces of masonry or concrete, in which a projection on one fits into a recess of the other ■ *v* (**-gles, -gling, -gled**) **1.** *vti* SHAKE to shake something gently, or be shaken ○ *The table joggled and my drink spilt all over the place.* **2.** *vt* FIX MASONRY WITH JOGGLE to join pieces of masonry or concrete with a joggle [Early 18C. Origin ?]

Jogjakarta /jóg jə káártə/ city in southwestern Indonesia, on the island of Java. Population: 477,073 (1997).

jog trot *n* **1.** a slow steady running pace **2.** a dull steady pace of life ○ *things going on at a jog trot*

Johannesburg /jō hánnəss burg/ city in northeastern South Africa, and the capital of Gauteng Province. It originally developed as the centre of a gold-mining region. Population: 3,225,796 (2001).

Johannine /jō hánnīn/ *adj* relating to the apostle John or to the books of the Bible attributed to him [Mid-19C. < late Latin *Joannes* 'John']

Johari window /jō hári-/ *n* a graphical representation of how people give and receive information, used to help people understand interpersonal communication [late 20C. After the first names of Joseph Luft and Harry Ingham, inventors of the system]

john /jon/ *n N Am* same as **toilet** (sense 1) (*informal*) [Early 20C. < the name *John*]

John /jon/ *n* **1.** a book of the Bible, the fourth of the gospels in which the life and teachings of Jesus Christ are described, traditionally attributed to St John **2.** a name for three books of the Bible, originally written as letters and traditionally attributed to St John ▶ see table at **Bible**

John /jon/, **St** (*d.* 101?) one of the 12 apostles of Jesus Christ. He helped organize the early church throughout Palestine and Asia Minor. By tradition he is the author of the fourth Gospel, three Epistles, and Revelations in the Bible.

John (1167–1216) king of England. The youngest son of Henry II, he succeeded his brother Richard I as king (1199–1216). He was forced to issue the Magna Carta in 1215 after demands by the barons of England for constitutional reform. Known as **John Lackland**

John II (1319–64) king of France. He came to the throne in 1350. He was captured by the English (1356) but allowed to return to France to raise a ransom. Failing to do so, he returned to captivity. Known as **John the Good**

John IV (1604–56) king of Portugal. He proclaimed himself king following the overthrow of Spanish rule (1640), and founded the Braganza dynasty.

John VI (1769–1826) king of Portugal. He fled to Brazil following Napoleon's invasion of Portugal (1807), became king in 1816, and returned to Portugal in 1821. He granted Brazil independence (1822).

John (of Gaunt) /-gáwnt/, **Duke of Lancaster** (1340–99) English soldier and politician. The fourth son of Edward III, he fought the French and Spanish

during the Hundred Years' War. In England, he acted as a peacemaker during the reign of his nephew Richard II.

John (of Salisbury) /jon/ (1115?–80) English cleric, philosopher, and humanist. He was a leader of the 12th-century literary renaissance, and wrote on government, philosophy, and education. Afterwards he became bishop of Chartres. He wrote about the lives of St Thomas à Becket and St Anselm.

John (of the Cross), St (1542–91) Spanish poet and mystic. With St Teresa of Ávila he founded the contemplative order of Discalced Carmelites (1568). His mystical poems include 'Dark Night of the Soul'. Born **Yepes y Álvarez, Juan de**

John (the Baptist), St (8? BC–AD 27?) Judaean prophet. He is described in the gospels as the cousin and precursor of Jesus Christ. He was beheaded at the behest of Salome.

John, Augustus (1878–1961) British painter. The brother of Gwen John, he is known for his portraits of contemporary figures. Full name **John, Augustus Edwin**

John, Sir Elton (*b.* 1947) British rock singer and pianist. His partnership with lyricist Bernie Taupin produced a string of international hits. His songs include 'Can You Feel the Love Tonight' (1994) and 'Candle in the Wind', which was revised and reissued in commemoration of Princess Diana in 1997 and became the bestselling single of all time. Born **Dwight, Reginald**. Full name **John, Sir Elton Hercules**

John, Gwen (1876–1939) British painter. The sister of Augustus John, many of her works are portraits of women.

John Barleycorn /-baárli kawrn/ *n* (*literary or humorous*) **1.** the personification of alcoholic drink **2.** *Scotland* barley personified as the source of malt liquor

John Birch Society /-búrch-/ *n* a right-wing political organization formed in the United States to combat Communism

John Bull /-bool/ *n* **1.** the personification of England and the English people **2.** an Englishman, especially one regarded as embodying Englishness [Late 18C. After a character in *Law is a Bottomless Pit* (1712), by J. Arbuthnot] —**John Bullish** *adj*

John Doe /-dó/ *n N Am* **1.** an average man affected by everyday events (*informal*) **2.** a man or boy in a legal proceeding whose identity is either not known or not revealed

John Dory /-dáwri/ *n* a deep-sea fish with a large flat olive-yellow body, long dorsal spines, and large jaws. Native to: eastern Atlantic, Mediterranean. Latin name: *Zeus faber*.

Johne's disease /yónəz-/ *n* a chronic disease of sheep, cattle, and other domestic animals, with symptoms of diarrhoea and loss of weight, caused by a bacterium that is related to the tuberculosis bacterium [Early 20C. After H. A. *Johne* (1839–1910), German veterinary surgeon]

John Hancock /-hán kok/ *n US* somebody's signature (*informal*) [After the first person to sign the US Declaration of Independence]

John Henry /-hénri/ *n* **1.** in US folklore, an African American hero renowned for his great strength. He died after beating a steam drill in a contest of endurance. **2.** *N Am* somebody's signature (*informal*) [Partly after JOHN HANCOCK]

johnny /jónni/ (*plural* **-nies**) *n* **1.** same as **condom** (*slang*) **2.** a man or boy (*dated informal*) **3.** *US* a short gown that ties at the back, worn in hospitals by patients [Late 17C. < *Johnny*, familiar form of the name *John*]

Johnny Canuck /jónni kə núk/ *n Can* a personification of Canada, in the form of a strong clean-cut young man, often a lumberjack

Johnny-come-lately (*plural* **Johnny-come-latelies** or **Johnnies-come-lately**) *n* a recent arrival at a place, group, position, or point of view (*informal*) ○ *these Johnny-come-latelies and their 'new' ideas*

Johnny Reb /-réb/ *n US* a Confederate soldier in the American Civil War (*informal*) [Mid-19C. Shortening of *Johnny Rebel*]

John o'Groats /-ə gróts/ tourist village on the northeastern tip of Scotland. The distance between John o'Groats and Land's End in Cornwall is the longest between two places in mainland Great Britain, 1,405 km/873 mi.

John Paul I /jón páwl/, **Pope** (1912–78) He died 34 days after becoming pope in 1978. Born **Luciani, Albino**

John Paul II, **Pope** (*b.* 1920) In 1978 he became both the first ever Polish-born pope and the first non-Italian pope since 1523. Born **Wojtyła, Karol**

'Science can purify religion from error and superstition. Religion can purify science from idolatry and false absolutes.' [John Paul II. Quoted in *Galileo, A Life*, James Reston; 1994]

Johns /jonz/, **Jasper** (*b.* 1930) US artist. His work was an important influence on pop art, and features such imagery as the US flag.

'Sometimes I see it and then paint it. Other times I paint it and then see it. Both are impure situations, and I prefer neither.' [Jasper Johns. Quoted in *Sixteen Americans*, Dorothy C. Miller (ed.); 1959]

Johnson /jónss'n/, **Amy** (1903–41) British aviator. She made record solo flights to Australia (1930), Tokyo (1931), and the Cape of Good Hope and back (1936), and flew the Atlantic in 1933 with her husband. She was killed in an air crash.

'Had I been a man I might have explored the Poles or climbed Mount Everest, but as it was my spirit found outlet in the air.' [Amy Johnson. Quoted in *Myself When Young*, Margot Asquith (ed.); 1938]

Johnson, Andrew (1808–75) 17th president of the United States (1865–69). A Democrat, he was Abraham Lincoln's vice president (1865), and succeeded to the presidency after Lincoln's assassination in April 1865. As president, he withstood an impeachment by Republicans opposed to his conciliatory Reconstruction policies. See table at **president**

'The only safety of the nation lies in a generous and expansive plan of conciliation.' [Andrew Johnson. Quoted in *The Critical Year: A Study of Andrew Johnson*, Howard K. Beale; 1930]

Johnson, Claudia Alta Taylor (*b.* 1912) US first lady (1963–69). She took an active interest in ecological issues and in her husband's war-on-poverty programme. Known as **Lady Bird**

Johnson, Jack (1878–1946) US boxer. He became the first African American to win the world heavyweight boxing championship (1908). Full name **Johnson, John Arthur**

'It was not the fights but the fights to get those fights that proved the hardest part of the struggle. It was my color.' [Jack Johnson. Quoted in *World's Great Men of Color*, Joel Augustus Rogers; 1947]

Lyndon B. Johnson and Lady Bird Johnson

Johnson, Lyndon B. (1908–73) 36th president of the United States. A Democrat, he was John F. Kennedy's vice president and became president when Kennedy was assassinated, winning a full term the following year. During his presidency (1963–69), increased US involvement in the Vietnam War made him unpopular, and diverted attention from

his programme of social reform, the 'Great Society'. See table at **president**. Full name **Johnson, Lyndon Baines**. Known as **LBJ**

> 'It is a common failing of totalitarian regimes that they cannot really understand the nature of our democracy. They mistake dissent for disloyalty. They mistake restlessness for a rejection of policy...They mistake individual speeches for public policy.'
> [Lyndon B. Johnson, *Speech, San Antonio, Texas*; 29 September 1967]

Johnson, Magic (*b.* 1959) US basketball player. He played guard for the Los Angeles Lakers (1979–91, 92, 96), and is regarded as one of the greatest players of the game. Born **Johnson, Earvin, Jr.**

Johnson, Philip (*b.* 1906) US architect. His eclectic designs include the AT&T headquarters (1984) in New York City. Full name **Johnson, Philip Cortelyou**

> 'Architecture is the art of how to waste space.'
> [Philip Johnson, *New York Times*; 27 December 1964]

Johnson, Robert (1911–38) US blues singer and guitarist. His songs influenced Chicago blues and 1960s rock.

Johnson, Samuel (1709–84) British critic, poet, and lexicographer. His works include his *Dictionary of the English Language* (1755), an edition of Shakespeare (1765), and *Lives of the Poets* (1779–81). He founded two periodicals, *The Rambler* (1750–52) and *The Idler* (1758–60), and his witty conversation is recorded in James Boswell's biography of him. —**Johnsonian** /jon sṓni ən/ *adj*

> 'I am not yet so lost in lexicography as to forget that words are daughters of earth...'
> [Samuel Johnson. Preface, *A Dictionary of the English Language*; 1755]

> 'Language is the dress of thought.'
> [Samuel Johnson, 'Cowley', *Lives of the English Poets*; 1779–81]

Johnson grass *n* a coarse perennial variety of sorghum often grown as forage. Native to: Mediterranean. Latin name: *Sorghum halepense*. [After William *Johnson*, an Alabama planter]

Johnston /jónstən/, **George** (1912–70) Australian writer. His novels include *My Brother Jack* (1964) and *Clean Straw for Nothing* (1969). He was married to Charmian Clift. Full name **Johnstone, George Henry**

John Thomas *n* an offensive term for a penis (*slang*) [Origin ?]

Johor Strait /jə háwr-/ narrow strait running between Singapore and Malaysia

joie de vivre /zhwaá də veévrə/ *n* energy and love of life [Late 19C. < French, 'joy of living']

join /joyn/ *v* (**joins, joining, joined**) **1.** *vti* **BRING OR COME TOGETHER** to meet, or make two or more things meet, and become linked or united ○ *where the A4 joins the M4* **2.** *vt* **FIX THINGS TOGETHER** to put or fix two or more things together ○ *Join the wing to the body with glue.* **3.** *vt* **MAKE CONNECTION BETWEEN THINGS** to establish a connection between two or more things, e.g. by drawing a line between them ○ *join the dots* **4.** *vti* **BECOME PART OF GROUP** to become a member of something such as a club, social group, company, team, or other organization ○ *I've joined the Mountaineering Club.* **5.** *vt* **DO SAME AS SOMEBODY** to agree to do the same as somebody ○ *I'm sure my colleagues will want to join me in thanking you for your visit today.* **6.** *vt* **UNITE PEOPLE IN PARTNERSHIP** to bring two or more people into a partnership such as a marriage **7.** *vt* **MEET SOMEBODY** to go to meet somebody ○ *I'll join you later.* **8.** *vt* **SHARE SOMEBODY'S COMPANY** to enter into the company of another person ○ *Do you mind if I join you?* **9.** *vti* **BE ADJACENT** to be next to something or to each other ○ *This room joins the bathroom.* ■ *n* **JOINT** a place where two or more things have been joined ○ *You can hardly see the join.* [13C. Via Old French *joign-*, present stem of *joindre* < Latin *jungere* 'join'] —**joinable** *adj*

ORIGIN The Indo-European word from which *join* is ultimately derived is also the ancestor of English *adjust*, *conjugal*, *jostle*, *joust*, *jugular*, *juxtapose*, *subjugate*, *yoga*, *yoke*, and *zygo-*.

join in *vti* to take part in an activity along with other people ○ *Can I join in?*

join up *vi* **1.** to enlist as a member of one of the armed forces, especially at the outbreak of hostilities **2.** to meet somebody for a joint activity ○ *They join up with the same friends every year to go on holiday.*

joinder /jóyndər/ *n* **1. ACT OF JOINING** a joining or bringing together of two things (*formal*) **2. JOINING OF LEGAL PARTIES** a joining of two parties in a single lawsuit **3. COMBINING OF LEGAL PROCEEDINGS** a joining of two causes of action or two defences in a single lawsuit **4. ACCEPTANCE OF ISSUE IN LAWSUIT** a formal acceptance of an issue offered in a lawsuit [Early 17C. < Anglo Norman < Old French *joindre* 'to join' (see JOIN)]

joined-up *adj* **1.** describes handwriting in which each letter of a word is joined to the next, especially by children learning to write in this way **2.** having or showing coherence and logical connection in planning or execution ○ *joined-up thinking* ○ *joined-up government*

joiner /jóynər/ *n* **1.** somebody who makes wooden components for buildings, especially finished woodwork **2.** somebody who readily joins clubs, societies, or organizations (*informal*)

joinery /jóynəri/ *n* **1.** the visible finished woodwork in a building, e.g. door frames and window frames **2.** the work of a joiner, or the techniques that a joiner uses

joint /joynt/ *adj* **1. OWNED IN COMMON** owned in common by two or more people or concerns ○ *joint assets* **2. COMBINED** existing and operating in combination ○ *the joint ravages of the weather and pollution* **3. SHARING SAME ROLE** sharing the same role or position with another person or body ○ *My brother and I were appointed joint executors of her will.* **4. DONE TOGETHER** done or produced together with others ○ *A joint statement was issued by the three party leaders.* ■ *n* **1. JUNCTION BETWEEN BONES** a part of the body where bones are connected, e.g. the knee, elbow, or skull. Many joints have supporting ligaments, protective cartilage, and a particular range of movement, while others such as those between the bones of the vault of the skull are immobile. **2.** ZOOL **JUNCTION BETWEEN SEGMENTS OF INVERTEBRATE BODY** any of the points of connection between movable segments of the body in an insect, spider, crab, or other invertebrate **3.** BOT **DIVIDING POINT ON PLANT STEM** the place on a plant stem from which a leaf or branch grows **4. PLACE WHERE PARTS ARE JOINED** the place where parts or pieces of something are joined together **5. PIECE OF MEAT** a large piece of meat prepared and cooked for several people, especially one that is roasted **6. VENUE** a place of entertainment, e.g. a nightclub, especially one considered cheap or disreputable (*slang*) **7. PRISON** a prison or similar penal institution (*slang*) **8. CANNABIS CIGARETTE** a cigarette containing cannabis (*slang*) **9. TABOO TERM** a highly offensive term for a penis (*taboo slang*) **10.** GEOL **CRACK IN ROCK** a crack or fissure in rock, without any looseness or displacement of the surrounding mass **11.** PUBL **HINGE OF BOOK COVER** either of the creases between the spine and the front and back covers of a book, especially a hardback **12. PLACE** a building or dwelling of any kind (*slang*) ■ *v* (**joints, jointing, jointed**) **1.** *vt* **FIT PARTS TOGETHER** to fit or fix parts together by means of a joint **2.** *vt* **DIVIDE CARCASS INTO PIECES** to cut a carcass into pieces of meat for cooking **3.** *vt* **PLANE EDGE OF BOARD** to plane and shape the edge of a board so that it fits with another edge to form a joint **4.** *vi* **FORM JOINTS DURING GROWTH** to form joints in the stem during the growth process (*refers to cereal plants*) [13C. < French, past participle of *joindre* (see JOIN)] —**jointed** *adj* —**jointing** *n* ◇ **out of joint 1.** dislocated or painfully displaced **2.** disturbed or disrupted, usually as a result of some major change or upheaval

joint account *n* a bank account held in the names of more than one person, typically spouses or partners

Joint Chiefs of Staff *npl* the most important military advisory group to the president of the United States, consisting of the Chiefs of Staff of the Army and Air Force, the commandant of the Marine Corps, and the Chief of Naval Operations

joint defence *n* in legal proceedings, a defence strategy in which two or more defendants join and cooperate with one another so that their cases are heard together

jointer /jóyntər/ *n* **1.** a tool for pointing the mortar in brickwork or stonework after it has been laid **2.** a long plane used to shape the edges of planks into joints

jointly /jóyntli/ *adv* in conjunction with, or in co-operation with, a person or organization ○ *The copyright is jointly owned by the composer and the publisher.*

jointress /jóyntrəss/ *n* a woman on whom property has been settled by her husband at the time of their marriage

joint stock *n* stock held jointly, especially in a joint-stock company, a commercial enterprise whose capital is in shares that individual holders may transfer without the consent of the whole body

jointure /jóynchər/ *n* an estate or property settled by a husband on his wife at the time of their marriage, to take effect in the event of his death

joint venture *n* a business enterprise jointly undertaken by two or more companies, who share the outlay, risks, and profits (*hyphenated*) ■ *vi* to enter into a business enterprise jointly with another or others (*informal*) —**joint venturing** *n*

jointworm /jóynt wurm/ *n* the larva of some wasps that forms a weakening swelling at the stem joint of a cereal plant. Family: Eurytomidae.

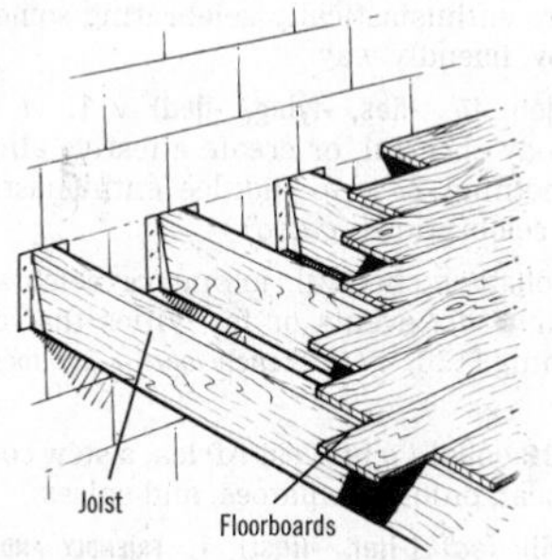

joist

joist /joyst/ *n* any of the parallel beams of wood, metal, or concrete that support a floor, roof, or ceiling [14C. < Old French *giste* 'beam supporting a bridge' < Latin *jacere* 'lie down']

jojoba /hō hṓbə/ (*plural* **-bas**) *n* **1.** a waxy oil derived from the seeds of a desert tree. Use: shampoos, cosmetics. (*often used before a noun*) **2.** a desert bush or small tree whose seeds yield jojoba. Native to: southwestern North America. Latin name: *Simmondsia chinensis*. [Early 20C. Via Mexican Spanish < a Native American language]

joke /jōk/ *n* **1. FUNNY STORY** a story, anecdote, or wordplay that is intended to amuse **2. CAUSE OF AMUSEMENT** anything said or done to make people laugh ○ *dressed up the dog in a hat and sunglasses as a joke* **3. SOMETHING INADEQUATE** somebody or something that is laughably inadequate or absurd (*informal*) ○ *The surroundings were pleasant enough but the food was a joke.* ■ *v* (**jokes, joking, joked**) **1.** *vti* **MAKE JOKES** to tell funny stories or say or do things to make somebody laugh **2.** *vi* **NOT TO BE SERIOUS** to be trying to be amusing, rather than serious or in earnest ○ *We knew he was only joking.* **3.** *vt* **TEASE SOMEBODY** to make fun of somebody (*archaic*) [Late 17C. < Latin *jocus* 'jest, wordplay'] ◇ **beyond a joke** having become a serious matter ◇ **be no joke** to be a serious or difficult matter (*informal*) ○ *It's no joke driving to work in the rush hour every day.*

joker /jṓkər/ *n* **1. TELLER OR PLAYER OF JOKES** a frequent teller or player of jokes **2. CARD BEARING PICTURE OF JESTER** an extra playing card in a pack, bearing a picture of a jester, that in some games can be substituted for other cards **3. AMUSING ECCENTRIC PERSON** an amusing, entertaining, or entertainingly eccentric person (*informal*) **4. THOUGHTLESS OR INCONSIDERATE PERSON** somebody whose thoughtless or inconsiderate action is highly annoying (*informal*) ○ *I'm looking for the joker who double-parked outside my front door.* ◇ **the joker in the pack** an unpredictable element that makes planning or projections difficult (*informal*)

jokey /jṓki/ (**-ier, -iest**), **joky** *adj* good-humoured and amusing, or full of jokes —**jokily** *adv* —**jokiness** *n*

jokingly /jṓkingli/ *adv* with the intention of making a joke rather than a serious comment or suggestion

joky *adj* another spelling of **jokey**

jol /jol/ *S Africa* (*informal*) *n* a party, or a good time ▪ *vi* to party or have a good time [Mid-20C. < Afrikaans, 'dance, party']

jolie laide /zhólli léd/ (*plural* **jolies laides** /*pronunc. same*/) *n* a woman whose facial features are not pretty in conventional terms, but nevertheless have a distinctive harmony or charm [< French < *jolie* 'pretty' + *laide* 'ugly']

Joliot-Curie /zhólli ō kyoóri/, **Frédéric** (1900–58) French physicist. Together with his wife, Irène Joliot-Curie (the daughter of Marie and Pierre Curie), he produced the first radioisotope artificially. They were joint winners of the Nobel Prize in chemistry (1935). Born **Joliot, Jean-Frédéric**

Joliot-Curie, **Irène** (1897–1956) French physicist. Together with her husband, Frédéric Joliot-Curie, she produced the first radioisotope artificially. They were joint winners of the Nobel Prize in chemistry (1935). Born **Curie, Irène**

Jolley /jólli/, **Elizabeth** (*b.* 1923) British-born Australian writer. Her works include radio plays, short stories, and novels, including *The Well* (1986). Full name **Jolley, Monica Elizabeth**

jollification /jóllifi káysh'n/ *n* the activities of people who are enthusiastically celebrating something in a happy, friendly way

jollify /jólli fī/ (**-fies, -fying, -fied**) *v* **1.** *vt* to make somebody cheerful, or create a festive atmosphere in something **2.** *vi* to indulge enthusiastically in happy celebrations (*dated*)

jollity /jólləti/ *n* cheerful, joking, or celebratory behaviour ▪ *npl* events or festivities that celebrate something [13C. < Old French *jolite* < *joli* 'merry, pleasant']

jollof rice /jóllǝf-/ *n* in West Africa, a stew containing rice, meat, onions, tomatoes, and spices

jolly /jólli/ *adj* (**-lier, -liest**) **1. FRIENDLY AND CHEERFUL** friendly and cheerful, especially in a hearty or exuberant way ○ *a jolly pink-cheeked woman* **2. HAPPY** happily festive in tone or mood (*dated*) **3. ENJOYABLE** bringing pleasure or enjoyment (*dated informal*) ○ *A picnic would be jolly.* ▪ *adv* **VERY** used to emphasize the extent to which something is good or bad (*dated informal*) ○ *Jolly nice of you to come.* [13C. < Old French *joli* 'merry, pleasant'] ◇ **get your jollies** *N Am* to get pleasure out of something (*slang*) ◇ **jolly well** a phrase used in annoyance to add emphasis (*dated*) ○ *I'm not jolly well going to stand for it.*

jolly along *vt* to keep somebody happy or cooperative by using flattery or encouragement (*informal*)

jolly up *vt* to make a person, place, or situation more lively or cheerful (*informal*) ○ *I thought some music might jolly things up a bit.*

jollyboat /jólli bōt/ *n* a small boat carried on a larger ship, often one kept hoisted at the stern of the ship [Late 17C. Origin ?]

Jolly Roger

Jolly Roger /-rójjǝr/ *n* the flag traditionally flown by a pirate ship, depicting a white skull and crossbones against a black background [Late 18C. Origin ?]

jollytail /jólli tayl/ (*plural* **-tails** or *same*) *n Aus* a small fish whose young are fried and eaten whole. Native to: Australasia. Latin name: *Galaxias maculatus*.

Jolson /jṓlssǝn/, **Al** (1886–1950) Russian-born US entertainer. He was known for his minstrel-style singing in blackface makeup. He starred in the first talking picture, *The Jazz Singer* (1927). Born **Yoelson, Asa**

> 'You ain't heard nothin' yet, folks.'
> [Al Jolson, *The Jazz Singer*; 1927]

jolt /jōlt/ *v* (**jolts, jolting, jolted**) **1.** *vti* **SHAKE OR JERK VIOLENTLY** to shake or jerk suddenly and violently, or make somebody or something shake or jerk suddenly and violently, especially as a result of a sudden movement **2.** *vi* **BUMP UP AND DOWN** to bump up and down or shake from side to side while moving **3.** *vt* **STARTLE SOMEBODY INTO REALITY** to startle somebody out of a daydream, fantasy, or other state of semi-awareness ▪ *n* **1. VIOLENT MOVEMENT** a sudden violent movement or blow ○ *The train moved off again with a series of jolts.* **2. SHOCK OR REMINDER** an emotional shock or a sharp reminder [Late 16C. Origin ?] —**joltingly** *adv* —**jolty** *adj*

Jon. *abbr* BIBLE Jonah

Jonah[1] /jṓnǝ/ *n* **1.** in the Bible, a Hebrew prophet of the 8th century BC who was swallowed by a great fish and vomited out three days later, unharmed **2.** a book of the Bible that tells the story of Jonah, whose preaching caused the Assyrians to repent their wickedness. See table at **Bible**

Jonah[2] /jṓnǝ/ *n* somebody who brings bad luck [Late 16C. < JONAH [1]] —**Jonahesque** /jṓnǝ ésk/ *adj*

Jonathan /jónnǝthǝn/ *n* in the Bible, the eldest son of King Saul and close friend of David, who was killed in battle against the Philistines (1 Samuel 13–2 Samuel 21)

jones /jōnz/ *n* **1.** *US* **ADDICTION** an addiction, especially a heroin addiction (*slang*) **2.** *US* **WITHDRAWAL** drug withdrawal symptoms, especially from heroin (*slang*) **3.** *US* **HABITUAL CRAVING** an all-consuming craving or desire for something (*slang*) **4.** *also* **Jones TABOO TERM** a highly offensive term for a penis (*taboo*) [Late 20C. Origin ?]

Jones, **Alan** (*b.* 1947) Australian motor-racing driver. He won the 1980 Formula One world championship.

Jones, **Inigo** (1573–1652) English architect and stage designer. He introduced the Palladian style into English architecture. His designs include the Queen's House at Greenwich (1616–35).

Jones, **John Paul** (1747–92) Scottish-born US naval officer. He captured or destroyed many British ships during the American War of Independence.

Joneses /jṓnziz/ *npl* neighbours, especially somebody's next-door neighbours [Late 19C. < *Jones*, common British surname] ◇ **keep up with the Joneses** to maintain a position of equal social status with your neighbours, especially in terms of possessions

jongleur /zhoN glúr/ *n* a wandering minstrel of medieval times who travelled about singing the compositions of troubadours or reciting epic poems in noble households or royal courts [Late 18C. Via French < Latin *joculator* 'jester' < *jocus* 'joke']

Jönköping /jõn chŏping/ city and capital of Jönköping County, in southern Sweden. Population: 115,897 (1998).

jonquil

jonquil /jóngkwil/ *n* **1.** a variety of narcissus. Flowers: small, fragrant, yellow. Native to: southern Europe. Latin name: *Narcissus jonquilla*. **2.** the golden-yellow colour of a jonquil [Early 17C. Via modern Latin

jonquilla or French *jonquille* < Spanish *junquillo* 'little rush' < *junco* 'rush'] —**jonquil** *adj*

Jonson /jónss'n/, **Ben** (1572–1637) English playwright and poet. His plays include brilliant comedies such as *Volpone* (1606) as well as classical tragedies. James I appointed him poet laureate in 1616. Full name **Jonson, Benjamin**

> 'Helter skelter, hang sorrow, care'll kill a cat, up-tails all, and a louse for the hang-man.'
> [Ben Jonson, *Every Man in His Humour*; 1598]

jook /joŏk/ (**jooks, jooking, jooked**), **juks** (**juks, juking, juked**) *vt* (*used in Black English*) **1. PRICK OR STAB SOMEBODY OR SOMETHING** to pierce somebody or something with a pointed or sharp implement such as a needle or a knife (*slang*) **2. JAB OR POKE SOMEBODY OR SOMETHING** to push somebody or something with a short jabbing or poking movement (*slang*) **3. TABOO TERM** a highly offensive term meaning to have penetrative sex with somebody (*taboo*) [Late 20C. Origin ?]

jootha /jṓothǝ/ *n S Asia* food that is considered polluted, usually because it has come in contact with somebody's saliva [< Hindi]

Joplin /jópplin/, **Janis** (1943–70) US rock singer. She is known for her raw and emotionally charged renditions of rock and blues songs.

Scott Joplin

Joplin, **Scott** (1868–1917) US composer. He is best known for his ragtime piano music.

joram *n* HIST another spelling of **jorum**

Jordaens /yawr daánss/, **Jacob** (1593–1678) Flemish painter. His large baroque works feature subjects such as banquets, revelry, and genre scenes.

Jordan

Jordan /jáwrd'n/ **1.** country in Southwest Asia, bordered by Syria, Iraq, Saudi Arabia, the Gulf of Aqaba, Israel, and the West Bank. Language: Arabic. Currency: Jordanian dinar. Capital: Amman. Population: 5,460,265 (2003). Area: 89,556 sq. km/34,578 sq. mi. Official name **Hashemite Kingdom of Jordan 2.** river in Southwest Asia that rises in the Anti-Lebanon Mountains of Lebanon and flows south through the Sea of Galilee before emptying into the Dead Sea. Length: 320 km/200 mi. —**Jordanian** /jawr dáyni ǝn/ *adj, n*

Jordan, **Michael** (*b.* 1963) US basketball player. He played for the Chicago Bulls from 1984 to 1993, and again from 1995 to 1998. He is considered by many to be the greatest player in basketball history. Known as **Air Jordan**

> 'Talent wins games, but teamwork and in-

telligence win championships.'
[Michael Jordan, *I Can't Accept Not Trying*; 1994]

Jordan curve *n* in mathematics, any simple closed curve, e.g. a circle or an ellipse [Early 20C. After M. E. C. Jordan (1838–1922), French mathematician]

Jordan curve theorem *n* in geometry, a theorem holding that every simple closed curve divides a plane into two regions and serves as their boundary

jorts /jawrts/ *npl* Carib light foods eaten between meals or in place of meals (*informal*)

jorum /jáwrəm/, **joram** *n* a large drinking bowl or its contents [Mid-18C. Origin ?]

Joseph /jōzif/ *n* in the Bible, the son of Jacob and Rachel, sold into slavery in Egypt by his jealous brothers

Joseph /jōzif/ **1.** ♦ **Akiba ben Joseph 2.** ♦ **Saadia ben Joseph**

Joseph, St (*fl* 1st century BC) According to the Bible, he was a carpenter of Nazareth and the husband of Mary, the mother of Jesus Christ

Joseph II (1741–90) Holy Roman Emperor. He was the son of Francis I and Maria Theresa. As emperor (1765–90), he saw his reforms frustrated by insurrection and the distractions of war.

'Convinced...of the...great benefits accruing to religion and the State from true Christian tolerance, we...grant the right of private worship to the Lutheran, Calvinist and non-Uniate Greek religions.'
[Joseph II, *Edict of Toleration*; 13 October 1781]

Joseph Bonaparte Gulf /jōsəf bónə paart-/ inlet of the Timor Sea on the north coast of Australia, extending from Western Australia into the Northern Territory. It is 320 km/200 mi. wide.

Joséphine /jōzə feen/ (1763–1814) empress of the French. She married the future Napoleon I in 1796 and was empress from 1804 until the childless marriage was dissolved in 1809. Born **Pagerie, Marie Joséphine Rose Tascher de la**

Joseph of Arimathea /-árrimə thee'ə/, **St** (*fl* AD 1st century) According to the Bible, he asked Pontius Pilate for the body of Jesus Christ, and buried it in his own tomb (Matthew 27)

Josephson effect /jōzifs'n-/ *n* the passage of an electric current through a thin insulating layer between two superconducting metals [Late 20C. After Brian David *Josephson* (b. 1940), British physicist]

Josephson junction *n* in electrical or electronic circuits, a junction that utilizes the Josephson effect, consisting of two superconducting materials separated by a thin insulating layer. In a computer memory, a Josephson junction acts as a high-speed switch.

Josephus /jō seéfəss/, **Flavius** (AD 37?–100?) Jewish historian and general. His works include a history of the Jewish revolt against Rome (AD 66) and a history of the Jews. Born **Matthias, Joseph Ben**

josh /josh/ *v* (*informal*) **1.** *vti* to make fun of somebody in a friendly, good-humoured way **2.** *vi* to joke or indulge in banter with somebody [Mid-19C. Origin ?] —**josher** *n* —**joshingly** *adv*

Josh. *abbr* BIBLE Joshua

Joshua /jóshoo ə/ *n* **1.** in the Bible, Moses' successor as leader of the Israelites **2.** a book of the Bible that describes the Hebrew invasion and partition of Canaan under Joshua's command. See table at **Bible**

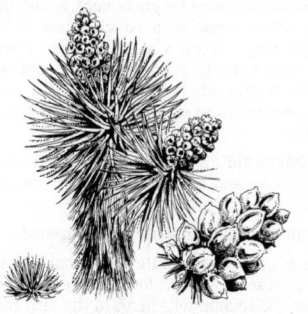
Joshua tree

Joshua tree *n* a small tree-shaped yucca with sword-shaped leaves. Flowers: white, in clusters. Native to: deserts of southwestern United States. Latin name: *Yucca brevifolia*. [Mid-19C. Probably after JOSHUA, because the tree's branching shape resembles somebody brandishing a spear (Joshua 8:18)]

Josiah /jō sí ə/ (648?–609 BC) king of Judah. He is credited in the Bible with restoring the worship of Yahweh, and was killed by the Assyrians at the Battle of Megiddo.

joss /joss/ *n* an image or statue representing a Chinese deity [Early 18C. Via Javanese *dejos* < Portuguese *deus* 'god' < Latin]

josser /jóssər/ *n* an offensive term for a man, especially one considered unintelligent or objectionable (*slang insult*) [Late 19C. < JOSS]

joss house *n* a Chinese shrine or temple containing images or statues of deities

joss stick *n* incense in the form of a stick of dried paste

jostle /jóss'l/ (-tles, -tling, -tled) *vti* to knock or bump against somebody, or push or elbow somebody deliberately, sometimes as an expression of aggression or hostility ○ *We managed to jostle our way to the front.* [Mid-16C. < JOUST] —**jostler** *n*

jot /jot/ *vt* (**jots, jotting, jotted**) to write something down hastily for later reference ○ *jotted down the title in her notebook* ■ *n* a very small amount [15C. Via Latin < Greek *iōta* (see IOTA)]

jota /khō taa, hō-/ *n* a fast Spanish dance performed with castanets in 3/4 time, usually to voice and guitar accompaniment. It is the traditional dance of Aragón. [Mid-19C. < Spanish]

jotter /jóttər/, **jotter pad** *n* **1.** a book or pad for making rough notes **2.** *Scotland* a school exercise book

jotting /jótting/ *n* a hastily written note, comment, or observation

Jotun /yōt'n, yō tōon/, **Jotunn** *n* in Norse mythology, a member of a race of giants with supernatural powers

Jotunheim /yōt'n haym, yō tōon-/ *n* in Norse mythology, the home of the giants [< Old Norse *Jotunheimar*]

Jotunn *n* MYTHOL another spelling of **Jotun**

joule /jool/ *n* the SI unit of energy or work, equal to the work done when the application point of a one newton force moves one metre in the direction of application. Symbol J [Late 19C. After James JOULE]

Joule /jool/, **James** (1818–89) British physicist. He determined the mechanical equivalent of heat. The joule, a unit of energy, is named after him. Full name **Joule, James Prescott**

Joule effect *n* an increase in heat resulting from the passage of a current through a conductor

jounce /jownss/ *vti* (**jounces, jouncing, jounced**) to bounce up and down and rock from side to side while moving, or make somebody or something move in this way ■ *n* a jolting, swaying, bouncing, or rocking movement [15C. Origin ?] —**jouncy** *adj*

jour. *abbr* **1.** journal **2.** journalist **3.** journeyman

journal /júrn'l/ *n* **1.** MAGAZINE OR PERIODICAL a magazine or periodical, especially one published by a specialist or professional body for its members, containing information and contributions relevant to their area of activity ○ *a medical journal* **2.** DETAILED PERSONAL DIARY somebody's written daily record of personal experiences, rather more elaborate and detailed than a diary, **3.** PRELIMINARY RECORD OF FINANCIAL TRANSACTIONS a book for recording daily transactions, especially in double entry book-keeping, using a formulaic style to ensure their correct entry in a ledger **4.** OFFICIAL RECORD the official daily record of proceedings kept by an association or body, especially a legislative body or parliament. The record in the British Parliament is called the Journals. **5.** MECH ENG SECTION OF SHAFT a cylindrical section of a shaft designed to rotate inside a bearing [14C. Via French, 'daily' < late Latin *diurnalis* (see DIURNAL)]

journal box *n* the metal housing of a journal and its bearing. It often serves as a lubricant store.

journalese /júrn'l eez/ *n* the style of writing supposedly associated with journalists, marked by the use of formulaic expressions (*disapproving*)

journalise *vti* another spelling of **journalize**

journalism /júrn'lizəm/ *n* **1.** the profession of gathering, editing, and publishing news reports and related articles for newspapers, magazines, television, or radio **2.** writing or reporting for the media as a literary genre or style

journalist /júrn'list/ *n* a writer or editor for a newspaper or magazine or for television or radio

journalistic /júrn'l ístik/ *adj* relating to journalism, or similar in style to journalism —**journalistically** *adv*

journalize /júrn'l īz/ (**-izes, -izing, -ized**), **journalise** (**-ises, -ising, -ised**) *vti* to keep a journal, or record something in a journal —**journalization** /júrn'l ī záysh'n/ *n* —**journalizer** *n*

~~journel~~ incorrect spelling of **journal**

journey /júrni/ *n* (*plural* **-neys**) **1.** EXPEDITION SOMEWHERE a trip or expedition from one place to another **2.** PROCESS OF DEVELOPMENT a gradual passing from one state to another regarded as more advanced, e.g. from innocence to mature awareness ○ *a spiritual journey* ■ *vi* (**-neys, -neying, -neyed**) TRAVEL SOMEWHERE to travel to a place or over a particular distance ○ *We are journeying into the unknown.* [12C. Via Old French *journee* 'day, day's work or travel' < Latin *diurnum* 'daily portion' < *diurnus* (see DIURNAL)] —**journeyer** *n*

journeyman /júrnimən/ (*plural* **-men** /-mən/) *n* (*often used before a noun*) **1.** a competent and reliable but unexceptional performer or exponent of something ○ *a good journeyman violinist* **2.** an artisan who has completed an apprenticeship and is fully trained and qualified but still works for an employer ○ *a journeyman electrician* [15C. Literally, somebody qualified to work for a daily wage rather than as an apprentice]

journo /júrnō/ (*plural* **-nos**) *n* same as **journalist** (*informal*) [Mid-20C. Contraction]

joust /jowst/ *n* MEDIEVAL TOURNAMENT a form of combat in medieval times held between two mounted knights in full armour who charged at and tried to unseat each other with a lance ■ *vi* (**jousts, jousting, jousted**) **1.** ENGAGE IN JOUST to take part in a joust **2.** ENGAGE IN CONTEST to take part in a contest against others ○ *candidates jousting for ninety minutes in a televised debate* [13C. < Old French *jouster* 'bring together' < Latin *juxta* 'close, beside'] —**jouster** *n*

J'Ouvert /zhoo váirt/ *n* Carib the Monday that is the eve of Mardi Gras, when the festivities begin [< French *jour ouvert* 'the day having been opened']

Jove /jōv/ *n* the Roman god Jupiter [14C. < Latin *Jov-*] —**Jovian** *adj* ◇ **by Jove** used to convey surprise, or to emphasize a conviction (*dated informal*)

jovial /jōvi əl/ *adj* cheerful in mood or disposition [Late 16C. Via French < Latin *jovialis* < *Jov-* 'Jove'] —**joviality** /jōvi álləti/ *n* —**jovially** *adv* —**jovialness** *n*

Jovian planet *n* any one of the four major planets, Jupiter, Uranus, Saturn, or Neptune

jowar /jə waár/ *n* S Asia PLANTS same as **sorghum** (sense 1) [Early 19C. < Hindi *jauār*]

jowl[1] /jowl/ *n* **1.** the jaw, especially the lower jaw **2.** a cheek, especially a prominent one [Old English *ceafl* < Germanic]

jowl[2] /jowl/ *n* **1.** a flaccid plump fold of flesh under somebody's chin **2.** a dewlap under the neck of cattle or a wattle on the neck of a bird [Old English *ceole* < Germanic]

jowly /jówli/ (**-ier, -iest**) *adj* with a fold of flesh hanging under the neck —**jowliness** *n*

joy /joy/ *n* **1.** GREAT HAPPINESS feelings of great happiness or pleasure, especially of an elevated or spiritual kind **2.** SOMETHING THAT BRINGS HAPPINESS a pleasurable aspect of something or source of happiness ○ *His little granddaughter was a great joy to him.* ■ *vi* (**joys, joying, joyed**) ENJOY SOMETHING to delight in something (*literary or archaic*) [12C. < French *joie* < Latin *gaudere* 'rejoice'] ◇ **no joy** no success (*informal*)

James Joyce

Joyce /joyss/, **James** (1882–1941) Irish novelist. His innovative techniques, as demonstrated in *Ulysses* (1922) and *Finnegans Wake* (1939), make him one of the most influential modern writers. Full name **Joyce, James Augustine Aloysius**

'The mystery of æsthetic like that of material creation is accomplished. The artist, like the God of the creation, remains within or behind or beyond or above his handiwork, invisible, refined out of existence, indifferent, paring his fingernails.'
[James Joyce, *A Portrait of the Artist as a Young Man*; 1916]

'Every life is many days, day after day. We walk through ourselves, meeting robbers, ghosts, giants, old men, young men, wives, widows, brothers-in-love. But always meeting ourselves.'
[James Joyce, *Ulysses*; 1922]

Joyce, William (1900–46) British traitor. He was found guilty of treason and hanged for broadcasting Nazi propaganda to Britain during World War II. Known as **Lord Haw-Haw**

joyful /jóyf'l/ *adj* **1.** full of joy, or feeling or expressing joy **2.** bringing or causing joy —**joyfully** *adv* —**joyfulness** *n*

joyless /jóyləss/ *adj* lacking in warmth or happiness —**joylessly** *adv* —**joylessness** *n*

joyous /jóy əss/ *adj* (*literary*) **1.** full of joy, especially of a fervent and unrestrained nature **2.** making people happy or joyful —**joyously** *adv* —**joyousness** *n*

joypad /jóy pad/ *n* a hand-held control mechanism for a computer game

joypop /jóy pop/ (-pops, -popping, -popped) *vi* to take illicit drugs occasionally rather than habitually (*slang*) —**joypopper** *n*

joyriding /jóy rīding/ *n* a crime that involves stealing a car and driving it dangerously at high speed —**joyride** *n*, *vi* —**joyrider** *n*

joystick /jóy stik/ *n* **1.** the control lever of an aircraft or of a small motor-powered vehicle **2.** a hand-held control stick that allows a player to control the movements of a cursor on a VDU screen or a symbol in a video game

jp *abbr* ONLINE Japan (*used in Internet addresses*) See table at **domain name**

JP *n* somebody appointed to judge minor criminal cases, perform marriages, administer oaths, and refer cases to higher courts. Full form **justice of the peace**

J particle *n* PHYS same as **J/psi particle**

jpeg /jáy peg/ *abbr* a file extension for a JPEG file. Full form **Joint Photographic Experts Group**

JPEG /jáy peg/ *n* a format for encoding high-resolution graphic images as computer files for storage and transmission. Full form **Joint Photographic Experts Group**

jpg *abbr* a file extension for a JPEG file. Full form **Joint Photographic (Experts) Group**

Jpn *abbr* **1.** Japan **2.** Japanese

J/psi particle *n* an unstable elementary particle of the meson group. It has a large mass, about 6,000 times that of an electron, and is thought to be formed from charmed quarks.

jr *abbr* junior

Jr *abbr* **1.** BIBLE Jeremiah **2.** Junior

JSD *abbr* LAW Doctor of Juristic Science [Latin *Juris Scientiae Doctor*]

JTLYK *abbr* ONLINE just to let you know (*used in e-mails or text messages*)

Juan Carlos /waán kaár loss/ (*b.* 1938) king of Spain. He became king following the death of General Franco (1975), presiding over Spain's rapid transition to democracy.

'I am very close to youth. I admire and share their desire to seek a better, more genuine world. I know that in the rebelliousness that worries so many people there can be found the great generosity of those who want open horizons.'
[Juan Carlos, *Speech, Madrid*; 1969]

Juan de Fuca, Strait of /joo ən də fyóoka/ body of water lying between Washington State, United States, and Vancouver Island, Canada, connecting the Strait of Georgia and Puget Sound to the Pacific Ocean. Length: 160 km/99 mi.

Juárez /waár ez/, **Benito Pablo** (1806–72) Mexican president and national hero. He fought against the government of General Antonio López de Santa Anna and served as president of Mexico (1861–63 and 1867–72).

Juba /jóobə/ city in southern Sudan on the River White Nile. Population: 114,980 (1993).

Jubbulpore /júbb'l poór/ former name for **Jabalpur**

jube /joob/ *n* ANZ a fruit-flavoured chewy sweet (*informal*) [Mid-20C. Shortening of JUJUBE]

jubilant /jóobilənt/ *adj* feeling or expressing great delight over a success, achievement, or victory [Mid-17C. < Latin *jubilant-*, present participle of *jubilare* 'call out, shout for joy'] —**jubilantly** *adv*

Jubilate /jóobi laáti, yóobi laá tay/ *n* Psalm 100, which is sung as a canticle in the Roman Catholic and Anglican churches. In the Latin version, it begins 'Jubilate Deo', meaning 'Rejoice in the Lord'.

jubilation /jóobi láysh'n/ *n* uninhibited rejoicing in the celebration of a victory or success [14C. < Latin *jubilation-* < *jubilat-*, past participle of *jubilare* 'call out, shout for joy']

jubilee /jóobilee, jóobi lée/ *n* **1.** SPECIAL ANNIVERSARY a significant anniversary of an important event such as a wedding or a monarch's succession **2.** JOYFUL TIME a time or season of celebration **3.** YEAR OF INDULGENCE SET BY POPE in the Roman Catholic Church, a period set by the pope, traditionally every 25 years, in which forgiveness of sins is granted in return for acts of piety or repentance **4.** JEWISH YEAR OF RESTITUTION in Jewish history, a year of restoration or restitution that was proclaimed every 50 years by a country-wide blast of trumpets. During the period, land was left uncultivated, slaves were emancipated, and land that had been sold reverted to its former owner. [14C. Via French *jubilé* < Latin *jubilaeus (annus)* '(year) of jubilee' < ecclesiastical Greek *iōbēlos* < Hebrew *yōbēl* 'ram'; from the ram's horn with which the year of jubilee was proclaimed]

Jubran /joo braán/ ▸ **Gibran, Khalil**

Jud. *abbr* BIBLE **1.** Judges **2.** Judith

Judaea /joo dée ə/, **Judah** /jóodə/ region in Southwest Asia, incorporating parts of Israel and the West Bank —**Judaean** *adj*, *n*

Judaeo- *prefix* Jewish, Judaism ○ *Judaeo-Christian* [< Latin *Judaeus* (see JEW)]

Judaeo-Christian *adj* in the shared tradition of Judaism and Christianity, or combining their common beliefs

Judaeo-Spanish *n*, *adj* LANGUAGE same as **Ladino** (sense 1)

Judah ▸ **Judaea**

Judaic /joo dáy ik/, **Judaical** /-ik'l/ *adj* belonging to or relating to Judaism or Jews [15C. Via Latin *Judaicus* < Greek *Ioudaikos* < *Ioudaios* (see JEW)] —**Judaically** *adv*

Judaica /joo dáy ikə/ *npl* the Jewish religion, customs, and culture, or artefacts and historical and literary materials that relate to them [Early 20C. < Latin, form of *Judaicus* (see JUDAIC)]

Judaical *adj* JUDAISM same as **Judaic**

Judaise *vti* another spelling of **Judaize**

Judaism /jóo day izəm/ *n* **1.** the religion of the Jews, which has its basis in the Bible and the Talmud. In Judaism, God is the creator of everything and the source of all goodness. **2.** Jewish religious practices, customs, and culture as a way of life [14C. Via ecclesiastical Latin < Greek *Ioudaismos* < *Ioudaios* (see JEW)] —**Judaistic** /jóo day ístik/ *adj*

Judaize /jóo day īz/ (-izes, -izing, -ized), **Judaise** (-ises, -ising, -ised) *v* **1.** *vi* to adopt the Jewish religion and Jewish cultural practices **2.** *vt* to give something a Jewish character [Late 16C. Via ecclesiastical Latin < Greek *ioudaizein* < *Ioudaios* (see JEW)] —**Judaization** /jóo day ī záysh'n/ *n*

judas /jóodəss/ *n* a peephole or very small window, e.g. in a door [Mid-19C. After JUDAS]

Judas /jóodəss/ *n* **1.** BIBLE same as **Judas Iscariot 2.** a traitor, especially somebody who betrays a close friend or a cause or belief (*literary*)

judas hole *n* same as **Judas**

Judas Iscariot /-is kárri ət/ *n* one of Jesus Christ's disciples, who betrayed him by identifying him with a kiss to the Jewish leaders in exchange for thirty pieces of silver (Luke 22)

Judas tree *n* a leguminous tree whose purplish-red flowers come out before the leaves. Native to: Europe, Asia. Latin name: *Cercis siliquastrum*. [Mid-17C. After JUDAS; from the popular notion that he hanged himself from this tree]

judder /júddər/ *vi* (-ders, -dering, -dered) to shake or vibrate violently and rapidly, or to move while shaking ○ *The car juddered along for a few more yards.* ■ *n* a violent, rapid vibration or shaking motion [Mid-20C. An imitation of the sound]

judder bar *n* NZ a ridge built across a road to slow down traffic. Same as **speed bump**

Jude /jood/ *n* a book of the Bible, originally a letter, probably written in the late 1st century AD, and traditionally attributed to St Jude. See table at **Bible**

Jude, St (*fl* AD 1st century) one of the 12 apostles of Jesus Christ. He is traditionally believed to have been martyred in Persia with St. Simon.

Judeo- *prefix* US another spelling of **Judaeo-**. US spelling of **Judaeo-**

Judezmo /joo dézmō/ *n* LANGUAGE same as **Ladino** (sense 1) [< Ladino, 'Jewish'] —**Judezmo** *adj*

Judg. *abbr* BIBLE Judges

judge /juj/ *n* **1.** ADJUDICATOR a person, sometimes one of several, appointed to assess entries or performances in a competition and decide who wins **2.** SOMEBODY GIVING INFORMED OPINION somebody who can give an informed opinion on something ○ *a good judge of character* **3.** JEWISH WARRIOR LEADER in Jewish history, any of a succession of warrior leaders who each temporarily held supreme power in Israel between Joshua's death and Saul's succession ■ *v* (judges, judging, judged) **1.** *vt* DECIDE LEGAL CASE to act as the judge of a legal case **2.** *vti* BE JUDGE IN CONTEST to act as a judge in a competition or, as an adjudicator, pronounce officially on the entries **3.** *vti* ASSESS to assess the quality of something or estimate probabilities ○ *Each proposal has to be judged on its individual merits.* **4.** *vt* FORM OPINION OF SOMEBODY OR SOMETHING to form an opinion of somebody or something, especially after thought or consideration ○ *She was judged to have the best qualifications.* **5.** *vti* ESTIMATE to measure by guesswork, using the eye or some other sense as a rough guide ○ *You can't always judge people's ages by their voices.* **6.** *vt* CONDEMN SOMEBODY to criticize or condemn somebody on moral grounds [12C. Via Old French *juge* < Latin *judex* 'somebody who speaks the law' < *jus* 'law, right'] —**judger** *n*

judge advocate *n* an officer appointed to oversee the proceedings and advise on points of law at a court martial

judgement *n* another spelling of **judgment**

Judges /jújiz/ *n* a book of the Bible that tells the story of the Israelites from Joshua's death in the 13th century BC to Samuel's birth in the 11th century BC (*takes a singular verb*) See table at **Bible**

a at; aa father; aw all; ay day; ai hair; ə about, item, edible, common, circus; e egg; ee eel; hw when; i it, happy; ī ice; 'l apple; 'm rhythm; 'n fashion; o odd; ō open; oo good; oo pool; ow owl; oy oil; th thin; th this; u up; ur urge;

judgment /júj'mənt/, **judgement** n **1. LEGAL VERDICT** the decision arrived at and pronounced by a court of law **2. OBLIGATION RESULTING FROM VERDICT** an obligation, e.g. a debt, that arises as a result of a court's verdict, or a document setting out an obligation of this kind (often used before a noun) **3. DECISION OF JUDGE** the decision reached by one or more judges in a contest ○ The judgment of the panel must be regarded as final. **4. DECISION ON DISPUTED MATTER** an opinion formed or a decision reached in the case of a disputed, controversial, or doubtful matter **5. DISCERNMENT OR GOOD SENSE** the ability to form sound opinions and make sensible decisions or reliable guesses ○ someone with shrewd commercial judgment **6. OPINION** an opinion formed or given after consideration ○ a snap judgment **7. ESTIMATE BASED ON OBSERVATION** an estimate of something such as speed or distance, made with the help of the eye or some other sense **8. JUDGING OF SOMETHING** the judging of a case or a contest **9. DIVINE PUNISHMENT** a misfortune regarded as a divine punishment for folly or sin (archaic or humorous) ○ The defeat was regarded as a judgment from God on the leader's pride. **10. ACT OF MAKING STATEMENT** in logic, the mental act of making or understanding a positive or negative proposition about something, e.g. in 'a chihuahua is a dog' or 'a lobster is not an insect' [13C. < Old French jugement < jugier 'to judge' < Latin judicare (see JUDICATURE)]

Judgment n **1.** in Roman Catholic belief, God's decision at the instant of somebody's death on whether the soul is to be saved or damned **2. RELIG** same as **Last Judgment**

judgmental /juj mént'l/ adj tending to judge or criticize the conduct of other people —**judgmentally** adv

judgment call n a decision that must be made on the basis of personal judgment, as neither alternative is clearly right or wrong

Judgment Day n in Jewish, Christian, and Islamic traditions, the day at the end of the world when God delivers his final judgment on humankind

judicable /jóodikəb'l/ adj capable of being or liable to be tried in a court of law [Mid-17C. < late Latin judicabilis < Latin judicare (see JUDICATURE)]

judicatory /jóodikətəri/ adj also **judicatorial** /jóodikə táwri əl/ **RELATING TO LEGAL SYSTEM** relating to a legal system or to judges or judgment ■ n (plural -**ries**) (formal) **1. LEGAL SYSTEM** a system of administering justice **2. LAW COURT** a court of law [Late 16C. < Latin judicare (see JUDICATURE)]

judicature /jóodikəchər, joo díkəchər/ n **1. ADMINISTERING OF JUSTICE** the dispensation of justice **2. JUDGE'S OFFICE** the power or office of a judge, or a judge's tenure of office **3. JUDGE'S AREA OF AUTHORITY** the area of authority of a judge or a court of law **4. BODY OF JUDGES** a body of judges or of people holding judicial power **5. SYSTEM OF LAW COURTS** a law court, or a system of law courts [Mid-16C. < medieval Latin judicatura < Latin judicare 'to judge' < judex (see JUDGE)]

judicial /joo dísh'l/ adj **1. RELATING TO JUDGES** relating or belonging to a body of judges or to the system that administers justice **2. RELATING TO COURT JUDGMENTS** relating to judges in performance of their duties or to judgment in a court of law **3. ENFORCED BY LAW COURT** enforced or sanctioned by a court of law **4. APPROPRIATE TO JUDGES** appropriate to a judge or expected of a judge [14C. < Latin judicialis < judicium 'legal proceedings' < judex (see JUDGE)] —**judicially** adv

judicial review n **1.** a reassessment or re-examination by judges of a decision or proceeding by a lower court or a government department **2.** a constitutional right of the court system in some countries to review and cancel government legislation that is held to have been passed illegally

judicial separation n LAW same as **legal separation**

judiciary /joo díshəri, -díshi əri/ n (plural -**ies**) **1. GOVERNMENT BRANCH DISPENSING JUSTICE** the branch of a country's central administration that is concerned with dispensing justice **2. COURT SYSTEM** a country's system of law courts **3. JUDGES IN GENERAL** a country's body of judges ■ adj **RELATING TO JUDGES** relating to courts, judges, and judgment [15C. < Latin judiciarius < judicium (see JUDICIAL)]

judicious /joo díshəs/ adj showing wisdom, good sense, or discretion, often with the underlying aim of avoiding trouble or waste ○ a little judicious

pruning [Late 16C. < French judicieux < Latin judicium (see JUDICIAL)] —**judiciously** adv —**judiciousness** n

Judith /jóodith/ n **1.** in the Bible, a Jewish woman who saved the city of Bethulia by beheading the general Holofernes **2.** a book of the Roman Catholic Bible and the Protestant Apocrypha that describes Judith's heroism in saving her people. See table at **Bible**

judo

judo /jóodō/ n a Japanese martial art in which opponents use balance and body weight, with minimal physical effort, to throw each other or hold each other in a lock. Judo was developed from jujitsu, a samurai art, by Jigoro Kano (1860–1938). [Late 19C. < Japanese jūdō < jū'gentle' (< Middle Chinese nˠuw) + dōʹway' (< Middle Chinese dawʹ)] —**judoist** n

judogi /joo dōgi/ n the costume worn by participants in judo, made of thick white cotton and consisting of a loose jacket secured by a belt and loose trousers. The colour of belt indicates the participant's grade, from the white belt worn by a beginner through various colours to black belt, the highest grade. [Mid-20C. < Japanese]

judoka /joo dō kaa/ (plural -**kas** or same) n an expert or practitioner in the art of judo [Mid-20C. < Japanese]

judy /jóodi/ (plural -**dies**), **Judy** n a girl or woman (dated slang; sometimes considered offensive) [Early 19C. < Judy, familiar form of the name Judith]

Judy /jóodi/ n the wife of Punch in a traditional Punch-and-Judy puppet show

jug¹ /jug/ n **1. POURING CONTAINER** a deep container for liquids that has a handle and has its rim shaped into a lip or spout for pouring **2.** N Am **LARGE CONTAINER FOR LIQUIDS** a large container for liquids, typically of earthenware or glass, with a handle and a narrow mouth usually closed with a cork **3. LIQUID CONTAINED IN JUG** the quantity of liquid held in a jug **4. GOOD HANDHOLD IN CLIMBING** a large, strong, and dependable handhold on a rock climb **5. PRISON** prison or jail (humorous) **6. OFFENSIVE TERM** an offensive term for a woman's breast (slang) ■ vt (**jugs**, **jugging**, **jugged**) **1. JAIL SOMEBODY** to put somebody in jail (humorous) **2. STEW MEAT IN EARTHENWARE POT** to stew meat in a deep earthenware pot [15C. Origin ?]

jug² /jug/ (**jugs**, **jugging**, **jugged**), **jug-jug** vi to make a call that sounds like 'jug' or 'jug-jug', as the nightingale and some other birds do [Early 16C. An imitation of the sound]

jugate /jóo gayt, jóogət/ adj **1.** describes leaves that consist of paired leaflets attached to a single leaf stalk **2.** describes heads or busts on coins that are superimposed in profile one on another [Late 19C. < Latin jugatus, past participle of jugare 'join together']

jug band n a blues or jazz band featuring jugs as instruments, played by blowing across their rims

jug-eared adj an offensive term meaning having large ears that stick out (informal)

Jugendstil /yóogənd shteel/ n the equivalent in Germany and Austria of art nouveau, a style of design that influenced all the visual arts in Europe during the late 19th and early 20th centuries. It is characterized by curvilinearity and the stylization of forms. [Early 20C. < German < Jugend 'youth' (title of a magazine) + Stil 'style']

jugful /júg fŏŏl/ (plural -**fuls**) n MEASURE same as **jug**¹ n (sense 3) ○ I found I was drinking jugfuls of water every day and still feeling thirsty.

jugged hare /jugd-/ n a stew of hare meat, traditionally cooked in an earthenware pot or

casserole dish. The sauce is usually thickened with the blood of the hare.

juggernaut /júggər nawt/ n **1.** a very large long lorry for transporting goods in bulk **2.** a force that is relentlessly destructive, crushing, and insensitive [Mid-19C. < JUGGERNAUT]

ORIGIN It used to be said, apocryphally, that worshippers of Krishna threw themselves under the wheels of the *Juggernaut* wagon in an access of religious ecstasy, so *juggernaut* came to be used metaphorically in English for an irresistible crushing force. The British application to large lorries did not become firmly established until the late 1960s.

Juggernaut /júggər nawt/ n in Hinduism, a form of the god Krishna. During a festival held each year in his honour, his statue is pulled through the Indian town of Puri on a huge chariot. [Early 19C. < Sanskrit Jagannātha 'protector of the world']

juggins /júgginz/ n an offensive term for somebody regarded as easy to trick or naive (dated) [Late 19C. Origin ?]

juggle /júgg'l/ (-**gles**, -**gling**, -**gled**) v **1.** vti **KEEP SEVERAL OBJECTS IN AIR** to keep several objects in motion in the air at the same time by throwing them and catching them in quick succession **2.** vt **HAVE DIFFICULTY HOLDING SOMETHING** to keep adjusting your grip or stance in order to balance objects being held ○ I was juggling coffee and a plate of sandwiches in one hand. **3.** vt **FIT THINGS INTO SCHEDULE** to try to make something fit into a satisfactory pattern or schedule by careful arranging ○ parents juggling careers and family life **4.** vt **REARRANGE DATA** to manipulate data in order to deceive ○ juggling the company's books [14C. Back-formation < JUGGLER] —**jugglery** n

juggler

juggler /júgglər/ n a professional entertainer who juggles [Pre-12C. Via Old French jogler < Latin joculator 'jester' < jocus 'joke']

juggling act n **1.** a skilful or precarious attempt to perform a variety of tasks at the same time **2.** a performance by a juggler

jug-jug vi BIRDS same as **jug**²

jugular /júggyŏŏlər/ n ANAT same as **jugular vein** ■ adj **1.** relating to or situated close to the neck or throat **2.** describes a fish that has pelvic fins in front of the pectoral fins [Late 16C. < late Latin jugularis < Latin jugulum 'collarbone, throat' < jugum 'yoke'] ◇ **go for the jugular** to make an attack that is intended to be highly destructive and conclusive (informal)

jugular vein n any one of four pairs of veins in the neck that drain blood from the head. A larger internal vein is flanked by an external vein on each side of the neck.

jugum /jóogəm/ n **1.** a lobe that sticks out from the base of the forewing of some insects in order to couple it with the hind wing during flight **2.** a pair of opposed leaflets in a compound leaf [Mid-19C. < Latin, 'yoke']

Jugurtha /jə gúrthə/ (160–104 BC) king of Numidia. He tried to free his northern African kingdom from Roman rule.

juice /jooss/ n **1. LIQUID FROM FRUIT OR VEGETABLES** the extractable liquid that is contained in fruit or vegetables, or a drink made from this liquid ○ lemon juice **2. BODILY FLUID** a natural fluid or secretion of the body ○ gastric juices **3. LIQUID FROM COOKING MEAT** the liquid that comes from a piece of meat when it is roasted or otherwise cooked **4. LIQUID EXTRACT** any

liquid extract or essence, especially from biological material ○ *Pure penicillin was isolated from mould juice.* **5.** FUEL OR POWER fuel, especially petrol for a vehicle, or electricity (*informal*) **6.** ALCOHOL alcoholic drink (*slang*) **7.** *N Am* MONEY OR INFLUENCE money or influence gained from or used in corrupt or criminal activities (*slang*) **8.** *US* LOAN OR INTEREST money lent at an extortionate rate of interest, or the interest extorted (*slang*) ■ *vt* (**juices, juicing, juiced**) TAKE JUICE FROM SOMETHING to extract the juice from a fruit or vegetable [13C. Via French *jus* < Latin, 'broth, sauce, vegetable juice'] ◇ **stew in your own juice** to have to suffer the consequences of your actions without any help from others

juice up *vt* to make something or somebody more lively, exciting, or interesting (*slang*) ○ *juice the party up by bringing in a live band*

juice bar *n* a café serving freshly prepared fruit juices and other healthy food and drinks

juice box *n N Am* a small box of fruit juice for one person that is sold with a straw attached to it

juiced /joost/ *adj* **1.** WITH JUICE REMOVED having had the juice extracted **2.** HAVING PARTICULAR JUICE containing juice of a particular kind or quality (*usually used in combination*) **3.** INTOXICATED drunk (*dated slang*)

juice extractor *n* HOUSEHOLD same as **juicer**

juicehead /jo͝oss hed/ *n N Am* a heavy drinker or an alcoholic (*slang*)

juicer /jo͝ossər/ *n* a kitchen appliance, usually electrically powered, for extracting the juice from fruit or vegetables

juicy /jo͝ossi/ (**-ier, -iest**) *adj* **1.** SUCCULENT containing a lot of juice **2.** PROVIDING INTEREST repaying effort by providing plenty of stimulation and food for thought ○ *I like getting my teeth into a nice juicy problem.* **3.** TITILLATING containing scenes or details that evoke interest because of their sensational nature (*informal*) **4.** LUCRATIVE extremely profitable or productive (*informal*) **5.** SEXUALLY DESIRABLE desirable in a sexual way (*slang*) —**juicily** *adv* —**juiciness** *n*

jujitsu /joo jítsoo/, **jiujitsu** *n* a Japanese system of unarmed fighting devised by the samurai, or the martial art based on it. Judo, aikido, and karate are all developments of jujitsu. (*often used before a noun*) [Late 19C. < Japanese *jūjutsu* < *jū* 'gentle' (< Middle Chinese *nʸuw*) + *jitsu* 'arts' (< Middle Chinese *zhwit*)]

juju /jo͞ojoo/ *n* **1.** OBJECT WITH SUPPOSED MAGICAL POWERS an object revered among some West African peoples for the magical powers that it is thought to possess **2.** SUPPOSED MAGIC POWER OF JUJU the magical or supernatural power associated with a juju **3.** SPELL EFFECTED BY JUJU a spell put on something or somebody by means of a juju [Early 17C. < Hausa] —**jujuism** *n*

jujube /jo͞o joob/ *n* **1.** DARK-RED FRUIT a plum-shaped dark-red fruit that is sometimes dried like a date **2.** TREE WITH RED FRUITS a tree that produces jujubes. Native to: Asia. Latin name: *Ziziphus jujuba*. **3.** CHEWY SWEET a chewy, usually fruit-flavoured, sweet made of gum or gelatin [14C. Directly or via French < medieval Latin *jujuba* < Greek *ziziphos*]

juk *vt* another spelling of **jook** (*slang; used in Black English*)

jukebox /jo͝ok boks/ *n* a coin-operated machine that automatically plays selected records or compact discs

juke joint *n N Am* a roadside café where music is played on a jukebox for dancing (*informal*) [Mid-20C. < slang *juke* 'roadhouse, brothel', probably < Gullah, 'disorderly, wicked' < a W African language]

jukskei /yo͝ok skay/ *n S Africa* an outdoor game in which skittle-shaped pegs are thrown at stakes set into the ground [Early 19C. < Afrikaans, 'yoke pin']

Jul. *abbr* CALENDAR July

julep /jo͞olip, jo͞o lep/ *n* BEVERAGES same as **mint julep** [14C. Via French or medieval Latin < Persian *gulāb* 'rose water']

Julian /jo͞oli ən/ *adj* **1.** relating to or associated with Julius Caesar **2.** relating to or reckoned according to the Julian calendar [Late 16C. < Latin *Julianus* < *Julius*]

Julian (of Norwich) /jo͞oli ən əv nórrich/ (1342–1416) English mystic. She wrote *Revelations of Divine Love*, an extraordinary record of medieval religious experience.

Juliana /jo͞oli aánə/ (1909–2004) queen of the Netherlands. She reigned as the queen of the Netherlands from 1948 to 1980, and abdicated in favour of her eldest daughter Beatrix.

Julian calendar *n* the twelve-month solar calendar introduced by Julius Caesar in 46 BC, consisting of 365 days, with an extra day every four years. It was replaced by the Gregorian calendar in 1582.

Julian date *n* in computer programming, a date expressed as the number of days since 1 January of the current year

julienne /jo͞oli én, zho͞oli-/ *adj* CUT THINLY cut into long thin matchstick strips ■ *n* CLEAR SOUP WITH VEGETABLE STRIPS a clear soup containing vegetables cut into thin matchstick strips ■ *vt* (**-ennes, -enning, -enned**) CUT VEGETABLES THINLY to cut vegetables into thin matchstick strips [Early 18C. < French < *Jules* or *Julien*, proper names]

Juliet /jo͞oli ət/ *n* **1.** a small inner natural satellite of Uranus, discovered in 1986 by the spacecraft Voyager 2. It is 84 km/52 mi. in diameter. **2.** a code word for the letter 'J', used in international radio communications

Juliet cap *n* a round close-fitting crocheted net cap for women, sometimes set with pearls. It was fashionable in the 1920s, 1930s, and 1950s for brides and bridesmaids. [Early 20C. < the heroine of Shakespeare's *Romeo and Juliet*]

Julius II /jo͞oli əss/, **Pope** (1443–1513) Becoming pope in 1503, he was a powerful ruler and lavish patron of the arts, commissioning Donato Bramante's design for St Peter's in Rome and Michelangelo's frescoes for the Sistine Chapel in the Vatican

Jullundur /júlləndər, jállən daar/ city in northwestern India, a major industrial centre. Population: 709,255 (2001).

July /jo͞o lī/ (*plural* **-lies**) *n* in the Gregorian calendar, the seventh month of the year, lasting 31 days. See table at **calendar** [12C. Via Anglo-Norman < Latin *Julius*, after *Julius* CAESAR]

Jumada /jo͞o maádə/ *n* in the Islamic calendar, either the fifth or the sixth month in the year. See table at **calendar** [Late 18C. < Arabic *jumādā* < *jamada* 'freeze']

jumar /jo͞omər/ *n also* **jumar clamp** a clip or clamp used in rock-climbing or ice-climbing that runs freely up a slack rope but tightens round the rope in response to weight applied from below ■ *vi* (**-mars, -maring, -mared**) to climb using jumar clamps [Mid-20C. Origin ?]

jumbal /júmb'l/, **jumble** *n* a light sweet crisp biscuit or cake, traditionally made in the shape of a ring or an S [Early 17C. Origin ?]

jumbie /júmbi/ *n Carib* a spirit or ghost [Late 19C. < Kongo *zumbi* 'fetish']

jumble[1] /júmb'l/ *vti* (**-bles, -bling, -bled**) **1.** PUT THINGS OUT OF ORDER to mix things together indiscriminately so that they are no longer neat or ordered, or become mixed together in this way **2.** CONFUSE THINGS to muddle things up in the mind, or become muddled ■ *n* **1.** MUDDLED MASS an untidy or disorganized mass of objects, images, or ideas ○ *His thoughts were all in a jumble.* **2.** ARTICLES FOR JUMBLE SALE unwanted possessions that people hand over for selling at a jumble sale. US term **rummage** [Early 16C. Origin ?]

jumble[2] *n* FOOD another spelling of **jumbal**

jumble sale *n* a sale of clothes and other goods, chiefly second-hand, usually to raise money for charity or for some specific purpose. N Am term **rummage sale**

jumbo /júmbō/ *n* **1.** something or somebody that is extra large (*often used before a noun*) ○ *a jumbo helping* **2.** AVIAT same as **jumbo jet** [Early 19C. < the name of a very large elephant at London Zoo, later sold to Barnum and Bailey circus]

jumboize /júmbō īz/ (**-izes, -izing, -ized**), **jumboise** (**-ises, -ising, -ised**) *vt* to increase the size of a ship, especially a tanker, by inserting a prefabricated central section

jumbo jet *n* a large wide-bodied commercial aircraft capable of carrying several hundred passengers

jumbuck /júm buk/ *n Aus* a sheep (*informal*) Same as **sheep** (sense 1) [Early 19C. Origin ?]

Jumna /júmnə/ former name for **Yamuna**

jump /jump/ *v* (**jumps, jumping, jumped**) **1.** *vi* LEAVE SURFACE WITH BOTH FEET to bend the knees and push the whole body quickly up off a surface or the ground **2.** *vt* GET OVER SOMETHING to pass from one side of something to the other by jumping ○ *jump the fence* **3.** *vti* JUMP AS SPORTING SKILL in various sports such as horse-riding and skiing, to perform a movement in which the whole body leaves the ground to travel over something ○ *Make sure you have your skis parallel before you attempt to jump.* **4.** *vi* MOVE QUICKLY to move quickly in a particular direction ○ *Jump in and I'll give you a lift home.* **5.** *vi* MAKE MENTAL LEAP to make an illogical mental leap ○ *His mind keeps jumping from one thing to another.* **6.** *vi* MOVE JERKILY to move in a jerky way that suggests a mechanical or electrical fault ○ *Interference was making the picture jump.* **7.** *vi* START IN SURPRISE to give a start of surprise or fright ○ *The noise made me jump.* **8.** *vi* RISE SUDDENLY to rise or increase suddenly by a large amount ○ *The Nikkei Index jumped 35 points.* **9.** *vti* LEAVE RAILS to come off the rails accidentally (*refers to trains*) **10.** *vi* MAKE PARACHUTE DESCENT to make a descent by parachute from an aircraft **11.** *vt* AMBUSH SOMEBODY to ambush somebody by attacking unexpectedly (*informal*) ○ *The guy jumped me.* **12.** *vt* VIOLATE ENGAGEMENT BY LEAVING to abscond or desert in violation of an engagement, contract, or undertaking ○ *jumped bail* **13.** *vti* OMIT SOMETHING to omit the intervening parts of something, especially passages of a text, sometimes inadvertently **14.** *vi* OBEY SOMEBODY IMMEDIATELY to carry out orders immediately (*informal*) ○ *When she speaks, you jump.* **15.** *vt* USURP OWNERSHIP to usurp ownership of a piece of land, especially a mining claim, on the grounds that the owner has abandoned it or not fulfilled the conditions of ownership ○ *jump a claim* **16.** *vti* RAISE BID to raise a partner's bid to indicate a strong hand **17.** *vt* PASS PIECE OVER OPPONENT'S PIECE in draughts, to capture an opponent's playing piece by passing a piece over it into an empty square **18.** *vt* DRIVE THROUGH TRAFFIC LIGHTS to fail to stop at a set of traffic lights, or start moving on a red traffic light (*informal*) **19.** *vt US* BOARD TRAIN ILLEGALLY to board a train surreptitiously with the intention of travelling on it without paying (*informal*) **20.** *vt* OFFENSIVE TERM an offensive term meaning to have sexual intercourse with a woman (*slang*) ■ *n* **1.** JUMPING MOVEMENT a jumping movement or the distance jumped ○ *a winning jump of 26 feet* **2.** OBSTACLE OR APPARATUS USED IN JUMPING a specially constructed obstacle or other piece of apparatus for use in competitive jumping, e.g. a fence in steeplechasing or a platform from which skiers take off **3.** LEAP OF PARTICULAR DISTANCE IN SPORTS in field events, a leap of a particular distance or height, or the action of attempting or completing such a leap **4.** SUDDEN RISE a sudden steep rise or increase in an amount ○ *a jump in property prices* **5.** START OF SURPRISE an involuntary movement made when startled **6.** SUDDEN TRANSITION a sudden transition or change of direction, representing a break in continuity or logical progression **7.** PARACHUTE DESCENT a descent by parachute from an aircraft **8.** CAPTURE OF OPPONENT'S PIECE in draughts, the move of jumping an opponent's piece and capturing it **9.** DISCONTINUOUS NUMERICAL INCREASE in mathematics, a point at which a function or a curve undergoes a sudden or major transition [Early 16C. Origin ?] —**jumpable** *adj* ◇ **jump to it** to hurry up and carry out orders or instructions (*informal*) ◇ **take a running jump** used dismissively as a blunt refusal or an instruction to go away (*informal*)

jump at *vt* to accept a chance or opportunity eagerly ○ *would jump at the chance*

jump on *vt* to make a sudden physical or verbal attack on somebody (*informal*) ○ *Pupils were jumped on for getting a question like that wrong.*

jump up *vi* to get to your feet immediately

jump ball *n* in basketball, a restarting of play, in which the referee throws the ball up high between two opponents who each try to tip it towards a team member

jump bid *n* in bridge, a bid of one more than is necessary to raise the existing bid

jump cut *n* in film and television, a sudden abrupt change from one sequence to another

jumped-up /júmpt-/ *adj* displaying an arrogance or self-importance that is completely unwarranted in somebody of such lowly status (*informal disapproving*)

jumper[1] /júmpər/ n **1.** PERSON OR ANIMAL THAT JUMPS a person or animal that jumps or is trained to jump competitively **2.** Can TYPE OF SLEDGE a sledge for use over rough terrain **3.** BORING TOOL a heavy drill used in quarrying that, because of its repeated-impact action, has a jumping motion **4.** WIRE FOR MAKING CONNECTION a short length of wire for making an electrical connection or for short-circuiting a portion of a circuit [Early 17C. < JUMP]

jumper[2] /júmpər/ n **1.** a knitted garment for the top half of the body, usually with sleeves, that is pulled on over the head. N Am term **sweater 2.** N Am CLOTHING same as **pinafore** (sense 1) [Mid-17C. Probably < jump 'man's short coat', alteration of jupe, via French < Arabic jubba]

jumper cables npl N Am ELEC ENG same as **jump leads**

jumping bean /júmping-/ n a seed of some Mexican bushes when it contains the larva of a small moth. The larva feeds on the seed pulp, making the seed move jerkily. The movements intensify if the seed is warmed, e.g. in the palm of the hand.

jumping gene n GENETICS same as **transposon**

jumping jack n **1.** a firework that has its gunpowder packed into a pleated tube, so that it jumps along the ground as each segment explodes **2.** N Am a warm-up exercise in which the legs are flung apart while the hands are clapped or swung above the head

jumping mouse n a rodent that looks like a mouse but has long hind legs and a long tail. Native to: northern temperate regions. Family: Zapodidae.

jumping-off place n a very remote place, especially a point at the edge of civilization beyond which lies the wilderness

jumping-off point n **1.** a place from which to begin a journey **2.** a basis on which to begin an enterprise or a discussion **3.** same as **jumping-off place**

jumping plant louse n a small insect that is a weak flier but has enlarged hind legs for jumping. Found worldwide, it feeds on the sap of plants. Family: Psyllidae.

jumping spider n a spider that fixes on its prey using an enlarged central pair of eyes, then pounces by rapidly extending its legs. The jumping is a result of a sudden increase in blood pressure, which causes the legs to extend rapidly, and the spiders can achieve distances of several centimetres. Family: Salticidae.

jump jet n a fixed-wing jet aircraft that takes off and lands vertically

jump jockey n a jockey specially trained to jump horses over fences and ride in steeplechases, as distinct from a flat-racing jockey

jump leads npl a pair of electric cables used to start the engine of a vehicle that has a dead battery by connecting it to an external live battery. N Am term **jumper cables**

jump-off n **1.** the start of something such as a race or a military attack **2.** a final extra round of a showjumping competition, in which all the riders who have had clear rounds compete against the clock —**jump off** vi

jump pass n in basketball, a pass that one player makes to another while in mid-jump

jump rope n US same as **skipping rope**

jump seat n a folding seat between the front and back seats of a taxicab or similarly large vehicle, or a seat like this for temporary use in an aircraft or train

jump shot n in basketball, a shot made with one or both hands by a player who is at the highest point of a jump —**jump shooter** n

jump-start vt to start a motor vehicle by attaching it to an external battery using jump leads ■ n a jump-starting of a motor vehicle

jumpstation /júmp staysh'n/ n a website whose primary function is to provide links to other websites, especially those relating to a particular subject

jumpsuit /júmp soot, -syoot/ n **1.** a woman's casual one-piece suit combining top and trousers **2.** a protective zip-up one-piece suit combining long trousers and jacket, worn by a parachutist when jumping

jumpy /júmpi/ (-ier, -iest) adj **1.** very nervous or anxious **2.** moving jerkily or erratically —**jumpily** adv —**jumpiness** n

jun. abbr junior

Jun. abbr June

Junagadh /joo naá gaad/, **Jūnāgadh** city in Gujarat State, western India. Population: 252,138 (2001).

junco /júngkō/ (plural **-cos**) n a small finch with greyish feathers, a pink beak, and white outer tail feathers. Native to: North America. Genus: Junco. [Early 18C. Via Spanish < Latin juncus 'rush (plant)']

junction /júngksh'n/ n **1.** PLACE WHERE THINGS JOIN a place where two or more structures such as roads or railroad lines meet or cross **2.** UK MOTORWAY EXIT a numbered point on a motorway at which traffic may join or leave **3.** ELECTRICAL CONNECTION a connection between electrical wires or cables **4.** PHYS LAYER BETWEEN METALS a layer of metal separating two metals with different properties and serving as a contact between them, especially in a thermocouple **5.** ELECTRONICS SEMICONDUCTOR CONTACT a point in a semiconductor device at which regions with different electrical properties come into contact with each other **6.** STATE OR ACT OF JOINING the joining of things, or their joined state [Early 18C. < Latin junction- < jungere 'join'] —**junctional** adj

junction box n an enclosed and protected box inside which electrical circuits are interconnected or branched for distribution

juncture /júngkchər/ n **1.** POINT IN TIME a point in time, especially an important or critical one **2.** JOINING PLACE a place where two or more things join (formal) **3.** JOINING OF THINGS the joining of one thing with another, or their joined state (formal) **4.** LING BREAK BETWEEN WORDS the break between one spoken word and another, or the pronunciation features that help a listener to recognize the break, distinguishing between groups of words such as 'grey day' and 'grade A' [14C. < Latin junctura 'joint' < jungere 'join']

June /joon/ n in the Gregorian calendar, the sixth month of the year, lasting 30 days. See table at **calendar** [Pre-12C. Via French juin < Latin (mensis) junius '(month) of Juno']

Juneau /joónō/ port and capital city of the state of Alaska, on the Gastineau Channel, opposite Douglas Island. Population: 30,751 (2002 estimate).

Juneberry /joon berri/ (plural **-ries**) n TREES, FOOD same as **serviceberry** (senses 1–2) [Mid-19C. < the month when it blooms]

June bug n a large brown flying beetle that is seen in late spring and feeds on leaves. Native to: North America. Subfamily: Melolonthinae.

Juneteenth /joon teénth/ n US a holiday commemorating the day on which slaves in Texas learned of the Emancipation Proclamation, which granted them freedom. Date: 19 June. [Blend of JUNE + NINETEENTH]

Carl Gustav Jung

AKG London

Jung /yoong/, **Carl Gustav** (1875–1961) Swiss psychiatrist. He broadened Freud's interpretation of the unconscious, and introduced the concepts of introvert and extrovert types and the collective unconscious. —**Jungian** adj, n

'Every form of addiction is bad, no matter whether the narcotic be alcohol or morphine or idealism.'

[Carl Gustav Jung, Memories, Dreams, Reflections; 1962]

Jung Chang /joong cháng/ (b. 1952) Chinese-born US author. She wrote Wild Swans (1991), an account of her family's experience in communist China.

'Gentleness was considered "bourgeois"...Over the years of the Cultural Revolution, I was to witness people being attacked for saying "thank you" too often, which was branded as "bourgeois hypocrisy".'

[Jung Chang, Wild Swans; 1991]

Jungfrau /yoong frow/ mountain in southern Switzerland. Height: 4,158 m/13,642 ft.

Junggar Pendi /joong gáir péndi/, **Dzungaria** /dzoong gáiri ə, zoóng-/ region in Northwestern China, west of the Republic of Mongolia and east of Kazakhstan, in Xinjiang Uygur Autonomous Region

jungle /júng g'l/ n **1.** TROPICAL FOREST an area of tropical rainforest covered with vegetation so dense that it is largely impenetrable **2.** THICKLY COVERED AREA any area covered with dense vegetation **3.** TANGLE a tangled or confused mass **4.** COMPLEX MATTER a frustratingly or impenetrably complex system **5.** HARSH PLACE a harsh environment characterized by fierce competitiveness or struggle for survival **6.** SYNTHESIZED MUSIC GENRE a rhythmically complex form of electronic dance music that is largely instrumental and shows the influence of jazz, dub, and techno [Late 18C. Via Hindi jangal 'wasteland' < Sanskrit jāngala 'dry']

jungle fever n a severe form of malaria common in tropical regions, especially Southeast Asia

junglefowl /júng g'l fowl/ (plural **-fowls** or same) n a wild bird related to pheasants that is thought to be the ancestor of the modern domestic fowl. Native to: Asia. Genus: Gallus.

jungle gym n ANZ, N Am a framework of interlocking metal, wooden, or plastic bars on which children can climb. UK term **climbing frame**

jungle juice n alcohol, especially home-made, poor quality, or very strong alcohol (informal)

jungli /júng gli/ adj S Asia wild in behaviour [Early 19C. < JUNGLE]

junior /joóni ər/ adj **1.** RELATING TO YOUTH OR CHILDHOOD relating to youth, childhood, or children **2.** also **Junior** YOUNGER younger in age, used especially when referring to the younger of two family members such as father and son who share the same name **3.** LOW IN RANK of relatively low rank or little experience ○ a junior minister **4.** SMALLER smaller than the standard or expected size **5.** OF THIRD-YEAR STUDENTS relating to or involving students in the third year of high school or college in the United States **6.** BOXING BOXING WEIGHT CATEGORY in boxing, used to describe a competitive category that has a slightly lower weight limit than the standard category ○ junior middleweight **7.** FOR CHILDREN BETWEEN 7 AND 11 relating to or involving schoolchildren between the ages of 7 and 11 ○ junior school ■ n **1.** YOUNGER PERSON somebody who is younger than another being referred to ○ My sister is three years my junior. **2.** LOW-RANKING PERSON somebody of relatively low rank or little experience **3.** JUNIOR-SCHOOL PUPIL a pupil in a junior school **4.** CHILD a young person, especially somebody younger than a teenager **5.** also **Junior** N Am WAY OF ADDRESSING BOY a form of address used for a boy or young man, affectionately to the son in a family or condescendingly to a stranger (informal; sometimes offensive) **6.** BARRISTER in England and Australia, a barrister who has not yet qualified as a Queen's Counsel **7.** THIRD-YEAR STUDENT in the United States, a student in the third year of high school or college [13C. < Latin, 'younger' < juvenis 'young']

junior college n N Am a college offering students a two-year course of study that either terminates in an associate degree or corresponds to the first two years at a four-year college

junior common room n in some colleges and universities, a room provided for general use by students, as distinct from the senior common room, reserved for staff

junior high, **junior high school** n N Am a school that is intermediate between primary school and high

school, embracing years six or seven to eight or nine

junior miss *n US* a girl or young woman in her teenage years (*dated*)

junior school *n* a state-run school for children between the ages of 7 and 11

juniper

juniper /jóonipər/ *n* **1.** an evergreen tree or bush with small purple cones resembling berries that are used in cooking and yield juniper oil. Genus: *Juniperus*. **2.** the oil from juniper berries. Use: to flavour gin. [14C. < Latin *juniperus*]

juniper tar, **juniper tar oil** *n* an oily brown substance. Source: wood of a species of juniper. Use: antiseptic soaps, pharmaceuticals.

junjo /jún jo/ (*plural* **-jos**) *n* same as **mushroom** (*humorous; used in Black English*) [< Krio *jonjo*]

junk[1] /jungk/ *n* **1.** RUBBISH discarded things, or things regarded as worthless or causing clutter (*informal*) **2.** USED GOODS FOR SALE second-hand goods offered for sale (*informal*) **3.** CHEAP STUFF cheap and poorly made goods (*informal*) **4.** NONSENSE meaningless or worthless talk (*informal*) **5.** HEROIN narcotics, especially heroin (*slang*) ■ *vt* (**junks**, **junking**, **junked**) DISCARD SOMETHING to get rid of something as useless (*informal*) [14C. Origin ?]

junk

junk[2] /jungk/ *n* a flat-bottomed sailing boat, popular in Chinese waters, that is high at the stern and has squarish sails, each supported on several battens [Mid-16C. Via Portuguese *junco* or Dutch *jonk* < Malay *jong*]

junk bond *n* an investment bond that offers the possibility of a high return but at a high risk

Junker /yóongkər/ *n* **1.** an aristocratic landowner in Prussia, with great political power **2.** an offensive term for a German army officer or official regarded as arrogant and dictatorial [Mid-16C. < German *Junker* 'young lord'] —**Junkerdom** *n* —**Junkerism** *n*

Junkers /yóongkərz/, **Hugo** (1859–1935) German aircraft engineer. His designs include the World War II dive-bomber the Junkers Ju 87, known as the Stuka.

junket /júngkit/ *n* **1.** EXPENSES-PAID TRIP a trip taken at somebody else's expense, especially one taken by a politician at public expense **2.** *N Am* ENTERTAINMENT an outing, excursion, or party of any kind **3.** SET MILK DESSERT a dessert made from milk that has been set with rennet ■ *v* (**-kets**, **-keting**, **-keted**) **1.** *vi* HAVE EXPENSES-PAID TRIP to go on an expenses-paid trip, especially one paid for with public money **2.** *vti US* HOLD PARTY to hold a party or entertain somebody with a party [14C. < French *jonquette* < *jonc* 'rush (plant)' < Latin *juncus*] —**junketer** *n*

junk food *n* food that does not form part of a well-balanced diet, especially highly processed, high-fat savoury snack items eaten in place of or in addition to regular meals

junkie /júngki/, **junky** (*plural* **-ies**) *n* **1.** a drug addict, especially somebody addicted to heroin (*slang*) **2.** somebody whose interest in or liking for something resembles an addiction (*informal*) ○ *a football junkie*

junk mail *n* unsolicited mail, especially advertising material

junk shop *n* **1.** a shop selling a variety of second-hand goods **2.** a second-rate antique shop

junky[1] /júngki/ (**-ier**, **-iest**) *adj* of very low quality or very little value (*informal*) [Mid-20C. < JUNK[1]]

junky[2] *n* another spelling of **junkie**

junkyard /júngk yaard/ *n US* a place where junk is collected before being sold or processed

Juno /jóonō/ (*plural* **-nos**) *n* **1.** in Roman mythology, the queen of the gods and wife of Jupiter. Greek equivalent **Hera 2.** a woman of queenly bearing and imposing beauty —**Junoesque** /jóonō ésk/ *adj*

junr, **Junr** *abbr* junior

junta /júntə, hóontə, jóontə/ (*plural* **-tas**) *n* (*takes a singular or plural verb*) **1.** NEW RULERS AFTER COUP a group of military officers who have taken control of a country following a coup d'état **2.** SECRET GROUP a small group of people, especially one secretly assembled for a common goal **3.** LATIN AMERICAN GOVERNMENT BODY in some parts of Central and South America, a council or other legislative body within the government [Early 17C. < Spanish or Portuguese < Latin *jungere* 'join']

junto /júntō, hóontō, jóontō/ *n POL* same as **junta** (sense 2) [Early 17C. Alteration]

jupa /jóopə/ *n Carib* BUILDINGS same as **ajoupa**

Jupiter /jóopitər/ *n* **1.** in Roman mythology, the king of the gods. Greek equivalent **Zeus 2.** the largest planet in the solar system, fifth in order from the Sun [12C. < Latin < *Jov-* 'Jove' + *pater* 'father']

Juppé /zhóoppay/, **Alain** (b. 1945) French politician. He was prime minister of France from 1995 to 1997. Full name **Juppé, Alain Marie**

Jura /jóorə/ **1.** department in east-central France, in the province of Franche-Comté. Area: 4,999 sq. km/1,930 sq. mi. **2.** island in western Scotland, the fourth largest of the Inner Hebrides. Population: under 200 (1998). Area: 272 sq. km/105 sq. mi.

jural /jóorəl/ *adj* **1.** relating to law or the administration of justice **2.** relating to rights or obligations (*formal*) [Mid-17C. < Latin *jur-* 'law'] —**jurally** *adv*

Jura Mountains /zhóorə-/ mountain range situated on the border between France and Switzerland. The highest point is Crêt de la Neige, 1,718 m/5,636 ft. Length: 320 km/200 mi.

Jurassic /joo rássik/ *n* the period of geological time, 206 million years to 144 million years ago, during which dinosaurs flourished and birds and mammals first appeared. It is the middle period of the Mesozoic era. See table at **geological time** [Mid-19C. < French *Jurassique* < *Jura* 'Jura', east-central France] —**Jurassic** *adj*

jurat /jóor at/ *n* **1.** a closing statement on an affidavit, giving details of the parties to it, the witnesses, and the place and time of signing **2.** a magistrate in France or the Channel Islands [15C. < medieval Latin *juratus* 'sworn man' < Latin *jurare* (see JURY)]

juridical /joo ríddik'l/, **juridic** /-ríddik/ *adj* relating to judges, to the administration of the law, or to law in general —**juridically** *adv*

juridical days *npl* days on which law courts are in session

jurisconsult /jóoriss kón sult/ *n* an expert in law who gives advice on legal matters, especially in relation to civil or international law [Early 17C. < Latin *jurisconsultus* 'skilled in law']

jurisdiction /jóoriss díksh'n/ *n* **1.** LEGAL AUTHORITY the authority to enforce laws or pronounce legal judgments **2.** RANGE OF LEGAL AUTHORITY the area over which legal authority extends **3.** AUTHORITY power or authority generally [13C. Via French < Latin *jurisdictio-*

< *jur-* 'law' + *diction-* 'saying'] —**jurisdictional** *adj* —**jurisdictionally** *adv* —**jurisdictive** *adj*

jurisprudence /jóoriss prood'nss/ *n* **1.** THEORY OF LAW the philosophy or science of law **2.** LEGAL SYSTEM a system of law, or the body of laws applied in a particular country or state **3.** BRANCH OF LAW a branch of law, or the law as it applies to a particular area of life [Early 17C. < late Latin *jurisprudentia* < Latin *jur-* 'law' + *prudentia* 'skill'] —**jurisprudential** /jóorisproo dénsh'l/ *adj* —**jurisprudentially** *adv*

jurist /jóorist/ *n* **1.** an expert in the science or philosophy of law, especially Roman or civil law **2.** a student or graduate of law [15C. Directly or via French < medieval Latin *jurista* < Latin *jur-* 'law'] —**juristic** /joor ístik/ *adj* —**juristical** *adj* —**juristically** *adv*

juror /jóorər/ *n* **1.** a member of a jury, especially in a court of law **2.** somebody who swears an oath such as an oath of allegiance (*formal or literary*) [14C. Via Anglo-Norman *jurour*, Old French *jureor* < Latin *jurator* < *jurare* (see JURY)]

jury /jóori/ (*plural* **-ries**) *n* **1.** a group of people, usually twelve people, chosen to give a verdict on a legal case that is presented before them in a court of law **2.** a group of people who judge a competition [14C. < Anglo-Norman, Old French *juree* 'oath, inquest' < Latin *jurare* 'swear' < *jur-* 'law'] ◇ **the jury is out** no conclusion has yet been drawn or no decision made about something disputed ○ *The jury is still out on whether the ban will limit pollution.*

jury box *n* the part of a court where the jury sits

jury duty *n N Am* LAW same as **jury service**

juryman /jóorimən/ (*plural* **-men** /-mən/) *n* a man who is a member of a jury in a court of law

jury nullification *n* the decision that a jury is, for whatever reason, incapable of sitting

jury-rig *vt* to build something in a makeshift way or fit something out, especially a boat, with makeshift equipment

jury service *n* service as a member of a jury in a court of law. N Am term **jury duty**

jurywoman /jóori wóomən/ (*plural* **-women** /-wimin/) *n* a woman who is a member of a jury in a court of law

jus gentium /júss jénti əm/ *n* international law (*technical*) [< Latin, 'law of nations']

jus sanguinis /júss sáng gwiniss/ *n* the principle in law according to which children's citizenship is determined by the citizenship of their parents [< Latin, 'right of blood']

jussive /jússiv/ *adj* GRAM same as **imperative** *adj* (sense 3) [Mid-19C. < Latin *juss-*, past participle of *jubere* 'command']

jus soli /júss sól ī/ *n* the principle in law according to which children's citizenship is determined by the place of their birth [< Latin, 'right of soil']

just /just/ *adv* **1.** IN IMMEDIATE PAST a very short time ago ○ *The train has just left.* **2.** AT THIS MOMENT indicating that somebody will begin doing something or something will start happening now (*used also with 'about to' and 'going to'*) ○ *I'll just go and get it.* ○ *I was just about to tell you.* **3.** ONLY only or merely the thing, amount, or situation mentioned ○ *This is just a warning.* **4.** BARELY by only a small degree or margin ○ *I arrived just in time.* **5.** USED FOR EMPHASIS used to emphasize a statement, usually in order to express an emotion ○ *It's just plain wrong.* **6.** EXACTLY precisely the thing, amount, or situation mentioned ○ *It's just what you need.* **7.** EXPRESSING AGREEMENT used as a comment on a statement that has just been made, in order to express agreement ○ *It was exactly what we needed. Wasn't it just!* ■ *adj* **1.** FAIR AND IMPARTIAL acting with fairness and impartiality **2.** MORALLY CORRECT done, pursued, or given in accordance with what is morally right **3.** REASONABLE valid or reasonable [14C. Via French < Latin *justus* < *jus* 'law, right'] —**justly** *adv* —**justness** *n* ◇ **just about** used to indicate that something is the case, but only by a very small degree or amount ○ *I can just about reach it.* ○ *These days, you can travel just about anywhere.* ◇ **just a moment** or **second** or **minute** used to ask someone to wait for a short time ◇ **just like that** without great effort, trouble, or inconvenience ○ *I can't move to another country just like that.* ◇ **just now 1.** a very short time ago **2.** at this very

moment ◇ **just so 1.** used to express agreement with or confirmation of a statement that has just been made **2.** done or arranged precisely ○ *They wanted the room decorated just so.*

justice /jústiss/ *n* **1.** FAIRNESS fairness or reasonableness, especially in the way people are treated or decisions are made **2.** SYSTEM OR APPLICATION OF LAW the legal system, or the act of applying or upholding the law **3.** VALIDITY validity in law **4.** GOOD REASON sound or good reason **5.** LAW same as **JP** [12C. Via French < Latin *justitia* < *justus* (see JUST)] ◇ **bring somebody to justice** to arrest somebody to be tried in a court of law ◇ **do justice to somebody** *or* **something 1.** to deal with somebody *or* something fairly **2.** to convey the true qualities, especially the merits, of somebody *or* something ◇ **do yourself justice** to display your own abilities fully or perform to your full potential (*often used in the negative*)

Justice Department *n* a department of the Scottish Executive, responsible for all aspects of the legal system and the police

justice of the peace *n* full form of **JP**

justiciable /ju stíshi əb'l/ *adj* **1.** able or required to be tried in a court of law **2.** able to be settled by applying the principles of law —**justiciability** /ju stíshi ə bíllǝti/ *n*

justiciary /ju stíshi əri/ *adj* relating to the administration of law ■ *n* (*plural* **-ies**) a judge or other officer who administers the law

justifiable /jústi fī əb'l/ *adj* capable of being shown as reasonable or merited according to accepted standards —**justifiability** /jústi fī ə bíllǝti/ *n* —**justifiableness** *n* —**justifiably** *adv*

justifiable homicide *n* killing that is deemed to be lawful, especially because it is carried out in self-defence or as the only way to prevent a crime

justification /jústifi káysh'n/ *n* **1.** SOMETHING THAT JUSTIFIES something, e.g. a reason or circumstance, that justifies an action or attitude **2.** GIVING OF REASONS FOR SOMETHING the act of justifying something **3.** ALIGNMENT OF MARGINS adjustment of the lengths of spaces between and within words in text in order to make both left and right margins align **4.** CHRISTIAN DOCTRINE the Christian belief that people are absolved from all sin if they believe in Jesus Christ [14C. Directly or via French < late Latin *justification-* < *justificare* (see JUSTIFY)]

justificatory /jústifi kaytəri/, **justificative** /-kaytiv/ *adj* serving or acting to justify something [Late 16C. < medieval Latin *justificatorius* < late Latin *justificare* (see JUSTIFY)]

justified /jústi fīd/ *adj* **1.** WITH GOOD REASON having an acceptable reason for the action taken ○ *was justified in not waiting* **2.** ACCEPTABLE acceptable or rea-

sonable in the circumstances ○ *a justified faith in her* **3.** PRINTING WITH MARGINS ALIGNED in printing, with both left and right margins aligned

justify /jústi fī/ (**-fies, -fying, -fied**) *vt* **1.** MAKE SOMETHING SEEM REASONABLE to serve as an acceptable reason or excuse for something (*often passive*) **2.** GIVE SOMEBODY REASON to give somebody an acceptable reason for taking a particular action (*often passive*) **3.** EXPLAIN SOMETHING to give a reason or explanation why something was done **4.** PRINTING PRINT TEXT WITH MARGINS ALIGNED to adjust the lengths of spaces between and within words in text in order to make both the left and right margins align **5.** CHR FREE SOMEBODY FROM SIN in Christianity, to free somebody from sinfulness through faith in Jesus Christ or by the grace of Jesus Christ (*refers to God*) **6.** LAW GIVE LEGAL REASON FOR SOMETHING to provide a good reason in law for something, especially for committing the offence that is the subject of a criminal charge [14C. Via French *justifier* < late Latin *justificare* 'act justly, justify' < Latin *justus* (see JUST)]

Justinian I /ju stínni ən/ (483–565) Roman emperor. During his reign (527–65), he restored Byzantine power in Rome, northern Italy, and Spain. He revised and systematized Roman law. Known as **Justinian the Great**

> 'Justice is the constant and perpetual wish to render to everyone his due.'
> [Justinian I, *Institutes*; 533?]

just-in-time *n* a manufacturing and stock-control system in which goods are produced and delivered as they are required. It is designed to eliminate waste and avoid the need for large stocks.

jut /jut/ *vti* (**juts, jutting, jutted**) to stick out, or make something stick out, especially beyond the surface or edge of something ■ *n* something that sticks out [Mid-16C. Alteration of JET [1]] —**jutting** *adj*

jute /joot/ *n* **1.** coarse fibre from the stems of an Asian plant. Use: sacking, rope. **2.** either of two main species of plant from which jute is produced. Native to: Asia. Genus: *Corchorus.* [Mid-18C. Via Bangla *jhuṭo* < Sanskrit *jūṭah* 'matted hair']

Jute /joot/ *n* a member of a Germanic people from around the Rhine estuary who invaded south-eastern England during the fifth century AD. They settled in Kent and the Isle of Wight, where they soon became the dominant people. [Pre-12C. < Latin *Jutae* < Germanic] —**Jutish** *adj*

Jutland /júttlənd/ peninsula in northern Europe, containing all of mainland Denmark. The base of the peninsula is part of Germany. Length: 338 km/210 mi.

Juvenal /joovǝnǝl/ (AD 65?–128?) Roman satirist. His sixteen extant *Satires*, which were famously translated into English by John Dryden, attack the follies and vices of Roman imperial society. Full name **Juvenalis, Decimus Junius**

'The people long eagerly for just two things—bread and circuses.'
[Juvenal, *Satires*; 98?–128?]

juvenescent /joovǝ néssn't/ *adj* (*literary*) **1.** youthful or young-looking **2.** growing out of infancy and into childhood [Early 19C. < Latin *juvenescent-*, present participle of *juvenescere* 'grow up'] —**juvenescence** *n*

juvenile /joovǝ nīl/ *adj* **1.** YOUTHFUL young or youthful **2.** RELATING TO YOUNG PEOPLE relating to, intended for, or suitable for young people ○ *a juvenile court* **3.** IMMATURE immature or childish ○ *juvenile behaviour* **4.** NOT YET MATURE describes a plant or animal that has not yet reached maturity **5.** SEXUALLY IMMATURE describes a bird that has developed contour feathers but is not yet sexually mature **6.** FROM WITHIN EARTH describes water or gas that has risen to the Earth's surface for the first time ■ *n* **1.** YOUNGSTER a young person **2.** IMMATURE ANIMAL OR PLANT an animal or plant that has not yet reached maturity **3.** ACTOR SUITED TO YOUTHFUL PARTS an actor who plays youthful roles **4.** BOOK FOR CHILDREN a book intended to be read by young people [Early 17C. < Latin *juvenilis* < *juvenis* 'young'] —**juvenilely** *adv* —**juvenileness** *n*

juvenile delinquent *n* a young person who habitually breaks the law, especially somebody repeatedly charged with vandalism or other antisocial behaviour —**juvenile delinquency** *n*

juvenile hormone *n* a hormone present in insect larvae that regulates the form of the larva after each moult. The levels of it eventually fall to allow the larva to be transformed into the adult insect.

juvenilia /joovǝ nílli ǝ/ *npl* works produced in a writer's, artist's, or composer's youth, especially before a mature style has developed [Early 17C. < Latin, form of *juvenilis* (see JUVENILE)]

juvenility /joovǝ nílləti/ *n* **1.** JUVENILE QUALITY juvenile quality or state **2.** IMMATURITY foolishly immature behaviour **3.** ACT OF IMMATURITY an act of foolishly immature behaviour (*often used in the plural*)

juxtapose /júkstǝ pōz/ (**-poses, -posing, -posed**) *vt* to place two or more things together, especially in order to suggest a link between them or emphasize the contrast between them [Mid-19C. < French *juxtaposer* < Latin *juxta* 'close' + French *poser* (see POSE [1])] —**juxtaposition** /júkstǝpǝ zísh'n/ *n* —**juxtapositional** *adj*

JV *abbr* COMM joint venture

Jy *symbol* MEASURE jansky

Jyaistha /jī ástǝ/ *n* in the Hindu calendar, the third month of the year, lasting 31 days and falling about the same time as May to June. See table at **calendar**

Kk

k¹ /kay/ (*plural* **k's**), **K** (*plural* **K's** or **Ks**) *n* **1.** the 11th letter of the English alphabet, representing a consonant sound **2.** a written representation of the letter 'k'

k² *abbr* **1.** MEASURE kilo- **2.** POL knight **3.** HANDICRAFT knit **4.** NAUT knot

K¹ /kay/ (*plural* **K's** or **Ks**) *n* **1.** something shaped like a letter 'K' **2.** MEASURE same as **kilometre** (*informal*) **3.** one thousand pounds (*informal*)

K² *symbol* **1.** PHYS kaon **2.** PHYS kelvin **3.** PHYS kinetic energy **4.** MATHS one thousand **5.** FIN one thousand pounds **6.** CHEM ELEM potassium

K³ *abbr* **1.** COMPUT kilobyte **2.** MEASURE kilometre **3.** CARDS, CHESS king **4.** POL knight **5.** MUSIC Köchel (*preceding a number in Köchel's catalogue of Mozart's works*) **6.** MONEY kopek **7.** MONEY krona **8.** MONEY krone **9.** MONEY kwacha **10.** MONEY kyat

K-1 *n* a sport in which competitors utilize standing techniques from sports such as karate, kick-boxing, kung fu, and tae kwon do to determine the world's strongest martial artist [< K¹ (sense 1) as the initial letter of KARATE, KUNG FU, and other martial arts + ONE, because of the event's single weight class]

K2 /kay toŏ/ second highest mountain in the world. It is situated in the Karakorum Range in the western part of the Himalayan system on the border between China and the disputed territory of Jammu and Kashmir. Height: 8,611 m/28,251 ft.

ka /kaa/ *n* in ancient Egypt, the soul of a dead person, said to be able to reside in a statue of that person after death [Late 19C. < Egyptian]

Kaaba /ka·ábə/ *n* a square building inside the great mosque in Mecca, containing a sacred stone (**Black Stone**) said to have been given by God. It is the most holy site in the Islamic religion. [Early 17C. < Arabic, 'the square house']

kabaddi /kə búddi/ *n S Asia* a chasing game played between teams, developed in northern India. One player at a time from each team enters the opposing team's court and tries to touch an opponent while repeating the word 'kabaddi'. [Mid-20C. Origin ?]

Kabardian /kə baárdi ən/ *n* **1.** a member of a people who live to the north of the Caucasus Mountains in southern European Russia **2.** a language spoken to the north of the Caucasus Mountains in southern European Russia, belonging to the Abkhaz-Adyghean group of Caucasian languages. Native speakers: 300,000. [Late 19C. < Russian *Kabarda*, placename] —**Kabardian** *adj*

Kabbalah /kə baálə, kábbələ/, **Kabbala**, **Qabalah**, **Cabala**, **Cabbala** *n* **1.** a body of mystical Jewish teachings based on an interpretation of the Hebrew scriptures as containing hidden meanings **2.** a set of secret or mystical beliefs [Early 16C. Via medieval Latin < Rabbinic Hebrew *qabbalah* 'tradition' < *qibbel* 'receive'] —**Kabbalism** *n* —**Kabbalist** *n* —**Kabbalistic** *adj* —**Kabbalistically** *adv*

kabeljou /kább'l yŏ/ (*plural same*), **kabeljauw** *n S Africa* FISH same as **kob** (sense 2) [Early 18C. Via Afrikaans < Dutch 'cod']

Kabinett /kábbi nét/ *n* the lowest grade of high-quality German table wine, typically dry to medium dry [Early 20C. < German *Kabinettwein* 'cabinet wine'; because it was kept in a special cellar]

kabob *n* FOOD same as **kebab**

kabuki

kabuki /kə boŏki/ *n* traditional Japanese drama in which male actors play both male and female parts [Late 19C. < Japanese < *ka* 'song' (< Middle Chinese) + *bu* 'dance' (< Middle Chinese *mu@*) + *ki* 'art' (< Middle Chinese *khi*)]

Kabul /ka·ábŏŏl/ capital city of Afghanistan, located in the centre of the country. Population: 700,000 (1993).

Kabyle /kə bĭl/ (*plural* **-byles** or *same*) *n* **1.** a member of a Berber people who live in northeastern Algeria **2.** a Berber language spoken in northeastern Algeria. Native speakers: 3 million. [Mid-18C. Probably < Arabic *kabā'il* 'tribes'] —**Kabyle** *adj*

kaccha *n* CLOTHING another spelling of **kuccha**

kachina /kə chée nə/ (*plural* **-nas**) *n* **1.** any of the spirits believed by the Native North American Hopi people to be the ancestors of human beings **2.** a representation of a kachina, usually either a carved wooden doll or a costumed performer in a ceremonial dance [Late 19C. < Hopi *katsina* 'supernatural being']

kadaitcha *n* CULTL ANTHROP same as **kurdaitcha**

Kádár /ka·ád aar/, **János** (1912–89) prime minister of Hungary (1956–58, 1961–65). He formed a pro-Soviet government in Hungary after the Soviet Union crushed the 1956 Hungarian uprising, and exercised supreme power until 1988. Born **Csermanck, János**

Kaddish /káddish/ (*plural* **-dishim** /-díshim/) *n* a prayer recited at the close of the sections of Jewish religious services, and by close relatives of a deceased person at times of mourning and anniversaries of the death [Early 17C. < Aramaic *qaddīs* 'holy']

kadooment /kə doŏ ment/ *n Carib* serious trouble or difficulty [< English dialect *ka* 'look' (contraction) + *dooment* 'commotion, disturbance' < DO¹]

Kaduna /kə doŏnə/ capital of Kaduna State, north-central Nigeria, situated about 145 km/90 mi. north of the national capital, Abuja. Population: 333,600 (1995).

kaffeeklatsch /káffay klach/, **kaffee klatch** *n N Am* LEISURE same as **coffee klatch** [Late 19C. < German < *Kaffee* 'coffee' + *Klatsch* 'gossip']

Kaffir /káffər/, **Kafir** *n* **1.** *S Africa* a highly offensive term for a Black African person (*taboo*) **2.** an offensive term for somebody who is not a Muslim (*slang*) **3.** LANG same as **Xhosa** (sense 2) (*dated*) [Mid-16C. < Arabic *kāfir* 'unbeliever, infidel'] —**Kaffir** *adj*

kaffir corn *n S Africa* a type of sorghum cultivated for its grain. Use: making beer, animal feed. (*sometimes considered offensive*)

kaffiyeh *n* CLOTHING another spelling of **keffiyeh**

Kafir *n* another spelling of **Kaffir**

Kafiri /káffəri/ *n* a language of northeastern Pakistan and Afghanistan, belonging to the Dardic branch of Indic [Early 20C. < Arabic *kāfir* 'unbeliever, infidel'] —**Kafiri** *adj*

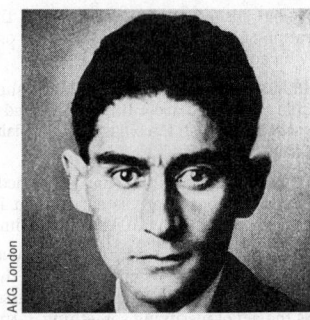

Franz Kafka

Kafka /káfkə/, **Franz** (1883–1924) Austrian (Czech) novelist. His dreamlike works such as *The Trial* (1925) and *The Castle* (1926) are full of oppression and despair. See Cultural note at **metamorphosis**, **trial**

'Gregory Samsa woke from uneasy dreams one morning to find himself changed into a giant bug.'
[Franz Kafka, 'The Metamorphosis', *Franz Kafka: Stories 1904–24*; 1981]

Kafkaesque /káfkə ésk/ *adj* **1.** relating to or characteristic of the work of Franz Kafka **2.** overly complex in seemingly pointless, impersonal, and often disturbing way

kaftan /káf tan/, **caftan** *n* **1.** a full-length tunic or robe for men, usually made of rich fabric, worn chiefly in eastern Mediterranean countries **2.** a western imitation of the kaftan, often brightly coloured and worn by men and women. It was popular in the 1970s and is still associated with hippy culture. [Late 16C. Via Turkish < Persian *kaftān*]

Kafue /kaa foŏ ay/ river in central Zambia, a tributary of the Zambezi. It rises near Zambia's northern border with the Democratic Republic of the Congo. Length: 950 km/590 mi.

Kagoshima /kággə shée mə/ seaport and capital of Kagoshima Prefecture on the southern coast of Kyushu, Japan. Population: 544,840 (2002).

kagu /ka·á goŏ/ *n* a large greyish flightless bird. Native to: New Caledonia. Latin name: *Rhynochetos jubatus*. [Mid-19C. < Melanesian]

kahawai /ka·áhə wī/ (*plural* **-wais** or *same*) *n* a large sea fish similar in appearance to a salmon. Native to: Australia, New Zealand. Latin name: *Arripis trutta*. [Mid-19C. < Maori]

kahikatea /kĭ́kə tee ə/ *n* a tall evergreen tree that is an important source of timber. Native to: New Zealand. Latin name: *Podocarpus dacrydioides*. [Early 19C. < Maori]

Kahiwa Waterfall /kə heéwə-/ *n* falls located on the island of Molokai, Hawaii, United States. Height: 533 m/1,748 ft.

---

a at; aa father; aw all; ay day; ai hair; ə about, item, edible, common, circus; e egg; ee eel; hw when; i it, happy; ī ice; 'l apple; 'm rhythm; 'n fashion; o odd; ō open; oŏ good; oo pool; ow owl; oy oil; th thin; th this; u up; ur urge;

AKG London

Frida Kahlo: photographed in 1930 by Edward Weston

~~kahki~~ incorrect spelling of **khaki**

Kahlo /ka'al ō/, **Frida** (1907–54) Mexican painter. She is known for her idiosyncratic self-portraits that incorporate features and subject matter inspired by Mexican folk art and her personal life. She was married to the Mexican painter Diego Rivera.

kahuna /kə hoōnə/ *n* **1.** a Hawaiian priest or traditional healer **2.** *N Am* an important or influential person (*informal*) ○ *the big kahuna* [Late 19C. < Hawaiian]

kai /kī/ *n NZ* FOOD same as **food** [Mid-19C. < Maori]

kaiak *n* CANOEING another spelling of **kayak**

Kaieteur Falls /kī ə toor-/ waterfall in central Guyana, on the Potaro branch of the River Essequibo. Height: 225 m/740 ft.

kaif *n* DRUGS same as **kif**

Kaifeng /kī fúng/ city in northern China, in the Huang He valley of northern Henan Province. Population: 508,224 (1991).

Kaikoura /kī koŏrə/ town on the northeastern coast of the South Island, New Zealand. It is a fishing, agricultural, and whale-watching centre. Population: 2,106 (2001).

Kaikoura Ranges twin mountain ranges near the northeastern coast of the South Island, New Zealand. The highest point is Tapuaenuku, 2,885 m/9,465 ft.

kail *n* FOOD another spelling of **kale**

kailyard *n* AGRIC another spelling of **kaleyard**

kainite /kīn īt, kayn-/ *n* a variously coloured mixed sulphate and chloride mineral containing potassium and magnesium. Use: source of potassium, fertilizer. [Mid-19C. < German *Kainit* < Greek *kainos* 'new']

Kaipara Harbour /kī paá raa-/ wide harbour on the northwestern coast of the North Island, New Zealand. Area: 520 sq. km/201 sq. mi.

Kairouan /kī ər waán/ city in northern Tunisia. Called 'the City of a Hundred Mosques', it is one of the holiest Muslim cities. Population: 110,280 (1999).

kaiser /kízər/ *n* formerly, a German, Austrian, or Austro-Hungarian emperor, especially the German emperor Wilhelm II, who ruled Germany during World War I [Early 19C. < German, via Germanic < Greek *kaisar* < Latin *Caesar*, family name of Gaius Julius CAESAR] — **kaiserdom** *n* —**kaiserism** *n*

Kaiser /kízər/, **Georg** (1878–1945) German dramatist. He is known for his plays in the expressionist style, including *From Morn to Midnight* (1916), *Gas I* (1918), and *Gas II* (1920).

kaiserin /kízərin/ *n* a German empress, or the wife of a German emperor [Late 19C. < German, form of *kaiser* (see KAISER)]

kaizen /kī zén/ *n* a Japanese business philosophy advocating the need for continuous improvement in somebody's personal and professional life [Late 20C. < Japanese, 'improvement']

kajal /ka'a yəl/ *n* lampblack or other black powder, worn as eye makeup or to make a mark on the forehead by some women and children in or from South Asia [< Hindi]

kak /kak/ *S Africa interj* a highly offensive term used as a swearword (*taboo*) ■ *n* something considered to be worthless or annoying (*slang*) [Late 20C. < Afrikaans, 'excrement' < Latin *cacare* 'defecate']

kaka /ka'a kaa/ *n* a parrot with a long grey beak and greenish-brown feathers. Native to: New Zealand. Latin name: *Nestor meridionalis*. [Late 18C. < Maori]

kaka beak *n* an evergreen climbing plant. Flowers: bright red, shaped like a parrot's beak. Native to: New Zealand. Latin name: *Clianthus puniceus*. [Because the leaves resemble the kaka's beak]

Kakadu National Park /kaakə doŏ-/ national park in the Northern Territory, Australia. Area: 20,000 sq. km/7,722 sq. mi.

kakapo

kakapo /ka'akə pō/ (*plural* **-pos**) *n* a large flightless nocturnal parrot with green feathers, now extremely rare. Native to: New Zealand. Latin name: *Strigops habroptilus*. [Mid-19C. < Maori]

kakemono /káki mōnō/ (*plural* **-nos**) *n* a Japanese wall hanging in the form of a tall narrow scroll, weighted at the base with a roller and decorated with a painting or with a text in ornamental handwriting [Late 19C. < Japanese < *kake-* 'hang' + *mono* 'thing']

kaki /káki/ *n* TREES, FOOD same as **Japanese persimmon** [Early 18C. < Japanese]

kakistocracy /káki stókrəssi/ (*plural* **-cies**) *n* government by the most unscrupulous or unsuitable people, or a state governed by such people [Early 19C. < Greek *kakistos* 'worst']

kala-azar /kállə ə za'ar/ *n* a severe, often fatal tropical fever caused by a parasite that enters the body via a sandfly bite. Symptoms include acute anaemia, weight loss, and an enlarged liver and spleen. [Late 19C. < Assamese < *kala* 'black' + *āzār* 'disease']

Kalachakra /ka'alə chukrə/ *n* a mandala, traditionally constructed out of grains of sand, depicting Buddhist deities in a portrayal of time. The mandala is destroyed shortly after construction to illustrate the Buddhist teaching of impermanence.

Kalahari Desert /kállə ha'ari-/ arid and semiarid region in southern Africa. It occupies much of Botswana and parts of Namibia and South Africa. Area: 260,000 sq. km/100,000 sq. mi.

kalamkari /kúlləm kaari/ *n* a hand-printed cotton cloth of a type originally made especially in Andhra Pradesh in southern India [< Hindi *kalamkārī* 'painting']

kalanchoe /kállən kō i/ *n* a cultivated succulent plant often grown as a pot plant for its shiny leaves. Flowers: small, bright red, pink, or white, in clusters. Native to: tropical Africa. Genus: *Kalanchoe*. [Mid-19C. Via modern Latin < French < Chinese *gāláncài*]

kalansuwa /kállən soŏwə/ *n* a white turban wrapped around a conical or spherical hat, worn by some Muslim spiritual leaders [< Arabic]

Kalashnikov /kə láshni kof/ *n* a Russian-manufactured semiautomatic assault rifle widely used as a weapon by terrorists and paramilitary organizations [Late 20C. < Russian, after M. T. *Kalashnikov* (b. 1919), Russian weapons designer]

Kalat /kə la'at/, **Kalāt** town in western Pakistan, principal town of the Kalat region, in Baluchistan Province. Population: 11,000 (1981 estimate).

kale /kayl/, **kail** *n* **1.** a hardy cabbage with dark green curly leaves and no heart. Latin name: *Brassica oleracea acephala*. **2.** *Scotland* cabbage of any kind **3.** *US* same as **money** (*slang*) [14C. Scottish variant of COLE]

kaleidoscope /kə lídəskōp/ *n* **1.** OPTICAL TOY an optical toy consisting of a cylinder with mirrors and coloured shapes inside that create shifting symmetrical patterns when the end is rotated **2.** COMPLEX

kale

SCENE OR PATTERN a complex, colourful, and shifting pattern or scene **3.** COMPLEX SET OF EVENTS a complex set of events or circumstances [Early 19C. < Greek *kalos* 'beautiful' + *eidos* 'form'] —**kaleidoscopic** /kə lídə skóppik/ *adj* —**kaleidoscopically** *adv*

kalends *npl* CALENDAR another spelling of **calends**

Kalevala /ka'alə va'alə/ *n* in Finnish legend, the land of the folk hero Kaleva, whose exploits are recorded in Finnish folk tales

kaleyard /káyl yaard/, **kailyard** *n Scotland* a kitchen garden

Kaleyard School /káyl yaard-/ *n* a group of Scottish writers, active in the late 19th and early 20th centuries, who wrote romantic portrayals of life in the Scottish Lowlands [< their portrayal of local town life]

Kalgoorlie-Boulder /kalgoŏrli-/ city in southern Western Australia, a gold-mining centre. Population: 29,506 (2002 estimate).

kali /ka'ali, calli/ *n* DRUGS same as **marijuana** (*slang*; used in Black English)

Kali /ka'ali/ *n* a Hindu goddess of destruction, one of the manifestations of the wife of the god Shiva, who destroys in order to recreate. She is depicted with wild red eyes, wears a necklace of severed heads, and wields a bloody sword. [< Sanskrit]

Kalidasa /kúlli da'assə/ (*fl* AD 5th century) Indian poet and dramatist. He is best known for his verse drama *Sakuntala*.

~~kaliedoscope~~ incorrect spelling of **kaleidoscope**

kalif, etc. ISLAM another spelling of **caliph, etc.**

Kalimantan /kálli mántən/ region of Indonesia covering the eastern, southern, southwestern, and central portions of Borneo. Population: 3,102,500 (1999). Area: 37,660 sq. km/14,541 sq. mi.

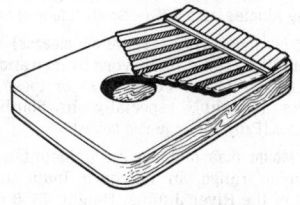

kalimba

kalimba /kə límbə/ *n* an African instrument consisting of a soundboard with tuned metal or bamboo bars of varying lengths that are plucked to give sound [Mid-20C. < Bantu]

Kalinin /kə leénin/ former name for **Tver** (1933–90)

Kaliningrad /kə leénin grad/ city in western Russia, on the River Pregolya. It is the capital of Kaliningrad Oblast. Population: 512,508 (1995). Former name **Königsberg** (until 1946)

Kaliyuga /ka'ali yoōgə/ *n* in Hindu philosophy, the age of decadence. It is the fourth and last age in the Hindu cycle of the world. [< Sanskrit]

kallikrein /kálli kreé in, kə líkri in/ *n* an enzyme present in blood, urine, and body tissue that, when

activated, dilates blood vessels [Mid-20C. < Greek *kallikreas* 'pancreas']

Kalmar /kál maar/ port and city in southern Sweden, the capital of Kalmar County. It is situated on Kalmarsund opposite the island of –land. Population: 56,863 (1994).

kalmia /kálmi ə/ *n* an evergreen bush that belongs to the heath family and has poisonous leaves. Native to: North America. Genus: *Kalmia*. [Mid-18C. < modern Latin, after Pehr *Kalm* (1716–79), Swedish botanist]

Kalmyck /kálmik/ (*plural* **-mycks** or same), **Kalmuk** /kál muk/ (*plural* **-muks** or same) *n* **1.** a member of a people who live in southwestern Russia. They migrated from northeastern China during the 17th century. **2.** a language spoken by the Kalmyck people, belonging to the Mongolian branch of Altaic. Native speakers: 150,000. [Early 17C. < Russian *Kalmyk*] —**Kalmyck** *adj*

kalpa /kálpə/ *n* in Hindu philosophy, an immeasurably long period of time. Its length is variable, sometimes described as one complete cycle of the world (**yuga**), sometimes as 1,000 cycles. [Late 18C. < Sanskrit]

kalpak *n* CLOTHING another spelling of **calpac**

Kaluza /kə loozə/, **Theodor F. E.** (1885–1945) German mathematician. In 1919 he suggested the existence of a fourth spatial dimension to unify electromagnetism with gravity. Full name **Kaluza, Theodor Franz Eduard**

kama /kaámə/ *n* sexual pleasure as the third of the four Hindu goals of life [< Sanskrit *kāma* 'love, desire']

kamaaina /kaámə ínə/ (*plural* **-nas**) *n Hawaii* a resident of Hawaii [Early 20C. < Hawaiian < *kama* 'child' + *āina* 'land']

kamacite /kámmə sīt/ *n* an alloy of nickel and iron. Source: meteorites. [Late 19C. < Greek *kamak-* 'vine pole']

Kamakura /kaámə koõrə/ city on southeastern Honshu Island, Japan, on Sagami Bay, in Kanagawa Prefecture. Population: 169,714 (2002).

kamala /kə maálə/ *n* **1.** a powder obtained from the seeds of a spurge. Use: dye, formerly to treat worm infestations. **2.** a tree belonging to the spurge family whose seeds yield kamala. Native to: South and Southeast Asia. Latin name: *Mallotus philippinensis*. [Early 19C. < Sanskrit, probably < Dravidian]

Kama Sutra /kaámə soõtrə/ *n* an ancient Sanskrit text giving instruction on the art of lovemaking [Late 19C. < Sanskrit < *kāma* 'love, desire' + *sūtra* 'precept']

Kamchatka Peninsula /kam chátkə-/ large peninsula of eastern Russia that separates the Sea of Okhotsk from the Bering Sea and the Pacific Ocean. Area: 518,000 sq. km/200,001 sq. mi.

kame /kaym/ *n* a ridge of sand and gravel left by a melting glacier [Late 18C. < Scottish form of COMB]

kameez /kə meez/ (*plural* same or **-meezes**) *n* a long garment like a tunic, often worn by men and women over tight trousers (**churidars**) or loose pleated trousers (**salwar**), especially in South Asian countries [Early 19C. < Arabic *kamīs*]

Kamet, Mount /kaá met, káa mayt/ mountain in the Himalayan range, in northern India, near the source of the River Jumna. Height: 7,756 m/25,446 ft.

kami /kaámi/ (*plural* same) *n* one of the sacred powers worshipped in the Shinto religion of Japan. Sometimes personified, they are generally regarded as being the forces that generate life. [Early 17C. < Japanese]

kamikaze /kámmi kaázi/ *n* **1.** JAPANESE SUICIDE PILOT a World War II Japanese pilot trained for the suicide mission of flying an aircraft packed with explosives into an enemy target, often a ship (*often used before a noun*) **2.** JAPANESE AIRCRAFT an aircraft used by a kamikaze, especially one designed specifically for suicide crashes (*often used before a noun*) **3.** RECKLESS PERSON a reckless person, often somebody whose actions seem self-defeating or self-destructive (*informal*) ■ *adj* RECKLESS reckless, especially in seeming to invite failure or self-destruction (*informal*) [Late 19C. < Japanese < *kami* 'divine' + *kaze* 'wind']

Kamilaroi /kámmələ roy/ (*plural* same) *n* **1.** a member of a group of Australian Aboriginal peoples living in northeastern New South Wales **2.** the language of the Kamilaroi people, now extinct [Mid-19C. < Kamilaroi]

Kampala /kam paálə/ capital city of Uganda, situated in the southern part of the country, near Lake Victoria. Population: 773,463 (1991 estimate).

Kampuchea /kámpoõ chée ə/ former name for **Cambodia** (1976–89) —**Kampuchean** *n, adj*

kamseen, kamsin *n* METEOROL another spelling of **khamsin**

Kamtok /kám tok/ *n* an English-based pidgin language used in Cameroon [Late 20C. < shortening of CAMEROON + *tok*, alteration of TALK]

kana /kaánə/ *n* **1.** either of two systems of symbols representing syllables, used in writing Japanese **2.** a syllabic symbol used in kana [Early 18C. < Japanese]

Kanak /kə naák/ *n* somebody who comes from the French overseas territory of New Caledonia in the South Pacific and supports independence from France [Early 20C. < French *canaque*] —**Kanak** *adj*

Kanaka /kə nákə/ *n* **1.** somebody who comes from Hawaii, especially somebody of Polynesian descent **2.** *Aus* HIST a Pacific islander, especially one brought to work as a labourer in northeastern Australia between the 1860s and the early 1900s [Mid-19C. < Hawaiian, 'person'] —**Kanaka** *adj*

kanamycin /kánnə míssin/ *n* an antibiotic obtained from a soil bacterium. Use: treatment of infections resistant to other antibiotics. [Mid-20C. < modern Latin *kanamyceticus*, bacterium species name]

Kananga /kə náng gə/ city in the southern Democratic Republic of the Congo, capital of Kasai-Occidental Region. Population: 393,030 (1994). Former name **Luluabourg**

Kanarese /kánnə reéz/ (*plural* same) *n* (*archaic*) **1.** PEOPLES same as **Kannadiga 2.** LANG same as **Kannada** —**Kanarese** *adj*

Kanazawa /kánnə zaáwə/ city and seaport in northern Honshu, Japan. Population: 438,272 (2000).

kanban /kán ban/ *n* **1.** in the just-in-time manufacturing and stock-control system, a card bearing an order for goods, sent to a manufacturer or supplier **2.** MANUF same as **just-in-time** [Late 20C. < Japanese, 'sign']

Kanchenjunga /kánchən júng gə/ third highest mountain in the world, in the Himalayan system, on the border between Nepal and India. Height: 8,598 m/28,209 ft.

Kandahar /kándə haár/ city in southern Afghanistan. It is the capital of Kandahar Province and the country's commercial centre. Population: 225,500 (1988 estimate).

Wassily Kandinsky: photographed at the Bauhaus, Dessau, Germany (1930?)

Kandinsky /kan dínski/, **Wassily** (1866–1944) Russian painter. One of the earliest exponents of pure abstraction in art, he wrote *Concerning the Spiritual in Art* (1912), the first treatise on this subject. He taught at the Bauhaus school of design in Weimar and Dessau, Germany (1922–33).

> 'Violet is red withdrawn from humanity by blue.'
> [Attributed to Wassily Kandinsky]

Kandy /kándi/ city in central Sri Lanka and the capital

of Central Province. Population: 104,000 (1990 estimate).

Kane /kayn/, **Paul** (1810–71) Irish-born Canadian artist. His paintings depict Native North American life in northwestern Canada.

kanga /káng gə/, **khanga** *n* a brightly coloured and decorated piece of cotton cloth for women to wrap around the body as a garment, worn originally and especially in East Africa [Mid-20C. < Kiswahili]

kangaroo

kangaroo /káng gə roó/ *n* (*plural* **-roos**) MARSUPIAL WITH POWERFUL HINDQUARTERS a large leaping marsupial with powerful hind legs, short forelegs, and a long tail. Native to: Australia, New Guinea. Family: Macropodidae. ■ **kangaroos** *npl* FIN AUSTRALIAN SHARES shares in Australian companies (*slang*) ■ *vi* (**-roos, -rooing, -rooed**) MOVE JERKILY to make jerky progress in a car as a result of improper use of the clutch or accelerator (*informal*) [Late 18C. < Aboriginal]

CULTURAL NOTE *Kangaroo*, a novel (1923) by the British writer D. H. Lawrence. Inspired by the author's 1922 visit to Australia, it tells the story of a settler and his wife who become reluctantly involved with local political organizations, including a right-wing political group and its charismatic leader, Kangaroo.

Kangaroo *n* a member of the Australian national rugby league team (*informal*) ■ **Kangaroos** *npl* the Australian national rugby league team (*informal*)

kangaroo court *n* an unofficial or mock court set up spontaneously for the purpose of delivering a judgment arrived at in advance, usually one in which a disloyal associate's fate is decided

kangaroo grass *n* a tall grass. Use: fodder. Native to: Australia. Latin name: *Themeda australis*.

Kangaroo Island /káng gə roó-/ island off the coast of South Australia. Population: 4,359 (2002 estimate). Area: 4,351 sq. km/1,680 sq. mi.

kangaroo paw *n* a tall hardy plant with downy green and red flowers. Native to: Australia. Genus: *Anigozanthos*.

kangaroo rat

kangaroo rat *n* a small nocturnal jumping rodent with a long tail and long hind limbs. Native to: deserts of the United States and Mexico. Genus: *Dipodomys*.

Kangaroo Valley 1. valley near the town of Nowra, New South Wales, Australia, noted for its rugged scenery **2.** the Earls Court area of London, where many young Australians live (*informal*)

kangaroo vine *n* a climbing vine with shiny green or mottled leaves. Native to: Australia. Latin name: *Cissus antarctica*.

kangha /kúnghə/ n a comb worn by baptized Sikhs as a symbol of religious loyalty [< Punjabi]

kanji /kánji, kaánji/ (plural same or **-jis**) n **1.** a writing system for Japanese that uses pictorial characters based largely on Chinese ideograms **2.** a character used in kanji [Early 20C. < Japanese < kan 'Chinese' + ji 'letter, character']

Kannada /kaánədə, kán-/ n a Dravidian language spoken in some states of southern India. Native speakers: 44 million. [Mid-19C. < Kannada Kannaḍa] —**Kannada** adj

LANGUAGE HERITAGE See *Dravidian*.

Kannadiga /kúnnə deégə/ n a member of a people living in the southern Indian state of Karnataka [< Kannada] —**Kannadiga** adj

Kano /kaánō, káynō/ capital of Kano State, northern Nigeria. Population: 657,300 (1995).

Kano Masanobu /kánnō mássa nóboo/ (1453–90) Japanese artist. He founded the school of painting named after him and based his style on that of Chinese ink painting.

Kano Motonobu /-mótō nóboo/ (1476–1539) Japanese artist. He continued the style of his father Kano Masanobu, and introduced the firm brush line used in later Kano painting.

kanooka (plural **-kas** or **-ka** /kə noókə/) n Aus TREES same as **water gum**

Kanpur /kaán poór/, **Kānpur** city in Uttar Pradesh State, northern India, on the River Ganges. Population: 2,690,486 (2001).

Kansas /kánzəss/ state in the western part of the central United States, bordered by Colorado, Missouri, Nebraska, and Oklahoma. Capital: Topeka. Population: 2,715,884 (2002 estimate). Area: 213,109 sq. km/82,282 sq. mi. —**Kansan** n, adj

Kansas City 1. city in northeastern Kansas. It is directly across the Missouri River from Kansas City, Missouri. Population: 146,978 (2002 estimate). **2.** largest city in Missouri, situated in the western part of the state, on both banks of the Missouri River at its confluence with the Kansas River. Located near the geographical centre of the United States, it is a major Midwestern transport and commercial centre. Population: 443,471 (2002 estimate).

Kansas City jazz n a style of big band jazz music characterized by blues motifs and a relaxed beat

Kant /kant/, **Immanuel** (1724–1804) German philosopher. He is a seminal figure in Western philosophy whose major work is *Critique of Pure Reason* (1781). —**Kantian** adj —**Kantianism** n

> 'Happiness is not an ideal of reason but of imagination.'
> [Immanuel Kant, *Fundamental Principles of Metaphysics*; 1785]

kanzu /kán zoo/ n a long garment resembling a robe, usually white and with long sleeves, worn by some men in East Africa [Early 20C. < Kiswahili]

Kaohsiung /ków shyoóng/ city in southwestern Taiwan, on the Taiwan Strait. It is the largest port on the island. Population: 1,462,302 (1999).

kaoliang /káyō lyang/ n **1.** a type of sorghum cultivated in China for its grain. Use: food grain, making liquor. Latin name: *Sorghum bicolor*. **2.** a strong alcoholic beverage made from the stalks of kaoliang [Early 20C. < Chinese gāoliang < gāo 'high' + liáng 'fine grain']

kaolin /káy əlin/, **kaoline** n a fine white clay. Use: porcelain, ceramics, medicines. [Early 18C. < Chinese gāolǐng, literally 'high hill', hill in Jiangxi province]

kaolinite /káy əli nīt/ n a white or grey aluminosilicate clay mineral. Source: kaolin, altered feldspars. Formula: $Al_2Si_2O_5(OH)_4$. —**kaolinitic** /káy əli níttik/ adj

kaon /káy on/ n an unstable elementary particle produced as a result of high-energy particle collision. It occurs in both charged and neutral forms and helps to hold protons and neutrons together inside a nucleus. Symbol **K** [Mid-20C. Contraction of K-MESON]

kapellmeister /kə pél mīstər/ n **1.** the director of a choir **2.** formerly, the director of the orchestra, choir, or opera in the household of a German prince [Mid-19C. < German < Kappelle 'court orchestra' + Meister 'master']

kaph /kawf/ n the 11th letter of the Hebrew alphabet, represented in the English alphabet as 'k' or, at the end of a word, as 'kh'. See table at **alphabet** [Early 19C. < Hebrew, 'palm of the hand']

Kapil Dev /káppil dév/ (b. 1959) Indian cricketer. A talented all-rounder, he captained India's World Cup winning side (1983) and holds the bowling world record of 434 Test wickets. Full name **Kapil Dev, Ramlal Nikhanj**

Kapiti /káppiti/ urban area in the southwestern part of the North Island, New Zealand. Population: 33,666 (2001).

kapok /káy pok/ n a silky fibre obtained from the seed covering of a tropical tree. Use: stuffing and padding material. [Mid-18C. < Malay]

kapok bush n a small deciduous tree. Flowers: bright yellow. Native to: Australia. Genus: *Cochlospermum*.

Kaposi's sarcoma /kə pózíz-/ n a cancer of connective tissue that causes purplish-red patches on the skin, most commonly found in equatorial Africa and in Aids patients [Late 19C. After M. K. *Kaposi* (1837–1902), Hungarian dermatologist]

kappa /káppə/ n the tenth letter in the Greek alphabet, represented in the English alphabet as 'k'. See table at **alphabet** [15C. < Greek]

Kaprow /kápprō/, **Allan** (b. 1927) US artist. His *18 Happenings in 6 Parts* (1959) established the happening as a new art form.

kaput /kə poót, ka-/ adj broken, incapacitated, or not functioning (informal) [Late 19C. Via German kaputt < French (être) capot '(be) without tricks in the game of piquet']

kara /kaárə/ n a steel bangle worn by baptized Sikhs as a symbol of religious loyalty [< Punjabi]

karabiner /kárrə beénər/, **carabiner** n a large oval or D-shaped metal ring with a spring clip that allows it to be attached to ropes, pitons, and other items of mountaineering equipment [Mid-20C. < German Karabinerhaken 'spring-hook']

Karachay-Cherkessia /kəru chí chair késsi ə/ autonomous republic in southwestern European Russia, bordering Georgia. Capital: Cherkessk. Population: 436,000 (1997). Area: 14,100 sq. km/5,440 sq. mi.

Karachi /kə raáchi/ seaport and largest city of Pakistan, located in the south of the country. Population: 9,269,265 (1998).

Karadzic /kárrəjich/, **Radovan** (b. 1945) Bosnian Serb leader (1992–96). He was indicted by the International War Crimes Tribunal (1995) for genocide and crimes against humanity for actions during his time as president of the self-declared Bosnian Serb Republic during the civil war in Bosnia and Herzegovina.

karahi /ku rí/ n a round frying pan with two handles used to prepare balti dishes, originally from Pakistan [Mid-20C. < Hindi]

Karaism /káirə izəm/ n the system of beliefs of a Jewish denomination founded in the 8th century whose members accept the Bible as the sole source of religious law and reject rabbinic interpretations [Late 19C. < Hebrew qēráīm 'Karaites' < qārā 'to read'] —**Karaite** n

Herbert von Karajan

Karajan /kárrə yaan/, **Herbert von** (1908–89) Austrian conductor. He was the music director of the Berlin Philharmonic Orchestra (1955–89) and director of the Vienna State Opera (1955–64).

Kara-Kalpak /kə raá kəl paák/ (plural **Kara-Kalpaks** or same) n **1.** a member of a people who live mainly in northwestern Uzbekistan **2.** a Turkic language spoken by the Kara-Kalpak people. Native speakers: 300,000. [Early 18C. < Kirghiz < kara 'black' + kalpak 'cap'] —**Kara-Kalpak** adj

Karakoram Range: view of the Sind Valley

Karakoram Range /kárrə káwrəm-/ mountain range in the western Himalayan system, in south-central Asia. Its highest peak is K2, 8,611 m/28,250 ft.

karakul /kárrək'l/, **caracul** n **1.** a soft curly black wool from central Asian lambs. Use: fur coats. **2.** a hardy sheep from central Asia, the lambs of which provide karakul [Mid-19C. < Russian, after an oasis in Uzbekistan and Kara Kul in Tajikistan]

Kara Kul /kárrə koòl/ dual lake system in eastern Tajikistan, on the Pamir plateau near the border with China. The two lakes are called Great Kara Kul and Little Kara Kul. Area: 363 sq. km/140 sq. mi. Depth: 238 m/780 ft.

Karamanlis /kárrə mánliss/, **Constantine** (1907–98) prime minister (1955–63, 1974–80) and president (1980–85, 1990–95) of Greece. He supervised Greece's transition from military to civilian rule in the 1970s.

Karamanlis, **Kostas** (b. 1956) prime minister of Greece (2004–). The son of Constantine Karamanlis, he represents the conservative New Democracy Party.

Karamea Bight /kárrəmi ə-/ large bay on the northwestern coast of the South Island, New Zealand

karaoke /kaárə ŏki, kárri-/ n a form of entertainment in which amateur singers sing popular songs accompanied by prerecorded music from a machine that may also display the words on a video screen [Late 20C. < Japanese < kara 'empty' + oke, shortening of ōkesutora 'orchestra' < English ORCHESTRA]

Kara Sea /kaárə-/ sea bordering the northwestern coast of Siberian Russia. It is an arm of the Arctic Ocean. Area: 777,000 sq. km/300,001 sq. mi.

karate

karate /kə raáti/ n a traditional Japanese form of unarmed combat, now widely popular as a sport, in which fast blows or kicks are used [Mid-20C. < Japanese < kara 'empty' + te 'hand']

karateka /kə raáti ka/ n somebody who practises or is an expert in karate [< Japanese, 'karate person']

Karbala /kaárbələ/, **Karbalā'** city in central Iraq, on the edge of the Syrian Desert. Population: 296,705 (1987).

Karelia /kə reéli ə/ **1.** autonomous republic in the

northwestern part of the Russian Federation. It is mainly covered by forest and has considerable mineral wealth. Language: Finnish, Russian. Currency: rouble. Capital: Petrozavodsk. Population: 766,400 (2000). Area: 180,500 sq. km/69,690 sq. mi. Official name **Republic of Karelia** **2.** historic region on the border between Finland and Russia in northeastern Europe, now divided between a Finnish province and the Republic of Karelia

Karelian /kə reéli ən/ n **1.** a dialect of Finnish spoken in Karelia. Native speakers: 120,000. **2.** somebody who comes from Karelia —**Karelian** adj

Karen /kə rén/ (plural **-rens** or same) n **1.** a member of a people who live mainly in southern and eastern Myanmar **2.** a Tibeto-Burman language spoken in southern and eastern Myanmar. Native speakers: 2 million. [Mid-18C. < Burmese ka-reng 'wild, unclean man'] —**Karen** adj

Kariba, Lake /kə reébə/ artificial lake on the border between Zambia and Zimbabwe, southern Africa. It was created by building the Kariba Dam across the River Zambezi. Area: 5,310 sq. km/2,050 sq. mi.

Karl-Marx-Stadt /kaarl maárks shtaat/ former name for Chemnitz (1953–90)

Karloff /kaár lof/, **Boris** (1887–1969) British actor. He appeared in numerous US horror films, notably as the monster in Frankenstein (1931). Born **Pratt, William Henry**

> 'The monster was indeed the best friend I could ever have.'
> [Boris Karloff. Quoted in Connoisseur; January 1991]

Karlovy Vary /kaár lawvi vaári/ city in the northwestern Czech Republic, situated on the River Ohře, west of Prague. Population: 55,000 (1997).

Karlsruhe /kaárlz roo ə/ industrial and university city in Baden-Württemberg State, southwestern Germany. Population: 277,011 (1997).

karma /kaármə/ n **1.** ACTIONS DETERMINING FUTURE STATE in Hindu and Buddhist philosophy, the quality of somebody's current and future lives as determined by that person's behaviour in this and in previous lives **2.** ATMOSPHERE the atmosphere radiated by a place, situation, person, or object (informal) **3.** DESTINY destiny or fate [Early 19C. < Sanskrit karman 'fate, action'] —**karmic** adj

Karnak /kaár nak/ village in eastern Egypt, on the River Nile, occupying part of the site of ancient Thebes

Karnatak /kər naátak/ adj relating to the linguistic region in south-central India between the Eastern Ghats and the Coromandel coast, now part of Madras state [Early 19C, < KARNATAKA (see CARNATIC)]

Karnataka /kər naátəkə/, **Karnātaka** state in southern India. Capital: Bangalore. Language: Kannada. Population: 52,733,958 (2001). Area: 191,791 sq. km/74,051 sq. mi.

Karnatak music /kər naátak-/, **Karnatic music** /kər naátik-/ n the classical music of southern India, which often accompanies dance

Karnatic /kər naátak/ adj GEOG same as **Karnatak**

Karoo /kə roó/, **Karroo** semidesert plateau region in Western Cape Province, South Africa. Area: 259,000 sq. km/100,000 sq. mi.

kaross /kə róss/ n a blanket made of animal skins, used in southern Africa as either a cloak or a mattress [Mid-18C. < Afrikaans karos]

Karratha /kə raáthə/ town on the western coast of Western Australia, an industrial centre. Population: 10,057 (1996).

karri /kárri/ n **1.** a durable wood from an Australian eucalyptus tree. Use: building. **2.** a eucalyptus tree that yields karri. Native to: Australia. Latin name: Eucalyptus diversifolia. [Late 19C. < Aboriginal]

Karroo ♦ **Karoo**

karsey n HOUSEHOLD same as **khazi** (slang)

karst /kaarst/ n a limestone landscape, characterized by caves, fissures, and underground streams [Late 19C. < German der Karst, plateau region in Slovenia] —**karstic** adj

kart /kaart/ n a small low engine-powered vehicle, like a miniature racing car, used in racing [Mid-20C. Shortening of GO-KART] —**karting** n

Karttika /kaártikə/, **Kartika** n in the Hindu calendar, the eighth month of the year, lasting 30 days. Date: October to November. See table at **calendar**

Kartvelian /kaart veéli ən/ n a family of languages including Georgian, spoken in the region south of the Caucasus Mountains. They are unrelated to the North Caucasian languages. Native speakers: 4 million. [< Georgian Kartvelebi 'Georgians'] —**Kartvelian** adj

Karumba /kərúmbə/ fishing port on the Gulf of Carpentaria in northwestern Queensland, Australia. Population: 1,043 (1996).

karyo- prefix cell nucleus ◊ karyoplasm [Via modern Latin < Greek karuon 'kernel']

karyogamy /kárri óggəmi/ n the fusion of cell nuclei that occurs during fertilization —**karyogamic** /kárri ə gámmik/ adj

karyogram /kárri ə gram/ n a photograph or diagram of the chromosomes of a cell in sequence

karyokinesis /kárri ōki neéssiss, -kī-/ n BIOL same as **mitosis** —**karyokinetic** /kárri ōki néttik, -kī-/ adj

karyology /kárri ólləji/ n the study of cell nuclei, especially with reference to chromosomes —**karyologic** /kárri ə lójjik/ adj —**karyological** adj —**karyologist** n

karyolymph /kárri ō limf/ n BIOL same as **nuclear sap**

karyoplasm /kárri ō plazəm/ n BIOL same as **nucleoplasm** —**karyoplasmic** /kárri ō plázmik/ adj

karyosome /kárri ō sōm/ n a thickened mass of chromatin in a cell nucleus

karyotype /kárri ō tīp/ n **1.** CHARACTERISTICS OF CELL CHROMOSOMES the appearance and characteristics of the chromosomes of a cell, especially size, number, and form **2.** PHOTOMICROGRAPH OF CELL CHROMOSOMES a photomicrograph in which a cell's chromosomes are arranged according to size and classification ■ vt (-types, -typing, -typed) FIND KARYOTYPE OF CELL to determine the karyotype of a cell —**karyotypic** /kárri ō típpik/ adj —**karyotypical** adj —**karyotypically** adv

Karzai /kaar zī/, **Hamid-** (b. 1955?) prime minister of Afghanistan. He was deputy foreign minister (1992–94) and chairman of the Interim Administration of Afghanistan (2001–02) before becoming prime minister in 2002.

karzy /kaárzi/ (plural **-zies**), **karsey**, **kazi** /kaázi/ (plural **-zis**) n HOUSEHOLD same as **khazi** (slang) [Mid-20C. Alteration of Italian casa 'house']

Kasavubu /kássə voó boo/, **Joseph** (1913?–69) Congolese politician. First president of the Republic of the Congo (now the Democratic Republic of the Congo, 1960–65), following independence from Belgium (1960), he was overthrown in a coup by Mobutu Sese Seko (1965).

kasbah /káz baa/, **casbah** n **1.** in North Africa, the older part of a city or town, often the market area **2.** in North Africa, a fortress or palace [Mid-18C. Via French < form of Arabic kaṣaba 'fortress']

kasha /káshə/ n a dish of cooked buckwheat resembling porridge, originally from eastern Europe [Early 19C. < Russian]

Kashmir /kash meér/ **1.** disputed territory in the Northern part of South Asia. All of the territory is claimed by India and Pakistan, and part of the territory is claimed by China. Area: 222,236 sq. km/85,806 sq. mi. **2.** ♦ **Azad Kashmir**

Kashmiri /kash meéri/ n **1.** somebody who comes from Kashmir **2.** the Dardic official state language of Kashmir, also spoken in neighbouring areas. Native speakers: 5 million. —**Kashmiri** adj

kashruth /káshrəth, kash roót/, **kashrut** n **1.** the body of Jewish laws that relate to the preparation and fitness of foods and to items such as textiles and ritual scrolls to be used by Jewish people **2.** the fitness of an item for use by Jews, as determined by reference to kashruth [Early 20C. < Hebrew, 'fitness']

Kaskaskia /kəss káski ə/ (plural **-as** or same) n a member of a Native North American people, one of the six peoples who formed the Illinois Confederacy —**Kaskaskia** adj

Kasparov /káspə rof/, **Garry** (b. 1963) Azerbaijani chess player. He became world champion following his defeat of Anatoly Karpov in 1985. Full name **Kasparov, Garry Kimovich**. Born **Weinstein, Garri**

Kassala /kə saálə/, **Kassalā** city in northeastern Sudan. Population: 234,270 (1993).

Kassel /káss'l/, **Cassel** industrial city in west-central Germany. It is known for its exhibitions of contemporary art that have been held there every four years since 1955. Population: 201,789 (1997).

kata /káttə/ n a sequence of movements in some martial arts such as karate, used either for training or to demonstrate technique [Mid-20C. < Japanese, 'model, pattern']

katabatic /káttə báttik/ adj describes a wind that moves down a slope as a result of the cooling of air at higher altitudes [Late 19C. < Greek katabatikos < katabainein 'go down']

katabolism n BIOCHEM another spelling of **catabolism**

katakana /káttə kaánə/ n a set of angular symbols representing syllables used in Japanese writing mainly for transliterating non-Japanese words [Early 18C. < Japanese < kata 'side' + kana, syllabic writing system]

Kata Tjuta /kaátə joótə/ group of monolithic rocks in southwestern Northern Territory, Australia, 26 km/16 mi. west of Uluru. Highest point 3507 ft/1,069 m. Former name **Olgas**

Kathak /kúttək/ n a form of classical dance from northern India that tells a story and is marked by fast footwork and pirouettes [Mid-20C. < Sanskrit kathaka 'storyteller' < kathā 'story']

Kathakali /kaáthə kaáli/ n a stylized form of drama from Kerala, southern India, that interprets stories from Hindu classical literature by combining dance and mime [Early 20C. < Malayalam < Sanskrit kathā 'story' + Malayalam kaḷi 'play']

Katharevousa /káthə révvoóssə/ n a form of modern Greek, used in literature as opposed to everyday speech and writing, that employs some of the features of classical Greek. ◊ **Demotic** (sense 1) [Early 20C. < Greek kathareuousa < katharos 'pure']

Katherine /káthrən/ town in north-central Northern Territory, Australia, a centre of beef production, fruit-growing, and tourism. Population: 8,824 (2002 estimate).

Katherine Gorge series of sandstone gorges cut by the River Katherine in the Northern Territory of Australia, northeast of Katherine

Kathmandu /kát man doó/, **Katmandu** capital city of Nepal, located in the central part of the country. It is situated about 89 km/55 mi. from the border with India. Population: 533,000 (1995).

katipo n a poisonous spider. Native to: New Zealand. Latin name: Latrodectus katipo.

Katmai, Mount /kát mī/ volcano in southwestern Alaska, in Katmai National Park and Preserve. Height: 2,047 m/6,716 ft.

Katmai National Park and Preserve national park in southwestern Alaska, on the Alaska Peninsula. Area: 16565 sq. km/6396 sq. mi.

Katmandu another spelling of **Kathmandu**

Katoomba /kə toómbə/ town in southeastern New South Wales, Australia. Population: 17,700 (1996).

Katowice /káttə veétsə/ city in southern Poland. It is an important mining and industrial centre. Population: 349,000 (1997).

Katsina /kátsinə/ city in northern Nigeria, the capital of Katsina State. Population: 201,500 (1995).

Kattegat /káttə gat/ strait between the southwestern coast of Sweden and the eastern coast of the Jutland peninsula, Denmark. Length: 225 km/140 mi.

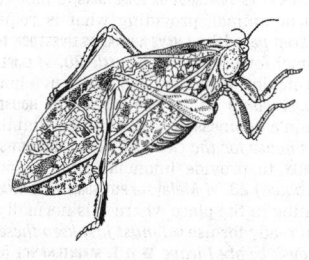

katydid

katydid /káyti did/ *n* a large green grasshopper with very long antennae. Native to: North America. Family: Tettigoniidae. [Late 18C. An imitation of the sound produced when the male rubs its front wings together]

Katyn Forest /kə teén-/ forest in western European Russia, near Smolensk, where the mass grave of thousands of Polish army officers murdered by Soviet security services was discovered in 1943

Katz /kats/, **Sir Bernard** (1911–2003) German-born British biophysicist. He was the joint winner of the Nobel Prize in physiology or medicine (1970) for his work on neurotransmitters.

katzenjammer /káts'n jamər/ *n* US (*dated informal*) **1.** MED same as **hangover 2.** a bewildered or discouraged state **3.** a loud and confused noise [Mid-19C. < German < *Katze* 'cat' + *Jammer* 'distress']

Kauai /kaa wí/ fourth largest island in Hawaii, the northernmost of the main islands. Population: 59,946 (2002 estimate). Area: 1,430 sq. km/552 sq. mi.

Kauffman /kówfmən/, **Angelica** (1741–1807) Swiss painter. Her essentially rococo paintings, often of historical or mythological subjects, incorporated aspects of neo-classicism. She was a founding member of the Royal Academy in London and worked with the British architect and interior designer, Robert Adam. Full name **Kauffman, Maria Ann Angelica**

Kaufman, Mount /kówfmən/ former name for **Lenin Peak**

Kaufman /kówfmən/, **George S.** (1889–1961) US playwright and director. He co-wrote many Broadway comedies such as *Animal Crackers* (1928), *Stage Door* (1936), and *The Man Who Came to Dinner* (1939). Full name **Kaufman, George Simon**

> 'Satire is what closes Saturday night.'
> [George S. Kaufman. Quoted in *George S. Kaufman and His Friends*, Scott Meredith; 1974]

kaumatua /kow má·a too ə/ *n* a Maori elder or leader [< Maori *kaumātua*]

Kaunas /kównəss/ industrial city in central Lithuania, situated about 100 km/60 mi. west of Vilnius. Population: 412,610 (2000).

Kaunda /kaa óondə/, **Kenneth** (*b.* 1924) Zambian politician. He was Zambia's first president after independence (1964–91). Full name **Kaunda, Kenneth David**

> 'I pray the Good Lord to give us courage to recognize our weaknesses and to give us wisdom to recognize the truth and, having recognized that truth, moral power to get committed to it through thick and thin.'
> [Kenneth Kaunda. Quoted in *Kenneth Kaunda*, Philip Brownrigg; 1989]

kauri /kówri/ *n* **1.** a strong light-coloured wood distinguished by fine speckling. Use: cabinetwork, boats, carving. **2.** an evergreen tree that yields kauri. Native to: New Zealand. Latin name: *Agathis australis*. **3.** INDUST same as **kauri gum** [Early 19C. < Maori]

kauri gum, kauri resin *n* the brittle resin of the kauri tree that is usually found in fossilized form. Use: varnishes.

kava /káavə/ *n* **1.** HERBAL REMEDY a herbal medicine made from the dried roots and rhizome of a bush. Use: to relieve anxiety, improve sleep. **2.** DRINK a narcotic drink made from the roots of a bush **3.** POLYNESIAN BUSH a bush of the pepper family whose root and rhizome are the source of kava. Flowers: small, clustered in spikes. Native to: Polynesia. Latin name: *Piper methysticum*. [Late 18C. < Polynesian, 'bitter']

Kavaratti /kúvvə rúttee/ island and capital of the Union Territory of Lakshadweep, southwestern India. Population: 10,113 (2001).

Kāveri another spelling of **Cauvery**

Kawabata /káwə báttə/, **Yasunari** (1899–1972) Japanese novelist. His works include *Snow Country* (1956) and *Thousand Cranes* (1959). He was the first Japanese writer to be awarded the Nobel Prize in literature (1968).

Kawaguchi /káawə goóchi/ city in southeastern Honshu, Japan, north of Tokyo in Saitama Prefecture. Population: 463,879 (2002).

Kawasaki /káawə saáki/ city in east-central Honshu, Japan, south of Tokyo, beside Tokyo Bay in Kanagawa Prefecture. Population: 1,245,780 (2002).

Kay /kay/, **John** (1704–64) British inventor. He invented the flying shuttle, patented in 1733, which contributed greatly to the mechanization of textile manufacture.

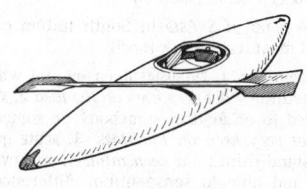

kayak

kayak /kí ak, kaiak/ *n* **1.** a lightweight fibreglass canoe propelled by a double-bladed paddle, used for leisure and in competitive sport **2.** a traditional Inuit boat that is narrow and pointed and consists of a light frame covered with skins. It is propelled by one or two people using double-bladed paddles. [Mid-18C. < Inuit *qayaq*] —**kayak** *vti* —**kayaker** *n* — **kayaking** *n*

kayo /káy ó/ (*slang*) *n* (*plural* -os) a knockout, especially in boxing ■ *vt* (-os, -oing, -oed) to knock somebody out, especially in boxing [Early 20C. < the pronunciation of KO]

Kayseri /kíssəri/ city in central Turkey, near Mount Argaeus. It is the capital of Kayseri Province. Population: 475,657 (1997).

kazachok /kaázə chók/ *n* a Ukrainian and Russian folk dance in which high kicks are made from a squatting position [Early 20C. < Russian, diminutive of *kazak* 'Cossack']

Kazakh /kí zák, ká zak/, **Kazak** *n* **1.** a member of a people of Central Asia living mainly in Kazakhstan **2.** the Turkic official language of Kazakhstan, also spoken in Mongolia, China, and Afghanistan. Native speakers: 8 million. [Mid-19C. Via Russian < Kazakh *kazak*] —**Kazakh** *adj*

Kazakhstan

Kazakhstan /kázzak staán/ country in Central Asia, bordered by Russia, China, Kyrgyzstan, Uzbekistan, Turkmenistan, and the Caspian Sea. Language: Kazakh. Currency: tenge. Capital: Astana. Population: 16,763,795 (2003). Area: 2,717,300 sq. km/1,049,200 sq. mi. Official name **Republic of Kazakhstan**

Kazan /kə zán/, **Elia** (1909–2003) Turkish-born US stage and film director and novelist. He won Academy Awards for directing *Gentleman's Agreement* (1947) and *On the Waterfront* (1954). Born **Kazanjoglous, Elia**

Kazantzakis /kázzan zaákiss/, **Nikos** (1883–1957) Greek writer. His novels include *Zorba the Greek* (1943) and *The Last Temptation of Christ* (1951).

kazatsky /kə zátski/ (*plural* -skies), **kazatske** *n* DANCE same as **kazachok**

Kazbek /kaaz bék/ peak on the border of Russia and Georgia in the Caucasus Mountains. Height: 5,037 m/16,526 ft.

kazi *n* HOUSEHOLD another spelling of **khazi** (*slang*)

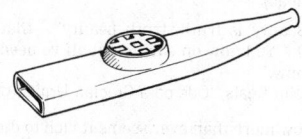

kazoo

kazoo /kə zoó/ (*plural* -zoos) *n* a toy instrument that makes a buzzing sound, consisting of a tube with a mouthpiece and a hole covered by a thin diaphragm [Late 19C. An imitation of its sound]

KB *abbr* **1.** COMPUT kilobyte **2.** King's Bench **3.** CHESS king's bishop **4.** Knight Bachelor

KBE *abbr* Knight Commander of the Order of the British Empire

KBP *abbr* CHESS king's bishop's pawn

kbyte /káy bīt/ *abbr* COMPUT kilobyte

kc *abbr* PHYS kilocycle

KC *abbr* **1.** Kennel Club **2.** LAW King's Counsel **3.** RELIG Knight of Columbus

kcal /káy kal/ *abbr* MEASURE kilocalorie

KCB *abbr* Knight Commander of the Order of the Bath

KCMG *abbr* Knight Commander of the Order of St Michael and St George

KCVO *abbr* Knight Commander of the Royal Victorian Order

ke *abbr* ONLINE Kenya (*used in Internet addresses*) See table at **domain name**

kea /keé ə/ *n* a large parrot with brownish-green feathers. Native to: mountainous regions of New Zealand. Latin name: *Nestor notabilis*. [Mid-19C. < Maori]

Kean /keen/, **Edmund** (1787–1833) British actor. He was noted for his tragic Shakespearean roles, principally Richard III, Hamlet, Othello, Iago, and Macbeth.

Keating /keéting/, **Paul** (*b.* 1944) Australian politician. He was Labor prime minister of Australia (1991–96). Full name **Keating, Paul John**. See table at **prime minister**

> 'Good economics is good politics.'
> [Paul Keating, *Sydney Morning Herald*; 27 August 1988]

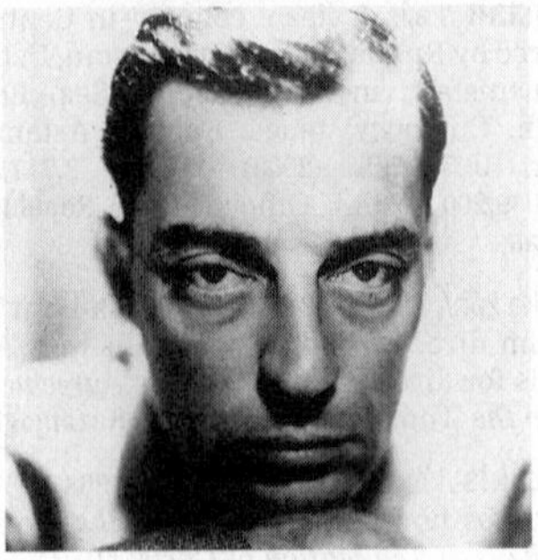

Buster Keaton

Keaton /kéet'n/, **Buster** (1895–1966) US silent film actor and director. He was a deadpan acrobatic clown in many classic silent films such as *The Navigator* (1924) and *The General* (1927). Born **Keaton, Joseph Francis**

Keats /keets/, **John** (1795–1821) British poet. His lyrical intensity made him one of the most influential of the romantic poets. His great odes were collected in *Lamia, Isabella, The Eve of St Agnes, and Other Poems* (1820). See Cultural note at **nightingale, urn** — **Keatsian** *adj*

> '"Beauty is truth, truth beauty",—that is all / Ye know on earth, and all ye need to know.'
> [John Keats, 'Ode on a Grecian Urn'; 1820]

> 'Now more than ever seems it rich to die, / To cease upon the midnight with no pain, / While thou art pouring forth thy soul abroad / In such an ecstasy!'
> [John Keats, 'Ode to a Nightingale'; 1820]

kebab /ki báb, kə báab/ *n* **1.** a selection of small pieces of tender food such as poultry, meat, seafood, or vegetables threaded onto a stick and grilled **2.** a pitta bread filled with small pieces of grilled meat, often with salad and a hot sauce [Late 17C. < Arabic *kabāb*]

Keble /kéeb'l/, **John** (1792–1866) British clergyman and poet. He helped to launch the Oxford Movement, and was also known for his book of poems, *The Christian Year* (1827). Keble College, Oxford, was named in his memory.

> 'Abide with me from morn till eve, / For without Thee I cannot live; / Abide with me when night is nigh, / For without Thee I dare not die.'
> [John Keble, 'Evening', *The Christian Year*; 1827]

Kechua *n, adj* PEOPLES, LANG another spelling of **Quechua**

Kedah /kéddə/ state in northwestern Malaysia, on the Malay Peninsula. Capital: Alur Setar. Area: 9,426 sq. km/3,639 sq. mi.

keddah *n* FIELD SPORTS another spelling of **kheda**

kedge /kej/ *vti* (**kedges, kedging, kedged**) to move a vessel by pulling on a rope or cable attached to a light anchor, or be moved in this way ■ *n also* **kedge anchor** a light anchor, especially one that is lodged some distance from a vessel so that the vessel can be pulled towards it [15C. Origin ?]

kedgeree /kéjjə ree/ *n* **1.** a dish of British origin consisting of rice with flaked smoked fish and hard-boiled eggs **2.** a spicy dish of South Asian origin made from lentils, rice, and sometimes fish [Mid-17C. < Hindi *khicṛī*]

keech /keech/ *n Scotland* an offensive term for human or animal excrement (*slang*) [Late 16C. Origin ?]

keek /keek/ *Scotland vi* (**keeks, keeking, keeked**) to look at something, usually in a quick furtive way or through a narrow opening ■ *n* a quick, often furtive look at something [14C. Origin ?]

keel /keel/ *n* **1.** NAUT **SHIP'S STRUCTURAL ELEMENT** the main structural element of a ship, stretching along the centre line of its bottom from the bow to the stern. It sometimes extends farther downwards into the water to provide extra stability. **2.** AVIAT **AIRCRAFT'S STRUCTURAL ELEMENT** a structure that looks or acts like a ship's keel, e.g. the main structural element of an aircraft's fuselage **3.** BIRDS **PART OF BIRD'S BREASTBONE** a ridge-shaped part in the breastbone of a bird to which the flight muscles are anchored. Technical name **carina 4.** BIOL **PART LIKE RIDGE** any ridge-shaped part of an organism **5.** same as **ship** (*literary*) ■ *vti* (**keels, keeling, keeled**) NAUT **CAPSIZE** to capsize a vessel, or capsize [14C. < Old Norse *kjölr*] ◇ **on an even keel** in a stable steady condition

keel over *v* **1.** *vi* to collapse or fall over, often through exhaustion or illness (*informal*) **2.** *vti* NAUT same as **keel**

keelage /kéelij/ *n* a docking fee for merchant ships, charged by a port

keelboat /kéel bōt/ *n* a covered river boat with a keel and shallow draught but no sail, propelled by rowing, poling, or towing, and used for transporting freight

keelhaul /kéel hawl/ (**-hauls, -hauling, -hauled**) *vt* **1.** to drag somebody on a rope from one side of a vessel to the other under the keel as a form of punishment **2.** to reprimand somebody severely (*informal*) [Mid-17C. < Dutch *kielhalen*]

keelie /kéeli/ *n Scotland* an offensive term for a man or boy from a town or city, especially Glasgow, who is regarded as being of low social class and tough or rough [Mid-19C. < Gaelic *gille* 'boy, servant']

keelson /kélss'n, kéelss'n/, **kelson** /kélss'n/ *n* a metal or wooden beam attached to the upper side of a boat's keel to reinforce it [13C. Probably < Old Norse *kjölsvīn* or Low German *kielsvīn*]

keema /kéemə/ *n S Asia* in South Indian cookery, minced meat [Late 20C. < Hindi]

keen[1] /keen/ *adj* **1.** **ENTHUSIASTIC** eager and willing to do something ○ *not very keen on the idea* **2.** **ATTRACTED** attracted to or fond of somebody or something ○ *He's not very keen on tomatoes.* **3.** **ACUTE** quick to understand things ○ *a keen mind* **4.** **SENSITIVE** finely tuned and able to sense minor differences, distinctions, or details ○ *a keen sense of smell* **5.** **INTENSE** intense and lively ○ *keen competition* **6.** **SHARP** having a sharp cutting edge (*literary*) ○ *a keen razor* **7.** **BITING** cold and penetrating ○ *a keen wind* **8.** COMM **COMPETITIVELY LOW** low and therefore competitive ○ *keen prices* **9.** *N Am* **VERY GOOD** fine or very good (*slang dated*) [Old English *cēne* 'brave, clever' < Germanic] — **keenly** *adv* —**keenness** *n*

keen[2] /keen/ *vi* (**keens, keening, keened**) to cry out or wail in grief, especially while lamenting the dead ■ *n* a lamentation for a dead person (*literary*) [Early 19C. < Irish *caoinim* 'I wail'] —**keener** *n*

~~keeness~~ incorrect spelling of **keenness**

keep /keep/ *v* (**keeps, keeping, kept** /kept/) **1.** *vti* **POSSESS SOMETHING** to hold or maintain something in your possession ○ *The sample is yours to keep.* **2.** *vt* **MAINTAIN CONDITION OF SOMETHING** to maintain somebody or something in a particular place or condition ○ *Keep your arm up.* **3.** *vt* **STORE SOMETHING** to store something in a place when it is not in use ○ *kept the keys in a drawer* **4.** *vti* **CONTINUE** to cause somebody or something to continue in a particular way or activity, or continue in a particular way ○ *kept working* **5.** *vt* **SAFEGUARD INFORMATION** to refrain from telling a secret or giving other information ○ *keep a secret* **6.** *vt* **SAVE SOMETHING** to save something for later use or withhold something from use ○ *kept some in reserve* **7.** *vt* **BE TRUE TO SOMETHING** to fulfil a promise or other verbal commitment ○ *kept his word* **8.** *vt* **FULFIL RELIGIOUS DUTY** to observe a religious obligation ○ *keep kosher* ○ *keep the Sabbath* **9.** *vt* **MAINTAIN RECORD** to create or maintain something as a written record ○ *keep a diary* **10.** *vi* **STAY** to remain in a particular condition ○ *keep warm* **11.** *vi* **MAINTAIN COURSE** to follow a particular course or direction ○ *Keep straight ahead until the roundabout.* **12.** *vi* **NOT SPOIL** to remain fresh or in a usable condition ○ *That fish won't keep in this hot weather.* **13.** *vi* **DO SOMETHING REPEATEDLY** to repeat an action a number of times ○ *He keeps calling me in the middle of the night.* **14.** *vi* **NOT REQUIRE ATTENTION** to be able to be postponed ○ *The dusting will keep until tomorrow.* **15.** *vi* **BE IN PARTICULAR CONDITION** to be or remain in a particular condition, especially in terms of health ○ *keeping well* **16.** *vt* **HAVE SOMETHING FOR SALE** to have something in stock in order to sell it ○ *keep a large selection of scarves* **17.** *vt* **DETAIN SOMEBODY** to make somebody wait or prevent somebody from going ○ *I won't keep you a moment.* **18.** *vt* **LOOK AFTER SOMEBODY OR SOMETHING** to take care of a person or animal, providing what is required to live ○ *keep pets* **19.** *vt* **HAVE ANIMAL AS LIVESTOCK** to breed an animal for profit ○ *keep cattle* **20.** *vt* **EMPLOY SOMEBODY** to employ somebody, especially in a household ○ *keep servants* **21.** *vt* **RUN BUSINESS OR HOUSEHOLD** to maintain a business, house, or other establishment ○ *keeps house for the General* **22.** *vt* **SUPPORT SOMEBODY FINANCIALLY** to provide financially for a spouse or lover (*dated*) **23.** *vt Malaysia* **PUT SOMETHING AWAY** to put something in the place where it is normally stored or kept ready for use ○ *I must just keep these papers in my desk before I leave.* ■ *n* **1.** **MAINTENANCE** food and lodging, or whatever somebody needs to live ○ *work for your keep* **2.** **CASTLE PART** a stronghold or the innermost fortified part of a castle [Old English *cēpan* 'take, observe', origin ?] ◇ **for keeps** permanently or forever (*informal*) ◇ **keep something to yourself** to refrain from revealing something ◇ **keep (yourself) to yourself** to avoid mixing or communicating with other people

keep at *vt* **1.** to persevere with something, especially something difficult or strenuous **2.** to persist in asking somebody to do something (*informal*) ○ *kept at me to put in longer hours*

keep away *v* **1.** *vt* to prevent somebody or something from going near somebody or something **2.** *vi* to avoid going near somebody or something

keep back *vt* **1.** **NOT TELL SOMETHING** to refrain from telling or revealing something **2.** **WITHHOLD SOMETHING FOR LATER USE** to hold something in reserve for later use or for another purpose **3.** **RESTRAIN SOMETHING** to restrain or confine something to a limit

keep down *v* **1.** *vt* **OPPRESS SOMEBODY OR SOMETHING** to maintain somebody or something in an inferior position or in a state of oppression **2.** *vt* **MAINTAIN SOMETHING AT LOW LEVEL** to maintain something at a low level, position, or number ○ *Keep the costs down.* **3.** *vi* **STAY LOW** to stay in a place or position where you cannot be seen **4.** *vt* **NOT VOMIT SOMETHING** to hold food or drink in your stomach without vomiting ○ *He hasn't been able to keep anything down since the operation.*

keep from *vt* **1.** **HIDE SOMETHING FROM SOMEBODY** to refrain from disclosing something to somebody **2.** **RESTRAIN SOMEBODY** to prevent somebody from doing something **3.** **SAFEGUARD SOMEBODY** to protect somebody from something ○ *kept us from harm*

keep in *vt* **1.** **REPRESS FEELING** to repress something that you feel ○ *keeps in her anger* **2.** **NOT LET SOMEBODY LEAVE** to make somebody stay in a place, e.g. to detain a schoolchild after class or keep a patient in hospital **3.** **PROVIDE SOMEBODY WITH SOMETHING** to provide somebody with a regular supply of something ○ *money to keep us in petrol*

keep in with *vt* to maintain a good relationship with somebody, often because this might be advantageous

keep off *v* **1.** *vt* **PREVENT SOMEBODY OR SOMETHING FROM TOUCHING** to prevent somebody or something from having direct contact with somebody or something else **2.** *vt* **NOT TOUCH SOMEBODY OR SOMETHING** to refrain from direct contact with something or somebody ○ *Keep off the grass!* **3.** *vt* **NOT CONSUME SOMETHING** to prevent somebody from consuming something, or refrain from consuming something ○ *kept off caffeine* **4.** *vt* **NOT TALK ABOUT SOMETHING** to prevent somebody from discussing something, or refrain from discussing something ○ *kept off the topic of money* **5.** *vi* **NOT BEGIN** to fail to start or appear ○ *Let's hope the rain keeps off until the games are over.*

keep on *v* **1.** *vi* **CONTINUE** to continue doing something ○ *kept on teasing the dog* **2.** *vt* **NOT TAKE SOMETHING OFF** to continue wearing something **3.** *vt* **NOT DISMISS SOMEBODY** to continue to employ somebody **4.** *vi* **PERSIST IN TALKING ABOUT SOMETHING** to talk repetitively or continuously about one thing in a way that makes others bored or annoyed (*informal*)

keep on at *vt* to pester or nag somebody about something (*informal*)

keep out *vti* to prevent somebody from entering a place, or refrain from entering a place

keep out of *vti* **1.** to prevent somebody or something from exposure to something, or avoid exposure to something ○ *keep it out of the rain* **2.** to prevent somebody from becoming involved in something, or avoid becoming involved in something ○ *Keep out of her way.*

keep to *vt* to adhere without deviation to a plan, course, or subject

keep up *v* **1.** *vt* MAINTAIN PRESENT LEVEL OF SOMETHING to maintain something at its present level ○ *Keep up the good work.* ○ *That's excellent. Keep it up.* **2.** *vi* STAY EVEN to go as fast or make the same progress as somebody else **3.** *vt* MAINTAIN SOMETHING IN GOOD CONDITION to make sure that something stays in good condition ○ *has a beautiful home but doesn't really keep it up* **4.** *vt* NOT LET SOMEBODY GO TO BED to prevent somebody from sleeping or going to bed at night ○ *The music from the party kept us up till dawn.*

keep up with *vt* **1.** REMAIN INFORMED ABOUT SOMETHING to remain abreast of something that undergoes continuous change or progress ○ *keeps up with technological developments* **2.** STAY IN CONTACT WITH SOMEBODY to stay in contact with somebody, especially by letter ○ *I still keep up with a few friends from school.* **3.** CONTINUE MAKING PAYMENTS to remain up to date with scheduled payments

keeper /keepər/ *n* **1.** MUSEUM GUARDIAN somebody who oversees a museum, gallery, or exhibition **2.** WARDEN somebody whose job is to look after or protect animals **3.** CARETAKER somebody in charge of a building (*usually used in combination*) ○ *a lighthouse keeper* **4.** PRISON GUARD somebody who is responsible for guarding other people, especially in a prison **5.** OCCUPATIONS same as **gamekeeper** **6.** SOMEBODY MAINTAINING SOMETHING somebody who keeps or maintains something ○ *a good record keeper* **7.** SPORTS same as **goalkeeper** (*informal*) **8.** CRICKET same as **wicketkeeper** (*informal*) **9.** HOLDING DEVICE a device used to keep something in place, e.g. a clip **10.** PHYS BAR ACROSS MAGNET'S POLES an iron or steel bar placed across the poles of a permanent horseshoe magnet when it is not in use, to close the magnetic circuit and prevent demagnetization **11.** AMERICAN FOOTBALL MOVE IN AMERICAN FOOTBALL in American football, a move in which the quarterback runs towards the goal with the ball —**keepership** *n*

Keeper of the Privy Purse *n* POL same as **Privy Purse** (sense 2)

keeper ring *n* JEWELLERY same as **guard ring**

keep fit *n* a programme of physical exercises designed to keep the body in good condition

keeping /keepiŋ/ *n* **1.** the act of looking after or caring for somebody or something **2.** somebody's charge, custody, or possession ○ *in his keeping* ◇ **in keeping with** consistent with or suitable for something ◇ **out of keeping with** not consistent with or suitable for something

keepnet /keep net/ *n* a long cylindrical net with wire hoops attached at regular intervals, placed in water and used to keep alive fish that have been caught

keepsake /keep sayk/ *n* a small item or gift kept because it evokes memories of somebody or something [Late 18C. Because kept 'for the sake of' the giver]

keeshond /káyss hond/ (*plural* -**honds** or -**honden** /-hondən/) *n* a dog with a dense shaggy blackish-grey coat and a tightly curled tail, belonging to a breed developed in the Netherlands [Early 20C. < Dutch, 'Kees dog' < Kees, pet form of *Cornelis* 'Cornelius']

keester *n* N Am ANAT another spelling of **keister**

kef *n* DRUGS same as **kif**

keffiyeh /kə feeyə, kaffiyeh/ *n* a cotton headdress fastened by a band and worn by some Arab men [Early 19C. < Arabic *kūfiyya*]

Keflavik /kéffləvik/ town in southwestern Iceland, situated about 35 km/22 mi. southwest of Reykjavik. Population: 7,637 (1996).

keg /keg/ *n* **1.** SMALL BARREL a small barrel used for storing liquids **2.** CONTENTS OF KEG the amount that a keg can hold **3.** BEER BARREL an aluminium barrel that is used for storing and transporting beer [Early 17C. Alteration of *cag* < Old Norse *kaggi*]

keg beer *n* beer that is stored in and served from a pressurized aluminium barrel

kegger /kéggər/ *n* US a party at which beer is served from kegs (*informal*)

keiretsu /kay rétsoo/ (*plural same*) *n* in Japan, a conglomerate headed by a major Japanese bank or made up of companies with a common supply chain linking wholesalers and retailers [< Japanese]

keister /keestər, kīstər/, **keester** /keestər/ *n* N Am the buttocks (*slang humorous*) [Late 19C. Origin ?]

Keitel /kīt'l/, **Wilhelm** (1882–1946) German field marshal. Hitler's chief military adviser during World War II, he was executed for war crimes in 1946.

Kejimkujik National Park /kéjim koojik-/ national park and wildlife preserve in southern Nova Scotia, Canada, established in 1974. Area: 403 sq. km/156 sq. mi.

Kekulé formula /kéka lay-/ *n* the representation of a benzene molecule as a hexagonal ring with alternating single and double bonds linking six carbon atoms, each linked to one hydrogen atom at the vertices [Mid-20C. After Friedrich August *Kekulé* (1829–96), German physicist]

Keller /kéllər/, **Helen** (1880–1968) US author and lecturer. An illness in her infancy left her unable to see or hear, and she was taught to read, write, and speak by Anne Sullivan in a process dramatized in the play and film *The Miracle Worker*. She lectured and wrote widely on political and social issues and her own life experience. Full name **Keller, Helen Adams**

> 'We could never learn to be brave and patient, if there were only joy in the world.'
> [Helen Keller, *Atlantic Monthly*; May 1890]

Kelly /kélli/, **Gene** (1912–96) US film actor, dancer, and director. He is best known for starring in and codirecting *Singin' in the Rain* (1952). Full name **Kelly, Eugene Curran**

> 'You learn to use the camera as part of the choreography. Film dancing will always be a problem because the eye of the camera is coldly realistic, demanding that everything looks natural, and dancing is unrealistic.'
> [Gene Kelly. Quoted in *The Films of Gene Kelly*, Tony Thomas; 1991]

Kelly, **Grace** (1929–82) US film actor. She starred in films such as *High Noon* (1952) and *Rear Window* (1954) before retiring in 1956 to marry Prince Rainier III of Monaco. Full name **Kelly, Grace Patricia**

Kelly, **Ned** (1855–80) Australian bushranger. Pursued by the police for two years, he was captured and hanged in 1880. He subsequently became a folk hero. Full name **Kelly, Edward**

kelly green /kélli-/ *adj* N Am of a bright green colour [Because green is associated with Ireland, where the surname *Kelly* is common] —**kelly green** *n*

keloid /kee loyd/ *n* an area of raised pink or red fibrous scar tissue at the edges of a wound or incision [Mid-19C. < French *kéloïde* < Greek *khēlē* 'crab claw'] —**keloidal** /kee loyd'l/ *adj*

kelp /kelp/ *n* **1.** a brown seaweed with thick broad fronds. Order: Laminariales. **2.** the ash from kelp or other seaweeds. Use: source of potash and iodine. [14C. Origin ?]

kelpie¹ /kélpi/, **kelpy** (*plural* -**pies**) *n* in Scottish folklore, a malicious water spirit that takes the form of a horse and lures people to death by drowning [Late 17C. Origin ?]

kelpie² /kélpi/ *n* a smooth-haired dog belonging to a breed of sheepdog. Native to: Australia. [Early 20C. After *King's Kelpie*, the female dog that founded the breed]

kelpy *n* another spelling of **kelpie¹**

kelson *n* NAUT same as **keelson**

kelt /kelt/ *n* a salmon that has returned to the river of its birth and recently spawned. In most species, the kelts do not survive, but Atlantic salmon can return to the ocean to spawn for another season. [14C. Origin ?]

Kelt *n* PEOPLES another spelling of **Celt**

kelvin /kélvin/ *n* the SI unit of absolute temperature, equal to 1/273.16 of the absolute temperature of the triple point of water, equivalent to one degree Celsius. A temperature in kelvin may be converted to Celsius by subtracting 273.16. Symbol **K** ■ *adj* relating to or measured on the Kelvin scale [Early 20C. After William Thomson, 1st Baron KELVIN]

Kelvin /kélvin/, **William Thomson, 1st Baron** (1824–1907)

British physicist. He did pioneering work in thermodynamics and electricity, and devised the absolute temperature scale. His work helped develop the law of the conservation of energy. Full name **Kelvin of Largs, William Thomson, 1st Baron**

Kelvin scale *n* a temperature scale on which zero is the lowest possible temperature and the triple point of water is defined as 273.16K. It is based on heat transfer between two sections of a reversible heat engine.

Kelvinside /kélvin sīd/ *n* Scotland an old-fashioned anglicized accent of Scottish English, considered affected [After *Kelvinside*, Glasgow]

Kemerovo /kémma róvə/ city in southern Siberian Russia, on the River Tom'. It is the capital city of Kemerovo Oblast. Population: 538,193 (1995).

kemp /kemp/ *n* a short coarse hair or fibre [14C. < Old Norse *kampr* 'beard, whisker'] —**kempy** *adj*

Kempe /kemp/, **Margery** (1373?–1440?) English mystic. She dictated *The Book of Margery Kempe*, an account of her visions and pilgrimages.

> 'I have oftentimes told thee, daughter, that thinking, weeping, and high contemplation are the best life on earth, and thou shalt have more merit in Heaven for one year of thinking in thy mind than for a hundred years of praying with thy mouth.'
> [Margery Kempe, *The Booke of Margery Kempe*; 1435?]

Kempe /kémpə/, **Rudolf** (1910–76) German conductor. He is known for his interpretations of Richard Strauss and Richard Wagner. He conducted the Royal Philharmonic Orchestra, London (1961–75).

Kempsey /kémpsi/ town in northeastern New South Wales, Australia, a centre of agriculture, timber production, and light industry. Population: 27,620 (2002 estimate).

Kemp's ridley /kémps-/ *n* a small endangered sea turtle with a drab greyish-green back and a prominent beak. Native to: Gulf of Mexico, Atlantic Ocean. Latin name: *Lepidochelys kempii*. [After Richard M. *Kemp*, who found a specimen in Key West, Florida, in 1880 and sent it to Harvard for identification]

kempt /kempt/ *adj* tidy and well looked after (*archaic*) [Old English *cemd*, past participle of *cemban* 'comb' < Germanic]

ken /ken/ *n* somebody's knowledge or understanding ○ *It's beyond my ken.* ■ *vti* (**kens, kenning, kenned** or **kent** /kent/) Scotland same as **know** [Old English *cennan* 'make known' < Indo-European]

Kendal /kéndəl/ market town in the Lake District, Cumbria, northwestern England. Population: 25,461 (1991).

Kendal green *n* **1.** a light greyish-green coarse thick woollen cloth similar to tweed, formerly worn by foresters **2.** a light greyish-green colour —**Kendal green** *adj*

Popperfoto

kendo

kendo /kéndō/ *n* a Japanese martial art in which people fence using bamboo sticks instead of swords [Early 20C. < Japanese, 'way of the sword']

Kendrew /kén droo/, **Sir John** (1917–97) British molecular biologist. He won a joint Nobel Prize in chemistry (1962) for his work on determining the structure of proteins. Full name **Kendrew, Sir John Cowdery**

Keneally /kə neéli, -nálli/, **Thomas** (*b.* 1935) Australian novelist. His book *Schindler's Ark* (1982) won the Booker Prize and was made into a film, *Schindler's List* (1993), by Stephen Spielberg. Full name **Keneally, Thomas Michael**

Kenilworth /kénn'l wurth/ market town in Warwickshire, central England. Its ruined castle dates from the early 12th century. Population: 21,623 (1991).

Kennedy /kénnədi/ (*b.* 1956) British violinist. He is known for his flamboyant style. His repertoire includes classical, jazz, and rock music. Born **Kennedy, Nigel**

Kennedy, Cape /kénnədi/ former name for **Canaveral, Cape** (1963–73)

Kennedy, Mount /kénnədi/ mountain in the St Elias Range in southwestern Yukon Territory, Canada. Height: 4,238 m/13,904 ft.

Kennedy, Charles (*b.* 1959) British politician. He was the youngest member of the British parliament when he was first elected in 1983. He became the party leader of the Liberal Democrats in 1999.

Kennedy, Edmund (1818–48) British-born Australian explorer. He was killed by Aboriginals while exploring northern Queensland, Australia. Full name **Kennedy, Edmund Besley Court**

Kennedy, Edward M. (*b.* 1932) US politician. He became a US senator in 1962 and unsuccessfully ran for the Democratic presidential nomination in 1980. John F. Kennedy and Robert F. Kennedy were his brothers. Full name **Kennedy, Edward Moore**. Known as **Ted Kennedy**

> 'I even opposed the death penalty for the man who killed my brother.'
> [Edward M. Kennedy, *Washington Post*; 29 April 1990]

John F. Kennedy Library
Jackie Kennedy

Kennedy, Jackie (1929–94) US first lady. She married John F. Kennedy in 1953 and as first lady (1961–63) became an international celebrity and style-setter. Born **Bouvier, Jacqueline Lee**. Full name **Kennedy-Onassis, Jacqueline Lee**

Popperfoto
John F. Kennedy

Kennedy, John F. (1917–63) 35th president of the United States. The youngest man elected president (1960), he promoted civil rights, established the Peace Corps, and in 1962 forced Nikita Khrushchev to remove Soviet ballistic missiles from Cuba. He was assassinated in Dallas, Texas, on 22 November 1963. Full name **Kennedy, John Fitzgerald**. Known as **Jack Kennedy**. See table at **president**

> 'And so, my fellow Americans: ask not what your country can do for you—ask what you can do for your country. My fellow citizens of the world: ask not what America will do for you, but what together we can do for the freedom of man.'
> [John F. Kennedy, *Inaugural address as president of the United States*; 20 January 1961]

Kennedy, Joseph P. (1888–1969) US business executive and government official. He was the father of John F., Robert F., and Edward M. Kennedy. He was ambassador to the United Kingdom (1938–40). Full name **Kennedy, Joseph Patrick**

Kennedy, Robert F. (1925–68) US attorney general (1961–64) during the Democratic administration of his brother John F. Kennedy. He was assassinated during his own presidential campaign. Full name **Kennedy, Robert Francis**. Known as **Bobby Kennedy**

> 'Some men see things as they are and say why? I dream things that never were and say "Why not?"'
> [Robert F. Kennedy, *Esquire*; 1969]

kennel /kénn'l/ *n* **1.** HUT FOR DOG a small outdoor structure like a hut, built for a dog to sleep in. N Am term **doghouse 2.** ANIMAL'S LAIR the lair of a wild animal such as a fox **3.** PACK OF DOGS a pack of hounds or dogs ▪ *vti* (**-nels, -nelling, -nelled**) PUT OR STAY IN KENNELS to put a dog into a kennels, or stay in a kennels [14C. < assumed Anglo-Norman *kenil* < Latin *canis* 'dog']

Kennelly-Heaviside layer /kénn'li hévvi sīd-/ *n* PHYS same as **E region** [Early 20C. After Arthur Edwin *Kennelly* (1861–1939), US electrical engineer, and Oliver *Heaviside* (1850–1925), British physicist]

kennels /kénn'lz/ (*plural same*) *n* a place where dogs are bred and trained and where people can leave their dogs while they are away from home

Kenneth I /kénnith/ (*fl* AD mid-9th century) king of Scotland. Around 846 he united the kingdoms of the Scots and the Picts, becoming the first king of Scotland. Known as **Kenneth MacAlpin**

kenning /kénning/ *n* a metaphorical expression, often a phrase, used to denote another word in Old Norse and Old English poetry [Late 19C. < Old Norse < *kenna* 'know']

Kenny, Elizabeth (1886–1952) Australian nurse and physical therapist. She pioneered alternative treatments for poliomyelitis. Her life story is told in the film *Sister Kenny* (1947). Known as **Sister Kenny**

> 'Some minds remain open long enough for the truth not only to enter but to pass on through by way of a ready exit without pausing anywhere along the route.'
> [Elizabeth Kenny, *And They Shall Walk*; 1951]

keno /keénō/ *n* Aus, N Am a game of chance in which players wager on a set of numbers to be drawn at random [Early 19C. Alteration of French *quine* 'set of five winning numbers' < Latin *quini* 'five each' < *quinque* 'five']

kenosis /ki nóssiss/ *n* according to Christian belief, Jesus Christ's act of partly giving up his divine status in order to become a man, as recorded in the Bible (Philippians 2:6–7) [Late 19C. < Greek *kenōsis* 'an emptying' < *heauton ekenōse* 'emptied himself', phrase in Philippians 2:7] —**kenotic** /ki nóttik/ *adj*

kenspeckle /kén spek'l/ *adj Scotland* easily seen or recognized, or well known [Mid-16C. Probably < Old Norse *kennispeki* < *kenna* 'know' + *spak* 'wise']

kent *Scotland* past participle, past tense of **ken**

Kent /kent/ county in the southeastern corner of England, and a former Anglo-Saxon kingdom. It contains the ports of Dover and Sheerness, and the terminus of the Channel Tunnel. Maidstone is the administrative centre. Population: 1,329,718 (2001). Area: 3,731 sq. km/1,441 sq. mi. —**Kentish** *adj*

Kent, William (1685–1748) English architect and landscape designer. He promoted the Palladian style in architecture and an informal style in garden design.

kente /kéntə/, **kente cloth** *n* a handwoven cloth from Ghana, usually with complex designs of very bright colours, traditionally worn on important ceremonial and religious occasions [Mid-20C. < Twi, 'cloth']

kentia /kénti ə/, **kentia palm** *n* a tall palm tree that is widely cultivated for its decorative foliage. Native to: Lord Howe Island. Latin name: *Howea forsterana*. [Late 19C. < modern Latin, after William KENT]

kentledge /kéntlij/ *n* scrap iron or other heavy material used as permanent ballast on ships [Early 17C. < Old French *quintelage* 'ballast' < *quintal* (see QUINTAL)]

Kentucky /ken túki/ **1.** state in the east-central United States, bordered by Illinois, Indiana, Missouri, Ohio, Tennessee, Virginia, and West Virginia. Capital: Frankfort. Population: 5,092,891 (2002 estimate). Area: 104,664 sq. km/40,411 sq. mi. **2.** river in central Kentucky that flows northwestwards to join the Ohio River at Carrollton. Length: 417 km/259 mi. —**Kentuckian** *n, adj*

Kentucky bluegrass *n* a grass widely used for pastureland and lawns. Native to: Africa, Europe, Asia, naturalized in North America. Latin name: *Poa pratensis*.

Kentucky Derby *n* a race for three-year-old horses that has been run annually since 1875 at Churchill Downs in Louisville, Kentucky. It is held on the first Saturday in May.

Kenya

Kenya /kénnyə, keényə/ country in eastern Africa. It became an independent member of the Commonwealth in 1963. Language: English, Swahili. Currency: Kenyan shilling. Capital: Nairobi. Population: 31,639,091 (2003). Area: 582,646 sq. km/224,961 sq. mi. Official name **Republic of Kenya** —**Kenyan** *n, adj*

Kenya, Mount extinct volcano in central Kenya, the second highest mountain in Africa. Height: 5,199 m/17,057 ft.

Kenyatta /ken yáttə/, **Jomo** (1891–1978) Kenyan politician. Following the outbreak of the Mau Mau uprising during Kenya's colonial period, he was imprisoned (1951–61). After independence he became Kenya's first prime minister (1963–64) and president (1964–78). Born **Kamau wa Ngengi**

> 'The African is conditioned, by the cultural and social institutions of centuries, to a freedom of which Europe has little conception, and it is not in his nature to accept serfdom forever.'
> [Jomo Kenyatta, *Facing Mount Kenya*; 1938]

Kenyon /kényən/, **Dame Kathleen** (1906–78) British archaeologist. She is known for her excavations at Jericho and Jerusalem.

kephalin *n* BIOL another spelling of **cephalin**

kepi /káypi/ (*plural* **-pis**) *n* a French military hat with

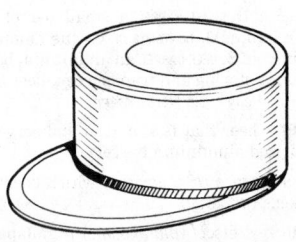
kepi

a round flat top and a horizontal peak [Mid-19C. Via French *képi* < Swiss German *Käppi* 'little cap']

Kepler /képplər/ crater on the Moon in Oceanus Procellarum, 32 km/20 mi. in diameter [After Johannes KEPLER]

Kepler /képplər/, **Johannes** (1571–1630) German astronomer. His three laws of planetary motion include his finding that the planets move around the Sun in elliptical orbits.

'Where there is matter, there is geometry.'
[Johannes Kepler. Quoted in *Solid Shape*, J. Koenderink; 1990]

Kepler's laws *npl* three mathematical statements that describe the movement of the planets in their orbits around the Sun. The first two laws were published in 1609 and the third a decade later.

kept /kept/ past participle, past tense of **keep**

kept man *n* a man who is financially supported by a lover (*often considered offensive*)

kept woman *n* a woman who is financially supported by a lover, especially by a married man (*often considered offensive*)

Kerala /kérrələ/ state in southwestern India. Capital: Trivandrum. Language: Malayalam. Population: 31,838,619 (2001). Area: 38,864 sq. km/15,005 sq. mi. — **Keralite** *adj, n*

kerat- *prefix* same as **kerato-** (*used before vowels*)

keratectomy /kérrə téktəmi/ *n* the surgical removal of part of the cornea

keratin /kérrətin/, **ceratin** *n* a fibrous insoluble protein that is the main structural element in hair, nails, feathers, and hooves [Mid-19C. < Greek *kerat-* 'horn'] — **keratinous** /ke ráttinəss/ *adj*

keratinise another spelling of **keratinize, etc**

keratinization /kérrəti nī záysh'n, ke rátti nī-/, **keratinisation** *n* the deposition of keratin in skin cells, e.g. in hair and nails, giving them the texture of horn

keratinize /kérrəti nīz, ke rátti nīz/ **(-izes, -izing, -ized)**, **keratinise** **(-ises, -ising, -ised)** *vti* to convert something into keratin, or become keratin

keratitis /kérrə tītiss/ *n* the inflammation and swelling of the cornea

kerato- *prefix* **1.** horny tissue ○ *keratose* **2.** cornea ○ *keratoplasty* [< Greek *kerat-* 'horn' < Indo-European]

keratoid /kérrə toyd/ *adj* like horn in texture or appearance

keratomileusis /kérrətō mī loóssis/ *n* eye surgery to change the shape of a cornea that refracts light wrongly [Late 20C. < KERATO- + Greek *smileusis* 'carving']

keratopathy /kérrə tóppəthi/ *n* a noninflammatory disorder of the cornea

keratoplasty /kérrətō plasti/ (*plural* **-ties**) *n* plastic surgery on the cornea, especially corneal grafting — **keratoplastic** /kérrətō plástik/ *adj*

keratose /kérrə tōss, -tōz/ *adj* describes sponges that have a horny skeleton

keratosis /kérrə tóssiss/ (*plural* **-toses** /-tōs seez/) *n* **1.** the growth of hard horny tissue on the skin **2.** a horny growth on the skin — **keratotic** /-tóttik/ *adj*

keratotomy /kérrə tóttəmi/ (*plural* **-mies**) *n* a surgical cutting of the cornea

kerb /kurb/ *n* a raised edge of stone or concrete separating the pavement from the road or street ■ *vt* (**kerbs, kerbing, kerbed**) to provide something with a kerb ▶ US spelling (all senses) **curb** [Mid-17C. Variant of CURB 'enclosing framework']

kerb appeal *n* the attractive appearance of a property for sale as seen from the roadside, creating a favourable first impression on a potential buyer

kerb crawling *n* the act of driving slowly beside a pavement looking for a prostitute to pick up — **kerb crawler** *n*

kerb drill *n* a procedure for crossing a road safely on foot, especially one that is taught to children

kerb market *n* a stock market that is separate from the stock exchange, originally one operating in the street

kerbside /kúrb sīd/ *n* the edge of a street or a pavement bordered by a curb

kerbstone /kúrb stōn/ *n* any of the large stones used to make a kerb

Kerch /kyurch/ seaport in southern Ukraine, on the east of the Crimean Peninsula. Population: 175,000 (1996).

kerchief /kúrchif, -cheef/ *n* a square scarf for women, worn round the neck or as a headscarf [13C. < Anglo-Norman *courchef* or Old French *cuevre-chef*, literally 'cover-head'] — **kerchiefed** *adj*

Kerensky /kərénski/, **Aleksandr Fyodorovich** (1881–1970) Russian revolutionary leader. He was the head of the 1917 provisional government of Russia from July until the Bolshevik takeover in November 1917.

kereru /kérrə roo/ *n NZ* BIRDS same as **kuku** [Late 19C. < Maori]

kerf /kurf/ *n* a cut or the width of a cut made by an axe, saw, or cutting tool [Old English *cerf* < W Germanic]

kerfuffle /kər fúff'l/, **carfuffle, kurfuffle** *n* a noisy disturbance or commotion (*informal*) ○ '*But [the group] didn't want to litigate, and it didn't want to walk away either. Instead it put out a press release and posted the details of the kerfuffle on the Web.*' (Brendan Miniter *Wall Street Journal*; 31 October 2003) [Early 19C. Origin ?]

Kerguelen Islands /kúrgilin-/ island group in the southern Indian Ocean, consisting of one main island and about 300 smaller islands and islets. Area: 6,000 sq. km/2,300 sq. mi.

Kermadec Islands /kúrmə dek-/ island group in the southern Pacific Ocean, a dependency of New Zealand. Area: 29 sq. km/11 sq. mi.

Kerman /kur máan/, **Kermān** city in southeastern Iran, the capital of Kerman Province. Population: 384,991 (1996).

kermes /kúr miz/ (*plural same*) *n* **1.** a purplish-red dye obtained from the dried bodies of female scale insects of the genus *Kermes*, or the dried bodies of these insects **2.** TREES same as **kermes oak** [Late 16C. Via French < Arabic *kirmiz* 'kermes beetle']

kermes oak *n* a small evergreen oak tree that provides a habitat for the scale insects used to make kermes. Native to: Europe, Asia. Latin name: *Quercus coccifera*.

kermis /kúr miss/, **kirmess, kermess** *n* in former times, an annual country fair held in the Netherlands and northern Germany [Late 16C. < Dutch, 'mass on the anniversary of the church's dedication' < *kerk* 'church' + *misse* 'mass']

kern[1] /kurn/, **kerne** *n* PART OF CHARACTER the part of a typographical character that projects beyond its body ■ *v* (**kerns, kerning, kerned; kernes, kerning, kerned**) **1.** *vti* BRING PRINTING TYPE TOGETHER to eliminate white space between adjacent printed letters that may appear too widely separated on a line **2.** *vt* OVERLAP ADJACENT CHARACTERS to join adjacent printed characters, or make them overlap [Late 17C. Via French *carne* 'corner' < Latin *cardin-* 'hinge']

kern[2] /kurn/, **kerne** *n* a medieval Irish or Scottish light infantryman [14C. < Irish *ceithearn*]

Kern /kurn/, **Jerome** (1885–1945) US composer. He wrote numerous Broadway musicals, including *Show Boat* (1927). His songs include 'Ol' Man River' and 'Smoke Gets in Your Eyes'. Full name **Kern, Jerome David**

'Irving Berlin *is* American music.'
[Jerome Kern. Quoted in *Guardian*; 25 September 1989]

kerne[1] *n, vti* PRINTING another spelling of **kern**[1]

kerne[2] *n* MIL, HIST another spelling of **kern**[2]

kernel /kúrn'l/ *n* **1.** EDIBLE CORE the edible content of a nut or fruit stone **2.** CEREAL GRAIN the grain of a cereal that contains a seed and husk **3.** CENTRAL PART the central or most important part of something ○ *a kernel of self-belief that never wavered* **4.** PHYS ATOM STRIPPED OF ITS ELECTRONS a positively charged atomic nucleus that has lost its valency electrons **5.** COMPUT KEY PORTION OF OPERATING SYSTEM the core of a computer's operating system that resides in the memory and performs essential functions such as controlling memory and files and allocating system resources [Old English *cyrnel* 'little seed' < CORN[1]]

SPELLCHECK See *colonel*.

Without kerning

A VOKO
Bad kerning

With kerning

AVOKO

kerning

kerning /kúrning/ *n* the addition or removal of space between adjacent characters in a piece of typeset text to improve its appearance or alter its fit [Late 17C. < KERN[1]]

kernite /kúr nīt/ *n* a colourless or white crystalline mineral consisting of hydrated sodium borate. Use: source of borax and other boron compounds. [Early 20C. After *Kern* County, California]

kernmantel rope /kúrn mant'l-/ *n* strong elastic rope made of sheathed nylon fibre [< German, 'core-casing']

kero /kérrō/ *n ANZ* same as **kerosene** (*informal*) [Mid-20C. Shortening]

kerogen /kérrəjən/ *n* a fossilized insoluble organic material found in some sedimentary rocks such as oil shales, yielding petroleum products when heated [Early 20C. < Greek *kēros* 'wax']

kerosene /kérrə seen/, **kerosine** *n* a colourless flammable oil distilled from petroleum. Use: fuel for jet engines, heating, cooking, and lighting. [Mid-19C. < Greek *kēros* 'wax']

Kerouac /kérrōō ak/, **Jack** (1922–69) US novelist. He was a leading figure in the 1950s Beat Generation, and his best-known novel is *On the Road* (1957). Full name **Kerouac, Jean Louis**. See Cultural note at **road**

'Because the only people for me are the mad ones...the ones who never yawn or say a commonplace thing, but burn, burn, burn, like fabulous yellow roman candles exploding like spiders across the stars and in the middle you see the blue centerlight pop and everybody goes "Awww!"'
[Jack Kerouac, *On the Road*; 1957]

kerplunk /kər plúngk/ *adv, interj* used to imitate the sound made by something heavy falling suddenly (*informal*) [Early 20C. An imitation of the sound.]

Kerr /kur/, **Sir John** (1914–90) governor general of Australia (1974–77). In 1975, he dismissed the Labour government led by Gough Whitlam. Full name **Kerr, Sir John Robert**

Kerr effect /kúr-/ *n* **1.** the property of some transparent substances that makes them refract doubly when placed in an electric field **2.** the elliptical polarization of plane-polarized or unpolarized light when reflected from the polished pole of a magnetized material [Early 20C. After John Kerr (1824–1907), Scottish physicist]

Kerry[1] /kérri/ (*plural* **-ries**) *n* a small black bull or dairy cow belonging to a breed that originated in Ireland [Mid-19C. After KERRY[2]]

Kerry[2] /kérri/ county in Munster Province, southwestern Republic of Ireland. Population: 126,130 (2002). Area: 4,701 sq. km/1,815 sq. mi.

Kerry, John (*b.* 1943) US politician. He has served as Democratic US senator from Massachusetts (1984–) and is the Democratic presidential candidate in 2004. A much-decorated Vietnam veteran, he co-founded Vietnam Veterans of America. Full name **Kerry, John Forbes**

Kerry blue terrier, **Kerry blue** *n* a terrier with a dense but soft wavy bluish-grey coat, belonging to a breed originating in Ireland [Early 20C. After KERRY[2]]

kersey /kúrzi/ *n* a smooth woollen fabric. Use: coats. [14C. After *Kersey*, village in Suffolk]

kerseymere /kérzi meer/ n a fine soft woollen cloth with a fancy twill weave [Late 18C. Alteration of *cassimere*, 'woollen fabric', alteration of CASHMERE, after KERSEY]

Kertész /kər tésh/, **André** (1894–1985) Hungarian-born US photographer. One of the founders of photojournalism, he is known for his realistic and sensitive scenes of everyday life.

kerygma /kə rígmə/ n the proclamation of Jesus Christ's teachings, especially as taught in the Gospels [Late 19C. < Greek *kērugma* < *kērussein* 'proclaim'] —**kerygmatic** /kérrig máttik/ adj

kesh /kaysh/ n the beard and uncut hair traditionally worn by baptized Sikh men as a symbol of religious loyalty [< Punjabi *kes*]

Kesselring /késs'lring/, **Albert** (1885–1960) German field marshal. During World War II he was the German commander in chief in Italy (1943–45) and on the western front (1945).

kestrel

kestrel /késtrəl/ n a small falcon that hovers before swooping on its prey of small mammals. Genus: *Falco*. [14C. Probably < French dialect *casserelle* < French *crécerelle* 'rattle' < Latin *crepitacillum* 'small rattle' < *crepitare* 'to rattle']

ket- prefix same as **keto-** (*used before vowels*)

ketamine /kéttə meen/ n a white crystalline powder. Use: general anaesthetic in human and veterinary medicine. Formula: $C_{13}H_{16}ClNO$.

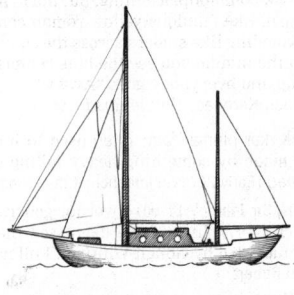

ketch

ketch[1] /kech/ n a small fore-and-aft rigged sailing ship with two masts, the forward mast taller than the other [Mid-17C. Probably < CATCH]

ketch[2] /kech/ (**ketches, ketching, ketched**) vt same as **catch** (slang; used in Black English) [Variant]

ketchup /kéchəp, -up/ n a thick savoury sauce, usually made with tomatoes, that is served cold as a condiment [Late 17C. Probably via Malay *kěchap* 'fish sauce' < Chinese (Cantonese) *k'ē chap* 'sauce']

ketene /kée teen/ n a strong-smelling colourless highly reactive toxic gas. Use: agent to attach an acetyl group to an organic compound. Formula: C_2H_2O. [Early 20C. < KETONE]

keto- prefix containing a ketone or ketone group ○ *ketonuria* [< KETONE]

keto form /kéetō-/ n one of two interconvertible forms of an organic compound, having a carbonyl group attached to two alkyl groups

ketogenesis /kéetō jénnəssiss/ n the formation or stimulation of the production of ketone bodies, as can happen in diabetes —**ketogenic** adj

ketone /kée'tōn/ n an organic compound containing a carbon atom connected to an oxygen atom by a double bond and to two carbon atoms. The simplest ketone is acetone, an important industrial solvent. ■ adj relating to the chemical group comprising a carbon atom connected to an oxygen atom by a double bond and to two carbon atoms [Mid-19C. < German *Keton*, alteration of *Aketon* 'acetone'] —**ketonic** /kee tónnik/ adj

ketone body n a mixture of ketones produced when body fat is broken down. The concentration of ketone bodies in blood and urine increases in starvation, diabetes, and pregnancy.

ketone group n the carbonyl group, containing carbon atoms doubly bonded to an oxygen atom and linked to the carbon atoms of two other organic groups, a characteristic of all ketones

ketonuria /kéetō nyoóri ə/ n the presence of ketones in the urine, a warning sign of severe and uncontrolled diabetes

ketose /kée tōss, -tōz/ n a carbohydrate that contains a ketone group

ketosis /kee tôssiss, ki-/ n the condition resulting from overproduction of ketone bodies —**ketotic** /-tóttik/ adj

ketoxime /kee tók seem/ n an organic compound containing a nitrogen atom bonded to a hydroxyl group and a carbon atom, which is bonded to two ketones. It is produced by the reaction between hydroxylamine and a ketone.

Kettering /kéttəring/ town in Northamptonshire, central England. Population: 81,844 (2001).

kettle /kétt'l/ n **1.** CONTAINER FOR BOILING WATER a plastic or metal container with a handle, spout, and lid, used for boiling water **2.** METAL POT a metal pot used for cooking, usually one with a lid ○ *a fish kettle* **3.** INDUSTRIAL CONTAINER a large container with no lid that is used for refining metals with a low melting point **4.** GEOL BASIN IN GLACIAL DRIFT DEPOSIT a steep-sided basin, often a lake or swamp, in a glacial drift deposit, caused by the melting of an ice mass left behind as the glacier retreated [Old English *cetel*, via Germanic < Latin *catillus* 'small cooking pot'] ◇ **a different kettle of fish** a different situation or person to be dealt with ◇ **a pretty** *or* **fine kettle of fish** an undesirable situation, usually one caused by somebody's negligence or incompetence

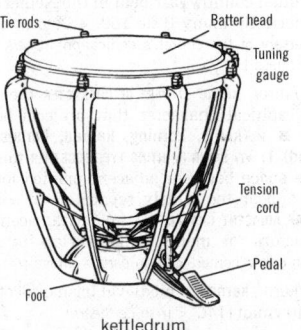

kettledrum

kettledrum /kétt'l drum/ n a percussion instrument consisting of a large copper or brass drum covered with a parchment skin that can be adjusted to alter the pitch. Pitch is altered by screws and pedals that increase or decrease the skin's tension. —**kettledrummer** n

kettle hole n GEOL same as **kettle** (sense 4)

keV abbr kilo-electron volt

kevel[1] /kévv'l/ n a sturdy bitt or bollard for securing the heavier cables on a ship [13C. Via Old N French *keville* 'pin, peg' < Latin *clavicula* 'small key']

kevel[2] /kévv'l/ n a two-headed hammer, one head with a sharp edge, the other with a point, used for breaking up or shaping stone [Origin ?]

Kevlar /kév laar/ tdmk a trademark for a reinforcing material used in tyres and bulletproof vests

Kew Gardens /kyoó-/ n an informal name for the Royal Botanic Gardens, Kew, located in western London. It holds the largest collection of plants in the world.

kewpie /kyoópi/ n a plump doll with rosy cheeks and a curl of hair on its head [Early 20C. Originally a trademark]

kex /keks/ n the dried stems of a large hollow-stemmed plant such as cow parsnip or chervil [14C. Origin ?]

key[1] /kee/ n (plural **keys**) **1.** INSTRUMENT FOR LOCKING a metal bar with notches or grooves that, when inserted into a lock and turned, operates the lock's mechanism **2.** DOOR OR LOCK OPENER a device that operates a door or lock, e.g. a plastic card with an encoded magnetic strip **3.** INSTRUMENT FOR WINDING UP a fitted tool that is turned repeatedly to wind up, set, or calibrate a mechanism **4.** IMPORTANT ASPECT the aspect of something that, once understood, provides a full understanding or explanation of the whole ○ *The key to this riddle lies in the subtle meanings of the words used.* **5.** MEANS a way or means of achieving something ○ *Continuity of effort is the key to success.* **6.** STRATEGIC PLACE a place that is strategically vital in gaining access to or controlling a larger area ○ *Istanbul is the key to the Bosporus.* **7.** LIST OF ANSWERS a list of the answers to a test or exercise **8.** ARTS EXPLANATORY TEXT a text that provides additional information on or an explanation of a work of literature, art, or music **9.** MUSIC TONAL CENTRE the relationship between the notes of a scale and the scale's main note **10.** MUSIC MAIN NOTE OF SCALE the note on which a musical scale begins **11.** MUSIC INSTRUMENT FEATURE the levers on a keyboard instrument that sound a note when pressed, or the metal buttons on a woodwind instrument that alter a note's pitch **12.** MUSIC MUSICAL SCALE a system of related notes in a scale beginning on a particular note ○ *in the key of E* **13.** KEYBOARD BUTTON a button on a typewriter's or computer's keyboard or keypad that performs an operation when pressed **14.** COMPUT DATABASE FEATURE a field in a database record that uniquely identifies that record **15.** ELEC ENG DEVICE FOR OPERATING CIRCUITS a small manual device for opening, closing, or switching circuits ○ *a telegraph key* **16.** ENG METAL PIN a metal wedge or pin used to lock together two structural or mechanical components such as a shaft and a hub to prevent movement relative to each other **17.** COMMUNICATION CRYPTOGRAPHIC FEATURE in cryptography, the sequence of symbols or characters that defines the makeup of an encoding mechanism **18.** BIOL OUTLINE OF CHARACTERISTICS an outline of the characteristics of an organism, used for taxonomic identification **19.** PHOTOGRAPHY, ART IMAGE FEATURE the tonal value of an image with regard to lightness, darkness, or colour intensity **20.** CONSTR SURFACE PREPARATION the process of preparing a surface, usually by making it rough or grooved, so that paint or some other finish will stick to it **21.** PITCH OR QUALITY the pitch or quality of an expressive sound, especially the voice ○ *answered in thoughtful key* **22.** MAPS EXPLANATORY LIST an explanatory list of the symbols or abbreviations used on a map or diagram **23.** ARTS MOOD OF ART WORK the general mood or style of a work of art, literature, or music **24.** ARCHIT same as **keystone** (sense 1) **25.** WINGED FRUIT a dry winged fruit like that of an ash or sycamore tree, usually growing in bunches. Technical name **samara 26.** BASKETBALL AREA AT END OF BASKETBALL COURT the area at the ends of a basketball court between the base line and the foul line ■ adj CRUCIAL vital in achieving understanding or success ○ *the key points in the report* ■ v (**keys, keying, keyed**) **1.** vti COMPUT TYPE to use the keyboard of a computer, or input data using it ○ *keyed for a solid hour* **2.** vt LOCK SOMETHING to lock or adjust something with a key **3.** vt PREPARE SURFACE to prepare a surface, usually by making it rough or grooved, so that paint or another finish will stick to it **4.** vt PROVIDE SOMETHING WITH EXPLANATION to provide something with an explanatory list or text **5.** vt MUSIC REGULATE INSTRUMENT'S PITCH to regulate the pitch of a musical instrument **6.** vt ADAPT SOMETHING to bring something in line with or make something consistent with something else (*often passive*) **7.** vt CONSTR LOCK ARCH WITH KEYSTONE to provide an arch with a keystone **8.** vt PRINTING MARK SOMETHING FOR CORRECT REPRODUCTION to mark artwork, or anything to be reproduced, with symbols that will allow different parts to be correctly aligned for reproduction **9.** vt BIOL IDENTIFY SOMETHING to identify an organism or specimen [Old English *cæg*, origin ?]

key in vt to enter data such as a password or PIN by typing on a keyboard or keypad

key up *vt* to make somebody nervous, tense, or excited (*informal*; *often used in the passive*)

key[2] /kee/ *n* a small low island of sand or coral, especially in the Gulf of Mexico or the Caribbean [Late 17C. < Old French *kay*, probably < Celtic]

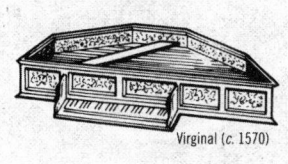

Virginal (*c.* 1570)

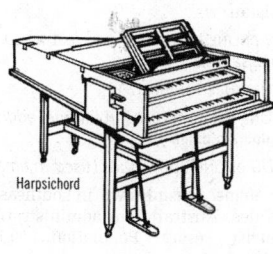

Harpsichord

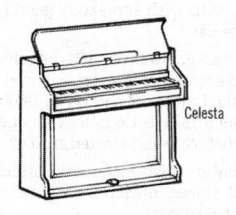

Celesta

Accordion

keyboard: instruments with keyboards

keyboard /kee bawrd/ *n* **1. SET OF KEYS** an array of keys in a row or rows used for operating something such as a computer or musical instrument **2. MUSIC MUSICAL INSTRUMENT** a musical instrument with a keyboard or keyboards, especially one with a horizontal keyboard, a soundboard and strings, e.g. a piano ■ *vti* (**-boards, -boarding, -boarded**) **INPUT DATA** to enter information into a computer using a keyboard ■ **keyboards** *npl* **MUSICAL INSTRUMENT WITH MULTIPLE KEY-BOARDS** an electronic musical instrument with a tier of two or more keyboards

keyboarder /kee bawrdər/ *n* an operator of the keyboard of a computer or typesetting machine

keyboardist /kee bawrdist/ *n* a musician who plays a keyboard instrument

key card *n* a card, usually made of plastic with an encoded magnetic strip, giving access to a door or mechanism

keychain drive /kee chayn-/ *n* a small plastic device functioning as a disk drive, key-sized, containing

memory chips that retain their contents without electrical power and that have a capacity of 16 megabytes and 2 gigabytes of data. On the end is a standard USB connector that fits into USB ports. [Early 21C.]

key database *n* a database that holds all keys used by a certificate authority

keyed up /keed-/ *adj* in a state of nervousness, tension or excitement (*informal*)

key escrow *n* a system for encrypting computer data in which the decoding key is held by a third party

key fruit *n* BOT same as **key**[1] *n* (sense 25)

key grip *n* the chief mover of equipment in a film or stage crew

keyhole /kee hōl/ *n* the small hole in a lock into which a key fits

keyhole saw *n* ANZ, N Am a handsaw with a stiff narrow pointed fine-toothed blade, used to make small-radius curved and internal cuts. UK term **padsaw**

keyhole surgery *n* surgery performed using instruments that can be introduced into the body through a very small hole and manipulated externally, thus avoiding the need for major incisions

Key Largo /key laargō/ one of the largest of the Florida Keys, in southeastern Florida, at Biscayne Bay. Length: 48 km/30 mi.

key light *n* the main studio or stage light that sets the overall level of light intensity for something that is being filmed, video-taped, or photographed

key lime, **Key lime** *n* a small tart lime grown in the Florida Keys and Caribbean islands

key lime pie *n* N Am a pie made from thickened sweetened condensed milk flavoured with juice from key limes

key money *n* a fee paid by a prospective tenant to a landlord or landlady in order to secure a tenancy

Keynes /kaynz/, **John Maynard, 1st Baron Keynes of Tilton** (1883–1946) British economist. He proposed the influential theory that government spending must compensate for insufficient business investment in times of recession. —**Keynesian** *n*, *adj*

'Modern capitalism is absolutely irreligious, without internal union, without much public spirit, often, though not always, a mere congeries of possessors and pursuers.'
[John Maynard Keynes, *Essays in Persuasion*; 1925]

Keynesianism /kaynzi ən izəm/ *n* the theory that government spending must compensate for insufficient business investment in times of recession

keynote /kee nōt/ *n* **1. MAIN THEME** the central or most important point or theme of something **2. MUSIC** same as **tonic** *n* (sense 4) ■ *adj* **MOST IMPORTANT** containing or outlining the most important themes or policies ■ *v* (**-notes, -noting, -noted**) **1.** *vti* **DELIVER KEYNOTE SPEECH** to deliver the most important speech at a conference or meeting **2.** *vt* **NOTE IMPORTANT POINTS** to outline an important policy in a speech or report

keynote address *n* same as **keynote speech**

keynoter /kee nōtər/, **keynote speaker** *n* a speaker who delivers the most important speech at a conference or political convention

keynote speech, **keynote address** *n* the most important speech at a conference or political convention

keypad /kee pad/ *n* **1.** a small keyboard, e.g. on a calculator or television remote control, usually with numbers on the keys **2.** the part of a computer keyboard in which the number and command keys are grouped

keypal /kee pal/ *n* US somebody with whom regular e-mail is exchanged [Late 20C. After PEN PAL]

key-punch *n* a machine, operated by keyboard, that punches holes in card or paper for use in a data-processing system, now largely obsolete ■ *vti* to use a key-punch to punch holes in a card or paper tape for data entry into a computer —**key-puncher** *n*

key ring *n* a metal ring used for keeping keys to-

gether, often with a decorative or identifying attachment

key signature *n* a group of sharps or flats printed on the staves at the beginning of a piece of music to show the key in which it is to be played

key stage *n* any of the four National Curriculum programmes of study that pupils are required to follow. Key stages 1, 2, 3, and 4 are for pupils aged 5 to 7, 8 to 11, 11 to 14, and 14 to 16, respectively.

keystone /kee stōn/ *n* **1.** the wedge-shaped stone at the highest point of an arch that locks the others in place **2.** something on which other interrelated things depend ○ *Alliances are the keystone of a country's security.*

CULTURAL NOTE *The Keystone Kops*, a group of comic characters who appeared in a number of silent films (1880–1960) by US director Mack Sennett. A bumbling police squad dressed in oversized uniforms, the Kops usually featured in slapstick chase sequences characterized by superb sight gags and acrobatic stunts.

keystroke /kee strōk/ *n* the pressing down of a key on a computer or typewriter keyboard, activating it

keyway /kee way/ *n* a longitudinal slot in two structural or mechanical components, e.g. in the hub or shaft of a wheel, into which a metal wedge or pin can be inserted. When the slots are filled, the two components are locked together so that they will not turn relative to one another.

Key West city in southern Florida, situated on the island of the same name. It is a port and a tourist resort. Population: 25,273 (2002 estimate).

keyword /kee wurd/ *n* **1. REFERENCE POINT** a word used as a reference point for further information or as an indication of the contents of a document **2. CODE WORD** a word that is used as a key to a code **3. COMPUT WORD WITH A SPECIAL MEANING TO A COMPUTER** a sequence of letters and numbers, often in the form of a common word, with special significance to a computer database or a programming or command language

kg[1] *symbol* MEASURE kilogram

kg[2] *abbr* ONLINE Kyrgyzstan (*used in Internet addresses*) See table at **domain name**

KG *abbr* Knight of the Order of the Garter

Kgalagadi Transfrontier Park /khállə khaadi transs frun teer paark/ cross-border game park and conservation area that combines South Africa's Kalahari Gemsbok Park and the Botswana Gemsbok Park. Established in 1999. Area: 37,991 sq. km/14,668 sq. mi.

KGB *n* the secret police of the former Soviet Union [< Russian, abbreviation of *Komitet Gosudarstvennoĭ Bezopasnosti* 'Committee of State Security']

kgf *symbol* MEASURE kilogram-force

kh *abbr* ONLINE Cambodia (*used in Internet addresses*) See table at **domain name**

Khabarovsk /kə baa rófsk/ city in eastern Russia, the administrative centre of Khabarovsk Territory. Population: 774,762 (1995).

khaddar /kaadər/, **khadi** /kaadi/ *n* a cotton cloth from South Asia that has a plain weave [Early 20C. < Punjabi *khaddar* or Hindi *khadar*]

Khakassia /kə kaasi ə/ autonomous republic in south-central Siberia, Russia. Capital: Abakan. Population: 584,000 (1994). Area: 61,900 sq. km/23,899 sq. mi.

khaki /kaaki/ *n* **1.** a dull brownish-yellow colour **2.** a tough yellowish-brown fabric. Use: military uniforms. [Mid-19C. < Urdu *kakī* 'dust-coloured' < Persian *kāk* 'dust'] —**khaki** *adj*

khalasi /kə lássi/ *n* S Asia somebody employed as a manual labourer [Late 18C. < Urdu]

khalif, etc. ISLAM another spelling of **caliph, etc.**

Khalsa /kaalssə/ *n* a strict Sikh religious order founded in 1699 by Guru Gobind Singh [Late 18C. Via Urdu < Arabic *kālis* 'pure']

Khaman'i /khaá me neé/, **Ali, Ayatollah** (*b.* 1939) supreme spiritual leader of Iran (1989–). A former deputy defence minister and Revolutionary Guard commander, he served as president (1981–89) before he was chosen to succeed Ayatollah Khomeini.

khamsin /kam seen, kámsin/, **kamseen, kamsin** *n* a dry dusty hot southerly wind that blows from the Sahara across Egypt and over the Red Sea from March to May [Late 17C. < Arabic *kamāsīn* < *kamsīn* 'fifty'; because it blows for about fifty days]

khan[1] /kaan/ *n* **1.** formerly in parts of Asia, a medieval title used by Mongol and Turkish rulers (*usually added to a name*) ○ *Genghis Khan* **2.** in Central Asian countries, a title of respect taken by some dignitaries ○ *the Aga Khan* [14C. Via Old French *chan* or medieval Latin *ca(a)nus* < Turkic *kān* 'lord, ruler']

khan[2] /kaan/ *n* in Turkey and some Central Asian countries, an inn [14C. < Persian *kān*]

Imran Khan

Khan /kaan/, **Imran** (b. 1952) Pakistani cricketer. He was four times captain of Pakistan's national team between 1982 and his retirement from cricket in 1992, and also played for Sussex and Worcestershire. Full name **Niazi, Imran Ahmad Khan**

Khan, Jahangir (b. 1963) Pakistani squash player. Holder of six world open titles (1981–85, 1988), he was undefeated from April 1981 until November 1986.

khana /kaánə/ *n S Asia* **1.** same as **food 2.** same as **meal**[1] [Early 19C. < Hindi]

khanate /kaá nayt/ *n* **1.** the territory governed by a medieval Chinese emperor or a Mongolian or Turkish khan **2.** the position or rank of a khan

khanga CLOTHING another spelling of **kanga**

khansama /kaánsə maa/ *n S Asia* a man who acts as cook and often also as steward or butler to a household [Early 17C. < Urdu, Persian *kānsāmān* < *kān* 'master' + *sāmān* 'household goods']

khapra beetle /kaáprə-/ *n* a beetle that is a pest of grain. Native to: Southeast Asia but now common elsewhere. Latin name: *Trogoderma granarium*. [Via Hindi < Sanskrit *khapara* 'thief']

kharif /kə reéf/ *n S Asia* a crop that is harvested at the beginning of winter [Early 19C. Via Persian or Urdu < Arabic *karīf* 'autumn']

Kharkiv /haákiv, khaár-/ second largest city in Ukraine, capital of Kharkiv Oblast. It is situated about 418 km/260 mi. east of Kiev. Population: 1,494,235 (1999). Former name **Kharkov**

Khartoum /kaar toóm/ capital city of Sudan and of Khartoum Province. It is situated just south of the confluence of the Blue Nile and White Nile rivers. Population: 924,505 (1993).

khat /kaat/, **qat** *n* **1.** the fresh leaves and twigs of a shrub that have a stimulating and euphoric effect when chewed or brewed as tea **2.** an evergreen bush whose leaves and twigs are used as khat. Native to: Arabia, Africa. Latin name: *Catha edulis*. [Mid-19C. < Arabic *kāt*]

Khatami /kaá taa mi/, **Mohammad** (b. 1943) president of Iran (1997–) and cleric. He entered parliament after the Iranian Revolution (1979) and held several government posts including minister of culture and Islamic guidance (1989–92). He has gained a reputation as a moderate and has pursued closer ties with the West.

khazi /kaázi/ (*plural* **-zis**), **kazi, karzy** /kaárzi/ (*plural* **-zies**), **karsey** (*plural* **-seys**) *n* a toilet, or a room or cubicle with a toilet (*slang*) [Mid-20C. Alteration of Italian *casa* 'house']

kheda /kédda/, **khedah, keddah** *n* in Karnataka, Myanmar, and other parts of South Asia, an en-closure used to capture wild elephants [Late 18C. < Assamese, Bangla *khedā*]

khedive /ki deév/ *n* the title of the Turkish viceroys who governed Egypt from 1867 to 1914 while it was under Turkish rule [Mid-19C. Via French < Ottoman Turkish *kediv* < Persian *kadiw* 'prince' < *kudā* 'god'] —**khedival** *adj* —**khedivate** /-vət, -vayt/ *n*

khi *n* another spelling of **chi**[1]

khichri /kíchree/ *n* a South Asian dish made from rice, pulses, onions, and spices [< Hindi *khicrī* < Sanskrit *khiccā* 'dish of boiled rice and sesame']

khir /keer/ *n* in South Asian cooking, a sweet rice pudding [< Hindi]

Khmer[1] /kmair, kə máir/ (*plural same* or **Khmers**) *n* **1.** MEMBER OF CAMBODIAN PEOPLE a member of the most populous people in Cambodia **2.** INHABITANT OF ANCIENT KINGDOM an inhabitant of an ancient kingdom that flourished in the Mekong valley between the 9th and 13th centuries **3.** OFFICIAL LANGUAGE OF CAMBODIA the official language of Cambodia, belonging to Mon-Khmer. Native speakers: 5 million. [Late 19C. < Khmer] —**Khmer** *adj*

Khmer[2] /kmair, kə máir/ ancient kingdom that flourished in the Mekong valley, Southeast Asia, between the 9th and 13th centuries. Its capital was the city of Angkor situated in the northwestern part of modern-day Cambodia.

Khmer Republic former name for **Cambodia** (1970–75)

Khmer Rouge /-roózh/ *n* the Cambodian Communist party that seized power in the civil war of 1975 and controlled the country until 1979 [< Khmer *Khmer* 'Cambodia' + French *rouge* 'red']

Khoikhoi /kóy koy/ (*plural same* or **-khois**) *n* **1.** a member of a formerly nomadic people now living mainly in Namibia **2.** *also* **Khoi Khoi** a language spoken in Namibia and some parts of western South Africa, belonging to Khoisan and characterized by the use of click consonants. Native speakers: 55,000. [Late 18C. < Nama, 'men of men'] —**Khoikhoi** *adj*

Khoisan /kóy saán/, **Khoi-San** *n* a family of African languages spoken in parts of Namibia and Botswana and notable for the use of click consonants [Mid-20C. Blend of KHOIKHOI + SAN[2]] —**Khoisan** *adj*

kho-kho /kókō/ *n* in South Asia, a form of tag played between two teams of 12 [< Marathi]

Khomeini /khóm ay neé/, **Ruhollah, Ayatollah** (1900?–89) Iranian Shiite head of state. He led an Islamic revolution that overthrew the shah (1979) and introduced a constitution and administration based on strict interpretation of Islamic law.

> 'Islam is the religion of militant individuals who are committed to truth and justice. It is the religion of those who desire freedom and independence. It is the school of those who struggle against imperialism.'
> [Ruhollah Khomeini, 'Islamic Government', *Islam and Revolution*; 1985]

khoum /koom/, **khum** *n* a subunit of Mauritanian currency. See table at **currency** [Late 20C. < Arabic *kums* 'one-fifth']

Khrushchev /króoss chof/, **Nikita** (1894–1971) premier of the USSR (1958–64). In 1953, after Stalin's death, he became first secretary of the Communist Party, and embarked on a programme of de-Stalinization. He was ousted in 1964. Full name **Khrushchev, Nikita Sergeyevich**

> 'Whether you like it or not, history is on our side. We will bury you.'
> [Nikita Khrushchev, *Speech in Moscow to Western diplomats*; 18 November 1956]

Khulna /koólnə/ city and river port in southwestern Bangladesh. It is situated about 145 km/90 mi. southwest of Dhaka. Population: 601,051 (1991).

khum *n* MONEY another spelling of **khoum**

khuskhus /kúskəss/, **khus-khus** *n S Asia* PLANTS same as **vetiver** [Early 19C. < Urdu, Persian *kaskas*]

Khyber Pass

Khyber Pass /kíbər-/ mountain pass in western Asia, the most important pass connecting Afghanistan and Pakistan

KHYF *abbr* ONLINE know how you feel (*used in e-mails or text messages*)

kHz *abbr* MEASURE kilohertz

ki *abbr* ONLINE Kiribati (*used in Internet addresses*) See table at **domain name**

KIA *abbr US* ONLINE know-it-all (*used in emails*)

Kiama /kī ámmə/ coastal town in southeastern New South Wales, Australia, an administrative centre and tourist resort. Population: 20,139 (2002 estimate).

kiang /ki áng/ *n* a large wild ass. Native to: Tibetan plateau, Himalayan region. Latin name: *Equus hemionus kiang*. [Mid-19C. < Tibetan *kyang*]

kia ora /keé ə áwrə/ *interj NZ* used as a greeting or farewell, or to wish somebody good luck [Late 19C. < Maori, 'be well']

Kibaki /ki baáki/, **Mwai** (b. 1931) president of Kenya. A trained economist and experienced politician, he founded the Democratic Party in 1991 and contested the presidential elections as its candidate in 1992 and 1997 before being elected in 2002.

kibbe /kíbbə/ *n* a dish made with minced lamb, pine nuts, and spices, of Southwest Asian origin [Mid-20C. < Arabic *kubbah*]

kibble[1] /kíbb'l/ *n* a large iron barrel used in wells or mines for lifting water, ore, or refuse to the surface [15C. Via German *Kübel* < medieval Latin *cupellus* 'drinking vessel' < late Latin *cuppa* (see CUP)]

kibble[2] /kíbb'l/ (**-bles, -bling, -bled**) *vt* to grind something such as grain into small pieces [Late 18C. Origin ?]

kibbutz /ki boóts/ (*plural* **-butzim** /-boot seem/) *n* a communal farm or factory in Israel run collectively and dedicated to the principle that production work and domestic work are of equal value [Mid-20C. < modern Hebrew *qibbūs* 'gathering']

kibbutznik /ki boótsnik/ *n* somebody who lives and works on a kibbutz

kibe /kīb/ *n* a chapped or swollen area of skin, usually on the heel and often ulcerated, caused by exposure to cold [14C. Origin ?]

Kibei /kee báy/ (*plural same*) *n US* somebody born in the United States of Japanese parents and educated in Japan [< Japanese, literally 'go home']

kibitka /ki bítkə/ *n* **1.** RUSSIAN SLEDGE a covered sledge or wagon in Russia **2.** TATAR TENT a tent made of felt used by the Tatars **3.** TATAR FAMILY a family of Tatars [Late 18C. < Russian]

kibitz /kíbbits/ (**-itzes, -itzing, -itzed**) *vi N Am* (*informal*) **1.** to interfere or give unwanted advice, especially when watching a card game **2.** same as **chat** [Early 20C. Via Yiddish < German *kiebitzen*] —**kibitzer** *n*

kiblah /kíbblə/, **kibla, qibla** *n* the direction of Mecca that Muslims must face when praying [Mid-17C. < Arabic *kibla* 'that which is opposite']

kibosh /kí bosh/ (**-boshes, -boshing, -boshed**) *vt* to put a stop to something (*informal*) [Mid-19C. Origin ?] ◇ **put the kibosh on something** to prevent something from happening or from being successful (*informal*)

kick /kik/ *v* (**kicks, kicking, kicked**) **1.** *vti* STRIKE WITH FOOT to strike something or somebody with the foot **2.** *vti* MOVE WITH FOOT to make something move by striking

it with the foot ○ *kick a ball around* **3.** *vti* **MAKE THRASHING MOVEMENT** to make a thrashing movement with the legs, e.g. when fighting or swimming ○ *Hold onto the side of the pool and kick your legs as hard as you can.* **4.** *vti* **RAISE LEG HIGH** to raise the leg up high in a swift movement, e.g. in a dance ○ *an entire chorus line kicking in unison* **5.** *vi* ARMS **RECOIL** to recoil when fired (*refers to firearms*) **6.** *vti* **SCORE GOAL** in various football games, to score a goal by kicking ○ *He kicked a conversion to win the game.* **7.** *vi* CRICKET **BOUNCE HIGH** to bounce up high and quickly (*refers to cricket balls*) ○ *On this wicket, a pace bowler should be able to make the ball really kick.* **8.** *vr* **BLAME YOURSELF** to be irritated with yourself (*informal*) ○ *I'm kicking myself for missing the deadline.* ■ *n* **1. FOOT MOVEMENT** a blow with the foot **2. LEG MOVEMENT** a thrashing movement with the leg ○ *a swimming kick* **3. RAISING OF LEG** a swift lift of the leg, e.g. in a dance ○ *a high kick* **4. KICKING OF BALL** the striking of a ball with the foot ○ *opted for a kick instead of a pass* **5. PLEASURE** an exciting, pleasurable, or satisfying feeling (*informal*) ○ *She really gets a kick out of appearing on stage.* **6. STIMULANT EFFECT** a sudden stimulant effect, especially one produced by alcohol (*informal*) **7. POWER** power or strength (*informal*) ○ *That sauce has quite a kick to it.* **8. TEMPORARY INTEREST** a temporary interest, especially a strongly absorbing interest (*informal*) ○ *They're on a real health kick at the moment.* **9.** ARMS **RECOIL OF GUN** the backward thrust of a gun when it is fired [14C. Origin ?] —**kickable** *adj* —**kicker** *n* ◇ **a kick in the pants** a reprimand given to somebody who is not showing enough enthusiasm or effort (*informal*) ◇ **a kick in the teeth** a humiliating setback (*informal*) ◇ **kick somebody upstairs** to promote somebody to a seemingly higher position that is actually less important or influential (*informal*)

kick against *vt* to show disapproval or resentment of a rule or institution by not complying or cooperating with it (*informal*) ○ *He kicked against the restrictions.*

kick around *v* **1.** *vt* **MISTREAT SOMEBODY** to treat somebody badly and unfairly (*informal*) **2.** *vt* **DISCUSS SOMETHING** to discuss a topic or range of topics in an informal way (*informal*) **3.** *vti* **TRAVEL AIMLESSLY** to travel around a place without any fixed plans **4.** *vi* **REMAIN UNNOTICED** to remain forgotten or neglected (*informal*)

kick back *v* **1.** *vti* **PAY BRIBE** to pay money illegally in order to gain concessions or favours (*informal*) **2.** *vi* **REACT SUDDENLY** to react strongly and violently (*informal*) **3.** *vi* ARMS **UNDERGO RECOIL** to recoil when fired (*refers to firearms*) **4.** *vt US* **RETURN SOMETHING STOLEN** to return stolen items or money to a shop or a person (*informal*) **5.** *vi US* **RELAX** to relax comfortably (*informal*)

kick in *v* **1.** *vi* to start to take effect or come into operation (*informal*) ○ *I'll feel better once the antibiotics kick in.* **2.** *vi US* same as **die**[1] (*slang*) **3.** *vti ANZ, N Am* to contribute towards the cost of something (*informal*)

kick off *v* **1.** *vi* in football, to start play by kicking the ball off the centre spot **2.** *vti* to start something, or begin (*informal*) ○ *Let's kick off tonight's show with our first guest.*

kick on *vi Aus* to continue or persevere in doing something (*informal*)

kick out *vt* to throw somebody out or send somebody away (*informal*)

kick up *v* (*informal*) **1.** *vt* **CAUSE SOMETHING** to cause or instigate something, usually something undesirable ○ *kicked up a fuss* **2.** *vi* **PROTEST** to protest or react in a way that causes trouble **3.** *vi US* **GIVE TROUBLE** to misbehave or malfunction

kickabout /kíkə bowt/ *n* an informal game of football

Kickapoo /kíkə poo/ (*plural same* or **-poos**), **Kikapoo** *n* **1.** a member of a Native North American people who lived in southwestern Wisconsin and now live in Kansas, Oklahoma, and Texas **2.** the Algonquian language of the Kickapoo people. Native speakers: 4,000. [Late 17C. < Kickapoo *kiikaapoa*] —**Kickapoo** *adj*

kick-ass *adj* an offensive term meaning forceful, aggressive, or ruthless (*taboo*)

kickback /kík bak/ *n* (*informal*) **1.** a sum of money paid illegally in order to gain concessions or favours **2.** a strong or violent reaction

kickboard /kík bawrd/ *n ANZ, N Am* SWIMMING a small buoyant board held by a swimmer in order to stay afloat while practising kicking techniques. UK term **float**

kickboxing /kík boksing/ *n* a form of boxing that involves kicking as well as punching —**kickboxer** *n*

kickdown /kík down/ *n* a way of changing gear in a car with automatic transmission, that involves pressing hard on the accelerator pedal

kicker /kíkər/ *n* somebody who kicks, especially a football player whose job in the team is to kick the ball

kicking /kíking/ *n* a severe beating (*informal*) ■ *adj* excellent, exciting, or very enjoyable (*slang*)

kickoff /kík of/ *n* **1. START OF MATCH** in football, the place kick from the centre spot that begins the match **2. STARTING TIME** the time at which a football match is due to start **3. START OF GAME** in American football, the kicking of the ball at the beginning of a game or half, or after a touchdown or field goal **4. START OF SOMETHING** the start of something, or the time when something starts (*informal*) ◇ **for a kickoff** to begin with, or as the first of several things (*informal*)

kick plate *n* a metal plate attached to a door at foot level to protect it

kick pleat *n* an inverted pleat at the lower back of a straight skirt to prevent the wearer from being hampered when walking

kick scooter *n* VEHICLES same as **micro scooter**

kickshaw /kík shaw/ *n* (*archaic*) **1.** a trinket of little value **2.** an exotic food delicacy [Late 16C. < French *quelque chose* 'something']

kicksin' /kíksin/ *n Carib* playing around and not acting serious (*informal*)

kickstand /kík stand/ *n* a pivoting metal bar on a bicycle or motorcycle that can be pushed down into contact with the ground to keep the vehicle upright when it is stationary [Mid-20C. Because raised and lowered with the foot]

kick-start *vt* **1. START MOTORCYCLE** to start the engine on a motorcycle by stepping down hard on the kick-starter **2. START SOMETHING QUICKLY** to quickly start or give new life to a process or activity ○ *policies designed to kick-start an ailing economy* ■ *n* **1.** MOTORCYCLES same as **kick-starter 2. SOMETHING THAT GIVES QUICK START** something that quickly starts or gives new life to a process or activity (*informal*) ○ *a development package to give the museum a £50,000 kick-start*

kick-starter *n* the pedal on a motorcycle that starts the engine when it is kicked downwards

kick turn *n* in skiing, a standing 180-degree turn made by swivelling each ski separately

kick wheel *n* a mechanical potter's wheel that is turned by a foot-operated treadle

kid[1] /kid/ *n* **1. CHILD** a young child (*informal*) **2. YOUTH** a young person (*informal*) **3.** *N Am* **TERM OF ADDRESS** used as a term of address (*informal*) ○ *Here's looking at you, kid.* **4. YOUNG GOAT** a young goat, antelope, or similar animal **5. SOFT LEATHER** soft leather made from the skin of a young goat ■ *adj* **YOUNGER** younger, especially of two siblings (*informal*) ○ *my kid sister* ■ *vti* (**kids, kidding, kidded**) **BEAR YOUNG** to give birth to a kid or kids (*refers to goats*) [12C. < Old Norse *kið*] ◇ **our kid** *N England* my or our younger brother

REGIONAL NOTE The use of **kid** to mean 'child' was regarded as 'low slang' until the 19th century. In parts of the north of England, **kid** is used as a term of address: *our kid* means 'my or our younger brother'.

SYNONYMS See *youth.*

kid[2] /kid/ (**kids, kidding, kidded**) *v* **1.** *vti* to tell somebody something that is not true, especially as a joke or tease **2.** *vt* to deceive or mislead another person or yourself (*informal*) ○ *Don't kid yourself.* [Late 16C. < KID[1]] —**kidder** *n*

kid[3] /kid/ *n* a small wooden tub, especially one used for serving food on ships (*archaic*) [Mid-18C. Origin ?]

Kidd /kid/, **William** (1645?–1701) Scottish-born American pirate. He was commissioned to suppress piracy in the Indian Ocean (1695), but made his own attacks on merchant vessels (1697–99) and was later hanged. Known as **Captain Kidd**

Kidderminster /kíddərminstər/, **Kidderminster carpet** *n* a type of ingrain carpet originally made in Kidderminster in west-central England

kiddie *n* another spelling of **kiddy**

kiddo /kíddō/ (*plural* **-dos** or **-does**) *n* **1.** used as a term of address, especially to a young person (*informal*) **2.** a child, young person, or friend (*slang*)

Kiddush /kíddəsh, kíddush/ (*plural* **-dushim** /-doo sheém/), **kiddush** (*plural* **-dushim**) *n* **1.** in Judaism, a special blessing, usually for wine, said before a meal on the eve of the Sabbath or a holiday in order to consecrate the festival **2.** a reception following the recitation of the Kiddush for the congregants, at which drinks and snacks are served [Mid-18C. < Hebrew *qiddūš* 'sanctification']

kiddy /kíddi/ (*plural* **-dies**), **kiddie** *n* a small child (*informal*)

kid glove *n* a glove of soft leather made from the skin of a young goat ◇ **handle** *or* **treat somebody** *or* **something with kid gloves** to use great care or delicacy when dealing with somebody or something

kidglove /kid glúv/ *adj* displaying tact and sensitivity

kidlit /kídlit/ *n N Am* literature for children (*informal*) [Late 20C. < KID[1] + *lit* shortening of LITERATURE]

Kidman /kídmən/, **Nicole** (*b.* 1967) Hawaiian-born Australian actor. She has starred in films such as *Portrait of a Lady* (1996) and *Eyes Wide Shut* (1999).

Kidman, Sir Sidney (1857–1935) Australian landowner. He owned vast plots of grazing land in Australia. Known as **the 'Cattle King'**

kidnap /kíd nap/ *vti* (**-naps, -napping, -napped**) to take somebody away by force and hold him or her prisoner, usually for ransom ■ *n* CRIME same as **kidnapping** [Mid-17C. < KID[1] + *nap* 'steal', origin ?] —**kidnapper** *n*

kidnapping /kíd naping/ *n* the action or crime of forcefully taking away and holding somebody prisoner, usually for ransom

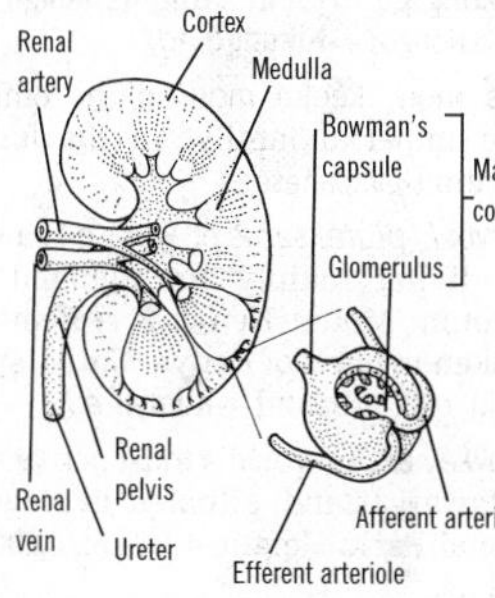

kidney

kidney /kídni/ (*plural* **-neys**) *n* **1. WASTE-REMOVING VERTEBRATE ORGAN** either of a pair of organs in the abdomen of vertebrates that filter waste liquid resulting from metabolism of the blood, which is subsequently excreted as urine **2. INVERTEBRATE ORGAN** the organ in invertebrates that filters waste material for excretion **3. ANIMAL KIDNEY AS FOOD** the kidney of a pig, calf, ox, or lamb, eaten as meat **4. KIND** a kind, type, or disposition (*dated*) ○ *a person of a very different kidney* [14C. Origin ?]

kidney bean *n* **1.** a small, kidney-shaped, usually dark red, edible bean **2.** a widely cultivated annual plant that produces kidney beans. Latin name: *Phaseolus vulgaris.*

kidney dish *n* a shallow kidney-shaped container used in hospitals and doctors' surgeries to hold soiled dressings, fluids, needles, or the instruments needed for a minor procedure

kidney-shaped *adj* in the shape of an oval with a concavity in one side

kidney stone *n* a small hard mass that forms in the kidney, consisting mainly of phosphates, oxalates, and urates

kidney vetch *n* PLANTS same as **okra** (sense 2)

kidology /ki dólləji/ *n* the use of bluffing or deception (*informal*) [Mid-20C. < KID[2]]

kidskin /kíd skin/ *n* same as **kid**[1] *n* (sense 5)

kids' stuff *n* (*informal*) **1.** something considered suitable only for children or immature people **2.** something that is very easy or very boring

kidult /kíddult/ *n* an adult who enjoys entertainment

such as films or computer games intended mainly for children (*slang*) [Mid-20C. Blend of KID[1] + ADULT]

kidvid /kíd vid/ *n* US a video for children (*informal*)

Kiel /keel/ city and seaport in north-central Germany, the capital of the state of Schleswig-Holstein, situated north of Hamburg. Population: 246,586 (1997).

kielbasa /keel bássə/ *n* a spicy smoked Polish sausage [Mid-20C. Via Polish < Turkic *kül bastî* 'roast pressed meat']

Kiel Canal canal in northwestern Germany connecting the North and Baltic seas. Length: 98 km/61 mi.

kier /keer/ *n* a vat in which yarn or cloth is bleached or dyed [Late 16C. < Old Norse *ker* 'tub']

Kierkegaard /keérkə gaard/, **Søren** (1813–55) Danish philosopher. His religious philosophy is concerned with individual existence, choice, and commitment, and has profoundly influenced theology and the existential philosophers. His books include *The Concept of Irony* (1841) and *Either/Or* (1843). Full name **Kierkegaard, Søren Aabye**

kieserite /keézə rīt/ *n* a white-to-yellow crystalline hydrated magnesium sulphate mineral. Source: salt residues. [Mid-19C. After Dietrich *Kieser* (1779–1862), German physician]

Kiev /keéy ef/ capital and largest city of Ukraine, located in the north-central part of the country. Population: 2,600,000 (1998).

kif /kif/, **kef** /kef/, **kaif** /kayf/ *n* marijuana, especially in North Africa [Early 19C. < Arabic *kayf, kef* 'pleasure']

Kigali /ki gaáli/ capital city of Rwanda, situated on a plateau in the centre of the country, just south of the equator. Population: 286,000 (1995).

kike /kīk/ *n* N Am a highly offensive taboo term for a Jew (*taboo*) [Early 20C. Origin ?]

Kikongo /kee kóng gō/ *n* LANG same as **Kongo**[1] (sense 2) [Late 19C. < Kongo] —**Kikongo** *adj*

kikumon /kíkə mon, keékə mon/ *n* the emblem of the Japanese imperial family, in the form of a chrysanthemum [< Japanese]

Kikuyu /ki koó yoo/ (*plural same* or **-yus**) *n* 1. a member of a people living mainly in highland Kenya, especially around Mount Kenya 2. a Benue-Congo language spoken in parts of Kenya. Native speakers: 5 million. [Mid-19C. < Bantu] —**Kikuyu** *adj*

Kilauea /keé low áy ə/ the world's most active volcano, on central Hawaii Island, situated in Hawaii Volcanoes National Park. Height: 1,247 m/4,090 ft.

Kild. *abbr* Kildare

Kildare /kil dáir/ county in the province of Leinster, eastern Republic of Ireland. The county town is Naas. Population: 134,992 (2002). Area: 1,694 sq. km/654 sq. mi.

kilderkin /kíldər kin/ *n* 1. an obsolete British measurement for liquids, equivalent to about 18 gallons or 68 litres 2. a cask with a capacity of one kilderkin [14C. < Middle Dutch *kinderkin* 'small quintal']

kiley *n* Aus LEISURE another spelling of **kylie**

kilim /ki leém, ki lím, keélim/ *n* a woven rug with richly coloured geometric patterns, made in Southwest Asia [Late 19C. Via Turkish < Persian *gelīm*]

Mount Kilimanjaro: view from Amboseli National Park

Kilimanjaro, Mount /kíləmən jaárō/ the highest mountain in Africa, located in northeastern Tanzania. Height: 5,895 m/19,340 ft.

Kilkenny /kil kénni/ county in the province of Leinster, eastern Republic of Ireland. The county town

is Kilkenny. Population: 75,336 (2002). Area: 2,062 sq. km/796 sq. mi.

kill /kil/ *v* (**kills, killing, killed**) 1. *vti* CAUSE SOMETHING LIVING TO DIE to cause the death of a person, animal, or other organism ○ *They were killed in a car crash.* 2. *vt* RUIN SOMETHING to cause something to end or be ruined ○ *The remark killed the conversation.* 3. *vt* OVERPOWER SOMETHING SUBTLE OR LESS STRONG to destroy or severely damage an essential, often delicate quality in something by superimposing something stronger ○ *Her perfume killed the scent of the roses.* 4. *vt* BLOCK PLAN to prevent a proposal such as the passing of a parliamentary bill going through 5. *vt* HURT PART OF SOMEBODY'S BODY to cause severe physical pain or discomfort to somebody (*informal*) ○ *My feet are killing me!* 6. *vt* TIRE SOMEBODY OUT to exhaust somebody completely (*informal*) ○ *These stairs kill me every time.* 7. **kill yourself** *vr* OVEREXERT YOURSELF to push yourself too hard (*informal, often used ironically*) ○ *She was killing herself to get the job done on time.* 8. *vt* SWITCH SOMETHING OFF to disconnect the power to something electrical or mechanical so that it stops working (*informal*) ○ *Kill the engine.* 9. *vt* MAKE TIME PASS to use up spare time in some activity (*informal*) ○ *We had a couple of hours to kill before going to the airport.* 10. *vti* BOWL SOMEBODY OVER to have an overpowering effect on somebody, e.g. causing extreme admiration, helpless laughter, or utter amazement (*informal*) ○ *dressed to kill* 11. *vt* DRINK ALL OF SOMETHING to finish off a bottle of something, usually an alcoholic beverage (*slang*) 12. *vt* SOCCER CONTROL BALL in football, to bring a fast-moving ball under instant control 13. *vt* RACKET GAMES MAKE BALL UNRETURNABLE in racquet games, to hit the ball so hard, with such skill, or in such a direction that your opponent has no chance of returning it 14. *vt* US AMERICAN FOOTBALL MAKE BALL DEAD in American football, to stop the ball so that it is no longer in play (*informal*) 15. *vt* US HIT BALL HARD to hit a ball very hard 16. *vt* PUBL CUT TEXT to delete a piece of text from a publication or remove a particular amount from a text (*slang*) ○ *We had to kill half a column to make space for the ad.* ■ *n* 1. KILLING the moment or an act of killing an animal, especially prey or game, or the bull at the end of a bullfight 2. FIELD SPORTS PREY the prey killed by an animal or human being 3. MIL DESTRUCTION OF ENEMY VEHICLE the destroying of an enemy vehicle such as a plane, ship, or tank (*slang*) [13C. < assumed Old English *cyllan* < Germanic] ◇ **be in at the kill** to be present at the end of something or the achievement of an aim, especially when you have worked to cause it

---

SYNONYMS *kill, murder, assassinate, execute, put to death, slaughter, slay, put down, put to sleep, take somebody's life*

CORE MEANING: to deprive of life

kill to cause the death of a person, animal, or other organism ○ *Floods have killed at least three people and forced hundreds from their homes.* ○ *a resolution asking countries not to kill whales for scientific purposes* ○ *A severe frost killed all the seedlings.* **murder** to kill another person deliberately and not in self-defence or with any other extenuating circumstance recognized by law ○ *She was found guilty of murdering a nursing colleague.* **assassinate** to kill somebody, especially a political leader or other public figure, by a sudden violent attack ○ *A police spokesperson told reporters a plot to assassinate the pontiff had been foiled.* **execute** to kill somebody as part of a judicial or extrajudicial process ○ *Cromwell ordered the Abbot of Reading to be tried and executed immediately.* **put to death** to kill somebody, especially in accordance with a legal death sentence ○ *put to death for treason* **slaughter** to kill a person or large numbers of people brutally, or to kill farm animals for food ○ *accused of slaughtering hundreds of unarmed protesters* ○ *cattle sent to be slaughtered at two years old* **slay** (*formal or literary*) to kill a person or animal ○ *Cain plotted to slay his brother Abel.* **put down** or **put to sleep** to kill an animal in a humane way, especially because it is ill, injured, or in pain ○ *Some of the animals were beyond help and had to be put down.* ○ *I think I'll have to have my poor old dog put to sleep.* **take somebody's life** to kill a person or yourself ○ *They were accused of taking the lives of hundreds of innocent women and children.* ○ *The verdict of the enquiry into his death was that he had taken his own life.*

---

kill off *vt* 1. to destroy something or somebody

utterly, especially the remaining members of a group of people or animals ○ *The spray killed off all the aphids.* 2. to write in the death of a character, especially in a serial or soap opera

Killarney /ki laárni/ town and tourist centre in the southwestern Republic of Ireland, situated by the Lakes of Killarney. Population: 12,087 (2002).

killdeer /kíl deer/ (*plural same* or **-deers**) *n* a bird with brown and white feathers, two black breast bands, and a distinctive noisy cry. Native to: North America. Latin name: *Charadrius vociferus*. [Mid-18C. An imitation of its call]

killer /kíllər/ *n* 1. SOMEBODY OR SOMETHING THAT KILLS a person or animal that kills others intentionally, especially one that does this more than once (*often used before a noun*) ○ *a killer crocodile* 2. SOMETHING VERY DIFFICULT something that is very demanding or difficult (*informal*) ○ *This aerobics class is a killer.* 3. DESTRUCTIVE PERSON OR THING somebody or something that destroys or is fatal ○ *a cancer that is still a major killer* 4. EXCEPTIONAL THING something that is excellent or exceptional (*slang*) ■ *adj* EXCEPTIONAL excellent or exceptional (*slang*) ○ *a killer performance*

killer app *n* a highly popular computer application, seen as definitive (*slang*)

killer bee *n* an aggressive honeybee that was hybridized in Brazil from African and European strains and has spread north into Mexico and southern Texas (*informal*)

killer cell, **killer T cell** *n* a T cell that is part of the body's immune system and attacks cells having specific antigens on their surface such as cancer cells and those infected with a virus

killer instinct *n* 1. a tendency, capacity, or urge to kill 2. an overpowering drive to succeed, e.g. in business deals or sports, whatever the cost may be to other people

killer T cell *n* ANAT same as **killer cell**

killer whale

killer whale *n* a black-and-white toothed whale. It grows up to 7.62 m/25 ft long, has a tall dorsal fin, and feeds mainly on fish and squid. Native to: colder seas. Latin name: *Orcinus orca*.

kill fee *n* US a payment made to a writer, photographer, artist, or illustrator by a publisher who has decided not to publish the contracted work

killfile /kíl fīl/ *n* a list on an Internet newsreader of authors, subjects, or threads that the user is not interested in, enabling messages or articles relating to the persons or topics listed to be filtered out ■ *v* to add somebody's name to a killfile in order to block any e-mail from that sender

killick /kíllik/, **killock** /kíllək/ *n* a small anchor, especially one made of a heavy stone [Early 17C. Origin ?]

Killiecrankie, Pass of /kílli krángki/ wooded pass in Perth and Kinross, central Scotland. It was the site of a battle between Jacobites and forces of William III.

killifish /kíllifish/ (*plural* **-fishes** or *same*) *n* a freshwater fish about the size of a minnow, kept in aquariums or used as bait and in mosquito control. Family: Cyprinodontidae. [Early 19C. Origin ?]

killing /kílling/ *n* 1. SLAYING the act of causing the death of a person or animal 2. QUICK PROFIT a large and quick profit (*informal*) ■ *adj* 1. EXHAUSTING totally exhausting 2. FUNNY hilariously funny 3. FATAL causing or resulting in death —**killingly** *adv*

killing fields *npl* the site of mass slaughter, e.g. of civilians

CULTURAL NOTE *The Killing Fields*, a film (1984) by Roland Joffe. Through the true story of US journalist Sydney Schanberg's attempts to trace the Cambodian aide he was forced to leave behind after the fall of Phnom Penh in 1975, Joffe portrays the atrocities perpetrated on the Cambodian people by the Khmer Rouge regime between 1975 and 1978. References such as 'the killing fields of Bosnia' clearly take their linguistic cues from this film title.

killjoy /kíl joy/ *n* somebody whose behaviour prevents other people from having a good time

killock *n* NAUT same as **killick**

kill shot *n* US in racket games, a shot that is hit so hard or accurately that it cannot be returned

kill-time *n* an activity that helps to pass the time

Kilmarnock /kil maárnək/ industrial town in East Ayrshire, central Scotland. Population: 44,307 (1991).

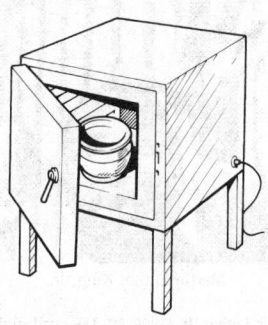

kiln: pottery kiln

kiln /kiln, kil/ *n* a specialized oven or furnace used for industrial processes such as firing clay for pottery or bricks and for drying materials such as hops or timber ■ *vt* (**kilns, kilning, kilned**) to dry, fire, or bake something in a kiln [Pre-12C. < Latin *culina* < *coquere* 'to cook']

Kilner jar /kílnər-/ *tdmk* a trademark for a glass jar that has an airtight lid and is used for preserving fruit and vegetables

kilo /keélō/ *n* MEASURE same as **kilogram** [Mid-19C. Shortening]

Kilo *n* a code word for K in military and police communications

kilo- *prefix* **1.** a thousand (10³) ○ *kilogram* Symbol **k 2.** in the binary system, a thousand (2¹⁰) ○ *kilobyte* [Via French < Greek *khilioi* 'thousand']

kilobit /kíləbit/ *n* 1,024 bits

kilobyte /kílə bīt/ *n* a unit of computer data or storage space equivalent to 1,024 bytes

kilocalorie /kílō kalləri/ *n* PHYS, MEASURE same as **calorie** (sense 2)

kilocycle /kílō sīk'l/ *n* MEASURE same as **kilohertz**

kiloelectronvolt /kílō i léktron vōlt/ *n* one thousand electron volts

kilogram /kílə gram/, **kilogramme** *n* the basic unit of mass in the SI system, equal to 1,000 grams or 2.2046 lbs. Symbol **kg**

kilohertz /kílō hurts/ *n* 1,000 hertz

kilojoule /kílə jool/ *n* 1,000 joules

kilometre /kílə meetər, ki lómmitər/ *n* 1,000 metres/0.621 miles

USAGE The traditional British English pronunciation of *kilometre* has the stress on the first syllable, as in other words beginning with *kilo-* and ending with *-metre*, for example *kilogram* and *millimetre*. An alternative pronunciation, with the stress on the second syllable (as in *barometer* and *thermometer*), is also heard, though it is disliked by some British people as an Americanism.

kiloparsec /kílō paar sek/ *n* 1,000 parsecs

kiloton /kílō tun/ *n* **1.** 1,000 tons **2.** an explosive force equal to 1,000 tons of TNT

kilovolt /kílə vōlt/ *n* 1,000 volts

kilowatt /kíllə wot/ *n* 1,000 watts

kilowatt-hour *n* a unit of energy equal to the work done by one kilowatt in one hour

kilt /kilt/ *n* SCOTTISH GARMENT a knee-length wrap-around tartan garment that is part of the traditional Scottish highland dress for men and is also worn by women and girls ■ *vt* (**kilts, kilting, kilted**) **1.** PLEAT GARMENT to form vertical pleats in the fabric of a garment, usually a skirt **2.** TUCK UP SKIRT to pull up a skirt and gather it into folds, so as to keep it out of water or mud or to allow more freedom of movement (*dated*) [Mid-18C. < dialect *kilt* 'tuck up, gird' < N Germanic] —**kilted** *adj*

kilter /kíltər/ *n* good working order or condition ○ *The well pump is out of kilter.* [Mid-17C. Variant of *kelter*, origin ?]

kiltie /kílti/ *n* a person wearing a kilt, especially a kilted soldier from a Highland regiment (*informal*)

Kimberley¹ /kímbərli/ capital of Northern Cape Province in central South Africa. It is located in a diamond-mining region. Population: 167,060 (1991).

Kimberley², **Kimberleys** /kímbərliz/ plateau region of northwestern Western Australia, near the border with the Northern Territory. The highest point is Mount Hann, 776 m/2,545 ft. Area: 360,000 sq. km/140,000 sq. mi.

kimberlite /kímbər līt/ *n* a form of igneous rock, found especially in South Africa, composed mainly of peridotite and often containing diamonds [Late 19C. After *Kimberley*, town in South Africa]

kimchi /kímchi/ *n* a pickle made with vegetables such as cabbage and white radish seasoned with chilli, garlic, and ginger, regarded as the national dish of Korea [Late 19C. < Korean *kimch'i*]

Kim Il Sung /kím il súng/ (1912–94) North Korean premier (1948–72) and president (1972–94) of North Korea. He encouraged a personality cult around himself and tried to extend Communist rule into South Korea, leading to the Korean War (1950–53). Born **Kim Song Ju**

Kim Jong Il /kím jong íl/ (b. 1941) North Korean head of state. He took over several major posts after the death of his father Kim Il Sung in 1994 but it was not until 1998 that he was officially made head of state. In 2000 he signed an agreement with the president of South Korea to work towards the reunification of the Korean peninsula.

kimono

kimono /ki mōnō/ (*plural* **-nos**) *n* **1.** a loose floor-length traditional Japanese garment that has wide sleeves, wraps in front, and is fastened with a sash **2.** a western garment, especially a dressing gown, similar to the Japanese kimono [Late 19C. < Japanese < *ki* 'wear' + *mono* 'thing'] —**kimonoed** *adj*

kin /kin/ *n* **1.** FAMILY GROUP somebody's relatives as a group (*takes a plural verb*) **2.** BLOOD RELATION somebody related by blood ○ *He's not kin but we consider him one of the family.* **3.** GROUP OR CLASS a member of a group that shares characteristics with another group ○ *the starfish and its kin the sea urchin* ■ *adj* RELATED related to somebody [Old English *cyn(n)* < Indo-European]

-kin *suffix* little, dear ○ *limpkin* [Probably < Middle Dutch *-ki(j)n*]

kina /keénə/ *n* the main unit of Papua New Guinean currency. See table at **currency** [Late 20C. < Tok Pisin]

Kinabalu, Mount /kínnəbə loó/ mountain in Malaysia

in the state of Sabah, in northern Borneo. It lies in Kinabalu National Park. Height: 4,101 m/13,455 ft.

kinaesthesia /kín eess theézi ə, kín eess-/, **kinaesthesis** /kín eess theéssiss, kín eess-/ *n* the perception or sensing of the motion, weight, or position of the body as muscles, tendons, and joints move [Late 19C. < Greek *kinein* 'to move' + *aisthēsis* 'sensation'] —**kinaesthetic** *adj* —**kinaesthetically** *adv*

kinase /kí nayss, -nayz/ *n* an enzyme that catalyses the transfer of a phosphate group from ATP [Early 20C. < KINETIC]

Kincardineshire /kin kaárdinshər/ former county in eastern Scotland, Now part of Aberdeenshire

kincob /kíng kob, -kəb/ *n* a South Asian silk fabric embroidered with gold or silver thread [Early 18C. < Urdu, Persian *kamkāb* 'gold or silver brocade', alteration of *kamkā* 'damask silk' < Chinese, 'gold flower']

kind¹ /kīnd/ *adj* **1.** COMPASSIONATE having a generous warm compassionate nature **2.** GENEROUS showing generosity or compassion ○ *a kind act* **3.** AGREEABLE OR SAFE not harsh, unpleasant, or likely to have destructive effects ○ *a detergent that is kind to the environment* **4.** CARING showing courtesy or caring about somebody (*formal*) ○ *my kindest regards to your family* **5.** LOVING full of love (*archaic*) [Old English *gecynde* 'innate, natural' < Germanic]

kind² /kīnd/ *n* **1.** △ GROUP OF INDIVIDUALS THAT SHARE FEATURES a group of individuals or items connected by shared characteristics ○ *What kind of fruit is this?* **2.** SOMETHING INFERIOR an example of something, especially if it is seen as inferior or doubtful ○ *Well, you could say it's a kind of tool, but how would you use it?* **3.** ESSENCE OF SOMETHING the primary character of something that determines the class to which it belongs [Old English *cynde* < Germanic] ◇ **in kind 1.** with goods or services, not with money **2.** with something of the same sort that was given ○ *If they attack us, they'll be paid back in kind.* ◇ **kind of** rather, to some extent, or in a way (*informal*) ○ *She seemed kind of upset when I talked to her.* ◇ **of a kind 1.** like something else in some respects but not enough to be satisfactory **2.** alike, or belonging to the same sort ○ *She's one of a kind, is Sarah.*

USAGE When *kind of* is followed by a plural word, there is a temptation to precede the whole phrase with a corresponding plural such as *these* or *those*, so that *this kind of thing* becomes *these kind of things*. However, such expressions (and ones on the same pattern employing *sort* or *type*) are widely regarded as ungrammatical. *These kinds of things* or *things of this kind* is to be preferred.

SYNONYMS See **type**.

kinda /kíndə/ *contr* kind of (*nonstandard*) ○ *It's kinda strange.*

kindergarten /kíndər gaart'n/ *n* ANZ, N Am a school or class for young children, usually between the ages of four and six, immediately before they begin formal education [Mid-19C. < German, 'children's garden']

kind-hearted /-haártid/ *adj* **1.** sympathetic and kind ○ *She's too kind-hearted to be angry with you for long.* **2.** showing or arising from a sympathetic and generous nature ○ *a kind-hearted gesture* —**kind-heartedly** *adv* —**kind-heartedness** *n*

Kindi /kíndi/, **al-** AD (801?–873?) Arabian Islamic philosopher. He translated the work of Aristotle into Arabic and formulated the theology of the Mutazilites.

kindie *n* ANZ EDUC another spelling of **kindy** (*informal*)

kindle¹ /kínd'l/ (**-dles, -dling, -dled**) *vti* **1.** START BURNING to set something alight, or begin to burn **2.** BRIGHTEN OR GLOW to begin to glow, or make something begin to glow **3.** IGNITE EMOTION OR INTEREST to become aroused, or arouse feelings or interest ○ *The programme kindled his interest in antiquarian books.* [12C. < Old Norse *kynda*; influenced by Old Norse *kyndill* 'torch, candle'] —**kindler** *n*

kindle² /kínd'l/ *n* a brood or a litter, e.g. of kittens ■ *vi* (**-dles, -dling, -dled**) to give birth, especially to baby rabbits [13C. Probably < KIND²]

kindling /kíndling/ *n* **1.** FIRE-LIGHTING MATERIAL something used to start a fire because it burns easily, e.g. a bunch of small dry twigs **2.** MAKING SOMETHING BURN the

act of making something start to burn **3.** STIRRING UP OF EMOTION the arousal of somebody's interest or feelings

kindly /kíndli/ adj (-lier, -liest) **1.** FRIENDLY AND GENEROUS BY NATURE sympathetic and kind **2.** SHOWING SYMPATHY arising from or showing a sympathetic and generous nature **3.** PLEASANT pleasant, mild, or comfortable ■ adv **1.** ⚠ PLEASE used in polite requests ○ *Kindly take your seats.* **2.** IN KIND WAY showing kindness and considerateness ○ *He kindly accompanied me home.* **3.** TOLERANTLY with tolerance and patience ○ *She kindly disregarded their lack of skill during the first few days.* —**kindliness** n

USAGE *Kindly* is not restricted just to *kindness* as such but may also mean, approximately, 'please'. In either case, it should modify the action or thing wished for, not some other part of the sentence. The intention of, for example, *May we kindly request that patrons take their seats,* is to encourage patrons to be so kind as to sit down. Thus the sentence should be reworded as *May we request that patrons kindly take their seats.*

kindness /kíndnəss/ n **1.** the practice of being or the tendency to be sympathetic and compassionate **2.** an act that shows consideration and caring ○ *How can we thank you for your many kindnesses?*

kindred /kíndrəd/ adj **1.** SIMILAR TO SOMEBODY OR SOMETHING close to somebody or something else because of similar qualities or interests ○ *the kindred relationship between neuroscience and neurology* **2.** OF SAME FAMILY related to somebody by blood (*formal*) ○ *the search for someone kindred to him* ■ n **1.** AFFINITY closeness to somebody that is based on something other than a blood relationship, e.g. on similarity of character or interests ○ *a sense of kindred between the two candidates* **2.** FAMILY RELATIONSHIP relationship by blood or, less strictly, by marriage ○ *occasions that reinforce the ties of kindred* **3.** SOMEBODY'S FAMILY somebody's relatives as a group (*takes a plural verb*) **4.** CLAN a family or group of closely related families, e.g. in the Celtic kin-based social system ○ *The Ui Neill were then the most powerful of the kindreds.* [12C. < KIN + Old English *ræden* 'condition'] —**kindredness** n —**kindredship** n

kindred spirit n somebody who resembles somebody else in character, interests, and temperament

kindy /kíndi/ (*plural* **-dies**), **kindie** n ANZ same as **kindergarten** (*informal*) [Mid-20C. Shortening and alteration]

kine /kīn/ npl cows or cattle (*archaic*) [Old English *cȳna*, form of the plural of *cū* (see COW¹)]

kinematics /kínni máttiks/ n a branch of physics that deals with the motion of a body or system without reference to force and mass (*takes a singular verb*) [Mid-19C. < Greek *kinēmat-* 'motion'] —**kinematic** adj —**kinematically** adv

kinescope /kínnəskōp, kínə-/ n US a cathode ray tube in a television [Mid-20C. Originally a trademark]

kinesics /ki néessiks, kī-, -néeziks/ n the study of the ways in which people use body movements such as shrugging to communicate without speaking (*takes a singular verb*) [Mid-20C. < Greek *kinēsis* (see KINESIS)]

kinesin /kī néessin/ n a protein that uses chemical energy from ATP to create movement within cells, e.g. separating chromosomes during division and transporting neurotransmitters inside nerve cells

kinesiology /ki néessi ólləji, kī-, -neé zi-/ n **1.** the study of the mechanics of motion with respect to human anatomy **2.** in alternative medicine, a system of muscle testing that reveals and corrects musculoskeletal imbalances and identifies food sensitivities [Late 19C. < Greek *kinēsis* (see KINESIS)] —**kinesiologist** n

kinesis /ki néessiss, kī-/ n the movement of a cell or organism in response to a stimulus such as light. Such movement can be in any direction and its rate depends on the intensity of stimulation. [Early 20C. < Greek *kinēsis* 'movement' < *kinein* 'to move']

-kinesis suffix **1.** motion, activity ○ *psychokinesis* **2.** cell division ○ *diakinesis* [< Greek *kinēsis* (see KINESIS)]

kinesthesia n PHYSIOL US spelling of **kinaesthesia**

kinetheodolite /kínnəthi óddə līt/ n an optical instrument that contains a cine camera and provides continuous footage of a moving target such as a missile or satellite along with its altitude and trajectory [Mid-20C. < KINESIS]

kinetic /ki néttik, kī-/ adj relating to, caused by, or producing motion [Mid-19C. < Greek *kinētikos* 'for putting in motion' < *kinein* 'to move']

kinetic art n art, especially sculpture, with parts that move, e.g. when blown by the wind or activated by electricity —**kinetic artist** n

kinetic energy n the energy that a body or system has because of its motion. Symbol T, E_k

kinetics /ki néttiks, kī-/ n (*takes a singular verb*) **1.** PHYS same as **dynamics 2.** the branch of chemistry that studies rates of reactions

kinetic theory n a theory of the behaviour of gases that assumes heat is a process of energy transfer and the internal energy of a gas is the total energy of its particles

kineto- prefix motion, movement ○ *kinetosome* [< Greek *kinetos* 'moving' < *kinein* 'to move']

kinetoplast /ki néttə plast, kī-/ n a small cell body outside the nucleus and near the base of the flagellum in some protozoans

kinetosome /ki néttə sōm, kī-/ n BIOL same as **basal body**

kinfolk /kín fōk/ npl somebody's relatives

king /king/ n **1.** MALE SOVEREIGN a man or boy who rules as a monarch over an independent state **2.** CHIEF a ruler of a group ○ *Jupiter was king of the Roman gods.* **3.** BEST EXAMPLE any animal considered as the best, strongest, or biggest of its kind ○ *The lion is variously called the king of beasts or the king of the jungle.* **4.** PRE-EMINENT MAN the principal man or pre-eminent male figure in a field ○ *king of the chat shows* **5.** HIGH COURT CARD a card in each suit of a pack that carries the picture of a king **6.** PRINCIPAL CHESS PIECE the most important piece in chess, whose capture wins the game **7.** CROWNED PIECE IN DRAUGHTS a piece in the game of draughts that has reached the far side of the board and has been crowned, and may therefore move in any direction ■ vt (**kings**, **kinging**, **kinged**) **1.** CROWN PIECE IN DRAUGHTS to make a piece into a king in the game of draughts **2.** CROWN SOMEBODY KING to make somebody a king [Old English *cyning* < Germanic] —**kingship** n

King n in Christianity, God or Jesus Christ

B. B. King

King /king/, **B. B.** (*b.* 1925) US blues musician. He led a blues revival in the 1960s and his rhythm-and-blues hits include 'The Thrill is Gone' (1970) and the album *Live at Cook County Jail* (1971). Born King, Riley B.

'Being a blues singer is like being black two times.'
[B. B. King. Quoted in *The Wit and Wisdom of Rock and Roll*, Maxim Jabukowski (ed.); 1983]

Billie Jean King

King, **Billie Jean** (*b.* 1943) US tennis player. Between 1961 and 1979 she won a record 20 Wimbledon titles. She also won numerous other titles in the United States, France, and Australia. She became the first president of the Women's Tennis Association in 1974. Born Moffat, Billie Jean

'It's really impossible for athletes to grow up. As long as you're playing, no one will let you.'
[Billie Jean King, *Billie Jean*; 1982]

King, **Coretta Scott** (*b.* 1927) US civil rights leader. The widow of Martin Luther King, Jr., she has continued her husband's civil rights advocacy and activism.

King, **Mackenzie** (1874–1950) prime minister of Canada. He became leader of the Liberal Party in 1919, and served three terms as prime minister (1921–26, 1926–30, 1935–48). Full name **King, William Lyon Mackenzie**. See table at **prime minister**

Martin Luther King, Jr.

King, **Martin Luther, Jr.** (1929–68) US civil rights leader and minister. His non-violent demonstrations against racial inequality led to civil rights legislation. He was awarded the Nobel Peace Prize (1964) and was assassinated four years later in Memphis, Tennessee.

'I have a dream that my four little children will one day live in a nation where they will not be judged by the color of their skin but by the content of their character.'
[Martin Luther King, Jr., *Speech at the Civil Rights March on Washington, DC*; 28 August 1963]

'A riot is at bottom the language of the unheard.'
[Martin Luther King, Jr., *Where Do We Go From Here?*; 1967]

King, **Stephen** (*b.* 1947) US writer. His horror stories such as *Carrie* (1973) and *Needful Things* (1991) have sold more than 100 million copies worldwide, and many have been made into films. Full name **King, Stephen Edwin**

King, **Thomas J.** (1921–2000) US embryologist. His research on frog embryos with Robert Briggs at the Institute for Cancer Research in Philadelphia led to the creation of the first amphibian clones in 1951.

kingbird /kíng burd/ (*plural same* or **-birds**) n a large songbird. Native to: Americas. Genus: *Tyrannus*.

kingbolt /kíng bōlt/ n a vertical bolt that joins the body of a carriage, wagon, or railway carriage to the front axle

King Charles spaniel n **1.** a small spaniel of a breed with a markedly domed head, snub nose, bulging eyes, floppy ears, and a tan or black coat with white patches **2.** a slightly larger breed of spaniel that has a longer nose [Late 19C. After CHARLES II, who was partial to the breed]

king cobra n a very large poisonous cobra that eats other reptiles and can reach a length of 5.5 m/18 ft. Native to: Southeast Asia. Latin name: *Ophiophagus hannah*. See illustration on next page

King Country region in the west of the North Island, New Zealand, lying south of the Waikato region between the western coast and Lake Taupo

king crab n MARINE BIOL same as **horseshoe crab**

kingcup /kíng kup/ n a plant of the buttercup family, especially a marsh marigold. Flowers: yellow.

king cobra

Native to: wetlands of Europe, North America. Family: Ranunculaceae.

kingdom /kíngdəm/ n **1.** MONARCH'S TERRITORY a state or people ruled over by a king or queen **2.** SPHERE OF ACTIVITY a realm or area of activity in which a particular thing is thought to dominate ○ *the kingdom of professional tennis* **3.** HIGHEST CLASSIFICATION FOR NATURAL THINGS each of the three groups, animal, vegetable, and mineral, into which natural organisms and objects are traditionally, as opposed to scientifically, divided

kingdom come n **1.** the next world or the state after death **2.** the point at which the world comes to an end (*informal*) [Late 18C. < *Thy kingdom come* (in the Our Father (Matthew 6:10)) 'may Thy kingdom come']

kingfish /kíng fish/ (*plural* **-fishes** or *same*) n **1.** a large game fish. Native to: warm Atlantic coastal waters. Genus: *Menticirrhus*. **2.** US FISH same as **king mackerel 3.** the flesh of a kingfish as food **4.** FISH same as **opah**

kingfisher

kingfisher /kíng fishər/ n a brightly coloured bird that usually has a short tail, a long strong beak, and sometimes a crest. It feeds on fish, insects, and other prey. Native to: mainly tropical, subtropical regions worldwide. Family: Alcedinidae. [15C. Originally *king's fisher*]

king-hit *Aus* (*informal*) vt (**king-hits, king-hitting, king-hit**) KNOCK SOMEBODY OUT to knock somebody out with a punch ■ n **1.** KNOCKOUT PUNCH a punch that knocks somebody out **2.** SETBACK a sudden major setback or misfortune

King Island island off the northwestern coast of Tasmania, Australia. It is known for its dairy produce. Population: 1,689 (2002 estimate). Area: 1,098 sq. km/424 sq. mi.

King James Bible, **King James Version** n N Am same as **Authorized Version**

kinglet /kínglət/ n **1.** a minor king, especially a contemptibly small or unimportant kingdom (*insult*) **2.** a small grey bird that has a black-edged yellow or reddish crown and feeds on insects. Native to: North America. Genus: *Regulus*.

kingly /kíngli/ (**-lier, -liest**) adj **1.** stately and grand, as befits a king ○ *a kingly posture* **2.** having or relating to the rank of king ○ *kingly duties* —**kingliness** n

king mackerel n US a mackerel often caught for sport. Native to: warm Atlantic waters. Latin name: *Scomber cavalla*.

kingmaker /kíng maykər/ n somebody with the power and connections to influence who is appointed to important positions, usually within a government

king-of-arms (*plural* **kings-of-arms**) n each of the principal heralds in the British colleges of arms

king of kings, **King of Kings** n **1.** in Christianity, God or Jesus Christ **2.** a male monarch who rules over other, subordinate kings

king of the castle n **1.** the most important person in a group or place (*informal*) **2.** UK, Can a game in which a child stands on a piece of higher ground and tries to prevent other children from taking it over. US term **king of the hill**

King Peak mountain in the St Elias Range of southwestern Yukon Territory, Canada. Height: 5,173 m/16,972 ft.

king penguin n a large penguin. Native to: Antarctic. Latin name: *Aptenodytes patagonica*.

kingpin /kíng pin/ n **1.** LEADER the most important person in a group or place (*informal*) **2.** PART OF AXLE a pivot pin that secures an axle to an axle beam and allows a vehicle to be steered **3.** CRUX OF ARGUMENT the most important point in an argument, upon which everything else depends **4.** FRONT PIN IN BOWLING the pin at the apex of a layout of the pins in tenpin bowling, which must be struck at a specific angle if all the pins are to be knocked down

king post n a vertical post that joins the apex of a triangular roof truss to the crossbeam

Kings /kingz/ n either of two books of the Bible that relate the histories of Israel and the kings of Judah (*takes a singular verb*) See table at **Bible**

king salmon n FISH same as **Chinook salmon**

King's Bench n a division of the High Court of Justice in England (*used when the reigning monarch is a man or boy*)

Kings Canyon /kingz-/ canyon in central Australia, near Alice Springs in the Northern Territory

King's Counsel n a senior barrister in England, entitled to wear a silk gown and sit inside the bar of a court (*used when the reigning monarch is a man or boy*)

King's English n standard written or spoken British English, considered as the most correct form of the language (*used when the reigning monarch is a man or boy*)

King's evidence n in English law, evidence for the prosecution given by somebody who took part in a crime, usually in exchange for leniency (*used when the reigning monarch is a man or boy*)

king's evil n MED same as **scrofula** (*archaic*) [< the belief that a king's touch could cure it]

Kingsford Smith /kíngsfərd smíth/, **Sir Charles Edward** (1897–1935) Australian aviator. In 1928, with Charles Ulm, he made the first flight across the Pacific Ocean.

King's highway n a public road, regarded as belonging ultimately to the monarch (*formal*; *used when the reigning monarch is a man or boy*)

king-size, **king-sized** adj **1.** EXTRA BIG larger, wider, or longer than the standard version of the same thing **2.** FULL-SIZE describes an extra-large size of bed, 1,930 x 2,032 mm/76 in x 80 in, or bedding made to fit this size of bed **3.** VERY GREAT very great in intensity, scope, or difficulty (*informal*) ○ *a king-size job to finish this weekend*

Kingsley /kíngzli/, **Charles** (1819–75) British writer and cleric. His novels include *Westward Ho!* (1855) and the children's book *The Water Babies* (1863). He was a chaplain to Queen Victoria.

> 'He did not know that a keeper is only a poacher turned outside in, and a poacher a keeper turned inside out.'
> [Charles Kingsley, *The Water Babies*; 1863]

King's Lynn /kingz lín/ historic town in Norfolk, eastern England, a major seaport in medieval times. Population: 41,281 (1991).

king snake n a nonpoisonous constricting snake that ranges from 0.6 m/2 ft to 1.8 m/6 ft in length and preys on small animals and other snakes. Native to: North America. Genus: *Lampropeltis*.

king's peace n in medieval England, the general peace of the kingdom secured by laws enforced in the king's name

King's Proctor n in the United Kingdom, an official of the High Court of Justice who has the right to intervene in some cases, including those involving divorces and wills, when there are charges of collusion among the people involved or suppression of facts (*used when the reigning monarch is a man or boy*)

king's ransom n an enormous sum of money

King's Regulations npl regulations that govern the armed forces of the United Kingdom and some Commonwealth countries (*used when the reigning monarch is a man or boy*)

king's shilling n in former times, a coin given to new military recruits as a symbol of enlistment into the British army (*used when the reigning monarch was a man or boy*) ◇ **take** or **earn the king's shilling** to enlist in the British army (*archaic*)

King's Speech n (*used when the reigning monarch is a man or boy*) **1.** a speech given by the monarch at the opening of Parliament each year, setting out the government's proposed legislation **2.** in the United Kingdom, a speech by the monarch to the nation and the Commonwealth broadcast on Christmas Day

Kingston /kíngstən/ **1.** largest city, chief seaport, and capital of Jamaica, situated on the southeastern coast of the island at the foot of the Blue Mountains. Population: 538,100 (1995). **2.** city on Lake Ontario, at the mouth of the St Lawrence River, in southeastern Ontario Province, Canada. Population: 108,158 (2001).

Kingston-upon-Hull ♦ Hull

Kingston-upon-Thames historic town on the River Thames in southeastern England. It is now part of Greater London. Population: 147,273 (2001).

Kingstown /kíngz town/ capital and principal port of St Vincent and the Grenadines, on the southwestern coast of St Vincent Island. It is the site of the oldest botanical garden in the western hemisphere, established in 1763. Population: 16,130 (1995).

Kingwana /king wáanə/ n a Bantu language related to Kiswahili, spoken in the Democratic Republic of the Congo and widely used as a lingua franca — **Kingwana** adj

kingwood /kíng wood/ n **1.** a hard fine-grained purplish wood. Use: cabinetwork. **2.** the leguminous tree that yields kingwood. Native to: Brazil. Latin name: *Dalbergia cearensis*.

kinin /kínin/ n **1.** a polypeptide that causes dilation in blood vessels and contraction of smooth muscle **2.** BIOCHEM same as **cytokinin** [Mid-20C. Origin ?]

kink /kingk/ n **1.** TIGHT COIL a tight twist or coil in an otherwise straight section of something such as rope, string, or wire **2.** MUSCULAR SPASM a sudden spasm in a muscle, especially a crick in the neck (*informal*) **3.** MINOR DIFFICULTY a slight difficulty or holdup in the progress of something (*informal*) **4.** ECCENTRICITY something that is eccentric or peculiar in somebody's personality or behaviour **5.** US ODD IDEA a quirky odd idea or impulse (*informal*) ○ *She got a kink in her head to swim across the Chesapeake Bay alone.* **6.** SEXUAL ODDITY an unusual sexual practice, especially one that might be considered deviant (*slang*) ■ **kinks** npl Scotland LAUGHTER convulsions of laughter (*nonstandard*) ○ *had us in kinks with his impressions* ■ vti (**kinks, kinking, kinked**) MAKE OR BECOME TWISTED to put a kink in something, or develop a kink [Late 17C. < Low German *kinke* 'twist in a rope']

kinkajou /kíngkə joo/ (*plural* **-jous** or *same*) n a tree-dwelling fruit-eating mammal related to the raccoon that has a long prehensile tail, brownish fur, and large eyes. Native to: Central and South America. Latin name: *Potos flavus*. [Late 18C. Via French *quincajou* 'wolverine' probably < a blend of Montagnais *kwa:hkwa:čè:w* and Ojibwa *gwiingwa'aage*]

kinky /kíngki/ (**-ier, -iest**) adj **1.** SEXUALLY DEVIANT being or engaging in unusual sexual practices that may be considered deviant (*informal*) **2.** SEXUALLY PROVOCATIVE intended to be provocative or sexually alluring, usually by being deliberately unusual or bizarre (*dated informal*) **3.** ECCENTRIC behaving in an unusual, idiosyncratic way (*informal*) **4.** TIGHTLY COILED full of tight coils ○ *kinky copper wire* —**kinkily** adv —**kinkiness** n

kinky boot *n* a woman's leather boot extending to the knee or mid-thigh (*dated informal*)

kinnikinnick /kínnikə ník/ *n* **1.** a mixture of dried leaves, bark, and sometimes tobacco, formerly smoked by some Native Americans **2.** a plant used for making kinnikinnick, e.g. sumach or dogwood [Late 18C. < Unami *kələkkəniikkan* 'receptacle for mixing']

Kinnock /kínnək/, **Neil** (*b.* 1942) British politician. He was the leader of the Labour Party from 1983 to 1992. He resigned as Leader of the Opposition after losing the 1992 general election. In 1995 he was appointed as a member of the European Commission, and in 1999 vice president. Full name **Kinnock, Neil Gordon**

> 'You don't play politics with people's jobs.'
> [Neil Kinnock, *Speech at the Labour Party Conference*; October 1985]

kino /keˈenō/ (*plural* **-nos**) *n* a red substance resembling resin, obtained by tapping several unrelated tropical trees. Use: locally, as an astringent and in tanning. [Early 19C. < a W African language, related to Mandingo *keno*, type of gum]

Kinross /kin róss/ historic market town in Perth and Kinross, central Scotland

kin selection *n* natural selection that favours self-sacrificing behaviour towards relatives because, even if the individual dies, those relatives that survive will carry some of its genes

Kinsey /kínzi/, **Alfred** (1894–1956) US biologist. He is best known for his studies of male (1948) and female (1953) sexuality (the *Kinsey Reports*). Full name **Kinsey, Alfred Charles**

kinsfolk /kínz fōk/ *npl* somebody's relatives

Kinshasa /kin shaˈassə/ capital of the Democratic Republic of the Congo, situated on the southern bank of the River Congo. Population: 4,655,313 (1994). Former name **Léopoldville** (until 1966)

kinship /kínship/ *n* **1.** relationship by blood or marriage to another or others **2.** relationship through common characteristics or a common origin ○ *kinship between Italic and Celtic languages*

Kinski /kínski/, **Klaus** (1926–91) Polish-born German actor. He is best known for his collaborations with the director Werner Herzog in films such as *Nosferatu* (1979) and *Fitzcarraldo* (1982).

kinsman /kínzmən/ (*plural* **-men** /-mən/) *n* a man or boy who is somebody's relative [12C. < Old English *cynnes* 'kin's']

kinswoman /kínz wŏomən/ (*plural* **-women** /-wimin/) *n* a woman or girl who is somebody's relative [14C. After KINSMAN]

kinteet /kín teet/ *vi* same as **smile** (*slang; used in Black English*) [< kin, form of SKIN + teet, form of TEETH]

Kintyre /kin tír/ peninsula of western Scotland, between the Firth of Clyde and the Atlantic Ocean. The Mull of Kintyre is its southernmost tip. Length: 64 km/40 mi.

kiore /kee áwri/ *n* ANZ a small brown rat, that has cultural significance for some Maori people. Native to: Asia and Pacific. Latin name: *Rattus exulans*.

kiosk /keˈe osk/ *n* **1.** SMALL ROOFED STREET STALL a small permanent or temporary structure in the street that sells items such as newspapers and sweets **2.** SMALL STRUCTURE FOR ADVERTISING a cylindrical structure that stands at a junction or on the street, used to post advertisements and announcements of events **3.** TELEPHONE BOOTH a small booth or shelter in which a public telephone is sited (*dated*) **4.** SW ASIAN GAZEBO formerly in Southwest Asia, a small open pavilion, especially in a garden [Early 17C. Via French < Turkish *köşk* 'villa' < Persian *kŭšk* 'villa, palace']

Kiowa /kíˈə waa/ (*plural* same or **-was**) *n* **1.** a member of a Native North American people who lived in Montana. Most Kiowa now live on a reservation in Oklahoma, which they share with a community of Kiowa Apache. **2.** the language of the Kiowa people, related to Tanoan [Early 19C. < American Spanish *Caygua* < Kiowa *kygú* (plural)] —**Kiowa** *adj*

Kiowa Apache *n* a member of a Native North American people who lived with the Kiowa people on the southern Great Plains, sharing a history and culture, but speaking a different language —**Kiowa Apache** *adj*

kip[1] /kip/ *UK n* **1.** SLEEP a sleep or a nap (*informal*) **2.** BED a bed or other place to sleep (*slang*) ○ *Is she still in her kip?* ■ *vi* (**kips, kipping, kipped**) TAKE NAP to sleep or take a nap, often in a makeshift bed (*informal*) [Mid-18C. < Danish *kippe* 'cheap inn']

kip[2] /kip/ *n* a unit of weight equivalent to 455 kg/1,000 lb [Early 20C. Contraction < KILO- + POUND[1]]

kip[3] /kip/ (*plural* same) *n* the main unit of currency of Laos. See table at **currency** [Mid-20C. < Thai]

kip[4] /kip/, **kipskin** /kípskin/ *n* a hide taken from an immature animal, especially a calf or a lamb [14C. < Middle Dutch or Middle Low German, 'bundle (of hides)']

Kipling /kípling/, **Rudyard** (1865–1936) British writer and poet. His books, many with Indian settings, include *The Jungle Books* (1894, 1895) and *Kim* (1901). He won the Nobel Prize in literature (1907). See Cultural note at **if**

> 'Oh, East is East, and West is West, and never the twain shall meet / Till Earth and Sky stand presently at God's great Judgment Seat...'
> [Rudyard Kipling, 'The Ballads of East and West'; 1892]

> 'The Devil whoops, as he whooped of old: "It's clever, but is it Art?"'
> [Rudyard Kipling, 'The Conundrum of the Workshops'; 1892]

kippa /ki paˈa/ (*plural* **-pot** /-pót/ or **-poth** /-pót/) *n* the skullcap worn by Jewish men and boys for prayer and by Orthodox Jewish men at all times [Mid-20C. < modern Hebrew *kippāh*]

kipper /kíppər/ *n* **1.** SMOKED HERRING a fish, usually a herring, that has been cleaned, split open, and then salted and smoked **2.** SALMON a male salmon during the spawning season ■ *vt* (**-pers, -pering, -pered**) SMOKE FISH to cure fresh fish, especially herring, by salting and smoking it (*usually passive*) [Old English *cypera* 'spawning salmon', origin ?] —**kipperer** *n*

kippot, kippoth JUDAISM, CLOTHING plural of **kippa**

kipskin *n* INDUST same as **kip**[4]

kir /keer/ *n* an alcoholic drink made by adding cassis to dry white wine [Mid-20C. After Canon Félix *Kir* (1876–1968), mayor of Dijon, France]

kirby grip /kúrbi-/ *n* a grip used to hold the hair in place. It consists of a piece of metal bent tightly over into two prongs, with the upper prong ridged. [Early 20C. < *Kirbigrip*™]

Kirchhoff /kúrk of, keˈerkh hof/, **Gustav** (1824–87) German physicist. With Robert Bunsen, he invented spectroscopy and discovered caesium and rubidium (1860). He formulated Kirchhoff's laws of electrical networks. Full name **Kirchhoff, Gustav Robert**

Kirchner /kúrknər, keˈerkhnər/, **Ernst Ludwig** (1880–1938) German artist. Known for his paintings and woodcuts, he was a leading figure in the German expressionist movement Die Brücke (1905–13).

Kirchner, Nestor (*b.* 1950) president of Argentina (2003–). A lawyer by training, he was governor of Santa Cruz until becoming president by default when former president Carlos Menem withdrew on the eve of the election.

Kirghiz, Kirgiz *n, adj* PEOPLES, LANG another spelling of **Kyrgyz**

Kiribati /kírri baˈati/ independent state in the west-central Pacific Ocean, part of Micronesia. It became an independent member of the Commonwealth in

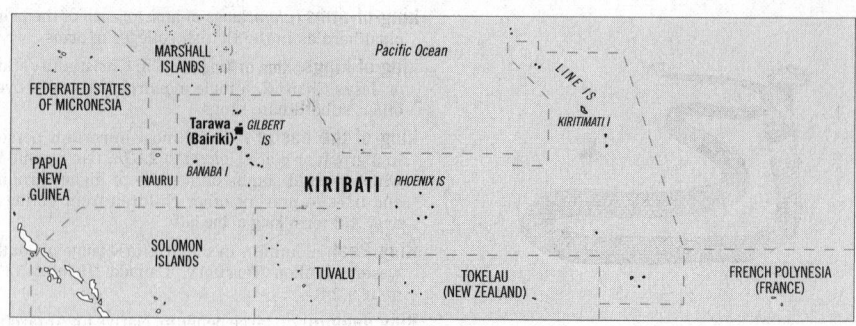

Kiribati

1979. Language: English. Currency: Australian dollar. Capital: Tarawa. Population: 98,594 (2003). Area: 811 sq. km/313 sq. mi. Official name **Republic of Kiribati**

kirigami /kírri gaˈami/ *n* the art of folding and cutting paper into ornamental shapes [< Japanese < *kiri* 'cut' + *gami* 'paper']

Kiritimati /kírri ti maˈati/ island forming part of Kiribati Republic. It is the largest atoll in the Pacific Ocean. Population: 2,537 (1990). Area: 609 sq. km/235 sq. mi.

kirk /kurk/ *n Scotland* same as **church** [12C. < Old Norse *kirkja* < Old English *cir(i)ce* (see CHURCH)]

Kirk *n Scotland* the Church of Scotland, the largest presbyterian church in Scotland

Kirk /kurk/, **Norman** (1923–74) prime minister of New Zealand (1972–74). He became president of the Labour Party in 1964 and served as foreign minister during his premiership. Full name **Kirk, Norman Eric**. See table at **prime minister**

Kirkcudbright /kur koˈobri/ town in Dumfries and Galloway Region, southwestern Scotland. Population: 3,588 (1991).

Kirkcudbrightshire /kur koˈobrishər/ former county in southwestern Scotland until 1975, now part of Dumfries and Galloway

Kirkwall /kúrk wawl/ capital and largest town of the Orkney Islands, northeastern Scotland, on the northern coast of Mainland Island. Population: 6,469 (1991).

Kirlian photography /kúr li ən-/ *n* a photographic process that records the radiation emitted by, or the aura surrounding, an object in a high-frequency electric field [Late 20C. After Semyon D. *Kirlian* 1900–80 and Valentina K. *Kirlian* d. 1971, Russian technicians]

Kirman /kər maˈan, keer-/ *n* a Persian carpet or rug of a type characterized by soft colours and naturalistic designs [Late 19C. After a province in Iran]

kirmess *n* LEISURE, HIST same as **kermis**

Kirov /keˈer of/ city in northeastern European Russia, capital of Kirov Oblast. Population: 633,395 (1995). Former name **Vyatka** (1780–1934)

Kirovohrad /ki róvvə grad/ city in central Ukraine, situated southeast of Kiev. Population: 270,000 (1998).

kirpan /keer paˈan/ *n* the short sword worn by baptized Sikh men as a symbol of religious loyalty [Early 20C. Via Punjabi, Hindi < Sanskrit *krpāna* 'sword']

Kirribilli House /kírrə bili-/ the Australian prime minister's official residence in Sydney

kirsch /keersh/, **kirschwasser** /keˈersh vassər/ *n* a clear brandy distilled from black cherries, especially in Germany and France [Early 19C. < German, shortening of *Kirschwasser* 'cherry-water' < *Kirsche* 'cherry' < assumed Vulgar Latin *cerasia*]

kirtle /kúrt'l/ *n* **1.** a long gown or skirt worn by women from the Middle Ages to the 17th century **2.** a long tunic or coat worn by men until the 16th century [Old English *cyrtel* 'short coat' < Germanic < Latin *curtus* 'short, cut short']

Kiruna /keˈeröonə/ city in Norrbotten County, northern Sweden, a region rich in high-quality iron ore. Population: 26,217 (1994).

Kirundi /ki roˈondi/ *n* a Bantu language that is the official language of Burundi —**Kirundi** *adj*

Kisangani /kíssang gáani/ capital of Orientale Region, in the northern Democratic Republic of the Congo. Population: 417,517 (1994).

Kishinev /kíshi nyof/ former name for **Chişinău**

kishke /kíshkə/ *n* a Jewish dish consisting of a chicken's or cow's intestine stuffed with flour meal, onion, and fat, and then boiled and roasted [Mid-20C. < Yiddish < Slavic]

Kislev /kísslәf, kiss lév/ *n* in the Jewish calendar, the ninth month of the religious year, lasting either 29 or 30 days and falling about the same time as November to December. See table at **calendar** [< Hebrew *Kislēw*]

kismet /kíz met, -mət/ *n* **1.** fate or destiny **2.** in Islam, the will of Allah [Mid-19C. Via Turkish < Persian *ķismat* < Arabic *ķisma(t)* 'lot, portion' < *ķasama* 'he divided']

kiss /kiss/ *v* (**kisses, kissing, kissed**) **1.** *vti* **CARESS WITH LIPS** to touch somebody or something with the lips, either gently or passionately **2.** *vti* **TOUCH BALL GENTLY** in cue games, to come into very light contact while passing each other, or touch another ball gently while passing it (*refers to balls*) **3.** *vt* **TOUCH SOMETHING GENTLY** to touch or brush against something lightly (*usually passive*) ○ *oranges kissed by the California sun* ■ *n* **1. CARESS DONE WITH LIPS** a gentle or passionate touch with the lips **2. GENTLE PASSING TOUCH** a very light, almost imperceptible touch in passing ○ *She felt the kiss of the evening breeze on her skin.* [Old English *cyssan* (verb) < *coss* (noun) < Germanic] —**kissable** *adj* ◇ **the kiss of death** something that is certain to destroy or ruin something

kiss off *v N Am* (*slang*) **1.** *vt* **REJECT SOMEBODY OR SOMETHING** to reject somebody or something abruptly ○ *The boss kissed off that idea fast.* **2.** *vt* **BE FORCED TO YIELD SOMETHING** to be compelled to give something up ○ *We had to kiss the trip off for lack of money.* **3.** *vi* **GO AWAY** to leave immediately or leave somebody alone

kiss up to *vt N Am* to try to please or win the favour of somebody by behaving in an obsequious or sycophantic manner (*slang*)

kissagram /kíssə gram/, **kissogram** *n* a delivery service in which the messenger delivers a kiss instead of or as well as the message

kiss and tell *n* a book, article, or broadcast interview in which the author or interviewee publicly relates past sexual intimacy with somebody

kiss-and-tell *adj* revealing an earlier sexual experience with somebody else, especially when the information, considered to be confidential, is made public (*informal*)

kiss curl *n* a small flat curl of hair pressed on the forehead or in front of the ear. N Am term **spit curl**

kisser /kíssər/ *n* **1.** somebody who kisses ○ *not much of a kisser* **2.** somebody's mouth (*slang*)

kissing ball /kíssing bawl/ *n US* mistletoe arranged in a ball shape, decorated with ribbons, and hung, e.g. in a hall or doorway during the Christmas season

kissing bug *n* a bloodsucking insect that feeds on other insects, inflicts painful bites on humans, and transmits diseases. Native to: Mexico, southern and western United States. Family: Reduviidae.

kissing cousin *n* **1.** somebody who is distantly related but can be kissed on meeting **2.** something closely related in kind to something else ○ *XML and its kissing cousin HTML*

kissing disease *n* same as **glandular fever** (*informal*)

Kissinger /kíssinjər/, **Henry** (*b.* 1923) German-born US secretary of state (1973–77). National security adviser and then secretary of state under US presidents Nixon and Ford, he helped to negotiate an end to the Vietnam War, for which he shared the Nobel Peace Prize (1973). His shuttle diplomacy was aimed at bringing peace between Israel and the Arab states. Full name **Kissinger, Henry Alfred**

> 'The conventional army loses if it does not win. The guerrilla wins if he does not lose.'
>
> [Henry Kissinger, 'The Vietnam Negotiations', *Foreign Affairs*; January 1969]

kissing gate *n* a gate in a V- or U-shaped frame that allows only one person at a time to pass through

kiss of death *n* something or somebody whose presence will bring failure or disaster to something [< the Bible passage (Mark 14:44–46) in which Judas kissed Jesus Christ, thereby betraying him]

kiss of life *n* (*informal*) **1.** mouth-to-mouth resuscitation **2.** something that revives or restores an enterprise or, less commonly, somebody's spirits

kiss of peace *n* a gesture, usually either a kiss or handshake, used as a sign of Christian fellowship during Communion

kissogram *n* another spelling of **kissagram**

kist[1] *n* ARCHAEOL another spelling of **cist**

kist[2] /kist/ *n Scotland, S Africa* a wooden storage chest used for blankets, linen, clothes, or a bride's trousseau [14C. < Old Norse *kista*, via Germanic < Latin *cista* (see CHEST)]

Kisumu /ki sóomoo/ city in southwestern Kenya, on Lake Victoria, a port and capital of Nyanza Province. Population: 185,100 (1989).

Kiswahili /kée swaa héeli/ *n* the Bantu national language of Tanzania and Kenya, widely used in Uganda, the Democratic Republic of the Congo, and neighbouring countries. Native speakers: 2 million. Other speakers: 20 million. [Mid-19C. < Bantu < *ki-*, prefix + *Swahili* (see SWAHILI)] —**Kiswahili** *adj*

kit /kit/ *n* **1. SET OF THINGS FOR USE TOGETHER** a set of articles, tools, or equipment used for a particular purpose **2. CONTAINER FOR SET** the container for a set of things ○ *a sewing kit* **3. SPECIAL CLOTHING AND EQUIPMENT** a special set of clothing and equipment assembled for a member of the armed forces or a sportsperson **4. SET OF PARTS FOR ASSEMBLING** a set of parts ready to be put together [14C. < Dutch *kitte* 'tankard, jug'] ◇ **get your kit off** to take your clothes off (*slang*)

kit out *vt* to provide somebody with the clothes, and sometimes also the equipment, needed to do something

Kitakyushu /kéetə kyóoshoo/, **Kitakyūshū** industrial city at the northern tip of Kyushu Island, in Fukuoka Prefecture, Japan. Population: 999,806 (2002).

Kitasato Shibasaburo /kée taa saáto shée baasə bóorō/ (1852–1931) Japanese bacteriologist. He isolated the bacteria that cause tetanus, anthrax, dysentery, and bubonic plague.

kitbag /kít bag/ *n* a canvas bag, usually cylindrical, for holding military kit, or a similar bag used by civilians, carried on the shoulder

kitchen /kíchin/ *n* a room or part of a room or building in which food is prepared and cooked [Pre-12C. < Latin *coquina* < *coquere* 'to cook']

REGIONAL NOTE All languages in the world have borrowed words from English, with ***kitchen***, *match*, and *school* being three of the commonest. In many UK dialects, ***kitchen*** retains an older meaning of 'sauce, savour', illustrating its link with cooking and such words as Latin *coquere* 'to cook': 'Hunger makes the best kitchen'.

---

kitchen cabinet *n* an informal unelected group of advisers to a head of government who are often believed to have more influence than the official cabinet

kitchen Dutch *n S Africa* same as **Afrikaans** (*dated disapproving*)

Kitchener /kíchənər/ industrial city located southwest of Toronto in southern Ontario, Canada. Population: 387,319 (2001).

Kitchener, Herbert, 1st Baron Kitchener of Khartoum and 1st Earl of Broome (1850–1916) British field marshal and politician. After successful campaigns in Sudan and South Africa, he became Britain's war secretary during World War I (1914–16). He was lost with HMS *Hampshire*, mined near the Orkney Islands. Full name **Kitchener, Horatio Herbert**. Known as **Lord Kitchener**

kitchenette /kíchi nét/ *n* a very small room, or part of another room, fitted out as a kitchen

kitchen garden *n* a garden in which vegetables, herbs, and sometimes fruit are grown for the use of a household —**kitchen gardener** *n*

kitchen midden *n* an area of an archaeological site that contains domestic refuse such as food waste, broken pottery, and pieces of other household artefacts, indicating long-term human occupation

kitchen paper, kitchen roll *n UK* absorbent paper on a roll of perforated sheets, used in the kitchen for various purposes, but especially for wiping up spills. ANZ, N Am term **paper towels**

kitchen roll *n* a roll of soft absorbent paper that can be torn off in sheets and used for a variety of purposes in the kitchen

kitchen sink ◇ **everything but the kitchen sink** everything possible, and much more than is advisable or necessary (*informal*)

kitchen-sink *adj* describes a type of drama, or less commonly a type of novel or film, that deals with the tribulations of domestic life in an unglamorous way

kitchen tea *n NZ* a women-only party held before a wedding, to which guests bring kitchen equipment as presents for the bride

kitchenware /kíchin wair/ *n* utensils used in the kitchen, including pots and pans, mixing bowls, chopping boards, knives, spoons, and gadgets

kite /kīt/ *n* **1. TOY FOR FLYING** a light framework covered in a thin light material, flown for fun in the wind at the end of a long string **2. SMALL HAWK** a small slim hawk with long pointed wings and a forked tail. Family: Accipitridae. **3. LIGHT SAIL** a light sail used in addition to a sailing ship's standard sails **4.** same as **aeroplane** (*slang dated*) ○ *a rickety kite that could barely get off the runway* **5. FAKE FINANCIAL TRANSACTION** a negotiable bill, e.g. a cheque, that is fraudulently used to sustain credit by representing a fictitious monetary transaction (*slang*) **6. BAD CHEQUE** a cheque that is fraudulently written against an account containing insufficient funds and dated so as to allow the perpetrator to take advantage of the time lag required for clearing ■ *v* (**kites, kiting, kited**) **1.** *vti* **PASS BAD CHEQUES** to write and pass bad cheques in order to sustain credit on a temporary basis, all the time using to advantage the period between writing them and their clearing (*slang*) **2.** *vi* **GLIDE AS IF FLYING** to glide and soar like a kite ■ *n* **LIGHTWEIGHT SAIL FOR KITEBOARDERS AND KITESURFERS** a large, often crescent-shaped, wind-catching device, like a large toy kite or a small parachute, with a harness, used by participants in kiteboarding or kitesurfing to provide propulsion and lift [< Old English *cȳta* 'kite (bird)', ultimately an imitation of its call] —**kiter** *n* ◇ **fly a kite** (*slang*) **1.** to do something or speak about something in order to test public opinion on it **2.** to issue a fraudulent financial document such as a cheque without having enough funds to cover it ◇ **high as a kite** (*informal*) **1.** extremely excited or elated **2.** extremely intoxicated or drug-affected

kiteboarding /kīt bawrding/ *n* **1.** a sport in which the participants ride on skateboards or snowboards with a kite attached to their bodies to give propulsion and lift **2.** *US* EXTREME SPORTS same as **kitesurfing** —**kiteboarder** *n*

Kitemark /kīt maark/ *n* the official mark of approval of the British Standards Institution, shaped like a stylized kite, indicating that a manufactured item meets specific standards of quality and reliability

kitesurfing /kīt surfing/ *n* a water sport in which the participants ride on surfboards with a kite attached to their bodies to give propulsion and lift —**kitesurfer** *n*

kit fox *n* a small slender fox that has large ears. Native to: western United States. Latin name: *Vulpes macrotis*. [Early 19C. Origin ?]

kith /kith/ *n* somebody's friends and acquaintances (*dated; takes a plural verb*) [14C. < Old English *cȳþ(þ)* 'knowledge, friends' < Germanic] ◇ **kith and kin** somebody's friends and relatives

kithara *n* MUSIC another spelling of **cithara**

kitsch /kich/ *n* **1.** sentimentality, tastelessness, or ostentation in any of the arts ○ *The book jackets were pure kitsch.* **2.** collectively, decorative items that are regarded as tasteless, sentimental, or ostentatious in style ○ *tourist shops full of kitsch* [Early 20C. < German < *kitschen* 'throw together'] —**kitschy** *adj*

kitten /kítt'n/ *n* the young of a cat ■ *vi* (**-tens, -tening, -tened**) to give birth to young cats [14C. < Old French *chitoun*, diminutive of *chat* 'cat'] ◇ **have kittens** to become angry, excited, or nervous about something (*informal*)

kitten heel *n* (*usually pl*) **1.** a low heel on a woman's shoe **2.** a woman's shoe with a low heel

kittenish /kítt'nish/ *adj* **1.** behaving in a lively and playful way, as a kitten does **2.** coyly flirtatious —**kittenishly** *adv* —**kittenishness** *n*

kittiwake /kítti wayk/ (*plural same* or **-wakes**) *n* a gull that nests on cliffs and winters on open oceans. Native to: northern regions. Latin name: *Rissa tridactyla* or *Rissa brevirostris*. [Mid-17C. An imitation of its call]

kittle /kítt'l/ *adj Scotland* difficult to deal with [15C. < Old Norse *kitla* 'to tickle']

kitty[1] /kítti/ (*plural* **-ties**) *n* a kitten or cat (*informal*) [Early 18C. Shortening and alteration of KITTEN]

kitty[2] /kítti/ (*plural* **-ties**) *n* **1.** JOINT POOL OF MONEY a fund of money contributed to by a group of people and used to buy something in common **2.** PROPORTION OF OVERALL POT IN POKER a portion of the total amount of money bet by all the players on each hand of poker **3.** POOL OF BETS the amount of money that has been bet by the players in a game **4.** BOWLS same as **jack**[1] *n* (sense 5) [Early 19C. Originally 'prison'. Origin ?]

kitty-cornered, **kitty-corner** *adv, adj N Am* same as **cater-cornered**

Kitty Hawk /kítti hawk/ town in northeastern North Carolina, on the Atlantic Ocean. On nearby Kill Devil Hill, the Wright brothers engaged in successful glider and aeroplane experiments between 1900 and 1903. It is the site of the Wright Brothers National Memorial. Population: 3,171 (2002 estimate).

Kitwe /kít way/ copper-mining city in north-central Zambia, north of Lusaka. Population: 338,207 (1990).

Kivu, Lake /keévoo/ freshwater lake in the Great Rift Valley of Africa, between western Rwanda and the eastern Democratic Republic of the Congo. Area: 2,700 sq. km/1,040 sq. mi.

Kiwano /ki waáno/ *tdmk* a trademark for a fruit from New Zealand that has bright yellow or orange spiky skin and pale yellow-green flesh with the texture of jelly

kiwi

kiwi /keéwi/ *n* (*plural same* or **-wis**) **1.** FLIGHTLESS BIRD a nocturnal flightless bird with a long slender beak and shaggy feathers. Native to: New Zealand. Genus: *Apteryx*. **2.** *also* **Kiwi** SOMEBODY FROM NEW ZEALAND somebody who comes from New Zealand (*informal*) **3.** FOOD same as **kiwi fruit 4.** CHINESE VINE WITH EDIBLE FRUIT a vine that produces kiwi fruit. Native to: China. Latin name: *Actinidia chinensis*. ■ *adj* OF NEW ZEALAND relating to New Zealand or its people (*informal*) [Mid-19C. < Maori, an imitation of the bird's call]

kiwi fruit

kiwi fruit *n* the fruit of the kiwi plant, which has a greenish-brown fuzzy skin and sweet green pulp

KKK *abbr* Ku Klux Klan

KKt *abbr* CHESS king's knight

KKtP *abbr* CHESS king's knight's pawn

KL *abbr* Kuala Lumpur

Klagenfurt /klaágən foort/ city and capital of Kärnten Province, southern Austria. It is situated about 100 km/62 mi. southwest of Graz. Population: 90,765 (1999).

Klaipeda /klípidə/ city in western Lithuania, on the coast of the Baltic Sea. Population: 202,480 (2000).

Klan /klan/ *n* POL same as **Ku Klux Klan** (*informal*) —**Klanism** *n*

Klansman /klánzmən/ (*plural* **-men** /-mən/) *n* a member of the Ku Klux Klan

klaxon /kláks'n/ *n* a loud electric horn [Early 20C. After *Klaxon*, the original manufacturers]

Klee /klay/, **Paul** (1879–1940) Swiss painter. His imaginative and often witty works, some inspired by children's paintings and drawings, had a great influence on modern art.

> 'Art does not reproduce the visible; rather, it makes visible.'
> [Paul Klee, 'Creative Credo (1920)', *Inward Vision*; 1958]

Kleenex /kleé neks/ *tdmk* a trademark for a soft facial tissue

Calvin Klein

Klein /klīn/, **Calvin** (*b.* 1942) US fashion designer. After establishing his own company in 1968, he became known for his understated sophisticated designs. Full name **Klein, Calvin Richard**

Klein, Melanie (1882–1960) Austrian psychoanalyst. She pioneered studies in child psychoanalysis using free-play therapy. She moved to England in 1926.

Klein bottle /klīn-/ *n* a one-sided surface formed by inserting the small open end of a tapered tube through the side of the tube and upward until it is contiguous with the larger end [Mid-20C. After Felix *Klein* (1849–1925), German mathematician]

Klemperer /klémpərər/, **Otto** (1885–1973) German conductor. Noted for his interpretations of Beethoven, Mozart, and Mahler, he moved to the United States in 1933, where he conducted the Los Angeles Symphony Orchestra. From 1959, he conducted the Philharmonia Orchestra of London.

klepht /kleft/ *n* any of the Greeks who resisted Turkish rule in Greece from 1456 to 1832 and who lived in the mountains as outlaws and brigands [Early 19C. < modern Greek *klephtēs* 'thief', later form of Greek *kleptēs*] —**klephtic** *adj*

kleptomaniac /kleptə máyni ak/ *n* somebody with an obsessive urge to steal, especially when there is no economic necessity —**kleptomania** *n* —**kleptomaniacal** /kleptə mə nī ək'l/ *adj*

Klerk ♦ de Klerk, F. W.

kletterschuh /klétter shoo/ (*plural* **-schuhe** /-shoo ə/ or **-schuhs**) *n* a lightweight climbing boot [Early 20C. < German, 'climbing shoe']

klezmer /klézmər/ *n* a traditional style of Jewish ensemble music with roots in Eastern Europe that features vocals and various instruments, especially the violin and the clarinet. It has had an influence on American popular music. [Mid-20C. Via Yiddish < Hebrew *kělēy zemer* 'musical instruments']

klick /klik/ *n N Am* same as **kilometre** (*informal*) [Mid-20C. Origin ?]

klieg light /kleég-/ *n* a powerful carbon-arc light formerly used in making films [Early 20C. After John H. *Kliegl* (1869–1959) and Anton T. *Kliegl* (1872–1927), German-born US inventors]

Klimt /klimt/, **Gustav** (1862–1918) Austrian painter. Founder of the Vienna Secession school of painting (1897), he created richly decorated portraits of women.

Klippel /klíppəl/, **Robert** (1920–2001) Australian sculptor. His works include assemblages made with scraps of metal. Full name **Klippel, Robert Edward**

klipspringer /klíp springər/ *n* a small agile antelope with large ears. Native to: mountainous regions of Africa. Latin name: *Oreotragus oreotragus*. [Late 18C. < Afrikaans, 'cliff-springer']

Klondike /klón dīk/ region of northwestern Yukon Territory, Canada, named after the Klondike River, which traverses it. After 1897, it was the site of a decade-long gold rush in which 30,000 prospectors streamed into the area. Gold was mined there until the mid-1960s.

kloof /kloof/ *n S Africa* a gorge or mountain pass, usually wooded [Mid-18C. Via Afrikaans < Dutch *clove*]

kloofing /kloófing/ *n S Africa* the extreme sport of following the course of a river through a gorge by climbing, swimming, and jumping. UK, ANZ term **canyoning** [Late 20C < Afrikaans *kloof*, 'gorge or ravine']

Kluane National Park Reserve /kloo áyn-/ national park in southwestern Yukon Territory, Canada. It includes Canada's highest peak, Mt Logan. Area: 22,000 sq. km/8,494 sq. mi.

kludge /klooj/, **kluge** (*slang*) *n* a makeshift combination of hardware and software put together to solve a computing problem that is effective but not suitable for manufacture ■ *vt* (**kludges, kludging, kludged; kluges, kluging, kluged**) to solve a computing problem using a makeshift combination of hardware and software [Mid-20C. After BOTCH, FUDGE] —**kludgy** *adj*

klutz /kluts/ *n* (*slang insult*) **1.** an offensive term that deliberately insults somebody's physical coordination or social skills **2.** an offensive term that deliberately insults somebody's intelligence [Mid-20C. Via Yiddish *klots* 'wooden beam' < German *Klotz* 'clod'] —**klutzy** *adj*

klystron /klī stron/ *n* an electron tube that uses an electric field to generate and amplify microwaves [Mid-20C. < Greek *klus-*, stem of *kluzein* 'wash over']

km *abbr* **1.** ONLINE Comoros (*used in Internet addresses*) See table at **domain name 2.** kilometre

K-meson *n* PHYS same as **kaon**

km/h, **kmph** *abbr* kilometres per hour

kn, kn. *abbr* **1.** NAUT knot **2.** MONEY krona **3.** MONEY krone **4.** ONLINE St Kitts and Nevis (*used in Internet addresses*) See table at **domain name**

KN *abbr* CHESS king's knight

knack /nak/ *n* **1.** an easy and clever way of doing something or handling a problem ○ *I can't get the knack of this software.* **2.** a particular skill, especially one that might be innate or intuitive and therefore difficult to teach ○ *You certainly have a knack with children.* [14C. Origin ?]

SYNONYMS See *talent*.

knacker /nákər/ *n* **1.** SOMEBODY WHO KILLS HORSES somebody who buys and slaughters old, worn-out, or injured horses for their body parts such as their flesh and hide **2.** DEMOLITION MERCHANT somebody who buys and demolishes unwanted buildings and sells their materials for scrap ■ **knackers** *npl* TESTICLES a man's or boy's testicles (*slang*) ■ *vt* (**-ers, -ering, -ered**) TIRE SOMEBODY OUT to exhaust somebody completely (*slang*) [Early 19C. Originally 'saddler, harness maker', origin ?] —**knackered** *adj*

knacker's yard *n* a place where old horses are slaughtered ◇ **ready for the knacker's yard** (*informal*) **1.** so old or worn-out that it is no longer of use **2.** so old and useless for work that it may as well be slaughtered (*refers to horses*)

knackwurst /nák wurst/, **knockwurst** /nók wurst/ *n* a spicy smoked Continental sausage similar to a

frankfurter but shorter and thicker [Mid-20C. < German, 'crack-sausage' (because its skin cracks open when bitten) < *knacken* 'to crack']

knag /nag/ *n* **1.** a knot in a piece of wood **2.** a peg made of wood [15C. < Low German *knagge* 'knot, peg']

knap /nap/ (**knaps, knapping, knapped**) *vt* to chisel or hammer something such as a stone so that it breaks into flakes [15C. Probably < Low German or Dutch *knappen* 'to crack', an imitation of the sound of breaking stone] — **knapper** *n*

knapping hammer /nápping-/ *n* a mason's hammer used for splitting and roughly shaping stone

knapsack /náp sak/ *n* a cloth or leather bag with shoulder straps, designed for carrying personal items and supplies on a hiker's back [Early 17C. < Low German < *knappen* 'bite, eat' + *Sack* 'sack']

knapweed

knapweed /náp weed/ (*plural* **-weeds** or *same*) *n* a wild or cultivated plant belonging to the daisy family, which is sometimes troublesome as a weed. Native to: Europe, Asia, introduced to North America. Genus: *Centaurea*. [Early 16C. Alteration of *knopweed* < variant of KNOB; from the shape of its cluster of flowers]

knar /naar/ *n* a knot on a tree or in wood [13C. Origin ?] —**knarred** *adj* —**knarry** *adj*

knave /nayv/ *n* **1.** a man who is considered dishonest and deceitful (*archaic*) **2.** a man of low social position or one who works as a servant (*archaic*) **3.** CARDS same as **jack**[1] *n* (sense 2) [Old English *cnafa* 'boy, male servant' < Germanic] —**knavery** *n* —**knavish** *adj* —**knavishly** *adv* —**knavishness** *n*

knawel /nawl, náw əl/ (*plural* **knawels** or *same*), **knawe** /naw/ (*plural* **knawes** or *same*) *n* a low-growing annual plant with narrow leaves, usually considered to be a weed. Native to: Europe, Asia. Latin name: *Scleranthus annuus*. [Late 16C. < German *Knauel* 'knot-grass']

knead /need/ (**kneads, kneading, kneaded**) *v* **1.** *vti* WORK DOUGH UNTIL SMOOTH to fold, press, and stretch a soft substance such as dough or clay, working it into a smooth uniform mass **2.** *vt* MASSAGE MUSCLES to rub, squeeze, or press a part of the body with the hands, e.g. in order to relax the muscles **3.** *vt* SHAPE SOMETHING WITH HANDS to make or shape something out of a soft substance by kneading it [Old English *cnedan* < W Germanic] —**kneadable** *adj* —**kneader** *n*

USAGE knead or **need**? Do not confuse the spelling of **knead** and **need**, which sound similar. **Knead** is a verb meaning 'to work dough' or 'to massage muscles'. **Need**, the more frequent of the two words, is a verb or noun referring to something that is required: *I need your help. There's no need to panic.*

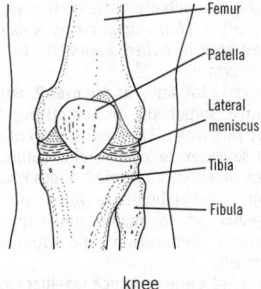

knee

(labels: Femur, Patella, Lateral meniscus, Tibia, Fibula)

knee /nee/ *n* **1.** MIDDLE JOINT OF HUMAN LEG the joint of the human leg between the thigh and the lower leg, where the femur and the tibia meet, covered in front by the kneecap (**patella**) **2.** AREA AROUND KNEE JOINT the general area surrounding the knee joint **3.** UPPER LEG the upper surface of the thigh of somebody sitting down ○ *Come and sit on my knee.* **4.** PART OF CLOTHING the part of a piece of clothing, especially trousers, that fits around the knee **5.** LEG JOINT IN ANIMALS the joint between the upper and lower parts of the hind legs in four-legged vertebrates and of the legs in birds **6.** GROWTH FROM ROOT a woody outgrowth from the roots of some trees that grow in saturated soils or standing water, which protrudes above the surface and enables them to breathe **7.** OBJECT LIKE KNEE something that resembles the human knee, e.g. a bent pipe ■ *vt* (**knees, kneeing, kneed**) HIT SOMEBODY WITH KNEE to strike somebody with the uplifted knee [Old English *cnēow* < Indo-European, 'to bend'] ◇ **bring somebody to his** *or* **her knees** to reduce somebody to a state of abject weakness and vulnerability, or force somebody to admit defeat

knee action *n* front-wheel suspension in a car that allows each wheel to move independently in a vertical direction

knee breeches *npl* CLOTHING same as **breeches** (sense 1)

kneecap /née kap/ *n* **1.** a flat triangular bone located at the front of the knee. It protects the knee joint. Technical name **patella** **2.** same as **kneepad** ■ *vt* (**-caps, -capping, -capped**) to shoot somebody deliberately in the knees as a punishment, in order to cause lasting difficulty in standing or walking (*informal*)

knee-deep *adj* **1.** IN AS HIGH AS KNEES standing or sunk in something that reaches up to the knees ○ *be knee-deep in mud* **2.** AS HIGH AS KNEES reaching up to the knees ○ *The river was only knee-deep.* **3.** EXTREMELY INVOLVED IN SOMETHING completely occupied by or entangled in something ○ *knee-deep in work*

knee drop *n* in wrestling, a move in which an opponent is lifted into the air and then dropped over the bent knee of the lifter

knee-high *adj* reaching up to the knees ■ *n* a sock or stocking that comes up as high as the knee

kneehole /née hōl/ *n* a hole made for the knees in a desk or other piece of furniture

knee jerk *n* an involuntary contraction of the thigh muscle that produces a sudden extension of the leg, usually in response to a light tap on the tendon below the kneecap

knee-jerk *adj* (*informal*) **1.** given or occurring immediately and automatically, without thought, and usually expressing habitual attitude or prejudice ○ *a knee-jerk opinion* **2.** tending to respond in a predictable and often unthinking way to a situation ○ *a knee-jerk political hack*

kneel /neel/ (**kneels, kneeling, knelt** /nelt/ *or* **kneeled**) *vi* to rest on, or get down on, one or both knees [Old English *cnēowlian* < *cnēow* (see KNEE)]

knee-length *adj* reaching up to or down to the knee ○ *a knee-length skirt* ○ *knee-length boots*

kneeler /née lər/ *n* CHR, FURNITURE, GARDENING same as **hassock** (sense 1)

kneepad /née pad/ *n* a covering that protects the knee from injury, especially during sports

kneepan /née pan/ *n* ANAT same as **kneecap** *n* (sense 1)

knee sock *n* a sock that reaches to the knee

knees-up *n* UK a lively noisy party, especially one with a lot of dancing (*informal*)

knee-trembler *n* an act of sexual intercourse performed standing up (*slang*, *sometimes offensive*)

knell /nel/ *n* **1.** SLOW BELL RING the sound of a bell rung slowly, associated with solemnity or mourning, used to announce a death or funeral **2.** OMINOUS SIGNAL something that signals death, disaster, or the end of something (*literary*) ■ *v* (**knells, knelling, knelled**) **1.** *vti* RING BELL to ring a bell slowly, or produce a slow ringing sound, especially as a sign of mourning or to announce a death or funeral **2.** *vt* SIGNAL SOMETHING OMINOUS to announce or signal something such as a death, disaster, or the end of something (*literary*) [Old English *cnyll* < *cnyllan* 'to strike' < Indo-European]

Kneller /néllər/, **Sir Godfrey** (1646–1723) German-born English painter. His portrait subjects included several monarchs and many other prominent figures.

knelt past participle, past tense of **kneel**

Knesset /knéss et, knéssit/, **Knesseth** *n* the parliamentary legislature of Israel. It has one legislative chamber with supreme authority. [Mid-20C. < Hebrew, 'gathering']

knew past tense of **know**

Kngwarreye /kəng wúrray/, **Emily Kame** (1910?–96) Australian Aboriginal painter. Her works were part of Australia's contribution to the Venice Biennale in 1997.

Knickerbocker /níkər bokər/ *n* US **1.** somebody descended from the early Dutch settlers of New York **2.** somebody who comes from the state of New York (*informal*) [Early 19C. After Diedrich *Knickerbocker*, fictitious author of Washington Irving's *History of New York*]

knickerbocker glory /níkər bokər-/ *n* a dessert consisting of layers of different flavours of ice cream, fruit, jelly, and cream, served in a tall conical glass dish

knickerbockers /níkər bokərz/ *npl* loose-fitting short breeches gathered at or just below the knee [Mid-19C. Origin ?]

knickers /níkərz/ *npl* **1.** an undergarment worn by women and girls that covers the body from the waist to the tops of the legs or below and has separate legs or leg-holes **2.** N Am CLOTHING same as **knickerbockers** ■ *interj* used as a mild or self-consciously humorous swearword (*informal*) [Late 19C. Shortening of KNICKERBOCKERS] ◇ **get your knickers in a twist** to become agitated, excited, or anxious (*informal*)

knick-knack /ník nak/, **nick-nack** *n* a small decorative ornament or object [Late 16C. < reduplication of KNACK] —**knick-knackery** *n*

knickpoint /ník poynt/ *n* a point along a river's length at which it suddenly begins to flow in a steeper course [Early 20C. Partial translation of German *Knickpunkt* < *Knick* 'bend' + *Punkt* 'point']

knife /nīf/ *n* (*plural* **knives** /nīvz/) **1.** TOOL FOR CUTTING a tool, usually with a sharp blade and a handle, used for cutting, slicing, or spreading **2.** STABBING WEAPON a knife with a handle and a sharpened blade specifically made to be a weapon ■ *v* (**knifes, knifing, knifed**) **1.** *vt* STAB SOMEBODY to stab or cut somebody with a knife **2.** *vi* MOVE WITH SWIFT SMOOTH MOTION to move quickly, forcefully, and cleanly through something ○ *The hawk knifed through the air.* [Old English *cnīf* < Germanic] **knife-like** *adj* —**knifer** *n* ◇ **have your knife in** *or* **into somebody** to feel hostility and malice towards somebody and wish to do him or her harm ◇ **the knives are out (for somebody)** there is general hostility towards somebody and a desire to cause that person difficulties or harm ◇ **twist** *or* **turn the knife (in the wound)** to try to make a difficult or painful situation even worse for somebody ◇ **under the knife** undergoing surgery (*informal*)

knife-edge *n* **1.** CRITICAL TIME IN SITUATION a decisive and precarious point at which a situation is finely balanced between different possibilities or outcomes ○ *with the future of the project on a knife-edge* **2.** KNIFE'S CUTTING EDGE the cutting edge of the blade of a knife **3.** OBJECT LIKE EDGE OF KNIFE an object that is sharp, thin, and narrow **4.** TECH FULCRUM FOR PRECISE INSTRUMENT a metal wedge whose narrow edge is used as a fulcrum for a scale beam or a lever in a precision instrument

knife pleat *n* a narrow sharply creased pleat, usually one of several folded in the same direction, especially in a skirt

knifepoint /nīf poynt/ *n* the sharp tip of a knife ◇ **at knifepoint** while being threatened with a knife

knife switch *n* an electric switch in which a hinged blade is placed between two contact clips

knight /nīt/ *n* **1.** HIST MEDIEVAL SOLDIER OF HIGH RANK in late medieval Europe, a noble in the military, promoted by the king after serving as a page and squire **2.** HIST MEDIEVAL MOUNTED SOLDIER OF LOW RANK in early medieval Europe, a tenant of a feudal lord who was required to serve as a soldier on horseback **3.** POL MAN WITH TITLE 'SIR' a man who holds a nonhereditary title

conferred by a ruler for personal achievement or public service. A British knight has the title 'Sir' before his name. **4.** CHESS **HORSE'S HEAD CHESSPIECE** a chesspiece shaped like a horse's head that moves two squares horizontally and one vertically or two vertically and one horizontally. Symbol **N** **5.** **MEMBER OF BROTHERHOOD** a man who belongs to a special group or organization, especially a religious or secret brotherhood **6.** **CHAMPION OF CAUSE** a fervent supporter or defender of a cause or belief **7.** **PROTECTOR OF WOMAN** a man who is protective of and devoted to a woman ■ *vt* (**knights, knighting, knighted**) **MAKE MAN KNIGHT** to bestow a knighthood on a man [Old English *cniht* 'boy, male attendant' < Germanic] ◇ **a knight in shining armour** a man who gallantly comes to the rescue of somebody in danger or difficulty

SPELLCHECK knight or **night**? Do not confuse the spelling of ***knight*** and ***night***, which sound similar. A ***knight*** is a medieval soldier or a man with the title 'Sir', as in *the knights of King Arthur*. ***Knight*** is also used as a verb, meaning 'bestow a knighthood on'. The word ***night*** is a noun or adjective referring to a period of darkness, as in *spend the night at a hotel, the night shift*.

knight bachelor (*plural* **knights bachelors** or **knights bachelor**) *n* a knight who is not a member of a specific order of knighthood

knight-errant (*plural* **knights-errant**) *n* **1.** a medieval knight who travelled around looking for adventure **2.** a man preoccupied with ideas of adventure and romance —**knight-errantry** *n*

knighthead /nīt hed/ *n* either of two upright timbers supporting the inner end of the bowsprit of a sailing ship, to which mooring cables or ropes are sometimes attached [Early 18C. Because it often had a carving of a man's head]

knighthood /nīt ho͝od/ *n* **1.** **POSITION OF KNIGHT** the rank, title, or occupation of a knight **2.** **CHIVALRY AND HONOUR** the qualities of chivalry, bravery, and honour, thought to be characteristic of a knight **3.** **KNIGHTS** knights considered as a group

knightly /nītli/ (**-lier, -liest**) *adj* relating to knights, or characteristic of a knight, especially in being noble and chivalrous —**knightliness** *n*

knight marshal (*plural* **knights marshal**) *n* HIST same as **marshal** *n* (sense 3)

Knight of Columbus *n* a member of a benevolent and fraternal organization of Roman Catholic men, founded in the United States in 1882 [Late 19C. After Christopher COLUMBUS]

Knights Hospitallers, Knights of St John of Jerusalem, Knights of the Hospital of St John of Jerusalem *npl* a military and religious order founded by crusaders in the 12th century to protect a hospital in Jerusalem

Knights of the Round Table *npl* an order of knights said to have been created by King Arthur that figures prominently in Arthurian legends and chivalric poems [Because the knights sat at a round table, where no one could be seated in a position of superiority]

Knight Templar (*plural* **Knights Templar**) *n* a member of a Christian military order that was founded in Jerusalem in 1119 to protect pilgrims after the First Crusade of 1096. The order grew wealthy and influential from banking activities before being suppressed by the pope in 1312.

kniphofia /ni fōfi ə/ (*plural* **-as** or *same*) *n* PLANTS same as **red-hot poker** [Mid-19C. After Johann Hieronymus *Kniphof* (1704–63), German botanist]

knish /kə nísh, knish/ *n* a piece of dough filled with meat, cheese, or potato and eaten as a snack or appetizer, especially in Jewish-American cooking [Mid-20C. Via Yiddish < Russian]

knit /nit/ *v* (**knits, knitting, knitted** or **knit**) **1.** *vti* **INTERLOCK WOOL LOOPS** to interlock loops of wool, using either long needles or a machine, or make a garment or other item by this method **2.** *vti* **USE PLAIN STITCH** to use a basic plain stitch that forms a flat vertical loop on the front of a piece of knitting ○ *Knit one, purl one.* **3.** *vti* **UNITE** to bring people or things together in a close association, or come together in this way **4.** *vi* MED **BECOME HEALED** to grow together again after a fracture (*refers to a bone*) **5.** *vti* **BRING BROWS CLOSER TOGETHER** to draw the brows together in a frown, or be drawn together in a frown ■ *n* **1.** **SOMETHING MADE BY KNITTING** a knitted garment or fabric **2.** **WAY OF KNITTING** a method or style of knitting a garment or fabric **3.** **PLAIN STITCH** a basic knitting stitch that forms a flat vertical loop on the front of something being knitted [Old English *cnyttan* 'tie in knots' < Germanic] —**knittable** *adj* —**knitter** *n*

SPELLCHECK knit or **nit**? Do not confuse the spelling of ***knit*** and ***nit***, which sound similar. ***Knit*** is chiefly used as a verb, meaning 'to interlock loops of wool' or 'to join' or 'to bring together', as in *knit a scarf, when the bones have knitted together, knitting his brow*. ***Knit*** is also occasionally used as a noun, referring to something knitted. The word ***nit*** is only used as a noun denoting an egg of a louse, or as an offensive term.

knitting /nítting/ *n* **1.** the act or process of making knitted items or fabric by hand-held needles or by machine **2.** an item that is in the process of being knitted

knitting needle *n* a long slim rod with a dull point, used in pairs in knitting

knitwear /nít wair/ *n* garments made from knitted fabric

knives plural of **knife**

knob /nob/ *n* **1.** **ROUNDED HANDLE OR DIAL** a rounded projecting part attached to a door, drawer, appliance, or other object, used as a handle or a dial or switch **2.** **ROUNDED PROJECTION** any rounded lump or part projecting from the surface of something **3.** **SMALL PIECE** a small piece of something ○ *a knob of butter* **4.** **RAISED ORNAMENTAL CARVING** a raised ornament in carved woodwork **5.** **HILL** a rounded hill **6.** **TABOO TERM** a highly offensive term for a penis (*taboo*) ■ *vti* (**knobs, knobbing, knobbed**) **TABOO TERM** a highly offensive term meaning to have sexual intercourse with somebody (*taboo; refers to a man*) [14C. < Middle Low German *knobbe* 'knot, knob, bud'] —**knobbed** *adj* ◇ **with knobs on** (*informal*) **1.** used as a way of returning an insult and supposedly adding greater force to it (*usually used by children*) **2.** to a great degree

knobbly /nóbbli/ (**-blier, -bliest**), **knobby** /nóbbi/ (**-bier, -biest**) *adj* having small hard rounded parts sticking out from the surface [Mid-17C. < *knobble* 'small knob' < KNOB]

knobkerrie /nób kerri/, **knobstick** /nób stik/ *n* a short wooden stick with a knob at one end, used by some South African peoples as a weapon [Mid-19C. < KNOB + *kierie* 'club' (< Nama), after Afrikaans *knopkierie*]

knock /nok/ *v* (**knocks, knocking, knocked**) **1.** *vi* **HIT REPEATEDLY** to strike loudly against something such as a door with the knuckles or an object in order to attract attention ○ *Someone's knocking at the door.* **2.** *vi* **MAKE LOUD NOISE BY COLLIDING** to produce a loud and usually repetitive noise by hitting something ○ *was disturbed by a branch knocking against the window all night* **3.** *vt* **DEAL SOMEBODY OR SOMETHING BLOW** to strike somebody or something with a hard blow ○ *knocked in a nail* **4.** *vt* **AFFECT SOMEBODY OR SOMETHING WITH BLOW** to cause something or somebody to be in a particular state with a blow ○ *He knocked me off balance.* **5.** *vti* **COLLIDE WITH SOMETHING** to hit against something, especially accidentally, or cause something to hit against something else ○ *The glass broke when I knocked it against the table.* **6.** *vt* **MAKE SOMETHING BY STRIKING** to produce something, especially a hole, by means of repeated blows ○ *knocked a hole in the partition* **7.** *vt* **CRITICIZE SOMEBODY OR SOMETHING** to criticize or find fault with somebody or something (*informal*) ○ *Don't knock it until you've tried it.* **8.** *vi* AUTOMOT **PRODUCE REPEATED RAPPING SOUND** to make a regular rapping noise that is usually caused by faulty fuel combustion (*refers to a vehicle or its engine*) **9.** *vt* **OFFENSIVE TERM** an offensive term meaning to have sexual intercourse with somebody (*slang*) ■ *n* **1.** **BLOW OR COLLISION** a blow struck against somebody or something, or a collision with somebody or something **2.** **SOUND OF KNOCKING** the sound made by a person or object hitting something, especially repeatedly **3.** **BAD EXPERIENCE** a painful, damaging, or distressing experience (*informal*) **4.** **CRITICISM** a disparaging or critical comment about somebody or something (*informal*) **5.** AUTOMOT **REPEATED RAPPING SOUND IN ENGINE** a regular rapping noise made by an engine, usually caused by faulty fuel combustion **6.** CRICKET **INNINGS** a cricket batsman's innings (*informal*) [Old English *cnocian*, ultimately an imitation of the sound] ◇ **knock it off** used to demand that somebody stop doing or saying something (*informal*) ◇ **knock somebody dead** to amaze and delight somebody with the quality of a performance (*informal*) ◇ **take the knock** to suffer financial loss (*informal*)

knock about *v* (*informal*) **1.** *vt* **BEAT SOMEBODY** to abuse somebody physically **2.** *vti* **TRAVEL AROUND** to travel to different places, or to different places within an area, especially without a specific itinerary **3.** *vi* **HAVE RELAXING TIME** to relax by doing nothing in particular **4.** *vi* **SPEND TIME** to spend time habitually in the company of somebody **5.** *vi* **BE IN SOME PLACE** to be somewhere in a place or area, though the exact whereabouts are uncertain ○ *I'm sure it's knocking about somewhere in the office.* **6.** *vt* **DISCUSS SOMETHING SPECULATIVELY** to discuss something casually in order to hear different views **7.** *vt* **KICK BALL AROUND** to kick, hit, or throw a ball in an informal game

knock around *v* same as **knock about**

knock back *vt* (*informal*) **1.** **GULP DRINK DOWN** to drink something, especially alcohol, very quickly **2.** **COST SOMEBODY MUCH MONEY** to cost somebody a large amount of money ○ *The repairs knocked me back £500.* **3.** **TAKE SOMEBODY ABACK** to come as an unwelcome surprise to somebody ○ *The news really knocked me back.* **4.** *Scotland, ANZ* **REJECT SOMEBODY OR SOMETHING** to dismiss or reject somebody or something

knock down *vt* **1.** **HIT SOMEBODY WITH VEHICLE** to hit and injure or kill somebody with a moving vehicle **2.** **MAKE SOMEBODY OR SOMETHING FALL** to cause somebody or something to fall to the ground by striking or pushing **3.** **DESTROY STRUCTURE** to demolish a building or part of a building **4.** **DISMANTLE SOMETHING** to take something apart for shipping or storage **5.** **PRONOUNCE SOMETHING SOLD** to show that something has been sold at an auction by striking a surface with a gavel **6.** **CUT PRICE OF SOMETHING** to reduce the price of something (*informal*) ○ *furniture knocked down by 50%* **7.** **MAKE SOMEBODY CUT PRICE** to persuade somebody to reduce the price of something ○ *He wanted £75 but I knocked him down to £60.*

knock off *v* **1.** *vti* **STOP WORKING** to finish work at the end of the day, or stop working or doing something in order to take a break (*informal*) **2.** *vt* **CUT PRICE** to decrease the price of something by a particular amount **3.** *vt* **DEDUCT AMOUNT OR POINTS** to deduct something from something, especially an amount from a price or a number of points from a score or total **4.** *vt* **PRODUCE SOMETHING WITH EASE OR SPEED** to make or deal with something easily and quickly (*informal*) ○ *knocks off six or seven articles a month* **5.** *vt* CRIME **KILL SOMEBODY** to kill somebody, especially intentionally (*slang*) **6.** *vt* CRIME **ROB OR STEAL SOMETHING** to rob a bank, shop, or other business, or to steal something (*slang*) **7.** *vt N Am* COMM **MAKE CHEAP COPY OF PRODUCT** to produce a cheap, sometimes illegal copy of a well-known product (*slang*) **8.** *vt* **OFFENSIVE TERM** an offensive term meaning to have sexual intercourse with somebody (*slang*)

knock on *vti* in rugby, to make illegal use of the hand or arm to move the ball forwards

knock out *vt* **1.** **MAKE SOMEBODY UNCONSCIOUS BY HITTING** to cause somebody to lose consciousness by striking him or her **2.** **DEFEAT OPPOSING BOXER WITH PUNCH** in boxing, to knock an opponent down for a count of ten, thus winning the match **3.** **STUPEFY SOMEBODY WITH DRUGS OR ALCOHOL** to cause somebody to lose consciousness or fall asleep by means of drugs or alcohol **4.** **ELIMINATE OPPONENT FROM TOURNAMENT** to eliminate an opponent or team from a competition by winning a match or game **5.** **MAKE SOMETHING USELESS** to destroy something, or make something inoperable ○ *The storm knocked out our electricity.* **6.** **TIRE SOMEBODY OUT** to exhaust somebody completely (*informal*) **7.** **PRODUCE SOMETHING WITH EASE OR SPEED** to make or do something easily or quickly (*informal*) **8.** **PLEASE OR IMPRESS SOMEBODY GREATLY** to overwhelm somebody with excitement or pleasure (*informal*) ○ *That music really knocks me out.* **9.** **SHOCK SOMEBODY** to cause somebody to be greatly shocked (*informal*)

knock over *vt* **1.** *UK* same as **run over** **2.** **MAKE SOMEBODY FALL** to cause somebody or something to fall by striking or pushing ○ *knocked my cup of coffee over* **3.** **ASTOUND SOMEBODY** to overwhelm somebody with amazement or shock (*informal*) **4.** **ROB PLACE** to rob a bank, shop, or other business (*informal*)

knock together *vt* to make something quickly, without much preparation, and often with little care (*informal*)

knock up *v* **1.** *vt* same as **knock together** (*informal*) **2.**

vt KNOCK ON DOOR TO WAKE SOMEBODY to wake somebody up by knocking on the door (*informal*) **3.** *vt* TIRE SOMEBODY OUT to make somebody very tired or ill (*slang*) **4.** *vi* HIT BALL IN PRACTICE in racquet games, to hit the ball back and forth in practice with an opponent, especially before beginning a match **5.** *vt* SCORE RUNS in cricket, to score a particular number of runs **6.** *vt* OFFENSIVE TERM an offensive term meaning to make a woman pregnant (*slang*)

knockabout /nókə bowt/ *n* **1.** COMIC PERFORMANCE comedy characterized by boisterous physical activity, or an actor who specializes in this type of comedy **2.** INFORMAL GAME an informal ball game, especially an informal game of football (*informal*) ■ *adj* **1.** USING SLAPSTICK characterized by boisterous physical activity **2.** STURDY AND INFORMAL suitable for rough or casual activities

knock-back *n Scotland, NZ* a rejection or slighting (*informal*)

knockdown /nók down/ *n* **1.** OVERWHELMING BLOW a powerful emotional or physical blow **2.** PRICE DROP a reduction in the price of something **3.** *ANZ* INTRODUCTION an introduction to somebody (*slang*) ■ *adj* **1.** VERY POWERFUL having an overwhelmingly powerful or very damaging effect ○ *a knockdown blow* **2.** EASILY DISASSEMBLED made to be taken apart easily **3.** DISCOUNTED for sale at a reduced or very low price ○ *a knockdown price*

knock-em-down rains *npl Aus* torrential downpours that occur at the end of the wet season in central northern Australia (*informal*)

knocker /nókər/ *n* **1.** FIXTURE FOR KNOCKING ON DOOR a metal fixture attached with hinges to the door of a house, used for knocking on the door **2.** CRITIC a carping or unfair critic (*informal*) ■ **knockers** *npl* OFFENSIVE TERM an offensive term for a woman's breasts (*slang*) ◇ **on the knocker** *ANZ* promptly (*dated informal*)

knock-for-knock *adj* describes an agreement between two insurance companies whereby each pays out for damage sustained by its policyholder in an accident involving a policyholder of the other company

knocking copy /nóking-/ *n* advertising material aimed at persuading prospective customers of the inferiority of a rival product or service

knocking-shop /nóking-/ *n* an offensive term for a brothel (*slang*) [< KNOCK 'have sexual intercourse with']

knock-knee *n* a condition in which the legs are permanently bent so that the knees are close together and the ankles are spread far apart ■ **knock-knees** *npl* the knees of somebody with knock-knee —**knock-kneed** *adj*

knockoff /nók of/ *n N Am* an inexpensive, sometimes illegal copy of a piece of well-known or popular merchandise (*informal*)

knock-on *adj* progressively affecting other people or things related directly or indirectly to whatever was first affected ○ *The knock-on effect will almost certainly cause further factory closures in the area.* ■ *n* in rugby, an illegal use of the hand or arm to move the ball forwards

knockout /nók owt/ *n* **1.** PUNCH WINNING BOXING MATCH in boxing, a punch that knocks an opponent down for a count of ten and so wins a contest **2.** WIN BY KNOCKOUT a victory in a boxing match by a knockout **3.** BLOW CAUSING UNCONSCIOUSNESS a blow that knocks somebody unconscious **4.** ELIMINATION COMPETITION a sports competition in which a person or team beaten in one game or match is eliminated from the entire competition **5.** SOMEBODY OR SOMETHING STUNNING somebody or something extremely attractive, good-looking, or enjoyable (*informal*)

knockout drops *npl* a solution, usually containing chloral hydrate, secretly put in a drink to render the drinker unconscious (*informal*)

knock-up *n* in racket games, a practice period with an opponent, especially before the beginning of a match

knockwurst *n* FOOD same as **knackwurst**

~~knoledge~~ incorrect spelling of **knowledge**

knoll[1] /nōl/ *n* a small rounded hill or mound [Old English *cnoll* < Germanic] —**knolly** *adj*

knoll[2] /nōl/ *n, vti* (**knolls, knolling, knolled**) same as **knell** (*archaic*) [14C. Ultimately < Germanic]

knop /nop/ *n* a small decorative knob [14C. < Middle Low German or Middle Dutch *knoppe* 'knob, knot'] —**knopped** *adj*

Knossos /nóssəss, knóssəss/ ruined city in northern Crete, the centre of the Minoan civilization from about 3000 BC to 1100 BC

knot[1] /not/ *n* **1.** OBJECT MADE BY TYING a usually hard, lump-shaped object formed when a strand of something such as string or rope is interlaced with itself or another strand and pulled tight **2.** WAY OF TYING a way of joining or securing lengths of rope, thread, or other strands by tying the material together or around itself **3.** TANGLED MASS a tightly tangled mass of strands that are hard to separate **4.** TIGHT GROUP a number of people or things grouped closely together **5.** TENSE FEELING a feeling of tightness or anxiety ○ *a knot in my stomach* **6.** CLOSE EMOTIONAL TIE a deep bond, especially marriage **7.** DECORATION a piece of material such as ribbon or braid tied in a knot or bow and used as a decoration **8.** PROBLEM a difficult or complex problem **9.** LUMP ON TREE a lump on a tree trunk or branch **10.** HARD PATCH ON TREE a hard patch on a tree out of which a branch or stem grows **11.** WOODWORK DARK WHORL IN TIMBER a hard dark-coloured patch in cut wood at a point where a branch or stem formerly grew out of the tree **12.** MED LUMP IN BODY a node, ganglion, lump, or swelling in the body **13.** MEASURE UNIT OF SPEED a unit of measurement for the speed at which a ship or aircraft travels, equivalent to one nautical mile per hour, approximately 1.85 kph/1.15 statute mph. Symbol **kn** **14.** NAUT INDICATOR MEASURING SHIP'S SPEED a division on a log line used for calculating the speed of a ship ■ *v* (**knots, knotting, knotted**) **1.** *vti* MAKE KNOT to tie something in a knot, or be tied with a knot **2.** *vti* ENTANGLE to tangle something, or become tangled **3.** *vt* MAKE SOMETHING WITH PATTERN OF KNOTS to produce something such as a piece of macramé that consists of a pattern of decorative knots **4.** *vti* BECOME TENSE to become tight or tense with anxiety or fear, or cause something to become so ○ *My stomach knotted up.* [Old English *cnotta* < Germanic, 'round lump'] —**knotter** *n* ◇ **get knotted** an offensive term expressing disagreement or impatience with somebody (*slang*) ◇ **tie somebody (up) in knots** to confuse somebody completely, especially in trying to explain something ◇ **tie the knot** to get married (*informal*)

USAGE knot or **not**? Do not confuse the spelling of ***knot*** and ***not***, which sound similar. ***Knot*** is a verb or noun referring to the tying of rope, thread, etc.; as a noun it also denotes a round patch on wood, a measure of speed, or a tight group of people. ***Not*** is an adverb used to form a negative: *I hope not. Not all children like ice cream.*

knot[2] /not/ *n* a small migratory sandpiper. Native to: Arctic. Latin name: *Calidris canutus* or *Calidris tenuirostris*. [15C. Origin ?]

knot garden *n* a herb or flower garden that has its plants arranged in an intricate pattern and sometimes also has trees and bushes trimmed in decorative designs

knotgrass /nót graass/ (*plural* **-grasses** or *same*) *n* a creeping plant with small pink flowers and prominent nodes on its stems, considered a troublesome weed. Native to: Europe. Latin name: *Polygonum aviculare*. [Early 16C. < its knotted stem]

knothole /nót hōl/ *n* a hole in wood where a knot has fallen out or been removed

knotted /nóttid/ *adj* **1.** tied in a knot, tangled up in knots, or made using decorative knots **2.** WOODWORK same as **knotty** (sense 2) **3.** BOT describes a plant that has stems with swellings resembling knots

knotting /nótting/ *n* decorative weaving produced by interlacing and tying knots in wool or thread, e.g. macramé or tatting

knotty /nótti/ (**-tier, -tiest**) *adj* **1.** PUZZLING OR COMPLEX very difficult to understand or solve **2.** MARKED WITH KNOTS used to describe wood that contains or is marked with many knots **3.** FULL OF KNOTS full of tied or tangled knots —**knottily** *adv* —**knottiness** *n*

knotty pine *n* pine wood that has many knots in it. Use: panelling, furniture.

knotweed /nót weed/ (*plural* **-weeds** or *same*) *n* PLANTS same as **knotgrass**

knotwork /nót wurk/ *n* decorative weaving produced by interlacing and tying knots in cords

knout /nowt/ *n* a leather whip formerly used in imperial Russia for flogging ■ *vt* (**knouts, knouting, knouted**) to flog somebody using a knout [Mid-17C. Via French < Russian *knut* < Old Norse *knútr* 'knot']

know /nō/ (**knows, knowing, knew** /nyoo/, **known** /nōn/) *v* **1.** *vti* HOLD INFORMATION IN MIND to have information firmly in the mind or committed to memory ○ *They know the names of all the US presidents.* **2.** *vti* BE CERTAIN ABOUT SOMETHING to believe firmly in the truth or certainty of something ○ *I know she wouldn't be late without a good reason.* **3.** *vti* REALIZE SOMETHING to be or become aware of something ○ *I didn't know you cared.* **4.** *vt* COMPREHEND SOMETHING to have a thorough understanding of something through experience or study ○ *know computers* **5.** *vt* HAVE ENCOUNTERED SOMEBODY OR SOMETHING BEFORE to be acquainted, associated, or familiar with somebody or something ○ *I have known John for years.* **6.** *vt* RECOGNIZE DIFFERENCES to be able to perceive the differences or distinctions between things or people ○ *old enough to know right from wrong* **7.** *vt* IDENTIFY SOMEBODY OR SOMETHING BY CHARACTERISTIC to recognize somebody or something by a distinguishing characteristic or attribute ○ *I'd know him anywhere by his peculiar laugh.* **8.** *vt* HAVE SEX WITH SOMEBODY to engage in sexual intercourse with somebody (*archaic*) [Old English *cnāwan* < Indo-European] —**knowable** *adj* —**knower** *n* ◇ **in the know** possessing information that is secret or known only to a small group of people ◇ **know something back to front** *or* **know something backwards** to be completely familiar with all the details of or facts about something. US term **know something backward and forward** ◇ **know something backward and forward** *N Am* same as **know something back to front** *or* **know something backwards** ◇ **not know where to put yourself** to feel acutely embarrassed (*informal*) ◇ **you know** used to fill a pause, add emphasis to a statement, or elicit a response from a listener (*informal*) ◇ **you never know** used to indicate that the outcome of events is uncertain and it is possible that something that seems unlikely could happen

SPELLCHECK know or **no**? Do not confuse the spelling of ***know*** and ***no***, which sound similar. ***Know*** is chiefly used as a verb, meaning 'to have in the mind' (as in *know what to do next*), or as a noun in the phrase *in the know*. The word ***no*** indicates a negative response or a lack of something: *No, I won't! There's no coffee left in the pot.*

know-all *n* somebody who professes to know more or better than anyone else about everything (*informal*) N Am term **know-it-all**

know-how *n* the practical skill and knowledge necessary to do something (*informal*)

knowing /nō ing/ *adj* **1.** INDICATING PRIVATE KNOWLEDGE suggesting that somebody knows a secret or something that others are unaware of ○ *a knowing smile* **2.** ASTUTE aware of things and able to act cleverly and judge shrewdly **3.** INTENTIONAL done on purpose —**knowingly** *adv* —**knowingness** *n*

know-it-all *n N Am* same as **know-all** (*informal*)

knowledgable *adj* another spelling of **knowledgeable**

knowledge /nóllij/ *n* **1.** INFORMATION IN MIND general awareness or possession of information, facts, ideas, truths, or principles ○ *Her knowledge and interests are extensive.* **2.** SPECIFIC INFORMATION clear awareness or explicit information, e.g. of a situation or fact ○ *I believe they have knowledge of the circumstances.* **3.** ALL THAT CAN BE KNOWN all the information, facts, truths, and principles learned throughout time ○ *With all our knowledge, we still haven't found a cure for the common cold.* **4.** COMMUNICATION TRANSMISSION OF INFORMATION information services and the storage and transmission of information, especially within a large organization **5.** INTERCOURSE sexual intercourse (*archaic*) [14C. Probably < obsolete *knowledge* 'acknowledge' < KNOW + Old English *-lǣcan* < *-lāc* 'practice']

SYNONYMS ***knowledge, erudition, information, learning, scholarship, wisdom***

CORE MEANING: general awareness or possession of information, facts, ideas, truths, or principles

knowledge awareness of information, either general or specific ○ *They had a lifetime of experience and involvement with primary schools, and were able to distil that lifetime's knowledge very rapidly.* **erudition**

knowledge acquired through study and reading ○ *A master storyteller, he draws together elements of classical erudition.* **information** the collected facts and data about a specific subject. ○ *The organization provides the public with information about alcohol to help them make informed choices.* ○ *the increasing use of the media as a source of information* **learning** knowledge or skill gained through education ○ *A man of obvious learning with a great admiration for classical civilization.* **scholarship** academic learning or achievement ○ *a multi-volume work of scholarship that took more than a decade to complete* **wisdom** accumulated knowledge of life or of a sphere of activity that has been gained through experience ○ *We admired the wisdom she showed in refusing to agree to their requests too readily.* ○ *another health report challenging the conventional wisdom about high blood pressure*

knowledgeable /nóllijəb'l/, **knowledgable** *adj* possessing or showing a great deal of knowledge, awareness, or intelligence —**knowledgeability** /nóllijə bílləti/ *n* —**knowledgeableness** *n* —**knowledgeably** *adv*

knowledge base *n* **1.** the computerized data in an expert system required for solving problems in a specific area **2.** the facts required for solving problems

knowledge industry *n* businesses that specialize primarily in data processing or the development and use of information technology

knowledge management *n* the organization of intellectual resources and information systems within a business environment

knowledge transfer *n* the communication of specialized knowledge developed in part of an organization to a wider group such as another part of the organization or business customers

knowledge worker *n* somebody working in an industry such as management consultancy or computer programming that produces information rather than goods

~~knowlegable~~ incorrect spelling of **knowledgeable**

known /nōn/ past participle of **know** ■ *adj* **1.** ACKNOWLEDGED generally recognized as or proved to be something ○ *a known criminal* **2.** FAMILIAR belonging to an established body of knowledge ○ *the limits of the known universe* ■ *n* CERTAINTY a fact or piece of information that is certain ○ *separate the knowns from the unknowns*

Knox /noks/, **John** (1513?–72) Scottish religious reformer. He was chaplain to Edward VI of England. He helped to found the Presbyterian Church of Scotland (1560), and opposed the rule of the Roman Catholic Mary, Queen of Scots.

> 'A man with God is always in the majority.'
> [John Knox, *Inscription on Reformation monument, Geneva, Switzerland*; 16th century]

Knoxville /nóks vil/ city and county seat of Knox County in eastern Tennessee, situated on the Tennessee River, northeast of Chattanooga. It is an industrial centre and home to the University of Tennessee. Population: 173,661 (2002 estimate).

KNP *symbol* CHESS king's knight's pawn

Knt *abbr* CHESS knight

knuckle /núk'l/ *n* **1.** FINGER JOINT a joint of a finger, especially a joint connecting a finger to the hand **2.** ROUNDED PROJECTION WHEN FIST IS MADE one of the rounded projections above a knuckle that appears on the back of a hand when a fist is made (*often used in the plural*) **3.** FOOD PIECE OF MEAT NEAR KNEE a cut of meat consisting of the lower joint from the hind leg of a calf, pig, or lamb **4.** MECH ENG HINGE PIVOT the cylindrical part of a hinge through which the pin passes **5.** MECH ENG same as **knuckle joint** (sense 2) ■ *v* (**-les**, **-ling**, **-led**) **1.** *vt* APPLY KNUCKLES TO SOMETHING to rub, hit, or press something with the knuckles ○ *knuckled her eyes in disbelief* **2.** *vi* LEISURE HAVE KNUCKLES ON GROUND PLAYING MARBLES to have the knuckles on the ground when shooting a marble with the thumb pressed into the bent forefinger [14C. < Middle Low German *knökel* 'small bone' < Germanic] —**knuckly** *adj* ◇ **go the knuckle** *Aus* to have a fight or punch-up (*informal*) ◇ **near the knuckle** rather indecent

knuckle down *vi* to work hard and conscientiously at something (*informal*)

knuckle under *vi* to give in to force or pressure

knuckleball /núk'l bawl/ *n* in baseball, a slow pitch with little spin and an unpredictable flight, produced by releasing the ball from the knuckles and the thumb or the tips of two or three fingers —**knuckleballer** *n*

knucklebone /núk'l bōn/ *n* a knobbly bone forming part of a joint in the human finger (*informal*)

knucklebones /núk'l bōnz/ *n* LEISURE same as **jacks** (*takes a singular verb*)

knuckle-duster *n* a piece of metal worn over the knuckles and used to make a punch inflict greater injury. N Am term **brass knuckles**

knucklehead /núk'l hed/ *n* an offensive term that deliberately insults somebody's intelligence or consideration for others (*slang insult*) —**knuckleheaded** *adj*

knuckle joint *n* **1.** a joint of the human finger **2.** a hinge with a pin that fastens the ends of two rods together, allowing movement in one plane only

knuckler /núklər/ *n* BASEBALL same as **knuckleball**

knuckle sandwich *n* a blow with the fist to the mouth (*slang*)

knur /nur/, **knurr** *n* a bump or knot on a tree trunk or in wood [15C. Origin ?]

knurl /nurl/ *n* **1.** BUMP OR KNOB a small hard knob or protuberance **2.** RIDGE USED FOR GRIPPING a ridge, especially one in a series that runs along the edge of something such as a thumbscrew that makes it easier to grip ■ *vt* (**knurls, knurling, knurled**) MAKE SOMETHING RIDGED to put ridges on something, especially to make it easier to grip [Early 17C. Probably < KNUR] —**knurly** *adj*

knurr *n* BOT another spelling of **knur**

Knut another spelling of **Canute**

KO (*informal*) *n* (*plural* **KO's**) a knockout, especially in boxing ■ *vt* (**KO's, KO'ing, KO'd**) to knock somebody out, especially in boxing [Early 20C. < the initial letters of *knock out*]

koa /kố ə/ (*plural* **-as** or *same*) *n* a tree with grey bark that yields a valuable reddish- to yellowish-brown hardwood used in furniture-making. Native to: Hawaii. Latin name: *Acacia koa.* [Early 19C. < Hawaiian]

koala

koala /kō áalə/, **koala bear** *n* a marsupial that resembles a small bear and has grey fur, a round face, and large ears. It lives in eucalyptus trees, feeding almost exclusively on their leaves. Native to: Australia. Latin name: *Phascolarctos cinereus.* [Late 18C. < Dharuk *kūl(l)a*]

koan /kố an/ (*plural* **-ans** or *same*) *n* a Zen Buddhist riddle used to focus the mind during meditation and to develop intuitive thinking [Mid-20C. Via Japanese < Chinese *gōngàn* 'official business']

kob /kob/ (*plural* **kobs** or *same*) *n* **1.** a large antelope with an orange-brown coat. Native to: open grasslands near swamps or rivers in Central and West Africa. Latin name: *Kobus kob.* **2.** *S Africa* a large edible fish that is taken commercially and for sport. Native to: warm southern oceans. Latin name: *Argyrosomus hololepidotus.* [Late 18C. < Wolof *kooba*]

Kobe /kốbi/, **Kōbe** capital of Hyogo Prefecture, and port on Osaka Bay, southern Honshu Island, Japan. Population: 1,478,380 (2002).

Koblenz /kō blénts/ city in the Rhineland-Palatinate, west-central Germany, south of Bonn. Population: 109,550 (1997).

kobo /kố bō/ (*plural same* or **-bos**) *n* a subunit of Nigerian currency. See table at **currency** [Late 20C. < Nigerian English, alteration of COPPER [1]]

kobold /kóbbōld/ *n* in German folklore, a mischievous elf that lives in houses or a gnome that haunts underground places, especially mines [Mid-19C. < German, variant of *Kobalt* (see COBALT)]

Kobuk Valley National Park /kố búk-/ national park located entirely north of the Arctic Circle in northwestern Alaska. Area: 7085 sq. km/2735 sq. mi.

Koch /kokh/, **Robert** (1843–1910) German bacteriologist. He discovered the tuberculosis bacillus (1882) and the cholera bacillus (1883). He was awarded the Nobel Prize in physiology or medicine (1905).

kochia /kốki ə/ *n* US a bushy annual plant with narrow light green leaves that turn red in autumn. It spreads rapidly as a weed and is toxic to grazing animals. Native to: Europe and western Asia, naturalized elsewhere. Latin name: *Bassia scoparia.* Same as **summer cypress** [Late 19C. After Wilhelm D. J. Koch (1771–1849), German botanist]

Kodály /kốd ī/, **Zoltán** (1882–1967) Hungarian composer. His works are influenced by the folk songs he collected. He developed an influential system of music education for children.

Kodiak /kốdi ak/ (*plural* **-aks** or *same*), **Kodiak bear** *n* a brown bear that can grow to a very large size. Native to: coastal areas and nearby islands of Alaska and British Columbia. Latin name: *Ursus middendorffi.* [Late 19C. After KODIAK ISLAND]

Kodiak Island /kốdi ak īlənd/ island in the Gulf of Alaska, southwestern Alaska, noted for its bears and marine life. Area: 8,974 sq. km/3,465 sq. mi.

koeksister /kốok sistər/ *n* S Africa a twisted or plaited doughnut, deep-fried in oil then dipped into cold sugar syrup and sometimes dried coconut [Early 20C. < Afrikaans]

koel /kố əl/ (*plural* **koels** or *same*) *n* a cuckoo, of which the male has black feathers. Native to: Asia, Australia. Genus: *Eudynamys.* [Early 19C. < Hindi *koël*]

Koetsu Hon'Ami /ko ətsoố hōnáami/ (1558–1637) Japanese artist. A founder member of the revivalist Rimpa school, he was noted for his paintings, calligraphy, pottery, and patronage of the arts.

kof *n* another spelling of **qoph**

kofta /kóftə/ (*plural same* or **-tas**) *n* in South Asian cooking, a dish consisting of minced meat, fish, or vegetables cooked in small balls [Late 19C. < Urdu, Persian *koftah* 'pounded meat']

koftgari /kốftgəri/ *n* South Asian decorative metalwork made from steel etched with gold [Late 19C. < Urdu, Persian *kuft-garī* 'beaten work']

kohen *n* JUDAISM another spelling of **cohen**

Kohima /kō heémə/ capital of Nagaland State in northeastern India. Population: 67,200 (1991).

Kohinoor[1] /kố i noór/ *n* an extremely large South Asian diamond that is among the British crown jewels [Early 19C. < Persian *kūh* 'mountain' + *i* 'of' + Arabic *nūr* 'light']

Kohinoor[2] /kố i noór/ *tdmk* a trademark for pens and pencils

kohl /kōl/ *n* especially in South Asia and North Africa, a chemical preparation used by women to darken the rims of their eyelids. It usually consists of powdered antimony sulphide or lead sulphide. [Late 18C. < Arabic *kuḥl*]

Kohl /kōl/, **Helmut** (b. 1930) chancellor of the Federal Republic of Germany (1982–98). As Christian Democratic chancellor, he played the leading role in German reunification (1990).

> 'Only through resolute commitment to the realization of European unification can we obviate a relapse into the destructive nationalism of the past.'
> [Helmut Kohl, *Speech to the Bundestag, Bonn*; 17 June 1992]

> 'The policy of European integration is in reality a question of war and peace in the

kohlrabi

21st century.'
[Helmut Kohl, *Speech at Louvrain University*; 2 February 1996]

kohlrabi /kōl raˊabi/ *n* **1.** (*plural* **kohlrabies**) a swollen turnip-shaped stem of a plant, eaten as a vegetable **2.** a plant of the cabbage family whose swollen stems are kohlrabies. Latin name: *Brassica oleracea* var. gongylodes. [Early 19C. Via German < plural of Italian *cavolo rapa* < medieval Latin *caulorapa* < Latin *caulis* 'cabbage' + *rapa* 'turnip']

Kohoutek /kə hoˊot ek/ *n* a comet that passed around the Sun in late 1973 and early 1974

koi /koy/ (*plural same*), **koi carp** *n* a carp with red-gold or white colouring, kept as an aquarium or ornamental pond fish. Native to: Japan, temperate regions of East Asia. Latin name: *Cyprinus carpio*. [Early 18C. < Japanese]

koine /kóy nee/ *n* **1.** LANGUAGE same as **lingua franca** (sense 1) **2.** a dialect or regional variant of a language that becomes the standard language for a wider population of speakers [Late 19C. < KOINE]

Koine /kóy nee/ *n* the form of Greek, mostly derived from the Attic dialect, that became the standard language for Greek-speaking people during the Hellenistic period [Late 19C. < Greek *koinē* 'common'] —**Koine** *adj*

Koizumi /koy zoˊomi/, **Junichiro** (*b.* 1942) Japanese prime minister. A member of the Liberal Democratic Party, he was elected to the Lower House in 1972 and took up ministerial office in 1988. He was elected prime minister in 2001.

kokanee /kō kánni/ (*plural* **-ees** or *same*), **kokanee salmon** *n* a small nonmigratory sockeye salmon. Native to: landlocked lakes from western North America to Siberia and Japan. Latin name: *Oncorhynchus nerka kennerlyi*. [Late 19C. < Salish *kəknǽxʷ*]

Koki pen /kóki-/ *tdmk S Africa* a trademark for a felt-tip pen

Kokoda Trail /kə kōdə-/ a trail in Papua New Guinea linking Port Moresby with the village of Kokoda in the Owen Stanley Range. During World War II, Australian and Papuan soldiers successfully defended the trail, thereby preventing a Japanese invasion of the island.

Koko Nor /kókō nawr/ GEOG ♦ **Qinghai Hu**

Kokoschka /ko kóshkə/, **Oskar** (1886–1980) Austrian-born painter and writer. He is best known for his expressionist portraits and landscapes. He lived in Britain (1938–53) before settling in Switzerland.

kola *n* TREES another spelling of **cola**[1] (sense 2)

Kola Peninsula /kólə-/ peninsula in northwestern European Russia, between the Barents Sea and the White Sea. Area: 100,000 sq. km/40,000 sq. mi.

Kolar Gold Fields /kō laˊar-/ city in southern Karnataka State, southern India, near Bangalore. Population: 156,398 (1991).

Kolhapur /kōl haa poˊor/ city in Maharashtra State, southwestern India. Population: 497,554 (2001).

kolinsky /kə línski/ (*plural* **-skies**) *n* **1.** the dark tawny fur of a weasel **2.** a weasel whose fur is kolinsky. Native to: northern Europe and Asia. Latin name: *Mustela sibirica*. [Mid-19C. < Russian *kolinskiĭ* 'of Kola' (port in NW Russia)]

Kolkata /kol kúttə/ capital of Bangla State and one of India's largest cities. It is a major commercial and industrial city and port, situated on the River Hoogly, an arm of the Ganges about 100 km/60 mi. from its mouth at the Bay of Bengal. Population: 4,580,544 (2001). Former name **Calcutta**

kolkhoz /kól kóz, -káwz, -háwz/ (*plural* **-khozes** or *same* or **-khozy** /-zi/), **kolkoz** (*plural* **-kozes** or *same* or **-kozy**) *n* a collective farm in the former Soviet Union [Early 20C. < Russian < *kol(lektivnoe) khoz(yaĭstvo)* 'collective farm']

kolkhoznik /kól kóznik, -káwznik, -háwznik/ *n* a worker on a collective farm in the former Soviet Union

kolkoz *n* AGRIC another spelling of **kolkhoz**

Kol Nidre /kól níddray/ *n* **1.** in Judaism, the prayer recited at the opening of the service on the eve of Yom Kippur. It asks that all unfulfilled vows to God be nullified and that all transgressions be forgiven. **2.** the service on the eve of Yom Kippur [Late 19C. < Aramaic *kol niḏrē* 'all the vows', its opening words]

kolo /kólō/ (*plural* **-los**) *n* **1.** a Serbian folk dance in which one or more dancers perform inside a circle of other dancers **2.** the music for a kolo [Late 18C. < Serbo-Croatian, 'wheel']

Kolonia /kə lóni ə/ largest town in the Federated States of Micronesia, and capital of Pohnpei island state. Population: 6,600 (1994).

Kolyma Range /kólli maˊa-/ mountain range in northeastern Siberian Russia. Length: 2,100 km/1,300 mi.

komatik /kó matik/ *n* an Inuit sledge with wooden crossbars tied to the runners with rawhide [Early 19C. < Inuit *qamutik*]

kombu /kóm booˊ/ *n* a kelp sold dried. Use: in Japanese cooking. [Late 19C. < Japanese]

Komi /kómi/ (*plural same* or **-mis**) *n* **1.** a member of a Uralic people who live in northeastern European Russia **2.** the Finnic language of the Komi people, belonging to the Finno-Ugric branch of Uralic. Native speakers: 400,000. [Late 19C. < Komi] —**Komi** *adj*

Komodo dragon

Komodo dragon /kə mōdō-/, **Komodo lizard** *n* a large monitor lizard, growing to a length of 3 m/10 ft. Native to: island of Komodo, east of Java. Latin name: *Varanus komodoensis*. [After an island east of Java]

komondor /kómmən dawr/ *n* a large dog with a long matted white coat, belonging to a Hungarian breed that is traditionally used for herding sheep or as a watchdog [Mid-20C. < Hungarian]

Komsomol /kómssə mol, kómssə mól/ *n* a Communist organization for young people in the former Soviet Union [Mid-20C. < Russian < *Kommunisticheskiĭ Soyuz Molodëzhi* 'Communist Union of Youth']

Komsomolsk /kómssə molsk/ city in far eastern Russia, on the River Amur. Population: 355,634 (1995).

koneki /kónn eki/, **koneke** *n NZ* a sledge with runners at the front and wheels at the back, used by farmers and forestry workers [Early 20C. < Maori]

Kongo[1] /kóng gō/ (*plural* **-gos** or *same*) *n* **1.** a member of a people who live along the lower River Congo in west-central Africa **2.** the Bantu language spoken by the Kongo people in southern Congo and northern Angola. Native speakers: 7 million. Other speakers: 2 million. [Mid-19C. < Kongo] —**Kongo** *adj*

Kongo[2] /kóng gō/ former kingdom in central Africa that flourished between the 14th and 16th centuries in the area between present-day Gabon and Northern Angola

Königsberg /königz burg/ former name for **Kaliningrad**

konimeter /kō nímmitər/ *n* an instrument for measuring the amount of dust in the air [Early 20C. < Greek *konis* 'dust']

koniology /kóni ólləji/ *n* the study of airborne dust and its effects on the environment [< Greek *konis* 'dust']

Konkani /kóngkə nee/ *n* a dialect of Marathi spoken in coastal Maharashtra in western India [Late 19C. < Marathi *kōkṇi*] —**Konkani** *adj*

kook /kook/ *n* **1.** *N Am* an offensive term for somebody whose behaviour is regarded as unpleasantly eccentric (*informal insult*) **2.** a snowboarder who is a beginner or inexperienced (*slang*) [Mid-20C. Probably shortening of CUCKOO]

kookaburra

kookaburra /kooˊkə burrə/ (*plural* **-ras** or *same*) *n* a large bird of the kingfisher family with a loud call that sounds like laughter. Native to: Australia and nearby islands. Latin name: *Dacelo novaeguineae* or *Dacelo leachii*. [Mid-19C. < Wiradhuri *gugubarra*]

kooky /kooˊki/ (**-ier, -iest**) *adj N Am* an offensive term meaning thought to be unpleasantly eccentric (*informal insult*) —**kookily** *adv* —**kookiness** *n*

Kooning ♦ **de Kooning, Willem**

Koons /koonz/, **Jeff** (*b.* 1955) US artist. He transforms everyday and often kitsch objects into works of art. His controversial *Made in Heaven* series (1989–91) deliberately challenges the boundaries between pornography and art.

Koori /kooˊri/ (*plural* **-ries**), **Koorie, koori, koorie** *n Aus* an Aboriginal of southeastern Australia (*informal*) [Mid-18C. < Awakabal *guri* 'man'] —**Koori** *adj*

Kootenai *n, adj* PEOPLES, LANG another spelling of **Kutenai**

Kootenay[1] /kooˊtə nay/, **Kootenai** river of the northwestern United States and southwestern Canada. It rises in the Rocky Mountains of southeastern British Columbia, flows into the United States, then re-enters Canada through Kootenay Lake and joins the Columbia River. Length: 655 km/407 mi.

Kootenay[2] *n, adj* PEOPLES, LANG another spelling of **Kutenai**

kop /kop/ *n S Africa* **1.** a prominent crest of a hill **2.** intelligence or common sense (*informal*) ○ *Use your kop!* [Mid-19C. Via Afrikaans < Dutch, 'head']

kopek /kó pek/, **kopeck, copeck** *n* a subunit of Russian currency. See table at **currency** [Early 17C. < Russian *kopeika*, literally 'little lance'; from the figure of a tsar bearing a lance on the coin]

koph *n* another spelling of **qoph**

kopiyka /kō peˊeka/ *n* a subunit of currency in the Ukraine. See table at **currency** [< Ukrainian]

kopje *n S Africa* GEOG another spelling of **koppie**

koppa /kóppə/ *n* the 17th letter of the ancient Greek alphabet, later adopted by the Romans as the letter 'q'. See table at **alphabet** [Late 19C. < Greek]

koppie /kóppi/, **kopje** *n S Africa* a small hill [Mid-19C. Via Afrikaans *kopje* < Dutch, 'small head' < *kop* 'head']

Kor. *abbr* **1.** Korea **2.** PEOPLES, LANG Korean

kora /káwrə/ (*plural* **-ras**) *n* a West African 21-string lute that has a gourd resonator [Late 18C. < a W African language]

koradji /kə ráaji/ (*plural* **-djis**) *n Aus* a traditional healer in Australian Aboriginal culture [Late 18C. < Dharuk]

Koran /kaw ráan, kə-/, **Qur'an** *n* the sacred text of Islam, believed by Muslims to record the revelations of God to Muhammad [Early 17C. < Arabic *ḳur'ān* 'recitation' < *ḳara'a* 'recite'] —**Koranic** /-ránnik/ *adj*

Kordofan /kawr dō fáan/ former province in central Sudan

Kordofanian /káwrdō fáyni ən/ *n* AFRICAN LANGUAGE GROUP a small group of languages spoken in southern Sudan that may be distinct from other African languages or a branch of Niger-Congo ■ *adj* **1.** OF KORDOFANIAN relating to Kordofanian **2.** OF KORDOFAN relating to Kordofan, central Sudan

kore /káw ray/ (*plural* **-rai** /-rī/) *n* a Greek sculpture of a clothed standing young woman dating from the period 650 to 480 BC [Early 20C. < Greek *korē* 'maiden']

Korea /kə reé ə/ peninsula in East Asia, divided since 1948 into the Democratic People's Republic of Korea (North Korea) and the Republic of Korea (South Korea). Area: 219,806 sq. km/84,868 sq. mi.

Korea, North ◊ **North Korea**

Korea, South ◊ **South Korea**

Korean /kə reé ən/ *n* **1.** somebody who comes from North or South Korea **2.** the Altaic official language of North and South Korea, also spoken in China, Japan, and Asia of the former Soviet Union. Native speakers: 60 million. Other speakers: 60 million. —**Korean** *adj*

Korean War *n* a war that lasted from 1950 to 1953 between North Korea, and its ally China, and South Korea, supported by United Nations troops, especially from the United States

korfball /káwrf bawl/ *n* a game similar to basketball that is played by two teams of twelve players, each team having six men or boys and six women or girls [Early 20C. < Dutch *korfbal* < *korf* 'basket' + *bal* 'ball']

Kōrin /kṓrin/ (1658?–1716) Japanese artist. He is known for his bird, flower, and landscape paintings. Full name **Ogata Kōrin**

korma /káwrmə/ (*plural* **-mas**), **qorma** *n* in South Asian cooking, a mildly spiced dish of meat, seafood, or vegetables cooked in a cream or yoghurt sauce [Late 19C. < Urdu *ḳormā*]

Koror /kə ráwr/ island and administrative centre of the Republic of Palau, in the western Pacific Ocean. Population: 11,552 (1997). Area: 21 sq. km/8 sq. mi.

Korsakoffian /káwrssə kóffi ən/ *adj* relating to the Wernicke-Korsakoff syndrome ■ *n* an offensive term for somebody who is affected by Wernicke-Korsakoff syndrome [After Sergei Sergeevich *Korsakov* (see WERNICKE-KORSAKOFF SYNDROME)]

koruna /ko róonə/ (*plural* **-nas**) *n* the main unit of Czech and Slovak currency. See table at **currency** [Early 20C. < Czech, 'crown']

kos /kōss/ (*plural same*) *n* in South Asia, a unit of measurement used for land distances that varies in length from region to region, ranging from 1.6 to 4.8 km/1 to 3 mi [Early 17C. Via Hindi < Sanskrit *krośa* 'cry']

Kos another spelling of **Cos**

Kosciuszko, Mount /kóssi úsk ō/ highest mountain in Australia, located in the Snowy Mountains in southeastern New South Wales. Height: 2,228 m/7,310 ft. Former name **Kosciusko**

Kościuszko /kóssi úsk ō/, **Thaddeus** (1746–1817) Polish soldier and revolutionary. He served with George Washington in the American War of Independence, and in 1794 led a revolt for Polish independence. Born **Kościusko, Tadeusz Andrzej Bonawentura**

kosher /kṓshər/ *adj* **1.** RITUALLY PURE describes food that has been prepared so that it is fit and suitable under Jewish law **2.** PREPARING OR SELLING KOSHER FOOD preparing or selling foods that are fit and suitable under Jewish law **3.** REAL genuine, not false or fake (*informal*) **4.** LAWFUL OR PROPER allowed by law, or regarded as correct or proper (*informal*) ○ *Something's not kosher about his handling of the situation.* ■ *vt* (**-shers, -shering, -shered**) PREPARE KOSHER FOOD to prepare food in a way that is fit and suitable under Jewish law [Mid-19C. < Hebrew *kāšēr* 'fit, proper']

Kosovo /kóssəvə, -vō/ former autonomous province in southwestern Serbia, in the Federal Republic of Yugoslavia. The administrative centre is Priština. Large numbers of the majority Albanian population were displaced by a Serbian programme of ethnic cleansing. Since 1999 Kosovo has become a United Nations supervised region. Population: 1,956,196 (1991). Area: 10,887 sq. km/4,203 sq. mi. Albanian name **Kosova** —**Kosovan** *n, adj* —**Kosovar** /-vaar/ *n, adj*

Kossuth /kóssooth, kósh oot/, **Lajos** (1802–94) Hungarian politician and nationalist. A leader of the Hungarian Revolution (1848), he was appointed provisional governor of Hungary (1849) but was deposed shortly afterwards.

Kosuth /kóssooth/, **Joseph** (*b.* 1945) US conceptual artist. His installations such as *One and Three Chairs* (1965) challenge the aesthetic value of art and emphasize its concept and meaning.

> 'Being an artist now means to question the nature of art.'
> [Joseph Kosuth. Quoted in *Arte Povera*, Germano Celant; 1968]

Kosygin /kə seégin/, **Aleksey** (1904–80) Soviet premier. In this capacity, he was chairman of the Council of Ministers of the Soviet Union (1964–80). Full name **Kosygin, Aleksey Nikolayevich**

Kota Baharu /kṓtə baároo/ city on the northeastern coast of the Malay Peninsula, Malaysia, and capital of Kelantan State. Population: 219,582 (1996).

Kota Kinabalu /kṓtə kinəbə lóo/ city in eastern Malaysia. It is the capital of Sabah State, on the South China Sea. Population: 76,120 (1996). Former name **Jesselton** (until 1968)

koto /kṓtō/ (*plural* **-tos**) *n* a Japanese musical instrument resembling a zither, with strings stretched over a convex wooden sounding board. It is plucked using three plectra worn on the thumb, index finger, and middle finger. [Late 18C. < Japanese]

kotuku /kṓtŏŏ koo/ (*plural* **-kus**) *n NZ* a white heron. Native to: New Zealand. Latin name: *Egretta alba modesta.* [Mid-19C. < Maori]

kotwal /kot wáal/ *n S Asia* a police officer [Late 16C. Via Hindi *koṭvāl* < Sanskrit *koṭṭapāla*]

kotwali /kot wáali/ *n S Asia* a police station [Mid-19th. < Hindi < *koṭvāl* (see KOTWAL)]

koulibiac /kóoli byák/, **koulibiaca** /-byákə/, **coulibiac**, **coulibiaca** *n* a Russian-style fish pie, usually consisting of layers of cooked rice, fish, and eggs in pastry [Late 19C. < Russian *kulebyaka*]

koumiss, **koumis**, **koumyss** *n* FOOD another spelling of **kumiss**

kouprey /kóo pray/ (*plural* **-preys** or *same*) *n* an endangered species of wild ox with a blackish-brown body and white markings on its back and feet. Native to: Cambodia, Vietnam. Latin name: *Bos sauveli.* [Mid-20C. < Khmer]

kouros /kóor oss/ (*plural* **-roi** /-roy/) *n* a Greek sculpture of a naked, standing young man dating from the period 650 to 480 BC [Early 20C. < Greek, variant of *koros* 'boy']

Kowloon /kow lóon/ city in Hong Kong Special Administrative Region, southeastern China, on the northern side of Hong Kong harbour. Population: 2,030,683 (1991).

Kow Swamp /kow-/ a significant archaeological site in northern Victoria, Australia, where the remains of early human settlers have been found

kowtow /ków tów/ *vi* (**-tows, -towing, -towed**) **1.** BE SERVILE to behave in an extremely submissive way in order to please somebody in a position of authority **2.** KNEEL TO SHOW RESPECT formerly, in China, to kneel and touch the forehead to the ground in order to show respect, awe, or submission ■ *n* **1.** SERVILE ACT an extremely submissive act aimed at pleasing somebody in a position of authority **2.** ACT OF KNEELING TO SHOW RESPECT a show of respect or worship made by kneeling and touching the forehead to the ground [Early 19C. < Chinese *kòutóu* 'strike (the) head'] —**kowtower** *n*

Kozhikode /kṓzhə kōd/ city and seaport in Kerala State, southwestern India. It has been an important textile centre since the 16th century. Population: 419,531 (1991).

kp *abbr* ONLINE North Korea (*used in Internet addresses*) See table at **domain name**

KP *abbr* Knight (of the Order) of St Patrick ■ *symbol* CHESS king's pawn

kpc *abbr* kiloparsec

kph *abbr* MEASURE kilometres per hour

kr *abbr* ONLINE South Korea (*used in Internet addresses*) See table at **domain name**

Kr *symbol* CHEM ELEM krypton ■ *abbr* MONEY krona

KR *symbol* CHESS king's rook

kr. *abbr* MONEY **1.** krona **2.** króna **3.** krone

kraal /kraal/ *n S Africa* **1.** a traditional rural village, usually consisting of a number of huts surrounded by a stockade **2.** a pen or other enclosure for livestock, especially cattle [Mid-18C. Via Afrikaans < Portuguese *curral* < Nama]

Krafft-Ebing /kráft ébbing/, **Richard, Freiherr von** (1840–1902) German neuropsychologist. He is known for his pioneering studies into sexual psychopathology. His major work is *Psychopathia Sexualis* (1886).

kraft /kraaft/, **kraft paper** *n* tough, usually brown paper made from chemically treated wood pulp. Use: bags, wrapping paper. [Early 20C. < Swedish, shortening of *kraftpapper* 'strength paper']

krait /krīt/ *n* an extremely poisonous snake with brightly coloured bands on its back. Native to: Southeast Asia. Genus: *Bungarus.* [Late 19C. < Hindi *karait*]

Krajina /krī eénə/ region of central Croatia on the border with Bosnia and Herzegovina. Its predominantly Serbian population opposed Croatia's secession from Yugoslavia, declaring the Serbian Republic of Krajina in 1991. It fell to Croatian forces in 1995.

Krakatau /krákə tów/, **Krakatoa** /-tṓ ə/ **1.** small volcanic island in southwestern Indonesia, in the Sunda Strait between Java and Sumatra. Area: 15 sq. km/6 sq. mi. **2.** volcano on the island of Krakatau, whose eruption in 1883 destroyed most of the island and caused tens of thousands of deaths. Height: 813 m/2,667 ft.

kraken /kráakən/ *n* in Norwegian folklore, a huge sea monster shaped like a giant squid. Norwegian fishermen have periodically reported sightings since the 16th century. [Mid-18C. < Norwegian]

Kraków /krákow, -ō, -of/, **Cracow** university city on the River Vistula in southern Poland. Its medieval architecture attracts many tourists, but it is also an important industrial centre. Population: 740,500 (1997).

krans /kraanss/, **krantz** /kraants/ *n S Africa* a sheer rock face, typically occurring in the form of a band of exposed rock around the summit of a mountain [Late 18C. Via Afrikaans < Dutch, 'coronet, chaplet']

Krasnodar /krássnə dáar/ city and port in southwestern Russia. It is the administrative centre of Krasnodar Territory. Population: 761,681 (1995). Former name **Yekaterinodar** (until 1922)

Krasnoyarsk /krássnə yáarsk/ city in southern Siberian Russia. It is the administrative centre of Krasnoyarsk Territory. Population: 1,122,874 (1995).

Kraut /krowt/ *n* an offensive term for a German (*slang*) [Early 20C. < German, 'vegetable, cabbage'] —**Kraut** *adj*

Krebs /krebz/, **Sir Hans** (1900–81) German-born British biochemist. He discovered the citric acid cycle (**Krebs cycle**), for which he shared the Nobel Prize in physiology or medicine (1953) with Fritz Albert Lipmann. Full name **Krebs, Sir Hans Adolf**

Krebs cycle /krébz-/ *n* a sequence of biochemical reactions occurring in cells that is part of the metabolism of carbohydrates to produce energy

Kreisler /krī́zlər/, **Fritz** (1875–1962) Austrian-born US violinist and composer. He was one of the most noted violinists of his generation, and wrote numerous pieces for the violin.

kremlin /krémlin/ *n* a fortress or citadel in a Russian city [Mid-17C. Via French < Russian *kreml* 'citadel']

Kremlin *n* **1.** the walled citadel in Moscow in which cathedrals, palaces, and the offices of the Russian government are located. The outer walls date back to the 15th century. **2.** the government of the former Soviet Union

Kremlinology /krémli nólləji/ *n* the study of the government and policies of the former Soviet Union —**Kremlinological** /krémlinə lójjik'l/ *adj* —**Kremlinologist** *n*

kreplach /krép laak, -laakh/ *npl* a Jewish dish consisting of triangles or squares of pasta filled with liver or meat that are boiled and served in soup [Late 19C. < Yiddish *kreplech*, plural of *krepel* < German dialect *Kräppel* 'fried pastry']

kreutzer /króytsər/, **kreuzer** *n* a small silver or copper coin used in Germany, Austria, and Hungary between the 13th and the mid-19th centuries [Mid-16C. < German *Kreuzer* < *Kreuz* 'cross'; after medieval Latin *denarius crucigerus* 'cross-bearing penny']

kriegspiel /kreég speel/ *n* **1.** *also* **Kriegspiel** a military game played on a map or mock battlefield with figures representing troops, ships, and other equipment, originally developed to teach tactics to officers **2.** a way of playing chess in which players can only see their own board and must remember the other player's moves as reported to them by a referee [Late 19C. < German < *Krieg* 'war' + *Spiel* 'game']

krill /kril/ (*plural same*) *n* a tiny ocean crustacean resembling a shrimp that is the primary food of baleen whales and other animals that filter their food from seawater. Order: Euphausiacea. [Early 20C. < Norwegian *kril* 'small fry of fish']

krimmer /krímmər/ *n* pale fur made from the soft curly wool of lambs from the Crimean Peninsula [Mid-19C. < German < *Krim* 'Crimea']

Krio /kreé ō/ (*plural* **-os**) *n* **1.** a creole language spoken in Sierra Leone, based on English and with a strong Yoruba influence. Native speakers: 50,000. Other speakers: 200,000. **2.** somebody who speaks Krio [Mid-20C. Probably alteration of CREOLE] —**Krio** *adj*

Kriol /kreé ol/ *n Aus* an English-based creole spoken by many Aboriginal people in northern Australia [Mid-20C. < Kriol, alteration of CREOLE] —**Kriol** *adj*

kris /kreess, kriss/ *n* a Malay and Indonesian dagger with a wavy two-edged blade [Late 16C. < Malay *keris*]

Krishna /kríshnə/ *n* in Hinduism, the eighth incarnation of the god Vishnu, often depicted as a young cowherd [< Sanskrit *kṛṣṇa*] —**Krishnaism** *n*

Krishna Jayanti /-jī únti/ *n* a Hindu festival celebrating Krishna's birthday. Date: late Sravana. [*Jayanti* < Hindi, 'birthday']

kriss /kriss/ *adj* smartly or neatly dressed (*slang*; *used in Black English*) [Probably form of CRISP]

Kristeva /kris teévə/, **Julia** (*b.* 1941) Bulgarian-born French psychoanalyst, linguist, and writer. Her early works on linguistics and semiotics appeared in the journal *Tel Quel*, an important forum for post-structuralist pioneers. Her training as a psychoanalyst, completed in 1979, has influenced her later works, including *Desire and Language: A Semiotic Approach to Literature and Art* (1980).

Krivoy Rog /kri vóy rawk/, **Krivoi Rog** city and major iron-producing centre in south-central Ukraine. Population: 715,000 (1998).

KRL *abbr* COMPUT knowledge representation language

kromesky /krə méski/ (*plural* **-kies**) *n* **1.** in Polish or Russian cooking, a thin pancake containing a savoury or sweet filling. The pancake is sometimes coated thinly in egg and breadcrumbs and then deep-fried. **2.** in Polish or Russian cooking, a small fritter or croquette of minced meat or fish wrapped in bacon [Mid-19C. < Polish *kromeczka* 'small slice']

krona[1] /krṓnə/ (*plural* **-nor** /-nawr/) *n* the main unit of Swedish currency. See table at **currency** [Late 19C. < Swedish, 'crown']

krona[2] /krṓnə/ (*plural* **-nur** /-nawr/) *n* the main unit of Faroese currency. See table at **currency** [< Faroese, 'crown']

króna /krṓnə/ (*plural* **-nur** /*pronunc. same*/), **krona** *n* the main unit of Icelandic currency. See table at **currency** [Late 19C. < Icelandic, 'crown']

krone /krṓnə/ (*plural* **-ner** /-nər/) *n* **1.** the main unit of currency in Denmark **2.** the main unit of currency in Norway ▶ see table at **currency** [Late 19C. < Danish, German, 'crown']

Kronecker delta /krónnikər-/ *n* a mathematical function of two variables that takes on only two values, 0 when the variables are unequal, and 1 when the variables are equal [Early 20C. After Leopold *Kronecker* (1823–91), German mathematician]

kroner MONEY plural of **krone**

kronor MONEY plural of **krona**[1]

Kronos *n* MYTHOL another spelling of **Cronus**

Kronstadt /krṓnshtat/, **Kronshtadt** military port on Kotlin Island in the Gulf of Finland, situated in northwestern European Russia. It was founded by Peter I. Population: 40,525 (1995).

kronur MONEY plural of **krona**[2]

krónur MONEY plural of **króna**

kroon /kroon/ (*plural* **kroons** or **krooni** /króoni/) *n* the main unit of Estonian currency. See table at **currency** [Early 20C. < Estonian, 'crown']

Kropotkin /krə pótkin/, **Pyotr Alekseyevich, Prince** (1842–1921) Russian revolutionary. He was a leading theorist of the anarchist movement. He devoted himself to life as a revolutionary, advocating the abolition of governments and the founding of a society based on mutual trust.

Kroto /krṓtō/, **Sir Harold Walter** (*b.* 1939) British chemist. Together with Richard Smalley and Robert Curl, he discovered the family of carbon molecules called fullerenes, and shared the Nobel Prize in chemistry (1996).

kroužek /króozhek/ *n* in Czech, a mark (°) placed over the letter u to indicate the vowel is long. See table at **diacritic** [< Czech]

KRP *symbol* CHESS king's rook's pawn

Krsna-jayanti *n* another spelling of **Krishna Jayanti**

Kru /kroo/ (*plural same* or **Krus**) *n* **1.** a member of an African people inhabiting mainly the coastal regions of Liberia and Côte d'Ivoire **2.** the language of the Kru people, belonging to the Kwa group of Niger-Congo languages. Kru has a large number of different dialects. [Mid-19C. < Kru]

Kruger /króogər/, **Paul** (1825–1904) South African soldier and politician. During his period as president of the Transvaal, South Africa (1883–1902), his discriminatory policies directed at non-Boers led to the Second Boer War (1899–1902). Full name **Kruger, Stephanus Johannes Paulus**

Kruger National Park national park in northeastern South Africa, bordering Mozambique, established in 1926. Area: 19,485 sq. km/7,523 sq. mi.

Krugerrand /króogər rand/ *n* a South African gold coin weighing one ounce, intended mostly to be purchased as an investment [Mid-20C. After Paul KRUGER]

Krugersdorp /króogərz dawrp/ city in Gauteng Province, northeastern South Africa, near Johannesburg. Population: 93,000 (1991 estimate).

kruller *n US* FOOD another spelling of **cruller**

krumhorn *n* MUSIC another spelling of **crumhorn**

krummholz /króom hōlts/ (*plural same*) *n* **1.** stunted trees that grow just above the timberline on a mountain **2.** a high-altitude zone in which krummholz grows [Early 20C. < German, 'crooked wood']

krummhorn *n* MUSIC another spelling of **crumhorn**

Krupp /kroop/, **Alfred** (1812–87) German industrialist and arms manufacturer. He expanded his father's steel-manufacturing business into arms manufacture.

Krupp, Friedrich (1854–1902) German industrialist and arms manufacturer. He was the son of Alfred Krupp. Under his supervision the Krupp empire extended its dealings all over the world.

krypton /kript on, kríptən/ *n* a colourless inert gaseous element, constituting one millionth by volume of the atmosphere. Use: fluorescent lamps, lasers. Symbol **Kr**. See table at **element** [Late 19C. < Greek *krupton* 'hidden']

KStJ *abbr* RELIG Knight of the Order of St John

K selection *n* a process of natural selection that leads to a lowering of the birthrate when the population of a species approaches the maximum number that the environment can sustain [< *K*, the constant for carrying capacity in the population growth equation]

Kshatriya /kshátri ə/ *n* **1.** the second of the four Hindu castes, originally a royal and warrior caste. In modern times its members are professionals, administrators, or military personnel. **2.** a member of a Kshatriya caste [Late 18C. < Sanskrit *kṣatriya* < *kṣatra* 'rule']

kt *abbr* MEASURE, PHYS kiloton

Kt, kt *abbr* CHESS knight

KT *abbr* **1.** Knight (of the Order) of the Thistle **2.** HIST, CHR Knight Templar

Kuala Lumpur /kwaálə lóompoor/ capital of Malaysia, located on the southern Malay Peninsula. Population: 1,297,526 (2000).

Kublai Khan /kóoblī kaán/ (1215–94) Mongol leader and emperor of China. He completed the conquest of China begun by his grandfather Genghis Khan, and founded the Yuan dynasty (1279).

Kubrick /kyóobrik/, **Stanley** (1928–99) US film director. His varied films include *Lolita* (1962), *Dr Strangelove* (1964), *2001: A Space Odyssey* (1968), and *Eyes Wide Shut* (1999).

> 'The great nations have always acted like gangsters, and the small nations like prostitutes.'
> [Stanley Kubrick, *Guardian*; 5 June 1963]

> 'The very meaninglessness of life forces man to create his own meaning. If it can be written or thought, it can be filmed.'
> [Stanley Kubrick, *Halliwell's Filmgoer's and Video Viewer's Companion*; 1999]

kuccha /kúchə/, **kaccha** *n* a pair of short trousers worn by baptized Sikhs as a symbol of religious loyalty [< Punjabi]

kuchen /kóokhən/ (*plural same*) *n* a cake that has been raised with yeast [Mid-19C. < German, 'cake']

Kuching /kóo ching/ city in Malaysia. It is the capital of Sarawak State, on the island of Borneo. Population: 148,059 (1996).

kudos /kyóo doss/ *n* praise, credit, or glory for an achievement (*takes a singular verb*) [Late 18C. < Greek, 'praise, renown']

USAGE Careful writers and speakers avoid the form *kudo*, created in the erroneous belief that ***kudos*** is a plural.

kudu /kóo doo/ (*plural* **-dus** or *same*), **koodoo** (*plural* **-doos** or *same*) *n* a large antelope, the male of which has long spiralling horns. Native to: Africa. Latin name: *Tragelaphus strepsiceros* or *Tragelaphus imberbis*. [Late 18C. Via Afrikaans *koedoe* < Xhosa *i-qudu*]

kudzu /kóod zoo/ *n* a hardy vine that has compound leaves and purplish flowers, and roots that contain a nourishing starch used medicinally. It is an invasive weed in the southeastern United States. Native to: eastern Asia. Latin name: *Pueraria lobata*. [Late 19C. < Japanese *kuzu*]

Kuffar ISLAM plural of **Kaffir** (sense 2) (*slang offensive*)

Kufic /kóofik, kyóo-/, **Cufic** *adj* having an early angular style of Arabic writing used for Koranic manuscripts and inscriptions ■ *n* the Arabic alphabet written in Kufic script [Early 18C. After *Kufa*, ancient city south of Baghdad]

Kufuor /koo fwáwr/, **John** (*b.* 1938) president of Ghana (2001–). A graduate in law at Oxford University and leader of the New Patriotic Party, he served as deputy foreign minister and minister for local government before winning the presidential elections on his second attempt. Full name **Kufuor, John Kofi Agyekum**

kugel /kóog'l/ *n* in Jewish cookery, a savoury pudding often made of noodles or potatoes [Mid-19C. < Yiddish, 'ball' < Middle High German; probably from its traditional mound shape]

Kuiper belt /kīpər-/ *n* a ring of small astronomical objects orbiting through the outer solar system, beyond the farthest planets, Neptune and Pluto. It is believed that the Kuiper belt is a source of comets. [After Gerald Peter (Gerrit Pieter) *Kuiper* (1905–73), Dutch-born US astronomer]

Ku Klux Klan /kóo kluks klán/ *n* **1.** a terrorist secret society organized in the southern United States after the Civil War that used violence and murder to promote its white supremacist beliefs **2.** a white supremacist organization founded in Georgia in 1915. Its secret membership, supremacist views, and

terrorist methods are similar to those of the 19th-century Ku Klux Klan. [Mid-19C. Origin ?]

kukri /koŏkri/ n a large knife with a sharp curved blade that gets broader towards the point, used by the Gurkhas in Nepal for hunting and fighting [Early 19C. < Nepali *khukuri*]

kuku /koŏ koo/ n NZ 1. a large fruit-eating pigeon. Native to: forests of New Zealand. Latin name: *Hemiphaga novaeseelandiae*. 2. a mussel

kukui nut /koŏ koŏ i-/ n Hawaii the nut from the candlenut tree [< Hawaiian]

kukukumu /koŏkoŏ kooma/ (plural **-mus** or same) n NZ FISH same as **gurnard** [Origin ?]

kulak /koŏ lak/ n a wealthy landowning peasant in Russia during the time between the emancipation of the serfs and the Stalinist era [Late 19C. Via Russian, 'fist, tight-fisted person' < Turkic *kol* 'hand']

kulcha /koŏlcha/ n in South Asian cooking, bread made with flour, milk, yeast, and butter, baked in small rounds and usually stuffed with meat or vegetables [< Persian *kulīka*]

kulfi /koŏlfi/ (plural **-fis**) n in South Asian cooking, a rich ice cream [< Hindi *kulfī*]

Kultur /koŏl toŏr/ n German culture, regarded as superior and used as a vehicle of German imperialism during the period of the German Empire and under the Nazi regime [Early 20C. Via German < Latin *cultura* or French *culture* 'culture']

Kulturkampf /koŏl toŏr kampf/ n the struggle between the German government under Bismarck and the Roman Catholic Church over control of education, marriage, and Church appointments. It lasted from 1871 to 1887 and ended in compromise. [Late 19C. < German < *Kultur* 'culture' + *Kampf* 'struggle']

Kumamoto /koŏma mōtō/ city on the west of Kyushu Island, Japan, the capital city of Kumamoto Prefecture. Population: 653,835 (2002).

kumara n ANZ PLANTS, FOOD another spelling of **kumera**

Kumaratunga /koo maǎra toŏngǎ/, **Chandrika** (b. 1945) Sri Lankan politician. The daughter of S.W.R.D. Bandaranaike, she was elected president of Sri Lanka in 1994. Full name **Kumaratunga, Chandrika Bandaranaike**

Kumasi /koo maássi/ capital of the Ashanti Region, central Ghana. It is situated northwest of Accra. Population: 399,300 (1990 estimate). Former name **Coomassie**

kumera /koŏmǎrǎ/ (plural **-as**), **kumara** n NZ same as **sweet potato** [Late 18C. < Maori]

kumiss /koŏmiss/, **koumiss**, **koumis**, **koumyss** n a slightly alcoholic, fermented, and sour-tasting milk from a mare or camel, drunk by some of the peoples of central and western Asia [Late 16C. Via French *koumis*, German *Kumiss*, Polish and Russian *kumys* < Tatar *kumiz*]

kumkum /koŏmkoŏm/ n S Asia a red round decorative mark worn on the forehead by Hindu women and girls, but traditionally not by widows [Mid-20C. < Sanskrit *kuṅkuma* 'saffron']

kümmel /koŏmm'l/, **kummel** n a colourless liqueur or cordial that is flavoured with cumin and caraway seeds and is made primarily in the Baltic region [Mid-19C. < German, 'caraway seed' < Old High German *kumīn* 'cumin']

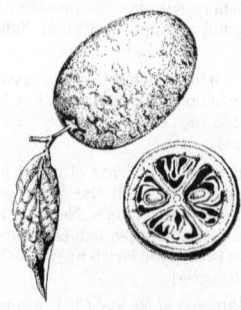
kumquat

kumquat /kúm kwot/, **cumquat** n 1. a small oval orange fruit, related to citrus fruits, with sweet skin and tart flesh, eaten whole or preserved 2. an evergreen

tree related to citrus species that produces kumquats. Native to: China. Genus: *Fortunella*. [Late 17C. < Chinese (Cantonese) *kam kwat* 'gold orange']

Kun /koon/, **Béla** (1886–1939?) Hungarian revolutionary. A Communist, he set up a short-lived Soviet republic in Hungary (1919), and later died during Stalin's purges.

kuna /kŏnǎ/ (plural **-ne** /-ne/) n the main unit of Croatian currency. See table at **currency** [Late 20C. < Serbo-Croatian]

Kuna n, adj LANG another spelling of **Cuna**

kundalini /koŏndǎ leéni/ n vital energy that Hindus believe lies dormant at the base of the spine until it is called into action, e.g. through yoga, to be used in seeking enlightenment [Late 19C. < Sanskrit *kundalinī*, literally 'snake'; because likened to a coiled snake]

Kundera /kúndǎrǎ/, **Milan** (b. 1929) Czech writer. His novels include *The Joke* (1967) and *The Unbearable Lightness of Being* (1984). He moved to France in 1975.

> 'The struggle of man against power is the struggle of memory against forgetting.'
> [Milan Kundera, *The Book of Laughter and Forgetting*; 1982]

> 'Mankind's true moral test, its fundamental test (which lies deeply buried from view) consists of its attitudes toward those who are at its mercy: animals.'
> [Milan Kundera, *The Unbearable Lightness of Being*; 1984]

kundiman /koŏndi man/ n Philippines a love song [< Tagalog]

kune MONEY plural of **kuna**

Kung /koŏong/ (plural same), **!Kung** n 1. a member of a San people who live in eastern Namibia and western Botswana 2. the Khoisan language of the Kung people [Early 20C. < Khoikhoi *!Kung*, literally 'people'] —**Kung** adj

kung fu

kung fu /kúng foŏ, koŏng-/ n a Chinese form of self-defence in which fluid, circular movements of the arms and legs are used to attack an opponent [Late 19C. < Chinese *gongfu*, literally 'merit master']

Kunlun Mountains /koŏn loŏn-/ mountain range in western China. India claims territory in the western area. Height: 7,723 m/25,338 ft. Length: 3,000 km/2,000 mi.

Kunming /koŏn míng/ capital city of Yunnan Province, southwestern China, a trade and transport centre. Population: 1,740,000 (1995).

Kununurra /kúnnǎ núrrǎ/ town in northeastern Western Australia, built in the 1960s to accommodate workers on nearby irrigation schemes. Population: 4,062 (1991).

Kunwinjku /kun wínj koo/ n an Australian Aboriginal language spoken in Arnhem Land and adjacent areas. Native speakers: 960. —**kunwinjku** adj

kunzite /koŏnts īt/ n a reddish-purple semiprecious stone that is a variety of spodumene. Use: gems. [Early 20C. After George F. *Kunz* (1856–1932), US gem expert]

Kuomintang /kwŏmín táng/ n the political party that established China as a republic in 1911, ruled China from 1928 to 1947 until defeated by the Communists, and then withdrew to rule in Taiwan [Early 20C. < Chinese *guómíndǎng* 'national people's party']

Kura /koŏ raá/ river in Transcaucasia, flowing through Turkey, Georgia, and Azerbaijan, and emptying into the Caspian Sea. Length: 1,500 km/940 mi.

kurchatovium /kúrchǎ tōvi ǎm/ n the name given to the element rutherfordium in the former Soviet Union [Mid-20C. After I. V. *Kurchatov* (1903–60), Russian nuclear physicist]

Kurd /kurd/ n a member of a largely Muslim people who live in Southwest Asia, in an area comprising parts of Iraq, Turkey, and Iran [Early 17C. < Kurdish]

kurdaitcha /kǎr dĭchǎ/, **kadaitcha** /kǎ dĭchǎ/ n among Aboriginal peoples of central Australia, a sorcerer who was responsible for avenging the death of a kinsman [Late 19C. < Aboriginal]

Kurdish /kúrdish/ n an Iranian language spoken in Turkey, Iraq, Iran, Armenia, and Syria, belonging to the Indo-Iranian branch of Indo-European languages. Native speakers: 10 million. ■ adj relating to the Kurds, or their language or culture

Kurdistan

Kurdistan /kúrdi staán/, **Kurdistān** region in Southwest Asia, encompassing parts of Turkey, Iraq, Iran, Armenia, and Syria, considered the homeland of the Kurdish people. Population: 26,000,000 (early 1990s).

kurfuffle n another spelling of **kerfuffle** (informal)

kurgan /koor gaán, -gán/ n a burial mound built by a prehistoric culture of eastern Europe and northern Iran [Late 19C. < Russian]

kuri /koŏori/ (plural **-ris**) n NZ 1. MONGREL a mongrel dog 2. EXTINCT DOG a dog belonging to an extinct breed 3. OFFENSIVE TERM an offensive term for somebody who is regarded with dislike [Mid-19C. < Maori]

Kuril Islands /koŏ reél-/, **Kurile Islands** island chain extending from northeastern Hokkaido in Japan to southern Kamchatka Peninsula in Russia. The islands were settled by Russians and Japanese in the 18th century, and are the subject of dispute between the two countries. Population: 25,000 (1990). Area: 15,590 sq. km/6,020 sq. mi.

Kurosawa /koŏrǎ saáwǎ/, **Akira** (1910–98) Japanese film director. He is known for such classic films as *Rashomon* (1950) and *The Seven Samurai* (1954).

> 'In all my films, there's three or maybe four minutes of real cinema.'
> [Akira Kurosawa]

Kuroshio /koŏ rōshi ō/ warm current in the Pacific Ocean, flowing from the Philippines northeastwards along the eastern coast of Japan

kurrajong /kúrrǎ jong/ n a tree that has yellowish or red bell-shaped flowers and yields a tough fibre. Native to: eastern Australia. Latin name: *Brachychiton populneum*. [Early 19C. < Aboriginal]

Kurri Kurri-Weston /kúrri kuri wéstǎn/ urban area in the Hunter Valley region of southeastern New South Wales, Australia. Population: 12,555 (1996).

Kursk /koorsk/ city in western Russia, the capital of Kursk Oblast, and a mining centre. Population: 578,671 (1995).

kurta /koŏrtǎ/ n a long loose collarless shirt worn by some men and women in or from South Asia [Early 20C. < Urdu, Persian *kurtah*]

kurtosis /kər tṓssiss/ (*plural* **-toses** /-tṓsseez/) *n* in statistics, a measure of the extent to which a frequency distribution is concentrated about its mean [Early 20C. < Greek *kurtōsis* 'curvature' < *kurtos* 'bent']

kuru /kŏórroo/ *n* a fatal degenerative disease of the central nervous system similar to Creutzfeldt-Jakob disease that affects some peoples in New Guinea. It is believed to derive from the practice of eating the brains of an ancestor. [Mid-20C. < a dialect of New Guinea, 'trembling']

Kush *n* BIBLE another spelling of **Cush**

Kuskokwim /kúskə kwim/ river in southwestern Alaska, rising in the Alaska Range and flowing into the Bering Sea. Length: 1,170 km/724 mi.

Kutch, Rann of ▶ Rann of Kutch

Kutenai /kŏót'n ay, -ee/ (*plural same* or **-nais**), **Kootenai**, **Kootenay** (*plural same* or **-nays**) *n* **1.** a member of a Native North American people living mainly in Montana, Idaho, and British Columbia **2.** the language of the Kutenai people, which has no known linguistic affiliations. Native speakers: 200. [Early 19C. < Blackfoot *Kotonáai*-] —**Kutenai** *adj*

Kuwait

Kuwait /kŏŏ wáyt/ country in Southwest Asia, at the northwestern tip of the Persian Gulf. It is bordered by Iraq and Saudi Arabia. Language: Arabic. Currency: Kuwaiti dinar. Capital: Kuwait City. Population: 2,183,161 (2003). Area: 17,818 sq. km/6,880 sq. mi. Official name **State of Kuwait** —**Kuwaiti** *n, adj*

Kuwait City capital of Kuwait, in the east of the country, on Kuwait Bay. Population: 28,259 (1995).

kV *abbr* MEASURE kilovolt

kvass /kvaass, kvass/, **kvas**, **quass** *n* an alcoholic drink similar to beer, made in Russia and eastern European countries from rye or barley or from stale bread [Mid-16C. < Russian *kvas*]

kvetch /kvech/ (*informal*) *vi* (**kvetches, kvetching, kvetched**) COMPLAIN INCESSANTLY to grumble and complain about things all the time ▪ *n* **1.** SOMEBODY INCESSANTLY COMPLAINING a constant grumbler or complainer **2.** COMPLAINT a complaint about something [Mid-20C. Via Yiddish *kvetsh* (noun), *kvetshn* (verb) < German *Quetsche* 'crusher', *quetschen* 'to crush']

kw *abbr* **1.** *also* **KW** MEASURE kilowatt **2.** Kuwait (*used in Internet addresses*) See table at **domain name**

Kwa /kwaa/ *n* a group of languages in the Niger-Congo family that are spoken in West Africa, and include Yoruba and Ibo [Mid-19C. < Kwa] —**Kwa** *adj*

kwacha /kwaáchə/ *n* the main unit of currency in Malawi and Zambia. See table at **currency** [Mid-20C. < Bantu, 'dawn']

kwaito /kwī́tō/ *n* a South African style of house music containing features of disco, hip-hop, rhythm and blues, and ragga [Late 20C. < Afrikaans *kwaai* 'bad; hot, kicking']

Kwakiutl /kwaákĭ ŏót'l/ (*plural same* or **-utls**) *n* **1.** a member of a Native North American people who live on Vancouver Island and on the adjacent coast of British Columbia **2.** the Wakashan language of the Kwakiutl people [Mid-19C. < Kwakiutl *Kwáguł*] —**Kwakiutl** *adj*

kwali /kwaáli/ (*plural* **-lis**) *n Malaysia* same as **wok** [< Malay]

Kwangju /kwung jŏó/ city in southwestern South Korea. It is the capital of South Chŏlla Province. Population: 1,334,000 (1998 estimate).

kwanza /kwánzə/ (*plural* **-zas** or *same*) *n* the main unit of Angolan currency. See table at **currency** [Late 20C. < Bantu]

Kwanzaa /kwaánzə/, **Kwanza** *n* a cultural and harvest festival celebrated by African Americans. Date: 26 December to 1 January. [Late 20C. < Kiswahili, literally 'first']

kwashiorkor /kwóshi áwr kawr, kwáshi-/ *n* malnutrition in children caused by inadequate intake of protein, common in impoverished African children weaned onto a cornmeal diet [Mid-20C. < a name in Ghana, 'red boy'; from the symptomatic reddening of the hair]

Kwasniewski /kvash nyéfski/, **Aleksander** (*b.* 1954) Polish politician. A founding member of the Democratic Left Alliance, he has twice been elected president (1995 and 2000).

KwaZulu /kwaá zooloo/ former homeland in South Africa, part of the province of KwaZulu-Natal since 1994

KwaZulu-Natal province in South Africa, in the southeastern part of the country. Capital: Pietermaritzburg. Population: 9,426,018 (2001). Area: 92,100 sq. km/35,560 sq. mi.

kwela /kwáylə/ *n* a style of urban South African pop music [Mid-20C. < Afrikaans]

kWh *abbr* MEASURE kilowatt-hour

KWIC /kwik/ *abbr* COMPUT, LING key word in context

KWIM *abbr* know what I mean (*used in e-mails or text messages*)

Kwinana /kwə naánə/ town in southwestern Western Australia, south of Perth. Population: 22,118 (2002 estimate).

KWOC /kwok/ *abbr* COMPUT key word out of context

kwyjibo /kwí jeé bō/ (*plural* **-bos**) *n* an offensive term for a person who is regarded as being big, clumsy, stupid, and resembling an ape (*slang*) [Late 20C. From its use during a Scrabble game on an episode of the television sitcom 'The Simpsons']

ky *abbr* Cayman Islands (*used in Internet addresses*) See table at **domain name**

kyanise *vt* CONSTR another spelling of **kyanize**

kyanite /kī́ ə nīt/, **cyanite** /sī́ ə-/ *n* a bluish aluminosilicate mineral found in thin-bladed crystals or in masses. Source: metamorphic rocks. Use: gems, refractory. [Late 18C. < Greek *kuan(e)os* 'dark blue']

kyanize /kī́ ə nīz/ (**-nizes, -nizing, -nized**), **kyanise** (**-nises, -nising, -nised**) *vt* to preserve wood against decay by treating it with a corrosive sublimate [Mid-19C. After J. H. *Kyan* (1774–1850), Irish inventor]

kyat /cha/ *n* the main unit of currency in Myanmar. See table at **currency** [Mid-20C. < Burmese]

Kyd /kid/, **Thomas** (1558–94) English playwright. His best known work is *The Spanish Tragedy* (1580?), which established the genre of revenge tragedy.

KYFC *abbr* ONLINE keep your fingers crossed (*used in e-mails or text messages*)

kyle /kīl/ *n Scotland* a narrow passage of water between two areas of land [Mid-16C. < Gaelic *caol* < *caol* 'narrow']

Kyle of Tongue /-túng/ inlet of the sea on the northern coast of Scotland. It is designated a National Scenic Area.

Kyles of Bute stretch of water in the Firth of Clyde, western Scotland, separating the island of Bute from the mainland. It is a National Scenic Area. Area: 119 sq. km/46 sq. mi.

kylie /kī́li/, **kiley** (*plural* **-leys**) *n Aus* a boomerang

that has one convex and one flat side [Mid-19C. < Aboriginal]

kylix /kíliks, kílliks/ (*plural* **-lices** /-li kees/) *n* in ancient Greece, a shallow two-handled cup, often with a footed stem [Mid-19C. < Greek *kulix*]

kymograph /kī́mō graaf, -graf/ *n* a device for recording variations in motion or pressure, e.g. of blood, consisting typically of a stylus and a rotating drum [Mid-19C. < Greek *kuma* 'wave'] —**kymographic** /kī́mō gráffik/ *adj* —**kymography** /kī móggrəfi/ *n*

Kyoto /ki ṓtō/ city on southern Honshu Island, Japan. It is a manufacturing centre and capital of Kyoto Urban Prefecture. Population: 1,387,264 (2002).

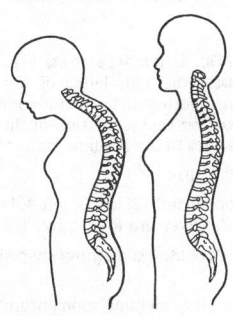

kyphosis

kyphosis /kī fṓssiss/ *n* a permanent curving of the spine that makes somebody look hunched over [Mid-19C. < Greek *kuphōsis* < *kuphos* 'bent'] —**kyphotic** /kī fóttik/ *adj*

Kyprianou /kípri aán oo/, **Spyros** (1932–2002) president of Cyprus (1977–88). He succeeded Archbishop Makarios as president.

Kyrgyz /kúr giz/ (*plural same*), **Kirghiz**, **Kirgiz** *n* **1.** a member of a people living in Kyrgyzstan and Siberia **2.** the Turkic language of the Kyrgyz — **Kyrgyz** *adj*

Kyrgyzstan

Kyrgyzstan /keérgi staan/ country in Central Asia, bordered by Kazakhstan, China, Tajikistan, and Uzbekistan. Language: Kyrgyz, Russian. Currency: som. Capital: Bishkek. Population: 4,892,808 (2003). Area: 198,500 sq. km/76,640 sq. mi. Official name **Kyrgyz Republic**

Kyrie /kírri ay, keéri-/, **Kyrie eleison** /-i láy son/ *n* **1.** a form of prayer that begins with the words 'Lord, have mercy', used in the Roman Catholic, Greek Orthodox, and Anglican churches **2.** a musical setting for the Kyrie, often forming part of a sung Mass [< medieval Latin *Kyrie eleison* < Greek *Kurie eleēson* 'Lord, have mercy']

Kyushu /kyoŏ shoō/, **Kyūshū** southernmost of the four major islands of Japan. Population: 13,269,000 (1990). Area: 36,554 sq. km/14,114 sq. mi.

kz *abbr* ONLINE Kazakhstan (*used in Internet addresses*) See table at **domain name**

l¹ /el/ (*plural* **I's**), **L** (*plural* **L's** or **Ls**) *n* **1.** 12TH LETTER OF ENGLISH ALPHABET the 12th letter of the English alphabet, representing a consonant sound **2.** LETTER 'L' WRITTEN a written representation of the letter 'L' **3.** ROMAN NUMERAL FOR 50 the Roman numeral for 50

l² *abbr* MEASURE litre

l³ *abbr* **1.** GEOG latitude **2.** law **3.** left **4.** length **5.** AVIAT lift **6.** line **7.** MONEY lira **8.** ELEC live (*used on plugs*)

L¹ /el/ (*plural* **L's** or **Ls**) *n* something shaped like a letter 'L'

L² *symbol* **1.** PHYS angular momentum **2.** PHYS inductance (sense 1) **3.** PHYS latent heat **4.** PHYS luminance **5.** ASTRON luminosity

L³ *abbr* **1.** MAPS Lake **2.** large **3.** Latin **4.** *also* **L.** League **5.** AUTOMOT learner **6.** POL **L.** *also* **L.** Liberal **7.** *also* **L.** EDUC Licentiate

L8R *abbr* ONLINE later (*used in e-mails or text messages*)

la¹ /laa, law/ *interj* US used to show surprise or to emphasize what is being said [Late 16C. Natural exclamation]

la² *n* MUSIC another spelling of **lah**

la³ *abbr* ONLINE Laos (*used in Internet addresses*) See table at **domain name**

La *symbol* CHEM ELEM lanthanum

LA *abbr* **1.** legislative assembly **2.** Library Association **3.** local agent **4.** Los Angeles

laager /laágər/, **lager** *n* a camp protected by a circle of wagons or other vehicles, formerly used by the Boers in South Africa ■ *vti* (**-gers, -gering, -gered**) to form wagons or other vehicles into a circle to make a protected camp [Mid-19C. Alteration of obsolete Afrikaans *lager*]

La Argentina /la aárjən teénə/ (1890?–1936) Argentine-born Spanish dancer. She re-established Spanish dancing as a popular art form in the 20th century. Born **Mercé, Antonia**

laari /laári/ (*plural* same or **-ris**), **lari** *n* a subunit of currency in the Maldives. See table at **currency** [Late 20C. Via Divehi < Persian *lārī*, after *Lār*, town north of the Persian Gulf]

lab /lab/ *n* same as **laboratory** (*informal*) [Late 19C. Shortening]

Lab. *abbr* **1.** POL Labour **2.** Labrador

Laban /laában/, **Rudolf von** (1879–1958) Hungarian dancer and choreographer. He devised a method of notating dance movements and founded several dance schools, including the Laban Centre, London.

labanotation /laábə nō táysh'n/ *n* a method of notating dance movements in detail, including the placement of the dancer's body, direction of movement, tempo, and dynamics [Mid-20C. Blend of LABAN + NOTATION]

labarum /lábbərəm/ (*plural* **-ra** /-rə/) *n* a military banner carried before Roman emperors, especially one with Christian symbols that was carried in front of Constantine the Great as a sign of his conversion to Christianity [Early 17C. < late Latin]

labasse /la báss/ *n Carib* a rubbish dump [Late 20C. < French *la basse* 'the flatlands, the shoal, the swampland', after an area near Port-of-Spain, Trinidad, where rubbish is dumped]

labdanum /lábdənəm/, **ladanum** /láddənəm/ *n* a bitter resinous gum extracted from various rockroses. Use: flavourings, perfumes. [Early 16C. < medieval

Latin, alteration of Latin *ladanum* < Greek *lēdanon* < *lēdon* 'mastic']

label /láyb'l/ *n* **1.** INFORMATIVE ITEM ATTACHED TO SOMETHING a piece of paper, fabric, or plastic attached to something to give instructions about it or identify it **2.** DESCRIPTIVE WORD OR PHRASE a word or phrase used to describe a person or group **3.** NAME OF RECORD COMPANY the name of a record company, especially when displayed on a record, CD, or cassette **4.** BRAND a brand name of some items of fashion ○ *always wore designer labels* **5.** IDENTIFIER FOR PART OF COMPUTER PROGRAM a number or word that acts as a unique identifier for a part of a computer program **6.** CHEMICAL IDENTIFIER a substance, usually a radioactive isotope or dye, that can be traced to identify a compound as it undergoes a chemical reaction or assimilation **7.** ARCHIT same as **dripstone** (sense 2) **8.** HERALDIC DESIGN a figure on a heraldic shield consisting of a horizontal band with pendants and identifying the person to whom it belongs as an eldest son ■ *vt* (**-bels, -belling, -belled**) **1.** PUT LABEL ON SOMETHING to attach a label to something as identification or to give instructions **2.** USE DESCRIPTIVE WORD FOR SOMETHING to describe somebody or something using a particular word or phrase ○ *resents being labelled as a troublemaker* **3.** ATTACH CHEMICAL LABEL TO SOMETHING to make a chemical substance identifiable with a marker such as a radioactive isotope or dye [13C. < Old French, 'ribbon, fillet'] —**labeller** *n*

labellum /lə bélləm/ (*plural* **-la** /-lə/) *n* **1.** the petal of an orchid that is its lowest and largest and forms a lip **2.** the lobe at the end of an insect's proboscis that it uses for feeding on liquids [Early 19C. < Latin, 'small lip' < *labrum* 'lip']

labia /láybi ə/ ANAT plural of **labium**

labial /láybi əl/ *adj* **1.** INVOLVING LIPS OR LABIA in, on, close to, or involving the lips or the labia **2.** PRONOUNCED WITH LIPS CLOSED pronounced with the lips closed or nearly closed as, e.g. in the sounds 'b' and 'p' **3.** SOUNDED BY MOVING AIR ACROSS EDGE describes an instrument or organ pipe that produces sound by the movement of air across a sharp edge ■ *n* **1.** SOUND PRONOUNCED WITH LIPS CLOSED a speech sound pronounced with the lips closed or nearly closed as, e.g. in 'b' and 'p' **2.** MUSICAL INSTRUMENT an instrument or organ pipe in which sound is produced by the movement of air across a sharp edge [Late 16C. < medieval Latin *labialis* < Latin *labia* 'lips'] —**labially** *adv*

labialize /láybi ə līz/ (**-izes, -izing, -ized**), **labialise** (**-ises, -ising, -ised**) *vt* to pronounce a sound with the lips rounded —**labialization** /láybi ə lī záysh'n/ *n*

labia majora /-mə jáwrə/ *npl* the two thick outer folds of skin that surround the clitoris, the opening of the urethra, and the opening of the vagina of women and girls [< modern Latin, 'larger lips']

labia minora /-mi náwrə/ *npl* the two small folds of skin that lie immediately inside the labia majora of women and girls and join at the front to form the hood of the clitoris [< modern Latin, 'smaller lips']

labiate /láybi ət, -ayt/ *adj* **1.** WITH DIVIDED SET OF PETALS describes a flower such as a snapdragon that has its set of petals (**corolla**) divided into two unequal and overlapping parts **2.** OF MINT FAMILY belonging to the mint family ■ *n* PLANT OF MINT FAMILY a plant of the mint family. Family: Labiatae. [Early 18C. < modern Latin *labiatus* < Latin *labium* 'lip']

labile /láy bīl, láyb'l/ *adj* **1.** liable to change **2.** readily or frequently undergoing chemical or physical

change ○ *a labile compound* [15C. < late Latin *labilis* 'prone to slip' < Latin *labi* 'to fall']

labio- *prefix* lips, labial ○ *labiodental* [< Latin *labium* 'lip']

labiodental /láybi ō dént'l/ *adj* pronounced with the upper teeth resting on the inside of the lower lip, as in the sounds 'f' and 'v' —**labiodental** *n*

labionasal /láybi ō náyz'l/ *adj* pronounced with the lips closed and the air being pushed through the nose, as in the sound 'm' —**labionasal** *n*

labiovelar /láybi ō veélər/ *adj* pronounced by constricting the back of the mouth and closing the lips, as in the sound 'kw' —**labiovelar** *n*

labium /láybi əm/ (*plural* **-bia** /-bi ə/) *n* **1.** FOLD ROUND WOMEN'S GENITALS a fold that surrounds a woman's or girl's genital organs. There are two inner (**labia minora**) and two outer (**labia majora**) folds. **2.** MOUTHPART OF INSECT a mouthpart of some insects, formed from a fused pair of appendages **3.** LIP OF FLOWER the lower lip of the corolla of a labiate flower **4.** PART LIKE LIP any part that looks or functions like a lip [Late 16C. < Latin, 'lip']

lablab /láb lab/ *n* BOT same as **hyacinth bean** [Early 19C. < Arabic *lablāb*]

labor /láybər/ *n*, *vti* Aus, US another spelling of **labour** —**Labor** *adj*

SYNONYMS See **work**.

Labor *n* the Australian Labor Party ■ *adj* supporting, belonging to, or associated with the Australian Labor Party

laboratory /lə bórrətəri/ (*plural* **-ries**) *n* **1.** a place where research and testing is carried out **2.** a room or place with appropriate equipment for teaching science or doing scientific work [Early 17C. < medieval Latin *laboratorium* 'place for work' < Latin *laborare* 'to work' < *labor* 'toil']

Labor Day *n* **1.** a national holiday in the United States and Canada honouring working people. Date: 1st Monday in September. **2.** Aus another spelling of **Labour Day** (sense 2)

laborious /lə báwri əss/ *adj* **1.** requiring much unwelcome, often tedious effort **2.** showing signs of effort or difficulty rather than naturalness or fluency, especially in speech or writing —**laboriously** *adv* —**laboriousness** *n*

SYNONYMS See **hard**.

Laborite /láybə rīt/ *n* a member or supporter of the Australian Labor Party

labor union *n N Am* POL same as **trade union**

labour /láybər/ *n* **1.** PHYSICAL WORK work done using the strength of the body ○ *sentenced to two years' hard labour* **2.** WORKERS COLLECTIVELY the workers, especially manual workers, in a country, company, or industry considered as a group (*often used before a noun*) ○ *labour relations* **3.** SUPPLY OF WORK the supply of work or workers for a particular job, industry, or employer ○ *outlawed child labour* **4.** PARTICULAR PIECE OF WORK a piece of work of a particular type, especially a difficult or long one (*often used in the plural*) ○ *a labour of love* ○ *the labours of Hercules* **5.** PROCESS OF CHILDBIRTH the process of giving birth to a baby from when the contractions start to the baby's delivery, or the time taken for this process (*often used before a noun*) ○ *labour pains* ■ *v* (**-bours, -bouring, -boured**) **1.** *vi* WORK HARD to work hard,

especially at physical work ○ *laboured all day in the hot sun* **2.** *vi* STRUGGLE TO DO SOMETHING to struggle to do something very difficult or very tiring ○ *laboured over the questions* **3.** *vi* OPERATE WITH DIFFICULTY to have difficulty in running or functioning smoothly, e.g. because of being overloaded or defective (*refers to engines or machines*) **4.** *vi* MOVE WITH DIFFICULTY to move with difficulty or great effort ○ *laboured up to the summit* **5.** *vt* OVEREMPHASIZE SOMETHING to continue trying to express or emphasize something when it is unnecessary ○ *Don't labour the point.* **6.** *vi* GIVE BIRTH to be in the process of giving birth to a baby **7.** *vi* PITCH AND ROLL to pitch and roll heavily at sea (*refers to boats*) [14C. Via French < Latin *labor* 'toil, pain']
◇ **a labour of love** something demanding or difficult that is done just for pleasure rather than for money

CULTURAL NOTE *Love's Labour's Lost*, a play by dramatist William Shakespeare (1594–95). Ferdinand, king of Navarre, and three of his lords agree to forgo the company of women in order to devote themselves to study. The arrival of the Princess of France and three of her ladies upsets their plans, giving rise to lively comedy and witty and poetic dialogue.

SYNONYMS See **work**.

labour under *vt* to be at a disadvantage because of believing something to be true that is not ○ *She had been labouring under the misconception that the problem was solved.*

Labour *n* POL same as **Labour Party** (*takes singular or plural verb*) ■ *adj* supporting, belonging to, or associated with the Labour Party in the United Kingdom or New Zealand

labour camp *n* a prison where the prisoners have to do hard physical work under a harsh, typically cruel, regime

Labour Day *n* **1.** CALENDAR same as **May Day** (sense 2) **2.** in Australia, a public holiday to honour working people. Date: observed by all Australian states, but at different times of year. **3.** in New Zealand, a national public holiday to celebrate the achievement of an eight-hour working day. Date: fourth Monday in October.

laboured /láybərd/ *adj* **1.** done with obvious effort or difficulty ○ *laboured breathing* **2.** lacking natural ease and grace ○ *a laboured speaker*

labourer /láybərər/ *n* somebody who works in a job that requires physical strength and stamina

labour exchange *n* UK same as **Jobcentre** (*dated*)

labour force *n* HR same as **workforce**

labour-intensive *adj* involving a relatively high number of workers or greater costs for labour than for other areas such as materials, machines, or design ○ *a labour-intensive industry*

labourism /láybərizəm/ *n* a political or social movement that upholds the rights of workers, or support for this movement

labourist /láybərist/ *n* a supporter of the rights of workers

Labourite /láybə rīt/ *n* a member or supporter of the Labour Party in the United Kingdom or New Zealand

labour of love *n* something demanding or difficult done for pleasure rather than money

Labour Party *n* **1.** a British political party founded in 1900 to support the rights and interests of working people **2.** a party with similar objectives in another country such as New Zealand

labour-saving *adj* designed or made to require less physical effort

labra ZOOL plural of **labrum**

Labrador[1] /lábbrə dawr/ *n* a large dog with a short thick black, brown, or yellow coat, belonging to a breed originally developed to fetch killed or injured game during a shoot. Labradors were first bred in Newfoundland, Canada, and later imported into the United Kingdom. [Early 20C. After LABRADOR[2]]

Labrador[2] /lábbrə dawr/ mainland portion of Newfoundland, eastern Canada, on the Labrador Sea. It abuts Quebec to the west and south and the Atlantic Ocean on the east. Area: 296,860 sq. km/114,618 sq. mi.

Labrador Current cold ocean current that flows south

past western Greenland and eastern Labrador and Newfoundland, Canada, to join the Gulf Stream

labradorite /lábbrə dáwr īt/ *n* a variety of plagioclase feldspar, the colour of which shifts between blue and green depending on the angle it is seen from [After LABRADOR[2]]

Labrador Peninsula large peninsula in eastern Canada, including much of Quebec and the mainland portion of Newfoundland. Area: 1,619,000 sq. km/625,100 sq. mi.

Labrador retriever *n* BREED same as **Labrador**[1]

Labrador Sea arm of the Atlantic Ocean that separates Labrador in eastern Canada from Greenland and the Atlantic Ocean. It is about 900 km/550 mi. wide.

Labrador tea *n* a low-growing evergreen bush with bell-shaped flowers and leaves that are used in making a tea. Native to: northern North America. Latin name: *Ledum groenlandicum.*

~~labratory~~ incorrect spelling of **laboratory**

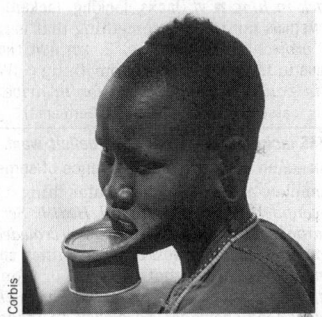
Corbis
labret

labret /láy bret/ *n* an ornament made of bone, shell, steel, or other material that is worn pierced through the lower lip or in the skin just below the lower lip. They are worn by some peoples in East Africa and South America and by people elsewhere who engage in body piercing. [Mid-19C. < Latin *labrum* 'lip']

labrish /lábbrish/ *n* same as **gossip** (*slang*; *used in Black English*) [< *labbermouth* 'boastful person', alteration of BLABBERMOUTH]

labrum /láybrəm, láb-/ (*plural* **-bra** /-brə/) *n* a projecting upper mouthpart of some arthropods [Early 18C. < Latin, 'lip']

Labuan /lə bóō ən, lábyóō ən/ island in Malaysia, off the northern coast of Borneo, northeast of Singapore. Population: 54,307 (1991). Area: 100 sq. km/40 sq. mi.

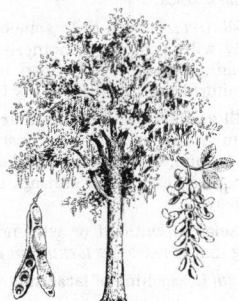
laburnum

laburnum /lə búrnəm/ *n* a tree with poisonous leaves, bark, and seeds. Flowers: yellow, drooping. Native to: Europe, Asia. Genus: *Laburnum.* [Mid-16C. < Latin]

labyrinth /lábbərinth/ *n* **1.** CONFUSING NETWORK a place with a lot of crisscrossing or complicated passages, tunnels, or paths in which it would be easy to become lost **2.** SOMETHING VERY COMPLICATED something that is made up of many different parts that is complicated and hard to understand ○ *a labyrinth of insurance regulations* **3.** ANAT SET OF CONNECTED TUBES a structure consisting of connected cavities or canals, especially the inside of the ear [14C. Directly or via French < Latin *labyrinthus* < Greek *laburinthos*]

Labyrinth *n* in Greek mythology, the maze designed by Daedalus for King Minos of Crete to confine the Minotaur

labyrinth fish *n* a fish with a specialized labyrinthine breathing organ that allows it to breathe air out of water. Family: Anabantidae.

labyrinthine /lábbə rín thīn/, **labyrinthian** /-rínthi ən/ *adj* **1.** consisting of or resembling a labyrinth of passages or paths ○ *a labyrinthine maze of backstreets* **2.** extremely complicated and therefore difficult to understand

labyrinthitis /lábbərin thítiss/ *n* an illness in which the inner ear becomes inflamed, causing a loss of balance and nausea

labyrinthodont /lábbə rínthə dont/ *n* an extinct amphibian resembling the crocodile that lived in the Late Palaeozoic and Early Mesozoic eras. Order: Labyrinthodontia. [Mid-19C. < modern Latin *Labyrinthodontia*, literally 'labyrinth-toothed' < Greek *laburinthos* 'labyrinth']

lac[1] /lak/ *n* a resinous substance secreted by some insects (**lac insects**). Use: formerly, source of shellac. [15C. Via Portuguese *lac(c)a* < Persian *lāk*, Hindi *lākh* < Sanskrit *lākṣā* 'red dye']

lac[2] *n* MEASURE another spelling of **lakh**

LAC *abbr* AIR FORCE leading aircraftman

Lacan /lə ka‑an, lə ka‑aN/, **Jacques** (1901–81) French psychoanalyst. A lifelong advocate of a traditional Freudian approach to psychoanalysis, he published a notoriously difficult collection of papers, *Escrits* (1966), that has had considerable influence on linguistics, critical theory, and psychology. Full name **Lacan, Jacques Marie Émile** —**Lacanian** /lə káyni ən/ *n*, *adj* —**Lacanianism** *n*

'How can we be sure that we are not impostors?'
[Jacques Lacan, *The Four Fundamental Concepts of Psycho-Analysis*; 1977]

laccolith /lákəlith/ *n* a massive intrusion of igneous rock between beds of sedimentary rock, creating a dome-shaped structure [Late 19C. < Greek *lakkos* 'pond, pit'] —**laccolithic** /lákə líthik/ *adj* —**laccolitic** /lákə líttik/ *adj*

Barnaby's
lace

lace /layss/ *n* **1.** DELICATE FABRIC WITH PATTERNED HOLES a delicate fabric made by weaving cotton, silk, or a synthetic yarn in a pattern that leaves small holes between the threads (*often used before a noun*) ○ *a lace shawl* **2.** CORD USED TO TIE EDGES TOGETHER a long cord that is used to tie two parts of a garment, shoe, or boot together and is threaded through holes or around hooks **3.** BRAID ON MILITARY UNIFORMS ornamental gold or silver braid used on military officers' uniforms and hats ■ *vt* (**laces, lacing, laced**) **1.** FASTEN SOMETHING WITH LACES to tie the edges of something with holes or hooks together by threading laces through the holes or round the hooks, pulling the edges close, and knotting the laces **2.** PASS LACE THROUGH HOLES to thread a lace or cord through holes or round hooks **3.** ADD LACE TO SOMETHING to decorate or trim something with lace **4.** ADD ALCOHOL TO DRINK to add a small amount of alcohol or a drug to a drink or to food ○ *eggnog laced with rum* **5.** ADD SMALL AMOUNT TO SOMETHING to add an amount of something to something else to enhance it ○ *an intelligent article laced with wit* **6.** STREAK SOMETHING WITH DIFFERENT COLOUR to mark something with streaks of a different colour **7.** INTERTWINE SOMETHING to intertwine something with something else ○ *laced her fingers together* **8.** BEAT

SOMEBODY to beat or thrash somebody (*informal*) [12C. < Old French *laz* 'net, string' < Latin *laqueus* 'noose']

lace into *vt* **1.** to fasten a corset or close-fitting garment around somebody by lacing it up **2.** to attack somebody verbally or physically (*informal*)

lace up *vt* to fasten or tighten the laces of something such as a boot or corset

lace bug *n* a small insect with a delicate lacy vein pattern on its wings. Family: Tingitidae.

Lacedaemonian /lássədi mőni ən/ *adj* relating to the ancient Greek city of Sparta [Mid-16C. < Latin *Lacedaemonius*, Greek *Lakedaimonios* 'of Lacedaemon (an ancient region)'] —**Lacedaemonian** *n*

lace pillow *n* **HANDICRAFT** same as **cushion** *n* (sense 7)

lacerate *vt* /lássə rayt/ (**-ates, -ating, -ated**) **1.** **CUT SKIN JAGGEDLY** to cut or gash the skin so that the wound is deep with irregular edges **2.** **CAUSE SOMEBODY DEEP DISTRESS** to distress somebody deeply or agonizingly ■ *adj* /lássərət/ **WITH JAGGED EDGES** describes leaves or petals that have jagged or irregular edges [15C. < Latin *lacerat-*, past participle of *lacerare* 'tear to pieces' < *lacer* 'torn'] —**laceration** /lássə ráysh'n/ *n*

lacerating /lássə rayting/ *adj* **1.** causing intense emotional or physical distress ○ *lacerating criticism* ○ *lacerating pain* **2.** cutting or gashing the skin in a way that leaves a deep jagged wound

lacers /láysserz/ *npl regional* shoe or boot laces (*informal*)

Lacerta /lə súrtə/ *n* a small constellation of the northern hemisphere. See illustration at **constellation** [Late 18C. < Latin, 'lizard']

lacertid /lə súrtid/ *n* a lizard with rough irregular scales and bony plates on its skull, e.g. the common wall lizard or green lizard. Family: Lacertidae. [Late 19C. < Latin *lacerta* 'lizard']

lace-up *n* a shoe or boot that fastens with laces —**lace-up** *adj*

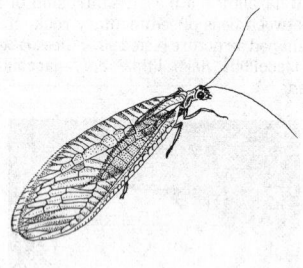

lacewing

lacewing /láyss wing/ *n* an insect with transparent wings and long antennae whose larvae feed on aphids and other insect pests. There are several species of lacewing, including the green lacewing and the brown lacewing. Superfamily: Hemerobioidea. [< the fine network of veins in its wings, likened to lace]

laches /láchiz, láy-/ *n* negligence or delay in doing something, especially in pursuing a legal claim [14C. < Anglo-Norman *laches(se)* 'negligence' < Old French *lasche* 'lazy' < Latin *laxus* 'loose']

Lachesis /lákississ/ *n* in Greek mythology, one of the three Fates who influenced human destiny. She determined the extent of the thread of life that was spun and cut by the other two.

Lachine /la sheen/ city in southern Quebec Province, Canada, on Montreal Island in the St Lawrence River. Population: 40,222 (2002).

Lachlan /láak lən/ river in south-central New South Wales, Australia. Length: 1,484 km/922 mi.

lachrymal /lákrim'l/ *adj* **1.** relating to tears or weeping (*literary*) **2.** **ANAT** same as **lacrimal** [Variant of LACRIMAL]

lachrymal bone *n* a small trangular bone of a pair that form part of the eye socket

lachrymation, etc. *n* **PHYSIOL** another spelling of **lacrimation, etc.**

lachrymatory /lákrimətəri, lákri máytəri/ *n* (*plural* **-ries**) a small bottle of a kind found in ancient tombs, thought in the past to have contained the tears of

mourners ■ *adj* **PHYSIOL** same as **lacrimatory** [Mid 17C. < Latin *lacrima* 'tear', after *chrismatory* 'vessel for the chrism']

lachrymose /lákrimōss, -mōz/ *adj* (*literary*) **1.** crying or tending to cry easily and often **2.** so sad as to make people cry [Early 18C. < Latin *lacrimosus* < *lacrima* 'tear'] —**lachrymosely** *adv* —**lachrymosity** /lákri móssəti/ *n*

lacing /láyssing/ *n* a beating or thrashing (*informal*)

laciniate /lə sínni ət, -ayt/, **laciniated** /-aytid/ *adj* describes a leaf that has a fringed, jagged, or lobed border [Mid-17C. < Latin *lacinia* 'fringe'] —**laciniation** /lə sínni áysh'n/ *n*

lac insect *n* an insect, the female of which secretes a substance (**lac**) that was formerly used to make shellac. Native to: South Asia. Latin name: *Laccifer lacca*.

lack /lak/ *n* **1.** **SHORTAGE** a complete absence of a particular thing ○ *Lack of sleep makes it difficult to concentrate.* **2.** **SOMETHING ABSENT** something that is needed but is in short supply or missing ○ *Courage is a lack in him.* ■ *vt* (**lacks, lacking, lacked**) **1.** **NOT HAVE SOMETHING** not to have something that is needed ○ *The project lacked funding.* **2.** **NOT HAVE ENOUGH OF SOMETHING** to have too little of something ○ *What he lacks in patience, he makes up for in drive.* [13C. Probably < assumed Old English *lac* < Germanic]

SYNONYMS *lack, shortage, deficiency, deficit, want, dearth*

CORE MEANING: an insufficiency or absence of something

lack a complete absence of a particular thing ○ *public lack of confidence in the National Health Service* ○ *The conditions are substandard and overcrowded, and there is a total lack of the most basic amenities.* **shortage** an absence of something that is needed or required ○ *a shortage of skilled labour* ○ *The drought is likely to cause severe food shortages.* **deficiency** an inadequate supply of something necessary, especially a nutrient, or a weakness in the provision or performance of something ○ *A diet of fast food and snacks can lead to nutritional deficiencies.* ○ *We accept responsibility for any deficiencies in the services we are contractually obliged to provide.* **deficit** the amount by which a total is less than it should be ○ *How does the government intend to cut the budget deficit without raising taxes?* ○ *Despite reducing the deficit to only one goal before the break, the home side was eventually beaten 3–1.* **want** or **dearth** an absence or scarcity of something ○ *exhausted from overwork and want of sleep* ○ *There is still a considerable dearth of knowledge on this disease.*

lackadaisical /lákə dáyzik'l/ *adj* without much enthusiasm, energy, or effort [Mid-18C. < *lackadaisy* 'alas', alteration of LACKADAY] —**lackadaisically** *adv*

lackaday /lákə day/ *interj* used to express regret, disapproval, or dismay (*archaic*) [Late 17C. Shortening of *alack-a-day* < ALACK]

lackey /láki/ (*plural* **-eys**) *n* **1.** somebody who is excessively willing to obey another's orders **2.** a man servant, especially a footman or valet who wears a uniform (*archaic*) [Early 16C. < French *laquais*]

lackey moth *n* a moth whose caterpillars are striped and live in a web on a tree or bush. Native to: England, Ireland. Latin name: *Malacosoma neustria*. [< the caterpillar's striped markings, suggestive of a footman's livery]

lacking /láking/ *adj* without or with not enough of something that is needed ○ *lacking in good taste*

lackluster *adj* US spelling of **lacklustre**

lacklustre /lák lustər/ *adj* lacking energy, excitement, enthusiasm, or passion

Laconia /lə kőni ə/ region in ancient Greece that occupied much of the Peloponnese. The capital city was Sparta.

laconic /lə kónnik/, **laconical** /lə kónnik'l/ *adj* using very few words [Mid-16C. Via Latin < Greek *Lakōnikos* 'of Laconia, Spartan'; from the reputation of Spartans for terseness] —**laconically** *adv*

laconism /lákənizəm/, **laconicism** /lə kónnissizem/ *n* **1.** the use of very few words **2.** something that is said in few words but is full of meaning [Late 16C. < Greek *lakōnismos* 'imitation of Spartan manners' < *Lakōn* 'Laconia']

La Coruña /la ko roónya/ city, port, and capital of La Coruña Province, in the autonomous region

of Galicia, northwestern Spain. Population: 236,371 (2002).

lacquer /lákər/ *n* **1.** **VARNISH** a varnish made from the sap of an eastern Asian tree. Use: protective coating, especially for wood. **2.** **GLOSSY SYNTHETIC COATING** a hard, glossy, clear or coloured coating made up of resins or cellulose derivatives and a plasticizer in a volatile solvent **3.** **HAIR** same as **hairspray** (*dated*) **4.** **ORNAMENTAL WOODEN OBJECTS** ornamental objects made of wood and coated with lacquer [Late 16C. < obsolete French *lacre* 'sealing wax', alteration of Portuguese *la(c)ca* (see LAC [1])] —**lacquer** *vt*

lacquer tree *n* a poisonous sumach tree whose sap is used to make lacquer. Native to: Southeast Asia. Latin name: *Rhus verniciflua*.

AKG London

lacquerware: Japanese lacquered box (1890)

lacquerware /lákər wair/, **lacquerwork** /-wurk/ *n* ornamental objects, usually of wood, that have been coated with lacquer and sometimes inlaid

lacrimal /lákrim'l/ *adj* **1.** relating to the glands that produce tears, or the ducts through which they drain **2.** **LITERAT** same as **lachrymal** (sense 1) [15C. < medieval Latin *lacrimalis* < Latin *lacrima* 'tear']

lacrimal duct *n* the passage carrying tears into the nose

lacrimal gland *n* a gland in the outer corner of the eye that produces tears

lacrimation /lákri máysh'n/, **lachrymation** *n* the production of tears in the eyes, especially excessive production as in crying or in reaction to a foreign body [Late 16C. < Latin *lacrimation-* < *lacrimat-*, past participle of *lacrimare* 'shed tears' < *lacrima* 'tear']

lacrimator /lákri maytər/, **lachrymator** *n* a substance that makes tears form in the eyes, e.g. tear gas [Early 20C. < Latin *lacrimat-* (see LACRIMATION)]

lacrimatory /lákrimətəri, -máytəri/ *adj* causing the eyes to produce tears [Mid 19C. Variant of LACHRYMATORY]

Popperfoto

lacrosse

lacrosse /lə króss/ *n* a sport in which two teams of ten players use sticks with a net pouch (**crosse**) at one end to throw and catch a small hard rubber ball. The aim is to score a goal by throwing the ball into the opposing team's goal net. Lacrosse was originated by Native North Americans. (*often used before a noun*) ○ *a lacrosse stick* [Early 18C. < Canadian French *(jeu de) la crosse* '(game of) the hooked stick' < Germanic]

lact- *prefix* same as **lacto-** (*used before vowels*)

lactalbumin /lak tálbyoōmin/ *n* a milk protein that contains all the essential amino acids

lactase /lák tayss, -tayz/ *n* an intestinal enzyme that

breaks down lactose into glucose and galactose [Late 19C. < LACTOSE]

lactate[1] /lak táyt, lák tayt/ (**-tates, -tating, -tated**) *vi* to produce milk in the body (*refers to female mammals*) [Late 19C. Back-formation < LACTATION]

lactate[2] /lák tayt/ *n* a chemical compound that is a salt or ester of lactic acid [Late 18C. < LACTIC]

lactation /lak táysh'n/ *n* **1.** the production of milk by the mammary glands **2.** the period during which milk is produced by the mammary glands [Mid-17C. Directly or via French < late Latin *lactation-* < Latin *lactare* 'suckle' < *lact-* 'milk'] —**lactational** *adj*

lacteal /lákti əl/ *adj* **1.** OF MILK relating to milk or milk production **2.** ANAT CARRYING MILKY FLUID carrying or containing a milky fluid (**chyle**) ○ *a lacteal vessel* ■ *n* ANAT LYMPHATIC VESSEL a lymphatic vessel that originates in the small intestine and carries a milky fluid (**chyle**) to the thoracic duct [Mid-17C. < Latin *lacteus* 'of milk' < *lact-* 'milk'] —**lacteally** *adv*

lactescent /lak téss'nt/ *adj* **1.** describes plants and insects that secrete a milky substance **2.** looking like milk, or becoming milky [Mid-17C. < Latin *lactescent-*, present participle of *lactescere* 'turn to milk' < *lactere* 'be milky' < *lact-* 'milk'] —**lactescence** *n*

lactic /láktik/ *adj* relating to or derived from milk [Late 18C. < Latin *lact-* 'milk']

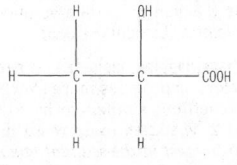

lactic acid

lactic acid *n* a colourless organic acid produced by muscles and found in sour milk. Use: preservative, in dyeing, manufacture of adhesives and pharmaceuticals. Formula: $C_3H_6O_3$.

lactiferous /lak tíffərəss/ *adj* **1.** describes a body part that carries or produces milk, or is capable of producing milk ○ *a lactiferous duct* **2.** describes a plant that produces a milky juice (**latex**) [Late 17C. < Latin *lact-* 'milk'] —**lactiferousness** *n*

lacto- *prefix* **1.** milk ○ *lactometer* **2.** lactic acid ○ *lactobacillus* **3.** lactose ○ *lactase* [< Latin *lact-* 'milk']

lactobacillus /láktō bə sílləss/ (*plural* **-li** /-lī/) *n* a rod-shaped bacterium that produces lactic acid through fermentation. Genus: *Lactobacillus*.

lactoflavin /láktō fláyvin/ *n* BIOCHEM same as **riboflavin**

lactogenic /láktō jénnik/ *adj* causing the mammary glands to produce milk

lactoglobulin /láktō glóbbyoŏolin/ *n* one of a group of globular proteins that occur in milk

lactometer /lak tómmitər/ *n* an instrument that is used to measure the density of milk. It is a kind of hydrometer.

lactone /láktōn/ *n* a chemical compound belonging to a group derived from hydroxy acids, often occurring as the odour-bearing component of a plant product —**lactonic** /lak tónnik/ *adj*

lactoprotein /láktō prōt een/ *n* a protein that is present in milk

lactose /lák tōss, -tōz/ *n* **1.** a sugar (**disaccharide**) composed of glucose and galactose. Source: milk. Formula: $C_{12}H_{22}O_{11}$. **2.** a white crystalline form of lactose. Source: whey. Use: in food products and pharmaceuticals. Formula: $C_{12}H_{22}O_{11}$.

lactovegetarian /láktō véjjə táiri ən/ *n* somebody who eats vegetables, grains, fruit, nuts, and milk products but not meat or eggs

lactulose /láktyoŏ lōss, -lōz/ *n* a synthetic sugar that is broken down by bacteria in the colon into products that draw water and ammonia into the colon. Use: treatment of constipation and symptoms

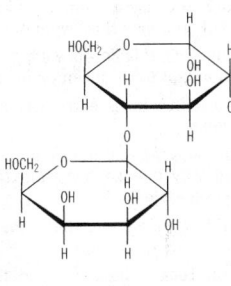

lactose

of liver disease. [Mid-20C. < LACTO-, probably after CELLULOSE]

lacuna /lə kyoónə/ (*plural* **-nae** /-nee/ or **-nas**) *n* **1.** a gap or place where something is missing, e.g. in a manuscript or a line of argument (*literary*) **2.** ANAT a small cavity, e.g. in bone or cartilage [Mid-17C. < Latin, 'hole' < *lacus* 'pond'] —**lacunal** *adj*

lacunar /lə kyoónər/ *n* **1.** CEILING WITH SUNKEN PANELS a ceiling that has sunken panels in it **2.** SUNKEN PANEL IN CEILING a decorative sunken panel in a ceiling ■ *adj* OF BODILY CAVITIES relating to pits or cavities in tissue, e.g. in bone or cartilage, especially ones that are atypical [Late 17C. < Latin < *lacuna* (see LACUNA)]

lacustrine /lə kúss trīn/ *adj* **1.** relating to lakes **2.** growing, living, or formed in or at the edge of a lake [Early 19C. < Latin *lacus* 'lake']

LACW *abbr* AIR FORCE leading aircraftwoman

lacy /láyssi/ (**-ier, -iest**) *adj* **1.** made of or decorated with lace **2.** having the appearance of lace ○ *lacy clouds* —**lacily** *adv* —**laciness** *n*

lad /lad/ *n* **1.** YOUNG MAN a boy or young man **2.** MAN a man of any age (*informal*) **3.** MAN WHO LOOKS AFTER HORSES a man whose job is to look after horses in a stable ○ *The head lad accompanies the horses when they go racing.* ■ **lads** *npl* MAN'S MALE FRIENDS the group of male friends or colleagues that a man socializes with [13C. Origin ?] ◇ **a bit of a lad** used in an affectionate way to describe a man who has a lively, even irresponsible, lifestyle

CULTURAL NOTE *A Shropshire Lad*, a collection of verse (1896) by poet A. E. Housman. Although they express a pessimistic world-view, these short poems about life in rural England are much loved for their sensitive handling of universal themes (the passing of time, the fleeting nature of existence, the trials and disappointments of life), as well as the poet's craftsmanship and musicality.

Ladakh /lə dáak/ dry mountainous region of NW India, Pakistan, and China. It is one of the highest inhabited regions of the world.

Ladakhi /lə dáaki/ *n* **1.** somebody who was born or brought up in Ladakh **2.** the form of Tibetan spoken in Ladakh [Mid-19C. < Tibetan] —**Ladakhi** *adj*

ladanum *n* INDUST same as **labdanum**

ladder /láddər/ *n* **1.** DEVICE WITH RUNGS TO CLIMB ON a portable piece of equipment with rungs fixed to sides made of metal, wood, or rope, used for climbing up or down **2.** PATH TO ADVANCEMENT a series of hierarchical levels on which somebody moves up or down within an organization or society ○ *working her way up the corporate ladder* **3.** LINE OF MISSING STITCHES IN TIGHTS a vertical line of stitches that have come undone in tights, a stocking, or a knitted garment, leaving only the horizontal stitches in place **4.** LIST OF RANKED PLAYERS a list of contestants in an ongoing sports or games competition, arranged according to ability ■ *vti* (**-ders, -dering, -dered**) DAMAGE TIGHTS OR OTHER GARMENT to damage tights, a stocking, or a knitted garment so that a line of vertical stitches have come undone, leaving only the horizontal stitches, or develop a ladder in this way [Old English *hlæd(d)er* < Indo-European, 'to lean']

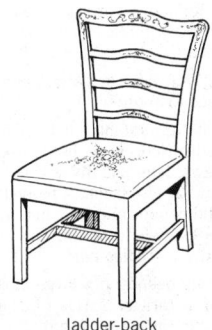

ladder-back

ladder-back *n* **1.** a chair with a back formed by horizontal slats between the two vertical parts that form the sides **2.** the tall back of a ladder-back chair —**ladder-back** *adj*

ladder tournament *n* a tournament based on a list of ranked players in a game or sport, in which each player may challenge any other player who is ranked one or two positions higher

laddie /láddi/ *n* a boy or young man (*informal*)

laddish /láddish/ *adj* conforming to a popular stereotype of male behaviour that includes an absorbing interest in sport and drinking alcohol, and a tendency to display sexist attitudes towards women (*informal*) —**laddishly** *adv* —**laddishness** *n*

laddism /láddizəm/ *n* the attitudes and behaviour of or associated with men, especially young men, who have an absorbing interest in sport, drinking alcohol, and sex

laddu /lúddoo/, **laddoo** (*plural* **-doos**), **ladoo** (*plural* **-oos**) *n* in South Asian cooking, a dessert made by frying a mixture of flour, sugar, and shortening, and then shaping it into a ball [< Hindi *laḍḍu*]

lade[1] /layd/ (**lades, lading, laded, laden** /láyd'n/ or **laded**) *v* **1.** *vti* PUT CARGO ON SHIP to take on cargo or freight, or load a ship with cargo or freight **2.** *vti* REMOVE LIQUID WITH LADLE to remove a measure of liquid using a ladle **3.** *vt* BURDEN SOMETHING OR SOMEBODY to place a load on something or a heavy burden on somebody (*dated*) [Old English *hladan* < Germanic]

lade[2] /layd/ *n* Scotland a stream, especially a mill-stream ○ *A wee boy was fishing in the lade.* [Early 18C. Probably variant of LEAD[1]]

la-de-da *adj* another spelling of **la-di-da**

~~ladel~~ incorrect spelling of **ladle**

laden /láyd'n/ past participle of **lade**[1] ■ *adj* **1.** carrying a load, usually a heavy load (*often used in combination*) ○ *He was laden down with shopping bags.* ○ *fruit-laden boughs* **2.** weighed down by a problem or an unpleasant feeling such as doubt or unhappiness ○ *laden with guilt*

Laden ♦ **Bin Laden, Osama**

ladette /la dét/ *n* a young woman with a lifestyle that is more characteristic of that of some young men, usually involving heavy drinking and boisterous behaviour (*informal*)

la-di-da /láa dee dáa/, **lah-di-dah**, **la-de-da** *adj* speaking or behaving in a way that is affectedly upper-class (*informal*) [Late 19C. An imitation of affected pronunciation]

ladies /láydiz/ *n* a women's public toilet (*informal*; *takes a singular verb*) ○ *I think she went to the ladies.* N Am term **ladies room**

ladies' fingers *npl* FOOD same as **okra** (sense 1)

ladies' gallery *n* an area of the public gallery of the UK House of Commons that is restricted to women only

ladies' man, lady's man *n* a man who enjoys being with women and flirting with them (*informal*)

ladies room, ladies' room *n* N Am same as **ladies**

ladies' tresses, lady's tresses *n* an orchid with slender spiral spikes of small white flowers. Genus: *Spiranthes*.

ladify *vt* another spelling of **ladyfy** (*offensive*)

Ladin /la deén/ *n* a language spoken in some valleys in northern Italy, belonging to the Rhaeto-Romance

subgroup of Romance languages. Native speakers: 25,000. [Mid-19C. Via Rhaeto-Romance < Latin *Latinus* (see LATIN)] —**Ladin** *adj*

lading /láyding/ *n* freight or cargo being transported from one place to another

Ladino /lə deenō/ (*plural* **-nos**) *n* **1.** a language based on Spanish with Hebrew elements, spoken by some Sephardic Jews. It is usually written in a form of Hebrew script. **2.** *also* **ladino** somebody of partially Spanish or indigenous ancestry in Central America who speaks Spanish [Late 19C. Via Spanish < Latin *Latinus* (see LATIN)] —**Ladino** *adj*

ladino clover /lə deenō-/ *n* a large variety of white clover grown as forage. Native to: North America. [Via Italian < Latin *Latinus* (see LATIN)]

ladle /láyd'l/ *n* a spoon with a long handle and a deep bowl, used to serve soup and other liquids ■ *vt* (**-dles, -dling, -dled**) to serve food such as soup onto a plate using a ladle [Old English *hlædel* < *hladan* (see LADE[1])]

ladle out *vt* to give out generous or overgenerous amounts of something, especially something intangible (*informal*) ○ *ladled out praise*

lad mag *n* a magazine containing articles, illustrations, and advertisements that appeal to young men who are chiefly interested in sport, alcohol, and sex (*informal*)

Ladoga, Lake /láadəgə/ largest lake in Europe, in northwestern Russia, northeast of St Petersburg. Its outlet is the River Neva, which connects it with the Gulf of Finland. Area: 18,390 sq. km/7,100 sq. mi.

ladoo *n* FOOD another spelling of **laddu**

lad's love *n* PLANTS same as **southernwood**

lady /láydi/ (*plural* **-dies**) *n* **1.** WOMAN a woman, especially when addressed as part of a group ○ *Ladies and gentlemen, please take your seats.* **2.** ARISTOCRATIC WOMAN an upper-class woman **3.** POLITE DIGNIFIED WOMAN a woman who behaves very politely and with dignity **4.** WIFE OR USUAL WOMAN COMPANION a man's wife or usual woman companion (*informal*) **5.** WOMAN FEUDAL SUPERIOR in medieval Europe, a woman who was a powerful land or property owner with authority over an area, castle, or community such as a manor **6.** DRUGS same as **cocaine** (*slang*) [Old English *hlæfdīge* 'bread-kneader' < *hlāf* 'bread', earlier form of LOAF[1]]

Lady *n* **1.** TITLE FOR WOMAN used as an alternative title for a marchioness, countess, viscountess, or baroness **2.** COURTESY TITLE FOR WOMAN used as a courtesy title for the daughter of an earl, marquess, or duke **3.** FORM OF ADDRESS FOR WOMAN used as a form of address for the wife of a viscount, earl, marquess, baron, baronet, or knight, and the daughter of a duke, marquess, or earl

ladybird /láydi burd/ *n* a small round flying beetle that has red or orange outer wings with black spots. It eats aphids and other insects. Family: Coccinellidae. N Am term **ladybug**

Lady Bountiful *n* a woman who makes generous and well-publicized charitable donations

ladybug /láydi bug/ *n* N Am same as **ladybird**

lady-candlestick *n* N England PLANTS same as **cowslip** (*informal*)

Lady Chapel, **lady chapel** *n* a chapel dedicated to Mary, mother of Jesus Christ, that is inside a cathedral or church

Lady Day *n* the day in the Christian calendar on which the feast of the Annunciation is celebrated, used as a quarter day in England, Wales, and Ireland. Date: 25 March.

lady fern *n* a large, delicate fern with bipinnate fronds. Native to: Great Britain. Latin name: *Athyrium filix-femina*. [< its delicate appearance]

ladyfinger /láydi fing gər/ *n* N Am a small finger-shaped sponge cake, several of which are often used to surround moulded desserts

ladyfish /láydi fish/ (*plural same* or **-fishes**) *n* **1.** a large silvery sea fish, related to the tarpon and prized as a game fish. Native to: tropics. Latin name: *Elops saurus*. **2.** US FISH same as **bonefish**

ladyfriend /láydi frend/ *n* a man's woman companion (*informal humorous; sometimes considered offensive*)

ladyfy /láydi fī/ (**-fies, -fying, -fied**), **ladify** *vt* an offensive term meaning to cause a woman or girl to affect the manners of an upper-class woman —**ladyfied** *adj*

lady-in-waiting (*plural* **ladies-in-waiting**) *n* a woman who is an attendant for a queen or princess

lady-killer *n* a man who is extremely attractive to women (*informal*)

ladylike /láydi līk/ *adj* behaving or done in a polite and dignified way ○ *not a very ladylike thing to whine* —**ladylikeness** *n*

ladylove /láydi luv/ *n* a woman that a man is in love with (*dated*)

lady luck, **Lady Luck** *n* luck or good fortune personified as a woman (*informal; sometimes considered offensive*)

Lady Mayoress, **lady mayoress** *n* the wife of a Lord Mayor

Lady Muck *n* an offensive term for a woman who is thought to have an exaggerated sense of her own importance (*informal*)

lady of the evening *n* US same as **prostitute** (*dated*)

Lady of the Lake *n* in Arthurian legend, a supernatural woman, sometimes considered to be the same person as Vivian, the lover of Merlin

lady of the night *n* same as **prostitute** (*dated*)

lady's bedstraw *n* a wild plant with narrow leaves. Flowers: small, yellow, in clusters. Native to: Europe, Asia. Latin name: *Gallium verum*.

Ladyship /láydi ship/, **ladyship** *n* a title used when addressing or referring to a woman with the title of 'Lady'

lady slipper *n* PLANTS same as **lady's slipper**

lady's maid *n* a woman who serves another woman, looking after her and her clothes and accessories

lady's man *n* same as **ladies' man**

lady's mantle *n* a low-growing plant of the rose family. Flowers: small, yellow-green, in clusters. Genus: *Alchemilla*. [< the round shape of its leaves]

Ladysmith /láydi smith/ town in KwaZulu-Natal Province, eastern South Africa. It was the scene of a famous siege (1899–1900) during the Boer War. Population: 25,102 (1985).

lady's slipper

lady's slipper, **lady slipper** *n* a wild orchid. Flowers: various colours, including pink, purple, yellow, resembling slippers. Native to: North America. Genus: *Cypripedium*.

lady's smock *n* PLANTS same as **cuckooflower**

lady's tresses *n* PLANTS same as **ladies' tresses**

Laënnec /la énnek/, **René** (1781–1826) French physician. He invented the stethoscope, and was a pioneer of thoracic medicine.

Laertes /lay úr teez/ *n* in Greek mythology, the father of Odysseus

laev- *prefix* another spelling of **laevo-** (*used before vowels*)

laevo- *prefix* **1.** leftwards, anticlockwise ○ *laevorotation* **2.** laevorotatory ○ *laevulose* [< French *lévo-* < Latin *laevus* 'left']

laevorotation /leevō rō táysh'n/ *n* a rotation to the left or anticlockwise, especially of the plane of polarized light

laevorotatory /leevō rō táytəri, -rótətəri/ *adj* **1.** turning or circling in a anticlockwise direction or to the

left **2.** turning the plane of polarized light in an anticlockwise direction

laevulose /lévvyoo lōss, -lōz/ *n* BIOCHEM same as **fructose** [Late 19C. < LAEVO- + -ULE]

Lafayette /lá fī ét/, **Marie Joseph Paul Yves Roch Gilbert du Motier, Marquis de** (1757–1834) French soldier and politician. He fought against the British in the War of American Independence, and then took part in the French Revolution. He became a member of the French post-revolutionary government.

La Fayette /lá fī ét/, **Marie Madeleine, Comtesse de** (1634–93) French novelist. She wrote the romances *Zaïde* (1670) and *La princesse de Clèves* (1678). Known as **La Fayette, Madame de**

laff /laaf/ *n* same as **laugh** (*nonstandard; often used ironically*) ○ *a lot of tasteless laffs* [Late 20C. Respelling]

Laffer curve /láffər-/ *n* a graph summarizing the fact that tax revenues are low for very high and for very low tax rates, thus demonstrating that raising tax rates beyond an optimum point will discourage investment and decrease tax revenues [Late 20C. After Arthur B. *Laffer* (b. 1942), US economist]

Laforgue /la fáwrg/, **Jules** (1860–87) Uruguayan-born French symbolist poet. The free verse and strikingly modern imagery of his poetry, e.g. *Les Complaintes* (Laments; 1885), influenced many 20th-century poets, including T. S. Eliot and Ezra Pound.

> 'O what an everyday business life is!'
> [Jules Laforgue, 'Complainte sur certains ennuis (Lament on certain vexations)', *Les Complaintes* (Laments); 1885]

lag[1] /lag/ *v* (**lags, lagging, lagged**) **1.** *vi* FALL BEHIND OTHERS to go, develop, or progress more slowly than somebody or something similar so as to fall back or fall behind **2.** *vi* SLACKEN to decrease in strength or intensity ○ *Interest in the scandal has never lagged.* **3.** *vi* DECIDE ORDER OF PLAY in billiards, to decide who is to play first by having each player rebound a ball from the top cushion as close as possible to the hand rail **4.** *vt* TOSS SOMETHING AT TARGET to pitch or shoot something such as a coin or marble at a target ■ *n* **1.** PERIOD BETWEEN EVENTS a period of time between one event and a related event **2.** POSITION OF HAVING FALLEN BEHIND the condition or an instance of having fallen behind **3.** LAGGING IN BILLIARDS in billiards, an act or instance of lagging [Early 16C. Origin ?]

lag[2] /lag/ *vt* (**lags, lagging, lagged**) to insulate something such as a pipe or hot water tank with lagging to prevent freezing or heat escaping ■ *n* a strip of wood, e.g. a stave of a barrel or a lath [Late 17C. Probably < N Germanic]

lag[3] /lag/ *n* (*slang*) **1.** PRISONER a current or former prisoner **2.** IMPRISONMENT a period of imprisonment ■ *vt* (**lags, lagging, lagged**) IMPRISON SOMEBODY to arrest somebody, or put somebody in prison (*dated slang*) [Late 16C. Origin ?]

lagan /lággən/, **ligan** /lígən/ *n* cargo or wreckage lying on the sea bed, often with a buoy attached so that it can be recovered [Mid-16C. < Old French]

Lagan Valley /lagan-/ region in southeastern Northern Ireland, near Belfast, and an Area of Outstanding Natural Beauty

Lag b'Omer /lag bōmər/ *n* a minor Jewish festival marking the day on which some of the restrictions on activities imposed during the Omer are lifted. Date: 18th day of Iyar, 33rd day of the Omer. [< Hebrew < *lāg* 'thirty-third' (pronunciation of the letters LG that symbolize this number) + *bā* 'in the' + *ōmer* 'Omer']

lager[1] /láagər/ *n* **1.** a light-coloured beer made with a low proportion of hops, usually stored for a period after brewing **2.** a drink of lager [Mid-19C. Shortened < German *Lager-Bier* < *Lager* 'storehouse' + *Bier* 'beer']

lager[2] *n*, *vti* MIL another spelling of **laager**

Lagerkvist /láagər kvist/, **Pär** (1891–1974) Swedish novelist, poet, and playwright. He won a Nobel Prize in literature (1951). Full name **Lagerkvist, Pär Fabien**

Lagerlöf /láagər löf/, **Selma** (1858–1940) Swedish novelist. A writer of works based on Swedish folk tales, she was the first woman to be awarded a Nobel Prize in literature (1909). Full name **Lagerlöf, Selma Ottiliana Louisa**

> 'If you have learned anything at all from

us, Tummetott, you no longer think that the humans should have the whole earth to themselves.'
[Selma Lagerlöf, *The Further Adventures of Nils*; 1911]

lager lout *n* a young man who is perceived as behaving violently or disruptively, usually as a result of drinking alcohol (*informal insult*)

laggard /lággərd/ *n* a person who or thing that does not keep up with others ■ *adj* slow or reluctant to do something (*dated*) [Early 18C. < LAG¹] —**laggardly** *adv*, *adj* —**laggardness** *n*

lagged out /lágd-/ *adj regional* affected by exhaustion [< LAG¹]

lagging /lágging/ *n* 1. insulating material used to keep heat from escaping, especially round a pipe or hot water tank 2. a wooden frame used in building, especially to support an arch while it is being built [Mid-19C. < LAG²]

lagniappe /lán yap, lan yáp/ *n* 1. *Carib, Southern US* a small present given by a shop to a customer who has just purchased something 2. *Southern US* an unexpected bonus or extra [Mid-19C. Via Louisiana French < American Spanish *la ñapa* 'the gift' < Quechua *yapay* 'give more']

lagomorph /lággə mawrf/ *n* a plant-eating mammal with two pairs of incisors in the upper jaw specifically adapted for gnawing. Rabbits, hares, and pikas are lagomorphs. Order: Lagomorpha. [Late 19C. < modern Latin *Lagomorpha* < Greek *lagōs* 'hare' + *morphē* 'shape'] —**lagomorphic** /lággə máwrfik/ *adj* —**lagomorphous** /lággə máwrfəss/ *adj*

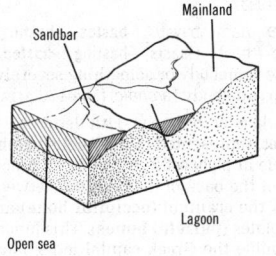
lagoon

lagoon /lə goón/ *n* 1. a coastal body of shallow water formed where low-lying rock, sand, or coral presents a partial barrier to the open sea 2. a small lake adjoining a larger one [Early 17C. Directly or via French < Italian, Spanish *laguna* < Latin *lacuna* (see LACUNA)] —**lagoonal** *adj*

Lagos /láy goss/ largest city, chief port, and former capital of Nigeria. Population: 1,484,000 (1995).

Lagos Escobar /láagoss éskō baar/, **Ricardo** (*b.* 1938) president of Chile. After a period of exile in the United States during the rule of General Pinochet, he returned to found the Party for Democracy (1987). He served as minister of education (1990–92) and minister of public works (1994–96) before winning the 2000 presidential elections.

Lagrange /lə graáNzh/, **Joseph Louis, Comte de l'Empire** (1736–1813) Italian-born French mathematician and astronomer. The author of *Mécanique analytique* (*Analytical Mechanics*) (1788), he pioneered many concepts in mechanics, algebra, and number theory.

'When we ask advice, we are usually looking for an accomplice.'
[Attributed to Joseph Louis Lagrange]

lah¹ /laa, la/ *n* a syllable that represents the sixth note in a musical scale when singing solfeggio. In fixed solfeggio it represents the note A. [14C. < medieval Latin, originally a syllable sung to this note in a hymn to St John the Baptist]

lah² /laa/ *adv* *Malaysia, Singapore* added to something said to indicate informality and intimacy (*informal*)

lahar /laa haar/ *n* a landslide or mudflow of volcanic debris, especially after a heavy rainfall [Early 20C. < Javanese]

lah-di-dah *adj* another spelling of **la-di-da** (*informal*)

Lahnda /laánda/ *n* a language spoken in Pakistan, related to Punjabi. It belongs to the Indic branch of the Indo-European family of languages. [Early 20C. < Punjabi *lahandā* 'western'] —**Lahnda** *adj*

Lahore /lə háwr/ city and capital of Punjab Province, northeastern Pakistan, about 257 km/160 mi. southeast of Islamabad. Population: 5,063,499 (1998).

Lahti /látti/ industrial city in southern Finland, north of Helsinki. Population: 96,666 (2000).

laic /láy ik/, **laical** /láy ik'l/ *adj* relating to or involving followers of a religion who are not clergy [Mid-16C. Via late Latin < Greek *laikos* 'of the people' < *laos* 'people'] —**laically** *adv*

laicize /láy i sīz/ (-cizes, -cizing, -cized), **laicise** (-cises, -cising, -cised) *vt* to remove something from control or governance by the church or the clergy and give control of it to the lay community —**laicization** /láy i sī záysh'n/ *n*

laid past participle, past tense of **lay¹**

laid-back *adj* very relaxed, easygoing, and unworried (*informal*) —**laid-backness** *n*

laid paper *n* a paper with a watermark of fine lines on it that are produced in the manufacturing process

laid work *n* embroidery based on a lattice of threads that is then decorated with filling stitches

laik /layk/ (laiks, laiking, laiked) *vti* *N England* to play, or play at something [14C. < Old Norse *leika* 'to play']

REGIONAL NOTE In parts of England where Viking influence was strongest, many words of Viking (Old Norse) origin persist. **Laik** means 'play', as in *There were children at bus stop laiking like*. In parts of Yorkshire, where this sentence comes from, it is estimated that about one third of the vocabulary is English, one third Viking (Old Norse), and the other third could be either English or Viking.

Lailat al-Baraah /láylat al bə raá/, **Lailat ul-Baraah** /-ṓōl-/ *n* an Islamic festival, the Night of Repentence, marking the night when God sets each person's path for the coming year and all who repent their sins are granted forgiveness. Date: 15th of Sha'ban. [< Arabic, 'night of the repentance']

Lailat al-Miraj /láylat al mi ráj/, **Lailat ul-Miraj** /-ṓōl-/ *n* an Islamic festival, the Night of Ascent, marking the ascent of Muhammad to heaven. Date: 27th of Rajab. [< Arabic, 'night of the ascent']

Lailat al-Qadr /láylat al ka'ādər/, **Lailat ul-Qadr** /-ṓōl-/ *n* an Islamic festival, the Night of Power, marking the sending down of the Koran to Muhammad. Date: 27th of Ramadan. [< Arabic, 'night of the power']

Laing /lang/, **R. D.** (1927–89) British psychiatrist. His radical views on schizophrenia were set out in *The Divided Self* (1960). Other books include *The Politics of Experience* (1967) and *The Politics of the Family* (1969). Full name **Laing, Ronald David**

'Children do not give up their innate imagination, curiosity, dreaminess easily. You have to love them to get them to do that.'
[R. D. Laing, *The Politics of Experience*; 1967]

lair¹ /lair/ *n* 1. WILD ANIMAL'S DEN a place where a wild animal rests or sleeps 2. PLACE TO BE ALONE IN a retreat or hideaway (*informal*) 3. CATTLE ENCLOSURE an enclosure for livestock 4. *Scotland* GROUND FOR GRAVE the ground for a single grave in a cemetery ■ *vti* (lairs, lairing, laired) RETURN TO LAIR to go to a lair, or take or drive an animal to a lair [Old English *leger* 'act of lying, bed' < Indo-European]

lair² /lair/ *Aus* (*dated informal*) *n* somebody regarded as vulgar or given to showing off ■ *vi* (lairs, lairing, laired) to show off or dress in a vulgar way [Mid-20C. Back-formation < LAIRY]

lairage /láirij/ *n* a place where livestock are kept temporarily, e.g. at docks or a market [Late 19C. < LAIR¹]

laird /laird/ *n* *Scotland* an owner of land, especially a large estate ○ *the laird of Shaws* [14C. Variant of LORD]

lairy /láiri/ (-ier, -iest) *adj* *Aus* (*informal*) 1. flashy, or brightly coloured in a garish way ○ *That's a lairy shirt!* 2. behaving in a flash or showy manner [Mid-19C. Probably alteration of LEERY]

laisser-faire *n* another spelling of **laissez-faire**

laisser-passer *n* another spelling of **laissez-passer**

laissez-faire /léssay fáir, láy say-/, **laisser-faire** *n* 1. the principle that the economy works best if private industry is not regulated and markets are free 2. refusal to interfere in other people's affairs, or the practice of letting people do as they please [< French, 'allow to do']

laissez-passer /léssay paá say, láy say-/, **laisser-passer** *n* a document that permits the holder to travel freely, especially one given in lieu of a passport [< French, 'allow to pass']

laity /láy əti/ *npl* 1. the followers of a religion who are not clergy 2. all the people who are not members of a specific profession, as distinguished from those who are members [15C. < LAY²]

Laius /lí əss/ *n* in Greek mythology, a king of Thebes mistakenly killed by his son Oedipus

---

WORLD'S LARGEST LAKES

1	Caspian Sea	Area [143,000 sq. mi. / 370,000 sq. km]	Location Europe/Asia
2	Lake Superior	Area [31,700 sq. mi. / 82,100 sq. km]	Location North America
3	Lake Victoria	Area [26,830 sq. mi. / 69,490 sq. km]	Location Africa
4	Lake Huron	Area [23,000 sq. mi. / 59,600 sq. km]	Location North America
5	Lake Michigan	Area [22,300 sq. mi. / 57,800 sq. km]	Location North America
6	Lake Tanganyika	Area [12,700 sq. mi. / 32,900 sq. km]	Location Africa
7	Great Bear Lake	Area [12,270 sq. mi. / 31,790 sq. km]	Location North America
8	Lake Baikal	Area [12,200 sq. mi. / 31,500 sq. km]	Location Asia
9	Aral Sea	Area [12,050 sq. mi. / 31,220 sq. km]	Location Asia
10	Lake Nyasa	Area [8,683 sq. mi. / 22,490 sq. km]	Location Africa

lake¹ /layk/ *n* 1. INLAND BODY OF WATER a large body of water surrounded by land 2. POOL OF LIQUID a large pool of liquid that has collected or spilled somewhere ○ *A lake of hot grease covered the floor by the cooker.* 3. SURPLUS OF LIQUID PRODUCT a large surplus of a liquid product, e.g. milk or wine, that is stored and not sold in order to prevent prices from becoming too low, especially in the European Union (*informal*; *usually used in combination*) ○ *a wine lake* [Pre-12C. Directly or via French < Latin *lacus* 'pond']

CULTURAL NOTE *The Lady of the Lake*, a poem (1810) by Scottish writer Sir Walter Scott. Set in early 16th-century Scotland, it describes the eventful courtship of Ellen, daughter of outlawed chieftain James of Douglas, who lives at Loch Katrine (the lake of the title). Regarded as one of Scott's finest works, it is admired for its satisfying plot, strong characterization, and charming songs.

lake² /layk/ *n* 1. a bright translucent pigment of various colours, made by combining an organic dye with a metallic hydroxide or other inorganic substance 2. a red pigment made by combining cochineal with a metallic compound [Early 17C. Variant of LAC¹]

Lake District /láyk-/ region of mountains and lakes in Cumbria, northwestern England. The district extends about 50 km/30 mi. from north to south and 40 km/25 mi. from east to west.

Lake District National Park national park in Cumbria, northwestern England, established in 1951. Its highest point is Scafell Pike, 978 m/3,208 ft. Area: 2,240 sq. km/866 sq. mi.

lake dwelling *n* a home or settlement built on a platform supported by wooden posts over or by a shallow lake or river edge, especially in prehistoric times —**lake dweller** *n*

lakefront /láyk frunt/ *n* the land along the shores of a lake

lake herring *n* a fish related to the whitefish. Native to: Great Lakes region of the United States. Latin name: *Coregonus artedii*.

Lakeland terrier

Lakeland terrier /láyklənd-/ *n* a wire-haired terrier with a black and tan coat, belonging to a breed originally developed for fox-hunting [Early 20C. After *Lakeland* 'the Lake District', NW England]

Lake Macquarie /-mə kwórri/ city in eastern New South Wales, Australia. Population: 188,717 (2002 estimate).

Lake of the Woods lake in central North America, on the border between the United States and Canada. It includes hundreds of wooded islands. Area: 4,390 sq. km/1,695 sq. mi.

Lake Poets *npl* the poets Wordsworth, Coleridge, and Southey, who lived in the Lake District in the early 19th century

laker /láykər/ *n N Am* 1. a boat or ship that is used on lakes rather than the sea 2. a fish living in a lake rather than the sea [Late 18C. < LAKE[1]]

lakeside /láyk sīd/ *n* the land at the edge of a lake

lake trout *n* FISH same as **brown trout**

lakh /laak/ (*plural* **lakhs** or *same*), **lac** (*plural* **lacs** or *same*) *n S Asia* the number 100,000, used especially for referring to sums of rupees [Early 17C. Via Hindi *lākh* < Sanskrit *lakṣam* 'mark, 100,000']

Lakota /lə kṓtə/ (*plural* **-tas** or *same*) *n* PEOPLES, LANG same as **Teton**[1] [Mid-19C. < Teton *lakhóta*] —**Lakota** *adj*

laksa /láksə/ *n* a Malaysian or Singaporean rice noodle, slightly thicker than spaghetti, often served in a spicy fish sauce or soup [< Malay]

Lakshadweep /lak shád weep, lúkshəd weèp/ Union Territory of southwestern India, comprising an archipelago of 36 islands in the Arabian Sea. Capital: Kavaratti Island. Population: 60,595 (2001). Area: 32 sq. km/12 sq. mi.

Lakshmi /lákshmi/, **Laksmi** *n* in Hinduism, the goddess of prosperity, wealth, and royalty, and wife of the god Vishnu

laky /láyki/ *adj* of a colour similar to a red form of the pigment lake [Mid-19C. < LAKE[2]]

Lala /laá laa/ *n S Asia* a title equivalent to 'Mr', used before men's names [< Hindi]

La-La /laá laa/ *n N Am* used as a nickname for Los Angeles (*slang*; *often used humorously*) ○ *moving to La-La* [< doubling of LA]

la-la land *n N Am* (*slang*) 1. a state of mind divorced from reality 2. a place where people live shallow, frivolous lives [< LA-LA]

lalang /laá laang/ *n* a tall coarse tropical grass. Native to: Malay Archipelago. Latin name: *Imperata arundinacea*. [Late 18C. < Malay]

lalapalooza *n N Am* same as **lollapalooza** (*informal*)

-lalia *suffix* speech, speech disorder ○ *echolalia* [< Greek *lalia* 'talk' < *lalein* 'to talk']

Lalique glass /la leék-/ *n* ornamental frosted glassware decorated with bas-relief figures, fruits, and flowers, designed by the French Art Nouveau craftsperson René Lalique (1860–1945)

Lallans /lállənz/, **Lallan** /lállən/ *n Scotland* the form of Lowland Scots used in revivals of Scots as a literary medium, especially in the 18th century and 20th centuries ■ *adj* relating to the Lowlands of Scotland, or any dialect of Scots spoken there [Early 18C. < a pronunciation of LOWLAND]

lallapalooza *n US* same as **lollapalooza** (*informal*)

lallation /la láysh'n/ *n* a mispronunciation of 'r', especially one that sounds like 'l' [Mid-17C. < Latin *lallation-* < *lallare* 'sing lullaby']

Lalor /láylər/, **Peter** (1827–89) Irish-born Australian civil engineer and politician. He led the Eureka Rebellion, a revolt by miners in Victoria, Australia, in 1854. He subsequently became a state politician.

lam /lam/ (*informal*) *v* (**lams, lamming, lammed**) 1. *vti* HIT HARD to hit somebody or something hard ○ *lammed into him with her fists* 2. *vi* SPEAK ANGRILY to speak angrily to somebody ○ *lammed into me for being late* 3. *vi N Am* ESCAPE HASTILY to escape or run away, especially from the law ■ *n N Am* HASTY ESCAPE a hasty escape, especially to avoid arrest [Late 16C. Origin ?]

lama /laáma/ *n* 1. a Tibetan or Mongolian Buddhist monk 2. in Buddhism, a title used for those people who are believed to be the reincarnations of a bodhisattva [Mid-17C. Representing the pronunciation of Tibetan *bla-ma*]

Lamaism /laáma izəm/ *n* a form of Mahayana Buddhism practised in Tibet and Mongolia that has non-Buddhist elements from South Asia and from an older nature-worshipping religion. Its monks (**lamas**) are led by the Dalai Lama, a temporal as well as spiritual ruler. —**Lamaist** *n, adj* —**Lamaistic** /laáma ístik/ *adj*

La Mancha /laa maánchə/ historic region occupying a high barren plateau in south-central Spain. Miguel de Cervantes set his Novel *Don Quixote* (1605–15) there.

Lamarck /la maárk/, **Jean-Baptiste Pierre Antoine de Monet, Chevalier de** (1744–1829) French naturalist and evolutionist. His theory that evolution proceeded by the inheritance of acquired characteristics was superseded by Darwin's theory of natural selection. —**Lamarckian** *adj, n*

Lamarckism /la maárkizəm/ *n* the evolutionary theory of Jean-Baptiste Lamarck that holds that evolution proceeds through the inheritance of characteristics acquired by individual organisms

Lamarr /la maár/, **Hedy** (1914–2000) Austrian-born US film actor. She starred in films in the 1930s and 1940s, including *Samson and Delilah* (1949) and, with co-inventor George Antheil (1900–59), patented a secret communication system for military use, which was a forerunner of mobile phone technology. Born **Kiesler, Hedwig Eva Maria**

Lamartine /la maar teén/, **Alphonse** (1790–1869) French poet, historian, and politician. A diplomat and French government minister during the 1848 revolution, he was the author of *Histoire des Girondins* (1847). Full name **Lamartine, Alphonse Marie Louis Prat de**

'At its birth the Republic gave voice to...three words, "Liberty, Equality, Fraternity"...If Europe is wise and just, each of these words signifies peace.'
[Alphonse Lamartine, 'A Manifesto to the Powers'; 4 March 1848]

lamasery /laáməssəri/ (*plural* **-ies**) *n* a Tibetan or Mongolian monastery of lamas [Mid-19C. < French *lamaserie* 'lama dwelling' < *lama* 'lama' < Tibetan *bla-ma*]

Lamaze /lə maáz/ *n N Am* a method of natural childbirth by which a woman is physically and psychologically prepared through prenatal training. Lamaze encourages the use of controlled breathing and the participation of the woman's partner during the process of childbirth. [Mid-20C. After Fernand *Lamaze* (1890–1957), French physician]

lamb /lam/ *n* 1. YOUNG SHEEP an immature sheep, especially one under a year old and without permanent teeth 2. MEAT OF LAMB the meat of an immature sheep that is under a year old 3. CLOTHING same as **lambskin** (sense 1) 4. SOMEBODY MEEK AND MILD a gentle and innocent person, especially a baby or small child 5. SOMEBODY EASILY DECEIVED somebody who is easily cheated, especially financially ■ *vti* (**lambs, lambing, lambed**) BEAR LAMB to give birth to a lamb [Old English < Germanic] ◇ **like a lamb to the slaughter** going to face something unpleasant, difficult, or dangerous calmly and without resistance

Lamb *n* CHR same as **Lamb of God**

Lamb /lam/, **Charles** (1775–1834) British essayist. He was a prose stylist of great clarity whose books include *Essays of Elia* (1823). Pseudonym **Elia**

'I love to lose myself in other men's minds. When I am not walking, I am reading; I cannot sit and think. Books think for me.'
[Charles Lamb, 'Detached Thoughts on Books and Reading', *Last Essays of Elia*; 1833]

Lamba /lámbə/ *n* a language spoken in Benin, belonging to the Gur branch of Niger-Congo. Native speakers: 29,000. [Early 20C. < Bantu] —**Lamba** *adj*

lambada /lam baádə/ *n* 1. a fast rhythmic dance of Brazilian origin in which partners hold each other close and gyrate their hips 2. the music for a lambada [Late 20C. < Brazilian Portuguese, 'a beating']

Lambaréné /lámbə reéni, loNbə ráynay/ capital of Moyen-Ogooué Region, western Gabon. Population: 42,316 (1993).

lambaste /lam báyst/ (**-bastes, -basting, -basted**), **lambast** /-bást/ (**-basts, -basting, -basted**) *vt* 1. to criticize somebody or something severely 2. to beat or whip somebody (*archaic*) [Mid-17C. < LAM + BASTE[2]]

lambda /lámdə/ *n* 1. the 11th letter of the Greek alphabet, represented in the English alphabet as 'l'. See table at **alphabet** 2. the point of junction at the centre of the back of the cranium between the rear plate of the cranium (**occipital bone**) and the two upper plates (**parietal bones**). This junction is said to resemble the Greek capital letter lambda. [Early 17C. < Greek]

lambda calculus *n* a descriptive theory of mathematical functions and the way they combine, used as the basis for some high-level computer programming languages

lambdacism /lámdəssizəm/ *n* the erroneous substitution of 'l' for 'r' in speech [Mid-17C. Via late Latin < Greek *lambdakismos* < *lambda* 'lambda']

lambda hyperon *n* a short-lived elementary particle that has a mass approximately 1.1 times that of the proton and zero electric charge

lambdoid /lám doyd/, **lambdoidal** /lam dóyd'l/ *adj* describes the suture that joins bones at the back of the skull, shaped like the Greek capitalized lambda

lambent /lámbənt/ *adj* 1. GLEAMING softly gleaming or glowing (*literary*) 2. PLAYING OVER SURFACE flickering or playing as a flame over a surface without burning it (*literary*) 3. BRILLIANTLY LIGHT having a light but brilliant touch ○ *lambent wit* [Mid-17C. < Latin *lambent-*, present participle of *lambere* 'lick'] —**lambency** *n* —**lambently** *adv*

lambert /lámbərt/ *n* an SI unit of surface brightness (**luminance**) equivalent to one lumen per square centimetre [Late 19C. After Johann Heinrich *Lambert* (1728–77), German scientist]

Lambeth walk /lámbəth-/, **Lambeth Walk** *n* a lively ballroom dance originating in England during the 1930s [Mid-19C. After a street in *Lambeth*, S London borough]

lamb fries *npl* FOOD same as **lamb's fry**

Lambic /loN bík/ *n* a strong sour-tasting draught beer brewed in Belgium from aged hops [Late 19C. < French *alambic*, modern form of Old French *alembic* (see ALEMBIC)]

lambie[1] /lámmi/ *n* a baby lamb (*baby talk*) [Early 18C. < LAMB]

lambie[2] /lámbi/ *n Carib* tenderized conch flesh used for food [Late 20C. < French *lambi* 'sea mollusc']

lambing /lámming/ *n* **1.** the birth of lambs, or the season when they are born **2.** the work of helping ewes give birth to lambs

lambkin /lámkin/ *n* **1.** a baby lamb **2.** used as a term of endearment for a baby or small child

Lamb of God *n* Jesus Christ, seen as a sacrifice whose crucifixion and resurrection redeemed humankind

lambrequin /lámbrikin, lámbər-/ *n* **1.** HOUSEHOLD **ORNAMENTAL HANGING** a decorative strip of drapery, hung along the top of a doorway, window, shelf, or mantelpiece **2.** HIST **SCARF ATTACHED TO KNIGHT'S HELMET** a veil, scarf, or piece of drapery attached to a knight's helmet to protect it from heat and rust **3.** HERALDRY same as **mantling 4.** CERAMICS **ORNAMENTAL BORDER ON VASE** a decorative border near the top of a vase [Early 18C. Via French < assumed Dutch, 'small veil' < *lamper* 'veil']

Lambrusco /lam bro͝osk ō/ *n* a sparkling wine, typically red and sweet, from the Emilia-Romagna district in northern Italy [Mid-20C. Via Italian < Latin *labruscum* 'fruit of the wild grape Vitis labrusca' < *labrusca* 'wild vine']

lamb's ears (*plural same*) *n* a perennial low-growing plant with silvery woolly leaves. Flowers: small, purple, on long stems. Latin name: *Stachys byzantina*. [< the resemblance of the leaves to a lamb's ears]

lamb's fry *n* **1.** lamb's testicles or internal organs, traditionally sold skinned and ready for cooking by frying **2.** *ANZ* lamb's liver cooked for food

lambskin /lám skin/ *n* **1.** the woolly pelt of a lamb. Use: making or trimming winter clothing. **2.** the hide of a lamb, prepared as leather

lamb's lettuce *n* a lettuce with small rounded leaves and a slightly sweet, nutty flavour. N Am term **corn salad** [Translation of Latin *lactuca agnina*]

lamb's tails *npl* the drooping catkins of the hazel tree

lambswool /lámz wo͝ol/, **lamb's wool** *n* fine soft wool sheared from a year-old lamb. Use: knitwear.

LAMDA /lámdə/ *abbr* London Academy of Music and Dramatic Art

lame[1] /laym/ *adj* (**lamer, lamest**) **1. WALKING UNEVENLY** walking unevenly because of a leg injury or motion impairment (*offensive when used of a person*) **2. DISABLED** injured or with impaired strength or motion (*offensive when used of a person*) **3. UNCONVINCING** inadequate, unconvincing, or unsatisfactory (*offensive in some contexts*) **4. INEFFECTIVE** ineffectual or inept (*offensive in some contexts*) ■ *vt* (**lames, laming, lamed**) **DISABLE PERSON OR ANIMAL** to cause a person or animal to be unable to walk evenly because of injury or impairment (*offensive when used of a person*) [Old English *lama* < Germanic, 'weak-limbed' < Indo-European, 'break by hitting'] —**lameness** *n*

lame[2] /laym/ *n* a thin plate of metal, especially one of the overlapping metal plates of which medieval armour was made from the mid-14th century [Late 16C. < French (see LAMÉ)]

lamé /laá may/ *n* a fabric with gold or silver threads interwoven with silk, wool, or cotton [Early 20C. < French, 'worked with silver and gold thread' < *lame* 'thin metal plate' < Latin *lamina* 'thin plate or layer']

lamebrain /láym brayn/ *n N Am* an offensive term that deliberately insults somebody's intelligence (*slang insult*) —**lamebrained** *adj*

lamedh /laámid, -med/, **lamed** *n* the 12th letter of the Hebrew alphabet, represented in the English alphabet as 'l'. See table at **alphabet** [Mid-17C. < Hebrew *lāmēdh*]

lame duck *n* **1. SOMEBODY OR SOMETHING WEAK** a person or thing considered as weak, inadequate, or unfortunate (*offensive when used of a person*) **2.** *US* POL **OFFICE HOLDER NOT RUNNING FOR RE-ELECTION** an elected official who either will not or may not legally run for another term in office and has reduced power or effectiveness **3.** *N Am* POL **OUTGOING OFFICE HOLDER** an elected office holder left seemingly powerless after a successor has been elected but has not yet taken office

lamella /lə méllə/ (*plural* **-lae** /-lee/) *n* **1.** ANAT **THIN PIECE OF BONE** any thin flat structure of bone or tissue **2.** FUNGI **PART OF FUNGUS** a gill of a fungus **3.** BIOL **MEMBRANE LAYER** a membrane layer in a plant chloroplast **4.** CONSTR **VAULT FRAMEWORK** a structural part of wood, metal, or reinforced concrete that is crisscrossed to form a vault [Late 17C. < Latin, 'small thin plate' < *lamina* 'thin plate or layer'] —**lamellar** *adj* —**lamellarly** *adv* —**lamellate** /lámmələt, lə méllət/ *adj*

lamelli- *prefix* lamella ○ *lamelliform* [< LAMELLA]

lamellibranch /lə mélli brangk/ *n* ZOOL same as **bivalve** [Mid-19C. < modern Latin *Lamellibranchia* < Latin *lamella* (see LAMELLA) + Greek *bragkhia* 'gills'] —**lamellibranchiate** /lə mélli brángki ət/ *adj, n*

lamellicorn /lə mélli kawrn/ *adj* describes a beetle that has antennae composed of layered segments, e.g. a dung beetle [Mid-19C. < modern Latin *Lamellicornia* < Latin *lamella* (see LAMELLA) + *cornu* 'horn'] —**lamellicorn** *n*

lamelliform /lə mélli fawrm/ *adj* shaped like a thin plate or scale

lamely /láymli/ *adv* inadequately, unconvincingly, or ineptly

lament /lə mént/ *vti* (**-ments, -menting, -mented**) **1. EXPRESS SADNESS** to express grief or sorrow about something **2. EXPRESS REGRET** to express regret, annoyance, or disappointment about something ○ *She was lamenting the lack of funding for her project.* ■ *n* **1. EXPRESSION OF SADNESS** an expression of grief or sorrow **2. EXPRESSION OF REGRET** an expression of regret, annoyance, or disappointment **3. WORK LAMENTING DEATH** a song or poem of mourning [Mid-16C. Directly or via French < Latin *lamentari* < *lamenta* 'laments'] —**lamentation** /lámmən táysh'n/ *n* —**lamented** *adj* —**lamenter** *n* —**lamentingly** *adv*

lamentable /lámməntəb'l/ *adj* **1.** unsatisfactory, pitiful, or deplorable **2.** sad and mournful (*literary*) —**lamentableness** *n* —**lamentably** *adv*

USAGE The traditional pronunciation of ***lamentable*** has the stress on the first syllable. It is often pronounced with the stress on the second syllable, as in the word *lament*, but this alternative pronunciation is more acceptable in American English than in British English.

Lamentations /lámmən táysh'nz/ *n* a book of the Bible written in the form of elegies, traditionally attributed to Jeremiah (*takes a singular verb*) See table at **Bible**

lamia /láymi ə/ (*plural* **-mias** or **-miae** /-mi ee/) *n* in classical mythology, a blood-sucking witch who takes the form of a serpent, used as a bogey with which to threaten children [14C. Via Latin < Greek, mythical monster]

lamina /lámminə/ (*plural* **-nae** /-nee/ or **-nas**) *n* **1. THIN LAYER** a thin plate, layer, or flake **2.** BOT **LEAF BLADE** the blade or flat part of a leaf **3.** ZOOL **PROTECTIVE PLATE INSIDE HOOF** in hoofed mammals, any of the parallel layers of sensitive tissue just inside the hard exterior of the hoof [Mid-17C. < Latin, 'thin plate or layer, leaf']

laminal /lámmin'l/ *adj* describes speech sounds articulated using the blade or flat part of the tongue

laminar flow /lámminər-/ *n* a flow in a liquid or gas in which neighbouring layers do not mix but flow at different velocities

laminaria /lámmi náiri ə/ *n* a large brown seaweed (**kelp**) that has broad flat fronds. Genus: *Laminaria*. [Mid-19C. < modern Latin *Laminaria* < Latin *lamina* 'thin plate or layer']

laminarin /lámmi naárrin/ *n* a carbohydrate occurring in brown algae [Mid-20C. < modern Latin *Laminaria* (see LAMINARIA)]

laminate *v* /lámmi nayt/ (**-nates, -nating, -nated**) **1.** *vt* **COVER SOMETHING WITH THIN LAYER** to cover something with a thin sheet of protective material such as plastic or metal **2.** *vt* **BOND LAYERS TOGETHER** to bond sheets or layers together so as to produce a strong and durable composite material ○ *Wood veneers were laminated to produce a cheap and durable alternative to expensive hardwoods for furniture-making.* **3.** *vt* **FORM METAL INTO THIN LAYERS** to roll or beat metal into thin sheets **4.** *vti* **SEPARATE INTO LAYERS** to split something into thin layers, or be split into thin layers ■ *n* /lámminət/ **MATERIAL MADE UP OF BONDED LAYERS** a product composed of layers or sheets bonded together —**laminable** *adj* —**laminated** *adj* —**laminator** *n*

lamination /lámmi náysh'n/ *n* **1. PROCESS OF BONDING LAYERS** the bonding together of thin layers of materials to form a composite material **2. FORMATION OF LAYERS** the formation of layers in something **3. THINLY LAYERED STRUCTURE** a structure composed of thin layers **4. THIN LAYER** a thin layer in something (*technical*) **5.** ELEC ENG **THIN STEEL PLATE IN TRANSFORMER CORE** one of a number of thin steel or iron plates that are held together to form a transformer core

laminectomy /lámmi néktəmi/ (*plural* **-mies**) *n* a surgical operation to remove one or more sides of the rear arches of a spinal vertebra and gain access to the spinal cord or spinal nerve roots

lamington /lámmingtən/ *n ANZ* a small square sponge cake covered in chocolate icing and dried coconut [Early 20C. After Lord *Lamington*, governor of Queensland, Australia, 1895–1901]

Lamington National Park /lámmingtən-/ national park in southeastern Queensland, Australia

Lamington Plateau high mountain plateau situated in the Macpherson Range, Lamington National Park, Queensland, Australia

laminitis /lámmi nītiss/ *n* inflammation of the sensitive plates of tissue in a hoof, especially a horse's hoof, usually causing lameness. It is one of the most serious equine hoof diseases.

Lammas /lámməss/ *n* **1.** formerly, a Christian religious feast marking St Peter's deliverance from prison. Date: 1 August. **2.** a day formerly celebrated in England as a harvest festival. Date: 1 August. [Old English *hlāfmæsse* < earlier forms of LOAF [1] + MASS; by association with LAMB]

Lammastide /lámməss tīd/ *n* the season of Lammas (*archaic*) [< TIDE 'period of time']

lammergeier /lámmər gī ər/, **lammergeyer** *n* a large vulture with dark wings and dark feathers that resemble a beard around its beak. It drops bones on rocks to break them in order to obtain marrow. Native to: mountains of southern Europe, Africa, Asia. Latin name: *Gypaetus barbatus*. [Early 19C. < German *Lämmergeier* 'lambs' vulture'; because it commonly feeds on their carcasses]

lamming /lámming/ *n* a thorough whipping or beating (*informal*)

lamp /lamp/ *n* **1. ELECTRIC LIGHT** a device that produces electric light **2. DEVICE PRODUCING LIGHT** a device that burns oil, gas, or wax to produce light **3. RADIATION SOURCE** a device that supplies ultraviolet light or infrared heat radiation, especially for medical or cosmetic treatment ○ *a sun lamp* **4. SOURCE OF ENLIGHTENMENT** a source of enlightenment or inspiration (*literary*) [12C. Via French *lampe* < Latin *lampas* < Greek, 'torch' < *lampein* 'to shine']

lampas[1] /lámpəss/ *n* an ornately patterned fabric resembling damask. Use: upholstery. [Mid-19C. < French]

lampas[2] /lámpəss/ *n* the swelling of the mucous membrane covering the roof of the mouth in horses, often due to tooth eruption and therefore transient [Early 16C. < French]

lampblack /lámp blak/ *n* a fine powdery form of carbon that is deposited when oils containing carbon are burned. Use: pigment, printing ink, in electrodes.

lampbrush chromosome /lámp brush-/ *n* an enlarged chromosome covered with fine loops of chromatin, observed during the early part of reproductive division (**meiosis**) [Because it resembles a brush for the inside of a glass lampshade]

lamp chimney *n* a glass cover that is placed over the wick of an oil or kerosene lamp to protect and control the flame

Lampedusa /lámpi do͞ozə/, **Giuseppe Tomasi di** (1896–1957) Italian author. A member of the Sicilian aristocracy, he wrote only one novel, *Il Gattopardo* (1958), translated into English as *The Leopard* (1960), which was published posthumously to critical acclaim.

lampern /lámpərn/ (*plural* **-perns** or *same*) *n* a river fish of the lamprey family that resembles an eel. Native to: Europe. Latin name: *Lampetra fluviatilis*. [14C. < Old French *lampreion* 'small lamprey' < *lampreie* (see LAMPREY)]

lamp glass *n* HOUSEHOLD same as **lamp chimney**

lampion /lámpi ən/ *n* a small oil lamp, usually with a tinted glass chimney, formerly popular as a car-

riage light [Mid-19C. Via French < Italian *lampione* 'large lamp' < *lampa* 'lamp' < French *lampe* (see LAMP)]

lamplight /lámp līt/ *n* the light cast by a lamp —**lamplit** *adj*

lamplighter /lámp līter/ *n* **1.** formerly, an employee who lit gas streetlamps **2.** *N Am* a device used to light lamps

lamp oil *n* oil suitable as lamp fuel

lampoon /lam poón/ *n* a piece of satirical writing or verse ridiculing somebody or something ■ *vt* (**-poons**, **-pooning**, **-pooned**) to use ridicule as a way of satirizing somebody or something in a piece of writing [Mid-17C. < French *lampon*] —**lampooner** *n* —**lampoonery** *n* —**lampoonist** *n*

lamppost /lámp pōst/ *n* **1.** a post or pillar that supports a streetlight **2.** *Malaysia* an unwanted single person with a couple or a group otherwise made up of couples (*informal*) ○ *I don't want to play lamppost.*

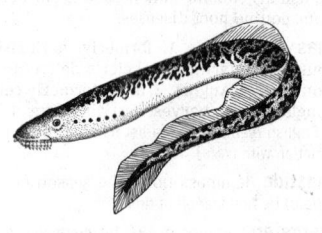

lamprey

lamprey /lámpri/ (*plural* **-preys**) *n* a freshwater jawless fish with a round sucking mouth for attaching itself to other fish and, in the case of adults, feeding parasitically on their blood. Family: Petromyzontidae. [13C. Via Old French *lampreie* < medieval Latin *lampreda*]

lamprophyre /lámprə fīr/ *n* an igneous rock that occurs mainly as an intrusion or dyke containing large crystals, especially of biotite and mica [Late 19C. < German *lamprophyr*, literally 'shining purple' < Greek *(por)phureos* 'purple']

lampshade /lámp shayd/ *n* a cover, typically decorative, used to moderate and direct artificial light from a lamp

lamp shell *n* MARINE BIOL same as **brachiopod** [< its resemblance to an ancient oil lamp and its wick]

lamp standard *n* same as **lamppost** (sense 1)

lampworking /lámp wurking/ *n* the process or technique of forming glass items made of rods and tubes by heating them with an oxygen-gas flame

lamsiekte /lámm sikta/, **lamziekte** *n S Africa* botulism in cattle and sheep [Late 18C. < Afrikaans, 'lame disease']

Lamut /lə moot/ *n* a language spoken in parts of eastern Siberia, belonging to the Tungusic branch of Altaic. Native speakers: 12,000. [Early 18C. Via Russian < Evenki, 'those living by the sea' < *lamu* 'sea'] —**Lamut** *adj*

lamziekte /lámsiktə/ *n S Africa* another spelling of **lamsiekte**

LAN /lan/ *abbr* COMPUT local area network

lanai /lə nī/ (*plural* **-nais**) *n* in Hawaii, an open roofed porch or veranda, often used as a living room [Early 19C. < Hawaiian]

Lanark /lánnərk/ town in central Scotland, in South Lanarkshire council area. Population: 8,877 (1991).

Lanarkshire /lánnərkshər/ former county in southern Scotland, until 1975

lanate /láy nayt/ *adj* covered with or consisting of woolly hairs [Mid-18C. < Latin *lanatus* < *lana* 'wool']

lançado /lán sádō/ (*plural* **-dos**) *n* a collection point in the interior of Africa for Portuguese trade, from the 16th century onwards, that linked African economies to the commercial centres on the Atlantic coast [< Portuguese, 'launching point']

Lancashire /lángkəshər/ coastal county in north-

western England. Population: 1,134,974 (2001). Area: 2,896 sq. km/1,183 sq. mi.

Lancaster[1] /lángkəstər/ *n* the branch of the Plantagenet dynasty that ruled England from 1399 to 1461, founded by Henry, duke of Lancaster (**Henry IV**)

Lancaster[2] /lángkəstər/ historic city in the county of Lancashire, northwestern England. Population: 133,914 (2001).

Lancaster, Burt (1913–94) US actor. His films include *From Here to Eternity* (1953), *Elmer Gantry* (1960), *The Swimmer* (1968), and *Local Hero* (1983). Full name **Lancaster, Burton Stephen**

Lancaster, Sir Osbert (1908–86) British cartoonist and writer. He created the cartoon character Lady Maudie Littlehampton for the *Daily Express* (1939), and wrote many books on architecture.

Lancastrian /lang kástri ən/ *adj* **1.** relating to Lancashire or Lancaster **2.** belonging to or supporting the royal house of Lancaster, especially during the 15th-century Wars of the Roses —**Lancastrian** *n*

lance /laanss/ *n* **1.** ARMS CAVALRY WEAPON a long weapon with a metal point carried by cavalry in battle **2.** FIELD SPORTS SPEAR FOR HUNTING OR FISHING a long pointed spear used in hunting or fishing **3.** METALL METAL-PIERCING DEVICE a thin metal tube or pipe through which a stream of oxygen is directed at a heated metal surface in order to pierce it **4.** TUBE FOR SPRAYING LIQUID a long rigid tube on the end of a hose, used for spraying water or other liquids ■ *vt* (**lances, lancing, lanced**) MED PIERCE WITH SHARP INSTRUMENT to pierce flesh with a sharp instrument to let out pus ○ *lance a blister* [13C. Via French < Latin *lancea*]

lance corporal *n* **1.** an Army or Royal Marines noncommissioned officer of a rank above private **2.** a noncommissioned officer in the US Marine Corps in the US Marine Corps of a rank above private first class [< obsolete *lancepesade* 'officer of the lowest rank', via French < Old Italian *lancia spezzata* 'broken lance']

lancelet /laánsslət/ *n* a small slender translucent animal living in the sea that is related to the ancestors of all vertebrate animals and lives buried in sand. Subphylum: Cephalochordata.

Lanceley, Colin (*b.* 1938) New Zealand-born Australian painter and sculptor. His colourful assemblages combine painting with collages and found objects.

Lancelot /laánssə lot/ *n* in Arthurian legend, the most famous of King Arthur's knights and the lover of Queen Guinevere

lanceolate /laánssi ə layt/ *adj* tapering to a point like the head of a lance ○ *lanceolate leaves* [Mid-18C. < late Latin *lanceolatus* < Latin *lanceola* 'small lance' < *lancea* 'lance'] —**lanceolately** *adv*

lancer /laánssər/ *n* a soldier on horseback armed with a lance

Lancer *n* a member of a cavalry regiment that was formerly armed with lances and keeps the title

lance rest *n* a support for a lance attached to a medieval breastplate or saddle and used during a charge

lancers /laánssərz/ *n* (*takes a singular verb*) **1.** a square dance for 8 or 16 couples, originally a 19th-century quadrille **2.** the music for a lancers

lance sergeant *n* a noncommissioned officer in some regiments of the British Army of a rank equivalent to corporal

lancet /laánssit/ *n* **1.** SURG same as **scalpel 2.** ARCHIT same as **lancet arch 3.** ARCHIT same as **lancet window**

lancet arch *n* a narrow arch that comes steeply to a point, typical in Gothic architecture

lanceted /laánssitid/ *adj* **1.** built with lancet arches or lancet windows, as in Gothic architecture **2.** having an arched, steeply pointed top

lancet fish *n* a long-bodied carnivorous deep-sea fish with a long dorsal fin and sharp teeth. Latin name: *Alepisauridae*. [< the sharpness of the fins]

lancet window

lancet window *n* a window formed as one or more slender pointed arches

lancewood /laánss wŏŏd/ (*plural* **-woods** or *same*) *n* **1.** a tough flexible wood. Use: fishing rods, bows, cabinetmaking. **2.** a tree that yields lancewood. Native to: tropical America, Caribbean. Latin name: *Oxandra lanceolata*.

Lan-chou another spelling of **Lanzhou**

lanciform /laánssi fawrm/ *adj* shaped like a lance

Lancs /langks/ *abbr* Lancashire

land /land/ *n* **1.** SOLID EARTH the solid part of the Earth's surface not covered by a body of water **2.** PART OF EARTH a part of the Earth's surface of a particular kind or that is used for a particular purpose ○ *low-lying land* ○ *agricultural land* **3.** COUNTRYSIDE ground used for agriculture, or rural or agricultural areas as distinguished from villages, towns, or cities ○ *He had worked on the land all his life.* **4.** OWNED GROUND an area of ground that somebody owns ○ *public land* ○ *What are you doing on my land?* **5.** HOMELAND a territory, country, or nation inhabited by those who regard it as their home ○ *her native land* **6.** IMAGINED PLACE an imagined place ○ *She's living in the land of make-believe.* **7.** SMOOTH PARTS OF GROOVED AREA the unindented parts of a grooved surface, e.g. a ridge between grooves in the bore of a rifle **8.** UNFURROWED SOIL the parts of the ground between furrows in a ploughed field ■ *v* (**lands, landing, landed**) **1.** *vi* ARRIVE BY PLANE to arrive by aircraft ○ *We land at 8:43.* **2.** *vti* SET DOWN AIRCRAFT to come down onto solid ground or water, or bring an aircraft down onto solid ground or water, especially at an airport ○ *The Luton plane landed five minutes ago.* **3.** *vti* GO OR PUT SOMETHING ASHORE to arrive on shore from a ship, or put something ashore from a ship ○ *We decided to land and explore the port.* **4.** *vi* COME DOWN THROUGH AIR to come down from a height ○ *The ball shot up and landed on the roof.* **5.** *vt* OBTAIN SOMETHING to win, obtain, secure, or be awarded something desired ○ *He finally landed the job he wanted.* **6.** *vt* STRIKE BLOW to deliver a blow that hits somebody or something ○ *She landed a blow on his head.* **7.** *vti* END UP SOMEWHERE UNPLEASANT to end up in an undesirable place or situation, or cause somebody or something to end up in an undesirable place or situation ○ *It could land him in jail.* **8.** *vi* APPEAR UNEXPECTEDLY to appear in an undesired and unexpected way ○ *One problem after another landed in our lap.* **9.** *vt* CATCH AND BRING IN FISH to catch a fish and get it onto a boat or solid ground [Old English, < Germanic, 'particular (enclosed) area'] ◇ **be in the land of the living** to be alive or awake (*humorous*) ◇ **find out** *or* **see how the land lies** to assess a situation before taking action

land up *vi* to finally get to a place or situation after a series of events or circumstances (*informal*) ○ *land up on the streets*

land with *vt* to give somebody something to do or deal with, especially because no one else wants to do it (*informal*) ○ *I was landed with the bill.*

land agent *n* **1.** the manager or administrator of a landed estate **2.** an agent for the buying and selling of land —**land agency** *n*

land army *n* a collective unit of women recruited to do agricultural work in the United Kingdom during World War I and World War II

landau /lán daw/ (*plural* **-daus**) *n* a four-wheeled horse-drawn carriage with a top that may be let down or

folded back and a raised seat for the driver [Mid-18C. After *Landau*, town in Bavaria, Germany]

landaulet /lán daw lét/, **landaulette** *n* 1. a small horse-drawn landau 2. a car that has a convertible top for the back seat, while the front seat is either roofed or open

land bank *n* a bank that issues loans using the borrower's property as security

land-based *adj* 1. existing on or operating from land, rather than from the sea or the sky ○ *land-based missiles* 2. existing in a physical location rather than as a website ○ *a land-based bookstore*

land bridge *n* a tract of land that connects continents, permitting the passage of people and animals

land crab *n* any crab that lives mainly on land and breeds in the sea

landed /lándid/ *adj* 1. possessing land, especially a large rural property 2. consisting of a large area of land

lander /lándər/ *n* a spacecraft designed to land on the surface of the Moon or a planet

landfall /lánd fawl/ *n* 1. an arrival on or a sighting of land, especially after a long journey by sea 2. the first land that somebody reaches after a long journey, especially by sea

landfill /lánd fil/ *n* 1. a site where waste material has been buried 2. the disposal of waste material or refuse by burying it in natural or excavated holes or depressions

landfill gas *n* a gas that is generated by the decomposition of organic material in a landfill site, e.g. methane

land forces *npl* armed forces serving exclusively on land

landform /lánd fawrm/ *n* a natural physical feature of the Earth's surface, e.g. a valley, mountain, or plain

land girl *n* a woman who did farm work as a member of the Land Army during World War I or World War II (*sometimes offensive*)

landgrave /lánd grayv/ *n* 1. in Germany, from the 13th century to 1806, a count who had jurisdiction over a region 2. a title given to some princes in central Germany after 1806 [Early 16C. < Middle Low German < *land* 'land' + *grave* 'count']

landgraviate /land gráyvi ət/, **landgravate** /lándgrə vayt/ *n* formerly, in Germany, the office, jurisdiction, or territory presided over by a landgrave or landgravine [Early 17C. < medieval Latin *landgraviatus* < Middle Low German *landgrave* (see LANDGRAVE)]

landgravine /lándgrə veen/ *n* 1. a woman who held the rank of landgrave, a title given in central Germany after 1801 2. the wife or widow of a landgrave [Late 17C. < Dutch *landgravin*, feminine of *landgraaf* 'landgrave' < Middle Low German *landgrave* (see LANDGRAVE)]

landholder /lánd hōldər/ *n* the owner or occupant of a piece of land —**landholding** *n, adj*

landing /lánding/ *n* 1. ACT OF COMING TO GROUND the act of reaching, touching, or alighting on the ground, e.g. after a jump or fall 2. ARRIVAL ON LAND an arrival on the ground after having been in the air or at sea 3. PLACE FOR LOADING OR UNLOADING a place for loading or unloading passengers or goods, especially from a ship ○ *There is a good landing at most of the villages along the coast.* 4. LEVEL AREA BETWEEN STAIRS a platform between flights of stairs or the floor at the top or foot of a flight of stairs

landing beacon *n* a radio transmitter at an airfield that sends a beam to guide aircraft on landing

landing beam *n* a radio beam emitted by a beacon at a landing field that enables incoming aircraft to make a landing

landing craft *n* a low open flat-bottomed boat designed for landing troops and equipment on shore from a ship

landing field *n* a place where aircraft can land and take off

landing gear *n* the wheels or floats and related mechanisms that are used by an aircraft or spacecraft when taking off and landing

landing net *n* a net like a bag fitted on a frame that is used by anglers to scoop up a hooked fish

landing pad *n* AVIAT same as **helipad**

landing speed *n* the minimum speed at which an aircraft has to be flying in order to land safely

landing stage *n* a floating or fixed wooden platform, used for loading or unloading passengers and goods from a boat

landing strip *n* AVIAT same as **airstrip**

landlady /lánd laydi/ (*plural* -dies) *n* 1. WOMAN WHO RENTS OUT PROPERTY a woman who owns property that she rents to tenants 2. WOMAN WHO RENTS OUT LODGINGS a woman who owns or runs a place offering accommodation, e.g. a bed-and-breakfast, guesthouse, or lodging house 3. WOMAN RUNNING PUB a woman who manages a public house

landless /lándləss/ *adj* not owning any land —**landlessness** *n*

landline /lánd līn/ *n* 1. a telecommunications cable laid overland 2. a telephone that is not a mobile phone or satellite phone

landlocked /lánd lokt/ *adj* 1. closed in completely or almost completely by land 2. adapted to life in a freshwater environment, with no access to the sea, though being a species historically found in the ocean

landlord /lánd lawrd/ *n* 1. SOMEBODY WHO RENTS OUT PROPERTY a person or organization that owns property that is rented to tenants 2. MAN WHO RENTS OUT LODGINGS a man who owns or runs a place offering accommodation, e.g. a bed-and-breakfast, guesthouse, or lodging house 3. MAN RUNNING PUB a man who manages a public house

landlubber /lánd lubər/ *n* somebody who is clumsy aboard a ship due to lack of experience at sea —**landlubberly** *adj*

landmark /lánd maark/ *n* 1. SOMETHING PROMINENT THAT IDENTIFIES LOCATION a prominent structure or geographical feature that identifies a location and serves as a guide to finding it 2. IMPORTANT NEW DEVELOPMENT an event, idea, or item that represents a significant or historic development 3. BOUNDARY MARKER a conspicuous object, e.g. a tree or stone, that is recognized as marking the boundary of a piece of land 4. *N Am* SOMETHING PRESERVED FOR HISTORIC IMPORTANCE a structure or site identified and preserved because of its historical significance ■ *adj* HIGHLY SIGNIFICANT marking a significant change or turning point in something, especially the law ○ *a landmark ruling*

landmass /lánd mass/ *n* a very large unbroken area of land, e.g. a continent or large island

landmine /lánd mīn/ *n* an explosive mine that is laid just under the surface of the ground and detonates if disturbed by pressure or the proximity of something such as metal

land office *n N Am* a government office that administers and records sales and transfers of public land

land of milk and honey *n* 1. in the Bible, a land of prosperity and plenty promised by God to the Israelites 2. a rich and fertile area or region of plenty (*literary*)

land of Nod *n* an imaginary place where people who are sleeping are said to be (*informal humorous*) [Pun, after a place mentioned in *Genesis* 4:16]

landowner /lánd ōnər/ *n* an owner of land —**landownership** *n* —**landowning** *n, adj*

Landrace /lánd rayss/ (*plural same* or -races) *n* a northern European pig belonging to a white lean long-bodied breed developed in Denmark [Mid-20C. < Danish, 'land breed']

landrail /lánd rayl/ *n* BIRDS same as **corncrake** [< RAIL[3]]

land reform *n* the redistribution of agricultural land, especially by government measures, so that those owning none receive some of it

Land Registry *n* a government department in England and Wales at which land and its ownership are registered

land rights *npl* ANZ the claim of Aboriginal peoples to the ownership of an area of land, usually based on occupation before the arrival of immigrants

Land Rover *tdmk* a trademark for a four-wheel-drive vehicle

landscape /lánd skayp/ *n* 1. VISUALLY DISTINCT SCENERY an expanse of scenery of a particular type, especially as much as can be seen by the eye 2. PAINTING OF VIEW a painting, drawing, or photograph of scenery, especially rural scenery 3. ART OF PAINTING OR DRAWING SCENERY the branch of art dealing with the painting, drawing, or photographing of scenery 4. GENERAL SITUATION OF ACTIVITY the general situation providing the background to a particular type of activity ○ *the economic landscape* 5. RANGE OF MENTAL CONCERNS any characteristic group of intellectual or imaginative features (*literary*) ■ *adj* PRINTED WITH LONG SIDES HORIZONTAL photographed or printed so that the long sides of a picture or the lines of text are parallel to the long sides of a rectangular page ■ *vt* (-scapes, -scaping, -scaped) MAKE LAND LOOK BETTER to enhance the appearance of land by altering its contours and planting trees and shrubs for aesthetic effect (*often passive*) ○ *The property was beautifully landscaped.* [Late 16C. < Dutch *landschap*, literally 'condition of being land' < *land* 'land']

landscape architect *n* somebody who plans and designs environments, especially with the aim of making new buildings, roads, and other structures compatible with their natural surroundings —**landscape architecture** *n*

landscape gardener *n* a designer of grounds and gardens —**landscape gardening** *n*

landscaper /lánd skaypər/ *n N Am* a designer of grounds or gardens

landscaping /lánd skayping/ *n* 1. the enhancement of the appearance of land, especially around buildings, by altering its contours and planting trees, shrubs, and flowers 2. the profession of designing or creating landscapes by combining plants and other features to produce a pleasing overall effect

landscapist /lánd skaypist/ *n* an artist who specializes in painting landscapes

Land's End /lándz énd/ cliff and promontory in Cornwall that forms the extreme southwestern tip of Great Britain

landshark /lánd shaark/ *n* an unethical dealer in land (*informal insult*)

landside /lánd sīd/ *n* 1. the part of an airport farthest from the aircraft 2. the flat part of a plough that faces unbroken land as it moves

landsknecht /lándz knekt/ *n* a mercenary foot soldier in Europe during the 16th century, especially a German pikeman [Early 17C. < German, 'servant of the country']

landsleit JUDAISM plural of **landsman**[2]

landslide /lánd slīd/ *n* 1. SUDDEN COLLAPSE OF LAND the collapse of part of a mountainside or cliff so that it descends in a disintegrating mass of rocks and earth 2. MASS OF LOOSENED ROCK AND EARTH a disintegrating mass of rock and earth that suddenly descends from a mountainside or cliff 3. CONSPICUOUS TRIUMPH an overwhelming victory, especially in an election

landslip /lánd slip/ *n* GEOG same as **landslide** (sense 1)

landsman[1] /lándzmən/ (*plural* -men /-mən/) *n* somebody who lives and works on land rather than at sea

landsman[2] /lándzmən/ (*plural* **landsleit** /lándz līt/) *n* a fellow Jew from the same district or area, originally in Eastern Europe [Mid-20C. Via Yiddish < Middle High German *lantsman* 'man from the (same) country']

Landsturm /laánt shtoorm/ *n* 1. in some European countries, a general draft of people for conscription into the armed forces 2. in some European countries, a military force of people drafted from the general population [Early 19C. < German, 'land storm']

Landtag /laánt taak/ *n* the legislative assembly of a German or Austrian state [Late 16C. < German, literally 'land day']

land tax *n* 1. an annual tax levied on landed property in the United Kingdom, abolished in 1963 2. in Australia, a tax imposed by states and territories, except the Northern Territory, on landowners where the unimproved value of the landholding exceeds a specific threshold

landward /lándwərd/ *adj* facing towards the land ■ *adv* same as **landwards**

landwards /lándwərdz/ *adv* in the direction of land

Landwehr /láant vair/ *n* in German-speaking countries, a reserve military force [Early 19C. < German, 'national defence']

Landy /lándi/, **John** (*b.* 1930) Australian athlete and politician. A middle-distance runner, he was the second person to run a mile in under four minutes (1954). He was appointed governor of the state of Victoria in 2001. Full name **Landy, John Michael**

land yacht *n* a wind-driven vehicle resembling a boat with a mast, sails, and three wheels, for use on beaches or other hard surfaces

lane /layn/ *n* **1.** NARROW STREET a narrow path, road or street, typically in older town areas or in the countryside, often enclosed by walls or hedges **2.** TRACK INTO WHICH ROAD IS DIVIDED a division of a road, street, or motorway wide enough for a single line of motor vehicles **3.** TRACK ASSIGNED TO RACER a track assigned to a competitive runner on a racing track or a swimmer in a swimming pool **4.** SHIPPING ROUTE a route assigned to a ship on a journey, especially through a congested area of sea **5.** AVIAT same as **air lane 6.** STRIP OF FLOOR IN BOWLING ALLEY the long strip of polished wooden flooring along which bowls are rolled in a bowling alley **7.** DIVISION OF BASKETBALL COURT an area of a basketball court extending from the free-throw line to just below the basket [Old English < W Germanic] ◇ **in the fast lane** at a fast, hectic, or stressful pace associated with success and achievement

Lane /layn/, **William** (1861–1917) British-born Australian journalist and political activist. He wrote *The Workingman's Paradise* (1892), and in 1893 founded an Australian socialist colony in Paraguay.

lane discipline *n* the degree of care and restraint exercised by drivers when using busy multilane roads, avoiding constant lane changing, cutting-in, driving too closely to vehicles in front, and risk-taking

Fritz Lang
Popperfoto

Lang /lang/, **Fritz** (1890–1976) Austrian-born US film director. He made many Hollywood films, but is best known for the silent film *Metropolis* (1927) and the German-language film *M* (1931).

Lange /lóngi/, **David Russell** (*b.* 1942) prime minister of New Zealand (1984–89). He pursued a non-nuclear defence policy that led to a dispute with the United States. See table at **prime minister**

Langi *n* PEOPLES, LANG same as **Lango**

langlauf /láang lowf/ *n* **1.** SKIING same as **cross-country skiing 2.** a contest in cross-country skiing [Early 20C. < German < *lang* 'long' + *Lauf* 'a run' (< Germanic)] — **langlaufer** *n*

langley /lángli/ (*plural* **-leys**) *n* a unit of solar radiation equivalent to one calorie per square centimetre [Mid-20C. After Samuel P. *Langley* (1834–1906), US aviation pioneer]

Lango /láng gō/ (*plural* **-gos** or *same*), **Langi** /-gi/ (*plural* **-gis** or *same*) *n* **1.** a member of a Nilotic people who live in northern Uganda **2.** the language of the Lango people, belonging to the Chari-Nile branch of Nilo-Saharan. Native speakers: 500,000. [Early 20C. < Nilotic] — **Lango** *adj*

Langobard /láng gə baard/ *n* PEOPLES same as **Lombard** (sense 2) [Late 18C. < late Latin *Langobardus* 'Lombard']

Langobardic /láng gə baárdik/ *n* a dialect of Old High German spoken by the ancient Lombards — **Langobardic** *adj*

langouste /long goóst/ *n* ZOOL, MARINE BIOL same as

spiny lobster [Mid-20C. Via French < Old Provençal *lagosta* < Latin *locusta* 'locust, crustacean']

langoustine /lóng goŏ steen/ *n* a large prawn or small lobster. Native to: North Atlantic. [Mid-20C. < French < *langouste* (see LANGOUSTE)]

langrage /láng grij/, **langridge** *n* shot consisting of a case filled with fragments of iron, formerly used for tearing the sails and rigging of enemy ships [Mid-18C. Origin ?]

Langrenus /láng grinəss/ *n* a plain on the Moon with a complex central peak located on the eastern edge of the Mare Fecunditatis, 132 km/82 mi. in diameter

langridge *n* ARMS another spelling of **langrage**

langsyne /láng sín/, **lang syne** Scotland *adv* long ago (*literary*) ○ *It all happened langsyne.* ■ *n* a time long past (*literary or humorous*)

Langtry /lángtri/, **Lillie** (1853–1929) British actress. She was the first woman of high social standing to go on the stage in Great Britain. She became the mistress of the Prince of Wales (later Edward VII). Born **Le Breton, Emilie Charlotte**

language /láng gwij/ *n* **1.** COMMUNICATION WITH WORDS the human use of spoken or written words as a communication system **2.** SPEECH OF GROUP the speech of a country, region, or group of people, including its vocabulary, syntax, and grammar **3.** SYSTEM OF COMMUNICATION a system of communication with its own set of conventions or special words ○ *sign language* **4.** NONVERBAL COMMUNICATION BETWEEN ANIMALS a nonverbal form of communication used by birds and animals **5.** NONVERBAL COMMUNICATION BETWEEN HUMANS the use of signs, gestures, or inarticulate sounds to communicate something **6.** SPECIALIST VOCABULARY the forms of expression used by those in a particular group or sphere of activity **7.** STYLE OF VERBAL EXPRESSION the verbal style by which people express themselves ○ *the language of diplomacy* **8.** COMPUT same as **programming language** [13C. < French *langage* < *langue* 'tongue' < Latin *lingua*] ◇ **speak the same language** to have values and interests in common with somebody so that it is possible to communicate effectively

SYNONYMS *language, tongue, speech, dialect, idiolect*
CORE MEANING: communication by words

language the human use of spoken or written words as a communication system, or the speech of a country, region, or group ○ *a full account of how we use language to communicate* ○ *Persian was for centuries the official language of much of the Indian subcontinent.* **tongue** a language used by a specific country, nation, or community ○ *students whose mother tongue is not English* ○ *Neither of them could speak the other's native tongue.* **speech** spoken language, especially as distinct from the written language ○ *The natural communication system for humans is speech, not typing messages on keyboards.* ○ *a writer trying to capture the patterns of speech of traditional village life* **dialect** a regional variety of a language, or a form of a language spoken by members of a specific social class or profession ○ *a dialect poem of 1730* ○ *A kill is a waterway in the local dialect.* **idiolect** an individual person's vocabulary and unique way of using language ○ *the distinct idiolect of each member of the family* ○ *With its phantasmagoric idiolect and cruel humour, this is a quite extraordinary book.*

language laboratory *n* a room equipped with audio or multimedia equipment for use in learning languages

language police *npl* people who try to set limits on written language considered offensive, discriminatory, or inappropriate (*informal disapproving*)

langue /longg/ *n* language regarded as a communication system and the common property of a speech community (*technical*) [Early 20C. < French (see LANGUAGE)]

langue de chat /lóng də shaá/ (*plural* **langues de chat** /pronunc. same/) *n* a small narrow flat biscuit often coated with chocolate [< French, 'cat's tongue']

langue d'oc /lóngg dók/ *n* the group of French dialects, usually considered to include Provençal, spoken in southern parts of medieval France [< French, 'language of "oc"'; from the use of *oc* (< Latin *hoc*) for 'yes']

Languedoc /lóng gə dók/ historical region and former province in southern France, stretching from the Pyrenees eastwards along the Mediterranean coast to the River Rhône

langue d'oïl /lóngg dóy/ *n* the group of French dialects spoken in the northern part of medieval France [< French, 'language of "oïl"'; from the use of *oïl* (< Latin *hoc ille*) for 'yes']

languet /láng gwet/ *n* something, e.g. a part in a machine or instrument, that is shaped like a tongue (*technical*) [14C. < Old French *languete* 'small tongue' < *langue* (see LANGUAGE)]

languid /láng gwid/ *adj* **1.** lacking vigour and energy ○ *a languid gesture* **2.** moving slowly ○ *a languid afternoon breeze* [Late 16C. Directly or via French < Latin *languidus* < *languere* 'be weak'] — **languidly** *adv* — **languidness** *n*

languish /láng gwish/ /láng gwish/ (**-guishes, -guishing, -guished**) *vi* **1.** BE NEGLECTED OR DEPRIVED to undergo hardship as a result of being deprived of something, typically attention, independence, or freedom **2.** BECOME LESS SUCCESSFUL to decline steadily, becoming less vital, strong, or successful **3.** PINE to long for something that is being denied [14C. < Old French *languiss-*, stem of *languir* < Latin *languere* 'be weak or faint'] — **languisher** *n* — **languishing** *n, adj* — **languishingly** *adv* — **languishment** *n*

languor /láng gər/ *n* **1.** TIREDNESS a pleasant feeling of weariness or weakness **2.** LISTLESSNESS IN SPEECH OR BEHAVIOUR listlessness and indifference in speech or behaviour **3.** HEAVINESS IN ATMOSPHERE an oppressive heaviness or sultriness in the air [13C. Via French < Latin *languere* 'be weak or faint']

languorous /láng gərəss/ *adj* **1.** listless and indifferent **2.** moving slowly ○ *They performed a languorous dance of infinite restraint.* — **languorously** *adv* — **languorousness** *n*

langur /láng gər, lang goór/ *n* a slender, leaf-eating monkey with a long tail, bushy eyebrows, and a chin tuft. Native to: Southeast Asia. Genus: *Presbytis.* [Early 19C. < Hindi *langūr* < Sanskrit *lāngūla* 'having a tail']

laniard *n* MIL, CLOTHING, NAUT, ARMS another spelling of **lanyard**

laniary /lánni əri/ *adj* describes a tooth adapted for tearing food [Early 19C. < Latin *laniarius* 'of a butcher' < *lanius* 'butcher' < *laniare* 'to tear'] — **laniary** *n*

laniferous /lə níffərəss/ *adj* wool-bearing or wool-covered [Mid-17C. < Latin *lanifer* < *lana* 'wool']

lanigerous /lə níjjərəss/ *adj* same as **laniferous** [Early 17C. < Latin *laniger* < *lana* (see LANIFEROUS)]

lank /langk/ *adj* **1.** limp and straight ○ *lank hair* **2.** long and slender [Old English *hlanc* 'lean' < Germanic, 'flexible'] — **lankly** *adv* — **lankness** *n*

lanky /lángki/ (**-ier, -iest**) *adj* tall and thin in a bony, ungracefully angular way — **lankily** *adv* — **lankiness** *n*

lanner /lánnər/ (*plural* **-ners** or *same*) *n* a large falcon, the female of which is used especially in falconry. Native to: Africa, Middle East, Mediterranean. Latin name: *Falco biarmicus.* [13C. < French *lanier*]

lanneret /lánnə ret/ (*plural* **-ets** or *same*) *n* a male lanner, smaller than the female and used in falconry

lanolin /lánnəlin/, **lanoline** /-leen/ *n* a fat extracted from sheep's wool. Use: in skin ointments. [Late 19C. < Latin *lana* 'wool' + *oleum* 'oil']

lansfordite /lánzfərd īt/ *n* a crystallized hydrate of magnesium carbonate occurring as stalactites [Late 19C. After *Lansford*, Pennsylvania, USA]

Lansing /lánssing/ capital of Michigan, a manufacturing city in the south-central part of the state. Population: 118,588 (2002 estimate).

lantana /lan táynə, -taánə/ (*plural* **-nas** or *same*) *n* an ornamental evergreen bush of the vervain family. Native to: tropical America. Genus: *Lantana.* [Late 18C. Via modern Latin < Italian dialect, 'wayfaring tree', which it resembles]

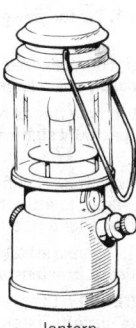

lantern

lantern /lántərn/ *n* **1.** PORTABLE LAMP a portable case with transparent or translucent sides that protects and holds a lamp **2.** LIGHTHOUSE ROOM a room containing the large lamp at the top of a lighthouse **3.** STRUCTURE WITH WINDOWS a structure with windows on all sides, resembling a lantern, e.g. one at the top of a dome **4.** STAGE LIGHT a light for illuminating a stage or part of a stage [13C. Via French < Latin *lanterna* < Greek *lamptēr* 'torch, lamp' < *lampein* 'to shine']

lantern fish *n* a small bony deep-sea fish with rows of luminous spots along its body. Family: Myctophidae.

lantern fly *n* a tropical insect with an elongated head that resembles a lantern and was formerly thought to emit light. Family: Fulgoridae.

lantern jaw *n* a long bony lower jaw, typically projecting beyond the upper jaw —**lantern-jawed** *adj*

lantern pinion *n* a gearwheel used in clocks and watches that has two circular discs connected by cylindrical pins

lantern slide *n* a transparent slide, typically made of glass, for projection onto a screen by a slide projector or magic lantern

lantern wheel *n* MECH ENG same as **lantern pinion**

lanthanide /lánthə nīd/ *n* an element of the lanthanide series of rare earths [Early 20C. < LANTHANUM]

lanthanide series *n* a group of the rare earths that range from lanthanum at atomic number 57 to lutetium at atomic number 71

lanthanum /lánthənəm/ *n* a silvery ductile metallic element resembling aluminium that belongs to the rare-earth group. Source: monazite, bastnaesite. Use: glass manufacture. Symbol **La**. See table at **element** [Mid-19C. < Greek *lanthanein* 'lie hidden'; because it was discovered hidden in cerium oxide]

lanugo /lə nyoogō/ (*plural* **-gos** or *same*) *n* a covering of soft downy hairs, especially those on a developing human foetus or newborn infant [15C. < Latin < *lana* 'wool'] —**lanuginous** /lə noojinəss/ *adj*

Lanús /la nooss/ city in Buenos Aires Province, eastern Argentina. It is a suburb of Buenos Aires. Population: 468,561 (1991).

lanyard /lányərd/, **laniard** *n* **1.** CORD WORN ROUND NECK a cord worn round the neck by military and naval personnel or by Scouts and Guides for carrying something such as a whistle or penknife **2.** SHORT ROPE ABOARD SHIP a short rope or cord used to hold or fasten something on a ship **3.** CORD FOR FIRING CANNON a cord tied to the breech mechanism of a cannon and used to fire it [14C. < French *lanière* 'strap'; influenced by YARD[1] 'spar']

Lanzarote /lánzə ráwti/ easternmost island of the Canary Islands, Las Palmas Province, Spain, situated northeast of Gran Canaria in the Atlantic Ocean. Population: 96,781 (2002). Area: 805 sq. km/311 sq. mi.

Lanzhou /lán jó/, **Lan-chou**, **Lanchow** capital of Gansu Province and a major transport and industrial centre on the Huang He (Yellow River), northern China. Population: 1,194,640 (1990).

Lao /low/ (*plural same*) *n* **1.** a member of a people of Laos and northeastern Thailand **2.** the language of the Lao and the official language of Laos, belonging to the Tai group of languages and closely related to Thai. Lao is spoken by about 3,000,000 people. [Mid-20C. < Lao] —**Lao** *adj*

Laoag /laa wáag/ town in the northwestern part of Luzon island in the northern Philippines. Population: 83,756 (1990).

Laocoön /lay ókō on/, **Laocoon** *n* in Greek mythology, a Trojan priest of Apollo who warned the Trojans about the Wooden Horse and was killed along with his two sons by sea serpents after he gave his warning

laodicean /láy ōdi seé ən/, **Laodicean** *adj* lacking in religious or political commitment ■ *n* somebody who has lukewarm or indifferent views, especially about religion or politics [Early 17C. < Latin *Laodicea*, city in modern-day Turkey, whose Christians were rebuked for indifference (Rev. 3:16)]

Laois /leesh/, **Leix** county in Leinster Province, Republic of Ireland. The county town is Port Laoise. Population: 52,945 (2002). Area: 1,720 sq. km/664 sq. mi.

Laos

Laos /lowss/ independent state of Southeast Asia, bordered by China, Vietnam, Cambodia, Thailand, and Myanmar. It is the only landlocked nation in Southeast Asia. Language: Lao. Currency: kip. Capital: Vientiane. Population: 5,921,545 (2003). Area: 236,800 sq. km/91,430 sq. mi. Official name **Lao People's Democratic Republic** —**Laotian** /lówsh'n, lay ōsh'n/ *n, adj*

Lao-tzu /lów tsóo/ (570?–490? BC) Chinese philosopher. He is credited with originating Taoism, described in the seminal *Tao-te Ching*. Known as **Master Lao**

lap[1] /lap/ *n* **1.** TOP OF SOMEBODY'S THIGHS WHEN SITTING the level area provided by the upper surface of the thighs of somebody who is seated **2.** PART OF CLOTHING RESTING ON THIGHS the part of a garment that hangs loosely across the thighs of somebody seated **3.** VALLEY a hollow in the contours of land, especially the gap between hills [Old English *læppa* 'flap of a garment, lobe' < Germanic] —**lapful** *n* ◇ **drop in** or **into your lap** to be given as something welcome and unexpected ◇ **drop something in somebody's lap** to become or make something somebody's responsibility ◇ **in the lap of luxury** in great luxury and comfort ◇ **in the lap of the gods** beyond human control or influence

lap[2] /lap/ *n* **1.** ONE CIRCUIT OF TRACK a single circuit of a racetrack or running track or one length of a swimming pool **2.** STAGE a phase in an extended project, enterprise, or journey **3.** OVERLAPPING PART an overlapping part of something **4.** LENGTH GOING ONCE ROUND REEL a length of fabric, thread, or rope that goes once round a roller, drum, or reel **5.** POLISHING DISC a rotating disc for cutting or polishing something such as glass or gemstones ■ *v* (**laps, lapping, lapped**) **1.** *vt* PASS COMPETITORS BY COMPLETE CIRCUIT to overtake a competitor on a racetrack or running track after having completed at least one circuit more than he or she has **2.** *vi* COMPLETE ONE TRACK CIRCUIT to run one complete circuit around a track **3.** *vt* WRAP SOMEBODY IN SOMETHING to enfold or enwrap somebody in something (*literary*; *often passive*) **4.** *vti* OVERLAP to overlap something (*literary*) **5.** *vt* POLISH OR CUT HARD SURFACES to polish or cut something hard such as glass, metal, or gemstones **6.** *vt* FORM FIBRES INTO BAND to arrange fibres so that they lie one against the other and form a band [14C. < LAP[1]] —**lapper** *n*

lap[3] /lap/ *vti* (**laps, lapping, lapped**) **1.** DRINK SOMETHING WITH TONGUE to drink a liquid by scooping it into the mouth with the tongue (*refers to animals*) **2.** WASH GENTLY AGAINST SURFACE to flow or splash gently against a surface ■ *n* **1.** PROCESS OF DRINKING SOMETHING WITH TONGUE the action of drinking liquid by scooping small amounts of it into the mouth with the tongue **2.** SOUND OF MOVING LIQUID the sound of a liquid gently flowing or splashing against something [Old English *lapian* < Germanic] —**lapper** *n*

lap up *v* **1.** *vti* same as **lap**[3] *v* (sense 1) **2.** *vt* to drink or eat something enthusiastically **3.** *vt* to enjoy something eagerly and uncritically

lap[4] /lap/ *n S Africa* a rag or small piece of cloth

lapa /laápə/, **lappa** *n S Africa* a fenced or thatched enclosure, used for outdoor meals or social gatherings [Early 20C. < Sotho *lelapa*, 'courtyard']

La Palma /la paálmə/ one of the Canary Islands, Spain, situated off the north coast of Africa. Population: 78,800 (2001). Area: 708 sq. km/273 sq. mi.

laparoscope /láppərə skōp/ *n* an instrument in the shape of a tube that is inserted through the abdominal wall to give an examining doctor a view of the internal organs

laparoscopy /láppə róskəpi/ (*plural* **-pies**) *n* examination of the internal organs of the abdomen using a laparoscope [Mid-19C. < Greek *lapara* 'flank'] —**laparoscopic** /láppərə skóppik/ *adj* —**laparoscopist** *n*

laparotomy /láppə róttəmi/ (*plural* **-mies**) *n* a surgical incision through the abdominal wall made to allow investigation of an abdominal organ or diagnosis of an abdominal disorder [Mid-19C. < Greek *lapara* 'flank']

La Paz /la páz/ **1.** capital city of Bolivia, located in the western part of the country. Population: 1,004,440 (2000). **2.** capital of Baja California Sur State, in western Mexico. Population: 170,366 (2000).

lap belt *n* a safety belt that is fitted to the seat of a motor vehicle and fastens across the lap

lapboard /láp bawrd/ *n* a thin flat board that is laid across the knees to serve as a table or writing surface

lap-chart *n* a record of each lap made by a motor vehicle in a race, showing each vehicle's exact position

lap dancer *n* a striptease artist who dances erotically close to or in the lap of a customer —**lap dancing** *n*

lapdog /láp dog/ *n* **1.** a small gentle-natured dog **2.** somebody who unthinkingly obeys somebody else's command, especially in an organization or institution

lapel /lə pél/ *n* either of the two folded-back front edges of a jacket that are continuous with the collar [Mid-17C. < LAP[1] 'part of a garment that projects'] —**lapelled** *adj*

lapidary /láppidəri/ *adj* **1.** ENGRAVED ON STONE engraved in stone or on a gemstone **2.** OF GEMSTONES relating to the art of cutting or engraving gemstones **3.** DIGNIFIED AND ELEGANT careful, elegant, and dignified in style (*formal*) ■ *n* (*plural* **-ies**) CUTTER OF PRECIOUS STONES an expert cutter, polisher, or engraver of gemstones [14C. < Latin *lapidarius* 'of stone' < *lapid-* 'stone']

lapidate /láppi dayt/ (**-dates, -dating, -dated**) *vt* (*literary*) **1.** to throw stones at somebody **2.** to stone somebody to death, especially as a punishment for wrongdoing [Early 17C. < Latin *lapidat-*, past participle of *lapidare* < *lapid-* 'stone'] —**lapidation** /láppi dáysh'n/ *n*

lapillus /lə pílləss/ (*plural* **-li** /-lī/) *n* a small fragment of lava thrown from a volcano [Mid-18C. < Latin, 'small stone' < *lapis* 'stone']

lapis lazuli /láppiss lázzyoo lī, -li/ *n* a deep blue semiprecious stone containing lazurite. Use: jewellery. ■ *adj* of the same deep brilliant blue as lapis lazuli [< Latin *lapis* 'stone' + medieval Latin *lazuli* 'of lapis lazuli' < Persian *lāžward* 'lapis lazuli']

Lapith /láppith/ (*plural* **-iths** or **-ithae** /-ith ee/) *n* in Greek mythology, a member of a people of Thessaly who fought the drunken centaurs at the wedding of their king, Pirithous. The contest of the Lapiths and centaurs was a frequent theme in Greek sculpture. [Early 17C. Via Latin < Greek *Lapithai* (plural)]

lap joint, **lapped joint** /lápt-/ *n* a joint made by overlapping the ends of two parts or pieces and fastening them together —**lap-jointed** *adj*

Laplace /laa pláss/, **Pierre Simon, Marquis de** (1749–1827) French astronomer and mathematician. He used Newton's theory of gravitation to account for the movement of planets in the solar system.

Lapland /láppland/ region largely within the Arctic Circle, extending across the northern parts of Norway, Sweden, Finland, and the Kola Peninsula of Russia —**Laplander** n

La Plata /la plaátə/ city and capital of Buenos Aires Province, eastern Argentina. Population: 676,128 (1991).

lap of honour n an extra lap round a racetrack or running track run by the winner of a race or game to acknowledge the presence and applause of spectators

Lapp /lap/ n **1.** an offensive term for a member of the Sami people of northern Europe **2.** an offensive term for the language of the Sami people [Late 16C. < Swedish] —**Lapp** adj

lapped joint n CONSTR same as **lap joint**

lappet /láppit/ n **1.** a loose fold or flap of fabric on a garment **2.** a lobe or hanging flap of flesh, e.g. a cow's dewlap or the wattle on a bird's head [15C. < LAP[1]]

lappet moth n a large purplish-brown moth whose furry larvae have flaps along their sides. Latin name: *Gastropacha quercifolia*.

lap pool n a pool designed for swimming laps, sometimes with a pump to create a current against which to swim

lap robe n N Am a small rug that wraps round the knees

lapsang souchong /láp sang soo shóng/ n a large-leafed type of black Chinese tea with a smoky flavour [Late 19C. *Lapsang* an invention]

lapse /laps/ n **1.** ERROR a momentary fault or failure in behaviour or morality **2.** GAP IN CONTINUITY a break in the continuity of something **3.** PERIOD a passage of time **4.** LAW FAILURE TO ACT IN TIME a failure to exercise a right within a specific period of time, e.g. the failure to buy a property before the termination of an option to buy ■ vi (**lapses, lapsing, lapsed**) **1.** GRADUALLY COME TO STOP to gradually come to an end or stop doing something **2.** DECLINE to decline in value, quality, or conduct ○ *Their standards have lapsed.* **3.** LOSE SIGNIFICANCE to decline gradually, becoming less important **4.** LAW BECOME VOID to become null and void through disuse, negligence, or death **5.** same as **elapse** [14C. < Latin *lapsus* 'falling, failure' < past participle of *labi* 'fall'] —**lapsable** adj —**lapser** n ◇ **a lapse from grace** a failure in moral conduct or religious belief
lapse into vi **1.** to revert to a previous state, especially of quiet or inactivity **2.** to revert to a previous habit or way of life, often an undesirable one

lapsed /lapst/ adj **1.** no longer committed to something, especially religious faith or observance **2.** expired or terminated

lapse rate n the rate at which the temperature of the atmosphere falls as altitude increases

lapstrake /láp strayk/ adj NAUT same as **clinker-built** ■ n a boat built with overlapping planks [Late 18C. < LAP[2] + STRAKE]

Laptev Sea /láptef-/ section of the Arctic Ocean, situated off the northern coast of Siberian Russia

laptop /láp top/ n a small portable personal computer, often battery operated, usually consisting of a case that opens to reveal a screen in the upper part and a keyboard in the lower part

Laputan /lə pyoót'n/ adj concentrating on absurdly impractical ideas or projects, often to the exclusion of things that need to be done [Mid-19C. < *Laputa*, island in *Gulliver's Travels* (1726) by Jonathan Swift whose people were like this]

lapware /láp wair/ n software for children that includes simple text and animation for telling stories

lapwing /láp wing/ n (plural -**wings** or same) n a long-legged bird that is noted for its shrill cry and erratic flight. Genus: *Vanellus*. [Old English *hleapewince* < LEAP + Germanic ancestor of WINK meaning 'move from side to side'; altered by association with LAP[1], WING]

~~laquer~~ incorrect spelling of **lacquer**

Lara /laárə/, **Brian** (b. 1969) Trinidadian cricketer. His score of 400 not out for the West Indies against England (2004) set the record as the highest ever score in test cricket.

larboard /laárbərd/ n the port or left side of a vessel (dated) [Late 16C. Alteration of *ladeboard* 'loading side']

~~larceny~~ incorrect spelling of **larceny**

larceny /laárss'ni/ n the unlawful taking and removal of another person's property (dated) [15C. < Anglo-Norman < Old French *larcin* < Latin *latrocinium* 'theft' < *latro* 'thief' < Greek *latron* 'pay, wages'] —**larcener** n —**larcenist** n —**larcenous** adj —**larcenously** adv

larch /laarch/ (plural **larches** or same) n **1.** a deciduous tree of the pine family with clusters of needle-shaped leaves and erect cones. Genus: *Larix*. **2.** the durable wood of a larch tree [Mid-16C. < Middle High German *larche* < Latin *larix*]

lard /laard/ n WHITE COOKING FAT white, slightly soft, pork fat. Use: cooking, in ointments and perfumes. ■ v (**lards, larding, larded**) **1.** vti ADD LARD TO MEAT BEFORE COOKING to thread strips of fat or fatty bacon through holes made in a lean cut of meat to keep the meat moist while cooking **2.** vt INCLUDE EXTRA WORDS IN TEXT to include an unnecessary or undesirable amount of additional material in a speech or piece of writing ○ *larded with quotations* [14C. < French, 'bacon' < Latin *lar(i)dum*] —**lardy** adj

lardass /laárd ass/ n N Am an offensive term that deliberately insults somebody's body weight (slang insult)

larder /laárdər/ n a cool place, especially a small room or large cupboard, used for storing food [13C. < Anglo-Norman < Old French *lard* (see LARD)]

larding-needle /laárding-/ n a long thick metal needle that grips one end of a strip of fat to allow it to be threaded through lean meat to keep it moist while cooking

Lardner /laárdnər/, **Ring** (1885–1933) US humorist and writer. He is known for his satirical short stories, particularly the baseball stories collected in the volume *You Know Me, Al* (1914). Full name **Lardner, Ringgold Wilmer**

'How do you look when I'm sober?'
[Ring Lardner. Quoted in *Ring*, J. Yardley; 1977]

lardy cake /laárdi-/ n a small, sweet, usually square or oblong cake made with yeast dough folded and rolled with lard, fruit, and sugar

Laredo /lə ráydō/ city in southern Texas, on the border with Mexico. Population: 191,538 (2002 estimate).

lares and penates /laá reez ənd pə naá teez, laí reez-/ npl **1.** in ancient Roman religion, the household deities. The lares were believed to protect the household from danger, while the penates were believed to bring wealth. **2.** a family's treasured or valuable possessions (dated) [Late 16C. < Latin]

large /laarj/ (**larger, largest**) adj **1.** VERY BIG comparatively big in size, number, or quantity, or bigger in size, number, or quantity than is usual or expected **2.** OF TALL HEAVY BUILD tall and well-built, heavy set, broad, or overweight **3.** IMPORTANT significant or general in scope, extent, or effect ○ *a large view of the subject* **4.** GENEROUS generous in spirit or attitude **5.** FAVOURABLE FOR SAILING describes a wind that is blowing in a favourable direction ○ *a large wind* [12C. Via French < Latin *larga*, form of *largus* 'abundant'] —**largeness** n ◇ **at large 1.** as a widely based and general group of people **2.** escaped or free and possibly dangerous ◇ **by and large** speaking generally ◇ **large it, live large** to live or celebrate in an extravagant way (informal)

large calorie n MEASURE same as **calorie**

large cap adj relating to a company with a large amount of share capital, especially when considered as one of a group of such companies on a stock market [< shortening of *capitalization*]

large copper n a butterfly with black and orange markings on its wings. Native to: Europe. Latin name: *Lycaena dispar*.

large-handed adj very generous or magnanimous —**large-handedness** n

large-hearted adj generous, kind, or understanding —**large-heartedness** n

large intestine n the end section of the alimentary canal reaching from ileum to anus and consisting of the caecum, colon, and rectum. Its function is to extract water and form faeces.

largely /laárjli/ adv **1.** for the most part **2.** on a big or grand scale

large-minded adj characterized by a liberal attitude —**large-mindedly** adv —**large-mindedness** n

large-print adj set in type that is bigger than normal for the benefit of partially sighted readers ○ *a large-print book*

larger-than-life adj very confident, impressive, flamboyant, and likely to attract attention (not hyphenated when used after a verb)

large-scale adj **1.** comparatively big in size and showing a lot of detail **2.** extensive in scope or scale

large-scale integration n the process of integrating a large number of circuits, often several thousand, on a silicon chip

largesse /laar jéss/, **largess** n **1.** GENEROSITY the generous giving of gifts, money, or favours **2.** GIFTS the gifts, money, or favours given as a result of somebody's generosity **3.** LIBERALITY generosity or liberality, especially in spirit or attitude [13C. < French < Latin *largus* 'abundant']

Large White n a large white pig belonging to a UK breed. Kept for: meat.

larghetto /laar géttō/ adv at a fairly slow tempo, but slightly faster than largo (used as a musical direction) ■ n (plural -**tos**) a larghetto movement or musical piece [Early 18C. < Italian, 'little largo' < *largo* 'broad'] —**larghetto** adj

largish /laárjish/ adj quite big, rather than enormous

largo /laárgō/ adv at a fairly slow and broad tempo, more slowly than lento but faster than grave (used as a musical direction) ■ n (plural -**gos**) a largo movement or musical piece [Late 17C. < Italian, 'broad'] —**largo** adj

lari[1] /laári/ (plural same or -**ris**) n the main unit of Georgian currency. See table at **currency** [Late 20C. < Georgian]

lari[2] /laári/ n MONEY another spelling of **laari**

lariat /lárri ət/ n N Am **1.** AGRIC same as **lasso 2.** a tethering rope, especially one used to hold a grazing animal in one place [Mid-19C. < Spanish *la reata* 'the rope' < *reatar* 'tie again' < Latin *aptare* 'adjust']

Larissa /lə ríssə/ n a small inner natural satellite of Neptune, discovered in 1989 by Voyager 2. It is irregular in shape and has a maximum dimension of approximately 210 km.

lark

lark[1] /laark/ n a small songbird with brownish feathers, noted for its song. Native to: worldwide. Family: Alaudidae. [Old English *láferce, læwerce* < W Germanic] ◇ **get up** or **rise** or **be up with the lark** to get up from bed very early

lark[2] /laark/ n **1.** MISCHIEVOUS ADVENTURE adventurous or risky fun ○ *did it for a lark* **2.** INNOCENT FUN a carefree or harmless piece of fun **3.** AREA OF ACTIVITY an activity, pastime, or job referred to as though it is not being taken very seriously (informal) ○ *have a go at the catering lark* ■ vi (**larks, larking, larked**) **1.** HAVE FUN to have fun, especially in a boisterous or good-humoured way **2.** ACT MISCHIEVOUSLY to behave in a mischievous, annoying, or irresponsible manner [Early 19C. Origin ?] —**larker** n —**larkiness** n —**larkish** adj —**larkishness** n —**larky** adj
lark about, lark around vi to have fun in a playful, childish, or irresponsible way

lark bunting n a small songbird related to the finch and sparrow with a black or brown body, white wing patch, and a large pale beak. Native to: south

central Canada and central United States. Family: Fringillidae.

Larkin /laárkin/, **Philip** (1922–85) British poet and jazz critic. He worked as a librarian at Hull University. His works include *The Whitsun Weddings* (1964) and *High Windows* (1974). Full name **Larkin, Philip Arthur**

> 'Nothing, like something, happens any-where.'
> [Philip Larkin, 'I Remember, I Remember', *Philip Larkin Collected Poems*; 1988]

larkspur /laárk spur/ *n* a delphinium plant. Flowers: pink, white, or blue, in spikes. Native to: cool regions worldwide. Genus: *Delphinium*. [Late 16C. < the resemblance of the spurred flowers to the lark's long hind claws]

Larne /laarn/ town in County Antrim, Northern Ireland. Population: 30,832 (2001).

La Rochelle /la ro shél/ seaport, tourist centre, and capital of Charente-Maritime Department, Poitou-Charentes Region, western France. Population: 76,584 (1999).

Larousse /la roóss/, **Pierre** (1817–75) French lexicographer. He compiled the 15-volume *Great Universal Dictionary of the Nineteenth Century* (1865–76).

larrigan /lárrigan/ *n* a knee-high boot with the leg part made of oiled leather, worn especially by lumberjacks, trappers, and woodsmen [Late 19C. Origin ?]

larrikin /lárrikin/ *n* ANZ **1. UNCONVENTIONAL PERSON** an unconventional or nonconformist person, especially in public life **2. SOMEBODY MISCHIEVOUS** a mischievous or playful person (*informal*) **3. LOUT** somebody regarded as behaving in an unruly or disruptive manner (*dated insult*) [Mid-19C. Origin ?] —**larrikinism** *n*

larrup /lárrap/ *vt* (**-rups, -ruping, -ruped**) to beat or flog a person or animal ■ *n* a blow, especially one delivered with a lot of force [Early 19C. Origin ?] —**larruper** *n*

Larson /laárss'n/, **Gary** (*b.* 1950) US cartoonist. His popular comic strip *The Far Side* (1980–95) is characterized by whimsical, absurd, and macabre animal and insect characters.

larva /laárva/ (*plural* **-vae** /-vee/) *n* **1.** the wingless immature worm-shaped form of many insects that develops into a pupa or chrysalis before becoming an adult insect **2.** the immature, early-stage form of frogs and other animals that undergo marked changes during metamorphosis [Mid-17C. < Latin, 'ghost'] —**larval** *adj*

larvicide /laárvi síd/ *n* a chemical used to kill larvae —**larvicidal** /laárvi síd'l/ *adj*

Larwood /laár wŏod/, **Harold** (1904–95) British cricketer. A fast bowler, he was key to the 'bodyline bowling' tactics in the 1932–33 England tour of Australia, which strained Anglo-Australian diplomatic relations.

laryng- *prefix* same as **laryngo-** (*used before vowels*)

laryngeal /la rínjəl, -rínji əl, lárrin jeé əl/ *adj* **1.** belonging to, relating to, situated in, or affecting the larynx **2.** describes a speech sound produced in the region of the larynx [Late 18C. < modern Latin *laryngeus* < *laryng-* (see LARYNGO-)] —**laryngeally** *adv*

laryngectomy /lárrin jéktəmi/ (*plural* **-mies**) *n* the surgical removal of all or part of the larynx

larynges ANAT *plural* of **larynx**

laryngitis /lárrin jítiss/ *n* inflammation of the larynx, usually accompanied by hoarseness and coughing —**laryngitic** /lárrin jíttik/ *adj*

laryngo- *prefix* larynx ○ *laryngotomy* [Via modern Latin *laryng-* < Greek *larugg-*, stem of *larugx*]

laryngology /lárring góllaji/ *n* a branch of medicine dealing with diseases and conditions of the larynx and vocal cords —**laryngologic** /lə ríng gə lójjik/ *adj* —**laryngologically** *adv* —**laryngologist** *n*

laryngopharynx /lə ríng gō fárringks/ (*plural* **-pharynges** /-fə rín jeez/ or **-pharynxes**) *n* the part of the throat immediately behind the voice box or larynx, and extending downwards to the top of the gullet or oesophagus

laryngoscope /lə ríng gə skōp/ *n* a medical instrument

consisting of a short metal or plastic tube fitted with a tiny light bulb, used when examining the larynx. Its commonest use is for viewing the entrance to the larynx when inserting a breathing tube during surgery.

laryngoscopy /lárring góskəpi/ (*plural* **-pies**) *n* an examination of the entrance to, or interior of, the larynx, for the purpose of diagnosis or to facilitate the passage of a tube through the larynx —**laryngoscopic** /lə ríng gə skóppik/ *adj* —**laryngoscopically** *adv* —**laryngoscopist** *n*

laryngotomy /lárring góttəmi/ (*plural* **laryngotomies**) *n* a surgical procedure in which an incision is made in the larynx

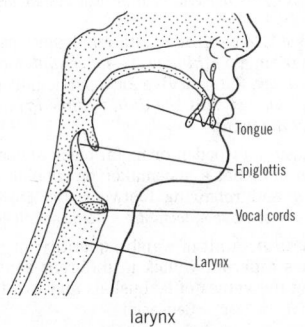

larynx

larynx /lárringks/ (*plural* **larynges** /lə rín jeez/ or **larynxes**) *n* the cartilaginous box-shaped part of the respiratory tract between the level of the root of the tongue and the top of the trachea. In humans and some other air-breathing vertebrates it is the organ of voice production, containing the vocal cords. [Late 16C. Via modern Latin < Greek *larugx*]

lasagne /lə zánnyə, -sánn-, -zaán-/ (*plural* **-gnes** or *same*), **lasagna** (*plural* **-gnas** or **-gne**) *n* **1.** a dish of Italian origin consisting of alternate layers of pasta sheets and filling, especially alternating pasta, a meat and tomato sauce, and a savoury white sauce, baked in the oven. Various other sauces or fillings may also be used. **2.** thin flat sheets of fresh or dried pasta, which are generally layered with sauces or other ingredients, then baked [Mid-19C. < Italian, plural of *lasagna* < Latin *lasanum* 'cooking vessel']

La Salle /la sál/, **René-Robert Cavelier, Sieur de** (1643–87) French explorer. He navigated the Mississippi River, North America, to its mouth, and tried to colonize the area for France.

lascar /láskər/, **Lascar** *n* a South or Southeast Asian sailor, army servant, or artilleryman (*dated*) [Early 17C. < Persian, Urdu *laškarī* 'soldier' < *laškar* 'army, camp']

Lascaux /láskō/ site of an underground cave, called Grotte de Lascaux, in southwestern France, that contains outstanding examples of Stone Age art

lascivious /lə sívvi əss/ *adj* **1.** showing a desire for, or unseemly interest in, sex **2.** provoking lust [15C. < Late Latin *lasciviosus* < Latin *lascivus* 'lustful'] —**lasciviously** *adv* —**lasciviousness** *n*

Lasdun /lázdən/, **Sir Denys** (1914–2001) British architect. His works include the National Theatre (1967–76) in London and the University of East Anglia in Norwich (1962–68).

lase /layz/ (**lases, lasing, lased**) *vi* to emit the type of single-wavelength radiation produced by a laser [Mid-20C. Back-formation < LASER]

LASEK /láyzek/ *n* laser surgery performed to correct short-sightedness, long-sightedness, or astigmatism by making a flap in the topmost layer of the cornea before reshaping the tissue underneath [Acronym < *laser epithelial keratomileusis*]

laser /láyzər/ *n* a device that utilizes the ability of some substances to absorb electromagnetic energy and re-radiate it as a highly focused beam of synchronized single-wavelength radiation [Mid-20C. Acronym < *light amplification by stimulated emission of radiation*]

laser card *n* COMPUT same as **smart card**

laser disk *n* COMPUT same as **optical disk**

laser printer *n* a computer printer using a focused laser beam to place an image on a photosensitive

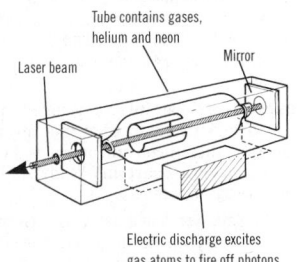

Tube contains gases, helium and neon

Laser beam

Mirror

Electric discharge excites gas atoms to fire off photons

laser

drum, which uses electrostatic charge to print the image

laser ring gyro *n* a navigation system for aircraft that uses measurement of laser light in a closed circuit

laser surgery *n* surgery performed using a laser to remove exact amounts of tissue without harming surrounding tissue, e.g. to improve eyesight or remove skin blemishes

laser welding *n* the process of using a laser to join tissues together in order to seal up wounds

lash[1] /lash/ *n* **1. STROKE WITH WHIP** a stroke with a whip or some other long flexible object, often one of several given as a punishment **2.** same as **eyelash 3. MOVEMENT LIKE WHIP** a movement like that of a whip being cracked ○ *The lion gave a lash of its tail.* **4. END OF WHIP** the flexible end of a whip **5. SEVERE SCOLDING** a severe reproof or verbal attack ○ *He felt the full lash of his father's tongue.* **6. IMPACT OF SOMETHING** a strong or powerful, often continuous, impact of something, especially a natural element, against a surface ○ *the lash of waves onto the beach* ■ *v* (**lashes, lashing, lashed**) **1.** *vti* **SMASH ONTO SOMETHING** to have a strong or powerful, often continuous, impact on a surface ○ *Heavy seas lashed the shore.* **2.** *vti* **CRITICIZE SOMEBODY** to criticize somebody or something severely ○ *She lashed into her critics.* **3.** *vt* **WHIP SOMEBODY** to hit somebody or something with a whip or an object like a whip, often repeatedly as a form of punishment ○ *Prisoners were lashed severely.* **4.** *vti* **FLICK TO AND FRO** to flick something from side to side sharply so that it moves like a whip, or move in this way ○ *The cat lashed its tail angrily.* **5.** *vt* **INCITE PEOPLE** to encourage somebody, especially a crowd of people, to feel a strong emotion such as anger ○ *The fans had lashed themselves into a fever of enthusiasm.* —**lasher** *n*

lash out *vi* **1. ATTACK SOMEBODY VERBALLY** to attack somebody verbally and suddenly **2. ATTACK SOMEBODY PHYSICALLY** to start suddenly to attack somebody with uncontrolled movements **3. SPEND MONEY** to spend money extravagantly on something (*informal*)

lash[2] /lash/ (**lashes, lashing, lashed**) *vt* to tie something tightly or securely to another object [15C. Origin ?] —**lasher** *n*

lashing[1] /láshing/ *n* **1. FLOGGING** a beating with a whip or something resembling a whip **2. SEVERE SCOLDING** a severe rebuke or critical attack ■ **lashings** *npl* **LARGE QUANTITY** generous or plentiful amounts of something [15C. < LASH[1]]

lashing[2] /láshing/ *n* rope or cord used for securing things [Mid-17C. < LASH[2]]

lash-up *n* an object hastily made or put together, especially in order to meet emergency needs

LASIK /láyzik/ *n* laser surgery performed to correct short-sightedness, long-sightedness, or astigmatism by cutting a flap in the cornea and removing tissue underneath [Acronym < *laser-assisted in situ keratomileusis*]

lasket /láskit/ *n* a loop on a sail for fastening an extra sail [Early 18C. Origin ?]

Las Palmas /lass pálməss/ city, seaport, and capital of Las Palmas Province, northeastern Grand Canary Island, Spain. Population: 352,641 (1998).

La Spezia /la spétsi ə/ naval base, port city, and capital of La Spezia Province, Liguria Region, northwestern Italy. Population: 91,391 (2001).

lass /lass/ *n* **1.** YOUNG WOMAN a girl or young woman (*sometimes considered offensive*) **2.** GIRLFRIEND a girlfriend or sweetheart **3.** N England, Scotland WOMAN a woman of any age [14C. Probably related to Old Norse *laskura* 'unmarried']

Lassa fever /lássə-/ *n* an infectious, often fatal, viral disease of West Africa marked by high fever, muscle pain, ulcers of the mucous membranes, headaches, haemorrhaging, and heart and kidney failure [Late 20C. After a village in Nigeria]

Lassalle /la sál/, **Ferdinand** (1825–64) German politician. A socialist, he founded the Universal German Working Men's Association, which later became the German Social Democratic Party.

Lassen Volcanic National Park /lássən-/ national park in Northeastern California, established in 1907. Its main feature is the volcanic Lassen Peak, 3,187 m/10,457 ft high. Area: 430 sq. km/166 sq. mi.

Lasseter /lássətər/, **Harold Bell** (1880–1931) Australian prospector. His claim that an enormous reef of gold lay in northwestern Australia led to several expeditions to the area. Born **Lasseter, Lewis Hubert**

lassi /lássi/ *n* a South Asian drink consisting of flavoured yoghurt or buttermilk diluted with water [Late 20C. < Hindi]

lassie /lássi/ *n* N England, Scotland (*informal*) **1.** a girl or young woman (*sometimes considered offensive*) **2.** a girlfriend or sweetheart **3.** same as **daughter** *n* (sense 1)

lassitude /lássi tyood/ *n* a state of weariness accompanied by listlessness or apathy [15C. Via French < Latin *lassitudo* < *lassus* 'weary']

lasso /lə soó, la-, lássō/ *n* (*plural* -**sos**) a long stiff piece of rope or cord with a sliding noose at one end, used especially for catching horses and cattle ■ *vt* (-**sos, -soing, -soed**) to use a lasso or other length of rope to catch a horse, cow, or other animal [Mid-18C. Representing the American Spanish pronunciation of Spanish *lazo* < Latin *laqueus* 'noose'] —**lassoer** *n*

last[1] /laast/ CORE MEANING: a grammatical word indicating that something is the most recent or final of all ○ (adj) *She was married last April.* ○ (adj) *John turned and took a last look at the band.* ○ (adv) *Allow me to apologize for the uncomfortable circumstances under which we last met.* ○ (adv) *He got to the meeting last.* ○ (pron) *Her new album's even better than the last.*

1. *adj, pron* MOST RECENT occurring most recently ○ (adj) *I saw him last Tuesday.* ○ (pron) *This flood may turn out to be even worse than the last.* **2.** *adj, pron* AFTER ALL OTHERS being or occurring after all the others ○ (adj) *He is believed to be the last person to see her before she left.* ○ (pron) *Your first complaint may well be your last.* **3.** *adj, pron* ONLY REMAINING the final or only person, thing, or part remaining ○ (adj) *This machine just ate my last pound coin!* ○ (pron) *Here – finish up the last of the cake.* **4.** *adj, pron* LEAST SUITABLE least suitable, appropriate, or likely ○ (adj) *She's the last person we want on this project.* ○ (pron) *I am the last to criticize you in any way.* **5.** *adj* RELATING TO END relating to the end of somebody's life **6.** *adj* UK, *regional* INFERIOR inferior or unpleasant ○ *This food is last.* **7.** *adv* MOST RECENTLY on the most recent occasion ○ *When I last spoke to them they sounded fine.* **8.** *adv* AFTER ALL OTHERS after all the others in a series or order **9.** *adv* FINALLY as the final point ○ *Last, I'd like to mention all the people who helped to make this evening a success.* **10.** *n* FINAL MOMENT the final moment, especially of life ○ *She remained cheerful to the last.* [Old English *latost* (adverb) 'after all the others' < Germanic] ◇ **at last** finally or in the end ○ *I've found you at last – I've been looking everywhere.* ◇ **at long last** eventually, after a long delay or many difficulties ○ *They fought the case for years and at long last got some compensation.* ◇ **breathe your last** same as **die**[1] (sense 1) (*literary*) ○ *I was by her side when she breathed her last.* ◇ **every last** everything without exception ○ *They ate it up, every last piece of it.* ◇ **last but not least** the final thing to be mentioned but important nevertheless ○ *And of course, last but not least, we thank the staff of customer relations.* ◇ **the last of 1.** the last remaining person, thing, or part of something, or the last in a sequence ○ *That's the last of the bread – I'll get some more tomorrow.* **2.** somebody's final contact with or news of somebody or something ○ *You haven't heard the last of this – I'm going to complain.*

CULTURAL NOTE *The Last of the Mohicans*, a novel (1826) by US writer James Fenimore Cooper. The most popular of Cooper's evocative accounts of frontier life, it is set in mid-18th-century North America during the wars between Britain and France. It describes the attempts of frontiersman Hawkeye and his Mahican companions, Chingachook and Uncas, the last of their people, to protect a British family from the French and their Huron allies.

---

last[2] /laast/ (**lasts, lasting, lasted**) *vti* **1.** to continue to exist or happen for a period of time ○ *The festival lasted for three hours.* ○ *The voyage lasted eight days.* **2.** to continue to be used or available for a period of time ○ *The provisions lasted for ten days.* ○ *The fruit lasted us a week.* [Old English *læstan* 'last, follow' < Germanic]

last out *vt* **1.** to be an adequate supply for a particular length of time ○ *I think we've got enough food to last out the week.* **2.** to survive for a particular length of time ○ *The vet said she didn't think Prince would last out the night.*

last[3] /laast/ *n* a wooden or metal block shaped like a human foot that a shoemaker or cobbler uses for making and repairing footwear [Old English *læste* < *lāst* 'sole of the foot, footprint' < Germanic, 'follow']

last[4] /laast/ *n* a unit of weight, quantity, or capacity that has different values in different contexts including the values of 80 bushels and two tons [Old English *hlæst* 'load' < Germanic]

last-born *adj* youngest in a family

last call *n* N Am a bartender's request for last drink orders before closing time (*informal*)

last-ditch *adj* done or taken when all other options have been exhausted

last-gasp *adj* done as a last measure when all other options have failed and time is running out

last-in, first-out *n* **1.** a method of accounting in which it is assumed that the most recently purchased items in an inventory are the first to be sold **2.** the dismissal of staff beginning with those who were employed most recently, used as a way of reducing personnel (*informal*)

lasting /laásting/ *adj* continuing for a very long time or indefinitely ■ *n* a strong durable twill fabric. Use: shoe uppers. [14C. < LAST[2]] —**lastingly** *adv* —**lastingness** *n*

Last Judgment *n* in Jewish, Islamic, and Christian traditions, God's final judgment of humankind, which is to take place at the end of the world

lastly /laástli/ *adv* as the final thing at the end of a series [14C. < LAST[1]]

last minute *n* the latest time that it is possible to do something and still be in time —**last-minute** *adj*

last name *n* same as **surname**

last orders *npl, interj* the final opportunity to buy drinks before a pub, bar, or other place selling alcohol closes

last post *n* **1.** a bugle call given to signal the end of the day at a UK military establishment and the lowering of the flag at last light **2.** a bugle call that is given at a UK military funeral

last resort *n* something tried or done when everything else has failed

last rites *npl* **1.** in the Roman Catholic Church, religious rites performed for somebody who is close to death **2.** in Christianity, religious rites accompanying a burial or funeral

last spike *n* N Am the final section completing a rail line, symbolized by the final spike driven to secure the rails

last straw *n* a minor annoyance that, because it comes at the end of a series of other misfortunes, makes a situation unbearable [< the fable of the camel whose back was broken by the last straw added to its load]

Last Supper *n* the last meal that Jesus Christ ate with his disciples before his crucifixion, commemorated by Christians in the Communion ceremony

last thing *adv* immediately before going to bed for the night

last time *adv* Malaysia, Singapore during or at an earlier period, but no longer ○ *Last time I lived in Ipoh.* [Probably translation < Chinese]

last word *n* **1.** FINAL REMARK IN DISCUSSION the final thing to be said, especially at the end of an argument, disagreement, or discussion **2.** ULTIMATE DECISION the final decision on something **3.** BEST the best of its kind ○ *the last word in convenience* ■ **last words** *npl* DYING STATEMENT the final remarks spoken by somebody who is dying, often thought to be very personal and sometimes of great significance

Las Vegas /lass váygəss/ city in southern Nevada, a centre for tourism and gambling. It is famous for the extravagant neon-lighted resort hotels, casinos, and bars that line its main street, known as 'The Strip'. Population: 508,604 (2002 estimate).

lat[1] /laat/ (*plural* **lati** /látti/ or **lats**) *n* the main unit of Latvian currency. See table at **currency** [Late 20C. < Latvian, shortening of *Latvija* 'Latvia']

lat[2] /lat/ *n* ANAT same as **latissimus dorsi** (*informal*) [Shortening]

lat. *abbr* GEOG latitude

Lat. *abbr* **1.** LANG Latin **2.** Latvia **3.** PEOPLES, LANG Latvian

Latakia /lə táki ə/ city and seaport, capital of Latakia Governorate, northwestern Syria. Population: 311,784 (1994).

latch /lach/ *n* **1.** DEVICE FOR KEEPING DOORS SHUT a device for holding a door, gate, or other opening closed consisting of a movable bar that drops into a hole or notch **2.** DOOR LOCK a door lock that needs a key to be opened from the outside but not the inside ■ *vt* (**latches, latching, latched**) FASTEN SOMETHING WITH LATCH to close or lock something with a latch [Old English *læccan* 'to grasp' < Indo-European]

latch on *vi* to finally grasp something or understand (*informal*)

latch onto *vt* (*informal*) **1.** to remain constantly in somebody's company even if the person would prefer other company or solitude **2.** to adopt something enthusiastically ○ *latched onto the idea*

latchet /láchit/ *n* a leather thong for tying a shoe or sandal (*archaic*) [14C. < Old French *lachet* 'little string' < *laz* (see LACE)]

latchkey /lách kee/ (*plural* -**keys**) *n* a key for lifting a latch, especially one on an outside door or gate

latchkey child *n* a child who returns from school to an empty home because the adults in the family are still at work

latchstring /lách string/ *n* a string attached to a latch and passed through a hole in a door to allow somebody to open it from the other side

late /layt/ *adj* (**later, latest**) **1.** AFTER EXPECTED TIME happening or arriving after an expected or arranged time ○ *Hurry up or we'll be late!* **2.** AFTER USUAL TIME happening or done after the normal or usual time ○ *a late lunch* **3.** NEAR END OF PERIOD near the end of a particular period of time ○ *The meeting is scheduled for late morning.* **4.** INTO NIGHT well into the evening or night ○ *It's late – time for bed.* **5.** ⚠ DEAD having died, especially fairly recently ○ *my late grandfather* **6.** UP UNTIL RECENTLY having recently done something, lived somewhere, or belonged to a group or organization but no longer doing so ○ *That reporter, late of the European bureau, is now moving to Southeast Asia.* **7.** DONE TOWARDS END OF CAREER produced near the end of somebody's career or life ○ *a late Degas* ■ *adv* (**later, latest**) **1.** NOT ON TIME after an expected or arranged time ○ *He arrived late.* **2.** BEYOND USUAL TIME after the usual or normal time ○ *She had to work late.* **3.** NEAR END OF PERIOD towards the end of a period of time ○ *These birds tend to nest late in the year.* **4.** WELL INTO EVENING at or until a point well into the evening or night ○ *Their flight is due late on Friday.* **5.** RECENTLY relatively recently ○ *She didn't pack her bags until as late as yesterday.* [Old English *læt* < Indo-European, 'let go'] —**lateness** *n* ◇ **of late** recently

---

USAGE **late** meaning 'dead': In obituaries or death announcements the person in question is hardly ever described as *the late...* Nor is it usual for somebody who died centuries ago to be described that way. In references to a deceased person, when is it time to start and stop using *late*? The word's purpose is to serve as a reminder that the person in question is no longer living. In an obituary, that much is obvious, so *late* is not needed. Nor is it needed in historical contexts, except

---

to indicate that somebody was dead by a particular time: *In 1553 Mary Tudor was entitled to the crown by her late father's testament.*

SYNONYMS See *dead*.

late adopter *n* somebody who is slow to embrace a new product, technology, or idea. ◊ **early adopter**

late blight *n* a disease of potatoes, caused by a fungus, in which both tubers and foliage decay

latecomer /láyt kumər/ *n* **1.** somebody who arrives late for an event **2.** somebody who has recently become involved with or interested in something ○ *a latecomer to Bach*

late developer *n* a child whose potential in some or all aspects of school work develops later than is the case for the majority of his or her contemporaries

lateen /lə téen/ *adj* describes a triangular sail hung on a yard attached to a small mast, or a ship with such a sail [Mid-16C. < French *(voile) latine* 'Latin (sail)' < Latin *Latinus* (see LATIN); because it was used in the Mediterranean]

lateen-rigged *adj* using a lateen sail

late Greek *n* the form of Greek used between the 3rd and the 9th centuries AD

late Hebrew *n* the form of Hebrew used between the 12th and the 18th centuries AD

late Latin *n* the written form of Latin used between the 3rd and the 7th centuries AD

lately /láytli/ *adv* within the last few days or weeks, or not too long ago

laten /láyt'n/ (**-ens, -ening, -ened**) *vti* to grow late, or make something late (*literary*)

latency /láyt'nssi/ *n* the state or condition of being latent

latency period *n* PSYCHOANAL same as **latent period**

La Tène /la tén/ *adj* relating to an Iron-Age culture that flourished in Europe between the 5th and the 1st centuries BC [Late 19C. After a district in Switzerland]

late-night *adj* **1.** done or happening at or until a relatively late hour of the evening or night ○ *late-night shopping* **2.** open for business at a late hour of the night ○ *a late-night club*

latent /láyt'nt/ *adj* **1.** HIDDEN present or existing, but in an underdeveloped or unexpressed form **2.** BIOL DORMANT dormant or undeveloped but able to develop normally under suitable conditions **3.** PSYCHOANAL PRESENT BUT UNEXPRESSED present in the unconscious but not consciously expressed [Early 17C. < Latin *latent-*, present participle of *latere* 'be hidden']

latent content *n* in psychoanalysis, the content of a dream that is hidden or repressed, and is represented in symbols

latent heat *n* the heat that is absorbed or emitted when a substance undergoes a physical phase change but that does not make the substance change temperature. Symbol *L*

latent image *n* the invisible image recorded on light-sensitive materials such as photographic film or paper but not yet developed

latent learning *n* learning that is not apparent when it occurs, but that can be inferred later from improved performance

latent period *n* **1.** MED DISEASE INCUBATION PERIOD the incubation period of a disease **2.** PHYSIOL TIME BETWEEN STIMULUS AND RESPONSE the interval between the application of a stimulus and the start of a response **3.** PSYCHOANAL THEORETICAL CHILDHOOD DEVELOPMENTAL STAGE in Freudian theory, a period between five or six years of age and adolescence when sexual interest is suppressed

latent print *n* a fingerprint that is left at a crime scene and remains invisible until chemically treated

latent time *n* PHYSIOL same as **latent period** (sense 2)

later /láytər/ comparative of **late** ■ *adv* after a particular period of time, the present time, or the time being discussed ■ *interj* used to say goodbye for now (*informal*)

lateral /láttərəl/ *adj* **1.** AT SIDE relating to, located at, or affecting the side **2.** SIDEWAYS IN CAREER, RATHER THAN UP involving transfer to a position in an organization

or career that has the same status or pay as the previous one **3.** OF LATERAL THINKING involving or relating to the use of lateral thinking **4.** PHON PRODUCED WITH INCOMPLETE OBSTRUCTION OF AIR describes a speech sound produced with the tip of the tongue touching the alveolar ridge so that air moves around one or both sides of the tongue. The only lateral sound in English is /l/. **5.** GENETICS same as **horizontal** *adj* (sense 7) ■ *n* **1.** PART AT SIDE a part, appendage, movement, or object at the side of something **2.** PHON LATERAL CONSONANT a lateral speech sound, e.g. /l/ in English [15C. < Latin *lateralis* < *later-* 'side'] —**laterally** *adv*

lateral bud *n* a bud that develops in the angle between a leaf and a stem

lateralization /láttərə lī záysh'n/, **lateralisation** *n* the localization of the control centre for a specific function, e.g. speech, on the right or left side of the brain

lateral line *n* a line of sensory pores along the head and sides of fish and some amphibians that detect pressure, current variations, and vibrations

lateral thinking *n* a way of solving problems by unconventional or apparently illogical means rather than by a traditionally logical approach

laterite /láttə rīt/ *n* a reddish mixture of clayey iron and aluminium oxides and hydroxides formed by the weathering of basalt under humid, tropical conditions. There are extensive deposits in India. [Early 19C. < Latin *later* 'brick'] —**lateritic** /láttə ríttik/ *adj*

laters /láytərz/ *interj* used to say goodbye for now (*informal*)

latest /láytist/ superlative of **late** ■ *adj* newest, most recent, or most up-to-date ■ *n* the newest, most recent, or most up-to-date news, fashion, or version of something (*informal*)

late tackle *n* in a game such as football, a foul resulting from an attempt to tackle an opposing player after the ball has been passed. This can be a bookable offence, especially if the player making the tackle comes into physical contact with the player who had possession of the ball.

latex /láy teks/ (*plural* **-texes** or **-tices** /-ti seez/) *n* **1.** a milky white liquid produced by some plants such as the rubber tree, whose sap is used to make rubber **2.** a suspension of rubber or plastic (**polymer**) particles in water. Use: manufacture of emulsion paints, adhesives, other products. [Mid-17C. < Latin, 'liquid']

lath /laath, lath/ *n* **1.** WOODEN STRIP USED IN FRAMEWORK one of the thin strips of wood used to form a framework to support plaster, tiles, or slates **2.** SUPPORT FOR PLASTERING a sheet of metal or a framework of wire mesh used as a support for plasterwork **3.** THIN STRIP OF WOOD a thin strip of wood, especially one used in the building trades ■ *vt* (**laths, lathing, lathed**) ATTACH LATHS TO SURFACE to attach or nail laths to a surface before plastering, tiling, or fixing slates [Old English *lætt* < Germanic]

Latham /láythəm/, **Mark** (*b.* 1961) Australian politician. He was elected to parliament as an Australian Labor Party MP in 1994 and became leader of his party in 2003.

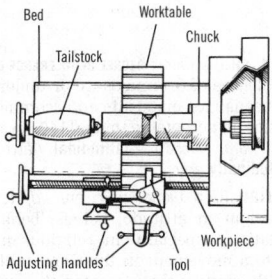

lathe

lathe[1] /layth/ *n* a machine for working wood or metal, in which the piece being worked is held and rotated while a cutting tool is applied to it ■ *vt* (**lathes, lathing, lathed**) to shape wood or metal using a lathe [14C. Probably < Old Danish *lad* 'stand, framework']

lathe[2] /layth/ *n* a former administrative division of the English county of Kent [Old English *læp* < Germanic, 'land']

lather /laáthər, láthər/ *n* **1.** SOAPY FROTH foam that is produced by soap or detergent used with water **2.** SWEATY FROTH white foam produced during periods of extremely heavy sweating, especially by horses **3.** AGITATED STATE a state of agitation or nervous anxiety (*informal*) ■ *v* (**-ers, -ering, -ered**) **1.** *vti* CREATE LATHER to produce a lather using a soap or detergent, or cause something to produce a lather **2.** *vt* PUT LATHER ON SOMETHING to coat something with soapy lather [Old English *læpor* < Indo-European, 'to wash'] —**lathery** *adj*

lathi /laáti/ (*plural* **-this**) *n* S ASIA in South Asia, a long heavy stick used as a weapon, especially by police [Mid-19C. < Hindi *lāṭhī*]

lathy /láythi/ *adj* regional tall and excessively thin [Late 17C. < LATH]

lathyrism /láthirizəm/ *n* a neurological disease of humans and domestic animals, caused by eating some types of legume and characterized by lack of strength in the legs or inability to move the legs. The legumes responsible for the disease are of the genus *Lathyrus*. [Late 19C. < modern Latin *Lathyrus* < Greek *lathuros*, species of vetch]

lati MONEY plural of **lat**[1]

latices INDUST plural of **latex**

laticifer /lə tíssifər/ *n* a duct in some plants that produces latex [Early 20C. < Latin *latici-*, stem of *latex* 'liquid'] —**laticiferous** /látti síffərəss/ *adj*

latifundium /látti fúndi əm/ (*plural* **-dia** /-di əl/) *n* in ancient Rome, an agricultural estate, especially one that was worked by slaves [Mid-17C. < Latin < *latus* 'broad' + *fundus* 'landed estate']

Latin /láttin/ *n* **1.** ANCIENT ROMAN LANGUAGE the extinct Indo-European language of ancient Rome and its empire, adopted in medieval Europe as the language of education, culture, religion, and government. The Romance languages developed from Vulgar Latin, and its prominence during medieval times led to Latin-derived words entering the vocabularies of other European languages. See panel on next page **2.** SOMEBODY FROM ANCIENT LATIUM somebody who came from ancient Latium in west central Italy **3.** SOMEBODY SPEAKING ROMANCE LANGUAGE somebody who speaks a language derived from Latin, especially somebody living in Latin America or southern Europe ■ *adj* **1.** OF LATIN relating to Latin **2.** OF PEOPLE SPEAKING ROMANCE LANGUAGES relating to a people using a language derived from Latin, especially a people living in Latin America or southern Europe **3.** OF ROMAN CATHOLIC CHURCH belonging or relating to the Roman Catholic Church **4.** WRITTEN IN ROMAN ALPHABET written in or relating to the Roman alphabet [Pre-12C. < Latin *Latinus* 'of the people of Latium, Roman' < *Latium*, ancient region in Italy]

Latin alphabet *n* LANGUAGE same as **Roman alphabet**

Latin America *n* **1.** the countries of the Americas that developed from the colonies of Spain, Portugal, and France **2.** the entire western hemisphere south of the United States —**Latin American** *adj, n*

Latin American Integration Association *n* a trade association formed by Argentina, Bolivia, Brazil, Chile, Columbia, Ecuador, Mexico, Paraguay, Peru, Uruguay, and Venezuela in 1980

Latinate /látti nayt/ *adj* derived from, relating to, or characteristic of Latin

Latin Church *n* CHR same as **Roman Catholic Church**

Latin cross *n* an upright cross in which the lowest limb is longer than the other three, often associated with Christianity

Latinise *vt* another spelling of **Latinize**

Latinism /láttinizəm/ *n* a word or phrase borrowed from Latin

Latinist /láttinist/ *n* an expert in or student of Latin

Latinity /lə tínnəti/ *n* a style or level of expertise in using Latin

Latinize /látti nīz/ (**-izes, -izing, -ized**), **Latinise** (**-ises, -ising, -ised**) *vt* **1.** TRANSLATE SOMETHING INTO LATIN to translate something into Latin, or give a Latin form to something such as a name **2.** TRANSCRIBE SOMETHING INTO ROMAN ALPHABET to transcribe words into the Roman alphabet from another alphabet **3.** MAKE

LANGUAGE HERITAGE *Latin* Much of English is made up of words from other languages, and a large proportion come from Latin, the extinct language of ancient Rome and its empire, inherited either directly, or indirectly through French (a Romance language developed from Latin). After it ceased to be a living first language, Latin nevertheless survived as the language of the Christian church and of scholarship, including science, where modern Latin still provides the taxonomic names for plants and animals. Latin has therefore been available as a source of new words for English throughout the history of the language.

Migrants direct from Latin tend to be more formal and technical than those that made their way into English through French, though many everyday words are still of immediate Latin origin (for example **curve, except, motor, persuade, produce,** and **silent**). Words that came into English from Latin via French include **absent, benign, card, human, legal,** and **patient**. The picture is further complicated by the similarity of related French and Latin forms, making either language the possible source of words such as **addition, canine, normal, succeed,** and **valid**; moreover English words from French were often Latinized after their adoption, for example **ocular** (directly from French *oculaire* but now reformed as if from its source late Latin *ocularis*), and **serious** (directly from French *sérieux* but now as if from late Latin *seriosus,* from Latin *serius*). ('Latin' alone usually refers to classical Latin, used between the end of the first century BC and the third century AD: later periods are specified as 'late Latin', 'modern Latin', etc. as appropriate.)

One large class of words clearly identifiable as being of Latin origin is that of verbs ending in *-ate* (**deviate, generate, liberate, vibrate,** etc.). Latin is a highly inflected language, with numerous different forms for the same word, and English tends to borrow such verbs from their past participles, whereas in French they have usually developed from the infinitive; for example **elevate** comes from *elevat-,* the past participle form of the Latin infinitive *elevare,* from which the equivalent French verb *élever* derives. Adjectives in *-ose* are also usually from Latin, and mostly late arrivals (early Latin words in *-osus* are usually anglicized as *-ous*), for example **bellicose** (15th century) and **religiose** (mid-19th). Certain types of irregular plural are also telltale signs of Latin migrant nouns: *-ae* for nouns in *-a* (**formula,** plural **formulae** alongside **formulas**), *-i* for nouns in *-us* (**stimulus,** plural **stimuli**), *-a* for nouns in *-um* (**ovum,** plural **ova**), a change of *-sis* to *-ses* (**emphasis,** plural **emphases** — though some words of this form may be directly from Greek), and in some technical words changes of *-x* to *-c-* or *-g-* (**calyx,** plural **calyces** alongside **calyxes, larynx,** plural **larynges** alongside **larynxes**). These irregular plurals have often caused difficulty and change in English: see, for example, **agenda, data,** and **media**; others have maintained their plural status, for example **impedimenta, memorabilia,** and **viscera**.

Some Latin words have changed grammatical status in the voyage into English: **alibi,** for example, was an adverb meaning 'elsewhere' in Latin and for the first century of its use in English, but during the late 18th century the adverbial use became obsolete and the current noun use took over; **tandem** was also an adverb, meaning 'at length', but was humorously applied to a vehicle; **veto** meant 'I forbid' in Latin, but in English became a noun and a fully inflected verb.

Up to the time of the Reformation, in the early 16th century, the main category of Latin words entering English belonged to the Christian church; from the late 16th century emphasis changed to scholarly and legal terms, and there was a conscious attempt to elevate and improve the English language and create a Latinate formal and literary stratum. Latin phrases and tags were introduced (including **a fortiori, caveat emptor, cui bono,** and **ne plus ultra**). *Exempli gratia* arrived in the mid-17th century, was abbreviated to **e.g.** before the century was out, and its Latin origin receded into the background. Latin alternatives to older English words were advocated, for example **terminate** (late 16th century) instead of 'end' or 'finish'; some found a regular useful place in the language, but others, for example **sequacious,** were always formal and are now often archaic. The vocabulary of science remains, however, resolutely Latinate, though English is now the usual vehicle of scientific publication. Chemical elements are given Latin forms, for example **aluminium** (early 19th century) and **lutetium** (early 20th); anatomical terms often derive from Latin, as in the **hippocampus, medulla oblongata,** and **pia mater** of the brain. Although the main waves of migration were over, the 20th century continued to receive Latin words in technical areas: in psychoanalysis, for example, **ego** and **id,** and in the same field of human observation **gravitas, libido,** and **persona**; in phonetics **fortis** and **lenis** consonants; in biology **mutant** and **predator**; and in **academia** (mid-20th century) **curriculum vitae**. In addition Latin elements have continued to be combined with others to create new terms, for example in the late 20th century in **lentivirus** (from *lentus* 'slow') and **nutraceutical** (another word for 'functional food', from *nutrire* 'nourish').

SOMETHING LIKE ROMAN CATHOLIC CHURCH to cause something to resemble the practices of the Roman Catholic Church **4.** ANCIENT HIST **MAKE PEOPLE MORE ROMAN** to make people adapt to Roman customs and styles —**Latinization** /látti nī záysh'n/ *n* —**Latinizer** *n*

Latin-Jazz *n* a form of jazz music that is a mixture of Afro-Cuban music and Fusion

Latino /la teénō/ (*plural* **-nos**) *n N Am* **1.** somebody who comes from a country of Latin America **2.** somebody of Latin American descent who comes from the United States [Mid-20C. Via American Spanish < Spanish, 'Latin, a Latin' < Latin *Latinus* (see LATIN)]

USAGE See *Hispanic.*

Latin Quarter *n* an area in central Paris on the Left Bank, noted for educational and cultural pursuits

latish /láytish/ *adj* fairly late, or later than is desirable or expected ○ *a latish supper* ■ *adv* at a fairly late time, or later than is desirable or expected ○ *They arrived latish.*

latissimus dorsi /la tíssimæss dáwr sī/ (*plural* **latissimi dorsi** /-mee-/) *n* either of the two broad triangular muscles along the sides of the back [Shortening of modern Latin *musculus latissimus dorsi* 'broadest muscle of the back']

latitude /látti tyood/ *n* **1.** IMAGINARY LINE AROUND EARTH an imaginary line joining points on Earth's surface that are all of equal distance north or south of the equator **2.** AREA OF EARTH'S SURFACE a region of the Earth's surface near a particular latitude (*often used in the plural*) ○ *snow showers in the northerly latitudes* **3.** ROOM TO MANOEUVRE enough scope or leeway for some freedom of choice, action, or thinking ○ *It's a very creative job, allowing me a great deal of*

latitude

latitude. **4.** PHOTOGRAPHY **DEGREE OF TOLERANCE OF EXPOSURE ERROR** the degree of overexposure or underexposure that light-sensitive material can accommodate and still provide an acceptable image [14C. < Latin *latitudo* 'breadth' < *latus* 'broad'] —**latitudinal** /látti tyoódin'l/ *adj* —**latitudinally** *adv*

latitudinarian /látti tyoodi náiri ən/ *adj* **1.** allowing some freedom in attitude, beliefs, behaviour, or interpretation, especially in religious matters **2.** relating to a movement in the Church of England in the 17th century that accepted the authority of bishops but denied that this was divine in origin. The movement placed emphasis on reason and individual judgment rather than divine authority. [Mid-17C. < Latin *latitudin-,* stem of *latitudo* (see LATITUDE)] —**latitudinarian** *n*

latke /látkə/ *n* a fried flat cake of grated potato with beaten egg. It is an Eastern European and par-

ticularly a Jewish speciality, traditionally served sprinkled with sugar, or as a savoury with a little grated onion added. [Early 20C. Via Yiddish < Russian *latka* 'earthenware cooking vessel']

Latona /lə tṓnə/ *n* in Roman mythology, the mother of Apollo and Diana by Jupiter. Greek equivalent **Leto**

latosol /láttə sol/ *n* a soil variety that is common in tropical or subtropical regions and is rich in iron and aluminium [Mid-20C. < LATERITE + Latin *solum* 'ground']

La Tour /la toór/, **Georges de** (1593–1652) French painter. The simplicity of his religious paintings, often depicting a candlelit scene, differentiates him from his contemporary baroque painters.

latrine /lə treén/ *n* a toilet, especially a communal one on a military base [13C. < Latin *latrina,* contraction of *lavatrina* < *lavare* 'to wash']

-latry *suffix* worship ○ *iconolatry* [< Greek *latreia*]

latte /láttay/ *n* an espresso coffee with frothy steamed milk [< Italian, 'milk']

latter /láttər/ *n* **SECOND OF TWO** the second of two people or things that have been mentioned, or that are being considered or referred to ○ *She went out with Joe and Sam, eventually marrying the latter.* ■ *adj* **1.** CLOSING near or relatively near the end of something ○ *spent the latter part of the day relaxing by the pool* **2.** LATER more recent, or more advanced in time ○ *In his latter years he became very forgetful.* [Old English *lætra* (adjective), *lator* (adverb), comparatives of *læt* (see LATE)]

latter-day *adj* resembling a particular person or type of person from the past ○ *a latter-day Churchill*

Latter-Day Saint *n* a member of the Church of Jesus Christ of Latter-Day Saints, founded by Joseph Smith in 1830 in the United States and centred in Salt Lake City, Utah

latterly /láttərli/ *adv* recently or in the most recent period ○ *He was quite ill for a while, but latterly seems to have returned to normal.*

lattice /láttiss/ *n* **1.** CRISSCROSS FRAMEWORK an interwoven open-mesh frame made by crisscrossing strips of wood, metal, or plastic to form a pattern **2.** SOMETHING MADE FROM LATTICE something, e.g. a door, gate, or fence, that is made from or consists of a lattice **3.** INTERWOVEN FORM a representation of a lattice framework, especially a heraldic one **4.** ARRANGEMENT OF POINTS a regular geometrical arrangement of points or objects such as the atoms in a crystal ■ *vti* (**-tices, -ticing, -ticed**) PROVIDE LATTICE to interweave strips to form a lattice, or decorate or provide something with a lattice [14C. < Old French *lattis* < *latte* 'lath' < Germanic]

lattice energy *n* the energy that would be required to separate the ions of a crystalline structure so that they would be an infinite distance apart

latticework /láttiss wurk/ *n* open mesh made by crisscrossing strips of wood, metal, or plastic to form a pattern, or a frame made of this

Latvia

Latvia /látvi ə/ country bordering the Baltic Sea in northeastern Europe. It is one of the Baltic States and became a member of the European Union in 2004. Language: Latvian. Currency: lat. Capital: Riga. Population: 2,348,784 (2003). Area: 63,700 sq. km/24,600 sq. mi. Official name **Republic of Latvia**

Latvian /látvi ən/ *n* **1.** somebody who comes from Latvia **2.** the official Balto-Slavonic language of

Latvia, also spoken in western European Russia. Native speakers: 3 million. —**Latvian** *adj*

laud /lawd/ *vt* (**lauds, lauding, lauded**) **PRAISE SOMEBODY** to glorify somebody, or praise somebody highly ■ *n* **1. GREAT PRAISE** high praise, acclaim, or glorification (*literary*) **2.** MUSIC **SONG OF PRAISE** a hymn of praise or glorification **3.** CHR **FIRST PRAYER OF DAY** in the Roman Catholic Church, the first prayer of the seven separate hours (**canonical hours**) that are set aside for prayer each day (*often used in the plural*) [14C. Noun via French < Latin *laud-* 'praise'; verb < Latin *laudere* 'to praise' < *laud-*] —**laudatory** /láwdətəri/ *adj* —**lauder** *n*

SPELLCHECK laud or **lord**? Do not confuse the spelling of ***laud*** and ***lord***, which sound similar. The verb and noun ***laud***, meaning 'praise', is largely restricted to formal or religious contexts, as in *laud their attempt to rescue the company; glory, laud, and honour.* ***Lord***, the more frequent of the two words, is chiefly used as a noun denoting an aristocrat, a powerful person, or the God of Christianity and Judaism, as in *Lord Byron, the lord of the manor, praise the Lord.* ***Lord*** is also used as a verb, meaning 'act in a superior way': *She lorded it over her colleagues.*

Laud /lawd/, **William** (1573–1645) English cleric. He was appointed archbishop of Canterbury in 1633. A close adviser to Charles I, he encouraged the king's desire to impose absolute monarchy in opposition to his Puritan Parliament and provoked the Bishops' War in Scotland (1639) by introducing the Anglican liturgy. He was impeached for treason and executed.

> 'Unity cannot long continue in the Church, when Uniformity is shut out at the Church door.'
> [William Laud, *Speech at his impeachment trial*; 12 March 1640]

Lauda /lówdə/, **Niki** (*b.* 1949) Austrian racing car driver. He became Grand Prix world champion in 1975, 1977, and 1984, despite a near-fatal crash in 1976. Full name **Lauda, Nikolas Andreas**

laudable /láwdəb'l/ *adj* admirable and worthy of praise —**laudability** /láwdə bílləti/ *n* —**laudableness** *n* —**laudably** *adv*

laudanum /láwd'nəm/ *n* a solution of opium in alcohol. Use: formerly, for pain relief. [Mid-16C. Origin ?]

laudatory /láwdətəri/, **laudative** /-tiv/ *adj* expressing praise or admiration

laugh /laaf/ *v* (**laughs, laughing, laughed**) **1.** *vti* **MAKE SOUNDS EXPRESSING AMUSEMENT** to make sounds from the throat while breathing out in short bursts or gasps as a way of expressing amusement **2.** *vt* **BRING SOMEBODY TO STATE BY LAUGHING** to cause somebody or yourself to be in a particular state by laughing ○ *We both laughed ourselves silly.* **3.** *vi* **RIDICULE** to make scornful fun of somebody or something ○ *They laughed when I said I'd enter the tournament, but I won it.* ○ *She laughed at her brother's attempts to balance on his skates.* **4.** *vi* **SHOW CONTEMPT** to express amusement, contempt, or disrespect for something ○ *laugh in the face of adversity* ○ *She has the ability to laugh at her own mistakes.* **5.** *vi* **MAKE NOISE LIKE LAUGHTER** to make a noise that sounds like somebody laughing (*refers to some birds and mammals*) ■ *n* **1. SOUND MADE WHEN LAUGHING** a series of sounds made when somebody laughs **2. SOMETHING FUNNY OR ENJOYABLE** a time of great fun and enjoyment, or something that gives fun and enjoyment (*informal*) ○ *had a real laugh with Bob and Patty* **3. SOMEBODY FUNNY** a funny or entertaining person ○ *You'll like him; he's a good laugh.* [Old English *hlæhhan* < Indo-European] —**laugher** *n* ◇ **have the last laugh** to be proved right or successful after being treated with disbelief, lack of confidence, or scorn

laugh down *vt* to reject something with contemptuous laughter ○ *The entire committee laughed down the new design.*

laugh off *vt* to trivialize or treat as amusing something serious or important ○ *Later we laughed the incident off as just a silly mistake.*

laughable /laáfəb'l/ *adj* so inadequate as to cause laughter or ridicule —**laughableness** *n* —**laughably** *adv*

laughing gas /laáfing-/ *n* CHEM same as **nitrous oxide** (*not in technical use*)

laughing jackass *n* BIRDS same as **kookaburra** (*dated*)

laughing kookaburra *n ANZ* BIRDS same as **kookaburra**

laughingly /laáfingli/ *adv* **1.** with laughter that shows amusement or contempt at something or somebody funny or ridiculous ○ *She laughingly dismissed this idea and changed the subject.* **2.** in a form of words that is amusingly or contemptibly inappropriate ○ *what the brochure laughingly calls 'spacious accommodation'*

laughing stock *n* somebody whose behaviour has made him or her an object of ridicule or fun

laughing thrush *n* a bird that makes a laughing call, often in groups, and usually has dark grey or brown plumage. Native to: South and Southeast Asia. Genus: *Garrulax.*

laugh lines *npl Aus, N Am* same as **laughter lines**

laughter /laáftər/ *n* **1.** the sound or an act of laughing **2.** happiness or fun expressed by laughing [Old English *hleahtor* < Germanic]

laughter lines *npl* wrinkles on the face at the outer corners of the eyes, associated with laughing or smiling. Aus, N Am term **laugh lines**

Laughton /láwt'n/, **Charles** (1899–1962) British-born US actor. He acted on stage and screen, winning an Academy Award for *The Private Life of Henry VIII* (1933).

laugh track *n* a recording of laughter added to the soundtrack of a radio or television programme

launce /lawnss/ *n* FISH same as **sand eel** [Early 17C. Variant of LANCE]

Launceston /láwn stən/ **1.** historic town in Cornwall, southwestern England. Population: 6,800 (1994). **2.** city and port in northern Tasmania, Australia, situated where the North Esk and South Esk rivers join to form the River Tamar. Population: 62,417 (2002 estimate).

launch[1] /lawnch/ *vt* (**launches, launching, launched**) **1. FIRE ROCKET INTO AIR** to send a rocket, missile, or spacecraft into the air or the upper atmosphere **2. PUT CRAFT TO SEA** to push or put a vessel into the water so that it is ready to sail **3. LAUNCH SHIP FOR FIRST TIME** to send a newly built vessel into the water for the first time, usually with a special ceremony **4. BEGIN CAMPAIGN** to begin an attack, campaign, investigation, or other carefully planned activity ○ *The police have launched an investigation.* **5. PUT PRODUCT ON SALE** to put a new product on sale to the public and begin promoting it **6. THROW SOMETHING WITH GREAT FORCE** to throw or propel something, especially forcefully **7. START PROGRAM** to start a computer program ■ *n* **1. START OF ACTIVITY** the start of something, especially a carefully planned activity such as a military offensive, an investigation, or a campaign **2. EVENT TO PRESENT NEW PRODUCT** an occasion, e.g. a party, at which a new product is launched ○ *the launch of her new book* **3. TIME WHEN ROCKET IS LAUNCHED** the occasion when a rocket, missile, or spacecraft is launched **4. TIME WHEN SHIP IS LAUNCHED** the occasion when a boat or ship is launched, especially for the first time [14C. < Anglo-Norman *launcher*, variant of Old French *lancier* 'pierce' < *lance* (see LANCE)]

launch into *vt* to begin an activity suddenly and enthusiastically ○ *The professor launched into yet another of his theories about how dinosaurs became extinct.*

launch out *vi* **1.** to start doing something new or untried **2.** to spend money extravagantly (*informal*)

launch[2] /lawnch/ *n* **1. LARGE MOTORBOAT** a large powerful motorboat **2. SMALL MOTORBOAT ON LARGE SHIP** a small motorboat carried on a large ship **3. LARGEST BOAT ON OLD WARSHIP** the largest boat formerly carried by a man-of-war [Late 17C. < Spanish *lancha* 'pinnace']

launch complex *n* a site containing the people and equipment needed for a rocket, missile, or spacecraft launch

launcher /láwnchər/ *n* a device or platform for firing something such as a rocket or missile

launch pad, launching pad /láwnching-/ *n* **1.** a platform, usually in a launch complex, from which a rocket, missile, or spacecraft is launched **2.** a starting point from which great or successful progress is made, e.g. in somebody's career

launch party *n* a party held to celebrate and to introduce a new book, author, book publisher, or retailer

launch shoe *n* a device on an aircraft used for launching a missile

launch vehicle *n* a rocket that is used to launch a spacecraft or satellite into space

launch window *n* the restricted period during which a rocket or other projectile can be successfully launched

launder /láwndər/ *v* (**-ders, -dering, -dered**) **1.** *vt* **MAKE MONEY APPEAR LEGAL** to pass illegally acquired money through a legitimate business or bank account in order to disguise its illegal origins **2.** *vt* **WASH AND IRON SOMETHING** to wash dirty clothes or linen and, often, iron them as well **3.** *vi* **BE WASHABLE** to be able to be washed ○ *It's a beautiful fabric, but I doubt that it would launder well.* ■ *n* MIN EXTRACT **TROUGH FOR WASHING ORE** a trough used for washing ore [Late 16C. < contraction of obsolete *lavender* 'washer of linen' < Old French *lavandier* < Latin *lavare* 'to wash'] —**launderable** *adj* —**launderer** *n*

launderette /láwndə rét, -drét/, **laundrette** /-drét/ *n* a laundry, usually self-service, containing coin-operated washing and drying machines

laundress /láwndrəss/ *n* a woman who does washing and ironing, especially one who does other people's washing and ironing as a way of earning a living (*dated*) [Mid-16C. < obsolete *launder* (see LAUNDER)]

laundrette *n* COMM same as **launderette**

Laundromat /láwndrə mat/ *tdmk Aus, N Am* a service mark for a self-service coin-operated commercial laundry

laundry /láwndri/ (*plural* **-dries**) *n* **1. DIRTY WASHING** dirty clothes or linen put aside to be washed and ironed **2. CLEAN WASHING** freshly washed clothes or linen **3. WASHING AND IRONING PLACE** a place, especially a commercial establishment or a communal room in a building, where clothes and linen can be washed and ironed [Early 16C. Contraction of obsolete *lavendry* < Old French *lavanderie* < Latin *lavare* 'to wash']

laundry basket *n N Am* same as **clothes basket** (sense 2)

laundry detergent *n N Am* same as **washing powder**

laundry list *n* a lengthy list of items, usually things wanted or needed

laundryman /láwndrimən/ (*plural* **-men** /-mən/) *n* **1.** somebody whose job involves working in a laundry or cleaners **2.** a man whose job involves collecting dirty washing and delivering it back after it has been washed and ironed or cleaned (*dated*)

laundrywoman /láwndri wŏŏmən/ (*plural* **-women** /-wimmin/) *n* a woman whose job involves working in a laundry or cleaners

Launfal /láwnfəl/ *n* in Arthurian legend, one of the knights at the court

Laurasia /law ráyzi ə, -ráyshə/ northern part of the ancient supercontinent of Pangaea, an ancient landmass thought to include what would become North America, Greenland, northern and central Europe, and most of Asia

laureate /láwri ət, lórr-/ *n* **1. AWARD WINNER** a recipient of a prize or honour for outstanding achievement in the arts or sciences **2.** LITERAT same as **poet laureate** ■ *adj* (*literary*) **1. CROWNED WITH LAUREL** crowned with laurel as a sign of honour **2. MADE OF LAUREL** made of laurel leaves or branches [14C. < Latin *laureatus* < *laurus* 'bay tree'] —**laureateship** *n*

laurel /lórrəl/ *n* **1.** PLANTS same as **bay**[3] (sense 1) **2. TREE OR BUSH RESEMBLING BAY** a tree or bush whose leaves, aroma, or berries are similar to those of the bay, e.g. the mountain laurel and cherry laurel **3. WREATH OF LEAVES** a wreath of woven bay leaves used as a mark of honour or victory in ancient times, e.g. to crown the winners of athletic events ■ **laurels** *npl* **HONOUR FOR ACHIEVEMENT** honour won for an achievement ■ *vt* (**-rels, -relling, -relled**) **1. GIVE SOMEBODY AWARD** to honour somebody with an award or prize **2. CROWN SOMEBODY WITH BAY** to crown somebody with a wreath of bay as a sign of honour (*literary*) [14C. Via Old French *lorier* < Latin *laureola* 'small bay branch' < *laurus* 'bay tree'] ◇ **look to your laurels** to be careful not to lose a successful or winning position because of a better performance by somebody else ◇ **rest on your**

laurels to be satisfied with your success and do nothing to improve on it

Laurel and Hardy

Laurel /lórrəl/, **Stan** (1890–1965) British-born US comedian. His partnership with Oliver Hardy was the first Hollywood film comedy duo. Laurel was the 'thin one' whose clumsiness was always getting them into trouble. Born **Jefferson, Arthur Stanley**

'Another nice mess you've gotten me into.'
[Stan Laurel, line in the film *Another Fine Mess*; 1930]

Laurentian Mountains /lo rénsh'n-/ range that runs north of the St Lawrence River in southern Quebec Province, Canada. Height: 1,190 m/3,905 ft.

Laurentian Plateau ♦ Canadian Shield

lauric acid /láwrik-, lórrik-/ *n* a crystalline fatty acid. Source: coconut, laurel oils. Use: manufacture of soaps, insecticides, cosmetics, lauryl alcohol. Formula: $C_{12}H_{34}O_2$. [Late 19C. < Latin *laurus* 'bay tree']

Laurier /lórri ər/, **Sir Wilfrid** (1841–1919) Canadian lawyer, journalist, and politician. He served as prime minister of Canada (1896–1911). See table at **prime minister**

'I am a subject of the British Crown, but whenever I have to choose between the interests of England and Canada it is manifest to me that the interests of my country are identical with those of the United States of America.'
[Sir Wilfrid Laurier, *Speech, Boston, Massachusetts*; 17 November 1891]

lauryl alcohol /láwrəl-, lórrəl-/ *n* a crystalline solid that is insoluble in water. Use: manufacture of detergents. Formula: $C_{12}H_{27}O$. [Early 20C. < shortening of *lauric* (see LAURIC ACID)]

Lausanne /lō zán/ capital of Vaud Canton, western Switzerland, on Lake Geneva. Population: 114,161 (1998).

lav /lav/ *n* same as **lavatory** (sense 1) (*informal*) [Early 20C. Shortening]

lava /laávə/ *n* **1.** molten rock that originates in the Earth's mantle and flows from a volcano or a fissure on land or the ocean floor **2.** rock formed from solidified lava, typically full of small air holes caused by escaping volcanic gases [Mid-18C. < Italian (originally Neapolitan)]

lavabo /lə vaábō, lə váy-/ (*plural* **-boes**) *n* **1. BASIN ATTACHED TO WALL** a basin with a water tank above attached to a wall, often used as a planter **2. WASHBASIN** a washbasin or washstand **3.** *also* **Lavabo RELIGIOUS RITUAL** a priest's ritual washing of the hands and reciting from the Psalms during the Communion service in some Christian churches **4. PLACE FOR WASHING** a place for washing in a monastery [Mid-18C. < Latin, 'I will wash', form of *lavare* 'to wash']

lavage /lávvij, la vaázh/ *n* the washing out of a hollow body organ such as the stomach using a flow of water [Late 18C. < French *laver* 'to wash' < Latin *lavare*]

Laval /lə vál/ **1.** city in le-Jésus County, southern Québec, Canada, situated on le-Jésus just north of Montreal. Population: 343,005 (2001). **2.** capital of Mayenne Department, western France, situated 250 km/160 mi. southwest of Paris. Population: 50,473 (1990).

Laval, Francois-Xavier de Montmorency (1623–1708) French-born Canadian cleric. He was the first Roman Catholic bishop of Quebec (1674–88).

Laval, Pierre (1883–1945) French politician. Three times prime minister of France (1931–32, 1936, 1942–44), he served as Marshal Pétain's deputy during the Vichy government, and was executed as a Nazi collaborator.

lava-lava /laávə laávə/ *n* a rectangular piece of printed cotton worn wrapped around the waist by the people of Samoa and other parts of Polynesia [Late 19C. < Samoan]

lavaliere /lə válli áir/ *n* a pendant on a chain worn around the neck [Late 19C. After Louise de *la Valière*, lover of Louis XIV of France]

lava sledding *n* in Hawaii, the traditional sport of riding a 50-lb., 12-ft.-long wooden sledge made of hardwood, crafted like a narrow ladder, down volcanic slopes. Riders can reach speeds of 50 mph. (*regional*)

lavatera /lávvə teérə, lə váttərə/ (*plural* **-ras** or *same*) *n* a plant or bush that is a type of mallow. Native to: Europe, naturalized in California. Genus: *Lavatera*. [Mid-18C. < modern Latin, after the brothers *Lavater*, 17 and 18C Swiss doctors and naturalists]

lavatorial /lávvə táwri əl/ *adj* **1.** containing childish references to faeces or urine (*disapproving*) ○ *lavatorial humour* **2.** relating to or suitable for a public lavatory

lavatory /lávvətri/ (*plural* **-ries**) *n* **1.** a toilet, or a small room or cubicle containing a toilet **2.** a room or building with washing and toilet facilities [14C. < late Latin *lavatorium* < Latin *lavare* 'to wash']

lave /layv/ *n Scotland* what is left of something [Old English *lāf* < Germanic]

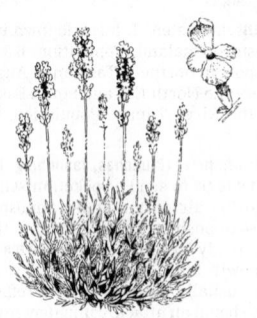

lavender

lavender /lávvəndər/ *n* **1. FRAGRANT PLANT** a low-growing aromatic bush with very thin grey leaves. Flowers: fragrant, bluish-purple, in clusters. Native to: Mediterranean region. Latin name: *Lavendula officinalis*. **2. FLOWERS AND LEAVES** the dried flowers and leaves of the lavender plant. Use: essential oil, perfume for clothes, linen, toiletries. **3. PALE PURPLE COLOUR** a pale bluish-purple colour [14C. Via Anglo-Norman *lavendre* < medieval Latin *lavendula*] —**lavender** *adj*

lavender water *n* perfume or toilet water made from the flowers of the lavender plant

laver[1] /láyvər/ *n* **1.** a large basin for ritual washing in the temple in Jerusalem and in modern synagogues **2.** a basin to wash in (*archaic*) [14C. Via Old French *laveor* < late Latin *lavatorium* (see LAVATORY)]

laver[2] /laávər/ *n* a dried edible seaweed of the red algae family. Genus: *Porphyra*. [12C. < Latin]

Laver, Rod (*b.* 1938) Australian tennis player. He is the only man to have won the tennis grand slam twice (1962 and 1969). Full name **Laver, Rodney George**

laver bread /laávər-/ *n* a Welsh dish made from boiled seaweed mixed with oatmeal, formed into cakes, and fried, traditionally in bacon fat. Sold as a dark green purée, laver bread is also used in sauces or served plain, heated with butter. [< LAVER[2]]

laverock /lávvərək/ *n N England, Scotland* BIRDS same as **skylark** (*archaic*) [Old English *lāferce* (see LARK[1])]

lavish /lávvish/ *adj* **1. ABUNDANT** given or produced in abundance or to excess **2. GENEROUS** giving or spending generously or to excess ■ *vt* (**-ishes, -ishing, -ished**) **BE EXTRAVAGANT WITH SOMETHING** to give or spend something generously or to excess ○ *lavished attention on the child* [15C. < Old French *lavasse*

'torrential rain' < *laver* 'pour' < Latin *lavare* 'to wash'] —**lavisher** *n* —**lavishly** *adv* —**lavishness** *n*

Lavoisier /lə vwaázi ay/, **Antoine Laurent** (1743–94) French chemist. He disproved the phlogiston theory of combustion and published the first proper table of the chemical elements. He was guillotined during the Reign of Terror.

law /law/ *n* **1. BINDING OR ENFORCEABLE RULE** a rule of conduct or procedure recognized by a community as binding or enforceable by authority **2. PIECE OF LEGISLATION** an act passed by a parliament or similar body **3. LEGAL SYSTEM** the body or system of rules recognized by a community that are enforceable by established process ○ *You are forbidden by law from entering the premises.* **4. CONTROL OR AUTHORITY** the control or authority resulting from the observance and enforcement of a community's system of rules ○ *Nobody is above the law.* **5. BRANCH OF KNOWLEDGE** the branch of knowledge or study concerned with the rules of a community and their enforcement ○ *went to university to study law* **6. AREA OF LAW** the body of law relating to a particular subject or area **7. SOC SCI** same as **common law 8. LAWYERS** the legal profession **9. LEGAL ACTION** legal action or proceedings **10. LAW ENFORCEMENT AGENT OR AGENCY** a person or organization responsible for enforcing the law, especially the police **11. GENERAL RULE OR PRINCIPLE** a general rule or principle that is thought to be true or held to be binding **12. STATEMENT OF SCIENTIFIC TRUTH** a statement of a scientific fact or phenomenon that is invariable under given conditions ○ *the laws of physics* **13. MATHEMATICAL PRINCIPLE** a general relationship that is assumed or proved to exist between mathematical expressions [Pre-12C. < Old Norse *lög* 'laws' < *lag* 'something set down' < Germanic, 'put'] ◇ **be a law unto yourself** to refuse to obey the rules, conventions, or suggestions made or upheld by others ◇ **lay down the law** to express an opinion in an overbearing or dogmatic way ◇ **take the law into your own hands** to try to obtain revenge or justice without involving the police, courts, or usual legal procedures

Law *n* **1.** the principles set out in the Bible, especially the Pentateuch, said to be the divine will **2.** JUDAISM same as **Pentateuch**

Law /law/, **Bonar** (1858–1923) Canadian-born British prime minister (1922–23). He served as Chancellor of the Exchequer in Lloyd George's coalition government (1916–18) and succeeded him as prime minister. He resigned after seven months in office because of ill health. Full name **Law, Andrew Bonar**. See table at **prime minister**

'If I am a great man, then a good many of the great men of history are frauds.'
[Attributed to Bonar Law]

law-abiding *adj* voluntarily and habitually obeying the law

law agent *n* in Scotland, a solicitor qualified to represent a client in a sheriff court

law and order *n* **1.** the strict enforcement of the law (*hyphenated when used before a noun*) ○ *law-and-order issues* **2.** the stability created by the observance and enforcement of the law within a community

lawbreaker /láw braykər/ *n* somebody who breaks the law —**lawbreaking** *n, adj*

law centre *n* a place where citizens can obtain legal advice free of charge, paid for out of public funds

law court *n* a court where legal cases are heard

law enforcement *n* an officer or agency responsible for enforcing the law ○ *Law enforcement is at the scene of the crime.*

lawful /láwf'l/ *adj* permitted or recognized by law —**lawfully** *adv* —**lawfulness** *n*

SYNONYMS See *legal*.

lawgiver /láw givər/ *n* **1.** a giver of a code of laws to a people **2.** LAW same as **lawmaker** —**lawgiving** *n*

lawks /lawks/ *interj* used to express surprise or concern (*dated or regional*) [Mid-18C. Alteration of LORD]

Lawler /láwlər/, **Ray** (*b.* 1921) Australian playwright. He wrote *The Summer of the Seventeenth Doll* (1954). Full name **Lawler, Raymond Evenor**

lawless /láwləss/ *adj* **1. UNREGULATED** uncontrolled or unregulated ○ *a disorderly and lawless gathering* **2.**

AGAINST LAW contrary to the law ○ *lawless conduct* **3. WITHOUT LAW** having no laws ○ *a lawless society* — **lawlessly** *adv* —**lawlessness** *n*

Law Lords *npl* those members of the House of Lords qualified to take part in judicial business

lawmaker /láw maykər/ *n* a drafter and enactor of laws —**lawmaking** *n, adj*

lawman /láw man, -mən/ (*plural* **-men** /-mən/) *n N Am* an officer responsible for enforcing the law, e.g. a sheriff

law merchant *n* the principles and rules governing commercial transactions, which originated in English common law and are codified in US law

lawn[1] /lawn/ *n* an area of closely mown grass, often part of a garden [Mid-16C. Alteration of obsolete *laund* 'woodland clearing, pasture' < Old French *launde* 'wooded district, heath' < Celtic]

lawn[2] /lawn/ *n* a fine light cotton or cotton-and-polyester fabric. Use: clothing, household linen. [15C. After *Laon*, town in France] —**lawny** *adj*

lawn bowling *n ANZ, N Am* SPORTS same as **bowls**

lawn bowls *n ANZ* SPORTS same as **bowls**

lawn mower *n* a machine, often power-operated, that cuts grass with rotating blades

lawn tennis *n* a game for two or four players played on a hard or grass court of standard dimensions in which the players hit balls with rackets across a central net

law of averages *n* **1.** the principle that over the long term laws of probability will influence all events that are subject to them **2.** the unscientific but reasonable assumption that things are bound to change some time

law of diminishing returns *n* the principle that a continual increase in effort or investment does not lead to a continual increase in output or results

law of effect *n* the theory that behaviour that is rewarded is more likely to be repeated than behaviour that is not rewarded. This theory was put forward by the US psychologist Edward Lee Thorndike.

Law of Independent Assortment *n* one of Mendel's laws stating that during meiosis, the alleles of a gene segregate independently of the alleles of other genes, so that the inheritance of an allele of one gene does not influence the inheritance of an allele of another gene. In practice, genes that are close together on a chromosome may be inherited together.

law of large numbers *n* the principle that a large sample is more likely than a smaller sample to have the characteristics of the whole

Law of Moses *n* RELIG same as **Mosaic Law**

law of nations *n* LAW same as **international law**

law of nature *n* a broadly applicable principle relating to natural phenomena

law of parsimony *n* SCI same as **Ockham's razor**

Law of Segregation *n* one of Mendel's Laws stating that during meiosis, the alleles of a gene pair segregate, each going to a separate gamete

law of supply and demand *n* the economic principle that the price charged for a product is determined by the level of demand and the quantity available

law of the jungle *n* aggressive or competitive behaviour based on the principle that self-interest and survival are of prime importance

law of the sea *n* the international rules that govern the use of the oceans, derived from custom, treaties, and judicial decisions

law of war *n* a rule or body of rules that governs the rights and duties of those engaged in international war

Lawrence /lórrənss/, **Bruno** (1941–95) British-born New Zealand actor. Among his films are *Smash Palace* (1981) and *Spotswood* (1991). Born **Lawrence, David Charles**

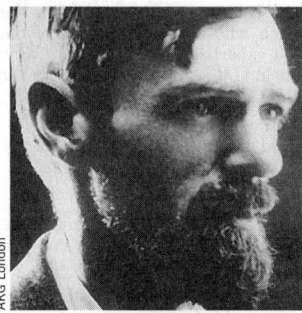

AKG London

D. H. Lawrence

Lawrence, D. H. (1885–1930) British writer. His novels include *Sons and Lovers* (1913), *Women in Love* (1921), and *Lady Chatterley's Lover* (1928). Full name **Lawrence, David Herbert**

'Some things can't be ravished. You can't ravish a tin of sardines.'
[D. H. Lawrence, *Lady Chatterley's Lover*; 1928]

'Why doesn't the past decently bury itself, instead of sitting and waiting to be admitted by the present?'
[D. H. Lawrence, *St. Mawr*; 1925]

Barnaby's

Gertrude Lawrence

Lawrence, Gertrude (1898–1952) British actor. She starred in comedies and musical revues in London and New York, including *Private Lives* (1931) and several other plays by her friend, Sir Noel Coward, as well as in the musical *The King and I* (1951). Born **Klasen, Gertrud Alexandra Dagmar Lawrence**

Lawrence, Marjorie (1908–79) Australian opera singer. She was a soprano with many leading international companies, and continued to perform after contracting poliomyelitis in 1941. Full name **Lawrence, Marjorie Florence**

Lawrence, T. E. (1888–1935) British soldier and author. Posted to Cairo at the start of World War I, he joined and later led the Arab revolt against the Turks (1916–18). His work *The Seven Pillars of Wisdom* (1926) is based on his travels in North Africa and Southwest Asia. Full name **Lawrence, Thomas Edward**. Known as **Lawrence of Arabia**

'All men dream: but not equally. Those who dream by night...wake in the day to find that it was vanity: but the dreamers of the day are dangerous men, for they may act their dream with open eyes, to make it possible.'
[T. E. Lawrence, *The Seven Pillars of Wisdom*; 1926]

lawrencium /lə rénssi əm/ *n* a short-lived radioactive metallic element. Source: produced artificially from californium and other elements. Symbol **Lr**. See table at **element** [Mid-20C. After Ernest O. *Lawrence* (1901–58), US physicist]

Lawson /láwss'n/, **Henry Hertzberg** (1867–1922) Australian writer. Among his poems and short stories the best-known book is the story collection *While the Billy Boils* (1896).

Lawson, Louisa (1848–1920) Australian writer, publisher, and feminist. In 1888 she founded *The Dawn*, Australia's first journal devoted to women's issues.

She was the mother of Henry Hertzberg Lawson. Born **Albury, Louisa**

Lawson, Nigel, Baron Lawson of Blaby (*b.* 1932) British politician. He was Chancellor of the Exchequer (1983–89) during Margaret Thatcher's administration.

Lawson, William (1774–1850) British-born Australian explorer. With Gregory Blaxland and William Wentworth he led the first crossing by Europeans of the Blue Mountains in New South Wales, Australia (1813).

lawsuit /láw soot, -syoot/ *n* a legal action brought between two private parties in a court of law

lawyer /láwyər, lóy ər/ *n* a qualified professional adviser on legal matters who can represent clients in court

lax /laks/ *adj* **1.** NOT STRICT not strict or careful enough **2.** NOT TENSE not tight or tense **3.** PHYSIOL WITH TENDENCY TO DIARRHOEA describes a bowel that is not easily controlled and produces loose faeces **4.** PHON PRONOUNCED WITH RELAXED MUSCLES pronounced with the muscles of the jaw relaxed rather than tense, as is the 'a' in 'hat' [14C. < Latin *laxus* 'loose'] —**laxly** *adv* —**laxness** *n*

laxation /lak sáysh'n/ *n* the action of making something loose, or the process of becoming loose

laxative /láksətiv/ *n* a drug or other substance that promotes bowel movements, either by irritating the lower colon or by bulking the stool [14C. < Old French *laxatif* < medieval Latin *laxativus* 'loosening' < Latin *laxare* 'loosen' < *laxus* 'loose'] —**laxative** *adj*

laxity /láksəti/ *n* the condition or fact of being not strict or careful enough

Laxness /láaks ness/, **Halldór** (1902–98) Icelandic novelist and playwright. He wrote *Salka Valka* (1931–32, translated into English 1936) and the Icelandic epic *Sjálfstaet Folk* (1934–35), and was awarded a Nobel Prize in literature (1955).

lay[1] /lay/ *v* (**lays, laying, laid**) **1.** *vt* SET SOMETHING DOWN to put something down, often carefully, in a horizontal position ○ *I laid the files on my desk.* **2.** *vt* PUT IN RESTING POSITION to place somebody or something in a position of rest ○ *It was time to lay the baby down for a nap.* **3.** *vt* BURY SOMEBODY to bury somebody or something in the ground ○ *They laid him in the family plot.* **4.** *vt* PLACE SOMETHING ON SURFACE to arrange, place, or spread something on, over, or along a surface ○ *They are laying the carpet tomorrow.* **5.** *vt* PRESS SOMETHING DOWN FLAT to smooth something down or make something lie flat ○ *The cat laid back its ears.* **6.** *vt* ARRANGE THINGS ON TABLE to prepare a table for a meal by setting out the required items ○ *lay the table for lunch* **7.** *vt* ARRANGE FUEL FOR FIRE to prepare a fire by arranging fuel, usually in a grate **8.** *vt* IMPOSE SOMETHING to impose something as a burden, duty, or penalty ○ *lay a tariff on imported products* **9.** *vt* ATTRIBUTE SOMETHING to impute or attribute something ○ *He laid the blame on me.* **10.** *vt* BRING SOMETHING TO BEAR to use something to bring about a desired outcome ○ *laid emphasis on the fact that we must study to excel* **11.** *vti* BET to place a bet with somebody on something **12.** *vt* CAUSE SOMETHING TO DECREASE to cause something to decrease or subside ○ *Our discussion laid everyone's fears.* **13.** *vt* DEVISE SOMETHING to devise, organize, or prepare something ○ *lay a trap* **14.** *vt* MAKE PREPARATIONS to prepare something as a basis **15.** *vti* PRODUCE EGGS to produce or deposit eggs ○ *All the hens are laying.* **16.** *vi* PUT EFFORT INTO SOMETHING to apply effort vigorously to a task ○ *The rowing team laid to their oars.* **17.** *vi* BE IN OR GO TO POSITION to put a boat in a particular position, or move in a particular direction **18.** *vi* LIE DOWN to be in or adopt a lying position (*nonstandard*) ○ *Lay down on the sofa and have a rest.* **19.** *vt* OFFENSIVE TERM an offensive term meaning to have sexual intercourse with somebody (*slang*) **20.** *vt* ARRANGE STRANDS OF ROPE to twist strands together to make a rope or cable **21.** *vt* PUT CANNON IN POSITION to establish the direction and elevation of a cannon or a battery of cannon **22.** *vt* TREAT HEDGE TO KEEP IT THICK to make partial cuts through some of the branches of a hedge, bending them over horizontally and pegging them to the ground to keep the hedge thick and dense ○ *hedge laying* ■ *n* **1.** WAY SOMETHING LIES the way or position in which something lies ○ *wanted to inspect the lay of the property* **2.** OFFENSIVE TERM an offensive term for a

partner in sexual intercourse (*slang*) 3. **OFFENSIVE TERM** an offensive term for sexual intercourse (*slang*) 4. **TWIST OF ROPE OR CABLE STRANDS** the arrangement of strands in a rope or cable, determined by the number, length, angle, and direction of twist 5. **SHARE OF PROCEEDS** a share in the proceeds of a whaling expedition [Old English *lecgan* < Germanic, 'put'] ◇ **be laid low** to become ill or incapacitated ◇ **lay it on (thick)** to exaggerate greatly, especially in order to flatter somebody ◇ **lay yourself open to something** to put yourself in a position that will make you liable to be blamed, criticized, or attacked

USAGE lay or **lie**? The verb ***lay*** is mainly transitive: it needs an object, as in *Lay the blanket across the bed.* ***Lay*** is sometimes used without an object in place of the intransitive verb ***lie***, but this is unacceptable in standard English: *Lie* [not *Lay*] *down on the bed. The letter was lying* [not *laying*] *on the table. The snow fell steadily but it did not lie* [not *lay*]. Confusion may arise because ***lay*** is the past tense of the verb ***lie***: *I lay down on the bed.* The past tense of the verb ***lay*** is *laid*: *I laid* [not *lay*] *the blanket across the bed.*

lay about *vti* to strike blows in all directions
lay aside *vt* 1. to give up on or abandon something ○ *'Be not the first by whom the new are tried, nor the last to lay the old aside.'* (Alexander Pope, *An Essay on Criticism*; 1711) 2. to put something away for the future
lay away *vt* 1. to put something away for the future 2. to set merchandise aside for future delivery
lay before *vt* to present something for consideration by somebody
lay by *vt* 1. to set something aside for the future 2. *ANZ* to purchase goods from a shop by placing a deposit then paying off the remainder in instalments, without interest. The shop retains the goods until full payment is received.
lay down *v* 1. *vt* **SURRENDER SOMETHING** to put down, surrender, or sacrifice something 2. *vt* **DECIDE ON RULE** to formulate a rule or principle 3. *vt* **STORE SOMETHING FOR FUTURE** to acquire and store something for future use 4. *vt* **PLACE BET** to place money as a bet 5. *vt* **DELIVER MILITARY FIRE** to deliver a concentration of military fire 6. *vi* **LIE DOWN** to lie down in a horizontal position (*nonstandard*)
lay in *vt* to acquire and store something for future use
lay into *vt* 1. to attack somebody forcefully with blows 2. to attack somebody forcefully with words (*informal*)
lay off *v* 1. *vt* **TERMINATE EMPLOYMENT OF SOMEBODY** to stop employing somebody, often temporarily, when there is insufficient work to be done 2. *vti* **STOP DOING SOMETHING** to stop doing or using something (*informal*) 3. *vti* **STOP IRRITATING SOMEBODY** to stop bothering somebody (*informal*) 4. *vt* **MEASURE OR MARK SOMETHING OFF** to measure off a distance or mark out the boundaries of something 5. *vt* **REDUCE RISK ON BET** to reduce risk as a bookmaker by placing all or part of a bet with another bookmaker
lay on *vt* 1. **APPLY SOMETHING** to apply something by spreading it 2. **USE SOMETHING TO EXCESS** to apply, administer, or use something in an exaggerated manner 3. **PROVIDE SOMETHING SPECIAL** to provide or arrange something, often in an elaborate or extravagant manner 4. **INSTALL AMENITY** to provide or install a supply of something such as gas or electricity
lay out *v* 1. *vt* **SPREAD SOMETHING OUT FOR DISPLAY** to arrange things or spread things out for display 2. *vt* **PLAN OR DESIGN SOMETHING** to plan or design something in detail 3. *vt* **PREPARE SOMEBODY FOR BURIAL** to prepare a body for burial 4. *vt* **MAKE SOMEBODY UNCONSCIOUS** to knock somebody unconscious (*informal*) 5. *vt* **SPEND MONEY** to spend money, especially in large quantities 6. *vr* **lay yourself out MAKE EFFORT** to make a considerable personal effort
lay over *vi N Am* to make a brief stop during a journey
lay to *vi* to make a ship or boat stop, e.g. by turning a sailing vessel into the wind
lay up *vt* 1. **STORE SOMETHING FOR FUTURE** to store something for future use 2. **CONFINE SOMEBODY WITH INJURY OR ILLNESS** to prevent somebody from leading a normal active life, usually temporarily because of injury or illness (*usually passive*) ○ *He was laid up with a bad back.* 3. **STOP USING SHIP OR BOAT** to take a ship or boat out of service, usually temporarily, e.g. by moving it to a dry dock for maintenance or repairs

lay[2] /lay/ *adj* 1. belonging to or involving the people of a church who are not members of the clergy 2. without expertise or professional training in a specific field [14C. < Old French *lai* < late Latin *laicus* (see LAIC)]

lay[3] /lay/ *n* 1. a short narrative poem that is sung 2. a medieval lyric or narrative song [13C. < Old French *lai*]

lay[4] /lay/ past tense of **lie**[1]

layabout /láy ə bowt/ *n* somebody regarded as lazy and given to loafing around and doing no work (*informal insult*)

lay attendant *n* in Buddhist monasteries, somebody who is responsible for taking care of tasks that the monks are forbidden to undertake

layaway /láy ə way/ *n* a method of purchasing something in which the purchaser pays a deposit and the seller keeps the goods until full payment is made

layback /láy bak/ *n* a way of climbing a vertical crack in a rock by leaning back and pulling on one side of the crack and pushing against the other side with the feet

lay brother *n* in a Christian religious order, a man who has taken vows, but does not take part in the full liturgical programme and serves as an ancillary or manual worker

lay-by (*plural* **lay-bys**) *n* 1. **STOPPING PLACE AT EDGE OF ROAD** a short strip of ground alongside a main road where vehicles can stop for a short time 2. *ANZ* **PAYING FOR GOODS IN INSTALMENTS** a method of purchasing goods by placing a deposit to secure an item and then paying off the full price in instalments, without interest, the goods being made available when full payment is received 3. *ANZ* **ITEM PAID FOR BY INSTALMENTS** an item purchased by placing a deposit and then paying in instalments

lay days *npl* the time allowed in port for a ship to load or unload its cargo without extra payment

lay-down *n US* an easy target or victim (*slang*)

layer /láy ər/ *n* 1. **FLAT COVERING OVER OR BETWEEN OTHERS** a single thickness of something that lies over or under something or between other similar thicknesses 2. **SOMEBODY WHO LAYS SOMETHING** somebody whose work is laying something such as tile or brick (*usually used in combination*) ○ *a bricklayer* 3. **LAYING HEN** a hen that lays eggs 4. GARDENING **ROOTED PLANT SHOOT** a branch or shoot that has been bent over and covered with soil to make it take root and grow into a new plant ■ *v* (**-ers, -ering, -ered**) 1. *vti* **MAKE LAYERS OF SOMETHING** to apply or arrange things as separate thicknesses, or form into separate thicknesses 2. *vt* **CUT HAIR IN DIFFERENT LENGTHS** to cut somebody's hair in overlapping sections of different lengths, usually in order to give shape to a hairstyle 3. *vti* GARDENING **PROPAGATE PLANT BY ROOTING SHOOTS** to bend a branch or shoot over and cover it with soil to make it take root as a new plant, or take root as a result of this procedure

layer cake *n* a sponge cake that consists of two or more layers sandwiched together with cream, jam, or other filling. The layers may be baked separately or cut horizontally.

layering /láyəring/ *n* a method of propagating plants by covering a branch or shoot with soil so that it takes root while still attached to the parent plant

layette /lay ét/ *n* a complete set of clothing and accessories for a newborn baby [Mid-19C. < French, literally 'small drawer' < Old French *laie* 'drawer, box' < Middle Dutch *laege* < Germanic, 'load']

lay figure *n* 1. a jointed model of the human body used by artists 2. a submissive or insignificant person

laying on of hands /láying-/ *n* a blessing involving placing the hands on somebody, especially on somebody's head, in a religious ceremony such as ordination or in faith healing

layman /láymən/ (*plural* **-men** /-mən/) *n* 1. somebody, especially a man, who is not trained or expert in a specific area ○ *a law book for the layman* 2. somebody, especially a man, who does not belong to the clergy

layoff /láy of/ *n* 1. a dismissal of employees, usually temporary 2. the time during which employees are out of work

lay of the land *n N Am* same as **lie of the land** (*informal*)

layout /láy owt/ *n* 1. **WAY THINGS ARE ARRANGED** the way component parts or individual items are arranged 2. **DESIGN SHOWING POSITIONS** a design or plan showing the way things are arranged 3. **DESIGN OF PRINTED MATTER** the design or arrangement of printed material such as an advertisement or the pages of a book 4. **PAGE SHOWING DESIGN** a page or pages showing the design for printed material 5. **DESIGNING OF PRINTED MATERIAL** the art of designing printed material 6. *N Am* **ESTABLISHMENT** a residence, business establishment, or other property, especially one that is large or elaborate ○ *a new high-tech manufacturing layout*

layover /láy ōvər/ *n N Am* a brief stop during a journey

layperson /láy purss'n/ (*plural* **-people** /-peep'l/) *n* 1. somebody who is not trained or expert in a specific area 2. somebody who does not belong to the clergy

lay reader *n* a lay member of a church, especially an Anglican church or the Roman Catholic Church, who is authorized to read some parts of the service

lay-up *n* in basketball, a shot made close to the basket, usually made one-handed and by bouncing the ball off the backboard

laywoman /láy wŏŏmən/ (*plural* **-women** /-wimin/) *n* 1. a woman who is not trained in a specific profession 2. a woman who does not belong to the clergy

lazar /lázzər, láyzər/ *n* a poor and sick person, especially somebody affected by leprosy (*archaic*) [13C. < medieval Latin *lazarus*, after *Lazarus*, a beggar in the Bible (Luke 16:20)]

lazaretto /lázzə réttō/ (*plural* **-tos**), **lazaret** /lázzə rét/, **lazarette** *n* 1. **QUARANTINE FACILITY** a building or ship used to hold people during a period of quarantine 2. **SHIP'S STORAGE SPACE** a storage space below deck near the stern of a ship 3. **HOSPITAL FOR CONTAGIOUS DISEASES** a hospital for the treatment of contagious diseases such as leprosy, especially in former times [Mid-16C. < Italian *lazzaretto*, blend of *lazzaro* 'leper' (< medieval Latin *lazarus*; see LAZAR) + *Nazareto*, hospital in Venice, after Santa Maria di *Nazaret* 'St Mary of Nazareth']

Lazarus /lázzərəss/ *n* in the Bible, a friend of Jesus Christ and the brother of Mary and Martha who died but was brought to life again by Jesus

laze /layz/ (**lazes, lazing, lazed**) *v* 1. *vi* to relax and do no work ○ *I just lazed in the shade with a book.* 2. *vt* to pass time idly ○ *laze the day away* [Late 16C. Back-formation < LAZY]
laze around, laze about *vti* to relax, doing nothing that requires effort

lazulite /lázzyŏŏ līt/ *n* a blue glassy rare phosphate mineral containing aluminium, iron, and magnesium. Use: gems. [Early 19C. < LAPIS LAZULI]

lazurite /lázzyŏŏ rīt/ *n* a deep violet-blue or greenish-blue rare aluminosilicate mineral that contains sodium and is the main constituent of lapis lazuli [Late 19C. < medieval Latin *lazur* < Arabic *lāžward* 'lapis lazuli']

lazy /láyzi/ (**-zier, -ziest**) *adj* 1. **NOT WANTING TO WORK** unwilling to do any work or make an effort 2. **CONDUCIVE TO IDLENESS** contributing to an unwillingness to work or make an effort ○ *a lazy spring day* 3. **SLOW** moving slowly ○ *a lazy river* 4. **SLOPING** shown as a brand on livestock as a letter or number rotated through 90° from an upright position ○ *a lazy H* [Mid-16C. Origin ?] —**lazily** *adv* —**laziness** *n*

lazy bed *n Ireland, Scotland* a bed about 2 m/6 ft wide where seed potatoes for cultivation are laid on the surface and covered with soil

lazybones /láyzi bōnz/ (*plural same*) *n* somebody who is regarded as lazy or without ambition (*informal*)

lazy daisy stitch *n* in embroidery, a single unattached chain stitch, often worked in a circle to resemble the petals of a flower

lazy eye *n* 1. an eye disorder in which vision is impaired for no apparent reason, or an eye affected by this disorder (*not in technical use*) Technical name **amblyopia** 2. a disorder in which the eyes appear to be looking in different directions, or an eye affected by this disorder

lazy Susan /-sŏŏz'n/ *n* a revolving tray holding a

selection of items such as cheeses or sauces, usually placed in the middle of a dining table

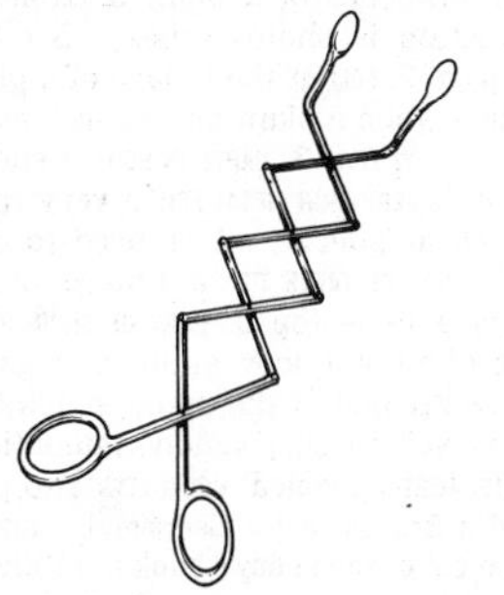

lazy tongs

lazy tongs *npl* tongs that can be used to grasp objects at a distance, usually by bringing together the handles to extend the jointed arms

lb[1] *abbr* **1.** CRICKET leg bye **2.** MEASURE pound or pounds (*of weight*)

lb[2] *abbr* ONLINE Lebanon (*used in Internet addresses*) See table at **domain name**

L-band *n* the range of frequencies of electromagnetic waves from 390 megahertz to 1550 megahertz, used for radar. Other bands in the microwave spectrum used for radar are designated S, X, and K.

LBD *abbr* CLOTHING little black dress

LBO *abbr* BUSINESS leveraged buyout

lbs *abbr* MEASURE pounds

LBV *abbr* WINE Late Bottled Vintage (*refers to port that is six years old*)

lbw *abbr* CRICKET leg before wicket

lc *abbr* **1.** THEATRE left centre (*of a stage*) **2.** BANKING letter of credit **3.** loco citato **4.** PRINTING lowercase **5.** St Lucia (*used in Internet addresses*) See table at **domain name**

LC *abbr* **1.** MIL Lance Corporal **2.** NAVY landing craft **3.** LIBRARIES Library of Congress

l/c, **L/C** *abbr* letter of credit

LCD *abbr* **1.** COMPUT liquid-crystal display **2.** *also* **lcd** MATHS lowest common denominator

l'chaim /lə khaá yim/, **lehayim**, **lechayim** *interj* a word used to express good wishes just before drinking an alcoholic drink ■ *n* a small drink of alcohol used to toast somebody or something [Mid 20C. < Hebrew *lĕḥayyīm* 'to life']

LCM *abbr* **1.** NAVY landing craft, mechanized **2.** *also* **lcm** MATHS lowest common multiple

L/Cpl *abbr* MIL lance corporal

ld *abbr* **1.** PRINTING lead **2.** load

Ld *abbr* **1.** COMM Limited (company) **2.** Lord

LD *abbr* **1.** EDUC learning disability **2.** EDUC learning-disabled **3.** PHARM lethal dose

LD50 *n* a toxicological test in which the dose that kills 50 per cent of a group of test animals is calculated. This test has been criticized by animal protection organizations and by many scientists, but it is still used.

LDC *abbr* ECON less-developed country

ldg *abbr* **1.** landing **2.** loading

Ldg *abbr* Leading

LDL *abbr* BIOCHEM low-density lipoprotein

L-dopa *n* a natural substance that stimulates the production of dopamine in the brain. Use: treatment of Parkinson's disease. [Mid-20C. < abbreviation of LAEVOROTATORY]

LDR *abbr* ONLINE long-distance relationship

L-driver *n* somebody who is learning to drive

LDS[1] *abbr* **1.** Latter-Day Saints **2.** Licentiate in Dental Surgery

LDS[2] *abbr* CHR praise be to God forever [Latin *laus Deo semper*]

lea /lee/ *n* **1.** a grassy field or meadow (*literary*) **2.** a field sown with grass [Old English *lēah* 'meadow, clearing' < Indo-European]

LEA *abbr* EDUC Local Education Authority

lea. *abbr* **1.** MEASURE league **2.** leather

leach[1] /leech/ *v* (**leaches, leaching, leached**) **1.** *vti* DRAIN AWAY to drain away from soil when dissolved in rainwater, or lose a mineral or chemical dissolved in rainwater ○ *herbicides that leached into the ground water* **2.** *vt* REMOVE SOMETHING BY DISSOLUTION to remove soluble components from a solid mixture by the use of a solvent **3.** *vi* LOSE SOLUBLE MATERIAL to lose soluble material by dissolution ■ *n* **1.** CONTAINER USED IN LEACHING a porous container used to hold a solid mixture through which a solvent is run in order to remove soluble components **2.** MIXTURE USED IN LEACHING a solid mixture through which a solvent is run in order to remove soluble components **3.** LIQUID CONTAINING LEACHED SUBSTANCE a solution containing a substance leached from a solid mixture [Old English *leccan* < Germanic] —**leachability** /leéchə bílləti/ *n* —**leacher** *n*

leach[2] *n* NAUT another spelling of **leech**[2]

Leach /leech/, **Bernard** (1887–1979) British potter. He revived the art of handmade pottery in Britain, setting up the Leach pottery in St Ives, Cornwall (1920). Full name **Leach, Bernard Howell**

> 'There can be no fullness or complete realization of utility without beauty, refinement and charm, for the simple reason that their absence must...be intolerable to both maker and consumer.'
> [Bernard Leach, *The Potter's Book*; 1940]

leachate /leé chayt/ *n* **1.** a liquid containing soluble material removed from a solid mixture through which the liquid has passed **2.** the liquid produced in a landfill from the decomposition of waste within the landfill

Leacock /leé kok/, **Stephen** (1869–1944) British-born Canadian writer. He is best known for his satirical short stories and essays, collected in volumes including *Literary Lapses* (1910). Full name **Leacock, Stephen Butler**

> 'Advertising may be described as the science of arresting human intelligence long enough to get money from it.'
> [Stephen Leacock, 'The Perfect Salesman', *The Garden of Folly*; 1924]

lead[1] /leed/ *v* (**leads, leading, led** /led/) **1.** *vti* GUIDE SOMEBODY to show the way to others, usually by going ahead of them ○ *He led us down the mountain.* **2.** *vti* BE THE WAY SOMEWHERE to be the route or direction that goes to a particular place or in a particular direction ○ *That street leads to the school.* **3.** *vt* BRING SOMEBODY OR SOMETHING to bring a person or animal along with physical guidance, e.g. by holding the person's hand or pulling a horse's reins **4.** *vt* COMMAND OTHERS to control, direct, or command others ○ *He led an infantry division in Burma during the war.* **5.** *vt* BE IN CHARGE OF SOMETHING to have a principal part or guiding role in something **6.** *vt* BE BETTER THAN OTHERS to be more successful than and an example to others ○ *They lead the world technologically.* **7.** *vti* BE AHEAD OF OTHERS to be ahead in a race or competition ○ *is leading in the election* **8.** *vt* INFLUENCE SOMEBODY TO DO SOMETHING to cause somebody to think or act in a particular way ○ *I was led to believe the house had been sold.* **9.** *vi* RESULT IN SOMETHING to bring about a particular outcome ○ *Her hard work ultimately led to widespread recognition.* **10.** *vt* LIVE LIFE to go through life or spend time in a particular way ○ *We all lead very busy lives.* **11.** *vt* BE AT START OF SOMETHING to be at the beginning or front of something ○ *Your name leads the waiting list.* **12.** *vt* BE PRINCIPAL MUSICIAN IN ORCHESTRA to be the principal performer of an orchestra or of a section of an orchestra **13.** *vti* DANCE GUIDE DANCE PARTNER to guide a partner in a ballroom dance **14.** *vt* ASK WITNESS LEADING QUESTION to suggest to a witness an answer to a question by phrasing the question in a way that will elicit the desired response **15.** *vt* CHANNEL OR CONVEY SOMETHING to guide something through a passage such as a conduit or channel **16.** *vti* PUT DOWN FIRST CARD to play the first card in a trick in a card game, often obliging others to play a card of the same suit if they can ○ *lead trumps* **17.** *vi* AIM FIRST BLOW to direct the first of a series of punches **18.** *vi* LEAVE BASE EARLY in baseball, to leave a base as a runner before a pitch **19.** *vt* AIM AHEAD OF SOMETHING to aim something such as a missile or ball at a point in front of a moving target to allow for the time of flight ■ *n* **1.** FRONT POSITION OR PRINCIPAL ROLE the front position, first place, or principal role ○ *The Prime Minister took the lead in condemning the attacks.* **2.** FORWARD POSITION a position ahead of all competitors ○ *Which party has the lead in the opinion polls?* **3.** FRONT RUNNER somebody or something ahead of all competitors **4.** DISTANCE BETWEEN FIRST AND SECOND the margin by which somebody or something is ahead of all competitors ○ *She had a narrow lead as the runners entered the last lap.* **5.** STARRING ROLE a principal role in a play, film, or show ○ *He will play the male lead in the film version.* **6.** SOMEBODY WITH STARRING ROLE somebody who has a principal role in a play, film, or show **7.** ROLE OF TAKING INITIATIVE the role of somebody who directs or guides others ○ *take the lead in a discussion* **8.** PRECEDENT an example or precedent ○ *follow his lead* **9.** TIP OR CLUE a piece of helpful or useful information ○ *The police are following up a number of leads.* **10.** MEDIA INTRODUCTION TO NEWS ITEM an introduction to a news story **11.** MEDIA HEADLINE ITEM the most important story in a newspaper or news broadcast ○ *The conflict should make the lead in all tomorrow's papers.* **12.** CARDS FIRST CARD PLAYED the first card played in a trick in a game **13.** CARDS RIGHT TO PUT DOWN FIRST CARD the right to play a card first in a trick in a game **14.** LINE USED TO CONTROL ANIMAL a strap, chain, or rope used to control the animal it is attached to, especially one used when walking a dog ○ *Dogs must be kept on a lead at all times.* N Am term **leash 15.** ELEC WIRE CONDUCTING ELECTRICITY an insulated electrical conductor used to connect two points in a circuit, e.g. a cable connecting an appliance to a source of electricity **16.** GEOL WATER CHANNEL THROUGH ICE a water channel through an ice field **17.** NAUT DIRECTION OF ROPE the direction in which a rope runs **18.** BASEBALL POSITION OF BASE RUNNER a position taken by a runner off one base of a baseball diamond towards another **19.** BOXING PUNCH an attacking punch **20.** MIL DISTANCE AHEAD OF MOVING TARGET the distance a missile, ball, or other projectile is aimed in front of a moving target to allow for the time of flight **21.** GEOL same as **lode** (sense 1) [Old English *lǣdan* < Germanic]

USAGE lead or **led**? ***Led***, the past tense and past participle of the verb ***lead***, 'to guide, command, be in charge', etc. is the correct choice in sentences like this: *The captain led* [not *lead*] *the troops into battle.* Confusion can arise because of the noun spelt ***lead***, 'a heavy metallic element', which is pronounced like ***led***: *found a high degree of lead* [not *led*] *in the paint.*

SYNONYMS See *guide*.

lead off *v* **1.** *vi* to begin doing something **2.** *vt* to be the first batter in a baseball or softball lineup or innings

lead on *vt* **1.** to lure somebody with an offer or promise that is later withdrawn **2.** to persuade somebody to do something foolish or wrong ○ *She doesn't let the older kids lead her on.*

lead up to *vt* **1.** to prepare the way for something **2.** to approach a subject gradually or indirectly

lead[2] /led/ *n* **1.** CHEMICAL ELEMENT a heavy bluish-grey metallic element that bends easily. Source: galena, cerussite. Use: car batteries, pipes, solder, radiation shields. Symbol **Pb**. See table at **element 2.** GRAPHITE IN PENCIL a long thin stick of graphite used in a pencil for writing or drawing **3.** DEVICE FOR MEASURING DEPTH a weight on the end of a line used to measure the depth of water **4.** WEIGHT FOR FISHING LINE a lead weight used on a fishing line **5.** AMMUNITION FOR GUNS bullets or shot for firearms (*informal*) **6.** STRIP BETWEEN LINES OF TYPE in traditional hot-metal printing, a thin strip of metal between lines of type that creates the space between lines on the printed page ■ **leads** *npl* **1.** LEAD STRIPS BETWEEN GLASS PANES strips of lead used to hold the small glass panes in place in a decorative window or art object **2.** SHEETS OF LEAD sheets of lead used to cover a roof **3.** ROOF COVERED WITH LEADS a roof covered with lead sheets ■ *vt* (**leads, leading, leaded**) **1.** PUT LEAD OVER SOMETHING to cover, fill, or weight something with lead **2.** INSERT STRIP BETWEEN LINES OF TYPE to put a thin strip of metal between lines of type to create a space on the printed page **3.** SECURE GLASS USING LEADS to hold small panes of glass together with strips of lead [Old English *lēad* < W Germanic] —**leady** *adj* ◇ **swing the lead** to avoid work, often by feigning illness

USAGE See *lead* [1].

lead acetate /léd-/ *n* a poisonous crystalline compound. Use: manufacture of paints, varnishes, mordant in dyeing, printing cottons. Formula: $Pb(C_2H_3O_2)_2 \cdot 3H_2O$.

lead arsenate /léd-/ *n* a poisonous crystalline compound. Use: insecticide. Formula: $Pb_3(AsO_4)_2$.

lead azide /léd-/ *n* a colourless crystalline compound. Use: detonator in explosives. Formula: $Pb(N_3)_2$.

lead balloon /léd-/ *n* a total failure ○ *went down like a lead balloon*

Leadbelly /léd beli/ (1888–1949) US singer and guitarist. His work influenced folk, jazz, and popular music. Born **Ledbetter, Huddie William**

lead carbonate /léd-/ *n* a poisonous white solid. Use: pigment in paints. Formula: $PbCO_3$.

lead chromate /léd-/ *n* a poisonous yellow crystalline substance. Use: pigment. Formula: $PbCrO_4$.

lead crystal /léd-/ *n* glass containing a high proportion of lead, used to make decorative items, especially tableware

lead dioxide /léd-/ *n* a poisonous brown crystalline compound. Use: batteries, explosives, textile dyeing. Formula: PbO_2.

leaded /léddid/ *adj* 1. containing or treated with lead or a compound of lead 2. containing many small panes of glass held together with strips of lead

leaden /lédd'n/ *adj* 1. DULL AND GREY of a dull grey colour, like lead ○ *leaden skies* 2. TIRED AND HEAVY tired, heavy, and hard to move ○ *My legs felt stiff and leaden from miles of walking.* 3. SLOW sluggish or laboured ○ *a leaden pace* 4. LIFELESS lacking spirit or vitality 5. OF LEAD made of lead —**leadenly** *adv* —**leadenness** *n*

leader /léedər/ *n* 1. SOMEBODY WHOM PEOPLE FOLLOW somebody who guides or directs others 2. SOMEBODY OR SOMETHING IN LEAD somebody or something in front of all others, e.g. in a race or procession 3. SOMEBODY IN CHARGE OF OTHERS the head of a nation, political party, legislative body, or military unit 4. MUSIC MUSICAL CONDUCTOR a conductor of a band or group 5. MUSIC PRINCIPAL MUSICIAN the principal performer of an orchestra or of a section of an orchestra 6. *also* **leading article** MEDIA ARTICLE EXPRESSING EDITORIAL OPINION a newspaper article expressing the opinion of the editor 7. *N Am* MARKETING same as **loss leader** 8. BOT MAIN STEM the main growing shoot of a tree or bush 9. RECORDING BLANK END OF TAPE a short strip of blank film or recording tape at the beginning or end of a reel, used for threading 10. FISHING LINE CONNECTING HOOK a short length of nylon or other material attached to a fishing line and used to connect a lure or hook 11. FISHING LINE AT END OF FISHING LINE a short length of heavy fishing line or wire tied to the end of the main line to prevent sharp-toothed fish from breaking off the hook ■ **leaders** *npl* PRINTING GUIDE IN PRINTED MATTER dots or dashes in printed material used to guide the eye across a page

Leader of the House *n* a member of the British government who is responsible for initiating legislative business in the House of Commons or the House of Lords

leadership /léedər ship/ *n* 1. OFFICE OR POSITION OF LEADER the office or position of the head of a political party or other body of people 2. ABILITY TO LEAD the ability to guide, direct, or influence people 3. GUIDANCE guidance or direction 4. LEADERS a group of leaders

lead-free /léd-/ *adj* containing no lead or harmful compounds of lead ○ *lead-free paint*

lead glass /léd-/ *n* glass that contains a high proportion of lead oxide. Use: decorative objects, optical components.

lead-in /léed-/ *n* 1. an introduction to something such as an item on television or a topic for discussion 2. a wire that connects an outside aerial with a transmitter or receiver

leading [1] /léeding/ *adj* 1. most important or well known 2. ahead of all others, e.g. in a race or procession [Late 16C. < LEAD [1]]

leading [2] /lédding/ *n* 1. lead strips around small panes in windows or art objects 2. the spacing between lines of type in traditional hot-metal printing [Early 19C. < LEAD [2]]

leading aircraftman /léeding-/ *n* a man in the Royal Air Force of a rank above aircraftman

leading aircraftwoman /léeding-/ *n* a woman in the Royal Air Force of a rank above aircraftwoman

leading article /léeding-/ *n* MEDIA same as **leader** (sense 6)

leading dog /léeding-/ *n NZ* a dog in New Zealand trained to run ahead of a flock of sheep and control them

leading economic indicator /léeding-/ *n* an economic variable that tends to show the direction of future economic activity

leading edge /léeding-/ *n* 1. MOST ADVANCED POSITION the forefront of development in technology, science, or some other field (*hyphenated when used before a noun*) ○ *at the leading edge of technology* 2. FRONT EDGE the forward edge of an aircraft wing, propeller, or aerofoil 3. INNER EDGE OF CURTAIN the vertical edge of a curtain that faces the middle of the window

leading lady /léeding-/ *n* the actor who has the principal female role in a play or film

leading light /léeding-/ *n* an influential or exemplary person in a field of endeavour

leading man /léeding-/ *n* 1. the actor who has the principal male role in a play or film 2. a man who is at the forefront of a specific sphere or activity, especially in politics or business

leading note /léeding-/ *n* in music, the seventh note of the diatonic scale. N Am term **leading tone**

leading question /léeding-/ *n* a question asked in a way that prompts the desired answer, e.g. 'Do you think the government should be wasting taxpayers' money on such a venture?'

leading rate /léeding-/, **leading rating** *n* a non-commissioned officer in the Royal Navy of a rank above a rating

leading seaman /léeding-/ *n* a noncommissioned naval officer in the Canadian Navy of a rank between able seaman and petty officer

leading woman /léeding-/ *n* 1. a woman who is at the forefront of a specific sphere or activity, especially in politics or business 2. ARTS same as **leading lady**

lead line /léd-/ *n* a line, weighted at one end, used to measure the depth of water. The line is usually marked at intervals to make measurement easier.

lead monoxide /léd-/ *n* a poisonous yellow or reddish-yellow lead compound. Use: manufacture of storage batteries, pottery, glass, rubber, pigment in paints. Formula: PbO.

lead oxide /léd-/ *n* an oxide of lead, e.g. litharge or red lead

lead poisoning /léd-/ *n* poisoning from the absorption of lead into the body, which over time can cause damage to the nervous system, brain, liver, and gastrointestinal tract

lead replacement petrol /léd-/ *n* lead-free petrol for compulsory use in vehicles that were designed to be used with leaded petrol, introduced as a way of improving air quality and protecting the environment

lead screw /léed-/ *n* a threaded shaft that controls the movement of a machine part such as the tool carriage of a lathe

leadsman /lédzmən/ (*plural* **-men** /-mən/) *n* somebody on a boat who uses a lead line to measure the depth of water

lead tetraethyl /léd-/ *n* CHEM same as **tetraethyl lead**

lead time /léed-/ *n* 1. the length of time in advance of a deadline that somebody must know or have something 2. the time needed to do something measured from start to finish, e.g. from design to production or from placing an order to delivery of the goods ○ *How much lead time do you need?*

lead-up /léed-/ *n* the period of time or series of events that precede an important event or occasion ○ *in the lead-up to the election*

leadwort /léd wurt, -wawrt/ *n* an evergreen garden plant. Flowers: blue, white, red, in spikes. Native to: tropics. Genus: *Plumbago.*

leaf /leef/ *n* (*plural* **leaves** /leevz/) 1. PLANT PART a flat green part that grows in various shapes from the stems or branches of a plant or tree and whose main function is photosynthesis. See illustration on next page 2. FOLIAGE the foliage of a plant or tree, or the time when a plant or tree has leaves ○ *when the trees are in leaf* 3. PAPER IN BOOK a sheet of paper in a book 4. VERY THIN METAL FOIL a very thin sheet of metal such as gold or silver used to decorate an object 5. PART OF TABLE TOP a hinged or removable section of a table top 6. PART OF DOOR a hinged or sliding section of a door, shutter, or gate 7. PART OF SPRING IN VEHICLE one of the metal strips that form a spring in a vehicle suspension system (**leaf spring**) ■ *vi* (**leafs**, **leafing**, **leafed**) GROW LEAVES to put out new leaves [Old English *lēaf* < Germanic] —**leafless** *adj* ◇ **take a leaf out of somebody's book** to follow somebody else's usually good example ◇ **turn over a new leaf** to start to behave in a more acceptable way

leaf through *vt* to turn the pages of a book or magazine quickly and casually

leafage /léefij/ *n* leaves or foliage

leaf beetle *n* a beetle that feeds on the leaves of plants and can be destructive to cultivated crops, e.g. the Colorado beetle or the flea beetle. Family: Chrysomelidae.

leafbird /léef burd/ *n* a bird with bold black and green or yellow markings. Native to: forests of Southeast Asia. Family: Aegithinidae.

leaf butterfly *n* a butterfly that resembles a leaf. Native to: South and Southeast Asia. Genus: *Kallima.*

leaf curl *n* a disease of plants that causes the leaves to curl

leafcutter ant /léef kuttər-/ *n* an ant that cuts leaves into pieces to use as fertilizer for the fungi it grows in its nest for food. Native to: tropical America. Genus: *Atta.*

leafcutter bee *n* a common solitary bee that usually nests in the ground or in a natural cavity and lines its nest with pieces of leaves. Family: Megachilidae.

leaf fat *n* the dense layers of fat surrounding the kidneys, especially a pig's kidneys, often used for making lard

leaf fish *n* a tropical freshwater fish that is laterally flat so that it appears to be a floating dead leaf. Family: Nandidae.

leafhopper /léef hoppər/ *n* a slender spindle-shaped leaping insect that sucks the sap from plants and spreads plant diseases. Native to: worldwide. Family: Cicadellidae.

leaf insect *n* an insect with a flat body that resembles a leaf in shape and colour. Native to: South Asia. Family: Phylliidae.

leaf lard *n* a high-quality lard made from the fat surrounding the kidneys of pigs (**leaf fat**)

leaflet /léeflat/ *n* 1. FREE PRINTED MATERIAL a sheet of printed paper, usually folded, that is distributed free as part of an advertising or information campaign 2. SMALL LEAF a small or young leaf 3. PART OF LEAF a division of a compound leaf ■ *vti* (**-lets**, **-leting**, **-leted**) DISTRIBUTE LEAFLETS to distribute leaflets in a particular place or to a particular group of people

leafleteer /léefla teer/, **leafleter** /léeflətər/ *n* somebody who writes or distributes leaflets

leaf miner *n* an insect of a type whose larvae tunnel into and feed on leaf tissue, including several species of very small moths and a species of fly. Family: Agromyzidae.

leaf monkey *n* a leaf-eating monkey related to the langurs. Native to: South Asia. Genus: *Presbytis.*

leaf mould *n* 1. nitrogen-rich compost or soil that consists mainly of decomposed leaves 2. a fungal growth on leaves

leaf primordium *n* a group of cells that develop into a leaf

leaf roll *n* a viral disease of potatoes that is transmitted by aphids and causes the leaves to curl upwards

leaf roller *n* a small moth whose larvae roll leaves to protect themselves while they eat them

leaf scar *n* the mark left on a stem when a leaf falls

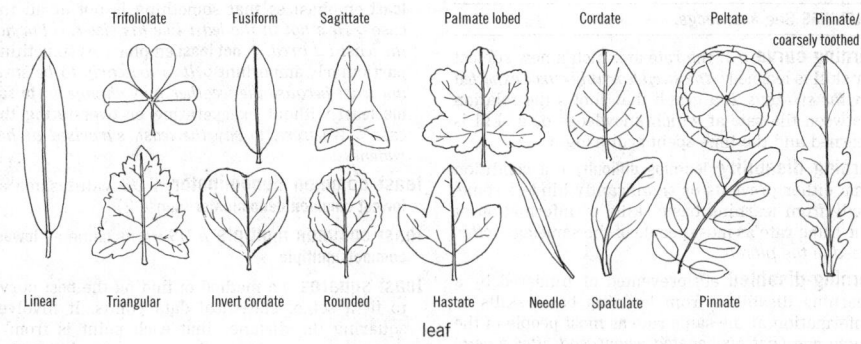

Trifoliolate · Fusiform · Sagittate · Palmate lobed · Cordate · Peltate · Pinnate/coarsely toothed

Linear · Triangular · Invert cordate · Rounded · Hastate · Needle · Spatulate · Pinnate

leaf

leaf sheath *n* the part at the bottom of the leaf that surrounds the stem in grasses

leaf spot *n* a fungal or bacterial plant disease that causes discoloured spots to develop on leaves

leaf spring *n* a spring made of several curved metal strips of different lengths (**leaves**) bracketed together, used in motor vehicle suspension systems

leafstalk /leef stawk/ *n* a stalk by which a leaf is attached to a stem. Technical name **petiole**

leaf trace *n* the structure that carries fluid between the main stem and the base of the leaf in plants

leaf tyer *n* INSECTS same as **leaf roller**

leafy /leefi/ (**-ier, -iest**) *adj* **1.** WITH MANY LEAVES covered with or having many leaves **2.** WITH MANY TREES with many trees and therefore a lot of foliage **3.** PRODUCING LEAVES producing broad leaves as distinct from blades or needles **4.** WITH EDIBLE LEAVES having edible, usually relatively large, leaves ○ *leafy vegetables* —**leafiness** *n*

~~**leag, leage**~~ incorrect spelling of **league**

league[1] /leeg/ *n* **1.** GROUP WITH COMMON GOALS an association of nations, states, organizations, or businesses with common interests or goals **2.** GROUP OF SPORTS CLUBS an association of sports clubs or teams that compete with each other **3.** LEVEL OF SKILL a level of performance or skill ○ *Her painting is not in the same league as yours.* **4.** *Aus* same as **rugby league** (*informal*) ■ *vti* (**leagues, leaguing, leagued**) FORM INTO LEAGUE to join with others for a common interest or goal, or bring people together for such a purpose [15C. Via French *ligue* 'pact' < Italian *liga* < Latin *ligare* 'bind'] ◇ **be in league (with somebody)** to collaborate with somebody, usually for a questionable purpose ◇ **be (way) out of your league** to be in a place, situation, or group where you do not belong or cannot cope (*informal*)

league[2] /leeg/ *n* a measure of distance of variable length, usually about 5 km/3 mi., no longer in general use [14C. < late Latin *leuga* < Gaulish]

league football *n Aus* same as **rugby league** (*informal*)

League of Nations *n* an alliance of nations that was established in 1920 to promote world peace and cooperation and replaced by the United Nations in 1946. It was first proposed by President Woodrow Wilson after World War I, though the United States never joined, and it became increasingly ineffective in the 1930s.

leaguer /leegər/ *n N Am* a member of a sports league

league table *n* **1.** LIST OF TEAMS OR PLAYERS a list of the members of a sports league arranged in order of rank **2.** LIST OF RANKING ORDER a comparison of performance in any area involving competition ■ **league tables** *npl* WRITTEN REPORT OF SCHOOLS' EXAM RESULTS a comparison of UK schools' performance in National Curriculum tests and other public examinations (*informal*)

leak /leek/ *n* **1.** HOLE OR CRACK an unintentional hole or crack that permits something such as liquid, gas, or light to escape or enter **2.** ACCIDENTAL ESCAPE OR ENTRY the accidental escape or unwanted entry of something, usually by way of an unintentional hole or crack **3.** ESCAPING LIQUID OR GAS something such as liquid or gas that escapes through an unintentional hole or crack **4.** MEANS OF ESCAPE a means of escape, or the resulting loss by means of it ○ *We need to plug the leak in our finances.* **5.** DISCLOSURE OF SECRETS an unofficial release of confidential information, usually to the media **6.** ACCIDENTAL ESCAPE OF ELECTRICITY a place through which an electric current escapes accidentally, or the resulting loss of electricity **7.** URINATION an act of urination (*slang*) ■ *vti* (**leaks, leaking, leaked**) **1.** LET SOMETHING IN OR OUT to let something escape or enter accidentally, or escape or enter in this way **2.** DISCLOSE SECRETS, OR BE DISCLOSED to release confidential information unofficially or covertly, usually to the media, or become publicly known in such a way ○ *She leaked the details of the deal to the press.* ○ *The news has leaked.* [15C. Origin ?] —**leaker** *n*

SPELLCHECK Do not confuse the spelling of **leak** and **leek** (the vegetable), which sound similar. **Leak** is a noun meaning 'accidental escape of a liquid or gas' or 'a disclosure of confidential information'; it is also used in these meanings as a verb. **Leek** denotes a green and white vegetable with an onion flavour.

leak out *vi* to become known unintentionally, or be disclosed unofficially

leakage /leekij/ *n* **1.** UNINTENTIONAL GRADUAL ESCAPE OR ENTRANCE a gradual escape or entrance of something such as oil, gas, or electric current by a leak **2.** SOMETHING THAT ESCAPES OR ENTERS an amount of something that escapes or enters by leaking **3.** DISCLOSURE OF SECRETS the unofficial release of confidential information, usually to the media

Leakey /leeki/, **Louis** (1903–72) British archaeologist and palaeontologist. He pioneered research into human ancestry at Olduvai Gorge in Tanzania, discovering several key hominid fossils. Full name **Leakey, Louis Seymour Bazett**

Leakey, Mary (1913–96) British archaeologist and palaeontologist. Her fieldwork in Africa yielded discoveries of early hominid fossils including *Zinjanthropus*, now reclassified as *Australopithecus boisei* (1959) and *Homo habilis* (1960). She was the wife of Louis Leakey, with whom she collaborated, and the mother of Richard Leakey. Born Nicol, Mary Douglas

Leakey, Richard (*b.* 1944) Kenyan-born British archaeologist and palaeontologist. The son of Louis and Mary Leakey, he continued his parents' research into human ancestry in Africa, becoming director of the Kenyan Wildlife and Conservation Management Service (1989). Full name **Leakey, Richard Erskine Frere**

leakproof /leek proof/ *adj* **1.** designed to prevent any of the contents of something from escaping or anything unwanted from entering **2.** not allowing breaches in secrecy or confidentiality (*informal*)

leaky /leeki/ (**-ier, -iest**) *adj* **1.** letting liquid or gas in or out accidentally through holes or cracks **2.** allowing breaches in secrecy or confidentiality (*informal*) —**leakily** *adv* —**leakiness** *n*

leal /leel/ *adj Scotland* loyal and true (*archaic*) [14C. < Anglo Norman *leal*, Old French *leel*, earlier form of *loial* (see LOYAL)]

Leamington Spa /lémmingtən spaa/ spa town in Warwickshire, central England, known for its mineral springs. Population: 55,396 (1991). Official name **Royal Leamington Spa**

lean[1] /leen/ *v* (**leans, leaning, leant** /lent/ or **leaned**) **1.** *vi* BEND OR INCLINE to be in or move to a position that is at an angle to the vertical **2.** *vti* REST SOMETHING OR BE SUPPORTED to rest against or on something for support, or rest something against something else **3.** *vi* TEND TOWARDS SOMETHING to have a preference or inclination for a particular thing or course of action ○ *leaning towards a more tolerant approach* ■ *n* TILTED POSITION a position that is at an angle to the vertical [Old English *hleonian* < Indo-European, 'slope']

lean on *vt* **1.** DEPEND ON SOMEBODY to be dependent on somebody **2.** GET SUPPORT FROM SOMEBODY to gain moral support from somebody ○ *You can always lean on me.* **3.** INTIMIDATE SOMEBODY to put pressure on somebody to do something (*informal*)

lean[2] /leen/ *adj* **1.** WITHOUT EXCESS FAT having no excess body fat and looking muscular and fit ○ *a tall lean physique* **2.** NOT FATTY having little or no fat ○ *lean meat* **3.** NOT PRODUCTIVE not productive or profitable ○ *a lean harvest* **4.** ECONOMICAL AND EFFICIENT not using any more resources than necessary ○ *runs a lean business* **5.** LOW IN COMBUSTIBLE MATERIAL describes a mixture of fuel and air that is low in combustible material ○ *a lean fuel mixture* **6.** MIN EXTRACT WITH FEW MINERALS low in mineral content ○ *lean ore* ■ *n* MEAT WITHOUT FAT meat with little or no fat [Old English *hlæne* < Germanic] —**leanly** *adv* —**leanness** *n*

SYNONYMS See *thin.*

Lean /leen/, **Sir David** (1908–91) British film director. He won Academy Awards for *The Bridge on the River Kwai* (1957) and *Lawrence of Arabia* (1962).

lean-burn *adj* designed to run on a mixture that has a high proportion of air to fuel in order to reduce air pollution ○ *a lean-burn engine*

Leander /li ándər/ *n* in Greek mythology, Hero's lover, who drowned in the Hellespont while swimming to visit her

leaning /leening/ *n* an inclination or tendency towards something such as a particular set of opinions

-leaning *suffix* showing a tendency towards ○ *a left-leaning think tank*

Leaning Tower of Pisa

Leaning Tower of Pisa *n* the bell tower of Pisa Cathedral, Italy, built between 1173 and 1350 and well known for its tilt. It is 55 m/180 ft high and after extensive corrective work between 1990 and 2001 leans more than 4.5 m/14.5 ft from the perpendicular.

leant past participle, past tense of **lean**[1]

lean-to (*plural* **lean-tos**) *n* **1.** an outbuilding with a slanted roof that rests against the wall of a larger building **2.** a shed or shack with a roof that slopes in one direction

leap /leep/ *v* (**leaps, leaping, leapt** /lept/ or **leaped**) **1.** *vi* JUMP FORCEFULLY to make a jump with a long or high arc ○ *leapt over the stream with ease* **2.** *vi* MOVE AS IF BY JUMPING to move abruptly, as if by jumping up or across something ○ *The dog leapt into her arms.* **3.** *vi* ABRUPTLY SWITCH TO SOMETHING to move abruptly to a new thought or action ○ *immediately leapt to the wrong conclusion* **4.** *vi* GO UP SUBSTANTIALLY to increase suddenly and sizably ○ *Stock prices leapt to new highs.* **5.** *vt* JUMP OVER SOMETHING to jump over an obstacle ○ *didn't think he could leap the fence* **6.** *vt* MAKE ANIMAL JUMP to cause an animal to jump over something ■ *n* **1.** FORCEFUL JUMP a long and high jump **2.** DISTANCE OF JUMP the distance covered by a leap ○ *a leap of almost three metres* **3.** PLACE TO JUMP a place over or from which to leap **4.** LARGE INCREASE a sudden and sizable increase ○ *a leap in profits* **5.** MUSIC MUSICAL INTERVAL a large interval in music [Old English *hléapan* < Germanic, 'run'] —**leaper** *n* ◇ **a leap in the dark** an action taken without knowing what the

outcome or consequences will be ◇ **in** *or* **by leaps and bounds** extremely rapidly

leap at *vt* to be quick to accept or take advantage of something ○ *leapt at the chance to play the lead in the film*

leap out *vt* to be suddenly or immediately obvious to somebody ○ *The answer just leaps out at you.*

leapfrog /leep frog/ *n* VAULTING GAME a game in which players take turns bending over so that another player can vault over them with the legs wide apart and the hands placed on their backs ■ *v* (**-frogs, -frogging, -frogged**) **1.** *vt* VAULT OVER SOMEBODY OR SOMETHING to vault over somebody in leapfrog, or over something in a manner similar to that used in leapfrog **2.** *vti* PASS EACH OTHER ALTERNATELY to take turns overtaking each other ○ *The two drivers were leapfrogging down the racetrack.* **3.** *vi* ADVANCE QUICKLY to advance quickly in status or position, usually bypassing competitors or colleagues ○ *She started the day in seventh place but soon leapfrogged into first.* **4.** *vt* CIRCUMVENT SOMETHING to evade something by passing around it

leap second *n* a second added at the end of June or December to a timekeeping system in order to keep measured time synchronized with the movement of Earth around the Sun [After LEAP YEAR]

leapt past participle, past tense of **leap**

leap year *n* a year with an extra day, 29 February, added to make up the difference between the 365-day calendar and the actual duration of the Earth's orbit of the Sun. Leap years occur every four years, except for years ending in 00 that are not divisible by 400. [Probably because any given date falls two days later than in the preceding year, instead of one]

Lear /leer/, **Edward** (1812–88) British writer and artist. His limericks and cartoons for children were first published in *A Book of Nonsense* (1846).

'The Owl and the Pussy-Cat went to sea /
In a beautiful pea-green boat, / They took
some honey, and plenty of money, /
Wrapped up in a five-pound note.'
[Edward Lear, 'The Owl and the Pussy-Cat',
Nonsense Songs; 1871]

learn /lurn/ (**learns, learning, learned** *or* **learnt** /lurnt/) *v* **1.** *vti* ACQUIRE INFORMATION OR SKILL to acquire knowledge of a subject or skill through education or experience ○ *I'm learning to play the piano.* **2.** *vti* FIND OUT to gain information about somebody or something ○ *learned that they're arriving tomorrow.* **3.** *vt* MEMORIZE SOMETHING to memorize something such as facts, a poem, a piece of music, or a dance ○ *learn the periodic table* **4.** *vt* TEACH SOMEBODY SOMETHING to teach a topic or skill to somebody (*nonstandard*) [Old English *leornian* < Indo-European, 'track'] —**learnable** *adj*

learned /lúrnid/ *adj* **1.** HIGHLY EDUCATED well educated and very knowledgeable ○ *a learned professor* **2.** SCHOLARLY showing or requiring much education and knowledge ○ *a learned journal* **3.** LAW HONOURABLE used in addressing or referring to a lawyer in court ○ *my learned friend* **4.** /lurnd/ PSYCHOL ACQUIRED, NOT INSTINCTUAL describes behaviour or knowledge that is acquired through training or experience rather than being instinctual [14C. Past participle of LEARN 'teach'] —**learnedly** *adv* —**learnedness** *n*

learned helplessness /lúrnd-/ *n* somebody's failure to take action to make his or her life better, arising from a sense of not being in control

learner /lúrnər/ *n* **1.** somebody who studies or learns to do something **2.** *also* **learner driver** somebody who is learning to drive a motor vehicle

learner's licence *n Aus* a driving licence for people who have not yet passed a driving test and are subject to various restrictions. UK term **provisional licence**

learner's permit *n N Am* AUTOMOT same as **provisional licence**

learning /lúrning/ *n* **1.** ACQUIRING OF KNOWLEDGE the acquisition of knowledge or skill **2.** ACQUIRED KNOWLEDGE knowledge or skill gained through education ○ *a man of great learning* **3.** PSYCHOL CHANGE IN KNOWLEDGE a relatively permanent change in, or acquisition of, knowledge, understanding, or behaviour

SYNONYMS See *knowledge*.

learning curve *n* **1.** the rate at which a new subject or skill is learned ○ *the steep learning curve expected by the syllabus* **2.** a graph that shows the relation between the rate at which knowledge or a skill is learned and the time spent acquiring it

learning disability, **learning difficulty** *n* a condition that either prevents or significantly hinders somebody from learning basic skills or information at the same rate as most people of the same age (*often used in the plural*)

learning-disabled *adj* prevented or hindered by a learning disability from learning basic skills or information at the same rate as most people of the same age (*not hyphenated when used after a verb*) ○ *materials aimed specifically at learning-disabled children*

learning theory *n* the theory that behaviour can be explained in terms of how people and animals learn to respond to a stimulus, especially learning by rewards and punishments (**operant conditioning**) and learning by association (**classical conditioning**)

learnt past participle, past tense of **learn**

leary *adj* another spelling of **leery**

lease /leess/ *n* **1.** RENTAL CONTRACT a legal contract allowing somebody exclusive possession of another's property for a specific time in return for a payment **2.** LENGTH OF LEASE the period of time covered by a lease ○ *Our lease is six months.* ■ *vt* (**leases, leasing, leased**) **1.** RENT PROPERTY TO SOMEBODY to allow somebody to use property under the terms of a lease **2.** RENT PROPERTY FROM SOMEBODY to rent property from somebody under the terms of a lease ○ *We've leased a cottage from friends.* [14C. < Anglo-Norman *les* < *lesser* 'to lease', variant of Old French *laissier* (see LEASH) —] **leasable** *adj* —**leaser** *n* ◇ **a new lease of life** renewed freshness or vigour, usually resulting from a minor change

leaseback /leess bak/ *n* a business arrangement in which a property is sold and then leased to its former owner by its new owner

leased line /leest-/ *n* TELECOM, ONLINE same as **dedicated line**

leasehold /leess höld/ *n* **1.** the holding of a property through a lease **2.** a property that is leased — **leaseholder** *n*

leash /leesh/ *n* **1.** N Am DOG'S LEAD a lead for an animal, especially a dog **2.** RESTRAINT something that controls or restrains somebody ○ *Our supervisor keeps us on a short leash.* **3.** THREE ANIMALS TOGETHER a set of three animals of one type, especially hounds ■ *vt* (**leashes, leashing, leashed**) RESTRAIN FEELINGS to restrain your emotions or impulses, or control the emotions or impulses of somebody else ○ *I tried to leash my anger.* [13C. < Old French *laisse* < *laissier* 'let go' < Latin *laxare* 'loosen' < *laxus* 'loose']

least /leest/ CORE MEANING: the smallest or lowest quantity or degree
1. *adj, adv, pron* SMALLEST AMOUNT POSSIBLE a smaller amount than anything or anyone else ○ *He went up the steps without showing the least anxiety.* ○ *what I liked least of all* ○ *The least said the soonest mended.* **2.** *adv* TO LESSER DEGREE THAN OTHERS having less of a particular quality than most other people or things ○ *one of the least appealing films of the year* **3.** *adj* EXTREMELY SMALL used to emphasize that something is so small as to be almost nonexistent ○ *She had not the least idea of what was going on with me.* **4.** *adv* TO SMALLEST EXTENT indicates that something happens or is true to a smaller degree than at any other time ○ *I had been appointed to take charge while I least expected anything of the sort.* **5.** *pron* MINIMUM used to indicate the minimum that should be done in a situation ○ *The least you can do is to make yourself thoroughly acquainted with the procedure.* [Old English *læst*, contraction of *læsest* < *læs* 'less'] ◇ **at least 1.** not less than an amount ○ *It'll take at least two days to finish.* ○ *We travelled at least 45 miles without a rest.* **2.** in any case and despite anything else ○ *At least you still have a job.* **3.** indicates a correction or change ○ *I know the answer, at least I think I do.* ◇ **least of all** emphasizes that a negative applies to one case in particular ○ *No one must know of our discovery – least of all our competitors.* ◇ **not (in) the**

least emphasizes that something is not at all the case ○ *He's not in the least like his sister.* ○ *I'm not the least bit tired.* ◇ **not least** emphasizes something particularly important ○ *It is too early to be sure, not least because the weather may change.* ◇ **to say the least** without exaggerating or overstating the case ○ *We were, to say the least, surprised at her rudeness.*

least common denominator *n US* MATHS same as **lowest common denominator** (sense 2)

least common multiple *n US* MATHS same as **lowest common multiple**

least squares *n* a method of finding the best curve to fit a set of statistical data points. It involves squaring the distance that each point is from a given curve, summing the squares, and choosing the curve for which the sum has the minimum value.

leastways /leest wayz/ *adv* in any case and despite anything else (*informal*)

leastwise /leest wīz/ *adv regional* same as **leastways**

leat /leet/ *n* a trench that brings water to a mill or factory [Old English *gelæt* 'channel' < Germanic]

leather /léthər/ *n* **1.** TANNED AND DRESSED HIDE the processed hide of animals with the fur or feathers removed **2.** POLISHING CLOTH a piece of leather used for polishing something **3.** MATERIAL LIKE LEATHER something that is like leather in appearance or texture ○ *fruit leather* **4.** SOMETHING MADE OF LEATHER an item or part of an item that is made of leather **5.** DOG'S EARFLAP the flap of a dog's ear ■ **leathers** *npl* MOTORCYCLISTS' LEATHER CLOTHING the protective leather jacket, trousers, boots, and gloves worn by motorcyclists ■ *adj* **1.** MADE OF LEATHER made of leather or a material that looks like leather **2.** INVOLVING SADOMASOCHISM OR FETISHISM wearing, or intended for people who wear, leather clothing as a symbol of interest in sadomasochism or as a fetish ■ *vt* (**-ers, -ering, -ered**) **1.** COVER SOMETHING IN LEATHER to give something a covering of leather **2.** PUNISH SOMEBODY PHYSICALLY to beat a person or animal severely, especially by using a leather strap (*dated informal*) [Old English *leper-* < Indo-European]

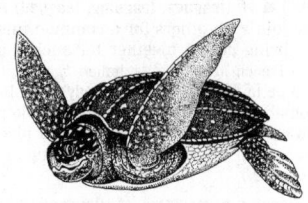

leatherback

leatherback /léthər bak/ *n* the largest of the living sea turtles, which has a flexible shell ridged with bone and covered with leathery skin. Native to: warm seas worldwide. Latin name: *Dermochelys coriacea.*

Leatherette /léthə rét/ *tdmk* a trademark for a product that is coloured and textured to resemble leather

Leatherhead /léthər hed/ town in Surrey, southern England, on the River Mole. Population: 42,903 (1991).

leatherjacket /léthər jakit/ *n* the tough-skinned larva of some crane flies that is considered to be a pest because it destroys grass roots

leatherneck /léthər nek/ *n US* a member of the US Marine Corps (*slang*) [< the leather collar that was part of the uniform]

leatherwear /léthər wair/ *n* clothing and accessories made of leather

leatherwood /léthər wōod/ *n* **1.** a deciduous tree with pliable branches and bark. Native to: eastern North America. Latin name: *Dirca palustris.* **2.** PLANTS same as **titi**[2] (sense 2)

leatherwork /léthər wurk/ *n* **1.** the craft of sculpting, cutting, or burning designs into leather **2.** items

made from leather, especially decorated leather — **leatherworker** *n* —**leatherworking** *n*

leathery /léthəri/ *adj* looking or feeling like leather, especially having a grainy surface or a tough unyielding consistency —**leatheriness** *n*

leave[1] /leev/ (**leaves, leaving, left** /left/) *v* **1.** *vti* DEPART to go away from a person or place ○ *I leave the office at five o'clock daily.* **2.** *vt* LET SOMEBODY CONTINUE DOING SOMETHING to go away from somebody in order to allow that person to do something ○ *You run along and leave me to my paperwork.* **3.** *vt* CAUSE SOMETHING TO REMAIN to give something to somebody or put something in a place before departing ○ *I left my number with Dan.* **4.** *vt* LET SOMETHING REMAIN BEHIND ACCIDENTALLY to forget to bring something away from a place ○ *I must have left my keys at the office.* **5.** *vt* GIVE SOMETHING IN WILL to bequeath something as a legacy ○ *He plans to leave all his money to charity.* **6.** *vt* PRODUCE SOMETHING THAT REMAINS to cause a residue, trace, or mark to remain ○ *The snails left trails on the path.* **7.** *vt* NOT CHANGE CONDITION OF SOMETHING to allow something or somebody to remain unchanged in a particular state ○ *I left my coat on.* ○ *Leave your sister alone.* **8.** *vt* HAVE SOMETHING REMAINING to cause an amount to remain by removing some amount or part ○ *6 minus 4 leaves 2.* **9.** *vt* SET SOMETHING ASIDE to save or keep something for somebody's use ○ *I left some cake for you.* **10.** *vt* DESERT SOMEBODY OR SOMETHING to abandon a person or place ○ *She has left the city to live in the country.* **11.** *vt* HAVE SOMEBODY AS SURVIVOR to be survived by somebody after death ○ *He leaves a wife and two young sons.* **12.** *vti* GIVE UP POSITION IN SOMETHING to end participation in a group or activity ○ *She left that job for a better one.* **13.** *vt* GIVE JOB TO ANOTHER to transfer control of or responsibility for something to somebody ○ *Leave it to me.* **14.** *vt* REJECT SOMETHING to reject something offered ○ *That's the best I can offer, take it or leave it.* [Old English *læfan* < Indo-European, 'to stick'] —**leaver** *n* ◇ **leave go** *or* **hold of somebody** *or* **something** (*nonstandard*) **1.** to stop bothering somebody, or stop interfering in a situation **2.** to stop holding somebody or something ○ *Leave go of my arm!* ◇ **leave it at that** to do or say no more about something ◇ **leave much to be desired** to be highly unsatisfactory ◇ **leave somebody to himself** *or* **herself** to go away and allow somebody to be alone (*often passive*) ◇ **leave well (enough) alone** to leave a situation as it is rather than risk making it worse

USAGE **leave** or **let**? Either **leave** or **let** is correct if you mean 'avoid or stop bothering somebody in order to allow that person to continue to do something': *Leave/let your sisters alone. Leave me to get on with my work. Let me get on with my work.* **Let** is the only choice if you mean 'allow or permit somebody to do something': *Let me finish this first. Let* [not *leave*] *us be.*

leave behind *vt* **1.** to move ahead of somebody or something proceeding at a slower pace (*often passive*) **2.** to dismiss something from the mind ○ *leaving your cares behind you*
leave off *v* **1.** *vi* to stop doing something ○ *Leave off chatting and listen for a change!* **2.** *vt* to stop doing or making use of something ○ *You can leave your coats off since it's so warm.*
leave out *vt* to fail to include somebody or something, whether by choice or accident ○ *I felt left out of the party.* ◇ **leave it out!** used to tell somebody to stop saying or doing something annoying (*informal*)

leave[2] /leev/ *n* **1.** PERIOD OF PERMITTED ABSENCE time off from work or duty, with official permission ○ *He'll get a month's paternity leave.* **2.** FAREWELL the act of saying goodbye to somebody ○ *took our leave* **3.** PERMISSION permission to do something (*formal*) ○ *He was given leave to present his proposal.* [Old English *lēaf* 'pleasure, approval' < Indo-European, 'desire'] ◇ **take leave of your senses** to become entirely irrational or lose all sense of reality

leave[3] /leev/ (**leaves, leaving, leaved**) *vi* to grow foliage ○ *The oak has started to leave.* [13C. < LEAF]

leaven /lévv'n/ *n* **1.** *also* **leavening** /lévv'ning/ RAISING AGENT a substance used to make dough rise, especially yeast or another fermenting agent **2.** *also* **leavening** /lévv'ning/ SOMETHING ENLIVENING something that lightens the weight or mood of something (*literary*) ○ *with a leaven of wit* ■ *vt* (**-ens, -ening, -ened**) **1.** MIX YEAST IN SOMETHING to add leaven to dough **2.** MAKE FOOD RISE to cause bread or cake to rise using

leaven **3.** ENLIVEN SOMETHING to lighten the atmosphere or mood of something (*literary*) ○ *His story leavened the mood of the gathering.* [14C. < Old French *levain* < Latin *levare* 'to raise']

Leavenworth /lévv'n wurth/ city in northeastern Kansas. It is home to Fort Leavenworth, a US military post, and to Leavenworth Federal Penitentiary. Population: 35,410 (2002 estimate).

leave of absence *n* **1.** permission to have time off from work or another duty for a period ○ *I requested a leave of absence so that I could take a finance course.* **2.** the time spent away from work or another duty with leave of absence ○ *His leave of absence included the holidays.*

leaves plural of **leaf**

leave-taking *n* a saying of goodbye before leaving somebody (*literary*) ○ *After a tearful leave-taking, we set off.*

leavings /léevingz/ *npl* something that somebody has left behind or that is left over, usually of little value

Leavis /léeviss/, **F. R.** (1895–1978) British literary critic. He stressed the moral value of the study of literature. He edited the journal *Scrutiny* (1932–53) and wrote *The Great Tradition* (1948), as well as studies of Charles Dickens and D. H. Lawrence. Full name **Leavis, Frank Raymond**

Lebanon

Lebanon /lébbənən/ country in Southwest Asia, on the eastern coast of the Mediterranean Sea. Language: Arabic. Currency: Lebanese pound. Capital: Beirut. Population: 3,727,703 (2003). Area: 10,452 sq. km/4,036 sq. mi. Official name **Lebanese Republic** —**Lebanese** /lébbə néez/ *n, adj*

lebensraum /láybənz rowm/ *n* **1.** additional land in Eastern Europe that the Nazi government claimed was necessary for the continued political and economic development of Germany **2.** adequate room for life or development [Early 20C. < German, 'living space']

lebkuchen /láyb kookən, -khən/ (*plural same*) *n* a rich decorated German gingerbread, traditionally baked in a wide variety of shapes and sizes for Christmas and other celebrations [Early 20C. < German, modern form of Middle High German *lebekuoche* < *lebe* 'loaf' + *kuoche* 'cake']

Lebowa /lə bṓ ə/ former homeland in northern South Africa, now part of Northern Province

Lebrun /lə brún, lə brṓN/, **Albert** (1871–1950) president of France. He became president of the French Third Republic (1932), but retired to make way for Marshal Pétain in 1940.

Le Carré /lə kárray/, **John** (*b.* 1931) British novelist. His popular spy novels include *Tinker, Tailor, Soldier, Spy* (1974) and *Smiley's People* (1980). Pseudonym of **Cornwell, David John Moore**

'A committee is an animal with four back legs.'
[John Le Carré, *Tinker, Tailor, Soldier, Spy*; 1974]

lech /lech/, **letch** (*informal*) *n* **1.** same as **lecher 2.** INTENSE DESIRE a lustful desire for somebody **3.** INSTANCE OF LECHERY an act or instance of lechery ■ *vi* (**leches, leching, leched; letches, letching, letched**) BEHAVE LEWDLY to behave lewdly towards somebody [Late 18C. Probably back-formation < LECHER]

Le Châtelier's principle /lə sha tél yayz-/ *n* the principle that a change affecting a chemical equilibrium is offset by compensatory changes in

other components of the equilibrium, thus producing little overall effect [Early 20C. After Henri Louis *Le Châtelier* (1850–1936), French chemist]

lechayim *interj* another spelling of **l'chaim**

lecher /léchər/ *n* a man who behaves lewdly and lustfully in a way regarded as distasteful [12C. < Old French *lecheor* < *lechier* 'to lick' < Germanic]

lecherous /léchərəss/ *adj* expressing or displaying lewdness and lust in a way regarded as distasteful —**lecherously** *adv* —**lecherousness** *n*

lechery /léchəri/ *n* lewd and lustful behaviour, especially by a man, that is regarded as distasteful

lechwe /láychwi/ *n* **1.** an antelope with long narrow hooves and long backward-pointing horns. Native to: marshes and riverbanks in Botswana and Zambia. Latin name: *Kobus leche.* **2.** an antelope with a white shoulder patch. Native to: wetlands of the upper Nile valley. Latin name: *Kobus megaceros.* [Mid-19C. Probably < Sesotho *lets'a*]

lecithin /léssithin/ *n* a phospholipid found in cell membranes that also plays a role in fat metabolism [Mid-19C. < French *lécithine* < Greek *lekithos* 'egg yolk']

lecithinase /lə síthi nayss, -nayz/ *n* BIOCHEM same as **phospholipase**

Leclanché cell /lə klaán shay-/ *n* a primary cell, the common dry cell, having a carbon anode, zinc cathode, and sal ammoniac as the electrolyte [Late 19C. After Georges *Leclanché* (1839–82), French chemist]

AKG London
Le Corbusier

Le Corbusier /lə káwr boozi ay/ (1887–1965) Swiss-born French architect and designer. He pioneered functionalist architecture and his use of reinforced concrete and views on urban living influenced reconstruction after World War II. Pseudonym of **Jeanneret, Charles-Édouard**

'A house is a machine for living in.'
[Le Corbusier, *Vers une architecture (Towards a New Architecture)*; 1925]

lect /lekt/ *n* a variety within a language, having its own rules [Late 20C. Back-formation < DIALECT]

lect. *abbr* EDUC **1.** lecture **2.** lecturer

lectern

lectern /léktərn/ *n* a stand with a sloping top on which a book or notes can rest in front of a standing reader or speaker [14C. Via French < late Latin *lectrum* < Latin *lect-* (see LECTURE)]

lectin /léktin/ *n* a protein found mainly in seeds and grains and their products, belonging to a group that binds to carbohydrates and causes blood cells to clump together. Lectins may be a factor in some immune reactions and dietary intolerance. Use:

testing for blood type. [Mid-20C. < Latin *lect-* (see LECTURE)]

lection /lékshʹn/ *n* **1.** a variant reading of a text in a specific edition or translation **2.** a passage from the Bible that is set to be read on a specific day as part of the liturgy of a Christian service [Early 17C. < Latin *lection-* 'reading' < *lect-* (see LECTURE)]

lectionary /lékshʹnəri/ (*plural* **-ies**) *n* a schedule of scriptural readings to be read at Christian church services over the course of the year

lector /lék tawr/ *n* **1.** a university teacher, especially a man who is a foreign language instructor in his own language **2.** a public reader of scriptural passages to a Christian congregation or a religious community [14C. < Latin, 'reader' < *lect-* (see LECTURE)]

lectrice /lek treéss/ *n* a woman who is a university teacher, especially a woman who is a foreign language instructor in her own language [Late 19C. < French, form of *lecteur* < Latin *lector* (see LECTOR)]

lecture /lékchər/ *n* **1.** INSTRUCTIONAL SPEECH an educational speech on a subject made before an audience ○ *I missed the lecture on Shakespeare's use of irony.* **2.** TEACHING SESSION a class meeting at which a lecture is given ○ *two lectures and two lab sessions per week* **3.** REPRIMAND a speech intended as a reprimand ■ *v* (**-tures, -turing, -tured**) **1.** *vti* GIVE EDUCATIONAL SPEECH TO SOMEBODY to deliver a lecture to a group of people as a method of instruction ○ *He lectures on stress management all over the country.* **2.** *vi* BE UNIVERSITY LECTURER to be employed as a lecturer at a university or college of higher education ○ *She lectures at the University.* **3.** *vt* REPRIMAND SOMEBODY to reprimand somebody by making a speech about how a person should behave ○ *lecturing the congregation about church attendance* [13C. Via French < medieval Latin *lectura* 'reading' < Latin *lect-*, past participle of *legere* 'read']

lecture hall *n* N Am same as **lecture theatre**

lecturer /lékchərər/ *n* **1.** a teacher at a university or college of higher education who ranks lower than a professor **2.** an informative speaker on a specific topic, especially as a professional ○ *a lecturer's tour*

lectureship /lékchər ship/ *n* a post at the rank of lecturer in a university or college of higher education ○ *The University has three lectureships open.*

lecture theatre *n* a large room with a stage for a speaker and desks and chairs for an audience, arranged so that the whole audience can see the speaker. N Am term **lecture hall**

led /led/ past participle, past tense of **lead**[1] (*often in combination*) ○ *The concern for safety is consumer-led rather than industry-led.*

USAGE See **lead**[1].

LED *n* a semiconductor that emits light when a current passes through it. Use: indicator lights on electronic equipment. Full form **light-emitting diode**

Leda /leédə/ *n* **1.** in Greek mythology, a queen of Sparta. She was the mother of Helen of Troy, Clytemnestra, and Castor and Pollux. **2.** a very small natural satellite of Jupiter. It is approximately 10 km/6 mi. in diameter.

lederhosen

lederhosen /láydər hōzʹn/ *npl* Bavarian leather shorts, usually with braces, worn by men and boys [Mid-20C. < German, 'leather trousers']

ledge /lej/ *n* **1.** FLAT SURFACE PROJECTING FROM ROCK FACE a narrow flat projecting rock shelf, e.g. on the vertical

surface of a cliff **2.** OCEANOG UNDERWATER RAISED SURFACE a raised surface underwater, e.g. a reef or ridge, especially one found near a shore **3.** NARROW SHELF AGAINST WALL a narrow shelf or moulding fixed to a wall that serves a decorative or protective purpose **4.** MIN EXTRACT ROCK LAYER a layer of ore-bearing rock [Mid-16C. Origin ?] —**ledged** *adj* —**ledgy** *adj*

ledger /léjjər/ *n* **1.** FINANCIAL RECORD BOOK a book or page with columns for debits and credits, on which to transcribe financial records **2.** HORIZONTAL GRAVESTONE a gravestone that lies flat on the ground **3.** CONSTR SCAFFOLDING BEAM a horizontal beam in a scaffolding that is attached to the uprights and supports the beams (**putlogs**) **4.** FISHING same as **ledger-tackle** ■ *vi* (**-ers, -ering, -ered**) USE LEDGER-TACKLE to fish using ledger-tackle [Early 16C. Probably < *leggen*, earlier form of LAY]

ledger board *n* **1.** a horizontal board, especially the top rail of a fence **2.** a narrow horizontal board attached to a row of studs to support joist ends

ledger line, **leger line** *n* a short line added above or below a musical staff to accommodate notes that are higher or lower than those on the staff

ledger-tackle *n* a fishing line with a weight attached near its end, used to anchor the line so that the bait floats near the bottom of the water

Leduc /lədoók/ town in Alberta, Canada, situated 32 km/20 mi. south of Edmonton. Population: 15,032 (2001).

lee /lee/ *n* **1.** SHIP SIDE AWAY FROM WIND the side of a ship away from the source of the wind **2.** PROTECTIVE COVER shelter from the wind ○ *in the lee of the wall* ■ *adj* AWAY FROM WIND on or towards the side of a ship, natural feature, or object that is away from the wind [Old English *hlēo* 'shelter' < Indo-European, 'warm']

Lee /lee/, **Gypsy Rose** (1914–70) US entertainer and novelist. The musical *Gypsy* (1959) was in part based on her life as a striptease artist. Born **Hovick, Rose Louise**

'God is love, but get it in writing.'
[Attributed to Gypsy Rose Lee]

Lee, Harper (*b.* 1926) US novelist. She was awarded the Pulitzer Prize in 1961 for her only novel, *To Kill a Mockingbird* (1960). See Cultural note at **mockingbird**

'Folks don't like to have somebody around knowin' more than they do. It aggravates 'em. You're not gonna change any of them by talkin' right, they've got to want to learn themselves.'
[Harper Lee, *To Kill a Mockingbird*; 1960]

Lee, John A. (1891–1982) New Zealand politician and writer. As well as being active in New Zealand's Labour Party, he wrote the novel *Children of the Poor* (1934). Full name **Lee, John Alfred Alexander**

Lee, Laurie (1914–97) British poet and writer. He wrote film scripts and several volumes of poetry, but is best known for his autobiographical novel *Cider with Rosie* (1959). See Cultural note at **cider**

'But the horse was king, and almost everything grew around him…This was what we were born to, and all we knew at first. Then, to the scream of the horse, the change began. The brass-lamped motorcar came coughing up the road.'
[Laurie Lee, 'Last Days', *Cider With Rosie*; 1959]

Library of Congress
Robert E. Lee

Lee, Robert E. (1807–70) US Confederate general. He commanded the Confederate army during the last three years of the American Civil War, and surrendered to Ulysses S. Grant at Appomattox. Full name **Lee, Robert Edward**

'It is well that war is so terrible; else we would grow too fond of it.'
[Attributed to Robert E. Lee, remarks made after the battle of Fredericksburg; December 1862]

Lee, Spike (*b.* 1957) US film writer and director. His films, including *Do the Right Thing* (1989) and *Malcolm X* (1992), are concerned with racial issues. Born **Lee, Shelton Jackson**

'I agree that agents are necessary, but they're still one of the lowest forms of life.'
[Spike Lee, *Do the Right Thing*; 1989]

leeboard /lee bawrd/ *n* either of two movable wooden or metal shelves on the outside of a ship's hull that prevent sideways movement caused by the wind

leech[1] /leech/ *n* **1.** BLOOD-SUCKING WORM a worm that sucks blood or eats flesh. One species has been used in medical treatments to bleed patients or to eat away putrid flesh from a wound. Native to: warm shallow fresh water. Class: Hirudinea. **2.** EXPLOITER OF OTHERS somebody who clings to or exploits somebody else, e.g. for financial support **3.** same as **physician** (*archaic informal*) ■ *v* (**leeches, leeching, leeched**) **1.** *vt* MED TREAT SOMEBODY WITH LEECHES to bleed a patient using leeches **2.** *vi* EXPLOIT SOMEBODY to cling to or take advantage of somebody, e.g. for financial support (*informal*) [Old English *lǣce*] —**leech-like** *adj*

leech[2] /leech/, **leach** *n* **1.** a vertical edge of a square sail **2.** the edge of a fore-and-aft sail that is farthest from the mast or stay [15C. Origin ?]

Leeds /leedz/ university and industrial city in Yorkshire, northern England. Population: 715,402 (2001).

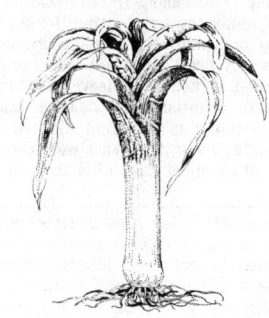
leek

leek /leek/ *n* an edible plant with dark green leaves rising from a close-set white base, related to the onion. The leek is one of the national symbols of Wales. Latin name: *Allium porrum*. [Old English *lēac* < Germanic]

SPELLCHECK See **leak**.

Leek /leek/ market town in Staffordshire, central England. Population: 18,167 (1991).

Lee Kuan Yew /lee kwaán yoó/ (*b.* 1923) prime minister of Singapore (1959–90). He was Singapore's first prime minister.

leer /leer/ *vi* (**leers, leering, leered**) to look or smile in a way that suggests unpleasantly lustful or malicious intent ■ *n* an unpleasantly lustful or malicious look or smile [Mid-16C. Probably < obsolete *leer* 'cheek' < Old English *hlēor*]

leery /leéri/ (**-ier, -iest**), **leary** *adj* **1.** regarding somebody or something with suspicion (*informal*) ○ *I'm leery of anyone who approaches me in the street.* **2.** regional same as **hungry** [Early 18C. Origin ?] —**leerily** *adv* —**leeriness** *n*

lees /leez/ *npl* sediment that settles in wine or other alcoholic beverages during fermentation [14C. Plural of obsolete *lee*, via French < medieval Latin *lia*]

lee shore *n* a shore that is in the direction away from the wind, relative to a ship

leet[1] /leet/ *n* formerly, a court held at regular intervals by the lords of English manors [13C. < Anglo-Norman *lete*]

leet[2] /leet/ *n Scotland* a list of applicants or candidates for a post or office [15C. Origin ?]

Leeuwarden /láy vaard'n, -waard'n/ capital of Friesland Province, in the northern Netherlands. Population: 87,495 (1994).

Leeuwin, Cape /lóo ən/ promontory in southwestern Western Australia, the most southwesterly point on the continent

leeward /léeward/; *nautical* /lóo ərd/ *adj* **AWAY FROM WIND** situated away from the wind, or on the side of something, especially a boat, that is away or sheltered from the wind ■ *adv* **AWAY FROM WIND** away from where the wind is coming from ■ *n* **PLACE AWAY FROM WIND** a place or direction away or sheltered from the wind

Leeward Islands /léeward-/ group of islands in the northeastern Caribbean. The principal islands include Antigua and Barbuda, Guadeloupe, Montserrat, and St Kitts. Area: 3,297 sq. km/1,273 sq. mi.

leeway /lée way/ *n* **1. LATITUDE FOR VARIATION** the permissible margin for variation or deviation from something **2. FALLING BEHIND** falling behind in progress or performance ○ *He's got a lot of leeway to make up at work after his holiday.* **3. DEVIATION FROM COURSE** the sideways movement of a ship or aircraft from its course, caused by strong winds

Le Fanu /léffə nyoo/, **Sheridan** (1814–73) Irish novelist and journalist. His 14 novels include *Uncle Silas* (1864), and he also owned and edited the *Dublin University Magazine*. Full name **Le Fanu, Joseph Sheridan**

left[1] /left/ *adj* **1. WEST WHEN FACING NORTH** on or towards the west when somebody or something is facing north ○ *Her left leg is broken.* **2.** *also* **Left** POL **ADVOCATING POLITICAL AND SOCIAL CHANGE** supporting liberal, socialist, or communist political and social changes or reform **3.** GEOG **ON LEFT WHEN LOOKING DOWNSTREAM** on the river bank to the left of somebody facing downstream **4.** THEATRE **TO RIGHT OF AUDIENCE** on or relating to that part of a stage that is to the left of somebody standing on it and facing the audience ○ *Exit stage left.* ■ *adv* **ON LEFT SIDE** on or towards the left side of somebody or something ○ *The pole is leaning left a bit.* ■ *n* **1. LEFT SIDE** the left side of somebody or something ○ *The house is on your left.* **2.** *also* **Left** POL **LIBERALS, SOCIALISTS, AND COMMUNISTS** people who support liberal, socialist, or communist political and social changes or reform **3.** BOXING **LEFT-HANDED PUNCH** a blow delivered with the left hand ○ *took a hard left to the jaw* **4.** BOXING **LEFT-HANDED PUNCHING ABILITY** a boxer's left hand with respect to its ability to deliver a punch ○ *He's got a good left.* [13C. < Old English *lyft-* 'weak' < W Germanic]

left[2] /left/ past participle, past tense of **leave**[1]

left atrioventricular valve *n* ANAT same as **mitral valve**

Left Bank *n* area in central Paris, south of the River Seine

left-brain *adj* relating to or involving skills or knowledge such as analytical or linguistic ability that are believed to be associated with the left half of the cerebrum —**left brain** *n*

left-click *vti* to press and release the left-hand button on a computer mouse

~~**leftenant**~~ incorrect spelling of **lieutenant**

left-face *US vi* to turn 90° to the left (*usually used as a command*) ■ *n* a turn 90° to the left

left field *n* **1. SECTION OF OUTFIELD** in baseball, the part of the outfield that is to the batter's left **2. OUTFIELDER'S POSITION** in baseball, the position held by the player who is responsible for fielding balls that are hit to left field **3.** *N Am* **VERY UNUSUAL POSITION** a position that is so different from mainstream beliefs that it is not generally taken seriously (*informal*) ■ *adj* MUSIC **UNCONVENTIONAL** going beyond the bounds of a genre, especially in modern popular music ◇ **out in left field** *N Am* in an erroneous or very unconventional position or state (*informal*)

left fielder *n* a baseball player who is responsible for fielding balls hit to left field

left-footer *n* **1.** somebody who has a natural tendency to lead with or use the left foot, especially in playing sports such as football **2.** an offensive term for a Roman Catholic (*informal*)

left-hand *adj* **1.** on or towards the left **2.** intended for or done by the left hand

left-hand drive *adj* describes a motor vehicle driven by somebody sitting in the left-hand front seat — **left-hand drive** *n*

left-handed *adj, adv* **1. USING LEFT HAND** using the left hand, rather than the right, for tasks such as writing and manipulating objects **2. STARTING SWING FROM LEFT** in sports, swinging from the left to the right ■ *adj* **1. DONE WITH LEFT HAND** done using the left hand **2. NOT SINCERE** ironic and insincere ○ *a left-handed compliment* **3. CLUMSY** lacking skill or grace **4. TURNING RIGHT TO LEFT** spiralling towards the left **5.** LAW same as **morganatic**

left-hander /-hándər/ *n* somebody who uses chiefly the left hand for ordinary tasks

leftie *n* another spelling of **lefty** (*informal*)

leftish /léftish/, **Leftish** *adj* tending to be relatively left-wing in politics

leftism /léftizəm/, **Leftism** *n* the advocating of liberal, socialist, or communist political and social change or reform —**leftist** *adj, n*

left-luggage office *n* a room in a railway or bus station where luggage can be temporarily deposited. ANZ term **baggage storage**. N Am term **baggage check**

leftmost /léftmōst/ *adj* in the position farthest to the left

left-of-centre *adj* holding or expressing political views that are slightly left-wing

leftover /léft ōvər/ *adj* **REMAINING UNUSED** remaining after the rest of something has been used or eaten ■ *n* **SOMETHING REMAINING** something that remains from a previous period of time while everything else associated with that period has disappeared ■ **leftovers** *npl* **SAVED FOOD** food remaining from a previous meal or meals, saved and served again or made into a new dish ○ *I made this soup from leftovers.*

leftward /léftwərd/ *adj* moving towards or located on the left ■ *adv* same as **leftwards**

leftwards /léftwərdz/ *adv* towards the left

left wing *n* **1. MEMBERS OF ORGANIZATION MOST FAVOURING CHANGE** a subgroup of a larger organization that advocates greater political and social change or reform than the rest of the organization **2. FIELD LEFT OF OPPONENT'S GOAL** the side of a playing field that is to the left of a player facing the opponent's goal **3. SOMEBODY PLAYING ON LEFT WING** a player whose position in a team is on the left wing —**left-wing** *adj* —**left-winger** *n*

lefty /léfti/ (*plural* **-ies**), **leftie** *n* (*informal*) **1.** somebody with left-wing beliefs **2.** *N Am* somebody who is left-handed ○ *How many lefties are on the team?*

leg /leg/ *n* **1. LOWER LIMB** a limb that animals and people use for standing, walking, running, or jumping, either including or excluding the foot **2. SUPPORTING POLE** a part of an object that looks like a human or animal lower limb and is used for support ○ *a table leg* **3. CLOTHING FOR LEG** the portion of a piece of clothing that covers all or part of the human leg ○ *a trouser leg* **4. MEAT FROM ANIMAL'S OR FOWL'S LEG** the meat, including the bone, from the back hindquarter of a four-legged mammal, or from the leg of a bird, that is cooked and eaten as food **5. BRANCH OF OBJECT** one of the extensions of a branched or jointed object **6. SECTION OF JOURNEY** a part of a journey that is separated from other parts by a period of rest or by a change in direction or the manner of travel **7.** SPORTS **RELAY RACE PORTION** one of the parts of a relay race that a single athlete completes **8.** SPORTS **PORTION OF SPORTS COMPETITION** one of several stages, events, or games that is part of a larger competition but is treated independently of the other parts and has its own winner **9.** FOOTBALL **ONE OF TWO FOOTBALL GAMES** either of two games in a competition played between two football teams, one game being played at home, the other away. The aggregate score of the two games determines the overall winner of the round. **10.** SAILING **SAILING COMPLETED ON ONE TACK** the distance travelled by a sailing boat on a single tack **11.** CRICKET **LEFT-HAND PART OF CRICKET FIELD** the part of a cricket field that lies on the left of and behind a right-handed batsman as he or she stands in position to hit the ball **12.** MATHS **RIGHT-ANGLE SIDE OF TRIANGLE** either of the two sides of a right-angled triangle that extend from the right angle ■ **legs** *npl* WINE **TRAILS OF WINE ON SIDE OF GLASS** the vertical trails of wine that cling to the side of a glass after wine has been swirled around in it. The length and movement of these trails are taken as an indication of the wine's body. [13C. < Old Norse *leggr*] ◇ **get your leg over** to have sex (*slang*) ◇ **have legs** *US* to be likely to enjoy a sustained period of popularity or success (*informal*) ◇ **leg it** (*informal*) **1.** to run away, especially in order to escape from somebody or something **2.** to walk or run ◇ **not have a leg to stand on** to have nothing to justify or support an attitude or position (*informal*) ◇ **on your last legs** on the verge of collapse or breakdown ◇ **pull somebody's leg** to tell somebody something untrue as a tease or for fun (*informal*) ◇ **shake a leg 1.** to hurry up (*usually used as a command*) **2.** same as **dance** *v* (sense 1) (*dated informal*) ◇ **show a leg** to get out of bed in the morning (*dated informal; usually used as a command*) ◇ **stretch your legs** to go for a walk after a period of being seated or stationary ◇ **talk the hind legs off a donkey** to talk a great deal (*informal*)

leg. *abbr* **1.** LAW legal **2.** CHR, POL legate **3.** MUSIC legato **4.** LAW, GOV legislation **5.** LAW, GOV legislative **6.** LAW, GOV legislature

legacy /léggəssi/ *n* (*plural* **-cies**) **1. BEQUEST MADE IN WILL** money or property that is left to somebody in a will **2. SOMETHING FROM PAST** something that is handed down or remains from a previous generation or time ■ *adj* **OUTDATED OR DISCONTINUED** associated with something that is outdated or discontinued ○ *legacy software* ○ *legacy currency* [14C. Via Old French *legacie* 'office of a delegate' < medieval Latin *legatia* < Latin *legatus* (see LEGATE)]

legal /léeg'l/ *adj* **1. LAW-RELATED** relating to the law or to courts of law ○ *took legal action* **2. OF OR FOR LAWYERS** relating to lawyers or to law as a profession **3. PERMITTED BY LAW** allowed under the law ○ *Parking on the grass isn't legal.* **4. UNDER LAW** established under the law ○ *the legal age of consent* **5. ESTABLISHED BY LAW COURT** recognized or established by a court of law, rather than a court of equity [15C. Via French < Latin *legalis* < *leg-* 'law'] —**legally** *adv*

ORIGIN The Latin stem *leg-* 'law', from which ***legal*** is derived, is also the source of English *colleague, college, delegate, legacy, legate, legislate, legitimate, loyal, privilege,* and *relegate*.

SYNONYMS ***legal, lawful, decriminalized, legalized, legitimate, licit***

CORE MEANING: describes something that is permitted, recognized, or required by law

legal established or allowed under the law ○ *It is perfectly legal to charge a reasonable interest rate on unpaid accounts.* ○ *Your spouse will still have a legal right to inherit from you.* **lawful** a less common word meaning legal ○ *a lawful act such as killing in self-defence* ○ *He believed he had lawful authority to ride the bike.* **decriminalized** no longer categorized as a criminal offence ○ *decriminalized activities* **legalized** previously categorized as illegal and now declared legal ○ *an opponent of legalized abortion* **legitimate** complying with the law, or having official status defined by law ○ *When the culprits were identified, it turned out that their activities were perfectly legitimate.* ○ *She had refused to sign the treaty recognizing Elizabeth as legitimate Queen of England.* **licit** allowed by law ○ *What had been licit and reasonably commonplace practices were now forbidden.*

legal age *n* the age established by law at which somebody is considered to be an adult

legal aid *n* **1.** legal advice or representation that is provided by an organization at low or no cost to people who cannot afford to pay for legal services **2.** public funds used for legal advice and representation for people who cannot afford private lawyers ○ *Legal aid paid for his defence.*

legal cap *n US* ruled white writing paper measuring 216 mm/8½ in by 350 mm/14 in to 406 mm/16 in, with the fold at the top, typically used by lawyers

legal eagle *n* a lawyer, especially a skilful or successful one (*slang*)

legalese /léegə léez/ *n* language that is typically used in legal documents and is generally considered by lay people to be difficult to understand

legal holiday *n N Am* a day established as a holiday by law, when government offices, schools, and post offices are typically closed

legalise *vt* LAW another spelling of **legalize**

legalism /leegəlizəm/ *n* **1.** strict adherence to a literal interpretation of a law, rule, or religious or moral code **2.** a word or phrase in legal jargon —**legalist** *n* —**legalistic** /leegə lístik/ *adj* —**legalistically** *adv*

legality /li gállәti/ (*plural* **-ties**) *n* **1.** the state of being in accordance with the law ○ *the legality of the corporation's activities* **2.** something required by law, especially a technical detail (*often used in the plural*) ○ *We have to take care of certain legalities before opening the business.*

legalize /leegə līz/ (**-izes, -izing, -ized**), **legalise** (**-ises, -ising, -ised**) *vt* to make an activity legal by introducing or changing a law that governs it —**legalized** *adj* —**legalization** /leegə lī záysh'n/ *n*

SYNONYMS See *legal.*

legal medicine *n* LAW same as **forensic medicine**

legal reserve *n US* an amount of money that a financial organization such as a bank or insurer is required to keep as security against debts (*often used in the plural*)

legal separation *n* **1.** separation of a married couple that is recognized by a court of law. This is often required as a first step towards divorce. **2.** the court decree establishing the separation of a married couple

legal tender *n* currency that is valid for the payment of a debt and must be accepted by a creditor

Legaspi /lə gásspi/, **Legazpi** city and capital of Albay Province, the Philippines, situated at the head of Albay Gulf. Population: 160,501 (1999).

legate /léggət/ *n* **1.** an emissary of the pope, especially one who represents the Vatican in another country **2.** an official representative of a government, especially a diplomat [12C. Via French < Latin *legatus* < *legat-* past participle of *legare* 'send as an envoy, bequeath'] —**legateship** *n* —**legatine** /-tīn/ *adj*

legatee /léggə tee/ *n* a recipient of a bequest made in a will [Late 17C. < *legate* 'bequeath' < Latin *legat-* (see LEGATE)]

legation /li gáysh'n/ *n* **1.** DIPLOMAT'S RESIDENCE the official local residence of a senior diplomat assigned to a country. It ranks below an embassy in importance. **2.** DIPLOMATIC STAFF the staff of a legation **3.** DIPLOMATS ON MISSION a group of representatives sent on a mission, especially a diplomatic mission **4.** SENDING OF DIPLOMATIC REPRESENTATIVE the sending of a representative on a diplomatic mission **5.** DIPLOMATIC MISSION a mission performed by a diplomatic representative **6.** LEGATE'S POSITION the status or office of a papal legate [14C. Directly or via French < Latin *legation-* < *legat-* (see LEGATE)]

legato /li gaátō/ *adv* in a smooth even manner, often indicated in a musical score by a curved line (**slur**) connecting the notes to be so played (*used as a musical direction*) ■ *n* (*plural* **-tos**) a piece of music, or a section of a piece, played legato [Mid-18C. < Italian, 'tied together'] —**legato** *adj*

legator /li gáytər/ *n* somebody who has made a will to bequeath something [Mid-17C. < Latin < *legat-* (see LEGATE)]

Legazpi another spelling of **Legaspi**

leg before wicket *adj, adv* forced to end a cricket innings as a result of being hit on the leg by a ball that the umpire adjudges would otherwise have hit the wicket ■ *n* in cricket, the dismissal of a batsman as a result of the leg obstructing a ball that the umpire adjudges would otherwise have hit the wicket

leg-break *n* in cricket, a ball with a bounce that spins from the leg side to the off side

leg bye *n* in cricket, a run scored after the ball has hit some part of the batsman's body other than the hand, without touching the bat

legend /léjjənd/ *n* **1.** OLD STORY a story that has been passed down for generations, especially one that is presented as history but is unlikely to be true **2.** OLD STORIES a group of stories presented as history but unlikely to be true **3.** MODERN MYTH a popular myth that has arisen in modern times **4.** CELEBRITY somebody famous admired for a skill or talent **5.** INSCRIPTION an inscription, especially a title or motto, on an object **6.** PUBL CAPTION a caption for an illustration **7.** MAPS MAP KEY an explanation of the symbols used on a map [14C. Via French *légende* < medieval Latin *legenda* 'things to be read' < Latin *legere* 'to read']

legendary /léjjəndəri/ *adj* **1.** BELONGING TO LEGEND described or commemorated in a legend ○ *the legendary figure of Hercules* **2.** CONTAINING LEGENDS retold for generations as history but unlikely to be completely or even partially true ○ *the legendary tales of ancient warriors* **3.** LIKE SOMETHING IN LEGEND appropriate for a legend ○ *an organization of legendary size* **4.** FAMOUS very famous in contemporary society ○ *Her generosity is legendary.* —**legendarily** *adv*

legendry /léjjəndri/ (*plural* **-ries**) *n* a collection or group of legends

Léger /láy zhay/, **Fernand** (1881–1955) French painter. One of the founders of the cubist movement, he developed a personal style that used rounded and cylindrical forms.

legerdemain /léjjərdə máyn/ *n* **1.** a display of skill or cleverness, especially for deceitful purposes ○ *a dazzling display of political legerdemain* **2.** ARTS same as **sleight of hand** (sense 1) (*dated*) [15C. < French *léger de main* 'light of hand']

leger line *n* MUSIC another spelling of **ledger line**

leges LAW plural of **lex**

-legged *suffix* **1.** /léggid/ with a particular number of legs ○ *four-legged* **2.** /legd/ with a particular type or position of legs ○ *bandy-legged* ○ *cross-legged*

legging /légging/ *n* PROTECTIVE COVERING FOR LOWER LEG a protective covering made of a strong material that is wrapped around the lower leg by labourers and players in some sports ■ **leggings** *npl* **1.** CLOSE-FITTING TROUSERS women's trousers or footless tights made of stretchy material that fit very closely to the legs and hips **2.** PROTECTIVE OUTER TROUSERS waterproof or insulated outer trousers that are worn for protection from snow, rain, and cold

leggy /léggi/ (**-gier, -giest**) *adj* **1.** WITH LONG LEGS having very long legs in relation to the rest of the body **2.** WITH SHAPELY LEGS having long good-looking legs ○ *a leggy supermodel* **3.** BOT SPINDLY IN GROWTH with long thin stems that have few and widely spaced leaves

leghorn /lég hawrn/ *n* **1.** BLEACHED STRAW fine bleached straw made from a type of Italian wheat **2.** STRAW FABRIC a fabric made from plaited leghorn straw **3.** STRAW HAT a hat made from leghorn straw [Mid-18C. After LEGHORN [2]]

Leghorn[1] /lég hawrn/ *n* a small domestic fowl. Kept for: white eggs. [Mid-19C. After LEGHORN [2]]

Leghorn[2] /lég hawrn/ ➧ **Livorno**

legible /léjjəb'l/ *adj* clear enough to be read [15C. < late Latin *legibilis* < Latin *legere* 'to read'] —**legibility** /léjjə bílləti/ *n* —**legibleness** *n* —**legibly** *adv*

ORIGIN The Latin word *legere* 'to collect, choose, read', from which ***legible*** is derived, is also the source of English *coil, collect*[1], *cull, elect, elegant, intelligent, lecture, legend, legion, lesson, neglect,* and *select.*

legion /leejən/ *n* **1.** MULTITUDE a large number of people or things (*often used in the plural*) ○ *Their complicated affairs are managed by a legion of accountants.* **2.** ANCIENT HIST ROMAN ARMY DIVISION in ancient Rome, an army division of 3,000 to 6,000 soldiers, including cavalry **3.** MIL LARGE BODY OF SOLDIERS a large military unit, especially an army ○ *the French Foreign Legion* **4.** MIL ORGANIZATION OF EX-MILITARY PERSONNEL an association of ex-servicemen and ex-servicewomen ○ *the Royal British Legion* ■ *adj* MANY very numerous (*literary*) ○ *dissatisfied customers and their legion complaints* [12C. Via French < Latin *legion-* < *legere* 'choose']

legionary /leejənəri/ *adj* belonging to, associated with, or forming a legion ■ *n* (*plural* **-ies**) a member of a legion, especially a Roman legion

legionnaire /leejə náir/, **Legionnaire** *n* **1.** SOMEBODY IN LEGION a soldier in a legion, especially the French Foreign Legion **2.** SOMEBODY IN ROYAL BRITISH LEGION a member of the Royal British Legion **3.** SOMEBODY IN AMERICAN LEGION a member of the American Legion [Early 19C. < French *légionnaire* < *légion* (see LEGION)]

legionnaires' disease *n* a virulent and sometimes fatal form of pneumonia caused by a bacterium and spread mainly by the water droplets in air conditioning systems [< its first recognized occurrence at an American Legion convention in Philadelphia in 1976]

Legion of Honour *n* a French order of merit awarded for illustrious military or civil service

Legion of Merit *n* a US military decoration awarded to military personnel from any country for exceptional and outstanding service

legis. *abbr* LAW, GOV **1.** legislation **2.** legislative **3.** legislature

legislate /léjji slayt/ (**-lates, -lating, -lated**) *v* **1.** *vi* to write and pass laws **2.** *vt* to make laws or rules designed to bring about an action or condition ○ *The candidates all promise to legislate change.* [Early 18C. Back-formation < LEGISLATOR, LEGISLATION]

legislation /léjji sláysh'n/ *n* **1.** the process of writing and passing laws **2.** a law or laws passed by an official body [Mid-17C. < late Latin *legis latio-* 'proposing of a law' < forms of *lex* 'law' + *latus,* past participle of *ferre* 'bring']

legislative /léjjislətiv/ *adj* **1.** RELATING TO LAW-MAKING involved in the writing and passing of laws **2.** RELATING TO LAW-MAKING BODY relating to or being part of a legislature **3.** ENACTED BY LAW created by governmental legislation ○ *There is no legislative solution to this problem.* [Mid-17C. < LEGISLATOR, LEGISLATION] —**legislatively** *adv*

legislative assembly *n* an official body with law- or rule-making powers

Legislative Assembly *n* **1.** US LAW-MAKING BODY the two-chamber legislature of some US states **2.** SINGLE-CHAMBER COMMONWEALTH LEGISLATURE the single-chamber legislature of most Canadian provinces and some Australian states **3.** LOWER HOUSE OF COMMONWEALTH LEGISLATURE the lower house of a two-chamber state legislature in some Commonwealth countries, especially that of some Australian states

Legislative Council *n* **1.** *also* **legislative council** COMMITTEE OF STATE SENATORS AND REPRESENTATIVES a permanent committee consisting of members of both houses of a two-chamber state legislature who discuss issues of common concern and plan legislative programmes **2.** UPPER HOUSE OF BRITISH COMMONWEALTH LEGISLATURE the upper house of the two-chamber legislature in some Commonwealth countries, e.g. in most South Asian and Australian states **3.** LEGISLATURE IN FORMER BRITISH COLONY the single-chamber legislature of some former British colonies

legislator /léjji slaytər/ *n* a writer of or voter on laws, especially as a member of a legislature [15C. < Latin *legis lator* 'proposer of a law' < forms of *lex* 'law' + *latus,* past participle of *ferre* 'bring'] —**legislatorial** /léjjislə táwri əl/ *adj* —**legislatorship** *n*

legislature /léjjisləchər/ *n* LAW, GOV an official body, usually chosen by election, with the power to make, change, and repeal laws [Late 17C. < LEGISLATOR]

legist /leejist/ *n* a specialist in law, especially Roman or civil law [15C. < French *légiste* < Latin *leg-* 'law']

legit /lə jít/ *adj* (*slang*) **1.** same as **legitimate** *adj* (sense 1) **2.** telling the truth and not trying to deceive ○ *Is his story legit?* **3.** THEATRE same as **legitimate** *adj* (sense 5) [Late 19C. Shortening of LEGITIMATE]

~~**legitamate**~~ incorrect spelling of **legitimate**

legitimate *adj* /lə jíttimət/ **1.** LEGAL complying with the law, or having official status defined by law ○ *legitimate tax deductions* ○ *a legitimate claim to the land* **2.** CONFORMING TO ACKNOWLEDGED STANDARDS complying with recognized rules, standards, or traditions **3.** WELL-FOUNDED well reasoned and sincere ○ *We have legitimate reasons for worrying about the quality of our water.* **4.** BORN IN WEDLOCK born of legally married parents **5.** THEATRE RELATING TO SERIOUS PROFESSIONAL DRAMA performing or involving professionally produced dramatic works that are considered to be serious art, in contrast to such forms as revues and musical comedy ■ *vt* (**-mates, -mating, -mated**) /lə jítti mayt/ LAW same as **legitimize** (senses 1–2) [15C. < medieval Latin *legitimatus,* past participle of *legitimare* 'make legal' < Latin *legitimus* 'lawful' < *lex* 'law'] —**legitimacy** *n* —**legitimately** *adv* —**legitimateness** *n* —**legitimation** /lə jítti máysh'n/ *n* —**legitimator** /-maytər/ *n*

SYNONYMS See *legal.*

legitimatize /lə jíttimə tīz/ (**-tizes, -tizing, -tized**), **legitimatise** (**-tises, -tising, -tised**) *vt* LAW same as **legitimize** —**legitimatization** /lə jíttimə tī záysh'n/ *n*

legitimise *vt* LAW another spelling of **legitimize**

legitimist /lə jíttimist/ *n* **1.** a believer in monarchy through inheritance or in a specific person's claim to inherit a throne **2.** in the 19th century, a supporter of the Bourbon claimants to the French throne [Mid-19C. < French *légitimiste* < *légitime* 'legitimate' < Latin *legitimus* (see LEGITIMATE)] —**legitimism** *n* —**legitimist** *adj*

legitimize /lə jítti mīz/ (**-mizes, -mizing, -mized**), **legitimise** (**-mises, -mising, -mised**) *vt* **1.** to make something lawful, by making, changing, or repealing laws or by decree **2.** to argue or prove that a claim or action is lawful or reasonable [Mid-19C. < Latin *legitimus* (see LEGITIMATE)] —**legitimization** /lə jítti mī záysh'n/ *n* —**legitimizer** *n*

legless /léggləss/ *adj* **1.** having no legs **2.** extremely drunk, especially too drunk to stand (*informal*)

legman /lég man/ (*plural* **-men** /-mən/) *n* US **1.** somebody employed in an office to run errands and gather information **2.** a reporter who gathers information for a story, especially from firsthand sources

Lego /léggō/ *tdmk* a trademark for a toy consisting of plastic building blocks and other components

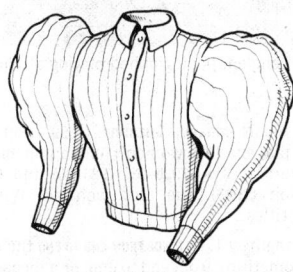

leg-of-mutton sleeve

leg-of-mutton, leg-o'-mutton *adj* shaped like a sharply tapered triangle ○ *a blouse with leg-of-mutton sleeves*

leg-pull *n* an amusing deception or practical joke (*informal*) [< *pull somebody's leg*] —**leg-puller** *n* —**leg-pulling** *n*

legroom /lég room, -rŏŏm/ *n* space in front of a seat for somebody's legs, especially enough space to stretch out and move the legs

Le Guin /lə gwín/, **Ursula** (*b.* 1929) US writer. Her science fiction novels include *The Left Hand of Darkness* (1969). Born **Kroeber, Ursula**

> 'He had grown up in a country run by politicians who sent the pilots to man the bombers to kill the babies to make the world safe for children to grow up in.'
> [Ursula Le Guin, *The Lathe of Heaven*; 1971]

legume /léggyoom/ *n* **1.** a seed, pod, or other part of a plant such as a pea or bean, used as food **2.** a plant that has pods as fruits and roots that bear nodules containing nitrogen-fixing bacteria. Peas and beans are legumes. [Mid-17C. Via French *légume* < Latin *legumen* 'bean']

leguminous /li gyoominəss/ *adj* **1.** belonging to or typical of the family of plants that has pods as fruits and roots that bear nodules containing nitrogen-fixing bacteria **2.** resembling a legume or a leguminous plant [Mid-17C. < Latin *leguminosus* < *legumin-* stem of *legumen* 'bean']

leg up *n* (*informal*) **1.** UPWARDS BOOST help for somebody to get onto something such as a horse or a wall by lifting the person's leg upwards or using your linked hands as a support **2.** CAREER HELP help for somebody to move up in a hierarchy or a field of activity **3.** *N Am* POSITION OF SUPERIORITY an advantage that other people do not have in an activity

legwarmer /lég wawrmər/ *n* a knitted tube that covers the calf of the leg and sometimes also the top of the foot, and is typically worn by a dancer during practice (*usually used in the plural*)

legwork /lég wurk/ *n* preparatory research for a project that is usually physically demanding or involves a lot of walking (*informal*)

Le Havre /lə haavrə/ city in Seine-Maritime Department, Haute-Normandie Region, northwestern France. Population: 190,905 (1999).

lehayim *n, interj* JUDAISM another spelling of **l'chaim**

Lehrer /laírər/, **Tom** (*b.* 1928) US teacher and songwriter. A university professor, he became a successful entertainer in the 1960s with his humorous songs, many of them political satires. Full name **Lehrer, Thomas Andrew**

> 'Life is like a sewer. What you get out of it depends on what you put into it.'
> [Tom Lehrer, *We Will All Go Together When We Go*; 1953]

lei[1] /lay/ (*plural* **leis**) *n* a garland of flowers, especially one worn around the neck in Hawaii and other parts of Polynesia [Mid-19C. < Hawaiian]

lei[2] /lay/ MONEY plural of **leu**

Leibniz /líb nits/, **Leibnitz, Gottfried Wilhelm von, Baron** (1646–1716) German philosopher and mathematician. The first president of the Prussian Academy of Sciences, he discovered calculus (independently of Newton) and contributed to the sciences of mechanics, optics, and logic, and to probability theory. —**Leibnizian** /līb nítsi ən/ *adj, n*

> 'There is nothing waste, nothing sterile, nothing dead in the universe; no chaos, no confusions, save in appearance.'
> [Gottfried Wilhelm von Leibniz, *Monadology*; 1714]

Leibovitz /léebə vitz/, **Annie** (*b.* 1949) US photographer best known for her portraits of celebrities, including musicians. She has worked for magazines such as *Rolling Stone*, *Vogue*, and *Vanity Fair*. Born **Leibovitz, Anna-Lou**

Leicester /léstər/ industrial city in Leicestershire, central England. Population: 279,921 (2001).

Leicester, Robert Dudley, 1st Earl of (1532–88) English courtier. A favourite adviser to and unsuccessful suitor of Queen Elizabeth I, he helped involve England in the Protestant struggle against Philip II of Spain.

Leicestershire /léstərshər/ county in central England. Population: 609,578 (2001). Area: 2,553 sq. km/986 sq. mi.

Leichhardt /lík haart/, **Ludwig** (1813–48?) Prussian-born Australian naturalist and explorer. He led three major expeditions into the Australian interior, and he disappeared while attempting to cross the continent from east to west. Full name **Leichhardt, Friedrich Wilhelm Ludwig**

Leics *abbr* Leicestershire

Leiden /láydən/, **Leyden** university city in Zuid-Holland Province, western Netherlands. Population: 117,196 (2000).

Leigh /lee/, **Mike** (*b.* 1943) British playwright and film director. His plays and films, including *Abigail's Party* (1977) and *Secrets and Lies* (1996), are developed with the actors in improvisation.

Vivien Leigh

Leigh, Vivien (1913–67) British actor. She won Academy Awards for her performances in *Gone with the Wind* (1939) and *A Streetcar Named Desire* (1951).

> 'In Britain, an attractive woman is somehow suspect. If there is talent as well it is overshadowed. Beauty and brains just can't be entertained; someone has been

too extravagant.'
> [Vivien Leigh, *Light of a Star*; 1967]

Leighton Buzzard /láyt'n búzzərd/ market town in Bedfordshire, central England. Population: 32,610 (1991).

Leinster /lénstər/ historic province in the eastern Republic of Ireland

Leipzig /lípsig/ city and cultural and university centre in east-central Germany, known for its international trade fairs. Population: 481,526 (1997).

leishmaniasis /léeshmə nī əssiss/ *n* an infection such as kala-azar and some other skin diseases caused by a protozoan that is a parasite in the tissue of vertebrates [Early 20C. < modern Latin *Leishmania*, after Sir William Boog *Leishman* (1865–1926), Scottish pathologist]

leister /léestər/ *n* a stick with three prongs, used for spearing fish ■ *vt* (**-ters, -tering, -tered**) to catch fish using a three-pronged spear [Mid-16C. < Old Norse *ljóstr* < *ljósta* 'to strike']

leisure /lézhər/ *n* time during which somebody has no obligations or work responsibilities, and therefore is free to engage in enjoyable activities [13C. < Anglo-Norman *leisour* < Old French *leisir* 'be permitted' < Latin *licere*] ◇ **at your leisure** at the time and pace that suits you ◇ **gentleman** or **lady of leisure** a man or woman who does not have to work for a living (*humorous*)

leisure centre *n* a public establishment that provides the space and equipment for recreational activities such as sports, games, and hobbies

leisured /lézhərd/ *adj* **1.** having a lot of free time, especially because of not having to work for a living **2.** same as **leisurely**

leisurely /lézhərli/ *adj* relaxed, unhurried, and enjoyable, e.g. because done during free time ○ *a leisurely stroll in the park* ■ *adv* in a slow and relaxed manner —**leisureliness** *n*

leisure society *n* a society in which a greater proportion of people's time is spent at leisure than at work

leisure visitor *n* same as **tourist**

leisurewear /lézhər wair/ *n* comfortable informal clothing such as a tracksuit, appropriate for relaxation or play

Leith /leeth/ seaport of Edinburgh, Scotland, situated on the Firth of Forth

leitmotif /lítmō teef/, **leitmotiv** *n* **1.** a musical theme that recurs in the course of a work to evoke a particular character or situation. Leitmotifs are typical of the operas of Richard Wagner. **2.** a recurring theme, e.g. in literature or history [Late 19C. < German < *leiten* 'to lead' + *Motiv* 'motif']

Leitrim /léetrim/ county in Connacht Province, northern Republic of Ireland. The county town is Carrick-on-Shannon. Population: 25,000 (1996). Area: 1,525 sq. km/589 sq. mi.

leiu incorrect spelling of **lieu**

Leix ♦ **Laois**

Leizhou Peninsula /láy jō-/ peninsula in Guangdong Province, southeastern China, stretching from Guangdong Bay in the east to the Gulf of Tonkin in the west

lek[1] /lek/ *n* the basic currency unit of Albania. See table at **currency** [Early 20C. < Albanian, after *Lek* Dukagjin, Albanian lawyer]

lek[2] /lek/ *n* an area used for the performance of communal breeding displays and courtship during the mating season by birds such as the black grouse or other animals [Late 19C. Origin ?]

lekgotla /lə kóttlə/ *n* S *Africa* a strategic meeting of senior political, corporate or union leaders [Late 20C. < Sotho, < *le-* singular prefix + 'council; assembly']

lekker /lékər/ S *Africa* (*informal*) *adj* enjoyable and pleasing ■ *adv* used to express pleasure or approval ○ *The team is playing lekker!* [Early 20C. Via Afrikaans < Middle Dutch]

LEM /lem/ *abbr* AEROSP lunar excursion module

Lemaître /lə méttrə/, **Georges-Henri** (1894–1966) Belgian astrophysicist and priest. He was a proponent of the big bang theory of the universe.

leman /lémmən, leémən/ (plural **-ans**) n somebody loved, e.g. a sweetheart or lover (archaic) [12C. Contracted < LIEF + MAN]

Le Mans /lə maáN/ capital of Sarthe Department, Pays de la Loire Region, northern France. Population: 146,105 (1999).

lemma[1] /lémmə/ (plural **-mas** or **-mata** /-mətə/) n 1. LOGIC **ASSUMPTION FOR SAKE OF ARGUMENT** a proposition that is assumed to be true in order to test the validity of another proposition 2. PUBL **SUBJECT HEADING** a heading that indicates the topic of a work or passage 3. LING **DICTIONARY HEADWORD** the headword of a dictionary entry [Late 16C. Via Latin < Greek *lēmma* 'something taken (for granted)']

lemma[2] /lémmə/ n the lower of two dry membranous leaves (**bracts**) protecting a single flower in a flower head of a plant of the grass family [Mid-18C. < Greek, 'husk' < past participle of *lepein* 'peel']

lemmata LOGIC, PUBL, LING plural of **lemma**[1]

lemme /lémmi/ contr let me (nonstandard)

lemming

lemming /lémming/ n 1. a rodent with a small thick furry body and furry feet that lives in subarctic regions. Lemmings are noted for their mass migrations in search of food during population explosions, which has given rise to the myth that they flock to the sea to drown themselves. Native to: Arctic and northern regions. Genus: *Lemmus* or *Dicrostonyx*. 2. a member of a large group of people who blindly follow one another on a course of action that will lead to destruction for all of them [Early 18C. < Norwegian]

Lemmon /lémmən/, **Jack** (1925–2001) US actor. His many films include the Academy Award-winning *Mister Roberts* (1955) and *Some Like It Hot* (1959). Full name **Lemmon, John Uhler, III**

lemniscus /lem nískəss/ (plural **-ci** /-si, -kee/) n a bundle of fibres, especially a bundle of nerve fibres [Mid-19C. Via Latin < Greek *lēmniskos* 'ribbon']

Lemnos /lémnoss/ island in eastern Greece, in the Aegean Sea, near the Dardanelles. Population: 15,721 (1981).

lemon

lemon /lémmən/ n 1. YELLOW OR GREEN CITRUS FRUIT a yellow or, in some climates, green oval citrus fruit with a thick fragrant rind and sour juicy flesh 2. TREE THAT BEARS LEMONS a tree with glossy leaves and spiky branches that is widely cultivated to produce lemons. Native to: southeastern Asia. Latin name: *Citrus limon*. 3. PALE YELLOW COLOUR a pale yellow colour typical of the rind of a lemon 4. LEMON DRINK a drink made from lemon juice 5. DEFECTIVE PRODUCT something that is defective or disappointing, especially a car

that does not run properly (informal) 6. SILLY PERSON somebody regarded as unintelligent or thoughtless (informal) ○ *I feel a lemon now.* 7. Aus OFFENSIVE TERM an offensive term for a lesbian (slang) [14C. Via French < Arabic *līmūn*] —**lemon** adj —**lemony** adj

lemonade /lémmə nayd/ n 1. FIZZY DRINK a sweet fizzy clear soft drink with a lemon flavour 2. DRINK MADE FROM LEMONS a still soft drink made from fresh lemons, sugar, and water 3. DRINK OF LEMONADE a drink of lemonade ○ *ordered a lemonade and two coffees*

lemonade berry n an evergreen bush with leathery leaves, clusters of small pink flowers, and acidic dark red fruits that are used in flavouring drinks. Native to: California. Latin name: *Rhus integrifolia*.

lemon balm n a widely cultivated plant of the mint family that has lemon-scented leaves. Flowers: small, white or pinkish. Native to: southern Europe.

lemon curd, **lemon cheese** n a thick sweet creamy-yellow spread made from lemons, sugar, eggs, and butter and usually eaten on bread

lemon drop n a small lemon-flavoured boiled sweet

lemon grass n a tropical grass cultivated for a lemon-scented oil distilled from its leaves, and for use as a flavouring in cooking. Native to: southern India. Latin name: *Cymbopogon citratus*.

lemon sole n 1. a common flatfish, prized as a food fish. Native to: northeastern Atlantic, North Sea. Latin name: *Microstomus kitt*. 2. the flesh of a lemon sole used as food

lemon-squeezer n a device for extracting juice from lemons, usually consisting of a raised fluted cone onto which a halved lemon is pressed, set in a shallow bowl where juice collects. N Am term **reamer**

lemon verbena, **lemon vervain** n a widely cultivated bush with leaves that produce a fragrance resembling lemons when crushed. Flowers: small, lavender. Native to: South America. Latin name: *Lippia triphylla*.

lemon yellow n COLOURS same as **lemon** (sense 3) — **lemon-yellow** adj

lempira /lem peérə/ n the main unit of Honduran currency. See table at **currency** [Mid-20C. After *Lempira*, 16C chieftain who fought against the Spanish conquerors of Honduras]

lemur

lemur /leénər/ n a primate with a long snout, large ears, and a long tail. Native to: Madagascar and nearby islands. Family: Lemuridae. [Late 18C. Via modern Latin < Latin *lemures* 'the spirits of the dead'; because it is nocturnal]

lemures /lémmyōo reez/ npl in ancient Rome, the spirits of the dead (literary) [Mid-16C. < Latin]

Lena /leénə/ river in Siberian Russia that rises in southern Siberia and flows northwards before emptying into the Laptev Sea, an arm of the Arctic Ocean. Length: 4,400 km/2,730 mi.

Lenape /lénnəpi/ n PEOPLES same as **Delaware**[1] [Early 18C. < Algonquian, 'people'] —**Lenape** adj

lend /lend/ (**lends**, **lending**, **lent** /lent/) v 1. vt LET SOMEBODY BORROW SOMETHING to allow somebody to take or use something on the understanding that it will be returned later 2. vti GIVE SOMEBODY MONEY FOR LIMITED TIME to allow a person or business to use a sum of money for a particular period of time, usually on condition that a charge (**interest**) is paid in return 3. vt ADD SOMETHING to give a particular quality or character to something ○ *The candles lend an air of intimacy*

to the room. [Old English *lǣnan* < Germanic] —**lendable** adj —**lender** n ◇ **lend itself to something** to be suitable for a particular purpose or occasion

USAGE See **borrow**.

lending library /lénding-/ n a library or department of a library where the public can borrow books and often audio tapes, videotapes, CDs, and DVDs

Lendl /lénd'l/, **Ivan** (b. 1960) Czechoslovakian-born US tennis player. Between 1981 and 1987 he won many international tournaments, including the French Open, the US Open and the Grand Prix Masters.

lenes PHON plural of **lenis**

Popperfoto

Suzanne Lenglen: photographed playing at Wimbledon (1922)

Lenglen /laaN glaáN/, **Suzanne** (1899–1938) French tennis player. The women's champion of France for several years (1920–23, 1925–26) and Olympic champion (1920), she also won six Wimbledon singles titles.

length /length/ n 1. DISTANCE FROM END TO END the distance along something from end to end, or a measurement taken of this distance ○ *The length of the garden is 25 metres.* 2. QUALITY OF BEING LONG the condition or state of being long ○ *The garden is designed to give a sense of length and openness.* 3. HOW LONG SOMETHING TAKES the time something lasts or takes from beginning to end ○ *The length of the second act is about 75 minutes.* 4. SIZE FROM BEGINNING TO END the extent of something from beginning to end ○ *The second volume is a massive 400 pages in length.* 5. LONG PIECE OF SOMETHING a piece of something long and narrow ○ *a length of copper piping* 6. UNIT OF MEASUREMENT a piece of something such as cloth that is measured or bought in units of a standard size ○ *bought three lengths of fabric* 7. SWIMMING END TO END IN SWIMMING POOL the distance from one end of a swimming pool to the other 8. FASHION HOW LONG GARMENT IS how high the hem of a coat, skirt, or dress is above the ground or below the wearer's waist, or how much of the wearer's legs it shows 9. SPORTS WINNING DISTANCE in something such as a boat race or horse race, the distance between two competitors, measured according to how long a single boat or horse is ○ *two lengths ahead with only 100m to go* 10. PHON HOW LONG SOUND TAKES TO MAKE the amount of time required to articulate a vowel or syllable 11. CRICKET DISTANCE BALL BOUNCES FROM BATSMAN in cricket, the distance from the batsman at which the ball bounces [Old English *lengþ* < Germanic] ◇ **at length** 1. in great detail and for a long time 2. after some time or following a delay

-length suffix extending all the way to a particular part of something ○ *shoulder-length hair*

lengthen /léngth'n/ (**-ens**, **-ening**, **-ened**) vti to make something longer, or become longer ○ *The weeks lengthened into months and still no news came.* — **lengthener** n

lengthways /léngth wayz/, **lengthwise** /-wīz/ adv, adj in relation to something's length from end to end ○ *attempting to force the suitcase into the boot lengthways*

lengthy /léngthi/ (**-ier**, **-iest**) adj lasting for a long time, especially for an excessively long time —**lengthily** adv —**lengthiness** n

lenient /leéni ənt/ adj showing tolerance or mercy in dealing with crime or misbehaviour [Mid-17C. < Latin *lenient-*, present participle of *lenire* 'soothe' < *lenis* 'smooth'] —**leniency** n —**leniently** adv

Vladimir Ilyich Lenin

AKG London

Lenin /lénnin/, **Vladimir Ilyich** (1870–1924) Russian revolutionary leader. Founder of the Soviet Union, he led the Bolshevik revolution in 1917. He was the first leader of the Soviet Communist regime, but became less active after suffering a stroke in 1922. Born **Ulyanov, Vladimir Ilyich**

'Under capitalism we have a state in the proper sense of the word, that is, a special machine for the suppression of one class by another.'
[Vladimir Ilyich Lenin, *The State and Revolution*; 1919]

Leninakhan /lénninə kaán/ former name for **Gyumri** (1924–90)

Leningrad /lénnin grad/ former name for **St Petersburg** (1924–90)

Leninism /lénninizəm/ n the political, social, and economic theories of Lenin, which he developed from Marxist theory —**Leninist** n, adj —**Leninite** n, adj

Lenin Peak /lénnin-/ mountain in the Trans-Alai Range of the Pamirs, situated in Tajikistan. Height: 7,134 m/23,406 ft. Former name **Kaufman, Mount**

lenis /leéniss/ adj describes a consonant produced using little breath and muscle power ■ n (plural **-nes** /-neez/) a consonant that is produced using little breath and muscle power [Early 20C. < Latin, 'smooth']

lenition /li nísh'n/ n the use of little breath and muscle power when articulating consonants [Early 20C. < Latin *lenit-*, stem of *lenis* 'smooth']

Lennon /lénnən/, **John** (1940–80) British singer, songwriter, and musician. A member of the Beatles, he had a songwriting partnership with Paul McCartney that revolutionized popular music. His most distinctive solo recording was 'Imagine' (1971). He was murdered in 1980. Full name **Lennon, John Winston**

'Imagine there's no heaven / It's easy if you try / No hell below us / Above us only sky / Imagine all the people / Living for today.'
[John Lennon, 'Imagine'; 1971]

leno /leénō/ n 1. an open weave created in textiles by twisting together pairs of warp threads to lock the weft threads in place 2. a fabric made using a leno weave [Late 18C. < French *linon* < *lin* 'flax' < Latin *linum*]

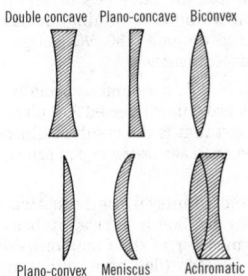

Double concave   Plano-concave   Biconvex

Plano-convex   Meniscus   Achromatic

lens: cross-sections of different lenses

lens /lenz/ n 1. OPTICS **TRANSPARENT PIECE OF GLASS FOR FOCUSING** a piece of curved and polished glass or other transparent material that forms an image by refracting and focusing light passing through it 2. OPTICS **SYSTEM OF LENSES** a system of two or more lenses

that is used in an optical instrument such as a telescope or camera 3. OPHTHALMOL same as **contact lens** 4. ANAT **LIGHT-FOCUSING PART OF EYE** the part of the eye that focuses light to produce an image on the light-sensitive cells of the retina. It is nearly spherical and convex on both sides, and sits behind the pupil. 5. PHYS **BEAM-FOCUSING DEVICE** a device that focuses a beam of electrons or radiation other than light [Late 17C. < Latin, 'lentil'; from its shape]

lensing /lénzing/ n the bending of light as it passes through the gravitational field of a large astronomical object such as a galaxy

lent past participle, past tense of **lend**

Lent /lent/ n the period of 40 weekdays before Easter observed in some Christian churches as a period of prayer, penance, fasting, and self-denial. This period, starting on Ash Wednesday in Western churches, commemorates the 40 days that Jesus Christ spent fasting in the wilderness. [13C. Shortening of LENTEN]

Lenten /léntən/, **lenten** adj happening in or suitable for Lent, especially in being meagre [Old English *lencten* 'spring' < Germanic]

~~lenth~~ incorrect spelling of **length**

lentic /léntik/ adj relating to or inhabiting still or slow-moving water [Mid-20C. < Latin *lentus* 'slow']

lenticel /lénti sel/ n a pore in the outer layer of a woody plant stem, through which gases pass from inside the stem to the atmosphere, or vice versa [Mid-19C. < modern Latin *lenticella*, literally 'little lentil' < Latin *lens* 'lentil'] —**lenticellate** /lénti séllət/ adj

lenticular /len tíkyoÒlər/ adj 1. shaped like a biconvex lens in having two convex faces 2. relating to a lens or lenses [15C. < Latin *lenticularis* < *lenticula* (see LENTIL)]

lentil /lént'l/ n 1. an edible seed that is lens-shaped, brown, grey, green, or black on the outside and yellow or orange inside, and rich in protein 2. a plant of the pea family grown to produce lentils. Native to: Mediterranean, western Asia. Latin name: *Lens culinaris*. [14C. Via French *lentille* < Latin *lenticula* 'little lentil' < *lens* 'lentil']

lentisk /léntisk/ n TREES same as **mastic tree** [14C. < Latin *lentiscus*]

lentissimo /len tíssimō/ adv very slowly (used as a musical direction) [Early 20C. < Italian, superlative of *lento* 'slow'] —**lentissimo** adj

lentivirus /lénti vīrəss/ n a retrovirus causing illness that characteristically does not produce symptoms until some time after infection [Late 20C. < Latin *lentus* 'slow']

lent lily n PLANTS same as **daffodil** (literary or dated) [Because it often blooms during Lent]

lento /léntō/ adv at a slow tempo (used as a musical direction) ■ n (plural **-tos**) a piece of music, or a section of a piece, to be played lento [Early 18C. Via Italian < Latin *lentus* 'slow'] —**lento** adj

Lenya /lénnyə/, **Lotte** (1898–1981) Austrian actor and cabaret singer. She played a leading role in several works by her husband Kurt Weill, including *The Threepenny Opera* (1928). Born **Blamauer, Karoline Wilhelmine Charlotte**

Leo /leé ō/ (plural **-os**) n 1. **CONSTELLATION IN N HEMISPHERE** a zodiacal constellation of the northern hemisphere between Cancer and Virgo. See illustration at **constellation** 2. **5TH SIGN OF ZODIAC** the fifth sign of the zodiac, represented by the lion and lasting from approximately 23 July to 22 August. Leo is classified as a fire sign and is ruled by the sun. 3. **SOMEBODY BORN UNDER LEO** somebody whose birthday falls between 23 July and 22 August [Pre-12C. < Latin, 'lion'] —**Leo** adj —**Leonian** /lee ōni ən/ n

Leo I /leé ō/, **St** (400?–461) pope. He summoned the Council of Chalcedon in 451 and was proclaimed a doctor of the church in 1574. Known as **Leo the Great**

Leo III, **Emperor** (680?–741) Byzantine monarch. He revitalized the Byzantine Empire, founded the Isaurian dynasty, and issued a legal code, the *Ecloga*.

Leo IX, **St** (1002–54) pope. During his reforming reign (1049–54), papal authority was strengthened, and this led to the Great Schism of 1054. Born **Bruno of Egisheim**

Leo X, **Pope** (1475–1521) An important patron of the arts, as pope (1513–21) he initiated the rebuilding of

St Peter's Basilica, Rome. Born **de' Medici, Giovanni**

Leo XIII, **Pope** (1810–1903) During his papacy (1878–1903), he upheld the authority of the church and promoted learning. His encyclical of 1896 declared Anglican orders invalid. Born **Pecci, Vincenzo Gioacchino**

Leo Minor n a small inconspicuous constellation of the northern hemisphere between Ursa Major and Leo. See illustration at **constellation**

Leominster /lémstər/ town in Herefordshire, England. Population: 9,543 (1991).

León /lay ón/ 1. city and capital of León Province, in the Castile-León autonomous region of northwestern Spain. Population: 128,576 (2002). 2. industrial city in central Mexico, founded in 1576. Population: 109,872 (2000).

Leonard /lénnərd/, **Sugar Ray** (b. 1956) US boxer. He won various boxing titles in five different weight categories, mainly in the 1980s. Born **Leonard, Ray Charles**

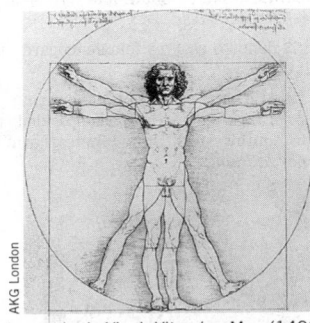

Leonardo da Vinci: Vitruvian Man (1490?)

AKG London

Leonardo da Vinci /leé ō naárd ō də vínchi/ (1452–1519) Italian painter, sculptor, architect, engineer, and scientist. One of the great masters of the High Renaissance, he painted the *Mona Lisa* (1503–06) and *The Last Supper* (1495–97). Many of his scientific observations and inventions, particularly in anatomy, optics, and hydraulics, were centuries ahead of their time.

'A bird is an instrument working according to a mathematical law, which instrument it is within the capacity of man to reproduce, with all its movements.'
[Leonardo da Vinci. Quoted in *The Notebooks of Leonardo da Vinci*, Edward McCurdy (tr.); 1928]

Leoncavallo /láy ong ka vállō/, **Ruggero** (1858–1919) Italian composer. An exponent of the verismo style in opera, he composed *I Pagliacci* (1892).

leone /lee ón/ n the main unit of Sierra Leonean currency. See table at **currency** [Mid-20C. < Sierra Leone]

Leonidas /li ónni dass/ (d. 480 BC) king of Sparta. He withstood the Persian army of Xerxes I at the Battle of Thermopylae in 480 BC.

'Go, stranger, and tell the Lacedaemonians that here we lie, obedient to their commands.'
[Leonidas, *Epitaph*; 480 BC]

leonine /leé ə nīn/ adj relating to or characteristic of a lion, e.g. in strength or appearance [14C. Directly or via French < Latin *leoninus* < *leo* 'lion']

leopard /léppərd/ n 1. a large slender member of the cat family with a fawn to orange-red coat spotted with black rosettes. Native to: Africa, Asia. Latin name: *Panthera pardus*. See illustration on next page 2. in heraldry, an image of a lion viewed from the side facing left, with its head turned towards the viewer and one front leg raised [13C. Via French < late Greek *leopardos* < Greek *leōn* 'lion' + *pardos* 'big cat' (see PARD [1])]

CULTURAL NOTE *The Leopard*, a novel (1958) by Italian writer Giuseppe Tomasi di Lampedusa. Set in late 19th-century Sicily, it describes the social and political changes resulting from the unification of Italy from the point of view of a local nobleman, Prince Salina. In addition to its political and historical insights, the novel is admired for its evocative descriptions of the Sicilian

leopard

landscape and its moving and poetic meditations on mortality.

leopard cat *n* a small wild cat with spots like those of a leopard. Native to: South and East Asia. Latin name: *Felis bengalensis*.

leopardess /léppərd ess/ *n* a female leopard, usually an adult one

leopard lily *n* an ornamental flowering plant. Flowers: orange-red with black-speckled petals. Native to: southwestern United States. Latin name: *Lilium pardalinum*.

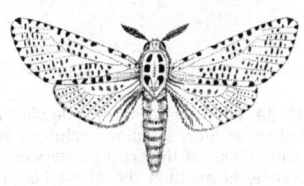

leopard moth

leopard moth *n* a large white moth with black spots whose caterpillars bore into trees, causing damage, and may be considered a pest. Native to: Europe, Asia, North Africa, North America. Latin name: *Zeuzera pyrina*.

leopard's bane *n* a plant with clusters of yellow flowers resembling daisies on long stalks. Native to: Europe, Asia. Genus: *Doronicum*.

leopard seal *n* a seal with a spotted dark grey back and paler belly that lives as a solitary hunter, feeding mainly on penguins. Native to: Antarctic waters. Latin name: *Hydrurga leptonyx*.

Leopold I /lée ə pṓld/, **Holy Roman Emperor, king of Bohemia, and king of Hungary** (1640–1705) As Holy Roman Emperor (1658–1705), king of Bohemia (1656–1705), and king of Hungary (1655–87) he led wars against France and the Ottoman Turks, and made efforts to extend Habsburg territory

Leopold II (1747–92) grand duke of Tuscany and Holy Roman Emperor. While Holy Roman Emperor (1790–92) he formed an alliance with Prussia against France to aid Marie Antoinette, his sister, during the French Revolution.

Leopold II (1835–1909) king of Belgium. During his reign (1865–1909), Belgium annexed the Congo Free State, which later became the Belgian Congo and is now the Democratic Republic of the Congo.

Leopold III (1901–83) king of Belgium. He became king in 1934, but went into exile after the invasion by Germany during World War II. He abdicated in 1951.

Léopoldville /lée ə pṓld víl/ former name for **Kinshasa**

leotard /lée ə taard/ *n* a tight-fitting one-piece elastic garment that covers the torso and is worn especially by dancers, gymnasts, and acrobats [Late 19C. After Jules Léotard (1830–70), French trapeze artist]

lep /lep/ *Ireland* (*informal*) *vi* (**leps, lepping, lept** /lept/) to leap ■ *n* an act of leaping [Variant of LEAP]

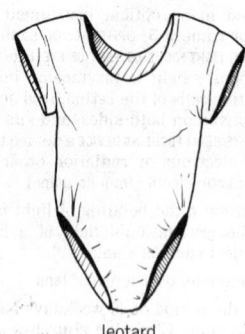

leotard

Lepautre /lə pṓtr/, **Pierre** (1648–1716) French interior designer. His decoration of the French royal house at Marly for Louis XV featured the arabesques and elegant curved designs that became the hallmarks of the rococo style.

Lepcha /lépchə/ (*plural* **-chas** or *same*) *n* **1.** a member of a people who live in the northeastern Indian state of Sikkim **2.** a Tibeto-Burman language spoken in the northeastern Indian state of Sikkim. Native speakers: 65,000. [Early 19C. < Nepali *lāpche*] —**Lepcha** *adj*

Le Pen /lə pén/, **Jean-Marie** (*b.* 1928) French politician. He was the founder of the French National Front (1972), and a presidential candidate (1988, 2002).

leper /léppər/ *n* **1.** somebody affected with leprosy **2.** somebody who is shunned by the rest of society [14C. < obsolete *leper* 'leprosy', via French < late Latin *lepra* < Greek *lepros* (see LEPROUS)]

lepido- *prefix* flake, scale ○ *lepidolite* [< Greek *lepid-*]

lepidolite /li píddə līt, léppidə-/ *n* a mica ranging in colour from pinkish-purple to grey. Use: an ore of lithium.

lepidopteran /léppi dóptərən/ *n* a butterfly or moth. Lepidopterans have four wings covered in tiny overlapping scales, and sucking mouthparts. Their larvae are caterpillars. Order: Lepidoptera. [Mid-19C. < modern Latin *Lepidoptera* < Greek *lepid-* 'scale' + *pteron* 'wing']

lepidopterist /léppi dóptərist/ *n* an expert in or student of butterflies and moths

lepidosiren /léppidō sírən/ *n* an eel-shaped freshwater fish that can breathe air using a pair of lungs that it has in addition to its gills. It spends the dry season lying dormant in a burrow. Native to: South America. Latin name: *Lepidosiren paradoxa*.

lepidote /léppi dōt/ *adj* covered in small scaly leaves [Mid-19C. Via modern Latin < Greek *lepidōtos* < *lepid-* 'scale']

leprechaun /léppri kawn/ *n* in Irish folklore, a small man with magical powers, often dressed in green, who works as a shoemaker and is believed to know where treasure is hidden [Early 17C. < Irish *leipreachán* 'small body']

leprosarium /lépprə sáiri əm/ (*plural* **-ia** /-i ə/) *n* a hospital for the treatment of patients with leprosy [Mid-19C. < late Latin *leprosus* (see LEPROUS)]

leprose /léppṓss/ *adj* MED same as **leprous** (sense 2) [Mid-19C. < late Latin *leprosus* or its source *lepra* (see LEPER)]

leprosy /lépprəssi/ *n* a tropical disease mainly affecting the skin and nerves that can cause tissue change and, in severe cases, loss of sensation and disfigurement. Leprosy is transmitted following close personal contact and has an incubation period of 1–30 years. It can now be cured if treated with a combination of drugs. [Mid-16C. < LEPROUS] —**leprotic** /le próttik/ *adj*

leprous /lépprəss/ *adj* **1.** having or relating to leprosy **2.** resembling the physical symptoms of leprosy, especially in being pale or scaly ○ *a leprous white deposit spreading across the cellar walls* [12C. Via French < late Latin *leprosus* < Greek *lepros* 'scaly' < *lepos* 'scale'; from the white scales that form on the skin]

-lepsy *suffix* seizure ○ *narcolepsy* [Via modern Latin *-lepsia* < Greek *lēpsis* < *lēp-*, stem of *lambanein* 'seize']

lept past participle, past tense of **lep**

lept- *prefix* same as **lepto-** (*used before vowels*)

leptin /léptin/ *n* a hormone produced by fat cells that indicates the degree of hunger to the hypothalamus of the brain

lepto- *prefix* thin, slender ○ *leptosome* [< Greek *leptos*, past participle of *lepein* 'peel']

leptocephalus /léptō séffələss/ (*plural* **-li** /-lī/) *n* the larva of some bony fishes such as the eel, the appearance of which is markedly different from that of the adult fish [Mid-18C. < modern Latin < Greek *leptos* 'small' + *kephalē* 'head']

lepton /lép ton/ *n* a fundamental subatomic particle that interacts only weakly with other particles, e.g. the electron, muon, neutrino, and their antiparticles [Mid-20C. < Greek *leptos* 'small'] —**leptonic** /lep tónnik/ *adj*

leptospirosis /léptō spī rṓssiss/ *n* an infectious disease occurring in human beings and domestic animals and affecting the kidneys and liver, caused by spiral-shaped bacteria (**spirochaetes**) of the genus *Leptospira*. In human beings a significant form of the disease is Weil's disease. [Early 20C. < modern Latin *Leptospira*, literally 'small coil']

Lepus /léppəss, leépəss/ *n* a small constellation of the southern hemisphere located directly south of Orion. See illustration at **constellation**

Lérida /lérridə/ capital of Lérida Province in the autonomous region of Catalonia, northeastern Spain. Population: 112,199 (2001).

Lermontov /lyérməntəf/, **Mikhail Yuryevich** (1814–41) Russian poet and novelist. His works include *A Hero of our Time* (1840) and *The Circassian Boy* (1840).

Lerner /lúrnər/, **Alan Jay** (1918–86) US playwright and lyricist. He collaborated with Frederick Loewe on several musicals, including *My Fair Lady* (1956) and *Camelot* (1960).

> 'You write a hit the same way you write a flop.'
> [Attributed to Alan Jay Lerner]

Lerwick /lúr wik/ seaport and largest town of the Shetland Islands, northeastern Scotland, on Mainland Island. Population: 7,336 (1991).

lesbian /lézbi ən/ *n* a woman who is sexually attracted to other women ■ *adj* involving or relating to lesbians [Late 19C. LESBIAN, because the woman poet Sappho of Lesbos wrote poems to women]

Lesbian /lézbi ən/ *n* somebody who comes from the Greek island of Lesbos ■ *adj* relating to the Greek island of Lesbos [Mid-16C. < Latin *Lesbius*, Greek *Lesbios* < *Lesbos* 'Lesbos']

lesbianism /lézbi ənizəm/ *n* sexual attraction and sexual relations between women

Lesbos /léz boss/ island in eastern Greece, in the Aegean Sea, situated 10 km/6 mi. off the coast of Turkey. Population: 103,700 (1991). Area: 1,637 sq. km/632 sq. mi.

Les Cayes /lay káy/ town and seaport in southwestern Haiti, west of Port-au-Prince. Population: 45,904 (1995).

lese majesty /leéz májjəsti/, **lèse majesté** *n* **1.** disrespect towards the authority or dignity of somebody or something **2.** a criminal offence against a ruler or head of state [15C. Via French < Latin *laesa majestas* 'violated majesty']

lesion /leézh'n/ *n* **1.** a wound, especially an area of skin that is broken or infected **2.** a physical change in a body part that is the result of illness or injury [15C. Via French < Latin *laesion-* < past participle of *laedere* 'injure']

Lesotho /lə sṓtō/ country in southern Africa, bordered on all sides by South Africa. It became an independent member of the Commonwealth in 1966. Language: Sesotho (Southern Sotho) and English. Currency: loti. Capital: Maseru. Population: 1,861,959 (2003). Area: 30,355 sq. km/11,720 sq. mi. Official name **Kingdom of Lesotho**. See map on next page

lespedeza /léspə deézə/ (*plural* **-zas** or *same*) *n* a plant of the pea family with leaves that have three leaflets, grown for forage and to control erosion. Genus: *Lespedeza*. [Late 19C. < modern Latin, (erroneously) after

Lesotho

Doris Lessing

Vincente Manuel de *Céspedes*, 18C Spanish governor of E Florida]

less /less/ CORE MEANING: a grammatical word used to indicate a smaller amount of something

1. *det, pron* SMALLER AMOUNT a smaller amount or proportion of something ○ *New cars tend to emit less air pollution.* ○ *Last month less of her salary was taken up with household expenses.* **2.** *adv* TO SMALLER DEGREE to a smaller extent or degree ○ *Demanding? I've never known a less demanding patient!* ○ *I see her much less than I used to.* **3.** *prep* MINUS indicating that a number or amount is subtracted from a previously mentioned number or amount ○ *Total: £500, less £50 expenses.* ○ *I earned £45,000 last year, less tax and insurance.* [Old English *læssa* < Germanic] ◇ **less than** not having a particular quality ○ *Her whole attitude towards me has been less than pleasant.* ◇ **much** or **still** or **even less** emphasizing that something is done or happens to a smaller extent than something mentioned in the previous statement (*used after a negative statement*) ○ *She could not fix her attention on any object or feel sensations, much less have conscious thoughts.* ◇ **no less** used to express surprise or admiration (*often used ironically*) ○ *He had borrowed money at Homburg from no less a person than Lord Montbarry.*

USAGE See *few*.

-less *suffix* **1.** without, lacking ○ *headless* ○ *restless* **2.** unable to be ○ *fathomless* [Old English *-lēas* < *lēas* 'without' < Germanic]

lessee /le see/ *n* a person or organization that leases a property from another [15C. < Anglo-Norman, past participle of *lesser* (see LEASE)]

lessen /léss'n/ (**-ens, -ening, -ened**) *vti* to make something less, or become less

Lesseps /léssəps/, **Ferdinand Marie, Vicomte de** (1805–94) French diplomat and engineer. While holding diplomatic posts he planned the cutting of the Suez Canal, and started work on the Panama Canal, which was eventually abandoned.

lesser /léssər/ *adj, adv* less significant or smaller in size or amount

Lesser Antilles /lésser an tílleez/ island group in the Caribbean comprising the Virgin Islands, Leeward Islands, and Windward Islands and stretching from Puerto Rico southeastwards to the coast of Venezuela

Lesser Bairam *n* an Islamic festival held each year. Date: at the end of Ramadan.

lesser celandine *n* PLANTS same as **celandine** (sense 1)

lesser omentum *n* the fold of the peritoneum that connects to the liver

lesser panda *n* ZOOL same as **red panda**

Lesser Slave Lake /-slayv-/ lake in central Alberta, Canada, northwest of Edmonton. It empties through the Lesser Slave River into the Athabasca River. Area: 1,168 sq. km/451 sq. mi.

Lesser Sunda Islands ♦ **Sunda Islands**

Lessing /léssing/, **Doris** (*b.* 1919) British novelist. Her works such as *The Grass is Singing* (1950), *Children of Violence* (1952–69), and *The Golden Notebook* (1962) explore political and social themes. Born **Tayler, Doris May**

'When old settlers say "One has to understand the country", what they mean is,

"You have to get used to our ideas about the native". They are saying, in effect, "Learn our ideas, or otherwise get out; we don't want you".'
[Doris Lessing, *The Grass is Singing*; 1950]

Lessing, Gotthold (1729–81) German dramatist and critic. His plays and essays were highly influential in the development of the Enlightenment. Full name **Lessing, Gotthold Ephraim**

'What we find beautiful in a work of art is not found beautiful by the eye, but by our imagination through the eye.'
[Gotthold Lessing, *Laokoön*; 1766]

Les Six /lay séess/ *n* a group of six French composers, Louis Durey, Arthur Honegger, Darius Milhaud, Germaine Tailleferre, Francis Poulenc, and Georges Auric, who promoted an anti-Romantic aesthetic influenced by Erik Satie and the writer Jean Cocteau in the early 20th century [Early 20C. French, 'the six']

lesson /léss'n/ *n* **1.** INSTRUCTION PERIOD a period of time spent teaching or learning a subject **2.** MATERIAL TAUGHT material to be taught or studied **3.** USEFUL EXPERIENCE something that acts as an example, punishment, or warning by teaching something not previously understood or accepted ○ *I think there's a lesson there for all of us – think ahead.* **4.** NEW OR BETTER KNOWLEDGE some useful knowledge or sense that results from direct experience ○ *I think there's a lesson there for all of us – think ahead.* **5.** *also* **Lesson** BIBLE PASSAGE a passage from the Bible that is read out to the congregation during a church service ○ *Today's lesson is from the book of Matthew.* **6.** REBUKE a strong criticism or telling-off, usually instructing or re-minding somebody how to behave correctly ○ *I need to give him a lesson in how to behave properly.* ■ *vt* (**-sons, -soning, -soned**) (*archaic*) **1.** INSTRUCT SOMEBODY to teach somebody **2.** SCOLD SOMEBODY to scold somebody for doing something wrong [12C. Via French *leçon* < Latin *lection-* 'reading' < *legere* 'to read']

lessor /le sáwr, léssawr/ *n* a person or organization that leases a property to another [14C. < Anglo-Norman *lessour* < *lesser* (see LEASE)]

lest /lest/ *conj* in order to prevent something happening, especially something causing fear (*formal*) ○ *must stay out of sight lest we be discovered* [Old English *þȳ lǣs þe* 'by which less that']

let[1] /let/ *vt* (**lets, letting, let**) **1.** NOT PREVENT SOMETHING to allow something to happen or somebody to do something ○ *You should let him explain what happened.* ○ *I won't let anything get in the way of us living a happy life together.* ○ *I never let myself worry about the future.* **2.** GIVE SOMEBODY PERMISSION to give somebody permission to do something ○ *I want to go to the disco but Dad won't let me.* **3.** EXPRESSING SUGGESTION used to express a suggestion, an offer, or an order ○ *Let's eat – I'm starving.* ○ *Let me take that bag for you – you must be exhausted.* ○ *Let the show go on!* **4.** MAKE SOMETHING PASS SOMEWHERE to allow or cause something to pass from one place to another ○ *You need to let some air out of those tyres.* ○ *Open the window and let some fresh air in.* **5.** EXPRESSING RESIGNATION used to indicate indifference to what happens or what somebody does, even though it may be unpleasant ○ *Let them do their worst.* ○ *If he wants to leave then let him – see if I care!* **6.** RENT OUT PROPERTY to allow people to use land, rooms, or a building in return for rent **7.** *Ireland* SAY SOMETHING to utter something (*informal*) **8.** MATHS, LOGIC MAKE MATHEMATICAL ASSUMPTION used to introduce an as-

sumption or hypothesis ○ *Let the point P be on a line L.* **9.** *US* ENVIRON RELEASE WATER FROM POND to release or cause something to release water from a lagoon or pond by breaching a sandbar or other obstacle so that the water drains into a larger body such as the sea ■ *n* LAW **1.** GRANT OF LEASE the granting of a lease **2.** RIGHT TO RENT SOMETHING permission to lease a building or piece of property [Old English *lǣtan* 'leave behind, allow' < Indo-European, 'let go'] ◇ **let alone** used to introduce something that is even less likely or probable than what has just been mentioned ◇ **let go (of something)** to stop holding something ○ *She let go of her mother's hand and ran onto the playground.* ◇ **let somebody have it** to deliver a physical or verbal attack on somebody ◇ **let yourself go 1.** to start acting in a much more relaxed or less inhibited way than usual **2.** to stop caring about your appearance

USAGE See *leave*[1].

let down *vt* **1.** LOWER SOMETHING to move something, or allow something to move, to a lower position ○ *It was getting dark, so she let down the curtains.* **2.** DISAPPOINT SOMEBODY to disappoint somebody by not meeting expectations ○ *Sorry to let you down, but I won't be able to make it tonight.* **3.** MAKE AIR COME OUT OF SOMETHING to make the air come out of an inflated object until it goes flat **4.** LENGTHEN GARMENT to lengthen clothing or part of a piece of clothing by shortening the hem ○ *let down the sleeves of the coat* **5.** ALLOW HAIR TO HANG DOWN to undo long hair so that it falls to its full length

let in *vt* **1.** to allow somebody to enter somewhere such as a building or a room ○ *They refused to let her in.* **2.** to allow water or air into something that is meant to be sealed ○ *Their boat had hit a rock and was letting in water.*

let in for *vt* to become involved in something that turns out to be more difficult or complicated than expected (*informal*) ○ *I didn't realize quite what I was letting myself in for.*

let in on *vt* to allow somebody to know about something

let into *vt* **1.** SHARE INFORMATION WITH SOMEBODY to allow somebody to know about something ○ *I'll let you into a secret: we're getting married.* **2.** ALLOW TO ENTER to allow somebody to enter somewhere **3.** ALLOW TO JOIN CLUB to allow somebody to join an organization or club

let off *v* **1.** *vt* EXCUSE SOMEBODY FROM PUNISHMENT to allow somebody to avoid something such as an unpleasant task or a punishment ○ *I'll let you off this time, but you'd better behave from now on.* **2.** *vt* MAKE SOMETHING EXPLODE to fire shots from a gun or make a firework or explosive blow up **3.** *vt* LET PASSENGER GET OUT to allow somebody to get off a vehicle such as a bus or train **4.** *vti* BREAK WIND to break wind (*informal*)

let on *v* **1.** *vi* PRETEND to make somebody believe something that is not true ○ *She let on that she was upset, but she wasn't really that bothered.* **2.** *vt* LET PASSENGER GET ON to allow somebody to board a vehicle such as a bus or train **3.** *vi* SHARE SECRET to share a secret with somebody (*informal*) ○ *He didn't let on that he was very rich.*

let out *v* **1.** *vt* MAKE LOUD YELL to make a loud or piercing sound using the voice ○ *let out a scream* **2.** *vt* RELEASE SOMEBODY OR SOMETHING to set a person or animal free from being confined or trapped **3.** *vt* ALLOW SOMEBODY TO LEAVE to allow somebody to leave a place such as a building or room **4.** *vt* ENLARGE GARMENT to make a piece of clothing, or a specific part of it, wider than it was before **5.** *vt* SPREAD INFORMATION to allow previously secret information to become more widely known **6.** *vt* RENT OUT PLACE to make a place available for letting ○ *They have recently let out a suite of rooms on the third floor.* **7.** *vi* N Am END AND RELEASE STUDENTS to come to an end and release students at the end of a session or term ○ *classes let out in early June*

let through *vt* to allow somebody or something to pass through a crowd ○ *Cars were pulling over to let an ambulance through.*

let up *vi* **1.** to become slower, calmer, or quieter ○ *Once the rain lets up a bit we'll have a look outside.* **2.** to stop working hard or being angry

let up on *vt* to treat somebody or something in a more relaxed, gentle, or kind way

let[2] /let/ *n* **1.** REPLAYED SERVICE SHOT in games such as tennis and squash, a service in which the ball is obstructed and the shot has to be played again **2.**

REPLAYED POINT the point that is replayed because of a let **3. DIFFICULTY OR OBSTACLE** something that prevents somebody doing something or makes it more difficult (*formal*) ○ *without let or hindrance* [12C. < Old English *lettan* 'hinder' < Germanic]

-let *suffix* **1.** small one ○ *wavelet* **2.** something worn on ○ *necklet* [< Old French *-elet* < *-el* 'small one' (< Latin *-ellus*) + *-et* (see -ET)]

letch *n, vi* another spelling of **lech**

Letchworth /léch wurth/ town in Hertfordshire, southeastern England. It was the first garden city in the country. Population: 31,418 (1991).

letdown /lét down/ *n* **1.** an occasion when somebody or something disappoints expectations, or the feeling of disappointment that results ○ *After all the hype the concert was a bit of a letdown.* **2.** the descent of an aircraft in preparation for landing, before the actual landing approach

lethal /leéth'l/ *adj* **1.** certain to or intended to cause death **2.** causing disaster or destruction ○ *a move that was lethal to his career* [Late 16C. < Latin *lethalis* < *lethum*, alteration of *letum* 'death', by association with Greek *lēthē* 'forgetfulness'] —**lethality** /lee thálləti/ *n* —**lethally** *adv* —**lethalness** *n*

SYNONYMS See *deadly*.

lethal dose *n* the amount of a drug or other substance that will cause death when administered

lethal injection *n* **1.** a method of capital punishment that involves injecting a deadly drug into somebody's body **2.** an injection of a deadly drug administered as capital punishment

lethargic /lə thaárjik/ *adj* **1.** physically slow and mentally dull as a result of tiredness, disease, or drugs **2.** causing a state of physical slowness and mental dullness —**lethargically** *adv*

lethargy /léthərji/ *n* **1.** a state of physical slowness and mental dullness resulting from tiredness, disease, or drugs **2.** lack of energy, activity, or enthusiasm [14C. Via French < late Latin *lethargia* < Greek *lēthargia* < *lēthargos* 'forgetful' < *lēthē* 'forgetfulness']

Lethbridge /léth brij/ city in southern Alberta, Canada. It is the cultural and economic centre of the surrounding agricultural area. Population: 67,374 (2001).

Lethe /leéthi/ *n* in Greek mythology, a river in Hades whose water made those who drank it forget their past [Mid-16C. Via Latin < Greek *lēthē* 'forgetfulness'] —**Lethean** *adj*

Leto /leétō/ *n* in Greek mythology, the mother of Apollo and Artemis by Zeus. Roman equivalent **Latona**

let-out *n* a way of freeing yourself from or avoiding something you have committed yourself to

let's /lets/ *contr* let us ○ *Let's just wait and see what happens.*

Lett /let/ *n* PEOPLES same as **Latvian** (sense 1) [Late 16C. Via German *Lette* < Latvian *Latvi*]

letter /léttər/ *n* **1. MESSAGE SENT BY POST** a piece of handwritten or printed text addressed to a recipient and typically sent by post **2. SYMBOL USED TO SPELL WORDS** a written or printed symbol representing a sound or set of sounds in a language and used to spell words **3.** PRINTING **PRINTING STYLE** a style of typeface ■ *vt* (**-ters, -tering, -tered**) **WRITE LETTERS ON SOMETHING** to write letters or words on something such as a sign [13C. Via French *lettre* < Latin *littera* 'letter of the alphabet, (plural) document']

letter bomb *n* **1.** an envelope with an explosive device inside it, addressed and sent through the post and designed to blow up when it is opened **2.** an e-mail message with a destructive code attached to it

letterbox /léttər boks/ *n* **1. SLOT FOR DELIVERING MAIL THROUGH DOOR** a narrow opening in a door, through which letters and packages can be posted. Sometimes a basket or box is fitted on the inside of the door to catch anything that is delivered. N Am term **mail slot 2.** MAIL same as **postbox 3. BOX FOR LEAVING MAIL IN** a private box or other place to which mail for a specific person or organization is delivered **4.** *also* **letterbox format** MEDIA **FILM FORMAT FOR TV** a film format for television that shows a wider and shorter picture than usual to accommodate the aspect ratios of cinema films when shown on television

letter card *n* **1.** a card that is folded over and sealed before being posted, usually with perforations for tearing the sealed edges when opening it **2.** a long folding letter with postcard scenes printed down the back that can be folded, sealed, and then posted like a postcard

letter carrier *n* somebody employed to deliver letters or other mail (*formal*)

lettered /léttərd/ *adj* **1. WITH LETTERS WRITTEN ON IT** marked with letters of the alphabet **2.** EDUCATED knowledgeable and cultured, especially in literary matters **3.** LITERATE able to read and write

letterform /léttər fawrm/ *n* the shape of a letter of the alphabet

letterhead /léttər hed/ *n* **1.** a printed heading for official stationery, usually containing a company's name, address, telephone and fax numbers, and often including a logo and other details **2.** a piece of writing paper with a printed letterhead ○ *Send in a letterhead along with your invoice details.*

lettering /léttəring/ *n* **1.** letters of the alphabet written, printed, inscribed, or painted on something **2.** the physical process of forming letters, or the way they are formed

Letterman /léttərmən/, **David** (*b.* 1947) US television presenter. Host of the US television programme *The Late Show* from 1993, he is known for his offbeat style.

> 'New York now leads the world's great cities in the number of people around whom you shouldn't make a sudden move.'
> [David Letterman, *Late Night with David Letterman*; 9 February 1984]

letter of credit *n* a letter from a bank, usually for presentation to another branch or bank, authorizing it to issue credit or money to the person named

letter of intent *n* a signed statement outlining an intention to form an agreement or arrangement

letter of introduction *n* a letter written by somebody to introduce one person to another

letter opener *n* N Am same as **paperknife**

letter-perfect *adj* N Am same as **word-perfect** (sense 1)

letterpress /léttər press/ *n* **1. PRINTING BY USE OF PRESSURE** a printing technique that transfers ink by pressing raised type onto paper **2. PRINTED MATERIAL** material that is printed using the letterpress technique **3.** TEXT text as opposed to illustrations

letter-quality *adj* describes printer output of a quality high enough to be compared to conventional printing, or a printer capable of producing such output

letters /léttərz/ *n* (*takes a singular or plural verb*) **1.** literature or literary culture **2.** knowledge and education

letters credential *npl* LAW same as **letters of credence**

letters of administration *npl* an official court order appointing somebody as the administrator of a deceased person's estate when no valid will exists

letters of credence *npl* an official document presented to a government in order to authenticate the official status of a diplomatic representative of another country

letters of marque *npl* **1.** a formal document issued by one country authorizing one of its private citizens to take possession of goods, or sometimes citizens, belonging to another country **2.** an official document issued by one country authorizing one of its citizens to fit a ship with weapons in order to attack or seize another country's ships and cargo [*Marque* 'reprisals' via French < Provençal *marca* < *marcar* 'seize as a pledge']

letters patent *npl* an official document stating that somebody has been granted the exclusive right to make and sell a new product. Letters patent are issued by the government and specify the length of time a patent will remain valid.

letters testamentary *npl* an official document authorizing somebody to assume the responsibilities and duties of executor of the will of a deceased person

letting /létting/ *n* a property that is being let

Lettish /léttish/ *n* LANG same as **Latvian** (sense 2) — **Lettish** *adj*

lettre de cachet /léttrə də ká shay/ (*plural* **lettres de cachet** /*pronunc. same*/) *n* a letter sealed with the royal seal authorizing the arrest and indefinite imprisonment of somebody who has offended the monarch [Early 18C. < French, 'letter of seal']

lettuce /léttiss/ *n* a common plant that is widely grown for its edible leaves, which are usually eaten in salads. Genus: *Lactuca*. [13C. Via Old French *letuēs* (plural) < Latin *lactuca* < *lac* 'milk'; from the milky sap of its stalk]

let-up *n* a pause, especially in something unpleasant (*informal*)

leu /láy oo/ (*plural* **lei** /lay/) *n* the main unit of currency in Romania and Moldova. See table at **currency** [Late 19C. < Romanian, 'lion']

$$H_3C-CH-CH_2-CH-C-OH$$

(with CH₃ and NH₂ substituents, and C=O shown as $\overset{O}{\underset{}{\|}}$)

leucine

leucine /loó seen/, **leucin** /loóssin/ *n* an essential amino acid. Formula: $C_6H_{13}NO_2$. [Early 19C. < Greek *leukos* 'white']

Leucippus /loo síppəss/ (450?–370 BC) Greek philosopher. He is credited with founding the atomic theory of matter, later developed by Democritus. None of his writings survives.

leucite /loó sīt/ *n* a white or grey mineral that is a silicate of aluminium containing potassium. Source: igneous rocks. Use: source of aluminium and potash for fertilizers. [Late 18C. < Greek *leukos* 'white']

leuco-, **leuko-** *prefix* **1.** white, pale, colourless ○ *leucoplakia* **2.** leucocyte ○ *leucopenia* **3.** white matter of the brain ○ *leucodystrophy* [< Greek *leukos* 'white, clear' < Indo-European]

leucoblast /loókō blaast/, **leukoblast** *n* an immature white blood cell (**leucocyte**)

leucocyte /loókə sīt/, **leukocyte** *n* a white blood cell (*technical*) —**leucocytic** /loókə síttik/ *adj* —**leucocytoid** /-sī toyd/ *adj*

leucocytosis /loókə sī tóssiss/, **leukocytosis** *n* a marked increase in the number of white blood cells (**leucocytes**), usually because of infection or disease —**leucocytotic** /-tóttik/ *adj*

leucoderma /loókə dúrmə/, **leukoderma** *n* MED same as **vitiligo** [Late 19C. < LEUCO- + Greek *derma* 'skin']

leucodystrophy /loókō dístrəfi/, **leukodystrophy** *n* a degenerative disease of nerve fibres or white matter that impairs brain function, sight, and motion, leading to death, often at an early age. It involves progressive loss of the fatty myelin layer surrounding the nerve fibres.

leucoma /loo kōmə/, **leukoma** *n* a dense white scar on the cornea of the eye, caused by disease or injury [Early 18C. Via modern Latin < Greek *leukōma* 'white tumour' < *leukos* 'white']

leucopenia /loókō peéni ə/, **leukopenia** *n* an excessive reduction in the number of white blood cells (**leucocytes**) —**leucopenic** *adj*

leucoplakia /loókō pláyki ə, -plák-/, **leukoplakia** *n* a precancerous condition that is seen as small thickened white patches, usually inside the mouth or vulva. Oral leucoplakia may be caused by smoking or by alcohol abuse. [Late 19C. < LEUCO- + Greek *plak-* 'flat surface']

leucoplast /lóokə plast/, **leucoplastid** /lóokə plastid, lóokə plástid/ *n* a common minute colourless body (**plastid**) found inside plant cells and used for storing food

leucorrhoea /lóokə reé ə/ *n* thick whitish or yellowish discharge from the vagina —**leucorrhoeal** *adj*

leucosis *n* VET another spelling of **leukosis**

leucotomy /loo kóttəmi/ (*plural* **-mies**) *n* a surgical operation that involves cutting nerve fibres, especially in the frontal lobes of the brain. It is now rarely performed, and only as a treatment for severe psychiatric disorders.

leucotriene /lóokə treen/, **leukotriene** *n* a short-range chemical messenger in various tissues that plays a role in inflammation. Leucotrienes help regulate the state of blood vessels and airways, and influence the activities of some white blood cells. [Late 20C. < LEUCO- + *triene* 'chemical compound containing three double bonds']

leukaemia /loo keémi ə/ *n* an often fatal cancer in which white blood cells displace normal blood, leading to infection, shortage of red blood cells (**anaemia**), bleeding, and other disorders. Certain types of childhood leukaemia respond well to treatment, which includes drugs (**chemotherapy**) and radiotherapy. —**leukaemic** *adj, n*

leukemia *n* MED US spelling of **leukaemia**

leuko-, etc. MED another spelling of **leuco-, etc.**

leukosis /loo kṓsiss/, **leucosis** *n* any animal disease in which the blood contains an unusually high number of white blood cells (**leucocytes**) [Early 18C. < Greek *leukōsis* < *leukon* 'make white' < *leukos* 'white']

leukotomy *n* SURG US spelling of **leucotomy**

leukotriene *n* BIOCHEM another spelling of **leucotriene**

Leunig /lóonig/, **Michael** (*b.* 1945) Australian cartoonist. His wistful characters are prone to philosophical musings.

~~**leutenant**~~ incorrect spelling of **lieutenant**

lev /lev/ (*plural* **leva** /lévvə/) *n* the main unit of Bulgarian currency. See table at **currency** [Late 19C. < Bulgarian, variant of *lăv* 'lion', probably < Greek *leōn*]

LEV *abbr* AUTOMOT low emission vehicle

Lev. *abbr* BIBLE Leviticus

Levant /li vánt/ *n* the region in the eastern Mediterranean comprising modern-day Lebanon, Israel, and parts of Syria and Turkey (*archaic*) [15C. < French, literally 'rising'; because the sun appears to rise there] —**Levantine** /lévv'n tīn/ *n, adj*

levanter /li vántər/ *n* a strong easterly wind that blows in the western Mediterranean area, especially in the late summer [Late 18C. < LEVANT]

levator /lə váytər/ *n* **1.** a muscle that helps to lift the body part to which it is attached **2.** a surgical instrument used to lift up a body part, especially a bone or a tooth [Early 17C. < Latin, 'lifter' < *levare* (see LEVER)]

levee[1] /lévvi, lévvay/ *n* **1.** NATURAL EMBANKMENT BESIDE RIVER a natural embankment alongside a river, formed by sediment during times of flooding **2.** ARTIFICIAL EMBANKMENT BESIDE RIVER an artificial embankment alongside a river, built to prevent flooding of the surrounding land ■ *vt* (**-ees, -eeing, -eed**) BUILD LEVEE ON RIVER to provide a river with an embankment to prevent flooding [Early 18C. < French *levée*, form of past participle of *lever* (see LEVER)]

levee[2] /lévvi, lə váy/ *n* **1.** in former times, an occasion when a noble or royal person received visitors informally soon after getting up in the morning **2.** in former times, a court reception at which a prince or sovereign received male visitors. It is usually held in the early afternoon. [Late 17C. < French *levé*, variant of *lever* 'rising' < *lever* (see LEVER)]

level /lévv'l/ *n* **1.** AMOUNT the amount or concentration of something ○ *My job has a low stress level but few prospects.* **2.** ASPECT a quality or aspect of something ○ *It's a film that works well on a number of different levels.* **3.** RANK OR SCALE a particular position in a range of relative scales or values ○ *playing tennis at the professional level* **4.** COMPUT GAMES SECTION OF COMPUTER GAME a part of a computer game that must be completed before moving to the next, often more difficult, stage **5.** POSITION OF PARTICULAR FLOOR the relative position of a particular floor or other plane in a structure such as a building or bridge ○ *The storeroom is down on the second level.* **6.** HEIGHT FOR MEASUREMENT a position, line, or flat surface according to which height is measured ○ *10,000 feet above sea level* **7.** HEIGHT OF SURFACE FROM BOTTOM the height of a surface from the ground or from the bottom of its container ○ *The level of the river had fallen alarmingly during the summer.* **8.** STATED HEIGHT a particular height ○ *flying below the level of the tree tops* **9.** GEOG HORIZONTAL SURFACE a horizontal surface or area of land **10.** CIV ENG SURVEYING INSTRUMENT in surveying, an instrument used to measure the relative heights of different points in the landscape **11.** CIV ENG MEASUREMENT OF HEIGHT in surveying, a measurement taken of the relative heights of different points in a landscape **12.** *N Am* CONSTR same as **spirit level 13.** MIN EXTRACT HORIZONTAL MINE TUNNEL a horizontal tunnel in a mine ■ *adj* **1.** NOT SLOPING flat and horizontal, with an even surface or top **2.** EQUAL equal to or even with another individual or group in rank, ability, or condition ○ *The two teams have drawn level after six games.* **3.** ALONGSIDE next to or alongside somebody or something else ○ *His car drew level as we approached the bend.* **4.** STEADY steady, consistent, or unchanging ○ *maintaining a level pressure* **5.** CALM showing calmness and self-control ○ *keep a level head* **6.** OF PARTICULAR LEVEL relating to or characteristic of a particular rank or condition (*usually used in combination*) ○ *an entry-level job* ■ *v* (**-els, -elling, -elled**) **1.** *vt* FLATTEN SOMETHING EVENLY to make something even, flat, and horizontal ○ *We spent days levelling the ground before we could start building.* **2.** *vti* MAKE OR BECOME EQUAL to make two things or people equal in position or of the same standard or value, or become equal in position, standard, or value ○ *Another goal in the final few minutes levelled the scores again.* **3.** *vt* DEMOLISH AND FLATTEN SOMETHING to completely destroy a building, place, or area and leave it flattened ○ *The village had been levelled by the hurricane.* **4.** *vti* AIM GUN to aim or point a weapon ○ *He levelled his pistol at the target.* **5.** *vt* DIRECT ATTENTION AT SOMEBODY to direct criticism or an attack towards somebody in a purposeful way ○ *Criticism has been levelled at a number of prominent politicians.* **6.** *vti* MEASURE ELEVATION OF LAND in surveying, to measure the elevation of an area of land **7.** *vt* KNOCK SOMEBODY DOWN to knock somebody to the ground, especially with a punch or blow (*informal*) ○ *levelled him with one punch* **8.** *vi* BE HONEST WITH SOMEBODY to speak frankly and honestly to somebody (*informal*) ○ *I'd better level with you right now – I'm leaving the company and going it alone.* [14C. < Old French *livel* 'tool for determining levelness' < Latin *libra* 'balance, scales'] —**levelly** *adv* —**levelness** *n* ◇ **on the level** honest and trustworthy (*informal*)

level off *vti* **1.** *also* **level out** to fly level with the ground, especially after climbing or descending, or make an aircraft do this ○ *We passed through the clouds and eventually levelled off at about 10,000 feet.* **2.** to reach a level and become stable and unchanging, or make something do this ○ *Stock prices seem to have levelled off.*

level up *vti* **1.** same as **level** *v* (senses 1–2) **2.** to increase the capabilities of a character in a computer game

level crossing *n* a place where a road crosses a railway line, usually with a system of warning signals and barriers that close automatically when a train is approaching. N Am term **grade crossing**

leveler *n* SOC SCI, POL US spelling of **leveller**

level-headed *adj* remaining rational and fully in control in difficult situations or emergencies —**level-headedly** *adv* —**level-headedness** *n*

leveller /lévvələr/ *n* **1.** a factor that makes situations or people more equal, especially by removing distinctions based on status or privilege ○ *Time is the great leveller.* **2.** somebody who advocates equality in society for everyone

Leveller /lévvələr/ *n* a member or supporter of a radical Parliamentarian movement during the Civil War, calling for religious tolerance, legal equality, a universal male vote, and the abolition of the monarchy. The movement was later suppressed by Cromwell.

levelling screw /lévvəling-/ *n* one of usually several screws on the bottom of something such as a scientific instrument or a washing machine that can be adjusted to make the piece of equipment stand level

level of attainment *n* the level that a child has reached on the eight-point scale by which the National Curriculum assesses pupils between the ages of 5 and 14 in the United Kingdom. Pupils progress through the eight levels at different rates, although average pupils are expected to reach each level at a particular age.

level pegging *n* in a game or competition, the same position, score, or level of achievement as somebody else ○ *It's level pegging at the moment, though anything could happen in the next round.* [< the use of pegs in parallel rows in a board to show card players' scores]

Leven, Loch /leévən/ lake in east-central Scotland, north of the Firth of Forth. Area: 26 sq. km/10 sq. mi.

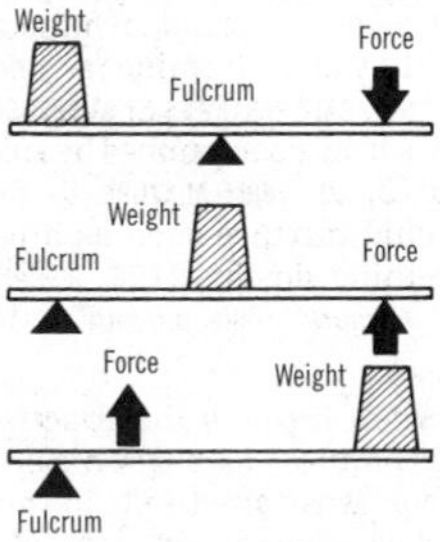

lever

lever /leévər/ *n* **1.** RIGID BAR USED FOR LEVERAGE a rigid bar that pivots about a point (**fulcrum**) and is used to move or lift a load at one end by applying force to the other end **2.** DEVICE OR MACHINE a mechanical device or machine that operates using leverage **3.** WAY OF ACHIEVING SOMETHING a device, tactic, or situation that can be used to advantage ■ *vt* (**-ers, -ering, -ered**) MOVE SOMETHING WITH LEVER to move something using a lever [13C. < Anglo-Norman, 'something that raises' < Old French, 'to raise' < Latin *levare* < *levis* 'light (in weight)']

Lever /leévər/, **William Hesketh, 1st Viscount Leverhulme** (1851–1925) British industrialist and philanthropist. Some of the fortune he made from manufacturing soap was used for the furtherance of higher education and for founding the industrial town of Port Sunlight.

leverage /leévərij/ *n* **1.** ACTION OF LEVER the action of a lever pivoting about a point **2.** MECHANICAL ADVANTAGE the mechanical advantage gained by using a lever **3.** POWER TO GET THINGS DONE power over other people, especially something that gives an advantage but is not referred to openly ○ *He uses the leverage of seniority with the more junior employees.* **4.** FIN BORROWING OF MONEY TO PURCHASE COMPANY the borrowing of money to purchase a company, in the hope that it will make enough profit to cover the interest payable on the loan **5.** *ANZ, N Am* FIN the ratio of a company's debt capital to the value of its ordinary shares. UK term **gearing** ■ *vti* (**-ages, -aging, -aged**) FIN BORROW MONEY HOPING TO MAKE MORE to borrow money in order to buy a company, relying on its making enough profit to cover the interest payable on the loan

leveraged buyout /leévərijd-/ *n* a takeover strategy in which a controlling proportion of a company's shares is bought using borrowed money, the collateral for which is assets belonging to the purchased company

leveret /lévvərət/ *n* a young hare, especially one less than a year old [14C. < Anglo-Norman, 'little hare' < *levre* 'hare' < Latin *lepus*]

Leverrier /lə vérri ay/, **Urbain** (1811–77) French astronomer. He predicted the existence of Neptune before it was discovered and improved the astronomical tables for Mercury. Full name **Leverrier, Urbain Jean Joseph**

Levi /leé vī/ *n* in the Bible, the third son of Jacob and patriarch of the house of Levi (Genesis 29:34)

Levi /lévvi/, **Primo** (1919–87) Italian novelist, poet, and scientist. His book *If This Is a Man* (1947) recorded his experiences in Auschwitz.

'Our language lacks words to express this offence, the demolition of a man.'
[Primo Levi, on a year spent as a prisoner in Auschwitz, *If This Is a Man*; 1947]

leviathan /lə ví əth'n/ *n* 1. *also* **Leviathan** MONSTER in the Bible, a large beast or sea monster 2. SOMETHING HUGE something extremely large and powerful in comparison with others of its kind 3. WHALE a whale or other large sea animal (*literary*) [14C. Via late Latin < Hebrew *liwyātān*]

CULTURAL NOTE *Leviathan*, a treatise (1651) by English philosopher Thomas Hobbes. Hobbes's major work is a defence of the principle of absolute monarchy. It argues that human beings can only live in peace if they agree to subject themselves to a single, absolute ruler. Since this ruler should be answerable only to God, the Church too must be subject to civil authority.

levigate /lévvi gayt/ (-**gates**, -**gating**, -**gated**) *v* 1. *vt* GRIND MINERAL INTO POWDER to grind a mineral into a fine powder with water, forming a smooth paste or slurry 2. *vt* SEPARATE PARTICLES BY SUSPENSION to separate fine particles from coarser ones by suspending them in a liquid 3. *vti* FORM MIXTURE to form a smooth uniform liquid mixture such as a paste or gel, or make something do this [15C. < Latin *levigat-*, past participle of *levigare* 'make smooth'] —**levigation** /lévvi gáysh'n/ *n*

levirate /léevirət, lévvi-/ *n* the practice by which a man may be required to marry his brother's widow. This custom was practised in ancient Jewish society and is common in parts of Africa today. [Early 18C. < Latin *levir* 'husband's brother'] —**leviratic** /léevi ráttik, lévvi-/ *adj*

Levi-Strauss /lévvi strówss/, **Claude** (*b.* 1908) French social anthropologist. A proponent of structuralism, he originated the thesis that all cultures have a common framework. Full name **Levi-Strauss, Claude Gustave**

levitate /lévvi tayt/ (-**tates**, -**tating**, -**tated**) *v* 1. *vti* to rise and float in the air, or make something rise and float in the air, seemingly in defiance of gravity 2. *vt* to support a patient on a cushion of air during treatment for severe burns [Late 17C. < Latin *levis* 'light (in weight)', after GRAVITATE] —**levitation** /lévvi táysh'n/ *n* —**levitator** *n*

Levite /lée vīt/ *n* a member of the Hebrew tribe of Levi, chosen to assist the priests of the Jewish Temple. The Levites were descended from Jacob's son Levi and constituted one of the twelve tribes of Israel. [14C. < ecclesiastical Latin *levita* < Greek *levitēs*, after *Levi* 'Levi']

Levitical /lə víttik'l/ *adj* 1. belonging or relating to the Levites 2. relating to the book of Leviticus, especially those portions containing laws relating to ritual or moral precepts

Leviticus /lə víttikəss/ *n* a book of the Bible that contains the priestly tradition of the Levites, traditionally attributed to Moses. It is the third book of the Pentateuch, continuing from the end of the book of Exodus. See table at **Bible** [14C. < late Latin, 'of the Levites' < Greek *levitēs* (see LEVITE)]

levity /lévvəti/ *n* remarks or behaviour intended to be amusing, especially when they are out of keeping with a serious occasion [Mid-16C. < Latin *levitas* < *levis* 'light (in weight)']

levo- *prefix* US spelling of **laevo-**

levodopa /léevō dṓpə/ *n* PHARM full form of **L-dopa**

levorotation, etc. *n* OPTICS US spelling of **laevorotation, etc.**

levulose *n* BIOCHEM US spelling of **laevulose**

levy /lévvi/ *v* (-**ies**, -**ying**, -**ied**) 1. *vt* OFFICIALLY DEMAND TAX PAYMENTS to use government authority to impose or collect a tax 2. *vt* RAISE ARMY to enlist troops for military service, often by force 3. *vt* DECLARE WAR to declare war on somebody 4. *vi* SEIZE PROPERTY TO FULFIL JUDGMENT to seize property in accordance with a legal ruling ■ *n* (*plural* -**ies**) 1. TAX money raised under government authority 2. RAISING OF TAX the act of collecting taxes under government authority 3. ARMY a group of soldiers drafted under government authority 4. CONSCRIPTION the act of drafting soldiers under government authority [15C. < French *levée* (see LEVEE¹)] —**leviable** *adj* —**levier** *n*

lewd /lood, lyood/ *adj* sexual in an offensive way [Old English *læw(e)de* 'lay, not in holy orders', origin ?] —**lewdly** *adv* —**lewdness** *n*

Lewes /lóo əss/ county town of East Sussex, south-eastern England. Its ruined Norman castle makes it a popular tourist destination. Population: 92,177 (2001).

lewis /lóo iss/ *n* an iron attachment consisting of linked pieces that fit into a dovetailed opening in a stone, used to grip heavy stones before lifting them [Mid-18C. Probably < French *lous*, plural of *lou(p)* 'kind of siege engine', literally 'wolf' < Latin *lupus*]

Lewis /lóo iss/, **Carl** (*b.* 1961) US athlete. He won nine Olympic gold medals for 100- and 200-metre races and the long jump between 1984 and 1996.

Lewis, C. S. (1898–1963) Irish-born British critic, scholar, and novelist. He wrote books on moral and religious issues, e.g. *The Screwtape Letters* (1942), and a children's book series known as *The Chronicles of Narnia* (1950–56). Full name **Lewis, Clive Staples**

'Telling us to obey instinct is like telling us to obey "people". People say different things: so do instincts. Our instincts are at war...Each instinct, if you listen to it, will claim to be gratified at the expense of the rest.'
[C. S. Lewis, *The Abolition of Man*; 1943]

Lewis, Edward B (*b.* 1918) US geneticist. He shared the Nobel Prize in physiology or medicine (1995) with Eric Wieschaus and Christiane Nüsslein-Volhard for his research into embryonic development.

Lewis, Sir Essington (1881–1961) Australian engineer and company director. He was general manager of a mining company (1921–50).

Lewis, Gilbert Newton (1875–1946) US chemist. He was noted for his study in chemical thermodynamics and theory of chemical attraction and valency.

Lewis, Jerry (*b.* 1926) US actor, screenwriter, film director, and film producer. He formed a comic duo with Dean Martin, with whom he made 16 films, and later starred in his own films. Born **Levitch, Joseph**

Lewis, Sinclair (1885–1951) US novelist. He wrote *Babbitt* (1922) and other novels that ridicule middle-class life in the United States, and won a Nobel Prize in literature (1930). Full name **Lewis, Harry Sinclair**

'In other countries, art and literature are left to a lot of shabby bums living in attics and feeding on booze and spaghetti, but in America the successful writer or picture painter is indistinguishable from any other decent business man.'
[Sinclair Lewis, *Babbitt*; 1922]

Lewis, Wally (*b.* 1959) Australian rugby league player. He captained the national team in 1984, 1986, and 1988.

Lewis, Wyndham (1882–1957) British painter, novelist, and critic. He was a noted portraitist, a war artist during World War I, the author of satirical novels, and founder of the Vorticist movement.

Lewis acid *n* a substance that can accept a pair of electrons from a base to form a covalent bond [Mid-20C. After Gilbert Newton LEWIS]

Lewis base *n* a substance that donates an electron pair to an acid during the formation of a covalent bond [Mid-20C. After Gilbert Newton LEWIS]

Lewis gun *n* a gas-powered machine gun with a circular magazine, first used in World War I [Early 20C. After Colonel Isaac Newton *Lewis* (1858–1931), US soldier]

lewisite /lóo i sīt/ *n* a colourless or brownish oily poisonous liquid. Use: in gaseous form in chemical warfare during World War I. Formula: $C_2H_2AsCl_3$. [Early 20C. After Winford Lee *Lewis* (1878–1943), US chemist]

Lewis rule of eight *n* the observation that chemical elements react together by losing, gaining, or sharing electrons so that they attain eight electrons in their outer shells [Mid-20C. After Gilbert Newton LEWIS]

lewisson /lóo iss'n/ *n* CONSTR same as **lewis**

Lewis with Harris /lóo iss with hárriss/ largest and northernmost island of the Outer Hebrides, western Scotland. Population: 21,737 (1991). Area: 2,134 sq. km/824 sq. mi.

LeWitt /lə wít/, **Sol** (*b.* 1928) US artist. An important figure in minimalist and conceptual art, he is best known for his wall drawings and geometric sculptures of cubes, grids, or pyramids.

'In Conceptual art the idea or concept is the most important aspect of the work...all planning and decisions are made beforehand and the execution is a perfunctory affair. The idea becomes the machine that makes the art.'
[Sol LeWitt, 'Paragraphs on Conceptual Art', *Artforum*; Summer, 1967]

lex /leks/ *n* a named law or set of laws [Late 18C. < Latin, 'law']

lexeme /léks eem/ *n* a fundamental unit of the vocabulary of a language that may exist in a number of different forms, e.g. 'make' existing as 'makes, making, maker, made' [Mid-20C. < LEXICON]

lexica plural of **lexicon**

lexical /léksik'l/ *adj* 1. relating to the individual words that make up the vocabulary of a language 2. relating to a lexicon or to lexicography [Mid-19C. < Greek *lexikos* (see LEXICON)] —**lexicality** /léksi kálləti/ *n* —**lexically** *adv*

lexicalize /léksikə līz/ (-**izes**, -**izing**, -**ized**), **lexicalise** (-**ises**, -**ising**, -**ised**) *vti* to form a single word from existing words, or be formed in this way, in order to express something previously conveyed by several words or a phrase. For example, 'front-runner' was lexicalized from 'runner at the front of the race'. —**lexicalization** /léksikə līz záysh'n/ *n*

lexical meaning *n* the meaning of the base word in the set of inflected forms (**paradigm**). In the paradigm 'throw, throws, throwing, threw, thrown', the lexical meaning is 'throw'.

lexicog. *abbr* 1. lexicographic 2. lexicography

lexicography /léksi kóggrəfi/ *n* the writing and editing of dictionaries [Mid-17C. < Greek *lexikos* (see LEXICON)] —**lexicographer** *n* —**lexicographic** /léksikə gráffik/ *adj* —**lexicographically** *adv*

lexicology /léksi kólləji/ *n* the branch of linguistics dealing with the use and meanings of words and the relationships between items of vocabulary [Early 19C. < Greek *lexikos* (see LEXICON)] —**lexicological** /léksikə lójjik'l/ *adj* —**lexicologically** *adv* —**lexicologist** *n*

lexicon /léksikən, -kon/ (*plural* -**cons** or -**ca** /-kə/) *n* 1. a reference book that alphabetically lists words and their meanings, e.g. of an ancient language 2. the entire stock of words belonging to a branch of knowledge or known by somebody [Early 17C. Via modern Latin < Greek *lexikon*, form of *lexikos* 'of words' < *lexis* 'word' < *legein* 'speak']

lexigraphy /lek síggrəfi/ *n* a system of writing in which each character stands for a word [Early 19C. < Greek *lexis* (see LEXICON)]

Lexington /léksingtən/ 1. city in Fayette County, in north-central Kentucky. The surrounding area is a leading world centre for horse breeding and sales. Population: 263,618 (2002 estimate). 2. town in northeastern Massachusetts, northwest of Boston. It is the site of the first battle of the War of American Independence in 1775. Population: 30,663 (2002 estimate).

lexis /léksiss/ *n* the entire stock of words in a language [Mid-20C. < Greek (see LEXICON)]

lex talionis /léks talli óniss/ *n* the legal principle that prescribes retaliating in kind for crimes committed [< Latin, 'law of retaliation']

ley¹ /lay, lee/ (*plural* **leys**) *n* any ancient path in Britain that led from hilltop to hilltop and touched on water sources and places of worship [Early 20C. Variant of LEA]

ley² /lay, lee/ (*plural* **leys**) *n* an area of arable land temporarily put down to grass [14C. < assumed Old English *læge* (see LEY FARMING)]

Leyden another spelling of **Leiden**

Leyden ♦ Lucas van Leyden

Leyden jar /láydən-/ *n* an early device for condensing static electricity consisting of a glass jar coated inside and outside with metal foil and with a conducting rod passing through an insulated stopper [Mid-18C. After the city of LEIDEN (in an alternative spelling)]

ley farming *n* the practice of growing grass in fields normally planted with grain or other tilled crops in order to prevent the soil from becoming exhausted [< assumed Old English *læge* 'fallow', related to LIE¹]

ley line /láy-, leé-/ *n* a straight line linking ancient landmarks and places of worship, believed to follow the course of former routes and popularly associated with mystical phenomena [< LEY¹]

Lezghian /lézgi ən/ *n* a Dagestanian language spoken in an area around the Caspian Sea. Native speakers: 300,000. [Mid-19C. < Russian *Lezgin*] —**Lezghian** *adj*

L-form *n* a bacterium that lacks cell walls [After the *Lister* Institute in London]

LGBT *abbr* lesbian, gay, bisexual, transgender (or transsexual)

LH *abbr* **1.** *also* **lh** left hand **2.** BIOCHEM luteinizing hormone

Lhasa /laássə/ city and capital of the autonomous region of Tibet, southwestern China. Population: 161,788 (1991).

Lhasa apso

Lhasa apso /laássə ápsō/ (*plural* **Lhasa apsos**) *n* a small dog belonging to a Tibetan breed with a long straight coat, hair that falls heavily over the eyes, and a fluffy tail that curls over the back [Early 20C. *Apso* < Tibetan, literally 'sentinel']

lherzolite /lúrzə līt/ *n* a coarse-grained rock containing minerals high in iron and magnesium that is believed to originate in the Earth's mantle [After the *Lherz* massif, French Pyrenees]

Lhotse /lótsi/ fourth highest mountain in the world. It is situated in the eastern part of the Himalayan system on the border between China and Nepal. Height: 8,516 m/27,940 ft.

LH-RH *abbr* BIOCHEM luteinizing hormone-releasing hormone

li /lee/ (*plural same*) *n* a traditional Chinese unit of distance, now standardized at 500 m/547 yd [Late 16C. < Chinese *lǐ*]

Li *symbol* CHEM ELEM lithium

liability /lī ə bílləti/ *n* (*plural* **-ties**) **1.** OBLIGATION UNDER LAW legal responsibility for something, especially costs or damages **2.** DEBT something for which somebody is responsible, especially a debt **3.** DISADVANTAGE something that holds somebody back or causes trouble **4.** SOMEBODY WHO IS BURDEN somebody who prevents a successful outcome or causes social embarrassment **5.** LIKELIHOOD OF SOMETHING likelihood or probability of something happening ■ **liabilities** *npl* MONEY OWED all debts and other financial obligations that appear on a balance sheet

liable /lī əb'l/ *adj* **1.** having legal responsibility for something, especially costs or damages **2.** likely to experience or do something, often something unpleasant or hazardous [15C. Probably < French *lier* (see LIAISON)]

liaise /li áyz/ (**-aises, -aising, -aised**) *vi* to establish or maintain close cooperation with somebody [Early 20C. Back-formation < LIAISON]

liaison /li áyz'n, -zon/ *n* **1.** COORDINATION the exchange of information or the planning of joint efforts by two or more people or groups, often of military personnel **2.** COORDINATOR somebody who coordinates communication between two or more people or groups **3.** UNMARRIED LOVE AFFAIR a romantic and sexual relationship between people who are not married to each other, especially when secret **4.** PRONOUNCED CONSONANT LINKING TWO WORDS in spoken French, the pronunciation of the usually silent final consonant of a word when it is followed by another word beginning with a vowel **5.** SOMETHING USED TO THICKEN LIQUID a thickening agent used in soups and sauces, e.g. egg yolks or flour [Mid-17C. < French *lier* 'bind' < Latin *ligare*]

liana /li aánə/, **liane** *n* a woody climbing tropical vine [Late 18C. < French *liane*, originally 'clematis'] —**lianoid** *adj*

Liao /lee ó/ river in northeastern China. Length: 1,345 km/836 mi.

Liaoning /lyów níng/ province in northeastern China. Capital: Shenyang. Population: 41,160,000 (1997). Area: 151,000 sq. km/58,301 sq. mi.

Liaoyang /lee ow júng/, **Liao-yang** city in Liaoning Province, northeastern China, situated 56 km/35 mi. south of Shenyang. Population: 559,719 (1991).

Liaquat Ali Khan /lee ə kwaat aáli kaán/ (1895–1951) prime minister of Pakistan (1947–51). Pakistan's first prime minister, he was assassinated while in office.

liar /lī ər/ *n* somebody who tells lies

liard /li aárd/ *n* a coin of small value formerly used in various European countries, including France [Mid-16C. < French]

Liard /lee ərd/ river of western Canada, rising in the Yukon Territory and flowing through British Columbia and the Northwest Territories, where it joins the Mackenzie River. Length: 1,115 km/700 mi.

~~**liase**~~ incorrect spelling of **liaise**

~~**liason**~~ incorrect spelling of **liaison**

Liassic /lī ássik/ *adj* belonging to or dating from the oldest division of the European Jurassic period, noted for its fossils of dinosaurs [Mid-19C. < French *liassique* < *Lias* 'division of the European Jurassic period' < Old French *liais* 'hard limestone'] —**Liassic** *n*

lib /lib/ *n* liberation of an oppressed group (*dated informal; used in combination in names of social campaigns*) ○ *gay lib* [Mid-20C. Shortening of *liberation*] —**libber** *n*

lib. *abbr* LIBRARIES **1.** librarian **2.** library

Lib. *abbr* POL Liberal

~~**libary**~~ incorrect spelling of **library**

libation /lī báysh'n/ *n* **1.** POURING OF LIQUID AS RELIGIOUS OFFERING the pouring out of a liquid, e.g. wine or oil, as a sacrifice to a god or in honour of a dead person **2.** SOMETHING POURED OUT AS SACRIFICE a liquid, e.g. wine or oil, poured out as a religious offering **3.** STRONG DRINK an alcoholic drink (*humorous*) [14C. < Latin *libation-* < *libare* 'pour out'] —**libational** *adj*

Lib Dem /líb dém/ *abbr* POL Liberal Democrat

libel /lib'l/ *n* **1.** DEFAMATION a false and malicious published statement that damages somebody's reputation. Libel can include pictures and any other representations that have public or permanent form. **2.** ATTACKING OF SOMEBODY'S REPUTATION the making of false and damaging statements about somebody **3.** WRITTEN STATEMENT the plaintiff's written statement in a case under admiralty law or in an ecclesiastical court ■ *vt* (**-bels, -belling, -belled**) **1.** DEFAME SOMEBODY to publish false and malicious statements about somebody that damage his or her reputation **2.** ATTACK SOMEBODY VERBALLY to give a false and damaging account of somebody **3.** SUE SOMEBODY FOR LIBEL to bring a suit for libel against somebody under admiralty law or in an ecclesiastical court [14C. Via French < Latin *libellus* 'little book' < *liber* 'book'] —**libeller** *n* —**libellist** *n*

SYNONYMS See *malign*.

libellous /lib'l əss/ *adj* constituting or containing a false and malicious published statement that damages somebody's reputation —**libellously** *adv*

Liber /lī bər/ *n* in Roman mythology, a god of wine identified with Bacchus

Liberace /libbər aáchi/ (1919–87) US entertainer. A performer of popular piano pieces, he was noted for his flamboyant attire and lavish presentations. Born **Liberace, Wladziu Valentino**

liberal /líbbərəl/ *adj* **1.** BROAD-MINDED tolerant of different views and standards of behaviour in others **2.** PROGRESSIVE POLITICALLY OR SOCIALLY favouring gradual reform, especially political reforms that extend democracy, distribute wealth more evenly, and protect the personal freedom of the individual **3.** GENEROUS freely giving money, time, or some other asset ○ *My great-aunt was liberal in her bequests.* **4.** GENEROUS IN QUANTITY large in size or amount ○ *a liberal helping* **5.** NOT LITERAL not limited to the literal meaning in translation or interpretation ○ *a liberal interpretation of the rules* **6.** CULTURALLY ORIENTED concerned with general cultural matters and broadening of the mind rather than professional or technical study ○ *a liberal education* **7.** OF BRANCH OF PROGRESSIVE JUDAISM relating or belonging to a branch of Progressive Judaism, characterized by radical revision of the liturgy and an emphasis on ethical teaching. Founded in England in the early 20th century, it accepts patrilineal descent as a qualification for membership of the Jewish religious community. **8.** OF POLITICAL LIBERALISM relating to a political ideology of liberalism ■ *n* LIBERAL PERSON somebody who favours tolerance or open-mindedness [14C. Via French < Latin *liberalis* < *liber* 'free']

SYNONYMS See *generous*.

Liberal *adj* supporting, belonging to, or associated with the Liberal Party in the United Kingdom, Canada, or Australia ■ *n* a member or supporter of the Liberal Party, e.g. in the United Kingdom, Canada, or Australia

liberal arts *npl* **1.** college and university subjects that are intended to provide students with general cultural knowledge, e.g. languages, literature, history, and philosophy **2.** the medieval studies known as the trivium and quadrivium

liberal democracy *n* a political system that has free elections, a multiplicity of political parties, political decisions made through an independent legislature, and an independent judiciary, with a state monopoly on law enforcement

Liberal Democrat *n* a member of the British Liberal and Social Democratic Party

liberalise *vti* another spelling of **liberalize**

liberalism /líbbərəlizəm/ *n* **1.** PROGRESSIVE VIEWS a belief in tolerance and gradual reform in moral, religious, or political matters **2.** POL POLITICAL THEORY STRESSING INDIVIDUALISM a political ideology with its beginnings in western Europe that rejects authoritarian government and defends freedom of speech, association, and religion, and the right to own property **3.** ECON FREE-MARKET ECONOMICS an economic theory in favour of free competition and minimal government regulation **4.** CHR CHRISTIAN THEOLOGICAL MOVEMENT a movement in Protestantism stressing intellectual freedom and the moral content of Christianity over the doctrines of traditional theology — **liberalist** *n* —**liberalistic** /líbbərə lístik/ *adj*

liberality /libbə rálləti/ *n* **1.** GENEROSITY generous provision of money, time, or another asset **2.** LARGENESS largeness in size or amount **3.** BROAD-MINDEDNESS tolerance of different views and standards of behaviour in others

liberalize /líbbərə līz/ (**-izes, -izing, -ized**), **liberalise** (**-ises, -ising, -ised**) *vti* to reform and become less strict, or reform something and make it less strict — **liberalization** /líbbərə lī záysh'n/ *n* —**liberalizer** *n*

liberally /líbbərəli/ *adv* **1.** with generosity in giving money, time, or another asset **2.** in large quantities or amounts

liberalness /líbbərəlnəss/ *n* same as **liberality**

Liberal Party *n* **1.** one of the main British political parties, which evolved from the Whigs, merged with the Social Democratic Party in 1988, and later became known as the Liberal and Social Democratic Party **2.** a major Canadian political party at both the national and provincial levels that first came to power nationally in 1873

Liberal Party of Australia *n* a conservative Australian political party founded in 1944 as an antisocialist organization that, except for 1972 to 1974, has always been in coalition with the National Party

liberal studies *n* a combined arts subject intended to provide students with general cultural knowledge, provided as an element of a more specialized, technical, or vocational course at school or college. It may include, e.g., the study of languages, literature, history, and philosophy. (*takes a singular verb*)

Liberal Unionist *n* a member of the former British Liberal Party who disagreed with Gladstone's policy on Irish Home Rule from 1886 onwards

liberate /líbbə rayt/ (**-ates**, **-ating**, **-ated**) *vt* **1.** SET SOMEBODY FREE PHYSICALLY to release a person, group, population, or country from political or military control or from severe physical constraint **2.** RELEASE SOMEBODY FROM SOCIAL CONSTRAINTS to set somebody free from traditional socially imposed constraints such as those arising from stereotyping by sex or age **3.** STEAL SOMETHING to take unlawfully something that belongs to somebody else (*informal*) **4.** CHEM RELEASE GAS DURING CHEMICAL REACTION to free something such as a gas from combination in a chemical compound during a chemical reaction [Late 16C. < Latin *liberat-*, past participle of *liberare* < *liber* 'free'] —**liberating** *adj* —**liberatingly** *adv* —**liberation** /líbbə ráysh'n/ *n* —**liberator** *n*

liberated /líbbə raytid/ *adj* **1.** RELEASED FROM SOCIAL CONSTRAINTS freed from traditional socially imposed constraints such as those arising from sexual or ageist stereotyping **2.** RELEASED FROM ENEMY freed from enemy control ○ *People lined the streets of the newly liberated city and greeted the soldiers with flowers.* **3.** CHEM RELEASED FROM CHEMICAL COMBINATION freed from combination in a chemical compound

liberation theology *n* a movement in Roman Catholic religious teaching that argues that the Church should work actively to combat social, political, and economic oppression. The movement is international but especially active in Latin America and bases its case on Jesus Christ's ministry to the poor and outcast in society. —**liberation theologian** *n*

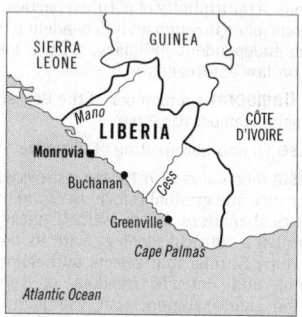
Liberia

Liberia /lī beeri ə/ country in West Africa, on the North Atlantic Ocean. Capital: Monrovia. Population: 3,317,176 (2003). Area: 99,067 sq. km/38,250 sq. mi. Official name **Republic of Liberia** —**Liberian** *adj, n*

libero /leebərō/ (*plural* **-ros**) *n* **1.** SOCCER same as **sweeper** (sense 3) (*informal*) **2.** in sports such as volleyball and ice hockey, a defensive player who operates freely across the whole playing area [Mid-20C. < Italian, 'free' < Latin *liber*]

libertarian /líbbər tairi ən/ *n* **1.** somebody who believes in the doctrine of free will **2.** somebody who believes in the principle that people should have complete freedom of thought and action [Late 18C. < LIBERTY] —**libertarianism** *n*

libertine /líbbər teen, -tīn/ *n* somebody, usually a man, who indulges in pleasures that are considered immoral and who has sexual relationships with many people [14C. < Latin *libertinus* < *libertus* 'somebody freed from slavery' < *liber* 'free'] —**libertinage** *n* —**libertinism** *n*

liberty /líbbərti/ (*plural* **-ties**) *n* **1.** RIGHT TO CHOOSE the freedom to think or act without being constrained by necessity or force **2.** FREEDOM freedom from captivity or slavery **3.** BASIC RIGHT a political, social,

and economic right that belongs to the citizens of a state or to all people (*often used in the plural*) **4.** BREACH OF ETIQUETTE an action or remark that violates the polite distance usually left between people and that may strike the person at whom it is directed as insultingly familiar [14C. Via French < Latin *libertas* < *liber* 'free'] ◇ **at liberty 1.** free or freed after a period of imprisonment or other constraint **2.** free or allowed to do something ◇ **take liberties with somebody** to behave inappropriately towards somebody, especially by way of excessive familiarity or sometimes sexual harassment (*disapproving*) ◇ **take liberties with something** to be deliberately inaccurate when dealing with facts (*disapproving*) ◇ **take the liberty** to be bold enough to do something, sometimes without permission

CULTURAL NOTE *On Liberty*, an essay (1859) by philosopher John Stuart Mill. A work that has inspired civil libertarians around the world, it examines the relationship between the rights of the individual and the power of the state. Mill argues for freedom of thought and expression, asserting that the only valid restrictions on the rights of individuals are those that protect the rights of others.

CULTURAL NOTE *Liberty Leading the People*, a painting (1830) by French artist Eugène Delacroix. Inspired by a scene witnessed by Delacroix during the antimonarchist uprisings in Paris in 1830, this mixture of allegory and realism shows a young woman leading a ragged band of rebels over razed barricades. Delacroix's declaration of solidarity with the revolutionary cause is also a powerful symbol of freedom and the struggle against oppression. The painting is sometimes called *Liberty on the Barricades*.

liberty bodice *n* a close-fitting sleeveless undergarment for the upper body made of thick soft cotton and worn by children, especially young girls. It was popular from the 1920s to the 1950s. [Because it was less restrictive than a corset]

liberty cap *n* a soft cone-shaped cap fitting tightly on the head and falling to one side, worn as a symbol of freedom by French revolutionaries and in the United States before 1800. It was first worn in ancient Rome, where it was given to people who were set free from slavery.

liberty hall, **Liberty Hall** *n* a place where people are free to do whatever they want (*informal*)

liberty horse *n* a horse that performs tricks in the circus in a group and without a rider

Liberty Island /líbbərti-/ island in New York Bay, southeastern New York State. It is the site of the Statue of Liberty. Area: 65 hectares/12 acres. Former name **Bedloe's Island** (until 1956)

liberty pole *n* a tall flagpole to the top of which a liberty cap or the flag of a new republic is attached

liberty ship *n* a cargo ship mass-produced in the United States during World War II

libidinous /li bíddinəss/ *adj* having or expressing strong sexual desires [15C. < Latin *libidinosus* < *libido* 'desire'] —**libidinously** *adv* —**libidinousness** *n*

libido /li beedō/ (*plural* **-dos**) *n* **1.** sexual drive **2.** in some psychoanalytical theories, the psychic and emotional energy in people's psychological make-up that is related to the basic human instincts, especially the sex drive [Early 20C. < Latin, 'desire'] —**libidinal** /li bíddin'l/ *adj* —**libidinally** *adv*

Li Bo /lee bố/, **Li Po** /lee pố/ (701–762) Chinese poet. His work is known for its lyrical beauty and precise imagery.

LIBOR /líˊ bawr/ *abbr* BANKING London Inter-Bank Offered Rate

Libra /leebrə/ *n* **1.** CONSTELLATION IN SOUTHERN HEMISPHERE a zodiacal constellation of the southern hemisphere. See illustration at **constellation 2.** 7TH SIGN OF ZODIAC the seventh sign of the zodiac, represented by a pair of scales and lasting from approximately 23 September to 22 October. Libra is classified as an air sign and its ruling planet is Venus. **3.** SOMEBODY BORN UNDER LIBRA somebody whose birthday falls between 23 September and 22 October [Pre-12C. < Latin, 'balance, scales'] —**Libra** *adj* —**Libran** *n, adj*

librarian /lī bráiri ən/ *n* a worker in or manager of a library [Late 17C. < Latin *librarius* (see LIBRARY)] —**librarianship** *n*

library /líbrəri, líbri/ (*plural* **-ies**) *n* **1.** PLACE WHERE BOOKS ARE KEPT a room, building, or institution where a collection of books or other research materials is kept **2.** COLLECTION OF THINGS a collection of books, newspapers, records, tapes, or other materials that are valuable for research **3.** COMPUT COLLECTION OF SOFTWARE a collection of things for use on a computer, e.g. programs or diskettes, or a collection of routines or instructions used by a computer program [14C. Via French < Latin *libraria* 'bookshop' < *librarius* 'of books' < *liber* 'book']

PRONUNCIATION The generally preferred pronunciation of *library* sound both of the two *r*s: /líbrəri/. A variant pronunciation, to which some people object, is /líbri/, in which the first *r* is dropped. This loss of the *r* is an example of a normal process that happens when some speakers are confronted with the repeated occurrence of the same sound within a word. Finding it difficult to articulate both sounds, especially when trying to say a word fast, some speakers will simply drop one of the two sounds.

library edition *n* a set of books, published in a series, either by a single author or on the same subject and with the same size and format

Library of Congress *n* the national library of the United States, located in Washington, DC and founded by an Act of Congress in 1800. It contains more than 28 million books and pamphlets as well as presidential papers, music, photographs, and recordings.

library science *n* the study of librarianship

libration /lī bráysh'n/ *n* a real or apparent oscillation in the orbit of one astronomical object as seen from the one around which it orbits, especially as seen in the Moon from Earth [Early 17C. < Latin *libration-* < *librare* 'to balance' < *libra* 'balance, scales'] —**librate** *vi* —**librational** *adj*

~~libray~~ incorrect spelling of **library**

libretti MUSIC, THEATRE plural of **libretto**

librettist /li bréttist/ *n* a writer of the words for a dramatic musical work such as an opera or musical

libretto /li bréttō/ (*plural* **-tos** or **-ti** /-ti/) *n* the words of a dramatic musical work such as an opera, including both the spoken and the sung parts [Mid-18C. < Italian, 'little book' < *libro* 'book' < Latin *liber*]

Libreville /leebrə vil/ chief port and capital of Gabon, on the Gulf of Guinea. Population: 365,650 (1993 estimate).

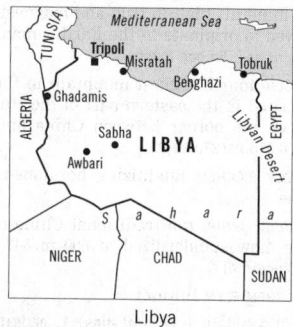
Libya

Libya /líbbi ə/ country in North Africa, south of the Mediterranean Sea. It was annexed by Italy in 1912, then became independent as a kingdom in 1951. In 1969 the monarchy was ousted in a coup led by Muammar al-Qaddafi. Language: Arabic. Currency: Libyan dinar. Capital: Tripoli. Population: 5,499,074 (2003). Area: 1,757,000 sq. km/678,400 sq. mi. Official name **Socialist People's Libyan Arab Jamahiriyah** —**Libyan** *n, adj*

Libyan Desert /líbbi ən-/ desert, the northeastern section of the Sahara, extending from eastern Libya into southwestern Egypt and the extreme northwestern part of Sudan

lice ZOOL plural of **louse**

licence /líss'nss/ *n* **1.** OFFICIAL PERMIT a printed document that gives official permission to a specific person or group to own something or do something **2.** LEGAL AUTHORIZATION official permission to do something,

either from a government or under a law or regulation **3. CHANCE TO DO SOMETHING** the opportunity to do something, especially when this goes beyond normal limits ○ *a licence to boss everybody around* **4. PERMISSION TO BEND TRUTH** the freedom of a writer or artist to rearrange the facts of ordinary life in order to make a more striking effect ○ *artistic licence* **5. LACK OF RESTRAINT** excessive freedom in behaviour or speech that gives a bad name to liberty **6.** *Scotland* **AUTHORITY TO PREACH** a permission to enter the ministry of a Presbyterian church following a period of probation [14C. Via French < Latin *licentia* 'freedom' < *licere* 'be allowed']

USAGE licence or **license**? Do not confuse **licence** with **license**, which has the same pronunciation. In British English, **licence** is the spelling of the noun and **license** is the spelling of the verb: *The restaurant has a licence to sell alcohol. The restaurant is licensed to sell alcohol.* (Note also the spelling of words derived from the verb, as in *licensing laws* and *licensed premises*.) In US English, **license** is the only spelling for verb and noun.

licence plate *n Can* same as **number plate**

license /líss'nss/ *vt* (**-censes, -censing, -censed**) to give official permission for somebody to do something or for an activity to take place (*often passive*) ○ *He was licensed to practise medicine in the United States.* ■ *n* US spelling of **licence** (senses 1–5) [Variant of LICENCE] —**licensed** *adj* —**licensor** *n*

USAGE See **licence**.

licensed premises *npl* an establishment that is legally permitted to sell alcoholic drinks

licensee /líss'n sée/ *n* a person or company that is officially permitted to do something, especially to sell alcohol

license plate *n US* same as **number plate**

licentiate /lī sénshi ət/ *n* **1. SOMEBODY AUTHORIZED IN PROFESSION** somebody who has been granted a licence to practise or teach a profession or skill **2. ACADEMIC DEGREE** a degree awarded by some European universities that ranks one step below that of a doctorate **3. SOMEBODY WITH LICENTIATE DEGREE** somebody holding the degree of licentiate **4. PRESBYTERIAN PREACHER** somebody licensed to preach but not perform the sacraments in a Presbyterian church, usually a trainee minister who has not yet been ordained [15C. < medieval Latin *licentiatus*, past participle of *licentiare* 'permit' < Latin *licentia* (see LICENCE)]

licentious /lī sénshəss/ *adj* pursuing desires aggressively and selfishly, unchecked by morality, especially in sexual matters [15C. < Latin *licentiosus* < *licentia* (see LICENCE)] —**licentiously** *adv* —**licentiousness** *n*

lichee *n FOOD* another spelling of **lychee**

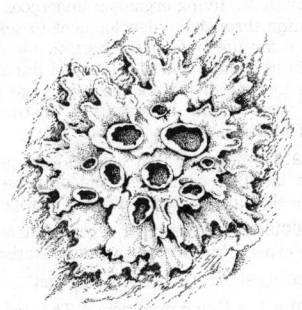

lichen

lichen /líkən, líchən/ *n* a complex organism consisting of fungi and algae growing together in symbiosis that often appears as grey, green, or yellow patches on rocks, trees, and other surfaces [Early 17C. Via Latin < Greek *leikhēn*] —**lichened** *adj* —**licheniform** *adj* —**lichenoid** *adj* —**lichenous** *adj*

lichen moth *n* a moth that has larvae that feed exclusively on lichen. Native to: Southeast Asia, Australia. Family: Lithosiidae.

Lichfield /lích feeld/ cathedral city in Staffordshire, central England. Population: 93,232 (2001).

lich-gate *n CHR, BUILDINGS* another spelling of **lych-gate**

Roy Lichtenstein

Lichtenstein /líktən stīn/, **Roy** (1923–97) US painter, graphic artist, and sculptor. A major figure in pop art, he is noted for his paintings featuring enlarged comic-strip images.

> 'Organized perception is what art is all about...It is a process. It has nothing to do with any external form the painting takes, it has to do with a way of building a unified pattern of seeing.'
> [Roy Lichtenstein. Quoted in 'What is Pop Art?' Interviews with Eight Painters', *Art News*, G. R. Swenson; February 1964]

licit /líssit/ *adj* allowed by law [15C. < Latin *licitus*, past participle of *licere* 'be allowed'] —**licitly** *adv* —**licitness** *n*

SYNONYMS See **legal**.

lick /lik/ *v* (**licks, licking, licked**) **1.** *vt* **PASS TONGUE OVER SOMETHING** to move the tongue across the surface of something, either to wet or clean it or as a way to move something into the mouth **2.** *vti* **BRUSH AGAINST SOMETHING** to touch or lightly move against something **3.** *vt* **BEAT SOMEBODY** to give somebody a physical beating (*informal*) **4.** *vt* **DEFEAT COMPETITOR** to defeat somebody easily or thoroughly (*informal*) ■ *n* **1. MOVEMENT OF TONGUE OVER SOMETHING** a movement of the tongue across the surface of something **2. QUICKLY APPLIED COATING** a quick coat of something, especially paint ○ *a lick of paint* **3. PUNCH** a punch or blow (*informal*) **4.** *MUSIC* **BRIEF IMPROVISATION** a distinctive few notes or short phrase in pop music or jazz, often improvised (*informal*) **5.** *GEOG* same as **salt lick** (sense 1) **6.** *VET* **MEDICINAL BLOCK FOR ANIMALS** a block of salt or chemical material to be licked by domestic animals as medicine ■ *adj* **GOOD** excellent or very pleasing (*slang; used in Black English*) [Old English *liccian* < Germanic] —**licker** *n*

lickerish /líkərish/, **liquorish** *adj* (*archaic*) **1.** taking an excessive or unfair amount, without concern for the needs of others **2.** continually thinking about sex or trying to make sexual contact with others [15C. Alteration of obsolete *lickerous* < Anglo-Norman variant of Old French *lecheros* 'lecherous' < *lecheor* (see LECHER)]

lickety-split /líkəti-/ *adv N Am* very quickly (*informal*) [*Lickety* < LICK]

licking /líking/ *n* (*informal*) **1.** a beating or spanking **2.** a severe defeat or setback

lickspittle /lík spitt'l/ *n* somebody who shows undue deference towards social superiors or powerful people (*literary*)

licorice *n FOOD Aus, US* spelling of **liquorice**

lictor /líktər/ *n* any of a group of minor officials in ancient Rome whose duties included carrying the fasces as a symbol of authority and clearing the way for the chief magistrates [14C. < Latin]

lid /lid/ *n* **1. TOP FOR CONTAINER** a cover of a container that can be removed or raised on a hinge to open the container **2.** *ANAT* same as **eyelid 3. RESTRAINT** a restraint or control on something that keeps it within acceptable bounds (*informal*) ○ *He promised to keep a lid on manufacturing costs.* **4.** *BIOL* same as **operculum** (sense 3) **5.** *US* **AMOUNT OF MARIJUANA** a quantity of marijuana, usually an ounce (*slang*) [Old English *hlid* < Indo-European, 'cover, something that bends over'] —**lidded** *adj* —**lidless** *adj* ◇ **flip your lid** to react to something or somebody in the strongest, most emotionally uncontrolled manner possible (*slang*)

lidar /lī daar/ *n* a device, similar in operation to radar, that uses pulses of laser light to analyse atmospheric phenomena [Mid-20C. Acronym < *light detection and ranging*, after RADAR]

Liddell Hart /lídd'l haárt/, **Basil Henry** (1895–1970) British journalist and military strategist. As a writer and personal adviser to the minister of war, he advocated the need to modernize military equipment.

Lidice /líddichi, líddissi/ village in western Czechoslovakia, in what is now the Czech Republic. It was the scene of a retaliatory massacre of villagers by Nazi German forces during World War II.

lido /léedō, līdō/ (*plural* **-dos**) *n* an outdoor swimming pool, or a section of beach, that is open to the public [Late 17C. After LIDO]

Lido /léedō/ island reef in northeastern Italy, separating the Venice Lagoon from the Adriatic Sea. It is a beach resort. Population: 20,950 (1980).

lidocaine /līdə kayn/ *n N Am PHARM* same as **lignocaine** [Mid-20C. < ACETANILIDE + -*caine*, INN stem]

lie[1] /lī/ *vi* (**lies, lying** /lī ing/, **lay** /lay/, **lain** /layn/) **1. RECLINE** to stretch out on a surface that is slanted or horizontal ○ *She was lying on the sofa.* **2. BE PLACED FLAT ON SURFACE** to be positioned on and supported by a horizontal surface ○ *A book lay open on his bedside table.* **3. BE LOCATED SOMEWHERE** to be located in a particular place ○ *Mexico lies south of the United States.* **4. BE BURIED** to be buried in a particular place ○ *Here lies Martha, beloved daughter of John and Mary.* **5. BE PLACED IN COMPETITION** to be in a particular position in a race or a competition ○ *She's lying third in the overall ratings.* **6. BE IN PARTICULAR STATE** to be or continue to be in a particular condition or state ○ *It lay hidden for years.* **7. BE IN PARTICULAR DIRECTION** to extend or be in a particular direction ○ *The city lies beneath us, glittering with a thousand lights.* **8. BE IN STORE** to be still to come ○ *A great deal of hard work lies ahead of us.* **9. STAY UNDISTURBED** to remain undiscussed or undisturbed ○ *Let sleeping dogs lie.* **10. BE ACCEPTABLE IN LAW** to be acceptable as an assertion or as evidence in court ■ *n* **1. ANIMAL'S RESTING PLACE** a place where an animal returns to rest or hide **2. POSITION OF GOLF BALL** the position of a golf ball after it comes to rest, as regards the ease with which the next shot can be taken ○ *The ball has quite a good lie, in spite of being in the rough.* [Old English *licgan* < Indo-European]

USAGE See **lay**[1].

lie around, lie about *vti* **1.** to sit around doing nothing in particular (*informal*) **2.** to be left lying and not cleared away

lie back *vi* to relax by stretching out flat on the back or reclining in a chair, especially one that tilts backwards

lie down *vi* **1. LIE ON SURFACE** to stretch out flat **2. REST** to rest with the body flat, especially in bed ○ *I need to lie down for an hour or two.* **3. REMAIN PASSIVE** to do nothing or make no response ○ *I'm not going to take this lying down.*

lie in *vi* to sleep or stay in bed past the time you usually get up (*informal*)

lie off *vti* to stay close to the shore or to another ship (*refers to ships*)

lie to *vi* to remain motionless, facing the wind (*refers to ships*)

lie with *v* **1.** *vti* to be the responsibility of somebody **2.** *vi* to have sexual intercourse with somebody (*archaic*)

lie[2] /lī/ *vi* (**lies, lying** /lī ing/, **lied**) **1. DELIBERATELY SAY SOMETHING UNTRUE** to say something that is not true in a conscious effort to deceive somebody ○ *He lied about his age in order to get into the army.* **2. BE DECEPTIVE** to give a false impression ○ *Don't forget that appearances can lie.* ■ *n* **1. FALSEHOOD** a false statement made deliberately ○ *She told me she wasn't seeing anyone else, but that was a lie.* **2. FALSE APPEARANCE** a situation based on deception or a false impression ○ *beginning to feel that my whole life is a lie* [Old English *lēogan* (verb), *lyge* (noun) < Germanic]

SYNONYMS lie, untruth, falsehood, fabrication, fib, white lie

CORE MEANING: something that is not true

lie a false statement made deliberately ○ *He described the evidence of his accusers as 'a pack of lies'.* A

police spokesperson declared that the allegation was 'a blatant lie'. **untruth** something that is presented as being true but is actually false ○ *This young woman was clearly quite able to tell untruths when it suited her.* **falsehood** an intentionally untrue statement ○ *The account was full of inaccuracies, even falsehoods.* **fabrication** an invented statement, story, or account devised with intent to deceive ○ *She claims that the infamous Richard III of Shakespeare and history books is a Tudor fabrication.* **fib** (*informal*) an insignificant or harmless lie ○ *That's a fib! I know you haven't been sick.* **white lie** a lie not intended to harm, but told in order to avoid distress or embarrassment ○ *telling little white lies in order to avoid conflict* ○ *Why hadn't she told a white lie and said the colour was flattering?*

Liebfraumilch /leéb frow milk, -milch/ n a slightly sweet white wine from southwestern Germany [Mid-19C. < German *lieb* 'dear' + *Frau* 'lady' (after Mary, mother of Jesus Christ, patron of the convent where it was produced) + *Milch* 'milk']

Liebig /leébig/, **Justus, Baron von** (1803–73) German chemist. Noted for his contribution to organic analysis and biochemistry, he established the first chemical research laboratory for students at Giessen, Germany.

> 'We are too much accustomed to attribute to a single cause that which is the product of several, and the majority of our controversies come from that.'
> [Attributed to Justus Liebig]

Liechtenstein

Liechtenstein /líkhtən shtīn/ small independent principality in central Europe, lying between Switzerland, with which it has close ties, and Austria. Language: German. Currency: Swiss franc. Capital: Vaduz. Population: 33,145 (2003). Area: 160 sq. km/62 sq. mi. Official name **Principality of Liechtenstein**

lied /leet/ (*plural* **lieder** /leédər/) n a German folk or art song, especially an art song of the 19th century with a solo voice part and interwoven piano accompaniment of equal importance. Schubert, Brahms, and Schumann were major composers of lieder. (*usually used in the plural*) [Mid-19C. < German, 'song']

lie detector n a device for finding out whether somebody is telling the truth during questioning. It has sensors that measure changes in blood pressure and pulse, which are supposed to reflect the uneasiness caused by lying.

lie-down n a short rest, especially in bed (*informal*)

lief /leef/ (*archaic*) adv **WILLINGLY** readily or without reluctance ■ adj 1. **WILLING** ready or desirous 2. **BELOVED** dear or treasured [Old English *lēof* < Germanic]

liege /leej/ n 1. a lord or sovereign who deserves loyalty and service under feudal law 2. a vassal or subject who owes loyalty and service to a lord or sovereign under feudal law [13C. Via French *lige* < medieval Latin *leticus* < *letus* 'colonist with limited freedom', probably < Germanic, 'free'] —**liegedom** n

Liège /li ézh/ city and capital of Liège Province, eastern Belgium. Population: 187,538 (1999).

liegeman /leéj man/ (*plural* -**men** /-mən/) n 1. **HIST** same as **liege** (sense 2) 2. a faithful or loyal follower

lie-in n a sleep or rest in bed until later than your usual time for getting up (*informal*)

lien /leen, leé ən/ n the legal right to keep or sell somebody else's property as security for a debt [Mid-16C. Via French < Latin *ligamen* 'bond' < *ligare* 'bind']

lie of the land n the general appearance or state of an area or situation presenting itself to somebody (*informal*) N Am term **lay of the land**

lierne

lierne /li úrn/ n a reinforcing rib in the vaulting of a Gothic cathedral or other roofed structure [Mid-19C. < French < *lier* 'bind' < Latin *ligare*]

~~**liesure**~~ incorrect spelling of **leisure**

lieu /lyoo, loo/ n place or stead (*archaic*) [Mid-16C. Via French < Latin *locus* 'place'] ◇ **in lieu** instead of something else already mentioned or that is usual in the current situation

Lieut *abbr* MIL Lieutenant

lieutenant /lef ténnənt/ n 1. **DEPUTY** an assistant to or substitute for somebody else 2. **NAVY OFFICER** an officer in the US Navy or Coast Guard of a rank above lieutenant junior grade, or an officer in the British or Canadian navies of a rank above sub-lieutenant 3. **POLICE OFFICER OR FIREFIGHTER** a US police or fire department officer of a rank above sergeant 4. **ARMY OFFICER** in the British and Canadian armies and in many other armed forces, a commissioned officer of a rank above second lieutenant [14C. < French, 'somebody who holds a place' < *lieu* (see LIEU) + *tenant* (see TENANT)] —**lieutenancy** n

lieutenant colonel n an officer in the US, British, or Canadian armies, the US and Canadian air forces, and the US Marine Corps of a rank above major

lieutenant commander n an officer in the US, Canadian, or British navies or the US Coast Guard of a rank above lieutenant

lieutenant general n an officer in the US, Canadian, or British armies and the US Marine Corps of a rank above major general

lieutenant governor n 1. an elected official in a US state government of a rank below governor 2. an official appointed by the Canadian federal government who acts for the Crown as the representative of the British monarch in a province —**lieutenant governorship** n

Lifar /li faár/, **Serge** (1905–86) Russian-born French dancer and choreographer. Director of the Paris Opéra Ballet, he created over 50 ballets, including *Prométhée* (1929) and *Icare* (1935).

life /līf/ (*plural* **lives** /līvz/) n 1. **EXISTENCE IN PHYSICAL WORLD** the quality that makes living animals and plants different from dead organisms and inorganic matter. Its functions include the ability to take in food, adapt to the environment, grow, and reproduce. 2. **LIVING INDIVIDUAL** a living being, especially a person, often used when referring to the number of people killed in an accident or a war (*usually used in the plural*) ○ *Two hundred lives were lost in the crash.* 3. **LIVING THINGS CONSIDERED TOGETHER** a group of living things, usually of a particular kind ○ *She was an expert on plant life in the Amazon.* 4. **WHOLE TIME SOMEBODY IS ALIVE** the entire period during which somebody is, has been, or will yet be alive ○ *All my life I've wanted to learn to fly.* 5. **TIME WHEN SOMETHING FUNCTIONS** the period during which something continues to function ○ *Cheap batteries usually have short lives.* 6. **PART OF SOMEBODY'S LIFE** a particular aspect of somebody's life ○ *social life* 7. **HUMAN ACTIVITY** human existence or activity in general ○ *real life* 8. **WAY IN WHICH SOMEBODY LIVES** the character or conditions of somebody's existence ○ *Most people in this city lead hard lives.* 9. **CHARACTERISTIC WAY OF LIVING** a way of living that is characteristic of a particular place or group ○ *country life* 10. **VITALITY** animation and vitality, or

something that produces animation or vitality ○ *We liked him because he was so full of life.* 11. **CHANCE IN GAME PLAYING** in various games, a chance to be unsuccessful without being put out of a game (*usually plural*) 12. **LIFE IMPRISONMENT** a sentence of life imprisonment (*informal*) 13. **BIOGRAPHY** an account of somebody's life, usually in writing, but sometimes in other media such as film, video, or radio ○ *He was the author of 'The Life of Aristotle'.* 14. **ARTIST'S SUBJECT** something real used as a subject by an artist, especially human models, who are often nude ○ *She always insisted on painting from life.* [Old English *līf* < Germanic] ◇ **get a life** to do something to improve your situation or change your lifestyle for the better (*informal*) ◇ **go for your life** Aus to do something with the greatest effort possible (*informal*) ◇ **take somebody's** *or* **your life** to kill somebody or yourself. see Synonyms at **kill**

> **CULTURAL NOTE** *The Life of Samuel Johnson*, a biography (1791) by Scottish writer James Boswell. Generally considered the finest biography in the English language, it is a rounded, revealing, and respectful portrait of one of the great scholars of the day. But its greatness also derives from its vivid descriptions of contemporary society and the candid revelations of its author.

life-and-death adj extremely important or serious, especially when somebody's life is at stake ○ *a life-and-death struggle*

life assurance n UK a plan under which regular payments are made to a company during somebody's lifetime, and in return the company pays a specific sum to the person's beneficiaries after the person's death. ANZ, N Am term **life insurance**

life belt n a belt or ring made of material that floats, worn to keep somebody from sinking or drowning

lifeblood /līf blud/ n 1. something that is vitally important to the welfare of a larger entity ○ *Donations are the lifeblood of this organization.* 2. blood when considered as necessary in maintaining life (*literary*)

lifeboat /līf bōt/ n 1. a small boat kept on the deck or railings of a larger ship, for use if the ship has to be abandoned 2. a boat used for rescuing people from ships in trouble at sea

life buoy n a float used in an emergency to keep somebody's head and shoulders above water until help arrives

life coach n somebody who provides advice and support to people who wish to improve their lives, helping them to make decisions, solve problems, and achieve goals

life crisis n a major disruptive event that happens in somebody's lifetime, e.g. bereavement or divorce

life cycle n 1. the series of changes of form and activity that a living organism undergoes from its beginning through its development to sexual maturity ○ *the life cycle of the snail* 2. the complete process of change and development during somebody's lifetime or during the useful life of something such as an organization, institution, or manufactured product

life estate n property that belongs to a particular person but that cannot be sold or passed on to anyone else until after the death of that person

life expectancy n the number of years that somebody can be expected to live, according to statistics

life force n PHILOSOPHY same as **élan vital**

life form n 1. a living organism ○ *They scanned the surface of the planet for life forms.* 2. the characteristic form of an organism at maturity

lifeguard /līf gaard/ n somebody trained in rescue techniques whose job is to watch over swimmers at a beach or swimming pool and save those in danger of drowning

Life Guards npl a cavalry regiment that together with the Horse Guards forms the Household Cavalry responsible for guarding the sovereign, especially during public ceremonies

life history n 1. **ENTIRE STAGES OF LIFE** all the changes experienced by a living organism, from its conception to its death 2. **SOMEBODY'S LIFE STORY** the story of somebody's life 3. **SOMEBODY'S LIFE STORY USED FOR RESEARCH** an account of somebody's life derived from

oral or documentary evidence and used in social research. It may shed light on issues of social concern or add to the sum of knowledge about society and social institutions.

life imprisonment *n* a punishment in which somebody convicted of a crime must remain in prison for the rest of his or her life, or for a very lengthy period. The period of imprisonment may be shortened for good behaviour.

life insurance *n* INSUR same as **life assurance**

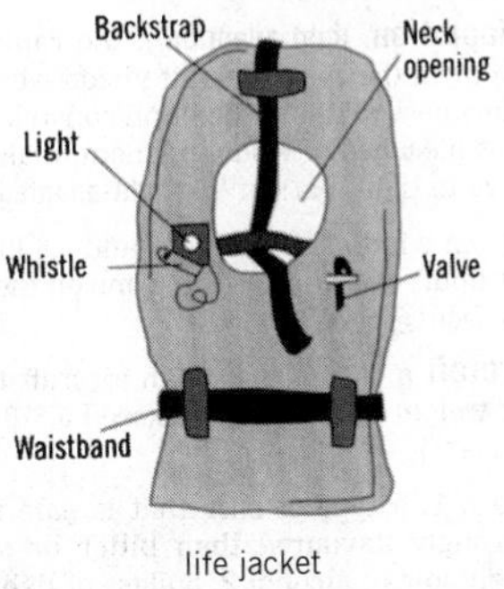
Backstrap
Neck opening
Light
Whistle
Valve
Waistband

life jacket

life jacket *n* a sleeveless jacket made of light material or filled with air, used to keep somebody afloat in water

lifeless /lífləss/ *adj* **1. DULL** lacking excitement or animation **2. DEAD** dead, or seeming to be dead **3. WITHOUT LIFE** not capable of supporting life —**lifelessly** *adv* —**lifelessness** *n*

SYNONYMS See *dead*.

lifelike /líf lìk/ *adj* looking alive or representing real life accurately

lifeline /líf lìn/ *n* **1.** a rope or cable used for safety in dangerous manoeuvres, especially at sea, e.g. attached to a diver's helmet or stretched along the deck of a boat **2.** a means of communication or support that is extremely important to the survival of an isolated person or group

life list *n* a birdwatcher's record of all the species of birds sighted in a lifetime

lifelong /líf long/ *adj* lasting the whole of a lifetime

life mask *n* a cast made of a living person's face, using plaster or another soft substance that hardens when it dries

life member *n* a member of an organization whose membership is valid for the rest of his or her life and does not require periodic renewal —**life membership** *n*

life-or-death *adj* same as **life-and-death**

life partner *n* the person with whom somebody has decided to spend the rest of his or her life in a sexual and romantic relationship ○ *'... makes people believe that somewhere there really is the life partner who will provide the ecstatic happiness depicted in opera...'* (*New York Times*; April 1999)

life peer *n* somebody who is granted a title and seat in the House of Lords that cannot be inherited. People are often made life peers when they have failed to be re-elected to the House of Commons, to allow them to continue to work on behalf of their political party. —**life peerage** *n*

life preserver *n* **1.** a hand weapon consisting of metal stitched into one end of a length of thick flexible leather, used to hit or batter somebody. N Am term **blackjack 2.** *N Am* a life belt or life jacket

lifer /lífər/ *n* somebody sentenced to life imprisonment (*informal*)

life raft *n* a raft usually made of inflatable plastic designed for use during an emergency at sea

lifesaver /líf sayvər/ *n* **1.** a provider or source of greatly needed help (*informal*) **2.** *ANZ* EMERGENCIES same as **lifeguard**

lifesaving /líf sayving/ *adj* **RESCUING OR REVIVING** used to rescue people or keep them alive ■ *n* **1. RESCUING OF PEOPLE** techniques or efforts to rescue people from danger, especially from drowning **2. MULTIACTIVITY WATER-BASED SPORT** in Australia, the activities of a lifesaver or a team of lifesavers formalized as a multiactivity sport. This forms the basis of the Iron Man and Iron Woman contests.

lifesaving club *n ANZ* SWIMMING same as **surf club**

life science *n* a branch of science that is concerned with plants, animals, and other living organisms, e.g. biology, botany, and zoology (*often used in the plural*)

life sentence *n* a court verdict that condemns a convicted criminal to spend the rest of his or her life, or a very lengthy period, in prison. It may be shortened for good behaviour.

life-size *adj* being the size of the original in life

life span *n* **1.** the length of time that a member of a particular species can be expected to remain alive **2.** the length of time that something can be expected to last or function

life span psychology *n* a field of psychology that studies human development from birth to death

life story *n* a detailed account of all the events of somebody's life

lifestyle /líf stìl/ *n* the way of life characteristic of a particular person, group, or culture

life-support *n* maintenance of vital body functions by a life-support system ■ *adj* designed to keep somebody alive in an environment such as space that does not support life, or designed to maintain breathing, heartbeat, and other vital functions in somebody who is seriously ill

life-support system *n* **1.** a piece of technical equipment that temporarily performs a vital body function such as respiration when somebody's own organ cannot because of injury or disease **2.** a piece of technical equipment that is designed to provide normal living conditions when these are not available, especially in space

life's work *n UK, ANZ, Can* something that is the product, result, or culmination of somebody's working life. US term **lifework**

life table *n* INSUR same as **mortality table**

life-threatening *adj* very dangerous or serious with the possibility of death as an outcome

lifetime /líf tìm/ *n* **1. TIME REMAINING ALIVE** the length of time that somebody or something remains alive **2. TIME REMAINING USEFUL** the length of time that something remains useful or in working order **3. LONG TIME** an extremely long time (*informal*) ◇ **chance** *or* **opportunity of a lifetime** a highly favourable situation that is unlikely to recur

lifework /líf wúrk/ *n N Am* same as **life's work**

LIFFE /líffi/ *abbr* London International Financial Futures and Options Exchange

Liffey /líffi/ river in the eastern part of the Republic of Ireland. It rises in the Wicklow Mountains southwest of Dublin and empties into Dublin Bay. Length: 80 km/50 mi.

LIFO /lífō/ *abbr* ACCT last in, first out

lift /lift/ *v* (**lifts, lifting, lifted**) **1.** *vt* **RAISE SOMETHING** to move something from one position to another, higher position **2.** *vi* **MOVE HIGHER** to move to a higher level than before **3.** *vt* **MOVE SOMETHING UPWARDS** to direct something upwards ○ *lifting her eyes from the book* **4.** *vi* **GO UPWARD** to move, especially mechanically, in an upward direction ○ *Just press the button, and the boot will lift automatically.* **5.** *vt* **TAKE SOMETHING FROM PLACE** to take hold of something and move it somewhere else ○ *She lifted the CD from the rack.* **6.** *vt* AVIAT **CARRY SOMEBODY OR SOMETHING IN AIRCRAFT** to transport somebody or something in an aircraft ○ *The rescue helicopter lifted the stranded climbers to safety.* **7.** *vt* **MAKE SOMETHING INVALID** to revoke something or make something no longer apply ○ *The government has decided to lift the trading restrictions.* **8.** *vti* **CHEER SOMEBODY OR BECOME CHEERED** to make somebody happier or more cheerful, or become happier or more cheerful ○ *A cup of hot tea will lift your spirits.* ○ *His low spirits lifted after a few songs.* **9.** *vi* **DIMINISH** to clear, disappear, or become less severe ○ *I think we should wait until this fog lifts.* **10.** *vt* **RAISE STATUS OF SOMEBODY OR SOMETHING** to have the effect of raising somebody or something in terms of status, respect, or public or official estimation ○ *Her latest novel has lifted her into the league of best-selling authors.* **11.** *vt* **IMPROVE SOMETHING** to raise the level of a performance or enhance a skill **12.** *vt* **MAKE SOMETHING BE HEARD** to increase the sound from something such as the voice to make it be heard or be heard more easily or clearly ○ *The choir lifted their voices in song.* **13.** *vt* AGRIC **HARVEST UNDERGROUND VEGETABLE** to dig up a plant for its edible underground tubers ○ *lift potatoes* **14.** *vt* GARDENING **DIG UP PLANT FOR TRANSPLANTING** to dig up a plant in order to transplant it **15.** *vt* **REMOVE WRINKLES SURGICALLY** to perform cosmetic surgery on a face to tighten the skin and so reduce wrinkling, or on a woman's breasts to reduce or eliminate sagging **16.** *vt* **STEAL SOMETHING** to steal something or take something away without the owner's permission or knowledge (*informal*) ○ *OK! Who's lifted my pen this time?* **17.** *vt* **PLAGIARIZE SOMEBODY'S WORK** to take and use somebody else's work without attributing it to its creator (*informal*) ○ *She was accused of lifting her first two paragraphs from a report on a webpage.* **18.** *vt* CRIME **ARREST SOMEBODY** to arrest somebody (*informal*) ○ *Max got lifted for causing a disturbance.* **19.** *vt* SPORTS **HIT BALL HIGH INTO AIR** to hit a cricket or golf ball high into the air ○ *lifting one straight down the fairway* **20.** *vt* MIL **STOP MILITARY ASSAULT** to cease the firing of artillery or naval guns during a combat operation or assault so as to allow ground personnel to move forwards ■ *n* **1.** *UK* **CAGE MOVING BETWEEN FLOORS OF BUILDING** a mechanically or electrically operated cage or platform, housed inside a shaft that runs vertically between the floors of a building or other construction, used for transporting people or things. ANZ, N Am term **elevator 2.** TRANSP **RIDE IN VEHICLE** a free ride as a passenger in somebody else's motor vehicle (*informal*) ○ *Do you want a lift to the airport?* **3. RISE IN SPIRITS** a rise in spirits, mood, or emotions that can often be attributed to a specific cause ○ *audiences turning to feel-good movies to give themselves a lift* **4. RAISING OF SOMEBODY OR SOMETHING** a placing of somebody or something in a higher position **5. FORCE NEEDED TO RAISE SOMETHING** the power or force available, necessary, or used for raising something **6. WEIGHT RAISED** a weight or an amount of something that is or can be raised **7. DEGREE OF RISE** the degree or distance by which something rises ○ *a moderate lift in temperature* **8.** AVIAT **UPWARD FORCE ACTING ON AIRCRAFT** the combination of forces that act to cause an aircraft to leave the ground and stay in the air **9.** PHYS **FORCE MAKING HOT-AIR BALLOON RISE** the force, usually provided by heated air, that makes a hot-air balloon or airship rise into the sky **10. RAISING OF PARTNER IN AIR** an act of raising a partner in pairs skating or ice dancing as part of a choreographed sequence **11.** CLOTHING same as **heeltap** (sense 2) **12. SOMETHING ADDED TO SHOE** a layer of material that is put inside a shoe or added to the heel of a shoe to make the wearer appear taller **13.** MIN EXTRACT **WATER PUMPS USED IN MINING** a set of pumps used to pump water out of a mineshaft to the surface **14.** MIN EXTRACT **AMOUNT OF EXTRACTED ORE** the amount of ore extracted from a seam **15.** *N Am* **OPERATION ALTERING BODY PART** a surgical operation to alter a part of the body for cosmetic effect (*informal*) ○ *Who did your lift?* [12C. < Old Norse *lypta* < Germanic] —**liftable** *adj* —**lifter** *n*

SYNONYMS See *raise*.

lift off *vi* to leave a launching pad and head upwards into the atmosphere (*refers to spacecraft*)

liftoff /líft of/ *n* **1.** the time when a rocket or spacecraft leaves the launching pad **2.** the initial thrust that sends a rocket or spacecraft upwards from the launching pad into the atmosphere

lig /lig/ (**ligs, ligging, ligged**) *vi* (*informal*) **1.** to do nothing habitually, often abusing the generosity of others **2.** to associate with powerful people, especially in the entertainment world, in order to benefit materially from the association, e.g. in the form of invitations to parties [Mid-20C. < N English dialect variant of LIE [1]] —**ligger** *n*

ligament /líggəmənt/ *n* **1.** a sheet or band of tough fibrous tissue that connects bones or cartilages at a joint or supports an organ, muscle, or other body part **2.** something that forms a connection or bond [14C. < Latin *ligamentum* < *ligare* 'bind'] —**ligamental** /líggə mént'l/ *adj* —**ligamentary** /-méntəri/ *adj* —**ligamentous** /-méntəss/ *adj*

ORIGIN The Latin word *ligare* 'to bind', from which *ligament* is derived, is also the source of English *ally*,

liaison, *lien*, *ligature*, *oblige*, and *rely*, and probably also of *liable* and *religion*.

ligan *n* NAUT same as **lagan**

ligand /líggənd, lígənd/ *n* an atom, molecule, group, or ion that is bound to a central atom of a molecule, forming a complex [Mid-20C. < Latin *ligandus* < *ligare* 'bind']

ligase /lī gayz, -gayss/ *n* an enzyme that joins two molecules, especially in living organisms [Mid-20C. < Latin *ligare* 'bind']

ligate /lī gayt, li gáyt/ (**-gates, -gating, -gated**) *vt* to bind something or tie something up (*technical*) [Late 16C. < Latin *ligat-* (see LIGATURE)] —**ligative** /líggətiv/ *adj*

ligation /lī gáysh'n/ *n* **1.** the tying of something with a surgical ligature **2.** something that is used for binding things or tying things up (*formal*)

ligature /líggəchər/ *n* **1. SOMETHING USED FOR TYING** something that is used for binding things or tying things up **2. TYING PROCESS** the process of binding something or tying something up **3. BOND** a unifying link or bond (*formal*) **4.** SURG **SURGICAL THREAD FOR TYING OFF DUCT** a piece of surgical thread used to tie off a duct or blood vessel in order to cut off the supply of body fluid normally running through it **5.** PRINTING **CHARACTER CONSISTING OF JOINED LETTERS** a character or piece of type that consists of two or more letters joined together, e.g. 'æ' **6.** MUSIC same as **tie** *n* (sense 8) **7.** MUSIC **SYMBOL IN MEDIEVAL MUSIC** in the notation of medieval music, a symbol indicating a group of notes to be sung to one syllable **8.** MUSIC **REED-HOLDER ON WOODWIND INSTRUMENT** on a woodwind instrument, a band, usually made of metal, that holds the reed to the mouthpiece [14C. Directly or via French < late Latin *ligatura* < Latin *ligat-*, past participle of *ligare* 'bind']

liger /līgər/ *n* the offspring that results from breeding a male lion with a female tiger [Mid-20C. Blend of LION + TIGER]

Ligeti /lígəti, li gétti/, **György** (*b.* 1923) Hungarian composer. His choral and orchestral works explore slowly moving colours and textures.

light[1] /līt/ *n* **1. ENERGY PRODUCING BRIGHTNESS** the energy producing a sensation of brightness that makes seeing possible **2. QUALITY OF LIGHT** a particular kind or quality of brightness ○ *We won't get good photographs in this fading light.* **3. ARTIFICIAL SOURCE OF LIGHT** an artificial source of illumination, e.g. an electric lamp or a candle ○ *switch the light on* **4. PATH TAKEN BY LIGHT** the path that light takes or somebody's share or access to light ○ *asked her to move out of my light* **5. DAYLIGHT** the condition of brightness created by the rays of the sun during the day ○ *keep filming while there's still some light left* **6. DAWN** the arrival of the sun's brightness at the beginning of the day ○ *get up before light to go running* **7. TRAFFIC SIGNAL** a signal that controls the movement of traffic ○ *Turn right at the first set of lights.* **8. GENERAL NOTICE** general or public notice, attention, or knowledge ○ *facts that only recently came to light* **9. WAY SOMETHING IS VIEWED** the manner in which somebody or something is regarded, especially by the public ○ *These actions have shown the committee in a particularly bad light.* **10. SOMETHING THAT IGNITES SOMETHING** a source of fire, especially a match ○ *Have you got a light?* **11. GLEAM IN SOMEBODY'S EYE** a glint in somebody's eye that is taken to indicate a particular mood or expression ○ *had a mischievous light in her eye* **12.** ARTS **REPRESENTATION OF LIGHT IN ART** the representation of light or the effect it has in a work of art **13.** BUILDINGS **WINDOW** a window or other opening in a building, designed to let sunlight in **14.** PHYS **VISIBLE ELECTROMAGNETIC RADIATION** electromagnetic radiation in the range visible to the human eye, between approximately 4,000 and 7,700 angstroms **15.** PHYS **ELECTROMAGNETIC RADIATION** electromagnetic radiation that has wavelengths of any length ■ *adj* **1. FULL OF BRIGHTNESS** full of illumination, or relatively well lit ○ *a light airy room* **2. PALE** of a relatively pale shade ○ *decorated in light green* ■ *v* (**lights, lighting, lit** /lit/ or **lighted**) **1.** *vti* **START BURNING** to begin to burn, or cause something to begin to burn ○ *Still trying to light the barbecue?* **2.** *vt* **ILLUMINATE SOMETHING** to illuminate, brighten, or shine on something ○ *A full moon lit the night sky.* **3.** *vt* **GIVE SOMETHING ANIMATED LOOK** to give somebody's eyes or face a happy or animated look ○ *A playful smile lit his face.* **4.** *vt* **LEAD SOMEBODY WITH LIGHT** to lead or direct somebody with a source of illumination such as a torch ○ *The usherette lit the way to our seats.* [Old English *lēoht* < Indo-European] ◇ **bring something to light** to reveal something, especially after an investigation ◇ **cast light on something** same as **shed** *or* **throw light on something** ◇ **come to light** to be revealed or made evident ◇ **go out like a light** to fall asleep very quickly and deeply (*informal*) ◇ **in the cold light of day, in the hard light of morning** when things are seen for what they really are rather than being seen in an unrealistically favourable light ◇ **in (the) light of something** taking into consideration what is known or what has just been said or found out ◇ **punch** *or* **put somebody's lights out** to give somebody a severe beating (*informal*) ◇ **see the light 1.** to have a sudden understanding or appreciation of something **2.** to be converted to a faith, belief, or point of view ◇ **see the light of day** to be published or made publicly known ◇ **shed** *or* **throw light on something** to make it possible or easier to understand something ◇ **strike a light** used to express surprise, shock, or disbelief (*dated informal*) ◇ **the light of somebody's life** the person somebody cherishes the most

light into *vt* to attack somebody or something, either verbally or physically (*informal*)

light out *vi US* to leave a place in a hurry (*informal*)

light up *v* **1.** *vti* **LIGHT CIGARETTE OR PIPE** to light something such as a cigarette, cigar, or pipe and begin smoking it **2.** *vt* **ILLUMINATE SOMETHING** to direct light on somebody or something **3.** *vti* **MAKE OR BECOME CHEERFUL** to become animated or cheerful, or cause something or somebody to become animated or cheerful **4.** *vi* **BEGIN SHINING** to start to shine

light[2] /līt/ *adj* **1. NOT HEAVY** weighing comparatively little **2. WEIGHING TOO LITTLE** weighing less than is correct or less than would be expected ○ *This sack is a couple of ounces light.* **3. LIGHTWEIGHT** made of thin fabric ○ *light summer apparel* **4. NOT DENSE** low in density or intensity ○ *only a light shower* **5. NOT FORCEFUL** performed with little physical force ○ *She felt a light tap on her shoulder.* **6. EASY TO DO** involving relatively little effort or exertion ○ *a little light weeding* **7. CONSUMING LITTLE OF SOMETHING** consuming something in small quantities only ○ *a light eater* **8. LESS SEVERE THAN POSSIBLE** considered less severe or harsh than might have been the case ○ *a light sentence* **9. UNIMPORTANT** of relatively little importance or seriousness ○ *a light throwaway remark* **10. NOT INTELLECTUALLY DEMANDING** not meant for serious study or contemplation ○ *some light holiday reading* **11. SHORT OF SOMETHING** lacking the usual or expected quantity of something ○ *a nice flavour but a bit light on salt* **12. UNWORRIED** not burdened by worries ○ *a light heart* **13. DIZZY** slightly dizzy or not quite thinking clearly, e.g. because of fatigue, alcohol, or drugs ○ *a light head* **14. NIMBLE** moving with grace and agility ○ *She's very light on her feet.* **15. EASILY DIGESTED** easily digested, or not very filling ○ *a light snack* **16.** FOOD **LOW IN CALORIES** low in calories, especially containing less than the usual amount of sugar or fat **17.** BEVERAGES **LOW IN ALCOHOL** having a very low alcohol content **18.** BEVERAGES **FLAVOURLESS** *S Asia* lacking in flavour or strength ○ *light tea* **19. FLUFFY AND WELL RISEN** of a light, flaky, fluffy, and well-risen consistency ○ *a very light pastry* **20. DELICATELY FLAVOURED** having a fresh delicate flavour ○ *a light rosé wine* **21. EASILY WOKEN** easily woken or disturbed when asleep ○ *a light sleeper* **22. EASILY WORKED** loose, well aerated, and therefore easily worked ○ *light soil* **23. CARRYING SMALL WEIGHTS** designed to carry something that is relatively low in weight or relatively small in bulk ○ *a light delivery van* **24. NOT LOADED** not containing or carrying a full load **25. MANUFACTURING SMALL PRODUCTS** involved in the manufacture of comparatively small products, especially consumer goods made without the use of heavy machinery **26.** CHEM **WITH LOW BOILING POINT** having a relatively low boiling point **27.** MIL **NOT HEAVILY ARMED** carrying only hand-held weapons ○ *a light infantry brigade* **28.** PHON **UNSTRESSED** describes a syllable that is not stressed or accented **29.** CARDS **OF LOW VALUE** describes a bid in bridge that is made on a lower-than-normal number of points **30.** CARDS **WITH TOO FEW TRICKS** describes a bridge player who has taken too few tricks to make a contract **31. IMMORAL** with low moral standards, especially relating to sexual behaviour (*archaic*) ■ *adv* **1. LENIENTLY** in a casual or lenient way **2. WITH LITTLE LUGGAGE** with only a small amount of luggage ○ *travelling light* ■ *vi* (**lights, lighting, lighted** or **lit** /lit/) **1. COME TO REST** to come to rest on a branch after flight (*refers to birds*) **2. GET DOWN FROM VEHICLE** to get down from a horse, vehicle, or other form of transport (*dated*) [Old English *lēocht*, *līht* < Indo-European] ◇ **make light of something** to treat something as unimportant

Light *n* **1.** God as a source of spiritual illumination and strength **2.** CHR same as **Inner Light**

Light /līt/, **William** (1786–1839) British-born Australian soldier and surveyor. In 1836 he selected the site for and planned the layout of the city of Adelaide, Australia.

light adaptation, **light adaption** *n* the rapid changes that occur in the eye to permit vision when moving from darkness to light. The pupil constricts and the retina is bleached of visual pigment, making it less sensitive to light. [< LIGHT [1]] —**light-adapted** *adj*

light air *n* a wind of between 1.6 and 4.8 km/1 and 3 mi. per hour, classified as force one on the Beaufort scale [< LIGHT [2]]

light aircraft *n UK, ANZ, Can* an aircraft that has a takeoff weight that does not exceed 5,670 kg/12,500 lbs [< LIGHT [2]]

light ale *n* **1.** a type of beer that is pale in colour, less strongly flavoured than bitter or stout, and relatively low in alcohol **2.** a glass of light ale

light breeze *n* a wind of between 6.4 and 11 km/4 and 7 mi. per hour, classified as force two on the Beaufort scale [< LIGHT [2]]

light bulb *n* a near-spherical glass case containing a filament that emits light when an electric current is passed through it. The filament is usually made of tungsten and is surrounded by argon or neon. [< LIGHT [1]]

light chain *n* the shorter of the two main polypeptides that make up an antibody molecule [< LIGHT [2]]

light-coloured *adj* of a pale shade or hue [< LIGHT [1]]

light-emitting diode *n* ELEC ENG full form of **LED** [< LIGHT [1]]

lighten[1] /līt'n/ (**-ens, -ening, -ened**) *vti* **1. REDUCE IN WEIGHT** to become less heavy, or make something less heavy **2. REDUCE IN UNPLEASANTNESS** to become less of a burden or chore, or cause something to become less of a burden or chore **3. INCREASE IN CHEERFULNESS** to become more relaxed or lively, or make somebody or something become more relaxed or lively ○ *The mood of the gathering lightened a little.* [14C. < LIGHT [2]]

SPELLCHECK See ***lightening***

lighten up *vi* to become less gloomy, serious, or angry (*informal*)

lighten[2] /līt'n/ (**-ens, -ening, -ened**) *v* **1.** *vti* **INCREASE IN PALENESS** to become pale or paler in colour, or cause something to become pale or paler in colour **2.** *vi* **GLOW** to give off shining or glowing illumination **3.** *vi* **FLASH** to flash across the sky (*refers to lightning*) [13C. < LIGHT [1]]

SPELLCHECK See ***lightening***

lightening /līt'ning/ *n* the process or time during late pregnancy when the foetal head begins to descend into the mother's pelvis, resulting in a lessening of pressure on the diaphragm [< LIGHTEN [1]]

SPELLCHECK lightening or **lightning**? Do not confuse the spelling of ***lightening*** and ***lightning***, which sound similar. ***Lightening*** is the present participle of either of the verbs *lighten* (as in *lightening the load, lightening his hair*), and as a verbal noun is also used with specific reference to a stage of pregnancy. The noun meaning 'a flash of light in the sky during a storm' is spelt ***lightning*** (as in *thunder and lightning*), as is the corresponding adjective meaning 'very fast or sudden' (as in *with lightning speed*).

light entertainment *n* entertainment that is not serious or highbrow in content, usually involving comedy, singing, dancing, or popular music

lighter[1] /lītər/ *n* **1.** a small typically gas-filled container with a flint or other spark-producer that produces a flame used for lighting something that is smoked, e.g. a cigarette, cigar, or pipe **2.** a person or device that lights, illuminates, or ignites some-

thing (*usually used in combination*) ○ *a lamplighter* [Mid-16C. < LIGHT ¹ (verb)]

lighter² /líːtər/ *n* a flat-bottomed open cargo boat or barge, used especially for taking goods to or from a larger vessel when it is being loaded or unloaded [14C. Origin ?]

lighter-than-air *adj* describes aircraft such as hot-air balloons and dirigibles that weigh less than the air they displace [< *lighter* comparative of LIGHT ² *adj*] —**lighter-than-air** *n*

lightface /líːt fayss/ *adj also* **light-faced** /-fayst/ describes printed type with characters formed from relatively narrow lines ■ *n* printed type that is lightface [< LIGHT ²]

lightfast /líːt faast/ *adj* describes a dye or dyed fabric whose shade or colour is unchanged by exposure to light, especially sunlight [Early 20C. < LIGHT ¹, after COLOURFAST] —**lightfastness** *n*

light-fingered *adj* 1. skilled at and likely to try shoplifting, pickpocketing, or petty stealing 2. able to move the fingers quickly and nimbly, and therefore good at doing intricate jobs [< LIGHT ²] —**light-fingeredness** *n*

light fitting *n* the part of an electric light that contains a socket for the light bulb and is attached to a ceiling or wall

light flyweight *n* 1. in amateur boxing, a weight category for competitors whose weight does not exceed 48 kg/106 lb 2. an amateur boxer who competes at light flyweight level [< LIGHT ²]

light-footed, **lightfoot** /líːt fŏŏt/ *adj* able to walk or run with light agile easy-flowing steps [< LIGHT ²] —**light-footedly** *adv* —**light-footedness** *n*

light globe *n ANZ* UTIL same as **light bulb** [< LIGHT ¹]

lightheaded /líːt héddid/ *adj* 1. slightly dizzy or euphoric, experienced as an effect of caffeine, alcohol, or fatigue 2. having a tendency to behave in a frivolous or immature way [15C. < LIGHT ²] —**lightheadedly** *adv* —**lightheadedness** *n*

lighthearted /líːt haártid/ *adj* 1. not weighed down with worries or troubles 2. entertaining in an amusing carefree way [15C. < LIGHT ²] —**lightheartedly** *adv* —**lightheartedness** *n*

light heavyweight *n* 1. WEIGHT CATEGORY IN PROFESSIONAL BOXING in professional boxing, a weight category for competitors who weigh between 72.5 and 79.5 kg/160 and 175 lb 2. WEIGHT CATEGORY IN AMATEUR BOXING in amateur boxing, a weight category for competitors who weigh between 75 and 81 kg/165 and 178 lb 3. BOXER COMPETING AT LIGHT HEAVYWEIGHT a professional or amateur boxer who competes at light heavyweight level 4. WEIGHT CATEGORY IN WRESTLING in wrestling, a weight category for competitors who weigh between 87 and 97 kg/192 and 214 lb 5. WRESTLER COMPETING AT LIGHT HEAVYWEIGHT a wrestler who competes at light heavyweight level [< LIGHT ²]

lighthouse

lighthouse /líːt howss/ (*plural* **-houses** /-howziz/) *n* a strategically placed coastal building, often a tall round tower, with a powerful flashing light, designed to guide sailors or warn them of dangers such as rocks [Early 17C. < LIGHT ¹]

CULTURAL NOTE *To the Lighthouse*, a novel (1927) by Virginia Woolf. Typical of Woolf's more experimental novels in its unusual structure and use of stream-of-consciousness narrative, it is set at the holiday home of the Ramsay family on a Scottish island. Through the relationship between Mrs Ramsay and a young painter,

Lily Briscoe, Woolf explores the changing roles and attitudes of contemporary women.

light-independent reaction *n* BOT same as **dark reaction** [< LIGHT ¹]

lighting /líːting/ *n* 1. TYPE OF LIGHT light of a particular quality or type, or the equipment that produces it ○ *subdued lighting* 2. EQUIPMENT FOR PROVIDING ARTIFICIAL LIGHT the equipment used for providing artificial light and light effects on a theatre stage or a television or film set 3. EFFECT PRODUCED BY LIGHTS the overall effect produced by the lights used on a theatre stage or a television or film set 4. QUALITY OF LIGHT IN ARTWORK the amount or type of light in a photograph, painting, or other artwork [Pre-12C. < LIGHT ¹]

lighting cameraman, **lighting cameraperson** *n* somebody responsible for the lighting and camerawork for a film

lighting-up time *n* the time, at night or in the late afternoon, when drivers of road vehicles are legally required to put their headlights on

lightly /líːtli/ *adv* 1. WITH LITTLE FORCE without exerting much pressure, force, or weight 2. WITH LEVITY without seriousness 3. SPARINGLY in small or sparing amounts 4. GRACEFULLY in an easy graceful way [Pre-12C. < LIGHT ²]

light meter *n* PHOTOGRAPHY same as **exposure meter** [< LIGHT ¹]

light middleweight *n* 1. in amateur boxing, a weight category for competitors who weigh between 67 and 71 kg/148 and 156 lb 2. an amateur boxer who competes at light middleweight level [< LIGHT ²]

light-minded *adj* not capable of thinking seriously, or not likely to think about serious issues [< LIGHT ²] —**light-mindedly** *adv* —**light-mindedness** *n*

lightness¹ /líːtnəss/ *n* 1. the illumination of something relative to its surroundings 2. OPTICS the attribute of an object or a colour that enables an observer to quantify the amount of light it appears to reflect [Pre-12C. < LIGHT ¹]

lightness² /líːtnəss/ *n* 1. RELATIVE SLIGHTNESS OF WEIGHT the condition of something that weighs relatively little 2. RELATIVE SLIGHTNESS OF FORCE the condition of something that has relatively little force ○ *lightness of touch* 3. EASE OR DELICACY the ease or delicacy with which something is done 4. NIMBLENESS ease and rapidity of movement 5. UNTROUBLED STATE total freedom from worry and trouble 6. LEVITY lack of the seriousness that is required or expected [12C. < LIGHT ²]

lightning /líːtning/ *n* flashes of light seen in the sky when there is a discharge of atmospheric electricity in the clouds or between clouds and the ground, usually occurring during a thunderstorm ■ *adj* very fast and often very sudden [14C. < LIGHTEN ²]

SPELLCHECK See *lightening*.

lightning arrester *n* a device, often an aerial, that protects a piece of electrical equipment from damage by lightning or some other electrical surge by diverting the electricity to the ground

lightning bug *n N Am* INSECTS same as **firefly**

lightning chess *n* a fast form of chess in which players either have a limited time to make each move or have to complete all their moves within a set time

lightning conductor *n* a metal rod attached to the highest point of a building or other structure to protect it from lightning by conducting the lightning to the ground. N Am term **lightning rod**

lightning rod *n N Am* same as **lightning conductor**

lightning strike *n* 1. an industrial strike that happens at short notice and often without union support 2. a military attack carried out suddenly and without warning

light opera *n* MUSIC same as **operetta** [< LIGHT ²]

light organ *n* ZOOL same as **photophore** [< LIGHT ¹]

light pen *n* 1. a pen-shaped light-sensitive device used to manipulate information on a computer screen by touching the screen directly 2. a device for reading bar codes on goods [< LIGHT ¹]

light pipe *n* 1. a refracting tube lined with reflective material, used to transmit natural light into an

otherwise dark interior space 2. a fibre-optic cable capable of transmitting light [Early 21C]

light plane *n US* same as **light aircraft** [< LIGHT ²]

light pollution *n* excessive artificial light, especially street lighting in towns and cities that prevents the night sky from being seen clearly [< LIGHT ¹]

lightproof /líːt proof/ *adj* designed so as not to be penetrated or affected by light [< LIGHT ¹]

light railway *n* a railway designed for light traffic, often with a narrower gauge or subject to lower-than-standard speed and weight limits [< LIGHT ²]

light reaction *n* the first stage of photosynthesis, when light energy is absorbed by chlorophyll and converted into chemical energy that is stored as ATP. It also generates NADPH, a substance that, like ATP, is essential for subsequent stages of photosynthesis. [< LIGHT ¹]

light reflex *n* the normal contracting of the pupil of the eye in response to increased light [< LIGHT ¹]

lights¹ /líːts/ *npl* the lungs of domestic animals, especially those of pigs, sheep, or cattle when they are used in making pet food or, occasionally, food for people [Pre-12C. < LIGHT ²; because the lungs are full of air]

lights² /líːts/ *npl* the ideas, theories, or principles peculiar to a particular person ○ *You must, in the end, act according to your lights.* [Early 16C. < LIGHT ²]

light sabre *n* an imaginary weapon that is used as a sword but has a blade of visible light, or a toy imitating this [< LIGHT ¹]

light-sensitive *adj* affected in some way by the presence of light, as are some materials such as photographic film or silicon sheets [< LIGHT ¹]

lightshade /líːt shayd/ *n* HOUSEHOLD same as **lampshade** [< LIGHT ¹]

light shelf *n* a device fitted to the inside of a window, used to reflect sunlight towards the ceiling of a room and then farther into the building [< LIGHT ¹]

lightship /líːt ship/ *n* a ship with a bright flashing light that functions as a lighthouse, especially one that is anchored in a place where a permanent structure would be impracticable [Mid-19C. < LIGHT ¹]

light show *n* 1. a spectacle in the form of a display of colourful moving lights, often a feature of a live pop or rock concert 2. a form of entertainment in which moving coloured lights are synchronized with recorded music, usually synthesized instrumental music [< LIGHT ¹]

lightsome /líːtsəm/ *adj* (*archaic or literary*) 1. feeling and displaying happiness and freedom from worry 2. with a graceful lightness of movement [15C. < LIGHT ²] —**lightsomely** *adv* —**lightsomeness** *n*

lights out *n* 1. TIME WHEN PEOPLE MUST SLEEP the time at night when people, especially those in the armed forces, prison, boarding schools, and other institutions, are supposed to go to sleep 2. SIGNAL SOUNDED AT LIGHTS OUT a bugle call, gong, or other signal sounded at lights out ■ *adj* AUTOMATED automated, or controlled from a remote location ○ *lights-out system administration*

lightstick /líːt stik/ *n* a plastic tube containing two chemicals that mix when the tube is bent to create a glow, used as an emergency light source or for amusement

light stylus *n* COMPUT same as **light pen** (sense 1) [< LIGHT ¹]

light water *n* ordinary water, as opposed to heavy water [< LIGHT ²]

lightweight /líːt wayt/ *adj* 1. NOT HEAVY IN WEIGHT OR TEXTURE relatively light in weight and in texture 2. LACKING INTELLECTUAL DEPTH fairly frivolous or trivial and requiring little or no intellectual effort ■ *n* 1. INSIGNIFICANT PERSON OR THING somebody or something regarded as insignificant or without influence, often in a particular area ○ *a political lightweight* 2. WEIGHT CATEGORY IN PROFESSIONAL BOXING in professional boxing, a weight category for competitors who weigh between 59 and 61 kg/130 and 135 lb 3. WEIGHT CATEGORY IN AMATEUR BOXING in amateur boxing, a weight category for competitors who weigh between 57 and 60 kg/126 and 132 lb 4. BOXER COMPETING AT LIGHTWEIGHT a professional or amateur boxer who competes at lightweight level 5. WEIGHT CATEGORY IN WRESTLING in

wrestling, a weight category for competitors who weigh between 52 and 57 kg/115 and 126 lb **6. WRESTLER WHO COMPETES AT LIGHTWEIGHT** a wrestler who competes at lightweight level [Late 18C. < LIGHT [2]]

light welterweight *n* **1.** in amateur boxing, a weight category for competitors who weigh between 60 and 63.5 kg/132 and 139 lb **2.** an amateur boxer who competes at light welterweight level [< LIGHT [2]]

light-year *n* a unit of distance in astronomy equal to the distance that light travels in a vacuum in one mean solar year, approximately 9.46 billion km/5.88 billion mi ■ **light-years** *npl* a very long way in time, distance, or other quantity or quality (*informal*) [< LIGHT [1]]

lign- *prefix* same as **ligni-** (*used before vowels*)

lignan /lígnən/ *n* a phenolic compound of a group found mainly in plants that are believed to protect human beings from tumours and viruses

ligneous /lígni əss/ *adj* consisting of or with the appearance or texture of wood [Early 17C. < Latin *ligneus* < *lignum* (see LIGNI-)]

ligni- *prefix* wood ○ *lignicole* [< Latin *lignum* 'wood, firewood' < Indo-European, 'to collect']

lignicole /lígni kōl/, **lignicolous** /lig níkələss/ *adj* living or growing in or on wood [Mid-19C. < LIGNI- + Latin *colere* 'inhabit']

lignify /lígni fī/ (**-fies, -fying, -fied**) *vti* to become woody and relatively rigid as lignin is deposited in cell walls, or make plant parts woody in this way [Early 19C. < Latin *lignum* (see LIGNI-)] —**lignification** /lígnifi káysh'n/ *n*

lignin /lígnin/ *n* the complex polymer in plant cell walls that gives the plant rigidity and strength, and is the major component of wood [Early 19C. < Latin *lignum* (see LIGNI-)]

lignite /líg nīt/ *n* GEOL same as **brown coal** —**lignitic** /lig níttik/ *adj*

ligno- *prefix* wood ○ *lignocellulose* [< Latin *lignum* (see LIGNI-)]

lignocaine /lígnō kayn/ *n* a strong local anaesthetic applied externally to the gums or given by injection. Use: in dentistry. N Am term **lidocaine**

lignocellulose /lígnō séllyoo̅ lōss, -lōz/ *n* a strengthening substance composed of lignin and cellulose, found in woody tissues of plants

lignum vitae /lígnəm vīti/ *n* TREES same as **guaiacum** [Late 16C. < Latin, 'wood of life'; from the medicinal uses of the wood and its resin]

ligroin /líggrō in/ *n* a solvent in the form of a flammable liquid mixture of hydrocarbons. Source: distillation of petroleum. [Late 19C. Origin ?]

ligula /líggyoo̅lə/ (*plural* **-lae** /-lee/ or **-las**) *n* **1.** the tip of the lower lip (**labium**) of an insect, which typically has four lobes **2.** BOT same as **ligule** (sense 1) [Mid-18C. < Latin, 'strap', variant of *lingula* 'little tongue' < *lingua* 'tongue'] —**ligular** *adj*

ligule /líggyool/ *n* **1.** an outgrowth at the junction of the leaf sheath and leaf blade in a grass, typically a membranous or scaly flap but in some grasses a ring of hairs **2.** the strap-shaped extension of florets found in the flower heads of some members of the daisy family and in some grasses [Early 19C. < Latin *ligula* (see LIGULA)] —**ligulate** *adj*

Ligurian Sea /li go̅ori ən-/ part of the Mediterranean Sea, lying between the northwestern coast of Italy and the islands of Corsica and Elba

likable /líkəb'l/, **likeable** *adj* pleasant and friendly and therefore easy to like —**likability** /līkə bílləti/ *n* —**likableness** *n* —**likably** *adv*

Likasi /li kaássi/ mining and industrial city in the southeastern part of the Democratic Republic of the Congo. Population: 299,118 (1994).

like[1] /līk/ CORE MEANING: a grammatical word indicating that two things or people are similar or share some of the same features, qualities, or characteristics; it also introduces an example of the set of things or people that have just been mentioned ○ *Vivid red phone booths, looking like London imports, stood nearby.*

1. *prep* **RESEMBLING** having a resemblance to somebody or something, or so as to have a resemblance to somebody or something ○ *She wrapped the towel like a turban on her head.* ○ *He looks like the hero type to me!* **2.** *prep* **SUCH AS** introduces a typical instance or an example of a particular category or type ○ *She won't go to loud places like bars.* ○ *I bought things like fishing tackle and waders.* **3.** *prep* **INDICATES CHARACTERISTICS** indicates qualities, characteristics, or features (*often used in questions*) ○ *What's it like, being a mother?* ○ *When you go on like this, do you know what you sound like?* **4.** *prep* **TYPICAL OF** characteristic of somebody or something (*often negative*) ○ *It's just like her to say catty things.* **5.** *prep* **INCLINED TOWARDS** having a tendency or desire to do something ○ *I felt like screaming when I found the kitchen floor flooded.* **6.** *prep* **WITH SUGGESTION OF** as though something might happen ○ *It looks like rain this morning.* **7.** ⚠ *conj* **AS** in the same way or manner that (*informal*) ○ *To ski like she does requires great athletic ability.* **8.** ⚠ *conj* **AS IF** as though or as if (*nonstandard*) ○ *Butch hops out of the car like it was on fire.* ○ *Like I'd tell you a secret!* **9.** ⚠ *adv* **USED AS FILLER OR FOR EMPHASIS** used especially in conversation as a filler, for emphasis, to indicate possible exaggeration, or to convey uncertainty or approximation (*informal*) ○ *You're, like, feeling stressed today, aren't you?* ○ *There were, like, hundreds of people there.* ○ *She has, like, six brothers and sisters.* **10.** *adv regional* **USED AS SENTENCE ENDING** used in conversation, tacked on to the end of an adjective, adverb, phrase, or clause, to modify its force or as a filler ○ *Can you lend me a fiver? Just till tomorrow, like.* **11.** ⚠ *adv* **INTRODUCES DIRECT SPEECH** used especially in conversation to introduce a quotation of what somebody said (*nonstandard*) ○ *Susan is like 'It's not for me' and Brandon is like, 'You had me worried' and Susan is like, 'Don't worry, I'm not going anywhere.'* **12.** *n* **SOMETHING SIMILAR** a thing or set of things similar to another ○ *window boxes, planters, flower pots, and the like* **13.** *n* **COUNTERPART** one person or thing that is regarded as similar or almost identical to another ○ *Have you ever tasted the like of this cheesecake?* ○ *We won't see his like again in this decade.* **14.** *adj* **ALIKE** having exactly the same or almost identical qualities or characteristics ○ *These two cats are as like as though they were of the same litter.* ○ *The new laws affect hospitals, nursing homes, clinics, and other like institutions.* [12C. < Old Norse *líkr*, shortening of *glíkr*, equivalent to Old English *gelīc* (see ALIKE)] ◇ **like as not** to a probable or likely extent (*informal*) ○ *Like as not he'll show up very late.* ◇ **like new** in pristine condition (*informal*) ○ *looked like new* ◇ **like so** in the manner demonstrated ○ *Spread the fabric out like so.* ◇ **the likes of** people or things of the particular sort ○ *Such luxuries aren't for the likes of us.*

USAGE like as a conjunction and a filler: In writing and formal contexts, it is best to avoid using ***like*** as a conjunction meaning 'as', 'as if', or 'as though' when introducing a fully developed clause (i.e. one with a subject and a verb). Constructions like these may be disapproved of: *It sounds like she may resign. This pizza smells and tastes like a good pizza should.* The sentences could be recast: *It sounds as if she may resign. This pizza smells and tastes good, just the way it should.* In comparisons, it is acceptable to use ***like*** as long as you do not include a verb in the matter following it: *She ran the company just like a tyrant.* ***Like*** is always relatively informal as a conjunction, and is even more so as a conversational filler: *'What were the main characters doing in Chapter One?' 'They were, like, trying to understand the reasons men make war.'* In such contexts, ***like*** often acknowledges that what follows is not strictly accurate, either because the speaker is exaggerating or because he or she is unsure: *It was like, 100 metres tall. It takes like, six or seven hours.* Another conversational use of ***like***, to introduce reported speech, is considered nonstandard: *She was like, 'Don't worry, I'll do it.'*

like[2] /līk/ *v* (**likes, liking, liked**) **1.** *vt* **ENJOY SOMETHING** to regard something as enjoyable ○ *I like cross-country skiing.* ○ *Do you like prunes?* **2.** *vt* **CONSIDER SOMEBODY PLEASANT** to regard somebody as pleasant and enjoy that person's company ○ *I like a man with a sense of humour.* ○ *Do you like your new teacher?* ○ *I really like her.* **3.** *vt* **WANT SOMETHING** to want to have or do something ○ *Would you like some coffee?* ○ *I'd like to meet your brother.* **4.** *vt* **REGARD SOMEBODY OR SOMETHING POSITIVELY** to have a positive opinion about something or somebody ○ *How do you like her prose style?* **5.** *vi* **HAVE PREFERENCE** to have a preference or inclination ○ *We can leave later than seven if you like.* ■ *n* **PREFERENCE** something that is preferred over others ○ *a full litany of her likes and dislikes* [Old English *līcian* 'to please' < Germanic, 'body']

CULTURAL NOTE ***As You Like It***, a play (1599?) by William Shakespeare. Based on Thomas Lodge's romance *Rosalynde* (1590), it is one of Shakespeare's most charming romantic comedies. Its complex plot revolves around Rosalind, daughter of Duke Ferdinand, and her love for a young knight, Orlando, which results in her being banished to the forest, where she is eventually reunited with her lover. The observation 'All the world's a stage' comes from this play.

like[3] /līk/, **liked** /līkt/ *vi Southern US* to have been on the verge or point of doing or almost doing a particular thing (*informal*; *only in the past tense*) ○ *I like to have died when I saw her in that getup.* [15C. < LIKE [1]]

-like *suffix* resembling or characteristic of ○ *workmanlike* [< LIKE [1]]

likeable *adj* another spelling of **likable**

liked *vi Southern US* same as **like** [3] (*informal*)

likelihood /líkli ho̅od/ *n* **1.** the chance of something happening **2.** something that is likely to happen ◇ **in all likelihood** very probably

likely /líkli/ *adj* (**-lier, -liest**) **1. PROBABLE** probably going to happen **2. PLAUSIBLE** fit to be believed (*often used ironically*) **3. SUITABLE** appropriate for a particular activity or purpose **4. PROMISING** with a good chance of success or victory ■ *adv* **PROBABLY** to a probable degree or extent ○ *It will very likely snow tomorrow.* [14C. < Old Norse *(g)líkligr* < *líkr* (see LIKE [1])] ◇ **(as) likely as not** very probably

~~**likelyhood**~~ incorrect spelling of **likelihood**

like-minded *adj* sharing the same or similar views, opinions, tastes, values, or outlook —**like-mindedness** *n*

liken /líkən/ (**-ens, -ening, -ened**) *vt* to compare something or somebody to another, especially in order to point out the similarities [14C. < LIKE [1]]

likeness /líknəss/ *n* **1.** similarity of appearance among or between people or things **2.** a representation of somebody or something, e.g. a painting or statue, often considered in terms of how accurately it represents the person or thing [Old English *(ge)līcnes* < *gelīc* (see ALIKE)]

Likert scale /líkurt-/ *n* a scale measuring the degree to which people agree or disagree with a statement, usually on a 3-, 5-, or 7-point scale [Mid-20C. After Rensis *Likert* (1903–81), US psychologist]

likewise /lík wīz/ *adv* **1.** in the same or a similar way **2.** used to state that the same applies in a second or subsequent case ○ *She works as a teacher; her brother likewise.* [15C. Contraction of *in like wise* 'in similar manner']

liking /líking/ *n* **1.** a feeling of enjoying something or finding something pleasant **2.** personal taste or choice [14C. < LIKE [2]]

SYNONYMS See ***love***.

~~**likly**~~ incorrect spelling of **likely**

likuta /li ko̅otə/ (*plural* **makuta** /ma-/) *n* a former subunit of currency of the Democratic Republic of Congo, 100 of which were worth one new zaïre [Mid-20C. < Kikongo, 'the cloth'; because a piece of cloth was a unit of currency]

lilac /líləк/ (*plural* **-lacs** or *same*) *n* **1.** an ornamental bush or small tree. Flowers: fragrant, white, mauve, or purple, in sprays. Native to: Europe, Asia. Genus: *Syringa*. **2.** a pale pinkish-purple colour tinged with blue [Early 17C. Via French < Persian *līlak* 'bluish'] —**lilac** *adj*

lilangeni /lee̅ lang gáyni/ (*plural* **emalangeni** /émmə-/) *n* the main unit of currency of Swaziland. See table at **currency** [Late 20C. < Bantu]

Lilburn /líl burn/, **Douglas** (1915–2001) New Zealand composer. Among his best-known works is *Aotearoa Overture* (1940). His later experimental work includes collaborations with leading poets. Full name **Lilburn, Douglas Gordon**

Lilburne /líl burn/, **John** (*c.* 1614–57) English political agitator and pamphleteer. A prominent member of

the Levellers, he was a Parliamentary officer in the Civil War, and advocated political reform.

liliaceous /lílli áyshəss/ *adj* belonging to the lily family of plants [Mid-18C. < late Latin *liliaceus* < Latin *lilium* 'lily']

Lilienthal /leéli ən taal/, **Otto** (1848–96) German inventor and aeronautical engineer. He was a pioneer of glider flight, and his study of aerodynamics led to advances in the design of aircraft wings.

Lilith /líllith/ *n* **1.** in Hebrew Scripture, the first woman, believed to have been created before Eve **2.** in Jewish folklore, an evil spirit of a woman, believed to lurk in deserted places and attack children

Liliuokalani /lee leé ōō ō kaa laáni/ (1838–1917) queen of the Hawaiian Islands. She was the last Polynesian sovereign to govern the Hawaiian Islands before its annexation by the United States, which she strongly opposed.

Lille /leel/ industrial city and capital of Nord Department, Nord-Pas-de-Calais Region, northern France. Population: 184,657 (1999).

Lillee /lílli/, **Dennis** (*b.* 1949) Australian cricketer. A fast bowler, he had taken a world-record 355 test wickets at his retirement in 1984. Full name **Lillee, Dennis Keith**

Lilliputian /lílli pyoósh'n/, **lilliputian** *n* **SMALL PERSON OR THING** a person or thing that is unusually small in height ■ *adj* **1. TINY** unusually small **2. TRIVIAL OR PETTY** of little or no importance or significance [Mid-18C. After *Lilliput*, country in *Gulliver's Travels* (1726) by Jonathan Swift whose people were only 15 cm/6 in. tall]

Lilo /lílō/ *tdmk* a trademark for an inflatable bed for use in swimming pools or on the sea

LILO /línlō/ *n* a data storage method in which data stored last is retrieved last. Full form **last in, last out**

Lilongwe /li lóng way/ capital and second largest city of Malawi. Population: 1,000,000 (1998).

lilt /lilt/ *n* **1. VARIATION IN VOICE PITCH** a pleasant rising and falling variation in the pitch of a person's voice **2. BOUNCY STEP** a light bouncy way of walking, often taken as an indication of a cheerful disposition **3. CHEERFUL PIECE OF MUSIC** a cheerful song or piece of music, especially one that is easy to sing along with (*archaic*) ■ *v* (**lilts, lilting, lilted**) **1.** *vti* **SAY OR SING SOMETHING CHEERFULLY** to say, sing, or play something in a cheerful way, often with pleasant variations in pitch **2.** *vi* **WALK BOUNCILY** to walk or move in a bouncy cheerful way [14C. Origin ?] —**lilting** *adj*

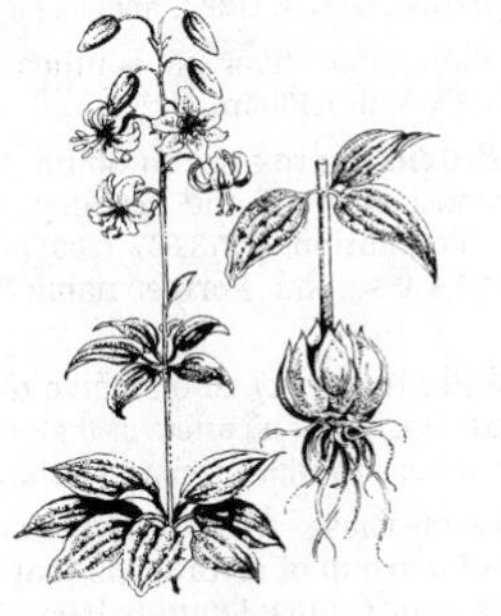

lily

lily /lílli/ *n* (*plural* **-ies**) **1. PERENNIAL PLANT** a perennial plant that grows from a bulb. Flowers: single, large, sometimes trumpet-shaped. Genus: *Lilium.* **2.** PLANTS **PLANT LIKE LILY** a plant that resembles a true lily **3. WHITE OR PURE THING** somebody or something that is particularly white or pure (*dated*) **4.** HERALDRY same as **fleur-de-lis** (sense 1) ■ *adj* **PALE** unusually pale in colour or shade [Pre-12C. < Latin *lilium*] ◇ **gild the lily** to try to improve something that is already good or beautiful enough

lily-livered /-livərd/ *adj* lacking courage (*dated*) [< the idea that a cowardly person's liver is pale through lack of bile, thought to engender courage]

lily of the valley (*plural* **lilies of the valley** or *same*) *n* a small poisonous ornamental plant with two long oval dark green leaves. Flowers: small, white or pale pink, sweet-scented, bell-shaped, drooping, growing from a single spike. Native to: North America, Europe, Asia. Genus: *Convallaria.* [Translation of Latin *lilium convallium*, unidentified plant]

lily pad *n* a floating leaf of a water lily

lily trotter *n* BIRDS same as **jaçana** [Because its elongated toes let it walk on floating vegetation]

lily-white *adj* **1.** unusually pale in tone and unblemished **2.** without any admixture

Lima[1] /leémə/ *n* a code word for the letter 'L', used in international radio communications

Lima[2] /leémə/ capital city of Peru, situated in the west-central part of the country, on the Pacific Ocean and adjacent to the River Rímac in a dry coastal region. Population: 7,443,000 (2000).

lima bean /límə-, leémə-/ *n* **1.** a pale green flattish edible seed produced by a cultivated plant of the bean family **2.** the plant that produces lima beans. Native to: Central America. Latin name: *Phaseolus limensis* or *Phaseolus lunatus.* [Mid-18C. After LIMA [2]]

limacine /límmə sīn, -sin, límə-/ *adj* **1.** belonging or relating to the slug family of invertebrate terrestrial molluscs **2.** resembling a slug in appearance or movement [Late 19C. < Latin *limac-* 'slug, snail']

limaçon /límmə son/ *n* a heart-shaped mathematical curve that is generated by a point on a line that intersects with a circle and rotates about a point on the circle [Late 19C. < French, 'snail shell' < Latin *limac-* 'slug, snail']

Limassol /líməsol/ city and port in southern Cyprus. It is the capital of Limassol District. Population: 152,900 (1997).

Limavady /límmə váddi/ town in County Londonderry, Northern Ireland. Population: 32,422 (2001).

limb[1] /lim/ *n* **1. BODY PART** an arm, leg, or similar appendage to the body such as a wing or flipper **2. LARGE BRANCH** a major branch of a tree **3. ASSOCIATED PERSON OR ORGANIZATION** somebody or something affiliated with a larger group or organization **4. PART STICKING OUT** a part that sticks out, e.g. on a building or a mountain range **5.** ARCHERY **PART OF BOW** either of the two halves of a bow used in archery [Old English *lim*] —**limbed** *adj* —**limbless** *adj* ◇ **be out on a limb** to be in an isolated position, without support ◇ **go out on a limb** to express a viewpoint that risks being controversial

limb[2] /lim/ *n* **1.** ASTRON **RIM OF PLANET** the illuminated edge of the Sun, the Moon, or a planet **2.** MATHS **ARC-SHAPED SCALE ON MEASURING DEVICE** an arc-shaped scale on an instrument such as a sextant that measures angles **3.** BOT **END OF PLANT PART** the expanded end of a plant part, especially of a sepal, petal, or leaf **4.** BOT **RIM OF FLOWER** the flared outer rim of a bell- or trumpet-shaped flower [14C. Directly or via French < Latin *limbus* 'edge']

limbate /lím bayt/ *adj* describes flowers that are a different colour at the edges ○ *limbate carnations* [Early 19C. < late Latin *limbatus* < Latin *limbus* 'edge']

limber[1] /límbər/ *adj* **1. SUPPLE AND AGILE** able to move with elastic ease and nimble quickness **2. FLEXIBLE** able to be bent easily ■ *vti* (**-bers, -bering, -bered**) **MAKE OR BECOME FLEXIBLE** to become flexible or supple, or cause something to become flexible or supple [Mid-16C. Probably < LIMBER [2], from its ease of movement] —**limberness** *n*

limber up *vi* to do gentle physical exercises to loosen and warm the muscles prior to taking part in more strenuous physical activity

limber[2] /límbər/ *n* a two-wheeled vehicle that forms the detachable front part of a gun carriage. It was also used for transporting ammunition and other supplies on the battlefield. ■ *vt* (**-bers, -bering, -bered**) to attach a gun or other piece of field equipment to a limber [Early 17C. Origin ?]

limbi ANAT plural of **limbus**

limbic /límbik/ *adj* **1.** belonging to a limbus, or situated in or near a limbus **2.** belonging to or situated in the limbic system [Late 19C. < French *limbique* < Latin *limbus* 'edge']

limbic system *n* an interconnected system of brain nuclei associated with basic needs and emotions such as hunger, pain, pleasure, satisfaction, sex, and instinctive motivation. The most primitive part of the brain, it is situated close to the inner wall of each cerebral hemisphere and includes the brain system concerned with the sense of smell.

limbo[1] /límbō/ *n* **1.** a state in which somebody or something is neglected or is simply left in oblivion **2.** *also* **Limbo** in Roman Catholic theology, the place that is believed to be home to the souls of children who died before baptism, and the souls of the righteous who died before Jesus Christ. Although they are barred from entry to heaven, they are not condemned to the eternal suffering of hell. [14C. < Latin, 'on the border (of hell)', form of *limbus* 'border, edge'] ◇ **in limbo** in a state of uncertainty or of being kept waiting

limbo[2] /límbō/ (*plural* **-bos**) *n* a Caribbean dance in which the body is bent backwards from the knees and moved under a horizontal boundary that is placed progressively lower. An expert at this dance needs very little clearance between the bar or rope and the floor. (*often used before a noun*) ○ *a limbo dancer* [Mid-20C. Alteration of LIMBER [1]] —**limbo** *vi*

Limbourg brothers /lím burg-/, **Pol**, **Herman**, and **Jehanequin** (*fl* 1400–16) Flemish illuminators. They are credited with the brightly coloured and highly detailed illustrations in the famous prayer book *Les Très riches heures du duc de Berry* (1413?–16), considered one of the finest examples of the French International Gothic style.

Limburger /lím burgər/, **Limburger cheese**, **Limburg cheese** /lím burg-/ *n* a soft white Belgian cheese with a strong smell and taste [Mid-19C. < Dutch or German, after *Limburg*, province of NW Belgium]

limbus /límbəss/ (*plural* **-bi** /-bī/) *n* the edge of various organs or body parts, e.g. the area in the eyeball where the cornea and sclera meet [15C. < Latin, 'edge']

lime[1] /līm/ *n* **1.** CHEM same as **calcium oxide** **2. CALCIUM USED FOR IMPROVING SOIL** a form of calcium that is added to soil with a low calcium content **3.** FIELD SPORTS same as **birdlime** ■ *vt* (**limes, liming, limed**) **1. SPREAD CALCIUM ON SOIL** to treat soil with calcium, often in the form of ground limestone, in order to reduce its acidity **2. PAINT WITH WHITEWASH** to cover a surface with whitewash **3. BLEACH WOOD** to treat wood with lime so that it has a pale bleached appearance ○ *kitchen cabinets of limed ash* **4.** FIELD SPORTS **SMEAR WITH BIRDLIME** to smear twigs or branches with birdlime in order to catch small birds **5.** FIELD SPORTS **CATCH BIRDS OR ANIMALS USING BIRDLIME** to catch small birds or animals using birdlime or some other sticky substance [Old English *līm* < Germanic]

lime[2] /līm/ *n* **1. SMALL GREEN FRUIT** a small acid-tasting citrus fruit with a thin green rind and green flesh (*often used before a noun*) ○ *lime juice* **2. EVERGREEN TREE** a small evergreen citrus tree that bears limes. Native to: Asia. Latin name: *Citrus aurantifolia.* **3. NONALCOHOLIC DRINK** a nonalcoholic drink made from or tasting of the juice of limes **4. LIME GREEN** the colour lime green [Mid-17C. Via French and Spanish < Arabic *līma* 'citrus fruit'] —**lime** *adj*

lime[3] /līm/ *n* **1.** *also* **lime tree** *UK, NZ, Can* a deciduous hardwood tree with heart-shaped leaves and clusters of white, yellowish, or green flowers, often planted for shade or ornament, or grown for timber. Native to: northern hemisphere. Genus: *Tilia.* Aus, US term **linden** **2.** the wood of the lime tree [Early 17C. Alteration of obsolete *line* < Old English *lind* (see LINDEN)]

lime[4] /līm/ (**limes, liming, limed**) *vi Carib* to spend time lazily (*slang*) [Late 20C. Back-formation < *limey* 'low-class white person']

limeade /līm áyd/ *n* a nonalcoholic, usually carbonated drink made from or tasting of lime juice [Late 19C. < LIME [2]]

lime-green *adj* of a pale green colour [< LIME [2]] —**lime green** *n*

limekiln /līm kiln/ *n* an oven that is used for heating limestone to produce quicklime [13C. < LIME [1]]

limelight /līm līt/ *n* **1. FOCUS OF ATTENTION** the focus of attention or public interest **2. LAMP IN WHICH QUICKLIME IS HEATED** a lamp used as an early form of stage lighting in which quicklime is heated to produce a brilliant light **3. LIGHT FROM LIMELIGHT** the light that a limelight lamp produces [Early 19C. < LIME [1]]

limerick /límmərik/ *n* a five-line humorous poem with a characteristic rhythm, often dealing with a risqué

subject and typically opening with a line such as 'There was a young lady called Jenny'. Lines one, two, and five rhyme with each other and have three metrical feet, and lines three and four rhyme with each other and have two metrical feet. [Late 19C. After LIMERICK, probably from nonsense songs with this rhyme scheme and the refrain 'will you come up to Limerick']

Limerick /límmərik/ **1.** port and chief city of Limerick County, southwestern Republic of Ireland. Population: 52,039 (2002). **2.** county in the southwestern Republic of Ireland, in Munster Province. Population: 165,042 (2002). Area: 2,686 sq. km/1,039 sq. mi.

limescale /lím skayl/ *n* a white deposit that forms on a surface such as the inside of a kettle or boiler because of the evaporation of water containing lime [< LIME [1]]

limestone /lím stōn/ *n* sedimentary rock formed from the skeletons and shells of sea organisms that consists chiefly of calcium carbonate. Use: in construction, in making lime and cement. [15C. < LIME [1]]

lime tree *n* TREES same as **lime** [3] (sense 1)

limewater /lím wawtər/ *n* **1.** a clear alkaline solution of calcium hydroxide in water. Use: in skin lotions, as an antacid. **2.** water that is naturally high in dissolved calcium carbonate or calcium sulphate [Late 17C. < LIME [1]]

limey /límí/ *ANZ, N Am n* **1.** OFFENSIVE TERM an offensive term for a British person (*slang*) **2.** BRITISH SHIP a British commercial or naval vessel (*slang disapproving*) ■ *adj* OFFENSIVE TERM an offensive term meaning coming from or relating to the United Kingdom (*slang*) [Late 19C. Shortening and alteration of *lime-juicer*, because sailors in the British Navy drank lime juice to prevent scurvy]

liminal /límmin'l/ *adj* belonging to the point of conscious awareness below which something cannot be experienced or felt [Late 19C. < Latin *limin-* 'threshold']

limit /límmit/ *n* **1.** FURTHEST POINT, DEGREE, OR AMOUNT the furthest point, degree, amount, or boundary, especially one that cannot or should not be passed or exceeded ○ *The car was tested to its limits on the test track.* **2.** MAXIMUM OR MINIMUM AMOUNT ALLOWED the maximum or minimum amount, or the largest or lowest quantity, that is available or allowed ○ *an upper age limit of 12 years* **3.** BOUNDARY OF AREA the boundary or edge of an area, or something that marks a boundary or edge (*often used in the plural*) ○ *the city limits* **4.** RESTRICTION a feature or circumstance that restricts what can be done ○ *a time limit* **5.** GAMBLING MAXIMUM MONEY ALLOWED IN BETTING the maximum amount of money that can be staked at any one time in various games of chance **6.** MATHS MAXIMUM OF MATHEMATICAL FUNCTION a numerical value approached by a mathematical function as the independent variable of the function approaches infinity or a specific value **7.** MATHS VALUE SPECIFYING INTEGRAL'S RANGE one of the two given values specifying the range over which a definite integral is evaluated ■ *vt* (**-its, -iting, -ited**) **1.** RESTRICT SOMETHING to restrict something or somebody in number or quantity, or restrict something to a particular group ○ *had to limit the number of guests because of space problems* **2.** BE BOUNDARY TO AREA to be or act as a boundary to an area [14C. < Latin *limit-* 'boundary'] —**limitable** *adj* ◇ **be the limit** to be so bad as to be almost beyond what somebody is able or prepared to tolerate ◇ **over the limit** with more alcohol in the bloodstream than the driver of a vehicle is legally permitted to have

limitary /límmitəri/ *adj* (*archaic*) **1.** on which limits are imposed **2.** imposing limits

limitation /límmi táysh'n/ *n* **1.** RESTRICTION an imposed restriction that cannot be exceeded or sidestepped ○ *limitations on the height of vehicles* **2.** RESTRICTING FLAW a disadvantage or weakness in somebody or something (*often used in the plural*) ○ *One of the limitations of the program is the amount of memory it requires.* **3.** SETTING OF LIMIT the act of limiting something ○ *damage limitation* **4.** LAW MAXIMUM DELAY ALLOWED a particular period of time within which a legal action must start **5.** LAW LEGAL RESTRICTION a legal restriction on the powers that somebody has

limit down *n* under futures exchange rules, the point reached by a commodity price that has fallen by the maximum amount allowed in a single day's trading

limited /límmitid/ *adj* **1.** WITH LIMIT IMPOSED on which some form of limit or restriction is imposed ○ *We have limited space available.* **2.** LACKING FULL SCOPE existing at or below the full degree or extent, usually far below ○ *limited powers* **3.** OF RELATIVELY LITTLE TALENT with talents or skills that fall short of what is expected or required **4.** POL LACKING FULL AUTHORITY lacking a full range of powers, especially because of constitutional or legal limitations **5.** COMM WITH RESTRICTED SHAREHOLDER LIABILITY describes a business enterprise whose shareholders' liability for any debts or losses is restricted —**limitedly** *adv* —**limitedness** *n*

limited company *n* a company in which the shareholders' liability for any debts or losses is restricted

limited edition *n* an edition, especially of a book or an art print, of which only a specific number of copies have been made. This has the effect of increasing the item's value. (*hyphenated when used before a noun*) ○ *limited-edition prints*

limited liability *n* an investor's liability for no greater a proportion of a company's debt than is represented by the value of his or her financial stake in the business

limited partner *n* a business partner who has no management responsibility and whose liability for company debts is limited to his or her financial stake —**limited partnership** *n*

limited war *n* a war in which it is not the aim of the participants to defeat or destroy the enemy totally, especially a war in which nuclear weapons are available but are not used

limiter /límmitər/ *n* **1.** an electronic circuit that limits the amplitude of an output wave to a specific value **2.** somebody or something that has a restricting effect

limiting /límmiting/ *adj* **1.** imposing limits, especially limits on the scope for development, progress, or improvement ○ *a limiting factor* **2.** describes an adjective that identifies rather than describes the referent of a noun, as the possessive 'your' does in 'your house'. The term 'limiting adjective' has now largely been superseded by the term 'determiner'.

limitless /límmitləss/ *adj* very great in amount, extent, or degree ○ *limitless resources* —**limitlessly** *adv* —**limitlessness** *n*

limit order *n* an order instructing an investment broker to buy or sell something at a specific price or one better than it within a limited period of time

limit point *n* a point in a set of mathematical points, such that for every neighbourhood around the point at least one other point in the set is contained in the neighbourhood

limit up *n* under futures exchange rules, the point reached by a commodity price that has risen by the maximum amount allowed in a single day's trading

limn /lim/ (**limns, limning, limned**) *vt* (*literary*) **1.** to draw or paint a picture of somebody or something, especially in outline **2.** to describe something in words [15C. Alteration of obsolete *lumine* 'illustrate a manuscript', via French < Latin *luminare* 'illumine' < *lumin-* 'light'] —**limner** *n*

limnetic /lim néttik/ *adj* relating to or living in the deep open water of a freshwater pond or lake [Late 19C. < Greek *limnētēs* 'living in marshes' < *limnē* 'marshy lake']

limnology /lim nólləji/ *n* the scientific study of lakes and other bodies of fresh water, including their physical and biological features [Late 19C. < Greek *limnē* 'marshy lake'] —**limnological** /límnə lójjik'l/ *adj* —**limnologically** *adv* —**limnologist** *n*

limo /límmō/ (*plural* **-os**) *n* same as **limousine** (*informal*) [Mid-20C. Shortening]

Limoges[1] /li mōzh/ *n* a fine porcelain made in the town of Limoges, France, since the 19th century

Limoges[2] /li mōzh/ capital of Haute-Vienne Department and Limousin Region, central France. Famous for its enamel work and porcelain, it is situated on the River Vienne, about 177 km/110 mi. northeast of Bordeaux. Population: 133,968 (1999).

limonene /límmə neen/ *n* a liquid unsaturated hydrocarbon that smells like lemon and is found in the essential oils of citrus fruits and peppermint. Use: a wetting agent and in making resins. Formula: $C_{10}H_{16}$. [Mid-19C. < German *Limonen* < *Limone* 'lemon']

limonite /límə nīt/ *n* a hydrated iron oxide ore that varies in colour from dark brown to yellow [Early 19C. < German *Limonit* < Greek *leimōn* 'meadow'] —**limonitic** /límə níttik/ *adj*

Limousin /límmoo zan, -zàN/ *n* a large hardy beef cow, belonging to a breed that originated in Limousin, a region of central France

limousine /límmə zeén, -zeen/ *n* **1.** a large luxurious car, usually chauffeur-driven, with a partition between the chauffeur and passengers **2.** *N Am* a vehicle used to transport passengers to and from an airport, usually between a hotel and airport [Early 20C. < French, form of *limousin* 'cloak with a cape', after *Limousin*, France]

limp[1] /limp/ *vi* (**limps, limping, limped**) **1.** WALK UNEVENLY to walk with an uneven step because of an injury or disability **2.** PROCEED WITH DIFFICULTY to move or continue with great difficulty ○ *The business limped through the recession.* ■ *n* IMPAIRED GAIT a way of walking or running that involves a degree of motion impairment (*sometimes offensive*) [Late 16C. Probably back-formation < obsolete *limphalt* 'walking unevenly' < Old English *lempheált* < *lemp-* (< Indo-European) + HALT [2]] —**limper** *n*

limp[2] /limp/ *adj* **1.** FLEXIBLE without stiffness or rigidity **2.** WEAK without strength, power, or firmness ○ *a limp handshake* **3.** LACKING FORCE without energy, vitality, or enthusiasm **4.** LACKING VOLUME OR SUBSTANCE without a firm or substantial feel or texture **5.** NOT STIFFENED BY BOARDS describes a book cover that is not stiffened by boards but is made of more durable material than a paperback **6.** UNCONVINCING not very convincing [Early 18C. Origin ?] —**limply** *adv* —**limpness** *n*

limpet /límpit/ (*plural* **-pets** or *same*) *n* a small invertebrate sea animal that has a low rough conical shell and clings to rocks. Native to: cool Atlantic and Pacific waters. Order: Archeogastropoda. [Pre-12C. Via medieval Latin *lampreda* < late Latin *lampetra*]

limpet mine *n* an explosive device that can be attached to the hull of a ship

limpid /límpid/ *adj* **1.** CLEAR clear and transparent **2.** LUCID expressing something in a way that is clear and easy to understand ○ *limpid prose* **3.** UNWORRIED emotionally calm and composed [Early 17C. Directly or via French < Latin *limpidus* 'clear'] —**limpidity** /lim píddəti/ *n* —**limpidly** *adv* —**limpidness** *n*

limpkin /límpkin/ (*plural* **-kins** or *same*) *n* a wading bird with a long neck, a long curved beak, long legs, and short rounded wings. Native to: South America, southeastern North America. Latin name: *Aramus guarauna.* [Late 19C. < LIMP [1]; from its limping walk]

Limpopo /lim pópō/ river in southeastern Africa. Length: 1,800 km/1,100 mi.

Limpopo Province province in South Africa, in the northernmost part of the country. Capital: Polokwane. Population: 5,273,647 (2001). Area: 47,830 sq. mi./123,910 sq. km. Former name **Northern Province**

limp-wristed /-rístid/ *adj* an offensive term meaning effeminate (*insult*) [< a posture of the wrists and hands offensively associated with effeminate men]

limulus /límmyōōləss/ (*plural* **-li** /-lī/ or *same*) *n* a member of a group of arthropods that includes the horseshoe crab. Genus: *Limulus.* [Mid-19C. Via modern Latin < Latin, 'somewhat sidelong' < *limus* 'oblique'; from the crab's motion]

limy /límí/ (**-ier, -iest**) *adj* **1.** smeared with birdlime **2.** consisting of, containing, or similar to lime

lin. *abbr* **1.** lineal **2.** linear

linac /línnak/ *n* PHYS same as **linear accelerator** [Mid-20C. Contraction]

Linacre /línnəkər/, **Thomas** (1460?–1524) English humanist and physician. He was an advocate of modern science and education, translated Galen, and founded the Royal College of Physicians in London.

> 'Either this is not the gospel or we are not Christians.'
> [Attributed to Thomas Linacre]

linage /línij/, **lineage** *n* **1.** the number of lines in a printed text **2.** a fixed payment per line of printed text made to the author

linalool

linalool /li nállō ol/, **linalol** /línnə lol/ *n* a colourless liquid with a pleasant smell. Source: essential plant oils. Use: manufacture of perfumes. Formula: $C_{10}H_{18}O$. [Late 19C. < Mexican Spanish *linaloĕ*, via Spanish < late Latin *lignum aloes* 'wood of the aloe']

Lin Biao /lín byów/ (1907?–71) Chinese military and political leader. He successfully commanded Communist forces during the Chinese Civil War, and died in an air crash after a failed coup attempt.

linchpin /línch pin/, **lynchpin** *n* **1.** somebody or something that is an essential element in the success of something such as a team or a plan **2.** a pin placed crosswise through an axle to prevent a wheel from coming off [14C. < obsolete *linch* 'linchpin' < Old English *lynis*]

Lincoln[1] /língkən/ *n* a heavy-fleeced sheep belonging to a breed originally developed in Lincolnshire. Kept for: mainly meat. [Mid-19C. After LINCOLNSHIRE]

Lincoln[2] /língkən/ **1.** historic cathedral city in eastern England. Population: 85,616 (2002). **2.** state capital of Nebraska and seat of Lancaster County, situated in the southeastern part of the state. It is home to the University of Nebraska, Union College, and Nebraska Wesleyan University. Population: 232,362 (2002 estimate).

Abraham Lincoln

Lincoln, Abraham (1809–65) 16th president of the United States. A Republican, he took office in 1861, led the North to victory in the US Civil War, and announced the emancipation of slaves in the southern Confederate states (1863). His Gettysburg Address, delivered on 19 November 1863, became one of the great texts of US history. Lincoln was assassinated by John Wilkes Booth while attending a performance at Ford's Theatre in Washington, DC. See table at **president**

> 'The world will little note, nor long remember, what we say here, but it can never forget what they did here. It is for us, the living, rather to be dedicated here to the unfinished work which they who fought here have thus far so nobly advanced. It is rather for us...that government of the people, by the people, and for the people, shall not perish from the earth.'
> [Abraham Lincoln, *Address*, Gettysburg; 19 November 1863]

Lincoln green *adj* of a bright green colour [After LINCOLN[2] (sense 1) where cloth of this colour was first manufactured] —**Lincoln green** *n*

Lincolnshire /língkənshər/ county in eastern England, bordering the North Sea and its inlet the Wash. Population: 646,646 (2001). Area: 5,885 sq. km/2,272 sq. mi.

Lincolnshire Wolds region of chalk hills in the northern and western parts of Lincolnshire, eastern England

Lincs. *abbr* Lincolnshire

linctus /língktəss/ *n* a medicinal syrup given to relieve coughs and soothe sore throats [Late 17C. < medieval Latin, '(medicine) for licking' < Latin *lingere* 'to lick']

Lind /lind/, **Jenny** (1820–87) Swedish soprano. The best-known singer of her day, she established the Mendelssohn Scholarships and various charities. Born **Johanna Maria Lind Goldschmidt**. Known as **the Swedish Nightingale**

lindane /lín dayn/ *n* a white poisonous crystalline powder that biodegrades very slowly. Use: insecticide, weedkiller. Formula: $C_6H_6Cl_6$. [Mid-20C. After Teunis van der *Linden*, 20C Dutch chemist]

Charles Augustus Lindbergh and Anne Lindbergh

Lindbergh /límd burg/, **Charles** (1902–74) US aviator and engineer. In 1927 he became the first person to fly solo across the Atlantic, which he described in *The Spirit of St Louis* (1953). Full name **Lindbergh, Charles Augustus**. Known as **Lucky Lindy**

linden /líndən/ (*plural* **-dens** or *same*) *n Aus, US* a deciduous hardwood tree with heart-shaped leaves and clusters of white, yellowish or green flowers, often planted for shade or ornament, or grown for timber. Native to: northern hemisphere. Genus: *Tilia*. UK, NZ, Can term **lime**[3] [Late 16C. < *linden* 'made of lime wood' < Old English *lind* 'lime tree' < Germanic]

Lindisfarne /líndiss faarn/ island off the northeastern coast of England, separated from the shore by tidal waters. It is the site of a seventh-century monastery founded by St Aidan. Area: 5 sq. km/2 sq. mi.

Lindrum /líndrəm/, **Walter** (1898–1960) Australian billiards player. He was the world champion (1933–50) and made a world-record break of 4,317 (1932). Full name **Lindrum, Walter Albert**

Lindsay /líndzi/, **Jack** (1900–90) Australian writer and historian. The eldest son of Norman Lindsay, he gained an international reputation for his writings on philosophy and art history. He also published novels, including *Rising Tide* (1953).

Lindsay, Norman (1879–1969) Australian artist and writer. He was noted for his paintings, drawings, and etchings of classical and erotic scenes, and for his children's story *The Magic Pudding* (1918). Full name **Lindsay, Norman Alfred William**

Lindsay, Vachel (1879–1931) US poet. He wrote *General Booth Enters into Heaven* (1913) and *The Congo and Other Poems* (1914). Full name **Lindsay, Nicholas Vachel**

> 'A nation of one hundred fine, mob-hearted, lynching, relenting, repenting millions.'
> [Vachel Lindsay, 'Bryan, Bryan, Bryan, Bryan', *Collected Poems*; 1923]

lindy /líndi/, **lindy hop** *n* a lively dance for couples that is similar to the jitterbug [Early 20C. After *Lindy*, nickname of Charles LINDBERGH]

line[1] /līn/ *n* **1.** LONG NARROW MARK a long narrow mark or stroke made on or in a surface **2.** ROW a row of people or things **3.** *N Am* PEOPLE WAITING a row of people or things waiting for a turn at something or for admittance to a place ○ *He's too impatient to wait in line.* **4.** DIRECTION a path or direction of movement ○ *The object was moving in a straight line towards us.* **5.** SHAPE the characteristic shape or contour of something (*often used in the plural*) ○ *the car's sleek lines* **6.** BORDER a boundary or division between two properties, jurisdictions, or political units **7.** SPORTS CONFINING BOUNDARY a long narrow mark that shows the boundary of any of the divisions of a playing area or race track **8.** LIMIT any limit or division ○ *a thin line between happiness and misery* **9.** SERIES OF PEOPLE a series of people, usually in the same family, who follow one another in the same job or role ○ *the last in a long line of musicians* **10.** SERIES OF EVENTS a series of related events or situations ○ *the latest in a long line of disasters for the company* **11.** FACIAL MARK a wrinkle or crease in the skin of the face (*often used in the plural*) **12.** APPROACH a course or approach followed in doing something ○ *his line of reasoning* ○ *We must decide what line to take before the meeting.* **13.** POLICY a policy, a way of thinking, or a version of something ○ *What's the government line on this?* **14.** DECEIVING TALK something said to deceive, impress, or attract somebody (*informal*) ○ *gave me that old line about the dog eating his homework* **15.** BRIEF MESSAGE a short written message ○ *Why not drop me a line?* **16.** CONNECTION a telephone connection **17.** TYPE OF MERCHANDISE a particular type of product or merchandise ○ *our new line of children's wear* **18.** THIN ROPE a length of rope or wire **19.** SPECIALIZED FIELD a particular area of interest, work, activity, or expertise ○ *in my line of work* **20.** USEFUL INFORMATION useful information or an insight into something **21.** ELECTRIC CABLE a cable used for transmitting electric power or electronic messages **22.** ROW OF PRINT a row of words or numbers on a page or other surface ○ *a few lines of doggerel* **23.** MEDIA PART OF TELEVISION PICTURE a horizontal scan that with many others forms the picture on a television screen **24.** RAIL TRACK the track on which a railway train runs **25.** RAIL FIXED RAILWAY ROUTE a particular part of a railway network **26.** TRANSP TRANSPORT COMPANY a company that runs a regular service of buses, ships, or aircraft on a route **27.** TRANSP ROUTE a rail, sea, or air route served by a transport organization **28.** AMERICAN FOOTBALL AMERICAN FOOTBALL PLAYERS in American football, either of the two rows of opposing players facing each other on either side of the line of scrimmage **29.** MUSIC MELODY the notes that make up a melody **30.** MUSIC PART OF STAVE a horizontal mark that is one of five that make up a stave **31.** MIL POSITIONED FORMATION a formation of troops, ships, weapons, or fortifications positioned in a place (*often used in the plural*) ○ *behind enemy lines* **32.** MIL FIGHTING FORCE the military or naval units of a country that actually go into battle **33.** MATHS ONE-DIMENSIONAL ELEMENT in mathematics, a straight geometrical element that has length but not width or thickness and whose identity is determined by two points **34.** MATHS TRACED PATH OF POINT in mathematics, an imaginary path that has length but not width, traced by a moving point **35.** ELECTRONICS NARROW BAND OF FREQUENCIES a narrow band of frequencies in an electromagnetic spectrum **36.** *US* SPORTS ODDS odds for wagering **37.** DRUGS AMOUNT OF DRUG a portion of a drug such as cocaine scraped into a long thin row to be inhaled (*slang*) **38.** GEOG EQUATOR the equator (*dated*) **39.** *Scotland* NOTE OF AUTHORIZATION a note of authorization, especially a medical certificate issued by a doctor (*informal*) **40.** *Ireland* ROAD a road, especially a new road ■ **lines** *npl* **1.** CERTIFICATE a certificate, especially a marriage certificate **2.** SCHOOL PUNISHMENT a phrase or sentence that a school pupil is made to write out a particular number of times as a punishment, or the material that is actually written out **3.** ACTOR'S WORDS the spoken words that make up an actor's part ■ *vt* (**lines, lining, lined**) **1.** MARK LINE ON SOMETHING to mark something with lines **2.** ARRANGE SOMETHING ALONG EDGE to arrange or be arranged along the edge or length of something ○ *shrubs lining the driveway* [Pre-12C. Directly or via French *ligne* < Latin *linea* 'linen string, line' < *linum* 'flax, linen'; partly < Old English *līne*, probably via Germanic < Latin *linea*] —**linable** *adj* ◇ **all along the line** throughout or at every stage in something ◇ **down** or **along the line 1.** at some time in the future ○ *looking for improvements down the line* **2.** at every stage ○ *poor communications all down the line* ◇ **draw the line** to restrict or set limits at a particular point ◇ **hold the line 1.** to keep a telephone connection open while waiting to speak to somebody **2.** to resist a military

attack without giving ground or allowing a formation to be broken ◇ **in line 1.** arranged in an orderly row **2.** in keeping with a policy or obedient to a set of rules ◇ **in line for** likely to receive something such as a promotion or position ◇ **in line with** in agreement or conformity with something ◇ **lay it on the line** to speak about something frankly (*informal*) ◇ **lay** *or* **put something on the line** to risk by some action the loss of something valuable (*informal*) ◇ **out of line** *US* (*informal*) **1.** rude and disrespectful **2.** unruly or out of control ◇ **read between the lines** to deduce something that is not made explicit (*informal*) ◇ **shoot a line** to exaggerate abilities or attributes in order to impress somebody (*informal*) ◇ **toe the line** to comply with what is expected

line up *v* **1.** *vti* **FORM ROW** to form a row, or form people or things into a row **2.** *vi* **FORM QUEUE** to form a queue to wait for a turn **3.** *vt* **PROVIDE SOMETHING** to organize, provide, or make something available to somebody ○ *had lined up a programme of entertainments for us* **4.** *vti* **ALIGN THINGS** to align two or more things, or be in alignment

line[2] /līn/ (**lines, lining, lined**) *vt* **1. REINFORCE SOMETHING** to cover or reinforce the inside or unexposed surface of something ○ *a jacket lined with silk* **2. COVER SOMETHING** to completely cover something with something else ○ *The walls were lined with books.* **3. FILL SOMETHING** to fill or supply something with something else ○ *a good hot meal to line your stomach* [14C. < obsolete *line* 'spun flax' < Old English *līn*, probably via Germanic < Latin *linum* 'flax'; from the use of linen to line garments]

lineage[1] /línni ij/ *n* **1.** the line of descent from an ancestor to a person or family **2.** a group of people related by descent from a common ancestor [14C. < French *lignage* < *ligne* (see LINE [1])]

lineage[2] /línij/ *n* MEDIA another spelling of **linage**

lineal /línni əl/ *adj* **1.** in a direct line from an ancestor ○ *a lineal descendant of Charlemagne* **2.** relating to or derived from direct descent ○ *a lineal claim to the throne* **3.** MATHS, ART, ELECTRONICS, BOT same as **linear** —**lineally** *adv*

lineament /línni əmənt/ *n* **1. FACIAL FEATURE** a feature or contour of a face (*literary*) **2. CHARACTERISTIC FEATURE** a characteristic feature, especially of something immaterial (*literary*) **3. FEATURE OF LAND** a major topographical feature such as a long fault plane that reveals something about its subsurface [15C. < Latin *lineamentum* 'line' < *lineare* 'make straight' < *linea* 'line']

linear /línni ər/ *adj* **1. RELATING TO LINES** relating to, consisting of, or using lines **2. RELATING TO STRAIGHT LINE** relating to a straight line or capable of being represented by a straight line **3. CHANGING PROPORTIONALLY** describes variables that change proportionally and are representable on a graph as a straight line ○ *There's no linear relation between mortality and size.* **4.** ART **WITH CLEARLY DEFINED LINES** relying for its visual effect on clearly defined lines rather than on colour **5.** MATHS **OF FIRST DEGREE** about or in the first degree relative to a mathematical variable **6.** ELECTRONICS **WITH OUTPUT VARYING AS INPUT DOES** with an output that varies directly with the input **7.** BOT **LONG AND NARROW** describes a leaf that is long and narrow —**linearity** /línni árrəti/ *n* —**linearly** *adv*

Linear A *n* an undeciphered writing system, dating from about 1500 BC and found on clay remains in Crete

linear accelerator *n* a device that propels charged particles in straight paths by using alternating high-frequency voltages

linear algebra *n* a branch of algebra dealing with linear transformations, vector spaces, matrices, and determinants

Linear B *n* an early form of Greek that dates from about 1400 BC, found on clay remains in Crete and the Greek mainland, and deciphered around 1952

linear equation *n* an equation with no variable raised to a power

linear function *n* MATHS same as **linear transformation**

linear induction motor *n* ENG same as **linear motor**

linearize /línni ə rīz/ (**-izes, -izing, -ized**), **linearise** (**-ises, -ising, -ised**) *vt* to form or project something into a line (*technical*) —**linearization** /línni ə rī záysh'n/ *n*

linear measure *n* any system or unit used to measure length

linear momentum *n* PHYS same as **momentum** (sense 3)

linear motor *n* an electric motor in which the motion between the rotor and stator is linear so that thrust is produced along a straight line

linear perspective *n* a form of perspective in which drawings or paintings are given apparent depth by showing parallel lines as converging on the horizon

linear programming *n* in mathematics, a method of finding the maximum and minimum values of a linear transformation using variables that are subject to constraints

linear transformation *n* a mathematical transformation in which the resulting variables are neither multiplied together nor raised to any power

lineation /línni áysh'n/ *n* **1.** division into or arrangement of lines **2.** the outline of an image

linebacker /līn bakər/ *n* in American football, a player who takes a position near and behind the defensive line —**linebacking** *n*

line breeding *n* the deliberate mating of closely related individuals in order to retain characteristics of a common ancestor

line cut *n* a photoengraving made from a line drawing

lined /līnd/ *adj* **1. WITH LINES** with marked horizontal lines ○ *Use lined paper.* **2. WRINKLED** with wrinkles and signs of age ○ *a lined face* **3. WITH LINING** having a lining ○ *a lined jacket*

line dancing *n* a style of dancing to country-and-western music in which dancers perform in rows —**line dance** *n, vi* —**line dancer** *n*

line drawing *n* a drawing done entirely in lines, with tones shown by the thickness or closeness of the lines

line engraving *n* an engraving in which lines are cut by hand into a metal plate from which the print is made

linefish /līn fish/ (*plural same*) *n S Africa* any edible sea fish caught by a hand-line either from a boat or the shore

line item *n* an item of important financial data presented on a separate line, e.g. in a ledger or an annual report

line judge *n* in sports such as tennis, an official who assists the umpire by signalling that the ball is out of play

Lineker /línnəkər/, **Gary** (*b.* 1960) British footballer. Noted for his skill as a goal scorer, he was top scorer in the 1986 World Cup. Full name **Lineker, Gary Winston**

lineman /līnmən/ (*plural* **-men** /-mən/) *n* **1.** *N Am* same as **linesman** (sense 3) **2.** in American football, a player on the forward line, especially a centre, guard, tackle, or tight end **3.** a surveyor's assistant who marks points or positions

line management *n* the managers in a company who are involved in production or the central part of the business, as opposed to managers of service sectors

line manager *n* a manager in a company who is involved in production or the central part of the business and to whom an employee below management level is directly answerable

linen /línnin/ (*plural same* or **-ens**) *n* **1.** a thread or durable fabric made from the spun fibres of flax **2.** clothes, table coverings, undergarments, or bedclothes made from linen or cotton (*often used in the plural*) [Old English *līnen* 'made of flax' < *līn* (see LINE [2])]

linen paper *n* fine paper that is made from flax fibres or given a finish to resemble linen

Line of Control *n* the line separating the areas of the disputed territory of Kashmir controlled by India and Pakistan. It was established in 1972 after a ceasefire agreement between the two sides.

line of credit *n* the amount of credit that a customer is allowed to draw on

line officer *n* an officer who serves in combat

line of fire *n* **1.** a position in which somebody is exposed to a threat, attack, or criticism **2.** the path taken by a bullet or missile fired from a weapon

line of force *n* an imaginary curve whose tangent at any point is that of the electric or magnetic field that is operating there

line of sight *n* **1.** an imaginary line from an observer to a distant object **2.** a straight path, unobstructed by the horizon, between a transmitting and receiving aerial

line-out *n* in rugby union, a restart of play in which the ball is thrown from the touchline for two lines of opposing forwards to jump and catch

line printer *n* a printing device that prints a line at a time rather than one character at a time

liner[1] /līnər/ *n* **1.** a passenger ship or aeroplane run by a shipping line or airline **2.** COSMETICS same as **eyeliner** [< LINE [1]]

liner[2] /līnər/ *n* **1.** something used as a lining or padding **2.** *US* RECORDING same as **sleeve** *n* (sense 2) **3.** a protective sleeve, usually made of metal, fitted inside or outside a cylindrical component [< LINE [2]]

liner notes *npl N Am* RECORDING same as **sleeve notes**

linesman /līnzmən/ (*plural* **-men** /-mən/) *n* **1. UMPIRE'S ASSISTANT** in sports such as tennis an official, especially a man, who assists the umpire by signalling that the ball is out of play **2. AMERICAN FOOTBALL OFFICIAL** in American football, an official who watches for infringements, marks the downs, and places the ball in position **3. REFEREE'S ASSISTANT** in football, an assistant referee positioned along a touchline (*dated*) **4. SOMEBODY MAINTAINING PHONE OR POWER LINES** somebody who installs or repairs telephone or power lines. N Am term **lineman**

line spectrum *n* a spectrum produced by a gas emitting light or a gas selectively absorbing light emitted by another source that consists of a series of distinct parallel lines

linesperson /līnz purss'n/ (*plural* **-sons**) *n* in sports such as tennis, football, and American football, an official who assists the referee or umpire, e.g. by signalling that a ball is out of play

line squall *n* a strong storm advancing along a weather front

lineswoman /līnz wŏŏmən/ (*plural* **-women** /-wimmin/) *n* in sports such as tennis, football, and American football, a woman official who assists the referee or umpire, e.g. by signalling that a ball is out of play

lineup /līn up/, **line-up** *n* **1. LIST OF PLAYERS** a list of players in a team together with the positions they play in **2. TELEVISION SCHEDULE** a programming schedule of a television network **3.** *N Am* CRIME same as **identification parade** **4. GROUP UNITED IN PURPOSE** a group of people or organizations recruited for a cause or common purpose such as raising funds for a charity **5.** *US* **SOMETHING FORMING LINE** a line of people or things

ling[1] /ling/ (*plural same* or **lings**) *n* **1. EUROPEAN SEA FISH** a fish related to cod. Native to: coastal waters of Greenland and northern Europe. Genus: *Molva*. **2. AUSTRALIAN FOOD FISH** a fish that lives near the sea floor. Native to: Australia. Genus: *Genypterus*. **3. LING AS FOOD** the flesh of a ling used as food [13C. Probably < Dutch or Low German]

ling[2] /ling/ *n* PLANTS same as **heather** (sense 1) [14C. < Old Norse *lyng*]

-ling[1] *suffix* **1.** one connected with or resembling ○ *hatchling* **2.** small one ○ *princeling* ○ *spiderling* [Old English, < Germanic]

-ling[2] *suffix* in a particular manner or condition ○ *darkling* [Old English, < Germanic]

Lingala /ling gáalə/ *n* a Bantu language used as a lingua franca in the Democratic Republic of Congo. Native speakers: 10 million. [Early 20C. < Bantu]

lingam /líng gəm/ *n* **1. PHALLIC SYMBOL** in Hinduism, a stylized phallus, used to represent the god Shiva **2. PENIS** a penis **3. SANSKRIT MASCULINE GENDER** the masculine gender in Sanskrit grammar [Early 18C. < Sanskrit *liṅga* 'mark, phallus']

lingcod /líng kod/ (*plural same* or **-cods**) *n* a spiny-finned large-mouthed game fish whose flesh is used as food. Native to: North Pacific Ocean. Latin name: *Ophidion elongatus*. [Mid-20C. < LING [1] + COD [1]]

linger /líng gər/ (**-gers, -gering, -gered**) *vi* **1. PUT OFF LEAVING** to delay leaving somewhere because of reluctance

to go **2. WAIT AROUND** to wait around or move about a place slowly and idly **3. BE BARELY ALIVE** to remain alive, although very weak, while gradually dying **4. TAKE TIME TO DO SOMETHING** to take longer than is usual to do something, e.g. to complete a task or look at somebody or something, usually because you are enjoying yourself ○ *Her eyes lingered on the letter.* **5. PERSIST** to remain fixed in the mind or noticed by the senses for a long time [13C. < obsolete *ling* 'delay, linger' < Old English *lengan* 'lengthen'] —**lingerer** *n*

lingerie /lánzhəri, lónzhəri, láNzhəri/ *n* women's underwear and nightdresses [Early 19C. < French, 'things made of linen' < *linge* 'linen' < Latin *lineus* 'made of flax' < *linum* 'flax']

lingering /líng gəring/ *adj* **1. DRAWN-OUT** long and drawn-out, especially with pain **2. SLOW** done slowly in order to prolong something as long as possible **3. PERSISTING IN MIND** remaining for some time in the thoughts or mind —**lingeringly** *adv*

lingo /líng gō/ (*plural* -**goes**) *n* (*informal*) **1.** a language that is not the speaker's native language **2.** a specialized set of terms requiring to be learned like a language ○ *the complicated lingo of lawyers* [Mid-17C. Origin ?]

SYNONYMS See *jargon*[1].

lingua /líng gwə/ (*plural* -**guae** /-gwee/) *n* the tongue or a part resembling one [Late 17C. < Latin, 'tongue']

lingua franca /líng gwə frángkə/ (*plural* **lingua francas** or **linguae francae** /-gwee-kee/) *n* **1.** a language or mixture of languages used for communication by people who speak different first languages **2.** the mixed language used chiefly by merchants throughout Mediterranean ports until the 18th century, consisting mainly of Italian with features of French, Spanish, Greek, Arabic, and Turkish [Late 17C. < Italian, 'Frankish tongue']

lingual /líng gwəl/ *adj* **1.** relating to, using, or similar to the tongue **2.** describes speech sounds formed with the tongue [Mid-17C. < medieval Latin *lingualis* < Latin *lingua* 'tongue'] —**lingually** *adv*

linguine /ling gwéeni/, **linguini** *n* pasta made in long narrow flat strips [Mid-20C. < Italian, plural of *linguina* 'little tongue' < *lingua* 'tongue' < Latin]

linguist /líng gwist/ *n* **1.** a speaker or adept learner of several languages **2.** an expert in or student of linguistics [Late 16C. < Latin *lingua* 'tongue']

linguistic /ling gwístik/ *adj* **1.** relating to language or languages **2.** relating to linguistics —**linguistically** *adv*

linguistic atlas *n* a collection of maps showing the distribution of varying language features in a region

linguistic form *n* an identifiable unit of speech, e.g. a word, prefix, phrase, or sentence

linguistic geography *n* the study of regional variation in speech —**linguistic geographer** *n*

linguistic philosophy *n* a form of philosophy prevalent during the 20th century, asserting that the function of philosophy is to clarify philosophical expressions by analysing and explaining them

linguistics /ling gwístiks/ *n* the systematic study of language (*takes a singular verb*)

lingulate /líng gyoōlat, -layt/, **lingulated** /-layted/ *adj* shaped like a tongue [Mid-19C. < Latin *lingulatus* < *lingula* 'little tongue' < *lingua* 'tongue']

liniment /línnəmənt/ *n* a liquid rubbed into the skin to relieve aches or pain, e.g. one containing alcohol and camphor [15C. < late Latin *linimentum* < Latin *linire* 'to smear']

linin /línin/ *n* a connective material in a cell nucleus [Mid-19C. < Greek *linon* 'thread']

lining /líning/ *n* a layer or a material used to cover, protect, or insulate the inner or unexposed surface of something [14C. < LINE[2]]

link[1] /lingk/ *n* **1. PART OF CHAIN** a ring that connects with others to make up a chain, or something resembling a ring in a chain **2. CONNECTION** something that ties, connects, or relates two or more things **3. TRANSP ROUTE** any part of a transport system, especially a connection between major routes **4. BROADCAST UNIT FOR COMMUNICATING BROADCASTS** a broadcasting unit or system used to relay radio or television signals, e.g.

a transmitter, receiver, or relay station **5. MEASURE SURVEYOR'S UNIT OF LENGTH** a unit of length used in surveying, equal to 20.12 cm/7.92 in and one hundredth of a chain ■ *vti* (**links, linking, linked**) **CONNECT THINGS, OR BE CONNECTED** to connect, join, or associate somebody or something with another, or become joined with another ○ *There was no evidence to link him to the crime.* [14C. < Old Norse *hlekkr* < Germanic, 'bending'] —**linker** *n*

link up *v* **1.** *vti* to join, connect, or unite somebody or something with another, or become joined with another **2.** *vi* to meet and join with somebody or something else

link[2] /lingk/ *n* a burning torch used in the past to give light [Mid-16C. Origin ?]

linkage /língkij/ *n* **1. LINK** a link or connection, or the fact of being connected **2. POL DIPLOMATIC PROCEDURE** a procedure in diplomacy that requires progress towards an overall objective to depend on concessions made by the various parties on other related issues **3. MECH ENG SYSTEM OF INTERCONNECTED PARTS** a system of interconnected rods, springs, or levers that transmit motion in a mechanism **4. GENETICS ASSOCIATED GENES** the proximity of two or more genes on a chromosome, which tends to cause them to be inherited together

linkage group *n* two or more genes on a chromosome that tend to be inherited as a group

linking verb /língking-/ *n* GRAM same as **copula** (sense 1)

Linklater /língk laytər/, **Eric** (1899–1974) British writer, journalist, and broadcaster. He wrote novels, plays, books for children, histories, and memoirs, which include *Fanfare for a Tin Hat* (1970). Full name **Linklater, Eric Robert Russell**

> 'With a heavy step Sir Matthew left the room and spent the morning designing mausoleums for his enemies.'
> [Eric Linklater, *Juan in America*; 1931]

linkman /língk man, -mən/ (*plural* -**men** /-men/) *n* BROADCAST same as **anchorman** (sense 1)

Linköping /líng chúrping/ industrial city and capital of Östergötland County, southeastern Sweden. Population: 131,948 (1998).

links /lingks/ *n* (*takes a singular or plural verb*) **1.** a golf course, especially one near the sea **2.** *Scotland* an area of gently undulating sandy ground near a seashore [Old English *hlincas*, plural of *hlinc* 'ridge']

linkup /língk up/ *n* a connection or association between two or more things or people

Linlithgow /lin líthgō/ town in West Lothian, eastern Scotland. Population: 11,866 (1991).

linn /lin/ *n regional* a waterfall, or a pool at the foot of a waterfall [Old English *hlynn* 'torrent'; later < Gaelic *linne* 'lake, pool']

Linnaeus /li née əss, -náy-/, **Carolus** (1707–78) Swedish naturalist. A pioneer of taxonomy, he devised the standard system of binomial nomenclature for plants and animals. Born **Carl von Linné** —**Linnaean** /li née ən, -náy-/ *adj*

> 'Nature does not proceed by leaps.'
> [Carolus Linnaeus, *Philosophia Botanica*; 1750]

linnet /línnit/ (*plural* -**nets** or *same*) *n* a small brownish songbird of the finch family, the male of which has a red breast and forehead. Native to: Europe, Africa, Asia. Latin name: *Carduelis cannabina*. [Early 16C. < Old French *linette* < *lin* 'flax' < Latin *linum*; from its diet of flax seed]

Linnhe, Loch /línni/ inlet of the sea in western Scotland, at the southern end of the Great Glen. Length: 50 km/31 mi.

lino /línō/ *n* same as **linoleum** (*informal*) [Early 20C. Shortening]

linocut /línō kut/ *n* a print made from a design that has been cut in relief into a piece of linoleum and mounted on a block of wood, or the design itself

linoleate /li nóli ayt/ *n* a salt or ester of linoleic acid [Mid-19C. < *linoleic* (see LINOLEIC ACID)]

linoleic acid /línnō lée ik-/ *n* an essential fatty acid, found in grains and seeds. Formula: $C_{18}H_{32}O_2$. [< Latin *linum* 'flax' + OLEIC]

linolenic acid /línnō lée nik-/ *n* a colourless liquid, essential to human nutrition. Source: linseed and other natural oils. Use: manufacture of paints and synthetic resins. Formula: $C_{18}H_{30}O_2$. [Translation of German *Linolensäure* < *Linolsäure* 'linoleic acid', with insertion of *-en* '-ene']

linoleum /li nóli əm/ *n* a tough washable floor covering, made from canvas or other material coated under heat and pressure with powdered cork, rosin, and linseed oil [Late 19C. < Latin *linum* 'flax' + *oleum* 'oil']

linsang /lín sang/ (*plural* -**sangs** or *same*) *n* **1.** a carnivorous mammal related to and resembling the civet and genet that has spotted or banded fur and a long tail. Native to: forests of South Asia. Genus: *Prionodon*. **2.** an animal similar to the Asian linsang. Native to: forests of West Africa. Genus: *Poiana*. [Early 19C. < Javanese *lingsang*]

linseed /lín seed/ *n* the seed of the flax plant, especially when used as the source of linseed oil [Old English *línsæd* 'flax seed' < *līn* (see LINE[2])]

linseed oil *n* oil obtained from the seeds of flax plants. Use: as a binder in linoleum, paints, inks.

linsey-woolsey /línzi woólzi/ *n* a coarse cloth made from linen interwoven with wool or cotton [15C. < *linsey* (probably after Lindsey, Suffolk) + WOOL + *-sey* for rhyme]

linstock /lín stok/ *n* a long staff with a forked end designed to hold a lighted match, used in the past to fire cannons [Mid-16C. < Dutch *lontstok* < *lont* 'match' + *stok* 'stick']

lint /lint/ *n* **1. MATERIAL FOR MEDICAL DRESSINGS** a soft absorbent material made from cotton or linen. Use: wound dressing. **2. THREAD OR FLUFF** little pieces of thread or fluff **3. COTTON FIBRES** the fibres that surround unprocessed cotton seeds [14C. Origin ?] —**linty** *adj*

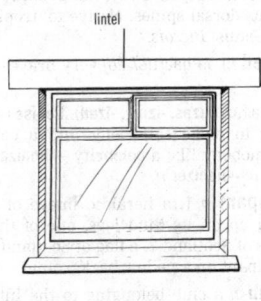

lintel

lintel /línt'l/ *n* a horizontal beam that supports the weight of the wall above a window or door [14C. < Old French < Latin *limit-* 'boundary'; influenced by Latin *limin-* 'threshold']

lintie /línti/ *n Scotland* BIRDS same as **linnet** [Late 18C. < Scots *lintwhite* 'linnet' < Old English < *līn* (see LINE[2]) + *-twige* 'plucker']

LINUX /línnəks, líněks/ *tdmk* a trademark for a computer operating system that is a free implementation of the UNIX operating system

Linz /lints/ capital of Upper Austria Province, northern Austria. Population: 189,073 (1999).

lion /líən/ *n* **1. BIG WILD PREDATORY CAT** a large wild member

lion

of the cat family that lives in extended family groups and hunts cooperatively for prey. It has a tawny yellow coat and the males have a shaggy mane. Native to: Africa, South Asia. Latin name: *Panthera leo.* **2. HERALDIC SYMBOL** the lion used as a symbol in heraldry, e.g. as the national emblems of Great Britain and of Scotland **3. SOMEBODY BRAVE AND STRONG** a brave, strong, or fierce person **4. CELEBRITY** an admired and celebrated person [13C. Via Anglo-Norman *liun* < Latin *leon* < Greek *leōn*]

Lion *n* **1.** ZODIAC same as **Leo** (sense 2) **2.** a member of a Lions Club

Lion, Gulf of /lĭ´ ən/ gulf in the Mediterranean Sea. It extends eastwards from the border between Spain and France to the French islands, les îles d'Hyères.

lion dance *n* a traditional Chinese ritual performed to bring good luck, especially at Chinese New Year, in which two men dance costumed in a large ornamental lion head and body

lioness /lĭ´ ə ness/ *n* a female lion

lionfish

lionfish /lĭ´ ən fish/ (*plural same* or **-fishes**) *n* a scorpion fish with a striped body, long spiny fins, and venomous dorsal spines. Native to: tropical Pacific Ocean. Genus: *Pterois*.

lionhearted /lĭ´ ən haártid/ *adj* very brave —**lionheartedness** *n*

lionize /lĭ´ ə nīz/ (**-izes, -izing, -ized**), **lionise** (**-ises, -ising, -ised**) *vt* to make somebody into a celebrity, or treat somebody like a celebrity —**lionization** /lĭ´ ə nī záysh'n/ *n* —**lionizer** *n*

Lion Rampant *n* **1.** a heraldic image of a red lion standing up on its hind legs, one of the national emblems of Scotland **2.** a flag of Scotland with a red lion rampant on a yellow background

Lions Club *n* a club belonging to the International Association of Lions Clubs, an organization founded in the United States in 1917 to promote fellowship and service in local communities

lion's share *n* the largest part or share of something [< Aesop's story in which a lion manages to get the whole kill in a hunt for himself]

lip /lip/ *n* **1. PART OF MOUTH** either of two fleshy folds around the mouth that help control eating, drinking, and the production of sounds by the mouth **2. SOMETHING LIKE LIP** something like a lip, especially an edge or rim of something hollow **3.** ANAT same as **labium** (sense 1) **4. IMPERTINENCE** impudent or disrespectful talk (*slang*) ■ *vt* (**lips, lipping, lipped**) **1. TOUCH SOMETHING WITH LIPS** to bring the lips into contact with something **2. FORM LIP OF SOMETHING** to form or be a lip of something [Old English *lippa* < Indo-European, 'lip'] ◇ **a stiff upper lip** a brave and composed bearing, with no giving way to emotion (*informal*) ◇ **bite your lip** (*informal*) **1.** to stop yourself from saying something you want to say **2.** to show that you are angry ◇ **button your lip** to stop speaking, not begin speaking, or keep a secret (*slang*)

lip- *prefix* same as **lipo-** (*used before vowels*)

lipa /leé pə/ (*plural same* or **-pas**) *n* a subunit of Croatian currency. See table at **currency** [< Croatian]

lipaemia /li peémi ə/ *n* the presence of excessive fat in the blood

Lipari Islands /líppəri-/ group of volcanic islands off the northern coast of Sicily in the Tyrrhenian Sea. Area: 114 sq. km/44 sq. mi.

lipase /lĭ´ payss, líppayss, lĭ´ payz, líppayz/ *n* a pancreatic enzyme that breaks down fats

lip balm *n* ANZ, N Am same as **lip salve**

lipectomy /li péktəmi, lĭ-/ (*plural* **-mies**) *n* the surgical removal of fatty tissue from beneath the skin

Li Peng /lĭ´ peng/ (*b.* 1928) prime minister of China (1987–98). Having become premier in 1987, he crushed the pro-democracy movement whose members had occupied Tiananmen Square (1989).

lip gloss *n* a cosmetic used on the lips to make them look shiny

lipid /líppid/, **lipide** *n* a biological compound that is not soluble in water, e.g. a fat. The group also includes waxes, oils, sterols, triglycerides, phosphatides, and phospholipids. [Early 20C. < French *lipide* < Greek *lipos* (see LIPO-) + French *-ide* '-id'] —**lipidic** /li píddik/ *adj*

Lipizzaner /líppit saánər/, **Lippizaner** *n* a compact, usually white or grey horse belonging to a breed often used in equestrian displays [Early 20C. < German, after *Lipizza*, near Trieste, Italy]

lip liner *n* a cosmetic, usually in soft pencil form, used to outline the lips before lipstick is applied

Lipmann /lípmən/, **Fritz Albert** (1899–1986) German-born US biochemist. He discovered the coenzyme that helps living cells derive energy from food, for which he shared the Nobel Prize in physiology or medicine (1953) with Sir Hans Krebs.

lip microphone *n* a microphone designed to be held close to the user's mouth to reduce background noise

Li Po /leé pó́/ ♦ **Li Bo**

lipo- *prefix* fat, fatty tissue ○ *lipolysis* [< Greek *lipos* 'fat' < Indo-European, 'to stick']

lipogenesis /líppō jénnəssiss, lĭ´pō-/ *n* the formation of fatty acids and other lipids in the body

lipoic acid /li pó́ ik-/ *n* a sulphur-containing fatty acid that plays a role in carbohydrate metabolism

lipoid /lípp oyd, lĭ´ poyd/ *adj* containing or resembling fat ■ *n* a substance resembling fat —**lipoidal** *adj*

lipolysis /li pólləssiss, lĭ-/ *n* the breakdown of fats into fatty acids and glycerol —**lipolytic** /líppō líttik, lĭ´pō-/ *adj*

lipoma /li pó́mə, lĭ-/ (*plural* **-mas** or **-mata** /-mətə/) *n* a benign tumour made up of fatty tissue —**lipomatous** /li pómmətəss, -pó́mətəss/ *adj*

lipophilic /líppō fíllik, lĭ´pō-/ *adj* having a chemical affinity for lipids

lipopolysaccharide /líppō pólli sákə rīd, lĭ´pō-/ *n* a complex of lipid and polysaccharide that forms the outer layer of some bacteria

lipoprotein /líppō pró́ teen, lĭ´pō-/ *n* a complex of lipids and proteins that carries lipids around the body

liposome /líppō sṓm, lĭ´pō-/ *n* a microscopic artificial sac whose walls are a double layer of phospholipids, used to carry substances such as drugs, vaccines, and enzymes to specific cells or organs of the body

liposuction /líppō suksh'n, lĭ´pō-/ *n* cosmetic surgery in which fat is removed from under the skin by vacuum suction

lipotropic /líppō tró́pik, lĭ´pō-, -tróppik/ *adj* preventing or reducing the accumulation of fat in the liver

lipotropin /líppō tró́pin, lĭ´pō-/ *n* either of two pituitary hormones that trigger the breakdown of fats in the body

-lipped *suffix* having a particular kind of lip or lips

Lippi /líppi/, **Fra Filippo** (1406?–69) Italian painter. The imposing formality of his early works gave way to a more decorative and informal style in his later works, e.g. *Madonna and Child* (1455).

lippie *n* COSMETICS another spelling of **lippy** (*informal*)

Lippizaner *n* SHOW JUMPING another spelling of **Lipizzaner**

lippy /líppi/ (*informal*) *adj* (**-pier, -piest**) tending to say impudent things ■ *n also* **lippie** same as **lipstick**

lip-read /-reed/ *vti* to understand what is said by watching how somebody's lips move rather than by listening —**lip-reader** *n*

lip-reading *n* understanding spoken words by watching lip movements, rather than by listening

lip salve *n* UK an ointment used on the lips, often in

stick form, especially to relieve chapping or dryness. ANZ, N Am term **lip balm**

Lipscomb /lípskəm/, **William** (*b.* 1919) US chemist. He conducted pioneering research on the molecular structure and chemical bonding of boron compounds and was awarded the Nobel Prize in chemistry (1976). Full name **Lipscomb, William Nunn, Jr.**

lip service *n* support or agreement that does not appear to be sincere because the words spoken are not followed up by appropriate action or behaviour

lipstick /líp stik/ *n* an oily cosmetic in stick form, in a plastic or metal tube, used to colour the lips

lipstick camera *n* a cylindrical digital device smaller than a packet of cigarettes, typically mounted on a military helmet, motor vehicle, or combat aircraft and used to make visual records of operations or potential targets

lipstick lesbian *n* a lesbian whose clothing and make-up are conventionally feminine and glamorous (*slang; sometimes considered offensive*)

lip-synch, **lip-sync** *vti* to pretend to sing or speak by moving the lips in synchronization with a recorded song or speech, or perform a song or speech in this way

lipuria /li pyoóri ə/ *n* the unusual presence of fat in the urine [Late 19C. < modern Latin < Greek *lipos* 'fat' + *ouron* 'urine']

liq. *abbr* **1.** SCI, PHON liquid **2.** BEVERAGES, COOK, PHARM liquor

liquate /li kwáyt/ (**-quates, -quating, -quated**) *vt* to heat an alloy or ore to a temperature high enough to separate the constituents with the lowest melting point from the rest [Mid-17C. < Latin *liquat-*, past participle of *liquare* 'liquefy'] —**liquation** /li kwáysh'n/ *n*

liquefacient /líkwi fáysh'nt/ *n* something that liquefies or helps to liquefy something else ■ *adj* capable of liquefying or helping to liquefy something [Mid-19C. < Latin *liquefacient-*, present participle of *liquefacere* (see LIQUEFY)]

liquefaction /líkwi fáksh'n/ *n* the process of liquefying something, or the state of having been liquefied [14C. < late Latin *liquefaction-* < Latin *liquefacere* (see LIQUEFY)]

liquefied natural gas /líkwi fīd-/ *n* a gas that is liquefied under pressure. Source: by-product of petroleum or natural gas. Use: fuel for heating, cooking, and transportation.

liquefied petroleum gas *n* a mixture of petroleum gases liquefied under pressure. Use: as heating or engine fuel.

liquefy /líkwi fī/ (**-fies, -fying, -fied**) *vti* to become liquid, or cause something to become liquid [14C. Via French *liquéfier* < Latin *liquefacere* < *liquere* 'be liquid' + *facere* 'make'] —**liquefiable** *adj* —**liquefier** *n*

liquer incorrect spelling of **liqueur**

liquescent /li kwéss'nt/ *adj* becoming or tending to become liquid [Early 18C. < Latin *liquescent-*, present participle of *liquescere* 'become liquid' < *liquere* 'be liquid'] —**liquesce** *vi* —**liquescence** *n* —**liquescency** *n*

liqueur /li kyoór/ *n* a sweet flavoured alcoholic drink usually considered an after-meal beverage [Mid-18C. Via French < Latin *liquor* 'fluid']

liquid /líkwid/ *n* **1. FLOWING SUBSTANCE** a substance in a condition in which it flows, that is a fluid at room temperature and atmospheric pressure, and whose shape but not volume can be changed **2.** PHON **CONSONANT PRONOUNCED WITHOUT FRICTION** a consonant that is pronounced without friction and is capable of being prolonged like a vowel. In modern English, 'l' and 'r' are liquids. ■ *adj* **1. CONSISTING OF LIQUID** relating to, characteristic of, or consisting of a liquid or liquids **2. SMOOTH AND FLUENT** moving or produced in a smooth and fluent way **3.** FIN **CONVERTIBLE TO CASH** easily converted into cash **4. CLEAR** clear and shining **5.** PHON **ARTICULATED WITHOUT FRICTION** describes a consonant that is articulated without friction and is capable of being prolonged like a vowel [14C. Via French < Latin *liquidus* 'fluid' < *liquere* 'be fluid'] —**liquidly** *adv* —**liquidness** *n*

liquid air *n* a pale blue mixture of gases, mainly oxygen and nitrogen, that has been cooled and liquefied to be used in manufacturing pure gases and as a refrigerant

liquidambar /líkwid ámbər/ (*plural* **-bars** or *same*) *n* a tree that exudes a yellowish aromatic balsam. Native to: North and Central America, Asia. Genus: *Liquidambar*. [Late 16C. < modern Latin < Latin *liquidus* (see LIQUID) + medieval Latin *ambar* 'amber']

liquid assets *npl* assets that can easily be converted into cash

liquidate /líkwi dayt/ (**-dates, -dating, -dated**) *v* **1.** *vti* **PAY DEBT** to pay a debt or other financial obligation **2.** *vti* **WIND UP BUSINESS** to wind up a business, paying off its liabilities from its assets, or cease trading as a business in this way **3.** *vt* **CASH ASSETS** to turn assets into cash **4.** *vt* **KILL SOMEBODY** to kill or dispose of somebody [Mid-16C. < late Latin *liquidat-*, past participle of *liquidare* 'melt' < Latin *liquere* 'be liquid'] —**liquidation** /líkwi dáysh'n/ *n*

liquidator /líkwi daytər/ *n* somebody appointed to oversee the liquidation of a business

liquid crystal *n* a liquid that changes between being clear and cloudy depending on variations in temperature or applied voltage. Use: visual display units.

liquid-crystal display *n* a display of numbers or letters in a calculator, watch, or other electronic device, created by applying electricity to cells made of liquid crystal to make some of them look darker

liquid glass *n* CHEM same as **water glass** (sense 2)

liquidise, etc. another spelling of **liquidize, etc.**

liquidity /li kwíddəti/ *n* **1.** the state or quality of being liquid **2.** assets that can easily be converted into cash

liquidize /líkwi dīz/ (**-izes, -izing, -ized**), **liquidise** (**-ises, -ising, -ised**) *v* **1.** *vti* to become liquid, or cause something to become liquid **2.** *vt* to make something solid into a liquid using a liquidizer

liquidizer /líkwi dīzər/, **liquidiser** *n* HOUSEHOLD same as **blender** (sense 1)

liquid lunch *n* alcoholic drinks consumed with little or no food, usually at a pub, in place of a midday meal (*humorous*)

liquid measure *n* a unit or system of units for measuring liquid volume or capacity

liquid paraffin *n* a clear oil distilled from petroleum and used as a laxative and skin softener. N Am term **mineral oil**

liquid refreshment *n* a drink or drinks, especially alcohol (*humorous*)

liquor /líkər/ *n* **1.** **ALCOHOLIC BEVERAGE** an alcoholic drink, especially of the type produced by distillation, e.g. whisky, rather than of the type produced by fermentation, e.g. wine or beer **2.** **COOKING LIQUID** a reduced liquid or juice left after cooking food, used as a sauce or as a basis for sauces **3.** **SOLUTION OF DRUG** a concentrated solution of a drug in a liquid, usually water **4.** **WATER IN WHICH MALT IS STEEPED** warm water added to malt in order to produce wort in the brewing process ■ *vti* (**-uors, -uoring, -uored**) **STEEP MALT IN WATER** to steep malt in warm water in order to form wort in the brewing of beer [13C. Via French < Latin]

liquor cabinet *n N Am* same as **drinks cabinet**

liquored up /líkərd úp/ *adj US* having drunk too much alcohol (*informal*)

liquorice /líkərish, -iss/ (*plural same*) *n* **1.** **DRIED BLACK PLANT ROOT** the dried black root of a perennial plant or an extract made from it. Use: laxative, confectionery, brewing. **2.** **KIND OF SWEET** a dense rubbery sweet that is usually made in black or red strips and flavoured with liquorice **3.** **PLANT WITH SWEET ROOT** a perennial plant with spiked blue feathery leaves and a root with a sweet flavour. Native to: Mediterranean. Latin name: *Glycyrrhiza glabra*. [12C. Via Anglo-Norman < late Latin *liquiritia* < Greek *glukurrhiza* < *glukus* 'sweet' + *rhiza* 'root']

liquorish *adj* another spelling of **lickerish** (*archaic*)

liquor store *n N Am* a shop that sells alcoholic beverages for consumption off the premises

lira /léerə/ (*plural* **-re** /léerə, -ray/) *n* **1.** the main unit of currency of Turkey and Malta. See table at **currency** **2.** the former unit of Italian currency [Early 17C. Via Italian < Latin *libra*, measure of weight]

Lisbon /lízbən/ capital and largest city of Portugal. Population: 564,657 (2001).

Lisburn /líz burn/ city near Belfast in eastern Northern Ireland. Population: 42,110 (1991).

lisinopril /lī sínnō pril/ *n* an oral drug that acts as an ace inhibitor. Use: treatment of high blood pressure and heart failure.

lisle /līl/ *n* a strong smooth fine cotton thread or fabric. Use: gloves, stockings. [Mid-16C. After LILLE (in former spelling)]

Lismore /líz mawr/ city in northeastern New South Wales, Australia, a dairy farming and educational centre. Population: 43,070 (2002 estimate).

lisp /lisp/ *n* **1.** **SPEECH DIFFICULTY** a minor speech difficulty in which the sounds 's' and 'z' are pronounced like the 'th' sound. Small children whose front teeth have not come through yet often have a temporary lisp. **2.** **SPEECH SOUND** the sound produced when 's' and 'z' are pronounced like the soft 'th' sound in 'third' or 'thick' ■ *vti* (**lisps, lisping, lisped**) **1.** **PRONOUNCE 'S' LIKE 'TH'** to pronounce something or speak so that 's' and 'z' are pronounced like the soft 'th' sound in 'third' or 'thick' **2.** **SPEAK LIKE CHILD** to speak in a childish or halting way [Old English *wlyspian* < Germanic, an imitation of the sound] —**lisper** *n* —**lisping** *adj, n* —**lispingly** *adv*

LISP /lisp/ *n* a high-level computer programming language, used in artificial intelligence, that converts data into lists [Mid-20C. Acronym < *list processing*]

Lissitzky /li síttski/, **El** (1890–1941) Russian artist, architect, typographer, and designer. His series of abstract geometric compositions, *Prouns* (1919–23), established him as a pioneer of the constructivist movement. Full name **Lissitzky, Eliezer Markovich**

lissom /líssəm/, **lissome** *adj* **1.** slender and able to bend easily and gracefully **2.** quick, light, and graceful in movement [Late 18C. Alteration of *lithesome*] —**lissomly** *adv* —**lissomness** *n*

list[1] /list/ *n* **1.** **ORDERED SERIES** a series of related words, names, numbers, or other items that are arranged in order, one after the other ○ *a list of people to call* **2.** COMPUT **SET OF DATA** an ordered set of data ■ *v* (**lists, listing, listed**) **1.** *vt* **ARRANGE ITEMS AS ORDERED SERIES** to arrange a series of related words, names, numbers, or other items one after the other ○ *She listed the things she intended to get done that afternoon.* **2.** *vt* **PUT SOMEBODY OR SOMETHING IN LIST** to include somebody or something in a series of words, numbers, or other items arranged one after the other ○ *He's listed among the founding members.* **3.** *vt* **CATEGORIZE SOMEBODY** to place somebody in a category or classification ○ *She lists herself as a club member but never attends meetings.* **4.** *vt* FIN **ADMIT SECURITY TO EXCHANGE** to admit a security for trading on an exchange ○ *is listed on the New York Stock Exchange* **5.** *vt* PUBLIC ADMIN **OFFICIALLY PROTECT BUILDING** to state officially that a building is one of a group that cannot be demolished or altered without government permission because they are of special architectural or historical importance **6.** *vti* MIL same as **enlist** (sense 1) (*archaic*) [Late 16C. < French *liste* < Germanic]

list[2] /list/ *n* **1.** AGRIC **FURROWS FORMING RIDGE** a ridge of earth formed by two furrows ploughed side by side **2.** ARCHIT same as **fillet** *n* (sense 3) **3.** TEXTILES same as **selvage** (*archaic*) ■ **lists** *npl* HIST, MIL **FENCED AREA IN TOURNAMENT** an area of combat in a medieval tournament enclosed by a fence of high stakes ■ *vt* (**lists, listing, listed**) **1.** **COVER SOMETHING WITH STRIP OF MATERIAL** to cover or border something with a band of cloth or other material **2.** AGRIC **FORM RIDGE FROM FURROWS** to plough together two furrows of earth to form a ridge [Old English *līste* < Germanic, 'band, strip'] ◇ **enter the lists** to begin to take part in a fight or argument (*formal*)

list[3] /list/ *vti* (**lists, listing, listed**) to lean to one side, or make a ship lean to one side ■ *n* an inclination to one side, especially one developed by a ship [Mid-17C. Origin ?]

list[4] /list/ (**lists, listing, listed**) *vt* to choose, wish, or like something (*archaic*) [Old English *lystan* < Indo-European, 'be eager'] —**list** *n*

list[5] /list/ (**lists, listing, listed**) *vti* to listen, or listen to something (*archaic*) [Old English *hlystan* < Germanic]

listed building /lístid-/ *n* a building on an official list of structures that cannot be demolished or altered without government permission because they are of special architectural or historical importance

listed company *n* a business whose securities may be traded on an exchange

listed security *n* a security that may be traded on an exchange

listel /líst'l/ *n* ARCHIT same as **fillet** *n* (sense 3) [Late 16C. < Italian *listello* 'small border' < *lista* 'border' < Germanic]

listen /líss'n/ *vi* (**-tens, -tening, -tened**) **1.** **MAKE CONSCIOUS EFFORT TO HEAR** to concentrate on hearing somebody or something ○ *We listened for the sound of the geese overhead.* **2.** **PAY ATTENTION** to pay attention to something and take it into account ○ *She wouldn't listen to my advice.* ■ *n* **ACT OF HEARING** an act of making an effort to hear something (*informal*) ○ *Why not give their new CD a listen?* [Old English *hlysnan* (influenced by LIST[5]) < Indo-European, 'hear']

listen in *vi* **1.** **EAVESDROP** to listen to other people, sometimes without their knowing it **2.** **LISTEN TO RADIO** to listen to a radio broadcast **3.** **MONITOR TELECOMMUNICATIONS** to monitor radio or telephone communications

listen up *vi* to pay attention, or listen carefully (*informal*)

listenable /líss'nəb'l/ *adj* pleasant to listen to, or suitable for listening to —**listenability** /líss'nə bílləti/ *n*

listener /líss'nər/ *n* somebody who listens, especially to a radio broadcast

listenership /líss'nər ship/ *n* the number or kind of people who listen to a radio broadcast, programme, or station (*takes a singular or plural verb*)

listening device /líss'ning-/ *n* a device that enables somebody to listen secretly to other people's conversations, e.g. in a room or on the telephone

listening post *n* **1.** **FORWARD POSITION** an advanced position near enemy lines from which troops can detect the enemy's movements **2.** **MONITORING PLACE** a post or area where information or intelligence is gathered **3.** MUSIC **POINT FOR LISTENING TO MUSIC** a module equipped with headphones and control buttons in record stores, where customers can listen to music before purchasing it

lister /lístər/ *n N Am* a plough that heaps earth on both sides of a furrow [Late 17C. < LIST[2]]

Lister /lístər/, **Joseph, 1st Baron** (1827–1912) British surgeon. His discoveries in antisepsis greatly reduced surgical mortality.

> 'There are people who do not...object to shooting a pheasant with the considerable chance that it may be only wounded and may have to die after lingering in pain...and yet who consider it something monstrous to introduce under the skin of a guinea pig a little inoculation of some microbe to ascertain its action.'
> [Joseph Lister, *British Medical Journal*; 1897]

listeria /li stéeri ə/ *n* a rod-shaped aerobic parasitic bacterium that causes disease, especially listeriosis. Genus: *Listeria*. [Mid-20C. < modern Latin, after Joseph LISTER]

listeriosis /li stéeri ṓssiss/ *n* a disease of the nervous system of mammals, birds, and occasionally humans that can cause fever, meningitis, miscarriage, or premature birth and is spread by eating food contaminated with listeria [Mid-20C. < LISTERIA]

listing /lísting/ *n* **1.** **SOMETHING ENTERED IN LIST** an entry in a list, catalogue, or directory **2.** **LIST** a list, catalogue, or directory **3.** COMPUT **PRINTOUT** a printout of a computer file or program **4.** FIN **PLACE ON OFFICIAL LIST OF SECURITIES** a place on an official list of securities that can be traded on an exchange ■ **listings** *npl* ARTS, COMMUNICATION **LISTS OF EVENTS** published lists of films, plays, or other cultural events, containing information such as times, locations, and ticket prices [Mid-17C. < LIST[1]]

listless /lístləss/ *adj* lacking energy, interest, or the willingness to make an effort [15C. < LIST[4] 'pleasure'] —**listlessly** *adv* —**listlessness** *n*

Liston /lístən/, **Sonny** (1932–70) US boxer. As world heavyweight champion (1962–64), he was noted for

his power and physical stature. Born **Liston, Charles**

list price *n* a published or advertised retail price of something that can often be discounted by the seller

Listserv /líst surv/ *tdmk* a trademark for a mailing list management system that allows subscribers to take part in e-mail discussions

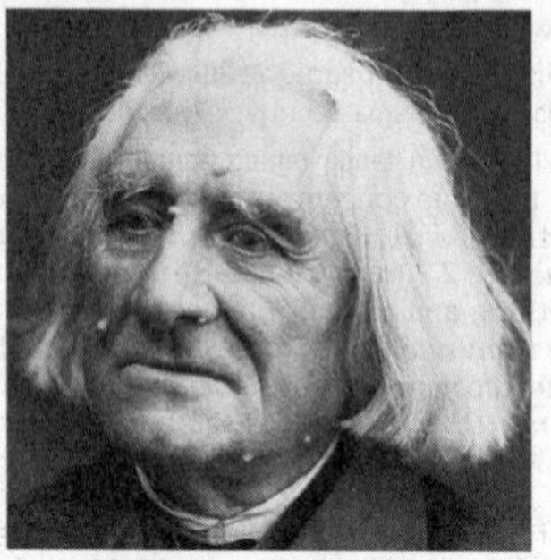

Franz Liszt

Liszt /list/, **Franz** (1811–86) Hungarian pianist, composer, and conductor. His compositions, including *A Faust Symphony* (1857), arrangements, and transcriptions for piano, influenced other composers. He was a brilliant virtuoso pianist.

lit[1] /lit/ past participle, past tense of **light**[1] ■ *adj* having drunk too much alcohol (*slang*)

lit[2] /lit/ past participle, past tense of **light**[2]

lit. *abbr* **1.** literal **2.** literally **3.** LITERAT literary **4.** LITERAT literature **5.** MEASURE litre

litany /líttəni/ (*plural* **-nies**) *n* **1.** a long and repetitious list of things such as complaints or problems ○ *recited a litany of grievances against the administration* **2.** in a Christian service, a series of sung or spoken liturgical prayers or requests for the blessing of God, including invocations from a priest or minister and responses from a congregation [13C. Via French < ecclesiastical Latin *litania* < Greek *litaneia* 'prayer' < *litanos* 'entreating' < *litē* 'supplication']

litas /lée taass/ (*plural same*) *n* the main unit of Lithuanian currency. See table at **currency** [Late 20C. < Lithuanian]

LitB *abbr* EDUC **1.** Bachelor of Letters **2.** Bachelor of Literature [Latin *Litterarum Baccalaureus*]

litchi *n* FOOD same as **lychee**

lit crit /lít krít/ *n* LITERAT same as **literary criticism** (*informal*) [Mid-20C. Shortening]

LitD *abbr* EDUC **1.** Doctor of Letters **2.** Doctor of Literature [Latin *Litterarum Doctor*]

lite /līt/ *adj* low in alcohol, calories, sugar, or fat (*used especially in labelling or advertising foods and beverages*) [Mid-20C. Respelling of LIGHT[2]]

-lite *suffix* mineral, rock, fossil ○ *halite* ○ *coprolite* [Via French < Greek *lithos* 'stone']

liter *n* MEASURE US spelling of **litre**

literacy /líttərəssi/ *n* **1.** the ability to read and write at a conventionally accepted level **2.** knowledge of or competence in a subject or area of activity ○ *computer literacy* ○ *emotional literacy*

literae humaniores /líttə rée hyoo mánni áwr eez/ *n* the faculty of classics and philosophy at Oxford University [Mid-18C. < Latin, literally 'more humane letters']

literal /líttərəl/ *adj* **1.** FOLLOWING BASIC MEANING adhering strictly and concisely to the basic meaning of a word or text ○ *a literal interpretation* **2.** WORD FOR WORD exactly following the order or meaning of a word or text ○ *a literal transcript* **3.** USED TO EMPHASIZE TRUTH OF STATEMENT used to emphasize that something is true ○ *It's the literal truth.* **4.** TAKING THINGS AT FACE VALUE understanding words, behaviour, and situations in a simple way that ignores context or implications **5.** FACTUAL AND UNIMAGINATIVE simple in an unimaginative way that sticks solely to the facts ○ *a literal account of the incident* **6.** USING ALPHABETICAL LETTERS involving or expressed by letters of the alphabet ■ *n* PUBL PRINTING ERROR a misprint, especially involving a single alphabetical letter [14C. Via French < Latin *literalis* < *littera* 'letter'] —**literalness** *n*

literalism /líttərə lizəm/ *n* **1.** strict adherence to the basic meaning of a word or text **2.** the realistic representation of something in art or literature —**literalist** *n* —**literalistic** /líttərə lístik/ *adj* —**literalistically** *adv*

literally /líttərəli/ *adv* **1.** STRICTLY ADHERING TO BASIC MEANING in a way based on the basic or explicit meaning of a word or text ○ *You shouldn't interpret these lyrics literally.* **2.** WITHOUT EXAGGERATION used to show that a statement is actually true and not exaggerated ○ *He had literally thousands of books in his home.* **3.** ⚠ USED FOR EMPHASIS used with figurative expressions to add emphasis (*informal*) ○ *I was literally freezing.*

USAGE literally used for emphasis: In formal contexts, avoid using ***literally*** in a consciously exaggerated way to add emphasis, especially in combination with a colourful figure of speech: *The manager is literally hopping mad.* Say instead *The manager is furious* or *The manager is really livid.*

literary /líttərəri/ *adj* **1.** RELATING TO LITERATURE relating to literature, writing, or the study of literature **2.** FORMALLY EXPRESSED typical of literature rather than everyday speech **3.** PROFESSIONALLY INVOLVED WITH LITERATURE involved with literature or writing as a profession **4.** KNOWLEDGEABLE ABOUT LITERATURE well-read or knowledgeable about literature [Mid-17C. < Latin *literarius* < *littera* 'letter'] —**literarily** *adv* —**literariness** *n*

literary agent *n* somebody whose job is to negotiate business contracts on behalf of an author

literary criticism *n* the process or art of analysing, commenting on, and judging the contents, qualities, and techniques of literary texts —**literary critic** *n*

literary executor *n* a manager of literary property on behalf of an author's estate

literary forensics *n* the scientific examination of documents of disputed authenticity (*takes a singular verb*)

literate /líttərət/ *adj* **1.** ABLE TO READ AND WRITE having the ability to read and write **2.** KNOWLEDGEABLE having a good understanding of a particular subject **3.** WELL-EDUCATED AND WELL-READ well-educated and cultured, especially with respect to literature or writing **4.** SKILFULLY WRITTEN showing skill in the techniques of writing ○ *a literate account of the voyage* ■ *n* **1.** SOMEBODY CAPABLE OF READING AND WRITING somebody who is able to read and write **2.** SOMEBODY WITH EXTENSIVE EDUCATION a well-educated, learned, or cultured person [15C. < Latin *litteratus* < *littera* 'letter'] —**literately** *adv*

literati /líttə ráa tee/ *npl* (*formal*) **1.** intellectuals or the educated class **2.** authors and other people closely or professionally involved with literature and the arts [Early 17C. Directly or via Italian < Latin *litterati* 'lettered people' < *littera* 'letter']

literation /líttə ráysh'n/ *n* the representation of sounds or words by means of alphabetical letters [Early 20C. < Latin *littera* 'letter']

literature /líttərəchər/ *n* **1.** WRITTEN WORKS WITH ARTISTIC VALUE written works, e.g. fiction, poetry, drama, and criticism, that are recognized as having important or permanent artistic value **2.** BODY OF WRITTEN WORKS the body of written works of a culture, language, people, or period of time ○ *Russian literature* **3.** WRITINGS ON SUBJECT the body of published work concerned with a particular subject ○ *scientific literature* **4.** BODY OF MUSIC the body of musical compositions for a particular instrument or group of instruments ○ *literature for the piano* **5.** PRINTED INFORMATION printed matter such as brochures or leaflets that give information ○ *the company's promotional literature* **6.** PRODUCTION OF LITERARY WORKS the creation of literary work, especially as an art or occupation [14C. Via French < Latin *litteratura* < *litteratus* (see LITERATE)]

lith. *abbr* PRINTING **1.** lithograph **2.** lithography

Lith. *abbr* **1.** Lithuania **2.** Lithuanian

lith- *prefix* same as **litho-** (*used before vowels*)

-lith *suffix* **1.** mineral, rock, stone ○ *batholith* **2.** stone structure or implement ○ *megalith* ○ *microlith* **3.** calculus, concretion ○ *otolith* [Via modern Latin *-lithus* < Greek *lithos* 'stone']

litharge /líth aarj/ *n* CHEM same as **lead monoxide** [14C. Via French < Latin *lithargyrus* < Greek *litharguros* < *lithos* 'stone' + *arguros* 'silver']

lithe /līth/ (**lither, lithest**), **lithesome** /līthsəm/ *adj* able to move or bend the body lightly and gracefully ○ *a lithe gymnast* [Old English *līþe* 'gentle' < Indo-European, 'flexible'] —**lithely** *adv* —**litheness** *n*

Lithgow /líthgō/ town in southeastern New South Wales, Australia, a centre of coalmining and light industry. Population: 20,389 (2002 estimate).

lithia /líthi ə/ *n* CHEM same as **lithium oxide** [Early 19C. < Greek *lithos* 'stone']

lithiasis /li thī əssiss/ *n* the formation or presence of stones formed by mineral concretions in the body, e.g. in the kidney, gall bladder, pancreas, or salivary glands [Mid-17C. Via modern Latin < Greek < *lithos* 'stone']

lithic[1] /líthik/ *adj* **1.** consisting of stone **2.** relating to undesirable mineral concretions in the body, e.g. kidney stones [Late 18C. < Greek *lithikos* < *lithos* 'stone']

lithic[2] /líthik/ *adj* relating to lithium [Early 19C. < LITHIUM]

-lithic *suffix* of a particular stage in human beings' use of stone implements ○ *Neolithic* [< Greek *lithos* 'stone']

lithify /líthi fī/ (**-fies, -fying, -fied**) *vti* to change from loose sediments into solid rock, or change something in this way [Late 19C. < Greek *lithos* 'stone'] —**lithification** /líthifi káysh'n/ *n*

lithium /líthi əm/ *n* a soft silver-white element that is the lightest metal known. Source: spodumene, lepidolite. Use: alloys, ceramics, batteries, in compounds as a medical treatment for bipolar disorder. Symbol **Li**. See table at **element** [Early 19C. < LITHIA]

lithium carbonate *n* a white crystalline salt. Use: in ceramics and glass, treatment of bipolar disorder. Formula: Li_2CO_3.

lithium fluoride *n* a white, slightly water-soluble powder. Use: manufacture of ceramics. Formula: LiF.

lithium hydride *n* a white translucent powder or crystal. Use: organic synthesis, production of hydrogen. Formula: LiH.

lithium oxide *n* a white alkaline solid that absorbs carbon dioxide and water vapour. Use: manufacture of ceramics and glass. Formula: Li_2O.

litho. *abbr* PRINTING **1.** lithograph **2.** lithography

litho- *prefix* **1.** stone ○ *lithosphere* **2.** calculus, concretion ○ *lithotomy* [< Greek *lithos* 'stone']

lithog. *abbr* PRINTING **1.** lithograph **2.** lithography

lithogenous /li thójjənəss/ *adj* describes organisms such as coral that secrete stony deposits

lithography /li thóggrəfi/ *n* a printing process using a plate on which only the image to be printed takes up ink. The area that is not to be printed is treated to repel ink. [Early 19C. < German *Lithographie* < Greek *lithos* 'stone' + *graphein* 'write'; because the plate was originally a porous stone] —**lithograph** /líthə graaf, -graf/ *n, vti* —**lithographer** *n* —**lithographic** /líthə gráffik/ *adj* —**lithographically** *adv*

lithoid /líth oyd/, **lithoidal** /li thóyd'l/ *adj* consisting of or resembling stone [Mid-19C. < Greek *lithoeidēs* < *lithos* 'stone']

lithology /li thólləji/ *n* **1.** the scientific study of rocks **2.** the physical characteristics of a rock or a rock formation —**lithological** /líthə lójjik'l/ *adj* —**lithologically** *adv* —**lithologist** *n*

lithophane /líthə fayn/ *n* a piece of thin translucent porcelain or china with an intaglio design

lithophyte /líthə fīt/ *n* **1.** a plant that grows on rock and absorbs nutrients from the atmosphere **2.** an organism that is composed in part of stony material, e.g. a coral —**lithophytic** /líthə fíttik/ *adj*

lithopone /líthə pōn/ *n* a white pigment that is a mixture of barium sulphate and zinc sulphide. Use: making paints and linoleum. [Late 19C. < LITHO- + Greek *ponos* 'product']

lithosphere /líthə sfeer/ *n* the solid outer layer of the Earth above the asthenosphere, consisting of the crust and upper mantle —**lithospheric** /líthə sférrik/ *adj*

lithotomy /li thóttəmi/ (*plural* **-mies**) *n* the surgical removal of a stone from an organ or duct of the body, especially the urinary tract or bladder —**lithotomic** /líthə tómmik/ *adj* —**lithotomist** *n*

lithotripsy /líthō tripsi/ *n* the fragmentation of a stone in the urinary system or gall bladder, e.g. with ultrasound shock waves, so that the gravel can be passed naturally [Mid-19C. < LITHO- + Greek *tripsis* 'rubbing']

lithotripter /líthə triptər/, **lithotriptor** *n* a device that breaks up kidney stones using ultrasound shock waves [Early 19C. Alteration of *litho(n)triptor* < Greek *lithōn thruptika* 'capable of pulverizing stones' < *lithos* 'stone' + *thruptein* 'to crush']

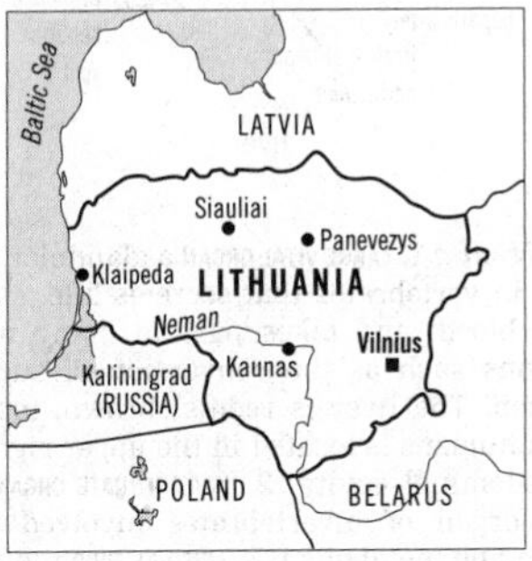

Lithuania

Lithuania /líthyoo áyni ə/ country bordering the Baltic Sea in northeastern Europe. Language: Lithuanian. Currency: litas. Capital: Vilnius. Population: 3,592,961 (2003). Area: 65,300 sq. km/25,200 sq. mi. Official name **Republic of Lithuania**

Lithuanian /líthyoo áyni ən/ *n* **1.** somebody who comes from Lithuania **2.** the official Balto-Slavic language of Lithuania, also spoken in western European Russia. Native speakers: 4 million. —**Lithuanian** *adj*

litigant /líttigənt/ *n* somebody engaged in a lawsuit [Mid-17C. Via French < Latin *litigant-*, present participle of *litigare* (see LITIGATE)] —**litigant** *adj*

litigate /lítti gayt/ (**-gates, -gating, -gated**) *vti* to contest or be involved in a lawsuit [Early 17C. < Latin *litigat-*, past participle of *litigare* < *lit-* 'lawsuit' + *agere* 'to drive'] —**litigable** *adj* —**litigator** *n*

litigation /lítti gáysh'n/ *n* **1.** the act or process of bringing or contesting a lawsuit ○ *The matter is in litigation.* **2.** same as **lawsuit** (*technical*)

litigious /li tíjjəss/ *adj* **1.** INCLINED TO GO TO LAW tending or wanting to take legal action ○ *a litigious person* **2.** OF LEGAL ACTION relating to litigation **3.** QUARRELSOME inclined to quarrel or argue (*formal*) [14C. < French *litigieux* < Latin *litigium* 'litigation' < *litigare* (see LITIGATE)] —**litigiously** *adv* —**litigiousness** *n*

litmus /lítməss/ *n* a powdery substance obtained from lichens, which turns red in acids and blue in bases. Use: indicator for acids or bases. [14C. < Old Norse *litmosi* < *litr* 'dye' + *mosi* 'moss']

litmus paper *n* a strip of paper treated with litmus. Use: to find out if something is an acid or a base.

litmus test *n* **1.** a test in which a single factor determines the outcome **2.** a test in which litmus is used to find out if something is an acid or a base

litotes /lítō teez, lī tốt eez/ (*plural same*) *n* a deliberate understatement, often expressed negatively, as in 'I am not unmindful of your devotion' [Late 16C. Via late Latin < Greek *litotēs* < *litos* 'simple']

~~litrature~~ incorrect spelling of **literature**

litre /léetər/ *n* a unit of volume equal to 1 cubic decimetre or 1.056 liquid quarts [Late 18C. Via French < medieval Latin *litra* < Greek, unit of measure]

LittB *abbr* EDUC **1.** Bachelor of Letters **2.** Bachelor of Literature [Latin *Litterarum Baccalaureus*]

LittD *abbr* EDUC **1.** Doctor of Letters **2.** Doctor of Literature [Latin *Litterarum Doctor*]

litter /líttər/ *n* **1.** SCATTERED RUBBISH pieces of rubbish that have been carelessly left on the ground, especially in a public place or outdoors **2.** MESSY STATE OR PLACE a large number of objects that have been scattered around untidily, or a place that is in an untidy state ○ *working away in the litter of her study* **3.** ANIMAL OFFSPRING a group of young animals born at the same time from the same mother **4.** BEDDING FOR ANIMALS material, e.g. hay or straw, that is used as bedding for animals **5.** MATERIAL FOR PET'S TOILET TRAY a dry absorbent substance, often in the form of granules, that is spread in a shallow container where a pet, especially a cat, can urinate or defecate when indoors **6.** GROUND SURFACE OF FOREST the surface layer of a forest floor, consisting of partly decomposed leaves and twigs **7.** COUCH FOR CARRYING PASSENGER a couch with poles on either side, used to transport a single passenger on people's shoulders or on animals **8.** STRETCHER WITH LONG SHAFTS a piece of cloth stretched between two long poles on each side that is used to carry a sick person or a dead body (*dated*) ■ *v* (**-ters, -tering, -tered**) **1.** *vti* MAKE PLACE UNTIDY to make a place, especially a public place or the outdoors, untidy by leaving or scattering rubbish **2.** *vt* BE SCATTERED OVER PLACE to lie or be scattered over a place, making it untidy, or put a place in disorder by leaving scattered objects in it ○ *Toys littered the playroom floor.* **3.** *vt* FILL SOMETHING WITH THINGS to fill something with many examples of something undesirable ○ *littered with mistakes* **4.** *vti* HAVE YOUNG to give birth to young (*refers to animals*) **5.** *vt* SUPPLY ANIMAL WITH BEDDING to provide an animal with hay or straw for bedding [14C. Via Anglo-Norman *litere* < medieval Latin *lectaria* < Latin *lectus* 'bed'] —**litterer** *n*

~~litterature~~ incorrect spelling of **literature**

litterbug /líttər bug/ *n ANZ, N Am* same as **litter lout** (*informal disapproving*)

litter lout *n UK* somebody who leaves litter in public places or outdoors (*informal disapproving*) ANZ, N Am term **litterbug**

littermate /líttər mayt/ *n* each of several animal young born or reared in the same litter

little /lítt'l/ (**-tler, -tlest**) CORE MEANING: an adjective meaning 'small' or 'young', or a grammatical word indicating that something exists in small quantities ○ (adj) *It was only a very little mistake!* ○ (adj) *He was helping the little boy put on his boots.* ○ (adj) *I'll bring my little sister with me.* ○ (det) *There was a little food left.* ○ (det) *There was little chance of winning.*

1. *adj* SMALL small, or of less than average size ○ *He gave her a little Christmas tree ornament.* **2.** *adj* YOUNG not yet grown up ○ *I met her when she was just a little girl.* **3.** *adj* YOUNGER refers to a younger sister or brother ○ *my little sister* **4.** *adj* SMALL AND PLEASANT small in a pleasant or good-looking way ○ *his cute little habits* **5.** *adj* SHORT short in duration, or executed quickly ○ *gave a little smile* **6.** *adj* TRIVIAL of no importance ○ *the little things he does that bother me* **7.** *det, pron* **a little** SMALL QUANTITY a small amount of something ○ *I only ate a little.* **8.** *det, pron* NOT MUCH only a very small amount ○ *had little or no effect* **9.** *adv* HARDLY hardly or not at all ○ *little did they know* **10.** *adv* NOT OFTEN on rare occasions ○ *visiting them little* [Old English *lȳtel* < Germanic, 'small'] —**littleness** *n* ◇ **little by little** gradually or by small degrees ○ *growing drowsy little by little* ◇ **no little** considerable ○ *ate with no little appetite* ◇ **not a little** a lot ○ *not a little embarrassed* ◇ **think little of somebody** *or* **something** to have a low opinion of somebody or something ○ *I have learned not to think little of anyone else's beliefs.*

little auk *n* a small squat seabird with a strong beak and, in winter, a white throat and breast. Native to: northern regions. Latin name: *Alle alle.* N Am term **dovekie**

Little Barrier Island /lítt'l bárri ər-/ uninhabited island in the Hauraki Gulf, off the northeastern coast of the North Island, New Zealand. It is a nature reserve. Area: 28 sq. km/11 sq. mi.

Little Bear *n* ASTRON same as **Ursa Minor**

Little Bighorn /-bíg hawrn/ river in southern Montana. General George Custer and his army were defeated by Native Americans on its banks in 1876. Length: 145 km/90 mi.

little black dress *n* a short black dress in any fashionable style for evening or party wear

little dawling /-dáwling/ *n regional* the smallest or weakest piglet in a litter [Alteration of DARLING]

REGIONAL NOTE See *underling*.

Little Dipper *n N Am* ASTRON same as **Ursa Minor**

little end *n* the part of a connecting rod that attaches to the gudgeon pin in an internal-combustion engine or reciprocal pump

Little Englander /-íng gləndər/ *n* somebody who emphasizes the interests of the United Kingdom rather than taking an international perspective (*disapproving*)

little finger *n* the smallest finger of the human hand, located farthest from the thumb

little folk *npl* same as **little people**

little grebe *n* BIRDS same as **dabchick**

little green man *n* an imaginary person from outer space (*humorous*)

little hours *npl* the hours of prime, terce, sext, and nones in the divine office to be recited every day by members of Roman Catholic orders

Little Ice Age *n* a period of colder weather marked by growth in alpine glaciers that began 5,000 years ago and lasted until the 19th century in some parts of the world

Little John *n* in English legend, a particularly tall and strong member of Robin Hood's band of men

Little League *n* a baseball league for boys and girls from 8 to 12 years old, divided into administrative bodies for the United States, Canada, South America, East Asia, and Europe —**Little Leaguer** *n*

little magazine *n* a literary magazine primarily made up of work by writers who have yet to become established, usually having a limited circulation and a small format

little man *n* **1.** an average person, as opposed to an important or wealthy one **2.** somebody who operates a small business or invests on a small scale

little office *n* a Roman Catholic office similar to but shorter than a divine office, especially a liturgical service of psalms and prayers to the Virgin Mary

little people *npl* tiny imaginary or mythological beings, e.g. fairies, elves, and leprechauns

Little Richard (*b.* 1935) US pianist and singer. A pioneer of rock and roll, his performance of songs such as 'Tutti Frutti' (1955) and 'Good Golly Miss Molly' (1958) made them classics of the genre. Born **Penniman, Richard Wayne**

Little Rock capital of Arkansas, in the central part of the state, on the Arkansas River. Population: 184,055 (2002 estimate).

Little Russia former region that included Carpathian Ruthenia, eastern Poland, Ukraine, and the western shores of the Black Sea

little slam *n* in the game of bridge, the winning of 12 out of the 13 tricks in a deal

little theatre *n N Am* **1.** a small, usually noncommercial theatre that produces experimental drama **2.** a form of noncommercial drama emphasizing experimental work

little toe *n* the fifth and smallest toe of the human foot, located farthest from the big toe

little woman *n Aus* an offensive term for a man's wife or de facto partner (*informal*)

Littlewood /lítt'l wood/, **Joan** (1914–2002) British theatre director. She founded the left-wing Theatre Workshop, for whose members she helped devise *Oh! What a Lovely War* (1963). Full name **Littlewood, Maudie Joan**

littlie /lítt'li/ *n Aus* a young child (*informal*) [Late 19C. < LITTLE]

littoral /líttərəl/ *adj* **1.** ON OR NEAR SHORE on or near a shore, especially the zone between the high and low tide marks **2.** SHORE-LIVING living on or near a shore ■ *n* SHORE a shore or coastal region, especially the zone between the high and low tide marks [Mid-17C. < Latin *littoralis* < *litor-* 'shore']

lit up *adj* having drunk too much alcohol (*slang*)

liturgical /li túrjik'l/, **liturgic** /-jik/ *adj* **1.** relating to liturgy **2.** relating to religious worship or to a service of worship, especially the celebration of Communion in a Christian service —**liturgically** *adv*

liturgics /li túrjiks/ *n* the study of public worship or liturgies (*takes a singular verb*)

liturgiology /li túrji óllәji/ *n* CHR same as **liturgics** —**liturgiologist** *n*

liturgist /líttərjist/ *n* **1.** SOMEBODY WHO STUDIES LITURGIES somebody who studies or compiles liturgies **2.** PRACTITIONER OF LITURGY somebody who performs the liturgy

3. SUPPORTER OF LITURGIES somebody who favours using liturgies —**liturgism** *n* —**liturgistic** /líttər jístik/ *adj*

liturgy /líttərji/ (*plural* **-gies**) *n* **1.** a form and arrangement of public worship laid down by a church or religion **2.** CHR another spelling of **Liturgy** [Mid-16C. Directly or via French < late Latin *liturgia* < Greek *leitourgia* 'service, worship' < *leitourgos* 'public servant' < *leitos* 'public']

Liturgy *n* the form of service used to celebrate Communion in a Christian denomination, especially in Eastern churches

Litvinov /lit véen of/, **Maksim** (1876–1951) Russian revolutionary and diplomat. A member of the Bolshevik Party, he worked for international recognition of the Soviet Union. He was ambassador to the United States (1941–43). Full name **Litvinov, Maksim Maksimovich**. Born **Wallach, Meier**

'Peace is indivisible.'
[Maksim Litvinov, *Speech to the League of Nations, Geneva*; 1 July 1936]

Liu Shaoqi /lyóo shów chée/, **Liu Shao-ch'i** (1898–1969) Chinese political leader. He became vice chairman of the Communist Party in 1959, but was forced from office during the Cultural Revolution (1966–69).

livable /lívvəb'l/, **liveable** *adj* **1.** COMFORTABLE comfortable or suitable for living in ○ *a very livable flat* **2.** BEARABLE endurable and worth continuing ○ *It's very tense at home, but still livable.* **3.** ENJOYABLE AS LIVING COMPANION enjoyable or easy to live with —**livability** /lívvə bílləti/ *n* —**livableness** *n*

live[1] /liv/ (**lives, living, lived**) *v* **1.** *vi* HAVE LIFE to be alive **2.** *vi* STAY ALIVE to remain alive ○ *lived through a serious illness* **3.** *vi* RESIDE to make your home in a particular place or condition or with a particular person ○ *lives alone* **4.** *vti* LEAD PARTICULAR TYPE OF EXISTENCE to spend your life in a particular way or under particular circumstances ○ *live comfortably* **5.** *vi* MAKE LIVING to earn or make a living ○ *lives by waiting tables* **6.** *vti* FULLY ENJOY LIFE to enjoy life to the fullest ○ *really knew how to live* **7.** *vi* CONTINUE to persist or continue in existence ○ *Her fame lives on.* **8.** *vt* EXPERIENCE SOMETHING to experience or go through something ○ *living a dream* **9.** *vti* MAKE LIFE CONFORM to make your life conform to something such as a philosophy or religion ○ *lived her faith* ○ *lived by strict rules* **10.** *vi* BE KEPT SOMEWHERE to be found or kept in a particular place (*informal*) ○ *The spare car keys live in this drawer.* [Old English *libban, lifian* < Indo-European, 'to stick'] ◇ **live and learn** to constantly gain new knowledge or learn from mistakes (*informal*) ○ *I thought it was safe to eat the berries, but you live and learn!* ◇ **live and let live** to be tolerant of others ◇ **live it up** to live or celebrate in an extravagant way (*informal*)

live down *vt* to live in a blameless or commendable way long enough for something shameful to be forgotten

live in *vi* to live at your place of work

live off *vt* to depend on somebody or something as a source of financial support or for a livelihood ○ *He lived off his parents.*

live on *vt* **1.** same as **live off 2.** to eat a particular type of food in order to survive or thrive ○ *The koala lives on eucalyptus leaves.*

live out *v* **1.** *vt* DO SOMETHING PREVIOUSLY IMAGINED to do in reality what had previously only been imagined or fantasized about ○ *live out a fantasy* **2.** *vt* LIVE UNTIL END OF PERIOD to spend the rest of your life or a period of time in a particular manner or place **3.** *vi* LIVE SOMEWHERE OTHER THAN WORKPLACE to live away from the place where you work

live through *vt* to experience and survive something difficult or dangerous

live together *vi* to share the same home and have a sexual relationship without being married

live up to *vt* to meet somebody's expectations or desires or match somebody's good example

live with *vt* **1.** PUT UP WITH to accept or tolerate something difficult or unpleasant ○ *The house is tiny, but we'll just have to live with it.* **2.** SHARE LIFE WITH SOMEBODY to share a home and have a sexual relationship with somebody without being married **3.** COPE WITH to cope with or match somebody or something (*slang*)

live[2] /līv/ *adj* **1.** LIVING alive rather than dead or inanimate **2.** BROADCAST AS IT HAPPENS broadcast while an event is happening ○ *Tonight's show is live from Paris.* **3.** IN PERSON appearing, performing, or performed in front of an audience or in person, rather than recorded or filmed ○ *I'd rather dance to live music.* **4.** RECORDED DURING PERFORMANCE recorded while a performance is happening ○ *live footage of the concert* **5.** ELEC CONNECTED TO POWER SOURCE connected to an electrical power source ○ *a live cable* **6.** CHARGED WITH EXPLOSIVE containing an explosive and able to be used ○ *live ammunition* **7.** CURRENTLY RELEVANT relevant to current interests or concerns ○ *a live issue* **8.** BURNING burning or glowing ○ *live coals* **9.** WITH LIVING BACTERIA made using living bacteria ○ *live yoghurt cultures* **10.** BRIGHT OR VIVID bright or brilliant, especially in terms of colour **11.** HIGHLY RESONANT with highly resonant or reverberant acoustics **12.** GEOL ACTIVE describes a volcano that is still active **13.** GEOL FOUND AS ORIGINAL ROCK describes a rock or mineral that is found free and not mined or quarried **14.** SPORTS IN PLAY in sports such as baseball or football, used to describe a ball that remains in play because officials have not halted action (*informal*) ■ *adv* **1.** IN PERSON in front of an audience or in person ○ *performing live here tomorrow night* **2.** WHILE EVENT HAPPENS so as to be broadcast at exactly the same time as a performance or event happens [Mid-16C. Shortening of ALIVE]

liveable *adj* another spelling of **livable**

live-bearer /līv-/ *n* a fish that gives birth to living young, rather than producing eggs —**live-bearing** *adj*

live birth /līv-/ *n* the birth of a living infant —**live-born** *adj*

lived-in /lívd-/ *adj* **1.** with a comfortable but slightly worn or untidy look that it is consistent with actual or current occupation **2.** showing the effects of life's experiences

livedo /li véedō/ (*plural* **-dos**) *n* a bluish-black patch of discoloured skin caused by the settling of blood, especially after death [< modern Latin < Latin *livere* 'be bluish in colour']

live-forever /lív-/ *n* PLANTS same as **orpine** [Because it lives for a long time]

live-in /līv-/ *adj* **1.** living in your place of employment ○ *a live-in nanny* **2.** sharing a home with a sexual partner

livelihood /līvlihood/ *n* something that provides income to live on, especially paid work [13C. Alteration of Old English *līflād* 'way of living' < *līf* 'life']

live load /līv-/ *n* the variable load or weight borne by a structure such as a bridge, in addition to its own weight

livelong[1] /lív long/ *adj* used to emphasize how long a period of time seems to last or how tedious it feels (*literary*) [14C. < LIEF; influenced by LIVE[1]]

livelong[2] /lív long/ *n* PLANTS same as **orpine** [Late 16C. < LIVE[1] + LONG[1]; because it lives for a long time]

lively /līvli/ (**-lier, -liest**) *adj* **1.** FULL OF ENERGY full of life and energy ○ *two lively children* **2.** ANIMATED animated, exciting, or intellectually stimulating ○ *a lively discussion* **3.** ENTHUSIASTIC active and enthusiastic ○ *takes a lively interest in everything* **4.** FULL OF MOVEMENT full of activity or movement ○ *a lively dance* **5.** VIVID clear, distinct, and vivid ○ *a lively recollection* **6.** BRILLIANT IN COLOUR bright and colourful in a good-looking way **7.** REFRESHING stimulating or refreshing ○ *a lively little breeze* **8.** SPRINGY bouncy or springy ○ *a lively rubber ball* **9.** NAUT RESPONSIVE TO STEERING describes a boat that is responsive to the helm [Old English *līflīc* 'lifelike'] —**livelily** *adv* —**liveliness** *n* ◇ **look** or **step lively** to hurry up and get going

~~**livelyhood**~~ incorrect spelling of **livelihood**

liven /līv'n/ (**-vens, -vening, -vened**) *v* **1.** *vti* same as **liven up** (sense 1) **2.** *vt* same as **liven up** (sense 2) [Early 18C. < LIFE] —**livener** *n*

liven up 1. *vti* to become lively or cheerful, or make somebody or something lively or cheerful ○ *What can we do to liven up the party?* **2.** *vt* to make something more attractive or interesting, e.g. by brightening its colour or intensifying its flavour ○ *livened up the sauce with some lemon juice*

live oak /līv-/ *n* a very large evergreen oak with a short broad trunk, leathery leaves, and hard timber, often grown for shade. Native to: Texas, east through the southeastern United States. Latin name: *Quercus virginianus*. [< LIVE[2]; from its being evergreen]

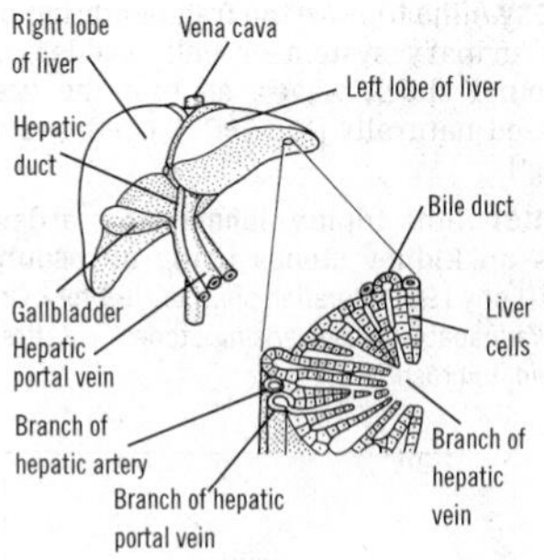

liver

liver[1] /lívvər/ *n* **1.** LARGE VITAL ORGAN a glandular vascular organ in vertebrates that secretes bile, stores and filters blood, and takes part in many metabolic functions such as the conversion of sugars into glycogen. The liver is reddish-brown, multilobed, and in humans is located in the upper right part of the abdominal cavity. **2.** INVERTEBRATE ORGAN a glandular organ of invertebrates involved with digestion and metabolism **3.** LIVER AS FOOD the liver of a mammal, bird, or fish eaten as food **4.** COLOURS DARK BROWN COLOUR a dark brown colour tinged with red or grey [Old English *lifer* < Germanic] —**liver** *adj*

liver[2] /lívvər/ *n* somebody who lives in a particular way ○ *a fast liver* [14C. < LIVE[1]]

liver-coloured *adj* of a reddish-brown colour resembling liver

liver fluke *n* a parasitic worm that infests the liver of mammals, including humans. Latin name: *Fasciola hepatica*.

liverish /lívvərish/ *adj* **1.** WITH LIVER DISORDER affected by a liver disorder **2.** IRRITABLE bad-tempered or irritable **3.** LIKE LIVER resembling liver, especially in colour (*informal*) —**liverishness** *n*

Liverpool /lívvər pool/ port and university city in northwestern England, on the River Mersey. Population: 439,473 (2001).

Liverpool Plains rich agricultural region of eastern New South Wales, Australia

Liverpool Range mountain range in eastern New South Wales, Australia. Its highest peak is Oxleys Peak, 1,372 m/4,500 ft.

Liverpudlian /lívvər púddli ən/ *n* somebody who comes from Liverpool [Mid-19C. < alteration of LIVERPOOL, substituting *puddle* for *pool*] —**Liverpudlian** *adj*

liver salts *n* a solution of mineral salts. Use: to relieve indigestion. (*takes a singular or plural verb*)

liver sausage *n* a sausage containing cooked minced liver, usually eaten cold as a spread. N Am term **liverwurst**

liver spot *n* a brown patch of pigmentation on the skin, usually occurring later in life [< its colour]

liverwort /lívvər wurt/ *n* a small dense green plant that grows on moist surfaces and resembles moss. Class: Hepaticae. [Old English *liferwyrt*, translation of medieval Latin *hepatica*; from its lobed shape]

liverwurst /lívvər wurst/ *n* *N Am* same as **liver sausage** [Mid-19C. Partial translation of German *Leberwurst* 'liver sausage']

livery[1] /lívvəri/ (*plural* **-ies**) *n* **1.** UNIFORM an identifying uniform worn by members of a group or trade, especially men and boys who are servants of a household or feudal retainers **2.** EMBLEM OR DESIGN a distinctive colour scheme or design used by a company to make its property and vehicles easily identifiable **3.** CHARACTERISTIC APPEARANCE a distinctive colouring, marking, dress, or outward appearance (*literary*) **4.** PROFESSIONAL CARE OF HORSES the care, feeding, and stabling of horses for money **5.** HIRING OF HORSES the business of hiring out horses [14C. < Old French *livree* 'delivery' < Latin *liberare* 'liberate' < *liber* 'free'] —**liveried** *adj*

livery[2] /lívvəri/ *adj* same as **liverish** (*informal*) [Mid-18C. < LIVER[1]]

livery company *n* any one of several chartered companies of the City of London entitled to wear an

identifying uniform. They started as craft guilds in the 14th century.

liveryman /lívvərimən/ (*plural* **-men** /-mən/) *n* **1.** a member of a livery company. Members are freemen of the City of London and are entitled to specific privileges. **2.** somebody who owns or works in a livery stable

livery stable *n* **1.** a stable that accommodates and looks after horses for their owners **2.** a stable where horses and carriages are kept for hire

livestock /lív stok/ *n* animals raised for food or other products, or kept for use, especially farm animals such as meat and dairy cattle, pigs, and poultry

live trap /lív-/ *n* a trap designed to catch a wild animal without injuring it

live wire /lív-/ *n* **1.** a wire connected to a source of voltage **2.** an enthusiastic and energetic person (*informal*)

livid /lívvid/ *adj* **1.** FURIOUS very angry **2.** WITH BLUISH BRUISED COLOUR bluish or discoloured as a result of bruising **3.** ASHEN very pale, especially unnaturally so **4.** GREYISH tinged with grey [15C. Directly or via French < Latin *lividus* < *livere* 'be bluish in colour'] — **lividity** /li víddəti/ *n* — **lividly** *adv*

living /lívving/ *adj* **1.** ALIVE having life, not dead or nonexistent ○ *every living thing* **2.** LIKE REAL THING realistic or true to life ○ *the living image of her grandmother* **3.** INTERESTING AND RELEVANT interesting in a way that is relevant and useful ○ *make a dry academic discipline into a living subject* **4.** SUITABLE FOR DOMESTIC LIFE designed for living in, especially for social and recreational activities ○ *lots of living space* **5.** STILL USED still used or in existence ○ *a living language* **6.** ABSOLUTE used to emphasize how real, intense, or thorough something is ○ *went through living torment* **7.** NATURAL in a natural condition or place ○ *living water* ■ *n* **1.** MONEY OR MEANS OF EARNING a means of earning money to live on, or the money somebody earns to live on ○ *What do you do for a living?* **2.** MAINTENANCE OF WAY OF LIFE the process of sustaining or maintaining a way of life ○ *the cost of living* **3.** MANNER OF LIFE quality of life, or a particular way of life ○ *healthy living* **4.** CHR same as **benefice** *n* (sense 1) ■ *npl* THOSE WHO ARE ALIVE people who are alive

living death *n* a life or period of time that is full of misery or pain

living fossil *n* an organism that is almost unchanged from early geological time and belongs to a group whose other members are extinct. Gingko trees and coelacanths are living fossils.

living hell *n* an extremely unpleasant situation that somebody is forced to endure, often for a considerable length of time (*informal*) ○ *The weeks of waiting were a living hell.*

living legend *n* somebody who becomes very famous within his or her own lifetime

living picture *n* THEATRE same as **tableau vivant**

living quarters *npl* the parts of a building, ship, or spacecraft where people eat, sleep, and spend their leisure time, as opposed to the parts where work is done

living room *n* a room in a house where people usually relax or entertain guests

living standards *npl* the conditions in which people live, especially in terms of their level of material comfort and disposable income

Livingston /lívvingstən/ town in West Lothian, Scotland. Population: 41,647 (1991).

Livingstone /lívvingstən/ city and tourist centre in southern Zambia, north of the Victoria Falls. Population: 82,218 (1990).

Livingstone, David (1813–73) British physician, missionary, and explorer. One of the most important explorers of the African interior, he was the first European to visit many areas of the continent.

Livingstone daisy *n* a cultivated mesembryanthemum. Flowers: brightly coloured, like large daisies. Latin name: *Mesembryanthemum criniflorum*. [Mid-20C. Origin ?]

living wage *n* a wage that will allow a worker to support a family in reasonable comfort

---

living will *n* a document, typically signed in advance while in good health, that specifies the decisions somebody wishes to be taken about his or her medical treatment in the event of becoming incapable of making or communicating them. It is usually a means of registering a desire not to be kept alive artificially by life-support systems.

Livonia /li vóni ə/ ancient Baltic region, comprising most of present-day Estonia and Latvia. Russia annexed it in 1721. —**Livonian** *adj, n*

Livorno /li váwrnō/ port and industrial city in northwestern Italy, on the Ligurian Sea. Population: 156,274 (2001). English name **Leghorn**

livre /leévrə/ *n* an old unit of French currency, equivalent to a pound of silver [Mid-16C. Via French < Latin *libra* 'pound']

Livy /lívvi/ (59 BC–AD 17) Roman historian. His *History of Rome*, ranging from the foundation of the city in 753 BC to 9 BC, was the basis for the Western tradition of historical writing, and remained the primary source of information about Rome until the 18th century. Full name **Livius, Titus**

lixiviate /lik sívvi ayt/ (**-ates, -ating, -ated**) *vti* CHEM same as **leach** (*archaic*) [Mid-17C. < late Latin *lixiviat-*, past participle of *lixiviare* < *lixivium* (see LIXIVIUM)] —**lixivial** *adj* —**lixiviation** /lik sívvi áysh'n/ *n*

lixivium /lik sívvi əm/ (*plural* **-iums** or **-ia** /-i ə/) *n* a solution obtained by leaching, e.g. lye [Mid-17C. < late Latin < Latin *lixivius* 'made into ashes or lye' < *lix* 'lye']

lizard

lizard /lízzərd/ *n* **1.** FOUR-LEGGED REPTILE a reptile with a long scaly body, movable eyelids, a long tapering tail, and four legs, typically living in hot dry regions. Lizards include the gecko, iguana, chameleon, and horned toad. Suborder: Sauria. **2.** LARGE REPTILE LIKE LIZARD a large reptile such as an alligator or crocodile that resembles a true lizard **3.** LEATHER FROM LIZARD SKIN leather made from the skin of a lizard [14C. Via Old French *lesard* < Latin *lacertus*]

Lizard /lízzərd/ peninsula in southwestern England. Its tip, Lizard Head or Lizard Point, is the southernmost point in England.

lizard fish *n* a slender, large-mouthed, predatory sea fish with a head shaped like that of a lizard. Family: Synodontidae.

Lizard Island island off the coast of Queensland, Australia

LJ *abbr* LAW Lord Justice

Ljubljana /lyŏŏ bli a'anə/ capital of Slovenia, in the central part of the country, near Trieste. Population: 330,000 (1997).

lk *abbr* Sri Lanka (*used in Internet addresses*) See table at **domain name**

'll *after a pronoun* /l/; *after a vowel* /əl/; *after a consonant* /'l/ *contr* **1.** shall **2.** will

LL *abbr* **1.** late Latin **2.** Lord Lieutenant

ll. *abbr* lines

llama /laámə/ *n* **1.** a domesticated long-haired South American animal related to camels. Kept for: load-carrying, wool. Latin name: *Llama glama*. **2.** wool or cloth made from llama hair [Early 17C. Via Spanish < Quechua]

Llandaff /lándəf, hlan dáf/ suburb of Cardiff, home of the ancient cathedral of Saints Dyfrig and Teilo

Llandrindod Wells /hlan drín dod wélz/ spa town in

llama

Powys, eastern Wales, known for its mineral springs. Population: 4,362 (1991).

Llandudno /hlan dúdnō/ town and seaside resort in Conwy, northern Wales. Population: 14,576 (1991).

Llanelli /hla néthli/ market town and port in Carmarthenshire, Wales, on the Burry Inlet of Carmarthen Bay. Population: 44,953 (1991).

Llanfair /hlan vír/ village in Anglesey, northwestern Wales. It is a terminus of the Welshpool and Llanfair Light Railway. Population: 3,101 (1991).

Llangefni /hlan gévni/ town in Anglesey, northwestern Wales. It is the island's administrative centre. Population: 4,643 (1991).

Llangollen /hlan góthlən/ town in Denbighshire, Wales, that is host to an international musical eisteddfod. Population: 3,267 (1991).

llano /laánō/ (*plural* **-nos**) *n* especially in Latin America and the southwestern United States, a large open grassy plain [Early 17C. Via Spanish < Latin *planus* 'flat']

LLB *abbr* LAW, EDUC Bachelor of Laws [Latin *Legum Baccalaureus*]

LLD *abbr* LAW, EDUC Doctor of Laws [Latin *Legum Doctor*]

Llewellyn /lə wéllin, hlə-/, **Richard** (1907–83) British author. His bestselling novel *How Green Was My Valley* (1939), the story of a Welsh mining family, was also turned into a successful film. Pseudonym of **Lloyd, Richard Doyle Vivian Llewellyn**

Llewellyn ♦ **Llywelyn**

Lleyn Peninsula /hlīn-/ peninsula in western Wales, lying between Cardigan Bay and Caernarvon Bay. Length: 45 km/28 mi.

LLM *abbr* LAW, EDUC Master of Laws [Latin *Legum Magister*]

Lloyd /loyd/, **Clive** (b. 1944) Caribbean cricketer. A fine batsman and fielder, he was captain of the West Indies and Lancashire cricket teams. Full name **Lloyd, Clive Hubert**

Lloyd, Harold (1893–1971) US comedian. He made almost 500 silent films and talking pictures, including *Safety Last* (1923), many of which featured stunts and chase sequences. Full name **Lloyd, Harold Clayton**

'I am just turning 40 and taking my time about it.'
[Harold Lloyd, *Times*; 23 September 1970]

Lloyd, Marie (1870–1922) British music-hall entertainer. Her Cockney songs won her great popularity. She performed in Britain, the United States, South Africa, and Australia. Born **Wood, Matilda Alice Victoria**

'Oh, mister porter, what shall I do? / I wanted to go to Birmingham, but they've carried me on to Crewe.'
[Marie Lloyd, 'Oh Mister Porter'; 1890?]

Lloyd George /lóyd jáwrj/, **David, 1st Earl of Dwyfor** (1863–1945) British prime minister (1916–22). As the last Liberal prime minister of the United Kingdom, he was a strong wartime leader during World War I. See illustration on next page and table at **prime minister**

Lloyd's Register /lóydz-/ *n* a society founded in London in 1760 that draws up specifications for the construction of merchant ships [After Edward *Lloyd*,

---

David Lloyd George

supplier of information about shipping at his London coffee house from the late 17C]

Lloyd Webber /-wébbər/, Andrew, Lord Lloyd Webber of Sydmonton (b. 1948) British composer. His popular stage musicals include *Jesus Christ Superstar* (1971), *Cats* (1981), *Phantom of the Opera* (1986), and *Sunset Boulevard* (1993).

Llywelyn ap Gruffudd /lə wéllin ap gríffith, hlə-/, **Llewelyn ap Gruffudd** (d. 1282) prince of Gwynedd. Grandson of Llywelyn ap Iorwerth, in 1258 he won recognition as Prince of Wales, and rebelled unsuccessfully against the English.

Llywelyn ap Iorwerth /-yáwr wurth/, **Llewelyn ap Iorwerth** (1173–1240) prince of Gwynedd. He extended his sovereignty over almost all of Wales and successfully fought against the English. Known as **Llewelyn the Great**

lm *symbol* PHYS lumen

LMDS *abbr* TELECOM, ONLINE Local Multipoint Distribution Service

LMK *abbr* ONLINE let me know (*used in e-mails*)

ln *symbol* MATHS natural logarithm

LNG *abbr* liquefied natural gas

lo /lṓ/ *interj* used to draw attention to something (*archaic or literary*) [Old English *lā*, natural exclamation]

loach /lṓch/ *n* a freshwater fish related to carp, with a long slender body and barbels around its mouth. Native to: Europe, Asia. Family: Cobitidae. [14C. < Old French *loche*]

load /lṓd/ *n* **1.** SOMETHING CARRIED OR TRANSPORTED something that is carried by an animal, person, or vehicle, especially something heavy or bulky **2.** AMOUNT CARRIED IN ONE TRIP the amount of material, goods, or people that are carried in one journey (*often used in combination*) ○ *delivered a boatload of passengers to the island* **3.** WORK DEMANDED OF SOMEBODY the amount of work that a person is required to do ○ *unhappy about his teaching load this term* **4.** MENTAL BURDEN something that makes somebody feel mentally weighed down, e.g. responsibility, worry, or guilt ○ *a heavy load to bear* **5.** QUANTITY THAT MACHINE CAN COPE WITH the amount that can be handled by a machine at one time, especially the amount of clothes that can be handled by a washing machine ○ *six loads of washing* **6.** SINGLE CHARGE FOR GUN a single charge of ammunition for a firearm **7.** ELEC AMOUNT OF DRAWN ELECTRICAL POWER the amount of electrical power that is drawn from a line or source **8.** ELEC ENG DEVICE DRAWING ELECTRICAL POWER any device to which electrical power is delivered **9.** MECH ENG FORCE AND WEIGHT ON STRUCTURE the total force and weight that a structure such as a bridge is designed to withstand. For a bridge, this includes the dynamic loads of traffic, wind, snow, and ice and the static load of the bridge's own weight. **10.** MECH ENG WORK REQUIRED OF MECHANICAL DEVICE the work required of or placed on an engine or machine, measured in kilowatts or horsepower **11.** FIN CHARGE ADDED TO MUTUAL SHARE PRICE a charge that is added to the price of some unit trust shares as a commission or marketing cost ■ **loads** *npl* LARGE AMOUNT OR NUMBER a large amount or a lot of (*informal*) ○ *We had loads of guests at the party.* ■ *adv* **loads** VERY MUCH very much or a great deal (*informal*) ○ *feeling loads better* ■ *v* (**loads, loading, loaded**) **1.** *vti* PUT SOMETHING ON VEHICLE to put cargo on or cause cargo to be placed on a vehicle, ship, or aircraft or to have cargo or passengers put on ○ *The aircraft is now loading.* **2.** *vt* PUT SOMETHING ON PERSON OR ANIMAL to put a load on an

animal or give a load to a person so that it can be carried **3.** *vt* PUT SOMETHING IN MACHINE to put into a machine the items that it will work on, e.g. clothes for washing **4.** *vti* PUT SOMETHING IN CAMERA to put a film, plate, or tape in a camera, or take in a film, plate, or tape **5.** *vt* PUT DISK IN DRIVE ON COMPUTER to put a disk or tape in a drive on a computer **6.** *vt* PUT PROGRAM IN COMPUTER to transfer data or a program to the main memory of a computer **7.** *vti* PUT ROUNDS IN GUN to put ammunition into a firearm ○ *loaded the rifle* **8.** *vt* GAMBLING WEIGHT ONE SIDE OF DICE to weight one side of a dice or roulette wheel to prevent it from operating randomly ○ *He must have loaded the dice.* **9.** *vt* FIN ADD EXTRA CHARGE TO INSURANCE PREMIUM to add an extra charge to an insurance premium, e.g. because of an increased risk **10.** *vt* ELEC INCREASE ELECTRIC OUTPUT OF GENERATOR to increase the output produced by or drawn from a circuit or generator **11.** *vt* MECH ENG INCREASE WORK REQUIRED OF ENGINE to increase the work required from an engine or motor [Old English *lād* 'course, way' < Indo-European, 'go ahead'] ◇ **a load of** used to say emphatically that something is ridiculous or nonsensical (*informal*) ○ *a load of nonsense* ◇ **a load off your mind** a relief from anxiety or worry ◇ **get a load of something** to look at or listen to something or somebody (*informal*)

loadbearing /lṓd bairing/ *adj* supporting the gravitational force exerted on a structure or part of one ○ *a loadbearing wall*

loaded /lṓdid/ *adj* **1.** WITH FULL LOAD carrying a full load **2.** CONTAINING AMMUNITION containing bullets or other ammunition and ready to fire **3.** WITH HIDDEN IMPLICATION having a hidden or secondary implication designed to trick somebody into making an admission or commitment ○ *That is a loaded question.* **4.** WEIGHTED UNFAIRLY with one side weighted to prevent dice or a roulette wheel from operating randomly **5.** RICH extremely rich (*slang*) ○ *Her parents are loaded.* **6.** *N Am* DRUNK very drunk (*slang*) **7.** *N Am* INTOXICATED BY DRUGS under the influence of drugs (*slang*)

Loader /lṓdər/, **Danyon** (b. 1975) New Zealand swimmer. He won a silver medal in the 200 metres butterfly at the 1992 Olympics and two gold medals in the 200 metres and 400 metres freestyle at the 1996 Olympics. Full name **Loader, Danyon Joseph**

load factor *n* **1.** the payload of an aircraft for a particular flight, expressed as a percentage of the maximum allowable payload **2.** an external load divided by the weight of an aircraft

loading /lṓding/ *n* **1.** WEIGHT CARRIED a load or weight carried **2.** FILLER material added to something to improve specific properties or add weight **3.** ADDITIONAL INSURANCE PREMIUM an additional insurance premium or higher rating incurred by items that are more valuable or at greater risk **4.** ADDITION OF INDUCTANCE the addition of inductance to a transmission line to improve its performance over a given frequency band **5.** *Aus* ADDITIONAL WAGE a payment made to workers over and above the basic wage in recognition of special skills or unfavourable conditions such as overtime or weekend work

loading bay *n* a parking bay, partly enclosed by a raised platform such as outside a warehouse, at which vans and lorries are loaded and unloaded. N Am term **loading dock**

loading bridge *n* a covered walkway from an airport departure-lounge gate that expands to connect to the door of a commercial aircraft, used by embarking and disembarking passengers and crew

loading dock *n N Am* TRANSP same as **loading bay**

loading gauge *n* the height and width limits that apply to trains, including external loads, on particular railways

load line *n* NAUT same as **Plimsoll line**

loadmaster /lṓd maastər/ *n* somebody who oversees the loading of cargo on a military or commercial transport aircraft

loadsa /lṓdzə/ *contr* loads of (*informal*) ○ *We need loadsa luck.*

load shedding *n* a temporary reduction in a supply of electricity as a method of reducing the demand on the generator

loadstar *n* ASTRON another spelling of **lodestar**

loadstone *n* GEOL another spelling of **lodestone**

loaf[1] /lṓf/ (*plural* **loaves** /lṓvz/) *n* **1.** QUANTITY OF BREAD a quantity of bread, shaped and baked as a whole, to be cut into slices for eating **2.** BLOCK OF FOOD SHAPED LIKE LOAF a quantity of food baked in a loaf tin or shaped to form a rectangular block and baked (*used in combination*) ○ *meat loaf* **3.** BRAIN common sense or intelligence (*slang*) ○ *Use your loaf!* [Old English *hlāf* < Germanic]

loaf[2] /lṓf/ (**loafs, loafing, loafed**) *vi* to do very little and spend time in a lazy, rather wasteful way [Mid-19C. Probably back-formation < LOAFER]

loafer /lṓfər/ *n* a lazy person who avoids work and wastes time [Mid-19C. Origin ?]

Loafer /lṓfər/ *tdmk* a trademark for a casual leather shoe that is like a moccasin but has a wide flat heel

loaf sugar *n* sugar in the shape of a large solid cone, formed using 19th-century methods of processing and purifying using large clay moulds

loam /lṓm/ *n* **1.** FERTILE WORKABLE SOIL an easily worked fertile soil consisting of a mixture of clay, sand, and silt and sometimes also organic matter **2.** CLAY AND SAND MIXED FOR BUILDING a mixture of moist clay and sand used for making bricks and in plastering ■ *vt* (**loams, loaming, loamed**) PUT LOAM IN OR ON SOMETHING to use loam in the process of covering, filling, or coating something [Old English *lām* 'clay, earth' < Indo-European, 'slippery'] —**loamy** *adj*

loan[1] /lṓn/ *n* **1.** MONEY LENT an amount of money given to somebody on the condition that it will be paid back later **2.** LENDING the act of letting somebody use something temporarily **3.** LING same as **loanword** ■ *vt* (**loans, loaning, loaned**) ⚠ LEND SOMETHING to allow somebody to borrow something on the condition that it is returned ○ *Loan me five pounds, will you?* [12C. < Old Norse *lán*] ◇ **on loan 1.** being lent or borrowed **2.** working at a temporary location because additional help or expertise is needed there

USAGE See **borrow**.

loan[2] /lṓn/ *n* **1.** *Scotland* a rural pathway or grassy track **2.** an open area used for milking cows [14C. Variant of LANE]

loanback /lṓn bak/ *n* the opportunity for a person to borrow from his or her own pension fund

Loan Council *n* a federal body set up in Australia in 1924 to monitor borrowing by state governments

loan shark *n* somebody who lends money at excessively high rates of interest (*informal; disapproving*)

loansharking /lṓn shaarking/ *n* the activity or business of lending money at excessively high rates of interest (*informal disapproving*)

loan translation *n* a word or expression that enters a language as a direct translation from another

loanword /lṓn wurd/, **loan word** *n* a word from one language that has become part of everyday usage in another, often with slight modification

loath /lṓth/, **loth** *adj* unwilling or reluctant to do something [Old English *lāp* 'loathsome' < Germanic]

SPELLCHECK loath, loth, or loathe? Do not confuse the spelling of *loath* (or its variant *loth*) and *loathe*. *Loath* (or *loth*) is an adjective meaning 'unwilling or reluctant' and is usually followed by *to*, as in *I was loath* [or *loth*] *to admit it.* It is also occasionally encountered in the fixed phrase *nothing loath* (or *nothing loth*). *Loathe* is a verb meaning 'dislike intensely': *I loathe this kind of music.*

SYNONYMS See **unwilling**.

loathe /lṓth/ (**loathes, loathing, loathed**) *vti* to dislike somebody or something intensely [Old English *lāpian* < Indo-European, 'despise'] —**loather** *n* —**loathingly** *adv*

SPELLCHECK See **loath**.

~~loathesome~~ incorrect spelling of **loathsome**

loathing /lṓthing/ *n* intense dislike of somebody or something

SYNONYMS See **dislike**.

loathsome /lṓthsəm/ *adj* arousing intense dislike and disgust —**loathsomely** *adv* —**loathsomeness** *n*

loaves plural of **loaf**[1]

lob /lob/ *v* (**lobs, lobbing, lobbed**) **1.** *vti* **HIT BALL IN HIGH ARC** to hit or throw a ball in a high curving trajectory **2.** *vt* **THROW SOMETHING CASUALLY** to throw something in a casual careless way **3.** *vi* **MOVE SLOWLY** to move slowly or heavily ■ *n* **1. HIGH ARCHING SHOT** a ball hit or thrown in a high curving path **2. BALL OVER TENNIS PLAYER'S HEAD** a ball that travels over the head of a tennis player [Late 16C. Probably < Low German] —**lobber** *n*
lob in *vi Aus* to arrive or turn up (*informal*)

Lobachevsky /lóbbə chéfski/, **Nikolay Ivanovich** (1793–1856) Russian mathematician. His system of non-Euclidian geometry undermined various previously held theories.

lobar /lṓbər/ *adj* relating to or affecting a lobe, e.g. in the lungs

lobate /lṓ bayt/ *adj* having or resembling a lobe or lobes —**lobately** *adv*

lobby /lóbbi/ *n* (*plural* **-bies**) **1. ENTRANCE AREA IN PUBLIC BUILDING** a large entrance hall or foyer immediately inside the door of a hotel, theatre, or other public building **2. PUBLIC AREA IN LEGISLATIVE BUILDING** a public area in or near a legislative building where people can meet and petition their political representatives **3. VOTING CORRIDOR** either of the two rooms in Parliament where members of both houses of Parliament vote for or against bills and proposals **4. GROUP TRYING TO INFLUENCE POLICY** a group of supporters and representatives of particular interests who try to influence political policy on a particular issue (*takes a singular or plural verb*) ○ *the environmental lobby* ○ *a lobby group* **5. ATTEMPT TO INFLUENCE POLICY** a visit to a legislative building to petition political representatives, organized by a campaign group as a protest or in an attempt to influence policy ■ *v* (**-bies, -bying, -bied**) POL **1.** *vti* **PETITION POLITICIANS OR INFLUENTIAL PEOPLE** to attempt to persuade a political representative or influential person to support or oppose a particular cause **2.** *vt* **CAMPAIGN ABOUT LEGISLATION** to campaign for or against a particular piece of legislation by attempting to influence politicians [Mid-16C. < medieval Latin *lobia* 'cloister, covered walk' < Germanic] —**lobbyer** *n*

lobby correspondent *n* in the United Kingdom, a journalist who receives briefings from government sources and reports on parliamentary activities

lobbyist /lóbbi ist/ *n* somebody who is paid to lobby political representatives on an issue —**lobbyism** *n*

lobby system *n* the system of employing professional lobbyists to attempt to influence political policy

lobe /lōb/ *n* **1.** ANAT same as **earlobe 2. ROUNDED BODY PART** a rounded division or projection of an organ or part in the body, especially in the lungs, brain, or liver **3. ROUNDED PROJECTING PART** a rounded part that projects from the main body of something **4. ROUNDED PLANT PART** a rounded segment on a leaf that is not divided all the way to the midrib [15C. Via late Latin < Greek *lobos*]

lobectomy /lō béktəmi/ (*plural* **-mies**) *n* the surgical removal of a lobe, e.g. of the lungs, liver, or thyroid

lobed /lōbd/ *adj* **1.** having lobes or shapes like lobes ○ *feather-lobed leaves* **2.** describes birds' toes that have a rounded flap on either side

lobefin /lṓbfin/ *n* FISH same as **crossopterygian** —**lobe-finned** *adj*

lobelia /lō beéli ə/ *n* a low-growing or trailing summer-flowering plant. Flowers: white to purple. Genus: *Lobelia*. [Mid-18C. After Matthias de *Lobel* (1538–1616), Flemish botanist]

Lobito /loo beétoo/ city and port in western Angola. Population: 150,000 (1983).

Lobito Bay arm of the Atlantic Ocean forming the harbour of the city of Lobito in western Angola

loblolly /lób loli/ *n* TREES same as **loblolly pine**

loblolly boy, loblolly man *n* in former times, a junior sailor acting as a medical assistant on board ship [< *loblolly* 'thick gruel', a shipboard remedy]

loblolly pine, loblolly *n* a pine with flaky bark, long needles grouped in threes, and oblong cones. Native to: southeastern United States. Genus: *Pinus taeda*. [< *loblolly* 'thick gruel']

lobola /lō bṓlə/, **lobolo** /lō bṓlō/ *n* payment, often in cattle, made by a groom's family to his bride's family before their wedding in some parts of southern and eastern Africa [Mid-19C. < Bantu]

lobotomize /lə bóttə mīz/ (**-mizes, -mizing, -mized**), **lobotomise** (**-mises, -mising, -mised**) *vt* **1.** to carry out a surgical operation in which nerves to the prefrontal lobe of the brain are severed **2.** to make somebody feel sluggish, mentally numb, or lacking in energy or vitality (*informal*)

lobotomy /lə bóttəmi/ (*plural* **-mies**) *n* same as **prefrontal lobotomy** [Mid-20C. < LOBE]

lobscouse /lób skowss/ *n* a stew of meat and vegetables thickened with ship's biscuits, traditionally eaten by sailors [Early 18C. Origin ?]

lobster /lóbstər/ *n* **1. HARD-SHELLED SEA CRUSTACEAN** a hard-shelled sea crustacean with a pair of large pincers, five pairs of limbs, eyes on stalks, and long antennae. Native to: Atlantic coasts of North America, Europe. Family: Homaridae. **2. CRUSTACEAN LIKE LOBSTER** a crustacean similar in appearance to the true lobster but without the two large pincers, especially the spiny lobster. Native to: subtropical, tropical coastal waters. Family: Palinuridae. **3. LOBSTER AS FOOD** the flesh of a lobster used as food. The tail meat and meat extracted from the claws is particularly valued for its fine, slightly sweet flavour. ■ *vi* (**-sters, -stering, -stered**) **CATCH LOBSTERS** to catch lobsters using a boat and pot [Old English *loppestre*, origin ?]

lobsterman /lóbstərmən/ (*plural* **-men** /-mən/) *n* **1.** somebody whose profession is fishing for lobsters **2.** a boat designed for catching lobsters

lobster Newburg /-nyoó burg/ *n* lobster meat cooked in a rich sherry sauce with butter and cream and usually served on small pieces of toast or croutons or in a pastry shell [Early 20C. Origin ?]

lobster pot *n* a trap in the form of a basket, used for catching lobsters

lobster thermidor /-thúrmi dawr/ *n* cooked lobster with a wine and cream sauce served in the shell with a topping of melted cheese [Late 19C. After *Thermidor* (1891), play by Victorien Sardou (1831–1908), French dramatist]

lobule /lóbbyool/ *n* **1.** a small lobe **2.** a section or division of a lobe [Late 17C. < LOBE] —**lobular** *adj* —**lobularly** *adv* —**lobulate** *adj* —**lobulose** *adj*

lobworm /lób wurm/ *n* **1.** ZOOL same as **lugworm** (sense 1) **2.** a large earthworm used by anglers as bait [Mid-17C. < LOB 'something hanging']

local /lṓk'l/ *adj* **1. IN NEARBY AREA** relating to, situated in, or providing a service for a particular area, especially the area near home or work ○ *the local school* **2. CHARACTERISTIC OF PARTICULAR AREA** characteristic of, or only found in, a particular area ○ *the local dialect* **3. NOT WIDESPREAD** confined to a fairly small area ○ *There have been local outbreaks of the disease.* **4. RELATING TO GOVERNMENTAL REGION** relating to a comparatively small region that controls some aspects of practical government such as housing or education ○ *local elections* **5. AFFECTING SMALL PART** affecting only a specific part of a human's or animal's body ○ *local infection* **6. STOPPING EVERYWHERE** stopping at all the stations or bus stops on a route ○ *local trains and buses* **7. TO PHONE NUMBER NEARBY** made to a phone number within a fairly small radius and therefore charged at a lower rate than long-distance calls ○ *a phone for local calls only* ■ *n* **1. SOMEBODY WHO COMES FROM PARTICULAR AREA** a native or long-term resident of a place **2. NEIGHBOURHOOD PUB** a pub close to where somebody lives that the person visits regularly (*informal*) ○ *I stopped at the local on the way home from work.* **3. STOPPING TRAIN OR BUS** a train or bus that stops at all the stations or stops on the route **4.** same as **local anaesthetic** (*informal*) **5.** *N Am* **BRANCH OF ORGANIZATION** a branch or office, especially of a labour union, situated in and serving members or clients only in one locale [14C. Via French < late Latin *localis* < Latin *locus* 'place'] —**locally** *adv* —**localness** *n*

local anaesthetic *n* a drug, usually given by injection, that eliminates pain, though not necessarily all sensation, in a particular area of the body without affecting consciousness

local area network *n* a network of personal computers and peripheral devices linked by cable and able to share resources

local authority *n* the body that has political and administrative powers to control a particular city or region. Aus, N Am term **local government**

local colour *n* unusual or traditional features of a particular place that make it interesting

locale /lō kaál/ *n* the place in which something happens or in which the action in a book or film takes place [Late 18C. Alteration of French *local* (see LOCAL), after MORALE]

local examination *n* a UK examination set by a national examination board but held at local schools and colleges around the country, e.g. the GCSE

local government *n* **1.** the government of a town, city, or region at a local level by locally elected politicians ○ *worked in local government all his life* **2.** *Aus, N Am* same as **local authority**

localise *vti* another spelling of **localize**

localism /lṓkəlizəm/ *n* **1.** a phrase, expression, or custom peculiar to the people in a particular area **2.** interest in local matters and customs rather than in national or global issues, sometimes resulting in a limited perspective —**localist** *n*

locality /lō kálləti/ (*plural* **-ties**) *n* **1. PARTICULAR PLACE** a particular place, district, or neighbourhood **2. SETTING FOR EVENT** the place or setting where something happens **3. SITUATION IN SPACE OR TIME** the fact of being situated at a particular point in space or time

localize /lṓkə līz/ (**-izes, -izing, -ized**), **localise** (**-ises, -ising, -ised**) *v* **1.** *vti* **CONFINE OR BE CONFINED TO PLACE** to become confined to, or restrict something to, a particular area **2.** *vt* **FIND LOCATION OF SOMETHING** to find the source or location of something **3.** *vt* **DECENTRALIZE CONTROL OF SOMETHING** to transfer power or control from a central authority to local bodies —**localizable** *adj* —**localization** /lṓkə lī záysh'n/ *n*

localized /lṓkə līzd/, **localised** *adj* restricted to a specific place or area ○ *a localized infection*

local option *n* the power granted to a local government to decide whether to implement a particular policy, especially with regard to the sale of alcohol

local time *n* the time in a particular region, calculated according to the time zone in which the place is situated

Locarno /lo kaárnō/ town and resort in Ticino Canton, southern Switzerland. Population: 14,312 (1998).

locate /lō káyt/ (**-cates, -cating, -cated**) *v* **1.** *vt* **FIND SOMETHING** to discover where something is **2.** *vi* **ESTABLISH BUSINESS IN PLACE** to establish a residence or business in a particular place **3.** *vt* **POSITION SOMETHING** to put something in a particular place [Early 16C. < Latin *locat-*, past participle of *locare* < *locus* 'place'] —**locatable** *adj* —**locater** *n*

location /lō káysh'n/ *n* **1. POSITION** the site or position of something **2. FILM SETTING** a place away from a studio where scenes for a film are shot ○ *The film was shot on location in Scotland.* **3. DISCOVERY** the discovery of something ○ *A metal detector is an essential aid in the location of buried treasure.* **4. POSITIONING OF SOMETHING** the positioning or siting of something or somebody in a particular place **5.** *S Africa* **URBAN SETTLEMENT FOR BLACK PEOPLE** an urban settlement planned for people classed as Black or of mixed ethnic origin by the apartheid system, usually with inferior facilities and services (*dated*) **6.** *Scotland* LAW **HIRING OUT OF SOMETHING** a contractual state under Scots law in which somebody has agreed to hire out either an object or his or her services —**locational** *adj*

locative /lókətiv/ *n* **1. GRAMMATICAL CASE** a grammatical case in some languages that indicates place or direction **2. FORM IN LOCATIVE** a word or phrase in the locative ■ *adj* **INDICATING PLACE OR DIRECTION** in or relating to the locative [Early 19C. < LOCATE]

locator /lō káytər/ *n US* **1.** somebody who establishes the boundaries of a piece of land or a mining claim **2.** a device that helps somebody locate something such as a table or index

loc. cit. *adv* in the place cited. Full form **loco citato**

loch /lo<u>kh</u>, lok/ *n Scotland* **1.** same as **lake**[1] (sense 1) **2.** a narrow arm of the sea stretching inland [14C. < Scottish Gaelic]

lochan /ló<u>kh</u>ən, lókən/ *n Scotland* a small lake or pool [Late 17C. < Scottish Gaelic, 'small loch']

Lochgilphead /lo<u>kh</u> gílp hed/ town in west-central

Scotland. It is the administrative centre of Argyll and Bute council area. Population: 2,421 (1991).

lochia /lóki ə/ *n* the normal vaginal discharge of cell debris and blood after childbirth [Late 17C. < Greek *lokhia* < *lokhos* 'childbirth'] —**lochial** *adj*

Loch Lomond and The Trossachs National Park /-tróssəks-/ national park, in western Scotland, established in 2002. Area: 1,865 sq. km/720 sq. mi.

Loch na Keal /lókh na keel/ sea loch classified as a National Scenic Area, on the island of Mull, Scotland

Loch Rannoch and Glen Lyon /lokh ránnəkh ənd glen líʹ ən/ National Scenic Area in central Scotland

loci LAW, MATHS, GENETICS plural of **locus**

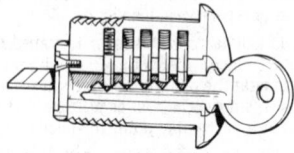

lock: cross-section of a key-operated lock

lock[1] /lok/ *n* **1.** FASTENING MECHANISM a mechanism used to fasten or secure a door, window, or lid, especially one operated by a key **2.** GATED SECTION OF CANAL a short section of a canal or river in which the water level can be altered to enable boats to pass to a higher or lower part of the waterway. The lock has gates at each end with a mechanism for letting water in or out. **3.** DEGREE OF WHEEL TURN the degree to which the wheels of a vehicle pivot as the car turns. A good lock means that the wheels can be turned a long way, making it easier to turn the vehicle in a small space. **4.** WRESTLING HOLD a wrestling hold in which a wrestler twists or puts pressure on part of the other wrestler's body **5.** GUN PART the part of a gun that makes the charge explode **6.** BLOCKING DEVICE a device that prevents an unauthorized person from using something, e.g. one operated by a password **7.** RUGBY PLAYER IN RUGBY SCRUM either of the two players in the second row in a rugby scrum **8.** ENG same as **airlock** ■ *v* (**locks, locking, locked**) **1.** *vti* FASTEN WITH LOCK to fasten something or become fastened using a lock **2.** *vt* PUT SOMETHING IN SECURE PLACE to put something into a safe place or container that can be locked ○ *Her diamonds are locked in a safe deposit box.* **3.** *vt* SECURE PLACE to make a building or vehicle secure by locking the doors and windows **4.** *vt* PREVENT UNAUTHORIZED USE to prevent something from being used by an unauthorized person, e.g. via software **5.** *vti* FIX OR BE FIXED IN PLACE to become fixed in one position, or fix something in one position, so that it cannot move normally **6.** *vt* HOLD SOMEBODY FIRMLY to hold somebody tightly ○ *locked in a passionate embrace* **7.** *vt* TRAP SOMEBODY IN DIFFICULT SITUATION to put somebody in a situation or conflict from which it is difficult to escape ○ *locked in a lengthy argument* **8.** *vt* BOATING PUT LOCKS ON WATERWAY to put locks on a stretch of canal or river **9.** *vi* BOATING GO THROUGH CANAL LOCKS to go through a series of locks on a boat, or take a boat through a series of locks **10.** *vt* PRINTING FIX TYPE IN PRINTING PRESS to secure metal type in a printing press **11.** *vt* FIN same as **lock up** (sense 4) [Old English *loc* < Germanic] —**lockable** *adj* ◇ **lock, stock, and barrel** completely

lock away *vt* CRIME, SAFETY same as **lock up** (senses 1–2)

lock in *vt* to prevent somebody from leaving a room or building by locking the door

lock on *vti* to find a target and track it automatically, or make a radar or missile find and track a target

lock out *vt* **1.** to prevent somebody from entering a place by locking the door **2.** to prevent workers from entering their workplace, usually as a strategy in an industrial dispute

lock up *v* **1.** *vt* IMPRISON SOMEBODY to put somebody into prison, a secure hospital, or other institution that deprives him or her of freedom **2.** *vt* STORE SOMETHING

IN SECURE PLACE to put valuables in a secure locked place **3.** *vti* SECURE BUILDING to make a building secure by locking all the doors and windows **4.** *vt* INVEST IN LONG-TERM PLAN to put money into a form of savings or investment that does not allow easy access to the funds

lock[2] /lok/ *n* **1.** PIECE OF HAIR a group of hairs that hang together, on somebody's head or cut off **2.** WISP OF FIBRE a small bunch of wool, cotton, or other fibre ■ **locks** *npl* **1.** HAIR somebody's hair (*literary*) **2.** HAIR same as **dreadlocks** (*slang; used in Black English*) [Old English *locc* < Germanic]

CULTURAL NOTE **The Rape of the Lock** a poem (1712) by Alexander Pope. Written in mock-heroic style, it satirizes a major quarrel between families that arose when a young man snipped off a lock of a young lady's hair. The poem's message is summarized in the opening lines: 'What dire offence from am'rous causes springs/ What mighty contests rise from trivial things.'

lockage /lókij/ *n* **1.** PASSAGE THROUGH LOCK the passage of a boat through a canal or river lock **2.** FEE a fee paid by a boat to pass through a lock **3.** LOCKS a number of locks on a canal or river

lockdown /lók down/ *n* **1.** COMPUTER LOCKING DEVICE a locking device that prevents a computer from being moved or stolen **2.** ONLINE COMPUTER SECURITY PROCEDURE the prevention of access by users of a computer network or intruders from the Internet to files essential to the integrity of a computer system **3.** US CONFINEMENT FOR SAFETY an emergency safety procedure in which people remain in a locked indoor space ○ *When an unknown intruder entered the building, the principal ordered the school into lockdown.* **4.** N Am CONFINEMENT TO PRISON CELL the state of being confined to a prison cell for all or most of the day (*slang*)

Locke /lok/, **John** (1632–1704) English philosopher. He developed the doctrine of empiricism according to which knowledge was acquired by experience, not by intuition.

> 'What can be more silly arrogant and mis-
> becoming, than for a Man to think that he
> has a Mind and Understanding in him, but
> yet in all the Universe beside, there is no
> such thing?'
> [John Locke, *An Essay Concerning Human*
> *Understanding*; 1690]

locked-in syndrome /lokt-/ *n* a condition resulting from massive brain stem damage that leaves the higher mental functions intact but prevents any movement except for that of the eyes and eyelids

locker /lókər/ *n* **1.** LOCKABLE COMPARTMENT a small lockable cupboard or compartment where personal belongings can be left, e.g. at a swimming pool, gym, school, or workplace **2.** TRUNK a trunk or low chest used for storage **3.** SOMEBODY OR SOMETHING THAT LOCKS somebody who or device that locks something

Lockerbie /lókərbi/ town in Dumfries and Galloway, southwestern Scotland. In 1988, an airliner was destroyed over the town by a terrorist bomb, killing all the passengers and crew and 11 of the town's residents. Population: 3,982 (1991).

locker room *n* a room containing lockers, where people change their clothes for sports or swimming

locker-room *adj* characteristic of or suitable only for a men's locker room ○ *telling locker-room jokes*

locket /lókit/ *n* a small decorative metal case with a hinged cover containing a picture or memento, worn on a neck chain or bracelet [14C. < Old French *locquet* 'small latch' < *loc* 'latch' < Germanic]

lockfast /lók faast/ *adj* Scotland fastened with a lock and consequently attracting a harsher penalty if broken into

lock forward *n* RUGBY same as **lock**[1] *n* (sense 7)

lock-in *n* **1.** DRINKING SESSION a session of after-hours drinking inside a pub (*informal*) **2.** FIN AGREEMENT FIXING RATE a written commitment fixing something at a particular level or rate ○ *got a lock-in on his mortgage rate* **3.** FIN RATE FIX a fixing of a rate of payment for a long period, or a fixed rate ○ *a mortgage lock-in*

lockjaw /lók jaw/ *n* MED **1.** same as **trismus 2.** same as **tetanus** (sense 1)

lockkeeper /lók keepər/ *n* somebody employed to look after or control a lock on a waterway and collect any fees payable

locknut /lók nut/ *n* **1.** a second nut tightened on a first to prevent it from loosening **2.** a nut designed to lock itself in place once tightened

lock-on *n* the point at which a radar or missile locates and starts to track a target

lockout /lók owt/ *n* an occasion when workers are prevented from entering their workplace, a tactic sometimes used by management in an industrial dispute

lockram /lókrəm/ *n* a coarse linen fabric [15C. < French *locrenan*, alteration of *Locronan*, village in Brittany]

locksmith /lók smith/ *n* somebody who makes, sells, installs, and repairs locks and keys. A locksmith can also open a lock when the owner has lost the key or has become locked out. —**locksmithing** *n*

lockstep /lók step/ *n* **1.** a form of military marching with soldiers close together and all moving forward with the same foot at the same time **2.** *N Am* a process or routine that is standardized and inflexible ○ *'It's a lockstep process, and if at any point the virus makes a mistake, the host will almost certainly kill it.'* (Virginia Morell, 'The Killer Cat Virus that Doesn't Kill Cats', *Discover Magazine*; July 1995)

lock stitch *n* the usual stitch made by a sewing machine, formed by the thread above the fabric interlocking with the bobbin thread

lockup /lók up/ *n* **1.** PLACE WITH PRISON CELLS a small prison, a block of cells at a police station, or a similar place where prisoners are kept for a short time **2.** GARAGE a garage, usually one of several grouped together, that can be rented (*often used before a noun*) ○ *a lockup garage* **3.** SHOP a small shop with no accommodation attached to it (*often used before a noun*) ○ *a lockup shop* **4.** SECURING OF BUILDING the securing of a building by locking it **5.** TIME FOR LOCKING BUILDING the time at which a building is locked

loco[1] /lókō/ *n* a railway locomotive (*informal*) [Mid-19C. Shortening]

loco[2] /lókō/ *adj* wildly irrational (*informal*) ■ *vt* (**-cos, -coing, -coed**) to poison an animal with locoweed [Late 19C. < Spanish, 'irrational']

loco[3] /lókō/ *adj* indicating that the performer should return to playing notes in the original register, negating a previous direction that they should be played an octave higher [Early 19C. < Italian, 'at the place'] —**loco** *adv*

loco citato /lókō si taʹatō/ *adv* full form of **loc. cit.** [< Latin, 'in the place cited']

loco disease *n* a disease of cattle, sheep, and horses in the western United States and Canada, caused by eating locoweed. It affects the animals' nervous systems, with symptoms of weakness, trembling, and inability to move.

locoman /lókōmən/ (*plural* **-men** /-mən/) *n* a train's engine driver or other engine crew (*informal*)

locomotion /lókə mósh'n/ *n* movement or the power to move from one place to another [Mid-17C. < Latin *loco* 'from a place']

locomotive

locomotive /lókə mótiv/ *n* RAIL ENGINE a railway engine ■ *adj* **1.** MOVABLE able to move about freely **2.** RELATING TO LOCOMOTION relating to, allowing, or aiding in the ability to move ○ *locomotive organs* [Early 17C.

< modern Latin *locomotivus* < Latin *loco* 'from a place' + late Latin *motivus* 'moving' (see MOTIVE)]

locomotor /lṓkə mṓtər/ *adj* relating to or aiding in locomotion ○ *locomotor hyperactivity* [Late 19C. < Latin *loco* 'from a place']

locomotor ataxia *n* MED same as **tabes dorsalis**

locomotory /lṓkə mṓtəri/ *adj* able to move independently

locoweed /lṓkō weed/ (*plural* **-weeds** or *same*) *n* **1.** a perennial plant of the pea family. Animals that eat it can contract loco disease. Native to: western North America. Genera: *Oxytropis* or *Astragalus*. **2.** *US* DRUGS same as **cannabis** (*slang*) [Late 19C. < LOCO²]

Locrian mode /lókri ən-/ *n* a medieval scale of notes that consists of the eight notes of the diatonic scale rising from B to B [Late 19C. < Greek *Locris*, region of ancient Greece]

locule /lókyool/, **loculus** /lókyŏŏləss/ (*plural* **-li** /-lī/) *n* a small cavity, chamber, or cell in a plant or animal [Late 19C. Via French < Latin *loculus* 'small place' < *locus* 'place'] —**locular** *adj*

locum /lṓkəm/, **locum tenens** /-ténnenz/ (*plural* **locum tenentes** /-te nén teez/) *n* somebody, especially a doctor or a member of the clergy, who stands in to do the job of another who is away or unwell [Mid-17C. < medieval Latin *locum tenens* 'somebody holding the place' < Latin *locus* 'place' + *tenere* 'to hold']

locus /lṓkəss/ (*plural* **-ci** /-sī/) *n* **1.** PLACE a place where something happens **2.** SET OF POINTS in mathematics, a set of points, the positions of which satisfy a set of algebraic conditions **3.** GENE POSITION the position of a gene on a chromosome [Early 18C. < Latin, 'place']

locus classicus /-klássikəss/ (*plural* **loci classici** /lṓ sī klássi sī/) *n* a much-quoted passage from an authoritative or standard text [< Latin, 'classical place']

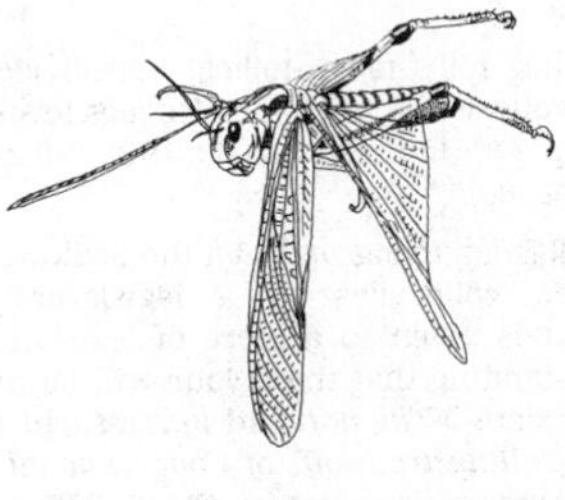

locust

locust /lṓkəst/ *n* **1.** SWARMING GRASSHOPPER a migratory grasshopper that often swarms and devours crops and vegetation. Native to: southern Europe, Asia, Africa, North America. Family: Acrididae. **2.** INSECTS same as **seventeen-year locust** **3.** POD-BEARING TREE a pod-bearing tree of the family that includes the honey locust, swamp locust, and carob. Family: Leguminosae. **4.** *ANZ, N Am* THORNY TREE a thorny deciduous tree with hanging clusters of fragrant flowers, compound leaves, and long seed pods. Native to: North America. Genus: *Robinia*. UK term **false acacia** **5.** HARD WOOD the hard yellowish wood of a locust tree [14C. Via French < Latin *locusta*]

locution /lə kyṓōsh'n/ *n* **1.** a phrase or expression typically used by a group of people **2.** the way in which somebody speaks [15C. Directly or via French < Latin *locution-* < *locut-*, past participle of *loqui* 'speak']

Lod /lod/ city in Israel, situated 37 km/23 mi. northwest of Jerusalem. Population: 61,100 (1999).

lode /lōd/ *n* **1.** DEPOSIT OF ORE a deposit or vein of ore **2.** *N Am* ABUNDANT SUPPLY an abundant supply of something **3.** FENS WATERWAY a waterway that acts as a drain off the land in an area of fenland [Old English *lād* (see LOAD)]

loden /lṓd'n/ *n* **1.** a thick waterproof woollen cloth. Use: coats, jackets. **2.** the dark-green colour of loden cloth [Early 20C. < German] —**loden** *adj*

lodestar /lṓd staar/, **loadstar** *n* **1.** the North Star **(Polaris)**, used for navigation or as a reference position in astronomy **2.** something that somebody uses as a model or principle to guide behaviour (*literary*) [14C. < LODE 'course']

lodestone /lṓd stōn/, **loadstone** *n* **1.** magnetite or a piece of magnetite with magnetic properties **2.** somebody or something that attracts others like a magnet [Early 16C. < LODE 'leading']

lodge /loj/ *n* **1.** SMALL GATEKEEPER'S HOUSE a small house in the grounds of a large country house, usually near the main gate, traditionally occupied by a gatekeeper, gardener, or estate worker **2.** COUNTRY BUILDING a cabin or other building in the country providing temporary accommodation, e.g. as a holiday home or a temporary shelter for campers, walkers, skiers, or hunters **3.** INN OR HOTEL a large house or hotel **4.** PORTER'S ROOM a room or set of rooms at the entrance to a university college for use by the college porter or caretaker **5.** BRANCH OF UNION OR SOCIETY a local branch or chapter of a society such as the Freemasons, or an organization such as a trade union **6.** MEETING HALL a hall or other meeting place used by a branch of a society **7.** NATIVE NORTH AMERICAN DWELLING a dwelling traditionally used by Native North American people, e.g. a wigwam, hogan, or long house **8.** BEAVER'S DEN a dome-shaped structure with an underwater entrance built by a beaver ■ *v* (**lodges, lodging, lodged**) **1.** *vt* REGISTER COMPLAINT OR APPEAL to make a formal complaint, accusation, or appeal by handing the documents to the appropriate authority **2.** *vt* DEPOSIT SOMETHING IN SAFE PLACE to put something somewhere or give it to somebody for safekeeping **3.** *vti* STICK OR GET STUCK to become jammed or embedded somewhere, or jam or embed something somewhere ○ *His head was lodged between the railings.* **4.** *vi* LIVE IN SOMEBODY'S HOUSE to live in somebody's house, free or as a paying guest (*dated*) ○ *She is lodging with her sister.* **5.** *vt* PUT SOMEBODY IN ACCOMMODATION to place somebody in temporary accommodation ○ *They were evacuated and lodged in a nearby school overnight.* **6.** *vt* GIVE SOMEBODY POWER TO ACT to invest somebody with the power or authority to do something ○ *powers that are lodged with the cabinet* **7.** *vti* BEAT CROPS FLAT to flatten crops, or be flattened by the wind and rain [13C. < Old French *loge* 'hut' < Germanic, 'roof made of bark']

Lodge *n Aus* the official residence of the Australian prime minister in Canberra

Lodge /loj/, **David John** (*b.* 1935) British novelist, critic, and scholar. Many of his novels, e.g. *Small World* (1984), are autobiographical, describing university life.

Lodge, Henry Cabot (1850–1924) US politician. As Republican leader in the Senate, he promoted US entry into World War I but opposed the League of Nations (1919).

lodgement *n* another spelling of **lodgment**

lodgepole pine /lój pōl-/ *n* a pine with two types of cones, one of which releases seeds only after a forest fire. Native to: western North America. Genus: *Pinus contorta*. [< Native North Americans' use of the trunks as supports for lodges]

lodger /lójjər/ *n* somebody who rents a room in somebody else's house ○ *'...the small kitchen in which she cooked the food for her lodgers'* (Jack London, *The People of the Abyss*; 1905)

lodging /lójjing/ *n* somewhere to stay temporarily ○ *We asked where we could find lodging for the night.* ■ **lodgings** *npl* a room or rooms in a boarding house or private home available for rent (*dated*)

lodging house *n* a private home or boarding house offering accommodation for rent (*dated*)

lodgment /lójmənt/, **lodgement** *n* **1.** PLACING OF SOMEBODY IN ACCOMMODATION the accommodation of somebody in a particular place (*formal*) **2.** PLACE TO STAY a temporary place to stay (*formal*) **3.** ACCUMULATION OR BLOCKAGE a build-up of something, especially when this causes a blockage **4.** FOOTHOLD IN ENEMY TERRITORY a small area of land that has been captured and held on the edge of enemy territory

lodicule /lóddi kyool/ *n* a tiny scale at the base of the ovary in a grass flower [Mid-19C. < Latin *lodicula* 'small coverlet' < *lodix* 'blanket']

Lodz /wooch/, **Łódź** /wooj/ industrial city in central Poland, situated about 121 km/75 mi. southwest of Warsaw. Population: 812,300 (1997).

Loeb /lōb/, **Jacques** (1859–1924) German-born US physiologist. He produced pioneering work in artificial parthenogenesis, and conducted important research in physiology and psychology.

loess /lṓ ess, löss/ *n* a fine-grained yellowish-brown deposit of soil left by the wind. The loess deposited by winds from Central Asia provided the basis for productive farming in early China. [Mid-19C. < German *Löss* < Swiss German *lösch* 'loose']

Loewe /lō/, **Frederick** (1904–88) US composer. His musical comedies, produced in collaboration with Alan Jay Lerner, include *My Fair Lady* (1956) and *Camelot* (1960).

Loewi /lṓ i/, **Otto** (1873–1961) German pharmacologist and physiologist. He shared a Nobel Prize in physiology or medicine (1936) for his work on the chemical transmission of nerve impulses.

lo-fi /lṓ fī/ *adj* (*informal*) **1.** ELECTRONICS relating to the production or reproduction of audio in which the sound is deliberately unpolished and rough **2.** of a quality and design that is neither advanced nor sophisticated [Shortening]

Lofoten Islands /lō fṓtən-/ chain of two groups of rock islands, northwestern Norway, in the Norwegian Sea. The southernmost group is the Lofoten, and the Vesterålen are to the north. Population: 26,241 (1970). Area: 4,044 sq. km/1,600 sq. mi.

loft /loft/ *n* **1.** ROOF SPACE the area between the ceiling of the top floor of a building and the roof (*often used before a noun*) ○ *We've got so much junk in the loft!* ○ *loft conversions* ○ *a loft ladder* **2.** UPPER FLOOR OF BARN the upper floor of a barn or stable, used for storing hay ○ *a hay loft* **3.** GALLERY a gallery or balcony, especially the gallery where the organ is situated in a church ○ *the organ loft* **4.** *N Am* UPPER FLOOR OF WAREHOUSE OR FACTORY an upper floor of a commercial building such as a factory or warehouse, typically converted to residential or studio use **5.** PIGEON COOP a shelter in which domesticated pigeons are kept ○ *a pigeon loft* **6.** SLANTING ANGLE ON GOLF CLUB the angle of the face of a golf club designed to drive the ball high into the air **7.** THICKNESS OF FABRIC the thickness and fluffiness of fabric, especially as an indication of its warmth ■ *vt* (**lofts, lofting, lofted**) **1.** HIT BALL HIGH in golf and cricket, to hit a ball in a high arching path **2.** KEEP SOMETHING IN LOFT to store something in a loft [Pre-12C. < Old Norse *lopt* 'air, upstairs room']

lofty /lófti/ (**-ier, -iest**) *adj* **1.** VERY HIGH very high or tall ○ *lofty peaks* **2.** EXALTED exalted and refined **3.** HIGH-RANKING of the highest rank or status **4.** HAUGHTY behaving in a falsely superior or haughty manner

log¹ /log/ *n* **1.** PIECE CUT FROM TREE a section of the trunk or a thick branch of a tree that has been cut for fuel or building material **2.** RECORD OF JOURNEY a record of a journey made by a ship or aircraft, detailing all events, or the book in which it is kept **3.** RECORD OF EVENTS any detailed record of events **4.** DEVICE FOR MEASURING SHIP'S SPEED a float attached to a ship by a line, formerly used for measuring the ship's speed ■ *v* (**logs, logging, logged**) **1.** *vt* INCLUDE EVENT IN LOG to record information or an event in a log ○ *The computer will log all these transactions automatically.* **2.** *vt* TRAVEL PARTICULAR DISTANCE OR SPEED to travel a particular distance, time, or speed that is then recorded in a log ○ *These checks are made routinely once the aircraft has logged 100,000 miles.* **3.** *vti* FELL TREES to cut down the trees growing on a particular area of land **4.** *vti* CUT UP TREE FOR LOGS to cut up a tree to produce logs for fuel or building [14C. Origin ?] ◇ **sleep like a log** to sleep very soundly

log in *vti* COMPUT same as **log on**

log off *vi* to end a session on a computer by typing in the appropriate command

log on *vti* to gain access to a computer system by entering a name and password or other appropriate commands

log out *vi* COMPUT same as **log off**

log² /log/ *n* MATHS same as **logarithm** (*informal*) [Mid-17C. Shortening]

Logan, Mount /lṓgən/ highest peak in Canada, located in the St Elias Range in southwestern Yukon Territory. Height: 5,959 m/19,551 ft.

loganberry

loganberry /lṓgənbəri/ (*plural* **-ries**) *n* **1.** a purplish-red fruit similar to a large raspberry **2.** a prickly trailing hybrid plant that bears loganberries. Native to: western United States, northwestern Mexico. Latin name: *Rubus ursinus loganobaccus*. [Late 19C. After James H. *Logan* (1841–1928), US horticulturist]

logaoedic /lṓggə eédik/ *adj* describes a poem or line of verse in which different metrical feet are mixed to give an effect like speech or prose [Mid-19C. Via late Latin < Greek *logaoidikos* < *logos* 'speech' + *aoidē* 'song']

logarithm /lṓggə rithəm/ *n* the power to which a base must be raised to equal a given number. For example, the logarithm of 8 to the base 2 is 3, since $2^3 = 8$. [Early 17C. < modern Latin *logarithmus* < Greek *logos* 'word, relation, ratio' + *arithmos* 'number'] —**logarithmic** /lṓggə ríthmik/ *adj* —**logarithmically** *adv*

logbook /lóg boŏk/ *n* **1.** a book containing a record of a journey made by a ship or aircraft **2.** formerly in the United Kingdom, a document giving details of a vehicle and its owners. This has now been replaced by the registration document, which some people still refer to informally as the logbook. [Late 17C. < LOG¹]

log cabin *n* **1.** a simple house made with logs **2.** a patchwork design formed from strips of fabric attached round each side of a central square

loge /lṓzh/ *n* **1.** a small private enclosure or box in a theatre **2.** *N Am* the area in a theatre at the front of the upper level [Mid-18C. < French (see LODGE)]

logger /lóggər/ *n N Am* a person or company in the business of harvesting trees for wood

loggerhead /lóggər hed/ *n* **1.** ZOOL same as **loggerhead turtle 2.** BIRDS same as **loggerhead shrike 3.** a tool consisting of a ball or bulb on a long handle that can be heated and used to melt pitch [Late 16C. Probably < *logger* 'block for hobbling a horse' < LOG¹] ◇ **at loggerheads** involved in a quarrel or feud

loggerhead shrike *n* a bird with grey feathers, black and white wings and tail, and a black facial mask. Native to: North America. Latin name: *Lanius ludovicianus*.

loggerhead turtle *n* a large flesh-eating sea turtle that lives in warm waters and has a large head and rounded shell. Latin name: *Caretta caretta*.

loggia

loggia /lójji ə, lṓ-/ (*plural* **-gias** or **-gie** /-jay/) *n* **1.** a covered open-sided walkway, often with arches, along one side of a building **2.** a balcony in a theatre [Mid-18C. Via Italian < Old French *loge* (see LODGE)]

---

logging /lógging/ *n* the job of felling, trimming, and transporting trees

logia CHR plural of **logion**

logic /lójjik/ *n* **1.** PHILOSOPHY **THEORY OF REASONING** the branch of philosophy that deals with the theory of deductive and inductive arguments and aims to distinguish good from bad reasoning **2.** SYSTEM OR INSTANCE OF REASONING any system of, or an instance of, reasoning and inference **3.** SENSIBLE ARGUMENT AND THOUGHT sensible rational thought and argument rather than ideas that are influenced by emotion or whim **4.** REASONING OF PARTICULAR FIELD the principles of reasoning relevant to a particular field **5.** RELATIONSHIP AND PATTERN OF EVENTS the relationship between specific events, situations, or objects, and the inevitable consequences of their interaction **6.** COMPUT **CIRCUIT DESIGN IN COMPUTER** the circuit design and principles used by a computer in its operation [14C. Via French *logique* < Greek *logikē (tekhnē)* '(art) of reason' < *logos* 'word, reasoning']

logical /lójjik'l/ *adj* **1.** SENSIBLE AND BASED ON FACTS based on facts, clear rational thought, and sensible reasoning **2.** ABLE TO THINK RATIONALLY able to think sensibly and come to a rational conclusion based on facts rather than emotion **3.** OF PHILOSOPHICAL LOGIC relating to philosophical logic —**logicality** /lójji kálləti/ *n* —**logically** *adv* —**logicalness** *n*

logical atomism *n* the philosophical theories of Bertrand Russell and Ludwig Wittgenstein's early period, which analyse a proposition in terms of its relation to some philosophically basic propositions

logical consequence *n* a proposition that is implied by valid reasoning from true propositions

logical constant *n* a connective expression that is used in formal logic, e.g. 'not', 'or', 'if … then' or 'if and only if'

logical positivism *n* a theory in linguistic philosophy that holds that in order for a sentence to be cognitively meaningful, it has to be verifiable

logical truth *n* a proposition that is necessarily true

logic bomb *n* a piece of software that interferes with the proper working of the computer's operating system

logic circuit *n* a computer switching circuit that performs operations on input signals

logician /lə jísh'n/ *n* somebody whose special training is in philosophical logic

logicism /lójjisizəm/ *n* the theory at the base of mathematics that mathematics is reducible to logic broadly construed to include set theory

Logie /lṓgi/ *n* in Australia, a statuette awarded annually to outstanding performers and practitioners in the television industry [After John *Logie* BAIRD]

login /lóggin/ *n* COMPUT same as **logon**

logion /lóggi on/ (*plural* **-gia** /-gi ə/) *n* a saying attributed to Jesus Christ that is not in the Bible [Late 19C. < Greek, 'oracle' < *logos* 'word']

logistic¹ /lə jístik/ *adj* relating to an uninterpreted calculus or system of symbolic logic [Early 17C. < medieval Latin *logisticus* < Greek *logos* 'word, reckoning'] —**logistician** /lójji stísh'n/ *n*

logistic² /lə jístik/, **logistical** /-tik'l/ *adj* **1.** involving the planning and management of how things are moved, especially military forces or industrial goods **2.** involving the planning and management of any complex task [Mid-20C. < French *logistique* (see LOGISTICS)] —**logistically** *adv*

logistics /lə jístiks/ *n* (*takes a singular or plural verb*) **1.** ORGANIZATION OF COMPLEX TASK the planning and implementation of a complex task **2.** MOVEMENT MANAGEMENT the planning and control of the flow of goods and materials through an organization or manufacturing process **3.** ORGANIZATION OF TROOP MOVEMENTS the planning and organization of the movement of troops, their equipment, and supplies [Late 19C. < French *logistique* < *loger* 'to lodge' < Old French *loge* (see LODGE)]

logjam /lóg jam/ *n* **1.** a situation where something is blocked or at a standstill and is unable to progress **2.** *N Am* a blockage caused by floating logs in a river

log line *n* a line from a ship trailing a floating log to determine the ship's speed

---

logo /lṓgō/ (*plural* **-gos**) *n* a design used by an organization on its letterhead, advertising material, and signs as an emblem by which the organization can easily be recognized [Mid-20C. Shortening of LOGOGRAM, LOGOTYPE]

logo- *prefix* word, thought, speech ○ *logotype* [< Greek *logos* 'word']

log of claims *n Aus* a list of claims regarding pay and working conditions presented to an employer by a group of employees or a trade union

logogram /lóggə gram/, **logograph** /lóggə graf, -graaf/ *n* a symbol that represents the meaning of a whole word or phrase, e.g. the symbols used in shorthand, or the symbol '&' used instead of the word 'and' —**logogrammatic** /lóggəgrə máttik/ *adj* —**logogrammatically** *adv*

logogriph /lóggō grif/ *n* a word puzzle, especially an anagram [Late 16C. < French *logogriphe* < Greek *logos* 'word' + *griphos* 'fishing-basket']

logomachy /lo gómməki/ (*plural* **-chies**) *n* an argument about the use or meaning of words [Mid-16C. < Greek *logomakhia* < *logomakhein* 'to fight with words' < *logos* 'word']

logon /lóggon/ *n* **1.** the act of logging on to a computer **2.** a name and password or other appropriate commands used for logging on to a computer

logorrhea *n* US spelling of **logorrhoea**

logorrhoea /lóggə reé ə/ *n* excessive talkativeness, especially when the words are uncontrolled or incoherent, as in some psychiatric conditions —**logorrhoeic** *adj*

Logos /lóggoss/ *n* **1.** Jesus Christ, so named in St John's Gospel, as the word of God, the personification of the wisdom of God, and divine wisdom as the means for human salvation **2.** in Judaism, the divine wisdom of the word of God [Late 16C. < Greek, 'word, reason']

logotype /lóggō tīp/ *n* **1.** a single piece of type that has different unconnected characters on it **2.** same as **logo**

logroll /lóg rōl/ (**-rolls**, **-rolling**, **-rolled**) *vti N Am* to trade votes with political colleagues to support one another's interests [Mid-19C. Back-formation < LOGROLLING]

logrolling /lóg rōling/ *n N Am* the striking of a deal between colleagues in a legislature whereby support is given to a piece of legislation on the understanding that the favour will be returned at a later date ○'*The national interest will lose out to the logrolling trade-offs of Congressional business.*' (*Bush speeches in campaign '92*; 1992) [Early 19C. < the US custom of neighbours helping each other to clear land by rolling logs to burn them]

-logue *suffix* speech ○ *monologue* [Via French < Greek *-logos* 'speaking' < *logos* 'word']

logwood /lóg woŏd/ *n* **1.** a spiny leguminous tree. Native to: Caribbean, Central America. Latin name: *Haematoxylon campechianum*. **2.** the wood of the logwood, which yields a purplish-red dye [Late 16C. Because the tree's wood was imported in log form]

logy /lṓgi/ (**-gier**, **-giest**) *adj N Am* with no energy or enthusiasm [Mid-19C. Origin ?]

-logy *suffix* **1.** speech, expression ○ *haplology* **2.** science, study ○ *musicology* [Directly or via French < Greek *-logia* < *logos* 'word, reason' and < *-logos* 'speaking']

loin /loyn/ *n* **1.** ANAT **BACK BETWEEN RIBS AND HIPS** the area on each side of the backbone of a human or other animal between the ribs and hips **2.** FOOD **MEAT CUT FROM LOIN OF ANIMAL** a prime cut of tender meat taken from the backbone and rib area of a pig, lamb, or calf ■ **loins** *npl* **AREA BELOW WAIST** the hips and the front of the body below the waist, considered as the part of the body that should be covered and as the site of the sexual organs (*literary*) [14C. Via Old French *loigne* < Latin *lumbus*] ◇ **gird (up) your loins** to prepare yourself to do something difficult and challenging

loincloth /lóyn kloth/ *n* a cloth covering the hips and the genital area typically worn by men in hot countries

Loire /lwaar/ longest river in France, rising in the Cévennes mountains, southeastern France. Length: 1,020 km/634 mi.

---

a at; aa father; aw all; ay day; ai hair; ə about, item, edible, common, circus; e egg; ee eel; hw when; i it, happy; ī ice; 'l apple; 'm rhythm; 'n fashion; o odd; ō open; oŏ good; oo pool; ow owl; oy oil; th thin; th this; u up; ur urge;

loiter /lóytər/ (**-ters, -tering, -tered**) *vi* **1.** to stand around without any obvious purpose **2.** to do something in a slow lazy way, stopping often to rest [15C. Origin ?] —**loiterer** *n*

loitering /lóytəring/, **loitering with intent** *n* formerly in English law, the offence of standing around in a public place with the apparent intention of committing a crime, especially soliciting

Loki /lṓki/ *n* in Norse mythology, a handsome giant god who was the embodiment of mischief or evil

Lok Sabha /lōk súbbə/ *n* the lower chamber of the Indian Parliament [< Hindi, 'people's assembly']

Lolita /lo leétə/ *n* a young teenage girl regarded or depicted as the object of sexual desire [Mid-20C. After the main character in *Lolita* (1958), novel by Vladimir Nabokov]

loll /lol/ (**lolls, lolling, lolled**) *vi* **1.** to relax in a reclining or leaning position **2.** to droop or hang down in a loose floppy way [14C. Origin ?]

Lolland /lóllənd/ island of southeastern Denmark, situated in the Baltic Sea. Population: 72,026 (1994). Area: 1,241 sq. km/479 sq. mi.

lollapalooza /lólləpə loózə/, **lalapalooza** /lálləpə loózə/, **lallapalooza** *n N Am* something that or somebody who is particularly wonderful and impressive or an outstanding example of something (*informal*) [Early 20C. Origin ?]

lollipop /lólli pop/ *n* a large boiled sweet, usually spherical or disc-shaped, fixed onto a stick [Late 18C. Origin ?]

lollipop lady *n* a woman employed to stop traffic to allow schoolchildren to cross a road (*informal*) [< the shape of the sign used]

lollipop man *n* a man employed to stop traffic to allow schoolchildren to cross a road (*informal*) [< the shape of the sign used]

lollipop person *n* somebody employed to stop traffic to allow schoolchildren to cross a road (*informal*)

lollop /lólləp/ (**-lops, -loping, -loped**) *vi* **1.** to move in a bouncy clumsy way **2.** to loll or lounge about [Mid-18C. < LOLL, influenced by GALLOP] —**lollopy** *adj*

lollo rosso /lóllō róssō/ *n* a variety of lettuce with curly red-tipped leaves [< Italian, literally 'red husk']

lolly /lólli/ (*plural* **-lies**) *n* **1.** same as **lollipop** (*informal*) **2.** *UK* same as **ice lolly** (*informal*) **3.** same as **money** (sense 1) (*informal*) **4.** *Aus* a sweet made from boiled sugar [Mid-19C. Shortening of LOLLIPOP]

lollygag /lólli gag/ (**-gags, -gagging, -gagged**), **lallygag** /lálli gag/ *vi N Am* to waste time in a pleasant idle way (*dated*) [Mid-19C. Origin ?] —**lollygagger** *n*

lolly water *n Aus* a soft drink

Lomax /lṓ maks/, **Alan** (1915–2002) US ethnomusicologist. He was noted for his work in the collection of American folk songs, in collaboration with his father John Lomax.

Lomax, John (1867–1948) US ethnomusicologist. He was noted for his work in the collection of American folk songs, in collaboration with his son Alan Lomax.

Lombard /lómbərd, -baard/ *n* **1.** somebody who comes from Lombardy in Italy **2.** a member of an ancient Germanic people who settled in northern Italy during the 6th century AD and soon became the dominant group there

Lombardy /lómbərdi/ region in northern-central Italy, a major commercial and industrial centre. Area: 23,861 sq. km/9,213 sq. mi. Population: 9,065,440 (2000). —**Lombardic** /lom baárdik/ *adj*

Lombardy poplar *n* a variety of poplar that has upright branches and a tall narrow shape. Latin name: *Populus nigra italica.*

Lombok /lómbok/ island of the Lesser Sunda Islands, West Nusa Tenggara Province, southern Indonesia, situated east of Bali. Population: 2,403,399 (1990). Area: 5,180 sq. km/2,000 sq. mi.

Lomé /lṓ may/ capital and largest city of Togo, situated on the Bight of Benin, close to the Ghana border. Population: 700,000 (1997).

loment /lṓ ment/, **lomentum** /lō méntəm/ (*plural* **-menta** /-tə/) *n* a pod or fruit that splits and separates at maturity into one-seeded segments [Mid-19C. < Latin *lomentum* 'cosmetic made of bean-meal' < *lavare* 'to wash']

Lomond, Loch /lṓmənd/ largest lake in Scotland, located north of Glasgow. Area: 71 sq. km/27 sq. mi.

Lomu /lṓmoo/, **Jonah** (*b.* 1975) New Zealand rugby union player. At the age of 19, he became the youngest-ever New Zealand international player.

London /lúndən/ **1.** capital city of the United Kingdom of Great Britain and Northern Ireland. It is one of the world's leading financial, industrial, and cultural centres. Population: 7,172,091 (2001). Area: 1,580 sq. km/610 sq. mi. **2.** city in Middlesex County, southwestern Ontario, Canada, on the Thames River. Population: 337,318 (2001). —**Londoner** *n*

London, Jack (1876–1916) US writer. He wrote realist and humanitarian novels, including *The Call of the Wild* (1903), which was inspired by his experiences in the Klondike. Born **Chaney, John Griffith**

> 'He must master or be mastered; while to show mercy was a weakness. Mercy did not exist in the primordial life. It was misunderstood for fear, and such misunderstandings made for death.'
> [Jack London, *The Call of the Wild*; 1903]

London Academy of Music and Dramatic Art *n* a leading institution for training students for careers in the theatre and music, based in London

Londonderry /lúndən deri/ **1.** city in northwestern Northern Ireland, officially called 'Derry' until it was fortified by people from London, England, in 1613. Population: 72,334 (1991). **2.** former county of Northern Ireland

London pride *n* a variety of saxifrage with rosettes of fleshy leaves. Flowers: pale pink in clusters on long stems. Latin name: *Saxifraga urbium.*

lone /lōn/ *adj* **1.** SOLITARY having no one else around **2.** ONLY only or sole ○ *a lone survivor* **3.** ISOLATED situated in an isolated position **4.** SINGLE without a husband, wife, or partner **5.** LONELY lonely and having no companions (*literary*) [14C. Shortening of ALONE]

lone hand *n* **1.** in some card games, a hand played without help from a partner, or a player without a partner **2.** somebody who lives or works alone

lonely /lṓnli/ (**-lier, -liest**) *adj* **1.** FEELING ALONE feeling sad through being without friends or company ○ *I felt so lonely after he'd gone.* **2.** ISOLATED isolated and rarely visited ○ *a lonely farmhouse in the middle of the moor* **3.** WITHOUT COMPANIONSHIP OR SUPPORT done or lived through without companionship or support from other people ○ *a lonely existence* **4.** same as **lone** (sense 2) (*informal*) ○ *one lonely pea left on the plate* —**loneliness** *n*

lonely hearts *adj* relating to people who are looking for a partner for a romantic relationship

~~**lonelyness**~~ incorrect spelling of **loneliness**

lone pair *n* a pair of unshared electrons in a molecule that are not involved in bonding in that molecule

loner /lṓnər/ *n* somebody who prefers to work or be alone

lonesome /lṓnssəm/ *adj N Am* **1.** SAD FROM BEING ALONE feeling sad, or causing a feeling of sadness, because of being alone **2.** DESOLATE isolated from human habitation **3.** ALONE having no one or nothing else around —**lonesomely** *adv* —**lonesomeness** *n*

lone wolf *n* same as **loner**

long[1] /long/ *adj* **1.** EXTENDING CONSIDERABLE DISTANCE extending a relatively great length or height **2.** GOING ON FOR LENGTHY PERIOD lasting for an extended period of time **3.** HAVING MANY ITEMS containing a relatively large number of parts or individual items ○ *a long list* **4.** OF PARTICULAR LENGTH of a particular length, height, total, number, or duration ○ *a book 300 pages long* **5.** LONGER THAN IT IS WIDE with a greater length than width ○ *Look in the long box, not the square one.* **6.** BEYOND WHAT IS WANTED extending in time or space beyond what is considered normal, reasonable, or desirable ○ *The speech was rather long, don't you think?* **7.** MORE DISTANT OR LENGTHY the more or most distant or lengthy of two or more things ○ *the long way home* **8.** ABLE TO REACH CONSIDERABLE DISTANCE capable of reaching or travelling far ○ *to have a long reach* **9.** SEEMING TO LAST FOREVER appearing to be or take more time than is really the case ○ *a long hour waiting* **10.** GOING FAR BACK IN TIME extending back in time ○ *a long memory* **11.** CONTAINING MUCH LIQUID containing a large quantity of liquid to drink, especially of a thirst-quenching kind ○ *a long cold drink on a hot day* **12.** EXTENSIVE exhaustive and critical ○ *Take a good long look at yourself.* **13.** RISKY with an uncertain outcome ○ *long odds* **14.** HAVING PLENTY OF SOMETHING possessing enough or more than enough of something (*informal*) ○ *a politician who is long on rhetoric* **15.** FIN HOLDING STOCK IN ANTICIPATION OF RISE describes shares and other securities or commodities that are held with the expectation that prices will rise **16.** PHON DRAWN OUT IN PRONUNCIATION describes a speech sound that is relatively drawn out **17.** PHON DESCENDED FROM LONG VOWEL describes an English vowel sound that is historically descended from vowels that were drawn out in pronunciation, e.g. the ones in English 'beet' and 'bite' **18.** LITERAT ACCENTED describes a syllable in accentual verse that is stressed **19.** LITERAT OF GREATER METRICAL DURATION describes a syllable in quantitative verse that is the one of the two types that is of greater duration ■ *adv* **1.** FOR LONG TIME for or during a lengthy period of time ○ *Have you been here long?* **2.** FAR at or over a great distance ○ *hit the ball long* **3.** FOR CERTAIN TIME for or during a particular length of time ○ *work all day long* **4.** AT ANOTHER TIME at a time much later or earlier than the time specified ○ *long after he left* **5.** FIN IN LONG STOCK POSITION in a long position in securities or commodities ○ *selling long* ■ *n* **1.** LONG TIME a lengthy period of time ○ *Will you be visiting for long?* **2.** PHON LONG SOUND a long syllable or sound **3.** CLOTHING SIZE FOR TALL PEOPLE a garment or garment size designed for somebody tall ■ **longs** *npl* **1.** CLOTHING LONG TROUSERS trousers with full-length legs (*informal*) **2.** FIN LONG-DATED GILT-EDGED SECURITIES gilt-edged securities with more than 15 years to run before redemption **3.** FIN SECURITIES HELD UNTIL PRICES RISE securities or commodities that are held with the expectation that prices will rise [Old English, < Germanic] —**longness** *n* ◇ **as** *or* **so long as 1.** for the whole of the time that **2.** provided that or on condition that **3.** because of the fact that ◇ **before long** before much time passes ◇ **longer term** insofar as a longer period of future time is concerned ◇ **long since** a long time ago ◇ **no longer** until the present but not for any further time ◇ **not long for** with little time remaining for ◇ **so long** good-bye (*informal*) ◇ **the long and the short of it** the basic idea or facts

long[2] /long/ (**longs, longing, longed**) *vi* to have a strong desire for a person, place, or thing, especially somebody or something unattainable or not within immediate reach ○ *She longed for a bit of excitement in her life.* [Old English *langian* < Germanic]

SYNONYMS See *want.*

Long /long/, **Richard** (*b.* 1945) British artist. His works often feature natural landscapes, either in photographs, *A Hundred Mile Walk* (1971–72), or materials, *Red Slate Circle* (1980). He was awarded the Turner Prize in 1989.

long. *abbr* GEOG longitude

long-ago *adj* relating to or existing in the distant past ○ *long-ago civilizations*

longan /lóngən/, **lungan** /lúngən/ *n* **1.** a small juicy fruit with a yellowish-brown exterior, white juicy flesh, and a large black seed **2.** an evergreen tree that produces longans. Native to: tropical and subtropical Asia. Latin name: *Euphoria longan.* [Mid-18C. < Chinese *lóngyan* 'dragon's eye']

long-awaited *adj* hoped for and expected for a considerable time

Long Beach city in Los Angeles County, southwestern California, situated on San Pedro Bay. Population: 472,412 (2002 estimate).

long black *n ANZ* a half-strength espresso in a standard-size cup

longboard /lóng bawrd/ *n* a surfboard that exceeds a specific length, longer than a shortboard —**longboarding** *n*

longboat /lóng bōt/ *n* **1.** the longest boat, usually a seaworthy rowing boat, carried on board a sailing ship, especially a merchant ship **2.** same as **longship**

long bone *n* any long cylindrical limb bone in vertebrates that contains marrow and ends in an enlarged head that unites to form a joint with another bone

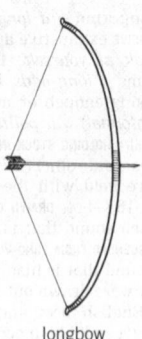

longbow

longbow /lóngbō/ n a large powerful hand-drawn bow made from a long piece of slightly curved wood and a bowstring, used, especially in medieval England, for hunting and in warfare —**longbowman** n

longcase clock /lóng kayss-/ n FURNITURE same as **grandfather clock**

long-chain adj describes a molecule or substance that has a relatively long chain of atoms, especially carbon atoms

long-dated adj describes a gilt-edged security that has more than 15 years to run before redemption

long-day adj describes plants requiring long periods of daylight, usually more than 12 hours, followed by short nights in order to mature and flower

long-distance adj **1.** FOR LONG WAY travelling or extending a relatively long way **2.** BETWEEN DISTANT PHONES relating to or providing a telephone service between places that are far apart **3.** BETWEEN DISTANT PLACES occurring between places that are far apart ○ a long-distance romance ■ adv USING LONG-DISTANCE CONNECTION using a long-distance telephone line

$$
\begin{array}{r}
71.3 \\
58\ \overline{)\ 4135.4} \\
-406 \\
\hline
75 \\
-58 \\
\hline
174 \\
174 \\
\hline
0
\end{array}
$$

long division

long division n a method or instance of dividing one number by another in which each step is written out in full

long dozen n a set of 13 items

long-drawn-out adj going on for an undesirably long period of time

long drink n a large cold refreshing drink, usually containing little or no alcohol

long drop n a pit latrine

longe n, vt RIDING same as **lunge**[2]

Long Eaton /-eet'n/ town in Derbyshire, central England. Population: 44,826 (1991).

longeron /lónjərən/ n a main structural component of an aeroplane's fuselage that runs from one end of the aeroplane to the other [Early 20C. < French]

long-established adj having existed for a long time in a position of general respect or widespread success

longevity /lon jévvəti/ (plural **-ties**) n **1.** LONG LIFE long duration of life **2.** DURATION OF LIFE the length of a person's or animal's life **3.** CAREER SPAN the length of somebody's employment or career [Early 17C. < late Latin longaevitas < Latin longaevus 'of a long age' < longus 'long' (< Germanic) + aevum 'age'] —**longevous** adj

long face n a facial expression showing unhappiness, disappointment, or seriousness —**long-faced** adj

Longfellow /lóng fel ō/, Henry Wadsworth (1807–82) US poet. He wrote many romantic verse narratives, including The Song of Hiawatha (1855) and Paul Revere's Ride (1863).

'Under a spreading chestnut tree / The village smithy stands; / The smith, a mighty man is he, / With large and sinewy hands; / And the muscles of his brawny arms / Are strong as iron bands.'
[Henry Wadsworth Longfellow, 'The Village Blacksmith'; 1839]

long finger n Ireland a state of being postponed for a long time (informal)

Longford /lóngfərd/ county in Leinster Province, central Republic of Ireland. Population: 30,166 (2002). Area: 1,044 sq. km/403 sq. mi.

Longford, Francis Aungier Pakenham, 7th Earl (1905–2001) British politician. Once a Conservative, he later held ministerial posts in Labour governments. He was an advocate of penal reform.

'On the whole I would not say that our Press is obscene. I would say that it trembles on the brink of obscenity.'
[Francis Aungier Pakenham Longford, Observer; 1963]

Longford, Raymond Hollis (1878–1959) Australian actor and director. His silent films include The Sentimental Bloke (1919). Born **Longford, John Walter**

longhair /lóng hair/ n **1.** CAT WITH LONG FUR a domestic cat with long fur **2.** N Am SOMEBODY DEDICATED TO ARTS AND MUSIC somebody dedicated to the arts and especially to classical music (informal) **3.** US LONG-HAIRED MAN somebody with long hair, especially a hippie man (dated informal disapproving) —**long-haired** adj

longhand /lóng hand/ n words and letters written by hand in full, rather than in shorthand

long haul n (informal) **1.** LONG DISTANCE a long journey or distance **2.** LOT OF WORK a long-lasting job or ordeal **3.** LENGTHY PERIOD a long period of time ◇ **for** or **over the long haul** US for a long period of time

long-haul adj relating to travel or transportation over long distances

long-headed /-héddid/ adj perceptive and wise (archaic or literary) [< the belief that a long head indicated wisdom]

long hop n in cricket, a short delivery that is very easy to hit

longhorn /lóng hawrn/ (plural **-horns** or same) n **1.** a red or variegated cow with long horns, belonging to a breed of beef cattle of Spanish origin that was once very common in the southwestern United States **2.** a cow belonging to a breed that has long horns

long-horned beetle n N Am INSECTS same as **longicorn**

long-horned grasshopper n a large, usually green grasshopper with long antennae and often a characteristic song. Family: Tettigoniidae

long house n **1.** N Am a long bark-covered communal dwelling place built by some Native North American peoples, especially the Iroquois. It had compartments for families around central meeting areas. **2.** a communal dwelling housing accommodating entire extended families and found especially in Borneo or Sarawak

long hundredweight n MEASURE same as **hundredweight** (sense 1)

longicorn /lónji kawrn/ n a beetle with long antennae, long legs, and a narrow, often brightly coloured body. The larvae of many species are wood borers. Family: Cerambycidae. N Am term **long-horned beetle** ■ adj having long antennae [Mid-19C. < modern Latin Longicornia 'long-horned ones' < Latin longus 'long' (< Germanic) + cornu 'horn']

longing /lónging/ n a persistent and strong desire, usually for somebody or something unattainable or not within immediate reach ■ adj expressing yearning or desire —**longingly** adv

Long Island largest island in the continental United States, in southeastern New York State. Queens and Brooklyn, two boroughs of New York City, are situated at the western end of the island. The Hamptons, a series of resort towns, are located on the island's eastern stretch. Population: 6,882,362 (2002 estimate). Area: 4,463 sq. km/1,723 sq. mi.

Long Island Sound body of salt water situated between the southern shore of Connecticut and the north shore of Long Island, New York. Area: 3,364 sq. km/1,299 sq. mi.

longitude /lónji tyood, lónggi-/ n **1.** the angular distance east or west of the prime meridian that stretches from the North Pole to the South Pole and passes through Greenwich, England. Longitude is measured in degrees, minutes, and seconds. **2.** a region near a particular longitude [14C. < Latin longitudo 'length' < longus 'long' < Germanic]

longitudinal /lónji tyoodin'l, lónggi-/ adj **1.** RUNNING LENGTHWAYS extending or placed along the length of something, as opposed to across it **2.** OVER TIME relating to development over a period of time **3.** OF LONGITUDE relating to longitude or length —**longitudinally** adv

longitudinal study (plural **longitudinal studies**), **longitudinal survey** n a study repeated over time, e.g. following the health of 20,000 people over the age of 50 over a period of 20 years

longitudinal wave n a wave such as a sound wave that is propagated in the same direction in which the particles of the medium vibrate

long jenny /-jénni/ n in billiards, a shot in which the ball goes into a far pocket after striking another ball [< JENNY 'losing hazard with the object ball near a cushion']

long johns /-jonz/ npl underpants with full-length legs, or one-piece underwear covering the torso, arms, and legs [< the name John]

long jump n an athletics event in which the contestants jump for distance, usually from a running start into a sand pit —**long jumper** n

long-lasting adj continuing for a long time

longleaf pine /lóng leef-/ n **1.** a pine tree with long needles, orange-brown bark, and dense resinous wood. Native to: southeastern United States. Latin name: Pinus palustris. **2.** the wood of the longleaf pine, used for timber

long lease n in England and Wales, a lease for a period of more than 21 years on a house that is the occupants' main residence

long leg n in cricket, a position on the leg side behind the batsman's wicket and close to the boundary, or a fielder occupying this position

long-legged /-legd, -léggid/ adj **1.** with long legs **2.** capable of running quickly

long-life adj specially treated to last for a long time ○ long-life milk

long list n a selection from a large number of items or people that will be used to form a short list

long-list vt to draw up a long list (often passive) ○ was long-listed for the Booker prize

long-lived adj living, lasting, or enduring for a long time

long-lost adj not seen for a long period of time

long measure n **1.** MEASURE same as **linear measure** **2.** LITERAT same as **long metre**

long metre n a four-line stanza in which the second and fourth lines always rhyme and the first and third sometimes rhyme. It is often used for hymns.

long moss n PLANTS same as **Spanish moss**

long-off n in cricket, a position on the off side, behind the bowler and close to the boundary, or a fielder occupying this position

long-on n in cricket, a position on the leg side, behind the bowler and close to the boundary, or a fielder occupying this position

long pig n human flesh as eaten by cannibals [Translation of a Polynesian name]

long-playing record n RECORDING full form of **LP**

long purse n a great deal of money (dated informal)

long-range adj **1.** EXTENDING WELL INTO FUTURE extending a long time into the future **2.** TRAVELLING LONG DISTANCES able to travel long distances **3.** ARMS ABLE TO HIT DISTANT TARGET relating to weapons that are capable of hitting a target a considerable distance away

Longreach /lóng reech/ town in central Queensland, Australia, a cattle-grazing centre. Population: 3,604 (1991).

long-running *adj* **1.** continuing for a long time ○ *a long-running war of words* **2.** having been performed or broadcast for many weeks, months, or years in succession ○ *a long-running Broadway musical*

long-service leave *n ANZ* extended paid leave awarded in some places of employment, especially in public service, in recognition of long service

longship /lóng ship/ *n* a narrow wooden ship with oars and a large square sail used by the Vikings

longshore /lóng shawr/ *adj* living, working, or situated on the coast [Early 19C. Shortening of ALONGSHORE]

longshoreman /lóng shawrmən/ (*plural* **-men** /-mən/) *n N Am* same as **docker**

long shot *n* **1.** SOMEBODY OR SOMETHING UNLIKELY TO WIN somebody or something that is unlikely to win a race or competition **2.** GAMBLING **BET UNLIKELY TO WIN** a bet on somebody or something that is unlikely to win a race or competition **3.** VENTURE UNLIKELY TO SUCCEED a venture that has little chance of success, although, if successful, an excellent chance of profit or reward **4.** PHOTOGRAPHY **CAMERA SHOT OF DISTANT OBJECT** a camera shot taken some distance from the object or scene ◇ **(not) by a long shot** (not) in any way at all (*informal*)

long-sighted *adj* **1.** able to see distant objects more easily than near objects, which can be seen clearly only by strongly focusing the eyes. N Am term **farsighted 2.** taking future problems or needs into consideration —**long-sightedly** *adv* —**long-sightedness** *n*

Longs Peak /lóngz-/ mountain in northern Colorado, the highest peak in Rocky Mountain National Park. Height: 4,345 m/14,255 ft.

longspur /lóng spur/ (*plural* **-spurs** or *same*) *n* a bird with brownish feathers and long-clawed hind toes. Native to: northern United States, Canada, the Arctic. Genus: *Calcarius*.

long-standing *adj* having existed or been going on for a long period of time

long-suffering *adj* patient and enduring in the face of suffering or difficulty ■ *n* patience and endurance in the face of suffering or difficulty —**long-sufferingly** *adv*

long suit *n* **1.** the suit to which the majority of cards in a player's hand belongs **2.** somebody's strongest quality or talent (*informal*)

long-tailed duck *n UK* a duck with a black back and wings, a white breast, a brown-and-white head, and a long pointed tail. Native to: Arctic seas. Latin name: *Clangula hyemalis*. ANZ, N Am term **oldsquaw**

long term *n* the period of time extending from the present far into the future

long-term *adj* **1.** IN FUTURE relating to or affecting a time long into the future **2.** ACCT **WITH LONGER ACCOUNTING PERIOD** with or relating to an accounting period of longer than one year **3.** FIN **MATURING IN NUMBER OF YEARS** maturing only after a long time, usually a number of years **4.** LONG-LASTING continuing for a long period of time

long-term memory *n* the part of the mind that retains information permanently or nearly so

longtime /lóng tīm/ *adj* having continued in existence for a long period of time

long tin *n* an oblong loaf of bread with a risen rounded crusty top, made in a long baking tin (*dated*)

long tom *n* **1.** LONG-BARRELLED CANNON USED BY NAVY a swivelling cannon with a long barrel, used in the past by the navy **2.** LONG-RANGE CANNON USED BY ARMY a long-range cannon used by the army **3.** AUTOMATIC ANTI-AIRCRAFT GUN a large-calibre automatic antiaircraft gun (*slang*)

long ton *n* MEASURE same as **ton**[1] (sense 1)

Longueuil /lóng gayl, loN göyi/ city in southern Quebec Province, Canada, situated on the St Lawrence River. Population: 128,016 (2001).

longueur /long gúr/ *n* a boring section, stretch, or period within something, e.g. a dull passage in a book or tedious scene in a play [Late 18C. < French, 'length' < *long* 'long' < Latin *longus* < Germanic]

long vacation, long vac *n* a period of approximately three months in the summer when law courts and universities are closed

long view *n* the consideration of how events or circumstances are likely to develop in the long term

long wave *n* (*hyphenated before a noun*) **1.** a radio wave with a wavelength of 1,000 m or more **2.** the broadcasting or receiving of radio waves of 1,000 m or more in length

longways /lóng wayz/ *adj, adv* same as **lengthways**

long weekend *n* a weekend with an extra day's holiday either on the Friday before, or the Monday after, or both

long-winded /-wíndid/ *adj* **1.** tediously wordy in speech or writing **2.** capable of doing physical exercise for a relatively long period of time without getting short of breath —**long-windedly** *adv* —**long-windedness** *n*

SYNONYMS See *wordy*.

longwise /lóng wīz/ *adj, adv N Am* same as **lengthways**

Longyearbyen /lóng yeer byen/ town in the Svalbard archipelago of Norway, north of the Arctic Circle

loo[1] /loo/ (*plural* **loos**) *n* same as **toilet** (senses 1–2) (*informal*) [Mid-20C. Origin ?]

ORIGIN The most widely claimed source of ***loo*** is *gardy loo* (based on pseudo-French *gare de l'eau* 'mind the water'), used in 18th-century Edinburgh to warn passers-by when a chamber pot was about to be emptied into the street below. However, this is chronologically unlikely, as there is no evidence of ***loo*** being used for 'lavatory' before the 1930s. Other possible candidates include *Waterloo* (the link with 'water' gives this some plausibility) and *louvre*, from the use of slatted screens for a makeshift lavatory. The likeliest source is perhaps French *lieux d'aisances*, literally 'places of ease', hence 'lavatory', possibly picked up by British service personnel in France during World War I.

loo[2] /loo/ (*plural* **loos**) *n* **1.** a gambling card game in which players place the money they are betting in a pool **2.** a bet placed in the pool in a game of loo [Late 17C. < French *lantur(e)lu*, refrain of a song]

looby /lóobi/ (*plural* **-bies**) *n* somebody considered to be unintelligent or lazy (*archaic insult*) [14C. Origin ?]

loofah /lóofə/ *n* **1.** a sponge made from the dried fibrous interior of an oblong fruit of a tropical gourd **2.** a vine of the gourd family that produces the large oblong fruits from which loofah sponges are made. Native to: tropical regions of the eastern hemisphere. Genus: *Luffa*. [Late 19C. < Arabic *lūfa*]

look /lòok/ *v* (**looks, looking, looked**) **1.** *vti* DIRECT EYES AT SOMETHING to turn the eyes towards or on something ○ *What are you looking at?* ○ *Look me in the eye.* **2.** *vi* USE EYES TO SEARCH to use the eyes to examine, watch, or find somebody or something ○ *We looked everywhere.* **3.** *vi* SEEM AS SPECIFIED to have the appearance of being or seem to be as specified ○ *He looks tired.* **4.** ⚠ *vi* CONSIDER SOMETHING to direct the attention towards something in order to consider it ○ *Let's look at the possible options.* **5.** *vt* APPEAR FITTING FOR SOMETHING to have an appearance that is in accordance with something ○ *He looks his age.* **6.** *vi* USE EYES IN SPECIFIED WAY to use the eyes in a particular way ○ *He looked intently at the ball.* **7.** *vi* FACE PARTICULAR WAY to face a particular direction or have a particular view ○ *The room looks over the lake.* **8.** *vt* EXPRESS SOMETHING to communicate something by an expression ○ *She looked her anger at all of us.* **9.** *vi* PAY ATTENTION used to tell somebody to pay attention or see something ○ *Look, why don't we split the difference?* ○ *Look! There he goes!* ■ *n* **1.** ACT OR INSTANCE OF LOOKING an act or instance of looking, e.g. to examine, watch, or find something ○ *Take a look at this.* **2.** WAY SOMEBODY OR SOMETHING APPEARS an impression conveyed by a manner or quality ○ *He has the look of someone enjoying himself.* **3.** EXPRESSION a facial expression that communicates something ○ *a meaningful look* **4.** FASHION an appearance, style, or fashion, especially of dress or hairstyle ■ **looks** *npl* OUTWARD APPEARANCE somebody's outward physical appearance, especially if it is pleasing ○ *good looks* [Old English *lōcian* < Germanic]

USAGE look at meaning 'consider'. Though often used orally and in informal writing, as in *Informed sources tell us that the court is going to look at the case*, some people object to this wording as vague and unacceptably casual when used in formal settings. Choose a more precise word such as *examine*, *study*, *investigate*, *analyse*, or *scrutinize*, depending on your intended meaning.

look after *vt* to care for or be responsible for somebody or something

look ahead *vi* to think about or plan for the future

look back *vi* **1.** to think about the past or past experiences **2.** to visit again later on (*informal*)

look down on, look down upon *vt* to regard or treat somebody or something as inferior or with contempt

look for *vt* **1.** to try to find somebody or something **2.** to hope for or anticipate something ○ *We're looking for a successful year.*

look forward to *vt* to anticipate a future event with excitement or pleasure

look in *vi* to pay a short visit (*informal*)

look into *vt* to carry out a careful investigation of something such as a possibility, problem, or crime

look on *v* **1.** *vi* to be a spectator or witness **2.** *also* **look upon** *vt* to regard somebody or something in a particular way

look out *v* **1.** *vi* to take care to avoid danger **2.** *vt* to search for and find something among a number of things, especially personal belongings

look out for *vt* **1.** to watch for somebody or something to appear (*informal*) **2.** to take particular care of somebody or something

look over *vt* **1.** to inspect a property by visiting it and walking round it **2.** to inspect or examine somebody or something either quickly or carefully

look through *vt* to fail to acknowledge somebody's presence, either intentionally or unintentionally ○ *I smiled at her, but she looked right through me.*

look to *vt* **1.** to hope or expect that somebody or something will do or provide something ○ *We always look to you for new ideas.* **2.** to want or hope to do something (*informal*) ○ *if you're looking to upgrade your computer*

look up *v* **1.** *vt* SEARCH FOR INFORMATION to search for information, e.g. by consulting a reference book **2.** *vi* IMPROVE to become better **3.** *vt* VISIT SOMEBODY to locate somebody, especially for a visit

look upon *vt* same as **look on** (sense 2)

look up to *vt* to have respect and admiration for somebody

lookalike /lóokə līk/ *n* somebody or something that looks like somebody or something else (*informal*)

looker /lóokər/ *n* **1.** a watcher, observer, or spectator **2.** a good-looking person, especially a girl or woman (*informal*; *sometimes considered offensive*)

looker-on (*plural* **lookers-on**) *n* same as **onlooker**

look-in *n* (*informal*) **1.** an opportunity to participate in something or be considered for something **2.** a visit of short duration

looking glass *n* a mirror for people to look at themselves in (*archaic*)

CULTURAL NOTE ***Through the Looking-Glass and What Alice Found There***, a children's story (1871) by Lewis Carroll. In this inspired sequel to *Alice's Adventures in Wonderland*, Alice climbs through a mirror into a magical world where chesspieces come alive, and flowers, insects, and animals all talk. The story features bizarre characters such as Tweedledum and Tweedledee and Humpty Dumpty, and the well-known poems 'Jabberwocky' and 'The Walrus and the Carpenter'.

looking-glass *adj* characterized by the complete reversal of everything normal (*dated*) [< *Through the Looking-Glass* (1871) by Lewis Carroll]

lookist *adj* involving judgments based on physical appearance, especially showing discrimination against people on this basis ■ *n* somebody who judges people on the basis of their physical appearance, especially somebody who discriminates against people in this way —**lookism** *n*

lookout /lóok owt/ *n* **1.** CAREFUL WATCH an act of watching carefully for somebody or something **2.** SOMEBODY WATCHING FOR DANGER somebody who watches carefully for signs of attack or danger **3.** PLACE GIVING GOOD VIEW a place or structure that affords a good view for

observation **4. PROBLEM** a problem or concern (*informal*) ○ *That's your lookout.* **5. PROSPECT** a prospect or outlook (*informal*)

lookover /loŏkōvər/ *n* a quick inspection or examination of something

look-see *n* a brief look or inspection (*informal*)

look-up *n* a computer procedure in which a term or value is matched against a table of stored information

loom[1] /loom/ *vi* (**looms, looming, loomed**) **1. BE ABOUT TO HAPPEN** to be imminent, often in a threatening way **2. BE SEEN AS LARGE SHAPE** to appear as a large or indistinct, and sometimes menacing, shape ■ *n* **APPEARANCE OF SOMETHING LARGE** an appearance of something, usually something large and threatening (*literary*) [Mid-16C. Origin ?]

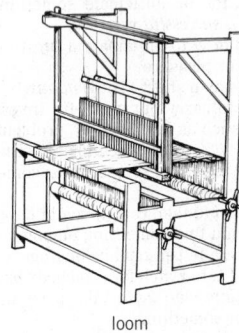

loom

loom[2] /loom/ *n* **1.** a hand-operated or machine-operated device for weaving thread or yarn into cloth **2.** the middle part of an oar between the blade and the handle [Old English *gelōma* 'tool']

loon[1] /loon/ *n* **1. ANZ, N Am** a fish-eating diving bird with a short tail, webbed feet, smooth black-and-white feathers, and a distinctive laughing call. Native to: northern hemisphere. Genus: *Gavia*. UK term **diver 2.** *Can* MONEY same as **loonie** (*informal*) [Mid-17C. Origin ?]

loon[2] /loon/ *n* **1.** an offensive term that deliberately insults somebody's mental condition or intelligence (*slang insult*) **2.** *Scotland* a boy or young man [15C. Origin ?]

looney *adj, n* another spelling of **loony**

loonie /loŏni/ *n Can* a Canadian one-dollar coin with an image of a loon on the back (*informal*) [Late 20C. < LOON[1]]

loons *npl* trousers made of cotton fabric with a low waist and widely flared legs that were fashionable in the late 1960s and early 1970s

loony /loŏni/, **looney, luny** *adj* (**-ier, -iest**) **1. OFFENSIVE TERM** an offensive term meaning irrational **2. SILLY** considered silly, thoughtless, or strange (*informal*) ○ *loony ideas* ■ *n* (**-ies; -eys, -ies**) **1. OFFENSIVE TERM** an offensive term that deliberately insults somebody's intelligence and ability to act rationally (*slang insult*) **2. SOMEBODY SILLY** somebody who behaves eccentrically or thoughtlessly (*informal; often offensive*) [Mid-19C. Shortening and alteration of LUNATIC] —**loonily** *adv* —**looniness** *n*

loony bin *n* an offensive term for a hospital for people who have psychiatric disorders (*informal*)

loony tune *n US* an offensive term for somebody who is regarded as highly eccentric or irrational (*informal insult*)

loop[1] /loop/ *n* **1. CIRCLE OR OVAL** a circular or oval shape formed by a line or something such as a piece of string that curves back over itself **2. CIRCULAR OR OVAL FASTENER OR HANDLE** something that has a closed or nearly closed circular or oval shape and is often used to carry or fasten something **3. CONTRACEPTIVE DEVICE** a contraceptive device in the shape of a loop of plastic or metal that is placed in a woman's womb **4. ELEC CLOSED CIRCUIT** a closed electric circuit **5. COMPUT SET OF COMMANDS IN COMPUTER PROGRAM** a set of instructions in a computer program that is repeated a particular number of times or until a specific objective has been achieved **6. AVIAT FLIGHT MANOEUVRE** a flight manoeuvre in which a plane flies up, over, and down again describing a circle vertically **7. RAIL**

RAILWAY BRANCH LINE a railway branch line that leaves the main line and then joins it again later on **8. CINEMA PIECE OF FILM OR TAPE** a piece of film or tape joined at both ends to allow repeated use of images or sound, especially in dubbing procedures **9. ELEC** same as **loop aerial 10. ANAT COMMON FINGERPRINT PATTERN** the commonest pattern of a human fingerprint formed by U-shaped ridges **11. ICE SKATING SKATING JUMP AND TURN** a jump in which a skater takes off from the outer back edge of a blade, turns in the air, and lands again on the same blade's outer back edge ■ *v* (**loops, looping, looped**) **1. vti MAKE LOOP** to form the shape of a loop, or make something form the shape of a loop **2. vt FIX SOMETHING WITH LOOP** to fasten, join, or arrange something using a loop **3. vi CURVE** to move in a curved path [14C. Origin ?] ◇ **in** or **out of the loop** *N Am* being *or* not being among the people who are decision-makers or are fully informed (*informal*) ◇ **knock** *or* **throw somebody for a loop** *N Am* to surprise, shock, or upset somebody (*informal*)

loop[2] /loop/ *n* a loophole in a wall (*archaic*) [14C. Origin ?]

loop aerial *n* an aerial consisting of a coil of wire wound around a frame

looped /loopt/ *adj* **1.** formed into a circular or oval shape **2.** *N Am* same as **drunk** (*dated slang*)

looper /loopər/ *n* **1.** a maker of loops **2. INSECTS** same as **measuring worm**

loophole /loop hōl/ *n* **1. GAP IN LAW** a small mistake or omission in a rule or law that allows it to be circumvented **2. MIL SLIT IN WALL** a small slit or hole in a wall, especially one in a fortified wall through which guns or other weapons are fired ■ *vt* (**-holes, -holing, -holed**) **MAKE LOOPHOLES IN WALL** to provide a wall with loopholes [< LOOP[2]]

loop knot *n* a square knot that leaves a single loop hanging free

loop line *n* RAIL same as **loop**[1] *n* (sense 7)

loop of Henle /-hénli/ *n* the part of the kidney tubule in birds and mammals that forms a loop between the cortex and medulla [Mid-19C. After Friedrich Gustav Henle (1801–85), German anatomist and pathologist]

loopy /loŏpi/ (**-ier, -iest**) *adj* **1.** an offensive term meaning considered to be irrational **2.** having or consisting of loops

Loos /looss/, **Adolf** (1870–1933) Austrian architect. He was a pioneer of functionalism in architecture, and his Steiner House in Vienna, Austria (1910) was a landmark of modernism and the use of concrete.

loose /looss/ *adj* (**looser, loosest**) **1. NOT FIRMLY FIXED** not firmly fastened or fixed in place ○ *a loose floorboard* **2. SLACK** not fastened or pulled tight ○ *a loose knot* **3. NOT TIGHT-FITTING** not fitting closely and thus baggy **4. FREE** allowed to move around freely without any restraint ○ *broke loose* **5. NOT PACKAGED** not enclosed in a container or bound together ○ *loose tea* **6. NOT FIRMLY PACKED** not compact or dense in texture or arrangement ○ *loose soil* **7. IMPRECISE** not exact, literal, or precise ○ *a loose translation* **8. FLEXIBLE** not strictly controlled or organized ○ *a loose arrangement* **9. AVAILABLE** not earmarked for a particular purpose ○ *loose funds* **10. IRRESPONSIBLE** lacking restraint or a sense of propriety ○ *loose talk* **11. TOO FLUID** too fluid in consistency ○ *characterized by stomach cramps and loose stools* **12. ACCOMPANIED BY PHLEGM** accompanied by the production of phlegm or mucus ○ *a loose cough* **13. RELAXED** relaxed or free from tension (*informal*) **14. PROMISCUOUS** having many sexual partners (*dated; disapproving*) ■ *adv* (**looser, loosest**) **FREELY** freely or without restraint ■ *v* (**looses, loosing, loosed**) **1. vt SET SOMEBODY OR SOMETHING FREE** to release a person or animal from restraint or confinement **2. vt UNTIE KNOT** to undo, untie, or unfasten something **3. vti MAKE SOMETHING LESS TIGHT** to make something less tight, or be made less tight **4. vt RELEASE SOMEBODY FROM OBLIGATION** to release somebody from an obligation or pressure **5. vti FIRE MISSILE** to fire an arrow, bullet, or other missile ■ *n* **RUGBY PLAY** any part of the play in rugby other than scrums, line-outs, or set kicks [12C. < Old Norse *lauss* < Germanic] —**loosely** *adv* —**looseness** *n* ◇ **be on the loose 1.** to be free from confinement, e.g. a prison **2.** to be free from responsibilities and having a good time (*informal*) ◇ **let loose** *N Am* to obtain relief from tension or worry (*informal*)

loosebox /looss boks/ *n* an enclosed compartment forming part of a stable in which the horse is not tied up but can move around. N Am term **box stall**

loose cannon *n* an unpredictable or indiscreet person, often causing trouble for colleagues or associates (*slang*)

loose change *n* a small amount of money in the form of coins

loose cover *n* a fitted cover for a sofa or an armchair that can be easily removed. N Am term **slipcover**

loose end *n* a small part of something such as a project or a story that has not been completed or fully explained (*informal; often used in the plural*) [Referring to the end of a string left hanging] ◇ **at a loose end** restless and a little bored because of having nothing to do

loose-fitting *adj* large, baggy, and not fitting closely to the body ○ *loose-fitting trousers*

loose head *n* the rugby prop forward occupying the position to the left of the hooker in the front row of a scrum

loose-jointed *adj* **1.** agile and supple in movement **2.** having joints that move freely —**loose-jointedness** *n*

loose-leaf *adj* with pages that can be removed and replaced easily

loose-limbed /-límd/ *adj* having supple legs and arms

loose man *n Aus* in Australian Rules, a player who is not being marked by an opposing player

loosen /looss'n/ (**-ens, -ening, -ened**) *v* **1. vti BECOME, OR MAKE SOMETHING, LESS TIGHT** to become less tight or less firmly fixed, or make something become less tight or less firmly fixed **2. vt UNTIE HAIR OR KNOT** to untie something such as hair or a knot **3. vt RELAX CONTROL** to lessen control, pressure, or strictness **4. vt MAKE BOWELS MORE REGULAR** to make somebody's bowel movements more fluid or regular

loosen up *v* **1. vti** to do exercises, or exercise muscles or joints, in order to become more limber, e.g. prior to strenuous activity **2. vi** to become less tense, strict, or serious

loose smut *n* a disease of cereal grasses in which powdery spore masses replace the grain head

loosestrife /looss strīf/ (*plural* **-strifes** or *same*) *n* **1.** a plant of the primrose family with clusters of yellow flowers. Native to: northern temperate regions. Genus: *Lysimachia*. **2.** a plant with spikes of purple flowers that has become an invasive species in North American wetlands. Native to: Europe. Latin name: *Lythrum salicaria*. [Mid-16C. Translation (wrongly, as if < Greek *lusimakhos* 'loosening strife') of Latin *lysimachia*, after *Lysimachus*, Greek physician]

loose-tongued *adj* liable to gossip or reveal information that should be kept secret (*informal*)

loosing /loossing/, **lowsening** /lówsəning/ *n N England* a 21st birthday celebration

loot /loot/ *n* **1. MIL SPOILS OF WAR OR RIOT** money or goods that have been pillaged during wartime or a riot **2. CRIME STOLEN GOODS** money or goods that have been stolen or obtained illegally **3.** same as **money** (sense 1) (*informal*) **4. LOT OF PRESENTS OR PURCHASES** a large amount of goods that have been bought or given on one occasion (*informal*) ■ *vti* (**loots, looting, looted**) **STEAL LOOT FROM PLACE** to steal valuables from a place during a time of disorder or confusion, e.g. during wartime or a riot [Mid-19C. < Hindi *lūṭ*] —**looter** *n*

lop[1] /lop/ *vt* (**lops, lopping, lopped**) **1. CUT BRANCH OFF TREE** to cut a branch off a tree cleanly **2. CUT OFF SOMETHING** to cut off something such as hair or a limb with one stroke **3. GET RID OF SOMEBODY OR SOMETHING** to eliminate somebody or something as superfluous **4. TAKE AMOUNT**

OFF PRICE to deduct an amount from a price ■ *n* **CUT-OFF BRANCH** a branch that has been cut off [Early 16C. Origin ?] —**lopper** *n*

lop[2] /lop/ (**lops, lopping, lopped**) *v* **1.** *vti* to hang, or allow something to hang, loosely **2.** *vi* to move with an awkward slouching posture [Late 16C. Probably suggesting the action of flopping about]

lop[3] /lop/ *n N England* INSECTS same as **flea** [14C. Probably < Old Norse *hlaupa* 'to leap']

lope /lōp/ *v* (**lopes, loping, loped**) **1.** *vi* **RUN IN LONG EASY STRIDES** to run in a relaxed and easy way, taking long strides **2.** *vti* **CANTER** to canter with a long easy stride, or make a horse canter with a long easy stride ■ *n* **LONG-STRIDING GAIT** a relaxed and easy gait with long strides [13C. < Old Norse *hlaupa* 'to leap'] —**loper** *n*

lop-eared /-eerd/ *adj* describes domestic rabbits, dogs, and goats that have loosely hanging ears

Lope de Vega /lōpay de váygə/ (1562–1635) Spanish playwright and poet. Considered the founder of Spanish national drama, he wrote 2,000 plays, more than 400 of which survive. Full name **Vega Carpio, Lope Félix de**

loperamide /lō pérrə mīd/ *n* an opiate drug that slows down the movements of the intestines. Use: treatment of acute and chronic diarrhoea. [Late 20C. Contraction of *chloroprophenyl piperidine butyramide*]

lophophore /lóffō fawr/ *n* a circular or horseshoe-shaped structure of tentacles round the mouth of a bryozoan or brachiopod that is used for capturing food [Mid-19C. < Greek *lophos* 'crest']

lopolith /lóppō lith/ *n* a basin-shaped body of igneous rock formed by the penetration of magma between existing layers of rock [Early 20C. < Greek *lopas* 'basin']

lopsided /lop sídid/ *adj* **1.** leaning or drooping to one side **2.** unevenly balanced because one side is larger, stronger, or heavier than the other [Early 18C. < LOP[2]]

loquacious /lo kwáyshəss/ *adj* tending to talk a great deal [Mid-17C. < Latin *loquaci-* < *loqui* 'speak'] —**loquaciously** *adv* —**loquaciousness** *n* —**loquacity** /lo kwássəti/ *n*

SYNONYMS See *talkative*.

loquat /lō kwot, -kwət/ (*plural* -**quats** or *same*) *n* **1.** a small pear-shaped orange-yellow sweet but slightly tangy fruit, eaten raw or cooked **2.** an evergreen tree that produces loquats. Native to: China, Japan. Latin name: *Eriobotrya japonica*. [Early 19C. < Chinese *luh kwat* 'rush orange']

loran /láwrən/ *n* a long-distance radio navigation system by which a ship or aircraft determines its position using radio signals sent out by two ground stations [Mid-20C. Acronym < *long-range navigation*]

lorazepam /lō rázzə pam/ *n* a mild tranquillizer. Use: relief of anxiety, often before surgery. [Late 20C. Contraction of *chlorodiazepam*]

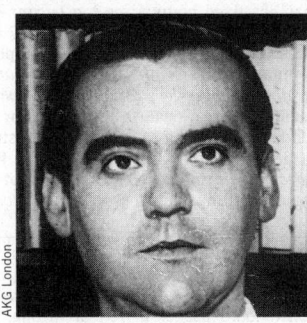

Federico García Lorca

Lorca /láwrkə/, **Federico García** (1898–1936) Spanish poet and playwright. A popular poet and powerful dramatist, he was assassinated by Nationalists during the Spanish Civil War. His works include *Blood Wedding* (1933) and *The House of Bernarda Alba* (1936).

lord /lawrd/ *n* **1.** **ARISTOCRAT** a man who is a member of the nobility, especially in Great Britain **2.** **FEUDAL SUPERIOR** in medieval Europe, a powerful land- or property-owner, with authority over an area, castle, or community, e.g. the lord of a manor **3.** **POWERFUL MAN** a man who has considerable power, authority,

or influence over others, e.g. a business tycoon **4.** **MASTER** a master, ruler, or head of a household, or a woman's husband regarded as her master (*archaic*) [Old English *hlāford*, contraction of *hlāfweard* 'loaf-guardian' < *hlāf*, earlier form of LOAF[1]] ◇ **lord it (over somebody)** to act in a superior, masterful, or bullying way towards somebody (*disapproving*)

SPELLCHECK See *laud*.

Lord *n* **1.** **CHRISTIAN GOD** in Christianity, God or Jesus Christ **2.** **JEWISH GOD** in Judaism, God **3.** **TITLE FOR GOD** used as a title for a deity in Hinduism and some other religions ○ *Lord Krishna* **4.** **TITLE FOR NOBLE** used as an alternative title for a marquess, earl, viscount, or baron **5.** **TITLE FOR NOBLE'S SON** used as a courtesy title for the younger son or sons of a marquess or duke **6.** **FORM OF ADDRESS FOR NOBLE** used as a form of address for an earl, viscount, or baron, and for the younger son of a duke or marquess **7.** **TITLE OF HIGH-RANKING OFFICIAL** a title given to some high-ranking British officials ■ *interj* **EXPRESSING SURPRISE** used to express surprise, concern, or annoyance about something (*informal*) ■ **Lords** *npl* GOV same as **House of Lords**

Lord Advocate *n* the chief law officer in Scotland, responsible for the public prosecution service and the administration of the criminal justice system

Lord Chamberlain *n* the official in charge of the British royal household

Lord Chancellor *n* the cabinet minister in the British government who is responsible for the administration of justice in England and Wales and is also the Speaker in the House of Lords. The post is to be abolished and the role will be undertaken by the Secretary of State for Constitutional Affairs.

Lord Chief Justice *n* in England, a judge who is the Lord Chancellor's deputy and president of the Queen's Bench Division of the High Court of Justice

Lord High Chancellor *n* GOV, LAW same as **Lord Chancellor**

Lord Howe Island /lawrd hów-/ island in the South Pacific Ocean, 700 km/435 mi. northeast of Sydney, Australia. Population: 369 (1996). Area: 145 sq. km/56 sq. mi.

Lord Justice of Appeal (*plural* **Lord Justices of Appeal**) *n* in England, a judge in the Court of Appeal

Lord Lieutenant *n* the representative of the sovereign in a UK county

lordling /láwrdling/ *n* a young, minor, or insignificant lord (*disapproving*)

lordly /láwrdli/ (-**lier**, -**liest**) *adj* **1.** arrogant, aloof, and behaving in a superior way **2.** very grand, magnificent, and suitable for a lord —**lordliness** *n*

Lord Mayor *n* the mayor of the City of London and some other large British boroughs and cities such as York

Lord Muck *n* an offensive term for a man who is thought to have an exaggerated sense of his own importance (*informal*)

Lord of Appeal *n* a judge who assists the House of Lords in hearing appeals

Lord of Hosts *n* in Christianity, God

Lord of Misrule *n* in Europe in the 15th and 16th centuries, somebody appointed to organize celebrations and sporting events, especially at Christmas

Lord of the Flies *n* JUD-CHR same as **Beelzebub**

lordosis /lawr dóssiss/ (*plural* -**doses** /-dō seez/) *n* **1.** an unusual inward curving of the spine in the lower part of the back, which may be medically significant **2.** an inward arching of the back of female mammals during sexual stimulation [Early 18C. Via modern Latin < Greek *lordōsis* < *lordos* 'bent backwards'] —**lordotic** /-dóttik/ *adj*

Lord President of the Council (*plural* **Lord Presidents of the Council**) *n* the cabinet minister in the UK government who presides over meetings of the Privy Council

Lord Privy Seal (*plural* **Lords Privy Seal**) *n* a senior cabinet minister in the British government with no specific portfolio

Lord Protector *n* HIST, POL same as **Protector**

Lord Provost *n* the chairman and head of the local authority in one of the five major Scottish cities, Edinburgh, Glasgow, Aberdeen, Perth, and Dundee

lords-and-ladies *n* PLANTS same as **cuckoopint** [Probably because some plants have dark spadices ('lords') and some light ('ladies')]

Lord's Day *n* in Christianity, Sunday, the Christian Sabbath

lordship /láwrd ship/ *n* **1.** the position held by a lord, or the period of tenure of a lord **2.** the land owned by a lord

Lordship *n* used as a respectful way to refer to or address a judge, a bishop, or some nobles

Lord's Prayer *n* the most important prayer in Christianity, which Jesus Christ taught to his disciples according to the Gospels of Luke and Matthew

Lords Spiritual *npl* the Anglican archbishops of Canterbury and York and the 24 most senior bishops of England and Wales, who are entitled to sit in the House of Lords

Lord's Supper *n* CHR same as **Communion** (sense 1)

Lord's Table *n* **1.** Communion in the Protestant Church **2.** the altar or Communion table in a Protestant church

Lords Temporal *npl* the UK peers sitting in the House of Lords who are not archbishops or bishops

lordy /láwrdi/ *interj* N Am used to express surprise, shock, or disappointment (*dated informal*)

lore[1] /lawr/ *n* **1.** acquired knowledge or wisdom on a subject such as local traditions, handed down by word of mouth and usually in the form of stories or historical anecdotes **2.** knowledge that has been acquired through teaching or experience (*archaic*) [Old English *lār* 'teaching, learning' < Germanic]

lore[2] /lawr/ *n* **1.** the part on each side of a bird's head between its eyes and the base of the beak **2.** the area on a snake's or a fish's face between its eyes and its mouth [Early 17C. < Latin *lorum* 'strap, thong']

Lorelei[1] /lórrə līt, láwrə-/ *n* in German legend, a beautiful woman said to live on a rock near the River Rhine and lure sailors onto the rocks with enchanting songs

Lorelei[2] /lórrə līt, láwrə-/ cliff overlooking the River Rhine between Mainz and Koblenz, west-central Germany. Height: 120 m/390 ft.

Loren /láwr en, law rén/, **Sophia** (b. 1934) Italian actor. Her film career includes both Italian comedies, often with Marcello Mastroianni, and work in Hollywood. Born **Scicolone, Sofia**

Lorentz /lórrənts/, **Hendrik Antoon** (1853–1928) Dutch theoretical physicist. He shared the Nobel Prize in physics with Pieter Zeeman (1902) for his work on electromagnetic radiation.

Lorentz-Fitzgerald contraction /lórrənts fits jérrəld-/ *n* the consequence of relativity that causes a reduction in length of an object travelling at a speed approaching that of light [Early 20C. After Hendrik Antoon LORENTZ and G. F. FITZGERALD]

Lorenz /láw rents/, **Konrad** (1903–89) Austrian zoologist and ethologist. He founded the science of ethology, and his research on animal behaviour included work on imprinting in birds and on human and animal aggression. He shared the Nobel Prize in physiology or medicine (1973). Full name **Lorenz, Konrad Zacharias**

'Just as the transmitting apparatus of animals is considerably more efficient than that of man, so also is their receiving apparatus.'
[Konrad Lorenz, *King Solomon's Ring*; 1949]

lo-res /lō rez/, **low-res** *adj* COMPUT same as **low-resolution** (*informal*) [Shortening and alteration]

lorgnette /lawr nyét/ *n* a pair of glasses or opera glasses held to the eyes by a short handle at one side. See illustration on next page [Early 19C. < French *lorgner* 'squint, peer at' < Germanic]

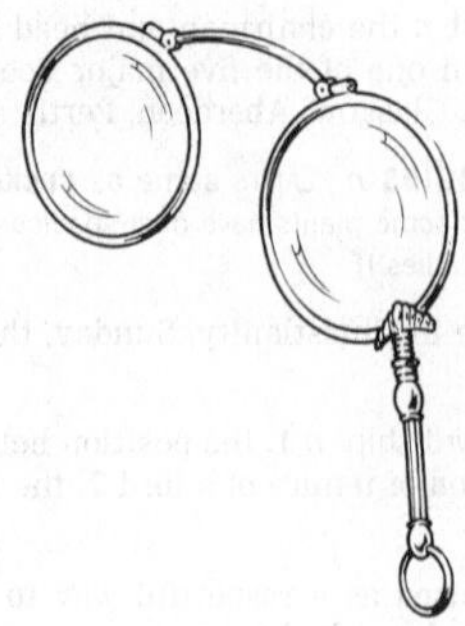

lorgnette

lorica /lórrikə/ (*plural* **-cae** /-kee/) *n* **1.** a light loose external shell that protects ciliated or flagellated protozoans **2.** a protective metal or leather garment covering the chest and back worn by ancient Romans [Early 18C. < Latin, 'breastplate' < *lorum* 'strap']

lorikeet /lórri keet, lórri keét/ (*plural* **-keets** or *same*) *n* a small brightly coloured parrot with a bristle-tipped tongue for extracting nectar and pollen from flowers. It is smaller than a lory. Native to: Australia, Pacific Islands. Subfamily: Loriinae. [Late 18C. < LORY, after PARAKEET]

lorimer /lórrimər/, **loriner** /lórrinər/ *n* formerly, a craftworker who made small metal accessories such as bits and spurs for horses [13C. < Old French *lorenier* < *lorain* 'harness strap' < Latin *lorum* 'strap']

loris /láwriss/ (*plural same*) *n* a small slow-moving tree-dwelling nocturnal primate with large eyes, dense woolly fur, a vestigial index finger, and no tail. Native to: tropical South Asia. Genera: *Loris* or *Nycticebus*. [Late 18C. < French]

Lorrain /lə ráyn/, **Claude** (1600–82) French painter. He was unsurpassed in his mastery of light effects in his idealized landscape paintings, often based on classical or biblical themes. Born **Gellée, Claude**

Lorraine /lə ráyn/ region in eastern France. Capital: Metz. Population: 2,310,376 (1999). Area: 23,540 sq. km/9,100 sq. mi.

lorry /lórri/ (*plural* **-ries**) *n* a large vehicle for transporting goods by road [Mid-19C Origin ?]

lory /láwri/ (*plural* **-ries** or *same*) *n* a small brightly coloured parrot with a bristle-tipped tongue for extracting nectar and pollen from flowers. Native to: Australia, New Guinea, Indonesia. Subfamily: Loriinae. [Late 17C. < Malay *lori*]

Los Alamos /los állə moss/ city in Los Alamos County, central New Mexico, situated approximately 55 km/35 mi. northwest of Santa Fe. Home to the Los Alamos National Laboratory, it was the site chosen in 1942 for research and development of nuclear weapons. Population: 18,305 (2002).

Los Angeles /los ánjələss, -leez/ city and county seat of Los Angeles County, southwestern California. Located on the Pacific Ocean, it is the second most populous city in the United States and home to the University of California at Los Angeles, or UCLA. Population: 3,798,981 (2002 estimate).

lose /looz/ (**loses, losing, lost** /lost/) *v* **1.** *vt* HAVE SOMETHING TAKEN AWAY to cease to possess or have something such as a job or home **2.** *vt* MAKE SOMEBODY FORFEIT SOMETHING to be the cause of somebody's failure to obtain, win, or maintain something ○ *a mistake that lost us the game* **3.** *vt* MISLAY SOMETHING to be unable to find something, often only temporarily **4.** *vti* FAIL TO WIN to fail to win a victory at something, e.g. in a contest, argument, war, game, or in court **5.** *vti* EARN LESS MONEY THAN YOU SPEND to be worse off, or worse off by a particular amount of money, as the result of a financial transaction or through expenditure exceeding income ○ *lost millions when the stock markets crashed* ○ *will lose on the deal* **6.** *vt* CEASE HAVING QUALITY to cease having a quality, belief, attitude, or characteristic ○ *He's lost the will to live.* **7.** *vt* CEASE HAVING ABILITY OR SENSE to cease having an ability or sense, e.g. through illness or an accident ○ *lose your sight* **8.** *vt* EXPERIENCE REDUCTION IN SOMETHING to experience a reduction in something such as weight or heat **9.** *vt* STRAY OFF TRACK to be unable to find the way ○ *lost his way* **10.** *vt* NOT USE SOMETHING TO ADVANTAGE to waste or fail to take advantage of something such as time or an opportunity **11.** *vt* BE UNABLE TO CONTROL SOMETHING to be unable to control an emotion or to maintain composure ○ *He loses his temper easily.* ○ *He finally lost patience with them.* **12.** *vt* HAVE LOVED ONE DIE to suffer the loss of somebody through death, e.g. a loved one, a patient, or a baby before term **13.** *vt* LEAVE SOMEBODY FOLLOWING BEHIND to escape from or leave behind somebody who is in pursuit **14.** *vt* NO LONGER SEE OR HEAR SOMEBODY to be unable to see or hear somebody or something any longer **15.** *vt* CONFUSE SOMEBODY to fail to make somebody understand something ○ *You've lost me there.* **16.** *vt* DISPOSE OF SOMETHING to get rid of something or somebody that is unwanted or undesirable ○ *Lose that extra space on the left.* **17.** *vti* RUN SLOW to be or become slow by an amount of time (*refers to timepieces*) [Old English *losian* 'perish, destroy, lose' < *los* (see LOSS)] —**losable** *adj* —**losableness** *n* ◇ **lose it** (*informal*) **1.** to become removed from reality **2.** to be unable to maintain emotional control or composure

USAGE See *loose*.

lose out *vi* to fail to win or obtain something in a competition or rivalry (*informal*)

~~**loseing**~~ incorrect spelling of **losing**

loser /lóozər/ *n* **1.** SOMEBODY WHO HAS NOT WON a person or team that has failed to win a specific contest **2.** SOMEBODY PUT AT DISADVANTAGE a person or thing adversely affected by a situation or course of action ○ *If this measure goes through, the real losers will be college-leavers.* **3.** TYPE OF LOSER somebody who accepts defeat in a particular way ○ *always was a bad loser* **4.** SOMEBODY UNSUCCESSFUL OR UNLUCKY an unsuccessful or unlucky person who seems destined to fail repeatedly (*informal insult*)

Losey /lṓzi/, **Joseph** (1909–84) US film director. Influential for its camerawork, his work encompassed political and social commentaries, thrillers, and psychological drama, and included *The Servant* (1963), *Accident* (1967), and *The Go-Between* (1971). Full name **Losey, Joseph Walton**

losings /lóozingz/ *npl* money or possessions that are lost, especially through gambling

loss /loss/ *n* **1.** FACT OF NO LONGER HAVING SOMETHING the fact of no longer having something or of having less of something **2.** DEATH the death of somebody **3.** SOMEBODY OR SOMETHING LOST somebody or something that has been lost **4.** MONEY SPENT IN EXCESS OF INCOME the amount of money by which a company's expenses exceed income (*often used in the plural*) **5.** SAD FEELING a feeling of sadness, loneliness, or emptiness at the absence of somebody or something **6.** REDUCTION a reduction in the level of something, especially in the body ○ *weight loss* **7.** INSTANCE OF LOSING CONTEST an instance of losing a competition, race, or contest **8.** ELEC DROP IN ELECTRICAL POWER a drop in power caused by resistance in an electric circuit **9.** INSUR INSTANCE OR AMOUNT OF CLAIM an instance or the amount of a claim made by an insurance policyholder [Old English *los* 'ruin, destruction' < Germanic] ◇ **at a loss** uncertain what to say or do ◇ **cut your losses** to withdraw from a situation in which there is no possibility of winning

loss adjuster *n* somebody employed by an insurance company to assess the financial losses incurred through an insurable event such as accident, theft, fire, or natural disaster and determine the amount of compensation. N Am term **adjuster**

loss leader *n* an item sold at a price below its cost in the hope that customers who buy it will also buy other things

lossmaker /lóss maykər/ *n* a business, organization, or industry that does not make a profit —**lossmaking** *adj*

loss ratio *n* the ratio of the losses paid out in a year by an insurance company to the income from premiums

lost /lost/ *v* past participle, past tense of **lose** ■ *adj* **1.** UNABLE TO FIND WAY unable to find the way to a place **2.** MISLAID unable to be found for the moment **3.** GONE no longer in existence or use **4.** NOT USED PROPERLY wasted or not taken advantage of ○ *a lost opportunity* **5.** CONFUSED BY SOMETHING COMPLICATED confused or bewildered by something complicated or poorly explained **6.** DESTROYED destroyed or killed ○ *The ship was lost in a storm.* **7.** PREOCCUPIED completely absorbed or involved in something ○ *lost in thought* **8.** LACKING CONFIDENCE unable to cope with a job or situation, usually because of inexperience or lack of confidence ○ *feels lost in front of an audience* **9.** UNAPPRECIATED not understood or appreciated by somebody ○ *His jokes were lost on me.* **10.** LACKING MORALS morally or spiritually past hoping for (*formal*) ◇ **get lost** used to tell somebody in a blunt and rude way to go away (*informal*)

lost and found *n NZ, N Am* same as **lost property** (sense 2)

lost cause *n* somebody who cannot be made to change, or something that cannot succeed

lost generation *n* **1.** the large numbers of young men who were killed in World War I **2.** the group of US authors, including Ernest Hemingway and F. Scott Fitzgerald, who rejected American values and lived in Paris in the 1920s.

lost property *n* **1.** personal possessions that have been accidentally left in a public place, e.g. in a cinema or on a train **2.** *also* **lost property office** a place in a public building such as a theatre or railway station, where personal possessions that have accidentally been left behind are kept for reclaiming by their owners ► NZ, N Am term **lost and found**

lost tribes *npl* the ten Hebrew tribes that separated from the other two to create a kingdom in northern Israel after Solomon's death. They were defeated by the Assyrians in 721 BC and may have become assimilated, but legend predicts their return.

lost wax *n* a method of casting metal in which a wax model is coated with a material with a high melting point. The wax is melted and replaced by the molten metal.

lot /lot/ *pron* **a lot, lots** /lots/ MUCH OR MANY a large amount, or a large number of people or things (*takes a singular or plural verb*) ○ *I learnt a lot.* ○ *A lot of people came.* ○ *Lots of exercise is what you need.* ○ *You have lots of choices.* ■ *adv* **a lot, lots** (*informal*) **1.** MUCH to a great extent or degree ○ *laughed a lot* ○ *I'm feeling lots better, thanks.* **2.** OFTEN often or much of the time ○ *went out to restaurants a lot* ■ *n* **1.** SET a set or group of things or people ○ *One lot of tourists has left the hotel already.* ○ *That lot go over there.* **2.** TYPE OF GROUP a group of people or things of a particular kind (*informal; takes a singular or plural verb*) ○ *They're a cheerful lot.* **3.** ITEMS IN AUCTION an item or group of items on sale at an auction ○ *I bought the silver as one lot.* **4.** DESTINY the things somebody has or experiences in life ○ *our lot in life* **5.** RANDOM CHOICE the process of choosing something at random, especially by taking from a set of pieces of paper or straws, one of which has a concealed mark or is shorter than the others ○ *chosen by lot* **6.** CINEMA FILM STUDIO a film studio together with the land that belongs to it **7.** *N Am* PIECE OF LAND a small area of land that has fixed boundaries ○ *a vacant lot* [Old English *hlot* 'object used to make decisions by chance, portion, destiny' < Germanic] ◇ **a bad lot** an unpleasant or disreputable person (*informal*) ○ *Don't have anything to do with him: he's a bad lot.* ◇ **a whole lot** very much or a great deal (*informal*) ◇ **draw** *or* **cast lots** to choose something at random, e.g. a straw or piece of paper, to determine an outcome ○ *We cast lots to decide who should go first.* ◇ **the lot** everything, or everything considered as one (*informal*) ○ *Personality, looks, brains... she's got the lot.*

USAGE a lot or alot? The superficial similarity of ***a lot*** to adjectives and adverbs like *alone* and *aloud* gives rise to a temptation to treat the expression as one word, but this is nonstandard usage. In formal writing, *much, many, a great deal of,* etc. can be substituted for ***a lot***.

Lot[1] /lot/ *n* in the Bible, the son of Haran, brother of Abraham. He is mentioned as Lut in the Koran.

Lot[2] /lot/ **1.** river in southwestern France. Length: 483 km/300 mi. **2.** department in Midi-Pyrénées Region, southwestern France, known for its scenic beauty. Population: 160,197 (1999). Area: 5,217 sq. km/2,014 sq. mi.

lota /lṓtə/, **lotah** *n* a small round water container, usually made of brass or copper, used in South Asia [Early 19C. < Hindi *loṭā*]

loth *adj* another spelling of **loath**

Lothair II /lō tháir/ (1075–1137) king of Germany and Holy Roman Emperor. His election as king of Germany (1125) led to a war between two rival families, the Guelphs and the Ghibellines.

Lothario /lō thaári ō, -thaíri ō/ (*plural* **-os**), **lothario** *n* a man who attempts to persuade women to enter sexual affairs with him [Mid-18C. After a character in *The Fair Penitent* (1703), tragedy by Nicholas Rowe]

Lothian /lṓthi ən/ former region of southeastern Scotland, approximately equivalent to the present-day council areas of East Lothian, Midlothian, West Lothian, and the City of Edinburgh

loti /lṓti/ (*plural* **maloti** /maa lṓti/) *n* the main unit of currency in Lesotho. See table at **currency** [Late 20C. < Sesotho, after the *Maloti* Mountains in Lesotho]

lotic /lṓtik/ *adj* describes ecological communities that live in swift-flowing water [Early 20C. < Latin *lot-* (see LOTION)]

lotion /lṓsh'n/ *n* a thick liquid preparation that is applied to the skin for cosmetic or medical reasons [14C. Directly or via French < Latin *lotion- < lot-*, past participle of *lavare* 'wash']

lotta /lótta/ *contr* lot of (*nonstandard*)

lottery /lóttəri/ (*plural* **-ies**) *n* **1.** a large-scale gambling game, usually organized to raise money for a public cause, in which numbered tickets are sold and a draw is held to select the winning numbers **2.** an activity, situation, or enterprise with an outcome dependent on chance [Mid-16C. Probably < Dutch *loterij* < *lot* 'lot' < Germanic]

lotto /lóttō/ *n* **1.** a game resembling bingo, in which numbers are called at random and players try to be the first to cover all the corresponding numbers on their cards **2.** *also* **Lotto** a state-run lottery in the United Kingdom, Australia and some other countries, and in some US states, in which players buy tickets bearing combinations of numbers. Periodically a combination of numbers is selected at random and people with matching tickets win cash prizes. [Late 18C. Directly or via French < Italian < assumed Frankish *lot* 'lot' < Germanic]

lotus

lotus /lṓtəss/ (*plural* **-tuses** or *same*) *n* **1.** SACRED PINK WATER LILY a water lily with large leaves, regarded as sacred in South Asia, China, and Tibet. Flowers: fragrant, pink. Native to: South Asia, Australia. Latin name: *Nelumbo nucifera*. **2.** SACRED WHITE WATER LILY a water lily sacred to the ancient Egyptians. Flowers: white. Native to: tropical Africa and South Asia. Latin name: *Nymphaea lotus*. **3.** PLANT OF PEA FAMILY a plant of the pea family. Flowers: yellow, pink, or white. Genus: *Lotus*. **4.** LOTUS FLOWER IN SACRED ART a representation of the flower of either of the sacred lotus plants, common in ancient Egyptian, Hindu, and Buddhist sacred art **5.** MYTHOLOGICAL FRUIT CAUSING DROWSINESS in Greek mythology, a fruit that made people who ate it feel a pleasant drowsiness **6.** MYTHOLOGICAL PLANT YIELDING LOTUS FRUIT in Greek mythology, a plant that produced the lotus fruit, thought to be the date or jujube [15C. Via Latin < Greek *lōtos*, applied to a variety of plants]

lotus-eater *n* **1.** a lazy, self-indulgent person **2.** in Greek mythology, somebody who lived in a state of idle stupor after eating the lotus fruit

lotus position: seated buddha, Uttar Pradesh, northern India

lotus position *n* a sitting position, used especially in yoga and meditation, in which the legs are crossed in such a way that each foot rests on top of the other leg's thigh [< its supposed resemblance to a lotus blossom]

Louangphrabang /loo áng prə báng/ city in northern Laos, on the Mekong River. Population: 68,000 (1995).

louche /loosh/ *adj* disreputable or of doubtful morality [Early 19C. Via French, 'cross-eyed, shady' < Latin *luscus* 'one-eyed']

loud /lowd/ *adj* **1.** HIGH IN VOLUME high in volume of sound **2.** EXPRESSING SOMETHING NOISILY expressing something forcefully and frequently ○ *loud protests* **3.** VISUALLY SHOCKING shockingly bright in colour or bold in design ○ *a loud shirt* **4.** OFFENSIVE noisy, coarse, and offensive [Old English *hlūd* < Indo-European, 'hear'] —**loudly** *adv*

louden /lówd'n/ (**-ens, -ening, -ened**) *vti* to become louder, or make a sound louder

loudhailer /lówd háylər/ *n* a portable device for amplifying the voice consisting of a loudspeaker with an integrated amplifier and microphone. N Am term **bullhorn**

loudmouth /lówd mowth/ (*plural* **-mouths** /-mowthz, -mowths/) *n* a loud and talkative person, especially a gossip or braggart (*informal*) —**loudmouthed** /lówd mowthd, -mowtht/ *adj*

loudness /lówdnəss/ *n* **1.** the degree of volume of sound **2.** PHYS the magnitude of the physiological effect produced when a sound stimulates the ear

loud pedal *n* MUSIC same as **sustaining pedal**

loudspeaker /lówd speékər/ *n* an electronic or electromagnetic device used to convert electrical energy into sound energy, providing the audible sound in equipment such as televisions, radios, CD players, and public-address systems

loudspeaker van *n* UK a van or other vehicle provided with a loudspeaker so that political or other messages can be delivered to people in the streets and adjacent houses. US term **sound truck**

Lou Gehrig's disease /loo gérrigz-/ *n* MED same as **amyotrophic lateral sclerosis** [Mid-20C. After Henry Louis ('*Lou*') Gehrig (1903–41), US baseball player who died from it]

lough /lokh, lok/ *n* Ireland **1.** same as **lake**¹ (sense 1) **2.** a long inlet of the sea [Pre-12C. Probably < Old Irish *loch* 'lake']

Loughborough /lúfbərə/ industrial and university town in Leicestershire, central England. Population: 46,867 (1991).

louis /loó i/ (*plural same*) *n* MONEY same as **louis d'or** [Late 17C. Shortening]

Louis XIV /loó i/ (1638–1715) king of France. He was a strong military leader and patron of the arts whose long reign (1643–1715) saw a great strengthening of the monarchy. Known as **the Sun King**

'The function of kings consists primarily of using good sense, which always comes naturally and easily. Our work is sometimes less difficult than our amusements.' [Louis XIV, *Memoir for the Instruction of the Dauphin*; 1661]

Louis XV (1710–74) king of France. His weak lead-

ership and despotic rule (1715–74) contributed to the crisis that led to the French Revolution.

Louis XVI (1754–93) king of France. Coming to the throne (1774) when France was impoverished, he was deposed during the French Revolution and executed.

Louis /loó iss/, **Joe** (1914–81) US boxer. He was the world heavyweight champion from 1937 to 1949. Born **Barrow, Joseph Louis**. Known as **the Brown Bomber**

'Once that bell rings you're on your own. It's just you and the other guy.' [Joe Louis. Quoted in *A Hard Road to Glory*, Arthur Ashe; 1988]

louis d'or /loó i dáwr/ (*plural same*) *n* **1.** a former gold coin of France used from the 17th century to the Revolution **2.** a former gold coin worth 20 francs used in France after the Revolution [Mid-17C. < French, 'louis of gold', after *Louis* XIII of France]

Louisiana /loo eézi áannə/ state in the southern United States bordered by the Gulf of Mexico, Texas, Arkansas, and Mississippi. Capital: Baton Rouge. Population: 4,482,646 (2002 estimate). Area: 128,595 sq. km/49,651 sq. mi. —**Louisianan** *n, adj*

Louisiana French *n* the dialect spoken by the French-speaking descendants of the early French settlers of Louisiana —**Louisiana French** *adj*

Louisiana Purchase *n* territory of the western United States purchased from France in 1803. The largest single territorial addition ever made to the United States, it comprised 2,100,000 sq. km/800,000 sq. mi., extending from the Gulf of Mexico northwards to the Canadian border and from the Mississippi River westwards to the Rocky Mountains.

Louis Philippe /loó i fee leép/ (1773–1850) king of France. Proclaimed king after the July Revolution (1830), he ruled as a constitutional monarch until the Revolution of 1848. Known as **the Citizen King**

Louisville /loó i vil/ city in northern Kentucky, on the Ohio River at Kentucky's border with Indiana. The largest city in the state, it is the site of Churchill Downs, home of the Kentucky Derby. Population: 251,399 (2002 estimate).

lounge /lownj/ *n* **1.** SITTING ROOM IN HOUSE a sitting or living room in a house **2.** PUBLIC ROOM FOR RELAXING a room in which people may relax or wait, e.g. in a public building such as a hotel or airport, or in a vehicle such as a ship **3.** LEISURE same as **lounge bar 4.** N Am LEISURE same as **cocktail lounge 5.** PERIOD OF LOUNGING a period of relaxation, laziness, or inactivity ○ *having a lounge on the sofa after lunch* **6.** BACKLESS COUCH WITH HEADREST a couch without a back but with a headrest at one end **7.** Aus SOFA a sofa or couch ■ *v* (**lounges, lounging, lounged**) **1.** *vi* LIE OR SIT LAZILY to sit or act in a casual, relaxed way **2.** *vti* PASS TIME LAZILY to pass time in a relaxed or lazy way ○ *lounged the afternoon away* [Early 16C. Origin ?]

lounge bar *n* an area in a pub or hotel with more comfortable or elegant furnishings than the public bar, and sometimes selling more expensive drinks

lounge lizard *n* **1.** a man who goes to places or events attended by the rich and famous, especially in order to approach wealthy women (*slang insult*) **2.** US a frequent patron of cocktail lounges (*slang*) [Probably < the negative associations of reptiles]

lounger /lównjər/ *n* **1.** an extendable chair or a lightweight, usually adjustable, couch designed to be comfortable for the user **2.** somebody who sits or walks in a casual relaxed way

lounge suit *n* a man's suit consisting of a jacket and trousers, occasionally also including a waistcoat, all made from the same cloth, worn as formal daywear

lounge suite *n* Aus a three-piece set of furniture, usually consisting of a couch and two armchairs

loungewear /lównj wair/ *n* clothing designed to be worn when relaxing, usually at home

loup /lowp, lowp/ *vti* (**loups, louping, louped; lowps, lowping, lowped**) N England, Scotland to leap or jump over an obstacle ■ *n* Scotland a leap or a jump [14C. < Old Norse *hlaupa* 'to leap' < Germanic]

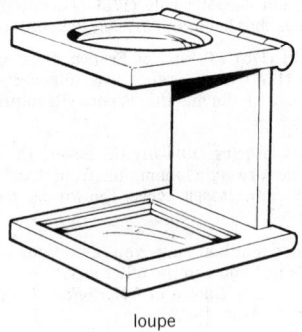

loupe

loupe /loop/ n a magnifying glass used especially by jewellers and watchmakers [Late 19C. < French, 'flawed gem']

loup-garou /lòo ga roo/ (plural **loups-garous** /pronunc. same/) n US same as **werewolf** (dated) [Late 16C. < French < Old French leu 'wolf' (< Latin lupus) + garoul 'werewolf' (< Germanic, 'man-wolf')]

louping ill /lówping-/ n a serious viral disease spread by ticks that damages the central nervous system, causing tremors and difficulty in mobility. It affects many animals, including sheep, cattle, goats, and pigs.

lour vi, n another spelling of **lower**[2]

Lourdes /loordz/ town in southwestern France, famous for its Roman Catholic shrine. Population: 15,203 (1999).

lourie /lówri/ n S Africa BIRDS **1.** same as **touraco 2.** same as **go-away bird** [Late 18C. Via Afrikaans < Dutch lori]

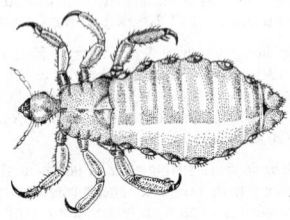

louse

louse /lowss/ n (plural **lice** /līss/) **1.** PARASITIC INSECT a small wingless insect that lives as a parasite on humans and other animals. There are sucking lice, e.g. head and body lice, and biting lice, e.g. bird lice. **2.** SMALL INVERTEBRATE ANIMAL a small invertebrate animal, e.g. a wood louse (often used in combination) **3.** (plural **louses**) OFFENSIVE TERM an offensive term that deliberately insults somebody's behaviour and attitude towards others (insult) ■ vt (**louses, lousing, loused**) MED same as **delouse** [Old English lūs < Indo-European]

louse up vti to mishandle a situation or task so that it is ruined (informal)

louse fly n a parasitic fly that clings to birds and mammals with its strong bristly legs and that is typically wingless. Family: Hippoboscidae.

lousewort /lówss wurt/ n a plant of the snapdragon family with feathery leaves. Flowers: white, yellow, or pinkish-purple, in spikes. Native to: northern regions. Genus: Pedicularis. [< the belief that sheep feeding on it became infested with lice]

lousy /lówzi/ (**-ier, -iest**) adj **1.** LOUSE-INFESTED infested with lice **2.** INFERIOR inferior or second-rate (informal) ○ lousy food **3.** UNPLEASANT unpleasant or unacceptable (informal) ○ a lousy way to treat somebody **4.** ILL painful or in bad health (informal) ○ I feel lousy today. **5.** N Am HAVING LOT OF SOMETHING having a large amount of something (informal) ○ lousy with money —**lousily** adv —**lousiness** n

lout /lowt/ n an offensive term that deliberately insults the behaviour and attitude of somebody, especially a young man (insult) [Mid-16C. Origin ?]

Louth 1. /lowth/ county in Leinster Province, the eastern Republic of Ireland. Population: 92,166 (2002). Area: 823 sq. km/318 sq. mi. **2.** /lowth/ ancient market town in Lincolnshire, eastern England. Population: 14,248 (1991).

loutish /lówtish/ adj marked by crude and unpleasant behaviour —**loutishly** adv —**loutishness** n

Louvain /loo váN/ town in central Belgium, near Brussels, famous for its old buildings and churches. Population: 88,245 (1999).

louvar /lòo vaar/ (plural **-vars** or same) n a large deep-sea fish with a blunt head, silvery-pink body, and bright red fins. Native to: tropics. Latin name: Luvarus imperialis. [Late 20C. Probably via modern Latin < Italian dialect (Sicilian) luvaru]

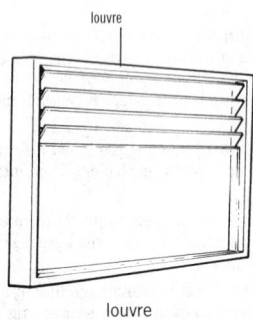

louvre

louvre /lòovər/, **louver** n **1.** FRAME WITH HORIZONTAL SLATS a frame on a door or window supporting spaced horizontal slats angled to admit air and light but not rain ○ a set of louvre doors **2.** SLAT IN FRAME an individual slat in a louvre **3.** SLATTED OPENING a slatted opening, generally for ventilation or cooling **4.** ROOF STRUCTURE RELEASING SMOKE a structure such as a lantern or turret on the roof of a building, especially a medieval building, that allows smoke to escape [14C. < Old French lover 'skylight' < Germanic] —**louvred** adj

Louvre /lòovrə/ n a museum in Paris that contains the French national art collection, including such famous works as the Mona Lisa and Venus de Milo

lovable /lúvvəb'l/, **loveable** adj attracting or worthy of love or affection —**lovability** /lúvvə bílləti/ n —**lovableness** n —**lovably** adv

lovage /lúvvij/ n a perennial herb cultivated for its aromatic seeds, leaves, and roots used in seasoning. Flowers: greenish. Native to: Mediterranean. Latin name: Levisticum officinale. [14C. Alteration of Old French levesche < late Latin levisticum, alteration of ligusticum, 'of Liguria', region in Italy]

lovat /lúvvət/ n a muted dusty yellowish or bluish-green colour [Early 20C. Probably after Lord Lovat (1802–75), Scottish nobleman who popularized tweeds in muted colours as hunters' dress] —**lovat** adj

love /luv/ v (**loves, loving, loved**) **1.** vti FEEL TENDER AFFECTION FOR SOMEBODY to feel tender affection for somebody such as a close relative or friend, or for something such as a place, an ideal, or an animal **2.** vti FEEL DESIRE FOR SOMEBODY to feel romantic and sexual desire and longing for somebody **3.** vt LIKE SOMETHING VERY MUCH to like something, or like doing, something very much ○ I love watching old movies on TV. **4.** vt SHOW KINDNESS TO SOMEBODY to feel and show kindness and charity to somebody ○ love your enemies **5.** vt VENERATE GOD to worship and venerate God **6.** vt HAVE SEX WITH SOMEBODY to have sexual intercourse with somebody (dated) ■ n **1.** PASSIONATE ATTRACTION AND DESIRE a passionate feeling of romantic desire and sexual attraction **2.** VERY STRONG AFFECTION an intense feeling of tender affection and compassion ○ Young children need unconditional love. **3.** ROMANTIC AFFAIR a romantic affair, possibly sexual **4.** SOMEBODY MUCH LOVED somebody who is loved romantically or sexually ○ He was her first real love. **5.** STRONG LIKING a strong liking for or pleasure gained from something ○ his love of music **6.** SOMETHING ELICITING ENTHUSIASM something that elicits deep interest and enthusiasm in somebody ○ Music was his greatest love but he also liked ballet. **7.** BELOVED used as an affectionate word to somebody loved (informal) **8.** TERM OF FRIENDLY ADDRESS used as a friendly term of address, usually to a woman

(informal) ○ Here's your change, love. **9.** KIND PERSON a kind or pleasant person (informal) ○ Be a love and pour me a cup of tea. **10.** SPORTS, LEISURE SCORE OF ZERO a score of zero in some sports and games, e.g. tennis, squash, and whist **11.** CHR GOD'S LOVE FOR HUMANITY in Christian belief, the mercy, grace, and charity shown by God to humanity **12.** CHR WORSHIP OF GOD in Christian belief, the worship and adoration of God [Old English lufian (verb) < lufu (noun) < Indo-European, 'to love'] ◇ **for love nor money** or **for love or money** used with a negative to indicate that something is quite impossible ○ You can't get a taxi after midnight for love nor money.

SYNONYMS *love, liking, affection, fondness, passion, infatuation, crush*

CORE MEANING: a strong positive feeling towards somebody or something

love an intense feeling of positive emotion towards, or enjoyment of, a person or thing, especially strong romantic or sexual feelings between people. ○ When Lynn met Derek it was love at first sight. ○ He was mortally ill, but his strength of will and love of life were indomitable. **liking** a feeling of enjoying something or or finding somebody or something pleasant ○ He sipped his coffee, which was just to his liking. ○ She'd begun to develop a liking for Maurice. **affection** fond or tender feelings towards somebody or something ○ a man with a deep affection for the countryside ○ Fifteen-year-old boys don't usually welcome displays of affection. **fondness** a feeling of affection or preference ○ gazing with fondness at the two blond-headed little boys ○ He developed a fondness for music as a child. **passion** intense or overpowering emotion, either love for somebody, usually of a strong sexual nature, or strong liking or enthusiasm for something ○ Begun from sheer sexual passion, her marriage had quickly gone sour. ○ His great passion was mountaineering. **infatuation** an intense but short-lived, often unrealistic love for somebody, usually of a romantic or sexual nature ○ her infatuation with a young English poet ○ She had thought herself in love, but it had only been an infatuation. **crush** (informal) a temporary romantic infatuation, especially in teenagers and young people ○ I was a silly little girl of eleven with a schoolgirl crush on Martin.

---

loveable adj another spelling of **lovable**

love affair n **1.** a sexual or romantic relationship between people who are not married to one another or who do not live together in a permanent relationship **2.** an intense liking or enthusiasm for something ○ her love affair with the cinema

love apple n PLANTS same as **tomato** (sense 1) [Translation of French pomme d'amour, German Liebesapfel]

love beads npl a necklace of coloured beads, first popular with hippies in the 1960s

lovebird /lúv burd/ n **1.** a lover, especially one who is publicly affectionate (usually used in the plural) **2.** a small greenish short-tailed parrot often kept as a cagebird, noted for close bonding and mutual preening between mates. Native to: Africa. Genus: Agapornis.

lovebite /lúv bīt/ n a small patch of bruised skin, often on the neck, caused by a partner's sucking kiss

love child n the child of parents who are not married to each other

loved one /lúvd-/ n a spouse, partner, or close family member (often used in the plural)

loved up adj feeling pleasurably empathic with and affectionate towards those around you (informal; hyphenated when used before a noun)

love feast n **1.** a meal held with the intention of stimulating goodwill **2.** a symbolic meal shared among Christians as a symbol of love and charity

love game n a game in tennis and some other sports in which the loser scores no points

love handles npl two regions of fat located at either side of the back just above the pelvis (informal humorous)

love-in n a relatively large gathering in which participants experience feelings of love and mutual support (dated)

love-in-a-mist n an annual flowering plant. Flowers: white or pale blue, surrounded by very fine bracts.

Native to: Mediterranean. Latin name: *Nigella damascena*. [Mist < the mass of fine bracts that surrounds the flower]

~~loveing~~ incorrect spelling of **loving**

love knot *n* a knot or bow of ribbon used to symbolize love

Lovelace /lúv layss/, **Ada** (1815–52) British writer and mathematician. Her *Sketch of the Analytical Engine* (1843) was the best account until recent times of Babbage's computing machine and included the pioneering use of 'programs'. Full name **Lovelace, Augusta Ada, Countess of**. Born **Byron, Ada**

Lovelace, Richard (1618–57) English poet. An ardent Royalist, he was one of the writers known as the Cavalier poets.

'Stone walls do not a prison make, / Nor iron bars a cage; / Minds innocent and quiet take / That for an hermitage; / If I have freedom in my love, / And in my soul am free, / Angels alone that soar above / Enjoy such liberty.'
[Richard Lovelace, 'To Althea, From Prison'; 1649]

loveless /lúvləss/ *adj* **1. EMPTY OF LOVE** devoid of feelings of love ○ *a loveless marriage* **2. NOT SHOWING LOVE** not exhibiting or giving love ○ *a loveless glance* **3. UNLOVED** not receiving love ○ *a loveless child* —**lovelessness** *n*

love-lies-bleeding *n* a tropical plant. Flowers: small, red, in drooping clusters. Native to: South Asia, Africa, South America. Latin name: *Amaranthus candatus*. [< the resemblance of the flowers to a flow of blood]

love life *n* the romantic or sexual relationships in somebody's life

Lovell /lúvv'l/, **Sir Bernard** (*b.* 1913) British astronomer. The director of Jodrell Bank Experimental Station near Manchester (1951–81), he was a pioneer of radio astronomy. Full name **Lovell, Alfred Charles Bernard**

'A study of history shows that civilizations that abandon the quest for knowledge are doomed to disintegration.'
[Sir Bernard Lovell, *Observer*; 14 May 1972]

lovelock /lúv lok/ *n* a long lock of hair separated from the rest by a ribbon, worn forward over the shoulder in the 16th century, or worn on the forehead in later periods

Lovelock /lúv lok/, **Jack** (1910–49) New Zealand athlete. He won the 1,500 metres at the 1936 Olympics in a world-record time of 3 minutes 47.8 seconds. Full name **Lovelock, John Edward**

lovelorn /lúv lawrn/ *adj* exceedingly unhappy because of unrequited love or difficulties with love —**lovelornness** *n*

lovely /lúvli/ *adj* (**-lier, -liest**) **1. BEAUTIFUL AND PLEASING** beautiful and pleasing, especially in a harmonious way ○ *a lovely view* **2. DELIGHTFUL** very enjoyable or pleasant ○ *We had a lovely time.* **3. CARING** loving or friendly and caring ○ *She's a lovely person.* **4. ATTRACTING LOVE** attracting or inspiring love in others ■ *n* (*plural* **-lies**) **SOMEBODY OR SOMETHING GOOD-LOOKING** an attractive or good-looking person or thing, especially a woman (*often used in the plural; sometimes considered offensive*) ○ *Farewell, my lovely!* —**loveliness** *n*

SYNONYMS See *good-looking*.

lovemaking /lúv mayking/ *n* **1.** sexual activity between lovers, especially sexual intercourse **2.** courtship or wooing (*dated*)

love match *n* a marriage based on love between the couple rather than economic or social considerations

love nest *n* a place where lovers can be together, e.g. a small flat or secluded house (*informal*)

love potion *n* a magical drink that supposedly causes the person who consumes it to feel sexual desire for the person who gives it

lover /lúvvər/ *n* **1. SEXUAL PARTNER** somebody's sexual partner, especially if the two are not married to each other **2. SOMEBODY HAVING LOVE AFFAIR** either of two people involved in a love affair (*often used in the plural*) **3. SOMEBODY DEVOTED TO SOMETHING** somebody who is devoted to or adores a particular thing (*often used in combination*) ○ *opera-lovers*

CULTURAL NOTE *Lady Chatterley's Lover*, a novel (1928) by D. H. Lawrence. Lawrence's last novel, it describes an aristocratic woman's search for love and sexual satisfaction after her husband is injured in war. The novel's notoriety, and the fact that the publishers of the first unexpurgated British edition were prosecuted for obscenity in 1960, has obscured its many qualities, including its insightful analysis of contemporary social and political values.

lover boy *n* an attractive young man, especially somebody's boyfriend or lover (*humorous*)

lover's knot *n* same as **love knot**

love seat *n* a small sofa that seats two people

lovesick /lúv sik/ *adj* listless or distracted because of love —**lovesickness** *n*

love triangle *n* same as **eternal triangle**

lovey /lúvvi/ (*plural* **-eys**) *n* used as an affectionate form of address, especially to a woman (*informal*)

lovey-dovey /-dúvvi/ *adj* showing affection in an excessive or excessively sentimental way (*informal*) [< pet forms of LOVE, DOVE [1]]

loving /lúvving/ *adj* **1.** showing or feeling affection **2.** done with enjoyment and careful attention —**lovingly** *adv* —**lovingness** *n*

loving cup

loving cup *n* **1.** a large drinking vessel with two or more handles, sometimes passed between people at a banquet **2.** an ornamental vessel with two handles awarded to the winner of a sports contest

loving kindness *n* tender compassion for other people

~~lovly~~ incorrect spelling of **lovely**

low[1] /lō/ *adj* (**lower, lowest**) **1. WITHOUT GREAT HEIGHT** relatively little in height between the top and bottom ○ *a low fence* **2. CLOSE TO GROUND** located close or closer than usual to the ground or the base of something ○ *The sinking sun was low in the sky.* **3. BELOW AVERAGE** below the average or expected degree, amount, or intensity ○ *The lowest rainfall in fourteen years.* **4. CONTAINING SMALL AMOUNT** having or containing a relatively small amount ○ *low in calories* **5. WITH LITTLE MONETARY VALUE** small in monetary value ○ *low prices* **6. OF BAD QUALITY** bad in quality, or having little value ○ *low standards* **7. OF LITTLE IMPORTANCE** having little importance or urgency ○ *low priority* **8. NEAR DEPLETION** approaching or near depletion ○ *We're low on supplies.* **9. TURNED DOWN OR DIMMED** adjusted so that there is less of something ○ *low lighting* **10. QUIET** at a quiet, soft, or hushed level ○ *a low murmur* **11. DEEP IN PITCH** with a relative pitch that is closer to bass than soprano sounds ○ *Her voice was gentle and low.* **12. SMALL** small or relatively small in degree ○ *a low risk* **13. NEAR BOTTOM OF SCALE** near the beginning or bottom of something measured on a scale ○ *The temperature was in the low 80s.* **14. DISPIRITED** melancholy, hopeless, or dispirited ○ *felt sad and low after the parting* **15. LACKING PHYSICAL STRENGTH** lacking in physical strength or vitality ○ *feeling low after her operation* **16. SHOWING NECK AND CHEST** cut to show more than usual of the wearer's neck and bosom ○ *a low neckline* **17. LACKING STATUS** lacking status or rank, or closer to the bottom of a class system **18. UNCOMPLIMENTARY** unfavourable or uncomplimentary ○ *a low opinion of someone* **19. UNPRINCIPLED** without principles or morals **20. VULGAR** full of vulgarity

or coarseness **21. LACKING MONEY** lacking resources, especially money (*informal*) ○ *Can you lend me some cash, I'm a bit low.* **22. GEOG NEAR EQUATOR** situated near to the equator **23. BIOL NOT COMPLEX** simple in organic structure **24. PHON PRONOUNCED LOW IN MOUTH** pronounced with the tongue lying low on the bottom of the mouth ○ *a low vowel* ■ *adv* (**lower, lowest**) **1. IN LOW POSITION** in or to a low position, state, degree, or level ○ *Turn the gas down low.* **2. NEAR GROUND** near or nearer to the ground ○ *flew low over the trees* **3. WITH DEEP PITCH** with a low or deep pitch ○ *Play it a semitone lower.* **4. QUIETLY** in a soft or quiet way **5. AT SMALL PRICE** at a low or small price ■ *n* **1. SOMETHING LOW** something, e.g. a position or degree, that is low ○ *Sales dropped to an all-time low.* **2. UNHAPPY PERIOD** an unhappy or unfortunate experience or period of somebody's life **3. METEOROL BAD WEATHER REGION** a region of low barometric pressure that results in bad weather [12C. < Old Norse *lágr*] —**lowness** *n* ◇ **lay somebody low** to cause somebody to feel overcome or helpless, e.g. with illness or exhaustion (*usually passive*) ○ *laid low with influenza*

SYNONYMS See *mean*[2].

low[2] /lō/ *vti* (**lows, lowing, lowed**) to make a mooing sound ■ *n* a characteristic mooing sound made by a cow or similar animal [Old English *hlōwan* 'bellow' < Indo-European, 'shout']

lowball /lō bawl/ (**-balls, -balling, -balled**) *vti* US to deliberately quote a price or estimate that is lower than the eventual cost [< *lowball*, game of draw poker in which the player with the lowest-ranking hand wins the pot]

low blow *n* an unfair comment or blow (*informal*) [< an illegal blow in boxing]

lowborn /lō báwrn/ *adj* being of common rather than aristocratic parentage

lowbred /lō bréd/ *adj* **1.** with a rude and vulgar manner (*insult*) **2.** same as **lowborn**

lowbrow /lō brow/ *adj* unsophisticated or trivial and not requiring intellectual effort to be understood or appreciated ■ *n* somebody considered to have unsophisticated or unintellectual tastes [Early 20C. After HIGHBROW]

low-cal /-kál/, **low-calorie** *adj* with few calories or fewer calories than usual

Low Church *n* a branch of the Church of England that favours less ritual and ceremony and prefers an evangelical approach to services

low-class *adj* **1.** belonging to or characteristic of a low social class **2.** of inferior quality

low comedy *n* comedy based on slapstick and coarse actions rather than more sophisticated forms of humour

Low Countries /-kúntriz/ region in northwestern Europe, made up of Belgium, the Netherlands, and Luxembourg. Population: 26,016,000 (1995). Area: 73,943 sq. km/28,550 sq. mi.

low-cut *adj* describes a woman's garment with a low neckline that shows the top part of the chest and cleavage

low-density *adj* having a low concentration of something in an area

low-density lipoprotein *n* the lipoprotein that carries cholesterol to cells and tissue

lowdown /lō down/ *n* significant information about somebody or something, especially information that is not widely known (*informal*) ○ *waiting for someone to give us the lowdown* [Early 20C. < *low down* 'very low' or *low-down* 'contemptible']

low-down *adj* mean and contemptible (*informal*) ○ *a low-down trick*

low earth orbit *n* an orbit that is nearer to Earth than a geostationary orbit

Lowell /lō əl/, **Amy** (1874–1925) US poet and critic. A leader of the imagist school, she wrote poems that exhibit a terseness of style and a use of free verse. Full name **Lowell, Amy Lawrence**

'All books are either dreams or swords, / You can cut, you can drug, with words.'
[Amy Lowell, 'Sword Blades and Poppy Seed'; 1914]

Lowell, Robert (1917–77) US poet. A lyric poet with a concern for social issues, he won the Pulitzer Prize

for *Lord Weary's Castle* (1946). Full name **Lowell, Robert Traill Spence, Jr**

'When the whale's viscera go and the roll / Beyond tree-swept Nantucket and Wood's Hole / And Martha's Vineyard, Sailor, will your sword / Whistle and fall and sink into the fat?'
[Robert Lowell, 'The Quaker Graveyard in Nantucket', *Poems 1938–49*; 1950]

'If we see light at the end of the tunnel, / It's the light of the oncoming train.'
[Robert Lowell, 'Since 1939'; 1977]

low-end *adj* inexpensive compared to a group of similar products

lower[1] /lṓ ər/ *adj* **1. BELOW SOMETHING** physically below another thing, especially one of the same type ○ *the lower lip* **2. REDUCED OR LESS** reduced or less in amount ○ *lower wages* **3. CLOSER TO BOTTOM** closer to the bottom or base of something ○ *the lower slopes* **4. OF LESS IMPORTANCE** of less importance or inferior status ○ *lower rank* **5.** GEOL **EARLIER IN GEOLOGICAL PERIOD** relating to the earlier part of a geological period or system **6.** ZOOL **LESS ADVANCED DEVELOPMENTALLY** describes organisms that are less advanced in terms of development or complexity ○ *a lower life form* **7. FARTHER FROM SOURCE** indicating that part of a river is farthest away from the source ○ *the lower river* ■ *adv* **SO AS TO BE BELOW** to or at a lower position ■ *v* (-ers, -ering, -ered) **1.** *vt* **BRING SOMETHING TO LOWER POSITION** to move something down to a lower level or to move something downwards ○ *lower the flag* **2.** *vti* **REDUCE OR FALL** to reduce something in quantity, quality, or value, or fall in quantity, quality, or value ○ *Interest rates have been lowered by the Bank of England.* **3.** *vt* **REDUCE SOMETHING IN DEGREE** to reduce something in degree **4.** *vt* **MOVE HEAD DOWNWARDS** to move the head or eyes downwards **5. lower yourself** *vr* **HUMILIATE YOURSELF** to reduce your dignity or the respect in which you are held ○ *I wouldn't lower myself to discuss it.* **6.** *vt* **REDUCE VOLUME OF SOUND** to reduce the volume of sound that something produces ○ *lower your voice* **7.** *vt* MUSIC **REDUCE SOUND PITCH** to bring a sound to a lower pitch **8.** *vt* PHON **MODIFY VOWEL SOUND** to change the sound of a vowel by pushing the tongue to the bottom of the mouth ■ *n* **SOMETHING LOWER** something that is the lower of two or more things [12C. Comparative of LOW[1]]

lower[2] /lówr ər/, **lour** /lowr/ *vi* (-ers, -ering, -ered; lours, louring, loured) **1. BE OVERCAST** to be overcast and threatening storms or heavy rain **2. LOOK ANGRY** to look angry or sullen ■ *n* **SCOWL** a scowl or miserable look [13C. Origin ?] —**lowering** *adj* —**loweringly** *adv*

lower bound *n* a number that is less than or equal to all the members of a set

Lower California /lṓ ər-/ ♦ **Baja California**

Lower Canada southern portion of present-day Quebec. It was a British province separate from Upper Canada from 1791 to 1840.

Lower Carboniferous *n* GEOL same as **Mississippian** (sense 2)

lowercase /lṓ ər káyss/ *n* **SMALL LETTERS NOT CAPITALS** the small rather than capital form of letters ○ *printed in lowercase* ■ *adj* **NOT CAPITAL** written or printed in small rather than capital form ○ *written with a lowercase 'p'* ■ *vt* (-cases, -casing, -cased) **PUT SOMETHING IN SMALL LETTERS** to put typescript or written material in lowercase form [Late 17C. Because types for small letters were kept in the lower of two type cases]

lower chamber *n* GOV same as **lower house**

lower class *n* the social group considered to occupy the lowest position in a hierarchical society, typically composed of manual workers and their families (*often used in the plural*) —**lower-class** *adj*

lower deck *n* **1.** the next deck in a ship above the hold **2.** a ship's ordinary seamen and petty officers considered as a group (*informal*)

lower ground floor *n* a storey of a building, especially a shop, that is below ground level. N Am term **basement**

lower house *n* one of two legislative houses, generally more directly representative and larger than the other house

Lower Hutt /-hút/ city in the southern part of the North Island, New Zealand. It is a suburb of Wellington. Population: 95,022 (2001).

lowermost /lṓ ər mōst/ *adj* very lowest

lower orders *npl* (*dated*) **1.** the lower classes of society **2.** people who belong to the lower orders

lower school *n* the younger pupils in a secondary school, usually those in the first three or four years

lower world *n* in mythology, the dwelling place of the dead, often considered to be beneath the ground

lowest common denominator /lṓ əst-/ *n* **1.** the mass of ordinary people, particularly when considered to have low critical standards and to lack taste **2.** *UK, ANZ, Can* the lowest multiple shared by all the denominators in a set of fractions. US term **least common denominator**

lowest common multiple *n UK, ANZ, Can* the lowest whole number that is divisible without a remainder by all of the members of a set of numbers. US term **least common multiple**

Lowestoft /lṓ iss toft, lṓ stoft/ seaside resort and fishing port in Suffolk, eastern England. Population: 55,200 (1994).

low-fat *adj* prepared with a reduced amount of fat

low-fi *n* another spelling of **lo-fi** (*informal*) [Shortening]

low frequency *n* a radio frequency ranging from 30 to 300 kilohertz

low gear *n* **1.** a gear such that the driven end of the drive shaft turns more slowly than the driving end, thus providing a relatively slow speed **2.** a state or period of little energy or activity

Low German *n* the German dialects that are spoken in northern Germany [Because spoken in the low-lying part of Germany]

low-grade *adj* **1.** bad or inferior in quality or grade **2.** describes a medical condition, especially a fever, that is mild and not serious

low-hanging fruit *n* a target that is easy to achieve, or a problem that is easy to solve ○ *Pick the low-hanging fruit first by identifying the most obvious opportunities.*

low-impact *adj* **1. NOT STRENUOUS** not requiring much energy or effort **2. EASY ON ENVIRONMENT** causing little or no damage to the surrounding environment **3. EASY ON JOINTS** describes exercise that involves little compression of the joints ○ *low-impact aerobics*

low-income *adj* having a relatively small income, or used by people on a relatively small income ○ *low-income families* ○ *low-income housing*

low-key, **low-keyed** *adj* **1. RESTRAINED** restrained and understated in character ○ *a relatively low-key campaign* **2. SUBDUED IN COLOUR** subdued or of low intensity, particularly in colour **3. DARK-TONED** describes a photograph or painting made up of dark tones and containing few highlights

lowland /lṓlənd/ *n* land that is relatively flatter or lower than adjacent land —**lowland** *adj*

Lowlander /lṓləndər/ *n* **1.** somebody who comes from the Scottish Lowlands **2.** somebody who comes from a lowland area

Lowlands /lṓləndz/ region of Scotland lying south of the Highlands, generally regarded as the area south of a line drawn between Dumbarton and Stonehaven —**Lowland** *adj*

low-level *adj* **1.** situated or done at a low or lower than usual level ○ *low-level aircraft* **2.** relatively low in terms of importance, status, expertise, or intensity ○ *low-level talks*

low-level language *n* a computer-oriented programming language, e.g. assembly language, in which instructions are in a code closer to machine code than to human language

lowlife /lṓ līf/ *n* **1. CRIMINAL** a criminal, or somebody who associates with criminals (*informal*) **2. SOMEBODY IMMORAL** a disreputable and immoral person (*informal insult*) **3. CRIMINAL OR IMMORAL PEOPLE** people who are thought to have criminal tendencies or extremely low morals, regarded as a group (*informal insult*) —**lowlife** *adj*

lowlights /lṓ līts/ *npl* strands of hair that are deliberately made darker than the rest of the hair —**lowlight** *vt*

low-loader *n* a truck or railway carriage built with a low platform so as to make it easier to load and unload heavy goods

lowly /lṓli/ *adj* (-lier, -liest) **1. LOW IN STATUS** low in rank, status, or importance **2. SIMPLE AND MODEST** simple, plain, and modest in character **3. MEEK** with a meek and humble way of behaving ■ *adv* (-lier, -liest) **1. IN MEEK WAY** in a humble or meek way **2. AT LOW VOLUME** at a subdued pitch or volume —**lowliness** *n*

low-lying *adj* at a lower level or closer to sea level than neighbouring ground

low-maintenance *adj* requiring only a little attention or effort to maintain (*informal*) ○ *As clients go, they're pretty low-maintenance.*

Low Mass *n* a plain Mass celebrated in a Roman Catholic or Anglican church that is recited, not sung

low-minded *adj* thinking or behaving in a coarse vulgar way —**low-mindedly** *adv* —**low-mindedness** *n*

low-necked *adj* cut to have a low neckline

lowp *vti, n N England, Scotland* another spelling of **loup**

low-paid *adj* receiving or offering relatively low wages, salary, or other remuneration

low-pass filter *n* an electronic filter that blocks signals above a specific cut-off frequency but allows those below it to pass through unchanged

low-pitched *adj* **1.** low in pitch or tonal range ○ *a low-pitched hum* **2.** with a shallow slope ○ *a low-pitched roof*

low point *n* the least successful, enjoyable, or important part of a period of time, activity, or experience ○ *the low point of the evening*

low-pressure *adj* **1.** having, exerting, or working under little physical pressure **2.** relaxed, easygoing, or presenting little stress

low profile *n* a way of behaving in which somebody deliberately seeks to avoid attention or publicity ○ *keep a low profile*

low-profile *adj* **1.** deliberately avoiding attention or publicity **2.** describes a tyre having a wide tread relative to its radial height

low relief *n* SCULPTURE same as **bas-relief** [Translation of French *bas-relief*]

low-rent *adj* **1.** having a low rental cost ○ *low-rent housing* **2.** *US* of low status, quality, or moral character (*informal*) ○ *a low-rent action movie*

low-res *adj* COMPUT another spelling of **lo-res** (*informal*)

low-resolution *adj* relating to a device such as a computer screen or printer in which the text or pictures are not sharply defined

low rise *n* a building consisting of only a few storeys ■ *adj* describes trousers, especially jeans, that sit low on the hips, usually revealing the navel [After HIGH-RISE] —**low-rise** *adj*

Lowry /lówri/, **L. S.** (1887–1976) British painter. His stylized depictions of the industrial north of England were deliberately executed in a childlike manner. Full name **Lowry, Laurence Stephen**

'A bachelor lives like a king and dies like a beggar.'
[Attributed to L. S. Lowry]

Lowry, Malcolm (1909–57) British writer and poet. He travelled extensively, and his most important work, *Under the Volcano* (1947), was inspired by his experience of living in Mexico. Full name **Lowry, Clarence Malcolm**. See Cultural note at **volcano**

'Where are the children I might have had? You may suppose I might have wanted them. Drowned to the accompaniment of the rattling of a thousand douche bags.'
[Malcolm Lowry, *Under the Volcano*; 1947]

low season *n* the period of the year when resorts or travel operators are least busy

lowsening *n N England* same as **loosing**

low-slung *adj* closer to the ground or the floor than usual

low spirits *npl* a state of unhappiness, hopelessness, or despondency ○ *The search party was in low spirits*

after three days. —**low-spirited** *adj* —**low-spiritedly** *adv* —**low-spiritedness** *n*

Low Sunday *n* in the Christian calendar, the Sunday after Easter [Probably in contrast to the 'high' feast of Easter Sunday]

low tech *n* same as **low technology** [Shortening] —**low-tech** *adj*

low technology *n* simple technology, especially that used to make basic items or perform basic tasks

low-tension *adj* capable of carrying low voltage or operating under low-voltage conditions

low tide *n* **1. LOWEST TIDE LEVEL** a tide at its lowest level **2. TIME OF LOWEST TIDE** the time of day when low tide occurs **3. WORST POINT** a lowest or worst point

low water *n* **1.** low tide, or the lowest level of water in a lake or river **2.** a very difficult situation or point

low-water mark *n* **1. LOWEST LEVEL OF WATER** the lowest level reached by a body of tidal or fresh water **2. LINE MARKING LOW-WATER MARK** a natural or artificial line marking a low-water mark **3. LOWEST POINT** a lowest or most difficult point

lox[1] /loks/ *n* smoked salmon [Mid-20C. Via Yiddish < German *Lachs* 'salmon']

lox[2] /loks/ *n* liquid oxygen, especially when used as an oxidizer for rocket fuel [Early 20C. < *l(iquid) o(xygen) (e)x(plosive)*; later interpreted as < *l(iquid) ox(ygen)*]

loxodrome /lóksə drōm/ *n* MAPS same as **rhumb line** (sense 1) [Late 19C. Back-formation < LOXODROMIC]

loxodromic /lóksə drómmik/, **loxodromical** /-drómmik'l/ *adj* relating to a map in which the rhumb lines appear straight, or to the rhumb lines on such a map [Late 17C. < French *loxodromique* < Greek *loxos* 'oblique' + *dromos* 'course'] —**loxodromically** *adv*

loxodromic curve *n* MAPS same as **rhumb line** (sense 1)

loyal /lóyəl/ *adj* **1.** remaining faithful to a country, person, ruler, government, or ideal **2.** expressing or relating to loyalty [Mid-16C. < French, modern form of Old French *loial*, variant of *leial* < Latin *legalis* (see LEGAL)] —**loyally** *adv* —**loyalness** *n*

loyalist /lóy əlist/ *n* a firm supporter of a country, ruler, or government —**loyalism** *n*

Loyalist *n* **1. SUPPORTER OF ULSTER UNION WITH BRITAIN** a Northern Ireland Protestant who wishes to continue Northern Ireland's political union with Britain **2. AMERICAN WHO SUPPORTED BRITISH** an American who supported the British during the War of American Independence **3. SPANISH CIVIL WAR SUPPORTER OF GOVERNMENT** a supporter of the republican government during the Spanish Civil War —**Loyalism** *n*

loyalty /lóyəlti/ (*plural* **-ties**) *n* **1.** the quality or state of being loyal **2.** a feeling of devotion, duty, or attachment to somebody or something (*often used in the plural*) [14C. < Old French *loialté* < *loial* (see LOYAL)]

loyalty card *n UK, ANZ, Can* a card issued to customers by a supermarket or chain store allowing them to qualify for rewards or discounts if they continue to shop there. US term **fidelity card**

lozenge /lózzinj/ *n* **1. MEDICATED TABLET** a medicated tablet that soothes the throat **2. DIAMOND SHAPE** a diamond-shaped figure **3. DIAMOND-SHAPED IMAGE** a diamond-shaped design or device on heraldic arms [14C. < Old French *losenge* 'windowpane, small square cake'] —**lozenged** *adj*

Lozi /lṓzi/ *n* a language of western Zambia, related to Sotho. Native speakers: 450,000. [Mid-20C. < Bantu] —**Lozi** *adj*

LP[1] *n* a long-playing gramophone record that turns at $33\frac{1}{3}$ revolutions per minute

LP[2] *abbr* **1.** Lord Provost **2.** low pressure

LPG *abbr* liquefied petroleum gas

L-plate *n* a small white square sign bearing a red letter 'L' displayed on vehicles driven by people who have not yet passed the driving test. By law, such a sign must be displayed on the front and rear of any vehicle driven by a learner. [*L* abbreviation of *learner*]

LPM, **lpm** *abbr* COMPUT lines per minute (*refers to computer printers*)

LPS *abbr* **1.** MICROBIOL lipopolysaccharide **2.** Lord Privy Seal

lr *abbr* ONLINE Liberia (*used in Internet addresses*) See table at **domain name**

Lr *symbol* CHEM ELEM lawrencium

LR *abbr* **1.** BUILDINGS living room (*in advertisements*) **2.** INSUR Lloyd's Register (of Shipping)

LRP *abbr UK* lead replacement petrol

LRV *abbr* RAIL light rail vehicle

ls *abbr* ONLINE Lesotho (*used in Internet addresses*) See table at **domain name**

LSD *n* a hallucinogenic drug made from lysergic acid that was used experimentally as a medicine and is taken as an illegal drug [< German *L(yserg)s(äure)-D(iäthylamid)* 'lysergic acid diethyl amide']

L.S.D, **l.s.d.** *abbr* MONEY pounds, shillings, pence [Latin *librae, solidi, denarii*]

LSE *abbr* EDUC London School of Economics

LSO *abbr* MUSIC London Symphony Orchestra

LSZ *abbr NZ* ROADS limited speed zone

lt *abbr* ONLINE Lithuania (*used in Internet addresses*) See table at **domain name**

LTA *abbr* TENNIS Lawn Tennis Association

Lt Cdr *abbr* NAVY Lieutenant Commander

Lt Col *abbr* MIL Lieutenant Colonel

Ltd, **ltd** *abbr* LAW limited (liability) (*used after the name of a British company*)

Lt Gen *abbr* MIL Lieutenant General

LTR *abbr* ONLINE long-term relationship

lu *abbr* ONLINE Luxembourg (*used in Internet addresses*) See table at **domain name**

Lu *symbol* CHEM ELEM lutetium

Lualaba /loo ə laábə/ headstream of the River Congo in southeastern Democratic Republic of the Congo. Length: 1,800 km/1,100 mi.

Luanda /loo ándə/ seaport and capital of Angola, situated in the northwestern part of the country, on the Atlantic Ocean. Population: 2,080,000 (1995).

luau /lóo ow/ *n* a Hawaiian feast, usually with music and entertainment [Mid-19C. < Hawaiian *lū'au*]

Luba /lóobə/, **Luba-Lulua** /-loo lóo ə/ *n* a group of Bantu languages or dialects of the southern Congo, around Kinshasa. Native speakers: 8 million. [Late 19C. < Bantu] —**Luba** *adj*

lubber /lúbbər/ *n* **1.** a big person who is regarded as clumsy or unintelligent (*insult*) **2.** same as **landlubber** [14C. Origin ?] —**lubberly** *adj, adv*

lubber line *n* a mark on a ship's compass that indicates the vessel's heading

lubber's hole *n* a space in a platform around a mast, allowing a sailor to climb through the space and stand on the platform

lubber's line *n* NAUT same as **lubber line**

Lubbock /lúbbək/ city and county seat of Lubbock County in north-central Texas, situated in the eastern part of the Llano Estacado region, south of Amarillo. It is a manufacturing and commercial centre. Population: 203,715 (2002 estimate).

lube /loob/ *Aus, N Am* (*informal*) *n* same as **lubricant** (sense 1) ■ *vt* (**lubes, lubing, lubed**) to apply lubricant to something

Lübeck /lóo bek/ port and city in Schleswig-Holstein State, north-central Germany. Population: 216,854 (1997).

Lubitsch /lóobich/, **Ernst** (1892–1947) German-born US actor and film director. He started making films in Germany, then moved to Hollywood as a director of comedies and costume epics.

Lublin /lóoblin/ city in southeastern Poland, situated about 153 km/95 mi. southeast of Warsaw. Population: 356,000 (1997).

lubricant /lóobrikənt/ *n* **1.** a substance, typically oil or grease, applied to a surface to reduce friction between moving parts **2.** somebody or something that eases or facilitates a solution to a potentially difficult or awkward situation —**lubricant** *adj*

lubricate /lóobri kayt/ (**-cates, -cating, -cated**) *v* **1.** *vti* **APPLY LUBRICANT** to apply an oily or greasy substance to something in order to reduce friction to moving parts **2.** *vt* **MAKE SOMETHING SLIPPERY** to make something slippery **3.** *vt* **MAKE SOMETHING RUN SMOOTHLY** to make something run smoothly and without problems [Early 17C. < Latin *lubricat-*, past participle of *lubricare* < *lubricus* 'slippery'] —**lubrication** /lóobri káysh'n/ *n* —**lubricational** *adj* —**lubricative** *adj* —**lubricator** *n*

lubricious /loo bríshəss/, **lubricous** /lóobrikəss/ *adj* (*literary*) **1.** lewd, obscene, or intended to be sexually exciting **2.** slippery or oily [Late 16C. < Latin *lubricus* 'slippery'] —**lubriciously** *adv*

lubricity /loo bríssəti/ *n* behaviour that is obscene or unchaste (*formal*) [15C. Directly or via French < late Latin *lubricitas* < Latin *lubricus* 'slippery']

lubricous *adj* same as **lubricious** (*literary*)

Lubumbashi /lóoboom báshi/ industrial city and mining centre in Shaba Administrative Region, southeastern Democratic Republic of the Congo. Population: 851,381 (1994). Former name **Elizabethville**

Lucania, Mount /loo káyni ə/ mountain in the St Elias Range, southwestern Yukon Territory, Canada, near the Alaskan border. Height: 5,226 m/17,146 ft.

lucarne /loo kaárn/ *n* a dormer window [Mid-16C. Via French < Provençal *lucana*]

Lucas /lóokəss/, **George** (*b.* 1944) US film director and producer. After making such successful films as *American Graffiti* (1973) and *Star Wars* (1977), he built up a pioneering special effects company.

Lucas van Leyden /-van lī́d'n/ (1494–1533) Dutch painter and engraver. One of the earliest painters of genre scenes, he also produced engravings of religious and allegorical subjects.

Lucca /lóokə/ historic city and capital of Lucca Province, Tuscany Region, north-central Italy. Population: 81,862 (2001).

Luce /looss/, **Maximilien** (1858–1941) French artist. A supporter of the anarchist movement and founder of the neoimpressionist school, he is best known for his industrial landscapes and paintings of Parisian street life.

lucent /lóoss'nt/ *adj* **1.** shining with a glowing light **2.** translucent or clear [15C. < Latin *lucent-*, present participle of *lucere* (see LUCID)] —**lucency** *n* —**lucently** *adv*

lucerne /loo súrn/ *n* PLANTS same as **alfalfa** [Mid-17C. Via French < modern Provençal *luzerno*, originally 'glowworm' < Latin *lucerna* 'lamp' < *lucere* (see LUCID)]

Lucerne /loo súrn/ city and capital of Lucerne Canton, central Switzerland. It is a tourist centre. Population: 57,193 (1998).

Lucerne, Lake of lake and popular tourist region in central Switzerland. Area: 114 sq. km/44 sq. mi.

lucid /lóossid/ *adj* **1. RATIONAL** rational, and mentally clear, especially only for a period between episodes of delirium or psychosis **2. EASILY UNDERSTOOD** clear and easily understood ○ *a lucid explanation* **3. SHINING** emitting light [Late 16C. < Latin *lucidus* < *lucere* 'to shine' < *luc-* 'light'] —**lucidity** /loo síddəti/ *n* —**lucidly** *adv*

lucifer /lóossifər/ *n* a friction match (*archaic*) [Mid-19C. < *lucifer match*, originally a trade name]

Lucifer /lóossifər/ *n* **1.** in Christianity, a rebellious archangel who is usually held to be the same as Satan **2.** the planet Venus appearing before sunrise as the morning star [Pre-12C. < Latin, 'the planet Venus', literally 'light-bearing' < *luc-* 'light']

luciferase /loo síffər ayz, -ayss/ *n* an enzyme that stimulates the oxidation of luciferin

luciferin /loo síffərin/ *n* a substance in the cells of bioluminescent organisms that emits light on enzymatic oxidation

luciferous /loo síffərəss/ *adj* bringing or emitting light (*literary*)

Lucina /loo sī́nə/ *n* in Roman mythology, Juno in her capacity as goddess of childbirth

~~**lucious**~~ incorrect spelling of **luscious**

luck /luk/ *n* **1. GOOD FORTUNE** success that seems to happen by chance ○ *a stroke of luck* **2. CHANCE** the arbitrary distribution of events or outcomes ○ *a game of luck* **3. FORTUNATE OR UNFORTUNATE EVENT** something fortunate or unfortunate that happens to somebody, or a series of such events ○ *Just my luck!*

zh vision. In foreign words: kh German Bach; aN French vin; aaN French blanc; ö German schön, French feu; oN French bon; öN French un; ü as in French rue. Stress marks: ´ as in secret /séekrət/, academic /ákə démmik/

4. SOMETHING BEARING LUCK an event, action, or object regarded as bringing good or bad luck ○ *It's said to be bad luck to walk under ladders.* [15C. Probably < Low German *luk*] ◇ **push your luck** to test how far you can go before running out of good fortune
luck into (lucks into, lucking into, lucked into) *vt N Am* to obtain something desirable or experience something pleasurable by chance
luck out *vi N Am* to be lucky enough to succeed by chance (*informal*)

luckenbooth /lúkən booth/ *n* a Scottish brooch design in the shape of a silver heart, given in the past as a token of love or betrothal [15C. *Lucken* past participle of obsolete *louk* 'lock' < Old English *lūcan* < Germanic; originally 'booth that can be locked' (where such brooches were sold)]

luckily /lúkili/ *adv* as a result of or the occasion for good luck

luckless /lúkləss/ *adj* without success or fortune — **lucklessly** *adv* —**lucklessness** *n*

Lucknow /lúk now/ capital of Uttar Pradesh State, northern India, situated in the Ganges valley, about 64 km/40 mi. northeast of Kanpur. Population: 2,266,933 (2001).

luckpenny /lúk peni/ (*plural* **-nies**) *n* a coin kept or given to bring good fortune

lucky /lúki/ (**-ier, -iest**) *adj* **1.** FORTUNATE having success or advantage, especially when it is unexpected ○ *You were lucky not to be seriously injured.* **2.** BRINGING GOOD FORTUNE producing or bringing good fortune ○ *lucky charm* **3.** RESULTING FROM GOOD LUCK as a result of good luck ○ *lucky escape* —**luckiness** *n*

SYNONYMS ***lucky, fortunate, happy, providential, serendipitous***

CORE MEANING: relating to advantage or good fortune

lucky having or producing success and advantage, especially when it is unexpected ○ *We were lucky to be born in prosperous times.* ○ *The ancient coins were a lucky find for the archaeologists.* **fortunate** happening as a result of good luck ○ *She was fortunate enough to win the prize.* **happy** resulting unexpectedly in something pleasant or welcome ○ *By happy coincidence my brother was there too.* **providential** so favourable that it seems determined by providence ○ *The firefighters' arrival was providential.* **serendipitous** favourable and happening entirely by chance ○ *Reading through the letters he made the serendipitous discovery of a small sketch of his great-great-grandmother.*

lucky-bone *n* same as **wishbone** (*regional*)

Lucky Country *n Aus* Australia seen as a comfortable country whose people can enjoy a pleasant life, particularly during the boom era of the 1960s and early 1970s

lucky dip *n* **1.** a game in which somebody takes a prize out of a container which is filled with soft material such as sawdust or shredded paper and within which prizes are hidden **2.** a situation or venture with a large element of chance (*informal*)

lucrative /lóokrətiv/ *adj* producing profit or wealth [15C. < Latin *lucrativus* < *lucrari* 'to gain' < *lucrum* 'gain'] — **lucratively** *adv* —**lucrativeness** *n*

lucre /lóokər/ *n* money, wealth, or profit (*dated or humorous*) ○ *filthy lucre* [14C. Directly or via French < Latin *lucrum* 'gain']

Lucretia /loo kréeshə/ (*fl* 6th century BC) Roman matron. After being raped by the son of Tarquinius Superbus, she committed suicide, leading to the expulsion of the Tarquin royal family from Rome.

Lucretius /loo kréeshəss/ (94?–55 BC) Roman poet and philosopher. His *De Rerum Natura*, based on the theories of Democritus and Epicurus, expounds his materialist philosophy. Full name **Carus, Titus Lucretius**

> 'Nothing can be created out of nothing.'
> [Lucretius, *De Rerum Natura (On the Nature of Things)*; 1st century BC]

lucubration /lóokyoo bráysh'n/ *n* **1.** a written work resulting from prolonged study, often having a scholarly or pedantic style (*usually used in the plural*) **2.** long hard study, especially at night [Late 16C. < Latin *lucubration-* < *lucubrare* 'compose at night' < *luc-* 'light'] —**lucubrate** /lóokyoo brayt/ *vi*

luculent /lóokyoolənt/ *adj* **1.** easy to understand **2.** shining or glowing [15C. < Latin *luculentus* < *luc-* 'light']

Lucullan /loo kúllən/ *adj* lavish or overindulgent, especially with regard to food [Mid-19C. < Latin *Lucullanus*, after Lucius Licinius LUCULLUS]

Lucullus /loo kúlləss/, **Lucius Licinius** (110?–56 BC) Roman general. A distinguished public career brought him great wealth. He was also a patron of artists and writers.

lud /lud/ *n* used to address a judge in court, either as 'm'lud' or 'my lud' [Early 18C. Representing a hurried pronunciation of LORD]

Luddite /lúddīt/ *n* **1.** an opponent of technological or industrial change **2.** a worker who was involved in protests in the United Kingdom in the 1810s against new factory methods of production and who favoured traditional methods of work [Early 19C. Perhaps after Ned *Ludd*, 18C Leicestershire farm worker, who destroyed machinery] —**Luddism** *n* —**Luddite** *adj*

luderick /lóodərik/ (*plural same*) *n* a food fish that is grey-brown in colour with dark vertical bands along its body. Native to: Australia. Latin name: *Girella tricuspidata.* [Late 19C. < an Aboriginal language]

Lüderitz /lóodərits/ port on the southern coast of Namibia. Population: 6,000 (1990).

ludic /lóodik/ *adj* playful in a way that is spontaneous and without any particular purpose (*literary*) [Mid-20C. < French *ludique* < Latin *ludere* 'to play' < *ludus* 'game']

ludicrous /lóodikrəss/ *adj* utterly ridiculous because of being absurd, incongruous, impractical, or unsuitable [Early 17C. < Latin *ludicrus* < *ludus* 'play'] — **ludicrously** *adv* —**ludicrousness** *n*

ORIGIN The Latin word *ludus* 'play', from which ***ludicrous*** is derived, is also the source of English *allude, collude, delude, elude*, and *illusion.*

Ludlow /lúdlō/ ancient market town in Shropshire, England. It was a Roman settlement, and later a Saxon town, and now part of the Ludlow rural district.

ludo /lóodō/ *n* a board game in which counters progress according to a player's dice throw [Late 19C. < Latin, 'I play', form of *ludere* (see LUDIC)]

Ludwigshafen /lóodvigs haafən/ port in Rhineland-Palatinate State, southwestern Germany, situated on the western bank of the River Rhine, opposite Mannheim. Population: 167,883 (1997).

lues /lóo eez/ *n* MED same as **syphilis** [Mid-17C. < Latin, 'plague']

luff /luf/ *v* (**luffs, luffing, luffed**) **1.** *vt* SAIL TOO CLOSE TO WIND to bring a boat closer in to the wind, or sail too close to the wind, so that the sails flap **2.** *vi* FLAP to flap when a boat is in a position too close to the wind (*refers to a sail*) ■ *n* SAIL'S FRONT EDGE the front edge of a sail [12C. < Old French *lof*]

Luftwaffe /lóoft vaffə/ *n* the German Air Force [Mid-20C. < German, 'air weapon']

lug[1] /lug/ *vt* (**lugs, lugging, lugged**) **1.** PULL SOMETHING WITH EFFORT to carry or pull something that is heavy or bulky, using great effort **2.** INTRODUCE SOMETHING IRRELEVANTLY INTO DISCUSSION to introduce irrelevant material into a discussion or conversation ■ *n* ACT OF PULLING LOAD the effort or action of pulling something very heavy [15C. Probably < N Germanic]

lug[2] /lug/ *n* **1.** PROJECTING PART a projecting part, especially one by which something can be moved, rotated, or supported **2.** PROJECTION FOR ELECTRICAL CONTACT a small metal projection to which an electrical conductor or wire may be attached, usually by soldering or using mechanical pressure **3.** SMALL PROJECTION IMPROVING TRACTION a small projection on a tyre or boot that helps provide traction **4.** FRUIT OR VEGETABLE BOX a box for vegetables or fruit **5.** EAR an ear, especially the external ear (*informal*) **6.** CLUMSY MAN a man who is regarded as unintelligent or clumsy (*informal insult*) [14C. Probably < N Germanic]

REGIONAL NOTE A **lug** was originally a lock of hair or something that could be pulled. It is uncertain when 'ear-pulling' became fashionable, but **lug** is still widely used as a word for 'ear': *Little jugs have big lugs* (Little children often hear more than they should).

lug[3] /lug/ *n* SAILING same as **lugsail** [Mid-19C. Shortening]

lug[4] /lug/ *n* ZOOL same as **lugworm** (sense 1) [Early 17C. Origin ?]

Luganda /loo gándə/ *n* LANG same as **Ganda** [Late 19C. < Bantu] —**Luganda** *adj*

Lugano /loo gaánō/ town and tourist centre in Ticino Canton, southern Switzerland. Population: 25,771 (1998).

Lugano, Lake lake in southern Switzerland and northern Italy. Area: 49 sq. km/19 sq. mi.

luge /loozh/ *n* a racing toboggan on which the riders lie on their backs with their feet pointing forwards ■ *vi* (**luges, luging, luged**) to race on a luge [Late 19C. Via Swiss French < medieval Latin *sludia*] —**luger** *n*

luggage /lúggij/ *n* suitcases, bags, and other items for carrying personal belongings during a journey (*often used before a noun*) ○ *the luggage compartment* [Late 16C. < LUG [1]]

luggage rack *n* **1.** an overhead frame in a train or bus for passengers to keep small items of luggage on **2.** *US* same as **roof rack**

luggage van *n* a railway carriage for storing rail users' luggage and bicycles. N Am term **baggage car**

lugger /lúggər/ *n* a small boat for fishing or pleasure sailing that is rigged with a lugsail [Mid-18C. Origin ?]

lughole /lúg hōl/ *n* an ear, especially the hole of the ear (*informal*)

lug nut *n* a large nut that screws onto a heavy bolt, especially one used to attach a wheel to a motor vehicle

Lugosi /loo góssi/, **Bela** (1882–1956) Hungarian-born US actor. He starred in numerous horror films, and was especially closely identified with the title role in *Dracula* (1931). Born **Blasko, Bela Ferenc Dezso**

lugsail /lúg sayl, lúgss'l/ *n* an irregularly shaped four-sided sail fixed to a beam that crosses the mast at an angle [Late 17C. Probably < LUG [3]]

lugubrious /lə góobri əss/ *adj* extremely mournful, sad, or gloomy [Early 17C. < Latin *lugubris* < *lugere* 'mourn'] —**lugubriously** *adv* —**lugubriousness** *n*

lugworm /lúg wurm/ *n* **1.** a segmented sea worm that burrows in sandy shores, has rows of tufted gills, and is often used as angling bait. Genus: *Arenicola.* **2.** MARINE BIOL same as **fanworm** [Early 19C. < LUG [4]]

Luhansk /loo hánsk/, **Luhans'k** industrial city in eastern Ukraine. Population: 475,000 (1998).

Luhrmann /lúrmən/, **Baz** (*b.* 1962) Australian film and theatre director. His films include *Strictly Ballroom* (1992) and *Moulin Rouge* (2001). Born **Luhrmann, Bazmark Anthony**

Lukács /lóo kach/, **György** (1885–1971) Hungarian philosopher, critic, and politician. Marxist in thought, his work *History and Class Consciousness* (1923) attempts to combine socialism and humanism.

Luke /look/ *n* a book of the Bible, the third of the gospels in which the life and teachings of Jesus Christ are described, traditionally attributed to St Luke. See table at **Bible**

Luke /look/, **St** (*fl* AD 1st century) evangelist companion to St Paul. Perhaps a physician, he was by tradition author of the biblical Acts of the Apostles and the third Gospel.

lukewarm /lóok wáwrm/ *adj* **1.** just slightly warm, especially when expected to be hot **2.** showing or having little enthusiasm, interest, support, or conviction [14C. < obsolete *luke* 'lukewarm', origin ?] — **lukewarmly** *adv* —**lukewarmness** *n*

Lula ➧ **Silva, Luis Inacio Lula da**

Luleå /lóolə ō, lóoli-/ seaport at the head of the Gulf of Bothnia, northern Sweden. Population: 71,238 (1997).

lull /lul/ *v* (**lulls, lulling, lulled**) **1.** *vt* SOOTHE OR CALM SOMEBODY to soothe or calm a person or animal, especially by using gentle sounds or motions **2.** *vt* MAKE SOMEBODY FEEL SAFE to give somebody a false sense of security so that an unpleasant situation takes the person by surprise ○ *They lulled us into thinking we still had time.* **3.** *vi* BECOME CALM to become calm or calmer ■ *n* PERIOD OF CALM a brief interval of calm or decreased activity [14C. Probably representing a sound made to soothe a child]

a at; aa father; aw all; ay day; aı hair; ə about, item, edible, common, circus; e egg; ee eel; hw when; i it, happy; ī ice; 'l apple; 'm rhythm; 'n fashion; o odd; ō open; oo good; oo pool; ow owl; oy oil; th thin; th this; u up; ur urge;

lullaby /lúllə bī/ n (plural **-bies**) **1.** GENTLE SONG a gentle song for soothing a child, especially into sleep **2.** MUSIC FOR LULLABY instrumental music in the style of a lullaby ■ vt (**-bies, -bying, -bied**) SING LULLABY TO CHILD to soothe a child with a lullaby [Mid-16C. < obsolete *lulla* 'lullaby' < a sound made to soothe a child + *-by* as in BYE-BYES]

Lully /loolli/, **Jean-Baptiste** (1633–87) Italian-born French composer. He wrote ballets and other musical entertainments for the court of Louis XIV of France.

lulu /loo loo/ n a remarkable or outstanding person, object, or idea (slang) [Late 19C. Alteration of *looly* in *looliest looly of the loolies*, said in admiration, origin ?]

Luluabourg /loo loo ə boorg/ former name for **Kananga**

lum /lum/ n Scotland a chimney or chimney stack (informal) [Early 16C. Origin?]

lumbago /lum báygō/ n pain in the lower or lumbar region of the back [Late 17C. < Latin *lumbus* 'loin']

lumbar /lúmbər/ adj relating to or situated in the loins or the small of the back [Mid-17C. < medieval Latin *lumbaris* < Latin *lumbus* 'loin']

SPELLCHECK lumbar or lumber? Do not confuse the spelling of **lumbar** and **lumber**, which sound similar. The adjective **lumbar** is used in medical expressions referring to the lower part of the back, as in *the lumbar vertebrae*, *a lumbar puncture*. **Lumber** is a noun meaning 'unwanted objects' or a verb meaning 'burden somebody with something unpleasant', as in *the lumber room*, *lumbered with the washing up*.

lumbar puncture n the insertion of a needle between two lumbar vertebrae into the spinal cord in order to obtain a sample of cerebrospinal fluid for diagnosis or to introduce medication

lumber[1] /lúmbər/ n **1.** N Am same as **timber** n (sense 1) **2.** UNWANTED OBJECTS large objects that are not being used and are stored out of sight ■ v (**-bers, -bering, -bered**) **1.** vt BURDEN SOMEBODY WITH SOMETHING to burden somebody with something unpleasant or unwanted, especially a responsibility or a task (informal) **2.** vt PILE THINGS TOGETHER to pile things together haphazardly **3.** vti N Am TURN TREES INTO TIMBER to cut down the trees in a region and convert them into saleable timber [Mid-16C. Origin ?] —**lumberer** n

SPELLCHECK See *lumbar*.

lumber[2] /lúmbər/ (**-bers, -bering, -bered**) vi to move clumsily or heavily [14C. Origin ?]

lumberjack /lúmbər jak/ n N Am **1.** a cutter and transporter of trees for timber **2.** CLOTHING same as **lumberjacket** [Mid-19C. < JACK[1]]

lumberjacket /lúmbər jakit/ n a work jacket made from thick, warm material, usually brightly coloured with a checked pattern [Mid-20C. < its being of a type worn by lumberjacks]

lumberyard /lúmbər yaard/ n N Am same as **timberyard**

lumen /loomin/ (plural **-mens** or **-mina** /-minə/) n **1.** UNIT OF LUMINOUS FLUX the SI unit of luminous flux, equal to the amount of light crossing a unit area at a unit distance from a light source of luminous intensity of one candela. Symbol **lm** **2.** SPACE WITHIN TUBE the space inside any tubular structure in the body such as an intestine, artery, or vein **3.** CAVITY IN PLANT the cavity within a plant cell wall [Late 19C. < Latin, 'light, opening']

Lumet /loo mét/, **Sidney** (b. 1924) US actor, director, and screenwriter. Among his greatest successes are *Murder on the Orient Express* (1974), *Dog Day Afternoon* (1975), and *Network* (1976).

lum hat n Scotland same as **top hat** (dated)

Lumière /loomi air/, **Auguste** (1862–1954) and his brother **Louis** (1864–1948), French inventors. They invented the cinema camera and projector, and made the first film, *Workers Leaving the Lumière Factory* (1895).

luminaire /loomi náir/ n a tungsten or fluorescent light fitting [Early 20C. < French < Old French *luminarie* (see LUMINARY)]

luminance /loominənss/ n **1.** the condition or quality of emitting or reflecting light. Symbol **L** **2.** a measure of the brightness of a surface, equal to the amount of luminous flux arriving at, passing through, or leaving a unit area of surface. It is

measured in candelas per square metre. [Late 19C. < *luminant* 'luminous' < Latin *luminant-*, present participle of *luminare* 'illuminate' < *lumin-* 'light']

luminaria /loomi náirə ə/ n Southwest US a small candle set inside a paper bag that has been weighted with sand, usually placed outdoors with others as a Christmas decoration [Mid-20C. Via Mexican Spanish < Spanish, 'decorative light' < late Latin, 'lamp', plural of *luminarium* (see LUMINARY)]

luminary /loominəri/ n (plural **-ies**) **1.** EMINENT PERSON an eminent or famous person **2.** SUN, MOON, OR STAR an object, especially an astronomical one, that emits light (literary) ■ adj CHARACTERIZED BY LIGHT relating to or characterized by light [15C. Directly or via Old French *luminarie* < late Latin *luminarium* < Latin *lumin-* 'light']

luminesce /loomi néss/ (**-nesces, -nescing, -nesced**) vi to emit light by phosphorescence, fluorescence, or bioluminescence [Late 19C. Back-formation < *luminescent* (see LUMINESCENCE)]

luminescence /loomi néss'nss/ n **1.** the emission of light produced by means other than heat (**incandescence**), e.g. by phosphorescence, fluorescence, or bioluminescence **2.** the light emitted by luminescence [Late 19C. < *luminescent* < Latin *lumin-* 'light'] —**luminescent** adj

luminiferous /loomi níffərəss/ adj generating or giving off light [Early 19C. < Latin *lumin-* 'light']

luminol /loomi nol/ n a white crystalline compound. Use: chemical testing. Formula: $C_8H_7N_3O_2$. [Mid-20C. < Latin *lumin-* 'light']

luminosity /loomi nóssəti/ n (plural **-ties**) n **1.** STATE OF BEING LUMINOUS the state or quality of being luminous **2.** ENERGY RADIATED BY ASTRONOMICAL OBJECT the energy radiated per second by an astronomical object. Symbol **L** **3.** STRENGTH OF LIGHT EMITTED the visual perception of the extent to which an object emits light **4.** SOMETHING LUMINOUS something that emits light

luminous /loominəss/ adj **1.** LIGHT-EMITTING emitting or reflecting light **2.** BRIGHT startlingly bright ○ *luminous orange* **3.** ILLUMINATED brightly illuminated **4.** UNDERSTANDABLE clear and easy to understand **5.** INSPIRING enlightened and inspiring **6.** PHYS RELATING TO LIGHT evaluated on the basis of the visual sensation produced in an observer rather than energy measurements [15C. Directly or via French < Latin *luminosus* < *lumin-* 'light, opening'] —**luminously** adv —**luminousness** n

luminous energy n the total amount of light emitted by a source. Symbol Q_v

luminous flux n the rate of emission of light evaluated by the visual sensation it produces. Symbol Φ_v

luminous intensity n the amount of light emitted by a source in a particular direction. Symbol I_v

lumme /lúmmi/, **lummy** interj used to express surprise or shock (dated informal) [Late 19C. Representing a pronunciation of (Lord) *love me*]

lummox /lúmməks/ n somebody considered clumsy or unintelligent (informal insult) [Early 19C Origin ?]

lummy interj same as **lumme** (dated informal)

lump[1] /lump/ n **1.** SOLID CHUNK a small irregularly shaped solid mass or piece **2.** TUMOUR a tumour or other swelling in the body **3.** SUGAR CUBE a small cube of solid sugar **4.** LARGE AND CLUMSY PERSON somebody regarded as large and unintelligent or clumsy (informal insult) **5.** CASUAL CONSTRUCTION WORKERS a collective term for workers in the building trade who are casual and do not belong to a union (informal) **6.** Scotland LARGE, SLOW-MOVING PERSON a big, fleshy, slow-moving person (informal) ■ **lumps** npl US HARDSHIP harsh, often undeserved, criticism, punishment, or hardship (informal) ○ *You have to take your lumps like everyone else.* ■ v (**lumps, lumping, lumped**) **1.** vt GROUP THINGS TOGETHER CARELESSLY to consider people, ideas, or objects as a single group, often without good reason ○ *All the students were lumped together as lazy.* **2.** vi MOVE HEAVILY to move in a heavy and clumsy manner ○ *He lumped along.* ■ adj IN LUMPS in small cubes or lumps ○ *lump sugar* [14C. Origin ?]

lump[2] /lump/ (**lumps, lumping, lumped**) vt to endure something unpleasant that cannot be changed (informal) ○ *like it or lump it* [Late 16C. Origin ?]

lumpectomy /lum péktəmi/ n (plural **-mies**) n a surgical operation for breast cancer in which the surgery is limited to the removal of the visible and palpable tumour only [Late 20C. < LUMP[1]]

lumpen /lúmpən, loom-/ (disapproving) adj **1.** MARGINALIZED living, or regarded as living, on the margins of society **2.** NOT EDUCATED OR ENLIGHTENED stupidly content with a life regarded as intellectually empty and socially inferior ■ npl **LUMPEN PEOPLE** people regarded by others as lumpen [Mid-20C. Back-formation < LUMPENPROLETARIAT]

lumpenproletariat /lúmpən prōlə táiri ət, loom-/ n (takes a singular or plural verb) **1.** in Marxist analysis, people regarded as living on the margins of society, particularly criminals, homeless people, and the long-term unemployed **2.** people from the lowest social class who are regarded as too content with a life that is supposedly intellectually empty and socially inferior (disapproving) [Early 20C. < German < *Lumpen*, plural of *Lump* 'ragamuffin' + French *prolétariat* (see PROLETARIAT)]

lumpfish /lúmpfish/ (plural **-fishes** or same) n a northern sea fish with a short scaleless body covered with rows of thorny lumps. Family: Cyclopteridae. [Early 17C. < Middle Dutch *lumpe* 'cod']

lumpish /lúmpish/ adj **1.** tending to move awkwardly or slowly and heavily **2.** regarded as having no intelligence, energy, or enthusiasm (insult) —**lumpishly** adv —**lumpishness** n

lumpsucker /lúmp sukər/ n FISH same as **lumpfish** [Mid-18C. < obsolete *lump* 'lumpfish' < Middle Low German *lumpen*, Middle Dutch *lumpe*]

lump sum n an amount of money that is given in a single payment, rather than being divided into smaller periodic payments

lumpy /lúmpi/ (**-ier, -iest**) adj **1.** WITH LUMPS having or filled with lumps, especially when lumps are unwanted, e.g. in the upholstery of a chair or the mattress of a bed **2.** LACKING SMOOTHNESS OF TEXTURE describes semiliquid foods such as sauces and soups that lack the normal appetizing smoothness of texture **3.** CUMBERSOME with a cumbersome quality or appearance **4.** CHOPPY having or exhibiting short choppy waves —**lumpily** adv —**lumpiness** n

Lumumba /loo moombə/, **Patrice** (1925–61) prime minister of the Republic of the Congo (now the Democratic Republic of the Congo). He was the first prime minister of the newly independent country (1960), but was overthrown in a military coup and assassinated the following year.

> 'Without dignity there is no liberty, without justice there is no dignity, and without independence there are no free men.'
> [Patrice Lumumba, letter to his wife, *Congo, My Country*; 1962]

Luna /loonə/ n in Roman mythology, the goddess of the Moon. Greek equivalent **Selene** [14C. < Latin, 'moon']

lunacy /loonəssi/ (plural **-cies**) n **1.** behaviour that is regarded as unintelligent, inconsiderate, or misguided, or an example of it **2.** an offensive term for any psychiatric disorder that rendered patients legally incompetent and required them to be taken into care. This term has never been used by physicians in medical or psychiatric contexts. (archaic) [Mid-16C. < LUNATIC]

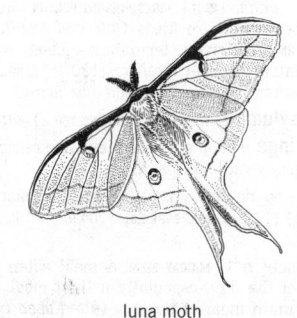

luna moth

luna moth /loonə-/ *n* a large moth that has spotted light-green wings with long thin extensions at the back that look like tails. Native to: North America. Latin name: *Actias luna*. See illustration on previous page [< Latin, 'moon'; from the crescent-shaped spots on its wings]

lunar: a lunar rover used by astronaut James Irwin on the Moon (1971)

lunar /loonər/ *adj* **1.** RELATING TO MOON relating to a moon or its movement around a planet, especially the Moon in relation to Earth **2.** USED FOR TRAVEL TO MOON for use in space travel to or on the Moon **3.** CRESCENT-SHAPED in the shape of a crescent moon **4.** PALE pale and cold-looking, as the Moon is compared to the Sun [15C. < Latin *lunaris* < *luna* 'moon']

lunar caustic *n* silver nitrate, especially when formed into small sticks (*archaic*)

lunar cycle *n* a means of establishing a calendar that is based on the cycles of the Moon. The Muslim calendar is based on the lunar cycle. It requires constant revision or intercalation, which the solar calendar does not.

lunar eclipse *n* an eclipse of the Moon caused by Earth passing between the Sun and the Moon and casting its shadow on the Moon

lunar excursion module *n* AEROSP same as **lunar module**

lunarian /loo náiri ən/ *n* in mythology and science fiction, an inhabitant of the Moon [Early 18C. < Latin *lunaris* (see LUNAR)]

lunar module *n* a small spacecraft used to travel from an orbiting command module to the surface of the Moon and back

lunar month *n* **1.** the time between one new moon and the next, a period of about 29.5 days. It is the time the Moon takes to make one complete orbit of Earth. **2.** a period of four weeks

Lunar New Year *n* the Chinese New Year, which usually occurs at a point between late January and mid-February

lunarscape /loonər skayp/ *n* a rugged barren landscape of strange rock formations, similar to the surface of the Moon

lunar year *n* a period of 12 lunar months

lunate /loon ayt/ *adj also* **lunated** /loo naytid/ shaped like a crescent moon ■ *n* ANAT same as **lunate bone** [Late 18C. < Latin *lunatus* < *luna* 'moon']

lunate bone *n* a bone of the wrist that articulates with the bones of the forearm [< its shape]

lunated /loo naytid/ *adj* same as **lunate**

lunatic /loonətik/ *adj* **1.** THOUGHTLESS considered thoughtless, ridiculous, or reckless **2.** OFFENSIVE TERM an offensive term meaning affected by a psychiatric disorder (*archaic*) ■ *n* **1.** IRRESPONSIBLE PERSON somebody considered wildly reckless (*informal insult*) **2.** OFFENSIVE TERM an offensive term for somebody who has a psychiatric disorder (*archaic*) [13C. Via French < late Latin *lunaticus* 'moonstruck' < Latin *luna* 'moon']

lunatic asylum *n* same as **asylum** (sense 3) (*offensive*)

lunatic fringe *n* people whose views are regarded as eccentrically radical (*insult*)

lunation /loo náysh'n/ *n* TIME same as **lunar month** (sense 1) [14C. < medieval Latin *lunation-* < Latin *luna* 'moon']

lunch /lunch/ *n* **1.** MIDDAY MEAL a meal eaten in the middle of the day, especially a light meal that is not the main meal of the day (*often used before a noun*) **2.** FOOD EATEN AT MIDDAY the food prepared and eaten at the midday meal ○ *Our lunch was soup and salad.* ■ *vi* (**lunches, lunching, lunched**) HAVE LUNCH to eat lunch, especially a particular type of lunch eaten somewhere other than at home [Early 19C. Shortening of LUNCHEON] ◇ **out to lunch** an offensive term that means displaying thoughtlessness or unusual behaviour in a way that suggests a loss of touch with reality (*insult*)

> CULTURAL NOTE *The Naked Lunch*, a novel (1959) by US writer William S. Burroughs. This controversial portrayal of drug abuse, written by Burroughs in Tunisia as he attempted to free himself of his own addiction, consists of a series of surreal episodes linked by themes and characters and described in language that is by turns clinical, hallucinatory, poetic, and scatological.

lunchbox /lúnch boks/ *n* a container for sandwiches or other foods carried somewhere, e.g. to work, to eat for lunch

luncheon /lúnchən/ *n* (*formal*) **1.** FOOD same as **lunch** *n* (sense 1) **2.** an organized gathering in the middle of the day, with invited guests being served a meal and often offered some form of entertainment, e.g. a guest speaker [Mid-17C. Probably alteration of archaic *nuncheon* 'snack' < NOON + obsolete *shench* 'drink' < Old English *scenc* < Germanic]

luncheonette /lúnchə nét/ *n* N Am a small fairly simple restaurant serving full lunch menus and snacks, and often breakfast

luncheon meat *n* processed meat, e.g. ham mixed with cereal, sold in a tin or sliced, and usually eaten cold

luncheon voucher *n* a voucher that can be exchanged for food in participating restaurants, sandwich bars, and other food establishments at lunchtime. Luncheon vouchers are offered by some firms to their employees as a bonus or incentive.

lunchroom /lúnch room, -room/ *n* N Am a room in a school or office where people can buy lunch or eat a packed lunch

lunchtime /lúnch tīm/ *n* the time, around the middle of the day, when lunch is usually eaten (*often used before a noun*)

Lund /loond/ historic city in southern Sweden, situated about 18 km/11 mi. northeast of Malmö. Population: 97,638 (1998).

Lunda /loondə/ *n* a Bantu language spoken in western central Africa, especially in Zaïre. Native speakers: 82,000. [Late 19C. < Bantu] —**Lunda** *adj*

Lundy /lúndi/ island in southwestern England, lying in the Bristol Channel off the Devon coast. Area: 4 sq. km/2 sq. mi.

lune /loon/ *n* **1.** in geometry, a crescent-shaped area on the surface of a plane or sphere defined by two semicircles whose common end points are diametrically opposed **2.** CHR same as **lunette** (sense 6) [Early 18C. Via French < Latin *luna* 'moon']

Lüneburg /loonə burg/ town in Lower Saxony State, north-central Germany. Population: 64,030 (1997).

Lunenberg bump /loonən burg-/ *n* Can in Nova Scotia, a jutting window on an upper floor of a multistorey house [Named after *Lunenberg*, a city in Nova Scotia.]

lunette /loo nét/ *n* **1.** CRESCENT-SHAPED OBJECT any object that has a crescent shape **2.** WINDOW IN DOMED CEILING an arch-shaped window at the height of a domed ceiling **3.** SEMICIRCULAR PANEL a semicircular panel on a wall, containing a window, painting, or frieze **4.** VEHICLE'S TOWING RING a metal ring on a vehicle to which a rope can be attached for towing **5.** GEOG CRESCENT-SHAPED MOUND OF SILT a crescent-shaped mound of fine silt or clay similar in form to a sand dune, found especially near the edge of a temporary lake **6.** CHR CONTAINER USED IN ROMAN CATHOLIC MASS in the Roman Catholic Church, a crescent-shaped container in which the consecrated bread is placed during a Mass [Late 16C. < French, literally 'little moon' < *lune* (see LUNE)]

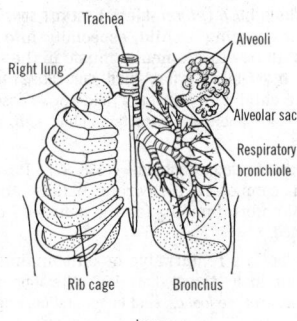

lung

lung /lung/ *n* **1.** in air-breathing vertebrate animals, either of the paired spongy respiratory organs, situated inside the rib cage, that transfer oxygen into the blood and remove carbon dioxide from it (*often used before a noun*) **2.** a respiratory organ found in invertebrate animals, especially the highly vascular region of the mantle cavity in some terrestrial snails [Old English, < Indo-European, 'light'] —**lungful** *n* ◇ **at the top of your lungs** extremely loudly (*informal*)

lungan *n* BOT, FOOD same as **longan**

lunge[1] /lunj/ *n* **1.** SUDDEN FORWARD MOVEMENT a sudden strong attacking movement forwards **2.** QUICK THRUST IN FENCING in fencing, a sudden thrust made at an opponent ■ *vi* (**lunges, lunging, lunged**) **1.** MOVE SUDDENLY FORWARDS THREATENINGLY to make a sudden attacking movement, thrusting forwards **2.** MAKE QUICK THRUST IN FENCING in fencing, to execute a sudden thrust at an opponent, especially with the sword or épée extended parallel to the floor [Mid-18C. Alteration of French *allonger* < Old French *alongier* 'lengthen' < Latin *longus* 'long']

lunge[2] /lunj/, **longe** /lunj, lonj/ *n* **1.** HORSE-TRAINING ROPE a long rope used to hold a horse while it is being trained **2.** HORSE-TRAINING AREA an enclosed circular area where young horses are trained ■ *vt* (**lunges, lunging, lunged; longes, longing, longed**) TRAIN HORSE to train a horse using a lunge [Early 18C. < French *longe* 'cord' < Old French *alongier* (see LUNGE[1])]

lungfish /lúng fish/ (*plural* **-fishes** *or same*) *n* a bony freshwater fish with one or two lungs for breathing air, as well as gills, that often becomes inactive during the dry season. Native to: swamps and pools in Australia, Africa, and South America. Order: Dipneusti.

lungi /loong gi/, **lungyi** *n* a long piece of cloth, often brightly coloured, traditionally worn like a skirt by men and women in Myanmar and as a loincloth by men in parts of South Asia [Early 17C. < Hindi *lungī*]

lungworm /lúng wurm/ *n* a parasitic nematode worm that inhabits the lungs of mammals and birds, sometimes causing coughs or respiratory distress

lungwort /lúng wurt/ *n* **1.** WOODLAND PLANT a perennial woodland plant. Flowers: tubular, purple or blue, often pink as buds. Native to: Europe, Asia. Genus: *Pulmonaria*. **2.** PLANT OF BORAGE FAMILY a plant of the borage family. Flowers: blue, in dangling clusters. Native to: northern temperate regions. Genus: *Mertensia*. **3.** LICHEN RESEMBLING LUNG TISSUE a lichen that has a superficial resemblance to lung tissue and is dark green when wet and pale greenish-brown when dry. It was used in the past to treat lung diseases. Latin name: *Lobaria pulmonaria*. [< the belief that such plants cured lung disorders]

lungyi *n* CLOTHING another spelling of **lungi**

lunisolar /looni sólər/ *adj* relating to both the Sun and the Moon, especially to the gravitational pull of both the Sun and the Moon

lunitidal interval /looni tíd'l-/ *n* the time between the Moon's passing a given point and the next high tide at that point

lunula /loonyoolə/ (*plural* **-lae** /-lee/), **lunule** /loo nyool/ *n* a semicircular mark, especially the white crescent-shaped area at the base of the fingernail (*technical*) [Late 16C. < Latin, 'small moon' < *luna* 'moon'] —**lunular** *adj* —**lunulate** *adj*

Luo /loo ō/ (*plural same or* **-os**) *n* **1.** a member of an African people who migrated from the Upper Nile

Valley, founding a dynasty among Bantu-speaking people in the lake region of eastern Africa **2.** a Nilotic language spoken in parts of Kenya and Tanzania. Native speakers: 6 million. [Early 20C. < Luo] —**Luo** *adj*

Luoyang /lṓ yáng/ city in Henan Province, northern China, situated on the River Luo. It alternated with Xi'an as the capital of ancient China, and after 1948 became a major industrial centre. Population: 1,370,000 (1995).

lupin /lóopin/ *n* an annual or perennial plant with seeds in pods. Flowers: various colours, in tall spikes. Native to: northern hemisphere. Genus: *Lupinus*. [14C. < Latin *lupinus* (see LUPINE [1])]

lupine[1] /lóo pīn/ *adj* **1.** relating to a wolf or wolves **2.** wildly hungry or greedy in behaviour or character [Mid-17C. < Latin *lupinus* < *lupus* 'wolf']

lupine[2] /lóopin/ *n* PLANTS US spelling of **lupin**

lupulin /lóopyoolin/ *n* a sticky yellow powder found in hop cones and containing the resins and essential oils that give beer its bitter taste. It was formerly used as a sedative. [Early 19C. < modern Latin *lupulus* < Latin, 'hop plant', literally 'little wolf' < *lupus* 'wolf']

lupus /lóopəss/ *n* MED **1.** same as **lupus erythematosus** **2.** same as **lupus vulgaris** [Late 16C. < Latin, 'wolf']

Lupus /lóopəss/ *n* a constellation of the southern hemisphere lying in the Milky Way, located between Scorpius and Centaurus. See illustration at **constellation**

lupus erythematosus /-érri theemə tṓssəss/ *n* either of two inflammatory diseases affecting connective tissue, one largely confined to the skin, the other affecting the joints and internal organs [*Erythematosus* < modern Latin < Greek *eruthēma* (see ERYTHEMA)]

lupus vulgaris /-vul gáiriss/ *n* tuberculosis of the skin in which reddish-brown patches develop on the face, leading to tissue destruction and scarring [< modern Latin, 'common lupus']

lurch[1] /lurch/ *vi* (**lurches, lurching, lurched**) **1.** MOVE VIOLENTLY to lean or pitch suddenly to one side **2.** MOVE UNSTEADILY to move along unsteadily, swaying from side to side ■ *n* SUDDEN SIDEWAYS MOVEMENT a sudden unbalanced movement to the side [Late 17C. Origin ?] —**lurchingly** *adv*

lurch[2] /lurch/ *n* in the card game cribbage, the state of being left with less than 30 points or half the winner's score at the end of a game [14C. Origin ?] ◇ **leave somebody in the lurch** to leave somebody in a difficult or embarrassing situation and offer no help

lurcher /lúrchər/ *n* a long-limbed crossbred dog that has predominant greyhound features, especially one used by poachers for catching rabbits [Early 16C. < obsolete *lurch* 'lurk', probably variant of LURK]

lure /lyoor, loor/ *vt* (**lures, luring, lured**) **1.** ENTICE SOMEBODY to persuade somebody to go somewhere or do something by offering something tempting **2.** RECALL FALCON to persuade a falcon to return by swinging a device in the air to attract its attention ■ *n* **1.** SOMETHING THAT ENTICES something that attracts or entices somebody to do something or go somewhere **2.** ATTRACTION the attractive or tempting quality that something has **3.** DEVICE ATTRACTING FISH a device attached to a fishing line to attract fish **4.** DEVICE FOR RECALLING FALCON a device swung through the air to attract or recall a falcon, usually a leather bag attached to the end of a line [13C. < Old French *luere* < Germanic] —**lurer** *n*

Lurex /lyóor eks, lóor-/ *tdmk* a trademark for a plastic-coated filament yarn or fabric made from this

lurgy /lúrgi/ *n* any illness or infection (*informal*) [Mid-20C. Origin ?]

Luria /lóori ə/, **Isaac ben Solomon** (1534–72) Palestinian mystic and scholar. He founded a school of Kabbalistic thought. Known as **The Lion**

lurid /lyóorid, lóor-/ *adj* **1.** HORRIFYING OR SHOCKING sensational and shocking, with graphic details of horror, devastation, or violence **2.** UNATTRACTIVELY BRIGHT of a sickeningly intense brightness or boldness of colour ○ *a lurid green* **3.** GLOWING UNNATURALLY glowing with an unnaturally vivid brightness **4.** PALLID with a pale sickly complexion [Mid-17C. < Latin *luridus* 'pale yellow, ghastly'] —**luridly** *adv* —**luridness** *n*

Lurie /lóori/, **Alison** (*b.* 1926) US novelist and scholar. Her best-known novel is *The War Between the Tates* (1974), which was made into a film (1977). She won the Pulitzer Prize for fiction for the novel *Foreign Affairs* (1985).

lurk /lurk/ *vi* (**lurks, lurking, lurked**) **1.** MOVE OR WAIT FURTIVELY to move about furtively, or wait in a concealed position or a shadowy corner, especially with the intention of doing something wrong ○ *a figure lurking in the bushes* **2.** EXIST UNSUSPECTED to exist as an unsuspected threat or danger **3.** ONLINE READ BUT NOT SEND ONLINE MESSAGES to read messages sent to an online discussion forum without contributing (*slang*) ■ *n ANZ* (*informal*) **1.** SCAM a sly or underhanded scheme **2.** AVOIDANCE OF WORK an underhand means of avoiding work [13C. Probably < Low German or N Germanic] —**lurker** *n* —**lurking** *adj*

Lusaka /loo saáka, -zaákə/ capital city of Zambia, situated in the south-central part of the country, about 145 km/90 mi. northeast of Kariba Dam, on the Zimbabwe border. Population: 1,640,000 (2000).

luscious /lúshəss/ *adj* **1.** SWEET AND JUICY with a rich, sweet, and juicy taste **2.** ROMANTIC AND EMOTIONAL written in a dramatic and romantic style with a strong appeal to the emotions and senses **3.** DESIRABLE very desirable physically, especially with a strong and direct sexual presence (*informal*) [14C. Alteration of obsolete *licious*, probably shortening of DELICIOUS] —**lusciously** *adv* —**lusciousness** *n*

lush[1] /lush/ *adj* **1.** GROWING VIGOROUSLY producing a lot of vigorous rich young growth **2.** WITH RICH TASTE tasting rich, sweet, and juicy **3.** LUXURIOUS with luxurious decoration and furnishings **4.** IN DRAMATIC STYLE written in a dramatic style that is intended to produce an emotional response **5.** SEXY voluptuously sensual in appearance or behaviour (*informal*) [15C. Probably alteration of obsolete *lash* 'loose, weak', via Old French, 'soft' < Latin *laxus* 'loose'] —**lushly** *adv*—**lushness** *n*

lush[2] /lush/ (*slang*) *n* **1.** *N Am* HEAVY DRINKER a drunkard **2.** *US* ALCOHOL alcoholic drink ■ *vi* (**lushes, lushing, lushed**) *N Am* DRINK HEAVILY to drink too much alcohol regularly [Late 18C. Origin ?]

Lushun /lóo shóon/, **Lü-shun** town and seaport in Liaoning Province, northeastern China, situated opposite the northern coast of Shandong. Former name **Port Arthur**

Lusitania /lóossi táyni ə/ ancient region and Roman province, corresponding approximately to present-day Portugal and the Spanish provinces of Salamanca and Cáceres —**Lusitanian** *adj, n*

lust /lust/ *n* **1.** SEXUAL DESIRE the strong physical desire to have sex with somebody, usually without associated feelings of love or affection **2.** EAGERNESS great eagerness or enthusiasm for something ○ *a lust for power* ■ *vi* (**lusts, lusting, lusted**) **1.** DESIRE SEXUALLY to feel a strong desire to have sex with somebody **2.** BE EAGER FOR SOMETHING to have a very strong desire to obtain something [Old English, 'pleasure, desire' < Indo-European, 'be eager'] —**lustful** *adj* —**lustfully** *adv* —**lustfulness** *n*

luster *n, vt* US spelling of **lustre**

lustra TIME, ANCIENT HIST plural of **lustrum** (*formal*)

lustral /lústrəl/ *adj* **1.** serving to purify the spirit, or relating to ceremonies of religious purification **2.** taking place once every five years [Mid-16C. < Latin *lustralis* < *lustrum* 'purification']

lustrate /lu stráyt, lús trayt/ (**-trates, -trating, -trated**) *vt* to make somebody or something spiritually pure by means of a special religious ceremony [Early 17C. < Latin *lustrat-*, past participle of *lustrare* (see LUSTRE)] —**lustration** /lu stráysh'n/ *n* —**lustrative** /lústrətiv/ *adj*

lustre /lústər/ *n* **1.** SOFT SHEEN a soft sheen of reflected light, especially from metal that has been polished gently **2.** SHININESS a bright and shiny condition or tone **3.** SPLENDOUR the glory and magnificence of a great achievement **4.** POLISH polish or wax used to give something a shiny finish **5.** CHANDELIER a chandelier or candelabrum made of cut glass, designed to reflect the light **6.** GLASS PENDANT ON CHANDELIER any decorative piece of cut glass hanging from a chandelier **7.** GLAZE ON POTTERY an opalescent metallic glaze on pottery, especially porcelain **8.** MINERALS LIGHT REFLECTED BY MINERAL the quality and amount of light reflected from the surface of a mineral. This is one of the ways in which a mineral is defined, the highest degree of lustre being splendent. **9.** TEXTILES GLOSSY FABRIC fabric with a sheen or glossy surface **10.** TIME same as **lustrum** (sense 1) (*formal*) ■ *vt* (**-tres, -tring, -tred**) **1.** IMPART GLOSSY FINISH TO SOMETHING to impart a glossy finish or coating to something **2.** GLORIFY SOMETHING to give something a glorious or magnificent quality [Early 16C. < French, < Latin *lustrare* 'brighten, purify by lustral rights' < *lustrum* 'purification']

lustrous /lústrəss/ *adj* with a soft shine or gloss —**lustrously** *adv*—**lustrousness** *n*

lustrum /lústrəm/ (*plural* **-trums** or **-tra** /-trə/) *n* (*formal*) **1.** a period of five years **2.** purification of the entire ancient Roman people, which took place every five years after the census [Late 16C. < Latin, 'purification']

lusty /lústi/ (**-ier, -iest**) *adj* **1.** STRONG AND HEALTHY in extremely good physical health, especially possessing great stamina and strength **2.** ENERGETIC full of energy, vitality, and enthusiasm **3.** LUSTFUL strongly desiring sex —**lustily** *adv* —**lustiness** *n*

lusus naturae /lóossəss nə tyóor ee/ (*plural same* or **lususes naturae**) *n* something that has developed in a typical way (*formal*) [< Latin, 'sport of nature']

lute

lute[1] /loot/ *n* a plucked musical instrument of the 14th to the 17th centuries resembling the guitar but with a flat, pear-shaped body [13C. Via Old French *lut* < Arabic *al-'ūd* 'wood']

lute[2] /loot/ *n* **1.** SEALANT USED IN BUILDING TRADE a substance, e.g. clay or cement, used in the building trade for sealing apertures, joints, or porous surfaces **2.** COOK FLOUR AND WATER PASTE a paste of flour and water used in cooking as a seal, e.g. to keep a casserole lid on tight **3.** DENT PASTE USED IN DENTISTRY a paste used in dentistry to attach a crown or cap onto a tooth ■ *vt* (**lutes, luting, luted**) SEAL SOMETHING WITH LUTE to seal, pack, or coat something using lute [14C. Directly or via French < medieval Latin *lutum* < Latin, 'mud, potter's clay']

luteal /lóoti əl/ *adj* relating to the stage of the menstrual cycle between the formation of a yellow mass of tissue (**corpus luteum**) after the release of an ovum and the start of the next period [Early 20C. < Latin *luteus* 'yellow']

lutein /lóoti in/ *n* **1.** a yellow carotenoid pigment found in many plants and egg yolks **2.** a powdered preparation of the tissue (**corpus luteum**) formed after the release of an ovum [Mid-19C. < Latin *luteus* 'yellow']

luteinizing hormone /lóoti inīzing-/, **luteinising hormone** *n* a hormone released by the pituitary gland that causes the ovary to produce one or more eggs, secrete progesterone, and form the corpus luteum, and causes the testes to secrete male sex hormones

luteinizing hormone-releasing hormone, **luteinizing hormone-releasing factor** *n* BIOCHEM same as **gonadotrophic-releasing hormone**

lutenist /lóotənist/ *n* somebody who plays a lute [Early 17C. < medieval Latin *lutanista* < *lutana* 'lute']

luteolin /lóoti ōlin/ *n* a yellow pigment found in some plants [Mid-19C. < French < modern Latin *luteola* < Latin *luteolus* 'yellowish' < *luteus* 'yellow']

lutetium /loo téeshəm, -shi əm/ *n* a silvery-white metallic element that belongs to the rare-earth group. Source: monazite. Use: catalyst in the nuclear industries. Symbol **Lu**. See table at **element**

[Early 20C. < Latin *Lutetia* 'Paris', native city of its discoverer, chemist Georges Urbains]

Luther /loóthər/, **Martin** (1483–1546) German theologian and religious reformer. His 95 theses against papal indulgences (1517) launched the Protestant Reformation.

'I shall never be a heretic, I may err in dispute; but I do not wish to decide anything finally; on the other hand, I am not bound by the opinions of men.'
[Martin Luther, *Letter*; 28 August 1518]

Lutheran /loótherən/ *n* a Christian who is a member of the Protestant church established by Martin Luther (**Lutheran Church**) ■ *adj* relating or belonging to Lutheranism

Lutheranism /loótherənizəm/ *n* the first form of Protestantism, founded by Martin Luther in 16th-century Germany. It focuses on the teachings of Jesus Christ and stresses individual faith over collective church authority. Spreading first through northern Europe, particularly Scandinavia, it now has adherents worldwide.

luthier /loóti ər/ *n* a maker and repairer of violins and other stringed instruments [Late 19C. < French < *luth* 'lute' < Old French *lut* (see LUTE¹)]

Luthuli /loo toóli/, **Albert** (1899–1967) South African political leader. As the president-general of the African National Congress (1952–67), he campaigned against apartheid in South Africa and won the Nobel Peace Prize (1960) for his steadfast opposition to violence. Full name **Luthuli, Albert John Mvumbi**

'The struggle must go on...to make the opportunity for the building to begin. The struggle will go on...God giving me strength and courage enough, I shall die, if need be, for this cause. But I do not want to die until I have seen the building begun.'
[Albert Luthuli, *Let My People Go*; 1963]

lutist /loótist/ *n US* MUSIC same as **lutenist**

Luton /loót'n/ town in Bedfordshire, central England. Population: 184,371 (2001).

Lutosławski /loóta slaávski/, **Witold** (1913–94) Polish composer and conductor. His use of the 12-tone system and of chance elements in his compositions produced works of considerable variety.

Lutyens /lúttyənz/, **Sir Edwin** (1869–1944) British architect. He designed houses, gardens, and furniture, but his most monumental work is the layout and design of new public buildings for the new national capital at New Delhi, India (1912–31). Full name **Lutyens, Sir Edwin Landseer**

lutz /loóts/ *n* a figure-skating jump from the back edge of one skate, landing on the back edge of the other, with one or more full rotations [Mid-20C. Probably after Gustave Lussi (1898–1993), Swiss figure skater and skating coach]

Lützen /loóts'n/ town in east-central Germany, the site of an important battle of the Thirty Years' War in 1632

luv /luv/ *n* (*informal*) **1.** another spelling of **love** (*used especially for the form of address*) **2.** used as a written representation of 'love', especially at the end of a message, in chat groups, or in e-mail or text messaging

luvvie /lúvvi/, **luvvy** (*plural* **-vies**) *n* an actor or somebody whose behaviour conforms to a stereotype of actors (*informal humorous or disapproving*) [Late 20C. Variant of *lovey*, stereotypically used by actors] —**luvviedom** *n* —**luvviness** *n*

Luwian /loó i ən/ *n* an extinct Anatolian language belonging to Indo-European [Early 20C. Alteration of German *Luwisch* < *Luwia* 'Luvia', region in Asia Minor] —**Luwian** *adj*

lux /luks/ (*plural same* or **luces** /loó seez/) *n* the SI unit of illumination, equal to one lumen per square metre. Symbol **lx** [Late 19C. < Latin, 'light']

Lux. *abbr* Luxembourg

luxate /luk sáyt, lúk sayt/ (**-ates, -ating, -ated**) *vt* to displace the bones of a joint (*technical*) [Early 17C.

< Latin *luxat-*, past participle of *luxare* < *luxus* 'dislocated'] —**luxation** /luk sáysh'n/ *n*

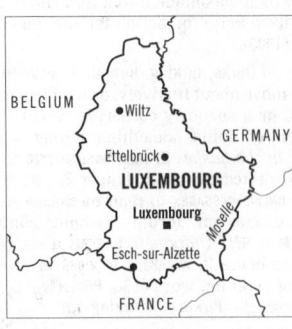
Luxembourg

Luxembourg /lúksəm burg/ **1.** country in Western Europe bordered by Belgium, Germany, and France. Language: French, German, Luxembourgish. Currency: Luxembourg franc. Capital: Luxembourg (City). Population: 454,157 (2003). Area: 2,586 sq. km/998 sq. mi. Official name **Grand Duchy of Luxembourg 2.** *also* **Luxembourg City** capital of Luxembourg, in the south-central part of the country. Population: 76,687 (2001). **3.** largest and southernmost province of Belgium. Capital: Arlon. Population: 246,820 (2000). Area: 4,440 sq. km/1,714 sq. mi. —**Luxembourger** *n*

Luxembourgish /lúksəm burg ish/ *n* the official language of Luxembourg, a form of German with many French features —**Luxembourgish** *adj*

Rosa Luxemburg

Luxemburg /lúksəm burg/, **Rosa** (1871–1919) Polish-born German political activist. She cofounded the Spartacus League (1916), which became the German Communist Party. She was murdered by German soldiers.

'Freedom is always and exclusively freedom for the one who thinks differently.'
[Rosa Luxemburg, *The Russian Revolution*; 1918]

~~luxery~~ incorrect spelling of **luxury**

Luxor /loók sawr, lúk-/ city in east-central Egypt, on the River Nile. Population: 146,000 (1992).

luxulyanite /luk soólyə nīt/ *n* a rare granite that contains needles of tourmaline in quartz and feldspar [Late 19C. After *Luxullian*, village in Cornwall]

luxuriant /lug zyoóri ənt, luk syoóri-, lug zhoóri-/ *adj* **1.** LUSH with a lot of young rich healthy growth ○ *luxuriant ground cover* **2.** GROWING PROFUSELY growing thickly and profusely ○ *a luxuriant mane of dark curly hair* **3.** ELABORATELY WRITTEN written in an elaborate, showy, and dramatic style **4.** PRODUCTIVE producing vast quantities of something [Mid-16C. < Latin *luxuriant-*, present participle of *luxuriare* (see LUXURIATE)] —**luxuriance** *n* —**luxuriantly** *adv*

USAGE **luxuriant** or **luxurious**? Both these adjectives are related to the noun **luxury**, but their meanings do not overlap. **Luxuriant** is used to describe something that grows in rich profusion, for example hair or vegetation. **Luxurious** means 'very comfortable', as in *a luxurious bedroom* or *a luxurious lifestyle*.

luxuriate /lug zyoóri ayt, luk syoóri-, lug zhoóri-/ (**-ates,**

-ating, -ated) *vi* **1.** to enjoy something in a self-indulgent way, taking great pleasure from the luxury and comfort that it offers **2.** to grow vigorously and successfully [Early 17C. < Latin *luxuriat-*, past participle of *luxuriare* < *luxuria* (see LUXURY)]

luxurious /lug zyoóri əss, luk syoóri-, lug zhoóri-/ *adj* **1.** very comfortable, with high-quality expensive fittings or fabrics **2.** with a liking for luxury, or used to living in luxury —**luxuriously** *adv* —**luxuriousness** *n*

USAGE See *luxuriant*.

luxury /lúkshəri/ *n* (*plural* **-ries**) **1.** GREAT COMFORT expensive high-quality surroundings, and the great comfort that they provide **2.** NONESSENTIAL ITEM an item that is desirable but not essential, and often expensive or hard to get (*often used before a noun*) **3.** PLEASURABLE SELF-INDULGENT ACTIVITY an activity that gives great pleasure, especially one only rarely indulged in ■ *adj* LUXURIOUS luxurious, or of the character of a luxury [14C. Via French < Latin *luxuria* 'profusion, excess' < *luxus* 'dislocated']

Luzon /loo zón/ largest island in the Philippines, in the northern part of the country. Population: 30,759,000 (1990). Area: 104,690 sq. km/40,421 sq. mi.

lv *abbr* ONLINE Latvia (*used in Internet addresses*) See table at **domain name**

Lviv /lə víf/, **L'viv, Lvov** /lə vóf/ industrial city in western Ukraine, capital of L'viv Oblast. Population: 794,000 (1998).

LW *abbr* **1.** MEDIA long wave **2.** low water

lwei /lə wáy/ (*plural* **lweis** or *same*) *n* a subunit of Angolan currency. See table at **currency** [Late 20C. < Bantu]

LWM, lwm *abbr* low water mark

lx *symbol* PHYS lux

ly *abbr* ONLINE Libya (*used in Internet addresses*) See table at **domain name**

-ly *suffix* **1.** like, having the characteristics of ○ *brotherly* ○ *kindly* **2.** in a particular manner ○ *briefly* **3.** recurring at a particular interval of time ○ *monthly* [< Old English *-līc* (adjective), *-līce* (adverb) < Indo-European, 'body']

USAGE See *adverb*.

lyase /lī ayz, -ayss/ *n* an enzyme that catalyses either the formation of a double bond, or the addition of a chemical group at a double bond [Mid-20C. < Greek *luein* 'loosen']

lycanthrope /líkənthrōp, lī kán-/ *n* same as **werewolf** (*literary*) [Early 17C. Via modern Latin < Greek *lukanthrōpos* < *lukos* 'wolf' + *anthrōpos* 'human being']

lycanthropy /lī kánthrəpi/ *n* in horror stories and legends, the transformation of a person into a wolf

lyceum /lī seé əm/ *n* **1.** a building where concerts, lectures, and other public events take place (*usually used in names of buildings*) **2.** *US* an organization that arranges or sponsors public events and entertainment [Late 16C. Via Latin < Greek *Lukeion* (*gymnasion*), school near Athens < *Lukeios*, epithet of Apollo]

lychee /lī chee, lí chee/, **litchi, lichee** *n* **1.** a small round fruit with a reddish skin, sweet whitish translucent pulp eaten fresh or dried, and a smooth hard seed **2.** a tree of the soapberry family that produces lychees. Native to: southern China. Latin name: *Litchi chinensis*. [Late 16C. < Chinese *lizhī*]

lych-gate /lích-/, **lich-gate** *n* a covered gateway into a churchyard. Traditionally, coffin-bearers would rest the coffin there before carrying it into the church. [15C. < Old English *līc* 'body, corpse' < Germanic]

Lycia /líssi ə/ ancient region on the coast of southwestern Asia Minor —**Lycian** *n, adj*

lycopene /líkə peen/ *n* a powerful antioxidant of the carotenoid group, found in tomatoes and used in many antioxidant dietary supplements [Mid-20C. < modern Latin *Lycopersicon* < Greek *lukos* 'wolf' + *persikos* 'peach']

lycopodium /līkə pódi əm/ *n* **1.** a plant that is a kind of club moss, with long branching stems covered in small leaves. It has small spore-carrying cones. Genus: *Lycopodium*. **2.** a flammable powder, composed of spores of lycopodium and other club

mosses. Use: formerly for coating for pills and suppositories, in fireworks, in foundry work. [Early 18C. < modern Latin < Greek *lukos* 'wolf' + *pod-* 'foot'; from its claw-shaped root]

Lycra /líkrə/ *tdmk* a trademark for a lightweight stretchy polyurethane fibre, or a fabric made from this

lyddite /líddīt/ *n* a powerful explosive consisting mainly of picric acid mixed with 10 per cent nitrobenzene and 3 per cent petroleum jelly. Use: in shells. [Late 19C. After *Lydd*, Kent, England, where first tested]

Lydgate /líd gayt/, **John** (1370?–1450?) English monk and poet. He wrote *The Troy Book* (1412–20), *The Siege of Thebes* (1420–22), and *The Fall of Princes* (1430–38).

> 'Woord is but wynd; leff woord and tak the dede.'
> [John Lydgate, 'Secretes of Old Philisoffres'; 1430?]

Lydia /líddi ə/ ancient country in present-day northwestern Turkey, on the Aegean Sea. It reached its peak of wealth in the 7th and 6th centuries BC before being conquered by Cyrus the Great of Persia about 546 BC. —**Lydian** *adj, n*

Lydian mode *n* a scale of notes originating in ancient Greek music and consisting of the eight notes of the diatonic scale rising from F to F

lye /lī/ *n* a strong solution of sodium hydroxide or potassium hydroxide in water. Use: industrial drain and oven cleaners. [Old English *lēag* < Indo-European, 'to wash']

Lye /lī/, **Len** (1901–80) New Zealand artist. He pioneered experimental films and kinetic sculpture.

Lyele /lyéllay/ *n* a language spoken in parts of Burkina Faso, belonging to the Gur branch of Niger-Congo. Native speakers: 60,000. —**Lyele** *adj*

Lyell /lī əl/, **Sir Charles** (1797–1875) British geologist. His theories and research influenced the development of modern geology.

> 'Amidst the vicissitudes of the earth's surface, species cannot be immortal, but must perish, one after another, like the individuals which compose them. There is no possibility of escaping from this conclusion.'
> [Sir Charles Lyell, *Principles of Geology*; 1830–33]

lygus bug /lígəss-/ *n* a plant-eating insect that is especially common in North America, where it is a pest of cotton and other crops. Genus: *Lygus*. [Via modern Latin < Greek *lugos* 'chaste tree, withy']

lying[1] present participle of **lie**[1]

lying[2] present participle of **lie**[2]

lying-in (*plural* **lyings-in**) *n* the period of time leading up to and immediately following childbirth, during which women used to be confined to bed (*archaic*; *often used before a noun*) [< LIE[1]]

lyke-wake /lík-/ *n* a vigil held over the body of somebody who has died, often accompanied by festivities (*archaic*) [14C. < Old English *līc* 'body, corpse' (< Germanic) + WAKE[1]]

Lyme disease /līm-/ *n* an infectious bacterial disease transmitted by ticks, in which skin rash, fever, and headache precede arthritis and nervous disorder [Late 20C. After *Lyme*, Connecticut, USA]

lyme grass /lím-/ *n* a perennial grass with broad bluish-green leaves that is found on sand dunes. Native to: northern temperate regions. Latin name: *Elymus arenarius*. [Origin ?]

Lyme Regis /līm reéjiss/ seaside resort in Dorset, southern England. Population: 3,851 (1991).

Lymington /límmingtən/ ancient town and seaport in Hampshire, southwestern England, on the edge of the New Forest. Population: 13,508 (1991).

lymph /limf/ *n* a fluid containing white cells, chiefly lymphocytes, that is drained from tissue spaces by the vessels of the lymphatic system. It can transport bacteria, viruses, and cancer cells. [Late 17C. Directly or via French < Latin *lympha* 'water']

lymph- *prefix* same as **lympho-** (*used before vowels*)

lymphadenopathy /lim fáddi nóppəthi, lím fadi-/ (*plural* **-thies**) *n* a disease, disorder, or enlargement of the lymph nodes

lymphatic /lim fáttik/ *adj* **1.** PHYSIOL **RELATING TO LYMPH SYSTEM** relating to lymph or the lymphatic system **2.** SLUGGISH without any energy or enthusiasm (*archaic*) ■ *n* ANAT **VESSEL TRANSPORTING LYMPH** a vessel that transports or contains lymph

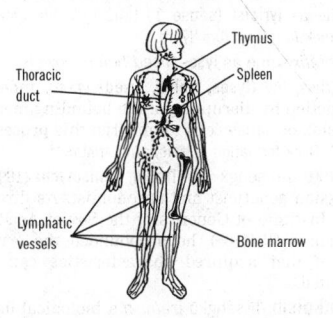

Thymus
Thoracic duct
Spleen
Lymphatic vessels
Bone marrow

lymphatic system

lymphatic system *n* a network of vessels that transport fluid, fats, proteins, and lymphocytes to the bloodstream as lymph, and remove microorganisms and other debris from tissues

lymph gland *n* ANAT same as **lymph node** (*not in technical use*)

lymph node *n* an oval body in the lymphatic system that produces and houses lymphocytes and filters microorganisms and other particles from lymph, thus reducing the risk of infection

lympho- *prefix* lymph, lymphocyte, lymphatic system ○ *lymphocytosis* [< LYMPH]

lymphoblast /límfō blast/ *n* an immature cell that develops into a lymphocyte

lymphoblastic /límfō blástik/ *adj* relating to the production of lymphocytes

lymphoblastic leukaemia *n* a disease in which there is great overproduction of immature lymphocytes

lymphocyte /límfō sīt/ *n* an important cell class in the immune system that produces antibodies to attack infected and cancerous cells, and is responsible for rejecting foreign tissue —**lymphocytic** /límfō síttik/ *adj*

lymphocytosis /límfō sī tóssiss/ *n* an increase in the number of lymphocytes in the bloodstream, occurring, e.g., in some persistent infections and forms of leukaemia

lymphogranuloma venereum /límfō gránnyōō lṓmə və neéri əm/ *n* a sexually transmitted disease caused by a bacterial infection, in which there is swelling of the genital lymph nodes and, especially in men, a genital ulcer [< modern Latin, 'venereal granuloma of the lymph nodes']

lymphoid /límf oyd/ *adj* relating to lymph, lymphatic tissue, or the lymphatic system

lymphokine /límfō kīn/ *n* a soluble substance released by lymphocytes that influences other immune cells [Mid-20C. < LYMPHO- + Greek *kinein* 'to move']

lymphoma /lim fṓmə/ (*plural* **-mas** or **-mata** /-mətə/) *n* a malignant tumour originating in a lymph node, e.g. hodgkin's disease or any of the range of cancers known as non-Hodgkin's lymphomas

lymphopoiesis /límfō poy eéssiss/ *n* the production of lymphocytes, which occurs mainly in the bone marrow, thymus, lymph nodes, spleen, and tonsils —**lymphopoietic** /-éttik/ *adj*

lymphotropic /límfō tróppik/, **lymphotrophic** /límfō trófik/ *adj* stimulating or acting on the lymphatic system

lynch /linch/ (**lynches, lynching, lynched**) *vt* to seize somebody believed to have committed a crime and put him or her to death immediately and without trial, usually by hanging [Early 19C. < LYNCH LAW] —**lyncher** *n* —**lynching** *n*

Lynch /linch/, **David** (*b.* 1946) US film director. His distinctively bizarre and surreal work includes the films *Eraserhead* (1977) and *Blue Velvet* (1986) and the cult television series *Twin Peaks* (1989–90).

Lynch, Jack (1917–99) Irish politician. Leader of the Fianna Fáil Party (1966–79), he was twice prime minister of Ireland (1966–73, 1977–79). He was also a noted Gaelic footballer. Born **Lynch, John**

> 'I have never and never will accept the right of a minority who happen to be a majority in a small part of the country to opt out of a nation.'
> [Jack Lynch. Referring to Loyalists in Northern Ireland. Quoted in *Irish Times*; 14 November 1970]

lynch law *n* the condemnation and punishment of somebody by a mob or self-appointed group without a legal trial [Early 19C. After Capt. William *Lynch* (1724–1820), Virginian planter and justice of the peace]

lynch mob *n* a group of people who capture and hang somebody without legal arrest and trial, because they think the person has committed a crime

lynchpin *n* ENG another spelling of **linchpin**

Lynn /lin/, **Dame Vera** (*b.* 1917) British singer. Her shows and radio broadcasts for UK service personnel during World War II enjoyed huge popularity. Known as **the Forces' Sweetheart**

lynx

lynx /lingks/ (*plural* **same** or **lynxes**) *n* a short-tailed cat with a lightly mottled yellowish- to reddish-brown coat and tufted ears. Native to: northern coniferous forests. Genus: *Lynx*. [14C. Via Latin < Greek *lugx*]

Lynx *n* a faint constellation of the northern hemisphere. See illustration at **constellation**

lynx-eyed *adj* with very good eyesight

lyo- *prefix* dissolution, dispersion ○ *lyophobic* [< Greek *luein* 'loosen, dissolve']

lyolysis /lī ólləssiss/ *n* the reaction of a salt with a solvent to form an acid and a base

Lyon another spelling of **Lyons**

Lyonnais /lee ən áy/ historic region of France, comprising the present-day Loire and Rhône departments

lyonnaise /leé ə náyz/ *adj* cooked with onions, or containing fried onions [Early 19C. < French (*à la*) *lyonnaise* 'in the manner of Lyons']

Lyons /lee óN/, **Lyon** city in east-central France, capital of the Rhône Department and the Rhône-Alpes Region. Population: 445,452 (1999).

Lyons /lī ənz/, **Dame Enid Muriel** (1897–1981) Australian politician. In 1943 she became one of the first two women to be elected to the Australian federal parliament. She was the wife of Joseph Aloysius Lyons. Born **Burnell, Enid Muriel**

Lyons, Sir Joseph (1848–1917) British business executive. He was a cofounder of a teashop that grew into a major UK catering firm.

Lyons, Joseph Aloysius (1879–1939) Australian politician. After founding the United Australian Party in 1931, he became prime minister (1932–39). See table at **prime minister**

lyophilic /lī ō fíllik/ *adj* describes a finely dispersed solid (**colloid**) that forms a stable dispersion

lyophilize /lī óffi līz/ (**-lizes, -lizing, -lized**), **lyophilise** (**-lises, -lising, -lised**) *vt* same as **freeze-dry** (*technical*) —**lyophilization** /lī óffi lī záysh'n/ *n* — **lyophilizer** *n*

lyophobic /lī ō fốbik/ *adj* describes a finely dispersed solid (**colloid**) that forms an unstable dispersion

Lyra /līrə/ *n* a small prominent constellation of the northern hemisphere between Cygnus and Hercules. It contains a very bright star (**Vega**) and a planetary nebula (**Ring Nebula**). See illustration at **constellation**

lyrate /līrət, -ayt/ *adj* **1.** in the shape of a lyre **2.** describes a leaf that has a broad rounded apex and small lateral lobes at the base [Mid-18C. < Latin *lyra* (see LYRE)]

lyre

lyre /līr/ *n* a plucked string instrument associated with ancient Greece and consisting of a U-shaped frame with a crossbar from which the strings stretch down to the soundbox [12C. Via French < Latin *lyra* < Greek *lura*]

lyrebird /līr burd/ *n* a ground-dwelling bird, the male of which has long tail feathers that form into the shape of a lyre during courtship. Native to: mountain forests of southeastern Australia. Family: Menuridae.

lyric /lírrik/ *adj* **1.** EXPRESSING PERSONAL FEELINGS relating to poetry that often has a musical quality and expresses personal emotions or thoughts ○ *a lyric poet* **2.** WITH LIGHTNESS OF VOICE singing with a voice that has a light quality and a vocally undramatic delivery ○ *a lyric tenor* **3.** WITH LIGHTNESS OF MUSICAL QUALITY having or played with a light smooth nondramatic quality that suggests singing **4.** RELATING TO LYRE relating to or written for the lyre, or for accompaniment by the lyre ■ *n* **1.** SONG WORDS the words of a song, especially a popular song (*often used in the plural*) **2.** SHORT PERSONAL POEM a short poem expressing personal feelings or thoughts [Late 16C. Via French < Greek *lurikos* 'singing to the lyre' < *lura* 'lyre']

lyrical /lírrik'l/ *adj* **1.** wildly enthusiastic and emotional about something ○ *critics waxing lyrical about the new exhibition* **2.** LITERAT, MUSIC same as **lyric** *adj* (senses 1–3) —**lyrically** *adv* —**lyricalness** *n*

lyricism /lírrissizəm/ *n* **1.** a lyric style in poetry or music **2.** emotional and enthusiastic expression of feelings or opinions

lyricist /lírrissist/ *n* **1.** a writer of words for songs, especially popular songs **2.** a writer of lyric poems

lyrist /līrist/ *n* **1.** somebody who plays a lyre **2.** MUSIC same as **lyricist** (sense 1) [Mid-17C. Via Latin *lyrista* < Greek *luristēs* < *lura* 'lyre']

lys- *prefix* same as **lyso-** (*used before vowels*)

lyse /līss, līz/ (**lyses, lysing, lysed**) *vti* to undergo destruction by disruption of the bounding membrane (**lysis**), or cause cells to undergo this process [Early 20C. Back-formation < LYSIS, after ANALYSE]

Lysenko /li séngk ố/, **Trofim Denisovich** (1898–1976) Russian geneticist and agronomist. As director of the Institute of Genetics of the Soviet Academy of Sciences (1940–65), he propounded the erroneous belief that acquired characteristics can be inherited.

Lysenkoism /lī séngkō izəm/ *n* a biological doctrine, presented by Trofim Denisovich Lysenko in the 1930s, maintaining that environmental characteristics acquired by an organism during its lifetime can be inherited by its offspring

lysergic acid /lī súrjik-, li-/ *n* a crystalline acid, soluble in most organic solvents. Source: ergot fungus. Formula: $C_{16}H_{16}N_2O_2$. [< LYSO- + ERGOT]

lysergic acid diethylamide /-dī ə thílə mīd/ *n* DRUGS full form of **LSD**

lysin /līssin/ *n* an agent, e.g. an enzyme or antibody, that is able to destroy cells by disruption of the bounding membrane (**lysis**) [Early 20C. < LYSIS]

lysine /lī seen/ *n* an essential amino acid that is a constituent of most proteins. Formula: $C_6H_{14}N_2O_2$. [Late 19C. < German *Lysin* < Greek *lusis* 'loosening' (see LYSIS)]

lysis /līssiss/ *n* **1.** the destruction of cells by disruption of the bounding membrane, allowing the cell contents to escape **2.** a gradual reduction in severity of a patient's signs and symptoms during the course of a disease [Mid-16C. Via Latin, 'loosening' < Greek *lusis* < *luein* 'loosen']

-lysis *suffix* **1.** dissolution, decomposition, disintegration ○ *thermolysis* **2.** hydrolysis ○ *proteolysis* [Via Latin < Greek *lusis* (see LYSIS)]

Lysithea /lī síthi ə/ *n* a very small natural satellite of Jupiter. It is approximately 35 km/22 mi. in diameter and occupies an intermediate orbit.

lyso- *prefix* lysis ○ *lysosome* [< LYSIS]

lysogen /līssəjən/ *n* **1.** a bacterium that is capable of releasing a bacterium-destroying virus (**bacteriophage**) **2.** an agent, particularly an antigen,

$$CH_2 - CH_2 - CH_2 - CH_2 - CH - C - OH$$
with NH₂ groups shown below the first and fifth carbons and a double-bonded O above the carboxyl carbon:
$$\underset{NH_2}{|} \qquad \underset{NH_2}{|} \quad \overset{O}{\overset{||}{C}}$$

lysine

that provokes the production of cell-destroying agents (**lysins**) by cells of the immune system

lysogenic /līssə jénnik/ *adj* describes a bacterium that is capable of producing and releasing a bacterium-destroying virus (**bacteriophage**) in response to specific stimuli

lysogenize /lī sójjə nīz/ (**-nizes, -nizing, -nized**), **lysogenise** (**-nises, -nising, -nised**) *vt* to convert a bacterium to a lysogenic state by infection with a bacterium-destroying virus (**bacteriophage**)

lysogeny /lī sójjəni/ *n* the ability of a bacterial cell to produce and release a bacterium-destroying virus (**bacteriophage**) in response to specific stimuli

lysosome /līssössōm/ *n* a membrane-bound cavity in living cells that contains enzymes that are responsible for degrading and recycling molecules — **lysosomal** /līssō sōm'l/ *adj*

lysozyme /līssō zīm/ *n* an enzyme in body secretions that can help destroy bacteria [Early 20C. < LYSO- + ENZYME]

-lyte *suffix* a substance that can be decomposed by a particular process ○ *electrolyte* [< Greek *lutos* 'soluble' < past participle of *luein* 'loosen'] —**-lytic** *suffix*

Lytham St Anne's /líthəm sənt ánz/ seaside resort in western Lancashire, on the northwestern coast of England. Population: 40,866 (1991).

lytic /líttik/ *adj* relating to, resulting from, or causing the destruction of cells by disruption (**lysis**) of the bounding membrane [Late 19C. < Greek *lutikos* 'able to loosen' < *luein* (see LYSIS)]

Lyttleton /lítt'ltən/, **Humphrey** (*b.* 1921) British jazz trumpeter, bandleader, broadcaster, and author. He formed his own band in 1948, which initially played traditional jazz but then moved to include modern jazz.

-lyze *suffix* to cause or undergo lysis ○ *plasmolyze* [Back-formation < -LYSIS]

m¹ /em/ (*plural* **m's**), **M** (*plural* **M's** or **Ms**) *n* **1.** 13TH LETTER OF ENGLISH ALPHABET the 13th letter of the English alphabet, representing a consonant sound **2.** LETTER 'M' WRITTEN a written representation of the letter 'm' **3.** 1,000 the Roman numeral for 1,000

m² *symbol* **1.** PRINTING em dash **2.** PHYS magnetic moment **3.** PHYS mass **4.** MEASURE metre¹ **5.** MATHS milli- **6.** MEASURE million

m³ *abbr* **1.** CRICKET maiden (over) **2.** male **3.** married **4.** GRAM masculine **5.** medium **6.** mile **7.** TIME minute *or* minutes **8.** CALENDAR month

M¹ /em/ (*plural* **M's** or **Ms**) *n* something shaped like a letter 'M'

M² *abbr* **1.** Majesty **2.** male **3.** CALENDAR March **4.** CHEM mass **5.** EDUC Master (*used in degree titles*) **6.** CALENDAR May **7.** medieval **8.** CLOTHING medium (*used of clothes size*) **9.** mega- **10.** Member **11.** LANGUAGE middle **12.** LOGIC middle term **13.** MONEY mill **14.** million **15.** CHEM molar **16.** CALENDAR Monday **17.** Monsieur **18.** ROADS motorway **19.** GEOG mountain

M³ *symbol* **1.** PRINTING em dash **2.** PHYS mutual inductance

M. *abbr* Monsieur

M'- *prefix* same as **Mac-**

M0 /ém zeerō/ *n* an assessment of the amount of money in public circulation, the money represented by banks' balances, and the money held in banks' tills (**narrow money**)

M1 *n* an assessment of the amount of money in coins, notes, and current and deposit accounts

M-1 rifle *n* a .30 calibre semiautomatic rifle invented by John C. Garand and adopted by the US Army in 1936.

M2 *n* an assessment of the amount of money in coins, currency, current and deposit accounts, savings accounts, and deposits

M3 *n* an assessment of the amount of money in M1, M2, and also large denomination repurchase agreements, institutional money market accounts, and some Eurodollar time deposits

M8 *abbr* ONLINE mate (*used in e-mails or text messages*)

ma /maa/ (*plural* **mas**) *n* **1.** same as **mother**¹ (*n* sense 1) (*informal*) **2.** a way of addressing or referring to a woman past middle age (*often offensive*) [Early 19C. Shortening of MAMA]

mA *symbol* MEASURE milliampere

MA *abbr* **1.** EDUC Master of Arts **2.** PSYCHOL mental age **3.** Military Academy

maaga *adj Carib* same as **mawger** (*also used in Black English*)

ma'am /mam, maam, məm/ *n* **1.** used when addressing royal women or other women of high status (*formal*) **2.** used when addressing a woman in a polite and respectful way (*dated informal*) [Mid-17C. Contraction of MADAM]

ma-and-pa *adj N Am* same as **mom-and-pop**

maar /maar/ (*plural* **maars** or **maare** /maári/) *n* a broad flat volcanic crater formed by a single explosive eruption and often filled with water [Early 19C. Via German dialect, 'crater lake' < Latin *mare* 'sea']

Ma'ariv /maáriv/, **Maariv** *n* in Judaism, the evening service of prayer [Late 20C. < Hebrew *ma'ărībh* 'evening prayer']

maas /maass/ *n S Africa* thick, naturally curdled milk [Early 19C. Via Afrikaans < Zulu *amasi* (plural)]

Maasai *n, adj* LANG, PEOPLES another spelling of **Masai**

maasbanker /maáss bangkər/ (*plural same* or **-ers**) *n S Africa* same as **horse mackerel** [Mid-19C. < Afrikaans < Dutch *marsbanker*]

Maastricht /maástrikt, -strikht/, **Maestricht** city in the southeastern Netherlands, the capital of Limburg Province. Population: 122,087 (2000).

Maastricht Treaty *n* a treaty signed in Maastricht in late 1991 by heads of the 12 member states of the European Community that set out a framework for increased political and economic integration. It was ratified in 1993.

Maat /maat/ *n* in Egyptian mythology, the goddess of the underworld who tested the value of a person's soul after death by weighing the heart on an ostrich feather

maatjes herring *n* FISH another spelling of **matjes herring**

Mab /mab/ *n* in Celtic mythology, the god of light, who mediated between humankind and the divine

mabela /mə beélə/ *n S Africa* **1.** a type of sorghum grown in southern Africa **2.** porridge made from ground sorghum [Mid-19C. < Bantu]

mabe pearl /máyb-, máybi-/ *n* a cultured pearl with a flat base and a rounded top [Origin ?]

Mabinogion /mábbi nóggi on/ *n* a collection of ancient Welsh stories of magic and mythology, including stories about King Arthur [< Welsh, plural of *mabinogi* 'youthful career' < *mab* 'youth' < Old Welsh *map* < Celtic, 'son']

Mabo /maábō/ *n* a landmark Australian legal ruling in 1992 confirming the land rights of Aboriginals [Late 20C. After Eddie MABO]

Mabo /maábō/, **Eddie** (1936–92) Australian land rights campaigner. He was the leader of a group of Torres Strait Islanders whose land rights claim led to a landmark Australian High Court ruling in 1992 that European settlement did not extinguish Aboriginal title. Born **Sambo, Edward Koiki**

mac /mak/, **mack** *n* same as **mackintosh** (sense 1) (*informal*) [Early 20C. Shortening]

Mac /mak/ *n Scotland, N Am* used as an informal way of addressing a man whose name is not known (*informal*) [Mid-20C. < MAC-]

REGIONAL NOTE See *man*.

MAC /mak/ *n* a system for transmitting pictures to colour televisions using satellites. Full form **multiplexed analogue component**

Mac. *abbr* BIBLE Maccabees

Mac-, Mc-, M'- *prefix* surname meaning 'son of' ○ *MacArthur* ○ *Macmillan* ○ *McCoy* [Via Scottish Gaelic and Irish < Old Irish *macc* 'son']

macabre /mə kaábrə, -bə/ *adj* including gruesome and horrific details of death and decay [15C. < French *(danse) macabre* 'dance of death', probably alteration of *danse Macabé* 'dance of the Maccabees'] —**macabrely** *adv*

macaco /mə kaákō/ (*plural* **-cos**) *n* a lemur, especially one belonging to a species in which the male is black and the female brown. Native to: Madagascar. Latin name: *Eulemur macaco macaco* or *Eulemur macaco flavifrons*. [Mid-18C. < French *mococo*]

macadam /mə káddəm/ *n* a smooth hard road surface made from small pieces of stone, usually mixed with tar or asphalt, in compressed layers [Early 19C. After John Loudon *McAdam* (1756–1836), Scottish civil engineer]

macadamia /mákə dáymi ə/ *n* **1.** same as **macadamia nut 2.** an evergreen tree cultivated for its macadamia nuts. Native to: Australia, Southeast Asia. Genus: *Macadamia*. [Early 20C. < modern Latin, after John *Macadam* (1827–65), Scottish-born Australian chemist]

macadamia nut *n* an edible, round, hard-shelled, waxy nut with a mild creamy flavour, produced by the macadamia tree

macadamize /mə káddə mīz/ (**-izes, -izing, -ized**), **macadamise** (**-ises, -ising, -ised**) *vt* to build or surface a road with macadam —**macadamization** /mə káddə mī záysh'n/ *n*

Macao another spelling of **Macau**

macaque

macaque /mə kaák, -kák/ (*plural* **-caques** or *same*) *n* a short-tailed sturdily built monkey. Native to: Asia, North Africa. Genus: *Macaca*. [Late 17C. Via French < Bantu *makaku* 'some monkeys']

macarena /mákə ráynə/ *n* a simple solo dance of Spanish origin mainly involving placing the hands on different parts of the body in sequence and swinging the hips [Late 20C. < *Macarena*, song to which it was performed]

macaroni /mákə rŏni/ *n* **1.** hollow tubular pasta, usually produced in short lengths **2.** (*plural* **macaronis** or **macaronies**) in 18th-century Britain, an affected, foppish young man who adopted the fashions, manners, and customs of the other countries he had visited [Late 16C. < Italian dialect *maccarone* 'macaroni, dumpling']

macaronic /mákə rónnik/ *adj* **1.** MIXING LANGUAGES IN VERSE describes verse containing words and phrases from everyday language mixed with Latin, other foreign words and phrases, or vernacular terms with Latinate endings, usually for comic effect **2.** RELATING TO MIXTURE OF LANGUAGES relating to or involving a combination of two or more languages ■ *n* MACARONIC VERSE a macaronic poem, or macaronic poetry in general [Early 17C. Via modern Latin < obsolete Italian *macaronico* < dialect *maccarone* 'macaroni, dumpling'] —**macaronically** *adv*

macaroni cheese *n* boiled macaroni in a cheese sauce, baked or grilled until golden

macaroon /mákə roón/ *n* a biscuit made from sugar and egg whites, with ground almonds or pieces of dried coconut folded in [Late 16C. Via French *macaron* < Italian dialect *maccarone* 'macaroni, dumpling']

Macarthur /mə kaárthər/, **John** (1767–1834) British-born Australian pioneer and wool merchant. He was a ringleader in the Rum Rebellion (1808–10), and as a pioneer of sheep-breeding established New South Wales, Australia, as a wool-exporting region.

---

zh vision. In foreign words: kh German Bach; aN French vin; aaN French blanc; ö German schön, French feu; oN French bon; öN French un; ü as in French rue. Stress marks: ´ as in **secret** /seékrət/, **academic** /ákə démmik/

MacArthur /mək aárthər/, **Douglas** (1880–1964) US general. He was the commander of Allied armed forces in the South Pacific during World War II. He lost the Philippines to the Japanese (1942), recaptured the islands (1944–45), and ultimately accepted the Japanese surrender in 1945. During the early stages of the Korean War, he was the UN commander in Korea (1950–51).

'There is no security on this earth; there is only opportunity.'
[Douglas MacArthur. Quoted in *MacArthur: His Rendezvous with History*, Courtney Weaver; 1955]

'It is fatal to enter any war without the will to win it.'
[Douglas MacArthur, *Speech to the Republican National Convention*; 7 July 1952]

Macassar /mə kássər/, **Macassar oil** *n* an oily substance formerly used to make the hair smooth and shiny [Early 19C. After MAKASSAR]

Macau /mə ków/, **Macao** Special Administrative Region in southeastern China, on the South China Sea, west of Hong Kong. Population: 453,733 (2001). Area: 21 sq. km/8 sq. mi.

macaw /mə káw/ (*plural* **-caws** or *same*) *n* a large parrot with a huge beak, a long tail and brilliant plumage. Native to: Central and South America. Genera: *Anodorhynchus* or *Ará*. [Early 17C. < Portuguese *macaó*]

Macbeth /mək béth/ (*c.* 1005–57) king of Scotland. After murdering Duncan I in 1040, he held the throne until he was killed by Duncan's son, Malcolm III.

Macc. *abbr* BIBLE Maccabees

Maccabees /mákə beez/ *npl* **1.** the followers of Judas Maccabeus, who led the revolt of the Jews against Syria in 168 BC **2.** four books of Jewish history, the first two of which are included in the Roman Catholic Bible and Protestant Apocrypha. See table at **Bible** [14C. Via Latin *Maccabaeus* < Greek *Makkabaios*, epithet of Judas] —**Maccabean** /mákə bee ən/ *adj*

maccaboy /mákə boy/ *n* rose-scented snuff from Martinique [Mid-18C. After *Macouba*, district in Martinique]

macchiato /máki aátō/ *n* a drink of espresso coffee with a small amount of steamed milk on top [Late 20C. < Italian, 'stained']

Macclesfield /mák'lz feeld/ manufacturing town in Cheshire, northwestern England. Population: 150,155 (2001).

MacDiarmid /mək dúrmid/, **Hugh** (1892–1978) Scottish poet, editor, and critic. A pioneer in the Scottish literary renaissance and active in reviving literary Scots, he was a founder of the Scottish National Party. Pseudonym of **Grieve, Christopher Murray**

'Post-Union Scottish history reminds me of a poor man with a pot-bellied grey mare, foaled by a famous dam and with a still more famous sire.'
[Hugh MacDiarmid, *Lucky Poet*; 1994]

Macdonald /mək dónn'ld/, **Flora** (1722–90) Scottish Jacobite. She helped Charles Edward Stuart, pretender to the British throne, escape to Skye after the uprising of 1745.

Ramsay MacDonald

MacDonald /mək dónn'ld/, **Ramsay** (1866–1937) British prime minister (1924, 1929–35). He was a founder member of the Labour Party and the United King-

dom's first Labour prime minister. Full name **MacDonald, James Ramsay**. See table at **prime minister**

'We hear war called murder. It is not: it is suicide.'
[Ramsay MacDonald, *Observer*; 4 May 1930]

MacDonnell Ranges /mək dónn'l-/ group of mountain ranges in the Northern Territory, central Australia. The highest peak is Mount Zeil, 1,510 m/4,953 ft.

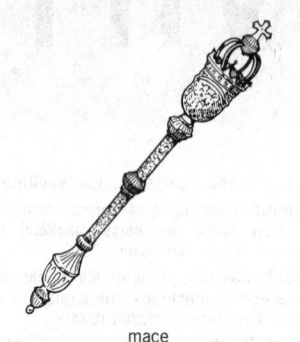
mace

mace[1] /mayss/ *n* **1.** CEREMONIAL STAFF OF OFFICE a stick or rod, usually with an ornamental head, carried by officials on ceremonial occasions as a symbol of authority **2.** same as **macebearer 3.** SPIKED METAL CLUB a medieval weapon in the form of a heavy club with a round spiked metal head **4.** CUE GAMES EARLY BILLIARD CUE an early form of the modern billiard cue [13C. < Old French < Latin *mateola* 'mallet']

mace[2] /mayss/ *n* a spice made from the covering of the nutmeg seed, used in the form of dried pieces or as a yellow-orange powder [13C. Via Anglo-Norman *macis* < Latin *macir*, an Asian spice]

macebearer /máyss bairər/ *n* an official who carries a mace on ceremonial occasions

macédoine /mássə dwaán/, **macedoine** *n* **1.** MIXED CHOPPED VEGETABLES a mixture of diced vegetables served hot or cold as a garnish, appetizer, or side dish **2.** MIXED CHOPPED FRUITS a salad of small diced pieces of fruit, often in syrup or jelly **3.** MEDLEY a mixed-up jumble or medley (*literary*) [Early 19C. < French *Macédoine* 'Macedonia'; because ALEXANDER THE GREAT ruled over many different peoples]

FYRO Macedonia

Macedonia /mássə dóni ə/ **1.** country in southeastern Europe. Formerly a constituent republic of Yugoslavia, it became independent in 1991. Language: Macedonian. Currency: dinar. Capital: Skopje. Population: 2,063,122 (2003). Area: 25,713 sq. km/9,928 sq. mi. Official name **Republic of Macedonia**. Former name **Former Yugoslav Republic of Macedonia 2.** mountainous region of northeastern Greece. Capital: Thessaloniki. Area: 34,177 sq. km/13,200 sq. mi. Population: 1,710,513 (1991). **3.** district in southwestern Bulgaria. Area: 6,465 sq. km/2,496 sq. mi. **4.** *also* **Macedon** /mássə don/ ancient kingdom in northern Greece, centralized under Philip II, who, with his son, Alexander the Great, created a vast empire in the 4th century BC —**Macedonian** *n, adj*

macerate /mássə rayt/ *vti* (**-ates, -ating, -ated**) **1.** SOFTEN BY SOAKING to soften something by soaking it in liquid, or become soft by soaking in liquid **2.** SEPARATE BY SOAKING to make something break up into pieces or into its various parts by soaking it in liquid, or break up in this way **3.** REDUCE OR WASTE AWAY to make somebody or something thin or lean, or become

thin or lean, especially by starvation or fasting ◼ *n* SOMETHING PRODUCED BY SOAKING something prepared by soaking in a liquid [Mid-16C. < Latin *macerat-*, past participle of *macere* 'soften'] —**macerater** *n* —**maceration** /mássə ráysh'n/ *n* —**macerative** /mássərətiv/ *adj*

Macgillicuddy's Reeks /mə gílli kudiz reéks/ mountain range in the southwestern Republic of Ireland. Highest peak: Carrantuohill 1,041 m/3,415 ft.

MacGuffin /mə gúffin/ *n* in a film, play, or book, something that starts or drives the action of the plot but later turns out to be unimportant [Mid-20C. Said to come from a story in which a man pretends to have a 'macguffin', a Scottish mountain lion, but admits it does not exist]

Mach /maak, mak/ *n* PHYS same as **Mach number**

Mach /makh/, **Ernst** (1838–1916) Austrian physicist and philosopher. He was noted for his pioneering work in ballistics. The Mach number is named after him.

'Physics is experience, arranged in economical order.'
[Ernst Mach, *The Economical Nature of Physical Inquiry*; 1882]

Machado de Assis /mə sháddoo də ə seéss/, **Joachim Maria** (1839–1908) Brazilian novelist, poet, and critic. Author of *Dom Casmurro* (1900), he founded the Brazilian Academy of Letters (1896).

machair /mákər, mákhər/ *n Scotland* a strip of grassland on a sandy shore, chiefly used for grazing livestock [Late 17C. < Scottish Gaelic]

machan /mə chaán/ *n* in South Asia, a raised platform, often in a tree, used to watch for tigers and other game [Late 19C. < Hindi]

mache /maash/, **mâche** *n* PLANTS same as **lamb's lettuce** [Late 17C. < French]

Machel /mə shél/, **Samora Moïses** (1933–86) president of Mozambique (1975–86). He fought for the independence of Mozambique from Portuguese rule and became the country's first president.

machete

machete /mə shétti, -chétti/ *n* a large heavy knife with a broad blade used as a weapon or as a tool for cutting through vegetation, especially in Central and South America and the Caribbean [Late 16C. < Spanish, 'little sledgehammer' < *macho* 'sledgehammer' < Latin *mateola* 'mallet']

Machiavelli /máki ə vélli, mákyə-/, **Niccolò** (1469–1527) Italian historian, politician, and philosopher. He wrote several works on statecraft, of which *The Prince* (1532) had a profound and lasting influence.

'Cunning and deceit will every time serve a man better than force.'
[Niccolò Machiavelli, *The Prince*; 1532]

Machiavellian /máki ə vélli ən/ *adj* **1.** using clever trickery, amoral methods, and expediency to achieve a desired goal, especially in politics **2.** relating to or characteristic of Niccolò Machiavelli or his political philosophy —**Machiavellian** *n* —**Machiavellianism** *n* —**Machiavellist** *n, adj*

Machiavellian intelligence *n* in psychology, social intelligence, especially the intelligence that involves deception and the formation of coalitions

machicolate /mə chíkō layt/ (**-lates, -lating, -lated**) *vt* to provide a castle wall with projecting galleries along its top [Late 18C. < Anglo-Latin *machicolare* < Provençal *machacol* 'neck-crusher']

machicolation

machicolation /mə chíkō láysh'n/ n **1.** GALLERY ON TOP OF CASTLE WALL a projecting gallery on top of a castle wall, supported by a row of arches and containing openings through which rocks and boiling oil could be dropped on attackers **2.** OPENING IN MACHICOLATION an opening in the floor of a machicolation **3.** ROW OF PROJECTING ARCHES an ornamental row of supported arches that project from a building

machinate /máki nayt, máshi-/ (-nates, -nating, -nated) vti to devise secret, cunning, or complicated plans and schemes to achieve a goal or to cause harm to others [Late 16C. < Latin *machinat*-, past participle of *machinari* < *machina* (see MACHINE)] —**machinator** n

machination /máki náysh'n, máshi-/ n **1.** the devising of secret, cunning, or complicated plans and schemes **2.** a secret, cunning, or complicated plan or scheme (usually plural)

machine /mə sheen/ n **1.** MECHANICAL DEVICE a device with moving parts, often powered by electricity, used to perform a task, especially one that would otherwise be done by hand ○ a washing machine **2.** SIMPLE UNPOWERED DEVICE a simple device used to overcome resistance at one point by applying force at another point, e.g. a lever, pulley, or an inclined plane **3.** POWERED FORM OF TRANSPORT an engine-driven means of transport, e.g. an aircraft, car, or motorcycle **4.** GROUP OF PEOPLE IN CONTROL an organized group of people that controls or directs something, especially a political group ○ the party machine **5.** COMPLEX SYSTEM a complex system structured so as to accomplish a particular goal ○ the war machine **6.** SOMEBODY WHO BEHAVES MECHANICALLY somebody who is regarded as behaving like a mechanical device, e.g. somebody who is efficient but uncreative ○ men trained as deadly machines **7.** THEATRE DEVICE TO PRODUCE STAGE EFFECTS a mechanical device used in the theatre, especially in classical drama, to create special effects such as the entrance of a supernatural being **8.** LITERAT LITERARY DEVICE a character or factor introduced into a work of literature to produce an effect or to resolve the plot ■ v (-chines, -chining, -chined) **1.** vti WORK WITH POWER-DRIVEN TOOL to cut, shape, or finish a piece of work using a power-driven tool such as a lathe or drilling device, or be cut, shaped, or finished in this way **2.** vt USE MACHINE ON SOMETHING to make or do something using a machine [Mid-16C. Via French < Latin *machina* 'device' < Greek *mēkhanē* < *mēkhos* 'means'] —**machinability** /mə sheenə bílləti/ n —**machinable** adj —**machineless** adj

machine bolt n a bolt with a square or hexagonal head, usually of heavy duty construction for use in aircraft and automobiles

machine code n COMPUT same as **machine language**

machine finish n PAPER same as **mill finish**

machine gun n an automatic weapon that fires rapidly and repeatedly without requiring separate squeezes on the trigger each time

machine-gun vt **1.** SHOOT SOMEBODY WITH MACHINE GUN to shoot or kill somebody with a machine gun, or fire a machine gun at somebody or something **2.** ADDRESS SOMEBODY RAPIDLY to speak rapidly to somebody (informal) ■ adj STACCATO rapid, abrupt, and staccato in delivery —**machine-gunner** n

machine language n instructions, usually written in binary code, telling a computer how to process data

machine pistol n a light automatic or semiautomatic submachine gun that can be discharged using only one hand

machine-readable adj in a form that is able to be used directly by a computer

machinery /mə sheenəri/ n **1.** MACHINES machines collectively or in general **2.** MECHANICAL PARTS the aggregate parts that make up a machine or group of machines **3.** SYSTEM OF MACHINES a system of machines working together ○ our office machinery **4.** SET OF PROCEDURES an interconnected series of parts or processes that works like a mechanical system to produce a result ○ the machinery of government **5.** LITERAT LITERARY DEVICES literary devices used for effect, especially in poetry, or to resolve the plot of a play or book

machine screw n a slotted or hexagonal-headed screw with a standardized thread. Use: to connect machine parts together.

machine shop n a workshop where various materials, especially metals, are cut, shaped and worked, often to tight specifications using machine tools

machine tool n a machine used for shaping and finishing metals and other solid materials, e.g. a lathe or grinder —**machine-tooled** adj

machine translation n the translation of text from one language to another by computer

machine-wash vt to wash something in a washing machine

machine-washable adj able to be washed in a washing machine without being damaged

machinist /mə sheenist/ n **1.** somebody whose job involves machining something or operating a machine or machine tool, especially in a factory **2.** somebody who makes or repairs machines

machismo /mə chízmō/ n an exaggerated sense or display of masculinity, emphasizing characteristics that are conventionally regarded as male, usually physical strength and courage, aggressiveness, and lack of emotional response [Mid-20C. < Mexican Spanish < *macho* (see MACHO)]

Machmeter /máak meetər, mák-/ n an instrument for measuring the Mach number of an aircraft

Mach number /maak-, mák-/ n the speed of an object relative to the speed of sound. An aircraft travelling at twice the speed of sound has a Mach number of 2. [Early 20C. After Ernst MACH]

macho /máchō/ adj having or showing characteristics conventionally regarded as male, especially physical strength and courage, aggressiveness, and lack of emotional response ■ n (plural -chos) a male who displays conventional masculine characteristics [Early 20C. Via Mexican Spanish, 'masculine' < Spanish < Latin *masculus*] —**machoism** n

machree /mə kree/ n Ireland used as an endearment [Early 19C. < Irish *mo chroidhe* 'of my heart']

Machu Picchu

Machu Picchu /máachoo peekchoo, -peechoo/ ruined ancient Inca city in the Andes in southern Peru. It is well known for its architecture and system of terraces.

machzor /maak záwr, maakh-/ (plural -zorim /maakh záwrim, maakh zaw reem/ or -zors), **mahzor** n a Jewish prayer book that details the rituals prescribed for festivals and holidays [Mid-19C. < Hebrew *mahzōr*]

Macias Nguema /mə see əss əng gwáymə/ former name for **Bioko** (1973–79)

macintosh n CLOTHING another spelling of **mackintosh**

mack n CLOTHING another spelling of **mac**

Mackay /mə kí/ **1.** salt lake in central Australia, on the border between Western Australia and the

Northern Territory. Area: 3,550 sq. km/1,370 sq. mi. **2.** coastal city in northeastern Queensland, Australia, a centre of sugar production. Population: 77,157 (2002 estimate).

Mackellar /mə kéllər/, **Dorothea** (1885–1968) Australian poet. She was the author of *My Country* (1908). Full name **Mackellar, Isobel Marion Dorothea**

Mackenzie /mə kénzi/ river in the Northwest Territories, Canada. It originates in Great Slave Lake. Length: 1,800 km/1,120 mi.

Mackenzie, Sir Alexander (1764–1820) Scottish-born Canadian explorer. He explored western Canada from the Arctic to the Pacific and was the first European to cross North America overland.

Mackenzie, Sir Compton (1883–1972) British novelist and playwright. His many books include *Carnival* (1912) and *Whisky Galore* (1947). During World War I, he served in the intelligence service. Full name **Mackenzie, Sir Edward Montague Compton**

Mackenzie, Sir Thomas (1854–1930) Scottish-born New Zealand politician. He briefly served as Liberal Party prime minister of New Zealand in 1912. See table at **prime minister**

~~mackeral~~ incorrect spelling of **mackerel**

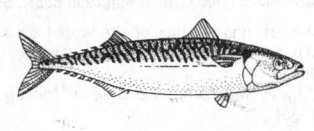

mackerel

mackerel /mákrəl/ (plural -els or same) n **1.** OILY FISH OF N ATLANTIC a bony oily fish with a greenish-blue body, dark blue bars, and a forked tail. Native to: North Atlantic coastal waters. Latin name: *Scomber scombrus*. **2.** FOOD MACKEREL AS FOOD the flesh of a mackerel used as food **3.** RELATED FISH a fish that is related to the true mackerel, e.g. the Spanish mackerel. Family: Scombridae. [13C. < Anglo-Norman]

mackerel shark n a large fierce shark with a pointed snout, related to the great white shark, mako shark, and porbeagle. Family: Lamnidae.

mackerel sky n a sky covered with cirrocumulus or altocumulus clouds in a pattern that resembles the markings on a mackerel (regional)

Mackerras /mə kérrəss/, **Sir Charles** (b. 1925) US-born Australian conductor and musical director. A conductor with a repertoire ranging from George Frederick Handel to Leos Janáček, he has held posts including the conductorship of the English National Opera, London (1970–79). Full name **Mackerras, Sir Alan Charles**

Mackillop /mə kílləp/, **Mary** (1842–1909) Australian nun. She founded the Sisters of St Joseph of the Sacred Heart in 1866. She was canonized, making her Australia's first saint. Known as **Mother Mary of the Cross**

mackinaw /máki naw/ n N Am **1.** a thick heavy woollen cloth, usually with a plaid design **2.** a short double-breasted coat made from mackinaw or a similar fabric [Early 19C. After a former trading post near *Mackinaw* City, Michigan, USA]

Mackinder /mə kíndər/, **Sir Halford John** (1861–1947) British geographer and politician. He established geography as an academic discipline.

Mackinnon /mə kínnən/, **Catherine** (b. 1946) US legal scholar. A pioneer in changing the legal attitude towards sex discrimination, she wrote the influential *Sexual Harassment of Working Women* (1979).

mackintosh /mákin tosh/, **macintosh** n **1.** a waterproof coat worn for protection against the rain (dated) **2.** a waterproof fabric, especially rubberized cotton [Mid-19C. After Charles *Macintosh* (1766–1843), Scottish inventor]

Charles Rennie Mackintosh

Mackintosh /mákin tosh/, **Charles Rennie** (1868–1928) British architect and interior designer. Noted for his art nouveau designs, he worked primarily on buildings and interiors in and around Glasgow.

mackle /mák'l/ *n* a blurred or double impression caused by the movement of paper or type during the printing process ■ *vti* (**-les, -ling, -led**) to cause a printed impression to blur, or appear blurred [Late 16C. Directly or via French < Latin *macula* 'spot, stain']

MacLaine /mə kláyn/, **Shirley** (*b.* 1934) US film actor. She won an Academy Award for her role in *Terms of Endearment* (1983). Born **MacLean Beaty, Shirley**

> 'We are not victims of the world we see. We are victims of the way we see the world.'
> [Shirley MacLaine, *Dancing in the Light*; 1985]

macle /mák'l/ *n* **1.** MINERALS same as **chiastolite 2.** a crystal that is composed of two mirror-image crystals sharing a common plane (**twinned**) **3.** a discoloured spot within a crystal [Early 19C. Via French < Latin *macula* 'spot, mesh']

Maclean /mə kláyn/, **Alistair** (1922–87) British novelist. Many of his adventure stories, set in different parts of the world, were made into films.

Maclean, Donald Duart (1913–83) British Soviet spy. He was an agent for the Soviet KGB while holding posts in the foreign office. He defected to Russia in 1951.

Macleod /mə klówd/, **John** (1876–1935) British physiologist. He discovered insulin with Sir Frederick Grant Banting and Charles Best, for which he shared the Nobel Prize in physiology or medicine (1923). Full name **Macleod, John James Rickard**

Harold Macmillan

Macmillan /mək míllən/, **Harold, 1st Earl of Stockton** (1894–1986) prime minister of the United Kingdom (1957–63). He served two terms as Conservative prime minister during which time many former colonies became independent. Full name **Macmillan, Maurice Harold**. See table at **prime minister**

> 'When you're abroad you're a statesman: when you're at home you're just a politician.'
> [Harold Macmillan, *Speech*; 1958]

MacMillan /mək míllən/, **Sir Kenneth** (1929–92) British choreographer. He created many ballets including *Romeo and Juliet* (1965) and was the holder of various posts in Europe and the United States, including the directorship of the Royal Ballet, London (1970–77).

MacNeice /mək neéss/, **Louis** (1907–63) British poet and playwright. His poetry, incorporating assonance and internal rhyme, shows great technical skill. He also wrote documentaries and plays for radio, notably *The Dark Tower* (1946).

> 'Time was away and somewhere else, / There were two glasses and two chairs / And two people with one pulse.'
> [Louis MacNeice, 'Meeting Point', *Holes in the Sky*; 1948]

maco /mákō/, **mako** *Carib n* (*plural* **-coes;** *plural* **-koes**) a gossip or busybody ■ *vi* (**-coes, -coing, -coed; -koes, -koing, -koed**) to gossip or be overly curious about other people's affairs [Late 20C. Shortening of French Creole *makomè* < French *macommère* 'my child's godmother, my intimate woman friend', hence 'gossip']

Mâcon[1] /maá koN/, **Macon** *n* a red or white wine from Burgundy, east-central France [Mid-19C. < MÂCON [2]]

Mâcon[2] /maá koN/ city in east-central France, the capital of Saône-et-Loire Department. Population: 34,469 (1999).

Macquarie, Lake /mə kwórri/ coastal lake in New South Wales, Australia. Area: 110 sq. km/43 sq. mi.

Macquarie, Lachlan (1762–1824) Australian colonial administrator. As governor of New South Wales, Australia, (1810–21), he turned the settlement into a prosperous colony and was noted for his progressive attitude towards the rehabilitation of convicts.

Macquarie Harbour large natural harbour in western Tasmania, Australia. Area: 285 sq. km/110 sq. mi.

Macquarie Island uninhabited Australian island located in the Southern Ocean, southeast of Tasmania. Area: 123 sq. km/47 sq. mi.

macr- *prefix* same as **macro-** (*used before vowels*)

macramé /mə kraámi, -may/ *n* pieces of string or cord knotted together to form a coarse ornamental lacy pattern, or something made using this method [Mid-19C. Via Turkish *makrama* 'towel' < Arabic *mikrama* 'bed cover']

Macready /mə kreédi/, **William Charles** (1793–1873) British actor. A leading actor of his day, he was noted for his stage theory and productions of Shakespearean tragedies.

macro /mákrō/ (*plural* **-ros**) *n* a computer instruction that initiates a series of additional commands [Mid-20C. < MACRO-]

macro- *prefix* **1.** large, inclusive ○ *macroeconomics* **2.** long ○ *macrobiotics* [< Greek *makros* < Indo-European, 'long, thin']

macrobiotics /mákrō bī óttiks/ *n* a vegan diet of seeds, grains, and organically grown fruit and vegetables, said to prolong life and balance the body's systems (*takes a singular verb*) [Late 18C. < Greek *makrobiotos* 'long life'] —**macrobiotic** *adj*

macrocarpa /mákrō kaárpə/ *n* an evergreen tree used as a windbreak. Native to: New Zealand. Latin name: *Cupressus macrocarpa*. [Early 20C. < modern Latin < Greek *makros* (see MACRO-) + *karpos* 'fruit']

macrocephaly /mákrō séffəli/, **macrocephalia** /-sə fáyli ə/ *n* the condition of having a head that is excessively large —**macrocephalic** /-si fállik/ *adj* —**macrocephalous** *adj*

macroclimate /mákrō klímət/ *n* the general climate of a large region such as a continent —**macroclimatic** /mákrō klī máttik/ *adj*

macrocosm /mákrō kozəm/ *n* a complex structure, e.g. the world or the universe, considered as a single entity that contains numerous similar smaller-scale structures [Early 17C. < medieval Latin *macrocosmus* < Greek *makro-* (see MACRO-) + *kosmos* 'world'] —**macrocosmic** /mákrō kózmik/ *adj* —**macrocosmically** *adv*

macrocyte /mákrō sīt/ *n* an unusually large red blood cell that commonly occurs in cases of anaemia —**macrocytic** /mákrō síttik/ *adj*

macrocytosis /mákrō sī tóssiss/ *n* the presence of unusually large red cells in the blood —**macrocytotic** /-sī tóttik/ *adj*

macroeconomics /mákrō ekə nómmiks, -eekə-/ *n* a branch of economics that focuses on the general features and processes that make up a national economy and the ways in which different segments of the economy are connected (*takes a singular*

verb) —**macroeconomic** *adj* —**macroeconomist** /-i kónnəmist/ *n*

macroeconomy /mákrō ikónnəmi/ *n* the economy viewed as a whole and in terms of all those factors that control its overall performance ○ *Employment rates did not respond to the macroeconomy as expected.*

macroevolution /mákrō eévə loósh'n/ *n* evolution theorized to occur over a long period of time, producing major changes in species and other taxonomic groups —**macroevolutionary** *adj*

macrofossil /mákrō foss'l/ *n* a fossil that is large enough to be observed or examined without the aid of a microscope

macrogamete /mákrō gammeet/ *n* the larger, usually female, sex cell (**gamete**) in a pair of conjugating cells of a heterogamous species

macroglobulin /mákrō glóbbyoōlin/ *n* a soluble protein in the blood with a high molecular weight

macroglobulinaemia /mákrō glóbbyoōli neémi ə/ *n* a medical condition marked by an increase in the blood of soluble proteins with high molecular weight

macroglobulinemia *n* MED US spelling of **macroglobulinaemia**

macrograph /mákrō graaf, -graf/ *n* a drawing, photograph, or other representation in which something appears at its actual size or larger —**macrographic** /mákrō gráffik/ *adj* —**macrography** /ma króggrəfi/ *n*

macroinstruction /mákrō in strúksh'n/ *n* COMPUT same as **macro**

macro lens *n* a lens used for close-up photography that produces a life-size or larger image on film, with a minimum of 1:1 object-to-image ratio

macromere /mákrō meer/ *n* a large yolk-filled cell (**blastomere**) formed from the unequal splitting of a fertilized egg [Late 19C. < MACRO- + BLASTOMERE]

macromolecule /mákrō mólli kyool/ *n* a large molecule such as that of a protein or polymer, made up of smaller components connected to one another —**macromolecular** /mákrō mə lékyoōlər/ *adj*

macron /mák ron/ *n* **1.** a short horizontal line placed over a vowel sound to indicate that it is long or stressed. Macrons are used in the spelling system of some languages, in some phonetic transcription systems, and in the study or analysis of poetic metre. **2.** a stressed or long syllable in a foot of verse, marked with a macron [Mid-19C. < Greek, 'long thing' < *makros* 'long']

macronucleus /mákrō nyoókli əss/ (*plural* **-clei** /-kli ī/) *n* the larger of two nuclei in most ciliate protozoans, involved in nonreproductive functions such as feeding and metabolism —**macronuclear** *adj*

macronutrient /mákrō nyoótri ənt/ *n* a chemical element needed in large amounts by plants for normal growth and development, e.g. nitrogen, carbon, or potassium

macrophage /mákrō fayj/ *n* a large cell that is present in blood, lymph, and connective tissues, removing waste products, harmful microorganisms, and foreign material from the bloodstream —**macrophagic** /mákrō fájjik/ *adj*

macrophotography /mákrō fə tóggrəfi/ *n* close-up photography that produces images on the film that are life-size or larger than life

macrophysics /mákrō fízziks/ *n* a branch of physics that studies systems and objects large enough to be easily observed (*takes a singular verb*)

macrophyte /mákrō fīt/ *n* a plant large enough to be studied and observed using the unaided eye, especially a water plant —**macrophytic** /mákrō fíttik/ *adj*

macropsia /mə krópsi ə/ *n* a medical condition in which everything perceived by the eye appears to be larger than it really is, often as a result of a retinal disease or a brain disorder [Late 19C. < MACRO- + Greek *opsia* 'seeing']

macroscopic /mákrō skóppik/, **macroscopical** /-skóppik'l/ *adj* **1.** large enough to be seen and examined without the aid of magnifying equipment **2.** relating to or concerned with large units [Late 19C. < MACRO-, after MICROSCOPIC] —**macroscopically** *adv*

macroscopic anatomy *n* ANAT same as **gross anatomy**

macrosociology /mákrō sōssi ólləji/ *n* the branch of sociology concerned with the study and analysis of societies in their entirety —**macrosociological** /-sōssi ə lójjik'l/ *adj*

macrosporangium /mákrōspə ránji əm/ (*plural* **-a** /-ji ə/) *n* BIOL same as **megasporangium** [Late 19C. < modern Latin < Greek *makros* (see MACRO-) + *spora* 'spore' + *aggeion* 'vessel']

macrospore /mákrō spawr/ *n* BIOL same as **megaspore**

macrostructure /mákrō strukchər/ *n* a structure such as that of a metal that is large enough to be seen or examined with little or no magnification —**macrostructural** /mákrō strúkchərəl/ *adj*

macula /mákyōōlə/ (*plural* **-lae** /-lee/) *n* **1.** PHYSIOL a small pigmented spot on the skin that is neither raised nor depressed **2.** OPHTHALMOL a small yellowish spot in the middle of the retina that provides the greatest visual acuity and colour perception **3.** ASTRON same as **sunspot** (*technical*) [14C. < Latin, 'spot, stain'] —**macular** *adj*

macula lutea /-loóti ə/ (*plural* **maculae luteae** /-ti ee/) *n* OPHTHALMOL same as **macula** (sense 2) [< Latin *luteus* 'yellow']

macular degeneration *n* MED breakdown or damage of the yellowish spot (**macula**) in the middle of the retina caused by leaking blood vessels. Symptoms include blurry central vision and diminished colour perception. Same as **age-related macular degeneration**

maculate /mákyōō layt/ (*literary*) *vt* (**-lates, -lating, -lated**) to mark somebody or something with a spot, blotch, or blemish ■ *adj also* **maculated** /mákyōōlaytid/ marked with spots, blotches, or blemishes [15C. < Latin *maculat-*, past participle of *maculare* < *macula* 'spot']

maculation /mákyōō láysh'n/ *n* **1.** the pattern of spots on some animals and plants **2.** the act of marking something with a spot, blotch, or blemish, or the state of being marked in this way (*archaic or literary*)

macule[1] /mákyōol/ *n* PHYSIOL same as **macula** (sense 1) [Mid-19C. Directly or via French < Latin *macula* 'spot, stain']

macule[2] /mákyōol/ *n* PRINTING same as **mackle** [15C. Directly or via French < Latin *macula* 'spot, stain']

Macusi /mə koóssi/, **Macushi** /mə koóshi/ *n* a Cariban language spoken in the border region between Brazil, Guyana, and Venezuela. Native speakers: over 10,000. [Early 20C. < Macusi] —**Macusi** *adj*

mad /mad/ *adj* (**madder, maddest**) **1.** ANGRY affected by great displeasure or anger ○ *She'll go mad when she finds out.* **2.** OFFENSIVE TERM an offensive term meaning affected with a psychiatric disorder **3.** VERY UNWISE OR RASH lacking common sense and not reasoning logically (*insult; offensive in some contexts*) **4.** WILDLY EXCITED completely unrestrained and out of control (*offensive in some contexts*) ○ *When the band finally appeared, the audience went mad.* **5.** FRANTIC done with great haste, excitement, or confusion (*offensive in some contexts*) ○ *There was a mad stampede to the fire exits.* **6.** EXCITING very exciting or boisterous (*sometimes offensive*) **7.** SEIZED BY UNCONTROLLABLE EMOTION overcome with a violent emotion (*sometimes offensive*) ○ *She was mad with jealousy.* **8.** PASSIONATE ABOUT SOMETHING very fond of, enthusiastic about, or interested in something, often to the exclusion of everything else (*often used in combination, offensive in some contexts*) ○ *I'm not mad about the colour.* ○ *football mad* **9.** MARKEDLY AGGRESSIVE unusually aggressive or ferocious (*refers to animals; offensive in some contexts*) ○ *a mad bull* **10.** RABID describes an animal that has rabies ■ *adv* UK EXTREMELY used for emphasis (*informal*) ○ *She's not mad keen on the idea.* [Old English *gemǣd* 'deprived of reason' < *gemād* 'irrational' < Indo-European, 'change'] ◇ **like mad** with great speed or energy (*offensive in some contexts*)

MAD /mad/ *abbr* **1.** PSYCHIAT major affective disorder **2.** *US* MIL mutual assured destruction

Madagascar /máddə gáskər/ *n* island country in the Indian Ocean, separated from southeastern mainland Africa by the Mozambique Channel. Language: Malagasy, French. Currency: Malagasy franc. Capital: Antananarivo. Population: 15,982,563 (2001). Area: 587,041 sq. km/226,658 sq. mi. Official name **Democratic Republic of Madagascar**. Former name **Malagasy Republic** (1958–75) —**Madagascan** *adj, n*

Madagascar aquamarine *n* a blue beryl found in Madagascar. Use: gems.

madam /máddəm/ *n* **1.** USED TO ADDRESS WOMAN a polite term of address for a woman, especially a customer

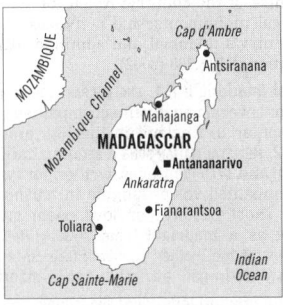
Madagascar

in a shop, restaurant, or hotel (*formal*) **2.** WOMAN RUNNING BROTHEL a woman who manages a brothel **3.** PRECOCIOUS GIRL a petulant or self-willed girl who expects everybody to do as she says (*informal*) [13C. < Old French *ma dame* 'my lady' < Latin *mea domina*]

Madam (*plural* **Mesdames** /máy dam, may dám/ or **Madams**) *n* **1.** used at the beginning of a formal letter to a woman, especially one whose name is not known (*formal*) **2.** used before the name of a woman's official position as a term of address ○ *Madam President*

Madame /ma dám/ (*plural* **Mesdames** /may dám/), **madame** (*plural* **mesdames**) *n* the title of a Frenchwoman or French-speaking woman, especially if married, used before her name or as a polite term of address [Mid-16C. < French < Old French *ma dame* (see MADAM)]

CULTURAL NOTE *Madame Bovary*, a novel (1857) by French writer Gustave Flaubert. It tells the story of Emma Bovary, a young married woman who seeks refuge from the mundaneness of her provincial life in a series of reckless and ultimately disastrous affairs. The novel's frank depiction of middle-class society and its almost scientific analysis of human behaviour made it a pioneering work of modern realism.

Madang /mə dáng/ *n* port on the northeastern coast of New Guinea in Papua New Guinea. Population: 27,057 (1990).

madcap /mád kap/ *adj* acting or behaving without caring or stopping to think about possible consequences [Late 16C. *Cap* represents the head] —**madcap** *n*

mad cow disease *n* VET same as **BSE** (*informal*)

madden /mádd'n/ *vti* (**-dens, -dening, -dened**) **1.** to make a person or animal extremely angry, or become extremely angry (*usually passive*) **2.** to make somebody irrational or cause somebody to have psychiatric problems, or become irrational

maddening /mádd'ning/ *adj* causing anger, annoyance, impatience, or frustration —**maddeningly** *adv*

madder[1] /máddər/ comparative of **mad**

madder[2] /máddər/ *n* **1.** PLANT a perennial plant with a fleshy red root. Native to: Europe, Asia. Latin name: *Rubia tinctorum*. **2.** ROOT YIELDING DYE the root of a madder plant. Use: formerly, red dye. **3.** RED DYE a red dye formerly obtained from madder roots **4.** RED PIGMENT a red pigment obtained from the dye alizarin. Use: dyes, inks, paints. **5.** REDDISH-PURPLE a deep reddish-purple colour [Old English *mædere* < Germanic] —**madder** *adj*

maddest /máddəst/ superlative of **mad**

madding /mádding/ *adj* acting in a way that suggests or reveals the presence of a psychiatric disorder (*literary*)

CULTURAL NOTE *Far from the Madding Crowd*, a novel (1874) by Thomas Hardy. The first of Thomas Hardy's Wessex novels, it is the story of a capricious, forceful young woman, Bathsheba Everdene, and the three men who want to marry her. It was made into a film by John Schlesinger in 1967.

made /mayd/ past participle, past tense of **make** ■ *adj* **1.** produced by artificial means **2.** certain of achieving success

Madeira[1] /mə deérə/ *n* a sweet or dry wine fortified with brandy, made in the Madeira islands and usually served as a dessert wine or after a meal

Madeira[2] /mə deérə/ river in western Brazil. It is the main tributary of the Amazon, flowing northeast from the Bolivian border and into the Amazon near Manaus. Length: 3,220 km/2,000 mi.

Madeira cake *n* a fine-textured plain cake, served without filling or icing

Madeira Islands group of islands with many resorts in the eastern North Atlantic Ocean. Population: 256,000 (1992). Area: 794 sq. km/307 sq. mi.

madeleine /mádd'lin, máddə layn/ *n* **1.** a small light whisked sponge cake baked in the form of a shell **2.** a sponge cake that is cooked in a small cup-shaped mould, coated in raspberry jam, rolled in desiccated coconut, and topped with a glacé cherry [Mid-19C. Probably after *Madeleine* Paulmier, 19C French pastry chef]

mademoiselle /máddəmwə zél/ (*plural* **mesdemoiselles** /máydəmwə zél/ or **mademoiselles** /máddəmwə zélz/) *n* **1.** a young Frenchwoman or French-speaking woman **2.** a female French teacher or French governess (*dated*) [Mid-18C. Use of MADEMOISELLE]

Mademoiselle /máddəmwə zél/ (*plural* **Mesdemoiselles** /máydəmwə zél/) *n* the title of a French woman or French-speaking young or unmarried woman, used before her name or as a polite term of address (*sometimes considered offensive*) [15C. < Old French *ma demoiselle* 'my damsel']

made-to-measure *adj* made by a tailor to fit a specific person

made-to-order *adj* **1.** made in accordance with a customer's specifications or requirements **2.** perfectly suitable or exactly as required

made-up *adj* **1.** UNTRUE lacking any basis in fact or reality **2.** WEARING COSMETICS having applied cosmetics to the face **3.** ASSEMBLED completely put together and prepared

madhouse /mád howss/ (*plural* **-houses** /-howziz/) *n* **1.** a place where there is much noise and activity and little order or control (*informal; sometimes considered offensive*) **2.** an offensive term for a hospital or residential facility for people who have psychiatric disorders (*dated*)

Madhya Pradesh /múddyə prə désh/ state in north central India. Capital: Bhopal. Population: 60,385,118 (2001). Area: 308,250 sq. km/118,985 sq. mi.

madison /máddiss'n/ *n* a cycling event in which competitors ride as teams, each rider relieving the other in turn

Madison /máddiss'n/ capital city of Wisconsin, in the south-central part of the state. It is home to the University of Wisconsin-Madison. Population: 215,211 (2002 estimate).

James Madison

Madison, James (1751–1836) 4th president of the United States. He played a leading role in the Constitutional Convention (1787) and served two terms as president (1809–17). See table at **president**

'Democracies...have in general been as short in their lives as they have been violent in their deaths.'
[James Madison, *Independent Journal*; 23 November 1787]

Madison Avenue *n* the centre of the US advertising and public-relations industries, or the US advertising industry itself [After the street in New York]

madly /mádli/ *adv* **1.** TO NO PURPOSE with great haste or activity but without accomplishing much ○ *She ran madly through the house looking for her keys.* **2.**

WILDLY in a wild and uncontrolled way ○ *He struck out madly in all directions.* **3. RASHLY** in a rash or thoughtless way ○ *I madly agreed to go with her.* **4. OFFENSIVE TERM** an offensive term meaning in the manner of somebody who is affected by a psychiatric disorder **5. INTENSELY** with an extraordinary degree of intensity or devotion ○ *madly in love*

madman /mádmən/ (*plural* **-men** /-mən/) *n* an offensive term for a man with a psychiatric disorder

madness /mádnəss/ *n* **1. OFFENSIVE TERM** an offensive term for a psychiatric disorder **2. RASHNESS** rash or thoughtless behaviour **3. ANGER** great anger or fury **4. EXCITEMENT** great enthusiasm or excitement

Madonna: Byzantine mosaic, Athens, Greece

Madonna /mə dónnə/ *n* **1.** Mary, the mother of Jesus Christ **2.** *also* **madonna** a picture, statue, or other artistic representation of Mary, the mother of Jesus Christ [Late 16C. < obsolete Italian *ma donna* 'my lady' < Latin *mea domina*]

Madonna

Madonna /mə dónnə/ (*b.* 1958) US pop singer and actor. Her career, which started in the early 1980s, shows an ability to change her style and image ahead of current trends. She has also written storybooks for children. Born **Ciccone, Madonna Louise Veronica**

Madonna lily *n* a tall lily. Flowers: white, trumpet-shaped. Native to: eastern Mediterranean. Latin name: *Lilium candidum.* [Traditional symbol of purity, often included in pictures of the Madonna, the mother of Jesus Christ]

madras /mə draáss, -dráss/ *n* **1. STRONG FINE CLOTH** a strong fine cotton or silk fabric, often with a woven striped or checked design **2. LIGHT CLOTH** a light cotton or rayon fabric. Use: curtains. **3. BRIGHTLY COLOURED SCARF** a scarf or handkerchief made from brightly coloured cotton or silk **4. FAIRLY HOT CURRY** a fairly hot curried dish made with meat, spices, chillies, and lentils [Early 19C. After MADRAS]

Madras /mə draáss/ former name for **Chennai**

madrasa /mə drássə/, **madrassa** *n* a school for the study of Islamic religion and thought, especially the Koran [Mid-17C. < Arabic, 'place to study']

madrepore /máddri pawr/ *n* a reef-building coral that lives in tropical waters. Genus: *Madreporaria.* [Mid-18C. Via French or modern Latin < Italian *madrepora* < *madre* 'mother' + either *poro* 'pore' or Latin *porus* 'calciferous stone' < Greek *poros*] —**madreporal** /máddri páwrəl/ —**madreporian** *adj* —**madreporic** *adj* —**madreporitic** /-pə ríttik/ *adj*

madreporite /máddri páw rīt/ *n* a porous plate in an echinoderm that takes in water to the vascular system [Early 19C. < MADREPORE]

Madrid /mə dríd/ capital and largest city of Spain, in the centre of the country. Noted for its museums, historical monuments, and active street life, it is the country's financial and administrative centre. Population: 3,016,788 (2002).

madrigal /máddrig'l/ *n* **1. ENGLISH PART SONG** a song with parts for several usually unaccompanied voices that was popular in England in the 16th and 17th centuries **2. MEDIEVAL ITALIAN SONG** a secular Italian song of the 13th and 14th centuries, written for two or three unaccompanied voices singing in harmony **3. LYRIC POEM** a short pastoral or love poem suitable for singing as a madrigal [Late 16C. < *Italian* < Latin *matricalis* 'of the mother' < *matrix* (see MATRIX)] —**madrigalian** /máddri gálli ən, -gáyli-/ *adj* —**madrigalist** *n*

madrilène /máddri lén, -láyn/, **madrilene** *n* a clear soup flavoured with tomato, usually served cold [Early 20C. Via French < Spanish *madrileño* 'of Madrid']

madroña /mə drónyə/, **madroño** /-nyō/ (*plural* **-ños**) *n* an evergreen tree with smooth crimson peeling bark, glossy leaves, and orange-yellow berries. Flowers: cream. Native to: North America. Latin name: *Arbutus menziesii.* [Mid-19C. < Spanish]

mad tom *n* a small common freshwater catfish with poisonous pectoral spines, a long adipose fin, and a rounded dorsal fin. Native to: central United States. Genus: *Noturus.* [Short for 'mad tom cat', since the fish inflicts nasty wounds with its poisonous spines]

Madura /mə doorə/ island in southwestern Indonesia, off the northeastern coast of Java. Population: 3,015,972 (1990). Area: 5,587 sq. km/2,157 sq. mi.

Madurai /máddyoorī/ historic city and pilgrimage centre in southern India. Population: 1,194,665 (2001).

maduro /mə doorō/ (*plural* **-ros**) *n* a dark strong cigar [Late 19C. < Spanish, 'ripe, mature']

madwoman /mád woomən/ (*plural* **-women** /-wimin/) *n* an offensive term for a woman with a psychiatric disorder

madwort /mád wurt/ (*plural* **-worts** or *same*) *n* a low-growing plant of the borage family. Flowers: small, blue. Native to: Europe, Asia. Latin name: *Asperugo procumbens.* [Late 16C. Translation of modern Latin *alyssum* 'removing rabies'; because it was believed to cure the bites of rabid dogs]

madzoon *n* FOOD another spelling of **matzoon**

Maecenas /mī seé nass/ (*plural same*) *n* a rich patron of the arts (*literary*)

Maecenas /mī seé nass, mee-/, **Gaius** (74?–8 BC) Roman politician. He was an adviser to Augustus and a generous patron of artists and writers, notably Horace and Virgil.

maelstrom /máyl strom/ *n* **1.** an exceptionally large or violent whirlpool **2.** a situation marked by confusion, turbulence, strong feelings, violence, or destruction [Late 17C. < early modern Dutch, < *maalen* 'whirl round' + *stroom* 'stream']

Maelstrom /máyl strəm/ marine whirlpool in northwestern Norway between two islands of the Lofoten Islands

maenad /meé nad/ *n* **1.** in ancient Greece, a woman who belonged to the cult of Dionysus and took part in orgiastic rites **2.** a woman affected by wild, uncontrollable emotion (*literary*) [Late 16C. Via Latin < Greek *Mainad-*, stem of *Mainas* < *mainesthai* 'rave'] —**maenadic** /mee náddik/ *adj*

maestoso /mī stóssō/ *adv* in a dignified or majestic manner (*used as a musical direction*) ■ *n* (*plural* **-sos**) a section of a piece of music played maestoso [Early 18C. < Italian, 'majestic' < Latin *majestas* (see MAJESTY)] —**maestoso** *adj*

Maestricht ▸ Maastricht

maestro /mī́strō/ (*plural* **-tros** or **-tri** /-tri/) *n* an expert in an art or skill, especially an accomplished musician, conductor, or composer [Early 18C. Via Italian, 'master' < Latin *magister*]

maestro di cappella /-di kə péllə/ (*plural* **maestri di cappella**) *n* formerly, especially in 17th-century Italy, the director of a group of musicians, especially a chapel choir or the private orchestra of a royal court or noble household [*Di capella* < Italian, 'of the chapel']

Maeterlinck /máytərlingk/, **Maurice, Comte** (1862–1949) Belgian poet and playwright. He was an exponent of symbolism, exemplified by his play *Pelléas et Mélisande* (1892) and a volume of poetry, *Hothouses*

(1889). Full name **Maeterlinck, Maurice Polydore Marie Bernard**

'The living are just the dead on holiday.'
[Attributed to Maurice Maeterlinck]

Mae West /máy wést/, **mae west** *n* (*informal*) **1.** an inflatable life jacket, especially one issued to US pilots during World War II **2.** a parachute malfunction in which a suspension line goes over the top of the canopy, creating what appears to be a huge bra [Mid-20C. Because the shape reminded airmen of Mae WEST's large bosom]

Mafeking /máffi king/ former name for **Mafikeng**

MAFF /maf/ *abbr* HIST Ministry of Agriculture, Fisheries, and Food

mafficking /máffiking/ *n* a boisterous and extravagant public celebration (*archaic*) [Early 20C. Based on MAFIKENG; from the celebrations after the siege was over in 1900] —**maffick** *vi* —**mafficker** *n*

mafia /maáfee ə/ *n* a close-knit or influential group of people who work together and protect one another's interests or the interests of a particular person [Mid-20C. < MAFIA]

Mafia /máffi ə/ *n* **1.** a secret criminal organization originating in Sicily that spread to mainland Italy and the United States and is involved in international drug-dealing, racketeering, gambling, and prostitution **2.** another spelling of **mafia** [Mid-19C. < Italian dialect (Sicilian), 'bragging']

mafic /máffik/ *adj* relating to dark-coloured minerals or rocks that are high in magnesium and iron [Early 20C. < MAGNESIUM + FERRIC]

Mafikeng /máffi keng/ capital of North West Province, South Africa. Its garrison, under Lord Robert Baden-Powell, was besieged by Boer troops between October 1899 and May 1900. Population: 6,900 (1994). Former name **Mafeking** (until 1980)

Mafioso /máffi óssō, -ōzō/ (*plural* **-si** /-ósee, -ōzee/ or **-sos**), **mafioso** *n* a member of the Mafia criminal organization [Late 19C. < Italian < *mafia* 'bragging']

mag /mag/ *n* PUBL same as **magazine** (sense 1) (*informal*) [Early 19C. Shortening]

mag. *abbr* **1.** magazine **2.** magnesium **3.** magnet **4.** magnetic **5.** magnetism **6.** magnitude **7.** magnum

magalogue /mággə lòg/ *n* a catalogue presented to look like a magazine, used as a marketing tool [Late 20C. Blend of MAGAZINE and CATALOGUE]

magazine /mággə zeén/ *n* **1. PERIODICAL PUBLICATION** a publication issued at regular intervals, usually weekly or monthly, containing articles, stories, photographs, advertisements, and other features, with a page size that is usually smaller than that of a newspaper but larger than that of a book **2. BULLET OR CARTRIDGE HOLDER** a detachable container for cartridges or bullets that can be quickly inserted or removed from a gun **3. STOREHOUSE FOR MILITARY SUPPLIES** a structure on land or a part of a ship where weapons, ammunition, explosives, and other military equipment or supplies are stored **4. STOCK OF AMMUNITION** a stock of ammunition or other supplies kept in a storehouse **5. SLIDE HOLDER** a container designed to hold a number of photographic slides and feed them automatically through a projector **6. FILM CONTAINER** a space or compartment in a camera from which film is loaded without exposing it to light **7. SUPPLY DEVICE** a device or container attached to a machine that holds or supplies necessary material **8. PROGRAMME CONTAINING ASSORTED ITEMS** a television or radio programme made up of an assortment of short factual items, often of interest to a particular group of people [Late 16C. Via French *magazin* < Italian *magazzino* < Arabic *makzan* 'storehouse']

magdalen /mágdələn/, **magdalene** /mágdə leéni, mágdə leen/ *n* **1.** a reformed prostitute (*archaic or literary*) **2.** a refuge for reformed prostitutes, or an institution where prostitutes are sent to be reformed (*literary*) [14C. < Mary *Magdalen*, reformed woman, in the Bible]

Magdalena /mágdə láynə/ major river of Colombia. It flows north from the Andes into the Caribbean Sea. Length: 1,540 km/957 mi.

Magdalene *n* BIBLE same as **Mary Magdalene**

Magdeburg /mágdə burg/ capital of Saxony-Anhalt State, north-central Germany. Population: 265,379 (1997).

mage /mayj/ *n* a magician or magus (*archaic*) [14C. An anglicization of MAGUS]

Magellan, Strait of /mə géllən/ channel separating mainland South America and Tierra del Fuego, between the Atlantic and Pacific oceans. Length: 560 km/350 mi.

Magellan /mə géllən/, **Ferdinand** (1480?–1521) Portuguese explorer. He sailed around South America through the Strait of Magellan and across the Pacific Ocean (1519–21). Although he died in the Philippines, his ship returned to Spain, completing the first circumnavigation of the Earth.

Magellanic Cloud /mággi lánnik-, májji-/ n either of two small galaxies near the south celestial pole that are irregularly shaped and closest to the Milky Way [Early 17C. After Ferdinand MAGELLAN]

Magen David /máwgən dáyvid/ n JUDAISM same as **Star of David** [< Hebrew, 'shield of David']

magenta /mə jéntə/ n 1. a brilliant purplish-pink colour that is one of the three subtractive colours 2. CHEM same as **fuchsin** ■ adj brilliant purplish-pink in colour [Mid-19C. After *Magenta*, N Italy]

maggid /maágid/ (plural -gidim /-gidim/) n a popular teacher travelling among the Ashkenazi Jewish communities of Eastern Europe [Late 19C. < Hebrew *maggīd* 'narrator']

maggiore /ma jáw ray/ n in music, a section of a fugue or set of variations in the major mode that occurs especially after a section in a minor mode [Late 19C. < Italian, 'major']

Maggiore, Lake /ma jáw ray/ lake that lies partly in the Ticino Canton, Switzerland, and partly in the Lombardy Region of northern Italy. Area: 212 sq. km/82 sq. mi.

maggot /mággət/ n 1. the worm-shaped larva of various members of the fly family, found in decaying matter and used as bait in fishing 2. a fanciful notion or idea (*archaic*) [14C. < maddock 'worm, maggot' < Germanic]

maggoty /mággəti/ (-ier, -iest) adj 1. FULL OF MAGGOTS full of or containing maggots 2. DRUNK extremely intoxicated by alcohol (*slang*) 3. Aus ANGRY extremely angry or irritated (*slang*)

Magha /múggə/ n in the Hindu calendar, the 11th month of the year, lasting 30 days and falling about the same time as January to February. See table at **calendar** [Late 20C. < Hindi]

Magherafelt /mákərə félt/ town in County Londonderry, Northern Ireland. Linen is made there. Population: 7,143 (1991).

Maghreb /múgrəb/, **Maghrib** loosely defined region in northwestern Africa, centred on Algeria, Morocco, and Tunisia

magi RELIG plural of **magus**

Magi /máy jī/ npl in the Bible, the group of three men who came to Bethlehem from the East to celebrate the birth of Jesus Christ. (Matthew 2:1–12). They are sometimes known individually as Caspar, Melchior, and Balthazar, and jointly as the Three Wise Men or the Three Kings. [Plural of MAGUS] —**Magian** /máyji ən/ adj, n —**Magianism** n

magic /májjik/ n 1. CONJURING TRICKS conjuring tricks and illusions that make apparently impossible things seem to happen, usually performed as entertainment 2. INEXPLICABLE THINGS a special, mysterious, or inexplicable quality, talent, or skill ○ *watched the dancer's feet work their magic* 3. SUPPOSED SUPERNATURAL POWER a supposed supernatural power that makes impossible things happen or gives somebody control over the forces of nature. Magic is used in many cultures for healing, keeping away evil, seeking the truth, and for vengeful purposes. 4. PRACTICE OF MAGIC the use of supposed supernatural power to make impossible things happen ■ adj 1. OF OR FOR MAGIC relating to magic or used in the working of magic ○ *a magic potion* 2. PARTICULARLY IMPORTANT particularly important or desirable ○ *reach the magic figure of 100 points* 3. EXCELLENT very good or enjoyable (*informal*) ○ *a great film and a magic dinner* ■ vt (-ics, -icking, -icked) SUBJECT SOMETHING TO MAGIC to make somebody or something seem to appear, disappear, change, or move by using magic [14C. Via Old French *magique* < Greek *magikē* < *magos* (see MAGUS)] ◇ **like magic 1.** rapidly **2.** without obstacles or difficulties

clinic. The clinic is a microcosm of European society at the time of World War I, with a cosmopolitan group of patients reflecting a range of contemporary political, philosophical, and scientific viewpoints.

magical /májjik'l/ adj 1. created by or as if by magic 2. so beautiful or pleasing as to seem supernaturally created —**magically** adv

magical realism n ART same as **magic realism**

magic bullet n 1. a drug that treats a serious disease with no undesirable side effects on the patient 2. a quick and easy solution for a difficult problem, or a means of accomplishing the impossible

magic carpet n in fairy stories, a carpet that flies through the air and is used as a form of transport

magic eye n a tiny cathode-ray tube used in a radio receiver to help tuning

magician /mə jísh'n/ n 1. CONJURER OR ILLUSIONIST an entertainer who performs conjuring tricks and illusions 2. SOMEBODY WHO PRACTISES SORCERY somebody who uses supposed supernatural powers 3. SOMEBODY WITH EXCEPTIONAL ABILITY an extraordinarily skilled or powerful person

Magic Marker tdmk a trademark for a felt-tip pen that comes in various colours of ink

magic mushroom n a fungus that contains a hallucinogenic substance (*informal*)

magic number n any of the numbers 2, 8, 20, 28, 50, 82, and 126 that represent the number of protons or neutrons in the nucleus of very stable atomic nuclei

magic pudding, **Magic Pudding** n Aus a resource that can be endlessly renewed (*informal*) ○ *The chattering classes think that public money is some kind of magic pudding.* [< *The Magic Pudding* (1918), children's book by Australian author Norman Lindsay, in which a pudding always replenishes itself and so can be eaten repeatedly]

magic realism, **magical realism** n a style of art or literature that depicts fantastic or mythological subjects in a realistic manner —**magic realist** n

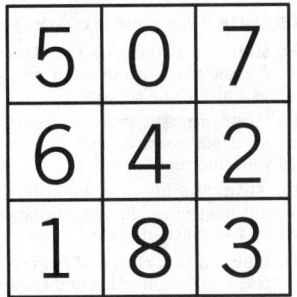

magic square

magic square n a square containing rows and columns of numbers arranged in such a way that each horizontal, vertical, and diagonal line has the same sum

magic wand n 1. a small thin stick used by a sorcerer or conjurer to perform magic 2. something fanciful or imaginary that would, if it existed, be able to solve a difficult or impossible problem immediately

magilp n ART another spelling of **megilp**

Maginot line /mázhi nō-/ n 1. a line of fortifications constructed by the French along the border between France and Germany before World War II that failed to stop the German army from invading 2. an ineffective defensive strategy that is relied on with unthinking confidence [Mid-20C. After André Maginot (1877–1932), French war minister]

magisterial /májji steéri əl/ adj 1. DIGNIFIED showing great dignity and authority 2. DOMINEERING behaving in an overbearing or dictatorial way 3. MASTERLY AND AUTHORITATIVE produced by or characteristic of a teacher, scholar, or expert 4. OF MAGISTRATE relating to or characteristic of a magistrate —**magisterially** adv —**magisterialness** n

magisterium /májji steéri əm/ n in the Roman Catholic tradition, the authority of the church to teach religious doctrine [Late 16C. < Latin < *magister* 'master']

magistracy /májjistrəssi/ (plural -cies), **magistrature** /-strəchər/ n 1. OFFICE OF MAGISTRATE the position or function of a magistrate 2. MAGISTRATE'S TERM OF OFFICE

the term of office of a magistrate 3. AREA OF MAGISTRATE'S JURISDICTION the district over which a magistrate has the power and authority to administer justice 4. MAGISTRATES COLLECTIVELY magistrates considered as a group

magistral /májjistrəl/ adj relating to or characteristic of an expert or scholar (*formal or archaic*) —**magistrality** /májji strálləti/ n —**magistrally** adv

magistrate /májji strayt, -strət/ n 1. LOWER COURT JUDGE a judge in a lower court whose jurisdiction is limited to the trial of misdemeanours and the conduct of preliminary hearings on more serious charges 2. LOCAL LAW OFFICER a minor law officer or member of a local judiciary with extremely limited powers, e.g. a justice of the peace who deals with traffic violations 3. Aus JUDGE OF AUSTRALIAN LOWER COURT a judicial officer appointed by the executive government to hear civil and criminal cases in a court of summary jurisdiction [14C. < Latin *magistratus* < *magister* 'master'] —**magistrateship** n

magistrates' court n 1. in England, a summary court presided over by a magistrate or two or more justices of the peace who make decisions about minor crimes, some civil actions, and preliminary hearings 2. in an Australian state, a court that tries minor offences without a jury

magistrature n LAW same as **magistracy**

maglev /mág lev/ n an electrically operated high-speed train that glides above a track by means of a magnetic field. ◊ **magnetic levitation** [Late 20C. Blend of MAGNETIC + *levitation*]

magma /mágmə/ (plural -mas or -mata /-mətə/) n 1. molten rock deep within the Earth from which igneous rock is formed by solidification at or near the Earth's surface 2. a soft paste or thick suspension made from fine solid particles mixed with liquid [15C. Via Latin < Greek < *massein* 'knead'] —**magmatic** /mag máttik/ adj

magma chamber n an underground cavity that contains magma, often located below a volcano

Magna Carta /mágnə kaártə/, **Magna Charta** /-chaártə/ n 1. a charter establishing the rights of English barons and free citizens, granted by King John at Runnymede in 1215 and regarded as the basis of civil and political liberty in England 2. a document that recognizes or guarantees rights, privileges, or liberties [< Latin, 'great charter']

magna cum laude /mágnə koŏm lów day, -di/ adv, adj with the second-highest level of academic honours at graduation [< Latin, 'with great praise'] —**magna cum laude** adj

Magna Graecia /mágnə greéssi ə, -greéshə/ n in ancient times, the parts of southern Italy and Sicily that contained numerous Greek colonies [< Latin, 'great Greece']

magnanimity /mágnə nímməti/ (plural -ties) n 1. great generosity or noble-spiritedness 2. a generous or noble-spirited act [14C. Via French *magnanimité* < Latin *magnanimitas* < *magnanimus* (see MAGNANIMOUS)]

magnanimous /mag nánniməss/ adj very generous, kind, and forgiving [Late 16C. < Latin *magnanimus* < *magnus* 'great' + *animus* 'mind'] —**magnanimously** adv

SYNONYMS See *generous*.

magnate /mág nayt, -nət/ n 1. somebody who has a lot of wealth and power, especially somebody in business or industry 2. a high-ranking member of the nobility [15C. < late Latin *magnat*- < Latin *magnus* 'great'] —**magnateship** n

magnesia /mag neéshə, -neézhə/ n CHEM same as **magnesium oxide** [14C. Via medieval Latin < Greek *magnēsia* 'mineral from *Magnesia*', Asia Minor] —**magnesial** adj —**magnesian** adj —**magnesic** /-neéssik/ adj

magnesite /mágni sīt/ n a white or colourless magnesium carbonate mineral. Use: source of magnesium oxide, insulation, refractory lining of furnaces. [Early 19C. < MAGNESIA]

magnesium /mag neézi əm/ n a light silver-white metallic element. Source: magnesite, dolomite, seawater. Use: alloys, metallurgy, photography, fireworks. Symbol **Mg**. See table at **element** [Early 19C. < MAGNESIA]

magnesium carbonate n a white crystalline salt. Source: dolomite, magnesite. Use: in antacids, glass, refractories. Formula: $MgCO_3$.

magnesium chloride *n* a colourless or white crystalline compound. Use: source of magnesium, in fireproofing, paper making, ceramics, fire extinguishers. Formula: $MgCl_2·6H_2O$.

magnesium hydroxide *n* a white crystalline powder. Use: antacid, laxative. Formula: $Mg(OH)_2$.

magnesium oxide *n* a white powder. Source: periclase. Use: antacid, laxative, refractories, cements, electrical insulation, fertilizers. Formula: MgO.

magnesium sulphate *n* a colourless crystalline salt. Use: in medicine, fertilizers, manufacturing. Formula: $MgSO_4$.

magnet /mágnət/ *n* 1. a piece of metal that has the power to draw iron or steel objects towards it and to hold or move them 2. same as **electromagnet** 3. somebody or something that has a great power of attraction over people [15C. Directly or via French < Latin *magneta* form of *magnes* < Greek *Magnēs lithos* 'stone from Magnesia', Asia Minor]

magnetar /mágnə taar/ *n* a neutron star with an extremely strong magnetic field that emits gamma rays and X-rays. A magnetar's magnetic field can be a thousand trillion times stronger than that of the Earth. [Late 20C. Blend of MAGNETIC and QUASAR]

magnetic /mag néttik/ *adj* 1. HAVING POWER OF MAGNET able to attract iron or steel objects 2. ABLE TO BE MAGNETIZED able to be magnetized, or attracted by a magnet 3. RELATING TO MAGNETISM relating to, involving, or produced by magnetism 4. USING MAGNET OR MAGNETISM containing or using a magnet or magnetism 5. POWERFULLY CHARMING having a great power of attraction over people ○ *a magnetic personality* 6. OF EARTH'S MAGNETISM relating to the Earth's magnetism —**magnetically** *adv*

magnetic bottle *n* a strong magnetic field. Use: to confine plasma in nuclear fusion experiments.

magnetic bubble *n* a small movable magnetic region in a thin film of magnetic material. Use: to store data in computer memory.

magnetic compass *n* an instrument used to indicate magnetic north and other directions, containing a magnetic needle that swings horizontally around a circle marked in degrees or with the points of the compass

magnetic declination *n* the angle between magnetic north and true north at a particular point on the Earth's surface

magnetic disk *n* a computer disk consisting of one or more thin magnetically etched plates

magnetic epoch *n* a long period of geological time between reversals of the Earth's magnetic field

magnetic equator *n* an imaginary line that lies near the geographical equator and passes through all points where a magnetic needle has no dip

magnetic field *n* a region of space surrounding a magnetized body or current-carrying circuit in which the resulting magnetic force can be detected

magnetic flux *n* the strength of a magnetic field represented by lines of force. Symbol ϕ

magnetic flux density *n* the strength of a magnetic field multiplied by the porosity of a medium, measured in teslas or gauss. Symbol B

magnetic head *n* an electromagnetic device that reads, writes, or erases data on a magnetic medium

magnetic induction *n* PHYS same as **magnetic flux density**

magnetic levitation *n* a system of high-speed rail travel using magnetism both to suspend and to propel trains above and along the track

magnetic meridian *n* an imaginary line around the Earth's surface that passes through both magnetic poles

magnetic mine *n* an underwater mine equipped with magnetic sensors that cause it to detonate when a large metal object, usually a ship, passes into its magnetic field

magnetic mirror *n* PHYS same as **magnetic bottle**

magnetic moment *n* a vector quantity representing the torque experienced by a magnetic system in a magnetic field. Symbol m

magnetic needle *n* a thin bar of magnetized metal used in navigational instruments, mounted or suspended so that it swings freely in a horizontal circle

and indicates the direction of the Earth's magnetic poles

magnetic north *n* the direction of the north magnetic pole, indicated by the needle of a magnetic compass

magnetic pole *n* 1. either of the two points at the end of a magnet where the magnet's field is most intense 2. either of the two regions on the Earth's surface near the geographical poles where the Earth's magnetic field is most intense

magnetic recording *n* 1. the storage of analogue or digital data on a magnetized medium such as audio, video, or computer data on tape, disk, or cards 2. a surface on which information has been magnetically recorded

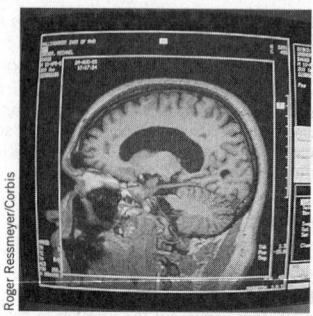

Roger Ressmeyer/Corbis

magnetic resonance imaging

magnetic resonance imaging *n* an imaging technique that uses electromagnetic radiation to obtain images of the body's soft tissues, e.g. the brain and spinal cord. The body is subjected to a powerful magnetic field, allowing tiny signals from atomic nuclei to be detected and then processed and converted into images by a computer.

magnetic reversal *n* the reversal of the Earth's magnetic poles that has occurred at irregular intervals averaging approximately one million years

magnetic sense *n* BIOL same as **compass sense**

magnetic storm *n* a disturbance in the Earth's magnetic field associated with charged particles from solar flares and sunspot activity

magnetic stripe, **magnetic strip** *n* a strip of magnetic medium on a plastic card such as a credit card, encoded with information

magnetic susceptibility *n* a number that characterizes the magnetization of a substance when it is subjected to a magnetic field

magnetic tape *n* a thin ribbon of material, usually plastic, coated with iron oxide and used to record sounds, images, or data. It is the tape used in audio and video cassettes, and on computers with tape drives.

magnetic transition temperature *n* PHYS same as **Curie point**

magnetic variation *n* PHYS same as **magnetic declination**

magnetise *vti* another spelling of **magnetize**

magnetism /mágnətizəm/ *n* 1. ATTRACTION OF MAGNETS FOR IRON the phenomenon of physical attraction for iron, inherent in magnets or induced by a moving electric charge or current 2. FORCE OF MAGNETIC FIELD the force exerted by a magnetic field 3. PERSONAL ATTRACTION the strong attractiveness of something, especially the power of somebody's personality to influence others ○*He was a born boon companion, with a magnetism which drew good humour from all around him.* (Arthur Conan Doyle, *The Valley of Fear*; 1915)

magnetite /mágnə tīt/ *n* a common black magnetic mineral consisting of iron oxide. Use: source of iron.

magnetize /mágnə tīz/ (**-izes**, **-izing**, **-ized**), **magnetise** (**-ises**, **-ising**, **-ised**) *v* 1. *vti* to become magnetic, or make an object or material magnetic 2. *vt* to hold a strong attraction for somebody ○ *prospectors magnetized by the possibility of finding gold in the hills* —**magnetizable** *adj* —**magnetization** /mágnə tī záysh'n/ *n* —**magnetizer** *n*

magneto /mag néetō/ (*plural* **-tos**) *n* a small alternator that uses permanent magnets to generate a spark in an internal-combustion engine, especially in

marine and aircraft engines [Late 19C. Shortening of *magneto-electric machine*]

magneto- *prefix* magnetic field ○ *magnetograph* [< MAGNET]

magnetoelastic /mag néetō i lástik/ *adj* describes a ferromagnetic material in which the elastic strain imposed on it determines its magnetization —**magnetoelasticity** /mag néetō ee lass tíssəti/ *n*

magnetoelectronics /mag néetō i lek trónniks, -elek-/ *n* PHYS same as **spintronics** —**magnetoelectronic** *adj*

magnetograph /mag néetō graaf, -graf/ *n* an instrument used to record variations in a magnetic field, usually that of the Earth

magnetohydrodynamics /mag néetō hídrō dī námmiks/ *n* the study of magnetic and electric fields in relation to the movement of electrically conducting fluids such as plasmas and molten metal (*takes a singular verb*) —**magnetohydrodynamic** *adj*

magnetometer /mágnə tómmitər/ *n* a device for measuring the direction and intensity of a magnetic field

magnetomotive /mag néetō mótiv/ *adj* relating to or producing a magnetic flux [Late 19C. After ELECTROMOTIVE]

magnetomotive force *n* a force that produces magnetic flux. Symbol F_m

magneton /mágnə ton/ *n* a unit that expresses the combined force and direction of a magnetic field (**magnetic moment**) such as that of an atom or elementary particle [Early 20C. < MAGNETIC]

magnetopause /mag néetō pawz/ *n* the region between the magnetosphere and outer space

magnetosphere /mag néetō sfeer/ *n* the region surrounding an astronomical object such as the Earth, in which charged particles are trapped and affected by the object's magnetic field —**magnetospheric** /mag néetō sférrik/ *adj*

magnetotactic /mag néetō táktik/ *adj* describes a cell or microorganism that is able to orient itself in relation to a magnetic field ○ *magnetotactic bacteria*

magnetotail /mag néetō tayl/ *n* the long tapering region of plasma that is driven away from an astronomical object's magnetosphere by the solar wind

magnetotaxis /mag néetō táksiss/ (*plural* **-taxes** /-ták seez/) *n* a movement of a cell or microorganism in response to a magnetic field

magnetotherapy /mag néetō thérrəpi/ *n* the use or wearing of magnets to prevent, alleviate, or remedy medical conditions

magnetron /mágnə tron/ *n* an electronic valve in which the flow of electrons is manipulated by electric and magnetic fields to generate microwaves. The microwave radiation produced is either pulsed, for use in radar applications, or continuous, as required for microwave cooking.

magnet school *n* N Am a state school that specializes in particular subjects, in addition to providing general education, and draws students from inside and outside the local area

~~**magnificant**~~ incorrect spelling of **magnificent**

Magnificat /mag níffi kat/ *n* 1. in the Bible, Mary's hymn of praise to God when she learns she is to be the mother of Jesus Christ, sometimes sung or chanted in church (Luke 1:46–55) 2. any hymn of praise sung or chanted in church [12C. < Latin, '(my soul) magnifies', a form of *magnificare* (see MAGNIFY), from the opening word of the Latin version]

magnification /mágnifi káysh'n/ *n* 1. INCREASE IN APPARENT SIZE the process of causing an object or image to appear larger than it really is, especially by using a lens or microscope 2. DEGREE OF ENLARGEMENT the amount by which an image is made bigger 3. RATIO INDICATING SIZE the size of the image of an object, expressed as a ratio of its actual size 4. INCREASING OF ACTUAL SIZE the process of increasing the actual size or magnitude of something 5. GROWTH IN IMPORTANCE the increasing of the importance attributed to somebody or something 6. ENLARGED COPY OF SOMETHING a copy of a map, photograph, or other image that has been made larger than the original

magnificence /mag níffiss'nss/ *n* 1. the impressive beauty or grandeur of somebody or something ○ *the magnificence of the palace and its formal gardens* 2. the great richness and splendour of somebody or something, usually indicating great wealth ○ *the magnificence of a royal wedding* [14C. Directly or via

Old French < Latin *magnificentia* < *magnificent-* (see MAGNIFICENT)]

magnificent /mag níffiss'nt/ *adj* **1.** beautiful and impressive ○ *a magnificent view of Rome from our balcony* **2.** exceptionally good of its kind ○ *The caterers had laid out a magnificent spread.* [15C. Directly or via Old French < Latin *magnificent-* 'performing great actions' < *magnus* 'great'] —**magnificently** *adv*

CULTURAL NOTE *The Magnificent Ambersons*, a film (1942) by US director Orson Welles. Based on a novel by Booth Tarkington, it is set in the midwestern United States during the Industrial Revolution and contrasts the declining fortunes of the upper-class Amberson family with the rise of a young entrepreneur. Despite suffering savage cuts at the hands of the studio, it is regarded as one of Welles's masterpieces.

magnifico /mag níffikō/ (*plural* **-coes**) *n* **1.** a rich or powerful person **2.** a nobleman of the Venetian Republic [Late 16C. < Italian, 'magnificent']

magnify /mágni fī/ (**-fies, -fying, -fied**) *v* **1.** *vt* INCREASE APPARENT SIZE OF SOMETHING to cause something to appear larger than it is, especially by a microscope or lens ○ *a virus magnified 50,000 times* **2.** *vt* INCREASE ACTUAL SIZE OF SOMETHING to increase the actual size or magnitude of something **3.** *vt* INCREASE IMPORTANCE OF SOMETHING to increase the importance attributed to somebody or something ○ *The complexities of today's medicine only magnify the need for better hospital management.* **4.** *vt* OVERSTATE IMPORTANCE to cause somebody or something to appear more important than is in fact the case ○ *The report was highly inaccurate, magnifying the dangers posed by the new vaccine.* **5.** *vi* HAVE ENLARGING ABILITY to have the ability to increase the size or magnitude of something **6.** *vt* PRAISE GOD to give praise or thanks to God (*formal*) ○ *'my heart doth magnify his holy name'* (*The Book of Mormon [part 1]*) [14C. Directly or via Old French *magnifier* < Latin *magnificare* 'make greater' < *magnus* 'great'] —**magnifiable** *adj* —**magnifier** *n*

magnifying glass /mágni fī ing-/ *n* a convex lens in a frame with a handle, used to make objects viewed through it appear larger

magniloquent /mag nílləkwənt/ *adj* employing impressive words and an exaggeratedly solemn and dignified style (*formal*) [Mid-17C. < Latin *magniloquus* < *magnus* 'great' + *-loquus* 'speaking'] —**magniloquence** *n* —**magniloquently** *adv*

Magnitogorsk /mágnitə gáwrsk/ city in southwestern Siberian Russia, on the River Ural. Population: 462,766 (1995).

magnitude /mágni tyood/ *n* **1.** GREATNESS OF SIZE greatness of size, volume, or extent ○ *computing the magnitude of heavenly bodies* **2.** IMPORTANCE the importance or significance of something ○ *the magnitude of the discovery* **3.** STATUS great personal importance or status ○ *a baseball star of unrivalled magnitude* **4.** GEOL MEASURE OF EARTHQUAKE SIZE a measure of the energy of an earthquake, specified on the Richter scale **5.** MATHS NUMBER ASSIGNED TO MATHEMATICAL QUANTITY a numerical value that describes the amount of something, usually expressed in terms of a multiple of standard units, or the item measured in this way **6.** ASTRON BRIGHTNESS OF ASTRONOMICAL OBJECT a numerical measure of the apparent brightness of an astronomical object, on a scale in which a lower number represents greater brightness [14C. < Latin *magnitudo* < *magnus* 'great'] —**magnitudinous** /mágni tyoodinəss/ *adj*

magnolia /mag nōli ə/ (*plural* **same** or **-lias**) *n* **1.** an evergreen or deciduous tree or bush with typically large simple leaves, widely cultivated as an ornamental. Flowers: yellow, white, pink, or green. Native to: North America, Asia. Genus: *Magnolia*. **2.** a creamy-white colour [Mid-18C. After Pierre *Magnol* (1638–1715), French botanist] —**magnolia** *adj*

Magnox /mág noks/ *n* **1.** an alloy of magnesium and other metals, especially aluminium, used to make casings for fuel in nuclear reactors **2.** an early type of gas-cooled nuclear reactor [Mid-20C. < MAGNESIUM + NO¹ + OXIDATION]

magnum¹ /mágnəm/ *n* **1.** a wine bottle that holds approximately 1.5 litres, the equivalent of two normal bottles **2.** the volume of liquid contained in a magnum [Late 18C. < Latin, a form of *magnus* 'large']

ORIGIN The Latin word *magnus* 'great', from which *magnum* is derived, is also the source of English *magnanimous*, *magnate*, *magnificent*, *magnify*, *magnitude*, *major*, *maximum*, and *mayor*.

magnum² /mágnəm/ *adj* describes firearms cartridges that have a larger charge and casing and are thus more high-powered than other gun cartridges of the same calibre ■ *n* a gun capable of shooting magnum cartridges [Mid-20C. Originally a proprietary name]

magnum opus *n* a great work of art or literature, especially the finest work produced by one artist or author [< Latin, 'great work']

Magog *n* BIBLE ♦ **Gog and Magog**

magot /ma gṓ, mággət/ *n* **1.** ZOOL same as **Barbary ape 2.** a crouching, often grotesque figurine in the Japanese or Chinese style [Early 17C. < Old French *magos*, a kind of monkey < *Magog* 'Magog' (see GOG AND MAGOG, used as emblems of ugliness in medieval romance)]

magpie

magpie /mág pī/ *n* **1.** BLACK AND WHITE BIRD a bird of the crow family with black and white feathers, a long wedge-shaped tail, and a chattering call. Genus: *Pica*. **2.** ASIAN BIRD a brightly coloured long-tailed bird of the crow family. Native to: mainly Southeast Asia. Genera: *Cissa* or *Urocissa* or *Cyanopica*. **3.** AVID COLLECTOR an enthusiastic or compulsive collector, especially of small objects (*informal*) **4.** AUSTRALIAN SONGBIRD a large black and white songbird. Native to: Australia. Latin name: *Gymnorhina tibicen*. **5.** TALKATIVE PERSON an incurable chatterer (*informal*) **6.** RING ON DARTBOARD the outermost but one ring on a dartboard **7.** HIT ON MAGPIE a hit on the magpie of a dartboard [Late 16C. < *Mag*, shortening of the name *Margaret* + PIE⁴]

Magritte /ma grēt/, **René** (1898–1967) Belgian painter. A leading member of the Belgian surrealists, his work consists of strange juxtapositions of ordinary objects and parodies of famous paintings. Full name **Magritte, René François Ghislain**

mag tape *n* same as **magnetic tape** (*informal*)

maguey /mə gáy, mág way/ *n* **1.** fibre made from the stalk of a tropical plant, or a rope made of this fibre **2.** a tropical plant that forms a cluster of 20–50 stiff upright leaves edged with prickles. Use: source of fibre, pulque production. Native to: Mexico. Genus: *Agave*. [Mid-16C. Via Spanish < Taino]

magus /máygəss/ (*plural* **-gi** /máy jī/) *n* **1.** in the ancient Persian religion of Zoroastrianism, a priest **2.** especially in ancient times, a man with supernatural or magical powers [Early 17C. Via Latin < Greek *magos* < Old Persian *maguš*] —**magian** /máyji ən/ *adj* —**magianism** *n*

CULTURAL NOTE *The Magus*, a novel (1966) by John Fowles. The plot concerns a young teacher, Nicholas Urfe, who takes a job on a Greek island and finds himself lured into an elaborate fiction staged by a wealthy resident, Maurice Conchis. Fowles uses this enigmatic story to explore the nature of individual identity and freedom of choice.

Magus *n* BIBLE ♦ **Magi** (*literary*)

Magyar /mág yaar/ (*plural* **-yars** or **same**) *n* **1.** a member of the Hungarian people that forms the largest population group of Hungary **2.** LANG same as **Hungarian** (sense 2) [Late 18C. < Hungarian] —**Magyar** *adj*

Mahabharata /mə haa báərətə/ *n* one of India's two great national epic poems, with nearly 100,000 verses, written in Sanskrit from about 300 BC. It tells of the great war in northern India between

the Pandava and Kaurava families. The 'Bhagavad-Gita' is the most celebrated section of the Mahabharata. [Late 18C. < Sanskrit, 'the great history of the Bharata dynasty']

Mahajanga /maáhə zhaángə/ port on the north-western coast of Madagascar. Population: 100,807 (1993).

maharajah /maáhə raájə/, **maharaja** *n* **1.** an Indian prince of a rank above a rajah, especially the ruler of one of the former Native States of India **2.** *S Asia* a person of aristocratic tastes and behaviour [Late 17C. < Sanskrit < *mahā* 'great' + *rājan* 'raja']

maharani /maáhə raáni/ *n* **1.** the wife or widow of a maharajah **2.** an Indian princess of a rank above a rani, especially the ruler of one of the former Native States of India [Mid-19C. < Hindi < Sanskrit *mahā* 'great' + *rājñnī*]

Maharashtra /maá hə ráshtrə/ state in western India, situated in the northwestern part of the Deccan plateau. Capital: Mumbai. Population: 96,752,247 (2001). Area: 307,690 sq. km/118,800 sq. mi. Language: mainly Marathi.

maharishi /maáhə ríshi/ *n* a Hindu religious teacher [Late 18C. < Sanskrit *maharṣi* < *mahā* 'great' + *ṛṣi* 'inspired sage']

mahatma /mə haátmə, -hát-/ *n S Asia* a title given to somebody who is deeply revered for wisdom and virtue [Late 19C. < Sanskrit *mahātman* < *mahā* 'great' + *ātman* 'soul']

Mahavira /maáhə véerə/ (599?–527 BC) Indian founder of Jainism. He was thought to be the last in a line of 24 great teachers.

Mahayana /maáhə yaánə/ *n* the branch of Buddhism that includes Tibetan, Chinese, and Zen Buddhism, developed around AD 1. It stresses compassion for all sentient beings and universal salvation. [Mid-19C. < Sanskrit < *mahā* 'great' + *yana* 'vehicle']

Mahdi¹ /maádi/ *n* in Islamic belief, a prophet or messiah who is expected to appear in the world sometime before it ends [Early 19C. < Arabic *al-mahdī* 'he who is rightly guided' < *hadā* 'lead in the right way'] —**Mahdism** *n* —**Mahdist** *n*

Mahdi² /maádi/ (1843–85) Sudanese religious leader. Claiming to be the Islamic spiritual saviour, he led a revolt in 1883, wresting control of Egyptian Sudan from General Charles Gordon. Born **Ahmad, Mohammad**

Mahé /maa háy/ largest island in the Seychelles, in the western Indian Ocean. Population: 59,500 (1987). Area: 148 sq. km/57 sq. mi.

Mahfouz /maa fóoz/, **Naguib** (*b.* 1911) Egyptian novelist and screenwriter. He is author of *The Cairo Trilogy* (1956–57) and other works that explore Egyptian society and culture. He won the Nobel Prize in literature (1988).

> 'Three years he had spent between fear and hope, death and expectation; three years spent in the telling of stories…Yet like everything, the stories had come to an end, had ended yesterday.'
> [Naguib Mahfouz, *Arabian Nights and Days*; 1982]

Mahican /mə héekən/ *n* **1.** a member of a Native North American confederacy of peoples who lived in the upper Hudson River Valley of New York State. Their descendants live in Wisconsin and Oklahoma. **2.** the Algonquian language of the Mahican people [Early 17C. < Mahican *muhheakunneuw* 'people of the tidal water'] —**Mahican** *adj*

mahi-mahi /maáhi maáhi/ *n* a tropical sea fish with a bright blue body and long dorsal fin. Latin name: *Coryphaena hippurus*. [< Hawaiian]

mahjongg /maá jóng/, **mahjong** *n* a game of Chinese origin using 144 small tiles bearing various designs, played by four people around a square table. The winning player is the first one who completes a particular pattern using 13 tiles. [Early 20C. < Chinese *má jiàng*]

Gustav Mahler

Mahler /máalər/, **Gustav** (1860–1911) Czech-born Austrian composer and conductor. He is best known for his songs and large-scale orchestral works, many of them involving voices, as in *Das Lied von der Erde* (*The Song of the Earth*) (1908).

Mahmud II /maa moöd/ (1785–1839) Turkish national leader. He was the sultan of the Ottoman Empire (1808–39).

Mahmud of Ghazna /maa moöd əv gaáznə/ (971–1030) Afghan sultan. He developed Ghazni, formerly Ghazna, into a centre of power and culture, through conquest.

mahogany /mə hóggəni/ (*plural* **-nies**) *n* **1.** REDDISH-BROWN HARDWOOD a hard reddish-brown wood. Use: construction, furniture-making. **2.** TROPICAL HARDWOOD TREE an evergreen hardwood tree cultivated for its timber. Native to: tropical America. Genus: *Swietenia*. **3.** REDDISH-BROWN a dark reddish-brown colour [Mid-17C. < obsolete Spanish *mahogani*] —**mahogany** *adj*

mahonia /mə hóni ə/ *n* an evergreen bush typically with spiny leaflets, widely cultivated as an ornamental. Flowers: small, yellow, in clusters. Native to: America, Asia. Genus: *Mahonia*. [Early 19C. After Bernard *McMahon* (1775–1816), US botanist]

mahout /mə hówt/ *n* in South and Southeast Asia, somebody who trains, drives, and looks after elephants [Mid-17C. Via Hindi *mahāut* < Sanskrit *mahāmātra* 'high official' < *mahā* 'great' + *mātra* 'measure']

Mahratta *n* PEOPLES another spelling of **Maratha**

Mahratti *n*, *adj* LANG, PEOPLES another spelling of **Marathi**

Mahy /máy hi/, **Margaret** (*b*. 1936) New Zealand writer. A children's author, her books include *The Change-over* (1984).

maid /mayd/ *n* **1.** WOMAN DOMESTIC WORKER a female domestic employee such as one working in a hotel or tourist accommodation **2.** YOUNG UNMARRIED WOMAN a young unmarried woman (*archaic or literary; sometimes offensive*) **3.** UNMARRIED WOMAN an unmarried woman past middle age (*archaic or literary; often offensive*) **4.** VIRGIN a woman who has never had sexual intercourse (*archaic or literary*) **5.** WOMAN SERVANT a female servant, especially one working in a large private house (*dated*) [12C. Shortening of MAIDEN]

maidan /mī daán/ *n* S Asia an open space where games are played and meetings are held [Early 17C. Via Persian, Urdu < Arabic *maydān*]

maiden /máyd'n/ *n* **1.** YOUNG UNMARRIED WOMAN a young unmarried woman (*archaic or literary; sometimes offensive*) **2.** VIRGIN a woman who has never had sexual intercourse (*archaic or literary*) **3.** HORSE YET TO WIN a horse that has never won a race **4.** CRICKET same as **maiden over 5.** GUILLOTINE in 16th- and 17th-century Scotland, a guillotine used to execute criminals **6.** N England FRAME FOR DRYING CLOTHES a frame on which wet laundry is hung to dry ■ *adj* **1.** FIRST done for the very first time (*sometimes offensive*) ○ *a maiden voyage* **2.** UNTOUCHED still in its original, unused, untouched, or unexplored condition (*literary; sometimes offensive*) ○ *maiden territory* **3.** FOR HORSES YET TO WIN for horses that have never won a race [Old English *mægden* < Germanic, 'young woman']

maidenhair fern /máyd'n hair-/ *n* an ornamental fern with slender dark stems and delicate fronds of numerous leaflets. Native to: warm moist regions worldwide. Genus: *Adiantum*.

maidenhair tree *n* TREES same as **ginkgo**

maidenhead /máyd'n hed/ *n* (*literary*) **1.** same as **hymen 2.** a woman's virginity [13C. < MAIDEN + *-head*, a variant of HOOD]

Maidenhead /máyd'n hed/ town and boating centre on the River Thames in southeastern England. Population: 59,605 (1991).

maidenhood /máyd'n hoŏd/ *n* the period of a woman's life before she marries or becomes sexually active (*archaic; sometimes considered offensive*)

maidenly /máyd'nli/ *adj* of, like, or thought suitable for a maiden —**maidenliness** *n*

maiden name *n* the former surname of a married woman who has assumed her husband's surname

maiden over *n* in cricket, an over in which no runs are scored

maiden speech (*plural* **maiden speeches**) *n* the first speech made in Parliament by a politician who has been elected for the first time

maid-in-waiting (*plural* **maids-in-waiting**) *n* a young, usually unmarried, lady-in-waiting

Maid Marian /-márri ən/ *n* **1.** in English legend, the beautiful young noblewoman loved by Robin Hood **2.** a character in morris dancing, played by a man dressed as a woman

maid of all work *n* a woman who does all kinds of domestic work (*often humorous*)

maid of honour *n* **1.** ROYAL ATTENDANT an unmarried woman of noble birth who attends a queen or princess **2.** INDIVIDUAL SPONGE CAKE a small individual cake with a base of short crust pastry topped with sponge cake **3.** N Am BRIDE'S ATTENDANT in the United States and Canada, the chief bridesmaid

maidservant /máyd survənt/ *n* same as **maid** (sense 5) (*dated*)

Maidstone /máydstən/ town in Kent, southeastern England, on the River Medway. Population: 138,948 (2001).

Maiduguri /máydo goöri/ city in Borno State, northeastern Nigeria. Population: 312,100 (1995).

maieutic /may yoötik, mī-/, **maieutical** /may oötik'l/ *adj* PHILOSOPHY same as **Socratic** [Mid-17C. < Greek *maieutikos* 'acting as midwife' < *maia* 'midwife']

maigre /máygər/ *adj* **1.** containing no meat and therefore suitable for eating on days when abstinence from meat is prescribed by the Roman Catholic Church **2.** describes a day when abstinence from meat is prescribed by the Roman Catholic Church [Late 17C. < French, 'lean']

mail[1] /mayl/ *n* **1.** ITEMS SENT THROUGH POST the letters, cards, periodicals, and packages that are handled and distributed in a postal system ○ *Is there any mail for me?* **2.** POSTAL SYSTEM the system that handles the collection and delivery of post (*often used before a noun*) ○ *send it by mail* **3.** SPECIFIC MAIL COLLECTION OR DELIVERY a particular collection or delivery of letters, cards, periodicals, and packages ○ *It came in yesterday's mail.* **4.** VEHICLE DELIVERING MAIL a car, train, ship, aircraft, or other vehicle used to collect and deliver mail **5.** same as **e-mail** (*informal*) ■ *vt* (**mails, mailing, mailed**) **1.** *Aus, N Am* SEND SOMETHING BY MAIL to send a letter, card, periodical, or package by mail **2.** E-MAIL SOMEBODY to send somebody a message by e-mail [13C. < Old French *male* 'bag, trunk' < Germanic, 'bag, wallet']

mail[2] /mayl/ *n* **1.** ARMOUR flexible armour made of interlocking metal rings or overlapping metal plates **2.** ANIMAL'S BODY COVERING the hard protective body covering of some animals such as turtles and crabs ■ *vt* (**mails, mailing, mailed**) PROTECT WITH ARMOUR to cover or protect the body with mail armour [13C. < French *maille* 'mesh' < Latin *macula* 'spot, holes in a net']

mailbag /máyl bag/ *n* **1.** a bag used for transporting mail, typically a sack made of coarse material **2.** *ANZ, N Am* a large bag, usually with a shoulder strap, used by a postman or postwoman. UK term **postbag 3.** *N Am* same as **postbag** (sense 2) [Early 19C. < MAIL[1]]

mail bomb *n* **1.** an explosive device sent by mail in a package or letter and set to explode when the package or letter is opened **2.** a form of electronic harassment in which massive amounts of e-mail are sent to a single system and crash it by filling up the available disk space —**mail-bomb** *vt*

mailbox /máyl boks/ *n* **1.** *ANZ, N Am* a container into which mail is delivered **2.** *N Am* same as **postbox 3.**

a storage area on a computer for e-mail or voice-mail messages [Early 19C. < MAIL[1]]

mail carrier *n* *N Am* a post office employee who delivers post to homes and businesses

maildrop /máyl drop/ *n* *N Am* **1.** a container into which delivered mail is placed **2.** a place where mail or messages can be left for later pick-up by somebody else, often secretly

mailed fist *n* the threat of military force (*literary*) [< MAIL[2]]

mailer /máylər/ *n* **1.** a packet or tube for sending objects of a particular kind through the post **2.** somebody whose job it is to address, stamp, weigh, and sort items for mailing [Late 19C. < MAIL[1]]

Mailer /máylər/, **Norman** (*b*. 1923) US writer. Famed for his World War II novel *The Naked and the Dead* (1948), he founded New Journalism with his coverage of 1960s political events, and shared a Pulitzer Prize for *Armies of the Night* (1968). See Cultural note at **naked**

> 'Once a newspaper touches a story, the facts are lost forever, even to the protagonists.'
> [Norman Mailer, *The Presidential Papers*; 1963]

mail form *n* a webpage designed to be used as an online order form

mailing /máyling/ *n* **1.** ACT OF SENDING BY POST the act of sending items for delivery by post **2.** SOMETHING SENT BY MAIL something sent through the post, especially as part of a mass advertising campaign ○ *send out a mailing advertising the service* ■ *adj US* RELATING TO MAIL suitable for or associated with mail ○ *a mailing label* ○ *mailing costs* [Late 19C. < MAIL[1]]

mailing list *n* a list, typically computerized, of names and addresses to which advertising material or information can be posted

maillot /mī ó/ *n* **1.** STRETCHY FABRIC a soft stretchable jersey fabric **2.** LEOTARD OR TIGHTS a leotard or a pair of tights made of maillot, worn for dancing or gymnastics **3.** SWIMSUIT a woman's one-piece bathing suit made of stretchy fabric, especially one with a high-cut leg **4.** CLOSE-FITTING TOP a tight-fitting knitted top or jersey [Late 19C. < French, 'swaddling clothes' < *maille* (see MAIL[2])]

mailman /máyl man/ (*plural* **-men** /-men, -mən/) *n* *N Am* same as **postman** [Late 19C. < MAIL[1]]

mail merge *n* the process of producing a personalized letter for each person on a mailing list by combining a database of names and addresses with a form letter created in a word processing program

mail order *n* **1.** a method of buying and selling goods, in which customers usually select what they want to buy from a catalogue, then send and receive their orders by post (*hyphenated when used before a noun*) ○ *a mail-order catalogue* **2.** an order for goods to be sent by post

mail-order bride *n* an offensive term for a woman brought from another country to be married, usually in return for a payment to a commercial agency (*informal*)

mailroom /máyl room, -roŏm/ *n* a room in an organization where mail is sorted, prepared, received, and distributed [Late 19C. < MAIL[1]]

mail server *n* a remote computer controlling the sending and receiving of e-mail

mailshot /máyl shot/ *n* **1.** the sending of unsolicited letters, advertisements, or brochures to a large number of people at one time **2.** a letter, advertisement, or brochure sent as part of a mailshot [Mid-20C. < MAIL[1]]

mail slot *n* *N Am* same as **letterbox** (sense 1) [Mid-20C. < MAIL[1]]

mailwoman /máyl woŏmən/ (*plural* **-women** /-wimin/) *n* *N Am* same as **postwoman**

maim /maym/ (**maims, maiming, maimed**) *vt* to inflict a severe and permanent injury on a person or animal, especially one that renders a limb useless ○ *maimed by a land mine* [14C. < Old French *mahaignier*]

main /mayn/ *adj* **1.** PRINCIPAL greatest in size or importance ○ *the main reason we're here* **2.** UTMOST exerted to the full or the utmost ○ *main force* **3.** NAUT OF MAINMAST on or relating to a sailing ship's mainmast ■ *n* **1.** LARGE PIPE OR CABLE a large and important pipe or line for the distribution of water,

gas, or electricity ○ *a ruptured water main* **2.** SEA the open sea (*archaic or literary*) [Old English *mægen*, influenced by Old Norse *magn* < Germanic, 'have power'] ◇ **in the main** largely or in general

Main /mīn, mayn/ river in south-central Germany. Length: 523 km/325 mi.

main chance *n* a good opportunity for personal gain or advantage ○ *have an eye to the main chance*

main course *n* the most substantial dish eaten at a meal with several courses

main drag *n N Am* the principal street of a town or city (*informal*)

Maine /mayn/ state in the northeastern United States, bordered by New Hampshire, Canada, and the Atlantic Ocean. Capital: Augusta. Population: 1,294,464 (2002 estimate). Area: 87,389 sq. km/33,741 sq. mi.

Maine coon, **Maine coon cat** *n* a large domestic cat with a long-haired coat that is usually brown with bold black stripes, belonging to a breed that developed in North America

mainframe /máyn fraym/ *n* a fast powerful computer with a large storage capacity that can accommodate several users simultaneously

mainland /máynlənd, -land/ *n* the principal landmass of a continent or country as distinct from its islands, and sometimes also excluding its peninsulas (*often used before a noun*) ○ *a ferry from the mainland* —**mainlander** *n*

Mainland /máynlənd/ **1.** largest of the Orkney Islands, northeastern Scotland. Population: 15,123 (1991). Area: 500 sq. km/195 sq. mi. **2.** largest of the Shetland Islands, northeastern Scotland. Fishing is the main occupation. Population: 17,562 (1991). Area: 1,053 sq. km/406 sq. mi.

main line *n* **1.** a major rail route between two cities, from which branch lines often lead off **2.** a major vein in the arm or leg into which drugs may be injected (*slang*)

mainline /máyn līn/ *vti* (**-lines, -lining, -lined**) (*slang*) **1.** TAKE DRUGS INTRAVENOUSLY to inject an illicit drug, especially heroin or cocaine, intravenously **2.** *N Am* CONSUME EXCESSIVELY to consume or do something excessively, or be affected by something excessively ■ *adj* OF MAIN RAIL LINE situated on or relating to a main rail line ○ *a mainline station* —**mainliner** *n* —**mainlining** *n*

mainly /máynli/ *adv* to a large extent or in most cases ○ *bacteria that live mainly in the small intestine*

mainmast /máyn maast/ *n* the principal mast on a sailing ship or sailing boat with more than one mast, usually either the foremost mast or the second from the bow

main memory *n* the random access memory of a computer, which executes instructions in real time

mains /maynz/ *npl* the central network of pipes or cables that distribute water, gas, or electricity from a local station to individual buildings in an area (*often used before nouns*) ○ *connected to a mains supply* [Early 17C. Plural of MAIN]

mainsail /máyn sayl, máynss'l/ *n* the largest and most important sail on a sailing ship or sailing boat

main sequence *n* a grouping of stars that consists of most of the known stars in the universe, represented on a graph of luminosity (**Hertzsprung-Russell diagram**) as a diagonal band

mainsheet /máynsheet/ *n* the rope that controls the angle of the mainsail on a sailing boat

mainspring /máyn spring/ *n* **1.** the largest and most important spring in the mechanism of a watch or clock **2.** the driving or motive force behind something ○ *It is the small companies that are the mainspring of this economy.*

main squeeze *n N Am* somebody's boyfriend or girlfriend (*slang*)

mainstay /máyn stay/ *n* **1.** somebody or something that plays the most important role in a particular group, place, or situation ○ *Tourism is the mainstay of the country's economy.* **2.** the strong rope or cable that secures the mainmast on a sailing ship

main stem *n* the principal waterway of a river, excluding its tributaries

mainstream /máyn streem/ *n* MAIN CURRENT OF THOUGHT OR BEHAVIOUR the ideas, actions, and values that are most widely accepted by a group or society, e.g. in politics, fashion, or music ○ *views well outside those of the mainstream* ■ *adj* REFLECTING NORM reflecting the most widely accepted views or tastes of a nation or culture and therefore not exceptional, extreme, or avant-garde ○ *The scandal, previously ignored by the mainstream media, is now on the front pages.* ■ *vti* (**-streams, -streaming, -streamed**) ENROL SPECIAL STUDENTS IN GENERAL CLASSES to enrol students with physical disabilities or learning difficulties in general school classes —**mainstreamer** *n* —**mainstreaming** *n*

main street *n* the most important street in a small town

Main Street *n US* people living in small towns, considered as a group and often described as conservative and unsophisticated ○ *Main Street will never accept those fashions.*

CULTURAL NOTE ***Main Street***, a novel (1920) by US writer Sinclair Lewis. This indictment of the narrow-minded complacency of small-town America is a satirical account of the stifling grip of Gopher Prairie, Minnesota, on Carol Milford, an intelligent young woman who marries a plodding local doctor. Her efforts to inject the townspeople with some of her own vitality are thwarted, and she runs away with a lover, only to be drawn back into the soul-destroying community she tried to leave behind.

maintain /mayn táyn, mən-/ (**-tains, -taining, -tained**) *v* **1.** *vt* MAKE SOMETHING CONTINUE to continue, or keep in existence, a situation, course of action, or condition without changing or impairing it ○ *They maintained production even with half the staff off sick.* ○ *The government maintained its confidence in the system despite teething troubles.* **2.** *vt* KEEP SOMETHING IN WORKING ORDER to ensure that something continues to work properly by checking it regularly and making repairs and adjustments if required ○ *The machine will give years of service if maintained properly.* **3.** *vt* PROVIDE SOMEBODY WITH FINANCIAL SUPPORT to provide somebody with the money required for a reasonable standard of living ○ *She maintains a big family on a tight budget.* **4.** *vt* ENABLE LIFE TO CONTINUE to sustain life in a person or animal ○ *nutrients essential to maintain life* **5.** *vt* DECLARE SOMETHING TO BE TRUE to insist on the truth of something in the face of challenge or disbelief ○ *He maintains that she knew all along.* **6.** *vt* DEFEND SOMETHING AGAINST CRITICISM to defend an opinion, idea, or argument against criticism ○ *The governor continues to maintain his position on cleaning up the environment.* **7.** *vi US* KEEP GOING to continue in the present state or situation without losing control (*informal*) ○ *Until the reorganization is complete, we're maintaining, and that's about it.* **8.** *vt* MIL DEFEND PLACE to continue to hold and defend a position when physically attacked ○ *The unit maintained its position in spite of heavy enemy shelling.* **9.** *vt* COMPUT UPDATE WEBSITE OR SOFTWARE to ensure that a website, a piece of software, or something similar is kept up to date and in good order for the benefit of users [13C. < Old French *maintener*, literally 'hold in the hand' < Latin *manus* 'hand'] —**maintainability** /mayn táynə bílləti, mən-/ *n* —**maintainable** *adj*

maintainer /mayn táynər/ *n* **1.** UPHOLDER OR PRESERVER OF SOMETHING somebody or something that preserves, upholds, or continues something such as a standard or tradition **2.** LONG-TERM EMPLOYEE an employee who is unwilling or unlikely to be lured away by a competitor or another company **3.** COMPUT SOMEBODY WHO UPDATES WEBSITE OR SOFTWARE somebody who is responsible for updating a website or software package

maintenance /máyntənənss/ *n* **1.** CONTINUING REPAIR WORK work that is done regularly to keep a machine, building, or piece of equipment in good condition and working order (*often used before a noun*) ○ *We take the car in for maintenance every six months.* **2.** UPKEEP the general condition of something with respect to repairs ○ *a car in a poor state of maintenance* **3.** CONTINUATION OF SOMETHING the continuation or preservation of something unchanged or unimpaired ○ *The maintenance of our security depends on constant vigilance.* **4.** PROVISION OF FINANCIAL SUPPORT the provision of enough money to ensure a reasonable standard of living ○ *responsible for the maintenance of two retired parents* **5.** MEANS OF SUPPORT the money that somebody has to pay to ensure a reasonable standard of living ○ *couldn't get by without the maintenance provided by their daughter* **6.** MONEY PAID TO SUPPORT EX-SPOUSE a sum of money paid regularly or in a lump sum by a divorced person, usually as part of a divorce settlement, to maintain the standard of living of the ex-spouse and any children **7.** LAW INTERFERENCE IN LEGAL ACTION formerly, unlawful interference in a lawsuit by an outsider who provides one party with the means to carry on the action

~~**maintenence**~~ incorrect spelling of **maintenance**

Mainz /mīnts/ historic city and river port in southwestern Germany, on the River Rhine. Population: 184,627 (1997).

maiolica *n* CERAMICS another spelling of **majolica**

maisonette /máyzə nét/, **maisonnette** *n* living accommodation with its own entrance, arranged on two floors of a larger building [Late 18C. < French, 'little house' < *maison* 'house']

Maistre /méstrə/, **Roy de** (1894–1968) Australian painter. He was the pioneer of postimpressionism, synchronism, and cubism in Australia. Full name **Maistre, Leroy Leveson Laurent de**

Maitland /máytlənd/ city in eastern New South Wales, Australia, a centre of coal mining, light industry, and agriculture. Population: 57,782 (2002 estimate).

maître d' /méttrə dée/ *n* OCCUPATIONS same as **maître d'hôtel** (sense 1) (*informal*)

maître d'hôtel /méttrə dō tél/ (*plural* **maîtres d'hôtel** /*pronunc. same*/) *n* **1.** a head-waiter in a restaurant or a hotel dining room **2.** same as **major-domo** (sense 1) [Mid-16C. < French, literally 'master of house']

maize /mayz/ *n* **1.** the grain of the maize plant. Use: vegetable, livestock feed, ground for flour, cooking oil. (*often used before a noun*) ○ *maize oil* **2.** an annual cereal grass that yields densely packed ears (**cobs**) of yellow grains. Native to: Central and South America. Latin name: *Zea mays*. ▶ N Am term **corn** [1] [Mid-16C. Directly or via French *maïs* < Spanish *maíz* < Taino *mahis*]

Maj. *abbr* MIL Major

majestic /mə jéstik/ *adj* **1.** greatly impressive in appearance ○ *the majestic plains* **2.** showing great dignity and grandeur ○ *her majestic bearing* —**majestically** *adv*

majesty /májjəsti/ *n* **1.** SPLENDOUR awesomely large size or great splendour ○ *the majesty of the Rocky Mountain peaks* **2.** DIGNITY a deeply impressive dignified quality ○ *a duchess whose majesty was clearly present in her every move* **3.** POWER supreme authority and power ○ *The full majesty of the Crown was brought to bear during the diplomatic mission.* [13C. Via Old French *majesté* < Latin *majestas* < *major* (see MAJOR)]

Majesty (*plural* **-ties**) *n* the title used to address or refer to a king or queen ○ *Her Majesty the Queen*

Maj. Gen. *abbr* MIL Major General

majlis /májjliss/ *n* in various countries in North Africa and Southwest Asia an assembly or parliament [Early 19C. < Arabic, 'place of session' < *jalasa* 'be seated']

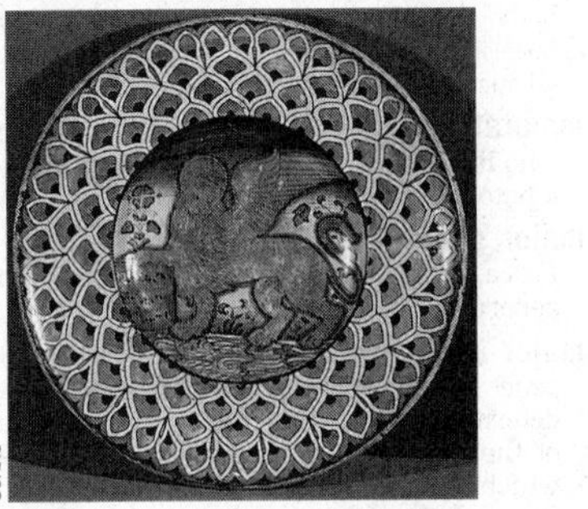

Corbis

majolica

majolica /mə jóllikə, -yólli-/, **maiolica** /mə yóllikə/ *n* Italian earthenware that is coated with a tin oxide glaze and highly decorated [Mid-16C. < Italian, old form of MAJORCA]

major /máyjər/ *n* **1.** MIL MILITARY RANK an officer in the US, Canadian, or British armies, the US or Canadian air forces, and the US Marine Corps of a rank above captain **2.** LAW SOMEBODY OF LEGAL AGE somebody who has reached the age at which a person is deemed

fully responsible for his or her actions **3.** *ANZ, N Am* EDUC **MAIN SUBJECT** the field of study in which a college or university student chooses to specialize ○ *a major in philosophy* **4.** *ANZ, N Am* EDUC **STUDENT IN SPECIALISM** a student studying a particular academic specialism ○ *a math major* **5.** MUSIC **MUSICAL KEY** a key or harmony based on a musical scale that has intervals of a semitone between the third and fourth and the seventh and eighth notes (**major scale**) **6.** FOOTBALL **GOAL** in Australian Rules football, a goal ■ *adj* **1. OF HIGH STANDING** greater in importance than most others ○ *a major recording artist* **2. SIGNIFICANT** of considerable size, extent, degree, or significance ○ *major bridge repairs* **3. SERIOUS** of great severity ○ *a major illness* **4. LARGE** great in number or proportion ○ *A major part of the meeting was devoted to agreeing on our report.* **5.** LAW **OF LEGAL AGE** of the age at which a person is deemed fully responsible for his or her actions **6.** EDUC **OF PRINCIPAL SUBJECT** relating to a subject studied as a specialism in a college or university **7.** MUSIC **DESCRIBES MUSICAL SCALE** describes a musical scale that has intervals of a semitone between the third and fourth and the seventh and eighth notes ○ *in a major key* ○ *a major sixth* **8.** MUSIC **DESCRIBES MUSICAL INTERVAL** describes the interval between the keynote of a major scale and any other note in it, excluding the perfect intervals ○ *a major sixth* **9.** MUSIC **DESCRIBES MUSICAL KEY** describes a key that is based on a major scale ○ *in B major* **10. ELDER** in British public schools, used after the surname to refer to the elder of two brothers (*dated*) ○ *Hobbs major* ■ *vi* (**-jors, -joring, -jored**) *ANZ, N Am* EDUC **STUDY AS MAIN SUBJECT** to make a particular subject the main field of study in a college or university ○ *She majored in economics.* [13C. < Latin, 'greater' < *magnus* 'great']

Major /máyjər/, **John** (*b.* 1943) British prime minister (1990–97). During his premiership he worked to set up peace talks in Northern Ireland, but in some areas of policy he was hampered by splits within the Conservative Party on the issue of closer European integration. See table at **prime minister**

> 'It is time to get back to basics: to self-discipline and respect for the law, to consideration for others, to accepting responsibility for yourself and your family, and not shuffling it off on the state.'
> [John Major, *Speech, Conservative party conference*, 8 October 1993]

Major, Dame Malvina (*b.* 1943) New Zealand opera singer. A soprano, she performed with numerous international companies. Full name **Major, Dame Malvina Lorraine**

Majorca /mə yáwrkə, -jáwr-/, **Mallorca** /mə yáwrkə/ largest of the Balearic Islands, an autonomous region of Spain, in the western Mediterranean Sea. Population: 676,516 (2001). Area: 3,624 sq. km/1,399 sq. mi. Spanish name **Mallorca** —**Majorcan** *n, adj*

major-domo /-dṓmō/ (*plural* **major-domos**) *n* **1.** the chief manservant in a large household, especially a royal or noble household, responsible for managing domestic affairs **2.** somebody responsible for managing affairs and making arrangements for somebody else (*humorous*) [Late 16C. Via French, Italian, Spanish < medieval Latin *major domus* 'chief of the house' < Latin *magnus* 'great' + *domus* 'house']

majorette /máyjə rét/ *n N Am* a girl or young woman who marches in front of a marching band, twirling a baton

major general *n* an officer in the US Army, Air Force, or Marine Corps of a rank above brigadier general

major histocompatibility complex *n* a cluster of genes occurring in humans and other animals that determines the recognizable pattern on the surface of the body's cells. This determines the extent to which an individual's immune system will accept or reject tissue from another individual.

majoritarian /mə jórri táiri ən/ *US adj* resulting from or based on rule by the majority in any given group ■ *n* somebody who believes that a group should be ruled in the way chosen by the majority of its members —**majoritarianism** *n*

majority /mə jórrəti/ (*plural* **-ties**) *n* **1. GREATER NUMBER OF PEOPLE OR THINGS** most of the people or things in a large group (*takes a singular or plural verb*) ○ *The majority of women now work.* **2. DIFFERENCE IN NUMBER OF VOTES** the number of votes by which the winning party or group beats the opposition ○ *swept to power with an overwhelming majority* **3.** POL **GROUP IN POWER** the most powerful party or group voting together in a legislature **4.** LAW **AGE OF LEGAL RESPONSIBILITY** the age, generally either 18 or 21, at which somebody is legally responsible and can assume civil duties and rights such as serving on a jury or voting **5.** MIL **RANK OF MAJOR** the rank and tenure of a major

USAGE majority as a singular or plural? When you use ***majority*** to refer to a group of people or things as a unit or whole, use a singular verb: *A majority of the House intends to support the motion.* When you use ***majority*** to refer to individuals within the group, use a plural verb: *The majority of our students live on campus, with a minority living in the surrounding district or area.* In that sentence, each student is under consideration; hence, the plural verb. Ensure that any pronouns referring to ***majority*** are in the same number denoted by ***majority***. Thus, it is incorrect to say *A majority of the House has cast their votes.* Say instead *A majority of the House has cast its vote*, or, if you are speaking of the members of parliament as individuals, say *A majority of the members have cast their votes.*

majority leader *n US* the head of the majority party in a legislature

majority minority *n US* a majority of people in an area who belong to a minority group overall ○ *a majority minority district*

majority rule *n* control of an organization or institution according to the wishes or votes of the majority of its members

major league *n* **1. MAIN BASEBALL LEAGUE** either of the two main professional baseball leagues in the United States **2. TOP SPORTS LEAGUE** a top league of professional football, ice hockey, or basketball teams in the United States ■ **major leagues** *npl N Am* **HIGH PLACES** the highest spheres of influence (*informal*) ○ *a politician operating in the major leagues* —**major-league** *adj*

majorly /máyjərli/ *adv* in a large degree or to a great extent (*informal*) ○ *an account that was majorly overdrawn*

Major Mitchell /-míchəl/ *n Aus* a pink cockatoo. Native to: dry regions of Australia. Latin name: *Cacatua leadbeateri.* [After *Major Thomas Mitchell* (1792–1855), explorer and Surveyor-General of New South Wales; because its cry was thought to resemble his name]

major order *n* in the Roman Catholic Church, one of the higher holy orders of bishop, priest, deacon, or subdeacon

major penalty *n* in sports such as ice hockey and lacrosse, a player's removal from the game for five minutes for a serious violation of the rules

major scale *n* a musical scale with intervals of a semitone between the third and fourth notes and the seventh and eighth notes and whole tones between all other consecutive notes. Major scales potentially have a bright and joyful quality.

major suit *n* in bridge and some other card games, spades or hearts, owing to their greater scoring potential

Majuro /mə jóōrō/ atoll and capital island of the Marshall Islands, in Micronesia, lying in the central North Pacific Ocean. Population: 19,664 (1988). Area: 10 sq. km/4 sq. mi.

majuscule /májjə skyool/ *n* a large letter used in writing or printing, e.g. a capital letter or any of the large rounded letters (**uncials**) used in ancient manuscripts [Early 18C. Via French < Latin *majuscula (littera)* 'somewhat larger (letters)' < *major* (see MAJOR)] —**majuscular** /mə júskyōōlər/ *adj*

Makalu /múkəloo/ mountain in the Himalayan range, on the Nepal-China border, estimated to be the fifth highest in the world. Height: 8,481 m/27,824 ft.

makan /má kan/ *n Malaysia, Singapore* food (*informal*) [Early 20C. < Malay]

makar /mákər/ *n Scotland* a writer, especially a poet (*archaic or literary*) [14C. Originally a variant of MAKER]

Makarios III /mə kaári oss/ (1913–77) Cypriot archbishop (1950–74) and first president of Cyprus (1959–77). He was noted for his efforts to unify Greek and Turkish Cypriots. Born **Mouskos, Mihail Christodolou**

Makarova /mə kaárəvə/, **Natalia** (*b.* 1940) Russian-born US dancer. A member of the American Ballet Theater, she excelled in classical roles, and later played a ballet dancer on Broadway in *On Your Toes* (1983).

Makassar /mə kássər/, **Macassar** former name for **Udjung Pandang**

Makassarese /mə kássə réez/ (*plural same*), **Makasarese** *n* **1.** somebody who was born or brought up in Makassar (now Udjung Pandang) in Sulawesi, Indonesia **2.** the Austronesian language of the Makassarese people. Native speakers: 1,600,000.

make /mayk/ *v* (**makes, making, made** /mayd/) **1.** *vt* **DO SOMETHING** used with a range of nouns to describe an action, where 'make' is used rather than a more specific verb ○ *She made no effort whatsoever to pass her exams.* **2.** *vt* **CONSTRUCT SOMETHING** to assemble something from constituent parts ○ *The exhibit contains items made out of recyclable materials.* **3.** *vt* **MANUFACTURE SOMETHING** to manufacture something as a business ○ *The company makes surgical instruments.* **4.** *vt* **PREPARE SOMETHING TO EAT OR DRINK** to prepare food or drink by mixing and usually cooking a number of ingredients ○ *Let's make soup.* **5.** *vt* **SHOW SOMETHING BY GESTURE** to perform movements or gestures that show the form of something or signal something ○ *She made the signs for 'I'll see you later'.* ○ *He made a circular motion with his hands.* **6.** *vt* **SAY SOMETHING** to say or deliver a statement or speech ○ *He made an emotional speech about his parents' struggle to get ahead in a new country.* **7.** *vt* **FORMULATE SOMETHING** to form something in the mind ○ *These politicians have made a commitment to try to solve the problem.* **8.** *vt* **UNDERSTAND SOMETHING** to comprehend the meaning or truth of something ○ *I couldn't make anything of her last remark.* **9.** *vt* **RECKON SOMETHING** to reckon or estimate something ○ *What time do you make it?* **10.** *vt* **BRING SOMETHING ABOUT** to cause a condition or situation to arise or exist ○ *The state made it illegal to sell fireworks.* ○ *Some people here have made this a personal issue.* **11.** *vt* **CHANGE SOMEBODY OR SOMETHING** to transform somebody or something into something else ○ *They made old clothes into patchwork quilts.* **12.** *vt* **APPOINT SOMEBODY** to appoint somebody to a particular role or position ○ *She's made me her deputy.* **13.** *vt* **PROVIDE SOMETHING** to provide something out of what already exists ○ *Make room for one more.* **14.** *vt* **CAUSE SOMEBODY TO ACT** to cause somebody to do something or act in a particular way ○ *I made him realize how wrong he'd been.* ○ *You made me lose my place.* **15.** *vt* **FORCE SOMEBODY TO ACT** to force somebody or something to do something or act in a particular way ○ *You can't make me wear that dress.* **16.** *vt* **BE MEANT TO BE SOMETHING** to cause somebody or something to exist for a particular reason (*usually passive*) ○ *She was made to be a star.* **17.** *vt* **EARN MONEY** to earn or be paid a sum of money ○ *He makes fifty thousand a year.* **18.** *vt* **CAUSE SOUND TO BE HEARD** to produce or give rise to a sound ○ *She made a choking noise in her throat.* **19.** *vt* **PREPARE SOMETHING FOR USE** to arrange something properly for later use ○ *He made the bed carefully.* **20.** *vt* **SCHEDULE MEETING** to fix a meeting or time ○ *Let's make a date for Friday.* **21.** *vt* **REPRESENT SOMETHING** to count as one in a series ○ *That makes the third time he's lied to me.* **22.** *vt* **TOTAL PARTICULAR AMOUNT** to amount to a total ○ *Five and three make eight.* **23.** *vt* **HAVE NECESSARY QUALITIES FOR SOMETHING** to have the qualities required to be something ○ *She'll make a very good doctor.* **24.** *vt* **DEVELOP RELATIONSHIP** to acquire a friend, enemy, or acquaintance ○ *They made friends straightaway.* **25.** *vt* **CAUSE SOMEBODY TO SUCCEED** to cause somebody to be successful, or cause something to seem successful ○ *the novel that made her career* **26.** *vt* **REACH PLACE** to reach or arrive at a place ○ *I'm not sure we can make the island in this boat.* **27.** *vt* **BE IN TIME FOR SOMETHING** to be in time to do something or for something to happen ○ *We can make the 10:05 train if we hurry.* **28.** *vt* **COVER DISTANCE** to travel a particular distance ○ *They made only five miles a day on the ascent.* **29.** *vt* **BE INCLUDED IN SOMETHING** to succeed in being included or mentioned in something ○ *stories that never make the national news* **30.** *vi* **SIGNAL INTENTIONS** to act so as to indicate what is coming ○ *They made as if to leave.* **31.** *vt* **HAVE SEX WITH SOMEBODY** to succeed in having sex with somebody (*dated slang*) **32.** *vt* CARDS **FULFIL BRIDGE CONTRACT** to fulfil a contract in a game of bridge by winning the required number of tricks **33.** *vt* CARDS **WIN TRICK IN CARDS** to win a trick in a card game **34.** *vt* ELECTRONICS **CLOSE CIRCUIT** to close an electrical circuit **35.** *vi* AGRIC **MATURE** to dry and mature (*refers to hay*) ■ *n* **1. BRAND** a brand of something such as an appliance, car, or machine ○ *Specify the make and model of the car.* **2.**

PROCESS AND OUTPUT the process of making something, or the amount or number made **3.** IDENTIFICATION the identification of somebody or something, usually made with the help of police records or information (*slang*) ○ *The police got a make on him from their records.* **4.** BUILD OR APPEARANCE the way that something has been made, or the size or shape it naturally has (*literary*) ○ *a woodland cabin of rustic make* [Old English *macian* < Indo-European, 'kneading'] —**makable** *adj* ◇ **have it made** to be in a position to succeed at something without obstacles or serious problems (*informal*) ◇ **made for somebody** *or* **something** ideally suited to somebody or something ◇ **make do (with something)** to use something that is an unsatisfactory substitute or temporary alternative for the real thing ◇ **make it 1.** to be successful (*informal*) ○ *You'll never make it as an actor.* **2.** to succeed in getting somewhere ○ *We finally made it to the top of the hill.* **3.** to be able to attend ○ *I can't make it to the party tonight.* ◇ **make like** to pretend (*informal*) ○ *She made like she was doing the breaststroke.* ◇ **make nice (to** *or* **with somebody)** *US* to be conciliatory and often ingratiatingly friendly towards somebody (*informal*) ◇ **on the make 1.** trying hard to gain a profit or advantage, especially using underhand or dishonest means (*informal*) **2.** looking for or making efforts to persuade somebody to be a sexual partner (*slang*)

make after *vt* to chase after somebody or something

make away *vi* same as **make off**

make away with *vt* **1.** STEAL SOMETHING to steal something and abscond with it ○ *They made away with the week's takings.* **2.** ABDUCT SOMEBODY to carry somebody off by force **3.** DESTROY SOMETHING INCRIMINATING to destroy or get rid of something incriminating ○ *We think someone's made away with the evidence.* **4.** KILL SOMEBODY to kill somebody (*dated*)

make for *vt* **1.** to move in the direction of somebody or something ○ *The reporters made for the courtroom.* **2.** to result in a particular situation ○ *This plan will make for a successful product launch.*

make off *vi* to leave a place quickly, usually with good reason

make off with *vt* same as **make away with**

make out *v* **1.** *vt* SEE OR HEAR SOMETHING INDISTINCTLY to see or hear somebody or something, but usually with difficulty or not clearly ○ *I could just make out her profile in the darkness.* **2.** *vt* COMPREHEND SOMETHING to identify or understand something ○ *I can't make out the suspect's motive.* **3.** *vt* COMPLETE SOMETHING IN WRITING to write necessary information such as the date and the recipient's name on a bill or similar document ○ *The deed is made out in my spouse's name.* **4.** *vt* INTIMATE SOMETHING to suggest or imply something that may not be true ○ *The kids make him out to be a real tyrant.* **5.** *vt* ARGUE IN SUPPORT OF SOMETHING to try to prove something is true or valid by giving good reasons ○ *made out a case for keeping the work in-house* **6.** *vi* MANAGE to perform in a situation (*informal*) ○ *How did you make out in the test?* **7.** *vi N Am* ENGAGE IN SEXUAL ACTIVITIES WITHOUT INTERCOURSE to kiss and caress somebody as an expression of sexual desire (*slang*)

make over *vt* **1.** MAKE SOMEBODY ELSE OWNER OF SOMETHING to transfer the ownership of money or property to somebody, usually by means of a legal document ○ *half of her estate was made over to her cousin* **2.** CHANGE APPEARANCE OF SOMEBODY OR SOMETHING to make major changes to the way somebody or something looks **3.** *N Am* REFASHION GARMENT to alter or remodel a garment

make up *v* **1.** *vt* PREPARE SOMETHING to get something ready, especially by putting a number of items together ○ *I've made up a packed lunch.* **2.** *vt* FORM WHOLE to be the constituent members or parts that together form a whole ○ *a group made up of four men and six women* **3.** *vt* CONSTITUTE SOMETHING to be a particular part or proportion of something ○ *Women make up more than half the country's workforce.* **4.** *vt* PROVIDE SUPPLEMENTARY QUANTITY to provide something, e.g. an additional sum of money, to raise an existing amount to the required amount ○ *You three pay £10 each and I'll make up the rest.* **5.** *vi* COMPENSATE to compensate for a failing such as a disappointment, deficiency, or shortcoming ○ *I'll buy lunch to make up for being late.* **6.** *vt* FABRICATE STORY to invent an excuse, fact, or story ○ *made the whole story up to shock her parents* **7.** *vt* PUT ON FACIAL COSMETICS to apply cosmetics to your own face or somebody else's face **8.** *vti* PREPARE APPEARANCE FOR PERFORMANCE to prepare somebody or yourself for an acting performance by applying cosmetics and fitting other accessories such as false hair, necessary for assuming a given role ○ *It takes her two hours to make up for the role.* **9.** *vti* RESOLVE QUARREL to become friends again after a quarrel ○ *Haven't you two made up yet?* **10.** *vt* CONSTR APPLY SURFACE TO ROAD to surface a road, e.g. with Tarmac™, concrete, or bitumen **11.** *vt* PRINTING ARRANGE LAYOUT OF PAGE to arrange columns of print and illustrations on a page ◇ **be made up** *regional* to be delighted

make up to *vt* **1.** to try to gain somebody's favour by behaving in a flattering and attentive way ○ *making up to the general manager's assistant* **2.** to flirt with somebody

make with *vt US* to start doing, using, or producing something (*dated slang*) ○ *Hey, let's make with the party, huh?*

Makeba /mə káybə/, **Miriam** (*b.* 1932) South African-born US jazz and folk singer. She introduced African song to international audiences. Born **Makeba, Zensile**

> 'Age is other things too. It is wisdom, if one has lived one's life properly. It is experience and knowledge. And it is getting to know all the ways the world turns, so that if you cannot turn the world the way you want, you can at least get out of the way so you won't get run over.'
> [Miriam Makeba, *My Story*; 1988]

make-believe *n* imaginary situations or events that somebody, especially a child playing, pretends are true (*often used before a noun*) ○ *watching them in their make-believe world*

make-do *adj* temporarily substituting for something else ○ *used a lid as a make-do plate* ■ *n* (*plural* **make-dos**) *N Am* a substitute, often an inferior one

makefast /máyk faast/ *n* a strong ring, post, or buoy to which a boat or ship is moored

make-nice *adj US* smoothly, often ingratiatingly friendly and conciliatory (*informal*)

make-or-break *adj* likely to result in either complete success or complete failure

makeover /máyk ōvər/ *n* **1.** an alteration of the way somebody looks, usually including changes of hairstyle, make-up, and clothing **2.** a remodelling of something that completely changes the way it looks

maker /máykər/ *n* **1.** CREATOR OR CAUSE a creator, source, or cause of something (*often used in combination*) ○ *a mischief-maker* **2.** PRODUCER OF GOODS a person or organization that produces goods (*often used in combination*) ○ *a maker of mid-priced textiles* **3.** LAW SIGNATORY OF DOCUMENT somebody who signs a legal document, especially a promissory note

Maker *n* in the Christian religion, God, regarded as the creator of everything

makeshift /máyk shift/ *adj* providing a temporary and usually inferior substitute ■ *n* a temporary and usually inferior substitute [Mid-16C. < *to make shift* 'try all means']

makeup /máyk up/, **make-up** *n* **1.** COSMETICS cosmetic products, especially for the face, e.g. lipstick and mascara **2.** THEATRICAL COSMETICS the cosmetics and other accessories such as false hair, that actors wear to alter their appearance on stage **3.** APPEARANCE WHEN MADE UP the appearance or effect produced by applying cosmetics, especially theatrical cosmetics, to the face ○ *He changed his makeup to reappear as an old man in the second act.* **4.** APPLYING ACTORS' COSMETICS the work of applying actors' cosmetics and other appearance-altering accessories such as false hair ○ *working in makeup* **5.** COMBINATION OF PARTS OR QUALITIES the way parts or qualities combine or are arranged, especially in somebody's personality ○ *Self-deprecation is an intrinsic part of her makeup.* **6.** PRINTING ARRANGEMENT OF TYPE the arrangement of typographical elements on a page

makeweight /máyk wayt/ *n* **1.** something placed on a scale to bring a weight up to a required level **2.** an extra person or object of no intrinsic importance introduced into a situation for the sole purpose of making up the required numbers ○ *invited her cousin along as a makeweight*

make-work *n N Am* unimportant or needless work assigned merely to keep workers busy

makimono /máki mṓnō/ (*plural* **-nos**) *n* a horizontal Japanese scroll decorated with paintings or calligraphy [Late 19C. < Japanese, 'a scroll, something rolled up']

making /máyking/ *n* **1.** CREATIVE ACTIVITY the activity of somebody who makes something ○ *during the making of the film* **2.** CAUSE OF SUCCESS something that causes somebody's success or progress ○ *a book that was the making of her career* ■ **makings** *npl* **1.** POTENTIAL the qualities required to become a particular thing ○ *He has the makings of a great musician.* **2.** NECESSARY INGREDIENTS the things required to make something, especially a dish of food ◇ **in the making** in the process of being made, formed, or developed ○ *a success story in the making*

mako[1] /maákō/, **mako-mako** *n* a small evergreen tree native to New Zealand that bears large clusters of reddish flowers. Latin name: *Aristotelia serrata*. [Mid-19C. < Maori]

mako[2] *n*, *vi Carib* another spelling of **maco**

mako shark /maákō-/ *n* a large slender blue-grey shark with a sharp nose and ferocious teeth that is prized as a game fish. Native to: southern oceans. Genus: *Isurus*. [Early 18C. < Maori]

Makurdi /mə kúrdi/ town in northern Benue State, eastern-central Nigeria. Population: 120,110 (1995).

makuta MONEY plural of **likuta**

Mal. *abbr* **1.** BIBLE Malachi **2.** Malay **3.** Malayan **4.** Malaysia **5.** Malaysian

mal- *prefix* **1.** bad, badly ○ *malpractice* **2.** improper or inadequate ○ *malnutrition* ○ *malfunction* [Via Old French < Latin *malus* 'bad', *male* 'badly']

Malabar Coast /mállə baar-/ region on the southwestern coast of India, that stretches from Goa southwards and includes most of Kerala State

Malabo /mállәbō/ capital, port, and largest city of Equatorial Guinea, on the northern coast of Bioko Island. Population: 30,000 (1995).

malabsorption /mál əb sáwrpsh'n, -záwrpsh'n/ *n* the inadequate absorption of nutrients from digested food in the alimentary canal, especially by the small intestine in coeliac disease

malac- *prefix* same as **malaco-** (*used before vowels*)

malacca /mə lákə/ *n* **1.** a walking stick made from the stem of the rattan palm **2.** the stem of the rattan palm, used to make walking sticks [Mid-19C. After MALACCA]

Malacca /mə lákə/ former name for **Melaka**

Malacca, Strait of strait in Southeast Asia connecting the Andaman Sea with the South China Sea. Length: 800 km/500 mi.

malacca cane *n* same as **malacca** (sense 1)

Malachi /mállə kī/ *n* **1.** in the Bible, a Hebrew prophet who wrote in the 5th century BC **2.** a book of the Bible that contains writings traditionally attributed to Malachi. See table at **Bible**

malachite /mállə kīt/ *n* a green copper carbonate mineral. Use: decorative stones, source of copper. [14C. < Old French *melochite* < Greek *molokhitis*, a stone similar in colour to the mallow leaf < *malakhē* 'mallow']

malacia /mə láyshi ə/ *n* the pathological softening of tissues or organs of the body such as bones or kidneys (*often used in combination*) [Early 18C. < Greek *malakos* (see MALACO-)]

malaco- *prefix* soft ○ *malacology* [< Greek *malakos* < Indo-European]

malacology /mállə kólləji/ *n* the branch of zoology that involves the study of molluscs [Mid-19C. < French < modern Latin *Malacozoa* 'soft-bodied creatures' < Greek *malakos* (see MALACO-)] —**malacological** /mállәkə lójjik'l/ *adj* —**malacologist** *n*

malacostracan /mállə kóstrəkən/ *n* a member of a common group of crustaceans that usually have stalked eyes, a carapace, and a tail fan formed from the rear limbs, e.g. a lobster. Subclass: Malacostraca. [Mid-19C. < modern Latin *Malacostraca* < Greek *malakos* 'soft' + *ostrakon* 'shell'] —**malacostracan** *adj*

maladapted /mállə dáptid/ *adj* unsuitable for or poorly adapted to a particular situation, function, or purpose —**maladaptation** /mál adap táysh'n/ *n*

maladaptive /mállə dáptiv/ *adj* **1.** poorly adapted, or unable to adapt well, to a particular situation, function, or purpose **2.** not facilitating or encouraging adaptation —**maladaptively** *adv*

maladjusted /mállə jústid/ *adj* unable to cope with everyday social situations and personal relationships —**maladjustment** *n*

maladministration /mállǝd mini stráysh'n/ *n* incompetent or dishonest management or administration, especially in public affairs — **maladministrator** /mállǝd mínni strayter/ *n* —**maladminister** /mállǝd mínnister/ *vt*

maladroit /mállǝ dróyt/ *adj* clumsy or insensitive in speech or behaviour [Late 17C. < French, 'not adept' < *adroit* (see ADROIT)] —**maladroitly** *adv* —**maladroitness** *n*

malady /mállǝdi/ (*plural* **-dies**) *n* **1.** a physical or psychological disorder or disease (*formal*) **2.** a condition or situation that is problematic and requires a remedy [13C. < French *maladie* < Latin *male habitus* 'in bad condition']

mala fide /mállǝ fīdi/ *adj*, *adv* done insincerely or dishonestly (*formal*) [Early 17C. < Latin]

Malaga /mállǝgǝ/, **Málaga** city, seaport, and holiday resort in southern Spain, on the Mediterranean Sea. It is the centre of the Costa del Sol, a major tourist region. Population: 535,686 (2002).

Malagasy /mállǝ gássi/ (*plural same or* **-ies**) *n* **1.** somebody who comes from Madagascar **2.** an Austronesian language, one of the official languages of Madagascar. Native speakers: 12 million. [Mid-19C. Variant of MADAGASCAR] —**Malagasy** *adj*

Malagasy Republic /mállǝ gássi-/ former name for **Madagascar** (1958–75)

malagueña /mállǝ gáynyǝ/ *n* **1.** a Spanish dance that is similar to a fandango **2.** a Spanish folk melody that is the music for a malagueña [Late 19C. < Spanish, 'from Málaga']

malaise /ma láyz/ *n* **1.** a general feeling of illness or sickness of no diagnostic significance **2.** a general feeling of worry, discontent, or dissatisfaction, often resulting in lethargy [Mid-18C. < French, 'ill ease' < *aise* 'comfort']

Malamud /mállǝmōōd/, **Bernard** (1914–86) US novelist and short-story writer. Known for his parables of Jewish life, he won a Pulitzer Prize for *The Fixer* (1966).

> 'I work with language. I love the flowers of afterthought.'
> [Bernard Malamud, *Writers at Work*, George Plimpton (ed.); 1984]

> 'If your train's on the wrong track, every station you come to is the wrong station.'
> [Bernard Malamud. Quoted in *Natural Born Winners*, Robin Sieger; 1999]

malamute /mállǝ moot, mállǝ myoot/, **malemute** *n* a dog with a thick grey, black, or white coat, belonging to a breed developed in Alaska for pulling sledges [Late 19C. < Inupiaq *Malimiut*, an Alaskan people]

Malang /mǝ laáng/ city in southwestern Indonesia, on the island of Java. Population: 720,534 (1997).

malapert /mállǝ purt/ *adj* impudent or bold in speech or behaviour (*archaic or literary*) [15C. < Old French, 'not experienced' < Latin *expertus* (see EXPERT)] —**malapert** *n* —**malapertly** *adv* —**malapertness** *n*

malapropism /mállǝ propizǝm/ *n* **1.** the misuse of a word through confusion with another word that sounds similar, especially when the effect is ridiculous **2.** an instance of using malapropism [Early 19C. After Mrs *Malaprop* (< MALAPROPOS), character in Richard Sheridan's play *The Rivals*] —**malapropist** *n*

malapropos /mál apprǝ pó/ (*formal*) *adj* OUT OF PLACE not appropriate to the situation in which something is done or said ■ *adv* INAPPROPRIATELY OR INOPPORTUNELY in an inappropriate way or at an inopportune moment ■ *n* INAPT OR UNTIMELY SPEECH OR ACTION something that is done or said in an inappropriate way or at an inopportune moment [Mid-17C. < French *mal à propos* 'ill-suited to the purpose']

malar /máylǝr/ *adj* relating to the cheek, the cheekbone, or the side of the head ■ *n* ANAT same as **cheekbone** [Late 18C. < modern Latin *malaris* < Latin *mala* 'jaw, cheekbone']

malar bone *n* ANAT same as **cheekbone**

Mälaren /méllǝren/ lake in southeastern Sweden. Stockholm lies on its eastern shore. Area: 1,140 sq. km/440 sq. mi.

malaria /mǝ láiri ǝ/ *n* an infectious disease caused by a parasite that is transmitted by the bite of infected mosquitoes. Common in tropical countries, the disease is characterized by recurring chills and fever. [Mid-18C. < Italian *malaria* 'bad air', once thought

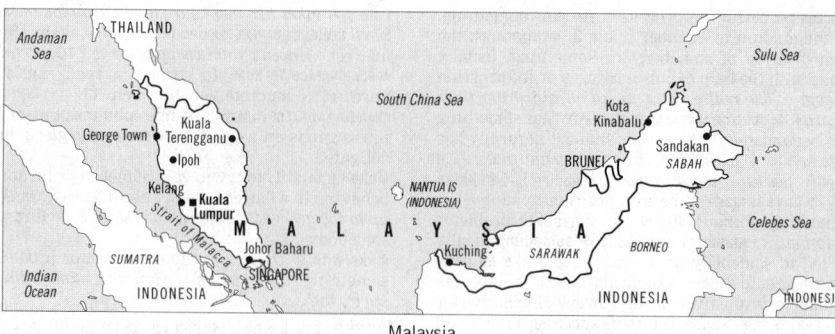
Malaysia

to be its cause] —**malarial** *adj* —**malarian** *adj* —**malarious** *adj*

malariology /mǝ láiri óllǝji/ *n* the scientific study of malaria —**malariologist** *n*

malarkey /mǝ laárki/, **malarky** *n* nonsense or rubbish, especially insincere talk (*informal*) [Early 20C. Origin ?]

malate /mállayt, máy layt/ *n* a chemical compound that is a salt or ester of malic acid

malathion /mállǝ thí on/ *n* a colourless solid organophosphorus insecticide. Formula: $C_{10}H_{19}O_6PS_2$. [Mid-20C. < MALATE + THIO-]

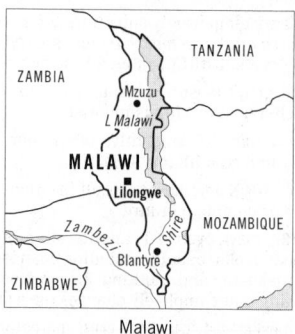
Malawi

Malawi /mǝ laáwi/ country in southeastern Africa. It became an independent member of the Commonwealth in 1964 and a republic in 1966. Language: English. Currency: kwacha. Capital: Lilongwe. Population: 11,651,239 (2003). Area: 118,484 sq. km/45,747 sq. mi. Official name **Republic of Malawi**. Former name **Nyasaland** —**Malawian** *n*, *adj*

Malawi, Lake same as **Nyasa, Lake**

Malay /mǝ láy/ *n* **1.** a member of a people who inhabit the Malay Peninsula, Indonesia, and other islands of the Malay Archipelago and the Philippines **2.** an Austronesian language spoken in Malaysia and in parts of Singapore, Borneo, Sumatra, Java, and surrounding areas. Native speakers: 22 million. Other speakers: 100 million. [Late 16C. < Malay *malayu*] —**Malay** *adj*

Malaya, Federation of /mǝ láy ǝ/ former state in the Malay Peninsula. It was incorporated into the Federation of Malaysia in 1963. —**Malayan** *adj*, *n*

Malayalam /málli aálǝm, mállay-/, **Malayalaam** *n* a Dravidian language that is the official language of the Indian state of Kerala. Native speakers: 30 million. [Early 19C. < Malayalam *Malayálam* 'mountain man'] —**Malayalam** *adj*

LANGUAGE HERITAGE See *Dravidian*.

Malay Archipelago world's largest system of island groups, comprising over 20,000 islands, mainly in Indonesia and the Philippines. Area: 2,800,000 sq. km/1,100,000 sq. mi.

Malayo-Polynesian /mǝ láyō-/ *n* LANG same as **Austronesian** —**Malayo-Polynesian** *adj*

Malay Peninsula peninsula in Southeast Asia that includes parts of Myanmar, Thailand, and Malaysia. Length: 1,210 km/750 mi.

Malaysia /mǝ láyzi ǝ, -zhǝ/ country in Southeast Asia, on the South China Sea, comprising the southern portion of the Malay Peninsula and parts of the Island of Borneo. It became an independent member

of the Commonwealth in 1957. Language: Bahasa Malaysia. Currency: ringgit. Capital: Kuala Lumpur. Population: 23,092,940 (2003). Area: 329,758 sq. km/127,320 sq. mi. Official name **Federation of Malaysia** —**Malaysian** *n*, *adj*

Malaysian English *n* a variety of English spoken in Malaysia. See panel on next page

Malbec /mál bec/ *n* a red grape variety from Argentina and Chile. Use: to make red wine.

Malcolm III /málkǝm/ (1031?–93) king of Scotland. He became king after killing Macbeth in 1057 and ruled until his death. He made peace with the king of England, William I (the Conqueror), in 1072.

Malcolm X

Malcolm X (1925–65) US political activist. He was a prominent member of the Black Muslims and founder of the Organization of Afro-American Unity (1964). Over time he moderated his views on Black separatism, and was later assassinated. Born **Little, Malcolm**

malcontent /mál kǝn tent/ *n* **1.** somebody who is discontented or dissatisfied, especially somebody who seems continually or chronically discontented **2.** somebody who opposes the established social or political system [Late 16C. < French, 'ill contented' < *content* 'content' < Latin *contentus* (see CONTENT [1])] —**malcontent** *adj* —**malcontented** /málkǝn téntid/ *adj* —**malcontentedly** *adv* —**malcontentedness** *n*

mal de mer /mál dǝ máir/ *n* seasickness [Late 18C. < French, 'sea sickness']

maldistribution /mál distri byóosh'n/ *n* unequal and unfair distribution of something, especially resources or wealth

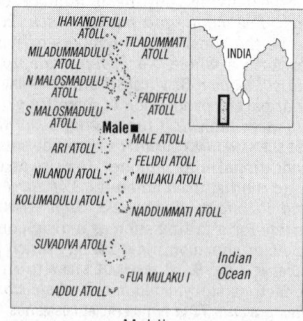
Maldives

Maldives /máwl deevz, -dīvz/ island country in South Asia, located southwest of the southern tip of India and consisting of a chain of almost 2000 small coral

malic acid

islands. It became an independent member of the Commonwealth in 1982. Language: Maldivian. Currency: rufiyaa. Capital: Male. Population: 329,684 (2003). Area: 298 sq. km/115 sq. mi. Official name **Republic of the Maldives**

Maldivian /mawl dívvi ən, mal-/ n **1.** somebody who was born or brought up in the Maldives off the coast of southwestern India **2.** the Indic language of the Maldives, also spoken in Minicoy Island, India. Native speakers: 200,000. —**Maldivian** *adj*

Maldon /máwldən/ historic town, river port, and local government district in Essex, eastern England. Population: 59,418 (2001).

male /mayl/ *adj* **1.** PRODUCING SPERM relating or belonging to the sex that produces sperm to fertilize female eggs **2.** RELATING TO MEN OR BOYS relating to, involving, or traditionally characteristic of men or boys **3.** BIOL FERTILIZING FEMALE SEX CELL capable of fertilizing a female reproductive cell (**gamete**) during sexual reproduction **4.** BOT BEARING ONLY STAMENS describes a flower or plant that bears stamens but not pistils and does not produce fruit or seeds **5.** ENG MACHINE PART OR FITTING describes a projecting part such as a bolt or plug that is designed to fit into a hollow part or socket that is the female counterpart ■ n **1.** BIOL MALE PERSON OR ANIMAL a person or animal belonging to the sex that produces sperm **2.** BOT PLANT WITH MALE FLOWERS ONLY a plant that has only male flowers [14C. < Old French < Latin *masculus* < *mas* 'male person'] —**maleness** n

Male /maá lay/ **1.** atoll in the Maldives in the northern Indian Ocean **2.** capital city of the Maldives, on the Male atoll. Population: 62,973 (1995).

male alto n MUSIC same as **countertenor**

maleate /málli ayt/ n any salt or ester of maleic acid

Malebo Pool /mə láybō-/ broad section of the River Congo. Area: 450 sq. km/170 sq. mi. Former name **Stanley Pool**

male chauvinist n a man who believes in the innate superiority of men over women (*disapproving*) —**male chauvinism** n

male chauvinist pig n an offensive term for a man who believes that men are innately superior to women, especially one who expresses his opinions in an aggressive or offensive way (*dated insult*)

Malecite /mállə sīt/ (*plural* -**cites** or *same*), **Maliseet** /-seet/ (*plural* -**seets** or *same*) n **1.** a member of a Native North American people who live in New Brunswick, Quebec, and Maine. The Malecites joined the Abenaki confederacy and fought against both the Iroquois confederacy and the British. **2.** the Algonquian language of the Malecite people [Mid-19C. < Mi'kmaq *malisiit* 'somebody who speaks an incomprehensible language'] —**Malecite** *adj*

malediction /málli díksh'n/ n (*formal*) **1.** a curse **2.** slander or evil talk about somebody [14C. < Latin *malediction-* < *maledicere* 'speak ill of' < *dicere* 'speak'] —**maledictive** *adj*

malefactor /málli faktər/ n a wrongdoer, especially a criminal [15C. < Latin < *male facere* 'do evil'] —**malefaction** /málli fáksh'n/ n

male fern n a fern that has creeping rhizomes and erect, spreading fronds with scaly stalks. The rhizomes produce an oil that is used to expel tapeworms. Native to: Europe, Asia, North America. Latin name: *Dryopteris filix-mas.*

malefic /mə léffik/ *adj* having a harmful or evil effect or influence (*literary*) [Mid-17C. < Latin *maleficus* 'evil-doing' < *male* 'badly']

maleficent /mə léffiss'nt/ *adj* causing harm or doing evil intentionally, or capable of such acts [Mid-17C. Back-formation < *maleficence* < Latin *maleficentia* 'evil doing' < *male* 'badly'] —**maleficence** n —**maleficently** *adv*

maleic acid /mə láyik-/ n a colourless crystalline solid. Use: manufacture of polymers. Formula: C₄H₄O₄. [< French *maléique*, alteration of *malique* (see MALIC)]

male menopause n a period in middle age when some men experience feelings of insecurity and anxiety about physical decline, sometimes compared to the effects of the menopause in women

malemute n ZOOL another spelling of **malamute**

Maler /maálər/ (*plural same* or -**lers**) n **1.** a member of a Dravidian people of northern India **2.** LANG same as **Malto** [Early 19C. < Dravidian, 'hill men' < *mala* 'mountain']

Malevich /mállivich/, **Kasimir** (1878–1935) Russian painter. He formulated an approach he called suprematism and contributed to the development of geometrical abstraction.

malevolent /mə lévvələnt/ *adj* **1.** having or showing a desire to harm others **2.** having a harmful or evil effect or influence [Early 16C. Directly or via Old French < Latin *malevolent-* < *male* 'badly' + *volent-*, present participle of *velle* 'wish'] —**malevolence** n —**malevolently** *adv*

malfeasance /mal féez'nss/ n **1.** conduct by a public official that cannot be legally justified or that conflicts with the law **2.** an act carried out by a public official that cannot be legally justified or that conflicts with the law [Late 17C. < Anglo-Norman *malfaisance* < Old French *malfaire* 'do ill' < Latin *malefacere*] —**malfeasant** *adj*, n

malformation /mál fawr máysh'n/ n variation from the usual structure or form of something, or an instance of this —**malformed** /mal fáwrmd/ *adj*

malfunction /mal fúngksh'n/ *vi* (-**tions**, -**tioning**, -**tioned**) to fail to function properly or normally, or stop functioning altogether, usually because of a fault or bad design ■ n a breakdown or failure to function properly or normally, usually because of a fault or bad design

Mali map

Mali

Mali /maáli/ landlocked country in West Africa. A former French colony, it gained independence in 1960. Language: French. Currency: CFA franc. Capital: Bamako. Population: 11,626,219 (2002). Area: 1,240,192 sq. km/478,841 sq. mi. Official name **Republic of Mali**

malic /mállik, máylik/ *adj* relating to or derived from malic acid [Late 18C. < French *malique* < Latin *malum* 'apple']

malic acid n a colourless crystalline solid. Source: fruits such as apples. Formula: C₄H₆O₅.

malice /málliss/ n **1.** the intention or desire to cause harm or pain to somebody **2.** LAW the intention to commit an unlawful and unjustifiable act that will result in harm to another [13C. Via French < Latin *malitia* < *malus* 'bad']

malicious /mə líshəss/ *adj* motivated by or resulting from a desire to cause harm or pain to another —**maliciously** *adv* —**maliciousness** n

malign /mə lín/ *vt* (-**ligns**, -**ligning**, -**ligned**) to criticize somebody or something in a spiteful and false or misleading way ■ *adj* harmful or evil in nature, effect, or intention [15C. Via French < Latin *malignus* 'of evil kind'] —**maligner** n —**malignly** *adv*

SYNONYMS *malign, defame, slander, libel, vilify*

CORE MEANING: to say or write something damaging about somebody

malign to criticize somebody in a spiteful and false or misleading way ○ *It was an old-fashioned firm and, as such, was much maligned by younger people.* ○ *You're maligning a man who was once your partner and a friend.* **defame** to attack somebody or somebody's reputation, character, or good name by making slanderous or libellous statements ○ *The lawyer claims his client defamed him in a television news programme.* ○ *The company spokesperson explained, 'Our rivals have defamed our character and called us pirates'.* **slander** to make a false and malicious oral statement about somebody ○ *Tensions remain high between the two families, with each side slandering the other.* ○ *The general sued, claiming she had slandered him by saying he helped cover up military atrocities.* **libel** to publish false and malicious statements about somebody ○ *The detective claimed that he was libelled in a television documentary.* **vilify** to make malicious and abusive statements about somebody ○ *There is nothing to be gained by vilifying these vulnerable homeless people.* ○ *The leader of the party has been vilified as a racist.*

malignancy /mə lígnənssi/ (*plural* -**cies**) n **1.** *also* **malignance** the condition or quality of being malignant **2.** a tumour that invades surrounding tissue and may spread to distant parts of the body by way of the lymphatic or circulatory system

malignant /mə lígnənt/ *adj* **1.** WANTING TO DO EVIL full of hate and showing a desire to harm others **2.** HARMFUL likely to cause harm **3.** MED LIKELY TO SPREAD describes a tumour that invades the tissue around it and may spread to other parts of the body **4.** MED LIKELY TO CAUSE DEATH used to describe a disease or condition that is liable to cause death or serious disablement unless effectively treated [Mid-16C. < late Latin, 'plotting against' < Latin *malignus* 'of evil kind'] —**malignantly** *adv*

malignity /mə lígnəti/ (*plural* -**ties**) n **1.** DESIRE TO DO EVIL intense hatred and a strong desire to do harm **2.** INTENTIONALLY HARMFUL ACT an intentionally harmful or evil act **3.** HARMFUL POTENTIAL potential to cause harm or death

malines /mə leén/ n **1.** thin stiff net with hexagonal holes. Use: dressmaking. **2.** TEXTILES same as **Mechlin** [Mid-19C. < French, after MALINES]

Malines /mə leén/ ♦ **Mechelen**

malinger /mə líng gər/ (-**gers**, -**gering**, -**gered**) *vi* to pretend to be ill, especially in order to avoid work [Late 18C. < French *malingre* 'sickly'] —**malingerer** n

Malinke /mə língki/ (*plural same* or -**kes**) n **1.** a member of a people who live in parts of West Africa, especially in Côte d'Ivoire, Mali, Senegal, and Gambia. They have traditionally used cowrie shells as a medium of exchange. **2.** the Mande language of the Malinke people. Native speakers: 4 million. [Late 19C. < Malinke] —**Malinke** *adj*

Malinowski /málli nófski/, **Bronislaw** (1884–1942) Polish-born British social anthropologist. He is regarded as the founder of the functional school of anthropology and was noted for his research into the formation of human culture. Full name **Malinowski, Bronislaw Kasper**

Maliseet *n*, *adj* PEOPLES, LANG another spelling of **Malecite**

malison /málliss'n, málliz'n/ *n* same as **curse** (*archaic*) [13C. Via Old French *maleiçon* < Latin *malediction-* (see MALEDICTION)]

maljo /máljō/ *n Carib* **1.** the belief that a conscious or unconscious look of envy or ill will can harm somebody **2.** a disease attributed to ill will, characterized by fever, changed colour, inability to urinate, a greenish stool, and loss of appetite and weight [Mid-20C. Probably < French *mal* 'evil' + *d'yeux* 'of the eyes' or Spanish *mal de ojo* 'evil of the eye']

malkin /máwlkin, máwkin, málkin/ *n regional* a domestic cat (*archaic*) [Late 17C. < *Malde*, early form of the name *Maude*]

mall /mawl, mal/ *n* **1.** *N Am* same as **shopping mall 2.** a sheltered and shady avenue or promenade **3.** in former times, an alley used for playing the game of pall-mall [Mid-17C. Shortening of PALL-MALL]

mallard

mallard /mállaard, -ərd/ (*plural* **-lards** or *same*) *n* a wild duck, the male of which has a dark green head with a white ring round the neck. Native to: northern hemisphere. Latin name: *Anas platyrhynchos*. [14C. < Old French]

Mallarmé /mál aar may/, **Stéphane** (1842–98) French poet. The author of *L'Après-midi d'un faune* (1876) and an originator of the symbolist movement, his work is characterized by obscurity and allusion.

> 'To *name* an object is to destroy three-quarters of the pleasure given by a poem, which is gained little by little: to *suggest* it, that is the ideal.'
> [Stéphane Mallarmé, *Réponses à des enquêtes: Sur l'évolution littéraire (On the Evolution of Literature)*; 1891]

mall crawl *n N Am* the act of going to a large number of different shops in a shopping centre (*informal*)

malleable /málli əb'l/ *adj* **1.** describes a metal or other substance that can be shaped or bent without breaking **2.** easily persuaded or influenced by others [14C. < Old French < Latin *malleus* 'hammer'] — **malleability** /málli ə bílləti/ *n* — **malleableness** *n* — **malleably** *adv*

SYNONYMS See *pliable*.

mallee /mállee/ *n* **1.** SHRUBBY EUCALYPTUS a low-growing eucalyptus tree. Native to: Australian deserts. Genus: *Eucalyptus*. **2.** GROUP OF MALLEE TREES a thicket of mallee trees **3.** *also* **Mallee** *Aus* AREA WITH MANY MALLEE TREES in southern Australia, land where mallee trees are the predominant vegetation [Mid-19C. < Australian Aboriginal]

Mallee /málli/ region in Northwestern Victoria, Australia, situated between the Murray and Wimmera rivers. Area: 41,000 sq. km/16,000 sq. mi.

mallee fowl *n* a large ground-dwelling bird that builds mounds of earth or sand to incubate its eggs. Native to: southern Australian deserts. Latin name: *Leipoa ocellata*. [Because it lives in mallee tree thickets]

mallee root *n* the thick underground stem (**rhizome**) of a mallee tree, often used as fuel

mallemuck /málli muk/ *n* BIRDS same as **mollymawk** [Late 17C. < *mal* 'foolish' + *mok* 'gull']

malleolus /mə lee əlass/ (*plural* **-li** /-lī/) *n* either of the hammer-shaped bony protuberances at the sides of the ankle joint that project from the lower end of the tibia and fibula [Early 17C. < Latin, 'little hammer' < *malleus* 'hammer'] — **malleolar** *adj*

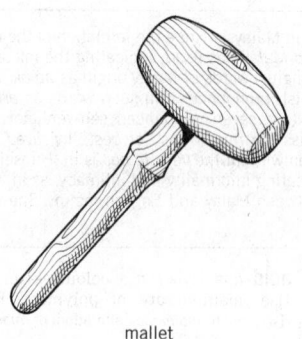

mallet

mallet /mállət/ *n* **1.** TOOL RESEMBLING HAMMER a tool with a large usually wooden or metal head that is used for driving another tool such as a chisel or for striking or moulding a material. The head of a mallet is larger than that of a hammer and usually cylindrical in shape. **2.** STICK USED IN CROQUET OR POLO a long stick with a cylindrical head, used to hit the ball in the games of croquet and polo **3.** HAMMER USED TO PLAY PERCUSSION INSTRUMENT a small hammer often with a padded head used for playing musical instruments such as the marimba and xylophone [15C. < French *maillet* 'small hammer' < *mail* (see MAUL)]

malleus /mɑ́lli əss/ (*plural* **-i** /-li ī/) *n* a hammer-shaped bone, the outermost of three small bones in the middle ear that transmit sound waves from the eardrum to the inner ear. ◊ **incus, stapes** [Mid-17C. < Latin, 'hammer']

Mallorca another spelling of **Majorca**

mallow /mállō/ (*plural* **-lows** or *same*) *n* **1.** a wild or cultivated plant with fine hairs on its stem and leaves, and disc-shaped fruit. Flowers: pink, purple, white. Genus: *Malva*. **2.** a plant such as lavatera that resembles or is related to mallow [Pre-12C. < Latin *malva*]

malm /maam/ *n* **1.** TYPE OF LIMESTONE a limestone that is greyish in colour and crumbles easily **2.** CHALKY SOIL a chalky soil produced by the crumbling of malm **3.** MIXTURE OF CLAY AND CHALK a mixture of clay and chalk used to make bricks [Old English *mealm* < Indo-European, 'pound, grind']

Malmesbury /máamzbəri/ ancient market town on the River Avon in Wiltshire, southwestern England. Population: 4,439 (1991).

Malmö /málmō/ industrial city and port in southwestern Sweden, opposite Copenhagen on the Danish side of the Øresund. Population: 254,904 (1998).

malmsey /máamzi/ *n* a dark fortified wine produced in Madeira, the sweetest type of Madeira wine [14C. Via Middle Dutch < medieval Latin *malmasia*, after *Monemvasia*, S Greece]

malnourished /mal núrrisht/ *adj* having a poor or inadequate diet — **malnourishment** *n*

malnutrition /mál nyoo trísh'n/ *n* a lack of healthy foods in the diet, or an excessive intake of unhealthy foods, leading to physical harm

malocclusion /mállə kloozh'n/ *n* an undesirable relative positioning of the upper and lower teeth when the jaw is closed — **maloccluded** *adj*

malodorous /mal ṓdərəss/ *adj* smelling unpleasant or offensive — **malodorously** *adv* — **malodorousness** *n*

malonic acid /mə lónik-, mə lónnik-/ *n* a colourless crystalline solid. Source: sugar beet. Use: manufacture of pharmaceuticals. Formula: $C_3H_4O_4$. [< French *malonique*, alteration of *malique* (see MALIC)]

Malory /málləri/, **Sir Thomas** (*d.* 1471) English writer and translator. He wrote *Le Morte d'Arthur* (1469–70), a retelling of the legends surrounding King Arthur, compiled from French and English sources.

maloti MONEY plural of **loti**

Malouf /mə loof/, **David** (*b.* 1934) Australian writer. His works include the novel *The Great World* (1990). Full name **Malouf, David George Joseph**

Malpighian corpuscle /mal píggi ən-/, **Malpighian body** *n* a cluster of small blood vessels enclosed in a capsule (**Bowman's capsule**) at the end of each of the tiny urine-secreting tubules (**nephrons**) of

the kidney [Mid-19C. After Marcello *Malpighi* (1628–94), Italian physician and anatomist]

Malpighian layer *n* the deepest layer of the outermost part of the skin (**epidermis**), now called the basal cell layer [See MALPIGHIAN CORPUSCLE]

Malpighian tubule, **Malpighian tube** *n* a narrow tube in the body of an insect that serves as an organ of excretion [See MALPIGHIAN CORPUSCLE]

malposition /málpə zísh'n/ *n* the undesirable position of something, especially a part of the body or a foetus in the womb — **malposed** /mal pṓzd/ *adj*

malpractice /mal práktiss/ *n* **1.** illegal, unethical, negligent, or immoral behaviour by somebody in a professional or official position, resulting in a failure to fulfil the duties or responsibilities associated with that position **2.** an act or instance of malpractice — **malpractitioner** /mál prak tísh'nər/ *n*

Malraux /mal rṓ/, **André** (1901–76) French novelist, art theorist, archaeologist, and public servant. Although known chiefly for his novels, his writings reflect the many fields in which he worked.

> 'Man knows that the world is not made on a human scale; and he wishes that it were.'
> [André Malraux, *Les Noyers de l'Altenburg (The Walnut Trees of Altenburg)*; 1945]

> 'Art is a revolt against fate.'
> [André Malraux, *Les Voix du silence (Voices of Silence)*; 1951]

malt /mawlt, molt/ *n* **1.** GRAIN USED TO MAKE ALCOHOLIC DRINKS cereal grain, especially barley, that has begun germination by being soaked in water. Use: brewing beer, distilling whisky. **2.** BEVERAGES same as **malt whisky 3.** BEVERAGES same as **malt liquor 4.** *N Am* BEVERAGES same as **malted milk** (sense 2) ■ *adj* CONTAINING MALT made from or containing malt ■ *v* (**malts, malting, malted**) **1.** *vti* CHANGE GRAIN INTO MALT change cereal grain into malt by soaking it in water to start germination and then drying it in a kiln, or to undergo this process **2.** *vt* MAKE OR MIX SOMETHING WITH MALT to make something with malt, or add malt to something [Old English *mealt* < Germanic]

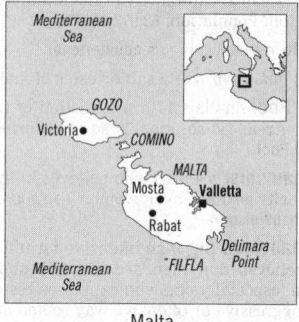

Malta

Malta /máwltə, móltə/ country consisting of two main islands and nearby islets in the central Mediterranean Sea. It became an independent member of the Commonwealth in 1964 and a member of the European Union in 2004. Language: Maltese, English. Currency: Maltese lira. Capital: Valletta. Population: 400,420 (2003). Area: 316 sq. km/122 sq. mi. Official name **Republic of Malta**

Malta fever *n* MED same as **brucellosis**

maltase /máwl tayz, -tayss, mol-/ *n* an enzyme that breaks down maltose into glucose

malted milk *n* **1.** a soluble powder made from dried milk and malted grain **2.** a drink made from malted milk, whole milk, ice cream, and flavouring

Maltese /máwl teéz, mól-/ (*plural same*) *n* **1.** somebody who comes from Malta **2.** an official language of Malta, belonging to the Semitic branch of Afro-Asiatic and featuring many words adopted from Italian. Native speakers: 300,000. **3.** (*plural* **Malteses**) BREED same as **Maltese dog** — **Maltese** *adj*

Maltese cross *n* a cross with four arms resembling arrowheads that taper towards the centre

Maltese dog *n* a small dog belonging to a breed with long white silky hair

malt extract *n* a sweet sticky substance produced from malt. Use: additive in cooking or brewing.

maltha /máltha/ n a black viscous bitumen that is a naturally occurring mixture of hydrocarbons [Early 17C. Via Latin < Greek, a mixture of pitch and wax]

Malthus /málthass/, **Thomas Robert** (1766–1834) British economist. His theory of population growth led to fears that the rising number of living people would produce widespread famine. He advocated birth control as a means of combating poverty. —**Malthusian** /mal thyóozi ən/ adj, n —**Malthusianism** n

'Population, when unchecked, increases in a geometrical ratio. Subsistence only increases in an arithmetical ratio.'
[Thomas Robert Malthus, *Essay on the Principle of Population*; 1798]

malt liquor n an alcoholic drink that is brewed from malt, especially one having a higher alcohol content than most beer or ale

Malto /mál tō/ n the Dravidian language of the Maler people. Native speakers: 100,000. [Late 19C. < Malto, 'language of the Maler'] —**Malto** adj

maltose

maltose /máwl tōz, -tōss, mól-/ n a sugar composed of two units of glucose. Formula: $C_{12}H_{22}O_{11}$. [Mid-19C. < MALT]

maltreat /mal tréet/ (-treats, -treating, -treated) vt to behave cruelly or unkindly towards a person or animal, especially by neglecting their welfare [Early 18C. < French maltraiter 'treat badly' < Old French traitier (see TREAT)] —**maltreater** n —**maltreatment** n

SYNONYMS See *mistreat*.

maltster /máwltstər, mólt-/ n somebody whose job involves producing or selling malt

malt sugar n BIOCHEM same as **maltose**

malt whisky n 1. a whisky distilled from malted barley, often one that is not a blend 2. a drink or measure of malt whisky

malvasia /málvə seé ə/ n the variety of grape that is used to make malmsey wine [Mid-19C. Via Italian < medieval Latin, variant of malmasia (see MALMSEY)] —**malvasian** adj

Malvern Hills /máwlvərn-/ range of hills in west-central England. Its highest peak is the Worcestershire Beacon, 425 m/1,395 ft.

malversation /málvər sáysh'n/ n dishonest or unethical conduct by somebody in a professional position or public office, often involving bribery, extortion, or embezzlement (formal) [Mid-16C. < French < Latin male versari 'behave badly']

malware /mál wair/ n software such as viruses or Trojans designed to cause damage or disruption to a computer system [Early 21C. Blend of MALICIOUS + SOFTWARE]

mam /mam/ n same as **mother**[1] n (sense 1) (informal or regional) [Late 16C. Probably < children's first attempts at speech]

mama /mə maá/, **mamma** n 1. same as **mother**[1] n (sense 1) (informal dated) 2. US a woman, especially somebody's girlfriend or wife (slang; sometimes considered offensive) [Late 16C. < children's first attempts at speech]

mamaguile /maámə gíl/ Carib n same as **mamaguy** ■ v (-guiles, -guiling, -guiled) same as **mamaguy** [Late 20C. Alteration of MAMAGUY, after GUILE]

mamaguy /maámə gí/ Carib vt (-guys, -guying, -guyed) to try to get something by flattery, especially by making exaggerated comments or compliments ■ n flattery or teasing [Late 20C. Alteration of Venezuelan

Spanish *mamar gallo* 'feed the cock', used to describe the behaviour of a cock that only pretends to fight]

mama's boy n N Am same as **mummy's boy** (insult)

mamba /mámbə/ n a large venomous snake, especially a green or black snake that lives in trees. Native to: tropical Africa. Genus: *Dendroaspis*. [Mid-19C. < Zulu *imamba*]

mambo /mámbō/ n (plural -bos) 1. DANCE RESEMBLING RUMBA a modern Latin American dance in 4/4 time that is similar to the rumba. It originated in Cuba. 2. MUSIC the music for a mambo ■ vi (-bos, -boing, -boed) DANCE MAMBO to dance the mambo [Mid-20C. < American Spanish]

Mameluke /mámmi look/ n a member of a former military caste, originally comprising enslaved Turks, that ruled Egypt between the 13th and the 16th centuries, remaining powerful until the early 19th century [Early 16C. Via French < Arabic *mamlūk* 'enslaved person' < *malaka* 'possess']

Mamet /mámmit/, **David** (b. 1947) US playwright and film director. His work, e.g. the play *Glengarry Glen Ross* (1992) is noted for its stylized dialogue and its focus on the alienation of lower middle-class life.

'We live in oppressive times. We have, as a nation, become our own thought police; but instead of calling the process by which we limit our expression of dissent and wonder "censorship", we call it "concern for commercial viability".'
[David Mamet, 'Radio Drama', *Writing in Restaurants*; 1986]

mamey /ma meé/ (plural -meys) n 1. a fruit with red skin, yellow flesh, and poisonous seeds 2. the tree that produces mameys. Native to: Caribbean. Latin name: *Mammea americana*. [Late 16C. Via American Spanish *mamei* < Taino]

mamilla /ma millə/ (plural -lae /-lee/) n 1. a nipple or teat 2. a protuberance or organ that resembles a nipple or teat [Late 17C. < Latin, 'little breast' < *mamma* 'breast'] —**mamillary** /mámmiləri/ adj —**mamillate** /mámmi layt/ adj

mamm- prefix same as **mammo-** (used before vowels)

mamma[1] /mámmə/ (plural -mae /-mee/) n the milk-secreting organ of female mammals, e.g. a woman's breast or a cow's udder. It includes the mammary gland and associated exterior structures such as the nipple or teat. (technical) [Pre-12C. < Latin] —**mammate** adj —**mammiform** adj

mamma[2] /mə maá/ n another spelling of **mama**

mammae ANAT plural of **mamma**[1]

mammal /mámm'l/ n a class of warm-blooded vertebrate animals that have, in the female, milk-secreting organs for feeding the young. The class includes human beings, apes, many four-legged animals, whales, dolphins, and bats. [Early 19C. < modern Latin *mammalia* < Latin *mamma* 'breast'] —**mammalian** /mə máyli ən/ adj

mammalogy /ma máləji/ n the branch of zoology that deals with the study of mammals —**mammalogical** /mámmə lójjik'l/ adj —**mammalogist** n

mammaplasty n SURG another spelling of **mammoplasty**

mammary /mámməri/ adj relating or belonging to the milk-secreting organ of a female mammal, e.g. the breast or udder [Late 17C. < MAMMA[1]]

mammary gland n a large milk-producing gland in female mammals that consists of a network of ducts and cavities leading to a nipple or teat. Mammary glands usually occur in pairs.

mammee /ma meé/ n TREES same as **mamey** (sense 2) [Variant]

mammee apple n PLANTS same as **mamey** (sense 1)

mammie n another spelling of **mammy** (informal)

mammiferous /ma míffərəss/ adj having mammary glands

mammilla n ANAT US spelling of **mamilla**

mammo- prefix breast ○ *mammogram* [< MAMMA[1]]

mammock /mámmək/ UK, regional (archaic) n a small piece of something ■ vt (-mocks, -mocking, -mocked) to tear something to shreds [Early 16C. Origin ?]

mammogram /mámmə gram/ n the procedure of taking an X-ray of all or part of the breast [Mid-20C. < MAMMA[1]]

mammography /ma móggrəfi/ n X-ray examination of the breast, used for the early detection of developing tumours, especially cancerous ones —**mammographic** /mámmə gráffik/ adj

mammon /mámmən/ n wealth and riches considered as an evil and corrupt influence [14C. Via late Latin < Aramaic *māmōnā* 'riches'] —**mammonish** adj —**mammonism** n —**mammonist** n

Mammon n in the Bible, the personification of wealth portrayed as a false god

mammoplasty /mámmə plasti/ (plural -ties), **mammaplasty** n plastic surgery performed on a woman's breast to alter the shape or size, e.g. as reconstruction following a mastectomy or as cosmetic surgery

mammoth /mámməth/ n (plural -moths or same) 1. EXTINCT ELEPHANT a large extinct elephant that had long curved tusks and was covered with hair. It existed mainly in the northern hemisphere and died out more than 10,000 years ago. Genus: *Mammuthus*. 2. SOMETHING ENORMOUS something that is a particularly large example of its kind ■ adj VERY LARGE of very great size or extent [Early 18C. < obsolete Russian *mámot*]

ORIGIN In its original Siberian language (possibly Ostyak) *mammoth* meant literally 'earth, soil': the first remains of *mammoths* to be found were dug out of the frozen soil of Siberia, and it came to be believed that the animals burrowed in the earth. The adjectival use of *mammoth* for 'huge' dates from the early 19th century.

mammy /mámmi/ (plural -mies), **mammie** n same as **mother**[1] n (sense 1) (informal; usually used by children) [Early 16C. Variant of MAMMA[2]]

mammy wagon n in West Africa, a bus with open sides that is used to carry both passengers and goods [Origin ?]

Mamoré /ma máw ray/ river in northern Bolivia, flowing northwards into the River Madeira on the Brazilian border. Length: 1,900 km/1,200 mi.

Mampruli /mam próoli/ n a Niger-Congo language spoken in Ghana and Togo. Native speakers: 200,000. [Mid-20C. < Mampruli] —**Mampruli** adj

mamzer /mámzər/ (plural -zers or -zerim /-zərim/), **momser** /mómzər/ (plural -sers or -serim), **momzer** n 1. in Jewish religious law, a child born of an adulterous or incestuous relationship 2. US an offensive term for somebody regarded as untrustworthy or contemptible (slang insult) [Mid-16C. Via late Latin < Hebrew *mamzēr*]

man /man/ n (plural men /men/) 1. ADULT MALE HUMAN an adult male human being 2. PARTICULAR TYPE OF MAN an adult male human being with a particular occupation, responsibility, background, or nationality (usually used in combination) ○ the TV repair man ○ I'm not a dogs man. 3. PERSON a person, regardless of sex or age (often offensive) ○ a six-man crew 4. HUMAN RACE the human race in general (often offensive) 5. MODERN OR EARLIER HUMAN BEING a member of the group that comprises modern humans and their ancestors. Genus: *Homo*. (sometimes considered offensive) 6. EMPLOYEE OR WORKER an employee or worker of either gender (often offensive) 7. MALE MEMBER OF ARMED FORCES a male member of the armed forces, especially one who is not an officer (usually used in the plural) 8. SERVANT a man who is a servant (dated) 9. VIRILE PERSON the personification of qualities traditionally associated with the male sex, including courage, strength, and aggression, or somebody with such qualities 10. HUSBAND OR MALE COMPANION a husband, or a man who is another person's companion or lover (slang) 11. TERM OF ADDRESS a term of address to a person of either sex (slang; sometimes considered offensive) ○ Cool it, man! 12. PIECE USED IN BOARD GAMES a piece used in playing board games such as draughts 13. MEDIEVAL VASSAL in feudal societies of the early Middle Ages, an adult male human who swore allegiance to a lord in return for help and protection 14. SHIP a ship, especially one of a particular kind (used in combination) ○ man-of-war 15. also **Man** US somebody in a position of authority, or a group that is seen as having an unfair advantage or undue power over others (dated slang; sometimes considered offensive) ○ in trouble with the Man ■ vt (mans, manning, manned) (often offensive) 1. SUPPLY SOMETHING WITH WORKERS to provide something with workers, operators, or military personnel 2. BE READY TO USE SOMETHING to be ready to

---
zh vision. In foreign words: kh German Bach; əN French vin; aaN French blanc; ö German schön, French feu; oN French bon; ôN French un; ü as in French rue. Stress marks: ´ as in secret /seékrət/, academic /ákə démmik/

operate or defend something ■ *interj* USED FOR EMPHASIS used to add emphasis (*slang*) ○ *Man, that was exciting!* [Old English *man(n)* < Indo-European, 'person, man'] —**man-like** *adj* ◇ **a poor man's...** a cheaper or inferior version of something, especially one that is more widely available than the original ◇ **as one man** unanimously or without exception (*often offensive if used of women*) ◇ **be your own man** to have the resources or confidence to be responsible for yourself or your actions (*often offensive if used of women*) ◇ **man and boy** throughout somebody's life ○ *He's lived in this house for 60 years, man and boy.* ◇ **to a man** everyone, without any exceptions (*often offensive if used of women*)

USAGE See *person.*

REGIONAL NOTE The use of address terms is both culture-specific and socially revealing. In the United Kingdom, there are a number of generic terms, all of which provide covert information on region or gender or ethnic origins. *Man* as in 'Are you coming, man?' is now occasionally addressed to females, as is 'you guys'. Terms such as *bo* and *mate* are still male and indicate a degree of friendship, whereas *Jimmy, Paddy, Mac(k),* or *Taf(fy)* can be condescending or offensive. Terms such as *kid* and *love* are addressed to all ages and both sexes, whereas *hen* and *cock* are gender specific.

ORIGIN The etymologically primary sense of *man* is 'human being, person', and that is what it generally meant in Old English: the sexes were usually distinguished by *wer* 'man' (which survives probably in *werewolf*) and *wīf* (source of modern English *wife*) or *cwene* 'woman'. But during the Middle English and early modern English periods 'male person' gradually came to the fore, and today *man*, meaning 'person', is decidedly on the decline (helped on its way by those who feel that the usage discriminates against women).

Man ➧ **de Man, Paul**

Man, Isle of ➧ **Isle of Man**

MAN /man/ *abbr* COMPUT metropolitan area network

man. *abbr* manual

Man. *abbr* **1.** PAPER Manila paper **2.** Manitoba

mana /maánə/ *n NZ* a life force associated with ritual power and high social status, especially in Polynesia and Melanesia [Mid-19C. < Maori]

man about town (*plural* **men about town**) *n* a sophisticated and cultured man who socializes in fashionable circles (*dated*)

manacle /mánnək'l/ *n* either of a pair of metal rings joined by a chain and fastened around the wrists of a prisoner to be restrained (*usually used in the plural*) ■ *vt* (**-cles, -cling, -cled**) to restrain somebody using manacles [14C. Via French *manicle* 'handcuff' < Latin *manicula* < *manus* 'hand']

manage /mánnij/ (**-ages, -aging, -aged**) *v* **1.** *vti* ADMINISTER OR RUN SOMETHING to be in charge of something such as a shop, department, or project and be responsible for its smooth running and for any personnel employed ○ *manages a department of 25 people* **2.** *vti* ACHIEVE SOMETHING WITH DIFFICULTY to succeed in doing something, especially something that seems difficult or impossible ○ *I finally managed to open the door.* **3.** *vt* HAVE ENOUGH ROOM FOR SOMETHING to have enough time or space for something ○ *couldn't manage a whole steak by himself* **4.** *vi* COPE IN DIFFICULT SITUATION to survive or continue despite difficulties, especially a lack of resources ○ *He manages with very little money.* **5.** *vt* HANDLE AND CONTROL SOMETHING to handle and keep control of something such as a weapon or tool ○ *could manage a computer without difficulty* **6.** *vt* DEAL WITH SOMETHING SUCCESSFULLY to deal with a situation or process that requires skilful control or handling ○ *managing patient care* **7.** *vt* DISCIPLINE OR CONTROL PERSON OR ANIMAL to keep control of a person or animal, or a number of people or animals, especially when they are wild or unruly **8.** *vt* BE SOMEBODY'S MANAGER to guide the career and control the business affairs of somebody such as a professional entertainer or athlete **9.** *vti* DIRECT TEAM ON PLAYING FIELD to direct the day-to-day operations, especially play on the field, of a sports team and its members (*used in professional baseball*) [Mid-16C. < Italian *maneggiare* 'train a horse' < Latin *manus* 'hand']

manageable /mánnijəb'l/ *adj* able to be handled or controlled without much difficulty —**manageability** /mánnijə bílləti/ *n* —**manageableness** *n* —**manageably** *adv*

managed fund /mánnijd-/ *n* a unit trust that makes considered investments rather than just following the performance of specific companies' shares

management /mánnijmənt/ *n* **1.** ADMINISTRATION OF BUSINESS the organizing and controlling of the affairs of a business or a sector of a business **2.** MANAGERS AS GROUP managers and employers considered collectively, especially the directors and executives of a business or organization **3.** HANDLING OF SOMETHING SUCCESSFULLY the act of handling or controlling something successfully ○ *crisis management* **4.** SKILL IN HANDLING OR USING SOMETHING the skilful handling or use of something such as resources

management accounting *n* ACCT same as **cost accounting**

management game *n* a computer game that simulates managing something such as a sports team or a business

management information system *n* a system for gathering the financial, production, and other information that managers need to operate a business, especially a system that is computerized

management sim *n* COMPUT GAMES same as **management game**

manager /mánnijər/ *n* **1.** ORGANIZER OF BUSINESS somebody who is responsible for directing and controlling the work and staff of a business, or of a department within it **2.** ORGANIZER OF SOMEBODY'S BUSINESS AFFAIRS somebody who organizes and controls the business affairs of somebody such as a professional entertainer **3.** ORGANIZER OF AFFAIRS OF ATHLETE somebody who organizes and controls the training of an athlete or a sports team **4.** COMPETENT HANDLER somebody who handles or controls something, especially somebody who works skilfully **5.** COMPUT PROGRAM FOR BASIC COMPUTER OPERATIONS a computer program designed to carry out the basic functions of a computer's operations **6.** LAW COURT APPOINTEE somebody who is appointed by a court to manage a business or organization in receivership **7.** GOV ORGANIZER OF PARLIAMENTARY AFFAIRS in Britain, a member of the House of Commons or the House of Lords appointed to organize matters of concern to both Houses of Parliament —**managership** *n*

managerial /mánni jéeri əl/ *adj* involving or characteristic of a manager or management, especially in business —**managerially** *adv*

managerialism /mánni jéeri əlizəm/ *n* the application of the techniques of managing a commercial business to the running of some other organization such as local government or public services —**managerialist** *n*

managing director /mánnijing-/ *n UK, ANZ, Can* somebody, usually the head of a board of directors, who has administrative control over a large company or other commercial organization

managing editor *n* an editor of books, newspapers, or other publications who oversees editorial process, budget, and schedules

~~**managment**~~ incorrect spelling of **management**

Managua /mə nágwə/ capital city of Nicaragua, located in the west of the country, near the Pacific Ocean. Population: 1,200,000 (1995).

Managua, Lake lake in western Nicaragua, the country's second largest. It is drained by the River Tipitapa. Area: 1,050 sq. km/405 sq. mi.

manakin /mánnəkin/ *n* a small bird with a short beak and bright colourful feathers. Native to: South and Central America. Family: Pipridae. ◊ **mannikin** [Early 17C. Variant of MANIKIN]

Manama /mə naámə/ capital city of Bahrain, situated in the northeastern part of the country. Population: 148,000 (1995).

mañana /man yaánə/ *adv* **1.** on the day following the present day **2.** at some unspecified time in the future [Mid-19C. < Spanish, 'morning, tomorrow' < Latin *mane* 'in the morning']

Manapouri, Lake /mánnə póori/ lake in the southwestern part of the South Island, New Zealand. At 444 m/1,455 ft deep, it is the deepest lake in New Zealand. Area: 142 sq. km/55 sq. mi.

Manaslu /múnnə sloo/ eighth highest mountain in the world. It is situated in the eastern part of the Himalayan system in the Gurkha massif of Nepal. Height: 8,163 m/26,781 ft.

Manassas /mə nássəss/ independent city in northeastern Virginia. It was the site of two Confederate victories at the US Civil War battles of Bull Run in 1861 and 1862. Population: 37,288 (2002 estimate).

manat /mánnat/ *n* the main unit of currency in Azerbaijan and Turkmenistan. See table at **currency** [Late 20C. < Azeri]

man-at-arms (*plural* **men-at-arms**) *n* a soldier, especially a medieval mounted soldier who was heavily armed

manatee /mánnə tée/ *n* a large plant-eating sea mammal with front flippers and a broad flattened tail. Native to: warm Atlantic coastal waters. Genus: *Trichechus*. [Mid-16C. Via Spanish *manatí* < Carib *manáti* 'breast']

Manaus /mə nówss/ city and river port in northwestern Brazil. It is the capital of Amazonas State. Population: 1,157,357 (1996).

Manawatu-Wanganui /mánnə waá too wong gə nóoi/ administrative region of New Zealand, situated in the southwestern part of the North Island. Population: 220,089 (2001). Area: 25,317 sq. km/9,775 sq. mi.

man bag *n* a bag in which a man carries small personal belongings

manche /maaNsh/ *n* in heraldry, a sleeve that hangs down (*technical*) [14C. < French < Latin *manicae* '(long) sleeves' < *manus* 'hand']

Manchego /man cháygō/ *n* a firm Spanish cheese that has a relatively high fat content and is made with ewes' milk [< Spanish, 'of La Mancha']

manchester /mánchistər/ *n ANZ* household linen or cotton goods, e.g. sheets and towels [Mid-16C. After MANCHESTER]

Manchester /mánchistər/ city in northwestern England. Population: 392,819 (2001).

Manchester terrier *n* a small terrier with a short-haired coat that is mainly black with tan patches

manchineel /mánchi néel/ (*plural* **-neels** or *same*) *n* a tree with poisonous apple-shaped fruit and milky sap that causes blistering. Native to: tropical America. Latin name: *Hippomane mancinella*. [Mid-17C. Via French *mancenille* < Spanish *manzanilla* 'little apple' < *manzana* 'apple' < Latin *matiana*, kind of apple, after *Matia*, a Roman gens]

Manchu /mán chóo/ (*plural* **-chus** or *same*) *n* **1.** a member of a people who invaded China from Manchuria in the 17th century, establishing a dynasty that lasted until the start of the 20th century **2.** a Tungusic language spoken in northeastern People's Republic of China. Native speakers: 20,000. [Late 17C. < Manchu, 'pure'] —**Manchu** *adj*

Manchuria /man chóori ə/ historical name for the mountainous region of northeastern China comprising the modern-day provinces of Heilongjiang, Jilin, and Liaoning —**Manchurian** *n, adj*

Manchu-Tungus *n* LANG same as **Tungusic** —**Manchu-Tungus** *adj*

manciple /mánssip'l/ *n* somebody responsible for buying food and other supplies for a college, Inn of Court, or monastery [13C. < Anglo-Norman < Latin *mancipium* 'purchase, enslaved person']

Mancunian /man kyóoni ən/ *n* somebody who comes from Manchester [Early 20C. < Latin *Mancunium* 'Manchester'] —**Mancunian** *adj*

-mancy *suffix* divination ○ *geomancy* [< Old French *-mancie* < Greek *mantis* (see MANTIC)]

M & A *abbr* BUSINESS mergers and acquisitions

Mandaean /man dée ən/, **Mandean** *n* **1.** a member of a Gnostic religious group who believe themselves to be descendants of John the Baptist. The group originated in Jordan and still exists in Iraq and Iran. **2.** a form of Aramaic used in the sacred writings of the Mandaeans [Late 18C. < Mandaean *mandaia* 'having knowledge' < *manda* 'knowledge'] —**Mandaean** *adj* —**Mandaeanism** *n*

mandala

mandarin duck

Nelson Mandela

mandala /mándələ, man daálə/ n 1. in Buddhism and Hinduism, a geometric or pictorial design usually enclosed in a circle, representing the entire universe and used in meditation and ritual 2. in Jungian psychology, a symbol representing the self and inner harmony [Mid-19C. < Sanskrit maṇḍalam 'circle'] —**mandalic** /man daálik/ adj

Mandalay /mándə láy/ city and transportation centre on the River Irrawaddy in central Myanmar. Population: 532,949 (1983).

mandamus /man dáyməss/ (plural -muses) n an order from a high court to a lower court, or to an authority, instructing it to perform an action or duty [Mid-16C. < Latin, 'we command']

Mandan /mán dan, mándən/ (plural same or -dans) n 1. a member of a Native American people of North Dakota who lived along the Missouri River and now mainly live near Lake Sakakawea 2. the language of the Mandan people, belonging to the Siouan branch of Hokan-Siouan languages. Native speakers: 1,200. [Late 18C. < N American French Mandane] —**Mandan** adj

mandapam /múndə pum/, **mandap** /mún dup/ n 1. the porch of a southern Indian temple 2. in southern India, a canopy erected temporarily so that a wedding or religious ceremony can be performed under it [< Sanskrit]

mandarin[1] /mándərin/ n 1. FORMER CHINESE OFFICIAL in the Chinese Empire, a member of any of the nine highest ranks of public officials, attained by examinations 2. CIVIL SERVANT a high-ranking civil servant or bureaucrat with wide-ranging powers 3. MEMBER OF ELITE GROUP an influential member of an elite group, especially a literary or intellectual group [Late 16C. < Spanish mandarín, Portuguese mandarim < Sanskrit mantrin- 'counsellor' < mantrah 'counsel'] —**mandarinate** n —**mandarinic** /mándə rínnik/ adj —**mandarinism** n

mandarin[2] /mándərin/ n 1. a small citrus fruit, similar to a tangerine but with easily peelable yellow-orange skin. The segments are commonly sold as tinned fruit. 2. a small citrus tree that produces mandarins. Native to: China. Latin name: Citrus reticulata. [Late 18C. Via French mandarine < Spanish mandarín (see MANDARIN[1]), because its colour is similar to that of mandarins' yellow robes]

Mandarin, Mandarin Chinese n, adj LANG same as **Modern Standard Chinese**

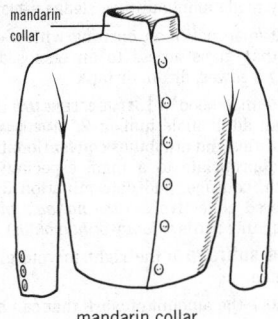

mandarin collar

mandarin collar

mandarin collar n a narrow collar that stands up from a close-fitting neckline and has an opening at the front

mandarin duck n a duck with a crested head and colourful feathers, the male of which has one enlarged orange feather on each wing for use in displays. Native to: Asia. Latin name: Aix galericulata.

mandarin orange n FOOD same as **mandarin**[2] (sense 1)

mandatary /mándətəri/ (plural -ies), **mandatory** n a person or state that has been given a mandate

mandate /mán dayt/ n 1. AUTHORITATIVE ORDER an official command or instruction from an authority 2. SUPPORT FROM ELECTORATE the authority bestowed on a government or other organization by an electoral victory, effectively authorizing it to carry out the policies for which it campaigned ○ The party in power has a clear mandate for reform. 3. INSTRUCTION FOR REGULAR TRANSFER OF FUNDS an instruction to a bank or building society to arrange for a regular payment such as a salary to be made into a customer's account 4. AGREEMENT FOR FREE SERVICE a contract by which somebody agrees to perform a service without payment 5. INSTRUCTION FROM SUPERIOR COURT an order from a superior court or official to a lower one 6. REGION RULED BY OUTSIDE POWER any territory that was placed by the League of Nations under the administration of one of its European member states after World War I 7. COMMISSION TO ADMINISTER STATE the power conferred by the League of Nations on a member state to administer a region ■ vt (-dates, -dating, -dated) 1. DELEGATE AUTHORITY TO SOMEBODY to delegate authority to somebody or require somebody to do something through use of a mandate 2. ASSIGN TERRITORY to assign a territory or region to a state under a mandate 3. US ORDER SOMETHING OFFICIALLY to require or order something officially or formally ○ The law mandates systematic tracking and reporting of hazardous wastes. [Early 16C. < Latin mandat-, past participle of mandare 'give into somebody's hand' < Indo-European, 'hand'] —**mandator** n

mandated territory /mán daytid-/ n HIST same as **mandate** n (sense 6)

mandatory /mándətəri/ adj 1. COMPULSORY needing to be done, followed, or complied with, usually because of an official requirement 2. WITH POWER OF MANDATE resembling or having the power of a mandate 3. AUTHORIZED TO ADMINISTER TERRITORY having a mandate to administer a region or territory ■ n (plural -ries) POL another spelling of **mandatary** —**mandatorily** adv

man-day n the work done by one person in one day (sometimes offensive)

Mande /maán day, mán-/ (plural same or -des) n 1. a group of around 20 languages spoken in West Africa, especially in Sierra Leone, Mali, Guinea, and the Côte d'Ivoire. It is a branch of the Niger-Congo family of languages. Native speakers: 9 million. 2. a member of a West African group of people who speak a Mande language [Late 19C. < Mande, 'little mother'] —**Mande** adj

Mandean n, adj RELIG, LANG another spelling of **Mandaean**

Mandela /man déllə, -dáylə/, **Nelson** (b. 1918) president of South Africa (1994–99). After a long incarceration as a political prisoner (1964–90), he became the first Black president of the Republic of South Africa (1994–99). He was awarded the Nobel Peace Prize with F. W. de Klerk (1993). Full name **Mandela, Nelson Rolihlahla**

'Years of imprisonment could not stamp out our determination to be free. Years of intimidation and violence could not stop us. And we will not be stopped now.'

[Nelson Mandela, Press conference; 26 April 1994]

'People...learn to hate, and if they can learn to hate, they can be taught to love, for love comes more naturally to the human heart than its opposite.'
[Nelson Mandela, Long Walk to Freedom; 1994]

Mandela, Winnie (b. 1934) South African political activist. She married Nelson Mandela in 1958 (divorced 1996), and continued his work after his imprisonment. She is an African National Congress (ANC) member of parliament and president of the ANC Women's League. Born **Madikizela, Nkosikazi Nomzamo**

Mandelstam /mánd'l stam/, **Osip Yemilyevich** (1891?–1938?) Russian poet. A critic of Joseph Stalin, he was arrested in 1934 and is believed to have died in a Soviet labour camp.

mandible /mándib'l/ n 1. LOWER JAW OF VERTEBRATE the lower jaw of a person or animal, usually containing a single bone (technical) 2. INSECT'S MOUTHPART either of a pair of parts in insects and similar animals used for biting and cutting food 3. BIRD'S BEAK the upper or lower part of a bird's beak [Mid-16C. Directly or via Old French < late Latin mandibula < Latin mandere 'chew'] —**mandibular** /man díbbyoōlər/ adj —**mandibulate** /man díbbyoōlit, -layt/ adj, n

Mandingo /man díng gō/ (plural -gos or -goes or same) n 1. a member of any of several peoples who live in parts of West Africa, especially along the Niger River valley 2. a group of Mande languages spoken in parts of West Africa, especially along the Niger River valley. Native speakers: 6 million. [Early 17C. < Mande] —**Mandingo** adj

Mandinka /man díng kə/ (plural same or -kas) n 1. a member of a West African people living in parts of the Gambia, Senegal, and Sierra Leone 2. the Niger-Congo language of the Mandinka people. Native speakers: 700,000. [Mid-20C. < Mande]

mandir /mún deer/ n S Asia a Hindu temple [Via Hindi < Sanskrit mandiram 'dwelling, mansion']

mandolin /mándə lín/, **mandoline** n 1. a stringed instrument of the lute family with a pear-shaped body and four or more pairs of strings, usually played with a plectrum 2. a kitchen tool for slicing vegetables, consisting of adjustable blades in a frame [Early 18C. Via French < Italian mandolino 'small lute' < mandola 'mandola' an early form of lute] —**mandolinist** n

mandorla /man dáwrlə/ n an oval area or panel in painting or sculpture, e.g. the area of light surrounding a representation of Jesus Christ after the Resurrection [Late 19C. < Italian, 'almond']

mandragora /man drággərə/ n PLANTS same as **mandrake** (sense 1) [Pre-12C. Directly or via French mandragore < medieval Latin mandragora < Greek mandragoras]

mandrake /mán drayk/ n 1. a plant with a forked root resembling a human body that was formerly believed to have magical powers and was made into a drug. Flowers: yellow, purplish. Native to: Europe, Asia. Latin name: Mandragora officinarum. 2. FOOD same as **May apple** (sense 1) [14C. Alteration of medieval Latin mandragora, influenced by MAN, DRAKE 'dragon' (from its emetic and narcotic properties)]

mandrel /mándrəl/, **mandril** n 1. TAPERED SHAFT FOR SECURING WORK TO a tapered shaft or arbor to which work is secured during machining or turning, e.g. on a lathe 2. CORE ROD a rod around which materials such

as metal or glass are moulded, forged, or shaped **3.** **SHAFT FOR MOUNTING TOOL** a shaft on which a tool such as a dentist's drill or machining tool is mounted **4.** **PICK** a miner's pick [Early 16C. Origin ?]

mandrill /mándril/ *n* a large baboon with a beard, mane, and crest. The male also has a brilliant ribbed blue, white, and scarlet muzzle. Native to: West Africa. Latin name: *Mandrillus sphinx*. [Mid-18C. Said to be < MAN + DRILL [4]]

manducate /mándyŏŏ kayt/ (**-cates, -cating, -cated**) *vt* to chew or eat something (*formal*) [Early 17C. < late Latin *manducat-*, past participle of *manducare* (see MANGER)] —**manducation** /mándyŏŏ káysh'n/ *n* —**manducatory** *adj*

Mandurah /mán dyoorə/ coastal town in southwestern Western Australia, on the Peel Inlet south of Perth. Population: 50,845 (2002 estimate).

mane /mayn/ *n* **1.** long hair on the head and neck of an animal such as a lion or horse **2.** a large amount of thick long hair on somebody's head (*literary or informal*) [Old English *manu* < Germanic] —**maned** *adj*

man-eater *n* **1.** an animal that eats or is thought to eat human flesh, e.g. a tiger or a great white shark **2.** same as **cannibal 3.** an offensive term for a woman who is thought to pursue men in order to make them her lovers and then discard them —**man-eating** *adj*

manège /ma náyzh, -nézh/, **manege** *n* **1.** **ART OF RIDING** the art of riding or training horses **2.** **HORSE MOVEMENTS** the movements that a horse has been trained to make **3.** **RIDING SCHOOL** a school where people are taught to ride and horses are trained [Mid-17C. < French < Italian *maneggio* < *maneggiare* (see MANAGE)]

manes /máa nayz/, **Manes** *n* the revered spirit of a dead person (*literary; takes a singular verb*) ■ *npl* in ancient Roman religion, the divine spirits of the dead (*takes a plural verb*) [14C. < Latin, 'good ones' < *manus* 'good']

Édouard Manet: portrait drawing by Edgar Degas

AKG London

Manet /mán ay/, **Édouard** (1832–83) French painter. His innovative work such as *The Bar at the Folies-Bergère* (1882) contributed to the development of impressionism.

maneuver *n*, *vti* US spelling of **manoeuvre**

man Friday (*plural* **man Fridays** or **men Friday**) *n* a man acting as an assistant or servant who is loyal and able to do many things [After the servant in *Robinson Crusoe* (1719) by Daniel Defoe]

manful /mánf'l/ *adj* brave, strong, and resolute, as a man is conventionally supposed to be —**manfully** *adv* —**manfulness** *n*

manga /máng gə/ *n* a Japanese style of comic books or animated cartoons, often very violent or erotic [Late 20C < Japanese < *man* 'indiscriminate' + *ga* 'picture']

mangabey /máng gə bay/ (*plural* **-beys** or *same*) *n* a large agile monkey with a long tail, slender body, and white eyelids. Native to: Africa. Genus: *Cercocebus*. [Late 18C. After *Mangabey*, Madagascar]

Mangalore /máng gə láwr/ city and seaport in Karnataka state in southwestern India, on the Arabian Sea. Population: 238,560 (2001).

mangan- *prefix* manganese ○ *manganous* [< MANGANESE]

manganate /máng gə nayt/ *n* any mixed-metal salt containing manganese and oxygen in the form of an anion

manganese /máng gə neez/ *n* a brittle greyish-white metallic element. Source: pyrolusite, rhodonite. Use: alloys, strengthening steel. Symbol **Mn**. See

table at **element** [Late 17C. Via French < Italian < medieval Latin *magnesia* 'magnesia']

manganese nodule *n* a stony nodule rich in manganese, found on the ocean floor

manganese steel *n* steel containing 11 to 14 per cent manganese. Use: manufacture of drills, blades, tools.

manganic /man gánnik/ *adj* containing or derived from manganese, especially with a valency of three or six

manganite /máng gə nīt/ *n* a greyish crystalline mineral consisting of manganese hydroxide

manganous /máng gənəss, man gánnəss/ *adj* containing or derived from manganese, especially with a valency of two

mange /maynj/ *n* an infectious skin disease of animals and sometimes humans that is caused by mites and results in hair loss, scabs, and itching [15C. < French *manjue* 'itch' < Old French *mangier* 'eat' < Latin *manducare* 'chew' < (see MANGER)]

mangel /máng g'l/, **mangel-wurzel** /-wurz'l/, **mangold** /máng gōld/, **mangold-wurzel** *n* a large yellow or reddish variety of beet that is grown as food for livestock [Late 18C. < German *Mangoldwurzel* 'beet root']

manger /máynjər/ *n* a trough from which livestock eat [14C. < Old French *mangeoire* < *mangier* 'eat' < Latin *manducare* 'chew' < *mandere*]

Lata Mangeshkar

Popperfoto

Mangeshkar /man gésh kaar/, **Lata** (*b.* 1929) Indian singer. She provided playback singing voices in Hindi films for more than 30 years, making over 30,000 recordings. Full name **Mangeshkar, Lata Dinanath**

mangetout /mónj toó, móNzh-/, **mangetout pea** *n* UK a variety of pea in which the whole pod is eaten. ANZ, N Am term **snow pea** [Early 19C. < French, 'eat-all']

mangey *adj* VET another spelling of **mangy**

mangle[1] /máng g'l/ (**-gles, -gling, -gled**) *vt* **1.** to mutilate or disfigure somebody or something by violent tearing, cutting, or crushing **2.** to spoil or ruin something through carelessness or ineptitude ○ *a reading that mangled the rhythm of the poem* [14C. < Anglo-Norman *mahangler*] —**mangler** *n*

mangle[2] /máng g'l/ *n* a machine for squeezing water out of wet clothes after washing by drawing them between two rotating cylinders. N Am term **wringer** [Late 17C. < Dutch *mangelstok* 'mangling roller'] —**mangle** *vt*

mango

mango /máng gō/ (*plural* **-goes** or **-gos**) *n* **1.** a red or green fruit with juicy, sweet, orange-yellow pulp and a large stone **2.** an evergreen tree that produces mangoes. Native to: tropical Asia. Latin name:

Mangifera indica. [Late 16C. Via Portuguese *manga* < Malay *mangga* < Tamil *mānkāy* 'mango-tree fruit']

mangold, mangold-wurzel *n* AGRIC same as **mangel**

mangonel /máng gənəl, máng gə nəl/ *n* a medieval military machine used for hurling stones at an enemy [13C. Via Old French *mangonel(le)* < medieval Latin *manganellus* 'little war engine' < Greek *magganon* 'war engine']

mangosteen /máng gō steen/ *n* **1.** a fruit with a hard reddish-brown rind and sweet juicy pulp **2.** an evergreen tree that has leathery leaves and produces mangosteens. Native to: Southeast Asia. Latin name: *Garcinia mangostana*. [Late 16C. < Malay *manggustan*, alteration of *manggis*]

mangrove

mangrove /máng grōv/ *n* an evergreen tree or bush with straight slender stems and intertwined roots that are exposed at low tide. Native to: tropical coasts. Families: Combretaceae, Verbenaceae, Rhizophoraceae. [Early 17C. Blend of Portuguese *mangue* or Spanish *mangle* (< Taino) + GROVE]

Mangue /máng gi, máng gwi/ *n* an extinct Native Central American language of Costa Rica, belonging to the Oto-Manguean family of languages [Late 18C. Origin ?] —**Mangue** *adj*

mangy /máynji/, **mangey** (**-ier, -iest**) *adj* **1.** **HAVING MANGE** affected by or caused by mange **2.** **SCRUFFY** having a dirty or shabby appearance (*informal*) **3.** *Ireland* **MISERLY** reluctant to spend or give money (*informal*) —**mangily** *adv* —**manginess** *n*

manhandle /mán hand'l, man hánd'l/ (**-dles, -dling, -dled**) *vt* **1.** to pull or push somebody or something around roughly **2.** to move something using human strength alone rather than machinery

Manhattan[1] /man hátt'n/, **manhattan** *n* a cocktail made from vermouth, whisky, and a dash of bitters [Late 19C. After MANHATTAN [2]]

Manhattan[2] /man hátt'n/ borough and main economic centre of New York City, occupying Manhattan Island at the northern end of New York Bay together with several adjacent areas. Population: 1,487,536 (2002 estimate). Area: 87 sq. km/34 sq. mi.

Manhattan Project *n* the top-secret research and development in several places in the United States that led to the successful construction and detonation of the first atomic bombs [Mid-20C. < *Manhattan District*, the code name it was given]

manhaul /mán hawl/ *vti* (**-hauls, -hauling, -hauled**) to pull a sledge along on foot or on skis, or pull equipment or supplies in a sledge in this way ■ *n* a journey made manhauling a sledge —**manhauler** *n*

manhole /mán hōl/ *n* an opening with a detachable cover that gives access to an enclosed area, especially a sewer, drain, or tank

manhood /mán hŏŏd/ *n* **1.** **STATE OF BEING MAN** the state of being an adult male human **2.** **TRADITIONAL MANLINESS** the qualities and attributes conventionally thought to be appropriate to a man, especially physical strength, courage, and determination **3.** **MEN** men considered collectively ○ *the nation's manhood* **4.** **PENIS** a man's penis (*literary or humorous*)

manhood suffrage *n* the right to vote given to all adult men

man-hour *n* the amount of work that can be done by one person in one hour, used as a means of assessing requirements, production, and performance (*sometimes offensive*) ○ *the number of man-hours lost through sickness*

manhunt /mán hunt/ *n* an organized search, especially

by the police, for an escaped criminal or other wanted person —**manhunter** *n*

mania /máyni ə/ *n* **1.** an excessive and intense interest in or enthusiasm for something **2.** a psychiatric disorder characterized by excessive physical activity, rapidly changing ideas, and impulsive behaviour [14C. Via late Latin < Greek, 'loss of reason' < *mainesthai* 'to rage']

-mania *suffix* excessive enthusiasm for or attachment to ○ *pyromania* [< MANIA]

maniac /máyni ak/ *n* **1.** OFFENSIVE TERM an offensive term for somebody who behaves in such an uncontrolled manner as to appear to be affected by mania **2.** ENTHUSIAST somebody who is obsessively interested in or enthusiastic about something **3.** OFFENSIVE TERM an offensive term for somebody affected by mania ■ *adj* PSYCHIAT same as **maniacal** (sense 2) (*offensive*) [Late 16C. Via late Latin *maniacus* < late Greek *maniakos* < *mania* (see MANIA)]

maniacal /mə nī ək'l/ *adj* **1.** an offensive term meaning so uncontrolled as to appear to be affected by mania **2.** an offensive term meaning characteristic of or indicative of mania —**maniacally** *adv*

manic /mánnik/ *adj* **1.** RELATING TO MANIA relating to or affected by mania **2.** HECTIC extremely or excessively busy (*informal; sometimes considered offensive*) **3.** OVEREXCITED in a state of unusually high excitement, especially because of tension (*informal*) [Early 20C. < MANIA] —**manically** *adv*

manic-depressive *n* somebody affected by bipolar disorder ■ *adj* characteristic of or affected by bipolar disorder

manic-depressive disorder, manic-depressive illness *n* MED same as **bipolar disorder**

Manichaeism /mánni kée izəm/, **Manicheism** *n* **1.** a religious doctrine based on the separation of matter and spirit and of good and evil that originated in 3rd-century Persia and combined elements of Zoroastrianism, Buddhism, Christianity, and Gnosticism **2.** a heretical Christian belief in the separate nature of matter and spirit [Early 17C. < late Latin *Manichaeus* < *Mani* (216?–276?), Persian sage] —**Manichaean** *adj* —**Manichee** /mánni kee/ *n*

manicotti /mánni kótti/ *n* a dish of large pasta tubes that are usually stuffed with a ricotta or meat filling and then baked, and often served with a tomato sauce [Mid-20C. < Italian, 'sleeves']

manicure /mánni kyoor/ *n* HAND AND NAIL COSMETIC TREATMENT a cosmetic treatment for the hands and nails that usually involves shaping and polishing the fingernails, pushing back the cuticles, and treating rough skin ■ *vt* (**-cures, -curing, -cured**) **1.** TREAT HANDS AND NAILS to treat the hands and fingernails by cutting, shaping, and polishing the nails, and softening the hands **2.** CUT AND SHAPE SOMETHING CAREFULLY to cut and shape something with great care and precision ○ *a neatly manicured lawn* [Late 19C. < French < Latin *manus cura* 'hand care']

manicurist /mánnikyoorist/ *n* somebody whose job is to give people manicures

manifest /mánni fest/ *adj* OBVIOUS clear to see or understand ■ *v* (**-fests, -festing, -fested**) **1.** *vt* SHOW SOMETHING CLEARLY to make something evident by showing or demonstrating it very clearly **2.** *vi* APPEAR to appear or be revealed **3.** *vt* INCLUDE SOMETHING IN CARGO LIST to include something in a ship's cargo list ■ *n* **1.** SHIP'S CARGO LIST a list giving details of a ship's cargo, its destination, and other particulars for customs purposes **2.** PLANE OR TRAIN CARGO LIST a list of cargo or passengers on a plane or train [14C. Directly or via French < Latin *manifestus* 'apprehensible' < *manus* 'hand' + *festus* 'seizable'] —**manifestable** *adj* —**manifestly** *adv*

manifestation /mánni fe stáysh'n/ *n* **1.** ACT OF SHOWING SOMETHING an act of showing or demonstrating something **2.** STATE OF BEING SHOWN the condition of being shown or being perceptible **3.** SIGN an indication that something is present, real, or exists ○ *one of the first manifestations of the disease* **4.** PUBLIC DEMONSTRATION a public demonstration, usually over a political issue **5.** MATERIALIZATION OF SPIRIT a supposed appearance in visible form by a spiritual being **6.** VISIBLE FORM OF DIVINE BEING a visible form in which a divine being, idea, or person is believed to be revealed or expressed —**manifestational** *adj*

manifest content *n* in dream analysis, the overt meaning of a dream remembered by the dreamer on waking that requires analysis to interpret its latent content or real meaning

Manifest Destiny *n* the 19th-century doctrine according to which the United States was believed to have the God-given right to expand into and possess the whole of the North American continent

manifesto /mánni féstō/ (*plural* **-toes** or **-tos**) *n* a public written declaration of principles, policies, and objectives, especially one issued by a political movement or candidate [Mid-17C. < Italian < *manifestare* 'make evident' < Latin *manifestus* (see MANIFEST)]

manifold /mánni fōld/ *adj* **1.** MANY AND VARIOUS of many different kinds ○ *The reasons for the crisis are manifold.* **2.** HAVING MANY FORMS having many parts, forms, or applications ○ *a manifold political system* ■ *n* **1.** CHAMBER WITH PORTS a chamber or pipe with several openings for receiving or distributing a fluid or gas, e.g. the intake or exhaust manifolds of an internal-combustion engine **2.** MATHS TOPOLOGICAL SPACE a topological space or surface satisfying specific conditions ■ *vt* (**-folds, -folding, -folded**) **1.** MULTIPLY SOMETHING to multiply something **2.** MAKE COPIES OF SOMETHING to make several copies of a book or page [Old English *manigfeald* < earlier forms of MANY + -FOLD] —**manifolder** *n* —**manifoldly** *adv* —**manifoldness** *n*

manikin /mánnikin/, **mannikin** *n* **1.** CLOTHING, COMM same as **mannequin** (sense 1) **2.** an anatomical model of the human body, used in teaching art or medicine **3.** an offensive term for a very short man [Mid-16C. < Dutch *manneken* 'little man' < *man* 'man']

manila /mə nílla/, **Manila** *adj* made of Manila paper ○ *a manila envelope* ■ *n* **1.** a cigar made in Manila **2.** TEXTILES same as **Manila hemp 3.** PAPER same as **Manila paper** [Late 17C. After MANILA]

Manila /mə níllə/ capital city of the Philippines, located on the coast of Luzon Island. Population: 1,673,000 (2000).

Manila Bay bay of the South China Sea in the northern Philippines, on Luzon Island. Area: 2,000 sq. km/770 sq. mi. Length: 60 km/37 mi.

Manila hemp, Manilla hemp *n* a strong fibre obtained from the Philippine abaca plant. Use: rope, paper. [Mid-19C. After MANILA]

Manila paper, Manilla paper *n* a strong pale-brown paper with a smooth surface, made from Manila hemp. Use: wrapping, envelopes. [Late 19C. After MANILA]

manille /mə níl/ *n* the second-best trump in the card games ombre and quadrille [Late 17C. < French < Spanish *malilla* 'little bad (card)']

man in the moon *n* the imaginary being behind the apparent face on the moon when it is full

man in the street *n* the average person, as opposed to an expert, celebrity, or prominent person (*sometimes considered offensive*)

manioc /mánni ok/, **manioca** /mánni ṓkə/ *n* PLANTS, FOOD same as **cassava** [Mid-16C. < Tupi *mandioca* (influenced by French *manihot*) < Guarani *mandio*]

maniple /mánnip'l/ *n* **1.** in the ancient Roman army, a subdivision of a legion, containing 60 or 120 men **2.** in the Christian church, a silk band or folded napkin formerly worn on the left arm of somebody administering Communion [Late 16C. < Latin *manipulus* 'handful' < *manus* 'hand']

manipular /mə níppyŏolər/ *adj* **1.** relating to an ancient Roman maniple **2.** relating to or constituting manipulation

manipulate /mə níppyoo layt/ (**-lates, -lating, -lated**) *vt* **1.** OPERATE SOMETHING to move, operate, or handle something ○ *manipulating the crane into position* **2.** CONTROL SOMEBODY OR SOMETHING to control or influence somebody or something in a clever or devious way **3.** FALSIFY SOMETHING to change or present something in a way that is false but personally advantageous **4.** TREAT BODY PART USING HANDS ONLY to treat a part of the body, or to move a part such as a joint during examination, using the hands only **5.** HANDLE NUMBERS to work with data on a computer [Early 19C. Back-formation < *manipulation* < French < *manipule* 'handful' < Latin *manipulus* (see MANIPLE)] —**manipulability** /mə níppyŏolə bílləti/ *n* —**manipulable** *adj* —**manipulatable** *adj* —**manipulation** /mə níppyŏo láysh'n/ *n* —**manipulator** *n* —**manipulatory** /-lətəri/ *adj*

manipulative /mə níppyŏolətiv/ *adj* **1.** using clever, devious ways to control or influence somebody or something ○ *a manipulative personality* **2.** relating to or involved in manipulation ○ *a manipulative technique* —**manipulatively** *adv* —**manipulativeness** *n*

Manipur /múnnə poŏr/ state in northeastern India. Capital: Imphal. Population: 2,388,634 (2001). Area: 22,327 sq. km/8,620 sq. mi.

manito *n* RELIG another spelling of **manitou**

Manitoba /mánni tṓbə/ province in south-central Canada, the easternmost of Canada's three Prairie provinces. Capital: Winnipeg. Population: 1,150,800 (2002). Area: 647,797 sq. km/250,116 sq. mi. —**Manitoban** *adj, n*

Manitoba, Lake lake in southern Manitoba, Canada. It discharges through the Dauphin River to Lake Winnipeg. Area: 4,659 sq. km/1,799 sq. mi.

manitou /mánni too/, **manitu, manito** /-tō/ (*plural* **-tos**) *n* a supernatural force or spirit believed by Algonquian peoples to exist within various living things and inanimate objects [Late 16C. < Narraganset *manittówock*]

Manitoulin Island /mánni toŏlin-/ world's largest freshwater island, in the Manitoulin Islands, an archipelago in northern Lake Huron on the border between the United States and Canada. Area: 2,766 sq. km/1,068 sq. mi.

manitu *n* RELIG another spelling of **manitou**

Manizales /mánni zaáless/ city in western Colombia. It is the capital of Caldas Department, in the Andes mountains. Population: 362,000 (1999).

mankind /man kínd/ *n* **1.** human beings considered collectively (*often considered offensive*) **2.** men considered collectively, as distinct from women (*dated*)

manky /mángki/ (**-kier, -kiest**) *adj* dirty, greasy, or otherwise unpleasant (*informal*) ○ *that manky old sweater of his* [Mid-20C. < Scots dialect *mank* 'mutilated, defective', via Old French *manc* 'maimed' < Latin *mancus*]

REGIONAL NOTE ***Manky*** is one of many dialect words that come from French. It would appear that many dialect speakers took the adage 'Cleanliness is next to godliness' seriously, for dialects abound in words meaning 'dirty'. These include *boggin, clarty, clabbery, cloggy, mucky,* and *smalmy.*

Manley /mánnli/, **Michael** (1923–97) Jamaican politician. He served twice as prime minister of Jamaica (1972–80 and 1989–92). Full name **Manley, Michael Norman**

> 'Where poverty is shared it may be endured. Where poverty is mocked by extravagance it becomes the condition within which resentment smoulders.'
> [Michael Manley, *Jamaica: Struggle in the Periphery*; 1982]

manly /mánnli/ (**-lier, -liest**) *adj* **1.** having or showing qualities conventionally thought to be characteristic of or appropriate to a man, especially physical strength or courage **2.** considered suitable or appropriate for a man —**manliness** *n*

man-made, manmade /mán máyd/ *adj* made by human beings and not occurring naturally (*often considered offensive*)

Mann /man/, **Heinrich** (1871–1950) German writer. The brother of the writer Thomas Mann, his book *Professor Unrat* (1904) was made into a film, *The Blue Angel* (1930).

> 'Each one of us is as nothing, but massed in ranks as Neo-Teutons, soldiers, bureaucrats, priests and scientists...we taper up like a pyramid to the point at the top where Power itself stands, graven and dazzling.'
> [Heinrich Mann, *Man of Straw*; 1918]

Mann, Thomas (1875–1955) German-born US novelist and critic. His work often explores the relationship between society and the creative artist, and includes *The Magic Mountain* (1924). He won the Nobel Prize in literature (1929). See Cultural note at **magic**

> 'Speech is civilization itself. The word, even the most contradictory word, preserves contact—it is silence that isolates.'
> [Thomas Mann, *The Magic Mountain*; 1924]

manna /mánnə/ *n* **1.** DIVINELY PROVIDED SUSTENANCE in the Bible, food provided miraculously to feed the Israelites in the wilderness **2.** UNEXPECTED BENEFIT something very welcome or of great benefit that comes

unexpectedly **3.** SWEET SUBSTANCE FROM ASH TREE a pale-yellow sugary gum exuded by the European ash tree. Use: formerly, as a laxative. **4.** SWEET SUBSTANCE FROM TAMARISK TREE a sweet substance exuded by a tamarisk tree when its bark is punctured by a scale insect [Pre-12C. Via late Latin and Greek < Hebrew *mān*]

mannan /mán an, mánnən/ n a polysaccharide composed of mannose [Late 19C. < MANNOSE]

Mannar, Gulf of /ma naár/ inlet of the Indian Ocean between the southern tip of India and western Sri Lanka

manned /mand/ adj (often offensive) **1.** having a human crew **2.** operated or attended by staff

mannequin /mánnikin/ n **1.** a usually life-size model of the human body used to display or fit clothes **2.** a fashion model (dated) **3.** ARTS same as **lay figure** (sense 1) [Mid-18C. Via French < Dutch *manneken* (see MANIKIN)]

manner /mánnər/ n **1.** WAY SOMETHING IS DONE the way in which something is done or happens ○ *His manner of doing things is often a little unconventional.* **2.** WAY OF BEING the characteristic way in which somebody behaves ○ *had a capricious manner about him* **3.** TYPE a type or kind (literary) ○ *What manner of insect makes this hole?* **4.** ARTS STYLE OF WORK OF ART the style in which a work of art is executed ○ *painted in the manner of Vermeer* ■ **manners** npl **1.** SOCIAL BEHAVIOUR social behaviour, especially in terms of what is considered correct or unacceptable **2.** CUSTOMS AND PRACTICES the customs and practices of a particular society or period in time [12C. < Anglo-Norman *manere* 'way of handling' < Latin *manuarius* 'of the hand' < *manus* 'hand'] ◇ **all manner of something** many different kinds of something ◇ **in a manner of speaking** in some ways, though not exactly or not in all ways ◇ **to the manner born** naturally adapted to something as though accustomed to it from birth ◇ **under manners** forced to behave properly, e.g. through parental pressure or school discipline (slang; used in Black English)

mannered /mánnərd/ adj **1.** affected or artificial ○ *spoke in mannered tones* **2.** behaving in a particular way or having manners of a particular kind (usually used in combination) ○ *an ill-mannered child*

Mannerheim /mánnər hīm/, **Carl** (1867–1951) Finnish president (1944–46). He ruled Finland as regent from 1918 to 1919 and was commander in chief of the Finnish army in the Russo-Finnish War (1939–40). Full name **Mannerheim, Baron Carl Gustaf Emil**

mannerism /mánnərizəm/ n **1.** IDIOSYNCRASY a distinctive gesture, habit, or way of doing something ○ *one of his odd little mannerisms* **2.** AFFECTED BEHAVIOUR affected or exaggerated speech, behaviour, or writing **3.** **Mannerism** STYLE OF ART AND ARCHITECTURE a style of art and architecture, predominant in Italy in the late 16th century, characterized by stylized and elongated forms and vivid colours —**mannerist** adj, n —**manneristic** /mánnə rístik/ adj —**manneristically** adv

mannerless /mánnərləss/ adj having or showing bad manners —**mannerlessness** n

mannerly /mánnərli/ adj well-mannered or polite —**mannerliness** n

Mannheim /mánn hīm/ city and river port in southwestern Germany, on the River Rhine. Population: 316,223 (1997).

Mannheim, Karl (1893–1947) Hungarian-born German sociologist. His main work was in the sociology of knowledge.

Mannheim school n a style of orchestral and string playing associated with the rise of the Classical period, developed at the court of Mannheim in the 18th century

mannikin n **1.** another spelling of **manikin 2.** a small bird of the waxbill family with brown, black, and white feathers that is often kept as a cagebird. Genus: *Lonchura*. ◊ **manakin**

manning /mánning/ n HR same as **staffing** (sense 2) (often offensive) ○ *a dispute over manning levels*

Manning /mánning/ river in eastern New South Wales, Australia. Length: 225 km/140 mi.

Manning, Frederic (1892–1935) Australian-born British writer. He was author of *Her Privates We* (1930), a novel based on his experience of World War I.

Manning, Henry, Cardinal (1808–92) British cleric. He converted from the Anglican Church to Roman Catholicism in 1851 and was made a cardinal in 1875.

Manning, Patrick (b. 1946) prime minister of Trinidad and Tobago (1991–95, 2001–). A member of the People's National Movement since the early 1970s, he held a variety of ministerial posts before winning the 1991 election. He was asked to form a government by the country's president in 2001 after the two parties contesting the election won the same number of seats. Full name **Manning, Patrick Augustus Mervyn**

mannish /mánnish/ adj **1.** resembling or suitable for a man rather than a woman (often considered offensive) ○ *a mannish haircut* **2.** considered characteristic of a man —**mannishly** adv —**mannishness** n

mannitol /mánni tol/, **mannite** /mánnīt/ n a sweet white alcohol found in many plants. Source: mannose. Use: sweetener. [Late 19C < MANNA]

Mannix /mánniks/, **Daniel** (1864–1963) Irish-born Australian cleric. He was archbishop of Melbourne (1917–63). His involvement in politics led to the founding of the Catholic Social Movement and the anticommunist Democratic Labour Party.

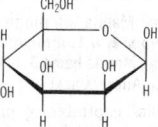

mannose

mannose /mánnōss, -nōz/ n a six-carbon sugar found in many plant cell walls. Formula: $C_6H_{12}O_6$. [Late 19C. < *manna*]

manny /mánni/ (plural **-nies**) n US a young man employed to look after children (informal) [Blend of MAN + NANNY]

mano a mano /mánnō ə mánnō/ n (plural **manos a manos**) **1.** US FACE-TO-FACE CONFRONTATION a face-to-face confrontation between opposing people or sides **2.** BULLFIGHT IN WHICH MATADORS TAKE TURNS a bullfight during which two competing matadors take turns fighting several bulls each ■ adj, adv US COMPETING DIRECTLY competing directly with somebody or something [Late 20C. < Spanish, 'hand to hand']

manoeuvre /mə nóovər/ n **1.** SKILLED MOVEMENT a movement or action that requires skill or dexterity **2.** MILITARY MOVEMENT a planned movement of one or several military or naval units **3.** DEVIOUS ACT an action, especially a devious or deceptive one, done to gain advantage ○ *one of his little manoeuvres to try to stay in total control* **4.** CHANGE OF COURSE a controlled change of course of a vehicle or vessel ■ **manoeuvres** npl MILITARY EXERCISES large-scale military exercises used for training or practice ■ v (**-vres, -vring, -vred**) **1.** vti MOVE SKILFULLY to move or cause something to move skilfully ○ *manoeuvred the boat into the berth* **2.** vti DO MILITARY EXERCISES to perform military manoeuvres, or cause somebody or something to perform military manoeuvres **3.** vt MANIPULATE SOMEBODY OR SOMETHING to manipulate somebody or something to gain advantage ○ *trying to manoeuvre her into agreeing* **4.** vi BEHAVE DEVIOUSLY to use devious means in order to gain advantage ○ *the various parties manoeuvring for the leadership* [15C. < French, 'manipulation', later form of Old French *maneuvre* 'manual labour' < medieval Latin *manuoperare* 'work with the hands' < Latin *manus* 'hand'] —**manoeuvrability** /mə nóovərə bílləti/ n —**manoeuvrable** adj —**manoeuvrer** n

man of God n **1.** a man who is a member of the clergy **2.** a saint or godly man

man of letters n a man who is a writer or scholar (formal)

man of straw n **1.** an issue or person of little importance or relevance, presented in order to be shown as an idea or adversary that can be easily

defeated **2.** somebody who acts as a front for somebody else's questionable or illegal activities ► N Am term **straw man**

man of the cloth n a man who is a member of the clergy

man of the hour (plural **men of the hour**) n a man, often a public figure, who is currently publicly admired because of his accomplishments or actions

man-of-war /mánnə wáwr/ (plural **men-of-war**), **man o' war** (plural **men o' war** /ménnə-/) n **1.** same as **warship 2.** MARINE BIOL same as **Portuguese man-of-war**

man-of-war bird, **man-o'-war bird** n BIRDS same as **frigatebird**

manometer /mə nómmitər/ n an instrument used to measure the pressure of a gas [Mid-18C. < Greek *manos* 'thin, rare'] —**manometric** /mánnə méttrik/ adj —**manometry** n

manor /mánnər/ n **1.** NOBLE'S HOUSE AND LAND a house and the land surrounding it, owned by a medieval noble **2.** BUILDINGS same as **manor house 3.** POLICE DISTRICT the area for which a particular local police station is responsible (slang) **4.** PERSONAL TERRITORY somebody's own local area or territory (slang) [13C. Via Anglo-Norman *maner* < Old French *maneir* 'dwelling-place' < Latin *manere* 'remain, stay'] —**manorial** /mə náwri əl/ adj

ORIGIN The Latin word *manere* 'to remain, to stay', from which **manor** is derived, is also the source of English *maisonette*, *manse*, *mansion*, *permanent*, and *remain*.

manor house n the residence of the lord or lady of a manor

~~manouver~~ incorrect spelling of **maneuver**

~~manouvre~~ incorrect spelling of **manoeuvre**

manpower /mán pow ər/ n (sometimes offensive) **1.** power in terms of the number of people available or needed to do something **2.** power supplied by the physical work of people rather than machines ○ *canals dug entirely by manpower*

manqué /móngk ay, maaN káy/ adj having wanted but failed to be or do something ○ *an artist manqué* [Late 18C. < French, past participle of *manquer* 'fail, lack']

mansard /mán saard, -ərd/ n the part of a building enclosed by a mansard roof [Mid-18C. < French, after the architect François *Mansard* (1598–1666)] —**mansarded** adj

mansard roof

mansard roof n a roof that slopes on all four sides, with each side divided into a gentle upper slope and a steeper lower slope

manse /manss/ n a house provided for a church minister by some Christian denominations [Late 15C. < medieval Latin *mansus* 'unit of land' < Latin *manere* 'remain']

Mansell /mánss'l/, **Nigel** (b. 1953) British motor racing driver. He won the World Grand Prix Formula One Championship (1992) and then started racing in the United States, where he won the Indy Car Championship (1993).

manservant /mán survənt/ (plural **menservants** /mén survənts/) n a man who is a servant, especially somebody's valet

Mansfield /mánss feeld/ town in Nottinghamshire, east-central England. Population: 98,181 (2001).

Mansfield, Jayne (1933–67) US film actor. She played leading roles in the comic films *The Girl Can't Help It* (1956) and *Will Success Spoil Rock Hunter?* (1957). Born **Palmer, Vera Jayne**

Mansfield, Katherine (1888–1923) New Zealand-born British writer. She was a major figure in the de-

velopment of the short-story form. Pseudonym of **Beauchamp, Katherine Mansfield**

'How idiotic civilization is! Why be given a body if you have to keep it shut up in a case like a rare, rare fiddle?'
[Katherine Mansfield, 'Bliss', *Bliss and Other Stories*; 1920]

Mansfield, Sir Peter (*b.* 1933) British physicist and biomedical scientist. He and Paul C. Lauterbur of the United States shared the 2003 Nobel Prize in Physiology or Medicine for their work in magnetic resonance imaging.

mansion /mánsh'n/ *n* **1. LARGE HOUSE** a large and stately house **2. DIVISION OF ZODIAC** one of the 28 divisions of the zodiac through which the Moon passes successively each month ■ **mansions** *npl* **LARGE BUILDING DIVIDED INTO FLATS** a large building that is divided up into separate flats (*often used in names of buildings*) [14C. < French, 'dwelling-place' < Latin *manere* 'remain']

mansion house *n* BUILDINGS same as **mansion** (sense 1)

Mansion House *n* the official residence of the Lord Mayor of London

man-sized, man-size *adj* **1.** larger than the ordinary size ○ *a man-sized appetite* **2.** the same size as or big enough for a man ○ *a man-sized hole in the fence*

manslaughter /mán slawtər/ *n* the unlawful killing of one person by another without advance planning

man's man (*plural* **men's men**) *n* a man who prefers the company of other men to that of women (*informal*)

Manson /mánssən/, **Charles** (*b.* 1934) US cult leader and murderer. Founder of the 'Manson Family', he was sentenced to death for ritual murders carried out in California in 1969, but his sentence was later commuted to life imprisonment by a Supreme Court ruling.

mansuetude /mánsswi tyood/ *n* a meek or gentle attitude or behaviour (*archaic*) [14C. Via French or directly < Latin *mansuetudo* < *mansuetus* 'tame', literally 'accustomed to the hand' < *suescere* 'accustom']

Mansura /man sóorə/ city in northeastern Egypt, in the Nile delta. Population: 371,000 (1992).

manta /mántə/ *n N Am* FISH same as **manta ray** [Late 17C. < Spanish, 'blanket' (from its shape)]

manta ray *n* a large warm-water ray with wide pectoral fins, a long tail, and two fins resembling horns that project from the head. Family: Mobulidae. N Am term **manta**

Mantegna /man tényə/, **Andrea** (1431–1506) Italian painter. He was a master of illusionistic perspective and foreshortening.

mantel /mánt'l/, **mantle** *n* an ornamental frame around a fireplace, usually made of stone or wood [15C. < Old French *mantel* (see MANTEL)]

mantelet /mántələt/, **mantlet** /mántlit/ *n* a short cape worn by women in the 19th century

mantelpiece /mánt'l peess/, **mantlepiece** *n UK, Can, Northeast US, Southern US* the mantel of a fireplace, especially its projecting top

mantelshelf /mánt'l shelf/ (*plural* **-shelves** /-shelvz/), **mantleshelf** (*plural* **-shelves**) *n* the projecting top of the mantel of a fireplace, used as a shelf

manteltree /mánt'l tree/, **mantletree** *n* a stone or beam that acts as a support for the masonry above a fireplace

mantic /mántik/ *adj* relating to or having powers of divination or prophecy [Mid-19C. < Greek *mantikos* < *mantis* 'prophet' < *mainesthai* 'to rage'] —**mantically** *adv*

mantid /mántid/ *n* INSECTS same as **mantis**

mantilla /man tíllə/ *n* **1.** a lace scarf that covers the head and shoulders, often worn by women in church, in countries such as Spain and Latin America **2.** a short light cape [Early 18C. < Spanish, 'little mantle']

mantis /mántiss/ (*plural* **mantises** or **mantes** /mán teez/) *n* a large, usually green insect that feeds on other insects and has a long body, large eyes, and strong grasping front legs that it holds up at rest. Family: Mantidae. [Mid-17C. Via modern Latin < Greek (see MANTIC)]

mantissa /man tíssə/ *n* the fractional part of a logarithm, to the right of the decimal point [Mid-17C. < Latin, 'makeweight']

mantis shrimp *n* MARINE BIOL same as **squilla**

mantle /mánt'l/ *n* **1. SLEEVELESS CLOAK** a loose sleeveless cloak **2. WIRE MESH FOR LIGHT** a small circle of wire mesh in a gas or oil lamp that gives out incandescent light when heated by the flame it surrounds **3. TRANSFERRED POSITION** a role or position, especially one that can be passed from one person to another (*formal*) ○ *assumed the mantle of the presidency* **4. COVERING** something that envelops or covers something else (*literary*) ○ *a mantle of snow* **5.** ZOOL **SHELL-PRODUCING GLAND** a layer of epidermis in a mollusc or brachiopod with glands that secrete a shell-producing substance **6. BIRD'S BACK AND SHOULDER** the upper back of a bird, lying between the scapulars **7.** GEOL **CENTRAL PART OF EARTH** the part of Earth or another planet that lies between the crust and core **8.** ARCHIT another spelling of **mantel** ■ *v* (**-tles, -tling, -tled**) **1.** *vt* **COVER SOMETHING** to cover something with a mantle or something resembling a mantle ○ *hilltops mantled with snow* **2.** *vi* **TO BECOME FLUSHED** to be filled or suffused with something (*refers to the face*) ○ *His puffy face mantled in angry red blotches.* [Pre-12C. Via Old French *mantel* < Latin *mantellum* 'cloak']

mantlepiece, etc. *n* FURNITURE another spelling of **mantelpiece, etc.**

mantlet *n* CLOTHING another spelling of **mantelet**

mantling /mántling/ *n* ornamental drapery round a shield on a coat of arms

man-to-man *adj* **1.** honest, intimate, and treating somebody as an equal ○ *a man-to-man talk* **2.** in sports such as football, hockey, or basketball, having each defender of one team mark a corresponding attacker of the other team ○ *man-to-man marking* —**man-to-man** *adv*

Mantoux test /mán too-/ *n* a test to determine whether somebody has ever had the tuberculosis infection and so has a measure of immunity to the disease [Mid-20C. After Charles *Mantoux* (1877–1947), French physician]

mantra /mántrə/ *n* **1.** in Hindu and Buddhist religious practice, a sacred word, chant, or sound that is repeated during meditation to facilitate spiritual power and transformation of consciousness **2.** an expression or idea that is repeated, often without thinking about it, and closely associated with something ○ *the mantra of marketing being 'new, improved'* [Late 18C. < Sanskrit, 'thought' < *man* 'think']

mantrap /mán trap/ *n* an illegal trap set to catch poachers or trespassers on private land, usually in the form of a metal device that snaps shut onto somebody's leg

mantua /mántyoo ə/ *n* a woman's gown, fitted above the waist, with an open front and draped skirt to show the underskirt, worn in Europe in the late 17th and 18th centuries [Late 17C. Alteration of *manteau* (< French, later form of *mantel*: see MANTLE), after MANTUA]

Mantua /mán tyoo ə/ historic city in central northern Italy, a tourist and agricultural centre. Population: 47,790 (2001). Italian name **Mantova**

manual /mánnyoo əl/ *adj* **1. USING HANDS** relating to, done with, or involving the hands ○ *manual dexterity* **2. PHYSICAL** involving physical rather than mental exertion ○ *manual tasks* **3. OPERATED BY HUMAN BEING** operated by a person rather than a machine or computer, or by human effort rather than electricity or another type of power ○ *switching to manual control* ■ *n* **1. HANDBOOK** a book that contains information and instructions about the operation of a machine or how to do something **2.** MUSIC **KEYBOARD PLAYED WITH HANDS** an organ or harpsichord keyboard that is played with the hands alone **3.** ARMS **RIFLE DRILL** a drill or exercise in the use of a hand-held weapon ○ *cadets practising the manual of arms* [15C. Directly or via French *manuel* < Latin *manualis* 'of the hand' < *manus* 'hand'] —**manually** *adv*

ORIGIN The Latin word *manus* 'hand', from which ***manual*** derives, is also the source of English *amanuensis, command, demand, manacle, manage, mandate, manifest, manipulate, manner, manoeuvre, manufacture, manure, mastiff, maundy,* and *remand.*

manual alphabet *n* an alphabet in which finger movements and positions stand for letters, used with other hand signs by hearing-impaired people

manual transmission *n* a vehicle transmission that requires the driver to change gear using a clutch

manubrium /mə nyóobri əm/ (*plural* **-bria** /-bri ə/ or **-briums**) *n* a handle-shaped anatomical part, e.g. the upper part of the sternum or part of the inner ear [Mid-17C. < Latin, 'handle' < *manus* 'hand'] —**manubrial** *adj*

Manuel I Comnenus /man wél kom néenəss/ (1122–80) Byzantine emperor. He reigned from 1143 to 1180 and expanded his empire to the west.

Manueline /mánnyoo ə līn/ *adj* built in or characteristic of a style of architecture that developed in early 16th-century Portugal and was characterized by lavish ornamentation, derived largely from marine and nautical forms [Early 20C. After *Manuel* I of Portugal (1469–1521)]

manuf., manufac. *abbr* **1.** manufacture **2.** manufactured **3.** manufacturer

manufactory /mánnyoo fáktəri/ (*plural* **-ries**) *n* MANUF same as **factory** (*archaic*) [Early 17C. < MANUFACTURE]

manufacture /mánnyoo fákchər/ *v* (**-tures, -turing, -tured**) **1.** *vti* **PRODUCE SOMETHING INDUSTRIALLY** to make something into a finished product using raw materials, especially on a large industrial scale ○ *a business manufacturing lightweight metal goods* **2.** *vt* **PRODUCE SOMETHING MECHANICALLY** to produce something in the manner of a machine, without creativity **3.** *vt* **INVENT SOMETHING** to invent or make something up ○ *manufactured an excuse to get out of the meeting* **4.** *vt* BIOCHEM **MAKE BODY CHEMICAL** to produce a substance needed by the body ○ *Bile is manufactured in the liver.* ■ *n* **1. PRODUCTION OF GOODS** the production of finished goods from raw materials, especially on a large industrial scale ○ *engaged in the manufacture of arms for the military* **2. PRODUCT** something that has been produced from raw materials, especially on a large industrial scale (*often used in the plural*) **3.** BIOCHEM **MAKING OF BODY CHEMICAL** the production of a substance needed by the body [Mid-16C. Via French < Italian *manifattura* 'something made by hand' < Latin *manu factum* 'made by hand' < *manus* 'hand'] —**manufacturable** *adj* —**manufacturing** *n, adj*

SYNONYMS See *make*.

manufacturer /mánnyoo fákchərər/ *n* a factory, person, or organization that produces finished goods from raw materials, especially on a large industrial scale

manuka /mə nóokə, maánəkə/ *n* a tree of the myrtle family with aromatic leaves sometimes used for tea. Native to: New Zealand. Latin name: *Leptospermum scoparium*. [Mid-19C. < Maori]

Manukau City /mánnə kow-/ city in the northwest of the North Island, New Zealand, near Auckland. Population: 283,197 (2001).

Manukau Harbour bay on the northwestern coast of the North Island, New Zealand. The city of Auckland lies on its northern shore. Area: 350 sq. km/150 sq. mi.

manumit /mánnyoo mít/ (**-mits, -mitting, -mitted**) *vt* to free somebody from slavery (*formal*) [14C. < Latin *manumittere* < *manu emittere* 'send out from your hand'] —**manumission** /mánnyoo mísh'n/ *n* —**manumitter** *n*

manure /mə nyóor/ *n* **1. FERTILIZER MADE FROM DUNG** animal excrement, often mixed with straw, used as fertilizer for soil **2. ANY FERTILIZER** any fertilizer or compost ■ *vt* (**-nures, -nuring, -nured**) **FERTILIZE WITH MANURE** to spread manure on land or soil to fertilize it [14C. < Anglo-Norman < Old French *manouvrer* 'work with the hands' < medieval Latin *manuoperare* (see MANOEUVRE)]

ORIGIN When English originally took the word ***manure*** over from Anglo-Norman, its connotations of manual labour had been channelled into the management of land, and in particular the cultivation of land. It was not until the middle of the 16th century that the noun ***manure*** came to denote 'fertilizer made from dung'. The related *manoeuvre*, reborrowed from French in the 18th century, has remained in more refined use. See also ***manual***.

manus /máynəss/ (*plural same*) *n* the wrist and hand of humans or the carpus and forefoot of other vertebrates (*technical*) [Early 16C. < Latin, 'hand']

manuscript /mánnyooskript/ *n* **1. HANDWRITTEN BOOK** a book or other text written by hand, especially one written before the invention of printing ○ *rare medieval manuscripts* **2. AUTHOR'S ORIGINAL TEXT** an author's text for a book, article, or other piece of written

work as it is submitted for publication **3. HANDWRITING** handwriting as opposed to the printed word ○ *a manuscript of the text* [Late 16C. < medieval Latin *manuscriptus* 'written by hand' < *scribere* 'write']

Manx /mangks/ *adj* **OF ISLE OF MAN** relating to the Isle of Man or its former Celtic language ■ *n* **LANGUAGE** a language formerly spoken on the Isle of Man, belonging to the Goidelic group of Celtic languages. The last native speaker died in the 1970s, but it survives especially in legal documents and is kept alive as the second language of the island by the Manx Society. ■ *npl* **MANX PEOPLE** the people of the Isle of Man [Early 16C. Alteration of assumed Old Norse *manskr* < Old Irish *Manu* 'Isle of Man'] —**Manxman** *n* —**Manxwoman** *n*

Manx cat, manx cat *n* a short-haired tailless domestic cat [< the origin of the breed in the Isle of Man]

Manx shearwater *n* a seabird with black feathers on its upper parts and white feathers on its underparts that nests in burrows on rocky islands. Native to: Atlantic. Latin name: *Puffinus puffinus*.

many /ménni/ CORE MEANING: a grammatical word referring to a considerable number of people or things ○ (det) *Many people own their homes.* ○ (pron) *Many believe that the matter will never come to trial.* ○ (pron) *Many of you may have heard this.* ○ (adj) *He was among the many visitors to this town.*
1. *det, pron* **CONSIDERABLE NUMBER** a considerable number of people or things ○ (det) *Many children are in the park today.* ○ (pron) *He is a friend to many.* ○ (pron) *Many of us agree with you.* ○ (det) *Among his many faults is self-importance.* **2.** *adj, pron* **LARGE NUMBER** a large number of people or things (used after 'so', 'too', 'not', 'as', 'the', 'that', and possessives) ○ (adj) *She has so many clocks, she can't be sure exactly what time it is.* ○ (adj) *I've just seen too many government studies that don't move quickly enough.* ○ (adj) *There aren't that many people who would agree with you.* ○ (adj) *Among his many interests is mountaineering.* ○ (pron) *Help yourself – you can have as many as you like.* **3.** *adj* **EACH OF A CONSIDERABLE NUMBER** each of a considerable number (used before 'a', 'an', or 'another') ○ *The situation has caused them many a sleepless night.* ○ *We did better than many another regiment.* **4.** *pron* **MAJORITY** the majority of people ○ *All these advantages should be available to the many – not just the few.* [Old English *manig* < Indo-European, 'many, often']

manyfold /ménni fōld/ *adv US* many times over

manyplies /ménni plīz/ (*plural same*) *n* ZOOL same as **omasum** [Late 18C. < MANY + PLY ²; from its many folds]

many-sided *adj* having a large number of sides, aspects, or abilities —**many-sidedness** *n*

many-valued logic *n* a system of logic in which propositions may have values in addition to true or false

manzanilla /mánzə níllə/ *n* a pale dry Spanish sherry [Mid-19C. < Spanish, 'camomile', because its smell resembles camomile]

Manzoni /man zóni, -dzóni/, **Alessandro** (1785–1873) Italian novelist, poet, and playwright. His historical novel *The Betrothed* (1825–27), with its colloquial language, laid the basis for modern Italian fiction. Full name **Manzoni, Alessandro Francesco Tommaso Antonio**

Mao ♦ **Mao Zedong**

MAOI *abbr* MED monoamine oxidase inhibitor

Maoism /mów izəm/ *n* the Marxist-Leninist doctrines, teachings, and policies of the former Chinese leader Mao Zedong —**Maoist** *n, adj*

Mao jacket /mów-/ *n* a plain tunic-style jacket with a stand-up collar often worn by Chairman Mao Zedong and the Chinese people under his regime

Maori /mówri/ (*plural same* or **-ris**) *n* **1.** a member of a Polynesian people living in New Zealand and on the Cook Islands. The Maori are believed to have originated on various Polynesian islands and to have migrated to New Zealand using canoes before the 14th century AD. **2.** the Austronesian language of the Maori people. Native speakers: 300,000. [Mid-19C. < Maori] —**Maori** *adj*

Maoridom /mówridəm/ *n NZ* the world of the Maori people, including their culture, society, and language

Maori hen *n NZ* BIRDS same as **weka**

Maori oven *n NZ* COOK same as **hangi** (sense 1)

Maori rat *n ANZ* same as **kiore**

Maoritanga /mówri tángə/ *n NZ* the culture and way of life of the Maori people [Mid-20C. < Maori]

Maori warden *n NZ* somebody appointed within a Maori community to offer advice and settle minor disciplinary disputes

Mao suit *n* a style of suit consisting of plain loose-fitting trousers and a tunic-style jacket with a stand-up collar often worn by Chairman Mao Zedong and the Chinese people under his regime

AKG London

Mao Zedong

Mao Zedong /mów dzee doöng/, **Mao Tse-tung** /-tsay toöng/ (1893–1976) chairman of the People's Republic of China (1949–76). The leader of the Long March in the Chinese Civil War (1934), he became head of the Chinese Communist Party in the same year. He defeated Chiang's Nationalists after World War II and declared the People's Republic of China in 1949. Known as **Chairman Mao**

'We are advocates of the abolition of war, we do not want war; but war can only be abolished through war, and in order to get rid of the gun it is necessary to take up the gun.'
[Mao Zedong, 'Problems of War and Strategy'; 6 November 1938]

map /map/ *n* **1.** **GEOGRAPHICAL DIAGRAM** a visual representation that shows all or part of the Earth's surface with geographical features, urban areas, roads, and other details **2.** **DIAGRAM OF STARS** a representation of the stars or the surface of a planet, usually in the form of a diagrammatic drawing **3.** **DRAWING SHOWING ROUTE OR LOCATION** a diagrammatic drawing of something such as a route or area made to show the location of a place or how to get there **4.** MATHS same as **function** *n* (sense 7) ■ *vt* (**maps, mapping, mapped**) **1.** **CREATE MAP OF SOMETHING** to re-

present a geographical or other defined area on a map ○ *mapping the heavens* **2.** **DISCOVER AND SHOW SOMETHING** to discover something and create a visual representation of it **3.** GENETICS **NOTE GENE SEQUENCE** to determine and record the sequence of encoded information on a gene or chromosome **4.** MATHS **MATCH SET ELEMENTS** to assign an element in one set to an element in another through a mathematical correspondence [Early 16C. < medieval Latin *mappa* (*mundi*) 'sheet (of the world)' < Latin *mappa* 'towel'] —**mappable** *adj* —**mapper** *n* ◇ **off the map** so as to be no longer famous or important (*informal*) ◇ **on the map** so as to be famous or important (*informal*) ○ *a festival that will put our town on the map*

map out *vt* to arrange or devise something such as a plan in detail

Map /map/, **Mapes** /maps, máy peez/, **Walter** (1140?–1210) English cleric and writer. He was a clerk to Henry II and author of *De Nugis Curialium* (1181–93), a book of satirical anecdotes and reflections.

'The rustics vie with each other in bringing up their ignoble and degenerate offspring to the liberal arts.'
[Walter Map, *De Nugis Curialium*; 1181–93]

maple

maple /máyp'l/ *n* **1.** **TREE** a deciduous tree with winged seeds and lobed leaves. Native to: northern temperate regions. Genus: *Acer*. **2.** **WOOD** the hard wood of the maple tree. Use: furniture, flooring. **3.** **FLAVOUR** the flavour of the processed sap of the sugar maple [Old English *mapul-* < W Germanic]

Maple Leaf *n* the Canadian flag, showing a stylized red maple leaf on a white background between vertical red bars

maple sugar *n* a sugar made by boiling down the sap of the sugar maple

maple syrup *n* a sweet syrup made from the sap of the sugar maple, or from various other sugars and artificial flavouring

mapmaker /máp maykər/ *n* somebody who makes maps —**mapmaking** *n*

mapping /mápping/ *n* **1.** the act or process of making maps **2.** MATHS same as **function** *n* (sense 7)

Mapplethorpe /máyp'l thawrp/, **Robert** (1946–89) US photographer. Acclaimed for his elegant photographic technique and experimentation with printing, light, and colour, he was controversial for the sexually explicit content of his work.

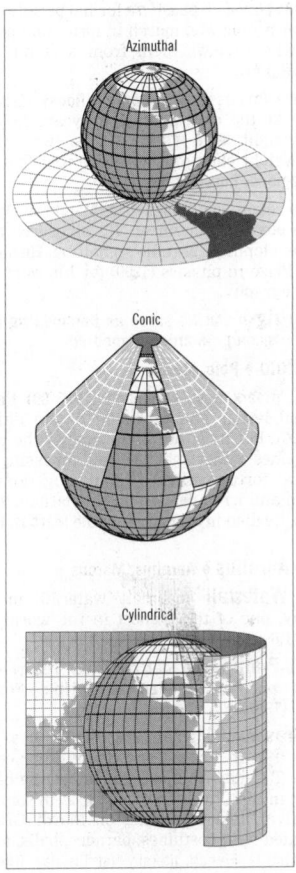

map projection

map projection *n* a representation of or way of representing a three-dimensional object, especially part of the Earth's surface, on a two-dimensional surface

Mapuche /ma póochi/ (*plural same* or **-ches**) *n* **1.** a member of a subgroup of the Araucanian people of central Chile and areas of western Argentina **2.** the Araucanian language of the Mapuche people. Native speakers: 400,000. [Early 20C. < Mapuche, 'country people'] —**Mapuche** *adj*

Maputo /mə póotō/ capital of Mozambique, in the southeast of the country on the Indian Ocean. Population: 1,098,000 (1991 estimate).

maquette /ma két/ *n* a small model of a planned sculpture or architectural work [Early 20C. Via French < Italian *macchietta* 'little spot' < Latin *maculare* 'to spot']

maquiladora /mákilə dáwrə/ *n* an assembly plant in Mexico run by US or other foreign interests. Parts are shipped to Mexico, products are assembled, and finished goods are returned for sale in the markets of origin. [Late 20C. < Mexican Spanish < *maquilar* 'assemble']

maquillage /máki aázh/ *n* **1.** make-up **2.** the art of applying make-up [Late 19C. < French < *maquiller* 'make up the face' < Old French *masquiller* 'to stain']

maquis /ma kée/ (*plural same*) *n* **1.** DENSE COASTAL VEGETATION dense shrubby vegetation of Mediterranean coastal regions **2.** *also* **Maquis FRENCH RESISTANCE** the underground French Resistance movement that fought against the German occupying forces during World War II **3.** *also* **Maquis FRENCH RESISTANCE FIGHTER** a member of the World War II French Resistance movement [Mid-19C. Via French < Italian *macchia* 'spot' < Latin *macula* (from the vegetation's resemblance to spots)]

Maquisard /máki zaár, -zaárd/ *n* HIST same as **maquis** (sense 3) [Mid-20C. < French < *maquis* (see MAQUIS)]

mar /maar/ (**mars, marring, marred**) *vt* to spoil or detract from something [Old English *merran* 'waste, spoil' < Germanic]

mar. *abbr* **1.** maritime **2.** married

Mar. *abbr* March

mara /mə raá/ (*plural* **-ras** or **same**) *n* a large long-legged member of the cavy family that resembles a hare. Native to: Argentine pampas. Latin name: *Dolichotis patagonum*. [Mid-19C. < American Spanish *maráy*]

Mara /maárə/ *n* in Buddhism, a force of evil, sometimes conceived of as a being [Late 19C. < Sanskrit *Māra* 'death' < *mṛ-* 'die']

marabou

marabou /márrəboo/, **marabout** *n* **1.** LARGE AFRICAN STORK a large stork that has dark-grey feathers and a short naked neck with a pink pouch at the front. Marabous are closely related to adjutants. Native to: Africa. Latin name: *Leptoptilos crumeniferus*. **2.** MARABOU FEATHERS down taken from the tail of the marabou. Use: trimming for clothes. **3.** RAW SILK a fine white raw silk [Early 19C. Via French < Arabic *murābit* 'holy man']

marabout[1] /márrəboo/ *n* **1.** a Muslim hermit, monk, or holy man, especially in North Africa **2.** the tomb or a shrine of a marabout, often a destination for pilgrims [Early 17C. Via French < Portuguese *marabuto* < Arabic *murābit* < *ribāt* 'frontier post', because hermits would go to such places to gain merit]

marabout[2] /márrəboo/ *n* BIRDS another spelling of **marabou**

marabunta /márrə búntə/ *n Carib* a red-brown wasp that nests in trees and house eaves. Family: Vespidae. [Late 19C. < a Guyanan name]

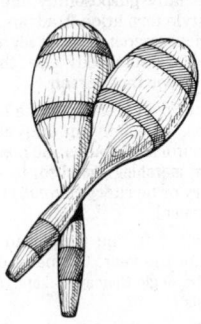

maraca

maraca /mə rákə/ *n* a percussion instrument consisting traditionally of a hollow gourd filled with small pebbles or beans. Maracas are usually shaken in pairs as an accompaniment to Latin American music. [Early 17C. Via Portuguese *maracá* < Tupi *maráka*]

Maracaibo, Lake /márrə kíbō/ largest lake in South America, in northwestern Venezuela, connected by a channel with the Gulf of Venezuela. Area: 13,300 sq. km/5,140 sq. mi.

Maracay /márrə káy/ city in northern Venezuela, near Lake Valencia. Population: 354,196 (1990).

Maradona /marrə dónnə/, **Diego** (*b.* 1960) Argentine footballer. An outstanding midfielder and goalscorer, he captained Argentina to World Cup victory in 1986. Full name **Maradona, Diego Armando**

> 'The goal was scored a little bit by the hand of God and a little bit by the head of Maradona.'
> [Diego Maradona, *Interview*, *Observer*; 28 December 1986]

marae /mə rí/ (*plural same*) *n NZ* **1.** an enclosed space or courtyard in front of a house **2.** in a Maori community, a meeting place [Late 18C. < Polynesian]

maraging steel /máa rayjing-/ *n* a strong low-carbon steel formed by ageing and heating and containing up to 25 per cent nickel with lesser amounts of titanium, aluminium, and niobium [< blend of MARTENSITE + AGE]

Marajó /márra zhő/ island in northeastern Brazil, in the delta of the River Amazon. Area: 40,100 sq. km/15,500 sq. mi.

Marañón /márra nyőn/ river in northern South America, flowing northwards from the Andes into the River Amazon. Length: 1,600 km/990 mi.

maranta /mə rántə/ *n* a plant with variegated thin leaves. Native to: tropical America. Genus: *Maranta*. [Early 19C. < modern Latin, after Bartolomeo Maranta (1500–71), Italian herbalist]

marasca /mə ráskə/ *n* a cultivated variety of sour cherry tree whose fruit is used to make maraschino. Latin name: *Prunus cerasus*. [Mid-19C. < Italian, alteration of *amarasca* < *amaro* 'bitter']

maraschino /márrə skéēnō, -shéēnō/ *n* a sweet liqueur distilled from marasca cherries [Late 18C. < Italian < *marasca* (see MARASCA)]

maraschino cherry *n* a bright red cherry preserved in a sweet syrup flavoured with maraschino or an imitation of this. Use: in cocktails, cake decoration.

marasmus /mə rázməss/ *n* a gradual wasting away of the body, generally associated with severe malnutrition or inadequate absorption of food and occurring mainly in young children [Mid-17C. < modern Latin < Greek *marasmos* 'decay' < *marainein* 'waste away'] —**marasmic** *adj*

Marat /má raa/, **Jean-Paul** (1743–93) French journalist and politician. He was a radical leader of the French Revolution. He was murdered in his bath by Charlotte Corday.

Maratha /mə raátə/, **Maratta, Mahratta** *n* a member of a people living mainly in the Deccan plateau in the Indian state of Maharashtra [Mid-18C. < Marathi *marāthā*, or Hindi *marhattā* < Sanskrit *Mahārāṣtra* 'great kingdom']

Marathi /mə raáti/, **Mahratti** *n* an official language of the Indian state of Maharashtra, belonging to the Indo-Iranian branch of Indo-European. Native speakers: 70 million. ■ *adj* relating to the Indian state of Maharashtra, or its people, language, or culture [Late 17C. < Marathi *marāṭhī* < Sanskrit *Mahārāṣtrī* < *Mahārāṣtra* 'great kingdom']

marathon /márrəth'n, -thon/ *n* **1.** LONG-DISTANCE RACE a long-distance footrace run over a distance of 42.195 km/26 mi. 385 yds **2.** DIFFICULT UNDERTAKING a lengthy and difficult task, event, or activity **3.** ENDURANCE TEST a test of endurance, especially in a competition ○ *a dance marathon* [Late 19C. After MARATHON] —**marathoner** *n*

ORIGIN According to tradition, when the Greek army defeated the Persians at Marathon in 490 BC, the runner Pheidippides was dispatched to bring the good news to Athens (in fact there is no contemporary evidence for the story, which is not recorded until 700 years after the event). When the modern Olympic Games were first held, in Athens in 1896, a long-distance race was introduced to commemorate the ancient feat, run over a course supposedly equal in distance to the journey from Marathon to Athens (about 35 km/22 mi.). The present distance was established at the 1948 London Olympics.

Marathon /márrə thon/ plain in southeastern Greece that was the site of an important Athenian military victory over the Persians in 490 BC

Maratta *n* PEOPLES another spelling of **Maratha**

maraud /mə ráwd/ (**-rauds, -rauding, -rauded**) *vti* to rove around carrying out violent attacks or looking for plunder, or raid a place in search of plunder [Late 17C. < French *marauder* < *maraud* 'rogue, vagabond'] —**marauder** *n* —**marauding** *adj*

Marbella /maar béllə/ resort town in Andalusia, southern Spain, on the Costa del Sol. Population: 110,847 (2001).

marble /maárb'l/ *n* **1.** DENSE CRYSTALLIZED ROCK a form of limestone transformed through the heat and pressure of metamorphism into a dense, variously coloured, crystallized rock. Use: building, sculpture,

monuments. **2. MARBLE SCULPTURE** a sculpture made from marble ○ *the Elgin Marbles* **3. SMALL GLASS BALL** a small hard ball, usually made of glass, used in the game of marbles **4. SOMETHING RESEMBLING MARBLE** something that resembles marble in being cold, hard, smooth, or white (*literary*) ■ *vt* (**-bles, -bling, -bled**) **COLOUR SOMETHING WITH MOTTLED STREAKS** to colour something, usually paper, with mottled streaks to give the appearance of marble [12C. Via French *marbre* < Latin *marmor* < Greek *marmaros* 'hard, shiny stone' (influenced by *marmairein* 'to shine')] —**marbly** *adj*

Marble Bar /maárb'l-/ mining town in northwestern Western Australia. It has the highest average monthly temperatures in Australia. Population: 384 (1991).

marble cake *n* a cake made with two different flavours of sponge, often chocolate and plain, dropped into the same tin and very lightly mixed before baking

marbled /maárb'ld/ *adj* **1. OF OR PATTERNED LIKE MARBLE** made of marble or resembling marble in colouring or mottling ○ *a marbled pediment* **2. COLOURED WITH MOTTLED STREAKS** describes paper or other material coloured with mottled streaks to create the appearance of marble ○ *an 18th-century volume with marbled endpapers* **3. STREAKED WITH FAT** describes lean meat that contains streaks of fat ○ *marbled steak*

marbles /maárb'lz/ *n* **1.** a game, played mainly by children, in which small hard balls are rolled on the ground with the aim of hitting the opponent's ball (*takes a singular verb*) **2.** mental abilities or sense of reality (*informal; takes a plural verb*)

marblewood /maárb'l wòod/ *n* **1.** a mottled black-banded wood. Use: cabinet-making. **2.** a tree of the ebony family that produces marblewood. Native to: Malaysia. Latin name: *Diospyros marmorata*.

marbling /maárbling/ *n* **1. COLOURING LIKE MARBLE** colouring or mottling that looks like marble **2. CREATION OF MARBLED EFFECT** the process of applying mottled streaks of colour to paper or other material to create the appearance of marble **3. STREAKS OF FAT** streaks of fat in lean meat

Marburg disease /maár burg-/ *n* a severe viral infection causing high fever, haemorrhaging, rashes, vomiting, and often death [Mid-20C. After *Marburg*, city in west central Germany]

marc /maark/ *n* **1.** brandy made from the skins and pulp that remain when grapes and other fruit have had their juice pressed out **2.** the skins and pulp remaining after grapes, apples, or other fruit have had their juice pressed out, e.g. for wine-making [Early 17C. < French < *marcher* 'trample' (see MARCH [1])]

Marc /maark/, **Franz** (1880–1916) German painter. He was a founder of the expressionist group Der Blaue Reiter (The Blue Rider). Semiabstract paintings of horses and deer are characteristic of his work.

marcasite /maárka sīt, -zeet/ *n* **1.** a yellowish iron sulphide mineral. Use: jewellery. **2.** polished steel or other white metal cut with facets and used in jewellery, or something made from this [15C. Via medieval Latin *marcasita* < Arabic *markašīṯa* < Persian or Aramaic]

marcato /maar kaátō/ *adv* with a heavy accentuation of individual notes that are often also played in a detached style (*used as a musical direction*) [Mid-19C. < Italian, 'marked, accented'] —**marcato** *adj*

marc brandy *n* BEVERAGES same as **marc** (sense 1)

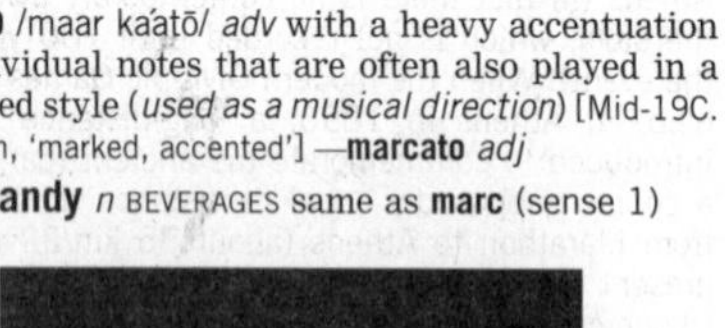

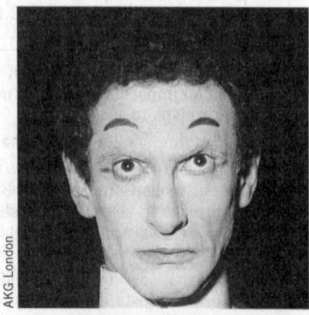

AKG London

Marcel Marceau

Marceau /maar sō/, **Marcel** (*b.* 1923) French mime artist. His white-faced character, Bip, became for a time synonymous with mime.

'Words can be deceitful, but pantomime necessarily is simple, clear and direct.'
[Marcel Marceau, *Theatre Arts*; March 1958]

marcel /maar sél/ *n also* **marcel wave** a women's hairstyle, popular in the 1920s, consisting of regular deep waves created with curling tongs ■ *vt* (**-cels, -celling, -celled**) to style somebody's hair in a marcel [Late 19C. After François *Marcel* Grateau (1852–1936), French hairdresser] —**marcelled** *adj*

marcescent /maar séss'nt/ *adj* remaining attached to a plant when withered ○ *marcescent blossom* [Early 18C. < Latin *marcescent-*, present participle of *marcescere* 'begin to wither' < *marcere* 'wither, decay']

march[1] /maarch/ *v* (**marches, marching, marched**) **1.** *vi* **WALK IN MILITARY FASHION** to walk with regular formalized movements of the arms and legs at a steady rhythmic pace, often in formation **2.** *vti* **MOVE IN MILITARY-STYLE FORMATION** to proceed somewhere, or direct a body of people or troops to proceed somewhere, on foot, in a disciplined military or military-style formation ○ *marched the troops off to battle* **3.** *vi* **SET OFF** to set off, usually on foot, on a military campaign or expedition ○ *Our orders are to march at daybreak.* **4.** *vi* **WALK WITH DETERMINATION** to walk quickly and with an air of determination ○ *marched in and demanded to see the manager* **5.** *vt* **FORCE SOMEBODY TO GO SOMEWHERE** to force somebody to accompany you, usually by physically taking hold of the person ○ *grabbed the boys and marched them into the house* **6.** *vi* **WALK TO PROTEST OR PUBLICIZE SOMETHING** to take part in a political demonstration or protest in the form of an organized walk in procession by a group of people to a place in support of a cause ○ *A huge crowd marched in support of the needy.* **7.** *vi* **PASS STEADILY** to pass steadily or inexorably ○ *Time marches on.* ■ *n* **1. ACT OR EXTENT OF MARCHING** a journey on foot, especially under military discipline or in a military formation ○ *a four-hour march back to the camp* **2. WALK FOR PROTEST OR PUBLICITY** a political demonstration or protest in the form of an organized walk in procession by a group of people to a place in support of a cause ○ *a protest march* **3. MARCHING SPEED** a particular speed or style of marching ○ *advanced at a slow march* **4. MOVEMENT FORWARDS** a steady forward movement or progression ○ *the march of time* **5. MUSIC IN MARCHING RHYTHM** a piece of music especially written or suitable to accompany marching, usually with a regular emphatic beat and in a military style [14C. < French *marcher* < Germanic, 'measure off'] —**marcher** *n* ◇ **on the march 1.** proceeding somewhere on foot, especially purposefully and in a military or military-style formation **2.** advancing or making progress ◇ **steal a march on somebody** to do or achieve something before somebody else, thereby gaining an advantage over that person

march[2] /maarch/ *n* an area along the border between two countries, especially an outlying area that is subject to territorial disputes and hostile incursions ■ *vi* (**marches, marching, marched**) to share a border with a country or territory (*formal*) [13C. < Old French *marche* < Germanic]

March /maarch/ *n* in the Gregorian calendar, the third month of the year, lasting 31 days. See table at **calendar** [< Anglo-Norman < Latin *Martius (mensis)* '(month) of Mars']

MArch *abbr* Master of Architecture

March. *abbr* Marchioness

Marches /maárchiz/ *npl* the areas of land around a national border, e.g. between England and Scotland or England and Wales

marchesa /maar káyza/ (*plural* **-se** /-zay/) *n* an Italian marchioness, holding the title either in her own right or as the wife or widow of a marchese [Late 18C. < Italian, form of *marchese* (see MARCHESE)]

marchese /maar káy zay/ (*plural* **-si** /-zi/) *n* an Italian marquis, a nobleman of a rank above count [Early 16C. < Italian < medieval Latin *(comes) marcensis* 'count of the border' < *marca* 'border' < Germanic]

marching band /maárching-/ *n* a band that plays while marching and performing manoeuvres

marching orders *npl* **1.** a summary dismissal or request to leave (*informal*) ○ *The manager was given his marching orders when the mistake came to light.* **2.** orders to soldiers to set off on a military campaign or expedition

marchioness /maársha néss, -shanəss/ *n* in the United Kingdom, a noblewoman of a rank above countess, or the wife or widow of a marquess [Late 16C. < medieval Latin *marchionissa* < *marca* 'borderland' < Germanic]

marchland /maárch land, -lənd/ *n* an area along the border between two countries [Mid-16C. < MARCH [2]]

marchpast /maárch paast/ *n* a formal parade by troops or other people who march in formation past somebody who reviews them from a stand or other vantage point

Marciano /maárssi aánō, -ánnō/, **Rocky** (1923–69) US boxer. At the end of his four years holding the heavyweight title (1952–56), he was the only heavyweight champion to retire undefeated. Born **Marchegiano, Rocco Francis**

Marconi /maar kṓni/, **Guglielmo, Marchese** (1874–1937) Italian electrical engineer. He pioneered the practical development of radio signalling. He shared the Nobel Prize in physics (1909) for his work in wireless telegraphy.

Marconi rig *n* SAILING same as **Bermuda rig** [After Guglielmo MARCONI] —**Marconi-rigged** *adj*

Marco Polo ♦ **Polo, Marco**

Marcos /maárk oss/, **Ferdinand** (1917–89) Philippine national leader and president of the Philippines (1965–86). For most of his presidency, he ruled the Philippines under martial law, amassing a large personal fortune. Ousted after allegations of corruption and irregularities in the national elections of 1986, he died in exile. Full name **Marcos, Ferdinand Edralin**

Marcus Aurelius ♦ **Aurelius, Marcus**

Mardal Waterfall /maárdəl-/ waterfall in western Norway, one of the highest in the world. Height: 517 m/1,696 ft.

Mar del Plata /maár del plaá taa/ resort city and fishing port in eastern Argentina. Population: 512,880 (1991).

Mardi Gras /maárdi graa/ (*plural* **Mardis Gras** /*pronunc. same*/) *n* **1.** in France and many other countries, Shrove Tuesday, the last day before the beginning of Lent in the Christian calendar **2.** in some places, a carnival held or ending on Mardi Gras, often celebrated with costumes, parades, balls, and other festivities [< French, literally 'fat Tuesday' (the day rich foods were used up before Lent)]

Marduk /maárdòok/ *n* in Babylonian mythology, the god who defeated the great goddess Tiamat and created humankind

mare[1] /mair/ *n* an adult female horse, or an adult female of a species closely related to the horse such as the zebra [Old English *mearh* < Indo-European, 'horse']

mare[2] /maá ray/ (*plural* **-ria** /-ri ə/) *n* a large dark plain on the surface of the Moon or Mars [Mid-19C. < Latin, 'sea']

Mare /mair/ ♦ **de la Mare, Walter**

mare clausum /maá ray klówssòom/ *n* a sea or other area of water that is under the jurisdiction of one country and closed to all others [< Latin, 'closed sea', title of a work (1635) by John Selden defending the right of a single nation to control parts of the sea]

Mare Crisium /maá ray kríssi əm/ lunar lowland plain visible in the northeast quadrant of the Moon, approximately 418 km/260 mi. across

Mare Fecunditatis /-fe kúndi taátiss/ lunar lowland plain visible in the southeast quadrant of the Moon, approximately 1,463 km/909 mi. across

Mare Frigoris /-fri gáwriss/ lunar lowland plain visible near the Moon's north pole, approximately 2,569 km/1,596 mi. across

Mare Humorum /-hyoo máwrəm/ lunar lowland plain visible in the southwest quadrant of the Moon, approximately 626 km/389 mi. across

Mare Imbrium /-ímbri əm/ lunar lowland plain visible in the northwest quadrant of the Moon, approximately 1,807 km/1,123 mi. across

mare liberum /maá ray leebəròom/ *n* an area of sea that is open to the ships of all countries [Mid-17C. < Latin, 'free sea', title of a treatise (1609) by Dutch jurist Hugo Grotius, defending free access to the ocean by all nations]

maremma /mə rémmə/ (*plural* **-me** /-mee/) *n* an area of marshy ground near the sea, especially in Italy [Mid-19C. Via Italian < Latin *maritimus* < *mare* 'sea']

Mare Nectaris /-nek taáriss/ lunar lowland plain visible in the southeast quadrant of the Moon, approximately 536 km/333 mi. across

Marengo /mə réng gō/ *adj* browned in oil and cooked in a sauce of tomatoes, mushrooms, garlic, onion, and white wine ○ *chicken Marengo* [Mid-19C. After *Marengo*, N Italy, where such a dish is said to have been served to Napoleon in 1800]

mare nostrum /maá ray nóstrŏŏm/ *n* an area of sea that is under the jurisdiction of one country or shared by two or more countries [< Latin, 'our sea' (name for the Mediterranean)]

Mare Nubium /-nyóobi əm/ lunar lowland plain visible in the southwest quadrant of the Moon, approximately 1,151 km/715 mi. across

Mare Orientale /-áwri en taáli/ lunar lowland plain on the side of the Moon that is furthest from the Earth, approximately 526 km/327 mi. across

Mare Serenitatis /-sə rénni taátiss/ lunar lowland plain, visible in the northeast quadrant of the Moon, approximately 1,138 km/707 mi. across. It is where Apollo 17 landed.

mare's nest /mairz-/ *n* **1.** a complicated or muddled situation **2.** a discovery at first thought to be important or valuable but subsequently found to be an illusion, a hoax, or valueless

mare's-tail /mairz-/ *n* **1.** a long wispy strand of cloud (*usually used in the plural*) **2.** a water plant with erect, partially submerged, narrow-leaved stems. Latin name: *Hippuris vulgaris*.

Mare Tranquillitatis /-trang kwílli taátiss/ lunar lowland plain visible in the northeast quadrant of the Moon, approximately 873 km/543 mi. across. It was the site of the the first crewed lunar landing, made by Apollo 11 in 1969.

Mareva injunction /mə ráyvə-, mə reévə-/ *n* an injunction allowing a court to freeze a defendant's assets to prevent them from being transferred abroad [Late 20C. After *Mareva* Compania Naviera SA, first plaintiff to be granted an injunction of this type]

Marfan syndrome /maár fan-/, **Marfan's syndrome** *n* a hereditary disorder that affects the body's connective tissues [Mid-20C. After A. B. J. *Marfan* (1858–1942), French paediatrician]

marg *n* FOOD another spelling of **marge** (*informal*)

marg. *abbr* **1.** margin **2.** marginal

Margaret /maárgrət, -ərət/, **St** (1046?–93) queen of Scotland. She was sister of Edgar (the Aetheling) and as wife of Malcolm Canmore, queen of Scotland (1070–93). She instituted reforms in the Celtic Church.

Margaret II, **Margrethe II** /maar gráytə/ (*b.* 1940) queen of Denmark. The Danish constitution was revised (1953) to allow her to become the first queen to rule the country in her own right. She acceded to the throne in 1972.

Margaret (of Anjou) (1430?–82) queen of England. She was the wife of Henry VI of England, and led the Lancastrians in the Wars of the Roses from 1455 until her final defeat in 1471.

Margaret, Princess, Countess of Snowdon (1930–2002) The younger sister of Elizabeth II, queen of the United Kingdom, she was the first president of the Royal Ballet. Born **Princess Margaret Rose**

margaric /maar gárrik/, **margaritic** /maárgə ríttik/ *adj* resembling a pearl or pearls (*formal*) [Early 19C. < French *margarique* < Greek *margaron* 'pearl']

margarine /maárjə reén, maárgə-/ *n* a yellow fat that usually consists of a blend of vegetable oils or animal fats mixed with water, flavouring, and other ingredients [Late 19C. < French]

margarita /maárgə reétə/ *n* a cocktail made with tequila, lemon or lime juice, and an orange-flavoured liqueur, typically served in a chilled glass whose rim has been dipped into salt [Early 20C. < Spanish < the name *Margarita*]

Margarita /maár gə reétə/ island in Nueva Esparta State, northern Venezuela, in the Caribbean Sea. Population: 117,700 (1979). Area: 1,072 sq. km/414 sq. mi.

margaritic *adj* JEWELLERY same as **margaric**

Margasirsa /maárgə séersə/ *n* in the Hindu calendar, the ninth month of the year, lasting 30 days and falling about the same time as November to December. See table at **calendar**

Margate /maár gayt/ seaside resort in northeastern Kent, southeastern England. Population: 51,268 (1998).

margay /maár gay/ *n* a wild cat slightly larger than a domestic cat, with colouring and markings similar to those of a leopard. Native to: rainforests of Central and South America. Latin name: *Felis wiedi*. [Late 18C. < French < Portuguese *maracaj'a* < Tupi *marakaya*]

marge /maarj/, **marg** *n* FOOD same as **margarine** (*informal*) [Early 20C. Shortening]

margin /maárjin/ *n* **1.** BLANK SPACE AT SIDE OF PAGE a blank space on the left or right edge, or at the top or bottom, of a written or printed page ○ *comments scribbled in the margin* **2.** LINE DOWN SIDE OF PAGE a straight line drawn down the left- or right-hand side of a page to separate a narrow section off from the main part ○ *Draw a margin an inch in from the edge.* **3.** OUTER EDGE the edge of something, especially the outer edge, or the area close to it ○ *dark-green leaves with reddish margins* **4.** PART FURTHEST FROM CENTRE a part of something such as a society or organization that is least integrated with its centre, least often considered, least typical, or most vulnerable (*often used in the plural*) ○ *on the margins of society* **5.** LIMIT a boundary indicating the limit beyond which something should not go or below which something should not fall (*often used in the plural*) ○ *beyond the margins of good taste* **6.** DIFFERENCE BETWEEN ONE AMOUNT AND ANOTHER the difference between two amounts or scores ○ *won by a small margin* **7.** ADDITIONAL AMOUNT an amount over and above what is strictly necessary, included for safety reasons or to allow for mistakes or delays ○ *no margin for error* **8.** COMM PROFIT the profit on a transaction, or the amount by which the price of something exceeds its cost ○ *We've cut our margins to the minimum.* **9.** ECON LOWEST VIABLE PROFIT the minimum profit that a business must make in order to remain viable **10.** FIN DIFFERENCE BETWEEN LOAN AND COLLATERAL VALUES the difference between the face value of a loan and the value of the collateral given to secure the loan **11.** FIN BROKER'S LOSS COVER the amount deposited with a stockbroker by a client to cover possible losses on transactions made on account **12.** *Aus* HR, FIN SUPPLEMENT TO WAGES OR SALARY an additional payment made to a worker in recognition of particular skills or to compensate for extra responsibilities ■ *vt* (**-gins, -gining, -gined**) **1.** CREATE MARGIN AROUND SOMETHING to create a margin around something **2.** FIN PLACE SOMETHING AS DEPOSIT WITH BROKER to place something such as collateral with a broker as a deposit [14C. < Latin *margin-* < *margo* < Indo-European, 'boundary, border']

margin account *n* an account with a brokerage that allows the investor to borrow money to buy securities, up to a permitted maximum

marginal /maárjin'l/ *adj* **1.** IN MARGIN written in a margin **2.** SMALL IN SCALE very small in scale or importance ○ *You can ignore any marginal discrepancies you find.* **3.** IRRELEVANT not of central importance or relevance ○ *ignored everything marginal to his main thesis* **4.** ON FRINGE operating or existing on the fringes of a group or movement ○ *a marginal artist* **5.** VERY LOW at or close to the lowest acceptable or viable limit ○ *a marginal standard of living* **6.** POL WON BY SMALL MAJORITY won by only a small majority at a previous election and therefore likely to provide a closely fought contest in any subsequent election ○ *a marginal constituency* **7.** ECON BARELY COVERING COSTS barely able to cover the costs of production when sold or when producing goods for sale **8.** AGRIC DIFFICULT TO CULTIVATE difficult to cultivate and therefore only brought into use if profits are high enough to make it worth the effort ○ *marginal land* ■ *n* POL MARGINAL SEAT a marginal political constituency —**marginality** /maárji nálləti/ *n*

marginal cost *n* the additional cost of producing one more item for sale

marginalia /maárji náyli ə/ *npl* notes written in a margin

marginalize /maárjinə līz/ (**-izes, -izing, -ized**), **marginalise** (**-ises, -ising, -ised**) *vt* to take or keep somebody or something away from the centre of attention, influence, or power —**marginalization** /maárjinə lī záysh'n/ *n*

marginally /maárjinəli/ *adv* **1.** very slightly **2.** only just or barely

marginal utility *n* the increase in utility prompted by one extra unit of a given service or product

marginate /maárji nayt/ *vt* (**-ates, -ating, -ated**) to add a margin to something, or provide something with a margin ■ *adj also* **marginated** /maárji naytid/ with a border or edge of a different colour or pattern ○ *a marginate leaf* —**margination** /maárji náysh'n/ *n*

margin call *n* a demand by a broker to an investor to provide cash or other assets to supplement a margin account

margin of safety *n* **1.** the difference between budgeted output level and the break-even output level **2.** the difference, e.g. in terms of time or space, between a dangerous situation and a state of safety

margravate /maárgrəvət, -vayt/, **margraviate** /maar gráyvi ət, -ayt/ *n* **1.** the territory ruled by a margrave or margravine **2.** the rank or position of a margrave or margravine

margrave /maár grayv/ *n* formerly, a German nobleman of a rank equivalent to a British marquess [Mid-16C. < Middle Dutch *markgrave* 'count of the border'] —**margravial** /maar gráyvi əl/ *adj*

margraviate *n* HIST same as **margravate**

margravine /maárgrə veen/ *n* formerly, a German noblewoman who was the wife or widow of a margrave or who held the rank in her own right [Late 17C. < Dutch *markgravin*, form of *markgraaf* 'margrave']

Margrethe II ♦ **Margaret II**

marguerite /maárgə reét/ *n* a widely cultivated garden plant. Flowers: white or pale yellow petals, yellow centre. Native to: Canary Islands. Latin name: *Chrysanthemum frutescens*. [Early 17C. < French < the name *Marguerite*]

Mari /maári/ (*plural same* or **-ris**) *n* **1.** a member of a people living around western and central stretches of the Volga River in Russia, and in Kazakhstan **2.** the Finno-Ugric language of the Mari people. Native speakers: 700,000. [Early 20C. < Mari] —**Mari** *adj*

maria ASTRON plural of **mare**[2]

mariachi /maári aáchi, márri-/ (*plural* **-chis**) *n* **1.** MEXICAN MUSIC traditional Mexican folk music as played by a mariachi band **2.** MEXICAN STREET BAND a Mexican street band that plays traditional folk music, traditionally consisting of stringed instruments, especially violins and guitars, brass instruments and singers **3.** MEXICAN BAND PLAYER a member of a mariachi band [Mid-20C. < Mexican Spanish]

~~**mariage**~~ incorrect spelling of **marriage**

mariage blanc /márri aazh blaáN/ (*plural* **mariages blancs** /*pronunc. same*/) *n* a marriage that has not been consummated [< French, literally 'white marriage'.]

mariage de convenance /márri aazh də koNvə naáNss/ (*plural* **mariages de convenance** /*pronunc. same*/) *n* same as **marriage of convenience** [< French, 'marriage for expediency or propriety'.]

Marian /máiri ən/ *adj* **1.** OF VIRGIN MARY relating to, characteristic of, or devoted to Mary, the mother of Jesus Christ **2.** OF QUEEN MARY relating to any Mary other than the Virgin Mary, especially Mary, Queen of Scots or Queen Mary I of England ■ *n* DEVOTEE OF VIRGIN MARY a Christian who is especially devoted to Mary, the mother of Jesus Christ

Mariana Islands /márri aánə-/ island group in the western North Pacific Ocean, east of the Philippines, comprising Guam and the Commonwealth of the Northern Mariana Islands. Population: 226,500 (2000). Area: 958 sq. km/370 sq. mi.

Marianao /maárya naá ō/ city in western Cuba, on the northern coast. Population: 133,016 (1989).

Mariana Trench deepest ocean trench in the world, in the western Pacific Ocean, east of the Mariana Islands. Length: 2,550 km/1,580 mi. Depth: 11,000 m/36,200 ft.

Marianne /márri án/ *n* an image of a woman personifying the French republic, e.g. on French coins, usually depicted in a light flowing robe and wearing the Phrygian cap of liberty [Late 19C. < French]

Maria Theresa /mə reé ə tə ráyzə/ (1717–80) archduchess of Austria and queen of Hungary and Bohemia (1740–80). Her succession as ruler of the Hapsburg dominions led to the War of the Austrian Succession (1740–48) and the Seven Years' War (1756–63).

Maria Theresa dollar *n* a silver coin minted in 1780 and used especially in North Africa and Southwest Asia [After MARIA THERESA]

mariculture /márri kulchər/ *n* the cultivation of sea animals and plants in their usual habitats, generally for commercial purposes [Early 20C. < Latin *mari-* (stem of *mare* 'sea')] —**maricultural** *adj* —**mariculturist** *n*

Marie Antoinette /márri antwə nét/ (1755–93) Austrian-born queen of France. The wife of Louis XVI, she was unpopular for promoting the interests of her native Austria and for her extravagance. After attempting to escape the French Revolution, she was captured, imprisoned, and guillotined.

Marie Byrd Land /maári búrd-/ region of western Antarctica, on the Amundsen Sea, east of the Ross Ice Shelf

Marie de Médicis /mə reé də méddi chee/ (1573–1642) queen of France. As widow of Henry IV of France, she became regent during Louis XIII's minority. Political intrigue resulted in her exile in 1630.

Marie-Galante /maa reé gaa lóNt/ island in the eastern Caribbean, a dependency of Guadeloupe. Population: 13,757 (1982). Area: 158 sq. km/61 sq. mi.

Marie-Louise (of Austria) /mə reé loo éez-/ (1791–1847) empress of France. She was Napoleon Bonaparte's second wife.

marigold

marigold /márri gōld/ *n* a common garden plant with stems with a strong smell sometimes thought unpleasant. Flowers: yellow, orange. Native to: tropical America. Genus: *Tagetes.* [14C. < the name *Mary* (referring to the Virgin Mary) + Old English *golde* 'marigold, corn marigold']

marigram /márri gram/ *n* a printed record of tide levels at a particular place [Late 19C. < Latin *mari-*, stem of *mare* 'sea']

marigraph /márri graaf, -graf/ *n* an instrument for recording tide levels [Mid-19C. < Latin *mari-*, stem of *mare* 'sea']

marijuana /márri waánə, -hwaánə/, **marihuana** *n* **1.** same as **cannabis** (sense 1) **2.** the Indian hemp plant that is the source of the drugs marijuana and cannabis. Latin name: *Cannabis sativa.* [Late 19C. < Mexican Spanish *mariguana*]

marimba /mə rímbə/ *n* a large musical instrument like a xylophone, with resonators made from metal or hollow gourds beneath the bars, used especially in African and Latin American music [Early 18C. Via Portuguese < Bantu] —**marimbist** *n*

marina /mə reénə/ *n* a harbour specially designed to cater for pleasure boats and their owners [Early 19C. < Italian or Spanish, 'seashore' < Latin *marinus* < *mare* 'sea']

marinade /márri náyd, -nayd/ *n* a liquid or paste made with ingredients such as vinegar, wine, oil, spices, and herbs, in which food is soaked or allowed to stand to give extra flavour and tenderness before cooking ■ *vti* (**-nades, -nading, -naded**) COOK same as **marinate** [Early 18C. < French < Italian *marinare* or Spanish *marinar* (see MARINATE)]

marinara /márri naárə/ *adj* **1.** made with tomatoes and garlic, often with other ingredients such as onions, parsley, capers, or olives, to serve on pasta or as a pizza topping ○ *marinara sauce* **2.** served with marinara sauce ○ *spaghetti marinara* [Mid-20C. < Italian *alla marinara* 'in sailor style' < *marinaro* 'sailor' < *marino* 'marine' < Latin *marinus* < *mare* 'sea'] —**marinara** *n*

marinate /márri nayt/ (**-nates, -nating, -nated**) *vti* **1.** to be placed or soaked in a marinade, or place or soak food in a marinade **2.** to be exposed to something for a long time, or cause somebody or something to be thoroughly immersed in something ○ *marinated in history* [Mid-17C. < Italian *marinare* or Spanish *marinar* 'pickle in brine' < Latin *(aqua) marina* 'sea (water)', form of *marinus* < *mare* 'sea'] —**marination** /márri náysh'n/ *n*

Marinduque /márrən dóoki/ island in the northwestern Philippines, south of Luzon and east of Mindoro. Population: 173,715 (1980). Area: 960 sq. km/370 sq. mi.

marine /mə reén/ *adj* **1.** OF SEA relating to, found in, or living in the sea **2.** NAUT OF SHIPS relating to ships or sailing **3.** MIL OF SEAGOING SOLDIERS relating to soldiers who serve at sea as well as on land ■ *n* **1.** *also* **Marine** MIL SEAGOING SOLDIER a soldier who serves at sea as well as in the air and on land, e.g. a member of the Royal Marines **2.** ART SEA SCENE a painting or photograph of a seascape, ship, or scene at sea **3.** SHIPPING NATION'S COMMERCIAL FLEET a fleet of merchant or naval ships and their crews (*formal*) [14C. Via French < Latin *marinus* < *mare* 'sea'] ◇ **tell that to the marines** used to express disbelief (*slang*)

marine architect *n* somebody specially trained to design ships —**marine architecture** *n*

marine biology *n* the branch of biology that deals with the plants and animals of the oceans —**marine biologist** *n*

Marine Corps *n* a branch of the US armed forces, trained to operate on land, at sea, and in the air, especially in amphibious assaults

marine engineer *n* somebody who attends to the engines and other heavy machinery of a ship or other offshore structure

mariner /márrinər/ *n* a sailor or navigator of vessels at sea [13C. Via Anglo-Norman or French *marinier* < Latin *marinarius* < *marinus* (see MARINE)]

CULTURAL NOTE ***The Rime of the Ancient Mariner,*** a poem (1798) by Samuel Taylor Coleridge. A cautionary tale of sin and redemption, it describes a curse placed on a sailor after he kills an albatross that has led his ship out of danger. The vessel is becalmed and the rest of the crew die of thirst. After his rescue, the sailor is compelled to recount his story for the remainder of his days. The expression 'Water, water, every where/ Nor any drop to drink' comes from this poem.

---

mariner's compass *n* a navigational ship's compass set within a binnacle

marine snow *n* small particles of organic and inorganic debris that drift down from the upper layers of the ocean to the bottom

Marinetti /márri nétti/, **Filippo** (1876–1944) Italian writer and political activist. His writings reflect the tenets of futurism, which he founded in 1909. Full name **Marinetti, Filippo Thommaso Emilio**

marinière /márrini áir/ *adj* cooked with a little wine, herbs, and chopped onion or shallot in a closed pan, so that the main ingredient, which is usually mussels, is partly poached and partly steamed [< French, 'sailor-style']

Mariolatry /máiri óllətri, márri-/ *n* in Christian doctrine, extreme devotion to Mary, the mother of Jesus Christ [Early 17C. < Latin *Maria* 'Mary'] —**Mariolater** *n* —**Mariolatrous** *adj*

Mariology /máiri ólləji, márri-/ *n* in Christianity, the study of the doctrines and beliefs concerning Mary, the mother of Jesus Christ [Mid-19C. < Latin *Maria* 'Mary'] —**Mariological** /máiri ə lójjik'l, márri-/ *adj* —**Mariologist** *n*

marionette /márri ə nét/ *n* a puppet operated by means of strings attached to its hands, legs, head, and body [Early 17C. < French, 'little Mary' < *Marion*]

mariposa /márri pōzə, -pōssə/ *n* a bulbous plant of the lily family. Flowers: brightly coloured, tulip-shaped. Native to: western North America. Genus: *Calochortus.* [Mid-19C. < Spanish, 'butterfly' (from its brightly coloured flowers)]

Marist /máirist/ *n* **1.** MEMBER OF SOCIETY OF MARY a member of the Society of Mary (**Marist Fathers**), a Roman Catholic order **2.** A MEMBER OF THE LITTLE BROTHERS OF MEMBER OF LITTLE BROTHERS OF MARY a member of the Little Brothers of Mary or (**Marist Brothers**), a Roman Catholic order **3.** *NZ* TEACHER OR PUPIL IN MARIST SCHOOL a teacher or pupil in a school run by the Society of Mary [Late 19C. < French *mariste* < *Marie* 'Mary'] —**Marist** *adj*

Maritain /márri táN, -táyn/, **Jacques** (1882–1973) French philosopher. An exponent of neo-Scholasticism, his greatest work was in epistemology, political philosophy, and aesthetics.

marital /márrit'l/ *adj* **1.** relating to marriage or the marriage of a particular couple **2.** relating to a husband or husbands (*formal*) [15C. < Latin *maritalis* < *maritus* 'married'] —**maritally** *adv*

marital status *n* the fact of somebody's being unmarried, married, or formerly married

maritime /márri tīm/ *adj* **1.** OF SEA relating to the sea, shipping, sailing in ships, or living and working at sea **2.** CLOSE TO SEA situated or living close to the sea ○ *the maritime region* **3.** METEOROL INFLUENCED BY SEA describes a climate influenced by the sea, and therefore generally temperate and with relatively small variations in temperatures [Mid-16C. Directly or via French < Latin *maritimus* < *mare* 'sea']

Maritime Provinces /márri tīm-/, **Maritimes** collective name for the eastern Canadian provinces of New Brunswick, Nova Scotia, and Prince Edward Island —**Maritimer** *n*

Maritsa /mə reétsə/ river in southeastern Europe, in the Balkan Peninsula. Length: 480 km/300 mi.

Mariupol /márri óo pol/ city in southeastern Ukraine, on the Sea of Azov. Population: 500,000 (1998).

Marius /márri əss, máiri-/, **Gaius** (157?–86 BC) Roman general and political leader. His political rivalry with Lucius Sulla led to the Roman civil war of 88–86 BC, in which Marius was victorious.

Marivaux /márri vō/, **Pierre Carlet de Chamblain de** (1688–1763) French playwright and novelist. His romantic comedies and novels portray 18th-century French middle-class life.

marjoram /maárjərəm/ *n* a herb with aromatic leaves and small purple or white flowers. Use: seasoning in cookery and salads. Native to: Mediterranean. Latin name: *Origanum majorana.* [14C. Via Old French *marjorane* < medieval Latin *majorana*]

mark[1] /maark/ *n* **1.** SPOT, SCRATCH, OR DENT a spot, scratch, or dent on the surface of something ○ *The hot plate left a mark on the table.* **2.** SYMBOL a recognizable sign or symbol used to indicate, e.g. ownership or the quality or origin of goods, or punctuation in a piece of writing (*often used in combination*) ○ *a question mark* **3.** SUBSTITUTE FOR SIGNATURE a cross or other symbol used in place of a signature by somebody who cannot write **4.** INDICATION OF FEELING an action, gesture, or other outward sign of somebody's feeling or attitude ○ *a mark of respect* **5.** SIGN OF INFLUENCE OR INVOLVEMENT evidence of the influence or involvement of somebody or something ○ *He left his mark on the firm.* **6.** IDENTIFYING FEATURE OR CHARACTERISTIC a distinctive and identifying feature or characteristic ○ *That perfect finish is the mark of the true professional.* **7.** INDICATION OF CORRECTNESS OR QUALITY a number, letter, or percentage indicating somebody's assessment of the correctness or quality of something such as answers to examination questions or somebody's performance in a contest ○ *She always gets top marks in English.* **8.** INDICATOR OF POSITION OR EXTENT an object, sign, or line that indicates the position, extent, or amount of something ○ *the high-water mark* **9.** AMOUNT the amount, distance, or level reached by something ○ *The temperature is way above the 80 degree mark.* **10.** STANDARD the desired or required standard for something ○ *Your work is simply not up to the mark these days.* **11.** TYPE a model or variety, e.g. of a car, aircraft, or weapon, usually distinguished from earlier or later models by a number **12.** TARGET a target or something that somebody aims at with a weapon ○ *He missed the mark.* **13.** GOAL a goal or standard that somebody wishes to achieve **14.** CRIME VICTIM OF CRIME the victim or intended victim of a theft or swindle (*slang*) ○ *a soft mark* **15.** ATHLETICS STARTING LINE the starting line for a race **16.** RUGBY INSTANCE OF PLAYER SHOUTING MARK in a game of rugby, an instance of a player within his or her 22 m line shouting 'mark' when intercepting the ball from an opponent's kick, entitling him or her to a free kick **17.** FOOTBALL CATCH OF BALL in Australian Rules football, a catch made after an opponent kicks the ball at least 9 m/10 yd without it touching the ground or another player. This entitles the catcher to a free kick. **18.** BOXING MIDDLE OF STOMACH in boxing, the middle of an opponent's stomach **19.**

same as **jack**[1] *n* (sense 5) **20.** NAUT **INDICATOR OF WATER DEPTH** a knot or other marker used to indicate intervals of fathoms on a sounding line **21.** NAVIG **GUIDE TO POSITION OR DIRECTION** a conspicuous object or another point of reference that serves as a visual guide **22.** HIST **COMMON LAND** in medieval Germany and England, land held in common by the members of a community ■ **marks** *npl* ATHLETICS **RUNNER'S STARTING POSITION** a runner's individual starting position for a race ■ *v* **(marks, marking, marked) 1.** *vti* **MAKE UNSIGHTLY MARK ON SOMETHING** to make a dent, scratch, or other mark on something, or become damaged in this way ○ *The mugs have marked the table.* **2.** *vt* **PUT SIGN OR SYMBOL ON SOMETHING** to put writing or a recognizable sign or symbol on something, e.g. to show ownership, to indicate price, or to give a warning or instruction ○ *All items of clothing must be clearly marked with the student's name.* **3.** *vt* **SHOW SOMETHING CLEARLY** to make something clearly visible, recognizable, or traceable by indicating it with a mark ○ *I've marked on the map where our house is.* **4.** *vt* **INDICATE LOCATION** to be an indicator showing where something is situated, how far it extends, or where an event took place ○ *This monument marks their last resting place.* **5.** *vt* **INDICATE POINT OF CHANGE** to indicate something, especially a significant point in time or in a process, has been reached ○ *It marks the end of an era in British theatre.* **6.** *vt* **COMMEMORATE EVENT** to give prominence to a particular event or anniversary, usually by holding a celebration ○ *a party to mark their 50th anniversary* **7.** *vt* **SELECT SOMEBODY FOR SPECIAL ATTENTION** to select or destine somebody or something for particular attention or treatment ○ *He was always marked out for success.* **8.** *vt* **MAKE SOMEBODY WORTHY OF NOTICE** to characterize, distinguish, or set somebody or something apart in some way ○ *The originality of her approach marks her as a candidate of real distinction.* **9.** *vti* **ASSESS QUALITY OR CORRECTNESS OF SOMETHING** to assess the quality or correctness of something and indicate the assessment by means of a mark such as a tick or cross, a letter, number, or percentage ○ *marking exam papers* **10.** *vt* **ASSESS WORK OF SOMEBODY** to assess somebody on the basis of the quality or correctness of his or her work or performance ○ *marked him high on the test* **11.** *vt* **TAKE NOTICE OF** to pay attention to something or somebody (*often used as a command*) ○ *Mark my words, this'll make them sit up and take notice.* **12.** *vt* **SEE SOMETHING** to see or notice something (*archaic*) **13.** *vt* **STAY CLOSE TO PLAYER** in games such as football and hockey, to stay close to an attacking player in the opposing team to prevent the player from receiving the ball or scoring **14.** *vti* **KEEP SCORE** to keep a note of the score **15.** *vt* FOOTBALL **MAKE MARK** in Australian Rules football, to catch the ball after it has been kicked at least 9 m/10 yds without having touched the ground or another player **16.** *vt* *ANZ* AGRIC **CASTRATE** to castrate a lamb or calf ■ *interj* RUGBY **SHOUT BY RUGBY PLAYER** in a game of rugby, the shout made by a player who catches the ball within his or her own 22 m line in order to claim a free kick [Old English *mearc* 'boundary, marker' < Indo-European, 'boundary'] ◇ **make your mark** to achieve recognition or success, usually in a particular field ◇ **mark you** used to call somebody's attention to a point or remark that you are making ◇ **on your marks** used as a command to runners to take up their starting positions for the start of a race ◇ **quick** *or* **slow off the mark** quick *or* slow to begin, react to, or understand something ◇ **up to the mark** of an acceptable standard or quality, or at an acceptable level ◇ **wide of the mark, off the mark** inaccurate or incorrect

SPELLCHECK Do not confuse the spelling of ***mark*** and ***marque*** ('a commercial brand'), which sound similar. The confusion may arise because of the sense of the noun ***mark*** meaning 'a model or variety of a car, weapon, etc., usually distinguished from an earlier or later one'. ***Marque*** denotes a make rather than a specific model of car, and is restricted to prestigious cars.

mark down *vt* **1. LOWER PRICE** to lower the price of something **2. MAKE WRITTEN NOTE OF SOMETHING** to make a written note of something somewhere **3. GIVE SOMEBODY OR SOMETHING LOWER MARK** to reduce the mark given to something or somebody in a test, examination, or contest ○ *You get marked down for bad spelling.* **4. FORM OPINION OF SOMEBODY** to make a judgment as to the character or likely behaviour of somebody

mark off *vt* **1. SEPARATE AREAS FROM ONE ANOTHER** to separate one area from another by means of a boundary line or barrier **2. MAKE SOMEBODY OR SOMETHING DIFFERENT** to make, or show somebody or something to be, different from others ○ *Her mathematical ability marks her off from the rest of her class.* **3. MARK SOMETHING AS DEALT WITH** to put a mark such as a tick, cross, or line beside, through, or around something, to show that it has been dealt with or to highlight it

mark out *vt* **1.** to draw lines, or use some similar method, to indicate the boundaries and divisions of something, especially the playing area for a game or a racecourse **2.** to make somebody or something noticeably different from and often superior to others

mark up *vt* **1.** BUSINESS **INCREASE PRICE OF SOMETHING** to increase the price of something, especially in order to provide the seller with a profit **2.** PUBL **CORRECT TEXT FOR PRINTING** to prepare a piece of written work for printing or rekeying by making corrections to it or adding instructions to the typesetters or keyboarders **3.** EDUC **INCREASE MARKS FOR SOMETHING** to increase the marks awarded to somebody or something in a test, examination, or contest

mark[2] /maark/ *n* **1.** MONEY, HIST same as **Deutschmark** **2.** a former unit of currency in England and Scotland that was worth 13 shillings and 4 pence, or two thirds of a pound **3.** a former unit of weight for gold and silver [Old English *marc*, a unit of weight < Germanic]

Mark /maark/ *n* a book of the Bible, the second of the gospels in which the life and teachings of Jesus Christ are described, traditionally attributed to St Mark. See table at **Bible**

Mark /maark/, **St** (*fl* 1st century) evangelist. A disciple of St Peter and one of the apostles of Jesus Christ, he is credited with writing the second Gospel in the Bible.

marka /múrkə/ *n* the main unit of currency in Bosnia and Herzegovina. See table at **currency** [< Serbo-Croatian < German *Mark* 'mark' (currency)]

Marka /múrkə/ port in southeastern Somalia. Population: 70,000 (1985).

Mark Antony ➧ **Antony, Mark**

markdown /maárk down/ *n* a reduction in price

marked /maarkt/ *adj* **1. NOTICEABLE** very noticeable ○ *a marked contrast* **2. SINGLED OUT** singled out for surveillance, suspicion, hostility, or an unpleasant fate ○ *a marked man* **3.** CARDS **WITH CONCEALED SYMBOL** having a concealed identifying mark that enables somebody to cheat in card games or perform conjuring tricks ○ *marked cards* **4.** LING **WITH DISTINCTIVE LINGUISTIC FEATURE** having an extra or less usual distinctive linguistic feature —**markedness** /maárkidnəss/ *n*

markedly /maárkidli/ *adv* to a significant extent or degree

marker /maárkər/ *n* **1. INDICATOR** an object or sign that indicates the position or presence of something or the direction in which somebody is to go **2. SOMETHING THAT MAKES MARKS** something used to make marks, especially a felt-tip pen **3. ASSESSOR OF SCHOOLWORK OR EXAMS** somebody who assesses examination papers or student exercises **4. PLAYER GUARDING ANOTHER** in games such as football and hockey, a player who stays close to an attacking player in the opposing team to prevent him or her from receiving the ball or scoring **5. SCOREKEEPER** in games such as snooker and billiards, somebody who records the score, or a record of the score

market /maárkit/ *n* **1. GATHERING FOR BUYING AND SELLING** a gathering in a public place for buying and selling goods or farm products, especially one held regularly ○ *a cattle market* **2. MARKET BUILDING OR PLACE** a building or open space where a market is regularly held **3. COLLECTION OF SHOPS OR STALLS** a number of small independently operated shops or stalls, housed in the same building and sometimes all selling the same type of goods **4.** ECON, POL **SUPPLY AND DEMAND** the whole area of economic activity in which the laws of supply and demand operate, often thought of as a regulatory force affecting both economic and political affairs ○ *market forces* **5. SHOP** a shop, especially one that sells goods or food of a particular type **6.** COMM **REGION OR GROUP AS CUSTOMERS** a geographical area or a section of the population, considered from the point of view of the amount of goods that can be sold to it ○ *the teenage market* **7.** COMM **DEMAND** the demand for goods or services being offered for sale ○ *You've got to go out and create a market if you want to succeed.* **8.** FIN **BUYING AND SELLING** the trade in a particular commodity ○ *the futures market* **9.** FIN same as **stock market** ○ *Prices rose on the New York and Chicago markets this morning.* **10.** FIN **TRADING IN STOCKS** trading in stocks, shares, and commodities ○ *The market was very slow this morning but picked up later.* **11.** FIN **PRICES OR EXCHANGE RATES** the prices or rates of exchange offered for stocks, shares, or commodities ○ *The market fell this morning but rallied later.* ■ *v* **(-kets, -keting, -keted) 1.** *vt* **PROMOTE PRODUCT** to use advertising and other promotional techniques to attract buyers for something when it is put on sale ○ *If this is marketed in the right way, it'll sell very well.* **2.** *vt* **OFFER SOMETHING FOR SALE** to offer something for sale, or sell something, in a market ○ *We market a wide range of goods.* **3.** *vi* *Malaysia, S Asia, Singapore* **SHOP AT MARKET** to go shopping at a market [Pre-12C. Via Old French dialect < Latin *mercat-*, past participle of *mercari* 'buy' < *merx* 'goods'] —**marketer** *n* ◇ **come onto the market** to become available for customers to buy ◇ **in the market (for something)** interested in buying or ready to buy something ◇ **on the market** available for customers to buy ◇ **on the open market** freely available and priced according to the law of supply and demand ◇ **price something out of the market** to charge so high a price for something as to make its sale unlikely ◇ **put something on the market** to offer something for sale

marketable /maárkitəb'l/ *adj* **1. SUITABLE FOR SELLING** fit to be sold ○ *a highly marketable property* **2. IN DEMAND** in demand and therefore relatively easy to sell ○ *skills that are readily marketable* **3.** FIN **CONVERTIBLE INTO CASH** able to be converted into cash quickly, but at a price that is determined by the market in that commodity ○ *marketable value* —**marketability** /maárkitə bíllәti/ *n*

market basket *n* **1.** *US* a shopping trolley **2.** *N Am* a selection of foods representing the theoretical requirements of a household of 3.2 people or a family of four, the cost of which is a factor in cost-of-living statistics

market capitalization *n* a method of assessing the value of a company by multiplying the number of shares by the stock market price

market economy *n* an economy in which prices and wages are determined mainly by supply and demand, rather than being regulated by a government

marketeer /maárki téer/ *n* **1.** a buyer or seller in a market **2.** an advocate or supporter of a specific type of market (*usually used in combination*) ○ *a free marketeer*

market garden *n* a plot of ground or small farm where fruit, vegetables, and sometimes flowers are grown for sale rather than for the grower's own use —**market gardener** *n* —**market gardening** *n*

marketing /maárkiting/ *n* the business activity of presenting products or services in such a way as to make them desirable

marketing board *n UK, Can* an organization set up by a government to promote and regulate the sale of a particular agricultural product

marketing mix *n* a mixture of marketing techniques such as pricing, packaging, and advertising used to promote the sale of a product

market leader *n* a company or brand that has a very large, or the largest, share of the market for a particular product

market maker *n* a dealer in securities who offers to buy and sell at a guaranteed price

market order *n* an order instructing a broker to buy or sell an asset immediately at the best prevailing price

marketplace /maárkit playss/ *n* **1. OPEN SPACE FOR MARKET** an open space where a market is held **2. SPHERE OF TRADING** the commercial sphere where buying and selling takes place and the laws of supply and demand operate **3. SET-UP WHERE IDEAS CAN BE DISCUSSED** a forum in which ideas are exchanged, discussed, and compete for recognition

market price *n* the price at which something is currently being bought by the majority of customers

market research *n* the gathering and analysis of information about what people want or like or what they actually buy —**market researcher** *n*

market share *n* the proportion of the total sales of a product secured by one particular company or brand

market town *n* a town in which a market is held regularly, usually the chief town of a farming area

market value *n* the amount that a seller could expect to obtain for property or goods sold on the open market

markhor /maár kawr/ (*plural* **-khors** or *same*) *n* the largest wild goat, which has a reddish-brown coat, spiral horns, and a shaggy beard on the male. Native to: Himalayan range. Latin name: *Capra falconeri*. [Mid-19C. < Persian *mār-kwār* 'serpent-eater']

marking /maár king/ *n* **1.** NATURAL PATTERN a mark or pattern of marks that occurs naturally, e.g. on an animal's coat (*often used in the plural*) **2.** AVIAT AIRCRAFT IDENTIFYING MARK an identifying mark, usually a coloured symbol, on an aircraft (*often used in the plural*) **3.** EDUC ASSESSMENT AND GRADING OF WRITTEN WORK a teacher's correction and assessment of students' written work **4.** EDUC WRITTEN WORK TO BE MARKED a quantity of written work that has to be corrected and assessed

marking ink *n* an ink used for writing on such things as clothes and bed linen because it does not wash out

markka /maár kaa, -kə/ (*plural* **-kaa** /-kaa/) *n* the main unit of the former Finnish currency [Early 20C. Via Finnish < Swedish *marka*]

Dame Alicia Markova: in *Mr Puppet* with Anton Dolin

Markova /maar kóvə/, **Dame Alicia** (*b.* 1910) British ballerina. She was a cofounder of the London Festival Ballet (1950) and director of the Metropolitan Opera Ballet (1963–69). Born **Marks, Lillian Alicia**

Markov chain /maár kof-/ *n* a random process in which events are discrete rather than continuous, and the future development of each event is independent of all historical events, or dependent only on the immediately preceding event [See MARKOV PROCESS]

Markov process /maárkof-/ *n* a continuous random process in which the probability of occurrence of each random event in a series is independent of all historical events, or dependent only on the immediately preceding event [After A. A. *Markov* (1856–1922), Russian mathematician]

Marks /maarks/, **Simon, 1st Baron Marks of Broughton** (1888–1964) British retailing magnate. He was the son of Michael Marks, the founder of Marks and Spencer. With Israel Seiff he transformed the company into a successful British retailing chain.

marksman /maárksmən/ (*plural* **-men** /-mən/) *n* **1.** somebody, especially a man, who is an accurate shooter, especially with a rifle **2.** somebody, especially a man, considered from the point of view of his or her ability to shoot accurately —**marksmanship** *n*

markswoman /maárks woòmən/ (*plural* **-men** /-wimin/) *n* **1.** a woman who is an accurate shooter, especially with a rifle **2.** a woman considered from the point of view of her ability to shoot accurately

markup /maárk up/ *n* **1.** the difference between the manufacturing cost or wholesale price of an item and its retail price **2.** the addition to a text that is to be printed of coding or instructions for layout and style

markup language *n* a computer coding system specifying the layout and format of a document

marl[1] /maarl/ *n* a naturally occurring fine crumbly mixture of clay and limestone, often containing shell remains and sometimes other minerals. Use:

fertilizer, water softener. ■ *vt* (**marls, marling, marled**) to add marl to soil as a fertilizer [14C. Via Old French *marle* < medieval Latin *margila* < Latin *marga*, after *argilla* 'white clay'] —**marly** *adj*

marl[2] /maarl/ (**marls, marling, marled**) *vt* to bind something with a marline [Early 18C. < Dutch *marlen* 'keep binding' < Middle Dutch *marren* 'to bind']

Marlborough /maárlbərə/ **1.** market town in Wiltshire, southwestern England. Population: 6,429 (1991). **2.** administrative region of New Zealand, occupying the northeastern corner of the South Island. It is chiefly an agricultural district. Population: 39,561 (2001).

Marlborough, John Churchill, 1st Duke of (1650–1722) English general. He won a string of brilliant victories as commander in chief of English forces during the War of the Spanish Succession (1701–14).

> 'I have not time to say more, but to beg you will give my duty to the Queen, and let her know her army has had a glorious victory. Monsieur Tallard and two other generals are in my coach, and I am following the rest.'
> [John Churchill Marlborough, *Message written on a tavern bill*; 13 August 1704]

Marley /maárli/, **Bob** (1945–81) Jamaican musician. His music, much of which he wrote himself, established reggae internationally as an important part of pop music. Full name **Marley, Robert Nesta**

> 'Reggae is a music that has plenty fight. But only the music should fight, not the people.'
> [Bob Marley. Quoted in *Bob Marley in His Own Words*, Ian McCann; 1993]

marlin /maárlin/ (*plural* **-lins** or *same*) *n* a large game fish with a very long thin upper jaw, like a spear. Native to: warm regions of the Atlantic and Pacific oceans. Family: Istiophoridae. [Early 20C. Shortening of *marlinspike*; from the shape of its upper jaw]

marline /maárlin/, **marlin** *n* a light two-stranded rope, used especially for binding the ends of larger ropes to prevent them from fraying [15C. < Dutch *marlijn* 'binding line', *marling* 'binding' < Middle Dutch *marren* 'to bind']

marlinespike /maárlin spīk/, **marlinspike** *n* a pointed metal tool used to separate strands of rope that are being spliced [Early 17C. Alteration (influenced by MARLINE) of *marlingspike* < MARL [2] + SPIKE [1]]

marlite /maár līt/ *n* a rock with the same composition as marl but with a harder, more resistant texture [Late 18C. < MARL [1]] —**marlitic** /maar líttik/ *adj*

Marlowe /maárlō/, **Christopher** (1564–93) English playwright. Often considered the first great English playwright, he wrote tragedies including *The Tragical History of Doctor Faustus* (1604?) and *Edward II* (1594).

> 'Was this the face that launch'd a thousand ships /And burnt the topless towers of Ilium? /Sweet Helen, make me immortal with a kiss.'
> [Christopher Marlowe, *Doctor Faustus*; 1592?]

marlstone /maárl stōn/ *n* GEOL same as **marlite**

marmalade /maármə layd/ *n* a clear thick preserve made with citrus fruits, usually containing the shredded rind of the fruit ■ *adj* describes cats with orange fur or orange fur streaked with yellow or brown [15C. Via French *marmelade* 'quince jam' < Portuguese *marmelada* < *marmelo* 'quince' < Greek *melimēlon* 'honey-apple', a kind of apple grafted onto the quince]

marmalade plum *n* FOOD same as **sapote** (sense 1)

marmalade tree *n* TREES same as **sapote** (sense 2)

Marmara, Sea of /maármərə/, **Marmora, Sea of** inland sea in northwestern Turkey, separating the Asian and European regions of the country. It is connected with the Black Sea by the Bosporus and with the Aegean Sea by the Dardanelles. Area: 11,350 sq. km/4,382 sq. mi.

marmite /maár mīt/ *n* a deep earthenware or metal cooking pot with a close-fitting lid, used for making soups, stews, or stock [Early 19C. Via French < Old French, 'hypocritical' < *marmouser* 'to murmur' + *mite* 'cat', imitations of sounds]

Marmite /maár mīt/ *tdmk* a trademark for a sticky

dark brown mixture of yeast and vegetable extracts, used as a spread and for flavouring

Marmolada /maármə laádə, maármo-/ highest mountain in the Dolomites, located in northeastern Italy. Height: 3,342 m/10,965 ft.

Marmora, Sea of another spelling of **Marmara, Sea of**

marmoreal /maar máwri əl/ *adj* made of marble, or like marble, especially in being white, cold, or aloof and impressive (*literary*) [Late 18C. < Latin *marmoreus* < *marmor* (see MARBLE)] —**marmoreally** *adv*

marmoset /maármə zét, -zet/ (*plural* **-sets** or *same*) *n* a small monkey that has soft thick fur, tufts of fur around its head and ears, a long tail, and clawed digits. Native to: Central and South America. Family: Callithricidae. [14C. < French *marmouset* 'grotesque figure']

marmot /maármət/ (*plural* **-mots** or *same*) *n* a large brownish rodent of the squirrel family that lives on the ground and in burrows. Native to: North America, Europe, northern Asia. Genus: *Marmota*. [Early 17C. < French *marmotte*]

Marne /maarn/ river in northern France. Length: 525 km/326 mi.

marocain /márrə kayn, -káyn/ *n* a ribbed crêpe fabric [Early 20C. < French, 'Moroccan']

Maronite /márrə nīt/ *adj* belonging or relating to the Christian Uniat Church of the Lebanon, an Eastern Catholic church [Early 16C. < medieval Latin *Maronita*, after *Maro*, 4C Syrian hermit] —**Maronite** *n*

Maroochydore /maroóchee dawr/ coastal town in southeastern Queensland, Australia, located at the mouth of the River Maroochy. Population: 36,406 (1996).

maroon[1] /mə roón/ *n* **1.** a deep purplish-red colour tinged with brown **2.** a small explosive device that makes a loud noise and is used for giving distress or warning signals [Late 18C. < French *marron* 'large sweet chestnut' < medieval Greek *maraon*] —**maroon** *adj*

maroon[2] /mə roón/ *vt* (**-roons, -rooning, -rooned**) **1.** LEAVE SOMEBODY ISOLATED to leave somebody or something somewhere with no means of getting away **2.** ABANDON SOMEBODY ON ISLAND to put somebody ashore on a lonely island or coast and leave him or her there with no means of escape ■ *n* **1.** also **Maroon** DESCENDANT OF ESCAPED SLAVES a descendant of people escaped from slavery in Guyana and the remoter parts of the Caribbean **2.** MAROONED PERSON somebody who has been marooned, especially on a desert island [Mid-17C < French *marron* 'fugitive from slavery', shortening of American Spanish *cimarrón* 'wild, untamed', probably < *cima* 'peak']

maroquin /márrə keén, -kin, -kwin/ *n* INDUST same as **morocco** [Early 16C. < French < *Maroc* 'Morocco']

Marq. *abbr* **1.** Marquess **2.** Marquis

marque /maark/ *n* a brand or make of product, especially a make of a luxury or high-performance car [Early 20C. < French < *marquer* 'to mark' < Germanic]

SPELLCHECK See *mark*[1].

marquee /maar keé/ *n* **1.** LARGE TENT a very large tent with straight sides that can be rolled up or removed, used for large gatherings such as parties, meetings, sales, and exhibitions **2.** *N Am* COVERING LIKE ROOF a permanent canopy, often of metal and glass, projecting out over the entrance to a large building such as a hotel or theatre **3.** ONLINE SCROLLING SCREEN MESSAGE a piece of text that scrolls across a screen horizontally or vertically in a highlighted band ■ *adj N Am* HAVING PUBLIC APPEAL having public appeal or considered in connection with public appeal ○ *a team with no marquee names* ○ *a star with great marquee value* [Late 17C. Alteration of French *marquise* 'canopy over a nobleman's tent' (see MARQUISE)]

Marquesas Islands /maar káyssəss-/ group of volcanic islands in French Polynesia, 1,200 km/740 mi. north of Tahiti, in the South Pacific Ocean. Population: 7,538 (1988). Area: 1,274 sq. km/492 sq. mi.

marquess /maárkwiss/ *n* in the United Kingdom, a nobleman ranking between a duke and an earl [15C. < Old French *marchis* < *marche* (see MARCH [2])] —**marquessate** *n*

Michael Boys/Corbis

marquetry

marquetry /maárkitri/, **marqueterie** n 1. designs or pictures made of thin pieces of wood, metal, shell, or other materials, inlaid in a wood veneer and often applied as decoration to pieces of furniture 2. the craft of making marquetry designs or pictures [Mid-16C. < French *marqueterie* < *marqueter* 'variegate' < *marquer* 'to mark']

Márquez ♦ García Márquez, Gabriel

marquis /maárkwiss, maar keé/ (*plural* -quises or -quis /-keéz/) n 1. in various European countries, a nobleman ranking above a count 2. same as **marquess** [14C. < Old French, alteration of *marchis* (see MARQUESS)] —**marquisate** /maárkwizit, -zayt/ n

marquise /maar keéz/ n 1. NOBLEWOMAN in various European countries, a noblewoman ranking above a countess, or the wife or widow of a marquis 2. POINTED OVAL GEM a gem cut into the shape of a pointed oval and usually faceted 3. RING WITH POINTED OVAL a ring set with a pointed oval gem or a cluster of stones arranged in a pointed oval shape 4. FRENCH CHOCOLATE DESSERT a French dessert consisting of either a rich chocolate mousse or a spongy chocolate cake, or a combination of chocolate mousse and cake 5. US COLD CREAMY FRENCH DESSERT a cold French dessert consisting of whipped cream folded into fruit-flavoured ice [Early 17C. < French, form of MARQUIS]

marquisette /maárki zét, maárkwi-/ n a fine woven fabric, often cotton or silk. Use: curtains, mosquito nets. [Early 20C. < French, 'little marquise']

~~marrage~~ incorrect spelling of **marriage**

Marrakesh /márrə késh/, **Marrakech** city in western Morocco. Population: 745,541 (1994).

marram /márrəm/, **marram grass** n a variety of grass that grows on sandy shores and is often planted to prevent erosion of sand dunes. Genus: *Ammophila*. [Mid-17C. < Old Norse *marálmr* 'sea haulm']

Marrano /mə raánō/ (*plural* -nos) n in the Middle Ages, a Jew from Spain or Portugal who converted to Christianity under duress and without conviction, and who continued to practise Judaism in secret [Late 16C. < Spanish, 'pig' (from the Jewish prohibition against pork)]

marriage /márrij/ n 1. LEGAL RELATIONSHIP BETWEEN SPOUSES a legally recognized relationship, established by a civil or religious ceremony, between two people who intend to live together as sexual and domestic partners 2. SPECIFIC MARRIAGE RELATIONSHIP a married relationship between two people, or a somebody's relationship with his or her spouse ○ They have a happy marriage. 3. JOINING IN MARRIAGE the joining together in marriage of two people 4. MARRIAGE CEREMONY the ceremony in which two people are joined together formally in marriage 5. UNION OF TWO THINGS a close union, blend, or mixture of two things ○ Civilization is based on the marriage of tradition and innovation. 6. CARDS KING AND QUEEN OF SAME SUIT in card games such as pinochle and bezique, a combination of the king and queen of the same suit [13C. < French *mariage* < *marier* (see MARRY)]

marriageable /márrijəb'l/ adj suitable or ready for marriage, or old enough to be married ○ of marriageable age —**marriageability** /márrijə bílləti/ n —**marriageableness** n

marriage bureau n an organization that sets up introductions and meetings between single people who are looking for somebody to marry

marriage commissioner n in Canada, a public official empowered by law to perform civil marriages and civil unions

marriage counselling, **marriage guidance** n advice given by professionals to help married couples resolve problems in their relationship

marriage lines npl a record of legal marriage, with the names of those marrying, the time and place, and other details (*informal*)

marriage of convenience n a marriage between two people that is intended to serve a practical, financial, or political purpose and is not based on their love for each other [Translation of French *mariage de convenance*]

married /márrid/ adj 1. HAVING SPOUSE having a wife or husband ○ married people 2. JOINED IN MARRIAGE joined together in marriage ○ get married ○ married couples 3. RELATING TO MARRIAGE arising from or relating to marriage ○ her married name 4. COMPLETELY DEDICATED TO SOMETHING completely dedicated to something and devoting a lot of time and effort to it ○ married to her job ■ **marrieds** npl MARRIED PEOPLE people who are married ○ young marrieds

marron glacé /márron glássay, márroN-/ (*plural* **marrons glacés** /pronunc. same/) n a chestnut cooked and preserved in sugar syrup, drained and then coated with a sugar glaze finish [< French, 'iced chestnut']

marrow /márrō/ n 1. LARGE LONG VEGETABLE a large long cylindrical vegetable with a tough green or green and yellow rind, creamy-white flesh, and a core of seeds that is usually scraped out before it is cooked and eaten. N Am term **marrow squash** 2. (*plural* **marrows** or *same*) MARROW PLANT a plant in the cucumber family that produces marrows as fruit. Latin name: *Cucurbita pepo*. N Am term **marrow squash** 3. SOFT TISSUE IN BONES soft red or yellow fatty tissue that fills the central cavities of bones. Red marrow is the site of blood cell production. 4. ESSENCE the essence, core, or key part of something (*literary*) [Old English *mærh* < Indo-European] ◇ **to the marrow (of your bones)** used to emphasize how intensely or deeply somebody is affected by something, especially the cold or an unpleasant experience ○ I was chilled to the marrow.

marrowbone /márrō bōn/ n a hollow bone that contains edible marrow, traditionally considered to be a culinary delicacy

marrowfat /márrō fat/, **marrowfat pea** n 1. a particularly large type of pea 2. a plant that produces marrowfats as its seed [Mid-18C. < MARROW 'substance like tallow, obtained by boiling down marrow', which the pea's texture resembles]

marrow pea n PLANTS, FOOD same as **marrowfat**

marrow squash n N Am same as **marrow** (senses 1–2)

marry /márri/ (-ries, -rying, -ried) v 1. vti TAKE SOMEBODY IN MARRIAGE to commit yourself to somebody, or yourselves to each other, formally in marriage 2. vt JOIN TWO PEOPLE IN MARRIAGE to officiate at somebody's marriage ceremony and give legal sanction or a religious blessing to the marriage 3. vt GIVE SOMEBODY IN MARRIAGE to give somebody, usually a child or ward, to somebody in marriage, or bring about his or her marriage to somebody 4. vt ACQUIRE SOMETHING BY MARRIAGE to acquire something, especially money, by marrying somebody who has it ○ wanted to marry wealth and power, and got both 5. vti COMBINE THINGS SUCCESSFULLY to brings things together, or to come together, to form a close and successful combination ○ The meat and the spices marry well. 6. vti same as **marry up** 7. vt NAUT MATCH TWO PIECES OF ROPE TOGETHER to equalize the strands of two pieces of rope, especially before splicing them [13C. Via French *marier* < Latin *maritare* < *maritus* 'married person, husband']

marry into vt to become part of something, or gain something, through marriage ○ married into a wealthy family

marry off vt to find a husband or wife for a daughter or son

marry up vti to fit and join together, or make two things fit and join together

marrying /márri ing/ adj likely or inclined to get married ○ Neither of them was the marrying kind.

Mars /maarz/ n 1. in Roman mythology, the god of war and the father of Romulus, the founder of Rome. Greek equivalent **Ares** 2. the third smallest planet in the solar system and the fourth planet from the Sun. Mars has two small satellites and its surface is reddish-orange in colour.

Popperfoto

Mars: View of the surface of Mars from the Sojourner rover (1997)

Marsala /maar saálə/ n a sweet or dry dark red fortified wine from Sicily [Early 19C. After a port in Sicily]

Popperfoto

Wynton Marsalis

Marsalis /maar saáliss/, **Wynton** (b. 1961) US musician and bandleader. His virtuosity on the trumpet has won him renown as both a jazz and a classical performer.

'Jazz is music that really deals with what it means to be American...Louis Armstrong, the grandson of a slave, is the one more than anybody else who could translate into music that feeling of what it is to be an American.'
[Wynton Marsalis, 'We Must Preserve Our Jazz Heritage', *Ebony (Chicago)*; February 1986]

Marsden /maárzdən/, **Samuel** (1765–1838) British-born Australian cleric and magistrate. Renowned as a harsh magistrate, he was also a leading figure in the development of agriculture in the colony of New South Wales, Australia.

Marseillaise /maár say éz, -áyz, maárssə láyz/ n the French national anthem, written in Strasbourg in 1792 by Claude-Joseph Rouget de Lisle, a captain in the French revolutionary army. Originally called 'War Song of the Army of the Rhine', its present name derives from its popularity with army units from Marseilles, the first to sing it in Paris.

marseille /maar sáy/, **marseilles** /maar sáy, -sáylz/ n a heavy cotton fabric with a raised pattern. Use: bedspreads. [Mid-18C. After MARSEILLES]

Marseilles /maar sáy/, **Marseille** chief port and capital of Bouches-du-Rhône Department, Provence-Alpes-Côtes d'Azur Region, southeastern France. Population: 798,430 (1999). [Late 18C. < French, 'of Marseilles']

marsh /maarsh/ n an area of low-lying waterlogged land, often beside water, that is poorly drained and liable to flood, difficult to cross on foot, and unfit for agriculture or building [Old English *merisc* < Germanic] —**marshy** adj

Marsh, **Graham** (b. 1944) Australian golfer. The brother of cricketer Rodney Marsh, he was winner of the 1977 World Matchplay championship.

Marsh, **Dame Ngaio** (1899–1982) New Zealand writer and theatre director. She wrote more than 30 crime novels, and played an important part in the development of live theatre in New Zealand. Full name **Marsh, Dame Edith Ngaio**

Marsh, **Rodney** (b. 1947) Australian cricketer. He was a Test wicketkeeper and batsman. At his retirement

zh vision. In foreign words: kh German Bach; aN French vin; aaN French blanc; ő German schön, French feu; oN French bon; őN French un; ü as in French rue. Stress marks: ´ as in secret /seékrət/, academic /ákə démmik/

in 1984, he was holder of a wicketkeeping world record of 355 Test dismissals.

'In England, soccer is a grey game played by grey people on grey days.'
[Rodney Marsh, *Remark*; 1979]

marshal /maársh'l/ *n* **1.** SOMEBODY IN CHARGE OF EVENT somebody in charge of or controlling an event or gathering such as a parade, ceremony, race meeting, or sports event **2.** HIGH-RANKING OFFICER the highest-ranking officer in some armed forces **3.** HIST HIGH ROYAL COURT OFFICIAL a high official in a royal court, formerly a military adviser and commander for the monarch, but nowadays having a ceremonial role **4.** LAW CIRCUIT JUDGE'S ASSISTANT a trained lawyer who assists a judge on circuit **5.** LAW US FEDERAL LAW OFFICER a US federal law enforcement officer who carries out court orders in a federal judicial district **6.** POLICE CITY LAW OFFICER a municipal law enforcement officer in some US cities **7.** PUBLIC ADMIN SENIOR FIRE OR POLICE OFFICER the head of the fire or police service in some US cities ■ *v* (-shals, -shalling, -shalled) **1.** *vt* ORGANIZE THINGS to arrange things in an appropriate order so that they can be used effectively ○ *marshal your thoughts* **2.** *vti* GATHER AND ORGANIZE TROOPS to gather troops together and organize them, or gather together and organize, before embarking on a military campaign or expedition **3.** *vt* GATHER PEOPLE TOGETHER to gather people together and organize them into an effective body ○ *marshal your supporters* **4.** *vt* GUIDE OR LEAD SOMEBODY to guide or lead somebody carefully or in an officious or ceremonious way **5.** *vti* ACT AS MARSHAL to act as a marshal at something such as a ceremony, parade, or sports event [13C. < Old French *mareschal* 'royal court official' < Germanic, 'groom', literally 'horse-servant'] —**marshaller** *n* —**marshalship** *n*

Marshall /maársh'l/, **George** (1880–1959) US army general and secretary of state (1947–49). He initiated the Marshall Plan (1947) to coordinate European economic recovery after World War II. He won the Nobel Peace Prize (1953) for this initiative. Full name **Marshall, George Catlett**

'If man does find the solution for world peace it will be the most revolutionary reversal of his record we have ever known.'
[George Marshall, *Biennial Report of the Chief of Staff, United States Army*; 1 September 1945]

Marshall, **Sir John Ross** (1912–88) prime minister of New Zealand (1972). A National Party politician, he held several ministerial posts from 1951 until he succeeded Keith Holyoake as prime minister. See table at **prime minister**

Marshall, **Thurgood** (1908–93) US civil rights lawyer and associate justice of the US Supreme Court. As chief counsel of the National Association for the Advancement of Colored People's Legal Defence Fund (1940–61), he won the landmark *Brown v. Board of Education* case (1954) that ended racial segregation in state schools. He was the first African American member of the US Supreme Court (1967–91).

'The United States has been called the melting pot of the world. But it seems to me that the colored man either missed getting into the pot or he got melted down.'
[Thurgood Marshall, *The Encyclopaedia of Black Folklore and Humor*, Henry D. Spalding; 1972]

'If the 1st Amendment means anything, it means that a State has no business telling a man, sitting alone in his own house, what books he may read or what films he may watch.'
[Thurgood Marshall, unanimous opinion in an obscenity case; 7 April 1969]

marshalling yard *n* an area occupied by many parallel railway tracks, where railway wagons are made up into trains

Marshall Islands /maársh'l-/ country consisting of 34 islands in the central North Pacific Ocean. Capital: Majuro. Population: 56,429 (2003). Area: 181 sq. km/70 sq. mi. Official name **Republic of the Marshall Islands**

Marshall Plan /maársh'l-/ *n* a programme of loans and other economic assistance provided by the US

government between 1947 and 1952 to help western European nations rebuild after World War II [Mid-20C. After George C. MARSHALL]

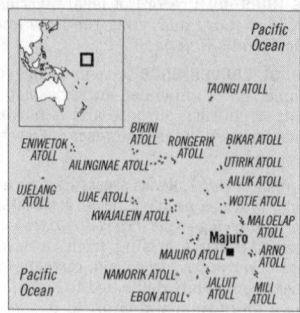
Marshall Islands

Marshal of the Royal Air Force *n* an officer in the Royal Air Force of the highest rank

marsh elder *n* a bush with unisexual flowers and greenish flower heads. Native to: marshes of central and eastern North America. Genus: *Iva*.

marsh fever *n* MED same as **malaria**

marsh gas *n* a mixture of gases, mostly methane, produced by decomposing plant matter in the absence of air. Spontaneous combustion of marsh gas is usually supposed to be the cause of the phenomenon known as a will-o'-the-wisp or ignis fatuus.

marshland /maársh land, -lənd/ *n* marshy ground, or an area or expanse of it

marsh mallow *n* a perennial shrubby plant that grows in marshes and has sticky roots that were used in the past to make marshmallow and are still used in some medicines. Flowers: pink. Native to: Europe. Latin name: *Althaea officinalis*.

marshmallow /maársh mállō/ *n* a soft spongy sweet made from sugar syrup, egg whites, and flavouring [Because formerly made from the root of the marsh mallow plant] —**marshmallowy** *adj*

marsh marigold *n* a plant of the buttercup family that has round or kidney-shaped leaves and grows in swampy areas. Flowers: bright yellow. Native to: Europe, North America. Latin name: *Caltha palustris*.

Marston /maárstən/, **John** (c. 1575–1634) English playwright and satirist. He is best known for his comedies such as *The Malcontent* (1604).

marsupial /maar syóopi əl, -sóo-/ *n* a mammal, e.g. a kangaroo, wombat, opossum, or koala, having no placenta and bearing immature young that are developed in a pouch on the mother's abdomen. Order: Marsupialia. [Late 17C. < modern Latin *marsupialis* < Latin *marsupium* (SEE MARSUPIUM)]

marsupial frog *n* a tree frog of which the female carries the eggs in a pouch on her back

marsupium /maar syóopi əm, -sóopi-/ (*plural* -pia /-pi ə/) *n* a pouch on the abdomen of most marsupials that encloses the mammary glands and in which the animal's newly born offspring complete their development [Mid-17C. Via Latin *marsupium* < Greek *marsupion* 'pouch', literally 'little purse' < *marsippos* 'purse']

mart /maart/ *n* a market, saleroom, or large shop [15C. < obsolete Dutch, variant of *markt* < Latin *mercat-* (see MARKET)]

Martaban, Gulf of /maártə baán-/ inlet of the Andaman Sea, east of the Irrawaddy delta, southern Myanmar

martagon /maártəgən/, **martagon lily** *n* an ornamental lily. Flowers: mottled, pinkish-purple, resembling turbans. Native to: Europe, Asia. Latin name: *Lilium martagon*. [15C. Via French < Turkish *martağan*, kind of turban, which the flower is thought to resemble]

martelé /maárte lay/, **martellato** /maárte laátō/ *adv* with the strings played in a strongly accented way (*used as a musical direction*) [Late 19C. < French, 'hammered']

Martello /maar téllō/ (*plural* -los), **Martello tower** *n* a fort in the form of a small circular tower, especially one built on the coast for defence against invasion during the Napoleonic Wars [Early 19C. Alteration, influenced by Italian *martello* 'hammer', of Cape *Mortella* in

Corsica, where such a tower was captured by the British fleet in 1794]

marten /maártin/ (*plural* -tens or same) *n* a short-legged bushy-tailed animal with a long slender body that lives in trees. Native to: northern forests. Genus: *Martes*. [13C. Via Middle Dutch *martren* < Old French *martre* < Germanic]

Martens /maártənz/, **Conrad** (1801–78) British-born Australian painter. He was one of the first professional artists in Australia. His works include many paintings of the New South Wales landscape.

martensite /maártin zīt/ *n* the hard solid solution of iron and carbon used in making hardened steel tools [Late 19C. After Adolf *Martens* (1850–1914), German metallurgist] —**martensitic** /maárt'n zíttik/ *adj*

Martha /maárthə/ *n* in the Bible, the sister of Mary and Lazarus, and friend of Jesus Christ (Luke 10: 38–42)

Martha's Vineyard /maárthəz-/ island in southeastern Massachusetts, in the Atlantic Ocean, near Cape Cod. It is a popular holiday resort. Area: 280 sq. km/100 sq. mi.

Martí /maártí/, **José** (1853–95) Cuban revolutionary leader and poet. He fought for Cuban independence from Spain and wrote many poems and essays on the theme of political freedom. Full name **Martí, José Julian**

'The dagger plunged in the name of Freedom is plunged into the breast of Freedom.'
[Attributed to José Martí]

martial /maársh'l/ *adj* **1.** characteristic of or suitable for soldiers, the military life, or war **2.** warlike and fierce [14C. Directly or via French < Latin *martialis* < *Mars*, the god of war] —**martialism** *n* —**martialist** *n* —**martially** *adv* —**martialness** *n*

martial art *n* a system of combat and self-defence, e.g. judo or karate, developed especially in Japan and Korea and now usually practised as a sport

martial law *n* the control and policing of a civilian population by military forces and according to military rules, imposed, e.g. in wartime or when the civilian government no longer functions

Martian /maársh'n/ *adj* found on, typical of, or originating from the planet Mars ■ *n* a supposed inhabitant of the planet Mars [14C. Directly or via Old French *martien* < Latin *Martianus* < *Mart-* 'Mars']

martin /maártin/ *n* a bird of the swallow family with a notched or square tail, which builds its nest on cliffs or houses [15C. Origin ?]

Martin /maártin/, **St** (316?–397?) Roman monk. The bishop of Tours, he spread Christianity throughout Gaul, establishing monasticism in the country, and became the patron saint of France.

Martin V (1368–1431) pope. His election in 1417, at the Council of Constance, ended the Great Schism. He reunified the Western Church and the Papal States.

Martin, Archer (1910–2002) British biochemist. He shared the Nobel Prize in chemistry (1952) for his study of protein structure and later developed chromatography for protein analysis. Full name **Martin, Archer John Porter**

Martin, Dean (1917–95) US singer and actor. He appeared in a number of films opposite Jerry Lewis, including *My Friend Irma* (1949). His television shows included *The Dean Martin Show* (1964–75). Born **Crocetti, Dino**

Martin, Paul (*b.* 1938) Canadian politician. A member of the Liberal Party, he was Minister of Finance (1993–2002) and became leader of the party and prime minister (2003). See table at **prime minister**

martinet /maárti nét/ *n* **1.** a military officer who demands absolute adherence to military rules and behaviour **2.** somebody who imposes strict discipline on others [Late 17C. After Jean *Martinet* (died 1672), French drillmaster] —**martinetism** *n* —**martinettish** *adj*

martingale /maártin gayl/ *n* **1.** PART OF HORSE HARNESS a strap of a horse's harness connecting the girth to the reins to keep the horse from throwing its head back **2.** *also* **martingale shroud** PART OF SHIP'S RIGGING a rope or cable that supports the forward-projecting spar (**bowsprit**) on some sailing ships **3.** GAMBLING SYSTEM gambling in which the stakes are doubled after each loss [Late 16C. < French]

martini /maar teeni/ *n* a cocktail made of gin or vodka with vermouth [Late 19C. < Italian *Martini*, surname of a winemaker]

Martini /maar teeni/ *tdmk* a trademark for an Italian vermouth

Martini /maar teeni/, **Simone** (1280?–1344?) Italian painter. One of the most influential artists of the 14th century, he painted mainly frescoes and altar panels, and introduced refinements of line, expression, and colour in works such as *The Annunciation* (1333).

Martinique /maarti neek/ island in the eastern Caribbean Sea, an overseas department of France. Population: 418,454 (2001). Area: 1,100 sq. km/425 sq. mi.

Martinmas /maartinməss, -mass/ *n* one of the Scottish quarter days. Date: 11 November. [13C. < St MARTIN + MASS]

Martinů /maarti noo/, **Bohuslav** (1890–1959) Czech composer. His music, ranging from operas to piano pieces, often combines a vibrant dissonance with elements of Czech folk music. Full name **Martinů, Bohuslav Jan**

martlet /maartlət/ *n* on coats of arms, a footless bird used to represent a fourth son [Early 16C. < French *martelet*, alteration of *martinet*, form of the name *Martin*]

martyr /maartər/ *n* **1.** SOMEBODY PUT TO DEATH somebody who chooses to die rather than deny a strongly held belief, especially a religious belief **2.** SOMEBODY WHO MAKES SACRIFICES somebody who makes sacrifices or suffers greatly in order to advance a cause or principle **3.** SOMEBODY IN PAIN somebody who experiences frequent or constant pain from something **4.** SOMEBODY SEEKING ATTENTION a frequent complainer who hopes to elicit sympathy from others ■ *v* (**-tyrs, -tyring, -tyred**) **1.** *vt* KILL SOMEBODY FOR HOLDING BELIEFS to kill somebody for refusing to deny a strongly held belief, especially a religious belief **2.** **martyr yourself** *vr* MAKE SACRIFICES FOR SOMETHING to bring difficulties, suffering, or hardship on yourself for something [Pre-12C. Via ecclesiastical Latin < Greek *martur* 'witness'] —**martyrdom** *n*

martyrology /maartə rólləji/ (*plural* **-gies**) *n* **1.** the study of the lives and history of religious martyrs **2.** a catalogue or list of religious martyrs, or a collection of stories about martyrs

Maruyama Okyo /márroo yaamə ŏki ŏ/ (1733–95) Japanese artist. He was founder of the Maruyama school of painting. Born **Maruyama Mondo**

~~marvalous~~ incorrect spelling of **marvellous**

marvel /maarv'l/ *n* **1.** WONDERFUL THING something that inspires awe, amazement, or admiration ○ *one of the marvels of the ancient world* **2.** SKILFUL PERSON somebody who does wonderful or astonishing things, especially somebody very skilled in something ○ *a marvel at machinery* ■ *vi* (**-vels, -velling, -velled**) BE AMAZED to be very impressed, surprised, or bewildered ○ *I could only marvel at her stamina.* [13C. < French *merveille* < Latin *mirabilis* 'wonderful' < *mirari* (see MIRACLE)]

Marvell /maarvəl/, **Andrew** (1621–78) English poet and politician. A metaphysical poet, he also wrote verse satires vigorously opposing the post-Restoration government.

'Let us roll all our strength and all / Our sweetness up into one ball, / And tear our pleasures with rough strife / Through the iron gates of life: / Thus, though we cannot make our sun / Stand still, yet we will make him run.'
[Andrew Marvell, 'To His Coy Mistress'; 1650?]

marvellous /maarvələss/ *adj* **1.** extraordinarily wonderful ○ *a marvellous example of Baroque architecture* **2.** very good or pleasing ○ *It was marvellous to see them all again.* —**marvellously** *adv* —**marvellousness** *n*

marvelous *adj* US spelling of **marvellous**

Karl Marx

Marx /maarks/, **Karl** (1818–83) German philosopher. His books, especially the *Communist Manifesto* (1848) and *Das Kapital* (1867, 1885, 1894), were the basis of Communism. Full name **Marx, Karl Heinrich** —**Marxian** *adj*

'The workers have nothing to lose but their chains. They have a world to gain.
WORKERS OF THE WORLD, UNITE.'
[Karl Marx, *The Communist Manifesto*; 1848]

Marx Brothers US comedians. Chico (born Leonard, 1891–1961), Groucho (born Julius Henry, 1895–1977), and Harpo (born Adolph, 1888–1964), the three most prominent of the brothers, appeared in comedy films such as *A Night at the Opera* (1935) and were known for their anarchic verbal and visual humour. Groucho later hosted the television game show *You Bet Your Life* (1950–61). Two other brothers, Gummo (born Milton, 1893–1977) and Zeppo (born Herbert, 1901–79), appeared in some of the Marx Brothers' early work.

Marxism /maarks izəm/ *n* **1.** the political and economic theories of Karl Marx and Friedrich Engels, in which class struggle is a central element in the analysis of social change in Western societies **2.** political ideology based on the theories of Karl Marx and Friedrich Engels —**Marxist** *n, adj*

Marxism-Leninism *n* Marxism with the inclusion of Lenin's idea that imperialism is the final stage of capitalism, and Lenin's shifting of the focus of class struggle from industrialized to nonindustrialized societies —**Marxist-Leninist** *n, adj*

Mary /máiri/ *n* in the Bible, the mother of Jesus Christ. Christian tradition holds that she conceived Jesus Christ without human contact, through the direct intervention of God. In Islam she is venerated as Maryan.

Mary /máiri/ (1867–1953) queen of the United Kingdom. A great-granddaughter of George III, she was the queen consort of George V and the mother of Edward VIII and George VI. She is remembered especially for her charitable and relief work during World War II. Known as **Mary of Teck**

Mary I (1516–58) queen of England and Ireland. She was the daughter of Henry VIII and Catherine of Aragon. As queen (1553–58) she tried to restore Roman Catholicism in England, and to cement union with Spain by marrying Philip II (1554). Known as **Bloody Mary**

'My father made the most part of you almost out of nothing.'
[Mary I, *Remark*; 1550?]

Mary II (1662–94) queen of England, Scotland, and Ireland. She was the daughter of James II. After the Glorious Revolution (1688) she was made coregent with her husband William III (Prince of Orange), during whose absences she governed as regent.

Mary, Queen of Scots (1542–87) queen of Scotland. Daughter of James V of Scotland, she was married successively to King Francis II of France, Lord Darnley, and the Earl of Bothwell. Her reign (1542–67) was marked by conflict between Catholics and Protestant reformers in Scotland. The Protestant lords forced her to abdicate in 1567 in favour of her son James VI, and she fled to England. Through her grandmother, she had a claim to the English throne, and became a focus for Catholic discontent. Elizabeth I imprisoned her after 1568 and signed the warrant under which she was executed for treason in 1587. Born **Stuart, Mary**

Mary, Queen of Scots: anonymous 16th-century portrait

'In my end is my beginning.'
[Mary, Queen of Scots. Motto embroidered on her canopy of state, quoted by William Drummond of Hawthornden in a letter to Ben Jonson; 1619]

Maryborough /máiribərə/ city and seaport in southeastern Queensland, Australia, an industrial and service centre. Population: 25,260 (2002 estimate).

Mary Jane /-jáyn/ *n* N Am same as **marijuana** (*slang*) [Early 20C. Origin ?]

Mary Janes /máiri jáynz/ *tdmk* a trademark for shoes and boots, especially low-cut patent-leather shoes for girls with a strap fastening near the ankle at the side

Maryland /máirilənd/ state in the eastern United States, bordered by Delaware, the District of Columbia, Virginia, West Virginia, Pennsylvania, and the Atlantic Ocean. Capital: Annapolis. Population: 5,458,137 (2002 estimate). Area: 31,849 sq. km/12,297 sq. mi. —**Marylander** *n*

Mary Magdalene /máiri magdə léni, -mágdələn/ *n* in the Bible, a follower of Jesus Christ, who cured her of evil spirits (Luke 8:2)

marzipan /maarzi pan, -pán/ *n* a sweet paste made of ground almonds and sugar, often with egg whites or yolks, used as a layer in cakes or moulded into ornamental shapes ■ *adj* relating or belonging to the upper-middle levels of the management hierarchy in an organization, just below the top executives [15C. Via German < Italian *marzapane* 'type of box', originally for sweets or coins]

ORIGIN Arabic *mawtabān* meant literally 'enthroned king'. It was used by the Saracens as the name of a medieval Venetian coin that had a figure of the seated Jesus Christ on it. In the Italian dialect of Venice the word became *matapan*, and eventually, in general Italian, *marzapane*; and its meaning supposedly progressed from the 'coin' via 'measure of weight or capacity', 'box of such capacity', and 'such a box containing confectionery' to 'the contents of such a box'. After English originally acquired the word (possibly via French) it became anglicized to *marchpane*, and that remained the standard form until the 19th century. Around this time *marzipan* was borrowed from German. This was an alteration of Italian *marzapane*, based on the misconception that it came from Latin *marci panis* 'St Mark's bread'.

Masaccio /mə saáchee ŏ/ (1401?–27) Italian painter. He is considered the first great painter of the Italian Renaissance, whose innovations in the use of scientific perspective inaugurated the modern era in painting. Born **Tommaso Cassai**

Masada /mə saádə/ ancient ruined fortress in Israel, on a mountaintop 48.3 km/30 mi. southeast of Jerusalem, southwest of the Dead Sea. It was used as a stronghold by the Jewish Zealots in the final two years of their rebellion against Roman rule (AD 66–73). After a siege lasting nearly two years, almost all the occupants of the fortress killed themselves rather than surrender to the Romans.

Masai /maa sĩ, maa sí, mássĩ/ (*plural same* or **-sais**), **Maasai** *n* **1.** a member of a pastoral people with strong warrior traditions who live in East Africa, mainly in Kenya and Tanzania. They are characteristically tall and slender in build. **2.** the Nilotic language of the Masai people. Native speakers: 700,000. [Mid-19C. < Masai] —**Masai** *adj*

masala /mə saálə, maa-/ *n* (*plural same* or **-las**) **1.** SPICY PASTE a mixture of spices ground into a paste, used

to flavour South Asian dishes, or a dish flavoured with such a paste **2.** *S Asia* GOSSIP gossipy embellishments in repeating a story (*informal*) ■ *adj S Asia* DESCRIBING SOUTH ASIAN FILMS describes South Asian popular films (*informal*) [Late 18C. < Urdu *maṣālaḥ*]

Masbate /maas baáti/ island in the central Philippines, in Masbate Province. Area: 4,000 sq. km/1,600 sq. mi. Population: 599,900 (1990).

masc. *abbr* GRAM masculine

Mascagni /mass kányi/, **Pietro** (1863–1945) Italian composer. His opera *Cavalleria Rusticana* (1890) is his best-known work. It exemplifies Roman verismo, a style of opera that dealt with stories of ordinary people.

mascara /ma skaárə, mə-/ *n* thick coloured paste applied to the eyelashes with a fine brush to darken them and give the appearance of greater length and thickness ■ *vt* (**-as, -aing, -aed**) to apply mascara to eyelashes [Late 19C. Probably < Italian *maschera* 'mask']

Mascarene Islands /máskə reén-/ group of islands east of Madagascar in the Indian Ocean, including Réunion, Mauritius, and Rodrigues. Population: 1,798,000 (1996). Area: 4,500 sq. km/1,700 sq. mi.

mascarpone /maáskər pōni, máskaar-/ *n* a rich fatty unsalted Italian cream cheese with a spreadable texture [Mid-20C. < Italian, 'rich whey cheese']

mascle /másk'l/ *n* a design on coats of arms in the form of a lozenge with a lozenge-shaped hole in the middle [13C. < Anglo-Norman < Latin *macula* 'mesh']

mascon /máss kon/ *n* an area of higher-than-normal gravity on the surface of the Moon [Mid-20C. Contraction of *mass concentration*]

mascot /máss kot, máskət/ *n* a person, animal, or thing that is believed to bring good luck, usually one that becomes the symbol of a particular group, especially a team [Late 19C. Via French *mascotte* < modern Provençal *mascotto* 'little witch']

masculine /máskyŏŏlin/ *adj* **1.** OF MEN AND BOYS relating or belonging to men and boys rather than women and girls **2.** OF TRADITIONAL MANLY CHARACTER having traits or qualities traditionally associated with men or boys rather than women or girls **3.** GRAM OF CERTAIN GRAMMATICAL GENDER relating to one of the classes that words and grammatical forms are divided into in some languages **4.** MUSIC CONCLUDING ON ACCENTED BEAT ending on a beat that is accented ■ *n* GRAM MASCULINE GENDER the masculine gender, or a word or form in the masculine gender [14C. Via French < Latin *masculinus* < *masculus*] —**masculinely** *adv*

masculine cadence *n* a closing section of music (**cadence**) that ends on a strong beat

masculine ending *n* **1.** a stressed syllable that ends a line of poetry **2.** an ending that marks a word as belonging to the masculine gender in some languages

masculine rhyme *n* a rhyme between two monosyllabic words, e.g. 'gab' and 'blab', or between the final stressed syllables of polysyllabic words, e.g. 'connive' and 'survive'

masculinise *vt* another spelling of **masculinize**

masculinity /máskyŏŏ línnəti/ *n* **1.** the state of being a man or boy **2.** those qualities conventionally supposed to belong to a man such as physical strength and courage

masculinize /máskyŏŏlin īz/ (**-izes, -izing, -ized**), **masculinise** (**-ises, -ising, -ised**) *vt* **1.** to give something or somebody features conventionally associated with maleness **2.** to cause a female animal or a plant to acquire male sexual characteristics, e.g. as a result of administering steroids —**masculinization** /máskyŏŏlin ī záysh'n/ *n*

Masefield /máyss feeld/, **John** (1878–1967) British poet. The author of vigorous narrative verse, collected in *Salt Water Ballads* (1902) and other volumes, he was named poet laureate in 1930.

> 'I must down to the seas again, to the lonely sea and the sky, / And all I ask is a tall ship and a star to steer her by, / And the wheel's kick and the wind's song and the white sail's shaking, / And a grey mist on the sea's face and a grey dawn breaking.'
> [John Masefield, 'Sea Fever', *Salt Water Ballads*; 1902]

maser /máyzər/ *n* **1.** a device used in radar and radio astronomy to boost the strength of microwaves **2.** a galactic source of polarized microwave radiation [Mid-20C. Acronym < *microwave amplification by stimulated emission of radiation*]

Maseru /mə sáiroo/ capital of Lesotho, situated on the River Caledon, near the border with South Africa. Population: 297,000 (1995).

mash /mash/ *n* **1.** MASHED POTATOES boiled potatoes that have been reduced to a pulp or purée, often with milk or butter added (*informal*) **2.** GRAIN AND WATER MIX a fermentable mixture of hot water and grain, usually barley or wheat, from which alcohol is brewed or distilled **3.** ANIMAL FOOD a mixture of ground feeds for livestock or poultry **4.** PULPY MASS the consistency of a soft pulp ■ *v* (**mashes, mashing, mashed**) **1.** *vt* MAKE SOMETHING INTO PULP to squash something into a pulpy mass **2.** *vt* SOAK GRAIN to soak grain in hot water to make a mash for brewing or for feeding to animals **3.** *vt* CRUSH SOMETHING to crush or grind something (*informal*) **4.** *vti regional* BREW TEA to soak tea leaves in hot water until the tea is ready to drink, or infuse in this way **5.** *vt Carib* STEP ON to step on something ○ *The driver had to mash brakes suddenly.* [Old English *masc* 'mash for brewing' < Indo-European] —**masher** *n*

MASH /mash/, **M.A.S.H.** *abbr* ARMY mobile army surgical hospital

---

CULTURAL NOTE ***M*A*S*H***, a film (1970) by US director Robert Altman. Set in a mobile army surgical hospital during the Korean War, this dark satire focuses on a group of eccentric medics who combat the horrors of war with cynicism, ribald humour, and practical jokes. The film, which was based on a novel, gave rise to a long-running television series.

---

masher /máshər/ *n* **1.** a utensil used for mashing food **2.** a man who inflicts his attentions on a woman (*dated slang*)

mashgiah /mash geé a<u>kh</u>/ (*plural* **-gihim** /-<u>kh</u>im/), **mashgiach** (*plural* **-gichim**) *n* an Orthodox rabbi, or a man appointed or approved by such a rabbi, who inspects slaughterhouses, meat markets, and restaurants to check that kosher food has been properly prepared and served [Mid-20C. < Hebrew *mašgīaḥ* 'supervisor']

mashie /máshi/ *n* an obsolete golf club similar to the modern five-iron [Late 19C. Origin ?]

mashie niblick *n* an obsolete golf club similar to the modern six-iron

Mashona /mə shṓnə/ *n* PEOPLES same as **Shona** (sense 1) —**Mashona** *adj*

mash up *adj* (*slang*; *used in Black English*) **1.** broken or no longer operating properly **2.** not in good health

mash-up[1] *n* a song in digital format created by combining parts of different songs, e.g. the music track of one song and the vocal track of another

mash-up[2], **mashed-up** *adj Carib* broken or damaged

masint /mássint/, **MASINT** *n* intelligence data acquired, typically electronically, about possible attacks using weapons of mass destruction. Full form **materials intelligence**

Masirah /ma zeérə/ island in the Arabian Sea off the southeastern coast of Oman

masjid /múss jid/ *S Asia* RELIG same as **mosque** [Mid-19C. < Arabic, 'place of prostration']

mask /maask/ *n* **1.** FACE COVERING TO HIDE IDENTITY a covering for the face, worn by somebody to conceal his or her identity ○ *a Halloween mask* ○ *two gunmen wearing masks* **2.** PROTECTIVE FACE COVERING a covering for the eyes, mouth, or face, worn for protection or for medical reasons ○ *an oxygen mask* **3.** CONCEALING THING something that conceals or disguises something else such as true motives or feelings **4.** ORNAMENT RESEMBLING FACE a representation of a face used as an ornament or decoration **5.** ZOOL ANIMAL'S FACE MARKINGS the face or facial markings of some animals such as foxes and raccoons **6.** MIL CONCEALMENT FOR TROOPS a natural or artificial feature that hides military troops and installations from an enemy **7.** ELECTRONICS TEMPLATE FOR ELECTRONIC CHIPS a template used to control the pattern of conducting material deposited or etched onto a semiconductor chip **8.** COSMETICS BEAUTY TREATMENT a facial preparation used to tighten the skin and remove impurities, applied to the skin as a paste and allowed to dry before being removed **9.** PHOTOGRAPHY PHOTOGRAPHIC GUARD a guard, often a sheet of paper, placed over areas of unexposed photographic film to stop light hitting it ■ *vt* (**masks, masking, masked**) **1.** PUT MASK ON SOMETHING to cover something with a mask ○ *masked their faces* **2.** CONCEAL SOMETHING to conceal something in order to protect or disguise it ○ *alleged that the company masked its true corporate identity* **3.** HIDE SOMETHING FROM VIEW to prevent something from being seen by covering it ○ *Thick vines masked the cave entrance.* **4.** SHIELD PART OF SOMETHING to cover part of a surface using masking tape before painting or spraying **5.** PHOTOGRAPHY SHIELD PHOTOGRAPHIC FILM FROM LIGHT to prevent stray or unwanted light from reaching areas of unexposed photographic film, either using hands or a special shield **6.** CHEM STOP CHEMICAL REACTING to prevent a chemical substance from reacting by the addition of another chemical [Early 16C. Via French *masque* < late Latin *masca* 'ghost, mask'] —**maskable** *adj*

masked /maaskt/ *adj* **1.** WEARING MASK with the face covered in order to prevent recognition **2.** MED NOT DETECTABLE describes diseases and symptoms that are present but not yet perceptible **3.** BOT same as **personate**[2] **4.** ZOOL WITH MARKINGS LIKE MASK with markings on the head or around the eyes that resemble a mask

masked ball *n* a ball at which people wear masks

masker /maáskər/ *n* somebody who wears a mask at a masked ball

masking /maásking/ *n* **1.** the hiding or screening of one sensory process such as hearing by another such as sight **2.** scenery that is used to hide a part of the stage from the audience

masking tape *n* easy-to-remove adhesive tape used to cover parts of a surface that are not meant to be painted

masochism /mássəkizəm/ *n* **1.** SEXUAL PLEASURE DERIVED FROM HUMILIATION sexual gratification achieved through humiliation and physical and verbal abuse **2.** PSYCHOLOGICAL DISORDER the psychological disorder in which somebody needs to be emotionally or physically abused in order to be sexually satisfied **3.** SEARCH FOR ABUSIVE SEXUAL PARTNERS the active seeking out of sexual partners who will dominate, humiliate, and physically and verbally abuse **4.** ENJOYMENT OF HARDSHIP the tendency to invite and enjoy misery of any kind, especially in order to be pitied by others or admired for forbearance [Late 19C. After Leopold von *Sacher-Masoch* (1836–95), Austrian novelist] —**masochist** *n*

masochistic /mássə kístik/ *adj* **1.** relating to or experiencing the desire to be humiliated and abused by others in order to feel sexually fulfilled **2.** tending to invite and enjoy misery —**masochistically** *adv*

mason /mayss'n/ *n* somebody who works with stone or brick, especially in the building trades ■ *vt* (**-sons, -soning, -soned**) to build or strengthen something using stone or brick [12C. < Old N French *machun* or Old French *masson*]

Mason *n* same as **Freemason**

Mason /máyss'n/, **Bruce** (1921–82) New Zealand playwright. He wrote the one-man show *The End of the Golden Weather* (1959).

mason bee *n* a solitary bee that builds nests of sand or clay held together with saliva

Mason-Dixon Line /máyss'n díks'n-/ *n* the boundary that separates Pennsylvania from Maryland and West Virginia, regarded as the dividing line between free and slave states before the American Civil War [After Charles *Mason* and Jeremiah *Dixon*, 18C surveyors]

masonic /mə sónnik/ *adj* relating to stonemasons or brick masons or their work —**masonically** *adv*

Masonic *adj* relating to Freemasons or Freemasonry

Masonite /máyssə nīt/ *tdmk* a trademark for hardboard products. Used for insulation, panelling, and building partitions.

Mason jar *n N Am* a wide-mouthed glass jar with a lid that screws or clips on and forms a vacuum seal, used for preserving food, especially fruits and vegetables [Late 19C. After John *Mason* (1832–1902), US metalworker]

masonry /máyss'nri/ *n* **1.** the trade of a mason **2.** the stone or brick parts of a building or other structure

Masonry *n* same as **Freemasonry** (sense 1)

mason wasp *n* a solitary wasp that builds mud nests or digs out nests in old mortar. Genus: *Odynerus.*

Masorete /mássə reet/, **Masorite** /-rīt/ *n* any of the scholars who produced the Masoretic text [Late 16C. Via French or modern Latin *Massoreta* < a misuse of Hebrew *māsōreṯ*] —**Masoretic** /mássə réttik/ *adj*

Masoretic text *n* the traditional text of the Hebrew Bible, revised and annotated by Jewish scholars between the 6th and 10th centuries AD

Masorite *n* JUDAISM, BIBLE same as **Masorete**

Masqat ♦ **Muscat**

masque /maask/ *n* **1.** a dramatic entertainment similar to opera, popular in England in the 16th and 17th centuries, in which masked performers represented mythological or allegorical characters **2.** the music and words written for a masque **3.** LEISURE same as **masquerade** *n* (sense 1) [Early 16C. < French (see MASK)]

masquer /maaskər/ *n* same as **masker**

masquerade /maàskə ráyd/ *n* **1.** PARTY WITH MASKS a party at which masks and costumes are worn, whether an informal gathering of friends or a formal ball **2.** DISGUISING COSTUME a costume worn to a masquerade **3.** DISGUISING PRETENCE a pretence or disguise ■ *vi* (**-ades, -ading, -aded**) **1.** PRETEND to pretend to be somebody or something else **2.** WEAR COSTUME to wear a particular costume to a party [Late 16C. Via French *mascarade* < Italian *mascherata* < *maschera* 'mask'] —**masquerader** *n*

mass /mass/ *n* **1.** LUMP a body of matter that forms a whole but has no definable shape **2.** COLLECTION a collection of many individual parts ○ *The garden is a mass of weeds.* **3.** GREAT UNSPECIFIED QUANTITY a large but unspecified number or quantity ○ *masses of work to do* **4.** MAJOR PART the greater part or majority ○ *The mass of respondents oppose the legislation.* **5.** PHYS PHYSICAL QUANTITY the property of an object that is a measure of its inertia, the amount of matter it contains, and its influence in a gravitational field. Symbol *m* **6.** ART AREA OF PAINTING a large area of a painting where the light, shade, or colour is uniform **7.** MIN EXTRACT DEPOSIT OF ORE an irregular deposit of ore that does not occur in veins ■ *npl* **1. masses** ORDINARY PEOPLE ordinary people in society, as distinct from political leaders, aristocracy, or educated people **2.** LOTS large amounts or large numbers (*informal*) ■ *vti* (**masses, massing, massed**) COLLECT to gather things in a mass, or be gathered in a mass ○ *Troops are massing on the border.* ■ *adj* **1.** OF LARGE NUMBER made up of or containing a large number ○ *a mass demonstration* **2.** GENERAL broadly general, in scope or effect ○ *The mass effect is rather disappointing.* [14C. Via French *masse* < Latin *massa* < Greek *maza* 'barley cake']
mass in *vt* to fill in areas of colour or shade in a drawing or painting

Mass /mass/, **mass** *n* **1.** in the Roman Catholic Church and some Protestant churches, the religious ceremony of Communion **2.** a part of the text of a Roman Catholic Mass set to music, to be sung by a choir [Pre-12C. < ecclesiastical Latin *missa* < Latin *mittere* 'send away']

Massachuset /mássə choǒsət/ (*plural same* or **-sets**), **Massachusett** (*plural same* or **-setts**) *n* **1.** a member of a Native North American people who lived in the Massachusetts Bay area **2.** an extinct Algonquian language formerly spoken in eastern Massachusetts —**Massachuset** *adj*

Massachusetts /mássə choǒssəts/ state in the northeastern United States, bordered by Vermont, New Hampshire, the Atlantic Ocean, Rhode Island, Connecticut, and New York. Capital: Boston. Population: 6,427,801 (2002 estimate). Area: 23,934 sq. km/9,241 sq. mi. Official name **Commonwealth of Massachusetts**

massacre /mássəkər/ *n* **1.** KILLING OF MANY PEOPLE the vicious killing of large numbers of people or animals **2.** BAD DEFEAT a contest in which one side is badly beaten (*informal*) ■ *vt* (**-cres, -cring, -cred**) **1.** KILL PEOPLE IN LARGE NUMBERS to kill large numbers of people or animals **2.** DEFEAT SOMEBODY COMPLETELY to defeat somebody completely, especially in a sporting contest (*informal*) [Late 16C. < French, 'butchery']

massage /mássaazh, -aaj/ *n* RUBBING OF BODY a treatment that involves rubbing or kneading the muscles, either for medical or therapeutic purposes or simply as an aid to relaxation ■ *vt* (**-sages, -saging, -saged**) **1.** RUB SOMEBODY'S MUSCLES to rub or knead somebody's muscles **2.** MANIPULATE INFORMATION DECEPTIVELY to manipulate statistics or other information in order to create a more suitable or falsely impressive result ○ *massaged their sales figures* **3.** ENHANCE SOMETHING to give something a boost with kind or uplifting treatment, especially somebody's ego with flattery [Late 19C. < French < *masser* 'apply massage to'] —**massager** *n*

massage parlour *n* **1.** a place that provides massages to paying customers **2.** a place that offers sex services for money, including sexual massages

massasauga /mássə sáwgə/ *n* a small rattlesnake that has variable colouring. Native to: North America. Latin name: *Sistrurus catenatus.* [Mid-19C. Alteration of *Mississagi*, river in SE Ontario, Canada]

mass balance *n* a mathematical equation, table, or quantitative chart showing the mass inputs and outputs of a process, plant, or machine, the principle being that what goes in must come out

mass communication *n* communication by means of broadcasting and newspapers, which reaches all or most people in society

masscult /máss kult/ *n* culture as it is presented and interpreted by the mass media (*informal*) [Shortening of *mass culture*]

mass defect *n* the difference between the mass of an isotope and the element's mass number

massé /mássi/ *n* in a cue game, a shot in which the cue is held almost vertically to strike the cue ball off-centre, making it curve round one ball to hit another [Late 19C. < French < *masse* 'large hammer']

Masséna /ma sáynə/, **André, prince of Essling and duke of Rivoli** (1758–1817) French soldier. He was a marshal of the Napoleonic empire, noted for his military victories, but switched loyalty to the Bourbons after the Restoration.

mass-energy equivalence *n* the principle in the theory of relativity that mass and energy are equivalent and interchangeable according to the equation $E = mc^2$

Massenet /mássə nay/, **Jules** (1842–1912) French composer. Famous for his opera *Manon* (1884), he also wrote oratorios, cantatas, and orchestral pieces. Full name **Massenet, Jules Émile Frédéric**

masseter /ma seétər/ *n* a muscle in the cheek that moves the jaws during chewing [Late 16C. < Greek *masētēr* < *masasthai* 'chew']

masseur /ma súr/ *n* a man who gives massages professionally [Late 19C. < French < *masser* 'apply massage to']

masseuse /ma sőz/ *n* a woman who gives massages professionally [Late 19C. < French, form of *masseur* (see MASSEUR)]

mass extinction *n* the destruction of a whole species by a force of nature such as climate change, volcanic eruption, or asteroid collision, thought by many scientists to have wiped out the dinosaurs

Massey /mássi/, **William** (1856–1925) Irish-born prime minister of New Zealand (1912–25). A Reform Party politician, he is the second longest-serving New Zealand prime minister after Richard Seddon. See table at **prime minister**. Full name **Massey, William Ferguson**

massicot /mássi kot/ *n* a yellow mineral consisting of lead oxide, or a powdered form of it used as a pigment [15C. < French]

massif /mássif, ma seéf/ *n* **1.** a large mountain mass, or a group of connected mountains that form a mountain range **2.** a part of the Earth's crust that is surrounded by faults and may be shifted or displaced by tectonic movements [Early 16C. < French (see MASSIVE)]

Massif Central /másseef son traál/ highland region in south-central France. Area: 93,000 sq. km/36,000 sq. mi.

massive /mássiv/ *adj* **1.** BULKY large, solid, and heavy **2.** COMPARATIVELY LARGE large in comparison to what is typical or usual ○ *gained a massive amount of weight* **3.** LARGE-SCALE extremely large in amount, degree, or scope **4.** DEVOID OF VISIBLE CRYSTALS describes a mineral that has no visible crystalline structure **5.** GEOL HOMOGENEOUS describes rock that is of the same composition throughout, as distinct from being layered **6.** EXCELLENT of the highest quality (*slang*) ■ *n* GANG a gang or small group (*slang; originally used in Black English*) [15C. Via French *massif* < Old French *massiz* < Latin *massa* (see MASS)] —**massively** *adv* —**massiveness** *n*

mass leisure *n* the everyday leisure pursuits of the majority of a population, constituting an aspect of popular culture. It is shaped by, and shapes the values, behaviours, and economics of societies, and cultures.

massless /másslǝss/ *adj* with a mass of zero

mass-market *adj* designed for sale to as wide a range of people as possible, rather than to a particular group in society

mass media *n* all of the communications media that reach a large audience, especially television, radio, and newspapers (*takes a singular or plural verb*)

mass noun *n* a noun representing something that cannot be counted, e.g. 'water', or something that can only be counted if the meaning is a single type or serving, e.g. 'coffee'

mass number *n* the number of protons and neutrons in the nucleus of an atom of a particular substance. Symbol **A**

mass observation *n* a method of observing how people act in social contexts by collating the subjects' own reports, diaries, and responses to questionnaires

mass-produce *vt* to manufacture a product in very large quantities in factories, especially using mechanization and assembly-line methods —**mass-producer** *n*

mass production *n* the manufacturing of products in very large quantities in factories, especially using mechanization and assembly-line methods

mass society *n* a society in which the national or global nature of the influences on life, e.g. mass production and the mass media, has stripped the population of its diversity

mass sociogenic illness /-sōsi ō jénnik-/ *n* PSYCHIAT a situation in which large numbers of people who, as a group, develop symptoms of physical illness as a result of intense perceived danger [Early 21C.]

mass spectrometer *n* an instrument that separates atoms and molecules according to their mass and that records the resulting mass spectrum —**mass spectrometry** *n*

mass spectrum *n* a record of the chemical constituents of a substance separated according to their mass and presented as a spectrum

mass transit *n US* TRANSP same as **public transport**

mass wasting *n* the downward movement of loose rock and soil along a slope

mast[1] /maast/ *n* **1.** VERTICAL SUPPORT FOR SAILS a vertical spar that supports sails, rigging, or flags on a ship **2.** UPRIGHT POLE a vertical pole, especially one that supports a flag **3.** BROADCAST TOWER a tall broadcasting aerial **4.** NAVY same as **captain's mast** ■ *vti* (**masts, masting, masted**) NAVY DISCIPLINE SAILOR, OR BE DISCIPLINED to subject somebody charged with a usually shipboard or on-base crime or infringement to a disciplinary hearing (**captain's mast**), or undergo such a hearing [Old English *mæst* < Indo-European] ◇ **at half mast 1.** partway down a flagpole, usually as a sign of respect following a death ○ *flags flying at half mast* **2.** partway up or down from the usual position at which something is worn (*informal humorous*) ○ *trousers at half mast* ◇ **before the mast** serving as an ordinary sailor or apprentice seaman

mast[2] /maast/ *n* the nuts of some trees, e.g. beech, oak, and chestnut, especially when used as food for pigs [Old English *mæst* 'fodder' < Germanic, 'meat']

mast- *prefix* breast, nipple, mammary gland ○ *mastitis* [< Greek *mastos*]

mastaba /mástəbə/, **mastabah** *n* in ancient Egypt, a brick tomb built with a flat base, sloping sides, and a flat roof. Its design inspired the pyramids. [Early 17C. < Arabic *maṣṭaba*]

mastalgia /ma stáljə/ *n* pain in the breast

mast cell *n* a large cell in connective tissue consisting of granules that release histamine and heparin during allergic reactions [< German *Mast* 'fattening, feeding']

mastectomy /ma stéktəmi/ (*plural* **-mies**) *n* the surgical removal of one or both breasts, usually as a

treatment for breast cancer [Early 20C. < Greek *mastos* 'breast']

master /maːastər/ *n* 1. **BOSS** especially formerly, a man in a position of authority, e.g. over a business or servants (*sometimes considered offensive*) 2. **SOMEBODY IN CONTROL** somebody or something controlling or influencing events or other things (*sometimes considered offensive*) 3. **ABSTRACT CONTROL** an abstract idea or force that is thought of as having control or influence (*sometimes considered offensive*) ○ *She believes strongly that fate is the master of our lives.* 4. **OWNER OF ANIMAL** a man who owns or has control of a horse, dog, or other domesticated animal 5. **SOMEBODY HIGHLY SKILLED** somebody highly skilled at something 6. **SKILLED WORKER** somebody who is highly skilled in a trade or craft and is qualified to teach apprentices (*usually used in combination*) ○ *master craftsman* 7. **PLAYER AT HIGH LEVEL** in some games, a player who has reached a high level of achievement, especially in chess or bridge 8. **ORIGINAL COPY** an original copy of something, e.g. a recording tape or a stencil, from which other copies can be made 9. **MAN TEACHER** a man who is a teacher, especially in a school (*dated*) 10. **LEADER** somebody whose philosophy or religious belief has attracted followers (*sometimes considered offensive*) 11. **SHIP'S CAPTAIN** the captain of a merchant ship 12. **LAW COURT OFFICER** a man who serves as an officer in the Supreme Court of Judicature, subordinate to a judge 13. **VICTOR** somebody who defeats somebody else (*literary*) 14. **COMPUT CONTROLLING MACHINE** a device or computer that controls the operation of one or more other connected devices or computers (*sometimes considered offensive*) ■ *adj* (*sometimes considered offensive*) 1. **MAIN** devised to operate on the broadest level ○ *a master plan* 2. **CONTROLLING** controlling the operation of everything or of all others ○ *the master switch* 3. **PRINCIPAL** biggest or primary among several ○ *the master bedroom* ■ *vt* (**-ters, -tering, -tered**) 1. **BECOME SKILLED IN SOMETHING** to become highly skilled in something or acquire a complete understanding of something 2. **CONTROL SOMETHING** to learn to control feelings or behaviour (*sometimes considered offensive*) 3. **MAKE SOMEBODY OR SOMETHING SUBMIT** to break the will of a person or animal (*sometimes considered offensive*) 4. **MAKE MASTER RECORDING** to produce a master recording of something [Pre-12C. < Old French *maistre* < Latin *magister* 'chief' < *magis* 'more'] —**masterless** *adj* —**mastership** *n*

Master *n* 1. **PREFIX TO BOY'S NAME** a title sometimes prefixed to a boy's surname in formal circumstances 2. **RELIGIOUS TEACHER** a title used to address a man who is a religious leader or teacher (*sometimes considered offensive*) 3. **SOMEBODY APPOINTED BY ROYALTY** a word that features in the title of various men who perform particular duties as officers in the royal household or who hold senior court positions

master-at-arms (*plural* **masters-at-arms**) *n* a noncommissioned officer aboard a naval vessel who is responsible for maintaining order and enforcing discipline in the ship's company

master builder *n* a self-employed builder who employs others as labour (*sometimes considered offensive*)

CULTURAL NOTE *The Master Builder*, a play (1845) by Norwegian dramatist Henrik Ibsen. Typical of Ibsen's more symbolic later works, it is the story of a successful architect, Halvard Solness, who is disturbed by his continued good fortune and fearful that he will eventually have to pay a price for it. His search for redemption eventually leads to his own death.

master chief petty officer *n* a noncommissioned officer in the US Navy or Coast Guard of a rank above senior chief petty officer

master class *n* a class for advanced students given by an acknowledged expert in a field (*sometimes considered offensive*)

master corporal *n* a noncommissioned officer in the Canadian Army, of a rank above corporal and below sergeant

masterful /maːastərfʼl/ *adj* (*sometimes considered offensive*) 1. demonstrating exceptional skill or ability 2. showing the ability or tendency to lead others —**masterfully** *adv* —**masterfulness** *n*

USAGE masterful or **masterly**? These two adjectives are interchangeable in the sense of 'exceptionally skilful'. Some people prefer to use **masterly** for this purpose, to prevent confusion with the other meaning of **masterful**,

'showing the ability or tendency to lead others', which has derogatory overtones. Others avoid both adjectives, in view of the masculine associations of the word *master*.

master key *n* a key that will open all the locks in a set or place

masterly /maːastərli/ *adj* demonstrating outstanding skill (*sometimes considered offensive*) —**masterliness** *n*

USAGE See **masterful**.

master mariner *n* NAUT same as **master** *n* (sense 11)

mastermind /maːastər mīnd/ (*sometimes considered offensive*) *n* somebody who plans, organizes, and oversees a complex operation ■ *vt* (**-minds, -minding, -minded**) to plan, organize, and oversee a complex operation

Master of Arts *n* an academic degree in a nonscience subject, usually awarded after one or two years of postgraduate study, but sometimes awarded as a first degree in place of a bachelor's degree

master of ceremonies *n* (*sometimes considered offensive*) 1. somebody who makes the opening speech and introduces speakers or performers at a formal event 2. a performer who acts as the host of a variety show performed in front of an audience

Master of Science *n* an academic degree in a science subject, usually awarded after one or two years of postgraduate study, but sometimes awarded as a first degree in place of a bachelor's degree

Master of Surgery *n* a postgraduate degree awarded for research in some area of medicine [Translation of Latin *Chirurgiae Magister*]

Master of the Rolls *n* the senior judge in England, who sits in the Court of Appeal and also has the official title of Keeper of the Records at the Public Record Office

masterpiece /maːastər peess/ *n* (*sometimes considered offensive*) 1. an exceptionally good piece of creative work, e.g. a book, film, or performance 2. the best piece of work by a particular artist or craftsperson [Early 17C. After Dutch *meesterstuk* or German *Meisterstück*]

master race *n* a group of people who consider themselves a race superior to all others, especially the Aryans in the ideology of Nazi Germany (*sometimes considered offensive*)

Master's degree *n* an academic degree, usually awarded after one or two years of postgraduate study

master sergeant *n* a noncommissioned officer in the US Army of a rank above sergeant first class, in the Marine Corps, of a rank above gunnery sergeant, and in the Air Force, of a rank above technical sergeant

mastersinger /maːastər singər/ *n* MUSIC same as **Meistersinger** [Early 19C. Anglicization]

masterstroke /maːastər strōk/ *n* a brilliant idea or very clever tactic (*sometimes considered offensive*)

master switch *n* a switch that controls the supply of electricity to a place or to a set of equipment

Masterton /maːastərtən/ town in the south of the North Island, New Zealand. Population: 19,497 (2001).

masterwork /maːastər wurk/ *n* ARTS same as **masterpiece** (*sometimes considered offensive*)

mastery /maːastəri/ *n* (*sometimes considered offensive*) 1. expert knowledge or outstanding ability 2. total control over somebody or something

masthead /maːast hed/ *n* 1. **TOP OF MAST** the top of a ship's mast 2. **MEDIA TITLE OF NEWSPAPER** the name of a newspaper or magazine as it appears in large letters on the front page or cover 3. **US MEDIA NEWSPAPER INFORMATION** the list in a newspaper or magazine that provides information about staff, owners, and circulation in a newspaper or magazine, usually printed on the first page

mastic /mastik/ *n* 1. **CEMENT** a flexible cement. Use: filler, adhesive, sealant in woodwork, plaster, brickwork. 2. **RESIN** an aromatic resin produced by a Mediterranean tree. Use: manufacture of lacquer, varnish, adhesives, condiments. 3. **LIQUOR** a liquor in which mastic gum is used as a flavouring 4. **TREES** same as **mastic tree** [14C. < French < Greek *mastikhan* 'grind the teeth']

masticate /masti kayt/ (**-cates, -cating, -cated**) *v* 1. *vti* to grind and pulverize food inside the mouth, using the teeth and jaws 2. *vt* to grind or crush something until it turns to pulp [Mid-17C. < Latin *masticat-*, past participle of *masticare* < Greek *mastikhan* 'grind the teeth'] —**masticable** *adj* —**mastication** /masti káyshʼn/ *n* —**masticator** *n*

masticatory /mastikətəri/ *adj* relating to chewing ■ *n* (*plural* **-ries**) a medicine made to be chewed in order to increase the production of saliva

mastic tree *n* a small evergreen bush of the cashew family, grown for its resin. Native to: Mediterranean. Latin name: *Pistachia lentiscus*.

mastiff

mastiff /mastif/ *n* a large powerful dog belonging to a breed with smooth-haired, often fawn or greyish coats, and dark faces [14C. < Old French *mastin* < Latin *mansuetus* 'used to the hand, tame' < *manus* 'hand']

mastiff bat *n* a snub-nosed bat. Native to: warm regions. Family: Molossidae.

mastigure /masti gyoor/ *n* a lizard that blocks its burrow with its very spiny tail. Native to: North Africa, Southwest Asia. Genus: *Uromastix*. [Mid-19C. < modern Latin *mastigura* < Greek *mastig-* 'whip' + *oura* 'tail']

mastitis /ma stítiss/ *n* inflammation of a woman's breast or an animal's udder, usually as a result of bacterial infection [Mid-19C. < Greek *mastos* 'breast'] —**mastitic** /ma stíttik/ *adj*

mastodon /mastə don, -dən/ *n* a large extinct mammal that resembled an elephant, with shaggy hair and two sets of tusks. Genus: *Mastodon*. [Early 19C. < Greek *mastos* 'breast' + *odōn* 'tooth'] —**mastodonic** /mastə dónnik/ *adj* —**mastodontic** /mastə dóntik/ *adj*

mastoid /mass toyd/ *adj* 1. shaped like a nipple or breast 2. relating to the mastoid process ■ *n* ANAT same as **mastoid process** [Mid-18C. Via French *mastoïde* or modern Latin *mastoides* < Greek *mastoeidēs* < *mastos* 'breast']

mastoid bone *n* ANAT same as **mastoid process**

mastoid cell *n* an air-filled space in the mastoid process

mastoidectomy /mass toyd éktəmi/ (*plural* **-mies**) *n* a surgical operation to remove part of an infected mastoid process

mastoiditis /mass toyd ítiss/ *n* inflammation of the mastoid process and mastoid cells

mastoid process *n* a bony protuberance on the skull, found behind the ear in many vertebrates, including humans

Mastroianni /mast roy yánni/, **Marcello** (1924–96) Italian film actor. Specializing in romantic or bittersweet comedy, he worked with many of the great Italian directors, including Federico Fellini in *La Dolce Vita* (1960).

'The less you do, the better you do it.' [Marcello Mastroianni, *Interview, Il Corriere della Sera*; 3 August 1985]

masturbate /mástər bayt/ (**-bates, -bating, -bated**) *vti* to give yourself or somebody else sexual pleasure by stroking the genitals, usually to orgasm [Mid-19C. < Latin *masturbat-*, past participle of *masturbari*] —**masturbation** /mástər báyshʼn/ *n* —**masturbator** *n* —**masturbatory** *adj*

masurium /mə soóri əm/ *n* CHEM ELEM same as **technetium** [Early 20C. < German, after *Masuria*, region of NE Poland]

mat[1] /mat/ *n* 1. **PIECE OF CARPET** a flat piece of material

placed on a floor for decoration or protection or for wiping the feet **2.** PIECE OF PADDED MATERIAL a piece of padded material placed on the floor for use in some sports and activities, e.g. to absorb the impact of falling in judo **3.** PROTECTIVE COVER a piece of fabric or board used to protect surfaces from damage by heat or scratching **4.** THICK MASS a thick or interwoven mass, e.g. a tangle of hair ■ *vti* (**mats, matting, matted**) FORM TANGLED MASS to make something into a thick tangled mass, or become a thick tangled mass [Pre-12C. < Latin *matta*]

mat[2] /mat/ *n, adj* PHOTOGRAPHY another spelling of **matt**

mat., **mat** *abbr* matinée

Matabeleland /màttə beéli land/ region in southern Zimbabwe, between the Limpopo and Zambezi rivers. The region's main city is Bulawayo. Area: 181,605 sq. km/70,118 sq. mi.

Matadi /mə taádi/ city in the western Democratic Republic of the Congo, on the River Congo. Population: 172,730 (1994).

matador /màttə dawr/ *n* **1.** BULLFIGHTER the main bullfighter in a bullfight, whose job is to kill the bull **2.** HIGH CARD one of the highest playing cards in some games, e.g. skat **3.** DOMINO GAME a variety of the game of dominoes in which the dots on adjacent halves must total seven [Late 17C. < Spanish < *matar* 'kill']

matagouri /màttə goóri/ (*plural* **-ris**) *n* a thorny bush that forms thickets in open areas. Native to: New Zealand. Latin name: *Discaria toumatou.* [Mid-19C. Alteration of Maori *tumatakuru*]

Mata Hari /maátə haári/ (1876–1917) Dutch dancer and spy. An intelligence agent for the Germans during World War I, she was executed by the French. Born **Zelle, Margaretha Geertruida**

'I am a woman who enjoys herself very much; sometimes I lose, sometimes I win.' [Mata Hari. Quoted in *Mata Hari, the True Story*, Russell Howe; 1986]

matai /maá tī/ (*plural* **-ais**) *n* a coniferous evergreen tree that has bluish bark. Use: wooden flooring. Native to: New Zealand. Latin name: *Podocarpus spicatus.* [Mid-19C. < Maori]

mataj /maátəj/ *n S Asia* a person's mother (*used as a respectful form of address for an older woman*) [< Hindi, form of *mata* 'mother' < Sanskrit *mātā*]

Matamoros /màttə máwrəss/ city and port in northeastern Mexico, near the mouth of the Rio Grande opposite Brownsville, Texas. Population: 418,141 (2000).

Mataura /mə tówrə/ river in the southern part of the South Island, New Zealand, that rises in the Eyre Mountains south of Lake Wakatipu and flows into the Foveaux Strait east of Bluff. Length: 240 km/149 mi.

match[1] /mach/ *n* **1.** CONTEST a contest between opponents, especially a sporting contest **2.** EQUAL somebody or something capable of competing equally with another person or thing **3.** SOMETHING SIMILAR a close likeness of somebody or something **4.** GOOD COMPLEMENT something that combines well with something else **5.** COUNTERPART somebody who or something that is identical to another person or thing or is one half of a pair **6.** MARRIAGE a relationship of marriage **7.** POTENTIAL PARTNER an appropriate marriage partner ■ *v* (**matches, matching, matched**) **1.** *vt* BE LIKE SOMEBODY OR SOMETHING to be similar or identical to somebody or something **2.** *vt* COMPETE EQUALLY WITH SOMEBODY OR SOMETHING to be as good, or sometimes as bad, as somebody or something else ○ *She knows she can match him for speed any day.* **3.** *vti* COMBINE WELL to make a suitable or pleasing combination, or put things together to make such a combination **4.** *vt* FIND SOMETHING THAT COMBINES WITH SOMETHING to find something that makes a suitable accompaniment **5.** *vti* JOIN CLEANLY to fit or join something smoothly, or fit or join together smoothly **6.** *vt* PLACE SOMEBODY OR SOMETHING IN OPPOSITION to provide somebody or something with an opponent **7.** *vti US* TOSS COINS to toss coins to see which sides land face up in order to determine a choice or decision [Old English *gemæcca* 'spouse, lover' < Germanic] —**matchability** /màchə bíllәti/ *n* —**matchable** *adj* —**matcher** *n*

match[2] /mach/ *n* **1.** a thin stick of wood whose tip is coated with a combustible material that ignites when scraped against a rough surface **2.** a slow-burning fuse used in cannons and explosives [14C. < Old French *meiche* < Greek *muxa* 'wick for a lamp']

matchboard /mách bawrd/ *n* a board that has a tongue along one edge and a groove along the other so that it can be fitted together with other boards [< MATCH [1]]

matchbook /mách bŏŏk/ *n* a small cardboard folder with safety matches inside and a striking surface usually on the outside [Mid-20C. < MATCH [2]]

matchbox /mách boks/ *n* a small cardboard box for matches, with a striking surface along one or both sides [Late 18C. < MATCH [2]]

matchless /máchləss/ *adj* so outstandingly great as to have no rival [Mid-16C. < MATCH [1]] —**matchlessly** *adv* —**matchlessness** *n*

matchlock /mách lok/ *n* **1.** formerly, a trigger mechanism in guns that ignited the powder with a slow-burning fuse **2.** a gun fitted with a matchlock [Mid-17C. < MATCH [2]]

matchmaker /mách maykər/ *n* somebody who arranges romantic partnerships or marriages [Mid-17C. < MATCH [1]] —**matchmaking** *n*

match play *n* in golf, a method of scoring in which the number of holes won is counted rather than the number of strokes taken [< MATCH [1]] —**match player** *n*

match point *n* **1.** the final point needed to win a match, especially in tennis and other racket games **2.** a unit used for scoring in bridge tournaments [< MATCH [1]]

matchstick /mách stik/ *n* STEM OF MATCH the wooden part of a match ■ *adj* **1.** MADE FROM MATCHES built of matchsticks **2.** THIN OR IN STRIPS as thin as matchsticks, or in the form of thin strips or simple lines [Late 18C. < MATCH [2]]

matchup /mách up/ *n US* a competition or contest between two people or two teams, e.g. in a competitive sport [< MATCH [1]]

matchwood /mách wŏŏd/ *n* fragments or splinters, especially resulting from the destruction of something [Late 16C. < MATCH [2]]

mate[1] /mayt/ *n* **1.** FRIEND a friend, also used as a friendly, or sometimes hostile, form of address to a man **2.** USED TO ADDRESS SOMEBODY used as a friendly, or sometimes hostile, form of address to a man (*informal; usually used in combination*) **3.** BREEDING PARTNER either of a pair of animals that breed together **4.** PARTNER IN SEX OR WEDLOCK a sexual or marriage partner (*informal*) **5.** SKILLED WORKER'S HELPER an assistant to a skilled worker ○ *a plumber's mate* **6.** OFFICER IN MERCHANT NAVY a deck officer of a rank below the master on a merchant ship **7.** *US* PETTY OFFICER a petty officer in the US Navy who assists a warrant officer **8.** SOMETHING THAT MATCHES either of a pair of things that belong together ■ *v* (**mates, mating, mated**) **1.** *vti* BREED to come together or bring animals together to breed **2.** *vi* HAVE SEX to engage in sex **3.** *vt* CONNECT TWO OBJECTS to combine or connect two things **4.** *vti* MARRY to join two people in marriage, or become joined in marriage (*informal or humorous*) [14C. < Middle Low German *gemate*] —**mateless** *adj*

REGIONAL NOTE See *man.*

mate[2] /mayt/ *n, vt* (**mates, mating, mated**), *interj* CHESS same as **checkmate** *n* (senses 1–2), *v* (sense 1), *interj* [14C. See CHECKMATE]

maté /maá tay, máttay/ *n* **1.** a milky drink popular South America that contains caffeine and is made from dried leaves **2.** an evergreen tree grown for its leaves, which are used to make maté. Native to: South America. Latin name: *Ilex paraguariensis.* [Early 18C. Via Spanish < Quechua *mati*]

matelote /mátt'lōt/ *n* a chunky fish stew made with wine [Early 18C. Via French, 'sailor' < Middle Dutch *mattenoot* 'bed companion']

mater /máytər/ *n* same as **mother**[1] *n* (sense 1) (*dated informal or humorous*) [Late 16C. < Latin]

ORIGIN The Latin word *mater* 'mother', from which ***mater*** is derived, is also the source of English *madrigal, material, maternal, matriculate, matrimony, matrix, matron,* and *matter.* Its Indo-European ancestor in turn gave rise to English *mammal, metropolis,* and *mother*[1].

materfamilias /máytər fə mílli ass/ *n* a woman described in her role as head of a household or as the mother of her children (*formal*) [Mid-18C. < Latin, 'mother of the family']

material /mə teéri əl/ *n* **1.** FABRIC woven flat cloth or fabric **2.** SOMETHING USED IN MAKING ITEMS the substance used to make things **3.** INFORMATION information such as facts, notes, and research used in the making of a book, film, or other work **4.** SOMEBODY SUITABLE somebody regarded in terms of his or her suitability to perform a particular job or task ○ *She's certainly executive material.* ■ **materials** *npl* EQUIPMENT the tools and other things needed to perform a particular task ■ *adj* **1.** PHYSICAL relating to or consisting of solid physical matter ○ *the material universe* **2.** WORLDLY relating to physical wellbeing rather than emotional or spiritual wellbeing ○ *material comforts* **3.** PERTINENT relevant or important **4.** LAW IMPORTANT IN COURT crucial to the outcome of a court case or to the validity of a legal document ○ *testimony that is material to the case* **5.** PHILOSOPHY OF CONTENT NOT FORM relating to the substance of reasoning rather than the form it takes [14C. Via French *matériel* < late Latin *materialis* < Latin *materia* (see MATTER)] —**materiality** /mə teéri álləti/ *n*

materialise *vti* another spelling of **materialize**

materialism /mə teéri əlizəm/ *n* **1.** devotion to material wealth and possessions at the expense of spiritual or intellectual values **2.** the philosophical theory that physical matter is the only reality and that psychological states such as emotions, reason, thought, and desire will eventually be explained as physical functions

materialist /mə teéri əlist/ *n* **1.** somebody who values material wealth and possessions rather than spiritual or intellectual things **2.** a supporter of the philosophical theory that physical matter is the only reality and that psychological states can be explained as physical functions ■ *adj* same as **materialistic**

materialistic /mə teéri ə lístik/ *adj* concerned with material wealth and possessions at the expense of spiritual or intellectual values —**materialistically** *adv*

materialize /mə teéri ə līz/ (**-izes, -izing, -ized**), **materialise** (**-ises, -ising, -ised**) *v* **1.** *vi* BECOME REAL to become real or become fact **2.** *vi* APPEAR to appear suddenly, as if out of nowhere **3.** *vti* ASSUME PHYSICAL FORM to assume a physical form, or cause a supposed ghost or spirit to assume a physical form —**materialization** /mə teéri ə lī záysh'n/ *n*

materially /mə teéri əli/ *adv* **1.** in a real sense or to a significant degree **2.** in terms of material wealth and possessions

materials science *n* the study of the features and applications of materials such as metals, plastics, and ceramics as used in science and technology

matériel /mə teéri él/, **materiel** *n* the supplies, weapons, and equipment associated with a military force [Early 19C. < French (see MATERIAL)]

maternal /mə túrn'l/ *adj* **1.** OF OR LIKE MOTHER belonging or relating to motherhood, a mother, or mothers in general ○ *maternal pride* **2.** CARING kind, caring, and protective in a motherly way ○ *a very maternal person* **3.** ON OR FROM MOTHER'S SIDE relating to or inherited from the mother or the mother's side of a family ○ *my maternal grandfather* [15C. < French *maternel* < Latin *maternus* < *mater* 'mother'] —**maternalism** *n* —**maternalistic** /mə túrnə lístik/ *adj* —**maternally** *adv*

maternity /mə túrnəti/ *n* **1.** TIME DURING OR AFTER PREGNANCY the period during pregnancy or around the time of childbirth (*usually used in combination*) ○ *maternity clothes* **2.** MOTHERHOOD the condition of being a mother (*usually used in combination*) **3.** MOTHERLY CHARACTERISTICS the characteristics and emotions traditionally associated with being a mother, e.g. loving kindness and protectiveness **4.** HOSPITAL SECTION CARING FOR NEWBORNS a ward, floor, or other section of a hospital where mothers and newborn babies are cared for [Early 17C. < French *maternité* < Latin *maternus* (see MATERNAL)]

maternity benefit, **maternity allowance** *n* a series of regular payments made by the state to a woman who has a baby, usually covering the 18 weeks around the child's birth

maternity leave *n* paid or unpaid leave from work that a woman is entitled to take before, at, and after the time that she has a child

mateship /máyt ship/ *n Aus* friendship, especially between two men or within a group of men, on terms of equality and mutual support (*informal*)

mates' rates *npl Aus* reduced prices for friends or regular customers

matey /máyti/, **maty** *adj* (**-ier, -iest**) friendly, especially in a way that is familiar or seems insincere ○ *Those*

two have been very matey lately. ■ *n* used by a man to address another man he does not know and, usually, feels hostile towards (*informal*) —**matily** *adv* —**matiness** *n*

matgrass /mát graass/ *n* a common European grass that grows in dense tufted clumps on peaty moorland. Latin name: *Nardus stricta.* [Late 18C. < its similarity to thick matting]

math /math/ *n N Am* same as **mathematics** (*informal*) [Late 19C. Shortening]

math. *abbr* **1.** mathematical **2.** mathematically **3.** mathematician **4.** mathematics

mathematic /máthə máttik/ *adj* same as **mathematical** (*archaic or literary*) ■ *n* same as **mathematics** (*archaic*) [14C. Directly or via French *mathématique* < Latin *mathematicus* < Greek *mathēmat-* 'something learned', related to *manthanein* 'learn']

mathematical /máthə máttik'l/ *adj* **1.** OF MATHEMATICS belonging to, relating to, or used in mathematics **2.** ACCURATE as accurate as if calculated by mathematics ○ *crafted the strategy with mathematical precision* **3.** WORKED OUT BY MATHEMATICS calculated or proved by mathematics ○ *It's a mathematical certainty that two numbers in the set will be the same.* **4.** GOOD AT MATHEMATICS skilled in mathematics ○ *more artistic than mathematical* —**mathematically** *adv*

mathematical expectation *n* STATS same as **expected value**

mathematical induction *n* MATHS same as **induction** (sense 8)

mathematician /máthəmə tísh'n/ *n* a student or expert in mathematics, or somebody whose job involves mathematics

mathematics /máthə máttiks/ *n* the study of the relationships among numbers, shapes, and quantities. It uses signs, symbols, and proofs and includes arithmetic, algebra, calculus, geometry, and trigonometry. (*takes a singular verb*) ■ *npl* the calculations involved in a process, estimate, or plan (*takes a plural verb*) ○ *It's a simple idea, though the mathematics of it are very complex.*

mathematize /máthəmə tīz/ (**-tizes, -tizing, -tized**), **mathematise** (**-tises, -tising, -tised**) *vt* to consider something in, or reduce it to, purely mathematical terms —**mathematization** /máthəmə tī záysh'n/ *n*

Mather /máythər, máth-/, **Cotton** (1663–1728) American puritan minister and theologian. He published works on witchcraft, ethics, religion, natural history, medicine, and science, and championed inoculations against smallpox. Increase Mather was his father.

> 'I write the wonders of the Christian religion, flying from the depravations of Europe, to the American strand: and, assisted by the Holy Author of that religion...I report the wonderful displays of His infinite power, wisdom, goodness, and faithfulness, wherewith his Divine Providence hath irradiated an Indian wilderness.'
> [Cotton Mather, *Magnalia Christi Americana*; 1702]

~~mathmatics~~ incorrect spelling of **mathematics**

maths /maths/ *n, npl* same as **mathematics** (*informal*) [Early 20C. Contraction]

Mathura /mu thoórə/ city in north-central India, on the River Yamuna. Population: 319,235 (2001).

Matilda /mə tíldə/ (1102–67) English princess. Though she was the daughter and acknowledged heir of Henry I of England, the throne was seized by her cousin Stephen, and she was never crowned queen.

matin /máttin/, **mattin, matinal** /máttinəl/ *adj* belonging or relating to matins, or taking place during matins [13C. < French *matines* (see MATINS)]

matinée /mátti nay/, **matinee** *n* **1.** a performance of a play, concert, or film that is given during the day, especially in the afternoon, often with cheaper seats than the evening performance **2.** an event or social occasion taking place at midday or in the afternoon ○ *The Senior Centre holds a matinée dance on the first Saturday of each month.* [Mid-19C. < French, 'morning' < *matin*, singular of *matines* (see MATINS)]

matinée coat *n* a flared top for a baby. It is usually long-sleeved and knitted and comes down to just on or below the level of the nappy.

matinée idol *n* an actor who is particularly attractive to women, especially a good-looking leading man in films of the 1930s and 1940s (*dated*)

matinée jacket *n* CLOTHING same as **matinée coat** (*dated*)

matins /máttinz/, **mattins** *n* **1.** MORNING LITURGY in the Roman Catholic Church, the morning hours of the divine office **2.** MORNING PRAYER in the Church of England, the ceremony of morning prayer **3.** HOURS BEFORE VIGIL in some Roman Catholic monastic communities, the hours before a vigil **4.** DAWN CHORUS a morning song, especially one sung by birds (*literary*) [13C. < French *matines* < Latin *matutinus* 'of the morning' < *Matuta* 'goddess of dawn']

AKG London

Henri Matisse: photographed in 1948 working on his paper cutouts

Matisse /mə teéss/, **Henri** (1869–1954) French artist. A leader of the fauve group from 1905, and an influential 20th-century artist, he used bold colour to create rhythmic forms and a flat perspective, later working with brightly coloured paper cutouts on canvas. Full name **Matisse, Henri Émile Benoît**

> 'An old brush has vitality, it's a brush that has lived, that has had a life of its own.'
> [Henri Matisse. Quoted in *Matisse, Picasso, Miro*, Rosamond Bernier; 1992]

matjes herring /máttyəz-/, **maatjes herring** *n* a fillet or fillets of herring, especially of a young herring that has not spawned, that is lightly salted, usually sweetened and flavoured, and eaten raw [Partial translation of Dutch *maatjesharing* 'maiden's herring' < *maatjes* 'maiden's' (from its use for young herring) + *haring* 'herring']

Matlock /mát lok/ town in Derbyshire, in the Peak District of central England. Population: 14,680 (1991).

Mato Grosso /máttō gróssō/ state in southwestern Brazil. Capital: Cuiabá. Population: 2,235,832 (1996). Area: 906,806 sq. km/350,120 sq. mi.

matoke /mə tṓki/ *n* banana or plantain flesh boiled and mashed and used in Uganda as a staple food [Mid-20C. < Bantu]

Matopo Hills /mə tṓpə-/ region of granite hills in southwestern Zimbabwe. Area: 3,240 sq. km/1,250 sq. mi.

~~matress~~ incorrect spelling of **mattress**

matri- *prefix* mother, maternal ○ *matriarchy* ○ *matrilineal* [< Latin *matr-*, stem of *mater* 'mother']

matriarch /máytri aark/ *n* **1.** WOMAN HEAD OF FAMILY a woman who is recognized as being the head of a family, community, or people **2.** STRONG SENIOR WOMAN a woman, usually a grandmother, who is highly respected by her family and to whom the family turn for advice and help **3.** WOMAN IN POWERFUL POSITION a woman who holds a position of dominance, authority, or respect [Early 17C. < Latin *matr-* 'mother', after *patriarch*] —**matriarchal** /máytri aárk'l/ *adj* —**matriarchic** *adj*

matriarchy /máytri aarki/ (*plural* **-chies**) *n* **1.** SOCIAL ORDER WHERE WOMEN HAVE POWER a form of social order where women are in charge and are recognized as the heads of families, with power, lineage, and inheritance passing, where possible, from mothers to daughters **2.** *also* **matriarchate** /máytri aarkayt/ COMMUNITY WHERE WOMEN HAVE POWER a community, society, or social group that is based on matriarchy **3.** ORGANIZATION WHERE WOMEN HAVE POWER an organization or government where women have power [Late 19C. After PATRIARCHY]

matric /mə trík/ *n* same as **matriculation** (*dated informal*) [Late 19C. Shortening]

matrices SCI plural of **matrix**

matricide /máytri sīd, máttri-/ *n* **1.** the act of murdering your own mother **2.** somebody who kills his or her own mother [Late 16C. Directly or via French < Latin *matricidium* < *matr-* 'mother'] —**matricidal** /máytri sīd'l, máttri-/ *adj*

matriclinous /máttri klīnəss/ *adj* having obvious characteristics that are inherited predominantly from the woman parent

matriculant /mə tríkyoolənt/ *n* EDUC same as **matriculate** [Mid-19C. < medieval Latin *matriculant-*, present participle of *matriculare* (see MATRICULATE)]

matriculate /mə tríkyoo layt/ *v* (**-lates, -lating, -lated**) **1.** *vt* ADMIT SOMEBODY AS STUDENT to admit a student to membership of a college or university **2.** *vi* BE ENROLLED AS STUDENT to be enrolled at a college or university, after meeting the academic standard required to be accepted for a course of further education ■ *n* SOMEBODY ENROLLED somebody who has matriculated [Late 16C. < medieval Latin *matriculat-*, past participle of *matriculare* < *matricula* 'little list' < *matrix* (see MATRIX)] —**matriculator** *n*

matriculation /mə tríkyoo láysh'n/ *n* **1.** the act or process of matriculating at a college or university **2.** an examination formerly taken in the United Kingdom as a school-leaving qualification

matrilineage /máttri línni ij/ *n* **1.** the line of genealogical relationship or descent that follows the female side of a family **2.** a group of people related by descent through mothers

matrilineal /máttri línni əl/ *adj* **1.** FEMALE describes the line of genealogical relationship or descent that follows the female side of a family **2.** RELATED THROUGH MOTHERS describes a group that is related by descent through mothers **3.** COMING THROUGH WOMEN'S LINE inherited or traced through the female line of descent —**matrilineally** *adv*

matrilocal /máttri lṓk'l/ *adj* **1.** describes a form of marriage in which, after the wedding, the bridegroom moves to his new wife's family home **2.** describes a culture in which young men live with their brides' families after marriage —**matrilocality** /máttri lō kálləti/ *n* —**matrilocally** *adv*

matrimonial /máttri mṓni əl/ *adj* belonging or relating to marriage or to a particular marriage [15C. Directly or via French < Latin *matrimonialis* < *matrimonium* (see MATRIMONY)] —**matrimonially** *adv*

matrimony /máttrimənì/ *n* **1.** MARRIED STATE the state or condition of being married **2.** MARRIAGE CEREMONY the religious ceremony of marriage **3.** CARD GAME a card game in which players try to hold a king and queen [13C. Directly or via Anglo-Norman *matrimonie* < Latin *matrimonium* 'state of motherhood' (because of the association of marriage with parenthood) < *matr-* 'mother']

matrimony vine *n* a sometimes thorny bush, some species of which are cultivated for their orange or red berries. Native to: Europe, Asia. Genus: *Lycium.*

matrix /máytriks/ (*plural* **-trices** /-tri seez/ or **-trixes**) *n* **1.** ARRANGEMENT OF CONNECTED THINGS an arrangement of parts that shows how they are interconnected **2.** SUBSTANCE CONTAINING SOMETHING a substance in which something is embedded or enclosed **3.** SITUATION IN WHICH SOMETHING DEVELOPS a situation or set of circumstances that allows or encourages the origin, development, or growth of something ○ *The matrix of video and computers is producing new forms of art.* **4.** TISSUE-FORMING SUBSTANCE the substance that exists between cells and from which tissue such as cartilage and bone develops **5.** TISSUE AT BASE OF NAIL the thickened tissue at the base of a fingernail, toenail, or tooth from which a new nail or tooth grows **6.** SOIL OR ROCK CONTAINING SOMETHING the soil or rock in which something such as a fossil, crystal, or mineral is embedded **7.** MAIN PART OF ALLOY the main metal component in an alloy **8.** ARRANGEMENT OF MATHEMATICAL ELEMENTS a rectangular array of mathematical elements, e.g. the coefficients of linear equations, whose rows and columns can be combined with those of other arrays to solve problems **9.** NETWORK OF CIRCUIT PARTS in computing, a network of circuit parts such as transistors and resistors **10.** METAL TYPE MOULD a metal mould from which type is cast in the hot-metal process **11.** MOULD MADE FROM RAISED SURFACE a mould made by taking the impression of a raised surface in a substance such

as plastic, used in stereotyping or electrotyping **12.** GRAMOPHONE RECORD MOULD a mould used in the production of gramophone records **13.** SURROUNDING MASS OF MATERIAL a bed or surround of material that gives protection or absorbs a force [14C. Directly or via French *matrice* < Latin *matrix* 'womb', later 'list' < *matr*- 'mother']

matrix sentence *n* the main clause in a complex sentence

matrix trading *n* a bond swap strategy designed to profit from yield curve differentials between bonds of different ratings or classes

matro- *prefix* ANTHROP same as **matri-**

matroclinous /máttrō klīnəss/, **matroclinal** /-klīnəl/ *adj* GENETICS same as **matriclinous**

matron /máytrən/ *n* **1.** HEAD NURSE a woman who is head of the nursing staff in a hospital, nursing home, or other medical institution, now called the senior nursing officer (*not in technical use*) **2.** SUPERVISOR a woman in charge of the medical and housekeeping arrangements in an institution such as a boarding school **3.** *N Am* WOMAN WARDEN a woman who is a warden in a women's correctional institution **4.** MATURE WOMAN a woman, especially a married woman of middle age or later, who has had children and is thought of as being mature, sensible, and of good social standing [14C. Directly or via French *matrone* < Latin *matrona* < *matr*- 'mother'] —**matronal** *adj* —**matronhood** *n* —**matronship** *n*

matronly /máytrənli/ *adj* **1.** LIKE MATRON having qualities associated with a matron, especially dignity and placidity **2.** MATURE AND FULL-FIGURED mature and plump, especially with a large bosom **3.** OF MATRON relating to or characteristic of a matron ○ *matronly duties* —**matronliness** *n*

matron of honour *n* a married woman who acts as chief bridesmaid at the wedding of a woman friend or relative

matronymic /máttrə nímmik/, **metronymic** /méttrə-/ *n* a name derived from a mother or a matrilineal ancestor [Late 18C. < Latin *matr*- 'mother']

mat salleh /mát sa láy/ *n Malaysia* a white foreigner [Early 20C. < Malay, alteration of English *mad sailor*, because drunken sailors were the Westerners that most Malayans had contact with]

Matsu Islands /mat sóo-/ island group in Taiwan, close to the Chinese mainland

matsutake /mátsoo taáki/, **matsutake mushroom** *n* an edible dark brown mushroom with a cinnamon fragrance. Native to: Japan. Latin name: *Tricholoma matsutake*. [< Japanese, 'pine mushroom']

Matsuyama /mát sōo yaámə/ industrial city in southwestern Japan, on the island of Shikoku. Population: 473,039 (2002).

matt /mat/, **matte**, **mat** *UK, ANZ, Can n* a dull or non-glossy finish, e.g. on paintwork or photographic prints ■ *adj* having a matt finish ▶ US spelling (all senses) [Mid-17C. < French *mat* 'dull']

Matt. BIBLE Matthew

mattamore /máttə mawr/ *n* an underground chamber, room, or storage place [Late 17C. Via French *matamore* < Arabic *maṭmūra* < *ṭamara* 'bury']

mattar /múttər/ *n S Asia* green peas [< Hindi]

matte[1] /mat/ *adj* ARTS another spelling of **matt**

matte[2] /mat/ *n* **1.** a mixture of metal sulphides formed during the smelting of sulphide ores such as ores of copper or nickel **2.** a mask used for obscuring part of an image so that another image can be put on top of the original [Mid-19C. < French, form of *mat* 'dull']

matted /máttid/ *adj* **1.** forming a thick tangled mass **2.** covered with mats or matting

matter /máttər/ *n* **1.** SOMETHING UNDER CONSIDERATION something that is being considered or needs to be dealt with ○ *This is a matter for serious thought.* **2.** CAUSE OF PROBLEM the reason why something is wrong or not working properly, or why somebody is annoyed, upset, or not feeling well ○ *What's the matter?* ○ *There's something the matter with the alarm.* **3.** SUBSTANCE a substance or material of a particular kind ○ *reading matter* **4.** SUBSTANCE CONSTITUTING UNIVERSE the material substance of the universe that has mass, occupies space, and is convertible to energy **5.** PRINTED TEXT text or other material that is printed ○ *cheaper rates for printed matter* **6.** SUBJECT OF SPEECH OR WRITING the subject that is dealt with in speech or writing, as opposed to its presentation **7.** WHAT IS PERCEIVED BY MIND in Cartesian philosophy, something that is extended in space and persists through time, and is contrasted with mind **8.** *US* SOMETHING TO BE PROVED a case to be proved or resolved in a court of law ○ *Who is the defendant in this matter?* **9.** BODILY DISCHARGE something that is discharged from the body, e.g. pus ■ **matters** *npl* CIRCUMSTANCES the current situation or circumstances ○ *We were both under a lot of stress, which didn't improve matters.* ■ *vi* (**-ters, -tering, -tered**) **1.** HAVE IMPORTANCE to be important ○ *The only thing that matters is for you to get better.* **2.** MAKE DIFFERENCE to make a difference ○ *It doesn't matter how you tell her, just make sure she knows.* **3.** PRODUCE PUS to form or discharge pus [12C. Directly or via Anglo-Norman *mater(i)e*, French *matière* < Latin *materia* 'timber, stuff' < *mater* 'mother'] ◇ **a matter of opinion** a subject about which there are varying views ◇ **as a matter of course** in accordance with normal procedure or expected events ◇ **for that matter** as far as that is concerned ◇ **no matter 1.** regardless of ○ *No matter how many we distribute, there are never enough.* **2.** it is not important ◇ **no matter what** used to express determination in the face of uncertain circumstances or consequences

SYNONYMS See ***subject***.

Popperfoto

Matterhorn

Matterhorn /máttər hawrn/ mountain in the Pennine Alps, on the Italian-Swiss border. Height: 4,478 m/14,692 ft.

matter of fact *n* **1.** something that is true and that cannot be denied ○ *Very few people here have jobs – it's a matter of fact.* **2.** a question to be decided by a court of law that involves deciding on the truth of a statement, rather than interpreting a point of law or forming an opinion ◇ **as a matter of fact 1.** used to add a statement that completes what you are saying or emphasizes its truth **2.** used to contradict what somebody else has said or to express disagreement

matter-of-fact *adj* **1.** straightforward and not fanciful or emotional ○ *I admired her matter-of-fact approach to life.* **2.** dealing with facts and not emotions or opinions ○ *a matter-of-fact account of the incident* —**matter-of-factly** *adv* —**matter-of-factness** *n*

matter of law *n* a question to be decided by a court of law that involves the interpretation of a point of law

mattery /máttəri/ *adj* secreting or discharging pus

matte shot *n* in filmmaking, a visual effect that is achieved by masking out part of an image using a matte and superimposing another image so that it combines with the rest of the original

Matthau /mát ow/, **Walter** (1920–2000) US actor. He is best known for his part in both stage and film versions of *The Odd Couple* (1965, 1968). He won an Academy Award for *The Fortune Cookie* (1966). Born **Matuschanskayasky, Walter**

Matthew /máthyoo/ *n* a book of the Bible, the first of the Gospels in which the life and teachings of Jesus Christ are described, traditionally attributed to St Matthew. See table at **Bible**

Matthew /máthyoo/, **St** (*fl* AD 1st century) one of the 12 apostles of Jesus Christ. By tradition he is considered to be the author of the first Gospel in the Bible.

Matthews /máthyooz/, **Sir Stanley** (1915–2000) British footballer. Noted for his skill as a dribbler, he played for Stoke City, Blackpool (1947–61), and England, winning 54 international caps.

Matthew Walker /máth yoo wáwkər/ *n* a knot made in the strands at the end of a rope [Mid-19C. Probably after the person who invented it]

Matthias /mə thī́ əss/ disciple chosen to replace Judas as one of the 12 apostles of Jesus Christ (Acts 1:15–26)

Matthias Corvinus /-kawr vī́nəss/ (1443–90) king of Hungary. His acquisition of Austria and various provinces made him a powerful ruler.

mattify /mátti fī/ (**-fies, -fying, -fied**) *vt* to remove or remedy oiliness or shininess of the complexion [< MATT]

mattin *adj* CHR another spelling of **matin**

matting[1] /mátting/ *n* **1.** MATERIAL WOVEN FROM NATURAL FIBRES a coarse material woven from natural fibres. Use: mats, coverings. ○ *coconut matting* **2.** MATS mats, taken collectively ○ *Matting is integral to Japanese interior design.* **3.** LAYER OF NATURAL MATERIALS a bed or layer formed by natural materials, e.g. by fallen leaves in a forest ○ *We walked through the pines on a matting of needles.* **4.** MAKING MATS the process of making a mat or mats [Early 17C. < MAT [1]]

matting[2] /mátting/ *n* **1.** a surface that is dull or without sheen **2.** the process of giving a surface, especially a metallic one, a dull finish [Late 17C. < MATT]

mattins *n* CHR another spelling of **matins**

mattock /máttək/ *n* a tool like a pickaxe with one end of its blade flattened at right angles to its handle, used for loosening soil and cutting through roots [Pre-12C. Origin ?]

mattress /máttrəss/ *n* **1.** PAD FOR SLEEPING ON a large pad on which to sleep, usually containing springs or a soft springy filling. Some modern mattresses have electronic controls that allow them to tilt into different positions. **2.** INFLATABLE PAD a large pad that can be filled with air or water and used as a bed or for floating on, e.g. in a pool **3.** FOUNDATION FOR BUILDING a slab or platform used as a foundation for a building **4.** INTERNAL METAL FRAMEWORK a metal framework inside reinforced concrete **5.** CIV ENG same as **blinding 6.** SHIELD FOR EMBANKMENTS a closely woven structure made from brushwood and poles and used for protecting dykes, embankments, dams, and other susceptible slopes from erosion [13C. < Old French *materas* < Arabic *al-matrah* 'cushion'; from the practice of sleeping on cushions]

maturate /máttyōō rayt, máchōō-/ (**-rates, -rating, -rated**) *vti* to mature, ripen, or develop, or develop or ripen something [Mid-16C. Either < Latin *maturat*-, past participle of *maturare* < *maturus* 'ripe' or back-formation < MATURATION] —**maturative** /mə tyóōrə tiv/ *adj*

maturation /máttyōō ráysh'n, máchōō-/ *n* **1.** PROGRESS TO MATURITY the process of becoming mature, ripe, or more developed **2.** PROCESS OF MAKING SOMETHING MORE MATURE the process of ripening or developing something or of making it more mature **3.** PROCESS OF CELL DEVELOPMENT the process in which immature cells in the ovary and testes develop into ova and spermatozoa [14C. Directly or via French < medieval Latin *maturation*- < *maturare* < *maturus* 'ripe'] —**maturational** *adj*

maturation division *n* the process of cell division by which the ova and spermatozoa are developed

mature /mə tyóōr, -chóōr/ *adj* **1.** ACTING OR SEEMING LIKE ADULT showing the mental, emotional, or physical characteristics associated with a fully developed adult person ○ *Philip is only 12 but he's very tall and already quite mature.* **2.** EXPERIENCED showing qualities gained by development and experience ○ *in the author's mature writings* **3.** ADULT adult or fully grown ○ *a mature animal capable of breeding* **4.** FULLY DEVELOPED describes an organism that is fully developed to a complete or final stage **5.** OLD AND OF GOOD FLAVOUR old enough to have acquired the maximum flavour ○ *mature Orkney cheddar* **6.** IN LATER LIFE no longer young ○ *the wisdom shown by the mature dramatist* ○ *The role is that of a mature woman with a successful career behind her.* **7.** INVOLVING SERIOUS THOUGHT involving or reached by a period of serious thought ○ *On mature reflection, I feel it would be wiser to sell.* **8.** DUE FOR PAYMENT describes a financial arrangement that has reached a previously set or mutually agreed-on time limit and is therefore due for payment or repayment ○ *mature bonds* **9.** NOT SUBJECT TO MAJOR CHANGE no longer subject to the instability of early development or

expansion ○ *Hydroelectric power is a mature industry in the region.* **10.** IN MIDDLE OF EROSION CYCLE describes a natural feature or landform that is in the middle stages of an erosion cycle ■ *v* (**-tures, -turing, -tured**) **1.** *vti* DEVELOP to go through a developmental process, or make something or somebody go through a developmental process ○ *Children begin to mature at different ages.* **2.** *vi* FALL DUE FOR PAYMENT to reach a previously set or mutually agreed-on time limit and therefore fall due for payment or repayment (*refers to financial arrangements*) **3.** *vti* DEVELOP INTO SOMETHING FINISHED to become fully worked out, or work something out fully, especially through long consideration ○ *The plan had matured over the intervening months.* [14C. Directly or via French < Latin *maturus* 'ripe'] —**maturely** *adv*

mature student *n* a student aged 25 or over who has gone into higher or further education later than is usual, especially after working or raising a family

maturity /mə tyoŏrəti, -choŏrəti/ *n* **1.** FULL GROWTH OR DEVELOPMENT the state of being fully grown or developed ○ *Girls tend to reach maturity earlier than boys.* **2.** MATURE STATE the condition of being ripe, fully aged, or fully grown, especially mentally or emotionally ○ *I'm amazed at the maturity shown by these young people.* **3.** TIME FOR REPAYMENT the time when a financial arrangement falls due for payment or repayment **4.** READINESS FOR REPAYMENT the state of a financial arrangement when it falls due for payment or repayment **5.** MATURE STATE OF LANDFORM the stage in the development of a landform at which there is maximum relief and drainage is well developed [15C. Directly or via French *maturité* < Latin *maturitas* < *maturus* 'ripe']

maturity-onset diabetes *n* MED same as **non-insulin-dependent diabetes**

matutinal /mǎttyoŏ tīn'l/ *adj* relating to or happening in the morning or the early part of the day (*formal*) [Mid-16C. < late Latin *matutinalis* < *Matuta*, goddess of the dawn] —**matutinally** *adv*

MATV *abbr* master antenna television

maty *adj, n* another spelling of **matey**

matzo /mótsə/, **matzoh** *n* (*plural* **-zos** or **-zoth** /mótsōt/; *plural* **-zohs** or **-zoth**) unleavened bread traditionally eaten during Passover in commemoration of the unleavened bread eaten by the ancient Hebrews escaping from slavery in Egypt ■ *adj* made from or like matzo, or used to make matzo ○ *matzo meal* ○ *matzo balls* [Mid-19C. Via Yiddish *matse* < Hebrew *massāh*]

matzo ball *n* a small dumpling made from matzo meal

matzoon /maat soŏn/, **madzoon** /maad zoŏn/ *n* a food similar to yoghurt, made from fermented milk [< Armenian *madzun*]

mauby /máwbi/ *n Carib* a drink made from the bark of a tree of the buckthorn family [Late 18C. < Carib *mabi* 'sweet potato (drink)']

maudlin /máwdlin/ *adj* tearfully or excessively sentimental, especially because affected by alcohol [Early 16C. Via French *Madeleine* 'Madeleine' < Greek *Mariaē Magdalēnē* 'Mary Magdalene', because she was commonly represented in medieval art weeping in repentance]

Mauger /máyjər/, **Ivan** (*b.* 1939) New Zealand speedway rider. He won the world championship a record six times (1968–70, 1972, 1977, 1979). Full name **Mauger, Ivan Gerald**

Maugham /mawm/, **W. Somerset** (1874–1965) British author best known for his short stories and novels such as *Of Human Bondage* (1915). Full name **Maugham, William Somerset**

'Impropriety is the soul of wit.'
[W. Somerset Maugham, *The Moon and Sixpence*; 1919]

'I [Death] was astonished to see him in Baghdad. I had an appointment with him tonight in Samarra.'
[W. Somerset Maugham, *Sheppey*, Act 3; 1933]

Maui /mów i/ second largest island of Hawaii, consisting of two oval peninsulas connected by an isthmus. Population: 134,007 (2002 estimate). Area: 1,884 sq. km/727 sq. mi.

maul /mawl/ *vt* (**mauls, mauling, mauled**) **1.** ASSAULT SOMEBODY to beat, batter, or tear at a person or animal ○

He got mauled in the ring by a better boxer. **2.** HANDLE SOMEBODY OR SOMETHING ROUGHLY to handle somebody or something too roughly or clumsily ○ *Children may need to be taught not to maul their pets.* **3.** CRITICIZE SOMEBODY OR SOMETHING FIERCELY to criticize somebody or something severely or mercilessly ○ *Despite being a box-office success, her new film was mauled by the critics.* ■ *n* **1.** MOVING SCRUM IN RUGBY in rugby, a loose scrum that members of both teams form around the player holding the ball or trying to run with the ball **2.** CROWD a crowd of people who are pushing, struggling, or fighting ○ *'The maul of medics holding bags and cords around the stretcher'* (Mark Lawson, *Idlewild*; 1995) **3.** PILE-DRIVING HAMMER a large heavy hammer, usually with a wooden head, used for driving in piles, stakes, or wedges **4.** LOG-SPLITTING HAMMER a heavy hammer that has one side of the head shaped like a wedge, making it suitable for splitting logs or wood [13C. < French *mail* 'hammer' < Latin *malleus*] —**mauler** *n*

Maulana /maw lǎanə/ *n* a title given to a man who is learned in Persian and Arabic [Mid-19C. < Arabic *mawlānā* 'our master' < *mawlā* 'mullah, master']

maulers /máwlərz/ *npl* the hands (*archaic slang*)

maulvi /mówl vee/ (*plural* **-vis**), **moulvi** /moŏlvi/ *n* a respected Muslim teacher or highly educated man, especially somebody with special knowledge of Islamic law [Early 17C. Via Urdu < Arabic *mawlawī* < *mawlā* 'mullah, master']

Mau Mau /mów mow/ *npl* a secret Kenyan organization set up in 1952 with the aim of forcing European settlers from the land and ending British rule in Kenya [Mid-20C. < Kikuyu]

mau-mau /mów mow/ (**mau-maus, mau-mauing, mau-maued**) *vt US* to confront somebody such as a public official or bureaucrat with the intent of gaining concessions, benefits, or advantage through intimidation (*slang*) [Late 20C. < MAU MAU]

maun /mawn, maan/, **man**, **mun** /mun/ *aux v regional* same as **must**[1] ○ *I maun get to the shops afore they shut.* [13C. < Old Norse *man*, a form of *munu* 'intend to']

Mauna Kea /mównə káy ə/ dormant volcano in Hawaii, on northern Hawaii Island. It is the highest peak in the state. Height: 4,205 m/13,796 ft.

Mauna Loa /-lŏ ə/ active volcano on Hawaii Island. It is one of the world's largest volcanoes. Height: 4,170 m/13,680 ft.

maund /mawnd/ *n* a unit of weight formerly used in South Asia, with a value that varies from place to place but is often equal to 37 kg/82 lb [Late 16C. < Arabic *mann*]

maunder /máwndər/ (**-ders, -dering, -dered**) *v* **1.** *vti* to talk or say something in a vague, rambling, or incoherent way **2.** *vi* to move or act in a vague or aimless way [Early 17C. Origin ?]

maundy /máwn di/ *n* a ceremony held in some Christian churches on Maundy Thursday that involves an actual or symbolic washing of people's feet in commemoration of Jesus Christ's washing of his disciples' feet (John 13:3–34) [13C. < Old French *mandé* < Latin *mandatum (novum)* '(new) commandment', first words of an antiphon sung in the ceremony]

Maundy *n* the distribution of Maundy money by the British sovereign

Maundy money *n* specially minted silver coins that the British sovereign distributes in a church ceremony on Maundy Thursday

Maundy Thursday *n* a Christian holy day marking the Last Supper. Date: Thursday before Easter Day.

Guy de Maupassant

Maupassant /mŏ pass oN, mŏ pass áaN/, **Guy de** (1850–93) French novelist and short-story writer. His short stories have been particularly influential and are written with a direct realism, portraying ordinary people in extraordinary situations. Full name **Maupassant, Henri René Albert Guy de**

'The least thing contains something unknown. Let us find it.'
[Guy de Maupassant, *Pierre et Jean*; 1887]

Mauriac /máw ri ak/, **François** (1885–1970) French poet, novelist, and playwright. Much of his work, coloured by his Roman Catholicism, centres on moral conflict and psychological analysis.

Maurier ♦ **du Maurier, Sir Gerald** ■ ♦ **du Maurier, Dame Daphne**

Maurist /máwrist/ *n* a member of a group of French Benedictine monks, founded in 1618 and dissolved during the French Revolution, who were renowned for their great scholarship, especially in hagiography [Late 18C. After St *Maur*, 6C disciple of St Benedict]

Mauritania

Mauritania /mórri táyni ə/ country in northwestern Africa, on the Atlantic Ocean. It became independent from France in 1960. Language: Arabic, French. Currency: ouguiya. Capital: Nouakchott. Population: 2,912,584 (2003). Area: 1,031,000 sq. km/398,000 sq. mi. Official name **Islamic Republic of Mauritania** —**Mauritanian** *n, adj*

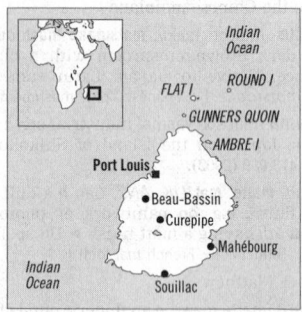

Mauritius

Mauritius /mə ríshəss/ island country in the southwestern Indian Ocean, east of Madagascar, consisting of the islands of Mauritius and Rodrigues and some islets. It became an independent member of the Commonwealth in 1968 and a republic in 1992. Language: English. Currency: Mauritian rupee. Capital: Port Louis. Population: 1,189,825 (2001). Area: 2,040 sq. km/788 sq. mi. Official name **Republic of Mauritius** —**Mauritian** *n, adj*

Maurya /mówri ə/ *n* a South Asian dynasty established in the 4th century BC after invasions by Alexander the Great, members of which included the emperor Ashoka [Late 19C. < Sanskrit, after *Maurya* Candragupta, its founder]

mausoleum /máwssə leé əm, máwzə-/ (*plural* **-leums** or **-lea** /-leé ə/) *n* **1.** TOMB a large tomb, especially one that is ornately decorated or made from expensive stone **2.** BUILDING CONTAINING TOMBS a building, often a highly decorated or elaborate one, that houses a tomb or several tombs **3.** GLOOMY INTERIOR a large gloomy oppressive room or building ○ *a huge mausoleum of a library* [15C. Via Latin < Greek *Mausōleion* 'tomb of Mausolus' (4C BC king of Caria in Asia Minor), built in 353 BC at Halicarnassus] —**mausolean** *adj*

mauve /mōv/ *n* a pale colour between purple and blue or pink [Mid-19C. Via French < Latin *malva* 'mallow plant'; from the colour of its flowers] —**mauve** *adj*

mav /mav/, **MAV** *interj* especially in Internet communication, used to indicate an apology after inadvertently causing a problem as the result of an error [Probably < a personal name]

maven /máyvən/, **mavin** *n* an expert or knowledgeable enthusiast [Mid-20C. Via Yiddish *meyvn* < Hebrew *mēbīn* 'somebody who understands']

maverick /mávvərik/ *n* **1.** an independent thinker who refuses to conform to the accepted views on a subject **2.** an unbranded animal, especially a calf that has become separated from its mother and herd. By convention, it can become the property of whoever finds it and brands it. [Mid-19C. Probably after Samuel Augustus *Maverick* (1803–70), Texas cattle-owner]

mavin *n* another spelling of **maven**

maving /mávving/ *n* especially in Internet communication, the inadvertent creation of confusion as the result of an error [< MAV]

mavis /máyviss/ *n* same as **song thrush** (*literary*) [14C. < French *mauvis*]

mavourneen /mə vóor neen/, **mavournin** *n Ireland* my darling [Early 19C. < Irish *mo mhuirnín* 'my little love']

maw /maw/ *n* **1.** ANIMAL'S MOUTH the mouth, jaws, throat, or stomach of an animal, especially a carnivorous animal that devours food greedily **2.** GREEDY PERSON'S MOUTH the mouth, throat, or stomach of a greedy person (*informal*) **3.** GAPING HOLE anything that seems like a gaping hole that devours things or people ○ *the ravenous maw of readers' expectations* [Old English *maga* 'stomach' < Germanic]

mawger /máwgər/, **mawga, maaga** /maágə/ *adj Carib* slim or lean (*also used in Black English*) [Late 20C. < Dutch *mager*]

mawkin /máwkin/ *n* **1.** same as **scarecrow** (sense 1) (*regional or archaic*) **2.** an offensive term that deliberately insults a woman's care for her appearance or her decency of speech and behaviour (*regional insult*) [13C. < the name *Matilda* or *Maud*, literally 'little Matilda']

mawkish /máwkish/ *adj* **1.** sentimental, especially in a contrived or off-putting way **2.** bland or unappetizing in taste or smell [Mid-17C. < *mawk* 'maggot' < Old Norse *maðkr*] —**mawkishly** *adv* —**mawkishness** *n*

Mawlid al-Nabi /máwlid al naábi/ *n* in Islam, the celebrations marking the prophet Muhammad's birthday. Date: 12th day of Rabi I. [< Arabic, 'birthday of the prophet']

Mawson /máwss'n/, **Sir Douglas** (1882–1958) British-born Australian geologist and explorer. He was a member of the first party to reach the South Magnetic Pole (1909) and was head of the Australasian Antarctic Expedition (1911–14).

max /maks/ *adv* AT MOST as a maximum (*slang*) ○ *We were offered £100 max.* ■ *adj* MOST most or highest (*slang*) ○ *Turn up the volume to get the max effect.* ■ *n* MAXIMUM the maximum limit or amount of something (*informal*) ○ *I could lend you 50 quid, but that's my max.* ■ *vi* (**maxes, maxing, maxed**) REACH HIGHEST LIMIT to come to the point that it is impossible to exceed (*slang*) ○ *The car maxes at 120 mph.* [Mid-19C. Shortening of MAXIMUM]

max out *vti N Am* to reach a limit in a personal attribute or ability, or reach the limit of a resource (*slang*) ○ *I maxed out my credit card last week.*

max. *abbr* maximum

maxi /máksi/ *n* ANKLE-LENGTH PIECE OF CLOTHING an ankle-length coat, skirt, or dress ■ *adj* **1.** ANKLE-LENGTH used to describe an article of clothing that is ankle-length **2.** UNUSUALLY LARGE larger than normal ○ *maxi tubs of ice cream* [Mid-20C. < MAXIMUM]

maxilla /mak síllə/ (*plural* **-lae** /-lee/) *n* **1.** either of a pair of bones that are fused at the midline and together form the upper jawbone in vertebrates **2.** a mouthpart that is one of one or two pairs behind the mandibles of arthropods [Late 17C. Directly and via Old French *maxille* < Latin *maxilla* 'little jaw' < *mala* 'jaw'] —**maxillar** *adj* —**maxillary** *adj*

maxilliped /mak sílli ped/ *n* one of the six specialized feeding appendages arranged in pairs and located just behind the maxillae on the heads of crustaceans [Mid-19C. < MAXILLA] —**maxillipedary** /mak sílli peédəri/ *adj*

maxillofacial /mak síllō fáysh'l/ *adj* relating to, located in, or affecting the face in the region of the upper jaw [Early 20C. < MAXILLA]

maxim /máksim/ *n* **1.** a succinct or pithy saying that has some proven truth to it **2.** a general rule, principle, or truth [15C. Via French < medieval Latin *maxima (propositio)* 'largest (proposition)', form of *maximus* (see MAXIMUM)]

Maxim /máksim/ *n* ARMS same as **Maxim gun**

Maxim /máksim/, **Sir Hiram** (1840–1916) US-born British engineer and inventor. He is best known for inventing the Maxim gun, an automatic machine gun.

maxima plural of **maximum**

maximal /máksim'l/ *adj* **1.** relating to or constituting a maximum **2.** the best or greatest possible —**maximally** *adv*

maximalist /máksimәlist/ *n* an uncompromising person who is determined to achieve a political aim, directly if necessary [Early 20C. < MAXIMAL after Russian *maksimalist*] —**maximalist** *adj*

Maximalist *n* a member of a Russian group that, in the early 20th century, advocated terrorist action to get rid of the tsar and the setting up of a temporary proletarian dictatorship

Maxim gun *n* an early single-barrelled machine gun that was cooled by an outer casing containing water [Late 19C. After Sir Hiram MAXIM]

Maximilian /máksi mílli ən/ (1832–67) archduke of Austria. He was made emperor of Mexico by Napoleon III of France in 1863, but was executed by Mexican republicans.

Maximilian I (1459–1519) Holy Roman Emperor. He made the Hapsburg dynasty a major power through diplomacy and marriage policy.

> 'My child, you are about to cheat the French and I the English, or at least I shall do my best.'
> [Maximilian I, *Remark*; Spring 1517]

maximin /máksimin/ *n* **1.** in mathematics, the largest of a set of minimum values **2.** in game theory, a strategy of attempting to maximize the smallest possible advantage [Mid-20C. Blend of MAXIMUM + MINIMUM; modelled on MINIMAX]

maximize /máksi mīz/ (**-mizes, -mizing, -mized**), **maximise** (**-mises, -mising, -mised**) *vt* **1.** INCREASE SOMETHING TO MAXIMUM to make something as great as possible ○ *maximize the chances of success* **2.** EMPHASIZE IMPORTANCE OF SOMETHING to attach the greatest importance to something ○ *Historians maximize the treaty's benefits to trade and tend not to mention its political costs.* **3.** COMPUT MAKE IMAGE LARGER to increase the size of a computer image **4.** MATHS FIND LARGEST VALUE OF FUNCTION in mathematics, to find or work out the largest value of a function —**maximization** /máksi mī záysh'n/ *n* —**maximizer** *n*

maximum /máksiməm/ *n* (*plural* **-mums** or **-ma** /-mə/) **1.** GREATEST POSSIBLE AMOUNT the largest amount, number, extent, or degree possible or allowed ○ *The stadium seats a maximum of 60,000.* **2.** LARGEST AMOUNT OR HIGHEST LEVEL REACHED the largest amount or value or highest level that something variable can reach or reaches during a period ○ *Even at its maximum, the noise did not exceed legal levels.* **3.** LARGEST NUMBER the largest number in a mathematical set **4.** GREATEST VALUE OF FUNCTION in mathematics, the greatest value that a continuous function can attain over a specific interval **5.** TIME OF GREATEST BRIGHTNESS OF STAR the interval during which a variable star is most luminous **6.** GREATEST MAGNITUDE OF STAR the magnitude of a variable star at its greatest ■ *adj* GREATEST POSSIBLE of the greatest possible or permitted amount or value ○ *visual effects with maximum impact* ○ *Maximum occupancy in this building is 235.* ■ *adv* AT MAXIMUM at the greatest extent ○ *The hall seats 400 maximum.* [Mid-16C. Directly or via French < modern Latin, form of Latin *maximus* 'greatest' < *magnus* 'great']

maximum-minimum thermometer *n* a special type of thermometer that logs the highest and lowest temperatures recorded during the period since it was last set

maximum-security *adj* protected or made secure by the most extensive and elaborate security arrangements that are available or in current use ○ *a maximum-security jail*

maxixe /mə shéesh, mak séeks/ *n* **1.** a Brazilian dance performed in duple time **2.** the music for a maxixe [Early 20C. < Brazilian Portuguese]

maxwell /máks wel/ *n* the centimetre-gram-second unit of magnetic flux, equal to the flux over one square centimetre perpendicular to a magnetic field of one gauss. Symbol **Mx** [Late 19C. After James Clerk MAXWELL]

Maxwell /máks wel, mákswəl/, **James Clerk** (1831–79) Scottish physicist. He did revolutionary work on electromagnetic fields and the electromagnetic theory of light.

> 'A molecule of hydrogen...whether in Sirius or in Arcturus, executes its vibrations in precisely the same time. Each molecule therefore throughout the universe bears impressed upon it the stamp of a metric system as distinctly as does the metre of the Archives at Paris, or the double royal cubit of the temple of Karnac.'
> [James Clerk Maxwell, *Discourse on Molecules*; 1873]

may[1] /may/ (**may, might** /mīt/) CORE MEANING: a modal verb indicating that something could be true, or could have happened, or will possibly happen in the future ○ *I may not be able to meet you.* ○ *He may have been working too hard.* ○ *A verdict may be announced today.*

modal v **1.** INDICATES POSSIBILITY indicates that something is possibly true ○ *That may be the best way to do it.* **2.** ⚠ INDICATES THAT SOMETHING COULD HAPPEN indicates that something could have happened, or could happen in the future ○ *The crash may well have been caused by faulty brakes.* ○ *The comet may be remembered best for its nonscientific impact.* **3.** INDICATES PERMISSION indicates that somebody is asking somebody for permission or giving somebody permission to do something (*formal*) ○ *'May I leave the table?' 'No, you may not'.* **4.** INDICATES RIGHT indicates that somebody has a legal or moral right to do something ○ *You may withdraw money from this account at any time.* **5.** INDICATES REQUESTS OR SUGGESTIONS indicates polite requests, suggestions, or offers ○ *May I remind you of our earlier agreement?* ○ *May I help you with that bag?* **6.** INDICATES WISH indicates that somebody wishes for something very strongly (*formal*) ○ *May God bless us, every one.* [Old English *mæg*, form of *magan* 'be able' < Indo-European] ◇ **be that as it may** indicates that somebody wants to go on to a new topic after conceding the possible truth of a previous statement ○ *'He doesn't earn much money'. 'Be that as it may, he's been successful in what he set out to do'.*

USAGE See *can*[1].

may[2] /may/ *n* **1.** TREES same as **hawthorn** **2.** PLANTS same as **may blossom** [< MAY; from the time it comes into flower]

May /may/ *n* in the Gregorian calendar, the fifth month of the year, lasting 31 days. See table at **calendar** [12C. Via French *mai* < Latin *Maius*, a form of *Maia* 'Maia' (a fertility goddess)]

maya /mī ə/ *n* **1.** in Hinduism, the material world, considered in reality to be an illusion **2.** in Hinduism, the ability to create illusion through supernatural, magical, or sacred power [Late 18C. < Sanskrit *māyā*] —**mayan** *adj*

Maya[1] /mī ə/ (*plural same* or **-yas**) *n* **1.** a member of a Native American people of Central America and southern Mexico whose classical culture flourished between the 4th and the 8th centuries AD **2.** a Mayan language spoken in Mexico, Guatemala, and Belize. Native speakers: 500,000. [Early 19C. Via Spanish < Maya] —**Maya** *adj*

Maya[2] /mī ə/ *n* the mother of the Buddha, in Buddhist belief by a miraculous virgin birth

Mayagüez /mī ə gwéz/ city and seaport in western Puerto Rico. Population: 100,371 (1990).

Mayakovsky /mī ə kófski/, **Vladimir** (1893–1930) Russian poet and propagandist. He wrote propaganda for the Bolsheviks after the Russian Revolution, but later fell from favour and committed suicide. Full name **Mayakovsky, Vladimir Vladimirovich**

> 'Today's poetry—is the poetry of strife. / Each word must, like a soldier in the army, be made of meat that is healthy, meat that is red! / Those who have it—join us!'

AKG London

Vladimir Mayakovsky

[Vladimir Mayakovsky, 'We Also Want Meat!'; 1914]

Mayan /mī ən/ *n* 1. a member of the Maya people 2. a group of Penutian languages spoken in Mexico, Guatemala, and Belize. Native speakers: 3 million. —**Mayan** *adj*

Mayapán /mī ə pán/ ruined ancient Maya city in southeastern Mexico, in Yucatán State

May apple *n* 1. an oval yellowish fruit with edible pulp 2. a poisonous plant of the barberry family that produces May apples. Flowers: single, white. Native to: eastern North America. Latin name: *Podophyllum peltatum*. [Because the fruit is produced in May]

maybe /máybi, -bee/ *adv* 1. PERHAPS expresses uncertainty ○ *Maybe I'm being too optimistic, but I really think we can get the best players.* ○ *'Can I have a new bike?' 'Maybe'.* 2. NEITHER YES NOR NO used to give a response that is neither yes nor no ○ *'So do you want to come with us or not?' 'Well, maybe'.* 3. INTRODUCES SUGGESTIONS used to introduce advice or suggestions ○ *Maybe you should ask her what she means before you jump to conclusions.* 4. APPROXIMATELY indicates an approximate estimation, e.g. of frequency or a number ○ *The coastal glacier gives off large icebergs maybe every three or four years.* ○ *The forests in this region are no more than 60, maybe 70, years old.* [14C. < (*it*) *may be*]

May beetle *n* INSECTS 1. same as **cockchafer** 2. same as **June bug** [Because they appear around May]

may blossom *n* the flower of the hawthorn

May bug *n* INSECTS 1. same as **cockchafer** 2. same as **June bug** [See MAY BEETLE]

mayday /máy day/ *n* the internationally recognized communications distress call, used especially by ships and aircraft [Early 20C. Representing the pronunciation of French *m'aider* in *venez m'aider* 'come and help me!']

May Day *n* 1. traditionally, a day for celebrating the coming of spring. Date: 1 May. 2. a national holiday in some countries that marks the importance of working people. Date: 1 May.

Mayer /máy ər/, **Sir Robert** (1879–1985) German-born British business executive and philanthropist. He founded the London Philharmonic Orchestra (1932) with Sir Thomas Beecham and promoted concerts for young people.

mayflower /máy flow ər/ (*plural* -**ers** or *same*) *n* 1. a plant that flowers in May, e.g. the cowslip or marsh marigold 2. the flower of the hawthorn

mayfly /máy flī/ (*plural* -**flies**) *n* 1. an insect that lives as an adult for only a few days, typically having two or four pairs of flimsy wings and two or three long slender tail appendages. The female lays her eggs in fresh water, where the larvae develop without a chrysalis stage. Order: Ephemeroptera. 2. a fishing fly that looks like a mayfly [Mid-17C. < the mistaken belief that they appear only in May]

mayhap /máy hap/ *adv* same as **perhaps** (*archaic*) [Mid-16C. < *it may hap* 'it may happen']

mayhem /máy hem/ *n* 1. absolute chaos or severe disruption ○ *Whenever the teacher left the room, it was mayhem.* 2. under old common law, the disabling or deprivation of a limb or other body part, with the result that the victim is unable to offer any defence or fight his or her adversary (*archaic*) [15C. Via Anglo-Norman *mahem*, Old French *mahaing* 'mutilating injury' < assumed Vulgar Latin *mahagnare* 'injure']

Mayhew /máy hyoo/, **Henry** (1812–87) British writer and editor. His book *London Labour and the London Poor* (1851–62) influenced social policy.

maying /máying/, **Maying** *n* May Day celebrations, or participation in them

mayn't /maynt, máy ənt/ *contr* may not

mayo /máy ō/ *n* same as **mayonnaise** (*informal*) [Mid-20C. Shortening]

Mayo /máy ō/ county in Connacht Province, northwestern Republic of Ireland. Castlebar is the county town. Population: 111,524 (2002). Area: 5,398 sq. km/2,084 sq. mi.

~~mayonaise~~ incorrect spelling of **mayonnaise**

mayonnaise /máy ə náyz/ *n* a rich creamy sauce or dressing made from egg yolks, vegetable oil, and flavourings [Early 19C. Probably < French]

ORIGIN There are several conflicting theories about the origin of *mayonnaise*, among them that it is an alteration of *bayonnaise*, as if the sauce originated in Bayonne, in southwestern France; that it was derived from the French verb *manier* 'to stir'; and that it goes back to Old French *mayou* 'egg yolk'. But the early variant spelling *mahonnaise* suggests that it originally meant literally 'of Mahon', and that the sauce was so named to commemorate the taking of Port Mahon, the capital of the island of Minorca, by the duc de Richelieu in 1756.

Mayon Volcano /ma yón-/ active volcano in the northeastern Philippines, on Luzon Island, beside the city of Legaspi. Height: 2,525 m/8,284 ft.

mayor /mair/ *n* somebody elected to be head of government in a city, town, or borough in many countries including the United States, and the United Kingdom except for Scotland [13C. Via French *maire* < Latin *major* 'more great' < *magnus* 'great'] —**mayoral** *adj* —**mayorship** *n*

CULTURAL NOTE *The Mayor of Casterbridge*, a novel (1886) by Thomas Hardy. It is the tragic story of Michael Henchard, a labourer whose success in business raises him to the position of mayor of his town, but who then loses his fortune as a result of a petty dispute with his assistant. A rich character study, it is also a revealing portrait of contemporary rural mores.

mayoralty /máirəlti/ (*plural* -**ties**) *n* 1. the official position held by a mayor 2. the length of time that a mayor holds office ○ *a five-year mayoralty*

mayoress /máir ess/ *n* 1. the wife of a mayor, or a woman chosen to assist an unmarried mayor at a social function 2. a woman elected to be head of government in a city, town, or borough in many countries including the United States, and the United Kingdom except for Scotland (*dated*)

Mayotte /ma yótt/ island in the western Indian Ocean near Madagascar, an overseas dependency of France. One of the Comoros Islands, it stayed under French control when the remaining islands declared independence in 1975. Language: French. Currency: French franc. Capital: Mamoudzou. Population: 163,366 (2001). Area: 374 sq. km/144 sq. mi.

maypole /máy pōl/ *n* a tall pole that is traditionally erected for May Day celebrations, usually decorated with flowers and with long coloured ribbons attached at the top. Dancers each take hold of the end of a ribbon and dance round the pole so that the ribbons become interlaced in coloured patterns round the pole.

May queen *n* a young woman chosen to preside over a May Day celebration

mayst /mayst/, **mayest** /máyist/ *modal v* 2nd person singular present of **may**[1] (*archaic*)

may tree *n* TREES same as **hawthorn**

may've /mayv/ *contr* may have (*informal*)

mayweed /máy weed/ *n* a straggly weed of the daisy family that has foul-smelling leaves. Flowers: white. Latin name: *Anthemis cotula*. [Mid-16C. May, alteration of *maythe* 'mayweed, camomile' < Old English *magoþe*]

mazaltov, **mazal tov** *interj* JUDAISM another spelling of **mazeltov**

Mazarin /mázzərin/, **Jules, Cardinal** (1602–61) Italian-born French cardinal. He controlled France during the minority of Louis XIV, when his absolutist policies resulted in the antiroyalist rebellions known as the Fronde (1648–53). He negotiated the

Peace of Westphalia (1648) and the Treaty of the Pyrenees (1659), ending major European wars. Born Mazzarino, Giulio Raimondo

> 'A woman will not go to sleep until she has talked over affairs of state with her lover or her husband.'
> [Attributed to Jules Mazarin]

Mazatlán /máthat lán/ city, seaport, and tourist resort in western Mexico. Population: 380,509 (2000).

Mazdaism /mázdə izəm/, **Mazdeism** *n* RELIG same as **Zoroastrianism** [Late 19C. < Avestan *mazdā* < *Ahura Mazda*, supreme god of ancient Persian religion]

maze /mayz/ *n* 1. PUZZLE MADE OF CONNECTING PATHS an area of interconnected weaving paths that it is difficult to find a way through, especially one in a garden with hedges between the paths or one designed for laboratory animals 2. ROUTE TRACING PUZZLE a diagrammatic version of a maze, where the object is to arrive at a finish point by tracing a route with a pen or pencil 3. CONFUSING NETWORK OF PATHS a network of paths, streets, or passageways that a walker or driver might easily become lost in ○ *a maze of narrow cobbled streets* 4. CONFUSING MUDDLE any confusing tangle or muddle, e.g. of regulations or procedures, that is difficult to negotiate ○ *a maze of official rules* ■ *vt* (**mazes, mazing, mazed**) *UK regional, Southern US* ASTONISH astonish, stun, or stupefy somebody [13C. Shortening of AMAZE]

mazeltov /mázz'l tov, -tof/, **mazel tov, mazaltov, mazal tov** *interj* used to express good wishes or congratulations [Mid-19C. < modern Hebrew *mazzāl ṭōb* 'good star']

Mazen /maáz'n/, **Abu** Prime Minister of the Palestine Territory (2003–)

mazer

mazer /máyzər/ *n* a large drinking cup or bowl, usually made from hardwood or metal [13C. < Old French *masere* 'kind of hardwood, maple' < Germanic]

mazourka *n* DANCE, MUSIC another spelling of **mazurka**

mazuma /mə zóomə/ *n* money, especially cash or loose change (*informal*) [Early 20C. < Yiddish]

mazurka /mə zúrkə/, **mazourka** *n* 1. a Polish national dance, similar to the polka 2. the music for a mazurka [Early 19C. Probably via Russian < Polish *mazurek* 'dance of an inhabitant of Mazovia (ancient part of Poland)' < *mazur* 'inhabitant of Mazovia']

mazy /máyzi/ (-**ier, -iest**) *adj* 1. LIKE MAZE tangled and interwoven like a maze 2. CONFUSING confusing or complicated 3. GIDDY giddy or confused (*archaic or literary*) —**mazily** *adv* —**maziness** *n*

mazzard /mázzərd/ *n* a wild sweet cherry tree often used as grafting stock for cultivated cherries. Latin name: *Prunus avium*. [Late 16C. Origin ?]

Mb *abbr* millibar

MB *abbr* 1. EDUC Bachelor of Medicine 2. MIL Medal of Bravery 3. COMPUT megabyte 4. message board

MBA *abbr* Master of Business Administration

Mbabane /am baa baáni/ capital of Swaziland, located in the western part of the country near the border with South Africa. Population: 73,000 (2000).

mbalax /am bálaa/ *n* a blend of Senegal's traditional percussion music and praise-singing with modern Afro-Cuban arrangements [Late 20C. < Wolof, 'rhythm']

mbaqanga /am baa káng gə/ *n* S Africa a rhythmic form of South African popular music [Mid-20C. < Zulu *umbaqanga*, literally 'steamed maize bread']

MBE *abbr* Member of the Order of the British Empire

Mbeki /əm békí/, **Thabo** (*b.* 1942) South African president. He was the first Black deputy president of the Republic of South Africa in 1994 and became leader of the African National Congress in 1997, before being elected president in 1999. Full name **Mbeki, Thabo Mvuyelwa**

mbira /əm beérə/ *n* an African musical instrument with a resonating box, often a hollow gourd, with tuned attached strips of wood or metal that are plucked [Late 19C. < Shona]

MBO *abbr* **1.** management buyout **2.** management by objectives

Mbps *abbr* megabytes per second

Mbuji-Mayi /əmboòjí mī i/ city in south-central Democratic Republic of the Congo, the capital of Kasai-Oriental Region. Population: 806,475 (1994).

Mbyte /ém bīt/ *abbr* COMPUT megabyte

mc *abbr* **1.** PHYS millicurie **2.** Monaco (*used in Internet addresses*) See table at **domain name**

MC[1] *abbr* **1.** MIL Medical Corps **2.** ASTRON Midheaven **3.** MIL Military Cross

MC[2] /em seé/ *n* **1.** RAP MUSICIAN a rapper whose role is to excite a crowd at a party or in a club and involve them in the music **2.** MASTER OR MISTRESS OF CEREMONIES a person in charge of the proceedings at an event or entertainment ■ *vi* (**MCs, MCing, MCed**) RAP TO MUSIC to speak rhythmically and often in rhyme over music [Abbreviation of MASTER OF CEREMONIES] —**MCing** *n*

Mc- *prefix* same as **Mac-**

MCA *abbr* E-COMMERCE merchant certificate authority

McAdam /mə káddəm/, **John Loudon** (1756–1836) British inventor and engineer. He developed an innovative method of road construction known as macadamization, in which foundations were raised to effect drainage.

McBride /mək bríd/, **Willie John** (*b.* 1940) Irish rugby union player. He was captain of Ireland and of the British Lions.

MCC *abbr* Marylebone Cricket Club

McCahon /mə káa ən/, **Colin** (1919–87) New Zealand painter. He produced works including religious paintings, expressionistic landscapes, and 'word paintings' incorporating biblical and Maori texts. Full name **McCahon, Colin John**

McCarthy /mə kaárthi/, **Joseph R.** (1908–57) US politician. While serving as a Republican US senator (1947–57), he instigated highly publicized Senate hearings in the early 1950s into alleged Communist subversion of the US government. His often unsubstantiated charges and extreme methods led to a Senate censure, and the period is often referred to as 'the McCarthy era'. Full name **McCarthy, Joseph Raymond**

McCarthy, Mary (1912–89) US writer and critic. She is best known for her novel *The Group* (1963). Full name **McCarthy, Mary Therese**

    '...a rebel demands a strong authority, a worthy opponent, God to his Lucifer.'
    [Mary McCarthy, *How I Grew*; 1986]

    'There are no new truths, but only truths that have not been recognized by those who have perceived them without noticing.'
    [Mary McCarthy, 'Vita Activa', *On the Contrary*; 1961]

McCarthyism /mə kaárthi izəm/ *n* **1.** the practice of publicly accusing somebody, especially somebody in government or the media, of subversive or Communist activities or sympathies, especially without real evidence to substantiate this **2.** the practice of using unsubstantiated accusations or unfair methods of investigation to discredit people [Mid-20C. After Joseph R. MCCARTHY] —**McCarthyist** *n, adj* **McCarthyite** *n, adj*

McCartney /mə kaártni/, **Sir Paul** (*b.* 1942) British singer, songwriter, and musician. He was a founder member, singer, and bass guitarist of the Beatles (1959–70), cowriting most of their songs with John Lennon. He later formed the band Wings (1971–81) with his first wife, Linda McCartney. Full name **McCartney, Sir James Paul**

    'The issues are the same. We wanted peace on earth, love, and understanding between everyone around the world. We have

learned that change comes slowly.'
    [Sir Paul McCartney, *Observer*; 7 June 1987]

McClintock /mə klínt ok/, **Barbara** (1902–92) US botanist and geneticist. Her research into 'jumping genes' (**transposons**) won her the Nobel Prize in Physiology or Medicine (1983).

    'I never thought of stopping, and I just hated sleeping. I can't imagine having a better life.'
    [Barbara McClintock, *Time*; 24 October 1983]

McColgan /mə kólgən/, **Liz** (*b.* 1964) British cross-country and marathon runner. An Olympic medallist, winning the New York (1991) and Tokyo (1992) marathons, she set a world record for 5,000 metres (1992). Born **Lynch, Elizabeth**

McConnell /mə kónn'l/, **Jack** (*b.* 1960) First Minister of Scotland (2001–). He is a former teacher, local council leader, and General Secretary of the Scottish Labour Party (1992–98).

McCormack /mə káwrmək, -ak/, **John** (1884–1945) Irish-born US tenor. He was noted for his solo performances of Irish folk songs, and also enjoyed a successful career as an opera singer.

McCoy /mə kóy/ [Early 20C. Origin ?] ◇ **the real McCoy** somebody or something that is genuine (*informal*)

ORIGIN Among the suggested origins of the phrase *the real McCoy* are that it may be an alteration of *the Reay Mackay*, a title applied to Lord Reay, the name of the chief of the northern branch of the Scots Mackay clan, the leadership of which was disputed by various branch factions; that it may be from *Mackay*, a whisky named after its makers A. and M. Mackay of Glasgow (once referred to as *the clear McCoy*); and that it may be from the professional name of the US welterweight boxing champion Kid McCoy (1873–1940), called 'Kid' to distinguish him from another boxer of the same name.

McCubbin /mə kúbbin/, **Frederick** (1855–1917) Australian painter. He was one of the founders of the Heidelberg School of Australian impressionists. Many of his works, e.g. *The Pioneer* (1904), depict the lives of early settlers in Australia.

McCullers /mə kúllərz/, **Carson** (1917–67) US writer. Her novels include Gothic tales set in the southern US states such as *Ballad of the Sad Café* (1951). Born **Smith, Lula Carson**

    'I suppose my central theme is the theme of spiritual isolation. Certainly I have always felt alone.'
    [Carson McCullers. Quoted in *The World We Imagine*, Mark Schorer; 1968]

    'He was a man watching a clock without hands.'
    [Carson McCullers, on someone terminally ill, *Clock Without Hands*; 1953]

McCullough /mə kúllək, -əkh/, **Colleen** (*b.* 1937) Australian novelist. Her novel *The Thorn Birds* (1977) was an international bestseller. Full name **McCullough, Colleen Margaretta**

McEnroe /mákənrō/, **John** (*b.* 1959) US tennis player. He was four times the winner of the US Open (1979, 1980, 1981, and 1984) and won the Wimbledon men's singles title three times (1981, 1983, and 1984). Full name **McEnroe, John Patrick, Jr.**

McEwen /mə kyoó ən/, **Sir John** (1900–80) Australian politician. He was the leader of the Country Party (1958–71) and caretaker prime minister 1967–68. See table at **prime minister**

MCG *abbr Aus* Melbourne Cricket Ground

McGrath /mə graáth/, **John** (1935–2002) British playwright. Founder of the 7:84 company (1971), he distanced himself from the theatrical establishment by his political stance.

McGraw /mə graáw/, **John** (1873–1934) US baseball manager. He led the New York Giants (1902–32) to three World Series™ titles (1905, 1921–22). Full name **McGraw, John Joseph**. Known as **Little Napoleon**

MCh *abbr* Master of Surgery [Latin *Magister chirurgiae*]

McIndoe /mákindō/, **Sir Archibald** (1900–60) New Zealand plastic surgeon. He was renowned for his pioneering work on injured pilots during the Battle of Britain. His patients were known as the Guinea Pig Club. Full name **McIndoe, Sir Archibald Hector**

McKay /mə kí/, **Heather** (*b.* 1941) Australian squash player. She won the British Open championship 16 consecutive times (1962–77) and was twice World Open champion (1975, 1979). Full name **McKay, Heather Pamela**

McKenna /mə kénnə/, **Siobhan** (1923–86) Irish stage and film actor. She was noted for her interpretation of the title role in *St Joan* by George Bernard Shaw. She also worked in film and television.

McKenzie /mə kénzi/, **Sir John** (1838–1901) Scottish-born New Zealand politician. As New Zealand's minister of lands and agriculture (1891–1900), he was a prominent defender of the rights of small farmers and a promoter of scientific agricultural methods.

Mount McKinley

McKinley, Mount /mə kínnli/ highest mountain in North America, in Denali National Park and Preserve, south-central Alaska. Height: 6,194 m/20,320 ft.

William McKinley

McKinley /mə kínnli/, **William** (1843–1901) 25th president of the United States (1897–1901). During many years in the US House of Representatives (1877–83 and 1885–91), he was instrumental in enacting protective tariffs. A Republican president, he presided over the Spanish-American War (1898), which made the United States a world power. He was assassinated by the anarchist Leon Czolgosz shortly after his election to a second term. See table at **president**

    'There was nothing left for us to do but to take them all, and to educate the Filipinos, and uplift and civilize and Christianize them, and by God's grace do the very best we could for them, as our fellowmen for whom Christ also died.'
    [Attributed to William McKinley]

McLaren /mə klárrən/, **Bruce** (1937–70) New Zealand motor racing driver. Runner-up in the 1960 Formula 1 world championship, he founded the McLaren Grand Prix racing team (1963). Full name **McLaren, Bruce Leslie**

McLeish /mə kleésh/, **Henry** (*b.* 1948) Scottish Labour politician. Appointed Minister of State and Scottish Office Minister for Devolution, Home Affairs and Local Government in 1997, he was elected First Minister of Scotland in October 2000.

McLuhan /mə klooən/, **Marshall** (1911–80) Canadian-born US critic and theorist. His writings dealt with the effects of media technology on the public. Full name **McLuhan, Herbert Marshall**

    'The new electronic independence re-creates the world in the image of a global village.'

[Marshall McLuhan, *The Gutenberg Galaxy*; 1962]

'The medium is the message.'
[Marshall McLuhan, on the pervasive influence of television, *Understanding Media*; 1964]

'Vietnam was lost in the living rooms of America and not on the battlefield.'
[Marshall McLuhan, *Montreal Gazette*; 16 May 1975]

McMahon /mək maáˈ ən/, **Sir William** (1908–88) Australian prime minister. A Liberal Party politician, he served as foreign minister (1969–71) before serving as prime minister of a coalition government (1971–72). See table at **prime minister**

McMurdo Sound /mək múrdō-/ bay in eastern Antarctica, in the southern Ross Sea. It is in the south of the Pacific Ocean.

McNaughten rules /mək náwt'n-/, **McNaghten rules** *npl* in English law, a legal ruling establishing that a defence of insanity depends on proving that the defendant was unaware or unable to understand that wrong was being done [Mid-19C. After Daniel M'Naghten, acquitted of murder in 1843]

MCom *abbr* Master of Commerce

m-commerce /ém komərss/ *n* business transactions conducted over the Internet using mobile phone technology [< abbreviation of MOBILE]

MCP *abbr* male chauvinist pig (*dated informal insult*)

McQueen /mə kweén/, **Steve** (1930–80) US actor. He achieved his greatest success in tough-guy and loner roles in films such as *The Magnificent Seven* (1960) and *Bullitt* (1968). Full name **McQueen, Terence Steven**

md *abbr* Moldova (*used in Internet addresses*) See table at **domain name**

Md *symbol* CHEM ELEM mendelevium

MD *abbr* **1.** MED Doctor of Medicine **2.** mailed (*used in e-mails or text messages*) **3.** managing director **4.** Maryland **5.** BANKING memorandum of deposit **6.** HOUSEHOLD minidisc **7.** MED muscular dystrophy **8.** MUSIC musical director

M/d *abbr* COMM months after date

Mda /əm daáˈ/, **Zakes** (*b.* 1948) South African novelist, playwright and academic. Among his works are *Ways of Dying* (1995) and *The Heart of Redness* (2000). Full name **Mda, Zanemvula Kizito Gatyeni**

MDF *abbr* medium density fibreboard

MDiv *abbr* Master of Divinity

MDMA *n* the drug Ecstasy. Full form **methylenedioxymethamphetamine**

MDS *abbr* Master of Dental Surgery

mdse *abbr* COMM merchandise

me[1] /mee/ *pron* **1.** used to refer to the speaker or writer (*used as the object or complement of a verb or preposition*) ○ *asked her to do me a big favour* ○ *Listen to me!* ○ *Was it me?* **2.** used to refer to the personality of the speaker or writer, or something that may express it (*informal*) ○ *I don't think I like this hat; it isn't really me.* **3.** N Am same as **myself** (*informal*) ○ *I'll get me a new boyfriend – see if I don't.* [Old English mē, me < Indo-European]

me[2] /mee/ *n* MUSIC another spelling of **mi**

Me *symbol* CHEM methyl

ME[1] *abbr* **1.** mechanical engineer **2.** CHR Methodist Episcopal **3.** LANG Middle English **4.** ENG mining engineer **5.** Most Excellent

ME[2] *n* chronic fatigue syndrome (*informal*) Full form **myalgic encephalomyelitis**

mea culpa /máy ə koólpa/ *interj* used to express an admission of your own guilt (*formal or humorous*) ▪ *n* a formal apology or acknowledgment of responsibility or guilt ○ *His grudging mea culpa failed to soothe feelings.* [< Latin, '(through) my fault', from the prayer of confession in the Roman Catholic Church's Latin liturgy]

mead[1] /meed/ *n* an alcoholic drink made by fermenting honey with water, often with added spices [Old English me(o)du < Indo-European, 'honey, sweet drink']

mead[2] /meed/ *n* same as **meadow** (sense 1) (*archaic or literary*) [Old English mæd (see MEADOW)]

Margaret Mead

Mead /meed/, **Margaret** (1901–78) US anthropologist. In such influential books as *Coming of Age in Samoa* (1928), she formalized her fieldwork research on child care, adolescence, and sexual behaviour in North American society and nonindustrial societies.

'The best way to learn is to learn from the best.'
[Margaret Mead, *Blackberry Winter*; 1972]

'Never doubt that a small group of thoughtful committed citizens can change the world. Indeed, it's the only thing that ever has.'
[Margaret Mead. Quoted in *Utne Reader*; March/April 1991]

Meade /meed/, **George** (1815–72) US Union general. He commanded the Army of the Potomac (1863–65) in the American Civil War. Full name **Meade, George Gordon**

Meade, James (1907–95) British economist. His writings on international economic policy were very influential. He won a Nobel Prize in economics (1977). Full name **Meade, James Edward**

meadow /méddō/ *n* **1.** a grassy field used for producing hay or for grazing domestic livestock **2.** an area of low-lying grassland, especially a marshy one near a river [Old English mædwe, form of mæd < Indo-European, 'cut grass with a scythe'] —**meadowy** *adj*

meadow brown *n* a very common brown butterfly that lives in grassy places throughout Europe. The female has an orange tinge to the underside of the wings. Latin name: *Maniola jurtina*.

meadow fescue *n* a perennial grass that has shiny leaves and stem bases that are surrounded by brown sheaths. Native to: Europe, Asia. Latin name: *Festuca pratensis*.

meadowland /méddō land/ *n* a large area of land that is made up of meadows

meadowlark /méddō laark/ (*plural* **-larks** or *same*) *n* a songbird with brown speckled feathers and a yellow breast with a black crescent-shaped mark across it. Native to: North America. Genus: *Sturnella*.

meadow mouse *n* a field mouse or vole

meadow nematode *n* a parasitic nematode worm that infests and destroys the roots of plants. Genus: *Pratylenchus*.

meadow rue *n* a plant related to the buttercup with small yellow flowers. Native to: northern temperate zones. Genus: *Thalictrum*.

meadow saffron *n* PLANTS same as **colchicum**

meadowsweet /méddō sweet/ (*plural* **-sweets** or *same*) *n* **1.** a tall perennial plant that grows in damp and marshy places. Flowers: tiny, creamy-white, sweet-smelling, in clusters. Native to: Europe. Latin name: *Filipendula ulmaria*. **2.** an ornamental bush. Flowers: small, white, in clusters. Native to: North America. Genus: *Spiraea*.

Meads /meedz/, **Colin** (*b.* 1936) New Zealand rugby union player. His 15-year career set a record as the longest of any member of the All Blacks.

meager *adj* US spelling of **meagre**

meagre /meégər/ *adj* **1.** UNSATISFACTORILY SMALL unsatisfactory in quantity, substance, or size ○ *a company that is notorious for paying meagre salaries* **2.** OF BAD QUALITY bad and unsatisfying in quality, strength, or effectiveness ○ *The street outside my window furnished meagre entertainment.* **3.** THIN very

thin, especially through malnutrition or illness [14C. Via Anglo-Norman megre, French maigre 'lean, thin' < Latin macr-] —**meagrely** *adv* —**meagreness** *n*

meal[1] /meel/ *n* **1.** a substantial amount of food, often more than one course, that is provided and eaten at one time **2.** any occasion, e.g. breakfast or lunch, when a substantial amount of food is provided and eaten [Old English mæl 'measure, mealtime' < Germanic] ◊ **make a meal of something** (*informal*) **1.** to put more time or effort into something than is usual or necessary **2.** to exaggerate the importance, intensity, or severity of something

meal[2] /meel/ *n* **1.** GROUND GRAIN the edible part of a cereal crop that has been ground to a powder **2.** GROUND-UP SUBSTANCE any substance ground to a fine or coarse powder ○ *fish meal* **3.** Scotland GROUND OATS ground oats, especially when used to make porridge [Old English melu < Indo-European, 'crush, grind']

mealie /meéli/ *n* S Africa an ear or cob of maize, or the plant on which it grows (*often plural*) [Early 19C. < Afrikaans mielie < Portuguese milho < Latin milium 'millet']

mealie meal *n* S Africa ground maize, used especially to make porridge (**mealie pap**)

mealie pap *n* S Africa a porridge made from ground maize [pap < Afrikaans pap 'porridge']

mealie pudding *n* Scotland FOOD same as **white pudding** [Because made from oatmeal]

mealie rice *n* S Africa crushed maize kernels, used in cooking in much the same way as rice

mealies /meéliz/ *n* S Africa maize plants or cobs (*takes a plural verb*)

meals on wheels *n* a service, usually provided by a social work department or charity, whereby hot meals are brought to senior citizens, people with disabilities, or housebound people (*takes a singular verb*)

meal ticket *n* **1.** somebody or something that can be counted on or exploited for money (*informal*) **2.** a voucher that entitles the holder to a meal

mealtime /meél tīm/ *n* the time when a meal is usually or regularly served

mealworm /meél wurm/ (*plural* **-worms** or *same*) *n* a larva that feeds on stored grain or flour and can cause severe damage and loss. Genus: *Tenebrio*.

mealy /meéli/ (**-ier, -iest**) *adj* **1.** LIKE MEAL powdery or granular, like meal or grain ○ *mealy potatoes* **2.** MADE OF MEAL containing, made of, or covered with meal **3.** DAPPLED having a spotted or dappled hide or coat **4.** PALE exceptionally pale, especially through malnutrition or illness —**mealiness** *n*

mealy bug *n* a scale insect that is covered with a white powdery secretion and feeds on plants, often causing significant damage to citrus crops and greenhouse plants. Family: Pseudococcidae.

mealy-mouthed *adj* overly wary of speaking plainly or openly, especially of admitting unpleasant truths

mean[1] /meen/ (**means, meaning, meant** /ment/) *vt* **1.** HAVE PARTICULAR SENSE to indicate or represent a particular sense ○ *I don't know what half these words mean.* ○ *When he raises his hand, it means he's making a bid.* **2.** INTEND TO EXPRESS SOMETHING to intend or be intended to express a particular idea in speech or writing ○ *That's not quite what I meant.* ○ *Just what's that supposed to mean?* **3.** INTEND TO DO SOMETHING to have an intention to do something ○ *I didn't mean to upset you.* ○ *I've been meaning to call you for weeks.* **4.** EXPRESS OPINION OR INTENTION to be serious in expressing a definite opinion or intention ○ *She says she's resigning, and I think this time she means it.* **5.** BE CAUSE OR SIGN OF SOMETHING to be a cause or indication of something ○ *The strike will mean a hard winter for many families.* ○ *A red sunset means fine weather.* **6.** GO WITH SOMETHING to accompany or be associated with something ○ *For Sam, summer meant golf.* [Old English mānan < Indo-European]

mean[2] /meen/ *adj* **1.** UNKIND unkind or malicious ○ *You hurt her feelings – that was a mean thing to do.* **2.** NOT GENEROUS unwilling to spend money on other people ○ *the meanest person I know* **3.** N Am BAD-TEMPERED behaving in an angry, often violent way ○ *He can be pretty mean at times.* **4.** SHABBY shabby and poor-looking ○ *streets full of small mean houses* **5.** US EXCELLENT excellent or skilful (*informal*) ○ *He plays a mean sax.* **6.** HUMBLE of low social position (*archaic*) ○ *living among the poor and mean* **7.** UNCOMFORTABLE

uncomfortable or disagreeable ○ *This is the meanest climate I've ever lived in.* [Old English *mǣne* < *gemǣne* 'shared by everyone' < Germanic] —**meanly** *adv* —**meanness** *n*

SYNONYMS ***mean, nasty, vile, low, base, ignoble***

CORE MEANING: below normal standards of decency

mean unkind or malicious ○ *All he does is give me a hard time. He's got to be the meanest man I've ever had the misfortune to work for.* **nasty** showing spitefulness or malice ○ *She's got a nasty streak.* ○ *a nasty snide way of putting things* **vile** despicable or shameful. ○ *vile manners* ○ *a vile unspeakable act* **low** without principles or morals ○ *How could he be so low as to make political mileage out of last week's tragedy?* **base** lacking proper social values or moral principles ○ *baser instincts* **ignoble** dishonourable and contrary to the high standards of conduct expected of somebody ○ *Can you assure us that these confidential communications were not ultimately put to any ignoble use?*

mean[3] /meen/ *n* **1. INTERMEDIATE VALUE** in mathematics, a value that is intermediate between other values, e.g. an average or expected value **2. MEDIUM TERM OF PROPORTION** in mathematics, either the second or third term of a proportion **3. MIDDLE WAY** a medium or moderate alternative or course of action, in the middle of a range of possibilities ○ *We need to find the mean between these extremes.* ■ *adj* **1. MEDIUM** medium or intermediate in size, strength, or quality **2. IN INTERMEDIATE POSITION** occupying an intermediate position in a range ○ *Speech was achieved in 74.3% of patients within a mean time interval of 63 days.* [14C. < Old French *meien* < Latin *medianus* (see MEDIAN)]

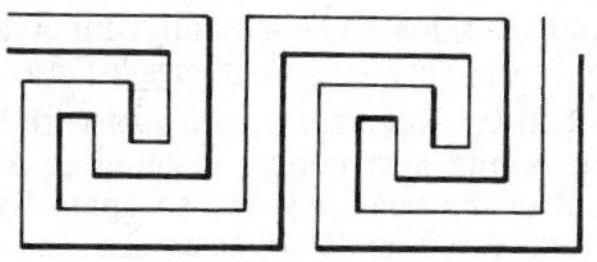

meander (sense 4)

meander /mi ándər/ *vi* (**-ders, -dering, -dered**) **1. FOLLOW TWISTING ROUTE** to follow an indirect route or course, especially one with a series of twists and turns ○ *The river meanders to the sea.* **2. WANDER SLOWLY AND AIMLESSLY** to move in a leisurely way, especially for pleasure or because of a lack of motivation ○ *meandering through the park* ■ *n* **1. RELAXED WALK** a slow leisurely walk or journey ○ *We went for a meander in the woods.* **2. TWIST OR BEND** a twist or bend in something, especially a river, path, or street **3. TWISTING ROUTE** an indirect course or route, especially one with a series of twists and turns ○ *We followed the meanders of the path.* **4. ORNAMENTAL DESIGN** an ornamental design, popular in ancient Greek art and architecture, made by a continuous line that forms square shapes by doubling back on itself [Late 16C. Directly or via French < Latin, 'winding course' < Greek *maiandros*, after a river (now the Büyük Menderes) in Turkey] —**meanderer** *n* —**meanderingly** *adv* —**meandrous** /mi ándrəss/ *adj*

mean deviation *n* in statistics, the mean of the absolute values of the differences between individual values and the mean or median, used as a measure of dispersion

mean distance *n* the average distance between an orbiting astronomical object and the object it is orbiting

mean free path *n* the average distance that a gas molecule travels before it collides with another molecule or with the containing vessel. Symbol λ

meanie /meéni/, **meany** (*plural* **-ies**) *n* an ungenerous or miserly person (*informal*)

meaning /meéning/ *n* **1. WHAT SOMETHING MEANS** what a word, sign, or symbol means ○ *Do you know the meaning of this word?* **2. WHAT SOMEBODY WANTS TO EXPRESS** what somebody intends to express, either in words or action ○ *I want to make my meaning very clear.* **3. WHAT SOMETHING SIGNIFIES** what something signifies or indicates ○ *I could not fathom the meaning of their glances.* **4. INNER IMPORTANCE** psychological or moral sense, purpose, or significance ○ *an empty life without meaning* ■ *adj* **SIGNIFICANT** conveying a significance that is not directly expressed ○ *A meaning silence followed these words.* —**meaningly** *adv*

meaningful /meéningf'l/ *adj* **1. WITH MEANING** having a discernible meaning ○ *To me, that is not a meaningful expression.* **2. SIGNIFICANT** conveying a meaning or significance that is not directly expressed ○ *She gave me a meaningful glance.* **3. ADDING VALUE TO LIFE** adding significance, meaning, or purpose to somebody's life ○ *I'm not claiming that we have a deep and meaningful relationship, but we do have fun.* —**meaningfully** *adv* —**meaningfulness** *n*

meaningless /meéningləss/ *adj* **1.** having no discernible meaning ○ *meaningless scrawl* **2.** lacking purpose or significance ○ *Offering to help now would be a meaningless gesture.* —**meaninglessly** *adv* —**meaninglessness** *n*

mean lethal dose *n* SCI same as **median lethal dose**

mean-minded *adj* ungenerous or malicious towards others —**mean-mindedly** *adv* —**mean-mindedness** *n*

means /meenz/ *n* something that is available and makes it possible for somebody to do something (*takes a singular or plural verb*) ○ *You can't live out there alone with no means of transport.* ■ *npl* the money and other resources that somebody has to live on (*takes a plural verb*) ○ *It'll be impossible to find a house in this area that's within their means.* [< MEAN [3]] ◇ **by all means** used as a polite way to give permission ◇ **by no means** used to emphasize a negative ○ *You were by no means the worst player.*

mean sea level *n* the sea level determined and used in mapmaking by the Ordnance Survey

means of production *npl* in Marxism, the raw materials, tools, machinery, and other necessities required in the manufacturing process

mean solar day *n* the constant interval between two successive transits of the mean sun across the meridian. Symbol **d**

mean-spirited *adj* malicious or bad-tempered —**mean-spiritedly** *adv* —**mean-spiritedness** *n*

mean square *n* the mean of the squares of a set of values

means test *n* an examination of somebody's income and savings, carried out in order to determine whether the criteria for a benefit or financial aid are met —**means-tested** *adj* —**means testing** *n*

mean sun *n* in timekeeping, an imaginary sun that moves uniformly in the celestial equator and takes the same time to complete a circuit as the real Sun takes in the ecliptic

meant past participle, past tense of **mean**[1]

mean time *n* time measured with reference to the mean sun crossing a given meridian

meantime /meén tīm/ *n* the intervening period of time between two events, or from now until something else happens ○ *I'll start dinner now and in the meantime you can have an apple.* ○ *I'll come as soon as I can; just wait there for the meantime.* ○ *Repairs will be done tomorrow and meantime please don't use the sink.*

mean value *n* MATHS, STATS same as **expected value**

meanwhile /meén wīl/ *adv* **1.** during the period of time between two events ○ *I'll meet you later; meanwhile I'll leave you to your food.* **2.** at the same time as something is happening ○ *I tried to keep everybody calm, meanwhile struggling to open the car door.*

meany *n* another spelling of **meanie** (*informal*)

meas. *abbr* **1.** measure **2.** measurement

measles /meéz'lz/ *n* a contagious acute viral disease with symptoms that include a bright red rash of small spots that spread to cover the whole body. Small white spots, known as Koplik's spots, appear in the mouth on the inside of the cheeks a few days before the rash appears and can be used in diagnosis. (*takes a singular or plural verb*) ■ *npl* the spots that are characteristic of measles (*takes a plural verb*) [14C. Probably < Middle Low German *masele* or Middle Dutch *masel* 'spot, blemish', and by folk etymology < *mesel* 'leper']

measly /meézli/ (**-slier, -sliest**) *adj* **1.** ridiculously or disappointingly small or inadequate (*informal*) ○ *He tipped me a measly 5p.* **2.** infected with measles

measurable /mézhərəb'l/ *adj* capable of being measured or perceived [13C. Via French *mesurable* < late Latin *mensurabilis* < Latin *mensura* (see MEASURE)] —**measurability** /mézhərə bílləti/ *n* —**measurably** *adv*

measure /mézhər/ *n* **1. SIZE** the size or extent of something, especially in comparison with a known standard **2. SYSTEM FOR DETERMINING SIZE** a particular system used to determine the dimensions, area, volume, or weight of something **3. UNIT IN SYSTEM** a unit in a system that is used to determine the dimensions, area, volume, or weight of something (*often used in the plural*) **4. WAY OF EVALUATING** a way of evaluating something, or a standard against which something can be compared **5. ACTION TAKEN** an action taken to make something happen or prevent something (*often used in the plural*) ○ *to take precautionary measures* **6. STANDARD AMOUNT OF SOMETHING** a standard amount of something, e.g. of a spirit poured into a glass for drinking **7. SOMETHING USED TO DETERMINE QUANTITY** something used to determine a quantity, e.g. a ruler, or a small container that holds a known volume **8. STANDARD USED FOR DETERMINING SIZE** a standard used for determining the dimensions, area, volume, or weight of something **9. DEGREE OF SOMETHING** an extent or amount that is limited, appropriate, or has its size specified ○ *Their help contributed in no small measure to our success.* **10. LIMITS** a limit or limits, especially one that is reasonable or appropriate ○ *His rage had no measure.* **11. LAW** a bill to be enacted into law, or a law that has been enacted **12. POETIC METRE** the rhythm of a piece of poetry **13. METRICAL FOOT** a unit of metre in poetry **14. WIDTH OF TYPE AREA** the width of the type area on a page or in a column ○ *In unjustified typesetting, not all lines extend to the full measure.* **15.** same as **dance** *v* (sense 1) (*archaic*) ■ **measures** *npl* MIN EXTRACT, GEOL **ROCK LAYERS** strata of rock, especially when they contain a particular material ■ *v* (**-ures, -uring, -ured**) **1.** *vt* **FIND SIZE OR QUANTITY OF SOMETHING** to find out the size, length, quantity, or rate of something using a suitable instrument or device **2.** *vt* **BE PARTICULAR SIZE, LENGTH, QUANTITY** to be a particular size, length, quantity, or rate **3.** *vt* **ASSESS SOMETHING** to assess the effect or quality of something, often against a standard ○ *You can't measure a hospital just by its facilities.* **4.** *vt* **DETERMINE SOMEBODY'S SIZE FOR CLOTHES** to determine somebody's size in order to make a garment or garments that will fit ○ *She was being measured for her wedding dress.* **5.** *vt* **COMPARE SOMETHING** to compare the size, effect, or quality of something with another thing ○ *The champion needs to measure his skill against a worthy challenger.* **6.** *vt* **ADJUST SOMETHING FOR EFFECT** to adjust something so that it is suitable or effective ○ *He measured his punch exactly to catch his opponent on the jaw.* **7.** *vi* **JOURNEY** to travel a particular distance (*archaic*) [12C. Via French *mesure* < Latin *mensura* < *mens-*, past participle of *metiri* 'measure'] —**measurer** *n* ◇ **beyond measure** very greatly or to an enormous extent ◇ **for good measure** as something extra to the amount required, especially to make sure of something ◇ **get** *or* **have somebody's measure** to arrive at an accurate assessment of somebody's qualities or abilities

CULTURAL NOTE ***Measure for Measure***, a play (1604) by William Shakespeare. Set in the court of the Duke of Vienna, this tragicomedy tells of a sister's attempts to win clemency for her brother, who has been condemned to death for the relatively minor crime of permissive behaviour. It deals broadly with morality and the nature of justice.

ORIGIN The Latin stem *mens-*, from which ***measure*** derives, is also the source of English *commensurate*, *dimension*, and *immense*.

measure off *vt* **1.** to determine a particular length of something so that this amount may be cut off **2.** to find or mark the limits of an area

measure out *vt* **1.** to take a particular amount from a larger amount of something for use **2.** to find or mark the limits of an area

measure up *v* **1.** *vi* to be good enough to meet a standard ○ *Her new play didn't measure up to expectations.* **2.** *vt* to find out the various dimensions of something using a suitable instrument or device

measured /mézhərd/ *adj* **1. UNHURRIED OR REASONABLE** slow, deliberate, or carefully considered ○ *spoke in measured tones* **2. ADJUSTED FOR EFFECT** adjusted to be suitable or effective ○ *a measured response to the criticism* **3.**

BY MEASUREMENT determined as a result of measuring ○ *a measured mile* —**measuredly** *adv*

measureless /mézhərləss/ *adj* too great to be measured ○*'Through caverns measureless to man'* (Samuel Taylor Coleridge, *Kubla Khan*; 1816)

measurement /mézhərmənt/ *n* **1. SIZE OF SOMETHING MEASURED** the size, length, quantity, or rate of something that has been measured. See table on next page **2. BODY DIMENSION MEASURED FOR CLOTHING** the size of a part of somebody's body, especially used to fit or make clothing (*often used in the plural*) **3. MEASURING OF SOMETHING** an act of measuring something

measuring worm /mézhəring-/ *n* the larva of a geometrid moth that has legs only at each end of its body and moves by bringing its rear forward, forming a loop, then moving its front. N Am term **inchworm**

meat /meet/ *n* **1. EDIBLE ANIMAL FLESH** the flesh of an animal that is considered edible, especially that of a mammal or bird **2. EDIBLE FRUIT OR NUT PART** the edible part of a fruit or nut, inside a shell or rind **3. IMPORTANT PART** the essence or important part of something ○ *the meat of the argument* **4. MATERIAL FOR THOUGHT** material that is interesting or stimulates thought ○ *There is plenty of meat in the book.* **5. FOOD** food or a meal (*archaic or literary*) [Old English *mete* 'food' < Indo-European, 'measure'] —**meatless** *adj* ◇ **meat and drink** something that somebody particularly enjoys ◇ **meat and potatoes** *N Am* the most basic or important idea or aspect of something

SPELLCHECK meat, meet or **mete**? Do not confuse the spelling of ***meat*** and ***meet***, which sound similar. ***Meat*** is chiefly used as a noun denoting edible flesh, as in *roast meat*. ***Meet*** is chiefly used as a verb meaning 'to encounter' or 'to come together': *I'll meet you outside the theatre. The lines meet at this point.* ***Meet*** is occasionally used as a noun, denoting a gathering of people for a sporting event or a hunt, and there is also an archaic adjective with this spelling, meaning 'appropriate': *It is meet to do so.* ***Mete*** appears mainly in ***mete out*** meaning 'to give out something such as punishment': *appalled at the mistreatment meted out to them.*

ORIGIN The sense of ***meat*** as 'animal flesh (eaten as food)' developed in the 13th century, but the original English sense 'food' still survives in phrases such as 'meat and drink' and 'one man's meat is another man's poison' (and is also seen in the word's relatives Danish *mad*, Icelandic *matur*, and Swedish *mat*).

meatball /meet bawl/ *n* **1.** a small round ball made from minced meat, usually with seasonings and a binding ingredient such as breadcrumbs or egg, that is then cooked **2.** *N Am* an offensive term that deliberately insults somebody's intelligence or energy level (*slang insult*)

meatbot /meet bot/ *n US* ONLINE same as **human being** (*slang*) [Late 20C. Blend of MEAT + ROBOT]

Meath /meeth, meeth/ county in Leinster Province, northeast of Dublin in the eastern part of the Republic of Ireland. The county town is Navan. Population: 109,732 (2002). Area: 2,336 sq. km/902 sq. mi.

meathead /meet hed/ *n* an offensive term that deliberately insults somebody's intelligence or perceptiveness (*slang insult*)

meat hook *n* a large hook used for hanging carcasses of meat

meat loaf *n* a mixture of minced meat and other ingredients, usually cooked in a loaf tin and served hot or cold

meat locker *n US* a large refrigerated store or storeroom for meat

meatus /mi áytəss/ (*plural* **-tuses** or *same*) *n* a body opening, e.g. the passage in the ear that leads to the eardrum [15C. < Latin, 'passage', past participle of *meare* 'go, pass']

meaty /meeti/ (**-ier, -iest**) *adj* **1. CONTAINING OR TASTING OF MEAT** containing a high proportion of meat or tasting strongly of meat **2. INTERESTING AND THOUGHT-PROVOKING** full of interesting and thought-provoking material ○ *a meaty role* **3. FLESHY OR MUSCLED** big and fleshy or muscular —**meatiness** *n*

mebos /mee boss/ *n S Africa* a confection made from apricots that have been pickled, sugared, and dried [Mid-19C. < Afrikaans]

mecca /mékə/ *n* a place that is an important centre for a particular activity or that is visited by a great many people [Mid-19C. < MECCA]

Mecca /mékə/ city in western Saudi Arabia, the birthplace of Muhammad. It is considered by Muslims the most sacred of the holy cities of Islam. Population: 770,000 (1995).

mech. *abbr* **1.** mechanical **2.** mechanics **3.** mechanism

mechan- *prefix* same as **mechano-** (*used before vowels*)

mechanic /mi kánnik/ *n* **1.** a skilled worker who is employed to repair or operate machinery or engines **2.** an unskilled worker or labourer (*archaic*) [Mid-16C. Directly or via French < Latin *mechanicus* < Greek *mēkhanē* (see MACHINE)]

mechanical /mi kánnik'l/ *adj* **1. MACHINE-OPERATED** operated by or using a machine or mechanism **2. INVOLVING MACHINE OR ENGINE** involving or located in or on a machine or engine ○ *mechanical failure* **3. DONE AS IF BY MACHINE** done automatically or as if by a machine instead of a human being ○ *His playing was mechanical.* **4. UNDERSTANDING MACHINES** having an aptitude for using or understanding machines ○ *I'm not very mechanical.* **5. INVOLVING PHYSICAL FORCES** relating to, involving, or done by physical forces such as wind and rain ○ *mechanical erosion* **6.** PHYS **OF MECHANICS** relating to, involving, or typical of the science of mechanics ○ *mechanical energy* ■ *n* HR same as **mechanic** (sense 2) (*archaic*) —**mechanically** *adv* —**mechanicalness** *n*

mechanical drawing *n* **1.** a drawing done to scale using specialized instruments and showing, e.g. machinery or an architectural plan **2.** the process of making mechanical drawings

mechanical engineering *n* the branch of engineering that deals with the design, production, and use of machinery and tools, as well as the generation and transmission of heat and mechanical power —**mechanical engineer** *n*

mechanical pencil *n N Am* same as **propelling pencil**

mechanical weathering *n* the breakdown of rocks and minerals by physical agents such as frost, wind, and tree roots, with no chemical alteration

mechanician /mékə nísh'n/ *n* somebody who makes machines or tools

mechanics /mi kánniks/ *n* **1. STUDY OF ENERGY AND FORCES** the branch of physics and mathematics that deals with the effect of energy and forces on systems (*takes a singular verb*) **2. MAKING AND RUNNING OF MACHINES** the application of the science of mechanics to the design, making, and operating of machines (*takes a singular or plural verb*) ■ *npl* **HOW SOMETHING WORKS** the details of how something works or the way it is done (*takes a plural verb*) ○ *She's a strategic player who really understands the mechanics of the game.*

mechanise *vt* MECH ENG, HR another spelling of **mechanize**

mechanism /mékənizəm/ *n* **1. MACHINE PART** a machine or part of a machine that performs a specific task **2. SOMETHING LIKE MACHINE** something that resembles a machine in having a structure of interrelated parts that function together ○ *the fragile mechanism of the planet's ecology* **3. METHOD OR MEANS** a method or means of doing something ○ *Interest rates are only one mechanism for controlling inflation.* **4. WAY THAT SOMETHING WORKS** the methods, procedures, or processes involved in the way something works or is done ○ *the mechanism of international diplomacy* **5.** PSYCHOL **INSTINCTIVE BEHAVIOURAL REACTION** a natural unconscious reaction or type of behaviour that comes into action when somebody is faced with a particular situation ○ *defence mechanisms* **6.** PHILOSOPHY **PHILOSOPHICAL THEORY** the philosophical theory that all natural phenomena, including human behaviour, can be explained by physical causes and processes [Mid-17C. < modern Latin *mechanismus* < Greek *mēkhanē* (see MACHINE)]

mechanist /mékənist/ *n* **1.** somebody who believes that all natural phenomena, including human behaviour, can be explained by physical causes and processes **2.** MECH ENG same as **mechanician** [Early 17C. < MECHANIC]

mechanistic /mékə nístik/ *adj* **1. LIKE MACHINE** typical of a machine rather than a thinking and feeling human being **2.** PHILOSOPHY **EXPLAINING BEHAVIOUR MECHANICALLY** explaining all natural phenomena, including human behaviour, in terms of physical causes and processes **3.** PHYS **OF SCIENCE OF MECHANICS** relating to, involving, or typical of the science of mechanics —**mechanistically** *adv*

mechanize /mékə nīz/ (**-nizes, -nizing, -nized**), **mechanise** (**-nises, -nising, -nised**) *vt* **1. USE MACHINERY TO DO SOMETHING** to change a process so that it is performed by machinery instead of human or animal labour **2. EQUIP SOMEBODY OR SOMETHING WITH MACHINERY** to equip a place of work or a workforce with machines to do work previously done by human or animal labour **3.** MIL **EQUIP ARMY WITH VEHICLES** to equip an armed force with trucks and armoured vehicles [Late 17C. < MECHANIC] —**mechanization** /mékə nī záysh'n/ *n* —**mechanized** *adj* —**mechanizer** *n*

mechano- *prefix* mechanical ○ *mechanoreceptor* [< Greek *mēkhanē* (see MACHINE)]

mechanochemistry /mékənō kémmistri/ *n* the branch of chemistry concerned with the conversion of chemical energy into mechanical work —**mechanochemical** *adj*

mechanoreceptor /mékənō ri séptər/ *n* a sensory receptor of a nerve that responds to pressure, vibration, or another mechanical stimulus —**mechanoreception** *n* —**mechanoreceptive** *adj*

mechanotherapy /mékənō thérrəpi/ *n* the treatment of injuries through mechanical means such as massage and exercise machines —**mechanotherapist** *n*

Mechelen /mékələn, mékh-/ city in northern Belgium, famous for the lace produced there since the 15th century. Population: 75,689 (1991). French name **Malines**

Mechlin /méklin/, **Mechlin lace** *n* a bobbin lace made at Mechelen, Belgium [15C. After *Mechlin*, former English name for MECHELEN]

MEcon *abbr* Master of Economics

meconium /mi kōni əm/ *n* the dark greenish faeces that have collected in the intestines of an unborn baby and are released shortly after birth [Early 17C. Via Latin, 'poppy juice' < Greek *mēkōnion* < *mēkōn* 'poppy']

mecopteran /mi kóptərən/ *n* an insect with long legs and wings and a structure resembling a beak at the front of the head, e.g. the scorpion fly. Order: Mecoptera. [< modern Latin *Mecoptera* < Greek *mēkos* 'length' + *ptera* 'wings'] —**mecopterous** *adj*

Med /med/ *n* the Mediterranean Sea (*informal*) [Mid-20C. Shortening]

MEd /ém éd/ *abbr* Master of Education

med. *abbr* **1.** medical **2.** medicine **3.** medieval **4.** medium

médaillon /méddī yóN/ *n UK* a round thin slice or portion of meat or another food. ANZ, N Am term **medallion** [Early 20C. < French (see MEDALLION)]

medaka /mə daakə/ *n* a small freshwater fish of the killifish family that is often kept in aquariums. Native to: Japan. Latin name: *Oryzias latipes*. [Mid-20C. < Japanese, 'eye-high']

medal /médd'l/ *n* **1. PIECE OF METAL GIVEN AS AWARD** a small flat piece of metal, usually shaped like a coin and stamped with an inscription or design, awarded to somebody for outstanding achievement or bravery or to commemorate something. See illustration on p.1170 **2. RELIGIOUS IMAGE WORN AS ACCESSORY** a cut and shaped piece of metal on which a religious image is often stamped, worn as a brooch or on a chain ■ *v* (**-als, -alling, -alled**) **1.** *vi N Am* **WIN MEDAL** to win a medal in a competition ○ *She medalled in the javelin throw.* **2.** *vt* **GIVE MEDAL TO SOMEBODY** to award somebody a medal (*archaic*) [Late 16C. < French *médaille* < assumed Vulgar Latin *medalia* 'coins worth half the value of a denarius' < late Latin *medialis* 'medial'] —**medallic** /mi dállik/ *adj*

medalist *n* US spelling of **medallist**

medallion /mə dálli ən/ *n* **1. MEDAL** a large medal **2. LARGE DECORATIVE METAL DISC** a large decorative metal disc worn on a chain round the neck **3. ROUND DECORATION** a round or oval decoration on something such as a building, vase, or piece of material **4.** *ANZ, N Am* COOK same as **médaillon** **5.** E-COMMERCE **MICROCHIP** the microchip inside a smart card [Mid-17C. Via French *médaillon* < Italian *medaglione* 'large medal' < *medaglia* 'medal']

medallist /médd'list/ *n* **1. SOMEBODY AWARDED MEDAL** somebody who has been awarded a medal, especially in a competition **2. SOMEBODY INVOLVED WITH MEDALS** somebody who designs, makes, collects, or is an expert on medals **3.** GOLF **WINNER OF STROKE PLAY TOURNAMENT** a golfer who wins a stroke play tournament

MEASUREMENTS

SI Metric System

The SI (Système Internationale d'Unités) is founded on seven base units that can be multiplied or divided by each other to yield derived units. Values of the base and derived units can be increased or decreased by using SI prefixes indicating decimal multiplication factors. Units and prefixes are assigned internationally accepted symbols.

Base Units

Name	Physical Quantity	Symbol
metre	length	m
kilogram	mass	kg
second	time	s
ampere	electric current	A
kelvin	thermodynamic temperature	K
mole	amount of substance	mol
candela	luminous intensity	cd

Derived Units With Special Names and Symbols

Name	Physical Quantity	Symbol
becquerel	radioactivity	Bq
coulomb	electric charge	C
degree Celsius	temperature	°C
farad	electric capacitance	F
gray	absorbed radiation dose	Gy
henry	inductance	H
hertz	frequency	Hz
joule	energy, work	J
lumen	luminous flux	lm
lux	illumination	lx
newton	force	N
ohm	electric resistance	Ω
pascal	pressure, stress	Pa
radian	plane angle	rad
siemens	electric conductance	S
sievert	radiation dose equivalent	Sv
steradian	solid angle	sr
tesla	magnetic flux density	T
volt	electric potential difference	V
watt	power	W
weber	magnetic flux	Wb

Some Derived Units Without Special Names and Symbols

Name	Physical Quantity	Symbol
ampere per metre	magnetic field strength	A/m
cubic metre	volume	m³
henry per metre	permeability	H/m
joule per kelvin	heat capacity, entropy	J/K
kilogram per cubic metre	mass density	kg/m³
metre per second	linear speed	m/s
metre per second squared	linear acceleration	m/s²
mole per cubic metre	concentration of substance	mol/m³
newton metre	moment of force, torque	N·m
radian per second	angular speed	rad/s
square metre	area	m²
volt per metre	electric field strength	V/m
watt per metre kelvin	thermal conductivity	W/(m·K)
watt per steradian	radiant intensity	W/sr

Prefixes

Multiplication Factor		Name	Symbol
1 000 000 000 000 000 000	or 10^{18}	exa-	E
1 000 000 000 000 000	or 10^{15}	peta-	P
1 000 000 000 000	or 10^{12}	tera-	T
1 000 000 000	or 10^9	giga-	G
1 000 000	or 10^6	mega-	M
1 000	or 10^3	kilo-	k
100	or 10^2	hecto-	h
10	or 10^1	deca- or deka-	da
0.1	or 10^{-1}	deci-	d
0.01	or 10^{-2}	centi-	c
0.001	or 10^{-3}	milli-	m
0.000 001	or 10^{-6}	micro-	μ
0.000 000 001	or 10^{-9}	nano-	n
0.000 000 000 001	or 10^{-12}	pico-	p
0.000 000 000 000 001	or 10^{-15}	femto-	f
0.000 000 000 000 000 001	or 10^{-18}	atto-	a

Other Units Used With the SI

Some units technically outside of the SI are nevertheless employed with it owing to their practical or special significance or because they are already in wide use. Excepting the electronvolt, litre, tex, and tonne, prefixes are not used with these units. The tonne does not take prefixes indicating a multiplication factor of less than ten.

Name	Symbol	Quantity	SI Equivalent
astronomical unit	–	length	$\approx 1.4960 \times 10^{11}$ m
barn	b	area	$= 10^{-28}$ m²
day, mean solar	d	time	$= 86{,}400$ s
degree	°	plane angle	$= (\Pi/180)$ rad
electronvolt	eV	energy	$\approx 1.6022 \times 10^{-19}$ J
hectare	ha	area	$= 10{,}000$ m²
hour, mean solar	h	time	$= 3{,}600$ s
knot	kn	linear speed	$= 1{,}852$ m/h
litre	L or l	volume	≈ 1 dm³ or 1,000 cm³
millibar	mbar	pressure	$= 100$ Pa
minute, mean solar	min	time	$= 60$ s
minute	'	plane angle	$= (\Pi/10{,}800)$ rad
nautical mile	M	length	$= 1{,}852$ m
parsec	pc	length	$\approx 3.0857 \times 10^{16}$ m
revolution	r	plane angle	$= 2\Pi$ rad
second	"	plane angle	$= (\Pi/648{,}000)$ rad
tex	tex	linear density	$= 1$ mg/m
tonne	t	mass	$= 1{,}000$ kg
unified atomic mass unit	u	mass	$\approx 1.6605 \times 10^{-27}$ kg
year	a	time	$= 3.1536 \times 10^7$ s (calendar)
			$= 3.155693 \times 10^7$ s (solar)
			$= 3.155815 \times 10^7$ s (sidereal)

Conversion of Common SI Units

Conversions for some common SI units or those used with the SI to imperial or US customary units are given below.

SI Unit	Conversion
length	
micrometre	= 0.00003937 inches
millimetre	= 0.03937 inches
centimetre	= 0.3937 inches
metre	= 39.37 inches or ≈ 1.094 yards
kilometre	≈ 0.621 miles
area	
square millimetre	≈ 0.00155 square inches
square centimetre	≈ 0.155 square inches
square metre	≈ 1.196 square yards or 10.76 square feet
hectare	≈ 2.471 acres
square kilometre	≈ 0.386 square miles
volume or capacity	
cubic millimetre	≈ 0.000061 cubic inches
cubic centimetre or millilitre	≈ 0.0610 cubic inches, 0.0352 Imp. fluid ounces, or 0.0338 US fluid ounces
cubic decimetre or litre	≈ 61.0 cubic inches, 0.880 Imp. quarts, 1.057 US liquid quarts, or 0.908 US dry quarts
cubic metre	≈ 1.308 cubic yards
mass	
gram	≈ 0.0353 oz avoirdupois or 0.0322 oz troy
kilogram	≈ 2.205 pounds avoirdupois
tonne	≈ 2,205 pounds avoirdupois
temperature	
degree Celsius	(°C × 1.8) + 32 = degrees Fahrenheit

Foot-Pound-Second and Troy Systems

The imperial and US customary systems are the last foot-pound-second systems still used nationally in everyday trade and commerce, while the troy system of weights continues to find use in the precious metals market, chiefly in North America. All have been supplanted by the SI in scientific and technical work and in nearly all international trade.

Imperial and US Customary System Units

Units of the imperial and US customary systems are equal except for some units of volume and capacity.

Unit	Relation	Conversion
length		
inch	–	≈ 25.4 mm
foot	12 inches	≈ 0.3048 m
yard	3 feet, 36 inches	≈ 0.9144 m
rod	5½ yards, 16½ feet	≈ 5.0292 m
furlong	220 yards, ⅛ mile	≈ 0.201 km
mile (statute)	1,760 yards, 5,280 feet	≈ 1.609 km
area		
square inch	–	≈ 645.16 mm²
square foot	144 sq. inches	≈ 929.0304 cm²
square yard	9 sq. feet	≈ 0.836 m²
acre	4,840 sq. yards	≈ 0.405 ha
volume or capacity		
cubic inch	–	≈ 16.387 cm³
cubic foot	1,728 cubic inches	≈ 28.316 dm³
cubic yard	27 cubic feet	≈ 0.765 m³
(Imperial)		
fluid ounce	–	≈ 28.413 cm³
pint	20 imp fl. oz	≈ 0.568 dm³
quart	2 imp. pints	≈ 1.136 dm³
gallon	4 imp. quarts	≈ 4.546 dm³
peck	8 imp. quarts	≈ 9.092 dm³
bushel	4 imp. pecks	≈ 36.369 dm³
barrel	36 imp. gallons	≈ 163.7 dm³
(US, liquid)		
fluid ounce	–	≈ 29.573 cm³
pint	16 US fl. oz	≈ 0.473 dm³
quart	2 US fl. pints	≈ 0.946 dm³
gallon	4 US fl. quarts	≈ 3.785 dm³
barrel, wine	31½ US gallons	≈ 119.2 dm³
barrel, oil	42 US gallons	≈ 0.159 m³
(US, dry)		
pint	–	≈ 0.551 dm³
quart	2 US dry pints	≈ 1.101 dm³
peck	8 US dry quarts	≈ 8.810 dm³
bushel	4 pecks	≈ 35.239 dm³
weight or mass		
ounce	–	≈ 28.349 g
pound	16 ounces	≈ 0.454 kg
(avoirdupois)		
stone (UK)	14 pounds	≈ 6.350 kg
hundredweight (UK)	112 pounds	≈ 50.80 kg
(long) ton (UK)	2,240 pounds	≈ 1.016 × 10³kg
(short) ton (US)	2,000 pounds	≈ 0.907 × 10³kg
(troy)		
ounce	–	≈ 31.103 g
pound	12 oz troy	≈ 373.242 g
temperature		
degree Fahrenheit	(°F – 32) ÷ 1.8 = degrees Celsius	

Some Volumetric Measurement Comparisons

Imperial Units	In US Units	In SI Units
1 UK fluid ounce	≈ 0.961 US fluid ounce	≈ 28.413 cm³
1 UK pint	≈ 1.201 US liquid pint	≈ 0.568 dm³
1 UK pint	≈ 1.032 US dry pint	≈ 0.568 dm³
1 UK gallon	≈ 1.201 US gallon	≈ 4.546 dm³

US Units	In Imperial Units	In SI Units
1 US fluid ounce	≈ 1.041 UK fluid ounce	≈ 29.573 cm³
1 US liquid pint	≈ 0.833 UK pint	≈ 0.473 dm³
1 US gallon	≈ 0.833 UK gallon	≈ 3.785 dm³
1 US dry pint	≈ 0.969 UK pint	≈ 0.551 dm³

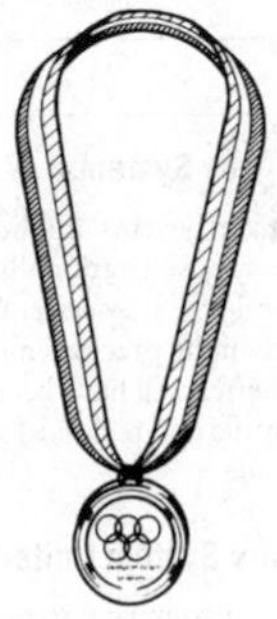

medal

medal play *n ANZ, US* a way of scoring in golf in which the total number of strokes taken for the round is counted rather than the number of holes won. UK, Can term **stroke play**

Medan /máy daan/ industrial city in western Indonesia on the island of northern Sumatra. Population: 1,974,300 (1997).

Medawar /méddəwər/, **Sir Peter** (1915–87) Brazilian-born British zoologist and immunologist. He shared a Nobel Prize in physiology or medicine (1960) for his work on immunology in organ transplants and skin grafts. Full name **Medawar, Sir Peter Brian**

> 'The human mind treats a new idea in the same way the body treats a strange protein; it rejects it.'
> [Attributed to Sir Peter Medawar]

meddle /médd'l/ (**-dles, -dling, -dled**) *vi* to become involved in somebody else's concerns or with somebody else's property in an intrusive or unwanted way ○ *I don't mean to meddle, only to offer advice.* ○ *Who's been meddling with the settings on my computer?* [13C. < Old French *me(s)dler*, variant of *mesler* < assumed Vulgar Latin *misculare* 'mix thoroughly'] —**meddler** *n*

meddlesome /médd'lsəm/ *adj* tending to interfere in other people's concerns —**meddlesomely** *adv* —**meddlesomeness** *n*

Mede /meed/ *n* a member of an Indo-European people who ruled an empire northwest of Persia in ancient times [< Latin *Medi*, plural of *Medus*]

Medea /mə dée ə/ *n* in Greek mythology, a woman with magical powers who was the daughter of the king of Colchis. She helped Jason to steal the Golden Fleece and, when he deserted her, killed their children in revenge.

~~medecine~~ incorrect spelling of **medicine**

~~medeival~~ incorrect spelling of **medieval**

Medellín /méddə yéen/ major city and capital of Antioquia Department in west-central Colombia. Population: 1,958,000 (1999).

medevac /méddi vak/ *n* **1.** MEDICAL EVACUATION OF INJURED the removal of injured people, especially military casualties, from the scene of their injury to the nearest hospital or place of treatment by helicopter or aeroplane **2.** *N Am* HELICOPTER USED TO EVACUATE INJURED an aircraft, especially a helicopter, used to take injured people, especially military casualties, from the scene of their injury to the nearest hospital or place of treatment ■ *vt* (**-vacs, -vacing, -vaced**) EVACUATE INJURED PERSON to remove somebody who is injured from the scene of his or her injury to the nearest hospital or place of treatment [Mid-20C. Blend of MEDICAL + EVACUATION]

media[1] /méedi ə/ *n* the various means of mass communication considered as a whole, including television, radio, magazines, and newspapers, together with the people involved in their production (*takes a singular or plural verb*) ■ plural of **medium** [Early 20C. Plural of MEDIUM]

USAGE media – singular or plural? Even though ***media*** is historically a plural of the Latin word *medium*, in some instances you can safely use ***media*** with a singular verb, depending on what is meant by ***media***. When ***media*** means the broadcast and print press in general, including all its personnel, equipment, and policies, a singular verb is acceptable. The word is also invariably preceded by *the* in such usages: *The media has covered the story ad nauseam.* If the writer's idea is to indicate, using ***media***, various separate journalistic outlets and their activities, a plural verb goes with ***media***: *The media have differed markedly in their approaches to coverage of the scandal.* Avoid using the plural ***media*** to refer to a single system or method of communication; use the singular *medium* instead: *Cable television is a relatively inexpensive advertising medium* [not *media*]. Never use the false plural 'medias' as in *new medias*. The correct form is ***media***, as in *new media*.

media[2] /méedi ə/ (*plural* **-diae** /-di ee/) *n* **1.** the middle, muscular layer of the wall of a blood or lymph vessel **2.** a primary vein in an insect's wing [Mid-19C. < Latin, 'middle', a form of *medius*]

Media /méedi ə/ ancient country corresponding to modern-day northwestern Iran —**Median** *adj, n*

media circus *n* a situation in which there is so much frantic activity by the news media around an event that the coverage overshadows the event and distorts its significance (*informal*)

mediacy /méedi əssi/ *n* the condition of being intermediate or of having an intermediate effect [Mid-19C. < MEDIATE]

mediae ANAT plural of **media**[2]

mediaeval, etc. *adj* HIST another spelling of **medieval, etc.**

media event *n* an event that attracts great attention from the news media, often arranged specifically for that purpose

mediagenic /méedi ə jénnik/ *adj US* appealing or attractive when covered by the media and thus highly suitable for media exposure

medial /méedi əl/ *adj* **1.** IN MIDDLE situated in or towards the middle **2.** ORDINARY not extreme or exceptional **3.** STATS same as **median** *adj* (sense 2) **4.** ZOOL NEAR MEDIAN PLANE near the median plane of an organism or body part **5.** LING IN MIDDLE OF LANGUAGE UNIT occurring between the first and last positions in a word or linguistic unit (**morpheme**) **6.** PHON CENTRAL pronounced in the middle of the mouth ■ *n* PHON SOUND BETWEEN STRONG AND SOFT SOUND a speech sound midway between a strong sound (**fortis**) and a soft sound (**lenis**) [Late 16C. < late Latin *medialis* < Latin *medius* 'middle'] —**medially** *adv*

media messaging *n* the sending of images, sound, and text from one mobile phone to another —**media message** *n*

median /méedi ən/ *n* **1.** MIDDLE POINT a point, line, part, or plane that is in the middle **2.** STATS MIDDLE IN SET OF ORDERED VALUES the middle value in a set of statistical values that are arranged in ascending or descending order **3.** STATS MIDPOINT IN FREQUENCY DISTRIBUTION the value in a frequency distribution above and below which values with equal total frequencies appear **4.** MATHS LINE DIVIDING TRIANGLE a line connecting a vertex of a triangle and the midpoint of the opposite side **5.** MATHS LINE DIVIDING TRAPEZOID a line connecting the midpoints of the nonparallel sides of a trapezoid ■ *adj* **1.** IN, TO, OR THROUGH MIDDLE located in, going towards, or passing through the middle **2.** STATS OF OR AS STATISTICAL MEDIAN relating to, involving, or constituting a statistical median **3.** ZOOL IN MIDDLE OF ANIMAL lying in the plane that divides a bilaterally symmetrical animal into right and left halves [14C. Directly or via French *(veine) médiane* 'median (vein)' < Latin *medianus* 'median' < *medius* 'middle'] —**medianly** *adv*

median lethal dose *n* the dose of a substance such as a drug or ionizing radiation that in a specific time period will kill half the experimental animals to whom it is given. Symbol $\mathbf{LD_{50}}$

median plane *n* a vertical plane that divides a bilaterally symmetrical animal or human body into right and left halves

median strip *n ANZ, N Am* a strip of land down the centre of a road that separates lanes of traffic travelling in opposite directions. UK term **central reservation**

mediant /méedi ənt/ *n* the third note of a major or minor musical scale, or the harmony built upon this note [Mid-18C. < French *médiante* < late Latin *mediare* 'be in the middle' < Latin *medius* 'middle']

mediastinum /méedi ə stínəm/ (*plural* **-na** /-nə/) *n* in mammals, the region of the chest between the lungs that contains the heart, trachea, and other organs [15C. < medieval Latin, form of *mediastinus* 'medial' < Latin, 'common servant' < *medius* 'middle'] —**mediastinal** *adj*

media studies *n* an academic subject in which the role and operation of the mass media are studied (*takes a singular or plural verb*)

mediate /méedi ayt/ *v* (**-ates, -ating, -ated**) **1.** *vi* INTERVENE TO RESOLVE CONFLICT to work with both sides in a dispute in an attempt to help them to reach an agreement ○ *mediating between the government and the rebels* **2.** *vt* OVERSEE AGREEMENT to oversee an attempt to solve a dispute by working with both sides to help them to reach an agreement ○ *appointed to mediate the talks* **3.** *vt* ACHIEVE AGREEMENT to achieve a solution, settlement, or agreement by working with both sides in a dispute ○ *Negotiators have mediated a ceasefire.* **4.** *vt* PHYSIOL TRANSFER SOMETHING to act as a medium that transfers something from one place to another in the body **5.** *vi* BE BETWEEN to be between two stages, ideas, times, or things ■ *adj* DEPENDING ON INTERMEDIATE ACTION involving or depending on an intermediary or an intermediate action [15C. < late Latin *mediat-*, past participle of *mediare* 'halve' < Latin *medius* 'middle'] —**mediately** *adv* —**mediation** /méedi áysh'n/ *n* —**mediative** /-ətiv/ *adj*

mediatize /méedi ə tīz/ (**-tizes, -tizing, -tized**), **mediatise** (**-tises, -tising, -tised**) *vt* to take control of another country but allow its ruler to retain his or her title and have some role in governing the country [Early 19C. < French *médiatiser* < late Latin *mediare* (see MEDIATE)] —**mediatization** /méedi ə tī záysh'n/ *n*

mediator /méedi aytər/ *n* **1.** somebody who works with both sides in a dispute in an attempt to help them to reach an agreement **2.** a substance that acts as a medium in transferring something from one place to another in the body [14C. Directly or via French < ecclesiastical Latin< late Latin *mediare* (see MEDIATE)]

medic[1] /méddik/ *n* **1.** a doctor or medical student (*informal*) **2.** *US* an enlisted person or noncommissioned officer in a military medical corps [Mid-17C. < Latin *medicus* (see MEDICINE)]

medic[2] /méddik/ *n* PLANTS another spelling of **medick**

Medicaid /méddi kayd/ *n* a programme funded by the US federal and state governments that pays the medical expenses of people who are unable to pay some or all of their own medical expenses [Mid-20C. Blend of MEDICAL + AID]

medical /méddik'l/ *adj* relating to, involving, or used in medicine or treatment given by doctors ■ *n* a physical examination by a doctor to check a patient's state of health [Mid-17C. Directly or via French < medieval Latin *medicalis* < Latin *medicus* (see MEDICINE)] —**medically** *adv*

medical certificate *n* a document signed by a doctor giving a judgment on somebody's state of health, especially certifying the person's fitness or unfitness for work

medical examination *n* HEALTH SERVICES same as **medical**

medical food *n* food specially processed or formulated to be given, under medical supervision, to patients who require a special diet

medical jurisprudence *n* MED same as **forensic medicine**

medical practitioner *n* MED same as **doctor** *n* (sense 1)

medical telematics *n* the development and use of computer networks for the international exchange and retrieval of medical data (*takes a singular verb*)

medicament /mə díkəmənt/ *n* a substance used to treat an illness [15C. Directly or via French < Latin *medicamentum* < *medicari* (see MEDICATE)]

medicare /méddi kair/ *n* in Canada, a government health insurance scheme funded by a tax levy in each province [Mid-20C. Blend of MEDICAL + CARE]

Medicare /méddi kair/ *n* **1.** in the United States, a health insurance programme under which medical care and hospital treatment for people over 65 is partly paid for by the government **2.** in Australia, a national health insurance scheme funded by a tax levy [Mid-20C. Blend of MEDICAL + CARE]

medicate /méddi kayt/ (**-cates, -cating, -cated**) *vt* **1.** to treat a patient with a drug (*often passive*) **2.** to add a drug to something, e.g. an antibacterial agent to a soap, or an anaesthetic to a throat lozenge [Early 17C. Either < Latin *medicari* 'heal' < *medicus* (see MEDICINE); or back-formation < MEDICATION] —**medicated** *adj* —**medicative** /-kətiv/ *adj*

medication /méddi káysh'n/ *n* **1.** a drug used to treat an illness **2.** the treatment of an illness using drugs [15C. Directly or via French < Latin *medication-* < *medicari* (see MEDICATE)]

Medicean /méddi sée̓ən/ *adj* relating to the Medici family and the period of their rule over Florence and Tuscany between the 15th and 17th centuries

Medici /méddichi, mə déechi/, **Cosimo de'** (1389–1464) Italian banker and political leader. He established the Medici as virtual rulers of Florence without holding public office himself and was a patron of the arts and learning. Known as **Cosimo the Elder**

Medici, Cosimo I de', 1st Grand Duke of Tuscany (1519–74) He became the sovereign ruler of Florence (1570) and established firm autocratic control over Florence and Tuscany.

Medici, Lorenzo de' (1449–92) Italian banker and politician. He was the virtual ruler of the Florentine Republic, a poet, and a patron of the arts. Known as **Lorenzo the Magnificent**

> 'How beautiful is youth, that is always slipping away! Whoever wants to be happy, let him be so: about tomorrow there's no knowing.'
> [Lorenzo de' Medici, 'The Triumph of Bacchus and Ariadne'; 15th century]

medicinal /mə díss'nəl/ *adj* **1.** CAPABLE OF TREATING ILLNESS having properties that can be used to treat illness ○ *a medicinal plant* **2.** INTENDED TO IMPROVE SOMEBODY'S WELLBEING intended to improve somebody's physical or emotional wellbeing in the way that a medicine does ○ *a drink taken for medicinal purposes* **3.** LIKE MEDICINE like medicine, especially in having a bitter taste [14C. Directly or via French < Latin *medicinalis* < *medicina* (see MEDICINE)] —**medicinally** *adv*

medicinal leech *n* a large freshwater leech that lives on blood, formerly used in bloodletting and still occasionally used to prevent coagulation. Native to: Europe. Latin name: *Hirudo medicinalis.*

medicine /médss'n, méddiss'n/ *n* **1.** DRUG FOR TREATING ILLNESS a drug or remedy used for treating illness, especially in liquid form ○ *cough medicine* **2.** TREATMENT OF ILLNESS the diagnosis and treatment of illnesses, wounds, and injuries **3.** TREATMENT USING DRUGS the treatment of illness or injury using drugs rather than surgery **4.** MEDICAL PROFESSION the profession of treating illness as a doctor **5.** CULTL ANTHROP RITUAL PRACTICE OR SACRED OBJECT a ritual practice or sacred object believed, especially by Native North Americans, to control supernatural powers or to work as a preventive or remedy of illness [12C. Directly or via French < Latin *medicina* 'practice of medicine' < *medicus* 'doctor' < *mederi* 'heal'] ◇ **a dose** *or* **taste of your own medicine** unpleasant treatment of the same kind that you have given others (*informal*)

medicine ball *n* a large heavy ball that people throw to each other as a strength-building exercise

medicine chest *n* a small cupboard or chest where medicines, bandages, and other things used in treating illness or injury are stored

medicine dance *n* a ceremonial religious dance performed by one or more Native North Americans to obtain supernatural assistance for something, e.g. to cure illness

medicine lodge *n* a wooden building used by some Native North American peoples for rituals such as ceremonial curing

medicine man *n* a man believed to be able to heal others by making use of supernatural powers, especially among Native North American peoples

medick /méddik/, **medic** *n* a plant of the pea family with three-lobed leaves. Use: fodder. Genus: *Medicago.* [14C. Via Latin *medica* < Greek *Mēdikē (poa)* '(poppy) of Media']

medico /méddikō/ (*plural* **-cos**) *n* a doctor or medical student (*informal*) [Late 17C. Via Italian < Latin *medicus* (see MEDICINE)]

medieval /méddi ée̓v'l/, **mediaeval** *adj* **1.** relating to, involving, belonging to, or typical of the Middle Ages **2.** old-fashioned, especially because lacking in modern enlightened attitudes ○ *Some of the working practices in the industry were positively medieval.* [Early 19C. < modern Latin *medium aevum* 'middle age'] —**medievally** *adv*

medieval Greek *n* the form of Greek used between the 7th and 13th centuries —**medieval Greek** *adj*

medievalism /méddi ée̓v'lizəm/, **mediaevalism** *n* **1.** CUSTOMS AND BELIEFS OF MIDDLE AGES the customs, practices, or beliefs of the Middle Ages **2.** DEVOTION TO MIDDLE AGES devotion to the spirit or beliefs of the Middle Ages **3.** SOMETHING FROM MIDDLE AGES a belief, custom, or style from or like one from the Middle Ages

medievalist /méddi ée̓v'list/, **mediaevalist** *n* somebody who studies, teaches the history of, or is an expert in the Middle Ages

medieval Latin *n* the form of Latin used in Europe during the Middle Ages —**medieval Latin** *adj*

medina /me déenə/, **Medina** *n* the oldest part of many North African cities [Early 20C. < Arabic, 'town']

Medina /me déenə/ city in western Saudi Arabia, the site of the Mosque of the Prophet that houses the tomb of Muhammad. Population: 608,300 (1992).

mediocre /mèedi ṓkər/ *adj* adequate or acceptable, but not very good [Late 16C. Directly or via French < Latin *mediocris* 'of middle height' < *ocris* 'rugged mountain'] —**mediocrely** *adv*

mediocrity /mèedi ókrəti/ (*plural* **-ties**) *n* **1.** a quality that is adequate or acceptable, but not very good ○ *His poetry seldom rises above the level of mediocrity.* **2.** somebody who lacks any special skill or flair [15C. Directly or via French *médiocrité* < Latin *mediocritas* < *mediocris* (see MEDIOCRE)]

Medit. *abbr* Mediterranean

meditate /méddi tayt/ (**-tates, -tating, -tated**) *v* **1.** *vi* EMPTY OR CONCENTRATE MIND to empty the mind of thoughts, or concentrate the mind on one thing, in order to aid mental or spiritual development, contemplation, or relaxation **2.** *vi* THINK CAREFULLY ABOUT SOMETHING to think about something carefully, calmly, seriously, and for some time **3.** *vt* PLAN SOMETHING to plan or consider doing something [Mid-16C. Either < Latin *meditat-*, past participle of *meditare* 'keep on measuring', related to *mederi* 'to cure'; or back-formation < MEDITATION] —**meditative** /-tətiv/ *adj* —**meditatively** *adv* —**meditativeness** *n* —**meditator** *n*

meditation /méddi táysh'n/ *n* **1.** EMPTYING OR CONCENTRATION OF MIND the emptying of the mind of thoughts, or the concentration of the mind on one thing, in order to aid mental or spiritual development, contemplation, or relaxation **2.** PONDERING OF SOMETHING the act of thinking about something carefully, calmly, seriously, and for some time, or an instance of such thinking **3.** SERIOUS STUDY OF TOPIC an extended and serious study of a topic [15C. Directly or via French < Latin *meditation-* < *meditari* (see MEDITATE)] —**meditational** *adj*

Mediterranean /médditə ráyni ən/ *n* **1.** MEDITERRANEAN SEA OR SURROUNDING AREA the Mediterranean Sea, or the lands bordering it ○ *holidaying in the Mediterranean* **2.** SOMEBODY FROM AROUND MEDITERRANEAN somebody who comes from a region bordering the Mediterranean Sea ■ *adj* **1.** IN OR NEAR MEDITERRANEAN located in the Mediterranean Sea, or in a region that borders it **2.** RELATING TO MEDITERRANEAN PEOPLE relating to or associated with the people living in a region that borders the Mediterranean Sea **3.** METEOROL WITH HOT SUMMERS AND WARM WINTERS having hot summers and warm winters, with most of the rainfall occurring in the winter **4.** ANTHROP WITH DARK HAIR AND OLIVE SKIN resembling people from countries around the Mediterranean Sea, who often have dark hair and olive complexions [Mid-16C. < Latin *mediterraneus* 'inland' < *medius* 'middle' + *terra* 'earth']

Mediterranean fever *n* MED same as **brucellosis** [Because it is common in that region]

Mediterranean flour moth *n* a small grey moth, common worldwide, whose larvae feed on grain and grain products. Latin name: *Anagasta kuehniella.*

Mediterranean fruit fly *n* a black-and-white two-winged fly that lays its eggs in citrus and other types of fruit, which the maggots then destroy. Native to: Mediterranean, but spread elsewhere. Latin name: *Ceratitis capitata.*

Mediterranean Sea /méddi tə ráy ni ən-/ inland sea of Europe, Asia, and Africa, linked to the Atlantic Ocean at its western end by the Strait of Gibraltar. Area: 2,509,000 sq. km/968,700 sq. mi.

Meditteranean incorrect spelling of **Mediterranean**

medium /mée̓di əm/ *adj* **1.** NEITHER LARGE NOR SMALL of middling size or dimensions, neither large nor small ○ *a man of medium build* **2.** NEITHER DARK NOR LIGHT not particularly dark or particularly light as a shade of a colour **3.** COOK BETWEEN RARE AND WELL DONE cooked so that the meat is brown on the outside but slightly pink and moist inside ■ *n* (*plural* **-dia** /-di ə/ or **-diums**) **1.** STATE BETWEEN EXTREMES an intermediate state or condition halfway between two extremes **2.** MEANS OF MASS COMMUNICATION a means of mass communication, e.g. television, radio, or newspapers **3.** VEHICLE FOR IDEAS a means of conveying ideas or information ○ *French is the medium of instruction in all subjects.* **4.** SUBSTANCE CARRIER a substance through which something is carried or transmitted **5.** MEANS TO END the means by which something is carried out or achieved **6.** COMPUT MATERIAL HOLDING DATA a material on which data is stored or printed, e.g. paper, tape, or disk **7.** BIOL PRESERVING SUBSTANCE a substance in which specimens of animals and plants are preserved or mounted **8.** PARANORMAL SOMEBODY SUPPOSEDLY COMMUNICATING WITH DEAD somebody believed to transmit messages between living people and the spirits of the dead **9.** BIOL NATURAL ENVIRONMENT a substance or environment in which an organism naturally lives or grows **10.** ARTS TYPE OF ART a method that an artist uses or a category such as sculpture in which an artist works **11.** ARTS ARTIST'S MATERIALS the materials that an artist uses in creating a work **12.** INDUST SOLVENT a solvent mixed with a pigment or paint to make it thinner **13.** PAPER PAPER SIZE a size of paper, especially 47 cm by 58.5 cm/18.5 in by 23 in ■ **mediums** *npl* FIN GILT-EDGED SECURITIES securities that are very safe as an investment [Late 16C. < Latin, neuter of *medius* 'middle']

ORIGIN The Latin word *medius* 'middle', from which *medium* is derived, is also the source of English *immediate, intermezzo, mean*³, *media*¹, *mediate, medieval, mediocre, meridian, mezzanine, mitten,* and *moiety.*

medium-dated *adj* describes gilt-edged securities redeemable after a period of between 5 and 15 years

medium frequency *n* a radio frequency lying between 300 and 3,000 kilohertz

medium of exchange *n* something commonly recognized in a country or community as a standard of value and used in the same way as money, e.g. gold

medium shot *n* a filmed view, midway between long shot and close-up, that shows a standing person from the waist up or the full body of a sitting person ○ *a medium shot of the two characters in conversation*

medium wave *n* a radio wave with a wavelength that lies between 100 and 1,000 m (*hyphenated when used before a noun*)

medlar /méddlər/ *n* **1.** a small apple-shaped fruit that is not edible until it is overripe. Use: preserves. **2.** a small fruit tree that produces medlars. Native to: Europe, Asia. Latin name: *Mespilus germanica.* [14C. < Old French *medler* < *medle* 'medlar fruit' (a variant of *mesle*) < Greek *mespilē*]

medley /méddli/ (*plural* **-leys**) *n* **1.** MIXTURE OF THINGS a mixture or assortment of various things **2.** MUSIC MUSICAL SEQUENCE OF DIFFERENT SONGS a continuous piece of music consisting of two or more different tunes or songs played one after the other **3.** SWIMMING RACE USING DIFFERENT STROKES a swimming race between individual swimmers or relay teams in which sections are swum using different strokes **4.** RELAY RACE WITH DIFFERENT LENGTHS a relay race in which each member of a team runs a different length [14C. < Old French *medlee*, variant of *meslee* 'melee' < medieval Latin *misculare* 'mix thoroughly' < *miscere* 'mix']

medley relay *n* **1.** a relay swimming race between teams of four swimmers, each of whom uses a different stroke **2.** ATHLETICS same as **medley** (sense 4)

medulla /mi dúllə/ (*plural* **-lae** /-lee/ or **-las**) *n* **1.** BIOL the innermost area of a part or organ of an animal or plant ○ *the adrenal medulla* **2.** ANAT same as **medulla oblongata** **3.** BOT same as **pith** *n* (sense 2) [14C. < Latin, 'pith'] —**medullar** *adj*

medulla oblongata /mi dúllə ób long gáatə/ (*plural* **medullae oblongatae** /-lee ób long gáa tee/ or **medulla oblongatas**) *n* the lowermost part of the brain in vertebrates. It is continuous with the spinal cord and controls involuntary vital functions such as those involved with the heart and lungs. [< Latin, literally 'prolonged marrow']

medullary ray /mi dúlləri-, médd'ləri-/ *n* any of the bands or sheets of connective tissue that radiate

between the pith and bark in the stems of some higher woody plants

medullary sheath *n* ANAT same as **myelin sheath**

medullated /médda laytid, mi dúllaytid/ *adj* **1.** ANAT same as **myelinated 2.** having a medulla ○ *medullated fibres*

medulloblastoma /mi dúllō bla stōmə/ (*plural* **-mas** or **-mata** /-mətə/) *n* a rapidly growing malignant tumour of the central nervous system arising in the brain, especially in children [Early 20C. < MEDULLA + BLASTO-]

medusa /mə dyóozə, -ssə/ (*plural* **-sas** or **-sae** /-zee, -ssee/) *n* **1.** the free-swimming reproductive stage of an animal such as a jellyfish, during which it has a transparent umbrella-shaped body with tentacles **2.** ZOOL same as **jellyfish** (sense 1) [Mid-18C. < modern Latin < Greek *Medousa* 'Medusa'; from the resemblance of the tentacles to the snakes on Medusa's head] —**medusan** *adj* —**medusoid** *adj*, *n*

Medusa: ancient Roman mosaic, Sousse, France

Medusa /mə dyóozə, -dyóossə/ *n* in Greek mythology, a Gorgon who could turn anyone who looked at her to stone. She was killed by Perseus. —**Medusan** *adj*

Medway /méd way/ river in southeastern England, flowing through Kent to the Thames Estuary. Length: 112 km/70 mi.

meek /meek/ *adj* **1.** showing mildness or quietness of nature **2.** showing submissiveness and lack of initiative or will [12C. < Old Norse *mjúkr* 'soft, pliant'] —**meekly** *adv* —**meekness** *n*

meerkat

meerkat /méer kat/ *n* a burrowing mongoose with four-toed feet and a greyish coat with faint black markings. Native to: southern Africa. Latin name: *Suricata suricatta*. [Early 19C. Via Afrikaans < Middle Low German *meerkatte* < *meer* 'sea' + *katte* 'cat']

meerschaum /méershəm/ *n* **1.** N Am MINERALS same as **sepiolite 2.** *also* **meerschaum pipe** a tobacco pipe with a bowl made of sepiolite [Late 18C. < German < *Meer* 'sea' + *Schaum* 'foam', translation of Persian *kef-i-daryā*; from its frothy appearance]

meet[1] /meet/ *v* (**meets, meeting, met** /met/) **1.** *vti* COME ACROSS SOMEBODY to encounter somebody without having arranged to do so beforehand ○ *Guess who I met in the supermarket.* **2.** *vti* GET TOGETHER to get together with somebody by arrangement ○ *We could meet for lunch tomorrow.* **3.** *vti* ENCOUNTER SOMEBODY FOR FIRST TIME to encounter somebody or each other for the first time ○ *They met exactly a year ago.* **4.** *vt* GREET SOMEBODY to go somewhere to greet or fetch somebody who is arriving there ○ *I'll come and meet you at the airport.* **5.** *vi* GATHER FOR DISCUSSION to gather in a place to discuss something ○ *The committee meets monthly.* **6.** *vti* JOIN SOMETHING to join, cross, or

be adjacent to something or each other ○ *where the two roads meet* **7.** *vti* TOUCH SOMETHING to bring something into contact with something else, or be brought into contact ○ *I can't get the two ropes to meet.* **8.** *vti* EXPERIENCE SOMETHING to experience something such as a difficulty, challenge, or success ○ *All our attempts met with failure.* **9.** *vt* SATISFY SOMETHING to cope with, satisfy, or fulfil what is required ○ *The new system meets all our computing requirements.* **10.** *vt* AGREE WITH SOMEBODY to come to an agreement with somebody on something ○ *I think we can meet you on that price.* **11.** *vti* LOOK AT SOMETHING to look at or confront something, or look at or confront each other ○ *Their glances met.* **12.** *vti* COMPETE OR FIGHT WITH SOMEBODY to come together to compete or fight with somebody or each other ○ *The two teams have already met this year.* **13.** *vt* RESPOND IN PARTICULAR WAY to respond to a situation with a particular type of behaviour ○ *He met success and failure with equal indifference.* **14.** *vi* OCCUR TOGETHER to happen or come together in the same place or person ○ *The extremes of creativity and irresponsibility meet in this genius.* ■ *n* **1.** SPORTING OCCASION an occasion at which numbers of competitors and spectators come together **2.** FIELD SPORTS GATHERING BEFORE HUNT the period before a hunt when the riders and hounds gather together [Old English *mētan* 'come upon' < Germanic, 'meeting']

SPELLCHECK See *meat*.

meet up *vi* to get together with somebody
meet with *vt* **1.** GET TOGETHER WITH to have a meeting with other people **2.** RECEIVE to get a particular reaction or result ○ *The suggestion met with his approval.* **3.** EXPERIENCE to experience something unpleasant (*formal*) ○ *He met with an accident.*

meet[2] /meet/ *adj* suitable or fitting (*archaic*) [Old English *gemǣte* < Germanic, 'measure'] —**meetly** *adv*

meeting /méeting/ *n* **1.** GATHERING OF PEOPLE FOR DISCUSSION an occasion when people gather together to discuss something **2.** GROUP AT MEETING the people attending a meeting ○ *The chairman stood up to address the meeting.* **3.** OCCASION WHEN PEOPLE MEET an occasion when somebody encounters somebody else, either accidentally or by arrangement **4.** SPORTING OCCASION an occasion when people get together for a sporting competition such as a set of horse races **5.** OCCASION FOR WORSHIP a regular occasion when a group of people, especially Quakers, gather for worship

meeting house *n* a room or building where some religious groups, especially Quakers, meet to worship

mefenamic acid /méffa námmik-/ *n* a drug that reduces inflammation. Use: pain relief from rheumatoid arthritis, menstruation. [< METHYL + *-fen-* (alteration and shortening of PHENYL) + *am-* (shortening of *amino-*) + *-ic* (shortening of *benzoic*)]

meg /meg/ *n* COMPUT same as **megabyte** (*informal*)

meg- *prefix* same as **mega-** (*used before vowels*)

mega /méggə/ *adj* extremely enjoyable, impressive, excellent, or large (*informal*) [Late 20C. < MEGA-]

mega- *prefix* **1.** one million (10^6) ○ *megavolt* Symbol **M 2.** COMPUT in the binary system, a million (2^{20}) ○ *megabyte* **3.** very large ○ *megadose* **4.** very great or excellent ○ *megastar* **5.** to a great extent (*slang*) ○ *megarich* [< Greek *megas* 'great' < Indo-European, 'large']

megabar /méggə baar/ *n* a unit of pressure equal to one million bars

megabit /méggə bit/ *n* COMPUT **1.** 1,048,576 bits **2.** one million bits

megabuck /méggə buk/ *N Am* (*slang*) *n* a million dollars ■ **megabucks** *npl* a large unspecified amount of money ○ *an actor earning megabucks in Hollywood*

megabyte /méggə bīt/ *n* **1.** a unit of computer data or storage space equivalent to 1,024 kilobytes **2.** one million bytes

megacephaly /méggə séffəli/ *n* MED same as **macrocephaly** —**megacephalic** /méggəsi fállik/ *adj* —**megacephalous** *adj*

megachurch /méggə church/ *n* a church with a very large membership, usually in the thousands, and often nondenominational and evangelical or charismatic in character

megadeath /méggə deth/ *n* one million deaths, used as a unit for recording deaths in a nuclear war

megadose /méggədōss/ *n* a very large dose of a medical drug or food supplement

Megaera /mə jeérə/ *n* in Greek mythology, one of the three Furies. The others were Alecto and Tisiphone.

megafauna /méggə fawnə/ *n* the animal life in a particular place that is larger than microscopic in size —**megafaunal** *adj*

megagamete /méggə ga meet/ *n* BIOL same as **macrogamete**

megahertz /méggə hurts/ (*plural same*) *n* one million hertz. Symbol **MHz**

megakaryocyte /méggə kárri ō sīt/ *n* a large cell in bone marrow that fragments to produce blood platelets

megal- *prefix* same as **megalo-** (*used before vowels*)

megalith /méggə lith/ *n* an enormous stone, usually standing upright or forming part of a prehistoric structure —**megalithic** /méggə líthik/ *adj*

megalo- *prefix* exceptionally large ○ *megalocardia* [< Greek *megal-*, stem of *megas* (see MEGA-)]

megaloblast /méggəlō blast/ *n* an unusually large red blood cell that has failed to mature properly, found especially in people affected by anaemia

megaloblastic anaemia /méggəlō blástik-/ *n* a form of anaemia in which the red blood cells are unusually large because they have failed to mature properly. It includes the type formerly known as pernicious anaemia.

megalocardia /méggəlō kaárdi ə/ *n* MED same as **cardiomegaly**

megalomania /méggəlō máyni ə/ *n* **1.** an excessive enjoyment in having power over other people and a craving for more of it **2.** a psychiatric disorder in which the patient experiences delusions of great power and importance —**megalomaniac** *n*, *adj* —**megalomaniacal** /-mə nī ək'l/ *adj* —**megalomaniacally** *adv*

megalopolis /méggə lóppəliss/ *n* **1.** an area in which there are several large cities whose suburbs meet or nearly meet **2.** an extremely large and populous city [Mid-19C. < MEGALO- + Greek *polis* 'city'] —**megalopolistic** /-loppə lístik/ *adj* —**megalopolitan** /-lə póllitən/ *adj*

megalosaur /méggəlō sawr/ *n* a very large carnivorous dinosaur of the Jurassic and early Cretaceous periods. Genus: *Megalosaurus*. [Mid-19C. Anglicization of modern Latin *megalosaurus* < MEGALO- + Greek *sauros* 'lizard'] —**megalosaurian** /méggəlō sáwri ən/ *adj*

-megaly *suffix* unusual enlargement ○ *hepatomegaly* [< modern Latin *-megalia* < Greek *megal-* (see MEGALO-)]

megamaser /méggə mayzər/ *n* an intense source of galactic maser radiation

Megan's Law /méggənz-/ *n* US an amendment to the Violent Crime Control and Law Enforcement Act of 1994, requiring community notification when a paroled or released sex offender moves into a locality [Late 20C. After *Megan* Kanka, seven-year-old girl killed by a convicted child molester]

megaphone /méggə fōn/ *n* a device shaped like a funnel, used to channel the voice in one direction and increase its volume —**megaphonic** /méggə fónnik/ *adj* —**megaphonically** *adv*

megapixel /méggə piks'l/ *n* a unit of graphics data transfer speed or image resolution equal to 1,048,576 pixels

megaplex /méggə pleks/ *n* **1.** a large cinema complex housing at least fifteen screens, often with the same film playing simultaneously in three or four of the theatres **2.** a very large complex of buildings

megapode /méggə pōd/ *n* a large ground-dwelling bird that builds a large mound of earth in which to incubate its eggs. Native to: Australasia. Family: Megapodiidae. [Mid-19C. < modern Latin *Megapodius* 'with big feet']

Megara /méggərə/ historic town in southern Greece. It once rivalled ancient Athens in power. Population: 25,061 (1991).

megarich /méggə rich/ *adj* extremely rich (*informal*) ○ *You need more than a million pounds to be considered megarich these days.*

megaron /méggə ron/ (*plural* **-ra** /-rə/) *n* the largest room in a house built during the Mycenaean period

of ancient Greek civilization [Late 19C. < Greek, 'large room']

megascopic /méggə skóppik/ *adj* PHYS same as **macroscopic** —**megascopically** *adv*

megasporangium /méggə spaw ránji əm/ (*plural* **-gia** /-ji ə/) *n* an organ in seed plants and ferns that produces large spores (**megaspores**) from which female gametophytes develop

megaspore /méggə spawr/ *n* the larger of two kinds of spore produced by seed plants and some ferns, which develops into a female gametophyte

megasporogenesis /méggə spáwrō jénnəssis/ *n* the formation and maturing of megaspores

megasprawl /méggə sprawl/ *n* a very large area of uncontrolled urbanization [20C.]

megastar /méggə staar/ *n* an extremely famous person, especially an entertainer

megastore /méggə stawr/ *n* an extremely large store that sells a range of goods

megathere /méggə theer/ *n* a large extinct American ground sloth that lived in the Miocene and Pleistocene epochs. Family: Megatheriidae. [Mid-19C. Anglicization of modern Latin *Megatherium* < Greek *mega-* 'large' + *thērion* 'animal'] —**megatherian** /méggə theéri ən/ *adj*

megaton /méggə tun/ *n* **1.** a unit of explosive power, e.g. in a nuclear weapon, that is equivalent to one million tons of TNT **2.** one million tons —**megatonic** /méggə tónnik/ *adj* —**megatonnage** *n*

megavitamin /méggə víttəmin, -vítəmin/ *n* a dose of a vitamin or vitamins that is much higher than the usual dose —**megavitamin** *adj*

megavolt /méggə vōlt/ *n* one million volts

megawatt /méggə wot/ *n* one million watts

Meghalaya /may gaálayə/ state in northeastern India. Capital: Shillong. Population: 2,306,069 (2001). Area: 22,429 sq. km/8,660 sq. mi.

Megiddo /mə gíddō/ ruined ancient city in northern Israel, thought to be the site of the predicted battle of Armageddon described in the Bible

megillah /mə gíllə/ (*plural* **-lahs** or **-loth** /-lót/) *n* **1.** a scroll containing part of the Hebrew Bible, especially the scroll containing the Book of Esther **2.** an overelaborate and unnecessarily lengthy account of something (*informal*) [Mid-17C. < Hebrew, 'roll, scroll' < *gālal* 'roll']

megilp /mə gílp/, **magilp** *n* a mixture of linseed oil and mastic varnish or turpentine. Use: solvent for oil paints. [Mid-18C. Origin ?]

megrim[1] /meégrim/ (*plural* **-grims** or *same*) *n* a sea flatfish related to the turbot. Native to: Europe. Latin name: *Lepidorhombus whiffiagonis*. [Mid-19C. Origin ?]

megrim[2] /meégrim/ (*archaic*) *n* **1.** MED same as **migraine** **2.** a sudden change of mind, or something about which somebody is briefly enthusiastic ▪ **megrims** *npl* a period of melancholy or low spirits [15C. Variant of MIGRAINE]

meibomian cyst /mī bómi ən-/ *n* a painless pea-shaped swelling in the eyelid, caused by the blockage of the outlet duct of a meibomian gland and the resulting accumulation of fatty secretion [See MEIBOMIAN GLAND]

meibomian gland *n* a sebaceous gland in the eyelid [Early 19C. After Heinrich *Meibom* (1638–1700), German anatomist]

Meighen /máygən/, **Arthur** (1874–1960) Canadian prime minister (1920–21 and 1926). A member of the Liberal-Conservative Party, he held a series of cabinet posts from 1915 until his election as prime minister in 1920. See table at **prime minister**

Meiji /máy jee, -jeé/ *n* the reign of the Japanese emperor Meiji Tenno (1867–1912), a period of extensive reform, including the abolition of feudalism [Late 19C. < Japanese, 'enlightened government']

Meiji Tenno /máyji ténnō/ (1852–1912) emperor of Japan. During a long reign (1867–1912), he modernized Japanese industry and introduced a new constitution that abolished feudalism (1889). Born **Mutsuhito**

meiny /máyni/ (*plural* **-nies**), **meinie** *n Scotland* a crowd or rabble [13C. < Old French *meinée* < Latin *mansion-* 'station, quarters' < *manere* 'remain, stay']

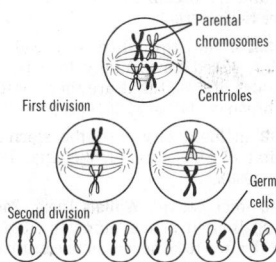

meiosis

meiosis /mī óssiss/ *n* **1.** in organisms that reproduce sexually, a process of cell division during which the nucleus divides into four nuclei, each of which contains half the usual number of chromosomes **2.** LITERAT same as **litotes** [Mid-16C. < modern Latin < Greek *meiōn* 'less'] —**meiotic** /mī óttik/ *adj*

Golda Meir

Meir /may eér/, **Golda** (1898–1978) Ukrainian-born Israeli politician. She served in the Labour government of Israel from 1949 and as prime minister from 1969 until 1974, when she resigned after the Yom Kippur War (1973). Born **Goldie Mabovich**

'We intend to remain alive. Our neighbors want to see us dead. This is not a question that leaves much room for compromise.'
[Golda Meir, 'The Indestructible Golda Meir', *Reader's Digest*; July 1971]

'We who have such an intimate knowledge of boxcars and deporation...cannot be silent.'
[Golda Meir, *Speech to the UN General Assembly on bellicose Soviet actions in Hungary*; 21 November 1956]

meishi *n* a business card carried by a Japanese businessman or businesswoman

Meissen[1] /míss'n/ *n US* CERAMICS same as **Dresden china** [Mid-19C. < MEISSEN [2]]

Meissen[2] /míssən/ town in east-central Germany, famous for its porcelain manufacture. Population: 32,900 (1997).

Meissner's corpuscle /míssnərz-/ *n* ANAT same as **tactile corpuscle** [Late 19C. After Georg *Meissner* (1829–1905), German anatomist]

-meister /mīstər/ *suffix* a highly skilled or prominent person (*humorous*) ○ *webmeister* ○ *spinmeister*

Meistersinger /mīstər singər/ (*plural* **-ers** or *same*) *n* a member of a German guild for poets and musicians in the 14th to 16th centuries who had completed an apprenticeship and composed original work [Mid-19C. < German, 'master-singer']

Meitner /mítnər/, **Lise** (1878–1968) Austrian physicist. She was the first scientist to identify nuclear fission, and discovered the element protactinium in association with Otto Hahn.

meitnerium /mīt neéri əm/ *n* a highly unstable radioactive chemical element. Source: produced artificially by nuclear fusion. Symbol **Mt**. See table at **element** [Late 20C. After Lise MEITNER]

Mejía /me heé a/, **Hipólito** (*b.* 1941) president of the Dominican Republic (2000–). A member of the left-wing Dominican Revolutionary Party, he has stated

that fighting poverty and corruption are his primary objectives.

Meknès /mek néss/ city and former capital of Morocco, located in the north of the country. Population: 530,171 (1994).

Mekong /mee kóng/ major river in Southeast Asia, flowing from SE China through the Indochinese peninsula and into the South China Sea in Vietnam. Length: 4,200 km/2,610 mi.

mela /máy laa/ *n S Asia* a large gathering [Early 19C. Via Hindi < Sanskrit *melā*]

melaena /mə leénə/ *n* a condition characterized by the production of black stools that are caused by bleeding into the bowel and the subsequent chemical changes in the blood effected by the bowel fluids [Early 19C. Via modern Latin < Greek *melaina*, feminine of *melas* 'black']

Melaka /mə lákə/ city and seaport in Malaysia, on the southern coast of the Malay Peninsula. Population: 75,909 (1996). Former name **Malacca**

melaleuca /méllə loökə/ *n* a tree or bush of the myrtle family that flourishes in wetlands and has become a pest in parts of North America. Native to: Australia. Genus: *Melaleuca*. [Early 19C. < modern Latin < Greek *melas* 'black' + *leukos* 'white']

melamine /méllə meen/ *n* **1.** a plastic made from copolymerizing a white crystalline solid with formaldehyde **2.** a white crystalline solid. Use: manufacture of synthetic resins, in leather tanning. Formula: $C_3H_6N_6$. [Mid-19C. Probably < German *Melamin*, substance obtained from the distillation of ammonium thiocyanate]

melan- *prefix* same as **melano-** (*used before vowels*)

melancholia /méllən kóli ə/ *n* depression as a form of psychiatric disorder (*dated*) [Early 17C. < late Latin (see MELANCHOLY)] —**melancholiac** *n, adj*

melancholic /méllən kóllik/ *adj* feeling or tending to feel a thoughtful or gentle sadness [14C. Either < MELANCHOLY or < French *mélancolique* < Greek *melankholia* (see MELANCHOLY)] —**melancholically** *adv*

melancholy /méllənkəli/ *adj* FEELING OR CAUSING SADNESS feeling or making somebody feel a thoughtful or gentle sadness ▪ *n* **1.** PENSIVE SADNESS a thoughtful or gentle sadness **2.** GLOOMY CHARACTER the gloomy character of somebody said to have an excess of black bile, one of the four bodily humours that were once thought to determine people's health and emotional state **3.** MED same as **black bile** (*archaic*) [14C. Directly or via French *mélancholie* < late Latin *melancholia* < Greek *melankholia* < *melan-* 'black' + *kholē* 'bile']

Melanchthon /mə lángkthən, me lánkh ton/, **Philipp** (1497–1560) German religious reformer. Working in association with Martin Luther, he produced some of the most important theological works of the Protestant Reformation, including *Commonplaces of Theology* (1521) and the Augsburg Confession (1530). Born **Schwartzert, Philipp**

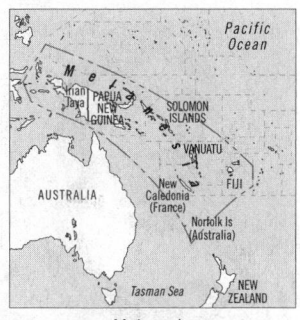

Melanesia

Melanesia /méllə neézi ə, -neézhə/ ethnographic grouping of Pacific islands, encompassing the islands of the western Pacific Ocean south of the equator, including New Guinea, the Solomon Islands, New Caledonia, Vanuatu, and Fiji

Melanesian /méllə neézi ən, -neézhən/ *n* **1.** a group of Austronesian languages, including Fijian, spoken in Melanesia. Native speakers: 300,000. **2.** a member of any people living on the islands of Melanesia —**Melanesian** *adj*

melange /may lónzh, -laánzh/, **mélange** *n* **1.** a collection of things of different kinds (*literary or formal*)

2. a region of rock that consists of a mixture of dissimilar rocky materials [Mid-17C. < French *mélange* < *mêler* 'to mix' < Latin *miscere*]

melanin /méllənin/ *n* a dark brown or black pigment that is naturally present to varying degrees in the skin, hair, eyes, fur, or feathers of people and animals as well as in plants —**melanic** /mə lánnik/ *adj* —**melanoid** *adj*

melanism /méllənìzəm/ *n* **1.** dark pigmentation of the skin, hair, fur, or feathers in a human being, animal, or plant, resulting from the presence of melanin **2.** MED same as **melanosis** —**melanistic** /méllə nístik/ *adj*

melanite /méllə nìt/ *n* a black andradite garnet containing titanium —**melanitic** /méllə níttik/ *adj*

melano- *prefix* black, dark ○ *melanocyte* [< Greek *melan-* 'black']

melanoblast /méllənō blàst/ *n* a cell that gives rise to either a melanocyte or melanophore, which produce the dark brown or black pigment melanin —**melanoblastic** /méllənō blástik/ *adj*

melanocyte /méllənō sìt/ *n* a cell in the epidermal layer of the skin that produces the dark brown or black pigment melanin

melanocyte-stimulating hormone *n* either of two hormones in vertebrates produced in the pituitary gland that darken the skin by regulating melanin dispersal

melanoid /méllə nòyd/ *adj* **1.** similar to melanin **2.** similar to melanosis

melanoma /méllə nṓmə/ (*plural* **-mas** or **-mata** /-mətə/) *n* a malignant tumour, most often on the skin, that contains dark pigment and develops from a melanin-producing cell (**melanocyte**)

melanophore /méllənō fàwr/ *n* a cell in fishes, amphibians, and reptiles that contains the dark brown or black pigment melanin

melanosis /méllə nṓssiss/ *n* an unexpected presence of dark pigmentation in the tissues [Early 19C. < modern Latin < Greek *melan-* 'black'] —**melanotic** /-nóttik/ *adj*

melanosome /méllənə sṓm/ *n* a small sac within an epidermal cell (**melanocyte**) in which the dark brown or black pigment melanin is synthesized

melanous /méllənəss/ *adj* having a dark complexion and dark hair [Mid-19C. < Greek *melan-* 'black'] —**melanosity** /méllə nóssəti/ *n*

melatonin /méllə tṓnin/ *n* a hormone derived from serotonin and secreted by the pineal gland that produces changes in the skin colour of vertebrates, reptiles, and amphibians and is important in regulating biorhythms [Mid-20C. Blend of MELANO- + SEROTONIN]

Melba /mélbə/ [After Dame Nellie MELBA] ◇ **do a Melba** ANZ to announce your retirement from a job or occupation repeatedly without actually leaving

Dame Nellie Melba

Melba /mélbə/, **Dame Nellie** (1859–1931) Australian opera singer. She was a soprano who won international acclaim for her performances in roles such as Mimì in *La Bohème*. Born **Mitchell, Helen Porter**

> 'Music is not written in red, white and blue. It is written in the heart's blood of the composer.'
> [Dame Nellie Melba, *Melodies and Memories*; 1925]

Melba sauce *n* a sauce consisting of puréed sweetened raspberries, served especially with poached

peaches and ice cream in peach Melba [Early 20C. After Dame Nellie MELBA]

Melba toast *n* very thin slices of bread toasted on both sides, sliced horizontally to expose two untoasted sides of bread that are then toasted too, so that the bread curls [Early 20C. After Dame Nellie MELBA]

Melbourne /mélbərn/ city in southeastern Australia, the capital of the state of Victoria. Population: 3,371,300 (1998).

Melbourne /mél bawrn/, **William Lamb, 2nd Viscount** (1779–1848) British prime minister (1834, 1835–41). A Whig MP after 1806, he was prime minister during the early years of Queen Victoria's reign, and was her political mentor.

Melbourne Cup /mélbərn-/ *n* the best-known horse race in Australia, which takes place each year on the first Tuesday in November. The first race was held in 1861.

Melburnian /mel búrni ən/ *n* somebody who comes from or lives in Melbourne, Australia [Mid-19C. < Latinized alteration of MELBOURNE] —**Melburnian** *adj*

Melchite /mél kìt/, **Melkite** *n* a member of any of several Christian churches in North Africa and Southwest Asia that use the Greek Orthodox liturgy but acknowledge the authority of the Roman Catholic Pope [Early 17C. Via ecclesiastical Latin < Byzantine Greek *Melkhitai* 'Melkites' < Syriac *malkāyē* 'royalists' < *malkā* 'king']

Melchizedek /mel kízzə dek/ *n* in the Bible, a priest and king of Salem who blessed Abraham

meld[1] /meld/ *vti* (**melds, melding, melded**) to cause things to combine or blend and become one thing or substance, or be combined or blended in this way ■ *n* a combination or blend of various things [Mid-20C. Origin ?]

meld[2] /meld/ *vti* (**melds, melding, melded**) in games such as canasta or pinochle, to show or declare some or all of a hand of cards in order to score points ■ *n* in games such as canasta or pinochle, a hand of cards that are shown or declared in order to score points, or an act of showing or declaring these cards [Late 19C. < German *melden* 'announce']

Meldrum /méldrəm/, **Max** (1875–1955) British-born Australian painter. He was a proponent of a scientific realist approach to painting.

melee /méllay/, **mêlée** *n* **1.** a noisy confused fight **2.** a confused, often noisy mixing of people or things, usually in a public place [Mid-17C. < French *mêlée*, later form of Old French *meslee* (see MEDLEY)]

melena *n* MED US spelling of **melaena**

melic /méllik/ *adj* describes an ancient Greek lyric poem that is meant to be sung rather than recited [Late 17C. Via Latin < Greek *melikos* < *melos* 'song']

Méliès /máyl yess/, **Georges** (1861–1938) French film director. A pioneer of cinematography, he built the first film studio, devised trick effects, and created his own production company.

Melilla /mə lílə/ Spanish enclave and port on the Mediterranean coast of Morocco. Population: 60,108 (1998). Area: 12 sq. km/4,63 sq. mi.

melilot /mélli lòt/ *n* a plant with compound leaves consisting of three oval leaflets, sometimes grown as forage. Flowers: small, yellow, fragrant on tall flower heads. Genus: *Melilotus*. [14C. Via French < Greek *melilōtos* < *meli* 'honey' + *lōtos* 'lotus, clover']

melinite /mélli nìt/ *n* an explosive made from picric acid [Late 19C. < French *mélinos* 'quince-coloured' < *mēlon* 'quince, apple'; from its yellow colour]

meliorate /méeli ə rayt/ (**-rates, -rating, -rated**) *vti* to become better, or make something better [Mid-16C. < late Latin *meliorare* < Latin *melior* 'better'] —**meliorable** *adj* —**melioration** /méeli ə ráysh'n/ *n* —**meliorative** *adj* —**meliorator** *n*

meliorism /méeli ərìzəm/ *n* the belief that human society has a natural tendency to improve and that people can consciously assist this process [Mid-19C. < Latin *melior* 'better'] —**meliorist** *n* —**melioristic** /méeli ə rístik/ *adj*

melisma /mə lízmə/ (*plural* **-mata** /-mətə/ or **-mas**) *n* **1.** a decorative phrase or passage in vocal music, especially one in which one syllable of a plainsong text is sung to a melodic sequence of several notes **2.** an embellishment or decoration of a melody **3.** MUSIC same as **cadenza** [Late 19C. Via modern Latin

< Greek, 'tune' < *melizein* 'sing' < *melos* 'song'] —**melismatic** /mélliz máttik/ *adj*

Melkite *n* CHR another spelling of **Melchite**

melli- *prefix* honey ○ *melliphagous* [< Latin *mel* < Indo-European]

melliferous /mə lífferəss/, **mellific** /mə líffik/ *adj* producing or bearing large quantities of honey [Mid-17C < Latin *mellifer* 'honey-bearing' < *mel* 'honey']

mellifluous /mə lífloo əss/, **mellifluent** /-ənt/ *adj* pleasant and soothing to listen to, and sweet or rich in tone [15C. < late Latin *mellifluus* 'flowing like honey' < Latin *mel* 'honey'] —**mellifluously** *adv* —**mellifluousness** *n*

Mellon /méllən/, **Andrew** (1855–1937) US industrialist, financier, and philanthropist. He endowed the Washington National Gallery of Art. Full name **Mellon, Andrew William**

mellophone /méllə fòn/ *n* a portable brass musical instrument similar in tone to a French horn, used mainly in brass bands and marching bands [Early 20C. < MELLOW]

mellow /méllō/ *adj* **1.** SOFT IN COLOUR OR TONE comfortingly soft, warm, and rich in colour or tone **2.** SMOOTH AND RICH IN TASTE matured to a long-lasting smooth rich taste **3.** FULLY RIPE soft, juicy, fully ripened, and sweet **4.** EASY-GOING good-humoured, tolerant, and approachable, especially as a result of maturity or a feeling of security **5.** MILDLY INTOXICATED mildly intoxicated by drink or drugs **6.** MOIST AND RICH IN TEXTURE describes soil that has a moist rich loamy texture ■ *vti* (**-lows, -lowing, -lowed**) **1.** BECOME OR MAKE SOMEBODY MORE EASY-GOING to become more good-humoured, tolerant, and approachable, or make somebody become so **2.** INCREASE IN OR GIVE SOMETHING RICHNESS to become richer, smoother, or softer in taste, colour, tone, or atmosphere, or make something become so [15C. Origin ?] —**mellowly** *adv* —**mellowness** *n*
mellow out *vti* N Am (*slang*) **1.** to become more relaxed and friendly, or make somebody more relaxed and friendly **2.** to become calm, or make somebody calm

melodeon /mə lṓdi ən/ *n* **1.** a small reed organ, similar to a harmonium, that uses suction bellows to draw air through its reeds **2.** a small accordion, used especially by German folk musicians [Mid-19C. Probably alteration of *melodium* 'small reed organ' < MELODY after HARMONIUM]

melodic /mə lóddik/ *adj* **1.** consisting of the melody of a piece of music ○ *the melodic line* **2.** relating to or characteristic of melody or the composition of melodies **3.** MUSIC same as **melodious** —**melodically** *adv*

melodic minor scale *n* a scale with the sixth and seventh notes raised a semitone when played in ascending order but in the natural minor pitch when played in descending order

melodious /mə lṓdi əss/ *adj* **1.** tuneful or varied and interesting in tone **2.** having the character of a melody —**melodiously** *adv* —**melodiousness** *n*

melodise *vti* MUSIC another spelling of **melodize**

melodist /méllə dist/ *n* **1.** somebody who composes melodies, especially beautiful or memorable melodies for song lyrics **2.** somebody who sings sweetly

melodize /méllə dìz/ (**-dizes, -dizing, -dized**), **melodise** (**-dises, -dising, -dised**) *v* **1.** *vti* to compose melodies or compose a melody to which lyrics can be sung **2.** *vt* to make something tuneful and pleasing to hear —**melodizer** *n*

melodrama /méllə draamə/ *n* **1.** SENSATIONALIZED DRAMATIC OR LITERARY WORK a dramatic or other literary work characterized by the use of stereotyped characters, exaggerated emotions and language, simplistic morality, and conflict **2.** DRAMATIC OR LITERARY GENRE melodramas collectively considered as a dramatic or literary genre **3.** HISTRIONIC BEHAVIOUR exaggerated behaviour or emotional displays, like those characteristic of a melodrama **4.** DRAMA INTERSPERSED WITH MUSIC formerly, a play with a sensational or romantic plot that is interspersed with musical numbers and often has music accompanying the action **5.** SPOKEN WORDS WITH MUSICAL ACCOMPANIMENT a piece of poetry or a scene in a dramatic or operatic work in which the text is recited to a musical accompaniment [Early 19C. < French *mélodrame* 'drama with songs' < Greek *melos* 'song']

melodramatic /mélladrə máttik/ *adj* **1.** behaving, speaking, done, or said in a way that is more dramatic, shocking, or highly emotional than the situ-

ation demands **2.** relating to or typical of melodrama [Early 19C. < MELODRAMA] —**melodramatically** *adv*

melodramatics /méllədrə máttiks/ *npl* exaggeratedly theatrical behaviour, speech, or writing

melodramatize /méllə drámmə tīz/ (**-tizes, -tizing, -tized**), **melodramatise** (**-tises, -tising, -tised**) *vti* to treat or react to something in an exaggeratedly theatrical way [Early 19C. < MELODRAMA, after DRAMATIZE] —**melodramatization** /méllə drámmə tī záysh'n/ *n*

melody /méllədi/ (*plural* **-dies**) *n* **1.** TUNE a series of musical notes that form a distinct unit, are recognizable as a phrase, and usually have a distinctive rhythm **2.** LINEAR MUSICAL STRUCTURE the linear structure of a piece of music in which single notes follow one another **3.** MAIN TUNE the primary and most recognizable part in a harmonic piece of music **4.** MUSICALLY EXPRESSIVE QUALITY the musically expressive quality of something, especially poetry **5.** MUSICAL LYRIC a poem that lends itself easily to being set to music or sung [12C. < French *mélodie* < Greek *melōidia* 'choral song' < *melos* 'tune' + *ōidē* 'song']

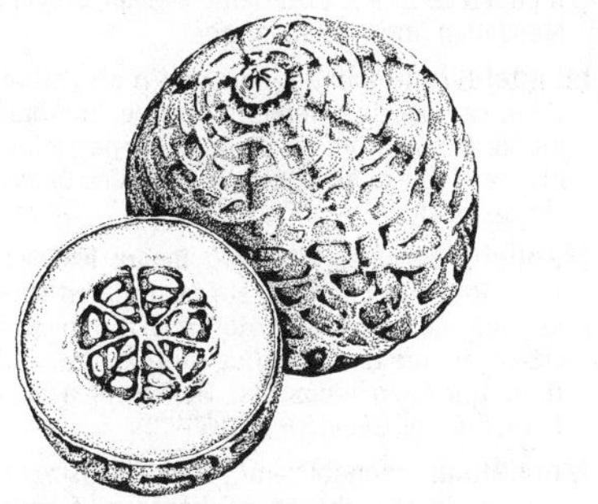

melon

melon /méllən/ *n* **1.** ROUND JUICY GOURD FRUIT the round edible fruit of vines belonging to the gourd family, with a tough rind and sweet juicy flesh ranging in colour from pale yellow to deep orange **2.** PLANT THAT PRODUCES MELONS a vine of the gourd family widely grown to produce melons. Latin name: *Cucumis melo* or *Citrullus lanatus*. **3.** SOUND ORGAN IN DOLPHIN'S HEAD a rounded waxy mass found in the head of some dolphins and toothed whales that is thought to play a part in the focusing of sound signals ■ **melons** *npl* OFFENSIVE TERM an offensive term for a woman's breasts, especially when large (*slang*) [14C. < late Latin *melon-* < Greek *mēlopepōn*, a kind of gourd < *mēlon* 'apple' + *pepōn* 'gourd']

Melos /mée loss/, **Mílos** island in southeastern Greece, one of the Cyclades. Population: 4,554 (1981). Area: 158 sq. km/61 sq. mi.

Melpomene /mel pómməni/ *n* in Greek mythology, the Muse of tragedy, one of the nine Muses believed to inspire and nurture the arts

Melrose /mél rōz/ historic market town on the River Tweed in southeastern Scotland. Population: 2,270 (1991).

melt[1] /melt/ *v* (**melts, melting, melted**) **1.** *vti* CHANGE FROM SOLID TO LIQUID STATE to change a substance from a solid to a liquid state by heating it, or be changed in this way **2.** *vti* DISSOLVE to dissolve something such as sugar in a liquid, or be dissolved in a liquid **3.** *vi* DISAPPEAR to disappear gradually and inconspicuously **4.** *vi* BECOME MERGED to change into, or blend with, something in such a way that the actual point of change or blending is almost imperceptible **5.** *vti* BE MOVED EMOTIONALLY to cause somebody to be moved emotionally so as to become gentler and more sympathetic, or be moved in this way **6.** *vi* FEEL HOT to feel uncomfortably hot (*informal*) ■ *n* **1.** MASS OF MELTED MATERIAL a mass or an amount of melted material, especially metal, produced in a single operation or during a specific period of time **2.** MOLTEN MATERIAL a material, e.g. metal or glass, in a molten state **3.** MELTING OF SOMETHING the process of melting something **4.** LIQUEFACTION the state or condition of being liquefied **5.** TOASTED CHEESE-TOPPED OPEN SANDWICH an open toasted sandwich, usually with cheese melted on top [Old English *m(i)eltan* < Indo-European] —**meltability** /méltə bíllәti/ *n* —**meltable** *adj* —**melter** *n*

melt down *vti* to liquefy metal or glass by heating in order to reuse it, or be liquefied in this way

melt[2] /melt/ *n* the spleen of a slaughtered animal, used mainly for animal food (*often used in the plural*) [Late 16C. Variant of MILT]

meltage /méltij/ *n* **1.** the process of melting something **2.** a liquefied substance produced by a heating process, or an amount of such a substance

meltdown /mélt down/ *n* **1.** MELTING OF NUCLEAR REACTOR FUEL RODS the melting of fuel rods in a nuclear reactor because of overheating that results in the escape of radioactive materials or radiation **2.** OVERLOAD OF COMPUTER NETWORK the shutdown of a computer network as a result of a deluge of illegal or wrongly routed packets that saturate the network and force multiple hosts to respond simultaneously **3.** COMPLETE COLLAPSE OF ORGANIZATION a situation of complete collapse of an organization or institution (*informal*) **4.** EXTREMELY ANGRY STATE a loss of composure, especially an extremely angry response to something (*informal*)

melting /mélting/ *adj* full of or causing sweet and tender or sentimental emotion —**meltingly** *adv*

melting point *n* the temperature at which a substance changes from a solid to a liquid form

melting pot *n* **1.** CONTAINER FOR MELTING AND MIXING a container in which substances, especially metals, are placed to be liquefied and mixed together **2.** SOCIETY COMPOSED OF MANY DIFFERENT CULTURES a place where people of different ethnic groups are brought together and can assimilate, especially a country that takes immigrants from many different ethnic backgrounds **3.** PROCESS THAT CREATES SOMETHING NEW a situation or process in which distinct elements can be brought together to produce something new

melton /méltən/ *n* smooth heavy wool cloth. Use: overcoats. [Mid-19C. After MELTON MOWBRAY]

Melton Mowbray /méltən mō bray/ ancient market town in Leicestershire, central England. It is famous for its pork pies. Population: 47,866 (1991).

meltwater /mélt wawtər/ *n* water formed by the melting of ice or snow, especially from a glacier

Melville /mélvil/, **Herman** (1819–91) US writer. His allegorical sea novel *Moby Dick* (1851) is sometimes held to be the greatest work of American fiction.

> 'I always go to sea a sailor, because they make a point of paying me for my trouble, whereas they never pay passengers a single penny.'
> [Herman Melville, *Moby Dick*; 1851]

Melville Island island located in the Timor Sea, off the northern coast of the Northern Territory of Australia. Population: 2,033 (1996). Area: 5,800 sq. km/2,239 sq. mi.

Melville Peninsula peninsula in Nunavut, northern Canada. Foxe Basin lies to its west, and Committee Bay to its east. Area: 65,000 sq. km/25,100 sq. mi.

mem /mem/ *n* the 13th letter of the Hebrew alphabet, represented in the English alphabet as 'm'. See table at **alphabet** [Early 19C. < Hebrew *mēm* 'water']

mem. *abbr* **1.** member **2.** memoir **3.** memorandum **4.** memorial

member /mémbər/ *n* **1.** ADHERENT OF PARTICULAR GROUP somebody who belongs to and participates in a particular group by birth or choice **2.** *also* **Member** POLITICAL REPRESENTATIVE somebody elected to a legislative body such as the UK Parliament or the US Congress **3.** LIMB a part or organ of a plant or animal body, especially a limb **4.** same as **penis** (*formal or humorous*) **5.** INDIVIDUAL PART a separate and distinct part of a whole, e.g. an object belonging to a mathematical set, a clause in a sentence, or a proposition in a syllogism **6.** STRUCTURAL UNIT a beam, wall, or similar structural unit in a building or other construction **7.** ELEMENT IN MATHEMATICAL EQUATION either of the expressions in a mathematical equation linked by an equals sign [14C. Via French *membre* < Latin *membrum* 'limb, part'] —**membered** *adj*

member firm *n* a company that trades in securities and belongs to an organized exchange

Member of Congress *n* somebody elected to the US Congress, especially to the House of Representatives

Member of Parliament *n* somebody who has been elected to a parliament

membership /mémbərship/ *n* **1.** the state or condition of belonging to a group such as a species, social class, team, club, or political party **2.** the members of a group such as a species, social class, organization, or mathematical set considered collectively (*takes a singular or plural verb*)

membrane /mém brayn/ *n* **1.** THIN LAYER OF TISSUE a thin flexible sheet of tissue connecting, covering, lining, or separating various parts or organs in animal and plant bodies, or forming the external wall of a cell **2.** THIN POROUS SHEET a thin, pliable, and often porous sheet of any natural or artificial material **3.** PIECE OF PARCHMENT a piece of parchment forming part of a roll [15C. Directly or via French < Latin *membrana* 'skin' < *membrum* 'limb, part'] —**membranaceous** /mémbrə náyshəss/ *adj*

membrane bone *n* a bone that develops directly out of membranous connective tissue rather than from cartilage, e.g. the clavicle and some cranial bones

membrane transport *n* the process by which substances in solution pass through a biological membrane

membranophone /mem bráynə fōn/ *n* a musical instrument that uses a stretched membrane to produce sound, e.g. a drum or kazoo

membranous /mémbrənəss/ *adj* **1.** relating to or similar to a membrane, especially in being thin, pliable, and often translucent **2.** resulting in the formation of a membrane or of a thin layer similar to a membrane

membranous labyrinth *n* the structure of fluid-filled sacs in the inner ear that are vital to hearing and balance

meme /meem/ *n* any characteristic of a culture, e.g. its language, that can be transmitted from one generation to the next in a way analogous to the transmission of genetic information [Late 20C. < Greek *mimēma* 'something imitated', after GENE]

memento /mə méntō, mi-/ (*plural* **-tos** or **-toes**) *n* an object given or kept as a reminder or in memory of somebody or something [Mid-18C. < Latin, 'remember!' (originally the first word in prayers for the dead) < *meminisse* 'remember']

memento mori /-máw ree/ (*plural same*) *n* **1.** an object, especially a skull, intended as a reminder of the fact that humans die **2.** a reminder of the fact that humans fail and make mistakes (*literary*) [< Latin, 'remember (that you have) to die']

Memling /mémmling/, **Hans** (1435?–94) Flemish painter. He chose mainly religious subjects, imbued with delicacy, harmony, and repose, and also painted idealized portraits.

Memnon /mém non/ *n* in Greek mythology, the Ethiopian king who fought for the Trojans in the siege of Troy and was killed by Achilles

memo /mémmō/ (*plural* **-os**) *n* **1.** a written communication similar to a letter but without the formal address blocks at the beginning, especially one that is circulated to people within an office or organization **2.** a note intended to serve as a reminder of something [Early 18C. Shortening of MEMORANDUM]

memoir /mém waar/ *n* **1.** BIOGRAPHY OR HISTORICAL ACCOUNT a biography or an account of historical events, especially one written from personal knowledge **2.** ESSAY ON SCHOLARLY SUBJECT a short essay, article, or report on a scholarly subject, usually one in which the writer is a recognized specialist ■ **memoirs** *npl* **1.** AUTOBIOGRAPHY somebody's written account of his or her own life or of events in which he or she took part **2.** PROCEEDINGS the records of the business and discussions of a learned society [Mid-17C. < French *mémoire* 'memory' < Old French *memorie* (see MEMORY)] —**memoirist** *n*

memorabilia /mémmərə bílli ə/ *npl* **1.** objects associated with a famous person or event, especially considered as collectors' items **2.** objects collected as souvenirs of important personal events or experiences [Late 18C. < Latin, 'memorable things' < *memorabilis* (see MEMORABLE)]

memorable /mémmərəb'l/ *adj* **1.** sufficiently interesting, exciting, or unusual to be worth remembering or likely to be remembered **2.** easy to remember [15C. Via French < Latin *memorabilis* < *memorare* 'bring to mind' < *memor* 'mindful'] —**memorability** /mémmərə bílləti/ *n* —**memorably** *adv*

memorandum /mémmə rándəm/ (*plural* **-dums** or **-da** /-də/) *n* **1.** BRIEF DIPLOMATIC COMMUNICATION a brief, often unsigned communication circulated among diplomats, especially one that summarizes a

country's position on an issue **2.** same as **memo** (sense 2) (*formal*) **3.** COMM same as **memo** (sense 1) **4.** SUMMARY OF LEGAL AGREEMENT a written statement summarizing the terms of a contract or a similar legal transaction **5.** CONSIGNOR'S STATEMENT a consignor's brief statement about a shipment of returnable goods [15C. < Latin, 'thing to be remembered' < *memorare* (see MEMORABLE)]

memorial /mə máwri əl/ *n* **1.** COMMEMORATIVE OBJECT OR EVENT something that is intended to remind people of somebody who has died or an event in which people died, e.g. a statue, speech, or ceremony **2.** STATEMENT OF FACTS ACCOMPANYING PETITION a written statement of facts accompanying a petition presented to a person or group in authority ■ *adj* COMMEMORATIVE intended as a reminder of a person or event or as a celebration of somebody's life and work [14C. < French < Latin *memoria* (see MEMORY)] —**memorially** *adv*

Memorial Day *n* in the United States, a public holiday to commemorate soldiers who died in war. Date: last Monday in May, formerly 30 May.

memorialise *vt* another spelling of **memorialize**

memorialist /mə máwri əlist/ *n* **1.** a writer of memoirs **2.** a writer, signer, or presenter of a memorial accompanying a petition

memorialize /mə máwri ə līz/ (**-izes, -izing, -ized**), **memorialise** (**-ises, -ising, -ised**) *vt* **1.** to serve as a memorial to somebody or something, or provide somebody or something with a memorial **2.** to present a written memorial accompanying a petition to a person or group in power —**memorialization** /mə máwri ə lī záysh'n/ *n* —**memorializer** *n*

memorize /mémmə rīz/ (**-rizes, -rizing, -rized**), **memorise** (**-rises, -rising, -rised**) *vt* to commit something to memory —**memorizable** *adj* —**memorization** /mémmə rī záysh'n/ *n* —**memorizer** *n*

memory /mémməri/ (*plural* **-ries**) *n* **1.** ABILITY TO RETAIN KNOWLEDGE the ability of the mind or of a person or organism to retain learned information and knowledge of past events and experiences and to retrieve that information and knowledge ○ *have a good memory for faces* **2.** SOMEBODY'S STOCK OF RETAINED KNOWLEDGE somebody's stock of retained knowledge and experience ○ *recite the poem from memory* **3.** RETAINED IMPRESSION OF EVENT the knowledge or impression that somebody retains of a person, event, period, or subject ○ *memories of a happy childhood* **4.** RECOLLECTION the act or an instance of remembering **5.** PRESERVATION OF KNOWLEDGE the preservation of knowledge of and, usually, celebration of a deceased person or past event ○ *a poem in memory of her father* **6.** POSTHUMOUS IMPRESSION the knowledge or impression of somebody retained by other people after that person's death **7.** TEMPORAL EXTENT OF RECOLLECTION the period of past time that a person or group is able to remember **8.** STORAGE AREA IN COMPUTER the area of storage in a computer that maintains information for instant retrieval and processing, as distinct from disk storage **9.** COMPUTER STORAGE CAPACITY the storage capacity of a computer that determines how much information can be maintained for instant retrieval and processing **10.** ABILITY TO RETURN TO ORIGINAL SHAPE the ability of some materials such as plastics and metals to return to their original shape after being subject to deformation [13C. Via French < Latin *memoria* < *memor* 'mindful'] ◇ **within living memory** in the time experienced and remembered by people now alive

memory bank *n* COMPUT same as **memory** (sense 8)

memory lane *n* the past, especially the past shared and remembered by a group of people, thought of as a path that can be travelled along to revisit former times

memory span *n* a measure of somebody's memory, often for units of information such as nonsense syllables or sequences of random numbers, over a short period of time

Memory Stick a trademark for a small flash drive that can store data for use in portable electronic devices such as handheld computers, digital cameras, and mobile phones

memory trace *n* PSYCHOL same as **engram**

Memphis /mémfiss/ **1.** ruined city and capital of ancient Egypt, located at the head of the Nile delta in the north of the country **2.** largest city in Tennessee, located in the southwestern corner of the state. Population: 648,882 (2002 estimate). —**Memphian** *n, adj*

Memphremagog, Lake /mémfrə máygog/ lake in Quebec, Canada, and Vermont. It is the second largest lake in Vermont. Length: 43 km/27 mi. Area: 102 sq. km/39 sq. mi.

MEMS *n* a computer chip that has integrated miniaturized mechanical devices for sensing, processing, or carrying out various functions. Full form **micro-electromechanical system**

memsahib /mem saáb, mém saab/ *n S Asia* a respectful form of address to a woman, formerly used by Indians to European married women [Mid-19C. < MA'AM + SAHIB]

men plural of **man**

men- *prefix* same as **meno-** (*used before vowels*)

menace /ménnəss/ *n* **1.** POSSIBLE SOURCE OF DANGER a possible source of danger or harm **2.** NUISANCE a constant source of trouble and annoyance (*informal*) **3.** THREATENING QUALITY a threatening quality, feeling, or tone **4.** THREATENING ACT a threatening act, gesture, or speech ○ *demanding money with menaces* ■ *v* (**-aces, -acing, -aced**) **1.** *vt* BE THREAT TO SOMEBODY OR SOMETHING to be a possible or actual source of danger or harm to somebody or something **2.** *vti* MAKE THREAT AGAINST SOMEBODY to behave towards or speak to somebody in a way that threatens injury or harm (*often passive*) [14C. < French < Latin *minac-* 'threatening' < *minari* 'threaten' < *minae* 'threats', literally 'projecting points'] —**menacer** *n* —**menacing** *adj* —**menacingly** *adv*

menadione /ménnə dī ōn/ *n* a yellow crystalline solid. Use: fungicide, vitamin K supplement in medicines and animal feedstuffs. Formula: $C_{11}H_8O_2$. [Mid-20C. Contraction of METHYL + NAPHTHALENE + DI- [1]]

ménage /máy naazh/ *n* (*formal*) **1.** a group of people living together as a household **2.** the running of a household [Late 17C. < French; < Latin *manere* 'dwell, stay']

ménage à trois /máy naazh aa trwaá/ (*plural* **ménages à trois** /*pronunc. same*/) *n* a sexual relationship involving three people [< French, literally 'household for three']

menagerie /mə nájjəri/ *n* **1.** DISPLAY OF CAPTIVE WILD ANIMALS a collection of wild animals kept in captivity for the curiosity and entertainment of the public, sometimes as part of a travelling show **2.** WILD ANIMAL ENCLOSURE an enclosure in which wild animals are kept for public exhibition **3.** DIVERSE OR EXOTIC GROUP a diverse, exotic, or unusual group of people or things [Late 17C. < French < *ménage* (see MÉNAGE)]

Menai Strait /ménnī stráyt/ narrow arm of the Irish Sea in northwestern Wales, separating the island of Anglesey from the mainland. Length: 23 km/14 mi.

menarche /me naárki/ *n* the first time that a girl or young woman menstruates [Early 20C. < MENO- + Greek *arkhē* 'beginning'] —**menarcheal** *adj*

menazon /ménnə zon/ *n* a colourless crystalline solid. Use: killing aphids. Formula: $C_6H_8N_5O_2PS_2$. [Mid-20C. Contraction of METHYL + AMINO- + AZO- + *thionate*]

Mencap *n* ➧ **Royal Mencap Society**

Mencius /ménshi əss, -shəss/ (371?–289 BC) Chinese philosopher. The successor of Confucius, he argued that humans are born good and are made better or worse by their environment. Born **Meng-tzu**

Mencken /méngkən/, **H. L.** (1880–1956) US journalist and critic. An authority on the American language, he was also an effective satirist. Full name **Mencken, Henry Louis**

> 'The public...demands certainties...But there *are* no certainties.'
> [H. L. Mencken, *Prejudices, First Series*; 1919]

> 'Conscience is the inner voice which warns us that someone may be looking.'
> [H. L. Mencken, *A Little Book in C Major*; 1916]

mend /mend/ *v* (**mends, mending, mended**) **1.** *vti* RESTORE SOMETHING TO SATISFACTORY CONDITION to restore something that is damaged or faulty to its original condition or a satisfactory condition **2.** *vt* REMOVE DAMAGE to fill, cover, or otherwise remove damage such as a hole or break **3.** *vti* IMPROVE SOMETHING to improve something or make it more acceptable, or be improved or made more acceptable ○ *You'd better mend your ways.* **4.** *vi* RECOVER OR HEAL to return to a healthy state after illness or injury ■ *n* REPAIR WORK an instance of repair work or a repaired place on a damaged object, especially a darn on a piece of clothing [12C. Partly shortening of AMEND, and partly < Anglo-Norman *mender*, shortening of *amender*; (see AMEND)] —**mendable** *adj* —**mender** *n* ◇ **on the mend** recovering or healing after illness or injury

mendacious /men dáyshəss/ *adj* **1.** having lied in the past, or prone to lying at any time **2.** deliberately untrue [Early 17C. < Latin *mendac-* 'lying'] —**mendaciously** *adv* —**mendaciousness** *n*

mendacity /men dássəti/ (*plural* **-ties**) *n* **1.** deliberate untruthfulness **2.** a lie or falsehood [Mid-17C. < French *mendacité* < Latin *mendax* 'lying']

Mende /méndi/ (*plural same* or **-des**) *n* **1.** a member of a people living in Sierra Leone **2.** the Niger-Congo language of the Mende people. Native speakers: 1 million. [Mid-18C. < Mende] —**Mende** *adj*

Mendel /ménd'l/, **Gregor** (1822–84) Austrian monk and scientist. Through his experiments he developed the principles of heredity, and so laid the basis of modern genetics. Full name **Mendel, Gregor Johann** —**Mendelian** /men deéli ən/ *adj*

mendelevium /méndə leévi əm/ *n* a synthetic short-lived radioactive element. Source: bombardment of einsteinium atoms with helium particles. Symbol **Md.** See table at **element** [Mid-20C. After Dmitry Ivanovich MENDELEYEV]

Mendeleyev /méndə láyef/, **Dmitry Ivanovich** (1834–1907) Russian chemist. He formulated the periodic law of elements and devised the periodic table (1869), using it to predict the existence of several then-unknown elements. He wrote a classic text, *Principles of Chemistry* (1868–70).

Mendelism /méndəlizəm/, **Mendelianism** /men deéli ənizəm/ *n* the theory of heredity formulated by Mendel, which explains how some characteristics are passed on from one generation to the next through genes

Mendel's Laws *npl* the laws of heredity formulated by Mendel to explain the transmission of characteristics from one generation to the next. There are two laws, the Law of Segregation and the Law of Independent Assortment.

Mendelssohn /ménd'lssən/, **Felix** (1809–47) German composer. His orchestral, choral, and keyboard works are key pieces of the romantic tradition. Full name **Mendelssohn-Bartholdy, Jakob Ludwig Felix**

> 'Anything but national music! May ten thousand devils take all folklore. Here I am in Wales...a harpist sits in the lobby of every inn of repute playing so-called folk melodies at you—i.e. dreadful, vulgar, fake stuff, and *simultaneously* a hurdy-gurdy is tootling out melodies...it's even given me a toothache.'
> [Felix Mendelssohn. Quoted in *A Life in Letters*, Rudolf Elvers (ed.), Craig Tomlinson (tr.); 1986]

Menderes /méndə ress/ river in southwestern Turkey, flowing west from the Anatolian Plateau into the Aegean Sea. Length: 584 km/363 mi.

mendicant /méndikənt/ *adj* LIVING ON CHARITY begging for and living on money given by strangers ■ *n* **1.** BEGGAR a beggar, especially somebody who begs in the street (*formal*) **2.** FRIAR WHO LIVES BY BEGGING a member of a religious order such as the Franciscans, Dominicans, Carmelites, or Augustinians that forbids the ownership of property and encourages working or begging for a living [14C. < Latin *mendicant-*, present participle of *mendicare* 'beg' < *mendicus* 'beggar' < *mendum* 'a defect']

mending /ménding/ *n* articles, especially clothes, to be mended

Mendip Hills /méndip-/ range of limestone hills in southwestern England. Its highest peak is Black Down, 326 m/1,068 ft.

Mendoza /men dṓzə/ city in western Argentina, the capital of Mendoza Province. Population: 121,620 (1991).

meneer /mə neér/ *n S Africa* in Afrikaans, the equivalent to 'Mr', or a respectful form of address equivalent to 'sir' [Mid-17C. Via Afrikaans < Dutch *mijnheer* 'my lord']

Menelaus /ménni láyəss/ *n* in Greek mythology, the king of Sparta and husband of Helen of Troy

Menelik II /ménnəlik/ (1844–1913) emperor of Ethiopia. He formed a united Ethiopian empire, resisting incursions by Italy and embarking on a programme of colonial expansion.

Menem /mén em/, **Carlos** (*b.* 1930) president of Argentina (1989–99). A Peronist politician, he was first elected president in 1989 and then allowed to stand for a second term in 1995 after a constitutional amendment in 1994. He ran for president again in 2003, but withdrew on the eve of the election. Full name **Menem, Carlos Saúl**

menfolk /mén fōk/ *npl* **1.** the male members of a family or group **2.** men in general or considered collectively

MEng /em éng/ *abbr* Master of Engineering

Mengistu Haile Mariam /meng gístoo hīli márri əm/ (*b.* 1937) Ethiopian politician. He served on the executive committee of the military government that succeeded Haile Selassie in 1974 and emerged as its leader in 1977. He made Ethiopia a Communist state and served as president from 1987 until he was forced to flee the country in 1991.

menhaden /men háyd'n/ (*plural* **-dens** or *same*) *n* a sea fish of the herring family. Use: mainly as a source of oil, fertilizer, bait. Native to: North America. Latin name: *Brevoortia tyrannus*. [Mid-17C. Origin ?]

menhir: le grand menhir, Dol, Brittany, France

menhir /mén heer/ *n* a large single upright stone, erected by prehistoric people and thought to have been used for astronomical observations, found in the British Isles and northern France [Mid-19C. Directly or via French < Breton *maen-hir* < *men* 'stone' + *hir* 'long']

menial /méeni əl/ *adj* **1.** UNSKILLED relating to or involving work that requires little skill or training, is not interesting, and confers low social status on somebody doing it **2.** RELATING TO SERVANTS suitable for, done by, or relating to a servant or servants ■ *n* **1.** DOMESTIC SERVANT a domestic servant, especially one of low status **2.** SOMEBODY WHO DOES MENIAL WORK somebody employed to do work that requires no skill or training (*formal*) [14C. < Anglo-Norman, 'of a household' < Latin *mansion-* < *manere* 'remain'] —**menially** *adv*

Ménière's disease /máyn yairz-/, **Ménière's syndrome** *n* a disorder caused by an accumulation of fluid in the labyrinths of the inner ear. Symptoms include vertigo, persistent ringing in the ears, and some loss of hearing. [Late 19C. After Prosper *Ménière* (1799–1862), French physician]

Menindee Lakes /mə níndi-/ group of reservoirs in New South Wales, southeastern Australia

mening- *prefix* same as **meningo-** (*used before vowels*)

meninges /mə nín jeez/ *npl* the three membranes that surround and protect the brain and the spinal cord, called the dura mater, the arachnoid mater, and the pia mater [Early 17C. Via modern Latin < Greek *mēnigg-* 'membrane'] —**meningeal** *adj*

meningi- *prefix* same as **meningo-**

meningioma /mə nínji ómə/ (*plural* **-mas** or **-mata** /-mətə/) *n* a slow-growing benign tumour that affects the meninges of the brain or spinal cord and may cause serious damage by compression [Early 20C. Shortening of *meningothelioma* < MENINGO- + ENDOTHELIOMA]

meningitis /ménnin jītiss/ *n* a serious, sometimes fatal illness in which a viral or bacterial infection inflames the meninges, causing symptoms such as severe headaches, vomiting, stiff neck, and high fever —**meningitic** /-jíttik/ *adj*

meningo- *prefix* meninges ○ *meningocele* [< Greek *mēnigg-*, stem of *mēninx* 'membrane']

meningocele /me níng gō seel/ *n* the protrusion of the meninges through the skull or backbone to form a cyst

meningococcus /mə níng gō kókəss/ (*plural* **-cocci** /-kók sī/) *n* a bacterium that causes cerebrospinal meningitis. Latin name: *Neisseria meningitidis*. —**meningococcal** *adj* —**meningococcic** /-kóksik/ *adj*

meningoencephalitis /mə níng gō en kéffə lítiss, -séffə-/ *n* an inflammation of the brain and the meninges —**meningoencephalitic** /-líttik/ *adj*

meninx /mónningks/ *n* ANAT singular of **meninges**

meniscus /mə nískus/ (*plural* **-ci** /-níssī/ or **-cuses**) *n* **1.** UPPER SURFACE OF LIQUID the curved upper surface of a still liquid in a tube, concave if the liquid wets the walls of the container, convex if it does not, caused by surface tension **2.** CARTILAGE DISC a crescent-shaped cartilage disc cushioning the end of a bone where it meets another bone in a joint, especially in the knee **3.** CONCAVO-CONVEX LENS a lens that is convex on one side and concave on the other **4.** CRESCENT SHAPE a crescent-shaped body or figure [Late 17C. Via modern Latin < Greek *mēniskos* 'little moon' < *mēnē* 'moon'] —**meniscal** *adj* —**meniscate** *adj* —**meniscoid** *adj* —**meniscoidal** /mónniss kóyd'l/ *adj*

Mennonite /ménnə nīt/ *n* a member of a Protestant denomination emphasizing adult baptism and pacifism and rejecting church organization and, in many cases, the holding of public office and the taking of oaths. There are many different bodies of Mennonites throughout the world, with especially large communities in the United States and Canada. [Mid-16C < German *Mennonit*, after *Menno* Simons (1496–1561), early Frisian leader of the group] —**Mennonitism** *n*

meno /ménnō/ *adv* less quickly or softly (*used as a musical direction*) [Late 19C. < Italian, 'less']

meno- *prefix* menstruation ○ *menopause* [< Greek *mēn(ē)* 'month' < Indo-European]

menology /mi nólləji/ (*plural* **-gies**) *n* a church calendar of the months, especially in the Eastern Orthodox Church, that shows saints' days and gives biographies of the saints [Early 17C. Via modern Latin < ecclesiastical Greek *mēnologion* 'month-reckoning' < *mēn* 'month']

Menominee /mə nómminee/ (*plural* same or **-nees**), **Menomini** (*plural* same or **-nis**) *n* **1.** a member of a Native North American people of northeastern Wisconsin **2.** the extinct Algonquian language of the Menominee people [Mid-18C. < Ojibwa *manōminī* 'wild-rice person'] —**Menominee** *adj*

meno mosso /ménnō móssō/ *adv* at a slower speed (*used as a musical direction*) [< Italian, 'less agitated']

Menon /ménnən/, **V. K. Krishna** (1896–1974) Indian politician. He was a leading member of the Indian nationalist movement in the 1920s and 1930s. He was forced to resign as India's defence minister (1957–62) after a border war with China. Full name **Menon, Vengalil Krishnan Krishna**

'The expression "positive neutrality" is a contradiction in terms. There can be no more positive neutrality than there can be a vegetarian tiger.'
[V. K. Krishna Menon, *New York Times*; 18 October 1960]

menopause /ménnō pawz/ *n* the time in a woman's life when menstruation diminishes and ceases, usually between the ages of 45 and 50 [Late 19C. < MENO- + Greek *pausis* 'pause' < *pausein* 'to stop'] —**menopausal** /ménnō páwz'l/ *adj* —**menopausic** *adj*

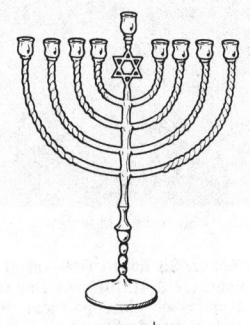
menorah

menorah /mə náwrə/ *n* **1.** a ceremonial candleholder consisting of a central stem surrounded by six curved branches, used in the Jewish Temple and as an emblem of Judaism and the state of Israel **2.** an eight-branched candleholder, lit during the Jewish festival of Hanukkah [Late 19C. < Hebrew *měnōrāh* 'candlestick']

Menorca /mi náwrkə/, **Minorca** Spanish island in the western Mediterranean Sea, the second largest of the Balearic Islands. Population: 66,900 (1989). Area: 695 sq. km/268 sq. mi. Spanish name **Menorca** —**Menorcan** *adj*, *n*

menorrhagia /ménnə ráyji əl/ *n* unusually heavy or prolonged bleeding during menstruation —**menorrhagic** *adj*

menorrhoea /ménnə rée əl/, **menorrhea** *n* normal bleeding during menstruation [Mid-19C. Back-formation < AMENORRHOEA]

Menotti /mə nótti/, **Gian-Carlo** (*b.* 1911) Italian-born US composer. He is known for his operas, including *The Consul* (1950) and *The Saint of Bleecker Street* (1954).

Mensa /ménssə/ *n* **1.** a faint constellation of the southern hemisphere that forms part of the larger Magellanic Cloud **2.** an international organization for people with a very high IQ. Members are admitted after passing an IQ test. [Mid-20C. < Latin, 'table']

mensal[1] /ménss'l/ *adj* occurring monthly [Mid-19C. < Latin *mensis* 'month']

mensal[2] /ménss'l/ *adj* used or done at the meal table, or connected with eating meals [15C. < late Latin *mensalis* < Latin *mensa* 'table']

mensch /mensh/ (*plural* **menschen** /-sh'n/ or **mensches**), **mensh** (*plural* **menshen** or **menshes**) *n N Am* somebody good, kind, decent, and honourable (*informal*) [Mid-20C. Via Yiddish < Old High German *mennisco* 'person, human']

menses /mén seez/ *n* (*technical; takes a singular or plural verb*) **1.** menstruation, or the period of time that it lasts **2.** the blood and other matter discharged from the womb during menstruation [Late 16C. < Latin, plural of *mensis* 'month']

mensh *n N Am* another spelling of **mensch** (*informal*)

Menshevik /ménshəvik/ (*plural* **-viks** or **-viki** /-víki/) *n* a member of the moderate minority faction of the Marxist Social Democratic Party in pre-revolutionary Russia that advocated a gradual approach to social reform, in contrast to the Bolsheviks [Early 20C. < Russian *men'shevik* < *men'she* 'less'; because the Socialist reform they favoured was less extreme than that favoured by the Bolsheviks] —**Menshevism** *n* —**Menshevist** *n*

mens rea /menz ráyə/ *n* prior intention to commit a criminal act, with the knowledge that the act is a crime. For all but some minor statutory offences, mens rea is basic to establishing the actual guilt of somebody alleged to have committed a crime. [< modern Latin, 'guilty mind']

men's room *n N Am* same as **gents**

mens sana in corpore sano /ménz saánə in káwpəri saánō/ *n* a healthy mind in a healthy body, as an ideal in living [< Latin]

menstrual /ménstroo əl/ *adj* occurring during, or connected with, menstruation

menstrual cycle *n* the monthly process of ovulation and menstruation that occurs between puberty and menopause in women and female primates who are not pregnant

menstruate /ménstroo ayt/ (**-ates**, **-ating**, **-ated**) *vi* to discharge blood and other matter from the womb as part of the menstrual cycle [Early 19C. < late Latin *menstruat-*, past participle of *menstruare* < Latin *menstruus* 'monthly, menstrual' < *mensis* 'month']

menstruation /mén stroo áysh'n/ *n* the monthly process of discharging blood and other matter from the womb that occurs between puberty and menopause in women and female primates who are not pregnant

menstruous /mén stroo əss/ *adj* PHYSIOL same as **menstrual**

mensurable /ménshərəb'l/ *adj* **1.** capable of being measured **2.** MUSIC same as **mensural** (sense 2) [Late 16C. < late Latin *mensurabilis* < Latin *mensura* (see MEASURE)]

mensural /ménshərəl/ *adj* **1.** relating to or involving measurement or measurable values **2.** describes notes, particularly in medieval music, that have a fixed length or time value relative to one another [Late 16C. < Latin *mensuralis* < *mensura* (see MEASURE)]

mensuration /ménshə ráysh'n/ *n* **1.** the calculation of geometric quantities such as length, area, and volume from dimensions and angles that are already known **2.** the act, process, or skill of measuring something (*formal*) [Late 16C. < late Latin *mensuration-* < Latin *mensura* (see MEASURE)]

menswear /ménz wair/ *n* **1.** clothing designed to be worn by men **2.** the department in a shop that sells menswear

-ment *suffix* **1.** action, process ○ *arraignment* ○ *betterment* **2.** result of an action, or condition resulting from an action ○ *bewilderment* **3.** instrument or agent of an action ○ *refreshment* **4.** place ○ *emplacement* ○ *escarpment* [Directly or via French < Latin *-mentum*]

mental /mént'l/ *adj* **1.** RELATING TO MIND relating to, found in, or occurring in the mind ○ *mental stimulation* **2.** CARRIED OUT IN MIND carried out in the mind without any physical action or the use of any physical aid ○ *mental arithmetic* **3.** PRODUCED BY MIND produced by the mind and visible only in the mind ○ *mental imagery* **4.** OFFENSIVE TERM an offensive term meaning having a psychiatric disorder **5.** OFFENSIVE TERM an offensive term meaning extremely unintelligent or silly (*insult*) [15C. < French < Latin *ment-* 'mind'] —**mentally** *adv* ◇ **chuck** *or* **throw a mental** *Aus* an offensive phrase meaning to become very angry or upset

mental age *n* a measure of intellectual development using norms against which children can be compared with other children of the same chronological age ○ *a four-year-old with a mental age of seven*

mental block *n* an inability to carry out a mental task such as remembering something, especially when caused by subconscious emotional factors

mental challenge *n* a condition that limits the ability to learn and to function independently, as a result of congenital causes, brain injury, or disease

mental cruelty *n* the infliction of psychological pain on somebody

mental disorder *n* in English law, a psychiatric disorder or impairment of mental faculties

mental handicap *n* an offensive term for a mental challenge

mental hospital *n* PSYCHIAT same as **psychiatric hospital** (*offensive*)

mental illness *n* any psychiatric disorder that causes untypical behaviour

mental impairment *n* in English law, a state of mental development that negatively affects somebody's intellectual capacity and ability to function

mentalism /mént'lizəm/ *n* the belief that all objects of knowledge, including the physical universe, ultimately have no existence except as creations of the mind —**mentalist** *n* —**mentalistic** /mént'l ístik/ *adj*

mentality /men tálləti/ (*plural* **-ties**) *n* **1.** a habitual way of thinking or interpreting events peculiar to a person or type of person, especially with reference to the behaviour that it produces **2.** somebody's intellectual ability

mental lexicon *n* the words of a language that somebody knows the meanings of, can use, or uses habitually

mentally challenged *adj* affected by a mental challenge

mental reservation *n* a tacit qualification of a statement or oath made when it would be unwise or disadvantageous to express doubt or disagreement openly ○ *agreed to testify without any mental reservation*

mental retardation *n* an offensive term for difficulty in learning or functioning independently (*dated*)

mentation /men táysh'n/ *n* (*formal*) **1.** mental activity, especially thinking **2.** somebody's state of mind or general attitude [Mid-19C. < Latin *ment-* 'mind']

mentee /men teé/ *n* somebody who is mentored [Late 20C. < MENTOR]

menthol /mén thol/ *n* an organic compound that has a cool minty taste. Source: peppermint oil. Use: flavourings, perfumes, mild anaesthetic. Formula:

$CH_3C_6H_9(C_3H_7)OH$. [Late 19C. < German, 'mint-oil' < Latin *mentha* (see MINT [1])]

mentholated /ménthə laytid/ *adj* flavoured with or containing menthol

mention /ménsh'n/ *v* (**-tions, -tioning, -tioned**) **1.** *vti* SAY OR WRITE SOMETHING to refer to something when speaking or writing, often in a brief or casual way ○ *I happened to mention your name to her.* ○ *He mentioned that the word was spelt wrongly.* **2.** *vt* CITE SOMEBODY FOR BRAVERY to refer to somebody by name in an official report as a way of acknowledging exceptional conduct, especially during a military action ■ *n* **1.** CASUAL REFERENCE a reference to a particular person or thing, often made in a brief or casual way **2.** ACKNOWLEDGMENT OF SOMEBODY'S EXCEPTIONAL CONDUCT an acknowledgment, especially in an official report, of somebody's exceptional conduct [14C. Via French < Latin *mention-* 'calling to mind'] —**mentionable** *adj* ◇ **don't mention it** used in reply to an expression of thanks as a polite way of saying that none is necessary ◇ **not to mention** used to emphasize a point by introducing somebody who or something that needs to be taken into consideration and is even more significant than what has been spoken of before

mento /méntō/ (*plural* **-tos**) *n Carib* **1.** Jamaican music similar Calypso that is based on a folk dance rhythm **2.** a composition or dance in mento style [Early 20C. Origin ?]

mentor /mén tawr/ *n* **1.** EXPERIENCED ADVISER AND SUPPORTER somebody, usually older and more experienced, who advises and guides a younger, less experienced person **2.** TRAINER a senior or experienced person in a company or organization who gives guidance and training to a junior colleague ■ *vt* (**-tors, -toring, -tored**) BE MENTOR TO SOMEBODY to act as a mentor to somebody, especially a junior colleague [Mid-18C. Via French < Latin < Greek *Mentōr* 'Mentor']

Mentor /mén tawr/ *n* in Greek mythology, the friend whom Odysseus left in charge of the household while he was at Troy and who was the teacher and protector of Telemachus, Odysseus's son

mentoring /méntəring/ *n* the task of acting as a mentor to somebody, especially a junior colleague, or the system of appointing mentors

menu /ménnyoo/ *n* **1.** LIST OF DISHES AVAILABLE a list of the dishes that can be ordered in a restaurant or that are to be served at a formal meal **2.** LIST OF PROGRAM OPTIONS a list on a computer screen of the options available to the user **3.** LIST OR COLLECTION a list of things available, or a collection of things from which a selection can be made [Mid-19C. < French, 'minute, detailed' < Latin *minutus* (see MINUTE [1])]

menu-driven *adj* describes computer software that is operated by selecting options from a menu

Menuhin /ményoo in/, **Yehudi, Baron Menuhin of Stoke d'Abernon** (1916–99) US-born British violinist. He was known as much for mentoring younger players as for his own virtuoso performances.

> 'Music creates order out of chaos; for rhythm imposes unanimity upon the divergent, melody imposes continuity upon the disjointed, and harmony imposes compatibility upon the incongruous.'
> [Yehudi Menuhin, *Sunday Times*; 10 October 1976]

Sir Robert Menzies

Menzies /ménziz/, **Sir Robert** (1894–1978) Australian prime minister (1939–41, 1949–66). During his premierships, he pursued close political ties with the United Kingdom and firmly aligned Australia eco-

nomically and militarily with the United States. Full name **Menzies, Sir Robert Gordon**. See table at **prime minister**

meow *n, vi* another spelling of **miaow**

MEP *abbr* **1.** EDUC Master of Engineering Physics **2.** POL Member of the European Parliament

mepacrine /méppəkrin/ *n* a synthetic drug. Use: formerly, treatment of malaria and worm infections. [Mid-20C. Blend of *methoxy + pentane + acridine*]

meperidine /mə pérri deen/ *n N Am* PHARM same as **pethidine** [Mid-20C. Blend of METHYL + PIPERIDINE]

Mephistopheles /méffi stóffə leez/, **Mephisto** /mə fístō/ *n* in medieval legend, a subordinate to the devil, one of the seven archangels cast out of heaven, to whom Faust sold his soul —**Mephistophelean** /méffistə feéli ən/ *adj*

mephitic /mi fíttik/, **mephitical** /-ik'l/ *adj* relating to or resembling a poisonous or foul smell (*formal*) [Early 17C. < late Latin *mephiticus* 'pestilential' < Latin *mephitis* 'foul smell'] —**mephitically** *adv*

mephitis /mi fítiss/ *n* **1.** a foul-smelling or poisonous vapour coming out of the ground **2.** a foul smell (*literary*) [Early 18C. < Latin]

meprobamate /mə próbə mayt, mépprō bámmayt/ *n* a bitter white powder. Use: tranquillizer, muscle relaxant. Formula: $C_9H_{18}N_2O_4$. [Mid-20C. Blend of METHYL + PROPYL + CARBAMATE]

mer. *abbr* GEOG meridian

mer- *prefix* same as **mero-** (*used before vowels*)

-mer *suffix* polymer ○ *oligomer* [Back-formation < -MERISM]

Merano /mə raánō/ city and health resort in Bolzano Province, Trentino-Alto Adige Region, northeastern Italy. Population: 33,504 (1996).

meranti /mi ránti/ *n* a tree that yields a white, yellow, or red hardwood. Native to: Southeast Asia. Genus: *Shorea*. [Late 18C. < Malay]

merbromin /mur brōmin/ *n* a green crystalline solid that forms a red solution when dissolved in water. Use: antiseptic. Formula: $C_{20}H_8Br_2HgNa_2O_6$. [Mid-20C. < MERCURIC + BROM-]

Mercalli scale /mur kálli-/ *n* a scale for measuring the intensity of earthquakes, ranging from 1 to 12, in which 1 denotes a weak earthquake and 12 one that causes complete destruction [Early 20C. After Giuseppe *Mercalli* (1850–1914), Italian geologist]

mercantile /múrkən tīl/ *adj* **1.** used for trade or by merchants, or characteristic of merchants or trading **2.** relating to or characteristic of mercantilism [Mid-17C. < French < Italian *mercante* 'merchant' < Latin *mercari* (see MERCHANT)]

mercantile marine *n* NAVY same as **merchant navy**

mercantilism /múrkəntilizəm, múrkən tīlizəm/ *n* **1.** an early modern European economic theory and system that actively supported the establishment of colonies that would supply materials and markets and relieve home nations of dependence on other nations **2.** the principles and methods of commerce —**mercantilist** *n, adj* —**mercantilistic** /múrkənti lístik, -tī-/ *adj*

mercaptan /mur káp tan/ *n* CHEM same as **thiol** [Mid-19C. < modern Latin (*corpus*) *mercurium captans* '(substance) that seizes mercury']

mercaptopurine /mur káptō pyoór een/ *n* a drug that interferes with the synthesis of purines. Use: treatment of leukaemia, other cancers. Formula: $C_5H_4N_4S$. [Mid-20C. < MERCAPTAN + PURINE]

Mercator /mur káytər/, **Gerardus** (1512–94) Flemish geographer, cartographer, and mathematician. His map projection allowed compass courses to be plotted as straight lines, and is widely used in navigation. Born **Kremer, Gerhard**

Mercator Projection *n* a method of making a map of the globe on a flat surface in which the meridians and latitudes are shown as straight lines that cross at right angles [Mid-17C. After Gerardus MERCATOR]

mercenary /múrss'nəri/ *n* (*plural* **-ies**) **1.** SOLDIER FIGHTING FOR MONEY a professional soldier paid to fight for an army other than that of his or her country **2.** SOMEBODY INTERESTED ONLY IN PROFIT an employee who works only for personal gain ■ *adj* **1.** MOTIVATED ONLY BY MONEY motivated solely by a desire for money **2.** RELATING TO MERCENARIES paid to serve in a foreign army, or consisting of mercenaries [14C. Directly or via

French *mercenaire* < Latin *mercen(n)arius* 'hireling' < *merces* 'wages'] —**mercenarily** *adv* —**mercenariness** *n*

mercer /múrssər/ *n* a dealer in silks and other fine cloth, especially formerly [13C. < Anglo-Norman < Latin *merc-* 'merchandise']

mercerize /múrssə rīz/ (**-izes, -izing, -ized**), **mercerise** (**-ises, -ising, -ised**) *vt* to treat cotton fabric or thread with an alkali to strengthen it and make it more lustrous and more receptive to dyes [Mid-19C. After John *Mercer* (1791–1866), British calico printer] —**mercerization** /múrssə rī záysh'n/ *n*

merchandise /múrchən dīz/ *n* GOODS goods bought and sold for profit ■ *v* **1. merchandise** (*3rd person present singular* **-dises,** *present participle* **-dising,** *past and past participle* **-dised**) *vti* TRADE COMMERCIALLY to trade in or buy and sell products for profit **2.** (*3rd person present singular* **merchandises,** *present participle* **merchandising,** *past and past participle* **merchandised**) *vt* MARKET PRODUCTS to promote a product by developing strategies for packaging, display, and publicity [13C. < French *marchandise* 'goods' < Old French *marchant* (see MERCHANT)] —**merchandisable** *adj* —**merchandiser** *n*

merchandising /múrchən dīzing/ *n* **1.** the promotion of a product by developing strategies for packaging, displaying, and publicizing it **2.** commercial products that are developed as spin-offs from the success of a film, TV programme, sports team, or event

merchant /múrchənt/ *n* **1.** COMMERCIAL DEALER somebody who buys and sells goods, especially as a wholesaler or internationally **2.** SOMEBODY NOTED FOR PARTICULAR ACTIVITY somebody who is noted for a particular activity or quality (*informal; usually used in combination*) ○ *a speed merchant in a souped-up car* ■ *adj* **1.** RELATING TO TRADE used for or relating to commerce, wholesalers, or retailers **2.** OF MERCHANT NAVY relating to, belonging to, or involving a merchant navy ■ *vt* (**-chants, -chanting, -chanted**) DEAL IN SOMETHING to trade or deal in products [12C. < Old French *marchant* < Latin *mercari* 'to trade' < *merc-* 'merchandise']

CULTURAL NOTE ***The Merchant of Venice***, a play (1596–97) by William Shakespeare. The story revolves around a loan made by Jewish usurer Shylock to Venetian merchant Antonio, and Shylock's subsequent attempts to claim the pound of flesh he has stipulated as security. Among the more serious issues raised in this blend of comedy, romance, and realism are the correct administration of justice and the power conferred by wealth. The well-known saying 'It is a wise father that knows his own child' comes from this play.

Merchant /múrchənt/, **Ismail** (*b.* 1936) Indian film producer and director. In partnership with James Ivory, he produced films set in South Asia and created adaptations of Western literary classics.

merchantable /múrchəntəb'l/ *adj* suitable or of a sufficiently high quality for buying and selling

merchant account *n* **1.** a bank account that enables a merchant to receive the proceeds of credit card purchases **2.** a bank account that enables the holder to deposit payments made by credit card, used especially in connection with trading on the Internet

merchant bank *n* a bank that provides financial services mainly for companies and large-scale investors —**merchant banker** *n* —**merchant banking** *n*

merchant certificate authority *n* in e-commerce, a certificate authority that provides certificates to merchants

merchantman /múrchəntmən/ (*plural* **-men** /-mən/) *n* SHIPPING same as **merchant ship**

merchant navy *n* a country's fleet of merchant ships, or the sailors who serve in them. N Am term **merchant marine**

merchant prince *n* an extremely wealthy, powerful, and prestigious merchant, especially in Renaissance Italy

merchant ship *n* a seagoing ship designed to carry goods, especially for international trade

Mercia /múrssi ə, múrshi ə/ ancient Anglo-Saxon kingdom of central England —**Mercian** *adj, n*

merciful /múrssif'l/ *adj* **1.** showing mercy or compassion to somebody **2.** welcome because of putting an end to something unpleasant or distressing —**mercifulness** *n*

mercifully /múrssif'li/ *adv* **1.** so as to show mercy or compassion **2.** ⚠ in a way or at a time that prevents or ends something unpleasant

USAGE See ***sentence adverb***.

merciless /múrssiləss/ *adj* **1.** LACKING MERCY showing no mercy or compassion towards somebody or something **2.** SEVERE very harsh in the judgment and treatment of others **3.** RELENTLESS continuing at a high level of violence or unpleasantness without pause or relief —**mercilessly** *adv* —**mercilessness** *n*

Merckx /murks/, **Eddy** (*b.* 1945) Belgian bicycle racer. Winner of five Tours de France (1969–74) and numerous other races, he also broke the world hour record (1972).

mercur- *prefix* mercury ○ *mercurous* [< MERCURY]

mercurate /múr kyŏŏ rayt/ (**-rates, -rating, -rated**) *vt* to treat or combine something with mercury —**mercuration** /múr kyŏŏ ráysh'n/ *n*

mercurial /mur kyóori əl/ *adj* **1.** LIVELY AND UNPREDICTABLE lively, witty, fast-talking, and likely to do the unexpected **2.** CONTAINING MERCURY containing or caused by mercury ■ *n* MEDICINE CONTAINING MERCURY formerly, a drug or chemical preparation containing mercury [Late 16C. < MERCURIAL] —**mercuriality** /mur kyóori álləti/ *n* —**mercurially** *adv* —**mercurialness** *n*

Mercurial /mur kyóori əl/ *adj* **1.** relating to the Roman god Mercury **2.** relating to the planet Mercury [14C. Directly or via French *mercuriel* < Latin *mercurialis* < *Mercurius* (see MERCURY)]

mercurialise *vt* another spelling of **mercurialize**

mercurialism /mur kyóori əlizəm/ *n* poisoning caused by ingesting mercury

mercurialize /mur kyóori əlīz/ (**-izes, -izing, -ized**), **mercurialise** (**-ises, -ising, -ised**) *vt* to treat somebody or something with mercury or with a compound containing mercury —**mercurialization** /mur kyóori ə lī záysh'n/ *n*

mercuric /mur kyóorik/ *adj* relating to or containing mercury with a valency of two

mercuric chloride *n* a white crystalline solid that is poisonous and soluble. Use: insecticide, fungicide, wood preservative, in photography. Formula: $HgCl_2$.

mercuric oxide *n* a poisonous orange-yellow solid. Use: pigment. Formula: HgO.

mercuric sulphide *n* a poisonous compound existing as a red or black solid. Use: pigment. Formula: HgS.

mercurous /múrkyŏŏrəss/ *adj* relating to or containing mercury with a valency of one

mercurous chloride *n* a white poisonous insoluble powder. Use: fungicide, formerly in medicines. Formula: Hg_2Cl_2.

mercury /múrkyŏŏri/ (*plural* *same* or **-ries**) *n* **1.** LIQUID METALLIC ELEMENT a poisonous heavy silver-white metallic element that is liquid at room temperature. Source: cinnabar. Use: thermometers, barometers, pharmaceuticals, dental amalgams, lamps. Symbol **Hg**. See table at **element** **2.** TEMPERATURE OR PRESSURE the mercury in a weather thermometer or barometer, or the air temperature or pressure it indicates ○ *The mercury rose steadily throughout the early part of the day.* **3.** WEEDY PLANT a weedy plant of the spurge family. Genus: *Mercurialis.* [14C. < Latin *Mercurius* (see MERCURY)]

Mercury /múrkyŏŏri/ *n* **1.** in Roman mythology, the god of commerce and rhetoric, who also acted as a messenger between humans and gods. His symbol is the caduceus, a staff with two snakes entwined around it. Greek equivalent **Hermes** **2.** the smallest planet in the solar system and the one nearest the Sun [12C. < Latin *Mercurius* < *merc-* 'merchandise']

mercury chloride *n* CHEM same as **mercuric chloride**

mercury-vapour lamp *n* an electric lamp whose bluish-green light is generated when electricity is passed through a vapour of low-pressure mercury. Its light has a strong ultraviolet component, and these rays are used for cosmetic and therapeutic treatment.

mercy /múrssi/ (*plural* **-cies**) *n* **1.** COMPASSION kindness or forgiveness shown especially to somebody a person has power over ○ *The judge showed mercy and imposed the shortest sentence he could.* **2.** COMPASSIONATE DISPOSITION a disposition to be compassionate or forgiving of others ○ *a killer completely without mercy* **3.** SOMETHING TO BE THANKFUL FOR a welcome event or situation that provides relief or prevents something unpleasant from happening ○ *It was a mercy that no one was hurt in the accident.* **4.** EASING OF DISTRESS the easing of distress or pain ○ *The supply convoy was on a mission of mercy.* [12C. Via French *merci* 'thank you' < Latin *merces* 'reward, wages'] ◇ **at the mercy of somebody** *or* **something** completely unprotected against whatever somebody or something does

mercy flight *n* an aircraft flight undertaken to bring medical help to an ill or injured person in a remote area or to transport the person to hospital

mercy killing *n* **1.** euthanasia regarded as motivated by compassion **2.** an act of killing somebody out of compassion, often at that person's request, in order to end his or her pain or distress

mercy seat *n* **1.** in Judaism, the gold covering on the Ark of the Covenant, regarded as God's resting place **2.** in Christianity, the throne of God in heaven

mere[1] /meer/ (*superlative* **merest**) *adj* **1.** just what is specified and nothing more, usually emphasizing the smallness, humbleness, or unimportance of the thing or person designated ○ *She was no mere journalist.* ○ *The merest hint of danger sent them all running for cover.* **2.** by itself and without anything more ○ *The mere mention of Arthur's name would make him upset.* [14C. Directly or via Anglo-Norman *meer*, Old French *mier* < Latin *merus* 'pure, unmixed']

mere[2] /meer/ *n* a body of standing fresh water, especially a lake (*archaic or literary; often used in placenames*) [Old English, 'sea' < Indo-European]

mere[3] /mérri/ *n* a short flat curved club used as a weapon by Maoris [Early 19C. < Maori]

-mere *suffix* part, segment ○ *centromere* [< Greek *meros* 'part']

Meredith /mérrə dith/, **George** (1828–1909) British novelist and poet. His novels are noted for their psychological analysis and distinctive style. They include *The Egoist* (1879) and *Diana of the Crossways* (1885).

> 'A kiss is but a kiss now! and no wave / Of a great flood that whirls me to the sea / But, as you will! we'll sit contentedly, / And eat our pot of honey on the grave.'
> [George Meredith, 'Modern Love'; 1862]

> 'Speech is the small change of silence.'
> [George Meredith, *The Ordeal of Richard Feverel*; 1859]

merely /méerli/ *adv* no more than as described, or doing no more than what is described ○ *I was merely pointing out where you had gone wrong.* ○ *merely a temporary setback*

merengue /mə réng gay/ *n* **1.** a ballroom dance, originally from the Dominican republic, characterized by hip and shoulder movements **2.** the music for a merengue [Mid-20C. Via American Spanish < Haitian creole *méringue* 'meringue' < French]

meretricious /mérrə tríshəss/ *adj* **1.** SUPERFICIALLY ATTRACTIVE attractive in a superficial or vulgar manner but without real value (*formal*) ○ *meretricious extras that don't really add to the car's value* **2.** MISLEADINGLY PLAUSIBLE seemingly plausible or significant, but actually insincere or false (*formal*) ○ *Don't be swayed by this meretricious argument in the project's favour.* **3.** OF PROSTITUTES relating to or like a prostitute (*archaic*) [Early 17C. < Latin *meretricius* < *meretric-* 'prostitute' < *mereri* 'serve for hire'] —**meretriciously** *adv* —**meretriciousness** *n*

merganser

merganser /mur gánssər/ (*plural* **-sers** or *same*) *n* a fish-eating diving duck with a crested head and a long beak notched like a saw blade. Genus: *Mergus.* See illustration on previous page [Mid-17C. < modern Latin < Latin *mergus* 'diver' + *anser* 'goose']

merge /murj/ **(merges, merging, merged)** *vti* **1.** to combine or unite with something to form a single entity, or make two or more things do this ○ *Two of the country's largest banks have decided to merge.* **2.** to blend, or make two or more things blend, gradually ○ *The sky and sea seem to merge at the horizon.* [Mid-17C. < Latin *mergere* 'to plunge, dip'] —**mergence** *n* —**merging** *n*

merger /múrjər/ *n* **1.** the joining together of two or more companies or organizations **2.** a blending, combining, or joining of something with something else, or the state of being blended, combined, or joined together [Early 18C. < Anglo-Norman < Latin *mergere* 'to plunge']

merguez /máir gez, mər géz/ (*plural same*) *n* a highly spiced North African sausage, usually made with lamb or mutton

Mérida /mérridə/ **1.** city in western Spain, in Badajoz Province. Population: 50,790 (2002). **2.** city in southeastern Mexico, the capital of Yucatán State. It was founded by the Spanish on a Maya site in 1542. Population: 705,055 (2000).

meridian /mə ríddi ən/ *n* **1.** GEOG **LINE OF LONGITUDE** an imaginary line between the North and South poles that crosses the equator at right angles. A meridian is designated by the degrees of longitude that it is west or east of the prime meridian. **2.** GEOG **HALF OF CIRCLE BETWEEN POLES** either half of the circle of the meridian, from pole to pole **3.** ASTRON **CELESTIAL GREAT CIRCLE** a great circle of the celestial sphere that passes through the celestial poles and the zenith of the observer **4.** ALTERN MED **LINE OF ACUPUNCTURE POINTS** in acupuncture, one of the pathways in the body along which the body's energy is believed to flow and along which acupuncture points are located **5.** **HIGHEST POINT** the peak or a high point, e.g. of development or success (*literary*) ○ *the decade when the empire's power reached its meridian* [14C. Directly or via French < Latin *meridianum* < *meridies* 'midday', alteration of *medidies* < *medius* 'middle' + *dies* 'day']

meridian circle *n* ASTRON same as **transit circle**

meridional /mə ríddi ən'l/ *adj* **1.** **OF MERIDIAN** along, belonging to, relating to, or like a meridian **2.** **OF SOUTHERN REGIONS** characteristic of or located in the south, especially southern Europe **3.** **OF SOUTHERN PEOPLES** relating to or characteristic of people who live in the south, especially southern Europe ■ *n* **SOUTHERN PERSON** somebody who comes from the south, especially southern France [14C. Via French < late Latin *meridionalis* < Latin *meridies* (see MERIDIAN)] —**meridionally** *adv*

Mérimée /mérri may/, **Prosper** (1803–70) French writer. His works include the novella *Carmen* (1846), the basis of Bizet's opera. He was also a historian.

> 'Like most men he was much more eloquent in asking than in thanking.'
> [Prosper Mérimée, *La Double Méprise (A Slight Misunderstanding)*; 1833]

meringue /mə ráng/ *n* **1.** a mixture of egg whites and sugar beaten until stiff, cooked, and used as a topping for tarts or to make biscuits and shells **2.** a cake, biscuit, or shell made of meringue, often with a cream filling [Early 18C. < French]

merino /mə reénō/ *n* (*plural* **-nos**) **1.** *also* **merino sheep** **SHEEP BRED FOR WOOL** a sheep belonging to a breed originally developed in Spain that is kept for its wool in many parts of the world, especially Australia **2.** **WOOL** the long fine white wool of the merino sheep **3.** **YARN OR FABRIC** a fine yarn or fabric made from the wool of the merino sheep, often mixed with cotton ■ *adj* **OF MERINO WOOL** made of merino wool ○ *a merino shawl* [Late 18C. Via Spanish < Arabic *(banū) marīn*, a Berber people]

-merism *suffix* denoting a relationship between chemical constituents ○ *isomerism* [< Greek *meros* 'part']

meristem /mérri stem/ *n* embryonic plant tissue that is actively dividing, as found at the tip of stems and roots [Late 19C. < Greek *meristos* 'divided' < *merizein* 'to divide' < *meros* 'part'] —**meristematic** /mérristə máttik/ *adj* —**meristematically** *adv*

meristic /mə rístik/ *adj* **1.** divided into or having segments **2.** involving a change in the number or arrangement of body parts or segments [Late 19C. < Greek *meris, meros* 'part'] —**meristically** *adv*

merit /mérrit/ *n* **1.** **VALUE** value that deserves respect and acknowledgment ○ *a work of considerable technical and artistic merit* **2.** **GOOD QUALITY** a good or praiseworthy characteristic that somebody or something has (*often used in the plural*) **3.** **ABILITY** proven ability or accomplishment ○ *She got her promotion based on merit.* **4.** RELIG **SPIRITUAL CREDIT** spiritual worthiness achieved by doing good works ■ **merits** *npl* **FACTS OF CASE** the facts of a matter considered without regard for emotional, procedural, or other issues ○ *to consider a proposal on its merits* ■ *vt* **(-its, -iting, -ited)** **DESERVE SOMETHING** to be worthy of or earn something ○ *Some people feel the award wasn't merited.* ○ *This merits closer inspection.* [12C. Via French *mérite* < Latin *meritum* 'price', form of the past participle of *merere* 'earn']

meritocracy /mérri tókrəssi/ (*plural* **-cies**) *n* **1.** **SYSTEM BASED ON ABILITY** a social system that gives opportunities and advantages to people on the basis of their ability rather than, e.g. their wealth or seniority **2.** **ELITE GROUP** an elite group of people who achieved their positions on the basis of ability and achievement **3.** **LEADERSHIP BY ELITE** leadership by an elite group of people who are chosen on the basis of their abilities and achievements —**meritocratic** /mérritō kráttik/ *adj*

meritorious /mérri táwri əss/ *adj* deserving honour and recognition ○ *She was awarded a medal for meritorious service.* [15C. < Latin *meritorius* < *merere* 'earn'] —**meritoriously** *adv* —**meritoriousness** *n*

merle /murl/, **merl** *n* same as **blackbird** *n* (sense 1) (*archaic or literary*) [15C. < French < Latin *merula*]

Merleau-Ponty /múrlō póNti/, **Maurice** (1908–61) French philosopher. An existentialist, he was noted for his critical writings on behaviourism and the phenomenology of perception.

> 'We should not ask ourselves if we perceive the world truly; on the contrary: the world is that which we perceive.'
> [Maurice Merleau-Ponty, *Phenomenology of Perception*; 1945]

merlin

merlin /múrlin/ *n* a small dark falcon with a broad black band on the end of its tail. Native to: northern hemisphere. Latin name: *Falco columbarius.* [14C. < Anglo-Norman *merilun*, alteration of Old French *esmirillon* 'large merlin' < *esmiril* 'merlin']

Merlin /múrlin/ *n* in Arthurian legend, a magician and adviser to King Arthur

merlon /múr lon/ *n* a solid part between two openings **(crenels)** in a battlement, e.g. on a castle [Early 18C. Via French < Italian *merlone* 'large battlement' < *merlo* 'battlement']

Merlot /múrlō/, **merlot** *n* **1.** a red wine made from a variety of black grape originally grown in France **2.** a black grape that is used to make Merlot wine [Early 19C. < French, 'small blackbird' < *merle* 'blackbird', probably from the colour of the grape]

mermaid /múr mayd/ *n* a mythical sea creature with the head and upper body of a woman and the tail of a fish instead of legs [14C. < MERE [2]]

merman /múr man/ *n* a mythical sea creature with the head and upper body of a man and the tail of a fish instead of legs [Early 17C. < MERE [2]]

mero- *prefix* part, partial ○ *merozoite* ○ *meroplankton* [< Greek *meros* 'part']

meroblastic /mérrō blástik/ *adj* used to describe an egg undergoing only partial division after being fertilized, with the undivided cells becoming the yolk —**meroblastically** *adv*

merocrine /mérrō krīn/ *adj* relating to or produced by glands that make secretions without cell damage or disintegration [Early 20C. < MERO- + Greek *krinein* 'to separate']

Meroë /mérrō i/ **1.** ruined city in northern Sudan, on the River Nile **2.** ancient kingdom of Nubia, in present-day northern Sudan

meroplankton /mérrō plángktən/ (*plural* **-tons** or *same*) *n* organisms that are plankton only for part of their life cycle, usually during the larval stage —**meroplanktonic** /mérrō plangk tónnik/ *adj*

-merous *suffix* having a particular number or kind of parts ○ *tetramerous* ○ *heteromerous* [< Greek *meros* 'part']

Merovingian /mérrō vínji ən/ *adj* belonging or relating to a dynasty of Frankish kings that was founded by Clovis I and reigned in Gaul and Germany from about AD 500 to 751 ■ *n* a member of the Merovingian dynasty [Late 17C. < French *mérovingien* < Latin *Meroveus* 'Merowig' (d. 458), grandfather of Clovis]

merozoite /mérrō zṓ īt/ *n* any protozoan cell produced by the fission of a schizont, e.g. that of the malaria protozoan

merperson /múr purss'n/ (*plural* **-people** /-peep'l/ or **-persons**) *n* in legends and fairy tales, a mermaid or merman [After MERMAID]

Merrick /mérrik/ hill in southwestern Scotland, the highest peak in the south of the country. Height: 843 m/2,765 ft.

merriment /mérrimənt/ *n* fun and enjoyment marked by noise and laughter

merry /mérri/ **(-rier, -riest)** *adj* **1.** **LIVELY AND CHEERFUL** full of or showing lively cheerfulness or enjoyment ○ *a merry laugh* **2.** **TIPSY** mildly drunk (*informal*) **3.** **FUNNY** very funny or amusing (*dated*) ○ *a merry quip* **4.** **DELIGHTFUL** tending to produce cheerfulness or happiness in people (*archaic*) ○ *the merry month of May* [Old English *myrige* 'pleasant' < Germanic, 'short'] —**merrily** *adv* —**merriness** *n* ◇ **make merry** to enjoy yourself, especially by taking part in a celebration or festivity ◇ **the more the merrier** extra people are welcome to come along or join in

CULTURAL NOTE ***The Merry Wives of Windsor***, a play (1600–01) by William Shakespeare. Shakespeare's only play wholly in prose was written to exploit the popularity of Falstaff, a comic character in *Henry IV.* It tells of Falstaff's attempts to seduce two married women in order to gain access to their wealth, the wives' discovery of his plan, and their imaginative revenge.

merry bone *n N England* a bird's wishbone

merry-go-round *n* **1.** a fairground or amusement park ride with a rotating circular platform fitted with seats that are usually shaped like animals such as horses and move up and down to music **2.** a busy or continuous cycle of fast-paced activities or events ○ *a merry-go-round of press interviews and promotional events* **3.** *N Am* same as **roundabout** *n* (sense 2)

merrymaking /mérri mayking/ *n* lively celebration, fun, or enjoyment —**merrymaker** *n*

merry men *npl* somebody's followers (*humorous*)

merse /murss/ *n Scotland* an area of flat, often marshy, alluvial land near a river or estuary [Early 19C. < Old English *mersc*]

Merse /murss/ rich agricultural region of the Scottish Borders

Mersey /múrzi/ river in NW England, flowing into the Irish Sea near Liverpool. Length: 110 km/70 mi.

Mersey beat /múrzi-/ *n* pop music of the 1960s that originated in the Merseyside area, especially Liverpool, and was performed by groups such as the Beatles

Merseyside /múrzi sīd/ former metropolitan county of northwestern England from 1974 to 1986

Mersey sound *n* MUSIC same as **Mersey beat**

Merthyr Tydfil /múrthər tídvil/ town in southern Wales, formerly an important centre of coalmining and iron smelting. Population: 55,981 (2001).

merwoman /múr wŏŏmən/ (*plural* **-women** /-wimin/) *n* in

legends and fairy tales, an older or mature mermaid [Early 19C. After MERMAID]

mes- *prefix* same as **meso-** (*used before vowels*)

mesa: Devil's Tower, Wyoming, United States

mesa /máyssə/ *n Southwest US* a relatively flat elevated area with steep sides that is less extensive than a plateau [Mid-18C. < Spanish, 'table' < Latin *mensa*]

Mesa /máyssə/ city and holiday resort in south-central Arizona, southeast of Phoenix. Population: 426,841 (2002 estimate).

Mesa, Carlos (*b.* 1953) president of Bolivia (2003–). He was vice president (2002–3) when conflict over the country's natural gas reserves forced his predecessor to resign. Full name **Gisbert, Carlos Diego Mesa**

mésalliance /me zálli ənss/ *n* a marriage with somebody of a lower social position, regarded as a bad match [Late 18C. < French, 'bad alliance' < *alliance* 'alliance' < Old French *aliance*]

mesarch /méssaark, méz-/ *adj* describes a succession of plant or animal communities (**sere**) that originates in a moist habitat [Late 19C. < MESO- + Greek *arkhē* 'beginning, origin']

Mesa Verde National Park /máyssə vúrdi-/ national park in southwestern Colorado, established in 1906. It is noted for its well-preserved ancient cliff dwellings. Area: 211 sq. km/81 sq. mi.

mescal /més kal/ (*plural* **-cals** or *same*) *n* **1.** a colourless Mexican spirit distilled from the fermented sap of some species of agave plant **2.** *Southwest US* DRUGS, PLANTS same as **peyote** [Early 18C. Via Spanish *mezcal* < Nahuatl *mexcalli* 'mescal liquor']

Mescalero /méskə láirō/ (*plural same* or **-ros**) *n* a member of a Native North American people who lived in Mexico, New Mexico, and Texas, and now live mainly in southern New Mexico [Mid-19C. < Spanish < *mezcal* (see MESCAL)]

mescaline /méskəlin, -leen/, **mescalin** /-lin/ *n* a hallucinogenic drug that is extracted from the button-shaped nodules on the stem of the peyote cactus [Late 19C. < German *Mezcalin* < Spanish *mezcal* (see MESCAL)]

mescla /mésklə/ *n* a drug made from the residue of processing cocaine, which is mixed with marijuana and smoked [< American Spanish, 'mixture']

mesclun /méssklən/ *n* a green salad made from several types of young leaf, typically including rocket, dandelion, radicchio, and endive [Late 20C. < Provençal *mesclar* 'to mix' < Old French *mescler* < Latin *miscere*]

Mesdames 1. plural of **Madame 2.** plural of **Madam**

mesdemoiselles plural of **mademoiselle**

mesembryanthemum /mi zémbri ánthiməm/ (*plural* **-mums** or *same*) *n* a small succulent plant with thick fleshy leaves. Flowers: like daisies, in many colours. Native to: southern Africa. Genus: *Mesembryanthemum*. [Late 18C. < modern Latin < Greek *mesēmbria* 'noon' + *anthemon* 'flower']

mesencephalon /méss en séffə lon/ *n* same as **midbrain** (*technical*) —**mesencephalic** /méss enssi fállik/ *adj*

mesenchyme /méss eng kīm/ *n* the cells within the embryo that develop into connective tissue, bone, cartilage, blood, and the lymphatic system [Late 19C. < Greek *mesos* 'middle' + *egkhuma* 'infusion'] —**mesenchymal** /mi séngkim'l/ *adj* —**mesenchymatous** /méss eng kímmətəss/ *adj*

mesentera ANAT plural of **mesenteron**

mesenteritis /me séntə rítiss/ *n* inflammation of the mesentery of the peritoneum

mesenteron /me séntə ron/ (*plural* **-tera** /-tərə/) *n* the middle section of the embryonic intestine, which develops into the stomach, small intestine, and most of the large intestine —**mesenteronic** /me séntə rónnik/ *adj*

mesentery /méss'ntəri/ (*plural* **-ies**) *n* **1.** a membrane that supports an organ or body part, especially the double-layered membrane of the peritoneum attached to the back wall of the abdominal cavity that supports the small intestine **2.** a supportive membrane surrounding and giving structure to the inner organs of invertebrates [15C. Via modern Latin *mesenterium* < Greek *mesenteron* 'middle intestine' < *enteron* 'intestine'] —**mesenteric** /méss'n térrik/ *adj*

mesh /mesh/ *n* **1.** MATERIAL LIKE NET material, or a piece of material, made of plastic, thread, or wire woven together like a net ○ *wire mesh* **2.** OPENING IN NET the open space between the threads or wires of a net **3.** STRANDS OF NET the threads or wires that make up a net **4.** TRAP something that holds or entangles like a net or a trap (*often used in the plural*) ○ *caught in the meshes of the criminal underworld* **5.** SOMETHING INTERWOVEN an interwoven or interlinked arrangement or construction ○ *the mesh of the girders against the sky* **6.** INTERLOCKING METAL LINKS a material consisting of interlocking metal links, used in jewellery **7.** MECH ENG ENGAGEMENT OF GEARS engagement of the teeth on gearwheels **8.** INDUST OPENING IN SCREEN a measure of the number of openings in a screen for sorting things into different sizes, usually per inch. A 20-mesh screen has 20 openings per inch. ■ *vti* (**meshes, meshing, meshed**) **1.** FIT TOGETHER to fit or work closely or well together, or make things work closely or well together ○ *Her vision of the company's future meshes perfectly with ours.* **2.** CATCH OR ENTANGLE to catch or entangle somebody or something, or become caught or entangled, in a mesh **3.** MECH ENG ENGAGE GEARWHEELS to engage together, or make the teeth on gearwheels engage together [14C. Probably < Middle Dutch *maesche* < Indo-European, 'knot'] —**meshy** *adj*

meshuga /mə shoóggə/, **meshugah** *adj* totally unreasonable or thoughtless (*slang insult*) [Late 19C. Via Yiddish *meshuge* < Hebrew *mĕshuggā*]

meshuggener /mə shoóggənər/, **meshugana** /mə shoógganə/ *n* somebody considered to be entirely unreasonable or thoughtless (*slang insult*) [Early 20C. Variant of MESHUGA]

meshwork /mésh wurk/ *n* material consisting of meshes

mesial /méezi əl/ *adj* relating to or occurring along the dental arch near the middle of the front of the jaw [Early 19C. < Greek *mesos* 'middle'] —**mesially** *adv*

mesic[1] /méezik/ *adj* growing in or characterized by moderate moisture [Early 20C. < Greek *mesos* 'middle'] —**mesically** *adv*

mesic[2] /méezik/ *adj* relating to a meson [Mid-20C. < MESON]

Mesic /máysich/, **Stjepan** (*b.* 1934) president of Croatia (2000–). The last president of the former Yugoslavia before its breakup (1991), he joined the centrist Croatian People's Party (1997) but left after being elected, in order to be 'president of all Croats'.

mesmeric /mez mérrik/ *adj* completely absorbing somebody's attention [Early 19C. < *Mesmer* (see MESMERIZE)] —**mesmerically** *adv*

mesmerise *vt* another spelling of **mesmerize**

mesmerism /mézmərizəm/ *n* **1.** the power to fascinate somebody in a way that is almost hypnotic **2.** hypnotism, formerly believed to involve animal magnetism [Late 18C. < *Mesmer* (see MESMERIZE)] —**mesmerist** *n*

mesmerize /mézmə rīz/ (**-izes, -izing, -ized**), **mesmerise** (**-ises, -ising, -ised**) *vt* **1.** to fascinate somebody or absorb all of somebody's attention ○ *The speaker mesmerized the audience with his dramatic tale.* **2.** to hypnotize somebody, especially by a method formerly believed to involve animal magnetism [Early 19C. After F. A. *Mesmer* (1734–1815), Austrian physician] —**mesmerization** /mézmə rī záysh'n/ *n* —**mesmerizer** *n* —**mesmerizingly** *adv*

mesne /meen/ *adj* in law, happening or appearing between two other things, especially assignments

of property [Mid-16C. < legal French, a variant of Anglo-Norman *meen* 'middle']

mesne profits *npl* intermediate profits received by a tenant who is in wrongful possession of an estate, which the landlord is entitled to recover

meso- *prefix* middle, intermediate ○ *mesopelagic* [< Greek *mesos* < Indo-European]

Mesoamerica /méssō ə mérrikə/ region of Central America and southern North America that was occupied by several civilizations, especially the Maya, in pre-Columbian times —**Mesoamerican** *adj*, *n*

mesoblast /méssō blast/ *n* BIOL same as **mesoderm**

mesocarp /méssō kaarp/ *n* the middle layer of a fruit wall (**pericarp**), e.g. the fleshy part of some fruits

mesocratic /méssō kráttik/ *adj* describes igneous rock containing as much as 60 per cent of heavy dark ferromagnesian minerals in its composition

mesoderm /méssō durm/ *n* the middle of the three cell layers in an embryo, from which connective tissue, muscle, blood, dermis, and bone develop —**mesodermal** /méssō dúrm'l/ *adj* —**mesodermic** /méssō dúrmik/ *adj*

mesoglea /méssō glee ə/, **mesogloea** *n* a layer of gelatinous substance separating the inner and outer walls of a coelenterate such as a jellyfish [Late 19C. < modern Latin, 'middle glue' < Greek *glia* 'glue'] —**mesogleal** *adj*

Mesolithic /méssō líthik/, **mesolithic** *n* the middle period of the Stone Age, between the Palaeolithic and Neolithic —**Mesolithic** *adj*

mesomorph /méssō mawrf/ *n* a large muscular body, or somebody who has such a body

meson /mée zon/ *n* an elementary particle such as a pion or kaon that has a rest mass between that of an electron and a proton and participates in the strong interaction. Mesons consist of a quark and an antiquark, and have a spin that is zero or an integer. —**mesonic** /mi zónnik/ *adj*

mesopause /méssō pawz/ *n* the upper boundary of the mesosphere, approximately 80 km/50 mi. above the Earth's surface

mesopelagic /méssōpə lájjik/ *adj* found in or relating to the intermediate oceanic depths between approximately 100 and 1,000 m/300 and 3,300 ft

mesophyll /méssōfil/ *n* the soft tissue (**parenchyma**) containing chlorophyll between the epidermal layers of a plant leaf —**mesophyllic** /méssō fíllik/ *adj* —**mesophyllous** /méssō fílləss/ *adj*

mesophyte /méssō fīt/ *n* a land plant that needs moderate amounts of moisture for growth —**mesophytic** /méssō fíttik/ *adj*

mesopore /méssō pawr/ *n* a tiny pore, between 2 and 50 nanometres in diameter, in a material such as carbon used to filter objects —**mesoporosity** /méssō paw róssəti/ *n* —**mesoporous** *adj*

Mesopotamia /méssəpə táymi ə/ ancient region located between the rivers Tigris and Euphrates in modern Iraq and Syria. It was the site of several early urban civilizations, including Babylonia. —**Mesopotamian** *n, adj*

mesosome /méssō sōm/ *n* an indentation in the cell membrane of some bacteria

mesosphere /méssō sfeer/ *n* the layer of the Earth's atmosphere in which temperature decreases rapidly, located between the stratosphere and thermosphere —**mesospheric** /méssō sférrik/ *adj*

mesothelioma /méssō theeli ómə/ (*plural* **-mata** or **-mas** /-ōmətə/) *n* a benign or malignant tumour of the lining of the lungs, heart, or abdomen. The malignant form is often the result of exposure to asbestos and may take more than 30 years to develop.

mesothelium /méssō theeli əm/ (*plural* **-liums** or **-lia** /-ə/) *n* a cell layer derived from mesoderm that lines the body cavity of a vertebrate embryo and develops into epithelia and muscle tissue —**mesothelial** *adj*

mesothorax /méssō tháwraks/ (*plural* **-raxes** or **-races** /-rə seez/) *n* the middle of the three segments of an insect's thorax, from which the middle pair of legs and first pair of wings grow —**mesothoracic** /méssō thaw rássik/ *adj*

Mesozoic /méssō zō ik/ *n* the era of geological time, 248 million to 65 million years ago, during which

dinosaurs, birds, and flowering plants first appeared. See table at **geological time** —**Mesozoic** *adj*

mesquite /me skéet/ (*plural same* or **-quites**) *n Southwest US* **1.** a hard wood often burned in a barbecue to flavour food **2.** a small spiny leguminous tree or bush with hard wood, the pods of which are sometimes used as fodder. Native to: southwestern United States, Mexico. Genus: *Prosopis*. [Mid-18C. Via Mexican Spanish *mezquite* < Nahuatl *mizquitl*]

mess /mess/ *n* **1. UNTIDY CONDITION** a dirty or untidy state ○ *The flat was left in a terrible mess after the party.* **2. CHAOTIC STATE** a chaotic, confused, or troublesome state or situation ○ *Their business affairs were in a complete mess.* ○ *The workmen have made a complete mess of the repairs.* **3. UNTIDY PERSON OR THING** somebody or something in a confused, dirty, or untidy state (*informal*) **4. EXCREMENT** animal excrement (*informal*) ○ *Someone had tramped dog mess on the front steps.* **5. PLACE FOR COMMUNAL MEALS** a place where a group of people, especially members of the armed forces, have meals together **6. PEOPLE WHO EAT TOGETHER** a group of people, especially members of the armed forces, who have meals together (*takes a singular or plural verb*) **7. COMMUNAL MEAL** a meal eaten together by a group of people, especially members of the armed forces **8. QUANTITY OF FOOD** a serving or quantity of food, especially of soft or soggy food ■ *v* (**messes, messing, messed**) **1.** *vti* **MAKE SOMETHING DIRTY** to make something dirty, muddled, or disordered ○ *She messed her jacket while checking the oil.* **2.** *vi* **MEDDLE** to interfere in something ○ *Don't mess in their business.* **3.** *vi* **USE SOMETHING CARELESSLY** to use something carelessly, causing a problem or damage as a result ○ *Who's been messing with my computer?* **4.** *vi* **EAT TOGETHER** to take meals along with a particular group of people, especially members of the armed forces ○ *I used to mess with the three of them.* ○ *We messed together in the army.* [13C. < Old French, 'portion of food' < Latin *mittere* 'send, put']

mess around, mess about *v* **1.** *vi* **WASTE TIME** to waste time in an unproductive or aimless manner (*informal*) **2.** *vi* **RELAX** to spend time in a leisurely and pleasant manner (*informal*) **3.** *vt* **INTERFERE** to interfere or meddle in something (*informal*) ○ *Don't mess in their business.* **4.** *vi* **BEHAVE IN UNSERIOUS WAY** to joke or behave playfully (*informal*) ○ *I thought he was just messing around.* **5.** *vt* **TREAT SOMEBODY BADLY** to treat somebody badly or unfairly, e.g. by continual changes of mind or lack of honesty (*informal*) ○ *Neil felt that he was being messed around by his manager.* **6.** *vi US* **ASSOCIATE WITH SOMEBODY** to associate with somebody, especially somebody who is seen as undesirable (*informal*) ○ *She started messing around with that crowd last summer.* **7.** *vi N Am* **BE SEXUALLY UNFAITHFUL** to have sexual activity with somebody other than a spouse or regular sexual partner (*slang*)

mess up *v* (*informal*) **1.** *vti* **RUIN SOMETHING** to spoil or bungle something, or make a mistake ○ *The rain messed up our plans to go for a picnic.* **2.** *vt* **MAKE SOMETHING MESSY** to make something dirty or disordered **3.** *vt* **UPSET SOMEBODY** to confuse or upset somebody

mess with *vt* (*informal*) **1.** to interfere or meddle in something in a way that may have bad consequences **2.** to try to thwart or deceive somebody

message /méssij/ *n* **1. COMMUNICATION** a communication in speech, writing, or signals, usually a brief one, and often one left for a recipient who cannot be directly contacted at the time **2. MEANING** a lesson, moral, or important idea communicated, e.g. in a work of art **3. ERRAND** the mission or errand of a messenger (*dated*) ○ *sent on a message to her grandmother's* **4.** *US* **ADVERTISEMENT** an advertisement, especially one on television, paid for by the sponsors of a programme or event ○ *and now a message from our sponsor* ■ **messages** *npl Scotland* **SHOPPING** shopping, especially the everyday necessities ○ *I'm away to get the messages.* ■ *vt* (**-sages, -saging, -saged**) **1. COMMUNICATE WITH SOMEBODY** to send a message to somebody ○ *Can you message me about that?* **2. COMMUNICATE SOMETHING TO SOMEBODY** to send something as a message ○ *to message the news to your boss* [13C. < French < Latin *missus*, past participle of *mittere* 'send'] ◇ **get the message** to take something in and understand it (*informal*)

message board *n* ONLINE same as **bulletin board** (sense 2)

message code authentication *n* the cryptographic verification of the author and integrity of an e-mail message

Messager /méssa zhay/, **André** (1853–1929) French composer. He was noted chiefly for his operettas such as *Véronique* (1898). Full name **Messager, André Charles Prosper**

message stick *n Aus* a wooden stick carved with symbols, traditionally carried by Aborigines as a form of identification or to help the bearer remember an important message

messaging /méssijing/ *n* **1.** a system for sending messages to people, e.g. by computer, telephone, or pager **2.** the process of sending a message using a messaging system

messaline /méssə léen/ *n* a soft shiny lightweight silk fabric. Use: clothing. [Early 20C. < French, after Valeria *Messalina*, wife of the Roman emperor Claudius]

~~**messanger**~~ incorrect spelling of **messenger**

Messeigneurs plural of **Monseigneur**

messenger /méss'njər/ *n* **1. SOMEBODY CARRYING MESSAGE** somebody who carries messages between people **2. PAID COURIER** an employee who carries and delivers messages, especially a courier **3. SOMEBODY RUNNING ERRAND** somebody who runs an errand **4.** NAUT **LIGHT ROPE** a lightweight rope used to haul a heavier one, e.g. from one ship to another [12C. < French *messager* < *message* (see MESSAGE)]

Messenger /méss'njər/, **Dally** (1883–1959) Australian rugby league player. He scored a record-breaking 155 points during the first Australian rugby league tour of England in 1908. Born **Messenger, Herbert Henry**

messenger bag *n* a satchel-shaped bag, usually made of synthetic material, used for carrying documents or small items

messenger line *n* NAUT same as **messenger** (sense 4)

messenger RNA *n* a form of RNA that is transcribed from a strand of DNA and translated into a protein sequence at a cell ribosome

Messerschmitt /méssər shmit/ *n* a fighter aircraft, especially the Me-109 or the Me-262, used by the German Air Force in World War II

Messerschmitt /méssərshmit/, **Willy** (1898–1978) German aircraft designer. His Messerschmitt Me-109 set a world speed record (1939), and his Messerschmitt Me-262, used by the German Air Force in World War II, was the first jet fighter plane. Born **Messerschmitt, Wilhelm**

mess hall *n* a building or room where a group of people, especially members of the armed forces, eat their meals together

Messiaen /méssi oN, -ən/, **Olivier** (1908–92) French composer and organist. His works for organ, piano, voice, chamber ensemble, and orchestra have a mystic quality and a unique harmonic language. Full name **Messiaen, Olivier Eugène Prosper Charles**

messiah /mə sí ə/ *n* somebody regarded as or claiming to be a saviour or liberator of a country, people, or the world [Mid-17C. < MESSIAH] —**messiahship** *n*

Messiah /mə sí ə/ *n* **1.** in Christianity, Jesus Christ regarded as the Messiah prophesied in the Hebrew Bible **2.** in the Hebrew Bible, an anointed king who will lead the Jews back to the land of Israel and establish justice in the world [12C. < French *Messie* < Greek *Messias* < Aramaic *mĕšīhā* and Hebrew *māšīăh* 'anointed' < *māšah* 'anoint'] —**Messiahship** *n*

CULTURAL NOTE ***The Messiah***, an oratorio (1742) by German composer George Frederick Handel. Consisting of biblical scriptures selected by Charles Jennens set to music by Handel, this enduringly popular work is noted for the power of its (distinctively Anglican) religious expression. For a time in the 19th century, it became fashionable to perform the work with an enormous orchestra and chorus.

messianic /méssi ánnik/ *adj* **1.** *also* **Messianic** JUDCHR **RELATING TO MESSIAH** belonging or relating to the Messiah **2.** JUDAISM **OF JUDAIC GOLDEN AGE** relating to, belonging to, or constituting a Judaic golden age of peace, truth, and happiness **3. OF LIBERATOR** relating or belonging to an inspirational leader, especially one claiming to be or regarded as a saviour or liberator **4. INVOLVING GREAT ENTHUSIASM** done with or showing great enthusiasm or devotion ○ *preaching with messianic fervour* —**messianically** *adv*

messianism /mə sí ənizəm/, **Messianism** *n* belief in the coming of the Messiah or a messiah or messianic age

Messieurs plural of **Monsieur**

Messina /me séenə/ historic Italian city and seaport in northeastern Sicily. Population: 261,134 (1999).

Messina, Strait of strait between Sicily and the Italian mainland, linking the Ionian and Tyrrhenian seas. Length: 32 km/20 mi.

mess jacket *n* a waist-length jacket worn as part of a military uniform, especially on formal occasions

mess kit *n* **1.** a compact set of cooking and eating utensils, usually made of metal, used especially by soldiers or campers **2.** a dress uniform worn by officers and senior noncommissioned officers at formal dinners

messmate /méss mayt/ *n* **1.** somebody with whom somebody regularly eats, especially in a military mess **2.** *Aus* a eucalyptus tree found in southeastern Australia. Latin name: *Eucalyptus obliqua*.

Messrs /méssərz/ *npl* the customary title used before the name of more than one man or in names of companies named after a person ○ *Messrs Smith and Jones* ○ *bought from Messrs Wright* [Late 18C. Abbreviation of MESSIEURS]

messuage /mésswij/ *n* a dwelling with its outbuildings and the surrounding land that is used by the dwelling's occupants [14C. < Anglo-Norman]

mess-up *n* a complete mistake or totally unsuccessful attempt at something (*informal*)

messy /méssi/ (**-ier, -iest**) *adj* **1. DIRTY OR DISORDERED** involving, producing, or marked by dirt or disorder ○ *Repairing a car can be a messy business.* **2. DIFFICULT TO SORT OUT** complicated and unpleasant to resolve or deal with ○ *a messy divorce* **3. CARELESS** showing a lack of carefulness or precision ○ *an erroneous conclusion resulting from messy reasoning* —**messily** *adv* —**messiness** *n*

mestiza /mess téezə/ *n* a woman with mixed ancestry, especially a woman in Latin America of both Native American and European ancestry [Late 16C. < Spanish, form of MESTIZO]

mestizo /mess téezō/ (*plural* **-zos** or **-zoes**) *n* somebody with mixed ancestry, especially somebody in Latin America of both Native American and European ancestry. Mestizos form the largest population group in many Latin American countries. [Late 16C. Via Spanish < Latin *mixtus*, past participle of *miscere* 'mix']

mestranol /méstrə nol/ *n* a synthetic oestrogen. Use: oral contraceptives. [Mid-20C. < METHYL + ESTRANE]

met /met/ past participle, past tense of **meet**[1]

Met /met/ *abbr* **1.** Meteorological Office **2.** Metropolitan Opera House (in New York) **3.** Metropolitan Police

met. *abbr* **1.** METALL metallurgy **2.** LITERAT metaphor **3.** PHILOSOPHY metaphysics **4.** METEOROL meteorological **5.** METEOROL meteorology **6.** metropolitan

met- *prefix* same as **meta-** (*used before vowels*)

meta- *prefix* **1.** later, behind ○ *metaphase* ○ *metathorax* **2.** beyond, transcending, encompassing ○ *metagalaxy* ○ *metalanguage* **3.** change, transformation ○ *metaplasia* **4.** higher, more developed ○ *metaxylem* **5.** used in chemical names ○ *metaphosphate* [< Greek *meta* 'beside, after' < Indo-European, 'between']

metabolic /méttə bóllik/ *adj* relating to or typical of metabolism [Mid-19C. < Greek *metabolikos* 'changeable' < *metabolē* (see METABOLISM)] —**metabolically** *adv*

metabolic pathway *n* a sequence of energy-producing, biochemical reactions catalysed by enzymes

metabolic rate *n* the speed at which the biochemical reactions of metabolism in living cells take place

metabolise *vti* BIOCHEM another spelling of **metabolize**

metabolism /mə tábbəlizəm/ *n* **1.** the series of processes by which food is converted into the energy and products needed to sustain life **2.** the biochemical activity of a particular substance in a living organism [Late 19C. < Greek *metabolē* 'change' < *metaballein* 'throw differently' < *ballein* 'to throw']

metabolite /mə tábbə līt/ *n* a by-product of metabolism [Late 19C. < METABOLISM]

metabolize /mə tábbə līz/ (**-lizes, -lizing, -lized**), **metabolise** (**-lises, -lising, -lised**) *vti* to subject something to metabolism, or undergo metabolism [Late 19C. < Greek *metabolē* (see METABOLISM)] —**metabolizable** *adj*

metabolome /mə tábbə lōm/ *n* the full complement of molecules of low molecular weight present in cells in a particular physiological or developmental state [Late 20C. Blend of METABOLITE + GENOME] —**metabolomic** /mə tábbə lōmmik/ *adj*

metabolomics /mə tábbə lōmmiks/ *n* the measurement of the metabolites of low molecular weight in an organism's cells at a specific time under specific environmental conditions (*takes a singular verb*)

metacarpal /méttə ka'arp'l/ *n* any bone in the human hand between the wrist and digits, or a corresponding bone in a vertebrate animal's forefoot ■ *adj* relating or belonging to the metacarpals —**metacarpally** *adv*

metacarpus /méttə ka'arpəss/ (*plural* **-pi** /-pī/) *n* **1.** the set of five long bones (**metacarpals**) in the human hand between the wrist and fingers **2.** the region between the wrist and digits of the forefoot or hand of a vertebrate animal

metacentre /méttə sentər/ *n* the intersection of the vertical line through the centre of buoyancy of an object at equilibrium with the vertical line through the centre of buoyancy when the object is tilted

metacentric /méttə séntrik/ *adj* **1.** relating or belonging to a metacentre **2.** describes a chromosome whose centromere is located at or near the middle

metachromatic /méttəkrō máttik/ *adj* **1.** taking on a colour atypical of the staining solution **2.** able to produce a colour in different shades in tissue or cells [Late 19C. < META- + Greek *khrōmat-* 'colour']

metachromatism /méttə krōmətizəm/ *n* a change in colour caused by a change in physical conditions such as temperature

metacognition /méttə kog nísh'n/ *n* knowledge of your own thoughts and the factors that influence your thinking —**metacognitive** /méttə kógnətiv/ *adj*

metadata /méttə daytə, -daatə/ *n* descriptive statistical information about the elements of a set of data (*takes a singular or plural verb*)

meta-ethics /méttə-/ *n* the branch of linguistic philosophy that analyses and seeks to clarify the meaning and use of ethical expressions such as 'good' and 'ought' (*takes a singular verb*) —**meta-ethical** *adj*

metafemale /méttə feé mayl/ *n* a female organism with an extra female chromosome

metafiction /méttə fiksh'n/ *n* **1.** fiction writing that deals, often playfully and parodically, with the nature of fiction, the techniques and conventions used in it, and the role of the author **2.** a work of metafiction —**metafictional** /méttə fíksh'nəl/ *adj* —**metafictionist** /méttə fíksh'nist/ *n*

metagalaxy /méttə galləksi/ *n* the total of all galaxies making up the universe —**metagalactic** /méttəgə láktik/ *adj*

metage /meétij/ *n* **1.** the official measurement of the contents or weight of a load, e.g. of coal or grain **2.** a charge for making an official measurement of the contents or weight of a load [Early 16C. < METE]

metagnathous /mə tágnəthəss/ *adj* describes the condition in which a bird has the tips of its beak crossed —**metagnathism** *n*

metal /méttˈl/ *n* **1.** TYPE OF CHEMICAL ELEMENT a chemical element that is malleable and ductile, usually solid, has a characteristic lustre, and is a good conductor of heat and electricity, e.g. copper or iron **2.** MIXTURE OF METALS a mixture (**alloy**) of one or more metals **3.** MUSIC same as **heavy metal** (sense 1) (*slang*) **4.** PRINTING TYPE printer's type made of metal **5.** MOLTEN GLASS molten glass for use in glassmaking **6.** HERALDRY GOLD OR SILVER in heraldry, gold or silver **7.** NAVY WEIGHT FIRED IN BROADSIDE the collective weight of the projectiles a warship can fire in a broadside **8.** ROADS same as **road metal** ■ **metals** *npl* RAILS the rails of a railway track ■ *vt* (**-als, -alling, -alled**) **1.** FIT SOMETHING WITH METAL to cover, fit, or provide something with metal **2.** MAKE OR MEND ROAD to make or repair a road with broken stones (**road metal**) [13C. Directly or via French < Latin *metallum* 'mine, metal' < Greek *metallon*]

SPELLCHECK metal or **mettle**? Do not confuse the spelling of *metal* and *mettle*, which sound similar. *Metal* is chiefly used as a noun denoting a type of chemical element, but also sometimes as a verb, meaning 'to provide something with metal' or 'to put broken stones on a

road'. *Mettle* is only a noun, meaning 'spirit' or 'mental character'

metal. *abbr* **1.** metallurgical **2.** metallurgy

metalanguage /méttə lang gwij/ *n* a language or system of symbols used to describe or analyse another language or system of symbols

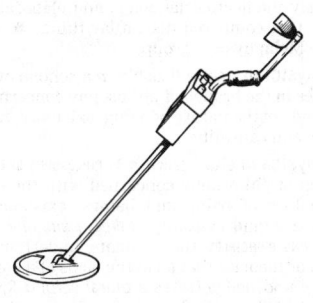

metal detector

metal detector *n* **1.** DEVICE FOR DETECTING BURIED METAL a portable electronic device with a search head that is swept over the ground and used to detect buried metal objects such as coins **2.** DEVICE FOR DETECTING WEAPONS an electronic device that registers the presence of metal, used, e.g. to detect metal weapons or to screen passengers at an airport **3.** DEVICE FOR DETECTING METAL IN FOOD an electronic device used in the food industry to check for the presence of pieces of metal that might have accidentally found their way into food during processing

metalinguistic /méttə ling gwístik/ *adj* relating to a metalanguage or to metalinguistics

metalinguistics /méttə ling gwístiks/ *n* (*takes a singular verb*) **1.** the branch of linguistics that deals with the study of metalanguages **2.** the branch of linguistics that deals with the relation between language and other aspects of culture

metalize *vt* MANUF US spelling of **metallize**

metall. *abbr* METALL **1.** metallurgical **2.** metallurgy

metall- *prefix* same as **metallo-** (*used before vowels*)

metallic /mə tállik/ *adj* **1.** CONTAINING OR BEING METAL made of, containing, or constituting metal or a metal **2.** OF METAL typical of a metal **3.** SHINY shiny and highly reflective ○ *a sports car with a metallic finish* **4.** TASTING OF METAL sharp and bitter to the taste ○ *This water has a slightly metallic taste.* **5.** SOUNDING LIKE STRUCK METAL like the sound of two metal objects knocking against each other **6.** HARSH-SOUNDING harsh and unpleasant in tone ○ *speaking with a metallic edge to her voice* —**metallically** *adv*

metallic bond *n* a chemical bond characteristic of metals, in which electrons are shared between atoms and move about in the crystal

metallicity /méttə líssəti/ *n* the amount of a specific metal contained in something such as a star, galaxy, or composite material. The ratio of iron to hydrogen in a star is used as a measure of its age.

metallic lens *n* a device consisting of louvres or slats, used to focus electromagnetic or sound waves

metalliferous /méttə lífferəss/ *adj* containing or yielding metal

metalline /méttə līn/ *adj* **1.** resembling a metal **2.** containing metal ions

metalling /méttˈling/ *n* **1.** ROADS same as **road metal 2.** the process of making or repairing roads with broken stones or other material

metallize /méttə līz/ (**-lizes, -lizing, -lized**) *vt* to coat or cover something with metal

metallo- *prefix* metal ○ *metallophone* [< Latin *metallum* (see METAL)]

metalloenzyme /mə tállōen zīm/ *n* an enzyme containing a bound metal ion incorporated into a protein

metallofullerene /mə tállō foóllə reen/ *n* a fullerene compound containing a metal atom or a metal oxide molecule

metallography /méttə lóggrəfi/ *n* the study of the composition and microscopic structure of metals —**metallographer** *n* —**metallographic** /mə tállə gráffik/ *adj* —**metallographically** *adv* —**metallographist** *n*

metalloid /méttə loyd/ *n* NONMETALLIC ELEMENT WITH METAL PROPERTIES a nonmetallic element such as silicon that has properties between those of a metal and nonmetal ■ *adj* **1.** *also* **metalloidal** /méttə lóyd'l/ OF METALLOID relating to or having the characteristics of a metalloid **2.** *also* **metalloidal** LIKE METAL resembling a metal

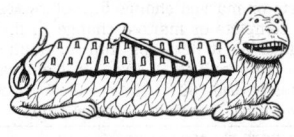

metallophone

metallophone /me tállə fōn/ *n* a musical instrument resembling a xylophone, with tuned metal bars that are struck with mallets

metallorganic /méttˈl awr gannik/ *adj* relating to or composed of an organic chemical compound with a metallic component

metallurgy /mə tállurji/ *n* the study of the structure and properties of metals, their extraction from the ground, and the procedures for refining, alloying, and making things from them —**metallurgic** /méttə lúrjik/ *adj* —**metallurgical** *adj* —**metallurgically** *adv* —**metallurgist** *n*

metalsmith /méttˈl smith/ *n* somebody who is skilled at making and repairing metal objects

metalware /méttˈl wair/ *n* objects that have been crafted from metal

metalwork /méttˈl wurk/ *n* **1.** MAKING OF METAL OBJECTS the craft of making objects out of metal **2.** METAL THINGS objects made of metal **3.** METAL PART OF SOMETHING the metal part of an object —**metalworker** *n* —**metalworking** *n*

metamale /méttə mayl/ *n* a male organism with an extra male chromosome

metamere /méttə meer/ *n* a segment into which the bodies of animals such as worms or lobsters are divided

metameric /méttə mérrik/ *adj* **1.** with a body divided into a series of similar segments (**metameres**) **2.** relating to or typical of metamerism —**metamerically** *adv*

metamerism /mə támmərizəm/ *n* the condition of having the body divided into a series of similar segments (**metameres**), or an embryonic stage in which the body is divided in this way

metamorphic /méttə máwrfik/, **metamorphous** /-máwrfəss/ *adj* **1.** relating to or involving a change in physical form, appearance, or character **2.** relating to or having undergone metamorphism —**metamorphically** *adv*

metamorphism /méttə máwrfizəm/ *n* a process of change in the physical structure of rock as a result of long-term heat and pressure, especially a change that increases the rock's hardness and crystalline structure

metamorphose /méttə máwrfōz/ (**-phoses, -phosing, -phosed**) *v* **1.** *vti* CHANGE PHYSICAL FORM to undergo a complete or marked change of physical form, structure, or substance, or make somebody or something undergo this ○ *The water had metamorphosed into ice.* **2.** *vti* CHANGE APPEARANCE OR CHARACTER to undergo a complete or marked change in appearance, character, or condition, or make somebody or something undergo this **3.** *vti* CHANGE SUPPOSEDLY BY MAGIC to undergo a transformation supposedly by magic, or make somebody or something undergo this **4.** *vi* ZOOL UNDERGO BODILY CHANGES DURING GROWTH to undergo a complete or marked change of bodily form while developing into an adult animal ○ *The tadpole has metamorphosed into a frog.* **5.** *vti* GEOL CHANGE ROCK STRUCTURE to undergo metamorphism, or make a rock undergo metamorphism [Late 16C. < French

métamorphoser < *métamorphose* 'metamorphosis' < Latin *metamorphosis* (see METAMORPHOSIS)]

metamorphosis /méttə máwrfəssiss/ (*plural* **-phoses** /-fə seez/) *n* **1.** CHANGE OF PHYSICAL FORM a complete or marked change of physical form, structure, or substance ○ *the overnight metamorphosis of the pond water into ice* **2.** CHANGE OF APPEARANCE OR CHARACTER a complete or marked change in appearance, character, or condition **3.** SUPPOSED SUPERNATURAL TRANSFORMATION a transformation caused by supposed supernatural powers **4.** TRANSFORMED PERSON OR THING somebody or something that has gone through a complete or marked change **5.** ZOOL CHANGE IN ANIMAL FORM a complete or marked change in the form of an animal as it develops into an adult, e.g. the change from tadpole to frog or from caterpillar to butterfly [Mid-16C. Via Latin < Greek *metamorphōsis* < *metamorphoun* 'transform' < *morphē* 'form']

CULTURAL NOTE ***The Metamorphosis***, a short novel (1915) by Austrian (Czech) writer Franz Kafka. The protagonist of this bizarre tale, Gregor Samsa, awakens to find himself transformed into an insect, then dies as a result of his family's neglect and his own failure to act. Gregor's metamorphosis can be read as both a portrayal of the author's troubled family life and a metaphor for the artist's power to transform life into art.

CULTURAL NOTE ***Metamorphoses***, a poem (AD 8) by the Roman poet Ovid. This long narrative work consists of a series of tales in which characters undergo some kind of transformation. The stories were based on Greek myths and legends and are presented in chronological order, but much of their liveliness derives from events, characters, and details invented by the poet.

metamorphous *adj* GEOL same as **metamorphic**

metanephros /méttə néffross/ (*plural* **-roi** /-roy/) *n* an embryonic organ of excretion in reptiles, birds, and mammals that develops into the kidney [Late 19C. < META- + Greek *nephros* 'kidney']

metaphase /méttə fayz/ *n* the second stage of cell division, during which chromosomes line up in preparation for separation

metaphase plate *n* the equatorial plane along which chromosomes line up during the second stage of cell division in preparation for separation

metaphor /méttəfər, -fawr/ *n* **1.** IMPLICIT COMPARISON the use to describe somebody or something of a word or phrase that is not meant literally but by means of a vivid comparison expresses something about him, her, or it, e.g. saying that somebody is a snake **2.** FIGURATIVE LANGUAGE all language that involves figures of speech or symbolism and does not literally represent real things **3.** SYMBOL one thing used or considered to represent another [15C. Via French or Latin < Greek *metaphora* < *metapherein* 'to transfer' < *pherein* 'to carry'] —**metaphoric** /méttə fórrik/ *adj* —**metaphorical** /méttə fórrik'l/ *adj* —**metaphorically** *adv*

metaphosphate /méttə fóss fayt/ *n* any salt or ester of metaphosphoric acid

metaphosphoric acid /méttə foss fórrik-/ *n* a glassy solid containing linked phosphate groups. Use: drying agent, in dental cements. Formula: HPO_3.

metaphrase /méttə frayz/ *n* LITERAL TRANSLATION a word-for-word translation of something ■ *vt* (**-phrases, -phrasing, -phrased**) **1.** TRANSLATE SOMETHING LITERALLY to translate something, especially word for word **2.** CHANGE WORDING OF SOMETHING to change the wording of a text [Mid-16C. < Greek *metaphrasis* < *metaphrazein* 'tell differently, translate' < *phrazein* 'tell']

metaphrast /méttə frast/ *n* somebody who changes the form of a text, e.g. from prose into verse [Early 17C. < Greek *metaphrastēs* < *metaphrazein* (see METAPHRASE)] —**metaphrastic** /méttə frástik/ *adj* —**metaphrastical** *adj* —**metaphrastically** *adv*

metaphysic /méttə fízzik/ *n* PHILOSOPHY same as **metaphysics**

metaphysical /méttə fízzik'l/ *adj* **1.** RELATING TO METAPHYSICS relating to the philosophical study of the nature of being and beings or a philosophical system resulting from such study **2.** SPECULATIVE based on speculative reasoning and unexamined assumptions that have not been logically examined or confirmed by observation **3.** ABSTRACT extremely abstract or theoretical ○ *metaphysical subjects removed from everyday life* **4.** INCORPOREAL without material form or substance ○ *the metaphysical realm of pure thought* **5.** SUPERNATURAL originating not in the physical world but somewhere outside it ○ *a metaphysical explanation of beauty and goodness* **6.** ARTS another spelling of **Metaphysical** —**metaphysically** *adv*

Metaphysical /méttə fízzik'l/ *adj* relating to the poetic style of John Donne, George Herbert, and other early 17th-century English poets who used consciously intellectual language and elaborate metaphors that compared dissimilar things ■ *n* a poet of the Metaphysical group

metaphysician /méttə fi zísh'n/ *n* a scholar who specializes in the branch of philosophy concerned with the study of the nature of being, existence, time and space, and causality

metaphysics /méttə fízziks/ *n* **1.** PHILOSOPHY OF BEING the branch of philosophy concerned with the study of the nature of being and beings, existence, time and space, and causality (*takes a singular verb*) **2.** UNDERLYING PRINCIPLES the ultimate underlying principles or theories that form the basis of a particular field of knowledge (*takes a plural verb*) ○ *Symmetry is part of the metaphysics of quantum mechanics.* **3.** ABSTRACT THINKING abstract discussion or thinking (*takes a singular verb*) [Mid-16C. < medieval Latin *metaphysica* (plural) < medieval Greek *(ta) metaphusika* '(the) metaphysics' < *ta meta ta phusika* 'the (works of Aristotle) after the "Physics"']

metaplasia /méttə pláyzi ə/ *n* the transformation of one kind of tissue into another undesirable type, as happens in tumour formation [Late 19C. < Greek *metaplassein* 'mould into a new form' < *plassein* 'to mould'] —**metaplastic** /méttə plástik/ *adj*

metapneumovirus /méttə pyoómō vīrəss/ *n* MICROBIOL same as **human metapneumovirus**

metapsychology /méttə sī kólləji/ *n* the philosophical study of those aspects of psychology that cannot be examined experimentally —**metapsychological** /méttə sīkə lójjik'l/ *adj*

metasomatism /méttə sṓmətizəm/, **metasomatosis** /-sṓmə tṓssiss/ *n* the gradual change in rock structure caused by the natural replacement of chemicals through interaction with liquids or gases [Late 19C. < META- + Greek *sōmat-* 'body'] —**metasomatic** /méttəsō máttik/ *adj* —**metasomatically** *adv*

metastable /méttə stáyb'l/ *adj* **1.** describes atoms and atomic nuclei in an apparent state of equilibrium, but likely to change to a more truly stable state if conditions change **2.** describes atoms and atomic nuclei that remain in an excited state for a relatively long time —**metastability** /méttəstə bílləti/ *n*

metastasis /me tástəssiss/ (*plural* **-tases** /-təs seez/) *n* **1.** the spread of a cancer from the original tumour to other parts of the body by means of tiny clumps of cells transported by the blood or lymph **2.** a malignant tumour that has developed in the body as a result of the spread of cancer cells from the original tumour [Late 16C. Via late Latin < Greek, 'removal, change' < *methistanai* 'remove' < *histanai* 'to place'] —**metastatic** /méttə státtik/ *adj* —**metastatically** *adv*

metastasize /me tástə sīz/ (**-sizes, -sizing, -sized**), **metastasise** (**-sises, -sising, -sised**) *vi* to spread in the body from the site of the original tumour by means of tiny cells transported by the blood or lymph (*refers to a cancer*)

metatarsal /méttə taárss'l/ *adj* belonging or relating to the bones between the toes and ankle ■ *n* any bone between the toes and ankle —**metatarsally** *adv*

metatarsus /méttə taárssəss/ (*plural* **-tarsi** /-taár ssī/) *n* **1.** the set of five long bones (**metatarsals**) in the human foot between the toes and ankle **2.** the region between the ankle and toes of the hind foot of a vertebrate animal

metatarsus adductus /-ə dúktəss/ *n* a condition found in newborn babies or young infants in which the front half of the foot is twisted inwards at an angle to the heel

metatherian /méttə theéri ən/ *adj* relating or belonging to marsupials ■ *n* same as **marsupial** [Late 19C. < modern Latin *Metatheria* 'wild animals between' < Greek *thēria*, plural of *thērion* 'wild animal']

metathesis /me táthəssiss/ (*plural* **-eses** /-ə seez/) *n* **1.** a reversal of the order of two sounds or letters in a word, either as a mispronunciation or as a historical development **2.** CHEM same as **double decomposition** [Late 16C. Via late Latin < Greek < *metatithenai* 'transpose' < *tithenai* 'to place'] —**metathetic** /méttə théttik/ *adj* —**metathetical** *adj* —**metathetically** *adv*

metathesize /me táthə sīz/ (**-sizes, -sizing, -sized**), **metathesise** (**-sises, -sising, -sised**) *vti* to change by metathesis, or make a word change by metathesis

metathorax /méttə tháw raks/ (*plural* **-raxes** or **-races** /-rə seez/) *n* the last segment of an insect's thorax, where the hind legs and hind wings are located —**metathoracic** /méttə thaw rássik/ *adj*

metaxylem /méttə zīləm/ *n* the rigid thick-walled tissue of plant parts that have matured

metazoan /méttə zṓ ən/ *n* an animal whose body consists of cells that are separated into different parts such as tissues and organs. All animals except for sponges and protozoans are classified as metazoans. Group: *Metazoa*. [Late 19C. < modern Latin *Metazoa* < Greek *meta-* 'beside, after' + *zoion* 'animal'] —**metazoan** *adj*

mete /meet/ (**metes, meting, meted**) *vt* same as **mete out** (*literary*) [Old English *metan* 'measure' < Indo-European]

SPELLCHECK See *meat*.

mete out *vt* to give out something such as punishment or justice, especially in a way that seems harsh or unfair

metempsychosis /méttem sī kṓssiss/ *n* the supposed passage of somebody's soul after death into the body of another person or an animal [Late 16C. Via late Latin < Greek *metempsukhōsis* < *meta* 'after' + *empsukhos* 'having a soul within']

metencephalon /métten séffə lon/ (*plural* **-lons** or **-la** /-lə/) *n* the part of an embryo's brain that develops into the cerebellum and the pons —**metencephalic** /métten si fállik/ *adj*

meteor /meéti ə, -awr/ *n* **1.** a mass of rock from space that burns up after entering the Earth's atmosphere **2.** the brief streak of light that a meteor creates, visible in the night sky [Late 16C. Via modern Latin *meteorum* 'atmospheric phenomenon' < Greek *meteōron*, form of *meteōros* 'raised up' < *meta* 'up' + *-aoros* 'lifted']

meteor. *abbr* METEOROL meteorology

meteoric /meéti órrik/ *adj* **1.** characterized by great speed or brilliance **2.** relating to or resembling meteors —**meteorically** *adv*

meteoric water *n* water in the ground that has come from the atmosphere as rain or condensation, rather than forming chemically underground

meteorite /meéti ə rīt/ *n* a piece of rock that has reached Earth from outer space

meteoritics /meéti ə ríttiks/ *n* the scientific study of meteors and meteorites (*takes a singular verb*) —**meteoriticist** *n*

meteoroid /meéti ə royd/ *n* a mass of rock in space, often a remnant of a comet, that becomes a meteor when it enters the Earth's atmosphere and a meteorite when it falls to Earth —**meteoroidal** *adj*

meteorol. *abbr* METEOROL meteorology

meteorology /meéti ə rólləji/ *n* the scientific study of the Earth's atmosphere, especially its patterns of climate and weather [Early 17C. < Greek *meteōrologia* < *meteōron* (see METEOR)] —**meteorological** /meéti ərə lójjik'l/ *adj* —**meteorologically** *adv* —**meteorologist** *n*

meteor shower *n* a number of meteors seen at regular intervals in the same area of the sky when a large group of meteors passes through the Earth's atmosphere

meter[1] /meétər/ *n* **1.** a device that measures and records the quantity or flow of something such as electricity, gas, water, distance, or time **2.** same as **parking meter** ■ *vt* (**-ters, -tering, -tered**) to measure the amount or flow of something such as electricity or water, using a meter [Early 19C. Origin ?] —**metered** *adj*

meter[2] *n* MEASURE US spelling of **metre**

-meter *suffix* measuring device ○ *heliometer* [Via French *-mètre* < Greek *metron* 'measure']

metered mail /meétərd-/ *n* mail that is franked privately by a machine licensed from the postal service

meter maid *n* a woman traffic warden (*dated informal*)

Meth. *abbr* CHR Methodist

meth- *prefix* methyl ○ *methicillin* [Shortening]

methacrylate /meth ákri layt/ *n* an ester derived from methacrylic acid

methacrylic acid /métha krillik-/ *n* a synthetic colourless liquid. Use: manufacture of plastic. Formula: $C_4H_6O_2$.

methadone /métha dōn/, **methadon** /-don/ *n* a synthetic narcotic drug similar in its painkilling effect to morphine. Use: substitute for heroin in the treatment of addiction. [Mid-20C. < METH- + AMINO + DI-[1]]

methaemoglobin /met heéma glóbin, me theéma/ *n* an altered form of haemoglobin that cannot bind oxygen, produced by some poisons or by a genetic disorder

methaemoglobinaemia /met heéma glóbi neémi ə, me theéma-/ *n* the presence in the blood of methaemoglobin

methamphetamine /méth am fétta meen/ *n* a derivative of amphetamine, used illegally as a drug. Formula: $C_{10}H_{15}N$.

methanal /métha nal/ *n* CHEM same as **formaldehyde** [Late 19C. < METHANE]

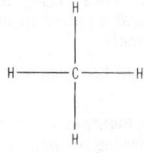

methane

methane /meé thayn/ *n* a colourless odourless flammable gas that is the main constituent of natural gas. Use: as fuel. Formula: CH_4. [Mid-19C. < METHYL]

methanoic acid /méthanō ik-/ *n* CHEM same as **formic acid** [< METHANE]

methanol /métha nol/ *n* a colourless volatile poisonous water-soluble liquid. Use: as solvent, fuel, in antifreeze for motor vehicles. Formula: CH_3OH. [Late 19C. < METHANE]

methaqualone /métha kwáylōn/ *n* a hypnotic drug that may become habit-forming. Use: treatment of anxiety, sleep disorders. Formula: $C_{16}H_{14}N_2O$. [Mid-20C. < METH- + contraction of *quinazolinon*, a derivative of quinoline]

methemoglobin *n* BIOCHEM US spelling of **methaemoglobin**

methicillin /métha síllin/ *n* a synthetic antibiotic. Use: treatment of penicillin-resistant infections. [Mid-20C. < METH- + -*cillin*, INN stem]

methicillin-resistant Staphylococcus aureus *n* MED, MICROBIOL full form of **MRSA**

methinks /mi thíngks/ (**-thought** /-tháwt/) *vi* it seems to me (*humorous or archaic*) [Old English *mē þyncþ* 'it seems to me' < *þyncan* 'seem' < Indo-European]

methionine

methionine /me thí ə neen, -nīn/ *n* an essential amino acid that contains sulphur [Early 20C. < METH- + THIO-]

metho /méthō/ (*plural* **-os**) *n* Aus (*informal*) **1.** same as

methylated spirit 2. somebody who drinks methylated spirits

method /méthad/ *n* **1. WAY OF DOING SOMETHING** a way of doing something or carrying something out, especially according to a plan ○ *a successful method of recruitment of new staff* **2. ORDERLINESS** orderly thought, action, or technique ○ *There is no method whatsoever in his approach to business.* **3. BODY OF TECHNIQUES** the body of systematic techniques used by a particular discipline, especially a scientific one [15C. Via Latin < Greek *methodos* 'pursuit, way' < *meta*- 'after' + *hodos* 'journey'] ◇ **there's method in somebody's madness** there is a good reason for somebody's apparently foolish, strange, or illogical action

Method *n* a theory and system of acting that involves the actor identifying strongly with the internal motivation of the character being portrayed. It is based on the teachings of Konstantin Stanislavsky.

methodical /mə thóddik'l/, **methodic** /-ik/ *adj* systematic or painstaking —**methodically** *adv* —**methodicalness** *n*

methodise *vt* another spelling of **methodize**

Methodism /méthadizam/ *n* the doctrines, principles, or organization of the Methodist Church

Methodist /méthadist/ *n* a member of the Methodist Church ■ *adj* relating to Methodism or membership of the Methodist Church [Mid-18C. Originally applied to members of a society founded at Oxford, from the methodical habits of life and worship it promoted] —**Methodistic** /métha dístik/ *adj* —**Methodistically** *adv*

Methodist Church *n* a group of Nonconformist Protestant denominations founded in 18th-century England by John Wesley and his followers

methodize /métha dīz/ (**-izes, -izing, -ized**), **methodise** (**-ises, -ising, -ised**) *vt* to reduce or arrange something according to a method —**methodization** /métha dī záysh'n/ *n* —**methodizer** *n*

methodology /métha dólləji/ (*plural* **-gies**) *n* **1. ORGANIZING SYSTEM** the methods or organizing principles underlying a particular art, science, or other area of study **2. STUDY OF ORGANIZING PRINCIPLES** in philosophy, the study of organizing principles and underlying rules **3. STUDY OF RESEARCH METHODS** the study of methods of research —**methodological** /méthadə lójjik'l/ *adj* —**methodologically** *adv* —**methodologist** *n*

methotrexate /métho trék sayt, meéthō-/ *n* a drug that inhibits cellular reproduction. Use: cancer treatment. Formula: $C_{20}H_{22}N_8O_5$. [Mid-20C. < METH- + -*trex*-, origin ?]

methought past tense of **methinks** (*humorous or archaic*)

methoxide /mi thók sīd/ *n* a chemical derivative of methanol that has some features of a salt, e.g. sodium methoxide. Formula: $NaOCH_3$. [Late 19C. < METH- + OXY-]

methoxychlor /mi thóksi klawr/ *n* a white crystalline compound used as an insecticide. Formula: $C_{16}H_{15}Cl_3O_2$. [Mid-20C. < METH- + OXY- + CHLORINE]

meths /meths/ *n* UK same as **methylated spirit** (*informal*; takes a singular verb) [Mid-20C. Contraction]

Methuselah /mə thyoòzələ/ *n* **1.** in the Bible, a man who was an ancestor of Noah and lived 969 years (Genesis 5: 21–27) **2.** *also* **methuselah** a wine bottle that holds the equivalent of eight normal bottles, approximately 6 litres/208 fl. oz

methyl /meé thīl, méth'l/ *adj* relating to the group of atoms derived from methane after the loss of a hydrogen atom. Formula: CH_3. [Mid-19C. < French *méthyl*, a back-formation < *méthylène* (see METHYLENE)] —**methylic** /mə thíllik/ *adj*

methyl acetate *n* a fragrant colourless liquid. Use: solvent in paint removers. Formula: $C_3H_6O_2$.

methylal /méthi lal/ *n* a colourless flammable liquid. Use: solvent, manufacture of perfumes and adhesives. Formula: $C_3H_8O_2$.

methyl alcohol /meé thīl-/ *n* CHEM same as **methanol**

methylamine /me thíla meen, mee-/ *n* a colourless flammable derivative of ammonia. Use: as a gas, in dyes, drugs, and herbicides. Formula: CH_5N.

methylate /méthi layt/ *n* CHEM same as **methoxide** ■ *vt* (**-ates, -ating, -ated**) **1.** to replace one or more hydrogen atoms in a molecule with the methyl group **2.** to mix something with methanol —**methylation** /méthi láysh'n/ *n* —**methylator** *n*

methylated spirit /métha laytid-/, **methylated spirits** *n* ethanol with methanol added, to make it undrinkable, and coloured with a violet dye. Use: fuel, in solvents.

methylbenzene /meéthīl bén zeen/ *n* CHEM same as **toluene**

methyl bromide *n* a poisonous colourless gas or liquid. Use: solvent, fumigant, refrigerant. Formula: CH_3Br.

methylcellulose /meéthīl séllyoō lōss/ *n* a greyish-white powder derived from cellulose that swells up in water. Use: food additive, manufacture of paints and cosmetics.

methyl chloride *n* a colourless poisonous gas. Use: refrigerant, local anaesthetic. Formula: CH_3Cl.

methyldopa /meé thīl dópə/ *n* a white powdered drug. Use: treatment of hypertension. Formula: $C_{10}H_{13}NO_4$.

methylene /métha leen/ *n* a bivalent group of atoms derived from methane. Formula: CH_2. ■ *adj* relating to the group of atoms derived from methane containing one carbon atom and two hydrogen atoms [Mid-19C. < French *méthylène* < Greek *methu* 'wine' + *hulē* 'wood, substance']

methylene blue *n* a crystalline compound that turns blue when dissolved in water. Use: dye, antiseptic, antidote for cyanide poisoning, stain in laboratories. Formula: $C_{16}H_{18}ClN_3S$.

methyl isocyanate *n* a flammable, colourless, extremely toxic liquid. Use: manufacture of herbicides. Formula: CH_3NCO.

methylmercury /meéthīl múrkyoori/ *n* an extremely toxic compound, derived from the action of microorganisms on metallic mercury. Use: seed disinfectant.

methyl methacrylate *n* a colourless flammable liquid that can be converted into clear plastic resins

methylnaphthalene /meéthīl náptha leen/ *n* either of two forms of naphthalene, a liquid used in making diesel fuels or a solid used in making insecticides. Formula: $C_{11}H_{10}$.

methyl orange

methyl orange *n* an alkaline dye that turns yellow when neutral and pink when acid. Use: chemical indicator.

methylphenidate /meéthīl fénni dayt/ *n* a drug that stimulates the central nervous system. Use: treatment of narcolepsy, attention deficit disorder. Formula: $C_{14}H_{19}NO_2$. [Mid-20C. Contraction of METHYL + PHENYL + PIPERIDINE + ACETATE]

methylprednisolone /meéthīl pred níssə lōn, méthil pred níssə lōn/ *n* a corticosteroid drug that reduces inflammation. Use: treatment of arthritis, allergies, and asthma.

metical /méttik'l/ (*plural* **-cais** /-kísh/ or **-cals**) *n* the main unit of Mozambican currency. See table at **currency** [Late 20C. Via Portuguese *matical* < Arabic *miṯkāl*, a unit of weight < *ṯakala* 'weigh']

meticulous /mə tíkyoōləss/ *adj* extremely careful and precise [Early 19C. < Latin *meticulosus* 'fearful, timid' < *metus* 'fear'] —**meticulously** *adv* —**meticulousness** *n*

SYNONYMS See *careful*.

métier /métti ay/, **metier** *n* **1.** somebody's occupation or trade **2.** an activity that somebody is particularly good at [Late 18C. < French < Latin *ministerium* (see MINISTRY)]

Metis /meétiss/ *n* the innermost known natural sat-

ellite of Jupiter. It is irregularly shaped and approximately 40 km/25 mi. in diameter.

metol /meé tol/ *n* a colourless soluble salt. Use: photographic developer. Formula: $C_{14}H_{20}N_2O_6S$. [Late 19C. Arbitrary]

Metonic cycle /mi tónnik-/ *n* a cycle of 235 lunar months, after which the phases of the Moon occur on the same days of the month as they did at the start of the cycle [Late 17C. After *Metōn*, 5C BC Athenian astronomer]

metonym /méttənim/ *n* a word or phrase used in a figure of speech in which an attribute of something is used to stand for the thing itself, e.g. 'laurels' when it is used to stand for 'glory' [Late 16C. Back-formation < METONYMY] —**metonymic** /méttə nímmik/ *adj* —**metonymically** *adv*

metonymy /me tónnəmi/ *n* a figure of speech in which an attribute of something is used to stand for the thing itself, e.g. 'laurels' when it stands for 'glory' or 'brass' when it stands for 'military officers' [Mid-16C. Via late Latin < Greek *metōnumia* 'change of name' < *meta*- 'beside, different' + *onuma* 'name']

me-too *adj* (*informal*) **1.** using products, methods, or policies copied from another person or a successful business competitor **2.** trying to emulate the success of others, or seeking to follow a trend —**me-tooer** *n* —**me-tooism** *n*

metope /méttōp, méttəpi/ *n* in a Doric frieze, a square space between two sets of three vertical grooves (**triglyphs**) [Mid-16C. < Greek *metopē* < *meta*- 'between' + *opē* 'hole']

metopic /me tóppik/ *adj* relating to the forehead [Late 19C. < Greek *metōpon* 'forehead' < *meta*- 'between' + *ōps* 'eye']

metr- *suffix* same as **metro-** (*used before vowels*)

metralgia /mi trálji ə/ *n* pain in the womb

metre[1] /meétər/ *n* the basic SI unit of length, equivalent to approximately 1.094 yd or 39.37 in. Symbol **m** [Late 18C. Via French < Greek *metron*]

metre[2] /meétər/ *n* **1.** an arranged pattern of rhythm in a line of verse **2.** the pattern of beats that combines to form musical rhythm [Pre-12C. Directly or via French < Latin *metrum* < Greek *metron* 'measure']

metre-kilogram-second *adj* using or based on the metre, kilogram, and second as the measuring units of length, mass, and time

metric /méttrik/ *adj* **1.** RELATING TO METRIC SYSTEM relating to or using the metric system of measurement **2.** same as **metrical** ■ *n* **1.** MATHEMATICAL FUNCTION a mathematical function defined for a coordinates system that assigns a value to each pair of elements equal to the distance between them, or to a property analogous to distance between points on a line **2.** STATS STATISTIC FOR MEASURING a standard or a statistic for measuring or quantifying something else ○ '"Today we lack metrics to know if we are winning or losing the global war on terror", Mr. [Donald] Rumsfeld wrote.' (Greg Jaffe *Wall Street Journal*; 23 October 2003)

metrical /méttrik'l/ *adj* relating to or using poetic metre —**metrically** *adv*

metricate /méttri kayt/ (**-cates**, **-cating**, **-cated**) *vt* to convert something from nonmetric to metric units of measurement —**metrication** /méttri káysh'n/ *n*

metric hundredweight *n* a unit of weight equal to 50 kg

metricize /méttri sīz/ (**-cizes**, **-cizing**, **-cized**), **metricise** (**-cises**, **-cising**, **-cised**) *vt* to express a measurement in metric units or change it into metric units

metrics /méttriks/ *n* the art or study of using metre in poetry (*takes a singular verb*)

metric system *n* a decimal system of weights and measures based on units such as the kilogram and metre

metric ton *n* a unit of weight equal to 1,000 kg. Symbol **t**

metrify /méttri fī/ (**-fies**, **-fying**, **-fied**) *vt* to put prose into verse or metre —**metrifier** *n*

metrist /méttrist/ *n* somebody who is skilled in using poetic metre

metritis /mi trítiss/ *n* inflammation of the womb

metro /méttrō/ (*plural* **-ros**) *n* **1.** an underground railway system in a town or city **2.** *Can* the

government of a large city **3.** same as **metropolis** (*informal*) [Mid-20C. Shortening of METROPOLITAN]

metro- *prefix* womb ○ *metrorrhagia* [< Greek *mētra*, related to *mētēr* 'mother' < Indo-European]

metrology /mi trólləji/ (*plural* **-gies**) *n* **1.** the scientific study of units of measurement **2.** a system of measurement [Early 19C. < Greek *metron* 'measure'] —**metrologic** /méttrə lójjik/ *adj* —**metrologist** *n*

metronidazole /méttrō nídəzōl/ *n* a yellow crystalline compound. Use: treatment of vaginal infections. Formula: $C_6H_9N_3O_3$. [Mid-20C. Contraction of METHYL + NITRO- + IMIDAZOLE]

metronome

metronome /méttrənōm/ *n* a device used to indicate a given tempo by means of a regularly recurring aural or visual signal [Early 19C. < Greek *metron* 'measure, metre' + *nomos* 'rule, division'] —**metronomic** /méttrə nómmik/ *adj* —**metronomically** *adv*

metronymic *n* LANGUAGE same as **matronymic**

metropolis /mə tróppəliss/ *n* **1.** LARGE CITY a very large city, often the capital or chief urban centre of a country, state, or region **2.** CENTRE OF ACTIVITY the centre or principal place for a particular activity **3.** MAIN DIOCESE in some Christian denominations, the principal diocese or see in an ecclesiastical province [Mid-16C. Via late Latin < Greek *mētropolis* 'mother city' < *mētēr* 'mother' + *polis* 'city']

metropolitan /méttrə póllitən/ *adj* **1.** FORMING LARGE CITY constituting a large urban area, usually one that includes a city and its suburbs and outlying areas **2.** CHARACTERISTIC OF METROPOLIS characteristic of a metropolis in scale, variety, or sophistication **3.** DOMESTIC AND INTERNAL relating to the home territory of a country rather than to its territories elsewhere **4.** RELATING TO ECCLESIASTICAL METROPOLIS relating to or constituting an ecclesiastical metropolis ■ *n* **1.** CITY-DWELLER an inhabitant of a metropolis **2.** HIGH-RANKING CHURCH OFFICIAL in some Christian denominations, a high-ranking church dignitary, e.g. an archbishop or head of an ecclesiastical province **3.** HEAD OF RUSSIAN ORTHODOX CHURCH the head of the Russian Orthodox Church, based in Moscow

metropolitan county *n* in England, any of the six large urban administrative units in the system of local government between 1974 and 1986

metropolitan district *n* in England, any of the districts that used to be metropolitan counties. They are the principal units of local government, each with an elected council

Metropolitan France *n* the mainland departments of France along with Corsica, excluding French overseas territories

metrorrhagia /meétrō ráyji ə/ *n* excessive discharge of blood from the womb —**metrorrhagic** *adj*

metrosexual /méttrō sékshoo əl/ *n* a young, straight, sensitive urban man who is unashamed to enjoy good clothes, stylish living, the art of decorating, and improving his personal appearance (*informal*) [mid-20C.] —**metrosexual** *adj*

-metry *suffix* measuring ○ *cephalometry* [< Greek *-metria* < *metron* 'measure']

Metternich /méttə nikh/, Klemens von (1773–1859) German-born Austrian chancellor of the Hapsburg Empire (1821–48). As an Austrian diplomat from 1814 and during his chancellorship, he was one of the most powerful political figures in Europe. He was driven from office in the Revolution of 1848. Full name **Metternich, Klemens Wenzel Nepomuk Lothar von, prince of Metternich-Winneburg-Beilstein**

mettle /métt'l/ *n* **1.** spirited determination **2.** the mental and emotional character unique to an individual person [Mid-16C. Variant of METAL] ◇ **on your mettle** ready or determined to do your best

SPELLCHECK See **metal**.

SYNONYMS See **courage**.

mettlesome /métt'lsəm/ *adj* spirited and courageous

Metz /mets/ city in eastern France, the capital of Moselle Department. Population: 123,776 (1999).

meunière /mɔ́ni áir/ *adj* dredged in flour, fried in butter, and sprinkled with lemon juice and chopped parsley ○ *sole meunière* [Mid-19C. < French *à la meunière* 'in the way of a miller's wife']

Meursault /múrsō/ *n* a dry white wine from east-central France [Mid-19C. < French, a village near BEAUNE, France]

Meuse /mōz/ river that flows through northeastern France, Belgium, and the Netherlands. Length: 925 km/575 mi.

MeV, Mev, mev *symbol* MEASURE million electron volts

mevrou /mə frṓ/ *n S Africa* in Afrikaans, a title equivalent to 'Mrs', or a respectful form of address equivalent to 'Madam' [Mid 19C. Via Afrikaans < Dutch]

mew[1] /myoo/ *vi* (**mews, mewing, mewed**) to give out a high-pitched cry (*refers to cats and kittens*) ■ *n* the high-pitched sound a cat or kitten makes [14C. An imitation of the sound]

mew[2] /myoo/ *n* a gull (*archaic*) [Old English *mæw* < Germanic]

mew[3] /myoo/ *n* CAGE FOR HAWKS a cage for keeping hawks in ■ *v* (**mews, mewing, mewed**) **1.** *vt* CONFINE HAWK OR FALCON to confine a hawk or falcon, especially by tying it to a perch **2.** *vi* MOULT to shed feathers [14C. < French *mue* < *muer* 'to moult' < Latin *mutare* 'to change']

mewl /myool/ (**mewls, mewling, mewled**) *vi* to whimper or cry weakly [Early 17C. Origin ?]

mews /myooz/ *n* (*takes a singular or plural verb*) **1.** a small street lined with former stables that have been converted into housing **2.** the houses in a mews [Early 19C. < MEW[3]]

ORIGIN In the latter part of the 14th century, the Royal Mews were built in London on the site of what is now Trafalgar Square, to house the royal hawks. By Henry VII's time, they were being used as stables, and from at least the early 17th century the term *mews* was used for 'stabling around an open yard'. The modern application to a 'street of former stables converted to housing' dates from the early 19th century.

Mex. *abbr* **1.** Mexican **2.** Mexico

Mexicali /méksə kaáli/ capital of Baja California State in northwestern Mexico, on the border with the United States. Population: 764,902 (2000).

Mexican American *n* an American of Mexican descent —**Mexican American** *adj*

Mexican bean *n US* FOOD same as **frijol**

Mexican bean beetle *n* a ladybird that feeds on the leaves of bean plants. Native to: North America. Latin name: *Epilachna varivestis*.

Mexican hairless *n* a tiny, mainly hairless dog belonging to a breed that originated in Mexico

Mexican jumping bean *n* PLANTS same as **jumping bean**

mexicano /méksi ka'a nō/ (*plural* **-nos**) *n US* a Mexican-born man or boy [< Spanish, 'Mexican']

Mexican Spanish *n* the form of the Spanish language used in Mexico —**Mexican Spanish** *adj*

Mexican standoff *n* a dispute or argument that cannot be won (*informal*)

Mexican War *n* a war between Mexico and the United States that lasted from 1846 to 1848, during which the United States won territory that now constitutes California and most of the states of the Southwest

Mexican wave *n* the rippling effect produced by rows of spectators at a sporting or musical event standing up, raising their arms, and then sitting down again in sequence. N Am term **wave** [Because first used at the 1986 World Cup finals in Mexico City]

Mexico

Mexico /méksikō/ country in North America, south of the United States. Language: Spanish. Currency: peso. Capital: Mexico City. Population: 104,1907,990 (2003). Area: 1,964,382 sq. km/758,452 sq. mi. Official name **United Mexican States** —**Mexican** /méksikən/ *adj, n*

Mexico, Gulf of arm of the Atlantic Ocean, bordered on the north by the United States, on the east by Cuba, and on the south and west by Mexico. Area: 1,500,000 sq. km/579,000 sq. mi.

Mexico City capital city of Mexico and of the Federal District, located in the south-central part of the country. With its surrounding suburbs it forms the most populous urban area in the world. Population: 8,591,309 (2000).

Meyerhof /míy ər hof, -hōf/, **Otto** (1884–1951) German-born US biochemist. He worked on the metabolism of muscles, for which he was joint winner of the Nobel Prize in physiology or medicine (1922). Full name **Meyerhof, Otto Fritz**

Meynell /mə nél/, **Alice** (1847–1922) British poet and literary critic. Her essay collections include *The Colour of Life* (1896) and *Hearts of Controversy* (1917).

> 'I must not think of thee; and, tired yet strong, / I shun the thought that lurks in all delight— / The thought of thee—and in the blue heaven's height, / And in the sweetest passage of a song.'
> [Alice Meynell, 'Renouncement'; 1875]

meze /mézzay/ (*plural* -**zes** or *same*), **mezze** (*plural* -**zzes** or *same*) *n* an assortment of snacks served with drinks as an appetizer or a light meal in Greece and Southwest Asia, e.g. stuffed vine leaves, small pastries, or grilled sausages [Early 20C. < Turkish < Persian *maza* 'taste, relish']

mezereon /mə zeéri ən/ *n* a poisonous deciduous bush that flowers before the leaves emerge, and bears crimson berries. Flowers: purple, in clusters. Native to: Europe, Asia. Latin name: *Daphne mezereum*. [15C. Via medieval Latin < Arabic *māzaryūn*]

mezuzah /mə zoózə, -zoó-/ (*plural* -**zahs** or -**zoth** /-zōt/) *n* a scroll with biblical passages on one side and a name of God on the other, inserted in a small case attached by religious Jews to doorposts in the home [Mid-17C. < Hebrew *mĕzūzāh* 'doorpost']

mezzanine /mézzə neen/ *n* **1.** *also* **mezzanine floor** INTERMEDIATE STOREY a low storey, especially one between the ground floor and the first floor in a building **2.** *N Am* THEATRE'S LOWEST BALCONY the lowest balcony in a theatre **3.** AREA UNDER STAGE a floor or room beneath the stage in a theatre ■ *adj* WITHIN INTERMEDIATE RANGE OF INVESTMENT describes an intermediate range of funding or investment that has a moderate degree of risk, such as some unsecured high-yielding loans [Early 18C. Via French < Italian *mezzanino* 'small one in the middle' < *mezzano* 'middle' < Latin *medianus* (see MEDIAN)]

mezza voce /métsə vóchi, -vō chay/ *adv* with moderate volume from the voice or instrument (*used as a musical direction*) [< Italian, literally 'half voice'] —**mezza voce** *adj*

mezze *n* FOOD another spelling of **meze**

mezzo /métsō/ *adv* moderately (*used as a musical direction*) ■ *n* (*plural* -**zos**) MUSIC same as **mezzo-soprano** [Mid-18C. < Italian, 'middle, half' < Latin *medius*]

mezzo forte *adv* moderately loud (*used as a musical direction*) [< Italian] —**mezzo forte** *adj*

mezzo piano *adv* moderately soft (*used as a musical direction*) [< Italian] —**mezzo piano** *adj*

mezzo-relievo /-ri leévō, -ri lyáyvō/ (*plural* **mezzo-relievos**) *n* SCULPTURE same as **half relief** [< Italian, 'half-relief']

mezzo-soprano *n* a woman whose singing voice is between a soprano and a contralto in range [< Italian, literally 'half soprano']

mezzotint /métsō tint/ *n* **1.** ENGRAVING PROCESS an engraving process that involves scraping and burnishing the roughened surface of a copper plate **2.** MEZZOTINT PRINT a print produced by the mezzotint process ■ *vt* (-**tints**, -**tinting**, -**tinted**) ENGRAVE PLATE USING MEZZOTINT to engrave a copper plate by using the mezzotint process [Mid-18C. Anglicization of Italian *mezzotinto* 'half-tint'] —**mezzotinter** *n*

mf *abbr* MUSIC mezzo forte

mF *abbr* MEASURE millifarad

MF *abbr* **1.** MEDIA medium frequency **2.** LANGUAGE Middle French

M/F, m/f *abbr* male or female (*in advertisements*)

MFA *abbr* EDUC Master of Fine Arts

mfd *abbr* manufactured

mfecane /əm fe kaáni/ *n* a series of wars in 19th-century southern Africa caused by Zulu expansion under Shaka, which revolutionized political organization in the region [Mid-20C. Origin ?]

mfg *abbr* manufacturing

mfr *abbr* **1.** manufacture **2.** manufacturer

mg[1] *abbr* MEASURE milligram

mg[2] *abbr* Madagascar (*used in Internet addresses*) See table at **domain name**

Mg *symbol* CHEM ELEM magnesium

MG *abbr* **1.** ARMS machine gun **2.** ARMY Major General

MGB *n* the secret police of the former Soviet Union from 1946 to 1954 [Mid-20C. Abbreviation of Russian *Ministerstvo Gosudarstvennoi Bezopasnosti*, 'Ministry of State Security']

mgmt *abbr* management

mgr *abbr* manager

Mgr *abbr* RELIG **1.** Monseigneur **2.** Monsignor

mgt *abbr* management

mh *abbr* Marshall Islands (*used in Internet addresses*) See table at **domain name**

mH *abbr* MEASURE millihenry

MH *abbr* **1.** MAIL Marshall Islands **2.** mental health

MHA *abbr* Member of the House of Assembly

MHC *n* a group of genes in mammals located next or near to one another that serve to make cells separate and distinguishable from those of other organisms. Full form **major histocompatibility complex**

MHD *abbr* PHYS magnetohydrodynamics

MHG *abbr* LANGUAGE Middle High German

MHL *abbr* EDUC Master of Hebrew Literature

MHz *abbr* MEASURE megahertz

mi /mee/, **me** *n* a syllable that represents the third note in a scale, used for singing solfeggio. In fixed solfeggio, it represents the note E. [15C. < medieval Latin]

MI *abbr* **1.** MIL Military Intelligence **2.** MED myocardial infarction

mi. *abbr* MEASURE mile

MI5 /ém ī fív/ *n* a former official and current popular name for Military Intelligence, section five, the British security and counterintelligence service

MI6 /ém ī síks/ *n* a former official and current popular name for Military Intelligence, section six, the British secret intelligence and espionage service

MIA *n* US a soldier who is reported missing during a military mission. Full form **missing in action**

Miami /mī ámmi/ port, city, and tourist resort in southeastern Florida, the county seat of Dade County. Population: 374,791 (2002 estimate).

Miami Beach city and tourist resort in southeastern Florida, on an island opposite Miami. Population: 89,575 (2002 estimate).

Miao /myow/ *n* PEOPLES, LANG same as **Hmong** [Early 20C. < Chinese *Miáo* 'people'] —**Miao** *adj*

miaow /mi ów/, **meow** *n* CHARACTERISTIC CRY OF CAT the characteristic cry made by a domestic cat ■ *vi* (-**aows**, -**aowing**, -**aowed**; -**ows**, -**owing**, -**owed**) UTTER

MIAOW to utter a miaow ■ *interj* DESIGNATING SPITEFUL OR MEAN COMMENT used to indicate that you think somebody's comment is spiteful or malicious (*informal*) [Late 16C. An imitation of the sound]

Miao-Yao /myów yow/ *n* a group of languages, including Hmong and Yao, spoken in the People's Republic of China, Vietnam, Laos, and Thailand. Native speakers: 6 million. —**Miao-Yao** *adj*

miasma /mi ázmə, mī-/ (*plural* -**mata** /-mətə/ or -**mas**) *n* **1.** a harmful or poisonous emanation, especially one caused by burning or decaying organic matter **2.** an unwholesome or menacing atmosphere [Mid-17C. Directly or via French *miasme* < Greek *miasma* 'defilement, pollution' < *miainein* 'pollute'] —**miasmal** *adj* —**miasmatic** /meé əz máttik/ *adj*

Mic. *abbr* BIBLE Micah

mica /mīkə/ *n* a shiny aluminosilicate mineral belonging to a group having varying compositions. Source: igneous and metamorphic rocks. Use: electrical insulators, heating elements. [Early 18C. < Latin, 'grain, crumb']

Micah /mīkə/ *n* **1.** in the Bible, a Hebrew prophet who lived during the 8th century BC **2.** a book of the Bible traditionally attributed to the prophet Micah. See table at **Bible**

Micawber /mi káwbər/ *n* a poor and idle person who remains cheerfully optimistic [Mid-19C. After Wilkins Micawber, character in *David Copperfield* (1850) by Charles Dickens] —**Micawberish** *adj*

Miccosukee, **Miccosuki** *n, adj* PEOPLES, LANG another spelling of **Mikasuki**

mice ZOOL, COMPUT plural of **mouse**[2]

CULTURAL NOTE *Of Mice and Men*, a novella (1937) by US author John Steinbeck. With great compassion and realism, Steinbeck recounts the tragic tale of two itinerant labourers, George Milton and Lennie Small. When Lennie, a giant with mental disabilities, accidentally kills a girl, George shoots his friend rather than surrender him to a lynch mob.

---

micelle /mi sél/ *n* an electrically charged particle formed by an aggregate of ions or molecules in soaps, detergents, and other suspensions [Late 19C. < modern Latin *micella* 'small crumb' < Latin *mica* 'grain, crumb'] —**micellar** *adj*

Mich. *abbr* CALENDAR Michaelmas

Michael /mīk'l/ (b. 1921) king of Romania. He held the throne from 1927 to 1930 and from 1940 to 1947, when he abdicated and went into exile. Born **Hohenzollern-Sigmaringen, Michael**

Michaelmas /mík'lməss/ (*plural* -**mases**) *n* a Christian holy day marking the feast of St Michael the Archangel. Date: 29 September. [Pre-12C. Contraction of *Michael's mass*]

Michaelmas daisy *n* a common aster that blooms in the autumn. Flowers: purple, pink, or white. Native to: North America.

Michaelmas term *n* the name used for the autumn term at Oxford and Cambridge Universities, the Inns of Court, and some other educational institutions

Michelangelo: engraving after a 16th-century portrait by Giuliano Bugiardini

Michelangelo /mík'l ánjəlō/ (1475–1564) Italian sculptor, painter, architect, and poet. One of the great masters of the High Renaissance, his major works, which include the ceiling of the Sistine Chapel in the Vatican, were executed for patrons in Florence and Rome. Full name **Buonarroti Simoni, Michelangelo di Lodovico**

'There is no clime or country outside the kingdom of Italy where one can paint well...We call good painting Italian, and if good painting be produced in Flanders or in Spain...it will still be Italian painting.' [Michelangelo. Quoted in *On Ancient Painting*, Francisco de Hollanda; 1548]

Michelin /míchəlin, méeshə laN/, **André** (1853–1931) French tyre manufacturer. He founded a tyre company with his brother Edouard Michelin in 1888, and initiated a series of road maps and influential guide books.

Michelson /mík'lssən/, **Albert** (1852–1931) German-born US physicist. He won a Nobel Prize in physics (1907) for his precise measurements of the velocity of light. Full name **Michelson, Albert Abraham**

'The most important fundamental laws of physical science have all been discovered, and these are now so firmly established that the possibility of their ever being supplemented in consequence of new discoveries is exceedingly remote.' [Albert Michelson. Quoted in *The Arrow of Time*, Peter Coveney and Roger Highfield; 1991]

Michelson-Morley experiment /mík'lss'n máwrli-/ *n* an attempt to measure the difference in speed between light beams travelling in different directions by using interference effects. The negative result is explained by special relativity. [Early 20C. After Albert MICHELSON and Edward *Morley* (1838–1923), US physicist]

Michigan[1] /míshigən/ state in the northern United States, consisting of two peninsulas situated among four of the Great Lakes. It borders the Great Lakes, Ohio, Indiana, Illinois, Wisconsin, and Minnesota. Capital: Lansing. Population: 10,050,446 (2002 estimate). Area: 250,465 sq. km/96,705 sq. mi. — **Michigander** /míshi gándər/ *n* — **Michiganite** /n, adj

Michigan[2] /míshigən/ *n US* same as **Newmarket**[1] (sense 1) [Early 20C. After MICHIGAN[1]]

Michigan, Lake lake in the northern United States, between Michigan and Wisconsin, one of the Great Lakes. Area: 57,800 sq. km/22,300 sq. mi.

Mick /mik/ *n* a highly offensive term that deliberately insults somebody's Irish origin (*taboo*) [Mid-19C. < *Mick*, nickname for *Michael*]

mickey /míki/ (*plural* **-eys**) *n* BEVERAGES same as **Mickey Finn** (*informal*) ◇ **take the mickey** to tease somebody (*informal*)

Mickey Finn *n* an alcoholic drink to which a strong sedative has been added to make the drinker unconscious (*informal*) [Early 20C. Origin ?]

Mickiewicz /mits kyáyvich/, **Adam** (1798–1855) Polish poet. A major figure in Polish romanticism, he also campaigned for his country's independence from Russia.

mickle /mík'l/ *Scotland adj* abundant or very large ■ *adv* greatly or much [Old English *micel* < Indo-European]

Micmac *n, adj* PEOPLES, LANG another spelling of **Mi'kmaq**

miconazole /míkə názōl/ *n* an imidazole drug. Use: to treat fungus infections of the skin and nails.

micro /míkrō/ *adj* very small ■ *n* (*plural* **-cros**) (*informal*) **1.** same as **microprocessor 2.** same as **microwave** (sense 1) **3.** same as **microcomputer** [Mid-19C. < MICRO-]

micro- *prefix* **1.** small, minute ○ *microcosm* **2.** using a microscope or requiring magnification ○ *microbiology* **3.** one millionth (10⁻⁶) ○ *microgram* ○ *microsecond* Symbol μ **4.** of a small area or on a small scale ○ *microhabitat* ○ *micromanage* **5.** involving microfilm or microphotography ○ *microform* [< Greek *mikros* 'small']

microaerophile /míkrō áirō fíl/ *n* a tiny organism such as a bacterium, that is capable of living in an environment where there is not much oxygen

microalga /míkrō álgə/ *n* a microscopic alga with an undifferentiated body, e.g. a diatom or dinoflagellate —**microalgal** *adj*

microampere /míkrō ám pair/ *n* one millionth part of an ampere

microanalysis /míkrō ə nállssiss/ (*plural* **-yses** /-əsseez/) *n* **1.** the chemical analysis of tiny samples of a substance **2.** an extremely detailed analysis of

something —**microanalyst** /míkrō ánnəlist/ *n* —**microanalytical** /míkrō anə líttik'l/ *adj*

microanatomy /míkrō ə náttəmi/ *n* ANAT same as **histology** —**microanatomical** /míkrō anə tómmik'l/ *adj*

microarray /míkrō ə ray/ *n* GENETICS same as **gene chip**

microbalance /míkrō balənss/ *n* a balance for precisely weighing extremely small quantities up to 0.1 g

microbar /míkrō baar/ *n* a unit of pressure equal to one millionth of a bar

microbarograph /míkrō bárrə graaf, -graf/ *n* a barograph that records tiny changes in atmospheric pressure

microbe /míkrōb/ *n* a microscopic organism, especially one that transmits a disease [Late 19C. < French < Greek *mikros* 'small' + *bios* 'life'] —**microbial** /mī krōbi əl/ *adj*

microbiology /míkrō bī ólləji/ *n* the scientific study of microscopic organisms and their effects —**microbiological** /míkrō bī ə lójjik'l/ *adj* —**microbiologically** *adv* —**microbiologist** *n*

microbrew /míkrō broo/ *n* a specialist beer produced in a microbrewery

microbrewery /míkrō broo əri/ (*plural* **-ries**) *n* a small, usually independently owned brewery that produces limited quantities of specialized beers, often selling them on the premises —**microbrewer** *n* —**microbrewing** *n*

microburst /míkrō burst/ *n* a strong localized air current that hits the ground and spreads, causing wind to rapidly change direction and speed

microbusiness /míkrō biznəss/ *n US* a small business, typically with fewer than six employees, that does not have access to conventional sources of capital

microcap /míkrō kap/ *adj US* relating to companies with very little share capital

microcapsule /míkrō kap syool/ *n* a tiny capsule used to release a drug, flavour, or chemical

microcarrier /míkrō kari ər/ *n* a microscopic particle to which something is attached, used especially in cell cultures and drug delivery systems

microcassette /míkrō kə sét/ *n* a small audiotape cassette designed to fit into a pocket-size tape recorder or dictation machine

microcephaly /míkrō séffəli/, **microcephalia** /-sə fáyli ə/ *n* the condition of having a small head or having reduced space for the brain in the skull, often associated with learning difficulties —**microcephalic** /míkrō sə fállik/ *adj*

microchemistry /míkrō kémmistri/ *n* the scientific study of extremely small quantities of substances —**microchemical** *adj* —**microchemist** *n*

microchip /míkrō chip/ *n* ELECTRONICS same as **chip** *n* (sense 5)

microcircuit /míkrō surkit/ *n* ELECTRONICS same as **integrated circuit** —**microcircuitry** /míkrō súrkitri/ *n*

microclimate /míkrō klímət/ *n* the climate of a confined space or small geographical area —**microclimatic** /míkrō klī máttik/ *adj* —**microclimatically** *adv* —**microclimatology** /míkrō klīmə tóllji/ *n*

microcline /míkrō klīn/ *n* a mineral of the feldspar group that contains potassium. Use: making glass, porcelain. [Mid-19C. < German *Mikroklin* < Greek *mikros* 'small' + *klinein* 'to lean'; because its angle of cleavage differs only slightly from 90°]

micrococcus /míkrō kókəss/ (*plural* **-cocci** /-kóksī/) *n* any mainly harmless spherical bacterium, e.g. the one that ferments milk. Genus: *Micrococcus*. —**micrococcal** *adj*

microcomputer /míkrō kəm pyootər/ *n* a small computer in which the central processing unit is a single silicon chip (**microprocessor**) [Late 20C. After MINICOMPUTER]

microcontinent /míkrō kontinənt/ *n* a small segment of the Earth's crust that has the same overall granitic composition as a continent but is much smaller

microcopy /míkrō kopi/ (*plural* **-ies**) *n* a photographic reproduction of something on microfilm or microfiche

microcosm /míkrō kozəm/ *n* a miniature copy of something, especially when it represents or stands for a larger whole ○ *Our classroom was a microcosm of the university.* [12C. < French *microcosme* < Greek *mikros*

kosmos 'little world'] —**microcosmic** /míkrō kózmik/ *adj* —**microcosmically** *adv*

microcosmic salt *n* a colourless odourless salt obtained from human urine and used to test metallic salts and oxides

microcosmos /míkrō kózmoss/ *n* SCI same as **microcosm**

microcredit /míkrō kreddit/ *n* the extension of credit to entrepreneurs and microenterprises too poor to qualify for conventional bank loans

microcrystal /míkrō krist'l/ *n* a crystal that can only be seen under a microscope —**microcrystalline** /míkrō krístə līn/ *adj*

microcurie /míkrō kyoori/ *n* a unit of radioactivity equal to one millionth of a curie

microcyte /míkrō sīt/ *n* an unusually small red blood cell —**microcytic** /míkrō síttik/ *adj*

microdissection /míkrō di séksh'n/ *n* dissection carried out using a microscope

microdot /míkrō dot/ *n* **1.** a tiny photographic reproduction of something, about the size of a dot or a pinhead **2.** a dose of LSD in a tiny tablet (*informal*)

microeconomics /míkrō eekə nómmiks, -ekə-/ *n* the study of particular aspects of an economy (*takes a singular verb*) —**microeconomic** *adj*

micro-electromechanical system *n* full form of **MEMS**

microelectronics /míkrō ilek trónniks, -elek-/ *n* the technology and techniques involved in the design, development, and construction of extremely small electronic circuits such as computers on a single silicon chip (*takes a singular verb*) —**microelectronic** *adj* —**microelectronically** *adv*

microelement /míkrō eləmənt/ *n* CHEM same as **trace element** (sense 1)

microencapsulate /míkrō in kápsyoo layt/ (**-lates**, **-lating**, **-lated**) *vt* to enclose a substance in microcapsules —**microencapsulation** /-in kápsyoo láysh'n/ *n*

microengineering /míkrō enjə neéring/ *n* the technology and techniques involved in integrating microelectronic circuitry into miniaturized mechanical devices for sensing, processing, or carrying out various functions —**microengineer** *n, vt*

microenterprise /míkrō entər prīz/ *n* BUSINESS same as **microbusiness**

microevolution /míkrō eevə loósh'n, -evə-/ *n* minor change within a species or small group of organisms, usually within a short period of time —**microevolutionary** *adj*

microfabrication /míkrō fabbri káysh'n/ *n* the production of electromechanical, mechanical, chemical, or optical devices on a microscopic scale —**microfabricated** /-fábbri kaytid/ *adj*

microfarad /míkrō farəd, -rad/ *n* one millionth part of a farad

microfauna /míkrō fawnə/ *npl* animals so small that they can be seen only under a microscope —**microfaunal** *adj*

microfibre /míkrō fībər/ *n* **1.** an extremely fine synthetic thread or yarn **2.** a wrinkle-resistant washable synthetic fabric made of microfibre. Use: clothing.

microfibril /míkrō fíbril/ *n* in cells, any extremely fine structure resembling a thread

microfiche /míkrō feesh/ *n* a sheet of microfilm containing information laid out in a grid pattern [Mid-20C. < French < Greek *mikros* 'small' + French *fiche* 'slip of paper']

microfilament /míkrō fílləmənt/ *n* a thin thread of protein found in muscle and the cytoplasm of all cells —**microfilamentous** /míkrō filə méntəss/ *adj*

microfilaria /míkrō fi láiri ə/ (*plural* **-ae** /-i ī/) *n* the early larval stage of a parasitic nematode worm (**filaria**), a cause of heartworm in dogs and elephantiasis in humans —**microfilarial** *adj*

microfilm /míkrō film/ *n* a strip of photographic film on which highly miniaturized reproductions have been recorded ■ *vti* (**-films**, **-filming**, **-filmed**) to photograph something on microfilm

microflora /míkrō flawrə/ *npl* plants that can be seen only under a microscope —**microfloral** *adj*

microform /míkrō fawrm/ *n* a piece of film or paper

such as microfilm or microfiche that contains miniature reproductions

microfossil /mī́krō foss'l/ *n* a fossil that can be studied only with a microscope, e.g. a bacterium fossil

microfungus /mī́krō fung gəss/ (*plural* **-gi** /-gī/ or **-guses**) *n* a fungus that has tiny or unobservable reproductive organs

microgram /mī́krō gram/ *n* one millionth part of a gram

micrograph /mī́krō graaf, -graf/ *n* **1.** a photograph or drawing of something as seen through a microscope **2.** a device that can produce engraving or writing using very fine lines —**micrographic** /mī́krō gráffik/ *adj* —**micrographically** *adv*

microgravity /mī́krō gravəti/ *n* a force of gravity so low that weightlessness occurs, e.g. during space travel

microgroove /mī́krō groov/ *n* the narrow spiral groove on a gramophone record

microhabitat /mī́krō hábbi tat/ *n* an environment that has a unique set of ecological conditions within a larger habitat and supports distinct flora and fauna

microhistory /mī́krō histəri/ *n* the study of and focus on a very small phenomenon in an effort to explain a larger event or an overall historical process

microinch /mī́krō inch/ *n* a unit of linear measurement equivalent to one millionth of an inch. Symbol μ**in**

microinjection /mī́kro in jeksh'n/ *n* the injection of a very small amount of liquid into individual cells, using a specialized instrument and a microscope for observation —**microinject** *vti*

microinstruction /mī́krō in struksh'n/ *n* a single instruction in a low-level computer program

microlending /mī́kro lending/ *n* same as **microcredit**

microlensing /mī́krō lenzing/ *n* the temporary focusing and brightening of light from a distant background star as a result of the gravitational effect of an astronomical object passing in the foreground —**microlens** *n*

microlepidopteran /mī́krō léppi dóptərən/ *n* a small or medium-sized moth, e.g. a leaf miner, that is of little interest to a collector

microlight /mī́krō līt/, **microlight aircraft**, **microlite**, **microlite aircraft** *n* a small low-speed lightweight aircraft, often with an open fuselage, that can carry one or two people and is used for flying for pleasure or reconnaissance

microlith /mī́krō lith/ *n* a tiny flint tool, usually triangular, found in Mesolithic sites in Europe and dating from 12,000 to 3,000 BC —**microlithic** /mī́krō líthik/ *adj*

microloan /mī́kro lōn/ *n* a small loan that enables a microenterprise or impoverished person to continue or start a business. Microloans are frequently made to impoverished people in developing countries as part of a programme to reduce poverty.

micromachining /mī́krō məsheening/ *n* the techniques used in fabricating the miniaturized devices and moving parts into which microelectronic circuitry is integrated —**micromachine** *vt*

micromanage /mī́krō manij/ (**-ages, -aging, -aged**) *vt* to control a person or a situation by paying extreme attention to small details —**micromanagement** *n* —**micromanager** *n*

micromanipulator /mī́krō mə níppyōō laytər/ *n* a device consisting of geared controls for the manipulation of extremely small dissecting tools or miniature surgical instruments under a microscope —**micromanipulation** /-mə níppyōō láysh'n/ *n* —**micromanipulative** *adj*

micromere /mī́krō meer/ *n* either of the cells (**blastomeres**) formed by the division of a fertilized egg

micrometeorite /mī́krō meeti ə rīt/ *n* a particle of cosmic dust that falls to Earth or onto the Moon's surface —**micrometeoritic** /-meeti ə ríttik/ *adj*

micrometeoroid /mī́krō meeti ə royd/ *n* an extremely small dust particle found in space that may land on Earth or the Moon as a micrometeorite

micrometeorology /mī́krō meeti ə rólləji/ *n* the study of weather conditions in the air immediately above ground level, especially in very small areas —

micrometeorological /-ərə lójjik'l/ *adj* —**micrometeorologist** *n*

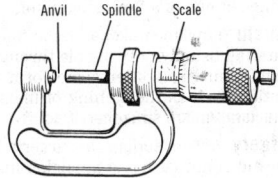

micrometer

micrometer[1] /mī krómmitər/ *n* a device for measuring small diameters, thicknesses, distances, or angles to a high degree of accuracy [Late 17C. < French *micromètre*] —**micrometric** /mī́krō méttrik/ *adj* —**micrometrically** *adv* —**micrometry** *n*

micrometer[2] *n* MEASURE US spelling of **micrometre**

micrometre /mī́krō meetər/ *n* a unit of linear measurement equivalent to one millionth of a metre. Symbol μ**m**

microminiaturization /mī́krō minnichə rī záysh'n/, **microminiaturisation** *n* the production and use of extremely small electronic components, especially semiconductors —**microminiaturize** /-mínnichə rīz/ *vt* —**microminiaturized** *adj*

micromole /mī́krō mōl/ *n* a molecular weight expressed in grams that is equivalent to one millionth of a mole. Symbol μ**mol** —**micromolar** *adj*

micromorphology /mī́krō mawr fólləji/ *n* the study of the fine detail in the external form and structure of organisms, or of other objects such as metal surfaces —**micromorphological** /-mawrfə lójjik'l/ *adj*

micron /mī́ kron/ *n* a unit of linear measurement equivalent to one millionth of a metre [Late 19C. < Greek *mikros* 'small' + -ON[1]]

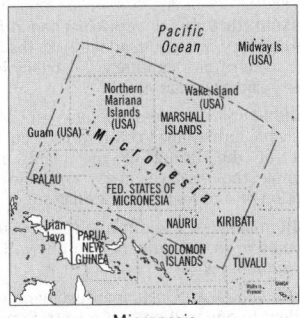

Micronesia

Micronesia /mī́krə nee͞ezi ə/ **1.** ethnographic grouping of Pacific islands, encompassing the islands of the western Pacific Ocean east of the Philippines and mainly north of the equator, including Kiribati, Guam, the Mariana Islands, the Federated States of Micronesia, and Palau **2.** island nation in the western Pacific Ocean, comprising more than 600 islands, about 60 of which are inhabited. Language: English. Currency: US dollar. Capital: Palikir. Population: 136,973 (2003). Area: 702 sq. km/271 sq. mi. Official name **Federated States of Micronesia** —**Micronesian** *adj, n*

micronize /mī́krə nīz/ (**-izes, -izing, -ized**), **micronise** (**-ises, -ising, -ised**) *vt* to reduce the particle size of a powder down to a few millionths of a metre

micronucleus /mī́krō nyōōkli əss/ (*plural* **-clei** /-kli ī/ or **-cleuses**) *n* the smaller of the two nuclei in the cells of ciliate protozoans. It contains genetic material and is involved in sexual reproduction. —**micronuclear** *adj*

micronutrient /mī́krō nyōōtri ənt/ *n* a substance that an organism requires for normal growth and development but only in very small quantities, e.g. a vitamin or mineral

microorganism /mī́krō áwrgənizəm/ *n* a tiny organism

such as a virus, protozoan, or bacterium that can only be seen under a microscope

micropalaeontology /mī́krō pálli on tóllaji/ *n* a branch of palaeontology that studies the microorganisms preserved as fossils in sedimentary rocks —**micropalaeontological** /mī́krō pálli ontə lójjik'l/ *adj* —**micropalaeontologist** *n*

microparasite /mī́krō párrə sīt/ *n* a microorganism that lives as a parasite on other organisms —**microparasitic** /-parrə síttik/ *adj*

microphage /mī́krə fayj/ *n* a small white blood cell, part of the immune system, that removes bacteria and other foreign bodies from blood and tissue —**microphagic** /mī́krə fájjik/ *adj*

microphagous /mī króffəgəss/ *adj* describes animals that live in water and feed on microscopic particles or microorganisms

microphone: cutaway view

microphone /mī́krə fōn/ *n* a device that converts sounds to electrical signals by means of a vibrating diaphragm. The signals can then be amplified, transmitted for broadcasting, or used for recording the sounds. [Late 17C. Originally a device for making faint sounds louder] —**microphonic** /mī́krə fónnik/ *adj*

microphonics /mī́krə fónniks/ *npl* the sound heard from an electronic device, especially a loudspeaker, caused by the vibration of some mechanical part

microphotograph /mī́krō fōtə graaf, -graf/ *n* **1.** a photographic image, e.g. on microfilm, so small that it has to be magnified in order to be viewed **2.** a photograph of an object viewed through a microscope —**microphotographer** /-fə tóggrəfər/ *n* —**microphotographic** /-fōtə gráffik/ *adj* —**microphotography** *n*

microphysics /mī́krō fízziks/ *n* the branch of physics that studies objects and systems such as molecules, atoms, and elementary particles that are observable only microscopically or indirectly (*takes a singular verb*) —**microphysical** *adj* —**microphysically** *adv* —**microphysicist** *n*

microphyte /mī́krō fīt/ *n* a plant observable only under a microscope, especially one that is parasitic —**microphytic** /mī́krō fíttik/ *adj*

micropipette /mī́krōpi pet/ *n* a very slender graduated tube that is used to measure, transfer, or remove minute amounts of something

micropower /mī́krō pow ər/ *n* electrical power generated or used in relatively small quantities, usually close to the location where it is needed

microprint /mī́krō print/ *n* printed text, e.g. on microfilm, so small that it has to be magnified in order to be viewed

microprism /mī́krō prizəm/ *n* a small prism that is part of the focusing screen of many single-lens reflex cameras

microprocessor /mī́krō pró sessər/ *n* the central processing unit that performs the basic operations in a microcomputer, consisting of an integrated circuit contained on a single chip

microprogram /mī́krō pró gram/ *n* a built-in program within a microprocessor, consisting of a series of arithmetical and logical steps that enable basic instructions to be carried out

microprogramming /mī́krō pró gramming/ *n* a means of programming the central processing unit of a computer by breaking down instructions into a series of small steps

micropropagation /mī́ krō propə gáysh'n/ *n* the propa-

gation of plants by cloning a small piece of plant tissue cultured in a growth medium

micropsia /mī krópsi ə/ *n* an eye condition in which the cones of the retina are separated by local swelling, making objects appear smaller than they really are [Mid-19C. < MICRO- + Greek *opsis* 'sight' + -IA]

micropyle /mī́krō pīl/ *n* **1.** a small opening in the covering of the ovule of a plant through which the pollen tube passes prior to fertilization **2.** a small pore in the membrane of an insect egg that allows sperm to enter and fertilize the egg [Early 19C. < French < Greek *micros* 'small' + *pulē* 'gate'] —**micropylar** /mī́krō pīlər/ *adj*

microradiography /mī́krō raydi óggrəfi/ *n* a technique that enlarges X-ray radiographs so that fine details can be examined —**microradiograph** /-ráydi ō graaf, -graf/ *n* —**microradiographic** /mī́krō ráydi ō gráffik/ *adj*

microreader /mī́krō reedər/ *n* a device that projects enlarged images and text from microfilm and microfiche onto a screen for easy reading

micro scooter *n* a small, often collapsible version of a child's foot scooter, used as a quick way of getting around on the pavements of city streets

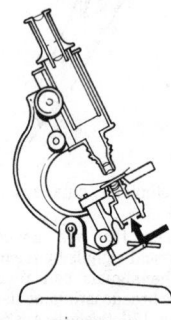

microscope

microscope /mī́krə skōp/ *n* a device that uses a lens or system of lenses to produce a greatly magnified image of an object. An optical microscope uses transmitted or reflected light to obtain the image. An electron microscope uses a beam of electrons and a system of electron-focusing lenses to obtain images.

microscopic /mī́krə skóppik/ *adj* **1.** VERY SMALL extremely small **2.** *also* **microscopical** /mī́krə skóppik'l/ INVISIBLE WITHOUT MICROSCOPE invisible without the use of a microscope **3.** *also* **microscopical** INVOLVING MICROSCOPE using or involving a microscope **4.** THOROUGH very thorough and meticulous —**microscopically** *adv*

Microscopium /mī́krō skópi əm/ *n* a small inconspicuous constellation of the southern hemisphere

microscopy /mī króskəpi/ (*plural* **-pies**) *n* **1.** the study and design of microscopes **2.** an investigation, observation, or experiment that involves the use of a microscope —**microscopist** *n*

microsecond /mī́krō sekənd/ *n* a measurement of time equivalent to one millionth of a second. Symbol μs

microseism /mī́krō sīzəm/ *n* a recurrent low-level earth tremor caused by phenomena such as the force of crashing waves rather than by movement of rock masses —**microseismic** /mī́krō sīzmik/ *adj* —**microseismicity** /mī́krō sīz míssəti/ *n*

microsmatic /mī́ kroz máttik/ *adj* having poorly developed olfactory organs [Late 19C. < MICRO- + Greek *osmē* 'smell' + -*atic* (form of -ATE)]

microsociology /mī́krō sóssi ólləji/ *n* the branch of sociology that studies small groups and units within a larger society

microsome /mī́krōsōm/ *n* a small particle obtained after isolating a cell using centrifugal action, typically consisting of ribosomes associated with fragments of endoplasmic reticulum —**microsomal** /mī́krō sōm'l/ *adj*

microsporangium /mī́krō spaw ránji əm/ (*plural* **-gia** /-ji ə/) *n* a part of the reproductive structure of some plants, especially ferns, that produces microspores —**microsporangiate** /mī́krō spaw ránji ət/ *adj*

microspore /mī́krō spawr/ *n* the smaller of two kinds of spore produced by seed plants and some ferns that develops into a male gametophyte

microsporocyte /mī́krō spáwrə sīt/, **microspore mother cell** *n* a plant cell that divides to produce four microspores

microsporophyll /mī́krō spáwrəfil/ *n* a leaf that bears a structure by which microspores are formed. In ferns, these are normal foliage leaves, the equivalent of the stamen of a flowering plant.

microstructure /mī́krō strukchər/ *n* the fine structure of a material, usually only visible through a microscope and sometimes after some form of surface preparation such as the etching of metal alloys —**microstructural** /mī́krō strúkchərəl/ *adj*

microsurgery /mī́krō súrjəri/ *n* surgery performed with the aid of miniaturized precision instruments, including scalpels, needles, and a specially designed optical microscope —**microsurgical** *adj*

microswitch /mī́krō swich/ *n* a very small sensitive switch that acts by the movement of a small lever and is used where rapid precise movements are required, especially in keyboards and automatic control devices

microteaching /mī́krō teeching/ *n* a training exercise used in teacher training in which a student or student teacher is videotaped during part of a class for subsequent analysis and evaluation

microtear /mī́krō tair/ *n* a minute tear in muscle-fiber tissue, seen in competitive cyclists and other distance athletes

microtome /mī́krōtōm/ *n* an instrument that is used to cut biological tissues into very thin transparent slices for microscopic examination

microtomy /mī króttəmi/ *n* the process of preparing thin slices of biological tissues using a microtome, so that they can be observed under a microscope —**microtomic** /mī́krō tómmik/ *adj* —**microtomist** *n*

microtone /mī́krōtōn/ *n* a musical interval smaller than a semitone, especially a quarter tone —**microtonal** /mī́krō tōn'l/ *adj* —**microtonality** /mī́krōtō nálləti/ *n* —**microtonally** *adv*

microtubule /mī́krō tyōob yool/ *n* a hollow tubular structure composed of the protein tubulin that helps to maintain the shape and movement of a living cell and the transport of material within it —**microtubular** *adj*

microvasculature /mī́krō váskyōōləchər/ *n* a part of the circulatory system made up of the smallest vessels such as capillaries, arterioles, and venules —**microvascular** *adj*

microvillus /mī́krō villəss/ (*plural* **-li** /-lī/) *n* a microscopic hair-shaped cell that projects from the surface of the lining of the small intestine, increasing the surface area available for the absorption of nutrients —**microvillar** *adj*

microvolt /mī́krōvōlt/ *n* a unit of electric potential or electromotive force equivalent to one millionth of a volt. Symbol μV

microwatt /mī́krō wot/ *n* a measurement of power equivalent to one millionth of a watt. Symbol μW

microwave /mī́krə wayv/ *n* **1.** OVEN USING ELECTROMAGNETIC RADIATION an oven that cooks or heats up food or beverages relatively quickly using high-frequency electromagnetic radiation **2.** HIGH-FREQUENCY ELECTROMAGNETIC WAVE an electromagnetic wave whose wavelength ranges from 1 mm to 30 cm. Use: radar, radio transmissions, cooking or heating devices. ■ *vt* (**-waves, -waving, -waved**) HEAT OR COOK SOMETHING IN MICROWAVE to heat or cook food or beverages in a microwave —**microwavable** *adj* —**microwaveable** *adj*

microwave oven *n* HOUSEHOLD same as **microwave** *n* (sense 1)

micturate /míktyōō rayt/ (**-rates, -rating, -rated**) *vi* same as **urinate** (*technical*) [Mid-19C. Back-formation < *micturition* 'urination' < Latin *micturire* 'want to urinate' < *mict*-, past participle of *meiere* 'urinate'] —**micturation** /míktyōō ráysh'n/ *n*

mid /mid/ *adj* **1.** found or occurring in or around the centre of or halfway through something ○ *She cut me off in mid sentence.* **2.** describes speech sounds produced with the tongue halfway between the high and low positions, like the vowels, e.g. in the words 'but' and 'bet' [Old English *midd* < Indo-European]

'mid /mid/, **mid** *prep* among a group (*literary*) [15C. Shortening of AMID]

mid. *abbr* middle

Mid. *abbr US* NAVY midshipman

mid- *prefix* middle ○ *midrange* ○ *midmost* [< MID]

midafternoon /mid aáftər noón/ *n* the part of the afternoon midway between noon and sunset —**midafternoon** *adj*

midair /mid áir/ *n* a point in the air above the ground or another surface ■ *adj* occurring or located at a point in the air above the ground or another surface

Midas /mídəss/ *n* in Greek mythology, a Phrygian king who befriended Silenus, a follower of Dionysus, and was rewarded by Dionysus with the gift of making everything he touched turn into gold

Midas touch *n* the ability to make large amounts of money, often with very little apparent effort

mid-Atlantic *adj* **1.** situated or occurring in the middle of the Atlantic Ocean **2.** influenced by both North America and Britain, especially in behaviour or speech

Mid-Atlantic Ridge submarine mountain range in the Atlantic Ocean, bisecting the ocean from north to south between Iceland and the Antarctic Circle. Its average height is 3,050 m/10,000 ft. Length: 15,000 km/9,300 mi.

Mid-Atlantic States *npl* same as **Middle Atlantic States**

midbrain /míd brayn/ *n* in vertebrates, the middle part of the three main divisions of either the embryonic or the adult brain. Technical name **mesencephalon**

midcourse /míd káwrss/ *n* the part of a missile's flight between the end of its launch and the beginning of its re-entry ■ *adj* present or occurring partway through a course or course of action

midday /mid dáy/ *n* twelve o'clock noon or the period around the middle of the day

midden /mídd'n/ *n* **1.** a pile of dung or refuse **2.** ARCHAEOL same as **kitchen midden 3.** *N England* same as **earth closet** [14C. < N Germanic]

middle /mídd'l/ *adj* **1.** CENTRAL AND EQUIDISTANT FROM LIMITS equidistant from the sides, edges, or ends of something **2.** BEING HALFWAY BETWEEN BEGINNING AND END occurring or located halfway between the start and finish of a period of time, an event, or a series ○ *in the middle years of the 19th century* **3.** OCCUPYING INTERMEDIATE POSITION situated in an intermediate position, e.g. in age or status ○ *below middle height* **4.** BEING MIDWAY BETWEEN EXTREMES lying between two extremes or opposites and, consequently, usually moderate **5.** GRAM CONCERNING VOICE EXPRESSING REFLEXIVE ACTION relating to the voice of verbs in some languages such as ancient Greek and Sanskrit that expresses the action of a subject on or for itself ■ *n* **1.** MIDWAY PART OR POSITION the part or position furthest from the sides, edges, or ends of something ○ *the middle finger* **2.** PART BETWEEN BEGINNING AND END the part between or halfway between the beginning and end of a period of time or an event ○ *in the middle of June* ○ *arrived in the middle of a diplomatic crisis* **3.** INSIDE PART the interior or central part of something ○ *Remove the seeds from the middle of the melon.* **4.** CENTRAL PART OF BODY the waist, stomach, or central area of the human body (*informal*) **5.** GRAM VOICE EXPRESSING REFLEXIVE ACTION the voice of verbs in some languages such as ancient Greek and Sanskrit that expresses the action of a subject on or for itself ■ *v* (**-dles, -dling, -dled**) **1.** *vti* PUT SOMETHING IN MIDDLE to place something equidistant from the sides, edges, or ends of something **2.** *vti* SAILING FOLD SAIL IN HALF to fold a sail in half, or to be folded in half **3.** *vt* CRICKET HIT BALL WITH MIDDLE OF BAT to hit a cricket ball firmly with the middle of the bat [Old English *middel*] ◇ **knock somebody into the middle of next week** to hit somebody very hard (*informal*)

Middle *adj* relating to a language or literature between its early and later stages of development

middle age *n* the period in somebody's life when that person is no longer considered young, usually between 40 and 60

middle-aged *adj* **1.** no longer considered young, but not yet considered old **2.** relating to the behaviour, attitudes, lifestyle, or interests considered characteristic of middle age, especially staidness, conventionality, or old-fashionedness

middle-aged spread *n* the excess fat sometimes accumulated around the waist during middle age (*humorous*)

Middle Ages *n* the period in European history between antiquity and the Italian Renaissance, often considered to be between the end of the Roman Empire in the 5th century and the early 15th century

middle-age spread *n* same as **middle-aged spread** (*humorous*)

Middle America *n* **1.** a section of the middle class in the United States considered by some to be politically conservative and to hold traditional social and moral values **2.** GEOG same as **Midwest 3.** *US* the area to the south of the United States and the north of South America that includes Mexico, Central America, and sometimes the Caribbean —**Middle American** *adj, n*

Middle Atlantic States *npl US* the states midway along the Atlantic coast of the United States, consisting of New York, New Jersey, and Pennsylvania, and usually Delaware and Maryland

Middleback Ranges /mídd'l bak-/ range of hills in South Australia. It forms the eastern section of the Gawler Ranges.

middlebreaker /mídd'l braykər/ *n* AGRIC same as **lister**

middlebrow /mídd'l brow/ *n* somebody who has moderate or conventional interests in cultural and intellectual matters (*informal*) [Early 20C. After HIGHBROW and LOWBROW] —**middlebrow** *adj*

middlebuster /mídd'l bustər/ *n* AGRIC same as **lister**

middle C *n* a note roughly in the middle of a piano keyboard, written in musical notation on the first ledger line below the treble staff or above the bass staff

Middle Chinese *n* the form of the Chinese language spoken and written during the Sui and Tang dynasties, AD 581–907

middle class *n* the section of society between the poor and the wealthy, including business and professional people and skilled workers —**middle-class** *adj*

middle common room *n* a room in some colleges and universities where postgraduate students can meet and relax

middle distance *n* the portion of space that is farther away from a viewer than the foreground but nearer than the background, especially in a landscape painting or photograph

middle-distance *adj* relating to foot races between 400 m/440 yd and 1,500 m/one mile long

Middle Dutch *n* the form of the Dutch language spoken and written between the 12th and the beginning of the 16th centuries AD

middle ear *n* the narrow air-filled space between the ear drum and the outer wall of the inner ear containing the three tiny bones that transmit sound vibrations

Middle Earth *n* MYTHOL same as **Midgard**

Middle East *n* **1.** the region stretching from the eastern Mediterranean to the western side of the Indian subcontinent, including Egypt, the Arabian Peninsula, Israel, Jordan, Lebanon, Syria, Turkey, Iran, and Iraq **2.** the area extending from Iran to Myanmar, including Afghanistan, South Asia, and Tibet (*dated*) —**Middle Eastern** *adj* —**Middle Easterner** *n*

Middle England *n* a section of the middle class in England considered to be politically conservative and to hold traditional social and moral values

Middle English *n* the form of the English language spoken and written between the 12th and the beginning of the 16th centuries. The leading dialects of this period were Kentish, West Saxon, West Midland, East Midland, and Northern.

middle finger *n* the longest finger of the human hand, next to the index finger

Middle French *n* the form of the French language spoken and written between the 14th and the beginning of the 17th centuries AD

middle game *n* the middle part of a game of chess, after the opening moves and before the endgame

Middle Greek *n, adj* LANG same as **medieval Greek**

middle ground *n* **1.** same as **middle distance 2.** an intermediate position between two opposing views or factions ○ *The two parties were unable to find any middle ground.*

Middle High German *n* the form of High German spoken and written between the 12th and the beginning of the 16th centuries

middle-income *adj* earning a wage or salary that is roughly the same as the average for a population

Middle Irish *n* the form of Irish Gaelic spoken and written between the 11th and the beginning of the 15th centuries

Middle Kingdom *n* **1.** PERIOD OF ANCIENT EGYPTIAN HISTORY a period of Egyptian history from the late 11th dynasty, approximately 2040 BC, to the 13th dynasty, 1670 BC **2.** FORMER CHINESE EMPIRE the former Chinese Empire, so called because it was supposedly at the centre of the world **3.** CENTRAL TERRITORY OF CHINESE EMPIRE the central territory held by most Chinese Empires, including the Huang and Yangtze river valleys, and eventually the 18 inner provinces of China

middle lamella *n* a thin membrane, composed of pectin and other polysaccharides, that cements the walls of two adjacent plant cells together

Middle Low German *n* the form of Low German spoken and written between the 12th and the beginning of the 16th centuries

middleman /mídd'l man/ (*plural* **-men** /-men/) *n* **1.** a trader, especially a man, who buys goods from a producer and then sells them to retailers or consumers **2.** somebody, especially a man, who is a negotiator or intermediary in a transaction

middle management *n* managers who are responsible for relatively small numbers of staff and are involved in the details of running an organization rather than in taking major decisions or setting policy —**middle manager** *n*

middlemost /mídd'l mōst/ *adj* same as **midmost**

middle name *n* the name between a first name and a surname ◇ **be somebody's middle name** to be a quality, attribute, or characteristic that somebody possesses a great deal of (*informal*) ○ *Tact's my middle name.*

middle-of-the-road *adj* **1.** OCCUPYING INTERMEDIATE POSITION taking a course of action or adopting a point of view that is midway between two extremes **2.** INTENDED TO HAVE BROAD MUSIC APPEAL intended to be musically appealing to the majority of people and avoid stylistic extremes, so often considered bland ■ *n* MUSIC AIMING FOR BROAD APPEAL music intended to appeal to many people that avoids stylistic extremes

Middle Palaeolithic *n* the period of geological time between the Lower and Upper Palaeolithic ages, from about 180,000 to 40,000 years ago

middle passage *n* the journey from western Africa across the Atlantic to the Caribbean or the Americas, formerly undertaken by many slave ships

middleperson /mídd'l purss'n/ (*plural* **-people** /-peep'l/ or **-persons**) *n* **1.** a trader who buys goods from a producer and then sells them to retailers or consumers **2.** a negotiator or intermediary in a transaction

Middlesbrough /mídd'lzbərə/ industrial town and port in northeastern England. Population: 134,855 (2001).

middle school *n* **1.** in the United Kingdom, a state-run school for children between the ages of about 8 and 13 years. The age range depends upon the local authority in which the school is situated. **2.** in the United States, a school for children between the ages of about 11 and 14 years, depending on the school's location

Middle Scots *n* the form of the Scots language written and spoken between the late 15th and the early 17th centuries

Middlesex /mídd'l seks/ former county in south-eastern England. In 1965 most of the county was absorbed into Greater London.

middle-sized *adj* neither very big nor very small

Middle Temple *n* in England, one of four legal societies of the Inns of Court in London

middle term *n* in logic, a term that appears in both premises of a syllogism but not in the conclusion

middleware /mídd'l wair/ *n* software that manages the connection between a client and a database

middle watch *n* on board a vessel, the watch from midnight until 4.00 am

middleweight /mídd'l wayt/ *n* **1.** WEIGHT CATEGORY IN PROFESSIONAL BOXING in professional boxing, a weight category for competitors who weigh between 66.5 and 72.5 kg/147 and 160 lb **2.** WEIGHT CATEGORY IN AMATEUR BOXING in amateur boxing, a weight category for competitors who weigh between 71 and 75 kg/157 and 165 lb **3.** BOXER COMPETING AT MIDDLEWEIGHT a professional or amateur boxer who competes at middleweight level **4.** WRESTLER OF INTERMEDIATE WEIGHT in various sports such as wrestling, a contestant of approximately the same weight as a middleweight boxer

Middle Welsh *n* the form of the Welsh language written and spoken between the 12th and the beginning of the 15th centuries

Middle West *n US* same as **Midwest** —**Middle Western** *adj* —**Middle Westerner** *n*

middlewoman /mídd'l wŏŏmən/ (*plural* **-men** /-wimin/) *n* **1.** a female trader who buys goods from a producer and then sells them to retailers or consumers **2.** a female negotiator or intermediary in a transaction

middling /míddling/ *adj* **1.** MEDIUM, MODERATE, OR AVERAGE of average size, quantity, quality, or position **2.** ORDINARY AND UNEXCEPTIONAL neither good nor bad, especially in health or mood ■ *adv* MODERATELY to a moderate and unremarkable degree (*informal*) [Late 16C. < MID + -LING [2]] —**middlingly** *adv*

middlings /míddlingz/ *npl* commodities or resources such as ore or petrol that are of average quality, grade, or price (*takes a plural verb*) ■ *n* poor-quality flour made from coarsely ground wheat and bran (*takes a singular or plural verb*)

Middx *abbr* Middlesex

middy /míddi/ (*plural* **-dies**) *n* **1.** NAVY same as **midshipman** (sense 2) (*informal*) **2.** *also* **middy blouse** a loose blouse with a sailor collar worn by women and children **3.** *Aus* in Western Australia, New South Wales, and Queensland, a medium-sized beer glass, containing 285 ml/10 fluid oz (*informal*)

Mideast /mid éest/ *n N Am* same as **Middle East** —**Mideastern** *adj* —**Mideasterner** *n*

midfield /mid feeld/ *n* **1.** the middle portion of a sports pitch, especially the area midway between the two penalty areas **2.** the group of players who contest control of the central area of the pitch between the two penalty areas (*takes a singular or plural verb*)

midfielder /mid feeldər/ *n* a member of a football team active in the central area of the playing field, often both in attack and defence

Midgard /mid gaard/, **Midgarth** /-gaarth/, **Midgarthr** /-gaarthər/ *n* in Norse mythology, the home of humankind, midway between Asgard and the underworld, encircled by a huge serpent and formed from the body of the giant Ymir

midge /mij/ *n* **1.** a small slender flying insect that occurs globally, particularly in swarms near bodies of standing water, or a related biting insect that can transmit blood-borne diseases. Family: Chironomidae or Ceratopogonidae. **2.** a person or animal of small stature [Old English *mycg* < Indo-European, probably an imitation of humming]

midget /míjjit/ *n* **1.** OFFENSIVE TERM an offensive term for a very short person whose skeleton and features are of standard proportions **2.** VERY SMALL VERSION OF SOMETHING a very small version of something such as a car or boat ■ *adj* MINIATURE OR SMALLER THAN USUAL miniaturized or belonging to a class smaller than the ordinary size [Mid-19C. < MIDGE, literally 'little midge']

midgut /mid gut/ *n* **1.** PART OF DIGESTIVE TRACT the central section of the digestive tract of a vertebrate, in which the processes of digestion and absorption take place **2.** PART OF INVERTEBRATE ALIMENTARY CANAL the middle section of the alimentary canal of an invertebrate **3.** PART OF EMBRYO'S GUT the middle portion of the gut of an embryo that develops into most of the small intestine and part of the large intestine

Midheaven /mid hévv'n/ *n* the point on the apparent annual path of the Sun in the celestial sphere where the meridian is crossed, or the sign of the zodiac that contains it

midi /míddi/ (*plural* **-is**) *n* a skirt or coat that comes down to just below the knee or halfway down the calf [Mid-20C. < MID after MINI-, MAXI] —**midi** *adj*

Midi /meédi/ *n* the south of France [French, literally 'midday']

Midi, Canal du /meédi-/ ♦ **Canal du Midi**

MIDI /míddi/ *n* the interface between an electronic musical instrument and a computer, used in composing and editing music to allow the computer to control an instrument or one instrument to control others. Full form **musical instrument digital interface**

midiron /míd ī ərn/ *n* in golf, a number 5, 6, 7, or 8 iron, used to give the ball a medium amount of lift

midi system *n* a compact hi-fi system, usually consisting of a CD-player, tuner, cassette deck, and amplifier, designed as a single unit with separate speakers

midland /mídlənd/ *n* the middle, inland, or interior part of a country ■ *adj* relating to or being in the middle or interior of a country

Midland *n* **1.** a variety of British English spoken in the Midlands of England, divided into East Midland and West Midland **2.** *US* a variety of US English spoken in states from New Jersey south to Georgia, especially in the Appalachian and Piedmont mountains and in the Shenandoah Valley —**Midland** *adj*

Midlands /mídləndz/ central, largely industrialized part of England, centred on Birmingham —**Midlander** *n*

midlife /míd líf/ *n* same as **middle age**

midlife crisis *n* feelings of self-doubt and a lack of confidence experienced by some people when they become middle-aged

midline /míd līn/ *n* a vertical line that divides a bilaterally symmetrical animal or human body into right and left halves

Midlothian /mid lṓthi ən/ council area in southeastern Scotland, on the Firth of Forth

midmorning /míd máwrning/ *n* the middle part of the morning —**midmorning** *adj*

midmost /mídmōst/ *adj* situated at or nearest the centre of something ■ *adv* in the very middle or midst of something [Old English *midmest*]

midnight /míd nīt/ *n* **1.** 12 o'clock at night or the period around the middle of the night **2.** a period of intense darkness or gloom (*literary*) —**midnightly** *adj, adv*

midnight blue *adj* of a very dark blue colour —**midnight blue** *n*

midnight sun *n* the Sun when it is visible from within the Arctic or Antarctic circles at midnight during their respective summer months

mid-ocean ridge *n* a long underwater mountain range of the Atlantic, Indian, or South Pacific oceans formed from volcanic rock released during the movement of tectonic plates

midpoint /míd poynt/ *n* **1.** the point on a line, journey, or distance that is halfway between the beginning and end **2.** the point of time halfway between the beginning and end of an event, course of action, or period

midrange /míd raynj/ *adj* **1.** occurring in the middle of a series, array, or range **2.** covering a distance midway between a short-range and long-range trajectory

Midrash /mídraash/ (*plural* **-rashim** /-róshim/) *n* a body of Rabbinic literature consisting of commentary on and clarification of biblical texts, first compiled before 500 AD [Early 17C. < Hebrew *midrāš* < *dāraš* 'expound'] —**midrashic** /mi dráshik/ *adj*

midrib /míd rib/ *n* the thick central vein that runs from the base of a leaf to its apex

midriff /mídrif/ *n* **1.** MIDDLE FRONT AREA OF HUMAN BODY the area of the human body between the chest and the waist **2.** ANAT same as **diaphragm** (sense 1) (*dated*) ■ *adj* **1.** NEAR MIDRIFF in the area of the midriff ○ *midriff bulge* **2.** EXPOSING MIDRIFF used to describe an article of clothing that exposes the midriff ○ *a midriff top* [Old English *midhrif* 'diaphragm' < *midd* (see MID) + *hrif* 'belly' (< Indo-European, 'body')]

mid-rise *US adj* relating to or consisting of buildings that are of moderate height, about five to ten storeys ■ *n* a building of moderate height, about five to ten storeys

midsagittal /míd sájjit'l/ *adj* relating to or situated along an imaginary plane that passes through the midline of the body or an organ

midsection /míd seksh'n/ *n* the middle part of some-

thing, especially the area of the human body between the chest and waist

midship /míd ship/ *adj* relating to or located in the middle section of a ship or vessel ■ *n* the middle section of a ship or vessel

midshipman /mídshipmən/ (*plural* **-men** /-mən/) *n* **1.** an officer in the British or other navies of a rank above naval cadet **2.** *US* a student who is training to be a naval officer, especially at a naval academy [Late 17C. Alteration of *midshipsman*, because originally stationed amidships]

midships /míd ships/ *adv, adj* NAUT same as **amidships** [Mid-19C. Shortening]

midsize /míd sīz/, **midsized** /míd sīzd/ *adj* of a size midway between large and small

midst /midst/ *n* the middle or central part of something ■ *prep* same as **amid** (*literary*) [15C. Alteration of earlier *middes* < MID] ◇ **in the midst of** in the middle of a situation, place, event, or period of time ◇ **in our midst** among us

midstream /míd streém/ *n* **1.** the middle part of a river or stream where the current is often very strong **2.** a point after the beginning and before the end of something such as a speech or course of action —**midstream** *adv*

midsummer /míd súmmər/ *n* the period of time in the middle of summer

Midsummer Day *n* the day of the summer solstice in the northern hemisphere marked by Christians as the feast of St. John the Baptist. It is one of the quarter days in England, Wales, and Ireland. Date: 24 June.

midsummer madness *n* eccentric, foolish, or frivolous behaviour that is traditionally supposed to occur around the middle of the summer

Midsummer's Day *n* CALENDAR same as **Midsummer Day**

midterm /míd túrm/ *n* **1.** MIDPOINT OF TERM the middle of an academic term or a term of office **2.** PERIOD MIDWAY THROUGH PREGNANCY the period halfway through a pregnancy **3.** *N Am* EXAM HALFWAY THROUGH ACADEMIC TERM an examination taken halfway through an academic term in North American colleges and universities (*often used in the plural*) ■ *adj* IN MIDDLE OF TERM OF OFFICE occurring in the middle of a term of office, especially that of a president of the United States ○ *midterm elections*

midtown /míd town/ *n N Am* the central area of a city between the uptown and downtown areas, especially in Manhattan

midway /míd wáy/ *adv, adj* **1.** HALF OF WAY halfway between two points, parts, or places **2.** HALFWAY THROUGH SOMETHING halfway through an event, course of action, or period of time ■ *n N Am* AREA OF SIDESHOWS AT FAIR an area in a fair, carnival, or circus for sideshows and other amusements [Old English *midweg*]

Midway Islands /míd way-/ coral atoll consisting of two islets in the central Pacific Ocean, administered by the United States. Area: 5 sq. km/2 sq. mi.

midweek /míd weék/ *n* the period of time in the middle of a week ■ *adj, adv* on a day in the middle of the week or relating to such a day —**midweekly** *adj, adv*

Midweek /míd week/ *n* the day of Wednesday, so called by members of the Society of Friends

Midwest /míd wést/ *n* the northern region of the central United States east of the Rocky Mountains, generally including the states of Illinois, Indiana, Iowa, Kansas, Michigan, Minnesota, Missouri, Nebraska, Ohio, and Wisconsin —**Midwestern** *adj* —**Midwesterner** *n*

mid-wicket *n* in cricket, the fielder or fielding position located between square leg and mid-on, usually on the batsman's left

midwife /míd wīf/ *n* (*plural* **-wives** /-wīvz/) **1.** SOMEBODY TRAINED TO DELIVER BABIES somebody trained to help deliver babies and offer support and advice to pregnant women **2.** SOMEBODY WHO HELPS TO CREATE SOMETHING somebody or something that assists in bringing something new into existence ■ *vt* (**-wifes**, **-wifing** or **-wiving** /-wīving/, **-wifed** or **-wived** /-wīvd/) *N Am* ASSIST IN BIRTH OF BABY to assist in the delivery of a baby [13C. Probably < obsolete *mid* 'with' + WIFE 'woman']

midwifery /míd wíffəri/ *n* the technique or practice of helping to deliver babies and offering advice and support to pregnant women

midwife toad *n* a toad that mates on land. The male carries a band of fertilized eggs wrapped round its back legs until they are ready to hatch. Native to: Europe. Latin name: *Alytes obstetricans*.

midwinter /míd wíntər/ *n* the period in the middle of winter

midyear /míd yeér/ *n* the period in the middle of an academic, calendar, or fiscal year

mien /meen/ *n* somebody's facial expression or general appearance, bearing, or posture, taken as an indication of his or her mood or character (*formal*) [Early 16C. Probably shortening of obsolete *demeine* 'demeanour' < Old French < *demener* 'lead away' < Latin *minare* 'drive a herd of animals']

Ludwig Mies van der Rohe

Mies van der Rohe /meéz van dər rṓ ə/, **Ludwig** (1886–1969) German-born US architect and designer. He was a pioneer in the design of glass-walled skyscrapers, in particular the Seagram Building, New York City (1958), on which he collaborated with Philip Johnson. His architecture and furniture are characterized by austere forms, elegant materials such as marble and chrome, and subtle proportion and detailing.

> 'Less is more.'
> [Ludwig Mies van der Rohe, *New York Herald Tribune*; 1959]

mifepristone /mi féppri stōn/ *n* a drug that blocks the hormone progesterone, which is essential for maintaining pregnancy. Use: foetus abortion in the first few weeks after conception. [Late 20C. Contraction of *aminophenyl* + *propyne* + *estradione* (elements of the drug's chemical name) + -ONE]

miff /mif/ (*informal*) *vt* (**miffs, miffing, miffed**) to annoy or offend somebody ■ *n* an angry mood or sulk [Early 17C. Origin ?]

miffed /mift/ *adj* annoyed or offended (*informal*)

miffy /míffi/ (**-fier, -fiest**) *adj* **1.** oversensitive, or too easily upset or offended (*informal*) **2.** describes plants that are difficult to propagate because they require particular environmental conditions

MiG /mig/ *n* a high-speed high-altitude fighter aircraft built in Russia [Mid-20C. Acronym < A. I. Mikoyan and M. I. Gurevich, Soviet aircraft designers]

MIG *abbr* mortgage indemnity guarantee

might [1] /mīt/ CORE MEANING: a modal verb indicating the possibility that something is true or will happen in the future ○ *She said that John might be living abroad now.* ○ *The meeting might be as early as next week.*
modal v **1.** used as a polite way of making suggestions and giving advice ○ *I thought we might go out tonight.* ○ *You might want to give him a ring first.* **2.** used to indicate that somebody ought to do something, often to show annoyance that it has not

been done ○ *You might at least have told me!* [Old English *mihte, meahte*, the past tense of *magan* (see MAY [1])]

SPELLCHECK might or **mite**? Do not confuse the spelling of ***might*** and ***mite***, which sound similar. ***Might*** is a verb meaning 'will possibly' or 'ought to': *It might rain. You might have warned me!* It is also noun meaning 'power' or 'strength': *the might of a multinational organization; with might and main.* ***Mite*** is a noun only, referring to a tiny eight-legged animal, a little child, or a small amount, as in *a spider mite, give the poor mite a drink,* or *feeling a mite jealous.*

might[2] /mīt/ *n* **1.** great power or influence ○ *up against the might of a huge organization* **2.** physical strength and determination ○ *We must push with all our might.* [Old English *miht* < Indo-European, 'be able']

SPELLCHECK See ***might*** [1].

might-have-been *n* an event or outcome that could have occurred but did not

mightily /mītili/ *adv* **1.** with considerable physical strength and effort ○ *struggle mightily* **2.** to a great extent or degree (*dated*) ○ *mightily relieved*

mightn't /mīt'nt/ *contr* might not (*informal*)

might've /mītəv/ *contr* might have (*informal*)

mighty /mīti/ *adj* (**-ier, -iest**) **1. STRONG AND POWERFUL** of great strength and power **2. BIG AND IMPRESSIVE** very impressive in size, scope, or extent ○ *a mighty oak tree* ■ *adv regional, N Am* **VERY MUCH SO** extremely or to a great degree ○ *mighty fine* [Old English *mihtig* < *miht* (see MIGHT [2])] —**mightiness** *n*

migmatite /mígmə tīt/ *n* a coarsely crystalline rock composed of a mixture of bands of metamorphic and igneous rocks and found in areas where high-grade metamorphic rocks are partly melted to form igneous rock [Early 20C. < Greek *migmat-*, stem of *migma* 'mixture' + -ITE [1]]

mignon /mín yon/ *adj* very delicate and pretty (*literary*) ■ *n* a small portion of prime beef, especially filet mignon [Mid-16C. < French, alteration of Old French *mignot*]

mignonette /mínyə nét/ (*plural* **-ettes** or *same*) *n* a plant with spiky leaves. Flowers: small, fragrant, greenish-white. Native to: Mediterranean. Genus: *Reseda*. [Early 18C. < French *mignon* 'dainty' (see MIGNON)]

~~**migrain**~~ incorrect spelling of **migraine**

migraine /mée grayn, mī-/ *n* a recurrent, throbbing, very painful headache, often affecting one side of the head and sometimes accompanied by vomiting or by distinct warning signs, including visual disturbances [14C. < French < Greek *hēmikrania* < *hēmi-* 'half' + *kranion* 'skull'] —**migrainous** *adj*

migrant /mīgrənt/ *n* **1. SOMEBODY MOVING FROM PLACE TO PLACE** somebody who moves from one place to another, often for employment or economic improvement **2. MIGRATORY ANIMAL** an animal, especially a bird, that moves from one region to another, often at the same times each year in order to breed or avoid unsuitable weather conditions **3.** *Aus* **RECENT IMMIGRANT** an immigrant, especially one who has entered the country recently [Late 17C. < Latin *migrant-*, present participle of *migrare* 'migrate'] —**migrant** *adj*

migrate /mī gráyt/ (**-grates, -grating, -grated**) *v* **1.** *vi* **MOVE FROM PLACE TO PLACE** to move from one region or country to another, often to seek work or other economic opportunities **2.** *vi* ZOOL **MOVE BETWEEN HABITATS** to move from one habitat or environment to another in response to seasonal changes and variations in food supply **3.** *vi* BIOL **MOVE POSITION WITHIN ORGANISM** to move from one part of an organism or substance to another, e.g. cells moving during the growth of an embryo **4.** *vt* COMPUT **MOVE BETWEEN COMPUTER SYSTEMS** to transfer a file from one computer system or database to another [Early 17C. < Latin *migrat-*, past participle of *migrare*] —**migrator** *n*

migration /mī gráysh'n/ *n* **1. MOVEMENT FROM ONE PLACE TO ANOTHER** the act or process of moving from one region or country to another **2. GROUP MOVING BETWEEN PLACES** a group of people, birds, or other animals that are moving together from one region or country to another **3.** CHEM **SHIFT OF IONS** the movement of ions under the influence of an electric field **4.** CHEM **MOVEMENT OF ATOMS** the movement of an atom, or a group of atoms or double bonds, from one part of a molecule to another **5. TRANSFERENCE BETWEEN COMPUTER SYSTEMS** a transfer of computer data, programs, or hardware from one system to another —**migrational** *adj*

migratory /mīgrətəri, mī gráytəri/, **migrative** /mīgrətiv/ *adj* **1. MOVING TO ANOTHER REGION EVERY YEAR** moving as part of a bird, fish, or other animal population from one region to another, usually at the same times every year, in order to breed or avoid unsuitable weather conditions **2. RELATING TO MOVEMENT FROM PLACE TO PLACE** relating to the movement of people from one place to another in order to achieve better living conditions **3. NOT SETTLING DOWN** tending to wander from one region or country to another without settling down in one place for any length of time

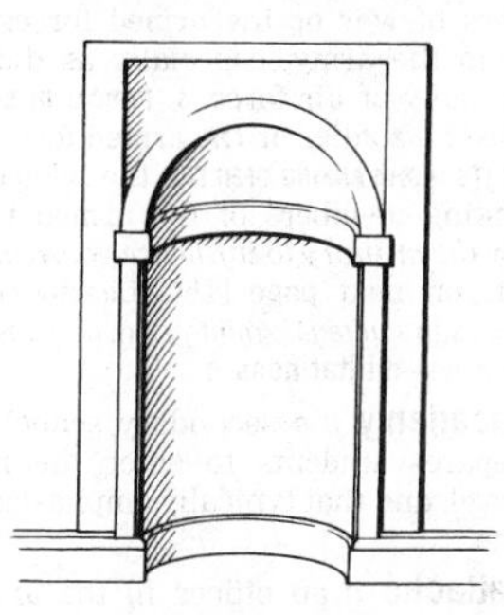

mihrab

mihrab /mée rab, méerəb/ *n* **1.** a small niche in a mosque that indicates the direction of Mecca **2.** a blank rectangular space in the middle of a prayer rug that faces Mecca during prayer [Early 19C. < Arabic *miḥrāb*]

mikado /mi kaád ō/ (*plural* **-dos**) *n* in former times, a title of a Japanese emperor [Early 18C. < Japanese, 'honourable gate']

Mikasuki /míkə sóoki/ (*plural same* or **-kis**), **Miccosukee** (*plural same* or **-kees**), **Miccosuki** (*plural same* or **-kis**) *n* **1.** a member of a Native North American people who lived in northern Florida and now live mainly in southern Florida **2.** the Muskogean language of the Mikasuki people [Mid-20C. < Mikasuki, after a lake in N Florida where they first settled] —**Mikasuki** *adj*

mike /mīk/ (*informal*) *n* same as **microphone** ■ *vt* (**mikes, miking, miked**) to supply somebody with, or transmit something through, a microphone [Early 20C. Shortening]

Mike /mīk/ *n* a code word for the letter 'm', used in international radio communications

Mi'kmaq /mík mak/ (*plural* **-maqs** or *same*), **Micmac** (*plural* **-macs** or *same*) *n* **1.** a member of a group of Native North American people living in Nova Scotia, New Brunswick, Prince Edward Island, and the Gaspé Peninsula in eastern Canada **2.** an Algonquian language spoken in eastern Canada. Native speakers: 3,000. [Early 18C. Via French < Mi'kmaq *migmac* 'allies'] —**Mi'kmaq** *adj*

mikvah /mik vaá, míkvə/, **mikveh, mikve** *n* among Orthodox Jews, a ritual bath for cleansing or purification, especially before the Sabbath or following menstruation, childbirth, or contact with a corpse [Mid-19C. Via Yiddish *mikve* < Hebrew *miqweh* 'mass (of water)']

mil[1] /mil/ *n* **1. ONE THOUSANDTH OF INCH** a unit of linear measurement equivalent to 0.0254 mm/one thousandth of an inch, often used in measuring the diameter of wires **2. UNIT OF ANGULAR MEASUREMENT FOR ARTILLERY** a unit of measurement equivalent to the angle subtended by 1/6400th of a circumference, used in aiming artillery **3. ONE MILLILITRE** a unit of volume equivalent to one millilitre or a cubic centimetre [Early 18C. Shortening of Latin *millesimus* 'thousandth' < *mille* 'thousand']

mil[2] *abbr* **1.** MIL military **2.** ONLINE military organization (*used in Internet addresses*) See table at **domain name 3.** militia

milady /mi láydi/ (*plural* **-dies**), **miladi** *n* (*archaic or humorous*) **1.** a British gentlewoman or a female member of the aristocracy **2.** a form of address for a gentlewoman or female member of the aristocracy [Late 18C. Via French < English *my lady*]

milage *n* MEASURE, TRANSP another spelling of **mileage**

Milan /mi lán/ capital of Milan Province and Lombardy Region, northern Italy. Population: 1,265,211 (2001). —**Milanese** /míllə néez/ *n, adj*

milch /milch/ *adj* producing milk

milch cow /mílch-/ *n* **1.** *UK, Can* a source of easily gained income (*informal*) **2.** a cow that produces milk (*dated*) [*Milch* < Old English *-milce* 'a milking' < Germanic]

milchig /mílkhik/, **milchik** *adj* under Jewish dietary laws, relating to, containing, or derived from dairy products and so not to be used with meat products [Early 20C. < Yiddish *milkhik* < *milkh* 'milk' < Old High German *miluh*]

mild /mīld/ *adj* **1. NOT HARSH** not severe or strong ○ *a mild sedative* ○ *mild disagreement* **2. LIGHTLY FLAVOURED** describes food that is lightly flavoured and not strong, hot, spicy, or bitter in taste ○ *a mild sauce* **3. PLEASANT AND TEMPERATE** pleasant and temperate in climate and not excessively hot or cold ○ *one of the mildest winters on record* **4. GENTLE AND AMIABLE** gentle, easy-going, and slow to get angry **5. NOT DANGEROUS** not serious enough to endanger life ○ *a mild earthquake* ○ *mild to moderate hypertension* **6. NOT CONTAINING HARMFUL CHEMICALS** feeling soft and gentle and not containing any chemicals that might harm the skin or clothes ○ *mild soap* ■ *n* **DRAUGHT BEER** a dark-brown draught beer with a blander taste than bitter [Old English *milde* < Indo-European, 'soft'] —**mildly** *adv*—**mildness** *n*

mildew /míl dyoo/ *n* **1. FUNGAL DISEASE OF PLANTS** a plant disease in which the parasitic fungus is visible as white or grey powdery deposits on the leaves or fruit **2. GREY OR WHITE FUNGUS** a grey or white fungus that grows on walls, paper, leather, and other similar materials in damp conditions ■ *vti* (**-dews, -dewing, -dewed**) **BE AFFECTED WITH MILDEW** to be affected, or affect something, with a grey or white fungus [Old English *mildēaw* 'honeydew, nectar' < Indo-European 'honey'] —**mildewed** *adj* —**mildewy** *adj*

mild language *n* mildly indecent language that might offend some people

mild-mannered *adj* having a polite gentle disposition

mild steel *n* a strong steel containing a low proportion of carbon [< its being easily worked]

mile /mīl/ *n* **1. UNIT OF DISTANCE** a unit of linear measurement on land, used in English-speaking countries, equivalent to 5,280 ft or 1,760 yd or 1.6 km **2.** MEASURE same as **nautical mile 3. UNIT OF MEASUREMENT COMPARABLE TO MILE** a unit of distance or length used in different historical periods or in non-English-speaking countries, e.g. the Roman mile **4. RACE OVER ONE MILE** a foot race that is a mile long ■ **miles** *npl* **A LONG WAY** a considerable distance ○ *We're miles from home.* ○ *We have miles to go before we sleep.* ■ *adv* **miles VERY MUCH** used with comparative adjectives to emphasize the degree of difference from something else, e.g. how very much better, longer, or more difficult something is (*informal*) ○ *His car's miles better.* [Old English *mīl* < Latin *milia (passuum)* 'a thousand (paces)' < *mille* 'thousand'] ◇ **be miles away** to be unaware of what is going on or being said through daydreaming or being preoccupied with your own thoughts (*informal*) ◇ **go the extra mile** to make an extra or special effort in order to achieve something ◇ **run a mile** used to emphasize how frightened somebody is of something, or how unwilling somebody is to do something (*informal*) ○ *He'd run a mile if he thought she was getting serious about him.* ◇ **see something a mile off** to recognize or be aware of something quickly ◇ **stick out a mile** to be extremely obvious (*informal*)

mileage /mīlij/, **milage** *n* **1. DISTANCE IN MILES** a distance or length measured in miles **2. NUMBER OF MILES VEHICLE HAS TRAVELLED** the total number of miles a vehicle has travelled **3. MILES VEHICLE TRAVELS ON FUEL** the total number of miles a vehicle can travel on a particular amount of fuel, such as a gallon or a litre **4. TRAVEL ALLOWANCE AT FIXED RATE** a travel allowance, usually set and paid per mile by somebody's employer **5. ADVANTAGE OR USEFULNESS OF SOMETHING** the amount of use, advantage, profit, or service that may be obtained from something (*informal*) ○ *It's amazing how much emotional mileage she can get out of a few simple words.*

~~**milennium**~~ incorrect spelling of **millennium**

mileometer /mī lómmitər/, **milometer** *n* a device built into the dashboard of a vehicle that records distance travelled. N Am term **odometer**

milepost /mīl pōst/ *n* **1.** a post on a racecourse one mile from the finishing line **2.** *N Am* a post by the

side of a road indicating the number of miles to a place, or placed a mile from a similar post

miler /mīlər/ *n* an athlete or horse that competes in a one-mile race

Miles /mīlz/, **Bernard, Baron** (1907–91) British stage actor and director. He was a member of the Old Vic company and founded the Mermaid Theatre, London, in 1951.

miles gloriosus /mée layz gláwri óssəss/ (*plural* **milites gloriosi** /mééli tayz gláwri ō sī/) *n* an arrogant, bragging, and often cowardly soldier, especially one who appears as a stock character in comedies (*literary*) [< Latin, 'boastful soldier', the title of a comedy by Plautus]

Milesian[1] /mī leézi ən/ *n* somebody who came from the ancient Greek city of Miletus [Mid-16C. < Latin *Milesius* < Greek *Milēsios* < *Milētos* 'Miletus'] —**Milesian** *adj*

Milesian[2] /mī leézi ən/ *n* in Irish legend, a member of a group of people from a royal Spanish family who invaded Ireland about 1300 BC and became the ancestors of the modern Irish [Late 16C. After *Milesius*, the legendary head of the family]

milestone /mīl stōn/ *n* **1.** a stone by the side of a road indicating the number of miles to a place **2.** a significant or important event, e.g. in the history of a country or in somebody's life

Miletus /mə leétəss/ ruined ancient Greek city of western Anatolia, in modern Turkey

milfoil /míl foyl/ (*plural* **-foils** or *same*) *n* PLANTS **1.** same as **yarrow 2.** same as **water milfoil** [13C. Via Old French < Latin *mil(l)efolium* 'thousand-leaf', a translation of Greek *muriophullon*; from the plant's feathery leaves]

Milford Haven /mílfərd háyv'n/ seaport in Pembrokeshire, southwestern Wales. Population: 13,194 (1991).

Milford Sound deep coastal inlet in the southwestern part of the South Island, New Zealand

Milhaud /mée ō/, **Darius** (1892–1974) French composer and teacher. He was a member of the Paris-based group of composers known as 'Les Six', and his work, e.g. *Le Boeuf sur le toit* (1919), was marked by polytonality and elements of jazz.

miliaria /mílli áiri ə/ *n* MED same as **prickly heat** (*technical*) [Early 19C. < modern Latin < Latin *miliarius* (see MILIARY)] —**miliarial** *adj*

miliary /mílli əri/ *adj* **1.** resembling millet seeds **2.** describes a medical condition consisting of or characterized by small nodules or lesions resembling millet seeds [Late 17C. < Latin *miliarius* < *milium* 'millet']

miliary fever *n* a highly infectious illness characterized by a high fever, excessive sweating, and a rash of small fluid-filled spots

miliary tuberculosis *n* an acute form of tuberculosis in which lesions resembling millet seeds occur in the affected organs after bacilli are spread by the blood from one point of infection

milieu /méel yö, meel yö́/ (*plural* **-lieus** or **-lieux** /-yöz, -yö́/) *n* the surroundings or environment that somebody lives in and is influenced by ○ *grew up in an artistic milieu* [Mid-19C. < French < *mi* 'mid' (< Latin *medius*) + *lieu* 'place']

milit. *abbr* MIL military

militant /míllitənt/ *adj* **1.** AGGRESSIVE extremely active in the defence or support of a cause, often to the point of extremism **2.** INVOLVED IN FIGHTING engaged in fighting or warfare ■ *n* SOMEBODY AGGRESSIVELY SUPPORTING CAUSE an aggressive defender or supporter of a cause [15C. Directly or via French < Latin *militant-*, present participle of *militare* 'be a soldier' < *milit-* (see MILITARY)] —**militancy** *n* —**militantly** *adv*

Militant Tendency *n* a former Trotskyite faction of the Labour Party, active in the 1970s and 1980s

militaria /mílli táiri ə/ *n* military objects, e.g. weapons, medals, and uniforms, that are collected as a hobby or for historical interest [Mid-20C. < MILITARY]

militarise *vt* MIL another spelling of **militarize**

militarism /míllitərizəm/ *n* **1.** PURSUIT OF MILITARY AIMS the pursuit or celebration of military ideals **2.** STRONG INFLUENCE OF MILITARY ON GOVERNMENT a high level of influence by military personnel and ideals on the government or policies of a country or state **3.** GOVERNMENT POLICY OF INVESTING IN MILITARY a government policy of investing heavily in and strengthening the armed forces

militarist /míllitərist/ *n* **1.** a zealous supporter and promoter of military ideals **2.** a student of military history and strategy —**militaristic** /míllitə rístik/ *adj* —**militaristically** *adv*

militarize /míllitə rīz/ (**-rizes, -rizing, -rized**), **militarise** (**-rises, -rising, -rised**) *vt* **1.** EQUIP OR TRAIN FOR WAR to equip or train a person or group of people for war **2.** CONVERT FOR MILITARY USE to convert something such as a piece of land or a building for military use **3.** PERSUADE TO SUPPORT MILITARISM to persuade somebody to support a policy of aiding and promoting the military —**militarization** /míllitə rī záysh'n/ *n*

military /míllitəri/ *adj* **1.** OF WAR OR ARMED FORCES relating to matters of war or the armed forces **2.** OF ARMY relating to the army, especially as distinguished from the navy or air force **3.** TYPICAL OF SOLDIER characteristic of a soldier or the armed forces ■ *n* ARMED FORCES OR ITS HIGH-RANKING OFFICERS the armed forces or high-ranking members of the armed forces ○ *attempts by the military to influence government policy.* See table on next page [15C. Directly or via French *militaire* < Latin *militaris* < *milit-*, stem of *miles* 'soldier'] —**militarily** *adv* —**militariness** *n*

military academy *n* a secondary school or college that prepares students to enter the military at officer level, and that typically emphasizes rigorous discipline

military attaché *n* an officer in the armed forces who has been assigned to the official staff of an ambassador in order to gather military intelligence

military honours *npl* ceremonies or ceremonial duties performed by the armed forces on special occasions such as a royal event or a soldier's funeral

military hotel *n S Asia* a restaurant that serves meat, fish, and poultry

military-industrial complex *n N Am* the military and the defence industries considered as a combined influence on US foreign and economic policy

military intelligence *n* **1.** information gathered about another country's military equipment and capabilities by means of observation, exchange of information, surveillance, or spying **2.** an armed forces agency whose duties include procurement, analysis, and use of tactical and strategic data required in decision-making

military law *n* the legal system, including statutes, regulations, and procedures, that applies to military personnel

military pace *n* the length of a single marching step, taken to be 76 cm/30 in in quick time

military police *n* a police force within the armed forces

military science *n* the academic study of the principles and procedures of warfare

militate /mílli tayt/ (**-tates, -tating, -tated**) *vi* to have an influence, especially a negative one, on something [Late 16C. < Latin *militat-*, past participle of *militare* 'be a soldier, wage war' < *milit-* (see MILITARY)]

USAGE militate or **mitigate**? These two often-confused words have different, mutually exclusive meanings and they function in different ways. ***Mitigate*** needs a noun object and means 'make an offence or crime less serious or more excusable' or 'make something less harsh, severe, or violent': *A six-month suspended sentence unfairly mitigates the seriousness of the offence. There were mitigating circumstances.* ***Militate*** does not take a noun object, but is followed by a preposition, often *against*, plus a noun. It means 'have an influence, especially a negative one, on something': *Trade sanctions militate* [not *mitigate*] *against international cooperation.*

militia /mə líshə/ *n* **1.** SOLDIERS WHO ARE ALSO CIVILIANS an army of soldiers who are civilians but take military training and can serve full-time during emergencies **2.** RESERVE MILITARY FORCE a reserve army that is not part of the regular armed forces but can be called up in an emergency **3.** UNAUTHORIZED QUASI-MILITARY GROUP an unauthorized group of people who arm themselves and conduct quasi-military training [Late 16C. < Latin, 'military service, body of soldiers' < *milit-* (see MILITARY)]

militiaman /mə líshəmən/ (*plural* **-men** /-mən/) *n* a man who serves in a militia

militiawoman /mə líshə wŏŏmən/ (*plural* **-women** /-wimin/) *n* a woman who serves in a militia

milium /mílli əm/ (*plural* **-ia** /-i ə/) *n* a whitehead on the skin (*technical*) [Mid-19C. < Latin, 'millet'; so called from the nodule's size and shape]

milk /milk/ *n* **1.** NUTRITIOUS FLUID PRODUCED BY MAMMALS a nutritious white fluid, rich in protein, fats, lactose, and vitamins, that women and other female mammals produce to feed their young immediately after birth **2.** DAIRY PRODUCT an opaque white fluid produced by cows, sheep, or goats and used by human beings as a drink, in cooking, and to make products such as butter and cheese **3.** PLANT SAP a white or off-white liquid from a plant, e.g. the liquid inside a coconut or the sap of some trees **4.** COSMETIC OR PHARMACEUTICAL PRODUCT a cosmetic or pharmaceutical product that is thick and white ○ *cleansing milk* ■ *v* (**milks, milking, milked**) **1.** *vti* TAKE MILK FROM COW to draw milk for use as a dairy product from the udder of a cow, goat, or sheep manually or by using a special machine **2.** *vi* PRODUCE MILK to yield or supply milk (*refers to dairy animals*) **3.** *vt* REMOVE LIQUID FROM SOMETHING to remove liquid from something, especially to drain the venom from a snake or the sap from a tree **4.** *vt* STEAL SOMETHING SLOWLY AND STEADILY to steal money from something such as a fund or an account in small quantities over a period of time (*informal*) **5.** *vt* EXPLOIT SOMETHING UNSCRUPULOUSLY to get as much benefit from something as possible, often in a calculating or unscrupulous way (*informal*) [Old English *milc* < Indo-European, 'to rub, milk']

CULTURAL NOTE ***Under Milk Wood***, a play (1953) by the Welsh poet Dylan Thomas. This play for voices, originally written for radio but occasionally presented as a stage play, describes a day in the life of a Welsh fishing village and is noted for its poetic prose, rich humour, and vivid characterization.

Milk /milk/ river that originates in Montana and flows into Alberta, Canada, before joining the Missouri River. Length: 1,010 km/625 mi.

milk bar *n* a café or snack bar that specializes in milk shakes and other milk drinks

milk chocolate *n* chocolate that has been made with milk and has a sweet creamy taste

milk cow *n* AGRIC same as **milch cow** (sense 2)

milker /mílkər/ *n* **1.** an animal that produces milk used for human consumption, especially a cow **2.** a milking machine, or somebody who milks animals, especially cows

milk fever *n* **1.** mild fever that some new mothers have around the time that they begin to produce breast milk **2.** a disease in cows, sheep, and goats that have recently given birth, caused by mineral depletion incurred during milk production. Symptoms include temporary loss of consciousness or ability to move.

milkfish /mílk fish/ (*plural* **-fishes** or *same*) *n* a large toothless silver fish related to herring and salmon. Native to: warm waters of the Pacific and Indian oceans. Latin name: *Chanos chanos*. [Early 20C. < its colour]

milk float *n* a small often electrically powered vehicle used for door-to-door deliveries of milk and other dairy products

milk glass *n* white or translucent whitish glass used in decorative glasswork

milking parlour, **milking shed** *n* a building with equipment for milking cows, usually part of a farm

milking stool *n* a short simple three-legged stool of a style formerly used when milking cows

milk leg *n* painful leg swelling that some women have following childbirth, caused by inflammation and clotting in the femoral vein

milkmaid /mílk mayd/ *n* a woman or girl who milks cows or does other jobs in a dairy (*dated*)

milkman /mílkmən/ (*plural* **-men** /-mən/) *n* a man who delivers or sells milk door to door

Milk of Magnesia *tdmk* a trademark for a milky mixture of magnesium hydroxide and water. Use: laxative, antacid.

milk pudding *n* a dessert consisting of a sweetened boiled or baked mixture of milk and grain, usually rice, semolina, tapioca, or sago

milk punch *n* a drink consisting of alcoholic spirit, milk, and sometimes sugar or spices

milk round *n* **1.** a regular route for door-to-door milk deliveries **2.** a regular tour with frequent stops

MILITARY RANKS

Military ranks of the United Kingdom, Australia, and New Zealand

Navy	Marines	Army	Air Force
Admiral of the Fleet	[1]	Field Marshal	Marshal of the Royal Air Force
Admiral	General	General	Air Chief Marshal
Vice Admiral	Lieutenant General	Lieutenant General	Air Marshal
Rear Admiral	Major General	Major General	Air Vice Marshal
Commodore	Brigadier	Brigadier	Air Commodore
Captain	Colonel	Colonel	Group Captain
Commander	Lieutenant Colonel	Lieutenant Colonel	Wing Commander
Lieutenant Commander	Major	Major	Squadron Leader
Lieutenant	Captain	Captain	Flight Lieutenant
Sub Lieutenant	Lieutenant	Lieutenant	Flying Officer
	Second Lieutenant	Second Lieutenant	Pilot Officer
Midshipman			
*			
Warrant Officer	Warrant Officer (1st, 2nd Class)	Warrant Officer (1st, 2nd Class)	Warrant Officer
Chief Petty Officer	Colour Sergeant	Colour/Staff Sergeant	Flight Sergeant
			Chief Technician
Petty Officer	Sergeant	Sergeant	Sergeant
Leading Rate[2]	Corporal	Corporal	Corporal
	Lance Corporal	Lance Corporal	
Able Rate[3]	Marine 1st Class	Private	Junior Technician/Senior Aircraftman
	Marine 2nd Class		Leading Aircraftman/Aircraftman

Notes

NB Ranks shown are not comparative between United Kingdom, Australia, New Zealand and the United States and Canada

* Indicates the end of officer rank

1 Marine service not applicable for Australia and New Zealand.

2 Leading Rate: also called 'Leading Seaman' in some forces.

3 Able Rate: also called 'Able Seaman' in some forces.

Military ranks of the United States and Canada

Navy	Marine Corps	Army	Air Force
Fleet Admiral (wartime)		General of the Army (wartime)	General of the Air Force (wartime)
Admiral	General	General	General
Vice Admiral	Lieutenant General	Lieutenant General	Lieutenant General
Rear Admiral Upper Half	Major General	Major General	Major General
Rear Admiral Lower Half	Brigadier General	Brigadier General	Brigadier General
Captain	Colonel	Colonel	Colonel
Commander	Lieutenant Colonel	Lieutenant Colonel	Lieutenant Colonel
Lieutenant Commander	Major	Major	Major
Lieutenant	Captain	Captain	Captain
Lieutenant Junior Grade	First Lieutenant	First Lieutenant	First Lieutenant
Ensign	Second Lieutenant	Second Lieutenant	Second Lieutenant
*			
	Chief Warrant Officer 5	Chief Warrant Officer 5	
Chief Warrant Officer 4	Chief Warrant Officer 4	Chief Warrant Officer 4	
Chief Warrant Officer 3	Chief Warrant Officer 3	Chief Warrant Officer 3	
Chief Warrant Officer 2	Chief Warrant Officer 2	Chief Warrant Officer 2	
Warrant Officer 1 (no longer in use)	Warrant Officer 1	Warrant Officer 1	
Master Chief Petty Officer of the Navy	Sergeant Major of the Marine Corps	Sergeant Major of the Army	Chief Master Sergeant of the Air Force
Fleet/Command Master Chief Petty Officer & Master Chief Petty Officer	Sergeant Major & Master Gunnery Sergeant	Command Sergeant Major & Sergeant Major	Command Chief Master Sergeant, Chief Master Sergeant & First Sergeant
Senior Chief Petty Officer	First Sergeant & Master Sergeant	First Sergeant & Master Sergeant	Senior Master Sergeant & First Sergeant
Chief Petty Officer	Gunnery Sergeant	Sergeant First Class	Master Sergeant & First Sergeant
Petty Officer 1st Class	Staff Sergeant	Staff Sergeant	Technical Sergeant
Petty Officer 2nd Class	Sergeant	Sergeant	Staff Sergeant
Petty Officer 3rd Class	Corporal	Corporal & Specialist	Senior Airman
Seaman	Lance Corporal	Private First Class	Airman First Class
Seaman Apprentice	Private First Class	Private	Airman
Seaman Recruit	Private	Private	Airman Basic

along the way, especially a tour of universities made by companies looking to recruit graduates

milk run *n* a routine trip, especially an airline's regular flight or an uneventful sortie made by a military aircraft (*informal*) [< the routine early-morning trips of trains delivering milk]

milk shake, **milkshake** /mílk shayk/ *n* a cold drink made by whisking or blending milk and flavouring

milk snake *n* a white or tan nonpoisonous king snake with red, yellow, brown, or black markings. Native to: North America. Genus: *Lampropeltis*. [*Milk* < its colour]

milksop /mílk sop/ *n* a man who is regarded as weak-willed or ineffectual (*dated insult*) [14C. The original meaning was 'bread soaked in milk']

milk stout *n* a sweet dark beer that contains lactose and has no bitter aftertaste

milk sugar *n* BIOCHEM same as **lactose** (sense 1)

milk thistle *n* 1. PLANTS same as **sow thistle** 2. a thistle that has dark-green leaves streaked with white veins. Flowers: purple. Use: in herbal medicine, to treat the liver. Latin name: *Silybum marianum*. [*Milk* < its milky sap]

milk tooth *n* a tooth in young mammals, including humans, that falls out in early life to be replaced by the adult tooth

milk vetch *n* a plant with seeds borne in pods, sometimes grown as fodder. Flowers: yellow, white, or purple. Genus: *Astragalus*. [Because thought by some to increase milk production in goats]

milkweed

milkweed /mílk weed/ *n* a flowering plant that secretes a milky latex and has seed pods that burst open to release silky-tufted seeds. Genus: *Asclepias*.

milkweed bug *n* a black crawling insect with red markings that feeds on the juice of the milkweed and is often used in scientific research. Latin name: *Oncopeltus fasciatus*.

milkwoman (*plural* **-men** /mílk woomən/) *n* a woman who delivers or sells milk door to door

milkwort /mílk wurt/ *n* a plant formerly believed to increase milk production in nursing mothers. Genus: *Polygala*.

milky /mílki/ (**-ier**, **-iest**) *adj* 1. MILK-COLOURED like milk in colour or consistency 2. CONTAINING MILK full of or containing milk 3. OPAQUE cloudy or translucent, as if milk had been added 4. LACKING COURAGE lacking courage, strength, or steadfastness (*dated*) —**milkily** *adv* —**milkiness** *n*

Milky Way *n* the spiral galaxy to which Earth and its solar system belong, appearing as a faint band of light in the night sky [14C. Translation of Latin *via lactea*]

mill[1] /mil/ *n* 1. FLOUR-MAKING FACTORY a building or group of buildings in which cereal grains are ground to make flour or meal 2. PROCESSING PLANT a building or group of buildings used for processing raw materials and manufacturing a product such as paper, fabric, or steel 3. ROTARY PROCESSING MACHINE a machine that processes materials, especially one that grinds, presses, or pulverizes raw materials using a rotary motion 4. SMALL DEVICE FOR GRINDING GRAINS a small device for grinding something such as coffee, pepper, or salt into granules 5. PROCESSING MACHINE a machine that repeats a simple manufacturing procedure, e.g. one that stamps or cuts metal 6. METAL ROLLER a metal roller used for impressing a design on something such as textiles or bank notes 7. INDUST same as **milling cutter** 8. INDUST same as **milling machine** 9. SOMETHING WORKING REPETITIVELY OR UNTHINKINGLY an in-

stitution, person, or process that operates in the same automatic, repetitive, or productive manner as a factory ○ *Our family is a regular rumour mill.* 10. TEDIOUS PROCESS a slow, unpleasant, or tedious process ○ *Getting the book through the editorial mill could take months.* 11. FIGHT a boxing match or other fist fight (*archaic slang*) ■ *v* (**mills**, **milling**, **milled**) 1. *vt* GRIND GRAIN BY MACHINE to grind grain or seed by machine 2. *vt* MANUFACTURE BY MACHINE to manufacture a product such as paper or fabric from raw materials by machine 3. *vt* PROCESS MATERIALS USING ROTARY MACHINERY to process materials using machinery that grinds, presses, or pulverizes raw materials using a rotary motion 4. *vt* SHAPE METAL BY MACHINE to use a milling cutter or milling machine to cut, shape, or finish metals 5. *vt* PUT RIDGES ON COIN EDGE to cut ridges or grooves into a metal object, especially the edge of a coin 6. *vi* CIRCLE RESTLESSLY to move around in a confused or restless group 7. *vt* MAKE CREAM FROTHY to whisk or shake something such as cream or chocolate until it is foamy [Pre-12C. < late Latin *molina* < Latin *molere* 'to grind'] —**millable** *adj* —**milled** *adj* ◇ **put somebody through the mill** to subject somebody to a difficult or unpleasant experience (*informal*)

CULTURAL NOTE *The Mill on the Floss*, a novel (1860) by George Eliot. Set in eastern England in the early 19th century, it describes the intellectual and emotional development of Maggie Tulliver, the daughter of a miller. By contrasting Maggie's independent spirit with the dreary conservatism of most of her family and acquaintances, Eliot highlights the obstacles faced by women in English society at the time.

---

mill about, **mill around** *vi* to wander about aimlessly, restlessly, or in confusion

mill[2] /mil/ (*plural same*) *n* MONEY same as **million** (sense 3) (*informal*) ○ *got over two mill from a bank job in London* [Mid-20C. Shortening]

mill[3] /mil/ *n* MEASURE same as **millimetre** (*informal*) [Mid-20C. Shortening]

mill[4] /mil/ *n* MEASURE same as **millilitre** (*informal*) [Shortening]

Mill /mil/, **James** (1773–1836) British philosopher and economist. Father of John Stuart Mill and an associate of Jeremy Bentham, he was one of the founders of utilitarianism.

Mill, John Stuart (1806–73) British philosopher and economist. The son of James Mill, he was one of the leading intellectuals of his day and a major proponent of utilitarianism. His most important works include *A System of Logic* (1843) and the essay *On Liberty* (1859).

> 'If all mankind minus one were of one opinion, and only one person were of the contrary opinion, mankind would be no more justified in silencing that one person, than he, if he had the power, would be justified in silencing mankind.'
> [John Stuart Mill, *On Liberty*; 1859]

Millais /míl ay, mi láy/, **Sir John Everett** (1829–96) British painter. A leading member of the Pre-Raphaelite movement, he painted many historical scenes and worked as a portraitist.

millboard /míl bawrd/ *n* thick paperboard used in binding books [Early 18C. Alteration of *milled board*]

milldam /míl dam/ *n* a dam built near a mill in order to raise the water level of a stream so that the flow is strong enough to turn a millwheel

millefeuille /meel fö´i, meel fö´i/ (*plural* **-feuilles**) *n* a dessert or pastry consisting of several layers of puff pastry with a filling of cream and jam, topped with icing sugar or icing [Late 19C. < French, literally 'a thousand leaves']

millefiori /mílli fi áwri/ *n* decorative glassware made by cutting and arranging cross sections of fused glass rods of varied colour and thickness [Mid-19C. < Italian, literally 'a thousand flowers']

millefleurs /meel flúr/ *adj* covered with a design of small flowers or plants [Early 20C. < French, literally 'a thousand flowers']

millenarian /mílli náiri ən/ *adj* 1. CHR RELATING TO JESUS CHRIST'S SECOND COMING relating to or believing in doctrines such as Jesus Christ's Second Coming, a final conflict between good and evil, or the end of the world, especially those based on the book of Revelation 2. RELATING TO FUTURE UTOPIA relating to or believing in the coming of some future utopian age 3.

RELATING TO END OF WORLD relating to or suggesting the end of the world 4. RELATING TO 1,000 relating to units of 1,000, especially 1,000 years [Mid-17C. < Latin *millenarius* < *mille* 'thousand'] —**millenarian** *n*

millenarianism /mílli náiri ənizəm/ *n* 1. BELIEF IN JESUS CHRIST'S SECOND COMING a belief in doctrines such as Jesus Christ's Second Coming, a final conflict between good and evil, or the end of the world, especially those based on the book of Revelation 2. BELIEF IN COMING UTOPIA a belief in the coming of a future utopian age, especially one created through revolution 3. BELIEF IN END OF WORLD a belief that the end of the world is near

millenary /mi lénnəri, míllinəri/ *adj* CHR, CALENDAR same as **millenarian** ■ *n* (*plural* **-ies**) CALENDAR same as **millennium** (sense 1) [Mid-16C. < Latin *millenarius* (see MILLENARIAN)] —**millenarism** /míllinərizəm/ *n*

mill end *n* either end of a roll of fabric or carpet that is finished instead of being cut

~~**millenium**~~ incorrect spelling of **millennium**

millennial /mi lénni əl/ *adj* relating to a millennium ■ *n* a member of the generation of children who were born between the years 1977 and 1994

millennium /mi lénni əm/ (*plural* **-niums** or **-nia** /-ni ə/) *n* 1. 1,000 YEARS a period of 1,000 years, especially a period that begins or ends in a year that is a multiple of 1,000 2. PROPHESIED RULE BY JESUS CHRIST the thousand-year period of peace that, according to one interpretation of prophecies in the book of Revelation, will follow the Second Coming of Jesus Christ 3. HOPED-FOR UTOPIAN AGE an imagined future utopian age of joy, peace, and justice, especially one created through revolution 4. THOUSANDTH ANNIVERSARY a thousand-year anniversary, especially the one in the year 2000 [Mid-17C. < modern Latin < Latin *mille* 'thousand' + *annus* 'year' (see ANNUAL)] —**millennialism** *n* —**millennialist** *n*

USAGE See *century*.

---

millennium bug *n* the problem posed by the year 2000 for computer software that coded dates by using only the last two digits of each year (*informal*)

Millennium Dome *n* a large dome-shaped structure by the River Thames in Greenwich, London, built to celebrate the year 2000

millepede *n* INSECTS another spelling of **millipede**

millepore /mílli pawr/ *n* a coral that forms white or yellow reefs [Mid-18C. < modern Latin *Millepora* < Latin *mille* 'thousand' + *porus* 'pore' (see PORE[1])]

miller /míllər/ *n* 1. MILL-OPERATOR somebody who owns, manages, or operates a mill 2. MILLING MACHINE a machine that mills materials 3. MOTH WITH POWDERY WINGS a moth whose wings have a powdery appearance

Arthur Miller

Miller /míllər/, **Arthur** (*b.* 1915) US playwright. He won a Pulitzer Prize for his tragedy *Death of a Salesman* (1949). His play *The Crucible* (1953) was a veiled critique of the House Un-American Activities Committee of the McCarthy era. His second wife was the film actor Marilyn Monroe. See Cultural note at **crucible, salesman**.

> 'For a salesman, there is no rock bottom to the life. He don't put a bolt to a nut, he don't tell you the law or give you medicine. He's a man way out there in the blue, riding on a smile and a shoeshine.'
> [Arthur Miller, 'Requiem', *Death of a Salesman*; 1949]

> 'The structure of a play is always the story

of how the birds come home to roost.'
[Arthur Miller, 'Shadows of the Gods', *Harper's Magazine*; August 1958]

Miller, George (*b.* 1945) Australian film director. His greatest successes include the *Mad Max* series of films (1979, 1981, 1985) and *The Witches of Eastwick* (1987).

Miller, Glenn (1904–44) US bandleader and composer. Leader of a big-band orchestra of the late 1930s and early 1940s, he was noted for swing music such as 'In the Mood' (1939). Full name **Miller, Alton Glenn**

Miller, Harry M. (*b.* 1934) New Zealand-born Australian entrepreneur. He is a producer of musicals and concerts, and a consultant to media personalities. Full name **Miller, Harry Maurice**

Henry Miller: photographed in 1932 by Brassaï

Miller, Henry (1891–1980) US writer. His novels *Tropic of Cancer* (1934) and *Tropic of Capricorn* (1939) are sexually explicit and were banned in the United States. Full name **Miller, Henry Valentine**. See Cultural note at **tropic**[1]

'The wallpaper with which the men of science have covered the world of reality is falling to tatters.'
[Henry Miller, *Tropic of Cancer*; 1934]

Miller, Hugh (1802–56) British geologist. He was the author of *The Old Red Sandstone* (1841) and *Footprints of the Creator* (1849), which stimulated popular interest in geology.

Miller, Leszek (*b.* 1946) prime minister of Poland (2001–). A former textile worker and trade unionist, he was elected chairman of the the Democratic Left Alliance (SLD) party when it was formed (1999).

millerite /mílla rīt/ *n* a nickel sulphide mineral that forms long wiry crystals. Use: source of nickel. [Mid-19C. After W. H. *Miller* (1801–80), British mineralogist]

miller's thumb *n* a small flat spiny freshwater fish. Native to: Europe, North America. Genus: *Cottus*. [< the shape of its body, alluding to the proverbial distrust of millers' methods of measurement]

millesimal /mi léssim'l/ *adj* **1.** OF THOUSANDTHS relating to thousandths **2.** DIVIDED BY THOUSAND divided by one thousand ■ *n* THOUSANDTH PART a thousandth part of something [Early 18C. < Latin *millesimus* 'thousandth' < *mille* 'thousand'] —**millesimally** *adv*

millet /míllit/ *n* **1.** GRAIN the pale shiny grain of a cereal plant. Use: flour, alcoholic drinks, birdseed, fodder. **2.** CEREAL PLANT a fast-growing cereal plant. Use: grain, fodder. Native to: warm regions. Latin name: *Panicum miliaceum*. **3.** GRASS PLANT a grass that is similar or related to millet, e.g. pearl millet. Use: grain. [15C. < Old French < Latin *milium*]

Millet /mée ay/, **Jean-François** (1814–75) French painter. Strong draughtsmanship and mellow colours characterize his realistic scenes of rural life.

mill finish *n* a particularly smooth surface on paper, made by a machine

milli- *prefix* one thousandth (10^{-3}) ○ *milligram* ○ *millisecond* Symbol **m** [< Latin < *mille* 'thousand']

milliampere /mílli ám peer, -ám pair/ *n* a unit of electric current equal to one thousandth of an ampere

milliard /mílli aard/ *n* one thousand million (*dated*) Now called **billion** [Late 18C. < French < Latin *mille* 'thousand']

milliary /mílli əri/ *adj* indicating or marking a distance of one Roman mile, measured as one thousand paces [Mid-17C. < Latin *milliarius* < *mille* 'thousand']

millibar /mílli baar/ *n* a unit of atmospheric pressure equal to one thousandth of a bar

millicurie /mílli kyoori/ *n* a unit of radioactivity equal to one thousandth of a curie

millieme /meel yém/ *n* **1.** a former minor unit of currency in Egypt and Sudan equal to one thousandth of a pound **2.** MONEY same as **millime** [Early 20C. < French *millième* (see MILLIME)]

millifarad /mílli farəd, -fa rad/ *n* a unit of electrical capacitance equal to one thousandth of a farad

milligram /mílli gram/ *n* a unit of mass and weight equal to one thousandth of a gram

millihenry /mílli henri/ (*plural* **-ries**) *n* a unit of electrical inductance equal to one thousandth of a henry

Millikan /míllikən/, **Robert A.** (1868–1953) US physicist. He measured the charge on the electron and coined the term 'cosmic rays'. He received a Nobel Prize in physics (1923). Full name **Millikan, Robert Andrews**

millilambert /mílli lambərt/ *n* a unit of luminance equal to one thousandth of a lambert

milliliter *n* MEASURE US spelling of **millilitre**

millilitre /mílli leetər/ *n* a unit of volume equal to one thousandth of a litre

millime /mee leém, mílleem/ *n* a subunit of Tunisian currency. See table at **currency** [Mid-20C. Via French *millième* 'thousandth' < Latin *millesimus* < *mille* 'thousand']

millimeter *n* MEASURE US spelling of **millimetre**

millimetre /mílli meetər/ *n* a unit of length equal to one thousandth of a metre

millimetrical /mílli méttrik'l/ *adj* progressing or moving extremely slowly by degrees

millimole /mílli mōl/ *n* a unit used to measure the amount of a chemical substance, equal to one thousandth of a mole

milline /míl līn, mil līn/ *n* **1.** a unit of advertising copy equal to one column line in agate type in one million copies of a newspaper or magazine **2.** COMM same as **milline rate** [Late 20C. Blend of MILLION + LINE[1]]

milliner /míllinər/ *n* somebody who designs, makes, or sells women's hats [Mid-16C. Alteration of earlier *Milaner* 'importer of fancy fabrics and wares from Milan, Italy']

milline rate *n* the cost per unit of advertising copy

millinery /míllinəri/ *n* **1.** hats and other accessories for women, sold by a milliner **2.** the design, manufacture, or sale of women's hats

milling /mílling/ *n* the ridged edge of a coin

milling cutter *n* a rotary tool used for cutting, shaping, or finishing metal objects

milling machine *n* a machine fitted with milling cutters to cut, shape, or finish metal objects

million /míllyən/ *n* **1.** THOUSAND THOUSAND a thousand thousand (10^6) **2.** LARGE NUMBER an unspecified very large number of people or things (*informal*; *often used in the plural*) **3.** MILLION UNITS OF CURRENCY a million units of a currency, especially pounds or dollars **4.** SEVENTH DIGIT TO LEFT OF DECIMAL the seventh digit to the left of the decimal point in the decimal number system ○ *In the number 7,654,321, the 7 is in the millions place.* [14C. Via French < obsolete Italian *millione* 'great thousand' < Latin *mille* 'thousand'] —**million** *adj*

millionaire /míllyə náir/ *n* somebody whose net worth or income is more than one million pounds, dollars, or another unit of currency (*often used before a noun*) [Early 19C. < French < *million* (see MILLION)]

millionairess /míllyə náirəss, míllyə náir ess/ *n* a woman whose net worth or income is more than one million pounds, dollars, or another unit of currency (*dated*)

~~millionnaire~~ incorrect spelling of **millionaire**

millionth /míllyənth/ *n* one of a million equal parts of something —**millionth** *adj*

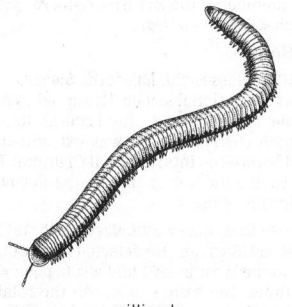

millipede

millipede /mílli peed/, **millepede** *n* a small plant-eating arthropod with a tubular body made up of segments, most of which have two pairs of legs. Class: Diplopoda. [Early 17C. < Latin *millipeda* 'woodlouse', literally 'with a thousand feet' < *ped-* 'foot']

millisecond /mílli sekənd/ *n* a unit of time equal to one thousandth of a second

millivolt /mílli vōlt/ *n* a unit of electrical voltage or potential difference equal to one thousandth of a volt. Symbol **mV**

milliwatt /mílli wot/ *n* a unit of electrical power equal to one thousandth of a watt. Symbol **mW**

millpond /míl pond/ *n* a pond created by damming a stream in order to create a flow of water to turn a millwheel

millrace /míl rayss/ *n* **1.** the stream of water that flows through a millwheel, making it turn **2.** a channel that directs water to and from a millwheel

millrun /míl run/ *n* **1.** INDUST same as **millrace 2.** a test to determine the quality of a mineral or the mineral content of an ore **3.** the quantity or quality of a mineral yielded by a millrun test

Mills /milz/, **Sir John** (*b.* 1908) British actor. His early roles were those of military or naval servicemen. He went on to play a great diversity of characters.

Mills and Boon /milz ənd boʻon/ *n* a romantic novel published by, or of the kind typically published by, the firm of Mills and Boon, publishers of popular romantic fiction

Mills bomb *n* an oval hand grenade [Early 20C. After Sir William *Mills* (1856–1932), English engineer]

millstone /míl stōn/ *n* **1.** either of two large circular stones used to grind grain in a mill **2.** a great burden or responsibility

millstream /míl streem/ *n* **1.** a stream whose water is used to turn a millwheel **2.** INDUST same as **millrace** (sense 1)

millwheel /míl weel/ *n* a wheel that powers a mill, usually turned by a flow of water

millwright /míl rīt/ *n* somebody who designs, builds, or maintains mills or mill machinery

Milne /miln/, **A. A.** (1882–1956) British writer. He created the character Winnie the Pooh to amuse his son Christopher Robin, and wrote four much-loved collections of children's poems and stories, including *Now We Are Six* (1927) and *The House at Pooh Corner* (1928). Full name **Milne, Alan Alexander**

'They're changing the guard at Buckingham Palace. / Christopher Robin went down with Alice. / Alice is marrying one of the guard. / "A soldier's life is terrible hard", / Says Alice.'
[A. A. Milne, 'Buckingham Palace', *When We Were Very Young*; 1924]

'"Good morning, Little Piglet", said Eeyore. "If it *is* a good morning", he said. "Which I doubt", said he. "Not that it matters", he said.'
[A. A. Milne, 'Eeyore Has a Birthday', *Winnie the Pooh*; 1926]

milo /mílō/ *n* a type of sorghum cultivated in the United States for its grain, known for growing early and resisting drought [Late 19C. Origin ?]

milometer *n* MEASURE another spelling of **mileometer**

milord /mi láwrd/ *n* **1.** a British gentleman or member of the aristocracy **2.** a form of address for a gentle-

man or member of the British aristocracy [Late 16C. Via French < English *my lord*]

Mílos ♦ **Melos**

Milosevic /mi lóssəvich/, **Milošević, Slobodan** (*b.* 1941) Yugoslavian national leader. He served as president of Serbia (1989–97) and the Federal Republic of Yugoslavia (1997–2000). He was extradited in 2001 to stand before the International Criminal Tribunal in The Hague for war crimes in the Former Yugoslavia in the 1990s.

Miłosz /mée losh, mée wosh/, **Czeslaw** (*b.* 1911) Lithuanian-born US writer. He defected from Communist Poland to the West in 1951 and wrote poetry, fiction, translations, and essays, often on the relationship between culture, morality, and politics. He won the Nobel Prize in literature (1980).

milreis /míl rayss, mil ráysh/ (*plural same*) *n* a former Portuguese or Brazilian unit of currency and coin equal to one thousand reis [Late 16C. < Portuguese < *mil* 'thousand' + *real* 'real' (a unit of currency)]

Milstein /míl stīn/, **Nathan** (1903–92) Russian-born US violinist. He studied at the St Petersburg Conservatory and lived in the United States from 1929.

milt /milt/ *n* **1.** the semen and seminal fluid of a fish **2.** the testis or sperm duct of a fish [Old English *milte* 'spleen']

milter /míltər/ *n* a fertile male fish during the mating season

Milton /míltən/, **John** (1608–74) English poet. His poems are considered to be among the greatest in English literature, and include the epic narrative of Adam and Eve's banishment from Paradise, *Paradise Lost* (1667). During the Civil Wars, he wrote powerful polemics that championed religious and civil liberty. See Cultural note at **paradise** —**Miltonian** /mil tōni ən/ *adj* —**Miltonic** /mil tónnik/ *adj*

> 'A dungeon horrible, on all sides round / As one great furnace flamed, yet from those flames / No light, but rather darkness visible / Served only to discover sights of woe, / Regions of sorrow, doleful shades, where peace / And rest can never dwell, hope never comes / That comes to all.'
> [John Milton, *Paradise Lost*; 1667]

> 'Who kills a man kills a reasonable creature, God's image; but he who destroys a good book, kills reason itself, kills the image of God, as it were in the eye.'
> [John Milton, *Areopagitica*; 1644]

Milton Keynes /-kéenz/ town in Buckinghamshire, southern England, designated a new town in 1967. Population: 207,063 (2002).

Milwaukee /mil wáwki/ largest city in Wisconsin, located in the southeastern corner of the state. Population: 590,895 (2002 estimate). —**Milwaukeean** *adj, n*

mim /mim/ *adj Scotland* excessively or affectedly shy or prim [Late 16C. An imitation of the gesture of pursing the lips]

Mimas /mī́ mass, mī́məss/ *n* a large natural satellite of Saturn

mimbar *n* ISLAM same as **minbar**

mime /mīm/ *n* **1.** ACTING USING ONLY GESTURE AND ACTION a style of performance in which people act out situations or portray characters using only gesture, facial expression, and action (*often used before a noun*) **2.** *also* **mime artist** PERFORMER WHO USES MIME a performer who does not speak, but relies solely on gesture, facial expression, and action to communicate with an audience **3.** THEATRICAL PERFORMANCE IN MIME a theatrical piece performed with gesture, facial expression, and action, and without words **4.** ANCIENT FARCE in ancient Greek and Roman theatre, a lewd comedy including dialogue, dance, and gesture ■ *vti* (**mimes, miming, mimed**) **1.** EXPRESS SOMETHING IN MIME to express something or act it out without words, using only gesture, facial expression, and action **2.** MOUTH WORDS OF SONG to mouth the words to a song silently [Early 17C. Via Latin *mimus* < Greek *mimos* 'imitator, mimic'] —**mimer** *n*

MIME /mīm/ *n* a set of Internet standards for handling multimedia and non-ASCII material. Full form **Multi-purpose Internet Mail Extensions**

mimeograph /mímmi ə graaf, -graf/ *n* **1.** COPYING MACHINE a machine that prints copies onto paper from an inked stencil rotated on a cylinder across the pages **2.** MIMEOGRAPHED COPY a copy made on a mimeograph ■ *vt* (**-graphs, -graphing, -graphed**) MAKE COPY OF SOMETHING WITH MIMEOGRAPH to make a copy of a document using a mimeograph [Late 19C. Originally a trademark < Greek *mimeisthai* (see MIMESIS) + -GRAPH]

mimesis /mi méessiss, mī-/ *n* **1.** ART'S IMITATION OF LIFE the imitation of life or nature in the techniques and subject matter of art and literature **2.** BIOL same as **mimicry** (sense 2) **3.** MED DISEASE SYMPTOMS IN HEALTHY PERSON the occurrence of the symptoms of a disease in somebody who does not have the disease, often produced psychosomatically **4.** RHETORICAL DEVICE the rhetorical use of what somebody else might have said [Mid-16C. < Greek *mimēsis* < *mimeisthai* 'imitate' < *mimos* 'mime']

mimetic /mi méttik, mī-/, **mimetical** /-méttik'l/ *adj* **1.** relating to or practising imitation, e.g. in artistic or literary mimesis **2.** relating to mimicry in animals and plants [Mid-17C. < Greek *mimētikos* < *mimēsis* (see MIMESIS)] —**mimetically** *adv*

mimic /mímmik/ *vt* (**-ics, -icking, -icked**) **1.** MOCK SOMEBODY THROUGH IMITATION to make fun of somebody by imitating him or her in an exaggerated way **2.** IMITATE SOMEBODY to adopt somebody else's voice, gestures, or appearance, in a deliberate and exaggerated way, especially to amuse people **3.** COPY SOMETHING to resemble something in a way that seems like a deliberate copy ○ *houses with facades that mimic the Tudor style* **4.** BIOL RESEMBLE OTHER SPECIES to take on the appearance of another plant or animal, e.g. to discourage predators ■ *n* IMITATOR somebody who imitates others, especially for comic effect ■ *adj* **1.** RELATING TO MIMICRY relating to mime, mimicry, or imitation **2.** SIMULATED simulated or pretend (*literary*) **3.** RESEMBLING SOMETHING imitating or resembling something (*literary*) [Late 16C. Via Latin *mimicus* < Greek *mimikos* < *mimos* 'imitator, mimic'] —**mimicker** *n*

SYNONYMS See ***imitate***.

mimicry /mímmikri/ *n* **1.** ART OF IMITATION the imitating of other people's voices, gestures, or appearance, often for comic effect **2.** BIOL SIMILARITY OF APPEARANCE IN NATURE the resemblance of a plant or animal to another species or to a feature of its natural surroundings, developed as protection from predators **3.** BIRDS BIRD CALL IMITATION the ability of some birds to imitate the songs of other species and use them in their own repertoire

miminy-piminy /mímmini pímmini/ *adj* same as **niminy-piminy** [Early 19C. Alteration]

Mimir /mée meer/ *n* in Norse mythology, the god of wisdom, a giant water demon who was said to reside at and drink from the well of wisdom at Yggdrasil

mimosa /mi mṓzə, -mṓssə/ *n* **1.** a tree or bush whose leaves are sensitive to touch. Flowers: white, yellow, or pink, in globular clusters. Native to: warm regions. Genus: *Mimosa*. **2.** TREES same as **silk tree** [Mid-18C. < modern Latin < Latin *mimus* 'imitator' (see MIME), because its leaves seem to flinch when touched, mimicking a recoiling animal]

mimulus /mímmyŏŏləss/ (*plural same*) *n UK, Can* a small wild or cultivated flowering plant. Flowers: shades of yellow and red, with two lips. Genus: *Mimulus*. ANZ, US term **monkey flower** [Mid-18C. < modern Latin, 'little mime' < Latin *mimus* (see MIME)]

min /min/ *n* a minute or a short while (*informal*) [Late 19C. Shortening of MINUTE [1]]

min. *abbr* **1.** SCI mineralogical **2.** SCI mineralogy **3.** MEASURE minim **4.** minimum **5.** *US* CHR, INTERNAT REL, GOV minister **6.** EDUC minor **7.** TIME minute [1]

Min. *abbr* **1.** POL Minister **2.** Ministry

mina /mī́nə/ (*plural* **-nae** /-nee/ *or* **-nas**) *n* a unit of weight and money used in ancient Greece and Asia Minor, usually equal to one sixtieth of a talent [Late 16C. Via Latin and Greek < Akkadian]

Minamata disease /mínnə maátə-/ *n* a severe degenerative disease of the nervous system caused by mercury contamination, especially from eating mercury-tainted seafood [Mid-20C. After a town in Japan]

Minamoto Yoritomo /mìnnəmṓtō yórri tṓmō/ (1147–99) Japanese leader. He founded the shogunate form of government and ruled most of Japan (1192–99).

minaret

minaret /mínnə ret, mínnə rét/ *n* a tall slender tower attached to a mosque, from which the muezzin calls the faithful to prayer [Late 17C. < French < Turkish *minārī* < Arabic *manāra* 'lighthouse, minaret']

Minas Basin /mī́nəss-/ tidal inlet on the coast of Nova Scotia, southeastern Canada. Length: 80 km/50 mi.

Minas Gerais /méenəss zhə ríss/ inland state in eastern Brazil. Much of its terrain is mountainous. Capital: Belo Horizonte. Population: 16,672,613 (1996). Area: 588,383 sq. km/227,176 sq. mi.

minatory /mínnətəri/, **minatorial** /mínnə táwri əl/ *adj* menacing or threatening (*formal*) [Mid-16C. < late Latin *minatorius* < Latin *minari* 'threaten' (see MENACE)] —**minatorially** /mínnə táwri əli/ *adv* —**minatorily** *adv*

minbar /mín baar/, **mimbar** /mím-/ *n* a pulpit in a mosque from which the sermon is delivered. It takes the form of a domed box with a door at the top of a staircase. [Mid-19C. < Arabic < *nabara* 'raise']

mince /minss/ *v* (**minces, mincing, minced**) **1.** *vt* SHRED FOOD to chop or grind meat or other food into very small pieces **2.** *vti* WALK DAINTILY to walk with small light steps in an affectedly dainty way **3.** *vti* SPEAK DAINTILY to speak, or say something, in an affectedly dainty way **4.** *vt* USE TACT to use words or deal with matters delicately in order not to offend or upset somebody (*in negatives*) ○ *She did not mince her words.* ■ *n* FINELY SHREDDED MEAT finely chopped or ground meat, especially beef [14C. < Old French *mincier* < *minutus* (see MINUTE [1])] —**mincer** *n*

mincemeat /mínss meet/ *n* **1.** a mixture of spiced and finely chopped fruits such as apples and raisins, usually cooked in pies **2.** minced meat [Mid-17C. Alteration of *minced meat*] ◇ **make mincemeat of somebody** *or* **something** to defeat somebody or something thoroughly (*informal*)

mince pie *n* an individual pie filled with mincemeat and served hot or cold, especially as a Christmas speciality

Minch /minch/, **Minches** /mínchiz/ sea channel in northwestern Scotland, separating the Outer Hebrides from the Inner Hebrides and the mainland. It is divided into the North Minch and the Little Minch.

Mincha /mínkhə, mín khaa/, **Minchah** *n* a daily Jewish prayer said in the afternoon [Early 19C. < Hebrew *minḥāh* 'offering']

Minches ♦ **Minch**

Mincho /mín chṓ, mínchō/ (1352–1431) Japanese artist and Buddhist priest. He was noted for his Buddhist icons and ink paintings. Full name **Kichizan Mincho**

mincing /mínssing/ *adj* affectedly dainty —**mincingly** *adv*

mind /mīnd/ *n* **1.** SEAT OF THOUGHT AND MEMORY the centre of consciousness that generates thoughts, feelings, ideas, and perceptions, and stores knowledge and memories **2.** THINKING CAPACITY the capacity to think, understand, and reason ○ *has a logical mind* **3.** CONCENTRATION concentration, or the ability to concentrate ○ *My mind was wandering.* **4.** WAY OF THINKING an opinion or personal way of thinking about something ○ *I've changed my mind about going with you.* ○ *Have you made up your mind about the job offer yet?* **5.** STATE OF THOUGHT OR FEELING the state of thought or feeling that is regarded as usual or desirable ○ *felt I was going out of my mind* **6.** DESIRE the desire or intention to act or behave in a particular way ○ *After such insults, I had a mind to leave right then.* **7.** INTELLECTUAL PERSON somebody considered in terms of his or her intellect or intelligence ○ *Einstein was*

one of the greatest minds of the modern era. **8. THINKING CHARACTERISTIC OF PARTICULAR GROUP** a pattern of thinking or feeling characteristic of a particular group ○ *Who knows what goes through the criminal mind?* **9.** PHILOSOPHY **NONMATERIAL THINGS** in the philosophy of Descartes, all things that are not matter ■ *v* **(minds, minding, minded) 1.** *vt* **PAY ATTENTION TO SOMETHING** to pay attention to something, especially so as to avoid danger or an accident ○ *Mind your step!* **2.** *vt* **CONTROL SOMETHING** to remain aware of the need to control something ○ *Mind your temper.* **3.** *vti* **OBJECT TO SOMEBODY OR SOMETHING** to have an objection to somebody or something ○ *Do you mind if we leave early?* **4.** *vt* **TEMPORARILY WATCH OVER SOMEBODY OR SOMETHING** to watch over and look after somebody or something, usually for a short time ○ *Will you mind the dog over the weekend?* **5.** *vt* **OBEY SOMEBODY** to listen to and obey somebody ○ *Be sure to mind your father while I'm away.* **6.** *vt* **REMEMBER SOMETHING** to remember or recall something ○ *Mind what I told you.* **7.** *vt Scotland, US regional* **REMIND SOMEBODY** to remind somebody of or about something [Old English *gemynd* < Indo-European 'think'] ◇ **bring something to mind** to remind somebody of something ○ *It brings to mind those horse-drawn carts they used to have.* ◇ **call something to mind** to remember something ○ *I can't quite call to mind the exact date they left.* ◇ **do you mind?** used to show that you object to something that somebody is doing ◇ **great minds think alike** used when two people coincidentally have the same idea ◇ **have it in mind to do something** to intend to do something ◇ **have somebody** *or* **something in mind** to be thinking of somebody or something as suitable for a specific purpose or role ◇ **keep something in mind** to remember something because it might be useful later ◇ **mind over matter** the act of making a mental effort to ignore, overcome, or control something physical ○ *They can lie on a bed of nails without feeling any pain – it's mind over matter.* ◇ **mind you** used to qualify something you have just said (*informal*) ◇ **speak your mind** to speak frankly and forthrightly

mind out *vi* to avoid something by keeping watch or being careful

mind-altering *adj* changing perceptions, moods, or thought patterns ○ *mild-altering drugs*

Mindanao /míndə nów/ island in the southern Philippines, the largest after Luzon. Population: 14,536,000 (1990). Area: 94,630 sq. km/36,540 sq. mi.

mind-bending *adj* (*informal*) **1.** PSYCHOL, DRUGS same as **mind-altering 2.** very complicated or difficult for the mind to deal with —**mind-bender** *n* —**mind-bendingly** *adv*

mind-blowing *adj* (*informal*) **1.** extremely exciting, surprising, or shocking **2.** PSYCHOL, DRUGS same as **mind-altering** —**mind-blower** *n* —**mind-blowingly** *adv*

mind-body problem *n* the philosophical question of whether the mind is part of the body or separate from it, first formulated as a problem by the French philosopher René Descartes

mind-boggling *adj* mentally overwhelming, e.g. because of great size or complexity (*informal*) —**mind-bogglingly** *adv*

mind candy *n N Am* something that is entertaining but not intellectually demanding (*slang*)

minded /míndid/ *adj* inclined to do a particular thing or act in a particular way

minder /míndər/ *n* **1.** same as **child minder 2.** a bodyguard or assistant who accompanies and protects a public figure, celebrity, or criminal (*informal*) **3.** a public-relations assistant to somebody in public life (*informal*)

mind-expanding *adj* **1.** describes drugs that heighten or intensify perceptions or moods **2.** expanding knowledge and awareness

mindful /mí̄ndf'l/ *adj* actively attentive, or deliberately keeping something in mind ○ *was mindful of the difficulties that lay ahead* —**mindfully** *adv* —**mindfulness** *n*

SYNONYMS See ***aware***.

mindfulness training *n* a programme designed to reduce the psychological and physical effects of stress that involves meditation, yoga, and other relaxation methods

mind game *n* a psychologically manipulative and deceptive practice intended to deceive or confuse somebody (*informal*; *often used in the plural*)

mindless /mí̄ndləss/ *adj* **1. BORING** uninteresting as a result of requiring little mental effort **2. PURPOSELESS** having no apparent purpose or rational cause **3. UNCONCERNED** not careful or concerned —**mindlessly** *adv* —**mindlessness** *n*

mind-numbing *adj* inspiring no interest or thought, especially because of dullness or repetitiveness —**mind-numbingly** *adv*

Mindoro /min dóorō/ island in the western Philippines, south of Luzon. Population: 282,593. Area: 9,738 sq. km/3,760 sq. mi.

mind-reader *n* somebody who claims or seems to be able to sense what others think without being told —**mind-reading** *n*

mindscape /mí̄nd skayp/ *n* **1.** a mental scene constructed from memory or imagination **2.** an artistic representation of a mental scene constructed from memory or imagination [After LANDSCAPE]

mindset /mí̄nd set/ *n* a set of beliefs or a way of thinking that determine somebody's behaviour and outlook

mind's eye *n* the mind as a place where visual images are conjured up from memory or imagination ○ *I can see in my mind's eye how the house will look after the renovations.*

mine[1] /mīn/ *n* **1. HOLE IN GROUND FOR EXTRACTING MINERALS** an excavated area from which minerals, often in the form of ore, are extracted **2. MINERAL-EXCAVATING BUSINESS** the industrial and commercial buildings, machinery, and personnel used to work a mine **3. MINERAL DEPOSIT** an area underground or at ground level where there is a deposit of ore, minerals, or precious stones **4. SOURCE** a rich source of something, especially information ○ *a mine of information* **5. HIDDEN EXPLOSIVE** an explosive device concealed underground or underwater that detonates on contact with a person, vehicle, or ship **6.** MIL **TUNNEL UNDER ENEMY TERRITORY** a tunnel dug under enemy territory in order to gain entry, undermine fortifications, or lay explosives **7.** ZOOL **INSECT BURROW** a tunnel made by a burrowing insect or larva, especially in a plant leaf ■ *v* **(mines, mining, mined) 1.** *vti* **REMOVE MINERALS** to extract minerals from the ground **2.** *vt* **LAY MINES IN GROUND OR WATER** to place explosive mines throughout an area of ground or water **3.** *vt* **CONSTRUCT TUNNEL** to dig a tunnel underground **4.** *vt* **MAKE USE OF RESOURCE** to make use of a particular resource ○ *Generations of scholars mined these archives.* [14C. Directly or via Old French < assumed Vulgar Latin *mina*] —**minable** *adj*

mine[2] /mīn/ *pron* refers to something that belongs to or relates to the speaker or writer ○ *He put on his coat, and told me to put mine on too.* ○ *She was a friend of mine.* ■ *det* belonging to or relating to me (*archaic*; *used before a vowel*) ○ *By mine eyes and by mine ears I swear.* [Old English *min* < Indo-European, 'me']

mine detector *n* an instrument used for finding explosive mines hidden under the ground or in water

mine dump *n S Africa* a heap of waste material from mines that looks like a hill

minefield /mí̄n feeld/ *n* **1.** an area of land or sea in which explosive mines have been placed **2.** a situation in which great care is needed to avoid the many hazards that exist in it

minelayer /mí̄n layər/ *n* a ship fitted with equipment for laying explosive mines under water

miner /mí̄nər/ *n* **1. MINEWORKER** somebody who works in a mine digging for minerals, especially coal **2. MINERAL-EXTRACTING MACHINE** a machine that extracts minerals, especially coal, from the ground **3. SOMEBODY LAYING EXPLOSIVE MINES** somebody whose job is to lay explosive mines underground or underwater **4.** *Aus* BIRDS **BIRD** a bird of the honeyeater family that has a loud call and nests in colonies. Genus: *Manorina.* **5.** INSECTS same as **leaf miner**

SPELLCHECK miner or **minor**? Do not confuse the spelling of ***miner***, ***minor***, or ***mynah***, which sound similar. A ***miner*** works in a mine; a ***minor*** is somebody below the legal age of adulthood; a ***mynah*** is a bird that can mimic human speech. The word ***minor*** has various other meanings and uses, principally as an adjective referring to something small or insignificant (as in *minor changes, a minor problem*) or describing a type of musical scale, key, or interval.

mineral /mínnərəl/ *n* **1. INORGANIC SUBSTANCE IN NATURE** a substance that occurs naturally in rocks and in the ground and has its own characteristic appearance and chemical composition **2. MINED SUBSTANCE** a naturally occurring substance that is mined or extracted from the ground **3. MATTER NOT ANIMAL OR VEGETABLE** something that is not made of animal or vegetable matter (*not in technical use*) **4. INORGANIC NUTRITIVE SUBSTANCE** an inorganic substance that must be ingested by animals or plants in order to remain healthy **5.** BEVERAGES same as **soft drink** (*dated; usually used in the plural*) [15C. < medieval Latin *minerale* < Old French *miniere* 'mine' < *mine* (see MINE [1])] —**mineral** *adj*

mineralize /mínnərə līz/ (**-izes, -izing, -ized**), **mineralise** (**-ises, -ising, -ised**) *v* **1.** *vt* to impregnate something such as water or organic matter with minerals **2.** *vti* to transform organic matter into a mineral, as happens in petrifaction, or to be transformed in this way —**mineralizable** *adj* —**mineralization** /mínnərə lī záysh'n/ *n*

mineralocorticoid /mínnərəlō káwrti koyd/ *n* a hormone (**corticosteroid**) such as aldosterone that controls electrolyte and fluid balance in the body and is secreted by the adrenal cortex [Mid-20C. < MINERAL + CORTICOSTEROID]

mineralogy /mínnə rálləji/ (*plural* **-gies**) *n* **1.** the scientific study of minerals and how to classify, distinguish, and locate them **2.** a profile of an area's mineral deposits —**mineralogical** /mínnərə lójjik'l/ *adj* —**mineralogically** *adv* —**mineralogist** *n*

mineral oil *n* **1.** an oil obtained from minerals, especially from petroleum **2.** *N Am* MED, COSMETICS same as **liquid paraffin**

mineral spring *n* a spring whose water has a high mineral or gas content

mineral tar *n* CHEM same as **maltha**

mineral water *n* a drinkable water with a high mineral salt or gas content, either obtained from a mineral spring or with minerals added. It is usually sold in bottles.

mineral wax *n* a wax made from a mineral, especially a hydrocarbon wax (**ozocerite**) found in veins in sandstone

mineral wool *n* a lightweight fibrous material made from slag or glass. Use: insulation, packing material, filters.

Minerva /mi núrvə/ *n* in Roman mythology, the goddess of wisdom and patron of arts, trade, and the art of war, who was born fully armed from the head of Jupiter. Greek equivalent **Athena**

mineshaft /mí̄n shaaft/ *n* a nearly vertical passageway that provides access or ventilation to an underground mine

minestrone /mínni strṓni/ *n* an Italian vegetable soup [Late 19C. < Italian < Latin *ministrare* 'serve' < *minister* 'servant']

minesweeper /mí̄n sweepər/ *n* a ship fitted with equipment for detecting and clearing underwater explosive mines

mineworker /mí̄n wurkər/ *n* somebody who works in a mine

Ming /ming/ *n* the Chinese dynasty that ruled from 1364 to 1644, under which arts, trade, and scholarship were greatly developed (*often used before a noun*) [Late 18C. < Chinese, 'bright, clear']

MING *abbr* ONLINE mailing (*used in e-mails or text messages*)

minge /minj/ *n* (*taboo*) **1.** a highly offensive term for a woman's genitals **2.** a highly offensive term for women collectively [Late 19C. Origin ?]

minger /míngər/ *n* an unattractive or unpleasant person (*slang*) [Origin ?]

minging /mínging/ *adj* unattractive or unpleasant (*slang*) [Origin ?]

mingle /míng g'l/ (**-gles, -gling, -gled**) *v* **1.** *vti* to mix together gently or gradually, or mix things together gently or gradually ○ *Heat gently to allow the flavours to mingle.* **2.** *vi* to circulate among a group of people such as guests at a party [15C. Alteration of obsolete *menglen* 'keep mixing' < Old English *mengan* 'to mix']

Mingrel /míng grəl/, **Mingrelian** /ming greéli ən/ *n* a Caucasian language closely related to Georgian that is spoken in the mountainous region to the northeast of the Black Sea. Native speakers: 500,000. [Mid-

17C < Latin *Mingrelia*, region of the Caucasus] —**Mingrel** *adj* —**Mingrelian** *adj*

ming tree *n* **1.** an evergreen tree used for bonsai, usually in a flat-topped asymmetrical arrangement **2.** an artificial bonsai tree [*Ming*, origin ?]

Mingus /míng gəss/, **Charlie** (1922–79) US double bassist and composer. He played in various jazz bands, establishing the double bass as a principal jazz instrument. Born **Mingus, Charles**

mingy /mínji/ (**-gier, -giest**) *adj* **1.** STINGY ungenerous or stingy (*informal*) **2.** INSUFFICIENT excessively or unacceptably small in quantity or amount (*informal*) ○ *a mingy helping* **3.** SHODDY IN QUALITY creating a negative impression on others because of being shoddy (*informal*) ○ *'Finally, they will have to change the mingy, defensive, consultant-driven style of recent campaigns.'* (Joe Klein *Newsweek*; 19 May 2003) [Early 20C. Origin ?]

mini /mínni/ (*plural* **-is**) *n* something that is small in comparison with other things of its type, especially a minicomputer or a miniskirt (*informal*) [Mid-20C. < MINI-]

mini- *prefix* small, short, miniature ○ *ministroke* [Shortening of MINIATURE]

miniature /mínnichər/ *n* **1.** SMALLER VERSION a smaller-than-usual version of something, e.g. a very small model or a smaller version of a particular breed of animal **2.** TINY PAINTING a very small, detailed, and well-finished painting, especially a portrait made to fit inside a locket or other piece of jewellery **3.** PAINTING OF MINIATURES the art of painting miniatures **4.** ILLUMINATED MANUSCRIPT ILLUSTRATION a small picture or decorative initial in an illuminated manuscript **5.** BEVERAGES SMALL BOTTLE OF SPIRITS a small bottle of alcoholic spirits, containing one or two measures only ■ *adj* SMALLER THAN USUAL smaller in size or scale than others of its type [Late 16C. Via Italian *miniatura* 'illumination' < Latin *minium* 'red lead'] ◇ **in miniature** on a small scale

ORIGIN Red lead was used in ancient and medieval times for making a sort of red ink with which manuscripts were decorated, and so the medieval Latin verb *miniare* was coined from *minium*, 'red lead', meaning 'to illuminate a manuscript'. Italian took this over and derived *miniatura* 'painting, illumination' from it. It referred particularly to the small paintings in manuscripts, and, after English acquired it, it was soon broadened to refer to any 'small image'. Association with *minute*, *minimum*, etc. led by the early 18th century to its adjectival use for 'small'.

miniature golf *n* a novelty version of golf played with a putter on a very small course with obstacles such as tunnels and bridges for the ball to avoid or go through

miniaturise *vt* another spelling of **miniaturize**

miniaturist /mínnichərist/ *n* an artist who paints miniatures or small pictures, e.g. in illuminated manuscripts

miniaturize /mínnichə rīz/ (**-izes, -izing, -ized**), **miniaturise** (**-ises, -ising, -ised**) *vt* to make a version of something in a much smaller size or on a greatly reduced scale —**miniaturization** /mínnichə rī záysh'n/ *n*

minibar /mínni baar/ *n* a small refrigerator in a hotel room stocked with alcoholic beverages and often also with soft drinks and snacks

mini-blind *n N Am* a Venetian blind with narrow slits

minibreak /mínni brayk/ *n* in a tennis match, a point won against the serve in a tie-break (*informal*)

minibus /mínni buss/ *n* a small bus for carrying around 10 to 15 passengers, usually on short journeys

minicab /mínni kab/ *n* an ordinary car used as a taxi, responding to telephone calls but not generally cruising the streets for business

minicompact /mínni kóm pakt/ *n* a passenger vehicle smaller than a subcompact in size

minicomputer /mínni kəm pyootər/ *n* a computer of a size, speed, and capacity intermediate between a standard personal computer and a mainframe

Miniconjou /mínni kón joo/ (*plural* **-jous** or *same*), **Minneconjou** *n* a member of a Native North American people who lived in Wyoming, South Dakota, and Nebraska, and who now live mainly in South Dakota

minidisc /mínni disk/, **MiniDisc** *n* a small recordable compact disc housed in a rectangular plastic case. It measures 5 cm/2 in in diameter.

minidress /mínni dress/ *n* a dress with a hemline above the knee

Minié ball /mínni ay-/ *n* a bullet with a cone-shaped head and a hollow base that expands when fired, used in muzzle-loading rifles of the 19th century [Mid-19C. After Claude-Étienne *Minié* (1804–79), French army officer]

minify /mínni fī/ (**-fies, -fying, -fied**) *vt* to understate or reduce the size or importance of something [Late 17C. Directly or via medieval Latin < Latin *minimus* 'least' after MAGNIFY] —**minification** /mínnifi káysh'n/ *n*

minikin /mínnikin/ *adj* small and delicate (*archaic*) [Mid-16C. < Dutch *minneken* 'darling' < *minne* 'love']

minim /mínnim/ *n* **1.** MUSICAL NOTE a musical note with the time value of half a semibreve or two crotchets. It is written as an open note head with a stem. N Am term **half note 2.** UNIT OF FLUID MEASURE a unit of fluid measure equal to one sixtieth of a fluid drachm, 0.0616 millilitres, or approximately one drop **3.** PEN STROKE a downward vertical stroke of the pen in handwriting [15C. Directly or via medieval Latin *minimus* < Latin 'least']

minima plural of **minimum**

minimal /mínnim'l/ *adj* **1.** VERY SMALL very small in amount or extent **2.** SMALLEST POSSIBLE smallest possible in amount or least possible in extent **3.** *also* **Minimal** RELATING TO MINIMALISM relating to or displaying attributes associated with minimalism [Mid-17C. < Latin *minimus* 'least'] —**minimality** /mínni mállәti/ *n* —**minimally** *adv*

USAGE Strictly speaking, ***minimal*** means 'smallest or least possible', just as *minimize* means 'reduce something to the lowest possible amount or degree'. Often, however, these words are used more generally: *a minimal amount of noise* may simply be the least amount of noise conveniently possible to make, rather than none at all. If the word is to retain any sense of being a superlative, it should not be used with modifiers such as *rather*, *somewhat*, and *slightly*. *Small*, *limited*, *reduced*, and *as little as possible* are all suitable alternatives to overextending ***minimal***; and *diminish*, *lessen*, and *reduce* do the job that *minimize* is sometimes inappropriately asked to do.

minimal art *n* **1.** ARTS same as **minimalism** (sense 1) **2.** minimalist works of art —**minimal artist** *n*

minimalise *vt* another spelling of **minimalize**

minimalism /mínnimәlizәm/ *n* **1.** *also* **Minimalism** ARTISTIC MOVEMENT a movement of abstract artists who produce uncluttered paintings and sculptures that make use of basic colours and geometric shapes in impersonal arrangements. The movement originated in New York in the 1960s. **2.** SIMPLICITY OF STYLE simplicity in artwork, design, interior design, or literature, achieved by using a few very simple elements to maximum effect **3.** MOVEMENT FOR SIMPLICITY IN MUSIC a trend in music towards simplicity of rhythm and tone, including sustained or repeated rhythmic and melodic patterns resulting in a hypnotic effect

minimalist /mínnimәlist/ *n* **1.** somebody whose works of art, literature, or music display the simplicity associated with minimalism **2.** somebody who advocates restricting the power and goals of something, especially somebody who wishes to limit the role of government **3.** POL another spelling of **Minimalist** (sense 1)

Minimalist /mínnәmәlist/ *n* **1.** POL same as **Menshevik 2.** ARTS another spelling of **minimalist** (sense 1) [Early 20C. In sense 1 translation of Russian *men'shevik*]

minimalize /mínnimә līz/ (**-izes, -izing, -ized**), **minimalise** (**-ises, -ising, -ised**) *vt* to reduce something to the minimum —**minimalization** /mínnimә lī záysh'n/ *n*

minimally invasive surgery *n* surgery performed with lasers and other high-tech devices that involves minimal trauma to the patient's body

minimal pair *n* in linguistics, a pair of words or other linguistic expressions that are the same except for one sound, e.g. 'bit' and 'pit'

minimax /mínnimaks/ *n* the lowest of a set of maximum values ■ *adj* describes options or strategies designed to minimize the risk of sustaining maximum loss in any situation that involves conflict or competition [Mid-20C. < MINIMUM + MAXIMUM]

mini-me *n* a miniaturized clone of somebody or something [Late 20C. < the name of a clone in the films based on the Austin Powers character]

minimill /mínni mil/ *n US* a small mill, especially a steel mill that processes scrap metal

minimize /mínni mīz/ (**-mizes, -mizing, -mized**), **minimise** (**-mises, -mising, -mised**) *vt* **1.** REDUCE SOMETHING TO MINIMUM to reduce something to the lowest possible amount or degree **2.** UNDERRATE SOMETHING to play down the extent or seriousness of something **3.** MAKE IMAGE SMALLER to reduce the size of a computer image —**minimization** /mínni mī záysh'n/ *n* —**minimizer** *n*

USAGE See ***minimal***.

minim rest *n* a musical rest with the time value of a minim. N Am term **half rest**

minimum /mínnimәm/ *n* (*plural* **-imums** or **-ima** /-imә/) **1.** LOWEST POSSIBLE DEGREE the lowest possible amount or degree of something **2.** LOWEST RECORDED DEGREE the lowest recorded amount or degree of something **3.** LOWEST PERMISSIBLE DEGREE the lowest amount or degree of something permitted by law, e.g. the lowest speed on a road or the youngest age at which something can be done legally **4.** MATHS LOWEST NUMBER the lowest number in a finite set **5.** MATHS FUNCTION'S LOWEST VALUE the smallest value of a continuous function over a particular interval ■ *adj* LOWEST POSSIBLE lowest possible, recorded, or permissible [Mid-17C. < Latin < *minimus* 'least']

minimum lending rate *n* the official lowest interest rate at which the Bank of England formerly lent to discount houses, replaced by the base rate in 1981

minimum-security *adj* describes places that have security measures appropriate to inmates or patients who are not considered dangerous or who are not likely to try to escape

minimum wage *n* the lowest rate of pay allowed by law or contract, either in general or for a specific type of work

minimus /mínnimәss/ *n* (*plural* **-imi** /-imī/) a very small or insignificant person (*archaic*) ■ *adj* a word sometimes placed after the surname of the youngest of several school pupils with the same surname, especially formerly in public schools (*dated*) [Late 16C. < Latin, 'least']

mining /míning/ *n* **1.** the process or business of removing minerals from the ground **2.** the process of laying explosive mines

minion /mínnyәn/ *n* **1.** a servile or slavish follower of somebody generally regarded as important **2.** a servant or slave (*archaic or literary*) [Early 16C. < French *mignon* 'darling' (see MIGNON)]

minipill /mínni pil/ *n* an oral contraceptive that contains progesterone but not oestrogen

mini roundabout *n* a small traffic roundabout at junctions of lesser roads, often no more than a white disc painted on the road surface

~~**miniscule**~~ incorrect spelling of **minuscule**

miniseries /mínni seeriz/ (*plural same*) *n* a short series of television programmes, often a serialized fictional story, usually broadcast on consecutive nights

miniskirt /mínni skurt/ *n* a skirt with a hemline well above the knee

minister /mínnistәr/ *n* **1.** MEMBER OF CLERGY a member of the clergy of a Christian church, especially a Protestant one **2.** SENIOR POLITICIAN a senior politician who heads a government department, especially in the parliamentary system of government **3.** INTERNAT REL DIPLOMAT RANKED UNDER AMBASSADOR a diplomat representing a country, especially of a rank below ambassador **4.** CHR HEAD OF ROMAN CATHOLIC ORDER the superior in some orders in the Roman Catholic Church **5.** RELIG SPIRITUAL ADVISER somebody who sees to the spiritual needs of others **6.** BUSINESS REPRESENTATIVE somebody's agent or representative (*formal or literary*) ■ *v* (**-ters, -tering, -tered**) **1.** *vi* HELP SOMEBODY to give help to somebody in need (*formal*) **2.** *vi* CHR DO RELIGIOUS MINISTER'S WORK to perform the duties of a member of the clergy **3.** *vt* GIVE SOMETHING to administer something such as aid, medicine,

or a sacrament (*archaic*) [13C. Via French < Latin, 'servant'] —**ministership** *n*

ministerial /mínni steéri əl/ *adj* **1.** RELATING TO CLERGY relating to a religious minister **2.** RELATING TO GOVERNMENT MINISTER relating to a government minister or the minister's department **3.** LAW REQUIRING FOLLOWING OF INSTRUCTIONS allowing no personal discretion, only the strict following of law **4.** INSTRUMENTAL playing an important part in achieving something (*formal*) **5.** *also* **Ministerial** BACKING GOVERNMENT supporting the government, not the opposition —**ministerially** *adv*

ministerialist /mínni steéri əlist/, **Ministerialist** *n* somebody who supports the government, not the opposition

Minister of State *n* an assistant minister in a government department who is usually not a member of the Cabinet

Minister of the Crown *n* a senior minister who is head of a government department and a member of the Cabinet

minister without portfolio *n* a senior government minister who is a member of the Cabinet but has no direct responsibility for a government department

ministrant /mínnistrənt/ *n* somebody who gives aid to others (*literary*) [Mid-16C. < Latin *ministrant-*, present participle of *ministrare* 'serve' < *minister* 'servant']

ministration /mínni stráysh'n/ *n* **1.** TREATMENT help, treatment, or service (*formal*; *often used in the plural*) **2.** RELIGIOUS MINISTER'S WORK the service provided by a religious minister **3.** ACT OF SUPPLYING the supplying or administering of something (*archaic*) [14C. < Latin *ministration-* < *ministrare* (see MINISTRANT)]

ministroke /mínni strók/ *n* a temporary blockage of blood circulation in some part of the brain, causing short-term stroke symptoms such as dizziness, inability to speak or move, or loss of senses. Technical name **transient ischaemic attack**

ministry /mínnistri/ (*plural* **-tries**) *n* **1.** *also* **Ministry** GOVERNMENT DEPARTMENT a government department headed by a minister **2.** GOVERNMENT BUILDING the building in which a government department headed by a minister is housed **3.** WORK OF RELIGIOUS MINISTER the profession and services of a religious minister **4.** PERIOD OF SERVICE a religious minister's career or period of service **5.** MINISTERS ministers collectively, especially religious ministers (*takes a singular or plural verb*) **6.** PRIME MINISTER'S SERVICE the period of government under a prime minister [14C. Via Old French < Latin *ministerium* < *minister* 'servant']

~~miniture~~ incorrect spelling of **miniature**

minium /mínni əm/ *n* CHEM same as **red lead** [Mid-17C. < Latin]

minivan /mínni van/ *n* a small van, often with seats that can be removed or rearranged to accommodate cargo

miniver /mínnivər/ *n* a white or light grey fur used as trim on ceremonial costumes [Late 16C. < Old French *menu vair* 'small vair']

mink

mink /mingk/ *n* **1.** (*plural* **minks** or *same*) WEB-TOED MEMBER OF WEASEL FAMILY a semiaquatic carnivorous member of the weasel family with webbed toes and a bushy tail. Kept for: fur. Native to: North America, Asia, Europe. Genus: *Mustela*. **2.** MINK FUR the thick shiny brown fur of a mink (*often used before a noun*) **3.** MINK FUR GARMENT a coat, stole, or other garment made of mink fur [15C. < Swedish]

minke whale /míngkə-, -ki-/ *n* a small grey and white whale with a pointed snout. It is the smallest of the rorqual family, growing to only 10 m/30 ft long. Native to: seas worldwide. Latin name: *Balaenoptera acutorostrata*. [Mid-20C. < Norwegian]

Minna /mínnə/ city in west-central Nigeria, the capital of Niger State, situated about 80 km/50 mi. northwest of Abuja. Population: 133,600 (1995).

Minneapolis /mínni áppəliss/ largest city in Minnesota, in the southeastern part of the state, close to the city of St Paul. Population: 375,635 (2002 estimate).

Minneconjou *n* PEOPLES another spelling of **Miniconjou**

Minnelli /mi nélli/, **Liza** (*b.* 1946) US stage and screen performer. Daughter of Judy Garland and Vincente Minnelli, she won an Academy Award for *Cabaret* (1972). Full name **Minnelli, Liza May**

> 'Reality is something you rise above.'
> [Liza Minnelli, *NY Newsday*; 23 February 1994]

minneola /mínni ólə/ *n* an orange-coloured citrus fruit that is a hybrid of a tangerine and a grapefruit [Mid-20C. After *Minneola*, town in Florida, US]

Minnesinger /mínni singər/, **minnesinger** *n* in Germany between the 12th and the 14th centuries, a travelling poet-musician who wrote and performed songs of courtly love [Early 19C. Via German < Middle High German, 'love singer']

Minnesota /mínnə sótə/ **1.** state in the north-central United States, bordered by Canada, Lake Superior, Wisconsin, Iowa, South Dakota, and North Dakota. Capital: St Paul. Population: 5,019,720 (2002 estimate). Area: 225,181 sq. km/86,943 sq. mi. **2.** river in southern Minnesota, flowing from Big Stone Lake into the Mississippi River. Length: 534 km/332 mi. —**Minnesotan** *adj, n*

Minnesota Multiphasic Personality Inventory *n* a standardized test that uses true-false questions to assess somebody's psychological and social adjustment. It is widely used in recruitment and screening. [After the University of MINNESOTA]

minnow /mínnó/ *n* **1.** BAIT FISH a small freshwater fish of the carp family, commonly used as fishing bait. Family: Cyprinidae. **2.** SMALL FISH a small silvery freshwater fish **3.** INSIGNIFICANT PERSON OR THING a person or organization of relatively low status or little importance [15C. Probably related to Old English *myne*]

Minoan /mi nó ən/ *adj* relating to the Bronze Age civilization on Crete that lasted from around 3000 to 1100 BC ■ *n* somebody who came from the island of Crete during ancient times, especially during the Minoan period [Late 19C. After *Minos*, legendary king of Crete]

Minogue /mi nóg/, **Kylie** (*b.* 1968) Australian actor and singer. She achieved fame in the Australian TV series *Neighbours* before launching a highly successful career as a pop singer.

minor /mínər/ *adj* **1.** SMALL relatively small in quantity, size, or degree **2.** LOW IN RANK relatively low in rank or importance **3.** LOW IN SEVERITY relatively low in severity or danger **4.** MUSIC DESCRIBES MUSICAL SCALE describes a musical scale that has a semitone interval between the second and third, fifth and sixth, and sometimes seventh and eighth notes **5.** MUSIC DESCRIBES MUSICAL INTERVAL describes a musical interval that is a semitone less than a major interval **6.** MUSIC DESCRIBES MUSICAL KEY describes a musical key that is based on a minor scale ○ *in B minor* **7.** LAW NOT LEGALLY ADULT younger than the legal age of adulthood **8.** *N Am* EDUC SECONDARY secondary to the major course of study **9.** YOUNGER WITH SAME NAME a word sometimes placed after the surname of the younger of two school pupils with the same surname, especially formerly in public schools (*dated*) ■ *n* **1.** LAW SOMEBODY NOT LEGALLY ADULT somebody who is not yet legally an adult **2.** MUSIC MUSICAL KEY OR HARMONY a key or harmony based on a musical scale whose third and, usually, sixth and seventh notes are lower by a semitone than those in the major scale ■ *vi* (**-nors, -noring, -nored**) *N Am* STUDY SECONDARY SUBJECT to have a second specialization in higher education, in addition to a major specialization ○ *She minors in Spanish.* [13C. < Latin, 'lesser']

SPELLCHECK See *miner*.

minor axis *n* the shorter axis of an ellipse

Minorca[1] /mi náwrkə/ *n* a white and black domestic chicken bred around the Mediterranean [Mid-19C. After MINORCA[2]]

Minorca[2] /mi náwrkə/ ◆ **Menorca**

minor element *n* CHEM same as **trace element** (sense 2)

minoritarianism /mī nórri tári ənizm/ *n* advocacy or political action on behalf of a minority

Minorite /mínə rīt/ *n* a friar of the Franciscan order [Mid-16C. < *Minor Friars*, translation of medieval Latin *Fratres Minores* 'lesser brethren', because the order stressed the virtue of humility]

minority /mī nórrəti, mi-/ *n* (*plural* **-ties**) **1.** SMALLER GROUP a group of people or things that is a small part of a much larger group **2.** GROUP WITH INSUFFICIENT VOTES TO WIN a group that has fewer votes in an organization than another group or groups **3.** SMALLER SOCIALLY DEFINED GROUP a group of people, within a society, whose members have different ethnic, racial, national, religious, sexual, political, linguistic, or other characteristics from the rest of society **4.** LAW NONADULTHOOD the state or period of being younger than the legal age of adulthood ■ *adj* **1.** OF MINORITY relating to or constituting a minority **2.** OFFENSIVE TERM an offensive term meaning belonging to, used or inhabited by, or involving a particular group of people within society who are different from the majority, especially ethnically or racially different ○ *minority schools*

minor key *n* a musical key based on a minor scale

minor league *n* in the United States, a league of professional baseball, football, ice hockey, or basketball teams that do not belong to the major leagues

minor-league *adj* **1.** relating to or being a team member of a minor sports league in the United States **2.** *N Am* mediocre in quality or position (*informal*)

minor scale *n* a scale whose third and, usually, sixth and seventh notes are lower by a semitone than those in the major scale, giving it a less bright, more emotionally suggestive quality

minor suit *n* in cards, either clubs or diamonds, which in bridge and similar games are ranked below hearts and spades

Minos /mín oss/ *n* in Greek mythology, the king of Crete and the son of Zeus, who kept a monster (**the Minotaur**) in a labyrinth

Minotaur /mínə tawr/ *n* in Greek mythology, a monster with the body of a man and head of a bull that lived in the Cretan labyrinth and was fed human sacrifices until it was killed by Theseus

minoxidil /mi nóksi dil/ *n* a drug that causes widening of the arteries. Use: treatment of high blood pressure and male-pattern baldness. [Late 20C. < shortening of AMINO- + OXIDE]

Minsk /minsk/ capital city of Belarus, situated in the north of the country. It is a major industrial city. Population: 1,699,000 (2001).

minster /mínstər/ *n* a large or important cathedral or church, usually one originally connected with a monastery [Old English *mynster* < ecclesiastical Latin *monasterium* (see MONASTERY)]

minstrel /mínstrəl/ *n* **1.** a medieval singer, musician, or reciter of poetry who travelled around from place to place giving performances **2.** any of a group of entertainers who wore black facial makeup and sang and performed in variety shows, a form of entertainment now usually considered racist and highly offensive [13C. Via Old French *menestral* 'entertainer, craftsman' < late Latin *ministerialis* 'official' < *ministerium* (see MINISTRY)]

minstrelsy /mínstrəlssi/ (*plural* **-sies**) *n* **1.** MINSTREL'S ART a minstrel's art or performance, or the profession of a minstrel **2.** MINSTRELS' POEMS AND SONGS the poems and songs written and performed by minstrels or by a particular minstrel **3.** MINSTREL TROUPE a troupe of medieval minstrels [14C. < Old French *menestralsie* < *menestrel* (see MINSTREL)]

mint

mint[1] /mint/ *n* **1.** a plant with aromatic leaves. Native to: northern temperate regions. Use: food flavouring. Genus: *Mentha*. **2.** a mint-flavoured sweet [Old English *minte*, via Germanic < Latin *mentha* < Greek *minthē*] —**minty** *adj*

mint[2] /mint/ *n* **1.** PLACE COINING MONEY a place where the coins used in a currency are manufactured under government control **2.** MUCH MONEY a large amount of money (*informal*) ■ *vt* (**mints, minting, minted**) **1.** MAKE COINS to make coins by stamping metal **2.** INVENT SOMETHING to create or invent something, especially a new word or phrase ■ *adj* IN PERFECT CONDITION in perfect condition as when first made ○ *in mint condition* [Old English *mynet*, via Germanic < Latin *moneta* (see MONEY)]

mintage /míntij/ *n* **1.** COINS FROM MINT coins made in a mint, especially a quantity of coins minted at the same time **2.** MINTING COINS the minting of coins **3.** FEE FOR MINTING a fee paid to a mint by a government for minting its coins

mint jelly *n* a jelly made chiefly from mint, green in colour, and served typically as a garnish for roast lamb

mint julep *n* a drink made by pouring spirits, usually bourbon whiskey, and sugar over crushed ice and flavouring or garnishing with mint

mintmark /mínt maark/ *n* a letter or symbol stamped on a coin that identifies the mint where it was made

mintmaster /mínt maastər/ *n* somebody responsible for supervising the minting of coins

Mintoff /mínt of/, **Dom** (*b.* 1916) Maltese prime minister (1955–58 and 1971–84). His call for independence during his first premiership led to the suspension of the constitution in 1959. In his second term he followed a policy of severing ties with Britain. Full name **Mintoff, Dominic**

mint sauce *n* a sauce made from mint, sugar, and vinegar, and traditionally served with roast lamb

minuend /mínnyoo end/ *n* the number from which another number (**subtrahend**) is to be subtracted [Early 18C. < Latin *minuendus* 'be made smaller' < *minuere* 'diminish']

minuet /mínnyoo ét/ *n* **1.** a slow French court dance of the 17th century, performed in triple time **2.** the music for a minuet [Late 17C. < French *menuet* 'small, dainty' < Latin *minutus*; from the steps taken in the dance]

minus /mínəss/ *prep* **1.** LESS reduced by the subtraction of a number ○ *Seven minus four is three.* **2.** WITHOUT lacking in or deprived of something ○ *Minus the tools, he cannot do the work required.* ■ *adj* **1.** SHOWING SUBTRACTION relating to or showing subtraction ○ *a minus sign* **2.** LESS THAN ZERO relating to or showing a value less than zero ○ *temperatures of minus 20 degrees* ○ *a minus amount* **3.** HAVING DETRIMENTAL EFFECT having a negative or detrimental effect ○ *a minus factor* **4.** SLIGHTLY BELOW STANDARD LEVEL used in marking or assessing something to show that it is slightly below the average standard indicated by a particular symbol ○ *a grade of C minus* ■ *n* **1.** MATHS same as minus sign ○ *The minus shows that it's a subtraction.* **2.** NEGATIVE QUANTITY a quantity below zero ○ *If we take that away we're left with a minus.* **3.** DISADVANTAGE something that is detrimental or disadvantageous ○ *The power problem may prove to be a minus.* [15C. < Latin < *minor* 'less']

minuscule /mínnəss kyool/ *adj* **1.** EXTREMELY SMALL extremely small or completely insignificant **2.** LOWER CASE in lower case letters ■ *n* **1.** SMALL LETTER a lower

case letter **2.** MEDIEVAL WRITING STYLE a small cursive style of writing used in medieval manuscripts **3.** LETTER WRITTEN IN MINUSCULE a letter of the alphabet written in minuscule style [Early 18C. Via French < Latin *minusculus* 'rather small' < *minus* 'less' (see MINUS)] —**minuscular** /mi núskyōōlər/ *adj*

minus sign *n* a symbol (–) used to indicate subtraction or a negative quantity

minute[1] /mínnit/ *n* **1.** 60 SECONDS a period of 60 seconds or a 60th part of an hour **2.** VERY SHORT TIME a very short period of time ○ *I'll only be gone a minute.* **3.** MOMENT a particular moment ○ *The minute we got there the show began.* **4.** SHORT DISTANCE a distance that can be travelled in a minute ○ *The villa is only a couple of minutes from the beach.* **5.** UNIT OF ANGULAR MEASURE a unit of measurement of angles equivalent to a 60th of a degree. Symbol **'** **6.** BRIEF NOTE a brief note or memorandum ■ **minutes** *npl* RECORD OF MEETING an official record of what is said or done during a meeting ■ *vt* (**-utes, -uting, -uted**) WRITE DOWN MEETING'S PROCEEDINGS to record or summarize officially what happens during a meeting, or make a note in the minutes of a particular thing that is said or done [14C. Directly or via Old French < Latin *minuta* < *minutus*, past participle of *minuere* 'make small'] ◇ **up to the minute** aware of, taking account of, or reporting the very latest developments

minute[2] /mī nyoot/ (**-nuter, -nutest**) *adj* **1.** VERY SMALL extremely small in size or scope **2.** INSIGNIFICANT so very small as not to matter **3.** CONCERNED WITH EVERY DETAIL extremely or laboriously thorough and painstaking, and concerned with every detail [Early 17C. < Latin *minutus* (see MINUTE [1])] —**minuteness** *n*

minute gun /mínnit-/ *n* a gun fired every minute as a distress signal or sign of mourning

minute hand /mínnit-/ *n* the longer pointer on a watch or clock that indicates the minutes

minutely /mī nyóotli/ *adv* **1.** IN GREAT DETAIL very thoroughly, carefully, and in great detail **2.** SLIGHTLY to a very small extent **3.** INTO SOMETHING VERY SMALL into a very small shape or very small pieces

minuteman /mínnit man/ (*plural* **-men** /-men/) *n* an armed fighter in the American War of Independence pledged to be ready to fight for the American cause at a minute's notice

minute steak /mínnit-/ *n* a piece of frying steak sliced so thinly that it can be cooked very quickly

minutiae /mī nyóoshi ee/ *npl* small or trivial details [Mid-18C. < Latin, 'small things' < *minutus* (see MINUTE [1])]

minx /mingks/ *n* an offensive term that deliberately insults a woman or girl as being impertinent or flirtatious [Mid-16C. Origin ?] —**minxish** *adj*

Minya, Al- ♦ **Al-Minya**

minyan /mínnyən/ (*plural* **-yanim** /-yə ním/ *or* **-yans**) *n* the minimum number, ten, of adult Jews required to be present to hold a religious service, or of Jewish men required for an orthodox religious service [Mid-18C. < Hebrew, 'count, reckoning']

Miocene /mī ə seen/ *n* the epoch of geological time, 24 million to 5 million years ago, during which the modern ocean currents were established and Antarctica became frozen. See table at **geological time** [Mid-19C. < Greek *meiōn* 'less' + *kainos* 'recent'] —**Miocene** *adj*

mioga /mi óggə/ *n* in Japanese cuisine, the shoot of a member of the ginger family that resembles a bud. It is sliced and used as a garnish. [Late 20C. < Japanese]

miosis /mī óssiss/ (*plural* **-oses** /-ósseez/), **myosis** *n* a contraction of the pupil of the eye, e.g. a contraction caused by a reaction to a drug [Early 19C. < Greek *muein* 'shut the eyes'] —**miotic, myotic** /mī óttik/ *adj*

MIP *abbr* **1.** INSUR marine insurance policy **2.** FIN monthly investment plan

MIPS /mips/, **mips** *abbr* COMPUT million instructions per second

Miquelon Island ♦ **St-Pierre and Miquelon**

mir /meer/ *n* a peasant commune in tsarist Russia [Late 19C. < Russian]

Mir: photographed from the space shuttle Atlantis (1997)

Mir *n* a space station launched by the former Soviet Union in 1986, designed to be permanently crewed

Mira /mírə/ *n* a variable red giant in the constellation Cetus that is only visible a few weeks a year when it becomes the brightest star in the constellation

mirabile dictu /mi rábbi lay dík too/ *interj* used to introduce the announcement of something the speaker, genuinely or ironically, considers to be amazing [< Latin, 'amazing to relate']

miracidium /mírə síddi əm/ (*plural* **-ia** /-i ə/) *n* the free-swimming first-stage larva of a trematode worm that hatches from an egg and then reproduces asexually [Late 19C. Via modern Latin < Greek *meirakidion* 'little boy'] —**miracidial** *adj*

miracle /mírrək'l/ *n* **1.** ACT OF GOD an event that appears to be contrary to the laws of nature and is regarded as an act of God **2.** AMAZING EVENT an event or action that is amazing, extraordinary, or unexpected ○ *It'll be a miracle if we get there on time.* **3.** MARVELLOUS EXAMPLE something admired as a marvellous creation or example of a particular type of science or skill ○ *a miracle of modern engineering* [12C. Via French < Latin *miraculum* 'object of wonder' < *mirari* 'wonder at' < *mirus* 'wonderful']

miracle drug *n* a drug, usually a new one, that is extraordinarily effective and seems to represent a breakthrough in the treatment of disease

miracle play *n* a medieval play broadly depicting miracles taken from the life of a saint or a story from the Bible

miraculous /mə rákyōōləss/ *adj* **1.** REGARDED AS CAUSED BY SUPERNATURAL INTERVENTION apparently contrary to the laws of nature and caused by a supernatural power **2.** EXTRAORDINARY unexpected, extraordinary, and marvellous **3.** ABLE TO PERFORM MIRACLES believed to have the power to perform miracles [15C. < French *miraculeux* < Latin *miraculum* (see MIRACLE)] —**miraculously** *adv* —**miraculousness** *n*

mirador /mírrə dáwr/ *n* a window, balcony, or turret designed to command a wide view [Late 17C. < Spanish < *mirar* 'to look' < Latin *mirare* (see MIRAGE)]

Miraflores, Lake /meeərə fláwrayz/ lake in central Panama, through which the Panama Canal passes

mirage /mírraazh, mə ráazh/ *n* **1.** an optical illusion of a sheet of water appearing in the desert or on a hot road, caused by light being distorted by alternate layers of hot and cool air **2.** something that appears to be real but is unreal or merely imagined [Early 19C. < French < *mirer* 'look at' < Latin *mirare* 'wonder at', variant of *mirari* (see MIRACLE)]

Miranda /mi rándə/ *n* a large natural satellite of Uranus

Carmen Miranda

Miranda /mi rándə/, **Carmen** (1909–55) Portuguese dancer and singer. Star of Brazilian and Hollywood musicals, she is remembered particularly for her elaborate costumes and headdresses made from tropical fruit. Born **Cunha, Maria do Carmo Miranda da**. See illustration on previous page

MIRAS /mīrəss/ *abbr* HIST mortgage interest relief at source

mirch /meerch/ *n S Asia* chilli, used either fresh or dried and ground into powder

mire /mīr/ *n* **1. BOG** an area of very marshy ground or deep slushy mud **2. THICK MUD** thick slimy mud **3. DIFFICULT SITUATION** a troublesome or oppressive situation or state that is very difficult to escape from ■ *v* (**mires, miring, mired**) **1.** *vti* **GET STUCK IN MUD** to sink into mud and become stuck, or make something sink into mud and become stuck **2.** *vt* **MAKE SOMETHING MUDDY** to make something muddy or dirty **3.** *vt* **ENTANGLE SOMEBODY OR SOMETHING** to involve somebody or something in difficulties (*often passive*) [13C. < Old Norse *myrr* 'bog'] —**miry** *adj*

mirepoix /meér pwaá/, **mirepois** *n* mixed finely diced vegetables, typically carrot, onion, and celery, lightly fried and used as a base for casseroles, savoury dishes, or on which to lay meat for roasting or braising [Late 19C. < French, after the Duc de Mirepoix, 1699–1757, French diplomat and general]

Miriam /mírri əm/ *n* in the Bible, a Hebrew prophet, poet, and the sister of Moses

mirin /mírrin/ *n* a sweet liquid flavouring made from fermented sake, widely used in Japanese cooking [Mid-20C. < Japanese]

mirk, etc. another spelling of **murk, etc.**

Miró /meérō, mee rṓ/, **Joan** (1893–1983) Spanish painter, sculptor, and printmaker. A leading surrealist, he developed a form of abstraction that produced dreamlike, ethereal compositions.

> 'I work like a gardener or a wine grower. Everything takes time. My vocabulary of forms, for example, did not come to me all at once. It formulated itself almost in spite of me.'
> [Joan Miró, *Interview, XXe Siècle (Paris) (20th Century)*; 15 February 1959]

mirrnyong /múrn yong/ *n Aus* the accumulated residue of a cooking fire used by Australian Aboriginals, made up of shells, ashes, and other fragments [Late 19C. < Aboriginal]

mirror /mírrər/ *n* **1. HIGHLY REFLECTIVE SURFACE** a surface, e.g. glass or polished metal, that reflects light without diffusing it so that it will give back a clear image of anything placed in front of it **2. GLASS FOR REFLECTING IMAGE** a piece of reflective material, especially glass coated on one side with metal, mounted in a frame for use, e.g. in the home or a vehicle **3. SOMETHING ACCURATELY REPRESENTING SOMETHING ELSE** something that accurately reproduces, describes, or represents something else ○ *the debate whether TV shows are a mirror of our culture* **4.** ONLINE same as **mirror site** ■ *vt* (**-rors, -roring, -rored**) **1. REFLECT SOMETHING IN SURFACE** to reflect something clearly in a surface (*often passive*) ○ *The mountains were mirrored in the lake.* **2. BE SIMILAR TO SOMETHING** to be very similar to or correspond closely with something else, or to reproduce it accurately ○ *These developments are now mirrored on the other side of the world.* **3. MAINTAIN COPY OF DATA OR WEBSITE** to maintain an exact copy of a program, data, or website, usually on another file server [13C. < Old French *mirour* < Latin *mirari* (see MIRACLE)]

mirror carp *n* a carp with very small scales that give its body a smooth shiny appearance. Latin name: *Cyprinus carpio*.

mirror image *n* something that, like a reflection in a mirror, is identical to something else but reversed

mirror site *n* a copy of a website maintained on a different file server so as to spread the distribution load or to back up data

mirth /murth/ *n* happiness or enjoyment, especially accompanied by laughter [Old English *myrgzz* < Germanic, 'pleasant, joyful'] —**mirthful** *adj*

mirthless /múrthləss/ *adj* not feeling or expressing amusement, good humour, or gladness —**mirthlessly** *adv* —**mirthlessness** *n*

MIRV /murv/ *abbr* MIL multiple independently targeted re-entry vehicle

Mirza /múrzə/ *n* an Iranian title of respect signifying a learned man or official when placed before a name, or, formerly, a royal prince when placed after a name [Early 17C. < Persian]

MIS *abbr* COMPUT management information system

mis- *prefix* **1.** badly, wrongly ○ *mishandle* **2.** bad, wrong ○ *misdeed* **3.** opposite, lack, failure ○ *mislike* [Partly Old English, and partly via Old French *mes-* < Germanic, 'go wrong']

misaddress *vt*
misadminister *vt*
misadministration *n*
misadvise *vt*
misaim *vt*
misalign *vt*
misalignment *n*
misallocate *vt*
misallocation *n*
misally *vt*
misanalyse *vt*
misanalysis *n*
misappraisal *n*
misassemble *vt*
misassumption *n*
misattribute *vt*
misattribution *n*
misbalance *vt*
miscatalogue *vt*
mischannel *vt*
mischaracterization *n*
mischaracterize *vt*
mischarge *vt*
misclassification *n*
misclassify *vt*
miscode *vt*
miscommunicate *vti*
miscompute *vt*
misconnect *vt*
misconnection *n*
misdate *vt, n*
misdeal *vti, n*
misdealer *n*
misdefine *vt*
misdescribe *vt*
misdescription *n*
misdiagnose *vt*
misdiagnosis *n*
misdivide *vt*
misdivision *n*
miseducate *vt*
miseducation *n*
misemploy *vt*
misemployment *n*
misevaluate *vt*
misfile *vt*
misfunction *n*
misgovern *vti*
misgovernment *n*
misgrade *vt*
mishear *vti*
mishit *n, vt*
misidentification *n*
misidentify *vt*
misimpression *n*
misinform *vt*
misinformant *n*
misinformation *n*
misinformer *n*
misinterpret *vt*
misinterpretation *n*
misinterpreter *n*
miskick *vti*
mislabel *vt*
mislearn *vt*
mislocate *vt*
misnumber *vt*
misorder *vt*
misorientation *n*
misperceive *vt*
misperception *n*
misplay *vt, n*
misprogram *vt*
misproportion *n*
misproportioned *adj*
misquotation *n*
misquote *vti*
misquoter *n*
misreckon *vti*
misrecord *vt*
misremember *vti*
misstate *vt*
misstatement *n*
missuit *vt*
misterm *vt*
mistime *vt*
mistranslate *vti*
mistranslation *n*
mistype *vti, n*
misvalue *vt*
misword *vt*
miswrite *vt*

misadventure /míssəd vénchər/ *n* **1.** an unfortunate event, especially something untoward, unlucky, or amusing that happens to somebody **2.** an accidental cause of death, not involving a crime or negligence on the part of somebody else [13C. < Old French *mesaventure* < *mesavenir* 'turn out badly' < *avenir* 'happen' < Latin *advenire* 'come to']

misalliance /míssə lī́ ənss/ *n* an unsuitable alliance, especially a marriage between mismatched partners

misandry /miss ándri/ *n* hatred of men as a sexually defined group [Early 20C. < Greek *andr-* 'man', after MISOGYNY] —**misandrist** *n* —**misandrous** *adj*

misanthrope /míss'n thrōp/, **misanthropist** /miss ánthrəpist/ *n* somebody who hates humanity, or who dislikes and distrusts other people and tends to avoid them [Mid-16C. < French < Greek *misanthrōpos* < *misein* 'to hate' + *anthrōpos* 'man'] —**misanthropic** /míss'n thróppik/ *adj* —**misanthropically** *adv* —**misanthropy** /miss ánthrəpi/ *n*

misapply /míssə plī́/ (**-plies, -plying, -plied**) *vt* **1.** to use something badly, incorrectly, or improperly **2.** to use money for an improper or dishonest purpose —**misapplication** /míss apli káysh'n/ *n*

misapprehend /míss apri hénd/ (**-hends, -hending, -hended**) *vt* to fail to understand something

misapprehension /míss apri hénsh'n/ *n* a false impression or incorrect understanding, especially of the nature of a situation or somebody's intentions —**misapprehensive** *adj*

misappropriate /míssə prṓpri ayt/ (**-ates, -ating, -ated**) *vt* to take something, especially money, dishonestly, or in order to use it for an improper or illegal purpose —**misappropriation** /míssə prōpri áysh'n/ *n*

SYNONYMS See *steal*.

misbegotten /míssbi gótt'n/ *adj* **1. ILL-CONCEIVED AND GENERALLY BAD** from a bad source, badly thought out, or generally deplorable from start to finish **2. DISHONESTLY OBTAINED** obtained by dishonest means **3. ILLEGITIMATE** born to parents who are not married to each other

misbehave /míssbi háyv/ (**-haves, -having, -haved**) *vi* **1.** to be naughty and troublesome, or otherwise behave in an unacceptable way **2.** to function badly or not at all, or to cause problems (*informal*) —**misbehaver** *n*

misbehavior *n* US spelling of **misbehaviour**

misbehaviour /míssbi háyvyər/ *n* unacceptable behaviour, especially naughtiness, disobedience, or troublesomeness on the part of children

misbelief /míssbi leéf/ *n* a belief that is or is considered to be false or unorthodox

misbelieve /míssbi leév/ (**-lieves, -lieving, -lieved**) *vi* to hold beliefs that are or are considered to be false or unorthodox, especially on religious matters (*disapproving*) —**misbeliever** *n*

misc. *abbr* **1.** miscellaneous **2.** miscellany

miscalculate /miss kálkyoo layt/ (**-lates, -lating, -lated**) *vti* **1.** to calculate something incorrectly **2.** to judge or assess somebody or something incorrectly, or form false expectations as to the consequences of an action —**miscalculation** /míss kalkyoo láysh'n/ *n* —**miscalculator** *n*

miscall /miss káwl/ (**-calls, -calling, -called**) *vt* to use the wrong or an inappropriate name for somebody or something —**miscaller** *n*

miscanthus /miss kánthəss/ *n* a tall perennial grass with a thick stem. Native to: eastern Asia. Use: fuel, bedding, thatching. Latin name: *Miscanthus giganteus*.

miscarriage /miss kárrij, míss karij/ *n* **1.** an involuntary ending of a pregnancy through the discharge of the foetus from the womb at too early a stage in its development for it to survive. Technical name **abortion 2.** the mishandling or failure of something such as a plan or project (*formal*)

miscarriage of justice *n* a failure of the legal system to come to a just decision

miscarry /miss kárri/ (**-ries, -rying, -ried**) *vi* **1. HAVE SPONTANEOUS ABORTION** to lose a foetus, especially a human foetus, through a miscarriage **2. BE SPONTANEOUSLY ABORTED** to be expelled from the womb at too early a stage in development to be able to survive **3. FAIL** to result in failure (*formal*) **4. BE LOST IN TRANSIT** to become lost or go astray before reaching an intended destination

miscast /míss kaást/ (**-casts, -casting, -cast**) *vt* (*often passive*) **1.** to choose somebody to play a stage or film part to which he or she is unsuited **2.** to give a role in a play or film to an unsuitable actor

miscegenation /míssijə náysh'n/ *n* (*offensive when used disapprovingly, as often formerly*) **1.** sexual relations between people of different races, especially of different skin colours, leading to the birth of children **2.** marriage or cohabitation between people of different races [Mid-19C. < Latin *miscere* 'to mix' + *genus* 'race'] —**miscegenational** *adj*

~~**miscelaneous**~~ incorrect spelling of **miscellaneous**

miscellanea /míssə láyni ə/ *npl* miscellaneous things, especially pieces of writing, brought together as a collection [Late 16C. < Latin < *miscellaneus* (see MISCELLANEOUS)]

miscellaneous /míssə láyni əss/ *adj* **1.** made up of many different things or kinds of things that have no necessary connection with each other **2.** each being different or having different abilities or qualities from the others ○ *a task force of miscellaneous specialists* [Early 17C. < Latin *miscellaneus* < *miscere* 'to mix'] —**miscellaneously** *adv* —**miscellaneousness** *n*

miscellanist /mi séllənist/ *n* a compiler or writer of miscellanies

miscellany /mi sélləni/ (*plural* **-nies**) *n* **1.** a miscellaneous collection of things **2.** a collection of miscellaneous pieces of writing in one volume, often by different authors on various subjects and

in different genres [Late 16C. Via French *miscellanées* < Latin *miscellanea* (see MISCELLANEA)]

mischance /míss cháanss/ *n* **1.** the occurrence of unfortunate events by chance **2.** something that happens through bad luck [14C. < Old French *mescheance* < late Latin *cadentia* (see CHANCE)]

~~mischeif~~ incorrect spelling of **mischief**

mischief /mísschif/ *n* **1. NAUGHTY BEHAVIOUR** behaviour, especially by children, that is undesirable or troublesome without being wicked **2. TENDENCY TO NAUGHTY BEHAVIOUR** a tendency to mildly troublesome or undesirable behaviour such as teasing or practical jokes **3. INJURY OR DAMAGE** injury or damage caused by the actions of somebody or something **4. SOURCE OF HARM OR TROUBLE** something or somebody that causes serious harm or trouble to others (*dated*) **5. HARMLESS TROUBLEMAKER** somebody who causes or enjoys causing harmless trouble (*dated*) [13C. < Old French *meschef* < *meschever* 'meet with misfortune' < *chever* 'come to an end' < *chef* 'head']

mischief-maker *n* a troublemaker who sets people against each other, especially by spreading malicious gossip —**mischief-making** *n*

~~mischievious~~ incorrect spelling of **mischievous**

mischievous /mísschivəss/ *adj* **1. PLAYFULLY NAUGHTY OR TROUBLESOME** behaving or likely to behave in a naughty or troublesome way, but in fun and not meaning serious harm **2. TROUBLESOME OR IRRITATING** intended to tease or cause trouble, though usually in fun or without much malice **3. FULL OF MISCHIEF** expressing somebody's intention or inclination to have fun by teasing, playing tricks, or causing trouble **4. DAMAGING** causing or meant to cause serious trouble, damage, or hurt (*formal*) —**mischievously** *adv* —**mischievousness** *n*

misch metal /mísh-/ *n* an alloy of cerium and rare metals used, e.g., in the flints of cigarette lighters [Early 20C. < German *Mischmetall* 'mix-metal']

miscible /míssəb'l/ *adj* describes two or more liquids that can be mixed together [Late 16C. < medieval Latin *miscibilis* < Latin *miscere* 'to mix']

miscommunication /mísskə myóoni káysh'n/ *n* **1.** failure to communicate something clearly or correctly **2.** a communication that is unclear or likely to be misinterpreted

miscomprehend /mís kompri hénd/ (**-hends, -hending, -hended**) *vt* to mistake the meaning or nature of something

misconceive /mísskən séev/ (**-ceives, -ceiving, -ceived**) *vt* to fail to understand something correctly, or form a false conception of something

misconceived /mísskən séevd/ *adj* resulting from a wrong or faulty understanding or idea of something and consequently doomed to failure

misconception /mísskən sépsh'n/ *n* a mistaken idea or view resulting from a misunderstanding of something

misconduct *n* /míss kóndukt/ **1. IMMORAL, UNETHICAL, OR UNPROFESSIONAL BEHAVIOUR** behaviour that is not in accordance with accepted moral or professional standards **2. INCOMPETENCE** incompetent or dishonest management of something, especially on behalf of others ■ *v* /mísskən dúkt/ (**-ducts, -ducting, -ducted**) **1. misconduct yourself** *vr* **ACT IMMORALLY** to act in an immoral or improper way **2.** *vt* **MANAGE SOMETHING BADLY** to manage something in an incompetent or dishonest way ○ *guilty of misconducting the whole affair*

misconstruction /mísskən strúksh'n/ *n* **1.** a faulty understanding or interpretation of something **2.** a faulty grammatical construction

misconstrue /mísskən stróo/ (**-strues, -struing, -strued**) *vt* to understand or interpret something incorrectly

miscount *vti* /míss kównt/ (**-counts, -counting, -counted**) to make a mistake when counting something ■ *n* /míss kownt/ an incorrect count or calculation

miscreant /mísskri ənt/ *n* **1.** somebody who behaves in a dishonest, malicious, or otherwise contemptible way (*literary*) **2.** somebody whose religious faith is frowned upon or loathed (*archaic insult*) [13C. < Old French, present participle of *mescroire* 'disbelieve' < Latin *credere* 'believe']

miscreate /mískri áyt/ (**-ates, -ating, -ated**) *vt* to make something badly or imperfectly —**miscreation** *n*

miscue /míss kyóo/ *n* **1.** CUE GAMES **FAULTY SHOT IN BILLIARDS** in billiards or snooker, a shot that fails because the cue does not strike the cue ball properly **2. MISTAKE** a mistake, especially one that involves giving somebody the wrong cue to say or begin something or giving a cue at the wrong time (*informal*) ■ *v* (**-cues, -cuing, -cued**) **1.** *vti* CUE GAMES **MAKE FAULTY SHOT** in billiards or snooker, to fail to strike the cue ball properly, or to play a miscue **2.** *vti* **MISS CUE** to fail to respond to a cue, to give the wrong cue for something, or to give a cue at the wrong time **3.** *vi* **ERR** to make a mistake (*informal*)

misdeed /míss déed/ *n* a wicked, blameworthy, or unlawful act

misdemeanant /míssdi méenənt/ *n* somebody convicted of a misdemeanour

misdemeanor *n* US spelling of **misdemeanour**

misdemeanour /míssdi méenər/ *n* **1.** in the United States and before 1967 in England and Wales, a crime less serious than a felony and resulting in a less severe punishment **2.** a relatively minor misdeed

misdial /miss dī́ əl/ (**-als, -alling, -alled**) *vti* to dial a telephone number incorrectly —**misdial** /míss dī əl/ *n*

misdirect /míssdə rékt/ (**-rects, -recting, -rected**) *vt* **1. GIVE SOMEBODY WRONG DIRECTIONS** to give somebody wrong directions or instructions **2. WRONGLY ADDRESS MAIL** to put a wrong address on an item of mail **3. AIM SOMETHING INACCURATELY** to aim something such as a punch or bullet inaccurately, or direct something such as a comment or insult at the wrong person **4. GIVE JURY WRONG INSTRUCTIONS** to give a jury incorrect information about the facts or laws pertaining to a case —**misdirection** *n*

mise en scène /méez on sáyn/ (*plural* **mises en scène** /*pronunc. same*/) *n* **1.** CINEMA, THEATRE **ARRANGEMENT OF ACTORS AND SCENERY** the positioning of actors, scenery, and properties on a stage or film set **2. STYLE OF FILM DIRECTING** a style of film directing characterized by long scenes, little camera movement, and few changes of camera position **3. SETTING FOR SOMETHING** the physical environment in which an event takes place [< French, literally 'putting on stage']

miser /mī́zər/ *n* **1.** somebody who hates spending money and lives as though he or she were poor **2.** somebody regarded as ungenerous, greedy, or selfish [Mid-16C. < Latin, 'unfortunate']

miserable /mízzərəb'l/ *adj* **1. VERY UNHAPPY** experiencing a serious lack of contentment or happiness ○ *feeling miserable* **2. VERY UNPLEASANT** causing or accompanied by discomfort, unpleasantness, or unhappiness ○ *a miserable weekend* **3. CONTEMPTIBLE** deserving contempt or condemnation **4. INADEQUATE** inadequate, often insultingly or embarrassingly inadequate, in quantity or quality ○ *a miserable score* **5. DIRTY OR SQUALID** dirty, squalid, and lacking any comfort **6.** *Scotland, ANZ* **STINGY** mean or stingy **7.** *Carib* **BADLY BEHAVED** troublesome and badly behaved (*especially used of children*) [15C. Via Old French < Latin *miserabilis* 'pitiable' < *miser* 'unfortunate'] —**miserableness** *n* —**miserably** *adv*

CULTURAL NOTE ***Les Misérables***, a novel (1862) by French writer Victor Hugo. Set in mid-19th-century France, it tells the story of Jean Valjean, whose attempts to escape his criminal past are dogged by guilt, fate, and the persistent police inspector Javert. This epic tale is noted for its gripping plot and vivid descriptions of events such as the battle of Waterloo.

misère /mi záir/ *n* **1.** a call in some card games, especially solo whist, indicating that a hand is expected to win no tricks **2.** a hand that is expected to win no tricks [Early 19C < French, literally 'poverty, misery']

miserere /mízzə ráiri/ *n* CHR same as **misericord** [Late 18C. < Latin, 'have mercy!' < *misereri* 'have mercy' < *miser* 'unfortunate']

Miserere /mízzə ráiri/ *n* **1.** the 50th or 51st Psalm, depending on the version of the Bible **2.** a musical setting of the Miserere [13C. < the first word of the Latin text, beginning *Miserere mei, Deus* 'have mercy on me, O God' (see MISERERE)]

misericord /mi zérri kawrd/ *n* a projecting ledge often with elaborate carving on the underside of a seat in a church stall that, when the seat is turned up, gives a standing person something to rest against [14C < Old French < Latin *misericord* 'merciful, compassionate' < *miser* 'unfortunate' + *cor* 'heart']

miserly /mī́zərli/ *adj* **1.** greedy for money and unwilling to share or to spend it **2.** contemptibly insufficient or inadequate —**miserliness** *n*

misery /mízzəri/ (*plural* **-ies**) *n* **1. GREAT UNHAPPINESS** a serious lack of contentment or happiness **2. SOURCE OF GREAT UNHAPPINESS** something that causes great unhappiness **3. POVERTY** a state of extreme poverty and squalor **4. GLOOMY PERSON** a consistently gloomy or brooding person (*informal*) [14C. Directly or via Anglo-Norman *miserie* < Latin *miseria* < Latin *miser* 'unfortunate'] ◇ **put somebody out of his** *or* **her misery** to put an end to somebody's suspense or anxiety, especially by revealing something that he or she is desperate to know (*humorous*) ◇ **put an animal out of its misery** to kill an animal in order to prevent it suffering further pain

misestimate /miss ésti mayt/ (**-mates, -mating, -mated**) *vt* **1.** to estimate something wrongly **2.** a wrong estimation —**misestimation** *n*

MI-SET *abbr* E-COMMERCE merchant initiated SET™

misfeasance /missféez'nss/ *n* in law, the abuse of lawful authority in order to achieve a desired result [Early 17C. < Anglo-Norman *mesfaisance* < *mesfaire* 'do ill' < *mes-* 'wrongly' + *faire* 'to do' < Latin *facere*] —**misfeasor** *n*

misfire *vi* /miss fī́r/ (**-fires, -firing, -fired**) **1. FAIL TO FIRE PROPERLY** to fail to shoot a bullet or shell when fired **2. FAIL TO OPERATE PROPERLY** to fail to ignite the fuel mixture in the cylinder, or to ignite it at the wrong time (*refers to an internal-combustion engine*) **3. GO WRONG** to fail to achieve a planned result ○ *the plot misfired* ■ *n* /míss fīr/ **MALFUNCTION IN FIRING** a failure to fire or function properly

misfit /míss fit/ *n* **1.** somebody who does not fit comfortably into a situation or environment ○ *a social misfit* **2.** something that fits badly

misfortune /miss fáwrchən/ *n* **1.** bad luck **2.** an undesirable or unhappy event or circumstance

misgive /miss gív/ (**-gives, -giving, -gave** /-gáyv/, **-given** /-gívv'n/) *vt* to feel apprehensive, or to cause a feeling of apprehension or foreboding in somebody (*literary*) [Early 16C. < GIVE in the obsolete sense 'suggest']

misgiving /miss gívving/ *n* a feeling of doubt or apprehension, especially about undertaking a course of action (*often used in the plural*) ○ *had misgivings about the plan*

misguide /miss gī́d/ (**-guides, -guiding, -guided**) *vt* to lead somebody in a wrong direction or into making a mistake —**misguidance** *n* —**misguider** *n*

misguided /miss gī́did/ *adj* motivated by or based on ideas that are mistaken, heedless, or inappropriate —**misguidedly** *adv* —**misguidedness** *n*

mishandle /miss hánd'l/ (**-dles, -dling, -dled**) *vt* **1.** to deal with something or somebody in an incompetent or ineffective way **2.** to treat something or somebody roughly

mishap /míss hap/ *n* **1.** an unfortunate accident or piece of bad luck **2.** an unfortunate circumstance or set of circumstances (*formal*)

Mishima /míshimə/, **Yukio** (1925–70) Japanese novelist. He celebrated Japan's nationalist and imperialist history, deploring the sterility of contemporary life, and committed ritual suicide. His novels include the tetralogy *The Sea of Fertility* (1965–70). Pseudonym of **Kimitake, Hiraoka**

mishmash /mísh mash/ *n* a disorderly collection or confused mixture of things [15C. < repetition of MASH]

Mishmi /míshmi/ (*plural same* or **-mis**) *n* **1.** a member of a people living in a mountainous region of Assam in northeastern India **2.** the Tibeto-Burman language of the Mishmi people —**Mishmi** *adj*

Mishnah /míshnə/, **Mishna** *n* **1. JEWISH LAW** the primary body of Jewish civil and religious law, forming the first part of the Talmud **2. JEWISH ORAL LAW** Jewish law from the oral tradition, as distinguished from law derived from the scriptures **3. JEWISH LEGAL TEACHING** the teaching of Jewish law by a rabbi or other authority on it [Early 17C. < Hebrew *mišnāh* 'repetition, teaching'] —**Mishnaic** /mish náy ik/ *adj*

misjoinder /miss jóyndər/ *n* an improper combining of plaintiffs, defendants, or causes of action in a single lawsuit

misjudge /miss júj/ (**-judges, -judging, -judged**) *v* **1.**

vti to make a mistake when judging or assessing something or when attempting to do something that requires accurate judgment **2.** *vt* to form an incorrect opinion about somebody or something, especially one that attributes bad qualities to somebody unjustly or mistakenly —**misjudger** *n* —**misjudgment** *n*

Miskito /mi skéet ō/ (*plural same or* **-tos**) *n* **1.** a member of a Native Central American people living along the Caribbean coasts of Nicaragua and Honduras **2.** the language of the Miskito people [Late 18C. < Miskito] —**Miskito** *adj*

Miskolc /méesh kōlts/ historic and industrial city in northeastern Hungary. Population: 176,629 (1999).

mislay /miss láy/ (**-lays, -laying, -laid** /-láyd/) *vt* to lose something temporarily, especially by forgetting where it was put —**mislayer** *n*

mislead /miss léed/ (**-leads, -leading, -led** /-léd/) *vt* **1.** INFORM SOMEBODY FALSELY to cause somebody to make a mistake or form a false opinion or belief, either by employing deliberate deception or by supplying incorrect information ○ *The defendant is trying to mislead the jury.* **2.** LEAD SOMEBODY INTO BAD ACTIONS to be responsible for making somebody, especially somebody younger, do wrong or adopt bad habits **3.** LEAD SOMEBODY IN WRONG DIRECTION to lead somebody in a wrong direction —**misleader** *n*

misleading /miss léeding/ *adj* likely or deliberately intended to confuse people or give them a false idea of something —**misleadingly** *adv*

misled past participle, past tense of **mislead**

mislike /miss lík/ (**-likes, -liking, -liked**) *vt* (*archaic*) **1.** to dislike or disapprove of somebody or something **2.** to offend or irritate somebody

mismanage /miss mánnij/ (**-ages, -aging, -aged**) *vt* to run, organize, or deal with something incompetently —**mismanagement** *n*

mismatch *n* /míss mach/ a pairing or combination of people or things that are incompatible with or apparently ill-suited to each other ■ *vt* /míss mách/ (**-matches, -matching, -matched**) to fail to match or pair people or things suitably (*usually passive*) ○ *mismatching the socks as usual*

Misnaged *n* JUDAISM same as **Mitnagged**

misname /mis náym/ (**-names, -naming, -named**) *vt* **1.** to call something by a wrong name **2.** to give somebody or something a wrong or inappropriate name

misnomer /miss nōmər/ *n* **1.** a wrong or unsuitable name or term for something or somebody **2.** a use of a wrong or unsuitable name or term to describe something or somebody [15C. < Old French < *mes-* 'wrongly' + *nommer* 'to name' < Latin *nominare*]

miso /méessō/ *n* Japanese fermented soya bean paste used mainly in vegetarian cooking [Early 18C. < Japanese]

misogamy /mi sóggəmi/ *n* an aversion to marriage and the married state [Mid-17C. < modern Latin *misogamia* < Greek *misein* 'to hate' + *gamos* 'marriage'] —**misogamic** /míssə gámmik/ *adj* —**misogamist** *n*

misogyny /mi sójjəni/ *n* a hatred of women, as a sexually defined group [Mid-17C. < Greek *misogunia* < *misein* 'to hate' + *gunē* 'woman'] —**misogynic** /míssə jínnik/ *adj* —**misogynist** *n, adj* —**misogynistic** /mi sójjə nístik/ *adj* —**misogynistically** *adv*

misology /mi sólləji/ *n* a hatred of reason, logical argument, or enlightenment [Early 19C. < Greek *misologia* < *misein* 'to hate' + *-logia* (see -LOGY)] —**misologist** *n*

misoneism /míssō née izəm/ *n* a hatred of new things or change [Late 19C. < Italian *misoneismo* < Greek *misein* 'to hate' + *neos* 'new'] —**misoneist** *n* —**misoneistic** /míssō nee ístik/ *adj*

~~**mispelling**~~ incorrect spelling of **misspelling**

mispickel /míss pik'l/ *n* MINERALS same as **arsenopyrite** [Late 17C. < German]

misplace /míss pláyss/ (**-places, -placing, -placed**) *vt* **1.** PUT SOMETHING IN WRONG PLACE to put something in a wrong place or position **2.** MISLAY SOMETHING to lose something, especially temporarily, through forgetting where it was put **3.** TRUST SOMEBODY OR SOMETHING UNWORTHY to put confidence, faith, or trust in somebody or something unsuitable or unworthy —**misplacement** *n*

misplaced modifier /míss pláysst-/ *n* a word or phrase positioned so that it is unclear what exactly it refers to, e.g. *lying in the gutter* in 'Lying in the gutter, we saw a dead rat'

USAGE See ***dangling participle*** and ***kindly***.

misplead /miss pleéd/ (**-pleads, -pleading, -pleaded, -pleaded** or **-pled** /-pléd/) *vti* to allege or claim something in a lawsuit in a manner not in accordance with procedure or the law

mispleading /miss pleéding/ *n* an error made or contained in the pleading in a lawsuit

misprint *n* /míss print/ an error in the printed copy of a text resulting from a mistake made when the text was being printed ■ *vt* /míss prínt/ (**-prints, -printing, -printed**) to print something wrongly

misprision[1] /miss prízh'n/ *n* **1.** the failure of somebody who knows of but is not involved in a felony or treason to report it to the authorities **2.** *US* neglect or wrong done by a public official in the performance of the duties of his or her office [15C. < Anglo-Norman *mesprisioun* 'error' < Old French *mesprendre* 'make a mistake']

misprision[2] /miss prízh'n/ *n* a misunderstanding of something, especially a failure to appreciate the true worth of somebody or something (*archaic*) [Late 16C. < MISPRIZE after MISPRISION [1]]

misprize /miss príz/ (**-prizes, -prizing, -prized**), **misprise** (**-prises, -prising, -prised**) *vt* (*formal*) **1.** to fail to appreciate the true worth of something or somebody **2.** to consider somebody or something unworthy of respect or admiration [14C. < Old French *mesprisier* 'misestimate value' < *prisier* 'to praise'] —**misprizer** *n*

mispronounce /míssprə nównss/ (**-nounces, -nouncing, -nounced**) *vti* to pronounce something incorrectly —**mispronunciation** /míssprə núnssi áysh'n/ *n*

misread /míss reéd/ (**-reads, -reading, -read** /-réd/) *vt* **1.** to make a mistake in reading something, e.g. reading aloud inaccurately, mistaking one word for another, or misunderstanding the sense of what is written **2.** to fail to understand the true meaning or nature of something ○ *misreading the public mood*

misreport /míssri páwrt/ *vt* (**-ports, -porting, -ported**) to report something in an inaccurate or distorted way ■ *n* an inaccurate or distorted report

misrepresent /míss repri zént/ (**-sents, -senting, -sented**) *vt* **1.** to give an inaccurate or deliberately false account of the nature of somebody or something **2.** not to be truly or typically representative of somebody or something —**misrepresentation** /míss repri zen táysh'n/ *n* —**misrepresentative** *adj* —**misrepresenter** *n*

misrule /míss roól/ *vti* (**-rules, -ruling, -ruled**) RULE BADLY to govern a people or place unjustly or inefficiently ■ *n* **1.** BAD GOVERNMENT unjust or inefficient government of a people or place **2.** PUBLIC DISORDER a state of public disorder or anarchy

miss[1] /miss/ *v* (**misses, missing, missed**) **1.** *vti* NOT HIT TARGET to fail to hit, reach, catch, or make contact with somebody or something that is being aimed at **2.** *vt* FAIL TO BE SOMEWHERE to fail to be present or on time for something **3.** *vt* NOT HEAR, SEE, OR COMPREHEND SOMETHING to fail to hear, see, or understand something, e.g. through inattention or being distracted **4.** *vt* NOT TAKE A CHANCE to fail to take an opportunity **5.** *vti* FAIL TO ACHIEVE to fail to achieve a set target or goal **6.** *vt* AVOID SOMETHING to escape or avoid a potentially harmful, dangerous, or unpleasant situation **7.** *vt* OMIT SOMETHING to leave something out **8.** *vt* REGRET ABSENCE OF SOMEBODY OR SOMETHING to feel sorry that somebody or something is absent ○ *missed her greatly while she was away* **9.** *vt* DISCOVER ABSENCE OF SOMEBODY OR SOMETHING to realize that a person or thing is not present at the expected time or in the expected place ○ *He was halfway home before he missed his wallet.* **10.** *vi* MISFIRE to fail to ignite the fuel mixture in the cylinder (*refers to an internal-combustion engine*) ■ *n* **1.** FAILURE TO MAKE CONTACT a failure to hit, reach, catch, or make contact with somebody or something aimed at **2.** A FAILURE something that does not succeed or fails to impress [Old English *missan* < Germanic, 'go wrong'] —**missable** *adj* ◇ **give something a miss** to choose not to do something or attend something (*informal*)

miss out *v* **1.** *vt* to omit or overlook something ○ *You missed out the best bit of the whole story.* **2.** *vi* to lose an opportunity of doing something

miss[2] /miss/ *n* **1.** WAY OF ADDRESSING YOUNG WOMAN a term of address for a girl or young woman, sometimes used in place of her name **2.** YOUNG WOMAN a girl or young woman ■ **misses** *npl* FASHION WOMEN'S CLOTHING SIZES a series of clothing sizes that fit women and girls of average height and build [Mid-17C. Shortening of MISTRESS]

Miss *n* **1.** TITLE PRECEDING NAME a title placed before the name of a girl or unmarried woman **2.** WINNER'S TITLE used together with a placename or another word in the winner's title awarded in a beauty contest or similar event ○ *Miss Panama* **3.** WAY OF ADDRESSING WOMAN TEACHER a term of address for or way of referring to a woman teacher

Miss. *abbr* **1.** mission **2.** missionary

missal /míss'l/ *n* a book that contains all the prayers, responses, and hymns used in the Roman Catholic Mass [13C. < medieval Latin *missale* < late Latin *missa* (see MASS)]

missel thrush *n* BIRDS another spelling of **mistle thrush**

missense /míss senss/ *n* a genetic mutation in which a genetic coding sequence (**codon**) for one amino acid is changed to one that codes for another

misshapen /míss sháypən/, **misshaped** /-sháypt/ *adj* having an undesirably unusual shape —**misshapenly** *adv* —**misshapenness** *n* —**misshape** *n, vt*

missile /míssīl/ *n* **1.** a weapon consisting of a warhead propelled by a rocket **2.** an object thrown or launched as a weapon, e.g. a stone or bullet [Early 17C. < Latin *missilis* < *mittere* 'send']

missilery /míssīlri/, **missilry** *n* **1.** missiles, considered collectively **2.** the designing, building, or operating of missiles

missing /míssing/ *adj* **1.** not present in an expected place ○ *There's a page missing from the book.* **2.** not yet traced and not known for certain to be alive, but not confirmed as dead ○ *missing persons* ◇ **go missing** to disappear or become lost, untraceable, or unaccounted for

missing link *n* **1.** an animal theorized or sought as a transitional evolutionary stage between apes and humans **2.** something that is absent from a sequence or series and is needed to connect up its various parts and complete it

missiology /míssi ólləji/ *n* the study of Christian missionary work [Mid-20C. < MISSION]

mission /mísh'n/ *n* **1.** ASSIGNED TASK a special task given to a person or group to carry out **2.** CALLING an aim or task that somebody believes it is his or her duty to carry out or to which he or she attaches special importance and devotes special care **3.** SPACE VEHICLE'S TRIP a single flight or voyage of a military aircraft or a spacecraft **4.** GROUP OF REPRESENTATIVES a group of people sent to a country to represent their government, a business, or other organization **5.** *US* DIPLOMATIC REPRESENTATION ABROAD a permanent diplomatic delegation in another country **6.** GROUP OF CHURCH WORKERS a body of people sent by a church to another part of the country or to a foreign country to spread their faith or do medical and social work **7.** CHURCH WORK IN COMMUNITY a campaign of religious work, often including community aid at home or abroad, carried out by a church **8.** COMMUNICATION OF BELIEFS the vocation or work of a church or other religious organization or of individual people in communicating their faith in a variety of ways to the wider community **9.** HOUSING USED BY MISSIONARIES a building or group of buildings belonging to a missionary organization **10.** MISSIONARY'S TERRITORY an area assigned to a missionary or missionary group **11.** PLACE THAT HELPS NEEDY a centre run by a religious or charitable organization offering food, shelter, aid, and spiritual comfort to needy people **12.** MINOR CHURCH a church that has no permanent clergy and is supported by a larger church ■ *adj also* **Mission** IN SPANISH MISSION STYLE relating to or influenced by a style of architecture or heavy dark oak furniture used in early Spanish missions in the southwestern United States ■ *vt* (**-sions, -sioning, -sioned**) **1.** SEND SOMEBODY ON MISSION to send somebody on or give somebody a mission **2.** OPERATE MISSION to establish or conduct a religious mission in a place or among a people [Late 16C. Directly or via French < Latin *mission-* < *mittere* 'send off']

ORIGIN The Latin word *mittere* 'to send off', from which ***mission*** is derived, is also the source of English *admit, commit, mess, message, missile, missive, permit, promise, remit, submit,* and *transmit*.

missionary /míshʹnəri/ *n* (*plural* **-ies**) **1.** SOMEBODY DOING CHURCH WORK ABROAD somebody sent to another country by a church to spread its faith or to do social and medical work **2.** PERSUADER somebody who tries to persuade others to accept or join something ■ *adj* OF OR LIKE MISSIONARY relating to or similar to a missionary

missionary position *n* a position for sexual intercourse in which the woman lies on her back and the man lies on top of and facing her [Because missionaries held it to be least reprehensible]

mission creep *n* a tendency of military operations in foreign countries to increase gradually in scope and demand further commitment of personnel and resources as the situation develops

missioner /míshʹnər/ *n* **1.** CHR same as **missionary** *n* (sense 1) **2.** somebody in charge of a mission church in a parish

mission statement *n* a formal document that states the aims of a company or organization

missis *n* another spelling of **missus** (*informal*)

Mississauga /míssi sáwgə/ city in southern Ontario, Canada, on the shore of Lake Ontario. Population: 612,925 (2001).

Mississippi

Mississippi /míssi síppi/ **1.** longest river in the United States. It flows southward from northern Minnesota to Louisiana, emptying into the Gulf of Mexico. Length: 3,770 km/2,340 mi. **2.** state in the southeastern United States, bordered by Tennessee, Alabama, the Gulf of Mexico, Louisiana, and Arkansas. Capital: Jackson. Population: 3,871,782 (2002 estimate). Area: 125,060 sq. km/48,286 sq. mi.

Mississippian /míssi síppi ən/ *n* **1.** somebody who comes from the US state of Mississippi **2.** the epoch of geological time, 360 million to 330 million years ago, during which land plants became larger and more varied, particularly in low-lying swampy areas —**Mississippian** *adj*

missive /míssiv/ *n* a letter or other written communication, often formal or legal communication (*formal*) [Early 16C. < medieval Latin *missivus* < Latin *mittere* 'send']

~~**missle**~~ incorrect spelling of **missile**

Missouri /mi zo͝ori/ **1.** major river in the United States. It flows from southwestern Montana southeastwards to join the Mississippi River in Missouri. Length: 3,726 km/2,315 mi. **2.** state in the central United States, bordered by Iowa, Illinois, Kentucky, Tennessee, Arkansas, Oklahoma, Kansas, and Nebraska. Capital: Jefferson City. Population: 5,672,579 (2002 estimate). Area: 180,545 sq. km/69,709 sq. mi. —**Missourian** *n, adj*

misspeak /miss spéek/ (**-speaks, -speaking, -spoke** /-spṓk/, **-spoken** /-spṓkən/) *v N Am* **1.** *vt* PRONOUNCE INCORRECTLY to pronounce something incorrectly **2.** **misspeak yourself** *vr* EXPRESS YOURSELF UNCLEARLY to speak or express yourself in a way that is inappropriate, inaccurate, or unclear ○ *Unfortunately the envoy misspoke himself on that particular issue.* **3.** *vi* SPEAK INCORRECTLY to speak incorrectly or imperfectly

misspell /miss spél/ (**-spells, -spelling, -spelt** /-spélt/ or **-spelled** /-spélt/) *vt* to spell a word incorrectly

misspelling /miss spélling/ *n* an incorrect spelling of a word

misspelt LANGUAGE past participle, past tense of **misspell**

misspend /miss spénd/ (**-spends, -spending, -spent** /-spént/) *vt* to spend money or time badly or wastefully —**misspender** *n*

misspoke LANGUAGE past tense of **misspeak**

misspoken LANGUAGE past participle of **misspeak**

misstep /miss stép/ *n* **1.** a bad or awkward step, or a step in a wrong direction **2.** an error in judgment or conduct

missus /míssəz, missis, míssiz/, **missis** /missis/ *n* (*informal*) **1.** used to refer to a man's wife or woman partner, usually either by the man himself or by another man (*sometimes considered offensive*) **2.** a term of address for a woman, often used in place of her name [Late 18C. Alteration of MISTRESS]

missy /míssi/ *n* used as a term of address for a girl or young woman, often expressing affection or reprimand (*informal; sometimes considered offensive*)

mist /mist/ *n* **1.** THIN FOG a thin grey cloud of water droplets that condenses in the atmosphere just above the ground **2.** CONDENSED WATER VAPOUR a film of water vapour that has condensed on a surface **3.** FINE SPRAY a fine spray of liquid, e.g. from an atomizer or aerosol **4.** LIQUID SUSPENSION IN GAS a suspension of liquid in a gas **5.** OBSCURING THING something that makes it difficult to see or understand something ■ *v* (**mists, misting, misted**) **1.** *vti* FILM OVER to cover or obscure something in a mist, or become covered in or obscured by mist ○ *misted over the windows* **2.** *vi* BECOME BLURRED BY TEARS to become blurred by tears **3.** *vt* SPRAY SOMETHING to apply a fine liquid spray to something [Old English < Indo-European, 'urinate']

mistake /mi stáyk/ *n* **1.** INCORRECT ACT OR DECISION an incorrect, unwise, or unfortunate act or decision caused by bad judgment or a lack of information or care ○ *It's an easy mistake to make.* **2.** ERROR something in a piece of work that is incorrect, e.g. a misspelling or a misprint **3.** MISUNDERSTANDING a misunderstanding of something ○ *There must be some mistake, I didn't order this.* ■ *vt* (**-takes, -taking, -took** /-to͝ok/, **-taken** /-táykən/) **1.** MISUNDERSTAND SOMETHING to misunderstand or misinterpret something ○ *I mistook the meaning of the phrase.* **2.** IDENTIFY SOMEBODY OR SOMETHING INCORRECTLY to identify somebody or something incorrectly, or fail to recognize somebody or something ○ *We tend to mistake infatuation for real love.* **3.** CHOOSE SOMETHING INCORRECTLY to choose something incorrectly or injudiciously [14C. < Old Norse *mistaka* 'take in error'] —**mistakable** *adj* —**mistakably** *adv* —**mistaker** *n* ◇ **by mistake** accidentally, without wishing or intending to do something

SYNONYMS ***mistake, error, inaccuracy, slip, blunder, faux pas, oversight***

CORE MEANING: something incorrect or improper

mistake an incorrect, unwise, or unfortunate act or decision caused by bad judgment or a lack of information or care ○ *He expects people to make occasional mistakes and plans accordingly.* ○ *He soon learnt he'd made a big mistake in marrying Bertha.* **error** something unintentionally done wrong ○ *If not detected, this error would have had disastrous consequences.* ○ *The leadership had made a serious error of military judgment.* **inaccuracy** something that is incorrect, especially something that has been measured, calculated, copied, or conveyed incorrectly ○ *The reports were riddled with inaccuracies.* ○ *The commission's findings were criticized for containing obvious inaccuracies.* **slip** a minor mistake, especially one caused by carelessness ○ *One slip would have betrayed all I was working for.* **blunder** a serious or embarrassing mistake, usually the result of carelessness or ignorance ○ *A series of staff blunders aided the two inmates in their escape from the jail.* ○ *The young Canadian scored another goal after a bad blunder by Switzerland's defence.* **faux pas** an embarrassing mistake that breaks a social convention ○ *She stopped smiling, as if I had committed a faux pas by referring to her dress.* **oversight** a mistake, especially as a result of a failure to do or notice something ○ *If the money still hasn't been transferred it's due to an oversight by my bank.*

mistaken /mi stáykən/ *adj* **1.** wrong or incorrect in an assumption, belief, or understanding of something ○ *If you think that'll work, then you're sadly mistaken.* **2.** based on incorrect information or values ○ *a mistaken sense of loyalty* —**mistakenly** *adv* —**mistakenness** *n*

Mistassini, Lake /místə séeni/ lake in central Canada, the largest in Quebec Province. Area: 2,200 sq. km/840 sq. mi.

mister /místər/ *n* (*informal*) **1.** used as a term of address for a man, usually in place of his name **2.** used to refer to a woman's husband or man partner, either by the woman or by another woman (*sometimes considered offensive*) [Mid-16C. Alteration of MASTER]

Mister *n* **1.** FORM OF 'MR' used as the full form of the courtesy title 'Mr' **2.** WAY TO ADDRESS JUNIOR OFFICERS used as the official term of address for male junior officers or warrant officers **3.** WAY TO ADDRESS SURGEON used as the usual title for a male surgeon **4.** WAY TO ADDRESS MERCHANT NAVY OFFICER used as the official term of address for any male officer in the merchant navy except the captain of a ship [Mid-18C. < MISTER]

misthrow /mis thrṓ/ (**-throws, -throwing, -threw** /-thro͞o/, **-thrown** /-thrṓn/) *vti* to throw something such as dice or a ball in a wrong or invalid way —**misthrow** /mís thrō/ *n*

Misti /méesti/ dormant volcano in the Andes, in southern Peru. Height: 5,822 m/19,101 ft.

mistle thrush /míssʹl-/, **missel thrush** *n* a large thrush with a spotted breast and greyish back that feeds on berries, especially those of mistletoe. Native to: Europe. Latin name: *Turdus viscivorus.* [Early 17C. < Old English *mistel* (See MISTLETOE)]

mistletoe /míssʹltō/ *n* **1.** PARASITIC BUSH an evergreen bush that grows as a parasite on trees such as apple and oak, has leaves in horseshoe-shaped pairs, and bears white berries in winter. Native to: Europe, Asia. Latin name: *Viscum album.* **2.** PLANT RESEMBLING MISTLETOE a bush that resembles true mistletoe. Native to: North America. Latin name: *Phoradendron flavescens.* **3.** CHRISTMAS DECORATION a sprig of mistletoe traditionally used as a decoration and for kissing under at Christmas [Old English *misteltān* < *mistel* 'mistletoe' + *tān* 'twig' < Germanic]

mistook past tense of **mistake**

mistral /místrəl/ *n* a powerful cold dry northeasterly wind that blows in the south of France [Early 17C. < French < Latin *magistralis* 'dominant'; from its power]

mistreat /miss tréet/ (**-treats, -treating, -treated**) *vt* to treat somebody or something badly or roughly —**mistreatment** *n*

SYNONYMS ***mistreat, abuse, ill-treat, maltreat, ill-use***

CORE MEANING: to treat somebody or something wrongly or badly

mistreat to treat somebody or something badly or roughly ○ *It was clear that some prisoners had been mistreated.* ○ *Children should be taught that mistreating animals is not okay.* **abuse** to treat a person or animal cruelly, whether physically, psychologically, or sexually, especially on a regular or habitual basis ○ *a clinic for men who have sexually abused children* ○ *She has been accused of abusing the animals in her care.* **ill-treat** to behave cruelly or unkindly towards a person or animal ○ *She felt let down by the broken promises, believing that she had been ill-treated by her employers.* ○ *There was evidence that the dogs were being ill-treated.* **maltreat** to behave cruelly or unkindly towards a person or animal, especially by neglecting their welfare ○ *If one child in a family is maltreated, others in the same family are at high risk.* **ill-use** to treat somebody or something harshly or inappropriately ○ *With a feeling of being ill-used he started to clear up the remains of last night's dinner.*

mistress /místrəss/ *n* **1.** EXTRAMARITAL LOVER OF MAN a woman with whom a man has a usually long-term extramarital sexual relationship, often one in which he provides financial support **2.** OWNER OF PET the woman owner of a pet animal **3.** ABLE WOMAN a woman who is highly skilled in a particular activity ○ *a mistress of the art of negotiation* **4.** TEACHER a female teacher **5.** OWNER OR CONTROLLER OF SOMETHING a woman who owns or controls something, e.g. a woman owner of an estate, head of a household, or employer of servants **6.** PERSONIFICATION AS WOMAN something that rules or controls, personified as a woman ○ *Venice, once mistress of the seas* **7.** LOVED WOMAN a woman with whom a man is in love (*archaic*) [13C. < Old French *maistresse*, form of *maistre* (see MASTER)]

Mistress *n* used as a courtesy title to address a married woman, usually in front of the surname (*archaic*)

mistress of ceremonies *n* a woman in charge of the proceedings at an event or entertainment

mistrial /míss trí əl/ n **1.** a trial that is invalid because a mistake such as an error in procedure has been made **2.** US a trial that does not come to a proper conclusion, e.g. because the jury cannot agree on a verdict

mistrust /míss trúst/ n suspicion about or lack of confidence in somebody or something ■ vt (**-trusts, -trusting, -trusted**) to be suspicious of and unable to trust or rely on somebody or something —**mistruster** n —**mistrustful** adj —**mistrustfully** adv —**mistrustfulness** n

misty /místi/ (**-ier, -iest**) adj **1.** COVERED IN MIST with a lot of mist in the air or surrounded or covered by mist ○ a misty mountain ○ a misty morning **2.** LIKE MIST like mist, especially in being in a cloud or spray of fine drops **3.** DIM AND INDISTINCT rather dim and indistinct, as if veiled by mist —**mistily** adv —**mistiness** n

misty-eyed adj **1.** with a film of tears in the eyes **2.** sentimental or dreamlike ○ a misty-eyed memoir

misunderstand /míss undər stánd/ (**-stands, -standing, -stood** /-stoód/) vti to fail to realize the real or intended meaning of something, the true nature of something, or what somebody is really like

misunderstanding /míss undər stánding/ n **1.** a failure to understand or interpret something correctly **2.** a minor disagreement or dispute

misunderstood /míss undər stoód/ past participle, past tense of **misunderstand** ■ adj not correctly understood, or not properly and sympathetically appreciated ○ a misunderstood teenager

misusage /miss yoóssij, miss yoózij/ n **1.** a wrong or inappropriate use of language **2.** same as **misuse** n (sense 1)

misuse n /míss yoóss/ **1.** WRONG USE the incorrect or improper use of something **2.** CRUEL TREATMENT the cruel treatment of a person or animal ■ vt /míss yoóz/ (**-uses, -using, -used**) **1.** USE SOMETHING WRONGLY to use something in an incorrect or improper way, or for a dishonest purpose **2.** TREAT SOMEBODY CRUELLY to treat a person or animal cruelly —**misused** adj

SYNONYMS misuse, abuse, misappropriate, ill-use, misapply

CORE MEANING: to use something for an inappropriate purpose

misuse to use something in an incorrect or improper way, or for a dishonest purpose ○ The former president is charged with misusing money from secret government funds during his presidency. **abuse** to use something in an improper, illegal, or harmful way ○ A handful of cynical local officials have behaved deplorably, abusing their powers. ○ She admits having abused drugs and alcohol. **misappropriate** to take something, especially money, dishonestly, or in order to use it for an improper or illegal purpose ○ He was sentenced to 12 years in jail on charges of misappropriating foreign aid for personal gain. **ill-use** to use something improperly ○ He was placed under investigation to determine how much of the $35 million that had been ill-used was his responsibility. ○ The writing is creative, in the true sense of that ill-used word. **misapply** to use something badly, incorrectly, or improperly ○ He said the appeals court 'disregarded the facts and misapplied the law'.

misuser /míss yoózər/ n somebody who uses a right, privilege, or position of authority in an incorrect or improper way or for a dishonest purpose

MIT abbr EDUC Massachusetts Institute of Technology

mitch /mich/ (**mitches, mitching, mitched**) vi UK regional, Ireland to stay away from school without permission (informal) [14C. Probably < Old French muchier 'hide, lurk']

Mitchell /míchəl/ river in northern Queensland, Australia, that rises in the Atherton Tableland and flows west to the Gulf of Carpentaria. Length: 560 km/348 mi.

Mitchell, Joni (b. 1943) Canadian singer and songwriter. Her albums include Clouds (1969), Blue (1971), and Wild Things Run Fast (1982). Born Roberta Joan Anderson

'To see teenagers sitting around trying to solve the problems of the world, I figured, all things considered, I'd rather be dancing.'
[Joni Mitchell. Quoted in 'Joni Mitchell', Off the Record: An Oral History of Popular Music, Joe Smith; 1988]

Mitchell, Keith (b. 1947) prime minister of Grenada (1995–). Head of the New National Party since 1989, as premier he has called for increased political and economic integration with neighbouring Caribbean states. Full name **Mitchell, Keith Claudius**

Mitchell, Margaret (1900–49) US writer. She wrote the enormously popular American Civil War novel Gone With the Wind (1936), which won a Pulitzer Prize. Full name **Mitchell, Margaret Munnerlyn**

'After all, tomorrow is another day.'
[Margaret Mitchell, closing words, Gone with the Wind; 1936]

Mitchell, R.J. (1895–1937) British aircraft designer. As chief designer at the Vickers Armstrong Supermarine Company, he developed seaplanes and created the Spitfire fighter. Full name **Mitchell, Reginald Joseph**

Mitchell, Sir Thomas (1792–1855) British-born Australian explorer and surveyor. He was leader of four major expeditions to the interior of eastern Australia. Full name **Mitchell, Sir Thomas Livingstone**

Mitchum /míchəm/, **Robert** (1917–97) US film actor. His many films include Night of the Hunter (1955), Farewell My Lovely (1975), and Cape Fear (1961).

'What's history going to say about the movies? All those rows of seats facing a blank screen. Crazy!'
[Attributed to Robert Mitchum, Filmgoer's Book of Quotes, Leslie Halliwell; 1973]

mite[1] /mīt/ n a tiny eight-legged invertebrate animal related to spiders and ticks. Some mites live freely and some as parasites that can carry disease, attack plants, and cause human allergies. Order: Acarina [Old English míte < Germanic, 'cut']

SPELLCHECK See **might**[1].

mite[2] /mīt/ n **1.** SMALL CHILD a small child or animal, especially one that inspires pity (informal) **2.** SMALL AMOUNT a small piece or small amount ○ You could show just a mite of concern. **3.** SMALL COIN a small coin of little value (archaic) [14C. < Middle Low German and Middle Dutch míte, a small Flemish coin, also 'tiny animal']

miter n, vt US spelling of **mitre**

Mitford /mítfərd/, **Jessica** (1917–97) British-born US writer. Her best-known book is The American Way of Death (1965). Hons and Rebels (1960) gives an account of her eccentric family, including her sister Nancy Mitford.

'I have nothing against undertakers personally. It's just that I wouldn't want one to bury my sister.'
[Jessica Mitford, Saturday Review; 1 February 1964]

Mitford, Nancy (1904–73) British writer. Author of Love in a Cold Climate (1949) and The Blessing (1951), she was the sister of Jessica Mitford.

'An aristocracy in a republic is like a chicken whose head has been cut off: it may run about in a lively way, but in fact it is dead.'
[Nancy Mitford, Noblesse Oblige; 1956]

mither[1] /míthər/ (**-thers, -thering, -thered**) v regional **1.** vt to pester or annoy somebody **2.** vi to worry or fuss [Late 17C. Origin ?]

mither[2] /míthər/ n Scotland same as **mother**[1] (sense 1) [Late 18C. Variant]

mithering /míthəring/ n regional an act of nagging at or scolding somebody

REGIONAL NOTE See **jawing**.

Mithraism /míth ray izəm/ n a religion originating in Persia and involving worship of the god Mithras. It became popular among Roman soldiers in the late Roman Empire. —**Mithraic** /mith ráy ik/ adj —**Mithraist** n

Mithras /míth rass/ n in the Zoroastrian tradition and Persian mythology, the god of light, truth, and goodness. He is often shown with a bull, which he is said to have slain before fertilizing the world with its blood. [Mid-16C. Via Latin Mithras < Old Persian and Avestan Mithra]

mithridate /míthri dayt/ n a substance believed in ancient medicine and folklore to be an antidote to every poison and a cure for every disease [Early

16C. < medieval Latin mithridatum < late Latin mithridatius 'relating to Mithridates', king of Pontus (132–62 BC), reputedly immune to poisons] —**mithridatic** /míthri dáttik/ adj —**mithridatism** n

miticide /mítti sīd/ n a substance that kills mites —**miticidal** /mítti sīd'l/ adj

mitigate /mítti gayt/ (**-gates, -gating, -gated**) vt **1.** to make an offence or crime less serious or more excusable **2.** to make something less harsh, severe, or violent [15C. < Latin mitigat-, past participle of mitigare 'make mild' < mitis 'gentle, soft' + agere 'make'] —**mitigable** adj —**mitigation** /mítti gáysh'n/ n

USAGE See **militate**.

mitigating /mítti gayting/ adj making an offence or a crime seem less serious or more excusable ○ mitigating circumstances

mitis /mítiss, meétiss/, **mitis metal** n a form of iron made malleable by having a small amount of aluminium added to it [Late 19C. Probably < Latin mitis 'mild']

Mitnagged /mít naa géd/ (plural **-dim** /-dím/), **Mitnaged Misnaged** /míss naa géd/ n in the 18th and 19th centuries, a Jew in central and eastern Europe who believed in rationalism and opposed Hasidism [Early 20C. < Hebrew mitnaggéd 'opponent']

mitochondria BIOL plural of **mitochondrion**

mitochondrial /mítō kóndri əl/ adj relating to a mitochondrion or mitochondria

mitochondrial DNA n a small circular DNA molecule found in the mitochondria of a cell. Mitochondrial DNA is inherited only from the mother.

mitochondrion /mítō kóndri ən/ (plural **-dria** /-dri ə/) n a small round or rod-shaped body that is found in the cytoplasm of most cells and produces enzymes for the metabolic conversion of food to energy [Early 20C. < Greek mitos 'thread' + khondrion < khondros 'granule, lump (of salt)']

mitogen /mítəjən/ n a substance or agent that induces mitosis [Mid-20C. < MITOSIS]

mitomycin /mítō míssin/ n an antibiotic produced by a soil bacterium that inhibits DNA synthesis and is used against tumours [Mid-20C. < mito-, origin ?]

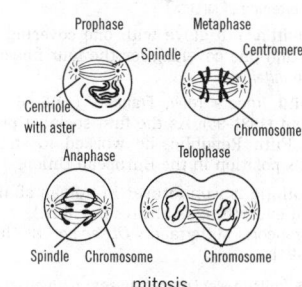

Prophase Metaphase
Spindle Centromere
Centriole
with aster Chromosome
Anaphase Telophase
Spindle Chromosome Chromosome

mitosis

mitosis /mī tóssiss/ n the process by which a cell divides into two daughter cells, each of which has the same number of chromosomes as the original cell [Late 19C. < Greek mitos 'thread'] —**mitotic** /mī tóttik/ adj

mitrailleuse /míttrī óz/ n an early machine gun with 35 barrels that could be fired simultaneously or in sequence, mounted on a carriage drawn by four horses. The gun was developed in France and first used in the Franco-Prussian War of 1870. [Late 19C. < French mitrailler 'fire mitraille' < mitraille 'small money, pieces of metal', alteration of Old French mitaille < mite, a small coin]

mitral /mítrəl/ adj relating to a bishop's mitre or like it in shape, especially in having separate front and back sections [Early 17C. < modern Latin mitralis < Latin mitra (see MITRE)]

mitral stenosis n the narrowing of the heart's mitral valve as the result of disease

mitral valve n the one-way valve between the upper and lower chambers, or atrium and ventricle, on the left side of the heart [< its shape]

mitre /mítər/ n **1.** BISHOP'S HAT the ceremonial headdress of a Christian bishop or abbot, consisting of a tall pointed hat creased across the top, with two ribbons

hanging down the back 2. CONSTR same as **mitre joint** 3. SURFACE OF MITRE JOINT either of the surfaces that are joined together to form a mitre joint 4. DIAGONAL JOIN AT CORNER BETWEEN HEMS in sewing, a diagonal join between the edges of two hems that meet at a corner of a piece of fabric ■ *vt* (**mitres, mitring, mitred**) 1. JOIN PIECES OF WOOD to join pieces of wood using a mitre joint 2. SHAPE WOOD FOR JOINT to shape the end of a piece of wood, especially by cutting it off at an angle of 45° when making a corner or mitre joint 3. DIAGONALLY JOIN HEMS AT CORNER in sewing, to make a diagonal join at a corner between two hems 4. GIVE MITRE TO SOMEBODY to confer a mitre on somebody, indicating promotion to the rank of bishop [14C. Via Old French < Latin *mitra* < Greek, 'belt, turban']

mitre block *n* a block with slots cut in it to guide a handsaw at the appropriate angle when cutting a mitre joint

mitre box *n* a box with open ends that is used to hold wood and guide a handsaw at the appropriate angle when cutting a mitre joint

mitre joint *n* a corner joint in woodwork, usually made by cutting two ends to be joined at 45° angles and gluing or nailing them together into a right angle

mitre square *n* a tool used in cutting wood at an angle that has a bevelled arm either fixed at an angle of 45° or adjustable to any angle

mitrewort /mītər wurt/ (*plural* **mitreworts** or **mitrewort**) *n* a plant with seed pods that resemble a bishop's mitre. Flowers: small, white, in clusters. Native to: Asia, North America. Genus: *Mitella*. [Mid-19C. < the shape of its capsule]

Mitsiwa /mi tséewə/ town and seaport in northern Eritrea, on the Red Sea. Population: 19,400 (1989).

mitsuba /mit so͝obə/ *n* in Japanese cuisine, a herb similar to flat-leaf parsley, having a mild flavour like that of chervil [Late 20C. < Japanese]

mitt /mit/ *n* 1. MITTEN a mitten, especially a child's mitten (*informal*) 2. HAND COVERING a covering for the hand and fingers, especially one shaped like a mitten ○ *an oven mitt* 3. HAND a hand, especially when large, clumsy, or dirty (*slang*) 4. BASEBALL PLAYER'S PADDED GLOVE in baseball, a large fingerless padded glove worn by the catcher or the first baseman 5. GLOVE WITHOUT FINGERS a woman's glove, popular in the 19th century, that left the fingers uncovered [Mid-18C. Shortening of MITTEN]

mitten /mítt'n/ *n* a glove with one covering for the thumb and one covering for the four fingers [14C. < French *mitaine*]

Mitterrand /méetə roN/, **François** (1916–96) French president (1981–95). As the first socialist president of the Fifth Republic, he worked to strengthen France's position in the European Union.

> 'Nothing is won forever in human affairs, but everything is always possible.'
> [François Mitterrand, *Observer*, 12 June 1994]

mittimus /míttiməss/ (*plural* **-muses**) *n* an official order to send somebody to prison [15C. < Latin, 'we send', first word of this order in Latin]

mitzvah /mítsvə/ (*plural* **-vahs** or **-voth** /-vōt/) *n* 1. a Jewish religious duty or obligation, especially one of the commandments of Jewish religious law 2. an act of kindness performed by or to a Jew [Mid-17C. < Hebrew *miṣwāh* 'commandment']

Miwok /mée wok/ (*plural* *same* or **-woks**) *n* 1. a member of a Native North American people living in central California from the Sierra Nevada foothills to the San Francisco Bay area 2. the language of the Miwok people, in some classifications belonging to the Penutian family of Native American languages. Miwok is now spoken by very few people. [Late 19C. < Miwok, 'people'] —**Miwok** *adj*

mix /miks/ *v* (**mixes, mixing, mixed**) 1. *vt* COMBINE INGREDIENTS to combine ingredients by putting them together or blending them to make a single new substance ○ *Mix the flour and dried fruit together.* 2. *vi* BE COMBINED to become combined, or be capable of becoming combined ○ *Oil and water don't mix.* 3. *vt* MAKE SOMETHING BY COMBINING to form or create something by combining separate ingredients ○ *Would you mix me a cocktail?* 4. *vt* ADD SOMETHING EXTRA to add something as an extra or later ingredient ○ *Mix the fruit into the batter.* 5. *vt* DO THINGS AT SAME TIME to do something at the same time as something else ○ *able to mix business with pleasure* 6. *vt* ARRANGE THINGS BESIDE EACH OTHER to arrange things next to or alongside each other ○ *mixing browns and golds to create a sense of warmth* 7. *vi* GO TOGETHER to go well together ○ *Reds and greens just don't mix.* 8. *vi* MEET PEOPLE to meet other people socially, or enjoy being with other people in social situations 9. *vi* PARTICIPATE to participate or become involved in something ○ *I heard them arguing but decided not to mix in.* 10. *vt* CONSUME THINGS TOGETHER to consume different drinks or foods on a single occasion 11. *vti* RECORDING BLEND MUSICAL SOUNDS to adjust and blend sounds from prerecorded tracks or live performers to create the desired combination of musical sounds. The process is done either by using a special deck (mixing deck) or a multitrack tape machine. 12. *vt* BIOL CROSSBREED PLANTS OR ANIMALS to breed one variety of a plant or animal with another in order to create a new variety ■ *n* 1. ACT OF MIXING SOMETHING an act of mixing something, or an occasion on which it is done ○ *Give all the ingredients a good mix.* 2. COMBINATION a combination or blend of things ○ *There's an intriguing mix of styles on her latest CD.* 3. SUBSTANCE USED TO PREPARE SOMETHING a substance, especially a number of dried ingredients in powder form, from which something is prepared ○ *cake mix* 4. RECORDING MUSICAL BLEND a balanced blend of live or prerecorded musical sound ○ *He thinks the drums are too low in the mix.* 5. RECORDING VERSION OF RECORDING a version of a musical recording that has been changed in some way to give it a different type of sound ○ *Their last hit has been rereleased in a disco mix.* 6. CONSTR RATIO OF MORTAR INGREDIENTS the ratio of sand and cement in mortar, or of sand, cement, and gravel in concrete [15C. < MIXED] —**mixable** *adj* ◇ **mix it up** to do something unexpected to stimulate or influence a situation in a beneficial way (*informal*)

mix down *vt* to blend parts that have been recorded separately to create a final finished sound recording

mix up *vt* 1. MISTAKE SOMEBODY OR SOMETHING FOR ANOTHER to confuse things or people and mistakenly identify one as the other ○ *People always mix her up with her sister.* 2. CHANGE ORDER OF THINGS to change the usual or previous order of things, either deliberately or by accident ○ *The pages got mixed up on the way to the printer's.* 3. INVOLVE SOMEBODY OR YOURSELF IN SOMETHING to involve somebody or yourself with a group of people or in an activity, especially one that is disapproved of (*usually passive*) ○ *She got herself mixed up with a bad crowd.* 4. MAKE SOMETHING FROM INGREDIENTS to prepare or make something by mixing different ingredients 5. MAKE SOMEBODY CONFUSED to make somebody confused and unsure of facts ○ *He got mixed up because the street names sounded so similar.*

mixdown /míks down/ *n* 1. the process of converting a multitrack recording, usually a master tape recorded in a studio, into a stereo recording, usually for public release 2. a new recording produced by a mixdown

mixed /mikst/ *adj* 1. CONSISTING OF VARIOUS THINGS consisting of a combination of different parts or different kinds of things 2. INVOLVING BOTH SEXES intended for, used by, or done by people of both sexes together 3. INVOLVING DIFFERENT RACES intended for, used by, or done by people of different races together 4. WITH INCONSISTENT ELEMENTS consisting of inconsistent or conflicting parts ○ *The play has had mixed reviews.* [15C. Via French *mixte* < Latin *mixtus*, past participle of *miscere* 'to mix']

mixed bag *n* a group of people or things of widely differing kinds

mixed blessing *n* something that has both advantages and disadvantages or good points and bad points

mixed doubles *n* in tennis, table tennis, or badminton, a match played by two pairs, each consisting of a man and a woman (*takes a singular verb*)

mixed drink *n N Am* a drink made by mixing two or more ingredients, at least one of which is alcoholic

mixed economy *n* an economy in which some industries and businesses are state-owned and some are privately owned

mixed farming *n* farming that combines growing crops and rearing livestock on the one farm

mixed grill *n* a dish consisting of a grilled meat chop or steak, kidneys, sausage, bacon, mushrooms, and tomatoes

mixed marriage *n* a marriage between people of different racial or religious backgrounds

mixed media *n* 1. the use of different artistic media, e.g. painting, photography, and collage, in a single composition or work 2. the use of different advertising media together, e.g. billboards, TV, and radio

mixed message *n* a confusing difference between the way somebody behaves and what somebody says

mixed metaphor *n* a combination of two or more metaphors that together evoke a strange or incongruous image, e.g. 'This thorn in my side has finally bitten the dust'

mixed nerve *n* a nerve that has both motor and sensory fibres, and thus has nerve impulses passing in both directions

mixed number *n* a figure that consists of a whole number and a fraction, e.g. the figure $2\frac{3}{4}$

mixed-race *adj* having or involving different racial backgrounds

mixed-up *adj* (*informal*) 1. in a disorganized state 2. in a state of emotional or psychological confusion

mixed-use *adj N Am* combining commercial and residential components in a single property, e.g. a block of flats with offices or shops

mixer /míksər/ *n* 1. MIXING DEVICE a machine or device for mixing food, cement, or another substance 2. BEVERAGES NONALCOHOLIC DRINK OFTEN MIXED WITH ALCOHOL a nonalcoholic drink such as fruit juice or soda water that is often mixed with alcoholic drinks 3. SOMEBODY WITH PARTICULAR DEGREE OF SOCIABILITY somebody considered in terms of his or her ability to socialize ○ *She's a good mixer.* 4. TROUBLEMAKER somebody who constantly causes trouble, especially by gossiping (*informal*) 5. RECORDING ELECTRONIC DEVICE FOR MIXING SOUNDS an electronic device used to adjust and combine various inputs, e.g. performed or broadcast sounds, to create a single output 6. BROADCAST, CINEMA SOMEBODY CREATING SOUND FOR FILM somebody who combines various sound recordings to create the final soundtrack of a film

mixer tap *n* a tap with separate controls for hot and cold water and a single outlet that combines both flows

Mixolydian mode /míksō líddi ən/ *n* a scale of notes originating in ancient Greek music and consisting of the eight notes of the diatonic scale rising from G to G [Late 16C. < Greek *mixoludios* 'half-Lydian' < *Ludios* 'Lydian']

mixte /míksti/ *adj* describes a frame for bicycles designed for women, consisting of two horizontal tubes connecting to the back axle without a crossbar [Late 20C. < French, 'mixed']

Mixtec /méess tek/ (*plural* **-tecs** or *same*), **Mixtecan** /meess tékən/ (*plural* **-ans** or *same*) *n* 1. a member of a Native American people who originally lived in southern Mexico and are now spread throughout Mexico. They are noted for their artistic and architectural skills. 2. an Oto-Manguean language spoken in Mexico. Native speakers: 400,000. [Late 18C. Via Spanish < Nahuatl *mixtecah* 'somebody from a cloudy place'] —**Mixtec** *adj*

mixter-maxter /míkstər mákstər/ *Scotland* (*informal*) *adj* in a disorganized or confused state ■ *n* a confused or disorganized collection of things [Late 18C. < reduplication of *mixt*, variant of MIXED]

mixture /míkschər/ *n* 1. ACT OF MIXING the combining or mixing of different ingredients 2. COMBINATION OF DIFFERENT PEOPLE OR THINGS a number of different components brought or existing together ○ *an interesting mixture of people* ○ *a mixture of old and new styles* 3. SUBSTANCE MADE OF DIFFERENT INGREDIENTS a substance containing several ingredients mixed together ○ *cake mixture* 4. PHARM LIQUID MEDICINE a medicinal preparation consisting of an insoluble solid suspended in a liquid, often with added flavouring and colouring 5. CHEM SUBSTANCE FORMED WITHOUT CHEMICAL REACTION a substance consisting of two or more substances that have been combined without chemical bonding taking place 6. ENG FUEL AND AIR MIX the combination of petrol vapour and air in an internal-combustion engine [15C. Directly or via French < Latin *mixtura* < *mixt-*, past participle of *miscere*]

SYNONYMS *mixture, blend, combination, compound, alloy, amalgam*

CORE MEANING: something formed by mixing materials

mixture a number of different components or features brought or existing together, or a substance containing several ingredients mixed together ○ *a chaotic mixture of emotions* ○ *Add the water and beat until the mixture is light and fluffy.* **blend** something formed by using together two or more things of different types, especially in a skilled way. ○ *his little-known first novel, a spirited and intricate blend of romance and mock-romance* ○ *a blend of passion fruit, peach juice, aromatic herbs, and spring water* **combination** an association of different things or factors ○ *a combination of beauty, wit, and charm* ○ *The combination of hardware and software provided a management tool that had never been available before.* **compound** a substance formed by the chemical combination of elements in fixed proportions, or anything composed of two or more separate parts ○ *volatile organic compounds* ○ *dictionaries of compounds, idioms, and common phrases* **alloy** a substance that is a mixture of two or more metals, or of a metal with a nonmetallic material ○ *Steel is basically an alloy of iron and carbon.* **amalgam** an alloy of mercury with another metal, or a combination of two or more characteristics ○ *The technique of 'mercury gilding' involved using an amalgam of gold and mercury.* ○ *The culture of the United States is a complicated amalgam of various traditions.*

mix-up *n* a state of confusion, or an error resulting from confusion ○ *an administrative mix-up*

Mizar /mí zaar/ *n* a multiple star in the constellation Ursa Major [< Arabic *Mi'zar* 'cloak, veil']

Mizoram /mízzō ram/ *n* state in northeastern India, between Bangladesh and Myanmar. Capital: Aizawl. Population: 891,058 (2001). Area: 21,081 sq. km/8,139 sq. mi.

mizuna /mi zoónə/, **mizuma** /-mə/ *n* a Japanese salad vegetable with a mild flavour and a delicate texture [Late 20C. < Japanese]

mizzen /mízz'n/ *n* **1.** a sail on a mizzenmast **2.** SAILING same as **mizzenmast** ■ *adj* relating to or used on a mizzenmast or its sail [15C. < French *misaine* 'foresail, foremast' < Latin *medianus* 'of the middle, median']

mizzenmast /mízz'n maast/ *n* **1.** on a ship with three or more masts, the third mast from the front **2.** on a boat such as a ketch or yawl, the mast nearest the back

mizzle[1] /mízz'l/ *regional n* a very fine rain ■ *vi* (-zles, -zling, -zled) to rain in very fine drops [15C. Origin ?] —**mizzly** *adj*

mizzle[2] /mízz'l/ (-zles, -zling, -zled) *vi* to leave suddenly or quickly (*dated slang*) [Late 18C. Origin ?]

mk *abbr* **1.** Macedonia (*used in Internet addresses*) See table at **domain name 2.** MONEY mark **3.** MONEY markka

Mk *abbr* **1.** BIBLE Mark **2.** AUTOMOT mark

mks, **MKS** *abbr* MEASURE metre-kilogram-second

mksA *abbr* MEASURE metre-kilogram-second-ampere

mks units *npl* the metric system of measurement, which has the metre, the kilogram, and the second as its basic units of length, mass, and time

mkt *abbr* COMM market

mktg *abbr* MARKETING marketing

ml[1] *symbol* MEASURE mile

ml[2] *abbr* MEASURE millilitre

ml[3] *abbr* ONLINE Mali (*used in Internet addresses*) See table at **domain name**

mL *abbr* MEASURE **1.** millilambert **2.** millilitre

ML *abbr* ONLINE more later (*used in e-mails or text messages*)

MLA *abbr* **1.** EDUC Master of Landscape Architecture **2.** Member of the Legislative Assembly **3.** LANGUAGE Modern Language Association

Mladic /mláddich/, **Ratko** (*b.* 1943) Yugoslavian general. He was indicted by the International War Crimes Tribunal (1995) for genocide and crimes against humanity for actions during his time as chief of the Bosnian Serb forces in the civil war in Bosnia and Herzegovina.

MLD *abbr* MED minimum lethal dose

MLF *abbr* MIL multilateral (nuclear) force

MLG *abbr* LANG Middle Low German

MLitt /ém lít/ *abbr* Master of Letters [Latin *Magister Litterarum*]

Mlle *abbr* Mademoiselle

Mlles *abbr* Mesdemoiselles

MLR *abbr* **1.** minimum lending rate **2.** MIL multiple-launch rockets

mm *abbr* **1.** MEASURE millimetre **2.** ONLINE Myanmar (*used in Internet addresses*) See table at **domain name**

MM *abbr* **1.** Messieurs **2.** MIL Military Medal

Mmabatho /əmbáʼato/ city in North-West Province in South Africa. Population: 13,544 (1995).

MMC *abbr* Monopolies and Mergers Commission

MMDS *abbr* MEDIA multipoint microwave distribution system

Mme *abbr* Madame

Mmes *abbr* Mesdames

mmf *abbr* PHYS magnetomotive force

mmHg *n* a unit for measuring atmospheric pressure. Full form **millimetre of mercury**

MMM *abbr* Member of the Order of Military Merit

MMORPG *abbr* COMPUT GAMES massively multiplayer online role-playing game

MMP *abbr* NZ POL Mixed Member Proportional

MMPI *abbr* PSYCHOL Minnesota Multiphasic Personality Inventory

MMR *n* a vaccine given to small children to protect them against measles, mumps, and rubella

MMS *n* a system that enables sounds, images, or animations to be incorporated into text messages sent, usually, from mobile phones. Full form **multimedia messaging service**

MMus *abbr* EDUC Master of Music

mn *abbr* ONLINE Mongolia (*used in Internet addresses*) See table at **domain name**

Mn *symbol* CHEM ELEM manganese

MN *abbr* **1.** GEOG magnetic north **2.** NAVY Merchant Navy

MNA *abbr* POL Member of the National Assembly (of Quebec)

MNC *abbr* COMM multinational company

mnemonic /ni mónnik/ *n* MEMORY AID a short rhyme, phrase, or other mental technique for making information easier to memorize ■ *adj* **1.** ACTING AS MNEMONIC acting as a memory aid **2.** RELATING TO MNEMONICS relating to the practice of improving the memory, or to systems designed to improve the memory [Mid-18C. < MNEMONICS, or < Greek *mnēmonikos* 'relating to memory' < *mnēmon*- 'mindful'] —**mnemonically** *adv*

mnemonics /ni mónniks/ *n* the practice of improving or helping the memory, or the systems used to achieve this (*takes a singular verb*) [Early 18C. < Greek *mnēmonika*, form of *mnēmonikos* (see MNEMONIC)]

Mnemosyne /nee mózzini, -móssini/ *n* in Greek mythology, the goddess of memory and mother of the Muses [Via Latin < Greek *Mnēmosunē*]

mngr *abbr* MANAGEMT manager

mo /mō/ *n* a moment or short while (*informal*) ○ *I'll be there in half a mo.* [Late 19C. Shortening of MOMENT]

Mo *symbol* CHEM ELEM molybdenum

MO *abbr* **1.** COMPUT magneto-optical **2.** mail order **3.** Medical Officer **4.** FIN money order

mo. *abbr* TIME month

m.o. *abbr* **1.** MAIL mail order **2.** *also* **M.O.** modus operandi **3.** FIN money order

-mo *suffix* used after numerals to indicate the number of pages made by folding a sheet of paper ○ *16mo* [< *12mo*, abbreviation of Latin *(in) duodecimo* '(in) a twelfth'; < *duodecimus* 'twelfth']

moa /mō ə/ *n* a large flightless bird similar to the ostrich that became extinct at the end of the 18th century. Native to: New Zealand. Family: Dinornithidae. [Mid-19C. < Maori]

Moab[1] /mó ab/ *n* in the Bible, the son of Lot and his eldest daughter, whose descendants were the enemies of Israel

Moab[2] /mó ab/ ancient kingdom situated on a plateau

to the east of the Dead Sea in modern-day Jordan — **Moabite** /mó ə bīt/ *n*, *adj*

MOAB /mó ab/ *n* a satellite-guided bomb weighing 9,525 kg/21,000 lb, the largest conventional bomb in the US arsenal, designed to detonate 1.8 m/6 ft from the ground. Full form **Massive Ordnance Air Blast** [Early 21C]

moan /mōn/ *v* (**moans, moaning, moaned**) **1.** *vi* MAKE LOW SOUND EXPRESSING PAIN to make a long low sound that expresses pain or misery **2.** *vti* COMPLAIN to complain about something, especially unreasonably or needlessly (*informal*) ○ *What's he moaning on about?* **3.** *vt* SAY SOMETHING IN PAINED VOICE to say something in a voice that expresses pain or misery ○ *'Oh no!', she moaned* **4.** *vi* MAKE SOUND LIKE SOMEBODY IN PAIN to make a long low sound similar to that made by somebody expressing pain or misery ○ *the wind moaning in the trees* ■ *n* **1.** SOUND OF PAIN a long low sound made by somebody expressing pain or misery **2.** SOUND LIKE MOAN a long low sound that resembles an expression of pain or misery, made by something such as the wind **3.** COMPLAINING SESSION a period of time during which somebody complains about something or about things in general (*informal*) ○ *had a good moan* **4.** COMPLAINT a complaint, especially one that is unreasonable or trivial (*informal*) [12C. < assumed Old English *mān* 'complaint' < Germanic] —**moaner** *n* —**moanful** *adj*

moat /mōt/ *n* **1.** DITCH AROUND CASTLE a wide water-filled ditch around a castle or fort, dug to give protection from attack **2.** DITCH ACTING AS BARRIER a water-filled ditch dug to prevent access or escape, e.g. to confine animals in a zoo **3.** *Ireland* ARCHAEOL same as **motte** ■ *vt* (**moats, moating, moated**) PUT MOAT AROUND CASTLE to surround a castle or other fortified place with a moat [14C. < Old French *mote* 'mound' or medieval Latin *mota*]

mob /mob/ *n* **1.** NOISY CROWD a large and unruly crowd of people **2.** GROUP a group of people (*informal*) **3.** ORDINARY PEOPLE ordinary people, especially when thought of collectively as unintelligent or irrational (*informal*) **4.** ANZ FLOCK OR HERD a flock of sheep or a herd of cattle (*informal*) **5.** *Aus* ABORIGINAL GROUP an Aboriginal community, or an extended family ■ *vt* (**mobs, mobbing, mobbed**) **1.** CROWD ROUND SOMEBODY OR SOMETHING to crowd round somebody or something noisily and excitedly **2.** CROWD INTO PLACE to crowd into and fill a place **3.** ATTACK SOMEBODY to attack somebody as a large group **4.** ZOOL ATTACK PREDATOR to surround and harass a potential predator [Late 17C. Shortening of archaic *mobile* < Latin *mobile (vulgus)* 'excitable (crowd)'] —**mobber** *n* —**mobbish** *adj*

Mob *n* a group of people who are involved in organized crime, or the world of organized crime (*informal*)

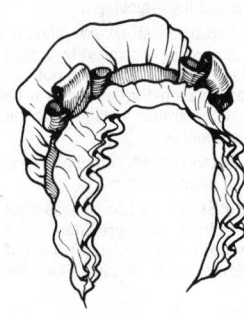

mobcap

mobcap /mób kap/ *n* **1.** a loose-fitting frilly cap often worn indoors by women in the 18th and early 19th centuries **2.** a soft hat shaped like a mobcap and worn especially by small children and babies [Mid-18C. < obsolete *mob* 'prostitute, negligée', variant of *mab* 'promiscuous woman', origin ?]

mob-handed *adj* in a large, often threatening group of people (*informal*)

mobile /mó bīl/ *adj* **1.** MOVING EASILY able to move freely or easily ○ *She's mobile again after her skiing accident.* **2.** OPERATING FROM VEHICLE operating from or set up in a vehicle that travels from place to place ○ *a mobile library* **3.** CHANGING EXPRESSION changing expressions quickly and easily ○ *a mobile face* **4.** PREPARED FOR CHANGE able or willing to change job, move home, or alter other arrangements at short

notice if necessary **5. CHANGING SOCIALLY** moving or able to move from one social or professional class or group to another, e.g. by changing jobs or moving to a new neighbourhood **6. WITH OWN TRANSPORT** able to go somewhere because of having transport available (*informal*) ○ *He's got his wife's car for the evening, so we're mobile.* ■ *n* **1.** TELECOM same as **mobile phone** (*informal*) **2. HANGING DECORATION** a hanging sculpture or decoration whose parts are balanced to move in response to air currents [15C. Via French < Latin *mobilis* 'movable' < *movere* 'to move']

Mobile /mō bēel/ city and port in southwestern Alabama, on the northwestern shore of Mobile Bay. Population: 194,862 (2002 estimate).

-mobile *suffix* automobile, vehicle ○ *snowmobile* [< AUTOMOBILE]

mobile home *n* a large caravan that can be transported on the back of a lorry but is usually connected to utilities and left on a single site

mobile library *n* a library operating from a bus or van and travelling from place to place, e.g. in rural areas

mobile phone *n* a portable telephone that works using a series of locally based cellular radio networks

Mobilian /mō bílli ən/ *n* a pidgin trading language containing elements of Choctaw that was used before the 20th century as a lingua franca in the Mississippi Valley and Gulf Coast [Mid-19C. < *Mobile*, town in Alabama] —**Mobilian** *adj*

mobilise *vti* another spelling of **mobilize**

mobility /mō bíllәti/ *n* **1. ABILITY TO MOVE** the ability to move about, especially to do work or take exercise **2. CHANGE TO ANOTHER SOCIAL GROUP** the ability of somebody to change from one social group or class to another **3. QUALITY OF BEING MOBILE** the quality of being mobile

mobility housing *n* housing built or adapted for people who have difficulty in walking or use wheelchairs

mobilize /mṓbə līz/ (**-lizes, -lizing, -lized**), **mobilise** (**-lises, -lising, -lised**) *vti* to organize people or resources in order to be ready for action or in order to take action, especially in a military or civil emergency, or to be organized for this purpose [Mid-19C. < French *mobiliser* < *mobile* 'movable' (see MOBILE)] —**mobilizable** *adj* —**mobilization** /mṓbə lī záysh'n/ *n*

Möbius strip /mṓbi əss-/ *n* a continuous single-sided surface formed by rotating one end of a strip through 180° and joining it to the other end [Early 20C. After August Ferdinand *Möbius* (1790–1868), German mathematician]

moblogging /mób logging/ *n* the use of a mobile phone or other hand-held digital device to post text and images to a weblog —**moblog** *n*

mobocracy /mo bókrəssi/ (*plural* **-cies**) *n* **1. CONTROL BY MOB** political control exercised by a mob **2. PLACE RUN BY MOB** a place where a mob has political control **3. MOB THAT RULES** a mob that rules in a mobocracy —**mobocrat** /móbbə krat/ *n* —**mobocratic** /móbbə kráttik/ *adj* —**mobocratical** *adj*

mobster /móbstər/ *n N Am* somebody who is involved in organized crime (*informal*)

Mobutu Sese Seko /mə bóotoo séss e sékō/ (1930–97) Congolese soldier and president of Zaïre (Democratic Republic of the Congo) from 1965 until he was forced into exile in 1997. Born **Mobutu, Joseph Désiré**

Moçâmedes /mə saámədish/ former name for **Namibe**

~~**mocassin**~~ incorrect spelling of **moccasin**

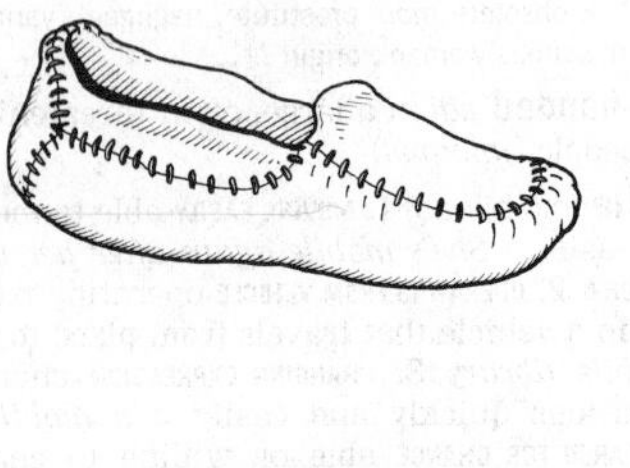

moccasin

moccasin /mókəssin/ *n* **1.** a Native North American heelless shoe made of deerskin or other soft leather wrapped around the foot and stitched on top **2.** a low-heeled leather shoe whose side panels are joined to the upper panel using prominent stitching to form a raised puckered seam **3.** REPT same as **water moccasin** (sense 1) [Early 17C. < Virginia Algonquian *mockasin*]

mocha /mókə/ *n* **1.** BEVERAGES **STRONG ARABIAN COFFEE** a dark-brown strong-tasting coffee from Yemen and some other countries on the Arabian peninsula **2.** FOOD **FLAVOURING OR DRINK** a flavouring or beverage made by mixing coffee and cocoa **3. LEATHER** a soft suede leather made from sheepskin or goatskin, originally from Africa **4.** COLOURS **DARK BROWN** a dark brown colour, like mocha coffee [Late 18C. After MOCHA] —**mocha** *adj*

Mocha /mṓkə, mókə/ town and seaport in southwestern Yemen, on the Red Sea, historically a coffee-exporting centre. Population: 1,163 (1977 estimate).

mochaccino /mṓkə chéen ō/ (*plural* **-nos**) *n* a cappuccino made from a mixture of coffee and chocolate

Moche /mō chay/ *adj* relating to the Mochica or their culture ■ *n* (*plural* **-ches** or *same*) PEOPLES same as **Mochica** [< archaeological site and valley in NW Peru]

Mochica /mō chéekə/ (*plural* **-cas** or *same*) *n* a member of an ancient Native South American people who lived along the coast of northern Peru, where their civilization lasted from the 6th century BC to the 2nd century BC. The Mochicas are particularly noted for their pottery, which was decorated with realistic paintings of human and animal forms. [Mid-19C. Via Spanish < a Native American language]

mock /mok/ *v* (**mocks, mocking, mocked**) **1.** *vti* **TREAT SOMEBODY OR SOMETHING WITH SCORN** to treat somebody or something with scorn or contempt **2.** *vt* **MIMIC SOMEBODY** to imitate somebody in a way that is intended to make that person appear silly or ridiculous **3.** *vt* **PREVENT SOMETHING** to prevent something from succeeding in a way that causes frustration or humiliation ○ *the wind mocking his efforts to light a fire* ■ *adj* **1. IMITATION** made to appear like something else, usually something older or more expensive ○ *mock leather* **2. PRETEND** done as an act, especially in order to amuse people ○ *frowned in mock disapproval* **3. PRACTICE** done as practice for the real thing ○ *mock exams* ■ *n* **1. IMITATION OBJECT** something made as an imitation **2. OBJECT OF SCORN** somebody or something ridiculed by others (*dated*) ■ **mocks** *npl* EDUC **PRACTICE EXAMINATIONS** in the United Kingdom, practice examinations given to school pupils to prepare them for their official examinations [15C. < Old French *mocquer*] —**mockable** *adj* —**mocking** *adj* —**mockingly** *adv*

SYNONYMS See ***ridicule***.

mock up *vt* to make a full-scale working model of something so that it can undergo testing or be used to aid research

mocker /mókər/ *n* somebody who mocks ◇ **put the mockers on somebody** *or* **something** to prevent somebody or something from being a success (*informal*)

mockernut /mókər nut/ *n* **1.** a large sweet hard-shelled nut, commonly gathered in the wild **2.** a hickory tree that produces mockernuts. Native to: North America. Latin name: *Carya tomentosa*.

mockery /mókəri/ (*plural* **-ies**) *n* **1. SCORN** words or behaviour intended to make somebody or something look silly or ridiculous **2. SOMETHING INADEQUATE** something that is ridiculously inadequate or wholly unsuccessful ○ *The investigation was a mockery from start to finish.* **3. OBJECT OF SCORN** somebody or something that is treated with scorn or contempt and made to look silly or ridiculous

mock-heroic *adj* describes poetry that satirizes the heroic style by using it to describe something trivial. Like heroic poetry, mock-heroic poetry traditionally used classical forms such as the iambic pentameter (**heroic couplet**) or the iambic hexameter (**alexandrine**). ■ *n* verse or a poem written in the mock-heroic style

mockingbird /móking burd/ *n* a bird of the thrasher family, some of which incorporate the songs and calls of other birds into their own songs. Native to: North America. Family: Mimidae.

CULTURAL NOTE ***To Kill a Mockingbird***, a novel (1960) by US writer Harper Lee. Set in the southern United States, it tells the story of a white lawyer who agrees to defend an African American man wrongly accused of the rape of a white girl. The events are narrated from the point of view of the lawyer's six-year-old daughter, Scout. It was made into a film by Robert Mulligan in 1962.

mock moon *n* ASTRON same as **paraselene**

mockney /mókni/, **Mockney** *n* an imitation of cockney speech adopted especially by somebody wanting to suggest they have a working-class background (*informal*) [Late 20C. Blend of MOCK + COCKNEY]

mock orange /mok/ *n* **1.** an ornamental bush or tree. Flowers: fragrant, white, resembling those of an orange tree. Genus: *Philadelphus*. **2.** a bush or tree that resembles an orange tree

mock sun *n* ASTRON same as **parhelion**

mock turtle *n N Am* FASHION, CLOTHING same as **turtleneck** (senses 1–2)

mock turtle soup *n* an old-fashioned soup made in imitation of turtle soup, using meat from a calf's head to replace the flesh of the green turtle. This soup was popular in Victorian times.

mock-up *n* **1.** a full-sized model of something, built to scale and with working parts, used especially for testing or research **2.** a preliminary layout of a newspaper, magazine, or other publication, showing the size and arrangement of material to be included

mod[1] /mod/, **Mod** *n* in the United Kingdom in the 1960s, a member of a youth group known for their fashionable dress, motor scooters, and fights with motorcycle gangs (**rockers**) [Mid-20C. Shortening of MODERN or MODERNISM]

mod[2] /mōd/, **Mod** *n* a festival of Gaelic music and poetry held annually in Scotland, usually in the Highlands [Late 19C. Via Gaelic *mòd* 'assembly, court' < Old Norse *mót*]

MoD *abbr* Ministry of Defence

mod. *abbr* **1.** moderate **2.** MUSIC moderato **3.** modern

modal /mṓd'l/ *adj* **1.** GRAM **EXPRESSING GRAMMATICAL MOOD** used to describe verbs and auxiliary verbs expressing a grammatical mood such as possibility or necessity **2.** MUSIC **RELATING TO MUSICAL MODES** relating to or using a mode, especially instead of a major or minor scale **3.** LOGIC **DESCRIBING LOGICAL MODALITIES** describes propositions involving necessity or probability, or those relating to knowledge, belief, and obligation [Mid-16C. Directly or via French < medieval Latin *modalis* < Latin *modus* 'measure'] —**modally** *adv*

modal auxiliary *n* a verb used with other verbs to express such ideas as permission, possibility, and necessity. The modal auxiliaries in English grammar are 'can', 'could', 'may', 'might', 'must', 'ought to', 'shall', 'should', 'will', and 'would'. Some classifications also include 'dare', 'need', and 'used'.

modality /mō dálləti/ (*plural* **-ties**) *n* **1.** GRAM **CONCEPT EXPRESSED BY MODAL VERB** the idea or concept that a modal auxiliary verb expresses **2.** PHILOSOPHY **PROPOSITIONS OF NECESSITY OR POSSIBILITY** the purely logical classification of propositions that relate to necessity or possibility **3.** MED **TREATMENT** something used in the treatment of a disorder, e.g. surgery or chemotherapy [Early 17C. Directly or via French *modalité* < medieval Latin *modalitas* < *modalis* (see MODAL)]

modal logic *n* the branch of logic that studies the relations between modal propositions

modal verb *n* GRAM same as **modal auxiliary**

mod cons /-kónz/ *npl* the facilities that make modern life easier and more comfortable, e.g. central heating, hot water, telecommunications, and household appliances (*informal*) [Mid-20C. Shortening of *modern conveniences*]

mode /mōd/ *n* **1. MANNER OR FORM** a way, manner, or form, e.g. a way of doing something, or the form in which something exists **2. STYLE OR FASHION** a style or fashion, e.g. in art or in dress **3. MACHINE SETTING** a setting or function on a machine such as a computer **4. TYPE OF AUTOMATIC BEHAVIOUR** a way of behaving, especially one that is instinctive, familiar, or habitual (*informal humorous*) ○ *in work mode* **5.** MUSIC **SET PATTERN OF NOTES** a musical scale that is one of the seven patterns of notes that can be played over an octave using only the white notes of the piano keyboard. Some modes were widely used in Euro-

pean religious, folk, and art music until around 1600, after which they were largely replaced by keys, while others were used in ancient Greece. **6.** MATHS, STATS **MOST FREQUENT VALUE** the value that has the highest frequency within a statistical range **7.** LOGIC **MODAL STATUS OF PROPOSITION** the modal status of a proposition, e.g. its being necessary or merely possible **8.** PHYS **RADIO FREQUENCY** one of the radio frequencies characteristic of a given resonator or oscillator **9.** PHILOSOPHY **COMBINATION OF IDEAS** a combination of ideas that cannot be worked out merely by analysis of its components [14C. < Latin *modus* 'measure']

model /módd'l/ *n* **1.** **COPY OF OBJECT** a copy of an object, especially one made on a smaller scale than the original (*often used before a noun*) **2.** MANUF **SPECIFIC VERSION OF ARTICLE** a particular version of a manufactured article ○ *had traded in her car for the latest model* **3.** **SOMETHING COPIED** something that is copied or used as the basis for a related idea, process, or system **4.** **SIMPLIFIED VERSION** a simplified version of something complex used in analysing and solving problems or making predictions ○ *a financial model* **5.** **PERFECT EXAMPLE** an excellent example that deserves to be imitated **6.** FASHION **SOMEBODY PAID TO WEAR CLOTHES** somebody who is paid to wear clothes or demonstrate merchandise, e.g. in fashion shows or in photographs **7.** ART **ARTIST'S SUBJECT** somebody who poses for a painter, sculptor, photographer, or other artist **8.** SCULPTURE **SMALL VERSION OF SCULPTURE** a small version of a sculpture, from which a finished work is copied **9.** ZOOL **ANIMAL SPECIES COPIED BY ANOTHER ANIMAL** an animal species repellent to predators that another animal mimics for protection **10.** LOGIC **INTERPRETATION** an interpretation of a theory arrived at by assigning referents in such a way as to make the theory true **11.** FASHION **ORIGINAL GARMENT** the first sewn example of a couturier's or clothing manufacturer's design, from which a new line of garments is produced ■ *v* (**-els, -elling, -elled**) **1.** *vti* **WORK AS FASHION MODEL** to work as a fashion model, or wear clothes, makeup, or other items in order to display them to others **2.** *vi* **BE ARTIST'S MODEL** to sit as a model for somebody such as a painter or photographer **3.** *vt* **BASE ONE THING ON SOMETHING ELSE** to base something, especially somebody's appearance or behaviour, on that of another person ○ *She modelled herself on her older sister.* **4.** *vt* **SHAPE SOMETHING** to make something by shaping a substance or material such as clay or wood **5.** *vti* **MAKE SIMPLIFIED VERSION OF PROCESS** to make a simplified version of a complex process or system as a way of analysing and solving problems or making predictions [Late 16C. Via French *modèle* < Italian *modello* 'model' < Latin *modulus* 'measure' < *modus*] —**modeller** *n*

model home *n* N Am CONSTR same as **show house**

modeling *n* US spelling of **modelling**

modelling /móddling/ *n* **1.** **FASHION MODEL'S WORK** the work of a fashion model **2.** **MAKING OF MODELS** the activity or hobby of making models **3.** PSYCHOL **DEMONSTRATION OF BEHAVIOUR** the demonstration of a way of behaving to somebody, especially a child, in order for that behaviour to be imitated

model theory *n* the branch of logic that deals with providing models for theories —**model-theoretic** *adj*

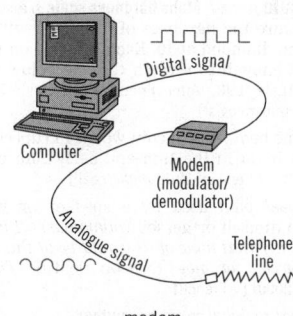
modem

modem /mó dem/ *n* an electronic device that connects computers via a telephone line, allowing the exchange of information. It consists of a modulator to convert computer information into a telephone signal and a demodulator to convert it back again. [Mid-20C. Blend of MODULATE + DEMODULATE]

Modena /móddinə/ historic city in northern Italy. It is an agricultural and industrial centre. Population: 165,502 (2001).

moderate *adj* /móddərət/ **1.** **SMALL OR SLIGHT** not large, great, or severe ○ *a moderate portion* **2.** **REASONABLE** not excessive or unreasonable ○ *a moderate eater* **3.** **MIDDLE-OF-THE-ROAD** not extreme or radical ○ *moderate views* **4.** **AVERAGE** neither particularly good nor particularly bad ○ *moderate results* ■ *n* /móddərət/ **SOMEBODY WITH MODERATE VIEWS** somebody who holds views that are not extreme, especially political views ■ *vti* /móddə rayt/ (**-ates, -ating, -ated**) **1.** **MAKE OR BECOME LESS EXTREME** to become less great, extreme, violent, or severe, or make something become so **2.** **PRESIDE OVER SOMETHING** to chair or preside over something such as a meeting or discussion **3.** **ACT AS EXAM MODERATOR** to act as a moderator in school examinations **4.** *Scotland* **PRESIDE OVER CHURCH ASSEMBLY** in the Presbyterian denominations of the Christian church, to preside over a formal meeting or assembly [14C. < Latin *moderat-*, past participle of *moderari* 'regulate'] —**moderately** *adv* —**moderateness** *n*

moderate breeze *n* a wind of between 20.9 and 29 km/13 and 18 mi. per hour, classified as force four on the Beaufort scale

moderate gale *n* a wind of between 51.5 and 61.2 km/32 and 38 mi. per hour, classified as force seven on the Beaufort scale

moderation /móddə ráysh'n/ *n* **1.** **STATE OF BEING MODERATE** the state or quality of being moderate ○ *moderation in all things* **2.** **ACTION OF MAKING SOMETHING MODERATE** the limiting, controlling, or restricting of something so that it becomes or remains moderate **3.** **JOB OF MODERATOR** the position or function of moderating something ◇ **in moderation** within reasonable limits, and never to excess

Moderations /móddə ráysh'nz/ *npl* EDUC same as **Honour Moderations**

moderato /móddə ra�/ *adv* at a moderate tempo (*used as a musical direction*) [Early 18C. < Italian < Latin *moderat-* (see MODERATE)] —**moderato** *adj*

moderator /móddə raytər/ *n* **1.** **SOMEBODY IN CHARGE OF DISCUSSION** somebody who presides over an assembly, especially a legislative assembly, or acts as a mediator in discussions or negotiations **2.** CHR **PRESIDING MINISTER** in the Presbyterian denominations of the Christian church, a minister presiding over a church court or other assembly **3.** *Scotland* CHR **PRESIDING MINISTER IN CHURCH OF SCOTLAND** in the Church of Scotland, the minister chosen to preside for one year over the General Assembly of the Church of Scotland and perform ceremonial duties **4.** PHYS **NEUTRON ABSORBER** a substance such as graphite or beryllium that slows neutrons in a nuclear reactor so that they can bring about the fission of uranium **5.** EDUC **EXTERNAL EXAMINER** an official responsible for making sure that standards of marking in public examinations are consistent from region to region —**moderatorship** *n*

modern /móddərn/ *adj* **1.** **BELONGING TO PRESENT DAY** relating or belonging to the present period in history **2.** **OF LATEST KIND** of the latest, most advanced kind, or using the most advanced equipment and techniques available ○ *modern medicine* **3.** **USING LATEST STYLES** relating to or using ideas and techniques that have only recently been developed or are still considered experimental **4.** LING **OF LANGUAGE'S LATEST STAGE** relating to or belonging to the most recent stage in the development of a language ■ *n* **1.** **MODERN PERSON** somebody living in the present period, especially somebody whose tastes and attitudes are regarded as nontraditional or strikingly new **2.** PRINTING **TYPEFACE** a typeface with heavy vertical strokes and straight serifs [Early 16C. Directly or via French *moderne* < Latin *modernus* < *modo* 'just now, in a (certain) manner' < *modus* 'measure'] —**modernly** *adv* —**modernness** *n*

SYNONYMS See *new*.

Modern Apprenticeship *n* a programme of work-based training for 16-to-17-year-olds, intended to include the achieving of an NVQ at level 3 within three years

modern dance *n* a free style of theatrical dancing that developed in the early 20th century

modern-day *adj* **1.** resembling a particular person or thing from the past **2.** relating to, belonging to, or existing in the present time

moderne /mə dáirn/ *adj* describes a style of architecture and design popular in the 1920s and 1930s and characterized by streamlined and curved forms [Mid-20C. < French *moderne* (see MODERN)]

Modern English *n* the English language from about 1500, when it began to develop a more standardized form compared with the dialects of Middle English. Modern English developed mainly from the East Midland dialect, and the standardization process was accelerated by the introduction of the printing press during the 1470s. —**Modern English** *adj*

modern Greek *n* the form of Greek spoken since around 1453, the year of the fall of Byzantium —**modern Greek** *adj*

Modern Hebrew *n* the form of the Hebrew language, a revival of the ancient form, that is the official language of the state of Israel —**Modern Hebrew** *adj*

modern history *n* **1.** the study of the period of history that extends from the end of the Middle Ages in Europe, around the middle of the 15th century, to the present day **2.** *US* the study of the period of European history after 1789

modernise *vti* another spelling of **modernize**

modernism /móddərnizəm/ *n* **1.** **LATEST THINGS** the latest styles, tastes, attitudes, or practices **2.** ARTS **EARLY 20C STYLES IN ART** the revolutionary ideas and styles in art, architecture, and literature that developed in the early 20th century as a reaction to traditional forms **3.** CHR **MOVEMENT WITHIN ROMAN CATHOLICISM** a movement in European Roman Catholicism in which scholars and theologians attempt to accommodate the contemporary world view within Roman Catholic theology and doctrine —**modernist** *n, adj* —**modernistic** /móddərn ístik/ *adj* —**modernistically** *adv*

modernity /mo dúrnəti/ (*plural* **-ties**) *n* **1.** **QUALITY OF BEING MODERN** the quality of being modern or up-to-date **2.** **SOMETHING MODERN** a modern thing **3.** SOC SCI **PERIOD SINCE ENLIGHTENMENT** the historical period from the Enlightenment to the present day, associated with the search for rational explanation of the universe and all things in it

modernize /móddərn īz/ (**-izes, -izing, -ized**), **modernise** (**-ises, -ising, -ised**) *vti* to change something in order to make it conform to modern tastes, attitudes, or standards, or be changed in this way —**modernization** /móddərn ī záysh'n/ *n* —**modernizer** *n*

modern jazz *n* a style of jazz that developed in the early 1940s, with rhythms and harmonies much more complex than those of traditional jazz

modern pentathlon *n* an athletics competition in which the contestants compete in five different events and are awarded points for each to find the best all-round athlete. The events are swimming, horse riding, cross-country running, fencing, and pistol shooting.

Modern Standard Chinese *n* the official language of the People's Republic of China, belonging to the Chinese branch of Sino-Tibetan languages. Native speakers: 800 million. Other speakers: 100 million. —**Modern Standard Chinese** *adj*

modest /móddist/ *adj* **1.** **HUMBLE** unwilling to draw attention to your own achievements or abilities **2.** **SHY** not confident or assertive, and tending to be easily embarrassed **3.** **REASONABLE** not large, extreme, or excessive ○ *a modest income* **4.** **SIMPLE** not showy, elaborate, or pretentious ○ *a modest dwelling* **5.** **NOT OVERTLY SEXUAL** reserved in appearance, manner, and speech, especially in relation to sexual matters [Mid-16C. Partly back-formation < MODESTY, partly via French *modeste* < Latin *modestus* 'kept within due measure'] —**modestly** *adv*

modesty /móddisti/ *n* **1.** **HUMILITY** unwillingness to draw attention to your own achievements or abilities **2.** **SEXUAL RESERVE** reserve in appearance, manner, and speech, especially in relation to sexual matters **3.** **SHYNESS** lack of confidence or assertiveness, with a tendency to embarrass easily **4.** **SIMPLICITY** lack of grandeur or ostentation **5.** **MODERATION** moderation in size, scale, or extent

modicum /móddikəm/ *n* a small amount, especially of something abstract such as a quality ○ *It only requires a modicum of common sense.* [Late 15C. < Latin, 'little way, short time', form of *modicus* 'moderate' < *modus* 'measure']

modif. *abbr* **1.** modification **2.** GRAM modifier

modification /móddifi káysh'n/ *n* **1.** **CHANGE** a slight change or alteration made to improve something or

make it more suitable ○ *made a few modifications to the original design* **2.** ACT OF MODIFYING the act or process of modifying something, or the condition of having been modified ○ *in need of modification* **3.** SOMETHING MODIFIED something that has been modified ○ *The new version is a modification and is based on existing software.* **4.** GRAM GRAMMATICAL RELATIONSHIP WITH MODIFIER in grammar, the relationship between a modifier and what it modifies [15C. Directly or via French < Latin *modificatio(n)-* < *modificat-*, past participle of *modificare* (see MODIFY)] —**modificative** /móddifi kaytiv/ *adj* —**modificator** /móddifi kaytər/ *n* —**modificatory** /móddifi kaytəri/ *adj*

modifier /móddi fī ər/ *n* **1.** somebody or something that makes slight changes to something, especially to improve it **2.** a word or phrase that affects the meaning of another, usually describing it or restricting its meaning. 'Pink' in the phrase 'the pink ribbon', 'fire' in the compound 'fire alarm', and 'in the morning' in the sentence 'She always goes jogging in the morning' are modifiers.

modify /móddi fī/ (**-fies, -fying, -fied**) *v* **1.** *vti* MAKE SMALL CHANGES TO SOMETHING to make a minor change or alteration to something, or change slightly, especially in order to improve **2.** *vt* LESSEN SOMETHING to make something less extensive, severe, or extreme **3.** *vt* GRAM AFFECT WORD'S MEANING to affect the meaning of another word, usually by describing or limiting it **4.** *vt* PHON CHANGE VOWEL SOUND to change the sound of a vowel from its usual sound, often in a way that is represented in writing by adding an umlaut [14C. Via French *modifier* < Latin *modificare* 'limit' < *modus* 'measure' + form of *facere* 'make'] —**modifiability** /móddi fī ə bíllәti/ *n* —**modifiable** *adj*

SYNONYMS See *change*.

Modigliani /móddil yaáni/, **Amedeo** (1884–1920) Italian painter and sculptor. His distinctive style, seen to best effect in his portraits, is characterized by graceful, elongated proportions.

modillion /mə díllyən/ *n* a small curved ornamental bracket under the corona of a Corinthian or Composite column [Mid-16C. Via French < Italian *modiglione* < Latin *mutulus* 'mutule']

modiolus /mō dī ələss/ (*plural* **-li** /-lī/) *n* the bony central pillar of the cochlea in the inner ear [Late 17C. < Latin, 'nave of a wheel' < *modius* 'measure']

modish /mṓdish/ *adj* in or conforming to the latest fashions or styles, especially those considered fads —**modishly** *adv* —**modishness** *n*

modiste /mō deést/ *n* a designer, maker, or seller of fashionable women's clothes (*dated*) [Mid-19C. < French < *mode* 'fashion']

Modred /mṓdrid/, **Mordred** /máwdrid/ *n* in Arthurian legend, a knight of the Round Table who killed his uncle, King Arthur

Mods /modz/ *npl* EDUC same as **Honour Moderations** (*informal*) [Mid-19C. Shortening of MODERATIONS]

modular /móddyōōlər/ *adj* **1.** made up of separate modules that can be rearranged, replaced, combined, or interchanged easily ○ *modular construction techniques* ○ *a modular course structure* **2.** relating to or resembling a modulus, or made up of moduli [Late 18C. < modern Latin *modularis* < Latin *modulus* (see MODULUS)] —**modularity** /móddyōō lárrəti/ *n* —**modularly** *adv*

modular arithmetic *n* a branch of arithmetic that deals with the remainders of whole numbers after the numbers have been divided by a modulus

modularized /móddyōōlə rīzd/, **modularised** *adj* made up of separate modules that can be rearranged, replaced, combined, or interchanged easily

modulate /móddyōō layt/ (**-lates, -lating, -lated**) *v* **1.** *vt* CHANGE SOUND to change the tone, pitch, or volume of sound, e.g. of a musical instrument or the human voice **2.** *vt* ALTER SOMETHING to make alterations in something to make it less strong, forceful, or severe **3.** *vti* MUSIC CHANGE KEY in tonal music, to change from one key to another through a harmonic progression, or change one key into another **4.** *vt* PHYS VARY WAVE CHARACTERISTICS to vary the frequency, amplitude, or other characteristics of a radio wave or another carrier wave in order to transmit information [Mid-16C. < Latin *modulat-*, past participle of *modulari* 'measure, adjust to rhythm' < *modulus* (see MODULUS)] —**modulability** /móddyōōlə bíllәti/ *n* —**modulable** *adj* —**modulation** /móddyōō láysh'n/ *n* —**modulative** /-lətiv/ *adj* —**modulator** *n* —**modulatory** /-lətəri/ *adj*

module /móddyool/ *n* **1.** SELF-CONTAINED INTERCHANGEABLE UNIT an independent unit that can be combined with others and easily rearranged, replaced, or interchanged to form different structures or systems **2.** EDUC SHORT COURSE OF STUDY a short course of study that forms part of a larger academic course or training programme, e.g. any of the elements that form part of a degree course **3.** AEROSP PART OF SPACE VEHICLE one of the self-contained units or craft that make up a space vehicle **4.** ARCHIT UNIT OF MEASUREMENT a unit of measurement or a standard, used especially in measuring architectural elements [Late 16C. Directly or via French < Latin *modulus* (see MODULUS)]

modulo /móddyōōlō/ *prep* with respect to a particular mathematical modulus ○ *9 and 30 are congruent modulo 7 because both leave the same remainder if they are divided by 7.* [Late 19C. < Latin, form of *modulus* (see MODULUS)]

modulus /móddyōōləss/ (*plural* **-li** /-lī/) *n* **1.** PHYS COEFFICIENT a coefficient expressing the degree to which a substance exhibits a particular property **2.** MATHS DIVISION NUMBER a number by which two other numbers can be divided so that both give the same remainder **3.** MATHS ABSOLUTE VALUE the absolute value of a complex number **4.** MATHS LOGARITHM FACTOR the factor by which a logarithm of one base must be multiplied to become the logarithm of another base [Mid-16C. < Latin, 'small measure' < *modus* 'measure']

modus operandi /mṓdəss óppə rán dee, -dī/ (*plural* **modi operandi** /mṓ dee óppə rán dee, mṓ dī óppə rán dī/) *n* a way of doing something [< Latin, 'mode of operating']

modus vivendi /mṓdəss vi vén dee, -dī/ (*plural* **modi vivendi** /mṓ dee vi vén dee, mṓ dī vi vén dī/) *n* **1.** a practical arrangement that allows conflicting people, groups, or ideas to coexist **2.** the way that a person or group of people lives [< Latin, 'mode of living']

MOF *abbr* ONLINE male or female (*used in e-mails or text messages*)

moffie /móffi/ *n S Africa* an offensive term for a man considered to be effeminate or homosexual (*slang*) [Mid-20C. < Afrikaans]

mog /mog/ *n* same as **cat** *n* (sense 1) (*informal*) [Early 20C. Shortening of MOGGY]

Mogadishu /móggə díshōō/ capital city and chief port of Somalia, situated in the southeast of the country. Population: 1,162,000 (1999).

Mogadon /móggə don/ *tdmk* a trademark for the drug nitrazepam

Mogen David /mṓgən-/ *n* JUDAISM same as **Star of David**

moggy /móggi/ (*plural* **-gies**), **moggie** *n* same as **cat** *n* (sense 1) (*informal*) [Late 17C. Variant of *Maggie* < *Mag*, shortening of *Margaret*]

Moghul *n* HIST same as **Mughal**

Mogollon /mṓgə yṓn/ (*plural* **-lons** or *same*) *n* a member of a Native North American people whose civilization in Arizona and New Mexico lasted from around the 2nd century BC to the 13th century AD. The Mogollons are particularly noted for their attractive pottery, traditionally decorated with black and white designs. [After placenames in Arizona and New Mexico after Juan Ignacio Flores *Mogollon*, governor of New Mexico (1712–15)]

mogul[1] /mṓg'l/ *n* an important or powerful person, especially somebody working in the media [Late 17C. < MOGUL]

mogul[2] /mṓg'l/ *n* a mound of hard compacted snow formed as an obstacle on a ski slope [Mid-20C. Origin ?]

Mogul *n, adj* HIST another spelling of **Mughal**

mohair /mṓ hair/ *n* **1.** the soft silky wool of the Angora goat **2.** silky yarn made from mohair [Late 16C. Alteration of *mocayre* < Arabic *mukayyar* 'cloth of goat's hair' < past participle of *kayyara* 'prefer']

Mohammed ISLAM another spelling of **Muhammad**

Moharram *n* ISLAM another spelling of **Muharram**

Mohave /mō haávi/ (*plural* **-ves** or *same*), **Mojave** *n* **1.** a member of a Native North American people who lived along the Colorado River valley on the border between California and Arizona **2.** the language of the Mohave people. It belongs to the Yuman branch of Hokan-Siouan languages. [Mid-19C. < Mohave *hàmakhá:v*] —**Mohave** *adj*

mohawk /mṓ hawk/ *n N Am* HAIR same as **mohican** [Late 19C. < MOHAWK]

Mohawk /mṓ hawk/ (*plural* **-hawks** or *same*) *n* **1.** a member of an Iroquois people who lived along the Mohawk and Hudson rivers, and who now live mainly in Ontario and New York State. The Mohawk were one of the five peoples who formed the Iroquois Confederacy, which later became known as the Six Nations. **2.** an Iroquoian language spoken in Quebec, Ontario, and northern New York. Native speakers: 3,000. [Mid-17C. < Narraganset *mohowawog* 'man-eaters'] —**Mohawk** *adj*

Mohegan /mō heégən/ (*plural* **-gans** or *same*) *n* **1.** a member of a Native North American people who lived in eastern Connecticut, and who now live mainly in southeastern Connecticut and Wisconsin **2.** an Algonquian language spoken in Connecticut and Wisconsin. Native speakers: 1,000. [Variant of MOHICAN] —**Mohegan** *adj*

mohel /mṓ hel, -el/ (*plural* **mohelim** /mṓ he leem/) *n* somebody who is qualified under Jewish religious law to carry out circumcisions [Mid-17C. < Hebrew *mōhēl*]

Mohenjo-daro /mə hénjō daárō/ ruined Bronze Age city in southern Pakistan. It formed part of the Indus Valley Civilization.

mohican /mō heékən, mṓ ikən/ *n* a hairstyle in which the sides of the head are shaved and the remaining hair is worn sticking up. It became associated with the punk movement and was often brightly coloured. N Am term **mohawk** [Mid-20C. < the topknots worn in illustrations of *Last of the Mohicans* (1826), a novel by James Fenimore COOPER]

Mohican /mō heékən, mṓ ikən/ *n* (*plural* **-cans** or *same*), *adj* PEOPLES, LANG same as **Mahican** (*dated*) [Variant] —**Mohican** *adj*

Mohock /mṓ hok/ *n* a member of a gang of ruffians from the upper classes who terrorized people in the streets of London in the early 18th century [Mid-17C. Variant of MOHAWK]

AKG London

László Moholy-Nagy

Moholy-Nagy /mō hṓli nój/, **László** (1895–1946) Hungarian-born US artist. He taught at the Bauhaus school (1923–28), founded the New Bauhaus in Chicago (1937), and was known for his artistic experiments involving modern technology.

Mohs scale /mṓz-/, **Mohs hardness scale** *n* a scale used to measure the hardness of minerals, with talc at zero and diamond at 10. Each mineral on the scale is hard enough to scratch the one below it in the scale. [Late 19C. After Friedrich *Mohs* (1773–1839), German mineralogist]

mohur /mṓ hər/ *n* a gold coin worth 15 rupees used in British India in the 19th and early 20th centuries [Late 17C. < Persian, Urdu *muhr* 'seal']

moi /mwaa/ *pron* used by a speaker or writer to refer to himself or herself (*humorous*) ○ *'I wanted to remind her that none of us would be at this juncture if it weren't for moi.'* (Nelson DeMille *The Lion's Game*; 2000) [< French]

moider *vti regional* same as **moither**

moidore /móy dáwr/ *n* an obsolete Portuguese or Brazilian gold coin [Early 18C. < Portuguese *moeda d'ouro* 'coin of gold']

moiety /móy əti/ (*plural* **-ties**) *n* **1.** either of two parts, not necessarily equal, into which something is or can be divided (*formal*) **2.** either of two halves into which some Native South American and Aboriginal

Australian societies are divided for ritual and marriage purposes. Marriages are forbidden within the same moiety. [15C. < French *moitié* 'half' < late Latin *medietas* < Latin *medius* 'middle']

moil /moyl/ n (*archaic*) **1.** TURMOIL a state of agitation or confusion **2.** DRUDGERY hard work ■ vi (**moils, moiling, moiled**) WORK HARD to work very hard ○ *toiling and moiling* [14C. < Old French *moillier* 'moisten, paddle in mud' < Latin *mollire* 'soften' < *mollis* 'soft'] —**moiler** n

Moirai /móy rī/ npl in Greek mythology, the Fates. Roman equivalent **Parcae** [< Greek]

moire /mwaar/ n a moiré fabric, especially silk but also, formerly, mohair [Mid-17C. < French, later form of *mouaire* 'mohair']

moiré /mwaʹa ray/ adj WITH WAVY PATTERN describes fabric with a shiny finish and wavy pattern on the surface ■ n **1.** TEXTILES WAVY PATTERN ON FABRIC a shiny finish and wavy pattern on fabric, especially silk, created by using engraved rollers **2.** WAVY PATTERN the wavy or shimmering effect created when two similar or identical geometric patterns are superimposed slightly out of alignment with each other **3.** TEXTILES same as **moire** [Early 19C. < French *moiré*, past participle of *moirer* 'water' < *moire* 'moiré fabric', probably alteration of *moire* (see MOIRE)]

moiré effect, **moiré pattern** n same as **moiré** n (sense 2)

moist /moyst/ adj **1.** DAMP slightly wet **2.** FRESH pleasantly fresh, rather than dry or stale ○ *a rich, moist fruitcake* **3.** TEARFUL full of tears ○ *moist eyes* **4.** RAINY humid or rainy, especially with light rain or drizzle [14C. < Old French *moiste* < Latin *mucidus* 'mouldy' < *mucus* 'slime', probably influenced by *musteus* 'new'] —**moistly** adv —**moistness** n

SYNONYMS See **wet**.

moisten /móyss'n/ (**-tens, -tening, -tened**) vti to make something moist, or become moist ○ *Moisten the mixture with a little beaten egg.* —**moistener** n

moisture /móysschər/ n wetness, especially as droplets of condensed or absorbed liquid, or in a vapour [14C. < Old French *moistour* < *moiste* (see MOIST)]

moisturize /móysschə rīz/ (**-izes, -izing, -ized**), **moisturise** (**-ises, -ising, -ised**) v **1.** vti to apply a cosmetic cream or lotion to the skin, especially on the face, to keep it from drying out **2.** vt to make something moist or more moist

moisturizer /móysschər īzər/ n a cosmetic cream or lotion used to make the skin, especially on the face, feel less dry

moither /móythər/ (**-thers, -thering, -thered**), **moider** /móydər/ (**-ders, -dering, -dered**) v regional **1.** vt to worry, bother, or confuse somebody **2.** vi to talk in an aimless or confused way [Late 17C. Origin ?]

Moja /mójə/ n US an arts festival featuring African American and Caribbean theatre, dance, music, arts, and crafts, especially one held annually in Charleston, South Carolina [Late 20C. < Kiswahili *moja*, literally 'one']

mojarra /mō haʹarə/ (*plural* **-ras** or same) n a small silvery sea fish with mouthparts that can be thrust outwards. Native to: shallow waters of tropical America. Family: Gerridae. [Mid-19C. < American Spanish]

Mojave n, adj PEOPLES, LANG another spelling of **Mohave**

Mojave Desert /mō haʹavi-/ dry region in southern California, part of the Great Basin region. Area: 52,000 sq. km/20,000 sq. mi.

mojo /mójō/ (*plural* **-joes** or **-jos**) n N Am (*slang*) **1.** MAGIC witchcraft or magic **2.** MAGNETIC QUALITY a quality that attracts or charms others **3.** MAGIC CHARM an object believed to have magical powers, especially the power to keep away evil spirits [Early 20C. Probably of African origin]

moke /mōk/ n same as **donkey** (*slang*) [Mid-19C. Probably from a personal name]

moko /mókō/ (*plural* **-kos**) n NZ **1.** tattooing practised by Maoris, especially on the face **2.** a pattern of tattoos used by Maoris [Mid-19C. < Maori]

moksha /mókshə/ n in Hinduism, the spiritual goal of release from reincarnation [Late 18C. < Sanskrit *mokṣa* < *muc* 'set free, release']

mol symbol CHEM mole [4]

mol. abbr CHEM **1.** molecular **2.** molecule

mola /mólə/ (*plural* **-las** or same) n FISH same as **sunfish** (sense 1) [Late 17C. < French *mole*]

molal /móləl/ adj describes a solution consisting of one mole of dissolved substance (**solute**) per 1,000 grams of solution [Early 20C. < MOLE [4]]

molality /mo láləti/ (*plural* **-ties**) n the concentration of a solution, expressed as the number of moles of a dissolved substance (**solute**) that can be found in 1,000 grams of solvent

molar [1] /mólər/ n a large back tooth in humans and other mammals, used for chewing and grinding. Human beings have twelve molars. [14C. < Latin *molaris* 'of a mill; grindstone, molar tooth' < *mola* 'mill']

molar [2] /mólər/ adj **1.** relating to or being a mole of a substance ○ *the molar volume of hydrogen* **2.** containing one mole of substance per litre of solution [Early 20C. < MOLE [4]] —**molarity** /mə lárrəti/ n

molar [3] /mólər/ adj relating to a body of matter rather than the properties of its molecules or atoms [Mid-19C. < Latin *moles* 'mass']

molar mass n the weight of one mole of any chemical substance [< MOLAR [2]]

molar tooth n DENT same as **molar** [1] [< MOLAR [1]]

molasses /mō lássiz/ n **1.** the thick dark bitter residue produced at the end of the sugar refining process **2.** N Am FOOD same as **treacle** (sense 1) [Late 16C. < Portuguese *melaços* < late Latin *mellaceum* 'new wine, must' < Latin *mel* 'honey']

mold, etc. US spelling of **mould, etc.**

Mold /mōld/ market town and administrative centre of Flintshire, Wales. Population: 8,745 (1991).

Moldavia /mol dáyvi ə/ former principality, located in what is now Romania and Moldova —**Moldavian** n, adj

molder vi US spelling of **moulder**

Moldova

Moldova /mol dóvə/ country in southeastern Europe. It was a republic of the former Soviet Union until 1991. Language: Romanian. Currency: leu. Capital: Chisinau. Population: 4,439,502 (2003). Area: 33,700 sq. km/13,000 sq. mi. Official name **Republic of Moldova** —**Moldovan** n, adj

moldy adj US spelling of **mouldy**

mole [1] /mōl/ n a small dark, sometimes raised growth on the human skin, sometimes with a hair or hairs growing from it [Old English *māl* 'discoloured mark' < Germanic, 'spot, mark']

mole [2] /mōl/ n **1.** BURROWING ANIMAL a small animal that usually lives underground and has large forelimbs for digging, no external ears, minute eyes, and dense velvety fur. Family: Talpidae. **2.** SPY somebody employed by a group or organization such as a government ministry who discloses sensitive information while keeping his or her own identity secret **3.** CONSTR TUNNELLING MACHINE a machine designed for boring through hard materials such as rock [14C. Probably < Middle Dutch *mol*]

mole [3] /mōl/ n **1.** a massive wall, usually made of stone, that extends into the sea and encloses or protects a harbour **2.** a harbour enclosed or protected by a mole [Mid-16C. Via French *môle* and medieval Greek *molos* < Latin *moles* 'mass, massive structure']

mole [4] /mōl/ n the basic SI unit of amount of a substance equal to the amount containing the same number of elementary units as the number of atoms in 12 grams of carbon-12. Symbol **mol** [Early 20C. < German *Mol*, shortening of *Molekul* 'molecule']

mole [5] /móli/ n a spicy Mexican sauce made with chocolate and a variety of chillies and spices, used especially for cooking poultry [Mid-20C. Via Mexican Spanish < Nahuatl *molli* 'sauce, stew']

Molech n BIBLE another spelling of **Moloch**

mole cricket n a cricket with a heavy body and short wings that burrows in the ground using front legs that are adapted for digging. It feeds primarily on plant roots. Family: Gryllotalpidae. [< MOLE [2]]

molecular /mə lékyōolər/ adj **1.** relating to or made up of molecules **2.** relating to or organized from simpler parts —**molecularity** /mə lekyōo lárrəti/ n —**molecularly** adv

molecular biology n the branch of biology concerned with the nature and function, at the molecular level, of biological phenomena such as RNA and DNA, proteins, and other macromolecules

molecular distillation n a technique of vacuum distillation in which the molecules of the distilled substance reach the condenser before colliding with each other

molecular film n CHEM same as **monolayer** (sense 1)

molecular formula n a chemical formula that specifies which atoms and how many of each atom there are in a molecule of a compound

molecular genetics n the branch of genetics that studies genes, chromosomes, and the transmission of hereditary characteristics at the molecular level (*takes a singular verb*)

molecular sieve n a crystalline compound with molecule-sized pores that can be used in separating larger molecules from smaller ones

molecular volume n the volume occupied by one mole of a substance when in the form of a gas

molecular weight n the total of all the atomic weights of the atoms in a molecule

molecule /mólli kyool/ n **1.** the smallest physical unit of a substance that can exist independently, consisting of one or more atoms held together by chemical forces **2.** a very small amount of something [Late 18C. Via French *molécule* < modern Latin *molecula* 'small mass' < Latin *moles* 'mass']

molehill /mól hil/ n a small mound of earth on the surface of the ground dug up by a burrowing mole [15C. < MOLE [2]]

mole rat n **1.** a tailless rodent that digs burrows with its enlarged incisors and powerful head. Native to: eastern Europe, southwestern Asia. Genus: *Spalax*. **2.** a rodent that has large protruding incisors for digging burrows. Native to: sub-Saharan Africa. Family: Bathyergidae. [< MOLE [2]]

mole run n a part of a network of tunnels and underground rooms built to provide shelter during a nuclear war (*informal*) [< MOLE [2]]

moleskin /mól skin/ n **1.** TEXTILES CLOTHING FABRIC a strong heavy cotton fabric with a brushed surface. Use: clothing. **2.** ZOOL FUR OF MOLE the short dense soft fur of a mole ■ **moleskins** npl CLOTHING MOLESKIN CLOTHING clothing, especially trousers, made of moleskin fabric [Mid-17C. < MOLE [2]]

molest /mə lést/ (**-lests, -lesting, -lested**) vt **1.** to force unwanted sexual attentions on somebody, especially a child or physically weaker adult **2.** to pester, bother, or disturb a person or animal [14C. Directly or via French < Latin *molestare* < *molestus* 'troublesome'] —**molestation** /mó le stáysh'n/ n —**molester** n

Molière /mólli air/ (1622–73) French dramatist. He satirized contemporary society in a series of witty plays including *Tartuffe* (1664). He also wrote *Le Bourgeois gentilhomme* (*The Bourgeois Gentleman*) (1670) and *Le Malade imaginaire* (*The Imaginary Invalid*) (1673). Pseudonym of **Poquelin, Jean-Baptiste**

'Most men die of their remedies, and not of their illnesses.'
[Molière, *Le Malade imaginaire* (*The Imaginary Invalid*); 1673]

moline /mō leén/ adj describes a heraldic cross that has arms of equal length that broaden at the ends by forking and curving backwards [Mid-16C. Probably < Anglo-Norman < *molin* 'mill' < late Latin *molinum*]

Molinism /mólənizəm/ n the doctrine in Christianity that a person has a choice in accepting divine grace [Mid-17C. After Luis de Molina (1535–1600), Spanish Jesuit who formulated it] —**Molinist** n

Molinos /mō leén oss/, **Miguel de** (1628–96) Spanish cleric and mystic. The founder of quietism, he was accused of heresy and immorality and in 1687 was sentenced to life imprisonment.

moll /mol/ *n* (*slang*) **1.** the woman companion of a gangster **2.** a woman prostitute [Early 17C. Shortening of *Molly*, a pet form of *Mary*]

MOLLE /mólli/, **Molle** *n* a water-repellent backpack with removable sections for carrying weapons and ammunition [Late 20C. Abbreviation of *modular lightweight load-bearing equipment*]

mollie *n* FISH another spelling of **molly**

mollify /mólli fī/ (**-fies, -fying, -fied**) *vt* **1.** PACIFY SOMEBODY to calm or soothe somebody who is angry or upset **2.** TEMPER SOMETHING to make something less intense or severe **3.** SOFTEN SOMETHING to make something less hard, rigid, or stiff [15C. Directly or via French *mollifier* < Latin *mollificare* < *mollis* 'soft'] —**mollifiable** *adj* —**mollification** /mólli fi káysh'n/ *n* —**mollifier** *n* —**mollifyingly** *adv*

mollusc: a snail

mollusc /mólləsk/ *n* an invertebrate with a soft unsegmented body, usually protected by a shell in one, two, or three pieces, e.g. the snails and the octopus. Most molluscs live in or near water. Phylum: Mollusca. [Late 18C. < French *mollusque* < Latin *molluscus* 'thin-shelled nut' < *mollis* 'soft'] —**molluscan** /mə lúskən/ *adj, n*

molluscicide /mə lúski sīd/ *n* a chemical that kills molluscs —**molluscicidal** /mə lúski sīd'l/ *adj*

molluscum contagiosum /mə lúskəm kən táyji ṓssəm/ *n* a benign viral skin infection characterized by numerous small round dimpled pearly-white nodules [Early 19C. < modern Latin, literally 'contagious fungus']

mollusk *n* ZOOL US spelling of **mollusc**

Mollweide projection /mól vīdə-/ *n* a projection of a map of the world showing lines of latitude as straight lines and lines of longitude as elliptical lines, used to show the distribution of land masses and oceans. This projection distorts shape but gives an indication of the relative size of countries and oceans. [Early 20C. After Karl B. *Mollweide* (1774–1825), German mathematician]

molly /mólli/ (*plural* **-lies**), **mollie** *n* a fish that bears live young and is often kept in aquariums. Native to: Central and South America. Genera: *Poecilia* or *Mollienisia*. [Mid-20C. Shortening of modern Latin *Mollienisia*, after Count F. N. *Mollien* (1758–1850), French statesman]

mollycoddle /mólli kod'l/ *vt* (**-dles, -dling, -dled**) to treat somebody in an overprotective and overindulgent way ∎ *n* a child, especially a boy, who is spoilt and overprotected [Mid-19C. < the name *Molly* (used for an effeminate boy or man) + CODDLE]

molly-dooker /mólli dookər/ *n* Aus a left-handed person (*informal*) [Mid-20C. < the name *Molly* or *mauley* 'hand, fist' (slang) + DUKE 'hand, fist']

Molly Maguire /mólli mə gwír/ *n* **1.** a member of a secret organization founded in Ireland in 1843 that used violent methods to stop evictions by the government **2.** a member of a secret Irish-American organization, active in the coal-mining districts of Pennsylvania from about 1865 to 1877, that used violent methods to try to get improved working conditions [Mid-19C. < a common Irish name, and because members of the original society disguised themselves as women]

mollymawk /mólli mawk/ *n* **1.** NZ an albatross, especially one of the smaller species. Family: Di-

omedeidae. **2.** a seabird, e.g. a fulmar, petrel, or albatross [Late 19C. < Dutch *mallemok* < *mal* 'foolish' + *mok* 'gull']

Molnár /mól naar, mōl-/, **Ferenc** (1878–1952) Hungarian playwright and novelist. His plays and short stories about fashionable society are underpinned by a concern for social justice.

moloch

moloch /mṓ lok/ *n* a lizard with large spiny scales covering its head and back. Native to: plains and deserts of central and southern Australia. Latin name: *Moloch horridus*. [Mid-19C. Via late Latin < Greek *Molokh* < Hebrew *Mōlek̄*, a Canaanite idol]

Moloch /mṓ lok/, **Molech** /mṓ lek/ *n* **1.** in the Bible, a Semitic deity to whom children were sacrificed **2.** somebody or something that requires a costly and painful sacrifice [Early 17C. Via late Latin < Greek *Molokh* < Hebrew *mōlek̄*, a Canaanite idol]

Molotov /mólla tof/, **Vyacheslav Mikhailovich** (1890–1986) Soviet politician. As a close associate and adviser of Joseph Stalin, he served as premier (1930–41) and foreign minister (1939–49, 1953–56) of the Soviet Union. He negotiated the German-Soviet non-aggression pact in 1939. Born **Scriabin, Vyacheslav Mikhailovich**

Molotov cocktail *n* a crude bomb, usually made of a bottle filled with a flammable liquid such as petrol and a wick that is set alight just before it is thrown

molt *vi, n* ZOOL US spelling of **moult**

molten /mṓltən/ *adj* **1.** MELTED changed into liquid form by heat **2.** MOULDED produced by melting a material and then shaping it in a mould **3.** GLOWING glowing with great heat [13C. Originally past participle of MELT[1]]

Moltke /móltkə/, **Helmuth Johannes Ludwig, Count** (1848–1916) German military commander. As chief of staff of the German army, he led Germany's unsuccessful invasion of France at the beginning of World War I.

molto /móltō/ *adv* used for emphasis before or after a musical direction derived from Italian [Early 19C. < Italian < Latin *multus* 'much']

Moluccas /mə lúkəz/ group of islands in eastern Indonesia, part of the Malay Archipelago. Population: 1,741,800 (1998). Area: 74,500 sq. km/28,800 sq. mi. —**Moluccan** *adj, n*

mol. wt. *abbr* CHEM molecular weight

moly /mṓli/ (*plural* **-lies**) *n* **1.** a plant of the garlic family. Flowers: yellow. Native to: southern Europe. Latin name: *Allium moly*. **2.** in Greek mythology, a magic herb with milky-white flowers and black roots that Hermes gave to Odysseus to protect him from Circe's spells [Mid-16C. Via Latin < Greek *mōlu*]

molybdate /mə líb dayt/ *n* a salt of molybdenum [Late 18C. < MOLYBDIC]

molybdenite /mə líbdə nīt/ *n* a greyish mineral consisting of molybdenum sulphide. Use: source of molybdenum. [Late 18C. < modern Latin *molybdenum* (see MOLYBDENUM)]

molybdenous /mə líbdənəss/ *adj* relating to or containing molybdenum, especially with a valency of 2 [Late 18C. < modern Latin *molybdenum* (see MOLYBDENUM)]

molybdenum /mə líbdənəm/ *n* a very hard silvery metallic element. Use: strengthening steel alloys. Symbol **Mo**. See table at **element** [Early 19C. < modern Latin < Greek *molubdaina* 'piece of lead' < *molubdos* 'lead']

molybdenum sulphide, **molybdenum disulphide** *n* a black crystalline powder that is insoluble in water. Use: lubricant. Formula: MoS_2.

molybdic /mə líbdik/ *adj* relating to or containing molybdenum, especially with a valency of 6 [Late 18C. < modern Latin *molybdenum* (see MOLYBDENUM)]

molybdous /mə líbdəss/ *adj* relating to or containing molybdenum, especially with a valency lower than 6 [Late 18C. < modern Latin *molybdenum* (see MOLYBDENUM)]

mom /mom/ *n* N Am same as **mother**[1] *n* (sense 1) (*informal*) [Late 19C. Shortening of MOMMA]

m.o.m. *abbr* US ACCT middle of month

mom-and-pop *adj* N Am describes a business that is owned and operated by a family, especially by a husband and wife ∘ *a mom-and-pop store*

Mombasa /mom bássə/ city and chief seaport of Kenya, in the southeast of the country on the Indian Ocean. It is also a tourist centre. Population: 465,000 (1989).

moment /mṓmənt/ *n* **1.** SHORT TIME a very short interval of time ∘ *Wait a moment.* **2.** PARTICULAR INSTANT a particular instant in time ∘ *At that moment she walked in the door.* **3.** PRESENT the present time ∘ *busy at the moment* **4.** SIGNIFICANT PERIOD an important or significant time or occasion ∘ *great moments in world history* **5.** SHORT PERIOD OF EXCELLENCE a brief period of excellence or interest (often used in the plural) ∘ *It's not a great opera, but it has its moments.* **6.** IMPORTANCE special importance or significance (*formal*) ∘ *a decision of great moment* **7.** PHILOSOPHY SPECIFIC STAGE a specific stage or aspect of something **8.** PHILOSOPHY same as **momentum** (sense 4) (*dated*) **9.** PHYS TENDENCY TO PRODUCE ROTATION a tendency to cause motion, especially rotation **10.** PHYS PRODUCT OF FORCE TIMES DISTANCE the product of a quantity such as a force multiplied by its perpendicular distance from a given point **11.** STATS MEAN IN FREQUENCY DISTRIBUTION the expected value of the deviations of a variable, compared to a fixed value, raised to a given power [14C. Via French < Latin *momentum* 'movement' < *movere* 'to move']

momentarily /mṓməntərəli/ *adv* **1.** BRIEFLY for a brief period of time **2.** PROGRESSIVELY with every passing moment **3.** N Am VERY SOON within a very short period of time ∘ *He'll be here momentarily.*

momentary /mṓməntəri/ *adj* **1.** VERY BRIEF lasting for a very short time **2.** CONSTANT present or happening at every moment **3.** WITH SHORT LIFE living or continuing for only a relatively short time —**momentariness** *n*

momently /mṓməntli/ *adv* US **1.** PROGRESSIVELY with every passing moment ∘ *growing momently more uneasy* **2.** VERY SOON within a very short period of time **3.** FOR INSTANT for a very short period of time

~~momento~~ incorrect spelling of **memento**

moment of inertia *n* a measure of resistance to changes in angular speed, calculated as the sum of the products of the component masses of an object multiplied by the square of their distance from the axis. Symbol *I*

moment of truth *n* **1.** a point in time when a crucial decision has to be taken or when somebody or something is put to an important test **2.** in a bullfight, the point at which the bull is about to be killed with the final blow

momentous /mō méntəss/ *adj* extremely important or crucial, especially in its effect on the future course of events —**momentously** *adv* —**momentousness** *n*

momentum /mō méntəm/ (*plural* **-ta** /-tə/ or **-tums**) *n* **1.** CAPACITY FOR PROGRESSIVE DEVELOPMENT the power to increase or develop at an ever-growing pace ∘ *The project was in danger of losing momentum.* **2.** FORWARD MOVEMENT the speed or force of forward movement of an object ∘ *the momentum gained on the downhill stretches of the course* **3.** PHYS MEASURE OF MOVEMENT a quantity that expresses the motion of a body and its resistance to slowing down. It is equal to the product of the body's mass and velocity. Symbol *p* **4.** PHILOSOPHY BASIC ELEMENT an essential part of a whole [Early 17C. < Latin *momentum* (see MOMENT)]

MOMI /mṓmi/ *abbr* Museum of the Moving Image (London)

momma /mómmə/ *n* N Am somebody's mother (*informal*) [Early 19C. Alteration of MAMA]

Mommsen /mómz'n/, **Theodor** (1817–1903) German historian. A specialist in Roman history, he was of outstanding importance in the foundation of modern Latin epigraphy. He was awarded a Nobel Prize in literature (1902).

'Bismarck has broken the spine of the nation.'
[Theodor Mommsen. Quoted in *Theodor Mommsen*, Albert Wucher; 1956]

mommy /mómmi/ (*plural* **-mies**) *n* N Am same as **mother**[1] *n* (sense 1) (*informal*) [Early 20C. Alteration of MAMMY]

mommy track *n* N Am a career route taken by a woman whereby she risks reducing her chances of career advancement by working flexitime or fewer hours in order to look after a child or children (*informal*)

momser *n* JUDAISM same as **mamzer**

Momus /mṓməss/ *n* in Greek mythology, the god of fault-finding and mockery. He is a son of Night. [Late 16C. Via Latin < Greek *Mōmos*]

momzer *n* JUDAISM same as **mamzer**

Mon /món/ (*plural same* or **Mons**) *n* **1.** a member of a people who live in adjacent parts of Thailand and Myanmar **2.** a Mon-Khmer language that is spoken in adjacent parts of Thailand and Myanmar. Native speakers: 700,000. [Late 18C. < Mon] —**Mon** *adj*

mon. *abbr* **1.** monastery **2.** monetary

Mon. *abbr* **1.** Monday **2.** CHR Monsignor

mon- *prefix* same as **mono-** (*used before vowels*)

mona /mṓnə/ *n* a monkey that has a dark back and white or yellow front and is capable of moving at speed through the trees. Native to: West Africa. Latin name: *Cercopithecus mona*. [Late 18C. Via Spanish < Portuguese < Italian *monna* 'monkey']

Mona /mṓnə/ *n* uninhabited island off the western coast of Puerto Rico. Area: 52 sq. km/20 sq. mi.

monachal /mónnək'l/ *adj* relating to a monastery or monks, or resembling monastic life [Late 16C. Directly or via French < ecclesiastical Latin *monachalis* < late Latin *monachus* (see MONK)] —**monachism** *n* —**monachist** *adj, n*

monacid, etc. CHEM same as **monoacid, etc.**

Monaco

Monaco /mónnəkō, mə náakō/ small independent principality of Europe, bordered by France and the Mediterranean Sea. Language: French. Currency: euro. Capital: Monaco. Population: 32,130 (2003). Area: 2 sq. km/0.75 sq. mi. Official name **Principality of Monaco** —**Monacan** *n, adj*

monad /mónnad/ *n* **1.** MICROBIOL SINGLE-CELLED MICROORGANISM a microorganism consisting of just one cell, especially a flagellate protozoan. Genus: *Monas*. **2.** CHEM ATOM WITH VALENCY OF ONE an atom or chemical group that has a valency of one **3.** PHILOSOPHY BASIC ENTITY IN METAPHYSICS OF LEIBNITZ in the metaphysics of Leibnitz, an indivisible indestructible unit that is the basic element of reality and a microcosm of it [Mid-16C. Directly or via French *monade* < late Latin *monad-* < Greek *monos* 'single'] —**monadic** /mo náddik/ *adj* —**monadical** *adj* —**monadically** *adv* —**monadism** *n*

monadelphous /mónnə délfəss/ *adj* **1.** describes stamens that have all the filaments united to form a single bundle in the shape of a tube **2.** describes a flower that has monadelphous stamens [Early 19C. < MONO- + Greek *adelphos* 'brother']

monadnock /mə nád nok/ *n* an isolated mountain or rock that has resisted the process of erosion and stands alone in an otherwise flat area [Late 19C. After *Monadnock*, peak in New Hampshire, United States]

Monaghan /mónnəhən/ *n* county in the northeastern part of the Republic of Ireland. Area: 1,291 sq. km/498 sq. mi.

monandrous /mo nándrəss/ *adj* **1.** WITH ONE MALE LOVER having a sexual relationship with only one man during a period of time **2.** BOT WITH ONE STAMEN describes a flower that has a single stamen **3.** BOT WITH MONANDROUS FLOWERS describes a plant that has monandrous flowers [Early 19C. < Greek *monandros* 'having one husband' < *monos* 'one, alone' + *andr-* 'man']

monandry /mo nándri/ *n* **1.** the practice of having only one husband at a time **2.** the practice of having a sexual relationship with only one man during a period of time

monanthous /mo nánthəss/ *adj* producing a single flower [Mid-19C. < MONO- + Greek *anthos* 'flower']

Mona Passage area of sea separating the islands of Hispaniola and Puerto Rico, linking the Atlantic Ocean to the Caribbean Sea

monarch /mónnərk/ *n* **1.** SUPREME RULER somebody, especially a king or queen, who rules a state or territory, usually for life and by hereditary right **2.** EXCEPTIONALLY POWERFUL PERSON somebody who possesses exceptional power or influence in an area of activity (*literary*) **3.** SOMETHING OUTSTANDING OR PREDOMINANT something that occupies a pre-eminent or predominant position (*literary*) **4.** INSECTS same as **monarch butterfly** [15C. Directly or via French < late Latin *monarcha* < Greek *monarkhos* 'rule alone' < *monos* 'one, alone' + *arkhein* 'to rule'] —**monarchal** /mə náark'l/ *adj* —**monarchally** *adv*

monarch butterfly *n* a large migrating orange and black butterfly whose caterpillars feed on milkweed plants. Native to: North America. Latin name: *Danaus plexippus*.

monarchic /mə náarkik/, **monarchical** /-ik'l/ *adj* relating to a monarch or monarchy —**monarchically** *adv*

monarchism /mónnərkizəm/ *n* **1.** belief in or support for monarchy as a system of government **2.** the system of government in which a monarch rules

monarchist /mónnərkist/ *n* an advocate or supporter of a system of monarchy ■ *adj* favouring or supporting a system of monarchy

monarchy /mónnərki/ (*plural* **-chies**) *n* **1.** SYSTEM OF RULE BY MONARCH a political system in which a state is ruled by a monarch **2.** ROYAL FAMILY a monarch and his or her family **3.** STATE RULED BY MONARCH a country ruled by a monarch

monarda /mə náardə/ *n* an aromatic plant of the mint family. Native to: North America. Genus: *Monarda*. [Late 18C. < modern Latin]

Monash /mó nash/, **Sir John** (1865–1931) Australian military commander, engineer, and administrator. He was commander of the Australian forces in France (1918–19).

monastery /mónnəstəri/ (*plural* **-ies**) *n* **1.** a building or buildings with grounds in which a group of people observing religious vows, especially monks, live together **2.** a group of people, especially monks, living together and observing religious vows [14C. Via ecclesiastical Latin *monasterium* < Greek *monazein* 'live alone' < *monos* 'one, alone'] —**monasterial** /mónnə steéri əl/ *adj*

monastic /mə nástik/ *adj also* **monastical** /mə nástik'l/ **1.** OF MONKS, NUNS, OR MONASTERIES relating to monks, nuns, or their way of life or the buildings in which they live ○ *monastic rule* **2.** RECLUSIVE OR AUSTERE characteristic of the life of a monk, especially in being reclusive, self-denying, or austere ■ *n* MONK somebody, especially a monk, who lives with others in a monastery and observes religious vows [15C. Directly or via French < late Latin *monasticus* < Greek *monazein* (see MONASTERY)] —**monastically** *adv*

monasticism /mə nástissizəm/ *n* the way of life characteristic of monks or nuns, in which they withdraw entirely or in part from society to devote themselves to prayer, solitude, and contemplation

~~monastry~~ incorrect spelling of **monastery**

monatomic /mónnə tómmik/, **monoatomic** /mónnō ə tómmik/ *adj* **1.** having only one atom in the molecule **2.** with one atom or chemical group that can be replaced during a chemical reaction **3.** CHEM same as **monovalent** (sense 1) —**monatomically** *adv*

monaural /mo náwrəl/ *adj* **1.** relating to or involving the hearing of sound by one ear **2.** ELECTRONICS same as **monophonic** —**monaurally** *adv*

monaxial /mon áksi əl/ *adj* BOT same as **uniaxial** (sense 1)

monazite /mónnə zīt/ *n* a reddish-brown phosphate mineral that contains cerium, lanthanum, and some

thorium [Mid-19C. < Greek *monazein* (see MONASTERY); because of its rare occurrence]

Monck /mungk/, **George, 1st Duke of Albemarle** (1609–70) English soldier. Initially a Royalist in the Civil War, he later served in the Parliamentary army under Oliver Cromwell, but regained royal favour after the Restoration.

mondain /mon dáyn, moN dáN/ *n* a man who belongs to fashionable society ■ *adj* same as **mondaine** [Late 19C. < French (see MUNDANE)]

mondaine /mon dáyn, moN dén/ *n* a woman who belongs to fashionable society ■ *adj* relating to fashionable society, especially in being worldly or sophisticated [Late 19C. < French, feminine of *mondain* (see MUNDANE)]

Monday /mún day, -di/ *n* the first day of the traditional working week, coming after Sunday and before Tuesday [Old English *mōnandæg* < Germanic, translation of Latin *lunae dies* 'day of the moon']

Monday Club *n* a club for right-wing Conservatives, founded in 1961. Their first meetings were over lunch on Mondays.

Mondayize /mún day īz/ (**-izes, -izing, -ized**), **Mondayise** (**-ises, -ising, -ised**) *vt* NZ to move a statutory holiday to the Monday falling closest to it so as to make a long weekend —**Mondayization** /mún day ī záysh'n/ *n*

Mondays /mún dayz, -diz/ *adv* every Monday

mondial /móndi əl/ *adj* relating to or involving the entire world [Early 20C. < French < *monde* 'world' < Latin *mundus*]

Mondrian /móndri áan, móndri aan/, **Piet** (1872–1944) Dutch painter. A leading figure of the De Stijl art movement, he was an advocate of pure geometric abstraction, with flat planes and straight lines, and the use of primary colours along with black and white. Born **Mondrian, Pieter Cornelis**

'Great masters of painting have emphasized the tension characterizing the contour...What I have in mind is the most extreme transformation of the tension of the line, until it finally becomes the absolutely straight line.'
[Piet Mondrian, 'Plastic Art and Pure Plastic', *Modern Artists on Art: 10 Unabridged Essays*; 1964]

monecious *adj* BOT another spelling of **monoecious**

Monégasque /mónnə gásk/ *n* somebody who comes from Monaco ■ *adj* relating to Monaco [Late 19C. < French < *Mounegue* 'Monaco']

monestrous *adj* ZOOL US spelling of **monoestrous**

Monet /món ay/, **Claude** (1840–1926) French painter. A leading figure of the impressionist movement, he is noted for his studies of the effects of light on scenes and subjects in nature. Full name **Monet, Claude Oscar**

'Could they have a title for the catalogue, it really couldn't pass for a view of Le Havre; I answered: "Put: 'Impression'". From this came Impressionism, and the jokes abounded.'
[Attributed to Claude Monet]

monetarism /múnnitərizəm/ *n* **1.** the theory that inflation and other economic variations are caused by changes in the money supply **2.** the policy of controlling an economic system by increasing or decreasing the money supply, especially in a gradual manner —**monetarist** *n, adj*

monetary /múnnitəri/ *adj* relating to or involving money or currency [Early 19C. Directly or via French *monétaire* < late Latin *monetarius* < Latin *moneta* (see MONEY)] —**monetarily** *adv*

monetary unit *n* the standard unit in a nation's currency system, e.g. the pound in the United Kingdom or the dollar in the United States

monetize /múnni tīz/ (**-tizes, -tizing, -tized**), **monetise** (**-tises, -tising, -tised**) *vt* **1.** MAKE SOMETHING LEGAL TENDER to make something the legal tender of a country **2.** COIN METAL to convert a metal into coins **3.** CONVERT DEBT INTO AVAILABLE MONEY to convert a government debt into available currency, especially by issuing securities [Late 19C. < Latin *moneta* (see MONEY)] —**monetization** /múnni tī záysh'n/ *n*

money /múnni/ *n* **1.** MEDIUM OF EXCHANGE a medium of exchange issued by a government or other public authority in the form of coins of gold, silver, or

other metal, or paper banknotes, used as the measure of the value of goods and services **2. DE-NOMINATION** a form or denomination of coin or paper money **3. SOMEBODY'S COINS AND BANKNOTES** the amount of coins and banknotes in somebody's possession ○ *Do you have money for lunch?* **4. SAVINGS OR CREDIT** the amount of money held in a bank account or available on credit to somebody **5. WAGES OR SALARY** the amount somebody is paid for working ○ *She earns good money.* **6. CONVERTIBLE ASSETS** assets or property that can be converted into cash **7. NATIONAL CURRENCY** the official currency of a country **8. RECOGNIZED MEDIUM OF EXCHANGE** a commodity, usually gold, that is officially recognized as a medium of exchange and a measure of value **9. RICH PEOPLE** a rich person, family, or class ○ *She married money.* ■ **monies** *npl* **SUMS OF MONEY** individual sums of money (*formal*) ○ *all monies payable* [13C. Via Old French *moneie* < Latin *moneta* 'mint, money' < *Moneta*, epithet of the goddess Juno, in whose temple coins were minted] ◇ **for somebody's money** in somebody's opinion or judgment ○ *For my money, he's easily their best player.* ◇ **have money to burn** to be able to spend money extravagantly ◇ **in the money** having a lot of money, especially as a change in circumstances ◇ **put your money where your mouth is** to take action to show that you truly mean what you have said (*informal*) ◇ **throw good money after bad** to put more money, better used elsewhere, into a bad investment ○ *If you have the car repaired again, you'll just throw good money after bad.* ◇ **throw money about** to spend money in an extravagant, ostentatious way (*informal*)

money-back *adj* refunding money paid for something if the product or service is unsatisfactory ○ *It comes with a money-back guarantee.*

moneybags /múnni bagz/ (*plural same*) *n* a conspicuously rich person (*informal*)

moneychanger /múnni chaynjər/ *n* an exchanger of currencies, usually for a commission

moneyed /múnnid/, **monied** *adj* **1.** possessing a great deal of money **2.** consisting of or resulting from money

moneygrubber /múnni grubər/ *n* somebody excessively concerned with making money from every possible opportunity —**moneygrubbing** *adj, n*

moneylender /múnni lendər/ *n* a lender of money in exchange for interest on the amount borrowed —**moneylending** *n*

moneymaker /múnni maykər/ *n* **1.** somebody who is skilled at making money **2.** a business, product, or project that makes a lot of money —**moneymaking** *n, adj*

moneyman /múnni man/ (*plural* **-men** /-men/) *n US* an expert on finance and economics (*informal*)

money market *n* the trade in low-risk securities that have a life of one year or less

money of account *n* a monetary unit that is used to keep accounts. It does not necessarily correspond to an actual currency unit.

money order *n* an order for a specific sum of money, usually purchased with cash at a bank or post office, that can be used to make payments

money shell *n* the shell of the butter clam, formerly used as money by Native Americans on the coast of western North America

money spider *n* a tiny brownish spider. Family: Linyphiidae. [< the folk belief that money will come to those on whom the spider crawls]

money-spinner *n* BUSINESS same as **moneymaker** (sense 2) (*informal*)

money supply *n* the total amount of money available in a given economy. One way of measuring the money supply is the total amount of currency in circulation combined with the money available in bank deposits.

money wages *npl* wages considered only in terms of how much money is paid and not in terms of what that money can buy. N Am term **nominal wages**

moneywort /múnni wurt/ *n Aus, US* an evergreen creeping plant with coin-shaped leaves. Flowers: yellow. Native to: Europe, eastern North America. Latin name: *Lysimachia nummularia.* UK, NZ, Can term **creeping Jennie**

mong /mung/ *n Aus* **1.** a dog, especially a mongrel (*informal*) **2.** an offensive term that deliberately

insults somebody's intelligence (*slang*) [Mid-20C. Shortening]

-monger *suffix* seller, dealer, promoter ○ *fishmonger* [Old English *mangere*, via Germanic < Latin *mango* 'peddler, swindler']

mongo /móng gō/ (*plural same* or **-gos**) *n* a subunit of Mongolian currency. See table at **currency** [Mid-20C. < Mongolian *möngö* 'silver']

mongol /móng g'l/ *n* a former term for somebody affected by Down's syndrome, now considered highly offensive (*dated offensive*) [Late 19C. < MONGOL]

Mongol /móng g'l, -gol/ *n* **1.** a member of the originally nomadic peoples who inhabit Mongolia and established an empire in the 13th century **2.** LANG same as **Mongolian** (sense 2) ■ *adj* relating to Mongolia, its people, or their language or culture [Late 17C. < Mongol]

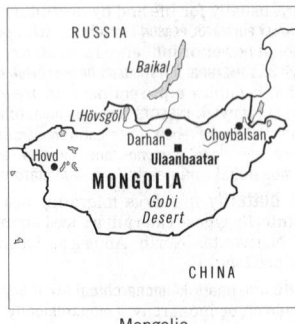

RUSSIA

L Baikal

L Hövsgöl

Darhan ■   ■ Choybalsan
Ulaanbaatar
Hovd ■

MONGOLIA

Gobi Desert

CHINA

Mongolia

Mongolia /mong góli ə/ country in Central Asia, bordered on the north by Russia and on the east, south, and west by China. Language: Mongolian. Currency: tugrik. Capital: Ulaanbaatar. Population: 2,712,315 (2003). Area: 1,566,500 sq. km/604,830 sq. mi.

Mongolian /mon góli ən/ *n* **1.** somebody who comes from Mongolia **2.** a language or group of dialects of the Altaic family spoken in Mongolia and in the Chinese region of Inner Mongolia. Native speakers: 6 million. —**Mongolian** *adj*

Mongolic /mon góllik/ *n* an Altaic group of languages that includes Mongolian, Buryat, and Santa ■ *adj* **1.** relating to Mongolic **2.** ANTHROP same as **Mongoloid** (*dated*)

mongolism /móng gəlizəm/ *n* a former term for Down's syndrome, now considered highly offensive (*dated*)

mongoloid /móng gə loyd/ *adj* a former term meaning affected by Down's syndrome, now considered highly offensive (*dated*)

Mongoloid /móng gə loyd/ *adj* in an obsolete classificatory system, relating or belonging to a racial group including the peoples of eastern Asia, the Inuit, and the Native Americans (*no longer used technically*) —**Mongoloid** *n*

mongoose

mongoose /móng gooss/ (*plural* **-gooses**) *n* a small short-legged carnivorous animal that resembles a ferret and is noted for its ability to kill poisonous snakes. Native to: South Asia. Genus: *Herpestes.* [Late 17C. < Marathi *maṅgūs*]

mongrel /múng grəl/ *n* **1. DOG OF MIXED BREED** a dog that is a mixture of different breeds **2. ANIMAL OR PLANT OF MIXED BREED** an animal or plant that is a mixture of different breeds or strains **3. OFFENSIVE TERM** an

offensive term for somebody who is of mixed racial ancestry **4. STRANGE MIXTURE** a combination or mixture of different people or things, especially one that seems particularly strange **5. *Aus* OBNOXIOUS PERSON** somebody regarded as obnoxious (*insult*) ■ *adj* **MIXED IN ORIGIN OR CHARACTER** of mixed breed, descent, type, or character (*offensive in some contexts*) [15C. Probably < Germanic, 'to mix'] —**mongrelism** *n* —**mongrelly** *adv*

mongrelize /múng grə līz/ (**-izes**, **-izing**, **-ized**), **mongrelise** (**-ises**, **-ising**, **-ised**) *vt* to make something or somebody become mongrel or mixed in character, type, or race (*offensive when used of people*) —**mongrelization** /múng grə lī záysh'n/ *n*

'mongst /mungst/ *prep* same as **among** (*literary*) [Late 16C. Shortening of *amongst*, variant of AMONG]

Monicagate /mónnikə gáyt/ *n N Am* a 1998–99 sex scandal involving US President Bill Clinton and a former White House intern, culminating in his impeachment and subsequent acquittal (*slang*) [< *Monica* S. Lewinsky, the intern]

monicker *n* another spelling of **moniker** (*slang*)

monied *adj* FIN another spelling of **moneyed**

monies plural of **money** (*formal*)

moniker /mónnikər/, **monicker** *n* somebody's name or nickname (*slang*) [Mid-19C. Origin ?]

moniliform /mə nílli fawrm/ *adj* describes a plant root or insect antenna that resembles a string of beads [Early 19C. Directly or via French < modern Latin *moniliformis* < Latin *monile* 'necklace'] —**moniliformly** *adv*

monism /mónnizəm/ *n* **1.** the philosophical theory that reality is a unified whole and is grounded in a single basic substance or principle **2.** a theory or point of view that attempts to explain everything in terms of a single principle [Mid-19C. < modern Latin *monismus* < Greek *monos* 'one, alone'] —**monist** *n, adj* —**monistic** /mo nístik/ *adj* —**monistically** *adv*

monition /mə nísh'n/ *n* **1. WARNING OF DANGER** a warning, especially a warning of danger **2. EXHORTATION TO CAUTION** a piece of advice counselling caution **3.** CHR **WARNING FROM BISHOP** an official warning from a bishop to refrain from doing something **4.** LAW **SUMMONS** an order to appear in court [14C. < French < Latin *monit-*, past participle of *monere* 'warn']

monitor /mónnitər/ *n* **1.** VDU a video device that displays data or images generated by a computer or terminal **2. CLOSED-CIRCUIT TELEVISION SET** a receiving device used in a closed-circuit television or video system **3. SOMEBODY ENSURING PROPER CONDUCT** somebody who checks for incorrect or unfair conduct **4.** EDUC **PUPIL WITH RESPONSIBILITY** a pupil who helps a teacher by being given a responsibility or special duty **5.** BROADCAST **VIEWING DEVICE IN STUDIO** a receiver in a television studio that enables the audience to watch the recorded portions of a show or performers to view parts of a programme **6.** ARTS **STAGE LOUDSPEAKER** a loudspeaker on a stage during a concert used to let performers hear what they are playing ○ *playing a guitar solo with one foot up on the monitor* **7.** BROADCAST **SOMEBODY WHO CHECKS BROADCASTS** somebody who listens to and checks broadcasts for a client or employer, e.g. to learn foreign news or discover secret plans **8.** COMPUT **COMPUTER PROGRAM** a computer program that observes and controls other programs in a system **9.** REPT **LARGE LIZARD** a large tropical carnivorous lizard. Native to: Asia, Africa, Australia. Family: Varanidae. N Am term **monitor lizard 10.** INDUST, EMERGENCIES **NOZZLE** a jointed device with a rotating nozzle that controls and aims a jet of water **11.** HIST **19C WARSHIP** a heavily armoured warship with gun turrets used in the 19th century in coastal manoeuvres ■ *vt* (**-tors**, **-toring**, **-tored**) **1. CHECK SOMETHING REGULARLY** to check something at regular intervals in order to find out how it is progressing or developing **2. WATCH FOR PROPER CONDUCT** to watch over somebody or something, especially in order to ensure that good order or proper conduct is maintained **3. LISTEN TO BROADCASTS OR TELEPHONE CONVERSATIONS** to use an electronic receiver to listen in on broadcasts or telephone conversations, especially in order to discover secret or illegal plans and activities **4.** BROADCAST **CHECK QUALITY OF SIGNALS** to use an electronic receiver to check the quality of transmitted audio or visual signals [Early 16C. < *monit-* (see MONITION)] —**monitorial** /mónni táwri əl/ *adj* —**monitorially** *adv* —**monitorship** *n*

ORIGIN The Latin word *monere* 'to warn', from which *monitor* is derived, is also the source of English *admonish*, *monument*, *premonition*, and *summon*.

monitor lizard *n N Am* REPT same as **monitor** *n* (sense 9) [< the belief that they warn of the proximity of crocodiles]

monitory /mónnitəri/ *adj* communicating a warning ■ *n* (*plural* **-ries**) a letter, usually from a bishop, that warns somebody to refrain from doing something

monk /mungk/ *n* a man who withdraws entirely or in part from society and goes to live in a religious community to devote himself to prayer, solitude, and contemplation [Old English *munuc*, via Germanic < late Latin *monachus* < Greek *monos* 'alone']

Thelonious Monk

Monk /mungk/, **Thelonious** (1920–82) US pianist and composer. An influential modern jazz musician, he was known for his compositions in the bebop style. Full name **Monk, Thelonious Sphere**

> 'I hit the piano with my elbow sometimes because of a certain sound I want to hear. You can't hit that many notes with your hands.'
> [Thelonious Monk. Quoted in 'Round About Monk', *Jazz People*, Valerie Wilmer; 1970]

monkery /múngkəri/ *n* (*disapproving*) **1.** the way of life led by monks in a monastery **2.** monks as a group

monkey /múngki/ *n* (*plural* **-keys**) **1.** NONHUMAN PRIMATE a medium-sized primate belonging to a group including baboons, marmosets, capuchins, macaques, guenons, and tamarins, but excluding apes, lemurs, and tarsiers. Native to: tropical regions. **2.** MISCHIEVOUS CHILD somebody, usually a child, who behaves badly, annoyingly, or high-spiritedly (*informal*) ○ *Did you hear what that cheeky monkey said?* **3.** CONSTR PILE-DRIVER RAM the ram of a pile-driver **4.** GAMBLING £500 the sum of £500, especially in betting (*slang*) ■ *vt* (**-keys, -keying, -keyed**) MIMIC SOMEBODY OR SOMETHING to copy or imitate somebody or something (*archaic*) [Mid-16C. Origin ?] ◇ **have a monkey on your back** *N Am* to have an addiction to drugs (*slang*) ◇ **I'll be a monkey's uncle** used to express surprise (*dated informal*) ◇ **make a monkey (out) of somebody** to make somebody look foolish (*informal*) ◇ **not give a monkey's (about somebody or something)** not to care at all about somebody or something (*informal*)

monkey around, **monkey about** *vi* to behave in a silly, casual, or careless way

monkey with *vt* to touch or move something casually or carelessly

monkey bars *npl* ANZ, *N Am* a structure, usually freestanding, consisting of metal or wooden poles and bars that children can climb on to play. UK term **climbing frame**

monkey bread *n* **1.** the gourd-shaped fruit of the baobab tree, whose pulp is eaten by monkeys **2.** *also* **monkey bread tree** TREES same as **baobab**

monkey business *n* (*informal*) **1.** silly or mischievous behaviour **2.** illegal, dishonest, or dubious activity

monkey flower *n* ANZ, *US* PLANTS same as **mimulus** [Because spots on the flowers form a pattern reminiscent of a monkey's face]

monkey in the middle *n N Am* LEISURE same as **piggy in the middle** (sense 1)

monkey jacket *n* a tight-fitting waist-length jacket, especially one worn by a sailor or as part of a military dress uniform [Because like the kind worn by an organ grinder's monkey]

monkey nut *n* a peanut while still in its shell (*informal*)

monkey orange *n* **1.** a hard-shelled edible fruit produced by a southern African evergreen tree **2.** an evergreen tree that produces hard-shelled edible fruit. Native to: southern Africa. Genus: *Strychnos*.

monkey orchid *n* a wild orchid that grows in grass and has an almost spherical flower head. Flowers: white with pink streaks, opening from the top to the bottom of the flower stem. Native to: Europe. Latin name: *Orchis simia*. [Because the shape of the lip of the flower is reminiscent of a monkey]

monkeypot /múngki pot/ *n* **1.** a large bulbous woody seed pod of a tropical tree **2.** a tree that produces monkey pots. Native to: tropical America. Genus: *Lecythis*.

monkey puzzle, **monkey puzzle tree** *n* a coniferous evergreen tree with spreading branches, sharp stiff leaves, and edible seeds. Native to: Chile. Latin name: *Araucaria araucana*. [Probably because of its long intertwining limbs and leaves]

monkeyshines /múnki shīnz/ *npl N Am* same as **monkey tricks** (*slang*)

monkey suit *n* (*dated informal*) **1.** a suit worn by a man as part of formal evening wear **2.** a uniform, especially a military one

monkey's wedding *n S Africa* an occasion on which sunshine and a light shower occur simultaneously (*informal*) [< The monkey and the moon are getting married, suggesting the union of two very different things]

monkey tricks *npl* silly or mischievous behaviour (*informal*) N Am term **monkeyshines**

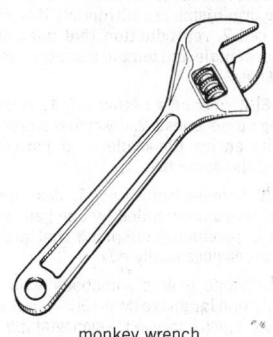

monkey wrench

monkey wrench *n* a spanner with a jaw that can be adjusted so that it can be used to turn nuts of different sizes

monkfish /múnk fish/ (*plural same* or **-fishes**) *n* **1.** a large bottom-dwelling anglerfish. Native to: Atlantic waters of Europe and Africa. Latin name: *Lophius piscatorius*. **2.** FISH same as **angel shark** [Early 17C. Origin ?]

Mon-Khmer *n* an Austro-Asiatic group of languages that includes Mon and Khmer, spoken in Southeast Asia —**Mon-Khmer** *adj*

monkish /múngkish/ *adj* **1.** relating to monks or their way of life **2.** characteristic of the life of a monk, especially in being reclusive, self-denying, or austere —**monkishly** *adv* —**monkishness** *n*

monk's cloth *n* a heavy cotton fabric with a basket weave. Use: curtains, bedcovers.

monk seal *n* a small dark brown subtropical seal that is now endangered. Native to: the waters of the Hawaiian Islands and the Mediterranean. Genus: *Monachus*.

monkshood /múngks hood/ (*plural same* or **-hoods**) *n* **1.** a poisonous perennial plant. Flowers: purplish. Native to: northern Europe. Latin name: *Aconitum napellus*. **2.** PHARM same as **aconite** (sense 1) [Late 16C. < the shape of its flowers]

Monmouth /mónməth/ market town in Monmouthshire, southeastern Wales. Population: 7,246 (1991).

Monmouthshire /mónməthshər/ county in southeastern Wales, known as Gwent from 1974 to 1996. The present-day administrative region occupies only part of the historic county of Monmouthshire. Population: 84,885 (2001). Area: 851 sq. km/329 sq. mi.

Monnet /món ay/, **Jean** (1888–1979) French diplomat and financier. He was the first deputy secretary of the League of Nations (1919–23) and founder of the Action Committee for a United States of Europe (1955).

mono[1] /mónnō/ *n* monophonic sound reproduction [Mid-20C. Shortening]

mono[2] /mónnō/ *n N Am* MED same as **glandular fever** (*informal*) [Mid-20C. Shortening]

mono- *prefix* **1.** one, single, alone ○ *monoculture* **2.** containing a single atom, radical, or group ○ *monoxide* **3.** monomolecular ○ *monolayer* [Via French and Latin < Greek *monos*]

monoacid /mónnō ássid/, **monacid** /mon ássid/ *n* an acid that has only one replaceable hydrogen atom ■ *adj* same as **monoacidic**

monoacidic /mónnō ə síddik/, **monacidic** /mónnə síddik/ *adj* describes a chemical base or alcohol that has only one hydroxyl group that can react with an acid

monoamine /mónnō áy meen/ *n* an amine compound that contains one amino group, especially the neurotransmitters adrenaline and serotonin

monoamine oxidase *n* an enzyme that breaks down monoamine neurotransmitters

monoamine oxidase inhibitor *n* a drug that blocks the breakdown of monoamines by monoamine oxidase in the brain. Use: antidepressant.

monoatomic *adj* CHEM same as **monatomic**

monobasic /mónnō báyssik/ *adj* describes an acid that has only one replaceable hydrogen atom in each molecule

monocarboxylic /mónnō kaar bok síllik/ *adj* describes an acid that has only one group. Formula: COOH.

monocarp /mónnō kaarp/ *n* a plant that flowers and bears fruit only once before dying [Mid-19C. < Back-formation MONOCARPIC]

monocarpellary /mónnō kaárpələri/ *adj* **1.** describes a flower that has only one carpel **2.** describes a plant gynoecium that consists of only one carpel

monocarpic /mónnō kaárpik/ *adj* describes a plant that flowers and bears fruit only once before dying [Mid-19C. < MONO- + Greek *karpos* 'fruit']

monocarpous /mónnō kaárpəss/ *adj* BOT **1.** same as **monocarpic 2.** same as **monocarpellary**

monocephalic /mónnō sə fállik/, **monocephalous** /mónnō séffələss/ *adj* describes a plant with a stalk that bears a single flower head, e.g. a tulip or dandelion

Monoceros /mə nóssərəss/ *n* a constellation near the celestial equator. See illustration at **constellation** [Late 18C. Via French < Greek *monokerōs* 'having one horn']

monochasium /mónnō káyziə m/ (*plural* **-sia** /-zi ə/) *n* a flower cluster in which each branch bears one other branch and ends in a single flower [Late 19C. < MONO- + Greek *khasis* 'separation'] —**monochasial** *adj*

monochlamydeous /mónnōklə míddi əss/ *adj* describes a flower that does not have a separate calyx and corolla [Mid-19C. < MONO- + Greek *khlamud-* 'cloak']

monochord /mónnə kawrd/ *n* an ancient acoustic device consisting of a single string stretched over an oblong sounding box, used to determine mathematical intervals between musical tones

monochromat /mónnō krō mat/, **monochromate** /-krō mayt/ *n* somebody who cannot perceive colours and sees only shades of grey [Early 20C. Back-formation < MONOCHROMATIC]

monochromatic /mónnōkrō máttik/ *adj* **1.** WITH ONLY ONE COLOUR having only one colour **2.** PHYS WITH ONLY ONE WAVELENGTH describes radiation that has only one wavelength, e.g. the light of a laser **3.** ART PAINTED IN ONE COLOUR painted or printed in a single colour **4.** MED RELATING TO TOTAL COLOUR BLINDNESS relating to or having total colour blindness (**monochromatism**) —**monochromatically** *adv* —**monochromaticity** /mónnōkrōmə tíssəti/ *n*

monochromatism /mónnō krōmətizəm/ *n* an eye condition in which the retina cannot distinguish any colours and a person sees only shades of grey

monochrome /mónnə krōm/ *adj* **1.** IN SHADES OF ONE COLOUR using or displaying only shades of one colour or black and white **2.** DULL dull, insipid, and lacking interest or distinctiveness **3.** ART CONSISTING OF ONE COLOUR painted or drawn in shades of a single colour

■ *n* 1. PHOTOGRAPHY **BLACK-AND-WHITE IMAGE** a black-and-white photograph or transparency 2. COLOURS **BLACK-AND-WHITE COLORATION** the condition of being only in black and white 3. ART **ARTWORK IN ONE COLOUR** a painting, drawing, or print in shades of a single colour 4. ART **ART TECHNIQUE USING ONE COLOUR** the art of painting, drawing, or printing in shades of a single colour 5. ART **CONDITION OF HAVING ONE COLOUR** the condition of being painted, drawn, or printed in shades of a single colour [Mid-17C. < medieval Latin *monochroma* < Greek *monokhrōmatos* 'of one colour' < *khrōma* 'colour'] —**monochromic** /mónnə krṓmik/ *adj* —**monochromist** *n*

monocle /mónnək'l/ *n* a lens for correcting the vision of one eye, held in position by the muscles around the eye socket [Mid-19C. Via French < late Latin *monoculus* 'single-eyed' < Greek *mono-* 'single' + Latin *oculus* 'eye']

monocline /mónnō klīn/ *n* a rock structure in which all the strata slope in one direction [Late 19C. < MONO- + Greek *klinein* 'to lean'] —**monoclinal** /mónnō klī́n'l/ *adj* —**monoclinally** *adv*

monoclinic /mónnō klínnik/ *adj* describes a crystal that has three unequal axes, with one pair not at right angles [Mid-19C. < MONO- + Greek *klinein* 'to lean']

monoclinous /mónnō klī́nəss/ *adj* describes a flower that has both pistils and stamens [Early 19C. < French *monocline* or modern Latin *monoclinus* 'in a single bed' < Greek *klinē* 'bed']

monoclonal /mónnō klṓn'l/ *adj* describes cells or products of cells that are formed or derived from a single clone

monoclonal antibody *n* an antibody with unique amino acid sequences derived from a single cell clone or cell line

monocoque /mónnō kok/ *n* 1. the metal outer shell of an aircraft, boat, or rocket that absorbs most of the stresses to which the craft is subjected 2. a design of motor vehicle in which the body and frame are integrated [Early 20C. < French, 'having a single shell' < *coque* 'shell']

monocot /mónnō kot/ *n* BOT same as **monocotyledon** (*informal*) [Late 19C. Shortening]

monocotyledon /mónnō kotə léed'n/ *n* a flowering plant that has a single leaf in the seed and floral parts in multiples of three. Monocotyledons include grasses and lilies. Class: Monocotyledones. —**monocotyledonous** *adj*

monocracy /mo nókrəssi/ (*plural* **-cies**) *n* a form of government in which one person alone rules —**monocrat** /mónnə krat/ *n* —**monocratic** /mónnə kráttik/ *adj*

monocular /mo nókyòolər/ *n* an optical device designed for use with one eye only, e.g. a field glass or a microscope ■ *adj* relating to, affecting, or having only one eye [Mid-17C. < late Latin *monoculus* (see MONOCLE)] —**monocularly** *adv*

monoculture /mónnō kulchər/ *n* the practice of growing a single crop in a field or larger area —**monocultural** /mónnō kúlchərəl/ *adj*

monocycle /mónnə sīk'l/ *n* VEHICLES same as **unicycle**

monocyclic /mónnō sī́klik/ *adj* 1. CHEM **WITH SINGLE-RING MOLECULAR STRUCTURE** describes a chemical compound that has a molecular structure in which there is only one ring 2. BOT **FORMING ONE WHORL** describes plant parts such as petals that form a single whorl 3. BOT **LIVING DURING ONE YEAR** describes a plant that completes its life cycle within a single year

monocyte /mónnō sīt/ *n* a large circulating white blood cell, formed in the bone marrow and in the spleen, that has a single well-defined nucleus and consumes large foreign particles and cell debris —**monocytic** /mónnō síttik/ *adj* —**monocytoid** /mónnō sī́ toyd/ *adj*

monocytosis /mónnō sī tṓssiss/ *n* an unusual increase in the numbers of monocytes

monodisperse /mónnō di spúrss/ *adj* describes a colloid that contains particles that are all of a uniform size

monodrama /mónnō draamə/ *n* a dramatic piece written for one actor —**monodramatic** /mónnōdrə máttik/ *adj*

monody /mónnədi/ (*plural* **-dies**) *n* 1. THEATRE **ODE SUNG BY ONE ACTOR** in Greek tragedy, an ode for one actor to sing alone 2. LITERAT **ELEGY** a poem that mourns somebody's death 3. MUSIC **MUSIC WITH SINGLE MELODIC LINE** a piece of music that has a single melodic line 4. MUSIC **17C ITALIAN VOCAL MUSIC** Italian vocal music of the 17th century for solo voice with instrumental accompaniment [Early 17C. < late Latin *monodia* < Greek *monōidos* 'singing alone' < *ōidē* 'song'] —**monodic** /mə nóddik/ *adj* —**monodically** *adv* —**monodist** *n*

monoecious /mo néeshəss/, **monecious, monoicous** /mo nóykəss/ *adj* describes a plant that has separate male and female flowers [Mid-18C. < modern Latin *Monoecia*] —**monoeciously** *adv*

monoestrous /mon éestrəss/ *adj* used to describe mammals that have only one oestrous cycle in a year or breeding season

monoethnic /mónnō éthnik/ *adj* relating to or belonging to the same ethnic group

monofilament /mónnə fílləmənt/ *n* an untwisted continuous single strand of natural or artificial fibre. Use: fishing lines.

monogamy /mə nóggəmi/ *n* 1. CULTL ANTHROP **MARRIAGE TO ONE PERSON** the practice of being married to only one person at a time 2. **PRACTICE OF HAVING ONE SEXUAL PARTNER** the practice of having a sexual relationship with only one partner during a period of time 3. ZOOL **PRACTICE OF HAVING ONE MATE** the practice of having only one mate at a time or during a lifetime [Early 17C. < French *monogamie* < Greek *monogamos* 'monogamous' < *gamos* 'marriage'] —**monogamist** *n* —**monogamous** *adj* —**monogamously** *adv*

monogenean /mónnə jeéni ən/ *n* a parasitic flatworm that spends its entire life cycle on the outside of the same fish. Order: Monogenea. [Mid-20C. < modern Latin *Monogenea* 'single generation' < Greek *genea* 'generation']

monogenesis /mónnō jénnəssiss/ *n* 1. the theory that all living organisms are ultimately descended from a single cell 2. reproduction that does not involve the fusion of male and female gametes —**monogenous** /mə nójjənəss/ *adj*

monogenetic /mónnōjə néttik/ *adj* 1. relating to or involving monogenesis 2. describes a nematode that spends its entire life cycle as a parasite on the outside of the same fish

monogenic /mónnə jénnik/ *adj* 1. describes a characteristic that is controlled by one gene or one pair of genes 2. producing offspring that are all of the same sex —**monogenically** *adv*

monoglot /mónnō glot/ *n* somebody who is able to speak only one language [Mid-19C. < Greek *monoglōttos* 'one tongue' < *glōtta* 'tongue'] —**monoglot** *adj*

monoglyceride /mónnō glíssə rīd/ *n* a compound derived from glycerol in which one hydroxyl group has been esterified

monogram /mónnə gram/ *n* a design of one or more letters, usually the initials of a name, used to decorate or identify an object —**monogram** *vt* —**monogrammatic** /mónnəgrə máttik/ *adj* —**monogrammed** *adj*

monograph /mónnə graaf, -graf/ *n* a scholarly article, paper, or book on a single topic —**monographer** /mə nóggrəfər/ *n* —**monographic** /mónnə gráffik/ *adj* —**monographically** *adv*

monogyny /mə nójjəni/ *n* 1. the practice of having only one wife at a time 2. the practice of having a sexual relationship with only one woman during a period of time —**monogynist** *n* —**monogynous** *adj*

monohull /mónnō hul/ *n* a boat that has a single hull

monohybrid /mónnō hī́brid/ *n* a hybrid from parents that are different only with respect to a single gene pair

monohydrate /mónnō hī́ drayt/ *n* a salt that is combined with one molecule of water

monohydric /mónnə hī́drik/ *adj* describes an alcohol that contains one replaceable atom of hydrogen

monohydroxy /mónnō hī dróksi/ *adj* describes a compound that contains one hydroxyl group

monoicous *adj* BOT same as **monoecious**

monolatry /mə nóllətri/ *n* the practice of worshipping only one god without, however, denying the existence of other gods —**monolater** *n* —**monolatrous** *adj*

monolayer /mónnō layər/ *n* 1. a film or other coating of a compound that is one molecule thick 2. a cultured layer of cells that is one cell thick

monolingual /mónnō líng gwəl/ *adj* 1. able to speak only one language 2. written, spoken, or produced in only one language —**monolingualism** *n*

monolith /mónnə lith/ *n* 1. **PILLAR OF ROCK** a tall block of solid stone standing by itself, whether a natural rock feature or a stone column shaped and erected by somebody, e.g. as a monument 2. **SOMETHING LARGE AND IMMOVABLE** something massive and unchanging, especially a large and long-established organization that is slow to change, uniform in character, and difficult to deal with on a human level 3. CONSTR **LARGE BLOCK OF BUILDING MATERIAL** a large uniform block of a single building material such as concrete pieced together with others to form a building or other structure

monolithic /mónnə líthik/ *adj* 1. **IN FORM OF LARGE STONE BLOCK** consisting of or formed into a tall block of solid stone 2. **BUILT USING LARGE BLOCKS** constructed using massive stones or large seamless blocks of material 3. **LARGE AND UNCHANGING** massive, uniform in character, and slow to change —**monolithically** *adv*

monolithic technology *n* a technology in electronic manufacturing in which all circuit components such as resistors, capacitors, and diodes are mounted on a single uniform piece of material

monologue /mónnə log/ *n* 1. CINEMA **LONG SPEECH BY ONE ACTOR** a long passage in a play or film spoken by one actor 2. CINEMA **PLAY FOR ONE ACTOR** an entire play or film in which only one actor appears and speaks 3. **LONG UNINTERRUPTED SPEECH BY SOMEBODY** a long tedious uninterrupted speech during a conversation 4. ARTS **PERFORMANCE BY COMEDIAN** a set of jokes or humorous stories following one another without a break, told by a solo entertainer —**monologic** /mónnə lójjik/ *adj* —**monologist** /mónnə logist, mə nólləjist/ *n* —**monologize** /mə nóllə jīz/ *vti*

monomania /mónnō máyni ə/ *n* an obsessive interest in a single thing, or a preoccupation with a single idea or thought —**monomaniac** *n* —**monomaniacal** /mónnō mə nī́ əkl/ *adj* —**monomaniacally** *adv*

monomark /mónnə maark/ *n* an identifying set of numbers or letters marked on an individual item, especially by a retailer ■ *vt* (**-marks, -marking, -marked**) to put a monomark on something

monomer /mónnəmər/ *n* a relatively light, simple organic molecule that can join in long chains with other molecules to form a more complex molecule or polymer —**monomeric** /mónnə mérrik/ *adj*

monometallic /mónnō mə tállik/ *adj* 1. describes a currency or monetary system that uses one type of metal, especially gold or silver, as a monetary standard 2. made of one type of metal only

monometallism /mónnō métt'lizəm/ *n* the use of just one metal, especially gold or silver, as a basic monetary standard

monomial /mo nṓmi əl/ *n* 1. an expression in algebra consisting of a single term, e.g. 3y, as distinct from one that contains two or more terms, e.g. 3x + 5y 2. a scientific name that consists of one element only, as do the names of most families of plants and animals [Early 18C. < MONO- after *binomial*] —**monomial** *adj*

monomolecular /mónnō mə lékyòolər/ *adj* 1. relating to or involving single molecules 2. describes a surface film that has a thickness of only one molecule. Monomolecular layers of alcohols or acids are used to retard water evaporation. —**monomolecularly** *adv*

monomorphic /mónnō máwrfik/, **monomorphous** /-máwrfəss/ *adj* 1. describes an organism or species that exists in a single discrete form, as distinct from one that changes form, as a caterpillar does when it becomes a butterfly 2. exhibiting only a single crystalline form —**monomorphism** *n*

Monongahela /mə nóng gə heélə/ river in the east-central United States. It flows north through West Virginia and Pennsylvania. Length: 210 km/130 mi.

mononuclear /mónnō nyóokli ər/ *adj* 1. describes a cell that has a single nucleus 2. describes an organic compound with a molecular structure containing only one ring of atoms

mononucleosis /mónnō nyóokli ṓssiss/ *n* 1. a significant rise in the number of atypical lymphocytes in the blood 2. MED same as **glandular fever**

mononucleotide /mónnō nyóokli ə tīd/ *n* a nucleotide that contains a phosphate group, a sugar, and a nitrogenous base

monophagous /mo nóffəgəss/ *adj* feeding on a single type of plant or animal —**monophagy** /mo nóffəji, mə-/ *n*

monophonic /mónnō fónnik/ *adj* using only one channel to carry sound from the source to the loudspeaker —**monophonically** *adv*

monophthong /mónnəf thong, mónnəp-/ *n* a vowel sound that keeps the same quality for the whole syllable [Early 17C. < Greek *monophthoggos* < *phthoggos* 'sound'] —**monophthongal** /mónnəf thóng g'l, mónnəp-/ *adj*

monophyletic /mónnō fī léttik/ *adj* describes a group of plants or animals that are descended from a single stock or ancestral form —**monophyletically** *adv* —**monophyletism** /mónnō fīlətizem/ *n*

Monophysite /mo nóffi sīt/ *n* somebody who believes that Jesus Christ has a single inseparable nature that is both human and divine [Late 17C. Via ecclesiastical Latin *Monophysita* < ecclesiastical Greek *monophusitēs* < *phusis* 'nature' (see PHYSICS)] —**Monophysitic** /mónnō fi síttik, mə nóffə síttik/ *adj* —**Monophysitism** *n*

monoplane

monoplane /mónnō playn/ *n* an aeroplane that has just one pair of wings

monoplegia /mónnō plé·eji ə/ *n* the inability to move a single limb or a single group of muscles —**monoplegic** *adj*

monopod /mónnə pod/ *adj* used to describe a structure whose only support is one central pillar. Such designs are used in drilling rigs in the Arctic where the shifting ice could damage conventional supports. ■ *n* a single-legged adjustable support used to steady a camera

monopode /mónnə pōd/ *n* **1.** BOT same as **monopodium 2.** a person or animal with a single foot, especially a member of a mythical African race of one-legged people [Early 19C. Via Latin *monopodius* < Greek *monopodios* < *pod-* 'foot'] —**monopodially** /mónnə pōdi əli/ *adv*

monopodium /mónnə pōdi əm/ (*plural* **-dia** /-di ə/) *n* the main axis of some plants such as the pine tree that extends to the tip of the plant and produces lateral branches

monopole /mónnə pōl/ *n* **1.** PHYS SINGLE MAGNETIC POLE OR ELECTRIC CHARGE an electric charge or hypothetical magnetic pole isolated from its opposite charge or pole **2.** PHYS HYPOTHETICAL PARTICLE a theoretical elementary particle that has only one magnetic pole, instead of the two present in ordinary magnetic bodies **3.** MEDIA RADIO ANTENNA a radio antenna made of an electrically charged conducting rod with an electrical connection at one end

monopolise *vt* ECON another spelling of **monopolize**

monopolist /mə nóppə list/ *n* **1.** somebody who controls a monopoly **2.** somebody who supports policies that favour monopolies —**monopolistic** /mə nóppə lístik/ *adj* —**monopolistically** *adv*

monopolize /mə nóppə līz/ (**-lizes, -lizing, -lized**), **monopolise** (**-lises, -lising, -lised**) *vt* **1.** to demand or take all of something such as somebody's time, attention, or affections, in a selfish way **2.** to have complete control of an industry or service and prevent other companies or people from participating or competing in it —**monopolization** /mə nóppə līzáysh'n/ *n* —**monopolizer** *n*

monopoly /mə nóppəli/ (*plural* **-lies**) *n* **1.** CONTROL OF MARKET SUPPLY a situation in which one company controls an industry or is the only provider of a product or service **2.** PERSONAL AND EXCLUSIVE POSSESSION an exclusive right to have or do something ○ *He seems to think he has a monopoly on common sense.* **3.** COMM CORPORATION WITH EXCLUSIVE CONTROL a company with a commercial monopoly **4.** ECON COMMODITY CONTROLLED BY ONE COMPANY a product or service whose supply is controlled by only one company **5.** LAW EXCLUSIVE LEGAL RIGHT a legal right to the exclusive control of an industry or service, as granted by a government [Mid-16C. Via Latin < Greek *monopōlion* < *pōlein* 'sell']

Monopoly /mə nóppəli/ *tdmk* a trademark for a property trading board game

monopsony /mə nópsəni/ (*plural* **-nies**) *n* a situation in which a product or service is only bought and used by one customer [Mid-20C. < MONO- + Greek *opsōnein* 'purchase provisions'] —**monopsonist** *n* —**monopsonistic** /mə nópsə nístik/ *adj*

monopteros /mo nóptə ross/ (*plural* **-teroi** /-tə roy/), **monopteron** /mo nóptə ron/ (*plural* **-tera** /-tər ə/) *n* a circular classical temple surrounded by a single ring of columns [Late 17C. Via Latin < Greek, 'having one wing' < *pteron* 'wing'] —**monopteral** *adj*

monorail /mónnə ráyl/ *n* a passenger railway transport system in which the carriages straddle or are suspended from a single beam

monosaccharide /mónnō sákə rīd, -rid/ *n* a simple sugar such as glucose or fructose that cannot be broken down into simpler sugars

monosemy /mo nóssəmi, mónnō seemi/ *n* the linguistic feature or fact of having only one meaning [Mid-20C. < MONO-, after POLYSEMY]

monoski /mónnō skee/ *n* a broad single ski on which a skier stands with both feet —**monoskier** *n* —**monoskiing** *n*

monosodium glutamate

monosodium glutamate /mónnə sōdi əm-/ *n* a sodium salt of glutamic acid. Use: flavour enhancer.

monosome /mónnə sōm/ *n* **1.** a single isolated chromosome, especially an unpaired X-chromosome **2.** a single protein-manufacturing particle (**ribosome**) combined with messenger RNA —**monosomic** /mónnə sōmik/ *adj* —**monosomy** *n*

monospermous /mónnō spúrməss/ *adj* describes a plant that produces only one seed

monostylous /mónnō stíləss/ *adj* describes a flower that has only one connecting stem (**style**) between the stigmas and the ovary

monosyllabic /mónnō si lábbik/ *adj* **1.** saying very little, often in a way that gives an impression of unfriendliness or lack of intelligence **2.** consisting of one syllable only —**monosyllabically** *adv*

monosyllable /mónnō siləb'l/ *n* a word or sentence consisting of only one syllable, e.g. 'Yes' or 'Me'

monotheism /mónnə thee izəm/ *n* the belief that there is only one God, as found in Judaism, Christianity, and Islam —**monotheist** *n, adj* —**monotheistic** /mónnə thi ístik/ *adj* —**monotheistically** *adv*

monotint /mónnə tint/ *n* ART same as **monochrome** *n* (sense 3)

monotone /mónnə tōn/ *n* **1.** UNCHANGING TONE a sound, especially a speech sound, that does not rise or fall in pitch, but stays on the same tone all the time **2.** SERIES OF IDENTICAL SOUNDS a sequence of sounds, e.g. a piece of speech, singing, or music, that stays at exactly the same pitch throughout **3.** UNVARYING QUALITY a complete lack of variety in colour, expression, or style **4.** MUSIC SINGER WITH NO SENSE OF PITCH somebody who cannot produce or distinguish between sounds of varying pitches when singing ■ *adj* **1.** WITH UNVARYING QUALITY lacking variety in pitch, colour, or another quality **2.** *also* **monotonic** /mónnə tónnik/ MATHS ASCENDING OR DESCENDING IN SEQUENCE describes a function or a sequence of real numbers that steadily increases or decreases —**monotonicity** /mónnə to níssəti/ *n*

monotonous /mə nóttənəss/ *adj* **1.** uninteresting or boring as a result of being repetitive and unvaried **2.** uttered or performed in one unvaried tone —**monotonously** *adv*

monotony /mə nóttəni/ *n* **1.** boredom or dullness arising from the fact that nothing different ever happens **2.** repetitiousness or lack of variation in pitch or tone, especially in relation to music or speech

monotropy /mónnə trōpi/ *n* a form of allotropy in which one form of an element is stable at all temperatures and pressures

monotype /mónnə tīp/ *n* **1.** a plant or animal that is the only member of the taxonomic category to which it belongs **2.** an artwork created by pressing on paper laid on an inked metal plate or sheet of glass. Although similar prints can be made, each one will be unique. —**monotypic** /mónnə típpik/ *adj*

Monotype /mónnə tīp/ *tdmk* a trademark for a typesetting machine run from a keyboard that activates a unit that sets type by individual characters

monounsaturated /mónnō un sáchə raytid/ *adj* describes a fatty acid with only one carbon double bond

monovalent /mónnō váylənt/ *adj* **1.** describes a chemical element or isotope that has a valency of one **2.** containing only one type of antibody —**monovalence** *n* —**monovalency** *n*

monoxide /mo nók sīd/ *n* a chemical compound with molecules that consist of one atom of oxygen and one or more atoms of another element

monozygotic /mónnō zī góttik/ *adj* describes twins derived from a single fertilized egg (**zygote**), e.g. human identical twins

James Monroe

Monroe /mən rố/, **James** (1758–1831) 5th president of the United States (1817–25). He held numerous state and national offices in nearly 50 years of public service, and was a popular Democratic-Republican president. He formulated the Monroe Doctrine (1823). See table at **president**

'The American continents, by the free and independent condition which they have assumed and maintain, are henceforth not to be considered as subjects for future colonization by any European powers...In the wars of the European powers in matters relating to themselves we have never taken any part, nor does it comport with our policy to do so.'
[James Monroe, 'The Monroe Doctrine'; 2 December 1823]

Marilyn Monroe

Monroe, Marilyn (1926–62) US actor. She starred in films such as *Bus Stop* (1956), *Some Like It Hot* (1959), and *The Misfits* (1961). She was married to the baseball player Joe DiMaggio and later the playwright Arthur Miller. Born **Mortenson, Norma Jean**. See illustration on previous page

'Hollywood is a place where they'll pay you a thousand dollars for a kiss and fifty cents for your soul.'
[Marilyn Monroe. Quoted in 'Acting', *Marilyn Monroe*, Guus Luijters; 1990]

Monroe doctrine *n* the political principle, as stated by President James Monroe in 1823, that Europe should no longer involve itself in the American continent by exerting influence. The policy was part of the US recognition of the independence of several Latin American countries. [Mid-19C. After James MONROE]

Monrovia /mon róvi ə/ capital city and chief seaport of Liberia, situated in the west of the country. Population: 479,000 (1999).

mons /monz/ (*plural* **montes** /món teez/) *n* a fleshy body part that sticks out, especially the one formed by a pad of flesh at the juncture of the pubic bones [Mid-20C. Shortening of MONS PUBIS]

Mons /moNs/ historic city in southwestern Belgium, situated about 48 km/30 mi. southwest of Brussels. Population: 91,187 (1999).

Monseigneur /móN see nyúr, -say-/ (*plural* **Messeigneurs** /máy see nyúr, -say-/) *n* a title given to some dignitaries, especially bishops and princes, in France and French-speaking countries [Early 17C. < French < *mon* 'my' + *seigneur* 'lord' < Latin *senior* 'older']

Monsieur /mə syúr/ (*plural* **Messieurs** /may syúr/), **monsieur** (*plural* **messieurs**) *n* 1. a title for a man in France or a French-speaking country, if he has no other special title 2. a form of address used when speaking or referring to a French or French-speaking man whose name is not known [Early 16C. < French < *mon* 'my' + *sieur* 'lord' < Latin *senior* 'older']

Monsignor /mon séenyər, -nyawr/ (*plural* **-signors** or **-signori** /-see nyáwri/) *n* a title used when speaking or referring to some members of the Roman Catholic clergy, especially bishops or officials of the papal court [Late 16C. Via Italian < French *monseigneur* (see MONSEIGNEUR)] —**Monsignorial** /món see nyáwri əl/ *adj*

monsoon /mon sóon/ *n* 1. RAINY SEASON a period of heavy rainfall, especially during the summer over South and Southeast Asia 2. HEAVY RAIN a very heavy fall of rain (*informal*) 3. WINDS THAT REVERSE DIRECTION SEASONALLY a large-scale wind system that seasonally blows in opposite directions and determines the climate of large regions. The reversal of wind direction is caused by the greater annual temperature differences over large land masses than over the adjacent waters. [Late 16C. Via obsolete Dutch *monssoen* < Portuguese *monção* < Arabic *mawsim* 'season'] —**monsoonal** *adj*

mons pubis (*plural* **montes pubis**) *n* a prominence caused by the pad of fat that overlies the junction of the pubic bones in women and girls [Late 19C. < Latin, 'mount of the pubes']

monster /mónstər/ *n* 1. UGLY TERRIFYING BEING a large ugly terrifying animal or person found in mythology or created by the imagination, especially something fierce that kills people. Monsters often feature in folklore and fairy tales as evil beings resembling a mixture of different animals. 2. EVIL PERSON somebody whose perceived inhumanity or vicious behaviour terrifies and disgusts people 3. HUGE THING something extraordinarily or unusually large (*informal*, *often used before a noun*) 4. BIOL IMPROPERLY FORMED FOETUS a foetus that is markedly improperly formed, especially one that cannot live outside the uterus (*sometimes considered offensive*) 5. OFFENSIVE TERM an offensive term for a person, animal, or plant that is undesirably formed (*archaic*) ■ *vt* (*informal*) 1. CRITICIZE SOMEBODY to criticize or rebuke somebody harshly 2. HARASS SOMEBODY to harass or pester somebody (*often passive*) [13C. Via French *monstre* < Latin *monstrum* 'monster, divine omen' < *monere* 'warn, remind']

monstered /mónstərd/ *adj* extremely drunk (*informal*)

monstrance

monstrance /mónstrənss/ *n* a large gold or silver container in which the Host is placed and then shown to the congregation for adoration in a Roman Catholic Mass [13C. < medieval Latin *monstrantia* < Latin *monstrare* 'to show' < *monstrum* (see MONSTER)]

monstrosity /mon stróssəti/ (*plural* **-ties**) *n* 1. an object, animal, or person that is very unpleasant or frightening to look at, often because it is large and strangely shaped 2. frightening size, shape, and ugliness ○ *a figure of overwhelming monstrosity* [Mid-16C. < late Latin *monstrositas* < Latin *monstruosus* (see MONSTROUS)]

monstrous /mónstrəss/ *adj* 1. SHOCKING AND MORALLY UN-ACCEPTABLE wicked, cruel, or unpleasant to an extent that is morally unacceptable 2. EXTREMELY LARGE extremely large, often in a way that seems ugly and frightening 3. LIKE MONSTER resembling a monster of the type found in folklore and fairy tales [14C. Via French < Latin *monstruosus* < *monstrum* (see MONSTER)] —**monstrousness** *n* —**monstrously** *adv*

mons veneris /-vénnəriss/ (*plural* **montes veneris**) *n* ANAT same as **mons pubis** [Early 17C. < Latin, 'the mount of Venus']

montage /mon taázh/ *n* 1. ARTWORK CREATED FROM SMALL PIECES a picture or other work of art composed by assembling, overlaying, and overlapping many different materials or pieces collected from different sources, e.g. photographs, magazines, and other pictures 2. ARTS CREATION OF MONTAGE the technique of creating a montage 3. CINEMA SEQUENCE OF OVERLAPPING FILM CLIPS a film sequence consisting of a series of dissolves, superimpositions, or cuts used to condense time or to suggest memories or hallucinations 4. CINEMA FILM-MAKING STYLE a style of film-making that makes extensive use of cuts, camera movements, and changes of camera position, particularly to set up new meanings not conveyed by the filmed action itself [Early 20C. < French < *monter* 'to mount' (see MOUNT¹)]

Montagnais /mónta nyáy/ (*plural same*) *n* 1. a member of a Native North American people who live in parts of Quebec and Labrador 2. the Algonquian language of the Montagnais. Native speakers: 4,000. [Early 18C. < French < *montagne* 'mountain'] —**Montagnais** *adj*

Montagnard /mónta nyaárd, -nyaár/ (*plural same* or **-gnards**) *n* a member of a people who live in the border region between Vietnam, Laos, and Cambodia [Mid-19C. < French, 'mountaineer' < *montagne* 'mountain']

Montaigne /mon táyn, mon ténya/, **Michel Eyquem de** (1533–92) French essayist. He invented the essay form in his *Essais (Essays)* (1580, 1588), original pieces on the ideas and personalities of his time.

'To make judgments about great and lofty things, a soul of the same status is needed; otherwise we ascribe to them that vice which is our own.'
[Michel Eyquem de Montaigne, *Essais (Essays)*; 1580]

Montana /mon tánnə, -taánə/ state in the northwestern United States, bordered by Canada, North Dakota, South Dakota, Wyoming, and Idaho. Capital: Helena. Population: 909,453 (2002 estimate). Area: 380,847 sq. km/147,046 sq. mi. —**Montanan** *n*, *adj*

montane /mon tayn/ *adj* growing or living in mountainous regions [Mid-19C. < Latin *montanus* < *mont-* 'mountain']

montan wax /món tan-/ *n* a brittle white to dark brown wax extracted from lignite and substituted in polishes and candles for carnauba and beeswax [Early 20C. < Latin *montanus* (see MONTANE), because extracted from lignite, a mountain ore]

Montauk /món tawk/ (*plural same* or **-tauks**) *n* a member of a Native North American people who lived in the eastern part of Long Island, New York [Mid-19C. < local place name]

Mont Blanc /móN blaáN/ highest mountain in western Europe, in the western Alps on the border of France and Italy. Height: 4,807 m/15,771 ft.

Montcalm /mont kaám, moN kálm/, **Louis-Joseph de, Marquis de Montcalm** (1712–59) French soldier. He was commander of the French forces in North America during the Seven Years' War and he was mortally wounded fighting the British in the battle of the Plains of Abraham.

monte /mónti/ *n* 1. a game in which a player chooses between two cards and bets on being dealt a card of that same suit before being dealt a card of the other suit 2. *Aus* something that is sure to happen or sure to be had or achieved [Early 19C. Via Spanish < Latin *mont-* 'mountain'; from the heap of cards on the table]

Monte Carlo /mónti kaárlō/ tourist resort with a famous casino in Monaco, on the Mediterranean Sea. Population: 13,154 (1982).

Monte Corno /-káwrnō/ highest mountain in the Apennines, located in central Italy. Height: 2,912 m/9,554 ft.

Montego Bay /mon teégō-/ 1. inlet of the Caribbean Sea in northwestern Jamaica 2. city, seaport and tourist resort in Jamaica, located on the bay of the same name. Population: 83,446 (1991).

monteith /mon teéth/ *n* a silver or pewter basin with notches around the edge, made to hold punch or to cool punch glasses by resting their bases over the scalloped edge [Late 17C. Probably after a Scotsman *Monteith*, known for his capes with scalloped hems]

Montélimar /món tay li maár/ town in Drôme Department, central France, situated about 129 km/80 mi. south of Lyon. Population: 31,344 (1999).

Montenegro /mónta neégrō/ smaller constituent republic of Serbia and Montenegro, in southeastern Europe. Capital: Podgorica. Population: 677,177 (2003). Area: 13,812 sq. km/5,333 sq. mi. —**Montenegrin** *n*, *adj*

Monterey /mónta ráy/ city and port in western California, on Monterey Bay. Population: 29,649 (2002 estimate).

Monterey Jack *n* a semihard cheese that is mild when young and becomes stronger and drier as it ages [Mid-20C. After *Monterey* County, California]

Monterey pine *n* a widely planted pine tree. Native to: Monterey Peninsula of California. Use: timber. Latin name: *Pinus radiata*.

Monte Rosa /mónti rōzə/ massif in the Pennine Alps, on the Swiss-Italian border, south of Zermatt. Height: 4,634 m/15,203 ft.

Monterrey /mónta ráy/ industrial city in northeastern Mexico, capital of Nuevo León State. Population: 1,108,499 (2000).

Montes Alpes /món tayz ál páyz/ extensive range of mountains on the Moon arching around the northeast of Mare Imbrium. Height: 3,658 m/12,000 ft.

Montes Apenninus /-áppa nínəss/ extensive range of mountains on the Moon surrounding the southeastern edge of Mare Imbrium

Montes Jura /-jóora/ range of mountains on the Moon north of Mare Imbrium. Height: 4,500 m/15,000 ft.

Montesquieu /món təskyə, -təskyoo/, **Charles Louis de Secondat, Baron de la Brède et de** (1689–1755) French jurist and writer. His works, including his seminal comparative political study *L'Esprit des lois (The Spirit of Law)* (1748), contributed to the European Enlightenment and helped create the political climate that led to the French Revolution.

'Liberty is the right to do everything which the laws allow.'
[Charles Louis de Secondat Montesquieu, *L'Esprit des lois (The Spirit of Law)*; 1748]

Maria Montessori

Monument Valley

Montessori /móntə sáwri/, **Maria** (1870–1952) Italian physician and educationalist. She devised a system for educating young children.

'The task of the educator of young children lies in seeing that the child does not confound good with immobility, and evil with activity.'
[Attributed to Maria Montessori]

Montessori method *n* a system of educating young children devised by Maria Montessori that aims to develop the child's natural interests and activities and does not use formal teaching methods

Monteverdi /mónti váirdi/, **Claudio** (1567–1643) Italian composer. His secular and sacred choral works and his operas mark the transition from Renaissance to baroque music. Full name **Monteverdi, Claudio Giovanni Antonio**

Montevideo /móntivi dáy ō/ capital city of Uruguay, located on the Atlantic Ocean in the south of the country. Population: 1,378,707 (1996).

Montez /mon téz/, **Lola, Baroness Rosenthal and Countess of Lansfield** (1818–61) Irish dancer. She enjoyed an international career and in 1847 became the mistress of Louis I of Bavaria, who ennobled her. Pseudonym of **Gilbert, Marie Dolores Eliza Rosanna**

Montezuma II /mónti zoomə/ (1480?–1520) Aztec emperor. His empire was brought down by Spanish invaders (1520).

Montezuma's revenge *n* an offensive term for diarrhoea and sickness experienced when visiting another country, originally Mexico, and eating unfamiliar food (*informal*) [Mid-20C. After MONTEZUMA II]

Montfort /móntfərt/, **Simon de, Earl of Leicester** (1200?–65) English aristocrat and soldier. Having captured Henry III in 1264, he set up a short-lived parliamentary-style assembly.

Montgolfier /mont gólfi ər, moN gólfyay/, **Joseph Michel** (1740–1810) and his brother **Jacques Etienne** (1745–99) French industrialists and inventors. Their development of the hot-air balloon led to the first balloon flight with human passengers, launched from Paris (1783).

Montgomery /mənt gómməri/ **1.** market and former county town in Powys, Wales. Population: 1,035 (1981). **2.** capital city of Alabama, in the centre of the state. It is a port on the Alabama River. Population: 201,425 (2002 estimate).

Montgomery, Bernard Law, 1st Viscount Montgomery of Alamein (1887–1976) British military commander. In World War II, he commanded the Eighth Army in North Africa, defeating Erwin Rommel, and became chief of the land forces in the Normandy invasion. After the war, he was deputy supreme commander of NATO forces (1951–58).

Montgomeryshire /mənt gómmərishər/ former county in central Wales, now part of Powys

month /munth/ *n* **1.** MAJOR DIVISION OF YEAR a major named division of the year in various calendar systems, e.g. in the Gregorian calendar there are 12 months, varying in length from 28 to 31 days **2.** FOUR WEEKS OR 30 DAYS a period of time equivalent to about four weeks or 30 days **3.** INTERVAL BETWEEN DATES IN CONSECUTIVE MONTHS a time lasting from a date in one calendar month until the same date in the next calendar month **4.** ASTRON same as **solar month 5.** ASTRON same as **lunar month 6.** ASTRON same as **sidereal month ■ months** *npl* LONG PERIOD OF TIME a long time, often an excessively or unacceptably long time [Old English *mōnap* < Indo-European, 'to measure'] ◇ **not** or **never in a**

month of Sundays used to emphasize that you think that something will never happen (*informal*)

monthly /múnthli/ *adj* **1.** HAPPENING EACH MONTH done, held, or arranged once every month ○ *a monthly meeting* **2.** PRODUCED EVERY MONTH published or issued once a month ○ *a monthly periodical* **3.** LASTING MONTH valid for one month ○ *a monthly pass ■ adv* ONCE EVERY MONTH at intervals of one month ■ *n* (*plural* **-lies**) **1.** PUBL MAGAZINE ISSUED EVERY MONTH a publication or periodical that is produced once a month **2.** WOMAN'S MENSTRUAL PERIOD a woman's monthly menstruation (*informal*; *usually used in the plural*)

monticule /mónti kyool/ *n* **1.** a subordinate volcanic cone **2.** a mound or small hill [Late 18C. Via French < late Latin *monticulus* < Latin *mont-* 'mountain']

Montmorency /móntmə rénssi/ river in southern Quebec, Canada. It flows south to join the St Lawrence River. Length: 97 km/60 mi.

Montmorency Falls highest waterfall in Quebec, Canada. They are located east of Quebec City where the Montmorency River empties into the St Lawrence River. Height: 84 m/275 ft.

montmorillonite /móntmə ríllə nīt, -reé ə nīt/ *n* a soft clay mineral. Source: bentonite clays. [Mid-19C. After *Montmorillon*, France] —**montmorillonitic** /móntmə ríllə níttik, -reé ə-/ *adj*

Montpelier /mont peélyər/ city and capital of Vermont, situated on the Winooski River in the north-central part of the state. Population: 8,026 (2002 estimate).

Montpellier /mont pélli ər, moN pə lyáy/ city in southern France, capital of the Hérault Department and administrative and commercial centre of the Languedoc-Roussillon Region. Population: 225,392 (1999).

Montreal /móntri áwl/ second largest city in Canada, situated on Montreal Island in the St Lawrence River, Quebec. Population: 1,039,534 (2001).

Montreux /mon trö/ major resort area in western Switzerland, on the northeastern shore of Lake Geneva. Population: 21,476 (1998).

Mont-Saint-Michel /móN saN mi shél/ steep granite hill off the Normandy coast in northern France. It becomes an island when the tides are high.

Montserrat /móntsə rát/ island in the eastern Caribbean Sea, a dependency of the United Kingdom. It was economically devastated by volcanic eruptions in 1997. Population: 12,771 (1996). Area: 102 sq. km/39 sq. mi.

monument /mónnyōomənt/ *n* **1.** LARGE STONE STATUE OR CARVING something designed and built as a lasting public tribute to a person, a group of people, or an event **2.** FAMOUS PLACE OR BUILDING a site or structure that is preserved because of its historical, cultural, or aesthetic importance **3.** CARVED HEADSTONE a tombstone, plaque, or ornamental stone structure placed on somebody's grave. A monument in a cemetery is usually inscribed with the name and dates of birth and death of the deceased person. **4.** WORTHY REMINDER OF SOMETHING something that remains as a reminder of something, especially something fine or distinguished **5.** MEMORIAL TRIBUTE a memorial to somebody in the form of a written or spoken tribute **6.** BOUNDARY MARKER an object that marks a boundary, e.g. a stone [13C. Via French < Latin *monumentum* < *monere* 'remind']

monumental /mónnyōo ment'l/ *adj* **1.** LARGE great in size, importance, or intensity **2.** DESERVING SPECIAL ADMIRATION so important or enduring that people cannot fail to notice or be impressed ○ *a monumental contribution to peace* **3.** MAKING CARVED HEADSTONES related to or involved in the making of tombstones and memorial items to go in cemeteries and churches **4.** OF MONUMENTS relating to monuments or taking the form of a monument —**monumentality** /mónnyōo men tálləti/ *n* —**monumentally** *adv*

Monument Valley /mónnyōomənt-/ region in northeastern Arizona and southeastern Utah, notable for its scenic rock formations

monuron /mónnyōo ron/ *n* a white crystalline odourless solid. Use: herbicide. [Mid-20C. Blend of MONO- + UREA]

Monza /mónzə, mōntsa/ city in northern Italy known for its motor racing course, situated about 13 km/8 mi. northeast of Milan. Population: 120,204 (2001).

monzonite /mónzə nīt/ *n* a visibly crystalline, granular igneous rock composed chiefly of equal amounts of two feldspar minerals, plagioclase and orthoclase, and small amounts of a variety of coloured minerals [Late 19C. After Mount *Monzoni* in the Tyrol] —**monzonitic** /mónzə níttik/ *adj*

moo /moo/ *vi* (**moos, mooing, mooed**) MAKE NOISE LIKE COW to produce the deep drawn-out sound that a cow makes ■ *n* (*plural* **moos**) **1.** NOISE THAT COW MAKES a deep drawn-out sound made by a cow, or by somebody imitating this sound **2.** OFFENSIVE TERM an offensive term that deliberately insults a woman's intelligence or abilities [Mid-16C. An imitation of the sound]

MOO /moo/ *n* a virtual online space in which several participants can meet at a given time to discuss a given topic. Full form **multi-user domain, object-oriented**

mooch /mooch/ (**mooches, mooching, mooched**) *v* **1.** *vti* GET SOMETHING FOR NOTHING to get something for nothing from somebody by asking directly for it, without making any personal effort for it (*informal*) ○ *He's always mooching off friends.* **2.** *vi* WANDER AIMLESSLY to wander or linger in an aimless way (*informal*) ○ *just mooching around* **3.** *vi US* SNEAK AROUND SUSPICIOUSLY to move around or wait somewhere quietly and secretly, trying not to be noticed (*slang*) [15C. < Old French *muchier* 'to hide'] —**moocher** *n*

mood[1] /mood/ *n* **1.** STATE OF MIND somebody's state of mind ○ *a good mood* **2.** GENERAL FEELING OF GROUP the way a group of people think and feel about something ○ *The mood of the country after the war was generally optimistic.* **3.** BAD TEMPER a feeling or display of sullen anger or irritability, especially one that begins suddenly or lasts a relatively short time ○ *He's in a mood.* [Old English *mōd* 'mind, courage' < Germanic] ◇ **in the mood** in the right or best state of mind for a particular activity or experience

mood[2] /mood/ *n* **1.** a group of verb forms expressing a particular attitude. English has the indicative mood, expressing factual statements, the imperative mood, expressing commands, and the subjunctive mood, expressing possibilities and wishes. **2.** LOGIC same as **mode** (sense 7) [Mid-16C. Alteration of MODE]

mood music *n* **1.** background music intended to induce a particular mood or atmosphere **2.** unofficial statements, hints, and rumours, emanating from especially political sources, that indicate the direction that policy or action is likely to take (*informal*)

mood swing *n* a sudden and extreme change in somebody's mood

moody /móodi/ (**-ier, -iest**) *adj* **1.** UNPREDICTABLY GRUMPY OR GLOOMY tending to change mood unpredictably from cheerful to bad-tempered **2.** CHANGEABLE unusually changeable or difficult to predict **3.** DISPLAYING MOOD displaying emotions, especially unhappiness or anger, clearly and intensely —**moodily** *adv* —**moodiness** *n*

Moody /móodi/, **Dwight L.** (1837–99) US evangelist. He founded Northfield Seminary girls' school (1879) and Mount Hermon School for boys (1881). Full name **Moody, Dwight Lyman**

moola /móolə, moó laa/, **moolah** *n N Am* same as **money** (*informal*) [Mid-20C. Origin ?]

mooli /móoli/ (*plural* **-lis** or **same**) *n UK* a large long white radish that can be eaten raw, cooked, or pickled, and is used especially in Japanese, Chinese, and other Asian cuisines. ANZ, N Am term **daikon** [Mid-20C. < Hindi *mūlī*]

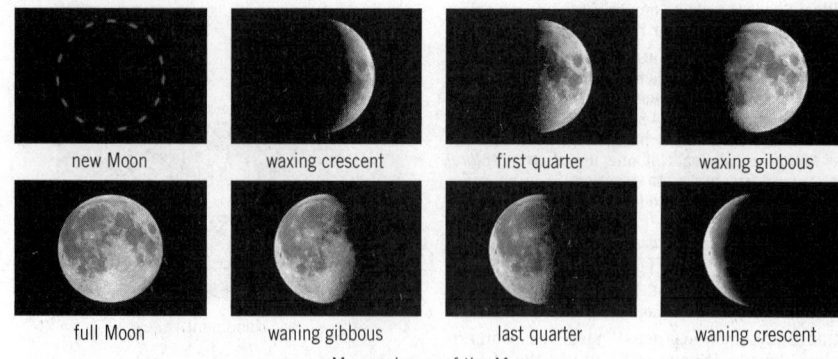

new Moon waxing crescent first quarter waxing gibbous

full Moon waning gibbous last quarter waning crescent

Moon: phases of the Moon

moon /moon/ *n* **1.** ASTRON another spelling of **Moon 2.** MOON'S SHAPE AS SEEN FROM EARTH a form or view of the Moon (**phase**) at a point in the lunar cycle. Since it shines only by reflected sunlight, the phases of the Moon depend on its position in relation to the Earth and the Sun. **3.** MOONLIGHT the light given out by the Moon **4.** SYMBOLIC REPRESENTATION OF MOON a simple or stylized representation of the Moon, usually in the form of a circle or crescent **5.** ASTRON NATURAL SATELLITE OF PLANET a natural satellite revolving around a planet. Mars, Jupiter, Saturn, Uranus, and Neptune each have more than one moon. **6.** PERIOD OF TIME a month, either as a rough estimate of time or as the time it takes for the Moon to complete its cycle around Earth (*archaic or literary*) ▪ *v* (**moons, mooning, mooned**) **1.** *vi* WANDER AIMLESSLY to wander around in a dreamy or listless state, unable to concentrate on anything **2.** *vi* YEARN FOR LOVED ONE to be stricken with longing for an absent loved one, and rendered dreamy or listless as a result (*literary or humorous*) **3.** *vti* EXPOSE BUTTOCKS TO SOMEBODY to bend over and deliberately expose the bare buttocks to somebody, either as a rude joke or as an act of defiance and disrespect (*informal*) [Old English *mōna* < Germanic] —**moonless** *adj*

Moon *n* Earth's only natural satellite. It is the astronomical body nearest to Earth, except for some artificial satellites and occasional meteors

Moon /moon/, **William** (1818–94) British inventor. In 1845 he developed a system of embossed line type, based on Roman letters, designed to be read by visually impaired people.

moonbeam /moon beem/ *n* a pale, milky, or iridescent beam of light reflected to the Earth by the Moon at night

moon blindness *n* periodic episodes of impaired vision in horses that often lead to permanent loss of sight

mooncalf /moon kaaf/ (*plural* **-calves** /-kaavz/) *n* somebody regarded as unintelligent or thoughtless (*archaic insult*)

moon dog *n* ASTRON same as **paraselene**

mooneye /moon ī/ *n* a silvery freshwater fish resembling a herring with very large eyes. Native to: North America. Latin name: *Hiodon tergisus*.

moon-faced *adj* having a large round face

moonflower /moon flowər/ *n* a plant whose flowers open at night, especially a climbing plant related to the morning glories

Moonie /mooni/ *n* a member of the Unification Church (*informal; often considered offensive*) [Late 20C. After Sun Myung **Moon**, the church's founder]

moonlight /moon līt/ *n* the pale cool light that shines from the Moon on a clear night, often considered eerie or romantic. Moonlight is light from the Sun reflected from the Moon's surface. ▪ *vi* (**-lights, -lighting, -lighted**) to have a second job in addition to a main job, often one done at night and kept secret for purposes of tax evasion (*informal*) —**moonlighting** *n*

CULTURAL NOTE *Moonlight Sonata*, a piano sonata (1801) by the German composer Ludwig van Beethoven. This nickname for Beethoven's sombre piano sonata in C# minor, op. 27 no. 2, was coined by the poet Heinrich Renstab. In his review of the composition, he described how the first movement brought to his mind the image of moonlight on Lake Lucerne.

moonlight flit *n* an act of secretly abandoning a rented house during the night, in order to avoid paying rent that is owed (*informal*)

moonlit /moon lit/ *adj* brightened or illuminated by light from the Moon

Moonlite /moon līt/, **Captain** (1842?–80) Irish-born Australian bushranger. A former religious minister turned thief, he was captured by police and hanged. Born **Scott, Andrew George**

moon pool *n* an open shaft in a deep-sea drilling vessel, usually located in the centre of the hull, through which the drilling takes place

moonraker /moon raykər/ *n* a small sail sometimes set above the skysail on a square-rigged ship [Early 19C. Probably < its great height]

moonrise /moon rīz/ *n* **1.** the time of day when the Moon rises over the horizon **2.** the rising of the Moon in the sky over the horizon

moonscape /moon skayp/ *n* **1.** the general appearance of the surface of the Moon as seen or portrayed **2.** a view or place that looks as rough, grey, and bleak as the surface of the Moon

moonset /moon set/ *n* **1.** the time of day when the Moon disappears below the horizon **2.** the disappearance of the Moon below the horizon [Mid-19C. < MOON after *sunset*]

moonshee *n* S Asia another spelling of **munshi**

moon shell *n* a carnivorous sea mollusc with a smooth rounded shell. Native to: mainly tropical waters. Family: Naticidae.

moonshine /moon shīn/ *n* **1.** whisky or other strong spirits produced and sold illegally **2.** talk, opinions, or ideas dismissed as senseless (*informal*) **3.** same as **moonlight** —**moonshiner** *n*

moonshot /moon shot/ *n* the launch of a crewed or uncrewed spacecraft to orbit or land on the Moon

moonstone /moon stōn/ *n* a lustrous bluish-white semiprecious stone that is a translucent variety of feldspar. Use: gems.

CULTURAL NOTE *The Moonstone*, a novel (1868) by Wilkie Collins. The first British detective novel, it involves the disappearance of a priceless Indian diamond and a subsequent puzzling murder. All the classic elements of the genre are present, including red herrings, alibis, and sufficient clues for the reader to solve the crime ahead of its hero, Sergeant Cuff of Scotland Yard.

moonstruck /moon struk/ *adj* **1.** acting in a rather irrational, dreamy, confused way, often out of love (*informal humorous*) **2.** behaving in a wild or confused way (*dated literary*)

moonwalk /moon wawk/ *n* **1.** INSTANCE OF WALKING ON MOON an exploratory walk or expedition across part of the Moon's surface, carried out by an astronaut. The first person to walk on the Moon was Neil Armstrong on 20 July 1969. **2.** GLIDING DANCE MOVEMENT a dance done using gliding walking movements of the feet and legs ▪ *vi* (**-walks, -walking, -walked**) **1.** GO ON FOOT ACROSS MOON'S SURFACE to walk away from a spacecraft for some distance across the surface of the Moon **2.** DANCE PERFORM GLIDING DANCE to perform a dance with gliding walking movements of the feet and legs —**moonwalker** *n*

moony /mooni/ (**-ier, -iest**) *adj* **1.** in a distracted or dreamy state, with little energy or concentration (*informal*) **2.** relating to or resembling the Moon —**moonily** *adv* —**mooniness** *n*

moor[1] /moor, mawr/ *n* a large uncultivated treeless stretch of land covered with bracken, heather, coarse grasses, or moss (*often used in the plural*) [Old English *mōr* < Germanic]

moor[2] /moor, mawr/ (**moors, mooring, moored**) *vti* to secure a boat, ship, or aircraft to one place with cables, chains, ropes, or an anchor, or be secured in this way [15C. Probably < Middle Low German *mōren*]

Moor /moor, mawr/ *n* a member of a nomadic people of Arab and Berber descent whose civilization flourished in North Africa between the 8th and the 15th centuries. They also settled in Spain during this period. [14C. Via Old French *More* < Latin *Maurus* < Greek *Mauros*]

moorage /moórij, máwrij/ *n* **1.** NAUT, AVIAT same as **mooring** (sense 1) **2.** the fee charged for mooring somewhere

Moore /moor, mawr/, **Bobby** (1941–93) British footballer. A skilled defensive player, he captained England to victory in the 1966 World Cup. Full name **Moore, Robert Frederick**

Moore, Dudley (1935–2002) British actor, comedian, and pianist. After working in partnership with comedian Peter Cook, he appeared in Hollywood film comedies.

Moore, G.E. (1873–1958) British philosopher. Author of *Principia Ethica* (1903), he is noted for his contribution to ethical theory and modern philosophical realism. Full name **Moore, George Edward**

'The assertion "I am morally bound to perform this action" is identical with the assertion, "This action will produce the greatest possible amount of good in the Universe".'
[G.E. Moore, *Principia Ethica*; 1903]

Moore, Gerald (1899–1987) British pianist. He was a leading accompanist of singers and instrumentalists.

Moore, Henry (1898–1986) British sculptor and printmaker. He is noted for his large-scale stylized representations of the human body, many made for outdoor locations.

'There is a right physical size for every idea.'
[Attributed to Henry Moore]

Moore, Mike (b. 1949) New Zealand prime minister (1990). A Labour Party politician, he held a number of cabinet posts from 1984 before taking over the premiership after Geoffrey Palmer's resignation. See table at **prime minister**. Full name **Moore, Michael Kenneth**

Moore, Patrick (b. 1923) British astronomer. He popularized astronomy with his regular television programme *The Sky at Night* and in books and lectures.

Mòoré /moó ə ray/, **Mooré, More** /máwri/ *n* LANG same as **Mossi** (sense 2) [< Mossi] —**Mòoré** *adj*

moorhen /moor hen, máwr-/ *n* a medium-sized water bird with black feathers and a red beak. Native to: marshy areas. Latin name: *Gallinula chloropus*.

Moorhouse /moor howss, máwr-/, **Frank** (b. 1938) Australian writer. His collections of short stories include *The Americans, Baby* (1972) and his novels include *Grand Days* (1993). Full name **Moorhouse, Frank Thomas**

mooring /moóring, máwr-/ *n* **1.** PLACE FOR SECURING BOAT OR AIRCRAFT a place where a boat, ship, or aircraft can be moored **2.** CABLE SECURING BOAT OR AIRCRAFT a cable, chain, or rope used to stop a boat, ship, or aircraft from drifting away **3.** PHYSICAL OR EMOTIONAL TIE something that gives a feeling of emotional or physical security, e.g. a family bond (*usually used in the plural*)

mooring tower *n* a permanent structure built as a place to moor airships. The structure provides facilities for transferring passengers, crew, and freight, for refuelling, and for replenishing ballast and lifting gas.

Moorish /moórish, máwr-/ *adj* **1.** relating to the Moors or their culture **2.** built or designed in an architectural style popular in Spain between the 8th and the 16th centuries, noted for its use of ornate curving decoration

Moorish idol *n* a tropical sea fish that has broad black and yellow stripes on its sides. Native to: Indo-Pacific reefs. Latin name: *Zanclus canescens*.

a at; aa father; aw all; ay day; ai hair; ə about, item, edible, common, circus; e egg; ee eel; hw when; i it, happy; ī ice; 'l apple; 'm rhythm; 'n fashion; o odd; ō open; oo good; oo pool; ow owl; oy oil; th thin; th this; u up; ur urge;

[Because its markings resemble those found in Moorish art]

moorland /moórlənd, máwr-/ *n* countryside, or a piece of countryside, consisting of a moor

moose /mooss/ (*plural same*) *n N Am* same as **elk** (sense 1) [Early 17C. < Abenaki *mos*]

SPELLCHECK moose, mouse, or **mousse**? Do not confuse ***moose*** and ***mousse***, which have a similar sound, or ***mousse*** and ***mouse***, which have a similar spelling. A ***moose*** is a large animal with long legs and large antlers, whereas a ***mouse*** is a small animal with short legs and a long tail (or a computer input device of similar shape). ***Mousse*** is a light rich food containing whipped cream and eggs (as in *chocolate mousse, salmon mousse*) or a foamy substance used in hairdressing.

moot /moot/ *adj* **1. ARGUABLE** open to argument or dispute ○ *Whether nutritional supplements are beneficial is a moot question.* **2. NOT RELEVANT** irrelevant or unimportant ○ *Her resignation was a moot issue, since she was going to have to leave her employment in any case.* **3.** LAW **NOT LEGALLY RELEVANT** legally insignificant because of having already been decided or settled ○ *Whether he was entitled to do business under that name was moot, because his company had ceased trading.* ■ *v* (**moots, mooting, mooted**) **1.** *vt* **SUGGEST TOPIC** to offer an idea for consideration or a topic for discussion (*usually passive*) **2.** *vi* LAW **HAVE FORMAL ARGUMENT** to take part in a debate, especially one organized as an academic exercise, e.g. a hypothetical case argued among law students ■ *n* **1.** LAW **DEBATE ON HYPOTHETICAL ISSUE** an academic discussion in which people such as law students argue hypothetically or plead a hypothetical legal case **2.** HIST **ANGLO-SAXON LOCAL COURT** in Anglo-Saxon England, a formal gathering for settling legal and administrative matters [Old English *mōt* 'assembly' < Germanic, 'meeting'] —**mootness** *n*

moot court *n* a court in which imaginary legal cases are conducted and tried by law students as part of their training

mop /mop/ *n* **1. TOOL FOR WASHING FLOORS** a long-handled tool for washing floors, with a washing head consisting of a large sponge or a thick mass of absorbent threads or fabric strips **2. TOOL FOR WASHING DISHES** a short-handled tool for washing dishes with a head consisting of a mass of twisted cotton threads **3. UNTIDY MASS** a thick or scruffy-looking tangle ○ *a mop of hair* ■ *vt* (**mops, mopping, mopped**) **1. WASH SOMETHING WITH MOP** to use a mop to wipe a floor surface clean, usually using warm soapy water **2. WIPE BODY TO REMOVE PERSPIRATION** to wipe perspiration from a part of the body [15C. Origin ?]

mop up *v* **1.** *vti* **GET RID OF LIQUID WITH CLOTH** to wipe or rub a piece of material over a liquid to soak it up **2.** *vt* MIL **DEAL WITH REMAINING ENEMY FORCES** to capture or kill remaining enemy troops in order to secure an area after a victory **3.** *vt* **CLEAR UP FINAL DETAILS** to complete or carry out the final details of a task (*informal*)

MOP *n* somebody who has assets such as shares that are nominally worth a million pounds or dollars but that may never be realizable in cash. Full form **millionaire on paper**

mopboard /móp bawrd/ *n US* CONSTR same as **skirting board**

mope /mōp/ *vi* (**mopes, moping, moped**) **1. BE MISERABLE** to be full of self-pity or sulky unhappiness and lose interest in everything else **2. WANDER ABOUT SADLY** to move in a listless or aimless way, especially one that is self-consciously sad or unhappy ■ *n* **MISERABLE PERSON** somebody who tends to mope and who depresses others (*informal*) ■ **mopes** *npl* **GLOOMY MOOD** a bout of melancholy or sulkiness (*informal*) [Mid-16C. Probably < N Germanic] —**moper** *n* —**mopy** *adj*

moped /mṓ ped/ *n* a lightweight pedalled motorcycle with an engine of less than 50 cc [Mid-20C. Blend of MOTOR + PEDAL [1]]

mopoke /mṓ pōk/ *n* BIRDS same as **boobook** [Early 19C. An imitation of its call]

MOPP *abbr* MIL Mission Oriented Protective Posture

moppet /móppit/ *n* (*informal*) **1.** a small child **2.** used as an affectionate form of address to a child [Early 17C. < obsolete *mop* 'baby, doll', origin ?]

moquette /mo két, mō-/ *n* thick velvety fabric. Use: carpeting, upholstery. [Mid-19C. < French]

MOR *abbr* MUSIC middle-of-the-road (*used especially in radio programming*)

mor. *abbr* INDUST morocco

Mor. *abbr* **1.** Moroccan **2.** Morocco

moraine /mə ráyn/ *n* a mass of earth and rock debris carried by an advancing glacier and left at its front and side edges as it retreats [Late 18C. Via French < French dialect *morena* 'mound'] —**morainal** *adj* —**morainic** *adj*

moral /mórrəl/ *adj* **1. INVOLVING RIGHT AND WRONG** relating to issues of right and wrong and to how individual people should behave **2. DERIVED FROM PERSONAL CONSCIENCE** based on what somebody's conscience suggests is right or wrong, rather than on what rules or the law says should be done **3. ACCORDING TO COMMON STANDARD OF JUSTICE** regarded in terms of what is known to be right or just, as opposed to what is officially or outwardly declared to be right or just ○ *a moral victory.* **4. ENCOURAGING GOODNESS AND DECENCY** giving guidance on how to behave decently and honourably **5. GOOD BY ACCEPTED STANDARDS** good or right, when judged by the standards of the average person or society at large **6. ABLE TO TELL RIGHT FROM WRONG** able to distinguish right from wrong and to make decisions based on that knowledge **7. BASED ON PERSONAL CONVICTION** based on an inner conviction, in the absence of physical proof ○ *moral certainty* ■ *n* **1. VALUABLE LESSON IN BEHAVIOUR** a conclusion about how to behave or proceed drawn from a story or event **2. FINAL SENTENCE OF STORY GIVING ADVICE** a short precise rule, usually written in a rather literary style as the conclusion to a story, used to help people remember the best or most sensible way to behave ■ **morals** *npl* **STANDARDS OF BEHAVIOUR** principles of right and wrong as they govern standards of general or sexual behaviour [14C. < Latin *moralis* < *mor-*, stem of *mos* 'custom', in plural 'morals'] —**morally** *adv*

SPELLCHECK Do not confuse the spelling of ***moral*** and ***morale*** ('level of confidence'). ***Moral*** is most often encountered as an adjective meaning 'based on or involving what is right or wrong', or 'generally accepted to be good or right': *moral standards; moral education.* It is also used as a noun meaning 'a valuable lesson', and in the plural 'principles of right and wrong': *the moral of the story; upholding society's morals.* ***Morale*** is stressed on the second rather than the first element and is used only as a noun meaning 'level of enthusiasm among a group': *Morale was high as the team set off.*

morale /mə raál/ *n* the general level of confidence or optimism felt by a person or group of people, especially as it affects discipline and motivation [Mid-18C. Via French *moral* < Latin *moralis* (see MORAL)]

SPELLCHECK See ***moral***.

moral fibre *n* courage and resilience in the face of pressure or disapproval from other people

moral hazard *n* the tendency of people who are insured against a specific hazard to cease to exercise caution to avoid the hazard

moral imperative *n* a thing that must be done because it is right, regardless of opposition or difficulty

moralise *vti* another spelling of **moralize**

moralism /mórrəlizəm/ *n* **1. PIECE OF MORAL ADVICE** a conventional moral maxim or saying **2. MORAL BEHAVIOUR** behaviour conforming to a system of moral standards that do not depend on religion **3. MORALIZING** criticism of other people's moral standards (*formal*)

moralist /mórrəlist/ *n* **1. SOMEBODY WITH HIGH MORAL STANDARDS** a follower of a strict moral code **2. CRITIC OF MORAL STANDARDS** somebody who seeks to regulate the moral standards and behaviour of others **3. SPECIALIST WHO STUDIES MORALITY** a student or teacher of morals as an academic discipline —**moralistic** /mórrə lístik/ *adj* —**moralistically** *adv*

morality /mə rálləti/ (*plural* **-ties**) *n* **1. ACCEPTED MORAL STANDARDS** standards of conduct that are generally accepted as right or proper **2. HOW RIGHT OR WRONG SOMETHING IS** the rightness or wrongness of something as judged by accepted moral standards **3. VIRTUOUS BEHAVIOUR** conduct that is in accord with accepted moral standards **4. MORAL LESSON** a lesson in moral behaviour

morality play *n* a play intended to teach a moral lesson, especially a medieval play written in verse in which the characters embody human virtues and vices such as Mercy and Lust

moralize /mórrə līz/ (**-izes, -izing, -ized**), **moralise** (**-ises, -ising, -ised**) *v* **1.** *vi* **CRITICIZE MORALS OF OTHERS** to criticize other people's conduct or standards of behaviour, or give advice on how general moral standards should be improved **2.** *vt* **ANALYSE SOMETHING IN TERMS OF MORALITY** to consider and explain something in terms of its moral significance **3.** *vt* **MAKE SOMETHING MORE MORAL** to change something to make it conform, or conform better, with society's ideas of what is good, right, or decent —**moralization** /mórrə lī záysh'n/ *n* —**moralizer** *n* —**moralizingly** *adv*

moral majority *n* the bulk of the population, who are thought to hold conservative religious beliefs and to approve of strict and traditional standards of sexual propriety (*takes a singular or plural verb*)

moral philosophy *n* PHILOSOPHY same as **ethics**

moral support *n* personal support and encouragement intended to bolster somebody's courage or determination

moral theology *n* the academic study of moral and ethical questions from a Christian viewpoint

Morant /mə ránt/, **Breaker** (1864?–1902) British-born Australian soldier and poet. He was court-martialled and executed by the British army in South Africa, an act which aroused protest and indignation in Australia. Full name **Morant, Harry Harbord**. Born **Murrant, Edwin Henry**

morass /mə ráss/ *n* **1.** a frustrating, confusing, or unmanageable situation that impedes or prevents progress **2.** an area of low-lying ground that is soft and wet to a great depth and therefore difficult to walk on [Mid-17C. Via Dutch *moeras* < French *marais*]

moratorium /mórrə táwri əm/ (*plural* **-riums** or **-ria** /-ri ə/) *n* **1.** a formally agreed period during which an activity is halted or a planned activity is postponed **2.** a period during which a person, usually a debtor, has the right to postpone meeting an obligation [Late 19C. < modern Latin < late Latin *moratorius* 'delaying' (see MORATORY)]

moratory /mórrətəri/ *adj* giving somebody the right to delay making payments on a debt [Late 19C. < late Latin *moratorius* 'delaying' < Latin *morat-*, past participle of *morari* 'to delay' < *mora* 'delay']

Morava /mə raávə/ river in the east-central Federal Republic of Yugoslavia. Length: 351 km/218 mi.

Moravia /mə ráyvi ə/ historic region of the eastern Czech Republic

Moravian /mə ráyvi ən/ *n* **1.** PEOPLES **SOMEBODY FROM MORAVIA** somebody who comes from Moravia **2.** CHR **MORAVIAN CHURCH MEMBER** a member of the Moravian Church **3.** LANG **DIALECT OF CZECH** the dialect of the Czech language spoken in Moravia —**Moravian** *adj*

Moravian Church *n* a Protestant church founded in Moravia in 1722 whose members place a strong emphasis on evangelism, ecumenism, and the authority of the Bible

moray /mórr ay, mo ráy/ *n* a brightly coloured sharp-toothed voracious eel that has no pectoral fins. Native to: rocky crevices or reefs of tropical coastal waters. Family: Muraenidae. [Early 17C. Via Portuguese *moréia* < Latin *murena* < Greek *muros* 'sea eel']

Moray /múrri/ council area in northeastern Scotland. The administrative centre is Elgin.

Moray Firth arm of the North Sea, on the north-eastern coast of Scotland

morbid /máwrbid/ *adj* **1. INTERESTED IN GRUESOME SUBJECTS** showing a strong interest in unpleasant or gloomy subjects such as death, murder, or accidents **2. GRISLY** inspiring disgust or horror **3.** MED **RELATING TO DISEASE** relating to or resulting in illness [Early 17C. < Latin *morbidus* 'diseased' < *morbus* 'sickness'] —**morbidly** *adv* —**morbidness** *n*

morbid anatomy *n* the study of diseased organs and tissues, especially as discerned by the naked eye in the course of postmortem examination

morbidity /mawr bíddəti/ *n* **1.** the presence of illness or disease **2.** the relative frequency of occurrence of a disease (*often used before a noun*)

morceau /máwr sō, mawr sṓ/ (*plural* **-ceaux** /*pronunc. same*/) *n* **1.** a short musical or literary composition **2.** a tiny piece, e.g. a small mouthful of food [Mid-18C. < French, later form of Old French *morsel* (see MORSEL)]

morcha /máwrchə/ *n S Asia* a demonstration or march organized to express a strongly held view on some issue [< Hindi *morcā*]

mordacious /mawr dáyshəss/ *adj* 1. deliberately bitter or critical, and intended to hurt somebody's feelings (*formal or literary*) 2. capable of biting, or tending to bite (*archaic or literary*) [Mid-17C. < Latin *mordac-* 'biting' < *mordere* 'to bite']

mordant /máwrd'nt/ *adj* 1. SARCASTIC sharply sarcastic or scathingly critical 2. CORROSIVE having a corrosive effect ■ *n* 1. INDUST SUBSTANCE THAT FIXES DYES a substance that fixes a dye in and on textiles or leather by combining with the dye to form a stable insoluble compound (**lake**) 2. ART ACID USED IN ETCHING a corrosive substance used to etch treated areas on a metal plate ■ *vt* (**-dants, -danting, -danted**) INDUST APPLY MORDANT TO SOMETHING to apply a mordant to fabric or leather in order to fix a dye [15C. < French, present participle of *mordre* 'to bite' < Latin *mordere*] —**mordancy** *n* —**mordantly** *adv*

mordent /máwrd'nt/ *n* a musical embellishment, similar to a short trill, in which either the note above or the note below the written note is played in addition to the principal note [Early 19C. Via German < Italian *mordente* < *mordere* 'to bite' < Latin]

Mordred *n* same as **Modred**

Mordvin /máwrdvin/ (*plural same* or **-vins**) *n* 1. a member of a Finnish people who live mainly in the middle of the Volga region of western Russia 2. the Finno-Ugric language of the Mordvin. Native speakers: 1 million. [Mid-18C. < Russian] —**Mordvin** *adj*

more /mawr/ CORE MEANING: a grammatical word, the comparative of 'much' and 'many', used to indicate a greater number of something, either a greater number than before, than average, or than something else ○ (det) *a need for more adult education programs* ○ (pron) *As regards benefits, this job offers me more.*
1. *adv* TO GREATER EXTENT to a greater extent, or in a larger number or amount (*forming the comparative of some adjectives and adverbs*) ○ (adv) *This problem is more complex than the other one.* ○ *is more beautiful* ○ *behaved more sensibly* 2. *adv* FOR LONGER TIME for a longer period of time ○ *chatted a bit more* 3. *adv, pron* WITH GREATER FREQUENCY OR INTENSITY used as the comparative of 'much' to mean 'with greater frequency or intensity' ○ (adv) *We are now going to the theatre more* ○ (adv) *It inspires me more now than ever.* ○ (pron) *The more you listen, the more you hear.*
4. *det, pron* ADDITIONAL indicates something additional or further (*pronoun + singular or plural verb*) ○ (det) *I need more light.* ○ (pron) *There aren't any more of these.* ○ (pron) *No more is expected.* [Old English *māra* < Germanic] ◇ (**all the**) **more** so to an even greater extent or degree ◇ **more or less** 1. approximately 2. essentially or basically ◇ **no** *or* **neither more nor less (than something)** simply, or exactly the same as something ◇ **the more** *Ireland* same as **although** (*nonstandard*) ◇ **what is more** used to introduce an additional or reinforcing point

More /mawr/, **Sir Thomas** (1478–1535) English politician and scholar. He resigned as Henry VIII's Lord Chancellor (1529–32) in protest against the king's break with the Roman Catholic Church, and was executed after refusing to recognize Henry as the head of the English Church. His literary works include *Utopia* (1516). He was canonized as St Thomas More in 1935.

> 'For men use, if they have an evil turn, to write it in marble; and whoso doth us a good turn we write it in dust.'
> [Sir Thomas, *Richard III and His Miserable End*; 1543]

Moreau /mo rṓ/, **Gustave** (1826–98) French painter. He is noted for his literary, mythological, and biblical scenes, which he depicted in a colourful symbolist style.

Morecambe /máwrkəm/ seaside resort on Morecambe Bay, Lancashire, northwestern England. Population: 46,657 (1991).

Moree /maw reé/ town in northern New South Wales, Australia, a major cotton-growing centre. Population: 16,242 (2002 estimate).

moreen /mo reén/ *n* a thick ribbed material made of wool, cotton, or a mixture of both. Use: curtains, upholstery. [Mid-17C. Origin ?]

moreish /máwrish/, **morish** *adj* so good to eat or drink that you keep wanting more of it (*informal*)

morel /mo rél/ *n* an edible mushroom with a brown pitted spongy cap. Genus: *Morchella*. [Late 17C. < French *morille*]

morello /mə réllṓ/ (*plural* **-los**) *n* a small sour cultivated cherry with dark red skin [Mid-17C. Origin ?]

morendo /mə réndṓ/ *adv* growing continuously softer and sometimes slower (*used as a musical direction*) [Early 19C. < Italian, 'dying', form of *morire* 'die'] —**morendo** *adj*

moreover /mawr ṓvər/ *adv* used to add a further piece of information that supports a previous statement

morepork *n* BIRDS same as **boobook**

mores /máwr ayz, -eez/ *npl* the customs and habitual practices that a group of people accept and follow, especially as they reflect moral standards, [Late 19C. < Latin, plural of *mos* 'manner, custom']

Moresque /maw résk/ *adj* ARCHIT same as **Moorish** (sense 2) [Early 17C. Via French < Italian *moresco* < *Moro* 'Moor' < Latin *Maurus* (see MOOR)]

Moreton Bay /máwrt'n-/ bay in southeastern Queensland, Australia, bordered in the east by two large islands, Moreton Island and North Stradbroke Island. Area: 800 sq. km/309 sq. mi.

Moreton Bay chestnut *n* TREES same as **black bean** (sense 4)

Moreton Bay fig *n* a large fig tree that has massive buttresses at the foot of its trunk and huge spreading roots. Native to: eastern Australia. Latin name: *Ficus macrophylla*.

Moreton Island island in Moreton Bay, off the coast of Queensland, Australia. Population: 455 (1996). Area: 170 sq. km/66 sq. mi.

MorF *abbr* ONLINE male or female (*used in e-mails or text messages*)

~~morgage~~ incorrect spelling of **mortgage**

morgan /máwrgən/ *n* a unit of chromosome length [Early 20C. After Thomas Hunt MORGAN]

Morgan /máwrgən/ *n* a black, bay, brown, or chestnut horse with a full mane and tail, short deep body, and slender legs, belonging to a US breed popular for hunting, jumping, and recreation [Mid-19C. After Justin *Morgan* (1747–98), owner of the stallion from which the breed descends]

Morgan /máwrgən/, **Sir Henry** (1635?–88) Welsh buccaneer. He carried out attacks on Spanish settlements and vessels from a base in Jamaica. He later became lieutenant governor of Jamaica.

Morgan, John Pierpont (1837–1913) US financier. He was the founder of J. P. Morgan and Company (1895), and a noted art collector and philanthropist.

> 'A man always has two reasons for doing anything—a good reason and the real reason.'
> [John Pierpont Morgan. Quoted in *Roosevelt: The Story of a Friendship*, Owen Wister; 1930]

Morgan, Rhodri (*b.* 1939) First Secretary of the Welsh Assembly (2000–). He was the head of the European Commission for Wales (1980–87) and Labour MP for Cardiff West (1987–2001).

Morgan, Thomas Hunt (1866–1945) US geneticist and biologist. He discovered that chromosomes are the carriers of genetic information. He received the Nobel Prize in physiology or medicine (1933).

morganatic /máwrgə náttik/ *adj* describes a marriage in which neither the spouse of lower social rank nor any children of the marriage may inherit the title or possessions of the higher-ranking spouse [Late 16C. Directly or via French or German < medieval Latin (*matrimonium ad*) *morganaticam* ('marriage for the) morning-gift' (the bridegroom's gift to the bride, which relieved him of further responsibility)] —**morganatically** *adv*

morganite /máwrgə nīt/ *n* a pink variety of beryl. Use: gems. [Early 20C. After John Pierpont MORGAN]

Morgan le Fay /máwrgən lə fáy/ *n* in Arthurian legend, an evil sorceress who was the half-sister and enemy of King Arthur

morgen /máwrgən/ *n* a unit of measurement for land area formerly used in various parts of the world and still in use in South Africa [Early 17C. < Dutch and German, 'area that can be ploughed in a morning']

morgue /mawrg/ *n* 1. PLACE FOR DEAD BODIES a room or building in which dead bodies are kept until a postmortem has been carried out or until they are buried or cremated 2. DISMAL PLACE a gloomy place that lacks warmth or cheer (*informal*) 3. MEDIA COLLECTION OF INFORMATION a room or file in a newspaper office containing miscellaneous pieces of information kept for future reference, e.g. for writing obituaries [Mid-19C. < French *Morgue*, building in Paris]

CULTURAL NOTE *The Murders in the Rue Morgue*, a novel (1841) by US writer Edgar Allan Poe. Regarded as the world's first detective story, it begins with the brutal murder of an old woman and her daughter, a crime that perplexes the police since the women's apartment is sealed from the inside. Amateur sleuth C. Auguste Dupin comes to their aid, providing an explanation based on a brilliant analysis of scattered clues.

MORI /máwri, mórri/, **Mori** *abbr* Market and Opinion Research Institute

moribund /mórri bund/ *adj* 1. OBSOLESCENT in the process of becoming obsolete 2. STAGNANT having lost all sense of purpose or vitality 3. DYING nearly dead [Early 18C. < Latin *moribundus* < *mori* 'die'] —**moribundity** /mórri búndəti/ *n* —**moribundly** *adv*

Moriori /mórri áwri/ (*plural same* or **-is**) *n* 1. a member of an extinct indigenous people who lived in New Zealand 2. the extinct Austronesian language of the Moriori [Mid-19C. < Polynesian] —**Moriori** *adj*

Morisco /mə rískṓ/ (*plural* **-cos** or **-coes**), **Moresco** /mə réskṓ/ *n* 1. in medieval Spain, a Muslim who was forcibly converted to Christianity and often continued the secret practice of Islam, or a descendant of such a person 2. a morris dance, or a morris dancer [Mid-16C. < Spanish < *Moro* 'Moor'] —**Morisco** *adj*

morish *adj* FOOD another spelling of **moreish** (*informal*)

Berthe Morisot: portrait by Marcellin Desboutin

AKG London

Morisot /mórri sṓ/, **Berthe** (1841–95) French painter. Her paintings, in a subtle and delicate impressionistic style, often depict landscapes or women and children.

> 'The truth is that our value lies in feeling, in intention, in our vision that is subtler than that of men, and we can accomplish a great deal provided that affectation, pedantry, and sentimentalism do not come to spoil everything.'
> [Attributed to Berthe Morisot]

Morley /máwrli/, **Thomas** (1557–1603) English composer. Noted for his madrigals, lute songs, and instrumental music, he helped to establish the madrigal in England as a distinctive musical form.

Mormon /máwrmən/ *n* CHR same as **Latter-Day Saint** (*sometimes considered offensive*) ■ *adj* relating to the Church of Jesus Christ of Latter-Day Saints [Mid-19C. After the prophet said to be the author of the *Book of Mormon*, a sacred history of the Americas] —**Mormonism** *n*

morn /mawrn/ *n* same as **morning** (*literary*) [Old English *morgen* < Germanic] ◇ **the morn** *Scotland* same as **tomorrow**

mornay /máwr nay/ *adj* served in a white sauce containing grated cheese ○ *cod mornay* [Early 20C. Probably after Philip de *Mornay* (d. 1623), French writer]

morning /máwrning/ *n* 1. EARLY PART OF DAY the early part of the day, from dawn until noon or lunchtime 2. MIDNIGHT TO MIDDAY the part of the day between midnight and midday 3. DAWN dawn or daybreak 4. EARLY PART the beginning of something ■ *interj* same as **good morning** (*informal*) [13C. < MORN + -*ing*, after EVENING]

morning-after pill *n* a contraceptive pill designed to be taken after sexual intercourse

morning coat *n* a man's jacket, usually black, cut away at the front below the waist and with a long divided tail, worn on formal occasions as part of morning dress

morning dress *n* a man's suit worn to formal daytime events such as weddings, consisting of a black morning coat, striped black trousers, usually a waistcoat, and sometimes a top hat

morning glory *n* a climbing plant of the bindweed family. Flowers: trumpet-shaped, blue, purple, pink, or white, closing in the evening. Native to: tropical regions. Genus: *Ipomoea*.

morning line *n* a list of entrants and their odds for a race, estimated by a bookmaker and posted before betting begins

Morning Prayer *n* the morning service of worship in the Anglican Church

morning roll *n Scotland* a plain bread roll made from white flour

mornings /máwrningz/ *adv* during the morning, or every morning (*informal*)

morning sickness *n* nausea and vomiting experienced by many pregnant women, usually in the morning and during the early months of pregnancy

Morningside /máwrning sīd/ *n Scotland* an anglicized accent of Scottish English, often considered affected [Late 19C. After a district of Edinburgh]

morning star *n* a planet, especially Venus, seen in the eastern sky around dawn

morning tea *n ANZ* a mid-morning snack or drink

Mornington Island /máwrnington-/ island in the Gulf of Carpentaria, Australia. It is the largest of the Wellesley islands. Population: 1,114 (1996). Area: 1,002 sq. km/387 sq. mi.

Mornington Peninsula peninsula in southern Victoria, Australia, near the city of Melbourne

morning watch *n* the period of watch between four o'clock and eight o'clock in the morning

Moro /máwrō/, **Aldo** (1916–78) Italian prime minister (1963–64, 1964–66, 1966–68, 1974–76, and 1976). A Christian Democrat, he held a number of ministerial posts before he became prime minister of a coalition government for the first time in 1963. In 1978 he was kidnapped and murdered by the Red Brigades.

morocco /mə rókō/, **morocco leather** *n* a soft leather made from goatskin, or a leather made in imitation of it from sheepskin or calfskin. Use: covering books, for shoes. [Mid-17C. After MOROCCO]

Morocco

Morocco /mə rókō/ country in northwestern Africa. Language: Arabic. Currency: dirham. Capital: Rabat. Population: 31,689,265 (2003). Area: 453,730 sq. km/175,186 sq. mi. Official name **Kingdom of Morocco** —**Moroccan** *n, adj*

morocco leather *n* INDUST same as **morocco**

moron /máwr on/ *n* **1.** an offensive term that deliberately insults somebody's intelligence (*insult*) **2.** a former term for somebody with significant learning difficulties and impaired social skills, now considered offensive (*dated offensive*) [Early 20C. < Greek *mōron* 'unintelligent, thoughtless'] —**moronic** /mə rónnik/ *adj* —**moronically** *adv* —**moronism** *n* —**moronity** /mə rónnəti/ *n*

Moroni /mə róni/ capital of Comoros, on Grande Comore Island. Population: 49,000 (2001).

morose /mə róss/ *adj* having a withdrawn gloomy personality [Mid-16C. < Latin *morosus* 'peevish' < *mos*

'manner, disposition'] —**morosely** *adv* —**moroseness** *n* —**morosity** /mə róssəti/ *n*

Morpeth /máwrpəth/ market town in Northumberland, northeastern England. Population: 14,393 (1991).

morph[1] /mawrf/ *n* an element of speech or writing that represents and expresses one or more morphemes [Mid-20C. Shortening of MORPHEME]

morph[2] /mawrf/ *n* one of two or more variant forms of an animal or plant [Mid-20C. < Greek *morphē* 'form']

morph[3] /mawrf/ (**morphs, morphing, morphed**) *vti* **1.** to transform one electronic graphic image into another or others, through the use of sophisticated computer software, or be transformed in this way **2.** to cause something to change its outward appearance completely and instantaneously, or undergo this process [Late 20C. < METAMORPHOSIS]

morph. *abbr* BIOL, LING **1.** morphological **2.** morphology

-morph *suffix* something that has a particular form, shape, or structure ○ *mesomorph* [< Greek *morphē* 'form'] —**morphic** *suffix* —**morphism** *suffix* —**morphous** *suffix* —**morphy** *suffix*

morphactin /mawrf áktin/ *n* a substance affecting plant growth and development [Mid-20C. Probably < Greek *morphē* 'form' + ACTIVE]

morphallaxis /mawrfə láksiss/ *n* the process whereby an organism regenerates body parts by the reorganization and transformation of existing tissue, rather than by the formation of new tissue [Late 19C. < Greek *morphē* 'form' + *allaxis* 'exchange']

morpheme /máwr feem/ *n* the smallest meaningful element of speech or writing [Late 19C. < French < Greek *morphē* 'form', after PHONEME] —**morphemic** /mawr feémik/ *adj* —**morphemically** *adv*

morphemics /mawr feémiks/ *n* (*takes a singular verb*) **1.** the way in which morphemes combine to form words in a language **2.** the study and description of the ways in which morphemes combine in languages

Morpheus /máwr fi əss, -fyooss/ *n* in classical mythology, the god of dreams and sleep, mentioned by the Roman poet Ovid [14C. < Latin] —**Morphean** *adj*

morphia /máwrfi ə/ *n* same as **morphine** (*dated*) [Early 19C. < MORPHEUS]

morphine /máwr feen/ *n* an alkaloid drug that may become addictive with prolonged use. Source: opium. Use: relief of severe pain. [Early 19C. < French < *Morphée* 'Morpheus' < Latin *Morpheus*]

morphinism /máwrfinizəm/ *n* addiction to morphine and the related health problems of such addiction (*dated*) —**morphinist** *n*

morpho /máwrfō/ (*plural* **-phos**) *n* a large butterfly with iridescent blue wings. Native to: tropical America. Genus: *Morpho*. [Mid-19C. Via modern Latin < Greek *Morphō*, epithet of APHRODITE]

morpho- *prefix* form, shape, structure ○ *morphogenesis* [< Greek *morphē*]

morphogen /máwrfəjən, -jen/ *n* a substance that influences the differentiation and growth of embryonic cells

morphogenesis /máwrfō jénnəssiss/ *n* **1.** the origin and development of an organism or of a part of one, as it grows from embryo to adult **2.** the development of an organism or of some part of one, as it changes as a species —**morphogenetic** /máwrfōjə néttik/ *adj* —**morphogenetically** *adv* —**morphogenic** *adj*

morphol. *abbr* BIOL, LING **1.** morphological **2.** morphology

morphology /mawr fólləji/ (*plural* **-gies**) *n* **1.** BIOL STRUCTURE OF ORGANISM the form and structure of an organism or of a part of an organism **2.** BIOL STUDY OF STRUCTURE OF ORGANISMS the study of the form and structure of organisms **3.** LING STRUCTURE OF WORDS the structure of words in a language, including patterns of inflections and derivation **4.** LING STUDY OF WORD FORMATION the study of the structure of words in a language **5.** STRUCTURE OF SOMETHING'S PARTS the structure of anything made up of interconnected or interdependent parts **6.** STUDY OF STRUCTURE OF SOMETHING'S PARTS the study of the structure of anything made up of interconnected or inter-dependent parts —**morphologic** /máwrfə lójjik/ *adj* —

morphological *adj* —**morphologically** *adv* —**morphologist** *n*

morphometry /mawr fómmətri/ *n* the measurement of the outside of something —**morphometric** /máwrfə méttrik/ *adj* —**morphometrically** *adv*

morphosis /mawr fóssiss/ (*plural* **-phoses** /-fôs seez/) *n* a variation in the pattern of development (**morphogenesis**) of an organism as a result of changes in the external environment [Late 17C. < Greek *morphōsis* 'a shaping' < *morphē* 'form'] —**morphotic** /mawr fóttik/ *adj*

Morris /mórriss/, **William** (1834–96) British artist, poet, and social activist. His decorations and furnishings drew on medieval tradition and his love of craftsmanship, and laid the foundations for the Arts and Crafts movement and art nouveau. His poetry included classical translations, some published in fine editions by Kelmscott Press, which he founded in 1890.

> 'Art will make our streets as beautiful as the woods, as elevating as the mountainside: it will be a pleasure and a rest, and not a weight upon the spirits to come from the open country into a town. Every man's house will be fair and decent, soothing to his mind and helpful to his work.'
> [William Morris. Quoted in *The Arts and Crafts Movement*, Thomas Sanderson; 1905]

Morris chair *n* a light carved wooden armchair with removable cushions and a reclining back that can be set at varying angles [After William MORRIS]

morris dance *n UK, ANZ, Can* a lively English folk dance, traditionally performed by men who wear white costumes and use small bells, sticks, and handkerchiefs [15C. < Old French *morois* 'Moorish' < *More* 'Moor', because perhaps of Moorish origin] —**morris dancer** *n* —**morris dancing** *n*

Morrison /mórriss'n/, **Herbert Stanley, Baron Morrison of Lambeth** (1888–1965) British politician. He held various senior government posts, including that of deputy prime minister, in the first British Labour government after World War II (1945–51).

Morrison, James (*b.* 1962) Australian jazz musician. A performer on several instruments, he is known both for his solo and ensemble work.

Morrison, Jim (1943–71) US rock singer and songwriter. He was the lead singer of the Doors and attracted a cult following after his death. Full name **Morrison, James Douglas**

> 'When you make your peace with authority, you become an authority.'
> [Jim Morrison. Quoted in *In Their Own Words: The Doors*, Andrew Doe and John Tobler; 1988]

Toni Morrison

Morrison, Toni (*b.* 1931) US writer. Her novels deal with the experience of being an African American and include *Beloved* (1987), which won a Pulitzer Prize. She received the Nobel Prize in literature (1993). Born **Wofford, Chloe Anthony**. See Cultural note at **beloved**

> 'If you take a life, then you own it. You responsible for it. You can't get rid of nobody by killing them. They still there, and they yours now.'
> [Toni Morrison, *Song of Solomon*; 1977]

Morrison, Van (*b.* 1945) British singer and songwriter. Born in Northern Ireland, he is noted for a repertoire ranging from rhythm and blues to folk and jazz, and including elements of Celtic music. Born **Morrison, George Ivan**

'It's a marvellous night for a moondance / With the stars up above in the sky / A fantabulous night to make romance.'
[Van Morrison, 'Moondance'; 1970]

morro /mórrō/ (*plural* **-ros**) *n* a hill or headland with a rounded outline [< Spanish]

morrow /mórrō/ *n* (*literary*) **1.** NEXT DAY the day after today or after a particular day **2.** MORNING the early part of the day **3.** FOLLOWING PERIOD OF TIME the period of time following an event or occurrence [13C. < earlier form of MORN]

Mors /mawrz/ *n* in Roman mythology, the god of death. Greek equivalent **Thanatos** [< Latin, 'death']

Morse /mawrss/ *n* a system for representing letters and numbers by signs consisting of one or more short or long signals of sound or light that are printed out as dots and dashes [Mid-19C. After Samuel F. B. MORSE]

Morse, Helen (*b.* 1946) British-born Australian actor. She is a frequent stage performer, and her work also includes roles in films such as *Caddie* (1976).

Morse, Samuel F. B. (1791–1872) US inventor and artist. He invented the electric telegraph (1837) and Morse. Full name **Morse, Samuel Finley Breese**

Morse code *n* COMMUNICATION same as **Morse**

morsel /máwrss'l/ *n* **1.** SMALL PIECE OF FOOD a small piece of something, especially of food **2.** SMALL AMOUNT a small amount of something **3.** SOMEBODY OR SOMETHING PLEASING somebody or something that is particularly appealing or pleasing [13C. < Old French, 'little bite' < *mors* 'bite' < past participle of Latin *mordere* 'to bite']

Mort, Thomas (1816–78) British-born Australian merchant and shipbuilder. He was a pioneer of the use of refrigerated containers for shipping frozen meat. Full name **Mort, Thomas Sutcliffe**

mortadella /máwrtə déllə/ *n* a smoked, fried, or steamed Italian sausage consisting of pork and beef flavoured with wine, garlic, and pepper [Early 17C. < Italian < Latin *murtatum* '(sausage) seasoned with myrtle berries']

~~mortagage~~ incorrect spelling of **mortgage**

mortal /máwrt'l/ *adj* **1.** HUMAN relating to human beings **2.** EVENTUALLY DYING certain to die eventually **3.** FATAL causing death ○ *a mortal blow* **4.** CONTINUING UNTIL SOMEBODY DIES continuing, or intended to continue, until somebody dies ○ *mortal combat* **5.** OF DEATH relating to or accompanying death ○ *in mortal agony* **6.** EXTREMELY HATED being the object of somebody's unrelenting hatred ○ *his mortal enemy* **7.** INTENSE intensely felt ○ *mortal fear* **8.** CONCEIVABLE being within the bounds of what is imaginable or possible ○ *What mortal reason could there be for him to leave like that?* **9.** BORING tedious and dull (*slang*) ■ *adj*, *adv* USED FOR EMPHASIS used for emphasis, and sometimes indicating that the speaker is frustrated or annoyed (*dated*) ■ *n* **1.** HUMAN BEING a human being, who will eventually die **2.** PERSON a person (*informal*) [14C. Directly or via French < Latin *mortalis* < *mors* 'death']

SYNONYMS See *deadly*.

mortality /mawr tálləti/ *n* **1.** DEATH RATE the number of deaths that occur at a specific time, in a specific group, or from a specific cause **2.** MANY DEATHS great loss of life **3.** CERTAINTY TO DIE the condition of being certain to die eventually **4.** RATE OF FAILURE the rate of failure of something such as businesses or farms **5.** HUMAN BEINGS the human race

mortality rate *n* the number of deaths in a place or group compared with the total number of people in that place or group

mortality table *n* a table listing the life expectancy and death rate for people of various ages or occupations that is based on mortality statistics over a number of years

mortally /máwrt'li/ *adv* **1.** so badly that death follows **2.** in an extreme or intense way

mortal sin *n* in Roman Catholic theology, a sin considered to be so wicked that it causes a complete loss of grace and leads to damnation unless it is absolved

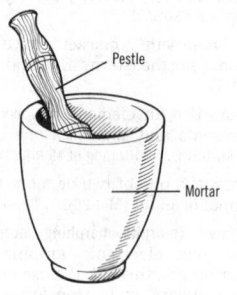

mortar (sense 4)

mortar /máwrtər/ *n* **1.** BONDING MATERIAL FOR BRICKS a mixture of sand, water, and cement or lime that becomes hard like stone. Use: in building to hold bricks and stones together. **2.** CANNON a cannon with a relatively short and wide barrel, used for firing shells at a high angle over a short distance **3.** GUN FIRING LIFELINE a gun for firing something other than a bullet, e.g. rope to somebody in need of rescue **4.** BOWL FOR GRINDING a hard heavy bowl designed to hold substances to be ground into small pieces or powder by means of a club-shaped tool (**pestle**) **5.** BOWL FOR CRUSHING ORE a cast-iron bowl in which ore is crushed ■ *vt* (**-tars, -taring, -tared**) **1.** FIRE MORTAR AT TARGET to fire at somebody or something with a mortar **2.** FIX MATERIALS WITH MORTAR to hold stones and bricks together with mortar [Pre-12C. Via French *mortier* 'bowl for mixing' < Latin *mortarium* 'bowl, substance prepared in it']

mortarboard

mortarboard /máwrtər bawrd/ *n* **1.** a hat often worn on formal academic occasions, consisting of a round cap with a hard square flat top and usually a tassel **2.** a square board with a handle in the centre of the underside, used by bricklayers for carrying mortar

mortgage /máwrgij/ *n* **1.** LOAN AGREEMENT SECURED BY PROPERTY an agreement by which somebody borrows money from a money-lending organization such as a bank or building society and gives that organization the right to take possession of property given as security if the loan is not repaid **2.** CONTRACT BETWEEN BORROWER AND LENDER a written contract describing the agreement between a borrower and a lending organization by which a loan is given against security **3.** TOTAL MONEY BORROWED the total amount of money lent to a borrower by a money-lending organization, with some of the borrower's property being given as security **4.** LOAN INSTALMENT TO BE REPAID the money paid by a borrower, usually monthly, to a lending organization until the entire sum borrowed by a mortgage agreement has been repaid ■ *vt* (**-gages, -gaging, -gaged**) **1.** GRANT CLAIM TO OWNERSHIP OF PROPERTY to give a claim to legal possession of property to a money-lending organization such as a bank or building society as security for a loan **2.** PUT SOMETHING AT RISK to pledge something when risk is involved (*informal*) [14C. < Old French < *mort* 'dead' + *gage* 'pledge', because property pledged as security may be lost] —**mortgageable** *adj*

mortgagee /máwrgi jee/ *n* an organization that lends money to a borrower by a mortgage agreement, e.g. a bank or building society

mortgager *n* FIN same as **mortgagor**

mortgage rate *n* the interest rate charged by organizations such as banks and building societies on mortgage loans

mortgagor /máwrgi jáwr, -jər/, **mortgager** /máwrgijər/ *n* a borrower of money under a mortgage agreement

mortice *n* CONSTR, PRINTING another spelling of **mortise**

mortician /mawr tish'n/ *n* N Am same as **undertaker** (sense 1) [Late 19C. < Latin *mort-* 'death']

mortification /máwrtifi káysh'n/ *n* **1.** SHAME deep shame and humiliation **2.** SOMETHING CAUSING MORTIFICATION something that causes a feeling of deep shame and humiliation **3.** RELIG SELF-IMPOSED HARDSHIP the use of self-imposed discipline, hardship, abstinence from pleasure, and especially self-inflicted pain in an attempt to control or put an end to desires and passions, especially for religious purposes **4.** MED DEATH AND DECAY OF LIVING TISSUE the death and decaying of a part of a living body, e.g. because the blood supply to it has been cut off [14C. Directly or via French < late Latin *mortificatio(n-)* 'destruction' < Latin *mortificat-* past participle of *mortificare* (see MORTIFY)]

mortify /máwrti fī/ (**-fies, -fying, -fied**) *v* **1.** *vt* SHAME SOMEBODY to make somebody feel deeply ashamed and humiliated **2.** *vt* RELIG IMPOSE HARDSHIP ON SELF to attempt to subdue the body or desires and passions by self-imposed discipline, hardship, abstinence from pleasure, and especially self-inflicted pain, usually for religious purposes **3.** *vi* MED DECAY to decay and die (*refers to living tissue*) [14C. Via Old French *mortifier* < Latin *mortificare* 'kill' < *mort-* 'death'] —**mortifier** *n* —**mortifying** *adj* —**mortifyingly** *adv*

Mortimer /máwrtimər/, **Roger de, 8th Baron of Wigmore, 1st Earl of March** (1287?–1330) English courtier. In 1327, following the deposition of Edward II, he became the virtual ruler of England. He was executed by Edward III.

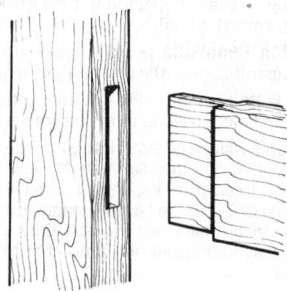

mortise

mortise /máwrtiss/, **mortice** *n* **1.** HOLE CUT TO HOLD OTHER PART a hole or slot cut into a piece of wood, stone, or other material, for a projecting part (**tenon**) to be inserted into it, in order to form a tight joint **2.** HOLE IN PRINTING PLATE a hole cut in a printing plate to receive type or another plate ■ *vt* (**-tises, -tising, -tised; -tices, -ticing, -ticed**) **1.** CUT MORTISE IN SOMETHING to cut a mortise in a piece of wood, stone, or other material **2.** JOIN PARTS USING MORTISE AND TENON to join two things or parts by means of a mortise and tenon **3.** CUT HOLE IN PRINTING PLATE to cut a hole in a printing plate to receive type or another plate [14C. < Old French, probably < Arabic *murtaj* 'locked'] —**mortiser** *n*

mortise lock *n* a lock inserted into a hole (**mortise**) cut into the side edge of a door so that when the door is closed the lock cannot be seen or removed

mortmain /máwrt mayn/ *n* the perpetual, nontransferable, and nonsaleable ownership of property by organizations such as churches [13C. Via Anglo-Norman, Old French < medieval Latin *mortua manus* 'dead hand']

Morton /máwrt'n/, **Jelly Roll** (1885–1941) US pianist and composer. He was a major figure in the development of jazz. Born **La Menthe, Ferdinand Joseph**

'It is evidently known, beyond contradiction, that New Orleans is the cradle of *jazz*, and I, myself, happened to be the creator in the year 1902...*Jazz* music is a style, not compositions; any kind of music may be played in *jazz*, if one has the knowledge.'
[Jelly Roll Morton, *Downbeat*; August 1938]

mortuary /máwrchoō əri/ *n* (*plural* **-ies**) a room or building in which dead bodies are kept until a postmortem has been carried out or until they are buried or cremated ■ *adj* relating to death or funerals [14C. Directly or via Anglo-Norman *mortuarie*

< Latin *mortuarius* < *mortuus* 'dead', past participle of *mori* 'die']

morula /máwryōōlə/ (*plural* **-las** or **-lae** /-lee/) *n* an early stage in the development of an animal embryo, consisting of a solid ball of cells derived by cleavage of the fertilized egg (**zygote**) [Mid-19C. < modern Latin, 'little mulberry' < *morum* 'mulberry'] —**morular** *adj* —**morulation** /máwryōō láysh'n/ *n*

Morwell /máwrwəl/ town in southeastern Victoria, Australia, a mining and dairy farming centre. Population: 15,423 (1991).

morwong /máwr wong/ (*plural* **-wongs** or *same*) *n* a large sea fish with a thick-lipped head, sharply tapering body, and extended dorsal fin. Native to: Australia, Asia. Family: Cheilodactylidae. [Late 19C. Probably < an Aboriginal language]

MOS *abbr* COMPUT metal oxide semiconductor

mos. *abbr* TIME months

mosaic: detail of mosaic floor at the Roman settlement of Verulamium, St Albans, England

mosaic /mō záy ik/ *n* **1.** PICTURE MADE WITH SMALL COLOURED PIECES a picture or design made with small pieces of coloured material such as glass or tile stuck onto a surface **2.** MAKING OF MOSAICS the art of making mosaics **3.** SOMETHING CONSISTING OF VARIETY OF COMPONENTS something consisting of a number of things of different types, forms, or colours **4.** MEDIA LIGHT-SENSITIVE SURFACE IN TV CAMERA a light-sensitive surface on a television camera tube, consisting of a thin sheet covered by particles that convert incoming light into an electric charge for scanning by an electron beam **5.** BOT VIRAL PLANT DISEASE a plant disease, often caused by a virus, in which the foliage develops irregular patches of discoloration **6.** BOT PLANT DISCOLORATION a pattern of light-green or yellowish mottling on the foliage of a plant, usually caused by a viral infection **7.** GENETICS same as **chimera** (sense 2) ■ *vt* (**-ics, -icking, -icked**) DECORATE SOMETHING WITH MOSAIC to make something into, or decorate something with, a mosaic [14C. < Old French < Latin *Musa* 'Muse'; from the decorations of medieval shrines dedicated to the Muses]

Mosaic /mō záy ik/, **Mosaical** /-ik'l/ *adj* relating to the biblical figure Moses [Mid-17C. Directly or via French < Latin *Mosaicus* < *Moses* 'Moses' < Hebrew *Mōšeh*]

mosaic disease *n* BOT same as **mosaic** *n* (sense 5)

mosaic gold *n* **1.** tin disulphide. Use: gilding. **2.** an alloy of copper and either zinc or tin that looks like gold. Use: to decorate such things as furniture and jewellery.

mosaicism /mō záy issizəm/ *n* the occurrence of genetically distinct cells within tissue or an individual organism

Mosaic Law *n* the code of law of the ancient Hebrews, beginning with the Ten Commandments, believed to have been set down by Moses and contained in the Pentateuch

mosasaur /mōssə sawr/, **mosasaurus** /-sáwrəss/ (*plural* **-sauri** /-sáw rī/) *n* an extinct lizard that lived in the sea and had a long slender body with limbs resembling paddles for steering, and a long flexible tail for propulsion. Family: Mosasauridae. [Mid-19C. < modern Latin *Mosaurus* < Latin *Mosa*, the River Meuse]

mosbolletjie /moss bólləki/ *n* S Africa a sweetish bun, eaten fresh or dried as a rusk, often flavoured with aniseed [Late 19C. < Afrikaans < *most* 'new wine' (because the yeast traditionally contains part-fermented grape juice) + *bolletjie* 'little ball']

moschatel /móskə tél/ (*plural* **-tels** or *same*) *n* a low-growing plant found in moist places. Flowers: small, yellowish-green, in cube-shaped clusters. Native to:

northern temperate regions. Latin name: *Adoxa moschatellina*. [Mid-18C. Via French < Italian *Moscatella* < *moscato* 'musk', from the scent of the flowers]

Moscow /móskō/ capital of Russia, located in the west-central European part of the country. It was also the capital of the former Soviet Union from 1922 to 1991. Population: 8,297,900 (1999).

Moseley /mōzli/, **Henry** (1887–1915) British physicist. Using X-ray diffraction, he showed that a chemical element's position in the periodic table is related to its nuclear electric charge. Full name **Moseley, Henry Gwyn-Jeffreys**

Moselle[1] /mō zél/ *n* a light typically dry white wine from west-central Germany [Late 17C. < MOSELLE[2]]

Moselle[2] /mō zél/ river in northeastern France and northwestern Germany. Length: 550 km/342 mi.

Moses /mōziz/ *n* in the Bible, a Hebrew prophet and the brother of Aaron who led the Israelites from slavery in Egypt to the Promised Land. He is believed to have written down the Ten Commandments (Exodus 20).

Moses /mōziz/, **Grandma** (1860–1961) US artist. She is known for her primitivist paintings of US rural life, which she began in her late seventies. Born **Moses, Anna Mary Robertson**

Moses basket *n* a portable wicker or straw cot for a baby [Because Moses was placed in such a basket (Exodus 2)]

mosey /mōzi/ (**-seys, -seying, -seyed**) *vi* to walk somewhere at a leisurely unhurried pace (*informal*) [Early 19C. Origin ?]

mosh /mosh/ (**moshes, moshing, moshed**) *vi* to dance to rock music in a frenzied way (*informal*) [Late 20C. Probably alteration of MASH]

moshav /mō shaáv/ (*plural* **-shavim** /-shaa veém/) *n* in Israel, a cooperative settlement consisting of independent small farms, or land farmed by the whole community with each family having its own house and garden [Mid-20C. < modern Hebrew *mōšāb* 'dwelling, colony']

mosh pit *n* an area in front of the stage at a rock concert where people dance wildly and energetically (*informal*)

Moslem /mózzləm, mōózzləm/ *n* (*plural* **-lems** or *same*), *adj* same as **Muslim** [Variant] —**Moslemic** /moz lémmik, mōōz-/ *adj* —**Moslemism** *n*

Mosley /mōzli/, **Sir Oswald** (1896–1980) British politician. He founded the British Union of Fascists in 1932. Full name **Mosley, Sir Oswald Ernald**

mosque: Delhi, India

mosque /mosk/ *n* a building in which Muslims worship [15C. Via French < Arabic *masjid* 'place of worship' < *sajada* 'bow down']

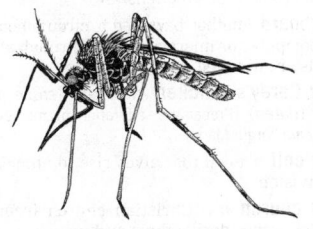

mosquito

mosquito /mə skeétō, mo-/ (*plural* **-toes** or **-tos**) *n* a small slender fly that feeds on the blood of mammals, including humans, and transmits diseases such as malaria, yellow fever, and dengue. Native to: tropics. Family: Culicidae. [Late 16C. < Spanish, 'little fly' < *mosca* 'fly' < Latin *musca*]

mosquito boat *n* NAVY same as **motor torpedo boat**

mosquito coil *n* a piece of coiled incense that is lit to repel mosquitoes

mosquito fern *n* a small fern that has branched stems with small leaves resembling scales and floats on freshwater ponds and lakes. Genus: *Azolla*.

mosquito net *n* a curtain of fine netting hung over a bed or across a window as a protection against mosquitoes

moss /moss/ *n* **1.** SIMPLE NONFLOWERING PLANT a simple nonflowering plant (**bryophyte**) that has short stems with small leaves arranged in spirals and resembling scales, and inhabits moist shady sites. Class: Musci. **2.** PLANT RESEMBLING MOSS a plant that resembles a true moss, e.g. a variety of seaweed known as irish moss **3.** MARSHY AREA in Scotland and northern England, an area of marshy ground or moorland, especially a peat bog (*often used in placenames*) [Old English *mos* 'swamp' < Germanic]

Moss /moss/, **Stirling** (*b.* 1929) British racing driver. He was winner of the British Grand Prix (1955, 1957) and the Mille Miglia (1955). An accident in 1962 ended his racing career. Full name **Moss, Stirling Crauford**

'One cannot really enjoy speed to the absolute limit if there's a destination involved.'
[Attributed to Stirling Moss]

Mossad /móssad/ *n* the intelligence service of Israel, established in 1951 (*takes a singular or plural verb*) [Mid-20C. < Hebrew *mosad* 'institution']

moss agate *n* a whitish agate containing dark-green patterns resembling moss

moss animal *n* MARINE BIOL same as **bryozoan**

mossback /móss bak/ *n* N Am **1.** (*plural* **mossbacks** or *same*) an old turtle, shellfish, or fish with algae growing on its back **2.** an offensive term for somebody regarded as old-fashioned or conservative (*insult*)

moss campion *n* a plant of the pink family that forms tufts of leaves resembling moss. Flowers: solitary, pink. Native to: cool alpine regions. Latin name: *Silene acaulis*.

moss green *adj* of a dull yellowish-green colour (*hyphenated when used before a noun*) —**moss green** *n*

mossgrown /móss grōn/ *adj* **1.** covered with moss **2.** old-fashioned or out of date

Mossi /móssi/ (*plural* same or **-sis**) *n* **1.** a member of a people living in West Africa, especially in Burkina Faso **2.** the Gur language of the Mossi people. Native speakers: 6 million. [Mid-19C. < an African name] —**Mossi** *adj*

mossie[1] *n* INSECTS another spelling of **mozzie**

mossie[2] /mózzi/ *n* S Africa BIRDS another word for **sparrow** [Late 19C. Via Afrikaans < Dutch *musje* 'little sparrow' < *mus* 'sparrow']

mosso /móssō/ *adv* in a quick and lively way (*used as a musical direction*) [Late 19C. < Italian, past participle of *muovere* 'to move']

moss pink, moss phlox *n* a garden plant of the pink family with spreading mats of tiny leaves. Flowers: lavender, pink, or white. Native to: eastern North America. Latin name: *Phlox subulata*.

moss rose *n* a rose with a mossy calyx and flower stalk. Flowers: fragrant, pink. Native to: Caucasia. Latin name: *Rosa centifolia* var. muscosa.

moss stitch *n* a basic knitting stitch consisting of alternating knit and purl stitches in one row, then alternating purl and knit stitches in the next row, producing a regular raised design

moss-trooper *n* in the 17th century, somebody involved in raiding, especially cattle-raiding, in the area around the Scottish-English border [< MOSS 'marshy area']

mossy /móssi/ (**-ier, -iest**) *adj* **1.** COVERED WITH MOSS covered or overgrown with moss **2.** RESEMBLING MOSS similar to moss, e.g. in texture or colour **3.** US OLD-

FASHIONED old-fashioned or out of date (*informal*) — **mossiness** *n*

mossy zinc *n* a form of zinc with a grainy texture. Source: pouring melted zinc into water.

most /mōst/ CORE MEANING: a grammatical word indicating nearly all or the majority of the people or things mentioned ○ *Most people enjoy watching a good film.* ○ *We'd finished off most of the work by lunchtime.* **1.** *det, pron* GREATEST indicates the greatest in number, amount, extent, or degree ○ (det) *the candidate winning the most votes* ○ (pron) *The most I can lend you is £50.* **2.** *adv* TO GREATEST EXTENT to the greatest extent, or in the largest number or amount (*forming the superlative of some adjectives and adverbs*) ○ *It works most effectively if you heat it first.* ○ *the most expensive* **3.** *adv* SUPERLATIVE OF 'MUCH' used as the superlative of 'much' to mean 'with the greatest frequency or intensity' ○ *He likes her most.* **4.** *adv* VERY in a high degree ○ *a most enjoyable day* **5.** *adv* N Am ALMOST nearly but not entirely (*informal*) ○ *Most everyone was invited.* [Old English *mæst* < Indo-European, 'big'] ◇ **at (the) most** at the maximum ○ *It'll take you two hours at the most.* ◇ **make the most of something** to take full advantage of something ◇ **the most** the best of all (*dated slang*) ○ *That song is the most!*

-most *suffix* **1.** nearest to or towards ○ *endmost* **2.** most ○ *nethermost* [Old English *-mest* < Germanic, taken as < MOST]

Mostaganem /mə stággə ném/ city and fishing port in northwestern Algeria. Population: 114,037 (1987).

Mostar /móss taar/ city in southern Bosnia and Herzegovina, on the Neretva River. It was the scene of intense fighting during the Bosnian-Croatian-Serbian War (1991–95), when a bridge was destroyed between the Bosnian Croats and Muslims living on either side of the river. It is situated about 80 km/50 mi. southwest of Sarajevo. Population: 24,606 (1991).

most favoured nation *n* a nation accorded the most favourable trading terms by another nation

Most Honourable *adj* in the United Kingdom, a title given to marquesses and marchionesses, and to members of the Order of the Bath

mostly /mōstli/ *adv* **1.** almost entirely ○ *The audience was mostly made up of younger fans.* **2.** on most occasions, or for the most part ○ *I swim mostly at weekends.*

Most Reverend *adj* a title given to Anglican and Roman Catholic archbishops, to Irish Roman Catholic bishops, to the Anglican Bishop of Meath, and to the Primus of the Episcopal Church in Scotland

mot /mot/ *n* Ireland a girl or young woman, especially a regular woman companion (*slang*) [Mid-16C. Origin ?]

MOT *n* **1.** ROADWORTHINESS TEST an inspection of a vehicle to test its roadworthiness **2.** ROADWORTHINESS CERTIFICATE a certificate of roadworthiness awarded to a vehicle that has passed its MOT test ■ *vt* (**MOTs, MOTing, MOTed**) CARRY OUT MOT ON VEHICLE to carry out an MOT test on a vehicle [Late 20C. Abbreviation of *Ministry of Transport*, which administers the test]

MOT certificate *n* AUTOMOT same as **MOT** *n* (sense 2)

MOTD *abbr* ONLINE message of the day (*used in e-mails or text messages*)

mote /mōt/ *n* a tiny speck or particle [Old English *mot*, origin ?]

motel /mō tél/ *n* a hotel intended to provide short-term accommodation for travelling motorists, usually situated close to a main road and having rooms accessible from the parking area [Early 20C. Blend of MOTOR + HOTEL]

~~moter~~ incorrect spelling of **motor**

motet /mō tét/ *n* a vocal composition with parts for different voices, usually based on a sacred text [14C. < Old French, 'little word' < Latin *muttire* 'to murmur']

moth /moth/ *n* an insect resembling a butterfly, typically with a duller colour and differently shaped antennae, active at night. Order: Lepidoptera. [Old English *moppe*, origin ?]

moth

mothball /móth bawl/ *n* MOTH-REPELLENT CHEMICAL BALL a small ball of a strong-smelling chemical such as camphor or naphthalene, used for keeping clothes moths away from clothing and other materials ■ *vt* (**-balls, -balling, -balled**) **1.** PUT SOMETHING OFF INDEFINITELY to postpone work or discussion on something for an indefinite time ○ *mothballed the expansion plans* **2.** INDUST SHUT DOWN FACTORY to take a factory out of operation but protect the equipment in it so that it can be used again at some time in the future **3.** NAUT, AEROSP SEAL CRAFT UP FOR STORAGE to seal all the openings in a ship or aircraft in order to protect it from corrosion while it is not in use ◇ **in mothballs** put aside or stored and not in use

moth bean *n* **1.** a yellowish-brown edible bean seed **2.** a plant of the pea family. Flowers: small, yellow. Use: forage, fertilizer, food. Native to: tropical regions, especially South Asia. Latin name: *Phaseolus aconitifolius.*

moth-eaten *adj* **1.** EATEN BY MOTH LARVAE damaged by clothes moth caterpillars **2.** SHABBY dilapidated and worn-out from use **3.** OUTDATED no longer usable or appropriate (*informal*)

mother[1] /múthər/ *n* **1.** FEMALE PARENT a woman who has a child, or a female animal that has produced young **2.** WOMAN ACTING AS PARENT a woman who acts as the parent of a child to whom she has not given birth **3.** CHARACTERISTICS OF MOTHER the qualities or feelings that are traditionally associated with being a mother ○ *brought out the mother in her* **4.** ORIGINATOR a woman regarded as the creator, instigator, or founder of something **5.** ORIGIN OF SOMETHING the cause, source, or origin of something ○ *Necessity is the mother of invention.* **6.** PROTECTOR something that protects and nourishes like a mother **7.** GOOD OR BAD EXAMPLE OF SOMETHING something very big, good, bad, or extreme, or particularly noteworthy in some other way (*slang; sometimes considered offensive*) ○ *a real mother of a headache* **8.** N Am TABOO TERM a highly offensive term for somebody regarded as objectionable or contemptible (*taboo*) ■ *vt* (**-ers, -ering, -ered**) **1.** LOOK AFTER SOMEBODY WITH CARE to look after somebody with great care and affection, sometimes to an excessive degree **2.** GIVE BIRTH TO BABY to give birth to and bring up a baby **3.** BRING SOMETHING ABOUT to give rise to something [Old English *modor* < Indo-European] —**motherhood** *n* ◇ **at your mother's knee** in early childhood ◇ **be mother** to pour out tea from a teapot for those present (*humorous*) ◇ **every mother's son** every man or boy (*dated*)

mother[2] /múthər/ *n* a slimy mass of bacteria and yeast cells that forms on the surface of alcohol being converted into acetic acid [Mid-16C. Probably < obsolete Dutch *moeder* < Middle Dutch *moeder* 'female parent'; from its part in the production of vinegar]

Mother *n* **1.** used as a title or form of address for a senior nun in a religious community **2.** used as a title of respect for a woman past middle age (*archaic; sometimes considered offensive*)

motherboard /múthər bawrd/ *n* a circuit board in a minicomputer or microcomputer through which all signals are directed

Mother Carey's chicken /-káiriz-/ *n* same as **storm petrel** (*dated*) [Probably < alteration of medieval Latin *mater cara* 'Virgin Mary']

mother cell *n* a cell that gives rise to other cells by cell division

mother church *n* a Christian church from which other churches derive their authority

mother country *n* **1.** the country of origin of people who have left to found a colony or colonies else-

where **2.** the country that somebody was born and grew up in

motherese /múthər eéz/ *n* the speech patterns and restricted vocabulary used by parents and caregivers when speaking to very young children

mother figure *n* a woman who embodies the qualities traditionally associated with a mother, especially support, advice, and affection

motherfucker /múthər fukər/ *n* N Am a highly offensive term of abuse for somebody regarded as objectionable or contemptible (*taboo*) —**motherfucking** *adj*

Mother Goose *n* the supposed author of a collection of nursery rhymes first published in the 18th century

mother hen *n* a woman who is regarded as over-protective and fussing

motherhouse /múthər howss/ *n* a Christian monastery or convent from which monks or nuns have gone out to found new monasteries and convents

Mother Hubbard /-húbbərd/ *n* a long loose-fitting shapeless dress [Late 16C. After a nursery-rhyme character depicted wearing such a dress]

Mothering Sunday /múthəring-/ *n* a day observed as a celebration of mothers. Date: fourth Sunday in Lent. Same as **Mother's Day**

mother-in-law (*plural* **mothers-in-law**) *n* the mother of a person's spouse

mother-in-law's tongue *n* PLANTS same as **sansevieria** [< its long pointed leaves]

motherland /múthər land/ *n* the country that somebody was born and grew up in

motherless /múthərləss/ *adj* without a mother, or having lost a mother through bereavement ■ *adv* Aus completely or thoroughly (*informal*) ○ *motherless broke*

mother lode *n* **1.** the main vein of ore in a mine **2.** a plentiful supply of something

motherly /múthərli/ *adj* having or showing qualities traditionally associated with mothers, especially kindness and protectiveness —**motherliness** *n*

mother-naked *adj* US completely nude

Mother Nature *n* the forces of nature personified as a wilful being

Mother of God *n* a title given to Mary, the mother of Jesus Christ, especially by Roman Catholics

Mother of Parliaments *n* the British parliament, thought of as the model for the parliaments of many other countries

mother-of-pearl *n* the hard pearly internal layer of the shells of some molluscs. Use: decorative inlays. [Early 16C. Translation of obsolete French *mère perle*]

mother of the chapel *n* in trade unions in the printing and publishing industries, the woman head of a workplace section (**chapel**) of a union

mother-of-thousands (*plural* **mothers-of-thousands** or **mother-of-thousands**) *n* a creeping or trailing plant that produces masses of small flowers, especially the ivy-leaved toadflax or the strawberry geranium

mother of vinegar *n* FOOD INDUST same as **mother**[2]

Mother's Day *n* **1.** UK same as **Mothering Sunday** **2.** a day observed as a celebration of mothers in the United States, Canada, Australia, and some other Commonwealth countries. Date: second Sunday in May.

mother ship *n* **1.** a ship or spaceship that provides services and supplies for a number of other, usually smaller ships **2.** an organization that oversees, or a place that acts as a base for, other activities (*informal*)

mother superior (*plural* **mother superiors** or **mothers superior**) *n* the head of a Christian convent or community of Christian nuns

mother-to-be (*plural* **mothers-to-be**) *n* a woman who is expecting a baby

mother tongue *n* **1.** the first language somebody learns as a child at home **2.** a language from which other languages have developed

Motherwell /múthərwel/ industrial town in North Lanarkshire, central Scotland. Population: 30,717 (1991).

Motherwell /múthərwəl, -wel/, **Robert** (1915–91) US

artist. He is known for his brilliantly coloured or black-and-white abstract expressionist paintings. Full name **Motherwell, Robert Burns**

> 'True painting is a lot more than "picture-making". A man is neither a decoration nor an anecdote.'
> [Robert Motherwell. Quoted in *The New Decade*, Whitney Museum of American Art, New York; 1955]

mother wit *n* natural intelligence or good sense

motherwort /múthər wurt/ (*plural* **-worts** or *same*) *n* a plant with deeply lobed leaves used in herbal medicine to treat gynaecological disorders. Flowers: white or pink, purple-spotted. Native to: Europe, Asia. Latin name: *Leonurus cardiaca*. [14C. < MOTHER [1] in the obsolete sense 'womb'; because formerly used as a medicinal herb during childbirth]

mothproof /móth proof/ *adj* treated with a substance designed to prevent damage by clothes moths —**mothproof** *vt*

mothy /móthi/ (**-ier, -iest**) *adj* **1.** damaged by the action of clothes moths **2.** full of or infested by moths

motif /mō téef/ *n* **1.** ARCHIT, DESIGN **REPEATED DESIGN** a repeated design, shape, or pattern **2.** HANDICRAFT, DESIGN **SEWN OR PRINTED DECORATION** a repetitive decorative design sewn into or printed on something such as a piece of clothing, or a single example of the pattern **3.** LITERAT **THEME IN WORK OF LITERATURE** an important and sometimes recurring theme or idea in a work of literature **4.** MUSIC **PROMINENT SEQUENCE OF NOTES** a short prominent sequence of notes forming the basis for development in a piece of music **5. CAR DECORATION** a decoration on a car that serves to identify the manufacturer [Mid-19C. < French (see MOTIVE)]

motile /mṓ tīl/ *adj* capable of or demonstrating movement by independent means [Mid-19C. < Latin *motus* 'motion' < past participle of *movere* 'to move'] —**motility** /mō tílləti/ *n*

motion /mṓsh'n/ *n* **1. ACT OF MOVING** the act or process of moving, or the way in which somebody or something moves ○ *walked with a swaying motion* **2. MOVEMENT** a movement, action, or gesture ○ *made a quick motion of the wrist* **3. POWER OF MOVEMENT** the power or ability to move something **4. PROPOSAL** a proposal put forward for discussion at a meeting **5.** LAW **APPLICATION TO JUDGE OR COURT** an application made to a court or judge for an order or ruling in a legal proceeding **6.** PHYSIOL **PASSING OF SOLID WASTE FROM BODY** the passing of solid waste matter out of the body through the anus **7.** PHYSIOL **ACT OF EMPTYING BOWELS** an act of emptying of the bowels, or the matter emptied (*dated; often used in the plural*) **8.** MUSIC **MOVEMENT FROM ONE NOTE TO ANOTHER** the movement from one note to the next by a voice or instrument ■ *vti* (**-tions, -tioning, -tioned**) **SIGNAL TO SOMEBODY** to gesture or signal something such as a request or intention to somebody ○ *motioned me over and told me to sit down* [14C. Via French < Latin *motion-* < past participle of *movere* 'to move'] ◇ **go through the motions** to do something in a perfunctory or mechanical way, without enthusiasm or commitment ◇ **put** *or* **set something in motion** to cause something to start moving, functioning, or happening

motionless /mṓsh'nləss/ *adj* not moving —**motionlessly** *adv*

motion picture *n N Am* CINEMA same as **film**

motion sickness *n ANZ, N Am* MED same as **travel sickness**

motion study *n* INDUST same as **time and motion study**

motivate /mṓti vayt/ (**-vates, -vating, -vated**) *vt* **1. GIVE SOMEBODY INCENTIVE** to give somebody a reason or incentive to do something **2. MAKE SOMEBODY WILLING** to make somebody feel enthusiastic, interested, and committed to something **3. CAUSE SOMEBODY'S BEHAVIOUR** to be the reason for something that somebody does ○ *motivated purely by greed* **4.** *S Africa* **DEFEND PROPOSAL** to prepare or present an argument in support of a proposal ○ *The report must contain enough data to motivate any decision or suggestion.* [Mid-19C. < MOTIVE, after French *motiver* 'motivate'] —**motivated** *adj* —**motivator** *n*

motivation /mṓti váysh'n/ *n* **1. GIVING OF REASON TO ACT** the act of giving somebody a reason or incentive to do something **2. ENTHUSIASM** a feeling of enthusiasm, interest, or commitment that makes somebody want to do something, or something that causes such a feeling **3. REASON** a reason for doing something or behaving in a particular way **4.** PSYCHOL **FORCES DETERMINING BEHAVIOUR** the biological, emotional, cognitive, or social forces that activate and direct behaviour **5.** *S Africa* **FORMAL DEFENCE OF PROPOSAL** a formal presentation, especially in writing, of arguments in support of a proposal —**motivational** *adj* —**motivationally** *adv* —**motivative** /mṓti vaytiv/ *adj*

motivational research, **motivation research** *n* the study of the motivation of consumers in their buying practices, used to plan marketing and sales

motive /mṓtiv/ *n* **1. REASON** the reason for doing something or behaving in a specific way **2.** ARTS same as **motif** (senses 1, 3) ■ *adj* **1. CAUSING MOTION** capable of causing or producing motion **2. CAUSING SOMEBODY TO DO SOMETHING** tending to make somebody want or be willing to do something ■ *vt* (**-tives, -tiving, -tived**) **MOTIVATE SOMEBODY** to make somebody want or be willing to do something [14C. Via Old French *motif* < late Latin *motivus* < past participle of Latin *movere* 'to move']

SYNONYMS ***motive, incentive, inducement, spur, stimulus, impetus***

CORE MEANING: something that prompts action

motive the reason for doing something or behaving in a specific way ○ *a crime that appears to have no motive* ○ *He stressed the need to maintain the highest standards in this new probe, fearing there were ulterior political motives for the investigation.* **incentive** something that encourages or motivates somebody to do something ○ *The economic insecurity experienced by lone mothers is another incentive for women to stay in the workforce and increase their skills.* ○ *financial incentives to reduce pollution* **inducement** something that persuades somebody to do something or attracts somebody to a course of action, especially something that is offered as a reward ○ *Debt relief was promised as an inducement to the country to make peace with its neighbour.* ○ *The committee expressed the hope that 'every inducement, direct or indirect, will be given to keep mothers at home'.* **spur** something that encourages a person or organization to take action or to make a greater effort, for example the hope of a reward or the fear of punishment ○ *Trade traditionally acts as a spur to economic expansion.* ○ *Shopkeepers saw the outsides of their properties improved, and that provided a spur for them to improve the insides.* **stimulus** something that encourages an activity or process to begin, increase, or develop ○ *The possibility of lowering interest rates acted as a stimulus to the economy.* ○ *Although the army knew that they were defending legality, they did not have the morale stimulus of winning battles which the rebels had.* **impetus** the energy or a driving force that prompts somebody to accomplish or undertake something ○ *In the early nineteenth century almost all the impetus for setting up schools came from the churches.* ○ *concerns that give fresh impetus to a growing environmentalist movement*

---

motiveless /mṓtivləss/ *adj* having no reason for doing something or behaving in a particular way ○ *a motiveless crime*

motive power *n* **1.** the power or energy that drives a piece of machinery, or the source of that power or energy **2.** the driving force behind an action or activity

motivic /mō tívvik/ *adj* relating to a musical motif or motifs

motivity /mō tívvəti/ *n* the power to move or to make something move

mot juste /mṓ zhóost/ (*plural* **mots justes** /*pronunc. same*/) *n* exactly the right word or words to express something [< French]

motley /móttli/ *adj* (**-lier, -liest**) **1. MADE UP OF DIFFERENT TYPES** consisting of people or things that are very different from one another and do not seem to belong together **2. OF VARIED COLOURS** made up of different colours ■ *n* (*plural* **-lies**) **1. JESTER'S COSTUME** the multicoloured clothing worn by a medieval jester **2. VARIED GROUP** a group of people or things that are very different from one another and do not seem to belong together [14C. Origin ?]

motmot /mót mot/ *n* a bird with a broad downward-curved beak, long tail, and usually greenish feathers with a black patch on the chest. Native to: Central and South America. Family: Momotidae. [Mid-19C. < American Spanish, an imitation of its call]

motocross /mṓtō kross/ *n* a motorcycle race, or the sport of racing motorcycles, over a rough course with steep hills, wet or muddy areas, and turns of varying difficulty [Mid-20C. < French < *moto* 'motorcycle' + English CROSS-COUNTRY]

motoneuron /mṓtō nyóor on/ *n* ANAT same as **motor neuron** [Early 20C. < MOTOR] —**motoneuronal** *adj*

motor /mṓtər/ *n* **1. MACHINE THAT CREATES MOTION** a machine that converts energy into motion and can be used as a power source, e.g. to drive another machine or to move some form of transport **2. CAR** a vehicle, especially a car, powered by a motor (*slang*) ■ *adj* **1. OF VEHICLES** relating to vehicles, especially cars, powered by a motor **2. MOTOR-DRIVEN** powered by a motor **3. CAUSING MOTION** causing or producing motion **4.** PHYSIOL **OF MUSCLE ACTIVITY** relating to muscle activity, especially voluntary muscle activity, and the consequent body movements ■ *vi* (**-tors, -toring, -tored**) **1. DRIVE IN CAR** to travel by car or another form of private vehicle, especially for pleasure (*formal*) **2. MOVE FAST** to move or progress at a fast pace (*informal*) [15C. < Latin, 'mover' < *movere* 'to move']

motorable /mṓtərəb'l/ *adj* able to be driven on by motor vehicles

motorbicycle /mṓtər bīssik'l/ *n* a motorcycle or moped

motorbike /mṓtər bīk/ *n* VEHICLES same as **motorcycle**

motorboat /mṓtər bōt/ *n* a small boat powered by an engine —**motorboater** *n* —**motorboating** *n*

motorbus /mṓtər buss/ *n* same as **bus** *n* (sense 1) (*dated*)

motorcade /mṓtər kayd/ *n* a procession of cars or other vehicles, especially one forming an escort for somebody important [Early 20C. < MOTOR + CAVALCADE]

motor camp *n NZ* a drive-in campsite for motorists with tents or caravans

motor car *n* AUTOMOT same as **car** (*dated or formal*)

motor caravan *n UK* a vehicle with cooking, living, and sleeping facilities like those of a caravan. ANZ, N Am term **motor home**

motor cortex *n* the region of the outer surface of the brain (**cortex**) where nervous impulses controlling voluntary muscle activity are initiated. The motor cortex in the right hemisphere of the brain is responsible for controlling muscles in the left side of the body, and vice versa for the left hemisphere.

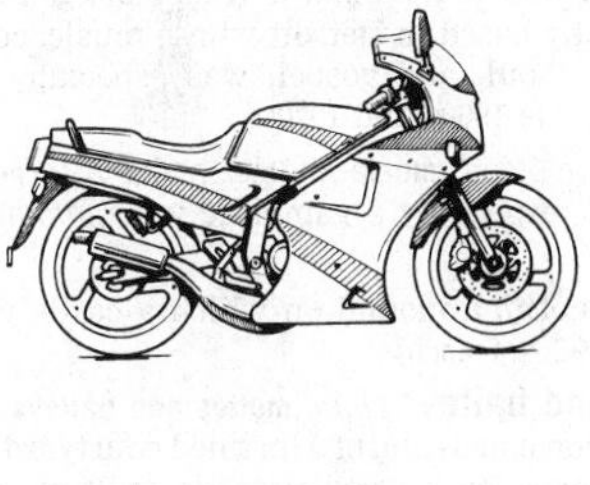

motorcycle

motorcycle /mṓtər sīk'l/ *n* a two-wheeled road vehicle powered by an engine ■ *vi* (**-cles, -cling, -cled**) to ride or travel on a motorcycle —**motorcyclist** *n*

motor drive *n* a motorized mechanism to advance film in a camera

motor home *n ANZ, N Am* VEHICLES, CAMPING same as **motor caravan**

motoric /mō tórrik/ *adj* relating to voluntary muscle movement —**motorically** *adv*

motorise *vt* ENG, MIL another spelling of **motorize**

motorist /mṓtərist/ *n* somebody who drives a car

motorize /mṓtə rīz/ (**-izes, -izing, -ized**), **motorise** (**-ises, -ising, -ised**) *vt* **1.** to fit something with a motor **2.** to provide troops with motor vehicles —**motorization** /mṓtə rī záysh'n/ *n*

motorman /mṓtərmən/ (*plural* **-men** /-mən/) *n* the driver of a tramcar or electric train

motormouth /mṓtər mowth/ (*plural* **-mouths** /-mowthz/) *n* somebody who talks too much or too fast (*informal insult*)

motor neuron, **motor neurone** *n* a nerve cell (**neuron**) that conveys nerve impulses from the spinal cord

or brain stem away from the central nervous system towards a muscle or gland

motor neuron disease *n* a progressive degenerative disease involving the motor neurons and causing weakness and wasting of the muscles

motor neurone *n* ANAT same as **motor neuron**

motor park *n W Africa* TRANSP same as **car park**

motor pool *n N Am* BUSINESS, TRANSP same as **car pool** (sense 2)

motor protein *n* any of a group of cell proteins that use chemical energy from ATP to create movement within cells, e.g. by separating chromosomes during cell division and transporting neurotransmitters inside nerve cells

motor racing *n UK, Aus, Can* the sport of racing in motor vehicles, especially in cars that are specially designed to travel at high speeds. US term **auto racing**

motor rhythm *n* a rhythmic motif in a piece of music maintaining a constant pulse, usually at a fast tempo, for an extended period

motorsailer /mṓtər saylər/ *n* a sailing boat equipped with a motor

motor scooter *n* a light motorcycle with small wheels, an enclosed engine, and a framework that includes a protective front plate and support for the rider's feet

motor ship *n* a ship powered by an engine

motorsport /mṓtər spawrt/ *n* a sport in which participants race motor vehicles, usually around a track

motor torpedo boat *n UK* a highly manoeuvrable vessel, 18 to 30 m/60 to 100 ft in length, carrying light armament and used to torpedo enemy shipping. ANZ, N Am term **PT boat**

motor unit *n* a motor neuron and the muscle fibres it acts on

motor vehicle *n* a car, lorry, or other road vehicle powered by an engine

motor vessel *n* a ship powered by an engine

motorway /mṓtər way/ *n UK* a limited-access road usually consisting of three lanes for vehicles in each direction, intended for travelling relatively fast over long distances

motor yacht *n* a yacht powered by an engine

Motown /mṓ town/ *tdmk* a trademark for a music company based in Detroit whose music, consisting of pop, soul, and gospel, was especially popular during the 1960s and 1970s

motser /mótsər/, **motza** /mótsə/ *n Aus* a large sum of money, especially a gambling win (*informal*) [20C. Origin ?]

motte /mot/ *n* a mound on which a castle was built [Late 19C. < French]

motte and bailey (*plural* **mottes and baileys**) *n* a fortification consisting of a fortified courtyard (**bailey**) overlooked by a wooden castle built on a mound of earth (**motte**). Such castles were built by the Normans in the 11th and 12th centuries.

MOT test *n* AUTOMOT same as **MOT** *n* (sense 1)

mottle /mótt'l/ *vt* (**-tles, -tling, -tled**) **MARK SOMETHING WITH DIFFERENT COLOURS** to mark something with an irregular pattern of patches or spots of different colours ■ *n* **1. IRREGULAR PATTERN OF COLOURS** an irregular pattern of patches or spots of different colours **2. PATCH OF COLOUR** a patch or spot of colour that forms part of an irregular pattern [Late 17C. Probably back-formation < MOTLEY]

mottled enamel /mótt'ld-/ *n* tooth enamel that is mottled as a result of swallowing excessive amounts of fluoride at the age when teeth harden

motto /móttō/ (*plural* **-toes** or **-tos**) *n* **1. RULE TO LIVE BY** a short saying that expresses a rule to live by ○ *'I heartily accept the motto, "That government is best which governs least"; and I should like to see it acted up to more rapidly and systematically.'* (Henry David Thoreau, *Civil Disobedience*; 1849) **2.** HERALDRY **SAYING ON COAT OF ARMS** a short saying that forms part of a coat of arms and expresses something about the family or place whose coat of arms it is **3.** LITERAT **QUOTATION AT BEGINNING OF WRITING** a short quotation at the beginning of a piece of writing such as a book, a chapter of a book, or a poem, related in some way to its contents **4.** MUSIC same as **motif** (sense 4) [Late 16C. < Italian, probably < assumed Vulgar Latin, 'word']

Motu /mṓ too/ (*plural same* or **-tus**) *n* **1.** a member of a Melanesian people of Papua New Guinea who live in the central province in and around Port Moresby **2.** the Austronesian language of the Motu. Native speakers: 14,000. [Late 19C. < Melanesian] —**Motu** *adj*

motu proprio /mṓ too prṓpri ō/ (*plural* **motu proprios**) *n* a decree issued by a pope acting independently and on his own initiative [< Latin, 'on your own initiative']

motza *n Aus* MONEY, GAMBLING another spelling of **motser** (*informal*)

moue /moo/ *n* a look of discontent in which the lips are pressed together and forward [Mid-19C. < French]

mouflon /mōō flon/ *n* a reddish-brown wild sheep with prominent curved horns. Native to: Sardinia, Corsica. Latin name: *Ovis musimon.* [Late 18C. Via French < Italian *muflone*]

mouillé /mwee ay/ *adj* describes a consonant pronounced with the tongue touching the palate [Mid-19C. < French, past participle of *mouiller* 'wet, moisten']

moulage /moo láazh/ *n* **1.** the process of making a mould or cast of something such as a footprint in the course of a criminal investigation **2.** a mould or cast made in the course of a criminal investigation [Early 20C. < French, 'moulding, moulded copy' < Old French *mouler* 'to mould']

mould[1] /mōld/ *n* **1. CONTAINER FOR MAKING SHAPE** a container that gives a shape to a molten or liquid substance poured into it to harden **2. FRAME** a frame on which something is formed or built **3. OBJECT MADE IN MOULD** an object formed using a mould **4. DISTINCTIVE TYPE** a particular type that has a distinctive character or nature ○ *a leader in the heroic mould* **5. SET OF ASSUMPTIONS** a fixed pattern or framework of assumptions, especially when regarded as restricting ○ *negotiators who break out of the traditional diplomatic mould* **6.** ARCHIT same as **moulding** (sense 1) ■ *v* (**moulds, moulding, moulded**) **1.** *vt* **MAKE SOMETHING IN MOULD** to shape or form something in a mould **2.** *vt* **GIVE SOMETHING SHAPE** to shape or give form to something **3.** *vt* **INFLUENCE SOMEBODY OR SOMETHING** to guide or influence the growth or development of somebody or something ○ *the childhood experience that helped mould her personality* **4.** *vti* **MAKE SOMETHING CLING** shape something, especially clothing, so that it clings to and follows the contours of the part it is fitted to, or be fitted to a part in this way **5.** *vt* METALL **MAKE MOULD FROM SOMETHING** to make a material into a mould to be used in casting metal **6.** *vt* ARCHIT **PUT MOULDING ON SOMETHING** to decorate something with a moulding [12C. Via Old French *modle* < Latin *modulus* 'little measure' < *modus* 'measure'] —**mouldable** *adj*

mould[2] /mōld/ *n* **1. FUNGUS** a fungus that causes organic matter to decay **2. GROWTH OF MOULD** a growth of mould on the surface of something, or the discoloration caused by the growth of mould ■ *vi* (**moulds, moulding, moulded**) **BECOME COVERED WITH MOULD** to become covered with or affected by mould [15C. < obsolete *moul* 'go mouldy' < assumed Old Norse *mugla*]

mould[3] /mōld/ *n* **1.** soil that is rich in humus and easily worked or crumbled **2.** the ground, especially surrounding a grave (*literary*) [Old English < Indo-European 'to grind']

mouldboard /mṓld bawrd/ *n* **1. BLADE OF PLOUGH** the curved metal blade of a plough that turns over the soil **2. BLADE OF BULLDOZER OR SNOWPLOUGH** the large curved blade on the front of a bulldozer or snowplough that pushes the soil or snow **3.** CONSTR **SIDE OF CONCRETE MOULD** a board that forms one side or one surface of a concrete mould

moulder[1] /mṓldər/ (**-ers, -ering, -ered**) *vti* to crumble or decay because of natural processes, or make something do this [Mid-16C. < *mold* 'loose soil' < Germanic, 'grind']

moulder[2] /mṓldər/ *n* somebody who moulds things or makes moulds [14C. < MOULD[1]]

moulding /mṓlding/ *n* **1.** a strip of wood or another material used to decorate or finish a surface of a wall or a piece of furniture **2.** something produced using a mould

mouldy /mṓldi/ (**-ier, -iest**) *adj* **1. WITH MOULD** containing or covered with mould **2. STALE FROM AGE OR ROT** stale and unpleasant from old age, neglect, or fungal growth **3. OLD** old-fashioned or out-of-date (*informal*) **4. BORING** dull, boring, or contemptible (*informal*) —**mouldiness** *n*

moules marinières /mool mari nyér/ *npl* a dish of mussels cooked and served in their shells with a wine sauce [< French]

moulin /mōōlin/ *n* an almost vertical shaft in a glacier, created by meltwater and debris boring into a crack in the surface of the ice [Mid-19C. Via French, 'mill' < late Latin *molinum*]

moult /mōlt/ *vti* (**moults, moulting, moulted**) **LOSE FEATHERS, HAIR, OR SKIN** to shed feathers, hair, or skin periodically, especially seasonally, in order to allow replacement of what is lost with new growth ■ *n* **1. LOSS OF FEATHERS, HAIR, OR SKIN** the process or time during which a bird or other animal sheds all or part of its feathers, hair, or skin **2. LOST FEATHERS, HAIR, OR SKIN** the feathers, hair, or skin shed by a bird or other animal [Pre-12C. < Latin *mutare* 'to change'] —**moulter** *n*

moulvi *n* ISLAM same as **maulvi**

mound /mownd/ *n* **1. SMALL HILL** a small rounded hill **2. CONSTRUCTED PILE OF SOMETHING** a pile of earth, stones, or other material built up for some purpose, e.g. to provide shelter, defence, or concealment **3. PILE OF OBJECTS** an untidy heap or pile of objects ○ *a mound of dirty laundry on the floor* **4. LARGE AMOUNT** a large amount of something ○ *a mound of mashed potatoes* ■ *vt* (**mounds, mounding, mounded**) **MAKE SOMETHING INTO MOUND** to form something into a mound [Early 16C. Origin ?]

moundbird /mównd burd/ *n* BIRDS same as **megapode** [Mid-19C. < its custom of depositing its eggs in a mound]

Mound Builder *n* a member of an early Native North American people who built burial mounds and earthwork fortifications in what is now the Midwest and Southeast of the United States

mound-builder *n* BIRDS same as **megapode** [See MOUNDBIRD]

mount[1] /mownt/ *v* (**mounts, mounting, mounted**) **1.** *vti* **CLIMB SOMETHING** to climb up something such as stairs or a hill **2.** *vti* **GET ONTO SOMETHING FOR RIDE** to get onto an animal or a form of transport such as a bicycle **3.** *vt* **PUT SOMEBODY ON FORM OF TRANSPORT** to put somebody onto an animal or a form of transport such as a bicycle **4.** *vt* **GET ONTO SOMETHING HIGHER** to get up onto a platform or other raised position **5.** *vi* **GO UP INTO AIR** to move upwards into the air **6.** *vt* **BEGIN COURSE OF ACTION** to put into operation a course of action such as a campaign, rescue, or attack **7.** *vt* **ORGANIZE ARTS PRODUCTION** to organize something such as an exhibition or a production of a play **8.** *vi* **INCREASE** to become greater, stronger, or more intense ○ *Tension was mounting.* **9.** *vt* **SECURE SOMETHING TO SOMETHING ELSE** to fix something securely to something else, e.g. a picture into a frame, a specimen onto a slide, a stamp into an album, or an exhibit onto a stand or support **10.** *vt* **PUT SOMETHING SOMEWHERE FOR USE** to put something onto a support or into a position so that it is ready for use ○ *mount a camera* **11.** *vt* **CLIMB ONTO ANIMAL TO COPULATE** to climb onto a female animal in order to copulate (*technical; refers to male animals*) ■ *n* **1. SOMETHING FOR FIXING SOMETHING IN PLACE** something on which or with which something else can be mounted, e.g. a stand, support, frame, or backing **2. ANIMAL FOR RIDING** an animal used for riding, e.g. a horse **3.** STAMPS **SOMETHING FOR MOUNTING STAMP** an envelope or card on which to mount a stamp [13C. < Old French *monter* 'go up' < Latin *mont-* 'mountain'] —**mountable** *adj* —**mounter** *n*

mount[2] /mownt/ *n* GEOG same as **mountain** (sense 1) (*archaic or literary; often used in placenames*) [Pre-12C. Via French < Latin *mont-* 'mountain']

mountain /mówntin/ *n* **1. HIGH POINT OF LAND** a high and often rocky area of a land mass with steep or sloping sides ○ *a plateau surrounded by mountains.* See table on next page **2. LARGE PILE** a large pile or heap of something ○ *a mountain of books* **3. LARGE AMOUNT** a large amount of something (*informal; often used in the plural*) ○ *a mountain of work* **4. SURPLUS** a large surplus of a particular commodity (*informal; usually used in combination*) ○ *a butter mountain* [13C. < Old French *montaigne* < Latin *mont-, mons*] ◇ **make a mountain out of a molehill** to treat something that is not important as if it were

mountain ash *n* TREES same as **rowan** (sense 1)

mountain avens *n* a small trailing plant of the rose family. Flowers: white. Native to: temperate mountainous and Arctic areas. Latin name: *Dryas octopetala.*

mountain beaver *n* a large thick-set rodent that lives

WORLD'S HIGHEST MOUNTAINS

World order (all in Asia)

1	Everest	*Himalayas*
Height	[29,035 ft / 8,850 m]	
2	K2	*Himalayas*
Height	[28,251 ft / 8,611 m]	
3	Kanchenjunga	*Himalayas*
Height	[28,209 ft / 8,598 m]	
4	Lhotse	*Himalayas*
Height	[27,940 ft / 8,516 m]	
5	Makalu	*Himalayas*
Height	[27,824 ft / 8,481 m]	
6	Cho Oyu	*Himalayas*
Height	[26,906 ft / 8,201 m]	
7	Dhaulagiri	*Himalayas*
Height	[26,811 ft / 8,172 m]	
8	Manaslu	*Himalayas*
Height	[26,781 ft / 8,163 m]	
9	Nanga Parbat	*Himalayas*
Height	[26,657 ft / 8,125 m]	
10	Annapurna	*Himalayas*
Height	[26,545 ft / 8,091 m]	

Highest in other continents

Europe

1	Mont Blanc	
Location	*Alps, France-Italy*	
Height	[15,771 ft / 4,807 m]	

Africa

1	Kilimanjaro	
Location	*Kibo Peak, Tanzania*	
Height	[19,340 ft / 5,895 m]	

North America

1	McKinley (Denali)	
Location	*Alaska Range, United States*	
Height	[20,320 ft / 6,194 m]	

South America

1	Aconcagua	
Location	*Andes, Argentina-Chile*	
Height	[22,834 ft / 6,960 m]	

Oceania/Australasia

1	Puncak Jaya	
Location	*Sudirman Range, Indonesia*	
Height	[16,502 ft / 5,030 m]	

in colonies made up of extensive burrows. Native to: northwestern North America. Latin name: *Aplodontia rufa*.

mountain bike *n* a bicycle built for rough terrain with wide thick tyres, straight handlebars, a strong frame, and more gears than a standard bicycle

mountain bluebird *n* a bird with a bright blue head, back, and wings and a pale-blue breast. Native to: western North America. Latin name: *Sialia currocoides*.

mountainboarding *n* the sport of travelling down hillsides on a board similar to a skateboard but with bigger wheels

mountain cat *n* a feline animal that lives in mountainous areas, e.g. a lynx or puma

mountain chain *n* a range of mountains or a string of adjacent mountain peaks

mountain devil *n Aus* ZOOL same as **moloch**

mountaineer /mównti néér/ *n* **1.** MOUNTAIN CLIMBER somebody who climbs mountains for sport **2.** MOUNTAIN INHABITANT somebody who lives in a mountainous area (*archaic*) ■ *vi* (**-eers, -eering, -eered**) CLIMB MOUNTAINS to climb mountains for sport

mountaineering /mównti nééring/ *n* the sport or pastime of climbing mountains

mountain goat *n* a large white wild goat with a woolly coat. Native to: North America, above the timberline in mountains from Alaska to Colorado. Latin name: *Oreamnus americanus*.

mountain hare *n* a hare with a coat that is brown in summer and white in winter. Native to: northern Europe, Asia. Latin name: *Lepus timidus*.

mountain laurel *n* an evergreen bush with shiny poisonous leaves. Flowers: pink or white, darker stamens. Native to: eastern North America. Latin name: *Kalmia latifolia*.

mountain lion *n Can, US regional* VERTEB same as **puma**

mountainous /mówntənəss/ *adj* **1.** characterized by many mountains **2.** very large or tall ○ *The ship was battered by mountainous waves.*

mountain range *n* a series of adjacent or interconnected mountains forming a distinct group and usually dating from the same geological period

mountain rescue *n* an organization of experienced climbers who go to the aid of people who get into difficulties in a mountainous place

mountain sheep *n* a wild sheep that lives in mountainous areas, e.g. the bighorn

mountain sickness *n* MED same as **altitude sickness**

mountainside /mówntən sīd/ *n* the sloping side of a mountain

Mountain Standard Time, **Mountain Time** *n* the standard time in the time zone centred on 105° W longitude, which includes the Rocky Mountain region of North America. It is seven hours behind Universal Time.

mountaintop /mówntən top/ *n* the summit of a mountain

mountainy /mówntini/ *adj* having many mountains, or forming part of a mountainous area

Mount Aspiring National Park /mównt ə spíring-/ national park in the southwestern part of the South Island, New Zealand. Situated in forested, mountainous terrain, the park was established in 1964 and expanded in 1989. Area: 2,873 sq. km/1,109 sq. mi.

Mountbatten /mownt bátt'n/, **Louis, 1st Earl Mountbatten of Burma** (1900–79) British naval commander and diplomat. After service in World War II as supreme allied commander in Southeast Asia (1943–46), he became the last viceroy of India (1947–48). He was killed by an IRA bomb.

Mount Cook lily *n* a large white buttercup. Native to: mountains of the South Island, New Zealand. Latin name: *Ranunculus lyallii*. [After the highest peak in the Alps of New Zealand]

mountebank /mównti bangk/ *n* (*literary*) **1.** somebody who deceives other people **2.** formerly, somebody who sold ineffective medicines in public places [Late 16C. < Italian *montambanco < monta in banco* (command) 'get up onto the bench'; from the quacks' practice of selling goods from a platform] —**mountebankery** *n*

mounted /mówntid/ *adj* **1.** riding on a horse ○ *mounted police* **2.** fixed onto something for use or display

Mount Gambier /-gámbi ər/ town in southeastern South Australia, built on the slopes of an extinct volcano. Population: 21,156 (1991).

Mountie /mównti/, **Mounty** (*plural* **-ies**) *n* a member of the Royal Canadian Mounted Police (*informal*) [Early 20C. < MOUNTED]

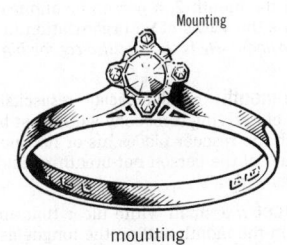

mounting

mounting /mównting/ *n* a support onto which something is fixed ■ *adj* becoming greater in size, number, or intensity ○ *We listened to the news with mounting alarm.*

mounting block *n* a block of stone on which somebody stands to get onto a horse

Mount Isa /-īzə/ city in western Queensland, Australia. Population: 20,785 (2002 estimate).

Mount Lofty Ranges /-lófti-/ range of hills in South Australia, situated east of Adelaide. It forms part of the Flinders Range. Length: 320 km/200 mi.

Mount of Olives /-óllivz/ ridge in central Israel, east of Jerusalem, with many biblical associations. It is separated from Jerusalem by the Valley of Kidron. Height: 834 m/2,737 ft.

Mount Rainier National Park /-ráyni ər-/ national park in western Washington State, established in 1899 and centred around Mount Rainier and its glacier system. Area: 953 sq. km/368 sq. mi.

Mount Rushmore ♦ **Rushmore, Mount**

Mount Vernon /-vúrnən/ city in southeastern New York State, on the Bronx River. It is a northern suburb of New York City. Population: 68,615 (2002 estimate).

Mounty *n* POLICE another spelling of **Mountie**

mourn /mawrn/ (**mourns, mourning, mourned**) *v* **1.** *vti* EXPRESS SADNESS AT SOMEBODY'S DEATH to feel and show sadness because somebody has died ○ *mourning the loss of his father* **2.** *vti* WEAR MOURNING CLOTHES to wear mourning clothes or other things that indicate grief over the death of somebody **3.** *vt* EXPRESS SADNESS AT SOMETHING LOST to feel and show sadness because something has been lost or no longer exists ○ *She mourned the loss of her independence.* [Old English *murnan* < Indo-European, 'remember'] —**mourner** *n*

Mourne Mountains /mawrn-/ granite mountain range in southern County Down, Northern Ireland. Its highest peak is Slieve Donard, 852 m/2,796 ft.

mournful /máwrnf'l/ *adj* **1.** expressing or feeling deep sadness ○ *a youth with a mournful face* **2.** causing or suggesting deep sadness ○ *a mournful anniversary* —**mournfully** *adv* —**mournfulness** *n*

mourning /máwrning/ *n* **1.** SHOW OF SADNESS AT SOMEBODY'S DEATH the feeling or showing of deep sadness following somebody's death ○ *was still in mourning over the death of her mother* **2.** CLOTHING FOR SOMEBODY WHO IS MOURNING clothing worn as a sign of sorrow following somebody's death, e.g. black clothes in Christian cultures ○ *wore mourning for a year* **3.** PERIOD OF SADNESS the period during which somebody's death is mourned ○ *The family observed a period of 40 days' mourning.* —**mourningly** *adv*

CULTURAL NOTE *Mourning Becomes Electra*, a play (1931) by US dramatist Eugene O'Neill. This drama in thirteen acts, lasting six hours, is a somewhat Freudian reworking of the *Oresteia* trilogy by the Greek author Aeschylus. Set in New England during the American Civil War (O'Neill's equivalent of the Trojan Wars), it portrays Lavinia Brant's attempts to avenge her mother's infidelity by turning the rest of the family against her.

mourning band *n* a band of black cloth worn on the arm as a sign of mourning

mourning cloak *n ANZ, N Am* a butterfly with purplish-brown wings that are spotted and rimmed with bright yellow. Native to: Europe, North America. Latin name: *Nymphalis antiopa*. UK term **Camberwell beauty**

mourning dove *n* a common dove with greyish-brown feathers, a long pointed tail, and a mournful call. Native to: North America. Latin name: *Zenaida macroura*.

mouse[1] /mowss/ *abbr* MIL minimum orbital unmanned satellite of the Earth
mouse over *vt* to move the cursor over text or an image on a computer screen using the mouse ○ *Simply mouse over the image and watch it change.*

mouse[2] /mowss/ *n* (*plural* **mice** /mīss/) **1.** SMALL RODENT a small rodent that has a brown or greyish-brown coat and a long, mostly hairless tail. Family: Muridae or Cricetidae. **2.** (*plural* **mouses** or **mice**) COMPUTER CONTROLLING DEVICE a hand-held input device with control buttons that is moved across a mat to control the movement of a cursor on a computer screen or is clicked to transmit instructions **3.** COWARD a timid or cowardly person (*insult*) **4.** BLACK

EYE a dark swelling under the eye that is caused by a blow (*dated slang*) ■ *vi* (**mouses, mousing, moused**) HUNT MICE to hunt for and kill mice (*refers to cats*) [Old English *mūs* < Indo-European]

SPELLCHECK See *moose*.

mousebird /mówss burd/ *n* BIRDS same as **coly** [Early 19C. < its soft hairlike plumage]

mouse button *n* a push button, usually one of two or three, on a computer mouse that transmits instructions to the computer

mouse-coloured *adj* of a dull nondescript brown or grey colour

mouse deer *n* ZOOL same as **chevrotain** [< the animal's small size and its similarity to a deer]

mouse-ear *n* either of two plant species with short hairy leaves supposedly resembling the ears of mice. Latin name: *Cerastium vulgatum* or *Hieracium pilosella*.

mouse mat, **mouse pad** *n* a small thin piece of material that provides a surface for a computer mouse to be moved on

mouseover /mówss ōvər/ *n* a feature on a webpage, e.g. a pop-up menu or graphic image, that is activated when a user moves the cursor over a contact point on the page. The feature is designed to encourage the user to select it. (*informal*)

mouse potato *n* somebody who spends an excessive amount of time sitting at a computer (*slang*) [Late 20C. After COUCH POTATO]

mouser /mówssər/ *n* a domestic animal that catches mice, especially a cat

mousetrap /mówss trap/ *n* a trap for catching and often killing mice

mousey *adj* another spelling of **mousy**

mousing /mówssing/ *n* a cord or bar across the opening of a hook to prevent its load from slipping

moussaka /moō saákə/ *n* a Greek baked dish with alternating layers of aubergine and minced meat in a tomato sauce, topped with a savoury white sauce [Mid-20C. Via Turkish *musakka* < Arabic *musakkā*]

mousse /mooss/ *n* **1.** LIGHT FOOD a light rich dish consisting mostly of whipped cream, eggs, or gelatin that is sweetened to serve as a dessert, or flavoured with vegetables, meat, or fish **2.** FOAMY HAIR PRODUCT a foamy substance used to set or style hair ■ *vt* (**mousses, moussing, moussed**) STYLE HAIR WITH MOUSSE to apply mousse to hair in order to style it [Mid-19C. < French, 'moss, foam' < Germanic]

SPELLCHECK See *moose*.

mousseline /moōss léen/ *n* **1.** a loosely woven fine fabric, resembling muslin and made from natural or synthetic fibres **2.** delicate blown glass **3.** COOK same as **mousseline sauce** [Late 17C. Via French < Italian *mussolina*, after *Mosul*, Iraq]

mousseline de laine /-də lén/ *n* a thin lightweight woollen fabric, often with a printed pattern [< French, literally 'muslin of wool']

mousseline de soie /-də swaá/ *n* a thin plain-woven rayon or silk fabric [< French, literally 'muslin of silk']

mousseline sauce *n* a hollandaise sauce to which whisked egg white or whipped cream has been added

moustache /mə staásh/ *n* **1.** facial hair allowed to grow on somebody's upper lip and often down the sides of the mouth or onto the cheeks **2.** hair, bristles, or feathers around the mouth or beak of an animal or bird [Late 16C. Via French < Italian *mostaccio* < Greek *mustak-* 'upper lip, moustache'] —**moustached** *adj*

moustache cup *n* an old-fashioned cup with a partial cover to prevent the contents from getting onto a drinker's moustache

Mousterian /moo stéeri ən/ *n* a prehistoric culture of the Palaeolithic period in Europe, North Africa, and southwestern Asia associated with the Neandertals and marked by the use of flint tools [Late 19C. < French *moustérien*, after *Le Moustier*, cave in SW France]

mousy /mówssi/ (**-ier, -iest**), **mousey** *adj* **1.** DULL BROWN dull brown in colour **2.** TIMID shy or uncommunicative, especially in a boring or irritating way **3.** FULL OF MICE overrun with mice **4.** RESEMBLING MOUSE having features that resemble a mouse, e.g. big front teeth or a pointed nose —**mousily** *adv* —**mousiness** *n*

mouth *n* /mowth/ (*plural* **mouths** /mowt͟hz/) **1.** FOOD AND VOICE ORGAN in people and animals, the opening in the head and its surrounding lips, gums, tongue, and teeth, through which food is taken in and through which sounds come out **2.** PART OF FACE the part of the mouth visible to others, including the lips and the opening between them ○ *She kissed him on the mouth.* **3.** SPEECH ORGAN the mouth regarded as the organ of speech ○ *You wouldn't believe some of the things that came out of his mouth.* **4.** WAY OF SPEAKING a way of using language that other people think is inappropriate or offensive ○ *a foul mouth* **5.** WATER JUNCTION the place where a stream or river enters a sea or lake **6.** OPENING IN THE GROUND an opening to a cave, tunnel, mineshaft, or volcano **7.** OPENING IN CONTAINER the opening of a container such as a jar, tube, or bottle **8.** OPENING BETWEEN PARTS OF TOOL the opening between the two sides of a device that can be closed to hold something, e.g. in a vice or clamp **9.** MUSIC OPENING IN PIPE the slit in the pipe of a pipe organ **10.** MUSIC OPENING IN FLUTE the hole in a flute that the player blows into **11.** RUDE ANSWERS impudent challenging speech in response to a question or order (*informal*) ○ *All I got from them was a lot of mouth.* **12.** GRIMACE a facial expression that shows displeasure, distaste, or sulkiness (*dated*) ○ *She made a mouth at him and quickly turned away.* ■ *vt* /mowt͟h/ (**mouths, mouthing, mouthed**) **1.** SAY SOMETHING INSINCERELY to speak or say something in a loud, affected, or insincere way ○ *How can you get up there and mouth such clichés?* **2.** FORM WORDS SILENTLY to form words with the tongue and lips without making a sound, usually in order to avoid being heard or to pretend to speak or sing something ○ *She mouthed a warning to the girl opposite as the teacher entered the room.* **3.** PUT SOMETHING IN MOUTH to put and hold something in the mouth as babies and young animals do **4.** CARESS SOMETHING WITH MOUTH to touch or caress something with the mouth **5.** ACCUSTOM HORSE TO BIT AND BRIDLE to train a horse to get used to a bit and bridle [Old English *mūþ* < Indo-European, 'to project'] ◇ **a mouth to feed** somebody who must be provided for, especially fed ◇ **be all mouth** to boast about doing something but never actually do it (*informal*) ◇ **down in the mouth** looking sad or gloomy (*informal*) ◇ **foam at the mouth** to produce foam from the mouth as a result of exertion, illness, or anger ◇ **give mouth to something** to express something in speech or writing (*formal*)

mouthbreeder /mówth breedər/, **mouthbrooder** /-broodər/ *n* a freshwater fish that carries its eggs and young in its mouth. Genus: *Haplochromis* or *Tilapia*.

-mouthed *suffix* **1.** having a particular kind of mouth ○ *wide-mouthed* **2.** speaking in a particular way ○ *foul-mouthed*

mouthful /mówthfoōl/ (*plural* **-fuls**) *n* **1.** QUANTITY OF FOOD OR DRINK the amount of food or drink that can comfortably be held in the mouth at one time **2.** SMALL AMOUNT OF FOOD only a very little amount to eat ○ *You can't go all day on a mouthful of food like that.* **3.** HARD-TO-PRONOUNCE WORD OR PHRASE a word or phrase that is hard to pronounce because of its unfamiliar sound combinations ○ *Her last name's a mouthful!* **4.** OFFENSIVE SPEECH something said that is offensive or impudent ○ *If you complain about the noise you only get a mouthful from them.*

mouth guard *n N Am* SPORTS same as **gumshield**

mouth organ *n* MUSIC same as **harmonica**

mouthpart /mówth paart/ *n* a body part near the mouth of an insect or other arthropod that it uses to gather or chew food

mouthpiece /mówth peess/ *n* **1.** the part of a musical instrument, telephone, or other device that is held to or in the mouth **2.** a person or publication that expresses the views of an organization (*sometimes disapproving*) ○ *He is the mouthpiece for big business in this city.*

mouth-to-mouth, **mouth-to-mouth resuscitation** *n* a method of reviving somebody who is not breathing in which the rescuer places his or her mouth over the mouth of the person not breathing and inflates the lungs with air

mouth ulcer *n* a small white ulcer that appears in groups in the mouth and on the tongue as a result of the fungal condition thrush (*usually used in the plural*) Technical name **aphtha**

mouthwash /mówth wosh/ *n* a medicated liquid that is gargled and swilled around the mouth to cleanse it and to freshen the breath

mouthwatering /mówth wawtəring/ *adj* stimulating the appetite by having a delicious smell or appearance —**mouthwateringly** *adv*

mouthy /mówt͟hi, mówthi/ (**-ier, -iest**) *adj* tending to talk rudely, loudly, or too much (*informal*) —**mouthiness** *n*

mouton /moō ton/ *n* sheepskin processed to resemble a fur such as seal or beaver [Mid-20C. < French]

mov /moov/ *abbr* a file extension for a film file. Full form **movie**

movable /moōvəb'l/, **moveable** *adj* **1.** EASILY MOVED able to move or be moved easily **2.** CHANGING DATE FROM YEAR TO YEAR falling on a different date each year ○ *Easter is a movable holiday.* ■ *n* LAW PROPERTY something that can be easily moved from one place to another, especially personal property such as an item of furniture (*often used in the plural*) —**movability** /moōvə bíllәti/ *n* —**movably** *adv*

movable feast *n* a religious festival that is not fixed but falls on a different day from year to year, as does Easter in the Christian calendar

move /moov/ *v* (**moves, moving, moved**) **1.** *vti* CHANGE POSITION to change position or location, or change the position or location of something ○ *Something moved behind that tree.* **2.** *vti* CHANGE RESIDENCE, JOB, OR SCHOOL to change your place of residence, work, or study, or make somebody do this ○ *move to the other side of town* **3.** *vti* TAKE ACTION to take action, or make somebody act ○ *It's due next week so we need to move quickly.* **4.** *vti* CHANGE VIEW to change a view or opinion, or make somebody do this ○ *She has moved to a more moderate position.* **5.** *vti* IMPROVE to make progress, or cause something to make progress ○ *Finally things have started moving.* **6.** *vi* ASSOCIATE WITH GROUP to associate with a particular group ○ *She moves among the yachting set.* **7.** *vi* PROPOSE ACTION to propose formally that something should happen or be done ○ *I move that the meeting be adjourned.* **8.** *vt* PRODUCE EMOTIONAL REACTION IN SOMEBODY to make somebody feel something, especially tender feelings ○ *Her performance moved all of us.* **9.** *vti* TAKE TURN IN GAME to change the position of one of the pieces in a board game as a turn in play ○ *Have you moved yet?* **10.** *vti* SELL WELL to sell well or effectively, or sell something well or effectively ○ *The souvenir mugs aren't really moving.* **11.** *vti* EMPTY BOWELS to empty the bowels ■ *n* **1.** ACT OF MOVING an act or instance of moving ○ *One false move and we're done for.* **2.** STEP IN SERIES an action considered as one of a series ○ *Keep your rivals guessing what your next move will be.* **3.** SOMEBODY'S TURN TO PLAY somebody's turn in a board game ○ *It's your move.* **4.** CHANGE OF LOCATION a change in your place of residence, work, or study ○ *I'm considering a move across town.* **5.** MANOEUVRE a manoeuvre or way of doing something ○ *If you're interested in martial arts, I could show you a few moves.* [13C. Via Anglo-Norman *mover* < Latin *movere*] ◇ **get a move on** to start doing something immediately, or do something faster (*informal*; *usually used as a command*) ◇ **make a move on somebody** to proposition somebody sexually (*slang*) ◇ **on the move 1.** going from one place to another **2.** busy doing one thing after another **3.** going forward, or making progress

ORIGIN The Latin word *movere* 'to move', from which *move* is derived, is also the source of English *commotion, emotion, mobile, moment, motif, motion, motive, motor, mutiny, promote*, and *remote*.

move in *v* **1.** *vti* to begin living or doing business in a place, or set somebody up in a place **2.** *vi* to approach closer to somebody or something, especially in order to make an attack ○ *move in for the kill*

move in on *vt* **1.** to attempt to take control of somebody or something, or take over from somebody ○ *He's trying to move in on our department* **2.** to approach closer to somebody or something, especially in order to make an attack ○ *The guards are moving in on the intruders.*

move into *vt* **1.** to begin living or doing business in a particular place ○ *move into a new flat* **2.** to begin dealing with something or doing business in a particular field ○ *The company is set to move into home banking.*

move on *vi* **1.** to leave a place and go somewhere else

○ *I think I'll be moving on.* **2.** to stop doing or dealing with something and start doing something else ○ *Let's move on to the next item on the agenda.*

move out *vi* to leave a place of residence or business, or help somebody do this

move over *vti* to move to one side in order to make room, or make somebody do this ○ *If you move over I'll be able to sit down.*

moveable *adj, n* another spelling of **movable**

movement /moóvmənt/ *n* **1.** ACT OF MOVING an act of changing location or position ○ *an instrument to detect subtle movements* **2.** WAY OF MOVING the way in which somebody or something moves ○ *the awkward movement of an injured arm* **3.** PHYSIOL ACT OF EMPTYING BOWELS an act of emptying the bowels, or the matter emptied **4.** POL EFFORT BY MANY TO ACHIEVE SOMETHING a collective effort by a large group of people to try to achieve something, especially a political or social reform ○ *the civil rights movement* **5.** POL PEOPLE ORGANIZED TO EFFECT CHANGE a large group of people who make a collective effort to achieve something, especially a political or social reform **6.** MUSIC SECTION OF MUSICAL WORK one of several self-contained sections that make up a large-scale musical work, usually differentiated from one another in tempo and character ○ *the concerto's third movement* **7.** MECH ENG MOVING PARTS the parts of a clock or watch mechanism that drive and regulate it **8.** FIN CHANGE IN PRICE a change in the prices of traded securities ○ *upward movement before the close of trading* **9.** LITERAT PLOT DEVELOPMENT the way in which a literary work develops as it progresses ○ *no movement in the plot for three chapters* **10.** LITERAT RHYTHM the cadence or rhythm of a piece of poetry **11.** ARTS SUGGESTED MOTION the illusion or suggestion of motion in a work of art such as a sculpture or painting **12.** MIL TACTICAL CHANGE OF POSITION a tactical change in the position or location of a military unit ■ **movements** *npl* ACTIVITIES AND LOCATION the things that somebody does and the places to which he or she goes, noted over a period of time ○ *The accused was asked to describe his movements on the day in question.*

mover /moóvər/ *n* **1.** SOMEBODY OR SOMETHING THAT CAUSES MOTION somebody or something that causes movement or accomplishes something ○ *She's the mover behind the project.* **2.** SOMEBODY PROPOSING MOTION somebody who formally proposes something at a meeting ○ *Does the mover of the motion consent to the amendment?* **3.** N Am MOVING COMPANY a company or person whose work is to transport the personal property of households or businesses from one location to another

movers and shakers *npl* people in society or in a particular sphere of activity who are powerful or influential ○ *one of the industry's movers and shakers*

movie /moóvi/ *n* **1.** N Am same as **film** (sense 2) **2.** COMPUT full form of **mov** ■ **movies** *npl* N Am **1.** the film industry, considered as a whole **2.** the showing of a film in a cinema ○ *We went to the movies last night.* [Early 20C. Shortening of *moving picture*]

movie camera *n* N Am CINEMA same as **cine camera**

movie film *n* N Am CINEMA same as **cine film**

moviegoer /moóvi gō ər/ *n* N Am CINEMA same as **filmgoer**

movie house *n* N Am CINEMA same as **cinema**

moviemaker /moóvi maykər/ *n* N Am CINEMA same as **filmmaker** —**moviemaking** *n*

movie star *n* N Am CINEMA same as **film star**

movie theater *n* US CINEMA same as **cinema** (sense 1)

moving /moóving/ *adj* **1.** AROUSING EMOTION producing a deep emotional reaction, especially sadness or compassion ○ *After such a moving speech we were all in tears.* **2.** MOVABLE able to move ○ *moving parts* **3.** IN MOTION in a state of movement (*usually used in combination*) ○ *slow-moving* **4.** CAUSED BY CHANGING PLACES involved in or caused by a change of residence or business location

SYNONYMS *moving, pathetic, pitiful, poignant, touching, heartwarming, heartrending*

CORE MEANING: arousing emotion

moving producing a deep emotional reaction, especially sadness or compassion ○ *a very moving description of life for children in these orphanages* ○ *the deeply moving funeral of a long-standing friend who had died of AIDS* **pathetic** arousing feelings of compassion and pity, often centred on somebody who is

vulnerable, helpless, or unfortunate ○ *Looking at her father, she saw a pathetic and solitary figure almost like a small boy.* ○ *There was a pathetic dignity about the old animal as she stood there, patient and undemanding.* **pitiful** arousing compassion and pity ○ *a picture of a pitiful starving kid* **poignant** causing a sharp sense of sadness, pity, or regret ○ *the opera's most poignant moment* ○ *The girl died just three days after our poignant pictures were taken.* **touching** causing feelings of warmth, sympathy, and tenderness ○ *He has been a tremendous support to me and my family in many small and touching ways.* **heartwarming** inspiring warm or kindly feelings, usually by showing life and human nature in a positive and reassuring light ○ *It is heartwarming that so many voters would like to see older members of society enjoying a better standard of living.* ○ *The former president recently found a heartwarming way to repay his childhood nanny – he helped build her a new house.* **heartrending** causing intense sadness or distress, especially in arousing sympathy with somebody else's unhappiness or hardship. ○ *heartrending handmade posters depicting victims who are still missing* ○ *These refugees often have heartrending stories to tell.*

moving-coil *adj* describes an electromechanical device or instrument that has a conducting coil freely suspended in a magnetic field. Current in the coil causes it to move or movement produces current.

movingly /moóvingli/ *adv* in a way that makes people feel deep emotions, especially sadness or compassion ○ *She spoke movingly about their plight.*

moving pavement *n* an endlessly circulating motor-driven belt that conveys people over a flat expanse of ground, especially in an airport. N Am term **moving sidewalk**

moving picture *n* CINEMA same as **film** (sense 2) (*dated*)

moving sidewalk *n* N Am TRANSP same as **moving pavement**

moving spirit *n* somebody who works hard to help to achieve something or inspires others to do this ○ *She was one of the moving spirits behind the campaign.*

moving staircase *n* ARCHIT, COMM same as **escalator** (sense 1)

moving van *n* N Am TRANSP same as **removal van**

mow[1] /mō/ (**mows, mowing, mowed, mown** /mōn/ or **mowed**) *v* **1.** *vti* to cut tall grass, hay, or grain with a scythe or machine **2.** *vt* to cut the grass, hay, or grain growing in a particular place ○ *Mow the front lawn today, please.* [Old English *māwan* < Germanic]

mow down *vt* **1.** to kill people quickly and in large numbers **2.** to knock somebody or something down by force

mow[2] /mō/ *n* US regional **1.** the part of a barn where hay or grain is stored when it has been harvested **2.** a pile of hay or grain, especially in a barn [Old English *mūga*, origin ?]

mower /mō ər/ *n* GARDENING same as **lawn mower**

mown AGRIC past participle of **mow**[1]

MOX /moks/ *n* a reactor fuel made from plutonium that has been separated from spent nuclear fuel by chemical reprocessing and mixed with natural or depleted uranium [Blend of MIXED + OXIDE]

moxa /móksə/ *n* in Eastern medicine, a cone or cylinder of downy or woolly material derived from various plants that is burned on the skin for its counterirritant effect [Late 17C. < Japanese *mogusa* 'burning herb']

moxibustion /móksi búsch'n/ *n* in Eastern medicine, the practice of burning a cone or cylinder of downy or woolly material derived from various plants on the skin for its counterirritant effect [Mid-19C. Blend of MOXA + COMBUSTION]

moxie /móksi/ *n* N Am courage combined with inventiveness (*slang*) [Mid-20C. After a brand of soft drink originally marketed as a 'nerve tonic']

Moynihan /móynihən/, **Daniel Patrick** (1927–2003) US academic and politician. He was ambassador to India (1973–74) and had a long and distinguished career in the US Senate (1976–2001).

'Somehow liberals have been unable to acquire from life what conservatives seem to be endowed with at birth: namely, a healthy skepticism of the powers of gov-

ernment agencies to do good.'
[Daniel Patrick Moynihan, *New York Post*; 14 May 1969]

Moz. *abbr* Mozambique

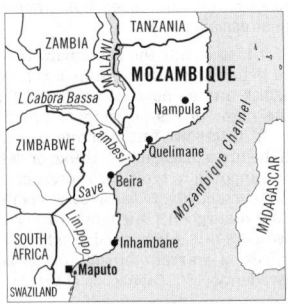

Mozambique

Mozambique /mố zam beék/ country in southeastern Africa. It became independent from Portugal in 1975 and joined the Commonwealth in 1995. Language: Portuguese. Currency: metical. Capital: Maputo. Population: 17,479,266 (2003). Area: 799,380 sq. km/308,642 sq. mi. Official name **Republic of Mozambique** —**Mozambican** *n, adj*

Mozarab /mō zárrəb/ *n* in Moorish Spain, a Christian who adopted some Arab customs without converting to Islam [Early 17C. Via Spanish *mozárabe* < Arabic *musta'rib* 'becoming an Arab'] —**Mozarabic** *adj*

Mozart /móts aart/, **Wolfgang Amadeus** (1756–91) Austrian composer. A figure of key importance in Western music, his compositions, in almost every musical genre, epitomize the classical style. —**Mozartian** /mōt saárti ən/ *n, adj*

'Music must never offend the ear; it must please the hearer. In other words, it must never cease to be music.'
[Attributed to Wolfgang Amadeus Mozart]

mozetta *n* CHR another spelling of **mozzetta**

mozzarella /mótsə réllə/ *n* a rubbery white unsalted Italian cheese used in salads, cooking, and especially on pizza [Early 20C. < Italian < *mozza*, type of cheese < *mozzare* 'cut off']

mozzetta /mō zéttə/, **mozetta** *n* a short hooded cape worn by the pope and other senior Roman Catholic clergymen [Late 18C. Via Italian < medieval Latin *almutia*]

mozzie /mózzi/, **mossie** *n* INSECTS same as **mosquito** (*informal*) [Mid-20C. Shortening and alteration]

mp *abbr* **1.** PHYS melting point **2.** MUSIC mezzo piano **3.** ONLINE Northern Mariana Islands (*used in Internet addresses*) See table at **domain name**

MP *abbr* **1.** GOV Member of Parliament **2.** Metropolitan Police **3.** MIL military police **4.** LAW mounted police

mp3 /ém pee threé/ *abbr* a file extension for an MP3 file. Full form **Motion Picture Experts Group, Audio Layer 3**

MP3 *n* a computer file standard for downloading compressed music from the Internet, playable on a multimedia computer with appropriate software. Full form **Motion Picture Experts Group, Audio Layer 3**

MPD *abbr* PSYCHIAT multiple personality disorder

mpeg /ém peg/ *abbr* a file extension for an MPEG file. Full form **Moving Pictures Experts Group**

MPEG /ém peg/ *n* **1.** a computer file standard for compressing, storing, and transmitting digital video and audio. Full form **Moving Pictures Experts Group 2.** a file containing digital video and audio in MPEG format

mpg[1] *abbr* MEASURE miles per gallon

mpg[2] *abbr* a file extension for an MPEG file. Full form **Moving Pictures (Experts) Group**

MPG *n* the basic salary scale for a teacher in Britain. Full form **main professional grade**

mph *abbr* MEASURE miles per hour

MPhil /ém fíl/ *abbr* EDUC Master of Philosophy

Mpumalanga /əm poómə láng gə/ province in South Africa in the northeastern part of the country. Capital: Nelspruit. Population: 3,122,977 (2001). Area: 79,490 sq. km/30,691 sq. mi.

MPV *n* a car similar to a van that can carry more

than five people, typically seven people in three rows of seats. Full form **multipurpose vehicle**

mq *abbr* ONLINE Martinique (*used in Internet addresses*) See table at **domain name**

mr *abbr* ONLINE Mauritania (*used in Internet addresses*) See table at **domain name**

Mr /místər/ *n* **1.** MAN'S TITLE the customary title of courtesy used before the name of a man ○ *Mr Smith* **2.** JOB OR FUNCTION TITLE a courtesy title used for a man before the name of his position or function ○ *Mr President* **3.** DESCRIPTIVE TITLE a humorous title used for a man before a place, name, thing, or description that he is supposed to typify or represent ○ *He's not exactly Mr Personality, is he?* **4.** SURGEON'S TITLE a title used before a surgeon's surname, rather than 'Dr' **5.** JUNIOR OFFICER'S TITLE a title used to address a junior naval officer, a warrant officer, or a cadet in a service academy [15C. Contraction of MASTER]

MR *abbr* Master of the Rolls

MRAM *abbr* COMPUT magnetic random access memory

Mr Big *n US* a powerful or important man, e.g. the chief of a criminal organization (*slang*)

MRBM *abbr* MIL medium-range ballistic missile

MRC *abbr* Medical Research Council

MRCA *abbr* MIL multirole combat aircraft

Mr Clean *n US* somebody, especially a public figure, who is seen as being admirably honest and moral (*informal*) [Mid-20C. After a cleaning solution trademark]

MRCS *abbr* Member of the Royal College of Surgeons

MRCVS *abbr* Member of the Royal College of Veterinary Surgeons

MRE *abbr* MIL meal, ready to eat

MRI *abbr* MED magnetic resonance imaging

MRIA *abbr* Member of the Royal Irish Academy

mridanga /mri dúng gə/, **mridang** /mri dúng/, **mridangam** /-gəm/ *n* a South Asian drum that is shaped like a barrel and used as an accompaniment in Karnatak music [Late 19C. < Tamil]

MRI scanner *n* a scanner that uses magnetic resonance imaging to obtain high-contrast detailed images in any plane of the tissues of the body

mRNA *abbr* GENETICS messenger RNA

MRP *abbr* manufacturer's recommended price

Mr Right *n* a man seen as being a perfect romantic or marriage partner for a specific woman (*informal*) ○ *One day Mr Right will come along.*

Mrs /míssiz/ *n* **1.** a customary title of courtesy for a married or widowed woman, used before her name ○ *Mrs Wright* **2.** a title used for a woman before a place name, thing, or description that she is supposed to typify or represent ○ *Mrs Cheerful* [Early 17C. Contraction of MISTRESS]

MRSA *n* a strain of a common infection-causing bacterium that has become resistant to treatment by the antibiotic methicillin and is therefore a hazard in places such as hospitals. Full form **methicillin-resistant staphylococcus aureus**

MRSC *abbr* Member of the Royal Society of Chemistry

Mrs Grundy /-grúndi/ *n* a very narrow-minded and prudish person [Late 18C. After a character in the play *Speed the Plough*, by Thomas Morton (1764–1838)]

Mrs Mop, **Mrs Mopp** *n* a woman employed to do domestic cleaning (*dated informal*)

ms *abbr* **1.** MEASURE millisecond **2.** ONLINE Montserrat (*used in Internet addresses*) See table at **domain name**

Ms /məz, miz/ *n* **1.** a customary title of courtesy used before the name or names of a woman without making a distinction between married and unmarried status ○ *Ms Bennett* **2.** a title used for a woman before a place, name, thing, or description that she is supposed to typify or represent ○ *Ms Efficiency* [Mid-20C. Blend of MISS + MRS]

MS[1] *abbr* **1.** *also* **ms.** LITERAT manuscript **2.** EDUC Master of Surgery **3.** Mississippi **4.** TRANSP motor ship **5.** MED multiple sclerosis

MS[2] *abbr* sacred to the memory of (*on gravestones*) [Latin *memoriae sacrum*]

MSBP *abbr* MED Münchausen syndrome by proxy

MSc *abbr* EDUC Master of Science [Latin *Magister Scientiae*]

MS-DOS /ém ess dóss/ *tdmk* a trademark for a widely used computer operating system

msec *abbr* MEASURE millisecond

MSG *abbr* CHEM monosodium glutamate

msg. *abbr* US message

Msgr *abbr* RELIG **1.** Monseigneur **2.** Monsignor

MSH *abbr* BIOCHEM melanocyte-stimulating hormone

MSI *abbr* ELECTRONICS medium scale integration

MSP *abbr* GOV Member of the Scottish Parliament

Ms Right *n* a woman seen as being the perfect romantic or marriage partner for a specific man ○ *tired of waiting for Ms Right to come along*

MSS, **mss.** *abbr* ARTS manuscripts

MST *abbr* TIME Mountain Standard Time

mt *abbr* **1.** ONLINE Malta (*used in Internet addresses*) See table at **domain name 2.** GEOG mount **3.** GEOG mountain

Mt[1] *abbr* **1.** BIBLE Matthew **2.** GEOG Mount **3.** GEOG Mountain

Mt[2] *symbol* CHEM ELEM meitnerium

MT *abbr* **1.** MIL, MEASURE megaton **2.** MEASURE metric ton **3.** TIME Mountain Time

mt. *abbr* **1.** MIL, MEASURE megaton **2.** GEOG mount **3.** GEOG mountain

Mtarazi Falls /əmtə ráatsi-/ waterfall in Zimbabwe, southeastern Africa, one of the highest in the world. Height: 762 m/2,500 ft.

MTB *abbr* motor torpedo boat

MTBE *n* a lead-free antiknock petrol additive. Full form **methyl tertiary-butyl ethyl**

MTBF *abbr* COMPUT mean time between failures

MTech /ém ték/ *abbr* EDUC Master of Technology

mtg *abbr* meeting

mtg. *abbr* **mtge.** FIN mortgage

mtn., **Mtn.** *abbr* US mountain

Mt Rev. *abbr* RELIG Most Reverend

mts, **mts.** *abbr* **1.** mountains **2.** US mounts

Mts, **Mts.** *abbr* **1.** Mountains **2.** US Mounts

MTTR *abbr* MANUF mean time to repair

mu[1] /myoo/ *n* the 12th letter of the Greek alphabet, represented in the English alphabet as 'm'. See table at **alphabet** [Late 19C. < Greek]

mu[2] *abbr* ONLINE Mauritius (*used in Internet addresses*) See table at **domain name**

MU *abbr* **1.** Mothers' Union **2.** Musicians' Union **3.** ONLINE multiuser

muah muah *n* another spelling of **mwah mwah**

Mu'awiya /moó ə weé ə/ (*d.* AD 680) leader of the Umayyad clan who became the first Umayyad caliph following civil war with Ali

Mubarak /moó báarək, moo-/, **Hosni** (*b.* 1928) Egyptian president. He became president after the assassination of Anwar Sadat in 1981 and continued Sadat's foreign policy of peace with Israel while mending strained relations with the Arab League. Full name **Mubarak, Muhammad Hosni Said**

muc- *prefix* same as **muco-** (*used before vowels*)

much /much/ *adv* **1.** LARGELY to a great extent, intensity, or degree (*often used in combination*) ○ *She hasn't changed much over the years.* ○ *It's a much more difficult game than the other.* ○ *a much-loved figure in British political life* **2.** OFTEN often or frequently ○ *I don't get out much these days.* ○ *Do you see your children much over the holidays?* **3.** NEARLY nearly or practically ○ *One day is much like the next when you're ill.* ○ *It's much the same problem all over again.* ■ *pron, det* LARGE AMOUNT a large amount or degree (*det*) *He doesn't have much free time because of the demands of work.* ○ (*pron*) *Much remains to be done.* ○ (*pron*) *She does much of her writing at home.* ■ *pron* IMPRESSIVE something impressive, important, or unusual ○ *The house isn't much to look at, but it's very comfortable.* [13C. Shortening of Old English *mycel* < Germanic] ◇ **as much** precisely that ○ *I wasn't surprised when she said she'd taken the money, as I'd suspected as much from the start.* ◇ **(as) much as** although, or even though ○ *As much as I'd like to join you, I'm afraid I can't.* ◇ **much as** to almost the same degree, or in a similar manner ○ *You cook it much as you would a potato.* ◇ **not much**

of not particularly good at something, or not a very good example of something ○ *It's not been much of a celebration, has it?* ◇ **not up to much** (*informal*) **1.** of a low standard **2.** not very active or energetic

muchness /múchnəss/ *n* greatness in quantity, extent, or degree (*archaic*) ◇ **much of a muchness** amounting to or being practically the same (*informal*)

muci- *prefix* same as **muco-**

mucic acid

mucic acid /myoóssik-/ *n* a colourless crystalline solid. Source: lactose. Use: manufacture of chemicals. Formula: $C_4H_4(OH)_4(COOH)_2$.

muciferous /myoo síffərəss/ *adj* producing or containing a lot of mucus

mucigen /myoóssijən/ *n* a substance in mucous cells that is converted into mucin

mucilage /myoóssilij/ *n* **1.** a thick water-based solution used as an adhesive **2.** a gummy substance secreted by some plants such as seaweed that contains protein and carbohydrates [14C. Via French < late Latin *mucillago* 'mouldy juice' < Latin *mucus*]

mucilaginous /myoóssi lájjinəss/ *adj* **1.** relating to or producing mucilage **2.** moist and sticky like glue —**mucilaginously** *adv* —**mucilaginousness** *n*

mucin /myoóssin/ *n* a complex protein present in mucus —**mucinous** *adj*

muck /muk/ *n* **1.** STICKY DIRT soft moist dirt or filth (*informal*) **2.** RUBBISH something that is distasteful, disgusting, or of very poor quality (*informal*) ○ *I don't know how they can publish such muck* **3.** AGRIC MANURE moist manure or compost, especially when used to fertilize land **4.** MIN EXTRACT MINE WASTE waste material from mining, e.g. earth or rubble ■ *vt* (**mucks**, **mucking**, **mucked**) **1.** CLEAN OUT PLACE to clean the muck out of a place such as a stable or barn **2.** MAKE SOMETHING DIRTY to pollute something or make something dirty (*informal*) **3.** AGRIC FERTILIZE LAND to fertilize land with manure or compost [13C. < N Germanic < Germanic, 'soft']

muck about *v* **1.** *vi* to waste time instead of doing something useful or important (*informal*) ○ *We'd get this job finished sooner if you two stopped mucking about.* **2.** *vt* to waste somebody's time, or fail to deal with somebody in a serious way ○ *The car people keep mucking me about.*

muck in *vi* to share something, especially work or accommodation, with other people (*informal*) ○ *It won't take long if everyone mucks in.* ○ *The house is a little overcrowded but we all just muck in together.*

muck up *v* **1.** *vt* DAMAGE SOMETHING to ruin or make a mess of something (*informal*) ○ *She's really mucked up her chances now.* **2.** *vt* MAKE SOMETHING DIRTY to soil or stain something (*informal*) ○ *He fell in the mud and mucked up his trousers.* **3.** *vi* Aus MISBEHAVE to act in an inappropriate or annoying way ○ *The kids have been mucking up all day.*

muckamuck /múkəmuk/ *n* N Am same as **high-muck-a-muck** (*informal*) [Early 20C. Shortening]

mucker /múkər/ *n* **1.** a friend (*dated slang*) ○ *This is my old mucker Charlie.* **2.** somebody whose job is to remove rocky mine waste

muckle /múk'l/ Scotland *adj* LARGE very big or great ○ *a muckle stone* ■ *adv* MUCH much or greatly ○ *not muckle clever* ■ *n* A LOT a large amount of something ○ *Many a mickle makes a muckle.* [Old English *mycel* (see MUCH)]

muckluck *n* CLOTHING another spelling of **mukluk**

muckrake /múk rayk/ *vi* (**-rakes**, **-raking**, **-raked**) to seek out and publicize misconduct by prominent people

■ *n* a rake used to spread manure or compost — **muckraker** *n* —**muckraking** *n*

muck sweat *n* heavy sweating, or a condition in which somebody sweats heavily (*informal*) ○ *I've been in a muck sweat over that lost file.*

muck-up day *n Aus* the last day of school before exams, on which pupils play practical jokes (*informal*)

mucky /múki/ (**-ier, -iest**) *adj* (*informal*) **1. FILTHY** very dirty or covered with muck **2. RUDE** rude or obscene **3. RAINY** rainy or stormy —**muckily** *adv* —**muckiness** *n*

REGIONAL NOTE See *manky*.

muco- *prefix* mucus, mucous membrane ○ *mucocutaneous* [< Latin *mucus*]

mucocutaneous /myoókō kyoo táyni əss/ *adj* involving both skin and mucous membrane

mucolytic /myoókō líttik/ *adj* able to break down mucus

mucopeptide /myoókō pép tīd/ *n* BIOCHEM same as **peptidoglycan**

mucopolysaccharide /myoókō pólli sákə rīd/ *n* a complex polysaccharide containing amino groups, found in connective tissues

mucoprotein /myoókō prṓ teen/ *n* a complex protein found in mucous secretions

mucopurulent /myoókō pyoórələnt/ *adj* containing both mucus and pus

mucosa /myoo kṓssə/ (*plural* **-sae** /-see/) *n* ANAT same as **mucous membrane** [Late 19C. < modern Latin (*membrana*) *mucosa* 'mucous membrane']

mucous /myoókəss/ *adj* containing, secreting, resembling, or covered with mucus [Mid-17C. < Latin *mucosus* < *mucus* 'mucus']

mucous membrane *n* a moist lining in the body passages of mammals that contains mucus-secreting cells and is open directly or indirectly to the external environment

mucro /myoókrō/ (*plural* **-cros**) *n* a sharp point projecting from an organ or plant part [Mid-17C. < Latin, 'sharp point, sword']

mucronate /myoókrə nayt/, **mucronated** /myoókrə naytid/ *adj* used to describe an organ or plant part that ends in a sharp point [Late 18C. < Latin *mucronatus* < *mucro* 'sharp point, sword'] —**mucronation** /myoókrə náysh'n/ *n*

mucus /myoókəss/ *n* the clear slimy lubricating substance consisting mostly of mucins and water that coats and protects mucous membranes [Mid-17C. < Latin] —**mucoid** *adj*

mud /mud/ *n* **1.** soil that is very wet, soft, and gummy **2.** defamatory things said or written about somebody (*informal*) [14C. Probably < Middle Low German *mudde*] ◇ **(as) clear as mud** not clear or understandable at all (*informal*) ◇ **here's mud in your eye!** used as a drinking toast (*informal*) ◇ **sling** *or* **throw mud at somebody** *or* **something** to make defamatory statements about somebody or something (*informal*)

MUD /mud/ *n* a virtual online space in which several participants can contribute to a communal project such as a collaboratively written story or a game for several players. Full form **multiuser domain**

mudbath /múd baath/ (*plural* **-baths** /-baathz/) *n* **1.** a bath in heated mud, thought to tone the skin and organs **2.** something, e.g. a football game, that takes place outdoors in very muddy conditions (*informal*)

mud dauber *n* a wasp that builds multicellular nests with mud. Family: Sphecidae. N Am term **mud wasp**

muddle /múdd'l/ *v* (**-dles, -dling, -dled**) **1.** *vt* MIX THINGS TOGETHER IN DISORDER to mix things together in a confused or disordered way ○ *They're arranged alphabetically, so don't muddle them.* **2.** *vt* CONFUSE THINGS to confuse things in the mind (*often passive*) ○ *They look so alike that it's easy to muddle them up.* **3.** *vti* CONFUSE OR BE CONFUSED to be confused or bemused, or cause somebody to be so ○ *Tell me again slowly - you're muddling me.* ■ *n* **1.** CONFUSED STATE something that is in such a confused condition that it is hard to organize or understand ○ *How did our records get into such a muddle?* **2.** MIX-UP a misunderstanding arising from or causing a confused situation or state ○ *There's been a muddle over the bookings.* [14C. Probably < Middle Dutch

moddelen < *modden* 'dabble in mud'] —**muddled** *adj* —**muddler** *n* —**muddly** *adj*

muddle through *vi* to succeed or manage to keep going despite being disorganized ○ *I expect we'll muddle through somehow.*

muddleheaded /múdd'l héddid/ *adj* **1.** unable to think clearly **2.** not clearly thought out —**muddleheadedly** *adv* —**muddleheadedness** *n*

muddy /múddi/ *adj* (**-dier, -diest**) **1.** MARKED WITH MUD full of, covered in, or dirtied with mud **2.** RESEMBLING MUD like mud in being cloudy or thick **3.** LACKING CLARITY lacking clarity, brightness, or transparency ○ *a muddy colour* **4.** CONFUSED hard to understand, or lacking in logical reasoning ■ *vt* (**-dies, -dying, -died**) **1.** MAKE SOMETHING MUDDY to cover or dirty something with mud **2.** MAKE SOMETHING UNCLEAR to make something confused and unclear —**muddily** *adv* —**muddiness** *n*

Mudéjar /moo dáy haar/ *n* (*plural* **-jares** /-haa ress/) a Moor who was allowed to stay in a part of Spain after it had been recaptured by the Christians ■ *adj* relating to the Mudéjares, especially their style of architecture [Mid-19C. < Spanish < Arabic *mudajjan*, past participle of *dajjana* 'permit to stay']

mud flap *n UK, ANZ, Can* a flap attached behind the wheel of a vehicle to prevent mud and water from splashing up onto the vehicle, or onto the vehicles following. US term **splashguard**

mudflat /múd flat/ *n* an area of low muddy land that is underwater only at high tide, especially one near an estuary

mudflow /múd flō/ *n* a fast-moving downhill flow of mud and soil loosened by rainfall or melting snow

mudguard /múd gaard/ *n* a curved rigid arch above the wheel of a bicycle or motorcycle designed to cut down the amount of water and mud thrown up by the wheel. N Am term **fender**

mudlark /múd laark/ *n* a child living on the streets and making money by selling objects found in tidal mud (*archaic*) [Late 18C. < MUD + LARK [1]]

mudpack /múd pak/ *n* a beauty treatment for the face that is allowed to dry before being removed

mud pie *n* a mass of mud shaped by children as a game

mud puppy *n* a salamander that lives on muddy banks and has dark red external gills. Native to: eastern North American. Genus: *Necturus*.

mudra /mə draá/ (*plural* **-dras**) *n* a symbolic position in which the hands are held in Hindu dancing and ritual [Early 19C. < Sanskrit *mudrā* 'seal, sign']

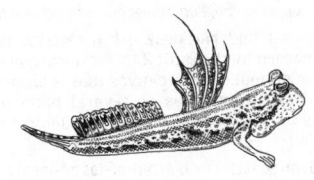

mudskipper

mudskipper /múd skipər/ *n* a tropical fish of the goby family that uses its pectoral fins to leave the water to feed. Native to: Asia, Africa. Genus: *periophthalmodon*.

mudslide /múd slīd/ *n* a slow-moving and often destructive mass of mud flowing down a slope

mudslinging /múd slinging/ *n* the making of defamatory remarks about somebody, especially a political opponent or other competitor ○ *The level of debate in this election has seldom risen above petty mudslinging.* —**mudslinger** *n*

mudstone /múd stōn/ *n* a grey sedimentary rock formed from mud, similar to shale but with less developed lamination

mud turtle *n* a small freshwater turtle that lives at the bottom of muddy ponds and streams. Native to: North and Central America. Genus: *Kinosternon*.

mud volcano *n* a conical mound of mud that forms around a hot spring or geyser

mud wasp *n N Am* INSECTS same as **mud dauber**

mudwrestling /múd ressling/ *n* a form of entertainment in which performers wrestle in a pit filled with mud in front of spectators —**mudwrestler** *n*

Mueller /múllər, múl/lər/, **Sir Ferdinand von** (1825–96) German-born Australian botanist and explorer. He was the author, with George Bentham, of *Flora Australiensis* (1863–78), and introduced the blue gum tree to Europe, North America, and Africa. Full name **Mueller, Sir Ferdinand Jakob Heinrich von**

Muenster /múnstər, moónstər/, **Munster** *n* a white to yellow semisoft mildly flavoured cheese that typically has an orange edible rind [Early 20C. After *Munster*, town in NE France]

muesli /myoózli/ *n* a mixture of cereal flakes and rolled oats with dried fruit and nuts, eaten with milk for breakfast [Mid-20C. < Swiss German, 'little purée' < German *Mus* 'purée']

muezzin /moo ézzin, myoo-/ *n* a mosque official who calls Muslims to prayer from a minaret five times a day [Late 16C. < dialect variant of Arabic *mu'addin*, form of *'addana* 'call to prayer' < *'udn* 'ear']

muff[1] /muf/ (*informal*) *vt* (**muffs, muffing, muffed**) **1.** FAIL TO CATCH SOMETHING to fail to catch a ball or make a shot ○ *He got right under the ball and still muffed it.* **2.** DO SOMETHING BADLY to do something badly or awkwardly ○ *The play got off to a bad start when the actors muffed the opening lines.* ■ *n* **1.** FAILED ACTION a badly performed catch, shot, or action **2.** BUNGLER somebody regarded as clumsy or bungling [Mid-19C. Origin ?]

muff

muff[2] /muf/ *n* **1.** an open-ended cylinder of fur or cloth used for keeping hands warm, one hand going in at each end **2.** either of the tufts of feathers on each side of the face of some types of domestic fowl [Late 16C. < Dutch *mof*, shortening of Middle Dutch *moffel* < medieval Latin *muffula* 'glove']

muffin /múffin/ *n* **1.** a small round thick savoury cake (**griddlecake**) made from yeasted batter and usually served split, toasted, and buttered. N Am term **English muffin** **2.** a small round cake for one person made from a thick batter and often containing fruit or nuts [Early 18C. Origin ?]

muffle[1] /múff'l/ *vt* (**-fles, -fling, -fled**) **1.** WRAP SOMETHING TO STIFLE SOUND to wrap or pad something with material in order to deaden the sound it makes **2.** MAKE SOUND LESS LOUD to make a sound quieter or less distinct ○ *He put his hands over his ears to muffle the noise of the sirens.* **3.** PREVENT SOMETHING BEING EXPRESSED to prevent something from being said or written ○ *a government that sought to muffle all opposition* **4.** KEEP SOMEBODY WARM to wrap somebody or a part of somebody's body in a garment or cloth for warmth ○ *She muffled herself up in a thick shawl.* ■ *n* **1.** SOMETHING MUFFLING SOUND something used to muffle a sound **2.** KILN a kiln in which objects being fired are protected from direct contact with the flames [15C. Origin ?] —**muffled** *adj*

muffle[2] /múff'l/ *n* the moist fleshy hairless upper lip of some rodents and ruminants [Early 17C. < French *mufle*]

muffler /múfflər/ *n* **1.** a scarf worn around the neck for warmth **2.** ACOUSTICS same as **muffle**[1] *n* (sense 1) **3.** *ANZ, N Am* a drum-shaped part of a car's exhaust pipe designed to reduce the amount of noise made by the engine. UK term **silencer**

mufti /múfti, moófti/ *n* ordinary clothes worn by somebody who usually wears a uniform [Early 19C. Origin ?]

Mufti /múfti, moŏfti/ *n* an expert on Islamic religious law [Late 16C. < Arabic *muftī*, past participle of *aftā* 'decide a legal point']

mufti day *n* a day on which school students are permitted to wear casual clothes rather than uniform, as a fundraising exercise

mug[1] /mug/ *n* **1.** a large round straight-sided cup typically made of earthenware and having a handle **2.** the contents of a mug, or the amount of liquid it can hold ○ *a mug of hot soup* [Early 16C. Origin ?] —**mugful** *n*

mug[2] /mug/ *n* (*slang*) **1.** SOMEBODY'S FACE somebody's face or mouth **2.** UNINTELLIGENT PERSON somebody regarded as unintelligent or easily deceived ■ *v* (**mugs, mugging, mugged**) **1.** *vt* ROB SOMEBODY to attack and rob somebody, especially a pedestrian in a public place **2.** *vi* MAKE FACES to make exaggerated facial expressions when performing or posing for a camera ○ *The actors were playing it for laughs, mugging in every scene.* [Early 18C. Probably < MUG[1], from the representation of faces on mugs] ◇ **a mug's game** something only gullible people would take part in (*informal*)

mug up *vi* to study hard, especially in preparation for an exam (*informal*)

Robert Mugabe
Popperfoto

Mugabe /moŏ ga´abi/, **Robert** (*b.* 1924) Zimbabwean politician. After leading the struggle against the white government of Rhodesia, he served as the first prime minister of Zimbabwe (1980–87) before becoming president in 1987. Full name **Mugabe, Robert Gabriel**

> 'Genuine independence can only come out of the barrel of a gun.'
> [Robert Mugabe. Quoted in *The Africans: Encounters from the Sudan to the Cape*, David Lamb; 1983]

mugaccino /múggə cheénō/ *n Aus* a large cappuccino served in a mug

muggar *n* REPT another spelling of **mugger**[2]

mugger[1] /múggər/ *n* somebody who attacks and robs somebody in a public place [Mid-19C. < MUG[2]]

mugger[2] /múggər/, **muggar, muggur** *n* a freshwater crocodile. Native to: South Asia. Latin name: *Crocodylus palustris.* [Mid-19C. < Hindi *magar*]

mugging /múgging/ *n* the crime of attacking and robbing somebody in a public place

muggins /múgginz/ *n* **1.** somebody regarded as gullible (*humorous insult*) **2.** a name people use to refer to themselves when they believe they are acting gullibly (*informal humorous*) ○ *I suppose muggins will have to come and pick you up?* [Mid-19C. Origin ?]

Muggle /múgg'l/ *n* in the Harry Potter novels by J. K. Rowling, somebody who is regarded unfavourably as a result of having no magical powers. [Late 20C. Coined by J. K. ROWLING, < ?]

muggur *n* REPT another spelling of **mugger**[2]

muggy /múggi/ (**-gier, -giest**) *adj* unpleasantly hot and humid [Mid-18C. < obsolete *mug* 'rain lightly' < N Germanic] —**muggily** *adv* —**mugginess** *n*

Mughal /moŏg'l, -gaal/, **Mogul, Moghul** *n* **1.** a member of a Muslim dynasty of Mongol origin that ruled large parts of India from 1526 to 1857 **2.** the Mughal emperor of Delhi [Late 16C. Via Urdu *mugal* < Persian *mugul* 'Mongol'] —**Mughal** *adj*

mugshot /múg shot/ *n* a photograph of somebody's face, especially one of a suspected criminal's face or profile taken by police

mugwort /múg wurt/ *n* a herbaceous perennial wormwood with aromatic leaves. Flowers: small, pale green. Native to: temperate regions of the northern hemisphere. Latin name: *Artemisia vulgaris.* [Old English *mucgwyrt* < earlier forms of MIDGE + WORT[1]]

mugwump /múg wump/ *n N Am* somebody who takes an independent or neutral position, especially in politics [Mid-19C. < Massachuset *mugquomp*, shortening of *muggumquomp* 'war leader'] —**mugwumpery** *n*

Muhammad /mə hámmid/, **Mohammed** (AD 570?–632) Arabian founder of Islam. According to Islamic tradition he received his first command from Allah in AD 610. In AD 628 he made Mecca the religious capital of Islam. He recorded his visions and teachings in the Koran.

Muhammad Ali ♦ Ali, Muhammad

Muharram /mə hárrəm/, **Moharram** /mō-/ *n* **1.** in the Islamic calendar, the first month of the year. See table at **calendar 2.** an Islamic festival that marks the martyrdom of the brothers Hussein and Hassan, grandsons of the prophet Mohammed. Date: in the month of Muharram. Same as **Ashora** [Early 19C. < Arabic *muharram* 'inviolable', past participle of *harrama* 'forbid']

muir /myoor, moor/ *n Scotland* GEOG same as **moor**[1] (*often in placenames*) [Variant]

Muir /myoor/, **Edwin** (1887–1959) British poet, translator, and critic. His work reflected his interest in psychoanalysis and his native Scotland. He is known for his English translations of Franz Kafka's works.

> 'Those lumbering horses in the steady plough, / On the bare field—I wonder why, just now, / They seemed terrible, so wild and strange, / Like magic power on the stony grange.'
> [Edwin Muir, 'Horses', *First Poems*; 1925]

Muir, Jean (1928–95) British fashion designer. She was noted for the classic cut and fluid shape of her designs. Full name **Muir, Jean Elizabeth**

Muir Glacier glacier in southeastern Alaska, flowing down Mount Fairweather and into Glacier Bay. It is nearly 3 km/2 mi. long and 40 to 65 m/135 to 210 ft high.

muishond /máys hont, máy sont/ (*plural same* or **-honds**) *n S Africa* a mongoose, or other small carnivorous mammal [Late 18C. < Dutch, 'weasel']

mujahedin /moŏjəhə deén/, **mujaheddin, mujahideen, mujahidin** *npl* Islamic guerrillas based in Iran and Pakistan who fought a holy war (**jihad**) against the Soviet forces occupying Afghanistan in the late 1970s and the 1980s [Mid-20C. < Persian or Arabic *mujāhidīn*, plural of *mujāhid* 'somebody who fights a jihad']

mukluk /múk luk/, **muckluck** *n* **1.** a sealskin boot originally worn by the Inuit **2.** *N Am* a waterproof boot made of animal skin or canvas that is large enough to be worn over shoes or several pairs of socks [Mid-19C. < Yupik *maklak* 'bearded seal', misunderstood as 'sealskin']

mulatto /myoŏ láttō, moŏ-/ (*plural* **-tos** or **-toes**) *n* (*dated*) **1.** an offensive term for somebody who has one Black and one white parent **2.** an offensive term for somebody who has both Black and white ancestors [Late 16C. < Spanish *mulato* 'young mule' < *mulo* 'mule' < Latin *mulus*]

mulberry

mulberry /múlbəri/ (*plural* **-ries**) *n* **1.** PURPLE FRUIT a small sweet fruit resembling a berry **2.** TREE WITH EDIBLE FRUIT a small deciduous tree, one species of which bears edible fruit and another species leaves that are fed to silkworms. Genus: *Morus.* **3.** PURPLE COLOUR a dark purple colour tinged with red or grey [Old English *mōrberie* < *mōr-* < Latin *morum* 'mulberry'] —**mulberry** *adj*

Mulberry Harbour *n* either of two preconstructed floating harbours that were towed across the English Channel to France as part of the Allied invasion in 1944 [< the operation's code name]

mulch /mulch/ *n* a protective covering of organic material laid over the soil around plants to prevent erosion, retain moisture, and sometimes enrich the soil ■ *vti* (**mulches, mulching, mulched**) to cover soil with mulch ○ *mulch with newspaper* [Mid-17C. Origin ?]

mulct /mulkt/ *vt* (**mulcts, mulcting, mulcted**) **1.** FINE SOMEBODY to fine somebody as a penalty **2.** CHEAT SOMEBODY to cheat somebody out of something (*archaic*) ■ *n* PENALTY a fine or penalty [15C. < Latin *mulctare* < *mulcta* 'fine']

Muldoon /mul doón/, **Sir Robert** (1921–92) prime minister of New Zealand (1975–84). Elected as a member of parliament for the National Party in 1960, he served in several ministries before becoming prime minister in 1975. Full name **Muldoon, Sir Robert David**

mule

mule[1] /myool/ *n* **1.** CROSS BETWEEN HORSE AND DONKEY the offspring of a female horse and a male donkey **2.** HYBRID ANIMAL OR PLANT the sterile offspring of two closely related species of animal or plant **3.** STUBBORN PERSON somebody regarded as stubborn or intractable (*informal*) **4.** DRUG COURIER somebody who transports illegal drugs for a dealer (*slang*) **5.** MANUF SPINNING MACHINE a machine that draws and spins cotton fibres into yarn and winds it onto spindles [Old English *mūl*, probably via Germanic < Latin *mulus*]

mule[2] /myool/ *n* a backless slipper or shoe [Mid-16C. Via French < Latin *mulleus (calceus)* 'reddish-purple (shoe)']

mule deer *n* a large deer that has a greyish-brown coat, some white underparts, a black tail, and long ears. Native to: western North America. Latin name: *Odocoileus hemionus.* [< MULE[1]]

muleta /myoŏ léttə/ (*plural* **-tas**) *n* a short red cape attached to a stick that a matador uses instead of the full cape in the final stages of a bullfight [Mid-19C. < Spanish, diminutive of *mula* 'female mule' < Latin *mulus* 'mule']

muleteer /myoŏlə teér/ *n* somebody whose occupation is driving mules [Mid-16C. < French *muletier* < *mulet*, diminutive of Old French *mul* 'mule' < Latin *mulus*]

mulga /múlgə/ *n* **1.** an acacia bush or small tree that forms dense thickets. Native to: dry regions of Australia. Genus: *Acacia.* **2.** *Aus* a part of Australia where there is little or no rainfall and mulgas are the dominant vegetation ○ *His car broke down out in the mulga.* [Mid-19C. < an Aboriginal language]

mulga snake *n* a large aggressive brown or tan snake. Native to: Australian interior. Latin name: *Pseudechis australis.*

Mulhacén /moŏlə tháyn/ highest peak on the Spanish mainland, situated in the Sierra Nevada, about 32 km/20 mi. southeast of Granada. Height: 3,477 m/11,407 ft.

Mulhouse /mü looz/ industrial city in Haut-Rhin Department, Alsace Region, northeastern France. Population: 110,359 (1999).

muliebrity /myoŏli ébbriti/ *n* (*literary*) **1.** the condition of being a woman **2.** the qualities conventionally associated with women [Late 16C. < Latin *muliebritas* < *mulier* 'woman']

mulish /myoŏlish/ *adj* obstinate and unwilling to co-

operate or listen to suggestions [Mid-18C. < MULE [1]] —
mulishly *adv* —**mulishness** *n*

mull[1] /mul/ *n* a period of deep thought [Mid-19C. Origin ?]

mull over *vt* to consider something thoroughly

mull[2] /mul/ (**mulls, mulling, mulled**) *vt* to heat, sweeten, and flavour wine, beer, or cider [Early 17C. Origin ?]

mull[3] /mul/ *n* soft cotton muslin. Use: dresses. [Late 17C. Shortening of Hindi *malmal*]

mull[4] /mul/ *n* nonacidic humus on a forest floor that eventually integrates into the soil beneath it [Early 20C. < Danish *muld* 'mould']

mull[5] /mul/ *n Scotland* GEOG same as **promontory** (*often used in placenames*) [14C < Celtic or N Germanic]

Mull /mul/ island in the Inner Hebrides, western Scotland. Population: 2,078 (1991). Area: 925 sq. km/353 sq. mi.

mullah /múllə, mŏŏlə/ *n* **1.** in Central and Southwest Asia, a Muslim cleric who specializes in the interpretation of Islamic religious law **2.** in Iran and Central and Southwest Asia, used as a term of respect for a Muslim man who is thought to be very wise [Early 17C. Via Persian or Urdu *mullā* < Arabic *mawlā*]

mullein /múllin/ *n* a tall plant with hairy leaves. Flowers: yellow, lavender, or white, in spikes. Native to: Europe, Asia, naturalized in the United States. Genus: *Verbascum*. [15C. < Old French *moleine*]

muller /múllər/ *n* a heavy smooth object made of stone, metal, wood, or glass, used for grinding paints or drugs on a flat surface [14C. Origin ?]

Müller /múllər, myŏŏlər/, **Paul** (1899–1965) Swiss chemist. He demonstrated the insecticidal properties of DDT, which was widely used from the 1940s to the 1970s. Full name **Müller, Paul Hermann**

Müllerian mimicry /moo leéri ən-/ *n* mimicry in which two or more animals that are inedible or harmful assume one another's appearance so that predators will leave them alone [Late 19C. After J. F. T. *Müller* (1821–97), German-born Brazilian zoologist]

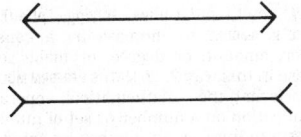

Müller-Lyer illusion

Müller-Lyer illusion /mŏŏlər lī ər-/ *n* an optical illusion in which a line with inward-pointing arrows is seen as longer than one of equal length with outward-pointing arrows [Late 19C. After Franz Carl *Müller-Lyer* (1857–1916), German sociologist and philosopher]

mullet /múllit/ *n* **1.** (*plural* **mullets** *or* same) FISH OF INSHORE WATERS a fish belonging to a large family that lives in fresh or salt water. Native to: temperate and tropical coastal waters. Family: Mugilidae. **2.** (*plural* **mullets** *or* same) ANZ, N Am a thick-bodied fish typically found in inshore waters. Family: Mugilidae. UK term **grey mullet 3.** FISH same as **red mullet 4.** MULLET AS FOOD the flesh of a mullet used as food **5.** (*plural* **mullets**) LONG HAIRSTYLE a hairstyle that is long at the back and short at the front and sides [15C. < Old French *mulet* < *mul* < Latin *mullus* 'red mullet' < Greek *mullos*, a sea fish]

mulligan /múlligən/ *n US* a shot that, against the rules, a golfer allows an opponent to take again [Mid-20C. Probably < the name *Mulligan*]

mulligan ballot *n US* a second ballot paper used if a voter records his or her vote wrongly at the first attempt (*informal*)

mulligatawny /múlligə táwni/ *n* a spicy meat and vegetable soup originally from eastern India [Late 18C. < Tamil *miḷaku-taṇṇi* 'pepper-water']

Mulliken /múllikən/, **Robert S.** (1896–1986) US chemist. He won the Nobel Prize in chemistry (1966) for

his molecular studies. He helped develop the atom bomb during World War II. Full name **Mulliken, Robert Sanderson**

Mullingar /múlling gaár/ town in Westmeath, central Republic of Ireland, situated west of Dublin. Population: 8,824 (2002).

mullion /múllyən/ *n* a vertical piece of stone, metal, or wood that divides the panes of a window or the panels of a screen [Mid-16C. Alteration of obsolete *monial* 'mullion' < Anglo-Norman *moinel* 'middle (part)' < *moien* 'in the middle, median'] —**mullioned** *adj*

mullite /múllīt/ *n* a colourless mineral consisting of crystalline aluminium silicate, able to withstand corrosion and very high temperatures [Early 20C. < MULL]

mullock /múllək/ *n regional* mess or rubbish [14C. < *mull* 'dust, rubbish' (< Dutch *mol, mul* < Germanic) + obsolete *-ock*, denoting smallness]

Brian Mulroney

Mulroney /mul rŏ́ni/, **Brian** (*b.* 1939) prime minister of Canada (1984–93). He led the Progressive Conservative Party from 1983, and signed the Canadian-US Free Trade Agreement in 1988. Full name **Mulroney, Martin Brian**. See table at **prime minister**

mult- *prefix* same as **multi-** (*used before vowels*)

Multan /mŏŏl taán/, **Multān** industrial city, district, and division of Punjab Province, eastern Pakistan. Population: 722,070 (1981).

multi- *prefix* many, multiple, more than one or two ○ *multilevel* ○ *multiparous* [Via French < Latin *multus* 'much, many']

multiactivity *adj*	**multimode** *adj*
multiarmed *adj*	**multimolecular** *adj*
multibank *adj*	**multimovement** *adj*
multibay *adj*	**multination** *adj*
multibillion *adj*	**multinuclear** *adj*
multibillionaire *n*	**multipage** *adj*
multibladed *adj*	**multipart** *adj*
multibranched *adj*	**multiparticle** *adj*
multicell *adj*	**multiparty** *adj*
multicelled *adj*	**multiphase** *adj*
multicellular *adj*	**multiphasic** *adj*
multicellularity *n*	**multiposition** *adj*
multichambered *adj*	**multirange** *adj*
multicommunity *adj*	**multiroomed** *adj*
multicourse *adj*	**multiscreen** *adj*
multicurrency *adj*	**multisense** *adj*
multidigit *adj*	**multisensory** *adj*
multidivisional *adj*	**multisided** *adj*
multidomain *adj*	**multisite** *adj*
multielement *adj*	**multispan** *adj*
multiemployer *adj*	**multispeed** *adj*
multiengine *adj*	**multistemmed** *adj*
multiethnic *adj*	**multistep** *adj*
multifilament *adj*	**multistomach** *adj*
multifocal *adj*	**multistranded** *adj*
multiform *adj*	**multistring** *adj*
multiformity *n*	**multisyllabic** *adj*
multifunction *adj*	**multitalented** *adj*
multifunctional *adj*	**multiterm** *adj*
multifunctioning *adj*	**multitiered** *adj*
multigenerational *adj*	**multitrack** *adj*
multiheaded *adj*	**multiunit** *adj*
multihued *adj*	**multiuse** *adj*
multijointed *adj*	**multiuser** *adj*
multilane *adj*	**multivalence** *n*
multilayered *adj*	**multivalency** *n*
multilobed *adj*	**multivolume** *adj*
multimember *adj*	**multiword** *n, adj*
multimillion *adj*	**multiyear** *adj*
multimodal *adj*	

multiaccess /múlti ák sess/ *adj* relating to a computer system that allows several users to access it at the same time

multiband /múlti band/ *adj* enabling more than one bandwidth of a signal to be processed separately in order to achieve higher fidelity

multicasting /múlti kaasting/ *n* the process of sending data across a network to several recipients simultaneously —**multicast** *vt*

multicentre /múlti sentər/ *adj* having two or more centres

multicentre bond *n* a chemical bond that consists of three or more atoms instead of the usual two, e.g. as found in boranes

multichannel /múlti chánnəl/ *adj* using or providing several channels in broadcasting or communication

multichannel communication *n* the existence or use of two or more communication channels over the same path, e.g. in radio transmission or within a communication cable

multicide /múlti sīd/ *n* the killing of many people at once (*formal*)

multicoloured /múlti kulərd/, **multicolour** /-kulər/ *adj* of many different colours

multiculti /múlti kúlti/ *adj* SOC SCI same as **multicultural** (*slang*) [Late 20C. Alteration of MULTICULTURAL]

multicultural /múlti kúlchərəl/ *adj* **1.** relating to, consisting of, or participating in the cultures of different countries, ethnic groups, or religions **2.** advocating or encouraging the integration of people of different countries, ethnic groups, and religions into all areas of society —**multiculturalism** *n* —**multiculturalist** *n*

multidimensional /múlti di ménsh'nəl, -dī-/ *adj* **1.** relating to or having more than three dimensions **2.** having several different aims, qualities, or aspects —**multidimensionality** /múlti di ménshə nálləti, -dī-/ *n*

multidirectional /múltidi réksh'nəl, -dī-/ *adj* **1.** having several aims or covering several aspects of a situation **2.** going, operating, or pointing in several different directions

multidisciplinary /múlti díssə plinəri/, **multidiscipline** /-plin/ *adj* studying or using several specialized subjects or skills

multievent *n* an athletic contest, e.g. the pentathlon or decathlon, that includes several different events

multifaceted /múlti fássitid/ *adj* **1.** with many different talents, qualities, or features **2.** having many facets or cut surfaces

multifactorial /múlti fak táwri əl/, **multifactor** /múlti fáktər/ *adj* **1.** involving several different factors **2.** relating to inheritance depending on more than one gene. Height and weight are examples of characters determined by multifactorial inheritance. —**multifactorially** *adv*

multifarious /múlti fáiri əss/ *adj* including parts, things, or people of many different kinds [Late 16C. < Latin *multifarius* 'varied, diverse' < *multi-* 'many' + *-farius* 'doing'] —**multifariously** *adv* —**multifariousness** *n*

multifid /múltifid/, **multifidous** /mul tíffidəss/ *adj* having many lobe-shaped segments

multiflora rose /múlti fláwrə-/ *n* a wild climbing rose that is the origin of many cultivated roses. Flowers: small, fragrant. Native to: Asia. Latin name: *Rosa multiflora*.

multiflorous /múlti fláwrəss/ *adj* having many flowers [Mid-18C. < late Latin *multiflorus* < Latin *multi-* 'many' + *flor-* 'flower']

multifoil /múlti foyl/ *n* in architecture, a flat shape, opening, or decorative design with many lobes or scallops at its edges

multigrade oil /múlti grayd-/, **multigrade** *n* engine oil that has a range of viscosities and is therefore effective over a range of temperatures

multigrain /múlti grayn/ *adj* describes bread that is made from several different types of grain

multigravida /múlti grávvidə/ *n* a pregnant woman who has had at least one previous pregnancy

multigym /múlti jim/ *n* an exercise apparatus with a range of weights, used for muscle toning

multihull /múlti hul/ *n* a sailing vessel with two or more hulls

multilateral /múlti láttərəl/ *adj* **1.** involving more than two parties or countries **2.** having many sides or flat surfaces [Late 17C. < medieval Latin *multilateralis* < Latin *multi-* 'many' + *lateralis* (see LATERAL)] —**multilaterally** *adv*

multilateralism /múlti láttərə lizəm/ *n* the principle or belief that several nations should be cooperatively involved in the process of achieving a goal, especially nuclear disarmament —**multilateralist** *n, adj*

multilevel /múlti levv'l/ *adj* **1. WITH SEVERAL LEVELS** having or operating on several layers or levels **2.** *also* **multilevelled** /-lévv'ld/ **WITH MANY LEVELS** having or operating on several or many different levels ■ *n* **STRUCTURE WITH MANY LEVELS** a building or structure with several or many levels

multilingual /múlti líng gwəl/ *adj* **1.** able to speak more than two languages fluently **2.** relating to the use of more than two languages —**multilingualism** *n* —**multilingually** *adv*

multilocular /múlti lókyoolər/ *adj* consisting of or having several different chambers or cavities [Early 19C. < LOCULE]

multimedia /múlti méedi ə/ *n* **1.** COMPUT **SOUND AND VIDEO ON COMPUTERS** programs, software, and hardware capable of using a wide variety of media such as film, video, and music as well as text and numbers **2.** ARTS **USE OF VARIOUS MATERIALS AND MEDIA** the use in art, especially the plastic arts, of different kinds of materials and media such as television, sound, and text **3.** MARKETING **USE OF ALL COMMUNICATIONS MEDIA** the use in advertising of a combination of media such as television, radio, and the press **4.** EDUC **USE OF MEDIA IN TEACHING** the use of film, video, and music in addition to more traditional teaching materials and methods —**multimedia** *adj*

multimedia messaging service *n* TELECOM full form of **MMS**

multimeter /múlti meetər/ *n* an instrument that reads and measures the values of several different electrical parameters such as current, voltage, and resistance

multimillionaire /múlti míllyə náir/ *n* somebody with money or assets worth several million pounds, dollars, or other units of currency

multinational /múlti nash'nəl/ *adj* **1. OPERATING IN SEVERAL COUNTRIES** operating or having investments in several countries **2. INVOLVING PEOPLE FROM SEVERAL COUNTRIES** relating to or including people from more than two countries ■ *n* **LARGE COMPANY OPERATING IN SEVERAL COUNTRIES** a large company that operates or has investments in several different countries —**multinationalism** *n*

multinomial /múlti nṓmi əl/ *n, adj* MATHS same as **polynomial**

multipack /múlti pak/ *n* a packet that contains more than two of an item of consumer goods such as batteries and is sold at a reduced price

multipara /mul típpərə/ (*plural* **-rae** /-ree/) *n* a woman who has borne a live child from each of two or more pregnancies [Mid-19C. < form of modern Latin *multiparus* (see MULTIPAROUS)]

multiparous /mul típpərəss/ *adj* **1.** describes an animal, especially a mammal, that normally gives birth to two or more offspring at one time **2.** describes a woman who has borne a child from each of two or more pregnancies, each pregnancy lasting for at least 20 weeks [Mid-17C. < modern Latin *multiparus* < Latin *multi-* 'many' + *-parus* '-bearing' (see -PAROUS)] —**multiparity** /múlti párrəti/ *n*

multipartite /múlti paar tīt/ *adj* **1.** involving more than two political parties or countries **2.** divided into many sections

multipath /múlti paath/ *adj* relating to television or radio signals that use more than one route from the transmitter to the receiver, causing picture or sound distortion

multiplane /múlti playn/ *n* an aircraft with more than one pair of wings

multiplayer /múlti pláyər/ *adj* describes a computer game that is played with other players, typically over a local area network or the Internet —**multiplayer** *n*

multiple /múltip'l/ *adj* **INVOLVING SEVERAL THINGS** involving or including several things, people, or parts ■ *n* **1.** MATHS **NUMBER DIVISIBLE BY ANOTHER** a number that can be divided exactly by a particular smaller number **2.** TELECOM **SYSTEM WITH MANY POSSIBLE ACCESS POINTS** a system of wiring so arranged that a group of communication lines are accessible at a number of points **3.** COMM same as **chain store** [Mid-17C. Via French < late Latin *multiplus*, alteration of Latin *multiplex* (see MULTIPLEX)]

multiple alleles *npl* three or more different forms of a gene. Any two of these forms can be present in a normal diploid cell or organism.

multiple-choice *adj* requiring the choice of the correct answer or answers out of several possible suggested answers ○ *a multiple-choice question*

multiple factor *n* GENETICS same as **polygene**

multiple fission *n* a form of asexual reproduction occurring in some single-celled organisms such as malaria parasites in which a single parent cell breaks up to yield numerous daughter cells

multiple fruit *n* a fruit that is produced from the ovaries of several flowers that merge to form a single structure, e.g. a pineapple or fig

multiple myeloma, multiple myelomatosis *n* a form of cancer of the bone marrow characterized by swellings, malformations, and fractures of various bones and accompanied by pain, anaemia, and weight loss. It affects the plasma cells that produce antibodies and can be diagnosed by the presence of unusual proteins in the blood.

multiple personality disorder *n* a psychological disorder, typically associated with childhood trauma, in which somebody appears to have two or more distinct personalities that are present at different times and dominate behaviour

multiplepoinding /múltip'l pínding/ *n Scotland* in Scottish law, an action brought by an owner to determine how something such as a property or a fund should be divided between several claimants [Late 17C. < Scottish form of POUND³]

multiple sclerosis *n* a serious progressive disease of the central nervous system, occurring mainly in young adults and thought to be caused by a malfunction of the immune system. It leads to the loss of myelin in the brain or spinal cord and causes muscle weakness, poor eyesight, slow speech, and some inability to move.

multiple shop *n* COMM same as **chain store**

multiple star *n* a group of three or more stars, usually with the same gravitational centre, that appears as one star to the naked eye

multiple store *n* COMM same as **chain store**

multiplet /múlti plet/ *n* **1.** a line in a spectrum made up of two or more component lines, caused by slight variations in atomic or molecular energy levels **2.** a group of elementary particles that have a different electric charge but have otherwise similar properties [Early 20C. < MULTIPLE, after DOUBLET, TRIPLET]

multiple unit *n* a passenger train with engines or motors in or beneath the coaches that require no separate locomotive

multiple voting *n* the fraudulent practice of voting in more than one constituency in an election

multiplex /múlti pleks/ *n* **1. CINEMA COMPLEX** a large cinema complex that has several separate units with screens as well as other facilities such as a restaurant or bar **2. MULTIPLE TRANSMISSION** the simultaneous transmission of two or more signals along one communications channel **3. SYSTEM FOR SIMULTANEOUS TRANSMISSION** a transmission system that carries two or more individual channels over a single communication path ■ *adj* **COMPLEX** involving or including several different things, parts, or factors ■ *vti* (**-plexes, -plexing, -plexed**) **SEND BY MULTIPLEX** to send two or more messages or signals along one communications channel at the same time [Mid-16C. < Latin < *multi-* 'many' + *-plex* '-fold']

multiplexer /múlti pleksər/, **multiplexor** *n* **1.** a device for sending several data streams down a communications line and for splitting a received multiple stream into components **2.** a device for transferring projected film to video

multiplexing /múlti pleksing/ *n* **1.** the sending of two or more signals along one communication channel **2.** a genetic sequencing approach that uses several pooled samples simultaneously, so increasing the sequencing speed

multiplexor *n* MEDIA, TELECOM another spelling of **multiplexer**

multiplicand /múltipli kánd/ *n* a number that is multiplied by another number (**multiplier**). The number 2 is the multiplicand in the statement $2 \times 4 = 8$. [Late 16C. < medieval Latin *multiplicandus*, form of Latin *multiplicare* (see MULTIPLY¹)]

multiplicate /múltipli kayt/ *adj* containing many parts [15C. < Latin *multiplicat-*, past participle of *multiplicare* (see MULTIPLY¹)]

multiplication /múltipli káysh'n/ *n* **1. ARITHMETIC OPERATION** a mathematical operation, symbolized by ×, that for integers is equivalent to adding a number to itself a particular number of times **2. MATHEMATICAL OPERATION** a mathematical operation equivalent to multiplication extended to expressions such as functions or matrices that are not numbers **3. INCREASE** a marked increase in number or amount ○ *a multiplication of claims* **4. REPRODUCTION** the act or process of reproduction in animals, plants, or people [14C. Directly or via French < Latin *multiplication-* < *multiplicat-*, past participle of *multiplicare* (see MULTIPLY¹)] —**multiplicational** *adj* —**multiplicative** /múlti plíkətiv/ *adj*

multiplication sign *n* the symbol × or •, used to indicate that one number is to be multiplied by another

multiplication table *n* a table giving a number from 1 to 10 or 12 multiplied by all the numbers from 1 to 10 or 12 in turn. Multiplication tables are used for teaching or remembering the basic facts of multiplication.

multiplicity /múlti plíssəti/ (*plural* **-ties**) *n* **1. GREAT VARIETY** a considerable number or variety ○ *Her style was shaped by a multiplicity of influences.* **2. COMPLEXITY** the state of being multiple or varied **3.** PHYS **NUMBER OF MOLECULAR ENERGY LEVELS** the number of energy levels of a molecule, atom, or nucleus that result from interactions between angular momenta **4.** PHYS **PARTICLES IN MULTIPLET** the number of elementary particles that form a multiplet [15C. < late Latin *multiplicatus* < Latin *multiplic-*, stem of *multiplex* (see MULTIPLEX)]

multiplier /múlti plī ər/ *n* **1.** somebody or something that multiplies or increases **2.** the number by which another number (**multiplicand**) is multiplied, e.g. the number 4 is the multiplier in the statement $2 \times 4 = 8$ **3.** PHYS same as **photomultiplier**

multiply¹ /múlti plī/ (**-plies, -plying, -plied**) *v* **1.** *vti* **INCREASE IN AMOUNT** to increase by a considerable number, amount, or degree, or make something increase in this way **2.** *vti* MATHS **PERFORM MULTIPLICATION** to perform the mathematical operation of multiplication on a number or set of numbers **3.** *vi* BIOL **BREED** to increase in number by breeding [12C. Via French *multiplier* < Latin *multiplicare* < *multiplic-* (see MULTIPLICITY)] —**multipliable** *adj* —**multiplicable** /-plikəb'l/ *adj*

multiply² /múltipli/ *adv* many times, or in many different ways [Late 19C. < MULTIPLE]

multipoint /múlti póynt/ *n US* TELECOM same as **multiple** *n* (sense 2)

multipolar /múlti pṓlər/ *adj* **1.** describes a nerve cell with more than two connecting fibres that carry impulses into the cell body **2.** having several poles or extremities —**multipolarity** /-pō lárrəti/ *n*

multiport /múlti pawrt/ *adj* describes a computer network with more than one point of access or connection

multipotent /mul típpətənt/, **multipotential** /múltipə ténsh'l/ *adj* capable of developing into various types of cell, depending on the surrounding conditions

multiprocessing /múlti prṓ sessing/ *n* the operation of a computer in which two or more processing units work on separate parts of the same program or set of instructions to reduce processing time

multiprocessor /múlti prṓ sessər/ *n* a system of linked central processing units on which two or more programs can be run simultaneously by parallel processing

multipronged /múlti próngd/ *adj* **1.** involving several different approaches or aspects **2.** having several prongs

multipurpose /múlti púrpəss/ *adj* designed or able to be used for several different purposes

multiracial /múlti ráysh'l/ *adj* relating to, made up of, or involving people from several races ○ *a multiracial society* —**multiracially** *adv*

multiracialism /múlti ráysh'l izəm/ *n* the principle or practice of ensuring that people of various races are fully integrated into a society —**multiracialist** *adj*

multiregionalism /múlti reéjənəlizəm/ *n* a theory of evolution holding that modern human beings are descended from several separate subspecies —**multiregionalist** *adj, n*

multirole /múlti ról/ *adj* having several roles or functions

multiskilled /múlti skíld/ *adj* trained and capable in a large variety of skills or activities

multiskilling /múlti skílling/ *n* the training of employees to do a large variety of tasks

multistage /múlti stayj/ *adj* divided into or taking place in several separate stages

multistage rocket *n* a rocket with two or more propulsion units that are used and discarded in succession

multistorey /múlti stáwri/ *adj* having several storeys ■ *n* (*plural* -**storeys**) a car park constructed on several levels (*informal*)

multitask /múlti taask/ (-**tasks**, -**tasking**, -**tasked**) *vi* to perform more than one task at the same time ○ *The best way to pass the time while exercising is to multitask – why just pedal when you can talk on your mobile at the same time.*

multitasking /múlti taasking/ *n* the simultaneous management of two or more tasks by a computer or a person

multiton /múlti tun/ *adj US* weighing or capable of carrying several tons

multitude /múlti tyood/ *n* **1.** CROWD a large crowd of people **2.** LARGE NUMBER a very large number of things or people (*often used in the plural*) **3.** MAJORITY the majority of ordinary people [14C. Via French < Latin *multitudo* < *multus* 'much, many']

multitudinous /múlti tyoódinəss/ *adj* **1.** very great in number **2.** including many parts, items, or features [Early 17C. < Latin *multitudin-*, stem of *multitudo* (see MULTITUDE)] —**multitudinously** *adv* —**multitudinousness** *n*

multiuser domain, object-oriented (*plural* **multiuser domains, object-oriented**) *n* ONLINE full form of **MOO**

multivariate /múlti váiri ət/, **multivariable** /-váiri əb'l/ *adj* relating to or used to describe a statistical distribution that involves a number of random but often related variables

multiverse /múlti vurss/ *n* a hypothetical cosmos that contains our universe as well as numerous other universes and space-times

multiversity /múlti vúrssəti/ (*plural* -**ties**) *n* a university that has many affiliated or associated institutions such as research centres and colleges [Mid-20C. < MULTI- + UNIVERSITY]

multivibrator /múlti vī bráytər/ *n* an oscillating electronic circuit consisting of pairs of tubes, transistors, or other components, whose oscillation is sustained by coupling the output of one to the input of the other

multivitamin /múlti vítəmin/ *n* a tablet or capsule containing several vitamins and sometimes minerals —**multivitamin** *adj*

multivocal /múlti vók'l/ *adj* with many different and valid meanings or interpretations

multum in parvo /moóltoóm in paárvō/ *n* the quality or fact of containing, implying, or expressing much in a little space or time [< Latin, 'much in little']

multure /múlchər/ *n Scotland* (*archaic*) **1.** a fee that a miller used to charge for grinding grain **2.** a miller's right to receive a fee for grinding grain [14C. Via Old French *mo(u)lture* < medieval Latin *molitura* < *molere* 'grind']

mum[1] /mum/ *n* same as **mother**[1] *n* (sense 1) (*informal*) [Mid-17C. Partly (especially in early use) variant of MAM, partly shortening of MUMMY[1]]

mum[2] /mum/ *adj* saying nothing, especially about a sensitive piece of information (*informal*) [15C. An imitation of the sound made when the lips are closed]

mum[3] /mum/ (**mums**, **mumming**, **mummed**), **mumm** (**mumms**, **mumming**, **mummed**) *vi* **1.** to act in a masked folk play or mime **2.** to participate in festivities wearing a mask or disguise [Mid-16C. < French *momer* 'act in a mime']

mum[4] /mum/ *n* PLANTS same as **chrysanthemum** (*informal*) [Late 19C. Shortening]

mum and dad investors *npl* people who purchase shares, but have little or no knowledge of the stock market (*informal*)

Mumbai /moóm bī/ capital of Maharashtra State and the largest city in India, situated on the Arabian Sea. Population: 11,914,398 (2001). Former name **Bombay**

mumble /múmb'l/ *vti* (-**bles**, -**bling**, -**bled**) **1.** MUTTER to speak or utter something quietly and indistinctly without opening the mouth very much **2.** CHEW WITH DIFFICULTY to chew food with difficulty ■ *n* INDISTINCT SPEECH a quiet indistinct utterance in which the mouth is not opened very much [14C. < obsolete *mum* 'make an indistinct sound with closed lips'] —**mumbler** *n* —**mumblingly** *adv*

mumbo jumbo /múmbō júmbō/ *n* **1.** CONFUSING LANGUAGE complicated and confusing language, especially technical jargon, that is difficult to understand (*informal*) **2.** WORTHLESS BELIEFS OR RITUALS religious beliefs, language, or rituals that appear pointless or meaningless to the speaker (*offensive in some contexts*) **3.** SUPPOSEDLY SUPERNATURAL OBJECT an object or effigy believed to hold supernatural powers [Mid-18C. Origin ?]

mu meson *n* PHYS same as **muon**

mumm *vt* THEATRE another spelling of **mum**[3]

mummer /múmmər/ *n* **1.** an actor in a pantomime, folk play, or mime show **2.** somebody who participates in festivities wearing a mask or disguise **3.** THEATRE same as **mime 4.** THEATRE same as **actor** (*humorous*) [15C. < Old French *momeur* < *momer* 'act in a mime']

Mummerset /múmmər set/ *n* a stereotypical West Country accent used in drama [Mid-20C. Probably blend of MUMMER + *Somerset*, county in the west of England]

mummery /múmməri/ (*plural* -**ies**) *n* **1.** a performance by a group of mummers **2.** a showy or hypocritical ceremony

mummify /múmmi fī/ (-**fies**, -**fying**, -**fied**) *v* **1.** *vt* PRESERVE CORPSE FOR BURIAL to preserve the corpse of a person or animal for burial by embalming it and wrapping it in cloth **2.** *vti* SHRIVEL to dry out and shrivel, or cause something to dry out and shrivel **3.** *vt* PRESERVE CUSTOM OR INSTITUTION to preserve something such as an old custom or an institution just for the sake of it and without making any effort to keep it alive [Early 17C. < MUMMY[2] after French *momifier*] —**mummification** /múmmifi káysh'n/ *n*

mummy[1] /múmmi/ (*plural* -**mies**) *n* same as **mother**[1] (sense 1) (*usually used by or to children*) [Late 18C. Dialectal variant of MAMMY]

mummy: detail of wall painting in the tomb of Sennudjem, Deir-el-Medinah, near Luxor, Egypt (1295–1186 BC)

mummy[2] /múmmi/ (*plural* -**mies**) *n* **1.** the body of a person or animal that has been embalmed and wrapped in cloth, especially as was the custom in ancient Egypt **2.** the body of an organism preserved by natural processes, e.g. by burial in peat or ice [Early 17C. Via Old French *momie* < Arabic *mūmiyā* 'embalmed body']

mummy's boy *n* an offensive term that deliberately insults a man's strength of character, courage, or independence (*insult*) N Am term **mama's boy**

mumps /mumps/ *n* an acute contagious disease, usually affecting children, that causes a fever with swelling of the salivary glands and sometimes also affects the pancreas and ovaries or testes. It is caused by a virus and can be prevented through vaccination. It may cause sterility if contracted by a man. (*takes a singular or plural verb*) [Late 16C. Plural of obsolete *mump* 'grimace', an imitation of the sounds made with a closed mouth]

mums and dads /múmz ən dádz/ *npl Aus* the uninformed general public, especially investors who know nothing about the stock market (*informal*)

mumsy /múmzi/ (-**sier**, -**siest**) *adj* **1.** unfashionable and dowdy (*informal*) **2.** kind and motherly in a gentle sweet-natured way [Late 19C. < MUM[1]]

mumu *n* CLOTHING another spelling of **muumuu**

mun *v regional* another spelling of **maun**

munch /munch/ (**munches**, **munching**, **munched**) *vti* to chew food purposefully, usually with visible movements of the jaw and sometimes with a crunching sound [14C. Origin ?] —**muncher** *n*

AKG London
Edvard Munch

Munch /moóngk/, **Edvard** (1863–1944) Norwegian painter. His work, suffused with melancholy and anguish, most famously in *The Scream* (1893), anticipates expressionism.

> 'The sky was suddenly blood-red—I stopped and leaned against the fence, dead tired. I saw the flaming clouds like blood and a sword—the bluish-black fjord and town—my friends walked on—I stood there, trembling with anxiety—and I felt as though Nature were convulsed by a great unending scream.'
> [Edvard Munch, *Letter*; 1892]

Münchausen /múnch owz'n/ *n* **1.** a fantastic story full of exaggeration, told to impress people **2.** somebody who makes up fantastic stories in order to impress others [Mid-19C. After the eponymous hero, Baron *Münchausen*, of a book of impossible adventures (1785) written in English by the German author Rudolf Eric Raspe]

Münchausen syndrome *n* a psychological disorder in which somebody pretends to have a serious illness in order to undergo testing or treatment or to be admitted to hospital

Münchausen syndrome by proxy *n* a diagnosis of child abuse asserting that a parent or carer induced symptoms of illness in a child

munchies /múnchiz/ *npl* a craving for snack food (*informal*)

munchkin /múnchkin/ *n N Am* (*informal*) **1.** a small child **2.** an insignificant person who keeps busy with trivial matters [Late 20C. < creatures invented by L. Frank Baum in *The Wizard of Oz* (1900)]

Munda /moóndə/ *n* **1.** one of the four major Indian language groups spoken in eastern parts of South Asia. Native speakers: 5 million., belonging to the Austro-Asiatic family of languages **2.** somebody who speaks Munda as a native language [Mid-19C. < Munda *Muṇḍā*] —**Munda** *adj*

mundane /mun dáyn/ *adj* **1.** commonplace, not unusual, and often boring **2.** relating to matters of this world [15C. Via French < late Latin *mundanus* < Latin *mundus* 'world'] —**mundanely** *adv* —**mundaneness** *n*

munga /múng gə/ *n ANZ* **1.** an army canteen (*informal*) **2.** FOOD same as **food** (*slang*) [Early 20C. Probably < French *manger* or Italian *mangiare* 'eat']

mung bean /múng-/ *n* **1.** a small green or yellow bean that is dried and sometimes split. It is also germinated to produce bean sprouts. **2.** a plant that produces mung beans. Native to: East Asia. Latin name: *Vigna radiata*. [< Hindi *mūng*]

mungo /múng gō/ *n* a cheap fabric made from waste wool and rags [Mid-19C. Origin ?]

Mungo, Lake /múng gō/ dry lake in western New South Wales, Australia. It is part of Mungo National Park.

muni /moŏni/ (*plural* **-nis**) *n* S *Asia* a Hindu or Jain ascetic noted for exceptional holiness, religious inspiration, piety, or knowledge [Late 18C. < Sanskrit, literally, 'silent' < *man* 'think']

Munich /myoónik/ capital and largest city in the state of Bavaria, southeastern Germany. Population: 1,210,100 (2001).

Munich Conference *n* a meeting about Germany's occupation of Czechoslovakia in 1938, at which Western leaders agreed to the division of Czechoslovakia after receiving Hitler's assurances that he would take no more land

municipal /myoŏ níssip'l/ *adj* relating to a town, city, or region that has its own local government [Mid-16C. Directly or via French < Latin *municipalis* < *municip-* 'holder of a civic office' < *munus* 'gift, service, duty' + *capere* 'take'] —**municipalism** *n* —**municipalist** *n* —**municipally** *adv*

municipal bond *n* US a bond or security issued by a city or other local government, usually to pay for public improvements

municipalise *vt* POL another spelling of **municipalize**

municipality /myoŏ níssi pálləti/ (*plural* **-ties**) *n* **1.** a city, town, or other area that has its own local government **2.** the appointed or elected members of a local government

municipalize /myoŏ níssipə līz/ (**-izes, -izing, -ized**), **municipalise** (**-ises, -ising, -ised**) *vt* **1.** to bring something such as a public service or area of land under the ownership or control of a city, town, or other area with its own local government **2.** to grant a city, town, or other area powers of government in local matters —**municipalization** /myoŏ níssipə līzáysh'n/ *n*

munificent /myoŏ níffiss'nt/ *adj* **1.** very generous in giving a lot of money **2.** characterized by generosity ○ *a munificent award* [Late 16C. < Latin *munificent-* < *munificus* 'generous' < *munus* 'gift, service, duty'] —**munificence** *n* —**munificently** *adv*

SYNONYMS See *generous*.

muniments /myoŏnimənts/ *npl* documents by which a claim to property or rights is supported, e.g. the title deeds to land [15C. < Latin *munimentum* 'fortification' < *munire* (see MUNITION)]

munition /myoŏ nísh'n/ *vt* (**-tions, -tioning, -tioned**) to supply somebody with weapons and ammunition ■ **munitions** *npl* military supplies, e.g. weapons and ammunition [Early 16C. Via French < Latin *munition-* < *munire* 'fortify' < *moenia* 'defensive walls'] —**munitioner** *n*

munitionize /myoŏ nísh'n īz/ (**-izes, -izing, -ized**), **munitionise** (**-ises, -ising, -ised**) *vt* ARMS same as **weaponize**

Munnings /múnningz/, **Sir Alfred** (1878–1959) British painter. He was a conservative stylist, noted for his equestrian scenes. He served as a war artist during World War I. Full name **Munnings, Sir Alfred James**

Munro /mən rố/ (*plural* **-ros**) *n* a mountain peak in Scotland over 914.4 m/3,000 ft high, one of 284 currently recognized [Early 20C. After Sir Hugh Thomas *Munro* (1856–1919), compiler of a list of such mountains]

Munro /mən rố/, **Alice** (b. 1931) Canadian writer, known for her short stories of rural Ontario life and sensitive portrayals of young girls. Her works include *Something I've Been Meaning to Tell You* (1974) and *Open Secrets* (1994). Pseudonym of **Laidlaw, Alice Anne**

Munsee /múnsee/ (*plural same* or **-sees**), **Munsi** (*plural same* or **-sis**) *n* **1.** the Algonquian language of the Delaware people. Munsee is nearly extinct. **2.** somebody who speaks Munsee as a native language [< Munsee] —**Munsee** *adj*

munshi /moŏn shee/, **moonshee** *n* S *Asia* somebody whose profession involves writing or language skills, e.g. a secretary or language teacher [Late 18C. Via Urdu and Persian < Arabic *mun ši* 'writer']

Munster[1] *n* FOOD another spelling of **Muenster**

Munster[2] /múnstər/ historic province in the southwest of the Republic of Ireland

Münster /myoŏnstər/ inland port on the Dortmund-Ems Canal, North Rhine-Westphalia State, northwestern Germany. Population: 264,887 (1997).

munt /moŏnt/ *n* S *Africa* an offensive term for a Black African person (*dated slang insult*) [Mid-20C. < Bantu *umuntu* 'person', singular of *abantu*]

munter /múntər/ *n* somebody who is considered unattractive (*slang insult*) [Origin ?]

muntin /múntin/ *n* a strip of wood or metal that separates and holds in place the panes of a window [Early 17C. Old French *montant* 'upright' < present participle of *monter* (see MOUNT[1])]

muntjac /múnt jak/ (*plural* **-jacs** or *same*), **muntjak** (*plural* **-jaks** or *same*) *n* a small deer with a reddish-brown coat, a cry like a dog's bark, and small antlers. Native to: Southeast Asia. Genus: *Muntiacus*. [Late 18C. < Sundanese *minchek*, Malay *menjangan* 'deer']

Muntz metal /múnts-/ *n* brass containing two parts of zinc to three parts of copper. Use: casting, extrusion. [Mid-19C. After George Frederick *Muntz* (1794–1857) British metallurgist]

muon /myoŏ on/ *n* an elementary particle with a mass about 200 times that of an electron. It is a lepton with a negative charge and a half-life of two-millionths of a second. [Mid-20C. Contraction of MU MESON] —**muonic** /myoo ónnik/ *adj*

muon neutrino *n* a lepton that exists in association with a muon. It has zero rest mass and no charge.

muppet /múppit/ *n* somebody who is considered silly or stupid (*slang insult*) [After puppets in *The Muppet Show*™]

Murad IV /myoŏr ad/ (1609–40) Arabian sultan. He succeeded Mustafa I as sultan of the Ottoman Empire (1623–40).

mural /myoŏrəl/ *n* a usually large picture painted directly onto an interior or exterior wall ■ *adj* relating to or like a wall [Mid-16C. Via French < Latin *muralis* < *murus* 'wall'] —**muralist** *n*

muramic acid /myoŏ rámmik-/ *n* an amino sugar found in the cell walls of blue-green algae. Formula: $C_9H_{17}NO_7$. [< Latin *murus* 'wall' + AMINE]

Murasaki /moŏr aa saáki/, **Shikibu** (978?–1026?) Japanese lady-in-waiting at the imperial court and writer. She is known for *The Tale of Genji* (?1010), considered one of the world's first novels.

Murat /myoŏr a, mü rá/, **Joachim** (1767–1815) king of Naples. The brother-in-law of Napoleon, he served under Napoleon in several campaigns and was awarded the monarchy of Naples by him in 1808.

Murchison /múrchiss'n/ river in Western Australia that rises in the Robinson Range and flows into the Indian Ocean near the town of Kalbarri. Length: 800 km/500 mi.

Murchison, Sir Roderick (1792–1871) British geologist. His study of early Palaeozoic rock strata and their fossils led to his formulation of the Silurian rock system. Full name **Murchison, Sir Roderick Impey**

Murcia /múrshə, múrssi ə/ capital of Murcia Province and Murcia Region, southeastern Spain. Population: 377,888 (2002).

Murcutt /múrkət/, **Glenn** (b. 1936) British-born Australian architect. He is known for simple, open domestic structures that blend modernist and traditional styles.

murder /múrdər/ *n* **1.** CRIME OF KILLING SOMEBODY the crime of killing another person deliberately and not in self-defence or with any other extenuating circumstance recognized by law **2.** SOMETHING DIFFICULT OR UNPLEASANT something that is very difficult or unpleasant and involves great effort or hardship (*informal*) ○ *This exam is murder!* ■ *v* (**-ders, -dering, -dered**) **1.** *vti* KILL SOMEBODY ILLEGALLY to kill one person deliberately and not in self-defence or with any other extenuating circumstance recognized by law **2.** *vt* SPOIL SOMETHING to spoil something such as a song or a piece of writing by performing it badly or changing it (*informal*) **3.** *vt* DEFEAT SOMEBODY COMPLETELY to defeat a person or team completely, especially in a sporting contest (*informal*) **4.** *vt* DESTROY SOMETHING to put an end to or destroy something (*informal*) ○ *The fire murdered their chances of selling the house.* **5.** *vt* PUNISH SOMEBODY to punish or be very angry with somebody (*informal*) ○ *My mother will murder me if I'm not on time.* [Old English *morþor*. < Indo-European] —**murderer** *n* —

murderess *n* ◇ **get away with murder** to escape punishment for or detection of wrongdoing

SYNONYMS See *kill*.

murder ball *n* a simple informal game using a medicine ball and two mats in which two teams of participants try to get the ball onto their opponents' mat

murderous /múrdərəss/ *adj* **1.** LIKELY TO MURDER capable of, guilty of, or likely to commit murder **2.** LIKELY TO CAUSE DEATH violent and likely to result in bloodshed or murder **3.** DIFFICULT very difficult, unpleasant, or dangerous (*informal*) —**murderously** *adv* —**murderousness** *n*

Dame Iris Murdoch

Murdoch /múr dok/, **Dame Iris** (1919–99) Irish-born British novelist and philosopher. Her many novels are noted for their thoughtful exploration of moral and philosophical problems. She is the author of *A Severed Head* (1961) and the Booker Prize-winning *The Sea, the Sea* (1978). Full name **Murdoch, Dame Jean Iris**

'We live in a fantasy world, a world of illusion. The great task in life is to find reality.'
[Dame Iris Murdoch, *Times*; 15 April 1983]

Murdoch, Sir Keith (1885–1952) Australian journalist and newspaper proprietor. He was chairman of an organization that owned several Australian newspapers. Full name **Murdoch, Sir Keith Arthur**

Rupert Murdoch

Murdoch, Rupert (b. 1931) Australian-born US media proprietor, son of Sir Keith Murdoch. He turned his family's newspaper empire into a global network of media organizations. Full name **Murdoch, Keith Rupert**

'There is no such thing as a global village. Most media are rooted in their national and local cultures.'
[Rupert Murdoch, *Business Review Weekly*; 17 November 1989]

murein /myoŏr een/ *n* BIOCHEM same as **peptidoglycan** [Mid-20C. < Latin *murus* 'wall' after PROTEIN; from its forming the walls of cells]

murex /myoŏr eks/ (*plural* **-rices** /-ri seez/) *n* an invertebrate sea animal that has a spiny shell. Native to: tropical waters. Genus: *Murex*. [Late 16C. < Latin]

muriatic acid /myoŏri áttik-/ *n* CHEM same as **hydrochloric acid** [< Latin *muriaticus* 'pickled in brine' < *muria* 'brine']

muricate /myoŏórikət/, **muricated** /-kaytid/ *adj* covered

in short spines or points [Mid-17C. < Latin *muricatus* 'shaped like a murex' < *murex*]

murices ZOOL plural of **murex**

Murillo /myoo rílló/, **Bartolomé Esteban** (1617–82) Spanish painter. He is noted for his religious subjects and genre scenes.

murine /myoór ĭn/ adj **1.** OF MOUSE AND RAT FAMILY relating to or belonging to the family of long-tailed rodents that includes rats and mice. Family: Muridae. **2.** LIKE RODENT resembling a mouse or a rat **3.** SPREAD BY RODENTS caused or transmitted by mice or rats [Early 17C. < Latin *murinus* < *mur-* 'mouse']

murine typhus n a relatively mild form of typhus that is transmitted from rats to humans by fleas or lice. Symptoms include fever, headaches, and muscular pain, and recovery is usually rapid. It is caused by the microorganism *Rickettsia typhi*.

murk /murk/, **mirk** n **1.** gloomy darkness caused by fog, mist, smoke, or cloud **2.** N England a mist or thin fog (informal) ■ adj same as **murky** (archaic or literary) [Old English *mirce*, *myrce* < N Germanic]

murky /múrki/ (**-ier, -iest**), **mirky** adj **1.** GLOOMY dark and gloomy **2.** HARD TO SEE THROUGH thick with fog, mist, smoke, cloud, or dirt, and difficult to see through **3.** OBSCURE unclear and difficult to understand ○ *offered several murky excuses* **4.** DISHONEST involving dishonesty or illegal activities —**murkily** adv —**murkiness** n

Murmansk /mur mánsk/ city and port in northwestern Russia, on the Kola Inlet, an arm of the Barents Sea. Population: 539,411 (1995).

~~murmer~~ incorrect spelling of **murmur**

murmur /múrmər/ n **1.** CONTINUOUS HUM a continuous low sound, often one that seems to be coming from some distance away **2.** SOMETHING SAID QUIETLY something said that is either very quiet or sounds indistinct **3.** COMPLAINT a complaint made in a discreet or secretive way **4.** MED SOUND IN CHEST a soft blowing or fluttering sound, usually heard via a stethoscope, that originates from the heart, lungs, or arteries and may indicate disease or structural concerns. It is caused by turbulent blood flow. ■ v (**-murs, -muring, -mured**) **1.** vti SAY SOMETHING SOFTLY to say something very quietly or indistinctly **2.** vi COMPLAIN DISCREETLY to complain in a discreet or secretive way **3.** vi MAKE CONTINUOUS LOW SOUND to make a continuous low sound, often one that seems to be coming from some distance away [14C. Via French < Latin *murmurare*] —**murmurer** n —**murmurous** adj

murmuration /múrmə ráysh'n/ n **1.** an act or sound of murmuring **2.** a flock of starlings

murmurings /múrmərĭngz/ npl quiet and subdued expressions of discontent

murphy /múrfi/ (plural **-phies**) n FOOD same as **potato** (dated informal) [Early 19C. < the Irish surname *Murphy*; from the stereotypical prominence of the potato in the Irish diet]

Murphy /múrfi/, **Audie** (1924–71) US actor and war hero. A Congressional Medal of Honor winner, he was the most decorated soldier of World War II and later starred in several films, including *The Quiet American* (1958) and *The Unforgiven* (1960).

Murphy, Graeme (b. 1950) Australian dancer and choreographer. He became artistic director of Australia's Sydney Dance Company in 1976.

Murphy bed n N Am a bed that can be folded or swung into a cupboard or wall recess when not in use [Early 20C. After William *Murphy* (1876–1959), US inventor]

Murphy's Law /múrfiz-/ n ANZ, N Am the law or principle that if anything can go wrong, it will (informal) UK term **Sod's Law** [Mid-20C. After Edward *Murphy* (b. 1917), US engineer]

murragh /múrrə/ (plural **-raghs** or same) n a caddis fly to which trout are particularly attracted. Latin name: *Phryganea grandis*. [Origin ?]

murrain /múrrĭn/ n **1.** an infectious disease that affects cattle, e.g. anthrax **2.** an infectious and fast-spreading disease (archaic or humorous) [14C. < Anglo-Norman *moryn*, Old French *morine* < *mourir* 'die' < Latin *mori*]

Murray /múrri/ major river in southeastern Australia. Length: 2,589 km/1,609 mi.

Murray, Gilbert (1866–1957) British scholar. He was a classicist noted for his translations of Greek plays

and for his critical editions of the works of Euripides and Aeschylus. Full name **Murray, George Gilbert Aimé**

Murray, Sir James (1837–1915) British philologist and lexicographer. He laid the foundations of what became the *Oxford English Dictionary* and edited half of the first edition. Full name **Murray, James Augustus Henry**

Murray, Les (b. 1938) Australian poet and critic. He is the author of *Subhuman Redneck Poems* (1996) and winner of the 1997 T. S. Eliot Prize for Poetry. Full name **Murray, Leslie Alan**

'A human is a comet streamed in language far down time.'
[Les Murray, 'From Where We Live on Presence', *Translations from the Natural World*; 1993]

Murray Bridge town in southeastern South Australia, an agricultural centre located on the Murray River. Population: 17,273 (2002 estimate).

Murray cod n a large freshwater fish. Native to: Australian inland waterways. Latin name: *Maccullochella peeli*.

murrelet /múrlit/ (plural **-lets** or same) n a small diving bird of the auk family. Genera: *Brachyramphus* or *Synthliboramphus*. Native to: coastal regions of north Pacific.

murrey /múrri/ adj of the colour mulberry (archaic) [15C. Via Old French *moré* < medieval Latin *moratus* < Latin *morum* 'mulberry']

murrhine /múrrĭn/, **murrine** n a substance, possibly fluorite, that the ancient Romans used to make vases, cups, and other similar objects [Late 16C. < Latin *murr(h)inus* < *murra* 'murrhine']

murrhine glass n glassware made from fluorspar and decorated with flecks of metal

murrine n ANCIENT HIST, INDUST another spelling of **murrhine**

Murrinh-Patha /moorrin paatə/ n an Australian Aboriginal language spoken in the northwestern Northern Territory. Native speakers: 1,160.

Murrumbidgee /múrrəm bíjji/ river in southeastern Australia. Length: 1,600 km/980 mi.

Murry /múrri/, **John Middleton** (1889–1957) British writer and literary critic. He edited several periodicals and wrote critical studies of British authors and a biography of his wife, Katherine Mansfield.

murther /múrthər/ (archaic) n same as **murder** n (sense 1) ■ vti (**-thers, -thering, -thered**) same as **murder** v (sense 1) [14C. Variant]

muryan /múrri ən/ n regional same as **ant** [Mid-19C. < Cornish]

REGIONAL NOTE See *ant*.

mus. abbr **1.** museum **2.** music **3.** musical **4.** musician

Musaf /moo sáf/ n in Judaism, a group of additional prayers that is included in morning services on Sabbaths, festivals, and Rosh Chodesh [< Hebrew, 'addition']

MusB, **MusBac** abbr EDUC, MUSIC Bachelor of Music [Latin *Musicae Baccalaureus*]

Musca /múskə/ n a small constellation of the southern hemisphere. See illustration at **constellation**

muscadel, muscadelle n WINE same as **muscatel**

Muscadet /múskə day/ n a dry white wine from western France [Early 20C. < French < *muscade* 'nutmeg' < *musc* (see MUSK)]

muscadine /múskə dīn/ n **1.** a purple grape variety with a thick skin and musky smell. Use: to make wine. **2.** a cultivated ancestor of a wild grapevine found in the southeastern United States that produces muscadine grapes. Latin name: *Vitis rotundifolia*. [Mid-16C. Probably variant of MUSCATEL]

muscae volitantes /múski vólli tán teez/ npl specks that appear to float before the eyes (technical) [Mid-18C. < Latin, 'flies flying about']

muscarine /múskərĭn/ n a toxic substance, found in fly agaric and some other fungi, that affects the nervous system when ingested. Among other effects it dilates the blood vessels, slows the heart rate, constricts the airways, and stimulates the gut. [Late 19C. < modern Latin *Muscaria*, species name of the fly agaric < Latin *musca* 'fly'] —**muscarinic** /múskə rínnik/ adj

muscat /mús kat/ n **1.** a sweet white grape variety. Use: to make wine, raisins. **2.** a grapevine producing muscat grapes [Mid-16C. Via French < Provençal < *musc* < Latin *muscus* (see MUSK)]

Muscat /mús kat/, **Masqat** /máss gat/ capital city of Oman, on the northeastern coast of the country, on the Gulf of Oman. Population: 635,000 (1995).

muscatel /múskə tél/, **muscadel** /-dél/, **muscadelle** n **1.** a sweet white wine made from muscat grapes **2.** FOOD same as **muscat** (sense 1) [Mid-16C. Via Old French < Provençal, 'little muscat' < *muscat* (see MUSCAT)]

muscavado n FOOD another spelling of **muscovado**

muscid /mússid/ n a fly of the family that includes the housefly and the stable fly. Family: Muscidae. [Late 19C. Back-formation < modern Latin *Muscidae* < Latin *musca* 'fly'] —**muscid** adj

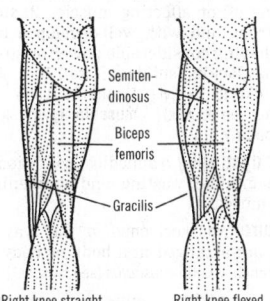

Right knee straight   Right knee flexed

muscle: muscles of the human knee

muscle /múss'l/ n **1.** BODY TISSUE PRODUCING MOVEMENT a tissue that can undergo repeated contraction and relaxation, so that it is able to produce movement of body parts, maintain tension, or pump fluids within the body. There are three types: voluntary (**striped muscle**), involuntary (**smooth muscle**), and branched or heart muscle. **2.** ORGAN COMPOSED OF MUSCLE an organ composed of bundles or sheets of muscle tissue, bound together with connective tissue and with tendons by which the contracting part is attached to the bones that it moves **3.** INFLUENCE power and influence, especially in the political, financial, or military spheres **4.** STRENGTH physical strength (informal) ○ *put some muscle into it* ■ vti (**-cles, -cling, -cled**) US MOVE USING STRENGTH to move using strength and force or effort, or make somebody or something move in this way (informal) ○ *muscled us aside to get to the head of the queue* [14C. Via French < Latin *musculus* literally 'small mouse' < *mus* 'mouse'; from the supposed resemblance of some muscles to mice] —**muscly** adj

SPELLCHECK Do not confuse the spelling of *muscle* and *mussel* ('a shellfish'), which sound similar. *Muscle* is a noun meaning 'a type of body organ', 'influence', and 'strength': *tired muscles*; *political muscle*; as a verb it means 'to move forcefully': *muscled his way past*. *Mussel* meaning 'a type of shellfish' is used only as a noun.

muscle in vi to become involved in or interfere in something by disregarding other people's wishes or by using strength, power, or influence (informal)

muscle-bound adj **1.** having muscles that are so bulky that they restrict movement **2.** too large, powerful, or overdeveloped to be capable of flexibility or a swift response

muscle candy n US a dietary supplement used by athletes to enhance bursts of high performance (slang)

muscle fibre n a basic contracting unit of striated muscle such as that in arms and legs, formed from several fused elongated cells (**myofibrils**) that contract when stimulated

muscleman /múss'l man/ (plural **-men** /-men/) n **1.** a very strong man with highly developed muscles **2.** a strong man hired by a criminal or gangster for protection and to intimidate enemies

muscle mary n an offensive term for a gay man with a muscular physique (slang)

muscle sense n PHYSIOL same as **kinaesthesia**

muscovado /múskə vaadō/, **muscavado** n a raw or unrefined sugar made by evaporating the molasses from sugar-cane juice [Early 17C. < Portuguese *mascabado* 'made badly']

muscovite /múskə vīt/ n a common mica mineral consisting of potassium aluminium silicate. Source: igneous and sedimentary rocks. [Mid-19C. < *Muscovy glass* 'mica' (from its being obtained from Russia)]

Muscovite /múskə vīt/ n somebody who comes from Moscow, Russia ■ adj PEOPLES same as **Russian** (*archaic*) [Mid-16C. < modern Latin *Muscovia* < Russian *Moskva* 'Moscow']

Muscovy /múskəvi/ former principality in western Russia, centred on Moscow

Muscovy duck /múskəvi-/ n a large duck with greenish-black feathers, white markings, and heavy red wattles. Kept for: food. Native to: Central America. Latin name: *Cairina moschata*. [Alteration (by association with archaic *Muscovy* 'of Moscow') of MUSK DUCK]

muscular /múskyōōlər/ adj 1. OF MUSCLES relating to, consisting of, or affecting muscles 2. STRONG physically strong and with well-developed muscles 3. VIGOROUS having considerable power or strength, but sometimes lacking subtlety [Late 17C. < obsolete *musculous*, directly or via French < Latin *musculosus* < *musculus* (see MUSCLE)] —**muscularity** /múskyōō lárrəti/ n —**muscularly** adv

muscular dystrophy n a medical condition in which there is gradual wasting and weakening of the skeletal muscles

musculature /múskōōləchər/ n the way that the muscles are arranged in a body or body part [Late 19C. < French < Latin *musculus* (see MUSCLE)]

musculo- prefix muscle, muscular ○ *musculocutaneous* [< Latin *musculus* (see MUSCLE)]

musculocutaneous /múskyōōlō kyōō táyni əss/ adj relating to or supplying the muscles and skin

musculoskeletal /múskyōōlō skéllit'l/ adj relating to or involving the muscles and the skeleton

MusD, **MusDoc** abbr Doctor of Music [Latin *Musicae Doctor*]

muse[1] /myōoz/ v (**muses, musing, mused**) 1. vti THINK ABOUT SOMETHING to think about something in a deep and serious or dreamy and abstracted way 2. vti SAY SOMETHING THOUGHTFULLY to say something in a thoughtful or questioning way 3. vi GAZE THOUGHTFULLY to gaze at somebody or something thoughtfully or abstractedly ■ n THOUGHTFUL STATE a state of deep thought (*literary*) [14C. < Old French *muser* 'meditate'] —**muser** n —**musingly** adv

muse[2] /myōoz/ n 1. SOMEBODY WHO INSPIRES ARTIST somebody who is a source of inspiration for an artist, especially for a poet 2. ARTIST'S INSPIRATION the source of inspiration that stimulates an artist, especially a poet 3. ARTIST'S PARTICULAR TALENT the gift or talent of an artist, especially a poet ○*With Donne, whose muse on dromedary trots/ Wreathe iron pokers into true-love knots'* (Samuel Taylor Coleridge, *On Donne's Poetry*; 1818) [14C. Directly or via French < Latin *musa* < Greek *mousa*]

Muse n in Greek mythology, one of the nine daughters of Zeus and Mnemosyne, goddess of memory. The Muses inspired and presided over the creative arts. They were Calliope, Clio, Erato, Euterpe, Melpomene, Polyhymnia, Terpsichore, Thalia, and Urania, responsible for epic poetry, history, love poetry, lyric poetry, tragedy, sacred song, dance, comedy, and astronomy, respectively.

museology /myōōzi ólləji/ n the study of how museums are designed, organized, and managed [Late 19C. < MUSEUM] —**museological** /myōōzi ə lójjik'l/ adj —**museologically** adv —**museologist** n

musette /myōo zét/ n 1. French bagpipes that make a relatively soft sound. The musette was popular in the 17th, 18th, and 19th centuries. 2. a piece of pastoral dance music that imitates the sound of bagpipes or has bagpipes playing the bass line [14C. < French, 'little bagpipes' < *muse* 'bagpipes']

museum /myōo zee əm/ n 1. a building or institution where objects of artistic, historical, or scientific importance and value are kept, studied, and put on display 2. ONLINE the domain name for a museum (*used in Internet addresses*) See table at **domain name** [Early 17C. Via Latin, 'library, academy' < Greek *mouseion* 'place of the Muses' < *mousa* 'muse']

museum piece n 1. an object that is so valuable, interesting, or old that it could or should be in a museum 2. somebody or something considered very old-fashioned (*informal*)

Musgrave Ranges /múss grayv-/ mountain range in central Australia, on the border between the Northern Territory and South Australia

mush[1] /mush/ n 1. PULP a soft pulpy mass 2. SENTIMENTAL WORDS OR IDEAS excessively romantic and sentimental words or ideas, e.g. in a book or film 3. MEDIA INTERFERENCE radio interference, especially a hissing noise 4. US FOOD PORRIDGE a thick mixture made from cornmeal and milk or water ■ vt (**mushes, mushing, mushed**) US MASH SOMETHING to mash something into a soft pulpy mass [Late 17C. Probably variant of MASH] —**mushy** adj

mush[2] /mush/ N Am interj COMMAND TO SLED DOGS used to make sled dogs start pulling or moving faster ■ n DOGSLED JOURNEY a journey on a dogsled ■ vti (**mushes, mushing, mushed**) TRAVEL BY DOGSLED to travel on a dogsled, or drive a dogsled or team of dogs [Mid-19C. < *Mush on!*, probably < French *marchons* 'let us march' < *marcher* 'to march'] —**musher** n

mush[3] /mŏosh/ n somebody's face or mouth (*dated slang*) [Mid-20C. Origin ?]

mush[4] /mŏosh/ n a familiar or disrespectful way of addressing somebody, usually a man (*slang*) [Mid-20C. Origin ?]

mushaira /mŏo shírə/ n S Asia an evening social event at which people read or recite their own Urdu poetry, often in competition with each other [< Hindi *muśaïra*]

mush area /músh-/ n a region where two or more radio signals overlap so that interference results [< MUSH[1]]

Musharraf /moo shárraf/, **Pervez** (*b.* 1943) president of Pakistan. An army general, he seized power in a bloodless coup in 1999, and declared himself president and formal head of state in 2001.

mushroom /músh room, -rŏom/ n 1. UMBRELLA-SHAPED FUNGUS the usually umbrella-shaped spore-producing body of a fungus that consists of a fleshy cap on a stalk. Class: Basidiomycetes. 2. EDIBLE FUNGUS an edible mushroom, especially the field mushroom 3. FAST-GROWING THING something that grows very fast ■ vi (**-rooms, -rooming, -roomed**) 1. GROW QUICKLY to grow or develop very rapidly 2. BECOME MUSHROOM-SHAPED to swell into a shape like a mushroom 3. PICK MUSHROOMS to go mushroom picking [15C. Via French *mousseron* < late Latin *mussirion*- a type of mushroom] —**mushroomy** adj

AKG London

mushroom cloud

mushroom cloud n the large mushroom-shaped cloud of dust and debris caused by an explosion, especially a nuclear explosion

Mushuau Innu /mŏo shŏo aw-/ n a member of a Native North American people who once lived and hunted in the Canadian bush, but who now live in communities in Newfoundland and Labrador [< Montagnais] —**Mushuau Innu** adj

music /myōozik/ n 1. SOUNDS THAT PRODUCE EFFECT sounds, usually produced by instruments or voices, that are arranged or played in order to create an effect 2. ART OF ARRANGING SOUNDS the art of arranging or making sounds, usually those of musical instruments or voices, so as to create an effect 3. TYPE OF MUSIC music of a particular type, place, time, instrument, or style ○ *rock-and-roll music* 4. WRITTEN MUSIC written notation indicating the pitch, duration, rhythm, and tone of notes to be played 5. PLEASING SOUND a sound or group of sounds that creates a desired effect ○ *the music of the wind in the trees* [13C. Via French *musique* < Greek *mousikē* 'art of the Muse, music' < *mousikos* 'of a Muse' < *mousa* 'muse'] ◇ **be (like) music to somebody's ears** to be very pleasant, satisfying, or reassuring to hear ◇ **face the music** to deal with a pressing, difficult, or unpleasant situation arising from something you have done previously

musical /myōozik'l/ adj 1. OF OR FOR MUSIC relating to or producing music 2. PLEASANT-SOUNDING sounding pleasant and melodious 3. GOOD AT MUSIC having a talent for or a keen interest in music 4. WITH MUSIC set to, consisting of, or involving music ■ n PLAY OR FILM WITH SONGS a light-hearted play or film that has singing, music, and often dancing in it as important devices for developing the story and characters —**musically** adv

musical box n a box that contains a mechanical device that plays music. N Am term **music box**

musicale /myōozi kaál/ n N Am a social occasion in which music is the featured entertainment [Late 19C. < French (*soirée*) *musicale* 'musical evening']

musicality /myōozi kálləti/ n 1. musical ability, especially a knowledge of or sensitivity to music 2. the quality of being musical

music box n N Am same as **musical box**

music centre n a one-piece hi-fi unit that has a turntable, amplifier, cassette deck, radio, and speakers (*dated*)

music drama n a type of opera, first composed by Richard Wagner in the late 19th century, in which the dramatic and musical content are intended to be of equal importance

music hall n 1. UK a type of entertainment, popular in the late 19th and early 20th centuries, that consisted of a variety of singing, dancing, and comic acts. ANZ, N Am term **vaudeville** 2. a theatre in which music hall shows were staged

musician /myōo zísh'n/ n somebody who plays, performs, conducts, or composes music —**musicianly** adj —**musicianship** n

music of the spheres n the perfect but inaudible music that Pythagoras and other later philosophers believed was created by the movement of astronomical objects

musicology /myōozi kólləji/ n the academic study of music and its history —**musicological** /myōozikə lójjik'l/ adj —**musicologist** n

music paper n paper with staves printed on it, used for writing music on

music roll n a roll of paper with carefully positioned holes in it, used for controlling a mechanical instrument such as a player piano

music stand n a height-adjustable frame for holding printed music that is being performed

music stick n Aus a traditional Aboriginal percussion instrument consisting of one or, more usually, two short pieces of eucalyptus or mulga wood, played by striking one stick against another or against the ground

music video n a short video or film made to accompany a song or piece of popular music, often as a cinematic or dramatic interpretation of it

Musil /mŏoss'l/, **Robert** (1880–1942) Austrian novelist. Much of his work drew on personal experiences and often reflected Austrian culture.

musings /myōozingz/ npl thoughts, especially when aimless and unsystematic ○ *philosophical musings*

musique concrète /myōo zeek kong krét/ n recorded music composed by electronically combining and enhancing natural and musical sounds [Mid-20C. < French, 'concrete music']

musk /musk/ n 1. GLANDULAR SECRETION OF DEER a pungent and greasy secretion from a gland in the male musk deer. Use: perfume manufacture. 2. SUBSTANCE LIKE MUSK a secretion similar to musk from other animals such as the civet or otter, or a synthetic substance with similar properties 3. PLANTS PLANT WITH MUSKY SCENT a plant that has a musky scent 4. SMELL OF MUSK the smell of musk, or a similar smell [14C. Via late Latin *muscus* < Persian *mušk*]

musk deer n a small mountain-dwelling deer, the male of which lacks antlers and possesses long canine teeth. Native to: central and northeastern Asia. Latin name: *Moschus moschiferus*.

musk duck n BIRDS same as **Muscovy duck** [< its smell]

muskeg /músk eg/ n 1. N Am an area of swamp or boggy land covered in sphagnum moss, leaves, and a mass of dead plant matter resembling peat 2. the dead plant matter resembling peat that covers areas of muskeg [Late 18C. < Cree *maske:k*]

muskellunge /múskə lunj/ (*plural* **-lunges** or *same*) n

1. *N Am* a large predatory freshwater fish of the pike family, caught as game. Native to: Great Lakes region of North America. Latin name: *Esox masquinongy*. **2.** the flesh of a muskellunge used as food [Late 18C. Via Canadian French *maskinongé* < Ojibwa *maashkinoozhe* 'big fish']

musket /múskit/ *n* a shoulder gun with a long barrel and a smooth bore, used between the 16th and 18th centuries [Late 16C. Via French *mousquet* < Italian *moschetto* 'crossbow bolt' < *mosca* 'fly' < Latin *musca*]

ORIGIN Early *muskets* could fire crossbow bolts as well as bullets. The name was probably reinforced by Italian *moschetto* 'sparrow hawk' (from its markings suggestive of flies), early guns being often named after birds of prey (e.g. *falconet*, a type of small cannon).

musketeer /múskə teér/ *n* **1.** an infantryman armed with a musket **2.** a member of a company of musketeers in the French royal household's personal troops in the 17th and 18th centuries

CULTURAL NOTE *The Three Musketeers*, a novel (1844) by French writer Alexandre Dumas. Set in France during the reign of Louis XIII, this historical romance tells the story of a young adventurer, D'Artagnan, who is taken under the wing of three musketeers, Athos, Porthos, and Aramis. The four become embroiled in a series of adventures involving love, politics, swordsmanship, and the machinations of the evil Cardinal Richelieu.

musketry /múskitri/ *n* **1.** a group of muskets or musketeers **2.** the technique or practice of using small arms

Muskhogean *n, adj* LANG another spelling of **Muskogean**

musk mallow *n* a plant of the mallow family with a hairy and often purple-spotted stem and a slight musky scent. Flowers: pink. Native to: Europe, North Africa. Latin name: *Malva moschata*.

muskmelon /músk mellən/ *n* **1.** a fruit with a ribbed or rough rind and white, yellow, or green flesh with a sweet full flavour and a pleasant, slightly musky smell **2.** a widely cultivated trailing vine that produces muskmelons. Latin name: *Cucumis melo*.

Muskogean /mus kógi ən/, **Muskhogean** *n* a Hokan-Siouan branch of languages, including Chickasaw, Choctaw, and Creek —**Muskogean** *adj*

Muskogee /mus kógi/ (*plural same* or **-gees**) *n* a member of a Native North American people who lived in southeastern North America [Late 18C. < Creek *ma:skó:ki*]

musk orchid *n* a small orchid. Flowers: musk-scented, greenish-yellow, in dense spikes. Native to: Europe, Asia. Latin name: *Herminium monorchis*.

musk ox *n* a large wild ox with a black or brown shaggy coat and flat downward-curving horns. Native to: northern Canada, Greenland. Latin name: *Ovibos moschatus*.

muskrat

muskrat /músk rat/ (*plural* **-rats** or *same*) *n* **1.** a large amphibious rodent, closely related to the vole and the lemming, with a thick brown coat and musk glands. Native to: North America, Europe. Latin name: *Ondatra zibethica*. **2.** the fur of the muskrat [Early 17C. < Algonquian *muscascus*, by association with MUSK and RAT]

musk rose *n* a late-flowering rose with white, musk-scented flowers. Native to: Mediterranean. Latin name: *Rosa moschata*.

musk thistle *n* a thistle with leaves divided into narrow spine-tipped lobes. Flowers: single, drooping, reddish-purple. Native to: temperate regions of Europe and Asia. Latin name: *Carduus nutans*.

musk turtle *n* a small freshwater turtle that gives off a pungent smell. Native to: eastern United States, Canada. Genus: *Sternotherus*.

musky /múski/ (**-ier, -iest**) *adj* having a sweet pungent smell similar to that of musk —**muskily** *adv* —**muskiness** *n*

~~**musle**~~ incorrect spelling of **muscle**

Muslim /moʻozləm/ *n* somebody whose religion is Islam ■ *adj* relating to the followers of Islam or to areas, cultures, or activities in which followers of Islam are especially numerous [Early 17C. < Arabic, 'somebody who surrenders (to God)', active participle of *'aslama* (see ISLAM)] —**Muslimism** *n*

Muslim Brotherhood *n* an Egyptian nationalist movement founded by Hasan al-Bannah in 1928 that is committed to the Islamic fundamentalist cause and opposes Western influence. The Muslim Brotherhood is active in several other countries throughout Southwest Asia, North Africa, South Asia, and Southeast Asia.

Muslim League *n* a Muslim political organization founded in India in 1906 that was instrumental in achieving the creation of Pakistan in 1947. It caused a division within the Indian nationalist movement.

muslin /múzlin/ *n* a thin plain-weave cotton cloth. Use: curtains, sheets, dresses. [Early 17C. Via French *mousseline* < Italian *mussolina*, < Arabic *mawsiliy* 'of Mosul', Iraqi city]

MusM *abbr* Master of Music [Latin *Musicae Magister*]

muso /myoʻozō/ (*plural* **-sos**) *n* (*informal*) **1.** a musician, especially in a pop group, who pays too much attention to technique **2.** *Aus* somebody who plays a musical instrument [Mid-20C. Shortening of MUSICIAN]

musquash /múss kwosh/ *n* ZOOL same as **muskrat** [Early 17C. < Massachuset < W Abenaki *môskwas*]

muss /muss/ *N Am* (*informal*) *vt* (**musses, mussing, mussed**) to make something, especially somebody's hair or clothes, untidy or ruffled ■ *n* a state of untidiness or disorder [Mid-19C. Probably variant of MESS]

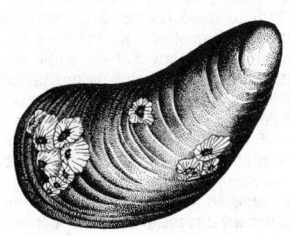

mussel

mussel /múss'l/ *n* **1.** an edible bivalve mollusc with a blue-black shell that lives attached to objects in the sea. Genus: *Mytilus*. **2.** a freshwater bivalve mollusc whose shell is a source of mother of pearl. Genera: *Anodonta* or *Unio*. [Pre-12C. < assumed Vulgar Latin *muscula*, alteration of Latin *musculus* 'small mouse' (see MUSCLE); from the mussel's supposed resemblance in shape and colour to a mouse]

SPELLCHECK See *muscle*.

Mussolini /moʻossə leéni/, **Benito** (1883–1945) Italian national leader. He founded the Italian Fascist Party in 1919 and served as prime minister from 1922 and dictator (1925–43). After forming an alliance with Germany in 1939, he brought Italy into World War II (1940). He was overthrown three years later, and eventually assassinated by the Italian Resistance. Full name **Mussolini, Benito Amilcaro Andrea**. Known as **Il Duce**

'For me Fascism is not an end in itself.
It was a means to re-establish national equilibrium.'
[Benito Mussolini. Quoted in *Fascist Italy*, John Whittam; 1995]

Mussorgsky /mə sáwrgski/, **Modest** (1839–81) Russian composer. His works, often inspired by Russian folk music, include the opera *Boris Godunov* (1868) and the piano suite *Pictures at an Exhibition* (1874). Full name **Mussorgsky, Modest Petrovich**

'Art is not an end in itself, but a means of addressing humanity.'
[Attributed to Modest Mussorgsky]

Mussulman /múss'lmən/ (*plural* **-men** /-mən/ or **-mans**) *n* same as **Muslim** (*archaic*) [Late 16C. < Persian *musulmān* 'Muslim' (adjective) < Arabic *muslim* (see MUSLIM)]

mussy /mússi/ (**mussier, mussiest**) *adj US* not tidy or in an orderly state (*informal*) —**mussily** *adv* —**mussiness** *n*

must[1] stressed /must/; unstressed /məst, məss/ (**must, plural musts**) CORE MEANING: a modal verb indicating that somebody is compelled to do something because of a rule or law, or that it is necessary or advisable to do something ○ *Accidents causing injury must be reported immediately.* ○ *Employment decisions must be based on ability.* ○ *We must improve our schools.* ○ *You must give him a chance to state his case.*
1. *modal v* BE COMPELLED to be compelled to do something because of a rule or law ○ *You must stop when the light is red.* ○ *All guests must vacate their rooms by 12 noon.* **2.** *modal v* BE NECESSARY to be important or necessary for doing something ○ *Henceforth, he said, the central organizing principle of all governments must be the environment.* ○ *Health care insurance must be affordable.* **3.** *modal v* BE CERTAIN indicates that somebody is sure that something is the case ○ *This must seem strange to you.* ○ *Those must be your footprints in the garden.* **4.** *modal v* INDICATES BELIEF indicates that somebody concludes that something is the case on the basis of the available evidence ○ *Palaeontologists know that primates must have immigrated to South America sometime before 28 million years ago.* **5.** *modal v* USED TO MAKE SUGGESTIONS used to make suggestions or invitations or to give advice ○ *You must see a doctor.* ○ *You must come round for dinner one evening.* **6.** *modal v* INTEND to intend or be determined to do something ○ *I must be going.* ○ *I must telephone my brother.* **7.** *n* SOMETHING ESSENTIAL something that is essential or obligatory ○ *Formal attire is a must at a state dinner.* **8.** *prefix* ESSENTIAL absolutely necessary or highly recommended for somebody (*informal*; added to a verb to form a noun or adjective) ○ *a must-win situation* [Old English *mōste*, past tense of assumed *mōtan* 'have to, be able to' < Germanic]

must[2] /must/ *n* the juice from grapes or other fruit that is to be fermented into wine [Pre-12C. < Latin *mustum*, form of *mustus* 'new, fresh']

must[3] /must/ *n* the condition of being musty or mouldy [Early 17C. Back-formation < MUSTY]

must[4] *n* ZOOL another spelling of **musth**

mustache *n* HAIR US spelling of **moustache**

mustachio /mə staáshi ō/ (*plural* **-os**) *n* a moustache that is thick or trimmed into a fancy shape (*archaic or humorous; often used in the plural*) [Mid-16C. Blend of Spanish *mostacho* + Italian *mostaccio* (see MOUSTACHE)] —**mustachioed** *adj*

mustang /mús tang/ *n* a small hardy wild horse living on the plains of North America, descended from Arab horses brought to the continent by Spanish soldiers [Early 19C. Via Mexican Spanish *mestengo* < Spanish, 'ownerless' < *mesta* 'ranchers who appropriated wild cattle' < Latin *mixta* 'mixed']

mustard /mústərd/ *n* **1.** SPICY CONDIMENT the powdered seeds of a brassica plant, or a hot spicy paste made from these, or sometimes whole seeds, water, and other ingredients, eaten in small quantities as a condiment **2.** PLANTS PLANT WITH PUNGENT SEEDS a plant with long thin seed pods containing mustard seeds. Flowers: small, yellow. Genus: *Brassica*. **3.** COLOURS DARK YELLOW COLOUR a brownish-yellow colour, like that of mustard **4.** *US* ENTHUSIASM enthusiasm or zest (*informal*) [12C. < Old French *mo(u)starde* < Latin *mustum* 'must, new wine' (originally mixed with the crushed seeds)] —**mustard** *adj* —**mustardy** *adj* ◇ **cut the mustard** to be up to the desired standard of performance, ability, or quality (*informal*)

mustard and cress *n* a salad of seedlings of white mustard and garden cress, cultivated indoors in small containers

mustard gas *n* an oily liquid that evaporates into a poison gas. Used in chemical warfare, it burns the

skin and causes often fatal respiratory damage. Formula: $(CH_2CLCH_2)_2S$. [Because its smell resembles mustard]

mustard oil *n* an oil obtained from mustard seeds. Use: making soap.

mustard plaster *n* a paste made from black mustard seeds and applied to the skin. Use: formerly, to stimulate blood flow and counter inflammation.

musteline /músti līn, -lin/ *adj* relating to, belonging to, or characteristic of the group of mammals that includes weasels, otters, badgers, and skunks. Family: Mustelidae. [Mid-17C. < Latin *mustelinus* < *mustel* 'weasel']

muster /mústər/ *v* (**-ters, -tering, -tered**) **1.** *vt* **CALL UP SOMETHING** to summon up something such as strength or courage that will help in doing something **2.** *vti* **ASSEMBLE SOLDIERS OR CREW MEMBERS** to bring together a group of soldiers or the members of a crew, e.g. for inspection, or be brought together in this way **3.** *vt* **GATHER PEOPLE OR THINGS** to gather people or things together **4.** *vt ANZ* AGRIC **ROUND UP LIVESTOCK** to round up livestock, especially cattle or sheep ■ *n* **1. MILITARY ASSEMBLY** a gathering of soldiers or a crew, e.g. for inspection **2.** MIL, NAVY same as **muster roll 3. GATHERING OR COLLECTION** a gathering of people or collection of things **4.** *ANZ* AGRIC **ROUND-UP OF ANIMALS** a round-up of animals, especially cattle or sheep [14C. Via Old French *mo(u)strer* 'to show', *moustre* 'showing' < Latin *monstrare* < *monstrum* '(evil) omen, sign'] ◇ **pass muster** to measure up to set standards or to expectations
muster in *vti US* to enrol somebody for military service, or be enrolled for military service
muster out *vti US* to discharge somebody from military service, or be discharged from military service

muster roll *n* a list of the members of a military or naval unit

musth /must/, **must** *n* a state of increased sexual activity accompanied by aggression in large male land mammals, especially male elephants, lasting 2 to 3 months [Late 19C. Via Urdu *mast* < Persian, 'drunk, intoxicated']

must-have *adj* absolutely necessary or highly recommended to possess ○ *a list of this year's must-have accessories* —**must-have** *n*

Mustique /mu steék, moō-/ island in the eastern Caribbean Sea. It is part of St Vincent and the Grenadines.

mustn't /múss'nt/ *contr* must not ○ *You mustn't worry.*

must-see *n* something that is considered so important, beautiful, or excellent that everyone should see it, e.g. a place, film, or work of art (*often used before a noun*)

musty /músti/ (**-ier, -iest**) *adj* **1. WITH OLD DAMP SMELL** smelling old, damp, and stale because of not having been used or exposed to fresh air for a long time **2. WITH STALE TASTE** tasting old, stale, and mouldy **3. OUTDATED AND UNINTERESTING** no longer relevant or interesting because of being old-fashioned [Early 16C. Origin ?] —**mustily** *adv* —**mustiness** *n*

Muswellbrook /mússəl brŏŏk/ town in eastern New South Wales, Australia, a coal mining and agricultural centre. Population: 15,352 (2002 estimate).

mutable /myoōtəb'l/ *adj* **1. CHANGEABLE** tending or likely to change **2. CAPABLE OF CHANGE** capable of changing, or subject to change **3.** GENETICS **TENDING TO UNDERGO MUTATION** describes a gene or organism that has a tendency to undergo mutation **4.** ASTROL **OF GEMINI, VIRGO, SAGITTARIUS, AND PISCES** describes the signs of the zodiac Gemini, Virgo, Sagittarius, and Pisces, thought to be characterized by adaptability [14C. < Latin *mutabilis* < *mutare* 'to change'] —**mutability** /myoōtə bílləti/ *n* —**mutableness** *n* —**mutably** *adv*

mutagen /myoōtəjən/ *n* an external agent that increases the rate of mutation of cells or organisms, e.g. radiation or some chemicals or viruses [Mid-20C. < MUTATION + -GEN] —**mutagenesis** /myoōtə jénnəssiss/ *n* —**mutagenic** /myoōtə jénnik/ *adj* —**mutagenically** *adv* —**mutagenicity** /myoōtə jə níssəti/ *n*

mutant /myoōt'nt/ *n* **1. SOMETHING THAT HAS MUTATED** an animal, organism, cell, or gene that has mutated **2. OFFENSIVE TERM** an offensive term for somebody who looks or appears strange (*slang insult*) **3. ODD THING** a strange-looking thing or animal (*slang*) ■ *adj* **1. RESULTING FROM MUTATION** undergoing or resulting from genetic mutation **2. APPEARING STRANGE** having an odd appearance or other qualities regarded as strange (*slang*) [Early 20C. < Latin *mutant-*, present participle of *mutare* 'to change']

Mutare /moo taári/ resort town and capital of Manicaland Province in eastern Zimbabwe, close to the Mozambique border. Population: 131,367 (1992).

mutase /myoō tayz, -tayss/ *n* an enzyme that promotes a change in the shape of a molecule [Early 20C. < Latin *mutare* 'to change']

mutate /myoo táyt/ (**-tates, -tating, -tated**) *vti* to undergo mutation, or make something undergo mutation [Mid-18C. Partly back-formation < MUTATION; partly < Latin *mutat-*, past participle of *mutare* 'to change'] —**mutative** /myoōtətiv, myoo táytiv/ *adj*

mutation /myoo táysh'n/ *n* **1. CHANGE IN GENETIC MATERIAL** a random change in a gene or chromosome resulting in a new trait or characteristic that can be inherited. Mutation can be a source of beneficial genetic variation, or it can be neutral or harmful in effect. **2.** BIOL same as **mutant** *n* (sense 1) **3. ALTERATION** the action or process of changing something or of being changed **4.** LING same as **umlaut** *n* (sense 1) **5.** PHON **PHONETIC CHANGE** a phonetic change found in Celtic languages in which the initial consonant of a word changes according to the preceding word —**mutational** *adj* —**mutationally** *adv*

mutation stop *n* a stop that controls a set of organ pipes that do not play the tones of the written notes, but usually a fifth or third above them

mutatis mutandis /moo taátiss moo tandiss/ *adv* with the necessary changes having been made [< Latin]

mutawaa /moo taá waa/ *npl* in some Muslim countries, a police force whose duty is to ensure that the population complies with the laws of Islam [< Arabic]

Mutazilite /moo taázi līt/ *n* a member of an ancient Muslim religious group who subsequently became part of the Shia group [Early 18C. < Arabic, 'those who keep to themselves']

mute /myoot/ *adj* **1. NOT SPEAKING** unwilling or unable to speak **2. MAKING NO SOUND** saying nothing, or making no sound **3. NOT EXPRESSED IN WORDS** felt or expressed without speech **4.** LAW **NOT ANSWERING CHARGE** refusing to answer a charge brought in a court of law **5.** PHON same as **plosive 6.** PHON **NOT PRONOUNCED** not pronounced, like the final 'e' in 'cheese' ■ *n* **1. OFFENSIVE TERM** an offensive term for somebody who is unable or unwilling to speak (*dated*) **2.** LAW **SOMEBODY REFUSING TO ANSWER CHARGE** somebody who refuses to answer a charge in a court of law **3.** PHON same as **plosive 4.** PHON **SILENT LETTER** a letter that is not pronounced **5.** MUSIC **DEVICE FOR ALTERING TONE OF INSTRUMENT** a pad, clip, or other device used to reduce or alter in some way the tone of a brass or stringed instrument **6. HIRED MOURNER** somebody who was formerly paid to act as a mourner at a funeral ■ *vt* (**mutes, muting, muted**) **1. TURN DOWN SOUND** to moderate the volume of a sound **2. MAKE SOMETHING LESS BRIGHT** to make a colour or light less bright or harsh **3.** MUSIC **ALTER TONE OF INSTRUMENT** to reduce or alter in some way the tone of a brass or stringed instrument using a pad, clip, or other device [14C. < French *muet* 'slightly mute' < Old French *mu* < Latin *mutus*] —**mutely** *adv* —**muteness** *n*

muted /myoōtid/ *adj* **1. NOT BRIGHT OR INTENSE** not bright, intense, or harsh in colour or tone **2. NOT LOUD** not loud or distinct enough to be heard clearly **3. UNDERSTATED** subdued and understated ○ *muted criticism* **4.** MUSIC **FROM INSTRUMENT WITH MUTE** fitted with a mute, or produced by an instrument fitted with a mute —**mutedly** *adv*

mute swan *n* a large white swan with an orange bill. Native to: Europe, Asia. Latin name: *Cygnus olor*.

muti /moōti/ *n S Africa* medicine, especially herbal medicine [Late 19C. < Zulu *umuthi* 'tree, plant']

mutilate /myoōti layt/ (**-lates, -lating, -lated**) *vt* **1. DESTROY BODY PART** to inflict serious injury on the body or a part of the body of a person or animal by removing or destroying parts of it **2. RUIN SOMETHING BY REMOVING PARTS** to damage or spoil something such as a piece of writing or a film by removing important parts of it **3. DAMAGE SOMETHING SERIOUSLY** to inflict serious damage on something [Mid-16C. Partly < Latin *mutilat-*, past participle of *mutilare* 'cut or lop off' < *mutilus* 'maimed'; partly < obsolete *mutilate* 'mutilated'] —**mutilation** /myoōti láysh'n/ *n* —**mutilative** *adj* —**mutilator** *n*

mutineer /myoōti neér/ *n* somebody who rebels against the legal authority of others, especially a soldier or sailor [Early 17C. < French *mutinier* < Old French *mutin* 'rebellious' (see MUTINY)]

mutinous /myoōtinəss/ *adj* **1.** plotting, participating in, or typical of a mutiny **2.** refusing to obey or submit to control, especially military control [Late 16C. < Old French *mutineus* < *mutin* 'rebellious' (see MUTINY), or < English *mutine*] —**mutinously** *adv*

mutiny /myoōtəni/ *n* (*plural* **-nies**) a rebellion against legal authority, especially by soldiers or sailors refusing to obey orders and, often, attacking their officers ■ *vi* (**-nies, -nying, -nied**) to take part in a rebellion against legal authority [Mid-16C. Via obsolete *mutine* 'rebellion' < French *mutiner* < Old French *mutin* 'rebellious' < *muete* 'revolt', via assumed Vulgar Latin *movitus* < Latin *motus* 'moved']

mutism /myoōtizəm/ *n* **1.** a refusal to speak either at all times or at some times, usually as a result of trauma or stress **2.** an offensive term for the inability to speak (*dated*)

muton /myoōt on/ *n* the smallest known unit of DNA in which mutation can take place, either spontaneously or as a result of an external agent [Mid-20C. < MUTATION]

mutt /mut/ *n* **1.** a dog that is of mixed or unknown breed (*slang*) **2.** an offensive term that deliberately insults somebody's intelligence or knowledge (*slang insult*) [Late 19C. Shortening of MUTTONHEAD]

mutter /múttər/ *v* (**-ters, -tering, -tered**) **1.** *vti* **SAY SOMETHING QUIETLY** to speak or say something quietly and indistinctly **2.** *vi* **GRUMBLE** to say something in a quiet voice, especially as a complaint or in annoyance ■ *n* **1. ACT OF UTTERING QUIETLY** an act of saying something quietly and indistinctly **2. SOMETHING SAID QUIETLY** a quiet and indistinct utterance [14C. Origin ?] —**mutterer** *n*

mutton /mútt'n/ *n* the flesh of a fully grown sheep, eaten as food [13C. Directly or via Old French *molton* 'ram, wether, sheep' < medieval Latin *multon-*] —**muttony** *adj* ◇ **mutton dressed as lamb** an offensive term for meaning dressing in a way considered to be more suitable for a younger person

muttonbird *n* a seabird traditionally hunted for food, e.g. a petrel or shearwater. Native to: Australasia. Family: Procellaridae. [Because its cooked flesh is said to resemble mutton]

mutton-birder *n NZ* somebody who hunts mutton birds

muttonchops /mútt'n chops/ *npl* facial hair trimmed into a narrow strip beside each ear, broadening out along the lower cheek and stopping at the side of the chin, which is kept bare [< the shape]

muttonhead /mútt'n hed/ *n* an offensive term that deliberately insults somebody's intelligence or knowledge (*dated informal insult*) —**muttonheaded** *adj*

mutual /myoōchoo əl/ *adj* **1. FELT BY EACH** done, felt, or expressed by each towards or with regard to the other ○ *mutual admiration* **2. WITH SAME FEELINGS** having or involving the same feelings towards each other ○ *mutual friendship* **3. SHARED BY PEOPLE** shared by or common to two or more people or groups **4.** INSUR **OF MUTUAL INSURANCE** relating to mutual insurance [15C. < French *mutuel* < Latin *mutuus* 'borrowed, reciprocal, done in exchange'] —**mutuality** /myoōchoo állәti/ *n* —**mutually** *adv*

mutual assured destruction *n* the enormous reciprocal damage that the superpowers and their allies would inflict on each other in the event of a nuclear war

mutual company *n* a company owned by its clients, e.g. an insurance company owned by its policyholders, who receive profits in the form of bonuses instead of in share dividends

mutual fund *n N Am* FIN same as **unit trust**

mutual inductance *n* a measure of the change in the electromotive force of a circuit caused by a change in the current flowing through an associated circuit. It is given as the ratio of the electromotive force induced to the rate of current change producing it. Symbol *M*

mutual induction *n* the production of an electromotive force in a circuit resulting from a change in the current flowing through another circuit to which it is magnetically linked

mutual insurance *n* a method of insurance in which the customers buying policies own the company, pay premiums into a common fund to cover claims, and share in the profits

mutualise *vti* another spelling of **mutualize**

mutualism /myoʻochoo əlizəm/ *n* a relationship between two organisms of different species that benefits both and harms neither. For example, lichens are a fungus and an alga living in mutualism: the fungus provides a protective structure, and the alga produces a carbohydrate as food for the fungus. —**mutualist** *n* —**mutualistic** /myoʻochoo ə lístik/ *adj*

mutualize /myoʻochoo ə līz/ (**-izes, -izing, -ized**), **mutualise** (**-ises, -ising, -ised**) *vti* to become mutual, or make something mutual —**mutualization** /myoʻochoo ə līzáysh'n/ *n*

mutual savings bank *n* a bank without shareholders in which the depositors are technically the owners

mutuel /myoʻotyoo əl/ *n N Am* GAMBLING same as **pari-mutuel** [Early 20C. Shortening]

mutule /myoʻo tyool/ *n* a projecting block that holds a conical ornament (**gutta**) under a Doric cornice [Mid-17C. Via French < Latin *mutulus*]

muumuu /moʻomoo/ (*plural* **-muus**), **mumu** (*plural* **-mus**) *n* a loose shapeless Hawaiian dress made of brightly coloured fabric [Early 20C. < Hawaiian *muʻu muʻu* 'cut off' (because there was originally no yoke)]

mux /muks/ *n* COMPUT same as **multiplexer** (*informal*) [Late 20C. Contraction]

Muzak /myoʻo zak/ *tdmk* a trademark for recorded background music played in shops, restaurants, lifts, and other public places

muzhik /moo zhík/ *n* a Russian peasant, especially during the tsarist era [Mid-16C. < Russian, 'small man' < *muzh* 'man, husband']

Muzorewa /moʻozzə ráywə/, **Abel** (*b.* 1925) prime minister of Rhodesia (1979–80). He was the Methodist bishop of Rhodesia and prime minister during its transition to majority rule as Zimbabwe. Full name **Muzorewa, Abel Tendekayi**

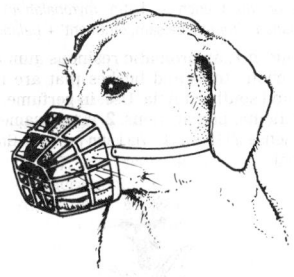
muzzle (sense 2)

muzzle /múzz'l/ *n* **1.** ANIMAL'S NOSE AND JAWS the projecting part of an animal's face, made up of its nose and jaws **2.** RESTRAINING DEVICE FOR ANIMAL a device that is strapped over the nose and jaws of an animal to prevent it from opening its mouth, e.g. to bite, bark, or eat **3.** END OF GUN BARREL the front open end of the barrel of a firearm **4.** CENSORSHIP something that is meant to prevent free expression ■ *vt* (**-zles, -zling, -zled**) **1.** PUT MUZZLE ON ANIMAL to put a muzzle over the nose and jaws of an animal **2.** CENSOR SOMEBODY to prevent a person or group from publicly expressing their views or opinions **3.** SAILING TAKE IN SAIL to roll up and secure a sail [14C. < Old French *musel* 'small muzzle' < *muse* 'muzzle'] —**muzzler** *n*

muzzle-loader /múzz'l lōdər/ *n* a firearm that is loaded through its muzzle —**muzzle-loading** *adj*

muzzle velocity *n* the speed of a bullet or other projectile as it leaves the muzzle of a firearm

muzzy /múzzi/ (**-zier, -ziest**) *adj* **1.** unable to think clearly, especially as a result of illness or drinking alcohol **2.** indistinct, vague, or confused [Early 18C. Origin ?] —**muzzily** *adv* —**muzziness** *n*

mv *abbr* **1.** ONLINE Maldives (*used in Internet addresses*) See table at **domain name 2.** MUSIC mezza voce

mV *abbr* MEASURE millivolt

MV *abbr* **1.** MEASURE megavolt **2.** SHIPPING merchant vessel **3.** SHIPPING motor vessel **4.** ARMS muzzle velocity

m.v. *abbr* **1.** COMM market value **2.** STATS mean variation

MVD *n* the Ministry for Internal Affairs of the former Soviet Union from 1946 to 1960, which acted as its secret police. Full form **Ministerstvo vnutrennikh dyel**

MVO *abbr* Member of the Royal Victorian Order

MVP *abbr* N Am SPORTS most valuable player (award)

MVS *abbr* Master of Veterinary Surgery

MVSc *abbr* Master of Veterinary Science

mw *abbr* ONLINE Malawi (*used in Internet addresses*) See table at **domain name**

mW *abbr* MEASURE milliwatt

MW *abbr* **1.** MEDIA medium wave **2.** MEASURE megawatt **3.** CHEM molecular weight

mwah mwah /mwaʻa mwaʻa/, **muah muah** *n* used as a humorous representation of the sound of ritual social kissing, which does not involve physical contact (*slang*)

Mwanawasa /mwaʻanə waʻasə/, **Levy Patrick** (*b.* 1948) president of Zambia (2002–). A former vice president, he became Zambia's third president in 2002 after the most closely fought presidential election since independence.

mx *abbr* ONLINE Mexico (*used in Internet addresses*) See table at **domain name**

Mx *abbr* PHYS maxwell

MX *abbr* MOTOR SPORTS motocross

mxd *abbr* mixed

my[1] *n* /mī/ *det* belonging or relating to the speaker (*first person possessive determiner*) ○ You can borrow my car. ○ I always keep my promises. ■ *interj* used to express sudden emotion such as surprise, fright, concern, or pleasure ○ My! What a mess! [12C. Shortening of MINE[2], originally only before consonants other than 'h']

my[2] *abbr* **1.** ONLINE Malaysia (*used in Internet addresses*) See table at **domain name 2.** million years

MY *abbr* motor yacht

my- *prefix* same as **myo-** (*used before vowels*)

myalgia /mī álji ə/ *n* pain or tenderness in a muscle or group of muscles —**myalgic** *adj*

myalgic encephalomyelitis /mī áljik-/ *n* MED full form of **ME**[2]

myalism /mī əlizəm/ *n* witchcraft practised in the Caribbean [Mid-19C. < *myal* 'myalism', origin ?] —**myalist** *n*

Myall Lake /mī əl-/ coastal lake in eastern New South Wales, Australia, north of Port Stephens. Area: 310 sq. km/120 sq. mi.

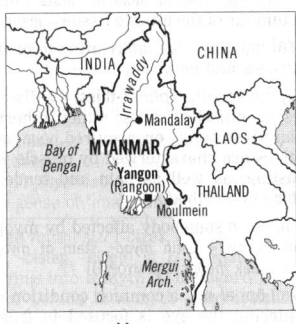
Myanmar

Myanmar /mī ən maa, myán maar/ country in Southeast Asia. It became independent from Britain as the Union of Burma in 1948. Language: Burmese. Currency: kyat. Capital: Yangon. Population: 42,510,537 (2003). Area: 676,552 sq. km/261,218 sq. mi. Official name **Union of Myanmar**. Former name **Burma** (until 1989)

myasthenia /mī əss theʻeni ə/, **myasthenia gravis** /-graʻaviss/ *n* an autoimmune disease involving extreme weakness of some muscles, caused by the blocking of the receptors for acetylcholine, the neurotransmitter that causes muscular contraction —**myasthenic** /-thénnik/ *adj*

my bad *interj* US used to apologize for a mistake (*slang*) ○ Whoops, my bad! You were right after all.

mycelium /mī seʻeli əm/ (*plural* **-lia** /-li ə/) *n* a loose network of the delicate filaments (**hyphae**) that form the body of a fungus, consisting of the feeding and reproducing hyphae [Mid-19C. < modern Latin

< Greek *mukēs* 'fungus' after *epithelium* (see EPITHELIUM)] —**mycelial** *adj* —**myceloid** /mīssə loyd/ *adj*

Mycenae /mī seʻe nee/ ancient Greek city in the Peloponnese that was a centre of Bronze Age culture until its destruction around 1100 BC —**Mycenaean** /mīssə neʻe ən/ *n, adj*

-mycete *suffix* fungus, fungi ○ *phycomycete* [Via modern Latin *-mycetes* < Greek *mukētes*, plural of *mukēs* 'fungus']

mycetoma /mīssi tōmə/ (*plural* **-mas** or **-mata** /-mətə/) *n* a chronic inflammation of tissues, caused by a fungal or bacterial infection, that usually occurs in the feet or legs, which swell and develop pus-discharging nodules [Late 19C. < modern Latin < Greek *mukēt-*, stem of *mukēs* 'fungus'] —**mycetomatous** /-tómmətəss/ *adj*

-mycin *suffix* a substance derived from a bacterium ○ *streptomycin* [< MYCO- + -IN; because the bacteria were originally thought to be fungi]

myco- *prefix* fungus, fungi ○ *mycotoxin* [< Greek *mukēs* < Indo-European, 'slimy']

mycobacterium /mīkō bak teʻeri əm/ (*plural* **-ria** /-ri ə/) *n* a rod-shaped Gram-positive aerobic bacterium that can form branching structures resembling filaments. Some diseases in humans are caused by mycobacteria, e.g. tuberculosis and leprosy. Genus: *Mycobacterium*. —**mycobacterial** *adj*

mycology /mī kólləji/ *n* **1.** STUDY OF FUNGI a branch of botany that specializes in the scientific study of fungi **2.** FUNGI OF PARTICULAR AREA the fungi that live in a particular area **3.** CHARACTERISTICS OF INDIVIDUAL FUNGUS the characteristics of a particular fungus —**mycologic** /mīkə lójjik/ *adj* —**mycological** *adj* —**mycologically** *adv* —**mycologist** *n*

mycophagist /mī kóffəjist/ *n* an animal that eats fungi [Mid-19C. < *mycophagy*]

mycophagous /mī kóffəgəss/ *adj* feeding on fungi —**mycophagy** /-kóffəji/ *n*

mycoplasma /mīkō plázmə/ *n* a microorganism of a genus considered to be the smallest known living cells. Some species cause respiratory diseases in animals and human beings. Regarded by some as primitive bacteria, they need sterols such as cholesterol for growth. Genus: *Mycoplasma*. —**mycoplasmal** *adj*

mycoprotein /mīkō prō teen/ *n* a food made by heating, draining, and texturing the fermentation product of a fungus *Fusaria graminearum*. It is a source of protein, fibre, biotin, iron, and zinc, is low in saturated fat, and is often used as a meat substitute.

mycorrhiza /mīkō rízə/ (*plural* **-zas** or **-zae** /-zee/), **mycorhiza** (*plural* **-zas** or **-zae** /-zee/) *n* a mutually beneficial association of a fungus and the roots of a plant such as a conifer or an orchid, in which the plant's mineral absorption is enhanced and the fungus obtains nutrients [Late 19C. < modern Latin < *myco-* (see MYCO-) + Greek *rhiza* 'root'] —**mycorrhizal** *adj*

mycosis /mī kōssiss/ (*plural* **-coses** /-kōsseez/) *n* a disease or infection of human beings or animals caused by a fungus

mycotoxin /mīkō tóksin/ *n* a poisonous substance produced by a fungus. Mycotoxins may affect foods such as peanuts.

mycotrophic /mīkō tróffik, -tróffik/ *adj* describes a plant that lives in association with a fungus, as do various orchids in which the fungus lives on the roots

mydriasis /mī drí əssiss, mi-/ *n* excessive dilation of the pupils of the eye, usually caused by prolonged drug therapy, coma, or injury to the eye [Early 19C. Via Latin < Greek *mudriasis*]

myel- *prefix* same as **myelo-** (*used before vowels*)

myelencephalon /mī ə len séffə lon/ *n* a part of the embryonic hindbrain formed by an extension of the spinal cord into the skull. It is the major pathway for nerve impulses leaving and entering the brain. —**myelencephalic** /mī ə len sə fállik/ *adj*

myelin /mī əlin/ *n* a whitish material made up of protein and fats that surrounds some nerve cells in concentric sheaths, insulating adjacent nerve fibres and enabling transmission of nerve impulses

myelinated /mī əli naytid/ *adj* describes nerve fibres that are surrounded by a sheath of myelin

myelin sheath *n* a layer of myelin that insulates some nerve cells. In multiple sclerosis, the myelin

n[1] /en/ (*plural* **n's**), **N** (*plural* **N's** or **Ns**) *n* **1.** the 14th letter of the English alphabet, representing a consonant sound **2.** a written representation of the letter 'n'

n[2] *symbol* **1.** PHYS amount of substance **2.** PRINTING en dash ■ *n* MATHS an indefinite whole number ■ *symbol* **1.** MEASURE nano- **2.** PHYS neutron **3.** PHYS, OPTICS refractive index

n[3] *abbr* **1.** COMM net **2.** GRAM neuter **3.** GRAM nominative **4.** TIME noon **5.** north **6.** northern **7.** MUSIC note **8.** GRAM noun **9.** number

n' /ən/, **'n'** *conj* same as **and** (*informal*)

N[1] *abbr* **1.** CHESS knight **2.** AUTOMOT neutral (*used on gear sticks*) **3.** GEOG New (*in placenames*) **4.** LANG Norse **5.** COMPASS north **6.** COMPASS northern **7.** CALENDAR November

N[2] /en/ (*plural* **N's** or **Ns**) *n* something shaped like a letter 'N'

N[3] *symbol* **1.** PHYS Avogadro's number **2.** PRINTING en dash **3.** PHYS, MEASURE newton **4.** CHEM nitrogen

n- *prefix* normal

na *abbr* Namibia (*used in Internet addresses*) See table at **domain name**

Na *symbol* CHEM ELEM sodium [Shortening of modern Latin *natrium* < Greek *nitron* 'nitre']

NA *abbr* North America

n/a *abbr* **1.** not applicable **2.** not available

NAACP *abbr* National Association for the Advancement of Colored People

NAAFI /náffi/, **Naafi** *n* **1.** an organization that provides canteens and shops for people who work in the armed forces. Full form **Navy, Army, and Air Force Institutes 2.** (*plural* **NAAFIs** or **Naafis**) a canteen or shop provided by the NAAFI

naan *n* FOOD another spelling of **nan**[1]

naartjie /naárchi/, **naartje, nartjie** *n* S Africa FOOD, TREES same as **tangerine** [Late 18C. Via Afrikaans < Tamil *nārattai* 'citrus']

Naas /nayss/ town in County Kildare in the eastern Republic of Ireland. Population: 18,288 (2002).

nab /nab/ (**nabs, nabbing, nabbed**) *vt* (*informal*) **1.** to seize, snatch, or take something suddenly **2.** to catch and arrest a criminal or fugitive [Late 17C. Probably variant of *nap* < N Germanic]

Nabataean /nábbə teé ən/, **Nabatean** *n* **1.** a member of an Arab people who in Roman times lived in part of Jordan **2.** the extinct language of the Nabataeans, a dialect of Aramaic [Early 17C. < Latin *Nabat(h)aeus*] —**Nabataean** *adj*

Nabis /naábi/ *npl* a group of 19th-century French artists, including Pierre Bonnard, who embraced symbolism rather than the naturalism of the impressionist painters [Mid-20C. Plural of *nabi* 'member of the Nabis' < Hebrew *nābī* 'prophet']

Nablus ♦ **Nabulus**

nabob /náy bob/ *n* **1.** a rich or powerful person (*informal*) **2.** formerly, a person from Europe who had made a fortune in the East, especially in South Asia **3.** HIST same as **nawab** (sense 1) [Early 17C. Via Portuguese *nababo* or Spanish *nabab* < Urdu *nawwāb* 'deputy governor']

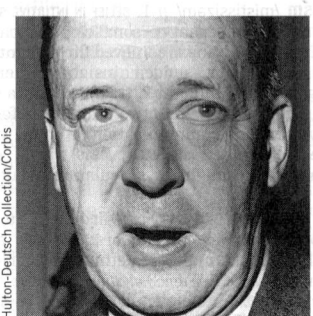
Vladimir Nabokov

Nabokov /nə bŏk of, -bók-, nábbə kof/, **Vladimir** (1899–1977) Russian-born US writer. He is known for the stylish wordplay and intellectual subtlety of his novels, which include *Lolita* (1955) and *Pale Fire* (1962), and he was acclaimed for his translations, memoirs, and literary criticism. He lived in Switzerland after 1959. Full name **Nabokov, Vladimir Vladimirovich**

'A novelist is, like all mortals, more fully at home on the surface of the present than in the ooze of the past.'
[Vladimir Nabokov, *Strong Opinions*; 1951]

Nabulus /nábbəlŏoss/, **Nablus** /naábləss/, **Nābulus** city in the West Bank territory, 48 km/30 mi. north of Jerusalem. Population: 100,231 (1997).

NAC *abbr* National Advisory Council

nacelle /nə sél/ *n* a separate streamlined enclosure on an aircraft for crew, cargo, or engines [Early 20C. Via French, 'dinghy, gondola' < late Latin *navicella* 'boat' < Latin *navis* 'ship']

nacho /nácho/ (*plural* **-chos**) *n* a tortilla chip, usually eaten in quantity covered with melted cheese, salsa, or sliced pickled jalapeño peppers (*often used in the plural*) [Mid-20C. < American Spanish]

NACODS /náy kodz/ *abbr* National Association of Colliery Overmen, Deputies, and Shotfirers

nacre /náykər/ *n* INDUST same as **mother-of-pearl** [Late 16C. Via French < Italian *naccaro* < Arabic *nāqūr* 'hunting horn']

nacreous /náykri əss/ *adj* **1.** relating to, typical of, or made of mother-of-pearl **2.** with the iridescent quality of mother-of-pearl

nacreous cloud *n* an iridescent cloud that looks like a cirrus and appears especially in the winter at high latitudes

NACRO /nákrō/, **Nacro** *abbr* National Association for the Care and Resettlement of Offenders

NAD *n* a coenzyme that plays a role in the electron transport chain, where it is vital in the production of energy. Formula: $C_{21}H_{27}N_7O_{14}P_2$. Full form **nicotinamide adenine dinucleotide**

Na-Dene /naá dáyni, nə deèn/, **Na-Déné** *n* a group of Native North American languages spoken in parts of Alaska, Canada, and the southwestern United States. Native speakers: 200,000. [Early 20C < Athabaskan *na* + *dene* 'people'] —**Na-Dene** *adj*

Nader /náydər/, **Ralph** (*b.* 1934) US lawyer and consumer-protection advocate. He was largely responsible for the rise of the consumer-protection movement in the United States following the publication of his book *Unsafe at Any Speed* (1965), about unsafe design and manufacture in the automobile industry. He ran unsuccessfully as a Green Party candidate for the presidency in 2000 and ran again as an Independent in 2004.

'Trying to control corporate power and abuse by American corporate law has proven about as effective as drinking coffee with a fork.'
[Ralph Nader. Quoted in *The Times*; 23 October 1976]

NADH *n* the reduced form of NAD that reverts to NAD during the generation of cellular energy [Mid-20C. < NAD + H[1] 'hydrogen']

nadir /náy deer, nád eer/ *n* **1.** the lowest possible point ○ *the nadir of despair* **2.** the point on the celestial sphere directly below the observer and opposite the zenith [14C. Via French and medieval Latin < Arabic *nazīr (as-samt)* 'opposite (the zenith)']

NADP *n* a coenzyme involved in anabolism, consisting of NAD with an extra phosphate group. It tends to participate in biochemical syntheses rather than energy-yielding reactions. Formula: $C_{21}H_{28}N_7O_{17}P_3$. Full form **nicotinamide adenine dinucleotide phosphate**

NADPH *n* the reduced form of NADP [< NADP + H[1] 'hydrogen']

nae /nay/ *adv* Scotland **1.** same as **no**[1] **2.** same as **not** [Early 18C. Variant of obsolete *na* < *ne* 'not' (< Germanic) + form of AYE[2]]

naevus /neévəss/ (*plural* **-vi** /-vī, -veel/) *n* a birthmark, mole, or any other kind of growth or mark on the skin that a person is born with [Mid-19C. < Latin *naevus*]

naff /naf/ *adj* lacking fashionable stylishness and appearing boring, tasteless, or unattractive (*informal*) [Mid-20C. Origin ?]

naff off (**naffs off, naffing off, naffed off**) *vi* used as a rude way of telling somebody to go away (*informal*)

NAFTA /náftə/ *n* a free trade agreement signed between the United States and Canada in 1989, and extended to include Mexico in 1994. Full form **North American Free Trade Agreement**

nag[1] /nag/ *v* (**nags, nagging, nagged**) **1.** *vti* ASK SOMEBODY REPEATEDLY to ask or urge somebody persistently and annoyingly to do something ○ *He keeps nagging me to go and see the doctor.* **2.** *vti* KEEP CRITICIZING SOMEBODY to find fault with somebody regularly and repeatedly **3.** *vi* BE PERSISTENTLY PAINFUL OR BOTHERSOME to be a persistent cause of discomfort, anxiety, or unease ○ *a nagging pain* ○ *a worry that nags into the late night hours* ■ *n* SOMEBODY WHO NAGS somebody, especially a woman, who is regarded as having a tendency to nag (*insult*) [Early 19C. Origin ?] —**nagger** *n* —**nagging** *n* —**naggingly** *adv*

SYNONYMS See *complain*.

nag[2] /nag/ *n* **1.** OLD HORSE an old horse, especially one that is worn out **2.** RACEHORSE a horse, especially a racehorse (*slang*) **3.** SMALL HORSE a small horse for riding (*archaic*) [15C. Origin ?]

naga[1] /naágə/ *n* S Asia **1.** a Hindu belonging to any of the groups whose members live wandering lives as ascetics and mendicants **2.** in the 19th century, a Hindu belonging to an armed group who served as mercenaries [Early 19C. < Hindi *nāgā* 'naked']

naga[2] /naágə/ *n* in Indian mythology, a creature that is part-human and part-cobra in appearance and is

associated with water. It is sometimes worshipped by women who want children. [Late 18C. < Sanskrit *nāga* 'snake']

Naga /naʹagə/ (*plural same* or **-gas**) *n* **1.** a member of a South Asian people who live in Nagaland, in northeastern India and western Myanmar. They were head-hunters until the 20th century and still maintain a traditional style of life. **2.** the Tibeto-Burman language of the Naga people. Native speakers: 120,000. [Mid-19C. Origin ?] —**Naga** *adj*

Nagaland /naʹagə land/ state in northeastern India, bordering Myanmar. Capital: Kohima. Area: 16,579 sq. km/6,401 sq. mi. Population: 1,988,636 (2001).

nagana /nə gaʹanə/, **n'gana** /əng gaʹanə/ *n* an often fatal disease caused by trypanosome protozoan parasites that affects hoofed animals such as cattle, horses, and goats in tropical Africa and is transmitted by the tsetse fly. It is related to sleeping sickness. [Late 19C. < Zulu *nakane*]

Nagano /nə gaʹanō/ city and port in Japan, on Honshu Island. It is the commercial centre and capital of Nagano Prefecture. Population: 359,045 (2002).

Nagari /naʹagəri/ *n* LING same as **Devanagari** [Late 18C. < Sanskrit *nagari* 'script of the city']

Nagarjuna /nág aar jóonə/ (*fl* AD mid-2nd or 3rd century) Indian philosopher. One of the greatest Buddhist thinkers, he founded the Madhyamika (Middle Path) school of Mahayana Buddhism.

Nagasaki /nággə saʹaki/ city and port in southern Japan, on Kyushu Island, and capital of Nagasaki Prefecture. It was destroyed by an atomic bomb in 1945. Population: 419,901 (2002).

Nagoya /na góy ə/ city in Japan, on Honshu Island. It is the capital city and industrial centre of Aichi Prefecture. Population: 2,109,681 (2002).

Nagpur /nag poʹor/ city in central India, in Maharashtra State, on the River Nag. Population: 2,122,965 (2001).

AKG London

Imre Nagy

Nagy /nój/, **Imre** (1896–1958) Hungarian prime minister (1953–55 and 1956). He was dismissed as prime minister in 1955 following disagreements with Stalin over policy issues. He led the Hungarian uprising (1956) and was later executed.

nah /na, naa/ *interj* same as **no**[1] (*nonstandard*) [Early 20C. Alteration]

Nah. *abbr* BIBLE Nahum

Nahanni National Park /nə haʹani-/ national park and preserve in Northern Canada, in southwestern Northwest Territories, on the South Nahanni River. It is a World Heritage Site. Area: 4,766 sq. km/1,840 sq. mi.

NAHT *abbr* National Association of Head Teachers

Nahuatl /naʹa waatʹl, naa waʹatʹl/ (*plural same* or **-tls**), **Nahua** /naʹa waa, naa waʹa/ (*plural same* or **-huas**) *n* **1.** a member of a Native Central American people who live in southern Mexico and Central America. The Nahuatl include the ancient Aztecs. **2.** *also* **Nahuatlan** /naa waʹatlən/ the Uto-Aztecan language of the Nahuatl people. Native speakers: 1 million. [Early 19C. Via Spanish < Nahuatl, singular of *Nahua* 'Nahuatl people'] —**Nahuatl** *adj*

LANGUAGE HERITAGE *Nahuatl* Much of English is made up of words from other languages, and Nahuatl is a small but significant contributor in this respect, especially in the matter of cuisine. The word *Nahuatl* itself shows some of the distinctive structure of the language, but most loanwords have been modified in their journey through other languages (especially Spanish) to English, and less obviously indicate their Central American origins. *Chocolate*, for example, goes back to Nahuatl *chocolatl* 'bitter water', but lost its distinctive ending on its way through Spanish, and perhaps also French; *avocado* started out as Nahuatl *ahuacatl*, literally 'testicle' (because of the shape of the fruit), but became *aguacate* in Spanish before assuming its familiar form; *cacao* (later also to be altered to *cocoa*) came via a Spanish shortening of Nahuatl *cacauatl* 'cacao tree'; *tomato* is an alteration of Spanish *tomate* from Nahuatl *tomatl*. Other culinary terms with a Nahuatl ancestry include *chilli*, *guacamole*, *mole*, and *pulque*, and *tamale*. Chewing gum would be unknown without its main ingredient *chicle* (via American Spanish from Nahuatl *tzictli*).

Numerous New World animals and birds that were unfamiliar to Europeans naturally acquired names from Nahuatl: *cacomistle*, *coyote*, *hoatzin*, *ocelot*, and *quetzal*, for example. Names of indigenous peoples were also adopted from Nahuatl: *Aztec* (via French *Aztèque* or Spanish *Azteca* from Nahuatl *aztecatl* 'somebody from Aztlan'), *Mixtec* (via Spanish from Nahuatl *mixtecah* 'somebody from a cloudy place'), and *Toltec* (via Spanish from Nahuatl *toltecatl* 'somebody from Tula', an ancient Toltec city).

Nahum /náyhəm/ *n* **1.** in the Bible, a Hebrew prophet who lived in the 7th century BC. He was one of the minor prophets. **2.** a book of the Bible that contains the prophecies traditionally attributed to Nahum, including the prophecy foretelling the siege and sack of the Assyrian capital of Nineveh in 612 BC. See table at **Bible**

NAI *abbr* nonaccidental injury

naiad /níʹ ad/ (*plural* **-ads** or **-ades** /níʹ ədeez/) *n* **1.** MYTHOL WATER NYMPH in Greek mythology, a nymph of lakes, rivers, springs, and fountains. The naiads were skilled in music and dancing, and were supposed to have healing powers. **2.** INSECTS WATER-DWELLING LARVA the immature water-dwelling form (**larva**) of a dragonfly, damselfly, mayfly, or stonefly **3.** PLANTS UNDERWATER PLANT an underwater plant with narrow leaves. Flowers: small, white. Genus: *Najas*. [14C. Via Latin *naiad*- < Greek, 'water nymph' < *naein* 'to flow']

Naiad *n* a small natural satellite of Neptune

naïf /ní eéf/ *n* a naive person ■ *adj* same as **naive** (senses 1–4) [Late 16C. < French *naïf* (see NAIVE)]

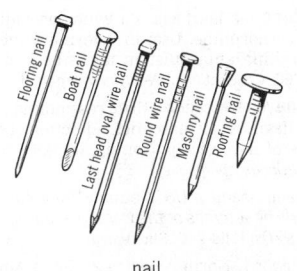

Flooring nail · Boat nail · Last head oval wire nail · Round wire nail · Masonry nail · Roofing nail

nail

nail /nayl/ *n* **1.** SHORT POINTED METAL ROD a strong metal pin with a flat round head and a pointed end that is hammered into wood or masonry and used to fasten objects together or hang something on **2.** SOMETHING LIKE NAIL something that is like a nail in its shape, in being sharp, or in the way it is used **3.** HARD AREA ON FINGER OR TOE in humans and other primates, the thin horny covering that grows on the upper surface of the end of each finger and toe **4.** CLAW the claw of a bird, mammal, or reptile **5.** UNIT OF MEASURE a former unit of measure for cloth that was equal to 5.7 cm/2.25 in ■ *vt* (**nails, nailing, nailed**) **1.** ATTACH SOMETHING WITH NAILS to fasten, attach, or secure something using nails **2.** FIX SOMETHING STEADILY to keep something fixed or focussed on something ○ *His gaze was nailed to the astonishing scene.* **3.** CATCH OR CONVICT GUILTY PERSON to catch somebody who is guilty of an offence, prove the person's guilt, or have the person convicted (*informal*) ○ *It took them five years to nail him for insider trading.* **4.** EXPOSE UNTRUTH to prove that something is not true or valid and so stop others from believing it (*informal*) **5.** HIT TARGET WITH PROJECTILE to hit or bring down somebody or something with a bullet or a projectile (*informal*) **6.** STOP PERSON to stop somebody and speak to him or her (*informal*) ○ *nailed me in the corridor and demanded an explanation* **7.** *N Am* DO SOMETHING PRECISELY OR WELL to catch, hit, seize, or execute something adroitly or precisely (*slang*) ○ *nailed the high dive and won the medal* **8.** *N Am* IDENTIFY SOMEBODY OR SOMETHING to identify somebody or establish something precisely (*slang*) ○ *I nailed him as a fraud as soon as he started*

talking about his wealthy background. [Old English *nægl* < Indo-European, 'fingernail, toenail'] —**nailer** *n* ◇ **a nail in somebody's coffin** an event or action that further weakens the position of somebody or something already in decline ◇ **hit the nail on the head** to be absolutely correct or accurate ◇ **on the nail** immediately, or paid immediately

nail down *v* **1.** *vt* to make somebody be definite about something **2.** to establish something clearly and conclusively ○ *an investigation that will attempt to nail down what really happened here*

nail bed *n* the layer of tissue at the base of a fingernail or toenail from which new nail material develops

nail-biter *n* **1.** somebody who habitually bites the ends of his or her fingernails **2.** a situation or contest that is extremely tense and exciting because its outcome remains uncertain until the end (*slang*) [< the stereotype of nail-biting as a sign of anxiety]

nail-biting *n* the habit of biting off the ends of the fingernails, especially out of anxiety, tension, or boredom ■ *adj* extremely tense and exciting because the outcome is uncertain [See NAIL-BITER]

nail bomb *n* a bomb packed with nails to cause widespread injuries among people who are near it when it goes off

nailbrush /náyl brush/ *n* a small brush used for cleaning the fingernails, with short stiff bristles on one or both sides

nail clippers *npl* a small pair of clippers used for trimming fingernails and toenails

nail enamel *n* COSMETICS same as **nail polish**

nail file *n* a small file used for smoothing and shaping the ends of the fingernails

nailhead /náyl hed/ *n* a decorative design that resembles the round head of a nail, used on furniture and leather

nail polish *n* a fast-drying coloured or transparent varnish used to decorate fingernails or toenails

nail punch *n* a tool that pushes a nail level with or lower than the surrounding surface

nail scissors *npl* small scissors, sometimes with curved blades, used for trimming fingernails or toenails

nail set *n* CONSTR same as **nail punch**

nail varnish *n* COSMETICS same as **nail polish**

nainsook /náynssŏok, nán-/ *n* a lightweight cotton fabric. Use: babywear, lingerie. [Late 18C. < Hindi *nainsukh* 'pleasure to the eye']

Naipaul /ní pawl/, **V. S.** (*b.* 1932) Trinidadian-born British novelist and cultural commentator of Indian descent. His novels include *A House for Mr Biswas* (1961) and the Booker Prize-winning *In a Free State* (1971), while his studies of culture include *India: A Million Mutinies Now* (1990) and *Beyond Belief* (1998). His works analyse suppressed histories of peoples. He was awarded the Nobel Prize in literature (2001). Full name **Naipaul, Sir Vidiadhar Surajprasad**

'Worse, to have lived without even attempting to lay claim to one's portion of the earth; to have lived and died as one had been born, unnecessary and unaccommodated.'
[V. S. Naipaul, *A House for Mr. Biswas*; 1961]

naira /níʹrə/ *n* the main unit of Nigerian currency. See table at **currency** [Late 20C. < Nigerian English, alteration of NIGERIA]

Nairnshire /náirnshər/ former county of northern Scotland, abolished in 1975, and incorporated into Highland Region

Nairobi /nī rṓbi/ capital city of Kenya, situated in the south-central part of the country. Population: 1,810,000 (1995).

Nairobi National Park national park in south-central Kenya, near the capital city. It was established in 1946. Area: 115 sq. km/44 sq. mi.

NAIRU /náy roo/ *abbr* nonaccelerating inflation rate of unemployment

naissance /náyss'nss/ *n* the birth or origination of something or somebody (*formal*) [15C. < French < *naissant* (see NAISSANT)]

naissant /náyss'nt/ *adj* in heraldry, describes a beast figure shown in the top half of a shield with only the upper part of its body visible [Late 16C. < French, present participle of *naître* 'be born']

naive /nī éev/, **naïve** (**-ïfer, -ïfest**) *adj* **1. EXTREMELY SIMPLE AND TRUSTING** having or showing an excessively simple and trusting view of the world and human nature, often as a result of youth and inexperience **2. NOT SHREWD OR SOPHISTICATED** showing a lack of sophistication and subtlety or of critical judgment and analysis ○ *a politically naive statement* **3. ARTLESS** admirably straightforward and uncomplicated or refreshingly innocent and unaffected **4.** ARTS **REJECTING SOPHISTICATED TECHNIQUES IN ART** not using the conventional styles and techniques of trained artists, e.g. in the treatment of perspective or light and shade **5.** SCI **NOT PREVIOUSLY EXPERIMENTED ON** not previously used in any scientific tests or experiments or not having previously used a particular drug ○ *naive laboratory mice* [Mid-17C. < French *naïve*, feminine of *naïf* < Latin *nativus* 'born'] —**naively** *adv* —**naiveness** *n*

naive realism *n* the theory of perception holding that when we look at an object what we see is the actual object, not a mental representation of it

naivety /nī éevəti/ (*plural* **-ties**), **naiveté** /nī éevə tay/ *n* **1.** a naive quality or naive behaviour **2.** a naive action or remark

Najd /najd, nejd/ region in central Saudi Arabia. Area: 1,158,000 sq. km/447,100 sq. mi.

NAK /nak/, **nak** *n* an ASCII control code used to indicate to the sender that a transmitted message has not been properly received. Full form **negative acknowledgment**

Nakasone Yasuhiro /nákə sṓni yássoo héerō/ (*b.* 1918) Japanese prime minister (1982–87). He was first elected to the Diet as a member of the Liberal-Democratic party in 1947 and held a series of cabinet posts before he became prime minister.

naked /náykid/ *adj* **1. WEARING NO CLOTHES** not covered by clothing, especially having no clothing on any part of the body **2. LACKING COVERING** lacking the usual covering or protection ○ *a naked flame* ○ *a naked light bulb* **3. NOT CONCEALED** openly displayed or expressed and often threatening or disturbing ○ *naked aggression* **4. FRANKLY UNVARNISHED** direct, frank, and without embellishment ○ *the naked truth* **5. UNARMED** unarmed and defenceless ○ *'If you carry this resolution you will send Britain's Foreign Secretary naked into the conference chamber.'* (Aneurin Bevan, 1957) **6. DEVOID OF SOMETHING** without or unaccompanied by a particular quality or thing ○ *naked of all pretensions to grandeur* **7.** BOT **HAVING NO NATURAL COVERING** having no natural covering in the form of earth, vegetation, or foliage **8.** ZOOL **LACKING HAIR, FUR, OR FEATHERS** having no hair, fur, scales, shell, or feathers **9.** BOT **NOT ENCLOSED IN OVARY** describes conifer seeds, which are not enclosed in an ovary **10.** BOT **LACKING SEPALS OR PETALS** describes flowers that have no sepals or petals [Old English *nacod* < Indo-European] —**nakedness** *n*

CULTURAL NOTE ***The Naked and the Dead***, a novel (1948) by US writer Norman Mailer. Set on a Pacific island during World War II, it is both a powerful account of the experience of war and, through its presentation of the conflicting political and philosophical views of the principal characters, a portrayal of some of the tensions in contemporary US society. It was made into a film by Raoul Walsh in 1958.

SYNONYMS ***naked, bare, nude, undressed, unclothed***

CORE MEANING: without clothes or covering

naked not covered or concealed, especially having no clothing on any part of the body ○ *a ceiling decorated with frescos of naked cherubs* **bare** without the usual furnishings or decorations, or not covered by clothing ○ *The three men sat around a bare wooden table.* ○ *bare legs* **nude** not wearing any clothes at all, especially in artistic contexts ○ *the nude statue in the courtyard* **undressed** not wearing any or many clothes, or having just removed clothes ○ *The children were undressed and ready to put on their nightclothes.* **unclothed** wearing little or no clothing ○ *a window full of unclothed dummies* ○ *He felt awkwardly unclothed in just a towel.*

naked eye *n* human sight without the aid of a microscope, telescope, or other optical instrument

naked ladies (*plural same*) *n* PLANTS same as **autumn crocus** [< its leafless flower stems]

nakedly /náykidli/ *adv* without any attempt at disguise or concealment ○ *a description of the state as a nakedly repressive machine*

naked option *n* a stock or commodity option sold by somebody who does not own the underlying asset, and who is exposed to considerable risk if the price of the underlying asset changes adversely

nakfa /nák fə/ *n* the main unit of Eritrean currency. See table at **currency** [After *Nakfa*, town in N Eritrea]

Nakh /naak/ *n* a language family of the North Caucasian group of Caucasian languages, including Chechen and Ingush [Mid-20C. Origin ?] —**Nakh** *adj*

Nakuru /nə ko͝o roo/ city in west-central Kenya. It is the capital of Rift Valley Province. Population: 150,000 (1991).

Nakuru, Lake lake in west-central Kenya, noted for its flamingos and other birds. Area: 62 sq. km/24 sq. mi.

nalbuphine /nal béw feen/ *n* a drug resembling morphine. Use: relief of moderate to severe pain. [Mid-20C. Blend of NALORPHINE + BUTYL]

NALGO /nálgō/, **Nalgo** *abbr* National Association of Local Government Officers

nalidixic acid /náyli díkssik-/ *n* an antibacterial drug. Use: treatment of urinary infections. [< rearranged elements of NAPHTHALENE + DI-[1] + *carboxylic*]

nalorphine /na láwrfeen/ *n* a white crystalline drug. Source: morphine. Use: in veterinary medicine as a morphine antagonist in anaesthetized animals. [Mid-20C. Contraction of *N-allylnormorphine*]

naloxone /nə lóksōn/ *n* a drug resembling morphine. Use: diagnosis of narcotics addiction, reversal of effects of narcotics poisoning. [Mid-20C. Contraction of *N-allylnoroxymorphone*]

Nam /nam, naam/ *n US* Vietnam (*informal*; *used particularly by veterans of the war there during the 1960s and 1970s*) [Mid-20C. Shortening]

N. Am. *abbr* **1.** North America **2.** North American

Nama /naáamə/ (*plural same* or **-mas**) *n* **1.** a member of a Khoikhoi people who live in southwestern Africa **2.** the San language of the Nama people. Native speakers: 25,000. [Mid-19C. < Nama] —**Nama** *adj*

namable *adj* another spelling of **nameable**

Namaqua /nə maákwə/ (*plural same* or **-quas**) *n* PEOPLES, LANG same as **Nama** (senses 1–2) [Late 17C. < Nama *nama gu a*] —**Namaquan** *adj*

Namaqualand /nə maákwə land/ coastal region in southwestern Africa, in southern Namibia and South Africa. It is the homeland of the Nama people. Population: about 66,000. Area: 47,962 sq. km/18,518 sq. mi.

namaste /númmə stay/, **namaskar** /nummə skaár/ *n* a polite bow of greeting or farewell used by Hindus, made with the hands held at chest height and both palms pressed together [Mid-20C. < Hindi, 'bowing to you']

Namatjira /námmət jéerə/, **Albert** (1902–59) Australian Aboriginal painter. His watercolours of Australia's heartland were much sought-after from the 1930s.

Nambour /nám boor/ town in southeastern Queensland, northeastern Australia. Population: 10,365 (1991).

namby-pamby /námbi pámbi/ *adj* (*informal*) **1. WEAK** feeble and lacking strength of character **2. SILLY** silly, sentimental, or overly sensitive ■ *n* (*plural* **namby-pambies**) **NAMBY-PAMBY PERSON** somebody regarded as weak or silly (*informal insult*) [Mid-16C. < nickname for the English poet *Amb(rose)* Philips (1674–1749)]

name /naym/ *n* **1. WHAT SOMEBODY OR SOMETHING IS CALLED** a word, term, or phrase by which somebody or something is known and distinguished from other people or things **2. UNCOMPLIMENTARY DESCRIPTION WORD ABOUT SOMEBODY** an uncomplimentary or abusive word or phrase used to describe somebody ○ *called him names behind his back* **3. REPUTATION** the reputation or standing of somebody or something ○ *She's made quite a name for herself in the music world.* **4. FAMOUS PERSON** a famous person ○ *All the big Hollywood names were there.* **5. MEMBER OF LLOYD'S** a member of Lloyd's, the London insurance house, who provides capital for a syndicate but is not involved in how it is run ■ *adj* **RESPECTED** having an established and good reputation ○ *name brands* ■ *vt* (**names, naming, named**) **1. GIVE NAME TO SOMEBODY** to give somebody or something a name ○ *They named the dog Sport.* **2. IDENTIFY SOMEBODY OR SOMETHING BY NAME** to identify somebody or something by giving his, her, or its name ○ *He says he can name all 50 state capitals.* **3. SPECIFY SOMETHING** to decide upon or specify something such as a date, time, or price ○ *would not name a figure* **4. APPOINT SOMEBODY TO OFFICE** to choose somebody for a particular office or honour ○ *They haven't yet named her successor.* **5. BAN MP FROM COMMONS** to refer formally by name to a Member of Parliament who has behaved in an unparliamentary manner, thereby temporarily banishing that MP from the House of Commons [Old English *nama* < Indo-European] —**namable** *adj* —**namer** *n* ◇ **a name to conjure with** a person or organization considered to be influential, powerful, or extremely famous ◇ **in name only** supposedly or officially, but not in any real sense ◇ **in the name of 1.** by the authority of **2.** for the sake of something ◇ **name names** to mention the names of specific people in order to blame or accuse them of an error or of wrongdoing ◇ **somebody's name is mud** somebody is in trouble or is the object of disapproval ◇ **name and shame** to reveal the name of a person or organization that has been unsatisfactory or has done something illegal or immoral in order to cause embarrassment and so provoke an improvement in performance or behaviour ◇ **the name of the game** what something is all about, its most important element, or the kind of thing that most commonly happens in it (*informal*) ◇ **to somebody's name** credited or belonging to somebody ○ *hasn't got a penny to his name* ◇ **you name it** used to suggest that an enormous number of things are involved or an enormous number of options are possible (*informal*) ○ *They experienced cold, chills, and frostbite–you name it!*

ORIGIN The Indo-European word from which ***name*** is ultimately derived is also the ancestor of English *anonymous, nomenclature, nominate, noun, pseudonym, renown*, and *synonym.*

nameable /náyməb'l/, **namable** *adj* able to be identified by name

name-calling *n* verbal abuse, especially as a substitute for reasoned argument in a dispute

namecheck /náym chèk/ (**-checks, -checking, -checked**) *vt* **1.** to mention the name of a product, brand, or performer publicly, especially in a song, a broadcast, or the press ○ *The company was delighted to be namechecked in the rap lyrics, gaining exposure to potential new consumers.* **2.** to check the name of somebody or something —**namecheck** *n*

name day *n* in the Roman Catholic and Eastern Orthodox churches, the feast day of the saint that somebody is named after

name-dropping *n* the practice of frequently mentioning the names of famous or influential people as friends or acquaintances in order to impress people —**name-drop** *vi* —**name-dropper** *n*

nameless /náymləss/ *adj* **1. LACKING NAME** not having a name **2. ANONYMOUS** having a name that is unknown or not revealed **3. INDESCRIBABLE** defying accurate description ○ *a nameless fear* **4. DISTRESSING BEYOND WORDS** too unpleasant or disgusting to be described or mentioned **5. ILLEGITIMATE** illegitimate or not legally entitled to a name —**namelessly** *adv* —**namelessness** *n*

namely /náymli/ *adv* used to introduce a description or explanation of something just referred to in a more general way ○ *She was given a new post, namely that of head of department.*

nameplate /náym playt/ *n* a plate or plaque, e.g. on a door, bearing a name and associating the named

person with the place or thing that the plate is attached to

namesake /náym sayk/ *n* somebody or something with the same name as somebody or something else [Mid-17C. Probably < *for your name's sake*]

name tag *n* a small piece of metal or plastic with somebody's name on, attached to his or her clothing for purposes of identification

name tape *n* a small strip of cloth with somebody's name on, sewn onto the inside of his or her clothing as proof of ownership

Namib Desert /nə míb-/ desert in southwestern Africa, mostly in Namibia. Length: 1,500 km/930 mi.

Namibe /na meéb/ city and port in southwestern Angola. It is the capital of Namibe Province. Population: 100,000 (1981). Former name **Moçâmedes** (until 1982)

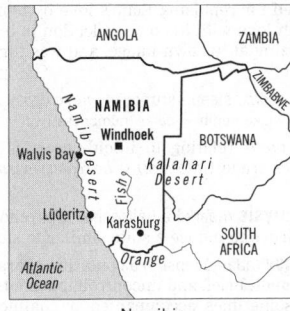

Namibia

Namibia /nə míbbi ə/ country in southwestern Africa, with its western coast on the Atlantic Ocean, directly north of South Africa. It became an independent member of the Commonwealth in 1990. Language: English, German, Afrikaans. Currency: Namibian dollar. Capital: Windhoek. Population: 1,927,447 (2003). Area: 824,269 sq. km/318,252 sq. mi. Official name **Republic of Namibia** —**Namibian** *n, adj*

naming ceremony /náyming-/ *n Aus* a ceremony held to mark the naming of a baby

namkin /num keén/, **namkeen** *n S Asia* any salty or spicy food eaten as a snack [< Hindi]

Namoi /nám oy/ river in northeastern New South Wales, southeastern Australia. Length: 845 km/525 mi.

nam pla /nám plaá/ *n* a thin sauce of fermented fish with a strong flavour and smell and a salty taste, widely used in Southeast Asian cookery [< Thai]

Namur /nə moór-/ city in southeastern Belgium. It is the capital city of Namur Province. Population: 104,994 (1999).

nan[1] /naan, nan/, **naan** *n S Asia* a flat round or oval bread served with South Asian food [Early 20C. < Persian, Urdu *nān*]

nan[2] /nan/ *n* same as **nana** (*informal*) [Mid-20C. Alteration of GRAN or shortening of NANA or NANNY]

nana /nánnə/, **nanna** *n* same as **grandmother** (sense 1) (*informal*) [Mid-19C. Alteration of GRANNY or NANNY]

Nanaimo /nə nímō/ city in southwestern Canada, on Vancouver Island, on the Strait of Georgia. Population: 77,845 (2001).

Nanak /naának/ (1469–1539) Indian religious leader. He founded the Sikh religion, and his teachings were collected as the *Adi Granth*, the Sikh scriptures. Known as **Guru Nanak**

nance *n* same as **nancy** (*slang offensive*)

Nanchang /nan chúng/ city in eastern China. It is the capital of Jiangxi Province. Population: 1,410,000 (1995).

nancy /nánssi/ (*plural* **-cies**), **nancy boy**, **nance** /nanss/ *n* an offensive term for an effeminate or gay man (*slang insult*) [Early 20C. < *Miss Nancy* in same sense]

Nancy /noN seé/ city in northeastern France, in Lorraine Region. It is the capital of Meurthe-et-Moselle Department. Population: 103,605 (1999).

NAND /nand/ (*plural* **NANDs**) *n* a logic operator used in computing that produces an output signal only if at least one of its inputs has no signal, thus being the

inverse of an AND operator [Mid-20C. Blend of NOT + AND]

Nanda Devi /núndə deévi/ second highest mountain in India after Kanchenjunga. It is in the extreme north of the country, in the Himalaya range, near the Tibetan border. Height: 7,817 m/25,646 ft.

NANDGATE *n* COMPUT same as **NAND**

nandrolone /nándrə lōn/ *n* a muscle-building anabolic steroid that athletes are banned from using by the rules of the International Amateur Athletics Federation [Late 20C. Contraction < NOR- + ANDRO- + -/- + -ONE]

Nanga Parbat /núng gə paár bat/ mountain in northwestern Kashmir, in the Himalaya range. Height: 8,125 m/26,657 ft.

Nanjing /nán jíng/ city in eastern China, on the Yangtze River. It is the capital of Jiangsu Province. Population: 2,960,000 (1995). Former name **Nanking**

nankeen /nan keén/ *n* a durable yellowish-brown cotton fabric [Mid-18C. After *Nanking* (NANJING)]

Nanking /nan kíng/ ♦ **Nanjing**

nanna *n* another spelling of **nana** (*informal*)

nannie *n, vt* another spelling of **nanny**

Nanning /nán níng/ city and capital of Guangxi Zhuangzu Autonomous Region, southeastern China, situated approximately 530 km/330 mi. west of Guangzhou. Population: 1,370,000 (1995).

nannofossil *n* another spelling of **nanofossil**

nanny /nánni/, **nannie** *n* (*plural* **-nies**) **1.** SOMEBODY EMPLOYED TO CARE FOR CHILDREN somebody who is paid to take care of one or more children in a family home, often also living there **2.** GRANDMOTHER somebody's grandmother (*informal*) ■ *vt* (**-nies, -nying, -nied**) BE OVERPROTECTIVE TOWARDS SOMEBODY to behave in an overprotective and patronizing way towards others, not allowing them to make their own decisions [Early 18C. Pet-form of the name *Ann(e)*]

nanny goat *n* a female domestic goat

nanny state *n* a government that brings in legislation that it considers is in the people's best interests but that is regarded by some as interfering and patronizing

nano- *prefix* **1.** extremely small ○ *nanofossil* ○ *nanotechnology* **2.** one thousand millionth (10⁻⁹) ○ *nanosecond* Symbol **n** [< Greek *nan(n)os* 'dwarf, little old man']

nanoanalysis /nánnō ə nálləssiss/ *n* the determination of the atomic structures of materials such as crystals —**nanoanalytical** /nánnō anə líttik'l/ *adj*

nanobot /nánnō bot/ *n US* a robot of microscopic proportions built using nanotechnology (*informal*) [Blend of NANO- + ROBOT]

nanocosm /nánnō kozəm/ *n* nanotechnology, including its developers, researchers, components, and products ○*In the world of the nanocosm, the tiny etchings on our densest microchips are vast highways.'* (Ron Bailey *Wall Street Journal*; 23 May 2003) [Late 20C. After MICROCOSM]

nanocrystal /nánnō krist'l/ *n* a crystal with dimensions in the nanometre range —**nanocrystalline** /nánnō krístə līn/ *adj*

nanofossil /nánnō foss'l/, **nannofossil** *n* a very small fossil, especially of nanoplankton

nanogram /nánnō gram/ *n* one billionth (one thousand-millionth) of a gram

nanometre /nánnō meetər/ *n* one billionth (one thousand-millionth) of a metre

nanoparticle /nánnō paartik'l/ *n* a particle of something such as a metal, polymer, or oxide, with dimensions in the nanometre range

nanophotonics /nánnō fō tónniks/ *n* the study of photonic phenomena and devices with dimensions in the nanometre range (*takes a singular verb*) —**nanophotonic** *adj*

nanoplankton /nánnō plangktən/, **nannoplankton** *n* very small plankton including bacteria, algae, and protozoans. They are usually in the size range 5–60 micrometres.

nanopore /nánnō pawr/ *n* a tiny pore in a material used to filter objects such as molecules or DNA strands that are less than several nanometres in

diameter —**nanoporosity** /nánnō paw róssəti/ *n* —**nanoporous** /nánnō páwrəss/ *adj*

nanoscience /nánnō sī ənss/ *n* the study of materials and their behaviour at the level of particles measured in nanometres —**nanoscientific** /nánnō sī ən tíffik/ *adj*

nanosecond /nánnō sekənd/ *n* one billionth (one thousand-millionth) of a second

nanoshell /nánnō shel/ *n* a tiny manufactured layered sphere with dimensions in the nanometre range, used in biotechnology

nanostructure /nánnō strukchər/ *n* an extremely small structure such as a semiconductor or optoelectronic device with dimensions of 0.1–50nm —**nanostructuring** *n*

nanotechnology /nánnō tek nólləji/ (*plural* **-gies**) *n* the art of manipulating materials on a very small scale in order to build microscopic machinery

nanotube /nánnō tyoob/ *n* an extremely thin metallic or semiconducting cylinder, capped at one end, consisting of a rolled-up layer of fullerene-structured carbon atoms

nanowire /nánnō wīr/ *n* a very thin strand of a material such as a polymer or metal with a diameter in the nanometre range

Nansen /nánss'n/, **Fridtjof** (1861–1930) Norwegian explorer. He led several expeditions to the Arctic and was also involved in humanitarian projects, for which he won the Nobel Peace Prize (1922).

nant /nant/ *n regional* same as **ant** (sense 1) [Alteration]

REGIONAL NOTE See *ant*.

Nantes /naant, naaNt/ city and major port on the Loire in western France. In 1598, Henry IV of France issued the Edict of Nantes there, granting partial religious freedom to the Protestant Huguenots. Population: 270,251 (1999).

Nantong /nan toŏng/ city and seaport in eastern China, in southeastern Jiangsu Province. Population: 323,941 (1991).

Nantucket /nan túkət/ island in southeastern Massachusetts, in the Atlantic Ocean, south of Cape Cod. Population: 10,416 (2002 estimate). Area: 148 sq. km/57 sq. mi.

Nantwich /nántwich/ market town in northwestern England, in Cheshire. Population: 11,695 (1991).

naoi ARCHIT plural of **naos**

Naomi /náyəmi/ *n* in the Bible, the mother-in-law of Ruth (Ruth 1:2)

naos /náyoss/ (*plural* **-oi** /-oy/) *n* ARCHIT same as **cella** [Late 18C. < Greek, 'temple']

nap[1] /nap/ *n* SHORT SLEEP a period of short light sleep, especially during the day ■ *vi* (**naps, napping, napped**) **1.** SLEEP LIGHTLY to have a short period of light sleep **2.** BE OFF GUARD to be inattentive or off guard ○ *caught napping* [Old English *hnappian*, origin ?]

nap[2] /nap/ *n* the small soft fibres that stick up slightly from the surface of a fabric such as velvet and that usually all lie in one direction only ■ *vt* (**naps, napping, napped**) to raise the nap of a fabric by brushing it [15C. < Middle Low German, Middle Dutch *noppe* < Germanic]

nap[3] /nap/ *n* **1.** CARD GAME a card game similar to whist, played with hands of five cards, in which players bid for the number of tricks they will take **2.** BID IN NAP a bid to win all five tricks in the game of nap **3.** GOOD TIP IN RACING in horse racing, a tip for a horse that is very likely to win ■ *vt* (**naps, napping, napped**) NAME LIKELY WINNER to name a horse as a likely winner of a race [Early 19C. Shortening of NAPOLEON]

NAP *n* the use of drugs by military personnel as protection against the effects of a nerve agent prior to exposure. Full form **nerve action pretreatment**

napa *n* TEXTILES another spelling of **nappa**

Napa /náppə/ city in west-central Florida. It is the administrative seat of Napa County. Population: 66,548 (1998 estimate).

napalm /náy paam, ná-/ *n* **1.** JELLY USED FOR FIRE BOMBS a highly flammable jelly produced by mixing a thickening agent with petrol. Use: in flamethrowers and fire bombs. **2.** THICKENING AGENT FOR JELLIED PETROL a thickening agent, consisting of aluminium soap. Use: manufacture of jellied petrol. ■ *vt* (**-palms, -palming, -palmed**) ATTACK SOMEBODY OR SOMETHING WITH

NAPALM to attack somebody or destroy something with napalm [Mid-20C. Blend of NAPHTHENE + PALMITATE]

Napa Valley region of west-central California, Northeast of San Francisco. Extending northwestwards from the city of Napa, its wineries lead the United States in grape production, and it is a major tourist destination.

nape /nayp/ *n* the back part of the neck [13C. Origin ?]

napery /náypəri/ *n* tablecloths and napkins, collectively (*archaic*) [14C. < Old French *naperie* < *nappe* (see NAPKIN)]

nap hand *n* a situation that appears to be favourable for taking risks [< NAP³]

Naphtali /náftə līʹ/ *n* in the Bible, the son of Jacob and Rachel's handmaid, Bilhah (Genesis 30: 7–8)

naphtha /náfthə, nápthə/ *n* a clear colourless flammable mixture of light hydrocarbons. Source: petroleum. Use: raw material for many petrochemicals and plastics. [Late 16C. Via Latin < Greek]

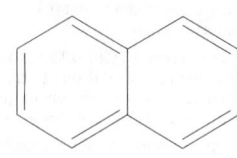

naphthalene

naphthalene /náfthə leen, nápth-/ *n* a white crystalline hydrocarbon. Source: coal tar. Use: moth repellent, in solvents, in the manufacture of dyes, resins, plasticizers, polyesters, and explosives. Formula: $C_{10}H_8$. [Early 19C. < NAPHTHA + -AL²] —**naphthalenic** /náfthə lénnik, nápthə-/ *adj*

naphthene /náf theen, náp-/ *n* an alicyclic hydrocarbon. Source: petroleum. Use: formerly, in the manufacture of napalm. [Late 19C. < NAPHTHA] —**naphthenic** *adj*

naphthol /náfthol, náp-/ *n* either of two derivatives of naphthalene that are isomers. Use: antiseptics, manufacturing. Formula: $C_{10}H_7OH$. [Mid-19C. < NAPHTHA]

Napier /náypi ər/ city in New Zealand, situated on the eastern coast of the North Island. Devastated by an earthquake in 1931, it was rebuilt in a distinctive art-deco style. Population: 54,537 (2001).

Napier, John (1550–1617) Scottish mathematician. He invented logarithms and a calculating device called Napier's bones.

Napier, Robert Cornelis, 1st Baron Napier of Magdala (1810–90) British field marshal. He served in India in the Sikh Wars and Indian Mutiny, and captured Magdala during an expedition to Ethiopia (1868).

Napierian logarithm /nə peéri ən-/ *n* MATHS same as **natural logarithm** [Early 19C. After John NAPIER]

Napier's bones /náypi ərz-/ *npl* a set of graduated rods based on the principles of logarithms, formerly used to perform multiplication and division but now used primarily for educational purposes [Mid-17C. After John NAPIER]

napiform /náypi fawrm/ *adj* being conical at one end and spherical at the other [Mid-19C. < Latin *napus* 'turnip']

napkin /nápkin/ *n* 1. a usually square piece of cloth or tissue paper used at mealtimes to protect clothes and wipe the mouth 2. full form of **nappy** (*formal*) [14C. < French *nap(p)e* 'tablecloth' < Latin *mappa* 'napkin, cloth']

Naples /náypʹlz/ city in southern Italy. It is the capital of Campania Region and of Napoli Province and an important seaport. Population: 1,004,500 (2001). Italian name **Napoli**

NAPO /náypō/ *abbr* National Association of Prison Officers

napoleon /nə poʹli ən/ *n* 1. a gold coin formerly used in France, equivalent to 20 francs 2. CARDS same as **nap³** [Early 19C. After NAPOLEON I]

Napoleon I, emperor of the French: portrait (1807) by Andrea Appiani

Napoleon I /nə poʹli ən/ (1769–1821) emperor of the French. He made his name as a general, was appointed first consul of France in 1799, and took the title of emperor in 1804. After conquering most of Europe, he was exiled after defeat at the battle of Waterloo (1815). Born **Bonaparte, Napoleon** — **Napoleonic** /nə poʹli ónnik/ *adj*

> 'I want the whole of Europe to have one currency; it will make trading much easier.'
> [Napoleon I, *letter to his brother Louis*; 6 May 1807]

> 'It is only one step from the sublime to the ridiculous.'
> [Napoleon I, *to the Polish ambassador, De Pradt, after his retreat from Moscow*; 1812]

Napoleon III (1808–73) emperor of the French. A nephew of Napoleon I, he became emperor after a coup d'état in 1851, but went into exile after defeat in the Franco-Prussian War (1870–71). Full name **Bonaparte, Charles Louis Napoleon**

Napoleonic code *n* same as **Code Napoléon**

nappa /náppə/, **napa** *n* a soft leather made from sheep or kid's skin [Late 19C. After *Napa*, county, town, and valley in California, USA]

nappe /nap/ *n* 1. SHEET OF WATER a sheet of water flowing over a dam or a weir 2. SHEET OF ROCK a large archshaped sheet of rock that has been forced over underlying rocks by internal stresses 3. MATHS PART OF CONE either of the two parts, or sheets, of a conical or pyramidal surface that are separated by a line through the vertex [Late 19C. < French (see NAPKIN)]

napper /náppər/ *n* a person's head (*dated informal*) [Late 18C. Origin ?]

nappy /náppi/ (*plural* **-pies**) *n* a piece of soft absorbent material, usually made of paper or cloth, that is wrapped around a baby's bottom and between its legs to absorb urine and excrement. N Am term **diaper** [Early 20C. Shortening and alteration of NAPKIN]

nappy rash *n* a sensitive red area on a baby's skin around the genitals and buttocks, caused by irritation from urine or faeces. N Am term **diaper rash**

naproxen /nə próksʹn/ *n* a drug that reduces inflammation and pain. Use: treatment of arthritis. [Late 20C. < *methoxynaphthylpropionic (acid)*]

Nara /náʹərə/ city in Japan, on southern Honshu Island. It is the capital of Nara Prefecture. Population: 364,411 (2002).

Naracoorte /nárrə kawrt/ agricultural town in southern South Australia. Population: 4,718 (1991).

~~narative~~ incorrect spelling of **narrative**

Narayan /nə ríʹyən/, **Jayaprakash** (1902–79) Indian politician. He was the uniting force in the Janata Party, which defeated the government of Indira Gandhi in 1977.

Narayan, R. K. (1906–2001) Indian writer. Many of his gentle novels, written in English, are set in the fictional southern Indian town of Malgudi. They include *The Vendor of Sweets* (1967) and *The World of Nagaraj* (1990). Full name **Narayan, Rasipuram Krishnaswamy**

> 'When he told the person before him, gazing at his palm, "In many ways you are not getting the fullest results for your efforts", nine out of ten were disposed to agree with him.'

> [R. K. Narayan, 'An Astrologer's Day', *An Astrologer's Day and Other Stories*; 1947]

narcissi PLANTS plural of **narcissus**

narcissism /náarssissizəm/ *n* 1. excessive self-admiration and self-centredness 2. in psychiatry, a personality disorder characterized by the patient's overestimation of his or her own appearance and abilities and an excessive need for admiration. In psychoanalytic theory, emphasis is placed on the element of self-directed sexual desire in the condition. [Early 19C. After NARCISSUS] —**narcissist** *n* —**narcissistic** /nárssi sístik/ *adj* —**narcissistically** *adv*

narcissus /naar síssəss/ (*plural* **-cissuses** or **-cissi** /-síssī/) *n* a spring-blooming plant with narrow leaves that grows from a bulb. Flowers: yellow or white, with a cup-shaped centre. Genus: *Narcissus*. [Mid-16C. Via Latin < Greek *narkissos* < *narkē* 'numbness'; from its narcotic properties]

Narcissus *n* in Greek mythology, a youth who was punished for repulsing Echo's love by being made to fall in love with his own reflection in a pool. He died gazing at his own image, and was turned into a flower.

narco-¹ *prefix* sleep, stupor ○ *narcolepsy* [< Greek *narkoun* 'make numb' < *narkē* 'numbness']

narco-² *prefix* relating to illicit narcotics and the narcotics trade (*informal*) ○ *narcoterrorism* [< NARCOTIC]

narcoanalysis /náarkō ə nálləssiss/ *n* psychoanalysis using drugs to induce a state similar to sleep

narcolepsy /náarkō lepsi/ *n* a condition characterized by frequent, brief, and uncontrollable bouts of deep sleep, sometimes accompanied by hallucinations and an inability to move [Late 19C. After EPILEPSY] —**narcoleptic** /náarkō léptik/ *adj, n*

narcosis /naar kóssiss/ *n* a state of unconsciousness or stupor caused by a narcotic or other drug [Late 17C. < Greek *narkōsis* < *narkoun* (see NARCOTIC)]

narcoterrorism /náarkō térrə rizəm/ *n* terrorist acts carried out by groups that obtain their funds directly or indirectly from the illicit drug trade —**narcoterrorist** *n, adj*

narcotic /naar kóttik/ *n* 1. DRUG a typically addictive drug, especially one derived from opium, that may produce effects ranging from pain relief and sleep to stupor, coma, and convulsions 2. N Am ILLEGAL DRUG a drug whose use is illegal, whether it is addictive or not 3. SOOTHING THING something that soothes, induces sleep, relieves pain or stress, or causes a sensation of mental numbness ■ *adj* 1. CAUSING SLEEP able to induce drowsiness, sleep, or stupor, or alter mental states through its chemical properties 2. SOOTHING having a generally soothing, numbing, or soporific effect 3. OF NARCOTICS relating to narcotic drugs and their use 4. OF ADDICTS relating to people addicted to narcotics [14C. Via French and medieval Latin < Greek *narkōtikos* 'numbing' < *narkoun* 'make numb' < *narkē* 'numbness'] —**narcotically** *adv*

narcotise *vt* DRUGS another spelling of **narcotize**

narcotization /náarkə tī záyshʹn/ *n* US the process by which a society falls under the control of drugs, drug traffickers, and the illegal drug business (*informal*)

narcotize /náarkə tīz/ (**-tizes, -tizing, -tized**), **narcotise** (**-tises, -tising, -tised**) *vt* 1. to treat somebody with a narcotic 2. to induce stupor in somebody, especially by administering a narcotic drug

nard /naard/ *n* PLANTS same as **spikenard** (senses 1–2) [14C. Via Latin *nardus* < Greek *nardos*, probably < Sanskrit *naladam* 'Indian spikenard']

nares /náir eez/ *npl* openings or passages leading out of the nose or nasal cavity. Most vertebrate animals have paired external nares, the nostrils, and a pair of internal nares opening into the mouth. [Late 17C. < Latin, plural of *naris* 'nostril']

narghile /náargə lay/, **nargileh** *n* DRUGS same as **hookah** [Mid-18C. Directly or via French and Turkish < Persian *nārgīl* 'coconut, hookah' < Sanskrit *nārikela* 'coconut']

Narita /nə reétə/ city in Japan, on southeastern Honshu Island, in Chiba Prefecture. Population: 95,850 (2002).

nark /naark/ *v* (**narks, narking, narked**) 1. *vt* ANNOY SOMEBODY to irritate, offend, or annoy somebody (*informal*) 2. *vi* COMPLAIN to complain in an irritating way (*informal*) 3. *vi* ACT AS INFORMER to act as an in-

former, especially for the police (*slang*) ■ *n* **POLICE INFORMER** somebody who acts as a decoy or informer, especially an ex-criminal who is working for the police (*slang*). < Romany *nāk* 'nose']

Narrabri /nárrə brī/ town in northeastern New South Wales, southeastern Australia. Population: 14,477 (2002 estimate).

Narraganset /nárrə gánssət/ (*plural* **-sets** or *same*), **Narragansett** (*plural* **-setts** or *same*) *n* **1.** a member of a Native North American people who lived in Rhode Island west of Narraganset Bay. They were among the largest and strongest of the northeastern Native American peoples until large numbers of them were killed in a war against the New England colonists in the late 17th century. **2.** the extinct Iroquoian language of the Narraganset people [Early 17C. < Narraganset] —**Narraganset** *adj*

Narragansett /nárrə gánssət/ town and summer resort in southeastern Rhode Island State, Washington County. Population: 16,809 (2002 estimate).

Narragansett Bay inlet of the Atlantic Ocean in southeastern Rhode Island. Length: 42 km/26 mi.

narrate /nə ráyt/ (**-rates**, **-rating**, **-rated**) *vt* **1.** to tell a story or give an account, usually in detail **2.** to provide the narration for a film or television programme [Mid-17C. < Latin *narrat-*, past participle of *narrare* < *gnarus* 'knowing'] —**narratable** *adj*

narration /nə ráysh'n/ *n* **1.** **ACT OF NARRATING** the act of telling a story or giving an account of something **2.** **SOMETHING NARRATED** a narrative or story **3.** **SOUNDTRACK VOICED BY ACTOR** the voiced soundtrack of a broadcast or film when given by an actor or commentator who does not appear

narrative /nárrətiv/ *n* **1.** **STORY** a story or an account of a sequence of events in the order in which they happened **2.** **PROCESS OF NARRATING** the art or process of telling a story or giving an account of something **3.** **STORY IN LITERARY WORK** the part of a literary work that is concerned with telling the story ■ *adj* **1.** **TELLING STORY** having the aim of telling a story ○ *narrative poetry* **2.** **RELATING TO NARRATION** relating to or involving the art of storytelling —**narratively** *adv*

narrator /nə ráytər/ *n* **1.** **STORYTELLER** somebody who tells a story or gives an account **2.** **TALKING CHARACTER** a character in a work of fiction who is presented as telling the story and who refers to himself or herself as 'I' **3.** **COMMENTATOR** somebody who provides narration, e.g. for a television programme

narrow /nárrō/ *adj* **1.** **SMALL IN WIDTH** having a small width, especially in comparison to height or length ○ *a narrow gap* **2.** **LIMITED IN SIZE** limited or restricted in size or scope ○ *a narrow range of options* **3.** **NARROW-MINDED** limited and usually inflexible in outlook ○ *a narrow view of events* **4.** **JUST ENOUGH FOR SUCCESS** only just sufficient for success ○ *a narrow victory* ○ *a narrow escape* **5.** *US* **NOT GENEROUS** unwilling to give things or help people **6.** **THOROUGH** close and thorough, leaving nothing uninvestigated ○ *a narrow investigation of the scene* **7.** **MEAGRE** small or limited in quantity ○ *a narrow provision* **8.** **PHON** same as **tense**[1] *adj* (sense 4) **9.** **AGRIC** **HIGH IN PROTEIN** describes animal feed that is very rich in protein ■ *n* **NARROW PASSAGE** a narrow place or passage ■ *vti* (**-rows**, **-rowing**, **-rowed**) **1.** **MAKE OR BECOME NARROW** to make something narrow or narrower, or become narrow or narrower **2.** **CONTRACT SOMETHING, OR BE CONTRACTED** to restrict or limit the scope or extent of something, or become restricted or limited in scope or extent ○ *narrowed the focus of their investigation to two individuals* [Old English *nearu* < Germanic] —**narrowness** *n*

narrowband /nárrō band/ *adj* functioning within a narrow band of broadcasting frequencies

narrowboat /nárrō bōt/ *n* a long canal barge with a width not exceeding 2.1 m/7 ft

narrowcast /nárrō kaast/ (**-casts**, **-casting**, **-cast** or **-casted**) *vt* to aim a radio or television transmission at a limited group of people such as cable subscribers or a specialized audience

narrow gauge *n* **1.** a distance between the two rails of a railway track that is less than the 143.5 cm/4 ft 8.5 in distance of the standard gauge railways **2.** a railway line with track of a narrow gauge, or a carriage or locomotive designed to run on one —**narrow-gauge** *adj*

narrowly /nárrōli/ *adv* **1.** **BY SMALL MARGIN** by a very small

margin or distance ○ *narrowly avoided capture* **2.** **INTENTLY** in a very concentrated, searching, or detailed way ○ *eyed him narrowly* **3.** **WITHIN NARROW LIMITS** in a way that allows little freedom or scope ○ *narrowly circumscribed*

narrow-minded /-míndid/ *adj* having or showing a limited and often prejudiced or intolerant outlook —**narrow-mindedly** *adv* —**narrow-mindedness** *n*

narrow money *n* money usable as a means of exchange, especially notes and coins, but also some bank balances

narrows /nárrōz/ *n* a narrow section of a river, or a narrow stretch of sea usually between two larger bodies of water (*takes a singular or plural verb*)

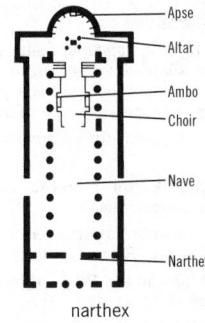

Apse
Altar
Ambo
Choir
Nave
Narthex

narthex

narthex /naár theks/ *n* **1.** an entrance hall at the west end of a Christian church between the porch and the nave **2.** an area at the west end of the nave of an early Christian church separated off by a screen or railing behind which women, catechumens, and penitents were admitted [Late 17C. < late Greek *narthēx* 'giant fennel', later 'casket' (because the plant was used to make boxes)]

nartjie *n S Africa* another spelling of **naartjie**

narwhal

narwhal /naár wayl/ (*plural same* or **-whals**), **narwal** (*plural same* or **-wals**), **narwhale** (*plural same* or **-whales**) *n* a small arctic whale, about 6 m/20 ft long, with a spotted body, short flippers, and, in the male, a long twisted ivory tusk. It was formerly hunted for oil and ivory. Latin name: *Monodon monoceros*. [Mid-17C. < Danish or Norwegian *narhval*]

nary /náiri/ *adj* not a single (*literary*) ○ *Nary a word was said.* [Mid-18C. Contraction of *ne'er a* 'never a']

NAS *abbr* **NAVY** naval air station

NASA /nássə/ *n* the US government agency responsible for nonmilitary programmes in the exploration and scientific study of space. Full form **National Aeronautics and Space Administration**

nasal /náyz'l/ *adj* **1.** **OF NOSE** forming part of or relating to the nose **2.** **PRONOUNCED THROUGH NOSE** describes a speech sound that is pronounced with breath escaping mainly through the nose rather than the mouth **3.** **WITH NASAL SOUNDS** characterized by nasal sounds ○ *a nasal accent* ■ *n* **1.** **NASAL SOUND** a nasal sound or a letter that represents it **2.** **HELMET PART** the nosepiece of a helmet [Mid-17C. Directly or via French < medieval Latin *nasalis* < Latin *nasus* 'nose'] —**nasality** /nay zálləti/ *n* —**nasally** *adv*

nasal cavity *n* either of the two open spaces, located between the floor of the cranium and the roof of the mouth, that form the inner nose

nasal concha *n* **ANAT** same as **turbinate** *n* (sense 1)

nasalize /náyzə līz/ (**-izes**, **-izing**, **-ized**), **nasalise** (**-ises**, **-ising**, **-ised**) *vti* to make a sound nasal by lowering the soft palate so that air flows through the nose —**nasalization** /náyzə līzáysh'n/ *n*

nascent /náss'nt, náyss'nt/ *adj* **1.** in the process of emerging, being born, or starting to develop **2.** in the process of being created in a reaction medium, often in a highly active form [Early 17C. < Latin *nascent-*, present participle of *nasci* 'be born'] —**nascence** *n*

NASDAQ /náz dak/ *tdmk* a service mark for an electronic communications system in the United States that links all over-the-counter securities dealers to form a single market. Full form **National Association of Securities Dealers Automated Quotation System**

naseberry /náyz berri/ (*plural* **-ries**) *n* **TREES** same as **sapodilla** (sense 1) [Late 17C. < Spanish *nispero* or Portuguese *nespera* < Latin *mespilus* 'medlar', by association with **BERRY**]

~~nash~~ incorrect spelling of **gnash**

Nash /nash/, **John** (1752–1835) British architect. His designs include the neoclassical Regent Street in London (begun 1812) and the elaborate Royal Pavilion in Brighton (1815–23).

Nash, Ogden (1902–71) US poet and lyricist. He is known for his comic verse and the musical *One Touch of Venus* (1943). Full name **Nash, Frederic Ogden**

'Professional men, they have no cares; /
Whatever happens, they get theirs.'
[Ogden Nash, 'I Yield to My Learned Brother'; 1935]

Nash, Paul (1889–1946) British painter. His landscapes reflect the influence of surrealism, and he worked as an official war artist during World War I and World War II.

Nash, Sir Walter (1882–1968) British-born prime minister of New Zealand (1957–60). Elected to Parliament for the Labour party in 1919, he held several ministerial posts, including finance minister (1935–40) before taking over as party leader (1949). As prime minister, he pursued a policy of social reform. See table at **prime minister**

nashi /náshi/ (*plural* **-is**) *n* **FOOD**, **TREES** same as **Asian pear** [Mid-20C. < Japanese, 'pear']

Nashville /násh vil/ capital city of Tennessee, situated in the north-central part of the state. It is a major centre for country-and-western music. Population: 570,785 (2002 estimate).

nasi goreng /naássi gə réng/ *n* a Malaysian dish of fried rice with other ingredients, usually including meat or fish [< Malay, 'fried rice']

nasion /náyzi ən/ *n* the point where the bridge of the nose meets the forehead [Late 19C. < French < *nasal* 'nasal', after INION] —**nasial** *adj*

naso- *prefix* nose, nasal ○ *nasogastric* [< Latin *nasus* < Indo-European, 'nose']

nasofrontal /náyzō frúnt'l/ *adj* relating to the nasal and the frontal bones jointly

nasogastric /náyzō gástrik/ *adj* passing through the nose to the stomach

nasolacrimal /náyzō lákrim'l/, **nasolachrymal** *adj* relating to or connecting the nose and the tear-producing sacs

nasopharyngeal /náyzō fə rínji əl/ *adj* relating to the nose and pharynx or to the nasopharynx

nasopharynx /náyzō fárringks/ (*plural* **-pharynges** /-fə rínjeez/ or **-pharynxes**) *n* the upper part of the pharynx, behind and above the soft palate, continuous with the nasal passages

Nasruddin /názrōō deen/ *n* in Islamic folklore, a trickster. He first appeared in stories used by Sufis to teach their students. [Mid-20C. < Turkish]

Nassau /nássaw/ capital city and principal port of the Bahamas, situated on the northeastern coast of New Providence Island. Population: 172,000 (1997).

Gamal Abdel Nasser

Nasser /nássər/, **Gamal Abdel** (1918–70) president of Egypt (1956–70). During his presidency, he promoted industrialization, built the Aswan High Dam, and nationalized the Suez Canal. He was the foremost Arab leader of his time.

> 'Power is not merely shouting aloud. Power is to act positively with all the components of power.'
> [Gamal Abdel Nasser, *The Philosophy of the Revolution*; 1952]

Nastase /nə stássi/, **Ilie** (*b.* 1946) Romanian tennis player. He won the US Open (1972) and French Open (1973), and many doubles titles.

nastic /nástik/ *adj* describes the movement of the parts of a plant in response to external stimuli, e.g. the opening of a crocus flower in response to temperature [Early 20C. < Greek *nastos* 'pressed together' < *nassein* 'to press']

nasturtium

nasturtium /nə stúrshəm/ *n* a plant with shield-shaped pungent edible leaves. Flowers: yellow, orange, red. Genus: *Tropaeolum*. [12C. < Latin]

nasty /naásti/ *adj* (**-tier, -tiest**) **1.** SPITEFUL showing spitefulness or malice ○ *a nasty trick to play on someone* **2.** REPUGNANT disgusting to the senses ○ *a nasty smell* **3.** UNPLEASANT generally disagreeable, unpleasant, or causing discomfort ○ *The weather turned nasty.* **4.** SERIOUS likely to cause harm or to be painful ○ *a nasty accident* ○ *a nasty bump on the head* **5.** MORALLY OFFENSIVE morally offensive or obscene (*informal*) ○ *nasty videos* **6.** DIFFICULT difficult to solve or deal with (*informal*) ○ *a nasty problem* ■ *n* (*plural* **-ties**) UNPLEASANT PERSON OR THING somebody or something that is very disagreeable, harmful, or offensive (*informal*) ■ *vt Carib* MAKE DIRTY to make something dirty or messy [14C. Origin ?] —**nastily** *adv* —**nastiness** *n*

SYNONYMS See *mean*².

-nasty *suffix* nastic response ○ *thermonasty* [< Greek *nastos* (see NASTIC)]

NAS/UWT *abbr* National Association of Schoolmasters/Union of Women Teachers

Nat /nat/ *n ANZ, S Africa* a member of the National Party in Australia or New Zealand, or of the former National Party in South Africa, or a member of parliament belonging to the National Party (*informal*) [Mid-20C. Shortening of *Nationalist*]

nat. *abbr* **1.** national **2.** native **3.** natural

natal¹ /náyt'l/ *adj* **1.** relating to birth or to the time and place of birth **2.** same as **native** *adj* (sense 3) (*literary*) [14C. < Latin *natalis* < *nasci* 'be born']

natal² /náyt'l/ *adj* relating to the buttocks [Late 19C. < Latin *natis* 'buttock']

Natal /nə taál/ **1.** city and seaport in northeastern Brazil. It is the capital of Rio Grande do Norte State. Population: 656,037 (1996). **2.** British colony which became a province in the Union of South Africa in 1910. In 1994 it became the province of Kwa-Zulu Natal.

natality /nay tálləti, nə-/ *n* STATS same as **birthrate**

natant /náyt'nt/ *adj* floating or swimming in water (*technical*) [15C. < Latin *natant-*, present participle of *natare* (see NATATORY)]

Nataraja /naátə raájə/ *n* in Hinduism, the god Shiva when represented as a dancing figure with several arms and legs [Early 20C. < Hindi, 'prince of dancers']

natation /nə táysh'n/ *n* the action or skill of swimming (*formal*) [Mid-16C. < Latin *natation-* < *natare* (see NATATORY)] —**natational** *adj*

natatory /nə táytəri/, **natatorial** /náttə táwri əl/ *adj* relating to or adapted for swimming (*formal*) [Late 18C. < late Latin *natatorius* < Latin *natator* 'swimmer' < *natare* 'keep on swimming' < *nare* 'to swim']

natch /nach/ *adv* naturally (*informal*) [Mid-20C. Shortening]

nates /náy teez/ *npl* the buttocks [Late 17C. < Latin, plural of *natis* 'buttock, rump']

NATFHE /nát fee/ *abbr* National Association of Teachers in Further and Higher Education

Nathan /náyth'n/ *n* in the Bible, a prophet at David's court (2 Samuel 7:1–17, 12:1–15)

Nathan /náyth'n/, **S. R.** (*b.* 1924) president of Singapore (1999–). A former social worker, he served as ambassador to the United States (1990–96) before becoming president. Full name **Nathan, Sellapan Ramanathan**

nation /náysh'n/ *n* **1.** PEOPLE IN LAND UNDER SINGLE GOVERNMENT a community of people or peoples living in a defined territory and organized under a single government **2.** PEOPLE OF SAME ETHNICITY a community of people who share a common ethnic origin, culture, historical tradition, and, frequently, language, whether or not they live together in one territory or have their own government **3.** NATIVE AMERICAN PEOPLE OR FEDERATION a Native American people or a federation of peoples ○ *the Apache nation* **4.** LAND OF NATIVE AMERICAN NATION a territory occupied by a Native American people or federation **5.** GROUP WITH COMMON INTEREST a group of people united by a common interest ○ *the hip-hop nation* [13C. Via French < Latin *nation-* 'birth, race' < *nat-*, past participle of *nasci* 'be born'] —**nationhood** *n* —**nationless** *adj*

national /násh'nəl/ *adj* **1.** OF NATION relating to, belonging to, representing, or affecting a nation, especially a nation as a whole rather than a part of it or section of its territory ○ *the national team* **2.** CHARACTERISTIC OF PEOPLE OF NATION relating to or characteristic of the people of a nation ○ *the British national character* **3.** OWNED OR CONTROLLED BY CENTRAL GOVERNMENT owned, maintained, or controlled by the central government of a nation ○ *a national film museum* **4.** REFERRING TO COALITION GOVERNMENT describes a coalition government consisting of members of all the major political parties ■ *n* **1.** CITIZEN OF PARTICULAR NATION a citizen of a particular nation, especially when living in another country ○ *a foreign national* **2.** MEDIA same as **national newspaper** **3.** SPORTS EVENT FOR CONTESTANTS FROM WHOLE COUNTRY a sports contest involving participants from every part of a country (*often used in the plural*)

National *n* HORSERACING same as **Grand National** (*informal*)

national anthem *n* a nation's official hymn or song, expressing patriotic sentiments and played or sung on public occasions

national assembly *n* a legislative body consisting of the elected representatives of a nation or country

National Assembly *n* the first legislative assembly set up during the French Revolution, ruling from 1789 to 1791

National Assembly for Wales *n* the centre of devolved government for Wales, made up of elected members. It has the power to introduce secondary legislation in areas such as health and education in Wales.

national bank *n* **1.** a bank that acts as banker to a government and performs duties relating to na-

tional finances, especially the country's fiscal and monetary policy **2.** *US* a bank in a system of privately owned commercial banks in the United States, operating under federal charter and legally required to be a member of the Federal Reserve System

National Certificate *n* EDUC full form of **NC**²

national code *n Aus* FOOTBALL same as **Australian Rules**

national colours *npl* the colours of a country's flag

national consciousness *n* the ideas, beliefs, and attitudes regarded as characteristic of a nation

national costume *n* CLOTHING same as **national dress**

National Curriculum *n* the curriculum for pupils aged 5 to 16 taught in state schools in England and Wales following the Education Reform Act of 1988. It comprises three 'core' subjects, English, maths, and science, and seven 'foundation' subjects, art, design and technology, geography, history, music, physical education, and a foreign language.

national debt *n* the total amount of money owed by a nation's central government as a result of borrowing

National Diploma *n* EDUC full form of **ND**²

national dress *n* clothes of a distinctive design that are, or were, characteristic of the people of a particular country

national emblem *n* an object that a country has adopted as its symbol, e.g. Canada's maple leaf or Scotland's thistle

National Gallery *n* a museum in Trafalgar Square, London, that contains more than 2,000 paintings from the national collection. Founded in 1824, it opened in its present building in 1838. A new Sainsbury Wing opened in 1991.

National Gallery of Art *n* a museum in Washington, DC that contains the national collection of paintings, prints, drawings, sculptures, photographs, and other works of art. It was founded in 1937 with the gift to the nation of the art collection of the financier Andrew W. Mellon.

National Gallery of Australia *n* a museum in Canberra that contains the national collection of Aboriginal, modern Australian, and world art. The collection was begun in 1911, and is housed in a building dating from 1982. Former name **Australian National Gallery**

National Gallery of Canada *n* a museum in Ottawa that contains the national collection of Canadian and European art. It was created by an Act of Parliament in 1913.

national grid *n* **1.** a network of high-voltage electric power lines linking major power stations throughout the United Kingdom **2.** a system of metric coordinates, shown as vertical and horizontal lines on maps, used for map reference purposes by the Ordnance Survey and other map-producing organizations

national guard *n* a military organization that operates as a national defence or police force

National Guard *n* in the United States, the military reserve units controlled by individual states and equipped by the federal government that can be called into service by either federal or state governments

National Health Service *n* in the United Kingdom, the state system for providing free or subsidized medical care, established in 1948 and financed mainly by taxation and national insurance

National Hunt racing *n* horseracing over distances up to 6.5 km/4¼ mi. in which horses jump over movable hurdles or fixed fences, as distinct from flat racing

national income *n* the total money earned or gained by all residents of a country over a period of time, including income from rent, profits, interest, government benefits, salaries, and wages

National Institutes of Health *n* an agency of the US federal government that conducts and supports medical research and programmes designed to improve the health of the nation (*takes a singular verb*)

National Insurance *n* in the United Kingdom, a state system based on compulsory contributions from employees and employers that provides medical

and financial assistance, including pensions, to people who are ill, retired, or unemployed

National Insurance number *n* in the United Kingdom, a unique reference number assigned to each person within the state insurance system. It remains the same throughout each person's life.

national interest *n* actions, circumstances, and decisions regarded as benefiting a particular nation

nationalise *vt* COMM another spelling of **nationalize**

nationalism /násh'nəlizəm/ *n* **1.** DESIRE FOR POLITICAL INDEPENDENCE the desire to achieve political independence, especially by a country under foreign control or by a people with a separate identity and culture but no state of their own **2.** PATRIOTISM proud loyalty and devotion to a nation **3.** EXCESSIVE DEVOTION TO NATION excessive or fanatical devotion to a nation and its interests, often associated with a belief that one country is superior to all others —**nationalist** *n, adj*

nationalistic /násh'nə lístik/ *adj* relating to or supporting nationalism, especially the kind that emphasizes fervent devotion to one nation and its interests above all others —**nationalistically** *adv*

nationality /náshə nálləti/ (*plural* **-ties**) *n* **1.** CITIZENSHIP OF PARTICULAR NATION the status of belonging to a particular nation by origin, birth, or naturalization **2.** PEOPLE FORMING NATION-STATE a people with a common origin, tradition, and often language, who form or are capable of forming a nation-state **3.** ETHNIC GROUP WITHIN LARGER ENTITY an ethnic group that is part of a larger entity such as a state **4.** NATIONHOOD political independence as a separate nation **5.** NATIONAL CHARACTER the character of a nation of people

nationalize /násh'nə līz/ (**-izes, -izing, -ized**), **nationalise** (**-ises, -ising, -ised**) *vt* **1.** to transfer a business, property, or industry from private to governmental control or ownership **2.** to make something national or to give a national character to something **3.** same as **naturalize** (sense 1) —**nationalization** /násh'nə lī záysh'n/ *n* —**nationalized** *adj* —**nationalizer** *n*

National Liberation Front *n* a radical nationalist movement in Algeria that launched a guerrilla war against France in the 1950s, leading to Algeria's independence in 1958

National Library of Australia *n* the national library of Australia, in Canberra, established as an independent institution by an Act of Parliament in 1960. It was founded in 1901 as part of the Commonwealth Parliamentary Library.

National Library of Canada *n* the national library of Canada, founded in Ottawa in 1953

National Library of New Zealand *n* the national library of New Zealand, in Wellington, created in 1966 by combining the collections of the General Assembly Library, the Alexander Turnbull Library, and the National Library Service

National Library of Scotland *n* the national library of Scotland, situated in Edinburgh and founded in 1925, having as its core the much older Library of the Faculty of Advocates. It is Scotland's only copyright deposit library.

National Library of Wales *n* the national library of Wales, situated in Aberystwyth in Ceredigion and founded by royal charter in 1907. It is Wales's only copyright deposit library.

nationally /násh'nəli/ *adv* in, to, or throughout an entire nation

national media *n* the nationally distributed or marketed broadcast and print products of a country, e.g. major newspapers and television programming

national monument *n* a structure or site of scenic, historical, or scientific significance that is protected and maintained by a national government

national newspaper *n* a newspaper that is distributed to and sold in all parts of a country

National Offender Management Service *n* a service merging the Prison and Probation services, responsible for improving the rehabilitation of offenders in order to reduce repeat offences and crime

national park *n* a large area of public land chosen by a government for its scenic, recreational, scientific, or historical importance and usually given special protection

National Party *n* **1.** former name for **National Party of Australia 2.** in New Zealand, a conservative political

party **3.** in South Africa until 1998, a conservative political party that developed from the Afrikaner nationalist movement, came to power in 1948, was largely responsible for instituting apartheid, and relinquished power in 1994. In 1998 it changed its name to the New National Party.

National Party of Australia *n* in Australia, a conservative political party that has strong support in rural areas and has usually formed a coalition with the Liberal Party of Australia

national product *n* the total value of all goods and services produced by a nation during a limited period, usually a year

National Record of Achievement *n* a record of a young person's achievements that, together with portfolios of evidence, will help in making a decision about the young person's future education, training, or employment

National Savings *n* in the United Kingdom, a savings bank that operates through local post offices and offers a variety of government-backed savings and investment schemes (*takes a singular verb*)

national security *n* the protection of a nation from attack or other danger by maintaining adequate armed forces and guarding state secrets

National Security Council *n* in the United States, a council consisting of the president, the secretary of state, the national security adviser, and top military and intelligence officers that decides on policies and measures to maintain national security

national service *n* compulsory service in the armed forces or in a civilian role, as prescribed in some countries

national socialism, **National Socialism** *n* the ideology and practices of the Nazi Party, in Germany's Third Reich, which included national expansion, state control of the economy, the totalitarian principle of government, and anti-Semitism —**national socialist** *n, adj*

National Trust *n* **1.** a charitable organization in England, Wales, and Northern Ireland concerned with the preservation of areas of great natural beauty and historic buildings and monuments for the benefit of the public **2.** an organization in Australia concerned with the preservation of areas of natural beauty and historic monuments

National Trust for Scotland *n* a Scottish charitable organization, established in 1931, concerned with the preservation of areas of natural beauty and historic buildings and monuments for the benefit of the public

National Vocational Qualification *n* EDUC full form of **NVQ**

nation language *n* Carib in the Caribbean, the popularly used English language, whether considered as a dialect of English or as an English-related creole language

Nation Language *n* LANG same as **Creole** (sense 3) (*slang; used in Black English*)

Nation of Islam *n* a movement of African Americans, founded in 1930, whose members follow Islamic religious practice out of a belief that Black Americans have Islamic origins. Malcolm X was a leading spokesman for the organization until he left it in 1964.

nation-state *n* a politically independent country, especially one in which the citizens share the same language, culture, and nationality

nationwide /náysh'n wīd/ *adj* applying to, happening in, or found in all parts of a nation ○ *a nationwide advertising campaign* —**nationwide** *adv*

native /náytiv/ *adj* **1.** INBORN existing in or belonging to somebody by nature ○ *her native intelligence* **2.** BORN OR ORIGINATING SOMEWHERE born or originating in a particular place ○ *native to the Southwest* **3.** RELATING TO SOMEBODY BECAUSE OF BIRTH relating or belonging to somebody or something because of the place or circumstances of birth ○ *She returned to her native land.* **4.** INDIGENOUS originating, produced, growing, or living naturally in a place **5.** CHARACTERISTIC OF LOCAL INHABITANTS characteristic of, belonging to, or relating to the indigenous inhabitants of a particular place, particularly those with a traditional culture (*dated; often considered offensive*) **6.** NOT EXTERNALLY AFFECTED unaffected by artificial or outside influences ○ *the native charm of the local fishing villages* **7.** CHEM

ELEM OCCURRING NATURALLY found in nature, especially in a pure or unadulterated form ○ *native copper* **8.** FISHERIES RAISED IN BRITISH WATERS describes oysters raised in British waters, especially in artificial beds **9.** COMPUT FOR PARTICULAR COMPUTER SYSTEM designed exclusively for a particular computer operating system ■ *n* **1.** SOMEBODY BORN IN PARTICULAR PLACE somebody born or brought up in a particular place ○ *a native of Cardiff* **2.** OFFENSIVE TERM an offensive term for an original inhabitant of a place belonging to an indigenous non-white people with a traditional culture, as distinct from a colonial settler and immigrant (*dated*) **3.** LONG-TERM LOCAL RESIDENT an established permanent local resident, as distinct from a visitor, temporary resident, or newcomer (*humorous*) **4.** INDIGENOUS PLANT OR ANIMAL SPECIES a plant or animal species that originates from a particular area **5.** OYSTER RAISED IN BRITISH WATERS an oyster raised in British waters, especially in an artificial bed ■ *adj* COMPUT READABLE BY PARTICULAR APPLICATION used to describe the format in which a software application normally saves its documents, usually readable only by that application [14C. Directly or via French *natif* < Latin *nativus* 'born' < *nasci* 'be born'] —**natively** *adv* —**nativeness** *n* ◇ **go native** to take up the customs and culture of the foreign place where you have settled (*humorous*)

USAGE Avoid use of the lowercase noun and adjective *native* to mean 'an indigenous inhabitant of a place' and 'relating to the indigenous people of a place', as in *the natives of …* and *the native people of …* Prefer the *indigenous* [or *original* or *aboriginal*] *people of …*

ORIGIN The Latin word *nasci* 'to be born', from which *native* is derived, and its past participle *natus* are also the source of English *cognate, impregnate, innate, naive, nascent, nation, nature, noel, pregnant, puny*, and *renaissance*.

SYNONYMS *native, aboriginal, indigenous, autochthonous*
CORE MEANING: originating in a particular place
native born or originating in a particular place ○ *the native peoples of Siberia* ○ *Native to the region are jaguars, giant anteaters, and caymans.* **aboriginal** existing in a place from the earliest known times ○ *a tiny aboriginal island community* **indigenous** originating in and naturally living, growing, or occurring in a region or country ○ *the indigenous population of the region* **autochthonous** originating where currently found, especially used of rocks and minerals that were formed in their present position, or flora, fauna, or inhabitants descended from those present in a region from earliest times ○ *Hummingbirds are autochthonous and exclusive birds of tropical America.* ○ *autochthonous Miocene claystones*

Native American *n* a member of any of the indigenous peoples of North, South, or Central America, belonging to the Mongoloid group of peoples ■ *adj* relating to any of the indigenous American peoples, their languages, or their cultures

USAGE See *Indian*.

native bear *n* Aus same as **koala**

native-born *adj* belonging to a place by birth

native bush *n* NZ forest made up of trees and bushes indigenous to New Zealand

native cat *n* Aus same as **dasyure**

Native Central American *n* a member of any of the indigenous peoples of Central America ■ *adj* relating to any of the indigenous Central American peoples, their languages, or their cultures

LANGUAGE HERITAGE See *Nahuatl*.

native frangipani *n* an evergreen tree with fragrant cream or yellow flowers. Native to: coastal eastern Australia. Latin name: *Hymenosporum flavum*.

native hen *n* Aus a moorhen that has mainly dark feathers and a greenish beak. Native to: Australia. Genus: *Gallinula*.

native land *n* the land to which somebody belongs by birth

Native North American *n* a member of any of the indigenous peoples of North America. See panel on next page ■ *adj* relating to any of the indigenous North American peoples, their languages, or their cultures

LANGUAGE HERITAGE ***Native North American*** Much of English is made up of words from other languages, and Native North American languages, especially those in the Algonquian family, are significant contributors in this respect, particularly to US and Canadian English. To begin with, many names of states and provinces, of rivers, lakes, and other geographical features are of Native American origin. Although the early European settlers preferred European names for their political divisions, during the 19th century state names with Native North American origins were adopted with increasing frequency, from ***Ohio*** in 1803, through ***Arkansas*** in 1836 and ***Oregon*** in 1859, to ***Utah*** (named after the ***Ute*** people) in 1896. All in all 26 US states and 6 Canadian provinces or territories have such names. The older, eastern states with Native American names, ***Massachusetts*** and ***Connecticut***, share them with a bay and a river respectively. Major rivers also give their names to the states of ***Arkansas***, ***Mississippi***, ***Missouri***, ***Ohio***, and ***Tennessee***. Other landscape terms of Native American origin include four of the five Great Lakes – ***Erie***, ***Huron***, ***Ontario***, and ***Michigan*** – as well as others such as the ***Susquehanna River***, the ***Niagara Falls*** and ***Yosemite Falls***, and the ***Adirondack***, ***Allegheny***, and ***Appalachian*** mountains. In Canada the name of the country itself is said to come from an Iroquoian word *kanata* meaning 'village, community', and, for example, ***Quebec***, ***Manitoba***, ***Yukon***, and ***Saskatchewan*** are of Native North American origin; in 1991 the Inuktitut name ***Nunavut*** (literally 'our land') was officially adopted for the larger part of Arctic Canada.

In identifying indigenous peoples the incoming Europeans often adopted Native North American names, either the people's own name, as ***Dakota*** (from Dakota, 'allies'), ***Haida*** ('people'), or ***Tsimshian*** (from Tsimshian *čamsián* 'inside the Skeena River'), or an ally's, enemy's, or stranger's name, as ***Arapaho*** (from Crow *alappahó* 'many tattoo marks'), ***Menominee*** (from Ojibwa *manōminī* 'wild-rice person'), or ***Mohawk*** (from Narraganset *mohowawog* 'man-eaters'). Sometimes the English name is mediated through North American French, for example ***Assiniboin*** (via French from Ojibwa), ***Cheyenne*** (via French from Dakota), and ***Sioux*** (from a shortening of French *Nadouessioux*, from Ojibwa *nātowēssiwak*), or through Spanish, as ***Comanche*** (ultimately from Southern Paiute or a related language), ***Navajo*** (via Spanish from Tewa *navahū* 'fields adjoining a ravine'), and ***Yaqui*** (via Spanish from Yaqui *Hiaki*). Sometimes a word is translated, for example ***Blackfoot***, from Blackfoot *Siksika*. Occasionally a European term was adopted by Native North Americans themselves and then passed to English, as ***Seminole***, which came from Creek *simanó:li* but goes back to American Spanish *cimarrón* 'wild, untamed'.

Words relating to Native North American artefacts and ways of life have become familiar to English-speakers, often extending far beyond their original cultural reference. The ***moccasin***, for example, (early 17th century, from Virginia Algonquian) is now a generic word for a type of shoe; ***powwow*** (from Narraganset) has come to be used informally for any meeting or gathering to discuss something; the ***tomahawk*** (from Virginia Algonquian) is now any small short-handled axe in North America, Australia, and New Zealand; ***totem*** (from Ojibwa *nindoodem* 'my totem') is used generally for something treated with the kind of respect normally reserved for religious icons. Names of foods adopted into English include ***samp***, which has moved into South African English as well, ***squash*** (a shortening of Narraganset *asquutasquash* 'green things that may be eaten raw'), and ***succotash***. Other terms from Algonquian languages remain in their original cultural context, for example ***manitou***, ***sagamore***, ***wendigo*** (a demonic creature of Algonquian folklore), and ***wickiup***. From other peoples and languages come ***tepee*** (Dakota), ***muckamuck*** (Chinook Jargon), and ***kachina*** (Hopi).

Flora and fauna naturally form important categories of words of Native North American origin. Algonquian-named animals include, for example, the ***chipmunk*** (from Ojibwa *ajidamoon'*, literally 'one that comes down trees headlong'), ***opossum***, ***raccoon***, ***terrapin*** (an alteration of Virginia Algonquian *torope*), and ***wapiti*** (from Shawnee). Altered by folk etymology to conform to English expectations are ***muskrat*** (from Algonquian *muscasus*) and ***woodchuck***. Showing the complexity of interaction between European and Native American languages is ***kinkajou***, from a French word *quincajou* 'wolverine' that is probably a blend of one Montagnais and one Ojibwa word. Algonquian is a significant source of shellfish and fish names: ***quahog***, ***muskellunge*** (via Canadian French *maskinongé* from Ojibwa *maashkinoozhe* 'big fish'), ***scup***, ***tautog***, and more. Representing other languages are, for example, ***abalone*** (via Spanish from Shoshonean) and ***quinnat salmon*** (first element from Chinook).

Trees and other plants, their fruits, wood, and other products have often retained or acquired Native North American names, for example from Algonquian ***chinquapin***, ***cohosh***, ***hackmatack***, ***hickory***, ***persimmon***, ***puccoon***, ***saskatoon***, ***tamarack*** (via Canadian French), and ***tuckahoe***.

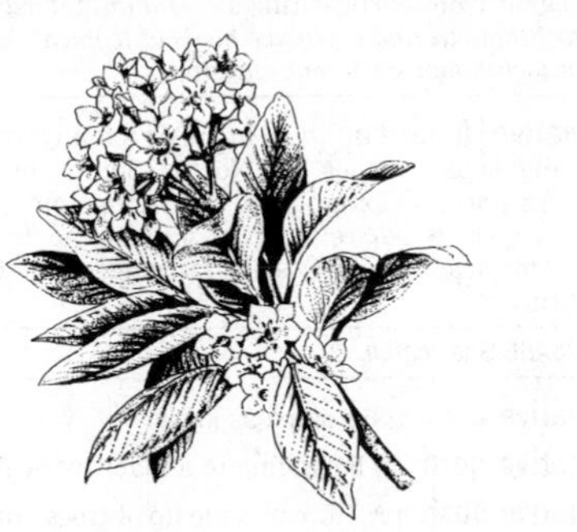

native frangipani

Native South American *n* a member of any of the indigenous peoples of South America ■ *adj* relating to any of the indigenous South American peoples, their languages, or their cultures

LANGUAGE HERITAGE See ***Tupi-Guarani***.

native speaker *n* a speaker of a language learned in infancy

native title *n ANZ* a right to an area of land claimed by aboriginal peoples whose ancestors were the original inhabitants before European settlement and who can prove a continuous association with that land

native tongue *n* the first language that somebody learns to speak

nativism /náytivizəm/ *n* **1.** POLICY OF FAVOURING INDIGENOUS INHABITANTS a policy, especially in the United States, of favouring the interests of the indigenous inhabitants of a country over those of immigrants **2.** POLICY OF REAFFIRMING INDIGENOUS CULTURE a policy of protecting and celebrating traditional cultures **3.** PHILOSOPHICAL DOCTRINE OF INNATE IDEAS the belief that the mind possesses some ideas that are inborn and not derived from external sources **4.** PSYCHOLOGICAL THEORY OF PERSONALITY in psychology, a theory claiming that personality and behaviour are determined from within, not externally —**nativist** *n, adj* —**nativistic** /náyti vístik/ *adj*

nativity /nə tívvəti/ (*plural* **-ties**) *n* **1.** birth or origin, especially the place, process, or circumstances of being born **2.** a horoscope based on the time of somebody's birth [14C. Via Old French < Latin *nativitas* < *nativus* (see NATIVE)]

Nativity (*plural* **-ties**) *n* **1.** BIRTH OF JESUS CHRIST the birth of Jesus Christ, which is celebrated by Christians at Christmas **2.** REPRESENTATION OF JESUS CHRIST'S BIRTH an artistic representation of the events surrounding the birth of Jesus Christ **3.** CHRISTMAS the festival of Christmas, which commemorates the birth of Jesus Christ

nativity play *n* a play, usually performed by children at Christmastime, that tells the story of the birth of Jesus Christ

natl *abbr* national

NATO /náytō/, **Nato** *n* an international organization established in 1949 to promote mutual defence and collective security that was the primary Western alliance during the Cold War. Full form **North Atlantic Treaty Organization**

natriuresis /náytriyoo reéssiss/ *n* the excretion of sodium in urine, especially in excessive amounts [Mid-20C. < *natrium* a name for sodium + Greek *ourēsis* 'urination'] —**natriuretic** /réttik/ *adj*

natrolite /náttrə līt/ *n* a white sodium aluminosilicate mineral of the zeolite group [Early 19C. < NATRON]

natron /náytrən, -tron/ *n* a white, yellow, or grey hydrous sodium carbonate mineral. Source: salt deposits. Use: formerly, embalming. [Late 17C. Via French, Spanish, and Arabic < Greek *nitron* 'potassium or sodium nitrate']

NATSOPA /nat sṓpə/, **Natsopa** *abbr* National Society of Operative Printers, Graphical and Media Personnel [Originally *of Printers and Assistants*]

natter /náttər/ (*informal*) *vi* (**-ters, -tering, -tered**) to talk about not very serious matters, often rapidly and at length and sometimes in an irritating way ■ *n* a trivial or gossipy conversation [Early 19C. Origin ?]

natterjack /náttər jak/ *n* a rare western European toad that inhabits sandy areas and has short hind legs and a skin colour ranging from yellow-green to olive-grey. It moves by running rather than hopping, inflates its body when alarmed, and has the loudest croak of all European toads. Latin name: *Bufo calamita*. [Mid-18C. Origin ?]

natty /nátti/ *adj* (**-tier, -tiest**) **1.** DAPPER neat and smart in appearance or dress **2.** IN DREADLOCKS describes hair worn in dreadlocks (*slang; used in Black English*) ■ *n* (*plural* **-ties**) SOMEBODY WITH DREADLOCKS somebody who wears his or her hair in dreadlocks (*slang; used in Black English*) [Late 18C. Origin ?] —**nattily** *adv* —**nattiness** *n*

natural /náchərəl/ *adj* **1.** OF NATURE relating to nature ○ *natural history* **2.** CONFORMING WITH NATURE in accordance with the usual course of nature ○ *natural signs of ageing* **3.** PRODUCED BY NATURE present in or produced by nature, not artificial or synthetic ○ *a natural sapphire* **4.** OF PHYSICAL WORLD relating to the physical rather than the spiritual world ○ *striking natural features* **5.** LIKE HUMAN NATURE in accordance with human nature ○ *It's only natural that they should want to be independent.* **6.** INNATE inborn, rather than acquired ○ *lots of natural charm* **7.** BEING SOMETHING BY NATURE having a particular character by nature ○ *a natural leader* **8.** NOT AFFECTED behaving in a sincere and unaffected way and not affected or adopted for a special purpose ○ *a natural manner* **9.** LIKE REAL LIFE representing something in a way that seems true to life **10.** BIOLOGICAL related by blood, rather than adoption ○ *her natural mother* **11.** NOT SHARP OR FLAT describes a note in music that is neither sharp nor flat **12.** WITHOUT SHARPS OR FLATS describes a musical key or scale containing no sharps or flats **13.** WITHOUT JOKER OR WILD CARD not made using a joker or a wild card ○ *a natural flush* **14.** ILLEGITIMATE born of unmarried parents (*archaic*) ○ *a natural child* ■ *n* **1.** SOMEBODY WITH INNATE SKILLS OR ABILITIES somebody who has seemingly innate skills or abilities ○ *a natural at bowling* **2.** MUSIC MUSICAL SIGN CANCELLING SHARP OR FLAT a sign placed before a musical note in order to cancel a previous sharp or flat **3.** MUSIC NOTE AFFECTED BY NATURAL SIGN a musical note affected by a natural sign **4.** CARDS, GAMBLING STAKE-WINNING RESULT OR COMBINATION a result or combination in some card and dice games such as craps and pontoon, that immediately wins the stake **5.** COLOURS LIGHT COLOUR a nearly white colour with tints of grey, yellow, or brown, like that of undyed fibres or yarn [13C. Via French < Latin *naturalis* < *natura* (see NATURE)] —**naturalness** *n*

natural childbirth *n* childbirth with little or no medication or medical intervention, in which the mother uses special techniques and exercises in order to minimize pain and assist in the delivery

natural death *n* death caused by disease or old age rather than by an act of violence or an accident

natural disaster *n* a disaster caused by natural forces rather than by human action, e.g. an earthquake

natural fibre *n* a fibre that forms naturally, e.g. cotton, wool, or silk

natural gas *n* a mixture of combustible hydrocarbon gases, mostly methane and ethane, found trapped in the pore spaces of some sedimentary rocks, often along with petroleum deposits

natural history *n* **1.** STUDY OF LIVING THINGS the study and description of living things, especially their behaviour and how they relate to one another **2.** STUDY OF WHOLE NATURAL WORLD the study and description of the natural world, including minerals and fossils **3.** NATURAL PHENOMENA OF TIME OR PLACE the natural phenomena, especially plants and animals, of a particular time or place **4.** NATURAL DEVELOPMENT OF SOMETHING the natural development of something such as an organism or a disease over a period of time ○ *the natural history of the leech* **5.** WRITTEN ACCOUNT OF ASPECT

OF NATURE a written account of a particular aspect of the natural world

naturalise *vti* another spelling of **naturalize**

naturalism /náchərəlìzəm/ *n* **1.** ARTISTIC MOVEMENT ADVOCATING REALISTIC DESCRIPTION in art or literature, a movement or school advocating factual or realistic description of life, including its less pleasant aspects. In literature, it is applied especially to Zola, Maupassant, and other 19th-century French writers. In the visual arts, it refers to the practice of faithfully representing subjects. **2.** BELIEF IN RELIGIOUS TRUTH FROM NATURE a belief that all religious truth is derived from nature and natural causes, and not from revelation **3.** DOCTRINE REJECTING SPIRITUAL EXPLANATIONS OF WORLD a system of thought that rejects all spiritual and supernatural explanations of the world and holds that science is the sole basis of what can be known

naturalist /náchərəlist/ *n* **1.** SOMEBODY STUDYING NATURAL HISTORY a student of or expert in natural history, especially botany or zoology. The term is particularly used to describe a field biologist. **2.** ADVOCATE OF NATURALISM a believer in or adherent of naturalism, especially in the arts ■ *adj* RELATING TO BELIEFS OF NATURALISM relating to or in accordance with the beliefs of naturalism

naturalistic /náchərə lístik/ *adj* **1.** REPRODUCING EFFECTS OF NATURE imitating or reproducing nature or perceived reality in a very exact and faithful way **2.** RELATING TO BELIEFS OF NATURALISM relating to, characteristic of, or in accordance with the tenets of naturalism, especially in art or literature **3.** OF NATURALISTS relating to naturalists or natural history —**naturalistically** *adv*

naturalize /náchərə lìz/ (**-izes, -izing, -ized**), **naturalise** (**-ises, -ising, -ised**) *v* **1.** *vti* GRANT OR ACQUIRE CITIZENSHIP to grant citizenship to somebody of foreign birth, or to acquire citizenship in an adopted country **2.** *vt* INTRODUCE SOMETHING FOREIGN INTO GENERAL USE to introduce something foreign such as a word or custom into general use or into the language of a community **3.** *vti* ACCLIMATIZE PLANT OR ANIMAL to cause a plant or animal from another region to become established in a new environment, or adapt successfully to new environmental conditions **4.** *vt* EXPLAIN SOMETHING IN NATURAL TERMS to explain a phenomenon in terms of natural causes, rather than supernatural causes **5.** *vt* MAKE SOMETHING NATURAL to make something natural or lifelike —**naturalization** /náchərə lì záysh'n/ *n* —**naturalized** *adj* —**naturalizer** *n*

natural killer cell *n* a white blood cell (**lymphocyte**) that can recognize microbes and tumour cells as 'foreign', without requiring prior exposure to them, and destroy them

natural language *n* **1.** a naturally evolved human language, as distinct from a created language such as a computer language **2.** naturally evolved human languages considered collectively

natural language processing *n* the branch of computational linguistics concerned with the use of artificial intelligence to process natural languages, as in machine translation

natural law *n* **1.** LAW OF MORALITY a law of morality believed to be derived from human beings' inherent sense of right and wrong, rather than from revelation or the legislation produced by society **2.** LAW OF NATURE a law that governs the behaviour of natural phenomena **3.** BELIEF IN UNIVERSAL JUSTICE SYSTEM the belief that general laws of nature can be applied as a system of justice for all societies, regardless of their individual culture or customs

natural light *n* light from a natural source, usually the sun, as distinct from artificial light

natural logarithm *n* a logarithm with the irrational number *e* as a base

naturally /náchərəli/ *adv* **1.** AS EXPECTED as might be expected ○ *They naturally objected to being treated in this way.* **2.** OF COURSE without any question or doubt ○ *'You'll go then?' 'Naturally'.* **3.** BY NATURE as a result of a natural feature, talent, or quality that somebody possesses ○ *a naturally gifted player* ○ *Writing seems to come naturally to her.* **4.** IN NORMAL WAY in a normal and unaffected manner ○ *People seldom act naturally when being filmed.* **5.** WITHOUT ARTIFICIAL AID OR TREATMENT occurring as a natural feature or quality without artificial aid **6.** REALISTICALLY in a manner that faithfully represents nature

natural medicine *n* MED same as **naturopathy**

natural number *n* any whole number greater than zero

natural philosophy *n* the study of nature and natural phenomena (*archaic*)

natural resource *n* a naturally occurring material, e.g. coal or wood, that can be exploited by people

natural scale *n* a musical scale that has no sharps or flats

natural science *n* any science that deals with phenomena observable in nature, e.g. biology, chemistry, and physics —**natural scientist** *n*

natural selection *n* the process, according to Darwin, by which organisms best suited to survival in their environment achieve greater reproductive success, thereby passing advantageous genetic characteristics on to future generations

natural theology *n* a theology that holds that knowledge of God can be derived by human reason alone, not requiring divine revelation

natural virtue *n* in theology, one of the four virtues of which people are capable without direct assistance from God, specifically fortitude, justice, prudence, and temperance

natural wastage *n* a gradual reduction in the workforce of an organization achieved by not replacing staff who leave through retirement or resignation

natural world *n* natural phenomena collectively, as distinct from supernatural or paranormal phenomena or those created by human activity

nature /náychər/ *n* **1.** PHYSICAL WORLD the physical world including all natural phenomena and living things **2.** *also* **Nature** FORCES CONTROLLING PHYSICAL WORLD the forces and processes collectively that control the phenomena of the physical world independently of human volition or intervention, sometimes personified as a woman called 'Mother Nature' **3.** COUNTRYSIDE the countryside or the environment in a condition relatively unaffected by human activity or as the home of living things other than human beings **4.** TYPE a type or sort of thing ○ *a detective novel or something of that nature* **5.** INTRINSIC QUALITIES OF SOMETHING OR SOMEBODY the intrinsic or essential qualities of somebody or something ○ *the intricate nature of this kind of work* **6.** TEMPERAMENT disposition or temperament in a person ○ *It's just not part of his nature to act unkindly.* **7.** REAL APPEARANCE OR ASPECT the appearance or aspect of a person, place, or thing that is considered to reflect reality ○ *The portrait was remarkably true to nature.* **8.** PRIMITIVE EXISTENCE a basic state of existence, untouched and uninfluenced by civilization **9.** NATURAL STATE OF HUMANKIND the natural and original condition of humankind, as distinguished from a state of grace **10.** UNIVERSAL HUMAN BEHAVIOUR the patterns of behaviour or the moral standards that are considered to be universally found and recognized among human beings **11.** GENETIC MATERIAL AFFECTING ORGANISM the inherited characteristics of an organism, as opposed to what is learnt from experience or the environment ○ *nature versus nurture* [13C. Via Old French < Latin *natura* 'birth, nature' < *nasci* 'be born'] ◇ **by nature** as a part of somebody's or something's essential character ○ *optimistic by nature* ◇ **in the nature of something** in the category of something ○ *Have you got anything in the nature of a computer table?*

-natured *suffix* having or showing a particular nature or disposition ○ *good-natured* —**-naturedly** *adv*

nature reserve, nature preserve *n* a managed and protected area of land usually containing rare or endangered plants or animals

nature strip *n Aus* a strip of vegetation such as trees, grass, or other plants along the edge of a pavement or between the lanes of a main road or highway

nature trail *n* a route through a natural area that is specially designed to draw attention to interesting natural features

naturism /náychərìzəm/ *n* **1.** the practice of going without clothes, usually in a communal setting or in designated areas, in the belief that nudity is a healthy natural state **2.** worship of nature in general, or of objects of nature such as trees and mountains —**naturist** *n* —**naturistic** /náychə rístik/ *adj* —**naturistically** *adv*

naturopathy /náychə róppəthi/ *n* a system of medicine founded on the belief that diet, mental state, exercise, breathing, and other natural factors are central to the origin and treatment of disease —**naturopath** /náychərō path/ *n* —**naturopathic** /náychərō páthik/ *adj* —**naturopathically** *adv*

naught /nawt/ *n N Am* same as **nought** ■ *pron* same as **nothing** *pron* (sense 1) (*archaic or literary*) ○ *Their efforts were all for naught.* ■ *adj* worthless in character or behaviour (*archaic*) [Old English *nāwiht* < *nā* NO[1] + *wiht* 'thing, being' (see WIGHT)]

naughty /náwti/ *adj* (**-tier, -tiest**) **1.** BADLY BEHAVED badly behaved, especially by being mischievous or disobedient **2.** MILDLY INDECENT mildly indecent or improper (*humorous*) ○ *standing with his hands over his naughty parts* ○ *a naughty smile* **3.** SINFUL mildly sinful (*humorous*) ○ *Would it be naughty of me to have another chocolate?* ■ *n* (*plural* **-ties**) *ANZ* ACT OF HAVING SEX an act of sexual intercourse (*slang*) ○ *They were upstairs having a quick naughty.* [14C. Literally 'having naught, poor'] —**naughtily** *adv* —**naughtiness** *n*

nauplius /náwpli əss/ (*plural* **-plii** /-pli ī/) *n* a free-swimming larva that is produced by many different crustaceans, with an unsegmented body, three pairs of limbs, and a single eye [Mid-19C. Via Latin, kind of shellfish < Greek *nauplios*]

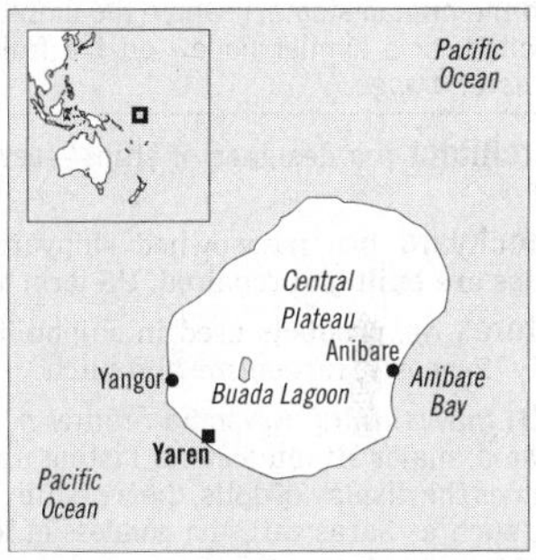

Nauru

Nauru /nə ròo, naa óoroo/ island country in the central Pacific Ocean, just south of the Equator. It became an independent member of the Commonwealth in 1968. Language: English, Nauruan. Currency: Australian dollar. Capital: Yaren. Population: 12,570 (2003). Area: 21 sq. km/8 sq. mi. Official name **Republic of Nauru**

Nauruan /nə ròo ən, naa óoroo ən/ *n* **1.** somebody who comes from Nauru **2.** an Austronesian language that is one of the official languages of Nauru — **Nauruan** *adj*

nausea /náwzi ə, -si ə/ *n* **1.** the unsettling feeling in the stomach that accompanies the urge to vomit **2.** deep disgust (*literary*) [15C. Via Latin < Greek *nausia* < *naus* 'ship']

nauseate /náwzi ayt, -si ayt/ (**-ates, -ating, -ated**) *vti* **1.** to have the unsettling feeling in the stomach that accompanies the urge to vomit, or make somebody have this feeling **2.** to feel deep disgust, or make somebody feel deep disgust

nauseating /náwzi ayting, -si ayting/ *adj* **1.** producing the unsettling feeling in the stomach that accompanies the urge to vomit **2.** deeply disgusting —**nauseatingly** *adv*

nauseous /náwzi əss, -si əss/ *adj* **1.** producing the unsettling feeling in the stomach that accompanies the urge to vomit **2.** suffering from the unsettling feeling in the stomach that accompanies the urge to vomit —**nauseously** *adv* —**nauseousness** *n*

naut. *abbr* nautical

nautch /nawch/ *n* in northern India, a professional performance of dancing by women, designed for the erotic entertainment of men [Early 19C. Via Hindi *nāc* < Sanskrit *nṛt* 'dance']

nautical /náwtik'l/ *adj* relating to sailors, ships, or seafaring [Mid-16C. Via Latin < Greek *nautikos* < *nautēs* 'sailor' < *naus* 'ship'] —**nautically** *adv*

nautical mile *n* an international unit of measurement of distance at sea equal to 1.852 km or about 6,076 ft. Symbol **M**

nautili MARINE BIOL plural of **nautilus**

nautiloid /náwti loyd/ *n* a mollusc that belongs to the group that includes the nautiluses and many fossil species. Subclass: Nautiloidea. [Mid-19C. < NAUTILUS]

nautilus /náwtiləss/ (plural **-luses** or **-li** /-lī/) n 1. a mollusc with numerous tentacles, a horny beak, and a spiral shell with gas-filled chambers for buoyancy. Native to: South Pacific and Indian oceans. Genus: *Nautilus*. 2. MARINE BIOL same as **paper nautilus** [Early 17C. Via Latin < Greek *nautilos* 'sailor, nautilus' < *nautēs* (see NAUTICAL)]

NAV abbr FIN net asset value

nav. abbr 1. NAUT naval 2. NAVIG navigable 3. NAVIG navigation

Navajo /návvəhō/ (plural same or **-jos** or **-joes**), **Navaho** (plural same or **-hos** or **-hoes**) n 1. a member of a Native North American people living mainly in northern New Mexico and Arizona 2. the Athabaskan language of the Navajo people. Native speakers: 225,000. [Late 18C. Via Spanish (*Apaches de) Navajó* '(Apaches of) Navajó' < Tewa *navahū* 'fields adjoining a ravine'] —**Navajo** adj

naval /náyv'l/ adj relating or belonging to a navy or to warships —**navally** adv

> **SPELLCHECK naval** or **navel**? Do not confuse the spelling of **naval** and **navel**, which sound similar. **Naval** is an adjective meaning 'of a navy or warships', as in *a naval officer, a naval battle*. **Navel** is a noun denoting the hollow on the human stomach where the umbilical cord was attached, or a similar hollow on the fruit that is called a *navel orange*.

naval architect n a designer of ships —**naval architecture** n

naval dockyard n a navy-owned shipyard where warships are built and repaired. US term **navy yard**

naval stores npl products used in shipbuilding, especially, formerly, turpentine and pitch

Navaratri /núvvə rúttri/, **Navaratra** /-rúttrə/ n a widely celebrated, major Hindu festival lasting nine days. It includes the display of dolls, the worship of female deities such as Saraswati, the goddess of learning, and Durga, the slayer of demons, and the burning of effigies. Date: autumn. [< Sanskrit, 'nine nights']

Navarre /nə vaár/ autonomous region in northeastern Spain, between the Basque Country and Catalonia. Capital: Pamplona. Population: 555,829 (2001). Area: 10,391 sq. km/4,012 sq. mi.

nave[1] /nayv/ n the long central hall of a cross-shaped church, often with pillars on each side, where the congregation sits [Late 17C. Via medieval Latin < Latin *navis* 'ship']

nave[2] /nayv/ n the hub of a wheel [Old English *nafu* < Germanic]

navel /náyv'l/ n a small rounded hollow on the surface of the human stomach, where the end of the umbilical cord was tied after being cut. Technical name **umbilicus** [Old English *nafela* < Indo-European] ◇ **examine** or **contemplate your navel** to spend too much time in pointless self-analysis (*informal*)

> **SPELLCHECK** See **naval**.

navel-gazing n pointless self-analysis as opposed to considering broader issues or making a decision (*informal*)

navel orange n a sweet seedless orange with a small navel-shaped depression or bump at its blossom end enclosing a smaller secondary fruit. Latin name: *Citrus sinensis*.

navelwort /náyv'l wurt/ n PLANTS same as **pennywort** (sense 1) [15C. < the navel-shaped indentation on its leaves]

navicular /nə víkyoolər/ n ANAT same as **navicular bone** (sense 1) ■ adj 1. shaped like a boat (*formal*) 2. relating to a navicular bone [15C. < late Latin *navicularis* < Latin *navicula* 'small ship' < *navis* 'ship']

navicular bone n 1. a small boat-shaped bone in the human wrist or ankle 2. a small bone in a horse's hoof. It is prone to disease (**navicular disease**), causing lameness.

navigable /návvigəb'l/ adj 1. PASSABLE BY SHIP passable by ship or boat, especially deep enough and wide enough to allow ships or boats to sail through 2. STEERABLE able to be steered or otherwise controlled 3. ONLINE FOLLOWABLE THROUGH LINKS describes a website that is designed to enable the user to move between or through sections by clicking on usually highlighted computer links —**navigability** /návvigə bílləti/ n —**navigably** adv

navigate /návvi gayt/ (**-gates, -gating, -gated**) v 1. vti FIND ROUTE to find a way through a place, or direct the course of something, especially a ship or aircraft, using a route-finding system ○ *navigating by the stars* 2. vt PASS THROUGH PLACE to follow a correct or satisfactory course along a route ○ *Even a champion paddler would have difficulty navigating those rapids.* 3. vi KEEP CAR ON RIGHT ROUTE to have responsibility for keeping a car on the right route, e.g. by following a map and giving the driver instructions 4. vi PROCEED to make your way over or through something, usually with difficulty ○ *navigated through the crowd* 5. vt FIND YOUR WAY to find a way to a place, usually with difficulty (*informal*) ○ *managed to navigate his way through the fog* 6. vti WALK to go somewhere on foot (*informal*) ○ *navigating with effort after his surgery* 7. vti ONLINE FOLLOW THROUGH LINKS to move between the different areas of a website by using the links provided in it [Late 16C. < Latin *navigat-*, past principle of *navigare* 'to sail' < *navis* 'ship' + *agere* 'drive']

navigation /návvi gáysh'n/ n 1. DIRECTING OF VEHICLE'S COURSE the plotting and directing of the course of a ship, aircraft, or other vehicle 2. MOVEMENT THROUGH PLACE the act or task of moving through a place or along a route, e.g. along a river or through a range of mountains 3. SCIENCE OF NAVIGATING the science of plotting and following a course from one place to another and of determining the position of a moving ship, aircraft, or other vehicle —**navigational** adj —**navigationally** adv

navigation light n a light on the outside of a ship or aircraft that alerts others to its position and direction

navigation satellite n an artificial satellite, used as an aid to navigation, that follows a fixed orbit made known to navigators on ships and aircraft

navigator /návvi gaytər/ n 1. somebody who navigates something, especially a ship or aircraft 2. a passenger of a motor vehicle who gives a driver information about a route

Martina Navratilova

Navratilova /na vrátti lṓvə/, **Martina** (b. 1956) Czech-born US tennis player. She set the women's record of 167 singles championships (1974–94), including nine Wimbledon titles.

> 'The moment of victory is much too short to live for that and nothing else.'
> [Martina Navratilova, *Guardian*; 21 June 1989]

NAVSAT /náv sat/ abbr NAVIG navigation satellite

navvy /návvi/ n (plural **-vies**) an unskilled labourer, especially somebody who does the heavy digging work involved in the building of roads, railways, and canals (*dated*) ■ vi (**-vies, -vying, -vied**) to work as a navvy [Early 19C. Shortening of NAVIGATOR in the archaic sense 'canal labourer']

navy /náyvi/ (plural **-vies**) n 1. the branch of a country's armed forces that crews, maintains, and fights on warships 2. a fleet of ships, especially one belonging to a country 3. COLOURS same as **navy blue** [14C. < Old French *navie* 'fleet' < Latin *navis* 'ship'] —**navy** adj

navy bean n a small white variety of kidney bean [< its former use as a food staple in the US Navy]

navy blue n a dark blue colour [< the colour of the British naval uniform] —**navy-blue** adj

navy cut n tobacco that has been cut into fine slices from a large block

navy yard n US same as **naval dockyard**

nawab /nə waáb/ n 1. in India during the Mughal empire, a title for a local nobleman 2. in Pakistan, a distinguished Muslim man [Mid-18C. Via Urdu *nawāb* < Arabic *nā'ib* 'deputy']

nay /nay/ n NO VOTE a vote of no, or somebody who votes no ■ adv INTRODUCING CORRECTION used to introduce a phrase that corrects something just said, often a phrase that states the truth in stronger terms (*archaic or literary*) ○ *It was a disappointing, nay, humiliating, outcome.* ■ interj NO used to refuse, deny, or disagree with something (*archaic*) [12C. < Old Norse *nei* < *ne* 'not' + *ei* 'ever']

naysay /náy say/ (**-says, -saying, -said** /-sed/) vt N Am to refuse, oppose, or criticize something

naysayer /náy sayər/ n N Am somebody who speaks against something, especially somebody who habitually expresses contrary opinions

Nazarene /názzə reèn/ n 1. SOMEBODY FROM NAZARETH somebody who comes from Nazareth 2. MEMBER OF PROTESTANT CHURCH a member of the Church of the Nazarene, a modern Protestant denomination 3. JESUS CHRIST Jesus Christ, as connected with Nazareth (*literary*) [13C. Via late Latin < Greek *Nazarēnos* < *Nazaret* 'Nazareth'] —**Nazarene** adj

Nazareth /názzərəth/ town in northern Israel. It is believed to be where Jesus Christ lived during his childhood. Population: 57,200 (1999).

Nazarite /názzə rīt/, **Nazirite** n a member of a Jewish religious group in biblical times whose members made various vows of abstinence, including a vow not to drink wine or cut their hair [Mid-16C. < late Latin *Nazaraeus* < Greek *Nazōraios* < *Nazaret* 'Nazareth']

Nazca Lines /názkə-/ n a group of long straight lines representing birds, fish, animals, or geometric figures carved into the desert near Nazca, southern Peru, believed to have been made around 200 BC and only visible from the air [After a place in S Peru]

Nazi /naátsi/ (plural **-zis**) n 1. FOLLOWER OF HITLER a member of the fascist German National Socialist Party that came to power under the leadership of Adolf Hitler in 1933 (*often used before a noun*) 2. RACIST somebody regarded as having right-wing political views, especially on race and immigration (*insult*) 3. also **nazi** BOSSY PERSON an authoritarian or dictatorial person (*insult; sometimes offensive*) [Mid-20C. < German, shortening of *Nationalsozialist* 'national socialist' or *Nationalsozialismus* 'national socialism'] —**Nazification** /naátsifi káysh'n/ n —**Nazify** vt

Naziism n POL, HIST same as **Nazism**

Nazirite n RELIG another spelling of **Nazarite**

Nazism /naátsizəm/, **Naziism** /naátsi izəm/ n the philosophy of the German National Socialist Party under the leadership of Adolf Hitler

nb abbr CRICKET no ball

Nb symbol CHEM ELEM niobium

NB, **N.B.** abbr New Brunswick

N.B., **NB**, **n.b.** interj used to draw somebody's attention to something particularly important, usually an addition to or qualification of a previous statement. Full form **nota bene**

NBA abbr 1. BASKETBALL National Basketball Association 2. BOXING National Boxing Association 3. PUBL, HIST Net Book Agreement

NBC abbr 1. National Broadcasting Company 2. MIL nuclear, biological, and chemical (*refers to weapons or warfare*)

NbE abbr COMPASS north by east

NBG, **nbg** abbr no bloody good (*informal*)

NBL abbr PUBL National Book League

NBV abbr ACCT, COMM net book value

NbW abbr COMPASS north by west

nc abbr ONLINE New Caledonia (*used in Internet addresses*) See table at **domain name**

NC[1] abbr 1. also **N.C.** EDUC National Curriculum 2. no charge

NC[2] n a UK qualification in a vocational subject that is roughly equivalent to a GCSE. Full form **National Certificate**

n/c abbr no charge

NCC abbr 1. National Consumer Council 2. National Curriculum Council 3. Nature Conservancy Council

NCO *abbr* MIL noncommissioned officer

NCT *abbr* National Childbirth Trust

NCU *abbr* National Communications Union

Nd *symbol* CHEM ELEM neodymium

ND[1], **N.D., n.d.** *abbr* no date

ND[2] *n* a UK vocational qualification that is roughly equivalent to two A levels. Full form **National Diploma**

NDE *abbr* near-death experience

Ndebele /əndə beéli, -báyli/ (*plural same* or **-les**) *n* **1.** a member of an African people who originated in northeastern South Africa, but now live mainly in southern Zimbabwe **2.** the Bantu language of the Ndebele people, which has distinct forms in Zimbabwe and South Africa. Native speakers: 1 million. [Late 19C. < Nguni] —**Ndebele** *adj*

N'Djamena /ən ja máynə/ capital of Chad, in the southwestern part of the country. Population: 530,965 (1993).

ndole /ən dōli/ *n W Africa* in African cuisine, a plant that must be scraped to remove bitter juice before being sliced, parboiled, and then cooked in stews and soup [< a Cameroon language, perhaps Duala]

NDP *abbr* ECON net domestic product

NDPB *n* full form **nondepartmental public body**

NDT *abbr* Newfoundland Daylight Time

ne *abbr* Niger (*used in Internet addresses*) See table at **domain name**

né /nay/ *adj* **1.** used to introduce a man's former or original name, e.g. the name of a newly titled peer ○ *Lord Healey, né Denis Healey* **2.** *US* used to introduce the name that something was formerly known under ○ *Zimbabwe, né Rhodesia* [Mid-20C. < French (see NÉE)]

Ne *symbol* CHEM ELEM neon

NE *abbr* **1.** *also* **N.E.** New England **2.** COMPASS northeast **3.** COMPASS northeastern

NEA *abbr* EDUC National Education Association

Neagh, Lough /nay/ inland lake in central Northern Ireland, the largest lake in the British Isles. Area: 396 sq. km/153 sq. mi.

Neandertal /ni ándər taal/, **Neanderthal** /ni ándər thaal/ *adj* **1.** OF NEANDERTAL MAN relating to Neandertal man **2.** *also* **neandertal** *or* **neanderthal** OFFENSIVE TERM an offensive term meaning displaying a lack of intellect, lack of sensitivity, and boorishness (*insult*) **3.** *also* **neandertal** *or* **neanderthal** OFFENSIVE TERM an offensive term meaning very old-fashioned or conservative (*insult*) ■ *n also* **neandertal** *or* **neanderthal** OFFENSIVE TERM an offensive term that deliberately insults somebody's intelligence, manners, or sensitivity, or somebody's ability to adopt modern ideas (*insult*) [Mid-19C. After a valley in W Germany]

Neandertal man *n* an extinct subspecies of human being that populated Europe, North Africa, and western Asia in the early Stone Age

Neanderthal *adj, n* same as **Neandertal**

neap /neep/ *n* GEOG same as **neap tide** ■ *adj* relating to or associated with a neap tide [15C. < Old English *nēp-*, origin ?]

Neapolitan /neé ə póllitən/ *adj* relating to the Italian city of Naples ■ *n* somebody who comes from Naples [15C. < Latin *Neapolitanus* < Greek *Neapolis*, literally 'new town']

Neapolitan ice cream *n* ice cream made in differently coloured and flavoured layers, usually served in a slice

neap tide *n* a tide that shows the least range between high and low and occurs twice a month between the first and third quarters of the moon

near /neer/ (**nears, nearing, neared; nearer, nearest**) CORE MEANING: a grammatical word that indicates that somebody or something is at or moving towards a point that is not far away in distance ○ (prep) *The art exhibition is near here.* ○ (adv) *He took a step nearer to the water.* ○ (adv) *as the car drew nearer* ○ (adj) *There must be a restaurant nearer than that.* ○ (adj) *Can you tell me where the nearest telephone is?* **1.** *adv, prep, adj* SHORT TIME AWAY at or to a time not far away ○ (adv) *as the time for her to leave drew near* ○ (prep) *near the end of the week* ○ (adj) *the near future* **2.** *adv, adj* CLOSE at a point that is not far away in state, resemblance, or number ○ (adv) *It was nearer two hours before he got through customs.* ○ (adv) *a sensation near to fear* ○ (adj) *the nearest thing to a champion* **3.** *adv, adj* ALMOST almost in a particular state or situation ○ (adv) *I damn near fainted.* ○ (adv) *near total failure* ○ (adj) *living in near poverty* **4.** *adj, n* ON LEFT on the left side, especially of an animal or a horse-drawn vehicle ○ *the near foreleg* **5.** *adj* CLOSELY RELATED closely related to somebody **6.** *adj* MISERLY reluctant to give or spend money (*archaic*) **7.** *v vti* APPROACH to approach, or approach a particular place, time, or state ○ *The project is nearing completion.* ○ *With the big event nearing, everyone was working hard.* [12C. < Old Norse *nær* 'nearer' < *nā* 'near'] —**nearness** *n* ◇ **near the bone** *or* **knuckle** rather vulgar or indecent (*informal*) ◇ **so near (and) yet so far** used to express frustration or regret at failure by a narrow margin

NEAR /neer/ *n* a binary operator used in searches of computer text that returns true if its operands (usually two words) occur within a specific proximity to each other, and false otherwise

nearby /neér bī/ *adj, adv* in, at, or to a place a short distance away ○ *a nearby grocer* ○ *His mother was waiting nearby.* ■ *adj* closest in time, especially to a stock-exchange transaction

Nearctic /ni áarktik/ *adj* relating to or located in the region of plant and animal life in the Arctic and temperate areas of Greenland and North America [Mid-19C. < NEO-]

near-death experience *n* a sensation that people on the brink of death have described as leaving their own bodies and observing them as though they were bystanders

near-earth object *n* an asteroid or comet that can approach, or is on course to approach, within 45 million km/28 million mi of the Earth's orbit

Near East *n* **1.** same as **Middle East** (sense 1) **2.** the countries on the Balkan peninsula, comprising Greece, Albania, Romania, Bulgaria, the states of the former Yugoslavia, and the European part of Turkey —**Near Eastern** *adj* —**Near Easterner** *n*

near gale *n* METEOROL same as **moderate gale**

near hand *adv regional* **1.** close in position **2.** almost or nearly

near letter quality *adj* describes the printing quality of a computer printer that produces printed characters as clear as a typewriter's

nearly /neérli/ *adv* **1.** almost but not quite the case ○ *We waited for nearly an hour.* **2.** closely, in time, proximity, or relationship ○ *'Brennan described to the police the man he saw in the window and then identified Oswald as the person who most nearly resembled the man he saw.'* (Earl Warren et al, *The Report of the Warren Commission*; 1964) ◇ **not nearly** used to emphasize that something stated, implied, or assumed is very far from being the case ○ *not nearly enough time to answer all the questions*

near miss *n* **1.** NEAR COLLISION a situation in which two vehicles or aeroplanes only narrowly avoid colliding with each other **2.** SHOT NEAR TARGET a shot or strike that comes very close to a target but does not quite hit it **3.** BARELY AVERTED DISASTER something, especially something undesirable, that is only narrowly avoided or averted (*informal*)

near point *n* the point nearest the eye at which an object remains in focus

nearside /neér sīd/ *n* **1.** the side of a vehicle that is opposite the driver's side and close to the kerb **2.** the left side of an animal's body (*often used before a noun*) ○ *the nearside foreleg*

nearsighted /neér sītid/ *adj N Am* same as **shortsighted** —**nearsightedly** *adv* —**nearsightedness** *n*

near thing *n* something only just avoided or only just achieved (*informal*)

neat[1] /neet/ *adj* **1.** ORDERLY IN APPEARANCE orderly and in a clean condition **2.** ORDERLY BY NATURE tending to keep things in an orderly and clean condition ○ *My husband's very neat in the kitchen.* **3.** ELEGANT simple, effective, and elegant ○ *a neat solution to a complex problem* **4.** SKILFULLY PERFORMED performed with skill, ingenuity, and apparent ease ○ *a neat pirouette* **5.** COMPACT appealingly regular or compact ○ *She stood admiring her own neat little figure in the mirror.* **6.** UNDILUTED describes drinks that are not diluted with water, ice cubes, or a mixer **7.** *N Am* EXCELLENT used as a general term of approval (*informal*) ○ *Her parents are really neat.* [Mid-16C. Via French *net* < Latin *nitidus* 'shiny' < *nitere* 'to shine'] —**neatly** *adv* —**neatness** *n*

neat[2] /neet/ (*plural* **neats** or *same*) *n* an animal in the cattle family, e.g. a cow or ox (*archaic*) [Old English *nēat* < Germanic, 'to use']

neaten /neét'n/ (**-ens, -ening, -ened**) *vt* to make something neat or orderly

neath /neeth/, **'neath** *prep* same as **beneath** (*literary*) [Late 18C. Shortening]

Neath /neeth/ industrial town in southern Wales. Population: 45,965 (1991).

neatnik /neét nik/ *n US* somebody who is extremely neat and orderly (*informal*)

neat's-foot oil *n* a pale yellow oil. Source: feet and shinbones of cattle. Use: treatment of leather. [< NEAT²]

neb /neb/ *n* **1.** *Scotland or N England* SOMEBODY'S NOSE somebody's nose (*informal or humorous*) ○ *told him to keep his neb out of my business* **2.** *N England* ANIMAL'S NOSE an animal's bill, beak, nose, or snout (*informal*) **3.** POINT OR PROJECTION something that sticks out, e.g. an overhanging rock or peak (*archaic*) [Old English *nebb* < Germanic]

NEB *abbr* **1.** National Enterprise Board **2.** CHR New English Bible

Nebbiolo /nébbi ōlō/ (*plural* **-los**) *n* **1.** a typically full-bodied red wine made from a variety of black grape grown mainly in northwestern Italy **2.** a black grape variety. Use: to make Nebbiolo. [Mid-19C. < Italian < *nebbia* 'mist'; because the grapes ripen in autumn]

nebbish /nébbish/ *n* an offensive term that deliberately insults somebody's courage, personality, and initiative (*insult*) [Late 19C. < Yiddish *nebekh* 'poor thing' < assumed Slavic *ne-bogŭ* 'poor']

NEbE *abbr* COMPASS northeast by east

NEbN *abbr* COMPASS northeast by north

Nebraska /nə bráskə/ state in the central United States, bordered by South Dakota, Iowa, Missouri, Kansas, Colorado, and Wyoming. Capital: Lincoln. Population: 1,729,180 (2002 estimate). Area: 200,356 sq. km/77,358 sq. mi. —**Nebraskan** *n, adj*

Nebuchadnezzar II /nébbyōōkəd nézzər/ (*fl* 6th century BC) Babylonian king. He conquered and destroyed Jerusalem in 586 BC, consigning its inhabitants to captivity. He is thought to have created the Hanging Gardens of Babylon.

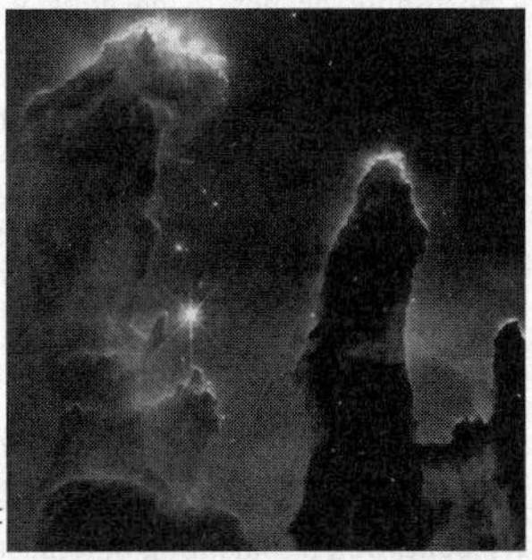

Popperfoto

nebula photographed by the Hubble Space telescope (1995)

nebula /nébbyōōlə/ (*plural* **-lae** /-lee/ or **-las**) *n* **1.** SPACE DUST a region or cloud of interstellar dust and gas appearing variously as a hazy bright or dark patch **2.** MED FLAW ON EYEBALL a faint cloudy area or scar on the cornea of the eye **3.** MED CLOUDY URINE cloudiness in the urine **4.** MED LIQUID FOR SPRAYING liquid prepared for use in any kind of atomizing sprayer, especially a nebulizer [Mid-17C. < Latin, 'mist, vapour'] —**nebular** *adj*

nebular hypothesis *n* a formerly held theory that the solar system evolved as a hot rotating flattened gaseous nebula. The theory states that as the nebula cooled, the Sun condensed at the centre and planets and their moons formed from contracting concentric rings at the rim.

nebuliser, etc. MED another spelling of **nebulizer, etc.**

nebulize /nébbyōō līz/ (**-lizes, -lizing, -lized**), **nebulise** (**-lises, -lising, -lised**) *vt* to reduce a liquid to a fine spray for medical use [Late 19C. < NEBULA] —**nebulization** /nébbyōō lī záysh'n/ *n*

nebulizer /nébbyoo̅ līzər/, **nebuliser** *n* a device, with a face mask attached, for administering a medicinal liquid in the form of a fine spray that is breathed in through the mouth or nose

nebulosity /nébbyoo̅ lóssəti/ (*plural* **-ties**) *n* ASTRON same as **nebula** (sense 1)

nebulous /nébbyoo̅ləss/ *adj* **1.** not clear, distinct, or definite **2.** relating to or resembling a nebula —**nebulously** *adv* —**nebulousness** *n*

NEC *abbr* **1.** National Executive Committee **2.** National Exhibition Centre (Birmingham)

neccesary incorrect spelling of **necessary**

necessarily /néssəssərəli, néssə sérrəli/ *adv* **1.** inevitably, or in every case ○ *This route isn't necessarily the best one.* **2.** following as an unavoidable result or consequence ○ *Voting was a necessarily slow and complex process.*

necessary /néssəssəri/ *adj* **1.** REQUIRED important in order to achieve a specific result, or desired by authority or convention ○ *Is it really necessary to contact the police?* **2.** FOLLOWING INEVITABLY inevitable given what has happened previously ○ *No doubt they will draw the necessary conclusion.* **3.** LOGIC LOGICALLY TRUE logically true because of being impossible to be false ■ *n* (*informal*) **1.** (*plural* **-ries**) SOMETHING ESSENTIAL an essential item ○ *I've packed the necessaries.* **2.** SOMETHING NEEDED the thing that is needed, especially an action or a sum of money ○ *Tell him to do the necessary.* [14C. Via Anglo-Norman < Latin *necessarius* < *necesse* 'unyielding' < *cess-* (see CESSION)]

SYNONYMS ***necessary, essential, vital, indispensable, requisite, required, needed***

CORE MEANING: important to have

necessary important in order to achieve a specific result, or desired by authority or convention ○ *Our son says he'll get a bank loan to buy the car if necessary.* ○ *Repairs are necessary in order to avert a danger to health and safety.* **essential** of the highest importance for achieving something ○ *Besides ability, the other essential element in political success is sheer luck.* ○ *It is absolutely essential that relatives have adequate warning so they can make arrangements for the patient's homecoming.* **vital** extremely important and necessary, or indispensable to the survival or continuing effectiveness of something ○ *The president's support for the negotiations was vital to their success.* ○ *The neighbourhood watch has a vital role to play in reducing crime.* **indispensable** extremely desirable or useful, or not to be done without ○ *Although not a popular leader, he created the belief that he was indispensable to political stability.* ○ *Online sources have become almost indispensable for today's history teaching.* **requisite** (*formal*) necessary for a specific purpose ○ *The resolution fell only four votes short of achieving the requisite two-thirds majority.* ○ *We ended up rejecting the majority of applicants because they didn't have the requisite skills.* **required** necessary or appropriate, or insisted upon or imposed as a condition ○ *They haven't got the required documents.* **needed** necessary or desired ○ *This generous donation allowed us to purchase some much-needed items.*

necessary condition *n* something that must happen or exist in order for something else to happen or exist

necessary evil *n* something that is unpleasant or undesirable but is needed to achieve a result

necessitarian /ni séssi táiri ən/ *n* somebody who believes that all events are determined by previous causes —**necessitarianism** *n*

necessitate /nə séssi tayt/ (**-tates, -tating, -tated**) *vti* **1.** to make something necessary or inescapable ○ *a dry climate that necessitates water conservation* **2.** to force or oblige somebody to do something (*formal*) —**necessitation** /nə séssi táysh'n/ *n* —**necessitative** /-tətiv/ *adj*

necessitous /nə séssitəss/ *adj* **1.** pressingly necessary **2.** in a state of poverty (*literary*) ○ *'grew necessitous, pawn'd his cloaths, and wanted bread'* (Benjamin Franklin, *The Autobiography of Benjamin Franklin*; 1788) —**necessitously** *adv*

necessity /nə séssəti/ (*plural* **-ties**) *n* **1.** SOMETHING ESSENTIAL something that is essential, especially a basic requirement ○ *food, shelter, and the other necessities* **2.** COMPELLING CIRCUMSTANCES circumstances that create a need or an obligation ○ *issuing replacements as necessity dictates* **3.** NEED the condition of being needed or required ○ *We'll hire new staff when the necessity arises.* **4.** PHILOSOPHY NECESSARY QUALITY the quality of being necessary or of not being able to be otherwise [14C. Via French < Latin *necessitas* < *necesse* (see NECESSARY)]

neck /nek/ *n* **1.** PART BETWEEN HEAD AND BODY the part of the body that joins the head to the rest of the body **2.** GARMENT PART ROUND NECK the part of a garment that goes round or lies below the wearer's neck **3.** CUT OF MEAT a cut of meat from the neck of an animal, especially a sheep **4.** LONG OPENING a long narrow opening ○ *the neck of a bottle* **5.** STRIP OF LAND OR WATER a long narrow strip of land or stretch of water **6.** LONG NARROW FINGERBOARD the long narrow fingerboard that projects out of the body or sound box of a hand-held string instrument such as a guitar or violin **7.** WINNING MARGIN in horseracing, a narrow winning margin equal to the distance between a horse's nose and its shoulder ○ *won the race by a neck* **8.** SOMETHING IMPORTANT RISKED OR SAVED somebody's life, job, reputation, or other important asset that has been placed at risk or saved from danger (*informal*) ○ *telling a lie to save her neck* **9.** CHEEK impudence or cheek (*informal*) ○ *had the neck to ask another favour* **10.** GEOL SOLIDIFIED LAVA a plug of solidified lava or igneous rock filling the vent of an extinct or dormant volcano **11.** MARINE BIOL same as **siphon** *n* (sense 3) **12.** ARCHIT BAND AROUND PILLAR a narrow band around the top of a pillar ■ *v* (**necks, necking, necked**) **1.** *vi* KISS AND CUDDLE to kiss and embrace sexually, usually sitting or lying with clothes on (*informal*) ○ *teenagers necking in the car* **2.** *vt* COOK KILL POULTRY to kill a bird to be cooked by breaking its neck or chopping its head off (*informal*) **3.** *vt* SWALLOW SOMETHING to swallow something, especially a drink (*slang*) [Old English *hnecca* 'nape' < Indo-European, 'high point, ridge'] —**necked** *adj* ◇ **be breathing down somebody's neck 1.** to be close behind somebody **2.** to be putting pressure on somebody to do something more quickly ◇ **be in something up to your neck** to be very much involved in something, often something dishonest or illegal ◇ **break your neck** to try very hard to achieve something (*informal*) ◇ **get it in the neck** to be punished or scolded severely (*informal*) ◇ **neck and neck** level in a competition and with an equal chance of winning (*informal*) ◇ **neck of the woods** a particular area or part of the country (*informal*) ◇ **neck or nothing** risking everything, or prepared to risk everything (*informal*) ◇ **stick your neck out** to take a risk by saying or doing something that could bring blame or censure (*informal*)

neckband /nék band/ *n* the part of a garment that fits or wraps round the neck

neckcloth /nék kloth/ *n* a cravat or scarf worn round the neck rather than round the collar, especially one worn by men between the 17th and mid-19th centuries

neckdown /nék down/ *n US* an outwards extension of the kerbs at an intersection, narrowing the width of roadway available to traffic and acting as a traffic-calming measure

neckerchief /nékər chif, -cheef/ (*plural* **-chiefs** or **-chieves** /-cheevz/) *n* a square of cloth worn tied round the neck as a scarf [14C. < NECK + KERCHIEF]

necking /néking/ *n* **1.** kissing and embracing sexually while sitting or lying with clothes on (*informal*) **2.** a moulding at the top of a pillar, below the capital

necklace /nékləss/ *n* a decorative chain or string of jewels worn around the neck

necklet /néklət/ *n* a small plain necklace

neckline /nék līn/ *n* the line formed by the edge of a garment at or under the neck, especially at the front

neckpiece /nék peess/ *n* a garment like a scarf, especially one made of fur

neck ring *n* a rigid necklace or ornamental band that fits snugly round the neck

necktie /nék tī/ *n N Am* CLOTHING same as **tie** *n* (sense 1)

neckwear /nék wair/ *n* garments or fashion accessories worn round the neck, e.g. ties, cravats, and scarves

necr- *prefix* same as **necro-** (*used before vowels*)

necro- *prefix* death, the dead, dead body ○ *necrophobia* [< Greek *nekros* 'corpse' < Indo-European]

necrobiosis /nékrō bī óssiss/ *n* the degeneration and death of the body's cells from natural processes —**necrobiotic** /-óttik/ *adj*

necrology /ne królləji/ (*plural* **-gies**) *n* (*formal*) **1.** a list of people who have died recently or during a specific period **2.** a notice of somebody's death [Early 18C. < medieval Latin *necrologium* < Greek *nekros* 'corpse'] —**necrological** /nékrə lójjik'l/ *adj* —**necrologist** *n*

necromancy /nékrō manssi/ *n* **1.** the practice of attempting to communicate with the spirits of the dead in order to predict or influence the future **2.** witchcraft or sorcery in general (*literary*) [13C. Alteration of *nigromancy*, via French < medieval Latin *nigromantia* < late Latin *necromantia* (influenced by Latin *niger* 'black') < Greek *nekromanteia* < *nekros* 'corpse' + *manteia* 'divination'] —**necromancer** *n* —**necromantic** /nékrō mántik/ *adj*

necrophilia /nékrō fílli ə/ *n* sexual feelings for or sexual acts with dead bodies —**necrophiliac** *n* —**necrophilic** *adj*

necrophobia /nékrō fóbi ə/ *n* an irrational fear of death or of dead bodies —**necrophobe** /nékrō fōb/ *n* —**necrophobic** *adj*

necropolis /nə króppəliss/ (*plural* **-lises** or **-leis** /-layss/) *n* a cemetery, especially a large, elaborate, or ancient one [Early 19C. < Greek < *nekros* 'corpse' + *polis* 'city']

necropsy /nékropsi/ (*plural* **-sies**) *n* MED same as **autopsy** *n* (sense 1) [Mid-19C. < NECRO- + AUTOPSY]

necrosis /ne króssiss/ *n* the death of cells in a tissue or organ caused by disease or injury [Mid-17C. Via modern Latin < Greek *nekrōsis* 'deadness' < *nekros* 'corpse'] —**necrotic** /ne króttik/ *adj*

necrotizing /nékrō tīzing/, **necrotising** *adj* causing or undergoing the death of cells (**necrosis**) ○ *necrotizing bacteria* [Late 19C. < *necrotize* 'become affected with necrosis' < *necrotic* 'of necrosis' < Greek *nekroun* 'to kill']

necrotizing fasciitis *n* a severe bacterial infection that causes cell tissue to decay rapidly

nectar /néktər/ *n* **1.** PLANT LIQUID the sweet liquid that flowering plants produce as a way of attracting the insects and small birds that assist in pollination **2.** ENJOYABLE DRINK an enjoyable or much appreciated drink (*informal*) **3.** DRINK OF GODS in Greek and Roman mythology, the drink of the gods that sustained their beauty and immortality **4.** *US* PULPY JUICE a thick drink made from puréed fruit ○ *mango nectar* [Mid-16C. Via Latin < Greek *nektar* 'drink of the gods'] —**nectarous** *adj*

nectarine /néktə reen/ *n* **1.** a fruit similar to a peach with a smooth skin **2.** a tree that produces nectarines. Latin name: *Prunus persica*.

nectary /néktəri/ (*plural* **-ries**) *n* the nectar-producing organ of a flowering plant —**nectarial** /nek táiri əl/ *adj* —**nectaried** *adj*

neddy /néddi/ (*plural* **-dies**) *n* **1.** *regional* ZOOL same as **donkey** (sense 1) **2.** *Aus* a horse, particularly a racehorse (*informal*) [Mid-16C. < *Ned*, pet form of the name *Edward*]

née /nay/, **nee** *adj* used to introduce a married woman's maiden name ○ *Jane Smith née Jones* [Mid-18C. < French form of *né*, past participle of *naître* 'be born' < Latin *nasci*]

need /need/ *v* (**needs, needing, needed**) *vti* REQUIRE SOMETHING require something in order to have success or achieve a goal ○ *Do you need any money?* ○ *He told me that I didn't need to know.* ○ *This shirt needs ironing.* ■ *modal v* BE NECESSARY used to indicate that a course of action is desirable or necessary (*used in negative statements*) ○ *You don't need to thank me; I'm happy to help whenever I can.* ○ *Studying medicine need not mean you can't study architecture later.* ■ *v* **1.** *vti* DESERVE SOMETHING to deserve something, especially as punishment (*informal*) ○ *That little boy needs to be given a good talking to.* ○ *Those troops need to be shown who's boss.* **2.** *vi* TO BE ESSENTIAL to be essential or necessary to something (*archaic*) ○ *'I think that we are all agreed in this matter, and therefore there needs no more words about it.'* (John Bunyan, *Pilgrim's Progress*; 1678) ■ *n* REQUIREMENT something that is a requirement or is wanted ○ *an economic system that recognizes the need for financial security* ○ *His needs are small.* [Old English *nē(o)d* < Indo-European] ◇ **in need 1.** not having enough of things essential for an adequate standard of living ○ *children in need* **2.** needing something ◇ **no need**

to *or* **for something** no reason or justification for something

SPELLCHECK See ***knead.***

needed /neéd id/ *adj* necessary or desired (*usually in combination*) ○ *a much-needed rest*

SYNONYMS See ***necessary.***

needful /neédf'l/ *adj* (*formal*) **1. REQUIRED** necessary or required **2. REQUIRING** lacking or requiring something ○ *a situation needful of common sense* ■ *n* **SOMETHING NEEDED** something that is needed, especially the sum of money required or the action that needs to be taken (*informal*) ○ *Make sure you bring the needful.* —**needfully** *adv* —**needfulness** *n*

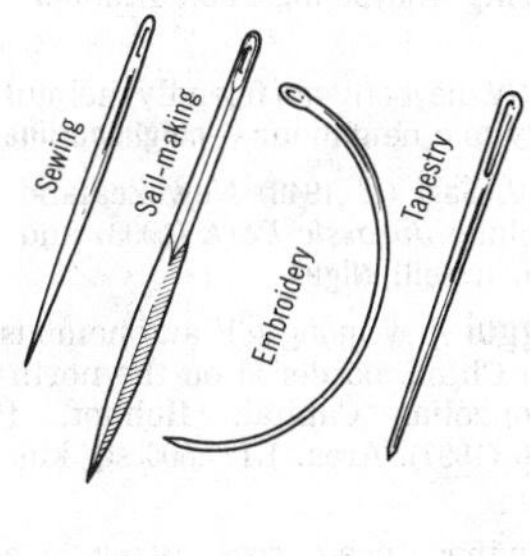

needle

needle /neéd'l/ *n* **1. SEWING TOOL** a small sharp metal pin used for sewing, with a hole at the blunt end for holding thread **2. KNITTING TOOL** a pointed rod used in knitting **3. POINTER** a pointed indicator on a dial, scale, or scientific instrument such as a compass or a car's speedometer **4. SYRINGE** a hypodermic syringe, or the hollow pointed end of one **5. ACUPUNCTURE TOOL** a small sharp metal pin used in acupuncture to stimulate points on the body **6. STYLUS** the stylus on a record player **7. CONIFER LEAF** a small pointed leaf of a conifer tree ○ *pine needles* **8. POINTED PART** a long thin pointed part of an animal's body, e.g. a porcupine quill or a sea urchin spine **9. ENMITY** a feeling of antagonism or hostility (*informal*) **10.** CRYSTALS **POINTED CRYSTAL** a long thin pointed crystal **11.** ARCHIT **OBELISK** a tall stone pillar **12.** HANDICRAFT **ENGRAVING TOOL** a sharp tool used in engraving **13.** CONSTR **SUPPORTING BEAM** a beam that passes through a wall as a temporary support ■ *vt* (**-dles, -dling, -dled**) **1. PROVOKE** to tease or provoke somebody, especially repeatedly in an indirect way (*informal*) **2.** HANDICRAFT **USE NEEDLE ON SOMETHING** to sew, prick, or pierce something with a needle [Old English *nǣdl* < Indo-European, 'sew'] —**needler** *n*

needlecord /neéd'l kawrd/ *n* corduroy fabric with very fine ribs

needlecraft /neéd'l kraaft/ *n* sewing as a skill or craft

needle exchange *n* a public health programme that allows drug addicts to exchange used hypodermic needles for new ones in an effort to stop the spread of disease and infection

needlefish /neéd'l fish/ *n* a carnivorous sea fish with a very long slender body and long jaws with sharp teeth. Native to: tropical and subtropical waters. Family: Belonidae.

needle grass *n* PLANTS same as **feather grass**

needle match *n* a bitterly fought contest between two competitors or teams who bear each other a grudge (*informal*)

needlepoint /neéd'l poynt/ *n* (*often used before a noun*) **1.** embroidery done with thick coloured threads on canvas or plain cloth, usually in uniform diagonal stitches **2.** lace made with a needle worked on a paper pattern

Needles /neéd'lz/ group of three chalk rocks in southwestern England, situated in the sea off the western tip of the Isle of Wight. Height: 30 m/100 ft.

needless /neédləss/ *adj* without reason or justification —**needlessly** *adv* —**needlessness** *n*

needle time *n* the amount of time that a radio station spends playing music [< the use of a record player]

needle valve *n* a valve in which the flow of a fluid or gas is precisely controlled by a needle-shaped insert in a conical seat

needlewoman /neéd'l wŏŏmən/ (*plural* **-women** /-wimin/) *n* HANDICRAFT same as **seamstress**

needlework /neéd'l wurk/ *n* **1.** a craft that involves the use of a needle, e.g. sewing, needlepoint, embroidery, quilting, crochet, or knitting **2.** an example of needlework —**needleworker** *n*

needn't /neéd'nt/ *contr* need not (*informal*)

needs /needz/ *adv* used before or after 'must' to reinforce necessity, urgency, or inevitability (*archaic*) ○ *'any abstract ideas that are once true must needs be eternal'* (John Locke, *An Essay Concerning Human Understanding*; 1690)

need-to-know *adj* **FOR AUTHORIZED RECIPIENTS ONLY** intended for or relating to people and agencies deemed as secure recipients of classified information, so that they can use the information in fulfilling a mission ■ *n* **1. AUTHORIZED PERSON** a person regarded as a secure recipient of classified information essential in the fulfilment of a mission **2.** *N Am* **IMPORTANT FACT** an essential fact about something ○ *a list of college need-to-knows*

needy /neédi/ (**-ier, -iest**) *adj* **1.** living in poverty ○ *gifts for needy children* **2.** feeling or showing a strong need for affection, love, or other emotional support —**needily** *adv* —**neediness** *n*

neem /neem/ *n* a tall evergreen tree grown for its bark, resin, and seed oil, which have medicinal and insecticidal properties. On Hindu New Year's Day, in southern India, its bitter leaves and flowers are symbolically savoured with jaggery to signal acceptance of the pleasant and the unpleasant in life. Native to: South Asia. Latin name: *Azadirachta indica*. [Early 19C. Via Hindi *nīm* < Sanskrit *nimba*]

neep /neep/ *n N England, Scotland* a turnip or swede [Pre-12C. < Latin *napus*]

ne'er /nair/ *adv* same as **never** (*archaic or literary*) [13C. Contraction]

Ne'erday /náir day/ *n Scotland* CALENDAR same as **New Year's Day** [Mid-19C. Contraction]

ne'er-do-well (*dated*) *n* a lazy and irresponsible person ■ *adj* lazy and irresponsible

nefarious /ni fáiri əss/ *adj* utterly immoral or wicked [Early 17C. < Latin *nefarius* < *nefas* 'sin' < *ne* 'not' + *fas* 'divine law'] —**nefariously** *adv* —**nefariousness** *n*

Nefertiti /néffər teéti/ (*fl* 14th century BC) queen of ancient Egypt. As the chief wife of King Akhenaton, she supported his religious and cultural reforms. Her carved and painted image is a famous surviving Egyptian artwork.

neg. *abbr* negative

negate /ni gáyt/ (**-gates, -gating, -gated**) *vt* **1.** to declare officially that something is invalid or ineffective, or make something invalid or ineffective (*formal*) ○ *Failure to disclose such a change of circumstances would automatically negate the policy.* ○ *a theory that negates all previous research* **2.** LOGIC to deny the truth of something, or prove something to be false [Early 17C. < Latin *negat-*, past participle of *negare* 'deny'] —**negator** *n*

SYNONYMS See ***nullify.***

negation /ni gáysh'n/ *n* **1. DENIAL OR ANNULMENT** the denying, disproving, or nullifying of something **2. NEGATIVE OF SOMETHING** the opposite of something regarded as positive, or the absence of such a thing ○ *The existence of happiness implies its negation.* **3.** LOGIC **LOGICAL DENIAL** a statement of denial or contradiction, especially an assertion that a particular proposition is false

negative /néggətiv/ *adj* **1. INDICATIVE OF 'NO'** indicating 'no', or refusing or denying something ○ *a negative response* **2. BAD** unhappy, discouraging, angry, or otherwise detracting from a happy situation ○ *negative feelings* **3. PESSIMISTIC** pessimistic, or tending to have a pessimistic outlook ○ *Don't be so negative; cheer up!* **4.** MED **SHOWING THAT SOMETHING IS NOT PRESENT** showing the absence of a disease or condition that is being tested for ○ *The test for cancer is negative.* **5.** MED same as **Rh negative** **6.** MATHS **LESS THAN ZERO** indicating a quantity that is less than zero ○ *a negative number* **7.** MATHS **OPPOSITE TO POSITIVE** describes something such as a quantity or angle of the same magnitude as, but opposite to, something considered positive **8.** PHYS **HAVING SAME CHARGE AS ELECTRON** with the same electric charge as that of an electron, shown by the symbol – **9.** PHYS **SHOWING DIRECTION OF CURRENT** indicating the direction towards which current flows in an external circuit **10.** PHOTOGRAPHY **WITH TONES AND COLOURS REVERSED** describes photographic film that has been exposed to light, used as a basis for preparing final prints **11.** LOGIC **OPPOSING** denying or contradicting a statement, proof, or argument **12.** BIOL **MOVING AWAY** moving or growing away from a source of stimulation such as heat or light ○ *negative tropism* ■ *n* **1. ANSWER OF 'NO'** an answer meaning 'no' ○ *answered in the negative* **2. SOMETHING OR SOMEBODY UNDESIRABLE** a person, thing, quality, or situation, that is bad, undesirable, discouraging, or otherwise detracts from satisfaction (*informal*) ○ *The area's harsh winters will be a negative for anyone who doesn't like snow.* **3. PHOTOGRAPHIC IMAGE** a photographic image, or the film containing it, that shows black and white tones reversed and colours as complementary **4.** GRAM **WORD IMPLYING 'NO'** a word that expresses the idea 'no', e.g. the words 'not', 'nothing', and 'never' **5.** LOGIC **NEGATING PROPOSITION** a statement that contradicts, denies, or disproves something **6.** ELEC **DESTINATION OF ELECTRONS** the part of an electric circuit to which the electrons flow, e.g. a terminal or the cathode where negative ions are formed in electrolytic applications **7.** MATHS **QUANTITY OPPOSITE TO POSITIVE** a number or quantity, e.g. speed, angle, or direction, that is less than zero or considered to be the opposite of positive ■ *interj* **NO** used to say 'no' to something or somebody (*formal*) ■ *vt* (**-tives, -tiving, -tived**) **1. SAY 'NO' TO SOMETHING** to refuse, reject, deny, cancel, or forbid something (*formal*) ○ *'a polite request that Elizabeth would lead the way, which the other politely and more earnestly negatived'* (Jane Austen, *Pride And Prejudice*; 1813) **2.** LOGIC **DISPROVE PROPOSITION** to contradict or invalidate a proposition (*informal*) —**negativeness** *n* —**negativity** /néggə tívvəti/ *n*

negative equity *n* a situation in which, as a result of falling prices, a piece of property is worth less than the amount of money that was borrowed to buy it

negative feedback *n* in an electronic or mechanical system, the redirecting of part of the output back to the input as a way of improving the quality of the output

negative gearing *n Aus* a tax reduction available to somebody who has borrowed money to pay for an investment such as shares or a house and whose income from that investment is less than the loan repayments

negatively /néggətivli/ *adv* **1. SAYING 'NO'** in a way that means 'no' **2. ADVERSELY** in an adverse way ○ *patients reacting negatively to the medication* **3. PESSIMISTICALLY** in a pessimistic or defeatist way **4.** PHYS **WITH NEGATIVE ELECTRICAL CHARGE** with the same electric charge as that of one or more electrons, shown by the symbol –

negative reinforcement *n* encouragement of a desired response by giving an unpleasant stimulus when the response is absent, or discouragement of an undesired response by an unpleasant stimulus when the response is present

negative staining *n* staining of an area around a biological subject, rather than the subject itself, so that the subject can be clearly seen against it

negativism /néggətivizəm/ *n* **1.** a strong tendency to be pessimistic, to assess situations in the worst light, or to be unreasonably sceptical about generally accepted beliefs **2.** persistent defiance of authority and refusal to obey instructions —**negativist** *n* —**negativistic** /néggəti vístik/ *adj*

Negeb ♦ **Negev**

Negeri Sembilan /néggri sem beélən/ state in southwestern Malaysia. Capital: Seremban. Population: 810,500 (1997). Area: 6,643 sq. km/2,565 sq. mi.

Negev /néggev/, **Negeb** /néggeb/ desert region in Israel, comprising the southern half of the country. Area: 12,800 sq. km/4,940 sq. mi.

neglect /ni glékt/ *vt* (**-glects, -glecting, -glected**) **1. NOT CARE FOR SOMETHING PROPERLY** to fail to give the proper or required care and attention to somebody or something **2. FAIL TO DO SOMETHING** to fail to do something, especially because of carelessness, forgetfulness, or indifference ○ *neglected to tell him* ■ *n* **1. WITHHOLDING OF PROPER CARE** the act of failing to give proper care or attention to somebody or something ○ *parents charged with criminal neglect* **2. LACK OF PROPER CARE** the effect of lack of proper care or

attention ○ *Soon the business began to suffer from neglect.* [Early 16C. < Latin *neglect-*, past participle of *neglegere* < *legere* 'choose'] —**neglecter** *n* —**neglectful** *adj*

SYNONYMS See ***overlook***.

negligée /néggli zhay/, **negligé** *n* **1.** a woman's dressing gown made of light often see-through fabric **2.** informal dress (*dated formal*) [Mid-18C. < French *négligé*, past participle of *négliger* (see NEGLIGIBLE)]

negligence /négglijənss/ *n* **1. CONDITION OF BEING NEGLIGENT** the condition or quality of being negligent **2.** LAW **CIVIL WRONG CAUSING INJURY OR HARM** a civil wrong (**tort**) causing injury or harm to another person or to property as the result of doing something or failing to provide a proper or reasonable level of care **3. CASUALNESS** casualness in matters of dress or general appearance, whether regarded as stylish or slovenly (*dated formal*) ○ *'clad in an artist's velvet, but with none of an artist's negligence'* (G. K. Chesterton, *The Wisdom of Father Brown*; 1914)

negligent /négglijənt/ *adj* **1. HABITUALLY CARELESS** habitually careless or irresponsible **2.** LAW **GUILTY OF NEGLIGENCE** guilty of failing to provide a proper or reasonable level of care **3. CASUAL IN APPEARANCE** casual in matters of dress or general appearance, whether considered stylish or slovenly (*literary*) [14C. Via French < Latin *negligent-*, present participle of *negligere*, variant of *neglegere* (see NEGLECT)] —**negligently** *adv*

negligible /négglijəb'l/ *adj* too small or unimportant to be worth considering [Early 19C. < obsolete French *négligible* < *négliger* 'to neglect' < Latin *neglegere* (see NEGLECT)] —**negligibility** /négglijə bílləti/ *n* —**negligibly** *adv*

negotiable /ni gṓshəb'l, -gṓshi əb'l/ *adj* **1. OPEN TO DISCUSSION** not fixed but able to be established or changed through discussion and compromise ○ *Salary is negotiable, according to age and experience.* **2. NAVIGABLE** able to be crossed, passed, or successfully dealt with **3.** FIN **EXCHANGEABLE FOR MONEY** describes financial instruments such as cheques and securities that can be transferred to another person in exchange for money ■ *n* FIN **SOMETHING EXCHANGEABLE FOR MONEY** a negotiable financial instrument (*usually used in the plural*) —**negotiability** /ni gṓshə bílləti, -gṓshi ə-/ *n* —**negotiably** *adv*

negotiant /ni gṓshi ənt/ *n* **1.** a dealer or trader, especially somebody in the wine trade **2.** somebody who negotiates (*archaic*)

negotiate /ni gṓshi ayt/ (**-ates, -ating, -ated**) *v* **1.** *vti* **DISCUSS TERMS OF AGREEMENT** to attempt to come to an agreement on something through discussion and compromise **2.** *vt* **NAVIGATE SOMETHING SUCCESSFULLY** to manage to get past or deal with something that constitutes a hazard or obstacle ○ *A canoe can negotiate these waters when the wind is calm.* **3.** *vt* FIN **SELL SOMETHING** to transfer ownership of a financial instrument such as a cheque or security to somebody else in exchange for money [Late 16C. < Latin *negotiat-*, past participle of *negotiari* 'do business' < *negotium* 'business' < *neg-* 'not' + *otium* 'leisure'] —**negotiator** *n*

negotiation /ni gṓshi áysh'n/ *n* **1. RESOLVING OF DISAGREEMENTS** the reaching of agreement through discussion and compromise ○ *matters still under negotiation* **2. NAVIGATION** the tackling of a hazard or problem (*formal*) ■ **negotiations** *npl* **DISCUSSION SESSIONS** one or more meetings at which attempts are made to reach agreement through discussion and compromise ○ *Negotiations are already under way between the opposing factions.*

Negress /neégress, -grəss/ *n* an offensive term for a Black woman (*dated*) [Late 18C. < French *négress* < *nègre* < Latin *nigr-* 'black']

Negrillo /ni gríllō/ (*plural* **-los** or **-loes**) *n* a member of a people of central and southern Africa [Mid-19C. < Spanish, 'small Black person' < *negro* (see NEGRO[1])]

Negrito /ni greétō/ (*plural* **-tos** or **-toes**) *n* a member of some of the peoples of Austronesia [Early 19C. < Spanish, 'small Black person' < *negro* (see NEGRO[1])]

negritude /néggri tyood/ *n* identity as a Black person, especially awareness of a distinct Black history and culture as something to be proud of [Mid-20C. Via French *négritude* < Latin *nigritudo* < *nigr-* 'black']

Negro[1] /neégrō/ (*plural* **-groes**) *n* an offensive term for a Black person, often considered an acceptable term in historically established phrases such as baseball's Negro Leagues [Mid-16C. < Spanish and Portuguese < Latin *nigr-* 'black']

Negro[2] /néggrō/ **1.** river in northwestern South America that rises in eastern Colombia and flows southeastwards to empty into the Amazon in northern Brazil. Length: 2,300 km/1,400 mi. **2.** river in central Argentina flowing eastwards into the Atlantic Ocean. Length: 640 km/400 mi.

Negroid /neé groyd/ *adj* an offensive term meaning belonging or relating to a group, in a former classification of humankind, that originated in Africa (*dated*)

negrophile /neégrō fīl/ *n* an offensive term for a person who favours the interests of Black people —**negrophilia** /neégrō filli ə/ *n* —**negrophilism** /ni gróffilizəm/ *n*

Negro spiritual *n* MUSIC, RELIG same as **spiritual** *n* (sense 1)

negus /neégəss/ *n* a hot drink made of port or sherry with water, sugar, lemon juice, and spices [Mid-18C. After Francis *Negus* (d.1732), English colonel]

Negus /neé gəss/ *n* a title formerly used for the king or emperor of Ethiopia [Late 16C. < Amharic *n'gus* 'kinged, king']

Neh. *abbr* BIBLE Nehemiah

Nehemiah /neé i mī ə/ *n* **1.** in the Bible, a Jewish leader and governor of Judaea. He was responsible for rebuilding Jerusalem in 444 BC. **2.** a book of the Bible that describes the rebuilding of Jerusalem in the 5th century BC and the reforms undertaken after its completion, traditionally attributed to Nehemiah. See table at **Bible**

Nehru /náir oo/, **Jawaharlal** (1889–1964) Indian politician. He became a leading member of the Indian National Congress and the political heir of Mohandas Karamchand Gandhi, taking an active part in the civil disobedience campaigns of the 1930s and 1940s leading to Independence. He was the first prime minister of independent India (1947–64) and a leader of nonaligned nations during the Cold War. Indira Gandhi was his daughter.

> 'At the stroke of the midnight hour, India will awake to life and freedom. A moment comes, which comes but rarely in history, when we step out from the old to the new, when an age ends, and when the sound of a nation, long suppressed, finds utterance.' [Jawaharlal Nehru, *Speech to the Lok Sabha, the lower house of the Indian parliament just before independence was declared*; 14 August 1947]

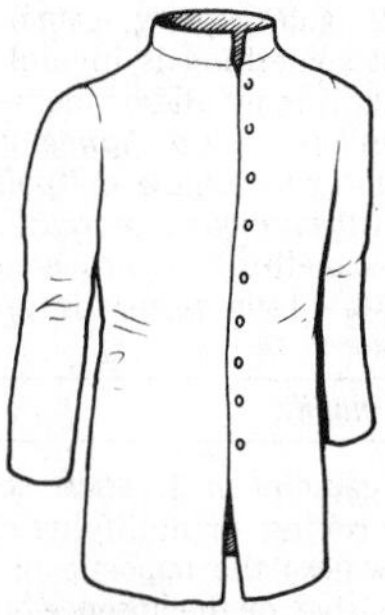

Nehru jacket

Nehru jacket *n* a long narrow jacket with a high stand-up collar [Mid-20C. After Jawaharlal NEHRU]

~~**neice**~~ incorrect spelling of **niece**

neigh /nay/ *n* the long high-pitched sound that a horse makes ■ *vi* (**neighs, neighing, neighed**) to make the high-pitched sound characteristic of a horse [Old English *hnǣgan*, origin ?]

neighbor, etc. US spelling of **neighbour, etc.**

neighbour /náybər/ *n* **1. SOMEBODY LIVING NEARBY** somebody who lives next door or close to somebody else **2. SOMETHING OR SOMEBODY NEARBY** a person, place, or thing located next to another or very nearby ○ *the Spanish and their Portuguese neighbours* **3. FELLOW HUMAN** a fellow human being (*archaic or literary*) ■ *vti* (**-bours, -bouring, -boured**) **BE NEAR TO SOMETHING OR SOMEBODY** to be located very close to something or somebody, or be close to something in character [Old English *nēahgebūr* < *nēah* 'near' + *gebūr* 'dweller']

neighbourhood /náybər hŏŏd/ *n* **1. COMMUNITY** a local community with characteristics that distinguish it from the areas around it **2. PEOPLE LIVING NEAR EACH OTHER** people who live near each other or in a specific neighbourhood ○ *The whole neighbourhood turned out for the picnic.* **3. VICINITY** the general vicinity or surrounding area of a place ○ *Stop by if you're in the neighbourhood.* **4. APPROXIMATION OF AMOUNT** an approximate amount, size, or range (*informal*) ○ *expenses in the neighbourhood of £175,000* **5.** MATHS **SURROUNDING POINTS** the set of all points within a given distance from an identified point

neighbourhood watch *n* a nationwide scheme to raise awareness of crime and crime prevention within local communities, with members taking part in various initiatives, including keeping watch on one another's homes

neighbouring /náybəring/ *adj* situated or located nearby

neighbourly /náybərli/ *adj* friendly, helpful, and kind, especially to a neighbour —**neighbourliness** *n*

Neill /neel/, **Sam** (*b.* 1948) New Zealand actor. His films include *Jurassic Park* (1993) and *The Piano* (1993). Born **Neill, Nigel**

Nei Monggol /náy mōng g'l/ autonomous region of northern China, bordered on the north by Russia and Mongolia. Capital: Hohhot. Population: 23,070,000 (1997). Area: 1,177,500 sq. km/454,640 sq. mi.

neither /nī*th*ər, neé-/ CORE MEANING: a negative grammatical word that introduces or connects two people, things, or situations, both of which are excluded ○ (det) *Neither shirt looks good on you.* ○ (pron) *Neither of the boys wants to go.* ○ (pron) *'Would you like pork or fish'? 'Neither, thank you'.* ○ (conj) *Neither my father nor my mother commented.* **1.** *det, pron* **EXCLUDES BOTH** not one or the other ○ (det) *Neither machine works.* ○ (pron) *I like neither of them.* ○ (pron) *Neither is true.* **2.** *conj* **INTRODUCES ALTERNATIVES** used preceding two alternatives joined by 'nor' to indicate that both did not happen or are not true ○ *Neither my boss nor his wife can cook.* **3.** *adv, conj* **INDICATES THAT ALSO EXCLUDED** used to indicate a second person or thing, or group of people or things, that can also be included in a negative statement just made, or that the previous negative statement ought to apply in the second case also ○ *'We've never been to Paris'. 'Neither have I'.* ○ *She doesn't want to go? Me neither!* ○ *She can't play today, and neither can her brother.* **4.** *adv* **INTRODUCES MODIFICATION OF NEGATIVE** used in a statement that indicates a modification or partial contradiction of a previous negative statement ○ *You won't find it hot, but neither will you be freezing cold.* [12C. Alteration (influenced by EITHER) of Old English *nawþer*, contraction of *nāhwæþer* < *nā* 'not' + *hwæþer* 'which of two']

USAGE neither meaning **none** Do not substitute ***neither*** for the pronoun ***none*** in the sense 'not one of several', as in *Neither of these (four) options has any appeal.* Say instead: *None* [or *Not one*] *of these (four) options has any appeal.* When you use ***neither*** as a conjunction, follow it with ***nor***, not *or*, and make the verb agree with the nearest noun: *Neither rain nor snow* [not *or snow*] *is* [not *are*] *going to stop mail delivery.*

nekton /nék ton/ *n* an organism such as a fish that lives in water and can actively swim against currents, as opposed to microorganisms that are simply carried along [Late 19C. < Greek *nēkton*, form of *nēktos* 'swimming' < *nēkhein* 'to swim'] —**nektonic** /nek tónnik/ *adj*

nelly /nélli/ (*plural* **-lies**), **nellie** *n* **1.** a man or boy who is regarded as weak or cowardly (*dated informal insult*) **2.** an offensive term for an effeminate or gay man (*insult*) [Mid-20C. < pet form of the name *Helen* or *Eleanor*]

nelson /nélss'n/ *n* a wrestling hold in which one arm (**half nelson**) or both arms (**full nelson**) are passed through the opponent's arms from behind and pulled back, levering against the opponent's back [Late 19C. Origin ?]

Nelson /nélss'n/ **1.** industrial town in Lancashire, northwestern England. Population: 29,120 (1991). **2.** city in New Zealand, on the northern coast of the South Island. Situated at the mouth of the River Matai, it is an agricultural and tourist centre. Population: 53,688 (2001). **3.** administrative region of New Zealand, located in the north of the South Island. It

is the site of Kahurangi, Nelson Lakes, and Abel Tasman national parks. Population: 41,568 (2001). Area: 1,114 sq. km/430 sq. mi.

Nelson, Horatio, Viscount (1758–1805) British naval commander. He defeated the French and Spanish naval forces at Trafalgar (1805) but was killed during the battle. His affair with Emma, Lady Hamilton caused a considerable scandal.

> 'England expects every man will do his duty.'
> [Horatio Nelson, at the Battle of Trafalgar. Quoted in *Life of Nelson*, Robert Southey; 1813]

Nelspruit /nélsproyt/ capital of Mpumalanga Province in northeastern South Africa. Population: 21,474 (1991).

nemat- *prefix* same as **nemato-** (*used before vowels*)

nematic /ni máttik/ *adj* describes a phase of liquid crystals in which the axes of the molecules become parallel in response to a magnetic field [Early 20C. < Greek *nēmat-* 'thread']

nematicide *n* BIOCHEM same as **nematocide**

nemato- *prefix* **1.** thread, resembling a thread ○ *nematocyst* **2.** nematode ○ *nematocide* [< Greek *nēmat-* 'thread' < Indo-European, 'spin']

nematocide /ne máttō sīd/, **nematicide** /ne mátti-/ *n* a substance that destroys nematodes —**nematocidal** /ne máttō sīd'l/ *adj*

nematocyst /némmə tō sist/ *n* a sting found in animals of the jellyfish family. It comprises a fluid-filled sac within which is a coiled hollow thread that is rapidly turned outwards (**everted**) to capture food or for defence.

nematode /némmə tōd/ *n* a worm, often microscopic, with a cylindrical unsegmented body protected by a tough outer skin (**cuticle**). Phylum: Nematoda. [Mid-19C. < modern Latin *Nematoda* < Greek *nēmat-* (see NEMATO-)]

nematology /némmə tólləji/ *n* the branch of zoology that is concerned with the study of nematodes — **nematological** /némmətə lójjik'l/ *adj* —**nematologically** *adv* —**nematologist** *n*

nem. con. /ném kón/ *adv* without opposition ○ *The motion was carried nem. con.* [< shortening of Latin *nemine contradicente* 'with no one contradicting']

Nemean lion /ni meé ən-/ *n* in Greek mythology, the huge lion that Heracles killed as the first of his twelve labours [Late 16C. After *Nemea*, district in ancient Greece]

nemertean /ni múrti ən/ *n* same as **ribbon worm** (*technical*) [Mid-19C. < modern Latin *Nemertes* < Greek *Nēmertēs* 'Nereid'] —**nemertean** *adj* —**nemertine** /némmər tīn, -teen/ *adj*

nemesis /némməssiss/ (*plural* **-eses** /-əsseez/) *n* (*literary*) **1.** a person or force that inflicts punishment or revenge **2.** punishment that is deserved, especially when it results in somebody's downfall [Late 16C. < Greek, 'Nemesis, righteous indignation' < *nemein* 'distribute what is due']

Nemesis /némməssiss/ *n* in Greek mythology, the goddess of just punishment or vengeance [< Greek (see NEMESIS)]

NEMS *n* a computer chip that has integrated devices on a molecular scale for sensing, processing, or carrying out various functions. Full form **nano-micro-electromechanical system**

nene /náy nay/ (*plural same* or **-nes**) *n* a rare wild goose with a greyish-brown body and a black face. Native to: Hawaiian Islands. Latin name: *Branta sandvicensis*. [Early 20C. < Hawaiian]

NEO *abbr* ASTRON near-earth object

neo- *prefix* new, recent ○ *neotype* ○ *neo-Darwinism* [< Greek *neos* < Indo-European]

neo-Confucian *adj, n*	**neoorthodox** *adj*
neo-Confucianism *n*	**neoorthodoxy** *n*
neo-Freudian *adj, n*	**neorealism** *n*
neo-Freudianism *n*	**neorealist** *n, adj*
neo-Georgian *adj*	**neorealistic** *adj*
neo-Gothic *adj, n*	**neoromantic** *adj*
neo-Malthusian *adj, n*	**neo-Scholastic** *adj*
neo-Malthusianism *n*	**neo-Scholasticism** *n*
neo-Marxism *n*	**neosurrealism** *n*
neo-Marxist *n, adj*	**neosurrealist** *n*
neo-noir *adj*	**neosurrealistic** *adj*

neoclassical: front porch of Monticello, Charlottesville, Virginia, USA (begun 1770)

neoclassical /neé ō klássik'l/, **neoclassic** /-klássik/ *adj* **1.** ARTS, ARCHIT OF REVIVAL OF CLASSICAL ART FORMS relating to or belonging to a style of art and architecture prevalent in the late 18th and early 19th centuries, characterized by the simple, symmetrical forms of ancient Greek and Roman art **2.** LITERAT OF CLASSICAL REVIVAL relating to or characteristic of the European revival of Greek and Roman literary forms **3.** MUSIC OF FORMAL MUSICAL STYLE relating to a movement in the late 19th and early 20th centuries that favoured the more formal style of composers before the Romantic movement **4.** ECON OF MACROECONOMIC MONETARIST THEORY relating to macroeconomic monetarist theories that emphasize the need for the free operation of market forces —**neoclassicism** *n* —**neoclassicist** *n, adj*

neocolonialism /neé ō kə lốni əlizəm/ *n* the domination by a powerful, usually Western nation of another nation that is politically independent but has a weak economy greatly dependent on trade with the powerful nation —**neocolonial** *adj* —**neocolonialist** *n, adj*

neoconservative /neé ō kən súrvətiv/ *n* somebody who, during the mid-1980s, began to support conservatism in society, and in politics in particular, as a reaction to the social freedoms sought throughout the 1960s and early 1970s —**neoconservative** *adj* —**neoconservatism** *n*

neocortex /neé ō káwr teks/ (*plural* **-tices** /-tə seez/ or **-texes**) *n* the roof of the cerebral cortex that forms the part of the mammalian brain that has evolved most recently and makes possible higher brain functions such as learning —**neocortical** /-káwrtik'l/ *adj*

neo-Darwinism *n* a theory of evolution that combines Darwin's theory and modern genetics, especially with regard to variations in populations as a result of genetic mutations —**neo-Darwinian** *adj* —**neo-Darwinist** *n, adj*

neodymium /neé ō dímmi əm/ *n* a silvery-white or yellowish metallic element that is one of the lanthanide series of rare-earth elements. Source: monazite, bastnaesite. Use: lasers, glass manufacture. Symbol **Nd**. See table at **element** [Late 19C. < NEO- + DIDYMIUM]

neo-expressionism *n* a 20th-century art movement, begun in Germany, Italy, and the United States, and based on expressionism, that focuses on the artist's inner experiences and often produces violent or erotic paintings —**neo-expressionist** *n, adj*

neofascism /neé ō fáshizəm/ *n* **1.** the modern-day revival of Fascist beliefs of the 1930s and 1940s, which assume that a supposed Aryan race is superior to all others and attempt to justify genocide **2.** the views or actions of any modern-day white group or movement that holds racist views, especially anyone involved in the violent intimidation of non-white people —**neofascist** *adj, n*

neofascist /neé ō fáshist/ *adj* **1.** OF MODERN-DAY FASCISTS relating to, or typical of, any modern-day movement inspired by the racial intolerance and militarism of the Fascists and Nazis of the 1930s and 1940s **2.** OF WHITE RACISTS relating to the members, views, or actions of any modern-day group or movement of white people with violently racist views, especially those involved in the violent intimidation of non-whites ■ *n* MODERN-DAY FASCIST OR WHITE RACIST somebody who currently holds fascist or white racist opinions

Neogene /neé ō jeen/ *n* a period of geological time from 23.3 million to 1.64 million years ago that

includes both the Miocene and Pliocene epochs [Late 19C. < NEO- + Greek *-genēs* 'born'] —**Neogene** *adj*

neogenesis /neé ō jénnəssiss/ *n* the regrowth of living tissue —**neogenetic** /-jə néttik/ *adj* —**neogenetically** *adv*

neoimpressionism /neé ō im présh'nizəm/ *n* a 19th-century movement in painting, led by the pointillist Georges Seurat, that favoured stricter and more formal techniques of composition than impressionism —**neoimpressionist** *adj, n*

neo-Lamarckism /neé ō lə maárkizəm/ *n* a theory of evolution that modifies Lamarckism by emphasizing the ways environment influences genetic variations —**neo-Lamarckian** *adj, n*

Neo-Latin *n, adj* LANG same as **New Latin** ■ *adj* relating to a language that has developed from Latin

neoliberalism /neé ō líbbərəlizəm/ *n* the political view, arising in the 1960s, that emphasizes the importance of economic growth and asserts that social justice is best maintained by minimal government interference and free market forces —**neoliberal** *adj, n*

neolith /neé ō lith/ *n* a stone tool from the Neolithic period

Neolithic /neé ō líthik/ *n* the latest period of the Stone Age, between about 8000 BC and 5000 BC, characterized by the development of settled agriculture and the use of polished stone tools and weapons —**Neolithic** *adj*

neologise *vi* LING another spelling of **neologize**

neologism /ni óllǝjizǝm/, **neology** /ni ólləji/ (*plural* **-gies**) *n* **1.** a recently coined word or phrase, or a recently extended meaning of an existing word or phrase **2.** the practice of coining new words or phrases, or of extending the meaning of existing words or phrases [Early 19C. < French *néologisme* < *néo-* 'new' + Greek *logos* 'word'] —**neologist** *n*

neologize /ni óllə jīz/ (**-gizes, -gizing, -gized**), **neologise** (**-gises, -gising, -gised**) *vi* to coin new words or phrases, or extend the meaning of existing words or phrases

neology *n* LING same as **neologism**

neo-Melanesian *n* a creole language based on English with borrowings from other languages that is used in island groups of the southwestern Pacific —**neo-Melanesian** *adj*

neomycin /neé ō míssin/ *n* an antibiotic with a wide range of effectiveness. Source: the bacterium *Streptomyces fradiae*. Use: treatment of skin, eye, and intestinal infections.

neon /neé on, -ən/ *n* **1.** a colourless odourless gaseous element that occurs in very small quantities in the air and glows orange when electricity is passed through it. Symbol **Ne**. See table at **element 2.** lighting produced by neon lights or by lamps containing similar gases such as argon or krypton **3.** (*plural* **-ons** or *same*) FISH same as **neon tetra** [Late 19C. < Greek, form of *neos* 'new']

neonate /neé ō nayt/ *n* a newborn child, especially one less than one month old [Early 20C. < NEO- + Latin *natus*, past participle of *nasci* 'be born'] —**neonatal** /neé ō náyt'l/ *adj*

neonatology /neé ō nay tólləji/ *n* the branch of medicine that deals with the care and development of newborn babies and the treatment of their diseases —**neonatological** /neé ō náytə lójjik'l/ *adj* —**neonatologist** *n*

neo-Nazi *n* **1.** a member of a modern-day movement that promotes the idea that a supposed race of Aryans is superior to all others and that genocide is justifiable **2.** a member of any modern-day group or movement of white people who hold racist views, especially those involved in violent attacks on non-white people —**neo-Nazism** *n*

neon light, neon lamp *n* a light with a bulb, usually tube-shaped, containing neon gas, that glows orange when a high-voltage electric current is passed through it. Neon lights are used for display signs and television tubes.

neon tetra *n* a small iridescent blue and red fish, often kept in aquariums. Native to: Amazon. Latin name: *Hyphessobrycon innesi*. [< its bright colours like neon glowing]

neopagan /neé ō páygən/ *n* a believer in a modernized version of the principles of old pre-Christian re-

ligions, especially reverence for nature and natural objects rather than worship of a transcendent supreme being —**neopaganism** n

neophilia /neé ō fílli ə/ n a liking for new things, change for the sake of change, or novelty —**neophile** /neé ō fíl/ n —**neophiliac** n, adj

neophyte /neé ō fít/ n 1. BEGINNER a beginner or novice at something 2. RECENT CONVERT a recent convert to a religion 3. RELIGIOUS NOVICE a new resident of a religious community who has not yet taken vows [14C. Via late Latin neophytus < Greek neophutos 'newly planted' < phuein 'plant, cause to grow'] —**neophytic** /neé ō fíttik/ adj

neoplasia /neé ō pláyzi ə/ n the formation or existence of tumours

neoplasm /neé ō plazəm/ n a tumour or tissue containing a growth [Late 19C. < NEO- + Greek plasma 'formation' < plassein 'to form']

neoplastic /neé ō plástik/ adj 1. relating to neoplasms or neoplasty 2. relating to neoplasticism

neoplasticism /neé ō plástissizəm/ n a style of abstract painting, as found in the work of Mondrian, using black, grey, white, and the primary colours, and horizontal and vertical lines and planes

neoplasty /neé ō plasti/ n the surgical construction of new tissue, or the repair of damaged tissue

neo-Platonism, Neoplatonism /neé ō pláytənizəm/ n a philosophical system combining Platonism with mysticism and Judaic and Christian ideas and positing one source for all existence, developed by Plotinus and his followers in the 3rd century AD —**neo-Platonic** adj —**neo-Platonist** n

neoprene /neé ō preen/ n a synthetic material resembling rubber, but slower to perish and more resistant to oil. Use: in the manufacture of equipment for which waterproofing is important. [Mid-20C. < NEO- + CHLOROPRENE]

neostigmine /neé ō stíg meen/ n a white crystalline compound. Use: treatment of myasthenia. [Mid-20C. < NEO- + PHYSOSTIGMINE]

neoteny /ni óttəni/ n the existence of juvenile features in an adult animal, e.g. the retention of gills in some salamanders [Late 19C. < NEO- + Greek teinein 'stretch, extend']

neoteric /neé ō térrik/ adj having a contemporary origin [Late 16C. Via Latin < Greek neōterikos 'youthful']

Neotropical /neé ō tróppik'l/, **Neotropic** /-tróppik/ adj relating to a geographical area of plant and animal distribution east, south, and west of Mexico's central plateau that includes Central and South America and the Caribbean

neotype /neé ō típ/ n a specimen of a plant or animal selected to replace an original representative example used in classification (**holotype**) that has been lost or destroyed —**neotypical** /neé ō típpik'l/ adj

NEPAD n S Africa an organization established in 2001 by Africa's political leaders to implement an integrated social and economic development programme for the whole continent. Full form **New Partnership for Africa's Development**

Nepal

Nepal /nə páwl/ country in South Asia, northeast of India, in the Himalayan range. Language: Nepali. Currency: rupee. Capital: Kathmandu. Population: 26,469,569 (2003). Area: 147,181 sq. km/56,827 sq. mi. Official name **Kingdom of Nepal** —**Nepalese** /néppə leéz/ n, adj

Nepali /ni páwli/ (plural same or **-is**) n 1. the Indic official language of Nepal, also spoken in Bhutan and northeastern India. Native speakers: 16 million. 2. somebody who comes from Nepal —**Nepali** adj

nepenthe /ni pénthi/ n 1. a supposed substance that people took in ancient times to forget their sadness or troubles, or the plant that produced the substance 2. something that eases pain or makes people forget their troubles (literary) ○ respite and nepenthe from thy memories of Lenore' (Edgar Allan Poe, The Raven; 1845) [Late 16C. < Greek nēpenthēs 'banishing pain' < nē 'not' + penthos 'grief'] —**nepenthean** adj

neper /neépər, náy-/ n a unit for comparing two currents, voltages, or related quantities, equal to the natural logarithm of the ratio of the quantities. Symbol Np [Early 20C. < Neperus Latinized name of John NAPIER]

nepheline /néffəlin, -leen/, **nephelite** /-līt/ n a white aluminosilicate of potassium and sodium. Source: igneous rocks. Use: manufacture of glass and ceramics. [Early 19C. < French < Greek nephelē 'cloud']

nephelinite /néffəli nīt/ n a fine-grained igneous rock that has nepheline and pyroxene as its main mineral ingredients

nephelite n MINERALS same as **nepheline**

nephelometer /néffə lómmitər/ n 1. an instrument that uses reflected light to measure the size or density of solid particles present in a liquid 2. an instrument used to measure the degree of cloudiness of the sky [Late 19C. < Greek nephelē 'cloud'] —**nephelometric** /néffəlō méttrik/ adj —**nephelometry** n

nephew /néffyoo, névvyoo/ n the son of somebody's brother, sister, brother-in-law, or sister-in-law [13C. Via French neveu < Latin nepot- 'sister's son, grandson']

nepho- prefix clouds ○ nephoscope [< Greek nephos 'cloud']

nephogram /néffō gram/ n a photograph of a cloud formation, especially one taken from a satellite, used in predicting weather patterns

nephograph /néffō graaf, -graf/ n a device for taking photographs of cloud formations

nephology /ne fólləji/ n the branch of meteorology concerned with the study of clouds —**nephological** /néffə lójjik'l/ adj —**nephologist** n

nephoscope /néffə skōp/ n an instrument for measuring the altitude, speed, and direction of movement of clouds

nephr- prefix same as **nephro-** (used before vowels)

nephralgia /ni fráljə/ n pain in the kidneys

nephrectomy /ni fréktəmi/ (plural **-mies**) n the surgical removal of a kidney

nephric /néffrik/ adj relating to or affecting the kidneys

nephridium /ni fríddi əm/ (plural **-ia** /-i ə/) n 1. a simple tube-shaped organ in earthworms and many other invertebrate organisms for releasing waste matter into the gut or out of the body 2. the organ that develops into the kidney in the embryo of a vertebrate animal [Late 19C. < NEPHRO- + modern Latin -idium 'small one' (< Greek -idion)] —**nephridial** adj

nephrite /néf rīt/ n a variety of jade that ranges in colour from white to dark green, containing calcium, magnesium, and iron

nephritic /ni fríttik/ adj 1. relating to or affected by nephritis 2. relating to or affecting the kidneys

nephritis /ni frítiss/ n severe inflammation of the kidney, caused by infection, degenerative disease, or disease of the blood vessels

nephro- prefix kidney ○ nephrogenous [< Greek nephros]

nephrogenous /ni frójjənəss/, **nephrogenic** /néffrō jénnik/ adj 1. located in or moving into a kidney 2. capable of developing into kidney tissue

nephrology /ni fróllǝji/ n the branch of medicine concerned with the study and treatment of diseases of the kidneys —**nephrological** /néffrō lójjik'l/ adj —**nephrologist** n

nephron /néf ron/ n a fine tubule in the kidneys of vertebrates that filters and excretes waste materials from the blood and produces urine

nephropathy /ni fróppəthi/ (plural **-thies**) n a disease or medical disorder of the kidney —**nephropathic** /néffrō páthik/ adj

nephroscope /néffrō skōp/ n a tube-shaped instrument inserted into an incision in the body wall in order to examine a patient's kidneys

nephrosis /ni fróssiss/ n a disease that causes the kidneys to degenerate without inflaming them, especially one that affects the nephrons —**nephrotic** /ni fróttik/ adj

nephrotomy /ni fróttəmi/ (plural **-mies**) n a surgical incision into a kidney

ne plus ultra /náy plooss ool traa, neé pluss úl trə/ n the highest level of excellence, or something that reaches it [Late 17C. < Latin, 'not farther beyond', supposed to have been inscribed on the Pillars of Hercules]

nepotism /néppətizəm/ n favouritism shown by somebody in power to relatives and friends, especially in appointing them to good positions [Mid-17C. < French népotisme < Latin nepot- 'grandson, sister's son'] —**nepotist** n —**nepotistic** /néppə tístik/ adj —**nepotistically** adv

Neptune /néptyoon/ n 1. the eighth planet from the Sun in our solar system 2. in Roman mythology, the god of the sea, son of Saturn, brother of Jupiter and Pluto. Greek equivalent **Poseidon** [15C. Directly or via French < Latin Neptunus]

Neptunian /nep tyoóni ən/ adj relating to the planet Neptune

neptunium /nep tyoóni əm/ n a silvery radioactive metallic element. Source: uranium ores, a by-product of plutonium production in nuclear reactors. Use: neutron detection. Symbol **Np**. See table at **element** [Late 19C. After the planet NEPTUNE, discovered after uranium (named after Uranus)]

NERC /nurk/ abbr Natural Environment Research Council

nerd /nurd/ n 1. an offensive term that deliberately insults somebody's physical appearance or social skills (slang insult) 2. somebody who is considered to be excessively interested in a subject or activity that is regarded as too technical or scientific (often used in combination; offensive in some contexts) [Mid-20C. Origin ?] —**nerdish** adj —**nerdy** adj

Nereid /neéri id/ n 1. in Greek mythology, a sea nymph, one of the 50 daughters of Nereus, a god of the sea 2. a large natural satellite of Neptune [Late 17C. Via Latin < Greek Nēreid- < Nēreus, a Greek god of the sea]

nereis /neéri iss/ (plural **-ides** /-ə deez/ or **-ises**) n a large segmented worm usually found living in saltwater, e.g. a ragworm. Genus: Nereis. [Mid-18C. Via modern Latin < Latin < Greek Nēreis form of nēreid- (see NEREID)]

neritic /nə ríttik/ adj relating to or found in shallow coastal waters [Late 19C. < Latin nerita, type of shellfish of shallow seas < Greek Nēreus, a Greek god of the sea]

Nernst /nurnst, nairnst/, **Walther** (1864–1941) German physical chemist. He developed the third law of thermodynamics and won the Nobel Prize in chemistry (1920). Full name **Nernst, Walther Hermann**

Nernst equation n an equation that shows the dependence of the electromotive force in a dry cell on the activities of the reacting chemicals and the temperature

Nero /neérō/ (AD 37–68) Roman emperor. He succeeded Claudius (AD 54), but his tyrannical and neglectful rule led to revolts against him, and he committed suicide. Born **Ahenobarbus, Lucius Domitius**. Full name **Nero, Claudius Caesar Drusus Germanicus**

nerol /neér ol, nérrol/ n a colourless alcohol. Source: neroli and other essential oils. Use: perfumes. [Early 20C. < NEROLI]

neroli /neéroli/, **neroli oil** n an oil distilled from the flowers of orange trees, especially the Seville orange. Use: aromatherapy, perfumes, food flavouring. [Late 17C. Via French < Italian, after an Italian princess who supposedly discovered the oil]

Neruda /ne roódə, -roóthə/, **Pablo** (1904–73) Chilean poet and diplomat. He is known for his socialist poetry and won the Nobel Prize in literature (1971). Pseudonym of **Reyes y Basoalto, Neftalí Ricardo**

'Peace goes into the making of a poem as flour goes into the making of bread.'
[Pablo Neruda, Memoirs; 1974]

Nerva /núrvə/ (AD 30–98) Roman emperor. He succeeded Domitian in 96, and introduced measures to help the poor. He was succeeded by his son Trajan. Full name **Nerva, Marcus Cocceius**

nerve /nurv/ n 1. FIBRE BUNDLE TRANSMITTING IMPULSES a bundle of fibres forming a network that transmits messages in the form of impulses between the brain

or spinal cord and the body's organs. Motor nerves carry impulses outwards to the muscles and glands, while sensory nerves carry inbound information about the body's movements and sensations. Mixed nerves perform both functions. **2.** COURAGE coolness, steadiness, and self-assurance ○ *lost his nerve* **3.** BOLDNESS boldness or impudence ○ *You've got a nerve!* **4.** DENT SENSITIVE PULP IN TOOTH the sensitive tissue inside the roots of a tooth **5.** BOT LEAF VEIN a vein in a leaf **6.** INSECTS VEIN IN INSECT'S WING a thin rib visible inside an insect's wing ■ **nerves** *npl* **1.** SOMEBODY'S ABILITY TO TOLERATE STRESS somebody's ability to tolerate emotional stress or excitement ○ *My nerves are shattered.* **2.** NERVOUSNESS a state of emotional agitation (*informal*) ○ *He had a bad case of nerves before every performance.* ■ *vt* **(nerves, nerving, nerved)** STEEL YOURSELF to cause somebody or yourself to muster courage or self-control in preparation for dealing with something difficult, stressful, or frightening [14C. Directly or via Old French *nerf* 'sinew' < Latin *nervus* 'nerve, sinew, tendon']

SYNONYMS See *courage*.

nerve block *n* the use of a local anaesthetic to numb a part of the body in order to prevent the transmission of pain messages to the brain

nerve cell *n* ANAT same as **neuron**

nerve centre *n* **1.** the place from which a large organization, system, or network is controlled **2.** a cluster of interconnected nerve cells that performs a specific function in the body

nerve cord *n* a strand of nerve tissue, e.g. the spinal cord, that runs the length of the body and forms a principal part of an animal's nervous system

nerve fibre *n* one of the long thin extensions of a neuron such as an axon or dendrite

nerve gas *n* a poisonous gas used as a weapon of war that attacks the central nervous system and stops people breathing

nerve impulse *n* a rapid and momentary change in electrical activity that passes along a nerve fibre to other neurons, muscles, or other body organs and signals instructions or information

nerveless /núrvləss/ *adj* **1.** NUMB having no sensation or strength **2.** FEARLESS showing calmness, courage, or confidence, especially in a dangerous situation **3.** COWARDLY lacking courage or determination —**nervelessly** *adv* —**nervelessness** *n*

nerve net *n* a simple nervous system, found in some invertebrates such as jellyfish, consisting of interconnecting nerve cells, but lacking a control centre such as a brain

nerve-racking *adj* causing great anxiety or distress

nerve trunk *n* a bundle of nerve fibres surrounded by a sheath of connective tissue that forms the main stem of a nerve

nerve-wracking *adj* same as **nerve-racking**

Nervi /náirvi/, **Pier Luigi** (1891–1979) Italian architect and engineer. His designs for large-scale public buildings, in Europe and in North and South America, make use of reinforced concrete.

nervous /núrvəss/ *adj* **1.** UNEASY having a feeling of dread or apprehension ○ *I was nervous about meeting his parents.* **2.** TIMID easily worried or frightened ○ *people of a nervous disposition* **3.** AFFECTING NERVES relating to somebody's ability to tolerate anxiety or stress ○ *a nervous illness* **4.** OF NERVES relating to or located in nerves or the nervous system ○ *nervous tissue* [14C. Originally 'sinewy'] —**nervosity** /nur vóssəti/ *n* —**nervously** *adv* —**nervousness** *n*

nervous breakdown *n* a psychiatric disorder, usually caused by intense stress or anxiety, in which somebody becomes incapable of coping with daily life and exhibits low self-esteem or depression

nervous system *n* the network of nerve cells and nerve fibres in most animals that conveys sensations to the brain and motor impulses to organs and muscles

nervous tic *n* an involuntary twitch of a muscle, especially of the face, that is sometimes a symptom of nervousness or a nervous disease

nervure /núr vyoor/ *n* **1.** a supporting structure resembling a rod that is visible inside an insect's wing **2.** BOT same as **vein** *n* (sense 4) [Early 19C. < French, 'strap' < Latin *nervus* 'nerve']

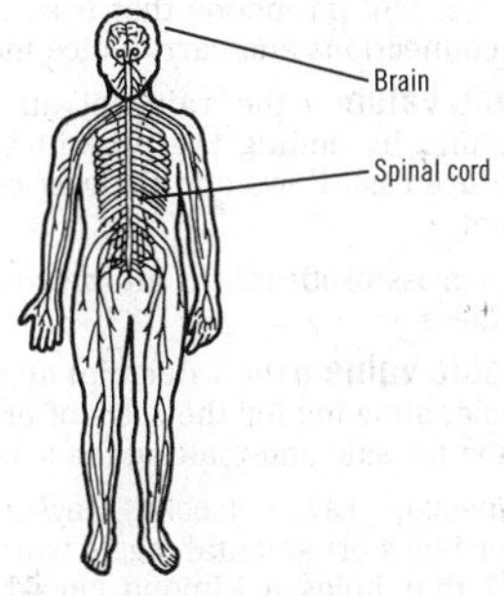

nervous system

nervy /núrvi/ (**-ier, -iest**) *adj* (*informal*) **1.** NERVOUS feeling or easily becoming worried, upset, or frightened **2.** *US* FEARLESS showing a lot of courage or foolhardiness **3.** *US* AGGRESSIVE acting in ways that show lack of respect for the boundaries or feelings of other people —**nervily** *adv* —**nerviness** *n*

Nesbit /nézbit/, **E.** (1858–1924) British novelist and poet. Her children's books include *Five Children and It* (1902), *The Phoenix and the Carpet* (1904), and *The Railway Children* (1906). Full name **Nesbit, Edith**

nesh /nesh/ *adj regional* **1.** very sensitive to cold temperatures **2.** lacking courage or self-confidence [Old English *hnesce* < Germanic]

ness /ness/ *n* a section of coastline that projects into the sea (*often used in placenames*) [Old English *næs(s)* < Indo-European]

Ness, Loch /ness/ long narrow lake in northern Scotland, forming part of the Caledonian Canal. It is believed by some people to be the home of an ancient monster. Length: 37 km/23 mi.

-ness *suffix* state, condition, quality ○ *callousness* [Old English *-nes* < Germanic]

nesselrode /néss'l rōd/, **Nesselrode** *n* a creamy frozen dessert containing puréed chestnuts, candied fruit, and usually a sweet wine or liqueur [Mid-19C. After Karl-Robert *Nesselrode* (1780–1862), Russian statesman, whose chef invented it]

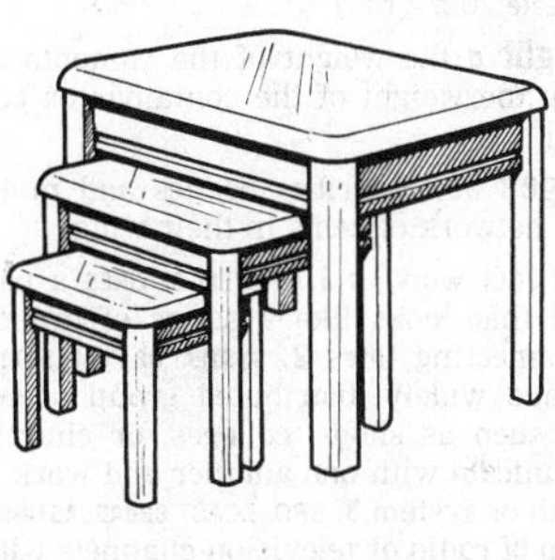
nest: nest of tables

nest /nest/ *n* **1.** BIRD OR ANIMAL HOME a structure that birds and other animals such as mice build to shelter themselves and their young, using available natural materials such as grass, twigs, and mud **2.** COMMUNITY OF ANIMALS the community of animals living in a nest **3.** SOMETHING SHAPED LIKE BIRD'S NEST something shaped more or less like a bird's nest, especially something that encloses or contains things ○ *a meringue nest* **4.** COSY PLACE a cosy, protected, or secluded place **5.** BAD PLACE a place where something bad such as crime or treason flourishes ○ *a nest of vice* **6.** CRIMINALS' SECRET PLACE a hideaway for criminals, or a group of criminals hiding away there ○ *a nest of thieves* **7.** SET OF THINGS a set of things such as tables or wooden eggs that fit one inside the other **8.** GUN EMPLACEMENT a protected or camouflaged place from which a gun or other weapon is fired ■ *v* **(nests, nesting, nested) 1.** *vi* BUILD NEST to make or live in a nest, especially in preparation for giving birth to young **2.** *vi* MAKE PLACE MORE HOME-LIKE to make a place more comfortable and home-like (*informal*) **3.** *vt* PUT THINGS TOGETHER to put one thing inside another, or group things together into a single unit, e.g. items in a reference book into a single entry or under a main heading [Old English < Indo-European 'place where a bird sits down']

nest box *n* a box for wild birds to use for breeding, placed in a park, forest, or other outdoor place

nest-building *n* **1.** the construction of a nest by a bird in preparation for having young **2.** the process of making a place more comfortable and home-like, often for an expected baby (*informal*)

nest egg *n* **1.** a sum of money put aside for future expenses or emergencies **2.** a real or artificial egg that is put in a hen's nest to encourage it to continue laying after the other eggs have been removed

nesting box /nésting-/ *n* BIRDS same as **nest box**

nestle /néss'l/ **(nestles, nestling, nestled)** *v* **1.** *vti* SETTLE INTO COMFORTABLE POSITION to settle into a position that feels comfortable, warm, and safe, or lay a part of the body in such a position **2.** *vi* BE SECLUDED to be in a sheltered or secluded place ○ *a village nestling in the foothills* **3.** *vt* CUSHION SOMETHING WITH SOFT MATERIAL to put something such as delicate china or glassware in a protected cushion of soft material [Old English *nestlian* < Germanic]

nestle-draf /néss'l draf/ *n regional* the smallest or weakest piglet in a litter [< *nestle-chick*, the weakling of a bird's brood + *draf*, origin ?]

REGIONAL NOTE See *underling*.

nestling /néstling/ *n* a young bird that does not yet have its flight feathers, and is therefore not yet able to leave the nest [14C. < NEST or NESTLE]

Nestorian /ne stáwri ən/ *adj* relating to a Southwest Asian Christian denomination that believes that two distinct persons, one divine and the other human, existed in Jesus Christ. This doctrine was declared heresy in AD 431. [15C. < late Latin *Nestorianus*, after *Nestorius* (AD 428–31), patriarch of Constantinople] —**Nestorian** *n* —**Nestorianism** *n*

net[1] /net/ *n* **1.** MESH a material made from threads or wires knotted, twisted, or woven to form a regular pattern with spaces between the threads **2.** MESHWORK BAG a piece of meshwork fabric in a shape resembling a bag that is used for holding, carrying, trapping, or confining something ○ *a fishing net* **3.** LIGHT MESHWORK FABRIC a fine light cotton or synthetic fabric with an open weave ○ *net curtains* **4.** SELECTING OR RESTRICTING SYSTEM a plan or system designed to select or restrict somebody or something ○ *those who slip through the net* **5.** SPORTS STRIP OF MATERIAL ACROSS PLAYING AREA in some sports such as tennis and volleyball, a strip of meshwork material that divides a court into halves and over which the players must hit a ball or shuttlecock **6.** SPORTS GOAL IN SOME SPORTS in some sports such as football and water polo, a goal with a backing made of meshwork material **7.** BASKETBALL PART OF BASKETBALL BASKET in basketball, an open-bottomed piece of meshwork material attached to the hoop of the basket **8.** CRICKET PRACTICE CRICKET PITCH in cricket, an indoor or outdoor practice pitch surrounded on three sides by nets that contain the ball after it has been hit (*often used in the plural*) **9.** CRICKET CRICKET PRACTICE SESSION in cricket, a session on a practice pitch (*often used in the plural*) **10.** BROADCAST BROADCASTING NETWORK a television or radio network **11.** COMPUT TELEPHONE OR COMPUTER NETWORK a telecommunications or computer network ■ *v* **(nets, netting, netted) 1.** *vt* TRAP SOMEBODY OR SOMETHING to catch or snare somebody or something in a net **2.** *vt* GET SOMETHING to manage to obtain or achieve something (*informal*) ○ *We may net ourselves several new clients this way.* **3.** *vt* PROTECT SOMETHING WITH NET to cover something with a net in order to keep something else out or away ○ *Net the cherry trees to keep birds out.* **4.** *vi* MAKE NET to make a net by knotting, twisting, or weaving threads or wires together **5.** *vt* HIT BALL INTO NET TO SCORE in games such as football and hockey, to hit the ball into the net so as to score **6.** *vt* SERVE BALL INTO NET in games such as tennis and volleyball, to hit the ball into the net so as to lose a serve, and sometimes a point [Old English, < Indo-European, 'to bind, tie']

net[2] /net/, **nett** *adj* **1.** LEFT AFTER DEDUCTIONS remaining from an amount, especially of money, after all necessary deductions have been made ○ *net pay* **2.** RELATING TO CONTENTS relating to contents only, excluding the container or the packaging ○ *net weight* **3.** HAVING ALL THINGS CONSIDERED general or overall, after positive and negative features have been weighed against each other ○ *the net result* ■ *vt* **(nets, netting, netted)** EARN SOMETHING AS PROFIT to earn or provide a sum of money as pure profit after all necessary deductions have been made ■ *n* **1.** NET AMOUNT a net profit or weight **2.** GOLFER'S SCORE a golfer's final score

after his or her handicap has been deducted [15C. Via Italian *netto* < Latin *nitidus* (see NEAT[1])]

net[3] *abbr* networking organization (*used in Internet addresses*) See table at **domain name**

Net /nét/, **net** *n* ONLINE same as **Internet** (*informal*) [Late 20C. Shortening]

Netanyahu /nétt'n yaáhoo/, **Binyamin** (*b*. 1949) Israeli prime minister (1996–99). As a Likud prime minister, he was criticized for failing to press for the implementation of the peace agreements with the Palestinians.

net asset value *n* the value of the securities owned by a unit trust, calculated as the total value of assets minus the total amount of liabilities divided by the number of shares issued

netball /nét bawl/ *n* an indoor or outdoor game usually played by girls or women in which goals are scored by throwing a ball through a raised net. Players can hand or throw the ball to each other but not run with it.

Net Book Agreement *n* an agreement in the British book trade, ended in 1995, that prevented booksellers from selling books at prices lower than those fixed by the publishers

net cord *n* **1.** a tennis shot, especially a serve, that touches the net before landing on the opponent's side. In the case of a serve, the server retakes the shot. **2.** the wire that holds up the net on a tennis court

net domestic product *n* the gross sum of domestic production minus the cost of depreciation of capital goods

Neth. *abbr* Netherlands

nether /néthər/ *adj* located in a low or lower position or under something [Old English *neopera* < Indo-European, 'down']

Netherlands

Netherlands /néthərləndz/ country in northwestern Europe, west of Germany, on the North Sea. Language: Dutch. Currency: guilder. Capital: Amsterdam. Population: 15,150,511 (2003). Area: 41,526 sq. km/16,033 sq. mi. Official name **Kingdom of the Netherlands** —**Netherlander** *n* —**Netherlandish** *adj*

Netherlands Antilles two Dutch island groups in the Caribbean Sea. One group is situated off the northern coast of Venezuela and the other lies east of Puerto Rico in the Leeward Islands. Capital: Willemstad. Population: 212,226 (2001). Area: 800 sq. km/309 sq. mi.

nethermost /néthərmōst/ *adj* lowest or farthest down

nether world *n* **1.** HELL in the belief system of some cultures, hell or the place where evil spirits live (*formal*) **2.** ABODE OF DEAD SOULS in classical mythology, the place below the earth's surface where the souls of the dead live **3.** CRIMINAL UNDERWORLD the world of organized crime, or the people involved in it (*literary*)

netiquette /nétti ket, -kət/ *n* a set of empirically derived rules for communication via the Internet (*informal*) [Late 20C. Blend of NET + ETIQUETTE]

Netizen /néttizən/ *n* somebody who uses the Internet frequently (*informal*) [Late 20C. Blend of NET + CITIZEN]

netlag /nét lag/ *n* a temporary loss of contact between an Internet user and a server, usually caused by network delays (*slang*) [Late 20C. After JET LAG]

net national product *n* the amount left after subtracting a depreciation allowance for capital goods from the gross national product

netphone /nét fōn/ *n* a phone that uses the Internet to make connections and carry voice messages

net present value *n* the value of an investment project found by adding the present value of expected future cash flows and the cost of the initial investment

net profit *n* gross profit minus all the costs incurred by a business

net realizable value *n* the value that an asset would have if sold, allowing for the costs of bringing it to a condition for sale and making the sale

netsuke /nétski, -kay, nétsoŏki, -kay/ *n* a carved wooden or ivory ornamental toggle worn at the end of a cord that holds a kimono closed, originally used to fasten a purse or pouch [Late 19C. < Japanese]

Net surfing *n* the activity of browsing through the information and sites available on the Internet, especially casually

nett /nét/ *adj* **1.** another spelling of **net**[2] **2.** Malaysia, Singapore describes a price that cannot be changed by bartering

netter /néttər/ *n* somebody with an Internet address (*slang*)

netting /nétting/ *n* fabric made from threads or wires knotted, twisted, or woven to form a regular pattern with spaces between the threads ○ *wire netting*

nettle /nétt'l/ *n* **1.** PLANT WITH STINGING LEAVES a wild plant with serrated-edged leaves covered with fine hairs or spines that sting when touched. Native to: found worldwide. Genus: *Urtica*. **2.** NONSTINGING PLANT RESEMBLING NETTLE a wild plant with serrated leaves like a stinging nettle, but without the stinging hairs, especially a dead nettle. Native to: northern temperate regions. Genus: *Lamium*. ■ *vt* (**-tles, -tling, -tled**) **1.** IRRITATE SOMEBODY to irritate or annoy somebody (*informal*) **2.** STING SOMEBODY to sting somebody with a nettle leaf [Old English *netele* < Indo-European, 'to tie']

nettle rash *n* MED same as **urticaria**

net ton *n* MEASURE same as **ton**[1] (sense 2) [< NET[2]]

netwar /nét wawr/ *n* nontraditional warfare carried out by dispersed groups of activists without a central command, often communicating electronically [Late 20C. < NET]

net weight *n* the weight of the contents only, excluding the weight of the container or packaging [< NET[2]]

net-winged *adj* describes beetles and midges that have a network of veins in their wings

network /nét wurk/ *n* **1.** SYSTEM OF LINES a pattern or system that looks like a series of branching or interconnecting lines **2.** SYSTEM OF PEOPLE OR THINGS a large and widely distributed group of people or things such as shops, colleges, or churches that communicate with one another and work together as a unit or system **3.** BROADCAST BROADCASTING CHANNELS a group of radio or television channels with a core of programmes that they all broadcast at the same time, with local or regional variations at other times **4.** COMPUT SYSTEM OF COMPUTERS a system of two or more computers, terminals, and communications devices linked by wires, cables, or a telecommunications system in order to exchange data. The network may be limited to a group of users in a local area (**local area network**), or be global in scope, as the Internet is. **5.** ELEC SYSTEM OF CIRCUITS a system of interconnected electrical circuits or components **6.** NETTING net or netting ■ *v* (**-works, -working, -worked**) **1.** *vi* MAINTAIN RELATIONSHIPS WITH PEOPLE to build up or maintain informal relationships, especially with people whose friendship could bring advantages such as job or business opportunities **2.** *vt* COMPUT LINK COMPUTERS to link a group of computers or their users so that information can be mutually accessed or exchanged **3.** *vt* BROADCAST BROADCAST SOMETHING SIMULTANEOUSLY to broadcast a programme simultaneously on all the channels that form a network

network-centric *adj* relating to warfare that employs instantaneous electronic cooperation among air, ground, and naval forces, smart munitions, spy planes, drones, and commandos equipped with computers and laser-guided weapons, all coordinated to orchestrate highly accurate attacks ○ *In war bad stuff happens. This is as true of network-centric warfare as the more traditional kind of an earlier*

day.' (Daniel Ford, *Wall Street Journal*; 12 August 2003)

networking /nét wurking/ *n* **1.** the act of linking computers so that users can exchange information or share access to a central store of information **2.** the process or practice of building up or maintaining informal relationships, especially with people whose friendship could bring advantages such as job or business opportunities —**networker** *n*

Network Rail *n* a statutory company that owns and operates the track, stations, signals, and other plant in the UK railway system, but does not run trains. It is limited by guarantee and has no shareholders, unlike Railtrack, which it superseded.

net worth *n* the difference between the assets and liabilities of a person or company ○ *services for high net worth investors*

neum *n* MUSIC another spelling of **neume**

Neumann ♦ **von Neumann, John**

neume /nyoom/, **neum** *n* in medieval Europe, an early musical notation that sometimes indicated only the approximate shape of a melody [15C. Via French < Greek *pneuma* 'breath'] —**neumatic** /nyoo máttik/ *adj*

neur- *prefix* same as **neuro-** (*used before vowels*)

neural /nyoŏrəl/ *adj* relating to or located in a nerve or the nervous system —**neurally** *adv*

neural arch *n* a bony or cartilaginous arch enclosing the spinal cord on the outward-facing side of a vertebra

neural computer *n* COMPUT same as **neurocomputer**

neural crest *n* a ridge of cells in the ectoderm of the vertebrate embryo that develops into cranial, spinal, and autonomic ganglia

neuralgia /nyoŏ ráljə/ *n* an intermittent and often severe pain in a part of the body along the path of a nerve, especially when there is no physical change in the nerve itself —**neuralgic** *adj*

neural net *n* a system of electrical circuits designed to perform in a similar way to the human nervous system, especially a computer system mimicking the human brain

neural network *n* **1.** an interconnecting system of nerve cells, e.g. the system that makes the brain function **2.** COMPUT same as **neural net**

neural spine *n* a projection that points backwards from the neural arch of a vertebra

neural tube *n* the hollow tube of tissue in the embryo of humans and other vertebrates that develops into the spinal cord and brain

neural tube defect *n* a disorder such as spina bifida that is present at birth and is caused by failure of the neural tube to close completely, resulting in loss of muscle function and various medical disorders

neurasthenia /nyoŏrəss theéni ə/ *n* a condition marked by chronic mental and physical fatigue and depression (*dated*) —**neurasthenic** /-thénnik/ *adj* —**neurasthenically** *adv*

neurectomy /nyoŏ réktəmi/ (*plural* **-mies**) *n* the removal of part of a nerve using surgery, e.g. as a treatment for neuralgia

neurilemma /nyoŏri lémmə/, **neurolemma** /nyoŏrō-/ *n* the outermost layer of the myelin sheath that surrounds the axon of a myelinated nerve cell [Early 19C. < NEUR- + Greek *eilēma* 'covering'] —**neurilemmal** *adj* —**neurilemmally** *adv*

neurilemmoma /nyoŏri le mōmə/ (*plural* **-mas** or **-mata** /-mətə/) *n* MED same as **neurofibroma**

neurinoma /nyoŏri nōmə/ (*plural* **-mas** or **-mata** /-mətə/) *n* MED same as **neurofibroma**

neuritis /nyoŏ rítiss/ *n* inflammation of a nerve, accompanied by pain, loss of reflexes, and muscle shrinkage —**neuritic** /-ríttik/ *adj*

neuro- *prefix* nerve, neural ○ *neurosurgery* [< Greek *neuron* 'nerve']

neuroactive /nyoŏrō áktiv/ *adj* having an effect on neural tissue or the nervous system

neuroanatomy /nyoŏrō ə náttəmi/ *n* **1.** the structure of the nervous system **2.** the branch of anatomy that studies the structure of the nervous system —**neuroanatomical** /-anə tómmik'l/ *adj* —**neuroanatomically** *adv* —**neuroanatomist** *n*

neurobehavioural /nyoŏrō bi háyvyərəl/ *adj* relating to the condition of the nervous system and its effects

on behaviour ○ *the neurobehavioural effects of exposure to solvents* —**neurobehaviour** *n* —**neurobehaviourally** *adv*

neurobiology /nyoŏrō bī óllәji/ *n* BIOL same as **neuroscience** (sense 2) —**neurobiological** /-bī ә lójjik'l/ *adj* —**neurobiologically** *adv* —**neurobiologist** *n*

neuroblast /nyoŏrō blast/ *n* an embryonic cell that develops into a nerve cell

neuroblastoma /nyoŏrō bla stṓmә/ (*plural* **-mas** or **-mata** /-mәtә/) *n* a malignant tumour of embryonic nerve cells (**neuroblasts**)

neurochemistry /nyoŏrō kémmistri/ *n* the study of the chemical composition of and reactions within the nervous system —**neurochemical** *adj* —**neurochemically** *adv* —**neurochemist** *n*

neurocomputer /nyoŏrō kәm pyootәr/ *n* a computer designed to imitate the human brain's ability to identify patterns, learn by trial and error, and find relationships in information. It is used in artificial intelligence research and to perform such tasks as machine translation, process control, handwriting recognition, and weather forecasting. —**neurocomputational** /nyoŏrō kómpyoŏ táysh'nәl/ *adj* —**neurocomputing** *n*

neurodegenerative /nyoŏrō di jénnәrәtiv/ *adj* relating to a disorder such as Alzheimer's disease or Parkinson's disease that causes nerve degeneration —**neurodegeneration** /nyoŏrō di jénnә ráysh'n/ *n*

neuroendocrine /nyoŏrō éndō krīn, -krin/ *adj* relating to or involving a nerve cell that releases a chemical messenger, especially a neurohormone, directly into the bloodstream

neuroendocrinology /nyoŏrō endōkri nóllәji/ *n* the study of the interrelationships between the nervous system, the endocrine system, and hormones —**neuroendocrinological** /-krinә lójjik'l/ *adj* —**neuroendocrinologically** *adv* —**neuroendocrinologist** *n*

neurofibril /nyoŏrō fíbril/ *n* a microscopic thin strand that occurs inside the cell body, axon, and dendrites of a nerve cell —**neurofibrillary** /nyoŏrōfi brílləri/ *adj*

neurofibroma /nyoŏrō fī brṓmә/ (*plural* **-mas** or **-mata** /-mәtә/) *n* a usually benign tumour growing on the sheath of a nerve

neurofibromatosis /nyoŏrō fī brōmә tṓssiss/ *n* an inherited disorder marked by coffee-coloured patches on the skin and neurofibromas formed along nerves, causing visual and hearing impairment, other nervous disorders, and sometimes major complications

neurogenesis /nyoŏrō jénnәssiss/ *n* the formation and development of nerve cells —**neurogenetic** /-jә néttik/ *adj* —**neurogenetically** *adv*

neurogenetics /nyoŏrō jә néttiks/ *n* the branch of medicine that studies the genetic influences involved in neurological disorders (*takes a singular verb*) —**neurogeneticist** *n*

neurogenic /nyoŏrō jénnik/ *adj* **1.** relating to the growth of nerve tissue **2.** arising in or stimulated by nerve tissue or the nervous system —**neurogenically** *adv*

neuroglia /nyoo róggli ә/ *n* *ANZ, US* the network of supporting tissue and fibres that nourishes nerve cells within the brain and spinal cord. It comprises several layers of cells and makes up about 40% of the total volume of nerve tissue. UK, Can term **glia** [Mid-19C. < NEURO- + Greek *glia* 'glue'] —**neuroglial** *adj*

neurohormone /nyoŏrō háwrmōn/ *n* a hormone secreted by specialized nerve cells —**neurohormonal** /-hawr mṓn'l/ *adj* —**neurohormonally** *adv*

neurohumour /nyoŏrō hyoŏmәr/ *n* BIOL same as **neurotransmitter** —**neurohumoral** /nyoŏrō hyoŏmәrәl/ *adj*

neurohypophysis /nyoŏrō hī póffississ/ (*plural* **-yses** /-is seez/) *n* the posterior lobe of the pituitary gland that secretes hormones such as vasopressin —**neurohypophyseal** /-hīpō fízzi әl, -hī pofi sée әl/ *adj*

neuroimaging /nyoŏrō ímmijing/ *n* the use of devices such as electroencephalographs or CT scanners to produce a cross-sectional image of the brain —**neuroimage** *n* —**neuroimager** *n*

neurol. *abbr* MED **1.** neurological **2.** neurology

neurolemma *n* MED same as **neurilemma**

neuroleptic /nyoŏrō léptik/ *adj* reducing nerve activity and producing a tranquillizing effect ■ *n* a tranquillizing drug that works by reducing nerve activity. Use: treatment of delirium and behavioural disturbances. [Mid-20C. < NEURO- + Greek *lēptikos* 'seizing' < *lambanein* 'seize, take'] —**neuroleptically** *adv*

neurolinguistic programming /nyoŏrō ling gwistik-/ *n* **1.** a theory and model of human behaviour and communication based on linguistic insights into how people avoid change and how to assist them in changing **2.** a system of therapy in which the brain is viewed as a computer that can be reprogrammed to think and feel in a way that helps people achieve goals

neurolinguistics /nyoŏrō ling gwístiks/ *n* the branch of linguistics that explores how the brain encodes language (*takes a singular verb*) —**neurolinguist** /-líng gwist/ *n* —**neurolinguistic** *adj* —**neurolinguistically** *adv*

neurology /nyoŏ róllәji/ *n* the branch of medicine that deals with the structure and function of the nervous system and the treatment of the diseases and disorders that affect it —**neurologic** /nyoŏrō lójjik/ *adj* —**neurological** *adj* —**neurologically** *adv* —**neurologist** *n*

neuroma /nyoŏ rṓmә/ (*plural* **-mata** /-mәtә/ or **-mas**) *n* MED same as **neurofibroma**

neuromuscular /nyoŏrō múskyoŏlәr/ *adj* **1.** relating to or affecting both nerve and muscle tissue **2.** having features common to both nerve and muscle tissue

neuromuscular junction *n* the connection between a nerve cell and a muscle, where nerve impulses are transmitted to initiate contraction of the muscle

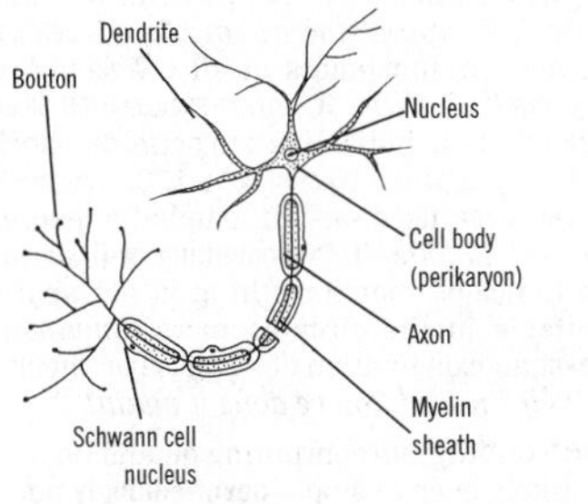

Dendrite
Bouton
Nucleus
Cell body
(perikaryon)
Axon
Myelin
sheath
Schwann cell
nucleus

neuron

neuron /nyoŏr on/, **neurone** /-ōn/ *n* a cell, usually consisting of a cell body, axon, and dendrites, that transmits nerve impulses and is the basic functional unit of the nervous system [Late 19C. Via German < Greek *neuron* 'sinew, cord, nerve'] —**neuronal** /nyoŏ rṓn'l/ *adj* —**neuronally** *adv*

neuropath /nyoŏrō path/ *n* somebody affected by a disorder of the nervous system

neuropathology /nyoŏrō pә thóllәji/ *n* the branch of medicine that studies diseases and disorders of the nervous system —**neuropathological** /-pathә lójjik'l/ *adj* —**neuropathologist** *n*

neuropathy /nyoŏ róppәthi/ (*plural* **-thies**) *n* a disease or disorder, especially a degenerative one, that affects the nervous system —**neuropathic** /nyoŏrō páthik/ *adj*

neuropeptide /nyoŏrō pép tīd/ *n* a peptide released by the nervous system that acts as a neurotransmitter

neuropharmacology /nyoŏrō faarmә kóllәji/ *n* the branch of medicine that studies the effects of drugs on the nervous system —**neuropharmacological** /-faarmәkә lójjik'l/ *adj* —**neuropharmacologist** *n*

neurophysiology /nyoŏrō fizzi óllәji/ *n* the branch of physiology that studies how the nervous system functions —**neurophysiological** /-fizzi ә lójjik'l/ *adj* —**neurophysiologist** *n*

neuroprosthesis /nyoŏrō pros théessiss/ *n* a prosthetic device that uses brain waves to stimulate muscle contraction —**neuroprosthetic** /-théttik/ *adj* —**neuroprosthetically** *adv*

neuroprosthetics /nyoŏrō pros théttiks/ *n* the branch of medicine that deals with prosthetic devices that are controlled by brain-wave activity (*takes a singular verb*) —**neuroprosthetist** /-prósthәtist/ *n*

neuropsychiatry /nyoŏrō sī kī́ әtri/ *n* the study of the neurological aspects of psychiatric disorders —**neuropsychiatric** /-sīki áttrik/ *adj* —**neuropsychiatrist** *n*

neuropsychology /nyoŏrō sī kóllәji/ *n* the branch of neurology that studies behaviour, especially in disorders such as epilepsy, memory loss, or speech impairment —**neuropsychological** /-sīkә lójjik'l/ *adj* —**neuropsychologist** *n*

neuropteran /nyoŏ róptәrәn/, **neuropteron** (*plural* **-tera** /-tәrә/) *n* an insect that has two large pairs of veined wings and mouthparts adapted for chewing, e.g. the ant lion or lacewing. Order: Neuroptera. —**neuropterous** *adj*

neuroradiology /nyoŏrō raydi óllәji/ *n* the use of X-rays to diagnose and treat physiological disorders and diseases of the nervous system, or the branch of medicine that deals with their use in this way —**neuroradiological** /-lójjik'l/ *adj* —**neuroradiologist** *n*

neuroscience /nyoŏrō sī әnss/ *n* **1.** a scientific discipline that studies nerve cells or the nervous system, e.g. neuroanatomy or neurophysiology, or all such disciplines collectively **2.** the scientific study of the molecular and cellular levels of the nervous system, of systems within the brain such as vision and hearing, and of behaviour produced by the brain —**neuroscientific** /nyoŏrō sī әn tíffik/ *adj* —**neuroscientist** /nyoŏrō sī́ әntist/ *n*

neurosensory /nyoŏrō sénssәri/ *adj* relating to the sensory activity of nerve cells or the nervous system —**neurosensorily** *adv*

neurosis /nyoŏ rṓssiss/ (*plural* **-roses** /-rṓ seez/) *n* a mild psychiatric disorder characterized by anxiety, depression, or hypochondria

neurosurgery /nyoŏrō súrjәri/ *n* surgery on any part of the nervous system, including the brain —**neurosurgeon** *n* —**neurosurgical** *adj*

neurotic /nyoo róttik/ *adj* **1.** AFFECTED BY NEUROSIS relating to, involving, affected by, or characteristic of a mild psychiatric disorder characterized by depression, anxiety, or hypochondria **2.** PSYCHIAT OVERANXIOUS OR OBSESSIVE overanxious, oversensitive, or obsessive about everyday things (*often considered offensive*) ■ *n* **1.** SOMEBODY AFFECTED BY NEUROSIS somebody diagnosed as affected by neurosis **2.** SOMEBODY OVERANXIOUS OR OBSESSIVE somebody regarded as overanxious, oversensitive, or obsessive about everyday things (*often considered offensive*) [Mid-17C. < Greek *neuron* 'nerve'] —**neurotically** *adv* —**neuroticism** /-sizәm/ *n*

neurotology /nyoŏrō tóllәji/ *n* the medical study of the nervous system as it affects the ear and hearing loss —**neurotologic** /nyoŏrәtә lójjik/ *adj*

neurotomy /nyoŏ róttәmi/ (*plural* **-mies**) *n* a surgical operation to cut a nerve, especially in order to relieve pain

neurotoxin /nyoŏrō tóksin/ *n* a substance that damages, destroys, or impairs the functioning of nerve tissue —**neurotoxic** *adj* —**neurotoxicity** /-tok síssәti/ *n*

neurotransmitter /nyoŏrō tranz míttәr/ *n* a chemical that carries messages between different nerve cells or between nerve cells and muscles, e.g. to trigger or prevent an impulse in the receiving cell. Excitatory neurotransmitters trigger a nerve impulse in the receiving cell, while inhibitory neurotransmitters act to prevent further transmission of an impulse.

neurotrophic /nyoŏrō trṓfik/ *adj* relating to the nutrition and maintenance of tissue of the nervous system —**neurotrophy** /nyoŏ róttrәfi/ *n*

neurotrophin /nyoŏrō trṓfin/ *n* a protein in the body that encourages the survival and growth of nerve cells

neurotropic /nyoŏrō tróppik/ *adj* affecting or having an affinity with nerve tissue —**neurotropism** /nyoŏ róttrәpizәm, nyoŏrә trṓpizәm/ *n*

neurovestibular /nyoŏrō ve stíbbyoŏlәr/ *adj* involving the sensory systems of the inner ear and eye, and the brain's response to input from them, e.g. during space travel

neurovirology /nyoŏrō vī róllәji/ *n* the scientific study of viruses such as HIV that occur in brain cells and of the diseases and mental illnesses caused by them —**neurovirological** /-vīrә lójjik'l/ *adj* —**neurovirologist** *n*

neurula /nyoŏryoŏlә/ (*plural* **-lae** /-lee/ or **-las**) *n* a vertebrate embryo in an early stage, when the nervous system is beginning to develop [Late 19C. < NEURO- + Latin *-ula* 'small' after BLASTULA, SCROFULA] —**neurulation** /nyoŏryoŏ láysh'n/ *n*

neuston /nyoŏst'n/ *n* a mass of minute organisms that float or swim on the surface of water [Early 20C. < German < form of Greek *neustos* 'swimming' < *nein* 'to swim']

neut. *abbr* GRAM neuter

neuter /nyóotər/ *vt* (**-ters, -tering, -tered**) **REMOVE TESTICLES OR OVARIES OF ANIMAL** to remove the testicles or ovaries of an animal ■ *adj* **1. WITHOUT SEX ORGANS** having undeveloped, nonfunctioning, or no sexual organs **2. NOT INDICATING SEX OR OTHER CHARACTERISTICS** not indicating the sex of a person, the qualities of a thing, or an attitude towards somebody or something **3.** GRAM **GRAMMATICALLY NEITHER MASCULINE NOR FEMININE** describes nouns and adjectives in languages such as Latin or German belonging to a separate gender that is neither masculine nor feminine **4.** GRAM **INTRANSITIVE** describes a verb that is neither active nor passive ■ *n* **1.** VET **CASTRATED OR SPAYED ANIMAL** an animal that has been castrated or spayed **2.** GRAM **GRAMMATICALLY NEUTER WORD** a grammatically neuter noun, adjective, or verb **3.** INSECTS **INSECT WITH UNDEVELOPED SEXUAL ORGANS** an insect with undeveloped sexual organs, e.g. a worker bee **4.** BOT **ASEXUAL FLOWER** an asexual flower without a stamen or pistil [14C. < Latin < *ne* 'not' + *uter* 'which of two']

neutral /nyóotrəl/ *adj* **1. TAKING NO SIDES** belonging to, favouring, or assisting no side in a war, dispute, contest, or controversy **2. WITHOUT DISTINCTIVE QUALITIES** possessing no distinctive quality or revealing no attitude or feeling ○ *She was careful to explain the problem in neutral terms.* **3. WITHOUT HUE** describes a colour such as white, black, or grey that is not in the spectrum **4. NOT STRONGLY COLOURED** not strongly or strikingly coloured and thus relatively inconspicuous and able to blend easily with other colours **5.** BIOL same as **neuter** *adj* (sense 1) **6.** CHEM **NOT ACID OR ALKALINE** neither acidic nor alkaline **7.** PHYS **WITH ZERO ELECTRIC CHARGE** having zero electric charge or potential **8.** MECH ENG **WITH NO MOTION TRANSMITTED** describes a gear or position in which no power is transmitted from the engine to the moving parts **9.** PHON **PRONOUNCED WITH TONGUE MIDWAY** describes a vowel articulated with the tongue relaxed and in the mid-central position, as, e.g., in the first syllable of 'away' ■ *n* **1.** AUTOMOT **GEAR WITH NO MOTION TRANSMITTED** a gear in which no power is transmitted from the engine to the moving parts **2.** POL **NONALIGNED PERSON OR THING** a person or country that remains neutral in a war, dispute, contest, or controversy [15C. < Latin *neutralis* 'of neuter gender' < *neuter* (see NEUTER)] —**neutrally** *adv*

neutral corner *n* either of the two corners of a boxing ring that are not used by boxers between rounds. If one boxer is knocked down during a round, the other must go to a neutral corner.

neutralise *vt* another spelling of **neutralize**

neutralism /nyóotrəlizəm/ *n* the policy of remaining neutral in wars and other disputes, or support for this policy —**neutralist** *n, adj* —**neutralistic** /nyóotrə lístik/ *adj*

neutrality /nyoo trálləti/ *n* the state of not taking sides, especially in a war or dispute

neutralize /nyóotrə līz/ (**-izes, -izing, -ized**), **neutralise** (**-ises, -ising, -ised**) *vt* **1. RENDER SOMETHING INEFFECTIVE** to make something ineffective, especially by removing its ability to act as a threat or obstacle **2.** POL **MAKE COUNTRY UNALIGNED** to make or declare a country unaligned in a war or dispute **3.** CHEM **MAKE SOMETHING NEITHER ACID NOR ALKALINE** to render a substance neither acid nor alkaline **4.** PHYS **MAKE CHARGE ZERO** to make the electric charge or potential of something zero —**neutralization** /nyóotrə lī záysh'n/ *n* —**neutralizer** *n*

neutral spirits *n US* alcohol distilled at or above 190 proof. Use: in blending alcoholic drinks. (*takes a singular or plural verb*)

neutral zone *n* in sport, the space between the areas of two competing teams, especially the area between the linemen of American football teams or the middle area of an ice hockey rink between the two blue lines

neutrino /nyoo treénō/ (*plural* **-nos**) *n* a stable neutral elementary particle of the lepton group with a zero rest mass and no charge. There are three types of neutrino, associated respectively with the electron, muon, and tau particle, and all have a spin of 1/2. [Mid-20C. < NEUTRAL + Italian *-ino* 'small']

neutron /nyóo tron/ *n* a neutral elementary particle of the baryon family with a zero electrical charge and a mass approximately equal to that of a proton [Early 20C. < NEUTRAL] —**neutronic** /nyoo trónnik/ *adj*

neutron bomb *n* a nuclear bomb designed to kill all life by a heavy bombardment with neutrons, but to cause little blast damage and leave relatively low radioactive contamination

neutron star *n* an astronomical object consisting entirely of a very dense compact mass of neutrons, the remnant of a star that has collapsed under its own gravity

neutrophil /nyóotrə fil/ *adj* describes cells or tissues that are readily stainable only with chemically neutral dyes, e.g. white blood cells ■ *n also* **neutrophile** /nyóotrə fīl/ the most common type of white blood cell in vertebrates, responsible for protecting the body against infection and stainable with neutral dyes [Late 19C. < Latin *neutr-*, stem of *neuter* (see NEUTER)] —**neutrophilic** /nyóotrə fíllik/ *adj*

Nevada /nə vaádə/ state in the western United States, bordered by Oregon, Idaho, Utah, Arizona, and California. Capital: Carson City. Population: 2,173,491 (2002 estimate). Area: 286,367 sq. km/110,567 sq. mi. —**Nevadan** *n, adj*

névé /névvay/ (*plural* **-vés**) *n* **1.** compacted granular snow, found at the top of a glacier, that has not yet become ice **2.** a field of compacted granular snow at the top of a glacier [Mid-19C. < Swiss French < Latin *nivatus* 'snow-cooled' < *niv-* 'snow']

never /névvər/ CORE MEANING: an adverb indicating that something will not happen at any time, or that somebody will definitely not do something ○ *The details will never be known.* ○ *I would never do anything to hurt her.*

1. *adv* **AT NO TIME** at no time in the past or the future ○ *The bird has never been seen in Iceland before. It may never appear there again.* **2.** *adv* **CERTAINLY NOT** not in any circumstances at all ○ *I would never turn my back on them.* **3.** *interj* **EXCLAMATION OF SURPRISE** an exclamation indicating surprise or shock ○ *'She's come top again'. 'Never!'* [Pre-12C. < *ne* 'not' + EVER] ◇ **never ever** used as an emphatic expression for 'never' (*informal*) ◇ **something will** *or* **would never do** indicates that something is not appropriate or suitable in the circumstances (*informal*) ◇ **well I never** an exclamation of surprise or shock (*informal*) ○ *Well I never! You've done it again!*

never-ending *adj* continuing on and on and seeming unlikely ever to stop —**never-endingly** *adv*

neverendum /névvər endəm/ *n* **1.** the holding of repeated referendums on the same subject **2.** a referendum on a subject on which there have been referendums before

never-married *adj* describes somebody who has never been married

nevermore /névvər máwr/ *adv* never again or in the future (*literary*)

never-never *n* **1.** FIN same as **hire purchase** (*dated informal*) ○ *They bought a three-piece suite on the never-never.* **2.** *Aus* the remote dry parts of central Australia

never-never land *n* an unreal or imaginary place, especially one where wonderful things happen ○ *The Opposition's budget policy springs from the same never-never land as their employment policy.* [< *Never Never Land* in J. M. Barrie's *Peter Pan* (1904)]

nevertheless /névvər*th*ə léss/ *adv* despite a situation or comment

Nevin /névvin/, **Robyn** (*b.* 1942) Australian actor. A stage and screen performer, she appeared in the film *The Chant of Jimmie Blacksmith* (1978). Full name **Nevin, Robyn Anne**

Nevis /neéviss/ island in St Kitts and Nevis, in the eastern Caribbean Sea, one of the Leeward Islands. Capital: Charlestown. Population: 10,080 (1989). Area: 93 sq. km/36 sq. mi.

Nevis, Ben /névviss/ ➧ **Ben Nevis**

nevus *n* ANAT US spelling of **naevus**

new /nyoo/ *adj* **1. RECENTLY MADE** recently made, created, or invented ○ *a new drug* **2. FIRST-HAND** not yet used by anyone else ○ *And motorists will continue paying higher registration fees for new cars.* **3. REPLACING EXISTING ONE** replacing or supplementing something of the same kind that already exists ○ *new rules to enhance security* ○ *I'll have a new boss from next week.* **4. RECENTLY DISCOVERED** recently discovered or noticed, though existing before ○ *The new comet will be visible at the beginning of July this year.* **5. WITH RECENTLY ACQUIRED STATUS** having recently acquired a particular status or position ○ *a new mother* ○ *the new medical school graduates* **6. PREVIOUSLY UNFAMILIAR** not seen, known, or experienced by somebody before and thus unfamiliar ○ *The city was completely new to me.* **7. UNUSED TO SOMETHING** unaccustomed to something, e.g. such as a place, job, or situation, through having only recently arrived there or experienced it for the first time ○ *He's not new to this city.* **8. CHANGED** changed, especially for the better ○ *I felt as if I had slept, and had now just awakened – a new woman, with a new mind.* **9.** *also* **New REVIVED OR DIFFERENT** constituting a revived, different, improved, or more advanced form of something, e.g. a political or artistic movement, that already exists or that existed before **10. EARLY** appearing early in the season ○ *new potatoes* ■ *n Aus* **BEER** a light-coloured beer produced by bottom fermentation [Old English *nēowe* < Indo-European] —**newness** *n*

SYNONYMS ***new, novel, innovative, fresh, newfangled, original***

CORE MEANING: never experienced before or having recently come into being

new recently made, created, or invented, or not previously known or encountered ○ *new technologies like DNA-fingerprinting* ○ *over 125,000 species of flora and fauna, many of which were entirely new to science* **novel** new and different, often in an interesting, unusual, or inventive way ○ *The company came up with a novel idea for a faster train.* ○ *The bank has introduced a novel way of detecting credit card crime.* **innovative** new and creative, especially in the way something is done ○ *a program to support flexible, innovative transportation alternatives* **fresh** excitingly or refreshingly different from what has been done or experienced previously ○ *a completely fresh approach* ○ *a fresh start in a different city* **newfangled** puzzlingly or worryingly new or different, especially because it seems gimmicky or overcomplicated ○ *one of those newfangled small cameras that do almost everything for you* ○ *A traditionalist at heart, he is instinctively suspicious of newfangled ideas.* **original** completely new and not copied or derived from something else ○ *Leonardo's highly original method of fresco working* ○ *On examination it is seen that these ideas are not so very original after all.*

New Age *adj* relating to a cultural movement dating from the 1980s that emphasizes spiritual consciousness, and often involves belief in reincarnation and astrology and the practice of meditation, vegetarianism, and holistic medicine ■ *n* a style of instrumental music with simple repetitive melodies, often synthesized or reproducing natural sounds, that is intended to promote mental tranquillity —**New Ager** *n*

New Age music *n* MUSIC same as **New Age**

New Age traveller *n* a member of a New Age cultural movement who travels, often in a group, to gather in spiritually significant places

Newark /nyóo ərk/ city in northeastern New Jersey. It is the county seat of Essex County, situated 14 km/9 mi. west of New York City. Population: 277,000 (2002 estimate).

Newark-on-Trent historic market town in Nottinghamshire, central England, on an arm of the River Trent. Population: 35,129 (1991).

new arrival *n* **1.** somebody or something that has recently arrived somewhere ○ *She's a new arrival at the firm.* **2.** a recently born baby (*informal*) ○ *I hear there's been a new arrival in the family.*

New Australian *n Aus* a recent immigrant to Australia

New Bedford /nyoo-/ city and port in southeastern Massachusetts, on Buzzards Bay, southeast of Taunton. It was a major whaling centre during the 1800s. Population: 94,088 (2002 estimate).

newbie /nyóobi/, **Newbie** *n* somebody who is new to an activity such as using the Internet or playing a computer game

new blood *n* a person or group bringing fresh ideas and enthusiasm to a place, situation, or organization

newborn /nyóo bawrn/ *adj* **1. NEWLY BORN** born very recently **2. NEWLY DISCOVERED OR RECOVERED** recently discovered, or recovered afresh ○ *newborn faith* ■ *n* **NEW BABY** a newborn child

New Britain largest island in Papua New Guinea and in the Bismarck Archipelago. It is divided into the districts of East New Britain and West New Britain.

Population: 311,955 (1990). Area: 36,500 sq. km/14,100 sq. mi.

new broom *n* a newly arrived person in a place or organization who is keen to make changes and improvements [< the saying *New brooms sweep clean*]

New Brunswick province in southeastern Canada, bordering the Gulf of St Lawrence and the Bay of Fundy. Capital: Fredericton. Population: 756,700 (2002). Area: 72,908 sq. km/28,150 sq. mi.

new build *n* newly built housing, or a newly built housing unit

Newburg /nyoo burg/ *adj* cooked and served with a rich sauce of cream, butter, sherry, and egg yolks ○ *lobster Newburg* [Early 20C. Origin ?]

Newbury /nyoóbəri/ town in central southern England. Population: 33,273 (1991).

New Caledonia island and overseas territory of France in the southwestern Pacific Ocean, east of Australia. Capital: Nouméa. Population: 204,863 (2001). Area: 19,103 sq. km/7,376 sq. mi.

Newcastle /nyoó kaass'l/ city in eastern New South Wales, southeastern Australia, located at the mouth of the Hunter River. Population: 143,238 (2002 estimate).

Newcastle, Thomas Pelham-Holles, 1st Duke of (1693–1768) prime minister of Great Britain (1754–56 and 1757–62). A member of the Whig Party, he was blamed for the initial failure of the British forces in the Seven Years War during his first premiership. His second was a coalition with William Pitt the Elder. Born **Pelham, Thomas**

Newcastle disease *n* a highly infectious viral disease that affects poultry and other birds, attacking the lungs and nervous system [Early 20C. After NEWCASTLE UPON TYNE]

Newcastle upon Tyne /nyoó kaass'l ə pon tín/ city and port on the River Tyne, northeastern England. It is situated at one end of Hadrian's Wall, and the Romans built a bridge over the river there. Population: 259,536 (2001).

Newcombe /nyoókəm/, **John** (*b.* 1944) Australian tennis player. He was singles champion at Wimbledon in 1967, 1970, and 1971. Full name **Newcombe, John David**

New Comedy *n* a form of Greek comedy that began near the end of the 4th century and used stock characters and plots from middle-class life

Newcomen /nyoó kumən/, **Thomas** (1663–1729) English inventor. He developed a steam engine that was used for pumping water from coalmines throughout Europe and North America.

newcomer /nyoó kumər/ *n* somebody who or something that has recently arrived, appeared, or been introduced

New Country *n* a form of country music, originating in the 1980s, that is influenced by pop music and is designed to appeal to an urban audience

New Criticism *n* a movement between 1930 and 1970 in the study of literature, especially poetry, that examined its structure, imagery, and ambiguities, rather than its historical setting or the author's intent

New Deal *n* **1.** the policies of social and economic reform introduced in the United States in the 1930s under the presidency of Franklin D. Roosevelt. **2.** the period during which Franklin D. Roosevelt's policies of social and economic reform were implemented. —**New Dealer** *n*

New Delhi capital city of India, situated in the National Capital Territory within the city of Delhi. It was built between 1912 and 1929 and inaugurated as the capital in 1931. Population: 11,680,000 (2000 estimate).

New Economic Policy *n* a programme implemented in the Soviet Union between 1921 and 1928 that permitted some private enterprise although the state retained overall economic control

new economy *n* the postindustrial economy considered by some to have emerged in the late 20th century, characterized by global competition, the exploitation of information technology, and the valuing of intangible assets such as ideas and knowledge

newel

newel /nyoó əl/ *n* **1.** a vertical pillar to which the steps of a spiral staircase are attached **2.** *also* **newel post** a post supporting the handrail of a staircase at the top or bottom or on a landing [14C. Via French *novel* 'knob' < assumed Vulgar Latin *nodellus* 'little knot']

New Eng. *abbr* New England

New England region of the northeastern United States, comprising the states of Maine, New Hampshire, Vermont, Massachusetts, Rhode Island, and Connecticut —**New Englander** *n*

New England Range mountain range in New South Wales, southeastern Australia. Its highest peak is Ben Lomond, 1,550 m/5,100 ft.

New English Bible *n* a version of the Bible in modern English translated by British scholars from various denominations and published in 1970

Newf *n Can* same as **Newfie** (*informal; offensive in some contexts*)

Newf. *abbr* Newfoundland

newfangled /nyoó fáng g'ld/ *adj* puzzlingly or worryingly new or different, especially because it seems gimmicky or overcomplicated [15C. < past participle of Old English *fōn* 'capture']

SYNONYMS See *new.*

new-fashioned *adj* up to date or modern (*informal*) [After OLD-FASHIONED]

Newfie /nyoófi/, **Newf** /nyoof/ *n Can* somebody who comes from Newfoundland (*informal; offensive in some contexts*) [Mid-20C. Shortening and alteration of *Newfoundland*]

New Forest region of heath, marsh, and forest in Hampshire, southern England. Area: 337 sq. km/130 sq. mi.

New Forest pony *n* a hardy pony with a short neck and sturdy body belonging to a breed originating from the New Forest region of England

newfound /nyoó fownd/ *adj* recently discovered or met

Newfoundland /nyoóofəndlənd/ *n* a large sturdy dog with a long straight back and a dense, usually black coat, belonging to a breed formerly used in water rescues [Early 19C. After the Island of NEWFOUNDLAND]

Newfoundland, Island of /nyoóofəndlənd/ island in the Atlantic Ocean. It is part of the province of Newfoundland and Labrador. Population: 538,099 (1991). Area: 108,860 sq. km/42,031 sq. mi. —**Newfoundlander** *n*

Newfoundland and Labrador easternmost province in Canada, comprising the Island of Newfoundland and Labrador on the mainland. Capital: St John's. Population: 531,600 (2002). Area: 405,212 sq. km/156,453 sq. mi.

New Georgia island group in the southwestern Pacific Ocean, in the central Solomon Islands, lying northwest of Guadalcanal. Area: 1,300 sq. km/500 sq. mi.

New Granada former Spanish colony in northwestern South America that included present-day Colombia, Ecuador, Venezuela, and Panama

New Guinea second largest island in the world, in the western Pacific Ocean, off the northern coast of Australia. It is divided between the Indonesian province of Irian Jaya in the west and Papua New Guinea in the east. Population: about 5,300,000 (1995). Area: 808,510 sq. km/312,170 sq. mi. —**New Guinean** *n, adj*

New Hampshire state in the northeastern United States, bordered by Canada, Maine, the Atlantic Ocean, Massachusetts, and Vermont. Capital: Concord. Population: 1,275,056 (2002 estimate). Area: 24,043 sq. km/9,283 sq. mi.

New Harmony village in Posey County, southwestern Indiana, situated 37 km/23 mi. northwest of Evansville. The Harmony Society and Robert Owen both established utopian communities there in the 19th century. Population: 905 (2002 estimate).

Newhaven /nyoó hayv'n/ town and seaport in East Sussex, southeastern England. It is a terminal for ferry services to Dieppe, France. Population: 11,208 (1991).

New Haven city in New Haven County, southern Connecticut, situated 58 km/36 mi. southwest of Hartford. It is the home of Yale University, founded in 1701. Population: 124,176 (2002 estimate).

New Hebrides former name for **Vanuatu** (until 1980)

new horizons *npl* new and promising prospects that seem to be opening up for somebody or something

Ne Win /náy wín/ (1911–2002) Burmese national leader. Dictator (1962–74) and president (1974–81) of Burma (now Myanmar), he nationalized the economy and suppressed dissent. Born **Maung Shu Maung**

New Ireland island in the Bismarck Archipelago, northeastern Papua New Guinea, in the southwestern Pacific Ocean. Population: 15,743 (1990). Area: 8,650 sq. km/3,340 sq. mi.

New Jersey state on the eastern coast of the United States, bordered by New York State, the Atlantic Ocean, Delaware, and Pennsylvania. Capital: Trenton. Population: 8,590,300 (2002 estimate). Area: 21,277 sq. km/8,215 sq. mi. —**New Jerseyan** *n, adj* —**New Jerseyite** *n*

New Journalism *n US* a style of journalism originating in the United States in the 1960s that emphasizes the subjective impressions of the reporter and uses techniques typically found in fiction writing

New Kingdom *n* a period in the history of ancient Egypt, from the 18th to the 20th dynasty (approximately 1580 to 1090 BC)

New Labour *n* the Labour Party as it evolved in the late 20th century, characterized by abandonment of the principle of state ownership and greater acceptance of the free-market economy

Newlands /nyoóoləndz/, **John** (1837–98) British chemist. By listing the elements according to atomic weight, he established the law of octaves, which led to the periodic table. Full name **Newlands, John Alexander Reina**

New Latin *n* the form of the Latin language used since about the beginning of the 16th century, especially for scientific and taxonomic classification —**New Latin** *adj*

New Left *n* a political movement, chiefly among students and intellectuals in the United States and Europe during the 1960s and 1970s, that sought radical social and economic change —**New Leftist** *n*

new look *n* a radical change in appearance, design, or style —**new-look** *adj*

New Look *n* a style in women's clothes introduced in 1947 by the designer Christian Dior that featured broad shoulders, narrow waists, and long full skirts

newly /nyoóoli/ *adv* **1.** LATELY recently or lately **2.** AGAIN again or once more **3.** DIFFERENTLY in a different or novel way

newlywed /nyoóoli wed/ *n* somebody who has recently been married —**newlywed** *adj*

Newman /nyoóomən/, **Barnett** (1905–70) US painter. His abstract expressionist works feature a colour field broken by one or more vertical lines.

Newman, John Henry, Cardinal (1801–90) British theologian. After converting in 1845, he became the leading British Roman Catholic and was made a cardinal in 1879.

> 'It is as absurd to argue men, as to torture them, into believing.'
> [John Henry Newman, 'The Usurpations of Reason (1831)', *Oxford University Sermons*; 1843]

Newman, Paul (*b.* 1925) US stage and film actor. A

popular leading man, he won an Academy Award for *The Color of Money* (1986).

'The second you step out of the confines of the personality the public has set up for you, they get incensed. Public reaction tends to keep actors as personalities instead of allowing them to act. It's a very corrupting influence.'
[Paul Newman, *Photoplay*; 1977]

New Man *n* modern man characterized by emotional sensitivity, recognition of women as equals, and a desire to share in domestic chores and the work associated with child rearing

Newmarket[1] /nyoŏ maarkit/ *n* **1.** a card game in which players win by playing cards that match those already on the table. US term **Michigan**[2] **2.** a long double-breasted close-fitting jacket with a full skirt worn in the 19th century as a riding coat or overcoat [Late 17C. After NEWMARKET[2]]

Newmarket[2] /nyoŏ maarkit/ market town in Suffolk, famous for its horseracing since the early 1600s. Population: 16,498 (1991).

new maths *n* a method of teaching mathematics, devised in the 1960s, in which children are introduced to elementary set theory at an early stage

New Mexico state in the southwestern United States, bordered by Colorado, Oklahoma, Texas, Mexico, and Arizona. Capital: Santa Fe. Population: 1,855,059 (2002 estimate). Area: 314,937 sq. km/121,598 sq. mi. —**New Mexican** *n, adj*

new money *n* recently acquired wealth, or people who have it ○ *It's largely new money that's buying this kind of property these days.*

new moon *n* **1.** MOON AS NARROW CRESCENT the Moon at the beginning of its cycle, when it is invisible from Earth or when only a narrow crescent on the right-hand side of its surface as seen from Earth is visible **2.** PERIOD OF NEW MOON the period during which there is a new moon **3.** PHASE OF MOON one of the four phases of the Moon, during which it is directly between Earth and the Sun and invisible or seen only as a narrow crescent

New National Party *n* in South Africa, a political party formed in 1998 when the National Party changed its name to distance itself from its apartheid past

New Netherland /-néthər land/ Dutch colony in North America between 1613 and 1664, when it was conquered by the English and divided into the states of New York and New Jersey

New Norwegian *n* LANG same as **Nynorsk** —**New Norwegian** *adj*

New Orleans /-awrli ənz, -awr leénz/ city in southeastern Louisiana, on the eastern bank of the Mississippi River. The largest city in the state, it is known for its annual Mardi Gras festival. Population: 473,681 (2002 estimate).

New Plymouth city on the southwestern coast of the North Island, New Zealand. It is a centre for dairy farming and oil and gas production. Population: 47,763 (2001).

Newport /nyoŏ pawrt/ **1.** city on the River Usk in southeastern Wales. Population: 137,011 (2001). **2.** town in southern England. It is the county town of the Isle of Wight. Population: 25,033 (1991). **3.** city in southeastern Rhode Island State, on Rhode Island itself, connected to the mainland by bridges. Population: 26,312 (2002 estimate).

Newport News city at the mouth of the James River in southeastern Virginia. It is home to one of the world's largest shipyards. Population: 180,272 (2002 estimate).

Newquay /nyoŏ kee/ town and seaside resort in Cornwall, southwestern England. Population: 17,390 (1991).

New Quebec district in northern and eastern Quebec, Canada. Area: 777,000 sq. km/300,000 sq. mi.

New Right *n* a conservative political movement that arose in the United States during the late 1960s and affirmed a commitment to established religion, patriotism, and smaller less interventionist government

Newry /nyoŏri/ city and port in Newry and Mourne

District, County Down, Northern Ireland. Population: 22,975 (1991).

Newry and Mourne /-máwrn/ local government district in Northern Ireland. Area: 894 sq. km/345 sq. mi.

news /nyooz/ *n* **1.** RECENT INFORMATION information about recent events or developments ○ *I phoned the hospital, and the news is good.* **2.** CURRENT EVENTS information about current events printed in newspapers or broadcast by the media ○ *She has been in the news a lot lately.* **3.** PROGRAMME a radio or television broadcast presenting the important events or developments that have taken place ○ *I heard about it on the radio news.* **4.** SOMEBODY OR SOMETHING INTERESTING somebody or something considered as being of interest to people in general ○ *The reporters considered that the Royal Family were always news.* **5.** SOMETHING PREVIOUSLY UNKNOWN something previously unknown to somebody that he or she is surprised to hear about ○ *They're divorcing? That's news to me!* [15C. Plural of NEW]

news agency *n* an organization that gathers information about current events and supplies it to the media

newsagent /nyoóz ayjənt/ *n* somebody who keeps a shop or stall selling newspapers and magazines, often together with confectionery, tobacco, and other items. US term **newsdealer**

newsboy /nyoóz boy/ *n* a boy who sells newspapers in the street or delivers them to houses

newsbreak /nyoóz brayk/ *n N Am* **1.** a short pause in a radio or television programme during which two or three news items are broadcast **2.** something that is newsworthy

newscast /nyoóz kaast/ *n* a television or radio broadcast consisting of news

newscaster /nyoóz kaastər/ *n N Am* BROADCAST same as **newsreader**

news conference *n* MEDIA same as **press conference**

newsdealer /nyoóz deelər/ *n US* same as **newsagent**

news desk *n* an area of a newspaper office or a radio or television studio where news is prepared for publication or broadcasting

news flash *n* a brief item of urgent news, often broadcast at short notice interrupting a scheduled programme

newsgirl /nyoóz gurl/ *n* a girl who sells newspapers in the street or delivers them to houses

newsgroup /nyoóz groop/ *n* a discussion group maintained on a computer network such as the Internet in which people leave messages on topics of mutual interest for other participants to read

newshound /nyoóz hownd/ *n N Am* a journalist, especially one who covers news in an aggressive way (*informal*)

New Siberian Islands uninhabited island group in northeastern Russia, lying in the Arctic Ocean between the Laptev Sea and the East Siberian Sea. Area: 38,000 sq. km/14,672 sq. mi.

newsletter /nyoóz lettər/ *n* a printed report or letter that contains news of interest to a specific group, e.g. the members of a society or employees of an organization, and is circulated to them periodically

news magazine *n N Am* **1.** a magazine, usually published weekly, containing news and news analysis from the preceding week **2.** a weekly radio or television programme of interviews, investigative reportage, features, and commentary on the news

newsman /nyoózmən, -man/ (*plural* **-men** /-mən, -men/) *n* a male journalist or broadcaster who reports news

newsmonger /nyoóz mung gər/ *n* somebody who gathers and spreads gossip —**newsmongering** *n*

New South Wales state in southeastern Australia. Capital: Sydney. Population: 6,686,600 (2003). Area: 801,600 sq. km/309,500 sq. mi.

New South Welshman *n* a man who comes from or lives in New South Wales, Australia

New South Welshwoman *n* a woman who comes from or lives in New South Wales, Australia

newspaper /nyoóss paypər, nyoóz-/ *n* **1.** PRINTED ACCOUNT OF NEWS a publication containing news and comment on current events, together with features and advertisements, that usually appears daily or weekly and is printed on large sheets of paper that

are folded together **2.** ORGANIZATION an organization that produces a newspaper **3.** PAPER FROM NEWSPAPER a sheet or sheets of a newspaper when used for a purpose other than reading ○ *wrapped in newspaper*

newspaperman /nyoóss paypər man, nyoóz-/ (*plural* **-men** /-men/) *n* **1.** a man who writes or edits for a newspaper ○ *Although he eventually built up a global media empire he remained a newspaperman at heart.* **2.** a man who owns or publishes a newspaper

newspaperperson /nyoóss paypər purss'n, nyoóz-/ (*plural* **-people** /-peep'l/ or **-persons**) *n* **1.** somebody who writes or edits for a newspaper **2.** somebody who owns or publishes a newspaper

newspaperwoman /nyoóss paypər wŏomən, nyoóz-/ (*plural* **-women** /-wimin/) *n* **1.** a woman who writes or edits for a newspaper **2.** a woman who owns or publishes a newspaper

newspeak /nyoó speek/ *n* language that is ambiguous and designed to conceal the truth, especially that sometimes used by bureaucrats and propagandists ○ *She said that to call sacking workers 'rationalization' was typical of modern newspeak.* [After the language of propaganda in *Nineteen Eighty-Four*, by George ORWELL, 1949]

newsperson /nyoóz purss'n/ (*plural* **-persons** or **-people** /-peep'l/) *n US* a journalist or broadcaster who reports news

newsprint /nyoóz print/ *n* a relatively cheap and low-quality paper made from recycled materials or wood pulp and used for printing newspapers

newsreader /nyoóz reedər/ *n* **1.** somebody who reads the news on a television or radio broadcast. N Am term **newscaster 2.** a computer program that allows somebody to read and post messages to Internet newsgroups

newsreel /nyoóz reel/ *n* a short cinema film about recent news events, formerly shown before a feature film

news release *n* MEDIA same as **press release**

newsroom /nyoóz room, -rŏom/ *n* a room in a radio or television studio or newspaper office where news is prepared for publication or broadcasting

news service *n* MEDIA same as **news agency**

newssheet /nyoóz sheet/ *n* COMMUNICATION same as **newsletter**

newsstand /nyoóz stand/ *n* a stall or booth where newspapers and magazines are sold

New Style *n* the reckoning of dates by the Gregorian calendar

newsvendor /nyoóz vendər/ *n UK, Can* a seller of newspapers

newswire /nyoóz wīr/ *n* an Internet service providing the latest information on current events

newswoman /nyoóz wŏomən/ (*plural* **-women** /-wimin/) *n* a female journalist or broadcaster who reports news

newsworthy /nyoóz wurthi/ (**-thier, -thiest**) *adj* interesting or important enough to be reported in the media —**newsworthily** *adv* —**newsworthiness** *n*

newswriting /nyoóz rīting/ *n* the craft of writing news stories —**newswriter** *n*

newsy /nyoózi/ (**-ier, -iest**) *adj* filled with news and gossip ○ *a newsy letter*

newt

newt /nyoot/ *n* a small amphibian of the salamander family with short legs and a well-developed tail.

Family: Salamandridae. [15C. < mistaken division of *an ewte, ewte* being a form of EFT]

REGIONAL NOTE *Newts* were originally *ewts* or *efts*, a name they retain in many British dialects. The opening *n-* is the result of 'an ewt' being incorrectly interpreted as 'a newt'. The reverse phenomenon occurred when 'a norange' (from Spanish *naranja*) became 'an orange' and 'a napron' (from Old French *naperon*) became 'an apron'.

New Territories /-térrətəriz/ area of Hong Kong situated mostly on the Chinese mainland north of Kowloon that was leased to Great Britain by China from 1898 to 1997. Area: 950 sq. km/365 sq. mi.

New Testament *n* the second section of the Christian Bible dealing with the life and teachings of Jesus Christ, containing the Gospels, the Acts of the Apostles, the Epistles, and the Book of Revelations

newton /nyoot'n/ *n* an SI unit of force equivalent to the force that produces an acceleration of one metre per second per second on a mass of one kilogram. Symbol **N** [Early 20C. After Sir Isaac NEWTON]

Newton /nyoot'n/, **Sir Isaac** (1642–1727) English scientist. He discovered gravitation, invented calculus, and formulated the laws of motion. He recognized that white light is a mixture of coloured lights, and wrote *Mathematical Principles of Natural Philosophy* (1687) and *Opticks* (1704). — **Newtonian** /nyoo tōni ən/ *adj*

> 'If I have seen further it is by standing on the shoulders of giants.'
> [Sir Isaac Newton, *Letter to Robert Hooke*; 5 February 1676]

Newtonian telescope *n* a reflecting telescope in which mirrors transfer an image to an eyepiece in the side of the telescope's body

Newton's cradle *n* a toy consisting of five metal balls hanging side by side in a frame. Swinging the ball at one end transmits force along the line so that the ball at the other end swings away. [After Sir Isaac NEWTON]

Newton's rings *n* a pattern of light interference created by the contact of a convex lens with a glass plate, appearing as a series of alternating bright and dark rings [After Sir Isaac NEWTON]

new town *n* a complete self-contained town with all the usual facilities, created with government funding on an open site, usually to accommodate excess population from existing urban areas

Newtown /nyoo town/ new town on the River Severn in Powys, Wales. It was designated in 1967. Population: 2,068 (1998).

Newtownabbey /nyoot'n ábbi/ town in County Antrim, northeastern Northern Ireland. Population: 79,995 (2001).

Newtownards /nyoótənərdz/ industrial town in County Down, Northern Ireland, at the head of Strangford Lough. Population: 24,301 (1991).

Newtown St Boswells /-sənt bózwəlz/ town in southern Scotland. It is the administrative headquarters of Scottish Borders Council. Population: 1,102 (1991).

new university *n* one of the former UK polytechnics or colleges of higher education designated as a university in the 1990s

new variant CJD *n* MED same as **variant CJD**

new vaudeville *n* US a form of variety entertainment performed on the street or in a theatre by jugglers, magicians, acrobats, clowns, comedians, and similar artists

new wave *n* **1.** POST-PUNK ROCK MUSIC rock music made in the late 1970s after the punk rock era **2.** FORM OF FRENCH CINEMA a form of film-making originating in France during the 1950s that emphasized spontaneity, unconventionality, and the individual styles of directors **3.** INNOVATIVE ARTS MOVEMENT any new and innovative movement in the arts

New World *n* North and South America as considered by Europeans following Columbus's discovery of the Americas

new year *n* the year following the current year, especially the early part of it ○ *We hoped that things would be better in the new year.*

New Year *n* the first day or first few days of a calendar year

WORLD ENGLISH *New York English* is the variety of English used in New York City, whose idiom has been influenced by waves of immigration, especially from Central Europe (notably Jewish and Italian immigrants) and from Latin America (notably Puerto Rican immigrants). Local pronunciation on the whole does not pronounce *r* in words such as *art, door,* and *worker.* There is a distinctive 'o'-sound in words such as *coffee* ('kawfee') and *ought* ('awt'). Although 'broad New York' tends to have low prestige in the United States (including among its own speakers), its everyday usage has had a marked influence nationwide and abroad, notably in Yiddish-derived words like *bagel, chutzpah, klutz, maven, s(c)hmaltz,* and *s(c)hlock,* and the humorously or ironically dismissive repeated element *s(c)h-* as in 'fancy-s(c)hmancy' (too fancy to be acceptable). New York English is also called New Yorkese.

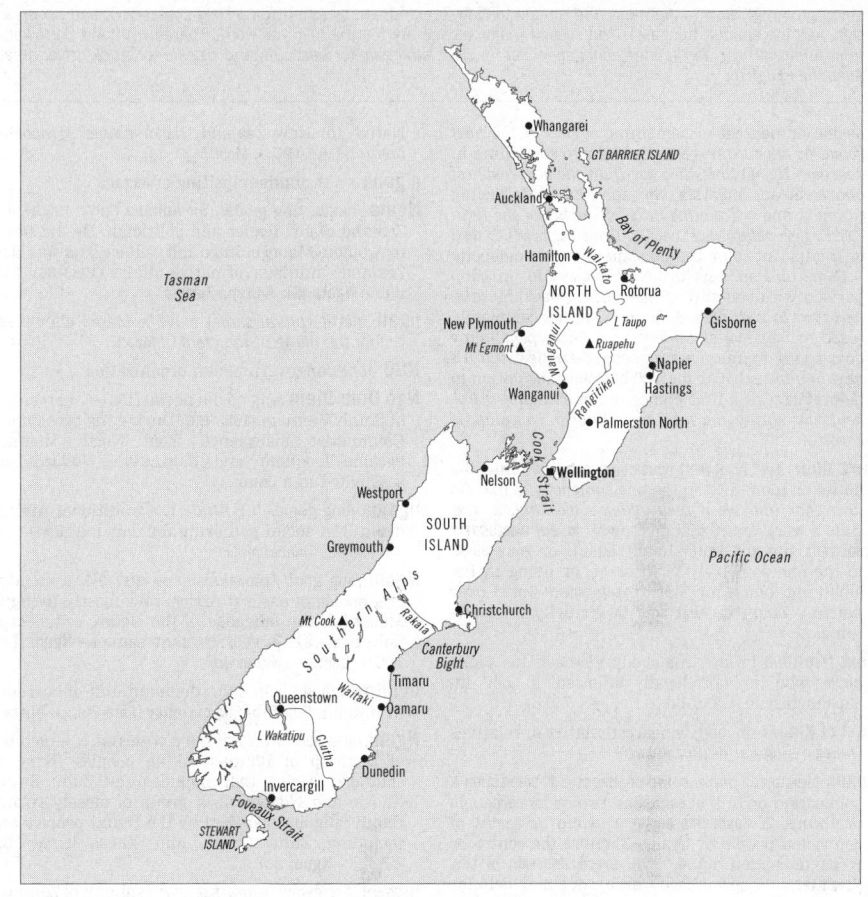

New Zealand

New Year's Day *n* the first day of the year in the Gregorian calendar, widely celebrated as a public holiday. Date: 1 January.

New Year's Eve *n* the last day of the year in the Gregorian calendar, or the evening of that day. Date: 31 December.

New Year's resolution *n* a decision to do or stop doing something, made or announced at the New Year, which is traditionally considered a time for a fresh start

New York 1. *also* **New York City** city and major port in southeastern New York State, at the mouth of the Hudson River. It is the most populous city in the United States. It comprises Manhattan, the Bronx, Brooklyn, Queens, and Staten Island boroughs. Population: 8,084,316 (2002 estimate). **2.** state in the northeastern United States, bordering Pennsylvania, the Atlantic Ocean, New Jersey, Canada, Vermont, Massachusetts, Connecticut, Lake Erie, and Lake Ontario. Capital: Albany. Population: 19,157,532 (2002 estimate). Area: 139,831 sq. km/53,989 sq. mi. —**New Yorker** *n*

New York Bay inlet of the Atlantic Ocean lying at the mouth of the Hudson River at New York City

New York English *n* a variety of English spoken in New York City

New Yorkese /nyoo yawr keez/ *n* same as **New York English** (*informal*)

new zaïre *n* MONEY same as **zaïre**

New Zealand /-zeeland/ country in the southwestern Pacific Ocean, southeast of Australia, comprising two large islands, the North Island and the South Island, and numerous smaller islands. Its Maori name is Aotearoa, meaning 'Land of the Long White Cloud'. It became an independent member of the Commonwealth in 1931. Language: English. Currency: New Zealand dollar. Capital: Wellington. Population: 3,951,307 (2003). Area: 270,534 sq. km/104,454 sq. mi. Maori name **Aotearoa** —**New Zealander** *n*

New Zealand English *n* a variety of English spoken in New Zealand. See panel on next page

New Zealand Time *n* the standard time in the time zone with an eastern border of 180° longitude that includes New Zealand. It is 12 hours later than universal time.

New Zild /nyoo zíld/ *n* NZ (*informal humorous*) **1.** same as **New Zealand 2.** same as **New Zealand English** [Contraction]

next /nekst/ CORE MEANING: a grammatical word indicating that something follows something else in a series or is immediately beside it ○ (adj) *He lives next door to me.* ○ (adj) *When I returned, my next patient was waiting.* ○ (adv) *Which patient do you want to see next?*

1. *adj, adv* IMMEDIATELY FOLLOWING following immediately after the present or previous one ○ (adj) *Our next meeting is on April 2nd.* ○ (adv) *Are you wondering what to do next?* **2.** *det* FOLLOWING THIS ONE used to describe the day, month, or year following this one ○ *The case is scheduled for trial next month.* ○ *There is no way of predicting whether this might happen next year or in 300 years.* **3.** *adj* ADJOINING immediately

beside or nearest to something ○ *He's in the next room.* **4.** *adj* CLOSEST IN DEGREE closest to something in degree ○ *It's 40 times heavier than the next heaviest quark.* **5.** *adj* Malaysia, Singapore SECOND following the next one ○ *Take the next left turn, not the first.* [Old English *nēhsta* 'most near' < Germanic, 'near'] ◇ **next to 1.** adjacent to or beside something or somebody ○ *Come and sit next to me.* **2.** closest to, in comparison with something else ○ *Cleanliness, he said, was next to godliness.* **3.** almost, but not completely (used in negative statements) ○ *I have spent many days trying to figure out a good alternative, and it's next to impossible.* ◇ **the next best thing** the option to be preferred if a first choice is not available ○ *For healthier eating the next best thing to chocolate is carob.*

next door *adv* **1.** IN NEXT HOUSE OR ROOM in or into the house or room next to the one somebody is in ○ *Go next door and see if their phone's working.* **2.** VERY CLOSE a very short distance away ■ *adj* IMMEDIATELY ADJACENT situated immediately beside or very close to the one somebody is in or at, or living in the adjoining house or flat (*hyphenated when used before a noun*) ◇ **next door to** virtually the same thing as

next friend *n* in law, somebody who acts for somebody who is not legally allowed to act independently, e.g. a child

next of kin *n* somebody's nearest relative or relatives (*takes a singular or plural verb*)

nexus /néksəss/ (*plural same* or **-uses**) *n* **1.** CONNECTION a connection or link associating two or more people or things **2.** CONNECTED GROUP a group or series of connected people or things **3.** CENTRE the centre or focus of something **4.** BIOL SPECIALIZED PART OF CELL MEMBRANE a specialized area of the cellular membrane that helps cells to communicate or adhere [Mid-17C. < Latin *nex-*, past participle of *nectere* 'bind']

Nez Percé /nez púrss, -páir say/ (*plural* **Nez Percés** or *same*) *n* **1.** a member of a Native North American people who lived along the Snake River, and who now live mainly in western Idaho and northeastern Washington state **2.** the Sahaptin-Chinook language of the Nez Percé. Native speakers: 5,000. [Early 19C. < French, 'pierced nose'] —**Nez Percé** *adj*

nf *abbr* Norfolk Island (*used in Internet addresses*) See table at **domain name**

NF *abbr* **1.** POL National Front **2.** GEOG Newfoundland **3.** *also* **N/F** BANKING no funds **4.** LANG Norman French

Nfd. *abbr* Newfoundland

NFER *abbr* EDUC National Foundation for Educational Research

NFL *abbr* US AMERICAN FOOTBALL National Football League

Nfld *abbr* Newfoundland

NFS *abbr* **1.** National Fire Service **2.** COMPUT network file service **3.** COMPUT network file system **4.** not for sale

NFT *abbr* **1.** National Film Theatre **2.** TIME Newfoundland Time

NFU *abbr* National Farmers' Union

NFWI *abbr* National Federation of Women's Institutes

ng *abbr* **1.** Nigeria (*used in Internet addresses*) See table at **domain name 2.** *also* **n.g.** *or* **NG** *or* **N.G.** no good

ngaio /nĭ́ ō/ (*plural* **-os**) *n* an evergreen tree that has white wood and leaves dotted with oil glands.

Native to: New Zealand. Latin name: *Myoporum laetum*. [Mid-19C. < Maori]

n'gana *n* VET another spelling of **nagana**

Ngata /naátə, əng gaátə/, **Sir Apirana** (1874–1950) New Zealand Maori leader and politician. He did much to promote Maori culture and welfare, and was New Zealand's minister of native affairs (1928–34). Full name **Ngata, Sir Apirana Turupa**

ngati /nátti/ (*plural same*) *n* NZ a Maori clan (*used before the name of the clan*) [< Maori]

NGO *abbr* nongovernmental organization

Ngo Dinh Diem /əng gố din deém/ (1901–63) president of South Vietnam (1955–63). During his presidency, Communist insurgence from North Vietnam became frequent and disruptive. He was assassinated in a coup.

ngoma /əng gốmə/ *n* E Africa **1.** a traditional African drum **2.** a social gathering for dancing [Early 20C. < Kiswahili, 'dance, music']

Ngoni /əng gốni/ (*plural same* or **-nis**) *n* **1.** a member of a people of eastern Africa, now mostly living in Malawi **2.** the language of the Ngoni, a dialect of Zulu or Swazi **3.** PEOPLES, LANG same as **Nguni** [Late 19C. < Bantu] —**Ngoni** *adj*

ngultrum /əng goóltrəm/ *n* the main unit of currency in Bhutan. See table at **currency** [Late 20C. < Tibetan]

Nguni /əng goóni/ (*plural same* or **-nis**) *n* **1.** a member of a group of Bantu-speaking peoples living in southern Africa that includes the Zulu, Swazi, Xhosa, and Ndebele **2.** a group of closely related Bantu languages spoken by the Nguni peoples and including Zulu, Swazi, and Xhosa [Early 20C. < Zulu] —**Nguni** *adj*

ngwee /əng gwáy/ (*plural same*) *n* a subunit of Zambian currency. See table at **currency** [Mid-20C. < Bantu]

NH *abbr* New Hampshire

NHI *abbr* HEALTH SERVICES National Health Insurance

NHS *abbr* National Health Service

ni *abbr* Nicaragua (*used in Internet addresses*) See table at **domain name**

Ni *symbol* CHEM ELEM nickel

NI *abbr* **1.** National Insurance **2.** Northern Ireland **3.** NZ North Island

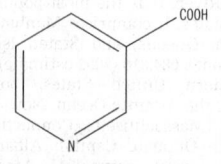

niacin

niacin /nĭ́ əssin/ *n* a B complex vitamin found in meat and dairy products. Deficiency of niacin causes pellagra. Formula: $C_6H_5NO_2$. [Mid-20C. < NICOTINE + ACID]

niacinamide /nĭ́ ə sínnə mīd/ *n* a B complex vitamin that is an amide of niacin

Niagara Falls

Niagara /nī ággrə, nī ággərə/ river in northeastern North America, in New York State and Ontario, flowing between Lake Erie and Lake Ontario via Niagara Falls. Length: 56 km/35 mi.

Niagara Falls waterfall in the Niagara River, divided by Goat Island into American Falls and Horseshoe, or Canadian, Falls. Height: 55–57 m/182–187 ft.

Niamey /ni aá may/ capital city of Niger, situated on the River Niger in the southwestern part of the country. Population: 587,000 (1995).

Niarchos /ni aárk oss/, **Stavros** (1909–96) Greek shipowner. He was a pioneer in the construction of supertankers and the owner of a large independent fleet. Full name **Niarchos, Stavros Spyros**

~~**niave**~~ incorrect spelling of **naive**

nib /nib/ *n* **1.** a shaped detachable metal tip on the end of a pen such as a fountain pen, by means of which the ink is transferred to the paper **2.** a sharp point or tip, especially the sharpened end of a quill pen **3.** BIRDS same as **beak** (sense 1) [Late 16C. Variant of NEB]

nibble /níbb'l/ *v* (**-bles, -bling, -bled**) **1.** *vti* TAKE SMALL QUICK BITES to take a series of small quick bites at something, or eat something in a series of small quick bites ○ *She nibbled an apple while she read.* **2.** *vti* BITE PLAYFULLY AND CARESSINGLY to take gentle playful little bites at part of somebody's body as a form of caress ○ *The lion cubs nibbled at each other playfully.* **3.** *vi* REDUCE GRADUALLY to reduce or wear away something gradually by taking a small amount at a time ○ *These day-to-day expenses nibble away at our funds.* **4.** *vi* SHOW MILD INTEREST to show a tentative interest in something ○ *Lower the price a little and the buyers will start to nibble.* ■ *n* **1.** ACT OF NIBBLING a series of small quick or gentle bites at something **2.** TINY AMOUNT OF FOOD a tiny amount of some type of food (*informal*) **3.** EXPRESSION OF MILD INTEREST an expression of tentative interest ○ *I've been trying to make a sale all day but not a nibble so far.* ■ **nibbles** *npl* SMALL THINGS TO EAT small pieces of food intended as appetizers, snacks, or party food, e.g. nuts or canapés ○ *Help yourself to some nibbles while I put away your coat.* [Early 16C. Origin ?] —**nibbler** *n*

Nibelung /neébəloong/ (*plural* **-lungs** or **-lungen** /-loongən/) *n* in medieval German mythology, a member of a race of dwarfs who owned a hoard of treasure that was captured by the heroic prince Siegfried [Mid-19C. < German]

niblick /níbblik/ *n* an obsolete golf club, similar to a modern nine-iron, having a short iron head with a steeply sloping face, used to give extra lift, e.g. when playing out of a bunker [Mid-19C. Origin ?]

nibs /nibz/ *n* used as a mock title when referring to an important or self-important person (*informal*) ○ *His nibs will doubtless be expecting the red carpet treatment.* [Early 19C. Origin ?]

Nic. *abbr* **1.** Nicaragua **2.** COMPUT Network Interface Card

nicad /nĭ́ kad/, **nicad battery** *n* a dry cell battery with electrodes of nickel and cadmium in an alkaline electrolyte [Mid-20C. < NICKEL + CADMIUM]

Nicaea /nī seé ə/ ancient Byzantine city of Asia Minor, on the site of present-day Iznik, northwestern Turkey. It flourished under the Romans.

Nicaragua

Nicaragua /níkə rággyŏŏ ə/ largest country in Central America, situated between the North Pacific Ocean and the Caribbean Sea. Capital: Managua. Population: 5,128,517 (2003). Area: 129,494 sq. km/49,998 sq. mi. Official name **Republic of Nicaragua** —**Nicaraguan** *n, adj*

niccolite /níkə līt/ *n* a nickel arsenide mineral. Use: source of nickel. [Mid-19C. < modern Latin *niccolum* 'nickel']

nice /nīss/ (**nicer, nicest**) *adj* **1.** PLEASANT pleasant or enjoyable **2.** KIND kind, or showing courtesy, friendliness, or consideration ○ *It was a nice gesture to return the money.* **3.** RESPECTABLE respectable, or of an acceptable social or moral standard ○ *She's made some nice friends at work.* **4.** GOOD-LOOKING pleasing to look at ○ *What a nice hat you're wearing!* **5.** ACCOMPLISHED skilful and accomplished **6.** SUBTLE subtle and involving delicacy or fine discrimination **7.** FASTIDIOUS AND FUSSY very concerned and careful about choosing, or being seen to do, the right thing ○ *You can't be too nice about your methods if you want to get the job done.* [13C. Via Old French < Latin *nescius* 'ignorant'] —**nicely** *adv* —**niceness** *n* ◇ **nice and** sufficiently or pleasingly ○ *It's nice and warm by the fire.*

Nice /neess/ city on the Mediterranean coast in southeastern France. A major tourist centre, it is known for its mild climate. Population: 342,738 (1999).

NICE /nīss/ *abbr* National Institute of Clinical Excellence

Nicene creed /ní seen-/ *n* a formal statement of Christian beliefs formulated at a council held in Nicaea in AD 325, subsequently altered and expanded, and still in use in most Christian churches [< late Latin *Nic(a)enus* < *Nic(a)ea* 'Nicaea']

nicety /níssəti/ (*plural* **-ties**) *n* **1.** REFINEMENT OR DETAIL a subtle distinction or point, or a small detail, especially of proper procedure or social etiquette (*often used in the plural*) **2.** REFINED FEATURE a feature that makes something particularly refined and pleasurable (*often used in the plural*) **3.** SUBTLETY a subtle, delicate, or fastidious quality, especially in somebody's feelings or taste **4.** PRECISION the ability to be precise and accurate and make fine distinctions ○ *the nicety of his powers of judgment* ◇ **to a nicety** with great precision or exactness

niche /neesh, nich/ *n* **1.** WALL RECESS a recess in a wall, especially one made to hold a statue **2.** HOLLOW PLACE any recess or hollow, e.g. in a rock formation **3.** SUITABLE PLACE FOR SOMEBODY a position or activity that particularly suits somebody's talents and personality or that somebody can make his or her own ○ *She carved out her own niche in the industry.* **4.** COMM SPECIALIZED MARKET an area of the market specializing in one type of product or service ○ *designed to undercut the competition in the same niche* ○ *'Thanks to the Internet, small niche companies can reach mass markets in a heartbeat.'* (*Forbes Global Business and Finance*; November 1998) **5.** ECOL PLACE IN NATURE the role of an organism within its natural environment that determines its relations with other organisms and ensures its survival ■ *vt* (**niches, niching, niched**) PUT SOMETHING IN NICHE to place something in a niche [Early 17C. < Old French *nichier* 'build a nest, nestle' < Latin *nidus* 'nest']

niche market *n* a market in which a limited and clearly defined range of products is sold to a specific group of customers

Nichiren /néech ee ren/ (1222–82) Japanese Buddhist monk. He established a form of Buddhism based on the Lotus Sutra, which has many followers in Japan today.

Nicholas /níkələss/, **St** (*fl* 4th century) prelate and saint from Asia Minor. He is the patron saint of Russia, children, and merchants.

Nicholas I (1796–1855) tsar of Russia. Autocratic and militaristic throughout his reign (1825–55), he put down the Decembrists' uprising that occurred upon his ascension in December 1825, waged successful wars against Persia (1826–28) and Turkey (1827–29), and entered into the Crimean War (1853–56), during which campaign he died.

Nicholas II (1868–1918) tsar of Russia. The last tsar of Russia (1894–1917), he was overthrown in the Russian Revolution and executed with his family.

Nicholas of Cusa /-ləss əv kyoozə/ (1401–64) German cardinal and scholar. He opposed scholasticism, suggested a reform of the calendar, and posited the theory that the Earth revolved around the Sun.

Nicholson /ník'lss'n/, **Ben** (1894–1982) British painter and sculptor. After experimenting with cubism, he evolved a more personal abstract style. Full name **Nicholson, Benjamin Lauder**

Nicholson, Jack (*b.* 1937) US film actor. He won Academy Awards for *One Flew Over the Cuckoo's Nest* (1975), *Terms of Endearment* (1983), and *As Good As It Gets* (1997).

> 'Men are boring to women because there's only about 12 types of us, and they know all the keys. And they're bored by the fact we never escape our types.'
> [Jack Nicholson, *Observer*; 21 August 1994]

nick /nik/ *n* **1.** NOTCH a small V-shaped cut or indentation in an edge or surface **2.** SMALL CUT a small cut on the skin **3.** PRINTING GROOVE ON TYPE a groove on the side of a piece of metal printing type, used to identify and orient it **4.** same as **police station** (*slang*) **5.** same as **prison** *n* (sense 1) (*slang*) ○ *He spent ten years in the nick.* **6.** CONDITION the particular condition of something or somebody (*slang*) ○ *What kind of nick is your motor in?* ■ *v* (**nicks, nicking, nicked**) **1.** *vt* NOTCH OR CUT SOMETHING SLIGHTLY to make a notch, indentation, or small cut in something ○ *The scythe blade had been nicked by a stone.* **2.** *vt* STEAL SOMETHING to steal something from its owner (*informal*) ○ *Somebody's nicked my bike.* **3.** *vt* ARREST SOMEBODY to place somebody under arrest (*slang*) ○ *A copper's job is to nick villains.* **4.** *vt* US CHEAT SOMEBODY to cheat or defraud somebody (*slang*) **5.** *vi* Aus GO QUICKLY to go somewhere quickly (*informal*) **6.** *vt* VET INCISE HORSE'S TAIL to make a cut in the tendons at the root of a horse's tail to make the tail stick up [15C. Origin ?] ◇ **in the nick of time** at the critical or last possible moment

nick off *vi* Aus to go away or leave (*informal; often used as a command*)

SYNONYMS See *steal*.

nickel /ník'l/ *n* **1.** SILVERY WHITE METALLIC ELEMENT a hard corrosion-resistant silvery-white metallic element. Source: sulphide and oxide ores. Use: in alloys, batteries, electroplating, catalyst. Symbol **Ni**. See table at **element 2.** *N Am* FIVE-CENT COIN a coin worth five cents ■ *vt* (**-els, -elling, -elled**) COAT SOMETHING WITH NICKEL to plate something with nickel [Mid-18C. Shortening of German *Kupfernickel* 'copper nickel' < *nickel* 'mischievous demon', because the ore yielded no copper]

nickel-and-dime US *adj* **1.** LOW-PAID paying or involving only a small amount of money (*slang*) ○ *a nickel-and-dime job* **2.** MINOR small-scale, or of little importance (*informal*) ■ *vt* (**-dimes, -diming, -dimed**) **1.** IMPOVERISH SOMEBODY THROUGH SMALL EXPENSES to get somebody or something into financial trouble by accumulating many small costs and expenses (*slang*) **2.** BOTHER SOMEBODY IN MANY SMALL WAYS to hinder or harass somebody with trivialities and insignificant matters

nickel-cadmium battery *n* ELEC ENG same as **nicad**

nickelic /ni kéllik/ *adj* containing nickel, especially nickel with a valency of three

nickeliferous /níkə líffərəss/ *adj* containing or yielding nickel

nickelodeon /níkə lŏdi ən/ *n N Am* **1.** EARLY JUKEBOX an early variety of coin-operated jukebox **2.** 5-CENT CINEMA an early 20th-century cinema, charging five cents for admission **3.** COIN-OPERATED PLAYER PIANO an early variety of player piano operated by inserting coins [Early 20C. < NICKEL + MELODEON]

nickelous /níkələss/ *adj* containing nickel, especially nickel with a valency of two

nickel plate *n* a thin coating of nickel applied to something, usually by electrolysis —**nickel-plated** *adj* —**nickel-plating** *n*

nickel silver *n* a hard durable white alloy of copper, zinc, and nickel. Use: making cutlery and wire.

nicker[1] /níkər/ (**-ers, -ering, -ered**) *vi* to make a soft neighing sound ○ *The pony nickered and shook its head.* [Late 16C. An imitation of the sound] —**nicker** *n*

nicker[2] /níkər/ (*plural same*) *n* a pound sterling (*slang*) [Early 20C. Origin ?]

Jack Nicklaus

Nicklaus /ník lowss/, **Jack** (*b.* 1940) US golfer. He dominated professional golf in the 1960s and 1970s, winning a record 20 championship titles. Known as **Golden Bear**. Full name **Nicklaus, Jack William**

> 'Last week I made a double bogey and didn't even get mad. Now that's bad.'
> [Jack Nicklaus, *New York Times*; 24 July 1977]

~~nickle~~ incorrect spelling of **nickel**

nick-nack *n* HOUSEHOLD same as **knick-knack**

nickname /ník naym/ *n* **1.** INVENTED NAME an invented name for somebody or something, used humorously or affectionately instead of the real name and usually based on a conspicuous characteristic of the person or thing involved **2.** SHORT NAME a shortened or altered form of a name, e.g. 'Billy' for 'William' or 'Peggy' for 'Margaret' ■ *vt* (**-names, -naming, -named**) CALL SOMEBODY BY NICKNAME to give a nickname to somebody or something ○ *They nicknamed him 'Spuds' because of his fondness for potatoes.* [15C. < mistaken division of *an eke name* 'an additional name']

Nicobarese /níkəbə reez/ (*plural same*) *n* **1.** somebody who comes from the Nicobar Islands **2.** a group of Austro-Asiatic languages spoken in the Nicobar Islands. Native speakers: fewer than 20,000. —**Nicobarese** *adj*

Nicobar Islands /níkə baar-/ island group in the Indian Ocean, east of Sri Lanka, part of the Indian union territory of the Andaman and Nicobar Islands. The Nicobar Islands consist of 19 islands. Population: 39,022 (1991). Area: 1,841 sq. km/711 sq. mi.

niçoise /nee swaáz/ *adj* made or garnished with tomatoes and olive oil, and often including black olives, capers, anchovies, tuna, hard-boiled eggs, and green beans (*used after the noun*) [Late 19C. < French, feminine of *niçois* 'of Nice']

Nicosia /níkə see ə/ capital city of Cyprus, situated on the Pedhieos River in the northern part of the island. In 1974 it was partitioned into Turkish and Greek Cypriot sectors. Population: 197,800 (2000).

nicotiana /ni kŏshi aánə, níkəti aánə/ (*plural* **-as** or *same*) *n* a perennial or annual flowering plant of a genus that includes the tobacco plant. Flowers: fragrant, white, yellow, or purple. Genus: *Nicotiana*. [Early 17C. After Jean *Nicot* (1530–1604), French ambassador to Lisbon, who introduced tobacco to France]

nicotinamide /níkə tínnə mīd/ *n* BIOCHEM same as **niacinamide**

nicotinamide adenine dinucleotide *n* BIOCHEM full form of **NAD**

nicotinamide adenine dinucleotide phosphate *n* BIOCHEM full form of **NADP**

nicotine /níkə teen/ *n* **1.** a toxic alkaloid. Source: tobacco. Use: insecticide. Formula: $C_{10}H_{14}N_2$. **2.** tobacco products, or the smoking of them (*informal*) [Early 19C. Shortening of NICOTIANA] —**nicotinic** /níkə tínnik/ *adj*

nicotine gum *n* chewing gum containing nicotine, used as a substitute for tobacco by people who are trying to give up smoking

nicotine patch *n* a small patch that when placed on the skin releases nicotine directly into the bloodstream, used by people who are trying to give up smoking

nicotinic acid /níkə tínnik-/ *n* BIOCHEM same as **niacin**

nicotinism /níkə tee nizəm/ *n* poisoning caused by an excessive intake of nicotine through smoking

nictitate /níkti tayt/ (**-tates**, **-tating**, **-tated**), **nictate** /nik táyt, níkt ayt/ *vi* to blink or wink (*technical*) [Early 19C. < medieval Latin *nictitat-*, past participle of *nictitare* 'wink repeatedly' < Latin *nictare* 'to wink'] —**nictation** /nik táysh'n/ *n* —**nictitation** /níkti táysh'n/ *n*

nictitating membrane /níkti tayting-/ *n* a thin transparent layer of skin underneath the eyelid that can cover the eye surface of birds, reptiles, and some mammals to moisten and protect it

NIDA /nídə/, **Nida** *n* Australia's premier drama school. Full form **National Institute of the Dramatic Arts**

Nidderdale /níddər dayl/ region in West Yorkshire, northern England, in the valley of the River Nidd. It is an Area of Outstanding Natural Beauty. Area: 603 sq. km/233 sq. mi.

nidi BIOL, MED plural of **nidus**

nidicolous /ni díkələss/ *adj* describes young birds that remain in the nest for some time after hatching [Early 20C. < Latin *nidus* 'nest']

nidificate /níddifi kayt/ *vi* BIOL same as **nidify** [Early 19C. < Latin *nidificat-*, past participle of *nidificare* (see NIDIFY) —**nidification** /níddifi káysh'n/ *n*

nidifugous /ni díffyŏŏgəss/ *adj* describes young birds that leave the nest a short time after hatching [Early 20C. < Latin *nidus* 'nest' + *fugere* 'flee']

nidify /níddi fī/ (**-fies**, **-fying**, **-fied**) *vi* to build a nest [Mid-17C. < Latin *nidificare* 'build a nest' < *nidus* 'nest']

nidus /nídəss/ (*plural* **-duses** or **-di** /-dī/) *n* **1.** SPIDER OR INSECT NEST a nest in which spiders or insects deposit eggs **2.** FOCUS OF INFECTION a place in the body at which an infection develops **3.** SPORE-DEVELOPING PLANT PART a place in a plant where its spores develop [Early 18C. < Latin, 'nest']

niece /neess/ *n* a daughter of somebody's brother, brother-in-law, sister, or sister-in-law [13C. Via Old French < Latin *neptis* 'granddaughter, niece']

~~**nieghbour**~~ incorrect spelling of **neighbour**

niello /ni éllō/ *n* (*plural* **-li** /-élli/ or **-los**) **1.** BLACK ALLOY USED AS INLAY a deep black alloy of sulphur and silver, lead, or copper, used to fill lines inlaid as decoration on a metal surface **2.** USE OF NIELLO the process of using niello to decorate a metal surface **3.** SOMETHING DECORATED WITH NIELLO something decorated with niello as an inlay ■ *vt* (**-los**, **-loing**, **-loed**) DECORATE SOMETHING WITH NIELLO to decorate something using niello as an inlay [Early 19C. Via Italian < Latin *nigellus* 'blackish', diminutive of *niger* 'black'] —**niellist** *n*

nielsbohrium /neelz báwri əm/ *n* an artificially produced radioactive element with the atomic number 105 [Late 20C. After *Niels* BOHR]

Nielsen /neelss'n/, **Carl** (1865–1931) Danish composer best known for his six symphonies. Full name **Nielsen, Carl August**

Niemeyer /nee mī ər/, **Oscar** (*b.* 1907) Brazilian architect. He is best known for designing the major buildings in Brasília (1956–64), the new capital of Brazil. Full name **Niemeyer Soares Filho, Oscar**

Niemöller /nee möllər/, **Martin** (1892–1984) German pastor. A veteran of World War I, he initially supported Hitler but during the 1930s was active in the German resistance against the Nazis. Arrested for treason, he spent seven years in Dachau and Sachsenhausen concentration camps before being released by the Allies at the end of World War II. During the postwar years, he was an outspoken pacifist and advocate of reconciliation and disarmament.

~~**niether**~~ incorrect spelling of **neither**

Friedrich Wilhelm Nietzsche

Nietzsche /neetshə/, **Friedrich Wilhelm** (1844–1900) German philosopher. Author of *Thus Spake Zarathustra* (1883–85) and one of the most influential thinkers of the 19th century, he founded his philosophy on the will-to-power and rejected religion. —**Nietzschean** *n*, *adj* —**Nietzscheanism** *n*

> 'Species do not evolve toward perfection, but quite the contrary. The weak, in fact, always prevail over the strong, not only because they are in the majority, but also because they are the more crafty.'
> [Friedrich Wilhelm Nietzsche, *The Twilight of the Idols*; 1888]

> 'Truths are illusions about which one has forgotten that this is what they are; metaphors which are worn out and without sensuous power; coins which have lost their pictures and now matter only as metal, no longer as coins.'
> [Friedrich Wilhelm Nietzsche, 'On Truth and Lie in an Extra-Moral Sense', *The Portable Nietzsche*; 1954]

nieve /neev/ *n Scotland* same as **fist** *n* (sense 1) [13C. < Old Norse *hnefi*]

nifedipine /nī féddi peen/ *n* a drug that stops the heart muscles from taking up calcium. Use: treatment of high blood pressure, angina pectoris. Formula: $C_{17}H_{18}N_2O_6$. [Late 20C. < NITRO- + *fe* (shortening and alteration of PHENYL) + -*dipine*, INN stem]

niff /nif/ (*slang*) *n* an unpleasant smell or odour ■ *vi* (**niffs**, **niffing**, **niffed**) to have an unpleasant or strong smell [Early 20C. Origin ?] —**niffiness** *n* —**niffy** *adj*

nifty /nífti/ (**-tier**, **-tiest**) *adj* (*informal*) **1.** VERY GOOD very good or effective **2.** AGILE good, quick, and clever at doing something or using something **3.** STYLISH AND GOOD-LOOKING fashionable and good-looking [Mid-19C. Origin ?] —**niftily** *adv* —**niftiness** *n*

Nig. *abbr* **1.** Nigeria **2.** Nigerian

nigella /nī jéllə/ *n* a member of a genus of flowering plants of the buttercup family that includes love-in-a-mist. Flowers: white, blue, yellow. Native to: Mediterranean, western Asia. Genus: *Nigella*. [14C. < modern Latin, feminine of *nigellus* (see NIELLO)]

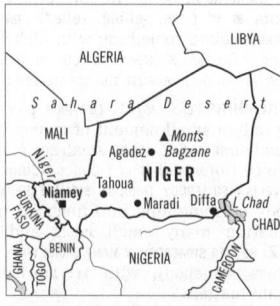
Niger

Niger /nījər/ **1.** country in West Africa, north of Nigeria and south of Libya. Language: French. Currency: CFA franc. Capital: Niamey. Population: 11,058,590 (2001). Area: 1,267,000 sq. km/489,200 sq. mi. Official name **Republic of Niger 2.** river in West Africa. The third longest river in Africa, it rises in southern Guinea, and flows northwards through Mali, then southeast into the Gulf of Guinea,

through Niger and Nigeria. Length: 4,180 km/2,600 mi.

Niger-Congo *n* a large family of languages spoken in central and southern parts of Africa. Native speakers: 200 million. —**Niger-Congo** *adj*

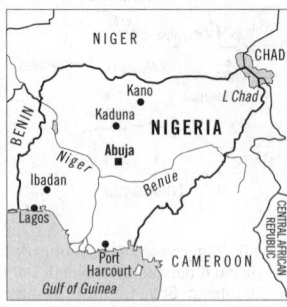
Nigeria

Nigeria /nī jeéri ə/ country in West Africa, on the Gulf of Guinea, south of Niger. It became an independent member of the Commonwealth in 1960. Language: English. Currency: naira. Capital: Abuja. Population: 133,881,700 (2003). Area: 923,768 sq. km/356,669 sq. mi. Official name **Federal Republic of Nigeria** —**Nigerian** *n*, *adj*

Nigerian English *n* a variety of English spoken in Nigeria. See panel on next page

niggard /níggərd/ *n* somebody regarded as stingy or miserly [14C. Alteration of *nigon*, perhaps < *nig* 'stingy' < N Germanic]

niggardly /níggərdli/ *adj* (**-lier**, **-liest**) **1.** NOT GENEROUS very reluctant to give or spend anything **2.** SMALL OR INADEQUATE very small or inadequate in quantity ■ *adv* in STINGY WAY in a miserly or stingy way —**niggardliness** *n*

nigger /níggər/ *n* (*taboo*) **1.** a highly offensive term for a Black person **2.** a highly offensive term for a dark-skinned person [Late 17C. Alteration of NEGRO[1]]

USAGE This term is arguably the single most racially offensive term in the English language. The fact that Black people sometimes use this word in reference to themselves (sometimes as *nigga*) does not excuse its present-day use by members of other ethnic groups. The term of choice is *Black person*.

USAGE See *insult*.

niggle /nígg'l/ *v* (**-gles**, **-gling**, **-gled**) **1.** *vi* CRITICIZE IN PETTY WAY to criticize or find fault continually, especially about small matters **2.** *vi* BE PREOCCUPIED WITH DETAILS to be preoccupied with petty details **3.** *vt* WORRY SOMEBODY to be a source of worry and irritation to somebody, especially in a small way over a long period of time ■ *n UK, Can* **1.** PETTY COMPLAINT a small or petty complaint, criticism, or point of detail or dispute ○ *Once we have a broad agreement, we can sort out these niggles.* **2.** NAGGING WORRY a small but continuing source of annoyance or worry [Early 17C. Origin ?] —**niggler** *n*

niggling /níggling/ *adj* **1.** too preoccupied with details **2.** irritating, painful, or worrying, especially in a small but persistent way —**niggling** *n* —**nigglingly** *adv*

nigh /nī/ *adv*, *adj* near in place or time (*archaic*) ○ (adv) *Daybreak drew nigh.* ○ (adj) *Morning was nigh.* ■ *adv* nearly ○ *We talked for nigh on two hours.* [Old English *nēah* < Germanic]

night /nīt/ *n* **1.** DAILY PERIOD OF DARKNESS the period of darkness occurring each day in most parts of the world, or the entire period between sunset and sunrise **2.** TIME BETWEEN BEDTIME AND WAKING the time between somebody's going to sleep in the evening and waking the next morning **3.** PERIOD OF EVENING ACTIVITIES the period between sunset and bedtime, especially when spent in entertainment or some other activity ○ *We had a great night at her birthday party.* **4.** *also* **Night** EVENING DEVOTED TO SPECIAL ACTIVITY any period after sunset devoted to a special activity, function, or observance ○ *Tomorrow night is Burns Night.* **5.** NIGHTFALL the period of time just after the sun goes down, when it gets dark **6.** PERIOD OF CULTURAL OR EMOTIONAL GLOOMINESS a period marked by grief, gloom, ignorance, or obscurity ○ *Europe slipped into the long night of the Dark Ages.* **7.** DARK OR DARKENED STATE a dark or darkened state, or an absence of

light, consciousness, or enlightenment (*literary*) ■ *adj* **1. OCCURRING AT NIGHT** occurring, appearing, or visible at night ○ *night terrors* **2. USED AT NIGHT** used chiefly at night ○ *Use the night entrance.* **3. WORKING AT NIGHT** working at night in a job also done during the day ○ *the night porter* **4. ACTIVE AT NIGHT** awake or active at night ○ *night feeders* ■ *interj* same as **goodnight** (*informal*) [Old English *niht* < Indo-European] ◇ **night and day** the entire time

SPELLCHECK See *knight*.

night blindness *n* an inability to see clearly in dim light while having normal vision in clear light. Technical name **nyctalopia** —**night-blind** *adj*

nightcap /nɪt kap/ *n* **1. DRINK BEFORE SLEEP** a drink, often alcoholic, taken before going to bed **2. CAP USED AS SLEEPWEAR** a soft cap worn in bed to keep the head warm, in use mainly until the late 19th century **3.** *US* **LAST EVENT** the last event of a day of sports, especially the second game of a baseball doubleheader

nightclothes /nɪt klōthz/ *npl* clothes designed to be worn in bed

nightclub /nɪt klub/ *n* a place of entertainment open late at night, offering live music, dancing, and drinks, and sometimes serving food and providing a floorshow

nightclubbing /nɪt klubbing/ *n* same as **clubbing** (sense 1)

night depository *n* *N Am* same as **night safe**

nightdress /nɪt dress/ *n* a loose dress of light material worn in bed by women and girls. N Am term **night-gown**

nightfall /nɪt fawl/ *n* the time of evening at which it becomes dark and night begins ○ *Be home by nightfall.*

night fighter *n* a fighter aircraft designed to fly at night

nightglow /nɪt glō/ *n* a dim light from the upper atmosphere seen at night

nightgown /nɪt gown/ *n* **1.** *N Am* same as **nightdress 2.** CLOTHING same as **nightshirt**

nighthawk /nɪt hawk/ *n* **1.** a bird of the nightjar family with long pointed wings and black, white, and buff feathers, that feeds on flying insects after dark. Native to: North America. Genus: *Chordeiles.* **2.** same as **night owl** (*informal*)

night-heron *n* a stocky heron with short legs and a thick beak that is active at night or twilight. Genus: *Nycticorax.*

nightie /nɪti/, **nighty** (*plural* **-ies**) *n* CLOTHING same as **nightdress** (*informal*) [Late 19C. Shortening and alteration]

nightingale /nɪting gayl/ *n* a migratory songbird of the thrush family with brownish feathers, the male of which is particularly known for its song. Latin name: *Luscinia megarhynchos*. [13C. Alteration of Old English *nihtegala* < Germanic, 'night-singer']

CULTURAL NOTE *Ode to a Nightingale*, a poem (1819) by John Keats. The poet recounts how on hearing the joyful song of the nightingale he is filled with an intense joy that provides an escape from his woes. But, as he considers the fact that the bird's song has been an inspiration throughout history, the sound fades and he is suddenly returned to reality.

AKG London

Florence Nightingale

Nightingale /nɪting gayl/, **Florence** (1820–1910) British nurse. She worked in the Crimean War, becoming known as 'The Lady with the Lamp'. Later she founded the Nightingale School of Nurses at St Thomas's Hospital, London.

> 'No *man*, not even a doctor, ever gives any other definition of what a nurse should be than this—"devoted and obedient". This definition would do just as well for a porter. It might even do for a horse. It would not do for a policeman.'
> [Florence Nightingale, *Notes on Nursing*; 1860]

nightjar /nɪt jaar/ *n* a bird with a short beak, large gaping mouth, and dark feathers that is active at night and twilight and feeds on insects caught in flight. Family: Caprimulgidae. [< JAR² 'quivering sound']

night latch *n* a door lock operated from inside by a knob and from outside by a key

nightlife /nɪt līf/ *n* the entertainment or social life that goes on in a place in the evenings ○ *Let's go out and check out the local nightlife.*

nightlight /nɪt līt/ *n* a small lamp or candle lit to give a dim light during the night, especially in a child's bedroom

nightlong /nɪt lóng/ *adj* lasting or occurring throughout the entire night —**nightlong** *adv*

nightly /nɪtli/ *adj* **1. HAPPENING EVERY NIGHT** taking place every night **2. OCCURRING AT NIGHT** typically occurring at night ■ *adv* EVERY NIGHT on or during each and every night ○ *The band is playing nightly this week.*

nightmare /nɪt mair/ *n* **1. BAD DREAM** a frightening or upsetting dream **2. TRAUMATIC EXPERIENCE** a traumatic, very upsetting, or extremely difficult and troublesome experience or situation **3. DREADED EVENT** a situation or event that somebody dreads **4. EVIL SPIRIT** a malign spirit formerly believed to suffocate or haunt people during sleep ■ *adj* EXTREMELY FRIGHTENING OR DIFFICULT extremely frightening, upsetting, or difficult to deal with [13C. < NIGHT + Old English *mære*

nightingale

'nightmare' < Germanic] —**nightmarish** *adj* —**nightmarishly** *adv*

night owl *n* somebody who stays up late at night, especially to work or socialize (*informal*)

nightrider /nɪt rīdər/ *n* a member of a group of masked horsemen who at night terrorized or intimidated African Americans and their sympathizers in the southern United States in the period after the Civil War

nights /nɪts/ *adv* during the night, or every night ○ *They work nights.*

night safe *n* a safe in the wall of a bank that can be opened from outside to allow people to deposit money at times when the bank is closed. N Am term **night depository**

night school *n* a school or college that holds classes in the evening, especially for people who are at work during the day

nightscope /nɪt skōp/ *n* an optical device, e.g. one using infrared radiation, that gives better vision in the dark

nightshade /nɪt shayd/ *n* a wild plant, related to potatoes, tomatoes, and aubergines, with flowers that have five petals, and small berries. Some are poisonous, e.g. deadly nightshade. Family: Solanaceae.

night shift *n* **1.** a set period of work during the night **2.** a group of people who work during a set period at night (*takes a singular or plural verb*) ○ *The night shift finish at seven in the morning.*

nightshirt /nɪt shurt/ *n* a long loose garment resembling a shirt, worn in bed by men

nightside /nɪt sīd/ *n* the side of a planet or moon that is not lit by the Sun

night sight *n* an infrared sight on a rifle used for taking aim in darkness

night soil *n* human excrement collected at night from toilets or cesspools, especially for use as fertilizer

nightspot /nɪt spot/ *n* same as **nightclub**

nightstand /nɪt stand/ *n* *N Am* FURNITURE same as **night table**

nightstick /nɪt stik/ *n* *N Am* a club carried by a police officer [Because traditionally carried especially at night]

night table *n* *N Am* a bedside table or stand

night terror *n* a sudden awakening from sleep in a condition of extreme fear that is not associated with a dream or nightmare

nighttime /nɪt tīm/ *n* the period of each day when it is dark, or the time between sunset and sunrise

night vision *n* somebody's ability to see in the dark ○ *They say eating carrots improves your night vision.*

night watch *n* **1.** a guard or watch kept during the night ○ *I'm on night watch this week.* **2.** same as **night watchman** (sense 1)

night watchman *n* **1.** somebody who guards or watches over something at night, especially a building site or factory **2.** in cricket, a lower-order batsman who is sent in out of order if a wicket falls near the end of a day's play, to play defensively and prevent the loss of another more important wicket

nightwear /nɪt wair/ *n* clothes for people to wear while sleeping. N Am term **sleepwear**

nighty *n* CLOTHING another spelling of **nightie** (*informal*)

nigrescence /nɪ gréss'nss/ *n* the process of becoming black or dark [Mid-19C. < Latin *nigrescent-*, present participle of *nigrescere* 'grow black' < *niger* 'black'] —**nigrescent** *adj* —**nigrescently** *adv*

nigrosine /nígrə seen, -sin/, **nigrosin** /-sin/ *n* a black aniline pigment or dye. Use: ink, polish, textile dye. [Late 19C. < Latin *niger* 'black']

NIH *abbr* GOV National Institutes of Health

NIHE *abbr* EDUC National Institute for Higher Education

nihilism /nɪ i lizəm, nɪhi-/ *n* **1. TOTAL REJECTION OF SOCIAL MORES** the general rejection of established social conventions and beliefs, especially of morality and religion **2. BELIEF THAT NOTHING IS WORTHWHILE** a belief that life is pointless and human values are worthless **3. DISBELIEF IN OBJECTIVE TRUTH** the belief that there is no objective basis for truth **4. BELIEF IN DESTRUCTION OF AUTHORITY** the belief that all established authority is corrupt and must be destroyed in order to rebuild a just society **5.** *also* **Nihilism** RUSSIAN POLITICAL MOVEMENT

a political movement in late 19th-century Russia that sought to bring about a socially just new society by destroying the existing one through acts of terrorism and assassination [Early 19C. < German *Nihilismus* < Latin *nihil* 'nothing'] —**nihilist** *n* —**nihilistic** /nĭ i lístik, nĭhi-/ *adj* —**nihilistically** *adv*

nihility /nī híllәti, nee-/ *n* the condition of being nothing [Late 17C. < medieval Latin *nihilitas* < Latin *nihil* 'nothing']

nihil obstat /níhil ób stat, níhil-/ *n* **1.** a statement by a Roman Catholic Church official that a publication is not offensive to religion or morals **2.** an official statement of nonopposition [Mid-20C. < Latin, 'nothing hinders']

NII *abbr* Nuclear Installations Inspectorate

Niigata /nyi ә gaátә/ city and port in Japan, on northern Honshu. It is the capital city of Niigata Prefecture. Population: 514,678 (2002).

Vaslav Nijinsky: performing in *Le Spectre de la Rose* (1911)

Nijinsky /ni jínski/, **Vaslav** (1890–1950) Russian ballet dancer. The leading dancer of the original Ballets Russes, he choreographed several innovative ballets including *The Rite of Spring* (1913).

-nik *suffix* somebody associated with or characterized by ○ *refusenik* [Directly or via Yiddish < Russian]

Nike /níki/ *n* in Greek mythology, the winged goddess of victory

Nikkei Index /ní kay-/ *n* an index of 225 leading shares traded on the Tokyo Stock Exchange [Late 20C. Abbreviation of Japanese *Nihon Keizai Shimbun* 'Japanese Economic Journal']

Nikko /neékō/ city in Japan, in Tochigi Prefecture, central Honshu, 145 km/90 mi. north of Tokyo. Population: 17,527 (2002).

nil /nil/ *n* nothing or zero, often used in the scores of games ○ *Our team won two-nil.* [Early 19C. Latin, contraction of *nihil* 'nothing']

Nile

Nile /nīl/ river in northeastern Africa. It is the longest river in the world. Rising in east-central Africa near Lake Victoria, it flows. Length: 6,695 km/4,160 mi.northwards through Uganda, Sudan, and Egypt before emptying into the Mediterranean Sea

Nile blue *adj* of a pale greenish-blue colour —**Nile blue** *n*

Nile green *adj* of a yellowish-green colour —**Nile green** *n*

nilgai /níl gī/ (*plural same* or **-gais**), **nilgau** /-gaw/ (*plural same* or **-gaus**), **nilghau** (*plural same* or **-ghaus**) *n* a large antelope, the male of which is bluish-grey and horned, the female brownish and hornless. Native to: South Asia. Latin name: *Boselaphus*

tragocamelus. [Late 18C. < Hindi *nīlgāe* < Sanskrit *nīla* 'blue' + *-gāvī* 'cow']

Nilo-Saharan /nílō-/ *n* a large family of languages spoken in central Africa. Native speakers: 15 million. —**Nilo-Saharan** *adj*

Nilotic /nī lóttik/ *adj* **1.** RELATING TO NILE relating to, living beside, or involving the River Nile **2.** OF NILE VALLEY LANGUAGE relating to a Nilo-Saharan group of languages spoken in parts of the Nile valley ■ *n* NILE VALLEY LANGUAGE GROUP a Nilo-Saharan group of languages spoken in parts of the Nile valley, mainly in Uganda and Sudan. Native speakers: 3 million. [Mid-17C. Via Latin < Greek *Neilōtikos* < *Neilos* 'Nile']

nim /nim/ *n* a game in which players remove small, differently arranged items from piles, the winner being the player who takes, or sometimes does not take, the final item [Early 20C. Origin ?]

nimble /nímb'l/ (**-bler**, **-blest**) *adj* **1.** agile, fast, and light in movement **2.** able to think quickly and cleverly [Old English *næmel, numol* 'quick at grasping' < *niman* 'to take'] —**nimbleness** *n* —**nimbly** *adv*

nimbostratus /nímbō stráytәss, -straátәss/ (*plural* **-ti** /-tī/) *n* a low dark layer of rain-bearing cloud covering all of the sky [Late 19C. < NIMBUS]

nimbus /nímbәss/ (*plural* **-buses** or **-bi** /-bī/) *n* **1.** METEOROL DARK RAIN-BEARING CLOUD a dense dark rain-bearing cloud **2.** RELIG CLOUD OF LIGHT AROUND DEITY a cloud of light surrounding a god, goddess, saint or holy person **3.** ART IMAGE OF HALO a bright halo or disc around the head of a deity, saint, or sovereign in a painting, icon, or medal **4.** AURA OF SPLENDOUR an aura or atmosphere of splendour surrounding somebody or something [Early 17C. < Latin, 'cloud, rain']

NIMBY[1] /nímbi/ (*plural* **NIMBYs**), **Nimby** (*plural* **-bys**) *n* **1.** somebody who objects to something unattractive or potentially dangerous being located near his or her home **2.** the attitude of a NIMBY [Late 20C. < NIMBY[2]] —**Nimbyism** *n*

NIMBY[2] *abbr* not in my back yard

niminy-piminy /nímmәni pímmәni/ *adj* affected and mincing [Late 18C. Based on NAMBY-PAMBY]

nimrod /ním rod/ *n* a skilful or enthusiastic hunter (*literary*) [Mid-16C. < *Nimrod* as a 'mighty hunter' (Genesis 10:9)]

Anaïs Nin

Nin /nin/, **Anaïs** (1903–77) French writer. Involved with surrealism and psychoanalysis, she is best known for her passionate and self-revelatory *Diaries* (1966–85).

'Each friend represents a world in us, a world possibly not born until they arrive, and it is only by this meeting that a new world is born.'
[Anaïs Nin, *The Diary of Anaïs Nin*, volume II; 1967]

'Life shrinks or expands in proportion to one's courage.'
[Anaïs Nin, *The Diary of Anaïs Nin*, volume III; June 1941]

nincompoop /níngkәm poop/ *n* an offensive term that deliberately insults somebody's intelligence or competence (*insult*) [Late 17C. Alteration of *nicompoop*, origin ?] —**nincompoopery** *n*

nine /nīn/ *n* **1.** 9 the number 9 **2.** SOMETHING WITH VALUE OF 9 something in a numbered series, e.g. a playing card, with a value of 9 ○ *a nine of clubs* ○ *to play the nine* **3.** GROUP OF NINE a group of nine objects or people **4.** BASEBALL BASEBALL TEAM a team of nine baseball players **5.** GOLF HALF OF GOLF COURSE half of the total

number of holes on a golf course, usually called the front nine or the back nine [Old English *nigon* < Indo-European] —**nine** *adj, pron* ◇ **dressed (up) to the nines** very elaborately or formally dressed

9/11 /nĭn i lévv'n/, **9–11** *n* the events of 11 September 2001, when planes hijacked by terrorists destroyed the World Trade Center in New York, damaged the Pentagon, and crashed into a field in Pennsylvania, with great loss of life [< the US convention of representing dates with the month before the day]

ninebark /nīn baark/ *n* a bush with bark that separates into many layers. Native to: eastern North America. Genus: *Physocarpus.*

nine days' wonder, **nine day wonder** *n* something that, or somebody who, briefly arouses great interest or excitement but is soon forgotten again [Refers to Lady Jane Grey (1537–54), who was proclaimed queen of England in 1553 but was deposed after nine days and subsequently beheaded]

911 /nīn wun wún/ *n* in the United States and Canada, the telephone number used to call for police, fire, or ambulance emergency services ○ *The teacher sent a child to call 911 and get an ambulance.*

ninefold /nīn fōld/ *adj* **1.** BY NINE TIMES of nine times the original figure ○ *a ninefold rise* **2.** WITH NINE PARTS made up of nine parts ○ *The problem is ninefold.* ■ *adv* BY NINE TIMES AS MUCH by nine times as much or as many ○ *The numbers increased ninefold.*

999 /nīn nīn nīn/ *n* in the United Kingdom, the telephone number used to call for police, fire, or ambulance emergency services ○ *When I heard the collision I dialled 999 right away.*

ninepin /nīn pin/ *n* N Am same as **skittle**

ninepins /nīn pinz/ *n* N Am same as **skittles** (*takes a singular verb*)

nineteen /nīn teén/ *n* **1.** 19 the number 19 **2.** SOMETHING WITH VALUE OF 19 something in a numbered series with a value of 19 **3.** GROUP OF 19 a group of 19 objects or people [Old English *nigontyne* < Germanic, 'nine-ten'] —**nineteen** *adj, pron*

nineteenth /nīn teénth/ *n* one of 19 equal parts of something ○ *My share came to three-nineteenths.* —**nineteenth** *adj, pron*

nineteenth hole *n* a place, especially the bar of a clubhouse, where players can drink and socialize after a round of golf (*slang*) [As after the conventional 18 holes]

~~nineth~~ incorrect spelling of **ninth**

ninetieth /nínti әth/ *n* one of 90 equal parts of something ○ *a ninetieth of the whole* —**ninetieth** *adj, pron*

nine-to-five *adj* requiring regular attendance, e.g. at an office job, especially between 9 a.m. and 5 p.m. (*informal*) ○ *without the self-discipline to hold down a nine-to-five job*

nine-to-fiver *n* N Am somebody who works regular hours, especially from 9 a.m. to 5 p.m. (*informal*) ○ *She took the morning train with the rest of the nine-to-fivers.*

ninety /nínti/ *n* 90 the number 90 ■ **nineties** *npl* **1.** NUMBERS BETWEEN 90 AND 99 the numbers between 90 and 99, particularly as a range of Fahrenheit temperatures **2.** YEARS FROM 90 TO 99 the years from 90 to 99 in a century **3.** PERIOD FROM AGE 90 TO 99 the period of somebody's life from the age of 90 to 99 [Old English *nigontig*, shortening of *hundnigontig* < *hund* 'hundred' + *nigon* 'nine' + *-tig* 'ten'] —**ninety** *adj, pron*

99 /nínti nīn/ *n* a cone of ice cream with a stick of layered flaky chocolate stuck in it

Nineveh /nínnәvә/ ancient capital of the Assyrian empire, situated on the River Tigris in northern Iraq. At the height of its importance from about 705 BC, it was destroyed by the Babylonians and Medes in 612 BC.

Ningbo /ning bō/ city in northeastern Zhejiang Province, eastern China, situated approximately 145 km/90 mi. southeast of Hangzhou. Population: 1,145,219 (1991).

Ningxia Hui /níng shyaá hweé/ autonomous region in north-central China. Capital: Yinchuan. Population: 4,655,451 (1990). Area: 66,400 sq. km/25,600 sq. mi.

Ninian /nínni әn/, **St** (360?–432?) Scottish bishop and missionary. He was the earliest known Christian missionary in Scotland.

ninja /nínjә/ (*plural* **-jas** or *same*) *n* a member of a group of mercenaries in feudal Japan who were

trained in stealth and the martial arts and employed as spies, saboteurs, or assassins [Mid-20C. < Japanese, 'spy' < *nin* 'endure' + *ja* 'person' (< Middle Chinese *tšia?*)]

ninjitsu /nin jít soo/ *n* a Japanese martial art that emphasizes stealth in movement and camouflage [Mid-20C. < Japanese, 'stealth art']

ninny /nínni/ (*plural* **-nies**) *n* an offensive term that deliberately insults somebody's intelligence, common sense, or effectiveness (*insult*) [Late 16C. Origin ?] —**ninnyish** *adj*

ninon /neé non, nī-/ *n* a sturdy sheer silk or synthetic fabric [Early 20C. < French]

ninth /nīnth/ *n* **1.** one of 9 equal parts of something **2.** a musical tone separated from another by an interval of an octave and a second, or the interval of this tone —**ninth** *adj, pron*

ninth chord *n* a musical chord containing four thirds, including the ninth, added above the root

~~**ninty**~~ incorrect spelling of **ninety**

Niobe /nī ə bi/ *n* in Greek mythology, the daughter of Tantalus, punished by Apollo and Artemis for claiming superiority over their mother Leto. Her children were killed and she herself was turned into stone.

niobic /nī ṓbik/ *adj* concerning or containing niobium with a valency of five [< NIOBIUM]

niobite /nī ə bīt/ *n* MINERALS same as **columbite** [< NIOBIUM]

niobium /nī ṓbi əm/ *n* a lustrous pale grey ductile metallic element that is a superconductor chemically resembling tantalum. Source: columbite. Use: steel alloys. Symbol **Nb**. See table at **element** [Mid-19C. < its association with tantalum, TANTALUS being the father of NIOBE]

niobous /nī ṓbəss/ *adj* concerning or containing niobium with a valency less than five [< NIOBIUM]

nip[1] /nip/ *v* (**nips, nipping, nipped**) **1.** *vt* PINCH SOMETHING to take hold of something and squeeze or compress it, often painfully, between two surfaces, e.g. to pinch skin between a forefinger and thumb **2.** *vti* TAKE BRIEF BITE AT SOMETHING to bite something briefly, often painfully, but without doing much damage **3.** *vt* SEVER SOMETHING to remove something by pinching, biting, or clipping ○ *nipped off the dead flower heads* **4.** *vt* AFFECT SOMEBODY WITH COLD to sting or chill a person or part of the body painfully with cold ○ *frost nipping his fingers and toes* **5.** *vt* STOP SOMETHING FROM DEVELOPING to halt the growth or development of something ○ *hoped to nip the conflict in the bud* **6.** *vt* MAKE SOMETHING NARROWER to make something narrower or tighter ○ *The dress is nipped in at the waist.* **7.** *vt US* STEAL SOMETHING to steal or snatch something (*informal*) **8.** *vi* GO QUICKLY to go somewhere quickly or briefly (*informal*) ○ *She nipped down to the shop for bread.* ■ *n* **1.** SHARP SQUEEZE a sharp or painful squeeze with the fingers or between two surfaces **2.** SMALL BRIEF BITE a small bite with the teeth that may be painful but does not do much damage ○ *The dog tried to give my ankle a nip as I passed.* **3.** SMALL CUT-OUT PIECE a small piece cut from something **4.** CHILL a chilly feeling caused by a marked drop in temperature ○ *There's a nip in the air tonight.* **5.** SHARP FLAVOUR a sharp or pungent flavour [14C. < Middle Low German *nipen*] ◇ **nip and tuck** *N Am* very closely and evenly contested so that the outcome remains in doubt (*informal*)

nip[2] /nip/ *n* a small portion or drink of something alcoholic ■ *vti* (**nips, nipping, nipped**) to drink an alcoholic beverage in small sips [Late 18C. Origin ?]

nipa /neépə, nīpə/ *n* **1.** LEAVES OF PALM TREE the long feathery leaves of a palm tree. Use: thatching, basketry. **2.** DRINK FROM PALM SAP an alcoholic drink made from the sap of a palm tree **3.** (*plural* **nipas** or *same*) ASIAN PALM TREE a palm tree that produces nipa leaves, edible fruit, and the sap from which the drink nipa is made. Native to: South Asia. Latin name: *Nipa fruticans.* [Late 16C. < Malay *nipah*]

Nipigon, Lake /níppi gon/ lake in west-central Ontario, Canada. It empties into Lake Superior via the Nipigon River. Area: 4,850 sq. km/1,870 sq. mi. Depth: 165 m/540 ft.

Nipissing, Lake /níppi sing/ lake in southeastern Ontario, Canada. It empties into Georgian Bay via the French River. Area: 832 sq. km/321 sq. mi.

nipper /níppər/ *n* **1.** PINCER a large claw of a crustacean, especially a lobster or crab **2.** CHILD a small child (*informal*) ■ **nippers** *npl* PLIERS a tool used to squeeze or clip something, e.g. pliers

nipping /nípping/ *adj* **1.** very cold and biting **2.** bitingly sarcastic —**nippingly** *adv*

nipple /nípp'l/ *n* **1.** a small knob in the centre of the breast that in female mammals is the outlet for the ducts that provide the young with milk **2.** *N Am* same as **teat** (sense 2) **3.** a small knob on a device that is the outlet for fluid such as oil or grease [Mid-16C. Origin ?]

Nippon /níppon/ the Japanese name for Japan —**Nipponese** /níppə neéz/ *adj*

nippy /níppi/ (**-pier, -piest**) *adj* **1.** CHILLY rather chilly **2.** SMALL AND FAST small, quick, and easy to manoeuvre ○ *a nippy little car* **3.** TENDING TO BITE describes a dog that is inclined to attempt to bite people or other animals —**nippily** *adv* —**nippiness** *n*

NIRC *abbr* National Industrial Relations Court

N. Ire. *abbr* Northern Ireland

NIREX /nī reks/ *abbr* Nuclear Industry Radioactive Waste Executive

Niro ♦ **De Niro, Robert**

nirvana /neer vaánə, nur-/ *n* **1.** *also* **Nirvana** in Hinduism, Buddhism, and Jainism, the attainment of enlightenment and freeing of the spiritual self from attachment to worldly things, ending the cycle of birth and rebirth **2.** an ultimate experience of some pleasurable emotion such as harmony or joy [Mid-19C. < Sanskrit < *nirvā-* 'be extinguished' < *nis-* 'out' + *vā-* 'to blow']

Nisan /neé saan/ *n* in the Jewish calendar, the first month of the religious year, lasting 30 days and falling about the same time as March to April. See table at **calendar** [15C. < Hebrew *Nīsān*]

nisgal /nízg'l/ *n regional* the smallest or weakest piglet in a litter [Origin ?]

REGIONAL NOTE See *underling.*

nisi /nī sī, neéssi/ *adj* scheduled to take effect on a specific date unless some cause can be shown for cancelling or changing the date [Mid-19C. < Latin, 'unless']

Nissen hut /níss'n-/ *n* a temporary shelter made of corrugated steel in the shape of a half cylinder that was first used by the British during World War I [Early 20C. After Lt-Col Peter Norman *Nissen* (1871–1930)]

nit /nit/ *n* **1.** the egg or larva of a parasitic insect, especially a louse **2.** an offensive term that deliberately insults somebody's common sense or intelligence (*insult*) [Old English *hnitu* < Indo-European.] —**nitty** *adj*

SPELLCHECK See *knit.*

nite /nīt/ *n* a spelling of the word 'night', not appropriate for use in formal writing (*informal*)

Niten /neét en, nee tén/ (1584–1645) Japanese artist and soldier. He is noted for his *sumi-e,* or black ink, paintings of birds, and was renowned for developing the technique of fencing with two swords. Born **Miyamoto Musashi**

niter *n* CHEM US spelling of **nitre**

Niterói /neetə róy/ city in southeastern Brazil, situated on the southeastern shore of Guanabara Bay, opposite the city of Rio de Janeiro. Population: 450,364 (1996).

nitpick /nít pik/ (**-picks, -picking, -picked**) *vti* to find insignificant details of something unsatisfactory, often unjustifiably —**nitpicker** *n* —**nitpicky** *adj*

SYNONYMS See *criticize.*

nitpicking /nít piking/ *n* trivial, detailed, and often unjustified faultfinding

nitr- *prefix* same as **nitro-** (*used before vowels*)

nitrate /nī trayt/ *n* **1.** CHEM CHEMICAL GROUP a salt or an ester of nitric acid **2.** AGRIC FERTILIZER a fertilizer that consists of sodium nitrate, potassium nitrate, or ammonium nitrate ■ *vt* (**-trates, -trating, -trated**) CHEM, INDUST USE NITRATE ON SOMETHING to treat something with a nitrate or nitric acid, usually in order to change an organic compound into a nitrate [Late 18C. < French < *nitre* 'nitre'] —**nitration** /nī tráysh'n/ *n*

nitrazepam /nī trázzi pam/ *n* a tranquillizer used in some sleeping pills. Formula: $C_{15}H_{11}N_3O_{35}$. [Mid-20C. < NITRO- + -*azepam,* INN stem]

nitre /nītər/ *n* CHEM **1.** same as **potassium nitrate 2.** same as **sodium nitrate** [14C. Via Old French < Latin *nitrum* < Greek *nitron*]

nitric /nī trik/ *adj* made from or containing nitrogen, especially in a high valency state

nitric acid *n* a corrosive colourless or yellowish liquid that is a highly reactive oxidizing agent. Use: manufacture of explosives, fertilizers, rocket fuels. Formula: HNO_3.

nitric oxide *n* a colourless poisonous gas. Source: ammonia, atmospheric nitrogen. Formula: NO.

nitride /nī trīd/ *n* a compound made up of nitrogen and another more electropositive element such as phosphorus or a metal [Mid-19C. < NITROGEN]

nitrify /nītri fī/ (**-fies, -fying, -fied**) *vt* **1.** CHEM TREAT SOMETHING WITH NITROGEN to treat or combine something with nitrogen or nitrogen compounds **2.** AGRIC FERTILIZE SOIL to introduce nitrogen or nitrogen compounds into the soil in order to increase fertility **3.** BIOCHEM OXIDIZE AMMONIA IONS to oxidize ammonia ions into nitrite or nitrate ions, as nitrobacteria do [Early 19C. < French *nitrifier* < *nitre* (see NITRE)] —**nitrification** /nītrifi káysh'n/ *n* —**nitrifier** *n*

nitrifying bacterium /nītri fī ing-/ *n* a soil bacterium that converts ammonia to nitrites and nitrates, making nitrogen available to plants

nitrile /nītrəl, -trīl/ *n* an organic cyanide. Use: rubber, especially in latex-free gloves.

nitrite /nī trīt/ *n* a salt or ester of nitrous acid

nitrite bacterium *n* a nitrifying bacterium that converts ammonia to nitrites by oxidation

nitro /nītrō/ *n* same as **nitroglycerine** (*informal*) [Early 20C. Shortening]

nitro- *prefix* **1.** nitrogen ○ *nitrify* **2.** nitre, nitrate **3.** containing a univalent NO_2 group ○ *nitroparaffin* [< Latin *nitrum* (see NITRE)]

nitrobacterium /nītrō bak teéri əm/ (*plural* **-ria** /-ri ə/) *n* same as **nitrifying bacterium**

nitrobenzene /nītrō bén zeen/ *n* a poisonous organic compound that occurs either as bright yellow crystals or as an oily liquid that smells like almonds. Use: manufacture of polishes, insulating compounds. Formula: $C_6H_5NO_2$.

nitrocellulose /nītrō séllyoo lōss, -lōz/ *n* a chemical compound produced by the reaction of nitric and sulphuric acids on cellulose. Use: manufacture of plastics, explosives, lacquers.

nitrochloroform /nītrō klórrə fawrm/ *n* CHEM same as **chloropicrin**

nitrofuran /nītrō fyoór an/ *n* a drug that inhibits the growth of bacteria. It has been banned from use in food-producing animals in many countries.

nitrofurantoin /nītrō fyoo rántō in/ *n* a drug that inhibits the growth of bacteria. Use: treatment of urinary infections.

nitrogen /nītrəjən/ *n* a nonmetallic element that occurs as a colourless odourless almost inert gas and makes up four-fifths of the Earth's atmosphere by volume. Use: manufacture of ammonia, explosives, fertilizers. Symbol **N**. See table at **element** [Late 18C. < French *nitrogène* < *nitre* (see NITRE) + *-gène* (see -GEN)] —**nitrogenous** /nī trójjənəss/ *adj*

nitrogenase /nī trójjə nayz, -nayss/ *n* an enzyme found in nitrogen-fixing bacteria that catalyses the conversion of nitrogen to ammonia. It is a key component of the nitrogen cycle, providing nitrogen compounds for plants.

nitrogen balance *n* **1.** the difference between the amount of nitrogen taken into the body and the amount excreted **2.** the difference between the amount of nitrogen absorbed by the soil and the amount lost

nitrogen cycle *n* the series of processes by which nitrogen is converted from a gas in the atmosphere to nitrogen-containing substances in soil and living organisms, then reconverted to a gas. The main chemical transformations are performed by microorganisms and include nitrogen fixation, nitrification, and denitrification. See illustration on next page

nitrogen dioxide *n* a highly poisonous brown gas often present in smog and exhaust from vehicles. Use: manufacture of nitric and sulphuric acids. Formula: NO_2.

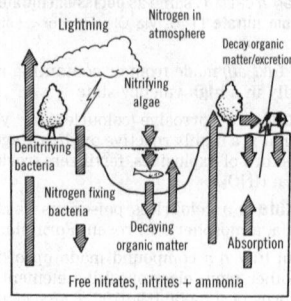

nitrogen cycle

nitrogen fixation *n* **1.** the natural conversion of atmospheric nitrogen by bacteria found in the nodules of legumes into compounds in the soil that plants and other organisms can use **2.** an industrial process in which nitrogen from the atmosphere is changed into compounds such as ammonia by chemical agents. Use: manufacture of fertilizers. — **nitrogen-fixer** *n* —**nitrogen-fixing** *adj*

nitrogenize /nī trójjə nīz/ (**-izes**, **-izing**, **-ized**), **nitrogenise** (**-ises**, **-ising**, **-ised**) *vt* to combine or treat something with nitrogen or one of its compounds — **nitrogenization** /nī trójjə nī záysh'n/ *n*

nitrogen mustard *n* a compound similar to mustard gas in which the sulphur is replaced by amino nitrogen. Use: treatment of some cancers.

nitrogen narcosis *n* light-headedness, confusion, or exhilaration caused by increased nitrogen in the blood. This occurs in deep-sea divers exposed to pressures several times that of the atmosphere.

nitroglycerine /nítrō glíssərin, -reen/, **nitroglycerin** /-rin/ *n* a colourless thick oily flammable and explosive liquid. Use: manufacture of explosives, treatment of angina. Formula: $C_3H_5N_3O_9$.

nitrohydrochloric acid /nítrō hīdrō klórrik-/ *n* CHEM same as **aqua regia**

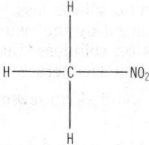

nitromethane

nitromethane /nítrō meé thayn/ *n* a poisonous colourless oily slightly water-soluble liquid. Use: manufacture of dyes, resins, rocket fuels, as a solvent and petrol additive. Formula: CH_3NO_2.

nitroparaffin /nítrō párrəfin/ *n* a colourless simple hydrocarbon containing the chemical group NO_2

nitrosamine /nī trōzə meen/ *n* an organic carcinogenic compound found in various foods. Formula: R_2NNO. [Late 19C. < Latin *nitrosus* 'nitrous']

nitrous /nítrəss/ *adj* made from or containing nitrogen, especially in a low valency state

nitrous acid *n* a weak inorganic acid found only in solution or in the form of its salts. Formula: HNO_2.

nitrous oxide *n* a colourless nonflammable sweet-smelling sweet-tasting gas. Use: anaesthetic. Formula: N_2O.

nitty-gritty /nítti grítti/ (*informal*) *n* BASICS the basic and most important details of something ■ *adj* **1.** BASIC AND IMPORTANT concerning or involving the most important aspects of a subject **2.** PRACTICAL useful and direct in a practical down-to-earth way ○ *a nitty-gritty approach to teaching* [Mid-20C. Origin ?]

nitwit /nít wit/ *n* an offensive term that deliberately insults somebody's common sense or intelligence (*insult*) [Early 20C. Origin ?]

Niue /nee oó ay/ island territory in free association with New Zealand, lying in the South Pacific Ocean, 563 km/350 mi. southeast of Samoa. Population: 2,000 (1995). Area: 263 sq. km/101 sq. mi.

Niuean /nee oó ay ən/ *n* **1.** a member of a Polynesian people who inhabit the Pacific island of Niue **2.** the Polynesian language of Niue, similar to Samoan and Tongan —**Niuean** *adj*

nival /nív'l/ *adj* growing in or under the snow [Mid-17C. < Latin *nivalis* < *niv-* 'snow']

niveous /nívvi əss/ *adj* resembling snow in colour [Early 17C. < Latin *niveus* < *niv-* 'snow']

nix /niks/ *N Am vt* (**nixes**, **nixing**, **nixed**) to refuse, forbid, or veto something (*slang*) ■ *n* same as **nothing** (*dated slang*) [Late 18C. < German, variant of *nichts* 'nothing']

nixie /níksi/, **nix** /niks/ *n* in Germanic mythology, a female water spirit that can appear in human form or as half-human, half-fish [Early 19C. < German *Nixe*, feminine of *Nix*]

Richard Nixon

Nixon /níks'n/, **Richard** (1913–94) 37th president of the United States. A Republican president (1969–74), he was forced to resign after the Watergate scandal (1974). He was responsible for ending the US commitment in Vietnam. See table at **president**. Full name **Nixon, Richard Milhous**

> 'I let down my friends, I let down my country. I let down our system of government.'
> [Richard Nixon, *Observer*; 8 May 1977]

> 'You won't have Nixon to kick around anymore, because, gentlemen, this is my last press conference.'
> [Richard Nixon, *remark to the media*; 7 November 1962]

Nizam /ni zaám/ *n* the title given to the hereditary ruler of the former Indian state of Hyderabad [Mid-18C. < Urdu *nizām-al-mulk* 'administrator of the realm']

Nizhniy Novgorod /nízhni nóvgərod/ industrial city and major river port in western Russia where the rivers Oka and Volga meet. Population: 1,840,212 (1995). Former name **Gorky** (1932–91)

Nizhny Tagil /nízhni taa gíl/ city in western Siberian Russia. Population: 391,737 (1995).

NJ *abbr* New Jersey

njamma-njamma /ən jámmə ən jámmə/ *n* in African cuisine, large- or small-leaf cooking greens resembling rocket

Nkomo /əng kṓmō/, **Joshua** (1917–99) Zimbabwean nationalist leader. He led the Zimbabwe African People's Union and other nationalist groups opposed to white rule in Rhodesia, and after the transition to majority rule in Zimbabwe held various government posts.

> 'The hardest lesson of my life has come to me late. It is that a nation can win freedom without its people becoming free.'
> [Joshua Nkomo, *The Story of My Life*; 1984]

Nkrumah /ən kroómə, əng-/, **Kwame** (1909–72) first prime minister (1957–60) and president (1960–66) of Ghana. He played a prominent role in the establishment of the independent state of Ghana in 1957 and was a strong supporter of pan-Africanism.

> 'Never in the history of the world has an alien ruler granted self-rule to a people on a silver platter.'
> [Kwame Nkrumah, *The Autobiography of Kwame Nkrumah*; 1959]

NKVD *n* the Soviet secret police from 1934 to 1946 [< Russian, abbreviation of *Narodny Kommissariat Vnutrennikh Del* 'People's Commissariat of Internal Affairs']

nl *abbr* **1.** Netherlands (*used in Internet addresses*) See table at **domain name** **2.** PRINTING new line

NL *abbr* LANG New Latin

NLF *abbr* POL National Liberation Front

NLP *abbr* **1.** COMPUT natural language processing **2.** PSYCHOL neurolinguistic programming

nm *abbr* **1.** MEASURE nanometre **2.** *also* **n.m.** MEASURE, NAUT nautical mile **3.** MEASURE nuclear magneton

NM *abbr* MEASURE nautical mile

NMR *abbr* PHYS, MED nuclear magnetic resonance

NNE *abbr* north-northeast

NNP *abbr* ECON net national product

NNW *abbr* north-northwest

no[1] /nō/ *adv, interj* **1.** INDICATING NEGATIVE RESPONSE indicates a negative response, used to refuse, deny, or disagree with something ○ '*Will you be taking the car?*' – '*No, not today*'. ○ '*Would you like a coffee?*' – '*No, I'm fine, thanks*'. **2.** ACKNOWLEDGING NEGATIVE STATEMENT used to express acceptance or understanding of a negative statement made by somebody else ○ '*Nobody seems to have the time to really listen these days*'. – '*No, they don't*'. **3.** INDICATING DISBELIEF used to indicate shock, disbelief, or disappointment at something somebody has said ○ '*The car's going to be in the garage for another week*'. – '*Oh no!*' ■ *n* (*plural* **noes** or **nos**) **1.** ANSWER OR VOTE an answer or vote of 'no' ○ *They all gave resounding noes to the proposition*. **2.** SOMEBODY VOTING 'NO' somebody who answers 'no' to a question or votes against something [Old English *nā* < *ne* 'not' + *ā* 'ever'] ◇ **not take no for an answer** not to accept a refusal ○ *I told her I couldn't do it, but she wouldn't take no for an answer.* ◇ **say no** to express disagreement or refusal ◇ **the noes have it** used to indicate that the majority have voted against something

SPELLCHECK See *know*.

no[2] /nō/ CORE MEANING: a determiner used to indicate that there is not any or not one person or thing ○ *There is nothing within walking distance: no post office, no bank*. ○ *I had no choice in the matter*. ○ *They pay no attention to me*.
det **1.** used to indicate that somebody or something does not have any of the characteristic or identity mentioned ○ *She's no fool*. **2.** not exceeding a particular amount or quality (*used with comparative adjectives and adverbs*) ○ *The issue was no less important to us than you*. [12C. Shortening of NONE]

no[3] *abbr* Norway (*used in Internet addresses*) See table at **domain name**

No[1] /nō/, **Noh** *n* a form of Japanese drama that presents a story in a highly stylized fashion, using music, dance, and elaborate costumes. It flourished in the 14th and 15th centuries, and its development was influenced by Zen Buddhism. [Late 19C. < Japanese *nō* 'talent, ability' < Middle Chinese *nəń*]

No[2] *symbol* CHEM ELEM nobelium

no., **No.** *abbr* **1.** north **2.** northern **3.** number

n.o. *abbr* CRICKET not out

Noachian /nō áyki ən/, **Noachic** /-áykik/, **Noachical** /-áykik'l/ *adj* **1.** characteristic of or relating to Noah or his time **2.** long out of date [Late 19C. < *Noach*, form of *Noah*]

Noah /nṓ ə/ *n* in the Bible, a Hebrew patriarch who, at God's command, built a ship and saved himself, his family, and a pair of every kind of animal from the Flood (Genesis 6–9)

Noah's ark *n* BIBLE same as **ark** (sense 1)

nob[1] /nob/ *n* somebody rich or socially powerful (*informal*) [Late 17C. Origin ?]

nob[2] /nob/ *n* **1.** the human head (*slang*) **2.** in cribbage, the jack of the suit that the dealer turns up, which scores one point for the player who holds it [Late 17C. Origin ?]

no ball *n* in cricket, a ball that has been bowled in a way not permitted by the rules of the game

nobble /nóbb'l/ (**-bles**, **-bling**, **-bled**) *vt* (*informal*) **1.** ACCOST SOMEBODY to make contact with somebody, especially in order to persuade that person to do something **2.** INFLUENCE SOMEBODY to influence or persuade somebody using underhand or illegal means such as lies, threats, or bribes ○ *an attempt to nobble the judges* **3.** DISABLE RACEHORSE to prevent a racehorse from winning a race by drugging or

disabling it **4. CHEAT SOMEBODY** to swindle or defraud somebody **5. STEAL SOMETHING** to steal something from its owner **6. SEIZE SOMEBODY** to seize hold of somebody [Mid-19C. Origin ?] —**nobbler** *n*

nobbut /nóbbət/ *adv N England* just or only ○ *They've nobbut had a bit of bread and milk.* [14C. < NO[1] + BUT[1]]

nobby /nóbbi/ *adj* fashionable or elegant (*informal*) [Late 18C. < NOB[1]]

Nobel /nō bél/, **Alfred** (1833–96) Swedish chemist. His development of dynamite brought him great wealth, which was used after his death to set up the Nobel Prizes. Full name **Nobel, Alfred Bernhard**

Nobelist /nō béllist/ *n* a winner of a Nobel Prize

nobelium /nō béeli əm/ *n* a radioactive element. Source: produced artificially from curium. Symbol **No**. See table at **element** [Mid-20C. After Alfred NOBEL]

Nobel Prize /nō bel-/ *n* an international award made annually for outstanding achievement in chemistry, literature, physics, physiology or medicine, economics, or promoting world peace [Early 20C. After Alfred NOBEL] —**Nobel prizewinner** *n* —**Nobel-prizewinning** *adj*

nobiliary /nō bílli əri/ *adj* relating to the nobility [Mid-18C. < French *nobiliaire* < *noble* (see NOBLE)]

nobiliary particle *n* a preposition used before a title or surname as a mark of rank, e.g. 'de' in French or 'von' in German

nobility /nō bílləti/ (*plural* **-ties**) *n* **1. NOBLE CHARACTER** high ideals or excellent moral character **2. ARISTOCRATS** a noble class or people of noble rank in a country **3. NOBLE RANK** aristocratic social position or rank **4. MAGNIFICENCE** impressiveness or magnificence [14C. Directly or via French < Latin *nobilitas* < *nobilis* 'noble']

noble /nṓb'l/ *adj* (**-bler, -blest**) **1. HAVING EXCELLENT MORAL CHARACTER** possessing high ideals or excellent moral character **2. ARISTOCRATIC** belonging or relating to an aristocratic social or political class **3. RELATING TO HIGH MORAL PRINCIPLES** based on high ideals or revealing excellent moral character **4. MAGNIFICENT** impressive in quality or appearance **5.** CHEM **NONREACTIVE** chemically inactive or inert ■ *n* **1. ARISTOCRAT** a titled aristocrat **2. FORMER ENGLISH COIN** a gold coin worth half a mark, formerly used in England [13C. Via French < Latin (*g*)*nobilis*] —**nobleness** *n* —**nobly** *adv*

noble gas *n* a chemically inert rare gas belonging to group 18 of the periodic table. Helium, neon, argon, krypton, xenon, and radon are noble gases.

nobleman /nṓb'lmən/ (*plural* **-men** /-mən/) *n* a man who belongs to a titled aristocracy

noble metal *n* a metal that is resistant to oxidation, e.g. gold, silver, or platinum

noble rot *n* a fungus that shrivels ripe grapes, increasing the proportion of sugar to liquid in them. It is desirable in the making of some wines, e.g. French Sauternes. Latin name: *Botrytis cinerea*.

noble savage *n* somebody belonging to a non-technological culture whose life is, according to an idea popularized by Rousseau, purer because it is closer to nature (*sometimes offensive*)

noblesse /nō bléss/ *n* **1.** aristocratic social position or rank **2.** the members of an aristocracy, especially the French aristocracy [13C. < French, 'nobility' < *noble* (see NOBLE)]

noblesse oblige /nō bléss ō bleézh/ *n* the idea that people born into the nobility or upper social classes must behave in an honourable and generous way towards those less privileged [< French, 'nobility obliges']

noblewoman /nṓb'l wòomən/ (*plural* **-women** /-wimin/) *n* a woman who belongs to a titled aristocracy

nobody /nṓbədi, -bodi/ *pron* not one single person ○ *Nobody can order the attack except the general.* ■ *n* (*plural* **-ies**) somebody regarded as unimportant or insignificant ○ *I felt like a nobody among so many important scientists.*

CULTURAL NOTE ***The Diary of a Nobody***, a fictional journal (1892) by George and Weedon Grossmith. Originally published in serial form in 'Punch', it is the diary of Charles Pooter, an anxious and hypersensitive middle-aged man who lives in the suburbs and works in the city of London. The text, which provides an amusing insight into the everyday life of the lower middle classes in late 19th-century London, is supplemented by Weedon Grossmith's illustrations, which add a wealth of detail about contemporary fashions and fads.

no-brain *adj* lacking intelligence, perception, or common sense (*informal*) ○ *Whose no-brain idea was that?*

no-brainer *n N Am* something, e.g. an idea or question, that is so easily understood or done that it requires little or no thought (*slang*)

nocent /nṓss'nt/ *adj* causing harm, injury, or damage [15C. < Latin *nocent-*, present participle of *nocere* 'to hurt'] —**nocently** *adv*

nociception /nṓssi sépsh'n/ *n* the perception of physical pain [Late 20C. < Latin *nocere* 'to hurt' + PERCEPTION]

nociceptive /nṓssi séptiv/ *adj* **1.** describes a stimulus that causes pain **2.** caused by or reacting to pain [Early 20C. < Latin *nocere* 'to hurt' + RECEPTIVE] —**nociceptively** *adv*

nock /nok/ *n* **1. GROOVE ON BOW** one of the grooves at each end of a bow that holds the bowstring **2. NOTCH ON ARROW** the notch at the end of an arrow that holds it on the bowstring ■ *vt* (**nocks, nocking, nocked**) **1. PREPARE TO FIRE ARROW** to place an arrow on a bowstring **2. CUT NOTCH IN BOW OR ARROW** to put a notch in a bow or an arrow [14C. Probably < Middle Dutch *nocke* 'projection, tip']

no claims bonus, no claims discount *n* a discount or reduction on an insurance premium, especially for a car, applied when the insured has not made a claim on the insurance during a specific period of time

noct- *prefix* same as **nocti-** (*used before vowels*)

nocti- *prefix* night, at night ○ *noctilucent* [< Latin *noct-* 'night' < Indo-European]

noctiluca /nókti lóokə/ (*plural* **-cae** /-kī/) *n* a plankton that produces light. When present in large groups they make the sea appear to glow. Genus: *Noctiluca*. [Mid-19C. < Latin, 'moon, lantern']

noctilucent /nókti lóoss'nt/ *adj* describes high clouds that are visible at night [Late 19C. < NOCTI- + Latin *lucere* 'to shine']

noctuid /nóktyoo id/ *n* a dull-coloured moth whose larvae, called army worms and cutworms, are destructive to young plants. Family: Noctuidae. [Late 19C. < Latin *noctua* 'night-owl'] —**noctuid** *adj*

noctule /nók tyool/ *n* a large reddish-brown bat that eats insects. Native to: Europe, Asia. Latin name: *Nyctalus noctula*. [Late 18C. Via French < Italian *nottola* 'bat']

nocturn /nók turn/ *n* in the Roman Catholic Church, one of the three divisions of the service of matins, previously held at midnight but now usually at daybreak [14C. Directly or via French *nocturne* < ecclesiastical Latin *nocturnus* < Latin, 'of the night' < *noct-* 'night']

nocturnal /nok túrn'l/ *adj* **1. AT NIGHT** occurring at night, as opposed to during the day **2.** ZOOL **ACTIVE AT NIGHT** describes animals that are active at night rather than during the day **3.** BOT **FLOWERING AT NIGHT** describes flowers that open at night and close during the day —**nocturnally** *adv*

nocturne /nók turn/ *n* **1.** a musical composition, especially for the piano, that suggests a tranquil dreamy mood. It evolved during the early 19th century, and Chopin was the most famous composer of nocturnes. **2.** a painting of a night scene [Mid-19C. < French (see NOCTURN)]

nocuous /nókyoo əss/ *adj* likely to cause injury or damage [Mid-17C. < Latin *nocuus* < *nocere* 'to hurt'] —**nocuously** *adv* —**nocuousness** *n*

nod /nod/ *v* (**nods, nodding, nodded**) **1.** *vti* **MOVE HEAD IN AGREEMENT** to lower and then raise the head quickly in order to show agreement or recognition or to give a signal ○ *He nodded discreetly to a man who was standing by the door.* **2.** *vt* **SIGNAL SOMETHING BY NODDING** to indicate or show something by nodding the head ○ *nodded approval* **3.** *vi* **DOZE** to let the head fall forward because of sleepiness **4.** *vi* **LOSE CONCENTRATION** to be momentarily careless or negligent **5.** *vi* **MOVE IN WIND** to droop, bend, or sway in a breeze ■ *n* **1. MOVEMENT OF HEAD TO SHOW AGREEMENT** a quick lowering and raising of the head in order to show agreement or recognition **2. ACKNOWLEDGMENT OF SOMETHING** a gesture, especially a token one, in recognition of something such as a convention or requirement ○ *an upbeat slogan that was a nod to the vogue for mission statements* [14C. Origin ?] —**nodder** *n* ◇ **a nod's as good as a wink (to a blind horse)** used to indicate that something expressed indirectly has been understood and that no further explanation is required ◇ **be on nodding terms (with somebody)** to know somebody slightly ◇ **give somebody** *or* **something the nod** to select or approve somebody or something ◇ **on the nod** agreed without formal discussion or procedures (*informal*)

nod off *vi* to fall asleep unintentionally or go into a drug-induced state of semiconsciousness

nod out *vi* to go into a state of drug-induced sleep or semiconsciousness (*slang*)

nod through *vt* **1.** to approve something without discussing it and voting on it **2.** to consider an MP as having voted in the House of Commons when he or she is unable to do so

nodding donkey /nódding-/ *n* a reciprocating pump for extracting oil [< DONKEY 'small pump or engine'; because it moves backwards and forwards]

noddle /nódd'l/ *n* the human head or brain (*dated informal*) [15C. Origin ?]

noddy /nóddi/ (*plural* **-dies**) *n* **1. TROPICAL SEABIRD** a dark-coloured seabird of the tern family. Native to: tropical coastal waters. Genera: *Anous* or *Procelsterna*. **2. OFFENSIVE TERM** an offensive term that deliberately insults somebody's intelligence or common sense (*dated insult*) **3. FOOTAGE OF INTERVIEWER NODDING** a short piece of film of a television interviewer nodding as if listening to the person interviewed that is spliced in with the main film of the interview. The technique is used especially when only one camera is available. (*informal*) [Early 16C. Origin ?]

noddy suit *n* a protective suit worn by military personnel likely to be exposed to nuclear, biological, or chemical weapons (*slang*)

node /nōd/ *n* **1.** ANAT **LUMP OR BULGE** a lump, knob, knot, or other kind of swelling that sticks out **2.** BOT **POINT ON PLANT STEM** the place on a plant stem where a leaf is attached or has been attached **3.** MATHS **POINT OF INTERSECTION** a point where lines meet or intersect in a diagram or graph **4.** MATHS **POINT WHERE PARTS OF CURVE INTERSECT** in geometry, a place on a curve where it crosses itself **5.** ASTRON **POINT WHERE ORBIT INTERSECTS ECLIPTIC** either of the two points where an orbit, e.g. that of a planet, crosses the ecliptic plane **6.** COMPUT **TERMINAL OR POINT IN NETWORK** a terminal or other point in a computer network where a message can be created, received, or transmitted **7.** PHYS **POINT ON WAVE** in physics, a place in a standing wave that has little or no amplitude **8.** LING **POINT IN SENTENCE STRUCTURE** in transformational grammars, a point in a sentence diagram where a category label, indicating the part of speech, appears and from which further branches may lead off [14C. < Latin *nodus* 'knot'] —**nodal** *adj*

node of Ranvier /-raánvi ay/ *n* a short gap in the myelin sheath that occurs at intervals along the length of a nerve fibre [After Louis Antoine *Ranvier* (1835–1922), French histologist]

nodose /nṓd ōss, nō dṓss/ *adj* having many points at which leaves join the stem —**nodosity** /nō dóssəti/ *n*

nodule /nóddyool/ *n* **1. SMALL LUMP** a small protruding knob, lump, or swelling on something **2.** BOT **ROOT PROTUBERANCE** a swelling or knob on the roots of legumes that contains bacteria **3.** ANAT **CELL OR TISSUE MASS** a small mass of cells or tissue, which may be a normal part of the body or a growth such as a tumour **4.** GEOL **LARGE ROUNDED MINERAL FORM** a form of a mineral that is massive with a rounded outer surface [15C. < Latin *nodulus* 'small knot' < *nodus* 'knot'] —**nodular** *adj* —**nodulose** *adj*

Noel /nō él/, **Noël** *n* Christmas, especially in carols or greetings [12C. < French < Latin (*dies*) *natalis* 'birth (day)' < *nasci* 'be born']

noetic /nō éttik/ *adj* characteristic of, coming from, or understood by the human mind [Mid-17C. < Greek *noētikos* < *noein* 'think' < *nous* 'mind'] —**noetically** *adv*

no-fault *adj* **1.** relating to a system of motor vehicle insurance in which insurance companies compensate accident victims without determining who is responsible for the accident **2.** relating to a form of divorce in which no blame is placed on either party for the breakdown of the marriage

no-fly list *n US* a computer-generated list of the names of people identified by the authorities as being so dangerous to civil aviation that they are denied permission to fly on commercial aircraft

no-fly zone *n* **1.** an area over which aircraft, especially those of another country, are forbidden to fly, and in which they will be attacked **2.** *US* a topic of questioning or conversation that is off-limits (*slang*) ○ *The press secretary declared that issue to be a no-fly zone for reporters.*

no-frills *adj* relating to a service or establishment that does not offer extra or special treatment (*informal*)

no-fuss *adj* involving little bother or few difficulties for the user

nog[1] /nog/ *n* **1.** a block of wood inserted into masonry or brickwork so that something can be nailed to it **2.** a wooden peg or pin [Early 17C. Origin ?]

nog[2] /nog/ *n* **1.** BEVERAGES same as **eggnog 2.** a strong ale formerly brewed in Norfolk [Early 17C. Origin ?]

noggin /nóggin/ *n* **1.** ONE-FOURTH OF PINT a measure of spirits equivalent to 0.148 litres/¼pint (*dated*) **2.** CUP a small cup or mug (*dated*) **3.** HEAD the human head (*dated informal*) [Mid-17C. Origin ?]

nogging /nógging/ *n* **1.** small stones, bricks, or bits of masonry used to fill the spaces between studs in a wall or partition **2.** one of the pieces of wood inserted between the main timbers of a half-timbered wall [Early 19C. < NOG[1]]

noggin-head *n* *regional* an offensive term that deliberately insults somebody's intelligence (*insult*) [Probably < NOGGING, from the same idea as BLOCKHEAD]

REGIONAL NOTE See *addle-headed*.

no-go *n* an event or situation that is prevented from occurring by adverse conditions (*informal*) ■ *adj* no longer going to happen or scheduled to occur

no-go area *n* **1.** a district where people are frightened or unable to go because of the violence and crime there **2.** an area that unauthorized people are forbidden to enter

no-good (*insult*) *adj* considered as lacking merit, virtue, worth, or morals ■ *n* somebody or something considered to lack merit, virtue, worth, or morals

Noguchi /nō góochi/, **Hideyo** (1876–1928) Japanese bacteriologist. He helped discover the spirochaete that causes syphilis, and devised a method to diagnose the disease.

CORBIS/Nathan Benn
Isamu Noguchi

Noguchi, Isamu (1904–88) US sculptor. He is known for his abstract sculptures and his sculpture gardens.

Noh *n* THEATRE another spelling of **No**[1]

no-hit *adj* relating to a baseball or softball game in which the opponents do not get a hit

no-hitter *n* a baseball or softball game in which the pitcher does not allow opponents a hit

no-holds-barred *adj* happening, or engaged in something, without restraint or control (*informal*) ○ *The debate was a no-holds-barred battle of wits.* [< a wrestling match in which any hold is permitted]

no-hoper *n* an offensive term that deliberately insults somebody's achievements and likelihood of future success (*insult*)

nohow /nó how/ *adv* not in any way (*nonstandard*)

NoI *abbr* POL, ISLAM Nation of Islam

noil /noyl/ *n* short fibres separated during combing from the long fibres of cotton, wool, silk, or another material [Early 17C. Probably < Old French *noel* < medieval Latin *nodellus* 'small knot' < Latin *nodus* 'knot']

noir /nwaar/ *adj* done or made in a style that is characteristic of film noir [< French, 'black']

noise /noyz/ *n* **1.** UNPLEASANT SOUND a loud, surprising, irritating, or unwanted sound **2.** ANY SOUND any sound or combination of sounds ○ *too much noise in the room* **3.** OUTCRY a loud clamour or commotion concerning something **4.** COMPLAINT a complaint or protest about something (*informal*) **5.** RUMOUR idle talk, rumour, or gossip (*informal*) **6.** PHYS ELECTRIC DISTURBANCE a random disturbance in an electric circuit that interferes with the reception of a signal **7.** COMPUT MEANINGLESS DATA unwanted or meaningless data intermixed with the relevant information in the output from a computer ■ *vt* (**noises, noising, noised**) SPREAD GOSSIP to spread a rumour or gossip ○ *an ugly story that was being noised about in newsrooms* [13C. Via French, 'uproar, brawl' < Latin *nausea* 'seasickness' < Greek *naus* 'ship'] ◇ **make noises** to do or say something intended to attract attention or indicate an intention ○ *He's making noises about a career change.*

noise abatement *n* the reduction of noise pollution

noiseless /nóyzləss/ *adj* not making any noise —**noiselessly** *adv* —**noiselessness** *n*

noisemaker /nóyz maykər/ *n* N Am a device used to make noise at a party or a celebration, e.g. a rattle or horn

noise pollution *n* irritating, distracting, or physically dangerous noise to which people are exposed in their environment and over which they usually have no control

noisette /nwaa zét/ *n* a piece of boned and rolled meat, especially the neck or loin of lamb [Late 19C. < French, 'little nut'; from its shape]

noisome /nóyssəm/ *adj* **1.** so offensive, especially to the senses, as to arouse feelings of disgust or repulsion **2.** extremely harmful [14C. < obsolete *noy*, shortening of ANNOY] —**noisomely** *adv* —**noisomeness** *n*

noisy /nóyzi/ (**-ier, -iest**) *adj* **1.** making a loud and annoying noise **2.** full of or characterized by loud sounds —**noisily** *adv* —**noisiness** *n*

noisy miner *n* a honey-eating bird that has grey and brown feathers with a black facial mask and yellow beak and legs, and is noted for its strident calls. Native to: Australia. Latin name: *Manorina melanocephala*. [< variant of MYNAH]

Nok /nok/ *n* a civilization located in the forests of central Nigeria that flourished between 500 BC and AD 300. It is known for its highly developed art style.

Popperfoto
Sir Sidney Nolan

Nolan /nólən/, **Sir Sidney** (1917–92) Australian painter. His colourful figurative works, often based on Australian folk history, include the *Ned Kelly* series. Full name **Nolan, Sir Sidney Robert**

nolens volens /nó lenz vó lenz/ *adv* whether willing or not willing [< Latin, 'unwilling willing']

noli-me-tangere /nóli may táng gəri, -tánjəri/ *n* **1.** PROHIBITION AGAINST TOUCHING a warning not to touch or interfere with somebody or something **2.** SOMEBODY OR SOMETHING NOT FOR TOUCHING somebody or something that must not be touched or interfered with **3.** ART PAINTING OF CHRIST WITH MARY MAGDALENE a depiction in art of Jesus Christ appearing to Mary Magdalene after his resurrection [< Latin, 'do not touch me'; from Jesus Christ's words to Mary Magdalene (John 20:17)]

nolle prosequi /nólli próssi kwī/ *n* an entry made in a court record when a plaintiff or a prosecutor decides not to proceed further with a case or action [< Latin, 'be unwilling to pursue']

nolo /nólō/ (*plural* **-los**) *n* US same as **nolo contendere** (*informal*) [Shortening]

nolo contendere /nólō kon téndəri/ *n* US in law, a plea entered by a defendant that does not explicitly admit guilt, but subjects the defendant to punishment, while allowing denial of the alleged facts in other proceedings [< Latin, 'I do not wish to contend']

no-lose *adj* certain to result in success or be beneficial, regardless of the outcome ○ *a no-lose proposition*

nol. pros. /nól próss/ *abbr* LAW nolle prosequi

nom. *abbr* GRAM nominative

noma /nómə/ *n* a severe gangrenous inflammation of the mouth or genitals, usually occurring in children who are malnourished or otherwise debilitated [Mid-19C. < modern Latin alteration of Latin *nome* < Greek *nom-*, stem of *nemein* 'to feed']

nomad /nó mad/ *n* **1.** a member of a people who move seasonally from place to place to search for food and water or pasture for their livestock **2.** somebody who wanders from place to place [Late 16C. < French *nomade* < Greek *nomas* 'wandering about to find pasture' < *nemein* 'to pasture'] —**nomadic** /nō máddik/ *adj* —**nomadically** *adv* —**nomadism** *n*

no-man's-land *n* **1.** TERRITORY BETWEEN OPPOSING FORCES the area of land that lies between two opposing armies and is held by neither side **2.** UNCLAIMED TERRITORY any area of land that no one has established a claim to **3.** AMBIGUOUS AREA any indefinite or ambiguous situation in which boundaries, rules, or authority are unclear or unfamiliar **4.** RACKET GAMES BAD POSITION ON TENNIS COURT in tennis and other court games, an area on a court in which a player is tactically at a disadvantage

nomarchy /nóm aarki/ (*plural* **-chies**) *n* any of the administrative provinces into which modern Greece is divided [Mid-17C. < Greek *nomarkhia* < *nomos* (see NOME) + *-arkhia* 'government']

nombril /nómbril/, **nombril point** *n* in heraldry, the midpoint of the lower half of an escutcheon, halfway between the fess point and the base point [Mid-16C. < French, 'navel']

nom de guerre /nóm də gáir/ (*plural* **noms de guerre** /*pronunc. same*/) *n* an assumed name that somebody uses, e.g. when fighting [< French, 'name of war']

nom de plume /nóm də plóom/ (*plural* **noms de plume** /*pronunc. same*/) *n* LITERAT same as **pen name** [< French, 'name of pen']

nome /nōm/ *n* **1.** a province of ancient Egypt **2.** POL same as **nomarchy** [Early 18C. < Greek *nomos* < *nemein* 'divide']

nomen /nó men/ (*plural* **nomina** /nómminə/) *n* in ancient Rome, a citizen's second name, which indicated the clan to which he or she belonged [Early 18C. < Latin, 'name']

nomenclator /nó men klaytər/ *n* an assigner of names in a scientific classification system (**taxonomy**) [Mid-16C. < Latin < *nomen* 'name' + *calare* 'to call']

nomenclature /nō méngkləchər, nómən klaychər, -kláychər/ *n* **1.** a system of names assigned to objects or items in a particular science or art **2.** the assigning of names to organisms in a scientific classification system (**taxonomy**) [Early 17C. Via French < Latin *nomenclatura* < *nomen* 'name' + *calare* 'to call'] —**nomenclatural** /nómən kláychərəl/ *adj*

nomenklatura /nó men kla tóorə/ *n* **1.** in Communist governments, the elite privileged class consisting of the people holding positions of authority in the bureaucracy (*takes a plural verb*) **2.** in the former Soviet Union and other Communist countries, the system for assigning senior positions in the bureaucracy, controlled by committees in the Communist Party (*takes a singular verb*) [Mid-20C. Via Russian < Latin *nomenclatura* (see NOMENCLATURE)]

nomina HIST plural of **nomen**

nominal /nómmin'l/ *adj* **1.** SO-CALLED acting or being something in name only, but not in reality **2.** VERY LOW IN COST representing very little cost when compared with the actual value received ○ *a nominal fee* **3.** BEARING SOMEBODY'S NAME assigned to a named person, and bearing that person's name **4.** OF NAMES relating to or consisting of a name or names **5.** GRAM OF NOUN relating to a noun or a group of words that functions as a noun **6.** ACCT RELATING TO CURRENT PRICES considered in terms of the stated or original value only, and ignoring changes due to inflation and other factors ■ *n* GRAM NOUN OR NOUN GROUP a word or group of words that functions as a noun [15C. Directly

or via French < Latin *nominalis* < *nomen* 'name'] —**nominally** *adv*

nominalise *vt* LING another spelling of **nominalize**

nominalism /nómminəlizəm/ *n* the philosophical doctrine that there are no realities other than concrete individual objects —**nominalist** *n, adj* —**nominalistic** *adj*

nominalize /nómminə līz/ (**-izes, -izing, -ized**), **nominalise** (**-ises, -ising, -ised**) *vt* **1.** to change a part of speech into a noun by the addition of a suffix **2.** to change an underlying clause in a sentence by a syntactic process or series of rules so that it functions like a noun —**nominalization** /nómminə lī záysh'n/ *n*

nominal quote *n* an approximate price given for a security when there is no firm bid or asking price

nominal value *n* FIN same as **par value**

nominal wages *npl N Am* same as **money wages**

nominate /nómmi nayt/ (**-nates, -nating, -nated**) *vt* **1.** PROPOSE SOMEBODY to suggest somebody for appointment or election to a position or for an honour or award **2.** APPOINT SOMEBODY to appoint somebody to a position, or make somebody responsible for a duty **3.** HORSERACING ENTER HORSE to enter a horse in a race [Mid-16C. < Latin *nominat-*, past participle of *nominare* 'to name' < *nomin-* 'name'] —**nominator** *n*

nomination /nómmi náysh'n/ *n* **1.** PROPOSAL a suggestion of somebody for appointment or election to a position or for receiving an honour or award **2.** SOMEBODY OR SOMETHING PROPOSED somebody or something suggested for appointment or election to a position or for receiving an honour or award **3.** APPOINTMENT the appointment of somebody to a position, or assignment of somebody to a duty

nominative /nómminətiv/ *n* GRAM **1.** GRAMMATICAL FORM a grammatical form (**case**) of nouns and pronouns that identifies the subject of a sentence or clause. Other words, e.g. adjectives, may be in the nominative in agreement with a noun. **2.** INSTANCE OF NOMINATIVE a word or phrase in the nominative ■ *adj* **1.** APPOINTED TO OR PROPOSED FOR OFFICE appointed or suggested for election to an office or position **2.** WITH OWNER'S NAME having the name of the owner on it **3.** GRAM OF NOMINATIVE in or relating to the nominative [14C. Directly or via French *nominatif* < Latin *nominativus (casus)* 'nominative (case)' < *nominat-* (see NOMINATE)]

nominee /nómmi neé/ *n* **1.** somebody who has been proposed for a position, honour, or office **2.** a person or group that holds title to a security or property but is not the true owner [Mid-17C. < NOMINATE]

nomograph /nómmə graaf, nṓmə-, -graf/, **nomogram** /-gram/ *n* **1.** a graph with three lines graduated so that a straight line intersecting any two of the lines at their known values intersects the third at the value of the related variable **2.** any graph that represents numerical relationships [Mid-18C. < Greek *nomos* 'law, custom'] —**nomographic** /nómmə gráffik, nṓmə-/ *adj* —**nomography** /no móggrəfi, nō-/ *n*

nomothetic /nómmə théttik, nṓmə-/, **nomothetical** /-théttik'l/ *adj* **1.** relating to the enactment of laws **2.** relating to the discovery of universal laws [Early 17C. < Greek *nomothetikos* < *nomothetēs* 'lawgiver' < *nomos* 'law'] —**nomothetically** *adv*

-nomy *suffix* system of rules, laws, or knowledge about a particular field ○ *gastronomy* [< Greek *-nomia* < *nomos* 'law, custom'] —**-nomic** *suffix* —**-nomical** *suffix* —**-nomically** *suffix*

non- *prefix* not, without, the opposite of ○ *nonaggression* ○ *nonassessable* [Via Old French < Latin *non* < Indo-European]

non-Aboriginal *n, adj*
nonabrasive *adj*
nonabsorbency *n*
nonabsorbent *adj*
nonabusive *adj*
nonabusively *adv*
nonabusiveness *n*
nonacademic *adj*
nonaccelerating *adj*
nonacceptance *n*
nonaccidental *adj*
nonaccredited *adj*
nonacid *adj*
nonacidic *adj*
nonacting *adj*
nonactor *n*
nonaddictive *adj*
nonadherence *n*
nonadhesive *adj*
nonadhesiveness *n*
nonadjacent *adj*
nonadjustability *n*
nonadjustable *adj*
nonadmission *n*
nonadmitted *adj*
nonadult *adj, n*
nonadulthood *n*
nonaerial *adj*
nonaerobic *adj*
non-African *adj, n*
nonaggressive *adj*
nonagricultural *adj*
nonair *adj*
nonalcoholic *adj*
non-Algonquian *adj*
nonallergenic *adj*
nonallergic *adj*
nonalphabetic *adj*
nonalphabetical *adj*
nonambiguous *adj*
non-American *adj, n*
nonanalytic *adj*
nonanswer *n*
nonapologetic *adj*
nonaquatic *adj*
non-Arab *adj, n*
nonarable *adj*
nonargument *n*
nonaromatic *adj*
nonart *n*
non-Aryan *adj, n*
non-Asian *adj*
nonassertive *adj*
nonassociative *adj*
nonastronaut *n*
nonathlete *n*
nonatomic *adj*
nonattendance *n*
nonattributable *adj*
nonattributably *adv*
nonavailability *n*
nonbaryonic *adj*
nonbeing *n*
nonbelief *n*
nonbeliever *n*
nonbelieving *adj*
nonbelligerence *n*
nonbelligerency *n*
nonbelligerent *adj, n*
nonbelligerently *adv*
nonbinary *adj*
nonbinding *adj*
nonbiodegradable *adj*
nonbiographical *adj*
nonbiological *adj*
nonbiting *adj*
non-Boer *adj, n*
nonbrand *adj*
nonbreakable *adj*
nonbreaking *adj*
nonbreeding *adj*
non-British *adj*
nonbroadcast *adj*
non-Buddhist *adj, n*
noncaking *adj*
noncaloric *adj*
noncalorific *adj*
noncancerous *adj*
noncanonical *adj*
noncarbon *adj*
noncarbonated *adj*
noncarcinogen *n*
noncarcinogenic *adj*
noncarnivorous *adj*
noncash *adj*
noncategorical *adj*
non-Catholic *adj, n*
non-Caucasian *adj, n*
noncausal *adj*
noncellular *adj*
noncertified *adj*
nonchemical *adj*
non-Chinese *adj, n*
non-Christian *adj, n*
nonchronological *adj*
non-Cistercian *adj, n*
noncitizen *n*
noncitrus *adj*
nonclassical *adj*
nonclerical *adj*
nonclimbing *adj*
noncling *adj*
nonclinical *adj*
noncoding *adj*
noncollegiate *adj*
noncombat *adj*
noncombative *adj*
noncombustibility *n*
noncombustible *adj, n*
noncommercial *adj*
noncommunicable *adj*
noncommunicating *adj*
noncommunicative *adj*
non-Communist *adj, n*
noncompatible *adj*
noncompetitive *adj*
noncomplying *adj*
noncompulsory *adj*
nonconcentric *adj*
nonconclusive *adj*
nonconcurrent *adj*
noncondensing *adj*
nonconducting *adj*
nonconductive *adj*
nonconductor *n*
nonconfidential *adj*
nonconfidentially *adv*
nonconforming *adj*
nonconjugated *adj*
nonconsecutive *adj*
nonconsensual *adj*
nonconstructive *adj*
nonconstructively *adv*
nonconstructiveness *n*
noncontagious *adj*
noncontentious *adj*
noncontentiously *adv*
noncontiguous *adj*
noncontinuous *adj*
noncontributing *adj*
noncontroversial *adj*
noncontroversially *adv*
nonconventional *adj*
nonconvertible *adj*
noncorporate *adj*
noncorroding *adj*
noncorrosive *adj*
noncoverage *n*
noncriminal *adj*
noncritical *adj*
noncrystalline *adj*
noncumulative *adj*
noncurrent *adj*
noncutting *adj*
nondairy *adj*
nondeductibility *n*
nondeductible *adj*
nondefining *adj*
nondegradable *adj*
nondegree *adj*
nondelinquent *adj*
nondelivery *n*
nondemocratic *adj*
nondemocratically *adv*
nondenominational *adj*
nondepartmental *adj*
nonderivative *adj*
nondevelopment *n*
nondiabetic *adj, n*
nondigestible *adj*
nondigital *adj*
nondiplomatic *adj*
nondiscretionary *adj*
nondiscrimination *n*
nondiscriminatory *adj*
nondisposable *adj*
nondisruptive *adj*
nondoctor *n*
nondoctoral *adj*
nondomestic *adj*
nondramatic *adj*
nondrinker *n*
nondrinking *adj*
nondriver *n*
nondrooping *adj*
nondrying *adj*
nondual *adj*
nondualism *n*
nonduality *n*
non-Dubliner *n*
nondurable *adj*
nonearning *adj*
nonecclesiastical *adj*
noneconomic *adj*
nonedible *adj*
noneducational *adj*
noneffective *adj*
nonelastic *adj*
nonelect *adj, npl*
nonelected *adj*
nonelection *n*
nonelective *adj, n*
nonelectric *adj*
noneligible *adj*
nonemergency *adj, n*
nonempty *adj*
nonenforceable *adj*
nonenforcement *n*
non-English-speaking *adj*
nonenzyme *n*
nonequilibrium *n*
nonestablished *adj*
nonethical *adj*
non-Euclidean *adj*
non-European *n, adj*
nonevidence *n*
nonexclusive *adj*
nonexempt *adj*
nonexpansion *n*
nonexpendable *adj*
nonexperimental *adj*
nonexpert *adj, n*
nonexplosive *adj*
nonexposure *n*
nonextinct *adj*
nonfactual *adj*
nonfading *adj*
nonfarmer *n*
nonfascist *adj, n*
nonfatal *adj*
nonfatally *adv*
nonfattening *adj*
nonfatty *adj*
nonfederal *adj*
nonfederated *adj*
nonferrous *adj*
nonfighting *adj*
nonfinancial *adj*
nonfinite *adj*
nonflexible *adj*
nonflowering *adj*
nonfluctuating *adj*
nonformal *adj*
nonformally *adv*
nonfraying *adj*
nonfreehold *adj*
nonfulfilment *n*
nonfunctional *adj*
nonfunctioning *adj*
nonfungal *adj*
nongaseous *adj*
nongeographical *adj*
nongloss *adj*
nonglossy *adj*
nongovernment *adj*
nongovernmental *adj*
nongranular *adj*
nongraphic *adj*
nongrasping *adj*
nongreasy *adj*
nongreen *adj*
nonhazardous *adj*
nonhereditary *adj*
nonhierarchical *adj*
non-Hispanic *adj, n*
nonhistorical *adj*
nonhomogeneous *adj*
nonhydrogen *adj*
nonidentical *adj*
nonideologue *n*
nonimitative *adj*
nonimpact *adj*
nonimportation *n*
noninclusive *adj*
nonincriminating *adj*
nonindependent *adj*
nonindictable *adj*
nonindigenous *adj*
noninductive *adj*
nonindustrial *adj*
nonindustrialized *adj*
noninfected *adj*
noninfectious *adj*
noninflammable *adj*
noninflammatory *adj*
noninflationary *adj*
noninflected *adj*
noninformative *adj*
noninhabitable *adj*
noninheritable *adj*
noninstinctive *adj*
noninsured *adj*
nonintegrated *adj*
nonintellectual *adj*
noninterchangeable *adj*
noninterest-bearing *adj*
noninterference *n*
nonintoxicating *adj*
noninvolvement *n*
nonionizing *adj*
nonirrigated *adj*
nonirritating *adj*
non-Italian *adj, n*
non-Jew *n*
non-Jewish *adj*
nonjudgmental *adj*
nonjudgmentally *adv*
nonjudicial *adj*
nonkosher *adj*
nonlawyer *n*
nonleafy *adj*
nonleague *adj*
nonlegal *adj*
nonlegally *adv*
nonlethal *adj*
nonlexical *adj*
nonlinguistic *adj*
nonliquid *adj, n*
nonliteral *adj*
nonliterally *adv*
nonliterary *adj*
nonliterate *adj*
nonliturgical *adj*
nonliving *adj*
nonloadbearing *adj*
nonlocal *adj*
nonlocally *adv*
nonlogical *adj*
nonluminous *adj*
nonlymphocytic *adj*
nonmagnetic *adj*
nonmainstream *adj*
nonmalicious *adj*
nonmalignant *adj*
nonmammalian *adj*
nonmanagement *adj, n*
nonmanipulative *adj*
nonmanual *adj*
nonmanufacturing *adj*
non-Maori *adj, n*
nonmarket *adj*
nonmarketable *adj*
nonmarried *adj*
nonmatching *adj*
nonmaterial *adj*
nonmaterialistic *adj*
nonmathematical *adj*
nonmeasurable *adj*
nonmedia *adj*
nonmedical *adj*
nonmedicinal *adj*
nonmetal *n*
nonmetallic *adj*
nonmetalliferous *adj*
nonmetric *adj*
nonmetropolitan *adj*
nonmicrobial *adj*
nonmigrant *adj, n*
nonmigratory *adj*
nonmilitant *adj*
nonmilitary *adj*
nonministerial *adj*
nonmobile *adj*
nonmolecular *adj*
nonmonastic *adj*
nonmonetary *adj*
nonmonogamous *adj*
non-Mormon *n, adj*
nonmotile *adj*
nonmotorized *adj*
nonmoving *adj*
nonmusical *adj*
nonmusician *n*
non-Muslim *adj, n*
non-narcotic *adj*
non-narrative *adj*
non-national *adj, n*
non-native *n, adj*
non-natural *adj*
non-naturalistic *adj*
non-naval *adj*
non-nervous *adj*
non-news *n*
non-numerical *adj*
nonnutrient *adj*
non-nutrient *adj, n*
nonobligatory *adj*
nonofficial *adj*
nonoily *adj*
nonoperatic *adj*

nonoperation n
nonoperational adj
nonoperative adj
nonopposition n
nonoptional adj
nonordained adj
nonorganic adj
nonorthodox adj
nonparallel adj
nonparasitic adj
nonparliamentary adj
nonparticipant n
nonparticipating adj
nonparticipation n
nonparty adj
nonpaternal adj
nonpayer n
nonpaying adj
nonpayment n
nonperforming adj
nonperishable adj, n
nonpermanent adj
nonpermeable adj
nonpersistent adj
nonpersonal adj
nonpetroleum adj
nonphilosophical adj
nonphysical adj
nonphysically adv
nonplant adj
nonplayer n
nonpoisonous adj
nonpolar adj
nonpolitical adj
nonpolluting adj
nonporous adj
nonpractising adj
nonprecious adj
nonpredatory adj
nonpregnant adj
nonprescription adj
nonprint adj
nonprinted adj
nonprinting adj
nonproductive adj
nonproductively adv
nonproductiveness n
nonproductivity n
nonprofessional n, adj
nonprofessionally adv
nonprofitable adj
nonprogrammer n
nonprogressive adj
nonproprietary adj
nonprotective adj
nonprotein adj, n
nonpsychological adj
nonpsychotic adj
nonpublic adj
nonpunitive adj
nonquantifiable adj
nonracial adj
nonradioactive adj
nonrandom adj
nonrapid adj
nonrational adj
nonreactive adj
nonreader n
nonrealistic adj
nonreceipt n
nonreciprocal adj
nonreciprocating adj
nonrecognition n
nonrecoverable adj
nonrecurring adj
nonrecyclable adj
nonredeemable adj
nonrefillable adj
nonreflecting adj
nonreflection n
nonreflective adj
nonrefundable adj
nonregulated adj
nonrelative adj, n
nonreligious adj
nonrenewable adj
nonrenewal n
nonrepayable adj
nonrepeating adj
nonreproducible adj
nonreproductive adj
nonrepudiation n

nonresemblance n
nonresidence n
nonresidency n
nonresident adj, n
nonresidential adj
nonresistance n
nonresistant adj
nonresolvable adj
nonresonant adj
nonresponse n
nonreturnable adj
nonreusable adj
nonreversible adj
nonrhotic adj
nonrhythmic adj
nonrigid adj
nonrotating adj
nonrural adj
nonsalaried adj
nonsaleable adj
nonschool adj
nonscience n
nonscientific adj
nonscientifically adv
nonscientist n
non-Scottish adj
nonscriptural adj
nonseasonal adj
nonsectarian adj
nonseeding adj
nonsegregated adj
nonselective adj
non-Semitic adj
nonseptate adj
nonsexist adj
nonsexual adj
nonsexually adv
nonshrink adj
nonsignificance n
nonsignificant adj
nonskater n
nonskid adj
nonskier n
nonskilled adj
non-Slav n
nonslave n, adj
non-Slavic adj
nonsocial adj
non-Socialist n, adj
nonsolar adj
nonsoldier n, adj
nonsoluble adj
nonspeaking adj
nonspecialist n, adj
nonspherical adj
nonspiritual adj
nonsporting adj
nonstaining adj
nonstanzaic adj
nonstatutory adj
nonstellar adj
nonstinging adj
nonstock adj
nonstore adj
nonstrategic adj
nonstructural adj
nonstudent adj, n
nonsubmissive adj
nonsubscriber n
nonsugar n
nonsupport n
nonsurgical adj
nonswimmer n
nonsynchronous adj
nonsystematic adj
nontalkative adj
nontangible adj, n
nontariff adj
nontarnishing adj
nontaxable adj
nonteaching adj
nontechnical adj
nontechnological adj
nontectonic adj
nonterminal adj
nonterritorial adj
nontext adj
nontextile adj
nontheatrical adj
nontheistic adj
nonthematic adj
nontherapeutic adj

nonthermal adj
nonthinking adj
nonthreatening adj
nonthreateningly adv
nontidal adj
nontoxic adj
nontradable adj
nontraditional adj
nontransparent adj
nontraveller n
nontrivial adj
nonunified adj
nonuniform adj
nonuniformity n
nonuniformly adv
nonurban adj
nonuse n
nonuser n
nonvascular adj

nonvegetable adj
nonvenomous adj
nonvirulent adj
nonviscous adj
nonvisible adj
nonvital adj
nonvocal adj
nonvolatile adj
nonvoter n
nonvoting adj
nonwage adj
non-Western adj
non-Westerner n
nonword n
nonwork adj
nonworker n
nonworking adj
nonwritten adj
nonzero adj

non-A, non-B hepatitis n an acute chronic viral disease of the liver, similar to hepatitis B but caused by neither the hepatitis A nor the hepatitis B virus. Among the several new hepatitis viruses discovered relatively recently, non-A, non-B hepatitis, in most cases, is thought to be due to hepatitis C virus.

nona- prefix nine ○ nonagon [< Latin nonus 'ninth' < Indo-European, 'nine']

nonage /nónij, nónn-/ n 1. the status of being under the requisite age for some legal entitlement (formal) 2. any time of immaturity [14C. < Anglo-Norman nounage, variant of Old French nonage 'not (the full) age' < age (see AGE)]

nonagenarian /nónəjə náiri ən, nónnə-/ n somebody who is between 90 and 99 years of age [Early 19C. < Latin nonagenarius 'consisting of ninety' < nonaginta 'ninety' < nonus 'ninth'] —**nonagenarian** adj

nonaggression /nón ə grésh'n/ n a policy of not attacking other countries ○ The two countries have signed a nonaggression pact.

nonagon /nónnə gon, nón-/ n a two-dimensional geometric figure formed of nine angles and sides —**nonagonal** /no nággən'l, nō-/ adj

nonaligned /nón ə línd/ adj not allied with any major world power —**nonalignment** n

nonanoic acid /nónnə nō ik-/ n UK, NZ, Can a colourless to yellow oil. Source: beets, potatoes. Use: in plastics, pharmaceuticals, synthetic flavours, additive in petrol. Formula: $CH_3(CH_2)_7COOH$. Aus, US term **pelargonic acid** [< nonane 'straight chain hydrocarbon containing nine carbon atoms']

nonappearance /nón ə peérənss/ n failure to appear or attend, especially the failure of an accused person or witness to turn up for a court appearance

nonarrival /nón ə rív'l/ n a failure to arrive or be delivered

nonassessable /nón ə séssəb'l/ adj impossible to estimate or determine ○ nonassessable losses

nonbank /nón bángk/ n a financial enterprise that is not a bank but performs a number of the functions of a bank —**nonbanking** adj

non-black /non blák/, **non-Black** adj relating to a person or to people with light skin tones, ultimately of European ancestry ■ n a light-skinned person whose ancestry can be traced ultimately to Europe

nonbook /nón boŏk/ adj not in the form of a book or books, or consisting of other things than books, e.g. as video tapes ○ the library's nonbook holdings

nonbusiness /nón bíznəss/ adj personal and not relating to business ○ details of nonbusiness expenditure

nonce[1] /nonss/ n the present time (archaic) [12C. < misanalysis of for then anes 'for the one (occasion)'] ◇ **for the nonce 1.** for the present occasion **2.** for the time being

nonce[2] /nonss/ n somebody who commits of a sexual offence against a child (slang insult) [Late 20C. Origin ?]

nonce word n a word that is coined for a single occasion

nonchalant /nónshələnt/ adj calm and unconcerned about things [Mid-18C. < French, 'not being concerned' < chalant, present participle of chaloir 'be concerned' < Latin calere 'be hot or roused'] —**nonchalance** n —**nonchalantly** adv

noncom /nón kom/ n same as **noncommissioned officer** (informal) [Late 19C. Shortening]

noncombatant /non kómbətənt/ n 1. somebody who is not in the armed forces during a war 2. a chaplain, medical officer, or other member of the armed forces who does not take part in battle

noncommissioned officer /nónkə mísh'nd-/ n a subordinate officer in any of the armed forces, e.g. a sergeant or corporal, who, instead of being given a commission, has been appointed from the lower ranks

noncommittal /nónkə mítt'l/ adj not making clear any personal opinions or feelings about something —**noncommittally** adv

noncompliance /nónkəm plī ənss/ n a refusal or failure to obey a law, rule, contractual agreement, or a doctor's order for medicine-taking —**noncompliant** adj

non compos mentis /nón kompəss méntiss/ adj in law, not mentally competent to understand what is happening and to make important decisions [< Latin, 'not having control of (your) mind']

nonconformist /nónkən fáwrmist/ adj UNCONVENTIONAL not conforming to an established pattern of behaviour ■ n 1. UNCONVENTIONAL PERSON somebody who does not conform to an accepted pattern of behaviour 2. also **Nonconformist** CHR MEMBER OF DISSENTING PROTESTANT CHURCH a member of a Protestant church not adhering to the doctrines or usage of a national or established church —**nonconformism** n

nonconformity /nónkən fáwrməti/ n 1. the practice of not conforming to an established pattern of behaviour 2. the state of being in disagreement with something

noncontributory /nónkən tríbbyŏŏtəri/ adj 1. describes a health insurance or pension scheme that does not require contributions from an employee or member ○ a noncontributory pension scheme 2. not contributing to a health insurance or pension scheme

noncooperation /nónkō oppə ráysh'n/ n 1. refusal or failure to cooperate 2. the practice of refusing to pay taxes or obey other government decrees, as a means of protest —**noncooperative** /nónkō óppərətiv/ adj

noncount noun /nón kownt-/ n a noun that refers to a mass of something or to a quality rather than to one thing, and that cannot usually be used with 'a' or 'an', with a number, or in the plural. Examples of English noncount nouns are 'milk', 'freight', and 'unhappiness'.

noncustodial /nón ku stódi əl/ adj not involving imprisonment or detention in custody ○ a noncustodial sentence

nondepartmental public body n an organization set up by the government to carry out a specific role within government responsibilities, but which is not a government department or part of one

nondescript /nóndiskript/ adj having no interesting or remarkable characteristics ■ n somebody with no interesting or remarkable characteristics [Late 17C. < NON- + Latin descriptus, past participle of describere (see DESCRIBE)]

nondestructive /nón di strúktiv/ adj not causing or capable of causing destruction

nondestructive testing n a technique used to test for flaws in materials, components, and joints without causing damage or destruction

nondirective /nóndə réktiv, -dī-/ adj describes a form of psychotherapy or counselling in which the patient is encouraged to speak freely with minimal input from the therapist

nondisclosure agreement /nón diss klózhər-/ n 1. an agreement, often required of new or departing employees, not to disclose any confidential or secret information relating to their new or previous employer 2. a contract that prohibits the signatory from sharing information about a project or other matter except under specific terms

nondisjunction /nón diss júngksh'n/ n a failure of paired chromosomes or sister chromatids to separate during cell division —**nondisjunctional** adj

nondistinctive /nóndi stíngktiv/ adj describes features of speech sounds that do not distinguish meanings

non dit /nón deé/ n US a taboo subject or fact that remains unspoken or is not discussed ○ His absence

was a non dit. [Late 20C. < French *le non-dit* 'what is left unsaid']

nondrip /nón dríp/ *adj* describes paint or varnish that is not likely to drip while being applied

none /nun/ *pron* **1.** not one person ○ *Wealth that is free for all is valued by none.* ○ *None of us wanted the situation to continue.* **2.** not any of something, not any part of something, or not a single one of something ○ *None of it seemed to matter any more.* ○ *We wrote last week demanding some answers, but so far have received none.* [Old English *nān* 'not one' < *ne* 'not' + *ān*, form of ONE] ◇ **have none of something** to refuse to tolerate something ○ *We asked him to explain himself, but he would have none of it.* ◇ **none the** in no degree (*used with comparative adjectives*) ○ *I'm still none the wiser.* ◇ **none too** not very

USAGE See *neither*.

nonelectrolyte /nón i léktrə līt/ *n* a substance that does not ionize readily in solution or in the molten state and is therefore a bad conductor of electricity

nonentity /no néntəti/ (*plural* **-ties**) *n* **1.** INSIGNIFICANT PERSON somebody regarded as unimportant, powerless, or insignificant **2.** SOMETHING NONEXISTENT something that does not exist in reality **3.** CONDITION OF NONEXISTENCE the condition or state of being nonexistent

nonequivalence /nón i kwívvələnss/ *n* **1.** the state of not being equal or equivalent **2.** a situation in which two propositions can have different truth values —**nonequivalent** *adj*

nones /nōnz/ *n* (*takes a singular or plural verb*) **1.** in the ancient Roman calendar, the ninth day before the ides of each month counting inclusively. The nones are the seventh day of March, May, July, and October, the fifth day of any other month. **2.** in the Roman Catholic Church, the fifth of the seven separate hours (**canonical hours**) that are set aside for prayer each day. This was originally held at the ninth hour after sunrise. [15C. In sense 1 via French < Latin *nonas*, plural of a form of; *nonus* 'ninth'. Sense 2 plural of *none* < Latin *nona*, feminine of *nonus*]

nonessential /nón i sénsh'l/ *adj* **1.** not absolutely necessary **2.** manufactured by the body and therefore not essential in the diet —**nonessential** *n* —**nonessentially** *adv*

nonet /no nét/ *n* **1.** a piece of music composed for nine voices or instruments **2.** a group of nine singers or instrumentalists [Mid-19C. < Italian *nonetto* 'small ninth' < *nono* 'ninth' < Latin *nonus*]

nonetheless /núnthə léss/ *adv* in spite of a situation or comment

nonevent /nón i vént/ *n* an occasion that is disappointingly unexciting

nonexchangeable /nón iks cháynjəb'l/ *adj* not able to be exchanged for an identical item or for something different

nonexecutive director /nón ig zékyōōtiv-/ *n* a director of a business organization who is not a full member of staff but whose duty is to advise the other directors

nonexistent /nón ig zístənt/ *adj* not in existence —**nonexistence** *n*

nonfat /nón fát/ *adj* without fat solids, or with the fat content removed

nonfeasance /nón feéz'nss/ *n* in law, the omission of some act that is expected to have been performed [Early 17C. < obsolete *feasance* 'doing' < Anglo-Norman *fesa(u)nce*, French *faisance* < *fais-*, present stem of *faire* 'to do' < Latin *facere*]

nonfiction /nón fíksh'n/ *n* writings that convey factual information and are not primarily works of the creative imagination ○ *her first nonfiction work* —**nonfictional** *adj*

nonfigurative /nón fíggərətiv/ *adj* **1.** LITERAT same as **literal** *adj* (sense 1) **2.** ARTS same as **nonrepresentational**

nonflammable /nón flámməb'l/ *adj* difficult to burn or ignite

USAGE See *flammable*.

nonfood /nón fóod/ *adj* describes something that is sold in a supermarket that is not for eating or drinking

nong /nong/ *n* Aus an offensive term for somebody

who is regarded as stupid (*slang insult*) [Mid-20C. Origin ?]

nongonococcal urethritis /nón gonō kók'l-/ *n* US same as **nonspecific urethritis**

nongovernmental organization *n* an independent organization that is not run or controlled by a government

nongraded /nón gráydid/ *adj* not sorted into different sizes ○ *nongraded rocks*

non grata /nón graátə/ *adj* not welcome [< PERSONA NON GRATA]

non-Hodgkin's lymphoma *n* a cancer of the lymph nodes that is distinguished from Hodgkin's disease by the absence of a type of cell with double nuclei

nonhuman /non hyōōmən/ *adj* relating to a thing or being that does not belong to the human race

nonillion /nō nílliən/ *n* the number equal to 10^{54}, written as 1 followed by 54 zeros [Late 17C. < French < Latin *nonus* 'ninth' + *-illion* as in MILLION] —**nonillionth** *adj, n*

nonimmigrant /non ímmigrənt/ *n* **1.** somebody who enters a country for a temporary stay **2.** somebody who returns to his or her own country after some time spent in another country

noninclusion /nón in klōozh'n/ *n* failure to include somebody or something, or to be included

non-insulin-dependent diabetes *n* diabetes mellitus that does not require insulin for its treatment

nonintervention /nón intər vénsh'n/ *n* failure or refusal to intervene in something, especially the policy on the part of a nation of abstaining from involvement in the affairs of other states —**noninterventionism** *n* —**noninterventionist** *n, adj*

noninvasive /nón in váyssiv/ *adj* **1.** not involving cutting into the body or entry into a body cavity such as the colon or stomach **2.** not spreading or likely to spread to other parts of the body

noniron /nón ī ərn/ *adj* not needing to be ironed because of being crease-resistant

nonissue /nón íssyoo, -íshyoo/ *n* something that is so unimportant that it is not worth considering or discussing

nonjoinder /nón jóyndər/ *n* failure to include a party in a lawsuit who should have been included

nonjuror /nón jōorər/ *n* somebody who refuses to take an oath, especially a member of the Church of England clergy who refused to take an oath of allegiance to William and Mary in 1689 —**nonjuring** *adj*

nonjury /nón jōori/ *adj* describes a trial in which the verdict is not the responsibility of a jury but of a judge

nonlinear /nón línni ər/ *adj* **1.** NOT IN LINE not lying on the same straight line **2.** NOT PREDICTABLE FROM PAST varying markedly as a result of individual factors or circumstances and so difficult to anticipate or likely to depart from previous patterns **3.** MATHS NOT IN DIRECT PROPORTION describes a relationship or function that is not strictly proportional

nonmember /nón mémbər/ *n* a person, group, or nation that does not belong to a specific organization —**nonmember** *adj*

nonmoral /nón mórrəl/ *adj* **1.** neither immoral nor moral, but unrelated to moral or ethical considerations **2.** not having or showing moral principles

non-negative *adj* in mathematics, relating to or being a real quantity that is positive or zero

non-negotiable *adj* **1.** not open to negotiation or arbitration ○ *non-negotiable demands* **2.** not legally transferable from one owner to another ○ *non-negotiable real property*

non-nuclear *adj* not using nuclear power or weapons

no-no /nōnō/ (*plural* **no-nos**) *n* something that is not allowed or is disapproved of (*informal*)

nonobjective /nónnəb jéktiv/ *adj* **1.** based on somebody's opinions or feelings, rather than on facts or evidence **2.** same as **nonrepresentational** —**nonobjectivity** /nón ob jek tívvəti/ *n*

nonobservance /nónn əb zúrv'nss/ *n* a failure to comply with something such as a law or practice, especially a religious practice —**nonobservant** *adj*

no-nonsense *adj* **1.** direct and practical in dealing with things or people **2.** basic and offering no extras, frills, or luxuries

nonoxynol-9 /non óksi nol nīn/ *n* a spermicide particularly used with barrier contraceptives such as diaphragms to improve their efficiency [< NONA- (in *nonyl*) + OXY- + PHENOL + 9 (because the compounds contained have an average of nine ethylene oxide groups per molecule)]

nonparametric /nón parrə méttrik/ *adj* relating to statistical methods that do not require assumptions about the form of the underlying distribution

nonpareil /nónpə ráy'l/ *n* **1.** SOMEBODY OR SOMETHING UNPARALLELED somebody or something without an equal **2.** PRINTING SIX-POINT TYPE a size of printers' type equivalent to six point (*dated*) ■ *adj* PEERLESS having no equal [15C. < French, 'not (having) equal' < *pareil* 'equal' < popular Latin *pariculus*, diminutive of Latin *par* 'equal']

nonpartisan /nón paarti zán/, **nonpartizan** *adj* not belonging to, supporting, or biased in favour of a political party —**nonpartisan** *n*

nonpenetrative /nón pénnitrətiv/ *adj* not involving penetration of the vagina or anus by the penis

nonperson /nón púrss'n/ *n* **1.** somebody who is ignored or not mentioned, usually because his or her views are disapproved of **2.** somebody regarded as of no importance or significance

non placet /nón pláyssət, nōn-/ *n* a negative vote in an ecclesiastical or academic assembly [< Latin, 'it does not please']

nonplaying /nón pláying/ *adj* not playing in a game or competition, but usually having a coaching or advisory role

nonplus /nón plúss/ *vt* (**-plusses, -plussing, -plussed**) to make somebody feel confused and unable to decide what to do ■ *n* a state of confusion and nervousness (*dated*) [Late 16C. < Latin *non plus* 'no more']

nonplussed /nón plúst/ *adj* **1.** surprised, confused, and uncertain what to do or say **2.** △ calm and unperturbed (*informal*)

USAGE The adjective **nonplussed** means 'surprised, confused, and uncertain what to do or say'. It is increasingly used in the almost opposite sense of 'untroubled', especially in US English (*Nonplussed by the criticism, she continued to direct her films in the very same offbeat manner for which she was famed.*). This new meaning is not yet accepted as standard, and it may cause ambiguity in sentences such as *He seemed nonplussed by the news*. It possibly derives from a misunderstanding of the *non-* element, perhaps also influenced by *nonchalant* which does mean 'calm and unconcerned'. But **nonplussed** goes back to Latin *non plus* 'no more', and does not have a positive or affirmative form *plussed*.

nonpoint source /non póynt-/ *n* a source of radiation or pollution that is diffuse rather than highly localized

nonprofit /nón próffit/ *adj* N Am same as **non-profit-making**

non-profit-making *adj* not operated with the primary aim of making a profit ○ *a non-profit-making organization* N Am term **nonprofit**

nonproliferation /nón prə líffə ráysh'n/ *n* the practice of limiting the production or spread of something, especially nuclear weapons or other weapons of mass destruction (*often used before a noun*) ○ *nonproliferation agreements*

nonpros /nón próss/ (*informal*) *n* (*plural* **-prosses**) LAW same as **non prosequitur** ■ *vt* (**-prosses, -prossing, -prossed**) to enter a judgment against a plaintiff who fails to appear in court [Late 17C. < shortening of NON PROSEQUITUR]

non prosequitur /nónprō sékwitər/ *n* a judgment in the defendant's favour when the plaintiff fails to appear in court [< Latin, 'he or she does not prosecute']

nonrecombinant /nón ri kómbinənt/ *adj* not produced by artificially manipulating genetic material

nonrelativistic /nón rélləti vístik/ *adj* not affected by the phenomena of relativity —**nonrelativistically** *adv*

non-REM sleep *n* BIOL same as **slow-wave sleep**

nonrepresentational /nón réppri zen táysh'nəl/ *adj* in art, not aiming to depict an object realistically and, usually, concerned more with form, pattern, or

colour for its own sake —**nonrepresentationalism** *n* —**nonrepresentationally** *adv*

nonresident Indian /non rèzzidənt-/ *n S Asia* an Indian who lives outside India

nonrestrictive /nón ri stríktiv/ *adj* with few or no restrictions

nonrestrictive clause *n* a relative clause that gives additional information about a noun or pronoun in the main clause but that is not essential to the understanding of the main clause. A nonrestrictive clause is usually separated from the rest of the sentence by commas, e.g. 'My partner, who is an artist, comes from Edinburgh'.

nonreturn valve /nón ri túrn-/ *n* ENG same as **check valve**

nonrun /nón rún/ *adj* designed not to ladder easily ○ *nonrun tights*

nonrunner /nón rúnnər/ *n* a nonstarter in a race

nonscheduled /nón shéddyoold/ *adj* **1.** not planned to happen as part of a schedule **2.** operating according to demand, rather than on a published schedule

nonsense /nónssənss/ *n* **1.** MEANINGLESS LANGUAGE OR BEHAVIOUR pointless or meaningless language or behaviour ○ *You're talking utter nonsense.* **2.** POINTLESS ACT OR UTTERANCE an instance of pointless or meaningless behaviour or language ○ *It would be a nonsense to lay people off now and hire them again later.* **3.** IRRITATING BEHAVIOUR disrespectful, obnoxious, or irritating behaviour ○ *the kind of judge who won't stand for any nonsense from barristers* **4.** LITERAT same as **nonsense verse** **5.** *also* **nonsense codon** GENETICS DNA SECTION PRODUCING NO AMINO ACID a set of three nucleotides (**codon**) in a DNA molecule that does not code for any amino acid. Codons are believed to signal the beginning and end of the synthesis of some protein molecules. ■ *interj* EXPRESSION OF CONTRADICTION used to contradict what somebody has said or written ◇ **make (a) nonsense of something** to make something seem pointless or absurd

CULTURAL NOTE ***A Book of Nonsense***, a collection of poems (1846) by British writer Edward Lear. Written for the grandchildren of the Earl of Derby, these songs, verses, and limericks, illustrated with Lear's own line drawings, conjure up a bizarre world where strange beings participate in surreal adventures. Although comic and fantastic, the verses are also tinged with a melancholy thought to reflect the author's depressive personality.

nonsense verse *n* poetry that is written in deliberately absurd language for humorous effect, mainly for children

nonsense word *n* a word with no meaning, usually created for humorous effect

nonsensical /non sénssik'l/ *adj* **1.** having no sense or meaning **2.** deserving ridicule —**nonsensicality** /non sénssi kálləti/ *n* —**nonsensically** *adv*

non sequitur /nón sékwitər/ *n* **1.** a statement that appears unrelated to a statement that it follows **2.** a conclusion that does not follow from its premises [< Latin, 'it does not follow']

nonslip /nón slíp/ *adj* designed to prevent people from slipping

nonsmoker /non smṓkər/ *n* **1.** somebody who does not smoke tobacco products **2.** a carriage or compartment in a train in which smoking is not allowed

nonsmoking /nón smṓking/ *adj* **1.** RESTRICTED TO NONSMOKERS reserved for people who do not want to smoke cigarettes, cigars, or pipes **2.** NOT SMOKING not smoking cigarettes, cigars, or a pipe ■ *n* AREA WHERE SMOKING IS FORBIDDEN an area of a public space such as a restaurant or aircraft cabin, where smoking is not permitted ○ *Do you want smoking or nonsmoking?*

nonspecific /nón spə síffik/ *adj* **1.** not particular or detailed **2.** not attributable to a specific medical cause or condition

nonspecific urethritis *n UK, ANZ, Can* inflammation of the urethra not caused by any identified infection. It is sexually transmitted but is not caused by gonorrhoeal organisms. US term **nongonococcal urethritis**

nonstandard /nón stándərd/ *adj* **1.** not conforming to an accepted standard **2.** not conforming to a standard accepted as grammatically correct by educated native speakers, or not used by educated native speakers

nonstarter /nón stáartər/ *n* **1.** SOMETHING OR SOMEBODY UNLIKELY TO SUCCEED something that or somebody who seems from the beginning to have no chance of success (*informal*) **2.** HORSE THAT DOES NOT COMPETE a horse that does not run in a race in which it has been entered **3.** COMPETITOR WHO WITHDRAWS BEFORE START a competitor who does not start a race, event, or competition in which he or she has been entered

nonstate actor /nón stayt-/ *n* an individual person or body acting independently of a state or government, e.g. a terrorist group

Non-Status Indian, **non-status Indian** *n* a member of an indigenous people not recognized by the federal government of Canada as having special rights and privileges, especially the right to live on a reserve

nonsteroid /nón stéer oyd, -stér royd/ *n* a drug that does not contain steroids ■ *adj also* **nonsteroidal** not containing or being a steroid

nonstick /nón stík/ *adj* with a coating or surface that prevents food sticking during cooking

nonstop /nón stóp/ *adj, adv* **1.** continuing without a stop ○ *a nonstop flight* **2.** continuing without interruption or rest ○ *a weekend of nonstop partying*

nonsuit /nón so͞ot, -syo͞ot/ *n* the dismissal of a suit by a judge when the plaintiff fails to make out a legal case or to produce adequate evidence

nontarget /nón táargit/ *adj* describes cells, tissues, or organisms that are not intended for treatment, e.g. by drugs or radiation, but may be affected by such treatment aimed elsewhere

nonterminating /non túrmi nayting/ *adj* **1.** having an infinite number of digits after the decimal point in a decimal fraction **2.** not having or coming to an end (*formal*)

nontitle /nón tīt'l/ *adj* not competed in to win a sports title or championship ○ *a nontitle fight*

nontransferable /nón transs fúr əb'l/, **nontransferrable** *adj* relating to a ticket, licence, or voucher that cannot be transferred to, or used by, anyone other than the person to whom it is sold or assigned

non-treaty Indian *n* PEOPLES same as **Non-Status Indian**

non troppo /nón tróppō/ *adv, adj* not too much (*used as a musical direction*) [< Italian]

non-U *adj* not belonging to or characteristic of the upper classes (*informal dated*) ○ *a non-U word for 'napkin'* [*U* abbreviation of *upper (class)*]

nonunion /nón yóonyən/ *adj* **1.** NOT IN UNION not belonging to a trade union **2.** NOT USING UNION MEMBERS not employing trade union members **3.** NOT MADE BY UNION MEMBERS not produced by trade union members —**nonunionized** *adj*

nonverbal /nón vúrb'l/ *adj* not using or involving words —**nonverbally** *adv*

nonverbal communication *n* communication by other means than by using words, e.g. through facial expressions, hand gestures, and tone of voice

nonviable /nón vī əb'l/ *adj* **1.** BIOL, MED incapable of growing and developing independently ○ *a nonviable foetus* ○ *nonviable seedlings* **2.** not capable of succeeding

nonvintage /nón víntij/ *adj* not belonging to an especially good year for a wine, or not identified by year

nonviolence /nón vī ələnss/ *n* **1.** the principle of refraining from using violence, especially as a means of protest **2.** the absence of or freedom from violence —**nonviolent** *adj* —**nonviolently** *adv*

non-white, **non-White** *n* a person whose ancestry cannot be traced ultimately to Europe (*sometimes considered offensive*) —**non-white** *adj*

nonwoody /non wo͝oddi/ *adj* **1.** not made of or containing wood or a material resembling wood **2.** describes a plant that does not form a woody stem

nonwoven /nón wṓv'n/ *adj* made of fibres that have been bonded or interlocked by mechanical, chemical, thermal, or solvent methods

nonya /nónnyə/ *adj* used to describe food or cuisine combining Chinese and Malay influences, in a style that originated in Melaka ■ *n Malaysia* a girl or woman of Chinese origin, born in Melaka and speaking Malay as a first language [< Malay, literally 'grandmother']

nonylphenol /nónnīl fée nol, nónnil-/ *n* a chemical compound that is a product of the breakdown of a surfactant commonly used in detergents and cleaning agents. It is reported to be an endocrine disrupter and is especially toxic to insects and aquatic organisms.

noodle[1] /no͝od'l/ *n* **1.** a long thin strip of pasta. Noodles are a staple of Italian and Chinese cookery. (*usually used in the plural*) **2.** *Aus* a long, narrow cylinder of polystyrene used as a flotation device for children [Late 18C. < German *Nudel*]

noodle[2] /no͝od'l/ *n* **1.** *N Am* the head or mind (*slang*) **2.** a term that deliberately, though perhaps affectionately, insults somebody's intelligence or common sense (*dated informal*) [Mid-18C. Origin ?]

noodle[3] /no͝od'l/ (**-dles, -dling, -dled**) *vti* to improvise on a musical instrument in a random meandering fashion, often in order to warm up (*slang*) [Mid-19C. Probably from likening such playing to the disorganized appearance of a dish of noodles]

noodle-noggin *n regional* a term that deliberately, though relatively humorously and affectionately, insults somebody's intelligence or common sense

REGIONAL NOTE See ***addle-headed***.

nook /no͝ok/ *n* **1.** a quiet private place **2.** a corner or small recess in a room [13C. Probably < Old Norse] ◇ **every nook and cranny** every tiny part of a place

nookie /no͝oki/, **nooky** *n* same as **sexual intercourse** (*slang; offensive*) [Early 20C. Origin ?]

noon /noon/ *n* **1.** 12 o'clock in the middle of the day **2.** the most important period of something (*literary*) [Pre-12C. < Latin *nona (hora)* 'ninth (hour) (of the Roman day, counted from sunrise)', feminine of *nonus*]

noonday /no͝on day/ (*literary*) *adj* relating to or happening at midday ■ *n* same as **noontime**

no one *pron* no person at all

noontide /no͝on tīd/ *n* same as **noontime** (*literary*)

noontime /no͝on tīm/ *n* the middle of the day, around 12 o'clock

Noonuccal /noo núk'l/, **Oodgeroo** (1920–93) Australian poet. Her collections include *We Are Going* (1964), the first book of poems published by an Aboriginal writer. Born **Kath Walker**

Noosa Heads /no͝ossə hedz/ town on the southeast coast of Queensland, Australia, a popular tourist resort. Population: 11,296 (1986).

noose /nooss/ *n* **1.** LOOP IN ROPE a loop at the end of a rope, tied with a knot so that it can be tightened and slackened, and used for trapping animals or hanging people **2.** ENTRAPMENT something that traps somebody in an unpleasant or unwanted situation ■ *vt* (**nooses, noosing, noosed**) **1.** CATCH SOMETHING WITH NOOSE to catch somebody or something with a noose **2.** TIE ROPE IN NOOSE to make a noose at the end of a rope or cord [15C. Probably via Old French *nos* (singular), *nous* (plural) < Latin *nodus* 'knot']

Nootka /no͝otkə, no͝ot-/ (*plural* **-kas** or *same*) *n* **1.** a member of a Native North American people of the coast of western Vancouver Island, British Columbia, and Cape Flattery, on the Olympic Peninsula in Washington State **2.** the Wakashan language of the Nootka people. Few people now speak Nootka. [Early 19C. After *Nootka* Sound, an inlet on the coast of Vancouver Island, British Columbia, Canada] —**Nootka** *adj*

NOP *abbr* National Opinion Polls

nopal /nṓp'l/ (*plural* **-pals** or *same*) *n* **1.** a cactus that is a host plant to the cochineal insect. Flowers: red, with long stamens. Latin name: *Nopalea cochinellifera*. **2.** the fleshy flattened stem of a nopal cactus, sliced and cooked after removal of the spines [Mid-18C. Via French < Nahuatl *nopalli* 'cactus']

no-par, **no-par-value** *adj* describes a security without a par or face value

nope /nōp/ *adv, interj* indicates a negative response refusing, denying, or disagreeing with something (*slang*) [Late 19C. Alteration of NO[1] (probably imitating the lips' emphatic closure)]

nopo *n* a train that is controlled automatically and needs no driver. Full form **no person operated train**

no-questions-asked *adj* given or granted unconditionally, whatever the reason or circumstances ○ *a no-questions-asked refund*

nor /nawr/ *conj* used to introduce an alternative, after a first alternative that is preceded by 'neither' (*used in negative statements*) ○ *Neither he nor his wife had*

profited in any way from the questionable investment. ■ *conj, adv* used to indicate that what has just been said also applies to somebody or something else, or to add extra information to what has just been said (*used after negative statements and followed by 'have', 'do', or 'be'*) ○ *He doesn't want to move to another town, and nor do I.* ○ *No surrounding tissue was damaged, nor did the infection spread.* ■ *prep, conj* same as **than** (*nonstandard*) ■ same as **neither** (sense 2) (*literary*) [13C. Contraction of obsolete *nouther* 'neither, nor']

NOR /nawr/ *n* a logical operator with two arguments that returns true if, and only if, both arguments are false [Mid-20C. Blend of NOT + OR[1]]

Nor. *abbr* **1.** HIST Norman **2.** North **3.** Norway **4.** Norwegian

nor- *prefix* an unaltered parent compound ○ *noradrenaline* [Shortening of NORMAL]

noradrenaline /náwrə drénnəlin/, **noradrenalin** *n* a hormone, secreted by the adrenal gland and similar to adrenaline, that is the principal neurotransmitter of sympathetic nerve endings supplying the major organs and skin. It increases blood pressure and rate and depth of breathing, raises the level of blood sugar, and decreases the activity of the intestines. N Am term **norepinephrine**

noradrenergic /náwr adrə núrjik/ *adj* releasing or involving noradrenaline in the transmission of nerve impulses

NOR circuit *n* a computer circuit with two inputs and one output where the output is on only when both inputs are off

Nordic /náwrdik/ *adj* **1.** SCANDINAVIAN relating to the countries of northwestern Europe, especially the Scandinavian countries and Iceland **2.** TALL, FAIR, AND BLUE-EYED tall, blonde, fair-skinned, and blue-eyed, in a way that is considered to be characteristic of people from Scandinavian countries **3.** *also* **nordic** INVOLVING CROSS-COUNTRY SKIING OR JUMPING describes ski events involving either cross-country racing or ski jumping or both ■ *n* SOMEBODY FROM SCANDINAVIA somebody from a Nordic country or of Nordic appearance [Late 19C. < French *nordique* < *nord* 'north' < Germanic]

Nord-Ostsee Kanal /nawrt óst zay ka nál/ ♦ **Kiel Canal**

nor'easter /náwr éestər/ *n* METEOROL same as **northeaster** [Mid-19C. Alteration]

norepinephrine /náwr epi néffrin/ *n N Am* same as **noradrenaline**

norethisterone /náwr e thístərōn/ *n* a progestogen drug. Use: oral contraceptives, hormone replacement therapy, treatment of premenstrual syndrome, menstrual disorders, endometriosis, cancer. [< NOR- + shortening and alteration of ETHYNE + *-ster*, INN stem]

Norf. *abbr* Norfolk

Norfolk /náwrfək/ **1.** county in eastern England, bordering on the Wash and the North Sea. Area: 5,360 sq. km/2,069 sq. mi. **2.** city in southeastern Virginia, situated southeast of Richmond at the mouth of the James and Elizabeth rivers. It is a major port and houses a number of large naval installations. Population: 239,036 (2002 estimate).

Norfolk and Suffolk Broads same as **Broads**

Norfolk Island island dependency of Australia, lying in the southwestern Pacific Ocean, 1,676 km/1,042 mi. northeast of Sydney. Population: 1,912 (1991). Area: 35 sq. km/13 sq. mi.

Norfolk Island pine *n* a tall symmetrical pine tree. Native to: Norfolk Island, off eastern Australia, but now also found on the mainland. Latin name: *Araucaria heterophylla.*

Norfolk jacket *n* a loose jacket with a belt and box pleats, first worn by men and later adapted to women's fashions [After NORFOLK, England]

Norfolk terrier *n* a small wire-haired dog, belonging to a breed with short tails and drop ears [After NORFOLK, England]

norg /nawrg/ *n Aus* an offensive term for a woman's breast (*slang*) [Mid-20C. Origin ?]

NOR gate *n* COMPUT same as **NOR circuit**

Norgay ♦ **Tenzing Norgay**

norgestrel /nawr jéstrəl/ *n* a progestogen drug. Use: oral contraceptives. [Late 20C. < NOR- + PROGESTOGEN]

nori /náwri/ *n* an edible preparation of dried pressed seaweed, often used to wrap sushi [Late 19C. < Japanese]

noria /náwri ə/ *n* a series of buckets on a water wheel, used for raising water from a stream [Late 18C. Via Spanish < Arabic *nā'ūra*]

Noriega /nórri áygə/, **Manuel** (*b.* 1934) Panamanian national leader. He took power in 1983, but was seized by US forces in 1989, and was later jailed for drug trafficking and other offences. Full name **Noriega Morena, Manuel Antonio**

norite /náwr īt/ *n* a coarse-grained igneous rock containing mainly plagioclase and orthopyroxene [Late 19C. < NORWAY] —**noritic** /naw ríttik/ *adj*

nork /nawrk/ *n Aus* an offensive term for a woman's breast (*slang*) [Mid-20C. Origin ?]

Norkay ♦ **Tenzing Norgay**

norm /nawrm/ *n* **1.** STANDARD PATTERN OF BEHAVIOUR a standard pattern of behaviour that is considered normal in a society **2.** USUAL SITUATION the customary situation or circumstances **3.** ACHIEVEMENT LEVEL a required level of achievement **4.** PSYCHOL EXPECTED RANGE OF FUNCTIONING the range of functioning that can be expected of members of a population such as babies of nine months or ten-year-old children. Psychologists use it to determine whether people functioning outside the expected range may need specialist help or support. **5.** MATHS REAL-VALUED FUNCTION the magnitude of a vector expressed as the square root of the sum of the squares of the absolute values of the components of the vector **6.** MATHS same as **mode** (sense 6) [Early 19C. Latin *norma* 'carpenter's square, rule']

Norm /nawrm/ *n Aus* an Australian man who enjoys watching sport on television while consuming large quantities of beer (*slang*) ○ *It's Grand Final week, so your average Norm will be glued to the box.* [< the forename *Norm*, short for *Norman*, influenced by NORM, NORMAL]

norm. *abbr* MATHS normal

Norm. *abbr* HIST, LANG Norman[1]

Norma /náwrmə/ *n* a small faint constellation of the southern hemisphere lying in the Milky Way, located between Ara and Lupus

normal /náwrm'l/ *adj* **1.** USUAL conforming to the usual standard, type, or custom **2.** HEALTHY physically, mentally, and emotionally healthy **3.** OCCURRING NATURALLY maintained or occurring in a natural state **4.** CHEM UNBRANCHED describes aliphatic hydrocarbons with unbranched chains of carbon atoms **5.** CHEM CONTAINING ONE GRAM PER LITRE describes a chemical solution containing an equivalent weight of solute in grams per litre of solution (*dated*) **6.** MATHS same as **perpendicular** *adj* (sense 1) ■ *n* **1.** USUAL STANDARD the usual standard, type, or custom **2.** MATHS PERPENDICULAR LINE OR PLANE a line or plane that is perpendicular to another line or plane [15C. Directly or via French < Latin *normalis* 'made according to the square' < *norma* 'carpenter's square']

normal curve *n* the symmetrical bell-shaped curve of a normal distribution

normalcy /náwrm'lssi/ *n N Am* same as **normality**

normal distribution *n* a probability frequency distribution for a random variable that theoretically takes on a bell shape symmetrical about the mean

normal fault *n* a geological fault in which the upper wall has slipped downward relative to the lower wall

normalise *vti* another spelling of **normalize**

normality /nawr mállәti/ *n* the way things are under normal circumstances

normalize /náwrmə līz/ (**-izes, -izing, -ized**), **normalise** (**-ises, -ising, -ised**) *v* **1.** *vti* MAKE SOMETHING NORMAL to make something normal or return something to normal, or become or return to normal **2.** *vt* MAKE SOMETHING OR SOMEBODY CONFORM to make something or somebody conform to a standard **3.** *vt* METALL HEAT STEEL to heat steel above a specific temperature and then cool it in order to reduce internal stress —**normalization** /náwrmə lī záysh'n/ *n*

normally /náwrm'li/ *adv* **1.** as a custom or habit ○ *Normally, we go swimming on Sundays.* **2.** in the usual or standard way ○ *The trains are running normally again.*

normal school *n* a school or college for training teachers, especially in France and, formerly, in England, the United States, and Canada [Mid-19C. After French *école normale*; from the first French school so named being considered a model for others]

Norman[1] /náwrmən/ *n* **1.** MEDIEVAL INHABITANT OF NORMANDY OR ENGLAND a member of a Viking people who raided and then settled in the French province later known as Normandy, and who invaded England in 1066 **2.** SOMEBODY FROM NORMANDY somebody who comes from the French region of Normandy **3.** LANG same as **Norman French** (sense 1) **4.** STYLE OF MEDIEVAL ARCHITECTURE a style of Romanesque architecture developed by the Normans in the Middle Ages, characterized by vaults separated by groins, heavy walls, and deeply recessed portals [13C. < Old French *Normans*, plural of *Normant* < Old Norse *Norðmaðr* (plural *Norðmenn*) < *norð* 'north'] —**Norman** *adj*

Norman[2] /náwrmən/ city in central Oklahoma, south of Oklahoma City. It is home to the University of Oklahoma. Population: 97,831 (2002 estimate).

Norman, Greg (*b.* 1955) Australian golfer. He was the winner of the British Open (1986, 1993), and the World Match Play Championship (1980, 1983, and 1986). Known as **Great White Shark**. Full name **Norman, Gregory John**

> 'It doesn't bother me what ball I use, what colour trousers I wear or what I ate the night before. How can that sort of stuff have any effect on my game?'
> [Greg Norman, *Sunday Times*; 23 September 1984]

Norman, Jessye (*b.* 1945) US operatic soprano. Her 1969 operatic debut in Berlin was the first of numerous international appearances in operas and concerts, where she was admired for her rich tone and dynamic range.

Norman Conquest *n* the invasion and conquest of England by the Normans, led by William the Conqueror, in 1066

Normandy /náwrməndi/ region in northwestern France, on the English Channel. Towards the end of World War II, in 1944, it was the scene of the D-day landings, the Allied invasion of German-occupied France. Capital: Rouen.

Norman French *n* **1.** a variety of French spoken by the Normans in the Middle Ages **2.** the French dialect spoken in modern Normandy —**Norman French** *adj*

normative /náwrmətiv/ *adj* (*formal*) **1.** relating to standards **2.** tending to create or prescribe standards [Late 19C. < French < Latin *norma* 'carpenter's square'] —**normatively** *adv* —**normativeness** *n*

norming /náwrming/ *n US* the practice of adjusting the scores on standardized tests in order to compensate for the possible effects that ethnic and cultural differences may have on the test results

normotensive /náwrmō ténssiv/ *adj* having or indicating normal blood pressure ■ *n* somebody with normal blood pressure [Mid-20C. < NORM or NORMAL]

normothermia /náwrmō thúrmi ə/ *n* the state of having a normal body temperature —**normothermic** *adj*

norm-referenced *adj* using a comparison of a pupil's performance in a test with the performance of other children in the same test —**norm-referencing** *n*

Norns /nawrnz/, **Nornir** /náwr neer/ *npl* in Scandinavian mythology, the three goddesses of destiny [Late 18C. < Old Norse]

norovirus /nórrō vīrəss/ *n* a single-stranded RNA virus that is highly contagious and causes gastroenteritis. Family: Caliciviridae. [Late 20C. Alteration of *Norwalk virus*, after a city in Ohio where the first outbreak occurred]

Norse /nawrss/ *adj* **1.** OF OLD SCANDINAVIA relating to ancient or medieval Scandinavia, or its people or culture **2.** LANG OF N GERMANIC LANGUAGES relating to the North Germanic languages, especially Danish, Icelandic, and Norwegian in their earlier forms ■ *npl* **1.** VIKINGS the Viking people of medieval Scandinavia **2.** SCANDINAVIANS the people of Scandinavia **3.** LANG N GERMANIC NATIVE SPEAKERS the people who speak one of the North Germanic languages as their native language ■ *n* LANG N GERMANIC LANGUAGE a North Germanic language, especially Danish, Icelandic, or Norwegian in their earlier forms [Late 16C. Via Dutch *Noorsch* < *noordsch* 'northern']

Norseman /náwrssmən/ (*plural* **-men** /-mən/) *n* a

member of a medieval Scandinavian group, especially a Viking

norteño /nawr táynyō/ n **1.** a type of Mexican dance music characterized by rolling accordion riffs **2. norteno** (*plural* **-nos**) N Am somebody from northern Mexico [Late 20C. Via American Spanish < Spanish, 'northern']

north /nawrth/ n **1.** DIRECTION the direction that lies directly to the left of somebody facing the rising Sun or that is located towards the top of a conventional map of the world **2.** COMPASS POINT one of the cardinal points on a compass. North is 90 degrees anticlockwise from east. **3.** *also* **North** AREA IN NORTH the part of an area, region, or country that is situated in or towards the north **4.** LEFT-HAND SIDE OF CHURCH the left-hand side of a church as you face the altar from the central section of the building **5.** *also* **North** POSITION EQUIVALENT TO NORTH the position equivalent to north in a diagram consisting of four points at 90-degree intervals ■ *adj* **1.** IN NORTH situated in, facing, or coming from the north of a place, region, or country **2.** BLOWING FROM NORTH describes a wind that blows from the north ○ *a north wind* ■ *adv* TOWARDS NORTH in or towards the north [Old English *norp* < Germanic]

North /nawrth/, **Frederick, 8th Baron North** (1732–92) British prime minister (1770–82). During his premiership, he pursued policies favoured by George III that led to the War of American Independence despite his own opposition to the war. Known as **Lord North**

North Africa /nawrth-/ northern part of the African continent, comprising Morocco, Mauritania, Algeria, Tunisia, Libya, and Northern Egypt —**North African** adj, n

Northallerton /náwrth állərt'n/ market town in North Yorkshire, northern England. Population: 13,774 (1991).

Northam /náwrthəm/ town in Devon, southwestern England, situated 76 km/47 mi. north of Plymouth. Population: 6,167 (1991).

North America continent in the western hemisphere, extending northwards from northwestern South America to the Arctic Ocean. It comprises Central America, Mexico, the United States, Canada, and Greenland. Population: 405,000,000 (2000). Area: 23,700,000 sq. km/9,200,000 sq. mi. —**North American** adj, n

USAGE See *America*.

Northampton /náwr thámptən/ county town of Northamptonshire, central England. Population: 194,458 (2001).

Northamptonshire /nawr thámptənshər/ county in central England. The county town is Northampton. Area: 2,370 sq. km/915 sq. mi.

Northants /náwrth ants/ *abbr* Northamptonshire

North Atlantic Conveyor, **North Atlantic Conveyor Belt** n an ocean current system that carries warm surface waters to the North Atlantic, where they cool and drop to a deeper level before flowing south again. It transfers heat to the atmosphere and gives western Europe its present temperate climate.

North Atlantic drift n the relatively warm current, originating as the Gulf Stream in the Gulf of Mexico, that flows across the surface of the North Atlantic Ocean from Newfoundland to northwestern Europe, influencing the latter's climate

North Atlantic Treaty Organization n INTERNAT REL full form of **NATO**

North Ayrshire council area in west-central Scotland that includes the Isle of Arran. The administrative centre is Irvine. Population: 136,875 (2001). Area: 884 sq. km/341 sq. mi.

North Borneo former name for **Sabah** (until 1963)

northbound /náwrth bownd/ adj leading, going, or travelling towards the north

north by east n the direction or compass point midway between north and north-northeast —**north by east** adj, adv

north by west n the direction or compass point midway between north and north-northwest —**north by west** adj, adv

North Cape promontory on Magerøya Island, northern Norway, on the Barents Sea

North Carolina state in the eastern United States, bordered by the Atlantic Ocean, South Carolina, Georgia, Tennessee, and Virginia. Capital: Raleigh. Population: 8,320,146 (2002 estimate). Area: 136,420 sq. km/52,672 sq. mi. —**North Carolinian** adj

North Caucasian n a group of language families spoken in the region of Caucasia, including the Abkhaz-Adyghean and Nakh languages. They are unrelated to Kartvelian, or South Caucasian. —**North Caucasian** adj

North Channel strait of the Atlantic Ocean separating northeastern Ireland and southwestern Scotland. Width: 37 km/23 mi.

northcountryman /náwrth kúntrimən/ (*plural* **-men** /-mən/) n a man who was born or brought up in the north of England

North Dakota state in the north-central United States, bordered by Minnesota, South Dakota, Montana, and Canada. Capital: Bismarck. Population: 634,110 (2002 estimate). Area: 183,123 sq. km/70,704 sq. mi. —**North Dakotan** adj, n

North Downs range of chalk hills in Surrey and Kent, southern England. Its highest peak is Leith Hill, 294 m/965 ft.

northeast /náwrth éest/; *nautical usage* /náwr éest/ n **1.** COMPASS POINT BETWEEN N AND E the direction or compass point midway between north and east **2.** *also* **Northeast** AREA IN NORTHEAST the part of an area, region, or country that is situated in or towards the northeast ■ *adj* **1.** IN NORTHEAST situated in, facing, or lying towards the northeast of a region, place, or country **2.** BLOWING FROM NORTHEAST describes a wind that blows from the northeast ○ *a northeast wind* ■ *adv* TOWARDS NORTHEAST in or towards the northeast

Northeast n **1.** northeastern England, especially the area from the River Tees northwards including Tyneside, Northumberland, and Durham **2.** *US* a part of the northeastern United States, usually thought of as consisting of the New England states, sometimes together with eastern New York, Pennsylvania, and New Jersey

northeast by east n the direction or compass point midway between northeast and east-northeast —**northeast by east** adj, adv

northeast by north n the direction or compass point midway between northeast and north-northeast —**northeast by north** adj, adv

northeaster /náwrth éestər/; *nautical usage* /náwr éestər/ n a storm or wind that blows from the northeast

northeasterly /náwrth éestərli/; *nautical usage* /náwr éestərli/ adj **1.** situated in or towards the northeast **2.** describes a wind that blows from the northeast ○ *a northeasterly wind* ■ n (*plural* **-lies**) METEOROL same as **northeaster** —**northeasterly** adv

northeastern /náwrth éestərn/; *nautical usage* /náwr éestərn/ adj **1.** IN NORTHEAST situated in the northeast of a region or country **2.** COMING FROM OR FACING NORTHEAST coming or blowing from, or facing towards the northeast **3.** BLOWING FROM NE blowing from the northeast **4.** *also* **Northeastern** OF NORTHEAST relating or native to the northeast of a region or country —**northeasternmost** adj

Northeast Passage sea passage extending from the North Sea eastwards along the northern coast of Europe and Asia to the Pacific Ocean. It was first successfully navigated by Adolf Erik Nordensköld in 1878–79.

northeastward /náwrth éestwərd/; *nautical usage* /náwr éestwərd/ adj towards or in the northeast ■ n a direction towards or a point in the northeast ■ adv same as **northeastwards** —**northeastwardly** adj, adv

northeastwards /náwrth éestwərdz/; *nautical usage* /náwr éestwərd/ adv in a northeasterly direction

northerly /náwrthərli/ adj **1.** IN NORTH situated in or towards the north **2.** BLOWING FROM NORTH describes a wind that blows from the north ○ *a northerly wind* ■ n (*plural* **-lies**) WIND FROM NORTH a wind that blows from the north —**northerly** adv

northern /náwrthərn/ adj **1.** IN NORTH situated in the north of a region or country **2.** NORTH OF EQUATOR lying north of the equator or north of the celestial equator **3.** FACING NORTH situated on the north side of something or facing north **4.** FROM NORTH blowing from the north ○ *a northern wind* **5.** *also* **Northern** OF NORTH relating or native to the north of a region or country

Northern Alliance n a loose coalition of Afghan military forces, operating mainly in the north of Afghanistan, that ended Taliban rule in Afghanistan in 2001

Northern Cape /náwrthərn-/ largest province in South Africa, in the northwestern part of the country. Capital: Kimberley. Population: 822,720 (2001). Area: 361,830 sq. km/139,670 sq. mi.

Northern Cross n a cross formed by six stars in the constellation Cygnus

Northern Crown n ASTRON same as **Corona Borealis**

northerner /náwrthərnər/, **Northerner** n somebody who comes from the northern part of a country or region

northern hemisphere n **1.** the half of the Earth that lies to the north of the equator **2.** the half of the celestial sphere north of the celestial equator

Northern Ireland province of the United Kingdom of Great Britain and Northern Ireland, situated in the northeastern part of the island of Ireland. Capital: Belfast. Population: 1,685,267 (2001). Area: 14,160 sq. km/5,467 sq. mi.

Northern Ireland Assembly n the centre of devolved government for Northern Ireland, made up of elected members, suspended from 14 October 2002

Northern Ireland Executive n the devolved government of Northern Ireland

Northern Ireland Office n during devolution, a UK government department responsible for constitutional and security issues in Northern Ireland

Northern Isles npl Orkney and Shetland islands

Northernism /náwrthərnizəm/, **northernism** n a pronunciation, word, or other linguistic construction characteristic of the northern region of a country

northern lights npl ASTRON same as **aurora borealis**

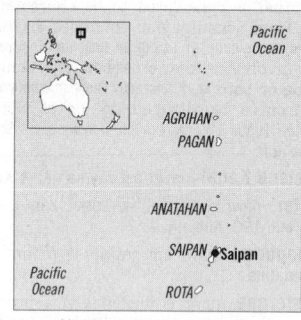

Northern Mariana Islands

Northern Mariana Islands /-márri ánnə-/ self-governing commonwealth of the United States, situated in the western Pacific Ocean and comprising all the Mariana Islands except Guam. Population: 71,912 (2000). Area: 457 sq. km/176 sq. mi.

northernmost /náwrthərn mōst/ adj situated farthest north

northern oriole n an oriole with two subspecies, the Baltimore oriole and Bullock's oriole, the males of each having black and orange plumage. Native to: North America. Latin name: *Icterus galbula*.

Northern Paiute, **Northern Piute** n **1.** a member of a Native North American people of Oregon, Nevada, and northeastern California **2.** a Uto-Aztecan language spoken in Oregon, Nevada, and northeastern California. Native speakers: 6,000. —**Northern Paiute** adj

northern pike n US regional FISH same as **pike**[1] (sense 1)

Northern Province former name for **Limpopo Province**

Northern Renaissance n a northern European cultural and intellectual movement of the 15th century in France, England, Scotland, the Low Countries, and Germany that placed more emphasis on religion than the Italian Renaissance did

Northern Rhodesia former name for **Zambia**

Northern Sotho n LANG same as **Pedi** —**Northern Sotho** adj

Northern Territory territory in north-central Australia. It became self-governing in 1978. Capital: Darwin. Population: 198,400 (2003). Area: 1,346,200 sq. km/519,770 sq. mi. —**Northern Territorian** n, adj

North Germanic *n* **1.** a group of Germanic languages that includes Danish, Faroese, Icelandic, Norwegian, and Swedish. Native speakers: 20 million. **2.** the language that is the ancestor of modern languages belonging to North Germanic —**North Germanic** *adj*

LANGUAGE HERITAGE See *Scandinavian.*

northing /náwrthing, -thing/ *n* **1.** MOVEMENT NORTH distance covered or movement made in a northerly direction, especially as measured by the difference in latitude between two points **2.** PROGRESS NORTH progress made in a northern direction **3.** LATITUDINAL GRID LINE ON MAP a grid line on a map that runs from east to west **4.** DISTANCE NORTHWARDS the distance northwards from an east-west grid line, shown in the second half of a map reference

North Island island in New Zealand, in the southwestern Pacific Ocean. It is the smaller and more northern of the country's two main islands. Population: 2,749,980 (1996). Area: 114,690 sq. km/44,282 sq. mi.

North Korea /-kə reé ə/ country in East Asia that occupies the northern portion of the Korean Peninsula. Language: Korean. Currency: won. Capital: Pyongyang. Population: 22,466,481 (2003). Area: 120,538 sq. km/46,540 sq. mi. Official name **Democratic People's Republic of Korea** —**North Korean** *n, adj*

North Lanarkshire council area in southern Scotland, established in 1996. Area: 474 sq. km/183 sq. mi.

northland /náwrth land/ *n* the northern part of a country

Northland[1] /náwrth land/ **1.** Scandinavian peninsula containing Norway and Sweden **2.** *Can* parts of Canada in the far north

Northland[2] administrative region in northern New Zealand, occupying most of the North Auckland Peninsula in the northwest of the North Island. Population: 140,131 (2001). Area: 30,105 sq. km/11,624 sq. mi.

north magnetic pole *n* the point on the Earth's surface to which the north-seeking pole of a compass needle is attracted

Northman /náwrthmən/ (*plural* -**men** /-mən/) *n* HIST, PEOPLES same as **Norseman**

north-northeast *n* the direction or compass point midway between north and northeast ■ *adj, adv* in, from, facing, or towards the north-northeast

north-northwest *n* the direction or compass point midway between north and northwest ■ *adj, adv* in, from, facing, or towards the north-northwest

North Pennines /-pénnīnz/ Area of Outstanding Natural Beauty in northern England, including parts of Cumbria, Durham, and Northumberland, established in 1988. Area: 1,983 sq. km/773 sq. mi.

north pole *n* **1.** GEOG, NAVIG same as **north magnetic pole 2.** the north end of the axis of rotation of a planet or other astronomical object **3.** the point at infinity along the northern extension of one end of the Earth's axis of rotation **4.** another spelling of **North Pole**

North Pole *n* the northern end of the Earth's axis at a latitude of 90° N

North Riding /-ríding/ former division in Yorkshire, northern England, now forming the county of North Yorkshire ■ ♦ **Tipperary**

North Saskatchewan river in Canada that rises in the Canadian Rocky Mountains and flows eastwards to join the South Saskatchewan River. It empties into Lake Winnipeg. Length: 1,200 km/760 mi.

North Sea arm of the Atlantic Ocean lying between the eastern coast of Great Britain and the continent of Europe. Area: 575,000 sq. km/222,000 sq. mi.

North-South Divide *n* **1.** the political and economic disparities between the northern and the southern regions of England **2.** the political and economic disparities between industrialized nations of the northern hemisphere and developing nations of the southern hemisphere

North Star *n* ASTRON same as **Pole Star**

North Stradbroke Island /-strád brook-/ island of northeastern Australia, in Moreton Bay, off the

coast of southeastern Queensland. Population: 2,290 (1994). Area: 319 sq. km/123 sq. mi.

North Uist /-yoo ist/ island in northwestern Scotland, in the Outer Hebrides, situated off the northwestern coast of the mainland. Population: 1,404 (1991).

Northumberland /nawr thúmbərlənd/ northernmost county of England, and one of the largest and most sparsely populated. Area: 5,033 sq. km/1,944 sq. mi.

Northumberland National Park national park in Northumberland, northeastern England. It includes the hilly country between Hadrian's Wall and the Scottish border. Area: 1,036 sq. km/400 sq. mi.

Northumbria /nawr thúmbri ə/ ancient region in northeastern England. It was one of the most powerful of the Anglo-Saxon kingdoms of England between the 7th and 10th centuries. —**Northumbrian** *adj, n*

North Vietnam former republic in Southeast Asia. Created by the French partition of Vietnam in 1954, it was reunited with South Vietnam in 1976 after the Vietnam War, and its capital of Hanoi became the national capital. —**North Vietnamese** *n, adj*

northward /náwrthwərd/ *adj* towards or in the north ■ *n* a direction towards or a point in the north ■ *adv* same as **northwards** —**northwardly** *adj, adv*

USAGE **northward** or **northwards**? **Northward** is the only form available for the adjective (*in a northward direction*), while **northwards** is commonly used as well as **northward** for the adverb: *The ship was moving slowly northward/northwards.*

northwards /náwrthwərdz/ *adv* in a northerly direction

North Wessex Downs Area of Outstanding Natural Beauty in southern England, including parts of Hampshire, Oxfordshire, and Wiltshire, established in 1972. Area: 1,730 sq. km/675 sq. mi.

northwest /náwrth wést/; *nautical usage* /náwr wést/ *n* **1.** COMPASS POINT BETWEEN N AND W the direction or compass point midway between north and west **2.** *also* **Northwest** AREA IN NORTHWEST the part of an area, region, or country that is situated in or towards the northwest ■ *adj* **1.** *also* **Northwest** IN NORTHWEST situated in, facing, or lying towards the northwest of a region, place, or country **2.** BLOWING FROM NORTHWEST describes a wind that blows from the northwest ○ *a northwest wind* ■ *adv* TOWARDS NORTHWEST in or towards the northwest

Northwest *n* **1.** AREA OF ENGLAND the northwestern region of England, especially Cumbria and Lancashire and including the Lake District **2.** NW UNITED STATES the northwestern area of the United States, including the states of Washington, Oregon, and Idaho **3.** FORMER AREA OF UNITED STATES formerly, a region of the United States west of the Mississippi River and north of the Missouri River **4.** CANADIAN REGION the area of Canada north and west of the Great Lakes

northwest by north *n* the direction or compass point midway between northwest and north-northwest —**northwest by north** *adj, adv*

northwest by west *n* the direction or compass point midway between northwest and west-northwest —**northwest by west** *adj, adv*

northwester /náwrth wéstər/; *nautical usage* /náwr wéstər/ *n* a wind that blows from the northwest

northwesterly /náwrth wéstərli/; *nautical usage* /náwr wéstərli/ *adj* **1.** situated in or towards the northwest **2.** METEOROL describes a wind that blows from the northwest ○ *a northwesterly wind* ■ *n* (*plural* -**lies**) METEOROL same as **northwester** —**northwesterly** *adv*

northwestern /náwrth wéstərn/; *nautical usage* /náwr wéstərn/ *adj* **1.** IN NORTHWEST situated in the northwest of a region or country **2.** FACING NORTHWEST coming or blowing from, or facing towards the northwest **3.** OF NORTHWEST relating to or native to the northwest of a region or country —**northwesternmost** *adj*

Northwest Passage /náwrth wést-/ sea passage through the Arctic regions of North America, connecting the Pacific Ocean and the Atlantic Ocean

North-West Province province in South Africa, in the north-central part of the country. Capital: Mmabatho. Population: 3,669,339 (2001). Area: 116,190 sq. km/44,850 sq. mi.

Northwest Territories region in northern Canada, and its largest political subdivision, constituting a

northern mainland region and numerous islands to the north. Capital: Yellowknife. Population: 441,400 (2002). Area: 1,346,106 sq. km/519,734 sq. mi.

Northwest Territory territory of the north-central United States ceded by England to the United States by the Treaty of Paris in 1783. The area of about 688,600 sq. km/265,900 sq. mi. extended from the Ohio and Mississippi rivers northwards to the Great Lakes, and included present-day Ohio, Indiana, Illinois, Michigan, Wisconsin, and eastern Minnesota.

northwestward /náwrth wéstwərd/; *nautical usage* /náwr wéstwərd/ *adj* towards or in the northwest ■ *n* a direction towards or a point in the northwest ■ *adv* same as **northwestwards** —**northwestwardly** *adj, adv*

northwestwards /náwrth wéstwərdz/; *nautical usage* /náwr wéstwərdz/ *adv* in a northwesterly direction

Northwich /náwrth wich/ market town in Cheshire, northwestern England, that has been a centre of salt extraction since Roman times. Population: 34,520 (1991).

North York Moors National Park national park in northern England, predominantly in Yorkshire. It consists largely of moorland and woodland. Area: 1,432 sq. km/533 sq. mi.

North Yorkshire county in northern England, created in 1974. Its administrative headquarters are in Northallerton. Area: 8,321 sq. km/3,213 sq. mi.

nortriptyline /nawr trípti leen/ *n* a tricyclic drug. Use: antidepressant, tranquillizer, pain reliever. Formula: $C_{19}H_{21}N$. [Mid-20C. < NOR- + *triptyline*, INN stem]

Norw. *abbr* **1.** Norway **2.** Norwegian

Norway

Norway /náwr way/ country in northern Europe, occupying the western and northern portions of the Scandinavian Peninsula. Language: Norwegian. Currency: krone. Capital: Oslo. Population: 4,546,123 (2003). Area: 385,639 sq. km/148,896 sq. mi. Official name **Kingdom of Norway**

Norway maple *n* a maple with broad five-lobed green or reddish leaves, widely grown as a shade tree. Native to: central and northern Europe. Latin name: *Acer platanoides.*

Norway rat *n* ZOOL same as **brown rat**

Norway spruce *n* a spruce tree with drooping branches and long cones, widely grown for its timber and as an ornamental. Native to: central and northern Europe. Latin name: *Picea abies.*

Norwegian /nawr weéj'n/ *n* **1.** somebody who comes from Norway **2.** the North Germanic language that is the official language of Norway. Native speakers: 5 million. [Early 17C. < medieval Latin *Norvegia* 'Norway' < Old Norse *Norvegr*] —**Norwegian** *adj*

LANGUAGE HERITAGE See *Scandinavian.*

nor'wester /náwr wéstər/ *n* **1.** METEOROL same as **northwester 2.** *NZ* in New Zealand, a hot dry wind that blows from the Southern Alps onto the Canterbury Plain in spring **3.** a strong alcoholic drink (*slang*) [Late 17C. Alteration]

Norwich /nórrich/ town and administrative centre of Norfolk, eastern England. Population: 121,550 (2001).

Norwich school *n* a British regional school of landscape painters that flourished in the early 19th century, inspired by the 17th-century Dutch realist tradition of landscape painting [Because associated with NORWICH]

Norwich terrier *n* a small short-legged dog with wiry fur and erect ears, belonging to a breed that originated in East Anglia

nos., Nos. *abbr* numbers

n.o.s. *abbr* not otherwise specified

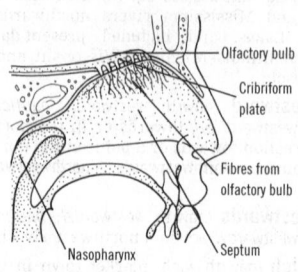

nose: cross section of the human nose

Labels: Olfactory bulb; Cribriform plate; Fibres from olfactory bulb; Nasopharynx; Septum

nose /nōz/ *n* **1. ORGAN OF SMELL** the part of the face or head through which a person or animal breathes and smells **2. SENSE OF SMELL** the sense of smell, especially the ability to recognize things by smell or to follow a scent **3. TALENT FOR DISCOVERY** an intuitive ability to discover, detect, or recognize something **4. PART RESEMBLING NOSE** a part that resembles the nose of a person or animal in appearance or function **5. PROJECTING FRONT PART OF VEHICLE** the pointed or rounded front end of an aircraft, spacecraft, boat, car, or other vehicle **6. DISTINCTIVE SMELL** the characteristic aroma of something such as wine or tobacco ■ *v* **(noses, nosing, nosed)** **1.** *vi* **SEARCH FOR BY SCENT** to try to find something by smelling or sniffing ○ *nosed out my secret hoard of chocolate* **2.** *vti* **ADVANCE WITH CAUTION** to move forward slowly, carefully, or cautiously, or make something move in this way ○ *nosed into the stream of traffic* **3.** *vt* **TOUCH SOMETHING WITH NOSE** to touch, rub, or push somebody or something with the nose (*refers to animals*) **4.** *vt* **SMELL SOMETHING** to smell or sniff something **5.** *vi* **PRY OR SNOOP** to try to make discoveries by searching or asking questions in an inquisitive, impertinent, or intrusive manner (*informal*) [Old English *nosu* < Indo-European] —**noseless** *adj* ◇ **as plain as the nose on your face** very obvious (*informal*) ◇ **follow your nose 1.** to go or continue straight ahead in the direction you are facing **2.** to act in accordance with your instincts or intuition ◇ **get up somebody's nose** to irritate or annoy somebody (*informal*) ◇ **keep your nose clean** to avoid getting into trouble (*informal*) ◇ **keep** *or* **have your nose to the grindstone** to keep working hard without taking a break ◇ **look down your nose at somebody** *or* **something** to regard somebody or something arrogantly or disdainfully as inferior or not worth your attention ◇ **nose to tail** so close together that the front of one vehicle almost touches the rear end of another ◇ **on the nose 1.** in betting on horse races, for a horse to win only, not to be placed second or third (*slang*) **2.** *N Am* absolutely on target, with total accuracy, or completely correctly (*informal*) ○ *at 10 o'clock on the nose* **3.** *Aus* foul-smelling (*informal*) **4.** *Aus* offensive ◇ **put somebody's nose out of joint** to make somebody feel thwarted or offended because you do, obtain, or achieve something that he or she was intending or hoping for ◇ **thumb your nose at somebody** *or* **something** to express defiance or contempt of somebody or something, especially by putting a thumb to the nose and extending the fingers ◇ **turn up your nose at something** to refuse to accept something because you feel it is inferior or unworthy of you (*informal*) ◇ **under somebody's nose** in full view of or very close to somebody

nose around, nose about *vti* to look or search through a place in an inquisitive and often intrusive way (*informal*)

nose out *v* **1.** *vi* **DRIVE CAUTIOUSLY FORWARDS** to move a vehicle very slowly and cautiously forwards out of a place **2.** *vt* **NARROWLY DEFEAT OPPONENT** to defeat an opponent by a very narrow margin **3.** *vt* **FIND SOMETHING OUT BY PRYING** to discover something by thorough and often cunning or intrusive searching or questioning (*informal*) **4.** *vt* **FIND SOMETHING BY SCENT** to discover something by smelling or sniffing, or as if by following a scent

nosebag /nōz bag/ *n* a cylindrical or bucket-shaped bag containing a horse's food that can be hung around its head, over its nose. *N Am* term **feedbag**

noseband /nōz band/ *n* the part of a horse's bridle that goes over its nose

nosebleed /nōz bleed/ *n* a flow of blood from the nose. Technical name **epistaxis** ■ *adj N Am* extremely high or excessive, e.g. in price or profit level (*informal*)

nose candy *n N Am* **DRUGS** same as **cocaine** (*slang*)

nose cone *n* the pointed front section of a missile, rocket, spacecraft, aircraft, or racing car, designed for aerodynamic efficiency

nose dive *n* **1.** a sudden very significant fall or decline in price, value, amount, or quality **2.** an extremely steep sudden plunge by an aircraft towards the ground

nose-dive *vi* **1.** to experience a sudden very significant fall or decline in price, value, amount, or quality **2.** to fall vertically or almost vertically with the front end pointing downwards (*refers to aircraft*) —**nose-diver** *n*

nose drops *npl* medicated liquid applied by a dropper into the nostrils

nose flute *n* a wind instrument of the South Pacific Islands, usually played by being breathed into through one nostril while the other one is plugged

nosegay /nōz gay/ *n* a small bouquet of flowers [< GAY 'ornament']

nose gear *n* a part of the landing gear of an aeroplane, consisting of a wheel and related mechanisms located forward of the plane's centre and the rest of the landing gear

noseguard /nōz gaard/ *n US* in American football, a defensive lineman who plays opposite the centre in the offensive line

nose job *n* a surgical operation to improve the shape or size of the nose (*informal*)

nose ornament *n* a decorative ring or stud worn through the nostril or septum

nosepiece /nōz peess/ *n* **1. PART OF GLASSES** the part of a pair of glasses that fits over the nose and connects the lenses **2. PART OF MICROSCOPE** the end piece of a microscope to which one or more objective lenses are attached **3. PROTECTION FOR NOSE** the part of a helmet or piece of armour that protects the nose **4.** RIDING same as **noseband**

nose rag *n* same as **handkerchief** (*slang*)

nose ring *n* **1.** a ring put through an animal's nose to lead or control it **2.** a ring worn for adornment through a hole pierced in the nostril or septum

nose stud *n* a small stud worn for adornment in a hole pierced in the nostril or septum

nose tackle *n US* FOOTBALL same as **noseguard**

nose wheel *n* a landing-gear wheel at the front end of an aircraft

nosey *adj* another spelling of **nosy** (*informal*)

nosh /nosh/ (*informal*) *n* **1. FOOD** same as **meal**[1] (sense 1) **2.** prepared food ■ *vti* **(noshes, noshing, noshed)** same as **eat** (sense 1) [Early 20C. Via Yiddish *nashen* 'to nibble' < Middle High German *naschen*] —**nosher** *n*

no-show *n* somebody who fails to appear or arrive when expected, without giving notice

nosh-up *n* a large, satisfying, and enjoyable meal (*informal*)

no-side *n* the end of a rugby match, as signalled by the referee's whistle

nosing /nōzing/ *n* **1. PROJECTING EDGE OF STAIR TREAD** the rounded edge of a stair tread that projects horizontally **2. PROTECTION FOR NOSE** a shield that protects a nosing on a staircase **3.** ARCHIT **PROJECTING EDGE OF MOULDING** the rounded projecting edge of an architectural moulding

no-smoking *adj* where smoking is not allowed, or that prohibits smoking

noso- *prefix* disease ○ *nosophobia* [< Greek *nosos*]

nosocomial /nóssō kṓmi əl/ *adj* describes a disease or infection that originates or occurs in a hospital [Mid-19C. < Greek *nosokomos* 'somebody who tends the sick' < *nosos* 'sickness']

nosography /no sóggrəfi/ (*plural* **-phies**) *n* a detailed classification and description of known diseases —**nosographer** *n* —**nosographic** /nóssə gráffik/ *adj* —**nosographically** *adv*

nosology /no sólləji/ (*plural* **-gies**) *n* **1.** the branch

of medicine concerned with the classification and description of known diseases **2.** a completed classification of known diseases —**nosological** /nóssə lójjik'l/ *adj* —**nosologically** *adv* —**nosologist** *n*

nosophobia /nóssō fṓbi ə/ *n* an irrational fear of catching diseases

nostalgia /no stáljə, -ji ə/ *n* **1. SENTIMENTAL RECOLLECTION** a mixed feeling of happiness, sadness, and longing when recalling a person, place, or event from the past, or the past in general **2. THINGS THAT AROUSE NOSTALGIA** something, or things, intended to arouse a feeling of nostalgia or to evoke the past in a way that arouses nostalgia **3. HOMESICKNESS** a longing for home or family when away from either (*dated*) [Late 18C. < modern Latin, 'homesickness' < Greek *nostos* 'homecoming' + *algos* 'pain'] —**nostalgic** *adj* —**nostalgically** *adv*

nostoc /nóss tok/ *n* a freshwater microorganism that lives in spherical colonies as coiled filaments and fixes atmospheric nitrogen. Genus: *Nostoc*. [Mid-17C. < modern Latin, invented]

nostology /no stólləji/ *n* MED same as **gerontology** [Mid-20C. < Greek *nostos* 'return home' (from the former idea that later life is like a return to early years)] —**nostologic** /nóstə lójjik/ *adj* —**nostologically** *adv* —**nostologist** *n*

Barnaby's

Nostradamus

Nostradamus /nóstrə dáaməss, -dáyməss/ (1503–66) French astrologer and physician. His prophecies, composed in rhyming quatrains and first published as *Centuries* in 1555, were consulted for hundreds of years. Born **Nostredame, Michel de**

nostril /nóstrəl/ *n* either of the two openings at the end of the nose of a person or animal [Old English *nospyrl* < *nosu*, form of NOSE + *pyrl* 'hole' < *purh*, form of THROUGH]

nostrum /nóstrəm/ *n* **1.** a remedy for a social, political, or economic problem, especially an idea or scheme that is often suggested but never proved to be successful **2.** a medicine prepared or prescribed by an unqualified person whose claims for its effectiveness have no scientific basis [Early 17C. < Latin *nostrum (remedium)* 'our (remedy)']

nosy /nṓzi/ (**-ier**, **-iest**), **nosey** *adj* too curious about other people's affairs (*informal*) —**nosily** *adv* —**nosiness** *n*

nosy parker /-paárkər/ *n* somebody who pries into other people's affairs, especially an impertinent or intrusive questioner (*informal*) [Said to refer to Elizabeth I's archbishop of Canterbury, Matthew *Parker*, who was noted for detailed enquiries concerning ecclesiastical affairs]

not /not/ *adv* **1. FORMING NEGATIVES** a negative adverb used to form structures indicating that something is to no degree or in no way or conveying the general notion 'no'. It is often used to express refusal, denial, or the negation of a statement just made. (*often contracted in spoken and informal written English to 'n't*) ○ *Don't you think we've done enough?* ○ *Not every household has a dishwasher.* ○ *There's nothing in my account; not one penny.* ○ *Not only was the meal expensive, the service was bad too.* **2. SENTENCE SUBSTITUTE** used as a sentence substitute when indicating denial, refusal or negation, in order to avoid repetition ○ *'Won't you come with us?' 'Certainly not'.* ○ *I don't think I'll be late, at least I hope not.* **3. INDICATING OPPOSITE** tagged onto the end of a statement to indicate that the truth is the opposite of what has been stated (*humorous*) ○ *You're really going to enjoy this – not!* [14C. Contraction of NOUGHT] ◇ **not at all** used as a polite way of acknowledging somebody's thanks ◇ **not that** used to

introduce a clause that explicitly denies something that the listener might infer from a previous or subsequent statement ○ *I'm actually seeing her tonight. Not that it's any of your business!*

SPELLCHECK See *knot*[1].

NOT /not/ *n* COMPUT same as **NOT circuit** [< NOT]

nota INSECTS plural of **notum**

nota bene /nốtə bénni, -nay/ *interj* full form of **N.B.** (*formal*) [< Latin < *nota*, imperative form of *notare* 'mark' + *bene* 'well']

notability /nốtə bílləti/ (*plural* **-ties**) *n* **1.** same as **notable 2.** the importance of somebody or something, or the quality that makes somebody or something worth paying attention to

notable /nốtəb'l/ *adj* **1.** WORTHY OF NOTE significant, or great enough to deserve attention or to be recorded ○ *a notable contribution to our understanding of this complex phenomenon* **2.** INTERESTING interesting, significant, and worth calling attention to ○ *more notable for what it leaves out than for what it includes* **3.** DISTINGUISHED particularly important, distinguished, or famous ■ *n* SOMEBODY IMPORTANT somebody who is particularly important or distinguished [14C. < Old French < Latin *notare* 'to note'] —**notableness** *n*

notably /nốtəbli/ *adv* **1.** especially, or in the most significant case ○ *There has been much opposition, notably from the farming community.* **2.** extremely or remarkably ○ *She seems notably unimpressed by all their arguments.*

notarial /nō táiri əl/ *adj* relating to or done by a notary public —**notarially** *adv*

notarize /nốtə rīz/ (**-rizes, -rizing, -rized**), **notarise** (**-rises, -rising, -rised**) *vt* to certify something such as a signature on a legal document as authentic or legitimate by affixing a notary's stamp and signature —**notarization** /nốtə rī záysh'n/ *n*

notary /nốtəri/ (*plural* **-ries**) *n* LAW same as **notary public** [14C. Via Old French *notarie* < Latin *notarius* 'shorthand writer, clerk']

notary public (*plural* **notaries public**) *n* somebody who is legally authorized to certify the authenticity or legitimacy of signatures and documents

notate /nō táyt/ (**-tates, -tating, -tated**) *vt* to write something down using notation, especially musical notation [Early 20C. Back-formation < NOTATION]

notation /nō táysh'n/ *n* **1.** SYMBOLIC REPRESENTATION a set of written symbols used to represent something such as the length and pitch of musical notes **2.** USE OF NOTATION the process of using a system of notation **3.** NOTING the act of making a note or writing something down **4.** NOTE a note or annotation [Late16C. Directly or via French < Latin *notation-* < *notat-*, past participle of *notare* 'to note']

notch /noch/ *n* **1.** NICK OR INDENTATION a small V-shaped cut in the edge or on the surface of something **2.** DEGREE ON SCALE a level or step on a scale, especially one measuring quality or achievement ○ *raise the tension on the wire another notch* **3.** NICK USED AS TALLY a cut made to record a score, a debt, or the number of times something has been done ■ *vt* (**notches, notching, notched**) **1.** MAKE V-SHAPED CUT IN SOMETHING to make a notch in or on something **2.** RECORD SOMETHING WITH NOTCHES to record a score or debt by making a series of cuts in a surface **3.** ACHIEVE OR SCORE SOMETHING to achieve a victory or success, or score a point or goal (*informal*) ○ *notched up another win* [Mid-16C. Origin ?] —**notchy** *adj*

NOT circuit *n* a logic circuit, used especially in computers, that produces a high-voltage output signal if the input signal is low or a low-voltage output signal if the input signal is high

note /nōt/ *n* **1.** JOTTED RECORD OR SUMMARY something written down, often in abbreviated form, as a record or reminder ○ *Fortunately, I'd made a note of her phone number.* **2.** INFORMAL LETTER a short written message or informal letter **3.** OFFICIAL LETTER a formal communication in writing, especially between governments **4.** ITEM OF SUPPLEMENTARY INFORMATION a piece of additional information about something in a printed text, usually given at the bottom of the page or at the end **5.** WRITTEN COMMENT a short written comment or item of information, e.g. one written in the margin of a book or piece of work **6.** MONEY same as **banknote 7.** FIN same as **promissory note 8.** MUSICAL OR VOCAL SOUND a sound of a distinct pitch,

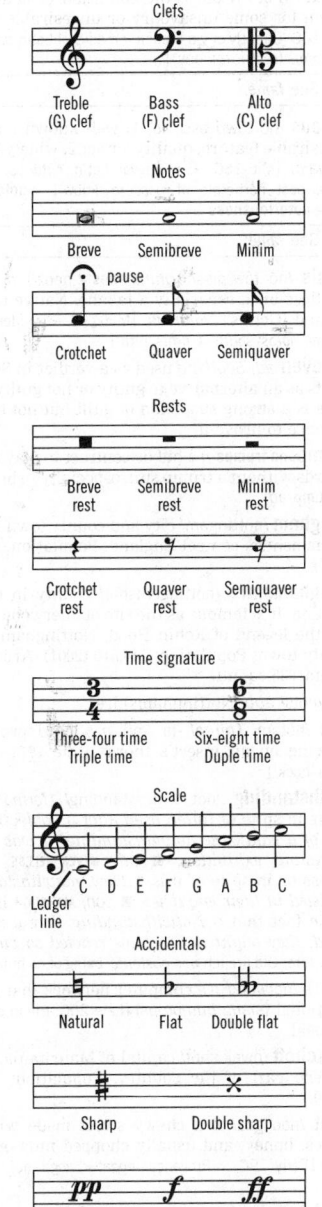

Clefs

Treble (G) clef   Bass (F) clef   Alto (C) clef

Notes

Breve   Semibreve   Minim
pause

Crotchet   Quaver   Semiquaver

Rests

Breve rest   Semibreve rest   Minim rest

Crotchet rest   Quaver rest   Semiquaver rest

Time signature

Three-four time / Triple time   Six-eight time / Duple time

Scale

C D E F G A B C
Ledger line

Accidentals

Natural   Flat   Double flat

Sharp   Double sharp

Pianissimo   Forte   Fortissimo

notation: musical notation

quality, or duration produced by a musical instrument or by the voice **9.** SYMBOL IN MUSIC in written or printed music, a symbol representing a specific sound **10.** KEY ON KEYBOARD a black or white key of a piano or other keyboard instrument **11.** INDICATION OF MOOD a tone in the voice or in writing, or an attitude or atmosphere, that indicates feelings or mood ○ *a note of urgency* ○ *The meeting closed on an optimistic note.* **12.** INTONATION SHOWING EMOTION a tone in the voice that indicates the speaker's feelings or adds to the meaning of what is said **13.** CHARACTERISTIC FEATURE a distinctive element, feeling, quality, or atmosphere **14.** HINT a hint or suggestion of something **15.** DISTINCTION distinction or excellence ○ *a writer of note* ■ **notes** *npl* SUMMARY FOR FUTURE REFERENCE a summary of important facts or points written down by a listener, e.g. by a student during a lesson ■ *vt* (**notes, noting, noted**) **1.** OBSERVE SOMETHING to notice or observe something, or to notice or remember something by paying special attention to it **2.** PERCEIVE SOMETHING to notice or become aware of something **3.** MENTION SOMETHING to mention something important **4.** WRITE SOMETHING DOWN to write down something important as a record or reminder [13C. Via Old French *note* 'sign' < Latin *nota* 'sign, mark'] —**noteless** *adj* —**noter** *n*

~~noteable~~ incorrect spelling of **notable**

notebook /nốt bŏŏk/ *n* **1.** a small book in which to write, containing blank or lined pages **2.** a small thin portable personal computer

note card *n* N Am same as **notelet**

notecase /nốt kayss/ *n* same as **wallet** (sense 1) (*dated*)

noted /nốtid/ *adj* **1.** well known and especially distinguished or admired for a particular thing or quality ○ *He is not noted for his generosity.* **2.** significant or distinctive enough to be noticeable ○ *a noted increase in applications* —**notedly** *adv* —**notedness** *n*

notelet /nốtlət/ *n* a folded sheet of paper or thin card with a picture on the front, used for writing short informal letters. N Am term **note card**

note of hand *n* FIN same as **promissory note**

notepad /nốt pad/ *n* a number of small sheets of blank or lined paper on which to write, fastened together in a way that makes it easy to detach a single page

notepaper /nốt paypər/ *n* paper for writing letters or making notes on

note row /-rō/ *n* MUSIC same as **tone row**

noteworthy /nốt wurthi/ (**-thier, -thiest**) *adj* deserving notice or attention, usually because of significance, excellence, uniqueness, or interest —**noteworthily** *adv* —**noteworthiness** *n*

not-for-profit *adj* BUSINESS same as **non-profit-making**

NOT gate *n* COMPUT same as **NOT circuit**

nothing /núthing/ *pron* **1.** NOT ANYTHING an indefinite pronoun indicating that there is not anything, not a single thing, or not a single part of a thing ○ *There is nothing more annoying than people who can't keep their personal lives private.* **2.** SOMETHING OF NO IMPORTANCE a thing or matter of no importance or significance ○ *It's nothing to me whether they win or lose.* **3.** NOT HAVING QUALITY used to indicate the complete lack of the quality mentioned in somebody or something ○ *He wore an ordinary dark blue jacket, with nothing special about it.* ○ *Nothing of any consequence was said.* **4.** ZERO AMOUNT a zero quantity or zero ○ *We won, three-nothing.* **5.** STATE OF NONEXISTENCE a condition of nonexistence, or the absence of any perceptible qualities ○ *vanished into nothing* ■ *n* SOMEBODY OR SOMETHING UNIMPORTANT somebody or something regarded as totally unimportant ■ *adj* UNDISTINGUISHED completely lacking in distinguishing qualities, interest, or significance (*informal*) ○ *a nothing product, despite all the hype* [Old English *nāðinc* < earlier forms of NO[1] + THING] ◇ **not for nothing** for a very good reason ◇ **nothing but** only ◇ **nothing doing** used to indicate a complete refusal to do something or to cooperate (*informal*) ◇ **nothing for it** used to indicate that there is no other course of action open to somebody ○ *There was nothing for it but for us to admit our error.* ◇ **nothing if not** definitely, undoubtedly, or at the very least ○ *He's nothing if not fair.* ◇ **nothing less than, nothing short of** used to emphasize forcefully that something truly, definitely, or amazingly is as described ○ *The things they've been saying about me are nothing less than slander.* ◇ **nothing like somebody** or **something** having no resemblance to somebody or something else ◇ **nothing much** no item or activity of importance, significance, size, value, or interest ○ *Nothing much happened in the first hour we were there.* ◇ **there's nothing to it** used to indicate that something is very easy

USAGE nothing – singular or a plural? *Nothing* is a singular indefinite pronoun, and so should be treated as a singular even if followed by a phrase introduced by words like *but* and *except for* and a plural noun: *Nothing but truthful answers is* [not *are*] *acceptable on this questionnaire. Nothing except for your boxes and bags has* [not *have*] *been removed from the apartment.* Moving the subject closer to its verb, however, reduces the chance of grammatical error and more closely follows the natural flow of speech: *Except for your boxes and bags, nothing has been removed from the apartment.*

nothingness /núthingnəss/ *n* **1.** ABSENCE OF EVERYTHING the absence of life, existence, and all discernible qualities **2.** EMPTY SPACE space with nothing in it **3.** COMPLETE WORTHLESSNESS complete worthlessness or insignificance **4.** SOMEBODY OR SOMETHING COMPLETELY WORTHLESS somebody or something without any worth or significance **5.** PHILOSOPHY LACK OF APPARENT MEANING the condition of lacking any apparent meaning

CULTURAL NOTE *Being and Nothingness*, an extended essay (1943) by French philosopher Jean-Paul Sartre. The fullest expression of Sartre's existential philosophy, it suggests that humans can be distinguished from the simple being or 'thing-ness' of objects and other creatures by their consciousness or 'no-thingness'. This awareness provides humans with their freedom, but it also leaves them searching for meaning in life.

~~noticeable~~ incorrect spelling of **noticeable**

notice /nótiss/ *n* **1. PUBLIC SIGN** a sign in a public place giving information, instructions, or a warning **2. WRITTEN ANNOUNCEMENT** a written or printed announcement or statement of information, often displayed on a board or wall, or published in a newspaper or magazine **3. WARNING** advance warning or notification of something ○ *gave us notice that the system would be changed* **4. PERIOD OF WARNING** the period of time between the giving of a warning or notification and its taking effect ○ *a day's notice of repairs to the water mains* **5. WARNING OF END OF EMPLOYMENT** official notification of the exercise of a right, especially the right to terminate employment, or the amount of time in advance that such notification is given **6. ATTENTION** somebody's attention, observation, or consideration ○ *How can such a glaring error possibly have escaped your notice?* **7. ARTS REVIEW** a written or published review of a book, play, or film ■ *v* (-**tices**, -**ticing**, -**ticed**) **1.** *vti* **OBSERVE SOMETHING** to see or catch sight of somebody or something and register the fact in the mind ○ *Did you notice what he had in his hand?* **2.** *vti* **PERCEIVE SOMETHING** to become aware of something or somebody and register the fact in the mind ○ *I noticed that he avoided mentioning her name.* **3.** *vt* **MENTION SOMETHING** to mention or remark on something **4.** *vt* **RECOGNIZE SOMEBODY** to recognize somebody, or indicate that you recognize somebody **5.** *vt* **TREAT SOMEBODY POLITELY** to treat somebody with polite attention **6.** *vt* **WRITE REVIEW OF SOMETHING** to write or publish a review of a book, play, or film **7.** *vt* **ANNOUNCE SOMETHING TO SOMEBODY** to give official notice to somebody (*formal*) [15C. Via French < Latin *notitia* 'fame, knowledge' < *notus* 'known']

noticeable /nótissəb'l/ *adj* **1.** easy to see, hear, feel, or detect **2.** important, distinctive, or worthy of comment —**noticeability** /nótissə bílləti/ *n* —**noticeably** *adv*

noticeboard /nótiss bawrd/ *n* a board fixed to a wall on which notices, announcements, or advertisements can be fastened for temporary display. N Am term **bulletin board**

notifiable /nóti fī əb'l/ *adj* describes an infectious disease of people or animals that must be reported to the appropriate authority when it occurs so that control or preventive measures can be taken

notify /nóti fī/ (-**fies**, -**fying**, -**fied**) *vt* **1.** to inform or warn somebody officially about somebody or something **2.** to announce or report something officially, or make something officially known [14C. Via Old French *notifier* < Latin *notificare* 'make known' < *notus* 'known'] —**notification** /nótifi káysh'n/ *n* —**notifier** *n*

no-tillage *n* a method of farming in which crops are planted in narrow slit trenches, without any ploughing, and weeds are controlled with chemical weedkillers

notion /nósh'n/ *n* **1. IDEA** an idea, opinion, or concept **2. IMPRESSION** a vague understanding or impression **3. DESIRE** a sudden desire or whim ■ **notions** *npl* N Am **ITEMS FOR NEEDLEWORK** small items used in sewing, e.g. needles, pins, thread, and buttons [14C. < Latin *notion-* 'concept' < *not-*, past participle of *noscere* 'know']

notional /nósh'nəl/ *adj* **1. IMAGINARY OR HYPOTHETICAL** existing only as an idea or in theory, not in reality **2. ABSTRACT OR SPECULATIVE** relating to or characteristic of ideas or concepts **3. LING USED WITH DEFINITE MEANING** used in a specific concrete sense as opposed to expressing a grammatical relationship. For example, 'did' in 'We did (= carried out) the work' is notional, whereas 'did' in 'Why didn't she come?' is not. —**notionally** *adv*

notochord /nótə kawrd/ *n* a long flexible rod of cells that supports the body of chordates and vertebrate embryos and is in effect a primitive backbone [Mid-19C. < Greek *notōn* 'back' + CHORD[2] 'line'] —**notochordal** /nótə káwrd'l/ *adj*

notoriety /nótə rī əti/ *n* the condition of being well known for some unsavoury or undesirable reason [Mid-16C. Directly or via French < medieval Latin *notorietas* < *notorius* (see NOTORIOUS)]

USAGE See *fame*.

notorious /nō táwri əss/ *adj* **1.** well known for some undesirable feature, quality, or act **2.** widely known (*archaic*) [Mid-16C. < medieval Latin *notorius* < Latin *notus*, past participle of *noscere* 'know'] —**notoriously** *adv* —**notoriousness** *n*

USAGE See *fame*.

notornis /nō táwrniss/ (*plural* -**nes** /-neez/) *n* a rare flightless bird, especially a takahe. Native to: New Zealand. Genus: *Notornis*. [Mid-19C. < modern Latin < Greek *notos* 'south' + *ornis* 'bird']

not proven *adj Scotland* used as a verdict in Scottish courts as an alternative to guilty or not guilty when there is a strong suspicion of guilt but not enough evidence to prove it

no trump, **no trumps** *n* a bid or contract to play a hand of cards without a trump suit, especially in bridge — **no-trump** *adj*

Nottingham /nóttingəm/ city and county town in Nottinghamshire, central England. Population: 266,988 (2001).

Nottinghamshire /nóttingəmshər/ county in central England. It is famous as the site of Sherwood Forest and the legend of Robin Hood. Nottingham is the county town. Population: 748,510 (2001). Area: 2,165 sq. km/835 sq. mi.

Notts /nots/ *abbr* Nottinghamshire

notum /nótəm/ (*plural* -**ta** /-ə/) *n* a hard protective covering on an insect's thorax [Late 19C. < Greek *nōton* 'back']

notwithstanding /nót with stánding/ (*formal*) *prep* **DESPITE** in spite of (*often used after its object*) ○ *The lack of a catalogue notwithstanding, it was a very interesting exhibition.* ■ *adv* **NEVERTHELESS** nevertheless or in spite of this ○ *They, notwithstanding, persisted in their enquiries.* ■ *conj* **ALTHOUGH** in spite of the fact that ○ *Notwithstanding they were provoked, they ought not to have reacted so violently.* [14C. After Old French *non obstante* 'being of no hindrance']

notwork /nótwurk/ *n* a computer network that is nonfunctional (*slang humorous*) [Late 20C. Blend of NOT + NETWORK]

Nouakchott /nwak shót/ capital of Mauritania, in the western part of the country. Population: 707,000 (1990).

nougat /nóo gaa/ *n* a chewy sweet made with egg whites, honey, and usually chopped nuts or dried fruit [Early 19C. < Provençal *nogat* < *noga* 'nut' < Latin *nux*]

nought /nawt/ *n* the number zero. N Am term **naught** [Old English *nōwiht* < *ne* 'not' + *ōwiht* 'anything', form of AUGHT]

Noughties /náwtiz/ *npl* the years from 2000 to 2009 (*humorous*) [< NOUGHT, punning on NAUGHTY]

noughts and crosses *n* a game in which two players alternately write '0' or 'X' on a grid of nine squares, until one player gets three of the same symbols in a line (*takes a singular verb*) N Am term **tick-tack-toe**

Nouméa /noo máyə/ capital of New Caledonia, on the southwestern coast of the island of New Caledonia, in the southwestern Pacific Ocean. Population: 65,110 (1989).

noumenon /nóomənən, -non, nów-/ (*plural* -**mena** /-mə nə/) *n* **1.** something beyond the tangible world that can only be known or identified by the intellect, not by the senses **2.** in Kantian philosophy, something that exists independently of intellectual or sensory perception of it, e.g. the soul in some beliefs [Late 18C. Via German < Greek < present participle of *noien* 'apprehend, conceive'] —**noumenal** *adj* —**noumenally** *adv*

noun /nown/ *n* a word or group of words used as the name of a class of people, places, or things, or of a specific person, place, or thing [14C. Via Anglo-Norman, 'name, noun' < Old French *nom* < Latin *nomen*]

noun phrase *n* a word or group of words that functions syntactically as a noun, e.g. as the subject, object, or topic, in a clause or sentence

nourish /núrrish/ (-**ishes**, -**ishing**, -**ished**) *vt* **1. GIVE FOOD TO SOMEBODY OR SOMETHING** to give people, animals, or plants the substances they require to live, grow, or remain fit and healthy **2. SUPPORT OR FOSTER SOMETHING** to encourage or strengthen a feeling or idea **3. HELP SOMETHING TO DEVELOP** to help something to grow or develop [13C. < Old French *norriss-*, a stem of *norir* < Latin *nutrire* 'suckle'] —**nourisher** *n*

nourishing /núrrishing/ *adj* providing people, animals, or plants with a substantial quantity of the substances they require to live, grow, or remain fit and healthy —**nourishingly** *adv*

nourishment /núrrishmənt/ *n* **1.** food, or the valuable substances in food that a person, animal, or plant requires to live, grow, or remain fit and healthy **2.** something that provides a stimulating and healthy emotional or intellectual environment for people or animals

nous /nowss/ *n* **1. COMMON SENSE** good sense or intelligence (*informal*) **2. INTELLECTUAL ABILITY** in ancient Greek philosophy, the capacity to reason and acquire knowledge, as distinguished from sensation **3. INTELLECT** in some philosophies, the part of the human spirit that is capable of rational thought [Late 17C. < Greek, 'intelligence']

nouveau /nóovō/ *adj* having recently appeared or become fashionable (*humorous*) [Early 20C. < French, 'new']

nouveau riche /nóovō réesh/ (*plural* **nouveaux riches** /pronunc. same/) *n* somebody with recently acquired wealth who likes to display it [Early 19C. < French, 'new rich'] —**nouveau riche** *adj*

nouveau roman /nóovō rō maáN/ (*plural* **nouveaux romans** /pronunc. same/) *n* LITERAT same as **antinovel** [Mid-20C. < French, 'new novel']

nouvelle cuisine /noó vel kwi zeén/ *n* a style of French cooking consisting of beautifully presented dishes made from fresh lightly cooked ingredients in less rich sauces than in traditional French cookery [Late 20C. < French, 'new cooking']

Nouvelle Vague /noó vel vaág/ *n* CINEMA same as **new wave** (sense 2) [Mid-20C. < French, 'new wave']

Nov. *abbr* November

nova /nóvə/ (*plural* -**vas** or -**vae** /-vee/) *n* a star that suddenly increases dramatically in brightness and then fades to its original luminosity over a short period of months or years [Late 19C. < Latin, form of *novus* 'new']

novaculite /nō vákyoō līt/ *n* a hard dense fine-grained sedimentary rock containing quartz and feldspar. Use: whetstones. [Late 18C. < Latin *novacula* 'razor']

novae ASTRON plural of **nova**

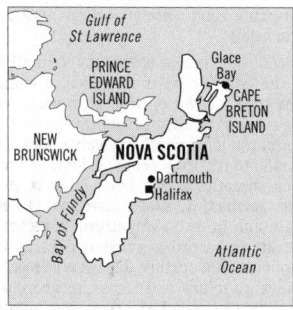

Nova Scotia

Nova Scotia /nóvə skóshə/ province in eastern Canada, bordering the Atlantic Ocean and comprising a mainland peninsula and Cape Breton Island. Capital: Halifax. Population: 944,800 (2002). Area: 55,284 sq. km/21,345 sq. mi. —**Nova Scotian** *n*, *adj*

novation /nō váysh'n/ *n* the replacement of an old contract or obligation with a new one [Early 16C. < late Latin *novation-* < Latin *novare* 'make new' < *novus* 'new']

novel[1] /nóvv'l/ *n* **1.** a fictional prose work with a relatively long and often complex plot, usually divided into chapters, in which the story traditionally develops through the thoughts and actions of its characters **2.** novels considered collectively as a literary genre [Mid-16C. < Italian *novella* (see NOVELLA)]

novel² /nóvv'l/ *adj* new and different, often in an interesting, unusual or inventive way [15C. Via Old French < Latin *novellus* 'slightly new' < *novus* 'new']

SYNONYMS See ***new***.

novel³ /nóvv'l/ *n* in Roman law, a new decree, or something that changes an existing statute [Early 17C. < late Latin *novella (constitutio)* 'new (constitution)', < form of Latin *novellus* (see NOVEL²)]

novelese /nóvvə leéz/ *n* a style of writing or language that is typical of inferior novels

novelette /nóvvə lét/ *n* **1. SENTIMENTAL NOVEL** a light romantic novel, especially one that is considered trite or sentimental **2. SHORT NOVEL** a long story or short novel **3.** MUSIC **SHORT LYRICAL MUSICAL COMPOSITION** a short piece of music written in a free lyrical style, usually for the piano —**novelettist** *n*

novelettish /nóvvə léttish/ *adj* having the qualities of an inferior piece of writing, especially triteness or sentimentality

novel food *n* a food that is produced by a novel process, e.g. a genetically modified food product

novelise *vt* LITERAT another spelling of **novelize**

novelist /nóvv'list/ *n* a writer of novels

novelistic /nóvvə lístik/ *adj* characteristic of a novel, especially in the treatment of real people or historical events —**novelistically** *adv*

novelize /nóvvə līz/ (**-izes, -izing, -ized**), **novelise** (**-ises, -ising, -ised**) *vt* **1.** to write the story of a film, play, or television series in the form of a novel **2.** to retell a true story in the form of a novel, sometimes adding fictional details —**novelization** /nóvvə lī záysh'n/ *n*

novella /nō véllə/ *n* a fictional prose work that is longer than a short story but shorter than a novel [Early 20C. < Italian *(storia) novella* 'new (story)' < Latin *novellus* (see NOVEL²)]

novelty /nóvv'lti/ (*plural* **-ties**) *n* **1. NEW THING OR EXPERIENCE** something new, original, and different that is interesting or exciting, though often for only a short time **2. NEWNESS AND ORIGINALITY** the quality of being new, original, and different **3. SMALL TOY OR TRINKET** a small inexpensive toy, ornament, piece of jewellery, or trinket

November /nō vémbər/ *n* **1.** in the Gregorian calendar, the 11th month of the year, lasting 30 days. See table at **calendar 2.** a code word for the letter 'N', used in international radio communications [13C. Via French < Latin, ninth month of the Roman calendar < *novem* 'nine']

novena /nō veénə/ (*plural* **-nas** or **-nae** /-nee/) *n* in the Roman Catholic Church, the recitation of prayers for nine consecutive days to achieve a specific purpose [Mid-19C. < medieval Latin, form of *novenus* 'ninefold' < *novem* 'nine']

novercal /nō vúrk'l/ *adj* relating to or said to be characteristic of a stepmother (*formal*) [Early 17C. < Latin *novercalis* < *noverca* 'stepmother']

Novgorod /nóvgə rod/ city in northwestern Russia, and the capital of Novgorod Oblast. Population: 288,910 (1995).

novice /nóvviss/ *n* **1.** somebody who is beginning or learning an activity and has acquired little skill in it **2.** somebody who has joined a religious order but has not yet taken final vows [14C. Via French < late Latin *novicius* < Latin *novus* 'new']

SYNONYMS See ***beginner***.

novitiate /nō víshi ət/, **noviciate** *n* **1.** the period of time during which somebody is a novice, especially in a religious order **2.** the part of a monastery or convent where novices live **3.** RELIG same as **novice** (sense 2) [Early 17C. < French *noviciat*, or medieval Latin *noviciatus* < late Latin *novicius* (see NOVICE)]

novocaine /nóvə kayn/ *n* PHARM same as **procaine** [Early 20C. < Latin *novus* 'new' + *-caine* as in COCAINE]

Novosibirsk /nóvō si beérsk/ city in southern Russia, and the capital of Novosibirsk Oblast. Population: 1,428,141 (1995).

Novyy Margelan /nóvvi maar jéllən/ former name for **Fergana**

now /now/ *adv* **1. AT PRESENT TIME** at the present time, often as opposed to in the past or in the future ○ *I've never done this before, and I'm not starting now.* **2. IMMEDIATELY** at once or at this exact time ○ *We'll miss our train if we don't go now.* **3. GIVEN CURRENT SITUATION** under the present circumstances ○ *It doesn't matter now.* **4. UP TO PRESENT TIME** used with statements of time to indicate that something has been happening for a particular length of time up to the present ○ *for six months now* **5. USED TO PREFACE OR CLARIFY REMARK** used to preface a remark, clarify a statement, get somebody's attention, or for emphasis ○ *Now, what would you like to drink?* **6. USED IN HESITATION** used in speech when hesitating and thinking of what to say next (*informal*) ○ *Now, where was I?* ■ *conj* **SINCE** since or in view of the fact that this is the present situation ○ *She can afford a decent car now that she's working.* ■ *n* **PRESENT TIME** the present time or moment ○ *Now would be a good time to tell her.* ■ *adj* **FASHIONABLE** in the latest fashion (*informal*) ○ *the now look in menswear* [Old English *nu* < Indo-European] ◇ **(every) now and then, (every) now and again** occasionally ◇ **for now** for the time being, as a temporary measure ◇ **just** *or* **right now 1.** a short time ago ○ *I was talking to her just now.* **2.** at the present moment ○ *Go away, I'm busy right now.* ◇ **now now** (*informal*) **1.** used as a friendly way of trying to comfort somebody **2.** used to warn or reprimand somebody gently ◇ **now then 1.** used to warn or reprimand somebody gently (*informal*) **2.** same as **now** *adv* (senses 5–6) ◇ **up to** *or* **up till** *or* **until now** up to the present time

NOW /now/ *abbr* National Organization for Women

nowadays /nów ə dayz/ *adv* in the present, or in the times in which we are now living, usually in contrast to the past [14C. < NOW + *adayes* 'during the day' < DAY]

noway *interj* /nō wáy/ *also* **no way** used to express emphatic refusal or denial (*informal*) ■ *adv* /nṓ way/ in no way, or not at all

~~**nowdays**~~ incorrect spelling of **nowadays**

nowhere /nṓ wair/; *occasional unstressed form* /nṓ wər/ *adv* not in or to any place ○ *Nowhere does it mention any side-effects.* ■ *n* a remote or insignificant place ◇ **get** *or* **go nowhere** to fail to make any progress with something you are trying to do ◇ **nowhere near** not at all, or a long way from being a particular thing (*informal*)

no-win *adj* in which there is no chance of a successful outcome for a participant (*informal*)

nowise /nṓ wīz/ *adv* in no manner, or by no means at all

now-now /nów now/ *adv S Africa* in the immediate past or the immediate future (*informal*) [Mid-20C. < Afrikaans *nou-nou* 'in a moment, a moment ago']

Nowra town on the southeast coast of New South Wales, Australia. It is an important regional service and commercial centre. Population: 19,553 (1986).

nowt /nowt, nōt/ *pron N England* same as **nothing** [Variant of NOUGHT]

REGIONAL NOTE The poet John Dryden was among the first to tell users of English that 'two negatives make an affirmative'. This rule did not actually apply to English. Indeed, Shakespeare often doubles up his negatives (*You'll lie like dogs, and yet say nothing neither.* 'The Tempest', III.i) and dialect speakers continue to use multiple negation for emphasis: *He said nowt to nobody didn't our kid.*

noxious /nókshəss/ *adj* **1. PHYSICALLY HARMFUL** harmful to life or health, especially by being poisonous **2. MORALLY HARMFUL** likely to cause moral, spiritual, or social harm or corruption **3. DISGUSTING** very unpleasant ○ *a noxious smell* [15C. < Latin *noxius* 'hurtful, damaging'] —**noxiously** *adv* —**noxiousness** *n*

Noyce /noyss/, **Phillip** (*b.* 1950) Australian film director. He was director of *Newsfront* (1978) and *Dead Calm* (1988). Full name **Noyce, Phillip Roger**

nozzle /nózz'l/ *n* **1.** a narrow or tapering part at the end of a tube or pipe, used to direct or control the flow of a liquid or gas **2.** a short tapered tube that directs or accelerates the flow of a fluid, e.g. in a jet engine [Early 17C. < NOSE + *-le*, literally 'appliance resembling a nose']

np *abbr* Nepal (*used in Internet addresses*) See table at **domain name**

Np *symbol* **1.** TELECOM neper **2.** CHEM ELEM neptunium

NP *abbr* **1.** *ANZ* National Party **2.** MED neuropsychiatry **3.** PRINTING new paragraph **4.** LAW notary public **5.** LING noun phrase

n.p. *abbr* PRINTING new paragraph

NPA *abbr* Newspaper Publishers' Association

NPD *abbr* new product development

npl *abbr* GRAM plural noun

NPL *abbr* National Physical Laboratory

NPN *abbr* CHEM nonprotein nitrogen

NPV *abbr* **1.** net present value **2.** FIN no par value

NPWS *abbr Aus* National Parks and Wildlife Service

NQA *abbr* no questions asked (*used in e-mails or text messages*)

nr *abbr* **1.** Nauru (*used in Internet addresses*) See table at **domain name 2.** near

NRA *abbr* **1.** *US* National Rifle Association **2.** National Rivers Authority

NRDS *abbr* neonatal respiratory distress syndrome

NREM *abbr* nonrapid eye movement

NREM sleep *n* BIOL same as **slow-wave sleep**

NRI *abbr* nonresident Indian

NRMA *n* the principle motoring organization of New South Wales, Australia, and the largest in the country, providing roadside assistance, travel information, and other motor-related services to its members, as well as insurance and travel services to the general public. Full form **National Roads and Motorists Association**

NRN *abbr* no reply necessary (*used in e-mails or text messages*)

NRV *abbr* net realizable value

ns *abbr* nanosecond

NS, N.S. *abbr* **1.** New Style **2.** BANKING not sufficient **3.** Nova Scotia **4.** nuclear ship

n.s. *abbr* **1.** nearside **2.** new series **3.** not specified

n/s *abbr* **1.** *also* **N/S** nonsmoker **2.** nonsmoking **3.** BANKING not sufficient (funds)

NSA *abbr US* National Security Agency

NSAID *n* a nonsteroid anti-inflammatory drug taken orally or applied externally. Use: relief of headaches, muscular and joint pain, inflammation. Full form **nonsteroid anti-inflammatory drug**

NSB *abbr* National Savings Bank

NSC *abbr* **1.** National Safety Council **2.** *US* National Security Council

nsec *abbr* nanosecond

NSF, N.S.F., n.s.f., N/S/F *abbr* BANKING not sufficient funds

NSG *abbr* EDUC nonstatutory guidelines

NSPCA *abbr US* National Society for the Prevention of Cruelty to Animals

NSPCC *abbr* National Society for the Prevention of Cruelty to Children

NSU *abbr* nonspecific urethritis

NSW *abbr* New South Wales

NT *abbr* **1.** National Trust **2.** BIBLE New Testament **3.** Nome Time **4.** Northern Territory **5.** *also* **N.T.** Northwest Territories **6.** CARDS no trump

nth /enth/ *adj* **1.** describes a very large, but unspecified, ordinal number, usually one that is the largest in a series of values **2.** last or latest in a long and often tedious series of similar occurrences (*informal*) ○ *This is the nth revision of the text.* [Mid-19C. < N² *n* 'indefinitely large or small amount']

NTP *abbr* MEASURE normal temperature and pressure

NTSC *abbr* National Television Systems Committee

nt wt, nt. wt. *abbr* net weight

nu¹ /nyoo/ (*plural* **nus**) *n* the 13th letter of the Greek alphabet, represented in the English alphabet as 'n'. See table at **alphabet** [Via Greek < Semitic]

nu² *abbr* Niue (*used in Internet addresses*) See table at **domain name**

Nu /nyoo/, **U** (1907–95) Burmese politician. He was the first prime minister of independent Burma (1948–58 and 1960–62) and a leader of the prodemocracy movement from 1988.

nu- *prefix* new, or modern (*used especially with styles of music*) ○ *nu-metal* [Alteration of NEW]

NUAAW *abbr* National Union of Agricultural and Allied Workers

nuance /nyoō aanss, noō oNss/ *n* **1.** a very slight difference in meaning, feeling, tone, or colour **2.** the use or awareness of subtle shades of meaning

or feeling, especially in artistic expression or performance [Late 18C. < French, 'slight difference of tone' < *nuer* 'show shading in colour' < Latin *nubes* 'cloud'] —**nuanced** *adj*

nub /nub/ *n* **1.** CENTRAL ISSUE the main point or most important part of a problem or argument **2.** SMALL LUMP a small lump or chunk **3.** SMALL PROJECTION a small protuberance **4.** TEXTILES FIBRE KNOT a knot of fibres in yarn [Late 16C. < Middle Low German *knubbe*, variant of *knobbe* 'knob'] —**nubbiness** *n* —**nubby** *adj*

Nuba /nyōōbə/ (*plural same* or **-bas**) *n* **1.** a member of a people inhabiting the mountains of central Sudan **2.** LANG same as **Nubian** (sense 2) [Early 19C. < Latin *Nubae* 'Nubians'] —**Nuba** *adj*

nubbin /núbbin/ *n* N Am **1.** a small undeveloped part of a fruit or vegetable, e.g. an ear of corn **2.** same as **nub** (sense 1) [Late 17C. < NUB, literally 'small nub']

nubble /núbb'l/ *n* a small lump or knob —**nubbliness** *n* —**nubbly** *adj*

nubecula /nyoo békyōōlə/ (*plural* **-lae** /-lī/) *n* ASTRON same as **Magellanic Cloud** (*technical*) [Late 17C. < Latin, 'small cloud' < *nubes* 'cloud']

Nubia /nyōōbi ə/ *n* region of northeastern Africa, in southern Egypt and northern Sudan, in the Nile valley

Nubian /nyōōbi ən/ *n* **1.** somebody who comes from ancient or modern Nubia **2.** a Nilo-Saharan language spoken in Sudan. Native speakers: 1 million. [15C. < medieval Latin *Nubianus* < *Nubia* 'Nubia'] —**Nubian** *adj*

nubile /nyōō bīl/ *adj* **1.** young and sexually desirable (*informal*) **2.** describes a young woman who is physically mature enough to have sexual intercourse and therefore suitable for marriage (*dated*) [Mid-17C. < Latin *nubilis* < *nubere* 'take a husband'] —**nubility** /nyoo bíllati/ *n*

nucellus /nyoo sélləss/ (*plural* **-li** /-lī/) *n* the central part of a plant ovule in which the embryo develops [Late 19C. < modern Latin, probably alteration of Latin *nucleus* (see NUCLEUS)]

nucl- *prefix* same as **nucleo-** (*used before vowels*)

nuclear /nyōōkli ər/ *adj* **1.** INDUST OF NUCLEAR ENERGY relating to, using, or producing nuclear energy through fission or fusion **2.** MIL OF NUCLEAR WEAPONS relating to or using weapons that produce a nuclear explosion **3.** PHYS OF ATOM NUCLEUS relating to the nucleus of an atom **4.** BIOL OF CELL NUCLEUS relating to, involving, or contained in the nucleus of a cell **5.** BIOL FORMING NUCLEUS forming or resembling a nucleus [Mid-19C. < NUCLEUS]

> PRONUNCIATION The word *nuclear* is correctly pronounced nyōōkli ər. The often-heard /nyōōkyələr/ is incorrect.

nuclear bomb *n* a bomb in which the explosive potential is controlled by nuclear fission or fusion

nuclear chemistry *n* the branch of chemistry in which nuclear reactions are studied

nuclear deterrent *n* the nuclear weapons possessed by a country or an alliance thought of as a means of discouraging enemy attack

nuclear disarmament *n* the reduction or elimination of a nation's nuclear weapons or its capacity to manufacture them

nuclear emulsion *n* a photographic emulsion used to identify and show the paths of subatomic particles after development

nuclear energy *n* the energy released by nuclear fission or fusion

nuclear envelope *n* BIOL same as **nuclear membrane**

nuclear family *n* a social unit that consists of a mother, a father, and their children

nuclear fission *n* PHYS same as **fission** (sense 1)

nuclear force *n* PHYS same as **strong interaction**

nuclear-free zone *n* an area, usually within a country, where all activities involving nuclear weapons or nuclear power are officially banned

nuclear fuel *n* a substance that undergoes fission in a nuclear reactor and is used to provide power for electricity and submarines, e.g. an isotope of uranium

nuclear fusion *n* the process in which light atoms such as those of hydrogen and deuterium combine and form heavier atoms, releasing a great amount

of energy, which primarily manifests itself in the form of heat

nuclearize /nyōōkli ə rīz/ (**-izes, -izing, -ized**), **nuclearise** (**-ises, -ising, -ised**) *vt* to provide or equip a military force with nuclear weapons —**nuclearization** /nyōōkli ə rī záysh'n/ *n*

nuclear magnetic resonance *n* the energy pulse released by an atomic nucleus exposed to high-frequency radiation in a magnetic field. It is used to provide data about the atom that can be transformed into an image by computer techniques. This phenomenon is the basis of devices used in medicine, where it is called magnetic resonance imaging, to produce images of tissues, and in physics and chemistry to study molecular structure.

nuclear medicine *n* the branch of medicine in which radioactive materials are used to diagnose and treat diseases

nuclear membrane *n* a two-layered membrane surrounding the nucleus of a living cell

nuclear physics *n* the branch of physics in which the structure, forces, and behaviour of the atomic nucleus are studied (*takes a singular verb*) —**nuclear physicist** *n*

nuclear pore *n* a complex opening in a nuclear membrane

nuclear power *n* the power, usually electrical or motive power, produced by nuclear fission or fusion —**nuclear-powered** *adj*

nuclear power station, **nuclear power plant** *n* a power station in which the heat for producing steam to drive electric turbogenerators is derived from a nuclear reactor

nuclear reaction *n* a process in which energy is produced by either the splitting of heavy atoms (**fission**) or the combining of light atoms (**nuclear fusion**)

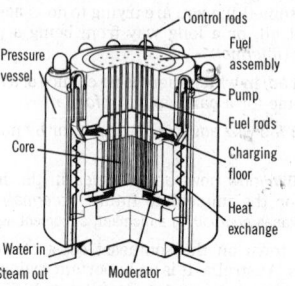

nuclear reactor

nuclear reactor *n* a device in which controlled nuclear fission takes place to produce heat energy

nuclear reprocessing plant *n* a facility in which various useful isotopes are removed from used rods of nuclear reactors

nuclear sap *n* the colourless liquid in the nucleus of a living cell

nuclear submarine *n* **1.** a submarine in which a nuclear reactor produces steam to drive turbines for propulsion **2.** a submarine that carries nuclear weapons

nuclear threshold *n* the point in a war being fought with conventional weapons when one of the opposing forces decides to use nuclear weapons

nuclear warhead *n* the forward part of a missile or other projectile whose explosive device derives its power from nuclear fission or fusion

nuclear waste *n* unwanted, often radioactive, material that is produced by nuclear reactors and reprocessing plants

nuclear weapon *n* a military weapon that derives its explosive power from nuclear fission or fusion

nuclear winter *n* a period of continual cold and darkness believed by some scientists to be a likely consequence of a nuclear war. It would be caused by the blocking of the Sun's rays by high-altitude dust clouds, and would have disastrous environmental consequences.

nuclease /nyōōkli ayz/ *n* an enzyme that breaks down nucleic acids [Early 20C. < shortening of *nucleic*]

nucleate *adj* /nyōōkli ət, -ayt/ *also* **nucleated** /nyōōkli aytid/ having a nucleus or nuclei ■ *vti* /nyōōkli ayt/ (**-ates, -ating, -ated**) to come together as a nucleus, or bring things together to form a nucleus [Mid-17C. < shortening of NUCLEAR] —**nucleator** /nyōōkli aytər/ *n*

nucleation /nyōōkli áysh'n/ *n* **1.** the process by which ice crystals and rain drops form in clouds round a solid core **2.** the formation of mineral crystals from a melt, often round a core of solid material

nuclei plural of **nucleus**

nucleic acid /nyoo klee ik-, -kláy-/ *n* an acid of high molecular weight, e.g. DNA or RNA, consisting of nucleotide chains that convey genetic information and are found in all living cells

nuclein /nyōōkli in/ *n* BIOCHEM same as **nucleoprotein**

nucleo- *prefix* **1.** nucleus, nuclear ○ *nucleoplasm* **2.** nucleic acid ○ *nucleocapsid* [< NUCLEUS]

nucleocapsid /nyōōkli ō kápsid/ *n* the basic viral structure consisting of a core of nucleic acid surrounded by a protein coat

nucleoid /nyōōkli oyd/ *n* the aggregated DNA of a bacterium, seen as a distinct region inside the cell ■ *adj* resembling a nucleus

nucleolar /nyōōkli ólər/ *adj* relating to a nucleolus or nucleoli

nucleolar organizer *n* a segment of a chromosome at which a nucleolus forms

nucleolus /nyōōkli óləss/ (*plural* **-li** /-lī/) *n* a small round body inside a cell nucleus, composed of protein and RNA and associated with the formation of ribosomes and ribosomal RNA [Mid-19C. < late Latin, 'little nucleus' < Latin *nucleus* (see NUCLEUS)] —**nucleolate** /nyōōkli ō layt/ *adj*

nucleon /nyōōkli on/ *n* a proton or neutron, especially when part of an atomic nucleus

nucleonics /nyōōkli ónniks/ *n* the branch of physics dealing with the properties of nucleons and the atomic nucleus (*takes a singular verb*)

nucleon number *n* PHYS same as **mass number**

nucleophile /nyōōkli ō fīl/ *n* a substance that becomes an electron donor in bonding during a chemical reaction —**nucleophilic** /nyōōkli ō fíllik/ *adj*

nucleoplasm /nyōōkli ō plazəm/ *n* the matter (**protoplasm**) contained in a cell nucleus

nucleoprotein /nyōōkli ō prō teen/ *n* a nucleic acid combined with a protein, as in a chromosome

nucleoside /nyōōkli ə sīd/ *n* a compound consisting of a purine or pyrimidine base linked to a sugar, especially ribose or deoxyribose [Early 20C. < NUCLEO- + GLYCOSIDE]

nucleosome /nyōōkli ə sōm/ *n* a structural unit of chromosomes, containing DNA. Nucleosomes fit together rather like a tightly condensed string of beads.

nucleosynthesis /nyōōkli ō sínthəssiss/ *n* the synthesis of heavier elements from lighter elements by fusion reactions within stars

nucleotide /nyōōkli ə tīd/ *n* a component of RNA and DNA, consisting of a nucleoside linked to a phosphate group [Early 20C. Alteration of NUCLEOSIDE]

nucleus /nyōōkli əss/ (*plural* **-i** /-kli ī/ or **-uses**) *n* **1.** IMPORTANT ELEMENT a central or most important item or part that has others grouped or built around it **2.** PHYS CENTRAL REGION OF ATOM the positively charged central region of an atom, consisting of protons and neutrons and containing most of the mass **3.** CHEM STABLE ATOMS IN MOLECULE a stable group of atoms in a molecule, e.g. a benzene ring, that forms the base structure of many compounds and remains unchanged in chemical reactions **4.** BIOL CENTRAL PART OF LIVING CELL the central body, usually spherical, within a eukaryotic cell, that is a membrane-encased mass of protoplasm containing the chromosomes and other genetic information necessary to control cell growth and reproduction **5.** BOT STARCH GRANULE'S CENTRE the central part of a starch granule **6.** BOT INNER KERNEL OF NUT the central kernel of a nut or seed **7.** ANAT GROUP OF NERVE CELLS a group of nerve cells in the central nervous system or a small mass of grey matter in the brain that has a specialized function **8.** ASTRON CORE OF COMET HEAD the central core in the head of a comet, consisting of ice, frozen gases, and dust **9.** ASTRON CENTRAL PART OF NEBULA OR GALAXY the central brighter portion of a nebula or galaxy **10.** PHON MOST RESONANT PART OF SYLLABLE

the most resonant part of a syllable, usually the vowel [Early 18C. < Latin, 'kernel' < *nuc-* 'nut']

nuclide /nyoó klīd/ *n* one or more atomic nuclei identifiable as being of the same element by having the same number of protons and neutrons and the same energy content [Mid-20C. < NUCLEUS]

NUCPS *abbr* National Union of Civil and Public Servants

~~nucular~~ incorrect spelling of **nuclear**

nuddy /núddi/ *n* a nude condition (*informal*) ○ *in the nuddy* [Mid-20C. Alteration of NUDE]

nude /nyood/ *adj* (**nuder, nudest**) **1.** UNCLOTHED wearing no clothes ○ *the nude figure of a man* **2.** FOR UNCLOTHED PEOPLE intended for, or done by, people wearing no clothes **3.** PLAIN bare or plain, with no covering or decoration **4.** LAW LACKING LEGAL REQUISITE lacking a legal requisite such as supporting evidence or a contract ■ *n* UNCLOTHED FIGURE an unclothed person, especially an unclothed figure in a painting or other artistic work [Mid-16C < Latin *nudus*] —**nudely** *adv* ◇ **in the nude** without clothes

SYNONYMS See ***naked.***

NUDETS *abbr* nuclear detection system

nudge /nuj/ *v* (**nudges, nudging, nudged**) **1.** *vt* PUSH OR POKE SOMEBODY to push or poke somebody gently, usually with a motion of the elbow **2.** *vt* MOVE SOMETHING to move something gently, especially by pushing it slowly and carefully **3.** *vt* APPROACH LEVEL to have very nearly reached a particular level or standard ○ *Their profits are nudging the 100 million mark.* **4.** *vt* GENTLY PERSUADE SOMEBODY to persuade somebody into an action, gently and delicately **5.** *vi* MOVE SLOWLY to move slowly or little by little ■ *n* **1.** GENTLE PUSH a gentle push to get somebody's attention **2.** PERSUASIVE ACT a gentle act of persuasion [Late 17C. Origin ?] ◇ **nudge nudge (wink wink)** used to hint or suggest that something is slightly lewd or sexually improper

nudism /nyoódizəm/ *n* LEISURE same as **naturism** (sense 1)

nudist /nyoódist/ *n* somebody who prefers not to wear clothes, especially somebody who does so in designated areas or communities —**nudist** *adj*

nudist colony *n* a place, especially a holiday camp, where the wearing of clothes is not allowed, intended for people who believe nudity is a healthy natural state

nudity /nyoódəti/ *n* **1.** the state of having no clothes on **2.** bareness or plainness, with no covering or decoration

nuée ardente /noó ay aar daánt/ *n* a thick, rapidly moving, deadly, gaseous cloud produced by a volcano and consisting of steam, ash, and rock segments [< French, 'burning cloud']

Nuevo Laredo /nwáyvō lə ráydō/ city in northeastern Mexico. Situated on the Rio Grande opposite Laredo, Texas, it is a major crossing point by road between the United States and Mexico. Population: 310,915 (2000).

Nuevo León /-lay ōn/ state in northeastern Mexico where the majority of the country's iron and steel industry is located. Capital: Monterrey. Population: 3,826,240 (2000). Area: 64,210 sq. km/24,792 sq. mi.

nuevo sol /nwáyvō sol/ (*plural* **nuevos soles** /nwáyvōs sólays/) *n* MONEY same as **sol**[2] [< Spanish, 'new sol']

nuff /nuf/ (*slang*) *adv, pron* same as **enough** ■ *det also* **nuffnuff** /núf nuf/ a large number or amount of (*used in Black English*) [Shortening and respelling of ENOUGH]

Nuffield /núf eeld/, **William Richard Morris, 1st Viscount** (1877–1963) British car manufacturer and philanthropist. He used his fortune for educational endowments and charitable causes.

nugatory /nyoógətəri/ *adj* **1.** having no importance whatsoever **2.** having no legal force [Early 17C. < Latin *nugatorius* < *nugae* 'trifling matters'] —**nugatorily** *adv*

nugget /núggit/ *n* **1.** LUMP OF PRECIOUS METAL a lump of gold or other precious metal in its natural state, dug up out of the ground **2.** SMALL PRECIOUS THING a small item or piece, especially of something abstract such as knowledge or information, regarded as very precious **3.** FOOD SMALL ROUND PIECE OF FOOD a small piece of food, usually coated with breadcrumbs and fried or baked in an oven [Mid-19C. Probably < an English dialect word, 'lump']

nuggety /núggiti/ *adj* **1.** occurring as nuggets **2.** *Aus* having a broad and strong-looking physique, and usually short in stature (*informal*)

nuisance /nyoóss'nss/ *n* **1.** an annoying or irritating person or thing **2.** something not allowed by law because it causes harm or offence, either to people in general (**public nuisance**) or to an individual person [15C. < Old French < Latin *nocere* 'injure']

nuisance call *n* a usually anonymous telephone call made to annoy, harass, upset, or scare somebody

nuisance value *n* the relative usefulness of something based on its potential to cause problems or difficulties for somebody

Nuits St Georges /nweé saN zháwrzh/ *n* a red wine from Burgundy, eastern France [After a district]

NUJ *abbr* National Union of Journalists

nuke /nyook/ *vt* (**nukes, nuking, nuked**) **1.** to attack somebody or something with nuclear weapons (*slang*) **2.** FOOD to cook something in a microwave oven (*informal*) ■ *n* ARMS same as **nuclear weapon** (*informal*) [Mid-20C. Shortening of NUCLEAR]

nukkad /nu kúd/ *n S Asia* a street corner or other place where people gather to chat [Late 20C. < Hindi]

Nuku'alofa /noókoo ə lṓfə/ capital of Tonga, on Tongatapu Island in the southern Pacific Ocean. Population: 34,000 (1990).

~~nukular~~ incorrect spelling of **nuclear**

null /nul/ *adj* **1.** INVALID having no legal validity **2.** VALUELESS having no value or importance **3.** AMOUNTING TO NOTHING amounting to nothing in terms of context or character **4.** AT ZERO LEVEL at the level of zero or nothing **5.** MATHS RELATING TO ZERO relating to or equal to zero **6.** MATHS EMPTY used to describe a mathematical set containing no elements ○ *the null set* **7.** MATHS ENDING IN ZERO converging to zero ○ *a null sequence* **8.** PHYS INDICATING READING OF ZERO indicating a reading of zero when a measured quantity is undetectable or equal to another in comparison ■ *n* same as **zero** (*literary*) [Mid-16C. Via Old French *nul* < Latin *nullus* 'not any'] ◇ **null and void** not legally valid

nullah /núllə/ *n S Asia* a ditch, irrigation canal, or ravine [Late 18C. < Hindi *nālā*]

nulla-nulla /núllə núllə/ *n* an Australian Aboriginal club made of hardwood and used as a weapon [Mid-19C. < Dharuk]

Nullarbor Plain /núllər bawr-/ dry plateau in southern South Australia. Area: 300,000 sq. km/115,831 sq. mi.

nullify /núlli fī/ (**-fies, -fying, -fied**) *vt* **1.** to make something legally invalid or ineffective **2.** to have the effect of cancelling something out —**nullifier** *n* —**nullification** /núll ifi káysh'n/ *n*

SYNONYMS ***nullify, abrogate, annul, repeal, invalidate, negate***

CORE MEANING: to put an end to the effective existence of something

nullify to make something legally invalid or ineffective ○ *Only the courts can nullify his decision.* ○ *The country's military rulers nullified national elections after pro-democracy candidates won a landslide victory.* **abrogate** (*formal*) to declare a legal document or agreement invalid ○ *Egypt and Somalia abrogated their friendship treaties with the USSR in the 1970s.* ○ *We condemn the levity with which certain politicians speak about abrogating our international obligations.* **annul** to declare a legal document or agreement invalid ○ *A court on Wednesday annulled the decree, saying it was illegal.* ○ *Many parties have called for the election results to be annulled because of alleged fraud.* **repeal** to officially end the validity of something such as a law ○ *We intend to repeal the act when alternative regulations are in place.* **invalidate** to deprive something of its legal force or value, e.g. by failing to comply with some terms and conditions ○ *Failure to disclose all relevant changes may invalidate your policy.* ○ *Does the result of this latest poll invalidate the findings of the earlier survey?* **negate** (*formal*) to declare officially that something is invalid or ineffective, or make something invalid or ineffective ○ *This argument does not negate the point I am making.* ○ *She used her speed and experience to negate her opponent's power, winning the match in straight sets.*

nullipara /nu líppərə/ (*plural* **-ras** or **-rae** /-ree/) *n* a woman who has never given birth to a child [Late 19C. < Latin *nullus* 'none' + English *-para* 'woman who has given birth' < Latin *parere* 'give birth']

nullity /núlləti/ *n* **1.** the state of being legally invalid **2.** a lack of effectiveness or usefulness

NUM *abbr* National Union of Mineworkers

num. *abbr* **1.** number **2.** numeral

Num. *abbr* BIBLE Numbers

numb /num/ *adj* **1.** WITH NO FEELING unable to feel or have sensations, e.g. as a result of extreme cold or the application of a local anaesthetic **2.** EMOTIONLESS unable to feel emotions ■ *vt* (**numbs, numbing, numbed**) **1.** TAKE SENSATION AWAY FROM SOMETHING to take away from a part of the body the power to feel or have sensations, or to take away the sensations themselves **2.** TAKE AWAY SOMEBODY'S FEELINGS to make somebody incapable of feeling emotion, or deaden somebody's emotions or feelings [15C. Past participle of Old English *niman* 'take'] —**numbly** *adv* —**numbness** *n*

numbat /núm bat/ *n* a marsupial that has a long snout, long tongue, and strong claws for feeding on ants and termites. Native to: southwestern Australia. Latin name: *Myrmecobius fasciatus.* [Early 20C. < Australian Aboriginal]

number /númbər/ *n* **1.** FIGURE USED IN COUNTING a figure, symbol, or word used in calculating quantities of individual things **2.** IDENTIFYING FIGURE a figure or group of figures identifying somebody or something, e.g. a set of figures identifying somebody as a telephone subscriber, or a figure identifying a sports player or competitor ○ *What's your fax number?* **3.** COUNTABLE QUANTITY a total or estimated total of people or things that can be individually counted ○ *We have received a number of complaints.* **4.** SINGLE THING IN SERIES a single one of a series of things produced in sequence, especially a single issue of a magazine **5.** COUNTING the concept of calculating quantities of individual things **6.** GRAM GRAMMATICAL QUANTITY quantity expressed, in some languages, by the form of a word ○ *The qualifying adjective agrees with the noun in gender and number.* **7.** PIECE OF MUSIC a self-contained piece of popular music, especially one of several that feature in a performance **8.** GARMENT an item of clothing, especially women's clothing (*informal*) ○ *a little silk number* **9.** THING a thing of any kind, especially something that gives pleasure or impresses (*informal*) **10.** PERSON somebody regarded in sexual terms (*informal; sometimes considered offensive*) **11.** CANNABIS CIGARETTE a cannabis cigarette (*slang*) ■ *v* (**-bers, -bering, -bered**) **1.** *vt* IDENTIFY SOMEBODY OR SOMETHING BY NUMBER to give somebody or something an identifying number ○ *Don't forget to number the pages.* **2.** *vti* ACHIEVE TOTAL to reach a particular total amount ○ *Supporters numbered over 300, while there were only 15 dissenters.* **3.** *vt* INCLUDE SOMEBODY OR SOMETHING to include somebody or something as one of a group ○ *It is numbered among the world's most prestigious hotels.* [13C. < Anglo-Norman *numbre* < Latin *numerus*] ◇ **do a number on somebody** to treat somebody unfairly or harshly, e.g. by deliberate and systematic criticism or ridicule (*slang*) ◇ **have (got) somebody's number** to understand somebody's true motives or character and so be well placed to deal with him or her ◇ **somebody's days are numbered** somebody's life or career is about to come to an end

USAGE number or **quantity**? Careful writers distinguish between ***quantity*** ('an amount of something') and ***number*** ('a total or estimated total of people or things that can be individually counted'), as in *A large number* [better than *quantity*] *of people had gathered in the square.* ***Quantity*** is best reserved for references to inanimate objects or inanimate uncountable nouns, as in *a huge quantity of rotten wheat; a large quantity of fuel.*

USAGE See ***amount.***

USAGE number – singular or plural? ***Number*** is a collective noun that can take a singular or plural verb depending on how you use it. If you put the definite article *the* in front of ***number***, you are stipulating one particular number, even if *of* and a series of things comes next. Therefore, you must use a singular verb with ***number*** preceded by '*the*': *The number of lab coats available is limited.* On the other hand, if you put the indefinite article *a* before ***number***, you must use a plural verb: *A number of lab coats are available.*

number-cruncher *n* (*informal*) **1.** somebody whose job consists of performing large quantities of arithmetical calculations **2.** a computer designed to perform large quantities of complex numerical calculations —**number-crunching** *n*

numbered account /númbərd-/ *n* a bank account

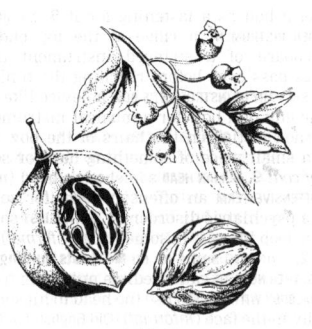
nutmeg

nutmeg /nút meg/ n **1.** COOK SPICE an aromatic spice made by grinding or grating the large hard seed of a tropical tree **2.** TREES TROPICAL EVERGREEN TREE an evergreen tree widely grown in tropical regions for its seeds, which yield nutmeg and mace. Native to: eastern India. Latin name: *Myristica fragrans*. **3.** SOCCER KICK OF BALL THROUGH OPPONENT'S LEGS in football, a move in which the ball is kicked between an opponent's legs and often regained behind him or her (*informal*) **4.** COLOURS LIGHT BROWN a light greyish-brown colour ■ vt (**-megs, -megging, -megged**) SOCCER KICK BALL THROUGH OPPONENT'S LEGS in football, to evade and take the ball past an opponent by kicking it through his or her open legs (*informal*) [13C. Probably < medieval Latin *nux muscata* 'nut smelling like musk' < *nux* 'nut' + late Latin *muscus* (see MUSK)]

nutraceutical /nyoótrə syoóti'l/, **nutriceutical** n PHARM same as **functional food** [Late 20C. < Latin *nutrire* 'nourish' + PHARMACEUTICAL]

nutria /nyoótri ə/ n **1.** the light brown fur of the coypu **2.** ZOOL same as **coypu** [Early 19C. Via Spanish < Latin *lutra* 'otter']

nutriceutical n PHARM another spelling of **nutraceutical**

nutrient /nyoótri ənt/ n a substance that provides nourishment, e.g. the minerals that a plant takes from the soil or the constituents in food that keep a human body healthy and help it to grow ■ adj providing nourishment [Mid-17C. < Latin *nutrient-*, present participle of *nutrire* 'nourish']

nutriment /nyoótrimənt/ n nourishment or nourishing substances [Mid-16C. < Latin *nutrimentum* < *nutrire* 'nourish']

nutrition /nyoo trísh'n/ n **1.** PROCESSING OF FOOD the process of absorbing nutrients from food and processing them in the body in order to keep healthy or to grow **2.** SCIENCE OF FOOD the science that deals with foods and their effects on health **3.** FOOD FOODS foods, or the minerals, vitamins, and other nourishing substances that they contain [Mid-16C. Via French < Latin *nutrition-* < *nutrire* 'nourish'] —**nutritional** adj — **nutritionally** adv

nutritional therapy n the alleviation of symptoms by dietary changes, sometimes using vitamin and mineral pills

nutritionist /nyoo trísh'nist/ n somebody who studies or is an expert on nutrition

nutritious /nyoo tríshəss/ adj containing minerals, vitamins, and other substances that promote health —**nutritiously** adv —**nutritiousness** n

nutritive /nyoótrətiv/ adj **1.** providing nutrients **2.** relating to nutrition [15C. Via French < medieval Latin *nutritivus* < the past participle of *nutrire* 'nourish'] —**nutritively** adv

nut roast n a vegetarian loaf made from chopped or ground-up nuts with onions, herbs, and seasonings, bound with breadcrumbs and baked

nuts /nuts/ (*slang*) adj **1.** OFFENSIVE TERM an offensive term meaning having a psychiatric disorder **2.** ENTHUSIASTIC wildly enthusiastic about something, or extremely fond of somebody (*offensive in some contexts*) ■ npl OFFENSIVE TERM an offensive term for testicles ■ interj EXPRESSION OF ANNOYANCE used to express annoyance, disbelief, or contempt (*sometimes offensive*)

nuts and bolts npl the most basic components, elements, or constituents of something (*informal*)

nutshell /nút shel/ n the hard outer shell of a nut that surrounds the edible inner seed ◇ **in a nutshell** in very few words, getting right to the main point

nutter /núttər/ n an offensive term for somebody with a psychiatric disorder (*informal*)

nutty /nútti/ (**-tier, -tiest**) adj **1.** CONTAINING NUTS containing a large amount of nuts **2.** LIKE NUTS like nuts in taste, appearance, texture, or smell **3.** OFFENSIVE TERM an offensive term meaning having or characterized by a psychiatric disorder (*informal*) —**nuttily** adv — **nuttiness** n

Nuuk /nook/ capital and largest city of the Danish Island of Greenland, situated on the southwestern coast. Population: 12,483 (1994). Former name **Godthåb** (until 1979)

nux vomica /núks vómmikə/ (*plural same*) n **1.** MEDICINE a medicine or homeopathic remedy made from the poisonous seeds of a South Asian tree **2.** POISONOUS SEEDS the seeds of a South Asian tree, which contain strychnine and other poisonous substances **3.** S ASIAN TREE a tree with orange-red berries and poisonous seeds. Native to: South Asia. Latin name: *Strychnos nux-vomica*. [< medieval Latin, 'emetic nut']

nuzzle /núzz'l/ v (**-zles, -zling, -zled**) **1.** vti RUB SOMETHING WITH NOSE to rub or push something gently with the nose, especially as a way of showing affection **2.** vi RUB SOMETHING WITH FACE to make affectionate rubbing or stroking movements with the face ■ n RUBBING MOVEMENT a rubbing or stroking movement with the nose or face [15C. Origin ?]

nuzzle-tripe n regional the smallest or weakest piglet in a litter [< *nuzzle* 'to nurse'; from the idea that a small piglet requiring special attention is almost worthless]

REGIONAL NOTE See *underling*.

NV abbr FIN nonvoting

N/V abbr BANKING no value

nvCJD abbr MED new variant CJD

NVQ n a UK qualification awarded at a variety of levels in a technical or vocational subject certifying the holder's proficiency in a range of work-related activities. Full form **National Vocational Qualification**

NW abbr **1.** northwest **2.** northwestern

NWbN abbr northwest by north

NWbW abbr northwest by west

Nwfld abbr Newfoundland

n.wt. abbr net weight

N.W.T. abbr Can Northwest Territories

NY abbr New York

nyabinghi /nya bínggi/ (*plural* **-ghis**), **nyabingi** (*plural* **-gis**), **nyahbingi** n (*slang; used in Black English*) **1.** a type of music popular among Rastafarians **2.** a Rastafarian religious service [After *Nyabinghi*, legendary Amazon queen around whom a cult grew in Uganda and Rwanda]

nyala /nyaálə/ (*plural same* or **-las**) n **1.** an antelope with vertical white stripes on its sides and, on the male, spiral horns. Native to: central Africa. Latin name: *Tragelaphus angasi*. **2.** an antelope with spiral horns on the males. Native to: mountainous regions in northeastern Africa. Latin name: *Tragelaphus buxtoni*. [Late 19C. < Zulu *i-nyala*]

nyam /nyam/ vti same as **eat** (*slang; used in Black English*) [< a W African language]

Nyanja /ni ánd jə/ n (*plural same* or **-jas**), adj LANG same as **Chewa** [Mid-19C. < Bantu *nyanja* 'lake']

Nyasa, Lake /nī ássə/ lake in southeastern Africa, lying between Malawi, Mozambique, and Tanzania. It is one of the world's largest lakes. Area: 22,490 sq. km/8,683 sq. mi.

Nyasaland /ni ássə land, nī-/ former name for **Malawi** (until 1966)

nybble /níbb'l/ n a unit of computer memory equal to half of one byte or four bits [Humorous play on the idea of a small bite]

NYC abbr New York City

nyctalopia /níktə lópi ə/ n the state of being unable to see well at night (*technical*) [Late 17C. < Late Latin < Greek *nuktalōps* 'sightless at night' < *nukt-* 'night' + *alaos* 'sightless' + *ōps* 'eye'] —**nyctalopic** /-lóppik/ adj

nyctitropism /nik títtrəpizəm/ n the movement of parts of a plant in response to light and temperature differences between night and day, e.g. the opening and closing of flowers and the folding together of leaves at night [Late 19C. < Greek *nukt-* 'night'] —**nyctitropic** /níktə trópik, -tróppik/ adj

nyctophobia /níktə fóbi ə/ n an irrational fear of the night or of darkness in general [Early 20C. < Greek *nukt-* 'night'] —**nyctophobic** adj —**nyctophobically** adv

nyetwork /nyét wurk/ n COMPUT same as **notwork** [Late 20C. Blend of Russian *nyet* 'no' + NETWORK]

nylon /nī lon/ n a tough synthetic material. Use: food containers, brush bristles, clothing. ■ **nylons** npl stockings made of a synthetic fibre such as nylon [Mid-20C. Origin ?]

NY-LON n a business executive working in both New York and London [< abbreviations NEW YORK and LONDON]

NYMEX /nī meks/ abbr New York Mercantile Exchange

nymph /nimf/ n **1.** SPIRIT OF NATURE in mythology, a minor goddess or spirit of nature inhabiting areas of natural beauty such as woods, mountains, and rivers and traditionally regarded as a beautiful young woman **2.** WOMAN a beautiful young woman (*literary*) **3.** INSECTS INSECT LARVA the larva of some insects such as mayflies, dragonflies, and grasshoppers that resembles the adult and develops into the adult insect directly, without passing through an intermediate pupa stage [14C. Via Old French < Greek *nymphē* 'bride, nymph']

nympha /nímfə/ (*plural* **-phae** /-fee/) n either of the small inner folds of skin (**labia minora**) that form the opening to the vagina [Late 17C. Via Latin < Greek *nymphē* 'nymph']

nymphalid /nímfəlid/ adj belonging to a family of butterflies that has brightly coloured wings and includes the tortoiseshell butterfly and the red admiral. Family: Nymphalidae. [Late 19C. Via modern Latin *Nymphalidae* < Latin *nympha* (see NYMPHA)]

nymphet /nímfit, nim fét/, **nymphette** /nim fét/ n a sexually aware and sexually desirable young woman, especially a woman in her early teens

nympho /ním fō/ (*plural* **-phos**) n same as **nymphomaniac** [Mid-20C. Shortening]

nymphomania /nímfə máyni ə/ n a compulsive desire to have sex with many different men, theorized to occur in some women (*often offensive*) [Late 18C. < modern Latin < Latin *nympha* (see NYMPH) + late Latin *mania* (see MANIA)]

nymphomaniac /nímfə máyni ak/ n **1.** a woman supposed to have a compulsive desire to have sex with many different men **2.** an offensive term for a woman regarded as being extremely active sexually (*informal*) —**nymphomaniacal** /nímfōmə nī ək'l/ adj

Nynorsk /neé nawrsk/ n the official form of the Norwegian language, derived from the rural dialects of Norwegian spoken in the west and north of the country and standardized during the mid-19th century [Mid-20C. < Norwegian, 'new Norwegian'] — **Nynorsk** adj

NYO abbr National Youth Orchestra

NYP abbr not yet published

NYSE abbr New York Stock Exchange

nystagmus /ni stágməss/ n an involuntary rhythmic movement of the eyes, usually from side to side, caused by some illnesses that affect the nerves and muscle behind the eyeball [Early 19C. Via modern Latin < Greek *nustagmos* 'drowsiness' < *nustazein* 'nod, be sleepy']

nystatin /nístətin/ n an antibiotic drug. Use: treatment of fungal infections, especially thrush. [Mid-20C. < N(ew) Y(ork) Stat(e)]

Nyungar /nyoóngə/, **Nyunga** n an Aboriginal language of southwestern Australia, now extinct [Mid-19C. < Nyungar *nungar* 'a man'] —**Nyungar** adj

nz abbr ONLINE New Zealand (*used in Internet addresses*) See table at **domain name**

NZBC abbr New Zealand Broadcasting Corporation

N Zeal. abbr New Zealand

NZMA abbr New Zealand Medical Association

NZRFU abbr New Zealand Rugby Football Union

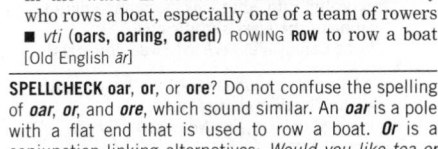

Oo

o¹ /ō/ (*plural* **o's**), **O** (*plural* **O's** or **Os**) *n* **1.** the 15th letter of the English alphabet, representing a vowel sound **2.** a written representation of the letter 'o'

o² *abbr* PHARM pint [Modern Latin *octarius*]

o³ *abbr* **1.** GEOG ocean **2.** PRINTING octavo **3.** old **4.** MATHS order **5.** BASEBALL out **6.** CRICKET over(s)

o' *stressed* /ō/; *unstressed* /ə/ *contr* of

O¹ /ō/ (*plural* **O's** or **Os**) *n* **1.** 'O'-SHAPED OBJECT something shaped like a letter 'O' **2.** ZERO the number zero **3.** MED HUMAN BLOOD TYPE a human blood type of the ABO system containing the O antigen. Somebody with this type of blood can donate to all other types in the group but can receive only type O blood.

O² /ō/ *interj* **1.** used to address a person or thing, or at the start of a plea or wish **2.** used to express surprise or great wonderment (*literary*) [12C. Natural exclamation]

O³ *symbol* CHEM ELEM oxygen

O⁴ *abbr* **1.** GEOG ocean **2.** PRINTING octavo **3.** old **4.** MATHS order **5.** BASEBALL out **6.** over (sense 16) (*used in e-mails or text messages*) **7.** CRICKET over(s)

-o *suffix* **1.** used to form abbreviated words ○ *aggro* ○ *demo* ○ *hypo* **2.** somebody or something associated with or having the characteristics of something ○ *dumbo* [Origin ?]

-o- *infix* connects words and suffixes [< Greek]

OA *abbr* MED osteoarthritis

o/a *abbr* on or about

oaf /ōf/ *n* somebody regarded as unintelligent, clumsy, or uncultured (*insult*) [Early 17C. < Old Norse *álfr* 'elf']

oafish /ṓfish/ *adj* unintelligent, clumsy, or uncultured (*insult*) —**oafishly** *adv* —**oafishness** *n*

Oahu /ō aáhoo/ island in Hawaii, the most populous and third largest of the Hawaiian Islands. Population: 870,761 (1995). Area: 1,546 sq. km/597 sq. mi.

oak

oak /ōk/ *n* **1.** HARD WOOD OF OAK TREE a hard rich-coloured wood. Use: furniture-making, flooring. **2.** TREE a deciduous or evergreen tree with acorns as fruit and leaves with several rounded or pointed lobes, grown for its shade and wood. Native to: northern hemisphere. Genus: *Quercus*. **3.** BUSH a bush with lobed leaves like those of an oak tree, e.g. a Jerusalem oak or poison oak **4.** OAK WREATH OR GARLAND a decoration made from the leaves of an oak tree, especially a wreath or garland ■ *adj* OF RICH BROWN COLOUR of a rich brown colour, similar to the colour of oak wood [Old English *āc* < Germanic]

oak apple *n* a rounded hollow growth on the trunk

of an oak tree caused by infestation with gall wasps, which use the growths as shelters for their larvae

oaken /ṓkən/ *adj* made of oak wood (*literary*)

oak fern *n* a light green woodland fern. Native to: northern regions. Latin name: *Thelypteris dryopteris*.

oak gall *n* BOT same as **oak apple**

Oakham /ṓkəm/ market town in central England. It has a Norman castle. Population: 8,691 (1991).

Oakland /ṓklənd/ city and county seat of Alameda County, western California, situated on the eastern side of San Francisco Bay. Population: 402,777 (2002 estimate).

oak leaf cluster *n* a small decoration shaped like a bunch of oak leaves and acorns, added to another military decoration to show that it has been awarded to the wearer more than once

Oakley /ṓkli/, **Annie** (1860–1926) US sharpshooter. She performed with Buffalo Bill's Wild West Show, and inspired the musical *Annie Get Your Gun* (1946). Full name **Moses, Phoebe Anne Oakley**

> 'I can shoot as well as you.'
> [Annie Oakley. Quoted in *Annie Oakley: Woman at Arms*, Courtney Ryley Cooper; 1927]

oakmoss /ṓk moss/ *n* a lichen that grows on oak trees and produces a resin used in the making of some perfumes. Native to: northern hemisphere. Latin name: *Evernia prunastri*.

oakum /ṓkəm/ *n* hemp or jute fibres, especially from old ropes unravelled and soaked in tar. Use: formerly, sealant for gaps between the planks in a wooden boat's hull. [Old English *ācumba* 'broken fibres', literally 'off-combing' < Indo-European, 'tooth']

Oakville /ṓkvil/ city in Halton Municipal Region, southeastern Ontario, Canada, situated 35 km/22 mi. southwest of Toronto. Population: 144,738 (2001).

oak wilt *n* a disease of oak trees caused by a fungus that kills their leaves

OAM *abbr* Medal of the Order of Australia

Oamaru /ómmə roo/ town and fishing port on the eastern coast of the South Island, New Zealand. Population: 12,696 (2001).

O & M *abbr* organization and method

OAP *n* somebody who is entitled to draw a pension from the government on reaching a specific age. Full form **old-age pensioner**

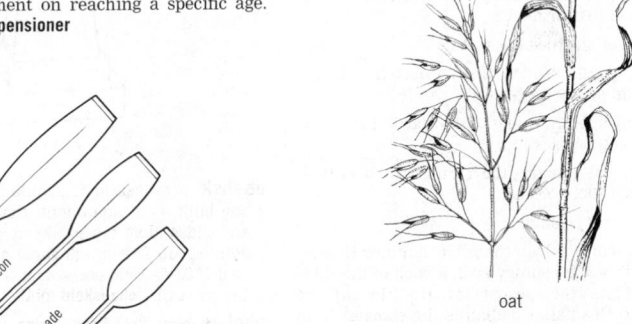

oar

oar /awr/ *n* **1.** BOATING POLE USED TO PROPEL BOAT a wooden pole with one broad flat end, used either singly or in pairs to propel a boat by dipping the broad end in the water **2.** ROWING SOMEBODY ROWING somebody who rows a boat, especially one of a team of rowers ■ *vti* (**oars, oaring, oared**) ROWING ROW to row a boat [Old English *ār*]

SPELLCHECK oar, or, or **ore**? Do not confuse the spelling of *oar*, *or*, and *ore*, which sound similar. An *oar* is a pole with a flat end that is used to row a boat. *Or* is a conjunction linking alternatives: *Would you like tea or coffee? Be quiet or leave the room!* *Ore* is a mineral from which metal is extracted, as in *iron ore*.

---

oarfish /áwr fish/ (*plural same* or **-fishes**) *n* a long, eel-shaped fish that grows up to 7 m/23 ft, with a red head fin and dorsal fin. Native to: tropical Atlantic waters. Latin name: *Regalecus glesne*. [Mid-19C. < the shape of its body]

oarlock /áwr lok/ *n N Am* ROWING same as **rowlock** [Old English *ārloc* < *ār* 'oar' + *loc* 'lock']

oarsman /áwrzmən/ (*plural* **-men** /-mən/) *n* a man who rows a boat, especially as part of a team of rowers — **oarsmanship** *n*

oarsperson /áwrz purss'n/ (*plural* **-people** /-peep'l/ or **-persons**) *n* somebody who rows a boat, especially as part of a team of rowers

oarswoman /áwrz wŏŏmən/ (*plural* **-women** /-wimin/) *n* a woman who rows a boat, especially as part of a team of rowers

oarweed /áwr weed/ *n* FUNGI same as **tangle²**

OAS *abbr* Organization of American States

oasis /ō áyssiss/ (*plural* **oases** /ō áy seez/) *n* **1.** fertile ground in a desert where the level of underground water rises to or near ground level, and where plants grow and travellers can replenish water supplies **2.** a place or period that gives relief from a troubling or chaotic situation [Early 17C. Via late Latin < Greek]

oast /ōst/ *n* **1.** a kiln used for drying hops, especially hops used to flavour beer **2.** FOOD INDUST same as **oasthouse** [Old English *āst* 'kiln' < Indo-European, 'be hot, burn']

oasthouse /ṓst howss/ (*plural* **-houses** /-howziz/) *n* a building constructed to contain hop-drying kilns that usually has conical or pyramid-shaped towers

oat

oat /ōt/ *n* a plant with edible seeds that is grown as a cereal crop. Native to: northern regions. Latin name: *Avena sativa*. ■ **oats** *npl* the seeds of the oat

---

zh vision. In foreign words: kh German Bach; aN French vin; aaN French blanc; ö German schön, French feu; oN French bon; ōN French un; ü as in French rue. Stress marks: ´ as in secret /seèkrət/, **academic** /ákə démmik/

oatcake /ót kayk/ *n* a hard unsweetened biscuit made from oatmeal, eaten with cheese or other savoury foods

grown as a cereal crop. Use: to make foods such as porridge, as livestock feed. [Pre-12C. Origin?]

oat-cell *adj* describes a highly malignant form of lung cancer (**oat-cell carcinoma**) characterized by the rapid growth of undifferentiated small round cells. Oat-cell carcinoma is usually related to smoking. [Because the cells look like grains of oats]

oaten /ót'n/ *adj* made from oats, oatmeal, or oat straw

oater /ótər/ *n* a film about cowboys, Native North Americans, and settlers in the American West (*informal humorous*) [Mid-20C. < the staple food of the horses featured]

Oates /óts/, **Joyce Carol** (*b.* 1938) US writer. Her naturalistic novels, often depicting violence in US society, include *Them* (1969), for which she won the National Book award.

> 'For what *is* passes so swiftly and irrevocably into what *was*, no human claim can be of the least significance.'
> [Joyce Carol Oates, *What I Lived For*; 1994]

> 'The use of language is all we have to pit against death and silence.'
> [Joyce Carol Oates, *New York Times*; 16 August 1987]

Oates, Titus (1649–1705) English conspirator. He fabricated the Popish Plot (1678), a fictitious plot to assassinate Charles II and restore Roman Catholicism in England. Initially rewarded, he was later found guilty of perjury and imprisoned.

oat grass *n* a wild grass that looks like the cultivated oat. Native to: Mediterranean, USA, Australia. Genera: *Arrhenatherum* or *Danthonia* or *Themeda* or *Enneapogon*.

oath /óth/ (*plural* **oaths** /óthz/) *n* 1. SOLEMN PROMISE a formal or legally binding pledge to do something such as tell the truth in a court of law, made formally and often naming God or a loved one as a witness ○ *took a solemn oath of loyalty* 2. WORDS OF PROMISE the words said when making a formal pledge, especially when reciting a conventional formula such as that used in a court of law 3. SWEARWORD a swearword, especially one that uses the name of God or another sacred name in a disrespectful way [Old English *áþ*] ◇ **my oath** *ANZ* used to express strong confirmation or agreement (*slang*)

oatmeal /ót meel/ *n* 1. oat grains ground or crushed into flakes or powder, used to make various foods such as porridge, flapjacks, and oatcakes ○ *oatmeal biscuits* 2. *N Am* FOOD same as **porridge** (sense 1) ■ *adj* COLOURS of a light greyish-brown colour

Oaxaca /wə haáká/ 1. state in southern Mexico. Capital: Oaxaca. Area: 3,438,765 (2000). Area: 93,136 sq. km/35,960 sq. mi. 2. historic city in southern Mexico, the capital of Oaxaca State. It was founded by the Aztecs. Population: 400,706 (2000).

Ob' /ob/ *river* in western Siberia that rises in the Altai Mountains, joins the Irtysh River, and then empties into the Arctic Ocean. Length: 3,680 km/2,290 mi.

OB *abbr* 1. MED obstetric 2. MED obstetrician 3. MED obstetrics 4. BROADCAST outside broadcast

ob.[1] *abbr* 1. MUSIC oboe 2. MED obstetric 3. MED obstetrician 4. MED obstetrics

ob.[2] *abbr* he or she died [Latin *obiit*]

Ob. *abbr* 1. BIBLE Obadiah 2. MED obstetric 3. MED obstetrician 4. MED obstetrics

ob- *prefix* inverse, inversely ○ *obvolute* [< Latin *ob* 'in the way, against, towards']

oba /óbə/ *n* a ruler among the Yoruba people of West Africa [Early 20C. < Yoruba]

Obad. *abbr* BIBLE Obadiah

Obadiah / óbə dí ə/ *n* 1. in the Bible, a minor Hebrew prophet of the 6th century BC 2. a book of the Bible that contains the prophecies traditionally attributed to Obadiah. Obadiah is the shortest book of the Bible. See table at **Bible**

Oban /óbən/ *town*, seaport, and tourist centre in western Scotland. Population: 8,120 (2001).

Obasanjo /óbbə saánjō/, **Olusegun** (*b.* 1937) president of Nigeria (1999–). His election in 1999 as a representative of the People's Democratic Party ended 15 years of military rule.

obb. *abbr* MUSIC obbligato

obbligato /óbbli gaátō/, **obligato** *adj* not to be omitted from a musical piece, either as an instrumental part in the piece or as an instrumental accompaniment to a singer (*used as a musical direction*) ■ *n* (*plural* **-tos** or **-ti** /-tee/) a musical part or accompaniment that is not to be left out [Early 18C. Via Italian, 'obliged' < Latin *obligare* (see OBLIGATE)]

OBC *abbr* S Asia Other Backward Classes

obcompressed /óbkəm prést/ *adj* used to describe a part of a plant that is flattened from back to front, like the fruits of yellow rattle

obconic /ob kónnik/, **obconical** /ob kónnik'l/ *adj* cone-shaped and attached to a plant by the pointed end ○ *an obconic fruit*

obcordate /ob káwr dayt/ *adj* heart-shaped and attached to a plant by the pointed end

obdurate /óbdyoōrət/ *adj* 1. not easily persuaded or influenced 2. not influenced by emotions, especially not inclined to feel sympathy or pity [15C. < late Latin *obduratus*, past participle of *obdurare* 'be hard' < *durus* 'hard'] —**obduracy** *n* —**obdurately** *adv* —**obdurateness** *n*

OBE *abbr* Officer of the (Order of the) British Empire

obeah /óbi ə/ *n* 1. a religion that involves witchcraft, originally practised in Africa and surviving now in parts of the Caribbean 2. an object believed to have magical powers, used in practising obeah [Mid-18C. < Twi *ōbayifo*]

~~obediance~~ incorrect spelling of **obedience**

obedience /ə beédi'nss/ *n* 1. the act or practice of following instructions, complying with rules or regulations, or submitting to somebody's authority 2. the religious authority exercised by a church, a priest, or another member of the clergy, or the people who are under this authority

obedient /ə beédi'nt/ *adj* carrying out, or willing to carry out, instructions, or submitting to somebody's will or authority [13C. < Old French < Latin *oboediens*, present participle of *oboedire* (see OBEY)] —**obediently** *adv*

obeisance /ō báyss'nss, ō bÉ-/ *n* 1. a gesture of respect or deference, e.g. a bow of the head (*formal*) 2. the attitude or behaviour of somebody who pays respect or homage to somebody or something [14C. < Old French < *obeir* (see OBEY)]

obeli PRINTING plural of **obelus**

obelia /ō beéli ə/ (*plural* **-lias**) *n* an ocean hydrozoan polyp that forms colonies that resemble moss on rocks, ships' hulls, and piles. Genus: *Obelia*. [Late 19C. < modern Latin < Greek *obelias* 'leaf baked on a spit' < *obelos* 'spit']

obelise *vt* PRINTING another spelling of **obelize**

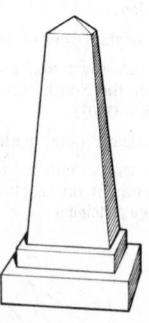

obelisk

obelisk /óbbə lisk/ *n* 1. a pillar of stone, especially one built as a monument, that has a square base and sides that taper like a pyramid towards a pointed top 2. PRINTING same as **dagger** *n* (sense 3) [Mid-16C. Via Latin *obeliscus* < Greek *obeliskos* < *obelos* (see OBELUS)] —**obeliskoid** /óbbə lísk oyd/ *adj*

obelize /óbbə līz/ (**-lizes, -lizing, -lized**), **obelise** (**-lises, -lising, -lised**) *vt* to mark a written or printed word or passage with a dagger or obelus [Mid-17C. < Greek *obelizein* < *obelos* 'spit']

obelus /óbbələss/ (*plural* **-li** /-lī/) *n* 1. PRINTING same as **dagger** *n* (sense 3) 2. a printed mark (†) used in modern editions of ancient manuscripts to indicate that the passage marked is thought not to be genuine [14C. Via late Latin < Greek *obelos* 'spit, obelisk']

obento /ō béntō/ (*plural* **-tos**), **bento** /bén tō/ *n* a Japanese meal that is packaged in a partitioned lacquer box [Late 20C. < Japanese]

Oberammergau /óbər ámmər gow/ *town* in Bavaria, southeastern Germany, famous for producing a Passion Play every ten years. Population: 5,225 (1997).

Oberon /óbə ron/ *n* 1. in medieval folklore, the king of the fairies and husband of Titania 2. a large natural satellite of Uranus

obese /ō beéss/ *adj* 1. extremely or unhealthily fat or overweight 2. having a body weight more than 20% greater than recommended for the relevant height and thus at risk from several serious illnesses, including diabetes and heart disease [Mid-17C. < Latin *obesus*, past participle of assumed *obedere* 'eat until overweight' < *edere* 'eat'] —**obesely** *adv* —**obeseness** *n* —**obesity** *n*

obesogenic /ōbeéssō jénnik/ *adj* tending to encourage excessive weight gain

obey /ə báy/ (**obeys, obeying, obeyed**) *vti* 1. to follow instructions or behave in accordance with a law, rule, or order 2. to be controlled by somebody or something [13C. Via Old French *obeir* < Latin *oboedire* 'listen to' < *audire* 'hear'] —**obeyer** *n*

obfuscate /ób fuss kayt, óbfəss-/ (**-cates, -cating, -cated**) *v* 1. *vti* to make something obscure or unclear, especially by making it unnecessarily complicated 2. *vt* to make somebody confused [Mid-16C. < late Latin *obfuscat-*, past participle of *obfuscare* 'darken' < *fuscus* 'dark'] —**obfuscation** /ób fu skáysh'n, óbfə-/ *n* —**obfuscator** *n* —**obfuscatory** /óbfə skáytəri/ *adj*

ob-gyn /ó bee jee wī én/, **ob/gyn** *n N Am* (*informal*) 1. the branch of medicine that deals with obstetrics and gynaecology 2. a specialist in obstetrics and gynaecology

obi[1] /óbi/ (*plural* **obis** or *same*) *n* a silk sash worn by a Japanese person in traditional dress to fasten the kimono [Late 19C. < Japanese, 'belt, band, girdle']

obi[2] /óbi/ *n* RELIG same as **obeah**

obi belt *n* a wide belt, sometimes fastened with buckles, in the style of the sash worn around a Japanese kimono

Ob'-Irtysh /ób eer tísh/ *river system* in western Siberia, and the longest in Asia, incorporating the rivers Irtysh and Ob'. Length: 5,410 km/3,362 mi.

obit /óbit, ō bít/ *n* same as **obituary** (*informal*) [14C. Via French < Latin *obitus* 'death' < (*mortem*) *obire* 'die', literally 'meet (death)' < *ire* 'go']

obiter dictum /óbbitər díktəm, ōbitər-/ (*plural* **obiter dicta** /-díktə/) *n* 1. an observation made by a judge that is incidental to the case being tried and, while being authoritative, is not binding on future courts under the doctrine of precedent 2. a comment made in passing [Early 19C. < Latin, 'said by the way, said in passing']

obituary /ə bíchoo əri/ *n* (*plural* **-ies**) an announcement, especially in a newspaper, of somebody's death, often with a short biography ■ *adj* relating to or recording a death [Early 18C. < medieval Latin *obituarius* < Latin *obitus* (see OBIT)]

obj. *abbr* 1. GRAM object 2. objection 3. GRAM objective

object *n* /óbb jikt/ 1. SOMETHING VISIBLE OR TANGIBLE something that can be seen or touched 2. FOCUS a focus of somebody's attention or emotion ○ *an object of public curiosity* 3. AIM an aim or purpose ○ *What is your object in pursuing this line of questioning?* 4. SOMEBODY OR SOMETHING RIDICULOUS somebody or something ridiculous or pitiable (*informal*) 5. GRAM NOUN AFFECTED BY VERB a noun, pronoun, or noun phrase denoting somebody or something that is acted on by a verb or affected by the action of a verb 6. GRAM NOUN GOVERNED BY PREPOSITION a noun, pronoun, or noun phrase that is governed by a preposition 7. PHILOSOPHY SOMETHING PERCEIVED AND NAMED AS SEPARATE something that is perceived as an entity and referred to by a name ○ *mental objects* 8. OPTICS SOURCE OF LIGHT RAYS the point or series of points that are or appear to be the source of light rays in an optical system

9. COMPUT **UNIT OF INFORMATION** a block of information containing text or graphics that can be shared among applications. Changes subsequently made to the original information are reflected in all the documents in which it appears. 10. COMPUT **UNIT OF COMPUTER PROGRAMMING** a collection of variables, data structures, and procedures stored as an entity and forming a basic building block of object-oriented programming ■ *v* /əb jékt/ (**-jects, -jecting, -jected**) 1. *vi* **BE OPPOSED** to be opposed to something, or express opposition to it ○ *I object to being treated like a lackey.* 2. *vt* **PUT SOMETHING FORWARD AS OBJECTION** to state something as a reason for being opposed to something ○ *She objected that she would have insufficient time to prepare for the interview.* [14C. < medieval Latin *objectum* 'thing presented (to the sight)' < Latin *obicere* 'present, throw against' < *jacere* 'to throw'] —**objector** *n* ◇ **something is no object** indicates that something is not a concern or difficulty ○ *I want the best room you have – money's no object.*

SYNONYMS ***object, protest, demur, remonstrate, expostulate***

CORE MEANING: to indicate opposition to something

object to be opposed or averse to something, or express opposition to it ○ *Two companies objected strongly to the proposals.* ○ *I don't object to people smoking in the privacy of their own homes.* **protest** to express strong disapproval of or disagreement with something, or to refuse to obey or accept something, often by making a formal statement or taking action in public ○ *a noisy demonstration of several hundred workers protesting against the proposed tax* ○ *On the other side of the door, he heard Anne protesting loudly at having to meet him.* **demur** to raise objections in a hesitant or tentative way ○ *In response to Alan's offer, they at first demurred politely, but finally succumbed to his persuasion.* ○ *Janet had demurred at her aunt's room being used, especially so soon after the woman's death.* **remonstrate** to reason or argue forcefully with somebody against something ○ *'You don't mean that!' she remonstrated.* ○ *The court heard that the shop owner had remonstrated with the couple for unruly behaviour on his premises.* **expostulate** to express disagreement or disapproval vehemently, or to attempt to dissuade somebody from doing something ○ *'Look here, Peter, don't talk nonsense!' expostulated Dan.* ○ *Now and again someone would try to expostulate with the judge, but he never went back on a decision.*

object ball *n* in billiards, pool, or snooker, the ball that a player intends to hit with the cue ball

object code *n* the binary version of a computer program that is used by the computer to run the program

object complement *n UK* a noun, pronoun, or adjective that is a complement of a verb and qualifies its direct object, e.g. *angry* in 'He makes me angry'. ANZ, N Am term **objective complement**

object glass *n* OPTICS same as **objective** *n* (sense 5)

objectify /əb jékti fī/ (**-fies, -fying, -fied**) *vt* 1. to think of or represent an idea or emotion as if it were something that actually exists 2. to reduce somebody, or something that is complex and multifaceted, to the status of a simple object

objection /əb jéksh'n/ *n* 1. a feeling or expression of opposition ○ *Several people raised very pertinent objections to the plan.* 2. a reason for a feeling or expression of opposition

objectionable /əb jéksh'nəb'l/ *adj* causing disapproval, offence, or opposition ○ *an objectionable habit* —**objectionableness** *n* —**objectionably** *adv*

objective /əb jéktiv/ *adj* 1. **FREE OF BIAS** free of any bias or prejudice caused by personal feelings 2. **BASED ON FACTS** based on facts rather than thoughts or opinions 3. MED **OBSERVABLE** describes disease symptoms that can be observed by somebody other than the person who is ill 4. PHILOSOPHY **EXISTING INDEPENDENTLY OF MIND** existing independently of the individual mind or perception 5. GRAM **BEING OBJECT OF VERB** in or relating to the grammatical form (**case**) that identifies a noun or pronoun as the object of a verb ■ *n* 1. **AIM** an aim or goal 2. **MILITARY TARGET** the target or goal of a military operation 3. GRAM **OBJECTIVE CASE** the objective grammatical case 4. GRAM **NOUN IN OBJECTIVE CASE** a noun or pronoun in the objective case 5. OPTICS **LENS NEAREST OBJECT** the lens or combination of lenses in an optical instrument nearest to and facing the object being viewed —**objectiveness** *n*

objective complement *n ANZ, N Am* same as **object complement**

objective correlative *n* something in a written or performed work that is associated with a particular emotion and used to evoke it in the reader or audience

objective lens *n* OPTICS same as **objective** *n* (sense 5)

objectively /əb jéktivli/ *adv* 1. without being influenced by personal feelings 2. on the basis of fact, experience, or some measurable quality ○ *objectively derived measures such as test scores*

objectivise *vt* another spelling of **objectivize**

objectivism /əb jéktivizəm/ *n* 1. the emphasizing of external realities rather than beliefs or feelings in literature or art 2. a philosophical belief that moral truths or external objects exist independently of the individual mind or perception —**objectivist** *n, adj*

objectivity /ób jek tívvəti/ *n* 1. **ABILITY TO VIEW THINGS OBJECTIVELY** the ability to perceive or describe something without being influenced by personal emotions or prejudices 2. **ACCURACY** the fact or quality of being accurate, unbiased, and independent of individual perceptions 3. PHILOSOPHY **ACTUAL EXISTENCE** the actual existence of something, without reference to people's impressions or ideas

objectivize /əb jékti vīz/ (**-vizes, -vizing, -vized**), **objectivise** (**-vises, -vising, -vised**) *vt* same as **objectify** (sense 1)

object language *n* 1. the language that a computer interprets in running programs 2. COMPUT same as **target language** (sense 3)

object lens *n* OPTICS same as **objective** *n* (sense 5)

object lesson *n* an incident that provides an opportunity for learning something, especially the best way to do something ○ *an object lesson in tact*

object-oriented graphics *npl* computer graphics images composed of individual geometric shapes such as circles and lines which, unlike bit maps, can be changed, added to, or deleted without disturbing those remaining (*takes a plural verb*)

object-oriented programming *n* a form of computer programming based on objects arranged in a branching hierarchy

object permanence *n* the knowledge that objects have an existence in time and space, independent of whether or not they can be seen or touched

object relations *npl* a psychoanalytic theory that sees a person as motivated by a desire to form bonds with appropriate objects or people, rather than merely satisfying impulses in order to discharge tension

objet d'art /ób zhay daár/ (*plural* **objets d'art** /*pronunc. same*/) *n* an object that has artistic value, especially a small piece [Mid-19C. < French, 'object of art']

objet trouvé /ób zhay troó vay/ (*plural* **objets trouvés** /*pronunc. same*/) *n* a natural or everyday object, e.g. a pebble from a beach, treated as something of artistic value or incorporated into a work of art [Mid-20C. < French, 'found object']

objurgate /ób jur gayt/ (**-gates, -gating, -gated**) *vt* to scold somebody angrily (*literary*) [Early 17C. < Latin *objurgat-*, past participle of *objurgare* 'quarrel against' < *jurgium* 'quarrel'] —**objurgation** /ób jur gáysh'n/ *n* —**objurgator** *n* —**objurgatory** /ob júrgətəri/ *adj*

obl. *abbr* PRINTING oblique

oblast /ób laast, óbbləst/ *n* a subdivision of a republic of the former Soviet Union [Late 19C. < Russian *óblast* 'authority on' < *vlast* 'authority, power']

oblate[1] /ób layt, o bláyt/ *adj* shaped like a sphere but with the length of the diameter at the equator greater than the length from pole to pole [Early 18C. < modern Latin *oblatus* 'brought against' < Latin *latus*, past participle of *ferre* 'bring'] —**oblately** *adv* —**oblateness** *n*

oblate[2] /ób layt/ *n* in the Roman Catholic Church, a lay person who is part of a religious community [Late 17C. Via French < medieval Latin *oblatus* 'brought to' < the past participle of Latin *offerre* (see OFFER)]

oblation /o bláysh'n/ *n* 1. **OFFERING OF GIFT TO DEITY** the offering of a gift or sacrifice to a deity 2. **COMMUNION OFFERING** the offering of bread and wine to God during the Christian service of Communion 3. **RELIGIOUS OR CHARITABLE GIFT** something offered in a religious rite or as a charitable gift [15C. Directly or via Old French < late Latin *oblation-* < Latin *offerre* (see OFFER)] —**oblational** *adj*

obligate /óbbli gayt/ *vt* (**-gates, -gating, -gated**) to compel somebody to do something as a legal or moral duty ■ *adj* describes an organism that can exist only in a particular role or under particular environmental conditions [15C. < Latin *obligatus*, past participle of *obligare* (see OBLIGE)] —**obligator** /-gaytər/ *n*

obligation /óbbli gáysh'n/ *n* 1. **DUTY** something that must be done because of legal or moral duty 2. **STATE OF BEING OBLIGATED** the state of being under a moral or legal duty to do something 3. **GRATITUDE OWED** something that somebody owes in return for something given, e.g. assistance or a favour 4. LAW **BINDING LEGAL AGREEMENT** a legal agreement by which somebody is bound to do something, especially pay a specified amount of money 5. LAW **LEGAL CONTRACT** a legal document such as a mortgage or bond that contains the terms of an obligation, usually including a penalty for failing to fulfil it —**obligational** *adj*

obligato *adj, n* MUSIC another spelling of **obbligato**

obligatory /ə blíggətəri/ *adj* 1. required by law or by a moral or religious rule 2. compulsory rather than optional —**obligatorily** *adv*

oblige /ə blíj/ (**obliges, obliging, obliged**) *v* 1. *vt* **REQUIRE SOMEBODY TO DO SOMETHING** to bind somebody morally or legally to do something 2. *vt* **FORCE SOMEBODY TO DO SOMETHING** to make it necessary for somebody to do something 3. *vt* **CAUSE SOMEBODY TO FEEL INDEBTED** to cause somebody to feel indebted by doing something for that person 4. *vt* **DO FAVOUR FOR SOMEBODY** to do a favour or service for somebody ○ *Would you oblige me by closing the door?* 5. *vi* **BE HELPFUL** to do something necessary or helpful ○ *was only too happy to oblige* [13C. Via Old French *oblig(i)er* < Latin *obligare* 'tie to' < *ligare* 'to tie'] —**obliger** *n*

obligee /óbbli jeé/ *n* somebody to whom another person is legally or morally bound, e.g. by a financial debt or obligation to do something

obligement /ə blíjmənt/ *n Scotland* a favour done for or owed to somebody else

obliging /ə blíjing/ *adj* willing to be helpful or do favours —**obligingly** *adv* —**obligingness** *n*

obligor /óbbli gáwr/ *n* somebody who legally agrees to do or pay something

oblique /ə bleék/ *adj* 1. **INDIRECT** not straightforward or direct ○ *an oblique reference to the lateness of the hour* 2. **SLOPING** sloping or joining something at an angle that is not a right angle 3. MATHS **NOT PARALLEL OR PERPENDICULAR** neither perpendicular nor parallel to another line or plane 4. MATHS **NOT RIGHT-ANGLED** not being or containing a right angle or a multiple of a right angle 5. GRAM **NOT BEING SUBJECT** of or being a grammatical case of a noun or pronoun other than the nominative or vocative 6. BOT **WITH SIDES OF DIFFERENT LENGTH** describes leaves that have sides of different length 7. ANAT **NOT BEING ON ANATOMICAL PLANE** slanting away from any of the anatomical planes of the body such as the horizontal or perpendicular plane 8. GEOG **BEING AT TANGENT TO EARTH'S SURFACE** relating to or from the point of view of an oblique projection ■ *adv* MIL **CHANGING DIRECTION AT 45°** changing direction to or at an angle of 45° ■ *n* 1. **SOMETHING SLANTING** something that is oblique, e.g. a slanting line 2. PRINTING same as **slash** *n* (sense 4) 3. NAVIG **COURSE CHANGE OF LESS THAN 90°** a change of course of less than 90° ■ *vi* (**obliques, obliquing, obliqued**) 1. **TAKE OBLIQUE DIRECTION** to move or slant in an oblique direction 2. MIL **ADVANCE IN OBLIQUE DIRECTION** to move forward at an angle of 45° in a military formation [15C. < Latin *obliquus* 'slanting, sidelong'] —**obliqueness** *n*

obliquely /ə bleékli/ *adv* 1. in a way that is not direct or straightforward 2. at an angle that is not a right angle

oblique projection *n* a map projection based on a plane of projection that is at a tangent to the Earth's surface at a point between the poles and the equator

oblique-slip fault *n* a fracture in a layer of rock in which the movement is both horizontal and vertical

obliquity /ə blíkwəti/ (*plural* **-ties**) *n* 1. **STATE OF BEING OBLIQUE** the condition of being oblique 2. **DEVIATION FROM PLANE** a deviation from the horizontal or

perpendicular **3.** CHARACTER FLAW a departure from morality or reason **4.** LACK OF DIRECTNESS a lack of directness or straightforwardness in speech or conduct **5.** *also* **obliquity of the ecliptic** ASTRON ANGLE BETWEEN EARTH'S ORBIT AND EQUATOR the angle between the plane of the Earth's equator and the plane of the Earth's orbit around the Sun, approximately 23.5°

obliterate /ə blíttə rayt/ (**-ates, -ating, -ated**) *vt* **1.** to destroy something so that nothing remains **2.** to erase or obscure something completely, leaving no trace [Late 16C. < Latin *oblitterat-*, past participle of *oblitterare* 'remove letters' < *littera* 'letter'] —**obliteration** /ə blíttə ráysh'n/ *n* —**obliterative** *adj* —**obliterator** *n*

oblivion /ə blívvi ən/ *n* **1.** STATE OF BEING FORGOTTEN a state of being utterly forgotten **2.** STATE OF FORGETTING a state of complete forgetfulness or unawareness **3.** LAW OVERLOOKING OF PAST OFFENCES the deliberate overlooking of past offences [14C. Via Old French < Latin *oblivion-* < *oblivisci* 'forget']

oblivious /ə blívvi əss/ *adj* **1.** unaware of or paying no attention to somebody or something **2.** forgetting about somebody or something —**obliviously** *adv* —**obliviousness** *n*

oblong /óbb long/ *adj* having a shape that is longer than it is wide, especially a rectangular or roughly elliptical shape ■ *n* something with a length greater than its width, especially a rectangle or distorted circle [15C. < Latin *oblongus* 'rather long' < *longus* 'long']

obloquy /óbbləkwi/ *n* (*formal or literary*) **1.** statements that severely criticize or defame somebody **2.** a state of disgrace brought about by being defamed [15C. < late Latin *obloquium* 'talking against' < *loqui* 'to talk']

obnoxious /əb nókshəss/ *adj* very offensive and unpleasant ○ *obnoxious stench* [Late 16C. < Latin *obnoxius* 'vulnerable to harm' < *noxa* 'harm'] —**obnoxiously** *adv* —**obnoxiousness** *n*

o.b.o. *abbr* or best offer (*used in advertisements*)

oboe /ṓbō/ *n* **1.** a woodwind instrument that produces a penetrating high sound and consists of a slim tube of conical bore with a double reed and keys operated by the fingers **2.** somebody who plays an oboe [Late 17C. Via Italian < French *hautbois* (see HAUTBOY)] —**oboist** *n*

oboe da caccia /-də káchə/ *n* an early form of oboe from which the cor anglais was developed [Late 19C. < Italian, 'hunting oboe']

oboe d'amore /-da máwray/ *n* an oboe used mainly in baroque music that has a lower pitch than the standard instrument [Late 19C. < Italian, 'oboe of love']

obol /óbbol/, **obolus** /óbbələss/ (*plural* **-li** /óbbə lī/) *n* a coin or unit of weight used in ancient Greece, equal to one sixth of a drachma [Mid-17C. Via Latin < Greek *obolos*, variant of *obelos* 'spit']

Obon /ō bón/ *n* in Japan, a Buddhist festival celebrating All Souls. Date: 13 to 31 July.

Obote /o bṓt ay, o bṓti/, **Milton** (*b.* 1925) prime minister (1962–66) and president (1966–71 and 1980–85) of Uganda. He was overthrown by Idi Amin in 1971 and ousted a second time in 1985, when he fled to Zambia. Full name **Obote, Apollo Milton**

obovate /ob ṓ vayt/ *adj* describes leaves that are oval with the narrow end at the base

obovoid /ob ṓ voyd/ *adj* describes fruits that are egg-shaped, with the narrow end at the base

obruk /ób rŏŏk/ *n* in the 18th century, work obligations owed by Russian peasants to either their aristocratic landlords or the state

obs. *abbr* **1.** obscure **2.** observation **3.** ASTRON observatory **4.** obsolete **5.** MED obstetrics

Obs. *abbr* ASTRON Observatory

obscene /əb séen/ *adj* **1.** INDECENT offensive to conventional standards of decency, especially by being sexually explicit **2.** DISGUSTING disgusting and morally offensive, especially through an apparent total disregard for others' rights or natural justice **3.** LAW LIKELY TO DEPRAVE AND CORRUPT describes publications that are considered likely to deprave and corrupt people [Late 16C. Via French < Latin *obscenus* 'ill-omened'] —**obscenely** *adv*

obscenity /əb sénnəti/ (*plural* **-ties**) *n* **1.** INDECENCY offensiveness to conventional standards of decency, especially as a result of sexual explicitness **2.** OBSCENE EXPRESSION a word, phrase, or statement that is offensive, especially because of being sexually explicit **3.** SOMETHING OBSCENE something that is disgusting and morally offensive

obscurantist /ób skyŏŏ rántist/ *adj* opposing or hindering the spread of new ideas and new social or political developments —**obscurant** /əb skyŏŏrənt/ *adj, n* —**obscurantism** *n* —**obscurantist** *n*

obscure /əb skyŏŏr/ *adj* **1.** HARD TO UNDERSTAND difficult to understand because of not being fully or clearly expressed ○ *an obscure passage in the manuscript* **2.** INDISTINCT not able to be seen or heard distinctly ○ *Its outlines are obscure, but the object seems roughly cigar-shaped.* **3.** UNIMPORTANT OR UNKNOWN not important or well-known ○ *an obscure portrait painter* **4.** KNOWN TO FEW PEOPLE unknown to most people, e.g. because of being hidden or remote **5.** DIM dark, shadowy, or clouded ○ *an obscure corner of the hall* **6.** LING UNSTRESSED describes a vowel that has a neutral, unstressed pronunciation (*technical*) ■ *vt* (**-scures, -scuring, -scured**) **1.** MAKE UNCLEAR to make something unclear, indistinct, or hidden **2.** DARKEN to make something dark or cover something with cloud [14C. Via Old French < Latin *obscurus* 'covered over' < *-scurus* 'covered'] —**obscuration** /ób skyŏŏ ráysh'n/ *n* —**obscureness** *n*

SYNONYMS ***obscure, abstruse, recondite, arcane, cryptic, enigmatic, esoteric***

CORE MEANING: difficult to understand

obscure difficult to understand because of not being fully or clearly expressed ○ *a rather obscure branch of mathematics called graph theory* ○ *a notion which may at first seem somewhat obscure* **abstruse** not easy to understand, often because it involves specialist knowledge or is expressed in specialist language ○ *songs with abstruse titles* ○ *He is so occupied with abstruse ideas that he is incapable of coping with everyday activities.* **recondite** requiring a high degree of scholarship or specialist knowledge to be understood ○ *an excellent tutor, with an obvious knowledge of an often recondite subject* **arcane** requiring information that is secret or known only to a few people in order to be understood ○ *The current pay structure is arcane and outdated.* ○ *He had drawn several arcane symbols round the boundary of the circle.* **cryptic** deliberately mysterious or ambiguous and seeming to have a hidden meaning ○ *cryptic clues* ○ *a fax in cryptic language* **enigmatic** having a quality of mystery and ambiguity that makes it difficult to understand or interpret ○ *his enigmatic smile* ○ *the brilliant and enigmatic figure of Thomas à Becket* **esoteric** understood by or intended for only an initiated few. ○ *He was employed as a church architect and was later dismissed because of his esoteric interest in Paganism and the occult.* ○ *dictionaries for more esoteric or specialist domains*

obscurely /əb skyŏŏrli/ *adv* **1.** UNCLEARLY in a way that is not clear, definite, or easy to understand **2.** DIMLY dimly or indistinctly **3.** AWAY FROM PEOPLE'S ATTENTION in a place or position that is remote, secluded, or not prominent or well known

obscurity /əb skyŏŏrəti/ (*plural* **-ties**) *n* **1.** STATE OF BEING UNKNOWN a state of being unknown or inconspicuous ○ *plucked from obscurity to star in a Broadway musical* **2.** UNCLEARNESS lack of clarity or difficulty in being understood **3.** SOMEBODY OR SOMETHING OBSCURE an obscure person or thing

~~obsene~~ incorrect spelling of **obscene**

obsequent /óbssikwənt/ *adj* describes a river, stream, or drainage system that flows into a subsidiary (**subsequent**) river in a direction contrary to that of the flow of the main (**consequent**) river [Late 19C. < Latin *obsequent-*, present participle of *obsequi* 'comply', literally 'follow towards' < *sequi* 'follow']

obsequies /óbssi kwiz/ *npl* rites or ceremonies carried out at a funeral [14C. Via Anglo-Norman < late Latin *obsequiae*, alteration (influenced by *obsequium* 'compliance') of *exequiae* 'those following out (to the grave)' < *exsequi* (see EXECUTE)]

obsequious /əb séekwi əss/ *adj* excessively eager to please or obey [15C. < Latin *obsequiosus* < *obsequium* 'compliance'] —**obsequiously** *adv* —**obsequiousness** *n*

observable /əb zúrvəb'l/ *adj* able to be seen or detected ■ *n* something that can be measured or observed directly, e.g. temperature —**observability** /əb zúrvə bíllәti/ *n*

observably /əb zúrvəbli/ *adv* in a way or to an extent that can be seen or detected

observance /əb zúrvənss/ *n* **1.** COMPLIANCE the execution of or compliance with laws, instructions, or customs **2.** RITUAL a custom, ritual, or ceremony, especially a religious one **3.** PERFORMANCE OF RELIGIOUS CEREMONIES the celebration of a religious occasion, or the practice of a religious rite, ceremony, or action **4.** RELIGIOUS RULE a rule of a religious order **5.** OBSERVATION careful watching or close attention

USAGE **observance** or **observation**? These two words share the meaning 'close attention', though ***observation*** is much more common: *our observation of the habits of the condor; the child's observance of the waving flags.* If you refer to 'compliance', 'ritual', 'celebration of religious rites', or 'a rule of a religious order', the only word to use is ***observance***, as in *observance* [not *observation*] *of the law; church observances* [not *observations*] *such as baptism and Communion; followed the observances* [not *observations*] *of the Jesuit order.* If you refer to 'a remark or comment' or 'a record of something seen or studied', ***observation*** is the correct choice: *made a few casual observations* [not *observances*] *about the foul weather; astronomical observations* [not *observances*] *in one volume.*

observant /əb zúrvənt/ *adj* **1.** paying such careful attention that little or nothing is unnoticed **2.** carrying out rituals or obeying laws, especially religious ones —**observantly** *adv*

observation /óbzər váysh'n/ *n* **1.** PAYING ATTENTION the attentive watching of somebody or something **2.** OBSERVING OF DEVELOPMENTS IN SOMETHING the careful watching and recording of something, e.g. a natural phenomenon, as it happens **3.** RECORD OF SOMETHING SEEN OR NOTED the result or record of observing something such as a natural phenomenon and noting developments **4.** REMARK OR COMMENT a remark or comment on something that has been noticed **5.** ACT OF OBSERVING OR OBEYING the act of observing a religious occasion or ritual or of obeying a law or rule **6.** NAVIG SIGHTING WITH NAVIGATIONAL INSTRUMENT a sighting with a navigational instrument to establish the observer's position in relation to an astronomical object such as the Sun **7.** NAVIG NAVIGATIONAL INSTRUMENT READING the reading taken from a navigational instrument that has been used to find the observer's position in relation to an astronomical object —**observational** *adj* —**observationally** *adv*

USAGE See ***observance***.

observation car *n* a railway carriage fitted with extra or larger windows and often a partly transparent roof to allow passengers a better view of passing scenery

observation post *n* a position from which soldiers can watch enemy movements and direct artillery fire

observatory /əb zúrvətəri/ (*plural* **-ries**) *n* **1.** a building, station, or artificial satellite used for scientific observation of natural phenomena such as astronomical objects, the weather, or earthquakes **2.** a place or building that commands an expansive view

observe /əb zúrv/ (**-serves, -serving, -served**) *v* **1.** *vt* NOTICE SOMETHING to see or notice something, especially while watching carefully ○ *You were observed entering the building.* **2.** *vti* WATCH SOMETHING ATTENTIVELY to watch somebody or something attentively, especially for scientific purposes ○ *I have been observing his movements for the last half hour.* **3.** *vti* OFFICIALLY WITNESS SOMETHING to be an official witness to something without taking an active part in it ○ *A UN delegation was present to observe the signing of the treaty.* **4.** *vi* BE SPECTATOR to watch something without taking part **5.** *vt* COMMENT ON SOMETHING to make a comment or remark on something seen or noticed ○ *'Your aim is definitely improving', she observed.* **6.** *vt* COMPLY WITH SOMETHING to carry out or comply with something such as a law or custom **7.** *vt* CELEBRATE FESTIVAL to celebrate or keep a religious or traditional festival [14C. Via Old French *observer* < Latin *observare* 'watch towards' < *servare* 'to watch']

observer /əb zúrvər/ *n* **1.** SOMEBODY WHO SEES OR WATCHES SOMETHING somebody who observes something that is

happening **2. NONPARTICIPATING WITNESS** somebody who acts as a witness to an event, often officially and at the invitation of the participants **3. SOMEBODY OBSERVING CEREMONY OR OBEYING LAW** somebody who duly celebrates a religious ceremony or ritual, or complies with a rule or law **4. AIR FORCE AIRCRAFT IDENTIFIER** somebody trained in identifying aircraft **5. MIL WATCHER OF ENEMY MOVEMENTS** a soldier who watches enemy movements or directs artillery fire

observingly /əb zúrvingli/ *adv* in an attentive or considering manner

obsess /əb séss/ (**-sesses, -sessing, -sessed**) *v* **1.** *vt* to occupy somebody's thoughts constantly and exclusively ○ *The desire for vengeance obsesses him.* **2.** *vi N Am* to think or worry about something constantly and compulsively [Early 16C. < Latin *obsess-*, past participle of *obsidere* 'besiege', literally 'sit opposite to' < *sedere* 'sit']

obsession /əb sésh'n/ *n* **1. PREOCCUPATION** an idea or feeling that completely occupies the mind ○ *His obsession with figures led him to make crucial economic mistakes.* **2. STATE OF BEING OBSESSED** the state of being obsessed by somebody or something ○ *Their devotion to each other borders on obsession.* **3. PSYCHIAT UNCONTROLLABLE PERSISTENCE OF IDEA** the uncontrollable persistence of an idea or emotion in the mind, sometimes associated with psychiatric disorder — **obsessional** *adj* —**obsessionally** *adv*

obsessive /əb séssiv/ *adj* **1.** amounting to an obsession or as strong as an obsession **2.** worrying compulsively about something or things generally —**obsessive** *n* —**obsessively** *adv* —**obsessiveness** *n*

obsessive-compulsive *adj* with or characteristic of obsessive-compulsive disorder ■ *n* somebody with obsessive-compulsive disorder

obsessive-compulsive disorder *n* a psychiatric disorder characterized by obsessive thoughts and compulsive behaviour such as continual washing of the hands prompted by a feeling of uncleanliness

obsidian /ob síddi ən/ *n* a jet-black volcanic glass, chemically similar to granite and formed by the rapid cooling of molten lava, that was used by early civilizations for manufacturing tools and ceremonial objects [14C. < Latin *(lapis) Obsidianus*, copyist's error for *Obsianus* '(stone) of Obsius', a Roman]

obsolesce /óbssə léss/ (**-lesces, -lescing, -lesced**) *vi* to become obsolete [Late 19C. < Latin *obsolescere* (see OBSOLESCENT)]

obsolescent /óbssə léss'nt/ *adj* in the process of becoming obsolete [Mid-18C. < Latin *obsolescent-*, present participle of *obsolere* 'wear out' < *solere* 'be accustomed'] —**obsolescence** *n* —**obsolescently** *adv*

obsolete /óbssə leet, óbssə léet/ *adj* **1. NOT USED ANY MORE** no longer in use **2. OUT-OF-DATE** superseded by something newer, though possibly still in use **3. BIOL UNDEVELOPED** describes a part or organ of an animal or plant that is undeveloped or no longer functional [Late 16C. < Latin *obsoletus*, past participle of *obsolescere* (see OBSOLESCENT)] —**obsoletely** *adv*

SYNONYMS See *old-fashioned.*

obstacle /óbstək'l/ *n* **1. HINDRANCE** somebody or something that hinders or prevents progress **2. SOMETHING IN WAY** something that blocks or impedes a road, passage, or somebody's way **3. HURDLE** a fence or hedge set up for horses to jump over in showjumping [14C. Via Old French < Latin *obstaculum* < *obstare* 'stand in the way' < *stare* 'to stand']

obstacle course *n* **1.** an area similar to a military assault course, used by competitors in an obstacle race **2.** *Aus, N Am* a training area where soldiers have to get past various obstacles such as ditches or high walls as quickly as possible. UK term **assault course**

obstacle race *n* a race in which competitors have to get past a range of obstacles

obstet. *abbr MED* **1.** obstetric **2.** obstetrics

obstetric /ob stéttrik/ *adj* relating to childbirth or obstetrics [Mid-18C. < Latin *obstetricius* 'of a midwife' < *obstetric-* 'midwife', literally 'woman who is present, stands before' < *stare* 'stand']

obstetrician /óbstə trísh'n/ *n* a doctor who specializes

in pregnancy, delivering babies, and the care of women after childbirth

obstetrics /ob stéttriks/ *n* the branch of medicine that deals with the care of women during pregnancy and childbirth, and for some six weeks following delivery (*takes a singular verb*)

~~**obsticle**~~ incorrect spelling of **obstacle**

obstinate /óbstinət/ *adj* **1. STUBBORN** determined not to agree to other people's wishes or accept their suggestions **2. REFUSING TO CHANGE** unwilling to change or give up something such as an idea or attitude **3. DIFFICULT TO CONTROL** difficult to control, get rid of, solve, or cure ○ *an obstinate blockage in the pipe* [14C. < Latin *obstinatus*, past participle of *obstinare* 'be resolved', literally 'stand by' < *stare* 'to stand'] —**obstinacy** *n* —**obstinately** *adv*

obstipation /óbsti páysh'n/ *n* severe constipation, often caused by a blockage in the intestines [Late 16C. < late Latin *obstipation-* 'pressing in the way of' < *stipare* 'to press']

obstreperous /əb stréppərəss/ *adj* **1.** noisily and aggressively boisterous **2.** strongly objecting to something or noisily refusing to be controlled [Late 16C. < Latin *obstreperus* 'clamorous', literally 'rattling against' < *strepere* 'to rattle'] —**obstreperously** *adv* —**obstreperousness** *n*

SYNONYMS See *unruly.*

obstruct /əb strúkt/ (**-structs, -structing, -structed**) *vt* **1. PREVENT CLEAR PASSAGE** to cause a blockage in a road, course, or passage **2. SLOW SOMEBODY OR SOMETHING DOWN** to cause a serious delay in action or progress **3. IMPEDE VIEW** to be in the way and prevent a clear view of something [Early 17C. < Latin *obstructus*, past participle of *obstruere* 'build up against' < *struere* 'heap up, pile'] —**obstructor** *n*

SYNONYMS See *hinder*[1].

obstruction /əb strúksh'n/ *n* **1. BLOCK OR HINDRANCE** somebody or something that causes or forms a blockage or hindrance **2. ACT OF BLOCKING** an act of blocking or hindering somebody or something **3. STATE OF BEING BLOCKED** the state of being obstructed **4. DELAYING OF SOMETHING** the deliberate delaying of the business of something such as a legislative body **5. UNFAIR IMPEDING OF OPPONENT** in football and other sports, the unfair impeding of an opposing player or competitor

obstructionist /əb strúksh'nist/ *adj* deliberately causing delay or impeding progress —**obstructionism** *n* —**obstructionist** *n* —**obstructionistic** /əb strúksh'n ístik/ *adj*

obstruction of justice *n US* the criminal offence of obstructing the administration and process of the law

obstructive /əb strúktiv/ *adj* **1.** hindering or preventing the progress of something **2.** relating to or caused by the obstruction of a passage in the body — **obstructively** *adv* —**obstructiveness** *n*

obstructive sleep apnoea *n* cessation or restriction of breathing during sleep that results in loud snoring

obstruent /óbb stroo ənt/ *adj* **1. MED OBSTRUCTING BODY PASSAGE** obstructing or closing a passage in the body such as the intestinal tract **2. PHON PRODUCED BY CUTOFF OF AIR** describes a speech sound produced by a stoppage of air from the lungs ■ *n* **1. MED OBSTRUCTION** something that obstructs or closes a passage in the body **2. PHON SOUND PRODUCED BY CUTOFF OF AIR** a speech sound produced by a stoppage of air from the lungs [Mid-17C. < Latin *obstruent-*, present participle of *obstruere* (see OBSTRUCT)]

obtain /əb táyn/ (**-tains, -taining, -tained**) *v* **1.** *vt* **GET SOMETHING** to get possession of something, especially by making an effort or having the necessary qualifications **2.** *vi* **BE ESTABLISHED** to be established, valid, or current ○ *under the regulations that obtained at the time* **3.** *vi* **RESULT** to follow as a result (*formal*) ○ *the unfortunate situation that obtains when such diverse characters are forced together* [15C. Via Old French *obtenir* < Latin *obtinere* 'hold to' < *tenere* 'to hold'] —**obtainer** *n* —**obtainment** *n*

SYNONYMS See *get*[1].

obtainable /əb táynəb'l/ *adj* able to be obtained or reached —**obtainability** /əb táynə bíll'ti/ *n*

obtrude /əb tróod, ob-/ (**-trudes, -truding, -truded**) *v* **1.** *vti* **IMPOSE** to impose something such as opinions or yourself on other people **2.** *vt* **MAKE SOMETHING STICK OUT** to push something out or forwards **3.** *vi* **APPEAR UNWELCOME** to appear or be present in a way that is unwelcome but cannot be ignored ○*Not a leaf stirred; not a sound obtruded upon great Nature's meditation.'* (Mark Twain, *The Adventures of Tom Sawyer*; 1875) [Mid-16C. < Latin *obtrudere* 'thrust against' < *trudere* 'to thrust'] —**obtruder** *n* —**obtrusion** /əb tróozh'n/ *n*

obtrusive /əb tróossiv/ *adj* **1. ANNOYING** tending to intrude or force opinions on other people ○ *plagued by an obtrusive photographer* **2. HIGHLY NOTICEABLE** highly noticeable, often with a bad or unwelcome effect **3. STICKING OUT** projecting or sticking out [Mid-17C. < Latin *obtrusus*, past participle of *obtrudere* (see OBTRUDE)] —**obtrusively** *adv* —**obtrusiveness** *n*

obtund /ob túnd/ (**-tunds, -tunding, -tunded**) *vt* to blunt, dull, or deaden something (*dated*) [14C. < Latin *obtundere* 'strike against' < *tundere* 'to strike'] —**obtundent** *adj*

obtuse /əb tyóoss/ *adj* **1. SLOW TO UNDERSTAND** slow to understand or perceive something **2. MATHS BETWEEN 90° AND 180°** describes an angle greater than 90° and less than 180° **3. MATHS WITH INTERNAL ANGLE GREATER THAN 90°** describes a triangle with one internal angle greater than 90° **4. BLUNT** not sharp or pointed **5. BOT WITH ROUNDED OR BLUNT TIP** describes a leaf that has a rounded or blunt tip [Early 16C. < Latin *obtusus* 'blunted', past participle of *obtundere* (see OBTUND)] —**obtusely** *adv* —**obtuseness** *n*

OBTW *abbr* oh, by the way (*used in e-mails or text messages*)

obverse /ób vurss/ *n* **1. MAIN SIDE OF COIN OR MEDAL** the side of a coin or medal that has the more important design on it, especially a head **2. COUNTERPART** a counterpart, complement, or opposite **3. LOGIC EQUIVALENT CATEGORICAL PROPOSITION** a proposition derived from another proposition by denying it and then negating the predicate. The obverse of 'Everything is possible' is 'Nothing is impossible'. ■ *adj* **1. VISIBLE** facing an observer **2. BEING COUNTERPART** forming a counterpart to something else **3. BOT NARROWER AT BASE** describes a leaf that is narrower at the base than the tip [Mid-17C. < Latin *obversus*, past participle of *obvertere* (see OBVERT)]

obversion /ob vúrsh'n/ *n* **1.** the process of turning something so that the other side is seen **2.** LOGIC the process of forming the obverse of a proposition

obvert /ob vúrt/ (**-verts, -verting, -verted**) *vt* **1.** to turn something such as a coin or medal so that the other side is seen **2.** LOGIC to convert a proposition to its obverse [Early 17C. < Latin *obvertere* 'turn towards' < *vertere* 'to turn']

obviate /óbvi ayt/ (**-ates, -ating, -ated**) *vt* **1.** to make something unnecessary (*formal*) **2.** to anticipate and so avoid something [Late 16C. < Latin *obviat-*, past participle of *obviare* 'withstand', literally 'stand in the way of' < *via* 'way'] —**obviation** /óbvi áysh'n/ *n*

USAGE obviate the need for: Because one of the meanings of *obviate* is 'to make unnecessary', it is sometimes argued that *obviate the need* (or *necessity*) *for* involves redundancy. An older but still current meaning, however, is 'to avoid an anticipated difficulty'. In a sentence like *Addressing these issues early can obviate any need for a joint resolution,* the need can be perceived as a difficulty — or early consideration can make the resolution unnecessary, in which case *any need for* is indeed redundant. There is little reason to prefer either interpretation to the other, except that the meaning 'to make unnecessary' allows much the same thought to be expressed with fewer words.

obvious /óbvi əss/ *adj* **1.** easy to see or understand because not concealed, difficult, or ambiguous **2.** lacking subtlety or any attempt at concealment [Late 16C. < Latin *obvius* 'in the way' < *via* 'way'] —**obviousness** *n*

obviously /óbvi əssli/ *adv* **1.** in a way or to an extent that is obvious **2.** used to suggest that there can be no doubt or uncertainty about something ○ *They want you to do it, obviously.*

obvolute /óbvə loot/ *adj* describes leaves or petals that are folded so as to overlap each other [Mid-18C. < Latin *obvolutus*, past participle of *obvolvere* 'wrap round']

< *volvere* 'to roll'] —**obvolution** /óbvə loósh'n/ *n* —**obvolutive** *adj*

OC *abbr* **1.** MIL Officer Commanding **2.** STAMPS original cover

Oc., oc. *abbr* GEOG Ocean

o.c. *abbr* in the work cited [Latin *opere citato*]

o/c *abbr* overcharge

oca /ókə/ *n* **1.** an edible tuber with firm white flesh **2.** a bushy plant whose edible tubers are oca. Native to: the Andes Mountains of South America. Latin name: *Oxalis tuberosa*. [Early 17C. Via Spanish < Quechua *ócca*]

OCAM *abbr* African and Malagasy Common Organization *n*

O Canada *n* the national anthem of Canada

ocarina /ókə reénə/ *n* a simple wind instrument related to the flute that has an oval body, finger holes, and a protruding mouthpiece [Late 19C. < Italian, 'little goose' (< its shape) < *oca* 'goose' < Latin *avis* 'bird']

~~occasionaly~~ incorrect spelling of **occasionally**

occ. *abbr* **1.** GEOG occident **2.** occupation

Occam's razor *n* PHILOSOPHY, SCI another spelling of **Ockham's razor**

occas. *abbr* **1.** occasional **2.** occasionally

occasion /ə káyzh'n/ *n* **1.** PARTICULAR TIME a particular time, especially a time when something happens **2.** CHANCE OR OPPORTUNITY a chance or opportunity to do something ○ *You might never have another occasion to do it.* **3.** CAUSE OR REASON a cause of or reason for something ○ *He has no occasion to criticize me.* **4.** NEED the need for something or to do something ○ *has never had occasion to use it* **5.** IMPORTANT EVENT an important or special event ■ *vt* (**-sions, -sioning, -sioned**) BRING SOMETHING ABOUT to cause or lead to something [14C. Via Old French < Latin *occasion-* 'falling down, happening' < *cadere* 'to fall'] ◇ **on occasion** from time to time

occasional /ə káyzh'nəl/ *adj* **1.** INFREQUENT occurring infrequently at irregular intervals **2.** RELATING TO SPECIAL EVENT done for or connected with a special event ○ *occasional verse* **3.** DESIGNED FOR USE FROM TIME TO TIME intended for use as needed, but not essential or in constant use ○ *an occasional table* **4.** CAUSING serving as the cause of something (*formal*)

SYNONYMS See *periodic*.

occasionally /ə káyzh'nəli/ *adv* from time to time, but not regularly or frequently

occident /óksidənt/ *n* the western part of the sky, where the sun sets (*formal*) [14C. Via French < Latin *occident-*, present participle of *occidere* 'fall down, set (of the sun)' < *cadere* 'to fall']

Occident *n* the western hemisphere, especially the countries in Europe and America (*dated formal*)

occidental /óksi dént'l/ *adj* western (*formal*)

Occidental (*dated formal*) *adj* relating to a country of the Occident, or its people or culture ■ *n* somebody who comes from the West

occidentalize /óksi déntə līz/ (**-izes, -izing, -ized**), **occidentalise** (**-ises, -ising, -ised**) *vt* to make somebody or something conform to the culture of the West (*dated formal*)

occipita ANAT plural of **occiput**

occipital /ok síppit'l/ *adj* relating to or located at the back of the head or skull ■ *n* ANAT same as **occipital bone** [Mid-16C. < medieval Latin *occipitalis* < Latin *occiput* (see OCCIPUT)]

occipital bone *n* the saucer-shaped bone at the rear of the skull that connects with the spinal column and has an opening at its base through which the spinal cord passes

occipital lobe *n* the pyramid-shaped area at the back of each hemisphere of the brain that deals with the interpretation of vision

occiput /óksi put, óksipət/ (*plural* **-ciputs** or **-cipita** /-síppitə/) *n* the back part of the head or skull [14C. < Latin, 'back of the head' < *caput* 'head']

occlude /ə klood/ (**-cludes, -cluding, -cluded**) *v* **1.** *vt* STOP UP SOMETHING to block or stop up something such as a passage **2.** *vt* CUT OFF FLOW OF SOMETHING to cut off or

prevent the flow or passage of something such as light or liquid **3.** *vti* DENT ALIGN TEETH PROPERLY to be in normal contact with another tooth when the mouth is closed, or align the upper and lower teeth for chewing or normal contact **4.** *vt* CHEM ABSORB OR ADSORB LIQUID to absorb or adsorb a liquid or gas on the surface of or within a solid **5.** *vti* METEOROL FORM OCCLUDED FRONT to form an occluded front, or undercut a mass of warm air so that it is no longer in contact with the Earth's surface [Late 16C. < Latin *occludere* 'close up' < *claudere* 'to close']

occluded front /ə kloodid-/ *n* a composite front formed when a cold air mass meets and undercuts a warm air mass, and forces the warm air upwards and away from contact with the Earth's surface

occlusal /ə klooz'l/ *adj* relating to the biting surface of a molar or premolar tooth

occlusion /ə kloozh'n/ *n* **1.** ACT OF OCCLUDING an act of occluding or the condition of being occluded **2.** OBSTRUCTION something that obstructs or occludes **3.** METEOROL same as **occluded front 4.** DENT MEETING OF UPPER AND LOWER TEETH the relation between the upper and lower teeth when the jaw is closed and their surfaces come in contact **5.** LING CLOSURE OF HOLLOW ORGAN the closure of a hollow organ such as the vocal tract in articulating a speech sound **6.** CHEM ABSORPTION OR ADSORPTION OF LIQUID the absorption or adsorption of a liquid or gas on or in a solid [Mid-17C. < Latin *occlus-*, past participle of *occludere* (see OCCLUDE)]

occlusive /ə kloossiv/ *adj* relating to, involving, or producing an occlusion ■ *n* a speech sound that involves a closure of the vocal tract

occult /ó kult, o kúlt/ *adj* **1.** SUPERNATURAL OR MAGIC relating to, involving, or characteristic of magic, witchcraft, or supernatural phenomena **2.** NOT UNDERSTANDABLE not capable of being understood by ordinary human beings **3.** SECRET secret or known only to the initiated **4.** MED HIDDEN describes a diseased condition that is hidden or difficult to detect **5.** MED DIFFICULT TO SEE not visible to the naked eye, and only detectable by microscope or chemical testing ■ *n* THE SUPERNATURAL the realm of magic, witchcraft, or supernatural phenomena ■ *vti* (**-cults, -culting, -culted**) **1.** ASTRON TEMPORARILY HIDE ASTRONOMICAL OBJECT to hide an astronomical object temporarily by moving between it and an observer, or be hidden in this way **2.** HIDE SOMETHING OR BE HIDDEN to hide something from view or be hidden from view [Early 16C. < Latin *occultus*, past participle of *occulere* 'conceal'] —**occultation** /ókul táysh'n, ók'l-/ *n* —**occultly** *adv* —**occultness** *n*

occultism /ó kultizəm, ók'ltizəm, o kúltizəm/ *n* the belief in and study of magic, witchcraft, or supernatural phenomena —**occultist** *n*

occupancy /ókyoopənssi/ (*plural* **-cies**) *n* **1.** ACT OF OCCUPYING the act or state of occupying something such as a building or an official position **2.** LEVEL OF OCCUPATION the rate or level of occupation of a place ○ *a block of flats with high occupancy* **3.** TIME OF OCCUPYING the period of time during which somebody occupies something such as a building or an official position **4.** LAW USE WITHOUT OWNERSHIP the use and possession of property without claiming ownership of it **5.** LAW POSSESSION OF UNOWNED PROPERTY the act of taking possession of property, especially land, that has no owner, with the intention of becoming its owner

occupant /ókyoopənt/ *n* **1.** a resident of a place or holder of a position **2.** somebody who takes possession of unclaimed property, especially land, with the intention of becoming its owner

occupation /ókyoo páysh'n/ *n* **1.** JOB the job by which somebody earns a living **2.** ACTIVITY an activity on which time is spent **3.** ACT OF OCCUPYING an act of occupying or the state of being occupied **4.** MIL INVASION the invasion and control of a country or area by enemy forces **5.** TIME OF OCCUPYING the period of time during which something is occupied

occupational /ókyoo pásh'nəl/ *adj* relating to or caused by somebody's job —**occupationally** *adv*

occupational disease *n* a disease that is directly caused by the conditions of somebody's work

occupational hazard *n* a risk associated with the work that somebody does

occupational medicine *n* the branch of medicine

that deals with work-related diseases and injuries incurred at work

occupational pension *n* a pension paid to an employee or former employee from a scheme set up by an employer, not the state

occupational therapy *n* the use of regular periods of suitable productive activity as part of the treatment of illness or medical condition —**occupational therapist** *n*

occupation groupings *npl* the categories, e.g. C1 or C2, that people can be put into according to their occupation, formerly used in the advertising industry to define target markets

occupy /ókyoo pī/ (**-pies, -pying, -pied**) *vt* **1.** LIVE IN PLACE to live in or be the established user of a place such as a home or office **2.** ENGAGE SOMEBODY'S ATTENTION to take up somebody's time or attention (*often passive*) ○ *something to occupy his leisure hours* **3.** FILL SPACE OR TIME to take up a space or an amount of time (*often passive*) ○ *His rambling speech occupied a good part of the hour.* **4.** MIL TAKE OVER PLACE to invade and take control of a country, area, or building **5.** HOLD POSITION to hold a post or rank [14C. Via Old French *occuper* < Latin *occupare* 'take over' < *capere* 'to take'] —**occupier** *n*

occur /ə kúr/ (**-curs, -curring, -curred**) *vi* **1.** HAPPEN to happen or come about **2.** EXIST to exist or be present **3.** ENTER MIND to come into somebody's mind ○ *It didn't occur to him to lock the door.* [Early 16C. < Latin *occurrere* 'run against' < *currere* 'to run']

~~occurance~~ incorrect spelling of **occurrence**

~~occured~~ incorrect spelling of **occurred**

occurrence /ə kúrrənss/ *n* **1.** something that happens **2.** the fact or act of something happening —**occurrent** *adj*

OCD *abbr* PSYCHIAT obsessive-compulsive disorder

WORLD'S LARGEST OCEANS AND SEAS

#	Ocean/Sea	Area
1	Pacific Ocean	[64 million sq. mi./165.7 million sq. km]
2	Atlantic Ocean	[31.8 million sq. mi./82 million sq. km]
3	Indian Ocean	[28.3 million sq. mi./73.4 million sq. km]
4	Arctic Ocean	[5.4 million sq. mi./14 million sq. km]
5	Gulf of Mexico and Caribbean Sea	[1.6 million sq. mi./4.2 million sq. km]
6	Mediterranean Sea	[0.97 million sq. mi./2.5 million sq. km]
7	Bering Sea	[0.87 million sq. mi./2.26 million sq. km]
8	Sea of Okhotsk	[0.59 million sq. mi./1.53 million sq. km]
9	Hudson Bay	[0.48 million sq. mi./1.2 million sq. km]
10	Sea of Japan	[0.39 million sq. mi./1 million sq. km]

ocean /ósh'n/ *n* **1.** LARGE SEA a large expanse of salt water, especially any of the Earth's five main seas, the Atlantic, Pacific, Indian, Arctic, and Antarctic oceans. The oceans occupy huge regions of the Earth's surface, and their boundaries are usually established by continental land masses and ridges in the ocean floor. **2.** EARTH'S SEAS TOGETHER the whole body of salt water on the Earth **3.** LARGE AMOUNT a vast amount or expanse of something [13C. Via French and Latin < Greek *ōkeanos*, the river surrounding the disc of the Earth]

oceanarium /ṓshə náiri əm/ (plural **-iums** or **-ia** /-i ə/) n a large saltwater aquarium for observing and exhibiting sea animals and plants [Mid-20C. Blend of OCEAN + AQUARIUM]

oceanaut /ṓshə nawt/ n an underwater swimmer in an ocean who uses an aqualung [Mid-20C. Blend of OCEAN + AQUANAUT]

oceanfront /ṓsh'n frunt/ n **1.** land along the seashore (often used before a noun) ○ oceanfront property **2.** the point at which two oceanic water masses of different thermal characteristics meet

oceangoing /ṓsh'n gō ing/ adj built, equipped, or used for travel on the ocean

ocean greyhound n a fast ocean liner

Oceania /ṓssi áaniə, ṓshi-/ geographical region consisting of most of the smaller islands of the western and central Pacific Ocean, sometimes also including Australia and New Zealand —**Oceanian** n, adj

oceanic /ṓshi ánnik, ṓssi-/ adj **1. IN OR FROM OCEAN** living, situated in, produced by, or taking place in an ocean, especially the depths of the open sea **2. VOLCANIC** resulting from volcanic activity in the ocean ○ an oceanic island **3. IMMENSE** immense, vast, or overwhelming [Mid-17C. < OCEAN]

Oceanic /ṓshi ánnik, ṓssi-/ n an Austronesian group of languages spoken mainly on the Pacific islands lying to the north and east of Australia. Native speakers: 2 million. ■ adj relating to the countries of Oceania [Mid-19C. < OCEANIA]

oceanic ridge n any section of a range of underwater mountains, found in all major oceans

oceanic trench n a long narrow deep furrow in the Earth's crust at the bottom of an ocean

Ocean Island former name for **Banaba**

ocean liner n an oceangoing passenger ship run by a shipping line

oceanography /ṓshə nóggrəfi, ṓshi ə-/ n the scientific study of oceans, including their chemistry, biology, and geology —**oceanographer** n —**oceanographic** /ṓsh'nə gráffik, ṓshi ənə-/ adj —**oceanographically** adv

oceanology /ṓshə nólləji, ṓshi ə-/ n the branch of oceanography that studies how oceans may be used for economic or technological purposes —**oceanological** /ṓsh'nə lójjik'l, ṓ shi ənə-/ adj —**oceanologically** adv

ocean racer n an oceangoing sailing boat suitable for racing

ocean tramp n NAUT same as **tramp steamer**

Oceanus Procellarum /ṓssi áanəss próssə láarəm/ vast lunar lowland plain stretching between Mare Imbrium and Mare Humorum, visible as a dark area in the northwestern quadrant of the Moon. Area: over 2,000,000 sq. km/775,000 sq. mi.

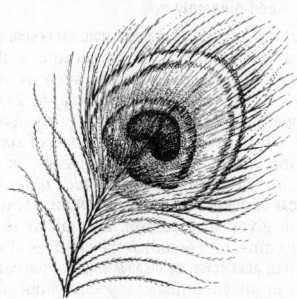

ocellus (sense 2): peacock feather

ocellus /ō sélləss/ (plural **-li** /-lī/) n **1. INSECTS SIMPLE EYE IN INVERTEBRATES** a simple eye in some insects and other invertebrates that is sensitive to light but unable to focus clearly **2. BIRDS EYE-SHAPED SPOT ON FEATHERS** an eye-shaped spot on the feathers of some birds such as peacocks **3. BOT EYE-SHAPED SPOT ON LEAF** an enlarged discoloured eye-shaped spot on a leaf **4. FISH EYE-SHAPED SPOT ON FISH** an eye-shaped spot on a fish, usually dark-ringed with a lighter colour inside, believed to deceive predators [Early 19C. < Latin, 'small eye' < oculus 'eye']

ocelot

ocelot /óssə lot/ (plural **-lots** or same) n a small wildcat with dark spots on a light brownish coat. Native to: southern United States, Central and South America. Latin name: Felis pardalis. [Late 18C. Via French < Nahuatl tlatlocelotl 'field jaguar']

och /okh/ interj Ireland, Scotland used to express disgust, disapproval, regret, weariness, or exasperation ○ Och, it's too late now. [Early 16C. Natural exclamation]

oche /óki/ n the line behind which a darts player must stand when throwing [Mid-20C. Origin ?]

ocher n, adj GEOL, COLOURS US spelling of **ochre**

ochlocracy /ok lókrəssi/ (plural **-cies**) n same as **mobocracy** (sense 1) [Late 16C. Via French ochlocratie < Greek okhlokratia < okhlos 'mob'] —**ochlocrat** /óklə krat/ n —**ochlocratic** /óklə kráttik/ adj —**ochlocratically** adv

ochre /ṓkər/ n **1.** a reddish or yellowish earthy iron oxide. Use: pigment. **2.** a brownish-yellow colour [14C. Via French < Latin ochra < Greek ōkhros 'pale, yellow'] —**ochre** adj —**ochreous** /ṓkri əss/ adj —**ochrous** /ṓkrəss, ṓkərəss/ adj —**ochry** /ṓkri, ṓkəri/ adj

ochrea n BOT another spelling of **ocrea**

-ock suffix something small or worthless ○ hillock [Old English -oc, -uc]

ocker /ókər/ ANZ n **1. OFFENSIVE TERM** an offensive term for an Australian regarded as boorish, uncultivated, and chauvinistic, especially a man with traditional views (slang insult) **2. TYPICAL WELL THOUGHT-OF AUSTRALIAN** a man who displays all the good qualities regarded as typically Australian (informal) ■ adj **1. OFFENSIVE TERM** an offensive term meaning boorish, uncultivated, or chauvinistic (slang) **2. TYPICALLY AUSTRALIAN** characteristically Australian (informal) ○ He's a real ocker Aussie. [Late 20C. Alteration of the forename Oscar, a character in an Australian television series]

Ockham /ókəm/, **William of** (1285?–1349) English philosopher. He revived nominalism and enunciated the principle known as Ockham's razor.

'Entities should not be multiplied unnecessarily. / No more things should be presumed to exist than are absolutely necessary.'
[William of Ockham, Quodlibeta Septem; 1320?]

Ockham's razor, Occam's razor n the philosophical and scientific rule that simple explanations should be preferred to more complicated ones, and that the explanation of a new phenomenon should be based on what is already known

o'clock /ə klók/ adv **1.** in telling the time, used to indicate an exact hour of the day or night, rather than some minutes past or before the hour ○ woke up at six o'clock in the morning **2.** in describing a position or direction of something, comparing it to the positions of numbers on a clock face, with the observer at the centre of the clock ○ Look at the man sitting to your right, at three o'clock. [15C. Contraction of of the clock]

O'Connell /ō kónn'l/, **Daniel** (1775–1847) Irish politician. A Roman Catholic, he succeeded in obtaining Catholic emancipation, becoming an MP at Westminster (1829). He agitated for repeal of the union of Ireland and Great Britain, and became Lord Mayor of Dublin (1841).

'The Union...was a crime, and it must still be criminal unless it shall be ludicrously

Daniel O'Connell

pretended that crime, like wine, improves by old age.'
[Daniel O'Connell, Repeal speech; 1809]

ocotillo /ókə teélyō, -teéyō/ (plural **-los** or same) n a spiny bush with red flowers at the tip of each branch. Native to: dry parts of southwestern United States, Mexico. Latin name: Fouqueria splendens. [Mid-19C. < American Spanish < ocote 'Mexican pine tree' < Nahuatl ocotl 'torch']

OCR abbr COMPUT **1.** optical character reader **2.** optical character recognition

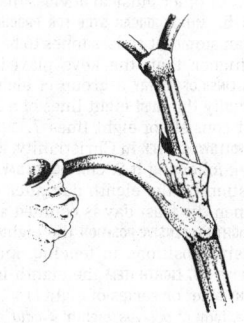

ocrea

ocrea /ókri ə/ (plural **-reae** /-ri ee/), **ochrea** n a cup-shaped sheath formed by appendages at the base of a leaf, as in rhubarb [Mid-19C. < Latin, 'soldier's leg-armour']

OCS abbr MIL Officer Candidate School

oct. abbr PRINTING octavo

Oct. abbr CALENDAR October

oct- prefix same as **octo-** (used before vowels)

octa- prefix same as **octo-**

octad /ók tad/ n a group or series of eight [Mid-19C. < Greek oktad- < oktō (see OCTO-)] —**octadic** /ok táddik/ adj

octagon /óktəgən/ n a two-dimensional geometric figure formed of eight sides and eight angles [Late 16C. Via Latin < Greek oktagōnon < oktagōnos 'eight-angled' < okto 'eight' + < gōnia 'angle'] —**octagonal** /ok tággən'l/ adj

octahedron /óktə heédrən/ (plural **-drons** or **-dra** /-drə/) n a three-dimensional geometric figure formed of eight faces —**octahedral** adj

octal /óktəl/ adj using or having a number system based on eight instead of ten ■ n **1.** COMPUT same as **octal notation 2.** a number with eight as its base

octal notation n a number system used in writing computer programs that is based on eight and uses numerals 0 to 7, one octal unit equalling three bits

octameter /ok támmitər/ n a line of verse consisting of eight metrical units or feet

octane /ók tayn/ n **1.** a liquid hydrocarbon found in petroleum that exists in 18 structurally different forms. Formula: C_8H_{18}. **2.** AUTOMOT same as **octane number** [Late 19C. < OCTO-; from the number of carbon atoms in the hydrocarbon]

octane number, octane rating n a number that measures the ability of a liquid motor fuel such as petrol to prevent preignition or knocking. Fuels with higher numbers are less likely to cause knocking.

octanol /óktə nol/ *n* a colourless oily aromatic liquid hydrocarbon. Use: solvent, in perfumes, in organic synthesis. Formula: $C_8H_{17}OH$.

Octans /ók tanz/ *n* a faint constellation of the southern hemisphere incorporating the south celestial pole. See illustration at **constellation**

octant /óktənt/ *n* **1.** ASTRON **EIGHTH OF ASTRONOMICAL CIRCLE** the position of one body in the sky one-eighth of a circle (45°) from another **2.** MATHS **EIGHTH OF CIRCLE** one-eighth of a circle, with or without the enclosed area **3.** MATHS **REGION OF SPACE IN CARTESIAN SYSTEM** any one of the eight regions into which space is divided by the three planes of the Cartesian coordinate system [Late 17C. < Latin *octant-* 'half-quadrant' < *octo* (see OCTO-)]

octapeptide /óktə pép tīd/ *n* a peptide consisting of eight amino acids

octavalent /óktə váylent/ *adj* describes an element, atom, or group that has a valency of eight

octave /óktiv/ *n* **1.** MUSIC **INTERVAL ON MUSICAL SCALE** an interval between two notes consisting of eight notes inclusive or seven steps on the diatonic scale **2.** MUSIC **NOTE AT EACH END OF OCTAVE** the note at each end of an octave, especially the higher one, considered in relation to the note at the other end **3.** MUSIC **NOTES AT END OF OCTAVE TOGETHER** the two notes at each end of an octave played together **4.** MUSIC **ALL NOTES INCLUDED WITHIN OCTAVE** the series of notes that fall within an octave, including the octave on each end, or the strings, keys, or other musical devices that produce these notes **5.** MUSIC **ORGAN STOP FOR PRODUCING HIGHER NOTES** an organ stop that causes tones to be produced an octave higher than the keys played alone **6.** LITERAT **EIGHT LINES OF POETRY** a group of eight lines of verse, especially the first eight lines of a sonnet, or a poem that consists of eight lines **7.** CHR **CHRISTIAN FEAST DAY AND FOLLOWING WEEK** in Christianity, a feast day and the week following it **8.** CHR **EIGHTH DAY AFTER FEAST DAY** in Christianity, the eighth day after an octave feast day when the feast day is counted as day one **9.** FENCING **EIGHTH DEFENSIVE POSITION** the eighth of eight basic defensive positions in fencing, known as a rotating perry **10.** **EIGHTH ITEM** the eighth in a series **11.** **SET OF EIGHT** a set or series of eight [14C. Via French < Latin *octava*, form of *octavus* 'eighth' < *octo* 'eight']

octave coupler *n* a mechanism on an organ or harpsichord that allows somebody simultaneously to play one note and another one an octave higher or lower

Octavia /ok táyvi ə/ (69?–11 BC) Roman aristocrat. The sister of Augustus, she married Mark Antony in a vain attempt to effect a reconciliation between the two men.

octavo /ok táyvō, -taavō/ (*plural* **-vos**) *n* **1.** a book with pages of a size traditionally created by folding a single sheet of standard-sized printing paper in half three times, giving 8 leaves or 16 pages **2.** the page size of an octavo book [Late 16C. < Latin, 'in an eighth (of a sheet)' < *octavus* (see OCTAVE); from the folding of a sheet eight times]

octennial /ok ténni əl/ *adj* **1.** occurring at intervals of eight years **2.** lasting for a period of eight years [Mid-17C. < late Latin *octennium* 'period of eight years' < Latin *octo* 'eight'] —**octennially** *adv*

octet /ok tét/ *n* **1.** a group of eight, especially eight singers or instrumentalists **2.** MUSIC a musical composition for a group of eight voices or instruments **3.** LITERAT same as **octave** (sense 6) [Mid-19C. Alteration of Italian *otteto* (< Latin *octo* 'eight')]

octet rule *n* CHEM same as **Lewis rule of eight**

octo- *prefix* eight ○ *octosyllable* [Directly or via Latin < Greek *oktō*]

October /ok tōbər/ *n* in the Gregorian calendar, the tenth month of the year, lasting 31 days. See table at **calendar** [Pre-12C. < Latin, 'eighth month' < *octo* 'eight']

octocentenary /óktō sen téenəri/ (*plural* **-ries**) *n* an 800th anniversary

octodecimo /óktō déssimō/ (*plural* **-mos**) *n* a book size of about 10 by 16 cm/4 by 6¼ in, or a book of this size [Mid-19C. < Latin, 'in an eighteenth (of a sheet)' < *octodecim* 'eight and ten'; from the folding of a sheet 18 times]

octogenarian /óktō jə náiri ən/ *n* somebody between 80 and 89 years of age [Early 19C. < Latin *octogenarius* < *octoginta* 'eighty', literally 'eight times ten']

octonary /óktənəri/ *adj* **1.** **BASED ON EIGHT** based on the number eight **2.** **MADE UP OF EIGHT** consisting of eight things ■ *n* (*plural* **-ies**) **1.** **GROUP OF EIGHT** a group or set of eight things **2.** COMPUT same as **octal** *n* (sense 2) [Mid-16C. < Latin *octonarius* 'containing eight' < *octo* (see OCTO-)]

octopi BIOL plural of **octopus**

octoploid /óktə ployd/ *n* a cell nucleus or an organism, especially a plant, containing eight haploid sets of chromosomes

octopod /óktə pod/ *n* a mollusc that has no shell and a large head and eyes and eight tentacles, e.g. the octopus. Order: Octopoda. [Early 20C. < modern Latin *Octopoda* < Greek *oktōpod-*, stem of *oktōpous* (see OCTOPUS)] —**octopodous** /óktə pōdəss/ *adj*

octopus /óktəpəss/ (*plural* **-puses** or **-pi** /-pī/ or *same*) *n* **1.** a sea animal with a big head, a soft oval body, well-developed eyes, and eight arms containing rows of suckers. It usually lives on the ocean floor. Genus: *Octopus*. **2.** something, especially an organization, that has many branches and forms of influence or control **3.** AUTOMOT same as **spider** (sense 3) [Mid-18C. < modern Latin < Greek *oktōpous* 'eight feet' < *oktō* 'eight' + *pous* 'foot']

octoroon /óktə ro͞on/ *n* an offensive term for somebody who has one Black great-grandparent and no other Black ancestors (*archaic*) [Mid-19C. < OCTO- after QUADROON]

octosyllable /óktə siləb'l/ *n* a language unit of eight syllables, usually a complete line of verse but occasionally just a word —**octosyllabic** /óktə si lábbik/ *adj*

octroi /ók trwaa/ *n* formerly, especially in France and Italy, a local tax levied on goods entering a town or city [Late 16C. < French *octroyer* 'to grant' < medieval Latin *auctorizare* (see AUTHORIZE)]

octuple /óktyo͝op'l, ok tyo͞op'l/ *adj* **1.** **EIGHT TIMES AS LARGE** eight times as large or effective **2.** **WITH EIGHT PARTS** consisting of eight parts ■ *vti* (**-ples, -pling, -pled**) **MULTIPLY BY EIGHT** to multiply something by eight, or be multiplied by eight ■ *n* **QUANTITY EIGHT TIMES GREATER** an amount that is eight times more than another amount

ocul- *prefix* same as **oculo-** (*used before vowels*)

ocular /ókyo͝olər/ *adj* relating to, perceived by, or performed by the eye ■ *n* an eyepiece in an optical instrument [Late 16C. Via French *oculaire* < late Latin *ocularis* < Latin *oculus* 'eye']

ORIGIN The Indo-European word from which ***ocular*** is derived is also the ancestor of English *atrocious, eye, ferocious, inoculate, optic,* and *window.*

oculist /ókyo͝olist/ *n* an optometrist or ophthalmologist (*dated*)

oculo- *prefix* eye ○ *oculomotor* [< Latin *oculus*]

oculogyric /ókyo͝olō jírrik/ *adj* relating to the movement of an eyeball in its socket

oculomotor /ókyo͝olō mōtər/ *adj* relating to or causing movement of the eyeball

oculomotor nerve *n* either of the third pair of cranial nerves that carry nerve fibres from the brain to the eye muscles and eyelids

~~**ocupation**~~ incorrect spelling of **occupation**

~~**ocurr**~~ incorrect spelling of **occur**

~~**ocurred**~~ incorrect spelling of **occurred**

~~**ocurrence**~~ incorrect spelling of **occurrence**

Od /od/ *interj* used euphemistically as an oath to mean 'God' (*archaic*) [Late 16C. Alteration of GOD]

OD¹ *abbr* **1.** MED Doctor of Optometry **2.** MIL Officer of the Day **3.** MIL olive drab **4.** GEOG ordnance datum **5.** BANKING overdraft **6.** BANKING overdrawn

OD² /ō dée/ (*informal*) *vi* (**ODs, OD'ing, OD'ed**) to take a dangerous amount of a drug, often causing hospitalization or death ■ *n* (*plural* **ODs**) an overdose of a drug [Mid-20C. Shortening of OVERDOSE]

o.d.¹ *abbr* **1.** MIL olive drab **2.** on demand **3.** MEASURE outside diameter

o.d.² *abbr* MED right eye [Latin *oculus dexter*]

O/D, o/d *abbr* BANKING **1.** overdraft **2.** overdrawn

odalisque /ódə lisk, óddə-/, **odalisk** *n* **1.** an enslaved woman or concubine, especially, formerly, in a Turkish harem **2.** a representation of an odalisque in art [Late 17C. Via French < Turkish *ōdalik* 'somebody who works in a chamber' < *ōda* 'chamber']

Oda Nobunaga /ódə nóbbyoo naagə/ (1534–82) Japanese feudal lord. He began the 16th-century reunification of Japan.

odd /od/ *adj* **1.** **UNUSUAL** peculiar or out of the ordinary ○ *There's something very odd about the letter.* **2.** **NOT DIVISIBLE EXACTLY BY 2** being a number that, when divided by 2, leaves a remainder of 1, e.g. 1, 3, 5, 7, 9, or 11 **3.** **LEFTOVER** leftover, and usually few in number ○ *a few odd coins* **4.** **SEPARATED FROM PAIR OR SET** left on its own without the other member or members of its pair, set, or series ○ *wearing odd socks* **5.** **IRREGULAR** irregular or occasional ○ *We get the odd day off here and there.* **6.** **SLIGHTLY GREATER THAN PARTICULAR NUMBER** used after a number to mean a little more than that particular number ○ *50-odd pounds* **7.** **REMOTE** not usually visited or reached by many people ○ *We found the papers lying about in odd corners of the house.* **8.** MATHS **HAVING CHANGING MATHEMATICAL SIGNS** used to refer to a function that changes sign but not value when the sign of each independent variable is changed at the same time ■ *n* **SOMETHING ODD IN NUMBER** something that is odd in number or numerical order [14C. < Old Norse *oddi* 'third or odd number'] —**oddish** *adj* —**oddly** *adv* —**oddness** *n*

oddball /ód bawl/, **odd bod** *n* somebody regarded as unusual or unconventional, but usually in a harmless way (*informal insult*)

Odd Fellow *n* a member of the Independent Order of Odd Fellows, a secret international social and charitable fraternity founded in England in the 18th century [< ODD 'remote, out-of-the-way'; from the Order's mystic practices]

oddity /óddəti/ (*plural* **-ties**) *n* somebody or something unique, unusual, or unconventional

odd job *n* an unspecialized job, e.g. a household repair, usually done casually and for low pay (*often used in the plural*) ○ *does odd jobs for a living* —**odd-job** *vi* —**odd-jobber** *n*

odd lot *n* a quantity or number of shares that is smaller than the usual trading unit, e.g. fewer than 100 shares when traded on a stock exchange, or less than one whole share when liquidated

odd man out *n* same as **odd one out**

oddment /ódmənt/ *n* something left over when most of something has been used or disposed of (*usually used in the plural*) ○ *By the time she arrived there were only oddments left in the sale.* [Late 18C. < ODD after FRAGMENT]

odd one out (*plural* **odd ones out**), **odd man out** (*plural* **odd men out**) *n* somebody in a group who differs from the rest of the group or is not treated as part of the group

odd-pinnate *adj* describes a plant leaf such as that of the rose that is pinnate with a single leaflet at the top —**odd-pinnately** *adv*

odds /odz/ *npl* **1.** **CHANCES OF SOMETHING HAPPENING** the likelihood or probability that something will occur, sometimes expressed as a ratio such as 10 to 1 ○ *The odds are that you'll never make it.* **2.** **PREDICTED CHANCES IN BETTING** a ratio of probability given to people placing a bet, usually the likelihood of something happening, or of a competitor, team, or animal winning ○ *The horse was given odds of four to one.* **3.** **HANDICAP OR ADVANTAGE IN COMPETITION** an advantage or handicap given to a person, animal, or team in a sporting contest, to equalize the chances of winning **4.** **PERCEIVED ADVANTAGE OR DISADVANTAGE** a perceived advantage or disadvantage, especially one that one person is believed to have over another in a competition [Early 16C. Plural of ODD] ◇ **at odds (with somebody)** in disagreement with somebody, especially over a period of time or about a particular issue ◇ **at odds (with something)** in conflict with something ◇ **over the odds** more than is usual or necessary ◇ **what's the odds?** used to indicate that something is of no importance

SYNONYMS See ***disagree.***

odds and ends *npl* a group of miscellaneous items

odds and sods *npl* miscellaneous people or items (*informal*)

oddsmaker /ódz maykər/ *n* an official calculator of betting odds

odds-on *adj* likeliest to win, succeed, or happen (*informal*) ○ *It was odds-on that he would succeed his father.*

ode /ōd/ *n* **1.** a lyric poem, usually expressing exalted emotion in a complex scheme of rhyme and metre **2.** an ancient Greek song written either for a chorus or for a solo singer [Late 16C. Via French < Greek *ōidē* 'song']

-ode *suffix* **1.** electrically conducting element ○ *electrode* **2.** electrode ○ *tetrode* [< Greek *hodos* 'way']

odea ARCHIT, MUSIC plural of **odeum**

Odense /ṓd'nssə/ city and port in south-central Denmark, on the island of Fyn. Population: 144,940 (1999).

odeon *n* ARCHIT same as **odeum**

Oder /ṓdər/ river in north-central Europe. Its northern course forms part of Poland's border with Germany. Length: 906 km/563 mi.

Odessa /ō déssə/, **Odesa** city and port in south-central Ukraine, on the Black Sea. Population: 1,027,000 (1998).

odeum /ṓdi əm/ (*plural* **odea** /ṓdi ə/), **odeon** /ṓdi ən/ *n* ARCHIT, MUSIC an ancient Greek or Roman building in which musical performances were held [Early 17C. Directly or via French < Latin *odeum* < Greek *ōideion* < *ōidē* 'song']

Odin /ṓdin/ *n* in Scandinavian mythology, the god of war and the king of the gods who held court in Valhalla, the final resting place of famous warriors

odious /ṓdi əss/ *adj* inspiring hatred, contempt, or disgust [14C. Via French < Latin *odiosus* < *odium* 'hatred, contempt'] —**odiously** *adv* —**odiousness** *n*

~~**odissey**~~ incorrect spelling of **odyssey**

odium /ṓdi əm/ *n* **1.** intense dislike, repugnance, or contempt for somebody or something ○ *incurred scorn and odium for his actions* **2.** the state of being hateful, contemptuous, or disgusting [Early 17C. < Latin]

odometer /ō dómmitər, o-/ *n N Am* same as **mileometer** [Late 18C. < French *odomètre*, or directly < Greek *hodos* 'way']

odonate /ṓdə nayt/ *n* an insect belonging to the order of insects that includes the dragonfly and damselfly. Order: Odonata. [Early 20C. < modern Latin *Odonata* < Greek *odōn*, variant of *odous* 'tooth']

odont- *prefix* same as **odonto-** (*used before vowels*)

-odont *suffix* having a particular kind of teeth ○ *acrodont* [< Greek *odont-*, stem of *odous* (see ODONTO-)]

odontalgia /óddon tálji ə/ *n* DENT same as **toothache** (*technical*)

-odontia *suffix* condition or treatment of teeth ○ *anodontia* [< Greek *odont-*, stem of *odous* (see ODONTO-)]

odonto- *prefix* tooth, teeth ○ *odontology* [< Greek *odont-* 'tooth' < Indo-European]

odontoblast /o dóntə blast/ *n* one of a layer of cells lining the pulp cavity of a tooth and taking part in the formation of dentine —**odontoblastic** /o dóntə blástik/ *adj*

odontoglossum /o dóntə glóssəm/ *n* a variety of orchid that grows on other plants and is widely cultivated for its clusters of brightly coloured flowers. Native to: mountainous areas from Bolivia to Mexico. Genus: *Odontoglossum*. [Late 19C < modern Latin, 'tooth tongue' < Greek *odont-* 'tooth' + *glōssa* 'tongue'; from the projection on the end of the flower, resembling a tooth]

odontoid /o dónt oyd/ *adj* resembling a tooth, especially in shape

odontoid process *n* a tooth-shaped peg that projects upwards from the second neck vertebra to engage with the first, acting as a pivot for side-to-side movements of the head

odontology /óddon tólləji/ *n* the branch of science that studies the teeth and their anatomy, development, and diseases —**odontological** /o dóntə lójjik'l/ *adj* —**odontologically** *adv* —**odontologist** *n*

odor *n* US spelling of **odour**

odorant /ṓdərənt/ *n* something that gives a characteristic smell to a product

odoriferous /ṓdə ríffərəss/ *adj* having or diffusing a strong odour (*technical*) —**odoriferously** *adv* —**odoriferousness** *n*

odorous /ṓdərəss/ *adj* same as **odoriferous** (*literary*) —**odorously** *adv* —**odorousness** *n*

odour /ṓdər/ *n* **1.** a smell, whether pleasant or unpleasant ○ *the delicious odour of baking bread* **2.** a quality or attitude that suggests or resembles a particular thing ○ *They had an odour of propriety.* ○ *the odour of sanctity* [13C. Via French < Latin *odor*] ◇ **be in bad** *or* **good odour (with somebody)** to be out of or in favour with somebody

SYNONYMS See ***smell***.

odourless /ṓdərləss/ *adj* having no smell that is strong enough to be detected by the human nose —**odourlessness** *n*

Odysseus /ō díssee əss/ *n* in Greek mythology, the king of Ithaca who is the main character in Homer's epic poem the *Odyssey*. Roman equivalent **Ulysses**

odyssey /óddissi/ (*plural* **-seys**) *n* a long series of travels and adventures [Late 19C. < the *Odyssey* < Greek *Odusseia* < ODYSSEUS]

CULTURAL NOTE ***The Odyssey***, an epic poem (?8th century BC) by the Greek writer Homer. The oldest surviving source of Greek mythology along with the *Iliad*, it describes Odysseus's ten-year journey home to Ithaca after the Trojan War. It provides both an insight into a long-lost civilization and a gripping narrative rich in evocative details, complex characters, and universal themes.

Oe *symbol* MEASURE oersted

OE *abbr* LANG Old English

OECD *abbr* COMM Organization for Economic Cooperation and Development

oedema /i deémə/ (*plural* **-mas** or **-mata** /-mətə/) *n* **1.** a buildup of excess serous fluid between tissue cells **2.** a swelling in a plant, chiefly caused by a buildup of excess water [15C. < Greek *oidēma* 'swelling tumour' < *oidein* 'swell'] —**oedematous** /i démmətəss, i deémətəss/ *adj*

Oedipus /eédipəss/ *n* in Greek mythology, a son of Jocasta and Laius, king of Thebes, who unwittingly killed his father and married his mother —**Oedipal** *adj*

Oedipus complex *n* according to the psychoanalytic theory of Sigmund Freud, feelings or desires originating when a child, especially a son, unconsciously seeks sexual fulfilment with the parent of the opposite sex

OEIC /oyk/ *n* a limited company managing a portfolio of investments for investors with holdings in the form of units representing a fraction of the value of the investments. Full form **open-ended investment company**

Ōe Kenzaburō /ṓ ay kenzə bóorō/ (*b.* 1935) Japanese writer. Perhaps the greatest Japanese novelist since World War II, he won the Nobel Prize in literature (1994).

OEM *abbr* original equipment manufacturer

oenology /ee nólləji/ *n* the scientific study of wine and the making of wine [Early 19C. < Greek *oinos* 'wine'] —**oenological** /eénə lójjik'l/ *adj* —**oenologist** *n*

oenomel /eénə mel/ *n* (*literary*) **1.** a drink of wine and honey made in ancient Greece **2.** words or ideas that combine strength and sweetness [Late 16C. Via late Latin *oenomeli* < Greek *oinomeli* 'honey wine' < *oinos* 'wine' + *meli* 'honey']

oenophile /eénə fīl/ *n* a lover of or expert on wine [Mid-20C. < French < *oeno-* < Greek *oinos* 'wine']

OEO *abbr US* Office of Economic Opportunity

o'er /ō ər, awr/ *prep, adv* same as **over** (*literary*) ○ *The sun rose o'er the mountain.* [14C. Contraction]

oersted /úr sted/ *n* the unit measure of magnetic field strength in the centimetre-gram-second system. It is equal to the magnetic field strength experienced by a magnetic pole when undergoing a force of one dyne in a free space. Symbol **Oe** [Late19C. After H. C. OERSTED]

Oersted /úrstid, ŏrstid/, **Hans Christian** (1777–1851) Danish physicist and chemist. He pioneered the study of electromagnetism, and was the first to isolate aluminium (1825).

oesophagus /i sóffəgəss/ (*plural* **-gi** /-gī/) *n* the passage down which food moves between the throat and the stomach [14C. Via medieval Latin *isophagus* < Greek *oisophagos*] —**oesophageal** /i sóffə jeé əl/ *adj*

oestradiol *n* BIOCHEM, PHARM another spelling of **estradiol**

oestral /eéstrəl, és-/ *adj* BIOL same as **oestrous**

oestriol /eéstri ol, és-/ *n* an oestrogen hormone produced in the ovaries and secreted in the urine during pregnancy [Early 20C. < OESTRUS + TRI- + -OL[1]]

oestrogen /eéstrəjən, és-/ *n* any steroid hormone produced mainly in the ovaries that stimulates oestrus and the development of female secondary sexual characteristics [Early 20C. < OESTRUS] —**oestrogenic** /eéstrə jénnik, éstrə-/ *adj*

oestrone /eéstrōn, és-/ *n* an oestrogenic hormone produced in the ovaries and synthesized for use in treating oestrogen deficiency and breast cancer. Formula: $C_{18}H_{22}O_2$. [Early 20C. < OESTRUS]

oestrous /eéstrəss, és-/, **oestral** /eéstrəl, és-/ *adj* **1.** relating to or happening at the time of oestrus **2.** describes a female mammal at the time of oestrus

oestrous cycle *n* a hormonally controlled reproductive cycle occurring in most female mammals, marked by a period of heat followed by ovulation and changes in the womb lining

oestrus /eéstrəss, és-/ *n* a regular period of sexual excitement in many female mammals during which the animal is receptive to mating [Late 19C. Via Latin, 'frenzy' < Greek *oistros* 'gadfly']

oeuvre /úrvrə, urvr/ *n* a work of art or literature, or such works considered as a unit, especially the complete work of a single artist [Late 19C. Via French < Latin *opera*, the plural of *opus* 'work']

of *stressed* /ov/; *unstressed* /əv, ə/ CORE MEANING: a preposition introducing a noun or noun phrase that provides more information about a preceding word or phrase, usually, but not always, also a noun ○ *Most software has complex sets of commands and options.* ○ *She let out a little squeal of delight.* ○ *I'm very fond of onions.* ○ *He thought of the consequences too late.*

prep **1.** AFFECTED BY ACTION used to indicate the person or thing affected by or performing an action ○ *the promotion of junior staff* ○ *the death of her father* **2.** USED IN MEASURING QUANTITIES used after words or phrases expressing quantities to indicate the substance or thing being measured ○ *millions of dollars* ○ *a herd of cows* ○ *10 gallons of oil* **3.** CONNECTED WITH used to indicate the place that somebody or something belongs to or is connected with ○ *the president of France* **4.** CONTAINING containing a particular substance ○ *a mug of coffee* ○ *a busload of schoolchildren* **5.** TAKEN FROM used to indicate a part of something that is normally considered as a whole ○ *a slice of cake* ○ *a square of fabric* **6.** MADE FROM made from or used as a material to form something ○ *ruled with a rod of iron* ○ *a paste of flour and water* **7.** INDICATING RELATIONSHIP OR ASSOCIATION used to indicate a relationship, association, or cause ○ *I'll be thinking of you.* ○ *accused of negligence* **8.** RELATING TO used after words describing feelings and qualities to indicate the person or thing they relate to ○ *He's very sure of himself.* ○ *It's very kind of you to come.* **9.** INDICATING PARTICULAR TYPE used to describe somebody or something in terms of a particular type or kind ○ *one heck of a gymnast* **10.** HAVING PARTICULAR QUALITY used to indicate a quality that somebody or something has, or the person or thing having a particular quality ○ *announcements of a general nature* ○ *a musician of great talent* ○ *the gentleness of his manner* **11.** INDICATING AMOUNT used to indicate an amount, age, or value ○ *There is a limit of eight characters in a computer user name.* ○ *a young boy of 12* **12.** ON EVERY used to indicate a day or other period of time when an activity regularly occurs (*informal*) ○ *We usually go out for a meal of a Friday.* **13.** *N Am* BEFORE before the hour of ○ *It was a quarter of ten before she returned.* [Old English < Germanic]

USAGE of and **'ve**: Note that *could've, should've,* and *would've* are contracted forms of *could have, should have,* and *would have.* The *'ve* contraction is sometimes wrongly interpreted as ***of***, because it sounds similar: *He*

could've [not *could of*] *been killed. You should've* [not *should of*] *followed the instructions. It would've* [not *would of*] *been quicker to walk.*

Ofcom /óf kom/ *n* **1.** a regulatory body with powers from 29 December 2003 to supervise the UK communications industries, including television, radio, telecommunications, and wireless communications. As telecommunications regulator it took over the functions of Oftel. **2.** regulatory body for the telecommunications and broadcasting industries set up to assume the responsibilities of five previous regulators [Early 21C. Contraction of *Office of Communications*]

off /of/ CORE MEANING: a grammatical word used to indicate separation or distance between two points, especially movement away from the speaker ○ (adv) *He ran off before I could stop him.* ○ (prep) *The bottle rolled off the ledge and fell to the floor.*
1. *prep, adv* **SO AS TO LEAVE** so as to come out of or leave a bus, train, or plane ○ *Check you have all your belongings before getting off the bus.* ○ *He got off at the next stop.* **2.** *prep, adv* **SO AS TO KEEP AWAY FROM** so as to keep away from, avoid stepping on, or be at a distance from or to the side of ○ *The sign said 'Please keep off the grass'.* ○ *I stepped off the kerb.* **3.** *prep, adv* **AWAY FROM WORK** away from work or usual duties owing to illness, holidays, or normal nonwork time ○ *trying to get time off work to visit her in hospital* ○ *I didn't see Jane – it must be her night off.* **4.** *prep, adv* **REDUCED BY** so as to be reduced by a particular amount ○ *10 per cent off all swimwear this week* ○ *She knocked £10 off for the slight stain on the sleeve.* **5.** *prep, adv* **IN FUTURE** a particular distance away in the future ○ *My fortieth birthday is only two years off!* **6.** *prep, adv* **SO AS TO REMOVE** so as to eliminate or remove something from view ○ *The dirt should wash off easily.* ○ *He was rubbing something off the board when I came in.* **7.** *adv* **TO DISTANT PLACE** so as to be away from the present location ○ *He hopped in the car, started it up, and took off.* **8.** *adv* **AWAY** at a particular physical distance away ○ *The nearest stop's about two miles off.* **9.** *adv* **MEASURED** so as to be divided or measured ○ *Measure the gap, mark it off with a pencil, and cut the wood to size.* **10.** *adv* **TO COMPLETION** to the point of completion ○ *We're trying to get our bills paid off.* **11.** *adv* **INTO PARTICULAR STATE** into a particular state, especially an unconscious state ○ *The baby dozed off on the way over here.* **12.** *adv* COMM **REQUIRED NUMBER** indicating the number of items required or produced (*preceded by a number*) ○ *a one off* **13.** *prep* **ABSTAINING FROM** no longer participating in or using ○ *I'm off caffeine for a week.* **14.** *prep* **ON DIET OF** using as a means of subsistence ○ *living off vegetables from our garden* **15.** *prep* **LEADING AWAY FROM** near or next to, and leading or branching away from ○ *He lives in a block of flats just off the square.* **16.** *prep* **NOT LIKING** no longer inclined towards ○ *I'm really off horror movies at the moment.* **17.** *prep* **FROM** used to show the initiator or source of an action (*nonstandard*) ○ *I got these sunglasses off my sister for my birthday.* **18.** *adv, adj* **NOT IN OPERATION** not functioning or in use ○ *Shall I switch the engine off?* ○ *Make sure the lights are off before you leave.* ○ *the off switch* **19.** *adv, adj* **CANCELLED** so as to be no longer taking place ○ *The deal's off.* **20.** *adj* **NO LONGER FRESH** smelling and tasting bad because of being no longer fresh ○ *We had to throw the fish away – it was going off.* **21.** *adj* **NOT ON MENU** no longer on the menu in a restaurant, or not being served at the moment ○ *I'm sorry sir, the steak is off.* **22.** *adj* **IN PARTICULAR CONDITION** in a particular condition with regard to something ○ *How are you off for cash?* **23.** *adj* **NOT CORRECT** in error or out of alignment **24.** *adj* **ON THE RIGHT OF** situated on the right side of a vehicle, farthest away from the kerb **25.** *adj* **UNACCEPTABLE** not up to normal or acceptable standards (*informal*) ○ *'She turned up two hours late'. 'Well I think that's a bit off'.* **26.** *n* CRICKET **PART OF CRICKET FIELD** the side of the cricket field facing the batsman taking strike [Old English. Originally an emphatic variant of OF] ◇ **off and on** occasionally

USAGE There are two usages of *off* that should be avoided in formal writing. The first involves *off* plus *of*: *The actors stepped off* [not *off of*] *the stage.* The second problem involves the use of *off* after certain verbs like *buy* or *borrow*, which mean 'obtain something from a source': *I bought the computer from* [not *off*] *my flatmate.*

off. *abbr* **1.** office **2.** officer **3.** official

Offa /óffə/ (730?–796) king of Mercia. He ruled from 757, took control of much of southern England, and built Offa's Dyke.

off-air *adj* spoken or occurring in broadcasting studios but not used during a broadcast —**off air** *adv*

offal /óff'l/ *n* **1.** the edible, mainly internal organs of an animal, e.g. the heart, liver, brains, and tongue, sometimes regarded as unpalatable **2.** something discarded as refuse [14C. < OFF + FALL]

Offaly /óffəli/ county in Leinster Province, Republic of Ireland. The county town is Tullamore. Population: 59,117 (2002). Area: 1,998 sq. km/771 sq. mi.

Offa's Dyke *n* a series of earthworks along the border between England and Wales, constructed by King Offa of Mercia between 784 and 796. It is 240 km/150 mi. long.

off beat *n* any unaccented beat in a bar of music

offbeat /óf beet/ *adj* not conforming to convention or to expectations

off-brand *adj N Am* made and sold inexpensively under a brand name that is not well-known

off-Broadway *n* in New York City, professional theatre productions, sometimes experimental or innovative in nature, that are staged outside the principal theatre district of Broadway

off-camera *adj* out of sight of the camera —**off camera** *adv*

off-campus *adj* done, taking place, or existing outside the area of a university, college, or other campus —**off campus** *adv*

off-centre *adj* **1.** not at the centre and therefore sometimes causing a lack of symmetry, balance, or evenness of movement **2.** slightly unconventional or eccentric —**off centre** *adv*

off chance, off-chance *n* a slight or remote possibility ◇ **on the off chance** just in case something happens

off-colour *adj* **1.** ILL ill or not very well ○ *I'm feeling a bit off-colour today.* **2.** **NOT COLOURED NORMALLY** not having the usual or desired colour **3.** **SLIGHTLY SMUTTY** mildly sexually indecent or suggestive (*informal*)

off-course *adj* occurring somewhere other than a racecourse. N Am term **off-track**

offcut /óf kut/ *n* a remnant left after the main pieces of something such as fabric or paper have been cut

off day *n* **1.** a day of not feeling or performing very well **2.** *Malaysia* a day on which somebody does not have to work

Offenbach /óff'n baak/ city in Hesse State, west-central Germany, on the River Main. Population: 116,482 (1997).

Offenbach, Jacques (1819–80) German-born French composer. He wrote witty satirical operettas, one of which includes the famous example of the cancan dance music, as well as the opera *The Tales of Hoffmann* (1880). Born **Eberst, Jacob**

offence /ə fénss/ *n* **1.** **LEGAL OR MORAL CRIME** an official crime, or a crime against moral, social, or other accepted standards ○ *He was convicted of a motoring offence* **2.** **ANGER OR RESENTMENT** anger, resentment, hurt, or displeasure ○ *'Please don't take offence'.* ○ *His remarks caused great offence.* **3.** **CAUSE OF DISPLEASURE OR ANGER** something that causes displeasure, humiliation, anger, resentment, or hurt ○ *The request was an offence to their dignity.* **4.** **ATTACK** an attack or assault, usually in the military or in sports ○ *The army launched its great offence that spring.* **5.** SPORTS **ATTACKING PLAYERS ON TEAM** the players making up the part of a team that attempts to score in a game, as distinct from the defence that tries to stop the other team from scoring ○ *We lacked a good offence last spring.* [14C. Via French < Latin *offens-*, past participle of *offendere* 'to strike']

offend /ə fénd/ (**-fends, -fending, -fended**) *v* **1.** *vti* to hurt somebody's feelings, or cause resentment, irritation, anger, or displeasure ○ *The book offended too many people.* **2.** *vi* to violate a law or code of conduct ○ *He offended against the club's rules of proper dress.* [14C. Directly or via French < Latin *offendere* 'to strike'] —**offender** *n* —**offending** *adj*

offense *n* US spelling of **offence**

offensive /ə fénssiv/ *adj* **1.** **UPSETTING, INSULTING, OR IRRITATING** causing anger, resentment, or moral outrage ○ *removed the offensive material from the play* **2.** **UNPLEASANT TO SENSES** causing physical repugnance ○ *an offensive smell* **3.** **USED WHEN ATTACKING** used, or designed to be used, when attacking ○ *an offensive weapon* **4.** **AGGRESSIVE** demonstrating aggression ○ *warned that this would be seen as an offensive action* ■ *n* MIL **ATTACK OR ASSAULT** an attack, assault, or siege ○ *The platoon braced itself for the dawn offensive.* —**offensively** *adv* —**offensiveness** *n*

offer /óffər/ *vt* (**-fers, -fering, -fered**) **1.** **PRESENT SOMETHING FOR ACCEPTANCE OR REJECTION** to attempt to give somebody something that may be taken or refused, usually something desirable ○ *They offered me the job.* **2.** **HAVE SOMETHING FOR USE OF OTHERS** to provide something, or make something available for those who want it ○ *The town offered many amenities.* **3.** **VOLUNTEER TO DO SOMETHING** to suggest doing something yourself as a favour for somebody else ○ *I offered to bring the salad.* **4.** **HAVE SOMETHING FOR SALE OR HIRE** to present or have something for sale or hire ○ *the first gym to offer professional trainers at a low cost* **5.** **GIVE SOMETHING AS WORSHIP** to present something to God, often as part of worship ○ *We offer hymns of praise to God.* **6.** **EXHIBIT QUALITY** to exhibit or demonstrate a particular quality ○ *The city offered little resistance against the army.* ○ *a plan that offers hope to millions* **7.** **MAKE BID** to make a bid or financial proposal for something ○ *They offered 40 pence a share.* **8.** **PRESENT PERFORMANCE** to present an exhibition or performance ○ *They offered two films each night.* ■ *n* **1.** **PROPOSAL OF SUGGESTED GIFT OR ACTION** a suggestion from somebody to give something or do something for somebody else ○ *A home-cooked meal and a place to stay: that's the best offer I've had all day!* **2.** **FINANCIAL PROPOSAL OR BID** a sum of money suggested as payment for something ○ *They made an offer for the house but we refused it.* **3.** **REDUCED PRICE** a reduced price for something, or something for sale at a reduced price ○ *this week's special offer* **4.** LAW **PROPOSAL LEADING TO BINDING CONTRACT** a proposal that, if accepted, creates a binding contract [Old English *offrian*, via Germanic < Latin *offerre* 'bring to' < *ferre* 'bring'] —**offerer** *n*
offer up *vt* RELIG same as **offer** *v* (sense 5)

offering /óffəring/ *n* **1.** **CONTRIBUTION** something that is offered, or the act of offering ○ *The restaurant had some pretty awful offerings.* **2.** **GIFT FOR GOD** something offered as a sacrifice to a deity **3.** **MONEY GIVEN DURING CHURCH SERVICE** a financial contribution to a church, often made during a church service

offer price *n* the price at which something, especially a share of a stock or mutual fund, is offered for sale

~~**offerred**~~ incorrect spelling of **offered**

offertory /óffərtəri/ (*plural* **-ries**) *n* **1.** **OFFERING OF COMMUNION BREAD AND WINE** the offering of the bread and wine during the Christian service of Communion **2.** **CHURCH COLLECTION** the offering of money or gifts made by a church congregation **3.** **PART OF CHRISTIAN SERVICE** a part of a church service during which prayers are said or sung while offerings are received [14C. Via ecclesiastical Latin *offertorium* 'offering place' < Latin *offerre* (see OFFER)]

off-glide *n* a sound produced by the vocal organs prior to their making another sound or assuming a neutral position

off-guard *adj* not anticipating a possible attack or approach (*not hyphenated when used after a verb*) ○ *caught the enemy off guard*

offhand /of hánd/ *adv* **1.** **CASUALLY** casually, thoughtlessly, or spontaneously **2.** **WITHOUT PREPARATION** without preparation or research ○ *Offhand, I'd say there must be 50 people in there.* ■ *adj also* **offhanded** /of hándid/ **1.** **UNCONCERNED AND UNCARING** so casual, uninterested, or blunt as to appear impolite or uncaring ○ *She was pretty offhand about the whole affair.* **2.** **CASUALLY DONE** taken or made casually or without planning, usually on the spur of the moment ○ *Only through her offhand comment did I realize who she was.* —**offhandedly** *adv* —**offhandedness** *n*

off-hour *n US* (*informal*) **1.** a period of time that is not crowded with cars or people (*often used before a noun*) ○ *We try to visit the zoo during off-hours.* **2.** a period of time outside normal business hours

office /óffiss/ *n* **1.** **ROOM USED FOR BUSINESS ACTIVITY** a room in which business or professional activities take

place, often occupied by a single person or a single section of the business **2.** PLACE OF BUSINESS the quarters in which a commercial, professional, or government organization carries out its activities **3.** OFFICIAL ORGANIZATION a commercial or professional organization **4.** STAFF IN OFFICE the people who work in an office ○ *get-well cards from the office* **5.** BRITISH GOVERNMENT DEPARTMENT a department in the British Government ○ *He works for the Home Office.* **6.** US GOVERNMENT AGENCY OR DEPARTMENT a US government agency or subdivision, especially an agency or subdivision of the federal government **7.** POSITION OF RESPONSIBILITY an official post or position of duty, trust, or responsibility ○ *The mayor has been in office four years now.* **8.** PLACE FOR TICKETS OR INFORMATION a booth or other place where tickets or information may be obtained **9.** CHR SET FORM OF CHRISTIAN SERVICE the prescribed order or form of a Christian church service, or of daily prayers **10.** TASK OR ASSIGNMENT a task, assignment, or chore (*formal; usually used in the plural*) ■ **offices** *npl* **1.** SOMETHING DONE ON BEHALF OF ANOTHER something said or done by somebody to or for another person (*formal*) ○ *I got the job through her kind offices.* **2.** AREAS OR BUILDINGS WHERE SERVANTS WORK the outbuildings or parts of a large house in which the servants work (*dated*) [13C. Via French < Latin *officium* 'doing work' < *opus* 'work' + *facere* 'do']

office-bearer *n* somebody who holds office in a society, club, or voluntary organization, e.g. the president or treasurer. N Am term **office holder**

office block *n UK, ANZ, Can* a large building holding offices. US term **office building**

office boy *n* a boy or man who does errands around an office (*dated*)

office building *n US* same as **office block**

office-free *adj US* relating to or involving a workforce that is not required to work from or at an office

office holder *n* **1.** an official in a government position **2.** *N Am* same as **office-bearer**

office hours *npl* the regular times during which a business or profession, or business as a whole, is conducted

office junior *n* a young office-worker entrusted only with minor clerical tasks

officer /óffissər/ *n* **1.** SOMEBODY OF RANK IN THE ARMED FORCES somebody in a military force authorized to command others **2.** ELECTED OR APPOINTED OFFICIAL an official who holds an administrative position **3.** POLICE same as **police officer** **4.** SOMEBODY IN AUTHORITY ON SHIP somebody with a position of authority on a civilian ship ■ *vt* (**-cers, -cering, -cered**) MIL, NAVY SUPPLY SOMETHING WITH OFFICERS to provide something such as a military unit or a ship with officers

officer of arms *n* a herald, especially one who devises, grants, or confirms coats of arms

official /ə físh'l/ *n* SOMEBODY HOLDING OFFICE a holder of office in an organization, corporation, or government department ■ *adj* **1.** OF GOVERNMENT OR AUTHORITY relating to the role of a government, public body, or authority ○ *official rules and regulations* **2.** AUTHORIZED BY AUTHORITY approved, recognized, or issued by a government, public body, or authority ○ *No official statement has been issued.* **3.** FORMAL formal or ceremonial ○ *invited to attend the official opening* —**officially** *adv*

official birthday *n* a date in June chosen as the occasion on which to celebrate the sovereign's birthday, with formal ceremonies taking place in London

officialdom /ə físh'ldəm/ *n* bureaucracy and those who work within it, especially when viewed as inefficient or pompous (*informal*) ○ *caught up in the red tape of officialdom*

officialese /ə físhə leéz/ *n* unclear, pedantic, and verbose language considered characteristic of official documents

officialism /ə físh'lizəm/ *n* excessive respect or adherence to official routines and regulations, considered to be characteristic of officials (*informal*)

Official Receiver *n* an official appointed to manage a bankrupt's property prior to the appointment of a trustee

Official Referee *n* in England and Wales, a circuit judge with authority from the High Court to try cases involving examination of accounts or other documents

Official Solicitor *n* in England and Wales, an officer of the Supreme Court of Judicature with special responsibilities for protecting the interests of people with disabilities

Official Unionist Party *n* same as **Ulster Unionist Party**

officiary /ə físhi əri/ *adj* derived from the holding of an office, or having a title that is derived from an office held ○ *an officiary title* ■ *n* an official, or an organized group of officials [Early 17C. < medieval Latin *officiarius* < Latin *officium* (see OFFICE)]

officiate /ə físhi ayt/ (**-ates, -ating, -ated**) *v* **1.** *vti* to preside in an official capacity, especially at a religious ceremony **2.** *vt* to act as a referee at a sports event [Mid-17C. Via medieval Latin *officiat-*, past participle of *officiare* 'conduct sacred service' < Latin *officium* (see OFFICE)] —**officiant** *n*

officinal /o físsinəl, óffi sínəl/ (*archaic*) *n* a stocked medicine rather than one specially prepared according to a prescription ■ *adj* having medicinal properties, especially those recognized by a pharmacopoeia [Late 17C. Via medieval Latin *officinalis* < *officina* 'workshop' (later 'storeroom for medicines') < Latin *officium* (see OFFICE)] —**officinally** *adv*

officious /ə físhəss/ *adj* **1.** characteristic of somebody who is eager to give unwanted help or advice ○ *whisked away our unfinished meal in an officious manner* **2.** unofficial or informal, especially in political or diplomatic dealings [Late 15C. < Latin *officiosus* < *officium* (see OFFICE)] —**officiously** *adv* —**officiousness** *n*

offie /óffi/ *n* same as **off-licence** (*slang*)

offing /óffing/ *n* the more distant part of the sea seen from the shore [Early 17C. Probably < OFF] ◇ **in the offing** expected or likely in the future

offish /óffish/ *adj* same as **standoffish** (*informal*)

off-key *adj* (*not hyphenated after a verb*) **1.** OUT OF TUNE not having the correct musical pitch **2.** INAPPROPRIATE not usual, conventional, or appropriate ■ *adv* OUT OF TUNE above or below the correct musical pitch

off-label *adj US* using or involving the use of a prescription drug to treat a condition for which the drug has not been approved by the US Food and Drug Administration

off-licence *n UK* a shop or a pub where bottles or cans of alcoholic beverages may be bought for consumption elsewhere

off-limits *adj* to which entry is forbidden or barred ○ *That part of town was off-limits to us.*

off-line *adj* **1.** describes a computer terminal or peripheral device that is disconnected or is functioning separately from an associated computer or computer network ○ *The printer was taken off-line for repairs.* **2.** involved in preparing but not transmitting material for broadcasting ○ *off-line editing* —**off line** *adv*

off-line newsreader *n* a piece of software that allows a user to read newsgroup articles when the computer is not connected to the Internet

offload /of lṓd, óf lōd/ (**-loads, -loading, -loaded**) *v* **1.** *vti* UNLOAD GOODS to unload goods or a cargo from a vehicle or container ○ *ships waiting to offload* **2.** *vt* GET RID OF SOMETHING to get rid of something unwanted by passing it on to somebody else ○ *managed to offload some of the work onto colleagues* **3.** *vti* UNBURDEN YOURSELF to relieve yourself of a stressful emotion such as anxiety or frustration by talking to somebody (*informal*) **4.** *vti* COMPUT TRANSFER DATA to transfer data from one computer to another to create spare capacity

off-message *adj* not following the official policy of a political party or other organization ○ *off-message MPs*

off-off-Broadway *n* in New York City, theatre productions that are considered to be fringe, experimental, or avant-garde

off-peak *adj* relating to the periods outside that of maximum use, frequency, or demand —**off peak** *adv*

off-piste *adj* relating to or taking place on fresh trackless snow that is away from the regular skiing runs —**off piste** *adv*

off-plan *adj* based only on the plans of a building that has not yet been built —**off plan** *adv*

offprint /óf print/ *n* a separate printing of a single article from a periodical, often given in small quantities to the contributor

off-putting *adj* arousing irritation, repugnance, or mild unease —**off-puttingly** *adv*

off-ramp *n N Am* a one-way road serving as an exit from a main highway

off-rhyme *n* a partial or near rhyme

off-road *adj* designed, manufactured, or used for travel off public roads, especially over rough terrain

off-road vehicle *n* a motorized vehicle designed or used for travel away from public roads or on rough terrain

off-sales *npl* the sales within a pub of alcoholic beverages for consumption elsewhere ○ *Off-sales amounted to about 10% of gross takings.*

offscourings /óf skowringz/ *npl* the leftover or discarded parts of something

off-screen *adj* **1.** NOT VISIBLE ON SCREEN not visible on a television or cinema screen ○ *an off-screen commentator* **2.** OCCURRING IN ORDINARY LIFE occurring in ordinary life, not as fiction on television or in a film ○ *Her off-screen life was just as exciting.* ■ *adv* IN ORDINARY LIFE aside from television or film performances ○ *Off-screen, he mostly played golf.*

off-season *n* **1.** TIME OF LESS ACTIVITY a time of year when activity or business is at a low level (*often used before a noun*) ○ *Hotel rooms were cheaper in the off-season.* **2.** PERIOD BETWEEN SEASONS a period after the end of one annual sports season and before the beginning of the next ○ *how players spend their time in the off-season* ■ *adv* IN OFF-SEASON during the off-season ○ *He liked to travel off-season.*

offset *n* /óf set/ **1.** SOMETHING COUNTERBALANCING SOMETHING ELSE something that counterbalances or compensates, or an allowance made in order to counterbalance something (*often used before a noun*) **2.** CONSTR ABRUPT BEND IN STRAIGHT LINE an abrupt bend put into an otherwise straight bar or pipe in order to avoid an obstruction **3.** PRINTING PRINTING PROCESS USING INK TRANSFER a method of printing in which inked impressions are transferred onto paper from another surface (*often used before a noun*) **4.** PRINTING UNINTENTIONAL MARKING FROM WET INK an accidental transfer of ink, usually from one piece of paper to another (*often used before a noun*) **5.** BOT OFFSHOOT CAPABLE OF PROPAGATION an offshoot or runner from the base of a plant that can propagate the plant **6.** GENETICS OFFSHOOT OR DESCENDANT something that has developed from something else, e.g. a collateral descendant or group of descendants of a family **7.** GEOL SPUR IN MOUNTAIN RANGE a projecting spur or ridge in a mountain range (*often used before a noun*) **8.** GEOL HORIZONTAL DISPLACEMENT OF ROCK the horizontal displacement that occurs as a result of the movement of a rock mass along a fault **9.** SOMETHING SET APART something set apart from other things (*often used before a noun*) **10.** MEASURE SURVEYING LINE a short distance measured at right angles from a main survey line, used in finding the area of a piece of land **11.** BEGINNING the beginning of something (*dated*) **12.** ARCHIT same as **setback** (sense 2) ■ *v* /of sét, óf set/ (**-sets, -setting, -set**) **1.** *vt* COUNTERACT SOMETHING to balance or make up for something (*often passive*) ○ *These improved sales were offset by last month's losses.* **2.** *vti* PRINTING PRINT SOMETHING BY TRANSFER to print something by offset printing, or to accidentally transfer ink by an offset **3.** *vti* CONSTR FORM OR BE OFFSET IN SOMETHING to make an offset in something such as a wall or pipe, or to be formed into an offset —**offset** /of sét/ *adv*

offshoot /óf shoot/ *n* **1.** a branch or shoot growing from the main stem of a plant **2.** something that springs or spreads from or that is a subsidiary of a main source or origin ○ *The company was an offshoot of their leisure empire.*

offshore *adv* /of sháwr/ **1.** FROM LAND TO WATER on or over land that is near water, especially away from the land towards the sea ○ *An icy wind blew offshore.* **2.** IN WATER SOME WAY FROM SHORE in a body of water at some distance from the shore ○ *anchored offshore* ■ *adj*

when predicative /of sháwr/; when attributive /óf shawr/ **1. BLOWING FROM LAND TO WATER** blowing or moving from land towards the sea ○ offshore breezes **2. AT SEA SOME WAY FROM SHORE** located at sea a considerable distance from shore **3. IN FOREIGN COUNTRY** based or registered in a foreign country, usually in order to avoid taxes

offside adj when predicative /of sīd/; when attributive /óf sīd/ illegally beyond or in advance of a ball or puck during play ■ n /óf sīd/ the side of a motor vehicle away from the edge of the road, which is the right side in countries where vehicles are driven on the left of the road. When driving on the right of the road, as in North America and continental Europe, it is the left side of the vehicle. ○ The offside wing mirror had been knocked off. —**offside** /of sīd/ adv

offsider /of sīdər/ n Aus an assistant or partner ○ Tony, my offsider, will meet you at the airport.

offsite /óff sīt/ adj not based or occurring in an organization's principal place of activity —**offsite** adv

offspring /óf spring/ (plural same) n **1.** a person's child or an animal's young, or sometimes a descendant of a plant **2.** the product, consequence, or effect of something

offstage /óf stáyj/ adv **1. OUTSIDE ACTING AREA** away from the area of the stage used for a performance, usually out of the view of the audience **2. IN PRIVATE LIFE** in private life, especially as opposed to the character an actor plays or the personality a performer projects **3. OUT OF PUBLIC VIEW** unseen by the public and media ■ adj **1. HAPPENING OFFSTAGE** happening or situated outside the area of the stage visible to the audience **2. PRIVATE** occurring in or characteristic of somebody's private life **3. HAPPENING UNSEEN** occurring out of the gaze of the public and the media

off-street adj not in a street but in a car park, driveway, or another place ○ off-street parking

off-the-books adj US **1.** not recorded in the accounts of a company **2.** not registered for the purposes of paying income tax

off-the-cuff adj delivered spontaneously or without preparation or notes [< the custom of scribbling extempore remarks on a starched shirt cuff] —**off the cuff** adv

off-the-peg adj ready-made and sold in standard sizes, not tailored for the individual customer. N Am term **off-the-rack** —**off the peg** adv

off-the-rack adj N Am same as **off-the-peg** —**off the rack** adv

off-the-record adj not intended for publication or to be attributed by name to the person who said it —**off the record** adv

off-the-shelf adj **1.** readily obtainable or taken from an existing stock of merchandise or supplies **2.** officially registered with the Registrar of Companies solely in order to be sold (not hyphenated after a verb) —**off the shelf** adv

off-the-shoulder adj describes a woman's dress or top with a wide neckline and short or long sleeves designed to reveal one or both shoulders

off-the-wall adj unusual or unconventional in a way that is particularly bizarre (informal) [Origin ?] —**off the wall** adv

off-track adj N Am same as **off-course**

off-white adj of a very pale colour that is a shade or two away from white —**off-white** n

offy (plural -**fies**) n another spelling of **offie** (slang)

OFGAS /óff gass/, **Ofgas** n a regulatory body set up to supervise the gas industry in the United Kingdom after privatization and deregulation. Full form **Office of Gas Supply**

O'Flaherty /ō fláhəti, ō fláa-/, **Liam** (1896–1984) Irish novelist. His works, notable for their realism and drama, include The Informer (1925).

> 'Then the sniper turned over the dead body and looked into his brother's face.'
> [Liam O'Flaherty, 'The Sniper'; 1937]

OFSTED /óff sted/, **Ofsted** n the government department that monitors educational standards in schools and colleges in England and Wales. Full form **Office for Standards in Education**

oft /oft/ adv same as **often** (archaic or literary; often used in combination) [Old English < Germanic]

OFT abbr Office of Fair Trading

Oftel /óf tel/, **OFTEL** n a former regulatory body that supervised the UK telecommunications industry until the end of 2003, when its functions were taken over by Ofcom. Full form **Office of Tele-communications**

often /óff'n, óftən, ófft'n/ adv at short intervals or repeatedly [13C. Alteration of OFT] ◇ **every so often** regularly but with fairly long intervals between each occurrence ◇ **more often than not, as often as not** fairly frequently, or in a majority of instances

PRONUNCIATION Pronunciation of **often**: 15th-century England saw a tendency among speakers of English to omit more consonants in an effort to pronounce some words more easily. Such was the case with the letter t in **often**. To this day, the preferred pronunciations of this word are /áwf'n, óff'n/, though some speakers do pronounce the t. Other words, such as listen, soften, hasten, and glisten, in which the t is never pronounced, reflect that same 15th-century trend.

oftentimes /óff'n tīmz, óftən-/, **ofttimes** /óft tīmz/ adv same as **often** (archaic)

OFWAT /óff wot/, **Ofwat** n a regulatory body set up to supervise water services in the United Kingdom after privatization and deregulation. Full form **Office of Water Services**

OG abbr **1.** Officer of the Guard **2. STAMPS** original gum

o.g. abbr **SPORTS** own goal

ogam n **LING** another spelling of **ogham**

Ogbomosho /ógbə mốshō/ city in Oyo state, southwestern Nigeria, situated approximately 201 km/125 mi. northeast of Lagos. Population: 711,900 (1995).

Ogdon /ógdən/, **John** (1937–89) British pianist and composer. He was an ebullient champion of neglected virtuoso pieces and of 20th-century music. Full name **Ogdon, John Andrew Howard**

ogee /ō jee/ n **1.** a decorative double curve like an elongated and flattened S **2.** a decorative moulding with an ogee-shaped profile **3. ARCHIT** same as **ogee arch** [Late 17C. Alteration of OGIVE]

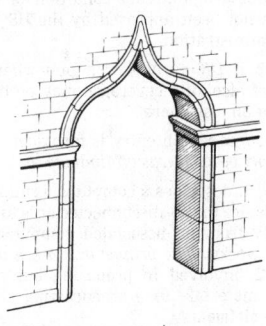

ogee arch

ogee arch n an arch whose sides curve gently inwards near the top and then curve upwards steeply to meet in a point

Ogen melon /ốgen-/ n a small melon with a green skin and sweet pale green flesh. Latin name: Cucumis melo. [After a kibbutz in Israel]

ogham /óggəm/, **ogam** n **1. ANCIENT CELTIC WRITING SYSTEM** an ancient British and Irish Celtic alphabet consisting of twenty characters formed by inscribing lines on either side of or across a long vertical baseline **2. CELTIC LETTER** a character used in the ogham alphabet **3. CELTIC INSCRIPTION** an inscription written in ogham, or something bearing such an inscription [Early 18C. Via modern Irish < Old Irish ogam, after Ogma, the Celtic god who supposedly invented it]

ogive /ō jīv/ n **1. ARCHIT RIB IN GOTHIC VAULT** a diagonal rib in a Gothic vault **2. ARCHIT POINTED ARCH** an arch that rises to a sharp point **3. STATS CUMULATIVE FREQUENCY GRAPH** a graph or curve that represents the cumulative frequencies of a set of values [Origin ?]

Oglala /og láalə/ (plural same or -**las**) n a member of a Native North American people, a branch of the

Teton, who live mainly in South Dakota [Mid-19C. < Dakota]

ogle /óg'l/ vti (**ogles, ogling, ogled**) to look at somebody for sexual enjoyment or as a way of showing sexual interest ■ n a prolonged flirtatious or lustful look at somebody [Late 17C. Origin ?] —**ogler** n

SYNONYMS See **gaze**.

ogonek /o gónnek/ n in some languages, a mark (˛) placed beneath vowels that signals a change in pronunciation. In Polish and in transcriptions of Native American languages it indicates nasalization. In Lithuanian it indicates a long vowel. [< Polish, literally 'little tail']

Ogooué /o gố way/ river in Gabon, west-central Africa. Length: 970 km/603 mi.

O grade n **1.** a former lower-level examination for the Scottish Certificate of Education, now replaced by Standard grade. Full form **Ordinary grade 2.** a subject studied, an examination taken, or a pass obtained at O grade

ogre /ốgər/ n **1.** in fairy tales, a wicked giant or monster especially one who eats people **2.** somebody who is particularly unpleasant and frightening —**ogreish** adj

ogress /ốgriss/ n **1.** in fairy tales, a wicked female giant or monster especially one who eats people **2.** an offensive term that deliberately insults a woman's appearance and temperament

Ogun /ō gốn/ state in southwestern Nigeria, north of Lagos State. Capital: Abeokuta. Population: 2,338,570 (1991). Area: 16,762 sq. km/6,472 sq. mi.

oh /ō/ interj **1. USED TO EXPRESS STRONG EMOTION** used to express a strong emotional reaction such as surprise, shock, pain, or extreme pleasure ○ Oh! That's wonderful news! **2. USED TO INTRODUCE STRONG REACTION** used to introduce short phrases that express a strong emotion such as anger, shock, delight, or triumph ○ Oh what a fool I've been! **3. USED TO INTRODUCE RESPONSE** used to introduce a response to what somebody has just said or asked ○ Oh, I'm fine. How are you? **4. USED TO SHOW THOUGHT** used to indicate thought or hesitation about what to say next ○ We've got, oh, fifteen minutes before the bus is due. **5. USED TO ATTRACT ATTENTION** used to attract somebody's attention or call attention to something ○ Oh, John, can you come over here? [Mid-16C. Alteration of O²]

OHG abbr **LANG** Old High German

O'Higgins /ō hígginz/, **Bernardo** (1778–1842) Chilean leader. He led Chile's fight for independence from Spain (1810–17) and established himself as a virtual dictator (1817–23). Known as **the Liberator of Chile**

Ohio /ō hí ō/ **1.** state in the north-central United States, bordered by Michigan, Lake Erie, Pennsylvania, West Virginia, Kentucky, and Indiana. Capital: Columbus. Population: 11,421,167 (2002 estimate). Area: 116,104 sq. km/44,828 sq. mi. **2.** major river of the eastern United States, originating from the confluence of two other rivers at Pittsburgh, Pennsylvania, and flowing southwards to join the Mississippi at Cairo, Illinois. Length: 1,580 km/981 mi. —**Ohioan** adj, n

ohm /ōm/ n the SI unit of electrical resistance, equal to the resistance between two points on a conductor when a potential difference of 1 volt produces a current of 1 ampere. Symbol Ω [Mid-19C. After Georg OHM]

Ohm /ōm/, **Georg** (1787–1854) German physicist. His research on electric currents led to the formulation of Ohm's law. The ohm is named after him. Full name **Ohm, Georg Simon**

ohmage /ố mij/ n electrical resistance measured in ohms

ohmmeter /ốm meetər/ n an instrument that measures electrical resistance in ohms

OHMS abbr On Her (or His) Majesty's Service

Ohm's law n the law of physics that states that electric current is directly proportional to the voltage applied to a conductor and inversely proportional to that conductor's resistance [After Georg OHM]

ohmygod /ốmī gód/, **ohmigod** (slang) interj used to express extreme dismay, shock, or surprise ■ adj relating to extreme dismay, shock, or surprise ○ In

an ohmygod moment, the conductor slipped and fell off the podium. [Respelling of *Oh, my God!*]

oho /ō hố/ *interj* used to express surprise or exultation, e.g. at making a discovery [14C. < o² + HO²]

OHP *abbr* overhead projector

OHV *abbr* **1.** off-highway vehicle **2.** *also* **o.h.v.** MECH ENG overhead valve

OIC *abbr* oh, I see (*used in e-mails or text messages*)

-oid *suffix* like, resembling, related to ○ *toxoid* ○ *rhomboid* [< Greek *-oeidēs* < *eidos* 'form, shape' (see IDOL)]

oidium /ō íddi əm/ (*plural* **-ia** /-i ə/) *n* a thin-walled egg-shaped fungal spore produced by the fragmentation of a hypha [Mid-19C. Via modern Latin < Greek *ōion* 'egg' (see OO-)]

oik /oyk/ *n* somebody, usually a man, who is considered to be ill-mannered, ignorant, and socially inferior (*informal insult*) [Early 20C. Origin ?]

oil /oyl/ *n* **1.** THICK GREASY LIQUID a liquid fat, obtained from plant seeds, animal fats, mineral deposits, and other sources, that does not dissolve in water and will burn. Oils are used for a wide variety of purposes, most commonly as lubricants and fuels and in cooking. **2.** PETROLEUM petroleum, the crude product that is distilled and refined to produce industrial oils and oil-based products (*often used before a noun*) ○ *oil prices* **3.** PETROLEUM DERIVATIVE a liquid extracted from petroleum and used as a domestic fuel or as a machinery and engine lubricant, e.g. paraffin or motor oil (*often used before a noun*) **4.** PETROLEUM INDUSTRY the worldwide industry that is based on petroleum extraction and refining (*often used before a noun*) ○ *oil companies* **5.** THICK LIQUID CONTAINING OIL a thick liquid containing oil or with the consistency of oil, especially a cosmetic **6.** ART same as **oil paint** (*usually used in the plural*) **7.** ART same as **oil painting** (sense 1) ■ *v* (**oils, oiling, oiled**) **1.** *vt* APPLY OIL TO SOMETHING to put oil into or onto something in order to lubricate, polish, preserve, or soften it ○ *oiling the rusty gears* **2.** *vti* NAUT GIVE OR GET FUEL to supply a ship with oil, or be supplied with oil **3.** *vti* TURN INTO OIL to turn a solid fat such as butter or lard into an oily liquid, or be turned into an oily liquid [12C. < Old French, via Latin *oleum* 'olive oil' < Greek *elaion* < *elaia* 'olive'] —**oiled** *adj* ◇ **burn the midnight oil** to work or study until very late at night

oil beetle *n* a beetle that emits a foul-smelling oily substance from the joints of its legs to deter predators. Family: Meloidae.

oilbird /óyl burd/ *n* a bird whose young have fatty flesh, formerly used as a source of oil for cooking and lighting. Native to: Central and South America. Latin name: *Steatornis caripensis*.

oil cake *n* the solid residue remaining after extraction of the oil from some seeds such as cottonseed and linseed. Use: livestock feed.

oilcan /óyl kan/ *n* a metal container with a long thin spout, used to squirt lubricating oil into machinery

oilcloth /óyl kloth/ *n* a cloth that has been treated with oil or a synthetic resin to make it waterproof. Use: table coverings.

oil-cooled *adj* fitted with a cooling system that uses oil

oilcup /óyl kup/ *n* a cup-shaped reservoir of oil that provides continuous lubrication for a bearing in a machine

oil drum *n* a large metal cylinder designed for transporting and storing oil. Empty oil drums may be used as refuse containers, flotation devices, and braziers and to make instruments for steel bands.

oiler /óylər/ *n* **1.** an oil tanker, especially one that refuels ships at sea **2.** a ship that uses oil as fuel **3.** INDUST same as **oil well** (*informal*)

oil field /óyl feeld/, **oilfield** *n* an area of land or sea under which there are substantial reserves of petroleum, especially such an area that is being exploited

oil-fired *adj* burning oil as a fuel

oil gland *n* **1.** BOT, ZOOL a gland that secretes oil **2.** BIRDS same as **uropygial gland**

oilman /óyl man, -mən/ (*plural* **-men** /-men, -mən/) *n* **1.** an executive in the petroleum industry **2.** somebody who works in an oil field

oil of cloves *n* an essential oil extracted from clove flowers. Use: relief of dental pain, component of temporary fillings.

oil of wintergreen *n* an aromatic oil extracted from a North American evergreen bush. Use: in liniments, as flavouring.

oil paint *n* a paint that consists of pigment mixed with a drying oil

oil painting *n* **1.** a picture painted with oil paints **2.** the art of painting with oil paints ◇ **be no oil painting** an offensive term meaning to lack appealing physical features, especially facial ones

oil palm *n* a palm tree widely cultivated for its fruit and seeds, which yield palm oil. Native to: West Africa. Latin name: *Elaeis guineensis*.

oil pan *n N Am* same as **sump** (sense 1)

oil rig *n* the equipment used for drilling for oil, including the platform that supports the drilling equipment

oilseed /óyl seed/ *n* a seed that is rich in oil, especially one grown as a crop for oil extraction, e.g. linseed, groundnut, or cottonseed ○ *fields of oilseed rape*

oil shale *n* a black or dark-brown shale from which petroleum can be extracted by distillation

oilskin /óyl skin/ *n* **1.** WATERPROOF FABRIC a cotton fabric that has been treated with oil to make it waterproof **2.** WATERPROOF GARMENT a garment, especially a coat, made of oilskin ■ **oilskins** *npl* WATERPROOF CLOTHING waterproof overgarments consisting of a coat and trousers made of oilskin

oil slick *n* a film of oil covering part of the surface of something, especially a large expanse of oil floating on the sea following a spillage of oil from an oil tanker

oilstone /óyl stōn/ *n* a fine-grained stone that is lubricated with oil and used to sharpen cutting tools

oil trap *n* a set of conditions within rock strata that blocks the upward movement of oil or gas, causing it to accumulate

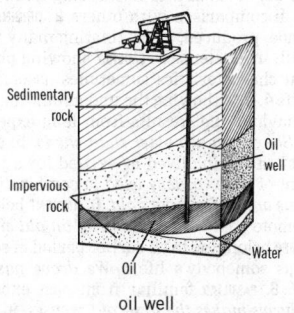

Sedimentary rock

Impervious rock

Oil well

Water

Oil

oil well

oil well *n* a shaft drilled into the ground or the bottom of the sea through which petroleum is extracted

oily /óyli/ (**-ier, -iest**) *adj* **1.** COVERED WITH OIL covered, smeared, or dirtied with oil ○ *don't want to get my hands oily* **2.** CONTAINING OIL containing or producing a lot of oil **3.** LIKE OIL resembling oil in texture, smell, or taste **4.** INGRATIATING unpleasantly eager to please or charm, or unpleasantly expert at doing this —**oiliness** *n*

oink /oyngk/ *interj*, *n* a representation of the nasal grunting sound made by a pig ■ *vi* (**oinks, oinking, oinked**) to make the nasal grunting sound of a pig [Mid-20C. An imitation of the sound]

ointment /óyntmənt/ *n* a smooth greasy substance used on the skin to soothe soreness or itchiness, help wounds heal, or make the skin softer [13C. Via Old French *oignement* < Latin *unguentum*]

Oireachtas /érrəktəss/ *n* the parliament of the Republic of Ireland, consisting of the president, the lower chamber (**Dáil Éireann**), and the upper chamber (**Seanad Éireann**) [Early 20C. < Irish, 'assembly']

OIRO *abbr* offers in the region of

Oise /waaz/ river in western Europe, flowing from southern Belgium through France and into the Seine. Length: 303 km/188 mi.

Oita /óytə/ city and seaport in Japan. It is the capital of Oita prefecture, on northeastern Kyushu Island. Population: 437,699 (2002).

OJ, oj *abbr* orange juice

Ojibwa /ō jíbbwə/ (*plural* **-was** or *same*), **Ojibway** /ō jíb way/ (*plural* **-ways** or *same*) *n* **1.** a Native North American people who originally lived north of Lake Huron and who later moved into territories ranging from Saskatchewan across to Michigan **2.** the Algonquian language of the Ojibwa people [Early 18C. < Ojibwa *ojibwe*] —**Ojibwa** *adj*

OJT *abbr* on-the-job training

OK /ố káy/, **okay** (*informal*) *interj* **1.** INDICATING AGREEMENT used to indicate agreement to or approval of what somebody has said or done ○ *'Can you help?' 'OK. What do you want me to do?'* **2.** USED TO CHECK FOR APPROVAL used at the end of a statement to enquire whether somebody has understood and agrees with or approves of what was said ○ *It's your job to make the arrangements, OK?* **3.** USED TO INDICATE FINISHING SOMETHING used to indicate that something is finished and that something else will now be done or discussed ○ *OK, let's move to the next item on the agenda.* ■ *adj* **1.** PASSABLE acceptable or tolerable but not exceptional ○ *It's OK for a first effort.* **2.** PHYSICALLY WELL in good health or condition ○ *I'll be OK if I can just sit down for a minute.* **3.** ALLOWABLE acceptable to somebody or permissible ○ *Is it OK for me to call home on the office phone?* **4.** FAIRLY GOOD OR PLEASANT better than just satisfactory or acceptable ○ *Her parents are OK; we get on quite well.* ■ *adv* FAIRLY WELL in an acceptable, tolerable, or satisfactory manner ○ *Everything's going OK, except that we're a little bit behind schedule.* ■ *vt* (**OK's, OK'ing, OK'ed; okays, okaying, okayed**) **1.** GIVE APPROVAL FOR SOMETHING to give approval for or agreement to something ○ *I just need you to OK the agenda.* **2.** OBTAIN SOMEBODY'S CONSENT to obtain somebody's approval for or agreement to something ○ *I'll need to OK that with my boss.* ■ *n* (*plural* **OK's**; *plural* **okays**) APPROVAL approval for doing something or agreement to do something ○ *As soon as she gives the OK, we'll start work.* [Mid-19C. Origin ?]

ORIGIN Of the many competing theories about the origins of *OK*, the one now most widely accepted is that the letters stand for *oll* or *orl korrect*, a facetious early-19th-century American phonetic spelling of *all correct*. This was reinforced by the fact that they were also coincidentally the initial letters of *Old Kinderhook*, the nickname of US president Martin Van Buren (who was born in Kinderhook, New York State), which were used as a slogan in the presidential election of 1840 (a year after the first record of *OK* in print).

Okanagan /ốkə naágən/ (*plural* **-gans** or *same*), **Okanogan** /ốkə nốgən/ (*plural* **-ans** or *same*) *n* **1.** a member of a Native North American people who live in southern British Columbia and Washington State **2.** LANG same as **Okinagan** —**Okanagan** *adj*

Okanagan, Lake /ốkə naágən/ lake in southern British Columbia, Canada. Area: 352 sq. km/136 sq. mi.

Okanogan *n, adj* PEOPLES, LANG same as **Okanagan**

okapi

okapi /ō káapi/ (*plural* **-pis** or *same*) *n* a plant-eating animal that resembles a small giraffe but has a short neck. It is chestnut brown with white stripes on its hindquarters. Native to: central Africa. Latin name: *Okapia johnstoni*. [Early 20C. < an African language]

Okavango /óka váng gō/ river in south-central Africa, rising in Angola, where it is called the Cubango, and flowing through Namibia and Botswana into the Okavango Swamp. Length: 1,800 km/1,120 mi.

Okavango Swamp marsh region in northwestern Botswana, southern Africa, occupying an inland drainage basin. Area: 15,000 sq. km/5,800 sq. mi.

okay *interj, adj, adv, vt, n* another spelling of **OK**

Okayama /óka yaáma/ city and port in Japan, on western Honshu Island, on the Inland Sea. Population: 621,809 (2002).

oke /ōk/ *n S Africa* same as **man** (*informal*) [Late 20C. Shortening of OKIE]

Okeechobee, Lake /óki chóbi/ lake in Florida, north of the Everglades National Park, forming part of the Cross-Florida Waterway. Area: 1,720 sq. km/663 sq. mi.

O'Keefe /ō keéf/, **Johnny** (1935–78) Australian singer. He is considered Australia's first rock and roll star. Full name **O'Keefe, John Michael**

Popperfoto

Georgia O'Keeffe

O'Keeffe /ō keéf/, **Georgia** (1887–1986) US artist. She is known for her stylized still lifes, especially of flowers and objects found in the desert.

'You paint *from* your subject, not what you see, so you can't be bothered with changes in light. I rarely paint anything I don't know very well.'
[Georgia O'Keeffe, *The Artist's Voice: Talks with 17 Artists*, Katherine Kuh; 1962]

Okefenokee Swamp /ókifi nóki-/ swamp in southeastern Georgia and northeastern Florida. It is noted for its rich wildlife. Area: 1,710 sq. km/660 sq. mi.

okeydokey /óki dóki/, **okeydoke** /-dók/ *interj* same as **OK** *interj* (sense 1) (*informal*) [Mid-20C. Alteration]

Okhotsk, Sea of /ō kótsk, ō khótsk/ sea lying off the eastern coast of Siberia, part of the northwestern Pacific Ocean. Area: 1,528,000 sq. km/590,000 sq. mi.

okie /óki/, **outjie** /óki, ótchi/ *n S Africa* same as **man** (*informal*; *also used as a patronizing form of address*) [Mid-20C. < Afrikaans *outjie* < *ou* 'old' + *-jie*, diminutive suffix]

Okie /óki/ *n US* **1.** an offensive term for a migrant farm labourer in the United States, especially one from Oklahoma or neighbouring Dust Bowl states during the 1930s (*slang insult*) **2.** somebody who comes from Oklahoma (*slang*) [Mid-20C. Shortening and alteration of OKLAHOMA]

Okinagan /óki naágən/ *n* the language of the Okanagan people, now with few speakers. It belongs to the Salishan branch of Algonquian-Wakashan languages. —**Okinagan** *adj*

Okinawa /óki naáwa/ **1.** city on south-central Okinawa Island, Japan. Population: 125,762 (2002). **2.** largest of the Ryukyu Islands in southwestern Japan, between the East China Sea and the North Pacific Ocean. Population: 1,229,000 (1991). Area: 2,255 sq. km/871 sq. mi. —**Okinawan** *adj, n*

Oklahoma /óklə hṓmə/ state in the south-central United States, bordered by Colorado, Kansas, Missouri, Arkansas, Texas, and New Mexico. Capital: Oklahoma City. Population: 3,493,714 (2002 estimate). Area: 181,048 sq. km/69,903 sq. mi. —**Oklahoman** *adj, n*

Oklahoma City capital city of Oklahoma, located in the central part of the state. Population: 519,034 (2002 estimate).

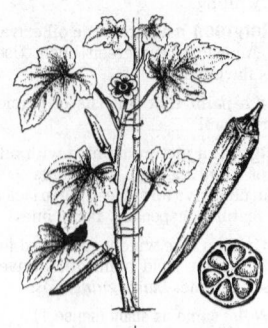

okra

okra /ókrə, ókrə/ (*plural same* or **okras**) *n* **1.** a green finger-length seed pod, cooked and eaten as a vegetable or used to thicken soups and stews **2.** a tall tropical plant that produces okra pods. Native to: Asia. Latin name: *Abelmoschus esculentus*. [Early 18C. Of West African origin, related to Igbo *okuro*]

okta /óktə/ *n* a unit of measure used to specify the amount of cloud cover, especially over an airfield, equivalent to enough cloud to cover one eighth of the sky [Mid-20C. Alteration of OCTO-]

-ol[1] *suffix* compound containing hydroxyl, especially an alcohol or phenol ○ *glycerol* [< ALCOHOL]

-ol[2] *suffix* another spelling of **-ole**

Olaf II /ṓ laf/, **Olav II** /ṓ lav/, **St** (995–1030) king of Norway. During his reign (1015–28), he completed the conversion of Norway to Christianity. He was ousted by the Danes and killed in battle. Full name **Haraldsson, Olaf**

—land /ṓ land/ island of Sweden, located in the southwestern Baltic Sea. Population: 25,382 (1992). Area: 1,344 sq. km/519 sq. mi.

Olav II ♦ **Olaf II**

old /ōld/ *adj* **1.** HAVING LIVED LONG having lived for many years in comparison with others **2.** ORIGINATING YEARS AGO made, produced, or originating many years ago and still in existence **3.** ELDERLY showing physical or mental characteristics sometimes associated with long life **4.** WISE showing the understanding, wisdom, or behaviour that results from long experience of life ○ *She acts much older than she is.* **5.** EXISTING FOR SPECIFIC TIME having lived or existed for a particular amount of time (*usually used in combination*) ○ *The day was only a few hours old.* **6.** ANCIENT belonging to the remote past ○ *the remains of an old civilization* **7.** FORMER belonging to an earlier period of something such as somebody's life ○ *We drove past my old school.* **8.** FAMILIAR familiar from past experience ○ *She always makes the same old excuses.* **9.** EXISTING OR USED OVER TIME having existed or been used for a long time, especially if showing wear or age ○ *Change into old clothes before gardening.* **10.** *also* **Old** EARLIER existing before one or all of the other stages, forms, or instances of something, especially a particular language ○ *Old English words* **11.** USED FOR EMPHASIS used as an intensifier (*informal*) ○ *any old reason* **12.** EXPRESSING FAMILIARITY used to express affection or familiarity (*informal*) ○ *Good old Charlie!* **13.** *US* ANNOYINGLY FAMILIAR annoyingly familiar, especially as a result of repetition (*informal*) ○ *the kind of routine that gets old fast* **14.** GEOL, GEOG ERODED reduced through erosion and weathering **15.** GEOL, GEOG SLOWER MOVING characterized by slower moving water and broad, flat floodplains ■ *n* **1.** PERSON OF PARTICULAR AGE somebody of a particular age (*used in combination*) ○ *childcare for three- and four-year-olds* **2.** OLD THINGS things or customs that are old ○ *to balance the old with the new* **3.** *Aus* DARK BEER a dark beer brewed by top fermentation ■ *npl* OFFENSIVE TERM an offensive term for people who have lived a long time [Old English *eald* < W Germanic < Indo-European, 'grow, nourish'] —**oldness** *n*

USAGE See *elder*[1].

ORIGIN *Old* is ultimately from an Indo-European word meaning 'to grow, nourish', which, through Latin *alere*, is also the ancestor of English *adolescent*, *adult*, *alimony*, and *alumnus*. In Latin the meaning evolved into 'high', as seen in the English derivatives *alto*, *exalt*, and *haughty*, whereas the Germanic languages preserved an old past participle meaning 'grown, old', which is also the ancestor of English *elder*[1], *eldest*, and *world*.

old age *n* the latter years of somebody's life lived out to its full term

Old Bailey *n* the chief criminal court in England and Wales, located in London on the site of Newgate Prison, which was demolished to make way for it in 1902

Old Bill *n* the police considered collectively, or an individual police officer or a group of police (*slang*) ○ *Better watch it, lads, here come the Old Bill.* [Probably from a cartoon character created by Captain Bruce Bairnsfather (1887–1959), who was used in a recruitment campaign for London's Metropolitan Police]

old boy *n* **1.** FORMER STUDENT a former student at a boys' or men's school, especially a British public school or college **2.** OFFENSIVE TERM an offensive term for a man who has reached an advanced age **3.** FAMILIAR ADDRESS TO MAN used as a familiar way of addressing a man or boy (*dated informal*) ○ *See here, old boy, you can't enter this club uninvited.*

old-boy network *n* a system of informal contacts between men who belong to the same social group, especially former members of a school or university, and use their influence to help one another

Old Church Slavonic *n* the earliest written Slavonic language, still used in religious services in some Eastern Orthodox churches

old country *n* an immigrant's country of origin

Old Dart *n Aus* Britain, especially England (*informal humorous*) [*Dart* from a dialect pronunciation of DIRT]

old dear *n* an offensive term that patronizes a woman of advanced age

olden /ṓldən/ *adj* in or from the distant past (*archaic or literary*) [14C. < OLD + -EN]

Oldenburg /ṓldən burg/ city and river port in Lower Saxony State, northwestern Germany, situated approximately 40 km/25 mi. west of Bremen. Population: 149,691 (1997).

Oldenburg /ṓldən burg/, **Claes** (*b.* 1929) Swedish-born US sculptor. A pioneer of pop art, he is known for his sagging 'soft sculptures' of everyday objects. Full name **Oldenburg, Claes Thure**

'I am for an art that tells you the time of day, or where such and such a street is. I am for an art that helps old ladies across the street.'
[Claes Oldenburg, *Statement for exhibition catalogue*; 1961]

Old English *n* **1.** the earliest form of the English language, used up to about AD 1150. It was first written using the runic alphabet. **2.** a form of blackletter typeface used by English printers up to the 18th century —**Old English** *adj*

Old English sheepdog

Old English sheepdog *n* a large dog with a long shaggy coat and dark grey and white markings [Because they were originally bred in England]

olde-worlde /ṓldi wúrldi/ *adj* quaintly historical in a way that may or may not be genuine [Alteration to resemble early English spellings]

old face *n UK* a typeface originating in the 18th century that shows little difference between light and heavy strokes and has slanting serifs. ANZ, N Am term **old style**

oldfangled /ṓld fáng g'ld/ adj antiquated or out of date [Mid-19C. After NEWFANGLED]

old fart n an offensive term for somebody, usually a person in authority, who is regarded as being set in his or her ways and lacking a sense of humour or fun (slang insult)

old-fashioned adj 1. OUT OF DATE characteristic of or belonging to a time in the past and no longer considered fashionable or suitable for the present 2. MAINTAINING OLD-STYLE WAYS favouring or deliberately maintaining ideas, behaviour, or ways of doing things from an earlier time ■ n N Am BEVERAGES WHISKY COCKTAIL a cocktail made with whisky, bitters, sugar, and lemon peel and garnished with fruit

SYNONYMS old-fashioned, outdated, antiquated, archaic, obsolete, passé, antediluvian

CORE MEANING: no longer in current use or no longer considered fashionable

old-fashioned characteristic of or belonging to a time in the past and no longer considered fashionable or suitable for the present ○ She drove an old-fashioned car with a running board. ○ He was old-fashioned enough to insist on silence at meals. **outdated** superseded by something better, more fashionable, or more technologically advanced ○ The information officers were relying on outdated sources and missed the crucial connection. **antiquated** in need of updating or replacing ○ The central heating was antiquated and broke down at the first sign of cold weather. **archaic** belonging or relating to a much earlier period ○ Much of the language of the poem is obscure or archaic. **obsolete** superseded by something newer, though possibly still in use ○ Spin-dry washing machines rendered the mangle obsolete. **passé** no longer current or fashionable ○ Coats like that are definitely passé: you need to buy a new one. **antediluvian** (humorous) extremely old-fashioned or outdated ○ condemned what he called the antediluvian attitudes of the union hierarchy

old-fashioned look n a quizzical or reproving look directed at somebody who has done or said something amiss

Old French n the earliest form of the French language, used until about AD 1400 or, in some analyses, AD 1600 —**Old French** adj

old fruit n a term of address between men, especially between friends (dated informal)

old girl n 1. FORMER STUDENT a former student at a girls' or women's school, especially a British public school or college 2. OFFENSIVE TERM an offensive term for a woman who has reached an advanced age 3. FAMILIAR ADDRESS TO WOMAN used as a familiar way of addressing a woman or girl (dated informal) ○ Sorry, old girl, didn't mean to lose my temper like that.

old-girl network n a system of informal contacts between women who belong to the same social group, especially former members of a school or university, and use their influence to help one another

Old Glory n a nickname for the flag of the United States

old gold adj of a dark dull yellow colour, sometimes tinged with brown —**old gold** n

old growth n a long-established forest or woodland that contains some large old trees and has a relatively stable and diverse community of plants and animals (hyphenated before a noun)

old guard, **Old Guard** n the members of a group or organization who have been in it longest, are the staunchest defenders of its traditions, and are the least amenable to change (takes a singular or plural verb)

Oldham /ṓldəm/ industrial town near Manchester, northwestern England. Population: 217,273 (2001).

old hand n somebody who is thoroughly experienced in a field of activity

old hat adj boringly familiar or old-fashioned (informal)

Old High German n the form of German used in written documents up to about AD 1200 —**Old High German** adj

oldie /ṓldi/ n (informal) 1. something old, especially an old popular song 2. an offensive term for somebody who has reached an advanced age

Old Kingdom n the period of ancient Egyptian history that comprises the third to sixth dynasties, from around 2700 to 2150 BC, when the capital was at Memphis and the great pyramids were built

Old Labour n the British Labour Party as it evolved during the greater part of the 20th century, characterized by adherence to traditional socialist principles such as state ownership and opposition to the free market economy

old lady n (informal) 1. an offensive term for somebody's mother 2. an offensive term for a man's wife or for a woman partner in a relationship

Old Latin n the form of the Latin language used until about the middle of the first century BC —**Old Latin** adj

old-line adj in existence for a long time and having a high social status or good reputation that has endured

old maid n 1. OFFENSIVE TERM an offensive term for a woman in or past middle age who has never been married and seems unlikely ever to marry 2. OFFENSIVE TERM an offensive term for a woman or man regarded as being excessively prim or fussy 3. CARDS CARD GAME a card game played with a pack from which one card has been removed. Players collect pairs of cards and the player left with the unpaired card loses. 4. CARDS LOSER IN OLD MAID the losing player in a game of old maid —**old-maidish** adj

old man n 1. OFFENSIVE TERM an offensive term for somebody's father (informal) 2. OFFENSIVE TERM an offensive term for a woman's husband or for a man partner in a relationship (informal) 3. COMMANDING OFFICER a man in a position of authority, especially a commanding officer (slang) ○ The old man is on the bridge, mad as can be. 4. FAMILIAR ADDRESS TO MAN used as a familiar way of addressing another man (dated informal) ○ Look here, old man, I'm in a spot of bother and wonder if you could help me out.

old man's beard n a plant that has trailing or hanging whitish growths, e.g. traveller's joy or Spanish moss

old master n 1. a great European painter of the period dating roughly from the late Middle Ages to the 18th century 2. a picture painted by an old master

Old Nick n a nickname for the devil (dated informal)

Old Norse n the North Germanic language from which the modern Scandinavian languages are derived, in use in Scandinavia from about AD 700 to 1350 —**Old Norse** adj

LANGUAGE HERITAGE See *Scandinavian*.

Old Red Sandstone n a sedimentary rock, usually red in colour, formed during the Devonian period and found in the United Kingdom and northwestern Europe

old rose adj of a deep greyish-pink colour —**old rose** n

old salt n a sailor who has years of experience at sea

Old Saxon n LANG same as **Saxon** (sense 2) —**Old Saxon** adj

old school n a group of people who adhere to traditional or old-fashioned values and practices ○ As a disciplinarian of the old school, he was horrified at the laxity of the new regime. —**old-school** adj

old school tie n 1. a tie whose colours indicate which school, especially which British public school, the wearer attended 2. the shared attitudes, traditions, and loyalties attributed to people who attended the same school, especially the same British public school

old skool /-skool/ adj reminiscent of or inspired by something from a slightly earlier period of popular culture, especially in music (slang) [Alteration of OLD SCHOOL]

old soldier n 1. VETERAN SOLDIER an experienced and long-serving soldier 2. FORMER SOLDIER somebody who formerly was a soldier 3. VETERAN somebody with a great deal of experience

oldsquaw /ṓld skwáw/, **old-squaw**, **old squaw** n ANZ, N Am same as **long-tailed duck**

old stager /-stáyjər/ n somebody with long experience in an activity

oldster /ṓldstər/ n an offensive term for somebody who has reached an advanced age (informal) [Early 19C. After YOUNGSTER]

old style n 1. ANZ, N Am PRINTING same as **old face 2.** a modern typeface that imitates the characteristics of old face

Old Style n the reckoning of dates by the Julian calendar

old-style adj characteristic of the past but now superseded by something else

old sweat n a veteran soldier (informal)

old-talk Carib vi to chat casually ■ n relaxed informal conversation [Perhaps < old people's talk]

Old Testament n the first part of the Christian Bible, corresponding to the Hebrew Bible, that recounts the creation of the world and the history of ancient Israel and contains the Psalms and the prophetic books

old-time adj 1. characteristic of or dating from a time in the past ○ the old-time music hall 2. in existence for a long time ○ the old-time families of the town

old-timer n 1. somebody who has been living in a place or involved in an activity for a long time 2. a senior citizen, especially a man (sometimes considered offensive)

Olduvai Gorge /ṓldə vī-/ ravine in northern Tanzania, where fossil remains of early humans and hominids have been found

oldwife /ṓldwīf/ (plural -wives /-wīvz/ or same) n an edible sea fish of several species, e.g. an alewife or a menhaden

old wives' tale n a traditional belief or story, passed down by word of mouth, that is now considered untrue or superstitious ○ Do what your doctor tells you and don't listen to old wives' tales. [< old wife 'old woman']

old woman n (slang) 1. an offensive term for somebody's mother 2. an offensive term for a man's wife or for a woman partner in a relationship 3. an offensive term for a man that deliberately insults his courage and decisiveness —**old-womanish** adj

Old World n the part of the world, consisting of Europe, Asia, and Africa, that was known to Europeans before Columbus made his first voyage to the Americas

old-world adj considered to be characteristic of a former and more gracious age

olé /ō láy/ interj used to express triumph, excited approval, or encouragement in Spanish. It is used especially at bullfights and during flamenco dancing. ■ n a cry or shout of olé [Early 20C. < Spanish]

OLE abbr COMPUT object linking and embedding

ole- prefix same as **oleo-** (used before vowels)

-ole suffix 1. a chemical compound containing a five-membered, usually heterocyclic, ring ○ carbazole 2. a chemical compound, usually an ether, that does not contain hydroxyl ○ anisole [Via French < Latin oleum (see OIL)]

olea CHEM plural of **oleum**

oleaginous /ṓli ájjənəss/ adj 1. CONTAINING OIL containing or producing oil 2. LIKE OIL similar to oil in nature or consistency 3. INGRATIATING unpleasantly eager to please, charm, or be of service ○ the oleaginous concierge [Mid-17C. Directly and via Old French oleagineux < Latin oleaginus 'of an olive tree, oily' < olea 'olive tree', alteration of oliva (see OLIVE)]

oleander /ṓli ándər/ (plural -ders or same) n a poisonous evergreen bush with leathery lance-shaped leaves and long seed pods. Flowers: sweet-smelling white, pink, or purple. Native to: Mediterranean region. Latin name: *Nerium oleander*. [Mid-16C. < medieval Latin]

olearia /ṓli áiri ə/ (plural -as or same) n TREES same as **daisy bush** [Mid-19C. < modern Latin, after J. G. Olearius (1635–1711), German horticulturist]

oleaster /ṓli ástər/ (plural -ters or same) n 1. an evergreen or deciduous bush with glossy leaves that are silvery underneath. Flowers: small, white, greenish-yellow. Genus: *Elaeagnus*. 2. the fruit of an oleaster, which resembles an olive [14C. Via Latin < olea 'olive tree', alteration of oliva (see OLIVE)]

oleate /ṓli ayt/ *n* a salt or ester of oleic acid

olecranon /ṓ lékrə non/ *n* the upper end of the ulna bone that extends beyond the joint of the elbow to form the elbow's hard projecting point [Early 18C. < Greek *ōlekranon* < *ōlenē* 'elbow' + *kranion* 'head']

olefin /ṓlə fin/, **olefine** /ṓlə feen/ *n* **1.** *also* **olefin fibre** *or* **olefine fibre** a synthetic fibre that is a long chain of polymers **2.** CHEM same as **alkene** [Mid-19C. < French *(gaz) oléfiant* 'oil-forming (gas)' < Latin *oleum* 'oil' (see OIL)]

oleic /ṓ lee ik/ *adj* **1.** relating to or derived from oil **2.** relating to or derived from oleic acid

oleic acid *n* a colourless oily liquid. Source: animal and vegetable fats. Use: manufacture of soap, ointments, cosmetics, and lubricating oils. Formula: $C_{18}H_{34}O_2$.

olein /ṓli in/, **oleine** /ṓli een/ *n* a yellow oily liquid that occurs naturally in most fats. Use: textile lubricant.

oleo /ṓli ō/ (*plural* **-os**) *n* PRINTING same as **oleograph** (*informal*) [Shortening]

oleo- *prefix* **1.** oil, oily ○ *oleograph* **2.** oleic acid ○ *oleate* [Via French *oléo-* < Latin *oleum* (see OIL)]

oleograph /ṓli ə graaf, -graf/ *n* a coloured lithographic print made on canvas with oil colours in order to imitate an oil painting —**oleographic** /ṓli ə gráffik/ *adj*

oleo oil *n* a yellow fatty substance extracted from beef fat. Use: manufacture of margarine, soap.

oleoresin /ṓli ō rézzin/ *n* a mixture of a resin and an essential oil, either obtained naturally from plants or produced synthetically

oleum /ṓli əm/ *n* a solution of sulphur trioxide in sulphuric acid [Early 20C. < Latin, 'oil' (see OIL)]

O level *n* **1.** a former school examination primarily for fifth-year students at secondary schools in England and Wales, now replaced by the General Certificate of Secondary Education (**GCSE**). Full form **Ordinary level 2.** a subject studied, an examination taken, or a pass obtained at O level [Shortening of ORDINARY]

olfaction /ol fáksh'n/ *n* **1.** the sense of smell **2.** the act of smelling something [Mid-19C. < Latin *olfacere* 'to smell']

olfactometer /ól fak tómmitər/ *n* an instrument for measuring the keenness of somebody's sense of smell [Late 19C. < OLFACTION + -METER]

olfactory /ol fáktəri/ *adj* used in smelling or relating to the sense of smell [Mid-17C. Via assumed Latin *olfactorius* 'used for smelling' < *olfacere* 'to smell' < *olere* + *facere* 'do']

olfactory bulb *n* the area of the brain from which the olfactory nerves extend

Olgas /ólgəz/ former name for **Kata Tjuta**

olibanum /o líbbənəm/ *n* CHEM same as **frankincense** [14C. Via medieval Latin *olibanum* and Greek *libanos* < Arabic *al-lubān* 'storax']

oligarch /ólli gaark/ *n* a ruler or leader in an oligarchy [Early 17C. < Greek *oligarkhēs* < *oligos* 'few' + -ARCH]

oligarchy /ólli gaarki/ (*plural* **-chies**) *n* **1.** SMALL GOVERNING GROUP a small group of people who together govern a nation or control an organization, often for their own purposes **2.** ENTITY RULED BY OLIGARCHY a nation governed or an organization controlled by an oligarchy **3.** GOVERNMENT BY SMALL GROUP government or control by a small group of people [Late 15C. Via French or medieval Latin < Greek *oligarkhia* < *oligos* 'few' + *-arkhia* '-archy' (see -ARCH)] —**oligarchic** /ólli gáarkik/ *adj*

oligo- *prefix* few ○ *oligophagous* [< Greek *oligos* 'small, little, few']

Oligocene /ólligō seen/ *n* the epoch of geological time, 38 million to 24 million years ago, during which primates first appeared. See table at **geological time** —**Oligocene** *adj*

oligoclase /ólligō klayss/ *n* a white, bluish, or reddish-yellow feldspar mineral of the plagioclase series. Source: igneous and metamorphic rocks. [Mid-19C. < OLIGO- + Greek *klasis* 'breaking' < *klan* 'break' (see CLASTIC), from its imperfect cleavage]

oligomer /ólli gōmər/ *n* a polymer consisting of fewer than five monomer units —**oligomeric** /ólligə mérrik/ *adj* —**oligomerization** /ólli gōmə rī záysh'n/ *n*

oligonucleotide /ólligō nyoóokli ə tīd/ *n* a polymeric chain containing ten nucleotides or fewer

oligopeptide /ólligō pép tīd/ *n* a peptide consisting of fewer than ten amino acids

oligophagous /ólli góffəgəss/ *adj* feeding on a restricted range of foodstuffs, usually a small number of different plants

oligopoly /ólli góppəli/ (*plural* **-lies**) *n* an economic condition in which there are so few suppliers of a product that one supplier's actions can have a significant impact on prices and on its competitors [Late 19C. < OLIGO- + MONOPOLY] —**oligopolistic** /ólli góppə lístik/ *adj*

oligopsony /ólli gópsəni/ (*plural* **-nies**) *n* an economic condition in which there are so few buyers for a product that one buyer's actions can have a significant impact on prices and the market in general [Mid-20C. < OLIGO- + MONOPSONY] —**oligopsonistic** /ólli gopsə nístik/ *adj*

oligosaccharide /ólligō sákkə rīd/ *n* a carbohydrate made up of a relatively small number of linked monosaccharides

oligotrophic /ólligō trṓfik, -tróffik/ *adj* describes bodies of water such as lakes that contain relatively little plant life or nutrients, but are rich in dissolved oxygen

olingo /o líng gō/ (*plural* **-gos**) *n* a small tree-dwelling nocturnal mammal similar in appearance to a slim sleek raccoon. Native to: tropical South and Central America. Latin name: *Bassaricyon gabbii*. [Early 20C. < American Spanish]

olio /ṓli ō/ (*plural* *same* or **-os**) *n* **1.** ASSORTMENT a miscellaneous collection of things **2.** SPICED STEW a highly spiced stew made from a variety of meats and vegetables, originally from Spain and Portugal **3.** ARTS MISCELLANY OR MEDLEY something made up of works of various kinds or works by different people, e.g. a literary miscellany or a musical medley [Mid-17C. Alteration of Spanish *olla* 'pot, stew' (see OLLA)]

Oliphant / óllifənt/, **Sir Mark** (1901–2000) Australian physicist. He discovered tritium (1934) and designed the first proton synchrotron accelerator. Full name **Oliphant, Sir Marcus Laurence Elwin**

olive

olive /ólliv/ *n* **1.** FOOD GREEN OR BLACK FRUIT a small oval bitter fruit with a stone, green when unripe and black when ripe, that yields olive oil **2.** TREES OLIVE TREE a widely cultivated evergreen tree that produces olives. Native to: Mediterranean region. Latin name: *Olea europaea*. (*often used before a noun*) **3.** INDUST OLIVE WOOD the wood of the olive tree. Use: decorative work. **4.** TREES TREE RESEMBLING OLIVE a tree or bush that resembles the olive tree **5.** COLOURS same as **olive green** [12C. Via Latin *oliva* < Greek *elaiwa*, a variant of *elaia* 'olive, olive oil']

olive branch *n* **1.** a gesture or offer intended to bring about a reconciliation **2.** a branch of an olive tree used as a symbol of peace [< Genesis 8:11]

olive drab *n* **1.** GREYISH GREEN a greyish-green colour **2.** *US* GREEN CLOTH a cloth dyed in an olive drab colour. Use: military uniforms. **3.** GREEN MILITARY UNIFORM a military uniform made of olive drab cloth, especially one worn in the United States army —**olive drab** *adj*

olive green *n* a deep yellowish-green colour —**olive-green** *adj*

olivenite /o lívvi nīt/ *n* a rare olive-green mineral that is a hydrated arsenate of copper. Formula:

$Cu_2(AsO_4)OH$. [Early 19C. < German *Olivenit* < *Olive* 'olive'; from its colour]

olive oil *n* a monounsaturated oil with a distinctive flavour extracted from olives. Use: salad dressings, cooking, manufacture of soap and cosmetics.

Oliver /ólliver/, **Isaac** (1560?–1617?) English painter of miniatures. He is noted for his naturalistic style, and painted portraits of the members of the court of James I.

olive ridley *n* a small endangered sea turtle with a drab green back and a prominent beak. Native to: Pacific Ocean. Latin name: *Lepidochelys olivacea*.

Olives, Mount of ♦ **Mount of Olives**

Laurence Olivier

Olivier /ə lívvi ay/, **Laurence, 1st Baron Olivier of Brighton** (1907–89) British actor and director. An influential Shakespearean actor, he was a founding director of the National Theatre (1961–73). Full name **Olivier, Laurence Kerr**

> 'Shakespeare—the nearest thing in incarnation to the eye of God.'
> [Laurence Olivier. Quoted in *Kenneth Harris Talking To Sir Laurence Olivier*, Kenneth Harris; 1971]

olivine /ólli veen/ *n* an olive-green magnesium-iron silicate mineral. Source: igneous rocks. Use: refractories, gems. —**olivinic** /ólli vínnik/ *adj* —**olivinitic** /óllivə níttik/ *adj*

olla /óllə/ *n* a large, usually unglazed pot with a spherical body and a wide mouth, used in Latin America and the southwestern United States for storing water and for cooking [Early 17C. Via Spanish < Latin *aulla* 'pot']

olla podrida /-po dreédə/ (*plural* **olla podridas** or **ollas podridas**) *n* **1.** a traditional Spanish and Latin American stew of meat and vegetables, usually containing sausage and chickpeas, and highly seasoned **2.** a miscellaneous mixture or assortment of things [< Spanish, 'rotten pot']

Olley /ólli/, **Margaret** (*b.* 1923) Australian painter. She is noted for her interiors and still life works. Full name **Olley, Margaret Hannah**

ollie /ólli/ *n* in skateboarding, a leap into the air on the board performed by pushing down on the rear end of the board (*slang*) [Late 20C. After the Florida skateboarder Alan 'Ollie' Gelfand]

olm /ōlm, olm/ *n* a sightless salamander, living in caves of southeastern Europe, that has a slender white body with a narrow head, tiny limbs, and red gills. The skin-covered vestigial eyes are sensitive to light. Latin name: *Proteus anguinus*. [Early 20C. < German]

Olmec /ól mek/ (*plural* **-mecs** or *same*) *n* **1.** a Central American civilization that arose around 1200 BC, before the Maya civilization. Notable features of this civilization were irrigated agriculture, urbanism, and the beginnings of calendar and writing systems. (*often used before a noun*) **2.** a member of one of the peoples who participated in the Olmec civilization [Late 18C. < Nahuatl *olmecatl* 'somebody who lives in the rubber country']

ology /ólla ji/ (*plural* **-gies**) *n* a science or academic field, especially one whose name ends in '-ology' (*informal*) ○ *people studying ologies you've never heard of* [Early 19C. < -OLOGY]

-ology *suffix* same as **-logy**

oloroso /óllə rṓssō/ *n* a golden-coloured full-bodied

sherry, usually medium-sweet in taste [Late 19C. Via Spanish, 'fragrant' < Latin *olere* 'to smell']

Olsen /óls's'n/, **John** (*b.* 1928) Australian painter. Primarily a landscape artist, he is known for works such as the *Journey into You Beaut Country* series (1961). Full name **Olsen, John Henry**

Olympia /ə límpi ə/ **1.** plain in southwestern Greece, in the western Peloponnese, near the Ionian Sea. It was an ancient religious site sacred to Zeus, and the first Olympic Games were held there in 776 BC. **2.** city and capital of Washington State, situated at the mouth of the Deschutes River on Puget Sound in the western part of the state. It has a deep-water port, and is a commercial and manufacturing centre. Population: 43,519 (2002 estimate).

Olympiad /ə límpi ad/ *n* **1.** an occasion when the modern Olympic Games take place **2.** the four-year interval between one Olympic Games and the next, used by the ancient Greeks as a way of calculating dates [14C. Via Latin < Greek *Olumpia*, where the games were held]

Olympian /ə límpi ən/ *adj* **1.** ENORMOUS extraordinarily great or demanding **2.** LIKE GREEK DEITY characteristic of a Greek god or goddess, or resembling one in power, majesty, or beauty (*literary*) **3.** MYTHOL OF MOUNT OLYMPUS relating to Mount Olympus, the home of the gods in Greek mythology **4.** ALOOF OR SUPERIOR so superior or grand as to be above everyday events and concerns ○ *his Olympian indifference to petty squabbles* **5.** OF OLYMPIA relating to Olympia, the ancient religious site in southwestern Greece ■ *n* **1.** OLYMPIC ATHLETE a competitor in the Olympic Games **2.** SUPERIOR PERSON somebody whose status is superior to everyday events and concerns **3.** MYTHOL GREEK DEITY in Greek mythology, one of the twelve major gods or goddesses who had their home on Mount Olympus **4.** PEOPLES SOMEBODY FROM OLYMPIA somebody who lived in ancient Olympia [15C. < Latin *Olympus* < Greek *olumpios*]

Olympic /ə límpik/ *adj* relating to the Olympic Games

Olympic Games *npl* **1.** a large-scale international sports contest intended to promote international goodwill. It has been held every four years since 1896 in different cities around the world. **2.** an ancient Greek religious festival held every four years at Olympia in honour of Zeus, with athletic, literary, and musical contests involving participants from all parts of Greece

Olympic Mountains /ə límpik-/ mountain range in northwestern Washington State, on the Olympic Peninsula, predominantly in Jefferson and Clallam counties. The highest peak is Mount Olympus, 2,428 m/7,965 ft.

Olympics /ə límpiks/ *n* the modern Olympic Games (*takes a singular or plural verb*)

Olympus, Mount /ə límpəss/ highest mountain in Greece, located in the north of the country. In Greek mythology it was believed to be the home of the gods. Height: 2,917 m/9,570 ft.

Olympus Mons /-mónz/ large volcano in the northern hemisphere of Mars. It is three times as high as Mount Everest. Height: 26 km/16 mi.

om *abbr* Oman (*used in Internet addresses*) See table at **domain name**

Om /ōm, om/, **Aum** /ōm/ *n* a sacred syllable that is chanted in Hindu and Buddhist prayers and mantras. It is symbolic of creation, destruction, and preservation, or of the primary trinities of Hinduism or Buddhism. [Late 18C. < Sanskrit]

OM *abbr* Order of Merit

-oma *suffix* tumour ○ *encephaloma* [Directly or via modern Latin < Greek *-ōma*]

Omagh /ōmə, ōm aa/ market town in central Northern Ireland. Population: 17,280 (1991).

Omaha[1] /ómə haa/ (*plural* **-has** or *same*) *n* **1.** a member of a Native North American people who live in northeastern Nebraska **2.** the Siouan language of the Omaha people, now with few speakers [Early 19C. < Omaha *umonhon* 'upstream people'] —**Omaha** *adj*

Omaha[2] /ómə haa/ city in eastern Nebraska, on the Missouri River. Population: 399,357 (2002 estimate).

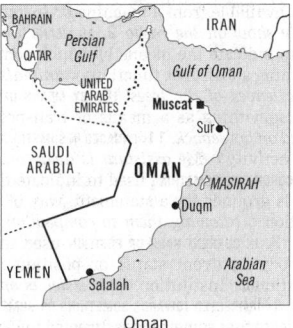

Oman

Oman /ō maan/ country on the southeastern Arabian Peninsula, on the Gulf of Oman. Language: Arabic. Currency: Omani rial. Capital: Muscat. Population: 2,807,125 (2001). Area: 309,500 sq. km/119,500 sq. mi. Official name **Sultanate of Oman** —**Omani** /ō maani/ *adj, n*

Oman, Gulf of arm of the Arabian Sea, situated between northern Oman and the southeastern coast of Iran

Omar Khayyam /ō maar kī aám, -ám/ (1050?–1122) Persian poet, mathematician, and astronomer. His *Rubáiyát* is an extensive collection of four-line stanzas, some of which were translated into English by Edward Fitzgerald (1859).

omasum /ō máyssəm/ (*plural* **-sa** /-sə/) *n* the third compartment of the stomach of a cow or other ruminant, situated between the abomasum and the reticulum. The inner surface has folds that break up food particles. [Early 18C. < Latin, 'bullock's tripe']

Omayyad *n* HIST, ISLAM another spelling of **Umayyad**

ombre /ómbər/ *n* a card game, popular in the 18th century, for three players, using forty cards, in which one player competes against the other two [Mid-17C. < Spanish *hombre* 'man, ombre' < Latin *homo* 'man']

ombudsman /ómboodzmən/ (*plural* **-men** /-mən/) *n* **1.** somebody, especially a man, responsible for investigating and resolving complaints from consumers or other members of the public against a company, institution, or other organization **2.** a government official responsible for impartially investigating citizens' complaints against a public authority or institution and trying to bring about a fair settlement [Mid-20C. Via Swedish < Old Norse *umboðsmaðr* 'manager, deputy' < *umboð* 'commission' + *maðr* 'man'] —**ombudsmanship** *n*

ombudsperson /ómboodz purs'n/ (*plural* **-persons** or **-people** /-peep'l/) *n* **1.** somebody responsible for investigating or resolving complaints from consumers or other members of the public against a company, institution, or other organization **2.** a government official responsible for impartially investigating citizens' complaints against a public authority or institution and trying to bring about a fair settlement [Late 20C. After OMBUDSMAN] —**ombudspersonship** *n*

ombudswoman /ómboodz woomən/ (*plural* **-women** /-wimin/) *n* **1.** a woman responsible for investigating and resolving complaints from consumers or other members of the public against a company, institution, or other organization **2.** a female government official responsible for impartially investigating citizens' complaints against a public authority or institution and trying to bring about a fair settlement [Mid-20C. After OMBUDSMAN] —**ombudswomanship** *n*

Omdurman /óm dur maan/ city in east-central Sudan, on the west bank of the River Nile, opposite Khartoum. Population: 1,267,077 (1993).

-ome *suffix* mass ○ *trichome* [Via modern Latin < Greek *-ōma*]

omega /ómigə/ *n* **1.** the 24th and final letter of the Greek alphabet, represented in the English alphabet as 'o'. See table at **alphabet 2.** the end, or the last thing in a series (*literary*) [Early 16C. < Greek *ō mega* 'great (i.e. long) o', as opposed to *o mikron* (see OMICRON)]

omega-3 *n* a long-chain polyunsaturated fatty acid with a double bond at the third carbon. Source: fish oils, seeds, and whole grains. Use: prevention of such conditions as high cholesterol, heart disease, and arthritis.

omega-6 oil *n* a long-chain polyunsaturated oil with a double bond at the sixth carbon, deficiency of which can cause skin problems and hormonal imbalances. Source: plants, seeds.

omega hyperon *n* a negatively charged elementary particle with a rest mass 3,272 times that of an electron

omega meson *n* an extremely short-lived neutral meson with a rest mass 1,532 times that of an electron

omega minus *n* PHYS same as **omega hyperon** [< the symbol for the particle]

omelet *n* FOOD US spelling of **omelette**

omelette /ómmlət/ *n* a dish consisting of beaten eggs fried over high heat until set, often served folded in half over a savoury filling such as cheese or mushrooms [Early 17C. Via French < Latin *lamella* 'small thin plate' < *lamina* 'thin plate']

omen /ō men, ōmən/ *n* something that happens that is regarded as a sign of how somebody or something will fare in the future ■ *vti* (**omens, omening, omened**) to be a sign of how somebody or something will fare in the future [Late 16C. < Latin]

omentum /ō méntəm/ (*plural* **-ta** /-tə/) *n* a fold of the peritoneum, especially the fold that covers the intestines (**greater omentum**) or the fold that connects to the liver (**lesser omentum**) [Mid-16C. < Latin]

omeprazole /o mépprə zōl/ *n* a drug that reduces the secretion of acid in the stomach. Use: treatment of ulcers and heartburn.

omer /ōmər/ *n* an ancient Hebrew unit of dry measure equal to one tenth of an ephah and roughly equivalent to 3.5 litres/3 quarts [Early 17C. < Hebrew *ōmer*]

Omer /ōmər/ *n* in Judaism, a seven-week period between the second day of Passover and the first day of Shavuoth, observed as a period of mourning, except on one day. Omer is named from the custom of offering an omer or sheaf of barley as a sacrifice in the Temple on the first day of this period. [Early 17C. < Hebrew *'ōmer*]

omerta /ō mair taá/, **omertà** *n* the code requirement alleged to apply to members of the Mafia, by which they must remain silent about any crimes of which they have knowledge [Late 19C. < Italian dialect < Latin *humilitas* 'humility' < *humilis* 'humble']

omicron /ō mī kron/ *n* the 15th letter of the Greek alphabet, represented in the English alphabet as 'o'. See table at **alphabet** [Mid-17C. < Greek *o mikron* 'small (i.e. short) o', as opposed to *ō mega* (see OMEGA)]

ominous /ómminəss/ *adj* suggesting or indicating that something bad is going to happen or be revealed ○ *I think it's rather ominous that they haven't replied to your letter.* [Late 16C. < Latin *ominosus* 'of an omen' < *omen* 'omen'] —**ominously** *adv* —**ominousness** *n*

omission /ō mísh'n/ *n* **1.** something that has been deliberately or accidentally left out or not done ○ *errors and omissions excepted* **2.** the act of omitting something, or the state of being omitted ○ *The omission of those three words changed the sense of the whole paragraph.* [14C. Via Old French < late Latin *omission-* < *omittere* 'OMIT']

omit /ō mít/ (**omits, omitting, omitted**) *vt* **1.** to fail to include or mention somebody or something, either deliberately or accidentally **2.** to fail to do something, either deliberately or accidentally [15C. < Latin *omittere* < *ob-* 'away' + *mittere* 'send'] —**omissible** /ō míssəb'l/ *adj*

SYNONYMS See *overlook*.

~~ommission~~ incorrect spelling of **omission**

~~ommited~~ incorrect spelling of **omitted**

omni- *prefix* all ○ *omnicompetent* [< Latin *omnis* < Indo-European, 'abundance, to produce']

omnibus /ómnibəss/ *n* **1.** BOOK COLLECTING SEPARATE WORKS a single book containing several works, usually by the same author, involving the same main character, or on the same subject, previously published separately **2.** *also* **omnibus edition** SINGLE BROADCAST OF PROGRAMMES a single continuous broadcast consisting

of several radio or television programmes previously broadcast separately as instalments of a serial or soap opera **3.** VEHICLES same as **bus** (*archaic or formal*) ■ *adj* **WITH MANY DIFFERENT THINGS** bringing many different things together as a single unit ○ *an omnibus education bill* [Early 19C. Directly or via French < Latin, 'for all' < *omnis* 'all' (see OMNI-)]

omnibus survey *n* a survey in which data on a wide variety of subjects is collected during the same interview

omnicompetent /ómni kómpitənt/ *adj* **1.** able to deal successfully with any task or situation **2.** competent to judge or try any kind of case

omnidirectional /ómnidi réksh'nəl, -dī-/ *adj* able to transmit or receive radio or sound waves in or from any direction

omnidirectional radio range *n* MEDIA same as **omnirange**

omnipotent /om nípəətənt/ *adj* possessing complete, unlimited, or universal power and authority [13C. Via French < Latin *omnipotent-* < *omnis* 'all' + *potens*, present participle of *posse* 'be able'] —**omnipotence** *n* —**omnipotently** *adv*

Omnipotent *n* RELIG same as **God**

omnipresent /ómni prézz'nt/ *adj* **1.** continuously and simultaneously present throughout the whole of creation **2.** present or seemingly present all the time or everywhere [Early 17C. < medieval Latin *omnipraesent-* < *omni-* 'omni-' + *praesens* 'present'] —**omnipresence** *n*

omnirange /ómni raynj/ *n* a very-high-frequency radio navigation network that enables aircraft pilots to choose and fly any bearing relative to a transmitter on the ground

omniscient /om níssi ənt/ *adj* knowing or seeming to know everything [Early 17C. < medieval Latin *omniscient-* < Latin *omni-* 'omni-' + *scire* 'know' (see SCIENCE)] —**omniscience** *n* —**omnisciently** *adv*

omnium-gatherum /ómni əm gáthə rəm/ (*plural* **omnium-gatherums**) *n* a collection of many different, often unsorted ideas or items (*humorous*) [< Latin *omnium* 'of all' + pseudo-Latin *gatherum*, alteration of *gathering*]

omnivore /ómni vawr/ *n* **1.** an animal that will feed on any type or many different types of food, including both plants and animals **2.** somebody who has wide-ranging and often undiscriminating interests or tastes [Late 19C. Via modern Latin *Omnivora* 'omnivores' < Latin *omnivorus* (see OMNIVOROUS)]

omnivorous /om nívvərəss/ *adj* **1.** eating any type or many different types of food, including both plants and animals **2.** wide-ranging and often undiscriminating in interests or tastes [Mid-17C. < Latin *omnivorus* < *omni-* (see OMNI-) + *-vorus* 'devouring'] —**omnivorously** *adv*

OMOV /ómov/, **Omov** *abbr* POL one member one vote

omphalos /ómfə loss/ (*plural* **-loses** or **-loi** /-loy/) *n* **1.** a conical stone with sacred significance in ancient Greek religion, especially the one at Delphi that was believed to mark the centre of the world **2.** the central or focal point around which everything else revolves (*literary*) [Mid-19C. < Greek, 'navel']

Omsk /omsk/ city and capital of Omsk Oblast, southwestern Russia, situated 772 km/480 mi. east of Chelyabinsk. Population: 1,437,781 (1995).

on /on/ *prep* **1.** **INDICATES POSITION** used to indicate a position above and in contact with the surface of something else ○ *sitting on the bed* **2.** **ATTACHED TO SOMETHING** used to indicate attachment to or suspension from a surface or object ○ *a wooden wheel mounted on the wall* **3.** **SUPPORTING WEIGHT** used to indicate what part of the body is supporting somebody's weight ○ *They sat there leaning on their elbows.* **4.** **CARRYING SOMETHING** carrying something that is therefore readily accessible ○ *I didn't have any cash on me at the time.* **5.** **INDICATES LOCATION OR VICINITY** located in a place or situated close to or alongside a place ○ *a town on the coast of Trinidad* **6.** **AT TIME** used to indicate when something happens ○ *just before noon on Tuesday* **7.** **RELATING TO SOMETHING** concerned with or relating to a particular subject, thing, or activity ○ *a talk on international relations* **8.** **WHERE SOMETHING IS AVAILABLE** used to indicate that some form of information or entertainment is currently available from a machine or instrument ○ *a comedy show on the radio* **9.** **AS MEANS OF FUNCTIONING** used to indicate the means by which somebody or something subsists or functions ○ *animals that feed on the leaves of the trees* **10.** **BY MEANS OF SOMETHING** using something as a means of transport ○ *They arrived on horseback.* **11.** **ENGAGED IN SOMETHING** engaged in an activity ○ *My assistant is away on a course.* **12.** **ACCORDING TO SOMETHING** used to indicate that something is grounds for a statement, way of thinking, or action ○ *allowing them to compete on an equal basis* **13.** **IN CURRENT RANK OR POSITION** used to indicate somebody's current status or position in an organization or institution ○ *My sister is on the committee.* **14.** **DIRECTED TOWARDS SOMETHING OR SOMEBODY** used to indicate that something is directed towards somebody or something ○ *I shone my torch on the inscription.* **15.** **CHARGED TO SOMEBODY** used to indicate that the cost of drinks or a meal is charged to a particular person ○ *The drinks are on me.* **16.** **IN DIRECT CONTACT** in direct conflict, competition, or contact with another (*informal*) ○ *spent many hours in one-on-one debate* ○ *white-on-white violence* ■ *adv* **1.** **IN CONTACT WITH SOMETHING** in contact with, attached to, or supported by something ○ *an envelope with a stamp on* **2.** **INTO CONDITION OF ATTACHMENT OR SUSPENSION** into a condition of being attached to or suspended from something ○ *sewing a button on* **3.** **INTO OPERATION** into the condition of operating or functioning ○ *turned the television on* **4.** **WITH CLOTHING** wearing clothes or placing clothing over a part of the body ○ *I pulled my tee-shirt on.* **5.** **PERSISTENTLY** in a continuous or persistent way ○ *decided to stay on in Cambridge* **6.** **IN PROGRESS** in activity or performance at the present time or at some implied time ○ *putting a play on* **7.** BASEBALL **INDICATING RUNNER'S POSITION** in baseball, used to indicate whether an offensive player is on the bases ○ *had left three runners on* **8.** GAMBLING **WAGERED** wagered as a bet ○ *put a bet on* ■ *adj* **1.** **TAKING PLACE** happening or being performed at the present time ○ *There's nothing good on tonight.* ○ *I've got a lot on at the moment.* **2.** **ARRANGED OR PLANNED** indicating that an activity is arranged and will happen ○ *Is the match still on?* **3.** **FUNCTIONING** indicating that a machine or device is functioning or in use ○ *There's a light on upstairs.* **4.** CRICKET **BOWLING** indicating that a particular bowler is bowling **5.** CRICKET **OF LEG SIDE** indicating or relating to the leg side of a cricket pitch **6.** CRICKET **IN CRICKET FIELDING POSITION** indicating some fielding positions on the leg side of a cricket pitch ■ *vt* (**ons, onning, onned**) *Malaysia, Singapore* **SWITCH SOMETHING ON** to switch on something such as a light or an electrical appliance (*usually used without inflections*) [Old English, < Indo-European] ◇ **be on about** used to indicate what somebody is talking about or what he or she means (*informal*) ◇ **be on it** *Aus* used to indicate that somebody is drinking alcohol (*slang*) ◇ **be on to somebody** *or* **something** to have information on or be aware of the real nature of somebody or something (*informal*) ◇ **it's not on** used to indicate that something is unacceptable ◇ **on and off** occasionally ◇ **on and on** in a continuous, persistent way ◇ **you're on** used to indicate that somebody is agreeing to do something proposed by somebody else (*informal*)

USAGE See ***onto***.

ON *abbr* **1.** LANG Old Norse **2.** Ontario

-on[1] *suffix* **1.** subatomic particle ○ *fermion* **2.** chemical substance ○ *fenuron* **3.** fundamental hereditary unit ○ *muton* **4.** unit, quantum ○ *chronon* **5.** inert gas ○ *radon* [< ION, influenced by the Greek neuter present participle *on* 'being' or neuter noun ending *-on*]

-on[2] *suffix* a biological or chemical substance ○ *parathion* ○ *interferon* [Alteration of -ONE]

on-again, off-again *adj* *N Am* happening or continuing intermittently (*informal*) ○ *an on-again, off-again romance*

onager /ónnəjər/ (*plural* **-gers** or **-gri** /-grī/) *n* **1.** a wild ass that is dark yellow with a stripe along its back. Native to: northern Iran and bordering areas. Genus: *Equus hemionus*. **2.** in former times, a war machine used to throw stones [14C. Via Latin < Greek *onagros* < *onos* 'ass' + *agrios* 'wild']

onanism /ṓnənizəm/ *n* (*literary*) **1.** the act of masturbating **2.** same as **coitus interruptus** [Early 18C. After *Onan*, a character in the Bible (Genesis 38:9), who spilled his semen onto the ground rather than impregnate his deceased brother's wife] —**onanist** *n* —**onanistic** /ṓnə nístik/ *adj*

onboard /ón báwrd/ *adj* carried or available on an aircraft, ship, or other vehicle or vessel

once /wunss/ *adv* **1.** **IN PAST** used to indicate that something happened or was the case at some time in the past ○ *The place must have been nice once.* ○ *a once comfortable lifestyle* **2.** **ONE TIME** on one occasion only **3.** **BY ONE STEP** distant by one place or degree ○ *a cousin once removed* **4.** MATHS **MULTIPLIED BY ONE** indicating that a number is multiplied by one ○ *once three is three* ■ *conj* **AS SOON AS** happening when something else has happened ○ *Once he got started, it was clear we were dealing with an expert.* ◇ **all at once** **1.** suddenly, often unexpectedly ○ *All at once he leapt up and ran from the room.* **2.** all at the same time ○ *She could not read the books all at once.* ◇ **at once** **1.** immediately ○ *Tell him at once.* **2.** all at the same time ○ *It's a lot to take in at once.* ◇ **for once** happening on this particular occasion, if at no other time ○ *For once my strategy worked.* ◇ **once and for all** completely, finally, or definitively ○ *We need to clear this up once and for all.* ◇ **once or twice** *or* **once and again** on a few occasions, but not often ○ *pausing once and again to listen* ◇ **once upon a time** used at the beginning of fairy tales and children's stories to indicate that something happened a long time ago or in an imaginary world

once-over *n* a rapid inspection or examination of somebody or something (*informal*) ○ *I'll give the car a quick once-over.*

onchocerciasis /óngkōsur kī́ əsiss/ *n* a disease caused by infestation with worms, especially a tropical disease of humans caused by a parasitic worm and transmitted by blackflies, causing skin nodules, lesions, and blindness [Early 20C. < modern Latin *Onchocerca*, genus of worms < Greek *ogkos* 'barb' + *kerkos* 'tail', from their shape]

onco- *prefix* tumour ○ *oncolysis* [< Greek *onkos* 'mass']

oncogene /óngkō jeen/ *n* a gene that can cause a cell to become malignant. Oncogenes are thought to be derived from normal cellular counterparts that have been taken up by viruses and altered so they malfunction when returned to the cell.

oncogenesis /óngkō jénnəssiss/ *n* the development of a tumour or tumours

oncogenic /óngkō jénnik/, **oncogenous** /ong kójjənəss/ *adj* relating to or causing the formation and growth of tumours —**oncogenicity** /óngkōjə níssəti/ *n*

oncology /ong kólləji/ *n* the branch of medicine that deals with the study and treatment of malignant tumours —**oncological** /óngkə lójjik'l/ *adj* —**oncologist** *n*

oncolysis /ong kólləssiss/ *n* the destruction of tumour cells, either spontaneously or, more usually, in response to drug or radiographic treatment

oncoming /ón kuming/ *adj* heading directly towards somebody or something ■ *n* the approach of something that is soon to occur

oncornavirus /ong káwrnə vīrəss/ *n* a virus containing single-stranded RNA and capable of causing cancer [Late 20C. < ONCO- + RNA + VIRUS]

oncost /ón kost/ *n* the general recurring expense of running a business, e.g. rent, maintenance, and utilities

Ondaatje /on daátyə/, **Michael** (*b.* 1943) Sri Lankan-

Isolde Ohlbaum

Michael Ondaatje

born Canadian writer. Among his many volumes of poetry and fiction is the Booker Prize-winning novel *The English Patient* (1992), which was made into a film.

'We die containing a richness of lovers and tribes, tastes we have swallowed, bodies we have plunged into and swum up as if rivers of wisdom, characters we have climbed into as if trees, fears we have hidden as if in caves.'
[Michael Ondaatje, *The English Patient*; 1992]

ondansetron /on dánssə tron/ *n* a drug that inhibits the production of serotonin. Use: control of nausea and vomiting caused by anticancer drug treatment and radiotherapy.

Ondes Martenot /óNd maártənō/ *n* an electronic musical instrument that can be played at a keyboard or with a finger slider, producing a sliding sound. The instrument was favoured by the composer Olivier Messiaen. [< French *Ondes (musicales)* '(musical) waves', its original name + (*Maurice*) *Martenot*, 1898–1980, French inventor]

on dit /oN deé/ (*plural* **on dits** /pronunc. same/) *n* a piece of gossip [< French, 'they say']

one /wun/ CORE MEANING: a grammatical word indicating a single thing or unit, and not two or more ○ (det) *just one accident out of thousands* ○ (det) *a one-legged man* ○ (pron) *The city used to have four hospitals and now has one.* ○ (pron) *Bill got one of his boxing gloves off.*
1. *det, pron* UNIQUE used to indicate the only thing or person with a specific characteristic ○ *the one exception to this* **2.** *det, pron* USED TO DISTINGUISH SOMETHING distinct from others of its kind ○ *from one thought to the next* **3.** *det* AT NONSPECIFIC TIME relating to an unspecified time in the past or future ○ *one August afternoon* **4.** *det* USED FOR EMPHASIS used instead of 'a' or 'an' to emphasize a following adjective or expression (*informal*) ○ *He's one cool customer!* **5.** *det* PARTICULAR introducing the name of somebody who is not known to the speaker ○ *a letter from one Thomas Atherton of Southport* **6.** *pron* TYPICAL INDIVIDUAL used to refer to people in general (*formal*) ○ *One can eat well here.* **7.** *pron* SOMEBODY OR SOMETHING UNSPECIFIED used to indicate somebody or something not specifically identified (*dated*) ○ *the voice of one crying in the wilderness* **8.** *pron* PREVIOUSLY MENTIONED used instead of a preceding noun to indicate somebody or something already mentioned ○ *nothing but an old vase, and a cracked one at that* **9.** *pron* JOKE OR STORY used to refer to a question, joke, or remark ○ *That's a good one!* **10.** *n* **1** the number 1. It is the smallest whole number, designating a single unit, and the first cardinal number. **11.** *n* SOMETHING WITH VALUE OF 1 something in a numbered series with a value of one ○ *to throw a one* **12.** *n US* DOLLAR BILL a one-dollar bill (*informal*) **13.** *n* TIME MEASURE used to indicate the time as one hour after twelve midday or midnight ○ *We'll stop for lunch at one.* **14.** *n* MUSIC MUSICAL NOTATION the numeral 1 used as the bottom figure in a time signature to indicate that the beat is measured in semibreves [Old English *ān* < Indo-European] ◇ **all one** not important enough to be of any consequence to somebody ○ *It's all one to me.* ◇ **as one** doing something at the same time or in the same way ◇ **at one** in harmony with somebody or something ◇ **be** *or* **get one up on somebody** to have or gain an advantage over somebody (*informal*) ◇ **one and all** everyone in a group ◇ **one and only 1.** unique and without comparison (*often used to introduce a performer on a show*) **2.** the person that somebody loves ◇ **one by one** happening individually in sequence ◇ **one or two** a few people or things ◇ **one time** *Carib* **1.** immediately **2.** completely **3.** used to add emphasis

USAGE **one of those people who is...** or **one of those people who are...?** Sense determines whether the verb in a construction of this type should be singular or plural, and in any given case one choice is right and the other wrong. To decide which verb form to choose, start with the *of*. For example, *He is one of those people who is/are always trying to impress* is not equivalent in meaning to *Of those people, he is one who is always trying to impress*. Rather, the idea is *Of those people who are always trying to impress, he is one*. Here the form of the verb *to be* is not governed by *one* but by

people, and therefore *one of those people who are* is right. In the following example the choice of the form of 'to be' is governed by 'only': *He is the only one of those people who is worth talking to*. Here the idea is *Of those people, he is the only one who is worth talking to*, so in this case *one of those people who is* is right.

1 *suffix* -one in pronouns, e.g. anyone (*used in e-mails or text messages*)

-one *suffix* ketone or related compound ○ *quinone* [Origin ?]

one-acter *n* a play that consists of only one act

one another *pron* each of several members of a group to the others ○ *neighbours helping one another*

USAGE See **each other**.

one-armed bandit *n* a gambling machine that is operated by inserting a coin or token in a slot and pulling down a lever on one side (*informal*)

one-dimensional *adj* **1.** existing in or possessing only one dimension **2.** presenting or perceiving only the most superficial aspects of something

Onega, Lake /o náygə/ second-largest lake in Europe, in northwestern Russia, east of Lake Ladoga, to which it is linked by the River Svir. Area: 9,610 sq. km/3,710 sq. mi.

one-horse *adj* **1.** VERY SMALL AND BORING describes a small place where nothing of interest or importance ever happens ○ *a one-horse town* **2.** HAVING ONE LIKELY WINNER fielding only one candidate or competitor who is likely to win ○ *a one-horse race* **3.** DRAWN BY SINGLE HORSE drawn by only one horse

Oneida /ō nídə/ (*plural* **-das** *or* same) *n* **1.** a member of a Native North American people who originally occupied lands in New York State and whose members now live mainly in Ontario, New York State, and Wisconsin. They were one of the five peoples who formed the Iroquois Confederacy, which later became known as the Six Nations. **2.** the Iroquoian language of the Oneida people [Mid-17C. < Oneida *onéryote*, the main Oneida settlement] — **Oneida** *adj*

Library of Congress

Eugene O'Neill

O'Neill /ō neél/, **Eugene** (1888–1953) US playwright. His realistic psychological dramas include *Mourning Becomes Electra* (1931), *The Iceman Cometh* (1946), and *Long Day's Journey into Night* (1956). He won the Nobel Prize in literature (1936). Full name **O'Neill, Eugene Gladstone**. See Cultural note at **mourning**

'None of us can help the things life has done to us. They're done before you realize it, and once they're done they make you do other things until at last everything comes between you and what you'd like to be, and you've lost your true self forever.'
[Eugene O'Neill, *Long Day's Journey into Night*; 1956]

oneiric /ō nī́ ərik/ *adj* relating to, in, or similar to dreams [Mid-19C. < Greek *oneiros* 'dream']

oneiromancy /ō nī́ ərō manssi/ *n* the practice of divining the future through the interpretation of dreams [Mid-17C. < Greek *oneiros* 'dream' + -MANCY] — **oneiromancer** *n*

one kind *adj* *Malaysia, Singapore* different from others in a way that makes somebody or something worthy of note

one-liner *n* a short joke or funny remark in one sentence

one-man *adj* consisting of, designed for, featuring, or performed by only one person ○ *a one-man tent*

one-man band *n* **1.** a performer who plays several musical instruments at once **2.** a business or organization in which one person does all or most of the work

oneness /wúnn nəss/ *n* **1.** SINGLENESS the quality of being one as opposed to many **2.** UNIQUENESS the quality of being unique **3.** AGREEMENT the condition of being united or agreed **4.** SAMENESS the quality of being the same or monotonous

one-night stand *n* **1.** a sexual encounter that lasts for only one night (*informal*) **2.** a single performance given at any one place for one night only

one-note *adj* *US* limited in ability, scope, or range (*informal*) ○ *a one-note writer*

one-off *adj* happening only once, not as part of a series ■ *n* a unique and unrepeatable or unrepeated thing or event

one-on-one *adj* *N Am* same as **one-to-one** (sense 1) — **one-on-one** *adv*

one-person *adj* consisting of, designed for, featuring, or performed by only one person

one-piece *adj* consisting of a single component, and not two or more ■ *n* a bathing suit consisting of a single piece

oner /wúnnər/ *n* a unique or extraordinary person or thing (*informal*)

onerous /ónərəss, ónnər-/ *adj* **1.** representing a great burden or much trouble **2.** involving obligations that are more disadvantageous than advantageous [14C. Via Old French *onéreux* < Latin *onerosus* < *oner-*, stem of *onus* 'burden'] — **onerously** *adv* — **onerousness** *n*

oneself /wun sélf/ *pron* (*formal*) **1.** REFERRING TO SUBJECT the reflexive form of 'one', meaning a person's own self ○ *The aim is to improve oneself and one's ability.* **2.** WITHOUT HELP FROM OTHERS used to indicate that something is done without help or interference from others ○ *One should always try and manage things oneself.* **3.** NORMAL SELF your usual or normal self ○ *In such situations one never feels oneself.* [Mid-16C. < *one's self*]

one-shot *adj* (*informal*) **1.** taking effect after only one application or attempt ○ *a one-shot solution to financial problems* **2.** *US* happening or doing something only once

one-sided *adj* **1.** UNFAIRLY WEIGHTED dominated by or favouring one side more than the other in a competition **2.** BIASED presenting or considering one side of a matter while ignoring other aspects of it **3.** BIGGER ON ONE SIDE larger, more prominent, or more developed on one side than the other **4.** BEING ON ONE SIDE occurring on or having only one side — **one-sidedly** *adv* — **one-sidedness** *n*

one-step *n* **1.** BALLROOM DANCE a ballroom dance similar to the foxtrot, in 2/4 time **2.** DANCE MUSIC the music for a one-step ■ *vi* DANCE ONE-STEP to perform the one-step

one-stop *adj* offering a wide variety of services or goods in one location so that a customer does not have to go from place to place ○ *a one-stop home design centre*

one-tailed *adj* describes a statistical test in which all values of the critical region either fall below or exceed a given value, but not both

onetime /wún tīm/, **one-time** *adj* **1.** having been something or played a particular role at a previous time ○ *the onetime world champion* **2.** done or occurring only once and unlikely to happen again

one-to-one *adj* **1.** INDIVIDUAL involving contact or communication between only two people ○ *a one-to-one conversation* N Am term **one-on-one 2.** MATCHING with one part that corresponds to or matches another **3.** MATHS WITH PAIRINGS THAT LEAVE NO REMAINDER describes a mathematical set in which each member can be paired with a member of another set leaving no remainder — **one-to-one** *adv*

one-track *adj* focused on, obsessed with, or restricted to only one issue or subject ○ *a one-track mind*

one-two *n* **1.** TWO SUCCESSIVE PUNCHES in boxing, a punch with one hand followed by a punch from the side

(cross) with the other hand ○ *I gave him the one-two.* N Am term **one-two punch** 2. QUICK SEQUENTIAL ACTIONS OR EVENTS two actions or events producing an effect because delivered or happening quickly and in sequence ○ *The incumbent could not survive the one-two of a sex scandal and defections by supporters.* N Am term **one-two punch** 3. PASS TO ANOTHER PLAYER THEN BACK in soccer, a pass made to another player on the same team who then immediately passes to a new position taken up by the original passer

one-two punch *n N Am* BOXING same as **one-two** (senses 1–2)

one-up (one-ups, one-upping, one-upped) *vt US* to gain an advantage over a rival or opponent (*informal*) ○ *Looks like I've been one-upped again.*

one-upmanship /-úpmənship/ *n* the practice of attempting to outdo or show yourself to be superior to a rival or opponent

one-way *adj* 1. GOING IN ONE DIRECTION moving or allowing movement in one direction only ○ *a one-way street* 2. NOT ALLOWING RETURN allowing somebody to travel to a destination but not to return ○ *a one-way ticket* 3. INVOLVING ONLY ONE OF TWO PEOPLE agreed on, felt by, or involving a contribution by only one of two people or parties ○ *a one-way agreement* 4. ALLOWING VIEWING FROM ONE SIDE made in such a way that it can be looked through from one side but not from the other ○ *one-way glass* ■ *n* ONE-WAY ROAD SYSTEM a one-way street or road system (*informal*)

one-way mirror *n N Am* same as **two-way mirror**

one-woman *adj* consisting of, designed for, featuring, or performed by one woman ○ *a one-woman show*

ongoing /ón gṓ ing, -gṓ-/ *adj* 1. having been developing or in progress for some time and continuing to do so 2. taking place at the present time

ONI *abbr* NAVY Office of Naval Intelligence

onigiri /ónni geéri/ *npl* Japanese rice balls, bite-sized or slightly larger, sometimes filled with seaweed or other foods and wrapped in seaweed [< Japanese]

onion

onion /únnyən/ *n* 1. EDIBLE BULB USED AS VEGETABLE a rounded edible bulb with hard pungent flesh in concentric layers beneath a flaky brown skin eaten raw or cooked as a vegetable 2. PLANT WITH PUNGENT BULBS a plant of the lily family that produces onions. Native to: Asia. Latin name: *Allium cepa*. 3. PLANT RELATED TO ONION any plant related to the onion, e.g. the Welsh onion [12C. < Latin *union-* 'onion'] —**oniony** *adj*

onion dome *n* a rounded dome resembling an onion in shape, typical of Russian and Byzantine church architecture

onionskin /únnyən skin/ *n* smooth thin translucent paper. Use: formerly, carbon copies.

Onitsha /ō níchə/ city in Anambra State, southeastern Nigeria, situated about 362 km/225 mi. east of Lagos. Population: 362,700 (1995).

-onium *suffix* a complex positively charged ion (**cation**) ○ *diazonium* [< AMMONIUM]

onium ion /ṓni əm-/ *n* a positively charged ion (**cation**) that is analogous to the ammonium ion. Formula: NH_4^+.

on-label *adj US* using or involving the use of a prescription drug to treat a condition for which the drug is approved by the US Food and Drug Administration

onlay *vt* /on láy/ (-lays, -laying, -laid /-láyd/) DECORATE SURFACE to apply something to a surface, especially for decorative purposes, so that it stands in relief ■ *n* /ónlay/ 1. MED SKIN GRAFT a skin graft surgically transferred to the surface of an organ or other part of the body 2. DENT INLAY IN TOOTH an inlay fixed to the biting surface of a tooth [15C. < ON + LAY[1] (verb)]

online /ón lī́n/ *adj* 1. CONNECTED VIA COMPUTER attached to or available through a central computer or computer network 2. DIRECTLY CONNECTED TO MEASURABLE PROCESS describes an instrument or sensor that is connected directly to a process being measured, thus obviating the need to take samples for analysis in a laboratory or elsewhere 3. US ONGOING currently going on or being done ■ *adv* WHILE CONNECTED TO COMPUTER while connected to a central computer or computer network

onliner /ón lī́nər/ *n* a user or a supplier of online computer services

onload /on lṓd/ (-loads, -loading, -loaded) *vti* to load freight onto a vehicle

onlooker /ón lŏŏkər/ *n* somebody who watches an event without participating in it —**onlooking** *adj*

only /ṓnli/ *adv* 1. SOLELY used to indicate the one thing or person that solely or exclusively happens or is involved in a situation ○ *facilities for club members only* ○ *I will act only in the best interests of our country.* ○ *The regulations apply only to new firms.* 2. INDICATING CONDITION used to indicate the condition that exists for something to happen or be true ○ *I'll go to the party, but only if you come with me.* 3. MERELY merely the situation, level, or amount indicated ○ *I could only stand and look.* ○ *That's only part of the picture.* 4. NO MORE AND NO LESS just the amount specified ○ *There are only 3.3 people at work for every person retired.* 5. AS RECENTLY AS considered as happening very recently ○ *only last March* 6. INDICATING EVENT HAPPENING IMMEDIATELY AFTER used to introduce a surprising or unpleasant event that happens immediately after the one mentioned ○ *We rushed the cat to the vet, only to find there was nothing wrong with it.* 7. *Ireland* EMPHASIZING used to emphasize a statement ○ *It was only terrible.* ■ *adj* 1. SINGLE PERSON OR THING used to indicate the single person or thing involved in a situation ○ *the only Democratic candidate* ○ *the only barrier between himself and the job* 2. WITH NO SIBLINGS with no brothers or sisters ○ *an only child* ■ *conj* BUT but or except ○ *It's the same product, only better.* [Old English *ānlic* < *ān* 'one' (see ONE)] ◊ **only too** used to emphasize the extent to which something is true ○ *Scenes like this are getting only too familiar.*

USAGE Avoid ambiguity in the placement of the limiting adverb **only**. The position of **only** within a sentence can determine the meaning of the entire sentence. As a general rule, put it next to the word you want it to modify: *She had only a pound. Only she had a pound.* or *She only had a pound.* Avoid putting **only** between a subject and a verb and between an auxiliary verb and a main verb: *He only does these things to get attention* where *He does these things only to get attention* is better. Similarly, *I will only stop the car once on the way there* is less desirable than *I will stop the car only once on the way there.*

on-message *adj* following the official policy of a political party or other organization ○ *The views expressed were most definitely not on-message.*

Yoko Ono and John Lennon

Ono /ṓnō/, **Yoko** (b. 1933) Japanese-born US artist. She is known for her avant-garde performance art, which after her marriage to John Lennon in 1969 included protests against the Vietnam War.

'Keep your intentions in a clear bottle and leave it on a shelf when you rap.'
[Yoko Ono, *Chicago Tribune*; 25 June 1978]

o.n.o. *abbr* or nearest offer (*used in advertisements*)

onomasiology /ónnō máyssi ólləjji/ *n* 1. the branch of linguistics that studies how meaning is expressed 2. LING same as **onomastics** (sense 1) [Early 20C. < Greek *onomasia* 'name' + -LOGY]

onomastic /ónnə mástik/ *adj* relating to, connected with, or explaining names [Late 16C. Via French < Greek *onomastikos* < *onoma* 'name']

onomastics /ónnə mástiks/ *n* 1. the study of proper names, their origins, and their formation (*takes a singular verb*) 2. the system underlying the creation and use of proper names in a specialized field (*takes a plural verb*)

onomatopoeia /ónnō matə peé ə/ *n* the formation or use of words that imitate the sound associated with something, e.g. 'hiss' and 'buzz' [Late 16C. Via late Latin < Greek *onomatopoiia* 'making of words' < *onoma* 'name' + *poiein* 'make' (see POEM)]

onomatopoeic /ónnə matə peé ik/ *adj* imitative of the sound associated with the thing or action denoted by a word —**onomatopoeically** *adv*

Onondaga /ónnən daágə/ (*plural* -gas or same) *n* 1. a member of a Native North American people who originally occupied lands in central New York State and whose members mainly continue to live there, as well as in Ontario. The Onondaga were one of the five peoples who formed the Iroquois Confederacy, which later became known as the Six Nations. 2. the Iroquoian language of the Onondaga people [Late 17C. < Onondaga *onóṭa?ke*, the main Onondaga settlement] —**Onondaga** *adj*

Onondaga, Lake /ónnən daágə/ lake in Onondaga County, central New York State. Area: 12 sq. km/5 sq. mi.

onrush /ón rush/ *n* a forward rush or push ○ *the onrush of enemy soldiers* ○ *the onrush of events* —**onrushing** *adj*

on-screen *adj, adv* while appearing on the screen in a television programme or film and therefore visible to the audience ○ *Their private life was very different from their on-screen relationship.*

onset /ón set/ *n* 1. the beginning of something, especially of something difficult or unpleasant ○ *the onset of winter* 2. an initial attack or assault in battle [Early 16C. < SET[1] (noun)]

onshore /ón sháwr/ *adj* 1. on land as opposed to at sea ○ *onshore drilling* 2. towards land from the sea ○ *onshore breeze* —**onshore** *adv*

onside /ón síd/ *adj, adv* in sports such as soccer or hockey, in a position that is allowed within the rules of the game

on-site *adj, adv* taking place or provided at the location where work or some other activity is being carried out

onslaught /ón slawt/ *n* 1. a powerful attack or force that overwhelms somebody or something 2. a very large quantity of people or things that is difficult to deal with ○ *faced with an onslaught of junk mail* [Early 17C. Via Dutch *aanslag* < Middle Dutch *aenslach* 'blow on' < *slach* 'blow']

onstage /ón stáyj/ *adj, adv* performing, happening, or existing on the stage as opposed to in the wings, backstage, or somewhere not visible to the audience

on-stream *adj, adv* in or into production or operation ○ *when the new system comes on-stream*

Ont. *abbr* Ontario

ont- *prefix* same as **onto-** (*used before vowels*)

-ont *suffix* cell, organism ○ *schizont* [< Greek *ont-* 'being' (see ONTO-)]

Ontario /on táiri ō/ Canadian province situated between the Great Lakes and Hudson Bay. Capital: Toronto. Population: 11,410,046 (2001). Area: 1,076,395 sq. km/415,598 sq. mi. Former name **Canada West** (1841–67) —**Ontarian** *n, adj*

Ontario, Lake lake in North America, the easternmost and smallest of the Great Lakes, straddling the US-Canadian border and bounded by New York State and Ontario Province. Its outflow is the St Lawrence River. Area: 19,010 sq. km/7,340 sq. mi.

on-the-job adj provided or obtained while working at a job ○ on-the-job training

ontic /óntik/ adj relating to real existence [Mid-20C. < the Greek stem ont- 'being' (see ONTO-)]

onto stressed /ón too/; unstressed /óntə, óntŏo/ prep 1. INDICATES POSITION used to indicate that somebody or something is located on something, or moves towards it so as to be on it ○ I splashed water onto my face. ○ hop onto a bus ○ shine a torch onto a wall ○ loading the data onto a disk ○ come onto the market 2. MAKING DISCOVERY making or about to make a discovery, often about something secret or illegal ○ I'm really onto something big here. ○ The police were onto them. 3. IN CONTACT in contact with a person or organization ○ Get onto the suppliers. [Early 18C. < ON + TO¹]

USAGE on, onto, or on to? Onto is usually preferable to on where movement is involved, as in I lifted the child onto [not on] my shoulders, and is always the better choice where on would be ambiguous: She jumped onto [not on] the platform. Unlike into, the preposition onto can be written as two separate words: He stepped onto [or on to] the pavement. Using onto, however, avoids the risk of confusion with the adverb on followed by the preposition to, which indicates progression and should not be joined together: We walked on to [not onto] the end of the road. Let us move on to [not onto] the next topic. See also into.

onto- prefix 1. being, existence ○ ontology 2. organism ○ ontogeny [< Greek ont-, present participle of einai 'be' < Indo-European]

ontogeny /on tójjəni/, **ontogenesis** /óntə jénnəssiss/ n the development of an individual from a fertilized ovum to maturity, as contrasted with the development of a group or species (**phylogeny**) — **ontogenic** /óntə jénnik/ adj —**ontogenically** adv

ontological /óntə lójjik'l/ adj relating to or derived from ontology —**ontologically** adv

ontological argument n an argument made by St Anselm and others to prove the existence of God by pointing to God's essence as a perfect, necessary being

ontology /on tólləji/ (plural -gies) n 1. the most general branch of metaphysics, concerned with the nature of being 2. a particular theory of being [Early 18C. < modern Latin, 'study of being' < Greek ont- 'being' (see ONTO-)] —**ontologist** n

onus /ónəss/ n 1. BURDEN a duty or responsibility ○ The onus is on her to make the first move. 2. BLAME the blame for something ○ He'll always bear the onus of having caused the accident. 3. LAW BURDEN OF PROOF OR PROCEEDING the burden of proof or responsibility for acting in a legal proceeding [Mid-17C. < Latin, 'burden, load']

onward /ónwərd/ adj directed or moving forward in space, time, or development ○ the great onward march of organization and life ■ adv same as **onwards**

onwards /ónwərdz/ adv towards a point or position ahead in space, time, or development

onya /ónyə/ interj Aus well done (informal) [Shortening and alteration of good on you!]

onycholysis /ónni kólləssiss/ n the separation of all or part of a fingernail or thumbnail from its bed, associated with psoriasis or a fungal skin condition [< modern Latin < Greek onukh-, stem of onux 'nail, claw']

onychophoran /ónni kóffərən/ n a small land invertebrate that has many pairs of unjointed legs and captures insects and similar prey by spraying them with adhesive mucus. Phylum: Onychophora. [Late 19C. < modern Latin Onychophora < Greek onukh- 'claw' + -phoros 'bearing'; from the curved claws]

-onym suffix name, word ○ pseudonym [< Greek onuma (see ONOMASTIC)]

onymous /ónnimess/ adj having a name rather than being anonymous [Late 18C. < ANONYMOUS]

onyx /ónniks/ n a semiprecious stone that is a fine-grained variety of chalcedony with bands of different colours. Use: gems, cameo work. [13C. Directly and via Old French and Latin < Greek onux 'fingernail, claw']

O.O., o/o abbr on order

oo- prefix ovum, egg ○ oospore [< Greek ōion < Indo-European, 'egg']

ooch¹ /ooch/ interj US same as **ouch** [Late 20C. Alteration]

ooch² /ooch/ (ooches, ooching, ooched) v 1. vi to try to make a sailing boat go faster by moving your body forward inside the boat and then stopping abruptly, thus imparting kinetic energy to the craft. Ooching is a controversial manoeuvre and sometimes regarded as cheating in yacht races. 2. vti US to move or make something move cautiously or slowly (slang) ○ told listeners the economy was just ooching along [Perhaps < OOCH¹]

oocyst /ṓ əssist/ n a fertilized gamete of parasitic organisms (**sporozoans**) that is enclosed in a thick wall

oocyte /ṓ ə sīt/ n a cell that develops into a female reproductive cell (**ovum**)

O.O.D. abbr NAVY officer of the deck

OODA Loop /ṓōdə-/ n in the armed forces and other defence-related agencies, a carefully worked-out chart or guide for use in making decisions throughout varying levels of policy and command [Late 20C. Acronym < observation, orientation, decision, accuracy]

O'Odham /ṓ ə dəm/ (plural same or -dhams) n PEOPLES, LANG same as **Papago** —**O'Odham** adj

oodles /ṓod'lz/ npl a large amount or number of something (informal) ○ She has oodles of friends. [Mid-19C. Origin ?]

OOG abbr COMPUT object-oriented graphics

oogamete /ṓ óggə meet/ n a female reproductive cell (**ovum**)

oogenesis /ṓ ə jénnəssiss/ n the formation and development of a female reproductive cell (**ovum**) — **oogenetic** /ṓ əjə néttik/ adj

oogonium /ṓ ə gṓni əm/ (plural -nia /-ni ə/ or -niums) n 1. a cell in the ovary that develops into an oocyte 2. the female sex organ of some algae and fungi that contains oospheres [Mid-19C. < OO- + Greek gonos 'generation, seed'] —**oogonial** adj

ooh /oo/ interj USED TO EXPRESS SURPRISE used as an exclamation of surprise, excitement, pleasure, or pain (informal) ■ vi (oohs, oohing, oohed) EXPRESS SURPRISE OR AWE to exclaim in surprise, excitement, pleasure, or pain, especially on first encountering something ○ When they went into the royal chambers, you could hear them oohing and aahing. ■ n EXCLAMATION OF SURPRISE an exclamation of surprise, excitement, pleasure, or pain [Early 20C. Natural exclamation] ◇ **ooh la la** used to show pleasant surprise or approval, or, humorously, to suggest that something is scandalous

oolite /ṓ ə līt/, **oolith** /ṓ ə lith/ n 1. a sedimentary rock, often shale, clay, or sandstone, that is made up of small spherical grains consisting of concentric layers 2. any small spherical grain in oolite [Early 19C. Via French ōōlithe < modern Latin oolites < Greek ōion 'egg' + lithos 'stone'] —**oolitic** /ṓ ə líttik/ adj

oolong /ṓo long/ n a dark Chinese tea that is partly fermented before being dried [Mid-19C. < Chinese wulong < wu 'black' + long 'dragon']

oom /oom/ n S Africa same as **uncle** (senses 1–2) (often used as a respectful form of address) [Mid-19C. Via Afrikaans < Dutch]

oompah /ṓom paa/, **oompah-pah** /ṓom paa paa/ n a representation of the sound made by a bass brass instrument, considered typical of some kinds of band music (often used before a noun) ○ an oompah band [Late 19C. An imitation of the sound]

oomph /ṓomf/ n 1. energy or enthusiasm ○ Put some oomph into it! 2. US strong or obvious sexual attractiveness (slang) [Mid-20C. Origin ?]

oonu /ṓonoo/, **oonoo**, **onnu** /ṓonoo/, **unnu**, **unna** /ṓonə/, **unu** pron used to address more than one person (slang; used in Black English) [Mid-20C. Probably < Ibo]

oophorectomy /ṓ əfə réktəmi/ (plural -mies) n SURG same as **ovariectomy** [Late 19C. < modern Latin oophoron 'ovary', literally 'egg-bearer' < Greek ōion 'egg']

oophoritis /ṓ əfə rítiss/ n inflammation of an ovary [Late 19C. < modern Latin oophoron 'ovary' (see OOPHORECTOMY)]

oops /ṓops, oops/ interj used as an exclamation on dropping something, doing something in a clumsy

or awkward manner, or making a mistake or blunder (informal) [Mid-20C. Natural exclamation]

Oort cloud /áwrt-, oórt-/ n a huge, roughly spherical, orbiting collection of comets thought to exist at the edge of the solar system [Late 20C. After Jan Hendrik Oort (1900–92), Dutch astronomer]

oose /ooss/ n Scotland fluff from textiles (informal)

oosphere /ṓ ə sfeer/ n an unfertilized female reproductive cell in algae and fungi [Late 19C. < OO- + SPHERE]

oospore /ṓ ə spawr/ n a fertilized female reproductive cell in algae and fungi [Mid-19C. < OO- + SPORE] — **oosporic** /ṓ ə spórrik/ adj —**oosporous** /ṓ óspərəss/ adj

ootid /ṓ ətid/ n the stage in the development of an egg cell that becomes the mature ovum immediately prior to fertilization. It is a haploid cell formed by division of the secondary oocyte [Early 20C. < OO-, after SPERMATID]

ooze¹ /ooz/ v (oozes, oozing, oozed) 1. vti FLOW OR LEAK SLOWLY to exude a liquid substance slowly and in small quantities, or flow in this way ○ Resin oozed from the trunk. 2. vti OVERFLOW WITH SOME QUALITY OR EMOTION to exude a quality or emotion in abundance, or be exuded in abundance ○ oozing charm and self-confidence 3. vi MOVE SLOWLY BUT STEADILY to move slowly but steadily forward or outward ○ The huge crowd oozed through the streets. 4. vi EBB to disappear or decline slowly and gradually ■ n 1. VERY SLOW FLOW a slow and gradual leakage or flow 2. TANNING SOLUTION an infusion used in tanning, made from oak bark and other plant materials [Old English wōs 'juice, sap' < Germanic]

ooze² /ooz/ n 1. SLUDGE thick mud or slime that is found at the bottom of a river or lake 2. BOG OR MARSH a soft or muddy area, e.g. a bog or marsh 3. MARINE BIOL SEDIMENT ON OCEAN FLOOR a layer of muddy sediment on the ocean floor consisting mainly of the remains of microscopic organisms such as plankton [Old English wāse]

ooze leather n a soft leather with a velvety finish [OOZE¹ 'tanning solution']

oozy¹ /oózi/ (-ier, -iest) adj leaking moisture [Pre-12C. < OOZE¹]

oozy² /oózi/ (-ier, -iest) adj wet and muddy [Pre-12C. < OOZE²]

op /op/ n a surgical operation (informal) [Early 20C. Shortening of OPERATION]

Op /op/ n same as **op art** [Late 20C. shortening]

OP abbr 1. MIL observation post 2. RELIG order of preachers (a title used by the Dominican order of friars) 3. CHEM organophosphate 4. PUBL out of print

op. abbr 1. MUSIC opera 2. SURG operation 3. opposite 4. OPTICS optical 5. MUSIC, LITERAT opus

Op. abbr MUSIC Opus

opacify /ṓ pássi fī/ (-fies, -fying, -fied) vti to become opaque, or make something opaque [Early 20C. < OPACITY] —**opacifier** n

opacity /ṓ pássəti/ n 1. BEING OPAQUE the quality, condition, or degree of being opaque 2. OBSCURITY the quality of being obscure in meaning 3. PHOTOGRAPHY, PHYS ABILITY OF MATERIAL TO STOP LIGHT the capacity of a material such as photographic film to stop light, expressed as a comparison between light striking the material and light transmitted 4. PHILOSOPHY PROPOSITIONS NOT ADHERING TO LEIBNIZ'S LAW propositions containing modal notions such as necessity or belief in which principles of logic such as Leibniz's law do not obtain [Mid-16C. Via French < Latin opacus 'shaded, dark']

opah /ṓpə/ n a brightly coloured sea fish that can be up to 1.8 m/6 ft long. Latin name: Lampris regius. [Mid-18C. < a West African language]

opal /ṓp'l/ n a variously coloured semiprecious stone that is a noncrystalline variety of silica. Use: gems. [Late 16C. Directly or via French < Latin opalus]

opalesce /ṓpə léss/ (-esces, -escing, -esced) vi to display shimmering milky colours [Early 19C. < OPAL + Latin -esce 'assuming a certain state']

opalescent /ṓpə léss'nt/ adj showing or possessing shimmering milky colours —**opalescence** n

opaline /ṓpə līn, -leen/ adj same as **opalescent** ■ n a semitranslucent glass made by adding fluorides

opaque /ō páyk/ *adj* **1.** NOT TRANSPARENT OR TRANSLUCENT impervious to light, so that images cannot be seen through it **2.** NOT SHINY dull and without lustre **3.** HARD TO UNDERSTAND obscure and unintelligible in meaning **4.** PHYS IMPENETRABLE BY RADIATION impenetrable by a specific form of radiation ■ *n* MATERIAL THROUGH WHICH LIGHT CANNOT PASS something opaque, especially a photographic pigment [15C. Directly or via French < Latin *opacus* 'shaded, dark'] —**opaquely** *adv* —**opaqueness** *n*

opaque projector *n N Am* OPTICS same as **episcope**

op art *n* a 20th-century school of abstract art that uses geometric patterns and colour to create the illusion of movement (*often used before a noun*) ○ *op art designs* [Shortening of OPTICAL ART, after POP ART] —**op artist** *n*

op. cit. /óp sít/ *abbr* in the text or texts quoted (*used in footnotes to refer to a source just mentioned*) [Latin *opus citatum* or *opere citato*]

ope /ōp/ (*archaic or literary*) *adj* open ■ *vti* (**opes, oping, oped**) to open, or open something [< OPEN]

OPEC /ō pek/ *n* an organization of oil-producing countries that share the same policies regarding the sale of petroleum. The members are Algeria, Gabon, Indonesia, Iran, Iraq, Kuwait, Libya, Nigeria, Qatar, Saudi Arabia, the United Arab Emirates, and Venezuela. Full form **Organization of Petroleum Exporting Countries**

op-ed /óp éd/ *n* **1.** a newspaper page, usually opposite the editorial page, that features signed articles expressing personal opinions (*often used before a noun*) **2.** an article expressing a personal viewpoint written for the op-ed section of a newspaper [Shortening of *opposite editorial (page)*]

open /ópən/ *adj* **1.** NOT CLOSED OR LOCKED allowing people or things to pass through freely ○ *an open window* **2.** ALLOWING ACCESS TO INSIDE with the lid, cork, or other device removed or in a position that allows access to the inside ○ *an open box* **3.** NOT SEALED not sealed, fastened, or wrapped ○ *an open envelope* **4.** APART OR WIDE with a part of the body widened or apart ○ *The kitten's eyes were open.* **5.** UNFOLDED OR APART having been unfolded, extended, or left apart ○ *A newspaper lay open on the table.* **6.** FRANK AND HONEST not trying to hide anything or deceive anyone ○ *open hostility* **7.** PUBLIC conducted in a public manner ○ *open hearings* **8.** RECEPTIVE ready and willing to accept or listen to something such as new ideas or suggestions ○ *I'm always open to suggestions.* **9.** VULNERABLE in a position in which blame, criticism, or attack are likely ○ *That remark left him open to criticism.* **10.** NOT ENCLOSED having no boundaries or enclosures ○ *open countryside* **11.** NOT COVERED having no cover or roof ○ *an open fire* **12.** AVAILABLE TO DO BUSINESS ready for business and available for use by customers or clients ○ *The garage is still open.* **13.** FREELY ACCESSIBLE accessible to all, with no restrictions on entry, membership, or acceptance ○ *an open meeting* **14.** ACCESSIBLE TO PARTICULAR GROUP accessible to a particular group of interested people ○ *This competition is open to all students under the age of 18.* **15.** VACANT ready for or available to applicants ○ *The vacancy is no longer open.* **16.** *US* TURNED ON switched on and ready to use ○ *an open microphone* **17.** NOT PREDETERMINED OR DECIDED remaining undecided or unresolved ○ *I'm trying to keep my options open.* **18.** ALERT in a state of focused attention and alertness ○ *Keep your eyes and ears open.* **19.** WITH NO TIME RESTRICTION with no restrictions on the period of use ○ *an open ticket* **20.** *US* GENEROUS very free or generous, especially with money ○ *She gave to charity with an open hand.* **21.** *US* NOT HAVING LEGAL RESTRICTIONS not having restrictions that limit activities such as gambling or drinking ○ *an open town* **22.** MED UNPROTECTED BY SKIN unprotected and exposed, with the skin cut, torn, or missing ○ *an open wound* **23.** MED NOT BLOCKED free from blockage and therefore allowing unobstructed passage **24.** TEXTILES HAVING GAPS having small gaps or intervals between the stitches or threads ○ *an open weave* **25.** OCEANOG FREE FROM ICE OR OTHER HAZARDS not covered by ice or containing objects dangerous to shipping ○ *open water* **26.** MUSIC NOT CLOSED OR MUTED not closed off at the end, stopped by a finger, or covered with a mute ○ *an open organ pipe* **27.** METEOROL WITHOUT FROST mild and free of frost **28.** MIL KNOWN TO BE UNDEFENDED publicly declared not to be garrisoned or defended in wartime ○ *an open city* **29.** FIN AVAILABLE WITHOUT LIMITATIONS freely available without restrictions ○ *open credit* **30.** FIN CURRENTLY ACTIVE active and with transactions being made ○ *an open bank account* **31.** PRINTING HAVING UNUSUALLY WIDE SPACES having wide spacing between printed lines **32.** PHON ENDING IN VOWEL describes a syllable that ends in a vowel **33.** GRAM HAVING SEPARATE ELEMENTS used to describe a compound word formed by two or more words that are spelled separately and without hyphenation **34.** CHESS WITHOUT PAWNS not having pawns as part of a file **35.** SPORTS UNGUARDED unprotected by the assigned player ○ *He left the goal wide open.* **36.** SPORTS HAVING FRONT FOOT BACK in sports, having the front foot farther from the line along which the ball is to be hit than the back foot ○ *Adopting an open stance, he began hitting the ball to the opposite field.* **37.** MATHS CONTAINING NO ENDPOINTS describes a mathematical interval that contains neither of a set's endpoints **38.** MATHS REFERRING TO SET QUALITY describes a mathematical set that has at least one neighbourhood of every point within the set **39.** MATHS SERVING AS COMPLEMENT TO CLOSED SET describes a mathematical set that is in a complementary relation to a closed set ■ *v* (**opens, opening, opened**) **1.** *vti* UNFASTEN FROM LOCKED OR CLOSED POSITION to change position or move so as to allow access, or change the position of or move something such as a door or window in order to allow access **2.** *vt* UNSEAL OR UNFASTEN SOMETHING to remove or unseal the lid, cork, or other device that keeps something such as a container closed **3.** *vt* UNWRAP SOMETHING to reveal the contents of something, e.g. by removing its wrapping ○ *I opened the parcel.* **4.** *vti* UNFOLD TO SHOW INSIDE to unfold or spread something apart so that the inner part is revealed, or become unfolded or spread in this way ○ *Open your books at page 75.* **5.** *vti* PART LIPS OR EYELIDS to move apart, or move the lips or eyelids apart **6.** *vti* START TRADING to start selling, trading, or doing business, or allow clients or customers access to premises in order to buy, trade, or do business **7.** *vti* GET UNDER WAY to start something formally, or get under way ○ *She opened the meeting with a speech about the environment.* **8.** *vt* START ACCOUNT to start an active banking or investment account **9.** *vt* DECLARE SOMETHING READY to make an official and usually public declaration that something is now ready for use or in session ○ *The sports centre was officially opened by the mayor.* **10.** *vi* BEGIN PUBLIC PERFORMANCE to start being shown to or performed for the general public for the first time ○ *The show opens on Friday.* **11.** *vti* BECOME ACCESSIBLE TO PUBLIC to be visited by the public, or become accessible to the public ○ *The house opens to the public in August.* **12.** *vt* REMOVE OBSTRUCTIONS to allow people free access to something when formerly this was denied or obstructed ○ *The country had finally opened its borders to the West.* **13.** *vi* GIVE ACCESS TO PLACE to provide access directly to another place (*refers to part of a building*) ○ *The bedroom opened onto a large living room.* **14.** *vti* BE READY FOR NEW IDEAS to become ready to accept new ideas, or make somebody ready to do this ○ *Try opening your mind a bit.* **15.** *vi* BEGIN TO RAIN to produce a downpour ○ *The heavens opened.* **16.** *vi* UNCURL to become fully developed or spread out (*refers to flowers or leaves*) ○ *The daffodils will open soon.* **17.** *vi* FIN START TRADING AT PARTICULAR VALUE to have a particular value at the start of a day's trading on a stock exchange **18.** *vt* MED EMPTY BOWELS to cause the bowels to evacuate **19.** *vt Malaysia, Philippines, Singapore* SWITCH SOMETHING ON to switch on something such as a light or an electrical appliance ■ *n* **1.** COMPETITION ANYONE CAN ENTER a competition or championship in which anybody, amateur or professional, can compete **2.** OUTSIDE a large and unobstructed outdoor space ○ *in the open* **3.** UNCONCEALED STATE the state of being no longer hidden or held back ○ *It's good to get all the facts out in the open.* **4.** COMPUT PUBLICLY AVAILABLE COMPUTER SYSTEM a product or system whose internal features and interfaces can be used or modified by users or developers in any way they wish [Old English, < Indo-European, 'up from under, over'] —**openness** *n*

open out *v* **1.** *vi* WIDEN to become wider ○ *The track opened out into a clearing.* **2.** *vti* UNFOLD to unfold or spread out something, or be unfolded or spread out **3.** *vti* DEVELOP FROM BUD TO FLOWER to uncurl from a bud into a fully open flower or leaf, or cause a bud to do this **4.** *vi* BECOME LESS INTROVERTED to become more sociable, outgoing, and communicative

open up *v* **1.** *vi* UNFOLD to become unclosed, unfold or expand, or offer a broader and freer view to a viewer ○ *Suddenly the valley opened up before us.* **2.** *vt* MAKE OPENING IN SOMETHING to make an opening in something, especially in order to get access **3.** *vt* REMOVE COVERING OR OBSTRUCTION FROM SOMETHING to remove anything that closes or covers something, or that blocks, obstructs, or restricts it **4.** *vti* MAKE SOMETHING ACCESSIBLE to make something more accessible or available to a wider range of people, or become more accessible ○ *The Internet has opened up a whole new world of information.* **5.** *vti* same as **open** *v* (sense 6) ○ *A new video store is opening up next week.* **6.** *vti* OPEN BUSINESS FOR TRADING to unlock something, especially a shop or business premises, so that trading can begin **7.** *vi* SPEAK FREELY to speak honestly, especially about personal feelings or experiences ○ *She opens up when she gets to know you.* **8.** *vi* TELL WHAT YOU KNOW to confess to a crime or give information about a crime under coercion (*informal*) **9.** *vi* START SHOOTING WEAPON to start firing or cause a gun or other weapon to start firing **10.** *vti* BECOME OR MAKE SOMETHING MORE EXCITING to become more free-flowing and more interesting or exciting, or cause something to become so ○ *After the first goal the match opened up.* **11.** *vi* MAKE VEHICLE GO FASTER to cause a motor vehicle to accelerate, or travel at an accelerated speed (*informal*)

open adoption *n* an arrangement concerning an adopted child by which contact between the child's adoptive and biological parents is maintained

open-air *adj* situated or happening outside a building

open-and-shut *adj* simple and easily resolved ○ *an open-and-shut case*

open bar *n* a bar at a party, wedding, or other social function where the drinks are served free of charge

open book *n* somebody or something that is very easy to understand or about which everything is known

open-cast *adj* describes a method of mining in which minerals or other materials are excavated from the surface rather than deep underground ○ *open-cast mining*

open chain *adj* an arrangement of atoms in a molecule in which the atoms are not joined at the ends to form a ring

open court *n* a trial or court that is open to members of the public, and whose proceedings are recorded

open day *n* a day on which an institution such as a school or university is open to the public for visitors to view aspects of its work and activities. N Am term **open house**

open door *n* (*hyphenated before a noun*) **1.** a policy whereby a nation allows free and unrestricted trade with all other nations **2.** free and unrestricted access at all times ○ *open-door management*

open-end *adj US* LAW same as **open-ended** (sense 4)

open-ended *adj* **1.** WITH NO PREARRANGED END with no planned or defined end **2.** EASILY MODIFIED not definite and easily changed ○ *We'd left everything pretty open-ended about the holidays.* **3.** NEEDING MORE THAN ONE WORD ANSWER requiring or allowing an answer that is fuller than a simple yes or no ○ *an open-ended question* **4.** *UK, ANZ, Can* HAVING NO LIMITS not having a fixed limit in either time or amount ○ *an open-ended contract* US term **open-end** —**open-endedly** *adv* —**open-endedness** *n*

opener /ópənər/ *n* **1.** OPENING DEVICE a device for opening containers such as tins, cans, or bottles **2.** INITIAL EVENT somebody or something that begins a discussion or event (*informal*) **3.** SPORTS FIRST MATCH the first match in a series or season **4.** SPORTS FIRST GOAL the first goal scored in a match **5.** CRICKET FIRST PLAYER TO BAT in cricket, the first player to bat at the beginning of a side's innings **6.** CARDS OPENING PLAYER in a card game, somebody who opens the bidding, betting, or play ■ **openers** *npl* CARDS STARTING POINT in some card games, a starting position or point, e.g. a set of cards that allow somebody to begin the betting ◇ **for openers** used to open a statement or discussion (*informal*)

open-eyed *adj* **1.** WATCHFUL alert to all that is happening **2.** WITH EYES WIDE IN WONDER having the eyes wide open in wonder or surprise **3.** ASSESSING REALISTICALLY realistic in knowing and accepting all aspects of a situation

open-faced *adj* with a face that suggests an honest, straightforward, and sincere character

open-faced sandwich *n N Am* FOOD same as **open sandwich**

open fracture *n* a bone fracture in which a broken bone pierces the skin or comes into contact with an open wound

openhanded /ṓpən hándid/ *adj* generous with money or other material things —**openhandedly** *adv* —**openhandedness** *n*

openhearted /ṓpən haártid/ *adj* sincere and generous in spirit towards other people —**openheartedly** *adv* —**openheartedness** *n*

open-hearth *adj* describes a steel-making process that uses a furnace with a shallow hearth and a low roof (**reverberatory furnace**) to produce high-quality steel

open-heart surgery *n* heart surgery during which the heart is exposed and blood is circulated outside the body by mechanical means

open house *n* **1.** a situation or occasion when visitors are welcome at any time ○ *It's open house here – come over whenever you like!* **2.** *N Am* EDUC same as **open day**

opening /ṓpəning/ *n* **1. GAP** a gap or hole in something, especially one through which you can see or through which people or animals can pass ○ *We found an opening in the fence.* **2. FIRST PART** the first part of something ○ *The film has a wonderful opening.* **3. FIRST TIME OF USE** the occasion on which something is formally opened or reopened for use (*often used before a noun*) ○ *the opening ceremony* **4. FIRST PERFORMANCE FOR GENERAL PUBLIC** the first public performance or showing of a play, exhibition, or other production (*often used before a noun*) **5. OPPORTUNITY** an opportunity to do something ○ *It gave her an opening to say how delighted she was.* **6. VACANCY** a job that is available ○ *We have an opening for a young person with drive and enthusiasm.* **7. ACT OF OPENING** the act of opening something **8.** *N Am* **CLEARING IN WOODS** an area in a wood or forest in which trees do not grow **9. BEGINNING OF GAME** the first moves of a game, especially in chess and draughts **10.** LAW **FIRST STATEMENT BY COUNSEL IN TRIAL** the initial statement made by the prosecuting and defending barristers in a trial, before witnesses are called to give evidence

opening night *n* ARTS same as **first night**

opening time *n* the time at which pubs in the United Kingdom are legally allowed to start serving alcohol

open interval *n* in mathematics, a set of real numbers consisting of all numbers between but excluding its endpoints, usually written (a,b) or]a,b[

open-jaw *adj* describes a flight or flight booking that goes to one destination and returns from another and is booked as a return ticket

open learning *n* a system of further education that allows people to learn on a flexible part-time basis (*often used before a noun*) ○ *open learning courses*

open letter *n* a letter that is addressed to a person or organization but is intended for everybody to read and is published in a newspaper or magazine

openly /ṓpənli/ *adv* without making any attempt at concealment ○ *Many members were openly hostile to the proposed plan.*

open market *n* a market with no commercial restrictions that allows free competition between buyers and sellers

open marriage *n* a marriage in which each partner agrees to allow the other to engage in sexual relationships with other people

open-minded *adj* free from prejudice and receptive to new ideas —**open-mindedly** *adv* —**open-mindedness** *n*

open-mouthed *adj* **1.** with the mouth wide open in surprise or wonder **2.** loudly and persistently demanding or complaining —**open-mouthedly** *adv* —**open-mouthedness** *n*

open-necked *adj* with the top button unfastened ○ *an open-necked shirt*

open-plan *adj* used to describe a large open undivided space, especially in a workplace

open-pollinated *adj* pollinated naturally, without human intervention

open prison *n* a prison with security measures that are appropriate to inmates who are not dangerous and are unlikely to try to escape

open punctuation *n* minimal punctuation, especially minimal use of commas

open sandwich *n* a sandwich consisting of a single slice of bread with filling on it but no second piece of bread on top, sometimes eaten with a knife and fork. N Am term **open-faced sandwich**

open season *n* **1.** a period during the year when restrictions on the hunting and killing of game or the catching of fish are lifted **2.** a period when the usual restraints are ignored, in particular, when a particular group or category of people come under unrestrained critical attack (*informal*) ○ *It seems to be open season on lawyers at the moment.*

open secret *n* something that is supposed to be secret but in actual fact is widely known

open sentence *n* in logic, a formula containing a free variable, e.g. 'X is human', that cannot be said to be true or false because the referent of the variable is not determined

open sesame /-séssəmi/ *n* a sure means of gaining access to or obtaining something [< the magical words used by Ali Baba, a character in the *Arabian Nights*, to open the door of the robbers' cave]

open set *n* a mathematical set that is included within a family of sets (**topology**)

open shop *n* a workplace where being a member of a union is not a condition of being employed

open side *n* in rugby, the side of the field that lies between a scrum and the farther touchline —**open-side** *adj*

open-skies, open-sky *adj* allowing aircraft belonging to any nation the freedom to fly over an area, and therefore placing no restrictions on aerial surveillance of military installations

open slather *n ANZ* a situation in which there are no limits or constraints on behaviour (*informal*)

open society *n* a society in which there is freedom of thought, ideas, speech, and communication

open system *n* a computer design system with uniform industry standards, compatible with any similar type of system or part

open ticket *n* **1.** a valid ticket for travel that does not specify a date or time, the actual date and time of travel being arranged later **2.** a request for technical assistance or customer support, especially with computer hardware or software, that has not yet been dealt with

open-toe, open-toed *adj* describes a shoe, especially a sandal, that is not closed at the front, allowing the toes to be seen

open-top, open-topped *adj* describes cars and buses that have no roof or that have the roof removed

open trading protocol *n* a standardized computer protocol for payment-related transactions such as purchase agreements, receipts, and payment methods (*used in e-commerce*)

Open University *n* a university, founded in 1969, offering degree courses primarily by correspondence to mature students studying part-time and having many classes that are broadcast on TV and radio. Local tutoring sessions and summer schools are also provided. (*often used before a noun*)

open verdict *n* in a coroner's court, the verdict given when the cause of death is not clear and no charge of murder or manslaughter can therefore be brought

open water *n* an expanse of water that is not enclosed or obstructed

openwork /ṓpən wurk/ *n* **1.** decorative items that make use of patterns of holes, e.g. wrought-iron work, fretwork, or lace **2.** an embroidery technique in which holes are formed in a fabric by cutting or pulling threads and embellished with various stitches, or embroidery made by this technique

opera[1] /óppərə/ *n* **1. MUSICAL DRAMA** a dramatic work where music is a dominant part of the performance, with the actors often singing rather than reciting their lines. It is usually highly stylized and typically has recurring themes intensified by musical repetitions developed as the piece progresses. **2. OPERAS IN GENERAL** operas thought of collectively or as an art form **3.** MUSIC **OPERATIC SCORE** the musical score or libretto of an operatic work **4.** same as **opera house** [Mid-17C. Via Italian < Latin, 'works' < *opus* (see OPUS)]

opera[2] /óppərə/ ARTS plural of **opus**

operable /óppərəb'l/ *adj* **1.** capable of being treated by surgery **2.** capable of being done or put into practice —**operability** /óppərə bílləti/ *n* —**operably** *adv*

opéra bouffe /óppərə bōof/ (*plural* **opéras bouffes** /*pronunc. same*/) *n* **1.** an opera with a comic or farcical theme **2.** opéra bouffes thought of collectively or as an art form [< French, 'comic opera'; translation of Italian *opera buffa*]

opera buffa /óppərə bōofə/ (*plural* **opera buffas** or **opere buffe** /óppə ray bōo fay/) *n* a comic opera of the kind that originated in Italy in the 18th century, using themes or characters from everyday life and usually having a happy ending. Mozart's *The Marriage of Figaro* is an example. [< Italian, 'comic opera']

opéra comique /óppərə ko meék/ (*plural* **opéras comiques**) *n* an opera on a light-hearted theme with spoken dialogue, especially popular in 19th-century France [< French, 'comic opera']

opera glasses *npl* small decorative low-powered binoculars for use by people in the audience at theatrical, operatic, or ballet performances

operagoer /óppərə gō ər/ *n* a regular attender at opera performances

opera hat *n* a man's collapsible top hat that is spring-operated

opera house *n* a theatre that is designed for putting on operas, often grander in style than an ordinary theatre

operand /óppə rand/ *n* **1.** a quantity, function, or other entity that is to have a mathematical operation performed on it **2.** the portion of a computer instruction that specifies the location in memory of the data to be manipulated [Late 19C. < Latin *operandum* 'thing to be worked on' < *operari* (see OPERATE)]

operant /óppərənt/ *n* **1. PERFORMER OF OPERATION** somebody or something that operates or that carries out some kind of operation **2.** PSYCHOL **VOLUNTARY ACTION** in learning theory, an action or other unit of behaviour that does not appear to have a stimulus ■ *adj* **HAVING EFFECT** producing a specific effect [Early 17C. < Latin *operant-*, present participle of *operari* (see OPERATE)] —**operantly** *adv*

operant conditioning *n* a form of learning that takes place when an instance of spontaneous behaviour is either reinforced by a reward or discouraged by punishment. The principles involved have had a strong influence on behaviour modification as well as on other kinds of therapy.

opera seria /óppərə seéri ə/ (*plural* **opere serie** /óppəray seéri ay/) *n* **1.** an opera that has a serious theme, often one taken from classical mythology, and usually a tragic ending. An example is Mozart's *The Clemency of Titus.* **2.** opere serie thought of collectively or as an art form [< Italian, 'serious opera']

operate /óppə rayt/ (**-ates, -ating, -ated**) *v* **1.** *vti* **FUNCTION OR MAKE SOMETHING FUNCTION** to function or work, or make something function or work **2.** *vti* BUSINESS **FUNCTION AS BUSINESS OR MANAGE SOMETHING** to exist as a working business or organization, or oversee the running of a working business or organization **3.** *vi* MED **PERFORM SURGERY** to perform surgery on a person or animal **4.** *vi* **EXERT EFFECT** to have an effect or influence on somebody or something **5.** *vi* MIL **CARRY OUT MILITARY OPERATIONS** to undertake military missions or activities, usually within a particular area or from a particular base **6.** *vi* FIN **TRADE IN FINANCIAL MARKET** to trade or deal in securities or commodities on the stock exchange **7.** *vi* **ENGAGE IN ILLEGAL ACTIVITIES** to be active in some illegal or underhand business [Early 17C. < Latin *operat-*, past participle of *operari* 'work' < *oper-*, stem of *opus* 'work']

~~**operater**~~ incorrect spelling of **operator**

operatic /óppə ráttik/ *adj* **1.** belonging or relating to opera **2.** overly or flamboyantly extravagant, especially in behaviour [Mid-18C. < OPERA[1], after DRAMATIC] —**operatically** *adv*

operatics /óppə ráttiks/ *n* flamboyantly exaggerated or extravagant behaviour (*takes a singular or plural verb*)

operating cycle *n* the period of time from when somebody purchases a product to when proceeds from its sale are received

operating room, **operating suite** *n N Am* MED same as **operating theatre**

operating system *n* the essential program in a computer that maintains disk files, runs applications, and handles devices such as the mouse and printer

operating table *n* a table on which somebody undergoing a surgical operation lies

operating theatre *n* a room in a hospital where surgical operations are performed. N Am term **operating room**

operation /óppə ráysh'n/ *n* **1. CONTROL** the act of making something carry out its function, or controlling or managing the way it works **2. FUNCTIONING STATE** the state of functioning or of being in effect ○ *The ban is to be put into operation from next week.* **3. SOMETHING DONE** something that is carried out, especially something difficult or complex ○ *the tricky operation of removing the sting* **4.** MED **SURGICAL INTERVENTION** any surgical procedure, e.g. one carried out to repair damage to a body part **5. ORGANIZED ACTION** an organized campaign, manoeuvre, or other form of action, especially one carried out by a rescue team, the police, or diplomatic personnel **6.** *also* **Operation** MIL **MILITARY ACTION** an action conducted by military forces that can range in scope from a reconnaissance mission to an entire campaign (*often used before a noun*) ○ *Operation Desert Storm* **7.** MATHS **MATHEMATICAL PROCESS** a mathematical process in which entities are derived from others through the application of rules, e.g. subtraction, multiplication, or differentiation **8.** COMPUT **SINGLE PART OF COMPUTER PROGRAM** a series of actions performed by a computer, defined by an instruction and forming part of a computer program **9. BUSINESS DEAL** a business deal or financial transaction **10. ILLEGAL BUSINESS** an illegal, dishonest, or underhand business ■ **operations** *npl* **CONTROLLING OF ORGANIZED ACTIVITIES** the supervising, monitoring, and coordinating of the activities of a military or civilian organization (*often used before a noun*)

operational /óppə ráysh'nəl/ *adj* **1. ABLE TO BE USED** in proper working order and able to be used ○ *The new transport link will be fully operational next month.* **2. OF OPERATING** relating to the operating of something or to the way it operates **3. OF ORGANIZATION'S ACTIVITIES** relating to the operations of an organization, especially its day-to-day activities or the basic management and control of these **4.** MIL **COMBAT-READY** ready for combat or manoeuvres —**operationally** *adv*

operational amplifier *n* an amplifier with high gain and high stability that is controlled by way of externally connected negative-feedback circuits

operationalism /óppə ráysh'nəlizəm/ *n* the view that terms for scientific concepts should be defined using the scientific operations such as measuring or observing performed to establish or disprove them —**operationalist** *n, adj* —**operationalistic** /óppə ráysh'nə lístik/ *adj*

operationalize /óppə ráysh'nəl īz/ (**-izes, -izing, -ized**), **operationalise** (**-lises, -lising, -lised**) *vt* to put something to use or into operation (*informal*)

operational research *n* MANAGEMT same as **operations research**

operationism /óppə ráysh'nizəm/ *n* PHILOSOPHY same as **operationalism**

operations research *n* analysis of the problems that exist in complex systems such as those used to run a business or a military campaign, designed to give a scientific basis for decision-making

operatise *vt* ARTS another spelling of **operatize**

operative /óppərətiv/ *adj* **1. IN EFFECT** in place and having an effect, especially the right or desired effect **2. SIGNIFICANT** carrying a special meaning or significance **3.** MED **OF SURGERY** relating to or resulting from a surgical procedure ■ *n* **1. SKILLED WORKER** a skilled worker, especially in a manufacturing industry **2. WORKER** somebody who performs a particular task or who works in a particular field (*formal or humorous*) ○ *a rodent operative* **3.** POL **POLITICAL WORKER** an employee of a political party who works in any behind-the-scenes capacity such as political troubleshooting or manipulation of media stories **4.** *US* **DETECTIVE** a private detective **5.** *N Am* **SPY** a spy or secret agent —**operatively** *adv* —**operativeness** *n* —**operativity** /óppərə tívvəti/ *n*

operatize /óppərə tīz/ (**-tizes, -tizing, -tized**), **operatise** (**-tises, -tising, -tised**) *vt* to make an opera out of an existing novel, play, or other text [Mid-19C. < OPERA[1], after DRAMATIZE]

operator /óppə raytər/ *n* **1. SOMEBODY OPERATING SOMETHING** somebody who operates machinery, an instrument, or other equipment **2. BUSINESS OWNER OR MANAGER** an owner or manager of a business or other commercial enterprise **3. STOCK-EXCHANGE DEALER** a dealer on the stock exchange or in a money market, especially somebody who is aggressive or speculative **4. MANIPULATIVE PERSON** somebody who behaves in a devious or manipulative way, especially in order to gain something (*informal*) ○ *a smooth operator* **5.** MATHS, COMPUT **SOMETHING EFFECTING MATHEMATICAL OPERATION** a mathematical symbol, term, or other entity that performs or describes an operation, e.g. a multiplication or subtraction sign **6. SOLDIER** a member of the US Army Special Forces

operculum /ō púrkyōōləm/ (*plural* **-la** /-lə/ or **-lums**) *n* **1.** ANAT **MUCUS PLUG IN CERVIX** the plug of mucus that fills the opening of a woman's cervix while she is pregnant. It helps to prevent infection. **2.** FISH **GILL-COVERING FLAP** the flexible bony flap covering the gills of bony fishes **3.** BOT **FLAP IN MOSSES AND FUNGI** a flap covering an aperture in the spore capsules of mosses and some fungi **4.** ZOOL **SEAL ON MOLLUSC'S SHELL** a rounded plate that seals the mouth of the shell of some gastropod molluscs when the animal's body is inside [Early 18C. < Latin, 'lid' < *operire* 'to cover'] —**opercular** *adj*—**operculary** *adv*—**operculate** /-lət/ *adj*—**operculated** /-laytid/ *adj*

operetta /óppə réttə/ *n* a theatrical production, usually with a comic theme, similar to opera but with much spoken dialogue and usually some dancing. Gilbert and Sullivan wrote many operettas. [Late 18C. < Italian, 'small opera' < *opera* (see OPERA[1])] —**operettist** *n*

operon /óppə ron/ *n* in bacteria, a segment of a chromosome containing the genes that specify the structure of a given protein, alongside the genes that regulate its manufacture. Operons are relatively simple units of genetic control and are found only in bacteria. [Mid-20C. < French *opéron* < *opérer* 'to work' < Latin *operari* (see OPERATE)]

operose /óppə rōss/ *adj* (*formal*) **1.** requiring a lot of effort **2.** busy, active, or hard working [Late 17C. < Latin *operosus* < *oper-*, stem of *opus* (see OPUS)] —**operosely** *adv*—**operoseness** *n*

Ophelia /ə féeli ə/ *n* a very small inner natural satellite of Uranus, discovered in 1986 by the Voyager 2 planetary probe. Its gravitational influence seems to help stabilize the outer ring of Uranus.

ophicleide /óffi klīd/ *n* a musical instrument resembling and superseded by the bass tuba [Mid-19C. < French *ophicléide* < Greek *ophis* 'snake' + *kleid-* 'key'; from its resemblance to an earlier instrument called a 'serpent']

ophidian /ō fíddi ən/ *adj* **1.** belonging or relating to snakes **2.** resembling a snake in appearance, habits, or movement [Early 19C. < modern Latin *Ophidia* < Greek *ophid-* 'snake'] —**ophidian** *n*

ophiolite /óffi ə līt/ *n* any igneous and metamorphic rock that was formed from deep-sea sediment. Ophiolites are rich in iron and magnesium. [Mid-19C. < Greek *ophis* 'snake' + -LITE; from its snaky texture]

ophite /ó fīt/ *n* a mottled green rock, e.g. diabase or dolerite, that is made up of small long plagioclase crystals surrounded by larger pyroxene crystals [Mid-17C. Via Latin < Greek *ophitēs* 'serpentine stone' < *ophis* 'snake'; from its markings, which are like a snake's]

ophitic /ō fíttik/ *adj* describes rocks consisting of small elongated plagioclase crystals completely enclosed by larger pyroxene crystals

Ophiuchus /o fyóokəss/ *n* a large constellation near the celestial equator. See illustration at **constellation**

ophthal. *abbr* MED **1.** ophthalmologist **2.** ophthalmology

ophthalm- *prefix* same as **ophthalmo-** (*used before vowels*)

ophthalmia /of thálmi ə/ *n* inflammation of the eye, especially of the conjunctiva and surrounding area [14C. Via late Latin < Greek < *ophthalmos* 'eye' (see OPHTHALMO-)]

ophthalmic /of thálmik/ *adj* relating to the eyes, or located in the region of the eye

ophthalmic optician *n* OPHTHALMOL same as **optician** (sense 1)

ophthalmitis /óf thal mítiss/ *n* inflammation of the eye

ophthalmo- *prefix* eye, eyeball ○ *ophthalmoscope* [< Greek *ophthalmos* < Indo-European, 'see']

ophthalmol. *abbr* MED **1.** ophthalmologist **2.** ophthalmology

ophthalmology /óf thal mólləji/ *n* the branch of medicine that is concerned with the diagnosis and treatment of eye diseases and conditions —**ophthalmological** /of thálmə lójjik'l/ *adj* —**ophthalmologist** *n*

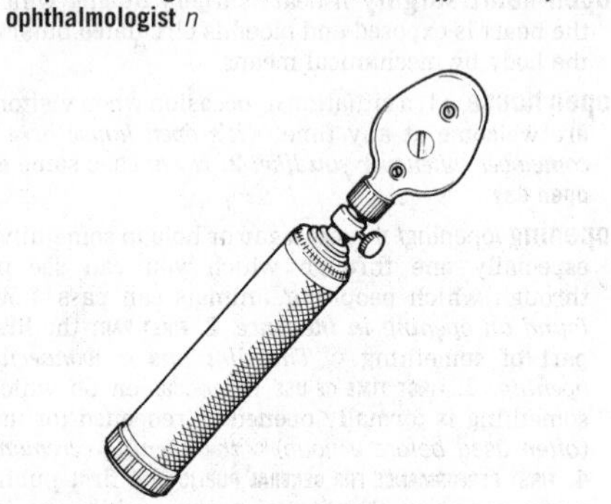

ophthalmoscope

ophthalmoscope /of thálmə skōp/ *n* a medical instrument used for examining the inside of the eye to detect changes to the retina such as those associated with diabetes and hypertension. A direct ophthalmoscope shines a fine beam of light into the eye and allows the examiner to see a magnified image of the spot where the beam falls. —**ophthalmoscopic** /of thálmə skóppik/ *adj*

ophthalmoscopy /óf thal móskəpi/ (*plural* **-pies**) *n* a medical examination of the inside of the eye using an ophthalmoscope to detect changes to the retina such as those associated with diabetes and hypertension

Ophuls /óff'lz/, **Opüls** /óppülss/, **Max** (1902–57) German-born French film director. His romantic, opulent films include *La Ronde* (1950) and *Madame de...* (1953). Born **Oppenheimer, Maximilian**

-opia *suffix* condition affecting vision ○ *hyperopia* ○ *protanopia* [< Greek < *ops* 'eye, face' < Indo-European, 'see']

opiate /ópi ət/ *n* **1. OPIUM-CONTAINING DRUG** a drug that contains opium or an opium derivative, e.g. morphine or heroin **2. SLEEP-INDUCING SUBSTANCE** a drug, hormone, or other substance capable of inducing drowsiness and other effects similar to those of opium or its derivatives **3. SOMETHING WITH DULLING EFFECT** something that has a relaxing, pacifying, or dulling effect ■ *adj* **1. CONTAINING OPIUM** containing opium or an opium derivative **2. BORING** mind-numbingly unexciting, especially because of being simplistic, cliché-ridden, or formulaic ■ *vt* (**-ates, -ating, -ated**) **1.** PHARM **TREAT SOMEBODY WITH OPIATE** to treat somebody, or somebody's symptoms, with an opiate **2. DULL PAIN** to dull or deaden pain, anguish, or some other unwanted condition [15C. < medieval Latin *opiatus* < Latin *opium* (see OPIUM)]

opine /ō pīn/ (**opines, opining, opined**) *vti* to express an opinion, or express something as your opinion (*formal*) [15C. < Latin *opinari* 'suppose, believe']

opinion /ə pínnyən/ *n* **1. PERSONAL VIEW** the view somebody takes about an issue, especially when it is based solely on personal judgment ○ *In my opinion it's all a waste of time.* **2. ESTIMATION** a view regarding the worth of somebody or something ○ *They had a pretty low opinion of me.* **3. EXPERT VIEW** an expert assessment of something ○ *I told the doctor I wanted a second opinion.* **4. BODY OF GENERALLY HELD VIEWS** the view or views held by most people or by a large number of people ○ *pundits and other opinion*

formers **5.** LAW **CONCLUSION OF FACT** a conclusion drawn from observation of the facts [14C. Via French < Latin *opinion-* < *opinari* 'suppose'] ◇ **be a matter of opinion** to be open to dispute or debate ◇ **be of the opinion that** to think that something is the case

opinionated /ə pínnyə naytid/ *adj* always ready to express opinions and tending to hold to them stubbornly, unreasonably dismissing other people's views

opinionative /ə pínnyənətiv/ *adj* (*formal*) **1.** relating to opinions or to the stating of them **2.** same as **opinionated** —**opinionatively** *adv*

opinion poll *n* a survey carried out to discover what the general public think about something

opioid /ōpi oyd/ *n* any opium-containing substance that is produced naturally in the brain ■ *adj* similar in effect or properties to opium but not derived from opium [Mid-20C. < OPIUM]

opioid peptide *n* a naturally occurring peptide that has pain-relieving and sedative effects. The endorphins are opioid peptides.

opisthobranch /ə pís thə brangk/ *n* an invertebrate sea animal that has gills, a small or nonexistent shell, and tentacles [Mid-19C. < modern Latin *Opisthobranchiata* < Greek *opisthen* 'behind' + *bragkhia* 'gills', because the gills are behind the heart]

opisthognathous /óppiss thógnəthəss/ *adj* having jaws that slope backwards or mouthparts that face backwards [Mid-19C. < Greek *opisthen* 'behind'] —**opisthognathism** *n*

opium /ōpi əm/ *n* **1.** a brownish gummy extract from the unripe seed pods of the opium poppy that contains several highly addictive narcotic alkaloid substances such as morphine and codeine **2.** something that has a stupefying, numbing, or sleep-inducing effect ○ *Soap operas she dismissed as the opium of a bored populace.* [14C. Via Latin < Greek *opion* 'poppy juice' < *opos* 'vegetable juice']

CULTURAL NOTE ***Confessions of an English Opium-Eater***, a memoir (1822) by Thomas de Quincey. This autobiographical work focuses on the author's chronic addiction to opium, which he first took to relieve rheumatic pains. Its vivid descriptions of uncontrollable urges and withdrawal-induced nightmares make it one of the first works in English literature to openly examine the dark side of the human psyche.

opium den *n* a place where opium is sold and smoked, especially one that has facilities where people using the drug can stay while under its influence

opium poppy *n* a poppy with greyish-green leaves, grown as a source of opium. Flowers: pink, red, or white. Native to: Europe, Asia. Latin name: *Papaver somniferum*.

~~oponent~~ incorrect spelling of **opponent**

Oporto ➧ **Porto**

~~oportunity~~ incorrect spelling of **opportunity**

~~oposite~~ incorrect spelling of **opposite**

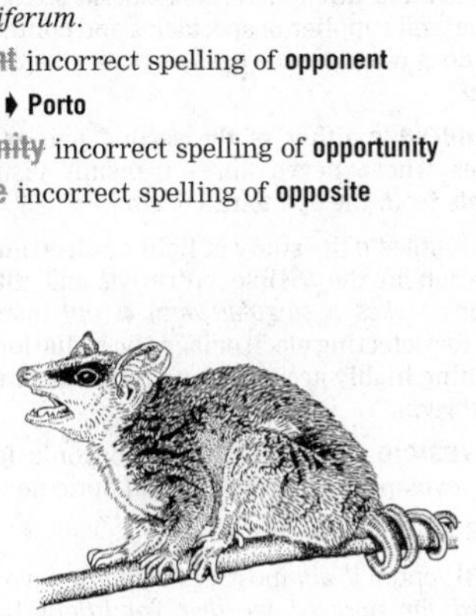

opossum

opossum /ə póssəm/ (*plural* **-sums** or *same*) *n* **1.** a small nocturnal tree-dwelling marsupial with dense fur, a long snout, and a hairless prehensile tail. Native to: United States, Central and South America. Latin name: *Didelphis marsupialis*. **2.** any one of several similar marsupials that are mostly nocturnal plant-eating tree-dwellers. Native to: Australia, New Zealand. Family: Phalangeridae. [Early 17C. < Virginia Algonquian *aposoum* 'white animal']

opossum shrimp *n* a crustacean that resembles a shrimp, the female of which carries the eggs and newly-hatched young in a pouch just below the thorax. Order: Mysidacae.

opp. *abbr* opposite

Oppenheimer /óppən hīmər/, **J. Robert** (1904–67) US nuclear physicist. He was the director of the Los Alamos atom bomb project (1943–45) and the United States Atomic Energy Commission (1946–53). He won the Enrico Fermi Award in 1963. Full name **Oppenheimer, Julius Robert**

> 'The atomic bomb...made the prospect of future war unendurable. It has led us up those last few steps to the mountain pass; and beyond there is a different country.'
> [J. Robert Oppenheimer. Quoted in *The Making of the Atomic Bomb*, Richard Rhodes; 1987]

> 'No man should escape our universities without knowing how little he knows.'
> [J. Robert Oppenheimer, *Partisan Review*; Summer 1967]

~~opperation~~ incorrect spelling of **operation**

Opperman /óppərmən/, **Sir Hubert** (1904–96) Australian cyclist. He was the first non-European to win the Paris-Brest-Paris marathon in France (1931). The following year he broke the world outdoor motor-paced speed record. Full name **Opperman, Sir Hubert Ferdinand**

OPP film *n* plastic film used for packaging. Full form **oriented polypropylene**

oppidan /óppidən/ (*formal*) *adj* belonging to, relating to, or found in a town, often the town in which a university is sited as distinct from the university itself ■ *n* a resident of a town [Mid-16C. < Latin *oppidanus* < *oppidum* 'fort, town']

oppilate /óppi layt/ (**-lates, -lating, -lated**) *vt* to block up a body passage such as a duct or a body opening such as a pore [15C. < Latin *oppilat-*, past participle of *oppilare* 'stop up' < *pilare* 'heap up' < *pila* 'heap of stones'] —**oppilation** /óppi láysh'n/ *n*

~~oppinion~~ incorrect spelling of **opinion**

opponent /ə pṓnənt/ *n* **1.** **ADVERSARY IN CONTEST** somebody who plays, fights, or competes against you in a contest **2.** **SOMEBODY OPPOSING SOMETHING** somebody who opposes a course of action, or a cause or belief ○ *a fierce opponent of reform of the voting system* **3.** ANAT **OPPOSING MUSCLE** any muscle that counteracts the motion of another ■ *adj* **1.** **CONTRARY** working or arguing against something **2.** **CONTRADICTORY** serving to contradict something [Late 16C. < Latin *opponent-*, present participle of *opponere* 'set against' < *ponere* 'to place']

opportune /óppər tyoon/ *adj* suitable for a purpose, or occurring at just the right time [15C. Via French < Latin *opportunus* 'favourable' (used of the wind) < *ob portum veniens* 'coming towards port'] —**opportunely** *adv* —**opportuneness** *n*

opportunist /óppər tyoonist/ *n* somebody who takes advantage of something, especially somebody who does so in a devious, unscrupulous, or unprincipled way ■ *adj* same as **opportunistic** (sense 1) —**opportunism** *n*

opportunistic /óppərtyoo nístik/ *adj* **1.** taking advantage of an opportunity, or exploiting opportunities and situations in general, especially in a devious, unscrupulous, or unprincipled way **2.** describes a microorganism or relatively minor disease that is not normally serious but that can become pathogenic or life-threatening when the host has a low level of immunity ○ *opportunistic infections* —**opportunistically** *adv*

opportunity /óppər tyoonəti/ (*plural* **-ties**) *n* **1.** a chance, especially one that offers some kind of advantage **2.** a combination of favourable circumstances or situations

opportunity cost *n* the cost of a commercial decision regarded as the value of the alternative that is forgone. For example, if the choice is between using a machine or scrapping it, the opportunity cost is the scrap value.

opportunity shop *n ANZ* full form of **op shop**

opposable /ə pṓzəb'l/ *adj* **1.** **RESISTIBLE** capable of being opposed or resisted **2.** **ABLE TO BE PLACED OPPOSITE SOMETHING** capable of being put in a position that is opposite something else **3.** ANAT **TOUCHING END OF ANOTHER DIGIT** describes a thumb or big toe that can face and touch the end of one or more of the other digits of the same hand or foot —**opposability** /ə pṓzə bílləti/ *n* —**opposably** *adv*

oppose /ə pṓz/ (**-poses, -posing, -posed**) *v* **1.** *vti* **BE AGAINST SOMETHING** to disapprove of something and wish to, or take action to, stop it ○ *They would not state openly that they oppose violence.* **2.** *vt* **COMPETE WITH OPPONENTS** to be in competition, conflict, or battle with another person, team, or fighting force **3.** *vt* **SET SOMETHING IN CONTRAST TO SOMETHING** to set something up as a contrast to something else **4.** *vt* **PUT SOMETHING OPPOSITE TO SOMETHING** to put one thing in a position directly facing another [14C. < French *opposer*, an alteration (influenced by *poser* 'place') of Latin *opponere* (see OPPONENT)] —**opposer** *n* —**opposing** *adj*

opposed /ə pṓzd/ *adj* disagreeing with or taking an active stance against somebody or something ○ *a government opposed to change of any sort* ◇ **as opposed to** used to introduce something that is a contrast to or the opposite of the first thing mentioned ○ *the acquisition of true knowledge, as opposed to mere memorizing*

opposed-cylinder engine *n* an engine in which cylinders or banks of cylinders are mounted on opposite sides of the crankcase in the same plane, with their connecting rods mounted on a common crankshaft. Piston strokes on each side of the camshaft work in a direction opposite to one another.

opposite /óppəzit/ *adj* **1.** **ON FACING SIDE** positioned so as to face somebody or something from the other side of an intervening space ○ *on the opposite side of the room* ○ *at the opposite end of the street* ○ *the house opposite* **2.** **FACING AWAY** pointing, facing, or moving away from each other ○ *went off in opposite directions* **3.** **TOTALLY DIFFERENT** different from or contrary to something or each other in every respect ○ *She thought the plan workable, I took the opposite view.* **4.** BOT **LEVEL WITH ON OTHER SIDE** describes plant parts, especially pairs of leaves or flowers, that grow at the same level on a stem but on either side of it **5.** MATHS **FACING ANGLE** describes the side of a triangle facing an angle **6.** MATHS **FACING EACH OTHER GEOMETRICALLY** describes sides or angles in an even-sided polygon that face each other ■ *n* **1.** **SOMEBODY OR SOMETHING DIFFERENT FROM ANOTHER** somebody or something that is completely different from or contrary to another or what is expected **2.** same as **opponent** *n* (sense 1) (*archaic or literary*) ■ *adv* **IN OPPOSITE POSITION** in or into a position that is opposite ○ *They live directly opposite.* ■ *prep* **1.** **ACROSS FROM SOMETHING** facing something or somebody across an intervening space ○ *They moved to a house opposite the museum.* **2.** **IN COMPLEMENTING ACTING ROLE TO SOMEBODY** in an acting role that is the counterpart to or complements another, especially when the two roles are played by people of different genders ○ *excited to be playing opposite the great star* [14C. Via French < Latin *oppositus*, past participle of *opponere* (see OPPONENT)] —**oppositely** *adv* —**oppositeness** *n*

opposite number *n* somebody with a similar job or post as somebody else, especially in another department or organization

opposite prompt *n* in a theatre, the side of a stage that is to the actors' right when they face the audience

opposite sex *n* people of the other sex, that is, men collectively from the point of view of women, or women collectively from the point of view of men

opposition /óppə zísh'n/ *n* **1.** **HOSTILE ATTITUDE OR ACTION** a disapproving attitude towards something and a wish to prevent it, or action taken to show disapproval of and prevent something ○ *Public opposition to the plan was growing.* **2.** **SPORTS OPPONENT** the person or team that you or another player or team have to play against (*takes a singular or plural verb*) ○ *He can expect stronger opposition in the semifinal.* **3.** *also* **Opposition** POL **POLITICAL GROUPS OPPOSING GOVERNMENT** a political party, or political parties or groups, opposed to the government in power in a country (*often used before nouns; takes a singular or plural verb*) **4.** *also* **Opposition** POL **PRINCIPAL PARTY OPPOSING GOVERNMENT** in a British-style parliamentary

system, the political party with the largest number of seats of those not in office, officially recognized as the government's main opponent (*often used before nouns; takes a singular or plural verb*) **5.** LING **LINGUISTIC CONTRAST** in linguistics, the contrast between two or more similar elements in a language **6.** PHON **PHONETIC CONTRAST BETWEEN SOUNDS** in phonetics, the contrast between two sounds that are articulated in a similar place in the mouth, e.g. between the voiced consonant /v/ and the voiceless consonant /f/ **7.** CHESS **ADVANTAGE NEAR END OF CHESS GAME** a situation towards the end of a game of chess in which the two kings are in such a position that the opponent must make a king move and is therefore at a disadvantage **8.** LOGIC **RELATIONS BETWEEN LOGICAL PROPOSITIONS** the way in which logical propositions sharing the same subject and predicate but differing in quantity or quality relate to each other **9.** ASTRON **MOON OR PLANET POSITION** the position of the Moon or one of the outer planets when it is on the opposite side of the Earth as seen from the Sun **10.** ASTRON **RELATIVE POSITION OF TWO ASTRONOMICAL OBJECTS** the position of two astronomical objects when they are diametrically opposite on the celestial sphere **11.** **ASTROLOGICALLY OPPOSING PLANETARY POSITION** in astrology, a situation when two planets are 180° from each other, believed to cause friction or symbolize confrontation — **oppositional** *adj*

opposition research *n US* research done in order to discover damaging or detrimental information about somebody

oppress /ə préss/ (**-presses, -pressing, -pressed**) *vt* **1.** to subject a person or a people to a harsh or cruel form of domination **2.** to be a source of worry, stress, or trouble to somebody [14C. < French *oppresser* < Latin *oppress-*, past participle of *opprimere* 'press against' < *premere* 'to press'] —**oppression** *n* —**oppressor** *n*

oppressive /ə préssiv/ *adj* **1.** **DOMINATING HARSHLY** imposing a harsh or cruel form of domination ○ *an oppressive regime* **2.** **HIGHLY STRESSFUL** exerting a worrying, troubling, or burdensome pressure on somebody **3.** **STIFLING** so hot and humid as to make people feel tired, irritable, or sluggish —**oppressively** *adv* —**oppressiveness** *n*

opprobrium /ə prṓbri əm/ (*plural* **-bria** /-bri ə/) *n* **1.** **SCORN** scorn, contempt, or severe criticism **2.** **DISGRACE** shame or disgrace that stems from disreputable behaviour **3.** **SOURCE OF SHAME** something or somebody that brings shame or disgrace (*archaic*) ○ *'would render him an object of scorn and an opprobrium of the religion with which he had diligently associated himself'* (George Eliot, *Middlemarch*; 1872) [Mid-17C. < Latin, 'infamy, reproach' < *opprobare* 'to reproach' < *probrum* 'disgrace'] —**opprobrious** *adj*

oppugn /ə pyóon/ (**-pugns, -pugning, -pugned**) *vt* to question the validity or truthfulness of something (*formal*) [15C. < Latin *oppugnare* 'fight against' < *pugnare* 'to fight'] —**oppugner** *n*

~~**opression**~~ incorrect spelling of **oppression**

ops /ops/ *npl* the controlling of organized military or civilian activities (*informal; often used before a noun*) ○ *Who's in the ops room tonight?* [Early 20C. Shortening of *operations*]

op shop *n ANZ* a charity shop selling second-hand goods donated by members of the public (*informal*) Full form **opportunity shop** [Shortening of OPPORTUNITY SHOP]

opsin /ópsin/ *n* a light-sensitive pigment found in the rod cells of the eye. It is a glycoprotein, and in the vertebrate eye it combines with retinal to form rhodopsin. [Mid-20C. Back-formation < RHODOPSIN]

opsonic /op sónnik/ *adj* relating to or involving opsonins

opsonic index *n* a measure of the number of bacteria destroyed by blood cells, expressed as the ratio of opsonin in the infected patient's blood to the amount found in a healthy person's blood

opsonify /op sónni fī/ (**-fies, -fying, -fied**) *vt* BIOL same as **opsonize**

opsonin /ópsənin/ *n* a protein fragment in blood that binds to the surface of an invading antibody and promotes its destruction by white blood cells [Early 20C. < Latin *opsonare* 'cater, buy provisions' < Greek *opsōnein* 'condiment']

opsonize /ópsə nīz/ (**-nizes, -nizing, -nized**), **opsonise** (**-nises, -nising, -nised**) *vt* to make foreign bodies such as bacteria susceptible to destruction by blood cells by coating them with opsonin —**opsonization** /ópsə nī záysh'n/ *n*

-opsy *suffix* examination ○ *biopsy* [< Greek *-opsia* 'sight' < *opsis* < Indo-European, 'see']

opt /opt/ (**opts, opting, opted**) *vi* to choose something or choose to do something, usually in preference to other available alternatives ○ *Offered tea or coffee, I opted for coffee.* [Late 19C. Via French *opter* < Latin *optare* 'choose, desire']

opt out *vi* **1.** to decide not to join in something or not to go along with something **2.** to choose to manage financial and administrative affairs without any input or control from the relevant local authority (*refers to schools and hospitals*)

opt. *abbr* **1.** GRAM optative **2.** OPTICS optical **3.** OPHTHALMOL optician **4.** OPTICS optics **5.** optimum **6.** optional

optative /óptətiv/ *adj* **1.** **OF CHOICE-MAKING** relating to the making of choices (*formal*) **2.** GRAM **OF GRAMMATICAL MOOD** describes a grammatical mood in Greek and some other languages that expresses wishes or desires, or a verb in this mood **3.** GRAM **CONTAINING VERB EXPRESSING WISH** describes a clause or sentence containing a verb expressing a wish or desire and in the subjunctive or optative mood ■ *n* GRAM **1.** **OPTATIVE MOOD** the optative mood of a verb **2.** **VERB IN OPTATIVE MOOD** a verb in the optative mood [Mid-16C. Via French < Latin *optativus* < *optare* 'choose, desire'] —**optatively** *adv*

~~**opthalmology**~~ incorrect spelling of **ophthalmology**

optic /óptik/ *n* **1.** any lens or reflecting part in an optical instrument **2.** same as **eye** *n* (sense 1) (*archaic*) ■ *adj* belonging or relating to the eyes, or situated in or near the eye [14C. Via French or medieval Latin < Greek *optikos* < *optos* 'seen, visible']

Optic /óptik/ *tdmk* a trademark for a device that fits over the neck of a bottle and dispenses a measure of spirits, used in pubs

optical /óptik'l/ *adj* **1.** **OF VISION** belonging or relating to the sense of sight **2.** PHYS **OF VISIBLE LIGHT** relating to or producing light that can be seen **3.** **LIGHT-SENSITIVE** describes an instrument or device that is sensitive to light **4.** OPHTHALMOL **OF CORRECTIVE LENSES** describes a lens designed to correct or enhance faulty vision **5.** PHYS **OF OPTICS** belonging or relating to the science of optics —**optically** *adv*

optical activity *n* the property of a crystal or a chemical solution of rotating the plane of polarized light that passes through it. In the case of solutions, the rotation is caused by asymmetrical molecules and the angle of rotation depends on the thickness of the substance.

optical art *n* ART full form of **op art**

optical brightener *n* a chemical substance used to make the whiteness or colour of fabrics brighter, e.g. in washing powders and liquids

optical character reader *n* a device for inputting material into a computer by digitizing the image of a printed page, identifying the characters, and storing them as machine code for further processing. Initially such devices could recognize only a specially designed typeface, but modern readers can recognize a wide variety of typefaces and even handwriting.

optical character recognition *n* the use of light-sensing methods to identify printed and handwritten material and encode it in machine-readable form for inputting into a computer

optical computer *n* a proposed computer that uses optical switches, fibres, and laser light instead of wires, transistors, and printed circuits to achieve processing speeds far higher than those of conventional computers

optical disk *n* a rigid computer storage disk with data stored as tiny pits in the plastic coating, readable by laser beam

optical double star *n* a pair of stars that appear to lie close together as viewed from Earth but are actually a long way apart, lying along the same line of sight

optical fibre *n* a fibre made of very pure glass or plastic that is used in modern communications systems to transmit information in the form of pulses of laser light. The core is usually of high refractive index and is enclosed in a sheath of lower refractive index, the light thus being transmitted by total internal reflection.

optical glass *n* any high-quality glass used in lenses for its superior refractive quality

optical illusion *n* **1.** a visual experience in which there is some kind of false perception of what is actually there **2.** something that causes an optical illusion, especially something drawn or designed deliberately to fool the eye

optical isomerism *n* the property exhibited by a pair of molecules that differ only in being mirror images of each other and rotate plane-polarized light in opposite directions when in solution —**optical isomer** *n*

optical mouse *n* a computer mouse that registers a change in position by detecting reflected light from a pair of light-emitting diodes and translating it into cursor movement

optical rotation *n* the rotation of plane-polarized light as it passes through an optically active medium

optical scanner *n* COMPUT same as **scanner** (sense 2)

optical semiconductor *n* an optoelectronic semiconductor device, e.g. a laser or photodiode

optical sound *n* a form of sound reproduction in films that employs a photographed pattern of light on the film that is read by a lamp in the projector. It has now largely been superseded by digital sound.

optic axis *n* a line passing through a lens, a curved mirror, or a crystal along which light can travel without undergoing double refraction

optic chiasma *n* the X-shaped nerve tract beneath the brain where the optic nerves from each eye meet and that enables some of their constituent nerve fibres to cross sides

optic cup *n* a two-walled depression in a human embryo that develops into the retina

optic disc *n* a small light-sensitive area of the retina marking the point where nerve fibres from the retinal cells converge to form the optic nerve

optician /op tísh'n/ *n* **1.** **QUALIFIED EYE EXAMINER** somebody who is qualified to examine eyes and prescribe corrective lenses. N Am term **optometrist** **2.** *also* **optician's** **SHOP SELLING SPECTACLES** a shop where eye examinations are carried out, corrective lenses are prescribed, and spectacles and contact lenses are supplied and fitted **3.** *N Am* **MAKER AND SELLER OF LENSES** a fitter and supplier of spectacles and contact lenses who does not examine eyes or prescribe corrective lenses

optic nerve *n* either of the second pair of cranial nerves whose nerve fibres transmit visual light signals from the eye to the brain

optics /óptiks/ *n* the study of light or electromagnetic radiation in the visible, infrared, and ultraviolet regions (*takes a singular verb*) ■ *npl* instruments used for detecting electromagnetic radiation and for attaining highly accurate long-range vision (*takes a plural verb*)

optic vesicle *n* a fold of the embryonic forebrain that develops into the retina and optic nerve

optima plural of **optimum**

optimal /óptim'l/ *adj* most desirable or favourable ○ *waited for optimal weather conditions* [Late 19C. < Latin *optimus* 'best'] —**optimality** /ópti mállәti/ *n* —**optimally** *adv*

optimise *vt* another spelling of **optimize**

optimism /óptimizəm/ *n* **1.** **TENDENCY TO EXPECT BEST** the tendency to believe, expect, or hope that things will turn out well **2.** **CONFIDENCE** the attitude of somebody who feels positive or confident **3.** PHILOSOPHY **DOCTRINE THAT OUR WORLD IS BEST** a philosophical doctrine, first proposed by Leibnitz, that ours is the best of all possible worlds **4.** PHILOSOPHY **BELIEF IN POWER OF GOOD** the belief that things are continually getting better and that good will ultimately triumph over evil [Mid-18C. < French *optimisme* < Latin *optimum* (see OPTIMUM)]

optimist /óptimist/ n 1. somebody who tends to feel hopeful and positive about future outcomes 2. a follower of a philosophical doctrine of optimism

optimistic /ópti místik/ adj tending to take a hopeful and positive view of future outcomes —**optimistically** adv

optimize /ópti mīz/ (-mizes, -mizing, -mized), **optimise** (-mises, -mising, -mised) vt 1. to make something function at its best or most effective, or use something to its best advantage 2. to write computer programming instructions for a task in as few lines as possible to maximize the speed and efficiency of program execution [Early 19C. < Latin optimus 'best'] —**optimization** /ópti mī záysh'n/ n

optimum /óptiməm/ n (plural -tima /-timə/ or -timums) the best out of a number of possible options or outcomes ■ adj most desirable or favourable ○ optimum trading conditions [Late 19C. < Latin, 'best thing' < optimus 'best']

USAGE Note that the word **optimum** refers to quality, not quantity – it means 'best', not 'greatest' or 'most': the optimum temperature for the storage of perishable foodstuffs. It often happens that the best is also the greatest or most, as in We are seeking the optimum return on our investment, which may be the reason for the confusion about the meaning of the word.

option /ópsh'n/ n 1. CHOICE a choice that is or can be taken, especially a course of action that remains open for somebody to choose ○ Several options were ruled out right away. 2. FREEDOM OF CHOICE the right, power, or freedom to make a choice ○ I'd no option but to refuse. 3. BUSINESS OPPORTUNITY AVAILABLE FOR LIMITED TIME an opportunity, usually a commercial opportunity, that has been made available for a limited period only 4. COMM OPTIONAL EXTRA an additional item or fitment, not part of the standard package, that can be purchased separately, e.g. when buying a car 5. FIN RIGHT TO BUY OR SELL the right to buy or sell something, especially a stock-market commodity, at a fixed price during a limited time period 6. POL same as **local option** ■ vt (-tions, -tioning, -tioned) COMM HAVE OR GIVE RIGHT TO SOMETHING to give or acquire an exclusive right to something [Mid-16C. Via French < Latin option- < optare 'choose, desire'] ◇ **keep** or **leave your options open** to put off making a decision or selection until a later time

optional /ópsh'nəl/ adj left to individual choice ○ It comes with optional air conditioning. —**optionally** adv

opto- prefix 1. eye, vision ○ optometry 2. optical ○ optoelectronics [< Greek optos 'seen, visible']

optoelectronics /óptō i lek trónniks, -ellek-/ n the branch of electronics dealing with devices that generate, modulate, transmit, and sense electromagnetic radiation in the visible-light, infrared, and ultraviolet ranges (takes a singular verb) [Mid-20C. < Greek optos 'seen, visible'] —**optoelectronic** adj

optometrist /op tómmətrist/ n N Am same as **optician** (sense 1)

optometry /op tómmətri/ n the practice of examining eyes in order to determine levels of vision and then prescribing and supplying any necessary corrective lenses [Late 19C. < Greek optos 'seen, visible'] —**optometer** n —**optometric** /óptə méttrik/ adj

~~optomist~~ incorrect spelling of **optimist**

~~optomistic~~ incorrect spelling of **optimistic**

optophone /óptə fōn/ n a device used especially by blind or visually impaired people that can convert written text into sounds

opt-out n 1. an option not to participate in something or be bound by something if it seems disadvantageous ○ opt-out clause 2. a decision taken by the administration of a hospital or school to remove itself from local authority control and administer its own affairs (often used before a noun)

opulent /óppyŏŏlənt/ adj 1. characterized by an obvious or lavish display of wealth or affluence 2. in richly abundant supply [Mid-16C. < Latin opulentus 'producing much'] —**opulence** n —**opulently** adv

Opüls ♦ **Ophuls, Max**

opuntia /ō púnshi ə/ n a cactus with orange, orange-red, or yellow flowers and oval fruits, e.g. the prickly pear or cholla. Native to: North and South America. Genus: Opuntia. [Early 17C. < modern Latin < Opunt-, stem of Opus, city in Greece]

opus /ópəss/ (plural **opuses** or **opera** /óppərə/) n 1. a musical work, especially one of a numbered series by the same composer arranged to show the order in which they were written or catalogued 2. a creative piece of work in any field of the arts [Early 18C. < Latin, 'work']

opus anglicanum /-ang gli káánəm/ n a form of English embroidery that was popular in the Middle Ages, usually seen on ecclesiastical robes [Mid-19C. < medieval Latin, 'English work']

opuscule /ō pús kyool/, **opusculum** /ə puskyŏŏləm/ (plural -**la** /-lə/) n a minor or insignificant creative work, especially a musical or literary work [Mid-17C. Via French < Latin opusculum 'little work' < opus 'work']

or¹ stressed /awr/; unstressed /ər/ CORE MEANING: a conjunction used to link two or more alternatives. In a series of alternatives, it is usually used only before the last alternative. ○ Which do you prefer, butter or low fat spread? ○ You can accept, refuse, or ignore the offer, as you see fit. conj 1. FOLLOWING 'EITHER' OR 'WHETHER' used to join two alternatives when the first is introduced by 'either' or 'whether' ○ Either you typed the wrong name, or something is wrong with the equipment. 2. INDICATING APPROXIMATION used between two numbers to indicate an approximate quantity or to imply a few of something ○ Hit the return key every three or four seconds until you get a greeting message. 3. REPHRASING STATEMENT used to introduce a rephrasing synonym or correction of a statement just made ○ foetal oxygen deprivation, or hypoxia ○ German measles, or rubella 4. OTHERWISE used to give an explanation of a statement just made ○ You'd better leave or you'll be late. 5. WHETHER OR EITHER a poetic word for 'either' or 'whether', preceding the first of two alternatives, with 'or' also preceding the second alternative (archaic or literary) [12C. Contraction of OTHER] ◇ **or other** used to show that the preceding words you use are not exact or definite ■ ○ For some reason or other, the house was crowded that night. ◇ **or so** approximately ○ I haven't seen her for a year or so.

SPELLCHECK See **oar**.

or² /awr/ adj describes an element of a coat of arms or other heraldic insignia that is coloured gold [15C. Via French < Latin aurum 'gold']

OR¹ /awr/ n a binary operator in Boolean algebra whose result is true if one or both of its operands are true and false otherwise

OR² abbr 1. BUSINESS operations research 2. MIL other ranks 3. INSUR owner's risk

-or¹ suffix somebody or something that does or performs ○ sailor [Via Old French -eor, -eur and Anglo-Norman -(o)ur < Latin -or and -ator]

-or² suffix condition, state, activity ○ horror [Via French < Latin]

ora BIOL plural of **os¹**

orache /órrəch/, **orach** n a wild plant with greyish-green edible leaves resembling spinach leaves. Native to: Europe. Genus: Atriplex. [13C. Via Anglo-Norman arasche < Latin atraphaxus, origin ?]

oracle /órrək'l/ n 1. SOURCE OF WISDOM somebody or something considered to be a source of knowledge, wisdom, or prophecy 2. WISE SAYING a wise or prophetic statement 3. SHRINE OF ANCIENT GOD in ancient Greece and Rome, a shrine dedicated to a particular god where people went to consult a priest or priestess in times of trouble or uncertainty. One of the most famous was the Delphic Oracle of Apollo. 4. GREEK OR ROMAN DEITY an ancient Greek or Roman deity that a priest or priestess would consult for advice on behalf of troubled or uncertain people 5. ADVICE FROM GREEK OR ROMAN DEITY a piece of advice, often in the form of a puzzle or an enigmatic statement, handed down by an ancient Greek or Roman deity 6. GOD-GIVEN MESSAGE a message believed to come from God in response to a request, plea, or petition 7. BIBLE AREA OF BIBLICAL TEMPLE the most sacred area in either of the Temples mentioned in the Bible, often referred to as the Holy of Holies ■ **oracles** npl BIBLE SCRIPTURE the books of the Bible [14C. Via French < Latin oraculum < orare 'speak' (see ORATE)]

oracular /o rákyŏŏlər/ adj 1. OF OR AS ORACLE relating to oracles, or in the form of an oracle 2. WISE knowing, wise, or prophetic 3. MYSTERIOUS puzzling, ambiguous, or enigmatic [Mid-17C. < Latin oraculum (see ORACLE)] —**oracularity** /o rákyŏŏ lárrəti/ n —**oracularly** adv

oracy /áwrəssi/ n UK, Can the ability both to convey thoughts and ideas orally in a way that others understand and to understand what others say [Mid-20C. < ORAL, after LITERACY]

ora et labora /áwrə et lə báwrə/ a Latin phrase meaning 'pray and work'

oral /áwrəl/ adj 1. OF THE MOUTH relating to or belonging to the mouth ○ oral hygiene 2. FOR THE MOUTH designed for use in the mouth 3. SPOKEN expressed in spoken form as distinct from written form 4. MED ADMINISTERED BY MOUTH describes medicines that are taken by mouth 5. PHON WITH RELEASE OF AIR THROUGH MOUTH describes a speech sound that is produced by means of an airstream that escapes through the mouth only, with the nasal cavity sealed off by the velum 6. PSYCHOANAL DERIVING PLEASURE VIA MOUTH in Freudian analysis, describes a stage in child development when erotic pleasure is derived from mouth-associated sensations, especially through feeding, thumb-sucking, and putting objects into the mouth 7. PSYCHOANAL DEPENDENT AND AGGRESSIVE in Freudian analysis, describes a dependent, selfish, and aggressive personality type with a tendency to derive pleasure from mouth-related activities such as eating, drinking, or smoking 8. BIOL WHERE MOUTH IS SITED describes the surface of the body of an animal on which the mouth is situated, e.g. the underside of a starfish ■ n EDUC TEST REQUIRING SPOKEN ANSWERS an examination or test that involves candidates giving spoken answers to spoken questions, as distinct from one where the questions and answers are in written form [Early 17C. < late Latin oralis < Latin or-, stem of os 'mouth'] —**orally** adv

USAGE See **aural**.

SYNONYMS See **verbal**.

oral contraceptive n a pill that is taken daily to prevent conception, especially one that combines an oestrogen and a progestogen

oral history n 1. HISTORY RECORDED BY PARTICIPANTS IN EVENTS the personal recollections of people who participated in historical events, recorded on audio or video tape or told to a younger generation 2. WRITTEN HISTORY BASED ON INTERVIEWS a written work of history based on interviews with or recordings of participants 3. STUDY OF HISTORY RECORDED ORALLY the branch of history that deals with personal accounts of historical events or periods recorded on audio or video tape —**oral historian** n

oral hygiene n DENT same as **dental hygiene** —**oral hygienist** n

Oral Law n Jewish religious law that developed out of interpretations of the Torah and was originally passed on orally by rabbis and sages before being recorded in writing, principally in the Mishnah and Talmud

oral rehydration solution n a liquid specially formulated to be given as a drink to correct the water, mineral, and nutritional deficiencies in an individual, especially an infant, who is affected by dehydration

oral sex n sexual activity that involves using the mouth and tongue to stimulate a partner's genitals

oral society n a community in which people do not read or write

Oral Torah n JUDAISM same as **Oral Law**

oral tradition n a community's cultural and historical background preserved and passed on from one generation to the next in spoken stories and song, as distinct from being written down

Oran /ə rán/ city and port in Algeria, on the northwestern coast of the country. Population: 590,000 (1987).

orang /aw ráng, ə-/ n ZOOL same as **orang-utan** [Late 18C. Shortening]

orange

orange /órrinj/ n 1. CITRUS FRUIT a round or oval citrus fruit with thick orange skin and juicy segmented flesh. As well as being eaten fresh, it is often squeezed for its juice. (often used before a noun) 2. TREE YIELDING JUICY FRUIT an evergreen tree with glossy leaves that bears oranges. Flowers: white, fragrant. Native to: Southeast Asia. Genus: *Citrus*. 3. COLOUR the bright colour of the skin of an orange, a mixture of red and yellow 4. INDUST same as **orangewood** 5. TREE WITH FRUITS SIMILAR TO ORANGE a tree or bush that produces flowers or fruits similar to a true orange tree, e.g. mock orange 6. BUTTERFLY THAT IS ORANGE a butterfly that is predominantly orange, e.g. a sulphur butterfly. Family: Pieridae. 7. PIGMENT MIXING YELLOW AND RED a pigment or dye that is a mixture of red and yellow 8. MATERIAL OF COLOUR ORANGE fabric or clothing that is orange in colour 9. ORANGE-COLOURED OBJECT something that is coloured orange [13C. < Old French *pomme d'orenge* < Italian *melarancia* 'orange fruit', via Arabic *nāranj* and Persian *nārang* < Sanskrit *nāraṅgaḥ*] — **orange** adj —**orangey** adj

Orange[1] /órrinj/ n DUTCH ROYAL HOUSE the royal house of the Netherlands from the accession of King William I in 1815. The family had earlier been Dutch princes and stadtholders, or magistrates. William of Orange became King William III of Great Britain and Ireland in 1689. ■ adj 1. OF HOUSE OF ORANGE relating to or belonging to the house of Orange 2. OF ORANGE ORDER relating to or belonging to the Orange Order [Mid-17C. After ORANGE[2] (sense 2) in SE France]

Orange[2] /órrinj/ 1. river in southern Africa. Its lower course forms the boundary between South Africa and Namibia. Length: 2,100 km/1,300 mi. 2. town in Vaucluse Department, Provence-Alpes-Côte d'Azur Region, southeastern France. Population: 27,989 (1999). 3. town in central New South Wales, Australia. It is a centre for fruit and vegetable growing and light industry. Population: 37,292 (2002 estimate).

orangeade /órrinj áyd/ n a still or fizzy nonalcoholic drink flavoured with orange or tasting like oranges [Early 18C. < ORANGE, after LEMONADE]

orange badge n an official sign displayed on vehicles of drivers with disabilities, entitling them to use reserved parking places

orange chromide n a tropical freshwater fish with distinctive orange spotty markings that is often kept in aquariums. Native to: Asia. Latin name: *Etropus maculatus*.

orange flower water n a sweet aromatic liquid flavouring made from orange blossom. It is used in cakes, confectionery, and desserts.

Orange Free State one of two independent Afrikaner-dominated territories in South Africa until becoming a province in the Union of South Africa in 1910. Now called: Free State Province.

Orange lodge n a local branch of the Orange Order, or the building in which the branch has its headquarters

Orangeman /órrinjmən/ (plural -men /-mən/) n 1. a member of the Orange Order 2. an Irishman of the Protestant faith [Late 18C. After the ORANGE ORDER]

Orange Order n a Protestant organization formed in 1795 with the aim of celebrating and defending Protestantism in Ireland, now especially in Northern Ireland, where it is prominent in Loyalist marches [Because formed out of loyalty to William of Orange (WILLIAM III)]

orange peel n the thick dimpled skin of an orange

orange-peel adj having a dimpled surface caused, e.g. by open pores or cellulite ○ *orange-peel skin*

orange-peel fungus n a widespread fungus that has an orange cup with a rough white underside resembling dry, curled-up orange peel. It grows singly or in groups, usually on decaying matter at the edge of woods, between September and January. Latin name: *Aleuria aurantia*.

orange pekoe n a high-quality black tea grown in South Asia and made using only the small, young, tender leaves growing at the tips of the stems

orangery /órrinjəri/ (plural -ries) n a building where orange trees are grown, especially a large greenhouse for use in cooler climates

orange squash n a sweet nonalcoholic drink made from oranges and other ingredients or tasting of oranges. It comes in concentrated form, to be diluted with water.

orange stick n a small stick used for manicuring the fingernails and cuticles that is usually wooden or plastic, with one pointed end and one rounded end [Because it is usually made from ORANGEWOOD]

orange-tip n a common European butterfly with predominantly white wings, mottled underneath, and the outer part of the forewing tipped with orange in the males. Latin name: *Anthocaris cardamines*.

orangewood /órrinj wood/ n the yellowish hard fine-grained wood of the orange tree. Use: furniture, carved objects.

orang-utan

orang-utan /aw ráng ə táng, -tán, ə ráng ə-/, **orang-utang** n a large tailless ape with reddish-brown coarse shaggy hair and long powerful arms. Native to: forests of Borneo and Sumatra. Latin name: *Pongo pygmaeus*. [Late 17C. < Malay *orang hutan* 'forest person']

orate /aw ráyt/ (orates, orating, orated) vi 1. to make a speech, especially a public, formal, or ceremonial speech (formal) 2. to speak in a pompous or boring way or for an inappropriately long time [Early 17C. < Latin *orat-* (see ORATOR)]

oration /aw ráysh'n/ n 1. FORMAL PUBLIC SPEECH a speech, lecture, or other instance of formal or ceremonial public speaking 2. POMPOUS SPEECH a speech that is considered pompous, boring, or inappropriately long 3. PUBLIC SPEECH SHOWING RHETORICAL SKILLS an academic speech that is designed to show the speaker's rhetorical skills, especially a speech given as an exercise in public speaking, often in a public speaking contest 4. STYLE OF SPEECH DELIVERY the way in which a speech is delivered, or a way of speaking [14C. < Latin *oration-* < *orat-* (see ORATOR)]

orator /órrətər/ n 1. a giver of speeches, especially somebody skilled in giving formal, ceremonial, or persuasive public addresses 2. somebody regarded as a pompous, boring, or overlong speaker [14C. Via Anglo-Norman < Latin, 'speaker, pleader' < *orat-*, past participle of *orare* 'speak, pray']

oratorio /órrə táwri ō/ (plural -os) n 1. a musical composition for voices and instruments that has a religious theme, often telling a sacred story but not using costumes, scenery, or dramatic staging. Handel's *Messiah* is an example of this genre. 2. oratorios as a musical genre [Mid-17C. < Italian, after the *Oratory* of St Philip Neri in Rome]

oratory[1] /órrətəri/ n 1. ART OF PUBLIC SPEAKING the art of speaking in public with style, cogency, and grace

2. RHETORICAL SKILL AND ELOQUENCE eloquence in public speaking, especially of the kind that shows the speaker's rhetorical skills 3. POMPOSITY IN SPEECH pompous, boring, or inappropriately long speech [Early 16C. < Latin (*ars*) *oratoria* ('art') of speaking' < *orator* (see ORATOR)] —**oratorical** /órrə tórrik'l/ adj —**oratorically** adv

oratory[2] /órrətəri/ (plural -ries) n a place for private prayer or worship, e.g. a small secluded chapel, usually set aside in a church [14C. < Anglo-Norman *oratorie* < Latin *orare* 'speak, pray']

Oratory n a religious society that has secular priests and is a branch of the Roman Catholic Church. It was founded in 1575 by Saint Philip Neri. [Mid-17C. < ORATORY[2]]

orb (sense 2)

orb /awrb/ n 1. SPHERE a sphere or spherical object 2. JEWELLED SPHERE OF KING OR QUEEN a small sphere usually made from a precious metal set with jewels and with a cross fixed to the top of it that forms part of a sovereign's ceremonial regalia 3. EYE an eye or eyeball (literary) 4. AREA OF INTEREST a sphere of interest, influence, or activity (literary) 5. ASTRON CONCENTRIC PLANET-HOLDING SPHERE one of the concentric spheres that were formerly believed by astronomers to hold the planets in their orbital paths 6. ASTRON SPHERICAL ASTRONOMICAL OBJECT a spherical astronomical object, especially the Sun, Moon, or Earth (archaic or literary) ■ v (orbs, orbing, orbed) 1. vt ENCIRCLE SOMETHING to encircle or surround something (literary) 2. vti MAKE OR BECOME CIRCULAR to become circular, or make something circular (archaic) [14C. < Latin *orbis* 'wheel, circle']

orbicular /awr bíkyōōlər/, **orbiculate** /-lət/ adj 1. having the form of a circle or sphere (formal) 2. describes plant parts, especially leaves, that are flat and round or roundish [14C. < late Latin *orbicularis* < Latin *orbiculus* 'small globe' < *orbis* 'globe'] —**orbicularity** /awr bíkyōō lárrəti/ n —**orbicularly** adv —**orbiculately** adv

orbit /áwrbit/ n 1. PATH OF PLANET, SATELLITE, OR MOON the path that an astronomical object such as a planet, moon, or satellite follows around a larger astronomical object such as the Sun 2. REVOLUTION OF ASTRONOMICAL OBJECT a single revolution of an astronomical object around a larger astronomical object 3. AREA OF INTEREST a sphere of interest, influence, or activity 4. ANAT EYE SOCKET the round cavity in which an eye is located in the skull of a vertebrate 5. PHYS ELECTRON PATH AROUND ATOM NUCLEUS the path that an electron takes as it moves around the nucleus of an atom ■ v (-bits, -biting, -bited) 1. vti MOVE AROUND ASTRONOMICAL OBJECT to move around an astronomical object in a path dictated by the force of gravity exerted by that body 2. vt PUT SOMETHING INTO ASTRONOMICAL ORBIT to send something, especially a spacecraft or an artificial satellite, into orbit 3. vi FOLLOW REGULAR PATH to move regularly or repeatedly along the same path, especially a circular path [Mid-16C. < Latin *orbita* 'wheel-track']

orbital /áwrbit'l/ adj relating to or belonging to an orbit ■ n 1. ROADS same as **ring road** 2. a subdivision of the available space within an atom for an electron to orbit the nucleus. An atom has many orbitals, each of which has a fixed size and shape and can hold up to two electrons. —**orbitally** adv

orbital space station n a spacecraft orbiting the Earth, designed to be occupied by a crew for extended periods and used as a base for the exploration, observation, and research of space

orbital space vehicle n a vehicle that transports

payloads to and from points in space with different orbits such as a space station, a satellite, and the Moon

orbiter /áwrbitər/ *n* a spacecraft or satellite designed to orbit an astronomical object but not to land on it

orb weaver *n* a spider that weaves a large circular web of silk to entrap its prey. Families: Araneidae or Tetragnathidae.

orca /áwrkə/ *n* MARINE BIOL same as **killer whale** [Mid-19C. Via modern Latin < Latin 'large sea creature']

Orcadian /awr káydi ən/ *n* somebody who comes from the Orkney Islands, Scotland [Mid-17C. < Latin *Orcades* 'Orkney Islands'] —**Orcadian** *adj*

orcein /áwrsi in/ *n* a brown dye. Source: orcinol. Use: as a biological stain. [Mid-19C. < *orcin* 'orcinol' < modern Latin *orcina* 'orchil']

orch. *abbr* MUSIC **1.** orchestra **2.** orchestrated by

orchard /áwrchərd/ *n* **1.** an area of land on which fruit or nut trees are grown, especially commercially **2.** all the fruit or nut trees growing in an area, planted for commercial reasons [Old English *ortgeard* < *ort*, origin ? + YARD[2]]

CULTURAL NOTE ***The Cherry Orchard***, a play (1903–04) by the Russian dramatist Anton Chekhov. Chekhov described his last play as a comedy, but it is often played as tragedy. It depicts the decline of the Ranyevskayas, a family of upper-class landowners, who, despite being faced with bankruptcy, refuse to contemplate the merchant Lopakhin's suggestion that they sell their beloved cherry orchard.

orchardist /áwrchərdist/ *n* somebody who owns or manages an orchard

orchestra /áwrkistrə/ *n* **1.** LARGE GROUP OF MUSICIANS a large group of musicians playing classical music, consisting of sections of string, woodwind, brass, and percussion players, and directed by a conductor **2.** GROUP OF MUSICIANS a group of musicians, especially a fairly large group usually but not always playing classical music **3.** *N Am* THEATRE, MUSIC same as **orchestra pit 4.** THEATRE PLACE FOR CHORUS the semicircular area in front of the stage in ancient Greek theatres, reserved for the chorus [Early 17C. Via Latin, 'space in front of the stage where the chorus danced' < Greek *orkhēstra* < *orkheisthai* 'to dance']

orchestral /awr késtrəl/ *adj* relating to orchestras, or intended for an orchestra, especially a symphony orchestra —**orchestrally** *adv*

orchestra pit *n* the part of a theatre where the musicians sit, immediately in front of the stage or under the front part of the stage. N Am term **orchestra**

orchestra stalls *npl* the front seats on the lower floor of a theatre, situated just in front of the orchestra

orchestrate /áwrki strayt/ (**-trates, -trating, -trated**) *vt* **1.** to arrange or compose music to be played by an orchestra **2.** to organize a situation or event unobtrusively so that a desired effect or outcome is achieved ○ *The press conference had clearly been carefully orchestrated.* —**orchestration** /áwrki stráysh'n/ *n* —**orchestrator** *n*

orchestrion /awr késtri ən/, **orchestrina** /áwrki streénə/ *n* a mechanical musical instrument resembling a barrel organ that can imitate the sounds of an orchestra [Mid-19C. < ORCHESTRA after *accordion*]

orchid /áwrkid/ *n* a perennial plant, some varieties of which grow on other plants. Flowers: showy, delicate, fragrant, with three petals. Native to: tropical climates. Family: Orchidaceae. [Mid-19C. < modern Latin *orchid-*, mistakenly < Latin *orchis* (see ORCHIS)] —**orchidaceous** /áwrki dáyshəss/ *adj*

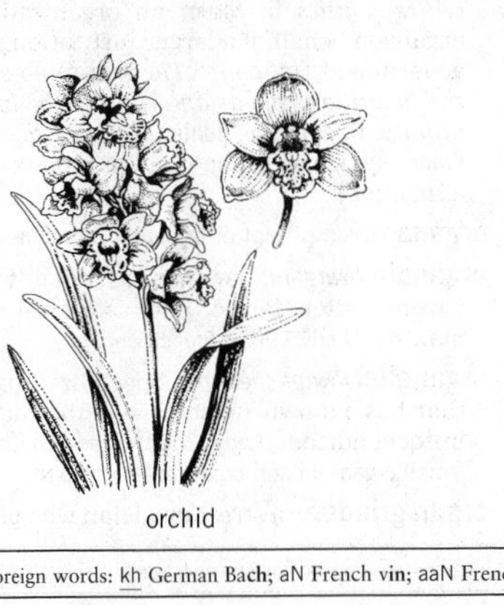

orchid

orchidectomy /áwrki déktəmi/ (*plural* **-mies**) *n* the surgical removal of one or both testicles [Late 19C. < Greek *orkhis* 'testicle']

orchil /áwrkil, -chil/ *n* **1.** a reddish dye derived from a lichen, obtained by treating the lichen with aqueous ammonia **2.** a lichen that yields orchil. Genera: *Roccella* or *Lecanora*. [15C. Via Spanish *orchilla* < Catalan *orxella* < Arabic]

orchis /áwrkiss/ *n* an orchid with a fleshy tuber belonging to many different species. Flowers: small, with spurred lips, growing in spikes. Native to: northern temperate regions. Genus: *Orchis*. [Mid-16C. Via Latin < Greek *orkhis* 'testicle' (from the tuber's shape)]

orchitis /awr kítiss/ *n* inflammation of one or both testicles, usually caused by infection. It can also develop in mumps, and if both testicles are affected, it may result in sterility. [Late 18C. < modern Latin < Greek *orkhis* 'testicle'] —**orchitic** /awr kíttik/ *adj*

orcinol /órsinawl/ *n* a colourless substance found in many lichens. Use: litmus dyes. Formula: $CH_3C_6H_3(OH)_2$. [Late 19C. < modern Latin *orcina* 'orchil']

OR circuit /áwr-/ *n* a logic circuit, used especially in computers, that gives a high-voltage output if all or one of its inputs carries a high voltage, and a low-voltage output otherwise

Ord /awrd/ river in northern Western Australia. It was dammed for irrigation in 1972, forming Lake Argyle. Length: 320 km/200 mi.

ord. *abbr* **1.** BIOL order **2.** ordinal **3.** BIOL ordinance **4.** ordinary **5.** MIL ordnance

ordain /awr dáyn/ (**-dains, -daining, -dained**) *vt* **1.** to appoint somebody officially as a priest, minister, or rabbi **2.** to order or establish something formally, especially by law or by some other authority ○ *laws of commercial transactions that had long been ordained by the government* [13C. Via Old French *ordener* < Latin *ordinare* 'set in order' < *ordo* 'order'] —**ordainer** *n*

ordeal /awr deél, áwr deel/ *n* **1.** a very difficult or harrowing experience, especially one lasting a long time **2.** formerly, a trial that involved subjecting a defendant to life-threatening danger, e.g. from fire or water, with the outcome regarded as reflecting divine judgment [Old English *ordāl* 'trial, judgment' < Germanic, 'share out']

order /áwrdər/ *n* **1.** INSTRUCTION an instruction to do something **2.** ARRANGEMENT OF ITEMS the way in which several items are arranged, as an indication of their relative importance or size or when each will be dealt with ○ *I will announce the winners in reverse order.* **3.** NEATNESS an organized condition, with items arranged properly, neatly, or harmoniously ○ *We all need a little order in our lives.* **4.** ABSENCE OF CRIME a peaceful condition in which laws are obeyed and misbehaviour or crime is not present or is prevented ○ *the establishment of law and order* **5.** FUNCTIONING CONDITION the condition something is in when it is functioning properly **6.** INSTRUCTION TO PROVIDE SOMETHING an instruction to bring or supply something, e.g. a spoken instruction to a waiter or waitress, or a written instruction to a manufacturer or supplier of goods ○ *Can I take your order now?* **7.** SOMETHING PROVIDED something provided in response to an instruction ○ *If you are not completely satisfied, you may return your order.* **8.** SOCIAL GROUPING the arrangement of society into groups or classes and the relationships between them ○ *a new world order* **9.** SOCIAL GROUP a group or class that is a division of society (*often used in the plural*) **10.** BIOL SET OF RELATED FAMILIES a taxonomic classification made up of related families of organisms ○ *the cat family, in the order Carnivora* **11.** TYPE a kind or type of something, often one judged on importance or worth ○ *Exactly what order of stupidity are we dealing with?* **12.** LAW INSTRUCTION FROM COURT an instruction issued by a judge or a court of law **13.** FIN FINANCIAL INSTRUCTION a written instruction to pay money **14.** *also* **Order** RELIG RELIGIOUS COMMUNITY a religious community in which members live according to principles that are often based on the writings of a particular saint ○ *the Order of Saint Francis* **15.** CHR RELIGIOUS RANK a grade or division of the ministry in some Christian denominations, e.g. that of a deacon, priest, bishop, or archbishop **16.** CHR RELIGIOUS SERVICE a form of Christian religious service used on particular occasions **17.** *also* **Order** GROUP OF HONOURED PEOPLE a prestigious group consisting of people who have been awarded an honour for services to their country, or the decoration indicating such an honour ○ *the Order of the Garter* **18.** ARCHIT ARCHITECTURAL STYLE one of the five major styles of classical architecture, the Doric, Ionic, Corinthian, Tuscan, or Composite. They differ in the shapes and styles of columns and entablatures. **19.** MATHS NUMBER OF ROWS AND COLUMNS the number of rows and columns in a matrix **20.** MATHS GROUP MEMBERS the number of items in a finite group **21.** MATHS NUMBER OF TIMES VARIABLE IS DIFFERENTIATED the number of times differentiation must be applied to a mathematical expression to obtain a specific derivative **22.** MATHS NUMBER OF DIFFERENTIATIONS NEEDED IN EQUATION in a differential equation, the number of successive differentiations required to reach the highest-order derivative **23.** CHEM CLASSIFICATION OF CHEMICAL REACTIONS a classification of chemical reactions based on the mathematical relationship between the rate of a given chemical reaction and the concentration of the reacting chemical compounds **24.** SCI same as **order of magnitude** ■ **orders** *npl* RELIG same as **holy orders** ■ *v* (**-ders, -dering, -dered**) **1.** *vt* GIVE SOMEBODY INSTRUCTIONS to command somebody to do something ○ *The colonel ordered the troops to move out.* **2.** *vti* REQUEST SOMETHING to give an instruction for something to be provided such as food in a restaurant or goods from a manufacturer or supplier **3.** *vt* ARRANGE ITEMS to arrange items in a particular way, especially in the sequence in which they are to be dealt with ○ *addresses ordered by postcode* **4.** *vt* PRESCRIBE SOMETHING to give an instruction for something to be done, e.g. for some type of medical test or treatment to be done **5.** *vt* ARRANGE THINGS NEATLY to put things into a neat, well organized state or into the required state ○ *ordered her business affairs prior to leaving for the summer* ■ *interj* CALL FOR CALM used to request calm or observance of correct procedure, e.g. by somebody chairing a debate [13C. Via French *ordre* < Latin *ordin-*, stem of *ordo*] —**orderer** *n* ◇ **a tall order** a request that is very difficult to fulfil (*informal*) ◇ **in order 1.** in a correct sequence or arrangement ○ *Put them in order alphabetically.* **2.** in a correct or appropriate condition ○ *The customs official was checking that the paperwork was in order.* ◇ **in order to** *or* **that** with the object or purpose of ◇ **of the order of** approximately ○ *of the order of 50,000 people in the crowd* ◇ **on order** requested, but not yet supplied or delivered ◇ **out of order 1.** not working properly or not working at all **2.** not in the correct sequence or place within a sequence **3.** not following accepted rules of procedure or conduct (*informal*) **4.** not done or behaving in a fair, appropriate, or tolerable way (*informal*) ◇ **to order** according to the requirements of a specific customer

USAGE The phrases ***in order that*** and ***so that*** have the same meaning, ***so that*** being a less formal alternative to ***in order that***. They should never be used in combination: *Please submit the original document in order that* [not *in order so that*] *its authenticity can be verified. I closed the gate so that* [not *in order so that*] *the dog could not follow me.*

order about, order around *vt* to subject somebody to domineering or bullying treatment ○ *Don't think you can order me about.*

order arms *n* an act of bringing a weapon, usually a rifle, from the shoulder to a resting position on the ground alongside the right leg, performed as part of a military drill ■ *interj* used as a command in a military drill to assume the order arms position

orderly /áwrdərli/ *adj* **1.** WELL-BEHAVED well-behaved or peaceful ○ *The meeting passed off in an orderly fashion.* **2.** NEATLY ARRANGED arranged or organized in a neat, sensible, or proper way ○ *orderly bookshelves* ■ *n* (*plural* **-lies**) **1.** ASSISTANT IN HOSPITAL a hospital worker with no medical training who is employed to do various ancillary jobs such as transporting patients **2.** SOLDIER WITH MINOR DUTIES a soldier acting as a senior officer's personal assistant who carries out a variety of minor duties such as carrying messages —**orderliness** *n*

Order of Australia *n* in Australia, an order awarded to somebody who is considered to have made an outstanding contribution to society. There are general and military awards.

order of battle *n* the way that military forces are organized in preparation for a battle

order of business *n* the order in which a number of items are to be discussed or dealt with, e.g. at a meeting

order of magnitude *n* the difference in size, usually expressed in powers of 10, between two quantities. For example, a quantity 100 times greater than another would be two orders of magnitude greater. ○ *The mass of the Earth is an order of magnitude greater than that of Mars.*

Order of Merit *n* a British honour awarded for eminence in any field

order of the day *n* 1. a programme of items to be discussed or dealt with on a particular day, e.g. by a legislative assembly 2. something that is regularly done, offered, chosen, or experienced ○ *Heroism was the order of the day during the last big battle of the war.*

Order of the Garter *n* the highest British order of knighthood

order paper *n* a printed list given out daily to British MPs showing the order and nature of business to be dealt with in Parliament

ordinal /áwrdin'l/ *adj* 1. MATHS SHOWING POSITION showing the relative position in a sequence of numbers 2. BIOL RELATING TO BIOLOGICAL ORDERS relating to a biological order in the classification of plants and animals ■ *n* 1. MATHS same as **ordinal number** (sense 1) 2. CHR BOOKLET LISTING ORDER OF CATHOLIC SERVICES in the Roman Catholic Church, an instruction booklet that lists the order of services in church worship 3. CHR BOOKLET FOR ORDINATION OF CHRISTIAN MINISTERS an instruction booklet that outlines rules and ceremony for the ordination of Christian ministers [Late 16C. < late Latin *ordinalis* 'ordered' < Latin *ordin-* (see ORDER)]

ordinal number *n* 1. a number used to show the relative position of somebody or something in a sequence, e.g. 'first', 'sixth', or '29th' 2. a measure of the size of an ordered set

ordinal scale *n* a list that shows only the relative positions of items on a scale, giving no measure of the difference between them

ordinance /áwrdinənss/ *n* 1. a law or rule made by an authority such as a local council 2. something regularly done because it is formally prescribed, especially a religious ceremony such as Communion (*formal*) [14C. < Old French *ordenance* < Latin *ordinare* (see ORDAIN)]

SPELLCHECK ordinance or **ordnance**? Do not confuse the spelling of *ordinance* and *ordnance*, which sound similar. An *ordinance* is a law or rule, or part of a religious ceremony. *Ordnance* denotes military weapons, or the department responsible for them. Maps of the United Kingdom are produced by the *Ordnance Survey*.

ordinand /áwrdi nand/ *n* somebody who is a candidate for ordination as a Christian minister [Mid-19C. < Latin *ordinandus* < *ordinare* (see ORDAIN)]

ordinarily /áwrd'nərəli/ *adv* usually or normally

~~ordinarily~~ incorrect spelling of **ordinarily**

ordinary /áwrd'nəri/ *adj* 1. COMMON of a common everyday kind 2. UNREMARKABLE not remarkable or special in any way, and therefore uninteresting and unimpressive ○ *He's just a pretty ordinary kind of guy.* 3. USUAL usual or customary 4. LAW WITH IMMEDIATE JURISDICTION having immediate jurisdiction, as opposed to jurisdiction by delegation or deputation 5. MATHS WITH TWO VARIABLES describes a differential equation that has only two variables ■ *n* (*plural* -**ies**) 1. LAW JUDGE a judge who acts in his or her own right 2. *also* **Ordinary** CHR MEMBER OF CLERGY WITH JUDGE'S POWERS a member of the clergy, especially a bishop, whose position brings with it the power to act as a judge in some ecclesiastical matters 3. *also* **Ordinary** CHR UNCHANGING PARTS OF RELIGIOUS MASS in the Roman Catholic Church, the parts of the daily Mass that do not change from day to day 4. *also* **Ordinary** CHR FORM FOR RELIGIOUS SERVICE in the Roman Catholic Church, the correct form that a religious service, especially Mass, should take, or a book that sets out the correct

form 5. HERALDRY SIMPLE DESIGN a simple shape or design used on a coat of arms 6. RESTAURANT an eating establishment or a dining room in a tavern (*archaic*) [14C. Via French < medieval Latin *ordinarius* 'following the usual course' < Latin *ordin-* (see ORDER)] —**ordinariness** *n*
◇ **out of the ordinary** unusual or extraordinary

Ordinary grade *n Scotland* EDUC full form of **O grade**

Ordinary level *n* EDUC full form of **O level**

ordinary rate *n* in the Royal Navy, a sailor of the lowest rank

ordinary shares *npl* shares that entitle the holder to a dividend in line with the company's profits, as distinct from preference shares that give the holder priority when dividends are paid. N Am term **common stock**

ordinate /áwrd'nət/ *n* the vertical or y-coordinate of a point on a two-dimensional graph or diagram in which pairs of numbers denote distances along fixed horizontal and vertical axes [Late 17C. < Latin *ordinare* (see ORDAIN)]

ordination /áwrdi náysh'n/ *n* (*plural* -**tions** or *same*) *n* an official investiture as a Christian priest or minister, or as a rabbi, or a ceremony during which somebody is consecrated as a priest, minister, or rabbi [15C. Directly or via French < Latin *ordination-* < *ordinare* (see ORDAIN)]

ordn. *abbr* ordnance

ordnance /áwrdnənss/ *n* 1. military weapons, including supplies for their use and equipment for their maintenance 2. the army or government department that has responsibility for military weapons and supplies [14C. Variant of ORDINANCE]

SPELLCHECK See *ordinance*.

ordnance datum *n* the sea-level standard adopted by the Ordnance Survey for mapmaking purposes. It is established as the sea level at Newlyn, in Cornwall.

Ordnance Survey *n* the government body responsible for mapmaking in the United Kingdom

ordo /áwrdō/ (*plural* -**dos** or -**dines** /-di neez/) *n* in the Roman Catholic Church, a calendar detailing the forms of Mass and other services to be followed for each day in the year [Mid-19C. < Latin, 'order']

ordonnance /áwrdənənss/ *n* the general arrangement of elements in architecture and in works of art and literature (*formal*) [Mid-17C. < French, alteration of Old French *ordenance* 'ordinance']

Ordovician /áwrdō víshi ən/ *n* a period of geological time, 495 million to 443 million years ago, during which primitive fish and other sea organisms appeared. See table at **geological time** [Late 19C. < Latin *Ordovices*, ancient Celtic people of N Wales] —**Ordovician** *adj*

ordure /áwr dyoor/ *n* 1. excrement or dung (*formal*) 2. obscene or immoral material or behaviour, or an example of it (*literary*) [14C. Via Old French < Latin *horridus* 'frightful' < *horrere* (see HORROR)]

ore /awr/ (*plural same* or **ores**) *n* a naturally occurring mineral from which constituents, especially metals, can be profitably extracted [Old English *ōra*, *ār* 'brass, bronze']

SPELLCHECK See *oar*.

öre /úrrə/ (*plural same*) *n* a subunit of Swedish currency. See table at **currency** [Early 18C. Via Swedish < Old Norse *aurar*]

øre /úrrə/ (*plural same*) *n* a subunit of Danish or Norwegian currency. See table at **currency** [Early 18C. Via Danish or Norwegian < Old Norse *aurar*]

oread /áwri ad/ *n* in Greek mythology, a mountain nymph [14C. Via Latin *Oread-* < Greek *Oreias* < *oros* 'mountain']

Örebro /úrrə brōō/ *city* and county seat of Örebro Province, central Sweden, situated 160 km/100 mi. west of Stockholm. Population: 122,641 (1998).

ore dressing *n* the separation of the mineral content of an ore from the unwanted rock

oregano /órri gaáno/ *n* 1. the fresh or dried leaves of an aromatic herb, used as a flavouring 2. a variety of wild marjoram that produces oregano. Native to: Mediterranean. Latin name: *Origanum vulgare*. [Late 18C. Via Spanish < Greek *origanon* 'wild marjoram']

Oregon /órrigən/ *state* in the northwestern United States, bordered by the Pacific Ocean, Washington, Idaho, Nevada, and California. Capital: Salem. Population: 3,521,515 (2002 estimate). Area: 251,571 sq. km/97,132 sq. mi. —**Oregonian** /órri gōni ən/ *n*, *adj*

Oregon Trail *n* a 19th-century route to the western United States extending from western Missouri to northern Oregon that was used by pioneers and settlers

Ore Mountains /áwr-/ range of mountains along the Czech-German border. Height: 1,244 m/4,080 ft.

Orenburg /órrən burg/ *city* in southwestern Siberian Russia, the capital of Orenburg Oblast. Population: 686,289 (1995).

Orense /aw rénss e/ *city* in northwestern Spain and capital of Orense Province, in the autonomous region of Galicia. Population: 107,510 (2002).

Orestes /o rést eez/ *n* in Greek mythology, the son of Agamemnon, whose death he avenged by killing his mother, Clytemnestra, and her lover, Aegisthus

Øresund /úrə sún, -sóond/ *channel* in northern Europe, between the Kattegat and the Baltic Sea. Length: 100 km/65 mi.

Oreti /ō ráyti/ *river* in the south of the South Island, New Zealand. It rises in the Southern Alps and flows south to the Foveaux Strait. Length: 203 km/126 mi.

orf /awrf/ *n* a pox caused by a virus, affecting sheep and goats and also transmittable to humans, in which pus-filled blisters form on the animals' lips [Mid-19C. Probably < Old Norse *hrufa*]

Orff /awrf/, **Carl** (1895–1982) German composer. He is noted for his highly rhythmic oratorio *Carmina Burana* (1937).

orfray *n* HANDICRAFT another spelling of **orphrey**

org /awrg/ *abbr* ONLINE noncommercial organization (*used in Internet addresses*) See table at **domain name**

org. *abbr* 1. organic 2. organization 3. organized

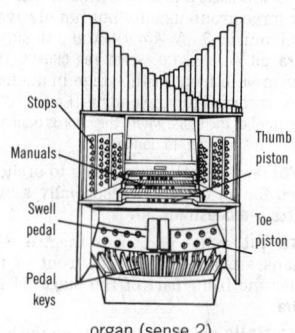

Stops
Manuals
Swell pedal
Pedal keys
Thumb piston
Toe piston

organ (sense 2)

organ /áwrgən/ *n* 1. BODY PART a complete and independent part of a plant or animal that has a specific function ○ *the organs of the digestive system* 2. KEYBOARD INSTRUMENT a large musical keyboard instrument producing sounds at different volumes using compressed air passed through pipes 3. INSTRUMENT SIMILAR TO ORGAN a musical instrument that makes sounds resembling the organ without using pipes, e.g. electronically or with reeds 4. MEANS OF COMMUNICATION a newspaper or magazine regarded as a means of communication, especially one communicating the views of a particular group such as a political party (*formal*) ○ *the daily organ of left-of-centre politics* 5. AGENCY an organization or body acting on behalf of a larger institution, especially a government (*formal*) ○ *There were no secrets about the institute's role as an organ of the business community.* 6. same as **penis** (*euphemistic*) [13C. Via Old French *organe* and Latin *organum* < Greek *organon* 'tool, instrument']

organa MUSIC plural of **organon, organum**

organdie /áwrgəndi, awr gándi/ *n* a lightweight transparent cotton fabric, often stiffened. Use: dressmaking. [Early 19C. < French *organdi*]

organelle /áwrgə nél/ *n* a specialized part of a cell that has its own function, e.g. the nucleus or the mitochondrion [Early 20C. < modern Latin *organella* 'small organ' < Latin *organum* (see ORGAN)]

organ grinder *n* a street musician who plays a barrel

organ, traditionally accompanied by a small monkey who circulates to collect money from bystanders [< the hand-cranked barrel organ]

organic /awr gánnik/ *adj* **1.** OF LIVING THINGS relating to, derived from, or characteristic of living things **2.** DEVELOPING NATURALLY occurring or developing gradually and naturally, without being forced or contrived **3.** INTRINSIC forming a basic and inherent part of something and largely responsible for its identity or makeup **4.** NATURALLY EFFICIENTLY ORGANIZED being made of parts that exist together in a seemingly natural relationship that makes for organized efficiency ○ *need to integrate the various functions of the department into an organic whole* **5.** AGRIC AVOIDING SYNTHETIC CHEMICALS relating to or employing agricultural practices that avoid the use of synthetic chemicals in favour of naturally occurring pesticides, fertilizers, and other growing aids **6.** FOOD PRODUCED WITHOUT SYNTHETIC CHEMICALS grown or reared without the use of synthetic chemicals ○ *a wide range of organic produce* **7.** MED OF BODY'S ORGANS relating to the organs of the body, specifically to basic changes in them brought about by physical disorders **8.** CHEM BASED ON CARBON belonging to a family of compounds that have chains or rings of carbon atoms linked to atoms of hydrogen and sometimes oxygen, nitrogen, and other elements ■ *n* ORGANIC SUBSTANCE an organic substance, especially a fertilizer or pesticide [15C. Directly or via French < Latin *organicus* < Greek *organikos* 'of an organ, instrumental' < *organon* 'tool, instrument']

organically /awr gánnikli/ *adv* **1.** in a natural or seemingly natural way ○ *paintings with key aspects organically arranged* **2.** without the use of synthetic chemicals, especially fertilizers and pesticides ○ *organically raised chickens*

organic brain syndrome *n* a psychiatric disorder caused by a permanent or temporary physical change in the brain

organic chemistry *n* the scientific study of carbon-based compounds, originally limited to compounds that are the natural products of living things, now including the study of synthetic carbon compounds such as plastics

organic disease *n* a disorder associated with physical changes in one or more organs of the body

organicism /awr gánnissizəm/ *n* **1.** the theory that all diseases are due to structural changes in the body's organs **2.** the theory that society is analogous to, or shares characteristics with, living organisms —**organicist** *n* —**organicistic** /awr gánni sístik/ *adj*

organise, etc. another spelling of **organize, etc.**

organism /áwrgənizəm/ *n* **1.** a living thing, e.g. a plant, animal, virus, or bacterium **2.** a functioning system of interdependent parts that resembles a living thing ○ *'Like any organism, public libraries and the people who run them must adapt and respond to change'* (Laurence Arnold, *Pulse of the People*; 1997) —**organismal** /áwrgə nízm'l/ *adj* —**organismic** /-nízmik/ *adj* —**organismically** *adv*

organist /áwrgənist/ *n* a musician who plays the organ

organization /áwrgə nī záysh'n/, **organisation** *n* **1.** GROUP a group of people identified by a shared interest or purpose, e.g. a business ○ *Each news organization sent its own photographer.* **2.** COORDINATION OF COMPONENTS the coordinating of separate components into a unit or structure ○ *in charge of the organization of international conferences* **3.** RELATIONSHIP OF COMPONENTS the relationships that exist between separate components in a coherent whole ○ *changes to the organization of the party* **4.** EFFECTIVENESS OF ARRANGEMENT the effectiveness of the arrangement of separate components in a coherent whole ○ *Your working method lacks organization.* —**organizational** *adj*

organizational psychology *n* PSYCHOL, INDUST same as **industrial psychology**

Organization of African Unity *n* an organization of African states founded in 1963 for mutual cooperation and the promotion of independence. It was superseded in 2002 by the African Union.

organization theory *n* the branch of sociology that deals with the structure of organizations and with the systems and processes that operate within them

organize /áwrgə nīz/ (**-izes, -izing, -ized**), **organise** (**-ises, -ising, -ised**) *v* **1.** *vti* FORM SOMETHING to form or establish something such as a club, by coming together or bringing people together into a structured group (*often passive*) **2.** *vt* COORDINATE SOMETHING to oversee the coordination of the various aspects of something **3.** *vt* ARRANGE to arrange the components of something in a way that creates a particular structure ○ *a society organized along democratic lines* ○ *candidates organized into groups of three* **4.** *vt* MAKE SOMEBODY MORE EFFECTIVE to apply or impose efficient working methods in order to work effectively or make somebody else work effectively ○ *Mature students are not necessarily better at organizing themselves.* **5.** *vti* FORM TRADE UNION to recruit the workers in a place or industry into a trade union, or come together to form a trade union [15C. Via French < medieval Latin *organizare* 'provide with bodily organs' < Latin *organum* (see ORGAN)]

organized /áwrgə nīzd/, **organised** *adj* **1.** working in a systematic and efficient way ○ *a motivated and organized self-starter* **2.** existing on a large scale and involving the systematic coordination of many different considerations ○ *organized religion*

organized crime *n* a powerful ruthless large-scale network of professional criminals, or such networks in general

organizer /áwrgə nīzər/, **organiser** *n* **1.** SOMEBODY WHO ORGANIZES somebody who sets up or organizes projects and motivates others to take part **2.** DIARY a small portable calendar and diary used for planning, or a hand-held computerized device with a simple database for managing appointments and other information **3.** CONTAINER WITH COMPARTMENTS a container with compartments for storing items in neat groups, e.g. a desktop container with compartments for pens, pencils, and other items of stationery **4.** BIOL EMBRYO PART a part of an embryo that controls the differentiation of cells and contributes to the formation of organs and all the other specialized parts that make up an individual organism

organo- *prefix* **1.** organ ○ *organography* **2.** organic ○ *organophosphate* [< Greek *organon* 'tool, instrument']

organochlorine /awr gánnō kláwreen, áwrgən/ *n* a hydrocarbon pesticide that contains chlorine. Organochlorine pesticides such as DDT were once widely used, but their use has markedly decreased owing to problems with toxicity.

organ of Corti /-káwrti/ *n* a part of the cochlea of the inner ear that transforms sound energy into nerve impulses and sends those impulses to the brain [Late 19C. After Alfonso *Corti* (1822–88), Italian anatomist]

organogenesis /awr gánnō jénnəssiss, áwgənō-/ *n* the formation and development of animal or plant organs that takes place during the development of an embryo —**organogenetic** /awr gánnō jə néttik, áwrgənō-/ *adj*

organography /áwrgə nóggrəfi/ *n* the scientific description of the organs and other main structures of plants and animals —**organographic** /áwrgənō gráffik/ *adj* —**organographical** *adj* —**organographically** *adv*

organoleptic /awr gánnō léptik, áwrgənō-/ *adj* affecting an organ, especially a sense organ [Mid-19C. < French *organoleptique* < Greek *organon* 'instrument' + *lēptikos* 'receptive'] —**organoleptically** *adv*

organology /áwrgə nóllə ji/ *n* the study of plant and animal organs —**organological** /áwrgənō lójjik'l/ *adj* —**organologist** *n*

organometallic /awr gánnō me tállik, áwrgənō-/ *adj* relating to an organic compound that contains one or more metal atoms, e.g. the petrol additive tetraethyl lead

organon /áwrgə non/ (*plural* **-gana** /-gənə/ or **-ganons**) *n* a set of principles for use in philosophical or scientific investigation (*formal*) [Early 17C. < Greek (see ORGAN)]

organophosphate /awr gánnō fóss fayt/ *n* an organic compound containing phosphate groups, which may be toxic. Use: pesticides.

organophosphorus /órganō fóssfərəss/, **organophosphorous** *adj* relating to organic compounds containing phosphate groups

organophosphorus compound /órganō fóssfərəss-/ *n* an organic compound containing phosphorus

organotherapy /awr gánnō thérrəpi/ (*plural* **-pies**) *n* the treatment of diseases by administering substances derived from animal organs, e.g. bovine insulin, which is used to treat diabetes in humans —**organotherapeutic** /awr gánnō thérrə pyo͞otik/ *adj*

organ-pipe cactus *n* a tall branched cactus. Native to: southwestern United States, northern Mexico. Latin name: *Lemaireocereus marginatus*. [< its tall pipe-shaped stems]

organ screen *n* an ornamental wooden or stone partition that separates the nave from the choir in a church or cathedral

organ stop *n* **1.** a set of pipes on a musical organ, used to vary the tone and sometimes to imitate the sounds of other instruments **2.** a knob or handle that controls the flow of air to an organ stop

organum /áwrgənəm/ (*plural* **-na** /-nə/ or **-nums**) *n* **1.** a style of composition in western music of the late medieval period that combines plainsong melody with other melodies **2.** a piece of music in the organum style [Early 17C. < Latin (see ORGAN)]

organza /awr gánzə/ *n* a stiff transparent fabric, usually silk, rayon, or nylon. Use: dressmaking. [Early 19C. Origin ?]

organzine /áwrgən zeen, awrgán zeen/ *n* a yarn made from strands of silk twisted together, or a fabric made from the yarn [Late 17C. Via French *organsin* < Italian *organzino*]

orgasm /áwr gazəm/ *n* the climax of sexual excitement, consisting of intense muscle tightening around the genital area experienced as a pleasurable wave of tingling sensations through parts of the body ■ *vi* (**-gasms, -gasming, -gasmed**) to experience sexual orgasm [Late 17C. Via French or modern Latin < Greek *orgasmos* < *organ* 'swell, be excited'] —**orgasmic** /awr gázmik/ *adj* —**orgasmically** *adv* —**orgastic** /-gástik/ *adj* —**orgastically** *adv*

OR gate *n* COMPUT same as **OR circuit**

orgeat /áwrji ət/ *n* a cooling drink made from almonds and orange-flower water. It was originally made from barley. [15C < French < Latin *hordeum* 'barley']

orgiastic /áwrji ástik/ *adj* **1.** relating to or similar to an orgy ○ *orgiastic gatherings* **2.** characterized by excessive indulgence in an activity or emotion, especially one that is disapproved of ○ *orgiastic shopping sprees* [Late 17C. < Greek *orgiastikos* < *orgiazein* 'celebrate secret rites' < *orgia* 'secret Dionysian rites'] —**orgiastically** *adv*

orgone /áwrgōn/ *n* a life force that is purported to exist in all living things. Some practitioners of alternative therapies claim it can be harnessed by patients sitting in specially designed booths. [Mid-20C. Probably < ORGANISM or ORGASM after HORMONE]

orgy /áwrji/ *n* **1.** GROUP SEX PARTY a gathering at which a group of people indulge in unrestrained sexual activity **2.** WILD PARTY a wild party or celebration characterized by excessive drinking and eating, with or without unrestrained sexual activity **3.** PERIOD OF OVERINDULGENCE a period of excessive indulgence in a particular activity or emotion, especially something that is disapproved of ○ *an orgy of self-pity* **4.** ANCIENT HIST WORSHIP OF ANCIENT GODS in ancient Greece and Rome, a secret rite in which the gods of pleasure, especially Dionysus or Bacchus, were worshipped with much dancing, drinking, and singing (*often used in the plural*) [Mid-16C. Via French < Greek *orgia* 'secret Dionysian rites']

oribi /órribi/ (*plural* **-bis** or *same*) *n* a small fawn-coloured antelope with long legs and, in the male, short horns. Native to: plains of southern and eastern Africa. Latin name: *Ourebia ourebi*. [Late 18C. Via Afrikaans < Khoikhoi]

oriel /áwri əl/ *n* **1.** *also* **oriel window** a bay window projecting from an outside wall and supported from beneath by a bracket. See illustration on next page **2.** a recess or small room formed by an oriel [15C. Via Old French *oriol* 'porch' < medieval Latin *oriolum* 'upper chamber']

orient /áwri ənt, órri-/ *v* (**-ents, -enting, -ented**) **1.** *vt* FAMILIARIZE SOMEBODY to accustom somebody or yourself to a new situation or set of surroundings ○ *It might take you a few weeks to orient yourself.* **2.** *vt* PUT SOMEBODY OR SOMETHING IN POSITION to position somebody or something facing a particular direction ○ *old stone buildings oriented north-south* **3. orient yourself** *vr* FIND YOUR POSITION to work out where you are and in

oriel

which direction you need to travel ○ *the seaman's skill of orienting himself by the stars* **4.** *vt* DIRECT SOMETHING to direct something in a particular way, e.g. towards a particular objective or audience ○ *advertising oriented towards teenage girls* **5.** *vt* POSITION SOMETHING TOWARDS EAST to position something so that it faces east, especially to build a church so that its length lies east to west, with the main altar at the eastern end ■ *n* **1.** EASTERN SKY the eastern part of the sky, where the sun rises (*archaic or literary*) **2.** same as **dawn** (*archaic or literary*) **3.** LUSTRE OF PEARL the lustre of a pearl, especially a pearl of high quality (*archaic*) **4.** PEARL a pearl, especially one of high quality (*archaic*) ■ *adj* **1.** same as **eastern** (*archaic*) **2.** RISING rising in the sky (*archaic or literary*) **3.** WITH GOOD LUSTRE describes pearls with an exceptionally rich lustre (*archaic*) ○*'These pearls are orient, but they yield in whiteness to your teeth.'* (Walter Scott, *Ivanhoe*; 1819) **4.** GLOWING glowing with a rich bright light (*archaic*) [14C. Via French < Latin *orient-*, present participle of *oriri* 'rise'; because the Sun rises in the east]

Orient *n* the countries of East Asia, especially China, Japan, and neighbouring countries (*dated*)

Oriental /áwri ént'l, órri-/, **oriental** *adj* **1.** RELATING TO EAST ASIA relating to the countries and peoples of East Asia, especially China, Japan, and neighbouring countries (*dated*) **2.** HIGH IN QUALITY describes pearls and gems that are high in quality and valuable ○ *an Oriental ruby* ■ *n* TABOO TERM a highly offensive term for somebody from East Asia (*dated*)

USAGE The adjective and noun ***Oriental***, with reference to people from East Asia, is now regarded as a relic of Western colonialism and should be avoided. The preferred substitute is *Asian*.

Oriental fruit moth *n* a small moth that in the larval stage is a damaging pest to fruit trees. Native to Asia, it has been introduced to other parts of the world. Latin name: *Grapolitha molesta*.

Orientalia /áwri en táyli ə, órri-/, **orientalia** *n* artefacts from countries in East Asia [Early 20C. < Latin, 'things from the Orient']

orientalism /áwri ént'lizəm, órri-/, **Orientalism** *n* **1.** a cultural feature associated with the countries, peoples, or cultures of East Asia **2.** the study of the civilizations of East Asia —**orientalist** *n* —**orientalistic** /áwri entə lístik, órri-/ *adj*

Oriental poppy *n* a perennial poppy, widely cultivated as a garden plant. Flowers: large, deep red. Native to: Southwest Asia. Latin name: *Papaver orientale*.

orientate /áwri ən tayt/ (**-tates, -tating, -tated**) *vti* same as **orient** [Mid-19C. Back-formation < ORIENTATION]

orientation /áwri ən táysh'n, órri-/ *n* **1.** POSITIONING the positioning of something, or the position or direction in which something lies ○ *slopes with a southerly orientation* **2.** DIRECTION OF DEVELOPMENT the direction in which something such as a scheme is developed or focused ○ *the programme's clear orientation towards the white middle class* **3.** LEANING the direction in which somebody's thoughts, interests, or tendencies lie ○ *irrespective of sexual orientation* **4.** PROCESS OF BECOMING ACCUSTOMED the process of becoming accustomed to a new situation or set of surroundings **5.** INTRODUCTORY SESSION a meeting at which introductory information or training is provided to somebody embarking on something new such as a course of study **6.** CHEM ARRANGEMENT IN CRYSTAL OR MOLECULE the arrangement of atoms, ions, radicals, or groups relative to each other in crystals or molecules **7.** BIOL REACTION TO STIMULUS movement or direction of growth in response to a stimulus, e.g. the way a plant grows in response to light —**orientational** *adj*

orientation week *n Aus* the week before classes begin at a university or further-education college, during which first-year students participate in activities designed to introduce them to their new environment

oriented /áwri entid, órri-/ *adj* openly supporting or favouring a particular point of view or set of beliefs (*often used in combination*) ○ *a Marxist-oriented approach to economics*

orienteering /áwri ən teéring, órri-/ *n* a sport that combines map-reading and cross-country running. Competitors make their way through unfamiliar terrain using a compass and a topographical map. [Mid-20C. Anglicization of Swedish *orientering* < *orientera* 'to orient' < French *orienter* < Latin *orient* (see ORIENT)] —**orienteer** *n, vi*

orifice /órrə fiss/ *n* an opening, especially the mouth, anus, vagina, or other opening into a cavity or passage in the body [Mid-16C. Via French < Latin *orificium* 'making a mouth' < *or-* 'mouth' + *-fic-*, stem of *facere* 'make']

oriflamme /órri flam/ *n* a red banner or flag that was adopted as the national flag of France in the Middle Ages [15C. < French *oriflambe*]

orig. *abbr* **1.** origin **2.** original **3.** originally

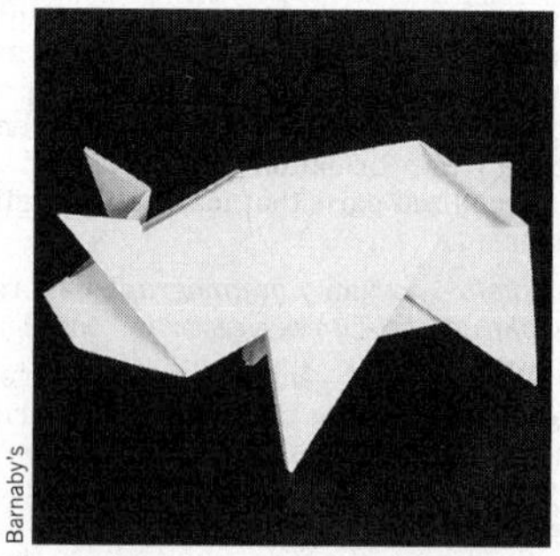

origami: an origami paper pig

origami /órri gaámi/ *n* the Japanese art of paper folding [Mid-20C. < Japanese, 'fold paper']

origin /órrijin/ *n* **1.** SOURCE the thing from which something develops, or the place where it comes from (*often used in the plural*) ○ *the origins of the universe* ○ *The expression has an uncertain origin.* ○ *customs that are French in origin* **2.** ANCESTRY the ethnic group, social class, or country that somebody belongs to or that somebody's family comes from (*often used in the plural*) ○ *a great family whose origins stretch back to the Middle Ages* **3.** ANAT ROOT OF MUSCLE the place where a muscle is attached **4.** ANAT ROOT OF NERVE OR BLOOD VESSEL the root of a nerve or blood vessel **5.** MATHS INTERSECTION OF AXES the point of intersection of all axes in a coordinate system. In a plane it has the coordinates (0,0), while in a three-dimensional space it has the coordinates (0,0,0). [Mid-16C. Directly or via French < Latin *origin-* < *oriri* 'arise']

CULTURAL NOTE ***On the Origin of Species by Means of Natural Selection***, a treatise (1859) by Charles Darwin. A highly controversial work, it challenged the established belief in the divine creation of life on Earth. Darwin put forward the theory that species evolved slowly in the struggle for existence: those best adapted to life in a particular environment would survive and reproduce by natural selection.

SYNONYMS ***origin, source, derivation, provenance, root***

CORE MEANING: the beginning of something

origin the thing from which something develops, or the place where something or somebody comes from ○ *Some of the concepts used now have their origins in the 19th century.* ○ *Researchers from overseas often decide not to return to their country of origin.* **source** the place, person, or thing through which something has come into being or from which it has been obtained ○ *It is important to trace the source of your error.* ○ *Inscriptions within mosaics provide a rich source of information.* **derivation** the origin or source of something such as a word or somebody's name ○ *The Latin word 'regula', meaning 'straight stick' is the derivation of the word 'rule'.* **provenance** the place of origin of something, especially a work of art or archaeological artefact ○ *an orange rug of Iranian provenance* ○ *Some experts have questioned the provenance and even genuineness of many of the museum's exhibits.* **root** the fundamental cause, basis, or essence of something, or the source from which something derives ○ *Various factors appear to be at the root of the inner city problem.* ○ *Lack of communication is the root of a wide range of problems.*

original /ə ríjj'nəl/ *adj* **1.** FIRST existing first, from the beginning, or before other people or things ○ *The original plan was to turn the site into a shopping centre.* **2.** NEW completely new and not copied or derived from something else ○ *She doesn't have a single original idea in her head.* **3.** CREATIVE possessing or demonstrating the ability to think creatively ○ *blessed with an original mind* **4.** NOT TRADITIONAL representing a departure from traditional or previous practise ○ *a refreshingly original interpretation of the classics* **5.** SOURCE FOR COPIES relating to or being something from which a copy or alternative version has been made ○ *the original document* ■ *n* **1.** FIRST VERSION the first or unique item from which copies or alternative versions are made ○ *The meaning of the original has been lost in translation.* **2.** AUTHENTIC PIECE OF ART a genuine work of art that is not a copy or forgery ○ *verified as an original* **3.** ECCENTRIC PERSON an unusual or eccentric person **4.** CREATIVE PERSON a person of outstanding creativity or revolutionary thinking [14C. Directly or via French < Latin *originalis* < *origin-* (see ORIGIN)]

SYNONYMS See ***new***.

originality /ə ríjjə nálləti/ *n* **1.** NEWNESS the quality of newness that exists in something not done before or not derived from anything else ○ *Improvised music lives on the tension between tradition and originality.* **2.** CREATIVITY the ability to think creatively and depart from traditional or previous forms **3.** (*plural* **originalities**) ORIGINAL THING something original, e.g. a new idea or approach ○*'That's always the case with my originalities – they are original to nobody but myself.'* (Thomas Hardy, *A Pair of Blue Eyes*; 1889)

originally /ə ríjj'nəli/ *adv* **1.** at first or from the beginning ○ *Originally a ballet dancer, she trained to become a circus acrobat.* **2.** in a creative or innovative way ○ *thoughtfully assembled and originally presented*

original sin *n* the sinful state, deriving from the disobedience of Adam and Eve, that Christians believe all people are born into

originate /ə ríjjə nayt/ (**-nates, -nating, -nated**) *v* **1.** *vi* HAVE ORIGIN to begin or develop somewhere or from something ○ *a custom that originated in the 19th century* **2.** *vt* INVENT SOMETHING to invent something, or bring something into being ○ *Einstein originated the theory of relativity.* **3.** *vt* CREATE FILM OF SOMETHING FOR REPRODUCTION to reproduce an image on film from which printing plates will be made ○ *Colour plates originated by Smith and Jones, plc.* [Mid-17C. < medieval Latin *originat-*, past participle of *originare* < Latin *origin-* (see ORIGIN)] —**origination** /ə ríjjə náysh'n/ *n* —**originator** *n*

originative /ə ríjjənətiv/ *adj* able to think of new ways of doing things —**originatively** *adv*

orinasal /áwri náyz'l/ *adj* describes a speech sound pronounced with both oral and nasal passages open, as the nasal vowels in French are [Mid-19C. < Latin *ori-* < *or-* 'mouth' + NASAL] —**orinasal** *n* —**orinasally** *adv*

O-ring /ō ring/ *n* a plastic or rubber ring used in machinery as a seal against air, oil, or high pressure [Mid-20C. < its shape]

Orinoco /órri nṓkō/ long river in Venezuela. Its main channel discharges into the Atlantic Ocean, but one branch flows into the Amazon river system. Length: 2,560 km/1,590 mi.

oriole /áwri ōl/ *n* **1.** a songbird with bold black and yellow markings. Native to: forests of Europe, Asia, Africa. Family: Oriolidae. **2.** an orange and black songbird. Native to: North America. Family: Ic-

teridae. [Late 18C. Via medieval Latin *oriolus* < Latin *aureolus* < *aurum* 'gold']

Orion /ə rī́ ən/ *n* **1.** in Greek mythology, a giant and hunter, the son of the sea god Poseidon, who was killed by the goddess Artemis and transformed into a constellation **2.** a constellation near the celestial equator containing the Great Nebula and more than 200 stars visible to the naked eye. See illustration at **constellation**

Orisha /ə ríshə/ *n Carib* RELIG same as **Shango**

Orissa /o ríssə/ state in eastern India bordering Bihar, Bangla, and the Bay of Bengal. Capital: Bhubaneshwar. Population: 36,706,920 (2001). Area: 155,782 sq. km/60,148 sq. mi.

Oriya /o rée ə/ (*plural same*) *n* **1.** a member of a people who live mainly in Orissa and neighbouring east Indian states **2.** an Indo-Iranian language spoken in eastern India, especially in Orissa and neighbouring states on the Bay of Bengal. Native speakers: 36 million. [Early 19C. Via Oriya < Sanskrit *Odra* 'Orissa'] —**Oriya** *adj*

Orkney Islands /áwrkni-/ island group and council area of Scotland, lying 32 km/20 mi. northeast of the Scottish mainland. Kirkwall is the administrative centre. Population: 19,612 (2001). Area: 905 sq. km/349 sq. mi.

Orlando /awr lándō/ city and capital of Orange County, northern Florida, 126 km/78 mi. northeast of Tampa. Population: 193,722 (2002 estimate).

orle /awrl/ *n* a border that runs inside and parallel to the edge of the shield of a coat of arms [Late 16C. < French < Latin *ora* 'border, edge']

Orleanist /awr lée ənist/ *n* a supporter of the family of the duke of Orléans and of its claim to the French throne, especially a supporter of King Louis Philippe, who reigned from 1830 to 1848 [Mid-19C. < French *Orléaniste* < *Orléans*, 'Orléans']

Orléans /awr lée ənz/ city in north-central France, the capital of Loiret Department and Centre Region. Population: 113,126 (1999).

Orléans /awr lée ənz, awr lay áaN/, **Louis Philippe Joseph, Duc d'** (1747–93) French nobleman. He supported the French Revolution but was executed during the Reign of Terror. He was father of the future king, Louis Philippe. Known as **Philippe Égalité**

Orly /áwrli/ southern suburb of Paris, location of an international airport. Population: 21,824 (1990).

Ormandy /áwrməndi/, **Eugene** (1899–1985) Hungarian-born US conductor. He worked with the Minneapolis Symphony Orchestra (1931–36) and the Philadelphia Orchestra (1936–80). Born **Blau, Eugene**

Ormazd /áwrməzd/ *n* RELIG same as **Ahura Mazda**

ormer /áwrmər/ *n* in the Channel islands, an abalone when eaten as seafood. Latin name: *Haliotis tuberculata.* [Mid-17C. Via Channel Islands French < Latin *auris maris* 'sea ear'; from its shape]

ormolu /áwrməloo/ *n* a gold-coloured alloy of copper, zinc, and sometimes tin. Use: decorating furniture, jewellery, mouldings. [Mid-18C. < French *or moulu* 'ground gold']

ornament *n* /áwrnəmənt/ **1.** SOMETHING THAT DECORATES something that decorates or adds beauty to something else **2.** DECORATIVE OBJECT a small decorative object displayed for its beauty **3.** DECORATION decoration or decorative quality ○ *manuscript pages entirely without ornament* **4.** MUSIC EMBELLISHING NOTE a note or set of notes added to embellish a melody or harmony **5.** VALUED PERSON somebody whose presence is a source of pride or honour (*archaic or literary*) ■ *vt* /áwrnə ment/ (**-ments, -menting, -mented**) DECORATE SOMETHING to make something more attractive by adding decorative items to it ○ *a stone facade ornamented with gargoyles* [14C. Via Old French < Latin *ornamentum* < *ornare* 'equip'] —**ornamented** /-mentid/ *adj*

ornamental /áwrnə mént'l/ *adj* **1.** DECORATIVE serving as a decoration and having no practical use ○ *The hitching post in the front yard was strictly ornamental.* **2.** GROWN FOR SHOW describes a plant grown for its beauty rather than for food ■ *n* ORNAMENTAL PLANT a plant grown for its beauty rather than for food —**ornamentally** *adv*

ornamentation /áwrnə men táysh'n/ *n* **1.** ADDITION OF DECORATION the addition of decoration that enhances beauty or visual appeal, especially in the arts **2.** DECORATION ADDED decoration added to enhance beauty or visual appeal, especially in the arts **3.** MUSIC ADDITION OF EMBELLISHING NOTES the addition of a note or set of notes that embellishes a melody or harmony

ornate /awr náyt/ *adj* **1.** having elaborate or excessive decoration **2.** using or consisting of elaborate language, especially language that is designed to impress with its complexity or literary quality ○ *expressions that are far too ornate for a TV soap opera* [Early 16C. < Latin *ornatus*, past participle of *ornare* 'equip'] —**ornately** *adv* —**ornateness** *n*

ornery /áwrnəri/ *adj* (*informal*) **1.** *N Am* uncooperative and irritable **2.** *US* meagre, whether out of poverty or lack of generosity [Early 19C. Dialectal variant of ORDINARY] —**orneriness** *n*

ornith. *abbr* **1.** ornithological **2.** ornithology

ornith- *prefix* same as **ornitho-** (*used before vowels*)

ornithine /áwrni theen/ *n* an amino acid formed in the liver as an intermediate in the manufacture of urea [Late 19C < its presence in birds' urine]

ornithischian /áwrni thíski ən/ *adj* relating to or belonging to an order of dinosaurs that had a backward-rotating pelvis similar to that of birds. The order includes the triceratops and stegosaur. Order: Ornithischia. ■ *n* an ornithischian dinosaur, e.g. an ankylosaur [Early 20C. < modern Latin *Ornithischia* < Greek *ornith-* 'bird' + *iskhion* 'hip joint']

ornitho- *prefix* bird ○ *ornithology* [< Greek *ornith-*, stem of *ornis* 'bird']

ornithology /áwrni thóllәji/ *n* the branch of zoology that deals with the scientific study of birds —**ornithological** /áwrnithə lójjik'l/ *adj* —**ornithologically** *adv* —**ornithologist** *n*

ornithopod /awr níthə pod/ *n* a plant-eating dinosaur that had hind feet similar to those of a bird, e.g. the hadrosaur or the iguanodon. Suborder: Ornithopoda. [Late 19C. < modern Latin *ornithopoda* < Greek *ornith-* 'bird' + *pod-* 'foot']

ornithopter /áwrni thoptər/ *n* an early flying machine that operated using flapping wings. Although many prototypes have been flown in the past 100 years, no ornithopter has ever been commercially successful. [Early 20C. < French *ornithoptère* < Greek *ornith-* 'bird' + *pteron* 'wing']

ornithosis /áwrni thṓssiss/ *n* the bacterial disease psittacosis, especially when contracted by humans from birds

oro- *prefix* mountain ○ *orography* [< Greek *oros*]

orogenesis /órrō jénnəssiss/ *n* GEOL same as **orogeny** —**orogenetic** /órrō jə néttik/ *adj* —**orogenetically** *adv*

orogenic /órrō jénnik/ *adj* relating to or formed by the folding, faulting, and uplift of the Earth's crust —**orogenically** *adv*

orogenic belt *n* a large linear feature on the Earth's surface that has undergone tectonic compression and uplift to form mountain ranges such as the Andes and the Alps

orogeny /o rójjəni/ *n* the folding, faulting, and uplift of the Earth's crust to form mountain ranges, often accompanied by volcanic and seismic activity

orography /o róggrəfi/ *n* the branch of physical geography involved with the study and mapping of variations in the Earth's surface, including mountains and mountain ranges

oroide /áwrō īd/ *n* an alloy of copper, zinc, tin, and iron that has a lustre similar to gold. Use: manufacture of inexpensive jewellery. [Late 19C. < French, 'like gold' < *or* 'gold' (see OR²)]

orology /o rólləji/ *n* GEOG same as **orography** —**orological** /órrə lójjik'l/ *adj* —**orologically** *adv* —**orologist** *n*

OROM /ṓ rom/ *abbr* COMPUT optical read-only memory

Oromo /o rṓmō/ (*plural* **-mos** or *same*) *n* **1.** a member of a people who originally occupied lands in Somalia and whose members now live in parts of eastern Africa, especially in Ethiopia and Kenya **2.** the Cushitic language of the Oromo people. Native speakers: 7 million. [Late 19C. < Oromo] —**Oromo** *adj*

Orontes /ə rónt eez/ **1.** mountain in Iran, just southwest of Hamadan. Height: 3,548 m/11,640 ft. **2.** river in Southwest Asia, flowing through Lebanon, Syria, and Turkey, and into the Mediterranean Sea. Length: 571 km/355 mi.

oropendola /órrə péndələ/ *n* a bird with black or greenish feathers and a yellow beak that nests in colonies of long bag-shaped woven nests. Native to: Central and South America. Family: Icteridae. [Late 19C. < Spanish *oropéndola* 'golden oriole' < *or* 'gold' + variant of *péñola* 'feather']

oropharynx /órrō fárringks/ (*plural* **-pharynxes** or **-pharynges** /-fə rín jeez/) *n* the part of the throat that is located below the soft palate and above the larynx [Late 19C. < Latin *or-* 'mouth' (see ORAL) + PHARYNX] —**oropharyngeal** /órrō fə rínji əl/ *adj*

orotund /órrō tund/ *adj* (*formal*) **1.** describes a tone or voice that is loud, clear, and strong **2.** describes language that is pompous or bombastic [Late 18C. < Latin *ore rotundo* 'with a round mouth'] —**orotundity** /órrō túndəti/ *n*

orphan /áwrf'n/ *n* **1.** CHILD WITHOUT PARENTS a child whose parents are both dead or who has been abandoned by his or her parents, especially a child not adopted by another family **2.** ANIMAL WITHOUT MOTHER a young animal whose mother is dead or has abandoned it **3.** PRINTING STRANDED FIRST LINE an opening line of a paragraph that is also the last line on a page, cut off from the rest of the paragraph by the page break ■ *vt* (**-phans, -phaning, -phaned**) DEPRIVE SOMEBODY OF PARENTS to make somebody an orphan ○ *a young boy orphaned by the war* ■ *adj US* **1.** MED AFFECTING VERY FEW PEOPLE describes a rare medical condition that affects only a small number of people and for which it is not commercially viable to develop drugs or therapies **2.** BUSINESS NOT COMMERCIALLY VIABLE describes a product that is not developed or marketed, often because of its perceived limited commercial potential ○ *orphan technologies* [14C. Via late Latin < Greek *orphanos* 'orphaned'] —**orphanhood** *n*

orphanage /áwrfənij/ *n* a home or other institutional setting for orphans, often operated by a local government or charitable organization

orphan assets *npl* assets held by life assurance and pension companies that are surplus to amounts needed to cover current or future payouts [Because deriving from policyholders who have died without making a claim or a full claim]

orphan drug *n* in the United States, a category for a medication used to treat a rare condition or disease that affects only a small number of people. Orphan drug status provides financial incentives for the pharmaceutical industry to develop medications for this sector. [< the idea that the drug is of little economic interest to a manufacturer]

orphan site *n* an area of contaminated land for which neither polluter nor owner will take responsibility. In such cases, the public sector normally assumes responsibility for decontaminating it.

orpharion /awr fárri ən/ *n* a large lute, popular during the Renaissance, played by plucking or strumming the strings [Late 16C. After ORPHEUS and *Arion*, musician in Greek mythology]

Orpheus /áwrfyooss, áwrfi əss/ *n* in Greek mythology, a poet and musician, who descended to the underworld to seek his wife, Eurydice, after her death, but failed to bring her back —**Orphean** *adj*

Orphic /áwrfik/ *adj* **1.** relating to the poems and mystical writings associated with Orpheus **2.** mystical or magical (*literary*)

Orphism /áwrfizəm/ *n* an artistic movement within Cubism that flourished briefly at the beginning of the 20th century, concentrating on achieving harmony of colour [Late 19C. < ORPHEUS] —**Orphist** *n* —**Orphistic** /awr fístik/ *adj*

orphrey /áwrfri/, **orfray** *n* elaborate embroidery, often done in gold [13C. Via Old French *orfreis* < medieval Latin *aurifrigium* 'Phrygian gold']

orpiment /áwrpi mənt/ *n* a bright yellow arsenic sulphide mineral. Use: dyeing, tanning. [14C. Via French < Latin *auripigmentum* 'gold pigment']

orpine /áwr pīn/, **orpin** /-pin/ *n* a low-growing succulent plant. Flowers: pink, purple. Native to: Europe, Asia. Latin name: *Sedum telephium.* [14C. < French *orpin* < *orpiment* (see ORPIMENT)]

Orpington /áwrpingtən/ *n* a heavy deep-chested domestic fowl with a single comb, of a breed developed in England [Late 19C. After a town in Kent, England]

orrery /órrəri/ (*plural* **-ries**) *n* a mechanical model of

the solar system that shows the orbits of the planets around the Sun at the correct relative velocities [Early 18C. After Charles Boyle, fourth Earl of *Orrery* (1676–1731)]

orris /órriss/ (*plural same* or **-rises**) *n* **1.** an iris with a fragrant root. Native to: central and southern Europe. Latin name: *Iris germanica.* **2.** same as **orrisroot** [Mid-16C. Probably alteration of IRIS]

orrisroot /órriss root/ (*plural* **-roots** or *same*) *n* the fragrant rootstock of orris. Use: perfumes, cosmetics.

ortanique /áwrtə néek/ *n* a hybrid fruit produced by crossing an orange with a tangerine [Mid-20C. Contraction < ORANGE + TANGERINE + UNIQUE]

Ortega y Gasset /awr táygə ee gas sét/, **José** (1883–1955) Spanish philosopher and writer whose lectures and essays contributed to the fall of the Spanish monarchy in 1931. His best-known work, *The Revolt of the Masses* (1930), argues for the necessity of an intellectual elite.

> 'He who wishes to teach us a truth should not tell it to us, but simply suggest it with a brief gesture, a gesture which starts an ideal trajectory in the air along which we glide until we find ourselves at the feet of the new truth.'
> [José Ortega y Gasset, *Meditations on Quixote*; 1914]

orth. *abbr* MED **1.** orthopaedic **2.** orthopaedics

ortho- *prefix* **1.** correct; correction, straightening ○ *orthography* ○ *orthodontics* **2.** straight, upright, vertical ○ *orthotropous* **3.** perpendicular ○ *orthorhombic* **4.** fully hydrated or hydroxylated ○ *orthophosphate* [Via French and Latin < Greek *orthos* 'straight, right']

orthocentre /áwrthō sentər/ *n* the point at which the three altitudes of a triangle intersect

orthochromatic /áwrthō krə máttik/ *adj* describes film that is sensitive to all the visible colours except red

orthoclase /áwrthō klayz, áwrthō klayss/ *n* a variously coloured feldspar. Source: igneous rock.

orthodontics /áwrthō dóntiks/, **orthodontia** /-dónti ə/ *n* the area of dentistry concerned with the prevention and correction of irregularities of the teeth (*takes a singular verb*) —**orthodontic** *adj* —**orthodontist** *n*

orthodox /áwrthə doks/ *adj* following the established or traditional rules of a political or religious belief, a philosophy, or a way of life [Late 16C. Via French *orthodoxe* and late Latin < Greek *orthodoxos* 'having the correct opinion' < *doxa* 'opinion'] —**orthodoxly** *adv*

Orthodox *adj* **1.** relating to the Orthodox Church **2.** relating to Orthodox Judaism

Orthodox Church *n* **1.** a Christian church that originated in the Byzantine Empire and recognizes the Patriarch of Constantinople as primate rather than the Pope **2.** a grouping of Christian churches including the Greek Orthodox Church, the Russian Orthodox Church, and also the national churches of Bulgaria, Romania, and Serbia

Orthodox Judaism *n* the branch of Judaism that accepts without reservation that the Torah was directly handed down from God to Moses

orthodoxy /áwrthə doksi/ *n* the practice of observing established social customs and definitions of appropriateness

Orthodoxy *n* **1.** the beliefs and practices of the Orthodox Church **2.** the beliefs and practices of Orthodox Judaism

orthoepy /áwrthō epi/ *n* **1.** the study of the ways that words are pronounced **2.** the usual pronunciation of words [Mid-17C. < ORTHO- + Greek *epe-* 'word, tale'] —**orthoepic** /áwrthō éppik/ *adj* —**orthoepically** *adv* —**orthoepist** /áwrthō epist/ *n*

orthogenesis /áwrthō jénnəssiss/ *n* an obsolete theory that evolution can proceed in a direction determined by internal genetic factors rather than the external forces of natural selection —**orthogenetic** /áwrthō jə néttik/ *adj* —**orthogenetically** *adv*

orthogonal /awr thóggən'l/ *adj* **1.** relating to or composed of right angles **2.** describes a set of axes all at right angles to each other in a crystal structure —**orthogonality** /awr thóggə nálləti/ *n* —**orthogonally** *adv*

orthogonal matrix *n* a matrix in which two rows or two columns are vectors whose scalar product is zero

orthogonal projection *n* a way of providing a two-dimensional graphic view of an object in which the projecting lines are drawn at right angles to the plane of projection

orthograde /áwrthō grayd/ *adj* describes primates that carry the body upright [Early 20C. < ORTHO- + Latin *gradus* 'walking']

orthographic /áwrthə gráffik/, **orthographical** /-gráffik'l/ *adj* **1.** RELATING TO SPELLING relating to the study of spelling **2.** CORRECT IN SPELLING correctly spelt **3.** MATHS MADE UP OF VERTICAL LINES composed of vertical lines —**orthographically** *adv*

orthographic projection *n* ENG same as **orthogonal projection**

orthography /awr thóggrəfi/ (*plural* **-phies**) *n* **1.** STUDY OF CORRECT SPELLING the study of established correct spelling **2.** STUDY OF HOW LETTERS ARE ARRANGED the study of letters of an alphabet and how they occur sequentially in words **3.** RELATIONSHIP BETWEEN SOUNDS AND LETTERS the way letters and diacritic symbols represent the sounds of a language in spelling

orthomorphic /áwrthō máwrfik/ *adj* GEOG same as **conformal** (sense 2)

orthopaedic /áwrthə peédik/, **orthopedic** *adj* **1.** relating to or used in orthopaedics **2.** relating to or marked by disorders of the bones, joints, ligaments, or muscles [Mid-19C. < French *orthopédique* 'of correct child-rearing' < Greek *paideia* 'child-rearing' < *paid-* 'child'] —**orthopaedically** *adv* —**orthopaedist** *n*

orthopaedics /áwrthə peédiks/, **orthopedics** *n* the branch of medicine concerned with the nature and correction of disorders of the bones, joints, ligaments, or muscles (*takes a singular verb*)

orthopedic, etc MED another spelling of **orthopaedic, etc**

orthophosphate /áwrthō fóss fayt/ *n* a salt or ester of phosphoric acid

orthophosphoric acid /áwrthō foss fórrik-/ *n* CHEM same as **phosphoric acid** (sense 1)

orthopsychiatry /áwrthō sī kí ətri/ *n* a cross-disciplinary method of diagnosing, preventing, and treating childhood psychological problems that involves psychiatrists, child psychologists, paediatricians, and social workers —**orthopsychiatric** /áwrthō sīki áttrik/ *adj* —**orthopsychiatrist** *n*

orthopteran /awr thóptərən/, **orthopteron** *n* a member of the order Orthoptera of primitive winged insects such as cockroaches, mantises, locusts, and crickets ■ *adj* INSECTS same as **orthopterous** [Late 19C. < modern Latin *Orthoptera* (plural) 'those with straight wings' < Greek *pteron* 'wing']

orthopterous /awr thóptərəss/ *adj* relating to the order Orthoptera of primitive winged insects such as cockroaches, locusts, mantises, and crickets

orthoptics /awr thóptiks/ *n* the study of eye disorders and their detection and correction, especially using nonsurgical treatments such as eye exercises (*takes a singular verb*) —**orthoptic** *adj* —**orthoptist** *n*

orthopyroxene /áwrthō pī rók seen/ *n* a member of a subgroup of the pyroxene silicate minerals. Enstatite is an example.

orthorhombic /áwrthō rómbik/ *adj* describes a crystal system that has three axes of different lengths that cross at right angles

orthoscopic /áwrthō skóppik/ *adj* **1.** able to see normally, without any visual distortion of images **2.** describes an optical instrument that gives normal vision

orthostatic /áwrthə státtik/ *adj* associated with or caused by standing in an upright position ○ *orthostatic hypotension* ○ *orthostatic intolerance*

orthotics /awr thóttiks/ *n* the branch of medical engineering concerned with the design and fitting of devices such as braces in the treatment of orthopaedic disorders (*takes a singular verb*) [Mid-20C. < *orthosis* 'artificial external device' < Greek *orthōsis* 'making straight' < *orthos* 'straight'] —**orthotic** *adj* —**orthotist** /áwrthətist/ *n*

orthotropic /áwrthə trópik, -tróppik/ *adj* involving or characterized by vertical growth along a vertical axis —**orthotropically** *adv* —**orthotropism** /awr thóttrəpizəm/ *n*

orthotropous /awr thóttrəpəss/ *adj* describes an ovule that grows straight

ortolan /áwrtələn/ (*plural same* or **-lans**) *n* a small brownish songbird of the bunting family that has a greyish head, a yellow throat, and an orange-brown body. It was formerly sometimes eaten as a delicacy. Native to: Europe, Asia, Africa. Latin name: *Emberiza hortulana.* [Early 16C. Via French < Provençal, 'gardener' < Latin *hortulanus* < *hortus* 'garden']

ORV *abbr* off-road vehicle

Orvieto /áwrvi áytō/ *n* a light white blended wine from central Italy [Mid-19C. After a city]

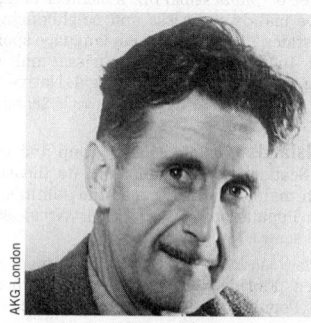
George Orwell

Orwell /áwr wel/, **George** (1903–50) British writer. A staunch critic of totalitarianism, he wrote political essays and fiction including the satirical political novels *Animal Farm* (1945) and *Nineteen Eighty-Four* (1949). Born **Blair, Eric Arthur.** See Cultural note at **farm** —**Orwellian** /awr wélli ən/ *adj*

> 'If you want a picture of the future, imagine a boot stamping on a human face—for ever...And remember that it is for ever.'
> [George Orwell, *Nineteen Eighty-Four*; 1949]

> 'All animals are equal, but some animals are more equal than others.'
> [George Orwell, *Animal Farm*; 1945]

-ory *suffix* **1.** of or relating to ○ *illusory* **2.** place or thing connected with or used for ○ *crematory* [Via Anglo-Norman and Old French dialect *-orie* < Latin *-orius* and *-orium*]

oryx /órriks/ (*plural same* or **oryxes**) *n* an antelope that has long horns, bold black and white markings on the face, and a hump above the shoulders. Native to: Africa, Arabia. Genus: *Oryx.* [14C. Via Latin < Greek *orux* 'spike, pickaxe, oryx']

orzo /áwrzō/ *n* pasta that is the size and shape of rice grains, often served with lamb in Greek cooking [Early 20C. Via Italian, 'barley' < Latin *hordeum*]

os[1] /oss/ (*plural* **ora** /áwrə/) *n* a mouth or similar opening in an organism [Mid-18C. < Latin, 'mouth, face, head' (stem *or-*)]

os[2] /oss/ (*plural* **ossa**) *n* ANAT same as **bone** (*technical*) [Mid-16C. < Latin, 'bone' (stem *oss-*)]

Os *symbol* CHEM ELEM osmium

OS *abbr* **1.** LAW old series **2.** Old Style **3.** COMPUT operating system **4.** NAVY ordinary seaman **5.** Ordnance Survey **6.** COMM out of stock **7.** CLOTHING outsize **8.** BANKING outstanding

o.s. *abbr* **1.** MED left eye **2.** LAW old series **3.** COMM out of stock **4.** *also* **O/S** BANKING outstanding [in sense 1 Latin *oculus sinister*]

O/S *abbr* COMM out of stock

OSA *abbr* Order of Saint Augustine

Osage /ō sáyj, ō sáyj/ (*plural same* or **Osages**) *n* **1.** a member of a Native North American people who originally lived in Ohio, Missouri, and Kansas, and who now live mainly in Oklahoma **2.** the Siouan language of the Osage people. Native speakers: 1,000. [Late 17C. Alteration of Osage *Wazhazhe*, one of the three Osage bands] —**Osage** *adj*

Osaka /ō saákə/ city and port in Japan, on southeastern Honshu Island. It is the capital of Osaka prefecture. Population: 2,484,326 (2002).

OSB *abbr* Order of Saint Benedict

Osborne /ózbən, óz bawrn/, **John** (1929–94) British play-wright and screenwriter. One of Britain's postwar generation of 'angry young men', he harshly criti-cized the British establishment in plays including *Look Back in Anger* (1956), *The Entertainer* (1957), and *Inadmissible Evidence* (1964). Full name **Osborne, John James**. See Cultural note at **anger**.

'There aren't any good, brave causes left.'
[John Osborne, *Look Back in Anger*, Act 3; 1956]

Oscan /óskən/ *n* an extinct Italic language formerly spoken in southern Italy [Late 16C. < Latin *Oscus* 'Oscan'] —**Oscan** *adj*

Oscar[1] /óskər/ *tdmk* a trademark for the golden statu-ette awarded annually by the Academy of Motion Picture Arts and Sciences to people in the film industry for achievement in the making of films

Oscar[2] /óskər/ *n* a code word for the letter 'O', used in international radio communications

CULTURAL NOTE *Oscar and Lucinda*, a novel (1988) by Australian writer Peter Carey. Set in early nineteenth century Britain and Australia, the novel tells the story of a young English clergyman who shares a passion for gambling with a young, independent-minded Australian woman. It won the Booker Prize in 1989.

Oscar II /óskər/ (1829–1907) king of Sweden and Norway. He came to the throne of Sweden and Norway in 1872, but relinquished Norwegian sov-ereignty in 1905 upon Norway's independence.

OSCE *abbr* POL Organization for Security and Co-operation in Europe

oscillate /óssi layt/ (**-lates, -lating, -lated**) *v* **1.** *vi* MOVE BACKWARDS AND FORWARDS to swing between two points with a rhythmic motion **2.** *vi* BE INDECISIVE to be unable to decide which is the better of two positions, points of view, or courses of action **3.** *vti* CAUSE SOMETHING TO CHANGE PREDICTABLY to cause something to produce rhythmic, predictable variations between two extremes, usually within a set period of time, or vary in this way [Early 18C. < Latin *oscillat-*, past participle of *oscillare* 'to swing' < *oscillum* 'swing, mask' (of Bacchus hung as a charm on a tree to swing) < *os* 'mouth, face, head'] —**oscillation** /óssi láysh'n/ *n* —**oscillator** *n* —**oscillatory** *adj*

oscillogram /o síllə gram/ *n* the record produced by an oscillograph or oscilloscope [Early 20C. After OSCILLOGRAPH]

oscillograph /o síllə graaf, -graf/ *n* a device that produces a visual record of variations between two points or states, e.g. of electric current [Late 19C. < French *oscillographe* 'that which swings while writing' < Latin *oscillare* 'swing' (see OSCILLATE)] —**oscillographic** /o síllə gráffik/ *adj* —**oscillographically** *adv* —**os-cillography** /óssi lóggrəfi/ *n*

oscilloscope /o síllə skōp/ *n* a device that uses a cathode ray tube to produce a visual record of an electrical current on a fluorescent screen. Use: testing of electronic equipment, measurement of electrical impulses of the heart or the brain. [Early 20C. < *oscillation*] —**oscilloscopic** /o síllə skóppik/ *adj*

oscine /óss īn, óssin/ *adj* relating to, typical of, or belonging to the large subgroup of passerine birds that includes most songbirds [Late 19C. < modern Latin *Oscines* < Latin *oscen* 'songbird' < *canere* 'sing']

oscitancy /óssitənssi/ (*plural* **-cies**), **oscitance** /-tənss/ *n* (*technical*) **1.** the act of yawning **2.** a state of drowsiness or dullness [Early 17C. < Latin *oscitant-*, present participle of *oscitare* 'yawn' < *os* 'mouth, face, head' + *citare* 'put in motion'] —**oscitant** *adj*

Osco-Umbrian /óskō-/ *n* a group of extinct Italic languages, including Oscan, Umbrian, and Faliscan, spoken in Italy during ancient times [< OSCAN] —**Osco-Umbrian** *adj*

oscular /óskyŏolər/ *adj* **1.** relating to or characteristic of an osculum **2.** relating to the mouth or activities of the mouth such as kissing (*technical*) [Early 19C. < Latin *osculum* (see OSCULUM)]

osculate /óskyŏo layt/ (**-lates, -lating, -lated**) *v* **1.** *vti* KISS SOMEBODY to kiss somebody or each other (*formal or humorous*) **2.** *vi* MAKE CONTACT to make contact or come together (*technical*) **3.** *vi* MATHS TOUCH AT TANGENCY POINT to touch at a point of common tangency to a line

passing between two branches of a curve, each branch continuing in both directions of the line (*refers to arcs*) [Mid-17C. < Latin *osculatus*, past participle of *osculari* 'kiss' < *osculum* (see OSCULUM)] —**osculant** *adj* —**osculation** /óskyŏo láysh'n/ *n* —**osculatory** *adj*

osculum /óskyŏoləm/ (*plural* **-la** /-lə/) *n* an opening like a mouth, through which a sponge expels water [Early 17C. Via modern Latin < Latin, 'little mouth, kiss' < *os* 'mouth']

OSD *abbr* **1.** Order of Saint Dominic **2.** GOV, MIL Office of the Secretary of Defense

-ose[1] *suffix* full of, having the qualities of, resembling ○ *verbose* [< Latin *-osus*]

-ose[2] *suffix* **1.** carbohydrate, sugar ○ *maltose* **2.** product of primary hydrolysis ○ *proteose* [< GLUCOSE]

OSF *abbr* **1.** COMPUT Open Software Foundation **2.** CHR Order of Saint Francis

Osh /awsh/ city in Kyrgyzstan east-southeast of Tash-kent, Uzbekistan. It is one of the most ancient settlements in Central Asia. Population: 225,600

O'Shane /ō sháyn/, **Pat** (*b.* 1941) Australian lawyer. She was Australia's first Aboriginal barrister and magistrate. Full name **O'Shane, Patricia June**

Oshawa /óshəwə/ city in southeastern Ontario, Canada, on Lake Ontario, northeast of Toronto. Population: 234,779 (2001).

Oshogbo /ə shóg bō/ capital city of Osun State, south-western Nigeria, situated approximately 190 km/120 mi. northwest of Lagos. Population: 465,000 (1995).

OSI *abbr* COMPUT open systems interconnection

osier /ózi ər/ *n* **1.** a willow tree with long flexible stems used in making baskets and furniture. Latin name: *Salix viminilis* or *Salix purpurea*. **2.** a branch or twig from a willow tree [14C. Via French < medieval Latin *auseria*]

Osiris /ō síriss/ *n* in Egyptian mythology, the god of the underworld and the dead, husband of Isis and father of Horus

-osis *suffix* **1.** unusual or diseased condition ○ *chlorosis* **2.** condition, action, or process ○ *osmosis* **3.** formation of or increase in ○ *thrombosis* [Via Latin < Greek]

Oslo /ózlō/ capital city of Norway, situated in the southeast of the country, at the head of Oslo Fjord. Population: 506,923 (2001).

Osman I /oz maʻan, ózmən/, **Othman** /óthmən, oth maʻan/ (1258–1324) Turkish warrior. He made himself ruler of a small state in northwestern Anatolia, from which grew the Ottoman Empire.

Osmanli /oz mánli/ *n* (*plural* **-lis** or same) **1.** SUBJECT OF OTTOMAN EMPIRE a subject of the Ottoman Empire **2.** TURKISH LANGUAGE OF OTTOMAN EMPIRE the Turkish language spoken in the Ottoman Empire, especially when written in Arabic script ■ *adj* RELATING TO OTTOMAN EMPIRE relating to the Ottoman Empire [Late 18C. < Turkish *Osmānli* < *Osman* 'Osman']

osmatic /oz máttik/ *adj* having or characterized by a sensitive sense of smell [Late 19C. < French *osmatique* < Greek *osmē* 'smell, odour']

osmic /ózmik/ *adj* **1.** connected with or containing the element osmium, especially in a high valence state **2.** relating to odours or the sense of smell (*technical*)

osmic acid *n* CHEM same as **osmium tetroxide**

osmiridium /ózmi ríddi əm/ *n* a very hard white or grey naturally occurring alloy of osmium and iridium, often with platinum and other metals. Use: pen nibs. [Late 19C. < German, blend of OSMIUM + IRIDIUM]

osmium /ózmi əm/ *n* a hard white crystalline metallic element, the densest known. Source: osmiridium. Use: catalyst, alloyed with iridium for pen nibs. Symbol **Os**. See table at **element** [Early 19C. < modern Latin < Greek *osmē* 'smell'; from the pungent smell of osmium oxides]

osmium tetroxide *n* a colourless or yellow crystalline solid with an unpleasant-smelling poisonous vapour. Use: biological stain. Formula: OsO_4.

osmoconformer /ózmō kən fáwrmər/ *n* a sea organism that varies the concentration of dissolved sub-stances inside its body in accordance with that of the surrounding seawater [Mid-20C. < OSMOSIS]

osmometer /oz mómmitər/ *n* an instrument that meas-ures osmotic pressure [Mid-19C. < OSMOSIS] —**os-mometric** /ózmə méttrik/ *adj* —**osmometry** *n*

osmoregulation /ózmō réggyŏo láysh'n/ *n* control of the concentration of dissolved substances in the cells and body fluids of an animal [Mid-20C. < OSMOSIS] —**osmoregulatory** /-réggyŏolətəri/ *adj*

osmoregulator /ózmō réggyoo layter/ *n* an organism that can maintain a concentration of dissolved sub-stances inside its body different from that of its surroundings [Mid-20C. < OSMOSIS]

osmose /oz mōz/ (**-moses, -mosing, -mosed**) *vti* to cause something to diffuse by osmosis, or undergo osmosis [Mid-19C. shortening of obsolete *endosmose, exosmose*, both < French < Greek *ōsmos* 'pushing']

osmosis /oz móssiss/ *n* **1.** the diffusion of a solvent through a semipermeable membrane from a dilute to a more concentrated solution **2.** the gradual, often unconscious, absorption of knowledge or ideas through continual exposure rather than deliberate learning ○ *She seemed to have picked up a working knowledge of Greek by osmosis.* [Mid-19C. Latinization of OSMOSE] —**osmotic** /oz móttik/ *adj*

osmotic pressure *n* the pressure that must be applied to a solution to stop osmosis

osmunda /oz múndə/ (*plural* **-das** or same) *n* a fern with large spreading fronds, e.g. the royal and cinnamon ferns. Genus: *Osmunda.* [13C. < modern Latin *Osmunda* < Old French *osmunde*]

osnaburg /óznə burg/ *n* a heavy coarse cotton cloth. Use: grain sacks, upholstery, draperies. [Mid-16C. After *Osnaburg*, Osnabrück, NW Germany]

osprey

osprey /óss pray, óspri/ (*plural* **-preys** or same) *n* a fish-eating hawk that has long wings and a white head with a dark strip around the eyes. Latin name: *Pandion haliaetus*. [15C. < Old French *ospres* probably < Latin (*avis*) *ossifraga*, a bird of prey mentioned by Pliny, identified with the lammergeier, literally 'bone-breaking']

ossa /óssə/ ANAT *plural* of **os**[2] (*technical*)

Ossa, Mount /óssə/ mountain in northern Tasmania, Australia. It is the highest mountain in Tasmania. Height: 1,617 m/5,305 ft.

ossature /óssə tyoor, -chər/ *n* the underlying structure or framework that supports a building or sculpture [Late 19C. < French < *os* 'bone', after MUSCULATURE]

ossein /óssi in/ *n* the protein component of bone [Mid-19C. < OSSEOUS]

osseous /óssi əss/ *adj* made of or resembling bone [Late 19C. < Latin *osseus* 'bony' < *os* 'bone']

Osset /óssit/, **Ossete** /ósseet/ *n* a member of a people who live in parts of southern European Russia and Georgia, especially Ossetia [Early 19C. < Russian *osetin* < Georgian *osetci* 'Ossetia']

Ossetic /o séttik/, **Ossetian** /o seé sh'n/ *n* the Iranian language of the Ossets. Native speakers: 300,000. ■ *adj* relating to the Ossets, their language, or culture

ossia /o seé ə, óssi ə/ *conj* used to introduce an alternative version given by a composer of a piece of music, often in order to solve technical dif-ficulties in the original version [Late 19C. < Italian *o sia* 'or let it be']

Ossian /óssi ən/ *n* a legendary Gaelic hero and poet supposed to have lived in the 3rd century AD —**Ossianic** /óssi ánnik/ *adj*

ossicle /óssik'l/ *n* a small bone, especially one of three bones of the middle ear in humans [Late 16C.

< Latin *ossiculum* 'little bone, ossicle' < *os* 'bone'] — **ossicular** /o síkyőőlər/ *adj* — **ossiculate** /o síkyőő lət, -layt/ *adj*

ossification /óssifi káysh'n/ *n* **1.** PROCESS OF BONE FORMATION the natural process of forming bone **2.** HARDENING OF SOFT TISSUE the hardening of soft tissue as a result of impregnation with calcium salts **3.** BONY MASS a mass or deposit of bony material in the human body **4.** PROCESS OF BECOMING INFLEXIBLE the process of becoming set and inflexible in behaviour, attitudes, and actions **5.** INFLEXIBLE CONFORMITY rigid, unthinking acceptance of social conventions

ossify /óssi fí/ (**-fies, -fying, -fied**) *vti* **1.** to change soft tissue such as cartilage into bone as a result of impregnation with calcium salts, or be changed in this way **2.** to become rigidly set in a conventional pattern of behaviour, beliefs, and attitudes, or make somebody become so [Early 18C. < French *ossifier* 'turn into bone' < Latin *os* 'bone']

osso buco /óssō bőőkō/ (*plural* **osso bucos** or **osso buchi** /-bőőkee/) *n* an Italian casserole of veal containing marrowbone, traditionally served with risotto [< Italian, 'bone marrow']

ossuary /óssyoo əri/ (*plural* **-ies**) *n* an urn or a vault used to hold the bones of the dead (*formal*) [Mid-17C. < late Latin *ossuarium* < Latin *os* 'bone']

ost- *prefix* same as **osteo-** (*used before vowels*)

osteal /ósti əl/ *adj* **1.** made of, containing, or resembling bone **2.** relating to bones or the skeletons of mammals [Late 19C. < Greek *osteon* 'bone']

osteitis /ósti ítiss/ *n* inflammation of a bone or bony tissue, caused by infection or injury

Ostend /o sténd/ port in West Flanders Province, western Belgium. Population: 67,304 (1999). Flemish name **Oostende**

ostensible /o sténssəb'l/ *adj* presented as being true, or appearing to be true, but usually hiding a different motive or meaning [Mid-18C. Via French < medieval Latin *ostensibilis* < Latin *ostensus*, past participle of *ostendere* 'show' < *tendere* 'stretch, spread']

ostensibly /o sténssəbli/ *adv* apparently for a particular reason, but not really for that reason ○ *He left the room, ostensibly to go and use the phone.*

ostensive /o sténssiv/ *adj* same as **ostensible** [Early 17C. < late Latin *ostensivus* < Latin *ostensus* (see OSTENSIBLE)] — **ostensively** *adv*

ostensorium /óss ten sáwri əm/ (*plural* **-ria** /-ri ə/), **ostensory** /o sténssəri/ (*plural* **-ries**) *n* CHR same as **monstrance** [Late 18C. < medieval Latin < past participle of Latin *ostendere* (see OSTENSIBLE)]

ostentation /óss ten táysh'n/ *n* conspicuous or vulgar display of wealth and success, especially designed to impress people [15C. Via Old French < Latin *ostentation-* < *ostentare* 'display, exhibit' < *ostendere* (see OSTENSIBLE)]

ostentatious /ós sten táysh əss/ *adj* marked by a vulgar display of wealth and success designed to impress people [Mid-17C. < OSTENTATION] — **ostentatiously** *adv* — **ostentatiousness** *n*

osteo- *prefix* bone ○ *osteotomy* [< Greek *osteon* < Indo-European]

osteoarthritis /ósti ō aar thrítiss/ *n* a form of arthritis characterized by gradual loss of cartilage of the joints, usually affecting people after middle age

osteoblast /ósti ō blast/ *n* a cell from which bone develops — **osteoblastic** /ósti ō blástik/ *adj*

osteoclasis /ósti ókləssiss/ (*plural* **-lases** /-əsseez/) *n* **1.** *also* **osteoclasia** /ósti ō kláyzi ə/ the process of disintegration and assimilation of bony tissue that occurs during normal growth of bone or as part of healing at a fracture site **2.** a surgical procedure in which a bone is broken in order to correct a natural malformation or a badly healed fracture [Early 20C. < OSTEO- + Greek *klasis* 'breaking' < *klan* 'to break']

osteoclast /ósti ō klast/ *n* **1.** a large cell with many nuclei, found in growing bone. It assimilates bony tissue and is active in the formation of canals and cavities. **2.** an instrument used to break bones during surgery to correct a natural malformation or a badly healed fracture [Late 19C. < OSTEO- + Greek *klastas* 'broken' < *klan* 'to break'] — **osteoclastic** /ósti ō klástik/ *adj*

osteogenesis /ósti ō jénnəssiss/ *n* the formation of bone in the body

osteogenesis imperfecta /-ímpər féktə/ *n* a rare hereditary disease in which poor connective tissue development causes fragile, brittle bones

osteogenic sarcoma /osti ō jénnik-/ *n* MED same as **osteosarcoma**

osteoid /ósti oyd/ *adj* resembling or having the characteristics of bone ■ *n* the tissue from which bone develops, especially before it has hardened

osteology /ósti ólləji/ (*plural* **-gies**) *n* **1.** the branch of anatomy concerned with the study of the structure and functions of bones **2.** the bone structure or skeleton of an animal — **osteological** /ósti ə lójjik'l/ *adj* — **osteologically** *adv* — **osteologist** *n*

osteolysis /ósti ólləssiss/ *n* the gradual disintegration of bone caused by disease

osteoma /ósti ōmə/ (*plural* **-mata** /-mətə/ or **-mas**) *n* a benign tumour made of bone, e.g. on the skull

osteomalacia /ósti ō mə láyshi ə/ *n* a disease occurring mainly in women that results from a lack of vitamin D or calcium, causing softening of the bones and resulting pain and weakness

osteomyelitis /ósti ō mí ə lítiss/ *n* inflammation of bone and bone marrow, caused by infection

osteopathy /ósti óppəthi/ *n* a system of medicine based on the theory that many diseases are caused by incorrect alignments of bones, ligaments, and muscles, and that correcting these through manipulation can cure the problems. It is often effective in treating joint and muscle disorders. — **osteopath** /ósti ə path/ *n* — **osteopathic** /ósti ə páthik/ *adj* — **osteopathically** *adv*

osteophyte /ósti ə fít/ *n* a small outgrowth of bone that occurs within joints or at other sites where there is degeneration of cartilage as in osteoarthritis — **osteophytic** /ósti ə fíttik/ *adj*

osteoplastic /ósti ə plástik/ *adj* **1.** relating to or typical of bone surgery **2.** relating to or important in the process of bone development

osteoplasty /ósti ə plásti/ *n* the surgical repair or correction of distortions of bones

osteoporosis /ósti ō pə róssiss/ *n* a disease occurring especially in women after the menopause in which the bones become very porous, break easily, and heal slowly. It may lead to curvature of the spine after the vertebrae collapse. [Mid-19C. < OSTEO- + Greek *poros* 'passage']

osteosarcoma /ósti ō saar kőmə/ (*plural* **-mata** /-mətə/ or **-mas**) *n* a malignant bone tumour

osteosis /ósti óssiss/ *n* the presence of bone-making nodules in the skin

osteotome /ósti ə tōm/ *n* a surgical instrument used to cut or divide bone

osteotomy /ósti óttəmi/ (*plural* **-mies**) *n* a surgical procedure in which bone is divided or sectioned — **osteotomist** *n*

ostia ANAT, ZOOL plural of **ostium**

Ostia /ósti ə/ ancient Roman port in Italy, at the mouth of the River Tiber, southwest of Rome

Ostiak *n, adj* PEOPLES, LANG another spelling of **Ostyak**

ostiary /ósti əri/ (*plural* **-ies**) *n* a doorkeeper in a Roman Catholic church [15C. < Latin *ostiarius* 'doorkeeper' < *ostium* 'opening']

ostinato /ósti naátō/ (*plural* **-tos**) *n* a short musical phrase or melody that is repeated over and over, usually at the same pitch [Late 19C. < Italian, 'stubborn, obstinate']

ostiole /ósti ōl/ *n* a small pore or opening in some algae or fungi, through which reproductive spores pass [Mid-19C. < Latin *ostiolum* 'little door' < *ostium* 'opening']

ostium /ósti əm/ (*plural* **-tia** /-ti ə/) *n* **1.** a small pore or opening in a passage or organ of the body **2.** a pore or small opening in a sponge, through which water passes [Mid-17C. < Latin, 'mouth of a river, opening']

ostler /ósslər/, **hostler** /hósslər/ *n* formerly, somebody employed to look after horses at an inn [14C. Variant of HOSTELLER]

ostmark /óst maark/ *n* the unit of currency used in the former German Democratic Republic [Mid-20C. < German, 'east mark']

ostomate /óstə mayt/ *n* somebody who has had a

stoma created, allowing the intestine to open at the body surface [Mid-20C. < OSTOMY]

ostomy /óstəmi/ (*plural* **-mies**) *n* a surgical procedure in which an artificial opening for excreting waste matter is created, e.g. a colostomy or ileostomy [Mid-20C. < terms like COLOSTOMY, ILEOSTOMY]

-ostosis *suffix* formation of bone ○ *hyperostosis* [< Greek *osteon* 'bone']

ostracize /óstrə síz/ (**-cizes, -cizing, -cized**), **ostracise** (**-cises, -cising, -cised**) *vt* **1.** to banish or exclude somebody from society or from a particular group, either formally or informally ○ *She was ostracized by all her former friends.* **2.** to banish somebody by a popular vote because that person is regarded as dangerous to society, as was the practice in ancient Greece [Mid-19C. < Greek *ostrakizein* < *ostrakon* 'shell, pottery fragment'] — **ostracism** *n*

ORIGIN In ancient Athens, when it was proposed that somebody should be sent into exile because of becoming a danger to the state, a vote was taken on the matter. The method of voting was to inscribe the name of the prospective exile on a piece of broken pottery (*ostrakon*). If enough votes were cast against him, he was sent away for ten years.

ostracod /óstrə kod/ (*plural* **same** or **-cods**) *n* a tiny crustacean that lives inside a hard outer shell made of two hinged halves. Subclass: Ostracoda. [Mid-19C. < modern Latin *Ostracoda* < Greek *ostrakōdēs* 'like a pottery fragment' < *ostrakon* 'shell']

Ostrava /óstrəvə/ city in the northeastern Czech Republic, situated about 16 km/10 mi. from the Polish border. Population: 322,111 (1999).

ostrich

ostrich /óstrich/ (*plural* **-triches** or **same**) *n* **1.** a two-toed fast-running bird with a long bare neck, small head, and fluffy drooping feathers. It cannot fly, and is the largest living bird. Native to: Africa. Latin name: *Struthio camelus.* **2.** somebody who tries to avoid unpleasant situations by refusing to acknowledge that they exist (*informal*) [13C. < Old French *ostrusce* < Latin *avis* 'bird' + Greek *strouthiōn-* < *strouthos* 'sparrow'. In sense 2 < the belief that ostriches bury their heads in sand if pursued]

Ostrogoth /óstrə goth/ *n* a member of the eastern branch of Gothic peoples who invaded Italy, where they ruled between the late 5th and the middle of the 6th centuries [14C. < late Latin *Ostrogothi* (plural) 'Ostrogoths' < Germanic] — **Ostrogothic** /óstrə góthik/ *adj*

Ostyak /ósti ak/ (*plural* **-aks** or **same**), **Ostiak** *n* **1.** a member of a people who live in western Siberia **2.** the Finno-Ugric language of the Ostyak people. Native speakers: 15,000. [Early 18C. Via Russian < Tatar *ustyak* 'one of another tribe'] — **Ostyak** *adj*

OSU *abbr* Order of Saint Ursula

Oswald /ózzwəld/, **St** (AD 604?–642) Anglo-Saxon monarch. He was king of Northumbria (AD 634–42), where, with the help of St Aidan, he re-established Christianity.

Oswald, Lee Harvey (1939–63) US alleged assassin. Accused of assassinating President John F. Kennedy (22 November, 1963), Oswald was fatally shot two days later by Jack Ruby while in police custody.

Oswestry /ózwəstri/ market town in Shropshire, west-central England. Population: 37,308 (2001).

Oświęcim /ósh vyén cheém/ town in Poland west of Krakow. It was the location of the biggest Nazi

concentration camp during World War II. Population: 43,300 (2003). Former name **Auschwitz**

OT *abbr* **1.** MED occupational therapy **2.** BIBLE Old Testament **3.** overtime

ot- *prefix* same as **oto-** (*used before vowels*)

Otago /ō táag ō/ administrative region of New Zealand, occupying the southeastern part of the South Island. Its principal city is Dunedin. Population: 181,539 (2001). Area: 38,638 sq. km/14,918 sq. mi.

Otago Peninsula peninsula on the southeastern coast of the South Island, New Zealand. It extends 25 km/16 mi. eastwards from Dunedin to Cape Saunders.

otalgia /ō tálji ə, -jə/ *n* pain in the ear (*technical*) [Mid-17C. < Greek *ōtalgia* < *ōt-*, stem of *ous* 'ear']

OTC *abbr* **1.** MIL Officers' Training Corps **2.** FIN, PHARM over-the-counter

OTE *abbr* on-target earnings (*used in advertisements for jobs that pay commission*)

other /úthər/ CORE MEANING: a grammatical word used to show that a thing, person, or situation is additional or different ○ (adj) *He does much to help the homeless and other people in need.* ○ (adj) *They met many other children there.* ○ (adj) *I went on ahead, and the other climbers struggled on behind.* ○ (pron) *This is one problem, but there are many others.* ○ (pron) *As much as I demand of others, I am much more demanding of myself.*
1. *adj, pron* FURTHER refers to an additional or further person or thing of the type already mentioned ○ (adj) *Let me make one other suggestion.* ○ (pron) *A couple of students failed the exam, but many others passed.* **2.** *adj, pron* DIFFERENT refers to a different thing or things from that or those already mentioned ○ (adj) *Are there any other items you'd like to take home?* ○ (pron) *This problem, more than any other, has divided the critics.* **3.** *adj, pron* SECOND OF TWO THINGS refers to the second of two things when the first is known or understood ○ (adj) *He threw his other glove out of the window.* ○ (pron) *She had a cup in one hand and a glass in the other.* **4.** *adj* THE REMAINING refers to the remaining people or things in a group, apart from the one mentioned ○ (adj) *She left earlier, with the other kids.* **5.** *pron* others OTHER PEOPLE OR THINGS other people or things (*takes a plural verb*) ○ *Others may think differently.* ○ *Put the others in the drawer.* [Old English *ōðer* < Indo-European] ◇ **other than** indicates an exception to a statement ○ *Was anyone there other than you?* ◇ **the other day** *or* **night** a few days or nights ago ○ *A funny thing happened to me the other day.*

Other Backward Classes *npl* in India, an official categorization of people involved in tasks regarded as menial or excluded from other castes, who are considered disadvantaged and granted special treatment

other-directed *adj* more concerned with what other people think than with personal values and standards

otherness /úthərnəss/ *n* the condition of being perceived as strange or different

otherwise /úthər wīz/ *adv* **1.** OR ELSE if things had been different ○ *He must have forgotten his mobile, otherwise he would have phoned.* **2.** DIFFERENTLY different from or opposite to something stated ○ *You may take your hand luggage with you unless otherwise requested.* **3.** IN OTHER WAYS in any other ways ○ *An otherwise dull day was enlivened by her arrival.* ■ *adj* OTHER THAN SOMETHING STATED different from or other than something specified ○ *lots of information, digital and otherwise* [Old English (*on*) *ōðre wīsan* '(in) (an)other wise or manner']

otherworld /úthər wurld/ *n* a world or life that is beyond the conventional perception of reality

otherworldly /úthər wúrldli/ *adj* **1.** OF MYSTICAL WORLD relating to a world or life beyond conventional perception of reality **2.** OF INTELLECTUAL MATTERS concerned with highly intellectual or academic matters **3.** CONCERNED WITH AFTERLIFE concerned with the supposed afterlife as opposed to this life in this world —**otherworldliness** *n*

Othman ♦ **Osman I**

otic /ốtik, óttik/ *adj* relating to or located near the ear

(*technical*) [Mid-17C. < Greek *ōtikos* < *ōt-*, stem of *ous* 'ear']

-otic *suffix* **1.** relating to a particular condition, action, or process ○ *hypnotic* **2.** having a particular disease or condition ○ *psychotic* [Via French and Latin < Greek *-ōtikos*]

otiose /ốti ōss, -ōz/ *adj* **1.** NOT EFFECTIVE with no useful result or practical purpose (*formal*) **2.** WORTHLESS with little or no value (*formal*) **3.** LAZY unwilling or disinclined to work or be active (*archaic*) [Late 18C. < Latin *otiosus* 'at leisure, idle' < *otium* 'leisure'] —**otiosely** *adv* —**otiosity** /ốti óssəti/ *n*

otitis /ō títiss/ *n* inflammation of the ear, caused by infection

otitis media /-méedi ə/ *n* a painful inflammation of the middle ear that can cause dizziness and temporary hearing loss

oto- *prefix* ear ○ *otolith* [Via modern Latin < Greek *ōt-*, stem of *ous*]

otocyst /ốtō sist/ *n* **1.** the structure from which the adult inner ear develops **2.** ZOOL same as **statocyst**

otol. *abbr* MED otology

otolaryngology /ốtō lárring gólləji/ *n* the branch of medicine concerned with the treatment and diagnosis of diseases of the ear, nose, and throat —**otolaryngological** /ốtō lə ríng gə lójjik'l/ *adj* —**otolaryngologist** *n*

otolith /ốtō lith/ *n* **1.** a particle of calcium carbonate found in the inner ear of vertebrates and involved in sensory perception **2.** ZOOL same as **statolith** (sense 1)

otology /ō tólləji/ *n* the branch of medicine concerned with the structure and function of the ear, its diseases, and their treatment —**otological** /ốtə lójjik'l/ *adj* —**otologist** *n*

Oto-Manguean /ốtō máng gee ən, -gwee ən/, **Oto-manguean** *n* a family of about 30 Native Central American languages spoken in a region extending from northern Mexico to Nicaragua [< OTOMI + MANGUE] —**Oto-Manguean** *adj*

Otomi /ốtə mée/ (*plural same* or **-mis**) *n* **1.** a member of a Native Central American people of central Mexico **2.** the Oto-Manguean language of the Otomi people. Native speakers: 200,000. [Late 18C. Via American Spanish < Nahuatl *otomih* 'unknown'] —**Otomi** *adj*

O'Toole /ō tóol/, **Peter** (*b.* 1932) Irish-born British actor. Among his numerous stage and screen appearances were starring roles in *Lawrence of Arabia* (1962), *The Lion in Winter* (1968), and *The Last Emperor* (1987). Full name **O'Toole, Peter Seamus**

otorhinolaryngology /ốtō rīnō lárring gólləji/ *n* MED same as **otolaryngology** —**otorhinolaryngological** /ốtō rīnō lə ríng gə lójjik'l/ *adj* —**otorhinolaryngologist** *n*

otosclerosis /ốtō sklə róssiss/ *n* a hereditary disease of the inner ear in which spongy bone growth leads to progressive hearing impairment

otoscope /ốtō skōp/ *n* an instrument incorporating a light and a magnifying lens, used to examine the external canal of the ear and the eardrum —**otoscopic** /ốtō skóppik/ *adj*

ototoxic /ốtō tóksik/ *adj* toxic to the ear and hence impairing hearing or balance —**ototoxicity** /-tok síssəti/ *n*

OTP *abbr* E-COMMERCE open trading protocol

Otranto, Strait of /ō tránt ō/ sea passage between the Adriatic and Ionian seas. It separates the heel of Italy from Albania. Length: 69 km/43 mi.

OTS *abbr* Officers' Training School

OTT *abbr* over the top (*informal*)

ottava /ō taávə/ *adj* sung or played at an octave higher or lower than the notes written on the staff, indicated by a sign placed above or below the staff [Early 19C. < Italian, 'octave, eighth' < *otto* 'eight' < Latin *octo*]

ottava rima /-réemə/ *n* a verse form made up of eight lines in iambic pentameter with the rhyme scheme abababcc [Early 19C. < Italian, 'eighth rhyme']

Ottawa /óttəwə/ **1.** river in Canada. It is the chief tributary of the St Lawrence River, forming part of the Ontario-Quebec border. Length: 1,120 km/696 mi. **2.** capital city of Canada, located in southeast

Ontario, on the Ontario-Quebec border. Population: 774,027 (2001).

otter

otter /óttər/ (*plural same* or **-ters**) *n* **1.** a fish-eating water animal with smooth dark brown fur and webbed feet that is related to weasels and minks. Native to: worldwide except Australia. Family: Mustelidae. **2.** the fur of the otter [Old English *ot(t)or* < Indo-European, 'water']

otter board *n* a board or plate attached to each side of the mouth of a purse seine or other trawl net to keep it open as it passes through the water

Otterburn /óttər burn/ village in Northumberland, northeastern England, site of the Scottish defeat of the English in the Battle of Otterburn in 1388

otter hound *n* a large dog belonging to an English breed developed for otter hunting

otto /óttō/ *n* PHARM, INDUST same as **attar** [Variant]

Otto I /óttō/ (912–973) Holy Roman Emperor (962–973) and king of Germany (936–973). He consolidated the kingdom of Germany and the Holy Roman Empire through a series of military victories and alliances. Known as **Otto the Great**

Otto cycle /óttō-/ *n* a thermodynamic process for the conversion of heat into work, e.g. the sequential suction, compression, ignition, and expulsion in a four-stroke engine [Late 19C. After Nikolaus August *Otto* (1832–91), German engineer and inventor]

ottoman /óttəmən/ *n* **1.** a low upholstered stool or long seat, often with storage space inside **2.** a heavy corded silk or rayon fabric. Use: coats, trimmings. [Early 19C. < French *ottomane*, feminine of adjective < *Ottoman* (see OTTOMAN)]

Ottoman /óttəmən/ *n* a member of a Turkish people who conquered Asia Minor in the 13th century [Late 16C. Via French or Italian < medieval Latin *ottomanus* < Arabic *'Uṭmān* 'Osman'] —**Ottoman** *adj*

Ottoman Empire *n* a Turkish empire established in the late 13th century in Asia Minor, eventually covering much of Southwest Asia, North Africa, and southeastern Europe. It ended in 1922.

Otway Ranges /ót way ráynjiz/ range of hills in southern Victoria, Australia, which extends from Anglesea to Cape Otway

ou /ō/ *n* S Africa same as **man** *n* (sense 1) (*informal*) [Mid-20C. < Afrikaans]

OU *abbr* Open University

ouabain /waá bay in, -bayn/ *n* a poisonous crystalline compound. Source: seeds of some African trees. Use: medicinally as a heart stimulant. [Late 19C. Via French *ouabaïo* < Somali *wabayo* 'arrow poison']

Ouagadougou /waágə dóogoo/ capital city of Burkina Faso, located in the centre of the country. Population: 634,479 (1991).

oubaas /ō baass/ *n* S Africa somebody who is above somebody else in age or rank [Mid-19C. < Afrikaans, 'old boss', origin ?]

oubliette /óobli ét/ *n* a dungeon made so that the only way in or out is through a trapdoor at the top [Early 19C. < French < *oublier* 'forget' < Latin *oblitus*, past participle of *oblivisci*]

ouch /owch/ *interj* an exclamation used to express sudden pain [Mid-19C. Origin ?]

oud /ood/ *n* a stringed instrument of southwestern Asia and North Africa that resembles a lute or a mandolin [Mid-18C. < Arabic *al-'ūd* 'the wood']

ought[1] /awt/ CORE MEANING: a modal verb indicating what somebody should do ○ *It seems to me that we ought to support their initiative.* ○ *You ought to tell her how you feel.*
modal v 1. **BE MORALLY RIGHT** indicates that somebody has a duty or obligation to do something or that it is morally right to do something ○ *You ought to be ashamed of what you have done.* 2. **BE IMPORTANT** indicates that something is important or a good idea ○ *You ought to see a doctor as soon as possible.* 3. **BE PROBABLE** indicates probability or expectation ○ *We ought to be there by now.* 4. **BE WISHED FOR** indicates a desire or wish ○ *You ought to come to dinner sometime.* 5. **SHOULD BE CASE** indicates that something should be the case but may not be ○ *That ought to be easy.* [Old English *āhte*, past tense of OWE]

USAGE didn't/hadn't/shouldn't ought Avoid in formal writing the regional constructions (called *double modal auxiliaries*) **didn't ought, hadn't ought** or **shouldn't ought**, as in *They didn't ought to have done that.* Use instead: *They ought not to have done that.*

ought[2] /awt/ *n* MATHS same as **zero** [Mid-18C. < erroneous division of *a nought*]

ouguiya /oo gée yə/ *n* the main unit of Mauritanian currency. See table at **currency** [Late 20C. Via French < Mauritanian Arabic *ūgiyya* < Greek *ougkia* < Latin *uncia* (see OUNCE[1])]

Ouija /wéejə/ *tdmk* a trademark for a board with letters and a pointer or planchette by which answers to questions are spelt out, supposedly by spiritual forces

ould /owld/ *adj Ireland* used to represent the Irish pronunciation of 'old', especially its use as an intensifier

Oulu /ó ōol ōō/ city and port on the Gulf of Bothnia, west-central Finland. Population: 117,670 (2000).

ouma /ó maa/ *n S Africa* 1. same as **grandmother** (sense 1) 2. an elderly woman [Early 20C. < Afrikaans, 'grandmother' < *ou* 'old' + *ma* 'mother']

ounce[1] /ownss/ *n* 1. **UNIT OF WEIGHT** a unit of weight in the avoirdupois system equal to one-sixteenth of a pound, approximately 28 g 2. **FLUID OUNCE** a unit for measuring liquid, equal to 0.0284 of a litre 3. **SMALL AMOUNT** a small amount of something ○ *Anyone with an ounce of common sense would take an umbrella on a day like this.* [14C. Via Old French *unce* < Latin *uncia* 'twelfth part, inch, ounce' < *unus* 'one']

ounce[2] /ownss/ (*plural same* or **ounces**) *n* ZOOL same as **snow leopard** [14C. < Old French *once*, variant of *lonce* (the *l* being mistaken for the definite article) < Latin *lync-* 'lynx']

oupa /ó paa/ *n S Africa* 1. same as **grandfather** (sense 1) 2. an elderly man [Early 20C. < Afrikaans, 'grandfather' < *ou* 'old' + *pa* 'father']

our /owr/ *det* 1. **BELONGING TO US** indicates that something belongs to or is associated with the speaker or writer and at least one other person (*first person plural possessive determiner*) ○ *Where are all our bags?* ○ *Our house is just a few hundred yards from yours.* 2. **BELONGING TO EVERYONE** indicates that something belongs to or is associated with people in general ○ *the dreams that inspire us to do our best* 3. **REFERS TO MEMBER OF FAMILY** refers to a member of the speaker's family (*informal*) ○ *Our John is an electrician now.* [Old English *ūre* 'of us', genitive plural of WE]

SPELLCHECK See *hour.*

Our Father *n* CHR same as **Lord's Prayer**

Our Lady *n* a title for Mary, the mother of Jesus Christ, used mainly in Catholic churches

ours /owrz/ *pron* refers to something or somebody belonging to or associated with the speaker and at least one other person (*first person plural possessive pronoun*) ○ *It's no surprise that their team is ahead of ours.* [13C. < OUR + -'s 'belonging to']

ourselves /owr sélvz, aar-/ *pron* 1. **BELONGING TO US** refers to the speaker or writer and at least one other person (*used as the object of a verb or preposition when the subject refers to the same people*) ○ *We blame ourselves for the accident.* 2. **REFERS TO PEOPLE IN GENERAL** refers to people in general ○ *Many of us have secrets that we find difficult to admit even to ourselves.* 3. **REFERS EMPHATICALLY TO US** refers emphatically to the speaker or writer and at least one other person ○ *We ourselves must bear the responsibility.* 4. **OUR USUAL SELVES** our usual selves ○ *At home with the family, we can really be ourselves.*

-ous *suffix* 1. full of or having the qualities of ○ *virtuous* ○ *traitorous* 2. CHEM having a lower valency than a corresponding compound or ion the name of which ends in *-ic* ○ *chromous* [Via Old French < Latin *-osus* and *-us*]

Ouse /ooz/ 1. river in eastern England that rises in Northamptonshire and empties into the Wash near King's Lynn, Norfolk. Length: 257 km/160 mi. 2. river in northeastern England that rises in North Yorkshire and empties into the Humber Estuary. Length: 92 km/57 mi. 3. river in southeastern England that rises in East Sussex and empties into the English Channel. Length: 48 km/30 mi.

oust /owst/ (**ousts, ousting, ousted**) *vt* 1. to remove or force somebody from an office or position 2. to use force to remove somebody from a place [15C. Via Old French *oster* < Latin *obstare* 'stand in the way' < *stare* 'to stand']

ouster /ówstər/ *n* 1. *N Am* the act of removing or forcing somebody out of a place or position 2. the illegal removal or forceful dispossession of somebody's property

out /owt/ (**outs, outing, outed**) CORE MEANING: a grammatical word indicating that somebody or something is away from a place or removed from somewhere ○ (adv) *The child raced out and got back onto the bike.* ○ (adv) *She yanked out the weeds.* ○ (adj) *She's been out late every night.*
1. *adv* **AWAY FROM PARTICULAR PLACE** away from a place, especially the inside of something ○ *He reached underneath the bed and hauled out a heavy box.* ○ *The child scampered out and jumped on the bike.* 2. *adv* **OUTSIDE** outside a place rather than inside ○ *It's cold out.* 3. *adv* **IN ANOTHER PLACE** in another place, usually far away ○ *She's out in Australia, I think.* 4. *adv* **INDICATES END POINT** indicates a goal or objective achieved in the action specified by the verb ○ *Stick it out – never give up.* 5. *adv* **EXISTING** in existence ○ *It's one of the best albums out.* 6. *adj, adv* **AWAY FROM HOME** away from home or your place of work ○ (adj) *He's not answering the doorbell, so he must be out.* ○ (adv) *She's not answering the phone; she must have gone out.* 7. *adj, adv* **FARTHER AWAY** refers to the tide when the sea moves away from the shore ○ (adj) *We can cross to the island when the tide is out.* ○ (adv) *The tide starts going out at around five o'clock.* 8. *adj, adv* **NO LONGER BURNING** no longer alight or no longer burning ○ (adj) *The fire is out.* ○ (adv) *The light has gone out.* 9. *adj, adv* **IN FLOWER** in flower ○ (adj) *The daffodils are out at last.* 10. *adj, adv* **AVAILABLE** available for people to buy ○ (adj) *Her new book is out in paperback.* 11. *adj, adv* **ON STRIKE** on strike ○ (adj) *The miners have been out for a month now.* ○ (adv) *Several hundred workers came out in protest over the benefit cuts.* 12. *adj* **NO LONGER IN GAME** unable to take part any longer in a game or sport 13. *adj* **CONSIDERING VERDICT** describes a jury that is considering its verdict 14. *adj* **INCORRECT** inaccurate or incorrect ○ *Look – the figures are way out.* 15. *adj* **UNACCEPTABLE** unacceptable or not worth considering ○ *That possibility is out, I'm afraid.* 16. *adj* **UNFASHIONABLE** no longer in fashion 17. *adj* **INTENT** determined or intent on something ○ *He's just out for what he can get.* 18. *adj* **UNCONSCIOUS** unconscious ○ *She was out cold.* 19. *adj* **USED UP** used up or exhausted ○ *All our rations are out.* 20. *adj* **NOT IN GOVERNMENT** no longer in power or office 21. *adj* **FINISHED** completed or concluded ○ *before the year is out* 22. *adj* **NOT OPERATIONAL** not in working order ○ *All the phones are out.* 23. *adj* **OPENLY GAY OR LESBIAN** open about being gay or lesbian ○ *He isn't out to his parents.* 24. *interj* **AWAY FROM HERE!** a command for somebody to leave a place ○ *Out! And don't come back!* 25. *vt* **EXPOSE SOMEBODY'S SEXUALITY** to expose somebody as gay, lesbian, or bisexual or reveal yourself as such ○ *The action group has outed many prominent celebrities.* 26. *n* **WAY OF AVOIDING BAD CONSEQUENCE** a way of escaping from a predicament or avoiding the undesirable consequences of something (*informal*) ○ *What's my out if things go wrong?* [Old English *ūt* < Germanic] ◇ **out of** 1. indicates that somebody leaves a place ○ *Three men came out of the store.* 2. indicates that somebody removes something from a place ○ *In her enthusiasm, she pulled the drawer right out of the desk.* 3. towards the outside ○ *She looked longingly out of the window.* 4. no longer available or in somebody's possession ○ *We're out of butter.* 5. using as a source or material ○ *Plastic products are made out of petroleum.* 6. indicates the proportion that something is true of ○ *This applies to one out of five adults.* 7. indicates that somebody gains an advantage from something ○ *I think I got a lot out of the course.* 8. indicates that somebody is sheltered from the weather ○ *Remember to keep out of the sun, or at least use sunblock.* 9. beyond the range of a sound ○ *I called her, but she was out of earshot.* 10. indicates the motivation behind an action ○ *He only did it out of spite.* 11. indicates that somebody is not or is no longer in a situation ○ *A police officer warned them to stay out of trouble.* ◇ **out of it** very drunk, or under the influence of drugs (*informal*) ○ *You were totally out of it last night!* ◇ **out with it** a command to somebody to let something be known immediately ○ *Come on, what's going on? Out with it!*

out- *prefix* 1. going beyond, overcoming, or outdoing ○ *outclass* 2. positioned outside, away, or separate ○ *outback* 3. moving or extending beyond or outwards ○ *outgoing* 4. completion or full extent ○ *outfit* [< OUT]

outact *vt*	**outprice** *vt*
outbid *vt*	**outproduce** *vt*
outdance *vt*	**outpunch** *vt*
outdrink *vt*	**outsail** *vt*
outeat *vt*	**outscore** *vt*
outfight *vt*	**outshout** *vt*
outfly *vt*	**outsing** *vt*
outhit *vt*	**outskate** *vt*
outlearn *vt*	**outsparkle** *vt*
outman *vt*	**outsprint** *vt*
outmanipulate *vt*	**outswim** *vt*
outmanoeuvre *vt*	**outtalk** *vt*
outmatch *vt*	**outthink** *vt*
outmatched *adj*	**outvote** *vt*
outperform *vt*	**outwear** *vt*
outplay *vt*	**outwrestle** *vt*
outpoll *vt*	**outyield** *vt*

outa *prep* another spelling of **outta** (*informal*)

outage /ówtij/ *n* 1. a temporary loss of function or interruption of a power source, especially a loss of electric power 2. an amount of something that is missing after delivery or storage

out-and-out *adj* being a thorough, uncompromising, or unapologetic example of something

out-and-outer *n* somebody who goes to extremes in an activity or endeavour

outback /ówt bak/ *n* a sparsely inhabited or wilderness region of a country, especially of Australia —**outback** *adj*

outbalance /owt bállənss/ (**-ances, -ancing, -anced**) *vt* to go beyond something in effect, influence, or importance

outboard /ówt bawrd/ *adj* 1. NAUT **ON OUTSIDE OF BOAT** located on the outside of the hull of a ship or boat 2. NAUT **TOWARDS SIDE OF BOAT** positioned away from the centre of a ship or boat 3. AVIAT **AWAY FROM FUSELAGE** away from the main body of an aircraft and towards the wing tips ■ *adv* NAUT, AVIAT **TOWARDS OUTSIDE OF CRAFT** in a direction away from the centre of a ship or aircraft ■ *n* 1. **BOAT WITH OUTBOARD MOTOR** a boat with an engine mounted outside the stern 2. NAUT same as **outboard motor**

outboard motor *n* a small or medium-sized engine

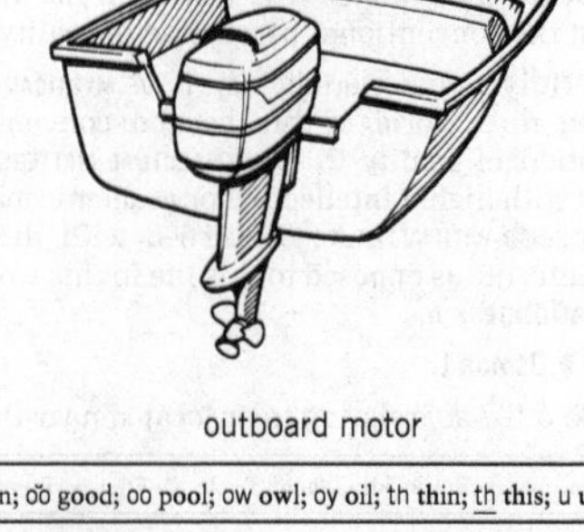

outboard motor

with a propeller that can be mounted outside the stern of a boat

outbound /ówt bownd/ adj travelling away from rather than towards a place ○ *an outbound journey*

out-box n 1. a location in which outgoing e-mail messages are stored until they are sent 2. *US* same as **out-tray**

outbrave /owt bráyv/ vt (archaic) 1. to face a threat with defiance 2. to be braver than somebody else

outbreak /ówt brayk/ n a sudden occurrence, usually of something unpleasant or dangerous such as illness or fighting ○ *the outbreak of war*

outbreed /owt breéd/ (-breeds, -breeding, -bred /-bréd/) vti to bring together distantly related members of a species in order to breed genetically varied offspring, or reproduce in this way [Early 20C. After INBREED]

outbuilding /ówt bilding/ n a barn, shed, or other structure that is situated away from the main building on a property

outburst /ówt burst/ n 1. a sudden display of strong emotion ○ *an outburst of grief* 2. a sudden burst of energy or growth

outcall /ówt kawl/ n a visit made by a doctor or other professional to the home of a client or patient

outcast /ówt kaast/ n somebody who has been rejected by a group or by society ○ *a social outcast* —**outcast** adj

outcaste /ówt kaast/ n 1. in South Asia, somebody who has been expelled from a Hindu caste for violating its rules or customs 2. in South Asia, somebody who does not belong to a Hindu caste

outclass /owt klaáss/ (-classes, -classing, -classed) vt to be so much better than others as to seem to be in a separate class altogether

outcome /ówt kum/ n 1. the way that something turns out in the end ○ *a satisfactory outcome* 2. an expected or likely final state, achievement, or result ○ *poorer health outcomes*

outcrop /ówt krop/ n the part of a rock formation that is exposed on the surface of the ground ■ vi (-crops, -cropping, -cropped) to stick out of the ground as an outcrop [Mid-18C. < crop out]

outcross vt /owt króss/ (-crosses, -crossing, -crossed) to mate two plants or animals not closely related but usually of the same breed in order to produce offspring ■ n /ówt kross/ the process of outcrossing plants or animals, or the progeny produced as a result

outcry /ówt krī/ (plural -cries) n 1. a strong, widespread public reaction against something 2. a loud cry from a crowd of people

outdated /ówt dáytid/ adj superseded by something better, more fashionable, or more technologically advanced ○ *outdated notions about how to bring up children*

SYNONYMS See **old-fashioned**.

outdid v past tense of **outdo**

outdistance /owt dístənss/ (-tances, -tancing, -tanced) vt 1. to be faster than other competitors in a race and leave them behind 2. to be considerably more successful than others

outdo /owt doó/ (-does, -doing, -did /-díd/, -done /-dún/) vt to do more or better than other people, or better than previously

outdoor /ówt dáwr/ adj 1. located in, belonging in, or suited to the open air ○ *outdoor activities* 2. enjoying activities that take place in the open air

outdoor relief n HIST same as **out relief**

outdoors /owt dáwrz/ adv outside, or in the open air ■ n the open air, especially when away from populated areas [Early 19C. < out of doors]

outdoorsman /owt dáwrzmən/ (plural -men /-mən/) n a man who spends much time doing outdoor activities such as camping, hunting, and fishing

outdoorsperson /owt dáwrz purss'n/ (plural -people /-peep'l/) n somebody who spends much time doing outdoor activities such as camping, hunting, and fishing

outdoorswoman /owt dáwrz woŏmmən/ (plural -women

/-wimmin/) n a woman who spends much time doing outdoor activities such as camping, hunting, and fishing

outdoorsy /owt dáwrzi/ adj suited to or fond of the open air (informal)

outdraw /owt dráw/ (-draws, -drawing, -drew /-droó/, -drawn /-dráwn/) vt 1. to draw a handgun faster than another person 2. to attract a larger audience than another performer or performance

outer /ówtər/ adj 1. ON OUTSIDE on or around the outside of something ○ *the outer surface of the spacecraft* 2. AWAY FROM CENTRE on the edge or away from the centre of something ○ *the outer islands* 3. OF BODY RATHER THAN SPIRIT concerning or belonging to external or worldly things rather than the life of the mind or spirit ◇ **on the outer** *Aus* EXCLUDED OR ONLY ON THE PERIPHERY on the periphery of things or excluded from a group (informal)

outer bar n in England and Wales, all the junior barristers practising at the bar

Outer Hebrides island group in Scotland, comprising the westernmost islands of the Hebrides

outermost /ówtər mōst/ adj farthest away from the centre [14C. < OUTER, after INNERMOST]

outer planet n one of the five planets that have orbits lying beyond the asteroid belt, i.e. Jupiter, Saturn, Uranus, Neptune, and Pluto

outer space n all space in the universe beyond Earth and its atmosphere, especially interplanetary and interstellar space, but including the region where astronauts walk and satellites orbit the Earth

outerwear /ówtər wair/ n clothing that is designed to be worn outdoors over other clothing

outface /owt fáyss/ (-faces, -facing, -faced) vt 1. to win a confrontation with somebody, especially by staring or not looking away 2. to confront somebody boldly or confidently

outfall /ówt fawl/ n the outlet of a sewer, drain, or stream, especially where it empties into a larger body of water

outfield /ówt feeld/ n 1. OUTER PART OF CRICKET PITCH the part of a cricket pitch farthest from the bowler and the player who is batting 2. AREA BEYOND INFIELD in baseball or softball, the part of a playing field beyond the diamond marked by the bases 3. PLAYERS IN OUTFIELD in baseball or softball, the players whose positions are in the outfield —**outfielder** n

outfit /ówt fit/ n 1. SET OF CLOTHES a set of clothes worn together 2. EQUIPMENT a set of tools or equipment for a particular task or occupation 3. SMALL ORGANIZATION a team or group of people who work closely together, e.g. a military unit (informal) ■ vt (-fits, -fitting, -fitted) 1. EQUIP SOMEBODY to provide somebody with all the equipment that is needed for a job or activity 2. DRESS SOMEBODY to provide somebody with a set of clothes

outfitter /ówt fitər/ n a shop that sells men's clothes

outflank /owt flángk/ (-flanks, -flanking, -flanked) vt 1. to go around the main body of an enemy force and attack it from the side or from behind 2. to outwit or bypass an opponent or competitor

outflow /ówtflō/ n 1. the process of flowing out or away 2. the flow, movement, or transfer of something such as gas, water, or money away from a place

outfox /owt fóks/ (-foxes, -foxing, -foxed) vt to defeat somebody by being more cunning

outgas /owt gáss/ (-gases, -gassing, -gassed) vti to remove or release trapped or absorbed gas, or be released as gas

outgeneral /owt jénnərəl/ (-als, -alling, -alled) vt to defeat somebody in battle through better leadership

outgo /owt gō/ vt (-goes, -going, -went /-wént/, -gone /-gón/) OUTDO SOMEBODY OR SOMETHING to go beyond or surpass somebody or something ■ n (plural -goes) 1. EXPENDITURE something that goes out, especially money that is paid out 2. SOMETHING THAT FLOWS OUT something that is flowing out

outgoing /ówt gō ing/ adj 1. LEAVING OR GOING OUT in the process of departing or going out of a building or place ○ *outgoing flights* 2. LEAVING JOB in the process of departing or being sent away after a period of office ○ *a dinner for the outgoing president* 3. SOCIABLE

confident and friendly in social situations ○ *a cheerful, outgoing child*

outgoings /ówt gō ingz/ npl money paid out, especially on a regular basis

outgone past tense of **outgo**

outgrew past tense of **outgrow**

out-group n a group of people excluded from another group with higher status

outgrow /owt grō/ (-grows, -growing, -grew /-groó/, -grown /-grōn/) vt 1. GET TOO LARGE FOR SOMETHING to grow too large for something 2. MOVE BEYOND PREVIOUS INTERESTS to change so that old ideas, interests, or ways of behaving are lost in favour of new ones 3. OUTSTRIP OTHERS to grow larger or faster than other things or people

outgrowth /ówt grōth/ n 1. a natural development or result of something else 2. something that is growing out from the main part

outguess /owt géss/ (-guesses, -guessing, -guessed) vt to get an advantage over somebody by anticipating what that person is thinking or planning to do

outgun /owt gún/ (-guns, -gunning, -gunned) vt 1. to have more guns or firepower than somebody else 2. to defeat a rival or competitor by being stronger or having better resources (informal)

outhaul /ówt hawl/ n a rope used to pull a sail taut along a boom or spar

out-Herod (-Herods, -Herodding, -Herodded) vt to behave more excessively than somebody else ○ *out-Herod Herod* [After HEROD (THE GREAT), presented in medieval mystery plays as an overdramatic character]

outhouse /ówt howss/ (plural -houses /-howziz/) n 1. a small building situated near the main building on a property 2. N Am an outdoor toilet consisting of a small building that encloses a seat with a hole in it built over a pit

outing /ówting/ n 1. EXCURSION a short pleasure trip usually lasting no more than a day 2. PARTICIPATION IN EVENT an appearance at or participation in a public event, especially an athletic competition 3. REVELATION OF SEXUAL PREFERENCE the practice of making public the fact of being gay, lesbian, or bisexual

outjockey /owt jóki/ (-eys, -eying, -eyed) vt to get an advantage over somebody by cleverness or trickery

outlander /ówt landər/ n somebody from another country or from a different region, and thus a stranger [Late 16C. After Dutch *uitlander*, German *Ausländer*]

outlandish /owt lándish/ adj 1. extremely unusual or bizarre 2. alien or foreign (archaic) —**outlandishly** adv —**outlandishness** n

outlast /owt laást/ (-lasts, -lasting, -lasted) vt to last or exist longer than somebody or something else

outlaw /ówt law/ n 1. FUGITIVE CRIMINAL a notorious criminal, especially one on the run 2. SOMEBODY WITHOUT LEGAL RIGHTS somebody, often a criminal, who has been officially deprived of legal rights and so is not protected by the law 3. REBELLIOUS PERSON somebody who is rebellious or flouts the law 4. VICIOUS ANIMAL a savage or uncontrollable animal ■ vt (-laws, -lawing, -lawed) 1. BAN SOMETHING to make something illegal 2. TAKE AWAY SOMEBODY'S LEGAL RIGHTS to deprive somebody officially of all their legal rights [12C. < Old Norse *útlagi* 'person outside the law' < *útlagr* 'outlawed, banished']

outlawry /ówt lawri/ n 1. refusal to obey the law 2. a state in which somebody has been deprived of his or her legal rights and is no longer protected by the law, or the legal process by which this happens

outlay n /ówt lay/ 1. SPENDING the expending of resources or spending of money 2. MONEY SPENT an amount of money spent ■ vt /owt láy/ (-lays, -laying, -laid /-láyd/) SPEND MONEY to spend a specific amount of money

outlet /ówt let, -lət/ n 1. STORE a shop that sells the products of a particular manufacturer, often at a discount 2. MARKET FOR GOODS a market providing goods or services 3. RELEASE FOR EMOTIONS a way of releasing emotions or impulses ○ *an outlet for creative expression* 4. VENT a passage or opening for letting something out, e.g. water or steam 5. N Am ELEC SOCKET an electric socket 6. RIVER MOUTH the mouth of a river where it flows into a lake or the sea 7. STREAM

DRAINING LAKE a stream or channel flowing from a larger body of water

outlier /ówt lī ər/ *n* 1. OUTLYING PART a separate part of a system, organization, or body that is at some distance from the main part 2. OUTSIDER somebody who chooses not to be a part of a group or community (*often used before a noun*) ○ *If we fail to ratify this treaty, we become associated with the outlier nations.* 3. SOMEBODY LIVING AT DISTANCE FROM WORK somebody who lives far from his or her workplace 4. STATS VALUE FAR FROM OTHERS a statistical value that is outside other values in a set of data 5. GEOL ROCK FORMATION an outcrop of rock that is separated from a main formation

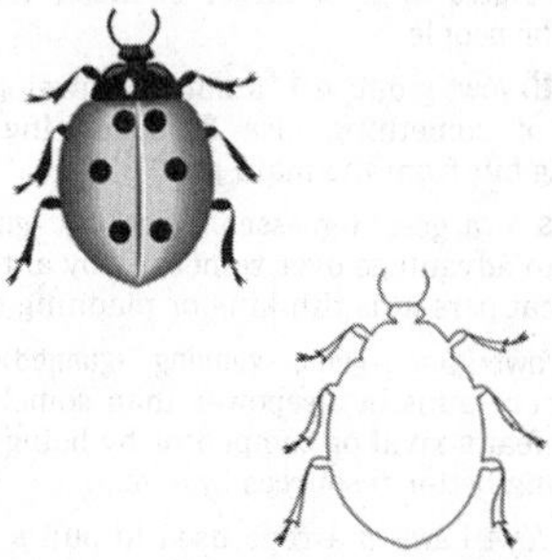

outline

outline /ówt līn/ *n* 1. LINE THAT SHOWS SHAPE the outer edge or edges of something thought of as a line defining its shape ○ *I could see the outline of the trees against the sky.* 2. LINE DEPICTING SHAPE OF SOMETHING a line drawn round or depicting the outside edges of something to show its shape 3. DRAWING WITHOUT SHADING a style or example of drawing in which an object or figure is shown as an outline (*often used before a noun*) ○ *an outline map* 4. ROUGH PLAN a general, preliminary, or rough plan or account of something, that concentrates on the main features and ignores detail, e.g. a list of the main points covered or to be covered in a speech (*often used before a noun*) ■ **outlines** *npl* MAIN FEATURES the most prominent or important aspects of something ○ *The outlines of the plan have already been agreed upon.* ■ *vt* (-lines, -lining, -lined) 1. DRAW MAIN FEATURES to draw a line showing or emphasizing the shape of something 2. GIVE ESSENTIAL POINTS to give the main points of an argument or plan

outlive /owt lív/ (-lives, -living, -lived) *vt* 1. to live longer than somebody else 2. to continue to exist beyond or last through something ○ *The policy has outlived its usefulness.*

outlook /ówt look/ *n* 1. ATTITUDE an attitude or point of view 2. LIKELY FUTURE expectations for the future, especially with respect to a particular situation 3. VIEW a view seen from a place

out loud *adv* in words that others can hear, rather than silently in the mind

outlying /ówt lī ing/ *adj* far from the central part of a place or region

outmigrate /ówt mī grayt/ (-grates, -grating, -grated) *vi* N Am to leave one region or community in order to settle in another —**outmigrant** *n* —**outmigration** *n*

outmoded /owt mṓdid/ *adj* 1. no longer fashionable or widely used 2. having been superseded by something newer or more efficient [Early 20C. Translation of French *démodé*] —**outmodedly** *adv* —**outmodedness** *n*

outmost /ówt mōst/ *adj* farthest away from the centre or main area [14C. Alteration of UTMOST]

outnumber /owt númbər/ (-bers, -bering, -bered) *vt* to be more numerous than another group or set of things

out-of-body *adj* describes an experience in which a person's consciousness appears to have an existence separate from the body, enabling the subject to see his or her own body from the outside

out of bounds *adj, adv* in or indicating a place that is beyond the established or official boundaries

out-of-court *adj* settled without going to court or without completing a court case

out-of-date *adj* old-fashioned or no longer current

out-of-doors *adv* same as **outdoors**

out-of-pocket *adj* 1. HAVING NO MONEY with less money than before, after spending some on something that did not produce good results 2. REQUIRING SOMEBODY TO SPEND CASH describes expenses paid for with cash ○ *out-of-pocket travel expenses* 3. WITH NO MONEY with no money to spend

out-of-the-way *adj* 1. far from a populated area or difficult to get to 2. uncommon or unconventional

out-of-town *adj* coming from or happening in another town or city

outpace /owt páyss/ (-paces, -pacing, -paced) *vt* to do better or go faster than something or somebody else

outpatient /ówt paysh'nt/ *n* a patient who receives treatment at a hospital without staying overnight

outplacement /ówt playssmənt/ *n* a service offered by a company to help employees who are being dismissed find new jobs

outpoint /owt póynt/ (-points, -pointing, -pointed) *vt* 1. to score more points than somebody else 2. to sail closer to the wind than another ship

outport /ówt pawrt/ *n* a secondary port near another port but in deeper water, used for larger vessels

outpost /ówt pōst/ *n* 1. TROOPS APART FROM MAIN FORCE a small group of troops stationed at a distance from the main body of an army and assigned to guard a place or area 2. MILITARY BASE a small military base in a remote area or different country 3. REMOTE SETTLEMENT a settlement in unfamiliar territory or on a frontier

outpour *vti* /owt páwr/ (-pours, -pouring, -poured) to flow out quickly and in large quantities, or make something flow out in this way ■ *n* /ówt pawr/ something that flows out rapidly and copiously, or the act of flowing out in this way

outpouring /ówt pawring/ *n* 1. an extravagant, passionate, or sometimes excessive display or expression of feeling ○ *an outpouring of generosity* ○ *an outpouring of lava* 2. same as **outpour**

output /ówt poot/ *n* 1. PRODUCTION the act of producing 2. YIELD an amount of something produced or manufactured, especially during a fixed period of time 3. CREATIVE OR ARTISTIC PRODUCTION creative or intellectual work produced by somebody ○ *her literary output* 4. ENERGY PRODUCED energy or power produced by a system 5. ELEC ENG ELECTRICAL POWER the electrical energy, measured in watts, delivered by a generator, light bulb, amplifier, or other electric device 6. COMPUT INFORMATION FROM COMPUTER information produced by a computer ■ *vt* (-puts, -putting, -put or -putted) COMPUT PRODUCE COMPUTER INFORMATION to display information from a computer on a monitor, or direct it to a printer or other device

output tax *n* in Australia, the amount of goods and services tax due to the Australian Taxation Office after the deduction of input tax credit

outrace /owt ráyss/ (-races, -racing, -raced) *vt* to do something better or faster than others

outrage /ówt rayj/ *n* 1. VIOLENT ACT an extremely violent or cruel act 2. OFFENSIVE ACT a very offensive or insulting act 3. FURY intense anger and indignation aroused by a violent or offensive act ■ *vt* (-rages, -raging, -raged) 1. AROUSE ANGER IN SOMEBODY to make somebody feel intense anger or indignation 2. VIOLATE to commit a flagrant violation or infringement of something 3. CRIME same as **rape**[1] *v* (sense 1) (*archaic*) [13C. Via French, 'excess, atrocity' < Old French *outrer* 'exceed' < Latin *ultra* 'beyond']

outrageous /owt ráyjəss/ *adj* 1. EXCESSIVE causing shock or indignation by exceeding the bounds of what is reasonable or expected ○ *outrageous prices* 2. MORALLY SHOCKING violating accepted standards of decency or morality in a flagrant or shocking way ○ *It's absolutely outrageous for a judge to take bribes.* 3. EXTRAORDINARY AND UNCONVENTIONAL extravagantly bold or unconventional, and likely to shock people ○ *She came in wearing the most outrageous hat.* 4. VIOLENT OR CRUEL violent or unrestrained in mood or action —**outrageously** *adv* —**outrageousness** *n*

~~**outragious, outragous**~~ incorrect spelling of **outrageous**

outrange /owt ráynj/ (-ranges, -ranging, -ranged) *vt* to have a greater range than something else of the same type

outrank /owt rángk/ (-ranks, -ranking, -ranked) *vt* to have a higher rank or status than somebody else

outré /oo tray/ *adj* peculiarly or shockingly unusual [Early 18C. Via French < Old French, past participle of *outrer* (see OUTRAGE)]

outreach *vt* /owt reéch/ (-reaches, -reaching, -reached) 1. REACH FARTHER THAN SOMEBODY to reach or extend farther than somebody or something else 2. EXCEED SOMETHING to exceed or go beyond a limit ■ *n* /ówt reech/ 1. PROVISION OF COMMUNITY SERVICES the provision of information or services to groups in society who might otherwise be neglected ○ *an outreach programme for people who cannot read* 2. EXTENT OF REACH the length or extent of the reach of somebody or something ○ *the outreach of a communications network*

out relief *n* formerly, money given by the state to people who needed financial support but were not living in a workhouse

outride /owt rīd/ (-rides, -riding, -rode /-rōd/, -ridden /-rídd'n/) *vt* 1. to ride better, farther, or faster than somebody else 2. to survive the violence of the wind and waves during a storm

outrider /ówt rīdər/ *n* 1. a rider in front of or at the side of a carriage, motor vehicle, or race horse, who acts as an escort 2. somebody who precedes a group and acts as a scout

outrigger /ówt rigər/ *n* 1. PART OF BOAT a beam or framework sticking out from the side of a boat, used to extend a rope or sail or as a brace for an oarlock 2. FRAMEWORK ON CANOE a long float attached to a framework that projects from the side of a seagoing canoe to prevent it from capsizing 3. KIND OF BOAT OR CANOE a boat or canoe fitted with an outrigger 4. STRUCTURE ON AIRCRAFT a projection attached to an aircraft or other vehicle or machine to stabilize it or to support something [Mid-18C. Origin ?]

outright *adv* /owt rīt/ 1. CANDIDLY openly and without reservation ○ *I told him outright that he was making a big mistake.* 2. WHOLLY completely, altogether, or as a whole in one transaction ○ *banned outright* ○ *bought the business outright* 3. INSTANTLY immediately and finally ○ *They refused our offer outright.* ■ *adj* /ówt rīt/ 1. TOTAL complete and utter ○ *an outright lie* 2. CANDID open and without reservation ○ *greeted us with outright enthusiasm* 3. WITHOUT QUALIFICATIONS without restrictions or limitations ○ *an outright gift*

outrival /owt rīv'l/ (-vals, -valling, -valled) *vt* to surpass somebody or something

outrun /owt rún/ (-runs, -running, -ran /-rán/, -run) *vt* 1. RUN FASTER THAN SOMEBODY to run faster or farther than somebody else 2. ESCAPE SOMEBODY to escape a pursuer by running or going faster than he, she, or it can ○ *outrun the bill collectors* ○ *The hare outran the wolf.* 3. EXCEED SOMETHING to develop faster than or exceed something ○ *Demand for petrol began to outrun supply.*

outsell /owt sél/ (-sells, -selling, -sold /-sṓld/) *vt* 1. to be sold faster or in greater quantities than something else 2. to sell more than another salesperson

outset /ówt set/ *n* the beginning or initial stage of an activity

outshine /owt shīn/ (-shines, -shining, -shone /-shón/) *vt* 1. to surpass somebody or something else, especially in terms of excellence or quality 2. to shine brighter than something else

outshoot /owt shoot/ (-shoots, -shooting, -shot /-shót/) *vt* to shoot a weapon better than somebody else

outside /ówt sīd/ CORE MEANING: a grammatical word indicating the outer surface or appearance of something ○ (noun) *Grill the chicken wings until the outsides are crisp.* ○ (adv) *The house still needs to be painted outside.*

1. *adv, prep, adj* BEYOND THE BOUNDARY OF SOMETHING located on or beyond the outer surface or edge of something ○ *standing outside the circle* 2. *adv, prep, adj* OUT OF DOORS in the open air rather than inside a building ○ (adv) *We should head outside soon if we're going to start the barbecue.* ○ (prep) *I'll meet you outside the post office.* ○ (adj) *an outside toilet* 3. *adv, prep, adj* BEYOND IMMEDIATE ENVIRONMENT happening, existing, or originating in places, people, or groups other than your own or those you are used to ○ (adj) *It was claimed that most of the substandard work had*

been done by outside contractors. ○ (adv) *in the world outside* ○ (prep) *married outside her religion* **4.** *adj* SLIGHT slight or remote ○ *There's an outside chance we may still be able to get tickets.* **5.** *adj* MAXIMUM the most extreme possible or probable ○ *an outside estimate of three months to complete the job* **6.** *adj* FARTHEST FROM SIDE OF ROAD farthest from the side of a road or the centre of a race track ○ *coming up fast in the outside lane* **7.** *prep* BEYOND SCOPE OF not included in the range or scope of something ○ *Such behaviour is completely outside my comprehension.* **8.** *n* EXPOSED SURFACE the outer surface or appearance of something ○ *The outside of the house needs painting.* **9.** *n* EXISTENCE NOT IN INSTITUTION existence in the community and not in an institution such as prison or a psychiatric hospital ○ *We wondered what life was like on the outside.* **10.** *n* AREA FARTHEST FROM SIDE OF ROAD the part farthest from the side of a road or the centre of a race track ○ *coming up fast on the outside* **11.** *n* HEAVILY POPULATED AREA OF CANADA the most populous areas of Canada along the coasts **12.** *adj* SPORTS FARTHER FROM CENTRE in football, hockey, and other sports, used to describe a position farther from the centre of the field than another of the same name ○ *outside left* ◇ **at the outside** at the maximum ○ *It shouldn't last longer than three hours at the outside.* ◇ **outside of** other than the person or thing mentioned

outside broadcast *n* a radio or television programme not recorded or filmed in a studio. US term **remote**

outsider /owt sídər/ *n* **1.** somebody who is not part of a group or organization **2.** a competitor or candidate who is considered unlikely to win

CULTURAL NOTE *The Outsider* A novel (1942) by French writer Albert Camus. This classic existentialist work, also known as *The Stranger*, is set in Algiers and recounts how a young man's extreme sense of alienation leads him to commit murder. During his trial, however, the absurdities of the judicial process compel him to acknowledge the value of human life.

outsight /ówt sīt/ *n* the ability to take note of or judge external things [Early 17C. After INSIGHT]

outsize /ówt síz, ówt sīz/ *n* a size that is larger than usual ■ *adj also* **outsized** much larger, heavier, or more extensive than is usual or expected ○ *an outsize ego*

outskirts /ówt skurts/ *npl* the areas at the edge of a town or city, farthest from the centre

outsmart /owt smaárt/ (-smarts, -smarting, -smarted) *vt* to use cunning or cleverness to get an advantage over somebody

outsold COMM past participle, past tense of **outsell**

outsole /ówt sōl/ *n* the outer sole of a boot or shoe [Late 19C. After INSOLE]

outsource /ówt sawrss/ (-sources, -sourcing, -sourced) *vt* to buy labour or parts from a source outside a company or business, usually as a means of cutting costs or to employ expertise not available within the company —**outsourcer** *n* —**outsourcing** *n*

outspan S Africa *n* /ówt spán/ formerly, a place for people travelling to stop to rest their animals ■ *vti* /owt spán/ (-spans, -spanning, -spanned) to remove a yoke or harness from an animal [Early 19C. Via Afrikaans *uitspan* 'unyoke, unharness' < Middle Dutch *uitspannen*]

outspend /owt spénd/ (-spends, -spending, -spent /-spént/) *vt* **1.** to spend more than somebody else **2.** to exceed fixed limits for something in spending ○ *outspent our budget*

outspoken /owt spókən/ *adj* expressing opinions directly, frankly, and fearlessly —**outspokenly** *adv* — **outspokenness** *n*

outspread *adj* /ówt spred/ STRETCHED OUT extended or spread out flat ■ *vt* /owt spréd/ (-spreads, -spreading, -spread) EXTEND SOMETHING to stretch out or extend something ■ *n* ACT OF SPREADING OUT the act or an example of extending outwards

outstand /owt stánd/ (-stands, -standing, -stood /-stoód/) *vi* to stand out or be prominent

outstanding /owt stánding/ *adj* **1.** CONSPICUOUSLY EXCELLENT clearly of very high quality or clearly superior to others in the same group or category ○ *outstanding work* **2.** NOT YET RESOLVED not yet paid, resolved, or dealt with ○ *outstanding debts* **3.** JUTTING OUT jutting

outwards or upwards **4.** FIN PUBLICLY SOLD publicly issued and sold as securities —**outstandingly** *adv*

outstare /owt staír/ (-stares, -staring, -stared) *vt* to make somebody look away or submit by staring hard

outstation /ówt staysh'n/ *n* a post or station in a remote unsettled spot ■ *adv* Malaysia in, at, or to a place that is not where you usually live or work, often one that is in a more rural area

outstay /owt stáy/ (-stays, -staying, -stayed) *vt* **1.** to stay longer than other people or beyond a limit ○ *outstayed their welcome* **2.** to show greater endurance than somebody ○ *outstayed their rivals*

outstep /owt stép/ (-steps, -stepping, -stepped) *vt* same as **overstep** (*literary*)

outstood past participle, past tense of **outstand**

outstretch /owt strech/ (-stretches, -stretching, -stretched) *vt* to hold out or extend something

outstrip /owt stríp/ (-strips, -stripping, -stripped) *vt* **1.** to achieve more or go faster than somebody, especially a competitor **2.** to be greater than something ○ *Demand for their products has already outstripped supply.*

outswing /ówt swing/ *n* the movement of a bowled cricket ball from the leg side to the off side

outta /ówttə/, **outa** *prep* out of (*informal*) ○ *I'm outta here.* [Mid-20C. Representing a pronunciation]

outtake /ówt tayk/ *n* **1.** a recorded scene or sequence that is not included in the final version of a film or television programme, usually because it contains mistakes ○ *The outtakes were funnier than the movie itself.* **2.** a recording not used in the final version of an album

out-there *adj* US outgoing and positively involved with life and the world (*slang*)

outthrust /ówt thrúst/ *adj* outstretched, or extending out beyond something ○ *the dog's outthrust paw* ■ *n* something that projects or extends outward

out-tray *n* a tray or container in an office for mail ready to be sent and completed items to be filed. US term **out-box**

outturn /ówt turn/ *n* the amount produced during a particular period [Late 18C. < turn out]

outward /ówtwərd/ CORE MEANING: a grammatical word indicating that something is outside or on or towards the exterior of something, or relates to the exterior of something ○ *A coconut shell is rough and hairy on the outward side.*
1. *adj* VISIBLE clearly observable ○ *She gave no outward indication that she was upset.* **2.** *adj* RELATING TO PHYSICAL BODY relating to the physical body rather than the mind or spirit ○ *His outward appearance reflected his inner turmoil.* **3.** *adj* APPARENT apparent or superficial ○ *can't judge by outward appearances* **4.** *adj* OUTBOUND heading away from a place **5.** *adv* same as **outwards 6.** *n* MATERIAL WORLD the reality of the external world (*literary*) —**outwardness** *n*

outward-bound *adj* making an outgoing journey or passage

outwardly /ówtwərdli/ *adv* in appearance rather than in reality

outwards /ówtwərdz/ *adv* towards the outside and away from the inside or middle

outwash /ówt wosh/ *n* sand and gravel deposited by streams that are flowing away from a glacier

outweigh /owt wáy/ (-weighs, -weighing, -weighed) *vt* **1.** to be more important or valuable than something else **2.** to weigh more than somebody or something else

outwit /owt wít/ (-wits, -witting, -witted) *vt* to use cunning or trickery to get an advantage over somebody

outwith /ówt with/ *prep* Scotland outside or beyond ○ *working outwith normal hours*

outwore past tense of **outwear**

outwork *vt* /owt wúrk/ (-works, -working, -worked) WORK HARDER THAN SOMEBODY to work harder or faster than somebody ■ *n* /ówt wurk/ **1.** MILITARY OUTPOST a trench or fortification built beyond the main line of defence **2.** WORK DONE AT HOME work done for a company outside the company's premises

outworker /ówt wurkər/ *n* a company employee who works from home rather than on the company's premises

outworn /ówt wáwrn/ past participle of **outwear** ■ *adj* outdated or no longer useful

ouzel /óoz'l/ *n* a small bird of the thrush family with dark feathers and a white band across its throat. Native to: Europe. Latin name: *Turdus torquatus.* [Old English *ōsle* 'blackbird' < Indo-European]

ouzo /óozō/ *n* a colourless aniseed-flavoured Greek alcoholic spirit flavoured with aniseed [Late 19C. < modern Greek]

ova ANAT plural of **ovum**

oval /óv'l/ *adj* EGG-SHAPED shaped like an egg or a flattened circle ■ *n* **1.** FLATTENED CIRCLE a two-dimensional shape like a stretched circle with slightly longer flatter sides **2.** EGG SHAPE something shaped like an egg or a flattened circle [Late 16C. < medieval Latin *ovalis* < Latin *ovum* 'egg'] —**ovally** *adv* —**ovalness** *n*

ovalbumin /ōv álbyōōmin, óv al byōómin/ *n* the main crystalline protein or albumin found in egg whites [Mid-19C. < Latin *ovi albumen* 'white of egg' < *ovum* 'egg' + *albumen* (see ALBUMEN)]

Oval Office *n* **1.** an oval-shaped room in the White House that is the private office used by the president of the United States **2.** the power and authority of the president of the United States

oval window *n* a membranous opening between the middle ear and the inner ear that transmits sound vibrations

Ovambo /ō vámbō/ (*plural same* or **-bos**) *n* **1.** a member of a people who live in parts of southern Africa, especially in Angola and Namibia **2.** the Bantu language of the Ovambo people. Native speakers: 700,000. [Mid-19C. < Bantu, 'people of leisure'] —**Ovambo** *adj*

ovariectomy /ō váiri éktəmi/ (*plural* **-mies**) *n* the surgical removal of one or both ovaries

ovariotomy /ō váiri óttəmi/ (*plural* **-mies**) *n* **1.** a surgical incision into an ovary **2.** SURG same as **ovariectomy**

ovaritis /óvə rítiss/ *n* same as **oophoritis**

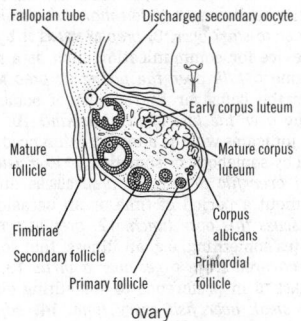

Fallopian tube   Discharged secondary oocyte

Early corpus luteum

Mature follicle   Mature corpus luteum

Fimbriae   Corpus albicans

Secondary follicle   Primordial follicle

Primary follicle

ovary

ovary /óvəri/ (*plural* **-ries**) *n* **1.** either of the two female reproductive organs that produce eggs and, in vertebrates, also produce the sex hormones oestrogen and progesterone **2.** the lower part of a pistil that bears ovules and ripens into a fruit [Mid-17C. < modern Latin *ovarium* < Latin *ovum* 'egg'] —**ovarian** /ō váiri ən/ *adj*

ovate /ó vayt/ *adj* **1.** shaped like an egg **2.** describes a leaf or petal that is broad and rounded at the base and tapers towards the tip [Mid-18C. < Latin *ovatus* 'egg-shaped' < *ovum* 'egg']

ovation /ō váysh'n/ *n* **1.** enthusiastic applause or cheering, especially from a crowd or large group of people **2.** an ancient Roman victory ceremony for a returning military hero [Mid-16C. Via Latin *ovation-* < *ovare* 'rejoice'; from an imitation of the sound of exulting] —**ovational** *adj*

oven /úv'n/ *n* a compartment warmed by a heat source and used for baking, roasting, or drying [Old English *ofen* < Indo-European, 'cooker']

ovenable /úvv'nəb'l/ *adj* heat-resistant, or in heat-resistant packaging and ready to be cooked without further preparation ○ *ovenable food packaging*

ovenbird /úvv'n burd/ *n* **1.** a warbler with a shrill call that builds a dome-shaped nest on the ground. Native to: North America. Latin name: *Seiurus aurocapillus*. **2.** a small brown bird that builds a dome-shaped nest from clay and dried leaves. Native to: South America. Genus: *Furnarius*. [Early 19C. < the shape of the birds' nests]

oven glove *n* a padded hand covering used as protection when putting hot dishes into, and taking them out of, an oven

ovenproof /úvv'n proof/ *adj* capable of being used in an oven without being damaged by the heat

oven-ready *adj* already prepared and ready to be cooked or heated before eating

ovenware /úvv'n wair/ *n* heat-resistant dishes that can be used for baking or roasting as well as for serving

over /óvər/ CORE MEANING: a grammatical word used to indicate a position directly above something, either resting on the top of something, or above the upper surface of something with a space in between ○ (prep) *a framed portrait over the fireplace* ○ (prep) *He wore a red flannel shirt over a T-shirt.* ○ (prep) *Julia was bent over the sink washing glasses.* ○ (adv) *flocks of geese flying over* ○ (adv) *Heat the milk and pour it over.*

1. *prep, adv* ON OR TO OTHER SIDE OF positioned on or moving to the other side of something such as a barrier, obstacle, or area of land ○ (prep) *To see the cathedral you need to cross over the river.* ○ (adv) *He climbed over into the next field.* **2.** *prep, adv* THROUGHOUT throughout the whole extent of ○ (prep) *travelling all over Europe* ○ (prep) *In the past few years, fifties diners have sprung up all over town.* ○ (adv) *People are the same the world over.* **3.** *prep, adv* MORE THAN more than a particular amount, measurement, or age ○ (prep) *go over your quota* ○ (adv) *people 30 and over* **4.** *adv* ACROSS INTERVENING SPACE positioned at, or moving to, a point on the other side of an intervening space ○ *She reached over and turned off the TV.* ○ *Jim sent a couple of guys over to help out.* **5.** *adv* SO AS TO FALL so as to change position, especially so as to become horizontal after being upright ○ *knocked over a pile of books* ○ *He rolled over and turned out the light.* **6.** *adv* REMAINING remaining or surplus after what was needed has been used ○ *There was plenty of food left over from the party.* **7.** *adv N Am* AGAIN doing something again, or again from the beginning ○ *If you make a mistake you'll just have to start over.* **8.** *prep* BY MEANS OF by means of a device for communication such as a radio or telephone ○ *talk over the phone* **9.** *prep* ABOUT indicates the cause or the subject of something ○ *grieving over the loss of her husband* **10.** *prep* AFFECTING indicates what is affected, influenced, or controlled by somebody or something ○ *exercising more control over file access* **11.** *prep* DURING during or throughout a period of time or an occasion ○ *We can discuss this over lunch.* **12.** *prep* RECOVERED FROM indicates something, e.g. an illness, that somebody has recovered from ○ *get over a virus* **13.** *prep* IN PREFERENCE TO in preference to something else ○ *I'd choose steak over fish every time.* **14.** *adj* FINISHED finished, or no longer in progress ○ *When all this is over I'm going on holiday.* **15.** *adv* VERY to a great extent or degree ○ *He's not over happy at the moment.* **16.** *interj* MEDIA INDICATING SOMEBODY'S TURN TO SPEAK used when communicating via radio to indicate that somebody has finished talking and it is the other person's turn to speak **17.** *n US* GAMBLING SCORE ABOVE PARTICULAR NUMBER IN WAGER in a wager, the score above a particular number of points, or an amount above a particular total ○ *bet the over in the play-off* **18.** *n* CRICKET BOWLING OF SIX BALLS in cricket, a series of six correctly bowled balls, or the play during this **19.** *vt* BUSINESS CARRY AGENDA ITEM FORWARD to postpone dealing with an item on an agenda until a later meeting [Old English *ofer* < Indo-European] ◇ **over again** once more ◇ **over against 1.** opposite to **2.** in contrast with, or in opposition to ◇ **over and above** in addition to or in excess of something ○ *benefits over and above the basic salary* ◇ **over and done with** completely finished or at an end ◇ **over and over** repeatedly, or a great deal

over- *prefix* **1.** excessively ○ *overconfident* ○ *overact* **2.** extremely ○ *overjoyed* **3.** going over something, extra ○ *overshoe* ○ *overtime* **4.** above, over, on top ○ *overcast* ○ *overlap* **5.** so as to turn over, completely ○ *overthrow* [< OVER]

overabundance *n*
overabundant *adj*
overabundantly *adv*
overaccentuate *vt*
overaggressive *adj*
overaggressively *adv*
overaggressiveness *n*
overambition *n*
overambitious *adj*
overambitiously *adv*
overambitiousness *n*
overanalyse *vt*
overanalysis *n*
overanalytical *adj*
overanxiety *n*
overanxious *adj*
overanxiously *adv*
overanxiousness *n*
overassertive *adj*
overassertiveness *n*
overassessment *n*
overattention *n*
overboil *vt*
overbold *adj*
overboldly *adv*
overboldness *n*
overbusy *adj*
overbuy *vti*
overcapitalization *n*
overcapitalize *vt*
overcareful *adj*
overcarefully *adv*
overcaution *n*
overcautious *adj*
overcautiously *adv*
overcautiousness *n*
overcentralization *n*
overcentralize *vt*
overcivil *adj*
overcivilized *adj*
overclean *adj*
overcommon *adj*
overcomplacency *n*
overcomplacent *adj*
overcomplex *adj*
overcomplexity *n*
overcomplicate *vt*
overcomplicated *adj*
overconcern *n*
overconcerned *adj*
overconfidence *n*
overconfident *adj*
overconfidently *adv*
overconscientious *adj*
overconscious *adj*
overconservative *adj*
overconsumption *n*
overcook *vt*
overcritical *adj*
overcritically *adv*
overcriticalness *n*
overcultivated *adj*
overcuriosity *n*
overcurious *adj*
overdecorate *vt*
overdecorative *adj*
overdelicacy *n*
overdelicate *adj*
overdemanding *adj*
overdependence *n*
overdependent *adj*
overdevelop *vt*
overdeveloped *adj*
overdevelopment *n*
overdramatic *adj*
overdramatically *adv*
overdress *vti, n*
overdressed *adj*
overdrink *vi*
overdrinking *n*
overdry *adj*
overeager *adj*
overeagerly *adv*
overeagerness *n*
overearnest *adj*
overeducate *vt*
overeducated *adj*
overeffusive *adj*
overelaborate *adj, vti*
overelaborately *adv*

overelaborateness *n*
overelaboration *n*
overembellish *vt*
overemotional *adj*
overemotionally *adv*
overenlargement *n*
overequipped *adj*
overexaggerate *vti*
overexaggeration *n*
overexcitable *adj*
overexcite *vt*
overexcited *adj*
overexcitement *n*
overexercise *vt*
overexert *vt*
overexertion *n*
overexpand *vti*
overexpansion *n*
overexpectation *n*
overexplain *vt*
overextravagant *adj*
overfar *adj, adv*
overfatigue *n*
overfed *adj*
overfeed *vti*
overfill *vt*
overfish *vti*
overfond *adj*
overfondly *adv*
overfondness *n*
overfull *adj*
overgarment *n*
overgenerous *adj*
overgraze *vt*
overhard *adj*
overharvest *vt*
overhasty *adj*
overhunt *vti*
overhydrate *vt*
overhydration *n*
overhype *vt*
overimaginative *adj*
overimaginatively *adv*
overimpress *vt*
overinflate *vt*
overinflated *adj*
overingenious *adj*
overintellectualize *vi*
overintense *adj*
overinterest *n*
overinvestment *n*
overladen *adj*
overlarge *adj*
overloud *adj*
overmany *adj*
overmature *adj*
overmatured *adj*
overmedicate *vt*
overmedication *n*
overmodest *adj*
overopinionated *adj*
overoptimism *n*
overoptimistic *adj*
overoptimistically *adv*
overorganization *n*
overorganize *vt*
overorganized *adj*
overpay *vti*
overpayment *n*
overpeopled *adj*
overpessimism *n*
overpessimistic *adj*
overpowerful *adj*
overpraise *vt*
overprescribe *vti*
overprescription *n*
overpressurization *n*
overpressurize *vt*
overprice *vt*
overprivileged *adj*
overprize *vt*
overproduce *vti*
overproduction *n*
overprotect *vt*
overprotection *n*
overprotective *adj*
overprotectively *adv*
overprotectiveness *n*
overpublicize *vt*
overrefine *vti*

overrefined *adj*
overrefinement *n*
overregulate *vt*
overregulation *n*
overreliance *n*
overreliant *adj*
overrepresentation *n*
overrepresented *adj*
overrich *adj*
overroast *vt*
overscrupulous *adj*
overscrupulously *adv*
overscrupulousness *n*
oversecretion *n*
oversensitive *adj*
oversensitively *adv*
oversensitiveness *n*
oversensitivity *n*
oversentimental *adj*
oversentimentality *n*
oversmart *adj*
oversophisticated *adj*
oversophistication *n*
overspecialization *n*
overspecialize *vi*
overspecialized *adj*

overstimulate *vt*
overstimulation *n*
overstrain *vti*
overstress *vt, n*
overstrict *adj*
overstuff *vt*
oversubtle *adj*
oversupplied *adj*
oversupply *n, vti*
oversusceptible *adj*
oversweet *adj*
overthin *adj*
overtire *vt*
overtired *adj*
overtiredness *n*
overtop *vt*
overtrain *vti*
overuse *n, vt*
overvaluation *n*
overvalue *vt*
overwater *vt*
overweary *adj, vt*
overwind *vt*
overzealous *adj*
overzealously *adv*
overzealousness *n*

overachieve /óvər ə cheév/ (-chieves, -chieving, -chieved) *vi* **1.** to perform better or be more successful than expected **2.** to be excessively or unhealthily dedicated to achieving success —**overachievement** *n* —**overachiever** *n*

overact /óvər ákt/ (-acts, -acting, -acted) *vti* to exaggerate movements or emotions, especially when acting in a performance

overactive /óvər áktiv/ *adj* excessively or unusually active —**overactivity** /óvər ak tívvəti/ *n*

overage[1] /óvər áyj/ *adj* **1.** older than the age fixed as a standard or considered appropriate for an activity **2.** of too great an age to be useful (*offensive if used of people*) [Late 19C. < OVER prep. + AGE]

overage[2] /óvərij/ *n* money, goods, or something else in excess of what is proper or shown in the records [Mid-20C. < OVER adj + -AGE]

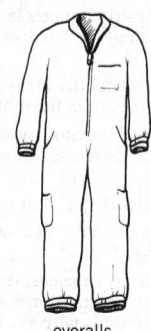

overalls

overall *adj* /óvər awl/, *adv* /óvər áwl/ **1.** END TO END from one extremity to the other **2.** TOTAL including everything ■ *adj* /óvər awl/ GENERALLY considered as a whole ○ *an overall impression* ■ *adv* /óvər áwl/ **1.** GENERALLY in general ○ *Overall, we were disappointed with the results.* **2.** CONSIDERING EVERYTHING taking everything into account ○ *The frozen foods side of the business overall saw a loss.* ■ *n* /óvər awl/ CLOTHING PROTECTIVE GARMENT a loose-fitting lightweight piece of clothing like a coat, worn over ordinary clothes to protect them ■ **overalls** *npl* **1.** ONE-PIECE PROTECTIVE GARMENT a one-piece garment with long sleeves and trousers worn to protect a worker's clothes from dirt or wear **2.** WORK TROUSERS WITH BIB loose-fitting trousers that have a bib and shoulder straps, originally worn over ordinary clothing as a protection from dirt and wear

overall majority *n* a majority of votes in an election when measured against the total combined votes of all other competing political parties

overarch /óvər áarch/ (-arches, -arching, -arched) *vt* to form an arch over something

overarching /óvər áarching/ *adj* embracing or overshadowing everything

overarm /óvər aarm/ *adj* **1.** WITH ARM ABOVE SHOULDER thrown or done with the arm raised above the

shoulder and rotating forward **2.** WITH ARM RAISED beginning a stroke in swimming with the arm raised above the shoulder and rotating forward ■ *adv* WITH HAND ABOVE SHOULDER with the hand coming forward in a semicircular motion from behind and above the shoulder. N Am term **overhand**

overate past tense of **overeat**

overawe /ṓvər áw/ (**-awes, -awing, -awed**) *vt* to make somebody feel subdued or inhibited by inspiring respect and some fear

overbalance /ṓvər bállənss/ *v* (**-ances, -ancing, -anced**) **1.** *vti* LOSE BALANCE to lose balance, or make somebody or something lose balance **2.** *vt* EXCEED SOMETHING IN IMPORTANCE to have greater weight or importance than something else ■ *n* PREPONDERANCE an excess of an amount, quantity, or weight

overbear /ṓvər báir/ (**-bears, -bearing, -bore** /-báwr/, **-borne** /-báwrn/) *v* **1.** *vt* OVERPOWER SOMEBODY to defeat somebody by having superior weight or strength **2.** *vt* SURPASS SOMETHING IN IMPORTANCE to be more important than other considerations **3.** *vi* PRODUCE TOO MUCH to produce too much fruit or too many offspring

overbearing /ṓvər báiring/ *adj* arrogant and tending to order people around —**overbearingly** *adv* —**overbearingness** *n*

overbid *v* /ṓvər bíd/ (**-bids, -bidding, -bid, -bidden** or **-bid**) **1.** *vti* BID MORE THAN WORTH OF SOMETHING to bid more than something is worth **2.** *vi* CARDS BID FOR TOO MANY TRICKS in bridge, to bid for more tricks than can be won ■ *n* /ṓvərbid/ HIGHER BID a bid that is higher than somebody else's bid —**overbidder** /ṓvər bíddər/ *n*

overbite /ṓvər bīt/ *n* a faulty alignment of the teeth in which the upper front teeth project too far over the lower teeth when the mouth is closed

overblanket /ṓvər blangkit/ *n UK* an electric blanket designed to be placed over somebody in bed rather than on the mattress. ANZ, N Am term **electric blanket**

overblouse /ṓvər blowz/ *n* a blouse designed to be worn outside the waistband of a skirt or trousers

overblow /ṓvər blṓ/ (**-blows, -blowing, -blew** /-blo͞o/, **-blown** /-blṓn/) *vti* to blow a wind instrument with extra force so as to produce an overtone

overblown /ṓvər blṓn/ *adj* **1.** EXAGGERATED done to excess and seeming exaggerated ○ *overblown stories that are barely credible* **2.** PRETENTIOUS showing pomposity or pretentiousness ○ *His style of writing is overblown and excessively wordy.* **3.** PAST BEST past full bloom and beginning to die ○ *an overblown rose*

overboard /ṓvər bawrd, ṓvər báwrd/ *adv* over the side of a ship or boat and into the water [Old English *ofer bord* 'over the side']

overbook /ṓvər bo͝ok/ (**-books, -booking, -booked**) *vti* to take more reservations than there are seats or places available

overbore past tense of **overbear**

overborne past participle of **overbear**

overbought /ṓvər báwt/ *adj* characterized by high prices on the stock exchange as the result of recent heavy trading, and so not likely to rise further in the near future

overbuild /ṓvər bíld/ (**-builds, -building, -built** /-bílt/) *v* **1.** *vti* BUILD TOO MUCH to construct more buildings than are necessary or desirable in an area **2.** *vti* BUILD OVERAMBITIOUSLY to construct something that is too large or elaborate **3.** *vt* BUILD ON SOMETHING ELSE to build something on top of a particular place or thing

overburden *vt* /ṓvər búrd'n/ (**-dens, -dening, -dened**) OVERLOAD to place too much weight or worry on somebody or something ○ *overburdened with debt* ■ *n* /ṓvər burd'n/ **1.** EXCESSIVE BURDEN an excessive or onerous burden **2.** SOIL LAYERED OVER ROCK soil or other material layered over bedrock or over a geological deposit

overcall /ṓvər káwl/ (**-calls, -calling, -called**) *vti* in bridge, to bid higher than an opponent before a partner has made a positive bid —**overcall** *n*

overcame past tense of **overcome**

overcapacity /ṓvər kə pássəti/ *n* an ability to produce goods or provide services that exceeds demand

overcast *adj* /ṓvər kaast/ **1.** CLOUDY very cloudy, with no sun showing **2.** SEWN WITH LONG STITCHES sewn along the edge with long loose stitches that prevent a piece of fabric from unravelling ■ *n* /ṓvər kaast/ **1.** HEAVY CLOUD COVER a heavy covering of clouds in the sky **2.** MIN EXTRACT MINE ARCH an arch in a mine supporting a passage above it ■ *v* /ṓvər káast/ (**-casts, -casting, -casted**) **1.** *vi* BECOME CLOUDY to become cloudy or dull **2.** *vt* SECURE EDGE WITH LOOSE STITCHES to sew the edge of a piece of fabric with an overcast stitch

overcasting /ṓvər kaasting/ *n* long slanting stitches sewn loosely across the edge of a piece of fabric to prevent it from unravelling

overcast stitch *n* a stitch used to bind a raw edge or to form a smooth raised line, e.g. in monogramming

overcharge *v* /ṓvər cháarj/ (**-charges, -charging, -charged**) **1.** *vti* CHARGE SOMEBODY TOO MUCH to charge somebody too much money for something **2.** *vt* PUT EXCESSIVE POWER INTO BATTERY to charge a battery or circuit with more electricity than it can safely hold **3.** *vt* OVERFILL OR OVERLOAD SOMETHING to fill or load something with more than it can hold or bear **4.** *vt* EXAGGERATE SOMETHING to make something seem greater or more important than it actually is (*literary*) ■ *n* /ṓvər chaarj/ **1.** EXCESSIVE CHARGE an excessively high charge for something **2.** ACT OF CHARGING TOO MUCH an act of charging too much for something

overclass /ṓvər klaass/ *n* a nation's elite governing or ruling class

overcloud /ṓvər klówd/ (**-clouds, -clouding, -clouded**) *vti* **1.** to cover something with clouds, or become covered with clouds **2.** to become dim and gloomy, or make something become dim and gloomy (*formal*)

overcoat /ṓvər kōt/ *n* **1.** a heavy coat worn over other outer clothes **2.** *also* **overcoating** an additional protective layer of something such as paint or varnish on top of a treated surface

overcome /ṓvər kúm/ (**-comes, -coming, -came** /-káym/, **-come**) *v* **1.** *vt* SURMOUNT DIFFICULTY to struggle successfully against a difficulty or disadvantage **2.** *vt* MAKE SOMEBODY HELPLESS to make somebody incapacitated or helpless, or break down somebody's normal self-control (*usually passive*) **3.** *vt* DEFEAT SOMEBODY to defeat somebody or something, especially in a conflict or competition **4.** *vi* WIN DESPITE OBSTACLES to win or be successful, especially in spite of obstacles

SYNONYMS See ***defeat***.

overcommit /ṓvər kə mít/ (**-mits, -mitting, -mitted**) *vti* to undertake more than can be accomplished, or make somebody or yourself do this (*often passive*) —**overcommitment** *n*

overcompensate /ṓvər kómpən sayt/ (**-sates, -sating, -sated**) *vti* **1.** to try too hard to make up for a disadvantage or shortcoming and fall into a fault of another kind **2.** to pay somebody too much in recompense or compensation for something done —**overcompensation** /-kómpən sáysh'n/ *n* —**overcompensatory** /-kómpən sáytəri/ *adj*

overcorrect /ṓvər kə rékt/ *vti* (**-rects, -recting, -rected**) to do too much when trying to correct a mistake or fault, usually so that a further mistake is made ■ *adj* excessively exact or proper

overcorrection /ṓvər kə réksh'n/ *n* **1.** LING same as **hypercorrection** **2.** the fact of overcorrecting a mistake or fault

overcrop /ṓvər króp/ (**-crops, -cropping, -cropped**) *vt* to make soil infertile by removing its nutrients through continuous cultivation

overcrowd /ṓvər krówd/ (**-crowds, -crowding, -crowded**) *vt* to put more people or things into an area than it is comfortably able to hold —**overcrowded** *adj* —**overcrowding** *n*

overdo /ṓvər do͞o/ (**-does** /-dúz/, **-doing, -did** /-díd/, **-done** /-dún/) *vt* **1.** DO SOMETHING TO EXCESS to do something too much, often with a harmful effect **2.** SPOIL EFFECT BY EXAGGERATION to spoil the effect of something by exaggerating it ○ *You rather overdid the sympathetic friend act on that occasion.* **3.** OVERCOOK SOMETHING to cook food for too long —**overdoer** *n* ◇ **overdo it** *or* **things 1.** to work too hard and tire yourself **2.** to do something to excess

overdose *n* /ṓvər dōss/ DANGEROUS AMOUNT OF DRUG a dangerously large dose of a drug, especially a narcotic, causing hospitalization or death ■ *v* /ṓvər dṓss/ (**-doses, -dosing, -dosed**) **1.** *vi* TAKE OVERDOSE to take an overdose of a drug **2.** *vt* GIVE SOMEBODY OVERDOSE to give somebody an overdose of a drug **3.** *vi* TAKE TOO MUCH to consume or experience an excessive amount of something (*informal*) ○ *had overdosed on soap operas*

overdraft /ṓvər draaft/ *n* **1.** the amount that an account holder owes a bank because he or she has withdrawn or debited from the account more than has been credited to it **2.** a limit up to which an account holder may borrow from a bank when there are no funds in his or her current account **3.** US spelling of **overdraught**

overdramatize /ṓvər drámmə tīz/ (**-tizes, -tizing, -tized**), **overdramatise** (**-tises, -tising, -tised**) *vti* to behave, or treat something, in an excessively dramatic way, e.g. by exaggerating feelings or the gravity of a situation

overdraught /ṓvər draaft/ *n* a current of air passed over a fire, e.g. in a furnace or kiln

overdraw /ṓvər dráw/ (**-draws, -drawing, -drew** /-dro͞o/, **-drawn** /-dráwn/) *v* **1.** *vti* WITHDRAW TOO MUCH FROM BANK ACCOUNT to withdraw or have debited more money from a bank account than it has credited to it, so that money is owed to the bank **2.** *vt* EXAGGERATE SOMETHING to exaggerate in describing or telling about something **3.** *vti* PULL BOW TOO TIGHT in archery, to pull a bow too tight

overdrawn /ṓvər dráwn/ *adj* **1.** owing money to a bank because an account has had more money withdrawn or debited from it than credited to it **2.** showing exaggeration in the description of something

overdrew *v* past tense of **overdraw**

overdrive *n* /ṓvər drīv/ **1.** HIGHEST ENGINE GEAR the highest gear in the engine of a motor vehicle that is used at high speeds for fuel economy and to save engine wear **2.** EXTRA HARD LEVEL OF ACTIVITY a particularly intense and productive mode of activity, usually possible only for short periods (*informal*) ○ *Production has gone into overdrive.* ■ *vt* /ṓvər drīv/ (**-drives, -driving, -drove** /-drṓv/, **-driven** /-drívv'n/) **1.** DRIVE SOMEBODY TOO HARD to drive somebody, something, or yourself too hard **2.** INCREASE ELECTRIC CURRENT TO to boost the supply of electrical current to a piece of electrical or electronic equipment beyond the recommended safe operating levels

overdub /ṓvər dub/ *vti* (**-dubs, -dubbing, -dubbed**) to add supplementary sound or music to a recording ■ *n* a supplementary layer of sound or music added onto a recording

overdue /ṓvər dyo͞o/ *adj* late or after the scheduled time, especially in arriving, occurring, or being paid ○ *The library said the books were overdue.*

overdye /ṓvər dī/ (**-dyes, -dying, -dyed**) *vt* **1.** to use too much dye on something **2.** to dye a fabric with another colour over the original one

overeat /ṓvər éet/ (**-eats, -eating, -ate** /-áyt, -ét/, **-eaten** /-éet'n/) *vi* to eat too much food, especially habitually —**overeater** *n* —**overeating** *n*

overemphasize /ṓvər émfə sīz/ (**-sizes, -sizing, -sized**), **overemphasise** (**-sises, -sising, -sised**) *vt* to give something too much importance, attention, or force —**overemphasis** *n*

overenthusiasm /ṓvər in thyo͞ozi azəm/ *n* more enthusiasm than is thought usual or appropriate —**overenthusiastic** *adj*

overenthusiastic /ṓvər in thyo͞ozi ástik/ *adj* more enthusiastic than is thought usual or appropriate

overestimate *vt* /ṓvər ésti mayt/ (**-mates, -mating, -mated**) **1.** GIVE EXCESSIVE MERIT OR IMPORTANCE TO to judge somebody or something to be better, greater, or more important than he, she, or it actually is **2.** CALCULATE SOMETHING TOO HIGHLY to calculate the amount, value, or quantity of something at too high a level ■ *n* /ṓvər éstimət, -mayt/ EXCESSIVELY HIGH ESTIMATE an estimate that is too high —**overestimation** /-esti máysh'n/ *n*

overexpose /ṓvər ik spṓz/ (**-poses, -posing, -posed**) *vt* **1.** to allow somebody, or expose somebody to, too much of something, especially to allow somebody to appear in public or in the media too often **2.** to expose a photographic medium such as film to too much light or for too long a time, so that the colours or tones in the resulting photograph are too light —**overexposure** /-ik spṓzhər/ *n*

overextend /ōvər ik sténd/ (**-tends, -tending, -tended**) *v* **1. overextend yourself** *vr* RISK FINANCIAL RUIN to risk financial ruin by borrowing excessively, spending too much, or overcommitting resources **2.** *vt* MAKE TOO GREAT DEMANDS ON SOMEBODY to force somebody, something, or yourself beyond a safe or reasonable limit **3.** *vt* PROLONG SOMETHING BEYOND EXPECTED DURATION to prolong something beyond its normal or expected duration

overfamiliar /ōvər fə mílli ər/ *adj* **1.** more friendly, informal, or intimate than is appropriate **2.** used so much or so well known as to be boring or ineffective —**overfamiliarity** /-fə milli árrəti/ *n*

overflew past tense of **overfly**

overflight /ōvər flīt/ *n* the flight of an aircraft over an area

overflow *v* /ōvər flṓ/ (**-flows, -flowing, -flowed**) **1.** *vti* FLOW OR POUR OVER to pour out over the limits or edge of a container because the container is filled beyond its capacity **2.** *vt* FLOOD SOMETHING to flood, cover, or flow over the surface of something **3.** *vt* SPREAD BEYOND LIMITS OF SOMETHING to spread beyond the area intended to contain it ○ *The crowd overflowed the hall into the street outside.* **4.** *vi* BE OVERWHELMED BY EMOTION to be so full of an emotion as to feel the need to express it ○ *overflowing with happiness* ■ *n* /ōvər flō/ **1.** EXCESS CONTENTS excess contents that flow over the edge of a container **2.** EXCESS PEOPLE OR THINGS people or things that cannot be contained in the space originally set aside for them **3.** OUTLET THAT PREVENTS FLOODING an outlet that allows something, usually a liquid, to escape before it runs over the top of its container **4.** AMOUNT IN EXCESS OF LIMIT the amount by which a limit is exceeded **5.** COMPUTER'S INABILITY TO HANDLE LARGE DATA the inability of a location in computer memory to handle data of an excessively large magnitude, or an instance of this ○ *an overflow error*

overfly /ōvər flī/ (**-flies, -flying, -flew** /-flōō/, **-flown** /-flṓn/) *vti* **1.** to fly over an area **2.** to fly past a fixed point ○ *The plane has overflown the runway.*

overfold /ōvər fōld/ *n* a geological fold that has turned over on itself so that both sides dip in the same direction, causing the middle strata to be upside down

overfunding /ōvər fúnding/ *n* the policy of selling more securities than are needed to finance government spending

overgeneralize /ōvər jénnərə līz/ (**-izes, -izing, -ized**), **overgeneralise** (**-izes, -ising, -ised**) *vti* to draw too general a conclusion about something on the basis of limited or incomplete evidence —**overgeneralization** /-jennərə lī záysh'n/ *n*

overglaze *n* /ōvər glayz/ **1.** EXTRA GLAZE ON POTTERY an additional coat of glaze applied to pottery or porcelain **2.** TOP LAYER OF DECORATION ON POTTERY a decoration applied to pottery or porcelain on top of the glaze ■ *vt* /ōvər gláyz/ (**-glazes, -glazing, -glazed**) APPLY GLAZE OR OVERGLAZE TO POTTERY to apply a glaze or overglaze to pottery or porcelain ■ *adj* /ōvər glayz/ APPLIED ON TOP OF GLAZE applied on top of a ceramic glaze ○ *overglaze colours*

overground /ōvər grównd/ *adj, adv* on or above ground level

overgrow /ōvər grṓ/ (**-grows, -growing, -grew** /-grōō/, **-grown** /-grṓn/) *vti* to grow so large, dense, or extensive as to cover the area of ground or container it is planted in and hinder the growth of other plants —**overgrowth** /ōvər grōth/ *n*

overgrown /ōvər grṓn/ *adj* **1.** COVERED WITH VEGETATION GROWING WITHOUT CHECK covered with plants or weeds that have been allowed to grow without check **2.** GROWN TOO MUCH FOR ALLOTTED SPACE grown too dense, large, or extensive for the area of ground or container in which it is planted **3.** IMMATURE grown to a large or adult size, but remaining immature ○ *behaving like an overgrown schoolboy*

overhand /ōvər hand/ *adj* **1.** SPORTS made with the hand coming forward in a semicircular motion from behind and above the shoulder **2.** sewn with small vertical stitches passing over the two edges that are being joined together to make a seam ■ *adv* *N Am* SPORTS same as **overarm**

overhand knot *n* a knot formed by passing one end of a cord or rope through a loop formed on another part of it, often used to prevent an end from fraying

overhang *v* /ōvər háng/ (**-hangs, -hanging, -hung** /-húng/) **1.** *vti* PROJECT OVER to project or extend over something leaving a sheltered space beneath **2.** *vt* LOOM OVER SOMEBODY to threaten or loom over somebody or something ■ *n* /ōvər hang/ **1.** PROJECTION something, e.g. part of a rock face or the edge of a roof, that projects out over the space beneath **2.** EXTENT OF PROJECTION the degree or amount by which something projects or extends over something **3.** AVIAT HALF DIFFERENCE IN WINGSPAN half the difference in the span of the two wings of a biplane **4.** AVIAT DISTANCE TO WING END ON MONOPLANE the distance from the last outer strut to the end of a monoplane's wing

overhaul *vt* /ōvər háwl/ (**-hauls, -hauling, -hauled**) **1.** CHECK SOMETHING FOR MECHANICAL FAULTS to examine a piece of machinery thoroughly to identify faults **2.** REPAIR MACHINE EXTENSIVELY to carry out comprehensive repairs and adjustments to a piece of machinery **3.** REVISE SOMETHING THOROUGHLY to examine and revise something thoroughly **4.** GRADUALLY OVERTAKE SOMEBODY to catch up with and overtake somebody or something **5.** NAUT SLACKEN OR RELEASE SOMETHING to slacken or release something such as a rope or the blocks of a tackle ■ *n* /ōvər hawl/ COMPREHENSIVE REPAIR a comprehensive examination and repair of something

overhead *adv* /ōvər héd/ DIRECTLY ABOVE directly above somebody or something, especially in the air ■ *adj* /ōvər héd/ **1.** POSITIONED DIRECTLY ABOVE positioned directly above somebody or something **2.** HIT WITH RACKET ABOVE HEAD describes a stroke in racket games played hard and downwards, with the racket held high above the head **3.** RELATING TO ONGOING COSTS relating to the general recurring costs of running a business such as rent, maintenance, and utilities ■ *n* /ōvər hed/ **1.** SHOT IN RACKET GAMES a shot in racket games played hard and downwards, with the racket held above head height **2.** *also* **overhead projection** *or* **overhead transparency** COMM TRANSPARENCY FOR OVERHEAD PROJECTOR a transparent sheet placed on an overhead projector so that its enlarged image can be projected on a screen or other surface **3.** SOMETHING LOCATED ABOVE something that is mounted or located in an overhead position, e.g. a light ■ **overheads** *npl* ONGOING BUSINESS COSTS the general recurring costs of running a business, excluding the costs of labour and materials, e.g. rent, maintenance, and utilities

overhead camshaft, overhead cam *n* a camshaft in an internal-combustion engine that is mounted above the cylinder heads and controls the operation, opening, and closing of the cylinder's valves

overhead compartment *n* a luggage compartment above the passenger seats for holding luggage in an aeroplane

overhead projection *n* **1.** COMM same as **overhead** *n* (sense 2) **2.** the use of or the image produced by the use of an overhead projector

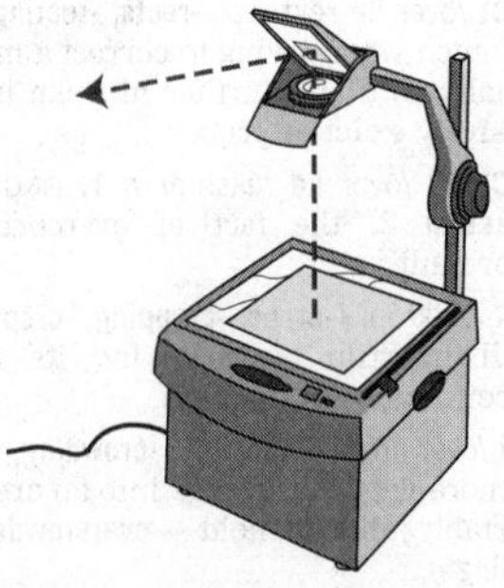

overhead projector

overhead projector *n* a projector with a flat transparent top on which a transparent sheet carrying an image is placed for projection onto a screen or other surface

overhead transparency *n* COMM same as **overhead** *n* (sense 2)

overhead-valve engine *n UK, ANZ, Can* MECH ENG same as **valve-in-head engine**

overhear /ōvər héer/ (**-hears, -hearing, -heard** /-húrd/) *vti* to hear what somebody is saying, either deliberately or accidentally, without the speaker's knowledge

overheat /ōvər héet/ (**-heats, -heating, -heated**) *vti* **1.** BECOME OR MAKE SOMETHING TOO HOT to become too hot, or make somebody or something become too hot **2.** ECON GROW TOO QUICKLY to experience too rapid growth in demand with a resultant increase in inflation, or cause too rapid growth in an economy **3.** BECOME OR MAKE SOMEBODY TOO EXCITED to become too excited, agitated, or angry, or make somebody become too excited, agitated, or angry —**overheated** *adj*

overhit /ōvər hít/ (**-hits, -hitting, -hit**) *vti* to hit a ball too hard, or put too much force into a stroke

overhung past participle, past tense of **overhang**

~~**overide**~~ incorrect spelling of **override**

overindulge /ōvər in dúlj/ (**-dulges, -dulging, -dulged**) *v* **1.** *vti* to indulge in something immoderately or too often, especially food or drink **2.** *vt* to allow somebody to do or have what he or she wants to an excessive degree —**overindulgence** *n* —**overindulgent** *adj* —**overindulgently** *adv*

overjoyed /ōvər jóyd/ *adj* extremely delighted

overkill /ōvər kil/ *n* **1.** EXCESS action that far exceeds what is needed in order to achieve a result **2.** GREATER DESTRUCTIVE CAPACITY THAN NEEDED the capacity of weaponry, especially nuclear weapons, to cause greater damage or destruction than is necessary to accomplish a mission ■ *vti* (**-kills, -killing, -killed**) DESTROY WITH EXCESS OF WEAPONS to use excessive force, especially far more nuclear weapons than necessary, to destroy an enemy or place

overlaid past tense of **overlay**[1]

overlain past participle of **overlie**

overland /ōvər land/ *adv* BY LAND by or across land ■ *adj* ACROSS LAND travelling across land ○ *take the overland route* ■ *vti* (**-lands, -landing, -landed**) *Aus* DRIVE LIVESTOCK to drive cattle or sheep long distances across land —**overlander** *n*

overlap *v* /ōvər láp/ (**-laps, -lapping, -lapped**) **1.** *vti* PLACE OR BE PLACED OVER to position things in such a way that the edge of one thing is on top of and extending past the edge of another, or be positioned in this way ○ *The roofers overlapped the slates.* **2.** *vt* EXTEND BEYOND SOMETHING to cover something such as a boundary or edge, and extend beyond it ○ *The tablecloth overlapped the table by several inches.* **3.** *vti* COINCIDE to coincide or correspond in part with something in time, function, or purpose, or make something coincide or correspond with something else ○ *Her area of responsibility to some extent overlaps mine.* ■ *n* /ōvər lap/ **1.** PARTIAL OVERLAY an edge that partly covers or is covered by something else **2.** EXTENT OF OVERLAP the amount by which something overlaps something else ○ *an overlap of six centimetres* **3.** PARTIAL COINCIDENCE a partial coincidence or correspondence of two things in time, function, or purpose **4.** GEOL YOUNGER SEDIMENTARY ROCK OVER OLDER LAYER a younger layer of sedimentary rock that extends over an older layer and conceals it completely [Early 18C. < LAP[2]]

overlay[1] *vt* /ōvər láy/ (**-lays, -laying, -laid** /-láyd/) **1.** PLACE SOMETHING AS COVERING to place a covering or covering layer of something on top of something else **2.** COVER SOMETHING to cover the surface of something with something else **3.** APPLY DECORATION TO SURFACE to apply a decorative material to a surface (*often passive*) **4.** *US* TELECOM CREATE NEW AREA CODE to create a new area code that applies within the same geographical region as an existing area code **5.** PRINTING EQUALIZE PRESSURE ON PRINTING PRESS to affix a piece of paper to the surface of an old-fashioned printing press to help make a uniform impression on a forme or plate ■ *n* /ōvər lay/ **1.** COVERING a covering or covering layer laid on top of something else **2.** EXTRA DECORATIVE LAYER a layer of decorative material applied to a surface **3.** TRANSPARENCY LAID ON TOP a transparent sheet containing additional details that is placed on top of another graphic **4.** *US* TELECOM NEW AREA CODE a new area code that applies to the same geographical region as an existing area code **5.** PRINTING PAPER TO EQUALIZE PRINTING PRESSURE in traditional methods of printing, a piece of paper used to equalize the pressure on a forme or printing plate before printing

overlay[2] past tense of **overlie**

overleaf /ṓvər léef/ *adv* on the other side of the page

overlie /ṓvər lī́/ (**-lies, -lying, -lay** /-láy/, **-lain** /-láyn/) *vt* **1.** to lie on top of somebody or something **2.** to kill a newborn baby or animal by accidentally lying on and smothering it —**overlying** *adj*

overload *vt* /ṓvər lṓd/ (**-loads, -loading, -loaded**) **1.** PUT EXCESSIVE LOAD ON SOMETHING to put too large or heavy a load on somebody or something or in something **2.** OVERBURDEN SOMEBODY to give somebody too much work, stress, or other difficulty **3.** FUSE ELECTRICAL SYSTEM to use more current than an electrical system can handle, e.g. by using too many electrical appliances simultaneously ■ *n* /ṓvər lōd/ **1.** EXCESSIVE ELECTRICAL LOAD a greater amount of electrical current than an electrical system can handle **2.** EXCESSIVE PHYSICAL WEIGHT something that is physically too heavy or too much to carry **3.** EXCESSIVE MENTAL OR EMOTIONAL BURDEN something that is mentally or emotionally too difficult to cope with **4.** *US* MENTAL OR EMOTIONAL EXHAUSTION the condition of having an excessive mental or emotional burden (*informal*) ○ *showed all the signs of overload and burnout*

overlock /ṓvər lok/ *n* a sewing technique using an invisible hem stitch made by a sewing machine or a special device

overlong /ṓvər lóng/ *adj* too long in extent or duration ■ *adv* for too long a time

overlook /ṓvər lŏŏk/ (**-looks, -looking, -looked**) *vt* **1.** MISS SOMETHING to fail to notice or check something as a result of inattention, preoccupation, or haste **2.** IGNORE SOMETHING to choose to disregard or ignore a shortcoming or fault **3.** PROVIDE VIEW OF SOMETHING to provide a view of something, especially from above **4.** LOOK DOWN AT SOMETHING to look at something from above **5.** BE ABOVE SOMETHING to be located high above something **6.** EXAMINE SOMETHING to look at something with care

---

SYNONYMS ***overlook, neglect, omit, forget***

CORE MEANING: to fail to do something

overlook to fail to notice or check something as a result of inattention, preoccupation, or haste ○ *You seem to have overlooked some important comments.* ○ *Despite the value of their work, carers' needs are often overlooked.* **neglect** to fail to do something, especially because of carelessness, forgetfulness, or indifference ○ *The survey neglected to ask how much consumers would be prepared to pay.* **omit** to fail to do something, either deliberately or accidentally ○ *The organizers somehow omitted to inform members of the time of the meeting.* **forget** to fail, or be unable, to remember something, or to do something ○ *I completely forgot to pick him up after work.*

---

overlord /ṓvər lawrd/ *n* **1.** a ruler with overall power, usually over several subservient rulers, especially somebody who ruled over other lords in a feudal system **2.** somebody of great power or influence —**overlordship** *n*

overly /ṓvərli/ *adv* to an extreme or excessive degree

overman *vt* /ṓvər mán/ (**-mans, -manning, -manned**) HR same as **overstaff** ■ *n* /ṓvər man/ (*plural* **-men** /-men/) **1.** PHILOSOPHY same as **superman** (sense 2) **2.** a man who supervises other workers (*archaic*) [In sense 1 of the noun translation of German *Übermensch*] —**overmanning** *n*

overmantel /ṓvər mant'l/ *n* an ornamental shelf above a mantelpiece

overmaster /ṓvər maástər/ (**-ters, -tering, -tered**) *vt* to conquer somebody's resistance, or break down somebody's self-control (*formal*) ○ *was overmastered by an urge to tell her precisely what I thought of her*

overmatch *vt* /ṓvər mách/ (**-matches, -matching, -matched**) *N Am* **1.** PROVIDE SOMEBODY WITH SUPERIOR OPPONENT to provide somebody with an opponent who is likely to defeat him or her easily **2.** DEFEAT SOMEBODY OR SOMETHING to be superior enough to defeat or surpass somebody or something ■ *n* /ṓvər mach/ *US* UNEQUAL CONTEST a contest in which one competitor is far superior to another

overmatter /ṓvər matər/ *n* copy that has been typeset but is in excess of the space available and is unable to appear in the final version

overmiked /ṓvər mīkt/ *adj* sounding too loud or artificial because of an imperfectly positioned or adjusted microphone

overmuch /ṓvər múch/ *adv* EXCESSIVELY to an excessive degree ■ *adj* EXCESSIVE too much ■ *n* EXCESSIVE QUANTITY an excessive quantity or amount

overnight *adv* /ṓvər nī́t/ **1.** DURING NIGHT throughout or at some point during the night **2.** VERY QUICKLY within a very short time ○ *It became a bestseller overnight.* ■ *adj* /ṓvər nīt, ṓvər nī́t/ **1.** OCCURRING AT NIGHT occurring during the night, or lasting throughout the night **2.** EXTREMELY SUDDEN happening in a very short time ○ *an overnight success* **3.** SPENDING NIGHT resident for the night **4.** USED WHEN SPENDING NIGHT used when staying overnight or for a short time somewhere ○ *overnight clothes* **5.** *N Am* INTENDED FOR NEXT-DAY DELIVERY guaranteed to get to the intended destination by the next day ○ *sent by overnight delivery* ■ *vi* /ṓvər nī́t/ (**-nights, -nighting, -nighted**) SPEND NIGHT to stay somewhere for the night

overnight bag, overnight case *n* a small piece of luggage used to carry necessities for a stay lasting one night

overnighter /ṓvər nī́tər/ *n* **1.** somebody who takes an overnight trip or stays somewhere overnight **2.** a stay lasting one night (*informal*)

overpass /ṓvər paass/ *n ANZ, N Am* a section of a road, or a bridge or passage, that crosses over another route. UK term **flyover**

overpersuade /ṓvər pər swáyd/ (**-suades, -suading, -suaded**) *vt* to persuade somebody to act contrary to his or her inclination or judgment

overpitch /ṓvər pích/ (**-pitches, -pitching, -pitched**) *vti* to bowl a ball in cricket so that it lands too close to the batsman

overplay /ṓvər pláy/ (**-plays, -playing, -played**) *v* **1.** *vt* OVERSTATE STRENGTH OF SOMETHING to exaggerate the importance or strength of something **2.** *vti* OVERACT PART to play a part or role in an exaggeratedly dramatic or theatrical way **3.** *vt* HIT BALL TOO HARD to hit or kick a ball too hard or too far

overplus /ṓvər pluss/ *n* a larger amount than is needed or appropriate [14C. Translation of French *surplus*]

overpopulate /ṓvər póppyŏŏ layt/ (**-lates, -lating, -lated**) *v* **1.** *vt* to increase the population of a place so much that the amount of space, food, water, or other resources available to support it is insufficient **2.** *vi* to increase to unsustainable or undesirable numbers by excessive reproduction —**overpopulation** /-póppyŏŏ láysh'n/ *n*

overpopulated /ṓvər póppyoo laytid/ *adj* containing too large a population to be sustainable

overpotted /ṓvər póttid/ *adj* growing in a pot too large for healthy development

overpower /ṓvər pów ər/ (**-ers, -ering, -ered**) *vt* **1.** SUBDUE SOMEBODY PHYSICALLY to use superior strength or force to defeat somebody, especially to make somebody physically helpless and unable to fight **2.** OVERWHELM SOMEBODY MENTALLY to have so strong an effect on somebody that he or she is unable to resist or control it **3.** GIVE EXCESSIVE POWER TO SOMETHING to supply something, especially a car, with more power than necessary

overpowering /ṓvər pów əring/ *adj* **1.** impossible to resist or control ○ *an overpowering urge to laugh* **2.** overwhelmingly superior in physical strength —**overpoweringly** *adv*

overpressure /ṓvər preshər/ *n* the amount by which atmospheric pressure exceeds normal levels, e.g. in a shock wave from an explosion or an accelerating aircraft

overprint *vti* /ṓvər prínt/ (**-prints, -printing, -printed**) ADD PRINTING TO SOMETHING to print something additional on an already printed surface, especially in order to add text, numbers, or another colour ■ *n* /ṓvər print/ **1.** ADDITIONAL PRINTING an additional printing on a surface, especially text, numbers, or another colour **2.** OVERPRINTED POSTAGE STAMP a postage stamp with additional information printed on its surface

overproof /ṓvər proof/ *adj* higher in alcohol content than proof spirit is

overproportion /ṓvər prə páwrsh'n/ (**-tions, -tioning, -tioned**) *vt* to make something larger than is usual or needed and out of proportion to other things

overqualified /ṓvər kwólli fīd/ *adj* with more academic or vocational qualifications or experience than is necessary or desirable for a job

overrate /ṓvər ráyt/ (**-rates, -rating, -rated**) *vt* to regard somebody as better or more capable, or something as greater, than is in fact the case —**overrated** *adj*

overreach /ṓvər réech/ (**-reaches, -reaching, -reached**) *v* **1.** *vr* FAIL THROUGH OVERAMBITION to fail through trying to do something that is too ambitious **2.** *vti* EXTEND TOO FAR to reach or extend too far or beyond something **3.** *vti* DEFEAT SOMEBODY BY TRICKERY to get the better of somebody by trickery or deception **4.** *vi* HURT ONE FOOT WITH ANOTHER to strike and injure the forefoot with the hind foot while moving forwards (*refers to horses*) **5.** *vi* SAILING SAIL ON TACK LONGER THAN NECESSARY to sail on a tack longer than is wanted or needed —**overreacher** *n*

overreact /ṓvər ri ákt/ (**-acts, -acting, -acted**) *vi* to react to something with disproportionate action or excessive emotion —**overreaction** *n* —**overreactive** *adj*

override *vt* /ṓvər rī́d/ (**-rides, -riding, -rode** /-rṓd/, **-ridden** /-rídd'n/) **1.** CANCEL SOMETHING to cancel or change an action or decision taken by somebody else **2.** OUTWEIGH SOMETHING to be more important than and take priority over something else **3.** TAKE MANUAL CONTROL OF SOMETHING to take manual control of an automatic control system **4.** RIDE HORSE OVER SOMETHING to ride a horse over or across an area **5.** RIDE HORSE TOO HARD to tire a horse by riding it too hard **6.** OVERLAP SOMETHING to extend over something, especially by overlapping it ■ *n* /ṓvər rīd/ **1.** ASSUMPTION OF MANUAL CONTROL the condition, process, or action of temporarily taking manual control of an automatic system **2.** SWITCH FOR MANUAL CONTROL a switch or some other manual control that temporarily cancels or reverses the effect of an automatic system **3.** REVERSAL OF DECISION the act or process of cancelling or changing an action or decision taken by somebody else

overrider /ṓvər rīdər/ *n* either of a pair of projections on the bumper of a motor vehicle, designed to prevent damage in a collision with the bumper of another vehicle

overriding /ṓvər rīding/ *adj* highest in priority —**overridingly** *adv*

overripe /ṓvər rīp/ *adj* too ripe and past its best flavour and texture —**overripen** *vti* —**overripeness** *n*

overrode past tense of **override**

overruff /ṓvər rúf/ (**-ruffs, -ruffing, -ruffed**) *vti* CARDS same as **overtrump**

overrule /ṓvər rool/ (**-rules, -ruling, -ruled**) *vt* **1.** RULE AGAINST SOMEBODY'S ARGUMENT to rule authoritatively that somebody's argument is unsound, especially in the case of a judge disallowing a barrister's arguments ○ *Objection overruled!* **2.** DECIDE AGAINST SOMEBODY to decide against somebody, or overturn a decision taken by somebody with lesser authority **3.** EXERCISE CONTROL OVER SOMEBODY to exercise dominion or control over somebody or something (*literary*)

overrun *v* /ṓvər rún/ (**-runs, -running, -ran** /-rán/, **-run**) **1.** *vt* SPREAD RAPIDLY AND INFEST SOMETHING to arrive in such large numbers or spread so rapidly in a place that it becomes infested or overcrowded (*often passive*) ○ *The cathedral square was overrun with tourists.* **2.** *vt* CONQUER ENEMY AND TERRITORY to attack an enemy force, defeat it conclusively, and take over the territory occupied by it ○ *The rebels overran the government forces.* **3.** *vti* EXCEED LIMIT to continue beyond a predetermined limit, especially a time limit or fixed budget **4.** *vt* OVERSHOOT SOMETHING to go on beyond an intended stopping point such as a boundary line or the end of an airport runway **5.** *vti* OVERFLOW to overflow or spill over something **6.** *vt* PRINTING PRINT MORE THAN PLANNED to print extra copies of a publication **7.** *vt* PRINTING MOVE TYPESET MATERIAL to transfer set type or illustrated material from one column, page, or line to another **8.** *vi* AUTOMOT RUN WITH THROTTLE CLOSED to run at higher revolutions than the throttle setting dictates. A vehicle engine most commonly overruns when the vehicle is running downhill with the throttle closed and the engine speed is dictated by the speed of the wheels. ■ *n* /ṓvər run/ **1.** AMOUNT EXCEEDING ESTIMATE the amount by which something exceeds a preset limit, an estimated cost, or a budget **2.** EXTRA QUANTITY PRODUCED an extra quantity of something produced, e.g. manufactured items or copies of printed matter **3.** ACT OF OVERRUNNING an instance of somebody or something overrunning, especially of going on

beyond the intended stopping point **4.** EXTRA AREA AT END OF RUNWAY a cleared level area at the end of a runway, available in case a plane overshoots

overrun brake *n* a brake on a vehicle being towed, to prevent it from running into the back of the vehicle towing it

oversaw past tense of **oversee**

overscale /ṓvər skayl/ *adj* larger than usual in size or scope ○ *an overscale portrait*

overscan /ṓvər skán/ *adj* describes an electronic image that extends beyond the viewing boundary of a computer screen —**overscan** *n*

overscore /ṓvər skáwr/ (**-scores, -scoring, -scored**) *vt* to draw a line over or through written text, usually so as to cancel or revise it

overseas *adv* /ṓvər seéz/ *also* **oversea** /ṓvər seé/ ACROSS SEA across or beyond a sea, especially in another country ○ *They live overseas.* ■ *adj* /ṓvər seez, ṓvər seéz/ *also* **oversea 1.** RELATING TO PLACE ACROSS SEA relating to, located in, or coming from a foreign country or place beyond a sea ○ *overseas visitors* **2.** TRAVELLING ACROSS SEA involving travel across a sea ○ *an overseas assignment* ■ *n* /ṓvər seéz/ SOMEWHERE BEYOND SEA a foreign country, or foreign countries and places beyond the sea collectively (*takes a singular verb*) ○ *come from overseas*

oversee /ṓvər seé/ (**-sees, -seeing, -saw** /-sáw/, **-seen** /-seén/) *vt* **1.** to watch over, manage, and direct somebody or a task done by somebody **2.** to observe something covertly or secretly while it is happening

overseer /ṓvər seer/ *n* somebody who supervises work done by somebody else

oversell /ṓvər sél/ (**-sells, -selling, -sold** /-sṓld/) *v* **1.** *vt* PRAISE SOMEBODY OR SOMETHING TOO HIGHLY to exaggerate the value or worth of somebody, something, or yourself to an implausible extent **2.** *vti* SELL TOO AGGRESSIVELY to use excessively aggressive sales techniques when selling a product **3.** *vti* SELL TOO MUCH to sell too much of a product, especially more than can be produced or supplied

overset /ṓvər sét/ (**-sets, -setting, -set**) *v* **1.** *vti* PRINTING TYPESET TOO MUCH COPY to set too much type or copy for the available space **2.** *vt* TIP SOMETHING OVER to tip or turn something over (*archaic*) **3.** *vt* DISTURB SOMEBODY to disturb or upset somebody (*archaic*)

oversew /ṓvər sṓ/ (**-sews, -sewing, -sewed, -sewn** /-sṓn/) *vt* to sew two edges together with small stitches that overlap both

oversexed /ṓvər sékst/ *adj* having an excessive preoccupation with or need for sex

overshadow /ṓvər sháddō/ (**-ows, -owing, -owed**) *vt* **1.** to take attention away from somebody or something by appearing more important or interesting **2.** to cast a physical shadow over something, or make something become gloomy

overshare *vti* /ṓvər sháir/ (**-shares, -sharing, -shared**) to give inappropriately personal or detailed information to somebody else, especially a stranger ○ *a retiring person, not usually inclined to overshare* ■ *n* /ṓvər shair/ a set of confidences that are inappropriately personal or detailed ○ *launched into a sudden overshare about his failed plans* —**overshare** /ṓvər shair/ *adj*

overshirt /ṓvər shurt/ *n* a loose shirt that is worn on top of another garment such as a sweater or another shirt

overshoe /ṓvər shoo/ *n* a shoe, usually made of rubber or plastic, that is worn over an ordinary shoe to protect it from dampness or dirt

overshoot *v* /ṓvər shoót/ (**-shoots, -shooting, -shot** /-shót/) **1.** *vti* SEND OR GO FARTHER THAN INTENDED to shoot a projectile beyond the target that was being aimed at, or be shot in this way **2.** *vti* EXCEED LIMIT to exceed a fixed or prearranged limit **3.** *vti* RUN OFF END OF RUNWAY to fail to complete a takeoff or landing before reaching the end of the runway and run off the end of it (*refers to aircraft*) **4.** *vt* MOVE QUICKLY OVER SOMETHING to move at a high speed over something ■ *n* /ṓvər shoot/ **1.** ACT OF OVERSHOOTING an instance of somebody or something overshooting an intended stopping point, especially the end of an airport runway **2.** AMOUNT OF EXCESS an instance of something exceeding a prearranged limit, or the amount or extent by which it exceeds it

overshot /ṓvər shot/ *adj* **1.** describes a jaw with an upper part that is longer than and sticks out over the lower part **2.** describes a water wheel driven by water flowing onto it from above

oversight /ṓvər sīt/ *n* **1.** a mistake, especially as a result of a failure to do or notice something **2.** the responsibility of supervising something (*formal*)

SYNONYMS See ***mistake***.

oversimplify /ṓvər símpli fī/ (**-fies, -fying, -fied**) *vt* to reduce something to such a level of simplicity that it becomes distorted or falsified —**oversimplification** /-simplifi káysh'n/ *n*

oversize *adj* /ṓvər sīz/ *also* **oversized** /-sīzd/ UNUSUALLY LARGE larger than is usual or necessary ■ *n* /ṓvər sīz/ **1.** UNUSUALLY LARGE SIZE a size that is larger than usual **2.** EXTRA-LARGE ARTICLE an article that comes in a larger size than usual

overskirt /ṓvər skurt/ *n* a skirt that is worn on top of another garment, often revealing part of the lower one

oversleep /ṓvər sleép/ (**-sleeps, -sleeping, -slept** /-slépt/) *vi* to continue sleeping for longer than desired or intended

oversold /ṓvər sṓld/ past participle, past tense of **oversell** ■ *adj* available at or characterized by prices that are excessively low as a result of previous heavy selling on the stock market ○ *indicators pointing to an oversold market*

overspend *v* /ṓvər spénd/ (**-spends, -spending, -spent** /-spént/) **1.** *vti* SPEND TOO MUCH to spend more money than can be afforded or has been budgeted **2.** *vt* EXHAUST SOMETHING to tire somebody or something out completely ■ *n* /ṓvər spend/ **1.** EXTRAVAGANCE an act or instance of spending more money than can be afforded or has been budgeted **2.** AMOUNT OVERSPENT an amount by which somebody overspends

overspill *n* /ṓvər spil/ **1.** SOMETHING SPILLED something that spills or has spilled over from something **2.** PEOPLE MOVING FROM CITY TO OUTSKIRTS the part of a crowded city's population that leaves to live in new housing areas outside it ■ *vti* /ṓvər spíl/ (**-spills, -spilling, -spilt** /-spílt/ or **-spilled**) SPILL OVER to spill over, or make something spill over

overspread /ṓvər spréd/ (**-spreads, -spreading, -spread**) *vt* to spread widely over or cover the surface of something

overstaff /ṓvər staáf/ (**-staffs, -staffing, -staffed**) *vt* to supply a workplace with too large a staff (*usually passive*)

overstand /ṓvər stánd/ (**-stands, -standing, -stood** /-stóod/) *vti* same as **understand** (*slang; used in Black English*) [Alteration]

overstate /ṓvər stáyt/ (**-states, -stating, -stated**) *vt* to exaggerate something in talking or writing about it —**overstatement** /ṓvər staytmənt, ṓvər stáytmənt/ *n*

overstay /ṓvər stáy/ (**-stays, -staying, -stayed**) *vti* to remain beyond the expected, planned, or desired time

oversteer *vi* /ṓvər steér/ (**-steers, -steering, -steered**) to turn more sharply than expected, especially in a motor vehicle ○ *We oversteered and landed in a ditch.* ■ *n* /ṓvər steer/ the tendency of a motor vehicle to turn more sharply than expected

overstep /ṓvər stép/ (**-steps, -stepping, -stepped**) *vt* to go beyond the limit of something

overstock *v* /ṓvər stók/ (**-stocks, -stocking, -stocked**) **1.** *vti* STOCK IN EXCESS to stock more of something than is necessary or desirable **2.** *vt* KEEP TOO MANY ANIMALS ON LAND to graze an area with more livestock than it can support ■ *n* /ṓvər stok/ *N Am* EXCESS an excessively large supply of something

overstored /ṓvər stáwrd/ *adj US* having more retail outlets than are required to meet consumer demand

overstretch /ṓvər stréch/ (**-stretches, -stretching, -stretched**) *v* **1.** *vt* STRETCH RESOURCES TOO FAR to make too heavy demands on a person or resource, with consequent strain and, usually, poor performance (*often passive*) ○ *Absenteeism is often a sign that employees are overstretched.* **2.** *vti* STRETCH SOMETHING TOO FAR to stretch something such as a muscle too much, so as to cause injury or damage **3.** *vt* STRETCH OVER SOMETHING to extend or stretch over something

overstrung /ṓvər strúng/ *adj* **1.** TOO NERVOUS excessively nervous and tense **2.** MUSIC WITH DOUBLE SET OF STRINGS describes a piano fitted with two sets of strings, one crossing the other at an angle **3.** ARCHERY STRUNG TOO TIGHTLY in archery, describes a bow with the bowstring fixed too tightly

oversubscribe /ṓvər səb skrīb/ (**-scribes, -scribing, -scribed**) *vt* to apply to participate in something in numbers in excess of the available number of places (*usually passive*) ○ *The course on modern poetry was heavily oversubscribed.* —**oversubscription** /-səb skrípsh'n/ *n*

overt /ō vúrt/ *adj* **1.** done openly and without any attempt at concealment **2.** done openly and intentionally, and therefore able to be taken as a sign of criminal intent [14C. < Old French, past participle of *ovrir* 'open' < Latin *aperire* (see APERTURE)] —**overtly** *adv* —**overtness** *n*

overtake /ṓvər táyk/ (**-takes, -taking, -took** /-tóok/, **-taken** /-táyk'n/) *v* **1.** *vti* GO PAST to draw level with and pass a person or vehicle travelling in the same direction **2.** *vt* DO BETTER THAN SOMEBODY to reach and then surpass a level achieved by somebody or something **3.** *vt* COME OVER SOMEBODY SUDDENLY to come over somebody suddenly, or catch somebody by surprise ○ *Sleep overtook them.* **4.** *vt* CATCH UP WITH SOMEBODY to go after and catch up with somebody

overtax /ṓvər táks/ (**-taxes, -taxing, -taxed**) *vt* **1.** to impose too great a strain on somebody, something, or yourself **2.** to levy more tax on somebody or something than is justified or considered fair —**overtaxation** /ṓvər tak sáysh'n/ *n*

over-the-air *adj* transmitted by radio or television —**over the air** *adv*

over-the-counter *adj* **1.** BUYABLE WITHOUT PRESCRIPTION sold directly to the customer without a doctor's prescription ○ *over-the-counter drugs* **2.** BOUGHT AND SOLD ELECTRONICALLY describes securities not quoted on an exchange, but bought and sold electronically **3.** DEALING IN OVER-THE-COUNTER SECURITIES relating to or dealing in over-the-counter securities —**over the counter** *adv*

over-the-hill *adj* **1.** past the point at which talent, energy, or physical performance is at its peak **2.** an offensive term meaning no longer young [< the idea of being past your peak]

over-the-shoulder shot *n* a cinematographic shot taken from over the shoulder of a character whose back can be seen at the side of the frame

over-the-top *adj* so exaggerated as to appear ridiculous or outrageous (*informal*)

overthrow *vt* /ṓvər thrṓ/ (**-throws, -throwing, -threw** /-thróo/, **-thrown** /-thrṓn/) **1.** REMOVE SOMEBODY FROM POWER BY FORCE to remove a person or group of people from a position of power by force **2.** THROW BALL TOO HARD to throw a ball too far so that it goes beyond the player or target it was intended to reach ■ *n* /ṓvər thrō/ **1.** REMOVAL FROM POWER BY FORCE the removal of a person or group of people from a position of power by force **2.** THROW THAT GOES TOO FAR a throw of a ball that goes beyond the player or the target such as the stumps in cricket that it was intended to reach **3.** CRICKET ADDITIONAL RUN FROM OVERTHROW in cricket, an additional run scored as a result of an overthrow by a fielder

overthrust fault /ṓvər thrust-/, **overthrust** *n* a rock fault produced by thrust action that causes older rocks to move long distances and eventually settle on top of younger rocks (**horizontal displacement**)

overtime /ṓvər tīm/ *n* **1.** ADDITIONAL TIME WORKED extra time worked beyond the normal hours of employment **2.** PAY FOR ADDITIONAL TIME WORKED payment, usually at a higher rate, for time worked beyond the normal hours of employment **3.** *N Am* SPORTS same as **extra time** ■ *adv* **1.** BEYOND NORMAL LENGTH OF TIME beyond the normal or contracted length of time **2.** VERY HARD using a great deal of energy and effort (*informal*) ○ *had been working overtime to try and make them see sense*

overtone /ṓvər tōn/ *n* **1.** a subtle additional meaning, nuance, or quality ○ *an overtone of malice in his manner* **2.** a musical tone whose frequency is a multiple of a fundamental tone and helps to determine the overall quality of the sound

overtook past tense of **overtake**

overtrade /ōvər tráyd/ (-trades, -trading, -traded) *vi* to trade something such as a stock beyond the level that can be supported by the trader's financial means or the market involved

overtrick /ōvər trik/ *n* in bridge, a trick taken in addition to the number needed to make a contract

overtrump /ōvər trúmp/ (-trumps, -trumping, -trumped) *vti* in a card game, to play a higher trump card than one already played by another player in a trick

overture /ōvər tyoor, -chər/ *n* 1. MUSICAL INTRODUCTION a single orchestral movement that introduces an opera, play, ballet, or longer musical work, often including the work's themes 2. MUSIC same as **concert overture** 3. INTRODUCTORY PROPOSAL OR INITIATIVE an introductory proposal or initiative made to mark the beginning of a discussion, agreement, or relationship ○ *made overtures to me* 4. INTRODUCTION TO LITERARY WORK an introduction to a written work such as a poem or play [15C. Via Old French, 'opening' < Latin *apertura* (see APERTURE)]

overturn *v* /ōvər túrn/ (-turns, -turning, -turned) 1. *vti* TIP OVER to turn somebody or something upside down, or be turned upside down 2. *vt* OVERTHROW SOMEBODY to remove a person or a group of people from a position of power 3. *vt* REVERSE PREVIOUS DECISION to reverse a previous decision, ruling, or law by using legal or legislative procedures ■ *n* /ōvər turn/ OVERTURNING OF SOMETHING an act of overturning something or somebody

~~overun~~ incorrect spelling of **overrun**

overview /ōvər vyoo/ *n* 1. a general or comprehensive outline of something 2. a brief summary of something

overvoltage /ōvər vōltij/ *n* a voltage that is in excess of the normal voltage for which an electrical circuit or system was designed

overweening /ōvər weening/ *adj* 1. intolerably arrogant or conceited 2. excessive, especially in an arrogant and conceited way [14C. < WEEN] —**overweeningly** *adv*

overweigh /ōvər wáy/ (-weighs, -weighing, -weighed) *vt* 1. same as **outweigh** (sense 2) 2. to oppress or burden somebody heavily

overweight *adj* (*v*) /ōvər wáyt/ 1. TOO HEAVY FOR GOOD HEALTH having more body weight than is considered healthy for the person's height, build, or age 2. ABOVE WEIGHT LIMIT heavier than the allowed weight limit ○ *an overweight letter* ■ *vt* (-weights, -weighting, -weighted) 1. OVEREMPHASIZE SOMETHING to give too much emphasis or consideration to something 2. OVERLOAD SOMETHING to weigh something down with an excessive load ■ *npl* /ōvər wayt/ OVERWEIGHT PEOPLE people who weigh too much for their height, build, or age (*sometimes considered offensive*)

overwhelm /ōvər wélm/ (-whelms, -whelming, -whelmed) *vt* (*often passive*) 1. OVERPOWER SOMEBODY EMOTIONALLY to affect somebody's emotions in a complete or irresistible way 2. PROVIDE SOMEBODY WITH HUGE AMOUNT to supply somebody with a very large or excessive amount of something 3. OVERCOME SOMEBODY PHYSICALLY to use superior strength, force, or numbers to defeat somebody, especially an enemy, completely 4. SURGE OVER SOMEBODY OR SOMETHING to flow over the top of and submerge or cover somebody or something

overwhelming /ōvər wélming/ *adj* 1. EXTREMELY LARGE extremely large in amount or proportion 2. EMOTIONALLY OVERPOWERING having such a great effect as to be emotionally overpowering 3. PHYSICALLY OVERPOWERING overpowering in strength, force, or numbers —**overwhelmingly** *adv*

overwinter /ōvər wíntər/ (-ters, -tering, -tered) *v* 1. *vti* to keep livestock or plants alive through the winter by sheltering them, or be kept alive in this way 2. *vi* to spend the winter by taking up residence in a particular place

overwork *v* /ōvər wúrk/ (-works, -working, -worked) 1. *vti* DO TOO MUCH WORK to work excessively, or make somebody, yourself, or an animal work excessively 2. *vt* OVERUSE SOMETHING to use something too often, especially a word or expression 3. *vt* WORK TOO MUCH ON SOMETHING to expend too much effort on something, especially so as to reduce its quality or effectiveness 4. *vt* DECORATE SURFACE OF SOMETHING to apply decoration to the surface of something ■ *n* /ōvər wurk/ EXCESSIVE WORK too much work

overwound past participle, past tense of **overwind**

overwrite /ōvər rīt/ (-writes, -writing, -wrote /-rōt/, -written /-rítt'n/) *v* 1. *vti* REPLACE COMPUTER FILE to replace an electronic file containing data or a computer program in memory or on a disk with a new file of the same name 2. *vti* WRITE TOO ELABORATELY to make a piece of writing too elaborate, polished, or decorative 3. *vt* COVER WRITING WITH MORE WRITING to cover a piece of writing by writing on top of it

overwrought /ōvər ráwt/ *adj* 1. VERY UPSET extremely upset, emotional, or agitated 2. TOO ELABORATE fashioned or decorated too elaborately 3. ORNAMENTED ON SURFACE ornamented on the surface with decoration

ovi- *prefix* egg, ovum ○ *oviform* [< Latin *ovum* 'egg']

Ovid /óvvid/ (43 BC–AD 17) Roman poet. His works include *Amores* and *Metamorphoses*, a collection of mythical and historical tales. See Cultural note at **metamorphosis** —**Ovidian** /o víddi ən/ *adj*

'It is the mind that makes the man, and
our vigour is in our immortal soul.'
[Ovid, *Metamorphoses*; 8? AD]

oviduct /óvi dukt/ *n* either of a pair of tubes in the body that transport eggs from the ovary to the uterus

Oviedo /óvvi áyd ō/ capital of Oviedo Province, northwestern Spain. Population: 202,938 (2002).

oviform /óvi fawrm/ *adj* shaped like an egg

ovine /ó vīn/ *adj* relating to or resembling a sheep [Early 19C. < late Latin *ovinus* < Latin *ovis* 'sheep']

oviparous /ō víppərəss/ *adj* 1. describes birds, fish, reptiles, and insects that reproduce by means of eggs that develop and hatch outside the mother's body 2. relating to the production of eggs that develop and hatch outside the mother's body —**oviparously** *adv*

oviposit /óvi pózzit/ (-its, -iting, -ited) *vi* to lay eggs (*refers usually to insects*) [Early 19C. < OVI- + Latin *posit-*, past participle of *ponere* 'to place']

ovipositor /óvi pózzitər/ *n* a tubular organ at the end of the abdomen of some female fish or other organisms, especially insects, that is used to deposit eggs

ovisac /óvi sak/ *n* a sac or capsule in the ovary of a mammal that contains a mature ovum

ovo- *prefix* same as **ovi-**

ovoid /ó voyd/ *adj* 1. WITH FORM OF EGG having the solid form of an egg 2. BOT SHAPED LIKE EGG describes a fruit or similar plant part that is shaped like an egg ■ *n* SOMETHING EGG-SHAPED something with the shape or form of an egg [Early 19C. < French *ovoïde* < Latin *ovum* 'egg']

ovolactovegetarian /óvō laktō vejjə táiri ən/ *n* a vegetarian who eats eggs and dairy products, but no products that involve the killing of animals

ovolo /óvələ ō/ (*plural* -li /-lī/) *n* a convex architectural moulding that resembles a quarter-circle or ellipse when viewed in cross section [Mid-17C. < Italian, 'little egg' < Latin *ovum* 'egg']

ovonic /ō vónnik/ *adj* relating to, consisting of, or using glassy materials that can rapidly and reversibly become electrical conductors after a minimum voltage is applied [Mid-20C. < OVSHINSKY EFFECT + ELECTRONIC]

ovonics /ō vónniks/ *n* the study or use of glassy materials that can rapidly and reversibly become electrical conductors after a minimum voltage is applied (*takes a singular verb*)

ovotestis /óvō téstiss/ (*plural* -testes /-tés teez/) *n* the sexual organ of a hermaphroditic animal such as the garden snail that produces both sperm and eggs

ovoviviparous /óvō vi víppərəss/ *adj* describes insects, fish, and reptiles that reproduce by means of eggs that develop within the female, deriving some nutrition from her but remaining encased within an egg membrane —**ovoviviparously** *adv*

OVP *abbr* GOV Office of the Vice President

Ovshinsky effect /ov shínski-/ *n* an effect that occurs in thin films of glass containing selenium and tellurium in which the resistance of the material drops rapidly when a specific voltage is applied across it [Mid-20C. After Stanford R. *Ovshinsky* (b. 1922), US physicist]

ovulate /óvvyoō layt/ (-lates, -lating, -lated) *vi* to ripen

and release an egg or eggs from the ovary for possible fertilization [Late 19C. < OVULE] —**ovulation** /óvvyoō láysh'n/ *n* —**ovulatory** *adj*

ovule /óvvyool/ *n* 1. a small structure in a seed plant that contains the embryo sac and develops into a seed after fertilization 2. a small or immature egg [Early 19C. Via French < modern Latin *ovulum* 'little egg' < Latin *ovum* 'egg'] —**ovular** /óvvyoōlər/ *adj*

ovum /óvvəm/ (*plural* **ova** /óvə/) *n* a female reproductive cell [Early 18C. < Latin, 'egg']

ow /ow/ *interj* used to represent an involuntary expression of pain [Early 20C. Natural exclamation]

owe /ō/ (owes, owing, owed) *v* 1. *vt* BE OBLIGATED TO PAY BACK MONEY to be under an obligation to pay or repay somebody an amount of money ○ *She owed a lot of money to the bank.* 2. *vti* BE FINANCIALLY IN DEBT to be financially in debt to somebody or for something ○ *She claims she doesn't owe anyone.* 3. *vt* BE INDEBTED FOR SOMETHING to have something, usually some desirable thing, only because of something or somebody else ○ *owed his success to her* 4. *vt* FEEL THAT RESPONSE IS DUE SOMEBODY to feel that something should be given to or done for somebody in recompense for something ○ *I owe myself a night out.* ○ *I owe you an explanation.* 5. *vt* BEAR GRUDGE TOWARDS SOMEBODY to feel a particular emotion, especially a grudge, towards somebody [Old English *āgan* < Indo-European, 'to own']

Owen /ó in/, **Michael** (*b.* 1979) British footballer. He has captained England, and is noted for his speed and skill as a goal scorer. Full name **Owen, Michael James**

Owen, Robert (1771–1858) British social reformer. A pioneer of socialist industrial communities, he wrote *Revolution in Mind and Practice* (1849).

'All the world is queer save thee and me,
and even thou art a little queer.'
[Attributed to Robert Owen]

Owen, Wilfred (1893–1918) British poet. Famous for his war poetry, he was killed in World War I a week before the armistice.

'I am the enemy you killed, my friend. / I knew you in this dark: for so you frowned / Yesterday through me as you jabbed and killed. / I parried; but my hands were loath and cold. / Let us sleep now.'
[Wilfred Owen, 'Strange Meeting'; 1918]

'My subject is War, and the pity of War. The Poetry is in the pity.'
[Wilfred Owen, Preface, *Poems*; 1918]

Jesse Owens: photographed in the long jump competition at the Berlin Olympics (1936)

Owens /ó inz/, **Jesse** (1913–80) US athlete. One of the greatest sprinters of all time, he won four gold medals at the 1936 Olympics, setting multiple Olympic and world records. Born **Owens, James Cleveland**

'I let my feet spend as little time on the ground as possible. From the air, fast down, and from the ground, fast up.'
[Attributed to Jesse Owens]

Owerri /ə wérri/ capital city of Imo State, southern Nigeria. Population: 35,010 (1983).

owing /ó ing/ *adj* due to be given, especially in payment or repayment of a debt ○ *amounts still owing* ◇ **owing to** as a result or consequence of something

USAGE See **due**.

owl

owl /owl/ n **1. NIGHT-HUNTING BIRD WITH HOOTING CALL** a predatory, usually nocturnal bird with a large head, large front-facing eyes, curved and feathered talons, a small hooked beak, and a distinctive hooting call. The owl is traditionally described as wise, perhaps because of its human-looking face and fixed gaze, as if it were considering something carefully. Order: Strigiformes. **2. SOMEBODY RESEMBLING OWL** somebody whose habits or qualities resemble those attributed to owls, e.g. wisdom, solemnity, or staying up late **3. FANCY PIGEON** a domestic pigeon belonging to a breed resembling an owl [Old English *ūle* < Germanic]

owl butterfly n a butterfly that has a spot like an owl's eye on the underside of each hind wing. Native to: South America. Genus: *Caligo*.

owlet /ówl ət/ n a young owl

owlet moth n INSECTS same as **noctuid** [Because its eyes shine in the dark when light strikes them]

owlet-nightjar n a bird related to the nightjar but resembling a small owl, that swoops down on insects from a perch. Native to: Australia, New Guinea. Family: Aegothelidae.

owlish /ówlish/ adj **1.** physically resembling an owl or a noticeable feature of an owl, especially its large round eyes or ear tufts ○ *owlish glasses* **2.** displaying a characteristic attributed to owls, e.g. wisdom or solemnity —**owlishly** adv —**owlishness** n

owl parrot n BIRDS same as **kakapo**

own /ōn/ adj, pron **1. EMPHASIZES POSSESSION** used to emphasize that somebody or something belongs to a particular person or thing and not to somebody or something else ○ (adj) *has her own business* ○ *Her own mother wouldn't have recognized her.* ○ (pron) *That's my paintbrush – get your own.* ○ *At last he had a house of his own.* **2. INDICATES THAT SOMEBODY DOES SOMETHING UNAIDED** used to indicate that somebody does something without help or interference ○ (adj) *makes his own clothes* ○ *I can make my own decisions.* ○ (pron) *I'd rather make my own than buy them ready-made.* ■ adj *Carib* **INDICATES SIMPLE POSSESSION** used after a possessive adjective, pronoun or name to indicate possession or ownership ○ *That could be anybody own.* ■ v (**owns**, **owning**, **owned**) **1.** vt **HAVE SOMETHING AS PROPERTY** to have something as your property ○ *He owns a chain of hotels.* **2.** vt **TAKE RESPONSIBILITY FOR SOMETHING** to acknowledge full personal responsibility for something ○ *encouraged us to own the project* **3.** vti **ACKNOWLEDGE** to acknowledge or admit something (*formal*) [Old English *āgen* 'your own', past participle of *āgan* (see **OWE**)] ◇ **come into your own** to start to be really effective, useful, or successful ◇ **hold your own 1.** to put up effective resistance in an argument or contest **2.** to remain in a stable condition after an illness or injury, often when it might not be expected ◇ **on your own 1.** alone **2.** without help or interference

own up vi to admit to having done something

own brand n an item for sale that has the trademark or label of the retailer, usually a large supermarket chain, instead of that of the manufacturer —**own-brand** adj

owner /ốnər/ n somebody who owns something —**ownerless** adj

owner-occupied adj used as a residence by the person who owns it

owner-occupier n somebody who owns or is buying the residence he or she is living in

ownership /ốnər ship/ n **1.** the legal right of possessing something **2.** the fact or condition of being an owner of something

own goal n **1.** a goal scored by mistake for the opposing team, usually by being miskicked or mishit by, or deflected off, a defender **2.** an action, especially one intended to damage somebody, that ends up harming its initiator (*informal*)

own label n COMM same as **own brand** —**own-label** adj

OWTTE abbr ONLINE or words to that effect (*used in e-mails or text messages*)

OX

OX /oks/ (*plural* **oxen** /óks'n/) n **1. BOVINE DRAUGHT ANIMAL** an adult castrated bull, sometimes used for pulling heavy loads and ploughs **2. COW OR BULL** a male or female bovine animal, especially one belonging to a domestic breed. Genus: *Bos*. **3. SOMEBODY UNINTELLIGENT AND CLUMSY** somebody who is regarded as unintelligent and clumsy, especially somebody with a large build (*insult*) [Old English *oxa* < Germanic]

OX- prefix oxygen ○ *oxime* [< OXYGEN]

oxacillin /óksə síllin/ n an antibiotic used to treat bacterial infections that are resistant to penicillin [Mid-20C. < *isoxazole* + PENICILLIN]

oxalate /óksə layt/ n a salt or ester of oxalic acid

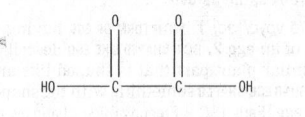

oxalic acid

oxalic acid /ok sállik-/ n a colourless poisonous acid. Source: plants, also made synthetically. Use: bleaching, dyeing, cleaning. Formula: $H_2C_2O_4$. [< Latin *oxalis* 'wood sorrel' (see OXALIS), because it occurs naturally in the plant's leaves]

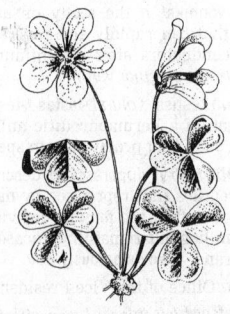

oxalis

oxalis /ok sálliss, óksəliss/ n a plant with leaves divided into three parts similar to those of clover, e.g. wood sorrel. Genus: *Oxalis*. [Early 17C. Via Latin < Greek, 'wood sorrel' < *oxus* 'sour', because of the taste of its leaves]

oxazepam /ok sázzə pam/ n a tranquillizer used to manage anxiety, insomnia, and alcohol withdrawal [Mid-20C. < HYDROXY + -*azepam*, INN stem]

oxblood /óks blud/, **oxblood red** adj of a dark brownish-red colour —**oxblood** n

oxbow /óks bō/ n **1. BEND IN RIVER** a bend in a river shaped like a 'U' **2. LAND IN RIVER BEND** the land that lies inside the bend of a river **3.** GEOG same as **oxbow lake 4. U-SHAPED COLLAR FOR OX** a collar for an ox used as a draught animal, consisting of a U-shaped piece of wood attached to a yoke

oxbow lake n a small curved lake developed on a river floodplain by a river abandoning its original meandering course and cutting a new channel

Oxbridge /óksbrij/ n the universities of Oxford and Cambridge, seen as forming an institution distinct from all the other more recently established universities in England [Mid-19C. Blend of OXFORD + CAMBRIDGE]

oxcart /óks kaart/ n a cart drawn by oxen, used for transporting heavy goods

oxen ZOOL plural of **ox**

oxeye /óks ī/ n **1. PLANTS** same as **daisy** (sense 2) **2.** a plant of the daisy family. Flowers: yellow. Native to: Europe, Asia, North America. Genera: *Buphthalum* or *Heliopsis*.

ox-eyed adj with big round eyes like those of an ox

oxeye daisy n PLANTS same as **daisy** (sense 2)

Oxfam /óks fam/ n an international charity dedicated to providing poverty and disaster relief [Mid-20C. Contraction of 'Oxford Committee for Famine Relief']

oxford /óksfərd/, **Oxford** n **1. STURDY LACE-UP SHOE** a sturdy leather shoe that laces over the instep **2. COTTON SHIRT** a shirt made of oxford cotton **3. COTTON FABRIC** a strong cotton fabric. Use: shirts. [Late 19C. After OXFORD]

Oxford /óksfərd/ n city in south-central England and administrative centre of Oxfordshire. Its university is the oldest in England. Population: 134,248 (2001).

Oxford accent n a way of speaking using the pronunciation associated with Oxford English

Oxford bags npl trousers with extremely loose baggy legs, popular during the 1920s [After *Oxford* University]

Oxford blue n **1.** a dark blue colour **2.** a student who has represented Oxford University in a sporting competition —**Oxford blue** adj

Oxford English n a variety of English, associated with Oxford University, that uses a form of Received Pronunciation, the standard educated speech of southern England

Oxford Movement n a movement in the Church of England that began in Oxford in the 1830s and advocated a renewal of Roman Catholic doctrine and practices

Oxfordshire /óksfərdshər/ n county in south-central England. Oxford is the administrative centre. Population: 605,488 (2001). Area: 2,610 sq. km/1,010 sq. mi.

oxidant /óksidənt/ n **1.** a substance that oxidizes other substances **2.** a substance in a bipropellant rocket fuel that contains oxygen to support the combustion of another substance, usually liquid oxygen, hydrogen peroxide, or nitric acid [Late 19C. < French < *oxide* (see OXIDE)]

oxidase /óksi dayz, -dayss/ n an enzyme that catalyses oxidation [Late 19C. < OXIDATION]

oxidation /óksi dáysh'n/ n **1.** a chemical reaction in which oxygen is added to an element or compound **2.** the process of losing electrons from a chemical element or compound [Late 18C. < French < *oxide* (see OXIDE)] —**oxidative** /óksi daytiv, -dətiv/ adj

oxidation-reduction n a chemical reaction in which one component loses electrons or is oxidized and another gains electrons or is reduced

oxidation state n the positive or negative difference between the number of electrons associated with an atom in a chemical compound and the same atom in an element

oxidative phosphorylation n the production of ATP from ADP and phosphate in the final stages of aerobic respiration

oxidative stress n impaired performance of cells

caused by the presence of too many oxygen molecules in them

oxide /óks īd/ *n* a compound containing oxygen, especially in combination with a metal [Late 18C. < French < *oxygène* 'oxygen', after *acide* 'acid']

oxidise, etc. CHEM another spelling of **oxidize, etc.**

oxidize /óksi dīz/ (**-dizes, -dizing, -dized**), **oxidise** (**-dises, -dising, -dised**) *vti* **1.** REACT OR MAKE REACT WITH OXYGEN to react with oxygen, or cause a chemical to react with oxygen, e.g. in forming an oxide **2.** LOSE OR MAKE LOSE ELECTRONS to lose electrons, or cause a chemical element or compound to lose electrons **3.** COVER WITH OXIDE COATING to form an oxide coating, or cover something with an oxide coating —**oxidizable** *adj* —**oxidization** /óksi dī záysh'n/ *n*

oxidizer /óksi dīzər/, **oxidiser** *n* CHEM same as **oxidant**

oxidizing agent /óksi dīzing-/ *n* a substance that oxidizes other substances and undergoes reduction in the process

oxidoreductase /óksidō ri dúk tayss, -tayz/ *n* an enzyme that catalyses the oxidation of one compound and reduction of another

oxime /óks eem, -īm/ *n* an organic compound containing a hydroxyl group bonded to a nitrogen atom [Late 19C. < OXY- + IMIDE]

oximeter /ok símmitər/ *n* an instrument that measures the amount of oxygen in something, especially in blood [Mid-19C. < OXY-] —**oximetry** *n*

oxlip /ókslip/ *n* a low-growing woodland plant. Flowers: small, yellow, in clusters on one side of a long stem. Native to: Europe, Asia. Latin name: *Primula elatior*. [Old English *oxanslyppe* 'ox dung' < *oxa* 'ox' + *slyppe* 'slime' (see SLIP³)]

Oxon. *abbr* Oxfordshire ■ *adj* of the University of Oxford (*used after titles of academic awards*) [Latin *Oxoniensis*]

Oxonian /ok sóni ən/ *adj* **1.** relating to or characteristic of Oxford University, or its students and staff **2.** relating to the city of Oxford or its inhabitants [Mid-16C. < *Oxonia*, Latinized form of Old English *Ox(e)naford* 'Oxford'] —**Oxonian** *n*

oxonium ion /ok sóni əm-/ *n* a cation consisting of an oxygen atom covalently bound to three other atoms or groups of atoms [< OXY- after AMMONIUM]

oxpecker /óks pekər/ *n* a bird of the starling family that climbs on the back of wild and domestic animals and eats parasites from their skin. Native to: Africa. Genus: *Buphagus*.

oxtail /óks tayl/ *n* the tail of a beef animal, skinned and chopped into short lengths for cooking. Oxtail is simmered for a long time to make rich soups or stews.

oxter /ókstər/ *n* regional a person's armpit [Old English *ōxta* < Indo-European, 'axis']

REGIONAL NOTE Old English speakers used *ohsta, oxta* for 'armpit', and dialect speakers in Ireland, Scotland, and the North of England have preserved the usage: *He had it hid under his oxter.* They have also created the verb *oxtercog*, meaning 'to go arm in arm', as in *They may be arguing now but they'll be oxtercogging tomorrow!*

oxtercog /ókstər kog/ (**-cogs, -cogging, -cogged**) *vi* regional to hold each other affectionately by linking arms

REGIONAL NOTE See *oxter*.

oxy- *prefix* oxygen ○ *oxyacid* [Shortening]

oxyacetylene /óksi ə séttə leen, -lin/ *n* a mixture of oxygen and acetylene. Use: cutting, welding metal.

oxyacid /óksi assid/ *n* an acid that contains oxygen

oxycephaly /óksi séffəli/ *n* a condition in which the skull becomes slightly pointed as a result of the premature closure of some connective bones (**sutures**) [Late 19C. < Greek *oxukephalos* < *oxus* 'sharp' + *kephalē* 'head']

oxycodone /óksi kódōn/ *n* an opiate drug related to codeine. Use: pain relief, sedative. [< *(dihydrohydr)oxycod(ein)one*, its chemical name]

oxygen /óksijən/ *n* a colourless odourless gas that is the most abundant element, forms compounds with most others, is essential for plant and animal respiration, and is necessary in most cases for com-

bustion. Symbol **O**. See table at **element** [Late 18C. < French, 'acid-former' (because it was thought to be a basic component of acids) < Greek *oxus* 'sharp, sour'] —**oxygenic** /óksi jénnik/ *adj*

oxygenase /óksijə nayz, -nayss/ *n* an enzyme that promotes the addition of oxygen to a compound

oxygenate /óksijə nayt, ok síjjə nayt/ *vti* (**-ates, -ating, -ated**) to combine something with oxygen, or be combined with oxygen ■ *n* a substance added to fuels, especially petrol, to make them burn more efficiently —**oxygenation** /óksijə náysh'n/ *n*

oxygen bar *n* a place similar to a café where customers can pay to breathe in oxygen through a face mask for its reviving effects

oxygen debt *n* the amount of oxygen needed to replenish the stores the body uses for its normal physiological processes after these have been depleted during strenuous physical exercise

oxygen demand *n* BIOCHEM same as **biochemical oxygen demand**

oxygen mask *n* a device fitting closely over the nose and mouth through which oxygen is supplied to assist breathing, e.g. at high altitudes

oxygen tent *n* a structure enclosing a patient in bed and resembling a transparent plastic tent, into which oxygen can be pumped to assist breathing

oxygen therapy *n* the inhaling of oxygen under pressure, often inside a pressurized chamber, as a treatment for respiratory conditions

oxyhaemoglobin /óksi heemə glóbin/ *n* the bright red form of haemoglobin containing bound oxygen molecules

oxyhydrogen /óksi hī drə jən/ *adj* using a mixture of oxygen and hydrogen gases, thus allowing hydrogen to burn in an oxygen atmosphere and giving a flame temperature of 2,400°C ○ *oxyhydrogen welding*

oxymetazoline /óksi méttə zólīn/ *n* a drug that constricts blood vessels, used as a nasal decongestant and usually administered as a spray [< HYDROXY + -azoline, INN stem]

oxymoron /óksi máw ron, -rən/ (*plural* **-ra** /-rə/ or **-rons**) *n* a phrase in which two words of contradictory meaning are used together for special effect, e.g. 'wise fool' or 'legal murder' [Mid-17C. < Greek *oxumōron*, form of *oxumōros* < *oxus* 'sharp' + *mōros* 'foolish']

oxyntic /ok síntik/ *adj* producing or secreting acid ○ *oxyntic cells* [Late 19C. < Greek *oxunteos* < *oxunein* 'sharpen, make acidic' < *oxus* 'sour']

oxysulphide /óksi súlfīd/ *n* a compound in which a chemical element is combined with sulphur and oxygen

oxytetracycline /óksi tettrə sī kleen/ *n* an antibiotic with a wide range of effectiveness. Source: the soil bacterium *Streptomyces rimosus*.

oxytocic /óksi tóssik/ *adj* inducing or speeding up childbirth by causing contractions in the muscles of the uterus ■ *n* a drug that induces or speeds up childbirth [Mid-19C. < Greek *oxutokia* 'sharp birth' < *tokos* 'birth']

oxytocin /óksi tóssin/ *n* a pituitary hormone that stimulates uterine contractions during childbirth and triggers lactation. Use: sometimes given to assist labour.

oxytone /óksi tōn/ *adj* **1.** WITH STRESS ON FINAL SYLLABLE describes a word with the stress on the final syllable **2.** WITH ACUTE ACCENT ON LAST SYLLABLE describes a classical Greek word with an acute accent on the final syllable ■ *n* WORD STRESSED ON FINAL SYLLABLE an oxytone word or syllable [Mid-18C. < Greek *oxutonos* 'sharp pitch' < *tonos* 'pitch, force']

oyer and terminer /óyər ənd túrminə/ *n* **1.** a commission from the British Crown empowering a judge to try cases in English courts of assize, abolished along with the assize system in 1972 **2.** a high court with general criminal jurisdiction in some states of the United States [Partial translation of Anglo-Norman *oyer et terminer* 'hear and determine']

oyez /ō yéz, -yéss, -yáy/, **oyes** *interj* used, usually three times in succession, to call for silence and indicate that an official announcement is about to be made, e.g. in court or by a town crier ■ *n* a cry of 'oyez' [< Anglo-Norman, imperative plural ('hear ye!') of *oyer* 'hear' < Latin *audire*]

oyster

oyster /óystər/ *n* **1.** SHELLFISH a shellfish with a rough irregularly shaped shell in two parts. Native to: seabed of coastal waters. Genera: *Ostrea* or *Crassostrea*. **2.** SHELLFISH SIMILAR TO OYSTER any shellfish similar to an edible oyster, e.g. a pearl oyster **3.** SLIGHTLY GREYISH OFF-WHITE a pale greyish-beige or pink colour **4.** PIECE OF DARK MEAT IN FOWL a small piece of dark meat found in a hollow on either side of the pelvic bone of a fowl such as a chicken or turkey **5.** UNCOMMUNICATIVE PERSON somebody who does not say much or is secretive (*informal*) ■ *vi* (**-ters, -tering, -tered**) GATHER OYSTERS to grow or gather oysters [Via Old French *oistre* < Latin *ostrea, ostreum* < Greek *ostreon*, related to *ostrakon* 'shell'] —**oyster** *adj*

oyster bed *n* an area of seabed where oysters grow or are grown

oystercatcher

oystercatcher /óystər kachər/ *n* a common large shorebird with a long flat, almost chisel-shaped red beak and black or black and white feathers that lives on shellfish and worms. Native to: found worldwide. Genus: *Haematopus*.

oyster crab *n* a small soft-bodied crab that lives harmlessly inside the shell of a live oyster or other mollusc. Latin name: *Pinnotheres ostreum*.

oysterman /óystər mən/ (*plural* **-men** /-mən/) *n* **1.** a grower, harvester, or seller of oysters **2.** a boat used in gathering oysters

oyster mushroom *n* an edible mushroom that grows on dead wood and has a soft flavourful grey cap. Latin name: *Pleurotus ostreatus*.

oyster plant *n* **1.** FOOD, PLANTS same as **salsify 2.** PLANTS same as **lungwort** (sense 2)

oyster sauce *n* a salty bottled sauce flavoured with oysters, used in Chinese cooking

oz[1] *abbr* MEASURE ounce [< Italian *ōz*, abbreviation of *onza* 'ounce' < Latin *uncia* 'twelfth part' (see OUNCE¹)]

oz[2] *abbr* ONLINE Australia (*used in Internet addresses*)

Oz /oz/ *n* Australia (*informal*) [Late 20C. Shortening and alteration]

Özal /ō za'al/, **Turgut** (1927–93) prime minister (1983–89) and president (1989–93) of Turkey. The founder of the Motherland Party, he is widely credited with reforming the Turkish economy and establishing boundaries between the state and the military.

Ozark Plateau /ő zaark-/, **Ozarks** /ő zaarks/, **Ozark Mountains** mountainous region in the southern United States, predominantly in Arkansas, Missouri, and Oklahoma. Area: 130,000 sq. km/50,000 sq. mi.

AKG London

Seiji Ozawa

Ozawa /ō za'áwə/, **Seiji** (*b.* 1935) Japanese conductor. He became the music director of the Boston Symphony Orchestra in 1973, and of the Vienna State Opera in 2002.

ozocerite /ˈōzō sírrit/, **ozokerite** /-kírrit/ *n* a waxy hydrocarbon substance occurring naturally in irregular veins in sandstone rock, ranging in colour from brown to jet black. Use: making candles, wax paper, and polishes. [Mid-19C. < German *Ozokerit* < Greek *ozein* 'to smell' + *kēros* 'beeswax']

ozone /ˈō zōn, ō zón/ *n* **1.** a gaseous form of oxygen with three oxygen atoms per molecule, formed by electrical discharge in oxygen. Use: water purification. Formula: O_3. **2.** fresh pure air, especially sea air (*informal*) [Mid-19C. Via German *Ozon* < Greek *ozon*, neuter present participle of *ozein* 'smell'; from its pungent smell]

ozone-friendly *adj* causing no harm to the ozone layer

ozone hole *n* an area of the upper atmosphere where the ozone layer is absent or has become unusually thin

ozone layer *n* the layer of the upper atmosphere, from 15 to 50 km/10 to 30 mi. above the Earth's surface, where most atmospheric ozone collects, absorbing harmful ultraviolet radiation from the Sun. In the 1980s it was realized that industrial pollutants such as CFCs were damaging the ozone layer and that holes had appeared in it, especially over the Antarctic.

ozonide /ˈō zōnīd/ *n* an explosive organic compound formed by the addition of ozone to any organic compound with a double or triple carbon bond

ozonize /ˈō zōnīz/ (**-nizes, -nizing, -nized**), **ozonise** (**-nises, -nising, -nised**) *vt* **1.** to convert oxygen into ozone **2.** to treat something with ozone, or add ozone to an organic compound with a double or triple carbon bond —**ozonization** /ˌōzō nī záysh'n/ *n*

ozonizer /ˈōzən īzzər/, **ozoniser** *n* a device that produces ozone from oxygen gas

ozonolysis /ˌōzō nólləssis/ *n* the technique of using ozone to oxidize an organic material in the process of identifying double bonds or synthesizing chemicals

ozonosphere /ˈō zónə sfeer, ō zónnə-/ *n* METEOROL same as **ozone layer**

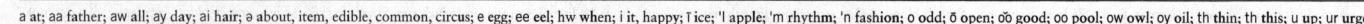

p[1] /pee/ (*plural* **p's**), **P** (*plural* **P's** or **Ps**) *n* **1.** the 16th letter of the English alphabet, representing a consonant sound **2.** a written representation of the letter 'p' ◇ **mind your p's and q's** to be careful to be polite, tactful, and well-behaved

p[2] *symbol* **1.** MONEY pence **2.** MONEY penny **3.** MUSIC piano[2] *adv* (*used as a musical direction*)

p[3] *abbr* **1.** page **2.** part **3.** GRAM participle **4.** GRAM past **5.** per **6.** MEASURE pint **7.** pipe **8.** population **9.** HANDICRAFT purl

P[1] *symbol* **1.** MONEY pataca **2.** MONEY peseta **3.** MONEY peso **4.** CHEM ELEM phosphorus **5.** MONEY pula

P[2] *abbr* **1.** PHYS parity **2.** AUTOMOT park (*used on gear sticks*) **3.** CHR Pastor **4.** CHESS pawn **5.** SPORTS played (*used in sports tables*) **6.** PHYS power **7.** President **8.** PHYS pressure **9.** CHR Priest **10.** Prince

P[3] /pee/ (*plural* **P's** or **Ps**) *n* something shaped like a letter 'P'

P2P /pée tə pee/ *adj* **1.** describes payments or linkups made between two people via the Internet. Full form **person-to-person 2.** describes software enabling commercial or private users of the Internet to communicate or share resources. Full form **peer-to-peer**

pa[1] /paa/ (*plural* **pa's** or **pas**) *n* father (*informal*) [Early 19C. Shortening of PAPA[1]]

pa[2] *abbr* ONLINE Panama (*used in Internet addresses*) See table at **domain name**

pa[3] /paa/ (*plural same*), **pah** *n* **1.** NZ a Maori village **2.** a fortified Maori settlement on a hilltop [Mid-18C. < Maori *på*]

Pa *symbol* **1.** PHYS pascal **2.** CHEM ELEM protactinium

PA[1] *n* an electronic amplification system used to increase the sound level of speech or music in a large or open space such as a stadium or auditorium. Full form **public-address system**

PA[2] *abbr* **1.** INSUR particular average **2.** *US* Pennsylvania **3.** BANKING personal account **4.** personal appearance **5.** HR personal assistant **6.** *US* MED physician's assistant **7.** MIL Post Adjutant **8.** LAW power of attorney **9.** CINEMA press agent **10.** PUBL Press Association **11.** *US* LAW prosecuting attorney

p.a. *abbr* per annum

P/A *abbr* LAW power of attorney

paan *n* BOT, FOOD another spelling of **pan**[3]

pa'anga /paáng gə, paa áang-/ *n* the main unit of Tongan currency. See table at **currency** [Mid-20C. < Polynesian]

PABA /pábbə, paábə/ *n* a form of aminobenzoic acid that is part of the B vitamin complex. Use: sunscreen. Full form **para-aminobenzoic acid**

pabulum /pábbyōōləm/ *n* **1.** a source of nourishment in an easily absorbable liquid, especially the nutrient intake of plants and lower animals **2.** material whose intellectual content is thin, trite, bland, or generally unsatisfying (*literary*) [Mid-17C. < Latin < stem of *pascere* 'to feed']

PABX *abbr* TELECOM private automatic branch exchange

paca

paca /paákə, pákə/ *n* a large burrowing plant-eating rodent with a large head and brown fur with white spots. Native to: rainforests of South and Central America. Genus: *Cuniculus*. [Mid-17C. Via Spanish and Portuguese < Tupi]

pace[1] /payss/ *n* **1.** SPEED OF MOVEMENT the speed at which somebody or something moves, especially when walking or running ○ *She quickened her pace.* **2.** SPEED OF EVENTS the rate or speed at which things happen or develop ○ *the pace of modern life* **3.** SPEED IN PERFORMANCE the degree of urgency, sharpness, or speed in the writing, composition, or performance of a dramatic or musical work **4.** STEP a step taken when walking or running **5.** DISTANCE COVERED IN STEP the distance covered in a single step or stride **6.** UNIT OF LENGTH any unit of distance, ranging from 0.76 to 1.52 m/30 to 60 in., based on the length of one or two human strides **7.** WAY OF WALKING a particular manner or style of walking ○ *an uneven pace* **8.** GAIT OF HORSE one of the distinctive ways in which a four-legged animal walks or runs at different speeds, e.g. a walk, trot, or canter, especially as executed by a trained horse **9.** 2-BEAT GAIT a two-beat gait of a four-legged animal where both legs on one side of the body move and are put down together. It is natural in camels but the product of training in horses. ■ *v* (**paces, pacing, paced**) **1.** *vti* WALK TO AND FRO to walk to and fro within a restricted area, especially in a state of nervous anxiety or deep thought ○ *paced up and down all night worrying* **2.** *vti* WALK ALONG SOMETHING to walk along or through something with regular strides **3.** *vti* MEASURE SOMETHING BY COUNTING STEPS to measure a distance by counting the paces taken to cover it ○ *I paced out the width of the room.* **4.** *vt* SET SPEED OF SOMETHING to set the speed at which somebody runs, moves, or does something ○ *I helped her train for the marathon by pacing her on a bicycle.* **5.** **pace yourself** *vr* DO SOMETHING AT CONTROLLED RATE to run or work at an even controlled speed so as not to waste energy ○ *Learn to pace yourself.* **6.** *vi* MOVE AT PACE to move at the distinctive two-beat gait known as the pace (*refers to horses*) [13C. Directly or via French *pas* 'step' < Latin *passus* 'stretch (of the leg)' < *pandere* 'stretch, extend'] ◇ **at somebody's own pace** at the rate that is natural or comfortable for somebody ◇ **force the pace** to do something to force somebody to go faster or to make something happen more quickly ◇ **off the pace** SPORTS behind the leader, or less than the score of the leading competitor ○ *three strokes off the pace* ◇ **put something through its paces** to make something demonstrate its capabilities, as a test or in order to impress other people ◇ **set the pace** to go at a speed or establish a standard that others

have to keep up with ◇ **stand** *or* **stay the pace** to be able to keep up with other people, especially when the pace is fast, the standard high, or the competition fierce

pace[2] /páyssi, paá chay/ *prep* used in front of a name or title as a gesture of real or ironic respect to somebody who is mistaken and about to be corrected ○ *Pace the critic of this newspaper, the character's name is Prospero, not Prosperus.* [Late 18C. < Latin, 'with peace, with permission', form of *pax* 'peace']

PACE *abbr* LAW Police and Criminal Evidence Act

pace bowler *n* in cricket, a fast bowler

pace car *n* a car that leads the competitors in a motor race through a pace lap before the start of a race but does not participate in the race itself

pace lap *n* a lap of the course driven by all the competitors in a motor race before the race begins, to warm up the engines

pacemaker /páyss maykər/ *n* **1.** DEVICE THAT REGULATES HEARTBEAT a battery-operated electrical device inserted into the body to deliver small regular shocks that stimulate the heart to beat in a normal rhythm **2.** NATURAL HEARTBEAT REGULATOR a small area of specialized heart-muscle tissue in the wall of the upper right chamber of the heart that sends out rhythmic electrical impulses to regulate the heartbeat **3.** COMPETITOR WHO SETS PACE a competitor in a race who sets the speed at which the whole or part of the race is run **4.** same as **pacesetter** (sense 1)

pacer /páyssər/ *n* **1.** MED same as **pacemaker** (sense 3) **2.** a horse trained to move at a pace in races

pacesetter /páyss setər/ *n* **1.** a person or group regarded as being a leader in any field and one whom others may emulate **2.** SPORTS same as **pacemaker** (sense 3)

pacey /páyssi/ (**-ier, -iest**), **pacy** *adj* with fast-moving action or a fast-moving exciting plot ○ *a pacey story*

pacha *n* HIST another spelling of **pasha**

pachinko /pə chíng kō/ *n* a Japanese gambling game similar to pinball played with the board vertical [Mid-20C. < Japanese]

pachisi /pə cheézi, paa-/ *n* an ancient South Asian four-handed game similar to backgammon, played on a cross-shaped board with six cowrie shells used as dice [Early 19C. < Hindi *pac(c)īsī* '(throw of) 25' (the highest in the game)]

Pachuca /pə chóokə/, **Pachuca de Soto** /-də sṓtō/ industrial city and capital of Hidalgo State, central Mexico. Population: 190,044 (2000).

pachyderm /páki durm/ *n* a large mammal with a thick skin, especially the elephant, rhinoceros, or hippopotamus [Mid-19C. < French *pachyderme* < Greek *pakhudermos* 'thick-skinned' < *pakhus* 'thick' + *derma* 'skin'] —**pachydermal** /páki dúrm'l/ *adj*

pachydermatous /páki dúrmətəss/ *adj* **1.** having the thick skin or some other physical characteristic typical of a pachyderm **2.** insensitive to other people and unworried by criticism or attack (*literary or humorous*) [Early 19C. < Greek *pakhus* 'thick' + *dermat-* 'skin']

pachysandra /páki sándrə/ (*plural* **-dras** or *same*) *n* a low-growing evergreen bush with toothed leaves and tiny white flowers, often used as ground cover. Genus: *Pachysandra*. [Early 19C. < modern Latin < Greek *pakhus* 'thick' + *andr-* 'man, male'; from the thick stamens]

pachytene /páki teen/ *n* the third stage of cell division, during which the paired chromosomes become shorter and thicker and divide into four chromatids [Early 20C. < French *pachytène* < Greek *pakhus* 'thick' + French *-tène* 'ribbon' (< Greek *tainia*)]

pacific /pə síffik/ *adj* 1. BRINGING PEACE leading to or promoting peace and an end to conflict 2. HAVING PEACEFUL TEMPERAMENT calm and peaceful by nature 3. UNAGGRESSIVE avoiding the use of force [Mid-16C. Directly or via French < Latin *pacificus* < *pac-*, stem of *pax* 'peace']

Pacific *n* the Pacific Ocean ■ *adj* relating to the Pacific Ocean, or to the territories that surround it or are surrounded by it

Pacific Islands /pə síffik-/ more than 25,000 islands spread over the western and central Pacific Ocean, usually divided into three subregions: Melanesia, Micronesia, and Polynesia —**Pacific Islander** *n*

Pacific Islands, Trust Territory of the former US trust territory of over 2,000 islands in the western Pacific Ocean, consisting of the Northern Mariana Islands excluding Guam (until 1986), the Federated States of Micronesia (until 1986), the Marshall Islands (until 1986), and Palau (until 1994)

Pacific Islands Forum *n* an annual meeting involving the heads of the 16 independent and self-governing states in the Pacific region, held for the purpose of promoting political and economic co-operation. It first took place in 1971 and has an administrative headquarters in Suva, Fiji. Former name **South Pacific Forum**

Pacific Northwest *n* a part of the northwestern United States on the Pacific coast that includes the states of Washington and Oregon and sometimes southwestern British Columbia, in Canada

Pacific Ocean largest ocean in the world, stretching from the Arctic Ocean in the north to Antarctica in the south, and from North and South America in the east to eastern Asia, the Malay Archipelago, and Australia in the west. Its deepest point is the Mariana Trench, 10,924 m/35,840 ft. Area: 165,700,000 sq. km/63,980,000 sq. mi.

Pacific Rim *n* the countries that border the Pacific Ocean, especially the countries of East Asia, considered as a political or economic unit

Pacific Solution *n Aus* the Australian federal government's policy of the late 1990s and early 2000s of placing asylum seekers in detention on Pacific islands while their applications for asylum are processed

Pacific Standard Time, Pacific Time *n* the standard time in the time zone centred on 120° west longitude, which includes the coastal regions of western North America. It is eight hours behind Universal Time.

pacifier /pássi fī ər/ *n* 1. somebody or something that calms a person or situation 2. *N Am* same as **dummy** *n* (sense 4)

pacifism /pássi fizəm/ *n* 1. BELIEF IN PEACEFUL RESOLUTION OF CONFLICTS the belief that violence, war, and the taking of lives are unacceptable ways of resolving disputes 2. REFUSAL TO PARTICIPATE IN WAR the refusal to take up arms or participate in war because of moral or religious beliefs 3. BELIEF IN DIPLOMACY OVER WAR the belief that international conflicts should be settled by negotiation rather than war

pacifist /pássi fist/ *n* 1. a believer in or advocate or practitioner of pacifism 2. somebody who refuses to perform military service or take part in a war —**pacifist** *adj*

pacify /pássi fī/ (**-fies, -fying, -fied**) *vt* 1. to calm somebody who is angry or agitated, or soothe violent or angry feelings 2. to bring peace to an area, people, or situation, often by using military force to end conflict or unrest [15C. Directly or via French *pacifier* < Latin *pacificare* 'make peace' < *pac-*, stem of *pax* 'peace'] —**pacifiable** *adj* —**pacification** /pàssifi káysh'n/ *n*

Pacinian corpuscle /pə sínni ən-/ *n* a pressure-sensitive nerve ending that resembles a tiny white onion and is connected to the end of nerve fibres in the skin, especially of the hands and feet, and in connective tissue [Mid-19C. After Filippo *Pacini* (1812–83), Italian anatomist]

Pacino /pə cheénō/, **Al** (*b.* 1940) US actor. He starred in *The Godfather* films and won an Academy Award for *Scent of a Woman* (1992). Full name **Pacino, Alfredo James**

pack[1] /pak/ *v* (**packs, packing, packed**) 1. *vti* PUT BELONGINGS INTO CONTAINER to put personal belongings into a bag or other container for transporting 2. *vti* PUT PRODUCTS IN CONTAINERS to put something into a container or fill a container with something for sale, transport, or storage 3. *vt* MAKE SOMETHING INTO PARCEL OR BUNDLE to make up a parcel or bundle, or wrap or roll something up in one 4. *vt* FILL SOMETHING WITH LARGE QUANTITY to fill something, especially a limited space, tightly (*often passive*) ○ *The case was packed with books and letters.* 5. *vti* CROWD INTO OR FILL PLACE to crowd into a place so that it is full or overfull, or to fill a place with people 6. *vt* FIT SOMETHING INTO LIMITED TIME to fit many different activities or events into a limited period of time ○ *packed a lot of sightseeing into one weekend* 7. *vt* COMPUT same as **compress** *v* (sense 3) 8. *vti* COMPACT SOMETHING OR BECOME COMPACTED to compact a substance such as snow or soil into a dense mass, or become densely compacted 9. *vt* PRESS SOMETHING AROUND OBJECT to wrap or press something in around an object to hold it firmly or protect it 10. *vt* MED USE PACK ON WOUND to apply a medical pack to a wound or insert one into a body cavity 11. *vt* MED APPLY COMPRESS TO BODY PART to apply cold compresses to part of a patient's body in order to control body temperature 12. *vt* MECH ENG SEAL SOMETHING TO PREVENT LEAKAGE to seal a mechanical joint by inserting a layer of compressible material between the moving parts to prevent leakage of fluid 13. *vt* MECH ENG FILL CAVITY WITH GREASE to fill a cavity containing bearings with grease 14. *vti N Am* CARRY GUN to carry a weapon, especially a gun (*informal*) 15. *vt* POSSESS SOMETHING AS FORCEFUL CAPABILITY to be capable of delivering something that has a powerful or devastating effect (*informal*) ○ *new computer packs a punch* 16. *vt* LOAD BAGGAGE ONTO ANIMAL to put goods or belongings onto a horse, donkey, or other animal in order to transport them 17. *vti* CARRY LOAD to be carrying something loaded usually on the back 18. *vi* RUGBY FORM SCRUM OR MAUL to get into a compact group for a scrum or maul ■ *n* 1. COMMERCIAL CONTAINER a container or piece of packaging holding several products or items of the same kind, or such a container and its contents 2. COLLECTION OF THINGS IN PACKAGE a set of documents or other materials relating to a subject that are packaged together ○ *a free information pack* 3. AMOUNT CONTAINED IN PACK the contents of a pack, or the amount of something that can be contained in a pack 4. SET OF CARDS a set of playing cards, comprising the four suits plus jokers ○ *a pack of cards* 5. BAG CARRIED ON BACK a bag or bundle, especially one designed to be carried on a person's or animal's back 6. PARACHUTE IN CONTAINER a parachute, rigged, folded, and in its container ready for use 7. LARGE AMOUNT a large amount of something (*informal*) ○ *a pack of lies* 8. ZOOL GROUP OF ANIMALS a group of animals that live and hunt together, especially wolves or dogs ○ *a pack of wolves* 9. LARGE GROUP OF PEOPLE ACTING TOGETHER a group of people who behave in the same way, especially a group whose behaviour appears to be threatening, predatory, or criminal ○ *always followed by a pack of photographers* 10. GROUP OF BROWNIES OR CUBS a local organized unit of Brownie Guides or Cub Scouts 11. RUGBY TEAM'S FORWARDS the forwards playing for a rugby team, or the forwards from both teams in a match, especially when involved in a scrum or maul 12. MAIN BODY OF COMPETITORS the main body of competitors in a race or competition 13. GROUP OF SUBMARINES OR AIRCRAFT a number of submarines, aircraft, or other military units who hunt and fight the enemy as a group 14. MED COMPRESS USED IN SURGERY a wad of soft absorbent material applied to a wound or temporarily inserted into a body cavity to control bleeding or keep tissues dry during surgery 15. MED HOT OR COLD PAD a compress placed on the body for medicinal purposes ○ *an ice pack* 16. COSMETIC PASTE a quantity of moist material applied to part of the body, especially the face, for cosmetic purposes ○ *a mud pack* 17. GEOG same as **pack ice** 18. AMOUNT OF FOOD PRESERVED an amount of food canned or preserved in a particular year or season [12C. < Dutch or Low German *pakken*] —**packable** *adj*

pack in *v* 1. *vt* ATTRACT PEOPLE IN LARGE NUMBERS to attract very large audiences ○ *The show has been running three years and is still packing them in night after night.* 2. *vti* STOP DOING SOMETHING to stop or give up doing something (*informal*) ○ *She's packed in her job.* 3. *vt* END RELATIONSHIP WITH SOMEBODY to end a sexual or romantic relationship with somebody (*informal*) ◇ **pack it in** to stop doing something (*informal; often used as a command*)

pack off *v* 1. *vt* to send somebody away unceremoniously to another place (*informal*) ○ *They were packed off to boarding school at the age of seven.* 2. *vi* to leave or go somewhere hastily or unceremoniously ○ *They packed off home as soon as the work was done.*

pack up *v* 1. *vti* STOP DOING SOMETHING to stop doing something ○ *I had to pack up playing the trombone because the neighbours were always complaining.* 2. *vi* BREAK DOWN to stop working properly (*informal*) ○ *The washing machine has packed up.* 3. *vi* FINISH WORK to finish work for the day (*informal*) ○ *I'm packing up and going home.*

pack[2] /pak/ (**packs, packing, packed**) *vt* to ensure that a group such as a jury or committee is made up wholly or mainly of supporters of one side [Early 16C. Probably alteration of PACT]

package /pákij/ *n* 1. PARCEL an object or set of objects wrapped, boxed, or tied in a bundle for transportation or mailing 2. DIFFERENT THINGS CONSTITUTING SINGLE ITEM a number of different components intended to constitute a single item ○ *a good severance package* ○ *a package of financial measures* 3. PIECE OF GENERAL ADAPTABLE COMPUTER SOFTWARE a piece of computer software that can be used for a range of related purposes such as word processing or financial analysis 4. TRAVEL same as **package holiday** 5. *N Am* COMM same as **pack**[1] *n* (sense 1) ○ *a package of chewing gum* ■ *vt* (**-ages, -aging, -aged**) 1. PUT SOMETHING INTO PACKAGE to put things into or wrap them up as a package 2. PRODUCE ATTRACTIVE PACKAGING FOR SOMETHING to create suitable or attractive packaging in which to sell a product 3. PROMOTE OR PRESENT SOMETHING to present somebody or something to others in a way intended to ensure appeal and acceptance ○ *It wasn't so much the policy that was wrong as the way it was packaged.* 4. GROUP SOMETHING AS PACKAGE to group or offer several different items together in a package 5. PRODUCE SOMETHING FOR OTHERS TO MARKET to produce a book or television programme or series in finished form ready to be published or broadcast by another company —**packager** *n*

package deal *n* a proposal or agreement comprising a number of different items that must all be accepted together

package holiday *n UK* a holiday or tour organized in advance by a travel company to whom the holidaymaker pays a single fee covering transport, accommodation, board, and often entertainment. ANZ, N Am term **package tour**

package tour *n ANZ, N Am* same as **package holiday**

packaging /pákijing/ *n* 1. WRAPPING OR CONTAINER the wrapping or container in which an item is presented for sale, or the materials used to make it 2. DESIGN OR STYLE OF WRAPPING the design or style of the wrapping or container in which something is offered for sale, especially from the point of view of its appeal to buyers 3. PRESENTATION the manner in which something or somebody is presented to the public in order to create a favourable image or impression 4. WORK OF BOOK PACKAGER the work of producing books or television programmes for others to market

pack animal *n* 1. an animal that is used to carry goods or equipment, e.g. a horse, donkey, or mule 2. an animal that lives in a pack

pack drill *n* a military punishment in which the offender has to march carrying a full load of equipment

packed /pakt/ *adj* 1. FULL OF PEOPLE full of people and extremely crowded ○ *played to a packed house every night* 2. CONTAINING MUCH OF SOMETHING containing or offering something in excitingly large quantities (*often used in combination*) ○ *a fun-packed adventure* 3. COMPRESSED pressed together to form a compact mass ○ *packed snow*

packed lunch *n UK* a lunch that has been prepared and put into a container to be eaten later, usually on a picnic or excursion. ANZ term **cut lunch**. N Am term **box lunch**

packed out *adj* crowded with or completely full of people (*informal*)

packer /pákər/ *n* **1.** a person or machine that packs goods in containers or in packaging **2.** a person or company involved in the processing and packing of goods, especially meat or fresh produce, for the wholesale market

Packer /pákər/, **Sir Frank** (1906–74) Australian journalist and newspaper proprietor. He was chairman of Australian Consolidated Press (1957–74), one of the country's largest media groups. Full name **Packer, Sir Douglas Frank Hewson**

Packer, Kerry (*b.* 1937) Australian media proprietor. His television coverage of cricket revolutionized the way the game is presented. Full name **Packer, Kerry Francis Bullimore**

> 'If a British guy saw someone at the wheel of a Rolls-Royce, he'd say "come the revolution and we'll take that away from you, mate", where the American would say "one day I'll have one of those, when I have worked hard enough". It's unfortunate we Australians inherited the British mentality.'
> [Kerry Packer, *Guardian*; 1 September 1977]

packet /pákit/ *n* **1.** SMALL CONTAINER FOR GOODS a small box, envelope, or bag in which goods are sold or stored **2.** CONTENTS OR QUANTITY IN PACKET the contents of a packet, or the quantity of goods contained in a packet ○ *still have half a packet of crisps* **3.** MAIL SMALL PARCEL a small parcel or package **4.** COMPUT DATA UNIT IN COMPUTER NETWORK a message or part of a message packaged as a fixed-size segment of data for transmission through a computer network **5.** *also* **packet boat** BOAT ON REGULAR SHORT RUN a small ship that provides a regular service carrying passengers, freight, and mail over a fixed short route ■ *vt* (**-ets, -eting, -eted**) PUT SOMETHING IN PACKET to put something into a packet or wrap it up as a parcel [15C. < PACK[1]] ◇ **catch** *or* **cop** *or* **get a packet** to be seriously injured (*slang*) ◇ **cost a packet** to cost a great deal of money (*informal*)

packet switching *n* the transmitting and routing of data as packet segments sent rapidly and sequentially over a channel that is occupied only during the actual transmission

packframe /pák fraym/ *n* a lightweight frame with shoulder straps to which equipment or unwieldy loads can be strapped to be carried on a person's back

packhorse /pák hawrss/ *n* a horse used for carrying goods or equipment

packhouse /pák howss/ *n* a company that packages fresh fruit or vegetables, e.g. for sale at supermarkets. N Am term **packinghouse**

pack ice *n* floating ice, especially in polar regions, that has formed itself into a solid mass covering a wide area

packing /páking/ *n* **1.** ACT OF PUTTING THINGS INTO CONTAINERS the task of putting things into containers, usually for storage or transport **2.** MATERIAL FOR PROTECTING PACKED OBJECT material used to surround and protect something packed inside a container **3.** WATERTIGHT OR AIRTIGHT MATERIAL material used to fill or surround something such as a joint in a pipe in order to make it watertight or airtight **4.** FOOD INDUST PROCESSING AND PACKAGING OF FOOD the processing and packaging of food such as meat or produce for sale **5.** MED ABSORBENT MATERIAL FOR MEDICAL PACKS absorbent material such as gauze for insertion in body cavities or wounds **6.** MECH ENG SPACERS BETWEEN CLAMPED SURFACES shims, washers, or other pieces of metal used to adjust the distance between component surfaces before they are secured

packing case *n* a large wooden box or crate in which objects are packed for transportation or storage

packing fraction *n* a measure of the stability of an atomic nucleus, arrived at by dividing the difference between its mass in atomic mass units and its mass number by that mass number

pack rat *n* a rat that lives in woodlands and collects and carries away objects to its nest, the best-known species of which has a long bushy tail and cheek pouches. Native to: North America. Latin name: *Neotoma cinerea.*

packsack /pák sak/ *n N Am* a bag with shoulder straps that can be carried on the back

packsaddle /pák sad'l/ *n* a saddle for carrying loads on a pack animal

packthread /pák thred/ *n* strong twine used for sewing up packages wrapped in sacking or other fabric

pack-up *n N England* FOOD same as **packed lunch**

pact /pakt/ *n* an agreement made between two or more people or groups, either formally or informally, to do something together or for each other [15C. Via French < Latin *pactum* < past participle of *pacisci* 'agree']

pacy *adj* ARTS another spelling of **pacey**

pad[1] /pad/ *n* **1.** PIECE OF SOFT MATERIAL a piece of soft material used to protect something or give it shape, to clean or polish articles, or to absorb moisture **2.** PROTECTIVE MATERIAL WORN BY SPORTS PLAYERS a specially shaped covering of impact-absorbing material used to protect part of the body, especially when playing a sport **3.** BLOCK OF PAPER SHEETS a number of sheets of paper of the same size fastened together along one edge **4.** INK-FILLED MATERIAL a thick firm piece of material saturated with ink onto which a rubber stamp is pressed so that ink is transferred to it **5.** AREA FOR TAKING OFF AND LANDING a place where a helicopter can land and take off or from which a rocket is launched **6.** SANITARY TOWEL a strip of absorbent material used externally during menstruation **7.** BACKING MATERIAL a firm backing or support for something that is laid on a surface **8.** FLESHY CUSHION OF ANIMAL'S PAW a small rounded fleshy cushion on the underside of an animal's paw **9.** FLESHY TIP OF FINGER OR TOE the rounded fleshy part at the end of a human finger or toe **10.** LIVING QUARTERS somebody's flat or house (*dated slang*) **11.** BOT FLOATING LEAF OF WATER PLANT the broad leaf of a plant such as a water lily that floats on the surface of the water **12.** ELEC ENG SET OF RESISTORS a fixed configuration of resistors designed to reduce the strength of an electrical signal without distorting the signal itself **13.** COMPUT GAMES same as **joypad** (*informal*) ■ *vt* (**pads, padding, padded**) **1.** COVER SOMETHING WITH SOFT MATERIAL to use soft material to give something shape, to make it more comfortable, or to protect it **2.** ADD UNNECESSARY MATERIAL TO SOMETHING to add unnecessary material to something, especially a piece of writing or a speech, in order to lengthen it ○ *padded out the speech with anecdotes* **3.** INFLATE SOMETHING BY ADDING BOGUS EXPENSES to add extra charges to a bill or expense account to make it higher than it should be [Mid-16C. Probably < Low Dutch]

pad[2] /pad/ *vti* (**pads, padding, padded**) **1.** WALK QUIETLY to walk, or to walk along or through somewhere, with soft or silent steps ○ *She padded along in her slippers.* **2.** WALK SLOWLY to walk along a route very slowly ■ *n* SOUND OF FOOTSTEPS the sound of soft steady footsteps [Mid-16C. Origin ?]

padded cell /páddid-/ *n* in former times, a room in a psychiatric hospital with its walls and floor covered with padding to prevent a patient from doing himself or herself physical harm

padding /pádding/ *n* **1.** THICK SOFT MATERIAL thick soft material used as a protective lining or covering or to fill and give shape to things **2.** UNNECESSARY ADDITIONS TO SPEECH OR WRITING unnecessary or irrelevant material added to a piece of writing or a speech to make it longer **3.** BOGUS ADDITIONS TO BILL extra charges added to a bill or expense account to make it higher than it should be

paddle[1] /pádd'l/ *n* **1.** SHORT FLAT-BLADED OAR a short oar with a flat blade at one or both ends used to propel a canoe or small boat **2.** ON PADDLE WHEEL a blade of a paddle wheel **3.** FLAT-BLADED STIRRING TOOL a tool with a flat blade used for shaping, stirring, or beating **4.** ZOOL same as **flipper** (sense 1) **5.** *N Am* TABLE TENNIS BAT a round wooden bat with a short handle used in table tennis **6.** *N Am* PIECE OF WOOD FOR SPANKING a usually short piece of wood with a flattened end used for physical punishment **7.** EARLY INPUT DEVICE FOR VIDEO GAMES an input device for early video games with a dial that allowed the user to move an on-screen object either up and down or from side to side ■ *v* (**-dles, -dling, -dled**) **1.** *vti* PROPEL CANOE WITH PADDLE to propel a canoe or small boat through water using a paddle **2.** *vt* CARRY SOMETHING IN CANOE to carry somebody or something somewhere in a canoe or paddleboat **3.** *vti* ROW AT EASY PACE to row a boat at an easy pace **4.** *vt* STIR WITH PADDLE to stir, beat, or shape something using a paddle **5.** *vt N Am* HIT SOMEBODY to hit somebody with a paddle or with the hand [15C. Origin ?] —**paddler** *n*

paddle[2] /pádd'l/ *v* (**-dles, -dling, -dled**) **1.** *vi* WALK ABOUT IN SHALLOW WATER to walk or play, usually with bare feet, in shallow water **2.** *vti* DABBLE HANDS OR FEET IN WATER to move the hands or feet about gently in shallow water **3.** *vi* WADDLE to walk along unsteadily like a very small child ■ *n* ACT OF PLAYING IN WATER an act or period of walking or playing in shallow water ○ *go for a paddle* [Mid-16C. Probably < Low Dutch] —**paddler** *n*

paddleball /pádd'l bawl/ *n* **1.** a game for two to four players played by hitting a ball against a wall with small bats **2.** the ball used in paddleball

paddleboard /pádd'l bawrd/ *n* a long narrow surfboard used especially in rescuing swimmers

paddleboat /pádd'l bōt/ *n* a boat propelled by one or more paddle wheels

paddlefish /pádd'l fish/ (*plural* **-fishes** or *same*) *n* a large freshwater fish with a long flat snout and a cartilaginous skeleton. Native to: Mississippi River valley, Yangtze River. Family: Polyodontidae.

paddle steamer

paddle steamer *n* a steamship propelled by paddle wheels on each side of the hull or by a single paddle wheel at the stern. N Am term **paddle wheeler**

paddle wheel *n* a wheel with flat blades fixed all round its edge, attached to the hull of a ship and usually turned by an engine to propel the ship through water

paddle wheeler *n N Am* same as **paddle steamer**

paddling pool /pádling-/ *n* a shallow pool filled with water for children to play in, usually a circular inflatable toy or a small pool near a larger swimming pool. Aus, N Am term **wading pool**

paddock[1] /páddək/ *n* **1.** ENCLOSED FIELD FOR HORSES a small field near a house or stable with grazing for horses **2.** AREA FOR MOUNTING RACEHORSES an area on a racecourse where the racehorses are paraded before a race and the jockeys mount **3.** AREA FOR RACING CARS BEFORE RACE an area near the pits on a motor-racing track where cars are worked on before a race **4.** *ANZ* FENCED AREA OF LAND a field or other fenced-off area of land **5.** *ANZ* PLAYING AREA the playing area for a sport, e.g. a football pitch ■ *vt* (**-docks, -docking, -docked**) KEEP HORSES IN PADDOCK to keep animals, especially horses, in a paddock [Early 17C. Alteration of dialect *parrock* < Old English *pearroc* 'fence, enclosed land' < Germanic]

paddock[2] /páddək/, **puddock** /púddək/ *n regional* a frog or toad [14C. < Old Norse *padda* 'toad']

paddy[1] /páddi/ (*plural* **-dies**) *n* **1.** *also* **paddy field** a field, usually kept covered with shallow water, in which rice is grown **2.** rice as a crop in the field or when harvested but not yet processed [Early 17C. < Malay *padi*]

paddy[2] /páddi/ (*plural* **-dies**) *n* a fit of rage or bad temper (*informal*) [Late 19C. < PADDY]

Paddy /páddi/ (*plural* **-dies**) *n* an offensive term for an Irish person (*slang*) [Late 18C. < pet form of Irish *Pádraig* 'Patrick']

REGIONAL NOTE See *man*.

paddy field *n* AGRIC same as **paddy**[1] (sense 1)

paddymelon *n* ZOOL another spelling of **pademelon**

paddy wagon *n ANZ, N Am* POLICE a police van (*informal*) [Late 19C. Probably < PADDY, referring to Irish policemen in New York and New England]

pademelon /páddi melən/ (*plural* **-ons** or *same*), **paddymelon** *n* a small wallaby that lives at the edges of forests in Australia. Genus: *Thylogale.* [Early 19C. Alteration of an Aboriginal name]

Paderewski /páddə réfski/, **Ignace Jan** (1860–1941) Polish pianist, composer, and prime minister (1919). An internationally renowned musician, he was prime minister of the newly independent Poland for ten months before resuming his musical career.

Padishah /páddi shaa/ *n* a title used by or to refer to the former shahs of Iran and sultans of Turkey [Early 17C. < Persian *pād(i)šāh* 'lord-shah' < *pati* 'lord, master' + *šāh* 'shah']

padlock /pád lok/ *n* a detachable lock with a movable semicircular bar at the top, the free end of which is usually passed through a hasp and then locked shut ■ *vt* (**-locks, -locking, -locked**) to secure something using a padlock [15C. Origin ?]

padparadscha /pád pə ráddshə/ *n* a rare orange-pink sapphire [Via German < Sinhalese *padmaraga* < Sanskrit *padma* 'lotus flower' + *raga* 'colour']

padre /paádri, -dray/ *n* **1.** a Christian clergyman who ministers to the armed forces **2.** used to address or refer to a Roman Catholic priest in a country where Spanish, Italian, or Portuguese is spoken [Late 16C. Via Italian, Spanish, or Portuguese < Latin *pater* 'father']

padrone /pə drṓni/ (*plural* **-nes** or **-ni** /-nee/) *n* the owner or manager of an Italian business, especially a restaurant or café [Late 17C. Via Italian < Latin *patronus* 'protector, patron' < *pater* 'father'] —**padronism** *n*

padsaw /pádd saw/ *n UK* a small narrow saw with a handle at one end only, used for cutting curves. ANZ, N Am term **keyhole saw** [Late 19C. < PAD[1] 'handle into which different tools can be fitted']

pad thai /pád tī/ *n* in Thai cooking, a dish of rice noodles stir-fried with various other ingredients, especially shrimp and chicken [< Thai]

Padua /páddyoō ə/ city in northeastern Italy, and the capital of Padua Province, Veneto Region. Population: 211,035 (1999). Italian name **Padova**

paduasoy /páddyoo ə soy/ *n* a rich heavy silk fabric [Late 16C. Alteration (influenced by PADUA) of French *pou-de-soie*]

paean /peé ən/ *n* a written, spoken, or musical expression of enthusiastic praise or rapturous joy [Late 16C. Via Latin, 'religious hymn (originally in honour of Apollo)' < Greek *paian* < *Paian*, name for Apollo]

paed-, **ped-** *prefix* same as **paedo-** (*used before vowels*)

paederast, etc. *n* SOC SCI another spelling of **pederast, etc.**

paediatrics /peédi áttriks/, **pediatrics** *n* the branch of medicine concerned with the care and development of children and with the prevention and treatment of children's diseases (*takes a singular verb*) —**paediatric** *adj* —**paediatrician** /peédi ə trísh'n/ *n* —**paediatrist** /peédi áttrist/ *n*

paedo-, **pedo-** *prefix* child, children ○ *paedophile* [< Greek *paid-* 'child, boy' < Indo-European, 'little']

paedodontics /peédə dóntiks/, **pedodontics** *n* the branch of dentistry concerned with dental care and treatment for children (*takes a singular verb*)

paedology /pi dólləji/, **pedology** *n* the scientific study of the physical and mental development of children —**paedologic** /peédə lójjik/ *adj* —**paedological** *adj* —**paedologically** *adv* —**paedologist** *n*

paedomorphosis /peédə máwrfəsiss, péddə-/, **pedomorphosis** *n* ZOOL same as **neoteny**

paedophile /peédə fīl/, **pedophile** *n* an adult who has sexual desire for children or who has committed the crime of sex with a child —**paedophilic** /peédə fíllik/ *adj*

paedophilia /peédə filli ə/, **pedophilia** *n* sexual desire felt by an adult for children, or the crime of sex with a child

paella /pī éllə/ *n* **1.** a dish made of saffron-flavoured rice with chicken, shellfish, and a variety of other ingredients cooked together, originally from Spain **2.** a large shallow frying pan, with a handle on each side, that allows rice to cook in a shallow depth of liquid that evaporates quickly and evenly [Late 19C. Via Catalan < Latin *patella* 'small dish' < *patina* 'shallow dish']

paeon /peé ən/ *n* a metrical foot of one long and three short syllables arranged in any order [Early 17C. Via Latin < Greek *paiōn*, variant of *paian* (see PAEAN)]

paeony *n* PLANTS another spelling of **peony**

Paestum /péstəm/ ancient city in southern Italy, noted for its Greek ruins

pagan /páygən/ *n* **1.** ADHERENT OF NONMAINSTREAM RELIGION a religious adherent who does not follow one of the world's main religions, especially somebody who is not a Christian, Muslim, or Jew (*sometimes considered offensive*) **2.** POLYTHEIST OR PANTHEIST a follower of an ancient polytheistic or pantheistic religion **3.** HEATHEN somebody without a religion (*disapproving*) ■ *adj* **1.** OF NONMAINSTREAM RELIGION believing in or relating to a religion that is not one of the world's main religions and is regarded as questionable **2.** FOLLOWING POLYTHEISTIC OR PANTHEISTIC RELIGION believing in or relating to an ancient polytheistic or pantheistic religion **3.** NONRELIGIOUS having no religion (*disapproving*) [14C. < late Latin *paganus* 'heathen, non-Christian', in classical Latin 'villager, civilian' < *pagus* 'rural district'] —**paganism** *n*

ORIGIN The Latin word *pagus*, from which ***pagan*** is derived, originally meant 'something stuck in the ground as a landmark'. It was extended metaphorically to 'rural district, village', and the noun *paganus* was derived from it, denoting 'country dweller, villager'. This shifted in meaning, first to 'civilian', and then (based on the early Christian notion that all members of the Church were 'soldiers' of Jesus Christ) to 'heathen'.

Paganini /pággə neéni/, **Niccolò** (1782–1840) Italian composer and violinist. He was renowned as a virtuoso, and his compositions include violin sonatas, caprices for solo violin, and concertos.

page[1] /payj/ *n* **1.** ONE SIDE OF SHEET OF PAPER one side of a single sheet of paper, especially one bound into a book, newspaper, or magazine, or forming part of a piece of written work **2.** SINGLE SHEET IN BOOK a single sheet of paper, especially one bound into a book, newspaper, or magazine ○ *a book with some pages missing* **3.** AMOUNT OF WRITING ON PAGE the amount of writing or printed matter that can be contained on a page **4.** COMPUTER DATA PRINTING OUT AS PAGE the amount of text or graphics in a computer document that will print out as a single page **5.** SCREENFUL OF COMPUTER DISPLAY the portion of text or graphics that can be seen on a computer screen at one time **6.** NOTEWORTHY PERIOD OR EVENT a period or event, especially a noteworthy one, in the history of something or somebody's life ○ *Antibiotics wrote an important page in the history of medical research.* ■ *v* (**pages, paging, paged**) **1.** *vi* LOOK THROUGH PAGES to turn and look over the pages of something **2.** *vt* LITERAT same as **paginate** [Late 16C. < French, shortening of *pagene* < Latin *pagina* 'strips of papyrus fastened together']

page[2] /payj/ *n* **1.** BOY ATTENDANT a youth acting as an attendant to somebody on a ceremonial occasion, e.g. to a bride at her wedding **2.** BOY WHO RUNS ERRANDS a youth employed to run errands or carry messages for guests in a hotel or club **3.** BOY SERVANT IN MEDIEVAL TIMES a youth who acted as a personal or household servant to somebody, especially a royal or noble person, in medieval times **4.** BOY APPRENTICED TO KNIGHT a youth who acted as the personal servant to a knight in medieval times as the first stage of his training to become a knight **5.** ERRAND RUNNER IN US CONGRESS somebody employed as a messenger, guide, and assistant in the US Congress ■ *vt* (**pages, paging, paged**) **1.** SUMMON SOMEBODY BY NAME to summon somebody by calling out his or her name, e.g. over a loudspeaker system **2.** CONTACT SOMEBODY ON PAGER to try to contact somebody on his or her pager **3.** HIST ACT AS PAGE TO SOMEBODY to serve somebody in the capacity of page [13C. < French]

Page /payj/, **Sir Earle** (1880–1961) Australian politician. He was founder and leader of the Country Party (1920–39), held various ministerial posts, and was prime minister for just 19 days in 1939. See table at **prime minister**. Full name **Page, Sir Earle Christmas Grafton**

pageant /pájjənt/ *n* **1.** a large-scale stage production representing historical or legendary events, especially local ones, in scenes or tableaux in which dramatic interest is less important than spectacle **2.** an elaborate and colourful procession, display, or ceremonial occasion [14C. < Anglo-Latin *pagina* 'scene, stage']

pageantry /pájjəntri/ *n* highly colourful, splendid, and stately display or ceremonies, usually with a historical or traditional flavour

pageboy /páyj boy/ *n* **1.** same as **page**[2] *n* (sense 1) **2.** a hairstyle in which the hair is cut to one length, usually jaw-length, and curls under slightly at the ends, with a fringe at the front

page break *n* a code or symbol on a computer screen that shows where a printer will start a new page, e.g. in a word processing document

~~**pagent**~~ incorrect spelling of **pageant**

pager /páyjər/ *n* a small electronic message-receiving device, often with a small screen, that beeps, flashes, or vibrates to let the user know that somebody is trying to contact him or her

Page Three *tdmk* a trademark for the page on which the *Sun* newspaper prints a large photograph of a bare-breasted woman

Paget's disease /pájjəts-/ *n* **1.** a disease in which the bones become enlarged and weakened and subject to fracture **2.** *also* **Paget's cancer** a cancerous inflammatory condition of the nipple and areola, associated with breast cancer [Late 19C. After Sir James *Paget* (1814–99), British surgeon]

page-turner *n* a book with a very gripping plot

page view *n* a count of the number of times a webpage is requested, assumed to be the number of times somebody has responded to an advertisement

paginal /pájjin'l/ *adj* **1.** exactly duplicating a previous edition or version, so that the same text appears on the same page in both **2.** consisting of, relating to, or like a page or pages [Mid-17C. < late Latin *paginalis* < Latin *pagina* 'strips of papyrus fastened together']

paginate /pájji nayt/ (**-nates, -nating, -nated**) *vt* to number the pages of a book or document [Late 19C. Probably back-formation < PAGINATION]

pagination /pájji náysh'n/ *n* **1.** the sequential numbers given to pages in a book or document **2.** the process or work of numbering pages [Mid-19C. < French *paginer* 'paginate' < Latin *pagina* 'strips of papyrus fastened together']

paging[1] /páyjing/ *n* the movement of a fixed-size block of computer data between faster main and slower auxiliary memories to optimize performance without the user being aware that the transfer has taken place [< PAGE[1]]

paging[2] /páyjing/ *n* a facility that enables somebody to be contacted via a pager (*often used before a noun*) ○ *a paging service* [< PAGE[2]]

Paglia /páyli ə/, **Camille** (*b.* 1947) US writer. Her books, which mainly examine art and culture, take an antifeminist position. Full name **Paglia, Camille Anna**

> 'Television is actually closer to reality than anything in books. The madness of TV is the madness of human life.'
> [Camille Paglia, *Harper's Magazine*; 1991]

Pagnol /pán yol/, **Marcel** (1895–1974) French playwright and film director. Many of his films, including *Manon des Sources* (1952), are set in southern France.

> 'Honour is like a match: you can only use it once.'
> [Marcel Pagnol, *Marius*; 1929]

pagoda

pagoda /pə gṓdə/ n 1. a Buddhist temple building, especially one in the form of a tower with several storeys, each with an upward curving roof that tapers slightly towards the top 2. a building that is shaped like a Buddhist pagoda but has a decorative rather than a religious purpose [Late 16C. < Portuguese *pagode*]

pagoda tree n a tree whose contorted branches can form a shape resembling a pagoda. Flowers: creamy-white, in clusters. Native to: China. Latin name: *Sophora japonica.*

pah /paa/ interj used to show disgust, contempt, or annoyance [Late 16C. Natural exclamation]

Pahlavi /paáləvi/, **Pehlevi** /páyləvi/ n a literary form of classical Persian used especially in Zoroastrian and Manichaean texts [Late 18C. < Persian *pahlawī* < *pahlav* < *parthava* 'Parthia' (country of ancient Asia)] —**Pahlavi** adj

Pahlavi /paáləvi/, **Muhammad Reza Shah** (1919–80) shah of Iran. During his reign (1941–79) he attempted to modernize and westernize Iran, but his dictatorial rule made him unpopular. He was overthrown in the 1979 Islamic revolution.

Pahlavi, **Reza Shah** (1877–1944) shah of Iran. He seized power in a coup (1921) and became shah (1925). He initiated westernization, and abdicated in favour of his son (1941).

pahoehoe /pə hṓ i hō i/ n a form of smooth dark-coloured glassy basaltic rock formed from lava flow [Mid-19C. < Hawaiian]

paid /payd/ FIN past participle, past tense of **pay**[1] ■ adj given money in return for work, or done for the purpose of earning money ○ *paid employment*

paid-up adj (not hyphenated when used after a verb) 1. NOT OWING ANYTHING having paid all the money owed to an organization or individual person 2. COMMITTED enthusiastic and committed 3. FULLY PAID FOR for which the full price or all instalments have been paid ○ *paid-up shares* 4. RECEIVED FROM SHAREHOLDERS constituting the amount of a company's capital that has actually been received from its shareholders ○ *paid-up capital*

paigle /páyg'l/ n PLANTS same as **oxlip** [Mid-16C. Origin ?]

pail /payl/ n HOUSEHOLD same as **bucket** n (senses 1–2) [14C. < Old French *paielle* 'warming pan, liquid measure']

paillasse /pal yáss/ n same as **palliasse** [Early 16C. Via French < Italian *pagliaccio* < Latin *palea* 'straw, chaff']

paillette /pal yét, páli ét/ n a sequin or spangle sewn onto a piece of clothing [Mid-19C. < French, literally 'small straw' < *paille* 'straw, chaff' < Latin *palea*]

pain /payn/ n 1. UNPLEASANT PHYSICAL SENSATION the acutely unpleasant physical discomfort experienced by somebody who is violently struck, injured, or ill ○ *cried out in pain* 2. FEELING OF DISCOMFORT a sensation of pain in a particular part of the body (often used in the plural) ○ *was complaining of pains in the lower abdomen* ○ *back pain* 3. EMOTIONAL DISTRESS severe emotional or mental distress ○ *the pain of rejection* 4. SOMEBODY OR SOMETHING TROUBLESOME somebody or something that is extremely annoying or causes many problems (informal) ■ **pains** npl 1. TROUBLE TAKEN TO DO SOMETHING conscientious effort or trouble taken, usually in tackling a piece of work 2. LABOUR PAINS the painful spasms experienced by a woman during childbirth, caused by the contraction of the uterus ■ v (**pains, paining, pained**) 1. vt SADDEN SOMEBODY to make somebody feel saddened or distressed ○ *It pains me to hear you speak like that.* 2. vti CAUSE OR FEEL PAIN to cause physical pain to somebody, or experience pain [13C. Via French < Latin *poena* 'penalty, punishment' < Greek *poinē* 'penalty'] ◇ **a pain in the arse** or **backside** an offensive term for somebody or something that is considered to be extremely annoying or troublesome (slang) ◇ **a pain in the neck** somebody or something that is considered extremely annoying or troublesome (informal) ◇ **feel no pain** to be very drunk (informal) ◇ **on** or **under pain of something** risking or threatened with something such as death or instant dismissal as punishment

SPELLCHECK pain or **pane**? Do not confuse the spelling of *pain* and *pane*, which sound similar. *Pain* is a noun and verb referring to an unpleasant physical sensation, emotional distress, or trouble, as in *a pain in my knee, if it pains you to see them suffer, taking great pains not to offend anybody. Pane* is a noun denoting a piece of glass in a window.

pain barrier n the point at which pain reaches its peak and begins to diminish, especially as experienced by an athlete

Library of Congress
Thomas Paine

Paine /payn/, **Thomas** (1737–1809) British-born American writer, political philosopher, and revolutionary. His pamphlet *Common Sense* (1776) influenced the move towards American independence. Known as **Tom Paine**

'Government, even in its best state, is but a necessary evil; in its worst state, an intolerable one.'
[Thomas Paine, *Common Sense*; 1776]

'These are the times that try men's souls. The summer soldier and the sunshine patriot will, in this crisis, shrink from the service of their country; but he that stands it *now*, deserves the love and thanks of men and women.'
[Thomas Paine, Introduction, *The Crisis*; December 1776]

pained /paynd/ adj expressing wounded feelings or a sense of being disappointed or offended by something that somebody has done ○ *a pained expression*

painful /páynf'l/ adj 1. CAUSING PAIN causing acute physical discomfort ○ *a painful cut* 2. HURTING hurting as a result of an injury or disease ○ *My arm's still quite painful.* 3. CAUSING DISTRESS causing emotional or mental distress ○ *painful memories* 4. DIFFICULT accomplished with laborious effort ○ *making painful progress with the work* 5. VERY BAD embarrassingly bad ○ *Her performance was painful to watch.* —**painfully** adv —**painfulness** n

painkiller /páyn kilər/ n something, especially a drug, that reduces pain —**painkilling** adj

painless /páynləss/ adj 1. not causing any pain 2. involving little or no difficulty or effort ○ *a painless solution to our problem* —**painlessly** adv —**painlessness** n

painstaking /páynz tayking/ adj involving or showing great care and attention to detail —**painstakingly** adv

SYNONYMS See *careful.*

paint /paynt/ n 1. COLOURED LIQUID APPLIED TO SURFACE a coloured liquid applied to a surface in order to decorate or protect it, or in order to create a painting 2. DRIED PAINT ON SURFACE a film of dried paint on a surface (often used before a noun) ○ *paint remover* 3. SOLID PIGMENT a solid block of pigment that forms liquid paint when moistened or dissolved 4. FACIAL MAKEUP makeup for the face (dated informal) 5. THEATRE same as **greasepaint** ■ v (**paints, painting, painted**) 1. vti COVER SOMETHING WITH PAINT to cover the surface of something with paint in order to decorate or protect it 2. vti CREATE PICTURE USING PAINT to create a picture, or create a picture of something, by applying paint in different colours to paper, canvas, or some other surface 3. vt ADD SOMETHING TO SURFACE USING PAINT to mark designs or words on a surface using paint ○ *The words 'No Parking' were painted on the wall.* 4. vt APPLY LIQUID WITH BRUSH to apply a liquid to a surface using a brush ○ *My father used to paint iodine onto our grazed knees.* 5. vt APPLY COSMETICS TO FACE OR NAILS to apply makeup to the face or lips, or varnish to the nails 6. vt DESCRIBE SOMETHING to describe something in words, especially vividly ○ *In his autobiography, he paints his uncle's home as a palace.* [12C. < French *peint*, past participle of *peindre* 'to paint' < Latin *pingere*]

paintball /páynt bawl/ n a team game in which each player has a gun that fires gelatin capsules filled with water-soluble marking dye, the object being to shoot members of the opposing team —**paintballer** n —**paintballing** n

paintbrush /páynt brush/ n a brush for putting paint onto surfaces or painting pictures

Painted Desert /páyntid-/ plateau region in Arizona noted for its vividly coloured rocks. Parts of it lie within Native American reservations. Area: 19,000 sq. km/7,500 sq. mi.

painted lady n a widely distributed migratory butterfly with reddish-brown, black, and orange wings. Latin name: *Vanessa cardui.*

painted turtle n a turtle found near slow-moving water that has red or yellow stripes on its legs, head, and tail and red markings on the margins of its shell. Native to: North America. Latin name: *Chrysemys picta.*

painter[1] /páyntər/ n 1. an artist who paints pictures ○ *a portrait painter* 2. somebody whose job is to cover surfaces with paint, especially to paint and decorate the interiors of buildings [14C. < PAINT]

painter[2] /páyntər/ n a rope attached to the front of a boat that is used to tie it to something such as a mooring [14C. Probably < Old French *penteur* 'rope running from a masthead' < *pendre* 'hang' < Latin *pendere*]

painterly /páyntərli/ adj 1. characterized by the use of colour rather than line to represent shapes or to structure a composition 2. characteristic of a good painter or good painting

painting /páynting/ n 1. a picture made using paint 2. the art or work of applying paint to surfaces

paintwork /páynt wurk/ n the painted surfaces of something, e.g. a vehicle's bodywork or the interior of a building

pair /páir/ n 1. TWO SIMILAR THINGS USED TOGETHER two matching objects that are designed to be used together ○ *a pair of socks* 2. THING WITH TWO JOINED PARTS a garment or article consisting of two matching or identical parts joined together ○ *a pair of binoculars* 3. TWO PEOPLE TOGETHER two people who are doing something together, or who are considered together because there is some connection between them 4. COUPLE two people in a relationship such as a marriage 5. 2 MATING ANIMALS a male and female animal of the same species who are together for mating 6. ONE OF TWO MATCHED ARTICLES one of two matched articles such as shoes or gloves ○ *lost the pair to his cuff link* 7. TWO HORSES HARNESSED TOGETHER two horses harnessed together to pull a carriage ○ *a coach and pair* 8. CARDS TWO PLAYING CARDS two playing cards that have the same value ○ *a pair of aces* 9. POL TWO OPPOSING MEMBERS MAKING VOTING AGREEMENT two members from opposing sides in a legislative body who each agree not to vote on issues if the other is not present and able to vote. The arrangement covers occasions when members cannot vote because of illness or other commitments, the effect being to maintain the usual balance of numbers between the two opposing sides. 10. POL AGREEMENT TO FORM PAIR an arrangement between two members on opposing sides in a legislative body to form a pair 11. ROWING same

as **pair-oar 12.** MATHS, LOGIC **TWO ORDERED ITEMS** a set consisting of two items in order **13.** CHEM **ELECTRON BOND** two electrons forming a bond between atoms **14.** CRICKET **ZERO IN BOTH INNINGS** a score of zero in both innings of a cricket match ■ *v* (**pairs, pairing, paired**) **1.** *vti* **PUT INTO GROUP OF TWO** to form a pair with somebody, or partner one person with another, for a shared activity or for romance or friendship **2.** *vt* **MATCH TWO THINGS TOGETHER** to put two matching articles together **3.** *vt* POL **FORM OPPOSING MEMBERS INTO LEGISLATIVE PAIR** to arrange a pair between two members of a voting assembly, or form a pair with another member **4.** *vi* ZOOL **FORM MATING PAIR** to form a mating pair with another animal of the same species [13C. Directly or via French *paire* < Latin *paria* 'equals', a plural of *par* 'equal, pair']

SPELLCHECK pair, **pare**, or **pear**? Do not confuse the spelling of *pair*, *pare*, and *pear*, which sound similar. *Pair* is a noun or verb referring to two things, parts, or people, as in *a pair of shoes, a pair of scissors, pair a novice with a more experienced partner*. *Pare* is only used as a verb, meaning 'to trim' or 'to peel', as in *pare down the number of candidates, pare the apples*. *Pear* is only used as a noun, denoting a fruit or the tree on which it grows.

USAGE pair as a singular or a plural: If *pair* means a unit, set, or whole, it takes a singular verb: *A pair of new leather riding boots is expensive*. If the people or things constituting the *pair* are regarded individually and not as a set, a plural verb is used: *A pair of volunteers are walking up and down various streets and alleys, picking up rubbish*. Here, the two people are thought of as working not only together on one street but also separately on other streets and alleys. If *pair* comes after a number over 1 (as in *16 pairs of boots*), *16 pairs*, not *16 pair*, is correct.

---

pair bond *n* a relationship between a male and female animal, formed either during courtship and breeding or for life, that excludes others of the same species —**pair-bond** *vi* —**pair bonding** *n*

pair-oar *n* a racing shell in which two rowers with one oar each sit one behind the other

pair production *n* the creation of a negative particle (**electron**) and a positive particle (**positron**) when a fast particle (**photon**) passes through a strong electric field such as that surrounding an atomic nucleus

pairs /pairz/ *n* CARDS same as **pelmanism** (*takes a singular verb*)

paisa /pī saa/ (*plural* **-se** /-say/ or *same*) *n* **1.** a subunit of currency in some South Asian countries. See table at **currency 2.** *S Asia* money in general [Late 19C. < Hindi *paisā*]

paisano /pī saʼanō, -zaʼanō/ (*plural* **-nos**) *n US* a friend or acquaintance (*informal; often used in direct address*) ○ *Well, paisano, how's it going today?* [Mid-19C. Via Spanish, 'peasant' < late Latin *pagensis* 'inhabitant of a district' < Latin *pagus* 'rural district']

paisley

paisley /páyzli/ (*plural* **-leys**) *n* **1.** a distinctive bold design consisting of multicoloured curving shapes, stylized cones, and feathers **2.** a fabric with a paisley design, especially a type of woollen shawl popular in the 19th century [Early 19C. After PAISLEY] —**paisley** *adj*

Paisley /páyzli/ town and administrative centre of Renfrewshire, Scotland. Population: 75,526 (1991).

País Vasco /pa éess váskō/ ♦ **Basque Country**

Paiute /pī oot/ (*plural* **-utes** or *same*), **Piute** *n* **1.** a member of either of two Native North American peoples, the Northern Paiutes and the Southern Paiutes **2.** the Uto-Aztecan language of the Paiute people. Native speakers: 12,000. [Early 19C. < Spanish *payuchi*] —**Paiute** *adj*

pajamas *npl* CLOTHING US spelling of **pyjamas**

Pak /pak/ *n* (*informal*) **1.** *US* somebody from Pakistan (*often used before a noun*) **2.** *S Asia* Pakistan ○ *Indo-Pak talks*

pak choi /pák chóy/ *n UK* a type of Chinese vegetable with tender wide white stems and bright green leaves, similar to Swiss chard in appearance. ANZ, N Am term **bok choy** [< Chinese (Cantonese) *paǎk ts'oi* 'white vegetable']

pakeha /paʼaki haa/ (*plural same* or **-has**) *n NZ* somebody who is not Maori, especially a white person [Early 19C. < Maori, 'somebody who is not a Maori']

Paki /páki/ (*plural* **-is**) *n UK, Can* a highly offensive term for somebody from Pakistan or South Asia, or with ancestors from those areas (*taboo*) [Mid-20C. Shortening of *Pakistani*]

Pakistan

Pakistan /paʼaki staʼan, páki-/ country on the Arabian Sea in the northwestern part of South Asia. It rejoined the Commonwealth in 1989 after withdrawing in 1972. Language: Urdu. Currency: Pakistani rupee. Capital: Islamabad. Population: 150,694,740 (2001). Area: 796,095 sq. km/307,374 sq. mi. Official name **Islamic Republic of Pakistan** —**Pakistani** *n, adj*

pakora /pə káwrə/ *n* a deep-fried South Asian fritter made by dipping pieces of vegetable, meat, or shellfish in a chickpea-flour batter and generally eaten as a snack [Mid-20C. < Hindi *pakorā*]

pal /pal/ *n* (*informal*) **1.** same as **friend** *n* (sense 1) **2.** used to address somebody, often in an unfriendly or aggressive way ○ *Listen, pal, you'd better watch out!* ■ *vi* (**pals, palling, palled**) to become friends with and spend time with somebody [Late 17C. Via English Romany, 'friend, brother' < Sanskrit *bhrātṛ* 'brother']

pal around *vi* to become friends with and spend time with somebody (*informal*)

pal up *vi* to form a friendship or friendly partnership (*informal*)

PAL /pal/ *n* the system used for broadcasting television programmes in the United Kingdom and many other European countries. Full form **phase alternation line**

palace /pálləss/ *n* **1.** a grand and imposing building that is the official residence of a king or queen, a head of state such as a president, or a high-ranking aristocrat or church dignitary **2.** a large public or private building with an imposing ornate style, used for entertainment or exhibitions ○ *an old movie palace fallen into disrepair* [13C. Via Old French *palais* < Latin *palatium*, after *Palatium* 'Palatine Hill', where the emperor Augustus built a house]

palace revolution *n* the overthrow of a ruler by those who are already in the ruling group, often carried out with little violence

paladin /pálladin/ *n* **1.** MEDIEVAL CHAMPION a champion or hero, especially in medieval legend or history **2.** CHAMPION OF CAUSE somebody known for championing a cause **3.** ONE OF CHARLEMAGNE'S COMPANIONS any one of the 12 legendary companions of Charlemagne [Late 16C. Via French < Latin *palatinus* (see PALATINE[1])]

---

palae- *prefix* same as **palaeo-** (*used before vowels*)

Palaearctic /páyli aʼarktik, pálli-/, **Palearctic** *adj* relating or native to the biogeographic region of the Arctic and immediately adjacent temperate regions of Europe, Asia, and Africa

palaeethnology /páyli eth nólləji, pálli-/ *n* the study of prehistoric human beings —**palaeethnological** /-ethnə lójjik'l/ *adj* —**palaeethnologist** *n*

palaeo- *prefix* **1.** ancient, prehistoric ○ *palaeozoology* **2.** primitive, early ○ *Palaeogene* [< Greek *palaios* < *palai* 'long ago']

palaeoanthropic /páyli ō an thróppik, pálli-/ *adj* relating to prehistoric human beings

palaeoanthropology /páyli ō ánthrə pólləji, pálli-/ *n* the study of early human beings and related species through fossil evidence —**palaeoanthropological** /-ō anthrəpə lójjik'l/ *adj* —**palaeoanthropologist** *n*

Palaeo-Asiatic /páyli ō-, pálli-/ *adj* LANG same as **Palaeosiberian**

palaeobiogeography /páyli ō bī̌o ji óggrəfi, pálli-/ *n* the study of the locations of prehistoric species on the basis of fossil evidence

palaeobotany /páyli ō bóttəni, pálli-/ *n* the study of prehistoric plants on the basis of fossil evidence —**palaeobotanical** /-bə tánnik'l/ *adj* —**palaeobotanist** *n*

palaeoceanography /páyli ōshə nóggrəfi, pálli-/ *n* the study of prehistoric oceans, especially their history, conditions, and life forms —**palaeoceanographer** *n* —**palaeoceanographic** /-ōshənə gráffik/ *adj*

Palaeocene /páyli ə seen, pálli-/ *n* the epoch of geological time, 65 million to 55 million years ago, during which various types of mammal flourished. See table at **geological time** [Late 19C. < PALAEO- + Greek *kainos* 'new'] —**Palaeocene** *adj*

palaeoclimatology /páyli ō klĭ̄mə tólləji, pálli-/ *n* the study of prehistoric climates on a global or regional scale from evidence preserved in glacial deposits, sedimentary structures, and fossils —**palaeoclimatological** /-klĭ̄mətə lójjik'l/ *adj* —**palaeoclimatologist** *n*

palaeocurrent /páyli ō kúrrənt, pálli-/ *n* a prehistoric current of water or wind, revealed by the study of the sedimentary structures and textures that it deposited

palaeoecology /páyli ō i kólləji, pálli-/ *n* the study of the interaction of prehistoric life forms and their environments —**palaeoecological** /-eʼekə lójjik'l, -ékə-/ *adj* —**palaeoecologist** *n*

palaeoethnobotany /páyli ō ethnō bóttəni, pálli-/ *n* the study of fossilized seeds and grain in order to gain information about prehistoric patterns of cereal growth —**palaeoethnobotanical** /-bə tánnik'l/ *adj* —**palaeoethnobotanist** *n*

Palaeogene /páyli ə jeen, pálli-/ *n* the early part of the Tertiary period of geological time, comprising the Palaeocene, Eocene, and Oligocene epochs, 65 million to 23 million years ago —**Palaeogene** *adj*

palaeogeography /páyli ō ji óggrəfi, pálli-/ *n* the study of the geographical features of past epochs —**palaeogeographer** *n* —**palaeogeographic** /-ō jee ə gráffik/ *adj* —**palaeogeographical** *adj*

palaeography /páyli óggrəfi, pálli-/ *n* **1.** the study of ancient handwriting and manuscripts **2.** an ancient manuscript or piece of handwriting —**palaeographer** /páyli óggrəfər/ *n* —**palaeographic** /páyli ə gráffik, pálli-/ *adj* —**palaeographical** /páyli ə gráffik'l, pálli-/ *adj*

Palaeo-Indian /páyli ō-, pálli-/ *adj* relating to the earliest inhabitants of the Americas, who arrived from Asia by the Bering land bridge that connected Alaska and Siberia. By 12,000 to 10,000 years ago they were hunting game and living in small groups throughout North America. —**Palaeo-Indian** *n*

palaeolith /páyli ə lith, pálli-/ *n* a stone tool from the Palaeolithic age

Palaeolithic /páyli ə líthik, pálli-/ *n* the early part of the Stone Age, when early human beings made chipped-stone tools, from 750,000 to 15,000 years ago —**Palaeolithic** *adj*

Palaeolithic man *n* a member of a people who lived in the Palaeolithic period, e.g. Neandertal, Cro-Magnon, or Java man

---

a at; aa father; aw all; ay day; ai hair; ə about, item, edible, common, circus; e egg; ee eel; hw when; i it, happy; ī ice; 'l apple; 'm rhythm; 'n fashion; o odd; ō open; oo good; oo pool; ow owl; oy oil; th thin; th this; u up; ur urge;

palaeomagnetism /páyli ō mágnitizəm, pálli-/ n 1. the polarity and intensity of residual magnetism in ancient rock 2. the study of changes in the intensity and direction of the Earth's magnetic field throughout geological time. The recurring reversals of the Earth's magnetic field and the changing configurations of the continents have been established through such studies. —**palaeomagnetic** /-mag néttik/ adj

palaeontography /páyli on tóggrəfi, pálli-/ n the branch of palaeontology concerned with describing fossils —**palaeontographic** /-ontə gráffik/ adj —**palaeontographical** adj

palaeontology /páyli on tólləji, pálli-/ n the study of life in prehistoric times by using fossil evidence —**palaeontological** /-ontə lójjik'l/ adj —**palaeontologist** n

palaeopathology /páyli ō pə thólləji, pálli-/ n the study of the evidence of disease processes in early human and animal remains, e.g. by using DNA analysis —**palaeopathological** /-pathə lójjik'l/ adj —**palaeopathologist** n

Palaeosiberian /páyli ō sī beéri ən, pálli-/, **Palaeo-Siberian** adj relating to a small group of languages spoken in eastern Siberia, including Chukchi, that do not belong to any of the major language families

Palaeozoic /páyli ə zó ik, pálli-/ n the era of geological time, about 570 million to 248 million years ago, during which fish, insects, amphibians, reptiles, and land plants first appeared. See table at **geological time** —**Palaeozoic** adj

palaeozoology /páyli ō zoo ólləji, pálli-/ n the study of ancient animals and animal life using fossils and other palaeontological evidence —**palaeozoological** /-ə lójjik'l/ adj —**palaeozoologist** n

palaestra /pə léstrə, -leéstrə/ (plural **-tras** or **-trae** /-tree/), **palestra** n a public sports ground or gymnasium in ancient Greece [14C. Via Latin < Greek palaistra < palaiein 'wrestle']

palaka /paa laá kaa/ (plural same) n a Hawaiian fabric woven in a checked pattern of white and one other colour, often blue [< Hawaiian]

palanquin /pállən keén/ n a covered seat carried on poles held parallel to the ground on the shoulders of two or four people, used in former times to transport an important person, especially in East Asia [Late 16C. Via Portuguese palanquim < Sanskrit palyaṅka 'bed, litter']

palatable /pállətəb'l/ adj 1. having a good enough taste to be eaten or drunk 2. acceptable to somebody's sensibilities —**palatability** /pállətə billəti/ n

palatal /pállət'l/ adj 1. ANAT FACING OR RELATING TO PALATE occurring at, facing, or relating to the palate 2. PHON PRONOUNCED WITH TONGUE AT PALATE describes a consonant sound that is produced by raising the tongue to or near the hard palate ○ The 'sh' sound is a palatal fricative. 3. PHON PRONOUNCED WITH TONGUE FORWARD describes a vowel sound that is produced with the tongue moved forward in the mouth ○ The vowel in 'meet' is palatal. ■ n PHON PALATAL SPEECH SOUND a speech sound pronounced with the tongue at or near the hard palate or with the tongue pushed forward, especially a palatal consonant —**palatally** adv

palatalize /pállətə līz/ (**-izes, -izing, -ized**), **palatalise** (**-ises, -ising, -ised**) vt 1. to make a speech sound by raising the tongue to or towards the hard palate 2. to alter a speech sound in pronunciation by placing the tongue closer to the hard palate rather than to the teeth, alveolar ridge, or velum —**palatalization** /pállətə līˈzáysh'n/ n

palate /pállət/ n 1. ROOF OF MOUTH the roof of the mouth, which separates it from the nasal cavity. It consists of a bony hard palate at the front and a muscular soft palate at the rear. 2. SENSE OF TASTE a personal sense of taste and flavour 3. AESTHETIC TASTE intellectual or aesthetic tastes or sensibilities [14C. < Latin palatum]

SPELLCHECK palate, palette, or pallet? Do not confuse the spelling of **palate**, **palette**, and **pallet**, which sound similar. A **palate** is the roof of the mouth, or a personal sense of taste, as in a cleft palate, dishes to please all palates. A **palette** is a board for an artist's paints, or the colours available on a computer display, and a palette knife is a broad-bladed kitchen implement. A **pallet** is a tray on which to stack loads, a board on which to dry

ceramics, a tool with which to mix clay, or a straw-filled mattress.

palatial /pə láysh'l/ adj 1. grand or luxurious ○ palatial mansions 2. appropriate for a palace [Mid-18C. < Latin palatium (see PALACE)] —**palatialness** n

palatinate /pə látti nayt, -nət/ n the territory, office, or responsibilities of a feudal palatine

Palatinate n a part of the German Empire ruled by the Count Palatine of the Rhine, or the part of modern Germany corresponding to this

palatine[1] /pállə tīn/ n 1. POWERFUL FEUDAL LORD a feudal lord in central Europe with sovereign powers within his territory 2. IMPERIAL COURT OFFICIAL a court official in the late Roman and Byzantine empires ■ adj 1. SUITABLE FOR PALACE relating to or suitable for a palace 2. HAVING POWER OVER TERRITORY describes an official or feudal lord who had sovereign power over a territory 3. RULED BY LORD describes a territory ruled by a sovereign feudal lord [15C. Via French < Latin palatinus 'of the palace, palace official' < palatium (see PALACE)]

palatine[2] /pállə tīn/ adj relating to the palate ■ n either of the two bones that form the hard palate [Mid-17C. < French palatin(e) < Latin palatum 'palate']

Palatine[1] /pállə tīn/ adj relating to the German Palatinate [Mid-17C. < PALATINE[1]]

Palatine[2] /pállə tīn/ n the central hill of the seven on which Rome was built, considered the oldest and the site of many of the imperial palaces [< Latin palatinus (see PALATINE[1])]

palatoalveolar /pállətō alvi ōˈlər, -alveé ələr/ adj describes a consonant sound that is produced with the tongue touching the upper part of the mouth where the back of the ridge behind the teeth joins the front of the hard palate —**palatoalveolar** n

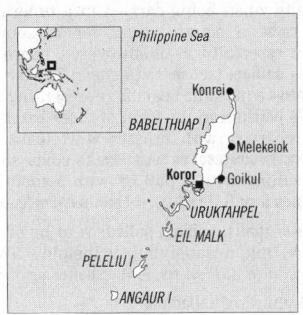

Palau

Palau /pə lów/, **Belau** /bə-/ country in the western Pacific Ocean comprising a group of volcanic islands that are part of the Caroline Islands. Capital: Koror. Population: 19,717 (2003). Area: 488 sq. km/188 sq. mi. Official name **Republic of Palau**

palaver /pə laávər/ n 1. INCONVENIENT BOTHER irritating and time-consuming activity and bother 2. EMPTY TALK idle, flattering, or time-wasting talk 3. CONFERENCE BETWEEN DIFFERENT PARTIES a conference or meeting between different parties (humorous) ■ vi (**-ers, -ering, -ered**) 1. TALK IDLY to talk idly, emptily, or with the intention of flattering 2. CONFER to confer, or hold a conference (humorous) [Mid-18C. Via Portuguese palavra 'speech' < Latin parabola (see PARABLE)]

Palawan /pə laáwən/ island and province of the Philippines, northeast of Borneo and southwest of Luzon. Area: 11,790 sq. km/4,550 sq. mi. Population: 528,290 (1990).

palazzo /pə látsō/ (plural **-zos** or **-zi** /-tsee/) n a large ornate building, e.g. a museum or an official residence, especially in Italy [Mid-17C. Via Italian < Latin palatium (see PALACE)]

palazzo pants npl women's loose-fitting lightweight trousers with flared legs

pale[1] /payl/ adj (**paler, palest**) 1. HAVING LITTLE COLOUR lacking colour or intensity ○ pale blue 2. PALLID FROM ILLNESS unusually light in skin complexion because of illness, shock, or worry 3. PRODUCING LITTLE LIGHT producing or reflecting little light 4. INADEQUATE inadequate or faint ○ a pale version of his former flamboyant self ■ v (**pales, paling, paled**) 1. vi BECOME

LESS IMPORTANT to be or become less important, remarkable, or intense, especially in comparison to something more important or serious 2. vi BECOME WHITER to become whiter or lose brilliance 3. vt CAUSE SOMEBODY OR SOMETHING TO FADE to cause somebody or something to lose colour or brilliance [14C. Via French < Latin pallidus (see PALLID)] —**palely** adv —**paleness** n

pale[2] /payl/ n 1. FENCE STAKE a pointed slat of wood for a fence 2. BOUNDARY FENCE a fence marking a boundary 3. FENCED-IN AREA an area fenced in, or the boundary of a fenced-in area 4. HERALDRY VERTICAL STRIPE ON SHIELD a wide vertical band down the centre of a shield ■ vt (**pales, paling, paled**) FENCE SOMETHING IN to surround an area with a fence [12C. Via French pal < Latin palus 'stake'] ◇ **beyond the pale** outside the limits of what is considered to be acceptable

Pale n 1. the area of Ireland, based around Dublin, that was controlled by England from the 12th century until the final conquest of the entire country in the 16th century 2. a restricted area in Imperial Russia where Jews were allowed to settle [PALE[2]]

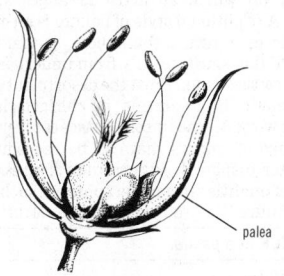

palea

palea /páyli ə/ (plural **-leae** /-li ee/) n 1. the upper of two dry membranous leaves (**bracts**) protecting a single flower in a flower head of a plant of the grass family 2. a dry membranous scale on the head of a composite flower such as a sunflower [Mid-18C. < Latin, 'chaff']

Palearctic adj GEOG another spelling of **Palaearctic**

paleethnology n ANTHROP US spelling of **palaeethnology**

paleface /páyl fayss/ n an offensive term for a white person (insult)

Palembang /paáləm baáng, paa lém baang/ city in Indonesia on southeastern Sumatra. Population: 1,481,000 (2003).

Palenque /pə lén kay/ ancient city in southern Mexico, southeast of Villahermosa. It is the site of a temple noted for its hieroglyphics.

paleo-, etc. US spelling of **palaeo-, etc.**

Palermo /pə láirmō/ city and port in Sicily, Italy. It is the largest city on the island, and is situated on the northwestern coast. Population: 686,722 (2001).

Palestine /pállə stīn/ area in Southwest Asia between the River Jordan and the eastern coast of the Mediterranean Sea. During biblical times it was the Jewish homeland, comprising the kingdoms of Israel and Judah, and was then successively occupied by the Romans, Arabs, and Ottoman Turks. In 1947 Palestine was partitioned between the new states of Israel and Jordan. Wars fought in 1948, 1967, and 1972 between Israel and the surrounding Arab states saw an increase in the land held by Israel. In 1987 a Palestinian uprising or intifada began in protest against the continued Israeli occupation. In 1993 and 1995 agreements were signed under which the Palestinian Arabs gained limited self-rule under the Palestinian National Authority in the Palestinian-Administered Territories in the Gaza Strip and on the West Bank of the River Jordan, but conflict and the Israeli presence continue. —**Palestinian** /pállə stínni ən/ n, adj

palestra n ANCIENT HIST, SPORTS another spelling of **palaestra**

Palestrina /pális treénə/, **Giovanni Pierluigi da** (1525–94) Italian composer. A prolific composer of re-

ligious and secular choral music, he wrote 250 motets and over 100 masses.

paletot /páltō/ n a fitted coat worn by women in the 19th century, usually over a bustle or crinoline [Mid-19C. < French]

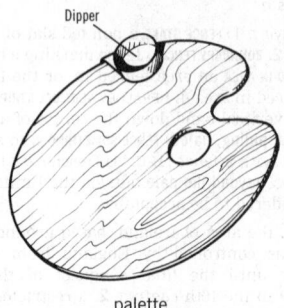

palette

palette /pállət/ n 1. ART **BOARD FOR ARTIST'S PAINTS** a board or tray on which an artist arranges and mixes paints. A traditional style of palette is an oval board that curves in near a thumbhole, so that the artist can hold the board steadily from underneath. 2. ART **RANGE OF COLOURS USED BY ARTIST** the assortment of colours on a palette, in a painting, or characteristic of an artist's work 3. COMPUT **COLOUR RANGE OF COMPUTER DISPLAY** the range of colours that can be reproduced on a computer display 4. ARTS **QUALITIES IN NONGRAPHIC ART** a range of qualities in a nongraphic art such as music or literature [Late 18C. < French (see PALLET[1])]

SPELLCHECK See *palate*.

palette knife n 1. a kitchen implement with a long flexible blunt-edged blade for lifting and turning food or for spreading, particularly when filling or icing cakes 2. a spatula-shaped implement with a slender flexible metal blade and a handle, used by an artist to mix and apply thick paints

palfrey /páwlfri, pól-/ (plural **-freys**) n a horse for everyday riding, especially one for a woman to ride (archaic) [12C. Via Old French palefrei < late Latin paraveredus 'extra horse' < Latin veredus 'light horse used by couriers' < Gaulish]

pali /paáli/ n Hawaii a high steep rock face [< Hawaiian]

Pali /paáli/ n an ancient Indo-European language derived from Sanskrit and formerly spoken in South Asia, surviving in Hinayana Buddhist scriptures [Late 18C. < Pali pāli 'canonical text' (as opposed to the commentary), shortening of Sanskrit pāli-bhāsā 'language of the line'] —**Pali** adj

palimony /pállimani/ (plural **-nies**) n N Am a maintenance allowance for an ex-lover or member of an unmarried couple, when required by a court of law [Late 20C. Blend of PAL + ALIMONY]

palimpsest /pállimp sest/ n a manuscript written over a partly erased older manuscript in such a way that the old words can be read beneath the new ■ adj describes a document that has been overwritten [Mid-17C. Via Latin < Greek palimpsestos 'something rubbed smooth again' < palin 'again, back' + form of psēn 'rub smooth']

palindrome /pállin drōm/ n 1. a word, phrase, passage, or number that reads the same forwards and backwards, e.g. 'Anna', 'Draw, o coward', or '23832' 2. a segment of DNA in which the nucleotide sequence in one strand read from one end is the same as the sequence in the complementary strand read from the opposite end. For example the sequence GGTACC is a palindrome when the complementary strand is CCATGG. [Early 17C. < Greek palindromos 'running back again' < palin 'again, back' + form of dramein 'to run'] —**palindromic** /pállin drómmik/ adj

paling /páyling/ n 1. a fence formed by a line of pointed stakes planted in the ground 2. CONSTR same as **pale**[2] n (sense 1)

palingenesis /pállin jénnassiss/ n 1. BIOL same as **recapitulation** (sense 2) 2. CHR spiritual rebirth by means of baptism 3. RELIG the supposed transmigration of the soul of somebody who has died into the body of another person or animal [Early

19C. < Greek palin 'again, back' + genesis 'birth'] —**palingenetic** /-jə néttik/ adj —**palingenetically** adv

palinode /pálli nōd/ n 1. a poem in which a poet retracts something written in a previous poem 2. a formal retraction of a statement (formal) [Late 16C. Directly or via French < Latin palinodia < Greek palinōdia < palin 'again, back' + ōidē 'song']

Palio /pálli ō/ n a traditional horse race run in Siena, Italy, twice a year, on 2 July and 16 August. Of medieval origin, it is accompanied by great pageantry. The race itself comprises three circuits of the Piazza del Campo and lasts little more than one minute. [Late 17C. Via Italian < Latin pallium 'covering'; from the cloth or banner awarded to the winner]

palisade /pálli sayd/ n 1. FENCE a fence made of pales driven into the ground 2. FENCE PALE a pale in a fence 3. BOT same as **palisade cell** ■ vt (**-sades**, **-sading**, **-saded**) FENCE PLACE IN to provide a place with a fence of pales as a means of defence [Early 17C. < French palissade < Latin palus 'stake']

palisade cell n a soft plant tissue (**parenchyma**) cell that is long and narrow, oriented on its vertical axis, and adjacent to the upper epidermis in a leaf

palisade layer, **palisade mesophyll**, **palisade parenchyma** n a layer of long cells under the upper epidermis of a leaf that are full of specialized chlorophyll-containing cell parts (**chloroplasts**)

Palk Strait /páwk-, páwlk-/ inlet of the Bay of Bengal, separating southeastern India from northwestern Sri Lanka. Length: 137 km/85 mi.

pall[1] /pawl/ n 1. DARK COVERING a covering that makes a place dark and gloomy ○ a pall of thick black smoke 2. GLOOMY ATMOSPHERE a prevailing gloomy mood or oppressive atmosphere ○ Her departure cast a pall over the weekend. 3. COFFIN COVERING a cloth covering for a coffin, bier, hearse, or tomb 4. COFFIN a coffin, especially when being carried in a funeral 5. CHR CHALICE COVER a square cover for a Communion chalice, especially a linen-covered board 6. CHR same as **pallium** (sense 1) (archaic) 7. HERALDRY HERALDIC BEARING a heraldic bearing representing an archbishop's pallium in the form of three bands in a Y-shape, charged with crosses ■ vt (**palls**, **palling**, **palled**) COVER SOMEBODY OR SOMETHING to cover somebody or something with a pall or with something that resembles a pall [Pre-12C. < Latin pallium 'covering']

pall[2] /pawl/ (**palls**, **palling**, **palled**) vi to be or become uninteresting, unsatisfying, or insipid ○ The music soon began to pall on us. [14C. Shortening of APPAL]

palladia plural of **palladium**[2]

Palladian[1] /pə láydi ən/ adj typical of or similar to the classical architectural style developed by Andrea Palladio in the 16th century [Early 18C. After Andrea PALLADIO]

Palladian[2] /pə láydi ən/ adj 1. relating to the goddess Pallas Athena 2. relating to wisdom or knowledge [Mid-16C. < Latin palladium (see PALLADIUM[2])]

Palladio /pə laádi ō/, Andrea (1508–80) Italian architect. Working in the classical tradition of ancient Rome, he produced symmetrical designs, many for villas, and wrote his Four Books on Architecture (1570), which influenced several generations of architects. Born **Gondola, Andrea di Pietro della**

palladium[1] /pə láydi əm/ n a malleable silvery-white metallic element resembling platinum. Source: ores of copper, gold, platinum. Use: catalyst, in electrical contacts, jewellery, dental alloys, medical instruments. Symbol Pd. See table at **element** [Early 19C. < Greek Pallad-, stem of Pallas, epithet of Athena and name given to an asteroid discovered shortly before the element] —**palladic** /pə láddik, -láy-/ adj —**palladous** /pə láydəss, pálledəss/ adj

palladium[2] /pə láydi əm/ (plural **-diums** or **-dia** /-di ə/) n 1. a protection or safeguard, especially one protecting social and civic institutions 2. also **Palladium** an object believed to have the power to protect a city or nation, especially the statue of Pallas Athena that was believed to protect Troy [14C. Via Latin < Greek palladion < Pallas, epithet of Athena]

Pallas /pálləss/ n 1. the second largest asteroid, discovered in 1802. It has an average diameter of approximately 530 km/330 mi. 2. also **Pallas Athena** MYTHOL same as **Athena**

Pallas's cat /pállssiz-/ n a small wild cat with small ears and luxurious grey fur with dark stripes. Native to: mountains of Tibet and Siberia. Latin name: Felis manul. [After Peter Pallas (1741–1811), German naturalist]

pallbearer /páwl bairər/ n a bearer or escort of a coffin at a funeral or burial

pallet[1] /pállət/ n 1. PLATFORM FOR LOADS a standardized platform or open-ended box, usually made of wood, that allows mechanical handling of bulk goods during transport and storage 2. CLAY-WORKING TOOL a wooden tool similar to a knife, used to mix and shape ceramic clay 3. BOARD FOR DRYING CERAMICS a board on which ceramic pieces are dried 4. GILDING TOOL a tool for manipulating gold leaf in gilding 5. MECH ENG REGULATING LEVER IN TIMEPIECE a lever that regulates a ratchet wheel, especially one that regulates the movement of the balance wheel or pendulum in a timepiece by transmitting movements from the escape wheel. The pallet's function is to convert rotary to reciprocating motion, or vice versa. 6. MUSIC VALVE ON ORGAN a valve on an organ that opens in order to let air into a pipe [15C. < French palette 'small blade or spade' < Latin pala 'spade, shovel']

SPELLCHECK See *palate*.

pallet[2] /pállət/ n 1. a straw-filled mattress 2. a temporary and usually uncomfortable bed, made from materials at hand [14C. < Anglo-Norman paillete < paille 'straw' < Latin palea]

palletize /pálle tīz/ (**-izes**, **-izing**, **-ized**), **palletise** (**-ises**, **-ising**, **-ised**) vt to put, transport, or store a load of something on a standardized platform

pallia plural of **pallium**

palliasse /pálli ass, -áss/ n a straw-filled mattress [Late 18C. Alteration of PAILLASSE]

palliate /pálli ayt/ (**-ates**, **-ating**, **-ated**) vt 1. MITIGATE INTENSITY OF SOMETHING to reduce the intensity or severity of something 2. PARTIALLY EXCUSE SOMETHING BAD to make or attempt to make an offence seem less serious by providing excuses or mitigating evidence 3. ALLEVIATE SYMPTOMS to alleviate a symptom without curing the underlying medical condition [15C. < Latin palliat- past participle of palliare 'cover, hide' < pallium 'covering'] —**palliation** /pálli áysh'n/ n —**palliator** n

palliative /pálli ətiv/ adj 1. SOOTHING soothing anxieties or other intense emotions 2. TREATING SYMPTOMS ONLY alleviating pain and symptoms without eliminating the cause ■ n SYMPTOM-TREATING MEDICINE something that palliates, especially a medicine that treats symptoms only —**palliatively** adv

palliative care n the treatment and relief of mental and physical pain without curing the causes, especially in patients suffering from a terminal illness

pallid /pállid/ adj 1. having an unhealthily pale complexion 2. lacking colour, spirit, or intensity [Late 16C. < Latin pallidus < pallere 'be pale'] —**pallidity** /pə líddəti/ n —**pallidly** adv

Palliser, Cape /pállissər/ southernmost point of the North Island, New Zealand, situated at the eastern end of the Cook Strait

pallium /pálli əm/ (plural **-lia** /-li ə/ or **-liums**) n 1. a white vestment that rests on the shoulders with pendants hanging at its front and back, worn by a pope, all Roman Catholic archbishops, and some bishops 2. ZOOL, BIRDS same as **mantle** n (sense 6), v (sense 2) 3. ANAT same as **cerebral cortex** (technical) 4. ANCIENT HIST a man's rectangular cloak worn in ancient Rome [Late 16C. < Latin, 'covering'] —**pallial** adj

pall-mall /páll máll/ n 1. a 17th-century game in which players used a mallet to hit a wooden ball through an iron hoop suspended at the end of a long alley 2. an alley in which pall-mall is played [Mid-16C. Via obsolete French palle maille < Italian pallamaglio < balla 'ball' + maglio 'mallet']

pallor /pállər/ n an unhealthy-looking paleness of complexion [14C. < Latin pallere 'be pale']

pally /pálli/ (**-lier**, **-liest**) adj having a friendly relationship (informal)

palm[1] /paam/ n 1. INNER SURFACE OF HAND the inner surface of the hand, extending from the base of the fingers

to the wrist **2. UNDERSIDE OF MAMMAL'S FOREFOOT** the part of a mammal's forefoot that is most often in contact with the ground **3. HAND-SIZED MEASURE** a unit of length, based on the length or width of a hand **4. COVERING FOR PALM OF HAND** something that covers the palm of the hand, e.g. the inner hand surface of a glove **5. BIOL FLAT PART OF BRANCHED STRUCTURE** the broad flat lobe of a branched structure such as the antler of a moose or deer or a cactus stalk **6. ROWING OAR BLADE** the blade of an oar **7. NAUT FACE OF ANCHOR POINT** the inner face of an anchor's point ■ *vt* (**palms, palming, palmed**) **1. HIDE ITEM IN HAND** to hide something in the hand, especially as part of a trick **2. TAKE SOMETHING STEALTHILY** to take something secretly by hiding it in the hand **3. TOUCH SOMETHING** to touch something with the palm **4. BASKETBALL HOLD BALL BRIEFLY** to let a basketball come to rest in the hands during a dribble, thereby committing a foul [12C. Via French *paume* < Latin *palma* 'palm of the hand'] ◇ **have somebody** *or* **something in the palm of your hand** to have complete power or influence over somebody or something
palm off *vt* **1.** to give or pass on something unwanted to somebody else ○ *Don't try to palm off that old armchair on me!* **2.** to shift something into another's possession in a deceitful way ○ *palmed off counterfeit money on unsuspecting shopkeepers.*

palm² /paam/ *n* **1. BOT** same as **palm tree 2.** a leaf from a palm tree, used as a symbol of victory or success **3.** a small decoration shaped like a palm leaf that is added to a military decoration to show that it has been awarded to the wearer more than once [Old English, via Germanic < Latin *palma* 'palm tree, palm of the hand' (because a cluster of palm leaves was thought to look like a hand and fingers)]

Palma /pálmə/ port on Majorca. It is the capital city of the Spanish Balearic Islands. Population: 319,181 (1998). Full name **Palma de Mallorca**

palmar /pálmər/ *adj* relating to the palm of the hand or to the underside of an animal's forefoot [Mid-17C. < Latin *palmaris* < *palma* 'palm of the hand']

palmate /pál mayt, -mət/, **palmated** /pál maytəd/ *adj* **1.** describes leaves that have five or more lobes arising from a single point, spreading like fingers from a hand **2.** describes birds' feet that have three webbed toes [Mid-18C. < Latin *palmatus* < *palma* 'palm of the hand'] —**palmately** *adv*

Palm Beach /paam-/ town in southeastern Florida on the Atlantic Ocean. It is a fashionable winter resort. Population: 9,766 (2002 estimate).

palmchat /paám chat/ *n* a gregarious bird that is olive-brown above and yellow with dark streaks below. Native to: open woodlands and cultivated fields in the Caribbean. Latin name: *Dulus dominicus.* [< PALM²]

palm civet *n* a mammal with short legs and sharp claws that lives in trees. Native to: Africa, Asia. Family: Viverridae. [< PALM²]

palmcorder /paám kawrdər/ *n* a small portable video camera and recorder that fits in the palm of the hand [Late 20C. < PALM¹ + RECORDER]

AKG London
Olof Palme

Palme /pálmə/, **Olof** (1927–86) prime minister of Sweden (1969–76 and 1982–86). A Social Democrat, he supported liberation movements and condemned superpower intervention in the developing world. He was killed by an unknown assassin. Full name **Palme, Sven Olof Joachim**

'It is an illusion to believe that you can meet demands for social justice with vio-

lence and military might. It is extremely difficult to gain people's loyalty with promises to defend a freedom which, in actuality, they have never been able to experience.'
[Olof Palme, *Speech, Social Democrat conference, Gävle, Sweden*; 1965]

palmer /paámər/ *n* a pilgrim, especially a medieval Christian pilgrim who carried or wore palm leaves as proof of a visit to the Holy Land [14C. Via Anglo-Norman < medieval Latin *palmarius* < Latin *palma* 'palm tree' (see PALM²)]

Express Newspapers
Arnold Palmer

Palmer /paámər/, **Arnold** (*b.* 1929) US golfer. He has won the US Masters (1958, 1960, 1962, and 1964), the US Open (1960), and the British Open (1961, 1962) tournaments.

Palmer, **Sir Geoffrey** (*b.* 1942) prime minister of New Zealand (1989–90). He joined the Labour Party in 1975 and was elected to Parliament in 1979. He succeeded David Russell Lange as prime minister but was defeated in the following year's elections. Full name **Palmer, Sir Geoffrey Winston Russell**. See table at **prime minister**

Palmerston /paámərstən/, **Henry John Temple, 3rd Viscount** (1784–1865) prime minister of Great Britain (1855–58 and 1859–65). Changing from Tory to Whig (1830), he served three terms as foreign secretary and two as prime minister. Known as **Firebrand Palmerston**

'We have no eternal allies and we have no perpetual enemies. Our interests are eternal and perpetual, and those interests it is our duty to follow.'
[Henry John Temple Palmerston, *Speech to Parliament*; 1 March 1848]

Palmerston North city in the south of the North Island, New Zealand, situated 140 km/87 mi. north of Wellington. Population: 72,681 (2001).

palmette /pal mét/ *n* a stylized palm leaf used as an ornament or in a decoration [Mid-19C. < French, literally 'small palm tree' < Latin *palma* 'palm tree' (see PALM²)]

palmetto /pal méttō/ (*plural* **-tos** *or* **-toes**) *n* **1.** a low-growing palm plant with fan-shaped leaves, especially the cabbage palmetto **2.** the blade of a palmetto leaf. Use: weaving. [Mid-16C. < Spanish *palmito* 'small palm tree' < Latin *palma* 'palm tree' (see PALM²)]

palmist /paámist/ *n* somebody who practises palmistry

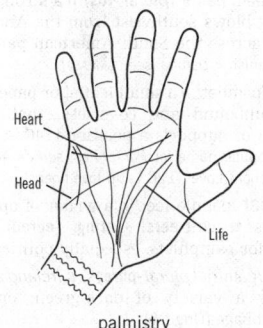
Heart
Head
Life
palmistry

palmistry /paámistri/ *n* the practice of examining the features of somebody's palms supposedly in order to predict that person's destiny [15C. < PALM¹]

palmitate /pálmi tayt/ *n* a salt or ester of palmitic acid

palmitic acid /pal míttik-/ *n* a waxy acid. Source: plant and animal fats and oils. Use: manufacture of soap, candles, food additives. Formula: $C_{15}H_{31}COOH$. [< French *palmitique* < *palme* (see PALMITIN)]

palmitin /pálmitin/ *n* an ester of palmitic acid and glycerol. Source: animal fats, palm oil. Use: soap-making. [Mid-19C. < French *palmitine* < *palme* 'palm tree' < Latin *palma* (see PALM²)]

palm oil *n* a yellowish oil extracted from the fruit of oil palms. Use: lubricants, soap, cosmetics, foods. [< PALM²]

Palm Springs town in southern California, a resort and residential centre. Population: 44,526 (2002 estimate).

palm sugar *n* sugar made from palm tree sap [< PALM²]

Palm Sunday *n* a Christian religious day marking Jesus Christ's triumphal entry into Jerusalem through a crowd waving palm branches. Date: Sunday before Easter. [< PALM²]

palmtop /paám top/ *n* a computer with a miniature keyboard and screen that fits into the palm of the hand [Late 20C. < PALM¹, after LAPTOP]

palm tree

palm tree *n* a tree, bush, or plant typically with a trunk without branches and a crown of pinnate or palmate leaves on top. Native to: tropics, subtropics. Family: Palmae. [< PALM²]

palm wine *n* an alcoholic drink made from fermented palm sap, common in parts of Africa [< PALM²]

palmy /paámi/ (**-ier**, **-iest**) *adj* **1.** relating to, consisting of, or abundant in palm trees **2.** prosperous or flourishing, especially formerly (*literary*) ○ *in her palmy days* [Late 16C. < PALM²]

palmyra /pal mírə/ (*plural* **-ras** *or* *same*) *n* a tall fan-leafed palm tree whose fronds, wood, and sap are harvested for various uses. Native to: Asia. Latin name: *Borassus flabellifer.* [Late 17C. Alteration (influenced by *Palmyra*, ancient city in Syria) of Portuguese *palmeira* 'palm tree' < Latin *palma* (see PALM²)]

Palo Alto /pállō áltō/ city in western California on San Francisco Bay. The city developed after the establishment of nearby Stanford University, and it is a centre for computing technology. Population: 57,543 (2002 estimate).

Palomar, Mount /pállə maar/ mountain in southern California, northeast of San Diego. It is the site of an astronomical observatory with one of the largest refracting telescopes in the world. Height: 1,871 m/6,138 ft.

palomino /pállə meénō/ (*plural* **-nos**) *n* a golden-coloured horse with a pale mane and tail, originally bred in the southwestern United States [Early 20C. Via American Spanish < Latin *palumbinus* 'like a dove']

palooka /pə loókə/ *n* (*slang*) **1.** *N Am* an offensive term that deliberately insults somebody's physical coordination and intelligence **2.** *US* an easily beaten athlete, especially a boxer [Early 20C. Origin ?]

Palouse /pə loóss/ (*plural* *same* *or* **-louses**) *n* a member of a Native North American people who lived in southern Washington and northern Idaho, and who now live mainly in northern Washington —**Palouse** *adj*

paloverde /pállō vúrdi/ (*plural* **-des** or *same*) *n South-west US* TREES same as **Jerusalem thorn** [Early 19C. < American Spanish, 'green tree']

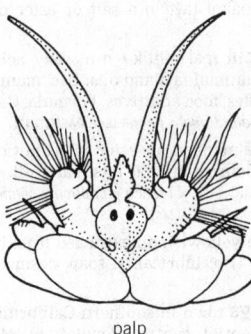

palp

palp /palp/ *n* a sensory appendage situated near the mouth of many invertebrate animals, used to assess or manipulate food before it is eaten [Mid-19C. Via French < Latin *palpus* < *palpare* 'touch gently, palpate']

palpable /pálpəb'l/ *adj* **1.** INTENSE so intense as to be almost able to be felt physically ○ *the palpable tension in the room* **2.** OBVIOUS obvious or easily observed ○ *a palpable need for change* **3.** MED ABLE TO BE FELT able to be felt by the hands, especially in a medical examination ○ *a palpable lump in the abdomen* [14C. < late Latin *palpabilis* < Latin *palpare* 'touch gently, palpate'] —**palpability** /pálpə bílləti/ *n* — **palpably** *adv*

palpate[1] /pal páyt/ (**-pates**, **-pating**, **-pated**) *vt* to examine a part of the body by feeling with the hands and fingers, especially to distinguish between swellings that are solid and those that are filled with fluid [15C. < Latin *palpat-*, past participle of *palpare* 'touch gently']

palpate[2] /pál payt/ *adj* describes an invertebrate organism that is equipped with one or more palps [Mid-19C. < PALP, PALPUS]

palpation /pal páysh'n/ *n* a method of clinical examination using gentle pressure of the fingers to detect growths, changes in the size of underlying organs, and unusual tissue reactions to pressure [Late 15C. < Latin *palpation-* 'stroking' < *palpat-* (see PALPATE[1])]

palpebral /pálpəbrəl/ *adj* relating to the eyelids [Mid-19C. < Latin *palpebra* 'eyelid']

palpi ZOOL plural of **palpus**

palpitate /pálpi tayt/ (**-tates**, **-tating**, **-tated**) *vi* to beat in an irregular or unusually rapid way, either because of a medical condition or because of exertion, fear, or anxiety (*refers to the heart*) [15C. < Latin *palpitat-*, past participle of *palpitare* < *palpare* 'touch gently, palpate'] —**palpitant** *adj*

palpitation /pálpi táysh'n/ *n* an irregular or unusually rapid beating of the heart, either because of a medical condition or because of exertion, fear, or anxiety (*usually used in the plural*)

palpus /pálpəss/ (*plural* **-pi** /-pee/) *n* ZOOL same as **palp** [Early 19C. < Latin (see PALP)]

palsgrave /páwlz grayv/ *n* a count palatine, especially in Germany [Mid-16C. < early Dutch *paltsgrave* < *palts* 'palatinate' + *grave* 'count']

palstave /páwl stayv/ *n* a metal axe that fits into a split handle, especially one of a distinctive bronze type found in ancient Europe [Mid-19C. < Danish *paalstav*]

palsy[1] /pálzi/ *adj* same as **palsy-walsy** (*slang*) [Mid-20C. < PAL]

palsy[2] /páwlzi/ *n* muscular inability to move part or all of the body (*archaic*) [13C. Via Old French *paralisie* < Latin *paralysis* (see PARALYSIS)]

palsy-walsy /pálzi wálzi/ *adj* very friendly, often in an insincere or unpleasant way (*slang*) [Mid-20C. Extension of PALSY[1]]

palter /páwltər/ (**-ters**, **-tering**, **-tered**) *vi* (*archaic*) **1.** to act or talk insincerely or deceitfully **2.** to haggle in bargaining [Mid-16C. Origin?] —**palterer** *n*

Paltrow /pál trō/, **Gwyneth** (*b.* 1972) US actor. A respected actor, she won an Academy Award for best

actress for *Shakespeare in Love* (1998) and *Sliding Doors* (1998).

paltry /páwltri, pól-/ (**-trier**, **-triest**) *adj* **1.** insignificant or unimportant ○ *a paltry sum of money* **2.** low and contemptible [Mid-16C. Probably < Scots, N English dialect *pelt* 'coarse cloth, rubbish'] —**paltrily** *adv* —**paltriness** *n*

paludal /pə lyoʻod'l, pállyoʻod'l/ *adj* relating to or living in swamps or marshes [Early 19C. < Latin *palud-* 'marsh']

paly /páyli/ *adj* describes a heraldic shield that is divided into equal-sized sections by vertical lines [15C. < French *palé* < *pal* (see PALE[2])]

palynology /pálli nólləji/ *n* the study of spores and pollen, including fossilized spores and pollen [Mid-20C. < Greek *palunein* 'to sprinkle'] —**palynological** /pállinə lójik'l/ *adj* —**palynologist** *n*

pam /pam/ *n* the jack of clubs in some card games such as loo, where it is the highest trump card [Late 17C. Shortening of French *pamphile* < Greek *Pamphilos*, personal name, literally 'loved by all']

Pama-Nyungan /paʻamə nyoʻongən/ *n* a large family of Aboriginal languages spoken in Australia. Native speakers: 100,000. [< two Aboriginal words for 'a man' (see NYUNGAR)] —**Pama-Nyungan** *adj*

~~**pamflet**~~ incorrect spelling of **pamphlet**

Pamirs /pə meʻerz/ mountainous region of Central Asia, located mainly in Tajikistan and extending to northeastern Afghanistan and northwestern China. The highest point is Ismail Samani Peak, 7,495 m/24,590 ft.

pampalam /pámpə lám/ *n Carib* confusion, fuss, or uproar [Late 20C. An imitation of the sound of noisy activity, perhaps after Twi *pam* 'sound of a gun', *pam pam* 'drive away']

pampas /pámpəss, -pəz/ *n* treeless grassy plains in temperate South America, especially Argentina (*takes a singular or plural verb*) [Early 18C. < Spanish, plural of *pampa* < Quechua, 'plain'] —**pampean** /pámpi ən, pam peʻe ən/ *adj*

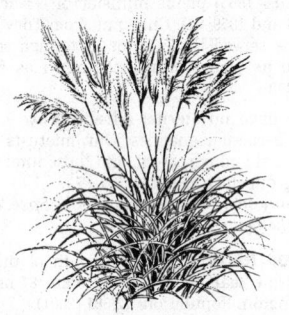

pampas grass

pampas grass *n* a tall grass with silky white flower plumes, often grown in parks and gardens. Native to: South America, naturalized in southern United States. Genus: *Cortaderia*.

pampelmoes /pámp'l moʻoss/ (*plural same*) *n S Africa* FOOD, TREES same as **pomelo** [Mid-18C. Via Afrikaans < Dutch]

pamper /pámpər/ (**-pers**, **-pering**, **-pered**) *vt* **1.** to lavish attention on somebody, indulging his or her taste for luxury **2.** to indulge or gratify a desire or need [14C. Probably < Low German or Dutch] —**pamperer** *n*

pampero /pam páirō/ (*plural* **-ros**) *n* a strong cold dry wind that blows southwest from the Andes to the Atlantic, across the South American pampas [Late 18C. < Spanish < *pampa* (see PAMPAS)]

pamphlet /pámflət/ *n* a small leaflet or paper booklet, usually unbound and coverless, that gives information or supports a position [14C. < *Pamphlet*, *Pamflet*, popular name for *Pamphilus, seu de Amore* 'Pamphilus, or about Love', 12C Latin love poem]

pamphleteer /pámflə teʻer/ *n* a writer of opinionated pamphlets ■ *vi* (**-eers**, **-eering**, **-eered**) to write material for pamphlets, especially political ones

pamphrey /pámfri/ (*plural* **-phreys**) *n Ireland* a cabbage, especially a variety of dark-green, open-leaved spring cabbage [Origin ?]

Pamplona /pam plóna/ city in northeastern Spain. It is the capital of the autonomous region of Navarre. Population: 198,364 (2002).

pan[1] /pan/ *n* **1.** COOKING POT a cooking pot, usually metal and with a handle, for use on the hob of a cooker **2.** CONTAINER FOR WASTE a shallow container that household waste is put into for easy disposal **3.** SHALLOW OPEN CONTAINER a shallow open container used to store, catch, or heat liquids or other substances ○ *drained the old oil into a pan* **4.** MIN EXTRACT DISH FOR SORTING MINERALS a flat metal dish, shaped like a pie plate, used to separate precious minerals, especially gold, from loose soil, gravel, or sediment **5.** MEASURE SCALE DISH either of the dishes suspended in a balance scale **6.** GEOG HOLLOWED PLACE IN DIRT a natural shallow sink or basin in the ground, usually filled with rainwater or mud **7.** GEOG same as **hardpan 8.** MIN EXTRACT SHALLOW AREA FOR EVAPORATING BRINE a natural or artificial concavity in the earth, in which brine is evaporated, leaving behind salt **9.** OCEANOG THIN ICE FLOE a small flat thin ice floe of the type that forms near a shore or in a bay **10.** ARMS PRIMING CONTAINER IN GUN the hollow part of a flintlock gun, into which the gunpowder is loaded **11.** MUSIC STEEL DRUM a metal drum played in steel bands ■ *v* (**pans**, **panning**, **panned**) **1.** *vt* CRITICIZE SEVERELY to criticize somebody or something severely, especially in a review (*informal*) **2.** *vi* MIN EXTRACT SORT THROUGH DIRT FOR MINERALS to use a shallow dish to separate valuable minerals from loose soil, gravel, or sediment by washing or shaking **3.** *vi* MIN EXTRACT YIELD PRECIOUS METALS to yield valuable metals when separating minerals and leavings by means of washing or shaking using a shallow dish ■ *prep* same as **on**, **upon** (*slang; used in Black English*) [Old English *panne* < Germanic]
pan out *vi* (*informal*) **1.** to turn out or result ○ *After all our careful planning, it's a shame that things didn't pan out as we had hoped.* **2.** to turn out well or successfully ○ *Her new career never panned out.* [< panning for gold]

pan[2] /pan/ *vti* (**pans**, **panning**, **panned**) to move a camera horizontally from a stationary point in order to capture a broad view or a moving object, or be moved in this way ■ *n* a horizontal movement of a camera from a fixed point, or the resulting filmed shot [Early 20C. Shortening of PANORAMA]

pan[3] /paan/, **paan** *n* in South and Southeast Asia, a betel leaf wrapped over a betel nut, often garnished with spices and lime, and chewed as a stimulant, especially after a meal [Early 17C. < Hindi *pān*]

Pan /pan/ *n* **1.** in Greek mythology, the god of nature, pastures, flocks, and forests, believed to have a human torso and head, and the hind legs, ears, and horns of a goat. Roman equivalent **Faunus 2.** the small innermost natural satellite of Saturn

PAN *abbr* E-COMMERCE primary account number

pan- *prefix* all, any, everyone ○ *panchromatic* ○ *Pan-Slavism* [< Greek]

panacea /pánnə seʻe ə/ *n* a supposed cure for all diseases or problems [Mid-16C. Via Latin < Greek *panakeia* < *panakēs* 'all-healing' < *akos* 'remedy'] —**panacean** *adj*

panache /pə násh/ *n* **1.** a sense or display of spirited style and self-confidence **2.** a plume or tuft of feathers, especially on a hat or helmet [Mid-16C. Via French < Italian *pennacchio* 'plume of feathers' < Latin *pinna* 'feather']

panada /pə naʻadə/ *n* a very thick paste of flour or another starchy ingredient and a liquid such as milk or stock. Use: base for sauces, binding for stuffing. [Late 16C. < Spanish or Portuguese < Latin *panis* 'bread']

Pan-African *adj* **1.** relating to the nations of Africa, collectively or in cooperation with one another **2.** advocating freedom and independence for African people —**Pan-Africanism** *n*

Panaji /púnnəji/ capital of Goa state in western India. Population: 51,872 (2001).

panama /pánnə maa, pánnə maʻa/ *n* CLOTHING same as **panama hat** [Mid-19C. < PANAMA]

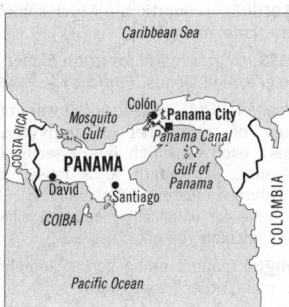

Panama

Panama /pánnə maa, -maá/ country in Central America. It has the Caribbean Sea to its north and the Pacific Ocean to its south, connected by the Panama Canal, and is situated between Costa Rica and Colombia. Capital: Panama City. Population: 2,960,784 (2001). Area: 75,517 sq. km/29,157 sq. mi. Official name **Republic of Panama**

Panama, Isthmus of isthmus connecting North and South America and separating the Pacific Ocean and the Caribbean Sea

Panama Canal canal across the Isthmus of Panama, completed in 1914. Length: 64 km/40 mi.

Panama City capital city of Panama, located in the centre of the country, on the Pacific Ocean. Population: 463,093 (2000).

panama hat *n* a brimmed men's hat made from the plaited leaves of the jipijapa, or an imitation of such a hat

Panamanian /pánnə máyni ən/ *n* somebody who comes from Panama ■ *adj* relating to Panama [Mid-19C. < PANAMA + -*n*- for euphony]

Pan-American *adj* relating to the nations of North, South, and Central America, collectively or in co-operation with one another —**Pan-Americanism** *n*

Pan-Arabism *n* a movement for greater cooperation among and self-reliance within Arab or Islamic nations —**Pan-Arab** *n, adj* —**Pan-Arabic** *adj* —**Pan-Arabist** *n, adj*

panatella /pánnə téllə/, **panatela** *n* a long thin cigar that does not bulge in the middle [Mid-19C. Via American Spanish, 'long thin biscuit' < Italian *panatello* 'small loaf' < Latin *panis* 'bread']

Panathenaea /pan áthə née ə/ *n* a summer festival held annually in ancient Athens but with an extra ceremony every fourth year. It involved games, sacrifices, and music and poetry contests. [Early 17C. < Greek *panathēnaia hiera* 'festival of all Athenians']

pancake /pán kayk/ *n* **1.** THIN FRIED CAKE a thin flat cake made by pouring batter onto a hot greased flat pan, and cooking it on both sides **2.** *Scotland* same as **drop scone 3.** AVIAT same as **pancake landing** ■ *v* (-**cakes**, -**caking**, -**caked**) **1.** *vti* MAKE PANCAKE LANDING to make a pancake landing, or cause an aircraft to make a pancake landing **2.** *vt US* POSITION SOMETHING FLAT to turn something parallel to the ground, especially a tennis racket in the course of a stroke

Pancake Day *n* CHR same as **Shrove Tuesday** [< the practice of making pancakes to use up eggs and fat before Lent]

pancake ice *n* a small flat thin piece of sea ice that drifts out into deeper water from near the shore or the bay in which it was formed

pancake landing *n* an aeroplane landing in which the aircraft drops abruptly straight to the ground from a low altitude, usually because of engine failure

pancake tortoise *n* a turtle with a flattened flexible shell, which can slip between rocks and narrow crevices and then slightly inflate to resist being pulled out. Native to: Tanzania. Latin name: *Malachersus tornieri*.

Pancake Tuesday *n* CHR same as **Shrove Tuesday**

pancetta /pan chéttə/ *n* a salt-cured and spiced form of belly of pork, used in Italian dishes [Mid-20C. < Italian, literally 'little belly' < Latin *pantix* 'bowel, intestine']

panchayat /pun chí ət/ *n S Asia* a village council [Early 19C. Via Hindi *pañcāyat* < Sanskrit *pañcāyatta* 'depending on five' (the original number of members)]

Panchen Lama /púnchən-/ *n* in Tibetan Buddhism, a lama of the second highest rank [< Tibetan, contraction of *pandi-tachen-po* 'great learned one']

panchromatic /pán krō máttik/ *adj* describes photographic film that is sensitive to all visible colours and some ultraviolet light

pancratium /pan kráyshi əm/ (*plural* -**tia** /-shi ə/) *n* in ancient Greece, an athletic event involving boxing and wrestling contests [Early 17C. Via Latin < Greek *pagkration* < *kratos* 'strength'] —**pancratic** /-kráttik/ *adj*

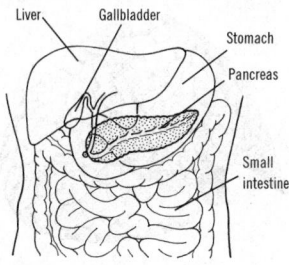

pancreas

pancreas /pángkri əss/ *n* a large elongated glandular organ lying near the stomach. It secretes juices into the small intestine and the hormones insulin, glucagon, and somatostatin into the bloodstream. [Late 16C. Via modern Latin < Greek *pagkreas* < *kreas* 'flesh'] —**pancreatic** /pángkri áttik/ *adj*

pancreat- *prefix* pancreas ○ *pancreatitis* [Via modern Latin < Greek *pagkreat-*, stem of *pagkreas* (see PANCREAS)]

pancreatectomy /pángkri ə téktəmi/ (*plural* -**mies**) *n* whole or partial removal of the pancreas by surgery

pancreatic duct *n* a duct that carries pancreatic juice and, in human beings, runs from the pancreas to join the common bile duct, which empties into the small intestine

pancreatic juice, pancreatic fluid *n* a watery alkaline fluid secreted by the pancreas. It contains enzymes that break down partially digested food in the small intestine.

pancreatin /pángkri ətin, pan krée-/ *n* **1.** a digestive aid made from a mixture of pancreatic enzymes extracted from domestic animals **2.** the mixture of digestive enzymes produced by the pancreas, including amylase, lipase, and trypsin

pancreatitis /pángkri ə títiss/ *n* inflammation of the pancreas

pancreozymin /pángkri ō zímin/ *n* BIOCHEM same as **cholecystokinin** [Mid-20C. < PANCREAS + *zymin*, enzyme < Greek *zumē* 'leaven']

pancytopenia /pán sītō péeni ə/ *n* MED same as **aplastic anaemia**

panda

panda /pándə/ *n* **1.** a large bamboo-eating mammal with bold black-and-white markings, including black patches over the eyes. Native to: central China. Latin name: *Ailuropodia melanoleuca*. **2.** ZOOL same as **red panda** [Mid-19C. Via French < Nepalese, 'red panda']

panda car *n* a police patrol car (*informal*) [< the resemblance of its paintwork to the giant panda's markings]

pandanus /pan dáynəss/ (*plural* -**nuses** or *same*) *n* a plant resembling a palm, with prop roots and a crown of narrow leaves. Use: mat-making. Native to: tropics. Genus: *Pandanus*. [Mid-19C. Via modern Latin < Malay *pandan*]

Pandean /pan dée ən/ *adj* relating to the mythological Greek god Pan [Early 19C. Irregularly < PAN]

pandect /pán dekt/ *n* **1.** a set of documents containing all the laws of a country or society **2.** a comprehensive treatise on a subject [Mid-16C. Directly or via French < Latin *pandecta* < Greek *pandektēs* 'all-receiving' < *dekhesthai* 'receive']

pandemic /pan démmik/ *adj* existing in the form of a widespread epidemic that affects people in many different countries. Aids is currently considered to be pandemic. ■ *n* a disease or condition that is found in a large part of a population [Mid-17C. < Greek *pandēmos* 'of all the people' < *dēmos* 'people']

pandemonium /pándə mōni əm/ *n* **1.** wild uproar and chaos **2.** a place or situation that is noisy and chaotic [Late 18C. < *Pandaemonium*, capital of Hell in Milton's *Paradise Lost* < modern Latin, 'home of all the demons' < Greek *daimōn* 'divine power, guiding spirit'] —**pandemoniac** *adj* —**pandemonic** /-mónnik/ *adj*

pander /pándər/ *vi* (-**ders**, -**dering**, -**dered**) **1.** INDULGE WEAKNESSES to indulge somebody's weaknesses or questionable wishes and tastes ○ *tired of pandering to their children's demands* **2.** PROCURE SEXUAL FAVOURS to procure sexual favours for somebody (*archaic*) ■ *n* **1.** *also* **panderer** INDULGENT PERSON somebody who indulges somebody else's weaknesses or questionable wishes and tastes **2.** *also* **panderer** ROMANTIC GO-BETWEEN a go-between in an illicit or secret romantic or sexual relationship (*dated*) **3.** same as **pimp** (*dated*) [14C. < *Pandare*, character in Chaucer's *Troilus & Criseyde* who procures Criseyde for Troilus]

P and H, p. and h., p&h *abbr US* MAIL postage and handling

pandit /pándit/ *n* a wise or learned Hindu man, especially a Brahman who is an expert in Hindu culture, law, and philosophy [Mid-19C. Variant of PUNDIT]

P & L *abbr* ACCT profit and loss

Pandora /pan dáwrə/ *n* **1.** in Greek mythology, the first woman, who was sent by the gods with a jar full of evils in order to avenge Prometheus's theft of fire. She opened the jar out of curiosity, thus releasing the evils into the world. **2.** a small inner natural satellite of Saturn, discovered in 1980 by Voyager 2. It is irregular in shape with a maximum dimension of 110 km/68 mi.

Pandora's box *n* **1.** in Greek mythology, the jar, later referred to as a box, from which Pandora allowed all the world's evils to escape **2.** the source of a great collection of ills that need not be faced unless an unwise action is taken ○ *If you criticize her work, you'll be opening a real Pandora's box.*

pandowdy /pan dówdi/ (*plural* -**dies**) *n US* a dish made of sliced apples and spices covered with a biscuit crust and baked in a deep pan [Mid-19C. Probably < PAN[1] + variant of DOUGH]

p & p *abbr* SHIPPING postage and packing

pane /payn/ *n* **1.** GLAZED SECTION OF WINDOW a glazed section of a window or door **2.** PIECE OF GLASS IN WINDOW a piece of plate glass in a window or door **3.** SECTION OF SURFACE a distinct section of a surface such as a door or wall **4.** SURFACE OF FACETED OBJECT a surface on a faceted object such as a metal nut or cut jewel **5.** SECTION OF SHEET OF STAMPS a rectangular section into which a sheet of postage stamps is divided before being sold [13C. Via French < Latin *pannus* 'piece of cloth']

SPELLCHECK See **pain**.

paneer /pa née r/, **panir** *n S Asia* a curd cheese used especially as an ingredient in cooking [< Hindi and Persian *panir* 'cheese']

panegyric /pánnə jírrik/ *n* extravagant praise delivered in formal speech or writing [Early 17C. Via French < Latin *panegyricus* 'public eulogy' < Greek *panēguris* 'public assembly' < *aguris* 'assembly, marketplace'] —**panegyrical** *adj* —**panegyrically** *adv* —**panegyrist** *n*

panel /pánn'l/ n **1.** FLAT RECTANGULAR PART a flat rectangular piece of hard material that serves as a part of something such as a door or wall, often raised above or sunk in the surface **2.** FENCE SECTION a section between two posts in a fence or gate **3.** STRIP OF FABRIC IN GARMENT a vertical section of fabric sewn onto other such sections in a flowing garment or drapery **4.** WOODEN SURFACE FOR PAINTING a thin piece of wood used as a surface for oil painting, or the painting on it **5.** COMIC STRIP FRAME a section depicting a single scene in a comic strip **6.** PART OF AIRCRAFT WING a section or surface of an aeroplane wing **7.** CLUSTER OF PERFORMANCE-MEASURING INSTRUMENTS a surface on which performance-measuring instruments such as gauges, dials, lights, and digital displays are clustered **8.** CONTROL AREA OF COMPUTER the collection of lights, digital displays, and switches used to monitor and control the operation of a computer **9.** DISPLAY ON COMPUTER SCREEN a display of related information on a computer screen, often a list of options **10.** GROUP OF JUDGES OR SPEAKERS a group of people who publicly discuss or judge something, usually in a situation where they sit in a row to face an audience or a competition arena **11.** LIST OF PEOPLE FOR JURY DUTY a list of people summoned as potential jurors, or the people themselves **12.** JURY a jury in a court proceeding **13.** Scotland ACCUSED PERSON an accused person or group of accused people brought into court to face charges ■ vt (**-els, -elling, -elled**) **1.** COVER SOMETHING WITH PANELS to furnish, cover, or decorate something with panels, especially wooden panelling for walls **2.** PUT JURORS ON PANEL to make a list of potential jurors or select a jury from such a list **3.** Scotland INDICT SOMEBODY to indict somebody for a crime [14C. < Old French, 'piece of cloth' < Latin pannus]

panel beater n a person or business that repairs car bodies, especially by beating out dents

panel heating n a domestic heating system in which heating elements are housed in panels attached to walls or floors

paneling n US spelling of **panelling**

panelist n US spelling of **panellist**

panelling /pánn'ling/ n **1.** thin boards or sheets of wood for covering walls, especially as decoration **2.** a panel-covered wall or other surface

panellist /pánn'list/ n a member of a panel

panel truck n N Am a small delivery van that is entirely enclosed, with access to the storage area from the driver's seat

panel van n ANZ a small van with rear doors, used for carrying goods and tools

panettone /pánnə tóni/ (plural **-nes** or **-ni** /-tóni/) n a tall Italian yeast cake flavoured with vanilla and dried and candied fruits, traditionally eaten at Christmas [Early 20C. < Italian pane 'bread' < Latin panis]

Pan-European adj relating to all the nations of Europe, collectively or in cooperation with one another

pan fish n N Am any small freshwater food fish, considered too small to be classed as a game fish, that is the right size to fry whole in a frying pan

pan-fry vt to fry food, usually fish or meat, in a frying pan with a little fat

pang /pang/ n **1.** a short sharp pain **2.** a sudden, intense, and usually distressing feeling [15C. Origin ?]

panga /páng gə/ n an African knife with a long broad heavy blade, often used for cutting down sugar cane [Mid-20C. < Kiswahili]

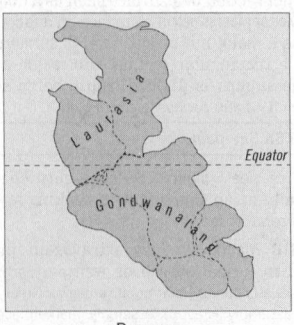

Pangaea

Pangaea /pan jeé ə/ n a hypothetical ancient supercontinent incorporating all the Earth's major landmasses. It is thought to have begun splitting up about 200 million years ago.

Pangasinan /pán gassi naán/ (plural same or **-nans**) n **1.** a member of a people who live in the province of Pangasinan in central Luzon in the Philippines **2.** the Austronesian language spoken by Pangasinan people [Mid-19C. < Pangasinan, 'region of salty ponds'] — **Pangasinan** adj

Panglossian /pan glóssi ən/ adj excessively and inappropriately optimistic (literary) [Mid-19C. After Dr Pangloss, philosopher in Voltaire's Candide (1759)]

pangolin

pangolin /páng gəlin, pang gólin/ n a mammal with horny scales, a long tapering snout and tail, and a long sticky tongue for catching ants and termites. Native to: Africa and Asia. Order: Pholidota. [Late 18C. < Malay peng-guling, literally 'roller'; because it rolls itself up when frightened]

panhandle[1] /pán hand'l/ n **1.** the handle of a cooking pan **2.** also **Panhandle** N Am a narrow section of land shaped like the handle of a cooking pan that extends away from the body of the US state or territory it belongs to ○ the Texas Panhandle [< PAN[1]]

panhandle[2] /pán hand'l/ (**-dles, -dling, -dled**) vti N Am to beg for money on the street by approaching and talking to passers-by [Late 19C. Probably < a supposed resemblance of an arm stretched out to beg to the handle of a pan] —**panhandler** n

Panhellenic /pán he lénnik/ adj relating to all Greek peoples or all of Greece

Panhellenism /pán héllənizəm/ n a philosophy or movement advocating a single political system for all Greek people

pani /paáni/ n S Asia water [Early 19C. Via Hindi pānī < Sanskrit pānīya]

panic[1] /pánnik/ n OVERPOWERING FEAR OR ANXIETY a sudden feeling of fear or anxiety, especially among many people, that comes on suddenly, is overwhelming, appears to be uncontrollable, and may seem to be unfounded ■ adj INVOLVING OR RESULTING FROM PANIC relating to, responding to, or resulting from panic or possible panic ○ panic selling on the stock market ■ vti (**-ics, -icking, -icked**) BE OR MAKE SOMEBODY EXTREMELY AFRAID to feel panic, or make a person or animal feel panic [Early 17C. < French panique < modern Latin panicus 'terrified' < Greek panikos < Pan, god of nature, thought to inspire fear] —**panicky** /pánniki/ adj

panic[2] /pánnik/, **pannick** n PLANTS same as **panic grass** [15C. < Latin panicum 'foxtail']

Panic /pánnik/ adj same as **Pandean** [< PAN (sense 1)]

panic attack n a sudden overpowering feeling of fear or anxiety that prevents somebody from functioning, often triggered by a past or present source of anxiety

panic bolt n a bolt released by a waist-high bar that is fitted on emergency exit doors in buildings used by large numbers of people

panic button n an alarm to call security staff or summon help in an emergency ◇ **hit** or **press** or **push the panic button** to react to a perceived emergency or crisis by panicking and responding too hastily (informal)

panic buying n the buying of a product in quantity by a large number of people who fear a possible shortage

panic disorder n a condition in which somebody has recurrent panic attacks

panic grass n a grass used for grain fodder and as a cereal, e.g. millet. Genus: Panicum. [< PANIC[2]]

panicle /pánnik'l/ n **1.** a cluster of flowers on a plant consisting of a number of individual stalks (**racemes**), each of which has a series of single flowers along its length **2.** a loose branching pyramid-shaped cluster of flowers [Late 16C. < Latin panicula 'little ear of millet' < panus 'swelling, ear of millet'] —**paniculate** /pə níkyoŏlət/ adj

panicmonger /pánnik mung gər/ n somebody who tends to make other people panic

panic room n a fortified room within a house, often equipped with high-tech security devices, where people can hide to protect themselves from attack or theft

panic stations n a state of panic, confusion, and commotion immediately following an unexpected event that requires immediate action (informal; takes a singular verb)

panic-stricken, **panic-struck** adj suddenly affected by or characterized by panic

~~**panicy**~~ incorrect spelling of **panicky**

panini /pa neéni/ npl Italian white bread rolls, or sandwiches made with them [Mid-20C. < Italian, plural of panino 'small bread' < pane 'bread']

Panislamism /pán iz laámizəm, pan ízləmizəm/ n a movement that aims to unify Islamic countries and spread the Islamic religion —**Panislamic** /pániz lámmik/ adj—**Panislamist** /pán iz laámist, pan ízləmist/ n, adj

Panjabi n, adj LANG, PEOPLES another spelling of **Punjabi**

panjandrum /pan jándrəm/ (plural **-drums** or **-dra** /-drə/) n somebody, especially an official, who is pompous or pretentious [Mid-18C. Invented word]

ORIGIN *Panjandrum* was coined in 1755 by the English actor and playwright Samuel Foote (1720–77) to test the memory of the actor Charles Macklin, who claimed to be able to memorize and repeat anything said to him (it was one of several inventions in the same vein that Foote put to him): 'And there were present the Picninnies, and the Joblillies, and the Garyulies, and the Grand Panjandrum himself, with the little round button at top'. It did not spread into general use until the 19th century.

Emmeline Pankhurst

Pankhurst /pángk hurst/, **Emmeline** (1858–1928) British suffragette. She founded the Women's Social and Political Union (1903) in Manchester. She was frequently imprisoned for destroying property, but during World War I she abandoned her campaign and encouraged women to do industrial war work.

'We have taken this action, because as women...we realize that the condition of our sex is so deplorable that it is our duty even to break the law in order to call attention to the reasons why we do so.' [Emmeline Pankhurst, Speech in court; 21 October 1908]

panleucopenia /pán lookō peéni ə/, **panleukopenia** n VET same as **feline distemper** (technical)

pan loaf n regional a baker's loaf of white bread with a thin soft crust all the way round it that is baked individually in a tin ■ adj, adv Scotland with an

affected way of speaking (*informal humorous*) [Because baked in a pan]

panmixia /pan míksi ə/, **panmixis** /-míksiss/ *n* random breeding and free interchange of genes within a population [Late 19C. Via modern Latin < German *Panmixie* 'all mixing' < Greek *mixis* 'mixing, mingling'] — **panmictic** *adj*

panne /pan/ *n* a lightweight silk or rayon fabric resembling velvet [Late 18C. < French]

pannick *n* PLANTS another spelling of **panic**[2]

pannier /pánni ər/ *n* 1. BASKET ON PACK ANIMAL a large basket, often one of a pair, that is placed on the back of a horse, donkey, or other pack animal 2. BAG ON BICYCLE one of a pair of bags carried on either side of the back or front wheel of a bicycle or motorcycle 3. FRAMEWORK TO WIDEN SKIRT a framework of cane worn by women in the 18th century at each side of the hips to widen a skirt 4. OVERSKIRT LOOPED UP AT HIPS an overskirt looped up at the hips to show the underskirt and give the impression of fullness, worn by women in the second half of the 19th century [13C. Via Old French *pannier* < Latin *panarium* 'breadbasket' < *panis* 'bread']

pannikin /pánnikin/ *n* a small metal drinking cup [Early 19C. < PAN[1], after CANNIKIN]

Panoan /pan ṓ ən/ *n* a group of languages spoken in Peru and western Brazil [Early 20C. < American Spanish *Pano*, a people of the upper Amazon basin] — **Panoan** *adj*

panoply /pánnəpli/ (*plural* -**plies**) *n* 1. FULL ARRAY an impressive and magnificent display or array of something 2. FULL CEREMONIAL DRESS ceremonial dress with all the necessary accessories 3. FULL ARMOUR a full suit of armour and equipment for a warrior 4. PROTECTIVE COVERING a covering that protects something [Late 16C. Via French < Greek *panoplia*, literally 'all weapons' < *hopla* 'weapons'] — **panoplied** *adj*

panoptic /pan óptik/, **panoptical** /-óptik'l/ *adj* taking in or showing everything in a single view [Early 19C. < Greek *panoptos* 'seen by all', *panoptēs* 'all-seeing' < *optos* 'visible'] — **panoptically** *adv*

panopticon /pan óptikən/ *n* a prison with cell blocks situated around a central area, ensuring that prisoners could be viewed at all times [Mid-18C. PAN- 'all' + Greek *optikon*, neuter of *optikos* 'optic'.]

panorama /pánnə ra'ámə/ *n* 1. ALL-ROUND VIEW an unobstructed view extending in all directions, especially of a landscape 2. COMPREHENSIVE SURVEY an all-encompassing survey of a particular topic or issue 3. PICTURE WITH WIDE VIEW a picture or photograph that has a wide view, especially one that is unrolled gradually in front of the spectator 4. ARTS same as **cyclorama** (sense 1) [Late 18C. < PAN- + Greek *horama* 'view' < *horan* 'to see'] — **panoramic** /-rámmik/ *adj* — **panoramically** *adv*

ORIGIN *Panorama* was coined in the late 1780s by an Irish artist called Robert Barker to describe a method he had invented for painting a scene on the inside of a cylinder in such a way that its perspective would seem correct to somebody viewing it from inside the cylinder. He put his invention into practice in 1793 when he opened his 'Panorama', a large building in Leicester Square, London, where the public could come and gaze at such all-encompassing scenes. The modern abstract meaning was in use by the early 19th century.

panoramic sight *n* a sight on a military weapon that gives the user a wide-angled view of the target area

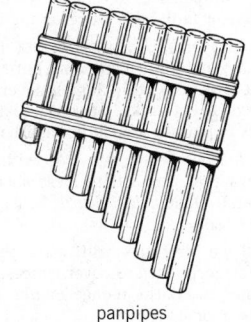

panpipes

panpipes /pán pīps/ *npl* a set of reeds of different lengths that are bound together in a row and played by blowing across the top of each pipe. Panpipes have been in use since ancient times and are today often associated with Peruvian music. [Early 19C. After PAN (sense 1)]

pansexual /pán sékshoo əl/ *adj* relating to a sexuality that expresses itself in many different forms — **pansexuality** /-sekshoo álləti/ *n*

Pan-Slavism *n* a 19th-century political and cultural movement advocating the union of all Slav people — **Pan-Slavic** *adj* — **Pan-Slavist** *n, adj*

panspermia /pan spúrmi ə/ *n* a theory that states that the universe is full of spores that germinate when they find a favourable environment [Mid-19C. < Greek, 'belief that the elements are made of all the seeds of things' < *sperma* 'seed']

pansy /pánzi/ (*plural* -**sies**) *n* 1. FLOWER WITH BRIGHT VELVETY PETALS a plant with brightly coloured velvety flowers that usually have black or dark centres. Native to: Europe. Genus: *Viola* or *Achimenes*. 2. DEEP VIOLET a deep violet colour 3. OFFENSIVE TERM an offensive term for an effeminate or gay man (*dated insult*) [15C. < French *pensée* 'thought' (from its lowered head), form of past participle of *penser* 'think'] — **pansy** *adj*

pant[1] /pant/ *v* (**pants**, **panting**, **panted**) 1. *vi* TAKE SHORT FAST SHALLOW BREATHS to take short fast shallow breaths, especially when excited, hot, or after physical exertion 2. *vt* SAY SOMETHING BREATHLESSLY to say something while trying to catch your breath 3. *vi* YEARN to have a strong desire and yearning for somebody or something 4. *vi* PULSATE QUICKLY to throb at a fast rhythm ■ *n* SHALLOW BREATH a short fast shallow breath [15C. Via assumed Anglo-Norman, 'gasp' < Vulgar Latin *phantasiare* 'gasp in horror' < Latin *phantasia* 'apparition' < Greek (see FANTASY)]

pant[2] /pant/ *n* N Am a pair of trousers [Late 19C. Back-formation < PANTS]

pant- *prefix* same as **panto-** (*used before vowels*)

pantalets /pántə léts/, **pantalettes** *npl* 1. long underpants extending below the skirt, usually with a frill round the bottom of each leg, worn by women in the first half of the 19th century 2. a pair of frills, one at the bottom of each leg, on a pair of pantalets [Mid-19C. < PANTALOON]

pantaloon /pántə loón/ *n* a character in pantomime who is the victim of the clown's jokes and tricks [Late 18C. < PANTALOON]

Pantaloon /pántə loón/ *n* a character in Italian commedia dell'arte, a very thin man of advanced years who is easily tricked and who wears pantaloons and slippers [Late 16C. Via French < Italian *Pantalone*, probably after *San Pantaleone* 'St Pantaleon', popular saint in Venice]

pantaloons /pántə loónz/ *npl* 1. WIDE TROUSERS GATHERED AT ANKLE loose-fitting trousers that are gathered at the ankle 2. 19C TIGHT-FITTING TROUSERS tight-fitting men's trousers fastened with buttons or ribbons at the ankle and sometimes held with a strap under the instep, worn in the early 19th century 3. 17C ENGLISH TROUSERS men's wide ankle-length breeches, worn especially in England during the reign of Charles II 4. BAGGY TROUSERS trousers that fit very loosely (*informal humorous*) [Mid-17C. After PANTALOON; because of a type worn by the stage character]

pantechnicon /pan téknikən/ *n* a large furniture-removal van (*dated*) [Late 19C. After *Pantechnicon*, a building in London built as a bazaar and later used for storing furniture < PAN- + Greek *tekhnikos* 'artistic']

ORIGIN The original *Pantechnicon* was a huge complex of warehouses, wine vaults, and other storage facilities in Motcomb Street, in London's Belgravia. Built in 1830 and supposed to be fireproof, it was almost totally destroyed by fire in 1874. It seems originally to have been intended to be a bazaar, hence its name, literally 'everything artistic', denoting that all sorts of manufactured wares were to be bought there. But it was its role as a furniture repository that brought it into the general language. Removal vans taking furniture there came to be known as 'pantechnicon vans', and by the 1890s *pantechnicon* was a generic term for 'removal van'.

pantheism /pánthi izəm/ *n* 1. the belief that God and the material world are one and the same thing and that God is present in everything 2. the belief in and worship of all or many deities [Mid-18C. < PAN- + Greek *theos* 'god'] — **pantheist** *n* — **pantheistic** /pánthi ístik/ *adj* — **pantheistically** *adv*

pantheon /pánthi ən, pan thée-/ *n* 1. TEMPLE a temple dedicated to all deities 2. ALL DEITIES OF SPECIFIC RELIGION all the deities of a people or religion considered collectively 3. MEMORIAL TO DEAD HEROES a monument or public building commemorating the dead heroes of a nation 4. GROUP OF IMPORTANT PEOPLE a group of people who are the most famous or respected in their field [15C. Via Latin < Greek *pantheion* 'of all the gods' < *theos* 'god']

Pantheon *n* a circular temple in Rome that was completed in 27 BC and dedicated to all the deities but which has been used as a Christian church since AD 609

panther /pánthər/ (*plural* -**thers** or *same*) *n* 1. a leopard, especially in its black unspotted phase 2. *N Am* VERTEB same as **puma** [13C. Via French < Greek *panthēr*]

pantie *adj* CLOTHING another spelling of **panty**

pantie girdle /pánti-/, **panty girdle** *n* a woman's undergarment with a sewn-in crotch like underpants, but made of elasticated material in order to give the abdomen a flatter appearance

panties /pántiz/ *npl* short light fitted underpants for women or girls (*informal*) [Mid-19C. < PANTS]

pantihose *npl* CLOTHING another spelling of **pantyhose**

pantile /pán tīl/ *n* a roof tile made in an 'S' shape so that the downward-curving tail of the 'S' overlaps the upward-curving head of the 'S' of the tile next to it [Mid-17C. < PAN[1]]

pantisocracy /pánti sókrəssi/ (*plural* -**cies**) *n* a planned utopian community in which everyone shares power and is equal [Late 18C. < PANTO- + Greek *isokratia* 'equality of power']

panto /pántō/ (*plural* -**tos**) *n* same as **pantomime** (sense 1) (*informal*) [Mid-19C. Shortening]

panto- *prefix* all ○ *pantograph* [< Greek *pant-*; form of *pan* 'all']

Pantocrator /pan tókrətər/ *n* in Christianity, Jesus Christ as ruler of the universe, creator, and saviour, represented in Byzantine church art with one hand upraised and the other holding a copy of the Gospels [Late 19C. < Greek *pantokratōr* 'almighty']

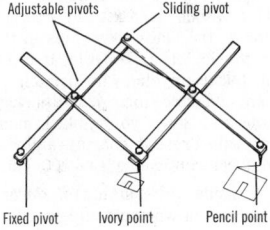

Adjustable pivots — Sliding pivot

Fixed pivot — Ivory point — Pencil point

pantograph

pantograph /pántə graaf, -graf/ *n* 1. COPYING INSTRUMENT a drawing instrument that consists of a set of adjustable interconnected bars forming a parallelogram and is used to copy line drawings or maps to any scale 2. FRAME OR BRACKET a device shaped like a pantograph and used as a frame or bracket 3. CURRENT-SUPPLY DEVICE FOR ELECTRIC TRAIN a device on the roof of electric trains and locomotives for picking up electric current from overhead wires — **pantographer** /pan tóggrəfər/ *n* — **pantographic** /pántə gráffik/ *adj* — **pantographically** *adv*

pantomime /pántə mīm/ *n* 1. HUMOROUS THEATRICAL ENTERTAINMENT a style of theatre, or a play in this style, traditionally performed at Christmas, in which a folktale or children's story is told with jokes, songs, and dancing. Pantomime stories include *Cinderella*, *Dick Whittington*, and *Aladdin*. 2. MIME ARTIST somebody who acts without speaking, using gesture and expression 3. ROMAN THEATRICAL PERFORMANCE in ancient Rome, a theatrical performance by one masked actor who played all the characters, using only

dance, gesture, and expression, and no words, while a chorus narrated the story **4.** ROMAN ACTOR an actor in a Roman pantomime **5.** LUDICROUS SITUATION a ridiculous and farcical situation that results from confusion and misunderstanding (*informal*) [Late 16C. Via Latin *pantomimus* 'mime artist' < Greek *pantomōmos* 'complete imitator' < *mōmos* 'imitator'] —**pantomimic** /pántə mímmik/ *adj* —**pantomimist** *n*

pantomime dame *n* the role in a pantomime of an ill-tempered comic woman of advanced years, traditionally played by a man

pantomime horse *n* a comic character in a pantomime played by two actors in a horse costume, with one occupying the front half of the horse and the other the back half

~~pantomine~~ incorrect spelling of **pantomime**

pantothenate /pántə thénnayt, pan tóthə nayt/ *n* an ester of pantothenic acid [Mid-20C. < PANTOTHENIC ACID]

pantothenic acid /pántə thénnik-/ *n* a B complex vitamin that is present in many foods and is essential for growth [< Greek *pantothen* 'from every side'; because widely found]

pantoum /pan tóom/ *n* a form of verse in which the second and fourth lines of each four-line verse are repeated as the first and third lines of the following verse [Late 18C. Via French < Malay *pantun*]

pantropic /pan trópik, -tróppik/, **pantropical** /-trópik'l, -tróppik'l/ *adj* found throughout the tropics

pantry /pántri/ (*plural* **-tries**) *n* **1.** a small closed space connected to a kitchen, often with a door, in which food and utensils for food preparation can be stored **2.** a highly ventilated cold small room or walk-in cupboard with shelves and a marble surface used for storing food [13C. < Old French *paneterie* 'cupboard for bread' < late Latin *panarius* 'bread-seller' < Latin *panis* 'bread']

pants /pants/ *npl* **1.** an item of clothing worn next to the skin that covers the buttocks and genital area **2.** *Aus, N Am* same as **trousers** ■ *adj* worthless, useless, or of low quality (*slang*) [Mid-19C. Shortening of PANTALOONS] ◊ **beat the pants off somebody** to defeat somebody decisively (*informal*) ◊ **bore** or **scare** or **charm the pants off somebody** to bore, scare, or charm somebody very much (*informal*) ◊ **wear the pants** *ANZ, N Am* to be the member of a household who makes the important decisions

pantsuit /pánt soot, -syoot/, **pants suit** *n N Am* same as **trouser suit**

pantsula /pant sóolə/ (*plural* **pantsulas** or **mapantsula** /maá-/) *n S Africa* **1.** DANCE an energetic dance originating in the black townships in the 1980s **2.** MUSIC the music for a pantsula, a forerunner of kwaito **3.** DANCER anyone who participates in the typical pantsula dance form **4.** STYLISH YOUNG BLACK MAN in the 1970s and '80s, a young black man from the townships who dressed sharply and displayed a challenging self-confidence [Late 20C. < Bantu]

panty /pánti/, **pantie** *adj* belonging to, concerning, suitable for, or part of women's underpants ○ *showing a panty line*

panty girdle *n* CLOTHING another spelling of **pantie girdle**

pantyhose /pánti hōz/, **pantihose** *npl N Am* same as **tights** (sense 1)

pantyliner /pánti līnər/ *n* a light thin sanitary towel

pantywaist /pánti wayst/ *n N Am* **1.** an offensive term for a man that deliberately insults his courage and masculinity (*slang*) **2.** a piece of clothing for children, consisting of a shirt and trousers that are buttoned together at the waist (*dated*)

panzer /pánzər/ *n* a German tank used in World War II [Mid-20C. Shortening of German *Panzerdivision* 'armoured unit' < Old French *pancier* 'armour for the belly' < *pance* 'belly' (see PAUNCH)]

Paolozzi /pow lótsi/, **Sir Eduardo** (*b.* 1924) Scottish sculptor. He was an important exponent of pop art during the 1950s, after which he turned to abstract sculpture incorporating mechanistic forms.

pap[1] /pap/ *n* **1.** SEMILIQUID FOOD soft semiliquid food, usually mashed or pulped, especially for babies or sick people **2.** TRIVIAL OR WORTHLESS MATERIAL something such as a book, film, or television programme that

is regarded as lacking in depth and substance and is considered worthless **3.** *S Africa* MAIZE MEAL PORRIDGE porridge, especially that made from maize meal [14C. Via French < Latin *pappa* 'food', children's word] —**pappy** /páppi/ *adj*

pap[2] /pap/ *n* **1.** a nipple or teat (*archaic*) **2.** *also* **Pap** a round, conical hill (*often used in placenames*) [12C. Origin?]

papa[1] /pə paá/ *n* same as **father** *n* (sense 1) (*dated*) [Late 17C. Via French and late Latin < Greek *pappas* 'father']

papa[2] /paápə/ *n* a soft blue-grey clay of marine origin [Late 19C. < Maori]

Papa /paápə/ *n* a code word for the letter 'P', used in international radio communications [< PAPA[1]]

papacy /páypəssi/ (*plural* **-cies**) *n* **1.** PAPAL POWER OR STATUS the power or position of the pope **2.** POPE'S PERIOD IN POWER the period of office of a pope **3.** PAPAL GOVERNMENT the system of government in the Roman Catholic Church with the pope as the head [14C. < medieval Latin *papatia* < late Latin *papa* (see POPE)]

papad /páppad/ *n S Asia* same as **poppadom** [Late 20C. Alteration of POPPADOM]

Papa Doc /páppə dók/ ♦ **Duvalier, François**

papadum *n* FOOD another spelling of **poppadom**

Papago /páppə gō/ (*plural same* or **-gos**) *n* **1.** a member of a Native North American people who lived in central Arizona, and now live mainly in northern Mexico and southern Arizona **2.** the Uto-Aztecan language of the Papago people, closely related to Pima. Native speakers: 9,000. [Mid-19C. Via Spanish *pápago* < Pima-Papago, 'bean eaters'] —**Papago** *adj*

papain /pə páy in, -pī́-/ *n* an enzyme found in the juice of papayas and used as a meat tenderizer and in medicine to promote digestion and healing of wounds [Late 19C. < PAPAYA]

papal /páyp'l/ *adj* relating to the pope or the papacy [14C. Via French < medieval Latin *papalis* < late Latin *papa* 'bishop, pope' (see POPE)] —**papally** *adv*

papal cross *n* a cross consisting of a long upright and three crossbars of successively decreasing length, with the shortest at the top

Papal States /páyp'l -/ former territories in Italy over which the pope had sovereignty between AD 754 and 1870

Papandreou /páppən dráy oo/, **Andreas** (1919–96) prime minister of Greece (1981–89 and 1993–96). The founder of the Pan-Hellenistic Socialist Movement (1974), he became the first socialist prime minister of Greece.

Papanicolaou test /páppə níkə loo-/, **Papanicolaou smear** *n N Am* MED same as **cervical smear** [Mid-20C. After G. N. *Papanicolaou* (1883–1962), Greek-born US anatomist]

paparazzi /páppə rátsō/ (*plural* **-zi** /-tsi/), **paparazzo** (*plural* **-zi**) *n* a freelance photographer who follows famous people hoping to catch a newsworthy story, especially something shocking or scandalous [Mid-20C. < Italian, surname of a photographer in the film *La Dolce Vita* (1959) by Federico Fellini]

USAGE The plural form *paparazzi* is used more often than the singular, even when referring to a single photographer.

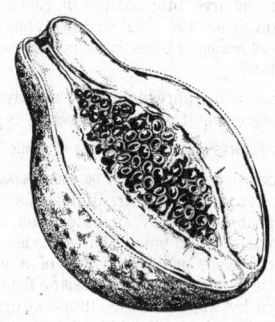

papaverine /pə pávvə reen, -páyvə-/ *n* a toxic white crystalline nonaddictive alkaloid. Source: opium, derived synthetically. Use: antispasmodic to treat

asthma and colic. Formula: $C_{20}H_{21}O_4N$. [Mid-19C. < Latin *papaver* 'poppy']

papaw *n* FOOD, TREES another spelling of **pawpaw**

papaya

papaya /pə pī́ ə/ *n* **1.** a large spherical or elongated fruit with yellow pulp and numerous seeds, eaten fresh or in salads and desserts **2.** a tropical evergreen tree with a crown of broad leaves, widely cultivated to produce papayas. Latin name: *Carica papaya*. [Late 16C. Via Spanish < Carib or Arawak]

paper /páypər/ *n* **1.** THIN FLAT MATERIAL FROM WOOD PULP a thin material consisting of flat sheets made from pulped wood, cloth, or fibre. Use: for writing and printing on, for wrapping things in, for covering walls. **2.** SHEET OR SHEETS OF PAPER one or more pieces or sheets of paper, for writing or drawing on **3.** MEDIA same as **newspaper** (sense 1) **4.** EXAMINATION a set of examination questions prepared on paper **5.** SET OF EXAM ANSWERS a written set of answers by a student to a set of examination questions **6.** ACADEMIC ARTICLE OR TALK an essay or article, particularly an academic one, read at a conference or to a society, or submitted for publication **7.** STUDENT'S ESSAY an essay written by a student for a class **8.** WRAPPER a piece of paper, especially one used to wrap a sweet or a cigarette (*often used in the plural*) **9.** GOVERNMENT DOCUMENT a white paper, green paper, or command paper **10.** COMMERCIAL NEGOTIABLE DOCUMENT a negotiable document, e.g. a bill of exchange or promissory note **11.** CONSTR same as **wallpaper** *n* (sense 1) (*informal*) **12.** FREE THEATRE TICKET a free ticket that is given out in order to fill up a theatre (*slang*) **13.** THEATREGOERS WITH FREE TICKETS members of the audience who have been given free tickets in order to fill up a theatre (*slang*) ■ **papers** *npl* **1.** PERSONAL IDENTITY DOCUMENTS a document or documents showing somebody's identity or status, e.g. a passport **2.** ASSORTMENT OF DOCUMENTS a collection of documents relating to an issue or subject ○ *official papers in the archives* **3.** SOMEBODY'S PERSONAL WRITINGS somebody's diaries, letters, and other personal writings **4.** NAUT same as **ship's papers** ■ *adj* **1.** MADE OF PAPER consisting of or made of paper **2.** RESEMBLING PAPER similar to paper, e.g. in flimsiness ○ *paper walls* **3.** EXISTING IN DOCUMENTARY FORM written in a document but not necessarily effective or useful in reality ○ *mere paper guarantees of peace* **4.** IN WRITING conducted in writing ○ *a paper war* ■ *vt* (**-pers**, **-pering**, **-pered**) **1.** COVER WITH WALLPAPER to cover a wall or room with wallpaper **2.** COVER SOMETHING WITH PAPER to cover something with paper **3.** FILL UP THEATRE to fill up a theatre by giving out free tickets (*slang*) [14C. Via Anglo-Norman *papir*, Old French *papier* < Latin *papyrus* (see PAPYRUS)] —**paperer** *n* ◊ **on paper 1.** in theory, but not in fact **2.** in writing

paper over *vt* **1.** to cover something up with paper, especially to cover a wall's imperfections or old paint with wallpaper **2.** to conceal something such as a mistake or fault without resolving it

paperback /páypər bak/ *n* SOFTCOVER BOOK a book that has a thin flexible cover instead of a hard cover ■ *adj* WITH FLEXIBLE COVER with a thin flexible cover, instead of a hard cover ■ *vt* (**-backs**, **-backing**, **-backed**) PUBLISH AS PAPERBACK to publish a book in paperback form

paperbark /páypər baark/ *n* a tree with pale thin papery bark that peels off in large sheets. Native to: Australia. Genus: *Melaleuca*. [< the colour and texture of the bark]

paper birch *n* a birch tree with white peeling bark that was formerly used to cover canoes. Native to: North America. Latin name: *Betula papyrifera*. [< the white colour of the bark]

paperboard /páypər bawrd/ *n* thick cardboard made from compressed paper

paperboy /páypər boy/ *n* a boy who delivers newspapers to people's homes, or who sells newspapers

paper chase *n* **1.** a cross-country race in which runners follow a trail of shredded paper that has been left by an earlier runner or runners **2.** an intense searching and collation of files, books, or documents

paperclip /páypər klip/ *n* a clip designed to be slipped over two or more sheets of paper to hold them together, especially a piece of wire that is bent into a long flat oval spiral

paper-cutter *n* a machine or device for cutting paper, especially a flat platform with a long arm containing a blade that can be raised and lowered in order to cut straight edges

papergirl /páypər gurl/ *n* a girl who delivers newspapers to people's homes, or who sells newspapers

paperhanger /páypər hangər/ *n* **1.** somebody who hangs wallpaper, especially as a profession **2.** *US* somebody who regularly passes bad cheques in order to obtain money (*slang*) —**paperhanging** *n*

paper jam *n* a situation in which paper becomes jammed in a printer or photocopier, causing it to stop working

paperknife /páypər nīf/ (*plural* **-knives** /-nīvz/) *n* a blunt knife for slitting open envelopes, or for slitting folded paper, especially leaves of books. N Am term **letter opener**

paperless /páypərləss/ *adj* using records or means of communication that are electronic rather than on paper ○ *the age of the paperless office*

paper money *n* currency in the form of banknotes, as opposed to coins

paper mulberry *n* a common shade tree whose inner bark was once used for making paper. Native to: Asia. Latin name: *Broussonetia papyrifera*.

paper nautilus *n* a cephalopod mollusc, the female of which has a thin delicate shell. Genus: *Argonauta*. [< the delicacy and whiteness of its shell]

paper profit *n* a profit that is not generated from the normal trading of a business and may or may not be realized (*often used in the plural*)

paper-pusher *n* somebody with a routine clerical job involving much paperwork (*informal*)

paper round *n* **1.** the job of delivering newspapers to people's homes **2.** the course followed from house to house by somebody delivering newspapers ▶ N Am term **paper route**

paper-thin *adj* extremely thin, like paper —**paperthin** *adv*

paper tiger *n* somebody or something, especially an organization or a nation, that appears to be very strong and powerful but is in fact weak and ineffectual

paper trail *n* a sequence of documents that can be used by an investigator as a record of someone's actions or decisions (*informal*)

paper wasp *n* a large slender wasp known for its elaborate nest that is made up of individual cells built of papery material. Genus: *Polistes*.

paperweight /páypər wayt/ *n* a small heavy usually ornamental object that is used to hold down papers and keep them in place

paperwork /páypər wurk/ *n* routine work that involves tasks such as filling in forms, keeping files up to date, or writing reports and letters

papery /páypəri/ *adj* similar to paper in texture or thickness —**paperiness** *n*

Paphian /páyfi ən/ *adj* **1.** RELATING TO PAPHOS relating to the village of Paphos **2.** RELATING TO APHRODITE relating to the goddess Aphrodite, who, in Greek mythology, rose fully formed from the sea at Paphos **3.** CONCERNING SEXUAL ACTIVITY relating to sexual love (*literary*) ■ *n* **1.** SOMEBODY FROM PAPHOS somebody who comes from Paphos (sense 1) (*literary*) **2.** *also* **paphian** same as **prostitute** *n*

Paphos[1] /pá foss/ town in southwestern Cyprus, on the site of the ancient city of Paphos. Population: 38,000 (1997).

Paphos[2] /páy foss/, **Paphus** /páyfəss/ *n* in Greek mythology, a king of Cyprus who was the son of Pygmalion and Galatea

Papiamento /páppi ə méntō/ *n* a Spanish-based creole of the Netherlands Antilles, derived from a Portuguese pidgin and including many Dutch words. Native speakers: 200,000. [Mid-20C. < Spanish, < Papiamento *papya* 'talk' + *-mentu* '-ment'] —**Papiamento** *adj*

papier collé /páppi ay kóllay/ *n* scraps of paper and other objects that are glued onto a sheet as an abstract artistic composition [< French, 'glued paper']

papier-mâché /páppi ay máshay, páypər-/ *n* sheets of paper pulp and glue stuck together in layers, usually onto a frame or mould, used to make various objects such as boxes, bowls, and masks [< French, 'mashed paper'] —**papier-mâché** *adj*

papilla /pə pílla/ (*plural* **-lae** /-lee/) *n* **1.** SMALL LUMP OF TISSUE a small nipple-shaped protuberance, e.g. on the tongue enclosing the taste buds, or at the root of a hair or feather **2.** NIPPLE a nipple or teat (*technical*) **3.** SMALL PROJECTION ON PETAL OR LEAF a small elevated pad on the surface of a stigma, petal, or leaf **4.** SMALL PROJECTION RESEMBLING NIPPLE a very small projection like a nipple on the surface of something [Late 17C. < Latin, 'little swelling' < *papula* 'swelling'] —**papillary** *adj* —**papillate** *adj* —**papilliferous** /páppi líffərəss/ *adj* —**papilliform** /pə pílli fawrm/ *adj*

papilloma /páppi lómə/ (*plural* **-mata** /-mətə/ *or* **-mas**) *n* a benign tumour of the skin or mucous membrane projecting from a surface, e.g. a wart —**papillomatous** *adj*

papillon /páppi lon/ *n* a small spaniel with a silky coat and heavily fringed tail and ears [Early 20C. < French, literally 'butterfly'; because its pointed ears resemble the shape of a butterfly's wings]

papillote /páppiyot/ [Mid-18C. < French < *papillon* 'butterfly'] ◇ **en papillote** baked in a wrapping of greaseproof paper, nonstick baking parchment, or foil

papist /páypist/ *n* an offensive term for a member of the Roman Catholic Church [Mid-16C. < French *papiste* or modern Latin *papista* < late Latin *papa* (see POPE)] —**papism** *n* —**papistic** /pə pístik/ *adj* —**papistry** *n*

papoose /pə póoss/, **pappoose** *n* **1.** an offensive term for a Native North American baby or young child **2.** a bag that fits over the shoulders, used for carrying a baby, especially in front of the body [Mid-17C. < Narragansett *papoòs* or Massachuset *pappouse*]

papovavirus /pə póvə vīrəss/ *n* a DNA-containing virus of a group that can cause cancers in animals, including those responsible for warts [Mid-20C. < first two letters of PAPILLOMA + POLYOMA + *vacuolation*]

pappardelle /páppər délli/ *n* pasta in the shape of broad flat ribbons [< Italian *pappare* 'eat ravenously']

pappoose *n* another spelling of **papoose**

pappus /páppəss/ (*plural* **-pi** /-pī/) *n* a covering of scales, bristles, and feathery hairs that surrounds the fruit of plants such as dandelions and thistles and helps to disperse the fruits [Early 18C. Via Latin < Greek *pappos* 'grandfather'] —**pappose** /páppōss/ *adj*

pappy /páppi/ (*plural* **-pies**) *n* *Can*, *US regional* same as **father** *n* (sense 1) (*dated*) [Mid-18C. < PAPA[1]]

pappyshow /páppi shō/ *n* *Carib* somebody who appears ridiculous or foolish [Early 20C. Alteration of Scottish dialect *puppy show* 'puppet show'] ◇ **make a pappyshow of somebody** *Carib* to ridicule somebody or make somebody appear foolish

paprika /pápprikə, pə préekə/ *n* **1.** MILD RED SPICE a mild red spice made from various sweet red peppers, used especially in Hungarian cooking **2.** SWEET RED PEPPER a sweet red pepper or the plant on which it grows. Genus: *Capsicum*. **3.** REDDISH-ORANGE COLOUR a bright reddish-orange colour [Late 19C. < Hungarian < Serbian *pàpar* 'pepper' < Latin *piper* (see PEPPER)] —**paprika** *adj*

Pap smear /páp-/, **Pap test** *n* *Aus*, *N Am* a test to detect cancerous or precancerous cells of the cervix, allowing for early diagnosis of cancer. UK, NZ term **cervical smear** [< shortening of *Papanicolaou* (see PAPANICOLAOU TEST)]

Papuan /páppŏo ən/ *n* **1.** somebody who comes from Papua New Guinea **2.** a group of languages spoken in Papua New Guinea and nearby islands, unrelated to the Austronesian languages. Native speakers: 2 million. —**Papuan** *adj*

Papua New Guinea

Papua New Guinea /páppŏo ə nyoo gínni/ independent nation in Oceania, situated north of Australia, in the southwestern Pacific Ocean, consisting of the eastern half of the island of New Guinea together with many other islands. It became an independent member of the Commonwealth in 1975. Language: English. Currency: kina. Capital: Port Moresby. Population: 5,295,816 (2003). Area: 462,840 sq. km/178,704 sq. mi. Official name **Independent State of Papua New Guinea** —**Papua New Guinean** *n*, *adj*

papule /páppyool/ *n* a small hard round protuberance on the skin [Early 18C. < Latin *papula*] —**papular** *adj* —**papuliferous** /páppyŏo líffərəss/ *adj*

papyri plural of **papyrus**

papyrology /páppə róllǝji/ *n* the study of ancient papyrus manuscripts —**papyrological** /páppərə lójjik'l/ *adj* —**papyrologist** *n*

papyrus /pə pírəss/ (*plural* **-ri** /-rī/ *or* **-ruses**) *n* **1.** MATERIAL RESEMBLING PAPER writing material used by the ancient Egyptians, Greeks, and Romans that was made from the pith of the stem of a water plant **2.** PAPYRUS DOCUMENT an ancient manuscript written on papyrus **3.** TALL MARSH PLANT a tall water plant. Flowers: small, like umbrellas. Use: writing material. Native to: southern Europe, Nile valley. Latin name: *Cyperus papyrus*. [14C. Via Latin < Greek *papuros* 'papyrus plant']

par /paar/ *n* **1.** AVERAGE LEVEL a level or standard considered to be average or normal **2.** STANDARD SCORE IN GOLF the standard score assigned to each hole on a golf course, or to the sum total of these holes **3.** ACCEPTED VALUE OF CURRENCY the accepted value of one country's currency in terms of the currency of another country that uses the same metal standard **4.** COMM same as **par value** ■ *adj* AVERAGE average or normal ■ *vt* (**pars**, **parring**, **parred**) SCORE PAR ON HOLE OR COURSE in golf, to score the equivalent of the par on a hole or course [Late 16C. < Latin, 'equal'] ◇ **be feeling below par** to feel slightly unwell or out of sorts (*informal*) ◇ **be on (a) par (with somebody** *or* **something)** to be on the same level as somebody or something, or generally have the same status or value ◇ **be par for the course** to be usual or to be expected under the circumstances (*informal*)

par. *abbr* **1.** paragraph **2.** MATHS, GRAM, GEOG parallel **3.** parenthesis **4.** parish

Par. *abbr* Paraguay

par- *prefix* same as **para-**[1]

para[1] /párrə/ *n* MIL same as **paratrooper** (*informal*; usually used in the plural) [Mid-20C. Shortening]

para[2] /páarə/ (*plural* **-ras** *or* **same**) *n* a subunit of Yugoslav currency. See table at **currency** [Late 17C. Via Turkish < Persian *pāra* 'piece, para']

para-[1] *prefix* **1.** beside, near, along with ○ *parataxis* **2.** beyond ○ *paranormal* **3.** isomeric or related compound ○ *paraldehyde* **4.** resembling ○ *paramyxovirus* **5.** faulty, undesirable ○ *paraphasia* **6.** assistant, auxiliary ○ *paralegal* **7.** occupying the para position in the benzene ring ○ *paradichlorobenzene* [< Greek *para* 'beside' < Indo-European, 'next to, in front of']

para-[2] *prefix* parachute ○ *paraskiing* [Shortening]

-para *suffix* a woman who has given birth to a particular number of children (*technical*) ○ *nullipara* [< modern Latin < Latin *parere* 'give birth']

para-aminobenzoic acid /párrə ə mĩnō ben zṓik-/ *n* BIOCHEM full form of **PABA**

para-aminosalicylic acid /párrə ə meé nō sállisilik-, -mĩ-/ *n* a drug similar to aspirin. Use: treatment of tuberculosis.

parabasis /pə rábbəsiss/ (*plural* **-ses** /-seez/) *n* in classical Greek comedy, a speech to the audience that is made by the chorus [Early 19C. < Greek < *parabainein* 'go aside' < *bainein* 'to step']

paraben /párrə ben/ *n* a chemical that mimics the hormone oestrogen. Evidence suggests that parabens can play a role in the development of breast tumours. Use: preservative in cosmetics, deodorants, food. [Late 20C. Shortening of *parabenzene* < PARA-¹]

parabiosis /párrə bĩ óssiss/ (*plural* **-oses** /-ṓseez/) *n* **1.** a state in which two people are joined together and share the same circulation of blood. This is the case for conjoined twins, and it can also be induced experimentally or to establish a blood supply for some grafts. **2.** the temporary suppression of nerve conduction [Early 20C. < PARA-¹ + Greek *biōsis* 'way of life' < *bios* 'life'] —**parabiotic** /párrə bĩ óttik/ *adj*

parablast /párrə blast/ *n* the yolk of a fertilized egg [Mid-19C. < PARA-¹ + Greek *blastos* 'a bud, shoot'] —**parablastic** /párrə blástik/ *adj*

parable /párrəb'l/ *n* **1.** a short simple story intended to illustrate a moral or religious lesson **2.** a parable that appears in the Bible, as told by Jesus Christ [14C. Via French < Latin *parabola* 'comparison' < Greek *parabolē* < *paraballein* 'put beside' < *ballein* 'throw']

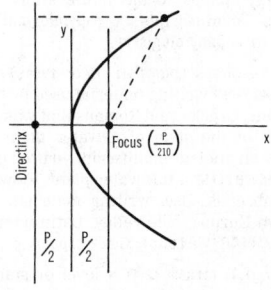

parabola

parabola /pə rábbələ/ *n* a curve formed by the intersection of a cone with a plane parallel to its side [Late 16C. Via modern Latin < Greek *parabolē* 'application, comparison' (see PARABLE); from the relationship between the section of a cone that forms the parabola and part of the cone's surface]

parabolic¹ /párrə bóllik/ *adj* **1.** relating to, resembling, or having the form of a parabola **2.** with the form of a paraboloid [Early 18C. < PARABOLA]

parabolic² /párrə bóllik/, **parabolical** /párrə bóllik'l/ *adj* relating to or resembling a parable [15C. Via late Latin < late Greek *parabolikos* 'figurative' < Greek *parabolē* (see PARABLE)] —**parabolically** *adv*

parabolic aerial *n* COMMUNICATION same as **dish aerial**

parabolize /pə rábbə lĩz/ (**-lizes, -lizing, -lized**), **parabolise** (**-lises, -lising, -lised**) *vt* to explain something or tell a story by means of a parable [Early 17C. < medieval Latin *parabolizare* 'speak in parables' < Latin *parabola* (see PARABLE)]

paraboloid /pə rábbə loyd/ *n* a mathematical surface in which intersections with planes produce parabolas, ellipses, or hyperbolas —**paraboloidal** /pə rábbə lóyd'l/ *adj*

para boots *npl* high-lacing boots worn by paratroopers that are popular in various street fashions

parabuntal /párrə búnt'l/ *n* fine straw made from the leaves of a palm tree. Use: making hats.

Paracelsus /párrə sélssəss/, **Philippus Aureolus** (1493?–1541) German physician and alchemist. His belief that disease is caused by outside agents and could be treated by chemical remedies defied the medical tenets of his time. Pseudonym of **Hohenheim, Theophrastus Bombastus von**

paracentesis /párrə sen teéssiss/ *n* MED same as **thoracentesis** [Late 16C. Via Latin, 'the removing of a cataract' < Greek *parakentēsis* < *parakentein* 'pierce at the side' < *kentein* 'prick, stab']

paracetamol /párrə seétə mol, -séttə-/ *n* **1.** a drug sold in tablet form. Use: relief of pain and fever. **2.** a tablet or capsule containing paracetamol ▶ N Am term **acetaminophen** [Mid-20C. < *par(a-)acet(yl)am(ino-phen)ol*, its chemical name]

parachronism /pə rákrənizəm/ *n* an error in assigning a date to something, especially when the date given is later than it should be [Mid-17C. < PARA-¹ + Greek *khronos* 'time', or alteration of ANACHRONISM]

parachute

parachute /párrə shoot/ *n* **1.** a device consisting of a canopy fitted to a harness that is used to slow the speed at which a person or object drops from an aircraft **2.** ZOOL same as **patagium** (sense 1) ■ *vti* (**-chutes, -chuting, -chuted**) to drop from an aircraft by parachute, or allow somebody or something to drop in this way [Late 18C. < French, 'protection against a fall' < *chute* 'a fall'] —**parachutist** *n*

parachute spinnaker *n* a very large light triangular sail used on a racing yacht

Paraclete /párrə kleet/ *n* in Christianity, the Holy Spirit [13C. Via French and ecclesiastical Latin < Greek *paraklētos* 'advocate, intercessor' < *parakalein* 'call to your side' < *kalein* 'to call']

parade /pə ráyd/ *n* **1.** CELEBRATORY PROCESSION an organized procession of people celebrating a special occasion and often including decorated vehicles or floats, a marching band, people twirling batons, and people on horseback **2.** DISPLAY a long moving line of people or things intended to be publicly displayed **3.** SUCCESSION a large number of people or things in succession ○ *a parade of visitors to the palace* **4.** FLAMBOYANT DISPLAY a showy or ostentatious exhibition or display of something **5.** PROCESSION OF TROOPS a march by troops along the streets or in a large area such as a square, usually as a celebration of an important event **6.** GATHERING OF TROOPS IN FORMATION a formal gathering of a troop of soldiers in a regimented formation for a ceremonial march, inspection, or training **7.** PEOPLE IN PARADE people marching in a parade **8.** MIL same as **parade ground 9.** *also* **Parade** STREET a street with a row of shops (*often used in placenames*) **10.** PARRY in fencing, a parry ■ *v* (**-rades, -rading, -raded**) **1.** *vti* GO ON FESTIVE PROCESSION to march in a festive public parade, or make somebody march in a parade **2.** *vti* ASSEMBLE FOR MILITARY PARADE to gather for and march in a military parade, or make troops take part in a parade **3.** *vt* SHOW SOMEBODY OR SOMETHING OFF to display somebody or something proudly and ostentatiously **4.** *vi* WALK ABOUT TO BE SEEN to walk or stroll about in public, especially in order to be seen or admired **5.** *vti* CLAIM TO BE SOMETHING ELSE to present something as better than it really is, or appear falsely as better ○ *parading old ideas as new reforms* [Mid-17C. Via French < Spanish *parada* 'stopping (a horse)' < Latin *parare* 'prepare'] ◇ **rain on somebody's parade** N Am to spoil things for somebody (*informal*)

parade ground *n* a place where troops regularly gather in formation for inspection or training

~~paradice~~ incorrect spelling of **paradise**

paradichlorobenzene /párrə dĩ kláw rō bén zeen/ *n* a white crystalline compound. Use: moth repellent. Formula: $C_6H_4Cl_2$.

paradiddle /párrə did'l/ *n* a drum roll in which left and right drumsticks alternate [Early 20C. An imitation of the sound]

paradigm /párrə dĩm/ *n* **1.** TYPICAL EXAMPLE a typical example of something **2.** MODEL THAT FORMS BASIS OF SOMETHING an example that serves as a pattern or model for something, especially one that forms the basis of a methodology or theory **3.** SET OF ALL FORMS OF WORD a set of word forms giving all of the possible inflections of a word **4.** RELATIONSHIP OF IDEAS TO ONE ANOTHER in the philosophy of science, a generally accepted model of how ideas relate to one another, forming a conceptual framework within which scientific research is carried out [15C. Via late Latin < Greek *paradeigma* 'example' < *paradeiknunai*, literally 'show beside' < *deiknunai* 'to show'] —**paradigmatic** /párrədig máttik/ *adj* —**paradigmatically** *adv*

paradigm shift *n* a radical change in somebody's basic assumptions about or approach to something

paradise /párrə dĩss/ *n* **1.** PLACE OR STATE OF PERFECT HAPPINESS a place, situation, or condition in which somebody finds perfect happiness **2.** *also* **Paradise** HEAVEN in some religions such as Christianity, Islam, and Judaism, the place where good people are believed to go after death, or the state they are believed to attain after death **3.** *also* **Paradise** GARDEN OF EDEN in the Bible, the perfect garden where Adam and Eve were placed at the Creation **4.** PLACE IDEALLY SUITED TO SOMEBODY a place where there is everything that a particular person needs for his or her interest (*informal*) ○ *a surfer's paradise* [12C. Via French and late Latin < Greek *paradeisos* 'enclosed place, park' < Avestan *pairidaeza* 'form around' < *diz* 'to form'] —**paradisaical** /párrədi sáy ik'l, -záy-/ *adj* —**paradisaically** *adv* —**paradisal** /párrə dĩss'l, -dĩz'l/ *adj* —**paradisally** *adv* —**paradisiacal** /párrədi sĩ ək'l, -zĩ-/ *adj* —**paradisiacally** *adv*

CULTURAL NOTE *Paradise Lost*, an epic poem (1667) by John Milton. This monumental work describes Satan's rebellion against God, his corruption of Adam and Eve, and their subsequent expulsion from the Garden of Eden. The sustained brilliance of its language, structure, characterization, and imagery makes it arguably the greatest epic poem in English literature. A sequel, *Paradise Regained*, was published in 1671.

paradise duck *n* a large duck, the male of which is dark-coloured with a black head, while the female is chestnut-coloured with a white head and wing patches. Native to: New Zealand. Latin name: *Tadorna variegata*. [< its bright colours]

paradise flycatcher *n* a brightly coloured bird of the flycatcher family, the male of which has a very long slender tail. Native to: Asia, Africa. Genus: *Terpsiphone*.

parador /párrə dawr/ *n* **1.** SPANISH TOURIST HOTEL in Spain, a hotel operated by the national government and usually located in a castle, monastery, convent, or other historic site **2.** LATIN AMERICAN HOTEL in Latin America, a privately owned and operated hotel or resort **3.** CARIBBEAN HOTEL in the Caribbean, a rural hotel with few amenities [Mid-19C. < Spanish *parar* 'stop, stay' < Latin *parare* 'prepare']

parados /párrə doss/ *n* a bank built up behind a trench or other fortification that gives protection from attack from the rear [Mid-19C. < French, literally 'defend the back' < *dos* 'back']

paradox /párrə doks/ *n* **1.** SOMETHING ABSURD OR CONTRADICTORY a statement, proposition, or situation that seems to be absurd or contradictory, but in fact is or may be true **2.** SELF-CONTRADICTORY STATEMENT a statement or proposition that contradicts itself **3.** PERSON OF OPPOSITES a person with seemingly self-contradictory qualities [Mid-16C. < Latin *paradoxum* < Greek *paradoxos* 'contrary to opinion' < *doxa* 'opinion' < *dokein* 'think'] —**paradoxical** /párrə dóksik'l/ *adj* —**paradoxically** *adv*

paradoxical frog *n* a frog of which the adult is less than a third the size of the tadpole. Native to: Amazon forest, the island of Trinidad. Latin name: *Pseudis paradoxa*.

paradoxical sleep *n* MED same as **REM sleep** [Because its electrical brain patterns resemble those of the waking state]

paradrop /párrə drop/ *n* the delivery of personnel, materials, or provisions to a place by attaching them to a parachute and dropping them from an aircraft ■ *vt* (**-drops, -dropping, -dropped**) to deliver somebody or something to a place by paradrop

paraesthesia /párress theéezi ə/ *n* an unusual or unexplained tingling, pricking, or burning sensation on the skin [Late 19C. < PARA-¹ + Greek *aesthēsis* 'feeling']

paraffin /párrəfin/ *n* **1.** a mixture of liquid hydrocarbons obtained from petroleum and used as a domestic heating fuel and as fuel for aircraft **2.** INDUST same as **paraffin wax 3.** CHEM same as **alkane** ■ *vt* (**-fins, -fining, -fined**) to treat something by saturating, impregnating, or coating it with paraffin or paraffin wax [Mid-19C. < Latin *parum* 'little' + *affinis* 'related'; because not closely related to any other substance]

paraffin oil *n* INDUST same as **paraffin** *n* (sense 1)

paraffin wax *n* a white waxy solid mixture of hydrocarbons. Source: petroleum. Use: in making candles, pharmaceuticals, cosmetics, as a sealing agent.

~~parafin~~ incorrect spelling of **paraffin**

paraformaldehyde /párrə fawr máldi hīd/, **paraform** /párrə fawrm/ *n* a white combustible polymer of formaldehyde. Use: disinfectant, fungicide, in contraceptive creams.

paragenesis /párrə jénnəsiss/, **paragenesia** /párrəjə neéezi ə/ *n* the order in which the mineral constituents of a rock are formed —**paragenetic** /párrəjə néttik/ *adj* —**paragenetically** /-néttikli/ *adv*

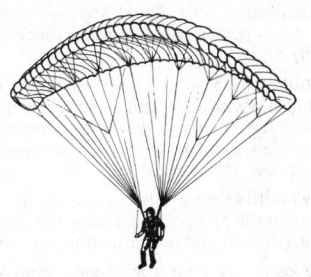
paragliding

paragliding /párrə glīding/ *n* a sport in which somebody jumps from an aircraft or a high place wearing a rectangular parachute that allows control of direction in the descent to the ground [< PARA-²] —**paraglider** *n*

paragoge /párrə gog/, **paragogue** *n* a letter, sound, or syllable added at the end of a word as the word develops, e.g. the 's' in 'towards' [Mid-16C. Via late Latin < Greek *paragōgē*, literally 'carrying beyond' < *agōgē* 'carrying'] —**paragogic** /párrə gójjik/ *adj* —**paragogically** *adv*

paragon /párrəgən/ *n* **1.** somebody or something that is the very best example of something **2.** a perfect diamond that weighs at least 100 carats [Mid-16C. Via French < Italian *paragone*, originally 'touchstone to test gold' < medieval Greek *parakonan* 'compare', literally 'sharpen against']

paragraph /párrə graaf, -graf/ *n* **1.** SECTION OF WRITING a piece of writing that consists of one or more sentences, begins on a new and often indented line, and contains a distinct idea or the words of one speaker **2.** SHORT NEWS STORY a short item of news or editorial comment in a newspaper ■ *vt* (**-graphs, -graphing, -graphed**) **1.** SET TEXT OUT IN PARAGRAPHS to arrange text in a series of paragraphs **2.** WRITE NEWS IN PARAGRAPH to report news or a story in a short paragraph [15C. Via French or medieval Latin < Greek *paragraphos* 'stroke marking a line in which there is a break in sense', literally 'writing beside' < *graphein* 'write'] —**paragrapher** *n*

paragraphia /párrə gráffi ə, -graáfi ə/ *n* the writing of words or letters different from the ones intended, as a result of a stroke or disease [Late 19C. < PARA-¹ + Greek *-graphia* 'writing']

Paraguay

Paraguay /párrə gwī/ **1.** country in South America, bordered by Bolivia, Brazil, and Argentina. Language: Spanish. Currency: guaraní. Capital: Asunción. Population: 6,036,900 (2001). Area: 406,752 sq. km/157,048 sq. mi. Official name **Republic of Paraguay 2.** river in central South America. The chief tributary of the River Paraná, it rises in western Brazil and flows south across central Paraguay to join the Paraná at the northern border of Argentina. Length: 2,550 km/1,580 mi. —**Paraguayan** /párrə gwī ən/ *n, adj*

Parahyba /párrə eébə/ former name for **João Pessoa**

parahydrogen /párrə hídrəjən/ *n* a form of molecular hydrogen in which the two atomic nuclei spin in opposite directions. Parahydrogen makes up about 25 per cent of hydrogen molecules.

para-influenza virus *n* a virus of a group of four similar to the influenza virus that causes respiratory illnesses, especially in children, with symptoms of severe sore throat, croup, and pneumonia

parakeet /párrə keet/ *n* a small tropical parrot that has a long tail and is usually very brightly coloured. Native to: tropics, subtropics. [Mid-16C. < Old French *paraquet*]

paralanguage /párrə lang gwij/ *n* nonverbal vocal nuances in communication that may add meaning to language as it is used in context, e.g. tone of voice or whispering

paraldehyde /pə ráldi hīd/ *n* a colourless liquid polymer of acetaldehyde. Use: sedative, solvent. Formula: $C_6H_{12}O_3$.

paralegal /párrə leég'l/ *n* somebody with specialist legal training who assists a fully qualified lawyer ■ *adj* relating to a paralegal or the work of a paralegal

paraleipsis *n* LITERAT same as **paralipsis**

~~paralel~~ incorrect spelling of **parallel**

paralinguistics /párrə ling gwístiks/ *n* the study of paralanguage (*takes a singular verb*) —**paralinguistic** *adj*

paralipomena /párrə lī pómmənə/ *npl* material added to a literary work as a supplement [Late 17C. Via late Latin < Greek *paraleipomena* '(things) left out' < *paraleipein* (see PARALIPSIS)]

Paralipomena /párrə lī pómmənə/ *npl* the title used for the Book of Chronicles in the Vulgate (*sometimes used in the sing*) [14C. < late Latin (see PARALIPOMENA); because it contains material omitted from the Books of Kings]

Paralipomenon /párrə lī pómmə non/ BIBLE singular of **Paralipomena**

paralipsis /párrə lípsiss/ (*plural* **-lipses** /-líp seez/), **paraleipsis** /-lípsiss/ (*plural* **-leipses** /-līp seez/) *n* a rhetorical technique in which you emphasize a topic by saying in some way that you will not talk about it, e.g. by using the phrase 'not to mention' [Mid-16C. Via late Latin < Greek *paraleipsis* 'omission' < *paraleipein* 'leave on one side' < *leipein* 'leave']

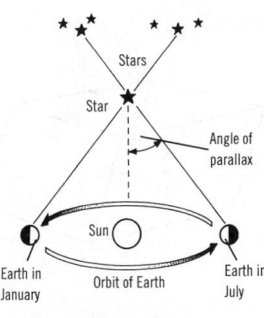
parallax (sense 2)

parallax /párrə laks/ *n* **1.** an apparent change in the position of an object when the person looking at the object changes position **2.** the angle between two imaginary lines from two different observation points meeting at an astronomical object, used to measure the object's distance from Earth [Late 16C. Via French < Greek *parallaxis* 'alternation, angle between two lines' < *parallassein* 'alter' < *allos* 'other'] —**parallactic** /párrə láktik/ *adj* —**parallactically** *adv*

parallax view *n* a viewpoint from which you can observe and study something or somebody from a new angle, thus gaining insights unavailable before

parallel /párrə lel/ *adj* **1.** RESEMBLING EACH OTHER relating to two things that are comparable because they are similar and share many characteristics **2.** MATHS ALWAYS SAME DISTANCE APART relating to or being lines, planes, or curved surfaces that are always the same distance apart and therefore never meet **3.** COMPUT USING SEVERAL ITEMS OF INFORMATION SIMULTANEOUSLY relating to a computer that processes several items of information at the same time **4.** GRAM OF IDENTICAL SYNTACTIC CONSTRUCTIONS describes two or more phrases or clauses in a single sentence that have identical syntactic constructions **5.** MUSIC KEEPING SAME MUSICAL INTERVAL THROUGHOUT describes the movement of two voices or melodies that match each other exactly in pitch, while preserving the same interval between them ■ *n* **1.** COMPARISON a comparison between two things that reveals their similarity ○ *It's easy to draw a parallel between their two careers.* **2.** SOMEBODY OR SOMETHING EQUIVALENT somebody or something that is very similar to another, sharing many characteristics **3.** MATHS PARALLEL LINE OR PLANE any of a set of parallel geometric forms, especially lines or planes **4.** GEOG LINE PARALLEL TO EQUATOR an imaginary line round the Earth that lies parallel to the equator and represents a specific degree of latitude from the equator **5.** GEOG LINE ON MAP a line on a map representing a parallel of latitude **6.** ELEC ENG CONFIGURATION OF ELECTRICAL COMPONENTS the way in which electrical components or circuits are connected so that the same voltage is applied across each component or circuit ○ *connected in parallel* ■ *vt* (**-lels, -leling, -leled**) **1.** CORRESPOND TO SOMETHING to be similar to something else, especially in following a similar course of events **2.** MATCH SOMEBODY OR SOMETHING to be equal to or as good as somebody or something else **3.** COMPARE SOMETHING TO SOMETHING ELSE to compare something with something else, or show something to be similar to something else **4.** BE PARALLEL to be or run parallel to something **5.** MAKE SOMETHING PARALLEL TO SOMETHING to make something be or run parallel to something else ■ *adv* ALONGSIDE in a parallel manner so as to keep the same distance away from something and never meet it [Mid-16C. Via French and Latin < Greek *parallēlos* 'beside each other' < *allēlōn* 'each other' < *allos* 'other'] ◇ **in parallel (with somebody or something)** in conjunction with and at the same time as somebody or something else

parallel bars *npl* a piece of gymnastic equipment consisting of two horizontal bars parallel to each other and supported on vertical posts (*takes a plural verb*) ■ *n* an event in a gymnastics competition that uses the parallel bars (*takes a singular verb*)

parallel broadcast *n* a broadcast that is transmitted simultaneously by radio or television and over the Internet

parallel cousin *n* a cousin who is the child of your mother's sister or your father's brother

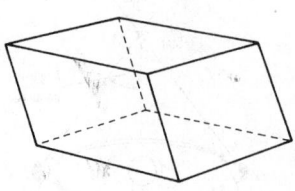

parallelepiped

Paralympic Games

parallelepiped /párrə lellə pí ped, -le léppi ped/ *n* a polyhedron consisting of six faces that are parallelograms [Late 16C. < Greek *parallēlepipedon* 'parallel surface' < *epipedon* 'surface' < *pedon* 'ground']

paralleling /párrə leling/ *n* the exploitation of differences in commercial markets by buying an expensive product in a place where prices are relatively low and selling it on in a place where prices are higher

parallelism /párrə lelizəm/ *n* **1.** PARALLEL STATE the condition of being parallel **2.** LITERAT REPETITION FOR EFFECT in writing, the deliberate repetition of words or sentence structures for effect **3.** PHILOSOPHY THEORY OF MIND-BODY RELATIONSHIP the philosophical theory that mind and body do not interact but follow separate parallel tracks, without any relationship of cause and effect existing between the two —**parallelist** *n*

parallel of latitude *n* GEOG same as **parallel** *n* (sense 4)

parallelogram /párrə léllə gram/ *n* a two-dimensional geometric figure formed of four sides in which both pairs of opposite sides are parallel and of equal length, and the opposite angles are equal [Late 16C. Via late Latin < Greek *parallēlogrammon* < *parallēlos* (see PARALLEL)]

parallel play *n* play in which two or more children who are in close proximity and possibly involved in similar activities do not interact with each other socially

parallel port *n* a connection point through which a computer sends and receives data simultaneously by means of a number of separate wires, commonly used for connecting a printer or external storage device. Computers transmit data through the parallel port at higher speeds and with fewer errors than through the serial port.

parallel processing *n* the use of two or more processors to run different parts of the same computer program concurrently and merge the results, with significantly faster program execution. Parallel processing is used when many complex calculations are required, e.g. in weather modelling and digital special effects.

parallel ruler *n* a ruler designed for drawing parallel lines, constructed with two linked straight edges that remain parallel although the distance between them may be varied

parallel turn *n* a skiing turn executed by shifting the body weight and keeping the skis parallel, rather than by adjusting the line of the skis

paralogism /pə rállǝjizǝm/ *n* in logic, an invalid argument that is unintentional or that has gone unnoticed [Mid-16C. Via late Latin < Greek *paralogismos* < *paralogos* 'contrary to reason' < *logos* 'reason'] —**paralogist** *n* —**paralogistic** /pə rállǝ jístik/ *adj*

Paralympic Games /párrǝ límpik-/, **Paralympics** /párrǝ límpiks/ *npl* an international sports competition for athletes with disabilities —**Paralympian** *n*

paralyse /párrǝ līz/ (-lyses, -lysing, -lysed) *vt* **1.** DEPRIVE SOMEBODY OF VOLUNTARY MOVEMENT to cause somebody to lose the ability to move a part of the body, either by damaging nerve or muscle function, or through the use of a drug **2.** MAKE SOMEBODY TEMPORARILY UNABLE TO MOVE to make somebody temporarily unable to move, e.g. with fear **3.** BRING SYSTEM TO STANDSTILL to bring a system or network to a stop or prevent it from

functioning effectively [Late 18C. < French *paralyser* < Latin *paralysis* (see PARALYSIS)]

paralysis /pǝ rállǝssiss/ *n* **1.** loss of voluntary movement as a result of damage to nerve or muscle function **2.** failure to take action or make progress [Pre-12C. Via Latin < Greek *paralusis* < *paraluesthai* 'be disabled' < *para-* 'on one side' + *luein* 'release']

paralysis agitans /-ájji tanz/ *n* MED same as **Parkinson's disease** [*Agitans* < Latin, present participle of *agitare* 'shake']

paralytic /párrǝ líttik/ *adj* **1.** DRUNK extremely drunk (*informal*) **2.** OF PARALYSIS relating to loss of voluntary movement ■ *n* OFFENSIVE TERM an offensive term for somebody affected by loss of voluntary movement [14C. Via French and Latin < Greek *paralutikos* < *paralusis* (see PARALYSIS)] —**paralytically** *adv*

paralyze *vt* US spelling of **paralyse**

paramagnetic /párrǝ mag néttik/ *adj* describes a substance that is weakly magnetized so that it will lie parallel to a magnetic field. The phenomenon results from the presence of unpaired electrons in the atoms of the substance, which cause the atoms to act as tiny magnets when a magnetic field is applied. —**paramagnetism** /-mágnǝtizǝm/ *n*

Paramaribo /párrǝ márribō/ port and capital city of Suriname, located in the north of the country near the Atlantic Ocean. Population: 289,000 (1997).

paramatta /párrǝ máttǝ/, **parramatta** *n* a lightweight fabric made from wool blended with silk or cotton [Early 19C. After PARRAMATTA]

paramecium /párrǝ meéssi ǝm/ (*plural* **-cia** /-si ǝ/ or **-ciums**) *n* a single-celled microscopic organism (**protozoan**) with fine appendages (**cilia**) around its body that it uses to move around in water and to capture bacteria. Genus: *Paramecium*. [Mid-18C. < modern Latin < Greek *paramēkēs* 'oval'; from its shape]

paramedic /párrǝ méddik/ *n* **1.** somebody trained to perform emergency medical procedures in the absence of a doctor, especially a member of an ambulance crew **2.** somebody whose work supports that of doctors and nurses, e.g. a radiologist or a laboratory technician —**paramedical** *adj*

parameter /pǝ rámmitǝr/ *n* **1.** LIMITING FACTOR a fact or circumstance that restricts how something is done or what can be done ○ *working within the parameters of cost and manpower* **2.** VARIABLE QUANTITY DETERMINING OUTCOME a measurable quantity, e.g. temperature, that determines the result of a scientific experiment and can be altered to vary the result **3.** ⚠ NOTABLE CHARACTERISTIC a distinguishing feature or notable characteristic **4.** MATHS VARIABLE MATHEMATICAL VALUE in a mathematical expression, a variable value that, when it changes, gives another different but related mathematical expression from a limited series of such expressions **5.** STATS OVERALL QUANTITY a general quantity that relates to an entire population, as distinct from an individual statistic that relates to a sample [Mid-17C. < modern Latin *parametrum* < Greek *para* 'beside' + *metron* 'measure'] —**parametric** /párrǝ méttrik/ *adj*

USAGE **Parameter**, which has special meanings in science, mathematics, and statistics, has taken on a general sense 'limiting factor', as in *had to adhere to all the parameters of tax law with regard to the establishment of family trusts and foundations*. This meaning, along with the others, is acceptable. Some people, however, object to yet another general meaning

of the word, 'a distinguishing feature or notable characteristic', as in *An important parameter in their culture is vegetarianism*, where *characteristic* or *feature* would be more precise and less pompous. Avoid confusing *parameter* with *perimeter* ('boundary'): *Guards patrolled the perimeter* [not *parameter*] *of the military installation*.

parametric equalizer *n* a device used with audio equipment to cut or boost selected frequencies of an output signal by continuously widening or narrowing the filtered frequencies of the signal. It is a more sophisticated version of the standard bass and treble controls on a stereo system.

parametric equations *npl* mathematical equations in which coordinates of points are explicitly expressed in terms of independent parameters

paramilitary /párrǝ míllitǝri/ *adj* **1.** USING MILITARY TECHNIQUES using military weapons and tactics to fight within a country against the official ruling power **2.** MILITARY IN STYLE similar to or modelled on the military but not belonging to it **3.** ASSISTING OFFICIAL MILITARY FORCES organized and staffed by civilians to provide support for the regular military services ○ *a paramilitary unit* ■ *n* (*plural* **-ies**) UNOFFICIAL SOLDIER a member of a paramilitary organization, especially one fighting against the official ruling power

paramnesia /párram neézi ǝ/ *n* **1.** false memories of events that did not really take place **2.** an inability to recall the meanings of common words

paramorph /párrǝ mawrf/ *n* a mineral formed by the conversion of one crystalline form (**polymorph**) into another. Calcite is a paramorph of aragonite. —**paramorphism** /párrǝ máwrfizǝm/ *n*

paramount /párrǝ mownt/ *adj* greatest in importance or significance [Mid-16C. < Anglo-Norman *paramont* < *par* 'by' + *amont* 'above'] —**paramountcy** —**paramountly** *adv*

paramour /párrǝ moor/ *n* a lover, especially one in a relationship with a married person (*literary*) ○ '*found thee out even in the arms of thy paramour*' (Sir Walter Scott, *Ivanhoe*; 1819) [14C. < obsolete *par amour* 'by way of love' < Old French]

paramyxovirus /párrǝ míksō vīrǝss/ *n* a virus belonging to the group that includes the mumps and measles viruses and the para-influenza virus

Paraná /párrǝ naá/ **1.** river in eastern South America, flowing through Brazil, along the border with Paraguay, and through Argentina, reaching the Atlantic Ocean at the Río de la Plata. Length: 2,800 km/1,740 mi. **2.** city in northeastern Argentina, on the River Paraná. Population: 207,041 (1991).

parang /paá rang/ *n* a large knife with a short straight-edged blade, used in Malaysia and Indonesia as a weapon and as a tool [Mid-19C. < Malay]

paranoia /párrǝ nóy ǝ/ *n* **1.** extreme and unreasonable suspicion of other people and their motives **2.** a psychiatric disorder involving systematized delusion, usually of persecution [Early 19C. < Greek, 'out of your mind' < *nous* 'mind']

paranoiac /párrǝ nóy ak/ *adj* characteristic of or resembling paranoia ■ *n* somebody affected by paranoia

paranoid /párrǝ noyd/ *adj* **1.** DISTRUSTFUL obsessively anxious about something, or unreasonably suspicious of other people and their thoughts or motives **2.** SHOWING CHARACTERISTICS OF PARANOIA relating to or showing the characteristics of the psychiatric disorder paranoia ■ *n* PARANOID PERSON somebody who is paranoid (*dated*)

paranormal /párrǝ náwrm'l/ *adj* unable to be explained or understood in terms of scientific knowledge ■ *n* paranormal events or phenomena —**paranormally** *adv*

paraparesis /párrǝpǝ reéssiss/ *n* a medical condition in which both legs, and often the bladder, have little voluntary control —**paraparetic** /-réttik/ *adj*

parapente /párrǝ pont/ *n* **1.** a lightweight parachute used by climbers to make descents from high mountains **2.** a modified parachute used for paraskiing and paragliding, with a framework of inflatable tubes that give it a semirigid structure, allowing it to be steered like a hang-glider [Late 20C. < French < *parachute* + *pente* 'slope']

parapenting /párrə ponting/, **paraponting** n EXTREME SPORTS same as **paragliding** [Late 20C. < *parapente* < PARACHUTE + French *pente* 'slope'] —**parapenter** n

parapet /párrəpət, -pet/ n **1.** a low protective wall built where there is a sudden dangerous drop, e.g. along the edge of a balcony, roof, or bridge. Some parapets are battlemented, especially on castles, and many are built as ornamental features. **2.** a bank of soil, rubble, or sandbags piled up along the edge of a military trench for protection from enemy fire [Late 16C. Via French < Italian *parapetto* < *parare* 'protect' + *petto* 'chest' (< Latin *pectus*)]

paraph /párrəf, pə ráff/ n a decorative flourish written under a signature to finish it off or, formerly, to protect against forgery [Late 16C. Via French < medieval Latin *paragraphus* (see PARAGRAPH)]

~~paraphanalia~~ incorrect spelling of **paraphernalia**

paraphasia /párrə fáyzi ə/ n a speech disorder of neurological origin in which the speaker's words are jumbled unintelligibly

paraphernalia /párrəfər náyli ə/ n (*takes a singular or plural verb*) **1.** ASSORTED OBJECTS assorted objects or items, especially of equipment required for a specific activity **2.** THINGS CHARACTERISTIC OF SOMETHING things usually associated with something ○ *banks, commercial buildings, department stores, and all the paraphernalia of a sophisticated modern city* **3.** WEDDING GIFTS TO WIFE formerly, items of property given to a wife on her wedding day by her new husband and regarded by law as belonging to her [Mid-17C. < medieval Latin < Latin *parapherna* < Greek *paraphernē* 'beside the dowry' < *phernē* 'dowry']

paraphilia /párrə fílli ə/ n the need for an extreme or dangerous stimulus such as a sadistic or masochistic practice in order to achieve sexual arousal or orgasm —**paraphiliac** n

paraphrase /párrə frayz/ vt (**-phrases, -phrasing, -phrased**) to restate something using other words, especially in order to make it simpler or shorter ■ n a rephrased, simplified, and usually shorter version of written or spoken material [Mid-16C. Via French and Latin < Greek *paraphrasis* < *paraphrazein*, literally 'explain alongside' < *phrazein* 'explain'] —**paraphraser** n —**paraphrastic** /párrə frástik/ adj

paraphysis /pə ráffississ/ n (*plural* **-physes** /-fi seez/) n an erect sterile filament that grows among the reproductive organs of fungi, algae, and mosses [Mid-19C. < modern Latin, literally 'growth beside' < Greek *phusis* 'growth'] —**paraphysate** /-sət, -sayt/ adj

paraplegia /párrə pléejə/ n total inability to move both legs and usually the lower part of the trunk, often as a result of disease or injury of the spine [Mid-17C. Via modern Latin < Greek *paraplēgiē* 'stroke on one side' < *paraplēssein* 'strike on one side' < *plessein* 'to strike'] —**paraplegic** adj, n

parapodium /párrə pódi əm/ n (*plural* **-dia** /-di ə/) n an appendage on the body of some sea worms, occurring in pairs on each segment of the worm's body, used for swimming, crawling, or holding onto things

paraponting n EXTREME SPORTS another spelling of **parapenting**

paraprofessional /párrəprə fésh'nəl/ n N Am a trained assistant to a professional person —**paraprofessional** adj

parapsychology /párrə sī kólləji/ n the study of supposed mental phenomena that cannot be explained by known psychological or scientific principles, e.g. extrasensory perception and telepathy —**parapsychological** /-sīkə lójjik'l/ adj —**parapsychologist** n

paraquat /párrə kwot/ n a widely used, fast-acting weedkiller that destroys green plant tissue on contact [Mid-20C. < PARA-[1] + QUATERNARY; from the position of its bonds]

Pará rubber tree /pə ráa-/ n a tree that yields latex for making rubber. Native to: tropical South America. Latin name: *Hevea brasiliensis*. [After a state in N Brazil]

parasailing /párrə sayling/ n a sport in which somebody wearing a parachute rises high into the air from a platform at the back of a moving motorboat

or from the water behind the boat and is towed along [Mid-20C. < PARA-[2]]

parascending /párrə sending/ n a sport in which somebody wearing an open parachute is towed along by a speedboat or land vehicle, rises into the air, and descends independently using the parachute [Late 20C. < PARA-[2] + ASCEND]

parascience /párrə sī ənss/ n the study of phenomena that cannot be explained or tested by conventional scientific methods

paraselene /párrəsi leéni/ n (*plural* **-nae** /-nee/) n an image of the Moon seen within a lunar halo [Mid-17C. < PARA-[1] + Greek *selēnē* 'moon'] —**paraselenic** /-lénnik/ adj

parasexual /párrə sékshoo əl/ adj describes a type of reproduction, seen in some fungi, in which the recombination of parental chromosomes takes place without the usual formation of sex cells by cell division (**meiosis**) —**parasexuality** /-sekshoo álləti/ n

Parashah /párrə shaa/ (*plural* **-shoth** /-shót/) n in Judaism, a passage from the Torah read during traditional weekly worship at the synagogue [Early 17C. < Hebrew *pārāšāh* 'division']

parasite /párrə sīt/ n **1.** a plant or animal that lives on or in another, usually larger, host organism in a way that harms or is of no advantage to the host **2.** somebody who exploits others without doing anything in return [Mid-16C. Via Latin < Greek *parasitos* 'somebody who eats from another's table' < *sitos* 'grain, food']

parasitic /párrə síttik/, **parasitical** /párrə síttik'l/ adj **1.** living in or on another host organism, usually causing it harm **2.** living off the generosity of others without offering anything in return —**parasitically** adv

parasiticide /párrə sítti sīd/ adj used or designed to destroy parasites ■ n a substance used to destroy parasites —**parasiticidal** /-sitti sīd'l/ adj

parasitise vt BIOL another spelling of **parasitize**

parasitism /párrə sītizəm/ n **1.** symbiosis in which one organism lives as a parasite in or on another organism **2.** VET same as **parasitosis**

parasitize /párrəssi tīz, -sī-/ (**-izes, -izing, -ized**), **parasitise** (**-ises, -ising, -ised**) vt to infest or live on an animal or plant as a parasite

parasitoid /párrəssi toyd, -sī-/ adj describes an insect that lays its eggs inside the living body of another animal or insect. The hatched newborns feed off the body, eventually killing the host. ■ n an insect that lays its eggs within a host, eventually causing the death of the host

parasitology /párrə sī tólləji/ n the scientific study of plants and animals that live as parasites —**parasitological** /-sītə lójjik'l/ adj

parasitosis /párrə sī tóssiss/ (*plural* **-toses** /-tós seez/) n a disease that develops as a result of infestation by parasites

paraskiing /párrə skee ing/ n the sport of skiing off high mountains and descending through the air using a light steerable parachute (**parapente**) made of inflatable tubes of fabric [Mid-20C. < PARA-[2]]

parasol /párrə sol/ n an umbrella made to provide shade from the sun [Early 17C. Via French < Italian *parasole* < *parare* 'protect' + *sole* 'sun']

parastatal /párrə stáyt'l/ adj performing a function usually associated with a government and under its indirect control ■ n a parastatal organization, business, or industry

parasuicide /párrə sóo i sīd/ n **1.** a suicide attempt or act of self-injury that is motivated by a desire to draw attention to personal problems rather than by a genuine wish to die **2.** somebody who carries out a parasuicide

parasympathetic /párrə simpə théttik/ adj relating or belonging to the parasympathetic nervous system [Early 20C. < PARA-[1]; because some of the nerves run beside sympathetic nerves]

parasympathetic nervous system n one of the two divisions in the part of the nervous system that controls involuntary and unconscious bodily functions (**autonomic nervous system**). Its actions

include slowing the heart, constricting the pupils, and relaxing the bowels.

parasynthesis /párrə sínthississ/ n the formation of words by a combination of smaller words and additional elements. For example, 'heavy-handed' is formed by parasynthesis, combining the adjective 'heavy' with 'handed', which in turn is 'hand' with '-ed' added. —**parasynthetic** /-sin théttik/ adj

parasyntheton /párrə sínthi ton/ (*plural* **-ta** /-tə/) n a word formed by the combination of smaller words and additional elements

parataxis /párrə táksiss/ n the combination of clauses or phrases without the use of conjunctions such as 'and' or 'so', e.g. in 'He saved my life – he deserves a medal' [Mid-19C. < Greek *parataxis* 'place side by side' < *tassein* 'arrange'] —**paratactic** /-táktik/ adj —**paratactically** adv

paratha /pə ráatə/ n a flat unleavened bread of South Asian origin, made from flour, water, and clarified butter, often eaten with a filling [Mid-20C. < Hindi *parāṭhā*]

parathion /párrə thí on/ n a colourless highly toxic oil. Use: insecticide. Formula: $C_{10}H_{14}NO_5PS$. [Mid-20C. < PARA-[1] + *thiophosphate* + -ON[2]]

parathyroid /párrə thí royd/ adj **1.** relating to or produced by the parathyroid glands **2.** in the area around the thyroid gland ■ n PHYSIOL same as **parathyroid gland**

parathyroid gland n a small gland of a group of four that lie in or near the walls of the thyroid gland and secrete a hormone that controls the depositing of calcium and phosphorus in bones

parathyroid hormone n a hormone secreted by the parathyroid glands that controls calcium and phosphorus balance in the body

paratrooper /párrə troopər/ n a soldier trained to go into battle by parachute, especially one who is also a member of an airborne unit —**paratroops** npl

paratyphoid fever /párrə tí foyd-/, **paratyphoid** n an infectious bacterial disease similar to typhoid but with much less severe symptoms, usually limited to a pink rash, diarrhoea, and some abdominal pain

Paravac /párrə vach/, **Borislav** (b. 1943) Serb representative of the presidency of Bosnia and Herzegovina (1998–), which rotates between a Serb, a Bosnian Muslim, and a Croat

paravane /párrə vayn/ n a torpedo-shaped device with sharp fins at the front, towed by a ship to cut the moorings of submerged mines [Early 20C. < *para-* 'protector' (after PARASOL)]

par avion /-ávvi on/ adv by air mail [< French, 'by aeroplane']

parazoan /párrə zố ən/ n (*plural* **-zoa** /-zố ə/) n a member of the subkingdom of invertebrate animals that includes sponges. Subkingdom: *Parazoa*. [Early 20C. < modern Latin *Parazoa* < Greek *para* 'beside', after *Protozoa*, *Metazoa*]

parboil /paár boyl/ (**-boils, -boiling, -boiled**) vt **1.** to boil something until it is partly cooked, usually before frying or roasting it **2.** to make somebody uncomfortably hot [15C. Via Old French *parboillir* 'boil thoroughly' < late Latin *perbullire* < Latin *bullire* 'boil']

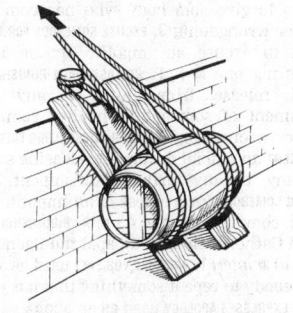

parbuckle

parbuckle /paár buk'l/ n a rope sling for lifting or lowering barrels, logs, or similar objects [Early 17C. Origin ?]

Parcae /paár see/ *npl* in Roman mythology, the Fates. Greek equivalent **Moirai** [Late 16C. < Latin]

parcel /paárss'l/ *n* **1.** SOMETHING WRAPPED UP one or more things wrapped up together in paper or other packaging **2.** PORTION a portion into which something is divided, especially a piece of land that was originally part of a larger area **3.** BATCH OF COMMERCIAL GOODS a quantity of wholesale merchandise treated as a unit, or a sales transaction for such a quantity of merchandise **4.** GROUP a collection of people or things (*archaic or literary*) ○ *'a parcel of rascals'* (Thomas Paine, *The Age of Reason*; 1794) ■ *vt* (**-cels, -celling, -celled**) **1.** MAKE PARCEL OF SOMETHING to wrap something or a group of things into a parcel **2.** NAUT PROTECT ROPE to bind canvas tightly round rope or cable to protect it [14C. Via French < Latin *particula* 'small part']

parcel out *vt* to divide and distribute something between a number of people

parcel-gilt *adj* partly gilded, often on the inside but not on the outside

parcel post *n* a postal service that collects, processes, and delivers parcels

parch /paarch/ (**parches, parching, parched**) *vt* to make somebody or something extremely dry through water deprivation or exposure to heat [14C. Origin ?]

parched /paarcht/ *adj* **1.** completely lacking in moisture because of hot conditions or lack of rainfall **2.** very thirsty (*informal*)

SYNONYMS See *dry*.

parchment /paárchmənt/ *n* **1.** FORMER WRITING MATERIAL a creamy or yellowish material made from dried and treated sheepskin, goatskin, or other animal hide, formerly used for books and documents **2.** DOCUMENT a manuscript or other work written, drawn, or painted on a sheet of parchment **3.** HIGH-QUALITY PAPER strong, smooth or textured, usually off-white paper used for special documents, letters, or artwork [13C. < Old French *parchemin* < alteration of Latin *pergamena*, after Greek *Pergamon* 'Pergamum']

parclose /paár klōz/ *n* a screen or railing that separates or encloses a side chapel, private tomb, or other special area within a large church [15C. < Old French, past participle of *parclore* 'close off' < Latin *claudere* 'to close']

parcourse /paár kawrss/ *n US* a training circuit in a park or other open space, where people can walk or run between stations carrying equipment and instructions as fitness exercises [Late 20C. < French *parcours* 'course' < medieval Latin *percursus*, literally 'running through' < *percurrere* 'run through' < Latin *currere* 'to run']

pard[1] /paard/ *n* a large cat, especially a leopard or a panther (*archaic*) [13C. Via French < Greek *pardos* < Iranian]

pard[2] /paard/ *n US* same as **pardner** (*slang*) [Mid-19C. Shortening]

pardner /paárdnər/ *n N Am* used as a term of address to a friend (*slang*) [Late 18C. Representing a pronunciation of PARTNER]

pardon /paárd'n/ *vt* (**-dons, -doning, -doned**) **1.** EXEMPT GUILTY PARTY FROM PUNISHMENT to officially release from any, or any further, punishment somebody who has committed a crime or wrongdoing **2.** FORGIVE GUILTY PARTY to forgive somebody who has committed a crime or wrongdoing **3.** EXCUSE SOMEBODY FOR SOMETHING IMPOLITE to excuse an impolite act or a person committing one ■ *n* **1.** RELEASE FROM PUNISHMENT the official release from any, or any further, punishment of somebody who has committed a crime or wrongdoing **2.** PAPER AUTHORIZING FREEDOM FROM PUNISHMENT an official document releasing somebody from any, or any further, punishment **3.** ACT OF EXCUSING SOMEBODY forgiveness of an impolite act or a person committing one **4.** CHR INDULGENCE in the Roman Catholic Church, a papal indulgence (*dated informal*) ■ *interj* **1.** WHAT DID YOU SAY? used as a request to somebody to repeat something that has just been said **2.** EXPRESSES APOLOGY used as an apology for doing something impolite or wrong [13C. < Old French *pardun* < *pardoner* 'grant thoroughly' < medieval Latin *perdonare* < Latin *donare* 'give, grant'] —**pardonable** *adj* —**pardonably** *adv* ◇ **pardon me 1.** used as an apology for doing something impolite or wrong **2.** *N Am* used as a request to somebody to repeat something that has just been said

pardoner /paárd'nər/ *n* **1.** a granter of a pardon **2.** somebody who, in medieval times, made a living by selling papal indulgences that were believed to free people from their sins

pare /pair/ (**pares, paring, pared**) *vt* **1.** to trim something such as fingernails or toenails **2.** to remove the skin or outer layer of something such as a vegetable or fruit thinly and neatly [13C. Via French *parer* 'prepare, trim' < Latin *parare*]

SPELLCHECK See *pair*.

pare down *vt* to reduce a total amount or number, usually an amount of money or a number of workers, slowly and steadily

paregoric /párrə górrik/ *n* a camphorated tincture of opium, once a major source of opium addiction. Use: formerly, nonprescription painkiller. ■ *adj* soothing or painkilling [Late 17C. Via late Latin < Greek *parēgorikos* 'soothing' < *para* 'beside' + *agoreuein* 'speak']

parenchyma /pə réngkimə/ *n* **1.** BOT PLANT TISSUE soft plant tissue made up of thin-walled cells that forms the greater part of leaves, stem pith, roots, and fruit pulp **2.** ANAT SPECIALIZED ORGAN TISSUE the tissue that makes up the specialized parts of an organ, rather than the blood vessels and connective or supporting tissue **3.** ZOOL WORM TISSUE the loose meshwork of cells that surrounds internal organs and fills spaces inside the body of animals such as flatworms [Mid-17C. Via modern Latin < Greek *paregkhuma* 'soft tissue' < *paregkhein* 'pour in beside' < *khein* 'pour'] —**parenchymatous** /párren kímmətəss/ *adj*

parent /páirənt/ *n* **1.** MOTHER OR FATHER somebody's mother, father, or legal guardian **2.** ORIGIN OF SOMETHING ELSE something from which one or more similar and separate things have developed, or to which they are attached (*often used before a noun*) ○ *money transferred from the parent fund* **3.** CHEM EARLIER ATOMIC FORM an atom, molecule, or ion that undergoes change to become a new product. The starting components in a chemical reaction are the parent molecules. (*often used before a noun*) **4.** PHYS PARTICLE'S EARLIER FORM a radioactive particle that disintegrates to give a new particle (**nuclide**) as a subsequent member of a radioactive decay series (*often used before a noun*) ■ *vt* (**-ents, -enting, -ented**) ACT AS PARENT TO SOMEBODY to be or act as a parent to somebody or something [15C. Via French < Latin *parent-* < present participle of *parere* 'give birth'] —**parenthood** *n* —**parentless** *adj*

parentage /páirəntij/ *n* **1.** a person's parents or ancestors, especially when regarded in terms of social characteristics or geographical origins ○ *of Irish parentage* **2.** the origins or sources that something has developed from

parental /pə rént'l/ *adj* **1.** relating to, belonging to, or provided by parents **2.** describes the original generation of individuals from which all subsequent generations have been bred —**parentally** *adv*

parental leave *n* time off from work, granted to a parent to care for a newborn or newly adopted child

parenteral /pa réntərəl/ *adj* **1.** describes drug administration other than by the mouth or the rectum, e.g. by injection, infusion, or implantation **2.** describes drugs that are administered by injection, infusion, or implantation [Early 20C. < PARA-[1] + Greek *enteron* 'intestine'] —**parenterally** *adv*

parenthesis /pə rénthississ/ (*plural* **-theses** /-this seez/) *n* **1.** PRINTING same as **bracket** *n* (sense 1) **2.** BRACKETED MATTER a word or phrase that comments on or qualifies part of the sentence in which it is found and is isolated from it by brackets or dashes **3.** DEPARTURE FROM TOPIC a piece of speech or writing that wanders off from the main topic **4.** INTERVAL something that acts as a pause or break in something (*formal*) [Mid-16C. Via late Latin < Greek *parentithenai* 'insert' < *tithenai* 'to place'] ◇ **in parenthesis** as an additional qualifying, explanatory, or otherwise separate comment

parenthesize /pə rénthə sīz/ (**-sizes, -sizing, -sized**), **parenthesise** (**-sises, -sising, -sised**) *v* **1.** *vt* PUT SOMETHING IN BRACKETS to enclose part of a written or printed passage in brackets **2.** *vt* ADD SOMETHING AS EXTRA COMMENT to add a word, phrase, or opinion as an extra comment that is not wholly related to what is being said **3.** *vti* INSERT EXTRA COMMENTS to break up speech or writing with extra comments added throughout

parenthetical /párrən théttik'l/, **parenthetic** /párrən théttik/ *adj* **1.** added as an extra comment or parenthesis **2.** describes writing that uses or contains additional comments or notes added as parentheses —**parenthetically** *adv*

parenting /páirənting/ *n* the experiences, skills, qualities, and responsibilities involved in being a parent and in teaching and caring for a child (*often used before a noun*) ○ *parenting skills*

parent metal *n* in welding, the metal of any of the components that are to be welded together

parents' evening *n* an evening meeting at which teachers make themselves available in school for parents to discuss their children's progress

Parent-Teacher Association *n* a school body run by teachers and parents to organize fundraising and social events and encourage cooperation and understanding

pareo *n* CLOTHING another spelling of **pareu**

Parer /párrər/, **Damien** (1912–44) Australian photographer and film director. His World War II documentary *Kokoda Front Line* (1942) was the first Australian film to win an Academy Award. Full name **Parer, Damien Peter**

parergon /pə rúr gon/ (*plural* **-ga** /-gə/) *n* one thing that exists as an addition or as an additional detail to something else, especially an employment or activity that is subsidiary to a person's main occupation (*archaic or literary*) [Early 17C. < Greek < *para* 'beside' + *ergon* 'work']

paresis /pə reéssiss, párrississ/ *n* muscular weakness or partial inability to move caused by disease of the nervous system [Late 17C. < Greek, 'letting go' < *para* 'aside' + *hienai* 'to throw']

paresthesia *n* MED US spelling of **paraesthesia**

pareu /paa ráy oo/, **pareo** /paa ráy ō/ (*plural* **-os**) *n* a length of fabric worn wrapped round the hips by both men and women in Polynesian countries, or a garment resembling this for wearing [Mid-19C. < Tahitian]

pareve /paárəvə/, **parveh** /paárvə/, **parve** *adj* describes a food that, under Jewish law, is neither a dairy nor a meat product and can therefore be eaten with either as part of the same meal [Mid-20C. < Yiddish]

par excellence /paar éksə laaNss, -éksə laáNss, -éksələnss/ *adj* of the very best kind or highest quality [< French, 'by virtue of pre-eminence']

parfait /paar fáy/ *n* a rich dessert consisting of frozen whipped cream or rich ice cream flavoured with fruit [Late 19C. Via French, 'perfect' < Latin *perfectus* (see PERFECT)]

parfleche /paár flesh/ *n N Am* **1.** the hide of an animal, soaked and scraped to remove the hair, then stretched and dried, but not tanned **2.** a shield, bag, or other item made of parfleche [Early 19C. < Canadian French < French *parer* 'defend' + *flèche* 'arrow']

pargana /pər gúnnə/ *n S Asia* a division of a district or estate in northern South Asia, usually made for financial purposes [Early 17C. < Urdu, 'district']

parget /paárjit/ *n* **1.** PLASTER FOR WALLS OR CHIMNEYS plaster, whitewash, roughcast, or any similar material used to coat walls or line chimneys **2.** PLASTERWORK ornamental plasterwork on a wall ■ *vt* (**-gets, -geting, -geted**) COAT SOMETHING WITH PARGET to cover walls, line chimneys, or decorate a surface with parget [14C. Alteration (influenced by Old French *parjeter* 'throw about') of Old French *porgeter* 'plaster a wall' < *jeter* 'to throw'] —**pargeting** *n*

parhelia ASTRON plural of **parhelion**

parhelic /paar heélik, -héllik/, **parheliacal** /paárhə lī́ ək'l/ *adj* relating to or characteristic of a parhelion

parhelic circle *n* a luminous horizontal band in the sky that passes through the Sun and is caused by the Sun's rays reflecting off ice crystals in the atmosphere

parhelion /paar heéli ən/ (*plural* **-lia** /-li ə/) *n* a bright coloured spot near the Sun, often seen in pairs and caused by ice crystals in the atmosphere diffracting

light [Mid-17C. Via Latin < Greek *parēlion* < *para* 'beside' + *hēlios* 'sun']

pari- *prefix* equal ○ *parisyllabic* [< Latin *par* 'equal']

pariah /pə rī ə/ *n* **1.** somebody who is despised and avoided **2.** in South Asia, somebody who has defied a social law and has therefore been rejected by a caste [Early 17C. < Tamil *paraiyan* 'drummer' < *parai* 'festival drum'; because hereditary drummers were outside the caste system]

pariah dog *n* VERTEB same as **pye-dog** [Because seen as belonging to the fringes of society]

Parian /páiri ən/ *adj* **1.** OF MARBLE FROM PAROS describes a fine white marble that was mined on the Greek island of Paros in ancient times **2.** OF PORCELAIN FROM PAROS describes a variety of fine porcelain used mainly to make figures and originally from the Greek island of Paros **3.** OF PAROS relating to the Greek island of Paros ■ *n* SOMEBODY FROM PAROS somebody who comes from the Greek island of Paros [Mid-16C. < Latin *Parius* 'of Paros']

parietal /pə rī ət'l/ *adj* **1.** BIOL OF WALLS OF HOLLOW PART relating to the walls of any hollow part of a plant or animal such as a plant's ovary or an animal's skull **2.** *US* EDUC OF IN-COLLEGE RESIDENCE relating to residence within a college ■ *n* BIOL PARIETAL PART a parietal part of a plant or animal [Early 16C. Directly or via French < late Latin *parietalis* < *paries* 'wall']

parietal bone *n* either of two bones, one on each side of the skull, that form a part of the sides and roof of the skull

parietal cell *n* any of the cells that make up the peptic glands of the stomach and secrete hydrochloric acid

parietal lobe *n* the middle region of either of the two hemispheres of the brain, lying beneath the crown of the skull

pari-mutuel /párri myoótyoo əl/ *n US* a system of betting on horse races using an electronic machine that totals all bets, deducts management charges and taxes, and determines the final odds and payouts [< French, 'mutual wager']

paring /páiring/ *n* something that has been pared or cut off something larger, e.g. a thin slice of fruit or vegetable peel

paring knife *n* a short tapered knife with a sharp blade designed for removing the outer skin of vegetables or fruit

pari passu /párri pássoo, paári-/ *adv* **1.** at an equal rate or in an otherwise fair way, with no one person or group taking precedence over another **2.** together, step for step (*literary*) [< Latin, 'with equal step']

Paris[1] /párriss/ *n* in Greek mythology, a Trojan prince whose abduction of Helen, the wife of Menelaus, started the Trojan War [Via Latin < Greek]

Paris[2] /párriss/; *French* /pa rée/ capital city of France, situated in the north-central part of the country. Population: 2,125,246 (1999). —**Parisian** /pə rízzi ən/ *adj, n*

Paris Commune *n* a French insurrectionary committee established in Paris in 1871 in opposition to the national government and the peace terms it negotiated to end the Franco-Prussian War. National troops were sent from Versailles to crush the Communards, which they did in a number of notoriously bloody conflicts.

Paris green *n* a bright blue-green toxic powder. Use: pigment in paints, insecticide, wood preserver. Formula: $(CuO)_3As_2O_3.Cu(Cu_2H_3O_2)_2$. [Mid-19C. After PARIS[2]]

parish /párrish/ *n* **1.** DISTRICT WITH OWN CHURCH in the Anglican, Roman Catholic, and some other churches, a division of a diocese that has its own church and member of the clergy (*often used before a noun*) ○ *the parish priest* **2.** SMALL LOCAL GOVERNMENT UNIT the smallest defined area of local government in rural areas of England, containing a village with its own elected council **3.** PEOPLE OF PARISH the people who live in a parish (*takes a singular or plural verb*) [13C. Via Old French *parroche* < ecclesiastical Latin *parochia, paroechia* < Greek *paroikos* 'neighbour', literally 'dwelling nearby' < *oikos* 'dwelling']

parish council *n* in England, a local government

body that meets regularly to make decisions concerning a civil parish

parishioner /pə rísh'nər/ *n* a resident of a religious or civil parish [15C. < obsolete *parishion* < Old French *parochien* < *parroche* (see PARISH)]

parish pump *adj* of local interest only

parish register *n* a book in which the births, baptisms, marriages, and burials in a parish are recorded

parisyllabic /párri si lábbik/ *adj* describes a noun or verb that contains the same number of syllables in all of its inflections

parity[1] /párriti/ *n* **1.** EQUALITY equality of status or position, especially in terms of pay or rank **2.** SIMILARITY BETWEEN THINGS the quality of being similar or identical **3.** MATHS RELATIONSHIP BETWEEN NUMBERS a relationship of oddness or evenness between two numbers (**integers**). If two numbers are both odd or both even, they are said to have the same parity. If one is odd and one is even, they have different parity. **4.** FIN EQUALITY OF EXCHANGE RATE equivalence in the rate of exchange between several currencies **5.** COMPUT INTEGRITY OF TRANSMITTED DATA equivalence between computer data transmitted, e.g. by fax or e-mail, and the data received. Errors are checked by comparing the number of 1s in the message sent with the number in the message received. [Late 16C. Directly or via French < late Latin *paritas* < Latin *par* 'equal']

parity[2] /párriti/ *n* **1.** the condition or fact of having given birth **2.** the number of children that a woman has given birth to [Late 19C. < PAROUS]

park /paark/ *n* **1.** AREA FOR PUBLIC RECREATION a publicly owned area of land, usually with grass, trees, paths, sports fields, playgrounds, picnic areas, and other features for recreation and relaxation **2.** PROTECTED AREA OF COUNTRYSIDE an area of land reserved and managed so that it remains unspoiled, undeveloped, and as natural as possible **3.** PRIVATE AREA OF LAND a large area of land attached to a country house that forms a private estate **4.** PRIVATELY OWNED RECREATION FACILITY an area of privately owned land, developed to offer recreation or amusements to paying customers **5.** BUSINESS BUSINESS SITE an area of land developed for a group of related commercial enterprises ○ *a science park* **6.** TOWN PLAN ROAD OR DISTRICT a street or district, especially in a suburban area (*often used in placenames*) **7.** MIL AREA HOUSING MILITARY VEHICLES a designated area where military vehicles are kept, within a military base **8.** AUTOMOT POSITION ON AUTOMATIC GEARBOX a position on the gear selector of an automatic gearbox that acts as a brake when parking a motor vehicle **9.** SOCCER GAMES PITCH a football pitch (*informal*) **10.** *N Am* SPORTS STADIUM OR SPORTS FIELD a sports stadium or sports field ○ *a ball park* **11.** *Aus* PARKING SPACE a space to park a vehicle in (*informal*) ○ *Did you get a park OK?* ■ *v* (**parks, parking, parked**) **1.** *vti* STOP AND LEAVE VEHICLE to stop a motor vehicle beside or off the road and leave it there for some time **2.** *vti* MANOEUVRE MOTOR VEHICLE INTO SPACE to manoeuvre a motor vehicle into a space in order to park it **3.** *vt* SETTLE SOMEWHERE to sit down somewhere, usually with the intention of staying there for some time (*informal*) ○ *Just park yourself over there.* **4.** *vt* LEAVE SOMETHING SOMEWHERE to place or leave something somewhere temporarily, especially something heavy, bulky, or unwanted (*informal*) **5.** *vt* AEROSP PLACE SPACECRAFT IN ORBIT to place a spacecraft or satellite in orbit, usually temporarily **6.** *vi N Am* KISS IN PARKED CAR to kiss and cuddle in a parked car in a quiet and secluded location (*slang*) **7.** *vt* PUT SOMETHING ON HOLD to stop pursuing or dealing with something temporarily [13C. Via French *parc* < medieval Latin *parricus* < Germanic, 'enclosure']

CULTURAL NOTE *Mansfield Park*, a novel (1814) by Jane Austen. It tells the story of young Fanny Price, who is sent to live with her wealthy relatives, the Bertrams. Fanny's warmth and moral strength, which are contrasted with her uncle's stern traditionalism and the irresponsible flirtations of her neighbours Mary and Henry Crawford, eventually win her the respect of the family and the hand of her cousin Edmund.

Park /paark/, **Sir Keith** (1892–1975) New Zealand air marshal. He was an RAF commander in World War II during the evacuation from Dunkirk and the Battle of Britain.

Park, **Mungo** (1771–1806) Scottish explorer. He explored the River Niger and wrote *Travels in the Interior Districts of Africa* (1799). In a subsequent expedition his party was attacked, and he was drowned.

Park, **Ruth** (*b.* 1923) New Zealand-born Australian novelist. Her works include *The Harp in the South* (1948), an account of life in Sydney, Australia.

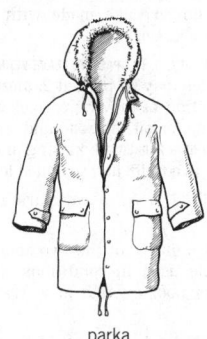

parka

parka /páarkə/ *n* **1.** a warm, knee- or thigh-length jacket that has a hood and is often lined with fur or imitation fur **2.** a thick, fur-lined, hooded outer garment for arctic conditions, pulled on over the head. Traditionally, parkas are made of animal hide and worn by the Inuit and Aleut people. [Late 18C. Via Aleut < Russian, 'pelt, skin jacket']

parkade /paár kayd/ *n Can* a multistorey car park [Mid-20C. < PARK, probably after ARCADE]

park-and-ride *n* a transport scheme, designed to reduce car use in city centres, in which motorists drive to out-of-town car parks from which buses or trains run regularly into the city

park day *n US* a day on which a group of people, usually parents and children, meet for communal activities in a public park

Parker /paárkər/, **Charlie** (1920–55) US jazz musician and composer. He was an alto saxophonist and pioneer of the bebop movement. Known as **Yardbird, Bird**. Full name **Parker, Jr, Charles Christopher**

'Music is your own experience, your thoughts, your wisdom. If you don't live it, it won't come out of your horn.'
[Charlie Parker. Quoted in *Hear Me Talkin' to Ya*, Nat Shapiro and Nat Hentoff; 1955]

Dorothy Parker

Popperfoto

Parker, **Dorothy** (1893–1967) US writer and critic. She is known for her sardonic stories, poetry, and reviews for *The New Yorker* magazine. Full name **Parker, Dorothy Rothschild**

'Sorrow is tranquility remembered in emotion.'
[Dorothy Parker, *Here Lies*; 1939]

'The best way to keep children at home is to make it pleasant—and let the air out of the tires.'
[Dorothy Parker. Quoted in *Utne Reader*; March/April 1991]

Parkes /paarks/ town in central New South Wales, Australia. It is the site of the Parkes Observatory. Population: 15,100 (2002 estimate).

Parkes, Sir Henry (1815–96) Australian politician. He was premier of New South Wales, Australia, five times between 1872 and 1891, and the architect of Australian federation.

park home *n* a small prefabricated bungalow-style dwelling located on a site similar to a caravan park

parkie /paárki/ *n* same as **park keeper** (*informal*)

parkin /paárkin/ *n* N England, Scotland, NZ a heavy moist dark ginger cake made with oatmeal and treacle [Early 19C. Origin ?]

parking /paárking/ *n* **1.** SPACE TO LEAVE VEHICLES spaces in which vehicles may be parked **2.** STOPPING AND LEAVING VEHICLE the action of driving a road vehicle into a position beside or off the road and leaving it there **3.** N Am KISSING IN PARKED CAR kissing and cuddling in a parked car in a quiet and secluded location (*slang*)

parking building *n* NZ a car park with multiple levels

parking light *n* either of the two small lights on a motor vehicle used in conditions where light is poor, but not poor enough to warrant the use of headlights

parking lot *n* N Am same as **car park**

parking meter *n* a coin-operated roadside meter that displays the length of time for which a vehicle may remain legally parked in a parking space

parking orbit *n* a temporary orbit of a spacecraft during which preparations are made for the next step in its programme. The orbit may be used while activities are being carried out aboard the craft or while waiting for the next phase of the programme to begin.

parking ramp *n* US a building or underground parking area having several levels reached by ramps, where cars can be parked temporarily

parking station *n* Aus a car park with multiple levels

Parkinsonism /paárkins'nizəm/ *n* a nervous disorder marked by symptoms of trembling limbs and muscular rigidity, e.g. Parkinson's disease. These disorders may be caused by the frequent use of some drugs or by exposure to chemicals.

Parkinson's disease /paárkins'nz-/ *n* a progressive nervous disorder marked by symptoms of trembling hands, lifeless face, monotone voice, and a slow shuffling walk. It is generally caused by the degeneration of dopamine-producing brain cells, and is the commonest form of Parkinsonism. [Late 19C. After James *Parkinson* (1755–1824), British physician]

Parkinson's law /paárkins'nz-/ *n* the observation that work always expands to fill the time set aside for it [Mid-20C. After C. Northcote *Parkinson* (1909–93), British historian]

park keeper *n* a public official who patrols, supervises, and maintains a public park

parkland /paárk land/ *n* the land contained within a park, especially when the grassland contains shrubs and trees

Parkman /paárkmən/, **Francis** (1823–93) US historian. He wrote literary studies of Native Americans and European settlers in North America.

> 'France built its best colony on a principle of exclusion, and failed: England reversed the system and succeeded.'
> [Francis Parkman. Introduction, *Montcalm and Wolf*; 1884]

Parks /paarks/, **Rosa** (*b.* 1913) US civil rights leader. Her arrest in Alabama for not relinquishing her bus seat to a white passenger (1955) led to Martin Luther King Jr's boycott campaign of the bus company and gave impetus to the campaign for civil rights. Full name **Parks, Rosa Louise**

parkway /paárk way/ *n* Aus, N Am a wide stretch of public highway with grassy areas on both sides, often divided by a grassy central reservation

parky /paárki/ (*-ier, -iest*) *adj* cold or chilly (*informal*) ○ *It does get a bit parky at night.* [Late 19C. Origin ?]

Parl. *abbr* GOV **1.** Parliament **2.** *also* **parl.** parliamentary

~~parlament~~ incorrect spelling of **parliament**

parlance /paárlənss/ *n* **1.** the style of speech or writing used by people in a particular context or profession **2.** speech, especially in a conversation [Late 16C. < Old French < *parler* 'speak' (see PARLEY)]

SYNONYMS See *jargon¹*.

parlando /paar lándō/ *adv* in a style of singing that suggests speech, usually without pitch or with less clear pitch (*used as a musical direction*) [Late 19C. < Italian, 'speaking'] —**parlando** *adj*

parlay /paárli, -lay/ N Am *vt* (*-lays, -laying, -layed*) **1.** BET WINNINGS to stake an original bet and its winnings on a subsequent bet **2.** USE ADVANTAGE to make good use of an asset or advantage to obtain success ○ *He parlayed his family connections into a prestigious job in the finance industry.* ■ *n* INSTANCE OF BETTING WINNINGS a bet in which winnings from a previous bet are gambled [Late 19C. Alteration of *paroli*, via French < Italian *parare* 'place a bet' < Latin, 'prepare']

parley /paárli/ *vi* (*-leys, -leying, -leyed*) to talk or negotiate, especially with an enemy ■ *n* (*plural -leys*) a round of talks or negotiations, especially between opposing military forces [Late 16C. < Old French *parlee* < *parler* 'speak' < late Latin *parabolare* < Latin *parabola* (see PARABLE)]

parliament /paárləmənt/ *n* **1.** LEGISLATIVE BODY a nation's legislative body, made up of elected and sometimes nonelected representatives **2.** ASSEMBLY OR CONFERENCE an assembly or conference held to make laws or discuss something **3.** ASSEMBLY OF PARLIAMENT an assembly of a parliament, created following a general election and dissolved before the next general election [13C. < Old French *parlement* < *parler* 'speak' (see PARLEY)]

Parliament *n* the supreme legislative body in various countries. In the United Kingdom, Parliament consists of the House of Commons and the House of Lords.

parliamentarian /paárlə men táiri ən/ *n* **1.** a member of a parliament **2.** an expert in parliamentary procedures and parliamentary history

Parliamentarian *n* during the English Civil War, a supporter or member of Oliver Cromwell's parliamentary army against King Charles I

parliamentarianism /paárlə men táiri ənizəm/ *n* government of a country by a parliament, or support for this kind of government

parliamentary /paárlə méntəri/ *adj* **1.** relating to parliaments, or in the form of a parliament ○ *parliamentary government* **2.** describes language and behaviour considered to conform to the standards that apply to a parliament

Parliamentary Commissioner, **Parliamentary Commissioner for Administration** *n* GOV same as **ombudsman** (sense 2)

parliamentary party *n* the members of a political party who are members of parliament

parliamentary private secretary *n* in the United Kingdom, a member of parliament who acts as an assistant to a government minister in parliamentary dealings, especially dealings with other members of parliament

parliamentary secretary *n* in the United Kingdom, a member of parliament, especially one appointed as a junior minister, who assists a government minister in the running of a department

parlor *n* US spelling of **parlour**

parlour /paárlər/ *n* **1.** WORK PREMISES a room or set of rooms equipped and used to provide particular goods or services (*often used in combination*) ○ *a beauty parlour* **2.** LIVING ROOM FOR ENTERTAINING GUESTS a living room that is set aside for entertaining guests **3.** SMALL QUIET ROOM a room in a hotel or pub that offers more privacy and comfort than the main or public bar areas (*dated*) [13C. < Old French *parler* 'to talk' (see PARLEY)]

parlour car *n* in the United States and Canada, a railway carriage containing individual reserved seats

parlour game *n* a game that can be played indoors (*dated or formal*)

parlourmaid /paárlər mayd/ *n* a maid employed to wait on a family and guests in the living room

and dining room of a large or wealthy household (*archaic*)

parlous /paárləss/ *adj* very unsafe, uncertain, or difficult (*archaic or humorous*) ○ *'Thou art in a parlous state, shepherd.'* (William Shakespeare, *As You Like It*; 1599) ■ *adv* used to emphasize the extreme or excessive nature of something (*archaic*) [14C. Shortening and alteration of *perilous*] —**parlously** *adv* —**parlousness** *n*

Parma /paármə/ city in northern Italy. It is the capital of Parma Province, in Emilia-Romagna Region. Population: 163,457 (2001).

Parmenides /paar ménni deez/ (*fl* 500 BC) Greek philosopher. He was a leader of the Eleatic school and the author of *On Nature*, which anticipates the idealism of Plato.

Parmesan /paármi zan, -zən, paármi zán/ *n* a pale yellow hard Italian cheese, often served grated as a garnish on pasta dishes [Mid-16C. Via French < Italian *parmigiano* 'from Parma']

parmigiana /paármi jaánə/ *adj* describes a dish that has been prepared using Parmesan cheese ○ *veal parmigiana* [Late 19C. < Italian, form of *parmigiano* 'of Parma']

Parmigianino /paármi ja neéno/, **Parmigiano** /paármi jaánō/ (1503–40) Italian painter. His use of graceful elongated figures influenced the development of mannerism.

Parnassian¹ /par nássi ən/ *adj* found in poetry, or associated with poetic works (*literary*) [Mid-17C. < Latin *Parnassius* < *Parnas(s)us* 'Parnassus' < Greek *Parnasos*]

Parnassian² /par nássi ən/ *n* a poet of a late 19th-century French school that advocated emotional detachment and purity of metrical form [< *Le Parnasse contemporain* (1866), French poetry anthology]

Parnassus /paar nássəss/ mountain in central Greece, directly north of Delphi. In ancient times it was sacred to Apollo and thought to be the home of the Muses. Height: 2,457 m/8,061 ft.

Parnell /paar nél/, **Charles Stewart** (1846–91) Irish politician. In 1880 he became leader of the Home Rule Party. He lost support after 1890, when he was involved in a divorce scandal.

> 'No man has a right to fix the boundary of the march of a nation; no man has a right to say to his country—thus far shalt thou go and no further.'
> [Charles Stewart Parnell, *Speech, Cork*; 21 January 1885]

parochial /pə rṓki əl/ *adj* **1.** concerned only with narrow local concerns without any regard for more general or wider issues **2.** relating or belonging to a parish or parishes [14C. Via French < ecclesiastical Latin *parochialis* < *parochia* (see PARISH)] —**parochialism** *n* —**parochialist** *n* —**parochially** *adv*

parochial school *n* N Am a private school that is affiliated with a church and provides children with religious instruction as well as a general education

parody /párrədi/ *n* (*plural -dies*) **1.** AMUSING IMITATION a piece of writing or music that deliberately copies another work in a comic or satirical way **2.** PARODIES IN GENERAL parodies as a literary or musical style or genre **3.** POOR IMITATION an attempt or imitation that is so poor that it seems ridiculous ■ *vt* (*-dies, -dying, -died*) IMITATE SOMEBODY OR SOMETHING COMICALLY to write or perform a parody of somebody or something [Late 16C. Via late Latin < Greek *parōidia* < *para* 'secondary, indirect' + *ōidē* 'song'] —**parodic** /pə rṓddik/ *adj* —**parodical** *adj* —**parodically** *adv* —**parodist** *n*

parol /pə rṓl, párrəl/ *adj* describes a legal contract that is oral, rather than written ■ *n* a legal contract that is made orally only [15C. < Anglo-French variant of French *parole* (see PAROLE)]

parole /pə rṓl/ *n* **1.** CONDITIONAL RELEASE OF PRISONER the early release of a prisoner, conditioned on good behaviour and regular reporting to the authorities for a set period of time ○ *He's out on parole.* **2.** PRISONER'S PROMISE the promise to fulfil set conditions, given by a prisoner released on parole **3.** CONDITIONAL PERIOD the period of time during which a released prisoner remains on parole **4.** US PRISONER OF WAR'S PROMISE a promise, given by a prisoner of war as a

condition of release, either not to escape or not to take up arms again **5.** LING **REAL-WORLD LANGUAGE** language considered as the utterances of real people, as distinct from the system of language (**langue**) that governs how those utterances are constructed ■ *vt* (**-roles, -roling, -roled**) **GIVE PRISONER PAROLE** to release a prisoner on parole [15C. Via French < Latin *parabola* 'speech, talk' (see PARABLE)] —**parolable** *adj*

paronomasia /párrənō máyzi ə/ *n* a play on words, especially a pun [Late 16C. < Latin < Greek *paronomazein* 'name differently' < *onomazein* 'to name'] —**paronomastic** /-mástik/ *adj* —**paronomastically** *adv*

paronym /párrənim/ *n* a word derived from the same root as another word. For example, 'folly' is a paronym of 'fool'. [Mid-19C. < Greek *parōnumon* < *para-* 'beside' + *onuma* 'name'] —**paronymic** /párrə nímmik/ *adj* —**paronymous** /pə rónniməss/ *adj* —**paronomously** *adv*

Paros /párross/, **Páros** Greek island in the southern Aegean Sea, one of the Cyclades. Since ancient times it has been noted for its marble quarries. The chief town is Parikia. Population: 12,783 (2001). Area: 197 sq. km/76 sq. mi.

~~parot~~ incorrect spelling of **parrot**

parotic /pə róttik/ *adj* ANAT same as **parotid** *adj* (sense 1) [Mid-19C. < Greek *para* 'beside' + *ōt-* 'ear']

parotid /pə róttid/ *adj* **1.** situated close to or beside the ear **2.** relating to the parotid gland ■ *n* ANAT same as **parotid gland** [Late 17C. Via French and Latin < Greek *parōtid-* 'beside the ear' < *ōt-* 'ear']

parotid gland *n* a salivary gland located below the ear in humans

parotitis /párrə títiss/, **parotiditis** /pə rótti dítiss/ *n* inflammation of a parotid gland or the parotid glands —**parotitic** /párrə títtik/ *adj*

parous /párrəss/ *adj* having given birth on at least one occasion [Late 19C. < -PAROUS]

-parous *suffix* giving birth to, producing ○ *uniparous* [< Latin *-parus* < *parere* 'give birth']

Parousia /pə roóssi ə/ *n* CHR same as **Second Coming** [Late 19C. < Greek, 'presence' < present participle of *pareinai* < *einai* 'be']

paroxetine /pə róksi teen/ *n* a drug that allows serotonin levels in the brain to increase. Use: treatment of anxiety and depression.

paroxysm /párrək sizəm/ *n* **1.** a sudden and uncontrollable expression of emotion ○ *paroxysms of grief* **2.** a sudden onset or intensification of a pathological symptom or symptoms, especially when recurrent [Late 16C. < medieval Latin < Greek *paroxunein* 'irritate', literally 'sharpen beyond' < *oxus* 'sharp'] —**paroxysmal** /párrək sízm'l/ *adj* —**paroxysmally** *adv* —**paroxysmic** /párrək sízmik/ *adj*

paroxytone /pə róksi tōn/ *n* **1.** **WORD WITH PENULTIMATE STRESS** a word in which the main stress is on the second-last syllable **2.** **GREEK WORD CATEGORY** in ancient Greek, a word with an acute accent on the second-last syllable ■ *adj* **WITH STRESSED PENULTIMATE SYLLABLE** with the main stress or accent on the second-last syllable [Mid-18C. < Greek *paroxutonos* < *para* 'beside' + *oxutonos* (see OXYTONE)] —**paroxytonic** /pə róksi tónnik/ *adj*

parp /paarp/ *n* a honking noise emitted by the horn of a vehicle [Mid-20C. An imitation of the sound] —**parp** *vti*

parpen /paárpən/, **parpend** /paár pənd/ *n* a stone or brick built into a wall to go from one side of the wall to the other and act as a binder. US term **perpend** [15C. Via French < medieval Latin *parpannus*]

parquet /paár kay, -ki/ *n* flooring consisting of blocks of wood laid in a decorative pattern ■ *vt* (**-quets, -queting, -queted**) to cover a floor in parquet [Early 19C. < French, literally 'small enclosed space' < *parc* (see PARK)]

AKG London

parquetry: parquetry floor in an anonymous painting (1860?)

parquetry /paàrkitri/ *n* flooring or a decorative inlay for furniture made with blocks of wood

parr /paar/ (*plural* **parrs** or *same*) *n* **1.** a young salmon up to two years old that has dark transverse bands (**parr marks**) and lives in fresh water **2.** the young of some fishes other than the salmon, e.g. of the trout [Early 18C. Origin ?]

Parr /paar/, **Catherine** (1512–48) queen of England. She married Henry VIII in 1543, becoming his sixth queen. After his death in 1547 she married Thomas Seymour.

parral *n* NAUT another spelling of **parrel**

~~parrallel~~ incorrect spelling of **parallel**

parramatta *n* TEXTILES another spelling of **paramatta**

Parramatta /párrə máttə/ city in New South Wales, Australia, a western suburb of Sydney. Population: 148,225 (2002 estimate).

parrel /párrəl/, **parral** *n* a ring, loop, or band that secures a boom to a mast while allowing it to move up and down [15C. Shortening of APPAREL 'rigging']

parricide /párri sīd/ *n* **1.** the murder of a parent or close relative **2.** somebody who murders his or her parent or close relative [Mid-16C. < Latin *parricidium* 'kin-slaying', *parricida* 'kin-slayer' < assumed *parri-* 'relative'] —**parricidal** /párri sīd'l/ *adj* —**parricidally** *adv*

Parrish /párrish/, **Maxfield** (1870–1966) US artist. He is best known for his illustrations, posters, and murals.

parrot

parrot /párrət/ *n* **1.** **BRIGHTLY COLOURED TROPICAL BIRD** a bird with a strong hooked beak and variously coloured, often brilliant plumage, some species of which can mimic speech. Native to: tropics, subtropics. Order: Psittaciformes. **2.** **SOMEBODY WHO COPIES OTHERS** a repeater of something that somebody else has said, without thought or understanding ■ *vt* (**-rots, -roting, -roted**) **COPY OTHER PEOPLE** to repeat what somebody else says or writes without having thought about it or understood it [Early 16C. Probably < French dialect *Perrot* 'little Pierre'] —**parroter** *n*

parrotbill /párrətbil/ *n* a small bird with a short strong beak for removing insects from bamboo or reed stems. Family: Psittacidae.

parrot-fashion *adv* mechanically and with no apparent understanding (*informal*) N Am term **parrotlike**

parrot fever *n* MED same as **psittacosis** [Because humans can contract it from pet birds such as parrots]

parrotfish /párrət fish/ (*plural same* or **-fishes**) *n* a brightly coloured sea fish with jaws shaped like a parrot's beak that it uses for scraping coral. Native to: tropics. Family: Scaridae.

parrotlike /párrət līk/ *adv* N Am same as **parrot-fashion**

parry /párri/ *v* (**-ries, -rying, -ried**) **1.** *vti* **TURN BLOW ASIDE** to block or deflect the damaging effect of a blow or weapon **2.** *vt* **AVOID ANSWERING QUESTION** to evade a question by cleverly saying something that does not answer it ■ *n* (*plural* **-ries**) **EVASION** an act of evading a blow, criticism, or question [Late 17C. Probably < French *parez* 'defend (yourself)!' < *parer* 'prepare' (see PARE)]

Parry, Cape /párri/ promontory in Canada, in the Northwest Territories, jutting into Amundsen Gulf between Franklin and Darnley bays

Parry, Sir William (1790–1855) British explorer. He mapped many areas in the Arctic but failed in his attempt to find the Northwest Passage or reach the North Pole. Full name **Parry, Sir William Edward**

parse /paarz/ (**parses, parsing, parsed**) *v* **1.** *vti* **DESCRIBE GRAMMATICAL ROLE OF WORD** to describe the grammatical role of a word in a sentence, or undergo this process **2.** *vti* **ANALYSE GRAMMATICAL STRUCTURE OF SENTENCE** to analyse and describe the grammatical structure of a sentence, or undergo this process **3.** *vt* COMPUT **ANALYSE COMPUTER INPUT** to analyse computer input in a specific language against the formal grammar of that language, both to validate the input and to create an internal representation of it for use in subsequent processing [Mid-16C. Perhaps < obsolete *pars* 'parts of speech' < Old French] —**parsable** *adj*

parsec /paár sek/ *n* an astronomical unit of distance equal to 3.262 light-years. A parsec is the distance from which the Earth's distance from the Sun would subtend one second of arc. Symbol **pc** [Early 20C. < PARALLAX + SECOND[2]]

Parsee /paár see, paar seé/, **Parsi** *n* a member of a Zoroastrian group living mainly in western India, descended from Persian refugees of the 7th and 8th centuries AD [Early 17C. < Persian *Pārsī* < *Pārs* 'Persia'] —**Parsee** *adj* —**Parseeism** *n*

parser /paárzər/ *n* **1.** a program that parses computer input. The parser determines how a sentence can be constructed from the grammar of the language, producing a tree (**parse tree**) about the statement as the output. **2.** somebody or something that analyses something into its component parts

Parsi *n, adj* RELIG another spelling of **Parsee**

parsimonious /paárssi mốni əss/ *adj* very frugal or ungenerous —**parsimoniously** *adv* —**parsimoniousness** *n*

parsimony /paárssiməni/ *n* **1.** great frugality or unwillingness to spend money **2.** economy in the use of means to achieve something, especially the principle of endorsing the simplest explanation that covers a case [15C. < Latin *parsimonia* < *pars-*, past participle of *parcere* 'spare']

parsley

parsley /paárssli/ *n* a widely cultivated plant of the carrot family with small compound leaves. Use: in cooking, as a garnish. Latin name: *Petroselinum crispum*. [Pre-12C. Via late Latin *petrosilium* < Greek *petroselinon* < *petra* 'rock' + *selinon* 'parsley']

parsley fern *n* a bright green fern with leaves that look like parsley leaves. Native to: Europe. Latin name: *Cryptogramma crispa*.

parsley piert /-peért/ *n* a small plant of the rose family with three-lobed leaves. Flowers: green, tiny. Latin name: *Aphanes arvensis*. [Late 16C. Alteration of French *perce-pierre* 'stone-piercer']

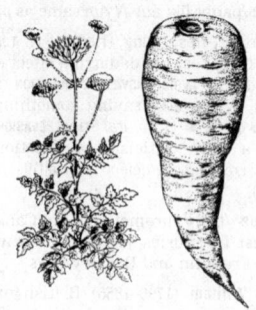

parsnip

parsnip /paárssnip/ *n* **1.** a long tapering cream-coloured root eaten cooked as a vegetable **2.** a plant of the carrot family that produces parsnips. Latin name: *Pastinaca sativa*. [14C. Alteration (influenced by NEEP) of Old French *pasnaie* < Latin *pastinaca* < *pastinum* 'gardening fork'; probably from its shape]

parson /paárss'n/ *n* **1.** an Anglican parish priest **2.** a member of the clergy, especially of the Protestant Church [13C. < variant of Old French *persone* (see PERSON)] —**parsonic** /paar sónnik/ *adj* —**parsonical** *adj*

parsonage /paárss'nij/ *n* the house, usually provided by the parish or congregation, where a parson lives

parson bird *n* NZ BIRDS same as **tui** [< the resemblance of its markings to the dark suit and white bands of a parson]

Parsons /paárss'nz/, **Sir Charles** (1854–1931) British engineer. He invented the first successful steam turbine engine, and built the first turbine-driven steamship (1897). Full name **Parsons, Sir Charles Algernon**

Parsons, Geoffrey (1930–95) Australian pianist. As an accompanist he performed with many of the world's leading singers. Full name **Parsons, Geoffrey Penwill**

parson's nose *n* the fatty piece of flesh at the rear end of a cooked chicken, turkey, or other bird, to which the tail feathers were attached. N Am term **pope's nose**

part /paart/ *n* **1.** PORTION a portion or section of something ○ *the early part of the century* **2.** COMPONENT a separable piece or component of something such as a machine, system, or device ○ *a motor with only three moving parts* **3.** EQUAL PORTION OF WHOLE a portion of something that with other portions of the same size makes up a whole ○ *pastry that is one part fat to three parts flour* **4.** IMPORTANT ELEMENT OF SOMETHING an integral and essential feature or component of something ○ *She wants to be part of the community.* **5.** ACTOR'S ROLE a role in a dramatic performance ○ *played the part of Hamlet in the school play* **6.** INVOLVEMENT IN EVENT somebody's participation in or influence on something ○ *What part did he have to play in all this?* **7.** SIDE somebody's side or viewpoint ○ *You're always taking her part.* **8.** ORGANIC CONSTITUENT an organ, system, or other discrete element of an organism ○ *the part of the plant that carries out photosynthesis* **9.** LOGICAL DIVISION a logical division of something such as a report, book, or presentation ○ *Part three of the paper deals with environmental issues.* **10.** SEPARATE MUSICAL ROLE the score for a single voice or instrument in a symphonic, orchestral, or choral work **11.** N Am HAIR same as **parting** *n* (sense 3) ■ **parts** *npl* **1.** AREA a region or area (*informal*) ○ *That's unheard of in these parts.* **2.** ABILITIES intellectual abilities or talents (*literary*) ○ *a man of parts* ■ *v* (**parts, parting, parted**) **1.** *vti* SEPARATE to move apart, or move two things or people in different directions so that there is a space between them ○ *They had to part the children to keep them from fighting.* ○ *The curtains parted.* **2.** *vti* DIVIDE INTO PARTS to divide something into parts, or undergo division into parts **3.** *vti* DIVIDE HAIR to make a line in the hair by combing in opposite directions from it, or separate naturally in this way **4.** *vi* END RELATIONSHIP to finish a relationship with somebody ○ *We parted on bad terms.* **5.** *vi* GO AWAY to go away from somebody

○ *They parted at the corner.* ■ *adj* PARTIAL partial or less than the whole ○ *part owner of a beach house* ■ *adv* PARTIALLY to some extent but not completely ○ *She's part Irish, part French.* [Pre-12C. Directly or via French < Latin *part-*] ◇ **for the most part** in general, or mostly ○ *She does OK at school, for the most part.* ◇ **in good part** without taking offence or becoming angry ◇ **in part** to an extent but not completely ◇ **on the part of** as far as somebody is concerned, or with regard to somebody ◇ **part and parcel** an essential element of something ◇ **part company** to go away in separate directions (*refers to two or more people*) ○ *They chatted for a while before parting company.* ◇ **take part (in something)** to be actively involved in something, usually as a member of a group

USAGE The idiom *part and parcel*, meaning 'an essential element of something', is correctly worded as shown here, e.g. *Driving is part and parcel of a sales representative's job*. *Part and partial* is incorrect.

part with *vt* to give something up or give something away, especially unwillingly

Pärt /paart/, **Arvo** (b. 1935) Estonian-born Austrian composer. He has written orchestral and choral works with worldwide appeal.

partake /paar táyk/ (**-takes, -taking, -took** /-took/, **-taken** /-táykən/) *vi* (*formal*) **1.** EAT OR DRINK SOMETHING to have something to eat or drink ○ *We're just about to have some tea. Would you care to partake?* **2.** HAVE OR SEEM TO HAVE to have or appear to have a quality or characteristic ○ *Somehow her help always partakes of do-goodery.* **3.** PARTICIPATE to share in or take part in something ○ *How many students partake in sports activities?* [Mid-16C. Back-formation < *partaker* < *part-taker, partaking* < *part-taking*, translations of Latin *particeps* 'participant', *participatio* 'participation'] —**partaker** *n*

partan /paart'n/ *n Scotland* an edible crab [15C. Probably < Scottish Gaelic, 'red']

parted /paártid/ *adj* **1.** SEPARATED separated or kept separate ○ *with parted lips* **2.** DIVIDED BY PARTING describes hair that has a parting ○ *a hairstyle parted on the left* **3.** IN PARTS divided into parts **4.** BOT DIVIDED TO BASE describes a leaf or plant part that is separated or cleft nearly to the base

parterre /paar táir/ *n* an ornamental garden laid out in a formal pattern that is usually marked out with low evergreen hedges and filled in with annual bedding plants [Early 17C. < French, 'ornamental garden' < *par terre* 'on the ground']

part exchange *n* a payment method by which a buyer gives something he or she owns to a seller as part payment for a more expensive item —**part-exchange** *vt*

parthenocarpy /paar theenō kaarpi/ *n* the production of fruits without fertilization or seeds [Early 20C. < German *Parthenocarpie* < Greek *parthenos* 'virgin' + *karpos* 'fruit'] —**parthenocarpic** /paar theenō kaárpik/ *adj* —**parthenocarpous** /paar theenō kaárpəss/ *adj*

parthenogenesis /paáthənō jénnəssiss/ *n* a form of reproduction, especially in plants, insects, and arthropods, in which a female gamete develops into a new individual without fertilization by a male gamete [Mid-19C. < Greek *parthenos* 'virgin'] —**parthenogenetic** /paáthənō jə néttik/ *adj* —**parthenogenetically** *adv*

Parthenon

Parthenon /paáthə non/ *n* a large temple on the Acropolis in Athens, Greece, built in the 5th century BC to the goddess Athena

Parthian /paárthi ən/ *n* somebody who came from Parthia, an ancient country in Southwest Asia that ruled an empire until the 3rd century AD —**Parthian** *adj*

Parthian shot *n* a final hostile remark or gesture made while leaving [< the Parthians' legendary tactic of firing arrows over their shoulders while retreating]

partial /paársh'l/ *adj* **1.** INCOMPLETE not complete or total ○ *only a partial success* **2.** AFFECTING PARTS affecting a part or parts but not the whole ○ *a partial restoration of the building* **3.** FOND OF SOMETHING having a liking for something ○ *very partial to chocolate cake* **4.** BIASED showing an unfair preference for one person or thing over another ■ *n* **1.** MATHS same as **partial derivative** (sense 2. **2.** MUSIC same as **overtone** (sense 2) [15C. Via French < late Latin *partialis* < Latin *part-* 'part'] —**partialness** *n*

partial derivative *n* the derivative of a function of two or more mathematical variables calculated with respect to one of the variables and on the assumption that the others are fixed

partial differential equation *n* a differential equation that involves partial derivatives of more than one variable

partial eclipse *n* an eclipse in which only part of something such as the Sun or Moon is darkened

partial fraction *n* any of a set of simpler fractions, the sum of which comprises a more complex fraction

partiality /paárshi álləti/ *n* **1.** a liking for something **2.** an unfair preference for one person or thing over another

partially /paársh'li/ *adv* **1.** to a degree but not completely **2.** in a way that shows an unfair preference for one person or thing over another

USAGE See **partly**.

partially sighted *adj* having a visual impairment that cannot be completely corrected by the use of glasses or contact lenses

partial pressure *n* the pressure that one gas in a mixture of gases would exert if it were the only gas present

partial product *n* the result when a mathematical quantity is multiplied by one digit of a number with two or more digits

partible /paártəb'l/ *adj* able to be divided ○ *a partible inheritance* [Mid-16C. < late Latin *partibilis* < Latin *partire* 'to divide' (see PARTITION)]

participant /paar tíssipənt/ *n* somebody who takes part in something ■ *adj* taking part in something [Mid-16C. < French, present participle of *participier* < Latin *participare* (see PARTICIPATE)]

participate /paar tíssi payt/ (**-pates, -pating, -pated**) *vi* to take part in an event or activity [15C. < Latin *participat-*, past participle of *participare* < *particeps* 'taking part' < *part-* 'part'] —**participation** /paar tíssi páysh'n/ *n* —**participative** *adj* —**participator** *n* —**participatory** *adj*

participating insurance /paar tíssi payting-/ *n* insurance in which the policyholders are entitled to a dividend from the insurance company's profits

participial /paárti síppi əl/ *adj* having the form or function of a verb that can be used as both adjective and verb [Late 16C. < Latin *participialis* < *participium* (see PARTICIPLE)] —**participially** *adv*

participle /paárti sip'l, paar tíssip'l/ *n* a form of a verb that is used to form complex tenses, as are 'loving' and 'loved' in English, and may also be used as an adjective [14C. < Old French < *participe* < Latin *participium* < *particeps* 'sharing' (see PARTICIPATE); because it shares qualities of both adjectives and verbs]

~~particlar~~ incorrect spelling of **particular**

particle /paártik'l/ *n* **1.** TINY PIECE a very small piece of something ○ *airborne particles* **2.** TINY AMOUNT a very small amount of something ○ *There wasn't a particle of truth in anything he said.* **3.** PHYS OBJECT WITH FINITE MASS a minute body that is considered to have finite mass but negligible size **4.** PHYS BASIC UNIT OF MATTER any of the basic units of matter, e.g. a molecule, atom, or electron **5.** PHYS SUBATOMIC UNIT a unit of matter smaller than the atom or its main components **6.** GRAM PART OF MULTIWORD VERB an adverb or preposition that occurs as part of a multiword verb,

e.g. 'up' in 'blow up' 7. CHR **PIECE OF CONSECRATED BREAD OR WAFER** in the Roman Catholic Mass, a small piece of consecrated bread or wafer [14C. < Latin *particula* 'small part' < *part-* 'part']

particle accelerator *n* same as **accelerator** (sense 2)

particle beam *n* a very narrow concentrated stream of charged particles such as electrons or protons, produced by a particle accelerator or a particle-beam weapon. Lenses are used to focus the beam and magnets change its direction.

particleboard /páartik'l bawrd/ *n NZ, N Am* a board made from sawdust or wood particles bonded with a resin binder. The particles of wood used in particle board tend to be smaller than those used in chipboard.

particle bombardment *n* a technique for inserting DNA from one organism into another by bombarding embryogenic cell cultures with DNA-coated metal particles

particle physics *n* the branch of physics that deals with the study of subatomic particles, particularly the many unstable particles produced in particle accelerators and high-energy collisions (*takes a singular verb*)

parti-coloured /páarti-/, **party-coloured** *adj* having different parts in different colours [< obsolete *party* 'multi-coloured', via French < Latin *partitus*, past participle of *partire* 'to divide' (see PARTITION)]

particular /pər tíkyŏŏlər/ *adj* **1. ONE OUT OF SEVERAL** relating to one person or thing out of several ○ *Which particular dress do you prefer?* **2. SPECIAL** special and worth mentioning ○ *had no particular objection to the plan* **3. EXCEPTIONAL** great or more than usual ○ *took particular care over it* **4. PERSONAL** belonging to one person and different from other people's ○ *a particular dislike* **5. FUSSY** having or demanding high standards ○ *She's very particular about standards of hygiene.* **6. CHOOSY** taking great care when making a choice ○ *They're very particular about the restaurants they go to.* **7. DETAILED** going into great detail about something (*formal*) **8.** LOGIC **NOT DEALING WITH ALL MEMBERS** in logic, used to describe a proposition that deals with some but not all members of a class ■ *n* **1. ITEM** an individual fact, item, or detail (*often used in the plural*) ○ *noted down his particulars* **2. SINGLE INSTANCE** an individual case or instance, as opposed to a more general theory **3.** PHILOSOPHY **REAL THING** in philosophy, an entity with definite spatial and temporal properties [14C. Via French < Latin *particularis* 'concerned with small parts or details' < *particula* (see PARTICLE)] ◇ **in particular** specifically or especially

particularise *vti* another spelling of **particularize**

particularism /pər tíkyŏŏlərizəm/ *n* **1. COMMITMENT TO ONE GROUP** exclusive commitment to one group, especially when detrimental to the interests or wellbeing of a larger group **2. SELF-RULE PRINCIPLE** a policy of allowing political divisions within a state or federation to be self-governing, without regard to what effect this may have on the larger body **3. BELIEF THAT GOD BESTOWS GRACE INDIVIDUALLY** the belief that God chooses to bestow grace and salvation on some people, but not all —**particularist** *n* —**particularistic** /pər tíkyŏŏlə rístik/ *adj*

particularity /pər tíkyŏŏ lárrəti/ (*plural* **-ties**) *n* (*formal*) **1. EXACTITUDE** attention to detail and concern for accuracy **2. FASTIDIOUSNESS** the practice of taking great care when making a choice **3. USE OF DETAIL** the use of great detail in describing something **4.** same as **particular** *n* (sense 1) **5. SOMETHING CHARACTERISTIC** a peculiarity or characteristic **6. INDIVIDUALITY** the condition of being peculiar to an individual person rather than a group

particularize /pər tíkyŏŏlə rīz/ (**-izes, -izing, -ized**), **particularise** (**-ises, -ising, -ised**) *v* **1.** *vt* **FOCUS ON INDIVIDUAL** to make something become particular, e.g. by focusing on a particular person or thing **2.** *vt* **PROVIDE SOMETHING WITH SPECIFIC EXAMPLES** to provide something with specific examples ○ *unable to particularize her account* **3.** *vti* **GO INTO DETAIL** to go into detail about something —**particularization** /pər tíkyŏŏlə rī záysh'n/ *n* —**particularizer** *n*

particularly /pər tíkyŏŏlərli/ *adv* **1. VERY MUCH** to a great degree ○ *Did you enjoy yourself? No, not particularly.* **2. MORE THAN USUALLY** more than usually or more than in other cases ○ *The trip to the museum was particularly interesting.* **3. SPECIFICALLY** as a specific example ○ *He particularly named you as one of the ringleaders.* **4. IN DETAIL** with great attention to detail

particulate /paar tíkyŏŏlət, -layt/ *adj* relating to or consisting of separate particles ■ *n* a substance that consists of separate particles, especially airborne pollution [Late 19C. < Latin *particula* (see PARTICLE)]

parting /páarting/ *n* **1. LEAVING** the act of leaving somebody or something, especially if the separation is sad or upsetting **2. SEPARATION** the process or action of separating or dividing **3. DIVIDING LINE IN HAIR** the line in a hairstyle from which the hair is combed or brushed in different directions. N Am term **part 4.** CRYSTALS **TENDENCY TO BREAK ALONG PLANE** the tendency of some crystals to break along a plane of weakness through deformation ■ *adj* **1. DONE WHILE LEAVING** done, made, or given when leaving ○ *a parting remark* **2. DEPARTING** leaving or coming to an end (*literary*) ○ *'The curfew tolls the knell of parting day...'* (Thomas Gray, *Elegy Written in a Country Churchyard*; 1751) **3. DIVIDING** used to divide or separate something ◇ **parting of the ways 1.** a separation of one person or group from another, e.g. after a disagreement **2.** a point at which a choice must be made between mutually exclusive courses of action

parting shot *n* a final, often hostile remark or gesture made by somebody who is leaving

parti pris /páarti prée/ (*plural* **partis pris** /*pronunc. same*/) *n* a preconceived opinion or bias [< French, literally 'side taken']

partisan[1] /páarti zán/, **partizan** *n* **1. BIASED SUPPORTER** a strong supporter of a person, group, or cause, especially one who does not listen to other people's opinions **2. RESISTANCE FIGHTER** a member of a group that has taken up armed resistance against occupying enemy forces ■ *adj* **SHOWING UNREASONING SUPPORT** showing strong and usually biased support for a cause, especially a political one [Mid-16C. Via French < Italian dialect *partisano* < Italian *parte* 'part, side' < Latin *part-*] —**partisanship** *n*

partisan[2] /páarti zán/, **partizan** *n* a weapon with a long shaft and a blade, used in the 16th and 17th centuries [Mid-16C. Via French < obsolete Italian dialect *partesana*, form (agreeing with *arma* 'weapon') of *partisano* (see PARTISAN[1])]

partita /paar téetə/ (*plural* **-te** /-tay/ or **-tas**) *n* a suite or set of musical variations, especially in baroque music [Late 19C. < Italian, 'composition divided into parts' < *partire* 'to divide' < Latin (see PARTITION)]

partite /páar tīt/ *adj* **1.** describes a plant part such as a leaf that is split almost to its base **2.** divided into or consisting of two or more parts (*usually used in combination*) [Late 16C. < Latin *partitus*, past participle of *partire* 'divide' (see PARTITION)]

partition /paar tísh'n/ *n* **1. SOMETHING THAT DIVIDES SPACE** a structure that divides a space, e.g. a wall built to make two rooms out of one **2. DIVISION OF COUNTRY** the division of a country into two or more separate states or countries ○ *the partition of India* **3. DIVISION INTO PARTS** the division of something into parts, or the state of being divided into parts (*formal*) ■ *v* (**-tions, -tioning, -tioned**) **1.** *vt* **DIVIDE AREA WITH PARTITION** to divide or separate an area such as a room by means of a partition **2.** *vti* **SPLIT COUNTRY** to divide a country into two or more separate states **3.** *vt* **DIVIDE SOMETHING** to divide something into separate parts [15C. Via French < Latin *partition-* < *partire* 'to divide' < *part-* 'part'] —**partitioner** *n* —**partitionist** *n* —**partitionment** *n*

partitive /páartətiv/ *adj* **1. SEPARATING** separating or dividing something (*formal*) **2.** GRAM **EXPRESSING PART OF SOMETHING** describes a grammatical construction expressing a part of something, e.g. 'of' in 'a lump of coal' or the possessive form in 'the dog's tail' ■ *n* GRAM **PARTITIVE CONSTRUCTION** a partitive construction [14C. Directly or via French < medieval Latin *partitivus* < Latin *partire* 'to divide' (see PARTITION)] —**partitively** *adv*

partizan *n* ARMS another spelling of **partisan**[2] ■ *n, adj* MIL another spelling of **partisan**[1]

partly /páartli/ *adv* to some extent, but not completely ○ *The road was partly blocked by a heavy snowfall.*

USAGE partly or **partially**? Both these adverbs mean 'in part', 'not completely', or 'to some extent', but they are not interchangeable in all contexts: *Our first attempt was only partly* [or *partially*] *successful. He left early, partly* [not *partially*] *because he was bored. Her mother is partially* [not *partly*] *sighted.* ***Partly*** is always preferred when there is a distinct division into parts: *The houses were built partly of wood and partly of stone.* ***Partially*** should, of course, be avoided where there is any risk of confusion with its other sense of 'in a biased way'.

partner /páartnər/ *n* **1. SOMEBODY WHO SHARES ACTIVITY** somebody who is involved in an activity with somebody else ○ *his partner in crime* **2. MEMBER OF RELATIONSHIP** either member of an established couple in a relationship **3. FELLOW PARTICIPANT IN SEXUAL ACTIVITY** either of two people who have sex together **4. ASSOCIATE IN DANCE OR GAME** somebody who dances with somebody else, or plays with somebody else on the same side in a game **5.** BUSINESS **BUSINESS ASSOCIATE** an owner of part of a company, usually a company he or she works in, who shares both the financial risks and the profits of the business **6. SOMETHING RELATED** something that is related in some way to something else **7.** NAUT **SUPPORTING TIMBER ON SHIP** one of the timbers on a ship underneath the deck that is used to support the mast (*often used in the plural*) ■ *vt* (**-ners, -nering, -nered**) **BE SOMEBODY'S PARTNER** to be somebody's partner, e.g. in a game or dance [14C. Alteration (influenced by PART) of obsolete *parcener* 'sharer' < Anglo-Norman < Latin *partition-* (see PARTITION)]

partnership /páartnər ship/ *n* **1. RELATIONSHIP BETWEEN PARTNERS** the relationship between two or more people or organizations that are involved in the same activity **2. COOPERATION** cooperation between people or groups working together ○ *scientists working in close partnership with colleagues overseas* **3. GROUP OF PEOPLE WORKING TOGETHER** an organization formed by two or more people or groups who work together for some purpose **4.** BUSINESS **COMPANY OWNED BY PARTNERS** a company set up by two or more people who put money into the business and share the financial risks and profits **5. PARTNERS** the people who make up a partnership, collectively

part of speech *n* a grammatical category or word group in a language to which words may be assigned on the basis of how they are used in sentences. The traditional main parts of speech in English are noun, verb, adjective, adverb, pronoun, preposition, conjunction, and interjection. Others sometimes used are article and determiner. [Translation of Latin *pars orationis*]

parton /páar ton/ *n* a postulated elementary particle, proposed as a constituent of neutrons and protons [Mid-20C. < PARTICLE]

Parton /páart'n/, **Dolly** (*b.* 1946) US singer, songwriter, and actor. She is known for her country-and-western songs, and for her appearances in several Hollywood films. Full name **Parton, Dolly Rebecca**

partook past tense of **partake**

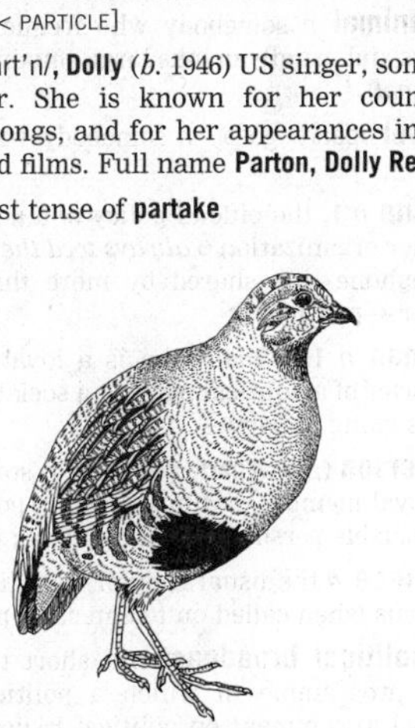

partridge

partridge /páartrij/ (*plural* **-tridges** or *same*) *n* **1.** a medium-sized, ground-nesting bird with variegated feathers, related to pheasants and grouse. Native to: Europe, Asia. Genera: *Alectoris* or *Perdix*. **2.** the flesh of the partridge as food [13C. Via Old French *perdriz* < Greek *perdix*]

partridgeberry /páartrij beri/ (*plural* **-ries**) *n* **1.** the scarlet relatively tasteless berry of a trailing plant **2.** a trailing evergreen plant with rounded leaves that bears partridgeberries. Flowers: small, white, fragrant. Native to: eastern North America. Latin name: *Mitchella repens*. [Early 18C. Because partridges eat the berries]

part song *n* a vocal musical composition with parts for different voices, usually performed without accompaniment

part-time *adj, adv* for less than the usual amount of time associated with a particular activity ○ *a part-time job* —**part-timer** *n*

parturient /paar tyoóri ənt/ *adj* **1. RELATING TO CHILDBIRTH** relating to the process or time of childbirth **2. GIVING BIRTH** about to give birth (*technical*) **3. ABOUT TO PRODUCE** on the verge of producing something or coming forth (*literary*) [Late 16C. < Latin *parturient-*, present participle of *parturire* (see PARTURITION)] —**parturiency** *n*

parturifacient /paar tyoóri fáysh'nt/ *adj* inducing birth or making it easier to give birth ■ *n* a drug that induces birth or makes it easier to give birth [Mid-19C. < Latin *parturire* 'be in labour' (see PARTURITION)]

parturition /paártyoō rísh'n/ *n* the act of giving birth to offspring (*formal or technical*) [Mid-17C. < late Latin *parturition-* < Latin *parturire* 'be in labour' < *parere* 'give birth']

partway /paárt way/ *adv* some but not all of the way through a process or distance

partwork /paárt wurk/ (*plural* **partworks** or **part works**) *n* a series of magazines published in weekly, fortnightly, or monthly instalments and intended to be collected to form a complete volume

party /paárti/ *n* (*plural* **-ties**) **1. SOCIAL GATHERING FOR FUN** a social gathering to which people are invited in order to enjoy themselves and often celebrate something ○ *Are you coming to my birthday party?* **2. POLITICAL ORGANIZATION** a nationally based organization of people who share the same broad political views and goals, usually one attempting to have members elected to government **3. GROUP ACTING TOGETHER** a group of people who are doing something together ○ *a search party* **4. PERSON** an individual (*formal*) **5.** LAW **ONE SIDE IN LEGAL MATTER** a person or a group of people acting together and forming one side in an agreement, contract, dispute, or lawsuit **6.** MIL **GROUP OF SOLDIERS** a detachment of soldiers given a particular task ■ *vi* (**-ties, -tying, -tied**) **BE AT PARTY** to socialize and have fun at a party or similar occasion (*informal*) ■ *adj* HERALDRY **OF TWO COLOURS** divided into parts of two different colours [13C. < French *partie* 'part, side in a contest' < Latin *partita*, form of past participle of *partire* 'divide' (see PARTITION)] —**partyer** *n* ◇ **be (a) party to something** to participate or be involved in a particular activity

party animal *n* somebody who frequently goes to parties and usually drinks large amounts of alcohol (*informal*)

partygoer /paárti gō ər/ *n* somebody who attends a party

party line *n* **1.** the official policy of a political party or other organization ○ *always toed the party line* **2.** a telephone line shared by more than one subscriber —**partyliner** *n*

party man *n* **1.** a man who is a loyal member or supporter of a political party **2.** a sociable man who enjoys going to parties

party person (*plural* **party people**) *n* **1.** somebody who is a loyal member or supporter of a political party **2.** a sociable person who enjoys going to parties

party piece *n* the usual song or turn that a person performs when called on to entertain people

party political broadcast *n* a short television or radio programme in which a political party is allowed to comment on political issues or to campaign, especially during an election

party politics *n* political activity as carried on by political parties, especially when devoted to furthering their own interests rather than the public's (*takes a singular or plural verb*) —**party-political** *adj*

party pooper /-poopər/ *n* somebody who spoils other people's fun, often by being unenthusiastic (*informal*)

party school *n US* a college, university, or similar institution where students are reputed to be more interested in fun and social activities than in academic study (*informal*)

party wall *n* a wall separating adjoining homes, buildings, or pieces of land

party woman *n* **1.** a woman who is a loyal member or supporter of a political party **2.** a sociable woman who enjoys going to parties

parulis /pə roóliss/ (*plural* **-lides** /-li deez/) *n* DENT same as **gumboil** (*technical*) [< modern Latin < Greek *para* 'beside' + *oulon* 'gums']

parure /pə roór/ *n* a matching set of jewellery that includes earrings, a brooch, ring, necklace, and bracelet, and sometimes other items such as buckles [Early 19C. < French < *parer* 'adorn, trim' (see PARE)]

par value *n* the value printed on a security such as a share certificate or bond at the time of issue. It is used to calculate interest or dividend payments.

Parvati /paárvəti/ *n* in Hinduism, a mother and fertility goddess, the wife of Shiva. She is thought of as the model Hindu wife and is often depicted with a conch, mirror, and lotus.

parve, parveh *adj* JUDAISM same as **pareve**

parvenu /paárvə nyoo/ (*plural* **-nus**) *n* somebody who has recently gained wealth or social status but who is still considered as inferior [Early 19C. < French < past participle of *parvenir* 'arrive' < Latin *pervenire* < *venire* 'come']

parvis /paárviss/, **parvise** *n* an enclosed area or portico at the front of a building, especially a church [14C. Via French < late Latin *paradisus* 'enclosed space' (see PARADISE)]

parvovirus /paárvō vīrəss/ *n* **1.** any of a group of viruses that have a single strand of DNA, especially those causing disease in mammals **2.** a contagious disease of dogs caused by a parvovirus and marked by fever, loss of appetite, and diarrhoea [Mid-20C. < Latin *parvus* 'small']

pas /paa/ (*plural* **pas** /*pronunc. same*/) *n* a step in dancing, especially in ballet [Early 18C. Via French < Latin *passus* 'step']

Pasadena /pássə deénə/ city in southwestern California, the home of the California Institute of Technology. Population: 139,712 (2002 estimate8).

pascal /pásk'l, pa skál/ *n* a unit of pressure or stress equal to one newton per square metre. Symbol **Pa** [Mid-20C. After Blaise PASCAL]

Pascal /pa skál, pásk'l/ *n* a high-level general-purpose computer language designed to encourage structured programming [Mid-20C. Acronym < French *programme appliqué à la sélection et la compilation automatique de la littérature*; also after Blaise PASCAL]

Pascal /pa skaál/, **Blaise** (1623–62) French philosopher and mathematician. He is considered one of the great minds in Western intellectual history. Among his achievements are the invention of the first mechanical adding machine and the development of the modern theory of probability.

> 'Had Cleopatra's nose been shorter, the whole face of the world would have changed.'
> [Blaise Pascal, *Pensées*; 1670]

Pascal's triangle /pa skaálz-/ *n* a triangular arrangement of numbers with a 1 at the top and at the beginning and end of each row, with each of the other numbers being the sum of the two numbers above it [After Blaise PASCAL]

paschal /pásk'l/ *adj* **1.** relating to Easter **2.** relating to Passover (*archaic*) [15C. Via French < ecclesiastical Latin *paschalis* < *pascha* 'Easter', ultimately < Greek *paskha*]

pas de deux /paá də dő/ (*plural* **pas de deux** /*pronunc. same*/) *n* a dance or dance sequence for two dancers [< French, 'step for two']

~~**pasenger**~~ incorrect spelling of **passenger**

paseo /paa sáy ō/ (*plural* **-os**) *n* **1.** the procession of matadors and other bullfighters into an arena before a bullfight begins **2.** *Southwest US* a stroll, especially in the evening [Mid-19C. < Spanish < *pasear* 'take a stroll' < *paso* 'step' < Latin *passus*]

pasha /paáshə, páshə/, **pacha** *n* formerly, in Turkey and the Ottoman Empire, an official of high rank [Mid-17C. < Turkish *paşa*]

pashm /páshəm/ *n* the fine soft wool of some goats, especially the Kashmir goat. Use: cashmere shawls, other garments. [Late 19C. < Persian *pašm* 'wool']

pashmina /pash meénə/ (*plural* **-nas**) *n* **1.** a fine woollen fabric made from the hair of goats raised in the Himalaya region **2.** a shawl made from pashmina [Late 19C. < Persian *pašmīn* 'woollen' < *pašm* 'wool']

Pashto /púshtō/ (*plural same* or **-tos**), **Pushto, Pushtu** /púsh too/ (*plural* **-tu** /*pronunc. same*/ or **-tus**) *n* **1.** an official language of Afghanistan, also spoken in northwestern Pakistan, belonging to the Indo-Iranian branch of Indo-European languages. Native speakers: 21 million. **2.** somebody who speaks Pashto as a native language [Late 18C. < Pashto *pəṣ̌tō*] —**Pashto** *adj*

Pashtun /push toón/ (*plural* **-tuns** or *same*) *n* a member of a people who live in eastern and southern Afghanistan and northwestern Pakistan [Early 19C. < Pashto *paštūn*]

Pasiphaë /pə síffi ee/ *n* **1.** in Greek mythology, the wife of Minos, King of Crete, who fell in love with a bull and gave birth to the Minotaur **2.** a small natural satellite of Jupiter, discovered in 1908 [Via Latin < Greek, literally 'all-shining']

paso doble /pássō dő blay/ (*plural* **paso dobles** /pássō dőblayz/) *n* **1.** a quick ballroom dance using Latin American marching movements. The movements of the man are intended to symbolize those of a bullfighter with the woman as his cape. **2.** the music for a paso doble [Early 20C. < Spanish, 'double step']

Pasolini /pássō leéni/, **Pier Paolo** (1922–75) Italian film director. His films include *The Gospel According to St Matthew* (1964) and *The Decameron* (1971).

> 'The cinema must be naturalistic. If I wish to express a dustman through the medium of cinema, I take a real dustman and reproduce him: body and voice.'
> [Pier Paolo Pasolini, 'Why that of Oedipus is a Story', *Oedipus Rex*; 1967]

pasqueflower /pásk flowər, paásk-/ *n* a small spring-flowering perennial plant with hairy leaves. Flowers: blue, purple, white. Native to: chalky grasslands of northern Europe and Asia or prairies of North America. Latin name: *Anemone pulsatilla* or *Anemone patens*. [Late 16C. Alteration of French *passefleur*, after French *pasque* 'Easter'; because it blooms in the spring]

pasquinade /pásskwi náyd/ *n* an often anonymous lampoon or satire that was traditionally displayed in a public place (*archaic*) [Late 16C. Via French < Italian *pasquinata* < *Pasquino*, statue in Rome where lampoons were posted] —**pasquinade** *vt* —**pasquinader** *n*

pass /paass/ *v* (**passes, passing, passed**) **1.** *vti* **MOVE PAST** to move past or through a place or past a person ○ *We passed several groups of refugees on our way.* ○ *dark clouds passing overhead* **2.** *vti* **OVERTAKE** to overtake somebody or something and move ahead **3.** *vti* **GIVE BALL TO PLAYER** to throw, kick, or hit a ball or other object to another player during a game **4.** *vt* **HAND SOMETHING OVER** to hand something to somebody ○ *Could you pass me the salt, please?* **5.** *vti* **TRANSFER SOMETHING, OR BE TRANSFERRED** to transfer something such as property, authority, or responsibility to somebody, or be transferred in this way ○ *The house will pass to his daughter when he dies.* **6.** *vti* **MOVE INTO DIFFERENT PLACE OR CONDITION** to make somebody or something move from one place or condition to another, or move from one place or condition to another **7.** *vti* **MOVE IN PARTICULAR WAY** to move in a particular way in relation to something else, or move something in this way ○ *He passed his hand along the banister.* **8.** *vt* **GUIDE SOMETHING** to guide something into a particular position ○ *Pass the wire over that hook.* **9.** *vi* **EXTEND PAST SOMETHING** to extend through, in front of, or along something such as a road or area ○ *The road passes by the cemetery.* **10.** *vi* **CHANGE** to go from one condition, stage, or state to another ○ *It sheds its skin before it passes to the pupal stage.* **11.** *vt* **SPEND TIME** to use up time doing something ○ *We passed the time playing cards.* **12.** *vi* **ELAPSE** to elapse or go by ○ *Time passes quickly.* **13.** *vi* **END** to come to an end ○ *The storm finally passed.* **14.** *vti* **BE SUCCESSFUL, OR DECLARE SOMEBODY SUCCESSFUL** to be successful in a test or examination, or officially decide that somebody has been successful in a test or examination **15.** *vti* **SUCCEED IN SUBJECT** to meet the requirements of a course of study **16.** *vi* **BE ACCEPTABLE** to be of an acceptable

standard ○ *It's not the best but it will pass.* **17.** *vti* APPROVE MEASURE OR BE APPROVED to approve something such as a law, measure, or proposal, or get official approval **18.** *vi* DIE to stop living (*formal*) ○ *She passed from this life in 1967.* **19.** *vi* HAPPEN BETWEEN PEOPLE OR THINGS to happen or be exchanged between two or more people or things ○ *A look passed between them.* **20.** *vi* NOT DO SOMETHING to decide not to do something that is suggested or not to accept something that is offered **21.** *vi* NOT RAISE BID to stop raising a bid in a card game **22.** *vt* EXCRETE SOMETHING to process and excrete something from the body ○ *had been passing blood* **23.** *vt* GIVE JUDGMENT to give a judgment **24.** *vt* STATE SOMETHING to say something or give an opinion ○ *She didn't pass any comment at all.* **25.** *vt* CIRCULATE FAKE MONEY to use fake money to pay for something ○ *passing counterfeit bills* ■ *n* **1.** DOCUMENT GIVING PRIVILEGES a document that entitles the holder to do something such as enter a place ○ *a press pass* **2.** ACT OF GIVING BALL TO PLAYER an act of throwing, kicking, or hitting a ball or other object to another player in a sport **3.** SUCCESSFUL GRADE a successful outcome in a test, examination, or course of study **4.** WAY THROUGH MOUNTAINS a way through or over mountains (*often used in placenames*) **5.** ATTEMPT TO KISS OR TOUCH SOMEBODY an uninvited attempt to kiss or touch somebody in a sexual way ○ *made a pass at her* **6.** ACT OF GOING BY an instance of something going past, through, over, or round a place **7.** MOVEMENT a movement of something such as the hand in conjuring tricks **8.** OPERATION a single cycle or complete operation of something such as machinery **9.** DOCUMENT EXCUSING SOMEBODY a document that excuses the holder from normal activities **10.** ACT OF NOT DOING SOMETHING an instance of not doing something that is suggested or not accepting something that is offered **11.** STATE OF AFFAIRS a state of affairs, usually of an undesirable nature ○ *How did we let things get to such a pass?* **12.** FAILURE TO BID IN CARDS an instance of not bidding or raising the bid in a card game **13.** SWORD THRUST a thrust with a sword ■ *interj* I DON'T KNOW used to indicate that you do not know the answer to a question or do not want to give an answer (*informal*) ○ *'Guess who I've just seen'. – 'Pass!'* ○ *'How would you rate him as a manager?' – 'Pass!'* [13C. < French *passer* < Latin *passus* 'step'] —**passer** *n* ◇ **let something pass** to make no comment or intervention ○ *It was a deliberate lie, but I let it pass.*

USAGE See ***past***[1].

pass as *vt* same as **pass for**

pass away *vi* **1.** to stop living (*often used as a euphemism for 'die'*) **2.** to come to an end or no longer exist

pass by *vt* to leave somebody or something unaffected or uninvolved ○ *The usual troubles of adolescence seemed to pass her by.*

pass for *vt* to be so like somebody or something as to be easily mistaken for the real person or thing

pass off *v* **1.** *vt* MAKE SOMETHING FALSE ACCEPTED to cause somebody or something to be accepted under a different, false identity ○ *She managed to pass herself off as a doctor for quite a while.* **2.** *vi* HAPPEN to have a particular outcome (*refers to planned events*) ○ *The ceremony passed off uneventfully.* **3.** *vi* DIMINISH to end or disappear gradually

pass on *v* **1.** *vi* to stop living (*often used as a euphemism for 'die'*) **2.** *vt* to convey or transmit something that has been received to somebody else

pass out *v* **1.** *vi* FAINT to lose consciousness **2.** *vt* DISTRIBUTE THINGS to distribute things among a number of people **3.** *vi* COMPLETE TRAINING to complete a course of training, especially as a military officer

pass over *v* **1.** *vt* IGNORE SOMEBODY to ignore somebody's right to be considered for something, especially a job or a promotion **2.** *vt* DISREGARD SOMEBODY OR SOMETHING to fail to consider or include somebody or something **3.** *vi* DIE to stop living (*dated*)

pass up *vt* to decide not to take advantage of an opportunity

passable /pa̋assəb'l/ *adj* **1.** ACCEPTABLE good enough but not excellent **2.** ABLE TO BE CROSSED capable of being crossed or travelled on **3.** ABLE TO BE ENACTED describes proposed legislation that is able to be passed or made law **4.** SUITABLE FOR CIRCULATION describes money that is suitable for circulation as legal and valid —**passably** *adv*

passacaglia /pássə kaályə/ *n* a baroque musical composition in slow triple time over a repeated bass line [Mid-17C. Via Italian < Spanish *pasacalle* < *pasar* 'to pass' + *calle* 'street'; because often played in the streets]

passade /pə sáyd/ *n* a movement in dressage in which a horse is made to move forwards and back again on the same spot [Mid-17C. Via French < Italian *passata* < Latin *passus* 'step']

passado /pə saádō/ (*plural* **-dos** or **-does**) *n* in fencing, a thrust made while stepping forwards [Late 16C. < Spanish *pasada* < Latin *passus* 'step']

passage[1] /pássij/ *n* **1.** CORRIDOR OR PATHWAY a corridor in an enclosed area or a path enclosed on both sides ○ *an underground passage* **2.** WAY THROUGH a path made for somebody through an obstruction such as a crowd of people **3.** PIECE OF WRITING OR MUSIC a section of a piece of writing, speech, or music **4.** CHANGE OF PLACE OR CONDITION the act of going from one place to another or changing from one condition to another (*formal*) ○ *the team responsible for easing the passage of the new President-elect into power* **5.** PROCESS OF TIME PASSING the process in which time goes by ○ *the passage of time* **6.** JOURNEY a journey, especially one made by sea or air **7.** FACT OF TRAVELLING the fact of travelling to a place or of being allowed to enter or pass through it ○ *The guides ensured our safe passage.* **8.** APPROVAL OF NEW LAW official approval of a new law or other proposal **9.** TUBE IN BODY a tube or channel in the body **10.** SEA CHANNEL a sea channel or strait (*often used in placenames*) **11.** BOWEL MOVEMENT the act or process of expelling something from the body, e.g. emptying the bowels or the bladder **12.** INTERCHANGE an exchange of words, blows, or information between people or parties (*formal*) **13.** /pa saázh/ BIOTECH BIOLOGICAL TECHNIQUE the technique of introducing a microorganism or cell into a host organism or culture medium as part of the process of maintaining or modifying it ■ *vt* (**-sages, -saging, -saged**) /pa saázh/ BIOTECH TRANSFER BIOLOGICAL MATERIAL to use the biological technique of passage to introduce a microorganism or cell [13C. < French *passer* (see PASS)]

CULTURAL NOTE ***A Passage to India***, a novel (1924) by E. M. Forster. In Forster's last and most highly regarded novel, an Englishwoman travelling in colonial India accuses a local doctor of assaulting her during a visit to the mysterious Marabar Caves. The conflicting responses of English expatriates and local Indians to the subsequent trial highlight the limitations of their belief systems and the problems of human understanding.

passage[2] /pássij, pə saázh/ *n* either of two movements in dressage, one being a sideways walk and the other a slow deliberate trot ■ *vti* (**-sages, -saging, -saged**) to perform a passage, or make a horse do this [Late 18C. Via French < Italian *passeggiare* 'to walk' < Latin *passus* 'step']

passage hawk, passager hawk /pássijər-/ *n* a hawk or falcon captured for hawking while on migration, especially a young bird in its first year of life

passageway /pássij way/ *n* BUILDINGS same as **passage**[1] *n* (sense 1)

passagework /pássij wurk/ *n* **1.** parts of a musical work that are thematically unrelated to the whole but enable a performer to display virtuosity **2.** the performance or execution of passagework

passant /páss'nt/ *adj* in heraldry, used to describe an animal shown walking to the left or right [15C. < French, present participle of *passer* (see PASS)]

passata /pə saátə/ *n* a thick tomato sauce with a rough texture, sometimes flavoured with herbs

passback /paáss bak/ *n* the act of passing the ball or puck to another player who is closer to the home goal

pass band *n* the range of frequencies that an electronic filter will allow to pass without attenuation. A voice band filter in a telephone exchange will pass a frequency band of approximately 3,000 cycles.

passbook /paáss bo͝ok/ *n* **1.** RECORD OF BANK TRANSACTIONS a book in which a record is kept of the money put into and taken out of a bank account or a building society account **2.** BOOK RECORDING CREDIT PURCHASES a book in which a trader records the items a customer has bought on credit **3.** IDENTITY DOCUMENT in South Africa during the apartheid era, a mandatory identification document issued to Black people that gave details of their ancestry and spelt out restrictions on their movement

Passchendaele /pásh'n dayl/, **Passendale** /páss'n dayl/ village in western Belgium. It was the scene of heavy fighting during World War I in October and November 1917.

passé /pássay, paá-/ *adj* **1.** no longer current or fashionable **2.** no longer in prime condition [Late 18C. < French, past participle of *passer* (see PASS)]

SYNONYMS See ***old-fashioned***.

passed pawn /paásst-/ *n* in chess, a pawn with no opposing pawn in front of it on its own or on either adjacent file that could become a queen

passementerie /pass méntri/ *n* **1.** a decorative trimming for clothing, e.g. one made of beads, braid, or lace **2.** the craft of making fringes, tassels, and cords to embellish soft furnishings and upholstery [Early 17C. < French < *passement* 'decorative lace or braid' < *passer* (see PASS)]

Passendale ➧ **Passchendaele**

passenger /pássinjər/ *n* **1.** a traveller in a motor vehicle, aircraft, train, or ship who is not a driver or crew member **2.** somebody in a team who does not do his or her fair share of the work [14C. Alteration of French *passager* 'somebody who makes a passage' < *passage* (see PASSAGE[1])]

passenger pigeon *n* a migratory pigeon that was abundant in the early 19th century but became extinct in the early 20th century from hunting and forest clearance. Native to: North America. Latin name: *Ectopistes migratorius.* [< PASSENGER in the obsolete sense 'migrating bird']

passenger profiling *n* the use of profiling to identify airline passengers who are deemed a potential threat to the safety of the flight, on the grounds of appearance, behaviour, and personal information gathered from databases

passenger seat *n* the seat in the front of a vehicle next to the driver's seat

passe-partout /páss paar to͞o/ (*plural* **passe-partouts** /*pronunc. same*/) *n* **1.** SOMETHING GIVING ACCESS something that gives unrestricted access to a building or area, e.g. a master key **2.** PICTURE FRAME a decorated mat round a framed picture **3.** ADHESIVE TAPE OR GUMMED PAPER adhesive tape or gummed paper used to fix pictures to mats before framing [< French, literally 'pass everywhere']

passer-by /paássər-/ (*plural* **passers-by**) *n* somebody who happens to be going past a place, especially on foot

passerine /pássə rīn, -reen/ *adj* relating or belonging to a group of mainly perching songbirds, which forms the largest order of birds including more than half of all bird species. Order: Passeriformes. ■ *n* any bird that belongs to the passerine order [Late 18C. < late Latin *passerinus* 'of sparrows' < Latin *passer* 'sparrow']

pas seul /paá sől/ (*plural* **pas seuls** /*pronunc. same*/) *n* a dance or passage performed by a single dancer [< French, 'solo step']

pass-fail *adj N Am* relating to a system of marking in which a student simply passes or fails, without a grade such as A, B, or C being awarded —**pass-fail** *n*

passible /pássəb'l/ *adj* emotionally sensitive, especially to the point of feeling pain (*formal*) [14C. Via French < Latin *passibilis* < past participle of *pati* 'feel, suffer'] —**passibility** /pássə bíllәti/ *n* —**passibly** *adv*

passim /pássim/ *adv* used especially in footnotes to indicate that what is being referred to occurs in various places in a book or other text [Early 19C. < Latin, 'so as to be scattered' < *passus*, past participle of *pandere* 'spread out']

passing /paássing/ *adj* **1.** GOING PAST moving past ○ *a passing car* **2.** TRANSITORY superficial and lasting only a short time **3.** BRIEF done briefly and without much attention being paid ○ *a passing interest* ■ *n* **1.** CEASING TO EXIST the fact or process of something becoming obsolete or ceasing to exist **2.** PROCESS OF TIME GOING BY the elapsing of time **3.** PLACE WHERE IT IS POSSIBLE TO PASS a place where it is possible to pass or cross

something **4.** same as **death** (sense 1) (*euphemistic*)

SYNONYMS See *temporary*.

passing bell *n* a bell rung to mark a death or a funeral

passing lane *n* a lane designated for drivers who want to pass slower traffic

passing note *n* a note played between two chords or pitches to provide a melodic transition from one to the other

passing out *n* the successful completion of a course of training, especially a military officer (*hyphenated when used before a noun*)

passing shot *n* in racket games such as tennis, a winning shot that passes beyond the reach of an opponent at the net

passion /pásh'n/ *n* **1.** INTENSE EMOTION intense or overpowering emotion such as love, joy, hatred, or anger ○ *Try and play it with a little more passion.* **2.** STRONG SEXUAL DESIRE strong sexual desire and excitement **3.** INTENSE ENTHUSIASM a strong liking or enthusiasm for a subject or activity ○ *a passion for music* **4.** OBJECT OF ENTHUSIASM the object of somebody's intense interest or enthusiasm ○ *Orchids are my passion.* **5.** OUTBURST OF EMOTION a sudden outburst of an emotion such as rage, hatred, or jealousy ○ *He flew into a passion.* ■ *passions npl* EMOTIONS strong emotions, especially as distinct from reason or intellect ○ *a meeting at which passions were running high* [12C. Via French < ecclesiastical Latin *passion-* 'suffering, affection' < Latin *pati* 'feel, suffer']

SYNONYMS See *love*.

Passion *n* **1.** in the Bible, the sufferings of Jesus Christ from the Last Supper until his crucifixion **2.** an account of the Passion in the Gospels

passional /pásh'nəl/ *adj* relating to passion or arising from passion (*literary*) ■ *n* a book that tells of the sufferings of Christian saints and martyrs [15C. < Latin *passionalis* < *passion-* (see PASSION)]

passionate /pásh'nət/ *adj* **1.** SHOWING SEXUAL DESIRE expressing or showing strong sexual desire ○ *a passionate kiss* **2.** SHOWING INTENSE EMOTION expressing intense feeling ○ *a passionate speech on human rights* **3.** ENTHUSIASTIC having a keen enthusiasm or intense desire for something ○ *a passionate golfer* **4.** HAVING STRONG EMOTIONS tending to have strong feelings, especially of love, desire, or enthusiasm ○ *a fiery, passionate personality* **5.** QUICK-TEMPERED easily made angry —**passionately** *adv*

passionflower

passionflower /pásh'n flow ər/ *n* a climbing vine with large flowers and edible fruit. Native to: Central, South America. Genus: *Passiflora*. [Mid-17C. Because parts of the flower are taken as symbols of Jesus Christ's Passion]

passion fruit *n* the edible fruit of a passionflower, especially a granadilla

passionless /pásh'nləss/ *adj* **1.** empty of romantic or sexual love ○ *a passionless film* **2.** feeling or expressing no emotion —**passionlessness** *n*

Passion play *n* a play that tells the story of the sufferings and crucifixion of Jesus Christ

Passion Sunday *n* **1.** the fifth Sunday in Lent, or the second Sunday before Easter, when Passiontide begins **2.** CHR same as **Palm Sunday**

Passiontide /pásh'n tīd/ *n* the last two weeks of Lent, from Passion Sunday to Easter

Passion Week *n* **1.** the second week before Easter, from Passion Sunday to the Sunday before Easter **2.** Holy Week (*archaic*)

passivate /pássi vayt/ (-**vates**, -**vating**, -**vated**) *vt* to coat the surface of a metal with a substance that protects it against corrosion

passive /pássiv/ *adj* **1.** NOT ACTIVELY TAKING PART tending not to participate actively, and usually letting others make decisions **2.** OBEYING READILY tending to submit or obey without arguing or resisting **3.** NOT OPERATIONAL not working or operating **4.** INFLUENCED BY SOMETHING EXTERNAL influenced, affected, or produced by something external ○ *passive solar heat gain* **5.** GRAM EXPRESSING ACTION DONE TO SUBJECT indicating that the apparent subject of a verb is the person or thing undergoing, not performing, the action of the verb, as in 'We were given work to do' **6.** CHEM UNREACTIVE chemically inactive or resistant to corrosion **7.** ELECTRONICS LACKING POWER SOURCE describes an electronic circuit or device that does not contain a source of energy **8.** FIN NOT PRODUCING INTEREST describes a form of investment that does not produce interest ■ *n* GRAM PASSIVE VOICE the passive voice, or a verb in the passive voice [14C. Directly or via French < Latin *passivus* < *pati* 'feel, suffer'] —**passively** *adv* —**passiveness** *n*

USAGE The **passive** voice In the active voice, the subject of the verb is the one who does the action described by the verb, and the object is the one acted upon: *The waiters will collect the plates.*

In the passive voice, this situation is reversed: the subject of the verb is the one acted upon by the verb, and the one who does the action – if mentioned at all – is relegated to a separate phrase, typically beginning with *by*: *The plates will be collected by the waiters.*

The passive can be used for a variety of purposes: for example, if the identity of the doer of the action is unknown, if the writer desires to conceal the identity of the doer of the action, as in *The vase was broken*, or if the writer wants to put special emphasis on what is affected by the action rather than on the doer of the action, as in *The bomb was defused by experts.*

Formal writing uses the passive more frequently than informal writing, and the passive is normal style in some scientific and technical writing. However, in many contexts too much use of the passive can seem wordy or pompous and the active is more direct and preferable. Compare: *Electrical goods may be found on the fourth floor* with *You can find electrical goods on the fourth floor*, or *Electrical goods are on the fourth floor*.

Avoid mixing passive and active voices in sentences like this: *Our commuter railway needs more money for major improvements and it will probably be raised by fare increases*. Say instead: *Our commuter railway needs more money for major improvements and will probably raise it by fare increases.*

A less commonly encountered but awkward construction is called the *double passive*. The writer has inserted two passive constructions close together in the same sentence: *No legal remedy was sought to be obtained by the victim*. Avoid such constructions and say instead *The victim did not seek to obtain any legal remedy*, or even *The victim did not seek any legal remedy*.

USAGE See *get¹*.

passive-aggressive *adj* describes a personality type or way of behaving that seeks to manipulate others indirectly and resist their demands rather than confronting or opposing directly —**passive-aggression** *n*

passive immunity *n* immunity from disease acquired by the transfer of antibodies from one person to another, e.g. through injections or between a mother and a fetus through the placenta

passive resistance *n* resistance to authority using only nonviolent methods such as peaceful demonstration or noncooperation —**passive resister** *n*

passive smoking *n* the involuntary breathing in of other people's tobacco smoke

passivity /pa sívvəti/ *n* passive behaviour, or the quality of being passive

passkey /paáss kee/ (*plural* -**keys**) *n* **1.** a key that gives the holder access via a restricted entrance **2.** same as **skeleton key**

pass law *n* in South Africa during the apartheid era, a law that restricted the movement of Black people within the country

Passmore /paáss mawr/, **John** (1904–84) Australian painter. He was a pioneer of abstract art in Australia.

Passmore, **John Arthur** (*b.* 1914) Australian philosopher and historian. His works include *A Hundred Years of Philosophy* (1957).

Passover /paáss ōvər/ *n* a Jewish festival marking the exodus of the Hebrews from captivity in Egypt. Date: seven or eight days from 14th day of Nisan. [Mid-16C. Translation of Hebrew *pesaḥ* (see PESACH)]

passport /paáss pawrt/ *n* **1.** IDENTIFICATION DOCUMENT an official document issued by the government of a country to a citizen that identifies the bearer and gives permission to travel to and from that country **2.** ANY AUTHORIZATION TO TRAVEL any authorization or official permission to travel in or through a country **3.** MEANS OF ACCESS something that grants somebody access to something ○ *Education can be the passport to a more fulfilling life.* [15C. < French *passeport* 'pass the seaport']

pass-through *n* *N Am* same as **serving hatch**

~~passtime~~ incorrect spelling of **pastime**

password /paáss wurd/ *n* **1.** a secret word or phrase that must be used by somebody who wants to be allowed in somewhere **2.** a sequence of characters that must be keyed in to gain access to all or part of a computer system or program ○ *Don't let anyone know your password.*

past¹ /paast/ CORE MEANING: a grammatical word describing movement that involves passing or going beyond somebody or something ○ (*prep*) *Walk past the library and you'll arrive at the park.* ○ (*adv*) *She walked right past without saying a word to us.* **1.** *prep, adv* LATER later than a particular time ○ *It's twenty past seven.* ○ *past his bedtime* **2.** *prep* ON FARTHER SIDE OF SOMETHING on the farther side of or beyond something ○ *the bakery past the school* **3.** *prep* BEYOND NUMBER, AMOUNT, OR POINT beyond a particular number, amount, or point, especially a point at which something can be done ○ *Do what you like; I'm past caring.* **4.** *adv* Scotland AWAY away, for the sake of tidiness or for future use (*informal*) ○ *Be a good wee soul and put your toys past.* [13C. Past participle of PASS] ◇ **not put it past somebody** to believe that somebody is quite capable of doing something, usually something disreputable or outrageous (*informal*) ◇ **past it** an offensive term meaning not as effective or capable of doing something as in former times (*informal*)

USAGE **past** or **passed**? Do not confuse these two words. Consider these examples: *He passed me at 80 mph; She is the past president of our student union.* In the first example, the past tense of the verb *pass*, which is **passed**, is required: *He passed me....* In the second sentence the adjective **past** ('one-time', former') is required: *She is the past president....*

past² /paast/ *adj* **1.** ELAPSED gone by or preceding or leading up to the present ○ *in times past* ○ *during the past few days* **2.** OF EARLIER TIME having existed, occurred, been done, or been gained in a previous time ○ *my past experience* **3.** ONE-TIME having formerly occupied a particular position ○ *a gathering of past presidents* ○ *a past love of his* **4.** GRAM EXPRESSING PREVIOUS ACTION describes a verb form or tense that expresses an action that took place previously ■ *n* **1.** TIME BEFORE PRESENT the time before the present or the events that happened during that time **2.** SOMEBODY'S PREVIOUS HISTORY everything that has happened previously to somebody or something ○ *She has a mysterious past.* **3.** SHAMEFUL HISTORY a shameful or scandalous earlier period in somebody's life **4.** GRAM PAST TENSE the past tense of a language, or a verb form in the past tense [13C. Past participle of PASS] —**pastness** *n*

pasta /pástə/ *n* **1.** a fresh or dried food of Italian origin made from a dough, usually of flour, eggs, and water, and produced in a variety of shapes and forms, e.g. in strings, ribbons, or sheets or as

spaghetti, macaroni, or lasagne **2.** a dish made with cooked pasta [Late 19C. Via Italian < late Latin (see PASTE[1])]

paste[1] /payst/ *n* **1. ADHESIVE MIXTURE** a soft mixture of flour and water or starch and water used as an adhesive, especially for sticking paper to something **2. SEMISOLID MIXTURE** a soft mass or mixture with a consistency between a liquid and a solid **3. FOOD SPREAD** a soft food product that can be spread on something such as bread ○ *anchovy paste* **4. PASTRY DOUGH** pastry dough usually made with shortening and used especially to make pie crusts **5. GLASS FOR IMITATION GEMS** a hard, brilliant glass used to make imitation jewels **6. PORCELAIN CLAY** the clay mixture used to make porcelain ■ *vt* **(pastes, pasting, pasted) 1. GLUE SOMETHING TO SOMETHING ELSE** to stick things together using paste **2. COVER SURFACE WITH PASTE** to cover a surface by sticking things to it with paste **3.** COMPUT **PLACE TEXT IN DOCUMENT ELECTRONICALLY** to place text, data, or an image into a document electronically [13C. Via French < late Latin *pasta* 'dough, paste' < Greek *pastē* 'barley porridge' < *passein* 'to sprinkle'] —**paster** *n*

paste up *vt* to take printed pages or proofs and stick them onto separate sheets of paper so that they can be read and amended

paste[2] /payst/ **(pastes, pasting, pasted)** *vt* to give somebody a severe beating or defeat somebody heavily (*informal*) [Mid-19C. Probably alteration of BASTE[2]]

pasteboard /páyst bawrd/ *n* **THICK STIFF PAPER** a stiff board made either of sheets of paper pasted together or of layers of paper pulp pressed together ■ *adj* **1. FLIMSY** not of good quality, or not very substantial ○ *pasteboard houses* **2. FAKE** intended to pass for the genuine article

pastel /pást'l, pa stél/ *adj* **PALE IN COLOUR** having a pale soft colour ■ *n* **1. PALE COLOUR** a pale soft colour **2. PASTE USED FOR MAKING CRAYONS** a paste of powdered pigment and gum, used for making crayons **3. CRAYON** an artist's crayon made of pastel **4. DRAWING** something drawn using pastel crayons **5. ART USING PASTELS** the technique or process of drawing with pastels [Late 16C. Directly or via French < Italian *pastello* 'small amount of paste' < *pasta* 'paste' < late Latin (see PASTE[1])] —**pastellist** *n*

pastern /pástərn/ *n* **1.** the part of a horse's foot between the fetlock and the top of the hoof **2.** either of two bones in a horse's foot that connect the hoof with the fetlock [13C. < Old French *pasturon* < *pasture* 'hobble for a pastured animal' < Latin *pascere* 'to feed']

Pasternak /pástər nak/, **Boris** (1890–1960) Soviet poet and author. His novel *Doctor Zhivago* (1956) was not published in Russia until 1987 because of its critical approach to Soviet Communism. The Soviet government forced him to decline the Nobel Prize in literature (1958). Full name **Pasternak, Boris Leonidovich**

> 'Man is born to live, not to prepare for life.'
> [Boris Pasternak, *Doctor Zhivago*; 1956]

paste-up *n* **1. SHEETS WITH PAGES FOR CHECKING** a number of sheets of paper onto which printed pages or proofs have been pasted for checking **2. PREPARATION FOR PRINTING PLATES** cards on which pieces of typesetting or artwork have been pasted to be photographed for making printing plates **3. TECHNIQUE OF MAKING PASTE-UPS** the technique or process of making paste-ups (*often used before a noun*) ○ *a paste-up artist*

Pasteur /pa stúr/, **Louis** (1822–95) French scientist. He invented the process of pasteurization and developed vaccines to induce immunity against viral diseases.

> 'When meditating over a disease, I never think of finding a remedy for it, but, instead, a means of preventing it.'
> [Louis Pasteur, *Address to the Fraternal Association of Former Students of the École Centrale des Arts et Manufactures, Paris*; 15 May 1884]

pasteurize /páaschə rīz, páschə-/ **(-izes, -izing, -ized), pasteurise (-ises, -ising, -ised)** *vt* to make a food product, especially milk, safer to drink or eat and improve its keeping qualities by heating it in order to destroy harmful bacteria [Late 19C. After Louis PASTEUR] —**pasteurization** /páaschə rī záysh'n, páschə-/ *n* —**pasteurizer** *n*

pasticcio /pa stíchō/ (*plural* **-ci** /-chi/ or **-cios**) *n* ARTS, LITERAT same as **pastiche** [Mid-18C. < Italian, 'pie, pasty' < late Latin *pasta* (see PASTE[1])]

pastiche /pa stéesh/ *n* **1. IMITATIVE WORK** a piece of creative work, e.g. in literature, drama, or art, that imitates and often satirizes another work or style **2. MIXTURE** a piece of creative work, e.g. in literature, drama, or art, that is a mixture of things borrowed from other works **3. USE OF PASTICHE** the creation or use of a pastiche [Late 19C. Via French < Italian *pasticcio* (see PASTICCIO)]

pastille /pást'l/ *n* **1.** a small flavoured or medicated sweet **2.** a substance, usually in tablet or paste form, that is burnt to scent or fumigate a room [Mid-17C. Via French < Latin *pastillus* 'lozenge, little loaf' < *panis* 'loaf']

pastime /páass tīm/ *n* an interest or activity that somebody pursues in his or her spare time [15C. < PASS + TIME]

pasting /páysting/ *n* a severe beating, or a complete defeat (*informal*)

pastis /pa stéess/ *n* a yellowish French liqueur flavoured with aniseed, often drunk as an aperitif [Early 20C. Via French, 'muddle, mixture' < late Latin *pasta* (see PASTE[1])]

pastitsio /pa stítsi ō/ *n* a Greek dish of minced meat mixed with cooked macaroni and topped with béchamel sauce, baked in a dish [Mid-20C. < Greek]

past master *n* **1.** somebody with great experience and skill in doing something **2.** a former holder of the position of master, e.g. in the Freemasons

pastor /páastər/ *n* **1. CHRISTIAN MINISTER** a Christian minister or priest in charge of a congregation **2. SPIRITUAL ADVISER** somebody who is not a minister or priest but who gives spiritual advice to a group of people **3. ASIAN STARLING** a starling with a black head and wings and a pink body that often feeds on swarming locusts. Native to: Asia. Latin name: *Sturnus roseus*. [14C. Via French < Latin, 'herdsman, shepherd' < *past-* (see PASTURE)] —**pastorship** *n*

pastoral /páastərəl/ *adj* **1. RURAL** relating to the countryside or to rural life ○ *pastoral living* **2. IDEALIZING RURAL LIFE** presenting an idealized image of rural life and nature ○ *pastoral poetry* **3. OF CLERGY** relating to Christian ministers or priests or their duties **4. GIVING ADVICE TO STUDENTS** involving the giving of personal advice and support to students on the part of a teacher as opposed to simply teaching them **5. USED FOR PASTURE** describes land that is used as pasture **6. OF SHEEP OR CATTLE** relating to or keeping sheep or cattle ■ *n* **1. DESCRIPTION OF RURAL LIFE** a literary work or painting that portrays rural life in an idealized way **2.** MUSIC same as **pastorale 3. LETTER FROM MINISTER** a letter written by a Christian minister or priest to his or her congregation **4. BISHOP'S STAFF** a staff carried by a Christian bishop as a symbol of office [15C. < Latin *pastoralis* < *pastor* (see PASTOR)] —**pastorally** *adv*

CULTURAL NOTE ***Pastoral Symphony,*** a composition (1808) by the German composer Ludwig van Beethoven. This is the name by which Beethoven's Symphony No. 6 in F major, op. 68, is popularly known. Beethoven described this widely performed work as a 'recollection of country life'. It describes a day's outing to countryside near Vienna and features peasant dances, bird song, and a storm.

pastorale /pástə ráal, pástə ráali/ (*plural* **-torales** or **-torali** /-ráali/ or **-torals**) *n* **1.** an opera with a rural story and setting, popular in western Europe in the 16th and 17th centuries **2.** a piece of music with a pastoral theme [Early 18C. Via Italian < Latin *pastoralis* (see PASTORAL)]

Pastoral Epistles *n* in the Bible, three epistles, the two to Timothy and the one to Titus, among those traditionally attributed to St Paul

pastoralism /páastrəlizəm/ *n* **1. LIVESTOCK RAISING** the raising of livestock, especially by traditional methods, as the main economic activity of a society **2. WAY OF LIFE DEPENDENT ON LIVESTOCK** a way of life that depends on raising livestock and living on its milk and meat **3. ARTISTIC TREATMENT OF RURAL LIFE** a style in literary work or painting that portrays rural life, especially that of shepherds, in an idealized way

pastoralist /páastrəlist/ *n* **1.** somebody who has a pastoral way of life **2.** *Aus* a cattle or sheep farmer, especially the owner of a large area of land in the Australian outback

pastorate /páastərət/ *n* **1.** the office, term of office, or jurisdiction of a pastor **2.** pastors considered as a group

past participle *n* a participle that expresses past time or a completed action. It is used with auxiliaries to form perfect tenses in the active voice and all tenses in the passive voice. In the sentence 'I waited until he had rung the bell', the past participle is 'rung'.

past perfect *n* a verb tense formed with 'had' that expresses an action completed at a more distant time in the past, that is, a time previous to the past time specified or implied elsewhere in the passage. In the sentence 'She had thought seriously about the implications of what she was doing', the verb 'think' is in the past perfect tense. —**past perfect** *adj*

pastrami /pə stráami/ *n* smoked and strongly seasoned beef, usually prepared from a shoulder cut, that is served cold in thin slices [Mid-20C. Via Yiddish < Romanian *pastramă*]

pastry /páystri/ (*plural* **-tries**) *n* **1. DOUGH FOR PIES** a dough made with flour, water, and shortening, used to make a base or covering for pies **2. FOODS MADE FROM PASTRY** sweet baked food made from pastry **3. SOMETHING MADE WITH PASTRY** a pie or small cake made with pastry [15C. < PASTE[1]]

pastry fork *n* a small delicate fork for eating pastries and cakes

pastry slice *n* a kitchen utensil with a flat triangular blade, used for serving pastries

past tense *n* a verb tense expressing something that happened or was done in the past. In the sentence 'I felt very proud of them', the verb 'felt' is in the past tense.

pasturage /páaschərij/ *n* **1.** AGRIC same as **pasture** *n* (sense 1) **2.** the grazing of livestock, or the right to graze livestock on a particular area of land

pasture /páaschər/ *n* **1. LAND FOR GRAZING** grass-covered land used for grazing livestock **2. PLANTS FOR GRAZING** grass and other growing plants that are suitable food for livestock ■ *vti* **(-tures, -turing, -tured) GRAZE** to graze, or put livestock somewhere to graze [13C. Via French < late Latin *pastura* < Latin *past-*, past participle of *pascere* 'feed, graze'] ◇ **pastures new** somewhere different to work or live (*informal*) ◇ **put somebody out to pasture** to impose early retirement on somebody (*informal*)

pastureland /páaschər land/ *n* an area of land that is used for grazing livestock

~~**pasturized**~~ incorrect spelling of **pasteurized**

pasty[1] /pásti/ (*plural* **-ties**) *n* a pie made from a folded-over round of pastry with a savoury or sweet filling in the middle [13C. < Old French *pasté(e)* < late Latin *pasta* (see PASTE[1])]

pasty[2] /páysti/ *adj* **(-ier, -iest) 1. UNHEALTHILY PALE** having a pale unhealthy appearance **2. RESEMBLING PASTE** resembling paste in consistency, colour, or texture ■ *n* (*plural* **-ies**) **NIPPLE COVERING** either of a pair of small adhesive coverings for a woman's nipples, worn usually by erotic dancers [Early 17C. < PASTE[1]] —**pastily** *adv* —**pastiness** *n*

PA system *n* same as **PA**[2]

pat[1] /pat/ *vt* **(pats, patting, patted) 1. STRIKE LIGHTLY** to strike something lightly with the palm of the hand or something flat **2. LAY HAND ON SOMETHING REPEATEDLY** to touch somebody or something repeatedly with the palm of the hand, e.g. to show affection or to congratulate somebody ○ *I patted the child's curly head.* **3. SHAPE SOMETHING WITH HANDS** to shape or smooth something with repeated light blows with the hands or with a flat object ○ *patted the dough into shape* ■ *n* **1. LIGHT BLOW** a light blow with the palm of the hand or with a flat object **2. LIGHT TOUCH** a light, usually repeated, touch with the hand to show affection or to congratulate somebody **3. SOFT SOUND** the sound made by a light blow with the hand or with a flat object, or by a light footstep **4. SMALL PIECE** a small piece of a soft substance, especially butter [14C. An

imitation of the sound made] ◇ **a pat on the back** an expression of praise or congratulation (*informal*) ◇ **pat somebody on the back** to praise or congratulate somebody (*informal*)

pat[2] /pat/ *adv* **1.** EXACTLY in an exact, accurate, or fluent way ○ *He has his lines off pat.* **2.** OPPORTUNELY at the most appropriate time or place ■ *adj* **1.** GLIB so easily and readily produced as to suggest lack of proper thought ○ *pat answers* **2.** CARDS NOT TO BE IMPROVED describes a poker hand that is not likely to be improved by drawing additional cards [Late 16C. Probably 'hitting the mark' < PAT[1]]

Pat /pat/ *n* an offensive term for an Irishman [Early 19C. Shortening of the name *Patrick*, common in Ireland]

pat. *abbr* **1.** patent **2.** patented

pataca /pə taákə/ *n* the main unit of currency of Macau. See table at **currency** [Mid-19C. Via Portuguese < Arabic *abū ṭāqah*, a coin]

patagium /pə táyji əm/ (*plural* **-gia** /-ji ə/) *n* **1.** a loose fold of skin between the fore and hind limbs in some mammals such as bats and flying lemurs, used as an aid to flying or gliding **2.** a thin fold of skin between a bird's wing and its shoulder [Early 19C. < Latin, 'gold edging on a tunic']

Patagonia /pàttə gṓni ə/ region of steppe and desert in southern Argentina and southeastern Chile, between the Andes Mountains and the South Atlantic Ocean. Area: 670,000 sq. km/260,000 sq. mi. —**Patagonian** *n, adj*

Patagonian Desert one of the largest deserts in the world, located in Patagonia, southern Argentina Area: 670,000 sq. km/260,000 sq. mi.

patch /pach/ *n* **1.** SOMETHING THAT COVERS OR MENDS a piece of material used to cover, strengthen, or mend a hole in something ○ *an elbow patch* **2.** SMALL AREA a small area of something within a larger one ○ *a patch of ice* **3.** SMALL GROWING AREA a small area of land used for growing a particular crop ○ *a cabbage patch* **4.** AREA OF CONTROL an area under somebody's control or jurisdiction ○ *They warned him to stay off their patch.* **5.** PERIOD a period of time in which a particular situation exists ○ *hit a bad patch* **6.** EYE SHIELD a pad worn over an injured or missing eye ○ *an eye patch* **7.** COVER FOR WOUND a piece of material used to cover a wound **8.** DRUG-IMPREGNATED MATERIAL a drug-impregnated adhesive pad worn on the skin to allow gradual absorption of the drug ○ *a nicotine patch* **9.** SEWN-ON BADGE a cloth badge sewn onto clothing as identification, a sign of rank, or to commemorate something **10.** SOFTWARE BUG CORRECTOR OR UPDATE a fragment of program code made available to fix a bug in a software application or to add a new feature before an updated version of the application is released ○ *a patch available on the Internet* **11.** TEMPORARY CONNECTION a temporary connection between parts of a communications system, especially to create a telephone hookup **12.** ARTIFICIAL BEAUTY SPOT a small piece of black silk or velvet worn on the face by men and women as an adornment in the 17th and 18th centuries ■ *vt* (**patches, patching, patched**) **1.** REPAIR SOMETHING WITH MATERIAL to cover or mend a hole in something or to strengthen a weak place using cloth or some other material **2.** MAKE SOMETHING FROM CLOTH PIECES to make something by sewing together pieces of fabric ○ *patched together a quilt* **3.** AMEND COMPUTER PROGRAM USING PATCH to fix or update software using a patch **4.** CONNECT CALL to connect one telephone or radio caller with another or transfer a call to somewhere else ○ *Patch me through to headquarters.* [14C. Origin ?] —**patcher** *n* ◇ **hit** *or* **strike a bad patch** go through a period of misfortune or difficulty ◇ **not a patch on somebody** *or* **something** not nearly as good as somebody or something (*informal*)

patch up *vt* **1.** MEND SOMETHING HURRIEDLY to mend or assemble something hurriedly or as a temporary measure **2.** BECOME FRIENDS AGAIN to become friends with somebody again after an argument **3.** GIVE TREATMENT TO SOMEBODY to give somebody medical treatment for an injury (*informal*)

patch board *n* an electrical panel with numerous sockets into which electrical cords (**patch cords**) can be plugged to form temporary circuits

patchouli /páchŏŏli, pə chŏŏli/, **pachouli** *n* **1.** an aromatic oil obtained from a tropical mint. Use: perfumes, aromatherapy. **2.** a bush of the mint family whose leaves produce patchouli. Native to: tropical Asia. Latin name: *Pogostemon cablin.* [Mid-19C. < Tamil *paccuḷi*]

patch panel *n* TELECOM same as **patch board**

patch pocket *n* a pocket made by sewing a patch of fabric onto the outside of a garment

patch test *n* a test for allergies in which small pads impregnated with allergens are applied to somebody's skin to check whether there is any negative reaction

patchwork /pách wurk/ *n* **1.** needlework in which pieces of fabric are sewn together in a decorative way ○ *a patchwork quilt* **2.** something made up of many different parts ○ *a patchwork of fields*

patchy /páchi/ (**-ier, -iest**) *adj* **1.** occurring only in patches rather than throughout an area, or consisting only of patches rather than a large expanse ○ *patchy fog* **2.** unpredictable and varying in quality depending on the place or time —**patchily** *adv* —**patchiness** *n*

patd *abbr* patented

pate /payt/ *n* the head, especially the top of the head (*archaic or humorous*) [14C. Origin ?]

pâté /páttay, pátti/ *n* a paste made from meat, fish, or vegetables, often served as an appetizer [Mid-19C. < French, modern form of Old French *paste* (see PASTE[1])]

pâté de foie gras /páttay də fwaá graá, pátti-/ *n* a rich pâté made from the livers of geese that are fattened specifically for this purpose [< French, 'pâté of fatty liver']

patella /pə téllə/ (*plural* **-lae** /-lee/ *or* **-las**) *n* ANAT same as **kneecap** *n* (sense 1) (*technical*) [15C. < Latin, literally 'small shallow dish' (from the shape) < *patina* (see PATEN)] —**patellar** *adj* —**patellate** *adj*

paten /pátt'n/, **patin, patine** *n* a shallow metal plate, often made of gold or silver, used to carry the bread at the celebration of the Christian Communion [13C. Directly or via French *patène* < Latin *patina* 'shallow dish' < Greek *patanē* 'plate']

patency /páyt'nssi/ *n* **1.** the obvious nature of something **2.** the naturally open and unblocked state of an artery, duct, or other tube in the body

patent /páyt'nt, pátt'nt/ *n* **1.** EXCLUSIVE RIGHT TO MARKET INVENTION an exclusive right officially granted by a government to an inventor to make or sell an invention **2.** DOCUMENT GRANTING PATENT an official document setting out the terms of a patent **3.** INVENTION PROTECTED BY PATENT an invention for which a patent has been granted **4.** DOCUMENT GRANTING RIGHT a official document that grants a right to somebody **5.** *N Am* GOVERNMENT GRANT a government grant that gives an individual title to public lands, or the land granted ■ *adj* **1.** CLEAR OR OBVIOUS very obvious and not open to doubt ○ *his patent discomfiture* **2.** OF PATENTS relating to or dealing in patents ○ *a patent lawyer* **3.** PROTECTED BY PATENT protected by a patent from being copied or sold by somebody else ○ *patent medicine* **4.** MED UNBLOCKED describes an artery, duct, or other tube in the body that is naturally open and unblocked **5.** BOT SPREADING describes plant parts that spread out widely from a centre **6.** LAW OPEN FOR INSPECTION describes a legal document that is accessible to anyone for inspection ■ *vt* (**-ents, -enting, -ented**) PROTECT RIGHTS TO SOMETHING BY PATENT to obtain a patent on or for something, especially an invention [14C. Directly or via French < Latin *patent-*, present participle of *patere* 'lie open']

patentee /páyt'n teé, pátt'n-/ *n* a person or group to whom a patent has been granted

patent leather *n* leather that has been treated with lacquer to give it a hard, glossy surface [< the idea of protection]

patent log *n* an instrument that measures a ship's speed or the distance it has travelled by means of fins that rotate as the instrument is dragged through the water behind the vessel [< PATENT 'patented']

patently /páyt'ntli, pátt'ntli/ *adv* in a way that can easily be seen or understood ○ *She was patently ill at ease.*

patent medicine *n* a medicine protected by a patent or trademark that can be bought without a prescription

Patent Office *n* a government office that evaluates patent claims and grants patents

patentor /páyt'n táwr, pátt'n-/ *n* a person or office that grants a patent

patent right *n* the exclusive right to make or sell something that is granted to somebody by a patent

Patent Rolls *npl* the register of patents granted in the United Kingdom

patent still *n* an alcohol still using steam heat and running continuously that produces very pure spirit [< PATENT 'patented']

pater /páytər/ *n* somebody's father (*informal dated*) [14C. < Latin, 'father']

ORIGIN The Latin word *pater* 'father', from which **pater** is derived, is also the source of English *paternal, patrician, patrimony, patron, pattern,* and *perpetrate.* Its Indo-European ancestor in turn also produced English *father, patriarch,* and *patriot.*

Pater /páytər/, **Walter** (1839–94) British essayist and philosopher. His *Studies in the History of the Renaissance* (1873) and phrase 'art for art's sake' had an important influence on the aesthetic movement. Full name **Pater, Walter Horatio**

> 'All art constantly aspires towards the condition of music.'
> [Walter Pater, 'The School of Giorgione', *Studies on the History of the Renaissance*; 1873]

paterfamilias /páytərfə mílli ass, páttər-/ *n* a man in the role of father and head of a household [15C. < Latin, 'father of a family']

paternal /pə túrn'l/ *adj* **1.** OF FATHERS OR FATHERHOOD relating to fathers or considered characteristic of a father **2.** RELATED THROUGH FATHER being on a father's side of a family ○ *her paternal grandfather* **3.** INHERITED FROM FATHER inherited or deriving from a father [15C. < late Latin *paternalis* < Latin *pater* 'father'] —**paternally** *adv*

paternalism /pə túrn'lizəm/ *n* a style of government or management, or an approach to personal relationships, in which the desire to help, advise, and protect may neglect individual choice and personal responsibility —**paternalist** *n* —**paternalistic** /pə túrnə lístik/ *adj* —**paternalistically** *adv*

paternity /pə túrnəti/ *n* **1.** FATHERHOOD a man's role or status as a father **2.** ANCESTRY descent from a father **3.** ORIGIN the origin or authorship of something (*literary*) [15C. Directly or via French < late Latin *paternitas* < Latin *pater* 'father']

paternity leave *n* time off work that an employer grants to a man whose partner has just had, or is about to have, a baby or who is adopting a child

paternity suit *n* a lawsuit brought by a woman against a man whom she claims is the father of her child and therefore liable for contributing to the child's financial support

paternity test *n* a medical test using DNA fingerprinting or other genetic information to determine whether or not a man is the father of a particular child

paternoster /páttər nóstər, -nostər/ *n* **1.** *also* **Paternoster** LORD'S PRAYER in Roman Catholicism, the Lord's Prayer, or a recitation of it **2.** LARGE BEAD IN ROSARY in Roman Catholicism, a large bead in a rosary, used to indicate when the Lord's Prayer is to be recited **3.** WORDS IN PRAYER OR ATTEMPTED MAGIC a set form of words used in prayer or in attempting magic **4.** NONSTOP LIFT a doorless lift in which compartments move continuously and people step on and off as they wish [Pre-12C. < Latin *pater noster* 'our father', first two words of the Lord's Prayer]

Paterson /páttərss'n/, **A. B.** (1864–1941) Australian poet. His works include *The Man from Snowy River and Other Verses* (1895) and the lyrics to the song 'Waltzing Matilda'. Full name **Paterson, Andrew Barton**. See Cultural note at **Snowy**. Known as **Banjo Paterson**

> 'Once a jolly swagman camped by a billybong, / Under the shade of a coolibah tree,

/ And he sang as he sat and waited for his billy-boil, / "You'll come a-waltzing, Matilda, with me".'
[A. B. Paterson, 'Waltzing Matilda', *Bulletin*; 1885]

path /paath/ *n* 1. **TRODDEN TRACK** a track that has been worn by the continual passage of feet 2. **SURFACED TRACK** a surfaced track made for walking or cycling 3. **COURSE** a route along which something moves ○ *the path of the Earth's orbit round the Sun* 4. **COURSE OF ACTION** a course of action or a way of living ○ *her path to freedom and independence* 5. **ROUTE TO COMPUTER FILE** the route that a computer operating system follows through the directories on a disk to locate a file, or the sequence of keyed characters that identifies this route [Old English *pæþ* < Indo-European, 'to tread'] ◇ **lead somebody up the garden path** to deceive or mislead somebody, often over a period of time (*informal*) ◇ **the primrose path** an enjoyable, easy way of life considered to lead to ruin or degeneration

-path *suffix* 1. somebody with a particular disorder ○ *neuropath* 2. somebody who practises a particular type of remedial treatment ○ *osteopath* 3. somebody who possesses a particular ability ○ *telepath* [Back-formation < -PATHY]

Pathan /pə taán/ (*plural same* or **-thans**) *n* a member of a people who live in Afghanistan, where Pathans are the largest ethnic group, and in parts of Pakistan [Mid-17C. < Hindi *Paṭhān*] —**Pathan** *adj*

pathetic /pə théttik/ *adj* 1. provoking or expressing feelings of compassion and pity 2. so inadequate as to be laughable or contemptible (*informal*) [Late 16C. Via French and late Latin < Greek *pathētikos* 'sensitive' < *pathos* 'feeling'] —**pathetically** *adv*

SYNONYMS See *moving*.

pathetic fallacy *n* the attribution of human characteristics to nature or to inanimate objects, as in the phrase 'the angry waves'

pathfinder /paáth fīndər/ *n* a discoverer of a route, especially through unmapped territories or uncharted areas of knowledge —**pathfinding** *n*

patho- *prefix* disease ○ *pathogen* [< Greek *pathos*]

pathogen /páthəjən, -jen/ *n* something that can cause disease, e.g. a bacterium or a virus

pathogenesis /páthə jénnəssiss/, **pathogeny** /pə thójjəni/ *n* the cause, development, and effects of a disease —**pathogenetic** /páthəjə néttik/ *adj*

pathogenic /páthə jénnik/ *adj* 1. causing disease, or able to cause disease 2. relating to the causes and development of diseases

pathognomonic /páthəgnə mónnik/ *adj* used to describe a symptom or sign that indicates almost beyond doubt the correct diagnosis of a disease [Early 17C. < Greek *pathognōmonikos* < *pathos* 'disease' + *gnōmōn* 'judge']

pathological /páthə lójjik'l/ *adj* 1. **OF PATHOLOGY** relating to pathology, or used in pathology 2. **OF DISEASE** relating to disease, or arising from disease 3. **EXTREME** uncontrolled or unreasonable ○ *a pathological fear of heights* [Late 17C. < Greek *pathologikos* < *pathos* 'disease'] —**pathologically** *adv*

pathology /pə thólləji/ (*plural* **-gies**) *n* 1. **STUDY OF DISEASE** the scientific study of the nature, origin, progress, and cause of disease ○ *plant pathology* 2. **PROCESSES OF A DISEASE** the processes of a disease, observable either with the naked eye or by microscopy, or, at a molecular level, as inferred from biochemical tests ○ *the pathology of cholera* 3. **DISEASE** a diseased condition ○ *a scan showing the area of suspected pathology* ○ *evidence of intestinal pathology* 4. **CONDITION THAT IS NOT NORMAL** a condition that is a deviation from the normal [Late 16C. < French *pathologie* or modern Latin *pathologia* < Greek *pathos* 'disease'] —**pathologist** *n*

pathophysiology /páthō fízzi ólləji/ *n* the disturbance of function that a disease causes in an organ, as distinct from any changes in structure that might be caused

pathos /páy thoss/ *n* 1. the quality in something that makes people feel pity or sadness 2. feelings of pity, especially when they are expressed in some way [Late 16C. < Greek, 'feeling, disease']

pathway /paáth way/ *n* 1. a path or route 2. a sequence of biochemical reactions involved in a metabolic process

-pathy *suffix* 1. disorder, disease ○ *retinopathy* 2. remedial treatment ○ *hydropathy* 3. feeling, perception ○ *telepathy* [< Greek *-patheia* < *pathos* 'feeling, disease'] —**-pathic** *suffix*

patience /páysh'nss/ *n* 1. the ability to endure waiting, delay, or provocation without becoming annoyed or upset, or to persevere calmly when faced with difficulties ○ *I was beginning to run out of patience.* 2. a card game for one player. N Am term **solitaire** [12C. Via French < Latin *patientia* < *patient-* (see PATIENT)]

patient /páysh'nt/ *adj* 1. **CAPABLE OF WAITING** able to endure waiting, delay, or provocation without becoming annoyed or upset 2. **CAPABLE OF PERSEVERING** able to persevere calmly, especially when faced with difficulties ■ *n* **SOMEBODY GIVEN MEDICAL TREATMENT** somebody who receives medical treatment [14C. Via French < Latin *patient-*, present participle of *pati* 'suffer'] —**patiently** *adv*

patina /páttinə/ *n* 1. **THIN GREEN LAYER ON COPPER** a thin layer formed by corrosion on the surface of some metals and minerals, especially the green layer that covers copper and bronze and is valued for its colour 2. **SURFACE SHEEN** a pleasing surface sheen that develops on an object with age or frequent handling 3. **SUPERFICIAL LAYER** a thin or superficial layer on something [Mid-18C. Via Italian < Latin (see PATEN)] —**patinated** /-naytid/ *adj*

patio /pátti ō/ (*plural* **-os**) *n* 1. a paved area adjoining a house, used for outdoor dining and recreation 2. a roofless inner courtyard typical of a Spanish-style house [Early 19C. < Spanish, 'courtyard of a house']

patio doors *npl* a pair of glazed doors in an outside wall of a house that open onto a patio

patisserie /pə téssəri, -tíssəri/ *n* 1. a bakery that specializes in pastries and cakes 2. sweet pastries or cakes collectively [Late 16C. < French *pâtisserie*, modern form of Old French *pastiserie* < *pasticier* 'make pastry' < late Latin *pasta* (see PASTE[1])]

Pátmos /pát moss/ Greek island in the southeastern Aegean Sea, one of the Dodecanese group. Population: 2,650 (1995). Area: 34 sq. km/13 sq. mi.

Patna /pátnə/ capital of Bihar State, northern India. Population: 1,707,429 (2001).

Patna rice /pátnə-/ *n* a variety of long-grained rice, used in savoury dishes

Pat. Off. *abbr* Patent Office

patois /pát waa/ (*plural* **-ois** /pát waaz/) *n* 1. a regional form of a language, used informally and usually containing nonstandard forms 2. the jargon used by a specific group [Mid-17C. < French, 'native speech']

Patois *n* 1. LANG same as **Creole** (sense 3) 2. *Carib* in the Caribbean, the local popularly used vernacular, usually a French- or English-related Creole —**Patois** *adj*

Paton /páytn/, **Alan** (1903–88) South African writer and politician. His novels, in particular *Cry, the Beloved Country* (1948), deal with the racial tensions in South Africa during the apartheid era. He helped establish the Liberal Party of South Africa in 1953 and served as its president until it was dissolved in 1968. Full name **Paton, Alan Stewart**. See Cultural note at **cry**

'Wise men write many books, in words too hard to understand. But this, the purpose of our lives, the end of all our struggle, is beyond all human wisdom.'
[Alan Paton, *Cry, the Beloved Country*; 1948]

pat. pend. *abbr* patent pending

patr- *prefix* same as **patri-** (*used before vowels*)

Patras /pə tráss, pátrəss/ port in southern Greece, on the northwestern Peloponnese. Population: 153,344 (1991).

patri- *prefix* father, paternal ○ *patrilineal* [Directly or via Latin < Greek *patr-* 'father']

~~**patriachal**~~ incorrect spelling of **patriarchal**

patrial /páytri əl, páttri əl/ *n* formerly, a person entitled to enter and stay in the United Kingdom without being regarded as an immigrant, e.g. somebody from a Commonwealth country [Early 17C. < French, or medieval Latin *patrialis* 'of your country' < Latin *pater* 'father']

patriarch /páytri aark, páttri-/ *n* 1. **HEAD OF FAMILY** a man who is the head of a family or group 2. **RESPECTED ELDERLY MAN** a respected and experienced elderly man within a group or family 3. **BIBLICAL ANCESTOR** in the Bible, a figure mentioned as the ancestor of the whole human race, e.g. Adam or Noah 4. **HEBREW LEADER** in the Hebrew Scriptures, especially the book of Genesis, an ancestor or religious leader of the Hebrew people, e.g. Abraham, Isaac, or Jacob 5. **OLDEST MEMBER** the oldest male member of something such as a community of people or a herd of livestock 6. **FOUNDER** a man who is a founder of something 7. **EASTERN ORTHODOX BISHOP** in the Eastern Orthodox Church, a bishop of the sees of Constantinople, Alexandria, Antakya, or Jerusalem, and also of Russia, Romania, or Serbia 8. **SENIOR ROMAN CATHOLIC BISHOP** in the Roman Catholic Church, a leading bishop in a Uniat church 9. **DIGNITARY OF LATTER-DAY SAINTS** a high dignitary of the Church of Latter-Day Saints with the power to invoke blessings [12C. Directly or via French < ecclesiastical Latin *patriarcha* < Greek *patriarkhēs* 'head of a family' < *patria* 'family']

patriarchal /páytri aárk'l, páttri-/ *adj* 1. **CHARACTERISTIC OF RULE BY MEN** relating to or characteristic of a culture in which men are the most powerful members 2. **RELATING TO PATRIARCH** relating to or held to be characteristic of a patriarch 3. **RULED BY BISHOP** in Roman Catholicism, governed by a bishop —**patriarchally** *adv*

patriarchal cross *n* a Christian cross with a second and shorter horizontal bar above the main bar

patriarchalism /páytri aárkəlizəm, páttri-/ *n* institutionalized domination by men, with women being regarded as socially or constitutionally inferior

patriarchate /páytri aarkət, páttri-/ *n* 1. the office, term of office, area of jurisdiction, or residence of a patriarch of a Christian church 2. SOC SCI same as **patriarchy** [Early 17C. < medieval Latin *patriarchatus* < ecclesiastical Latin *patriarcha* (see PATRIARCH)]

patriarchy /páytri aarki, páttri-/ (*plural* **-chies**) *n* 1. a social system in which men are regarded as the authority within the family and society, and in which power and possessions are passed on from father to son 2. a society based on a system of patriarchy [Mid-16C. Via medieval Latin < Greek *patriarkhia* < *patriarkhēs* (see PATRIARCH)]

patriate /páttri ayt/ *vt* to obtain control over a constitution that was formerly under the control of a colonial power (*refers to a former dependency*)

patrician /pə trísh'n/ *n* 1. **ARISTOCRATIC ROMAN** a member of an aristocratic family of ancient Rome whose privileges included the exclusive right to hold some high-status offices 2. **ARISTOCRAT** a member of an aristocracy 3. **SOMEBODY WITH UPPER-CLASS CHARACTERISTICS** somebody with the qualities and manners traditionally associated with the upper class 4. **NONHEREDITARY BYZANTINE TITLE** a nonhereditary honorary title bestowed by Byzantine emperors on people who had been of great service to the empire ■ *adj* 1. **OF PATRICIANS** relating to patricians, or belonging to a class of patricians 2. **ARISTOCRATIC** characteristic of aristocrats or the upper class [15C. < French *patricien* < Latin *patricius* 'of a noble father' < *pater* 'father']

patriciate /pə tríshi ət/ *n* 1. the position or rank of a patrician 2. the social class to which patricians belong [Mid-17C. < Latin *patriciatus* < *patricius* (see PATRICIAN)]

patricide /páttri sīd, páytri-/ *n* 1. the murder of a father by his child or children 2. somebody who murders his or her own father [Late 16C. < late Latin *patricidium* < Latin *pater* 'father'] —**patricidal** /páttri sīd'l, páytri-/ *adj*

Patrick /páttrik/, **St** (389?–461?) British-born Irish churchman. He spread Christianity throughout Ireland, and reorganized the church there. He is the patron saint of Ireland. Known as **the Apostle of Ireland**

'Christ beside me, Christ before me, Christ behind me, Christ within me, Christ beneath me, Christ above me.'
[St Patrick's Breastplate]

patriclinous /pə tríklinəss/, **patroclinous** adj descended or inherited from the male line [Early 20C. < PATRI- + Greek klinein 'lean']

patrilineal /páttrə línni əl/, **patrilinear** /-ər/ adj describes family relationships traced through the male line, or societies in which only such relationships are recognized —**patrilineally** adv

patrilocal /páttri lŏk'l/ adj describes a custom in which a wife goes to live with her husband's family or people after marriage, or a society in which this custom prevails —**patrilocally** adv

patrimony /páttriməni/ (plural **-nies**) n 1. INHERITANCE FROM FATHER an inheritance from a father or male ancestor 2. HERITAGE the objects, traditions, or values that one generation has inherited from its ancestors 3. CHR ESTATE BELONGING TO CHURCH an estate or endowment that belongs to a church [14C. Via French < Latin patrimonium < pater 'father'] —**patrimonial** /páttri mŏni əl/ adj —**patrimonially** adv

patriot /páttri ət, páy-/ n a proud supporter or defender of his or her country and its way of life [Late 16C. Via French < late Latin patriota 'fellow countryman' < Greek patris 'fatherland'] —**patriotic** /páttri óttik, páytri-/ adj —**patriotically** adv —**patriotism** n

patristic /pə trístik/, **patristical** /pə trístik'l/ adj relating to the early Christian writers such as St Augustine or St Ambrose whose works have helped to shape the Christian Church [Mid-19C. < German patristisch < Latin pater 'father'] —**patristically** adv

patristics /pə trístiks/ n the study of the writings and lives of the early Christian theologians (takes a singular verb) [Mid-19C. < German Patristik < Latin pater 'father']

patro- prefix same as **patri-**

Patroclus /pə trókləss/ n in Greek mythology, a friend of Achilles and a warrior in the Trojan War

patrol /pə trŏl/ n 1. REGULAR TOUR MADE BY GUARD a regular tour made of a place in order to guard it or to maintain order 2. SOMEBODY CARRYING OUT PATROL a person or group that carries out a patrol 3. MILITARY UNIT ON MISSION a military unit sent out for reconnaissance 4. SUBDIVISION OF SCOUT TROOP a subdivision of a troop of Scouts or Guides ▪ vti (**-trols, -trolling, -trolled**) GO ON PATROL to guard or protect a place by moving regularly around it and watching it ○ troops patrolling the border [Mid-17C. Directly or via German Patrolle < French patrouille < patroullier, originally 'walk through mud in a military camp' < Old French patte 'paw']

patrol car n same as **squad car**

patrolman /pə trŏlmən/ (plural **-men** /-mən/) n 1. an employee of a motoring organization who patrols an area and responds to calls from members 2. N Am a police officer who patrols a beat

patrology /pə trólləji/ n the study of the writings of the Fathers of the Christian Church [Early 17C. < Greek patēr 'father'] —**patrological** /páttrə lójjik'l/ adj —**patrologist** n

patrol wagon n ANZ, US an enclosed police vehicle for transporting prisoners

patrolwoman /pə trŏl wŏŏmən/ (plural **-women** /-wimin/) n US a policewoman who patrols a beat

patron /páytrən/ n 1. SPONSOR a giver of money or other support to somebody or something, especially in the arts 2. REGULAR CUSTOMER a customer, especially a regular one, of a shop or business 3. CHR same as **patron saint** 4. ROMAN SLAVE MASTER in ancient Rome, somebody who had given a slave his or her freedom but still retained some rights over the former slave 5. SOMEBODY ABLE TO MAKE CHURCH APPOINTMENTS a holder of the right to appoint a member of the clergy to an ecclesiastical benefice in the Church of England [14C. Via French < Latin patronus 'protector' < pater 'father'] —**patronal** /pə trŏn'l/ adj

SYNONYMS See *backer*.

patronage /páttrənij/ n 1. SUPPORT OF PATRON the encouragement, financial support, or influence of a patron 2. POWER TO MAKE APPOINTMENTS the political power to grant privileges or appoint people to pos-

itions 3. APPOINTMENTS ASSIGNED BY POLITICIAN the appointments or privileges that a politician can give to loyal supporters 4. RIGHT OF ECCLESIASTICAL APPOINTMENT in the Church of England, the right to appoint a member of the clergy to an ecclesiastical benefice 5. CONDESCENDING KINDNESS support or kindness offered in a condescending way 6. BUSINESS PROVIDED BY CUSTOMER the trade that a regular customer brings to a shop or business (formal) 7. N Am same as **custom** n (sense 4) [14C. < French < patron (see PATRON)]

patronise, etc. vti another spelling of **patronize, etc.**

patronize /páttrə nīz/ (**-izes, -izing, -ized**), **patronise** (**-ises, -ising, -ised**) v 1. vti BE CONDESCENDING TO to treat somebody as if he or she were less intelligent or knowledgeable than yourself 2. vt SUPPORT SOMEBODY to give money or other material support to somebody or something, especially in the arts 3. vt BE REGULAR CUSTOMER OF BUSINESS to be a regular customer of a shop or business (formal) —**patronizer** n

patronizing /páttrə nīzing/, **patronising** adj treating somebody as if he or she is less intelligent or knowledgeable than yourself —**patronizingly** adv

patron saint n a saint who is believed to be a special guardian, especially of a country, trade, or group of people

patronymic /páttrə nímmik/ adj describes a name derived from a male ancestor's name, especially one that adds a prefix such as 'Mac-', or a suffix such as '-son', to the earlier name [Early 17C. Via late Latin < Greek patrōnumikos < patrōnumos 'father's name' < patēr 'father' + onuma 'name'] —**patronymic** n

patsy /pátsi/ (plural **-sies**) n an easily victimized, cheated, or manipulated person (informal insult) [Late 19C. Origin ?]

pattée /páttay, pátti/ adj describes a cross with triangular arms that widen towards the ends [15C. < French < patte 'paw']

patten /pátt'n/ n a clog, sandal, or overshoe with a raised wooden sole to lift the wearer's feet above mud [14C. < French patin < patte 'paw']

patter[1] /páttər/ vi (**-ters, -tering, -tered**) 1. MAKE QUICK TAPPING SOUND to make a quick light tapping sound on something ○ The rain pattered against the window. 2. STEP LIGHTLY to move or run with short quick light steps ○ She pattered across the floor in her pyjamas. ▪ n TAPPING NOISE a quick light tapping sound [Early 17C. < PAT[1]]

patter[2] /páttər/ n 1. GLIB AND RAPID TALK the fast well-prepared talk of somebody such as a comedian or salesperson 2. JARGON the language of a specific group or class of people 3. SMALL TALK meaningless empty chatter ▪ v (**-ters, -tering, -tered**) 1. vi TALK QUICKLY to speak rapidly and glibly 2. vt REPEAT SOMETHING RAPIDLY to repeat something quickly in a mechanical way [14C. Shortening of PATERNOSTER]

pattern /páttərn/ n 1. DESIGN a repeated decorative design, e.g. on fabric ○ a zigzag pattern 2. REGULAR FORM a regular or repetitive form, order, or arrangement ○ a predictable pattern of behaviour ○ local variations in voting patterns 3. PROTOTYPE an original design or model from which exact copies can be made 4. PLAN OR MODEL a plan or model used as a guide for making something ○ a knitting pattern 5. GOOD EXAMPLE a model that is considered to be worthy of imitation 6. REGULAR MANNER OF PERFORMANCE a regular or standard way of moving or behaving ○ the flight patterns of birds 7. SAMPLE a specimen of a piece of fabric, wallpaper, or other material 8. MODEL USED FOR MAKING MOULD a wood, plaster, or metal shape used to make a mould for casting in a foundry. The original model is often slightly oversize to allow for contraction in the castings as they cool. 9. GUNSHOTS ON TARGET a series of marks made by shots from a gun on a target 10. SPREAD OF SPENT PROJECTILES the dispersal of projectiles such as artillery shells and shrapnel on the ground around a target ▪ vt (**-terns, -terning, -terned**) 1. MODEL SOMETHING ON SOMETHING to make something in such a way that it imitates the design, structure, or another quality of something else ○ patterned the scheme on an earlier immunization campaign 2. PUT PATTERN ON SOMETHING to make something into, or decorate something with, a repeated decorative design [14C. Alteration of French patron 'pattern, patron' (see PATRON)] —**patterned** adj —**patterning** n

pattern baldness n hair loss that takes place gradually and in a symmetrical pattern on the head, thought to be a result of both genetic and hormonal factors

pattern book n a collection of small samples of various fabrics, wallpapers, or similar products, made up in the form of a book

Patterson /páttərss'n/, **Percival** (b. 1935) prime minister of Jamaica (1992–). A member of the People's National Party, he became Jamaica's first Black prime minister. Full name **Patterson, Percival James**

patter song n a comic song, especially in the works of Gilbert and Sullivan, that consists of words sung together in rapid succession

George S. Patton

Patton /pátt'n/, **George S.** (1885–1945) US general. In World War II he commanded the Third Army in France. Full name **Patton, George Smith, Jr**

'The quickest way to get it over with is to get the bastards.'
[George S. Patton, Speech to troops; 1944]

patty /pátti/ (plural **-ties**) n 1. a small flat individual cake made from minced meat, vegetables, or other food 2. a small pie or pasty [Mid-17C. Anglicization of French pâté (see PÂTÉ), influenced by PASTY[1]]

pattypan squash n a variety of wheel-shaped summer squash with a ribbed edge. Latin name: Cucurbita pepo. [< PATTY + PAN[1]]

patulous /páttyŏŏləss/ adj describes branches that spread or expand from a central point [Early 17C. < Latin patulus 'standing open' < patere 'be open'] —**patulously** adv —**patulousness** n

Patwa /pát waa/ n Carib LANG another spelling of **Patois** [Form of PATOIS] —**Patwa** adj

patzer /pátsər, páátsər/ n US an inept player of chess (informal insult) [Mid-20C. Origin ?]

Pau /pō/ city in southwestern France. Population: 78,732 (1999).

PAU abbr Pan American Union

paua /pów əl/ (plural **-as** or same) n an edible abalone with an iridescent shell. Use: ornaments, jewellery. Native to: New Zealand. Latin name: Haliotis iris. [Mid-19C. < Maori]

paucity /páwssəti/ n 1. an inadequacy or lack of something 2. a small number of something [14C. Via French < Latin paucitas < paucus 'few, little']

Paul /pawl/, **St** (AD 3?–62?) early Christian missionary. He became a Christian after having a vision of Jesus Christ on the road from Jerusalem to Damascus. A major missionary of Christianity, he was also its first theologian. His life and teachings are described in the Epistles and the Acts of the Apostles in the Bible. Known as **Saul of Tarsus, Paul the Apostle** —**Pauline** /páwl īn/ adj

Paul III, Pope (1468–1549) As pope (1534–49), he excommunicated King Henry VIII of England (1538) and authorized the establishment of the Jesuits. Born **Farnese, Alessandro**

Paul VI, Pope (1897–1978) As pope (1963–78), he presided over the Second Vatican Council and travelled widely to extend the Vatican's influence. Born **Montini, Giovanni Battista**

pauldron /páwldrən/ n a piece of armour consisting of a metal plate worn on the shoulder [Late 16C. < Old French espauleron < espaule 'shoulder' < late Latin spatula 'shoulder blade']

Pauli exclusion principle /pówli-/ *n* a law of quantum physics stating that no two identical particles of a particular type (**fermions**) may occupy the same quantum state at the same time [Early 20C. After Wolfgang *Pauli* (1900–58), Austrian-born US physicist]

Pauling /páwling/, **Linus** (1901–94) US chemist and peace activist. He won the Nobel Prize in chemistry (1954) and the Nobel Peace Prize (1962) for his efforts to end nuclear testing. Full name **Pauling, Linus Carl**

> 'Science is the search for truth—it is not a game in which one tries to beat his opponent, to do harm to others.'
> [Linus Pauling, *No More War!*; 1958]

Paul Jones (*plural* **Paul Joneses**) *n* a dance in which partners are exchanged in a prearranged pattern [Early 20C. After John *Paul Jones* (1747–92), Scottish naval officer known for his victories in the American War of Independence]

paulownia /paw lṓni ə/ (*plural* **-as** or *same*) *n* a deciduous tree with large heart-shaped leaves. Flowers: purple, white, bell-shaped, in clusters. Native to: China. Latin name: *Paulownia tomentosa*. [Mid-19C. < modern Latin, after Anna *Paulowna* (1795–1865), wife of William II of the Netherlands and daughter of Tsar Paul I of Russia]

paunch /pawnch/ *n* **1.** a large round protruding stomach **2.** ZOOL same as **rumen 3.** a thick rope mat that protects against chafing [14C. Via Old French *pance, panche* < Latin *panticem* 'belly, bowels'] —**paunchy** *adj*

pauper /páwpər/ *n* **1.** an impoverished person **2.** formerly, an impoverished person who was eligible to receive aid from public funds [15C. < Latin, 'getting little' < *paucus* 'little' + *parare* 'get'] —**pauperism** *n* —**pauperize** *vt*

paupiette /pō pyét/ *n* a piece of meat or fish that is cut or rolled out very thin, topped with a stuffing, then rolled up into a neat shape and cooked [Early 18C. Via French < Italian *polpetta* < Latin *pulpa* 'pulp']

pauropod /páwrə pod/ *n* a small eyeless invertebrate with eleven segments and nine pairs of legs. Class: Pauropoda. [Late 19C. < modern Latin *pauropoda* 'small-footed' < Greek *pauros* 'small']

Pausa /páwzə/ *n* in the Hindu calendar, the tenth month of the year, lasting 30 days and usually falling within December and January. See table at **calendar**

pause /pawz/ *v* (**pauses, pausing, paused**) **1.** *vi* STOP BRIEFLY to stop doing something briefly before continuing ○ *He paused for a moment and then continued eating.* **2.** *vi* STAY BRIEFLY to halt somewhere for a short time ○ *I paused to glance into a shop window.* **3.** *vi* HESITATE to wait intentionally for a short period before doing or saying something ○ *Selena paused. There was no easy way of saying what had to be said.* **4.** *vt* CAUSE SOMETHING TO PAUSE to cause an electronic or mechanical device to stop operating temporarily, e.g. by pressing a pause button ○ *Can you pause the video for a moment?* ■ *n* **1.** BRIEF STOP a temporary break in an activity **2.** SHORT SILENCE a brief moment of silence between words, sounds, or musical notes **3.** HESITATION a brief moment of hesitation or uncertainty before something happens or is done **4.** *also* **pause button** PAUSING MECHANISM a control on an electronic or mechanical device such as a video recorder that brings it temporarily to a halt **5.** MUSICAL SYMBOL FOR TIME EXTENSION a musical symbol indicating that a note, chord, or rest is to be held longer than the indicated time value. It is represented by a full stop with an upside-down 'u' above it. **6.** LITERAT same as **caesura** (sense 1) [15C. Directly or via French < Latin *pausa* 'stopping, cessation' < Greek *pausis* < *pauein* 'stop, cease'] —**pausal** *adj* —**pausing** *n* ◇ **give somebody pause** to make somebody hesitate or reconsider

SYNONYMS See *hesitate*.

pav /pav/ *n* ANZ FOOD same as **pavlova** (*informal*)

pavane /pə ván, -vaán/ *n* **1.** a slow dance that was popular in European courts in the 16th and 17th centuries **2.** the music for a pavane [Mid-16C. Via French < Italian *pavana* 'Paduan' < *Pavo*, dialect name for Padua]

Luciano Pavarotti
AKG London

Pavarotti /pávvə rótti/, **Luciano** (*b.* 1935) Italian tenor. Known for his great vocal power and dramatic quality, he is associated with 19th-century Italian opera.

pave /payv/ (**paves, paving, paved**) *vt* **1.** PROVIDE SOMETHING WITH HARD SURFACE to cover a surface with stone, brick, concrete, or other hard materials in order to make it suitable for walking or travelling on **2.** BE SURFACE FOR WALKING ON to serve as a hard covering for the surface of something and make it suitable for walking or travelling on ○ *Large stone slabs paved the path.* **3.** COVER to cover a surface with a flat, uniform material such as leaves or flowers [14C. Via French < Latin *pavire* 'beat, tread down'] ◇ **pave the way (for something)** to prepare for and facilitate the progress of something

pavé /pávvay/ *n* a jewel setting in which small stones are set very close together so as to cover the surface of the piece and obscure the metal base [Late 19C. < French, 'paved']

pavement /páyvmənt/ *n* **1.** PATH FOR PEDESTRIANS a paved path for pedestrians alongside a street. N Am term **sidewalk 2.** CONSTR MATERIAL FOR PAVEMENTS material that is used to make a pavement, e.g. concrete or stone **3.** CIV ENG LAYERED SURFACE OF PATH the layered structure that forms the surface of a path, road, carriageway, or aircraft runway **4.** *N Am* ASPHALT SURFACE an asphalt surface, especially of a road **5.** GEOL LEVEL AREA OF ROCK a level area of bare rock that resembles a pavement [13C. Via French < Latin *pavimentum* 'beaten floor' < *pavire* 'beat, tread down']

paver /páyvər/ *n* **1.** a stone or slab used to pave an area such as a patio **2.** somebody who installs or lays a pavement

pavilion /pə vílli ən/ *n* **1.** OUTDOOR STRUCTURE a summer house or other ornamental building in a garden, **2.** SPORTS CLUBHOUSE a building at a cricket or other sports ground where players can change and where refreshments are served **3.** EXHIBITION TENT a large tent or other temporary structure used for displaying or exhibiting things **4.** BIG TENT a large and often extremely ornate tent **5.** ANNEX a detached building that forms part of a complex for a hospital or other large public building **6.** JEWELLERY FACET OF GEM a facet of a brilliant-cut gem that comes below the girdle ■ *vt* (**-ions, -ioning, -ioned**) **1.** SET SOMETHING IN PAVILION to enclose or house something inside a pavilion **2.** CONSTRUCT PAVILION FOR SOMETHING to construct a pavilion for something **3.** ENCLOSE SOMETHING to enclose or completely surround something (*literary*) ○ *'Pavilioned in splendour, And girded with praise'* (Sir Robert Grant, *O Worship the King*; 1833) [Pre-12C. Via French *pavillon* 'tent, canopy' < Latin *papilion-* 'butterfly, tent'; because a tent was thought to resemble a butterfly's wings]

~~pavillion~~ incorrect spelling of **pavilion**

paving /páyving/ *n* **1.** SURFACE FOR PATH OR ROAD a firm usually flat surface made of stone, brick, concrete, or other material **2.** MATERIAL FOR MAKING HARD SURFACE material used for making a firm hard surface, e.g. concrete or stones **3.** CONSTRUCTION OF PAVED SURFACE the act of making a paved surface

paving stone *n* a large flat rectangular slab, usually made from concrete or stone, used in making a paved surface

paviour /páyvyər/ *n* **1.** a stone, slab, or block used to pave an outdoor area such as a patio **2.** somebody whose occupation is laying external paving

Pavlov /páv lof/, **Ivan** (1849–1936) Russian physiologist. He became famous for his studies on conditioned reflexes with dogs. He won the Nobel Prize in physiology or medicine (1904). Full name **Pavlov, Ivan Petrovich**

pavlova /pav lṓvə/ *n* a dessert consisting of a large meringue shell filled with cream and fruit [Early 20C. After Anna PAVLOVA, in whose honour the dish was created]

Anna Pavlova
AKG London

Pavlova /pav lṓvə, pávləvə/, **Anna** (1882–1931) Russian ballet dancer. Admired for the poetic quality of her movement, she performed many classic roles. The solo dance 'The Dying Swan' was created for her.

> 'Happiness is like a butterfly which appears and delights us for one brief moment, but soon flits away.'
> [Anna Pavlova. Quoted in 'Pages of My Life', *Pavlova: A Biography*, A. H. Franks (ed.); 1956]

Pavlovian /pav lṓvi ən/ *adj* **1.** produced involuntarily in response to a stimulus **2.** relating to Ivan Pavlov and his work [Mid-20C. After Ivan PAVLOV]

Pavlovian conditioning *n* PSYCHOL same as **classical conditioning**

Pavo /paávō/ *n* a constellation of the southern hemisphere containing the bright star Peacock. See illustration at **constellation**

pavonine /pávvə nīn/ *adj* resembling a peacock, especially the colours and design of its tail (*literary*) [Mid-17C. < Latin *pavoninus* < *pavon-* 'peacock']

paw /paw/ *n* **1.** ANIMAL'S FOOT the foot of a four-legged mammal, usually having claws or nails **2.** HUMAN HAND a human hand, especially one that is large or clumsy (*informal*) ■ *vti* (**paws, pawing, pawed**) **1.** STRIKE SOMETHING REPEATEDLY WITH PAW to scrape or strike something repeatedly with a paw or hoof **2.** TOUCH SOMEBODY CLUMSILY to touch somebody or something, or caress somebody, roughly or rudely with the hands [13C. Via Old French *powe* < Frankish]

pawky /páwki/ (**-ier, -iest**) *adj regional* witty or shrewd in a dry or sly manner [Mid-17C. < *pawk* 'trick', origin ?] —**pawkily** *adv* —**pawkiness** *n*

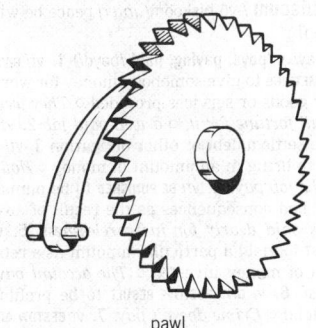
pawl

pawl /pawl/ *n* a hinged or pivoted catch, often spring-controlled, designed to engage with the teeth of a ratchet wheel to prevent reverse motion [Early 17C. Origin ?]

pawn[1] /pawn/ *n* **1.** a chess piece of the lowest value that can move one square forward at a time, with an optional first move of two squares. It can take other pieces by moving diagonally and can be ex-

changed for any other captured piece on reaching the farthest rank of the board. **2.** somebody or something that is being used for the advantage of another person or organization [14C. Via Anglo-Norman *poun*, Old French *peon* < medieval Latin *pedon-* 'foot soldier' < Latin *ped-* 'foot']

pawn[2] /pawn/ *vt* (**pawns, pawning, pawned**) **1.** DEPOSIT SOMETHING WITH PAWNBROKER to leave something with a pawnbroker as security against money borrowed **2.** PLEDGE SOMETHING to stake or pledge your honour, life, or word on something ■ *n* **1.** OBJECT DEPOSITED AS SECURITY an object that is left as security with a pawnbroker in exchange for a loan of money **2.** HOSTAGE somebody who is held as security, usually as a hostage **3.** ACT OF PAWNING the act of pawning something [15C. < Old French *pan(d)* 'pledge' < W Germanic] —**pawnage** *n* —**pawner** *n* ◇ **in pawn** left or held as security with a pawnbroker in exchange for a loan of money

pawnbroker /páwn brōkər/ *n* somebody who lends money at a fixed rate of interest in exchange for articles of personal property that are left as security

Pawnee /paw née/ (*plural same* or **-nees**) *n* **1.** a member of a confederation of Native North American peoples who lived in Nebraska and Kansas and who are now mainly dispersed **2.** the Caddoan language of the Pawnee people. Native speakers: 3,000. [Late 18C. Via Canadian French *Pani* < a Native N American language] —**Pawnee** *adj*

pawnshop /páwn shop/ *n* a shop where articles of personal property may be left as security in exchange for a loan of money

pawn ticket *n* a ticket that serves as a receipt for something that has been pawned

pawpaw /páw paw/, **papaw** /páw paw, pə páw/ *n* **1.** a yellow medium-sized oval fruit with sweet flesh and black seeds **2.** a deciduous tree with purple flowers that bears pawpaws. Native to: North America. Latin name: *Asimina triloba*. **3.** TREES, FOOD same as **papaya** (sense 2) [Early 17C. Alteration of PAPAYA]

pax /paks/ *interj* SCHOOLCHILDREN'S TRUCE a call for a truce or a break in a game used by children and usually signalled by holding up crossed fingers (*informal*) ■ *n* **1.** *also* **Pax** STABLE PERIOD UNDER POWERFUL EMPIRE a period of peace and stability under the influence of a powerful country or empire **2.** KISS OF PEACE IN CHURCH a kiss or other greeting given as a sign of peace during the Christian ceremony of Communion, especially in the Roman Catholic Mass **3.** TABLET KISSED AT CHRISTIAN COMMUNION a tablet bearing a representation of the Crucifixion that is kissed by participants in the Christian ceremony of Communion, especially during the Roman Catholic Mass [Pre-12C. < Latin, 'peace']

PAX *abbr* TELECOM private automatic exchange

Paxil /páks'l/ *tdmk* a trademark for the antidepressant drug paroxetine

Pax Romana /-rō máanə/ *n* the long period of peace and stability that existed under the Roman Empire, especially in the 2nd century AD [< Latin, 'peace of the Romans']

pax vobiscum /-vō bískōōm/ *interj* peace be with you [< Latin]

pay[1] /pay/ *v* (**pays, paying, paid** /payd/) **1.** *vti* GIVE MONEY FOR SOMETHING to give somebody money for work done or for goods or services provided ○ *They were paid a small fortune for it.* ○ *a well-paid job* **2.** *vti* SETTLE DEBT to settle a debt or other obligation **3.** *vti* BRING IN MONEY to bring in an amount of money ○ *How much will the job pay?* **4.** *vti* BE PUNISHED to be punished or suffer bad consequences as the result of an action ○ *He's paid dearly for his carelessness.* **5.** *vt* YIELD INTEREST to yield a particular amount as a return on a sum of money invested ○ *The account pays 12% interest.* **6.** *vi* GIVE POSITIVE RESULT to be profitable or beneficial ○ *Crime doesn't pay.* **7.** *vt* BESTOW ATTENTION to give something such as attention or a compliment to somebody or something ○ *pay a compliment* **8.** *vt* VISIT SOMEBODY to make a visit or call to see somebody **9.** *vt* same as **pay out** (sense 2) **10.** *vt* NAUT LET VESSEL GO LEEWARD to allow a vessel to make leeway **11.** *vt Aus* ACKNOWLEDGE SOMETHING IS TRUE to acknowledge the truth of a statement or that you were wrong (*informal*) ○ *OK, I'll pay that.* ■ *n* **1.** MONEY GIVEN IN RETURN FOR WORK money that is given in return for work or services provided, especially in the form of a salary or wages **2.** REWARD reward, recompense, or recognition granted to somebody **3.** MIN EXTRACT same as **pay dirt** (sense 2) ■ *adj* **1.** NEEDING INSERTION OF COIN TO FUNCTION requiring the insertion of coins or a card in order to function ○ *pay TV* **2.** MIN EXTRACT RICH IN METALS yielding metal or minerals valuable enough to make mining them profitable [12C. Via Old French *payer* 'pacify' < Latin *pacare* < *pax* 'peace'] ◇ **in the pay of somebody** employed by somebody, especially for a dishonest or criminal purpose ◇ **pay the piper** to bear the cost of something, and so to be in control ◇ **pay the price (for something)** to suffer the unpleasant consequences of something you have done ◇ **put paid to** to put an end to or ruin something (*informal*) ◇ **pay through the nose** to pay an exorbitant sum for goods or services

SYNONYMS See *wage*.

pay back *vt* **1.** to repay money that has been lent ○ *I'll pay you back on Friday.* **2.** to revenge yourself on somebody

pay down *vt* **1.** to pay an amount of money as a deposit or as the first instalment of a larger payment **2.** *N Am* to reduce the amount of a debt by repaying some of the money that has been borrowed ○ *'...should have paid down its debt or invested in microchip technology...'* (*Newsweek*; November 1998)

pay in *vt* to deposit money in a bank or other account

pay off *v* **1.** *vt* REPAY DEBT IN FULL to repay the full amount of a bill, debt, or other financial obligation, especially one that has been paid in instalments **2.** *vt* REPAY PART OF DEBT to repay a portion of a debt or other financial obligation **3.** *vt* BRIBE SOMEBODY to give somebody money as a bribe, usually to prevent that person from causing trouble (*informal*) **4.** *vt* PAY AND LAY OFF WORKERS to give employees or workers the money owing to them for work performed before dismissing them **5.** *vi* BE SUCCESSFUL to be successful or profitable ○ *All that preparation paid off in the end.* **6.** *vt* TAKE REVENGE ON SOMEBODY to take revenge on somebody for something he or she has done to you **7.** *vi* NAUT MAKE LEEWAY to make leeway

pay out *v* **1.** *vti* PAY MONEY to spend or pay money **2.** *vt* UNWIND to release a rope or cable gradually **3.** *vt* TAKE REVENGE to take revenge on somebody **4.** *vti Aus* CRITICIZE to criticize or abuse somebody (*informal*)

pay over *vi* to transfer money to somebody officially

pay up *vi* to pay money that is due

pay[2] /pay/ (**pays, paying, payed**) *vt* to make a ship's hull waterproof with pitch or tar [Early 17C. Via Old French *peier* < Latin *picare* < *pix* 'pitch']

payable /páy əb'l/ *adj* **1.** due or needing to be paid **2.** requesting payment to be made to a particular person ○ *Shall I make the cheque payable to you or to Jean?*

pay and display *n* a parking system in which motorists buy tickets from a machine in a car park and leave them on display in the windscreens or windows of their vehicles. Motorists pay for the amount of time they intend to stay, which is printed on the ticket.

pay-as-you-earn *n* FIN full form of **PAYE**

pay-as-you-go *n* **1.** the practice or system of paying debts or costs as they are incurred **2.** *Aus* FIN full form of **PAYG**

payback /páy bak/ *n* **1.** RETURN ON INVESTMENT a financial return on an investment equalling the initial capital invested **2.** TIME REQUIRED TO RECOVER OUTLAY the period of time required to recover the return on an initial investment **3.** REVENGE revenge or retaliation (*informal*) **4.** *US* REQUITAL FOR SERVICE RENDERED a benefit in exchange for an action or service performed (*informal*)

pay bed *n* a bed in a National Health Service hospital used by a private patient

pay cheque *n* **1.** a cheque issued to an employee as payment of salary or wages **2.** wages or salary

payday /páy day/ *n* the day on which employees are paid their wages or salary

pay dirt *n* **1.** *N Am* a discovery or idea that is likely to be useful or profitable **2.** gravel, sand, earth, or ore that is worth mining

paydown /páy down/ *n N Am* the repayment of part of a debt

PAYE *n* a system in which income tax is deducted as money is earned. Full form **pay-as-you-earn**

~~**payed**~~ incorrect spelling of **paid**

payee /pay ée/ *n* somebody to whom money is being paid or is due, especially the person to whom a cheque or money order is payable

pay envelope *n N Am* same as **pay packet**

payer /páyər/ *n* **1.** somebody who pays somebody or something **2.** the person named as responsible for the payment of a cheque, money order, or other financial paper when it is redeemed

PAYG *n* in Australia, the system in which income tax is deducted as money is earned. Full form **pay-as-you-go**

paying guest /páying-/ *n* somebody who pays to stay in another person's home for a temporary period, e.g. during a holiday

paying-in slip *n UK* a form for listing the contents of a bank deposit. ANZ, N Am term **deposit slip**

payload /páy lōd/ *n* **1.** QUANTITY OF CARGO the quantity of cargo or number of passengers that a plane, train, or other vehicle can carry, often expressed as weight or volume, or the revenue-producing portion of its cargo or passengers **2.** SPACECRAFT LOAD the passengers, equipment, or satellites carried by a spacecraft, or the weight of these **3.** EXPLOSIVE CHARGE the explosive charge of the warhead of a rocket or missile, or the total explosive charge of the bomb load carried by an aircraft

paymaster /páy maastər/ *n* the person who is responsible for paying wages or salaries in a business or government organization

Paymaster-General (*plural* **Paymasters-General**) *n* the government minister who heads the office that acts as paying agent for government departments

payment /páymənt/ *n* **1.** MONEY PAID an amount of money that is paid or is due to be paid **2.** ACT OF PAYING the act of paying money, or fact of being paid ○ *Payment will be made at the end of the month.* **3.** REWARD a reward or punishment given in return for something [14C. < Old French *paiement* < *payer* (see PAY[1])]

payment by results *n* a system of payment in which the salary paid depends on how well an employee does a job

payment gateway *n* a server or organization acting as an interface between the payment systems of retail seller, acquirer, and issuer with regard to Internet payments (*used in e-commerce*)

payment gateway certificate authority *n* a body issuing, renewing, or revoking certificates identifying an Internet payment gateway (*used in e-commerce*)

paymi /páymi/ *n Carib* FOOD same as **dukuna** [Late 20C. Via French Creole < French *pain de mie* 'bread made from crumb' (i.e. without a crust)]

paynim /páynim/ *n* (*archaic*) **1.** same as **pagan** *n* (sense 1) **2.** somebody who is not a Christian, especially a Muslim [13C. Via Old French *pai(e)nime* < ecclesiastical Latin *paganismus* 'paganism' < *paganus* 'pagan']

payoff /páy of/ *n* **1.** FULL PAYMENT full payment of a salary, wages, or a debt **2.** TIME FOR FULL PAYMENT the time when full and final payment of a debt, salary, or wage is due **3.** SETTLEMENT a final settlement, reward, or reckoning **4.** CLIMAX OF NARRATIVE the final climax of a narrative or sequence of events **5.** ADVANTAGE an ultimate benefit or advantage **6.** BRIBE a payment made to somebody as a bribe (*informal*) **7.** PSYCHOL HIDDEN BENEFIT OF NEGATIVE BEHAVIOUR an often unconscious or hidden benefit of a negative thought pattern or action

payola /pay ōlə/ (*plural* **-las** *informal*) *n N Am* a payment given in exchange for promoting a commercial product, or the system of making such payments, especially to disc jockeys [Mid-20C. < PAY[1]]

payout /páy owt/ *n* the act of paying out money or the sum of money paid

pay packet *n* **1.** an envelope containing an employee's wages **2.** wages received for a job or service ▶ N Am term **pay envelope**

pay-per-view *n* a cable or satellite television system in which individual programmes can be watched for a fee

payphone /páy fōn/ n a public telephone that operates only when coins or a card are used to pay for calls

payroll /páy rōl/ n **1.** a list of employees and their salaries or wages **2.** the total sum of money to be paid to employees at a given time

pay scale n a pay range for a particular type of work or for all types of work within a particular organization

payslip /páy slip/ n a printed statement of the amount an employee is paid, showing deductions for tax, pensions, and National Insurance. N Am term **paystub**

pay television n a system in which television programmes are transmitted in a scrambled form that can be decoded by viewers who have paid for the appropriate equipment

paytrain /páy trayn/ n a train on which passengers pay fares to the guard because there are no ticket offices open on the stations

pay TV n same as **pay television**

payware /páy wair/ n commercial software as opposed to freeware or shareware

Octavio Paz

Paz /pass, paz/, **Octavio** (1914–98) Mexican writer. Known for his poetry and essays, he was the first Mexican to be awarded the Nobel Prize in literature (1990).

‘Our democratic capitalist society has converted Eros into an employee of Mammon.’
[Octavio Paz, *Observer*; 19 June 1994]

Pb symbol CHEM ELEM lead² (sense 1)

PB abbr **1.** SPORTS personal best **2.** AUTOMOT power brakes **3.** CHR prayer book

PBX abbr TELECOM private branch exchange

pc¹ abbr **1.** per cent **2.** postcard

pc² abbr PHARM after meals (used in prescriptions) [Latin post cibum 'after food']

PC¹ abbr **1.** POL Parish Council **2.** POL Parish Councillor **3.** MIL Past Commander **4.** Police Constable **5.** politically correct **6.** MIL Post Commander **7.** Prince Consort **8.** ELECTRONICS printed circuit **9.** POL Privy Council **10.** POL Privy Councillor **11.** Can POL Progressive Conservative

PC² n **1.** COMPUT same as **personal computer 2.** a computer compatible with IBM™ personal computers and DOS [Abbreviation of PERSONAL COMPUTER]

p.c., **p/c** abbr **1.** BUSINESS petty cash **2.** FIN price current

PCB n a compound derived from biphenyl and containing chlorine that is a hazardous pollutant. Use: in electrical insulators, flame retardants, plasticizers. Full form **polychlorinated biphenyl**

PCI n a specification for extending the internal circuitry (**bus**) that transmits data from one part of a computer to another by inserting circuit boards. It allows the expansion of a computer by inserting printed circuit boards, or expansion boards, into sockets (**expansion slots**) inside the PCI bus. Full form **peripheral component interconnect**

pcm abbr **1.** per calendar month **2.** TELECOM pulse code modulation

PCMCIA n **1.** a specification for extending the internal circuitry (**bus**) that transmits data from one part of a computer to another, used to add memory or connect credit-card-sized peripheral devices. Full form **personal computer memory card interface adapter 2.** an international organization that has developed a standard for adding memory to personal computers and credit-card size devices. Full form **Personal Computer Memory Card International Association**

PCOS abbr MED polycystic ovarian syndrome

PCP abbr **1.** CHEM phencyclidine **2.** MED pneumocystis carinii pneumonia **3.** Can POL Progressive Conservative Party

PCR abbr BIOCHEM polymerase chain reaction

PCV abbr passenger carrying vehicle

pd abbr paid

Pd symbol CHEM ELEM palladium¹

PD¹ abbr **1.** POLICE police department **2.** MAIL postal district

PD² abbr public domain

p.d., **P.D.** abbr **1.** PHARM per diem **2.** PHYS potential difference

PDA abbr **1.** COMPUT personal digital assistant **2.** public display of affection (used in e-mails or text messages)

pdf¹ n a format for a computer document file that enables a document to be processed and printed on any computer using any printer or word-processing program. Full form **portable document format**

pdf² abbr a file extension for a file containing information in pdf format. Full form **portable document format**

PDN abbr ONLINE public data network (used in e-mails or text messages)

pdq adv at once or immediately (informal) Full form **pretty damn quick**

PDR abbr FIN price-dividend ratio

P-D ratio abbr FIN price-dividend ratio

PDSA abbr VET People's Dispensary for Sick Animals

PDT abbr TIME Pacific Daylight Time

pe¹ /pay/ n the 17th letter of the Hebrew alphabet, represented in the English alphabet as 'p' or 'f'. See table at **alphabet** [Early 19C. < Hebrew pē]

pe² abbr **1.** ONLINE Peru (used in Internet addresses) See table at **domain name 2.** PRINTING printer's error

PE abbr **1.** EDUC physical education **2.** PHYS potential energy **3.** CALENDAR Present Era **4.** Prince Edward Island **5.** STATS probable error **6.** CHR Protestant Episcopal

USAGE See *AD*¹.

p.e. abbr PRINTING printer's error

P/E abbr FIN price-earnings

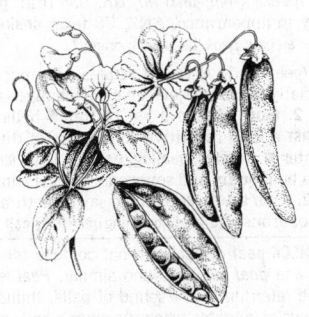

pea

pea /pee/ n **1.** SEED AS VEGETABLE a round green seed that grows in a pod, eaten as a vegetable **2.** PLANT PRODUCING PEAS an annual vine of the legume family with compound leaves that is widely grown for its edible seeds. Flowers: small, white. Native to: Europe, Asia. Latin name: *Pisum sativum.* **3.** PLANT RELATED TO PEA a plant related to or similar to the pea, e.g. the chickpea, sweet pea, or cowpea **4.** SOMETHING RESEMBLING PEA something resembling a pea in form or size [Mid-17C. Back-formation < pease (singular but taken as plural) < Old English pise, via Latin < Greek pison]

Peabody /pee bodi/, **George** (1795–1869) US businessman and philanthropist. He funded many educational institutions such as Baltimore's Peabody Institute and Yale's Peabody Museum, as well as new houses for workers in London.

~~**peacable**~~ incorrect spelling of **peaceable**

peace /peess/ n **1.** FREEDOM FROM WAR freedom from war, or the time when a war or conflict ends ○ the signing of the peace agreement **2.** TRANQUILLITY a calm and quiet state, free from disturbances or noise **3.** MENTAL CALM a state of mental calm and serenity, with no anxiety **4.** HARMONY freedom from conflict or disagreement among people or groups of people **5.** PEACE TREATY a treaty agreeing to an end of hostilities between two warring parties **6.** LAW AND ORDER the absence of violence or other disturbances within a state ○ Peace reigned throughout the land. ■ interj BE CALM OR SILENT used to tell somebody to be calm or silent or as a greeting or farewell [12C. Via Anglo-Norman pes < Latin pax] ◇ **at peace 1.** in a state of friendship and freedom from conflict **2.** dead (used euphemistically) **3.** in a state of calm and serenity ◇ **hold your peace** to refrain from speaking (dated) ◇ **keep the peace** to refrain from or prevent conflict or violence ◇ **make peace** to bring a disagreement or war to an end ◇ **make your peace with somebody** or **something** to resolve a disagreement with someone or become resigned to a situation that cannot be changed

---

SPELLCHECK **peace** or **piece**? Do not confuse the spelling of *peace* and *piece*, which sound similar. *Peace* is a lack of noise, disturbance, disagreement, or warfare, as in *peace and quiet*, a breach of the peace, make peace, not war. A *piece* is a part or item, as in *fall to pieces*, a *piece of music*.

---

peaceable /peéssəb'l/ adj **1.** inclined towards peace and avoiding contentious situations **2.** tranquil and free from strife and disorder —**peaceableness** n — **peaceably** adv

peace camp n a camp set up by antiwar demonstrators, usually in the vicinity of a military establishment

Peace Corps n a US government organization that trains volunteers to work in developing countries on educational and agricultural projects

peace dividend n savings on defence spending when a country is no longer at war or under threat of war

peaceful /peéssf'l/ adj **1.** QUIET AND CALM quiet, calm, and tranquil ○ a peaceful atmosphere **2.** MENTALLY CALM serene and untroubled in the mind **3.** APPROPRIATE FOR PEACETIME appropriate for a time of peace rather than war —**peacefully** adv —**peacefulness** n

peacekeeping /peéss keeping/ n the preservation of peace, especially as a military mission in which troops attempt to keep formerly warring armed forces from starting to fight again —**peacekeeper** n

peacemaker /peéss maykər/ n somebody who brings peace and reconciliation to others —**peacemaking** n

peace offering n something done for or given to an enemy or somebody you have quarrelled with in the hope of bringing about a reconciliation

peace officer n Aus, N Am somebody whose main duty is to preserve public order, e.g. a justice of the peace, police officer, or sheriff

peace pipe n a long-stemmed ceremonial pipe used by some Native North American peoples

peace sign n a sign used to indicate peaceful intentions, made by holding the palm upright and outwards and forming a V with the middle and index fingers

peacetime /peéss tīm/ n a time when there is no war

peach¹ /peech/ n **1.** LARGE FRUIT WITH STONE a sweet round juicy fruit with yellow flesh, a single stone, and a soft downy orange-yellow skin. See illustration on next page **2.** TREE WITH EDIBLE FRUIT a tree that bears peaches, widely grown in temperate regions. Flowers: pink. Native to: China. Latin name: *Prunus persica.* **3.** SOMEBODY OR SOMETHING EXCELLENT somebody or something that is particularly good or pleasing (informal) ○ That was a peach of a throw! **4.** ORANGE-YELLOW COLOUR a creamy yellowish-orange colour [13C. Via Old French pe(s)che < medieval Latin persica < Latin persicum < malum Persicum 'Persian apple'] —**peach** adj

peach

peach[2] /peech/ (**peaches, peaching, peached**) *vi* to inform against somebody, especially an accomplice (*dated informal*) [15C. Shortening of obsolete *appeach*, via Anglo-Norman < late Latin *impedicare* (see IMPEACH)]

peach melba *n* a dessert made with fresh or canned peaches, vanilla ice cream, and a raspberry sauce

peach palm *n* a dense spiny palm with an edible heart. Native to: Amazon basin. Latin name: *Bactris gasipaes*.

peachy /peechi/ (**-ier, -iest**) *adj* 1. resembling a peach in colour, taste, or texture 2. *US* very good or wonderful (*informal*) [Late 16C. < PEACH[1]] —**peachily** *adv* —**peachiness** *n*

peacoat /pee kot/ *n* CLOTHING same as **pea jacket**

peacock

peacock /pee kok/ *n* 1. MALE PEAFOWL a male peafowl with a crested head and a large fan-shaped tail with brilliantly coloured blue and green spots 2. PEAFOWL a peafowl, either male or female 3. VAIN PERSON a conspicuously vain person, especially as shown by his or her behaviour and dress [14C. < Old English *pēa* 'peacock' < Latin *pavo*] —**peacockish** *adj*

Peacock *n* the brightest star in the constellation Pavo

peacock blue *adj* of a brilliant greenish-blue colour, like a peacock's plumage —**peacock blue** *n*

peacock butterfly *n* a butterfly with bold iridescent colours and eyespots on its wings. Native to: Europe. Latin name: *Nymphalis io*.

peacock ore *n* a copper ore that becomes iridescent as it tarnishes, e.g. bornite

peafowl /pee fowl/ (*plural* **-fowls** or *same*) *n* a large pheasant, the male of which holds up its brilliant iridescent tail like a fan in courtship displays. Native to: South and Southeast Asia, Africa. Genera: *Pavo* or *Afropavo*. [Early 19C. After PEACOCK]

pea green *adj* of a medium yellowish-green colour —**pea green** *n*

peahen /pee hen/ *n* a female peafowl, with much plainer plumage than the peacock [14C. < Old English *pēa* (see PEACOCK)]

pea jacket *n* a heavy double-breasted jacket or short coat, made of mohair or thick wool and originally worn by sailors [Alteration of Dutch *pijjakker, pijjekker* 'coarse cloth jacket' < *pij* 'coarse cloth' + *jekker* 'jacket']

peak[1] /peek/ *n* 1. MOUNTAIN TOP the pointed summit of a mountain 2. MOUNTAIN a mountain with a pointed summit 3. POINTED PART a sharp projecting pointed part of something, e.g. the brim of a cap 4. HIGHEST POINT the point of greatest success, development, or

strength of a process or activity ○ *She's at the peak of her career.* 5. TOP OF CURVE the highest point in a curve, especially the curve of a wave 6. HAIR same as **widow's peak** 7. PHYS MAXIMUM VALUE OF QUANTITY a point at which a variable physical quantity such as temperature or voltage changes from rapidly increasing to rapidly decreasing, or the value of the quantity at such a point 8. NAUT EXTREME END OF HULL the narrow part at the front or back end of a boat's hull 9. SAILING CORNER OF FORE-AND-AFT SAIL the top rear corner of a fore-and-aft sail 10. SAILING GAFF END the outermost end of a gaff sail ■ *v* (**peaks, peaking, peaked**) 1. *vi* REACH HIGHEST POINT to reach the point of greatest success, development, intensity, or strength ○ *Sales peaked in July.* 2. *vi* FORM PEAK to form a peak or peaks ○ *The waves peaked as the storm grew.* 3. *vt* CAUSE PEAK IN SOMETHING to cause something to come to a high point ■ *adj* 1. HIGHEST being at a maximum or highest point ○ *peak efficiency* 2. OF GREATEST USE relating to the maximum use of something or the maximum demand on something ○ *peak viewing time* [Mid-16C. Back-formation < PEAKED[1], or variant of PIKE[3] or PIKE[4]]

SPELLCHECK **peak, peek,** or **pique**? Do not confuse the spelling of **peak, peek,** and **pique**, which sound similar. **Peak** is a noun, verb, or adjective referring to a high point, as in *a mountain peak, hoping that interest rates have peaked, peak viewing time*. **Peek** is a noun or verb referring to a quick look, as in *peek through the curtains, have a peek inside the box*. **Pique** is a noun or verb referring to a bad mood, as in *left in a fit of pique, piqued by their refusal*.

peak out *vi* to reach a peak or maximum level, often before beginning to decline

peak[2] /peek/ (**peaks, peaking, peaked**) *vi* to become thin, pale, and sickly in appearance (*archaic*) [Early 16C. Origin ?] —**peakish** *adj*

Peak District /pee k-/ region in central England forming the southern part of the Pennine Hills

Peak District National Park national park within the Peak District in central England, mainly in Derbyshire. It was founded in 1951. Area: 1,404 sq. km/542 sq. mi.

peaked[1] /peekt/ *adj* having a peak or point [15C. Variant of dialect *picked* 'pointed']

peaked[2] /peekt/ *adj* ANZ, US same as **peaky** [Mid-19C. < archaic *peak* 'be sickly', origin ?]

peak hour *n* ANZ the rush hour, when the greatest number of people are travelling to or from work

peak load *n* the maximum instantaneous rate of power consumption in a load circuit

peak season *n* N Am same as **high season**

peaky /peeki/ (**-ier, -iest**) *adj* UK, Can thin, pale, and sickly in appearance. ANZ, US term **peaked**[2] [Early 19C. < archaic *peak* 'be sickly', origin ?]

peal[1] /peel/ *n* 1. RINGING OF BELLS a ringing of bells, especially a change or series of changes rung on bells 2. GROUP OF BELLS a set of tuned bells 3. NOISY OUTBURST a loud repetitive sound, e.g. of thunder or laughter ■ *v* (**peals, pealing, pealed**) 1. *vti* RING BELL to ring a bell loudly and sonorously, or be rung in this way 2. *vt* SAY SOMETHING LOUDLY to say something loudly and sonorously [14C. Shortening of APPEAL 'call, request']

SPELLCHECK **peal** or **peel**? Do not confuse the spelling of **peal** and **peel**, which sound similar. **Peal** is a noun and verb referring to the sound of bells, thunder, etc., as in *peals of laughter, when the church bells peal*. **Peel** is a noun denoting an outer layer or skin, as in *orange peel*, or a verb referring to the removal of such a layer, as in *paint peeling from the walls*.

peal[2] /peel/ (*plural* **peals** or *same*) *n regional* FISH same as **grilse** [Mid-16C. Origin ?]

pean /peen/ *n* sable fur spotted with a gold or yellow colour [Mid-16C. Origin ?]

peanut /pee nut/ *n* 1. OILY EDIBLE SEED an oily edible seed with a thin shell that grows underground and is a source of vegetable oil 2. PLANT PRODUCING PEANUTS a low-growing annual plant of the legume family whose seeds are peanuts. Latin name: *Arachis hypogaea*. ■ **peanuts** *npl* SMALL AMOUNT OF MONEY a very small amount of money, especially when smaller than would be expected (*informal*) ○ *They're paid*

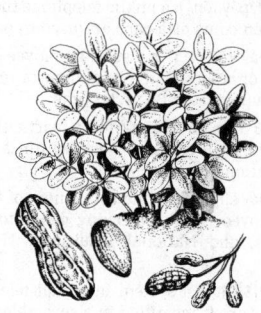

peanut

peanuts! [Early 19C. Because peanuts grow in a pod, as peas do]

peanut brittle *n* a hard sweet made of toffee and peanuts

peanut butter *n* an oily paste made from ground roasted peanuts and usually spread on bread or used in cooking

peanut oil *n* a combustible yellow oil extracted from peanuts. Use: cooking, medicine, soaps.

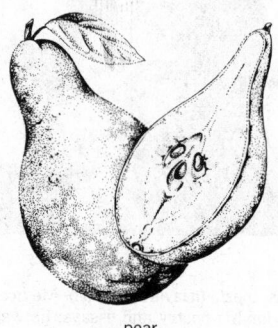

pear

pear /pair/ *n* 1. a sweet juicy fruit with a usually green skin, firm white flesh, and roughly teardrop shape, eaten fresh or canned 2. a tree with fine-toothed glossy leaves, widely grown to produce pears. Native to: Europe. Latin name: *Pyrus communis*. [Pre-12C. Via assumed Vulgar Latin *pira* < Latin *pirum*]

SPELLCHECK See **pair**.

pearl[1] /purl/ *n* 1. GEM FORMED IN MOLLUSC a small lustrous sphere of calcium carbonate that forms round a grain of sand in a sea organism such as an oyster. Use: gems. 2. HANDICRAFT same as **mother-of-pearl** 3. SOMEBODY OR SOMETHING MUCH VALUED somebody or something highly esteemed or valued 4. PALE GREYISH-WHITE COLOUR a pale greyish-white colour tinged with blue ■ *v* (**pearls, pearling, pearled**) 1. *vi* HARVEST PEARLS to fish or dive for pearls 2. *vti* MAKE BEADS to form drops shaped like pearls or take on a pearlized colour, or cause something to do this 3. *vt* DECORATE SOMETHING WITH PEARLS to decorate something with pearls or with things that resemble pearls [14C. < Old French *perle*, probably < assumed Vulgar Latin *pernula* 'little mollusc' < Latin *perna* 'ham'; because of the mollusc's shape] —**pearl-like** *adj*

pearl[2] /purl/ *n* HANDICRAFT another spelling of **purl**[1] *n* (senses 2–3)

pearl ash *n* the commercial form of potassium carbonate

pearl barley *n* grains of barley that have been polished and are used in soups and stews

pearler /purlər/ *n* 1. PEARL DIVER OR TRADER a diver for or dealer in natural pearls 2. BOAT USED FOR PEARL-DIVING a boat used for pearl-diving or for trading pearls 3. *also* **purler** *Aus* SOMETHING WONDERFUL something outstanding or exceptional (*dated informal*)

pearlescent /pur léss'nt/ *adj* with a lustrous surface like a pearl

pearl grey *adj* of a pale blue-grey colour —**pearl grey** *n*

Pearl Harbor /purl-/ inlet in Hawaii, on Oahu Island. The Japanese attack on the US naval base there in 1941 prompted the United States' entry into World War II.

pearlised *adj* another spelling of **pearlized**

pearlite /púrl īt/ *n* a microstructure of steel or cast iron made up of bands (**lamellae**) of pure iron (**ferrite**) and iron carbide (**cementite**) [Late 19C. < PEARL¹ + -ITE¹] —**pearlitic** /pur líttik/ *adj*

pearlized /púrl īzd/, **pearlised** *adj* having a pearly iridescent lustre

pearl millet *n* a tall cereal grass widely grown for its whitish seeds. Latin name: *Pennisetum americanum.*

pearl onion *n* a very small white onion that is often used for pickling

pearl oyster *n* a tropical sea mollusc that is a source of pearls. Genus: *Pinctada.*

pearly /púrli/ *adj* (**-ier, -iest**) 1. RESEMBLING PEARL resembling pearls or mother-of-pearl, particularly in having an iridescent lustre 2. DECORATED WITH PEARLS decorated with pearls or mother-of-pearl 3. PALE GREYISH-WHITE of a pale greyish-white colour tinged with blue ■ *n* (*plural* **-ies**) COCKNEY WEARING PEARL-DECORATED COSTUME a member of a Cockney family who, on ceremonial occasions, traditionally wears a special costume covered with pearl buttons arranged in ornamental patterns —**pearliness** *n*

pearly everlasting *n* a plant with woolly leaves and white flower heads. Native to: North America. Latin name: *Anaphalis margaritacea.*

Pearly Gates *npl* in Christianity, the gates of heaven (*informal*)

pearly king *n* a man from one of the Cockney families traditionally entitled to wear a pearl-covered costume, who is chosen as the one with the finest costume

pearly nautilus *n* a mollusc that has a spiral pearl-coloured multichambered shell. Genus: *Nautilus.*

pearly queen *n* a woman from one of the Cockney families traditionally entitled to wear a pearl-covered costume, who is chosen as the one with the finest costume

pearmain /páir mayn/ (*plural* **-mains** or *same*) *n* a variety of red-skinned apple [13C. < Old French *parmaine* < Latin *Parmensis* 'from Parma']

Pears /peerz/, **Sir Peter** (1910–86) British tenor. He is noted for his interpretation of music by Benjamin Britten, much of which Britten wrote for him. Full name **Pears, Sir Peter Neville Luard**

Pearse /peerss/, **Patrick** (1879–1916) Irish nationalist leader. He led the Irish Republican Brotherhood in the Easter Rising (1916), after which he was executed. Full name **Pearse, Patrick Henry**

Pearse, Richard (1877–1953) New Zealand inventor. He is said to have achieved a brief powered flight on 31 March 1902, 20 months before the flight of Wilbur and Orville Wright. Full name **Pearse, Richard William**

pear-shaped *adj* having a shape similar to that of a pear with a rounded bottom part and narrower top part ◇ **go pear-shaped** to get out of control or go wrong (*informal*)

Pearson /peerss'n/, **Lester** (1897–1972) prime minister of Canada (1963–68). He had a distinguished diplomatic career playing key roles at the UN and in the creation of Israel (1948) and NATO (1949). He received the Nobel Peace Prize (1957). Full name **Pearson, Lester Bowles**

> 'We prepare for war like ferocious giants, and for peace like retarded pygmies.'
> [Lester Pearson, *Nobel Prize acceptance speech*; 11 December 1957]

peart /peert/ *adj* lively and brisk [15C. Variant of PERT]

Peary /peeri/, **Robert** (1856–1920) US explorer. He is generally credited with leading the first expedition to reach the North Pole (1909). Full name **Peary, Robert Edwin**

peasant /pézz'nt/ *n* 1. AGRICULTURAL LABOURER an agricultural labourer or small farmer 2. RURAL PERSON somebody who lives in the country 3. OFFENSIVE TERM

an offensive term for somebody considered to be ill-mannered or uneducated [15C. < Anglo-Norman *paisant*, Old French *paisant* < Latin *pagus* 'rural district']

peasant blouse *n* ANZ, N Am a women's top with an elasticated low neckline, usually worn off the shoulders, and long or short sleeves. UK term **gypsy top**

peasantry /pézz'ntri/ *n* 1. peasants as a class in society 2. the status or characteristic behaviour of a peasant

peasant top *n* CLOTHING same as **gypsy top**

pease-brose /peéz brōz/ *n* Scotland a thick porridge made from dried peas [< pease (see PEA) + BROSE]

pease pudding /peéz-/ *n* a thick purée made from dried peas, usually served with ham, pork, or bacon [< pease (see PEA)]

peashooter /peé shootər/ *n* a toy in the form of a pipe through which dried peas or similar small pellets can be blown

pea soup *n* 1. soup made with fresh or dried peas 2. N Am same as **peasouper** (sense 1) (*informal*)

peasouper /pee soópər/ *n* 1. an extremely thick fog (*informal*) N Am term **pea soup** 2. Can an offensive term for a French Canadian (*slang*)

peat /peet/ *n* 1. a compacted deposit of partially decomposed organic debris, usually saturated with water 2. a cut and dried piece of peat used as fuel [14C. < Anglo-Latin *peta*, probably < Celtic, 'bit'] —**peaty** *adj*

peat bog *n* an area of land composed primarily of peat

peat moss *n* a moss that grows in wet places, and whose partially decomposed remains form peat. Genus: *Sphagnum.*

peau de soie /pṓ də swaá/ *n* a silk or artificial fabric with a smooth texture and a fine grainy or ribbed surface [< French, 'skin of silk']

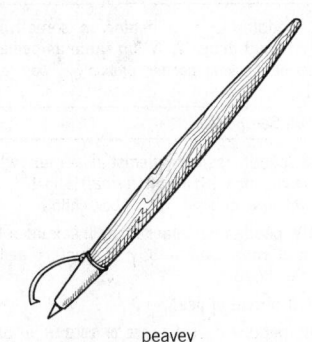

peavey

peavey /peévi/ (*plural* **-veys**), **peavy** (*plural* **-vies**) *n* a pointed lever with a hinged hook, used for handling logs [Late 19C. After Joseph *Peavey*, US inventor]

pebble /pébb'l/ *n* 1. SMALL ROUND STONE a small rounded stone that has been worn smooth by erosion 2. GEOL ROCK FRAGMENT a rock fragment with a diameter between 4 mm/0.16 in and 64 mm/2.51 in 3. GEOL QUARTZ USED FOR LENSES a colourless form of quartz (**rock crystal**) used for making lenses 4. OPTICS CRYSTAL LENS a lens made from colourless rock crystal 5. TEXTILES IRREGULAR SURFACE a rough grainy surface, especially on leather ■ *adj* THICK AND DISTORTING being or containing lenses that make the eyes of the wearer seem very large and distorted (*informal*) ○ *wearing thick pebble glasses* ■ *vt* (**-bles, -bling, -bled**) 1. COVER SOMETHING WITH PEBBLES to cover or pave something with pebbles 2. GIVE IRREGULAR SURFACE TO SOMETHING to give a rough grainy surface to something [Old English *papolstān*, origin ?] —**pebbly** *adj*

pebbledash /pébb'l dash/ *n* a finish for exterior walls, consisting of small stones set in plaster

pec /pek/ *n* same as **pectoral muscle** (*informal*; often used in the plural) ○ *exercises to strengthen the pecs* [Mid-20C. Shortening]

pecan /peékən, pi kán/ *n* 1. an edible nut resembling a long walnut with a thin dark red shell 2. a large hickory tree that has deeply furrowed bark and produces pecans. Native to: southern United States,

Mexico. Latin name: *Carya illinoensis.* [Late 18C. Via French *pacane* < Illinois *pakani*]

peccadillo /pékə díllō/ (*plural* **-loes** or **-los**) *n* a trifling offence [Late 16C. < Spanish, 'little fault' < *peccado* 'sin' < Latin *peccare* 'to sin']

peccant /pékənt/ *adj* (*formal*) 1. guilty of a sin 2. violating a rule or practice [Late 16C. < Latin *peccant-*, present participle of *peccare* 'to sin'] —**peccancy** *n* —**peccantly** *adv*

peccary /pékəri/ (*plural* **-ries**) *n* a wild pig with a rudimentary tail and small tusks on the upper jaw that grow downwards. Native to: Mexico, South America. Genus: *Tayassu.* [Early 17C. < Carib *pakira*]

peccavi /pe kaá vee/ (*plural* **-vis**) *n* an admission of sin or guilt (*literary*) [Early 16C. < Latin, 'I have sinned']

pech /pekh/ *Scotland n* a short, fast, and forceful breath ■ *vi* (**pechs, peching, peched**) to pant or struggle for breath from exertion [15C. An imitation of the sound]

Pechora /pi cháwrə/ river in northwestern European Russia, flowing northwards to the Barents Sea. Length: 1,809 km/1,124 mi.

peck¹ /pek/ *v* (**pecks, pecking, pecked**) 1. *vt* PICK SOMETHING UP WITH BEAK to take small bits of food using a beak 2. *vti* STRIKE SOMETHING WITH BEAK to strike somebody or something with a beak 3. *vt* MAKE HOLE IN SOMETHING to make a hole in something by repeatedly striking it with a beak 4. *vi* NIBBLE to eat small quantities of food with little interest ○ *She just pecked at her food.* 5. *vt* KISS SOMEBODY LIGHTLY to kiss somebody lightly and briefly 6. *vi* Aus, N Am NAG to nag or carp (*informal*) ■ *n* 1. SWIFT BITE WITH BEAK a quick light stroke, blow, or bite with a beak 2. HOLE MADE BY BEAK a mark or hole made by a beak or pointed object 3. LIGHT KISS a quick light kiss (*informal*) [14C. Probably variant of PICK¹]

peck² /pek/ *n* 1. UNIT OF DRY MEASURE a unit of dry measure equal to 9.09 litres/8 quarts 2. CONTAINER FOR PECK a container that holds a peck of material 3. LARGE QUANTITY a large amount or number of something (*informal*) [13C. Origin ?]

Peck /pek/, **Gregory** (1916–2003) US film actor. He was an appealing presence in a wide variety of films, including *Roman Holiday* (1953) and *To Kill a Mockingbird* (1962) for which he won an Academy Award for best actor. Born **Peck, Eldred Gregory**

pecker /pékər/ *n* 1. something that pecks, especially a woodpecker 2. N Am same as **penis** (*slang*; *sometimes considered offensive*) ◇ **keep your pecker up** used to tell somebody to keep his or her spirits up (*informal*)

pecking order *n* 1. a social hierarchy in which some members of a group are established as superior to others 2. a social hierarchy among domestic fowl in which each member maintains its place by dominance over the lower members

peckish /pékish/ *adj* UK, Can slightly hungry (*informal*)

Pecksniffian /pek sníffi ən/ *adj* hypocritical and making a show of having high moral principles [Mid-19C. After Mr *Pecksniff*, character in *Martin Chuzzlewit* (1844) by Charles Dickens]

pecorino /pékə reénō/ (*plural* **-nos**) *n* a hard pungent Italian cheese made from ewe's milk [Mid-20C. < Italian *pecora* 'sheep']

Pécs /paych/ capital of Baranya County, southwestern Hungary, situated about 170 km/105 mi. southwest of Budapest. Population: 159,607 (1999).

pectate /pék tayt/ *n* a salt or ester of pectic acid [Mid-19C. < PECTIC ACID]

pectic acid /péktik-/ *n* an insoluble component of pectin [< Greek *pēktikos* < *pēktos* 'curdled' < *pēgnunai* 'make solid']

pectin /péktin/ *n* a mixture of polysaccharides found in plant cell walls. Use: gelling agent. [Mid-19C. < French *pectine* < Greek *pektos* (see PECTIC ACID)] —**pectic** *adj* —**pectinous** *adj*

pectinesterase /pékti néstə rayz, -rayss/ *n* an enzyme that catalyses the breakdown of pectin

pectize /pék tīz/ (**-tizes, -tizing, -tized**), **pectise** (**-tises, -tising, -tised**) *vt* to change something into a gel —**pectizable** *adj* —**pectization** /pék tī záysh'n/ *n*

pectoral /péktərəl/ *adj* **1.** OF CHEST relating to or located in or on the chest **2.** WORN ON CHEST worn on the chest ○ *a pectoral medal* ■ *n* **1.** CHEST MUSCLE a chest muscle or organ ○ *an exercise for the pectorals* **2.** FISH same as **pectoral fin 3.** BREASTPLATE something that is worn on the chest as a decoration or ornament **4.** CHEST MEDICINE a medicine for chest or respiratory disorders (*dated*) [15C. Via French, 'something worn on the chest' < Latin *pectorale* 'breastplate' < *pectus* 'chest'] —**pectorally** *adv*

pectoral fin *n* either of a pair of fins of a fish located either directly behind the gill openings or below them

pectoral girdle *n* the part of the skeleton of a vertebrate animal that provides attachment points and support for the forelimbs

pectoral muscle *n* any of four flat muscles, two on each side of the front of the chest, that help to move the upper arm and shoulder

peculate /pékyoō layt/ (**-lates, -lating, -lated**) *vt* to appropriate money or property by embezzlement or theft (*formal*) [Mid-18C. < Latin *peculat-*, past participle of *peculari* < *peculium* (see PECULIAR)] —**peculation** /pékyoō láysh'n/ *n* —**peculator** *n*

peculiar /pi kyoóli ər/ *adj* **1.** UNUSUAL unusual, strange, or unconventional ○ *The situation was very peculiar.* **2.** UNIQUE belonging exclusively to or identified distinctly with somebody or something ○ *a form of wildlife peculiar to that region* ■ *n* CHURCH EXEMPT FROM DIOCESAN JURISDICTION a church or parish that is exempt from the jurisdiction of the diocese in which it is situated [15C. < Latin *peculiaris* 'of private property' < *peculium* 'private property' < *pecus* 'cattle'] —**peculiarly** *adv*

peculiarity /pi kyoōli árrəti/ (*plural* **-ties**) *n* **1.** the quality or state of being unusual or strange **2.** a characteristic that belongs distinctively to a particular person, place, or thing

~~peculier~~ incorrect spelling of **peculiar**

peculium /pi kyoóli əm/ *n* in Roman law, property that a father allowed his child, or a master his slave, to own independently [Late 17C. < Latin (see PECULIAR)]

pecuniary /pi kyoóni əri/ *adj* **1.** relating to or involving money **2.** involving a financial penalty such as a fine ○ *a pecuniary offence* [Early 16C. < Latin *pecuniarius* < *pecunia* 'money, wealth in cattle' < *pecus* 'cattle'] —**pecuniarily** *adv*

pecuniary advantage *n* in law, a financial benefit gained by fraud or deception

ped- *prefix* another spelling of **paed-**

-ped *suffix* foot ○ *biped* [< Latin *ped-, pes*]

pedagogue /péddə gog/ *n* **1.** a schoolteacher or educator (*formal*) **2.** a teacher who teaches in a particularly pedantic or dogmatic manner [14C. Via Latin < Greek *paidagōgos* 'slave who leads a child to school' < *paid-* 'child']

pedagogy /péddə goji/ *n* the science or profession of teaching [Mid-16C. Via French < Greek *paidagōgia* 'duties of a slave who leads a child to school' < *paidagōgos* (see PEDAGOGUE)] —**pedagogic** /péddə gójjik/ *adj* —**pedagogical** *adj* —**pedagogically** *adv*

pedal[1] /pédd'l/ *n* **1.** FOOT-OPERATED LEVER FOR MACHINE a lever operated by the foot that powers a mechanism such as a bicycle, sewing machine, or the foot controls of a car **2.** FOOT-OPERATED LEVER FOR MUSICAL INSTRUMENT a foot-operated lever used in playing the piano, organ, and other musical instruments **3.** MUSIC same as **pedal point** ■ *vti* (**-als, -alling, -alled**) **1.** MAKE BICYCLE MOVE to push down on the pedals to make a bicycle or other vehicle move forward **2.** OPERATE OR PLAY INSTRUMENT USING PEDALS to operate the pedals of a piano or organ while playing it, or those of a machine in order to make it work [Early 17C. Via French < Italian *pedale (d'organo)* '(organ) pedal' < Latin *pedalis* 'of the foot' < *ped-* 'foot'] —**pedaller** *n*

SPELLCHECK **pedal** or **peddle**? Do not confuse the spelling of **pedal** and **peddle**, which sound similar. The word **pedal** is chiefly used as a noun, denoting a part pressed by the foot, for example on a bicycle or a piano; it can also be used as a verb, meaning 'operate the pedals of', as in *pedal a bicycle*. The word **peddle** is only used as a

verb, meaning 'sell' or 'promote', as in *peddling books, peddling ideas.*

pedal[2] /peéd'l, pédd'l/ *adj* relating to the foot or feet [Early 17C. < Latin *pedalis* (see PEDAL[1])]

pedalfer /pi dálfər/ *n* soil without a layer of accumulated calcium carbonate, but in which iron and aluminium have tended to accumulate [Early 20C. Blend of PEDO-[1] + ALUMINIUM + Latin *ferrum* 'iron']

pedalo /péddəlō/ (*plural* **-los** or **-loes**) *n* a small pleasure boat that is powered by paddles and operated by pedals [Mid-20C. < PEDAL[1]]

pedal point *n* a note, usually in the bass, that is sustained while other musical parts and harmonies continue

pedal pushers *npl* calf-length trousers for women, originally designed for cycling

pedal steel, **pedal steel guitar** *n* an electrically amplified floor-mounted guitar that is fretted with a steel bar and usually has ten strings, whose pitch can be varied by the use of pedals

pedant /pédd'nt/ *n* **1.** somebody who unduly emphasizes unimportant details and rules **2.** somebody who displays his or her knowledge ostentatiously [Late 16C. Via French < Italian *pedante*]

pedantic /pi dántik/ *adj* too concerned with what are thought to be correct rules and details, e.g. in language —**pedantically** *adv*

pedantry /pédd'ntri/ (*plural* **-ries**) *n* a pedantic attitude or an example of pedantic behaviour

~~pedastool~~ incorrect spelling of **pedestal**

peddle /pédd'l/ (**-dles, -dling, -dled**) *v* **1.** *vti* SELL GOODS to sell goods, especially while travelling from place to place **2.** *vt* SELL ILLEGAL THINGS to sell something illegal, especially drugs (*dated*) **3.** *vt* PROMOTE IDEA to promote an idea or belief insistently [Mid-16C. Back-formation < PEDDLER]

SPELLCHECK See *pedal*[1].

peddler /péddlər/ *n* **1.** a dealer in something, especially illegal drugs **2.** *N Am* same as **pedlar** [14C. Alteration of dialectal *pedder*, probably < *ped* 'pannier', origin ?]

SPELLCHECK See *pedlar*.

pederast /péddə rast/, **paederast** *n* a man who has sexual relations with a boy (*formal*) [Mid-17C. < Greek *paiderastēs* 'lover of boys' < *paid-* 'boy, child']

pederasty /péddə rasti/, **paederasty** *n* sexual relations between a man and a boy (*formal*) —**pederastic** /péddə rástik/ *adj*

pedes ANAT plural of **pes**

pedestal /péddist'l/ *n* **1.** BASE OF COLUMN a base or support for a column or statue **2.** SUPPORTING BASE OF FURNITURE the column-shaped base of a piece of furniture such as a table or washbasin **3.** POSITION OF BEING EXALTED the position of being admired by somebody to the point of reverence or deification ○ *I don't want to be put on a pedestal – I just want to be treated as a normal person.* ■ *vt* (**-tals, -talling, -talled**) PUT SOMETHING ON PEDESTAL to provide somebody or something with a pedestal [Mid-16C. Via French *piédestal* < Italian *piedestallo*, literally 'foot of a stall'; altered after Latin *ped-* 'foot']

pedestrian /pə déstri ən/ *n* somebody who is travelling on foot, especially in an area also used by cars ■ *adj* ordinary, unimaginative, or uninspired [Early 18C. < French *pédestre* or its source Latin *pedester* 'going on foot' < *ped-* 'foot'] —**pedestrianism** *n* —**pedestrianly** *adv*

pedestrian crossing *n* a place marked on a road as a place for people to cross. N Am term **crosswalk**

pedestrianize /pə déstri ə nīz/ (**-izes, -izing, -ized**), **pedestrianise** (**-ises, -ising, -ised**) *vt* to change a street into an area for pedestrians only, by banning motor vehicles —**pedestrianization** /pə déstri ə nī záysh'n/ *n*

Pedi /péddi/ (*plural* **-dis** or *same*) *n* **1.** a member of a people who live in South Africa, mainly in the northern part of the country **2.** the Bantu language of the Pedi people. Native speakers: 3 million. [Mid-20C. < Sotho *Mopedi*] —**Pedi** *adj*

pedi- *prefix* foot, feet ○ *pedipalp* [< Latin *ped-* 'foot']

pediatrics *n* MED another spelling of **paediatrics**

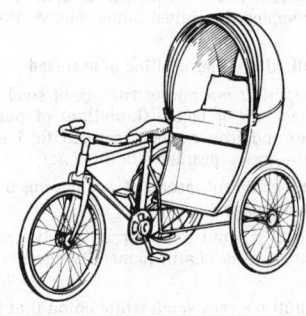

pedicab

pedicab /péddi kab/ *n* a pedal-operated tricycle with a seat in front for the driver and a passenger seat behind covered by a hood, available for hire in some Southeast Asian countries

pedicel /péddi sel, -s'l/, **pedicle** /péddik'l/ *n* **1.** BOT STALK OF INDIVIDUAL FLOWER a stalk bearing a single flower or spore-producing body within a cluster **2.** ANAT STALK-SHAPED BODY PART an anatomical part that resembles a stem or stalk **3.** ZOOL NARROW SEGMENT OF BODY a narrow anatomical part, e.g. the waist between the thorax and abdomen of wasps and related insects [Late 17C. < modern Latin *pedicellus* < Latin *pediculus* 'little foot' < *ped-* 'foot'] —**pedicellar** /péddi séllər/ *adj* —**pedicellate** /-séllit, -layt/ *adj*

pediculicide /péddi kyoóli sīd/ *n* a chemical substance that kills lice, used to treat infestations of humans and animals [Early 20C. < Latin *pediculus* 'louse']

pediculosis /pi díkyoō lóssiss/ *n* infestation with lice, specifically the head and body louse *Pediculus humanus*. It can cause insomnia, irritability, and depression. [Early 19C. < Latin *pediculus* 'louse'] —**pediculous** /pi díkyoōləss/ *adj*

pedicure /péddi kyoor/ *n* **1.** SESSION OF TREATMENT FOR FEET a session of cosmetic or medical treatment of the feet **2.** COSMETIC TREATMENT OF FEET cosmetic treatment of the feet, e.g. the application of nail varnish **3.** MEDICAL CARE OF FEET medical treatment of the feet, e.g. the removal of corns ■ *vt* (**-cures, -curing, -cured**) TREAT FEET OF SOMEBODY to give somebody a pedicure [Mid-19C. < French *pédicure* < Latin *ped-* 'foot' + *cura* 'care'] —**pedicurist** *n*

pedigree /péddi gree/ *n* **1.** LINE OF ANCESTORS the line of ancestors of an individual animal or person, especially a pure-bred animal **2.** LIST OF ANIMAL'S ANCESTORS a document recording the line of ancestors of an animal, especially a pure-bred animal **3.** FAMILY TREE a table showing the line of ancestors of a person, especially an aristocratic or upper class person **4.** BACKGROUND the background, history, or origin of something, especially a group ■ *adj* PURE-BRED descended from a line of animals whose purity of breed has been recorded over several generations [15C. < Anglo-Norman *pe de gru* 'crane's foot' (likened to the branches of a family tree)] —**pedigreed** *adj*

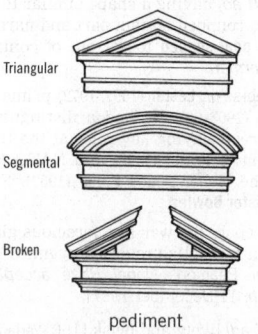

Triangular

Segmental

Broken

pediment

pediment /péddimənt/ *n* **1.** in classical architecture, a broad triangular or segmental gable surmounting a colonnade as the major part of a facade **2.** a broad flat rock surface of low relief adjacent to a steeper slope in a dry region, e.g. that of a mountain range, often covered with rock debris [Late 16C. Origin ?] —**pedimental** /péddi mént'l/ *adj*

pedipalp /péddi palp/ *n* either of a pair of appendages that are part of the mouths of spiders and other arachnids, used for various functions including manipulating food [Early 19C. < modern Latin *pedipalpi* < Latin *ped-* 'foot' + *palpus* 'palp']

pedlar /péddlər/ *n* somebody who travels from place to place or from door to door selling goods. N Am term **peddler** [Variant of PEDDLER]

SPELLCHECK *pedlar* or *peddler*? Do not confuse the spelling of *pedlar* and *peddler*, which sound similar. In UK English, the word denoting an itinerant seller of miscellaneous goods is spelt *pedlar*, and the spelling *peddler* is largely reserved for those who peddle drugs, ideas, etc.

pedo-[1] *prefix* soil ○ *pedology* [< Greek *pedon* 'ground']

pedo-[2] another spelling of **paedo-**

pedogenesis /peedə jénnississ/ *n* the natural process of soil formation, including erosion and leaching — **pedogenetic** /peedəjə néttik/ *adj* — **pedogenic** *adj*

pedology /pi dólləji/ *n* the scientific study of soil properties and the classification of soil types — **pedologic** /peedə lójjik/ *adj* — **pedological** *adj* — **pedologically** *adv* — **pedologist** *n*

pedometer /pi dómmitər/ *n* an instrument that measures the distance covered by a walker by recording the number of steps taken [Early 18C. < French *pedomètre* < Latin *ped-* 'foot' + French *-mètre* '-meter']

Pedro I /péddrō/ (1798–1834) emperor of Brazil. The son of the king of Portugal, he declared Brazil's independence in 1822, made himself emperor, and abdicated in 1831. He was also briefly king of Portugal (1826).

Pedro II (1825–91) emperor of Brazil. He was emperor from his father's abdication (1831) until his own abdication (1889). He abolished slavery in Brazil.

peduncle /pi dúngk'l/ *n* **1.** the stalk of a plant **2.** a part resembling a stalk in shape or function, e.g. the base of a fish's tail or a structure attaching an invertebrate animal to the place where it lives [Mid-18C. < modern Latin *pedunculus* 'small foot' < Latin *ped-* 'foot'] — **peduncled** *adj* — **peduncular** /pi dúngkyōōlər/ *adj* — **pedunculate** /pi dúngkyōōlət, -layt/ *adj*

pedway /péd way/ *n* N Am a walkway for pedestrians only

pee /pee/ (*informal; sometimes considered offensive*) *vi* (**pees, peeing, peed**) to pass urine ■ *n* **1.** same as **urine 2.** an act of urinating [Late 18C. < the first letter of PISS]

Peebles /peeb'lz/ town in southern Scotland, on the River Tweed. Population: 7,065 (1991).

peek /peek/ *vi* (**peeks, peeking, peeked**) to take a quick look at something, especially secretively or surreptitiously ○ *I peeked at the name at the foot of the letter.* ■ *n* a quick or secret look at something [14C. Origin ?]

SPELLCHECK See *peak*[1]

peekaboo /peekə boo, peekə boo/ *n* CHILDREN'S GAME a game played to amuse small children, in which the face is hidden in the hands and then suddenly uncovered as 'peekaboo!' is shouted ■ *interj* WORD SAID IN GAME the word used when playing a game of peekaboo ■ *adj* CLOTHING HAVING HOLES having holes or gaps intended to reveal parts of the body [Late 16C. < PEEK + BOO]

peel[1] /peel/ *v* (**peels, peeling, peeled**) **1.** *vt* REMOVE OUTER LAYER to cut away or pull off the skin or outer layer of something, especially a fruit or vegetable **2.** *vi* HAVE REMOVABLE SKIN to have a skin that can be removed **3.** *vt* PULL SOMETHING OFF to pull or strip off something, especially something that is stuck to a surface **4.** *vi* LOSE OUTER LAYER to lose or shed an outer layer or covering, e.g. of paint or sunburnt skin ○ *The skin on her nose was peeling.* **5.** *vi* COME OFF IN THIN PIECES to come off in flakes, small pieces, or thin strips **6.** *vt* PUT BALL THROUGH CROQUET HOOP in croquet, to make another player's ball go through a hoop ■ *n* **1.** FRUIT OR VEGETABLE SKIN the rind or skin of a fruit or vegetable ○ *apple peel* **2.** COSMETIC TREATMENT a beauty treatment that involves removing the top layer of skin, usually by means of abrasion or chemicals [13C. < Latin *pilare* 'deprive of hair' < *pilus* 'hair'] — **peelable** *adj*

SPELLCHECK See *peal*[1].

peel[2] /peel/ *n* a shovel with a long handle, used by bakers to move bread in and out of an oven [14C. Via Old French *pele* < Latin *pala* 'spade']

peel[3] /peel/ *n* a fortified tower of the type built in the border counties of Scotland and England in the 16th century to withstand raids [13C. Via Anglo-Norman *pel* < Latin *palus* 'stake']

Peel /peel/, **Sir Robert** (1788–1850) prime minister of Great Britain (1834–35 and 1841–46). As home secretary (1822–27 and 1828–30), he organized the London police force, later known as 'bobbies' or 'peelers'. He founded the modern Conservative Party and led it to victory in the 1841 elections.

peeler[1] /peelər/ *n* **1.** a device for removing the skin from fruit or vegetables, usually a hand-held utensil with a blade **2.** *US* a striptease dancer (*slang*) [14C. < PEEL[1]]

peeler[2] /peelər/ *n* a policeman [Early 19C. After Sir Robert PEEL]

peelie-wallie *adj* Scotland another spelling of **peely-wally** (*informal*)

peeling /peeling/ *n* a piece of something, especially fruit or vegetable skin, that has been peeled off (*often used in the plural*) ○ *potato peelings*

peely-wally /peeli wólli/, **peelie-wallie** *adj* Scotland pale, sickly, or feeling ill (*informal*) [Mid-19C. Origin ?]

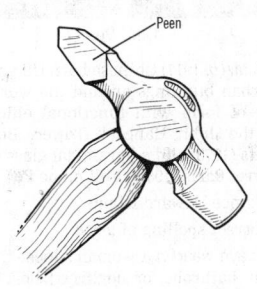

peen

peen /peen/ *n* the end of a hammer head opposite the flat face, often rounded or wedge-shaped, and used for bending and shaping ■ *vt* (**peens, peening, peened**) to bend or shape something by striking it with the peen of a hammer [Late 17C. Origin ?]

peep[1] /peep/ *v* (**peeps, peeping, peeped**) **1.** *vi* LOOK QUICKLY OR SECRETLY to look quickly or secretly, e.g. through a small opening or from a hiding place **2.** *vti* EMERGE, OR MAKE SOMETHING EMERGE to become partly visible or visible only for a short time, or make something become so ■ *n* **1.** QUICK LOOK a quick or secret look at something **2.** THE FIRST SIGHT OF SOMETHING the first appearance or sight of something [15C. Origin ?]

peep[2] /peep/ *vi* (**peeps, peeping, peeped**) **1.** MAKE SHORT, HIGH-PITCHED NOISE to make a short high-pitched noise like that made by a baby bird or a mouse **2.** SPEAK IN HIGH OR QUIET VOICE to speak in a quiet, weak, or high-pitched voice **3.** MAKE QUIET NOISE to make the quietest possible noise or remark ■ *n* **1.** SHORT HIGH-PITCHED SOUND a high-pitched sound like that of a baby bird or a mouse **2.** SMALLEST SOUND a very quiet utterance ○ *I don't want to hear another peep out of any of you!* [15C. An imitation of the sound]

peeper[1] /peepər/ *n* **1.** somebody who looks secretly at somebody or something **2.** somebody's eye (*dated slang; often used in the plural*) [Mid-17C. < PEEP[1]]

peeper[2] /peepər/ *n* AMPHIB same as **spring peeper** [Late 16C. < PEEP[2]]

peephole /peep hōl/ *n* **1.** a small crack or hole that somebody can look through **2.** a small hole in a door that allows somebody to see people on the other side without being observed

peeping Tom /peeping tóm/ *n* a man who gets sexual pleasure from secretly watching somebody undressing or watching sexual activity between other people [Early 19C. After a tailor in English legend who was the only person to look at Lady Godiva riding naked]

peeps /peeps/ *n* ONLINE same as **people** (*slang*) [Shortening and alteration]

peepshow /peep shō/ *n* **1.** an erotic or pornographic film or show viewed from individual booths **2.** a sequence of pictures viewed through a hole or lens in a box, regarded as a form of entertainment in former times

peep sight *n* a metal tab at the rear of a rifle barrel, containing a small circular opening through which the user looks to align the front sight with the target

peepul *n* TREES another spelling of **pipal**

peer[1] /peer/ (**peers, peering, peered**) *vi* **1.** to look very carefully or hard, especially at somebody or something that is difficult to see, often with narrowed eyes **2.** to be partially visible or appear briefly [Late 16C. Origin ?]

SPELLCHECK *peer* or *pier*? Do not confuse the spelling of *peer* and *pier*, which sound similar. *Peer* is a verb meaning 'to look carefully or hard' (as in *peering at the inscription on the weathered stone*) or a noun meaning 'an equal' or 'a member of the nobility' (as in *peer group, a peer of the realm*). *Pier* is a noun denoting a walkway jutting into the sea or a structural support.

peer[2] /peer/ *n* **1.** somebody who is the equal of somebody else, e.g. in age or social class **2.** a member of the nobility in Great Britain and Northern Ireland [13C. Via French < Latin *par* 'equal']

peerage /peerij/ *n* **1.** NOBLES AS GROUP peers considered as a class or group **2.** NOBLE RANK the rank, status, or title of a peer **3.** LIST OF NOBLES a book listing the members of the nobility and giving information about their families

peeress /peer ess/ *n* **1.** a woman who is a peer **2.** the wife or widow of a peer

peer group *n* a social group consisting of people who are equal in such respects as age, education, or social class ○ *Teenagers usually prefer to spend time with their own peer group.*

peerie /peeri/ *adj* Scotland same as **small** *adj* (sense 1) [Early 19C. Origin ?]

peerless /peerləss/ *adj* so good as to have no equal — **peerlessly** *adv* — **peerlessness** *n*

peer of the realm *n* in Great Britain and Northern Ireland, a member of the nobility who has the right to sit in the House of Lords

peer pressure *n* social pressure on somebody to adopt a type of behaviour, dress, or attitude in order to be accepted as part of a group

peer review *n* an assessment of an article, piece of work, or research by people who are experts on the subject — **peer-review** *vt* — **peer-reviewed** *adj*

peer-to-peer *adj* ONLINE full form of **P2P**

peeve /peev/ (*informal*) *vt* (**peeves, peeving, peeved**) ANNOY SOMEBODY to make somebody feel annoyed, irritated, or resentful ■ *n* **1.** SOMETHING THAT ANNOYS something that annoys or irritates somebody **2.** BAD MOOD an irritated or resentful mood [Early 20C. Back-formation < PEEVISH]

peevish /peevish/ *adj* bad-tempered, irritable, or tending to complain [14C. Origin ?] — **peevishly** *adv* — **peevishness** *n*

peewee[1] /pee wee/ *n* **1.** VERY SMALL PERSON OR THING somebody or something that is extremely small, especially a small child **2.** N Am CHILD PLAYING SPORT a child involved in a sport or sports league organized for children ■ *adj* **1.** TINY very small **2.** N Am FOR CHILDREN describes a sport or sports league that is organized for children ○ *played peewee baseball* [Late 19C. Reduplication of WEE[1]]

peewee[2] /pee wee/ *n* BIRDS another spelling of **pewee**

peewit /pee wit/ *n* BIRDS same as **lapwing** [Early 16C. An imitation of its cry]

peezle /peez'l/ *n* regional the penis of an animal, especially a bull or horse [Variant of PIZZLE]

~~peform~~ incorrect spelling of **perform**

peg /peg/ *n* **1.** PIN FOR FASTENING OR MARKING SOMETHING a small piece of metal, plastic, or wood used to secure or mark something, or to join two parts together **2.** HOOK FOR HANGING THINGS a hook or projecting piece of

wood or metal that is attached to a surface such as a door or wall and used to hang things on, especially clothes **3.** FASTENER FOR CLOTHES ON WASHING LINE a hinged piece of wood or plastic used to fasten washing to a clothes line. US term **clothespin 4.** PART OF INSTRUMENT FOR TUNING a screw or pin around which a string is wound in the head (**pegbox**) of a stringed instrument. The string can be tightened or loosened to raise or lower its pitch by turning the peg. **5.** REASON FOR DOING SOMETHING an excuse or reason for doing something, or a support for an argument **6.** DEGREE OR STEP a degree, notch, or step, especially in somebody's opinion of a person or thing **7.** SMALL DRINK OF SPIRITS a small drink of spirits such as brandy or whisky (*dated informal*) **8.** BASEBALL FAST THROW in baseball, a fast low throw of the ball that puts a base runner out **9.** LEISURE CROQUET PIN in croquet, a post that must be hit with a ball in order for a player to win the game ■ *vt* (**pegs, pegging, pegged**) **1.** SECURE SOMETHING WITH PEGS to fasten something with one or more pegs **2.** PUT PEG IN SOMETHING to insert a peg into something **3.** MARK SOMETHING WITH PEG to mark something such as the score in a game with a peg or pegs **4.** *N Am* CATEGORIZE SOMEBODY to classify somebody or something, especially as having a particular character **5.** COMM FIX SOMETHING AT CERTAIN LEVEL to fix the cost or value of something at a particular level **6.** BASEBALL THROW BASEBALL in baseball, to throw a low and fast ball (*informal*) [15C. Probably < obsolete Dutch *pegge*] ◇ **a square peg in a round hole** a person who is unsuited to the situation he or she is in ◇ **bring** *or* **take somebody down a peg (or two)** to make somebody more humble ◇ **off the peg** used to describe clothes that are ready to wear, not tailor-made

peg away *vi* to persist or continue working at something

peg down *vt* to fasten something such as a tent down with pegs

peg out *v* **1.** *vi* COLLAPSE FROM EXHAUSTION to collapse from exhaustion or to be too exhausted to continue (*informal*) **2.** *vt* FASTEN CLOTHES TO WASHING LINE to attach wet clothes to a washing line with pegs **3.** *vt* SECURE SOMETHING WITH PEGS to fasten something such as a tent with pegs **4.** *vi* same as **die**[1] (sense 1) (*informal*) **5.** *vt* MARK OUT LAND to mark out a piece of land with pegs **6.** *vi* WIN CROQUET GAME in croquet, to hit the peg, thereby winning the game **7.** *vt* EXCLUDE OPPONENT'S BALL IN CROQUET to make an opponent's croquet ball hit the peg, thereby causing it to be out of the game **8.** *vi* CARDS SCORE WINNING POINT IN CRIBBAGE in cribbage, to score the winning point

Pegasus /péggəsəss/ *n* **1.** in Greek mythology, a horse with wings, born of the shed blood of Medusa **2.** a large constellation of the northern hemisphere between Andromeda and Aquarius. See illustration at **constellation**

Pegasus Bay /péggəsəss-/ bay on the eastern coast of the South Island, New Zealand, situated between the Banks Peninsula to the south and Motunau Beach to the north

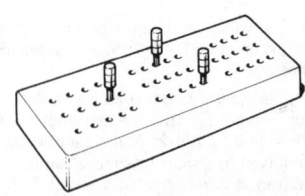

pegboard

pegboard /pég bawrd/ *n* **1.** a board with a pattern of holes into which pegs are placed in games such as solitaire **2.** a board with a pattern of holes into which pegs are placed to keep the score in some games, especially card games such as cribbage

pegbox /pég boks/ *n* the portion of a stringed instrument that holds the tuning pegs

peg leg *n* **1.** a prosthetic leg, especially a simple wooden one fitted at the knee (*offensive*) **2.** an of-

fensive term for somebody who has a prosthetic leg

pegmatite /pégmə tīt/ *n* a coarse-grained igneous rock, usually granite, that is characterized by large well-formed crystals and often contains rare elements [Mid-19C. < Greek *pēgmat-* 'something joined together'] —**pegmatitic** /pégmə títtik/ *adj*

peg top *n* a spinning top that is thrown from the hand and is caused to spin as a string quickly unwinds from around a central metal peg ■ **peg tops** *npl* trousers that are full and gathered at the hips and narrow at the ankle (*dated*)

peg-top *adj* describes a garment, especially a skirt or pair of trousers, that is wide at the hips and narrow at the hem (*dated*)

Pegu /pe góo/ city in Myanmar, formerly Burma. Between 1531 and 1635 it was the country's capital. Population: 150,528 (1983).

Pehlevi *n, adj* LANG another spelling of **Pahlavi**

I. M. Pei

Pei /pay/, **I. M.** (*b.* 1917) Chinese-born US architect. His major urban buildings around the world combine elegance of form with functional efficiency, and include the John Hancock Tower, Boston, Massachusetts (1973) and a pyramidal glass entrance to the Louvre, Paris (1989). Full name **Pei, Ieoh Ming**

PEI *abbr* Prince Edward Island

~~peice~~ incorrect spelling of **piece**

peignoir /páyn waar/ *n* a woman's loose-fitting dressing gown, bathrobe, or negligée [Mid-19C. < French *peigner* 'to comb' < Latin *pecten* 'comb']

~~peir~~ incorrect spelling of **pier**

Peirce /peerss/, **Charles S.** (1839–1914) US philosopher and physicist. A prolific writer on a wide range of mathematical, philosophical, and scientific subjects, he is best known for developing a system of philosophy that later came to be known as pragmatism. Full name **Peirce, Charles Sanders**

pejoration /peéjə ráysh'n/ *n* **1.** a worsening, deterioration, or decline in quality, status, or value (*formal*) **2.** a change over time in the meaning of a word so that it becomes less favourable or more negative. An example is the English word 'cunning', formerly used to mean 'learned' but now used to mean 'cleverly deceitful'. [Mid-17C. < medieval Latin *peioration-* < late Latin *peiorare* 'worsen' < Latin *peior* 'worse']

pejorative /pi jórrətiv/ *adj* expressing criticism or disapproval (*formal*) ■ *n* a word, expression, or affix that expresses criticism or disapproval [Late 19C. < French *péjoratif* < late Latin *peiorare* (see PEJORATION)] —**pejoratively** *adv*

peke /peek/, **Peke** *n* a Pekingese dog (*informal*) [Early 20C. Shortening]

Pekinese

Pekinese /peéki neéz/, **Pekingese** *n* (*plural same*) **1.** SMALL CHINESE DOG a small pet dog with a short flat nose, a long straight silky coat, and a tail that curls over its back, belonging to a breed originally developed in China **2.** SOMEBODY FROM BEIJING somebody who comes from Beijing **3.** LANG same as **Chinese** (sense 3) (*dated*) ■ *adj* OF BEIJING relating to Beijing, or its people or culture

Peking /pee kíng/ former name for **Beijing**

Peking duck *n* **1.** a Chinese dish in which small portions of duck meat, strips of crisp duck skin, cucumber, and spring onions are rolled in thin pancakes **2.** *Hong Kong* a student who is expected to deal with a large amount of school work and learn by rote

Peking man *n* the fossilized remains of an extinct human species that lived 400,000 to 500,000 years ago, originally classified as Pithecanthropus and now regarded as a subspecies of Homo erectus [Early 20C. After PEKING, because discovered in China]

pekoe /peékō/ *n* a high-quality black tea [Early 18C. < Chinese *pekho* 'white down']

pelage /péllij/ *n* a mammal's coat of fur, hair, or wool (*technical*) [Early 19C. < French < Old French *pel* 'hair' < Latin *pilus*]

Pelagianism /pi láyji ənizəm/ *n* the belief of the heretical Christian monk Pelagius that people can earn salvation through their own efforts, without relying on the grace of God, and the rejection of the concept of original sin [Late 16C. After PELAGIUS]

pelagic /pə lájjik/ *adj* **1.** relating to, living, or occurring in the waters of the ocean or the open sea as opposed to near the shore ○ *pelagic bird populations* **2.** describes sediments deposited beneath deep ocean waters that are rich in the remains of microscopic organisms [Mid-17C. Via Latin < Greek *pelagikos* < *pelagos* 'sea']

Pelagius /pi láyji əss/ (AD 360?–420?) Romano-British monk. His doctrine, known as Pelagianism, denies the existence of original sin and was condemned as heretical. —**Pelagian** *adj, n*

pelargonic acid /pélaar gonnik-/ *n Aus, US* same as **nonanoic acid**

pelargonium /péllə gốni əm/ *n* (*plural* **-ums** *or* same) *n* a flowering plant with rounded or lobed leaves. Flowers: red, pink, white, in clusters. Native to: southern Africa. Genus: *Pelargonium*. [Early 19C. < modern Latin < Greek *pelargos* 'stork' because its capsules resemble a stork's bill]

Pelasgian /pi lázji ən, -lázgi-/ *n* a member of an ancient people who lived in Greece and the islands of the Aegean Sea before the arrival of the Bronze Age Hellenic peoples ■ *adj also* **Pelasgic** /pi lázjik, -lázgik/ relating to the Pelasgian peoples or their cultures [15C. < Latin *Pelasgus* < Greek *Pelasgos*, the Pelasgians' mythical founder]

pelau /pi lów, pe-/ *n Carib* a spicy dish of browned meat, usually small pieces of beef or chicken, with rice, and sometimes peas [Mid-17C. Variant of PILAU]

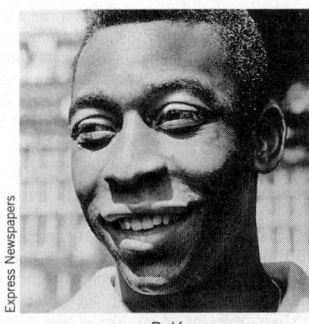

Pelé

Pelé /pél ay/ (*b.* 1940) Brazilian football player. He is considered one of the greatest players of all time. His Brazilian team won the World Cup in 1958, 1962, and 1970. He retired in 1977, having scored 1,281 goals during his career. Born **Nascimento, Edson Arantes do**

pelecypod /pi léssipod/ *n* MARINE BIOL same as **bivalve**

[Late 19C. < modern Latin *Pelecypoda* < Greek *pelekus* 'axe' + *-podos* 'footed']

pelerine /péllə reen, -rin/ *n* a woman's short narrow cape with long pointed ends that meet at the front [Mid-18C. Via French *pèlerine*, form of *pèlerin* 'pilgrim' < Latin *pelegrinus* (see PEREGRINE)]

Pele's hair /péllayz-/ *n* fine threads of volcanic glass formed by the action of the wind on jets of lava erupting into the air [Mid-19C. Translation of Hawaiian *lauoho o Pele*, after *Pele*, goddess of volcanoes]

Peleus /péeli əss, péel yoos/ *n* in Greek mythology, the king of the Myrmidons in Thessaly. He and the sea nymph Thetis were the parents of Achilles.

pelf /pelf/ *n* money, wealth, or riches, especially if obtained dishonestly (*archaic*) [14C. < Old N French variant of Old French *pelfre* 'booty']

pelham /péllám/ *n* a bit for a horse's bridle that is midway between the simple snaffle bit and the harsher curb bit [Mid-19C. After *Pelham*, surname]

pelican

pelican /péllikán/ *n* a large water bird that has webbed feet and a large flat beak with a hanging pouch that can be expanded to catch and store fish. Native to: warm-water coasts and lakes worldwide. Family: Pelecanidae. [Pre-12C. Via late Latin < Greek *pelekan*]

pelican crossing *n* a pedestrian crossing where people wishing to cross the road can stop the traffic by pressing a button that controls traffic lights at the side of the road [Alteration of acronym < *pedestrian light controlled*]

pelisse /pə léess/ *n* **1.** a cloak, coat, or jacket lined or trimmed with fur, often worn as part of a military uniform, e.g. by members of the Hussar regiments **2.** a woman's long fitted coat or dress that opens at the front and is often trimmed with fur [Early 18C. Via French < late Latin *pellicia* < Latin *pellis* 'skin']

pelite /pée līt/, **pelyte** *n* aluminium-rich metamorphic rock formed by the action of temperature and pressure on clay-rich sedimentary rocks [Late 19C. < Greek *pēlos* 'clay'] —**pelitic** /pi líttik/ *adj*

pellagra /pə lággrə, pə láygrə/ *n* a disease caused by a dietary deficiency of niacin and marked by dermatitis, diarrhoea, and disorder of the central nervous system [Early 19C. < Italian *pelle* 'skin' + *agra* 'rough' or *-agra* 'seizure'] —**pellagrous** *adj*

pellet /péllét/ *n* **1.** SMALL BALL OF COMPRESSED MATERIAL a small ball or piece of material that has been pressed tightly together, e.g. for animal feed or a medicine **2.** SMALL BULLET a small bullet or ball of metal fired from a gun, especially an air gun **3.** IMITATION BULLET an imitation bullet for use in a toy gun **4.** STONE MISSILE a ball, usually of stone, formerly used as a cannonball or as a missile fired from a catapult **5.** ZOOL ANIMAL FAECES a small round piece of the faeces of some animals such as sheep or rabbits **6.** BIRDS REGURGITATED MATTER an undigested mass of food, mostly bone and hair, that is regurgitated by owls and other birds of prey ■ *vt* (**-lets, -leting, -leted**) **1.** MAKE PELLETS OF SOMETHING to make or form something into pellets **2.** STRIKE SOMETHING WITH PELLETS to bombard or hit somebody or something with pellets [14C. < French *pelote* 'small ball' < Latin *pila* 'ball'] —**pelletization** /péllə tī záysh'n/ *n* —**pelletize** *vt* —**pelletizer** *n*

pellicle /péllik'l/ *n* **1.** a thin film, membrane, or skin **2.** a multilayered flexible sheath that lies immediately beneath the cell membrane of many protozoans

[Mid-16C. Via French < Latin *pellicula*, literally 'small skin' < *pellis* 'skin'] —**pellicular** /pə líkyoolər/ *adj*

pellitory /péllitəri/ (*plural* **-ries**) *n* a plant whose oil was formerly used for the relief of toothache. Native to: Mediterranean. Latin name: *Anacyclus pyrethrum*. [15C. < Old French *peletre*, alteration of *peretre* < Latin *pyrethrum* (see PYRETHRUM)]

pell-mell /pél mél/ *adv* **1.** IN DISORDERLY RUSH in a disorderly frantic rush **2.** UNTIDILY in a confused, jumbled, or untidy manner ■ *adj* DISORDERLY confused, frantic, or disorderly ■ *n* CONFUSION OR DISORDER a confused or disorderly condition or situation [Late 16C. < French *pêle-mêle*, modern form of Old French *pesle mesle* < *mesler* 'to mix']

pellucid /pə loóssid/ *adj* **1.** allowing all or most light to pass through (*literary*) **2.** easy to understand or clear in meaning (*formal*) [Early 17C. < Latin *pellucidus* < *pellucere* 'shine through' < *lucere* 'to shine'] —**pellucidly** *adv*

Pelly /pélli/ river in Canada. It is a tributary of the Yukon River in southeastern Yukon Territory and originates in the Mackenzie Mountains. Length: 530 km/329 mi.

pelmanism /pélmənizəm/, **Pelmanism** *n* a game in which a pack of cards is laid face down on a table and players try to select matching pairs by remembering their positions from previous attempts [Early 20C. After Christopher Louis *Pelman*, British psychologist]

pelmet /pélmət/ *n* a narrow piece of fabric or board fitted above a window for decoration and to hide the curtain rail [Early 20C. Probably alteration of French *palmette* 'stylized palm leaf' (see PALMETTE)]

pelobatid /péllō báttid, péelō-/ *n* a frog with the backbone development of more primitive frogs and the leg-muscle structure of more advanced ones, e.g. the European spade foot toad. Family: Pelobatidae. [Mid-20C. < Greek *pelos* 'mud' + *bates* 'walker']

Peloponnese /péllapə neess, péllapə neéss/ peninsula in southern Greece, linked to the rest of mainland Greece by the Isthmus of Corinth. Area: 21,440 sq. km/8,278 sq. mi. —**Peloponnesian** /péllapə neézh'n, -neésh'n/ *n, adj*

Pelops /pée lops/ *n* in Greek mythology, the son of Tantalus, killed by his father and served up as a meal to the gods. The gods punished Tantalus and restored Pelops to life.

pelorus /pi láwrəss/ *n* a device used to measure bearings relative to the direction in which a boat is travelling [Mid-19C. Origin ?]

Pelosi /pə lóssee/, **Nancy** (*b.* 1940) US minority leader of the House of Representatives. A Democrat and congresswoman for San Francisco since 1987, she became the first woman to lead a major party in the US Congress (2002).

pelota /pə lóttə, -lótə/ *n* **1.** a fast court game of Basque origin, in which two players use long wickerwork baskets strapped to their wrists to hurl a ball against a marked wall and catch it **2.** the ball used in pelota [Early 19C. < Spanish, 'ball' < Latin *pila*]

pelt[1] /pelt/ *n* **1.** ANIMAL SKIN the skin of an animal with the fur, hair, or wool still attached **2.** ANIMAL SKIN FOR TANNING the skin of an animal with the fur, hair, or wool removed so that it is ready for tanning into leather ■ *vt* (**pelts, pelting, pelted**) REMOVE ANIMAL'S SKIN to remove the skin of an animal [15C. Origin ?]

pelt[2] /pelt/ *v* (**pelts, pelting, pelted**) **1.** *vt* THROW THINGS AT SOMEBODY OR SOMETHING to bombard somebody or something with many blows or missiles **2.** *vt* BEAT AGAINST SOMETHING to beat against something continuously **3.** *vi* RAIN HEAVILY to fall fast and hard as hail or rain **4.** *vi* MOVE QUICKLY to hurry or move quickly ■ *n* A BLOW a strong blow [15C. Origin ?] —**pelter** *n* ◇ **at full pelt** extremely fast

peltast /pél tast/ *n* a foot soldier of ancient Greece armed with a light shield and a javelin [Early 17C. Via Latin < Greek *peltastēs* < *peltē* 'small light shield']

peltate /pél tayt/ *adj* describes a leaf that has its stalk attached to the lower surface in the centre rather than at the edge [Mid-18C. < Latin *peltatus*, 'armed with a light shield' < *pelta* 'small light shield' < Greek *peltē*] —**peltately** *adv* —**peltation** /pel táysh'n/ *n*

Peltier effect /pélti ay-/ *n* the production or absorption of heat at the junction of two metals when an electric current is passed from one metal to another. Heat is produced or absorbed depending on the direction and amount of current flow. [Mid-19C. After J. C. A. *Peltier* (1785–1845), French scientist]

Pelton wheel /pélt'n-/ *n* an impulse turbine in which cup-shaped buckets on the edge of a rotor are hit with a high-pressure jet of water, causing the rotor to turn [Late 19C. After L. A. *Pelton* (1829–1908), US engineer]

peltry /péltri/ *n* the skins of animals collectively, especially when the fur is still attached [15C. < Anglo-Norman *pelterie*, Old French *peleterie* < Old French *pel* 'animal skin, pelt' < Latin *pellis* 'skin, leather']

pelves ANAT plural of **pelvis**

pelvic /pélvik/ *adj* relating to, involving, or located in or near the pelvis

pelvic fin *n* either of a pair of fins on the lower surface of a fish that have skeletal support and are analogous to the hind limbs of land animals

pelvic inflammatory disease *n* an inflammation of a woman's reproductive organs in the pelvic area, which can cause infertility

pelvimetry /pel vímmətri/ *n* measurement of the inlet and outlet diameters of the pelvis, usually to assess whether there will be any difficulty during childbirth

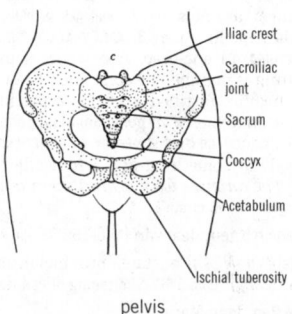

pelvis

pelvis /pélviss/ (*plural* **pelvises** or **pelves** /pél veez/) *n* **1.** the strong basin-shaped ring of bone near the bottom of the spine formed by the hip bones on the front and sides, and the triangular sacrum on the back **2.** any basin- or cup-shaped anatomical cavity, e.g. the region of the kidney into which urine is discharged before its passage into the ureter [Early 17C. < Latin, literally 'basin']

pelycosaur /péllikə sawr/ *n* a large extinct reptile that was common in Europe and North America during the Permian period, 245 to 290 million years ago. Order: Pelycosauria. [Mid-20C. < Greek *peluk-* 'bowl' + *sauros* 'lizard']

pelyte *n* GEOL another spelling of **pelite**

Pemba /pémbə/ island in northeastern Tanzania, in the Indian Ocean. Its main towns are Wete and Chake Chake. Population: 265,039 (1988). Area: 982 sq. km/379 sq. mi.

Pembroke /pém brook, pémbrək/ town in southwestern Wales, in Pembrokeshire. Population: 6,773 (1991).

Pembrokeshire /pémbrookshər/ county in southwestern Wales. It is the site of many prehistoric and Roman remains. Haverfordwest is its administrative centre. Population: 114,131 (2001). Area: 1,591 sq. km/614 sq. mi.

Pembrokeshire Coast National Park largely coastal national park, in southwestern Wales, established in 1952. It consists of four mainland areas and several islands. Area: 620 sq. km/240 sq. mi.

Pembroke table *n* a small four-legged table with a top that folds down on two sides and one or two drawers [Late 18C. Probably after PEMBROKE]

pemmican /pémmikən/, **pemican** *n* **1.** a traditional Native North American food made with strips of lean dried meat pounded into paste, mixed with melted fat and dried berries or fruits, and pressed into small cakes **2.** a nutritious food adapted from

traditional Native North American pemmican and used as emergency rations, e.g. by explorers [Late 18C. < Cree *pimihkan* 'he makes grease']

pemoline /pémmə leen/ *n* a synthetic stimulant of the central nervous system. Use: treatment of depression, attention deficit disorder in children. Formula: $C_9H_8N_2O_2$. [Mid-20C. < parts of *phenyliminooxooxazolidine*, its chemical name]

pemphigus /pémfigəss/ *n* an autoimmune disease characterized by large blisters on the skin and mucous membranes, often accompanied by itching or burning sensations [Late 18C. Via modern Latin < Greek *pemphig-* 'pustule']

pen[1] /pen/ *n* **1.** WRITING INSTRUMENT a long thin instrument used for writing or drawing with ink. Early examples were made from sharpened quill feathers, but modern pens usually consist of a metal or plastic shaft with a nib, point, or revolving ball at one end. **2.** WRITING the written word considered as a means of expression ○ *They say the pen is mightier than the sword.* **3.** MARINE BIOL SQUID'S INTERNAL SHELL the internal feather-shaped horny shell of a squid ■ *vt* (**pens, penning, penned**) WRITE SOMETHING to write something in letters or symbols, or compose something for others to read [13C. Via French < Latin *penna* 'feather'] —**penner** *n* ◇ **from the pen of somebody** composed or written by a particular author ○ *another novel from the pen of everybody's favourite thriller writer.*

pen[2] /pen/ *n* **1.** ENCLOSURE FOR ANIMALS a small fenced area of land, or an enclosure within a building, used to keep farm animals in **2.** ANIMALS IN PEN the farm animals kept in a pen **3.** AREA THAT CONFINES SOMEBODY OR SOMETHING an enclosed area where somebody or something is confined or controlled **4.** NAVY FORTIFIED DOCK a heavily fortified dock for repairing or servicing submarines ■ *vt* (**pens, penning, penned** or **pent** *archaic* /pent/) CONFINE SOMEBODY OR SOMETHING to keep somebody or something in a pen or other enclosed area ○ *The animals were penned up in a tiny space.* [Old English *penn*, origin ?]

pen[3] /pen/ *n* a female swan [Mid-16C. Origin ?]

pen[4] /pen/ *n* *N Am* a state, provincial, or federal prison (*slang*) [Late 19C. Shortening of PENITENTIARY]

Pen ♦ Le Pen, Jean-Marie

PEN /pen/ *abbr* International Association of Poets, Playwrights, Editors, Essayists, and Novelists

Pen. *abbr* Peninsula (used in placenames)

penal /péen'l/ *adj* **1.** OF PUNISHMENT relating to, forming, or prescribing punishment, especially by law ○ *the penal system* **2.** PUNISHABLE BY LAW subject to punishment under the law **3.** USED AS PLACE OF PUNISHMENT used as a place of imprisonment and punishment ○ *a penal institution* **4.** PAYABLE AS PENALTY required to be paid as a penalty [15C. Via French *pénal* < Latin *poenalis* < *poena* 'penalty']

penal code *n* a body or system of laws concerned with the punishment of crime

penal colony *n* a place of imprisonment and punishment at a remote location

penalize /péenə līz/ (**-izes, -izing, -ized**), **penalise** (**-ises, -ising, -ised**) *vt* **1.** SUBJECT SOMEBODY TO PENALTY to impose a penalty on somebody or something for breaking a law or rule **2.** DISADVANTAGE SOMEBODY to put somebody or something at a disadvantage, or treat him or her unfairly ○ *The tax system heavily penalizes people with high incomes.* **3.** PUNISH PLAYER FOR BREAKING RULE to punish a team or player for breaking a rule by giving an advantage to the opposing team or player **4.** MAKE SOMETHING PUNISHABLE to make something punishable by a law or rule —**penalization** /péenə līzáysh'n/ *n*

penal servitude *n* confinement in a penal colony as a result of conviction of a crime

penalty /pénn'lti/ (*plural* **-ties**) *n* **1.** PUNISHMENT FOR CRIME a legal or official punishment for committing a crime or other offence, e.g. a fine or imprisonment **2.** PUNISHMENT FOR BREAKING CONTRACT a punishment, e.g. a fine, for failing to fulfil the terms of a legal agreement **3.** UNPLEASANT CONSEQUENCE something unpleasant suffered as the result of an unwise action ○ *paying the penalty of being too lenient* **4.** DISADVANTAGE FOR BREAKING RULE a disadvantage imposed on a player or team for breaking a rule in a sport

or game, e.g. a free shot at the goal awarded to the opposing side **5.** SOCCER same as **penalty kick** (sense 1) **6.** GOAL FROM PENALTY in football, a goal scored from a penalty [15C. < assumed Anglo-Norman variant of French *pénalité* < Latin *poenalis* (see PENAL)]

penalty area *n* a rectangular area in front of a football goal within which the goalkeeper is allowed to handle the ball. A foul by the defending team within this area may result in a free shot at the goal being awarded to the opposing side.

penalty box *n* **1.** SOCCER same as **penalty area 2.** an area with a bench beside an ice-hockey rink where penalized players must stay during the period they have to serve as a time penalty

penalty kick *n* **1.** in football, a free kick from the penalty spot at the opposing team's goal, which is defended only by its goalkeeper. It is awarded for some types of foul within the penalty area. **2.** in rugby, a kick worth three points that can be aimed at the goal after a serious foul by a member of the opposing side

penalty rates *npl ANZ* rates of pay that are higher than normal rates and are paid for work performed outside normal working hours or in other exceptional conditions

penalty shoot-out *n* SOCCER same as **shoot-out** (sense 2)

penalty shot *n* SPORTS same as **penalty** (sense 4)

penalty spot *n* **1.** a designated spot on a football field, 11 m/12 yd from the goal line, from which penalty kicks are taken **2.** in hockey, a designated spot 7 m/23 ft from the goal line from which the shot is taken

penance /pénnənss/ *n* **1.** SELF-PUNISHMENT FOR SIN self-punishment or an act of religious devotion performed to show sorrow for having committed a sin **2.** DUTY IMPOSED BY PRIEST a duty or religious devotion imposed by a priest during the sacrament of confession in some Christian churches **3.** CHRISTIAN SACRAMENT OF RECONCILIATION a sacrament in some Christian churches in which a person confesses sins to a priest and is forgiven after performing a religious devotion or duty such as praying or fasting ■ *vt* (**-ances, -ancing, -anced**) IMPOSE PENANCE ON SOMEBODY to make somebody do penance for a sin [13C. Via French < Latin *paenitentia* 'regret' < *paenitere* 'to regret']

Penang /pə náng/, **Pinang** state in northwestern Malaysia, comprising Penang Island and a small mainland area on the Malay Peninsula. Capital: George Town. Population: 219,603 (1996). Area: 1,031 sq. km/398 sq. mi.

penannular /pen ánnyōōlər/ *adj* in the shape of an almost complete circle [Mid-19C. < Latin *paene* 'almost']

penates *npl* ♦ lares and penates

~~penatrate~~ incorrect spelling of **penetrate**

pence MONEY plural of **penny**

pencel /péns'l/, **pensil** *n* a small narrow flag (**pennon**) or streamer, especially one carried at the end of a lance [13C. < Anglo-Norman, contraction of Old French *penoncel* 'small pennon' < *penon* (see PENNON)]

penchant /póN shoN/ *n* a strong liking, taste, or tendency for something [Late 17C. < French, present participle of *pencher* 'incline' < assumed Vulgar Latin *pendicare* < Latin *pendere* 'hang']

pencil /péns'l/ *n* **1.** WRITING INSTRUMENT a thin cylindrical instrument used for drawing or writing. It consists of a rod of graphite or some other erasable marking material inside a wooden or metal shaft. **2.** SOMETHING RESEMBLING PENCIL something that has a similar shape, structure, or function to a pencil, e.g. a stick for applying cosmetics ○ *an eyebrow pencil* **3.** OPTICS CYLINDER OF LIGHT a long narrow cylinder or cone of light with a small angle of convergence **4.** MATHS SET OF LINES THROUGH POINT the set of all lines passing through a fixed point or of all lines parallel to a given line **5.** ART ARTIST'S INDIVIDUAL STYLE the individual drawing style or technique of an artist ■ *vt* (**-cils, -cilling, -cilled**) WRITE SOMETHING WITH PENCIL to draw, mark, write, or colour something with a pencil [14C. Via Old French *pincel* < Latin *peniculus* 'brush', literally 'small tail' < *penis* 'tail']

pencil in *vt* to note something provisionally such as

the time of a proposed engagement in an appointments book or on a calendar

pencil case *n* a small container for somebody's pens, pencils, and rubbers, used especially by school, college, and university students

pencil moustache *n* a very thin moustache

pencil pusher *n N Am* same as **penpusher** (*informal*)

pencil skirt *n* a narrow straight skirt

pen computer *n* a computer using pattern-recognition circuitry or software to enable it to accept handwriting as data input. Many personal digital assistants are pen computers.

pend[1] /pend/ (**pends, pending, pended**) *vi* **1.** to remain unsettled or wait to be judged **2.** to be suspended or drape from something (*literary*) [15C. Probably < French *pendre* (see PENDANT)]

pend[2] /pend/ *n Scotland* a vaulted or arched passageway, especially from the street to the back of a group of houses [15C. < French *pendre* 'hang', or its source Latin *pendere*]

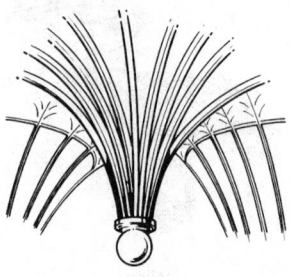

pendant (sense 4)

pendant /péndənt/ *n* **1.** HANGING ORNAMENT OR JEWELLERY an ornament or a piece of jewellery that hangs from a necklace, bracelet, or earring **2.** NECKLACE WITH ORNAMENT a necklace with a hanging ornament attached to it **3.** HANGING LIGHT a lamp, chandelier, or other lighting fixture that hangs from the ceiling **4.** ARCHIT ORNAMENT HANGING FROM CEILING an architectural ornament hanging from a vaulted ceiling or roof **5.** ARTS ONE OF MATCHING PAIR a piece of art that matches or goes with another piece **6.** NAUT LENGTH OF WIRE OR ROPE a length of wire or rope attached at the upper end to a spar or similar part and at the lower end to a block and tackle ■ *adj* ARCHIT, GRAM same as **pendent** [14C. < French < present participle of *pendre* 'hang' < Latin *pendere*]

pendent /péndənt/ *adj* **1.** HANGING OR SUSPENDED dangling, hanging, or suspended (*formal or literary*) **2.** OVERHANGING jutting, overhanging, or sticking out (*formal or literary*) **3.** PENDING not yet dealt with, decided, or settled (*formal or literary*) **4.** GRAM GRAMMATICALLY INCOMPLETE describes an incomplete grammatical structure ■ *n* JEWELLERY, ARCHIT, ARTS, NAUT same as **pendant** [13C. Variant of PENDANT] —**pendency** *n* — **pendently** *adv*

ORIGIN The Latin word *pendere* 'to hang', from which **pendent** is derived, is also the source of English *append*, *appendix*, *compendium*, *depend*, *impend*, *penchant*, *pendulum*, *penthouse*, *perpendicular*, and *suspend*.

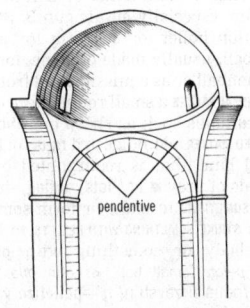

pendentive

pendentive /pen déntiv/ *n* a sloping triangular piece of vaulting between the arches that support a dome

and its rim [Early 18C. < French *pendentif* < Latin *pendere* 'hang']

Penderecki /péndə rétski/, **Krzysztof** (*b.* 1933) Polish composer. He is noted for his eerie, often random music. His works include *Threnody for the Victims of Hiroshima* (1961).

pending /pénding/ *adj* **1.** NOT YET TAKEN CARE OF not yet dealt with, decided, or settled **2.** ABOUT TO HAPPEN about to happen or come into effect ■ *prep* **1.** UNTIL until or while waiting for ○ *pending further enquiries* **2.** DURING during the course of something [Mid-17C. Anglicization of French *pendant* (see PENDANT)]

pendragon /pen drággən/ *n* a supreme leader of the ancient Britons [15C. < Welsh < *pen* 'head' + *dragon* 'military standard' (< Latin *dracon-*)] —**pendragonship** *n*

pendular /péndyŏŏlər/ *adj* swinging to and fro with the motion of a pendulum

pendulous /péndyŏŏləss/ *adj* **1.** hanging loosely or swinging freely **2.** undecided or wavering in making a decision (*literary*) [Early 17C. < Latin *pendulus* (see PENDULUM)] —**pendulously** *adv* —**pendulousness** *n*

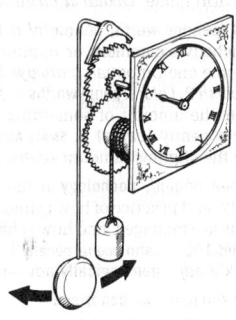

pendulum (sense 2)

pendulum /péndyŏŏləm/ *n* **1.** HANGING WEIGHT a weight hung from a fixed point so that it can swing freely to and fro under the influence of gravity **2.** ROD CONTROLLING CLOCK a rod with a weight at its base that swings from side to side and controls the mechanism of a clock **3.** SOMETHING THAT CHANGES REGULARLY something that changes its direction or position regularly, often alternating between two extremes ○ *The pendulum has swung back to more traditional teaching methods.* [Mid-17C. < modern Latin < Latin *pendulus* 'hanging' < *pendere* 'hang']

~~penecillin~~ incorrect spelling of **penicillin**

Penelope /pə nélləpi/ *n* in Greek mythology, the wife of Odysseus, who waited for his return from the Trojan War and was the mother of his son, Telemachus

peneplain /péeni playn/, **peneplane** *n* an area of nearly flat featureless land that is the result of a prolonged period of erosion [Late 19C. < Latin *paene* 'nearly, almost'] —**peneplanation** /péeniplə náysh'n/ *n*

penes ANAT plural of **penis**

penetralia /péni tráyli ə/ *npl* the innermost parts of a place, especially a sanctuary within a temple (*formal*) [Mid-17C. < Latin < *penetralis* 'innermost' < *penetrare* (see PENETRATE)] —**penetralian** *adj*

penetrance /pénnitrənss/ *n* the frequency with which a hereditary characteristic such as a genetic disease occurs among individuals carrying the gene or genes for that characteristic [Mid-20C. < German *Penetranz*]

penetrant /pénnitrənt/ *n* **1.** a substance that encourages a liquid to penetrate a porous material by lowering the surface tension of the liquid **2.** somebody or something that penetrates

penetrate /pénni trayt/ (**-trates, -trating, -trated**) *v* **1.** *vti* ENTER OR PASS THROUGH SOMETHING to enter or pass through something, e.g. by piercing it or forcing a way in ○ *The aim of the mission was to penetrate deep into enemy territory.* **2.** *vt* SPREAD THROUGH SOMETHING to enter and spread through something ○ *The fumes had penetrated the entire building.* **3.** *vt* GET SHARE OF MARKET to succeed in getting a share of a particular market **4.** *vt* INFILTRATE GROUP to enter something such as an organization or country, usually secretly, in order to influence or gather information from within **5.** *vt* SEE INTO SOMETHING to see into or through something

that is dark or obscuring **6.** *vt* DECIPHER MEANING to understand or discover the meaning of something ○ *an enigma few were able to penetrate* **7.** *vi* BE UNDERSTOOD to be understood or taken in by the mind ○ *It took a few seconds for the news to penetrate.* **8.** *vt* INSERT PENIS INTO SOMETHING to insert the penis into a vagina or anus [Mid-16C. < Latin *penetrat-*, past participle of *penetrare* 'penetrate' < *penitus* 'inner, innermost'] —**penetrability** /pénnitrə bílləti/ *n* —**penetrable** *adj* —**penetrator** *n*

penetrating /pénni trayting/ *adj* **1.** ABLE OR TENDING TO PENETRATE strong enough to enter or spread through something ○ *a penetrating odour* **2.** PIERCING OR PROBING apparently able to see or understand things that are hidden ○ *a penetrating glance* **3.** LOUD loud, piercing, shrill, or unpleasant to the ears **4.** PERCEPTIVE able to understand or accurately identify something ○ *a penetrating observation* —**penetratingly** *adv*

penetration /pénni tráysh'n/ *n* **1.** ENTERING OR PASSING THROUGH the action of penetrating, entering, or passing through something ○ *Penetration of the foundations by torrential rain resulted in structural damage.* **2.** ABILITY TO PENETRATE the ability or power to penetrate, enter, or pass through something **3.** UNDERSTANDING the ability to understand or perceive something **4.** INSERTION OF PENIS the insertion of the penis into a vagina or anus **5.** DEGREE OF SUCCESS IN MARKET the extent to which a commercial product or service is recognized or bought in a particular market ○ *The launch of the new product should improve the company's market penetration.* **6.** ATTACK ENTERING ENEMY TERRITORY an attack that succeeds in penetrating an enemy's territory or defences **7.** DEPTH PROJECTILE REACHES a measure of the depth a projectile reaches beneath the surface of its target

penetrative /pénnitrətiv, -traytiv/ *adj* **1.** PENETRATING piercing something or able to get through something **2.** KEEN mentally perceptive or insightful **3.** INVOLVING INSERTION OF PENIS describes sexual activity that involves putting the penis into a vagina or anus

penetrometer /pénni trómmitər/, **penetrameter** /-trám-/ *n* **1.** an instrument for measuring the penetrating power of electromagnetic radiation, e.g. gamma radiation in contaminated soils **2.** an instrument for measuring the penetrability of a solid material by measuring the depth to which it may be pierced with a standard needle [Early 20C. < PENETRATION]

pen friend *n* a person, especially one living in another country, with whom you establish a friendship through an exchange of letters and whom you may never meet in person. N Am term **pen pal**

penguin

penguin /péng gwin/ *n* an upright web-footed seabird with contrasting black and white feathers that cannot fly but uses its flipper-shaped wings for swimming. Native to: cold regions of the southern hemisphere. Family: Spheniscidae. [Late 16C. Origin ?]

penholder /pén hōldər/ *n* **1.** a handle for a pen point or nib, consisting of a metal, plastic, or wooden rod **2.** a holder for a pen or pens in the form of, e.g. a beaker, rack, or stand

-penia *suffix* deficiency ○ *thrombocytopenia* [Via modern Latin < Greek *penia* 'poverty, want']

penicillamine /pénni sílla meen/ *n* a chelating agent. Source: penicillin. Use: removal of toxic metals from the body. [Mid-20C. < PENICILLIN + AMINE]

penicillate /pénni síllət/ *adj* having or resembling a tuft of hair [Early 19C. < Latin *penicillus* (see PENICILLIUM)] —**penicillately** *adv* —**penicillation** /pénnissi láysh'n/ *n*

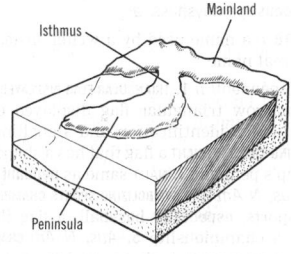

penicillin

penicillin /pénni síllin/ *n* an antibiotic belonging to a group originally derived from mould of the genus *Penicillium* but now produced synthetically. Formula: $C_{16}H_{18}N_2O_4S$. [Early 20C. < PENICILLIUM]

penicillinase /pénni sílli nayz, -nayss/ *n* an enzyme produced by some bacteria that inactivates penicillin. Use: treatment of adverse penicillin reactions.

penicillium /pénni sílli əm/ *n* a bluish-green fungus that grows on stale or ripening food. Use: in cheese-making, as a source of penicillin. Genus: *Penicillium*. [Mid-19C. < modern Latin < Latin *penicillus* 'paintbrush' < *peniculus* (see PENCIL)]

penile /pée nīl/ *adj* relating to, affecting, or resembling the penis

penillion /pe nílli ən/, **pennillion** *npl* Welsh songs, often improvised, sung to a set harp accompaniment [Late 18C. < Welsh, 'verses' < *pen* 'head']

Mainland

Isthmus

Peninsula

peninsula

peninsula /pə nínsyŏŏlə/ *n* a narrow piece of land that juts out from the mainland into an area of water [Mid-16C. < Latin *paeninsula* < *paene* 'almost' + *insula* 'island'] —**peninsular** *adj*

SPELLCHECK Do not confuse the spelling of **peninsula** (noun) and **peninsular** (adjective), which sound similar.

penis /péeniss/ (*plural* **penises** or **penes** /pée neez/) *n* the external male organ of copulation, used to transfer semen to the female. In most mammals, it is also used to expel urine from the body. [Late 17C. < Latin, 'tail, penis']

penis envy *n* in Freudian psychoanalysis, the theory that some girls' and women's psychological problems stem from a sense of deprivation about not having a penis. Very few psychologists now accept this concept.

penitent /pénnitənt/ *adj* FEELING REGRET FOR SINS expressing or feeling regret or sorrow for having committed sins or misdeeds ■ *n* **1.** SOMEBODY WHO FEELS REGRET a sinner or wrongdoer who feels regret or sorrow for misdeeds **2.** SOMEBODY DOING PENANCE somebody who does a penance as directed by a priest or minister after confessing his or her sins [14C. Via French < Latin *paenitent-*, present participle of *paenitere* 'regret'] —**penitence** *n* —**penitently** *adv*

penitential /pénni ténsh'l/ *adj* constituting or expressing penance or penitence —**penitentially** *adv*

menial tasks (*informal*) **2.** S Asia **LOW-PAID WORKER** formerly, in India and Sri Lanka, a low-paid office worker, soldier, or public servant **3.** **LABOURER** in Latin America and the southern United States, especially formerly, a farm labourer who was forced to work for a creditor until a debt was paid off [Early 17C. Via Spanish *peón*, Portuguese *peão* 'foot soldier' < medieval Latin *pedon-* < Latin *ped-* 'foot']

peonage /peé ənij/ *n* **1.** in Latin America and the southern United States, a former system under which a debtor was forced to work for a creditor until a debt was paid **2.** the status or condition of being a peon

peony /peé əni/ (*plural* **-nies**), **paeony** *n* a large ornamental shrubby plant. Flowers: large, globe-shaped, red, white, pink. Native to: Europe, Asia, North America. Genus: *Paeonia*. [Pre-12C. Via medieval Latin < Greek *paiōnia*, after *Paiōn* 'Paian', physician of the deities]

people /peép'l/ *n* **NATION** a nation, community, ethnic group, or nationality ○ *a proud people* ■ *npl* **1.** **HUMAN BEINGS COLLECTIVELY** human beings considered collectively or in general ○ *People tend not to mind if you ask them for help.* **2.** **SUBORDINATES** persons who are under the authority or leadership of somebody or something, e.g. employees, subjects, or followers ○ *I'll get one of my people to phone them.* **3.** **ORDINARY MEN AND WOMEN** the general population, as distinct from the government or higher social classes ○ *the will of the people* **4.** **POLITICAL UNIT** a group of persons comprising a political unit, electorate, or group **5.** **FAMILY MEMBERS** the members of somebody's family, especially somebody's close family (*informal*) ○ *My people were farmers.* ■ *vt* (**-ples, -pling, -pled**) **POPULATE AREA** to populate an area (*usually passive*) ○ *mountain regions that are sparsely peopled* [13C. Via Anglo-Norman and Old French < Latin *populus* < Etruscan]

USAGE people as singular or plural? In most places, *people* behaves as a plural, as in *People are funny; you never know what they will do.* However, when *people* means 'a nation, community, ethnic group, or nationality', it is regarded as a singular and when used in the plural, takes an *s* plural ending: *a Native American people of the Southwest, one of several such peoples noted for their peaceableness.* The possessive of *people* is formed by adding an apostrophe + *s* if one people is stipulated: *the people's choice of a new prime minister.* If many peoples are stipulated, the possessive is formed by adding an apostrophe after the *s*: *various Caribbean peoples' representatives at the conference.* *People* is the preferred form in designating human beings in the plural generally: *Thousands of people* [not *persons*] *jammed the stadium. What on earth will people* [not *persons*] *think if you do that?* Use *persons* only in certain narrow, typically legalistic or otherwise official, contexts: *the Bureau of Missing Persons; the arrest of three suspicious persons loitering outside the gates of Downing Street.*

people carrier *n* a large family car with three rows of seats, some of which can be temporarily removed or folded down to provide extra storage space

peoplehood /peép'l hood/ *n* identity as a member of a particular people, especially a nation or ethnic group

people mover *n* any automated means of transporting large numbers of people over short distances

people person *n* a sociable and communicative person

people's republic *n* a Socialist or Communist republic

Peoria /pi áwri ə/ city in southern Arizona, northwest of Phoenix. Population: 123,239 (2002 estimate).

pep /pep/ *n* liveliness or vigour (*informal*) [Early 20C. Shortening of PEPPER] —**peppy** *adj*
pep up *vt* to make somebody or something more lively, energetic, or interesting (*informal*)

PEP /pep/ *n* a tax-free investment plan that allows small investors to own shares in UK companies. Full form **Personal Equity Plan**

peperomia /péppə rṓmi ə/ *n* a plant often cultivated as a house plant for its heavily veined foliage. Native to: tropical and subtropical regions worldwide. Genus: *Peperomia*. [Late 19C. < modern Latin < Greek *peperi* (see PEPPER)]

pepino /pə peénō/ (*plural* **-nos**) *n* **1.** **OVAL FRUIT** an aubergine-shaped purple-streaked fruit with a flavour resembling that of a melon **2.** **SPINY PLANT** a plant with spiny foliage that bears pepinos. Native to: Peru. Latin name: *Solanum muricatum.* **3.** **CONE-SHAPED HILL** a steep conical hill, especially in Puerto Rico [Mid-19C. Via American Spanish < Spanish, 'cucumber' < Latin *pepo* (see PUMPKIN)]

Pepin the Short /pépin/ (714?–768) king of the Franks (751–768). He was the founder of the Carolingian dynasty and the father of Charlemagne.

pepla **CLOTHING** plural of **peplum**

peplos /péppləss/, **peplus** *n* a loose-fitting garment worn by women in ancient Greece, draped in folds around the shoulders and reaching the waist [Late 18C. < Greek]

peplum /péppləm/ (*plural* **-lums** or **-la** /-lə/) *n* a short flared ruffle attached to the waist of a jacket or blouse [Late 17C. < Latin < Greek *peplos* 'peplos']

pepo /peé pō/ (*plural* **-pos**) *n* a fruit of the gourd family, e.g. a melon, squash, pumpkin, or cucumber, that typically has a firm or hard rind, a large number of flat seeds, and soft watery flesh [Mid-19C. < Latin (see PUMPKIN)]

pepper (sense 2)

pepper /péppər/ *n* **1.** **SEASONING** a hot condiment or seasoning made from the ground dried berries of a tropical climbing plant. Black pepper is made from berries that are dried before they ripen, and white pepper from berries that ripen before being dried. **2.** **PLANT WITH BERRIES** a tropical climbing plant whose berries are dried for use as pepper, e.g. betel, cubeb, or kava. Genus: *Piper*. **3.** **HOLLOW VEGETABLE** a green, red, purple, or yellow fruit that is hollow with firm walls containing seeds and has mild or pungent flesh that can be eaten either raw or cooked as a vegetable **4.** **PLANT WITH EDIBLE PODS** a tropical plant of the nightshade family that produces mild or pungent peppers. Genus: *Capsicum*. **5.** **PUNGENT CONDIMENT** a seasoning such as cayenne pepper or chilli powder made from the more strongly pungent peppers ■ *v* (**-pers, -pering, -pered**) **1.** *vt* **SPRINKLE FOOD WITH PEPPER** to add or sprinkle pepper as a seasoning onto something **2.** *vt* **ASSAIL SOMEBODY OR SOMETHING** to bombard somebody or something with something **3.** **SPRINKLE SOMETHING AROUND** to scatter things liberally onto or among something (*often passive*) ○ *manuscripts peppered with typing errors* **4.** *vt* **MAKE SOMETHING LIVELY** to liven up something, e.g. a speech with wit [Old English *piper*, via W Germanic < Latin *piper* < Greek *peperi* < Sanskrit *pippalī* 'berry, peppercorn']

pepper-and-salt *adj* flecked with dark and light colours ○ *pepper-and-salt hair* N Am term **salt-and-pepper**

pepperbox /péppər boks/ *n* **1.** a cylindrical turret or cupola **2.** a small 18th-century pistol with several short revolving barrels

peppercorn /péppər kawrn/ *n* a small dried tropical berry that is ground to make pepper for use as a seasoning

peppercorn rent *n* a very low or nominal rent [< the custom of giving a peppercorn as a nominal rent]

peppered moth *n* a moth that is grey and speckled when found in rural areas and black in smoke-darkened industrial regions. Latin name: *Biston betularia.*

peppergrass /péppər graass/ *n* N Am same as **pepperwort** (sense 2)

pepperidge /péppərij/ *n* **TREES** same as **sour gum** [Mid-16C. Origin ?]

pepper mill *n* a kitchen utensil for storing and grinding peppercorns

peppermint

peppermint /péppər mint/ *n* **1.** **FLAVOURING** a flavouring prepared from the aromatic oil of a mint plant. Use: food industry, pharmaceuticals. (*often used before a noun*) **2.** **PEPPERMINT SWEET** a sweet flavoured with peppermint **3.** **AROMATIC HERB** a plant of the mint family whose dark-green downy leaves yield peppermint. Latin name: *Mentha piperita.*

pepperoni /péppə rṓni/ *n* a hard dry Italian sausage spiced with pepper, or a slice of this, often used on pizzas [Mid-20C. < Italian *peperone* 'red pepper' < Latin *piper* (see PEPPER)]

pepper pot *n* **1.** a small cylindrical container for ready-ground pepper with a perforated top for sprinkling. N Am term **peppershaker** **2.** a Guyanese or Caribbean stew made with meat, rice, and vegetables and seasoned with cassava syrup

peppershaker /péppər shaykər/, **pepper shaker** *n* N Am same as **pepper pot** (sense 1)

peppershrike /péppər shrīk/ *n* a small stocky bird with a thick hook-tipped beak. Native to: Central and South America. Genus: *Cyclarhis.*

pepper steak *n* a steak coated with crushed peppercorns before being fried or grilled

pepper tree *n* a tree of the cashew family that is cultivated for its bright red fruits. Native to: subtropical South America. Genus: *Schinus.*

pepperwort /péppər wurt/ *n* **1.** a freshwater fern with floating leaves and slender tangled stems that grows in marshes and ponds. Genus: *Marsilea.* **2.** a plant of the mustard family whose pungent lower leaves are used in salads and to season dishes. Genus: *Lepidium.* N Am term **peppergrass**

peppery /péppəri/ *adj* **1.** **CONTAINING PEPPER** strongly flavoured with pepper, or tasting of pepper **2.** **ANGRY** angry and critical **3.** **EASILY ANNOYED** easily annoyed — **pepperiness** *n*

pep pill *n* any pill that contains a stimulant drug, especially an amphetamine (*dated informal*)

pepsin /pépsin/ *n* an enzyme produced in the stomach that breaks down proteins into simpler compounds. It can be extracted from the stomachs of calves and pigs for use as a digestive aid and in the production of cheese. [Mid-19C. < Greek *pepsis* 'digestion' < *peptein* 'to digest']

pepsinogen /pep sínnəjən/ *n* a substance produced by stomach glands that is converted into pepsin after contact with hydrochloric acid during digestion

pep talk *n* a short speech designed to give advice and generate enthusiasm, e.g. in a sports team or among a company's employees (*informal*)

peptic /péptik/ *adj* **1.** **HELPING DIGESTION** relating to or helping digestion **2.** **INVOLVING PEPSIN** relating to, caused by, or producing pepsin **3.** **OF STOMACH** relating to or involving the stomach, especially any digestive actions or their results [Mid-17C. < Greek *peptikos* 'capable of digesting' < *peptein* 'to digest']

peptic ulcer *n* erosion of the mucous membrane that lines the upper digestive tract, caused by excess secretion of acid in the stomach

peptidase /pépti dayz, -dayss/ *n* an enzyme that splits amino acids from peptides

peptide /pép tīd/ n a linear molecule made up of two or more linked amino acids [Early 20C. < German *Peptid*, back-formation < *Polypeptid* 'polypeptide' < *Pepton* (see PEPTONE)] —**peptidic** /pep tíddik/ adj

peptide bond n a linkage formed between the amino group of one amino acid and the carboxylic acid group of another

peptidoglycan /pep tídə glī kan/ n a large structural molecule found in the cell walls of bacteria

peptize /pép tīz/ (**-tizes, -tizing, -tized**), **peptise** (**-tises, -tising, -tised**) vt to disperse fine particles of one substance evenly throughout another substance to create a state intermediate between a suspension and a solution (**colloid**) [Mid-19C. < PEPTONE] —**peptizable** adj —**peptization** /pép tī záysh'n/ n —**peptizer** n

peptone /péptōn/ n a fragment of protein formed by enzyme action in the first stages of digestion [Mid-19C. Via German < Greek *pepton*, form of *peptos* 'digested' < *peptein* 'to digest']

peptonize /péptə nīz/ (**-nizes, -nizing, -nized**), **peptonise** (**-tonises, -tonising, -tonised**) vt to digest protein using an enzyme —**peptonization** /péptə nī záysh'n/ n —**peptonizer** n

Pepys /peeps/, **Samuel** (1633–1703) English diarist. His *Diary* (1660–69) includes detailed descriptions of the Plague and the Fire of London. —**Pepysian** /peeps i ən/ adj

> 'Memoirs are true and useful stars, whilst studied histories are those stars joined in constellations, according to the fancy of the poet.'
> [Samuel Pepys. Quoted in *Samuel Pepys' Naval Minutes*, J.R. Tanner (ed.); 1926 edition]

Pequot /peé kwot/ (*plural same* or **-quots**) n 1. a member of a Native North American people of eastern Connecticut 2. the Algonquian language of the Pequot people. Native speakers: 7,000. [Mid-17C. < Narraganset *Pequtôog* 'Pequot people'] —**Pequot** adj

per /pər/ prep 1. for each or for every thing mentioned ○ *50 miles per hour* 2. by, through, or according to something ○ *per instructions* [14C. < Latin]

per- prefix 1. through ○ *permeate* 2. containing a large proportion of an element ○ *peroxide* 3. containing an element in its highest oxidation state ○ *perchlorate* 4. containing a peroxide group ○ *peracid* [< Latin *per* 'through']

peracid /pər ássid/ n an acid in which one element is in its highest possible state of oxidation, e.g. perchloric acid or permanganic acid —**peracidity** /pérrə síddəti/ n

peradventure /púrəd vénchər/ adv possibly or perhaps (*archaic*) ■ n chance, doubt, or uncertainty (*literary*) [13C. < Old French *par aventure* 'by chance']

perambulate /pə rámbyoŏ layt/ (**-lates, -lating, -lated**) vti to walk about a place (*formal*) [Mid-16C. < Latin *perambulat-*, past participle of *perambulare* < *ambulare* 'to walk'] —**perambulation** /pə rámbyoŏ láysh'n/ n —**perambulatory** adj

perambulator /pə rámbyoŏ laytər/ n a baby's pram (*formal*)

per annum /pər ánnəm/ adv in or for every year, or by the year [< modern Latin, 'by the year']

per ardua ad astra /pər aárdyoo ə ad ástrə/ adv by endeavour to the stars [< Latin]

p/e ratio abbr price-earnings ratio

perborate /pər báw rayt/ n a salt compound of borate. Use: bleaching agent in washing powder.

percale /pər káyl/ n a smooth-textured closely woven cotton or polyester fabric. Use: sheets, clothing. [Early 17C. < French]

per capita /pər káppitə/ adv, adj by or for each person ○ *earnings per capita* [< modern Latin, 'per head']

perceive /pər seév/ (**-ceives, -ceiving, -ceived**) vt 1. to notice something, especially something that escapes the notice of others 2. to understand or interpret something in a particular way ○ *the action was perceived as a conciliatory gesture* [13C. Via variants of Old French *perçoivre* < Latin *percipere*, literally 'seize completely' < *capere* 'seize'] —**perceivable** adj —**perceivably** adv —**perceiver** n

per cent, **percent** /pər sént/ adv AS EXPRESSED IN HUNDREDTHS used to express a proportion of an amount in hundredths, sometimes represented by the symbol % ■ n (*plural same*; *plural* **-cent** /pronunc. *same*/) 1. ONE HUNDREDTH one hundredth part of something 2. PERCENTAGE a part or percentage [< Latin *per centum* 'by a hundred']

USAGE **per cent** – singular or plural? If *per cent* stands alone without a subsequent prepositional phrase, you can use a singular or a plural verb with it: *Sixty per cent is accounted for; Sixty per cent are accounted for.* If a prepositional phrase following *per cent* contains a noun or pronoun object regarded as a unit or a whole, use a singular verb: *Sixty per cent of the electorate is accounted for.* If the object of the preposition in such a phrase is regarded as a number of people or things, use a plural verb: *Sixty per cent of the votes are accounted for.*

percentage /pər séntij/ n 1. PROPORTION IN ONE-HUNDREDTHS a proportion stated in terms of one-hundredths that is calculated by multiplying a fraction by 100 2. PROPORTION a proportion of a group or set ○ *A larger percentage of pupils are choosing to go on to college.* 3. COMMISSION an amount charged that is based on the total amount involved, e.g. a commission charged on a sale, especially the commission that an agent charges a client (*informal*) 4. ADVANTAGE advantage or benefit (*informal*) ○ *There's no percentage in accepting the proposal.*

USAGE **percentage** – singular or plural? If you put the definite article *the* before *percentage*, you are stipulating just one percentage and thus you must use a singular verb: *The percentage of errors in this paper is unacceptably large.* If you put the indefinite article *a* before *percentage*, use a plural verb when the noun or pronoun in any subsequent prepositional phrase is regarded as a countable plural, not a unit or a whole: *A large percentage of the errors remain uncorrected.* If the noun or pronoun object in such a phrase is singular or is regarded as a unit or a whole, use a singular verb: *A large percentage of the electorate remains undecided.*

USAGE Do not use *a percentage of* (or *a proportion of*) when you mean 'some', as in *A percentage of the students have laptop computers*. The words *percentage* and *proportion* are meaningless unless qualified by an adjective such as *large* or *small*, as in *a large proportion of the work*, and they are still best avoided where *many*, *much*, *a few*, or *a little* can be used instead.

percentile /pər sén tīl/ n in statistics, a value on a scale of one hundred that indicates whether a distribution is above or below it

percept /púr sept/ n something that is perceived by the senses [Mid-19C. < Latin *perceptum* 'something perceived' < past participle of *percipere* (see PERCEIVE)]

perceptible /pər séptəb'l/ adj large enough, great enough, or distinct enough to be noticed ○ *a perceptible difference* —**perceptibility** /pər séptə bílləti/ n —**perceptibly** adv

perception /pər sépsh'n/ n 1. PERCEIVING the process of using the senses to acquire information about the surrounding environment or situation ○ *the range of human perception* 2. RESULT OF PERCEIVING the result of the process of perception ○ *After watching the experiment closely, he noted his perceptions in his lab notebook.* 3. IMPRESSION an attitude or understanding based on what is observed or thought ○ *a news report that altered the public's perception of the issue* 4. POWERS OF OBSERVATION the ability to notice or discern things that escape the notice of most people 5. PSYCHOL NEUROLOGICAL PROCESS OF OBSERVATION AND INTERPRETATION any neurological process of acquiring and mentally interpreting information from the senses [14C. Via French < Latin *perception-* < *percipere* (see PERCEIVE)] —**perceptional** adj

perceptive /pər séptiv/ adj 1. possessing or showing keen insight and understanding 2. relating to perception, or capable of perceiving —**perceptively** adv —**perceptiveness** n —**perceptivity** /púr sep tívvəti/ n

perceptual /pər sépchoo əl/ adj relating to or involving sensory perception —**perceptually** adv

Perceval /púrssiv'l/, **John** (1923–2000) Australian painter and ceramicist. His early works were in-

fluenced by surrealism, and his later paintings are noted for their spontaneity and bright colours. Full name **Perceval, John de Burgh**

Perceval, **Spencer** (1762–1812) prime minister of Great Britain (1809–12). He served as chancellor of the exchequer (1807–09) before becoming prime minister. He was assassinated in the lobby of the House of Commons.

perch[1] /purch/ n 1. PLACE FOR BIRD TO SIT a place for a bird to land or rest on, e.g. a branch or a pole in a cage 2. RESTING PLACE any temporary resting place for a person or thing 3. SOLID MEASURE FOR STONE a unit of measure for the volume of stone, equal to about 0.7 cu. m/24 cu. ft 4. UNIT OF LENGTH a unit of length equal to 5.03 m/5½ yd 5. UNIT OF AREA a unit of area equal to 25.3 m²/30½ sq. yd 6. TEXTILES INSPECTION FRAME a frame that woven fabric is laid on to be inspected after weaving ■ v (**perches, perching, perched**) 1. vi SIT PRECARIOUSLY SOMEWHERE to sit or rest in a high or precarious position ○ *She perched on the edge of the desk.* 2. vt PUT SOMETHING IN HIGH PLACE to place something or somebody in a high or precarious position ○ *I looked up at the the old fort perched on the cliffs.* ○ *The child was perched on a high stool.* 3. vi SIT ON PERCH to land or rest on a perch (*refers to birds*) ○ *A pair of doves perched on the apple tree.* 4. vti TEXTILES LAY ITEM ON PERCH to place woven fabric on a perch to inspect after weaving, or be placed on a perch [13C. Via French < Latin *pertica* 'pole, stick'] —**percher** n ◇ **fall off your perch** to die (*informal*) ◇ **knock somebody off his** *or* **her perch** to make somebody feel less proud or superior

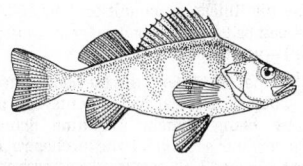

perch

perch[2] /purch/ (*plural* **perches** or *same*) n 1. a freshwater fish with rough scales and two dorsal fins, one spiny and one soft. Native to: North America, Europe. Genus: *Perca*. 2. the flesh of a perch used as food [14C. Via French < Latin *perca* < Greek *perkē*]

perchance /pər chaánss/ adv (*archaic or literary*) 1. possibly or perhaps 2. by chance [14C. < Anglo-Norman *par chance* 'by chance']

Percheron /púrshə ron/ n a large black or grey draught horse belonging to a breed originating in France [Late 19C. < French, 'of the Percheron breed', after *le Perche*, region of N France]

perching bird n BIRDS same as **passerine**

perchlorate /pər kláw rayt/ n a salt or ester of perchloric acid

perchloric acid /pər kláwrik-/ n a colourless acid of chlorine that is explosive under some conditions. Use: oxidizing agent in laboratory work. Formula: $HClO_4$.

perchloride /pər kláw rīd/ n a chloride of an element that contains more chlorine than all other chlorides of the same element

perchloroethylene /pər kláwrō éthə leen/ n a colourless toxic organic solvent. Use: in dry-cleaning fluid. Formula: C_4Cl_4.

perciatelli /púrchə télli/ n pasta in the form of long thin tubes [< Italian dialect, literally 'little pierced thing' < *perciato*, past participle of *perciare* 'pierce' < French *percer* (see PIERCE)]

Percier /pursi áy/, **Charles** (1764–1838) French architect. With his partner Pierre-François Fontaine, he introduced the Empire style of architecture with monumental projects such as the *Arc du Carrousel* (1806).

~~**perceive**~~ incorrect spelling of **perceive**

percipient /pər síppi ənt/ *adj* showing keen understanding, observation, or discernment ■ *n* somebody or something capable of perceiving [Mid-17C. < Latin *percipient-*, present participle of *percipere* (see PERCEIVE)] —**percipiently** *adv*

percoid /púr koyd/ *adj* belonging or relating to a large suborder of bony spiny-finned fishes that includes the perch, sea bass, sunfishes, and red mullet. Suborder: Percoidea. [Mid-19C. < modern Latin *Percoidea* < Latin *perca* (see PERCH²)] —**percoid** *n*

percolate /púrkə layt/ (**-lates**, **-lating**, **-lated**) *v* 1. *vti* PASS THROUGH FILTER to make a liquid or gas pass through a filter or porous substance, or filter through in this way 2. *vi* PASS THROUGH SLOWLY to pass slowly through something or spread throughout a place ○ *I let the idea percolate through my mind.* 3. *vti* MAKE COFFEE to prepare coffee in a percolator, or undergo preparation in a percolator [Early 17C. < Latin *percolat-*, past participle of *percolare* 'sieve through' < *colare* 'to sieve' < *colum* 'sieve'] —**percolable** *adj* —**percolation** /púrkə láysh'n/ *n* —**percolative** /-lətiv/ *adj*

percolator /púrkə laytər/ *n* a coffeepot in which boiling water rises repeatedly through a narrow stem, spills over into a sieve containing coffee grounds, mixes with them, and returns to the water below

per contra /pər kóntrə/ *adv* on the other hand or by way of contrast [< Italian, 'by the opposite side']

per curiam /pər kyoóri am/ *adj* relating to a unanimous decision or opinion by a court of law or one given without the need to retire to consider a verdict [< Latin, 'by the court']

percuss /pər kúss/ (**-cusses**, **-cussing**, **-cussed**) *vt* to gently tap a part of a patient's body in order to diagnose an illness or condition [Mid-16C. < Latin *percuss-*, past participle of *percutere* 'strike hard' < *quatere* 'to strike'] —**percussor** *n*

percussion /pər kúsh'n/ *n* 1. MUSICAL INSTRUMENTS THAT ARE HIT the group of musical instruments that produce sound by being struck, including drums and cymbals, or the section of the orchestra playing such instruments 2. ACT OF DETONATING PERCUSSION CAP the striking or detonating of a percussion cap in a firearm 3. IMPACT the impact of one object striking another, or the noise or shock created when two objects hit each other (*formal*) 4. MED TAPPING OF BODY examination of part of a patient's body by tapping with the fingers to assess the presence of fluid, the enlargement of organs, or the solidification of normally hollow parts [Mid-16C. < Latin *percussion-* < *percuss-* (see PERCUSS)]

percussion cap *n* a detonator consisting of a thin metal case or strip of paper containing explosive powder, formerly used to fire some pistols

percussion instrument *n* a musical instrument that is hit to produce sound, e.g. a drum, cymbal, or triangle

percussionist /pər kúsh'nist/ *n* a musician who plays one or more percussion instruments

percussion lock *n* a mechanism on a gun that fires by striking a percussion cap

percussion tool *n* any power tool that delivers repeated heavy blows, e.g. a pneumatic drill

percussive /pər kússiv/ *adj* having the effect of an impact or a blow —**percussively** *adv* —**percussiveness** *n*

percutaneous /púrkyoõ táyni əss/ *adj* describes medication that is administered or absorbed through the skin —**percutaneously** *adv*

Percy /púrssi/, **Sir Henry** (1366–1403) English military leader. The son of the Earl of Northumberland, he rebelled against Henry IV, and was killed at the Battle of Shrewsbury. Known as **Harry Hotspur**

per diem /pər deé em, -dí em/ *adv*, *adj* by the day or every day ■ *n* a daily payment or allowance [< Latin, 'by the day']

perdition /pər dísh'n/ *n* 1. in some religions, the state of everlasting punishment in hell that sinners endure after death 2. hell itself as a location [14C. Directly or via French < late Latin *perdition-* < Latin *perdere* 'put to destruction' < *dare* 'put']

Triangle · Tambourine · Castanets · Snare drum · High-hat cymbals · Cymbal · Tom-tom · Bass drum · Tenor drum · Tubular bells · Maraca · Conga

percussion

père /pair/ *n* 1. the title given to Roman Catholic priests in France and French-speaking countries 2. in France and French-speaking countries, used after a man's surname to distinguish him from his son ○ *Alexandre Dumas père* [Early 17C. Via French < Latin *pater* 'father']

Père David's deer *n* a large reddish-grey deer that survives in captivity only. Native to: China. Latin name: *Elaphurus davidianus*. [Late 19C. After *Père Armand David* (1826–1900), French missionary and naturalist]

peregrinate /pérrəgri nayt/ (**-nates**, **-nating**, **-nated**) *vti* to travel around a place or from place to place (*literary*) [Late 16C. < Latin *peregrinat-*, past participle of *peregrinari* < *peregrinus* (see PEREGRINE)] —**peregrinator** *n*

peregrination /pérrəgri náysh'n/ *n* a journey or voyage (*literary*) [15C. Directly or via French < Latin *peregrination-* < *peregrinari* (see PEREGRINATE)]

peregrine /pérrəgrin/ *adj* coming from another region or country (*archaic*) ■ *n* BIRDS same as **peregrine falcon** [14C. Via French < Latin *peregrinus* 'travelling' < *pereger*, literally 'through fields' < *ager* 'field']

peregrine falcon *n* a large falcon with a blue-grey back and whitish underparts that often catches other birds in flight. Family: Falconidae. [Because formerly captured for hawking while migrating, rather than taken from their nests]

peremptory /pə rémptəri/ *adj* 1. DICTATORIAL expecting to be obeyed and unwilling to tolerate disobedience, 2. EXPRESSING URGENCY communicating urgency, command, or instruction 3. LAW CLOSED TO FURTHER CONSIDERATION OR ACTION ending, or not open to, discussion, debate, or further action [13C. Via Anglo-Norman < Latin *peremptorius* 'decisive' < Latin *perimere* 'take away completely' < *emere* 'buy'] —**peremptorily** *adv* —**peremptoriness** *n*

Perendale /pérrən dayl/ *n* a sheep of a New Zealand breed that is a cross between a Romney Marsh and a Cheviot

~~**perenial**~~ incorrect spelling of **perennial**

perennate /pérrə nayt, pə rénnayt/ (**-nates**, **-nating**, **-nated**) *vi* to survive from one growing season to the next with reduced or arrested growth between seasons [Early 17C. < Latin *perennat-*, past participle of *perennare* 'last for years' < *perennis* (see PERENNIAL)] —**perennation** /pérrə náysh'n/ *n*

perennial /pə rénni əl/ *adj* 1. LASTING OVER 2 YEARS describes a plant that lasts for more than two growing seasons, either dying back after each season, as some herbaceous plants do, or growing continuously, as some shrubs do 2. RECURRING OR ENDURING constantly recurring, or lasting for an indefinite time ○ *the perennial problem of litter* ■ *n* PERENNIAL PLANT a plant that lasts for more than two growing seasons [Mid-17C. < Latin *perennis* 'through the year' < *annus* 'year'] —**perennially** *adv*

perentie /pə rénti/, **perenty** (*plural* **-ties**) *n* a large burrowing lizard that has brown skin with yellow patches and can reach 2.5 m/8 ft in length. Native to: semidry and desert regions of central and northern Australia. Latin name: *Varanus giganteus*. [Early 20C. < Aboriginal, probably Diyari *pirindi*]

Peres /pé res/, **Shimon** (*b.* 1923) Polish-born Israeli politician. First elected to the Knesset in 1959, he has twice served as prime minister (1984–86 and 1995–96). With Yasir Arafat and Yitzhak Rabin he shared the Nobel Peace Prize (1994) for his part in negotiating the Israeli-Palestinian peace agreement (1983).

'Peace is made with yesterday's enemies. What is the alternative?'
[Shimon Peres, *Observer*; 16 October 1994]

perestroika /pérrə stróykə/ *n* the political and economic restructuring in the former Soviet Union initiated by Mikhail Gorbachev from about 1986. The stated aims included decentralized control of industry and agriculture and some private ownership. [Late 20C. < Russian, 'rebuilding, reconstruction']

Pérez de Cuéllar /pé ress də kwáy yaar/, **Javier** (*b.* 1920) Peruvian diplomat. He was the fifth secretary-general of the United Nations (1982–91).

'I am like a doctor…If the patient doesn't want all the pills I've recommended that's up to him. But I must warn that next time I will have to come as a surgeon with a knife.'
[Javier Pérez de Cuéllar, *Guardian*; 10 May 1986]

perf. *abbr* 1. GRAM perfect 2. STAMPS perforated 3. performance

perfect *adj* /púrfikt/ 1. WITHOUT FAULTS without errors, flaws, or faults ○ *in perfect condition* 2. COMPLETE AND WHOLE complete and lacking nothing essential 3. EXCELLENT OR IDEAL excellent or ideal in every way ○ *That's the perfect word to describe him.* 4. ESPECIALLY SUITABLE having all the necessary or typical characteristics required for a given situation ○ *the perfect candidate for the job* 5. UTTER OR ABSOLUTE used to emphasize the extent or degree of something ○ *a perfect nuisance* ○ *perfect happiness* 6. EXACT AS REPRODUCTION exactly reproducing an original ○ *a perfect likeness* 7. BOT WITH STAMENS AND PISTILS TOGETHER describes a flower that has functional stamens and pistils in the same flower 8. MATHS EXACTLY DIVISIBLE exactly divisible into equal roots 9. GRAM WITH VERB ACTION FINISHED describes a verb or verb aspect for an

action that is brought to a close **10.** MUSIC **OF MUSICAL INTERVALS** describes the differences in pitch between the fourth, the fifth, and the octave, common to both major and minor scales **11.** FUNGI **WITH SEXUAL AND ASEXUAL REPRODUCTION** describes a fungus that reproduces both sexually and asexually during its life cycle **12.** INSECTS **SEXUALLY MATURE** describes an insect that is sexually mature and completely differentiated ■ *vt* /pər fékt/ (**-fects, -fecting, -fected**) **1. BRING SOMETHING TO COMPLETION** to make something as good as possible, or bring something to completion ○ *They perfected the process last year.* **2.** PRINTING **FINISH PAGE** to complete a printed page by printing its reverse side ■ *n* /púrfikt/ GRAM **1. PERFECT ASPECT OF VERB** the perfect aspect of a verb **2. VERB IN PERFECT ASPECT** a verb that is in the perfect aspect [13C. Directly or via French < Latin *perfectus* < *perficere* 'make completely, finish' < *facere* 'make'] —**perfecter** *n* —**perfectible** /pər féktəb'l/ *adj* —**perfectness** *n*

perfecta /pər féktə/ *n UK* a type of bet, especially on dogs or horses, that pays if the two entries chosen come in first and second in the order predicted. ANZ, US term **exacta** [Late 20C. < American Spanish *quiniela perfecta* 'perfect quinella']

perfect binding *n* a method of bookbinding in which a book's pages are cut and then bound to the spine with glue, as opposed to being stitched uncut — **perfect bound** *adj*

perfect competition *n* a market condition in which a product is traded freely by buyers and sellers in large numbers without any individual transaction affecting the price

perfect game *n* a game of bowling in which 12 consecutive strikes occur

perfect gas *n* PHYS, CHEM same as **ideal gas**

perfection /pər féksh'n/ *n* **1. PERFECT NATURE** the quality of something that is as good or suitable as it can possibly be ○ *to strive for perfection as a goal* **2. PROCESS OF PERFECTING** the process of becoming or making something perfect ○ *The perfection of the technique will require another two years' research.* **3. EXAMPLE OR INSTANCE OF BEING PERFECT** somebody or something that reaches the highest attainable standard, or an instance of this ○ *His cooking that evening was sheer perfection.* ◇ **to perfection** perfectly ○ *The piece showed off her talent as a pianist to perfection.*

perfectionism /pər féksh'nizəm/ *n* **1.** rigorous rejection of anything less than perfect **2.** the doctrine that perfection is possible in human beings

perfectionist /pər féksh'nist/ *n* **1.** somebody who demands or seeks to achieve nothing less than perfection **2.** a believer in the philosophical doctrine of perfectionism

perfective /pə féktiv/ *adj* **1. TOWARDS PERFECTION** tending towards perfection **2.** GRAM **DESCRIBING COMPLETED ACTION** describes a verb that reports a completed action as opposed to an incomplete or continuing one ■ *n* GRAM **PERFECTIVE VERB OR ASPECT** a verb in the perfective aspect, or the aspect itself —**perfectively** *adv*

perfectly /púrfiktli/ *adv* **1.** in exactly the way desired or required ○ *That will suit her perfectly.* **2.** used to emphasize the degree or extent of something ○ *They're perfectly capable of managing on their own.*

perfect number *n* a positive whole number that is equal to the sum of the numbers that can be multiplied to give it as a result, excluding itself

perfecto /pər féktō/ (*plural* **-tos**) *n* a medium-sized cigar with tapered ends and a thick centre [Late 19C. < Spanish, 'perfect']

perfect participle *n* GRAM same as **past participle**

perfect pitch *n* MUSIC same as **absolute pitch** (sense 1)

perfect rhyme *n* **1.** a rhyme of two words that are pronounced the same but spelt differently and have different meanings, e.g. 'flew' and 'flue' **2.** a rhyme in which the stressed vowel and the consonants following it are the same, e.g. 'alive' and 'contrive'

perfect square *n* a rational number equal to the square of another rational number

perfervid /pur fúrvid/ *adj* extremely passionate or enthusiastic (*literary*) [Mid-19C. < modern Latin *perfervidus* 'extremely vehement' < Latin *fervidus* (see FERVID)] —**perfervidly** *adv* —**perfervidness** *n*

perfidy /púrfidi/ *n* treachery or deceit (*formal*) [Late 16C. < Latin *perfidia* < *perfidus* 'treacherous' < *per fidem decipere* 'deceive through trustingness' < *fides* 'faith, trust'] —**perfidious** /pər fíddi əss/ *adj*

perfin /púrfin/ *n* a postage stamp with initials perforated in it by a business or other organization to prevent misuse [Mid-20C. Blend of PERFORATED + INITIAL]

perfoliate /pər fōli ət/ *adj* describes a leaf that encloses a stem so that the stem seems to pass through it [Late 17C. < modern Latin *perfoliatus* 'through a leaf' < Latin *folium* 'leaf'] —**perfoliation** /pər fōli áysh'n/ *n*

perforate *v* /púrfə rayt/ (**-rates, -rating, -rated**) **1.** *vt* **PUNCTURE SOMETHING** to make a hole or holes in something **2.** *vt* **MAKE HOLES FOR TEARING** to make a line of small holes in paper to make tearing it easier **3.** *vi* **PENETRATE SOMETHING** to penetrate or pass through something ■ *adj* /púrfərət/ **1.** BIOL **WITH SMALL HOLES** dotted with small holes **2.** BIOL **WITH TRANSPARENT SPOTS** dotted with transparent spots **3.** STAMPS same as **perforated** (sense 1) [Mid-16C. < Latin *perforat-*, past participle of *perforare* 'bore through' < *forare* 'to bore'] —**perforable** *adj* —**perforative** /-rətiv/ *adj* —**perforator** *n* —**perforatory** /-rətəri/ *adj*

perforated /púrfə raytid/ *adj* **1.** pierced with a hole or holes, especially with a line of small holes designed to make tearing easy **2.** in which a hole has developed ○ *a perforated eardrum*

perforation /púrfə ráysh'n/ *n* **1. HOLE** a hole made in something **2. HOLES FOR TEARING** a small hole or series of holes punched into a piece of paper to make tearing easy **3. MAKING HOLES OR HAVING THEM** the act of making a hole or holes in something or the state of being perforated **4.** MED **FORMATION OF HOLE** the formation of a hole in an organ, tissue, or tube, usually as a consequence of disease

perforce /pər fáwrss/ *adv* unavoidably or as forced by circumstances (*archaic or literary*) [14C. < Old French *par force* 'by force']

perform /pər fáwrm/ (**-forms, -forming, -formed**) *v* **1.** *vt* **ACCOMPLISH SOMETHING** to carry out an action or accomplish a task, especially one requiring care or skill ○ *the surgeon who performed the operation* **2.** *vt* **FULFIL REQUIREMENT** to do what is stated or required **3.** *vti* **PRESENT ARTISTIC WORK** to present or enact an artistic work such as a piece of music or a play to an audience **4.** *vi* **FUNCTION OR BEHAVE** to function, operate, or behave in a particular way or to a particular standard ○ *athletes who perform best under pressure* [14C. < Anglo-Norman *parformer*, alteration of Old French *parfornir* 'accomplish completely' < *fournir* 'accomplish'] —**performable** *adj* —**performer** *n*

SYNONYMS ***perform, do, carry out, fulfil, discharge, execute***

CORE MEANING: to complete an action or task

perform to carry out an action or accomplish a task, especially one requiring care or skill ○ *Six patients had the procedure performed under local anaesthesia.* ○ *Each child was asked to perform the specified task during the specified time.* **do** to take action or accomplish something ○ *I've got a load of paperwork to do tomorrow.* ○ *A robot will do anything you ask it.* **carry out** to complete a task or activity, especially something that has been ordered or planned ○ *claims of negligence in failing to carry out the duties imposed by the law* **fulfil** to do what is necessary to bring about or achieve something expected, desired, or promised ○ *Organizations are created because individuals need each other in order to fulfil goals that they consider worthwhile.* **discharge** (*formal*) to undertake a duty, responsibility, or promise successfully ○ *The people who are delegated must be competent to discharge those duties.* **execute** to put an instruction or plan into effect, or to complete an action or procedure that requires skill and expertise ○ *If a state failed to develop or execute a satisfactory plan, the agency had the authority to intervene directly.*

performance /pər fáwrmənss/ *n* **1. ARTISTIC PRESENTATION** a presentation of an artistic work such as a play or piece of music to an audience **2. MANNER OF FUNCTIONING** the manner in which something or somebody functions, operates, or behaves ○ *a high-performance car* **3. WORKING EFFECTIVENESS** the way in which somebody does a job, judged by its effectiveness (*often used before a noun*) ○ *performance-related pay* **4. THING ACCOMPLISHED** something that is carried out or accomplished **5. ACCOMPLISHMENT OF SOMETHING** the act of carrying out or accomplishing something such as a task or action **6. DISPLAY OF BEHAVIOUR** a public display of behaviour that others find distasteful, e.g. an angry outburst that causes embarrassment (*informal*) **7. IRRITATING PROCEDURE** an irritating or troublesome procedure (*informal*) **8.** LING **LANGUAGE PRODUCED** the language that a speaker or writer actually produces, as distinct from his or her understanding of the language

performance art *n* art that combines two or more artistic media, a traditionally static medium such as sculpture or photography, and a dramatic medium such as recitation or improvisation — **performance artist** *n*

performance enhancer *n* a dietary supplement used by athletes to enhance bursts of high performance

performative /pər fáwrmətiv/ *adj* describes speech that constitutes an act of some kind, e.g. the phrase 'I promise I'll do my best', which constitutes a promise in itself ■ *n* a performative utterance [Mid-20C. After DECLARATIVE] —**performatively** *adv*

performing arts /pər fáwrming-/ *npl* the forms of art that involve theatrical performance, especially drama, dance, and music

perfume /púr fyoom/ *n* **1. FRAGRANT LIQUID** a fragrant liquid that is sprayed or rubbed on the skin or clothes to give a pleasant smell **2. PLEASANT SCENT** a pleasant smell, especially of flowers or plants ■ *vt* (**-fumes, -fuming, -fumed**) **GIVE SOMETHING PLEASANT SCENT** to give something a pleasant or sweet smell [Mid-16C. < French *parfum* < *parfumer* 'fill with fumes or perfume' < obsolete Italian *parfumare*, literally 'smoke through' < *fumare* 'to smoke'] —**perfumed** *adj* —**perfumey** *adj*

SYNONYMS See ***smell.***

perfumer /pər fyoōmər/ *n* a manufacturer or seller of perfumes

perfumery /pər fyoōməri/ (*plural* **-ies**) *n* **1. PERFUMES** perfumes in general **2. PLACE MAKING OR SELLING PERFUMES** a place of business where perfumes are manufactured or sold **3. MAKING OF PERFUMES** the manufacture of perfumes, or the art of making perfumes

perfunctory /pər fúngktəri/ *adj* **1.** done as a matter of duty or custom, without thought, attention, or genuine feeling ○ *a perfunctory kiss* **2.** done hastily or superficially ○ *a perfunctory search* [Late 16C. < late Latin *perfunctorius* < Latin *perfungi* 'work through' < *fungi* 'perform'] —**perfunctorily** *adv* —**perfunctoriness** *n*

perfuse /pər fyoōz/ (**-fuses, -fusing, -fused**) *vt* **1.** to spread throughout something, or spread a substance or quality such as liquid, light, or colour throughout something **2.** to introduce a liquid into tissue or an organ by circulating it through blood vessels or other channels within the body [Early 16C. < Latin *perfus-*, past participle of *perfundere* 'pour over' < *fundere* 'pour'] —**perfused** *adj* —**perfusion** *n* —**perfusive** *adj*

Pergamum /púrgəməm/ ancient city in northwestern Asia Minor, in present-day Turkey. It was a major cultural centre in the 3rd and 2nd centuries BC.

pergola

pergola /púrgələ/ *n* a frame structure consisting of colonnades or posts with a latticework roof, designed to support climbing plants [Late 17C. Via Italian < Latin *pergula*]

perhaps /pər háps/; *informal* /praps/ CORE MEANING: an adverb expressing uncertainty, or indicating that something is possibly true or may possibly happen, often used to make remarks appear less definite ○ *Perhaps it will be warmer later.* ○ *He wondered if perhaps he had been mistaken.* ○ *Perhaps his best-known ceramic work is his public mural 'Voyage'.* *adv* **1.** used to show approximation ○ *The house is perhaps five miles from here.* **2.** used in requests and suggestions in order to sound more polite ○ *Perhaps we should help Dad in the kitchen.* [15C. < PER 'by' + plural of HAP[1] 'chance']

peri /peéri/ *n* **1.** in Persian mythology, a beautiful supernatural being descended from the fallen angels **2.** a graceful and beautiful girl or woman (*literary*) [Late 18C. < Persian *perī*]

peri- *prefix* **1.** around, surrounding ○ *pericarp* **2.** near ○ *perilune* ○ *perinatal* [< Greek *peri* 'around, about' < Indo-European]

perianth /pérri anth/ *n* the outer structure of a flower, made up of the corolla, the calyx, or both [Early 19C. Via French < modern Latin *perianthium* < Greek *peri* 'around' + *anthos* 'flower']

periapt /pérri apt/ *n* a charm worn to protect the wearer from harm [Late 16C. Via French < Greek *periapton* 'something fastened around' < *peri* 'around' + *haptein* 'fasten']

periastron /pérri ás tron/ *n* the points in space and time in the orbits of two stars in a binary system at which they are closest together [Mid-19C. < PERI- + Greek *astron* 'star', after PERIHELION]

pericarditis /pérri kaar dítiss/ *n* inflammation of the pericardium —**pericarditic** /-díttik/ *adj*

pericardium /pérri kaárdi əm/ (*plural* **-dia** /-di ə/) *n* a fibrous membrane that forms a sac surrounding the heart and attached portions of the main blood vessels [Late 16C. Via medieval Latin < Greek *perikardion* < *peri* 'around' + *kardia* 'heart'] —**pericardiac** *adj* —**pericardial** *adj*

pericarp /pérri kaarp/ *n* the part of a fruit that surrounds the seed or seeds, including the skin, flesh, and, in some fruits, the core —**pericarpial** /pérri kaárpi əl/ *adj* —**pericarpic** /pérri kaárpik/ *adj*

perichondrium /pérri kóndri əm/ (*plural* **-dria** /-dri ə/) *n* the fibrous membrane that covers the surface of cartilage except at joints [Mid-18C. < modern Latin < Greek *peri* 'around' + *khondros* 'cartilage'] —**perichondrial** *adj*

periclase /pérri klayss/ *n* a colourless, grey, green, or yellow magnesium oxide mineral. Source: limestone. [Mid-19C. Directly or via German *Periklas* < modern Latin *periclasia* < Greek *peri* 'around' + *klasis* 'breaking'; from its perfect cleavage] —**periclastic** /pérri klástik/ *adj*

Pericles /pérri kleez/ (495?–429? BC) Athenian political leader. He dominated Athens during its golden age by virtue of his oratory skills and honesty. He ordered the construction of the Parthenon and established Athens as a great centre of art and literature. —**Periclean** /pérri kleé ən/ *adj*

> 'Our love of what is beautiful does not lead to extravagance; our love of the things of the mind does not make us soft.'
> [Pericles, *Histories*, Rex Warner (tr.); 1961]

periclinal /pérri klín'l/ *adj* **1.** used to describe a fold in sedimentary rocks that appears as a regular dome on the surface of the Earth **2.** describes cell walls that are parallel to the outer surface of a plant part [Late 19C. < Greek *periklinēs* 'sloping all around' < *peri* 'all around' + *klinein* 'to slope']

pericline /pérri klīn/ *n* **1.** a dome-shaped fold in sedimentary rock **2.** a variety of the mineral albite that forms long white crystals [Mid-19C. < Greek *periklinēs* (see PERICLINAL)]

pericope /pə ríkəpi/ *n* an extract from a book, especially a passage from the Bible selected for reading during a Roman Catholic Mass [Mid-17C. Via late Latin < Greek *perikopē* 'section' < *peri* 'around' + *koptein* 'to cut'] —**pericopic** /pérri kóppik/ *adj*

pericranium /pérri kráyni əm/ (*plural* **-nia** /-ni ə/) *n* the membrane of connective tissue that surrounds the skull [Early 16C. Via modern Latin < Greek *perikranion* < *peri* 'round' + *kranion* 'skull'] —**pericranial** *adj*

pericycle /pérri sīk'l/ *n* the outer layer of plant tissue surrounding the inner core of the roots and stems of plants (**stele**) that conducts moisture and nutrients around the plant [Late 19C. Via French < Greek *perikuklos* 'circling around' < *peri* 'around' + *kuklos* 'circle'] —**pericyclic** /pérri síklik/ *adj*

periderm /pérri durm/ *n* the outer layer of plant tissue in woody roots and stems —**peridermal** /pérri dúrm'l/ *adj* —**peridermic** /pérri dúrmik/ *adj*

peridium /pə ríddi əm/ (*plural* **-ia** /-i ə/) *n* the covering of the spore-bearing organ in many kinds of fungi [Early 19C. Via modern Latin < Greek *pēridion* 'small leather wallet' < *pēra* 'wallet']

peridot /pérri dot/ *n* a pale green or yellowish-green semiprecious stone that is a transparent form of olivine. Use: gems. [Early 18C. < French]

peridotite /pérri dō tīt/ *n* a coarse-grained igneous rock that is rich in iron and magnesium. It is found in meteorites and also on Earth, where it is thought to form much of the Earth's core. —**peridotitic** /pérri dō títtik/ *adj*

perigee /pérri jee/ *n* the point in the orbit of a satellite, moon, or planet at which it comes nearest to the object it is orbiting [Late 16C. Via French < late Greek *perigeion* < *perigeios* 'close round the earth' < Greek *peri* 'around' + *gē* 'earth'] —**perigeal** /pérri jeé əl/ *adj* —**perigean** /pérri jeé ən/ *adj*

periglacial /pérri gláysh'l/ *adj* relating to or found in a region that borders on a glacier

Périgueux /pérri gō/ town in southwestern France, in Dordogne Department, Aquitaine Region. Population: 30,193 (1999).

perigynous /pə ríjjinəss/ *adj* describes a flower that has petals, stamens, and sepals arranged around a cup-shaped receptacle that contains the ovary, as have the flowers of cherries and roses —**perigyny** *n*

perihelion /pérri heéli ən/ (*plural* **-lia** /-li ə/) *n* the point in the orbit of a planet or other astronomical body at which it comes closest to the Sun [Mid-17C. Alteration of modern Latin *perihelium* < Greek *peri* 'around' + *hēlios* 'sun'] —**perihelial** *adj*

perikaryon /pérri kárri ən/ (*plural* **-ya** /-i ə/) *n* the part of a nerve cell that contains the nucleus —**perikaryal** *adj*

peril /pérrəl/ *n* **1.** exposure to risk of harm **2.** a source of possible or imagined harm [13C. Via French < Latin *periculum* 'experiment, risk' < Indo-European, 'try']

perilous /pérrələss/ *adj* involving exposure to very great danger [13C. Via Old French *perillous* < Latin *periculosus* < *periculum* (see PERIL)] —**perilously** *adv* —**perilousness** *n*

perilune /pérri loon/ *n* the point at which a planet or other body orbiting the Moon comes closest to the Moon's surface [Mid-20C. < PERI- + Latin *luna* 'moon']

perilymph /pérri limf/ *n* the fluid that fills the space between the membranous labyrinth and the bony labyrinth in the inner ear

perimeter /pə rímmitər/ *n* **1.** BOUNDARY ENCLOSING AREA a boundary that encloses an area **2.** OUTER EDGE OF TERRITORY the outer edge of an area of defended territory **3.** MATHS CURVE ENCLOSING AREA a curve enclosing an area on a plane, or the length of such a curve [Late 16C. Via Latin < Greek *perimetros* < *peri* 'around' + *metron* 'measure'] —**perimetric** /pérri méttrik/ *adj* —**perimetrical** *adj* —**perimetrically** *adv*

USAGE See *parameter*.

perimorph /pérri mawrf/ *n* a mineral that crystallizes around a grain of a different kind of mineral —**perimorphic** /pérri máwrfik/ *adj* —**perimorphism** *n* —**perimorphous** *adj*

perimysium /pérri mízzi əm/ (*plural* **-sia** /-zi ə/) *n* the sheath of connective tissue that surrounds bundles of muscle fibres [Mid-19C. < PERI- + Greek *mus* 'muscle']

perinatal /pérri náyt'l/ *adj* relating to or occurring during the period around childbirth, specifically from around week 28 of pregnancy to around one month after the birth —**perinatally** *adv*

perinatology /pérri nay tólləji/ *n* a medical speciality concerned with the care and treatment of mother and infant immediately prior to, during, and following childbirth —**perinatologist** *n*

perinephrium /pérri néffri əm/ (*plural* **-ria** /-ri ə/) *n* the fatty tissue that surrounds the kidney [Late 19C. < PERI- + Greek *nephros* 'kidney'] —**perinephric** *adj*

perineum /pérri neé əm/ (*plural* **-nea** /-neé ə/) *n* the region of the abdomen surrounding the urogenital and anal openings [Mid-17C. Via late Latin < Greek *perinaion* < *peri* 'around' + *inan* 'excrete'] —**perineal** *adj*

perineurium /pérri nyóori əm/ (*plural* **-ria** /-ri ə/) *n* the sheath of connective tissue that surrounds a bundle of nerve fibres [Mid-19C. < PERI- + NEURO-] —**perineurial** *adj*

period /peéri əd/ *n* **1.** LENGTH OF TIME an interval or portion of time **2.** IDENTIFIABLE TIME an interval of time that is identified by what happens or exists during it ○ *the early Victorian period* **3.** TIMETABLE SECTION a division of a schedule or timetable, e.g. a portion of the school day **4.** DIVISION OF GAME a division of playing time in some sports **5.** MENSTRUATION TIME an occurrence of menstruation **6.** GEOL UNIT OF GEOLOGICAL TIME a division of geological time shorter than an era and longer than an epoch **7.** *N Am* GRAM same as **full stop** (sense 1) **8.** PHYS TIME FOR SINGLE CYCLE the time required for one complete cycle of a repetitive system, e.g. the rotation of a star or the movement of an electromagnetic wave. Symbol **T** **9.** MATHS INTERVAL BETWEEN EQUAL VALUES the interval between the points at which the values of a periodic function are equal **10.** CHEM ROW IN PERIODIC TABLE a horizontal row of elements in the periodic table **11.** LITERAT UNIT OF POETIC RHYTHM one of the longer units in the classical system of analysing the rhythms of poetry **12.** MUSIC MUSICAL PASSAGE a long passage of music consisting of two or more contrasting musical phrases ■ *interj* SHOWING FINALITY a word added to the end of a statement to emphasize that the speaker will not discuss it further (*informal*) ○ *I'm not going, period!* ■ *adj* RELATING TO HISTORICAL TIME belonging to or intended to suggest a historical time ○ *actors in period costume* [14C. Via French < Greek *periodos*, literally 'way around' < *hodos* 'way']

periodic /peéri óddik/ *adj* **1.** OCCASIONAL recurring or reappearing from time to time **2.** REGULAR occurring or appearing at regular intervals or in regular cycles **3.** INVOLVING PERIODS associated with or occurring in periods [Mid-17C. Via French and Latin < Greek *periodikos* < *periodos* (see PERIOD)] —**periodically** *adv*

SYNONYMS ***periodic, intermittent, occasional, sporadic***

CORE MEANING: recurring over a period of time

periodic recurring or reappearing from time to time ○ *carry out periodic inspections* ○ *El Niño, a periodic weather pattern* **intermittent** occurring at irregular intervals ○ *The pain was usually intermittent, although in some patients it was continuous.* ○ *Thunder, lightning, and intermittent rain delayed the start of the tournament.* **occasional** occurring infrequently at irregular intervals ○ *Her family kept in contact by writing, telephoning, and occasional visits.* ○ *He sat silent, producing only an occasional suppressed grunt.* **sporadic** occurring at intervals that have no apparent pattern ○ *Despite a truce announced last month, sporadic fighting continues.* ○ *Prior to the mid-1960s, pollution issues received only limited and sporadic attention from the general public.*

periodic acid /pur ī óddik-/ *n* any strongly oxidizing acid of iodine [< PER- + IODIC]

periodical /peéri óddik'l/ *n* MAGAZINE a magazine or journal published at regular intervals, especially weekly, monthly, or quarterly ■ *adj* **1.** PUBLISHED REGULARLY published at regular intervals **2.** OCCASIONAL recurring or reappearing from time to time

periodic function *n* a mathematical function whose value is the same at regular intervals

periodicity /peéri ə díssəti/ *n* **1.** recurrence at regular intervals **2.** similarity between the properties of chemical elements that are close to each other in the periodic table

periodic law *n* the law stating that chemical elements fall into groups sharing similar properties when they are arranged according to atomic number

periodic sentence *n* in rhetoric, a complex sentence in which the main clause is left unfinished until

PERIODIC TABLE

Group → Period ↓	1	2	3	4	5	6	7	8	9	10	11	12	13	14	15	16	17	18
1	1 **H** 1.01																	2 **He** 4.00
2	3 **Li** 6.94	4 **Be** 9.01											5 **B** 10.81	6 **C** 12.01	7 **N** 14.01	8 **O** 16.00	9 **F** 19.00	10 **Ne** 20.18
3	11 **Na** 22.99	12 **Mg** 24.31											13 **Al** 26.98	14 **Si** 28.09	15 **P** 30.97	16 **S** 32.06	17 **Cl** 35.45	18 **Ar** 39.95
4	19 **K** 39.10	20 **Ca** 40.08	21 **Sc** 44.96	22 **Ti** 47.90	23 **V** 50.94	24 **Cr** 52.00	25 **Mn** 54.94	26 **Fe** 55.85	27 **Co** 58.93	28 **Ni** 58.71	29 **Cu** 63.55	30 **Zn** 65.38	31 **Ga** 69.72	32 **Ge** 72.59	33 **As** 74.92	34 **Se** 78.96	35 **Br** 79.90	36 **Kr** 83.80
5	37 **Rb** 85.47	38 **Sr** 87.62	39 **Y** 88.91	40 **Zr** 91.22	41 **Nb** 92.91	42 **Mo** 95.94	43 **Tc** 98.91	44 **Ru** 101.07	45 **Rh** 102.91	46 **Pd** 106.40	47 **Ag** 107.87	48 **Cd** 112.40	49 **In** 114.82	50 **Sn** 118.69	51 **Sb** 121.75	52 **Te** 127.60	53 **I** 126.90	54 **Xe** 131.30
6	55 **Cs** 132.91	56 **Ba** 137.34	* 57 **La** 138.91	72 **Hf** 178.49	73 **Ta** 180.95	74 **W** 183.85	75 **Re** 186.2	76 **Os** 190.2	77 **Ir** 192.22	78 **Pt** 195.09	79 **Au** 196.97	80 **Hg** 200.59	81 **Tl** 204.37	82 **Pb** 207.20	83 **Bi** 208.98	84 **Po** 209	85 **At** (210)	86 **Rn** (222)
7	87 **Fr** (223)	88 **Ra** (226)	** 89 **Ac** (226)	104 **Rf** (261)	105 **Db** (262)	106 **Sg** (266)	107 **Bh** (264)	108 **Hs** (269)	109 **Mt** (268)	110 **Ds** (271)	111 **Uuu** (272)	112 **Uub** (277)	113 **Uut** (284)	114 **Uuq**	115 **Uup** (288)	116 **Uuh**	117 **Uus**	118 **Uuo**

Chemical elements are indicated by their symbols. The numbers above the elements are the atomic numbers, and those below are the atomic weights (those in parentheses are for the longest-lived isotopes, while those for Np, Pa, and Tc are for the most technologically important isotopes). The lanthanides and actinides do not fit easily into any group and are thus shown separate from the main table.

Elements 113 and 115 are reported but unconfirmed; 117 is unknown; the report of 118 has been retracted, throwing doubt on 116.

Lanthanides *	57 **La** 138.91	58 **Ce** 140.12	59 **Pr** 140.91	60 **Nd** 144.24	61 **Pm** (145)	62 **Sm** 150.40	63 **Eu** 151.96	64 **Gd** 157.25	65 **Tb** 158.93	66 **Dy** 162.50	67 **Ho** 164.93	68 **Er** 167.26	69 **Tm** 168.93	70 **Yb** 173.04	71 **Lu** 174.97
Actinides **	89 **Ac** (226)	90 **Th** 232.04	91 **Pa** 231.04	92 **U** 283.04	93 **Np** 237.05	94 **Pu** (244)	95 **Am** (243)	96 **Cm** (247)	97 **Bk** (247)	98 **Cf** (251)	99 **Es** (254)	100 **Fm** (257)	101 **Md** (258)	102 **No** (255)	103 **Lr** (256)

the end in order to create the effect of anticipation or suspense

periodic system *n* the system of arranging chemical elements in a table according to the periodic law

periodic table *n* a table of the chemical elements arranged according to their atomic numbers

periodization /pèeri ə dī záysh'n/, **periodisation** *n* the dividing of history into distinct and identifiable periods

periodontal /pérri ō dónt'l/ *adj* relating to or affecting the tissues that surround the neck and root of a tooth [Mid-19C. < PERI- + Greek *odont-* 'tooth'] —**periodontally** *adv*

periodontics /pérri ō dóntiks/, **periodontology** /pérri ō don tólləji/ *n* the branch of dentistry concerned with the treatment of diseases of the gums and other periodontal tissues (*takes a singular verb*) —**periodontic** *adj*—**periodontical** *adj*—**periodontically** *adv*—**periodontist** *n*

period piece *n* something, especially a curio or a work of art, that dates from or evokes a historical period, often something with no other value

perionychium /pérri ō níki əm/ (*plural* **-chia** /-ki ə/) *n* the areas of skin that surround a fingernail or toenail [Early 20C. < modern Latin < Greek *peri* 'around' < *onukh-* 'nail']

periosteum /pérri ósti əm/ (*plural* **-tea** /-ti ə/) *n* the sheath of connective tissue that surrounds all bones except those at joints [Late 16C. Via modern Latin < Greek *periosteon* < *peri* 'around' + *osteon* 'bone'] —**periosteal** *adj*

periostitis /pérri o stítiss/ *n* inflammation of the periosteum —**periostitic** /pérri o stíttik/ *adj*

periostracum /pérri o óstrəkəm/ (*plural* **-ca** /-kə/) *n* the hard outer layer of the shell of some molluscs, especially freshwater molluscs [Mid-19C. < modern Latin < Greek *peri* 'around' + *ostrakon* 'shell']

periotic /pérri ótik/ *adj* involving the area around the ear, especially the bones around the inner ear

peripatetic /pérripə téttik/ *adj* travelling from place to place, especially working in several establishments and travelling between them ■ *n* a peripatetic worker, especially a teacher who travels between schools [Early 17C. Via French or Latin < Greek *peripatētikos* < *peripatein* 'walk around' < *patein* 'to walk'] —**peripatetically** *adv*

Peripatetic *adj* belonging or relating to the school of philosophy founded by Aristotle, who gave lectures while walking about the Lyceum in Athens ■ *n* a member of the Aristotelian school of philosophy

peripatus /pə ríppətəss/ *n* ZOOL same as **onychophoran** [Mid-19C. Via modern Latin < Greek *peripatos* < *peri* 'around' + *patos* 'way']

peripheral /pə rífferəl/ *adj* 1. AT EDGE at or relating to the edge of something, as opposed to its centre 2. NOT SIGNIFICANT minor or incidental in importance or relevance 3. ANAT NEAR SURFACE near the surface of an organ or the body ■ *n* COMPUT **PERIPHERAL PIECE OF HARDWARE** a piece of computer hardware such as a printer or a disk drive that is external to but con-

trolled by a computer's central processing unit — **peripherally** *adv*

peripheral nervous system *n* the part of the nervous system that lies outside the brain and spinal cord

periphery /pə ríffəri/ (*plural* **-ies**) *n* **1.** BOUNDARY the area around the edge of a place **2.** SURFACE the surface of an object **3.** POSITION OF LITTLE INVOLVEMENT the position or state of having only a minor involvement in something [Late 16C. Via late Latin < Greek *peripheria* < *peripherēs*, literally 'carrying around' < *pherein* 'carry']

periphrasis /pə ríffrəssiss/ (*plural* **-rases** /-rə seez/) *n* **1.** the use of excessively long or indirect language in order to say something **2.** an expression that states something indirectly [Mid-16C. Via Latin < Greek < *periphrazein*, literally 'explain around' < *phrazein* 'explain']

periphrastic /pérri frástik/ *adj* **1.** relating to or using periphrasis **2.** formed using two or more words rather than an inflected form, especially used to describe a verb tense formed using an auxiliary verb rather than by inflecting the main verb. 'Did you have' is a periphrastic equivalent of archaic 'had you'. [Early 19C. < Greek *periphrastikos* < *periphrazein* (see PERIPHRASIS)] —**periphrastically** *adv*

periphyton /pə ríffi ton/ *n* plants and animals that live in water attached to rocks and other submerged objects [Mid-20C. Probably < PERI- + Greek *phuton* 'plant', after *plankton*]

periplasm /pérri plazəm/ *n* the area of a cell that lies immediately inside the cell wall but outside the plasma membrane

periplast /pérri plast/ *n* a cell wall or cell membrane

periproct /pérri prokt/ *n* the area surrounding the anus of some invertebrate animals such as sea urchins [Late 19C. < PERI- + Greek *prōktos* 'anus']

peripteral /pə ríptərəl/ *adj* describes a classical building that has a single row of columns on all sides [Early 19C. < Greek *peripteros* 'with a wing around' < *pteron* 'wing']

perique /pə reék/ *n* a strongly flavoured tobacco grown in Louisiana. It is usually mixed with other tobaccos. [Late 19C. < Louisiana French]

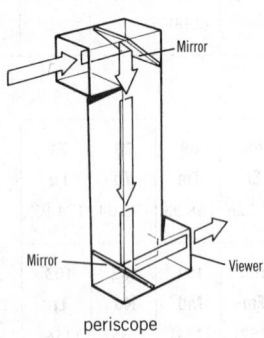

periscope

periscope /pérri skōp/ *n* a long tubular optical instrument, e.g. on a submarine, that uses lenses, prisms, and mirrors to allow a viewer to see objects not in a direct line of sight

periscopic /pérri skóppik/ *adj* **1.** describes a lens that has a wide field of view **2.** relating to or using a periscope —**periscopically** *adv*

perish /pérrish/ (**-ishes, -ishing, -ished**) *v* **1.** *vi* DIE to die, e.g. because of harsh conditions or an accident **2.** *vi* DISAPPEAR to come to an end or cease to exist (*formal*) **3.** *vti* DECAY to deteriorate or decay, or make a material such as rubber deteriorate or decay [13C. < French *périss-*, stem of *périr* < Latin *perire* 'go completely' < *ire* 'go']

perishable /pérrishəb'l/ *adj* liable to decay, rot, or spoil ■ *n* something that is perishable, especially an item of food —**perishability** /pérrishə bílləti/ *n* — **perishably** *adv*

perished /pérrisht/ *adj* feeling extremely cold (*informal*)

perisher /pérrishər/ *n* an annoying person, especially a naughty child (*dated informal*)

perishing /pérrishing/ *adj* **1.** extremely cold ○ *a perishing easterly wind* **2.** used to emphasize how an-

noying something or somebody is (*dated informal*) ○ *a perishing nuisance* —**perishingly** *adv*

perisperm /pérri spurm/ *n* nutritive tissue from a plant nucleus that surrounds the seed embryo — **perispermal** /pérri spúrm'l/ *adj*

perissodactyl /pə ríssō dáktil/ *n* a large animal that belongs to the order of mammals with hooves and an odd number of toes, which includes horses, rhinoceroses, and tapirs. Order: Perissodactyla. [Mid-19C. < modern Latin *Perissodactyla* < Greek *perissos* 'uneven' + *daktulos* 'finger, toe'] —**perissodactyl** *adj* — **perissodactylous** *adj*

peristalsis /pérri stálssiss/ (*plural* **-stalses** /-stáls seez/) *n* the waves of involuntary muscle contractions that transport food, waste matter, or other contents through a tube-shaped organ such as the intestine [Mid-19C. < modern Latin < Greek *peristaltikos* 'clasping, compressing' < *peristellein* 'place around' < *stellein* 'to place'] —**peristaltic** *adj* —**peristaltically** *adv*

peristome /pérri stōm/ *n* the mouthparts of an invertebrate such as an earthworm or echinoderm — **peristomal** /pérri stōm'l/ *adj* —**peristomial** *adj*

peristyle /pérri stīl/ *n* **1.** a line of columns (**colonnade**) that encircles a building or a courtyard **2.** a building or courtyard that has a peristyle [Early 17C. Via French < Greek *peristulos* 'having columns around' < *stulos* 'column'] —**peristylar** /pérri stīlər/ *adj*

perithecium /pérri theéssi əm/ (*plural* **-cia** /-si ə/) *n* in some kinds of fungus, a flask-shaped fruiting body that contains spores [Mid-19C. < modern Latin < Greek *peri* 'around' + *thēkē* 'case']

peritoneum /pérritō neé əm/ (*plural* **-nea** /-neé ə/ or **-neums**) *n* a smooth transparent membrane that lines the abdomen and doubles back over the surfaces of the internal organs to form a continuous sac [Mid-16C. Via late Latin < Greek *peritoneion* < *peritonos* 'stretched around' < *teinein* 'to stretch'] —**peritoneal** *adj* — **peritoneally** *adv*

peritonitis /pérritō nítiss/ *n* inflammation of the membrane that lines the abdomen (**peritoneum**). Symptoms can include swelling of the abdomen, severe pain, and weight loss. —**peritonitic** /pérri tō níttik/ *adj*

peritrack /pérri trak/ *n* AVIAT same as **taxiway** [Late 20C. < PERIMETER]

peritrich /pérri trik/ (*plural* **peritricha** /pə ríttrikə/) *n* a simple microscopic invertebrate (**protozoan**) covered in tiny filaments (**cilia**) that it uses to move around [Early 20C. < modern Latin *peritricha* < Greek *peri* 'around' + *trikh-* 'hair'] —**peritrichous** /pə ríttrikəss/ *adj*

periwig /pérri wig/ *n* a wig, especially of the kind that men wore in the 17th and 18th centuries [Early 16C. Alteration of an earlier form of PERUKE]

periwinkle[1] /pérri wingk'l/ *n* MARINE BIOL same as **winkle** [Mid-16C. Origin ?]

periwinkle

periwinkle[2] /pérri wingk'l/ *n* a trailing evergreen plant with dark green glossy leaves. Flowers: blue, white. Native to: Europe, Asia. Genus: *Vinca*. ■ *adj* of a pale bluish-purple colour [Pre-12C. < late Latin *pervinca* < Latin *vincapervinca*]

perjink /pər jíngk/ *adj Scotland* caring too much about neatness or unimportant details (*humorous*) [Early 19C. Origin ?]

~~**perjorative**~~ incorrect spelling of **pejorative**

perjure /púrjər/ (**-jures, -juring, -jured**), **perjure yourself** *vr* to tell a lie in a court of law and therefore be

guilty of perjury [15C. Via French < Latin *perjurare* 'swear falsely' < *jurare* (see JURY)] —**perjurer** *n*

perjured /púrjərd/ *adj* **1.** guilty of telling a lie in a court of law and therefore of committing perjury **2.** containing lies and therefore breaking an oath to tell the truth in a court of law

perjury /púrjəri/ (*plural* **-ries**) *n* **1.** the telling of a lie after having taken an oath to tell the truth, usually in a court of law **2.** a lie told in a court of law by somebody who has taken an oath to tell the truth [14C. Via Anglo-Norman < Latin *perjurium* < *perjurare* (see PERJURE)] —**perjurious** /pər joóri əss/ *adj* —**perjuriously** *adv* —**perjuriousness** *n*

perk[1] /purk/ *n* **1.** a benefit given to an employee in addition to a salary, e.g. the use of a car or membership of a club ○ *one of the perks of the job* **2.** anything that somebody gains incidentally or as a consequence of something else ○ *Taking time off whenever you want is one of the perks of being self-employed.* [Early 19C. Shortening of PERQUISITE]

perk[2] /purk/ (**perks, perking, perked**) *vti* to percolate, or percolate coffee (*informal*) [Mid-20C. Shortening.]

perk[3] /purk/ (**perks, perking, perked**) [14C. Probably < *perk* 'perch' (now dialectical) < Old French *perche* (see PERCH[1])] **perk up** *vti* **1.** to become more cheerful, positive, or active, or make somebody more cheerful, positive, or active **2.** to stick up, or make something stick up, especially quickly ○ *The dog's ears perked up.*

Perkins, **Charles** (1936–2000) Australian Aboriginal activist. He led antidiscrimination protests in the 1960s, and subsequently became head of Australia's Department of Aboriginal Affairs (1984–89). Full name **Perkins, Charles Nelson**

Perkins, **Kieran** (*b.* 1973) Australian swimmer. He won gold medals in the 1,500 m freestyle in the 1992 and 1996 Olympic Games.

perky /púrki/ (**-ier, -iest**) *adj* **1.** lively, cheerful, and energetic **2.** irritatingly self-confident —**perkily** *adv* —**perkiness** *n*

perlemoen /púrləmoŏn/ (*plural same*) *n S Africa* an abalone. Native to: South Africa. Latin name: *Haliotis midae*. [Mid-19C. Via Afrikaans < Dutch *perlemoder* 'mother-of-pearl']

perlite /púr līt/ *n* a greyish volcanic glass in the form of grains that resemble pearls. It is often added to potting compost as a soil conditioner and is also used as a heat insulator. —**perlitic** /pər líttik/ *adj*

Perlman, **Itzhak** (*b.* 1945) Israeli-born US violinist. He is considered one of the finest violinists of his generation.

perlocution /púr lō kyoósh'n/ *n* the effect that a speaker's words have on somebody's emotions and responses —**perlocutionary** *adj*

perm[1] /purm/ *n* a hair treatment that uses chemicals to give hair long-lasting curliness or waviness [Early 20C. Shortening of PERMANENT] —**perm** *vt*

perm[2] /purm/ (*informal*) *n* the selection of possible winners made by somebody making a bet, especially, in football pools, a number of matches thought likely to end in a score draw ■ *vt* (**perms, perming, permed**) to select a number of possible winners to bet on from a larger field, especially, in football pools, a number of matches thought likely to end in a score draw [Mid-20C. Shortening of PERMUTATION]

Perm /purm/, **Perm'** city in eastern European Russia. Population: 1,275,482 (1995).

permaculture /púrmə kulchər/ (*plural* **-tures** or *same*) *n* a system of agriculture that uses a mix of trees, bushes, other perennial plants, and livestock to create a self-sustaining ecosystem that yields crops and other products [Late 20C. Blend of PERMANENT + AGRICULTURE]

permafrost /púrmə frost/ *n* underlying soil or rock that remains permanently frozen, found mainly in the polar regions [Mid-20C. < PERMANENT]

permalloy /pər málloy/ *n* a nickel-iron alloy belonging to a group of alloys that are highly valued in the electronics industry because they allow magnetic fields to pass through them [Early 20C. < PERMEABLE]

~~**permanant**~~ incorrect spelling of **permanent**

permanence /púrmənənss/, **permanency** /púrmənənssi/ *n* existence in the same form for ever or for a very long time [15C. Directly or via French or medieval Latin *permanentia* < Latin *permanent-* (see PERMANENT)]

permanent /púrmənənt/ *adj* **1.** lasting for ever or for a very long time, especially without undergoing significant change **2.** never changing or not expected to change ■ *n N Am* HAIR same as **perm**[1] (*formal*) [15C. Directly or via French < Latin *permanent-*, present participle of *permanere* 'remain through' < *manere* 'remain'] —**permanently** *adv* —**permanentness** *n*

permanent health insurance *n* health insurance that provides a regular income in cases of absence from work owing to long-term illness

permanent magnet *n* a magnet that retains its properties after the magnetizing force has been removed from it. Permanent magnets are used in loudspeakers and small motors. —**permanent magnetism** *n*

permanent press *n* a chemical process used to give fabric shape and make it resistant to wrinkling (*hyphenated when used before a noun*)

Permanent Protection Visa *n Aus* a permanent visa awarded to an asylum seeker deemed to be a refugee

permanent set *n* a permanent plastic deformation of a test piece or structure once an applied load has been removed

permanent tooth *n* a tooth of the second and final set of teeth that grow to replace the milk teeth. A human adult has 32 permanent teeth.

permanent wave *n* same as **perm**[1]

permanent way *n* a railway track intended for long-term public use, laid with sleepers on a prepared bed of ground and supported by stones, as opposed to a lightweight or temporary track

permanganate /pər máng gə nayt/ *n* a chemical compound that is a salt of permanganic acid [Mid-19C. < PER- + MANGANESE]

permanganic acid /púr man gánnik-/ *n* an unstable acid that exists only in dilute solution. Formula: $HMnO_4$. [< PERMANGANATE]

permatan /púrmə tan/ *n* a year-round brown skin tone that has the appearance of a natural suntan but is artificially produced —**permatanned** *adj*

permeability /púrmi ə bílləti/ (*plural* -ties) *n* **1.** PERMEABLE NATURE the property of being permeable **2.** RATE SUBSTANCE PASSES THROUGH POROUS MEDIUM the rate at which something such as a liquid or a magnetic field passes through a membrane or other medium **3.** MAGNETIC PROPERTY the property of a material to alter a magnetic field in which it is placed, or a measure of this property. Symbol μ

permeable /púrmi əb'l/ *adj* allowing liquids, gases, or magnetic fields to pass through —**permeably** *adv*

permeance /púrmi ənss/ *n* **1.** the act of passing through a porous substance or membrane **2.** the ability of a magnetic component or assembly to be magnetized, measured in henries and calculated by dividing the magnetic flux by the magnetomotive force —**permeant** *adj, n*

permease /púrmi ayz, -ayss/ *n* a protein in bacterial cell membranes that allows a solute to enter the cell [Mid-20C. < PERMEATE]

permeate /púrmi ayt/ (-ates, -ating, -ated) *vti* **1.** to enter something and spread throughout it, so that every part or aspect of it is affected **2.** to pass through the minute openings in a porous substance or membrane, or make something such as a liquid pass through [Mid-17C. < Latin *permeat-*, past participle of *permeare* 'pass through' < *meare* 'to pass'] —**permeation** /púrmi áysh'n/ *n* —**permeative** *adj*

permenent incorrect spelling of **permanent**

Permian /púrmi ən/ *n* the period of geological time, 290 million to 248 million years ago, when many marine invertebrates disappeared and reptiles flourished. See table at **geological time** [Late 16C. After *Perm*, province in E Russia] —**Permian** *adj*

per mille /pər míllay/, **per mil** /-míl/ *adv* in every thousand, or by the thousand [*Mille* < Latin, 'thousand']

permissable incorrect spelling of **permissible**

permissible /pər míssəb'l/ *adj* allowable or permitted

[15C. < French < Latin *permiss-* (see PERMISSION)] —**permissibility** /-míssə bílləti/ *n* —**permissibly** *adv*

permission /pər mísh'n/ *n* agreement to allow something to happen or be done ■ *vt* (-sions, -sioning, -sioned) to give explicit permission for something, e.g. for marketing information to be sent automatically [15C. < French < Latin *permiss-*, past participle of *permittere* (see PERMIT)]

permissive /pər míssiv/ *adj* **1.** allowing or enjoying the freedom to behave in ways others might consider unacceptable, particularly in sexual matters **2.** granting permission [15C. < French, < Latin *permiss-* (see PERMISSION)] —**permissively** *adv* —**permissiveness** *n*

permit *v* /pər mít/ (-mits, -mitting, -mitted) **1.** *vti* ALLOW SOMETHING to allow something or give permission for it ○ *She will not permit talking in her class while she is speaking.* **2.** *vti* MAKE SOMETHING POSSIBLE to allow somebody the possibility of doing something ○ *New technologies will permit more people to work from home.* **3.** **permit yourself** *vr* ALLOW YOURSELF SOMETHING to allow yourself to have or do something, especially as a luxury or for a special occasion ■ *n* /púrmit/ **1.** DOCUMENT GIVING PERMISSION an official document or certificate giving permission for something **2.** PERMISSION permission granted, especially in written form (*formal*) [15C. < Latin *permittere* 'let go through' < *mittere* 'let go'] —**permittee** /púrmi teé/ *n* —**permitter** /pər míttər/ *n*

permited incorrect spelling of **permitted**

permittivity /púrmi tívvəti/ (*plural* -ties) *n* the measure of the ability of a nonconducting material to retain electric energy when placed in an electric field. Symbol v [Late 19C. < PERMIT, after *conductivity*]

permutate /púrmyoō tayt/ (-tates, -tating, -tated) *vt* to change the order of items in a group, especially to rearrange them in every possible way [Late 16C. < Latin *permutat-*, past participle of *permutare* (see PERMUTE)]

permutation /púrmyoō táysh'n/ *n* **1.** ARRANGEMENT an arrangement of items created by moving or reordering them **2.** REARRANGING the reordering or rearranging of items in a group **3.** TRANSFORMATION a change or transformation **4.** MATHS ORDER OF MATHEMATICAL ELEMENTS an ordered arrangement of elements from a set **5.** GAMBLING same as **perm**[2] (*formal*) —**permutational** *adj*

permute /pər myoot/ (-mutes, -muting, -muted) *vt* **1.** to change the order of items in a group, especially to rearrange them in every possible way **2.** to reorder the elements in a mathematical set [Late 19C. < Latin *permutare* 'change completely' < *mutare* 'to change'] —**permutability** /-myoōtə bílləti/ *n* —**permutable** *adj* —**permutably** *adv*

pernicious /pər níshəss/ *adj* **1.** wicked or meaning to cause harm **2.** causing great harm, destruction, or death [Early 16C. Via French < Latin *perniciosus* < *pernicies* 'complete destruction' < *nec-* 'destruction'] —**perniciously** *adv* —**perniciousness** *n*

pernicious anaemia *n* a severe form of anaemia, found mostly in older adults, that results from the body's inability to absorb vitamin B_{12}. Symptoms include weakness, breathing difficulties, and weight loss.

pernickety /pər níkəti/ *adj* (*informal*) **1.** excessively concerned about unimportant details **2.** requiring precise attention to detail ▶ US term **persnickety** [Early 19C. Origin ?] —**pernicketiness** *n*

perogative incorrect spelling of **prerogative**

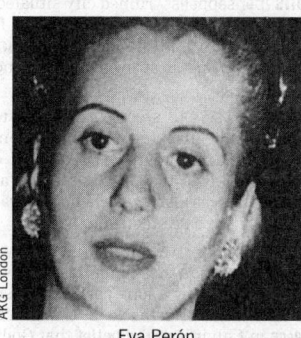
Eva Perón

Perón /pə rón/, **Eva** (1919–52) Argentine political figure. Married to President Juan Perón, she was adored by the Argentinian people for her charitable work. Born **Duarte, María Eva**. Full name **Duarte de Perón, Maria Eva**. Known as **Evita**

'Almsgiving tends to perpetuate poverty; aid does away with it once and for all. Almsgiving leaves a man just where he was before. Aid restores him to society as an individual worthy of all respect and not as a man with a grievance. Almsgiving is the generosity of the rich; social aid levels up social inequalities.'
[Eva Perón, *Speech to the American Congress of Industrial Medicine*; 5 December 1949]

Perón, **Isabel** (*b.* 1931) president of Argentina (1974–76). She was the third wife of Juan Perón, and after his death succeeded him as president. Born **Martínez Cartas, María Estela**. Full name **de Perón, Isabel**

Perón, **Juan** (1895–1974) president of Argentina (1946–55 and 1973–74). He rose to power by a military coup (1943) and enacted populist economic reforms during his presidencies. Full name **Perón, Juan Domingo** —**Peronist** /pə rónnist/ *n, adj*

peroneal /pérrə neé əl/ *adj* relating to the narrower of the two bones in the lower leg (**fibula**) [Mid-19C. < Greek *peronē* 'pin of a brooch, fibula']

perorate /pérrə rayt/ (-rates, -rating, -rated) *vi* (*formal*) **1.** to finish a speech by summarizing its main points **2.** to speak at length, especially in a formal or pompous way [Early 17C. < Latin *perorat-*, past participle of *perorare* 'speak all the way through' < *orare* 'speak']

peroration /pérrə ráysh'n/ *n* (*formal*) **1.** a conclusion to a speech in which the main points of the speech are summarized **2.** a long speech that makes much use of rhetorical devices —**perorational** *adj*

perovskite /pe róv skīt/ *n* a black, yellow, or brown calcium titanate mineral. Use: superconductive materials. [Mid-19C. After L. A. *Perovski* (1792–1856), Russian mineralogist]

peroxidase /pə róksi dayz, -dayss/ *n* an enzyme in animals and plants that helps neutralize harmful peroxides

peroxide /pə rók sīd/ *n* **1.** CHEMICAL COMPOUND a chemical compound that contains oxygen atoms in the group $-O_2$-, e.g. hydrogen peroxide **2.** HAIR COLOURING SUBSTANCE a solution of hydrogen peroxide used to lighten hair colour, giving a blonde tint that is almost white (*often used before a noun*) ○ *a peroxide blonde* ■ *vt* (-ides, -iding, -ided) **1.** COLOUR HAIR BLONDE to bleach hair using peroxide **2.** TREAT SOMETHING WITH PEROXIDE to treat something with peroxide or hydrogen peroxide

peroxisome /pə róksi sōm/ *n* a tiny part within a cell containing enzymes that oxidize toxic substances such as alcohol and prevent them from doing any harm. There are many peroxisomes in the cells of the liver and kidney. [Mid-20C. < PEROXIDE + -SOME[1]]

perp /purp/ *n N Am* somebody responsible for a crime (*slang*) [Late 20C. Shortening of *perpetrator*]

perpend /púr pənd/ *n US* same as **parpen** [15C. Variant]

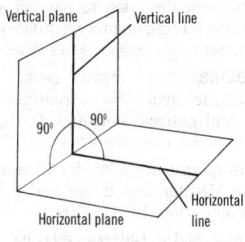
perpendicular

perpendicular /púrpən díkyoōlər/ *adj* **1.** AT RIGHT ANGLES at right angles to a line or plane **2.** VERTICAL perfectly vertical **3.** STEEP very steep **4.** *also* **Perpendicular** ARCHIT IN LATE GOTHIC STYLE relating to or typical of a style of Gothic architecture in which tall narrow facades, windows, and doors, and vaulted ceilings

are characteristic. It was popular in England in the 14th and 15th centuries. ■ *n* **1. PERPENDICULAR LINE** a perpendicular line or plane **2. DEVICE FINDING VERTICAL** any device used to establish a vertical line, e.g. a spirit level or a plumb line **3. SHEER ROCK** a sheer rock face **4.** *also* **Perpendicular** ARCHIT **ARCHITECTURAL STYLE** the perpendicular style of architecture [14C. Directly or via French < Latin *perpendicularis* < *perpendiculum* 'plumb line' < *perpendere* 'weigh thoroughly' < *pendere* 'weigh'] —**perpendicularity** /-dikyoŏ lárrəti/ *n* —**perpendicularly** *adv*

perpetrate /púrpi trayt/ (**-trates, -trating, -trated**) *vt* to commit or be responsible for something, usually something criminal or morally wrong [Mid-16C. < Latin *perpetrat-*, past participle of *perpetrare*, literally 'completely bring about' < *patrare* 'bring about' < *pater* 'father'] —**perpetration** /púrpi tráysh'n/ *n* —**perpetrator** *n*

perpetual /pər péchoo əl/ *adj* **1. LASTING FOR EVER** lasting for all time **2. LASTING INDEFINITELY** lasting for an indefinitely long time **3. OCCURRING REPEATEDLY** occurring over and over **4.** BOT **BLOOMING THROUGHOUT SEASON** describes flowers or flowering plants that bloom throughout the season [14C. Via French < Latin *perpetualis* < *perpetuus* 'continuous' < *perpes*, literally 'going towards throughout' < *petere* 'go towards']

perpetual calendar *n* a calendar set out in such a way that it can be used for several years or for any year

perpetual check *n* a situation in chess in which one player's king is placed in check with every move the other player makes, resulting in a draw

perpetually /pər péchoo əli/ *adv* **1.** for ever, or for a very long time **2.** repeatedly at very short intervals, and so appearing to be continuous

perpetual motion *n* **1.** the hypothetical continuous operation of a mechanism without the introduction of energy from an external source, known as perpetual motion of the first kind. A device demonstrating this would violate the first law of thermodynamics, which states that energy can neither be created nor destroyed. **2.** the hypothetical operation of a mechanism that would convert heat directly into work, known as perpetual motion of the second kind. A device demonstrating this would violate the second law of thermodynamics, which states that heat cannot be converted into work without producing some other effect.

perpetuate /pər péchoo ayt/ (**-ates, -ating, -ated**) *vt* **1.** to make something continue, usually for a very long time **2.** to make something or somebody be remembered [Early 16C. < Latin *perpetuat-*, past participle of *perpetuare* < *perpetuus* (see PERPETUAL)] —**perpetuation** /pər péchoo áysh'n/ *n* —**perpetuator** *n*

perpetuity /púrpi tyoŏ əti/ (*plural* **-ties**) *n* **1. PERPETUAL CONDITION** the state of continuing for a long time or indefinitely **2. ETERNITY** eternity or the rest of time ○ *a sacrifice honoured in perpetuity* **3.** LAW **TRANSFER OF PROPERTY FOR EVER** the transfer of property for an unlimited period of time, restricted in law by the rule against perpetuity. The maximum legal period of transferred ownership is based on the length of a life in existence at the time plus 21 years plus a nine month period of gestation. **4.** FIN **INVESTMENT** an investment designed to pay an annual return indefinitely, having no maturity date [15C. Via French < Latin *perpetuitas* < *perpetuus* (see PERPETUAL)]

perphenazine /pər fénnə zeen, -zin/ *n* an antipsychotic drug. Use: treatment of anxiety, tension and nausea. Formula: $C_{21}H_{26}ClN_3OS$. [Mid-20C. < PIPERIDINE + PHENOTHIAZINE]

Perpignan /púrp een yaaN/ *city in southern France, near the Mediterranean Sea and the border with Spain. Population: 105,115 (1999).*

perplex /pər pléks/ (**-plexes, -plexing, -plexed**) *vt* **1.** to puzzle or confuse somebody, especially causing doubt **2.** to make something excessively complicated or intricate [Late 16C. Back-formation from *perplexed* < obsolete *perplex* (adj), directly or via French < Latin *perplexus* 'intricate, involved' < *per-* 'through' + past participle of *plectere* 'plait, involve'] —**perplexed** *adj*

perplexing /pər pléksing/ *adj* disconcertingly difficult to understand or come to terms with —**perplexingly** *adv*

perplexity /pər pléksəti/ (*plural* **-ties**) *n* **1. BEING PERPLEXED** the state of being perplexed **2. PERPLEXING THING** something that is difficult to understand, especially because it is complex or part of a complicated whole (*often used in the plural*) **3. COMPLEX NATURE** the nature of something that is disconcertingly complex

per pro /pər pró/ *prep* a fuller form of the abbreviation 'pp' that is written in formal correspondence by somebody who is signing on behalf of another person [Shortening of Latin *per procurationem* 'by proxy']

perp walk *n* N Am an act of escorting a prisoner to confinement in full public view, especially in front of the media (*slang*)

perquisite /púrkwizit/ *n* **1.** same as **perk**[1] (sense 1) (*formal*) **2.** a tip that is customary on some occasions **3.** something considered to be an exclusive right [Early 18C. < medieval Latin *perquisitum* 'something searched for' < *perquirere* 'seek for' < *quaerere* 'seek']

Perrault /pérrō, pə ró/, **Charles** (1628–1703) French writer. In *Tales of Mother Goose* (1697) he set down from oral tradition such fairy tales as *Cinderella* and *Sleeping Beauty*.

~~**perrenial**~~ incorrect spelling of **perennial**

perron /pérrən/ *n* **1.** a raised platform at an entrance that is not at ground level **2.** an external stairway leading up to a perron [14C. < French, 'large stone' < Latin *petra* 'stone']

perry /pérri/ *n* a drink made from fermented pear juice, similar to cider or wine [14C. < Old French *pere* < Latin *pirum* 'pear']

Perry /pérri/, **Fred** (1909–95) British tennis player. He was winner of the US Open (1933, 1934, 1936), Wimbledon (1934, 1935, 1936), Australian Open (1934), and French Open (1935) singles titles. Full name **Perry, Frederick John**

per se /pər sáy/ *adv* in itself, by itself, or intrinsically [< Latin, 'by itself']

perse /purss/ *adj* of a dark bluish-grey or purplish-black colour [14C. Via French < medieval Latin *persus*] —**perse** *n*

Perse /purss/, **Saint-John** (1887–1975) French poet and diplomat. His poetry deals chiefly with the themes of solitude and exile. He won the Nobel Prize in literature (1960). Pseudonym of **Léger, Alexis Saint-Léger**

persecute /púrssi kyoot/ (**-cutes, -cuting, -cuted**) *vt* **1.** to systematically subject a race or group of people to cruel or unfair treatment, e.g. because of their ethnic origin or religious beliefs **2.** to make somebody the victim of continual pestering or harassment [15C. Via French < Latin *persecut-*, past participle of *persequi* 'keep following' < *sequi* 'follow'] —**persecutee** /púrssi kyoo teé/ *n* —**persecutive** *adj* —**persecutor** *n* —**persecutory** *adj*

persecution /púrssi kyoósh'n/ *n* **1.** the subjecting of a race or group of people to cruel or unfair treatment, e.g. because of their ethnic origin or religious beliefs **2.** the suffering felt by persecuted people

Perseid /púrssi id/ *n* a meteor in a meteor shower that appears around 12 August and seems to originate from near the constellation Perseus

Persephone /pər séffəni/ *n* in Greek mythology, the daughter of Demeter and Zeus who was abducted by Hades, king of the underworld. She spent half the year in the underworld and half on Earth. Her return to Earth symbolized the arrival of spring. Roman equivalent **Proserpina**

Persepolis /pər séppəliss/ *ruined city situated northeast of Shiraz in modern-day Iran. It was founded by Darius the Great in the 6th century BC as the Persian capital and destroyed by Alexander the Great.*

Perseus /púrssi əss, púr syooss/ *n* **1.** a constellation of the northern hemisphere. See illustration at **constellation 2.** in Greek mythology, the son of Zeus and Danae. He killed the Gorgon Medusa and also rescued the princess Andromeda as she was about to be sacrificed to a sea monster.

perseverance /púrssi véerəns/ *n* **1. DETERMINED CONTINUATION WITH SOMETHING** steady and continued action or belief, usually over a long period and especially despite difficulties or setbacks **2. CALVINIST CONCEPT OF DIVINE GRACE** in Calvinism, the belief that God's grace

brings selected people, the elect, to salvation **3. ROMAN CATHOLIC BELIEF IN GOD'S GRACE** in the Roman Catholic Church, the belief that God's grace lasts to the end of somebody's life if that person has maintained his or her good works and faith —**perseverant** *adj*

perseveration /pər sévvə ráysh'n/ *n* a tendency to repeat the response to an experience in later situations where it is not appropriate [Early 20C. < Latin *perseverare* (see PERSEVERE)]

persevere /púrssi veer/ (**-veres, -vering, -vered**) *vi* to persist steadily in an action or belief, usually over a long period and especially despite problems or difficulties [14C. Via French < Latin *perseverare* 'follow strictly' < *perseverus* 'very strict' < *severus* 'serious'] —**persevering** *adj* —**perseveringly** *adv*

~~**perseverence**~~ incorrect spelling of **perseverance**

Pershing /púrshing/ *n* a two-stage US Army ballistic missile capable of delivering a nuclear warhead [Mid-20C. After John J. PERSHING]

Pershing /púrshing/, **John J.** (1860–1948) US general. He led the American Expeditionary Force in Europe during World War I. Full name **Pershing, John Joseph**

> 'I hope that here on the soil of France and in the school of French heroes, our American soldiers may learn to battle and vanquish for the liberty of the world.'
> [John J. Pershing, *Speech, at Lafayette's tomb, Paris*; 4 July 1917]

Persia /púrshə, púrzhə/ **1.** former name for Iran **2.** ancient empire in Southwest Asia that, at its height under Darius the Great in the 6th century BC, stretched from the shores of the eastern Mediterranean to the River Indus in present-day Pakistan. It was conquered by Alexander the Great in 330 BC.

Persian /púrsh'n, púrzh'n/ *n* **1. SOMEBODY FROM IRAN** somebody who comes from Iran **2.** LANG same as **Farsi 3. SOMEBODY FROM ANCIENT PERSIA** a member of a people who lived in ancient Persia and who founded an empire around 500 BC **4. LANGUAGE OF ANCIENT PERSIANS** the Iranian language spoken by the ancient Persians ▶ See panel on next page —**Persian** *adj*

Persian carpet *n* a carpet consisting of a woven backing to which wool or silk threads have been hand-knotted, made in southwestern Asia and typically having rich colours and strong designs

Persian cat

Persian cat *n* a long-haired domestic cat belonging to a breed originally from southwestern Asia

Persian Gulf /púrsh'n-/ *gulf of the Arabian Sea, with Iran to its northeast and the Arabian peninsula to its southwest. Area: 230,000 sq. km/88,800 sq. mi.*

Persian Gulf War *n* ♦ **Gulf War** (sense 1)

Persian lamb *n* **1.** the soft curled usually black fur from the karakul lamb **2.** a lamb of the karakul sheep

Persian rug *n* TEXTILES same as **Persian carpet**

Persian wool *n* a loosely twisted three-strand wool yarn used in needlepoint, each strand being two-ply

persiennes /púrssi énz/ *npl* outside louvred shutters for blocking sunlight while allowing ventilation. N Am term **Persian blinds** [Mid-19C. < French < *persian* 'Persian']

persiflage /púrssi flaazh/ *n* **1.** light or teasing good-natured talk **2.** light-heartedness or frivolity in the

LANGUAGE HERITAGE ***Persian*** Much of English is made up of words from other languages, and some are from Persian, the earlier form of the language now known as Farsi. Persia once had a vast empire in Southwest Asia, and Persian left a legacy to many of the languages of the region. Though relatively few purely Persian words have moved directly into English, numerous words set out from Persian and found their way by a more circuitous route. A typical much-travelled example would be Persian *lāžward* 'lapis lazuli', which arrived in English in the 13th century as ***azure***, by way of Arabic *al-lāzaward* 'the lapis lazuli', medieval Latin *azzurum*, and finally Old French *azur*. Even earlier was the name of the game of ***chess***, known from the 12th century and a shortening of Old French *esches*, plural of *eschec* 'check in chess'; this is the word from which the English chess term ***check*** (14th century) immediately derives, though the French goes back to Persian *šāh* 'king', itself imported as ***shah*** in the mid-16th century; ***checkmate*** followed ***check*** in the 15th century, from Old French *eschec mat*, from Persian *šāh māt* 'the king is dead'.

Travel and trade brought English speakers more directly into contact with Persian, and this is reflected by early migrants, for example ***khan*** 'inn' (14th century), and ***caravanserai*** (late 16th), from Persian *kārwānsarāī*, formed from *kārwān* 'group of desert travellers' and *sarāī* 'inn' (***caravan*** itself also arrived from Persian in the late 16th century, by way of French). Luxury materials such as ***taffeta*** (14th century, via medieval Latin or Old French *taffetas* from Persian *tāftah* from *tāftan* 'to shine'), ***seersucker*** (early 18th, via Hindi from Persian *šīr o šakar* 'milk and sugar'), and ***pashmina*** (late 19th, from Persian *pašmīn* 'woollen', from *pašm* 'wool') continued to come from or through Persian.

A great proportion of words of Persian origin, however, migrated through the languages of northern South Asia such as Hindi and, especially, its close relative Urdu, the official language of Pakistan and of Bangladesh, which has many loanwords from Persian. Urdu and Persian gave, for example, familiar items such as ***pyjamas*** (early 19th century, from *pāy-jāmah* 'leg garment'), the ***shawl*** (early 17th, from *šāl*), and ***khaki*** (mid-19th, from Urdu *kakī* 'dust-coloured' from Persian *kāk* 'dust'). Through Persian and Urdu have migrated not only words relating to Islamic culture and religion such as ***burka***, ***chador***, ***mullah***, ***purdah***, and ***zakat*** ('tax that goes to charity'), but also the name for those of another great faith, ***Hindu*** (mid-17th century, via Urdu from Persian *Hindū* from *Hind* 'India'). South Asian terms of the military and of public administration include numerous words in *-dar*, from Persian *-dār* 'holder', for example ***havildar***, ***jamadar***, ***sardar***, ***subadar***, ***tahsildar***, and ***zamindar***.

During the 20th century, migration of people from South Asia has brought many more English-speakers into contact with its cultures, and nowhere more effectively than in its food. ***Biryani*** (via Hindi from Persian *biriyān* 'fried, grilled'), ***kofta*** (from Urdu and Persian *koftah* 'pounded meat'), ***nan*** (from Persian and Urdu *nān*), and the ***tandoori*** (from Persian and Urdu, from Urdu *tandūr*, Persian *tanūr* 'clay oven') are familiar pleasures of many non-Asian lives. See also ***Turkish***.

treatment of something [Mid-18C. < French < *persifler* 'to banter' < *siffler* 'to whistle' < Latin *sibilare* 'to hiss']

persimmon

persimmon /pər símmən/ *n* **1.** a juicy smooth-skinned orange-red fruit that is sweet only when fully ripe **2.** a tree that has hard wood and bears persimmons. Native to: Asia, Europe, eastern North America. Genus: *Diospyros*. [Early 17C. Alteration of Virginia Algonquian *pessemmins*]

persist /pər síst/ (**-sists, -sisting, -sisted**) *vi* **1. KEEP CARRYING ON** to continue steadily or obstinately despite problems, difficulties, or obstacles **2. CONTINUE TO BE BELIEVED WRONGLY** to continue being widely believed or accepted despite evidence or proof to the contrary ○ *a view that persists to this day* **3. CONTINUE** to continue happening [Mid-16C. < Latin *persistere*, literally 'stand through' < *sistere* 'make stand' < *stare* 'to stand'] —**persister** *n*

~~**persistant**~~ incorrect spelling of **persistent**

persistence /pər sístənss/, **persistency** /pər sístənssi/ *n* **1. QUALITY OF PERSISTING** the quality of continuing steadily despite problems or difficulties **2. ACT OF PERSISTING** the action of somebody who persists with something **3. LONG CONTINUANCE OF SOMETHING** continuance of an effect after its cause has ceased or been removed **4.** ZOOL **RESILIENCE OF ORGANISM** the ability of a living organism to resist being disturbed or altered

persistent /pər sístənt/ *adj* **1. CONTINUING DESPITE PROBLEMS** tenaciously or obstinately continuing despite problems or difficulties **2. INCESSANT OR UNRELENTING** existing or continuing for an unpleasantly long time **3.** BOT **PERSISTING BEYOND MATURATION** describes a plant part such as a scale on a pine cone that lasts beyond maturity without falling off **4.** ZOOL **SUSTAINING CONTINUAL GROWTH** describes a body part such as a tooth that grows throughout life **5.** ECOL, ENVIRON **ABLE TO REMAIN IN ENVIRONMENT** describes a chemical or a living organism that remains in the environment for months or years, usually because of resistance to attack by oxygen, light, and micro-organisms —**persistently** *adv*

persistent vegetative state *n* a medical condition in which a patient has severe brain damage and as a result is unable to stay alive without the aid of a life-support system, showing no response to stimuli

persnickety /pər sníkəti/ *adj N Am* same as **pernickety** (sense 1) (*informal*) [Early 20C. Alteration] —**persnicketiness** *n*

person /púrss'n/ (*plural* **people** /péep'l/ or **persons** *formal*) *n* **1. HUMAN BEING** an individual human being **2. HUMAN'S BODY** a human being's body, often including the clothing ○ *objects found on her person* **3. HUMAN'S APPEARANCE** an individual human being's general appearance (*formal*) **4. CHARACTER OR ROLE** a character or role, e.g. in a play (*archaic*) **5.** GRAM **FORM OF VERB AND PRONOUN** any one of three forms of verbs and pronouns used to denote the speaker, the person addressed, or somebody else being referred to ○ *the third person singular* **6.** ETHICS **OBJECT WITH SPECIAL MORAL VALUE** an object with special moral value because of some spiritual status, autonomous nature, or importance for other people **7.** LAW **INDIVIDUAL OR BODY OF INDIVIDUALS** a living human being or a group, either or both having legal rights and responsibilities [12C. Via French *persone* < Latin *persona* 'mask worn by an actor, character'] —**-person** *suffix* —**personhood** *n* ◇ **in person** personally, rather than being represented by somebody or something else

USAGE Terms that are not gender-specific have increasingly grown in prominence, and ones incorporating the suffix ***-person*** are now common (*chairperson*, *spokesperson*). The terms that have taken hold most strongly tend to be those that do not simply replace *-man* (or *-woman*) with ***-person*** but are more subtly neutral with respect to sex: *chair* rather than *chairperson*, *customer adviser* rather than *salesperson*. Despite the powerful trend towards inclusive terms, however, it remains true that when the members of the group at issue are predominantly male, the traditional term incorporating *-man* tends to be used more frequently (*fisherman*). Forms with *-woman* are also seen, though in most cases these are now less common than the form incorporating ***-person***. Choose gender-neutral words when they are available. See also ***people***.

Person *n* in Christianity, the Father, the Son, or the Holy Spirit, together being the Trinity

persona /pər sṓnə/ (*plural* **-nae** /-nee/ or **-nas**) *n* **1. ASSUMED IDENTITY OR ROLE** an identity or role that somebody assumes **2. CHARACTER IN LITERATURE** a character in a literary work, especially a play (*often used in the plural*) **3.** PSYCHOL, PSYCHOANAL **PERSONAL FACADE** the image of character and personality that somebody wants to show the outside world. This concept originated in Jungian psychology. [Early 20C. < Latin, 'mask worn by an actor, character']

personable /púrss'nəb'l/ *adj* having a pleasant personality and appearance —**personableness** *n* —**personably** *adv*

personage /púrss'nij/ *n* (*formal*) **1.** a distinguished, important, or famous person **2.** a historical figure, or a character in a work of literature [15C. < Old French < *persone* (see PERSON)]

persona grata /pər sṓnə graátə/ (*plural* **personae gratae** /pər sṓnee graá tee/) *n* somebody who is acceptable to others, especially as a diplomat [< late Latin, 'acceptable person'] —**persona grata** *adj*

personal /púrss'nəl/ *adj* **1. RELATING TO SOMEBODY'S PRIVATE LIFE** relating to the parts of somebody's life that are private ○ *personal relationships* **2. RELATING TO ONE PERSON** relating to a specific person rather than anyone else ○ *my personal opinion* **3. DONE BY ONE PERSON ONLY** done by a specific person rather than by that person's delegate ○ *that personal touch* **4. INTENDED FOR SOMEBODY** intended for or owned by a specific person rather than anyone else **5. REFERRING OFFENSIVELY TO SOMEBODY** referring, especially in an offensive way, to somebody's beliefs, actions, or physical characteristics ○ *That personal remark was definitely uncalled-for.* **6. UNFAIRLY REMARKING OR QUESTIONING ABOUT OTHERS** making unacceptable remarks or being too probing about other people ○ *There's no need to get personal.* **7. OF BODY** relating to somebody's body ○ *personal hygiene* **8.** RELIG **CONSCIOUS AND INDIVIDUAL** having the character or nature of a conscious and individual entity **9.** LAW **OF MOVABLE PROPERTY** relating to or constituting a person's movable property ○ *personal effects* ■ *n ANZ, N Am* MEDIA same as **personal ad** (*often used in the plural*) [14C. Via French < Latin *personalis* < *persona* 'mask worn by an actor, character']

personal ad *n UK* a usually classified newspaper or magazine advertisement in which somebody expresses interest in meeting others or sends a message of a personal nature to somebody else. ANZ, N Am term **personal**

personal allowance *n* an amount of money a person is entitled to earn before paying tax

personal appearance *n* **1.** the visual aspect of somebody, especially with regard to personal cleanliness and tidiness of clothing **2.** an occasion when an important or famous person takes part in a public event

personal assistant *n* somebody employed to perform secretarial and administrative tasks for somebody such as an executive who has many responsibilities

personal care *n* assistance with washing, dressing, and other personal needs, often provided at home by a paid helper for somebody who is unable to manage alone

personal column *n* a section of a newspaper or magazine in which personal ads are printed

personal computer *n* a computer with its own operating system and a wide selection of software, intended to be used by one person

personal digital assistant *n* a small hand-held computer with facilities for taking notes, storing information such as addresses, and keeping a diary, usually operated using a stylus rather than a keyboard

personal effects *npl* possessions that somebody carries or wears regularly

Personal Equity Plan *n* FIN full form of **PEP**

personal foul *n* a foul, especially one committed in football or basketball, involving illegal physical contact with an opponent during a game and also sometimes involving unnecessary roughness

personal identification number *n* FIN full form of **PIN**

personal information manager *n* a piece of software

that organizes random notes, contacts, and appointments for fast access

personal injury n US an actionable injury to an individual person, whether involving physical contact or not and whether fatal or not, but causing pain, discomfort, or injury

personalise vt another spelling of **personalize**

personalism /púrss'nəlizəm/ n a quirky or highly individualistic mode of expression or behaviour — **personalist** n, adj — **personalistic** /púrss'nə lístik/ adj

personality /púrssə nálləti/ (plural -ties) n 1. SOMEBODY'S SET OF CHARACTERISTICS the totality of somebody's attitudes, interests, behavioural patterns, emotional responses, social roles, and other individual traits that endure over long periods of time 2. CHARACTERISTICS MAKING SOMEBODY APPEALING the distinctive or very noticeable characteristics that make somebody socially appealing ○ a partner with real personality 3. SOMEBODY REGARDED AS EPITOMIZING TRAITS somebody regarded as epitomizing particular character traits 4. FAMOUS PERSON a famous person, especially an entertainer or athlete 5. UNUSUAL PERSON a distinctive and unusual person 6. QUALITY OF BEING PERSON the quality of existing as a person ○ Do you think that computers will ever achieve personality? 7. DISTINGUISHING CHARACTERISTICS the distinguishing characteristics of a place or situation [14C. Via French < late Latin personalitas < Latin personalis (see PERSONAL)]

personality disorder n a psychiatric disorder that makes it difficult for somebody to get on with other people or to succeed at work or in social situations but that does not involve loss of touch with reality

personality test n a standardized psychological test in which the subject is given questions about various aspects of personality, the answers supplying a character-trait profile unique to that person

personality type n a set of categories based on attitudes or behavioural tendencies into which people are grouped, e.g. introvert and extrovert

personalize /púrss'nə līz/ (-izes, -izing, -ized), **personalise** (-ises, -ising, -ised) vt 1. PUT INITIALS OR NAME ON SOMETHING to mark something such as a wallet, pen, or item of clothing with somebody's initials or name 2. CHANGE SOMETHING TO REFLECT PERSONALITY to change or modify something showing that it obviously originated from or belonged to you 3. TAKE REMARK PERSONALLY to take a remark in a personal way 4. same as **personify** (sense 3) — **personalization** /púrss'nə līzáysh'n/ n

personalized medicine n the prevention, detection, and treatment of disease taking into account a person's unique genetic profile

personally /púrss'nəli/ adv 1. AS OWN OPINION in one's own experience or showing one's own opinion ○ Personally, I would have given it back. 2. AS INDIVIDUAL in relation to a particular person ○ I'm sure the criticisms weren't directed at you personally. 3. WITHOUT OTHERS without intervention or assistance from others ○ I'll handle it personally. 4. AS PERSON IN SOCIAL CONTEXT as a person, considered in a social context ○ personally likable but professionally inept 5. AS SOMEBODY YOU HAVE MET by personal contact rather than by reputation ○ I never knew your brother personally.

personal organizer n 1. a diary that also contains personal information and has replaceable pages so that it can be kept up to date 2. a hand-held computer with a small keyboard and display that can function as a diary, an address book, a scheduler, and a calculator

personal pronoun n a pronoun that refers to the speaker, somebody being addressed, or another person, e.g. 'I', 'you', or 'she'

personal property n in law, somebody's tangible movable property, exclusive of land and including items such as automotive vehicles, boats, and money

personal shopper n a person, often an employee of a shop, who assists others in choosing what to buy, either accompanying them or buying for them

personal stereo n a small audio cassette or CD player used with earphones, designed to be carried in a pocket or worn attached to a belt

personal transporter n US a small lightweight motorized vehicle for one person, e.g. a two-wheeled vehicle similar to an upright scooter designed to be ridden while standing

personalty /púrss'nəlti/ (plural -ties) n LAW same as **personal property** [Mid-16C. Via Anglo-Norman < late Latin personalitas (see PERSONALITY)]

personal unconscious n in Jungian and related forms of psychotherapy, a section of somebody's unconscious mind that contains impulses, fears, and memories that have been repressed

personal watercraft n N Am a jet-propelled vehicle for one or two people, used for travelling on water. It is similar in appearance to a motorcycle.

persona non grata /pər sṓnə non graátə/ (plural personae non gratae /pər sṓnee non graá tee/) n 1. an unwelcome or unacceptable person 2. a diplomat who is unacceptable to the country to which he or she is sent [< late Latin, 'unacceptable person'] — **persona non grata** adj

personate[1] /púrssə nayt/ (-ates, -ating, -ated) vt (dated) 1. to play a dramatic role, especially in a play 2. to impersonate somebody in order to deceive or defraud [Late 16C. < late Latin personat-, past participle of personare < Latin persona 'mask worn by an actor, character'] — **personation** /púrssə náysh'n/ n — **personative** /púrss'nətiv/ adj — **personator** n

personate[2] /púrssə nayt/ adj describes a flower that has two lips, with one lip curling over the other to close the opening between them, e.g. a snapdragon [Late 16C. < Latin personatus 'masked' < persona 'mask worn by an actor, character']

~~**personell**~~ incorrect spelling of **personnel**

person-hour n a unit that measures the amount of work that can be done by one person in one hour and the cost of that hour's work

personification /pər sónnifi káysh'n/ n 1. SOMEBODY WHO EMBODIES SOMETHING an embodiment or perfect example of something 2. REPRESENTATION OF ABSTRACT QUALITY AS HUMAN a representation of an abstract quality or notion as a human being, especially in art or literature 3. ATTRIBUTION OF HUMAN QUALITIES TO ABSTRACTS the attribution of human qualities to objects or abstract notions

personify /pər sónni fī/ (-fies, -fying, -fied) vt 1. BE PERFECT EXAMPLE OF SOMETHING to be an embodiment or perfect example of something 2. REPRESENT SOMETHING ABSTRACT AS HUMAN to represent an abstract quality or notion as a human being, especially in art or literature 3. ASCRIBE HUMAN QUALITIES TO ABSTRACTS to ascribe human qualities to an object or abstract notion — **personifiable** adj — **personifier** n

personnel /púrssə nél/ n the department of an organization or business that deals with employing staff and staffing issues generally ■ npl the people employed in an organization, business, or armed force [Early 19C. < French < personne 'person' < Latin persona 'mask worn by an actor, character']

person-to-person adj 1. ONLINE, COMPUT full form of **P2P** 2. US used to describe a telephone call chargeable only when a specific person is reached

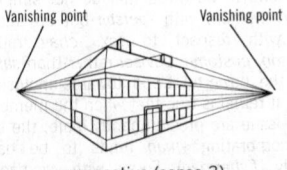

perspective (sense 3)

perspective /pər spéktiv/ n 1. PARTICULAR EVALUATION OF SOMETHING a particular evaluation of a situation or facts, especially from one person's point of view ○ a different perspective on the matter 2. MEASURED ASSESSMENT OF SITUATION a measured or objective assessment of a situation, giving all aspects their comparative importance ○ He's having trouble keeping things in perspective right now. 3. APPEARANCE OF DISTANT OBJECTS TO OBSERVER the appearance of objects to an observer allowing for the effect of their distance from the observer 4. ART ALLOWANCE FOR ARTISTIC PERSPECTIVE WHEN DRAWING the theory or practice of allowing for artistic perspective when drawing or painting 5. VISTA a vista or view [14C. Via French < late Latin perspectivus 'optical' < Latin perspicere 'look closely' < specere 'look at'] — **perspectively** adv

Perspex /púr speks/ tdmk a trademark for a tough transparent acrylic plastic that can be used in place of glass

perspicacious /púrspi káyshəss/ adj penetratingly discerning or perceptive [Early 17C. < Latin perspicac- < perspicere (see PERSPECTIVE)] — **perspicaciously** adv

perspicacity /púrspi kássəti/ n acuteness of discernment or perception

perspicuity /púrspi kyoó əti/ n 1. the quality of being perspicuous 2. same as **perspicacity**

perspicuous /pər spíkyoo əss/ adj clearly expressed and therefore easily understood [Late 16C. < Latin perspicuus < perspicere (see PERSPECTIVE)] — **perspicuously** adv

perspiration /púrspə ráysh'n/ n 1. fluid lost from the body both in the form of sweat secreted by the sweat glands and as water that diffuses through the skin 2. the process or act of excreting sweat — **perspiratory** /pər spírətəri/ adj

perspire /pər spír/ (-spires, -spiring, -spired) vti to secrete fluid from the sweat glands through the pores of the skin [Mid-17C. Via French < Latin perspirare, literally 'breathe through' < spirare 'breathe'] — **perspiringly** adv

Persson /páirss'n/, **Göran** (b. 1949) Swedish politician. A former minister of finance (1994–96), he became chairman of the Social Democratic Party and prime minister in 1996.

persuadable /pər swáydəbəl/ adj able to be persuaded to do or accept something ■ n an undecided voter who is regarded as being willing to vote for a candidate, given the right motivation and rationale

persuade /pər swáyd/ (-suades, -suading, -suaded) vt 1. to succeed in convincing somebody to do something, especially by reasoning, pleading, or coaxing 2. to make somebody believe something, especially by giving good reasons for doing so [Early 16C. < Latin persuadere 'urge strongly' < suadere 'to urge'] — **persuadability** /pər swáydə bílləti/ n

USAGE See **convince**.

persuader /pər swáydər/ n 1. somebody or something, e.g. a situation, that serves to persuade somebody to do something 2. a weapon, e.g. a gun, used to intimidate somebody (slang)

persuasion /pər swáyzh'n/ n 1. ACT OF PERSUADING the act of persuading somebody to do something 2. ABILITY TO PERSUADE the ability to persuade somebody 3. SET OF BELIEFS a set of beliefs, e.g. a set of religious or political beliefs ○ believers of all religious persuasions 4. GROUP WITH PARTICULAR BELIEFS a group whose members share a particular set of beliefs or views or a particular lifestyle ○ recent recruits to the hawkish persuasion 5. TYPE a group of people or things with a particular characteristic in common (informal humorous) ○ those of the long-legged persuasion [14C. Via French < Latin persuasion- < persuas-, past participle of persuadere (see PERSUADE)]

USAGE See **conviction**.

persuasive /pər swáyssiv/ adj having the ability to persuade people or the effect of persuading them [Late 16C. Directly or via French < medieval Latin persuasivus < Latin persuas- (see PERSUASION)] — **persuasively** adv — **persuasiveness** n

~~**persue**~~ incorrect spelling of **pursue**

~~**persuit**~~ incorrect spelling of **pursuit**

~~**persumably**~~ incorrect spelling of **presumably**

pert /purt/ adj 1. AMUSINGLY CHEEKY cheeky and lively in a pleasant or amusing way 2. JAUNTY jaunty and stylish in design ○ a pert hat 3. SMALL AND WELL-SHAPED small, well-shaped, and pretty ○ a pert nose [13C. Via

Old French *apert* 'open, frank' < Latin *apertus* 'open' < *aperire* 'to open'] —**pertly** *adv* —**pertness** *n*

PERT /purt/ *n* a method of charting and scheduling a complex set of interrelated activities that identifies the most time-critical events in the process. Full form **programme evaluation and review technique**

pertain /pər táyn/ (**-tains, -taining, -tained**) *vi* **1.** RELATE OR HAVE RELEVANCE to have relevance, reference, or a connection to something **2.** BE APPROPRIATE to be appropriate, fitting, or suitable **3.** BE PART OR BELONG to be part of something or belong to something, especially as an attribute or accessory [14C. Via French < Latin *pertinere*, literally 'hold to' < *tenere* 'hold, keep']

Perth /purth/ **1.** city on the River Tay in Perth and Kinross Council Area, central Scotland. Population: 41,453 (1991). **2.** capital city of Western Australia, located on the River Swan. Population: 1,341,900 (1998).

Perth and Kinross council area in north-central Scotland. Perth is its administrative centre. Area: 5,321 sq. km/2,019 sq. mi.

Perthite *n* ANZ somebody who comes from Perth in Western Australia —**Perthite** *adj*

pertinacious /púrti náyshəss/ *adj* determinedly resolute in purpose, belief, or action [Early 17C. < Latin *pertinac-* 'very tenacious' < *tenac-* (see TENACIOUS)] —**pertinaciously** *adv* —**pertinaciousness** *n* —**pertinacity** /-nássəti/ *n*

pertinent /púrtinənt/ *adj* relevant to the matter being considered [14C. Via French < Latin *pertinent-*, present participle of *pertinere* (see PERTAIN)] —**pertinence** *n* —**pertinently** *adv*

perturb /pər túrb/ (**-turbs, -turbing, -turbed**) *vt* **1.** to disturb and trouble somebody **2.** to cause a small deviation in the behaviour of a physical system, e.g. in the orbit of an electron or a planet [14C. Via French < Latin *perturbare* 'disturb thoroughly' < *turbare* 'disturb' < *turba* 'turmoil'] —**perturbable** *adj* —**perturbably** *adv* —**perturbing** *adj* —**perturbingly** *adv*

perturbation /púrtər báysh'n/ *n* **1.** BEING PERTURBED disturbance and trouble, a disturbed and troubled state, or the act of disturbing and troubling somebody or something **2.** CAUSE OF TROUBLE something that causes disruption, trouble, or disorder **3.** PHYS DISTURBANCE CAUSED BY SECONDARY INFLUENCE a slight disturbance of a system by a secondary influence within it **4.** ASTRON DEVIATION IN ORBIT CAUSED BY GRAVITY a deviation in an astronomical object's orbit or path caused by the gravitational attraction of another astronomical object

pertussis /pər tússiss/ *n* MED same as **whooping cough** (*technical*) [Late 18C. < modern Latin < Latin *per-* 'extreme' + *tussis* 'cough'] —**pertussal** *adj*

Peru

Peru /pə róo/ country in western South America, bordered by Ecuador, Colombia, Brazil, Bolivia, Chile, and the Pacific Ocean. It is the third largest country in South America. Language: Spanish. Currency: nuevo sol. Capital: Lima. Population: 28,409,897 (2003). Area: 1,285,216 sq. km/496,225 sq. mi. Official name **Republic of Peru**

Perugia /pə róojə/ city in central Italy. It is the capital of Perugia Province and Umbria Region. Population: 149,125 (2001).

peruke: Samuel Pepys wearing a peruke

peruke /pə róok/ *n* HAIR same as **periwig** (*archaic*) [Mid-16C. Via French < Italian *perrucca* 'head of hair']

peruse /pə róoz/ (**-ruses, -rusing, -rused**) *vt* **1.** to read or examine something, usually in a careful and thorough way or taking time to do it **2.** to read through or scan something quickly [Mid-16C. < Latin *per-* 'thoroughly' + USE] —**perusable** *adj* —**perusal** *n* —**peruser** *n*

Perutz /pə róots/, **Max** (1914–2002) Austrian-born British biochemist. He shared the Nobel Prize in chemistry (1962) for his work on haemoglobin, using X-ray crystallography. Full name **Perutz, Max Ferdinand**

Peruvian /pə róovi ən/ *adj* relating to or originating in Peru ■ *n* somebody who comes from Peru [Early 17C. < modern Latin *Peruvia* 'Peru']

Peruvian balsam *n* PHARM same as **balsam of Peru**

Peruvian bark *n* the bark of a cinchona tree. Use: formerly, to make quinine. [Because the trees grew in Peru]

perv /purv/, **perve** *n* **1.** same as **pervert** (*slang insult*) **2.** ANZ a voyeuristic glance or look (*slang*) ■ *vi* (**pervs, perving, perved**; **perves, perving, perved**) ANZ to give somebody a lustful look (*slang*) [Mid-20C. Shortening of PERVERT] —**pervy** *adj*

pervade /pər váyd/ (**-vades, -vading, -vaded**) *vt* to spread through or be present throughout something [Mid-17C. < Latin *pervadere* 'go throughout' < *vadere* 'go'] —**pervader** *n* —**pervasion** /-váyzh'n/ *n*

pervasive /pər váyssiv/ *adj* spreading widely or present throughout something [Mid-18C. < Latin *pervas-*, past participle of *pervadere* (see PERVADE)] —**pervasively** *adv* —**pervasiveness** *n*

perve *n, vi* ANZ another spelling of **perv** (*slang*)

perverse /pər vúrss/ *adj* **1.** contrary to what is regarded as normal or reasonable, often for reasons that seem unaccountable or self-defeating ○ *There's a kind of perverse logic that argues that only working longer and harder can get you more free time.* **2.** deliberately and doggedly behaving in a way that seems contrary to good sense or your own best interests ○ *He knew he was being perverse, but he still refused point blank to accept the offered help.* **3.** same as **perverted** (sense 2) [14C. Via French < Latin *perversus*, past participle of *pervertere* (see PERVERT)] —**perversely** *adv* —**perverseness** *n*

perversion /pər vúrsh'n/ *n* **1.** a sexual practice considered unusual or unacceptable **2.** the changing of something good, true, or correct into something bad or wrong, or a situation in which the change has occurred ○ *perversion of justice*

perversity /pər vúrssəti/ (*plural* **-ties**) *n* **1.** being perverse, especially wilfully persisting in actions that seem contrary to good sense or your own best interests **2.** something, e.g. an action or activity, that is perverse

perversive /pər vúrssiv/ *adj* tending or able to pervert something

pervert *vt* /pər vúrt/ (**-verts, -verting, -verted**) **1.** LEAD SOMEBODY AWAY FROM GOOD to lead somebody or something away from what is considered good, normal, moral, or proper **2.** MISINTERPRET OR DISTORT SOMETHING to misinterpret or distort something such as a piece of text **3.** USE SOMETHING IMPROPERLY to use something incorrectly or improperly **4.** DEBASE SOMETHING to bring something into a state regarded

as morally inferior or reprehensible ■ *n* /púr vurt/ SOMEBODY WHOSE SEXUAL BEHAVIOUR IS UNACCEPTABLE somebody whose sexual behaviour is considered unacceptably deviant [14C. Via French < Latin *pervertere* 'turn wrong' < *vertere* 'turn'] —**perverter** *n* —**pervertible** *adj*

perverted /pər vúrtid/ *adj* **1.** DEVIATING FROM WHAT IS PROPER deviating greatly from what is accepted as right, normal, or proper **2.** RELATING TO UNUSUAL SEXUAL ACTIVITIES relating to or practising sexual activities considered unusual or unacceptable **3.** DISTORTED misinterpreted or distorted —**pervertedly** *adv* —**pervertedness** *n*

pervious /púrvi əss/ *adj* **1.** able to be penetrated or permeated **2.** open to ideas, suggestions, and change [Early 17C. < Latin *pervius* < *per-* 'through' + *via* 'way'] —**perviously** *adv* —**perviousness** *n*

pes /pays, peez/ (*plural* **pedes** /peé deez/) *n* **1.** the foot, or a part resembling a foot **2.** a hind foot of a four-footed vertebrate [Mid-19C. < Latin, 'foot']

Pesach /páy saakh/ *n* the Passover festival [Early 17C. < Hebrew *pesaḥ* < *pāsaḥ* 'pass over'; because God passed over the Israelites' first-born (Exodus 12:11–27)]

peseta /pə sáytə/ *n* the main unit of the former Spanish currency [Early 19C. < Spanish, 'small peso' < *peso* (see PESO)]

pesewa /pay sáy waa/ *n* a subunit of the Ghanaian currency. See table at **currency** [Mid-20C. < Fanti and Twi, 'penny']

Peshawar /pə sháawər/, **Peshāwar** city near the Khyber Pass in the North-West Frontier District, Pakistan. Population: 988,055 (1998).

Peshitta /pə sheétə/, **Peshitto** /pə sheétō/ *n* the Syriac version of the Bible, written around the 4th century [Late 18C. < Syriac *pšīṭṭā* 'the simple one']

pesky /péski/ (**-kier, -kiest**) *adj* N Am troublesome or irritating (*informal*) [Late 18C. Probably < alteration of PEST] —**peskily** *adv* —**peskiness** *n*

peso /páyssō/ (*plural* **-sos**) *n* the main unit of currency in several South and Central American countries. See table at **currency** [Mid-16C. Via Spanish < Latin *pensum* 'weight' < past participle of *pendere* 'weigh']

pessary /péssəri/ (*plural* **-ries**) *n* **1.** a plastic device, e.g. a ring, placed in the vagina to keep the womb in position following a prolapse caused by weakened ligaments **2.** a suppository containing medication for insertion into the vagina [14C. < late Latin *pessarium* < Greek *pessos* 'pessary, oval stone used in board games']

pessimism /péssəmizəm/ *n* **1.** a tendency to see only the negative or worst aspects of all things and to expect only bad or unpleasant things to happen **2.** a doctrine that all things become evil or that evil outweighs good in life [Late 18C. < French *pessimisme* < Latin *pessimus* 'worst']

pessimist /péssə mist/ *n* somebody who always expects the worst to happen —**pessimistic** /pessə místik/ *adj* —**pessimistically** *adv*

pest /pest/ *n* **1.** DAMAGING ORGANISM an organism that is damaging to livestock, crops, humans, or land fertility **2.** ANNOYING PERSON OR THING somebody or something that is a nuisance (*informal*) **3.** OUTBREAK OF DISEASE an epidemic of infectious or contagious disease (*archaic*) [Mid-16C. Via French, 'pestilence' < Latin *pestis*]

Pestalozzi /péstə lótsi/, **Johann Heinrich** (1746–1827) Swiss educator. He developed teaching methods adapted to children's natural development, the basis of modern primary education.

> 'Perhaps the most fateful gift an evil genius could bestow upon our times is knowledge without skill.'
> [Johann Heinrich Pestalozzi. Quoted in *The Education of Man: Aphorisms*, Heinz and Ruth Norden (trs.); 1951]

pester /péstər/ (**-ters, -tering, -tered**) *vt* to be a constant source of annoyance to somebody, e.g. by harassing him or her with demands [Mid-16C. < French *empestrer* 'embarrass', influenced by PEST] —**pesterer** *n* —**pesteringly** *adv*

pesthouse /pést howss/ (*plural* **-houses** /-howziz/) *n* a hospital where patients suffering from infectious

disease were once treated [Early 17C. < PEST 'contagious disease']

pesticide /pésti sīd/ *n* a chemical substance used to kill pests, especially insects —**pesticidal** /pésti sīd'l/ *adj*

pestiferous /pe stíffərəss/ *adj* **1. ANNOYING** troublesome or annoying **2. CAUSING INFECTIOUS DISEASE** breeding or spreading a virulently infectious disease **3. CORRUPTING** wicked and corrupting (*formal*) [15C. < Latin *pestifer* 'plague-carrying' < *pestis* 'plague'] —**pestiferously** *adv* —**pestiferousness** *n*

pestilence /péstilənss/ *n* (*archaic*) **1.** an epidemic of a highly contagious or infectious disease such as bubonic plague **2.** a serious infectious disease

pestilent /péstilənt/ *adj* **1. DEADLY** causing or tending to cause death **2. ANNOYING** annoying or infuriating (*literary or humorous*) **3. DAMAGING** very harmful morally or socially (*archaic*) [14C. Via French < Latin *pestilent-* < *pestis* 'plague'] —**pestilential** /pésti lénsh'l/ *adj* —**pestilentially** *adv* —**pestilently** *adv*

pestle /péss'l/ *n* a rod-shaped object made from hard material with a rounded end that is used for crushing or grinding substances in a mortar ■ *vti* (**-tles, -tling, -tled**) to crush, grind, or pound a substance or object using a pestle [14C. Via French < Latin *pistillum*]

pesto /péstō/ *n* **1.** a sauce or paste made by crushing together basil leaves, pine nuts, oil, Parmesan cheese, and garlic. It is traditionally served hot or cold with pasta or on meat. **2.** a puréed or finely minced paste of herbs and vegetables, tomatoes, or olives, used as pasta sauce [Mid-20C. < Italian < past participle of *pestare* 'pound, crush' < late Latin *pistare* < Latin *pinsere* 'to beat']

pet[1] /pet/ *n* **1. ANIMAL KEPT AT HOME** an animal kept for companionship, interest, or amusement **2. FAVOURITE PERSON** an indulged or pampered person **3. LOVED PERSON** somebody whom others find lovable **4. AFFECTIONATE TERM OF ADDRESS** a term of affection or endearment used to address somebody (*informal*) ■ *adj* **1. KEPT AS PET** kept as a pet animal **2. SPECIAL OR FAVOURITE** cherished by or favourite to somebody ○ *a pet topic* ■ *v* (**pets, petting, petted**) **1.** *vt* **STROKE ANIMAL** to lovingly pat or stroke an animal, or touch a child similarly **2.** *vt* **TREAT SOMEBODY INDULGENTLY** to treat a person or animal indulgently **3.** *vi* **TOUCH FOR SEXUAL PLEASURE** to touch each other in a way that causes sexual pleasure [Early 16C. Origin ?] —**petter** *n*

pet[2] /pet/ *n* a fit of sulkiness or peevishness ■ *vi* (**pets, petting, petted**) to be peevish or sulky [Mid-16C. Origin ?]

PET[1] /pet/ *abbr* MED positron emission tomography

PET[2] *n* a type of plastic used for recyclable containers. Full form **polyethylene terephthalate**

Pet. *abbr* BIBLE Peter

peta- *prefix* **1.** one thousand million million (10^{15}) ○ *petabyte* Symbol **P 2.** in the binary system, a quadrillion (2^{50}) [Alteration of PENTA-; because it represents 1,000 to the fifth power]

petabyte /péttə bīt/ *n* one thousand million million bytes

Pétain /pe tán, pe táN/, **Philippe** (1856–1951) French general and head of the Vichy government (1940–42). He ruled the French-occupied territory as a dictator with the consent of the Nazi regime. He later stood trial for treason, and was sentenced to life imprisonment. Full name **Pétain, Henri Philippe Omer**

petal /pétt'l/ *n* one of the showy coloured parts of a flower in bloom. The ring of petals forms the corolla of a plant. [Early 18C. Via modern Latin < Greek *petalon* 'leaf'] —**petaline** /péttə līn/ *adj* —**petalled** *adj* —**petaloid** *adj*

-petal *suffix* moving towards ○ *centripetal* [< modern Latin *-petus* < Latin *petere* 'seek']

petaliferous /pétt'l íffərəss/, **petalous** /pétt'ləss/ *adj* having petals

pétanque /pay taángk/ *n* LEISURE same as **boules** [Mid-20C. < French]

petard /pe taárd/ *n* **1.** a small explosive charge or grenade used to blow a hole in a door, wall, or fortification **2.** a powerful firecracker [Mid-16C. < French *pétard* < *péter* 'break wind' < Latin *pedere*] ◇ **be hoist with your own petard** to be the victim of your own attempt to harm somebody else

Petavius /pə táyvi əss/ crater on the Moon with a prominent crack (**rill**) across the floor and a complex central peak, located south of Mare Fecundatis, 177 km/110 mi. in diameter

petcock /pét kok/ *n* a small manually operated valve or tap used to drain off waste material or excess fluid from the cylinder of an internal combustion engine [Mid-19C. < *pet*, origin ? + COCK 'spout']

petechia /pi teéki ə/ (*plural* **-chiae** /-ki ee/) *n* a tiny purplish-red spot on the skin caused by the release into the skin of a very small quantity of blood from a capillary [Late 18C. Via modern Latin < Italian *petecchie* 'spots on the skin' < Latin *impetigo* (see IMPETIGO)] —**petechial** *adj*

peter[1] /peétər/ (**-ters, -tering, -tered**) [Early 19C. Origin ?] **peter out** *vi* to dwindle and finally stop or disappear

peter[2] /peétər/ *n* (*slang*) **1.** a safe or cash box **2.** the witness box in a court **3.** *N Am* same as **penis** (*considered offensive by some people*) [Early 20C. < the name *Peter*]

peter[3] /peétər/ (**-ters, -tering, -tered**) *vi* in bridge and whist, to play a high card first, followed by a low card [Late 19C. Shortening of BLUE PETER in the obsolete sense 'higher card than necessary, played as a signal to your partner']

Peter /peétər/ *n* either of two books of the Bible, originally letters, traditionally attributed to St Peter. See table at **Bible**

Peter /peétər/, **St** (*d.* AD 64?) one of the 12 apostles of Jesus Christ. He was a leader and missionary in the early church, and traditionally the first Bishop of Rome. Born **Simon**

Peter I (1672–1725) tsar of Russia. During his reign (1682–1725), he did much to modernize and westernize his country, and his victory over Sweden established Russia as a major European power. He founded St Petersburg as his capital in 1703. Known as **Peter the Great**

Peterborough /peétərbərə/ **1.** city and unitary authority in eastern England. Population: 156,061 (2001). **2.** city in southeastern Ontario, Canada, approximately 40 km/25 mi. north of Lake Ontario. Population: 73,303 (2001).

Peterhead /peétər héd/ town and fishing port in Aberdeenshire. It is the most easterly town in Scotland. Population: 18,674 (1991).

Peterlee /peétər leé/ town in County Durham, northern England. It was built as a new town in 1948. Population: 31,139 (1991).

peterman /peétərmən/ (*plural* **-men** /-mən/) *n* a burglar who specializes in breaking safes (*slang*) [Early 19C. < *peter* 'safe, cash box', after the man's name *Peter*]

Peter Pan *n* a man who looks very young or behaves in a boyish way (*informal*) [Early 20C. After the hero of J. M. Barrie's play *Peter Pan, or The Boy Who Wouldn't Grow Up* (1904)]

Peter Pan collar *n* a flat collar attached to a round neck with rounded ends visible at the front

Peter Principle *n* the theory that all members of an organization will eventually be promoted to a level at which they are no longer competent to do their job [Mid-20C. After Laurence Johnston *Peter* (1919–90), US educationalist and author]

Peters /peétərz/, **Winston** (*b.* 1945) New Zealand politician. He founded the New Zealand First Party in 1993, and served as deputy prime minister and treasurer of New Zealand (1996–98). Full name **Peters, Winston Raymond**

petersham /peétərshəm/ *n* a strong ribbed ribbon used to reinforce parts of garments such as waistbands [Early 19C. After Viscount *Petersham* (1790–1851), British army officer]

Peterson /peétərss'n/, **Oscar** (*b.* 1925) Canadian pianist. He is known for his technical brilliance in jazz. Full name **Peterson, Oscar Emmanuel**

Peter's pence *n* **1.** a voluntary financial contribution made by some Roman Catholic dioceses to the Papal See **2.** a tax of one penny per household paid to the Papal See in medieval times until it was abolished by Henry VIII [After St PETER as the first bishop of Rome]

Peters' projection *n* a form of map projection that represents the relative size of land masses more accurately than Mercator's projection [Late 20C. After Arno *Peters* (b. 1916), German historian]

pethidine /péthi deen/ *n* a white crystalline compound. Use: painkiller, sedative. Formula: $C_{15}H_{21}NO_2$. N Am term **meperidine** [Mid-20C. Blend of P(IPER)IDINE + ETH(YL)]

pétillant /pétti oN, péttilənt/ *adj* describes wine that is slightly sparkling [Late 19C. < French, present participle of *pétiller* 'effervesce' < *péter* (see PETARD)]

petiolar /pétti ōlər/ *adj* relating to the growth of petioles

petiole /pétti ōl/ *n* same as **leafstalk** (*technical*) [Mid-18C. < modern Latin *petiolus*, variant of Latin *peciolus* 'little foot' < *pes* 'foot'] —**petiolate** /-ə layt/ *adj*

petiolule /pétti ə lyool/ *n* the stalk of a leaflet in a compound leaf [Mid-19C. < modern Latin *petiolulus* 'little petiole' < *petiolus* (see PETIOLE)]

petit bourgeois /pétti bóorzhwaa/ (*plural* **petits bourgeois** /*pronunc. same*/) *n* a member of the lower middle class [< French, 'little citizen']

petite /pə teét/ *adj* **1.** having a small and delicate build ○ *a petite woman* **2.** designed to fit smaller women or girls [Mid-16C. < French, 'little']

petite bourgeoisie /pə teét boor zhwaa zeé/ *n* people in the lower middle class, a group traditionally including small business operators and tradespeople

petit four /pétti fáwr/ (*plural* **petits fours** /pétti fáwr, -fáwrz/) *n* any one of a mixture of bite-size sweet biscuits or cakes served at the end of a meal with coffee [< French, 'little oven']

petition /pə tísh'n/ *n* **1. DEMAND FOR ACTION WITH SIGNATURES** a written request signed by many people demanding a specific action from an authority or government **2. APPEAL OR REQUEST TO HIGHER AUTHORITY** an appeal or request to a higher authority or being **3. SOMETHING REQUESTED** something requested or appealed for **4. ACT OF PETITIONING** the act of making a petition **5.** LAW **DOCUMENT INITIATING LEGAL ACTION** a written application for a legal action to be taken, particularly at the start of divorce proceedings ■ *vti* (**-tions, -tioning, -tioned**) **1. GIVE PETITION TO SOMEBODY** to give or address a petition to somebody, especially somebody in authority or a representative of an organization **2. MAKE DEMAND USING PETITION** to urge for or against a course of action by presenting a petition ○ *petitioning for his release* [14C. Via French < Latin *petition-* < *petere* 'seek, go towards'] —**petitionary** *adj* —**petitioner** *n*

ORIGIN The Latin word *petere* 'to seek', from which ***petition*** is derived, is also the source of English *appetite, compete, impetus, perpetual, petulant,* and *repeat.*

petitio principii /pə tíshi ō prin kíppi ī, -síppi ī/ *n* logically fallacious reasoning in which what has to be proved is already assumed [< Latin, 'assuming the first thing']

petit larceny /pétti-/ *n* the theft of something whose value lies below a locally set level

petit mal /pétti mál/ *n* a form of epilepsy marked by episodes of brief loss of consciousness without convulsions or falling. It is found most frequently in children and adolescents. [< French, 'small illness']

petit point /pétti póynt/ (*plural* **petits points** /*pronunc. same*/) *n* **1.** a small stitch used in needlepoint when creating details **2.** work embroidered using small stitches [< French, 'small stitch']

petits pois /pétti pwaá/ *npl* small sweet green peas [< French, 'small peas']

pet name *n* a special affectionate name used to address or refer to a family member or close friend

petnapping /pét naping/ *n* the theft of a pet animal [Late 20C. After KIDNAPPING] —**petnapper** *n*

Petra /péttrə/ ancient ruined city in southwestern Jordan, famous for its buildings and tombs that are carved out of solid rock

Petrarch /pét raark/ (1304–74) Italian lyric poet and scholar. He is best remembered for his series of love poems addressed to Laura, the *Canzoniere*

(after 1327). Born **Petrarca, Francesco** —**Petrarchan** /pi traárkən/ *adj*

Petrarchan sonnet *n* a form of poetry that has an eight-line stanza with the rhyme scheme abbaabba followed by six lines with various rhyme schemes, usually cdcdcd or cdecde [Early 19C. After Francesco PETRARCH]

petrel /péttrəl/ *n* a seabird such as the storm petrel, the diving petrel, or the fulmar. Petrels are widespread in ocean environments and move awkwardly on land. Families: Hydrobatidae or Pelecanoididae or Procellariidae. [Early 17C. Probably after St PETER, because it flies low with legs down giving the appearance of walking on water]

petri- *prefix* same as **petro-**

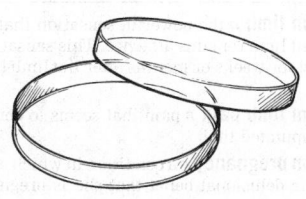

Petri dish

Petri dish /péttri-, peétri-/ *n* a shallow flat-bottomed dish with a loose cover, used especially to grow bacterial cultures in the laboratory [After Julius *Petri* (1852–92), German bacteriologist]

Petrie /peétri/, **Sir Flinders** (1853–1942) British archaeologist. He is noted for his work in Egypt and Palestine. He devised a method of relative dating based on pottery types. Full name **Petrie, Sir William Matthew Flinders**

petrifaction /péttri fáksh'n/, **petrification** /péttrifi káysh'n/ *n* **1.** the process in which the porous structure of organic material such as bone, shell, and wood is infiltrated by salt-bearing ground water, which preserves the structure when it solidifies. The Petrified Forest in Arizona contains whole tree trunks that have been turned into stone. **2.** the condition of being turned into stone

Petrified Forest National Park /péttri fíd-/ national park in eastern Arizona, established as a national monument in 1906, and as a national park in 1962. It is noted for its petrified trees and Native American ruins. Area: 379 sq. km/146 sq. mi.

petrify /péttri fí/ (-**fies**, -**fying**, -**fied**) *v* **1.** *vt* IMMOBILIZE SOMEBODY WITH FEAR to cause a person or animal to become immobile with terror **2.** *vti* TURN SOMETHING TO STONE to become stone, or cause something organic to turn into stone **3.** *vti* MAKE OR BECOME DEADENED to become dull, stiff, or deadened, or cause something to become dull, stiff, or deadened [15C. < French *pétrifier* or medieval Latin *petrificare*, both < Latin *petra* 'stone, rock' < Greek, 'rock'] —**petrifier** *n*

Petrine /peé trīn/ *adj* **1.** relating to or associated with St Peter **2.** in the Roman Catholic Church, relating to a dissolved marriage between somebody who has been baptized and somebody who has not [Mid-19C. < ecclesiastical Latin *Petrus* 'Peter']

petro- *prefix* **1.** rock, stone ○ *petrography* **2.** petroleum ○ *petrodollar* [< Greek *petros* 'stone', *petra* 'rock']

petrochemical /péttrō kémmik'l/ *n* a substance derived from petroleum or natural gas, e.g. petrol or paraffin wax ■ *adj* relating to or derived from petrochemicals —**petrochemically** *adv*

petrochemistry /péttrō kémmistri/ *n* **1.** the branch of chemistry that is concerned with petroleum and derivatives of petroleum **2.** the chemistry of rocks, especially with reference to their composition

petrodollar /péttrō dolər/ *n* a unit of foreign currency earned by an oil-exporting country

petrogenesis /péttrō jénnəssiss/ *n* the origin, formation, and history of rocks —**petrogenic** *adj*

petroglyph /péttrōglif/ *n* a prehistoric drawing done

on rock [Late 19C. < French *pétroglyphe* < Greek *petros* 'stone' + *glyphē* 'carving']

Petrograd /péttrə grád/ former name for **St Petersburg** (1914–24)

petrography /pe tróggrəfi/ *n* the systematic description of the texture of rocks and the minerals they contain, often using microscopy of thin slices of the rock to determine the mineral content —**petrographer** *n* —**petrographic** /péttrə gráffik/ *adj* —**petrographically** *adv*

petrol /péttrəl/ *n* a volatile flammable liquid made from petroleum, used as fuel in internal-combustion engines. N Am term **gasoline** [Mid-16C. Via French *pétrole* < medieval Latin *petroleum* (see PETROLEUM)]

petrol. *abbr* petrology

petrol blue *adj* of a greyish-blue colour tinged with green —**petrol blue** *n*

petrol bomb *n* a crude bomb usually made of a bottle filled with a flammable liquid such as petrol with a rag for a wick that is lit just before it is thrown ■ *vt* to use a petrol bomb on a target —**petrol bomber** *n*

petrol cap *n* a sealing device for the pipe that leads to the petrol tank of a motor vehicle

petroleum /pə tróli əm/ *n* crude oil that occurs naturally in sedimentary rocks and consists mainly of hydrocarbons. A wide variety of commercially important petrochemicals, including petrol and paraffin, are derived from it. [Early 16C. < medieval Latin < Latin *petra* 'stone, rock' + *oleum* 'oil']

petroleum jelly *n* a greasy gelatinous substance. Source: petroleum. Use: ointment base, lubricant, protective covering.

petrolhead /péttrəl hed/ *n* somebody whose principal interest is fast cars or motor racing (*slang*)

petrology /pə tróllaji/ *n* the study of sedimentary, igneous, and metamorphic rocks with respect to their occurrence, structure, origin, history, and mineral content —**petrological** /péttrə lójjik'l/ *adj* —**petrologically** *adv* —**petrologist** *n*

petrol pump *n* a device usually located at a petrol station for delivering fuel to a vehicle

petrol station *n UK* a place at which drivers can buy fuel, oil, and other motoring supplies. ANZ term **service station**. N Am term **gas station**

petronel /pétrə nel/ *n* a short firearm with a curved butt whose length was between that of a long pistol and a short carbine, used mostly by cavalry in the 16th and 17th centuries [Late 16C. < French *petrinal*, variant of *poitrinal* < *poitrine* 'chest' < Latin *pectus*; because the butt rested against the chest when the gun was fired]

petrosal /pə tróss'l/ *adj* affecting or belonging to the hard (**petrous**) portion of the temporal bone surrounding the inner ear [Mid-18C. < Latin *petrosus* (see PETROUS)]

petrous /péttrəss/ *adj* **1.** relating to or resembling rock or stone **2.** describes the hard portion of the temporal bone surrounding the inner ear [Mid-16C. < Latin *petrosus* 'rocky' < *petra* (see PETRIFY)]

PET scan /pét-/ *n* an image of a bodily cross-section, usually of the brain, that reveals metabolic processes and that is obtained by means of positron emission tomography —**PET scanner** *n* —**PET scanning** *n*

petticoat /pétti kōt/ *n* **1.** WOMAN'S UNDERGARMENT a woman's undergarment that is sometimes decorated and consists of an underskirt with or without a bodice **2.** CLOTHING SKIRT UNDER SARI a long skirt worn under a sari **3.** OFFENSIVE TERM an offensive term for a woman or girl, or women in general (*dated*) [15C. < PETTY 'small']

pettifogger /pétti fogər/ *n* somebody who quibbles or fusses about petty details [Mid-16C. Probably < PETTY + *fogger*, origin ?] —**pettifog** *vi* —**pettifoggery** *n*

pettifogging /pétti foging/ *adj* **1.** petty or trivial ○ *pettifogging details* **2.** quibbling or fussing over trivial matters

petting /pétting/ *n* touching between people that causes sexual pleasure but does not include sexual intercourse

pettish /péttish/ *adj* peevish, irritable, or sulky [Late 16C. < PET2] —**pettishly** *adv* —**pettishness** *n*

petty /pétti/ (-**tier**, -**tiest**) *adj* **1.** INSIGNIFICANT of little importance **2.** NARROW-MINDED narrow-minded in nature **3.** MEAN spiteful in character **4.** SUBORDINATE subordinate in rank or importance [14C. < Old French *peti, petit* 'small'] —**pettily** *adv* —**pettiness** *n*

Petty /pétti/, **Bruce** (*b.* 1929) Australian cartoonist and filmmaker. He won an Academy Award for his short animated film *Leisure '77* (1977). Full name **Petty, Bruce Leslie**

petty cash *n* a small amount of money kept, e.g. in an office, and used to cover minor everyday expenses

petty larceny *n* CRIME another spelling of **petit larceny**

petty officer *n* NAVY **1.** NAVAL OFFICER an officer in the British Navy of a rank above leading seaman **2.** NONCOMMISSIONED NAVAL OFFICER a noncommissioned officer in the US Navy or Coast Guard of a rank above seaman **3.** NAVAL OFFICER an officer in the Canadian Navy of a rank above master seaman

petty sessions *n* a court of summary jurisdiction in the United Kingdom, no longer used formally

petulant /péttyoŏlənt/ *adj* ill-tempered or sulky in a peevish manner [Late 16C. Via French < Latin *petulant-* 'insolent' < *petere* 'seek, go towards'] —**petulance** *n* —**petulantly** *adv*

petunia

petunia /pə tyoŏni ə/ *n* a flowering plant with sticky stems. Flowers: brightly coloured, funnel-shaped. Native to: tropical America. Genus: *Petunia*. ■ *adj* of a dark purple or violet colour [Early 19C. < modern Latin < obsolete French *petun* 'tobacco' < Tupi *pety*; because related to tobacco]

petuntse /pi túntsi, -toŏntsi/, **petunze** *n* a variety of feldspar that can be melted. Use: Chinese porcelain. [Early 18C. < Chinese *bāidūnzi*, literally 'white stone block']

Pevsner /pévsnər/, **Antoine** (1886–1962) Russian-born French sculptor. One of the founders of the constructivist school with his brother Naum Gabo, he emigrated to Paris (1923) and developed a highly personal style of sculpture.

pew /pyoŏ/ *n* **1.** a usually wooden bench with a straight back and often a kneeling bench attached to the one in front of it, used by worshippers in a church or synagogue **2.** a seat (*informal humorous*) ○ *take a pew* [14C. Via Old French *puie* 'balcony' < Latin *podium* (see PODIUM)]

pewee /peé wee/, **peewee** *n* a drab medium-sized bird of the tyrant-flycatcher family with a plaintive song. Genus: *Contopus*. [Late 18C. An imitation of its call]

pewit /peé wit/ *n* BIRDS same as **lapwing** [Early 16C. An imitation of its call]

pewter /pyoŏtər/ *n* **1.** TIN AND LEAD ALLOY a silver-grey alloy of tin and lead sometimes containing antimony and copper **2.** PEWTER OBJECTS COLLECTIVELY articles made from pewter **3.** DARK GREYISH COLOUR a dark dull grey colour tinged with blue or purple [14C. Via Old French *peutre* < assumed Vulgar Latin *peltrum*] —**pewter** *adj* —**pewterer** *n*

peyote /pay óti/ *n Southwest US* **1.** a spineless globe-shaped cactus that has small rounded nodules containing mescaline. Native to: Mexico, southwestern United States. Latin name: *Lophophora williamsii*. **2.** *also* **peyote button** a button-shaped nodule containing mescaline that forms on the stem of the peyote cactus [Mid-19C. Via American Spanish < Nahuatl *peyotl*]

pf *abbr* ONLINE French Polynesia (*used in Internet addresses*) See table at **domain name**

pF *symbol* MEASURE picofarad

pf. *abbr* **1.** GRAM perfect **2.** MONEY, HIST pfennig

PFD *abbr* **1.** NAUT personal flotation device **2.** FIN preferred (*used of shares*)

pfennig /fénnig/ (*plural* **-nigs** or **-nige** /-nigə/) *n* a subunit of the former German currency [Mid-16C. < German]

PFI *n* a government scheme to encourage private finance of public capital projects such as the building of hospitals and schools. Full form **Private Finance Initiative**

pg *abbr* ONLINE Papua New Guinea (*used in Internet addresses*) See table at **domain name**

PG[1] *tdmk* a rating indicating that a film may be seen by anyone, but parental guidance is suggested for children

PG[2] *abbr* EDUC postgraduate

P.G. *abbr* paying guest

PGA *abbr* Professional Golfers' Association

PGCA *abbr* E-COMMERCE payment gateway certificate authority

PGCE *n* in the United Kingdom, a teaching qualification taken by somebody who has already graduated from a university or college with a first degree. Full form **Postgraduate Certificate of Education**

PGP *n* a program to encrypt data for security purposes when transmitting over public networks such as the Internet. PGP uses public key encryption, a system that provides for privacy and authentication of both the sender and the receiver of the message. (*used in e-commerce*) Full form **Pretty Good Privacy**

PGx *abbr* PHARM **1.** pharmacogenetics **2.** pharmacogenomics

ph *abbr* ONLINE Philippines (*used in Internet addresses*) See table at **domain name**

pH *n* a measure of acidity or alkalinity in which the pH of pure water is 7, with lower numbers indicating acidity and higher numbers indicating alkalinity. Full form **potential of hydrogen**

Ph *symbol* CHEM phenyl group

PH, P.H. *abbr* PUBLIC ADMIN public health

phacoemulsification /fákō i múlssifi káysh'n/ *n* an ultrasonic technique using microsurgical instruments that allows a cataract-affected lens to be liquefied and removed by suction using a very small incision near the edge of the cornea. A foldable plastic lens is then inserted through the incision and unfolded. [Late 20C. < Greek *phakos* 'lentil'; because of the shape of the lens]

phaeton /fáytən/ *n* a small light four-wheeled carriage, usually with two seats and usually drawn by two horses [Late 16C. Via French < Greek *Phaethōn*, son of Helios in Greek mythology, killed by Zeus while trying to drive his father's chariot across the sky]

phage /fayj/ *n* MICROBIOL same as **bacteriophage** [Early 20C. Shortening]

-phage *suffix* something that eats ○ *xylophage* [< Greek *-phagos* < *phagein* 'eat' (see PHAGO-)]

phagedaena /fájjə deénə/, **phagedena** *n* an ulcer that spreads rapidly [Late 16C. Via Latin < Greek *phagedaina*]

-phagia *suffix* eating ○ *aerophagia* ○ *hyperphagia* [< Greek < *phagein* 'eat' (see PHAGO-)]

phago- *prefix* eating, consuming ○ *phagocyte* [< Greek *phagein* 'eat' < Indo-European, 'share out']

phagocyte /fággə sīt/ *n* a cell in the body's bloodstream and tissues, e.g. a white blood cell that engulfs and ingests foreign particles, cell waste material, and bacteria —**phagocytic** /fággə síttik/ *adj*

phagocytosis /fággə sī tṓssiss/ *n* the engulfing and ingesting of foreign particles or waste matter by phagocytes —**phagocytotic** /-sī tóttik/ *adj*

-phagous *suffix* eating ○ *polyphagous* [Via Latin < Greek *-phagos* (see -PHAGE)]

Phagwa /fágwa/ *n* HINDUISM same as **Holi** [Late 20C. < Hindi < PHALGUNA + *-wa*, masculine singular suffix]

-phagy *suffix* same as **-phagia**

Phalange /fə lánj/ *n* a Lebanese Christian paramilitary group [Mid-20C. Variant of FALANGE] —**Phalangist** *n, adj*

phalanger /fə lánjər/ *n* a small tree-dwelling marsupial with dense woolly fur and a long tail. Native to: Australia and nearby islands. Family: Phalangeridae. [Late 18C. < modern Latin < Greek *phalagg-* 'toe bone'; because of the webbed or fused toes on its hind feet]

phalanx /fállangks/ (*plural* **phalanxes** or **phalanges** /fə lán jeez/) *n* **1.** TIGHT GROUP a group of people, animals, or objects that are moving or standing closely together **2.** ANCIENT TROOP FORMATION especially in ancient Greece, a group of soldiers that attacked in close formation, protected by their overlapping shields and projecting spears **3.** (*plural* **phalanges**) FINGER AND TOE BONE a finger or toe bone of a human being or vertebrate animal [Mid-16C. Via Latin (stem *phalang-*) < Greek *phalagx* 'line of battle, finger or toe bone'] —**phalangeal** /fə lánji əl/ *adj*

phalarope /fállə rōp/ *n* a small wading bird that is related to the sandpiper but has lobed toes adapted for swimming. Genus: *Phalaropus*. [Late 18C. Via French < modern Latin *Phalaropus* < Greek *phalaris* 'coot' + *pous* 'foot']

Phalguna /fúl gŏŏnə/ *n* in the Hindu calendar, the 12th month of the year, lasting 30 days and falling about the same time as February or March. See table at **calendar**

phalli ARTS, ANAT plural of **phallus**

phallic /fállik/ *adj* **1.** OF PHALLUS relating to or resembling a phallus **2.** OF STAGE OF PSYCHOSEXUAL DEVELOPMENT in psychoanalytic theory, relating to a stage of psychosexual development during which a young child's sexual feelings are concentrated on the genitals **3.** OF PHALLICISM relating to phallicism [Late 18C. < Greek *phallikos* < *phallos* 'phallus']

phallicism /fállissizəm/ *n* the worshipping of the reproductive forces of life as symbolized by the penis —**phallicist** *n*

phallocentric /fállō séntrik/ *adj* centred on men or showing a preference for traditionally masculine qualities rather than traditionally feminine ones [Early 20C. < PHALLUS]

phallus /fálləss/ (*plural* **-luses** or **-li** /-lī/) *n* **1.** a picture, sculpture, or other representation of a penis, especially one regarded as a symbol of the reproductive force of life **2.** the human penis, especially when erect [Early 17C. Via late Latin < Greek *phallos*]

-phane, -phan *suffix* a substance having the appearance or qualities of ○ *cymophane* [< Greek *-phanēs* < *phainesthai* 'appear' < *phainein* 'bring to light']

phanerogam /fánnərō gam/ *n* a plant that produces seeds (*dated*) [Mid-19C. Via French < modern Latin *phanerogamus* < Greek *phaneros* 'visible' (< *phainein* 'bring to light') + *gamos* 'sexual union'] —**phanerogamic** /fánnərō gámmik/ *adj*

Phanerozoic /fánnərə zṓ ik/ *n* the present aeon of geological time, beginning 570 million years ago, that consists of the Palaeozoic, Mesozoic, and Cenozoic eras. See table at **geological time** [Late 19C. < Greek *phaneros* 'visible' + *zōē* 'life'] —**Phanerozoic** *adj*

phantasm /fán tazəm/ *n* **1.** a supposed being, e.g. a ghost or a disembodied spirit, that can be seen but does not have physical substance **2.** an understanding or perception that is not based on reality [13C. Via French *fantasme* < Greek *phantasma* < *phantazesthai* 'appear' < *phainein* 'bring to light'] —**phantasmal** /fan tázm'l/ *adj* —**phantasmally** *adv* —**phantasmic** /fan tázmik/ *adj* —**phantasmically** *adv*

phantasmagoria /fán tazmə gáwri ə/, **phantasmagory** /fan tázmə gawri/ (*plural* **-ries**) *n* **1.** a series or group of strange or bizarre images seen as if in a dream **2.** a scene or view that encompasses many things and changes constantly [Early 19C. < French *fantasmagorie* 'art of making optical illusions' < *fantasme* (see PHANTASM)] —**phantasmagoric** /-górrik/ *adj* —**phantasmagorical** *adj*

phantast *n* another spelling of **fantast**

phantasy /fántəssi/ (*plural* **-sies**) *n* another spelling of **fantasy** (*archaic*) [Variant]

phantom /fántəm/ *n* **1.** UNREAL BEING OR SENSATION something that can be seen or heard or whose presence can be felt, but that is not physically present **2.** GHOST a ghost or apparition **3.** ILLUSION somebody or something that does not exist, or whose existence is difficult to prove **4.** IMAGINARY SHAPE an imaginary embodiment in threatening form of an abstract thing or quality ○ *The phantom of disaster seemed to threaten their success.* ■ *adj* **1.** LIKE PHANTOM having the nature of a phantom, especially in being ghostly, illusory, or unreal ○ *phantom horsemen* **2.** NONEXISTENT nonexistent, but claimed to exist usually for purposes of fraud ○ *phantom voters* [13C. Via Old French *fanto(s)me* < Greek *phantasma* (see PHANTASM)]

CULTURAL NOTE ***The Phantom of the Opera***, a novel (1910) by French writer Gaston Leroux. This romantic melodrama about a disfigured musical genius who dwells in the passageways of a Paris opera house was not widely known until the appearance of Rupert Julian's film adaptation of 1925. This in turn inspired other film adaptations as well as Andrew Lloyd Webber's 1986 musical, one of the most successful musicals of all time.

phantom limb *n* the powerful sensation that an amputated limb remains attached. This sensation may persist for weeks or months after the limb has been lost.

phantom limb pain *n* pain that seems to come from an amputated limb

phantom pregnancy *n* a condition in which a woman has the delusional belief that she is pregnant and suffers symptoms and displays signs of pregnancy. N Am term **false pregnancy**. Technical name **pseudocyesis**

-phany *suffix* a manifestation of something ○ *epiphany* [< Greek *phan-*, stem of *phainesthai* 'appear' < *phainein* 'bring to light']

pharaoh /fáirō/ *n* **1.** a ruler of ancient Egypt **2.** somebody in a position of authority, especially somebody who is harsh, gives unreasonable orders, and expects unquestioning obedience [Pre-12C. Via ecclesiastical Latin < Greek *Pharaō* < Hebrew *par'ōh* < Egyptian *pr-'o* 'great house'] —**Pharaonic** /fai rónnik/ *adj*

Pharaoh ant, Pharaoh's ant *n* a small yellowish-red ant that is a household pest in many tropical countries. Latin name: *Monomorium pharaonis*. [Because common in warm parts of the world such as Egypt]

Pharisaic /fárri sáy ik/, **Pharisaical** /fárri sáy ik'l/ *adj* **1.** relating to or characteristic of the Pharisees **2.** *also* **pharisaic** *or* **pharisaical** acting with hypocrisy, self-righteousness, or obsessiveness with regard to the strict adherence to rules and formalities [Early 17C. Via ecclesiastical Latin < Greek *pharisaïkos* < *pharisaios* (see PHARISEE)] —**Pharisaically** *adv* —**Pharisaicalness** *n*

Pharisaism /fárri say izəm/ *n* **1.** the beliefs and practices of the Pharisees, especially the great attention they paid to the detailed rules of everyday life **2.** *also* **pharisaism** hypocritical, self-righteous, or obsessive behaviour or attitudes towards the observing of rules and formalities [Late 16C. < French *pharisaïsme* < ecclesiastical Latin *pharisaeus* (see PHARISEE)]

Pharisee /fárri see/ *n* **1.** a member of an ancient Jewish religious group who followed the Oral Law in addition to the Torah and attempted to live in a constant state of purity **2.** *also* **pharisee** a self-righteous, hypocritical, or sanctimonious person [Pre-12C. Via ecclesiastical Latin < Greek *pharisaios* < Aramaic *prīšayyā* 'those who are separate']

Phariseeism /fárri say izəm/ *n* JUDAISM, HIST same as **Pharisaism** (sense 1)

pharm /faarm/ (**pharms, pharming, pharmed**) *v* **1.** *vt* to produce medicinally valuable proteins in the milk of genetically modified cows and sheep **2.** *vti US* to mix and share prescription medications, especially narcotics and opiates, often with harmful effects (*slang*)

Pharm., pharm. *abbr* **1.** pharmaceutical **2.** pharmacist **3.** pharmacopoeia **4.** pharmacy

pharma /fáarmə/ *adj, n* same as **pharmaceutical**

pharmac- *prefix* same as **pharmaco-** (*used before vowels*)

pharmaceutical /fáarmə syŏŏtik'l/ *adj* involved in or related to the manufacture, preparation, dispensing, or sale of drugs used in medicine ■ *n* a drug used in medicine (*usually used in the plural*) [Mid-17C. < late Latin *pharmaceuticus* < Greek *pharmakeutēs* 'somebody who prepares drugs' < *pharmakon* 'drug'] —**pharmaceutically** *adv*

pharmaceutical chemist *n* PHARM same as **pharmacist**

pharmaceutics /faarmə syóotiks/ *n* the science of the preparation and dispensing of prescribed drugs (*takes a singular verb*) ▪ *npl* drugs prescribed as medicines (*takes a plural verb*)

pharmacist /faarməssist/ *n* somebody trained and licensed to dispense medicinal drugs and to advise on their use [Mid-19C. < PHARMACY]

pharmaco- *prefix* drugs, medicine ○ *pharmacodynamics* [< Greek *pharmakon* 'drug, poison']

pharmacodynamics /faarməkō dī námmiks/ *n* the study of the effects of drugs on living organisms (*takes a singular verb*) —**pharmacodynamic** *adj*

pharmacogenetics /faarmə kō jə néttiks/ *n* same as **pharmacogenomics** —**pharmacogenetic** *adj*

pharmacogenomics /faarməkō ji nómiks/ *n* the study of the relationship between a specific person's genetic makeup and his or her response to drug treatment (*takes a singular verb*) —**pharmacogenomic** *adj*

pharmacognosy /faarmə kógnəssi/ *n* the branch of pharmacology that deals with active substances found in plants [Mid-19C. < PHARMACO- + Greek *gnōsis* 'knowledge' (see GNOSIS)] —**pharmacognosist** *n* —**pharmacognostic** /faarmə kog nóstik/ *adj*

pharmacokinetics /faarməkō ki néttiks, -kī-/ *npl* the body's reaction to drugs, including their absorption, metabolism, and elimination

pharmacology /faarmə kólləji/ (*plural* -**gies**) *n* **1.** the science or study of drugs, especially of the ways in which they react biologically at receptor sites in the body **2.** the effects that a drug has when taken by somebody, especially as a medical treatment —**pharmacological** /faarməkə lójjik'l/ *adj* —**pharmacologically** *adv* —**pharmacologist** *n*

pharmacopoeia /faarməkə peé ə/, **pharmacopeia** *n* **1.** an official compendium of quality standards for pharmacologically active substances and drug products **2.** a stock or collection of drugs (*archaic*) [Early 17C. Via modern Latin < Greek *pharmakopoiia* 'preparing of drugs' < *pharmakon* 'drug'] —**pharmacopoeial** *adj* —**pharmacopoeic** *adj* —**pharmacopoeist** *n*

pharmacotherapy /faarməkō thérrəpi/ (*plural* -**pies**) *n* the use of drugs to treat conditions, especially psychiatric disorders

~~**pharmacuetical**~~ incorrect spelling of **pharmaceutical**

pharmacy /faarməssi/ (*plural* -**cies**) *n* **1.** the science or profession of dispensing medicinal drugs **2.** a place where medicinal drugs are dispensed or sold [14C. Via Old French *farmacie* < Greek *pharmakeia* 'use of drugs' < *pharmakon* 'drug']

pharyngeal /fə rínji əl, fárrin jeé əl/ *adj* found in, affecting, or relating to the throat [Early 19C. < modern Latin *pharyngeus* < *pharyng-* (see PHARYNX)]

pharynges *n* ANAT plural of **pharynx**

pharyngitis /fárrin jítiss/ *n* inflammation of the pharynx, commonly known as a sore throat

pharyngo- *prefix* pharynx ○ *pharyngoscope* [< modern Latin, *pharyng-* (see PHARYNX)]

pharyngology /fárring gólləji/ *n* the branch of medicine concerned with the throat, its diseases, and their treatment —**pharyngological** /fárring gə lójjik'l/ *adj* —**pharyngologist** /-góllajist/ *n*

pharyngoscope /fə ríng gə skōp/ *n* a medical instrument for examining the throat —**pharyngoscopic** /fə ríng gə skóppik/ *adj* —**pharyngoscopy** /fárring góskəpi/ *n*

pharynx /fárringks/ (*plural* **pharynges** /fə rín jeez/ or **pharynxes**) *n* **1.** the throat, the region of the alimentary canal in humans and in vertebrate animals that lies between the mouth and oesophagus **2.** a region between the mouth and the digestive system in sea anemones, worms, insects, and other invertebrate animals [Late 17C. Via modern Latin (stem *pharyng-*) < Greek *pharugx* 'throat']

phase /fayz/ *n* **1.** STAGE OF DEVELOPMENT a clearly distinguishable period or stage in a process, in the development of something, or in a sequence of events **2.** PATTERN OF BEHAVIOUR a period of time when a situation or particular pattern of behaviour persists and is often annoying or worrying **3.** PART OR ASPECT one of the many parts or aspects of something ○ *We needed to restructure all phases of our business.* **4.**

ASTRON RECURRING SHAPE OF MOON a recurring form of the Moon or a planet seen in the sky. The four principal phases of the Moon are the first quarter, full moon, last quarter, and new moon. **5.** PHYS PART OF REPEATING CYCLE a part of a repeated uniform pattern of occurrence of a phenomenon or process, relative to a fixed starting point or time **6.** PHYS STATE OF MATTER a state in which matter can exist, depending on temperature and pressure, e.g. the solid, liquid, gaseous, and plasmatic states **7.** ZOOL VARIATION IN ANIMAL FORM an alternative stage, appearance, or colouring that distinguishes a group of animals from most of their kind, or that an animal adopts under specific conditions **8.** BIOL STAGE IN LIFE CYCLE a stage in the life cycle of an organism ▪ *vt* (**phases, phasing, phased**) **1.** DO SOMETHING IN STAGES to plan or arrange something so that it is carried out in stages (*often passive*) ○ *a takeover that is being phased to minimize disruption* **2.** SYNCHRONIZE THINGS to cause two or more things to happen or operate simultaneously or in a coordinated way ○ *to phase the departure of one train with the arrival of another* [Early 19C. Partly via French < modern Latin *phasis*; partly back-formation < *phases*, plural of *phasis* 'phase', via modern Latin < Greek, 'appearance' < *phainein* 'to show'] —**phaseal** /fáyzi əl/ *adj* —**phasic** *adj* ◇ **in phase** in the same phase at the same time, or operating in a synchronized or coordinated way ◇ **out of phase** not in the same phase, or not synchronized or coordinated with each other

SPELLCHECK See *faze*.

phase in *vt* to introduce something in stages over a period of time

phase out *vt* to bring something to an end, or remove it, in stages over a period of time

phase alternation line *n* MEDIA full form of **PAL**

phase diagram *n* a graph on which parameters of a property such as temperature or pressure are plotted on perpendicular axes in such a way that a curve corresponds to a transition between physical states

phase modulation *n* a method of transmitting a voice or other signal in which the phase of a radio carrier wave is varied in accordance with the signal

phase music *n* a musical composition, associated with minimalism, in which the different parts use the same material at the same time but only sometimes in phase with each other

-phasia *suffix* speech disorder ○ *aphasia* [< Greek *phasis* 'utterance' < *phanai* 'to say' < Indo-European, 'speak']

phasmid /fázmid/ *n* a tropical plant-eating insect that has a body that looks like a twig with long legs and antennae. Stick insects and leaf insects are phasmids. Family: Phasmidae. ▪ *adj* belonging or relating to the phasmids [Late 19C. < modern Latin *Phasmida* < Greek *phasma* 'apparition' < *phainein* 'to show']

phat /fat/ *adj* of a very high quality or standard (*slang*) ○ '*music…set to the phat beats of hip-hop*' (*The New York Times*; November 1998) [Late 20C. Origin ?]

phatic /fáttik/ *adj* spoken in order to share feelings, create goodwill, or set a pleasant social mood, rather than to convey information. '*Have a nice day!*' is a phatic phrase. [Early 20C. < Greek *phatos* 'spoken' < *phanai* (see -PHASIA)]

PhB *abbr* EDUC Bachelor of Philosophy [Latin *Philosophiae Baccalaureus*]

PhD *abbr* EDUC Doctor of Philosophy [Latin *Philosophiae Doctor*]

pheasant /fézz'nt/ (*plural* -**ants** or same) *n* **1.** a large bird, the male of which often has a long tail and brightly coloured feathers. Pheasants are often bred for shooting. Native to: Asia, Europe, North America. Family: Phasianidae. **2.** the meat obtained from a pheasant [13C. Via Old French *fesan* < Greek *phasianos (ornis)* '(bird) from the river Phasis' in W Georgia, its supposed place of origin]

pheasant's eye (*plural* **pheasant's eyes** or same) *n* **1.** a plant of the buttercup family with very narrow twiggy leaves. Flowers: deep red with a dark centre, or yellow and cup-shaped. Genus: *Adonis*. **2.** a variety of narcissus with white petals surrounding a red-rimmed cup. Latin name: *Narcissus poeticus*.

phelloderm /féllə durm/ *n* a layer of plant cells produced by the inner surface of the cork cambium in woody plants, from which cork tissue develops [Late 19C. < Greek *phellos* 'cork'] —**phellodermal** /féllō dúrm'l/ *adj*

phellogen /félləjən/ *n* BOT same as **cork cambium** [Late 19C. < Greek *phellos* 'cork'] —**phellogenetic** /-jə néttik/ *adj* —**phellogenic** /-jénnik/ *adj*

phen- *prefix* CHEM, GEOL same as **pheno-**

phenacaine /fénnə kayn/ *n* a white crystalline compound. Use: local anaesthetic in ophthalmology. Formula: $C_{18}H_{22}N_2O_2$. [Early 20C. < PHEN- + -CAINE]

phenacite /fénnə kīt, fénnə sīt/, **phenakite** /fénnə kīt/ *n* a colourless glassy mineral that is composed of beryllium silicate. Use: gems. [Mid-19C. < Greek *phenak-* 'impostor'; because mistaken for quartz]

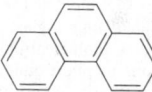

phenanthrene

phenanthrene /fə nánth reen/ *n* a colourless crystalline aromatic hydrocarbon. Use: manufacture of dyes, drugs, and explosives. Formula: $C_{14}H_{10}$. [Late 19C. < PHEN- + contraction of ANTHRACENE]

phencyclidine /fen síkli deen, -síkli-/ *n* a drug used as an anaesthetic in veterinary medicine and illegally as a hallucinogen. Formula: $C_{17}H_{25}N$. [Mid-20C. < PHEN- + CYCLO- + PIPERIDINE]

phenetics /fi néttiks/ *n* a system of biological classification based on overall similarities between organisms rather than on their genetic or developmental relationships (*takes a singular verb*) [Mid-20C. < Greek *phainesthai* 'appear' (see -PHANE)] —**phenetic** *adj* —**phenetically** *adv* —**pheneticist** *n*

pheno- *prefix* **1.** CHEM containing phenyl ○ *phenobarbitone* **2.** CHEM related to or derived from benzene ○ *phenol* **3.** GEOL appearing ○ *phenocryst* [< Greek *phainein* 'to show']

pheasant

phenobarbitone

phenobarbitone /feénō baárbitōn/ *n* a crystalline barbiturate. Use: sedative, hypnotic, anticonvulsant. Formula: $C_{12}H_{12}N_2O_3$. N Am term **phenobarbital**

phenocopy /féénō kopi/ (*plural* **-ies**) *n* a noninheritable change in an organism induced by its response to its environment but resembling a genetic mutation [Mid-20C. < PHENOTYPE]

phenocryst /féénə krist, fénnə-/ *n* a large embedded crystal in a porphyritic rock [Late 19C. < French *phénocryste* < *phéno-* 'appearing' (< Greek *phainein* 'to show') + Greek *krustallos* 'ice'] —**phenocrystic** /féénə krístik, fénnə-/ *adj*

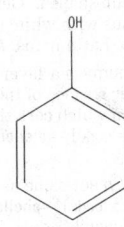

phenol

phenol /fée nol/ *n* **1.** a poisonous caustic crystalline compound. Source: coal, wood tar, benzene. Use: manufacture of resins, dyes, and pharmaceuticals, antiseptic, disinfectant. Formula: C_6H_5OH. **2.** a chemical compound that has one or more hydroxyl groups attached to a benzene ring

phenolic /fi nóllik/ *n* a resin that has high temperature stability. Use: in plastics, paints, adhesives. ■ *adj* derived from or containing phenol

phenolic resin *n* CHEM same as **phenolic**

phenology /fi nólləji/ (*plural* **-gies**) *n* **1.** the study of regularly recurring biological phenomena such as animal migrations or plant budding, especially as influenced by climatic conditions **2.** the relationship between a regularly recurring biological phenomenon and climatic or environmental factors that may influence it [Late 19C. < PHENOMENON] —**phenological** /féénə lójjik'l/ *adj* —**phenologist** *n*

phenolphthalein

phenolphthalein /fée nol thálleen, -tháy-/ *n* a colourless or yellowish compound. Use: chemical indicator, laxative. Formula: $C_{20}H_{14}O_4$.

phenol red *n* a red dye. Use: acid-base indicator, testing kidney function.

phenom /fə nóm/ *n* an outstanding or unusual person or thing (*slang*) [Late 19C. Shortening of PHENOMENON]

phenomena plural of **phenomenon**

phenomenal /fə nómminəl/ *adj* **1.** REMARKABLE remarkably and impressively good or great ○ *a phenomenal talent* **2.** OF PHENOMENON constituting or relating to a phenomenon **3.** PHILOSOPHY PERCEIVED BY SENSES perceived by or perceptible to the senses, rather than the mind, and thus having at least an apparent external existence —**phenomenally** *adv*

phenomenalism /fə nómminəlizəm/ *n* a philosophical theory stating that knowledge of the external world is limited to appearances, so that we know what our senses tell us about things, not what they are. Phenomenalism is chiefly associated with the work of the 18th-century British philosopher David Hume and his followers. —**phenomenalist** *n*, *adj* —**phenomenalistic** /fə nómminə lístik/ *adj* —**phenomenalistically** *adv*

phenomenology /fə nómmi nólləji/ *n* **1.** in philosophy, the science or study of phenomena, things as they are perceived, as opposed to the study of being, the nature of things as they are **2.** the philosophical investigation and description of conscious experience in all its varieties without reference to the question of whether what is experienced is objectively real —**phenomenological** /fə nómminə lójjik'l/ *adj* —**phenomenologically** *adv* —**phenomenologist** *n*

~~phenomenom~~ incorrect spelling of **phenomenon**

phenomenon /fə nómminən/ (*plural* **-na** /-nə/ or **-nons**) *n* **1.** SOMETHING EXPERIENCED a fact or occurrence that can be observed **2.** SOMETHING NOTABLE something that is out of the ordinary and excites people's interest and curiosity ○ *a strange phenomenon* **3.** (*plural* **phenomenons**) EXTRAORDINARY PERSON OR THING somebody or something that is, or is considered to be, truly extraordinary and marvellous **4.** PHILOSOPHY OBJECT OF PERCEPTION something perceived or experienced, especially an object as it is apprehended by the human senses as opposed to an object as it intrinsically is in itself [Late 16C. Via late Latin < Greek *phainomenon* 'that which appears' < *phainein* 'to show']

USAGE **phenomenon** or **phenomena**? Usage varies for the plural ending of nouns derived from Latin and Greek. For *phenomenon* never use the false singular *phenomena* as in *This phenomena occurs only in the southern hemisphere*; say instead *This phenomenon occurs....* Similarly, never attach an *-s* plural to the already plural *phenomena*, as in *These physiological phenomenas are fascinating.* Say instead *These physiological phenomena are...* The variant plural *phenomenons* is appropriate only outside scientific and philosophical contexts with the meaning 'extraordinary people, events, or things', as in *She is recognized as one of the greatest sporting phenomenons of our time.* Do not overuse *phenomenon* in nonscientific and nonphilosophical contexts. Restrict it to people, events, and things that are extraordinary, not merely interesting or vaguely out of the ordinary.

phenothiazine /féénō thí ə zeen, fénnō-/ *n* **1.** a yellowish crystalline compound used in veterinary medicine to destroy intestinal worms and as an insecticide. Formula: $C_{12}H_9NS$. **2.** a derivative of phenothiazine used as a tranquillizer and in the treatment of schizophrenia

phenotype /féénō tīp/ *n* the visible characteristics of an organism resulting from the interaction between its genetic makeup and the environment [Early 20C. < German *Phänotypus*, literally 'type that shows' < *phainein* 'to show'] —**phenotypic** /féénō típpik/ *adj* —**phenotypical** *adj* —**phenotypically** *adv*

phenoxide /fi nók sīd/ *n* a chemical compound that is a salt of phenol

phenyl /fée nīl, fénn'l/ *n* a chemical group derived from benzene by removing a hydrogen atom, thus having a valency of one. Formula: C_6H_5. [Mid-19C. < French *phényle* < Greek *phainein* 'to show'; because it was used to name compounds formed from lighting gas]

phenylalanine

phenylalanine /fée nīl állə neen, fénn'l-/ *n* an essential amino acid found in many proteins and converted to a nonessential amino acid (**tyrosine**) by the body. Formula: $C_9H_{11}O_2N$.

phenylbutazone /fée nīl byóotəzōn, fénn'l-/ *n* an anti-inflammatory drug. Use: treatment of arthritis, bursitis, gout. Formula: $C_{19}H_{20}N_2O_2$.

phenylephrine /féénīl éffreen, fénn'l-/ *n* a drug that constricts blood vessels. Use: nasal decongestant,

blood pressure regulator. [Mid-20C. Contraction of PHENYL + EPINEPHRINE]

phenylketonuria /fée nīl kéetə nyóóri ə, fénn'l-/ *n* a condition, resulting from a genetic mutation, in which the body lacks the enzyme to metabolize phenylalanine. If untreated, it results in developmental deficiency, seizures, and tumours.

phenylpropanolamine /fée nīl própə nóllə meen, fénn'l-/ *n* a drug that constricts blood vessels. Use: nasal and bronchial decongestant, appetite suppressant.

phenylthiocarbamide /fée nīl thī ō kaárbə mīd, fénn'l-/, **phenylthiourea** /fée nīl thí ō yoóri ə, fénn'l-/ *n* a crystalline compound that tastes extremely bitter to people who possess a specific dominant gene. Use: testing for that gene.

phenytoin /fénni tó in/ *n* a drug that controls convulsions. Use: treatment of epilepsy.

pheromone /férrəmōn/ *n* a chemical compound, produced and secreted by an animal, that influences the behaviour and development of other members of the same species [Mid-20C. < Greek *pherein* 'carry' + HORMONE] —**pheromonal** *adj*

phew /fyoo/ *interj* used to express tiredness, relief, surprise, or disgust [Early 17C. An imitation of blowing through partly closed lips]

phi /fī/ (*plural* **phis**) *n* the 21st letter of the Greek alphabet, represented in the English alphabet as 'ph'. See table at **alphabet** [Mid-20C. < late Greek, later form of Greek *pheî*]

PHI /fī/ *abbr* permanent health insurance

phial /fí əl/ *n* same as **vial** [14C. Via French < Latin *phiala* 'saucer' < Greek *phialē* 'broad flat vessel']

Phi Beta Kappa *n* **1.** an honorary society of American college and university students showing high academic achievement. It was founded in 1776. **2.** a member of Phi Beta Kappa

Phidias /fíddi ass/ (*fl* 490–430 BC) Greek sculptor considered the greatest of the classical period. His colossal statue of Zeus at Olympia was one of the Seven Wonders of the World.

phi effect *n* OPTICS same as **phi phenomenon**

PHIGS /figz/ *abbr* COMPUT programmers' hierarchical interactive graphics standard

phil. *abbr* **1.** philological **2.** philology **3.** philosopher **4.** philosophical **5.** philosophy

Phil. *abbr* **1.** MUSIC Philharmonic **2.** BIBLE Philippians **3.** Philippines

phil- *prefix* same as **philo-** (*used before vowels or l*)

-phil *suffix* same as **-phile**

Philadelphia /fíllə délfi ə/ largest city in Pennsylvania, situated on the Delaware River in the southeastern part of the state. It is known as the 'Birthplace of the Nation' because both the US Declaration of Independence and the Constitution of the United States were drawn up there. Population: 1,492,231 (2002 estimate).

philadelphus /fíllə délfəss/ *n* TREES same as **mock orange** (sense 1) [Late 18C. Via modern Latin < Greek *philadelphos* 'loving your brother' < *philos* 'loving' + *adelphos* 'brother']

Philae /fíl ee/ submerged island in southern Egypt, in the River Nile, south of Aswan. It was the site of ancient temples that were moved when the island was flooded after the building of the Aswan High Dam.

philander /fi lándər/ (**-ders, -dering, -dered**) *vi* to flirt with and have casual sexual affairs with many women, especially when married to another woman [Late 17C. < Greek *philandros* 'loving men' < *andr-* 'man'] —**philanderer** *n*

philanthropic /fíllən thróppik/, **philanthropical** /-ik'l/ *adj* **1.** showing kindness, charitable concern, and generosity towards other people **2.** devoted to helping other people, especially through giving charitable aid —**philanthropically** *adv*

philanthropy /fi lánthrəpi/ *n* **1.** a desire to improve the material, social, and spiritual welfare of humanity, especially through charitable activities **2.** general love for, or benevolence towards, the whole of humankind (*formal*) [Early 17C. Via late Latin < Greek

philanthrōpos 'humane' < philos 'loving' + anthrōpos 'human being'] —**philanthropist** n

philately /fi láttəli/ n the collection and study of postage stamps and related items [Mid-19C. < French philatélie < Greek philos 'loving' + ateleia 'exemption from tax' < telos 'tax'; from the freedom from charges that a stamped letter provides] —**philatelic** /fíllə téllik/ adj —**philatelically** adv —**philatelist** n

ORIGIN Monsieur Herpin, a French stamp collector, was looking for an impressive and learned-sounding term for his hobby. Because the Greeks and Romans did not have postage stamps, there was no classical term for them. So he went back a stage beyond stamps, to the days of franking with a postmark. In France, such letters were marked with the words franc de port 'carriage-free'. The nearest he could get to this in Greek was ateleia, and from it he created philatélie, the English form of which made its first recorded appearance in 1865.

Philby /fílbi/, **Kim** (1912–88) British intelligence agent and Soviet spy. During the 1940s and 1950s he penetrated the upper levels of British intelligence and passed vital information to the Soviet Union. Born **Philby, Harold Adrian Russell**

'To betray, you must first belong. I never belonged.'
[Kim Philby, Sunday Times; 17 December 1967]

-phile suffix **1.** somebody or something that loves or has an affinity for ○ bibliophile ○ acidophil **2.** loving or having an affinity for ○ homophile [Via Latin < Greek philos 'loving'] —**philic** suffix —**philous** suffix —**phily** suffix

Philemon /fi lée mən/ n a book of the Bible, originally a letter, that appeals to Philemon to take pity on his slave who had escaped and converted to Christianity, traditionally attributed to St Paul. See table at **Bible**

philharmonic /fíl haar mónnik, fíllər-/, **Philharmonic** adj describes an orchestra, choir, or society that promotes the study, performance, and appreciation of classical music ■ n a symphony orchestra, choir, or musical society that has the word 'philharmonic' in its title [Mid-18C. < French philharmonique < Greek philos 'loving' + harmonika (see HARMONIC)]

philhellene /fíl he leen, fil hélleen/, **philhellenist** /fil héllənist/ n an admirer of Greece, Greek history and culture, or the Greeks [Early 19C. < Greek philellēn < philos 'loving' + Hellēn 'a Greek'] —**philhellenic** /fíl he léenik, -lénnik/ adj —**philhellenism** /fil héllənizəm/ n —**philhellenistic** /fíl héllə nístik/ adj

-philia suffix **1.** intense or unusual attraction to ○ neophilia ○ zoophilia **2.** tendency towards ○ basophilia [Via modern Latin < Greek philia 'fondness' < philos 'loving'] —**philiac** suffix

philibeg n CLOTHING another spelling of **filibeg**

Philip /fílip/, **St** (fl 1st century AD) one of the 12 apostles of Jesus Christ. He was born in Bethsaida and was present at the feeding of the 5,000.

Philip I (1478–1506) duke of Burgundy and king of Castile. Father of Charles V and Ferdinand I, he founded the Hapsburg dynasty in Spain through his marriage to a Castilian princess. Known as **Philip the Handsome**

Philip II[1] (1527–98) king of Spain (1556–98). He ruled over a vast empire including the Netherlands, Naples and Sicily, the Philippines, and several South American colonies. His Armada was destroyed in an attempt to invade England (1588).

'England's chief defence depends upon the navy being always ready to defend the realm against invasion.'
[Philip II, Submission to the Privy Council; 1555?]

Philip II[2] (382–336 BC) king of Macedonia. After becoming king (359) he extended Macedonian power over the whole of Greece. He was the father of Alexander the Great.

Philip IV (1268–1314) king of France. He succeeded to the throne in 1285. His conflict with Pope Boniface VIII led to the residence of the popes in Avignon (1309–77). Known as **Philip the Fair**

Philip V (1683–1746) king of Spain. The grandson of Louis XIV of France, he was the first of the Spanish Bourbons. His accession to the throne (1700) led to the War of the Spanish Succession.

Philip, Prince, Duke of Edinburgh (b. 1921) The son of Prince Andrew of Greece and the great-great-grandson of Queen Victoria, he married Princess Elizabeth, later Queen Elizabeth II, in 1947

'Dentopedology is the science of opening your mouth and putting your foot in it. I've been practising it for years.'
[Attributed to Prince Philip]

~~Philipines~~ incorrect spelling of **Philippines**

Philippi /fi lípp ī, fílli pī/ n town in northern Greece. It was the site of a battle in 42 BC in which forces led by Mark Antony and Augustus defeated Marcus Brutus and Gaius Cassius Longinus.

Philippians /fi líppi ənz/ n a book of the Bible, originally addressed to the Christian church at Philippi and traditionally attributed to St Paul (takes a singular verb) See table at **Bible**

philippic /fi líppik/ n a verbal attack on somebody or something delivered in the most savage, bitter, and insulting terms, usually as a speech [Late 16C. Via Latin < Greek philippikos, speech of the 4C BC Greek orator Demosthenes urging the citizens of Athens to rise up against Philip of Macedon (see PHILIP II, king of Macedonia)]

Philippine /fíllə peen/ adj relating to the Philippines or its people or culture

Philippine English n a variety of English spoken in the Philippines

Philippines

Philippines /fíllə peenz/ country in Southeast Asia, in the western Pacific Ocean, in the Malay Archipelago. It comprises over 7,000 islands. Language: Filipino. Currency: Philippine peso. Capital: Manila. Population: 84,619,974 (2003). Area: 300,000 sq. km/115,831 sq. mi. Official name **Republic of the Philippines**

Philippine Sea /fíllə peen-/ section of the western Pacific Ocean, south of Japan and northeast of the Philippines. Area: 5,000,000 sq. km/2,000,000 sq. mi.

philistine /fíllə stīn/ (disapproving) n somebody who is regarded as being indifferent to artistic and intellectual achievements and values ■ adj regarded as being ignorant, uncultured, and indifferent or hostile to artistic and intellectual achievement [Early 19C. < PHILISTINE] —**philistinism** n

Philistine n a member of a people who settled in ancient Philistia in southern Palestine around the 12th century BC ■ adj relating to the ancient Philistines or their culture (disapproving)

Phillip /fíllip/, **Arthur** (1738–1814) British naval officer. He transported the first convicts to Australia in 1788, and was first governor of New South Wales (1788–92).

~~Phillipines~~ incorrect spelling of **Philippines**

Phillips screw /fíllips-/ tdmk a trademark for a screw with a cross-shaped slot on its head

Phillips screwdriver tdmk a trademark for a screwdriver that has a cross-shaped tip so that it can be used to turn a Phillips screw

phillumenist /fi lyoomənist/ n a collector of matchboxes and matchbooks as a hobby [Mid-20C. < PHILO- + Latin lumen 'light'] —**phillumeny** n

philo- prefix loving, having an attraction to or affinity for ○ philoprogenitive [< Greek philos 'loving']

Philoctetes /fíllək teé teez, fi lók ti teez/ n in Greek mythology, a friend of Achilles and the slayer of the Trojan prince Paris

philodendron /fíllə déndrən/ n (plural **-drons** or **-dra** /-drə/) n a climbing plant of the arum family, grown as a house plant for its evergreen leaves. Native to: tropical America. Genus: Philodendron. [Late 19C. Via modern Latin < Greek < philodendros 'loving trees' (because it climbs trees in its native habitat) < dendron 'tree']

philogyny /fi lójjəni/ n a positive and admiring attitude towards women in general (archaic) —**philogynist** n —**philogynous** adj

philology /fi lólləji/ n **1.** LING STUDY OF LANGUAGE IN TEXTS the scientific study of the relationship of languages to one another, and their history, especially based on the analysis of texts **2.** CULTL ANTHROP STUDY OF ANCIENT TEXTS the study and analysis of ancient texts, especially as an approach to the cultural history of a period or people **3.** LITERAT STUDY OF LITERATURE the study of literature in general (archaic) [14C. Via Latin < Greek philologia < philologos 'fond of words' < philos 'loving' + logos 'word'] —**philological** /fíllə lójjik'l/ adj —**philologically** adv —**philologist** n

philoprogenitive /fíllō prō jénnitiv/ adj **1.** producing a large number of offspring (formal) **2.** loving children, especially your own offspring (literary)

philosophe /fíllə sóf, -zóf/ n a leading writer or thinker of the Enlightenment in 18th-century France, who advocated a rational approach to philosophy and government and criticized the French social and political system [Late 18C. Via French < Latin philosophus (see PHILOSOPHER)]

philosopher /fi lóssəfər/ n **1.** SOMEBODY WHO STUDIES PHILOSOPHY somebody who seeks to understand and explain the principles of existence and reality **2.** THINKING PERSON a thinker who deeply and seriously considers human affairs and life in general **3.** CALM AND RATIONAL PERSON somebody who reacts calmly and rationally to events, especially adversity [14C. < Anglo-Norman philosophre, variant of Old French philosophe < Latin philosophus < Greek philosophos 'lover of knowledge' < philos 'loving' + sophia 'learning, wisdom']

philosopher's stone, **philosophers' stone** n a substance that medieval alchemists believed could be used to convert other metals into gold

philosophical /fíllə sóffik'l, -zóffik'l/, **philosophic** /-sóffik, -zóffik/ *adj* **1.** RELATING TO STUDY OF PHILOSOPHY concerned with the study of the nature of life and reality, or of related areas such as ethics, logic, or metaphysics **2.** CONCERNED WITH DEEP QUESTIONS OF LIFE concerned with or given to thinking about the larger issues and deeper meanings in life and events **3.** SHOWING CALMNESS AND RESIGNATION showing calmness, restraint, or resignation, especially reacting to adversity in a restrained or resigned way —**philosophically** *adv*

philosophize /fi lóssə fíz/ (**-phizes, -phizing, -phized**), **philosophise** (**-phises, -phising, -phised**) *v* **1.** *vi* DISCUSS NATURE OF REALITY to comment on or attempt to explain the nature of life and reality, or a part of it such as ethics, logic, knowledge, or existence **2.** *vi* EXPLAIN OR MORALIZE IN SUPERFICIAL WAY to express opinions of a supposedly philosophical nature in a superficial, tedious, or moralistic way **3.** *vt* PHILOSOPHY DEAL WITH SOMETHING FROM PHILOSOPHICAL STANDPOINT to consider, explain, or deal with something from a philosophical standpoint —**philosophization** /fi lóssə fī záysh'n/ *n* —**philosophizer** *n*

philosophy /fi lóssəfi/ (*plural* **-phies**) *n* **1.** EXAMINATION OF BASIC CONCEPTS the branch of knowledge or academic study devoted to the systematic examination of basic concepts such as truth, existence, reality, causality, and freedom **2.** SCHOOL OF THOUGHT a particular system of thought or doctrine **3.** GUIDING OR UNDERLYING PRINCIPLES a set of basic principles or concepts underlying a particular sphere of knowledge **4.** SET OF BELIEFS OR AIMS a precept, or set of precepts, beliefs, principles, or aims, underlying somebody's practice or conduct **5.** CALM RESIGNATION restraint, resignation, or calmness and rationality in somebody's behaviour or response to events [14C. Via French and Latin < Greek *philosophia* < *philosophos* (see PHILOSOPHER)]

philter *n* PARANORMAL US spelling of **philtre**

philtre /fíltər/ *n* a magical potion or charm, especially one that causes somebody to fall in love (*literary*) [Late 16C. Via French < Greek *philtron* < *philein* 'to love' < *philos* 'loving']

phimosis /fī mósiss/ *n* a narrowing of the opening in the foreskin that prevents its being drawn back over the penis. This makes washing difficult or impossible and often leads to irritation and infection. [Late 17C. Via modern Latin < Greek *phimōsis* 'muzzling']

phi phenomenon *n* an optical illusion in which the rapid appearance and disappearance of two stationary objects such as flashing lights are perceived as the movement back and forth of a single object

phish /fish/ (**phishes, phishing, phished**) *vi* to trick somebody into providing bank or credit-card information by sending a fraudulent e-mail purporting to be from a bank, Internet provider, etc. asking for verification of an account number or password [Late 20C. Alteration of FISH] —**phishing** *n*

~~phisical~~ incorrect spelling of **physical**

phiz /fiz/, **phizog** /fízzog, fi zóg/ *n* somebody's face (*slang*) [Late 17C. Shortening of PHYSIOGNOMY]

phleb- *prefix* same as **phlebo-** (*used before vowels*)

phlebitis /fli bítiss/ *n* inflammation of the wall of a vein

phlebo- *prefix* vein ○ *phlebotomy* [< Greek *phleb-* 'blood vessel']

phlebography /fli bóggrəfi/ *n* MED same as **venography**

phlebotomize /fli bóttə mīz/ (**-mizes, -mizing, -mized**), **phlebotomise** (**-mises, -mising, -mised**) *vt* to make an incision into a patient's vein in order to draw blood for testing

phlebotomy /fli bóttəmi/ (*plural* **-mies**) *n* a surgical incision made in a vein, or a puncture made by a needle to draw blood for testing —**phlebotomist** *n*

phlegm /flem/ *n* **1.** THICK MUCUS the thick mucus secreted by the walls of the respiratory passages, especially during a cold **2.** UNFLAPPABILITY calmness or composure that is not easily disturbed **3.** BODILY FLUID DETERMINING HEALTH AND EMOTIONS one of the four basic bodily fluids (**humours**). Phlegm was believed to be cold and moist in nature and to cause sluggishness and apathy. [14C. Via

French < late Latin *phlegma* 'clammy bodily moisture' < Greek, 'inflammation, heat' < *phlegein* 'to burn'] —**phlegmy** *adj*

phlegmatic /fleg máttik/, **phlegmatical** /-máttik'l/ *adj* generally unemotional and difficult to arouse [14C. Via French and Latin < Greek *phlegmatikos* < *phlegma* (see PHLEGM)] —**phlegmatically** *adv*

SYNONYMS See **impassive**.

~~phlem~~ incorrect spelling of **phlegm**

phloem /fló em/ *n* one of the two main types of tissue in vascular plants, which conducts synthesized nutrients to all parts of the plant. It is made up of sap-conducting tubes (**sieve tubes**) and the cells that lie alongside them (**companion cells**), elongated cells of soft tissue (**parenchyma**), and fibres. [Late 19C. < German < Greek *phloos* 'bark']

phlogiston /flə jístən, -gístən/ *n* a hypothetical element that some early scientists, before the discovery of oxygen, believed to be present in all combustible substances to make them burn [Mid-18C. < Greek, 'inflammable thing' < *phlogizein* 'set on fire' < *phlox* 'flame'] —**phlogistic** *adj*

phlogopite /flóggə pīt/ *n* a yellowish-brown or reddish-brown mineral form of mica. Source: marble, dolomite. [Mid-19C. < Greek *phlogōpos* 'fiery-faced' < *phlox* 'flame'; from its highly reflective flat crystals]

phlox

phlox /floks/ (*plural same* or **phloxes**) *n* a common garden plant that has slim stems with oval narrow leaves. Flowers: scented, white, red, purple, in clusters. Native to: North America. Genus: *Phlox*. [Early 18C. Via modern Latin < Greek, 'flame'; from its brightly coloured flowers]

Phnom Penh /nóm pén/ capital city of Cambodia, situated at the confluence of the Mekong and Tonle Sap rivers in the southern part of the country. Population: 999,804 (1999).

-phobe *suffix* fearing or disliking something or somebody ○ *claustrophobe* [Via French < Greek *phobos* 'fear']

phobia /fóbi ə/ *n* an irrational or very powerful fear and dislike of something such as spiders or confined spaces ○ *a phobia about travelling in lifts* [Late 18C. < -PHOBIA]

-phobia *suffix* an exaggerated or irrational fear ○ *claustrophobia* [Via Latin < Greek *phobos* 'fear']

phobic /fóbik/ *adj* **1.** INTENSELY FEARFUL OF SOMETHING having or showing an intense fear and dislike of something **2.** PSYCHIAT RELATING TO PHOBIAS affected with or arising out of a phobia ■ *n* PSYCHIAT SOMEBODY WITH PHOBIA somebody who fears or dislikes something strongly or irrationally

-phobic *suffix* with a strong or irrational fear or dislike of somebody or something ○ *claustrophobic*

Phobos /fó boss/ *n* the innermost of the two natural satellites of Mars, both of which are small. It was discovered in 1877 and is ellipsoidal in shape.

phocine /fó sīn/ *adj* relating to or resembling seals [Mid-19C. < modern Latin *Phocinae* < Greek *phōkē* 'seal']

phocomelia /fókō meéli ə/ *n* a condition, present at birth, characterized by an absent or underdeveloped upper section of a limb, with a normal-sized hand or foot attached to the trunk by a short broad flat limb [Late 19C. < Greek *phōkē* 'seal' + *melos* 'limb'; from the short limbs of seals]

Phoebe /feébi/ *n* **1.** TITAN GODDESS in Greek mythology, a Titan goddess who later became identified with

the goddess of the Moon, Artemis **2.** MOON PERSONIFIED a personification of the Moon (*literary*) **3.** ASTRON SMALL OUTERMOST MOON OF SATURN a small natural satellite of Saturn [14C. Via Latin < Greek *Phoibē*, form of *phoibos* 'bright, shining']

Phoebus /feébəss/ *n* **1.** also **Phoebus Apollo** in Greek mythology, the god Apollo when identified with the Sun **2.** a personification of the Sun (*literary*) [14C. Via Latin < Greek *Phoibos*, literally 'bright, shining']

Phoenicia /fə níshə, fə neéshə/ ancient region on the eastern coast of the Mediterranean Sea in modern Lebanon and Syria. It was the site of several city-kingdoms, whose people became the greatest traders and sailors of the ancient world.

Phoenician /fə nísh'n, fə neésh'n/ *n* **1.** a member of an ancient people who occupied Phoenicia, where they established trading ports **2.** an extinct Semitic language spoken in ancient Phoenicia —**Phoenician** *adj*

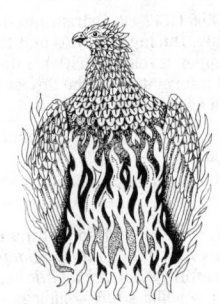

phoenix

phoenix /feéniks/ *n* **1.** in ancient mythology, a bird resembling an eagle that lived for 500 years and then burned itself to death on a pyre from whose ashes another phoenix arose. It commonly appears in literature as a symbol of death and resurrection. **2.** a supremely beautiful, rare, or unique person or thing (*literary*) ○ *a phoenix of princes* [Pre-12C. Via French and Latin < Greek *phoinix*]

Phoenix[1] *n* a constellation of the southern hemisphere situated between Sculptor and Eridanus. See illustration at **constellation**

Phoenix[2] /feéniks/ capital of Arizona and its largest city, located in the southern part of the state. Population: 1,371,960 (2002 estimate).

phon /fon/ *n* a unit of subjective measure of loudness level. The level in phons is equal in number to the sound intensity of a 1,000-hertz reference sound, measured in decibels, judged to be the same loudness as the measured sound.

phon- *prefix* same as **phono-** (*used before vowels*)

phonate /fó nayt, fō náyt/ (**-nates, -nating, -nated**) *v* **1.** *vt* to make a sound voiced by vibrating the vocal cords **2.** *vi* to produce sounds, especially speech sounds, with the voice —**phonation** /fō náysh'n/ *n* —**phonatory** /fō náytəri/ *adj*

phone[1] /fōn/ *n* same as **telephone** ■ **phones** *npl* a set of earphones or headphones (*informal*) ■ *vti* (**phones, phoning, phoned**) same as **telephone** *v* [Late 19C Shortening]

phone[2] /fōn/ *n* a single basic speech sound [Mid-19C. < Greek *phōnē* 'sound, voice']

-phone *suffix* **1.** a device that emits or receives sounds, e.g. a musical instrument ○ *diaphone* ○ *hydrophone* ○ *sousaphone* **2.** a telephone ○ *speakerphone* **3.** a speech sound ○ *isophone* **4.** a speaker of a particular language ○ *Francophone* [< Greek *phōnē* 'sound, voice'] —**-phonic** *suffix* —**-phony** *suffix*

phone book *n* TELECOM same as **telephone directory**

phone box *n* TELECOM same as **telephone box**

phonecard /fón kaard/ *n* a rectangular plastic card that can be used instead of money when making calls from some public telephones

phone-in *n* UK, ANZ, Can a radio or television programme in which audience members can participate by telephone and ask questions or take part in discussions with the host and any guests. US term **call-in**

phoneme /fṓ neem/ n a speech sound that distinguishes one word from another, e.g. the sounds 'd' and 't' in the words 'bid' and 'bit'. A phoneme is the smallest phonetic unit that can carry meaning. [Late 19C. Via French < Greek *phōnēma* 'sound produced' < *phōnein* 'produce a sound' < *phōnē* 'sound, voice']

phonemic /fə neémik, fō-/ adj 1. OF PHONEMES relating to a phoneme 2. OF DIFFERENT PHONEMES relating to speech sounds that belong to different phonemes rather than being different ways of pronouncing the same phoneme 3. OF PHONEMICS relating to the branch of linguistics that studies phonemes —**phonemically** adv

phonemics /fə neémiks, fō-/ n the branch of linguistics involved in the classification and analysis of the phonemes of a language (takes a singular verb) —**phonemicist** /fə neémissist, fō-/ n

phone phreak /-freek/ n somebody who breaks into telephone systems and other secure networks, often to make free long-distance telephone calls (slang)

phoner /fṓnər/ n 1. somebody who makes a telephone call 2. an interview conducted by telephone, especially on a radio or TV programme (informal)

phone sex n the act of talking in an erotic and explicit way to another person on the telephone for mutual or individual sexual pleasure

phonetic /fə néttik, fō-/ adj 1. OF SPEECH SOUNDS belonging to or associated with the sounds of human speech 2. SHOWING PRONUNCIATION representing the sounds of human speech in writing, often with special symbols or unconventional spelling 3. OF PHONETICS relating to the science of phonetics [Early 19C. Via modern Latin < Greek *phōnētikos* 'spoken' < *phōnein* (see PHONEME)] —**phonetically** adv

phonetic alphabet n 1. a set of letters and symbols used to represent the sounds of human speech in writing 2. a set of words representing alphabetical letters, e.g. 'Delta' for D and 'Tango' for T, used in radio or telephone communications. The phonetic alphabet is used to distinguish between letters that sound similar, to spell out words, and in code names or call signs.

phonetics /fə néttiks, fō-/ n (takes a singular verb) 1. the scientific study of speech sounds and how they are produced 2. the system or pattern of speech sounds used in a language —**phonetician** /fōnə tísh'n, fónnə-/ n

phoney /fṓni/, **phony** adj (-nier, -niest) 1. NOT GENUINE not genuine and used to deceive 2. GIVING FALSE IMPRESSION putting on a false show of something such as sincerity or expertise ■ n (plural -neys or -nies) SOMEBODY OR SOMETHING PHONEY a phoney person or thing [Late 19C. Origin ?] —**phonily** adv —**phoniness** n

phoney war n a period when enemies are officially at war but not actively engaged in armed conflict, e.g. the period of relative calm at the beginning of World War II

phonic /fónnik/ adj 1. USING PHONICS using or involving phonics as a method of teaching people to read 2. OF SOUND associated with sound or the scientific study of sound 3. OF SPEECH SOUNDS relating to the sounds used in speech [Early 19C. < Greek *phōnē* 'sound, voice'] —**phonically** adv

phonics /fónniks/ n a method of teaching reading in which people learn to associate letters with the speech sounds they represent, rather than learning to recognize the whole word as a unit (takes a singular verb) [Late 17C. < Greek *phōnē* 'sound, voice']

phono- prefix sound, speech, voice ○ *phonogram* [< Greek *phōnē* 'sound, voice' < Indo-European, 'speak']

phonocardiogram /fṓnō ka'ardi ə gram/ n a visual record of heart sounds and murmurs made by a phonocardiograph

phonocardiograph /fṓnō ka'ardi ə graaf, -graf/ n an instrument that amplifies heart sounds and converts them into a visual display —**phonocardiographic** /-ka'ardi ə gráffik/ adj —**phonocardiography** /-ka'ardi óggrəfi/ n

phonochemistry /fṓnō kémmistri/ n a branch of science and technology dealing with the effect of sound and ultrasonic waves on chemical reactions

phonogram /fṓnə gram/ n 1. a symbol that represents a word, part of a word, or an individual speech sound 2. a sequence of letters that have the same

pronunciation in several different words, e.g. 'ear' in 'earth', 'heard', and 'learn' —**phonogramic** /fṓnə grámmik/ adj

phonograph /fṓnə graaf, -graf/ n N Am a record player

phonography /fə nóggrəfi/ n 1. the use of symbols to represent speech sounds in writing 2. a method of writing in shorthand that uses symbols to represent speech sounds —**phonographer** n —**phonographic** /fṓnə gráffik/ adj —**phonographist** n

phonolite /fṓnə līt/ n a fine-grained light-coloured volcanic rock characterized by the presence of alkali feldspar and nepheline [Early 19C. < the resonance of the rock when hit with a hammer] —**phonolitic** /fṓnə líttik/ adj

phonology /fə nólləji, fō-/ (plural -gies) n 1. the study of the system or pattern of speech sounds used in a particular language or in language in general 2. the system or pattern of speech sounds used in a particular language —**phonological** /fṓnə lójjik'l, fónnə-/ adj —**phonologically** adv —**phonologist** n

phonon /fṓ non/ n a quantum of vibrational or acoustic energy in a crystal lattice

phonoscope /fṓnə skōp/ n a device that visually represents the vibrations of sound waves, used especially with musical instruments

phonotactics /fṓnō táktiks, fōnə-/ n the study of the sounds it is possible to put together to form words and parts of words in a language (takes a singular verb)

phony adj, n another spelling of **phoney**

phooey /fōo i/ interj used to express contempt, disbelief, disgust, or disappointment (informal) [Early 20C. Partly < phoo, natural exclamation; partly alteration of pfui < German]

phorate /fáwr ayt/ n an organophosphorus compound. Use: insecticide. Formula: $C_7H_{17}O_2PS_3$. [Mid-20C. Contraction of *phosphorodithioate* < PHOSPHORUS + DI-[1] + THIO- + -ATE]

-phore suffix something that carries ○ *sporophore* [< Greek *-phoros* 'bearing' < *pherein* 'carry' < Indo-European] —**-phorous** suffix

-phoresis suffix transmission ○ *diaphoresis* [< Greek *phorēsis* < *phorein* 'keep carrying' < *pherein* (see -PHORE)]

phosgene /fóss jeen, fóz-/ n a highly toxic colourless gas. Use: chemical weapons in World War I, manufacture of pesticides, plastics, dyes. Formula: $COCl_2$. [Early 19C. < Greek *phōs* 'light']

phosgenite /fóssji nīt, fózji-/ n a rare greyish fluorescent crystalline mineral consisting of a carbonate and chloride of lead. Formula: $Pb_2(Cl_2CO_3)$. [Mid-19C. Because formed from the same substances as phosgene]

phosph- prefix same as **phospho-** (used before vowels)

phosphatase /fóssfə tayz, -tayss/ n an enzyme that catalyses the hydrolysis of phosphate esters and the transfer of phosphate groups [Early 20C. < PHOSPHATE]

phosphate /fóss fayt/ n a salt or ester formed by the reaction of a metal, alcohol, or other radical with phosphoric acid. A tribasic acid, phosphoric acid forms three series of phosphates by replacement of one, two, or all three of its hydrogen ions. [Late 18C. < French *phosphate* < *phosphore* 'phosphorus'] —**phosphatic** /foss fáttik/ adj

phosphate rock n a sedimentary rock with a naturally high phosphate concentration. Use: fertilizer, manufacture of phosphorus compounds.

phosphatide /fóssfə tīd/ n BIOCHEM same as **phospholipid** —**phosphatidic** /fóssfə tíddik/ adj

phosphatidylcholine /fóssfəti dīl kṓ leen/ n BIOCHEM same as **lecithin** [Mid-20C. < PHOSPHATIDE + -YL]

phosphatidylethanolamine /fóssfəti dīl ethə nólla meen/ n BIOCHEM same as **cephalin** [Mid-20C. < PHOSPHATIDE + -YL]

phosphatize /fóssfə tīz/ (-tizes, -tizing, -tized), **phosphatise** (-tises, -tising, -tised) v 1. vt to treat something with phosphoric acid or with a phosphate, typically to protect ferrous metal against corrosion 2. vti to convert something into a phosphate or phosphates, or undergo this process —**phosphatization** /fóssfə tī záysh'n/ n

phosphene /fóss feen/ n a sensation of seeing light caused by pressure or electrical stimulation of the

eye [Late 19C. < French *phosphène* < Greek *phōs* 'light' + *phainein* 'to show']

phosphide /fóss fīd/ n a compound of phosphorus with a more electropositive element, e.g. a metal

phosphine /fóss feen/ n a colourless inflammable gas with a fishy smell. Use: pesticide. Formula: PH_3.

phosphite /fóss fīt/ n a salt or ester of phosphorous acid

phospho- prefix 1. phosphorus ○ *phosphate* 2. phosphate ○ *phosphocreatine* [< PHOSPHORUS]

phosphocreatine /fóssfō kreé ə teen/, **phosphocreatin** /-tin/ n a phosphate of creatine found in muscles, providing energy for muscle contraction

phosphofructokinase /fóssfō frúktō kí nayz, -kī nayz, -keé nayss/ n an enzyme that catalyses the transfer of phosphate to a fructose compound during the metabolism of glucose

phosphoglucomutase /fóssfō glóokō myoó tayz, -tayss/ n an enzyme that catalyses the breakdown and synthesis of glycogen, providing energy that can be used or stored

phospholipase /fóssfō lí payz, fóssfō lí payss/ n an enzyme that catalyses the hydrolysis of phospholipids in cell membranes

phospholipid /fóssfō líppid/ n a phosphorus-containing lipid found in double-layered cell membranes

phosphonic acid /foss fónnik-/ n CHEM same as **phosphorous acid** (sense 1)

phosphonium /foss fṓni əm/ n a univalent radical derived from phosphene. Formula: PH_4. [Late 19C. < PHOSPHO- + AMMONIUM]

phosphor /fóssfər/ n a substance that can emit light when irradiated with particles of electromagnetic radiation [Early 17C. < Latin *phosphorus* (see PHOSPHORUS)]

phosphorate /fóssfə rayt/ (-ates, -ating, -ated) vt to treat, combine, or impregnate something with phosphorus

phosphor bronze n one of several alloys containing copper, tin, and phosphorus that are resistant to wear and corrosion. Use: in bearings, gears, components exposed to sea water.

phosphoresce /fóssfə réss/ (-resces, -rescing, -resced) vi to continue to emit light without accompanying heat after exposure to and removal of a source of stimulating radiation

phosphorescence /fóssfə réss'nss/ n the continued emission of light without accompanying heat after exposure to and removal of a source of stimulating radiation —**phosphorescent** adj —**phosphorescently** adv

phosphoric /foss fórrik/ adj containing phosphorus with a valency state higher than that of the phosphorus ion or radical in an analogous phosphorous compound

phosphoric acid n 1. a water-soluble transparent solid acid. Use: fertilizer, rust-proofing, in soft drinks, pharmaceuticals, animal feeds. Formula: H_3PO_4. 2. an acid of a group formed by the combination of phosphorus pentoxide with water, each acid having one more oxygen atom than the corresponding phosphorous acid

phosphorite /fóssfə rīt/ n 1. a mineral deposit consisting of apatite and other phosphates 2. GEOL same as **phosphate rock** —**phosphoritic** /fóssfə ríttik/ adj

phosphorolysis /fóssfə róllississ/ n a process in which a phosphate group is added to a molecule, which then splits into two simpler fragments [Mid-20C. Blend of PHOSPHORUS and *phosphorylation* + HYDROLYSIS]

phosphorous /fóssfərəss/ adj relating to phosphorus with a valency state lower than that of the phosphorus ion or radical in an analogous phosphoric compound [Late 18C. < PHOSPHORUS]

phosphorous acid n 1. a white or yellowish crystalline solid that absorbs water from the atmosphere. Use: reducing agent, production of phosphite salts. Formula: H_3PO_3. 2. an acid of a group formed by the combination of phosphorus pentoxide with water, each acid having one less oxygen atom than the corresponding phosphoric acid

phosphorus /fóssfərəss/ *n* **1.** a poisonous nonmetallic chemical element that ignites in air and glows in the dark. Use: matches, fireworks, incendiary devices, fertilizers. Symbol **P**. See table at **element 2.** a phosphorescent substance or object [Early 17C. Via Latin < Greek *phōsphoros* 'morning star', literally 'light-bringing' < *phōs* 'light']

phosphorus pentoxide, **phosphorus oxide** *n* a flammable white solid that absorbs moisture from the air. Source: burning phosphorus in air. Use: manufacture of phosphoric acid. Formula: P_2O_5.

phosphoryl /fóssfəril/ *n* a chemical group, usually with a valency of three, consisting of one phosphorus atom and one oxygen atom

phosphorylase /foss fórri layz, -layss/ *n* an enzyme that catalyses the phosphorolysis of a molecule

phosphorylate /foss fórri layt/ (**-ates**, **-ating**, **-ated**) *vt* to add a phosphate group to an organic molecule in order to produce an organic phosphate —**phosphorylation** /fós forri láysh'n/ *n* —**phosphorylative** /-lətiv/ *adj*

phot /fōt, fot/ *n* the centimetre-gram-second unit of illumination equal to one lumen per square centimetre [Late 19C. Via French < Greek *phōt-* 'light']

phot- *prefix* same as **photo-** (*used before vowels*)

photic /fótik/ *adj* **1.** relating to light, especially when produced by living organisms **2.** describes the area of the ocean where light penetrates and photosynthesis occurs [Mid-19C. < Greek *phōt-* 'light']

Photius /fóti əss/ (820?–891?) Byzantine churchman and scholar. He was patriarch of Constantinople (858–867 and 877–886), initiating the spread of Orthodox Christianity in Eastern Europe.

photo /fótō/ *n* (*plural* **-tos**) PHOTOGRAPHY same as **photograph** ■ *vt* (**-tos**, **-toing**, **-toed**) to take a photograph or photographs of somebody or something [Mid-19C. Shortening]

photo- *prefix* **1.** light, radiant energy ○ *photochemistry* ○ *photic* **2.** photographic ○ *photomontage* **3.** photoelectric ○ *photocurrent* [< Greek *phōt-* 'light' < Indo-European, 'to shine']

photoactinic /fótō ak tínnik/ *adj* emitting radiation similar to visible and ultraviolet light in its chemical effects on substances such as photographic emulsions

photoactive /fótō áktiv/ *adj* exhibiting a reaction to electromagnetic radiation, especially visible light, either by chemical reaction or photoelectrically

photoautotroph /fótō áwtō trof/ *n* an organism that derives its energy exclusively from light and uses it to synthesize food —**photoautotrophic** /fótō áwtō tróffik/ *adj*

photobiology /fótō bī ólləji/ *n* a branch of biology concerned with the interaction of living organisms with light —**photobiological** /fótō bī ə lójjik'l/ *adj* —**photobiologist** *n*

photobiotic /fótō bī óttik/ *adj* describes organisms that need light in order to live and grow

photocall /fótō kawl/ *n* **1.** an occasion when celebrities pose for press and other photographers, usually for publicity purposes **2.** MEDIA same as **photo opportunity**

photocatalysis /fótō kə tállississ/ *n* the acceleration or deceleration of the speed at which a chemical reaction occurs, caused by electromagnetic radiation and especially visible light

photocathode /fótō káthōd/ *n* an electrode that emits electrons when exposed to electromagnetic radiation such as light. Use: in television and digital cameras and photoelectric cells.

photo CD *n* a compact disc that stores images from photographs that can be displayed on a computer or television screen

photocell /fótō sel/ *n* PHYS same as **photoelectric cell**

photochemical /fótō kémmik'l/ *adj* relating to photochemistry —**photochemically** *adv*

photochemical smog *n* air pollution caused by the effect of strong sunlight on nitrogen dioxide and hydrocarbons emitted by motor vehicles, creating a harmful haze of minute droplets in the air

photochemistry /fótō kémmistri/ *n* a branch of chemistry that studies the effect of radiation, especially of visible and ultraviolet light, on chemical reactions and the emission of radiation by chemical reactions —**photochemist** *n*

photochemotherapy /fótō keemō thérrəpi/ *n* MED same as **photopheresis** —**photochemotherapeutic** /-therə pyoótik/ *adj*

photochromic /fótō krómik/ *adj* changing colour or becoming darker or lighter in colour as light increases or decreases in intensity

photocoagulation /fótō kō aggyoŏ láysh'n/ *n* the use of a high-energy light source such as a laser to harden tissue for surgical repair, especially in eye injuries

photocomposition /fótō kompə zísh'n/ *n* ANZ, N Am PRINTING same as **filmsetting** —**photocompose** /fótō kəm póz/ *vt* —**photocomposer** /-pózər/ *n*

photoconduction /fótō kən dúksh'n/ *n* the conduction of electricity resulting from the absorption of electromagnetic radiation, especially visible light

photoconductivity /fótō kon duk tívvəti/ *n* an increase in the electrical conductivity of a substance on exposure to electromagnetic radiation, especially visible light —**photoconductive** /fótō kən dúktiv/ *adj* —**photoconductor** /-kən dúktər/ *n*

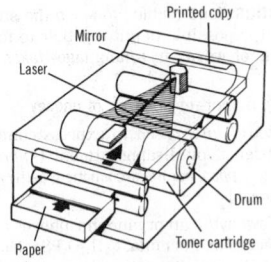

photocopier

photocopier /fótə kopi ər/ *n* a machine that uses a photographic process to produce an almost instant copy of something printed, written, or drawn

photocopy /fótə kopi/ *n* (*plural* **-ies**) a copy of something printed, written, or drawn that is produced almost instantly by a photographic process in a machine designed for this purpose ■ *vti* (**-ies**, **-ying**, **-ied**) to make a photocopy of something, or be photocopied

photocurrent /fótō kurənt/ *n* an electric current that is produced by and varies with the intensity of illumination. The current is a result of photoconductivity or of the photoelectric or photovoltaic effect.

photodecomposition /fótō dee kompə zísh'n/ *n* the breakdown of a chemical compound into simpler substances by means of incident electromagnetic energy, especially visible light

photodegradable /fótō di gráydəb'l/ *adj* able to be decomposed into simpler substances through prolonged exposure to incident electromagnetic energy, especially ultraviolet light

photodermatology /fótō durmə tólləji/ *n* a branch of photobiology dealing with the adverse effects of sunlight on the skin and the therapeutic use of artificial light —**photodermatologic** /-durmətə lójjik/ *adj*

photodiode /fótō dí ōd/ *n* a semiconductor device in which the flow of current is controlled by the intensity of light and that can therefore be used to detect light

photodisintegration /fótō diss inti gráysh'n/ *n* the ejection of a proton, neutron, or other elementary particle from an atomic nucleus as a result of its absorption of a photon, usually in the form of gamma radiation —**photodisintegrate** /-diss ínti grayt/ *vti*

photodriven /fótō drivv'n/ *adj* describes a physical or chemical reaction initiated by the absorption of photons

photodynamic /fótō dī námmik/ *adj* **1.** OF PHOTODYNAMICS relating to photodynamics or to the energy of light **2.** INVOLVING ADVERSE REACTION TO LIGHT bringing about or enhancing the toxic effects of some wavelengths of

light, especially ultraviolet, on living tissue **3.** OF LASER CANCER TREATMENT relating to or used to describe a cancer treatment in which the drug used is activated by a laser beam —**photodynamically** *adv*

photodynamics /fótō dī námmiks/ *n* a branch of biology dealing with the effects of light on living organisms (*takes a singular verb*)

photoelectric /fótō i léktrik/, **photoelectrical** /-trik'l/ *adj* relating to electrical effects that are due to the action of electromagnetic radiation, especially visible light —**photoelectrically** *adv* —**photoelectricity** /fótō ilek tríssəti, -ellek-/ *n*

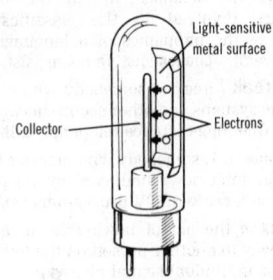

photoelectric cell

photoelectric cell *n* a solid-state device sensitive to varying levels of light that is used to generate or control an electric current, e.g. in burglar alarms, smoke detectors, and exposure meters

photoelectron /fótō i lék tron/ *n* an electron released from the surface of a substance that has been struck by a photon of electromagnetic radiation

photoemission /fótō i mísh'n/ *n* the release of electrons from a substance by incident electromagnetic radiation —**photoemissive** /fótō i míssiv/ *adj*

photoengraving /fótō ingráyving/ *n* **1.** PROCESS OF ETCHING PRINTING PLATE the process of making a printing plate by photographing an image onto a metal plate and then etching the image **2.** PRINTING PLATE MADE BY PHOTOENGRAVING a printing plate made by photographing an image onto a metal plate and then etching the image **3.** PRINT MADE BY PHOTOENGRAVING a print made by photographing an image onto a metal plate and then etching the image

~~photoes~~ incorrect spelling of **photos**

photoessay /fótō éssay/, **photo essay** *n* MEDIA same as **photo story**

photo finish *n* **1.** the end of a race in which two or more contestants are so close that the result must be determined from a photograph taken as they cross the finish line **2.** a race or competition won by a very small margin

photofission /fótō físh'n/ *n* nuclear fission induced by gamma rays

Photofit /fótō fit/ *tdmk* a trademark for a way of constructing a photograph of somebody using photographs of individual facial features arranged to fit a description closely. This method is often used to try to identify criminals.

photoflood /fótō flud/ *n* a very bright incandescent lamp used in photography and filming

photofluorogram /fótō floŏrə gram/ *n* a photograph of an image produced using X-rays

photofluorography /fótō floor róggrəfi/ *n* a technique that photographs an X-ray image onto a fluorescent screen for diagnostic purposes —**photofluorographic** *adj*

photog /fə tóg/ *n* a photographer (*informal*)

photogenic /fótə jénnik/ *adj* **1.** LOOKING ATTRACTIVE IN PHOTOGRAPHS tending to look good in photographs **2.** BIOL PRODUCING LIGHT describes an organism that produces its own light, especially by phosphorescence **3.** MED CAUSED BY LIGHT describes a physical reaction such as an epileptic episode that is caused or aggravated by light —**photogenically** *adv*

photogeology /fótō ji ólləji/ *n* the study and identification of landforms and other geological features by means of aerial and satellite photographs —

photogeologic /fótō jee ə lójjik/ adj —**photogeological** adj —**photogeologist** n

photogram /fótə gram/ n a photographic image produced without a camera, usually by placing an object on or near a piece of film or light-sensitive paper and exposing it to light

photogrammetry /fótō grámmətri/ n the making of measurements or scale drawings from photographs, especially using aerial photography in the construction of maps —**photogrammetric** /fótō grə méttrik/ adj —**photogrammetrist** n

photograph /fótə graaf, -graf/ n PICTURE PRODUCED WITH CAMERA an image produced on light-sensitive film or array inside a camera, especially a print or slide made from the processed image, or a reproduction in a newspaper, magazine, or book ■ v (-graphs, -graphing, -graphed) 1. vti TAKE PHOTOGRAPH OF SOMEBODY OR SOMETHING to produce an image of something or somebody using a camera 2. vi BE PHOTOGRAPHED WITH PARTICULAR RESULT to be able to be photographed, or to have a particular quality or appearance in a photograph ○ Scenes like this photograph best in bright sunlight. —**photographer** /fə tóggrəfər/ n

photographic /fótə gráffik/ adj 1. relating to, used in, or produced by photography 2. as accurate and detailed as a photograph ○ a witness who recounted the incident in photographic detail —**photographically** adv

photographic magnitude n the magnitude of a star determined by measuring its size on a photographic plate. Depending on the colour of the star, photographic magnitude and visual magnitude can differ because the eye and standard photographic plates have different colour sensitivities.

photographic memory n the ability to recall information, especially visual images, with great accuracy and clarity

photography /fə tóggrəfi/ n 1. the art, hobby, or profession of taking photographs, and developing and printing the film or processing the digitized array image 2. the process of recording images by exposing light-sensitive film or array to light or other forms of radiation

photogravure /fótō grə voyór/ n the process of using photography to make a printing plate with an image engraved into it [Late 19C. < French < photo- 'photo-' + gravure 'engraving' < graver 'engrave']

photoinduced /fótō in dyoóst/ adj initiated through exposure to light —**photoinduction** /fótō in dúksh'n/ n —**photoinductive** /-dúktiv/ adj

photoionization /fótō ī ə nī záysh'n/ n the removal of one or more electrons from an atom or molecule by absorption of a photon of electromagnetic radiation, especially visible and ultraviolet light. The free electrons in the ionosphere are believed to be a product of molecular absorption of ultraviolet radiation from the Sun. —**photoionize** /-ī ə nīz/ vti

photojournalism /fótō júrn'lizəm/ n a form of journalism in which photographs play a more important role than the accompanying text —**photojournalist** n —**photojournalistic** /-júrnə'l ístik/ adj

photokinesis /fótō ki néessiss, -kī-/ n the movement of an organism when stimulated by light —**photokinetic** /-ki néttik, -kī-/ adj —**photokinetically** adv

photolithography /fótō li thóggrəfi/ n 1. the process of creating lithographs using photographic methods 2. the process of producing integrated circuits and printed circuit boards by photographing the circuit pattern on a photosensitive substrate and then chemically etching away the background —**photolithograph** /fótō líthə graaf, -graf/ n —**photolithographer** n —**photolithographic** /fótō líthə gráffik/ adj —**photolithographically** adv

photoluminescence /fótō loomi néss'nss/ n the emission of light from a substance as a result of the absorption of electromagnetic radiation. The frequency of the light emitted is lower than that absorbed. —**photoluminescent** adj

photolysis /fō tólləssiss/ n the irreversible decomposition of a chemical compound as a result of the absorption of electromagnetic radiation, especially visible light —**photolytic** /fótō líttik/ adj —**photolytically** adv

photomap /fótō map/ n a map produced by marking placenames, grid lines, and other information on an aerial photograph ■ vti (-maps, -mapping, -mapped) to make a photomap of an area

photomask /fótō maask/ n ELECTRONICS same as **mask** n (sense 7)

photomechanical /fótō mi kánnik'l/ adj describes a method of producing printed text or images that uses photography —**photomechanically** adv

photo messaging n TELECOM same as **picture messaging**

photometry /fō tómmətri/ n 1. the measurement of the luminous intensities of visible light sources. This is sometimes expanded to include near-infrared and near-ultraviolet light. 2. the branch of physics concerned with the measurement of the intensity of light —**photometer** n —**photometric** /fótə méttrik/ adj —**photometrically** adv —**photometrist** n

photomicrograph /fótō míkrə graaf, -graf/ n a photograph made of something seen through a microscope —**photomicrographic** /fótō míkrə gráffik/ adj —**photomicrography** /fótō mī krógrəfi/ n

photomontage /fótō mon taázh/ n 1. the technique of combining a number of photographs or parts of photographs to form a composite picture, used especially in art and advertising 2. a composite picture made up of many photographs or parts of photographs, used especially in art and advertising

photomosaic /fótō mō záy ik/ n a large picture made up of many photographs, e.g. one combining aerial photographs to produce a detailed picture of an area

photomultiplier /fótō múlti plī ər/, **photomultiplier tube** n an evacuated electronic device used to convert low-intensity electromagnetic radiation, especially visible light, into an electrical current, and to amplify this current significantly

photon /fó ton/ n a quantum of visible light or other form of electromagnetic radiation demonstrating both particle and wave properties. A photon has neither mass nor electric charge but possesses energy and momentum. —**photonic** /fō tónnik/ adj

photonegative /fótō néggətiv/ adj 1. describes a conductive material whose electrical conductivity decreases in response to increasing illumination 2. describes organisms that move away from a source of light

photonics /fō tónniks/ n the scientific study of the properties and applications of light and other forms of radiant energy, including the generation of energy and information processing (takes a singular verb) —**photonic** adj

photonuclear /fótō nyoókli ər/ adj relating to a nuclear reaction caused by the absorption of a photon, usually in the form of gamma radiation, by an atomic nucleus

photo-offset n a method of offset printing in which plates are created using photographic methods

photo opportunity, **photo op** n an opportunity for the media to photograph a politician or other public figure doing something newsworthy, especially when it is deliberately staged to produce favourable publicity

photoperiod /fótō peéri əd/ n the daily cycle of light and darkness that affects the behaviour and physiological functions of organisms —**photoperiodic** /fótō peéri óddik/ adj —**photoperiodically** adv

photoperiodism /fótō peéri ədizəm/ n the influence of the daily cycle of light and darkness on the physiology and behaviour of an organism

photopheresis /fótəfə reéssiss/, **photophoresis** n a technique used to enhance the immune system in which a photoactive drug such as psoralen is injected into the body. Blood is removed, exposed to ultraviolet light to activate the drug, then returned to the body to fight the disease.

photophilous /fō tóffələss/ adj describes an organism such as a plant that grows well in strong light

photophobia /fótō fóbi ə/ n 1. very low tolerance of the eye for light, sometimes a symptom of disease or migraine 2. an irrational fear and avoidance of light or lighted spaces

photophobic /fótō fóbik/ adj 1. AFFECTED BY PHOTOPHOBIA relating to or having a condition in which the eye has very low tolerance to light 2. BEING AFRAID OF LIGHT

having an irrational fear of light 3. GROWING WELL IN REDUCED LIGHT describes an organism such as a plant that grows well in reduced light

photophore /fótə fawr/ n a luminous light organ on many deep-sea and some nocturnal fish, squids, and shrimps

photophoresis n MED same as **photopheresis**

photophosphorylation /fótō foss forri láysh'n/ n the process in photosynthesis that converts light energy to stored energy in plants and bacteria

photopia /fō tópi ə/ n normal vision during daylight, when the activity of the cones in the retina enables the eye to perceive colour —**photopic** /fō tóppik, fō tópik/ adj

photopigment /fótō pígmənt/ n a light-absorbing chemical that converts light into biochemical energy, e.g. in the rods and cones of the eye

photopolymer /fótō póllimər/ n a light-sensitive plastic whose physical properties change on exposure to visible or ultraviolet light

photopositive /fótō pózzətiv/ adj 1. describes a conductive material whose electrical conductivity increases in response to increasing illumination 2. describes organisms that move towards a light source

photorealism /fótō reé əlizəm/ n an artistic style, e.g. in painting or sculpture, that produces an accurate and detailed representation of the subject without attempting to conceal any unattractive aspects —**photorealist** adj, n —**photorealistic** /-ree ə lístik/ adj

photoreception /fótō ri sépsh'n/ n the perception, absorption, and use of light, e.g. for vision in animals or photosynthesis in plants —**photoreceptive** adj

photoreceptor /fótō ri séptər/ n a cell or organ that responds to light. Simple receptors may sense only changes in light intensity while more complex ones such as the eye may also form images of objects in the visual field.

photoreconnaissance /fótō ri kónniss'nss/ n reconnaissance undertaken using cameras, usually from an aircraft

photoresist /fótō ri zist, -zíst/ n a photosensitive material that is applied to a surface, exposed to visible or ultraviolet light, and developed prior to chemical etching during the photolithographic process

photorespiration /fótō respi ráysh'n/ n a pathway in photosynthesis in some plants in which oxygen is absorbed and carbon dioxide released

photosensitise vt SCI another spelling of **photosensitize**

photosensitive /fótō sénssətiv/ adj reacting to incident electromagnetic radiation, especially visible, infrared, and ultraviolet light —**photosensitivity** /fótō sénssə tívvəti/ n

photosensitize /fótō sénssə tīz/ (-tizes, -tizing, -tized), **photosensitise** (-tises, -tising, -tised) vt to increase the sensitivity of an organism or substance to electromagnetic radiation, especially visible light —**photosensitization** /fótō sénssə tī záysh'n/ n —**photosensitizer** /fótō sénssə tīzər/ n

photosphere /fótə sfeer/ n the intensely bright gaseous outer layer of a star, especially the Sun. Sunspots and faculae are features of the photosphere. —**photospheric** /fótə sférrik/ adj

Photostat /fótō stat/ tdmk a trademark for a photocopier

photo story n a collection of photographs in a magazine or book, often accompanied by a short commentary, that tells a story

photosynthesis /fótō sínthəssiss/ n a process by which green plants and other organisms turn carbon dioxide and water into carbohydrates and oxygen, using light energy trapped by chlorophyll —**photosynthetic** /fótō sin théttik/ adj —**photosynthetically** adv

photosynthesize /fótō sínthə sīz/ (-sizes, -sizing, -sized), **photosynthesise** (-sises, -sising, -sised) vti to produce carbohydrates and oxygen by photosynthesis [Early 20C. < PHOTOSYNTHESIS]

photosystem /fótō sistəm/ n either of two reactions

in the light phase of photosynthesis, the first (**photosystem I**) proceeding best with longer wavelengths of light, the second (**photosystem II**) with shorter wavelengths

phototaxis /fṓtō táksiss/, **photorxy** /fṓtō táksi/ n movement of an organism either towards or away from a source of light [Late 19C]—**phototactic** /-táktik/ adj—**phototactically** adv

phototherapy /fṓtō thérrəpi/, **phototherapeutics** /fṓtō thérrə pyóotiks/ n the use of light, especially ultraviolet light, in the treatment of disease—**phototherapeutic** /fṓtō thérrə pyóotik/ adj

phototoxic /fṓtō tóksik/ adj making the skin unusually sensitive to light and subject to damage by light, e.g. by sunburn—**phototoxicity** /fṓtō tok sssəti/ n

phototransistor /fṓtō tran zístər/ n a light-sensitive junction transistor that amplifies the base current as the illumination increases

phototrophic /fṓtō trṓfik, -tróffik/ adj describes organisms that can utilize light as a source of energy—**phototroph** /fṓtō trof/ n

phototropism /fṓtō trṓpizəm/ n the tendency of an organism to grow towards or away from a source of light

phototropy /fṓtō trṓpi/ n a property of some solids whereby they change colour in relation to the wavelength of the incident electromagnetic radiation, especially visible light

phototube /fṓtō tyoob/ n an electron tube that uses a cathode to convert visible light into electrical current at a rate proportional to the intensity of the illumination

phototypeset /fṓtō típ set/ (**-sets, -setting, -set**) vt to prepare text for printing by the use of filmsetting

phototypesetting /fṓtō típ setting/ n PRINTING same as **filmsetting**

photovoltaic /fṓtō vol táy ik/ adj able to generate a current or voltage when exposed to visible light or other electromagnetic radiation

photovoltaic cell n a photoelectric cell that detects and measures light intensity using the potential difference that arises between dissimilar materials when they are exposed to electromagnetic radiation

photovoltaic effect n the production of a potential difference across the junction of dissimilar materials or in a nonhomogeneous semiconductor material by the absorption of visible light or other electromagnetic radiation

phragmites /frag mí teez/ n an invasive reed of the grass family with stems that can grow as tall as 20 ft (6 m), found around the world in marshes and wetlands. Genus: *Phragmites*. [Early 20C. Via modern Latin < Greek *phragmitēs* 'growing in hedges' < *phragma* 'fence']

phrasal verb n a verb followed by an adverb, a preposition, or both, used with an idiomatic meaning that is often quite different from the literal meaning of the individual words. Examples include 'put up with', meaning 'tolerate', and 'stand for', meaning 'represent'.

phrase /frayz/ n 1. GRAMMATICAL UNIT a string of words that form a grammatical unit, usually within a clause or sentence 2. FIXED EXPRESSION a string of words that are used together and have an idiomatic meaning 3. BRIEF PITHY UTTERANCE a string of words, usually a short one, that memorably encapsulates something, e.g. a particular truth or sentiment or the character of a person or time ○ *We had certainly made progress, but this was still, in Churchill's phrase, only 'the end of the beginning'.* 4. LITERAT WORDS SPOKEN AS GROUP a group of words that form a unit of meaning or rhythm in prose or poetry, often separated by punctuation in writing and by pauses in speech 5. MUSIC MELODIC DIVISION a sequence of notes that form a unit of melody within a piece of music 6. DANCE PART OF CHOREOGRAPHIC PATTERN a short sequence of steps within a longer pattern of dance movements ■ v (**phrases, phrasing, phrased**) 1. vt EXPRESS SOMETHING IN PARTICULAR WAY to use a particular choice and order of words to express something in speech or writing ○ *She was saying more or less the same thing, but she phrased it differently.* 2. vt EXPRESS MEANING THROUGH PATTERNED SPEECH to show clearly in speech which groups of words belong together and how they are

to be understood, usually by pausing in appropriate places or by stress and intonation 3. vti MUSIC SEPARATE MUSIC INTO PHRASES to show clearly which sequences of notes belong together in a piece of music, especially when performing it [Mid-16C. Via Latin < Greek *phrasis* 'speech, way of speaking' < *phrazein* 'show, explain']

phrase book n a book of useful words and phrases in a foreign language, with translations, for the use of visitors to places where that language is spoken

phrasemaker /fráyz maykər/ n a maker of impressive phrases in speech or writing—**phrasemaking** n

phrase marker n a representation of the structure of a sentence, usually in the form of a tree diagram

phraseogram /fráyzi ə gram/ n a symbol used to represent a phrase in shorthand

phraseograph /fráyzi ə graaf, -graf/ n a phrase that is or can be represented by a symbol, usually in shorthand

phraseology /fráyzi ólləji/ n 1. the phrases used in a particular sphere of activity 2. the way words and phrases are chosen or used [Mid-17C. < modern Latin *phraseologia* < Greek *phrasis* (see PHRASE)]—**phraseological** /fráyzi ə lójjik'l/ adj—**phraseologist** n

phrase-structure grammar n a grammar that describes the structure and linear sequence of a sentence in terms of the phrases of which it is made up

phrasing /fráyzing/ n 1. the way words are chosen and put together to express something, or the words themselves 2. the way sequences of notes are grouped together to form units of melody in a piece of music, especially when it is performed

phratry /fráytri/ (*plural* **-tries**) n 1. a group of clans claiming descent from a common ancestor 2. in ancient Greece, a kinship group [Mid-19C. < Greek *phratria* < *phratēr* 'clansman, brother']—**phratric** adj

phreak /freek/ (**phreaks, phreaking, phreaked**) vi to use computer and telecommunications skills illegally to break into a telephone system to make free long-distance calls (*slang*) [Late 20C. Alteration of FREAK[1], after PHONE[1]]—**phreaking** n

phreatic /fri áttik/ adj 1. describes soil or rock below the water level, in which all the pores and intergranular spaces are full of water 2. describes an explosion caused by ground water coming into contact with ascending magma, e.g. in a volcano [Late 19C. < Greek *phreat-* 'well, cistern']

phreatomagmatic /fri áttō mag máttik/ adj describes a volcanic eruption caused by contact between magma and ground water in which magma, gases, and steam are expelled—**phreatomagmatism** /-mágmətizəm/ n

phrenic /frénnik/ adj 1. belonging to or supplying the diaphragm 2. belonging to or associated with the mind [Early 18C. < French *phrénique* < Greek *phrēn* 'mind, heart, diaphragm']

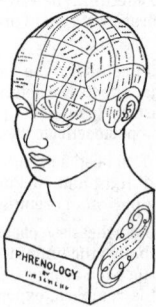

phrenology

phrenology /frə nólləji/ n the study of the bumps on the outside of the skull, based on the now discredited theory that these bumps reflect somebody's character [Early 19C. < Greek *phrēn* 'mind, heart, diaphragm']—**phrenological** /frénnə lójjik'l/ adj—**phrenologist** n

Phrygia /fríjji ə/ ancient country in Asia Minor, in present-day west-central Turkey. It reached the height of its importance in the 8th century BC.

Phrygian /fríjji ən/ n 1. somebody who came from ancient Phrygia 2. an extinct Anatolian language spoken in ancient Phrygia—**Phrygian** adj

Phrygian cap n same as **liberty cap** [Because worn by the ancient Phrygians]

Phrygian mode n a scale of notes originating in ancient Greek music and consisting of the eight notes of the diatonic scale rising from E to E

PHS abbr Public Health Service

phthalate /thálayt/ n a chemical compound used as a plastic softener and in many toiletries. It is reported to be a possible cause of reproductive or developmental problems because it mimics a natural hormone. [Mid-19C. < PHTHALIC ACID]

phthalein /tháy leen, tháy li in, thálleen, thálli in/ n an organic dye obtained by reacting phthalic anhydride with a phenol [Late 19C. < PHTHALIC ACID]

phthalic acid /thállik-/ n one of three isomers obtained by the oxidation of benzene derivatives. Use: dyes, perfumes, pharmaceuticals, synthetic fibres. Formula: $C_6H_4(CO_2H)_2$. [< shortening of NAPHTHALENE]

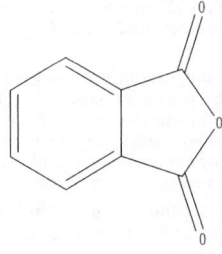

phthalic anhydride

phthalic anhydride n a white crystalline organic compound. Source: naphthalene. Use: manufacture of dyes, insecticides, plastics. Formula: $C_6H_4(CO)_2O$.

phthalocyanine /thállō sí ə neen, tháy lō-/ n 1. a bright greenish-blue crystalline compound. Source: phthalic anhydride. Use: pigment, coating for CD-ROMs, anticancer agent. Formula: $(C_6H_4C_2N)_4N_4H_2$. 2. a blue or green pigment developed as a metal-substituted form of phthalocyanine. Use: in enamels, plastics, printing inks, wallpaper, linoleum.

phthiriasis /thi rí əssiss/ n an infestation of the pubic hair of human beings with lice whose bite can irritate the skin [Late 16C. Via Latin < Greek *phtheiriasis* < *phtheirian* 'be infested with lice' < *phtheir* 'louse']

phthisic /thí sik, tí-/ n MED same as **phthisis** (sense 1) ■ adj also **phthisical** /thí sik'l, tí-/ relating to or having phthisis [14C. Via French and Latin < Greek *phthisikos* 'consumptive' < *phthisis* (see PHTHISIS)]

phthisis /thíssiss, tíssiss/ n 1. a disease or condition marked by wasting of the body 2. a disease of the respiratory system, especially asthma or tuberculosis (*archaic*) [Mid-16C. Via Latin < Greek *phthisis* 'consumption' < *phthinein* 'waste away']

Phuket /poo két/ 1. resort island off the western coast of Thailand. Population: 231,200 (2002). Area: 534 sq. km/206 sq. mi. 2. resort town and port on southeastern Phuket Island. Population: 60,000 (2002).

phulkari /pool kaári/ n 1. S Asia an embroidered shawl or cloth used on special occasions, especially associated with weddings 2. a style of embroidery using long thin stitches made close together [Late 19C. < Hindi]

phut /fut/ n a sound like a small explosion or a sudden expulsion of air (*informal*) [Late 19C. Probably an imitation of the sound] ◇ **go phut** (*informal*) 1. to stop working suddenly or break down completely 2. to collapse or come to nothing

phyco- prefix relating to seaweed or algae ○ *phycology* [< Greek *phukos* 'seaweed']

phycocyanin /fíkō sí ənin/ n a protein pigment in cyanobacteria

phycoerythrin /fíkō érrithrin/ n a red protein pigment in red algae

phycology /fī kólləji/ n BOT same as algology —**phycological** /fīkə lójjik'l/ adj —**phycologist** n

phycomycete /fíkō mī́ seet, fíkō mī seét/ n a mould resembling algae. Class: Phycomycetes. [Mid-20C. < Greek *phukos* 'seaweed' + *mukētes*, plural of *mukēs* 'fungus'] —**phycomycetous** /-mī seétəss/ adj

phyl- prefix same as **phylo-** (used before vowels)

phyla BIOL, LANGUAGE plural of **phylum**

phylactery

phylactery /fi láktəri/ (plural -ies) n 1. either of two small leather boxes containing slips of paper with scriptures written on them, traditionally worn by Jewish men during morning weekday prayers as reminders of their religious duties (often used in the plural) 2. a reminder of something important [14C. Via Latin < Greek *phulaktērion* 'amulet' < *phulaktēr* 'guard' < *phulassein* 'to guard']

phyle /fī́ li/ (plural -lae /-lī/) n any of a number of clans into which some peoples of ancient Greece were divided. The phylae formed political and administrative units within the large city-states. [Mid-19C. < Greek *phulē* 'tribe'] —**phylic** adj

phyletic /fī léttik/ adj relating to the hereditary descent of a species or its evolutionary development [Late 19C. < Greek *phuletikos* < *phulē* 'tribe'] —**phyletically** adv

phyll- prefix same as **phyllo-** (used before vowels)

-phyll suffix leaf ○ chlorophyll [< Greek *phullon* 'leaf'] —**-phyllous** suffix

phyllid /fíllid/ n a moss or liverwort leaf

phyllite /fíllīt/ n a fine-grained metamorphic rock with a distinctive shiny surface, containing large quantities of mica and resembling slate or schist [Early 19C. < Greek *phullon* 'leaf'] —**phyllitic** /fi líttik/ adj

phyllo- prefix leaf ○ phyllotaxis [< Greek *phullon* < Indo-European]

phylloclade /fíllō klayd/, **phylloclad** /-klad/ n BOT same as **cladophyll** [Mid-19C. < modern Latin *phyllocladium* < Greek *phullon* 'leaf' + *klados* 'shoot'] —**phyllocladous** /fi lókládəss/ adj

phyllode /fíllōd/, **phyllodium** /filṓdi əm/ (plural -dia /-di ə/) n a flat leaf stalk that functions as a leaf in some plants such as the acacia [Mid-19C. < modern Latin *phyllodium* < Greek *phullōdēs* 'resembling a leaf' < *phullon* 'leaf'] —**phyllodial** adj

phylloid /fílloyd/ adj like a leaf in shape or function [Mid-19C. < modern Latin *phylloides* < Greek *phullon* 'leaf']

phylloquinone /fíllō kwi nṓn/ n BIOCHEM same as **vitamin K₁**

phyllotaxis /fíllō táksis/ (plural -taxes /-tákseez/), **phyllotaxy** /-táksi/ (plural -ies) n 1. the way the leaves on a plant are arranged in relation to one another 2. the study of the factors that determine the growth patterns and arrangement of plant leaves —**phyllotactic** /-táktik/ adj

phylloxera /fi lóksərə/ (plural same or -ras or -rae /-rī/) n an aphid that is a major pest in wine-producing areas. Latin name: *Viteus vitifolii*. [Mid-19C. < modern Latin < Greek *phullon* 'leaf' + *xēros* 'dry'; from the insect's effect on leaves]

phylo- prefix race, kind, tribe, phylum ○ phylogeny [< Greek *phulon* 'race']

phylogeny /fī lójjəni/ (plural -nies), **phylogenesis** /fílō jénnəssiss/ (plural -eses /-əseez/) n the evolutionary history of a species, genus, or group, as contrasted with the development of an individual (ontogeny) —**phylogenetic** /fílō jə néttik/ adj —**phylo-**

genetically adv —**phylogenetics** n —**phylogenic** /fílō jénnik/ adj —**phylogenically** adv

phylum /fíləm/ (plural -la /-lə/) n 1. a major taxonomic group into which animals are divided, made up of several classes 2. a large group of languages or language stocks thought to be historically related, e.g. Afro-Asiatic or Indo-European [Late 19C. Via modern Latin < Greek *phulon* 'race']

physalis /fī sáyliss/ (plural -salises or -sales /-sáyleez/) n UK a tropical plant of the nightshade family that bears edible yellow berries. Native to: Americas. Latin name: *Physalis peruviana*. ANZ, N Am term **Cape gooseberry** [Early 19C. Via modern Latin < Greek *phusallis* 'bladder']

phys ed /fiz éd/ n EDUC same as **physical education** (informal)

physi- prefix same as **physio-** (used before vowels)

physiatrics /fízzi áttriks/ n US MED same as **physical medicine** (takes a singular verb) [Mid-19C. < Greek *phusis* 'nature' (see PHYSICS) + *iatrikos* 'medical']

physic /fízzik/ (archaic) n 1. PROFESSION OF MEDICINE medicine or healing as an art or profession 2. MEDICINE a medicine, especially a purgative ■ vt (-ics, -icking, -icked) TREAT SOMEBODY OR SOMETHING to treat somebody or something with a medicine or cure [13C. Directly or via Old French *fisique* < Latin *physica* (see PHYSICS)]

physical /fízzik'l/ adj 1. OF BODY relating to the body, rather than to the mind, the soul, or the feelings 2. REAL AND TOUCHABLE existing in the real material world, rather than as an idea or notion, and able to be touched and seen ○ physical evidence 3. NEEDING BODILY STRENGTH involving or needing a lot of bodily strength or energy ○ hard physical work 4. WITH BODILY CONTACT involving a lot of bodily contact or aggression ○ Some of the players were a little too physical. 5. INVOLVING TOUCHING tending to touch people or involving touching, especially in an affectionate or sexual way (informal) 6. NOT SOCIAL OR BIOLOGICAL describes sciences such as physics and chemistry that deal with nonliving things such as energy and matter ■ n MED same as **physical examination** (informal) ■ **physicals** npl COMM TANGIBLE GOODS items of trade or commerce that can be bought and used, as distinct from items bought and sold in a futures market —**physicality** /fízzi kálləti/ n —**physicalness** n

physical anthropology n the branch of anthropology that studies the evolutionary development of human physical characteristics and the differences in appearance among the peoples of the world, as distinct from cultural differences

physical challenge n 1. an inability to perform some or all of the tasks of daily life 2. a medically diagnosed condition that makes it difficult to engage in the activities of daily life

physical chemistry n the branch of chemistry that studies the physical and thermodynamic properties of substances in relation to their structures and chemical reactions

physical education n gymnastics, athletics, team sports, and other forms of physical exercise taught to children at school

physical examination n a doctor's general examination to determine somebody's state of physical health and fitness, sometimes as a requirement for a specific job or activity

physical geography n the branch of geography that studies the natural features of the Earth's surface as well as their formation

physicalise vt another spelling of **physicalize**

physicalism /fízzik'lizəm/ n in philosophy, a form of materialism that explains the phenomena of reality, including perceptual and intellectual processes, in terms of the physical —**physicalist** n, adj —**physicalistic** /fízzikə lístik/ adj

physicalize /fízzikə līz/ (-izes, -izing, -ized), **physicalise** (-ises, -ising, -ised) vt 1. to express or exhibit something such as emotion with the body 2. to represent something abstract in the form of a physical or concrete thing

physical jerks npl physical exercises of the kind done regularly to keep fit, e.g. press-ups (dated informal)

physically /fízzikli/ adv 1. relating to somebody's body or appearance ○ physically unattractive 2. in terms

of what is real or what exists in the material world, as opposed to what is theoretical or exists only in the mind ○ physically impossible

physically challenged adj describes somebody with a condition that makes it difficult to perform some or all of the basic tasks of daily life

physical medicine n the branch of medicine concerned with the diagnosis of injuries or physical disabilities and their treatment by external means, including heat, massage, or exercise, rather than by medication or surgery

physical science n a science that studies nonliving things, e.g. physics and chemistry

physical therapy n N Am same as **physiotherapy** —**physical therapist** n

physician /fi zísh'n/ n a doctor who diagnoses and treats diseases and injuries using methods other than surgery [13C. < Old French *fisicien* < *fisique* (see PHYSIC)]

physician-assisted suicide n ANZ, N Am the suicide of somebody with an incurable disease carried out with the help of a physician. Physician-assisted suicide is illegal in most countries. UK term **doctor-assisted suicide**

physicist /fízzissist/ n a student of physics or a scientist who specializes in physics [Mid-19C. < PHYSICS]

physicochemical /fízzikō kémmik'l/ adj 1. relating to both physical and chemical characteristics 2. relating to physical chemistry [Mid-17C. < Greek *phusikos* (see PHYSICS)] —**physicochemically** adv

physics /fízziks/ n the scientific study of matter, energy, force, and motion, and the way they relate to each other. Physics traditionally incorporates mechanics, electromagnetism, optics, and thermodynamics and now includes modern disciplines such as quantum mechanics, relativity, and nuclear physics. (takes a singular verb) ■ npl the physical processes, interactions, qualities, properties, or behaviour of something (takes a plural verb) [15C. < PHYSIC; translation of Latin *physica* (plural) < Greek *phusika*, plural of *phusikos* 'of nature' < *phusis* 'nature' < *phuein* 'make grow']

physio /fízzi ō/ (plural -os) n (informal) 1. a physiotherapist 2. MED same as **physiotherapy** [Mid-20C. Shortening]

physio- prefix physical ○ physiotherapy [< Greek *phusis* 'nature' (see PHYSICS)]

physiognomy /fízzi ónnəmi/ (plural -mies) n 1. FACIAL FEATURES the features of somebody's face, especially when they are used as indicators of that person's character or temperament 2. JUDGMENT OF CHARACTER FROM FACIAL FEATURES the use of facial features to judge somebody's character or temperament 3. CHARACTER OR APPEARANCE OF SOMETHING the character or outward appearance of something, e.g. the physical features of a landscape [13C. Via French < Greek *phusiognōmonia* < *phusis* 'nature' (see PHYSICS) + *gnomon* 'judge' (see GNOMON)] —**physiognomic** /fízzi ə nómmik/ adj —**physiognomically** adv —**physiognomist** n

physiography /fízzi óggrəfi/ n GEOG same as **physical geography** (dated) —**physiographer** n —**physiographic** /fízzi ə gráffik/ adj —**physiographically** adv

physiological /fízzi ə lójji'l/, **physiologic** /-lójjik/ adj 1. relating to the way that living things function, rather than to their shape or structure 2. relating to physiology —**physiologically** adv

physiological saline n an aqueous salt solution used to keep cells alive and to administer medication intravenously

physiology /fízzi ólləji/ n 1. the branch of biology that deals with the internal workings of living things, including functions such as metabolism, respiration, and reproduction, rather than with their shape or structure 2. the way a particular body or organism works [Mid-16C. Directly or via French < Latin *physiologia* < Greek *phusiologia* < *phusis* 'nature' (see PHYSICS)] —**physiologist** n

physiotherapy /fízzi ō thérrəpi/ n UK, ANZ, Can the treatment of injuries and physical disabilities by a trained person under the supervision of a specialist in physical medicine. US term **physical therapy** —**physiotherapeutic** /fízzi ō therə pyōōtik/ adj —**physiotherapeutically** adv —**physiotherapist** n

physique /fi zeék/ *n* the shape and size of somebody's body [Early 19C. < French < *physique* 'physical' < Greek *phusikos* (see PHYSICS)]

physostigmine /fīsō stíg meen/, **physostigmin** /-min/ *n* a crystalline alkaloid. Source: dried leaves of the vine that produces Calabar beans. Use: treatment of glaucoma, to counteract adverse effects of anticholinergic drugs on the central nervous system. Formula: $C_{15}H_{12}N_3O_2$. [Mid-19C. < modern Latin *Physostigma* < Greek *phusa* 'bladder' + *stigma* 'mark on the skin']

phyt- *prefix* same as **phyto-** (*used before vowels*)

-phyte *suffix* **1.** plant ○ *saprophyte* **2.** pathological growth ○ *osteophyte* [< Greek *phuton* (see PHYTO-)] —**-phytic** *suffix*

phyto- *prefix* plant ○ *phytohormone* [Via modern Latin < Greek *phuton* < *phuein* 'make grow' < Indo-European, 'be']

phytoaccumulation /fīto ə kyoomyóō láysh'n/ *n* ENVIRON same as **phytoextraction**

phytoalexin /fīto ə léksin/ *n* a chemical produced by a plant to protect it from infection by a pathogen or exposure to some agents of stress

phytochemical /fīto kémmik'l/ *n* a naturally occurring plant substance. Some phytochemicals have been shown in research to protect against disease.

phytochemistry /fīto kémmistri/ *n* the chemistry of plants and their metabolic processes —**phytochemical** *adj* —**phytochemically** *adv* —**phytochemist** *n*

phytochrome /fītōkrōm/ *n* a light-sensitive pigment in plants that controls flowering and germination of seeds [Late 19C. < PHYTO- + Greek *khrōma* 'colour']

phytoestrogen *n* BOT another spelling of **phytooestrogen**

phytoextraction /fīto ik stráksh'n/ *n* the process by which plants absorb metal contaminants in soil through their roots and store them in their upper parts, used as a means of cleaning the soil

phytogenesis /fīto jénnəssiss/, **phytogeny** /fī tójjəni/ *n* the evolutionary development of plants —**phytogenetic** /fīto jə néttik/ *adj* —**phytogenetically** *adv*

phytogenic /fīto jénnik/, **phytogenous** /fītójjənəss/ *adj* describes substances such as coal that are formed from plants

phytogeny *n* BOT same as **phytogenesis**

phytogeography /fītōji óggrəfi/ *n* the study of the geographical distribution of plants —**phytogeographer** *n* —**phytogeographic** /-jee ə gráffik/ *adj* —**phytogeographically** *adv*

phytohormone /fīto háwrmōn/ *n* BOT same as **plant hormone**

phytol /fī tol/ *n* an alcohol derived from chlorophyll from which plants synthesize vitamins E and K

phytology /fī tólləji/ *n* BOT same as **botany** (*archaic*)

phyton /fī ton/ *n* the smallest part of a plant, usually a leaf and its stem, that can grow when it has been cut from the parent plant [Mid-19C. < French < Greek *phuton* (see -PHYTE) + *-on* '-on']

phytooestrogen /fīto eéstrəjən, -éstrə-/, **phytoestrogen** *n* a sterol of a group found in plants that can have a similar effect on the body to that of a hormone

phytopathogen /fīto páthəjən/ *n* something that causes disease in plants

phytopathology /fīto pə thólləji/ *n* the branch of botany that studies plant diseases —**phytopathological** /fīto pathə lójjik'l/ *adj* —**phytopathologically** *adv* —**phytopathologist** *n*

phytophagous /fī tóffəgəss/ *adj* describes animals, especially insects, that feed on plants —**phytophagy** *n*

phytoplankton /fīto plángktən/ *n* very small free-floating plants, e.g. one-celled algae, found in plankton —**phytoplanktonic** /-plangk tónnik/ *adj*

phytoprotectant /fīto prə téktənt/ *n* a compound derived from plants that prevents the progression of diseases such as cancer

phytoremediation /fīto ri meédi áysh'n/ *n* the process of decontaminating soil by using plants to absorb heavy metals or other pollutants

phytosociology /fīto sōssi ólləji, -sōshi ólləji/ *n* the branch of ecology concerned with the identification, analysis, and classification of plant communities or plant associations —**phytosociological** /fīto sōssi ə lójjik'l, -sōshi-/ *adj* —**phytosociologically** *adv* —**phytosociologist** *n*

phytostabilization /fīto staybi lī záysh'n/ *n* the use of plant roots to immobilize soil contaminants and prevent them from polluting ground water

phytotoxic /fīto tóksik/ *adj* poisonous to plants —**phytotoxicity** /fīto tok síssəti/ *n*

phytotoxin /fīto tóksin/ *n* **1.** a poisonous substance obtained from plants, e.g. the drug digitalis **2.** something that is poisonous to plants

phytotron /fīto tron/ *n* a place in which plants can be grown under controlled conditions, e.g. a glasshouse or a more complex facility

pi[1] /pī/ *n* **1.** the 16th letter of the Greek alphabet, represented in the English alphabet as 'p'. See table at **alphabet 2.** a number approximately equal to 3.14159 that is the ratio of the circumference of a circle to its diameter and is represented by the symbol π [Early 19C. < Greek]

pi[2] /pī/, **pie** *n* **1.** JUMBLE OF PRINTERS' TYPE a pile of printing type that has been mixed up together **2.** DISORDERED MIXTURE a disorganized combination of things ■ *v* (**pies, piing, pied; pies, pieing, pied**) **1.** *vt* JUMBLE TYPE to mix printing type up together **2.** *vti* MAKE OR BECOME JUMBLED to mix things up in a confusing way, or become mixed up or confused [Mid-17C. Origin ?]

pi[3] /pī/ *adj* pretending to be very religious or virtuous (*dated informal*) [Mid-19C. Shortening of PIOUS]

PI *abbr* N Am private investigator

pia /pī/ *n* ANAT same as **pia mater** [Late 19C. Shortening] —**pial** *adj*

PIA *abbr* COMPUT peripheral interface adaptor

Piacenza /pya chéntsa/ capital city of Piacenza Province, Emilia-Romagna Region, northern Italy. Population: 95,594 (2001).

piacular /pī ákyoōlər/ *adj* **1.** done or offered in order to make up for a sin or sacrilegious action **2.** wicked or sinful and requiring the offender or sinner to atone [Early 17C. < Latin *piacularis* < *piaculum* 'atonement' < *piare* 'appease']

AKG London
Edith Piaf

Piaf /peé af/, **Édith** (1915–63) French singer. Her expressive performance of songs such as 'Je ne regrette rien' and 'La Vie en rose' led to international fame. Born **Gassion, Édith Giovanna**

piaffe /pi áf/ *n also* **piaffer** /pi áffər/ a dressage movement performed by a horse in which it trots in one place and raises its legs very high ■ *vi* (**piaffes, piaffing, piaffed**) to perform a dressage movement that involves trotting on the spot with the legs raised high [Mid-18C. < French < *piaffer* 'to strut']

Piaget /pi ázh ay/, **Jean** (1896–1980) Swiss psychologist. His pioneering study of intellectual development in children had a major impact on psychology and education.

> 'Psychoanalysis is a sort of individual history, an embryology of the personality.'
> [Jean Piaget, 'Psychoanalysis and its Relations with Child Psychology'; 1920]

pia mater /pīə máytər/ *n* the innermost and most delicate of the three membranes (**meninges**) that surround the brain and the spinal cord [14C. < Latin, 'tender mother', translated < Arabic *al-'umm ar-rakika*]

piani MUSIC plural of **piano**[2]

pianism /peé ənizəm/ *n* piano-playing skill or technique —**pianistic** /peé ə nístik/ *adj*

pianissimo /peé ə níssimō/ *adv* very softly and quietly (*used as a musical direction*) ■ *n* (*plural* **-mos** or **-mi** /-mee/) a part of a musical composition that is played very softly [Early 18C < Italian, 'very quiet' < *piano* (see PIANO[2])] —**pianissimo** *adj*

pianist /peé ənist/ *n* somebody who plays the piano

piano[1] /pi ánnō/ *n* (*plural* **-os**) a large musical instrument consisting of a keyboard fixed to a wooden case containing metal wires stretched across a frame. It is played by pressing the keys, each of which is attached to a small hammer that strikes one or more of the wires to sound a note. ■ *adj* relating to or played on a piano ○ *a piano sonata* [Early 19C. < Italian, shortening of PIANOFORTE]

CULTURAL NOTE *The Piano*, a film (1993) by New Zealand director Jane Campion. Set in the mid-nineteenth century, it is the story of the mute Scots wife of a New Zealand landowner who falls in love with a settler who has acquired her beloved piano. Holly Hunter won an Academy Award for her performance in the lead role.

piano[2] /pyaánō/ *adv* softly and quietly (*used as a musical direction*) ■ *n* (*plural* **-nos** or **-ni** /-nee/) a part of a musical composition that is played softly [Late 17C. Via Italian < Latin *planus* 'soft, flat'] —**piano** *adj*

piano accordion *n* an accordion with a keyboard on one side to play the notes of the melody on —**piano accordionist** *n*

piano bar *n* a bar, or a lounge in a hotel, where a pianist plays to entertain customers or provide background music

pianoforte /pi ánnō fáwrti/ *n* same as **piano**[1] (*formal*) [Mid-18C. < Italian < *gravecembalo col piano e forte* 'harpsichord with soft and loud']

piano hinge *n* a long narrow hinge that has a pin running the length of its joint

piano nobile /pyaánō nóbili/ *n* the first floor of a large residence or public building [< Italian, 'noble floor', because high above the ground]

piano quartet *n* an ensemble consisting of a piano and three other instruments, usually a violin, viola, and cello, or a piece of music written for this combination

piano quintet *n* an ensemble consisting of a piano and four other instruments, usually two violins, a viola, and a cello, or a piece of music written for this combination

piano roll *n* a roll of paper with patterns of perforations whose positions determine the sequence of notes played on a player piano

piano stool *n* an adjustable stool for a pianist to sit on, often with a hollow compartment under the seat for storing sheet music

piano trio *n* a musical ensemble consisting of a piano and two other instruments, usually a cello and a violin, or a piece of music written for this combination

piassava /peé ə saáva/, **piassaba** /-saába/ *n* **1.** a coarse fibre obtained from a Brazilian tree. Use: rope, brooms, brushes. **2.** a palm tree that produces piassava. Native to: Brazil. Latin name: *Attalea funifera* or *Leopoldinia piassaba*. [Mid-19C. Via Portuguese < Tupi *piaçába*]

piastre /pi ástər/ *n* a subunit of currency in several Middle Eastern countries. See table at **currency** [Late 16C. Via French < Italian *piastra (d'argento)* '(silver) plate' < Latin *emplastrum* (see PLASTER)]

Piave /pyaáv e/ river in northeastern Italy. Length: 220 km/137 mi.

piazza /pi átsə/ *n* (*plural* **-zas** or **-ze** /-tsay/) **1.** (*plural* **piazze** or **piazzas**) ITALIAN PUBLIC SQUARE a large open square, especially one in an Italian town **2.** OPEN-SIDED PASSAGEWAY a covered passageway that has arches on one or both sides and is usually attached to a building, e.g. along the inner walls of a courtyard or quadrangle **3.** *US regional* PORCH a veranda or porch, especially one attached to a house (*dated*) [Late 16C. Via Italian < Latin *platea* 'open space' (see PLACE)]

pi bond *n* a covalent bond between two atoms and a pair of electrons having orbitals whose greatest overlap is along a plane perpendicular to a line connecting the nuclei of the atoms —**pi-bonding** *adj*

pibroch /peeb rokh/ *n* a piece of music written for the Scottish Highland bagpipes, consisting of a theme and variations, often with a mournful tone [Early 18C. < Gaelic *piobaireachd* 'art of piping' < English PIPE[1]]

pic /pik/ (*plural* **pics** or **pix** /piks/), **pick** *n* (*informal*) **1.** a picture, especially a photograph or illustration **2.** a cinema film [Late 19C. Shortening of PICTURE]

pica[1] /píkə/ *n* a unit of measurement for printing type, equal to 12 points or 0.422 cm/0.166 in. [15C. < Anglo-Latin, 'church almanac'; from the resemblance to the handwriting in such books]

pica[2] /píkə/ *n* the indiscriminate craving for and eating of substances such as paint chips, clay, plaster, or dirt [Mid-16C. < Latin, literally 'magpie', translation of Greek *kissa*]

Picabia /pi cábbi ə/, **Francis** (1879–1953) French avant-garde artist who painted in most major 20th-century styles. He is best known for his Dadaist and surrealist works. Born **Picabia, François Marie Martinez**

picador /píkə dawr/ *n* a bullfighter on horseback, who attacks the bull with a spear early in the fight, making it easier for the main bullfighter (**matador**) to kill it with his sword [Late 18C. < Spanish < *picar* 'prick, pierce']

pica em *n* PRINTING same as **pica**[1]

picante /pi kán tay/ *adj* spicy, especially in being served with a sauce that contains tomatoes, onions, peppers, vinegar, and spices [< Italian *piccante* < present participle of *piccare* 'to sting']

Picard /píkaard/ *n* **1.** somebody who comes from Picardy in northern France **2.** the dialect of French spoken in Picardy [14C. < French]

Picardy /píkərdi/ region and former province of northern France, in an area between Calais and Paris and centred on the city of Amiens. There was heavy fighting there during World War I. French name **Picardie**

picaresque /píkə résk/ *adj* **1. OF LITERATURE HAVING ROGUE AS HERO** belonging to or characteristic of a type of prose fiction that features the adventures of a roguish hero and usually has a simple plot divided into separate episodes **2. RELATING TO ROGUES** relating to or characteristic of rogues or scoundrels ■ *n* **PICARESQUE FICTION** prose fiction featuring the adventures of a roguish hero [Early 19C. Via French < Spanish *picaresco* < *picaro* 'rogue' < assumed Vulgar Latin *piccare* 'to prick']

picaroon /píkə roón/, **pickaroon** *n* same as **rogue** *n* (sense 1) (*archaic or literary*) ■ *vi* (**-roons, -rooning, -rooned**) to live the adventurous life of a pirate, thief, swindler, or scoundrel (*archaic literary*) [Early 17C. < Spanish *picarón* 'great rogue' < *picaro* (see PICARESQUE)]

AKG London

Pablo Picasso: photographed in 1933 by Man Ray

Picasso /pikássō/, **Pablo** (1881–1973) Spanish painter and sculptor. An exceptionally versatile and prolific artist, he was the leading figure in the development of modern abstract art. Among his major works are the cubist masterpiece *Les Demoiselles d'Avignon* (1906–07) and *Guernica* (1937), which expresses his horror of war.

> 'Painting is a blind man's profession. He paints not what he sees, but what he feels, what he tells himself about what he has seen.'
> [Pablo Picasso. Quoted in 'Childhood', *The Journals of Jean Cocteau*, Wallace Fowlie (tr.); 1957]

picayune /píkə yoón/ *adj N Am* (*informal*) **1. TRIFLING** of very little importance **2. SMALL-MINDED** tending to fuss about unimportant things and to be childishly spiteful ■ *n* **1.** *N Am* **TRIFLING THING** something unimportant or of little value (*informal*) **2.** COINS **COIN FROM SPANISH AMERICA** a small silver coin formerly used in Spanish America, worth half of a real **3.** *US* COINS **SMALL COIN** a low-value coin, especially a five-cent piece (*archaic informal*) [Early 19C. Via French *picaillon*, Piedmontese coin < Provençal *picaioun*]

piccalilli /píkə lílli/ *n* pickle consisting of mixed vegetables, especially cauliflower, small whole onions, and cucumber, in a sauce containing mustard and vinegar [Mid-18C. Probably < PICKLE[1] + CHILLI]

piccaninny /píkə nínni/ (*plural* **-nies**) *n* (*taboo*) **1.** a highly offensive term for a small Black child **2.** *Aus* a highly offensive term for an Aboriginal child [Mid-17C. < Caribbean creole, probably < Portuguese *pequenino* 'very small' < *pequeno* 'small']

Piccard /pík aar/, **Auguste** (1884–1962) Swiss physicist. He is noted for his exploration of the deep sea and of the stratosphere, to which he made the first balloon ascent (1931).

piccata /pi kaátə/ *adj* describes meats sautéed in slices and served in a spicy lemon and butter sauce [< Italian < French *piqué*, past participle of *piquer* 'attach ingredients, lard', literally 'to prick']

piccolo /píkəlō/ (*plural* **-los**) *n* a musical instrument, the smallest member of the flute family, with a range one octave higher than the standard flute [Mid-19C. < Italian, 'small']

pice /pīss/ (*plural same*) *n* a subunit of currency formerly used in South Asia, four of which were worth an anna [Early 17C. < Hindi *paisā* 'paisa']

pichiciego /píchissi áygō/ (*plural same* or **-gos**), **pichiciago** *n* **1.** a very small armadillo with pink armour and silky hair. Native to: Argentina. Latin name: *Chlamyphorus truncatus*. **2.** a large armadillo with yellowish-brown armour and coarse whitish hair. Native to: South America. Latin name: *Burmeisteria retusa*. [Early 19C. < Spanish, probably < Guarani *pichey*, type of armadillo, literally 'small' + Spanish *ciego* 'sightless' < Latin *caecus*]

pick[1] /pik/ *v* (**picks, picking, picked**) **1.** *vt* **CHOOSE SOMETHING OR SOMEBODY** to take, or decide to take, one or more things or people from a larger number ○ *Pick three people for your team.* **2.** *vt* **REMOVE SOMETHING FROM PLANT** to remove something, especially in quantity and by hand, from a plant on which it has grown ○ *picking strawberries* **3.** *vt* **STRIP SOMETHING OF FRUIT OR FLOWERS** to strip a plant, or all the plants in a place, of fruit or flowers ○ *The bushes nearest the path had already been picked.* **4.** *vt* **REMOVE SOMETHING IN SMALL PIECES** to remove something bit by bit from the surface or middle of something using a sharp or pointed object such as a fingernail or a beak **5.** *vt* **SCRAPE BODY PART WITH FINGERNAIL** to use a fingernail to loosen and remove something, or to loosen and remove something attached to the surface of a part of the body ○ *pick a scab* **6.** *vt* **OPEN SOMETHING WITHOUT PROPER KEY** to use a special device or pointed instrument to open a lock, usually illegally ○ *pick a lock* **7.** *vt* **UNDO SOMETHING** to loosen, unfasten, or separate something into disconnected parts, especially something that was sewn together ○ *pick a seam apart* **8.** *vi* **FIND FAULT** to be petty or fault-finding **9.** *vt* **START FIGHT OR QUARREL** to begin a fight or quarrel with somebody, usually deliberately **10.** *vt* MUSIC **PLUCK OR PLAY BY PLUCKING** to pluck the strings of a stringed instrument or to play a tune on such an instrument in this way ■ *n* **1. CHOICE** the act or right of choosing somebody or something ○ *take your pick* **2. BEST** the very best of a wide selection of people or things ○ *the pick of the bunch* **3. CROP PORTION** the amount of a crop gathered by hand at one time [13C. Probably < assumed Old English *pīcian* 'to prick', Old Icelandic *pikka*] —**picker** *n* ◇ **pick and choose** to select only the best of what is on offer, or make a choice in a careful or fussy manner ◇ **pick your way** to step very carefully through a dirty, untidy, or dangerous area of ground

pick at *vt* **1. EAT LITTLE FOOD** to eat very little of a meal ○ *He only picked at his breakfast.* **2. SCRAPE SOMETHING WITH FINGERNAILS** to scrape away surface pieces of something with the fingernails **3. NAG SOMEBODY** to nag or criticize somebody in a petty way (*informal*)

pick off *vt* to shoot somebody or something selected as a target and deliberately aimed at, usually from a distance, or shoot a number of targets one by one

pick on *vt* **1.** to blame, criticize, or bully somebody repeatedly in a way that is considered unfair or unkind **2.** to choose somebody or something from among others

pick out *vt* **1. CHOOSE SOMETHING** to choose or select something or somebody from among others ○ *She picked out her favourite chocolate.* **2. IDENTIFY SOMEBODY FROM CROWD OR BACKGROUND** to recognize or distinguish somebody or something from among others or against a background that makes this difficult ○ *I couldn't pick him out in the crowd.* **3. MAKE SOMETHING STAND OUT** to make something stand out against its background, especially by giving it a strikingly different colour (*often passive*) ○ *The design was picked out in green.* **4.** MUSIC **PLAY SOMETHING NOTE BY NOTE** to play a tune slowly, note by note

pick over *vt* to go through something, selecting the best items or discarding unwanted items

pick up *v* **1.** *vt* **LIFT SOMETHING** to take hold of and raise or remove something or somebody **2.** *vt* **GATHER DROPPED THINGS** to collect things that have been dropped or have fallen to the ground **3. pick yourself up** *vr* **REGAIN UPRIGHT OR STRONGER POSITION** to stand up after falling down, or recover strength, courage, or a sense of purpose after a setback ○ *She picked herself up off the floor and staggered over to the phone.* ○ *They're still picking themselves up after narrowly avoiding bankruptcy.* **4.** *vti* **TAKE ON PASSENGERS** to stop a vehicle and let a passenger or passengers in ○ *picked up a hitchhiker* **5.** *vt* **CLAIM SOMETHING** to collect something such as an item left for repair or goods ordered from a shop ○ *pick up a library book* **6.** *vt* **PAY FOR SOMETHING** to take on the responsibility for paying something, especially a bill ○ *pick up the tab* **7.** *vt* **BUY SOMETHING ON IMPULSE** to buy something in a casual or unplanned way ○ *pick up a takeaway on the way home* **8.** *vt* **ACQUIRE SOMETHING CHEAPLY OR EASILY** to get or buy something cheaply or easily ○ *a book I picked up for a few dollars* **9.** *vt* **ACQUIRE SOMETHING CASUALLY** to acquire something casually, often without meaning to and without knowing it ○ *has picked up some bad habits* **10.** *vt US* **GAIN POINTS** to gain or win something such as an award, or points or runs **11.** *vt* **CATCH DISEASE** to become infected with a disease **12.** *vt* **RECEIVE SIGNAL** to receive something such as a radio or television signal or a radar image on a piece of equipment **13.** *vt* **NOTICE SOMETHING** to notice something or become aware of it **14.** *vt* **FIND SOMETHING** to find and follow something, especially a scent or trail ○ *pick up the scent* **15.** *vt* **UNDERSTAND SOMETHING** to understand something that is communicated indirectly **16.** *vt* **LEARN SOMETHING** to learn something in a casual or unsystematic way, e.g. by frequently hearing it, seeing it done, or trying to do it ○ *picked up a lot of Spanish on his trip* **17.** *vti* **ACCELERATE** to increase, or cause something to increase, in strength, speed, or intensity ○ *Her speed picked up.* **18.** *vti* **RETURN TO SOMETHING AGAIN** to continue, or continue something, at a later time, usually after an interruption or break ○ *We can pick up our discussion after the break.* **19.** *vt* **FIND SEXUAL PARTNER** to make the acquaintance of a stranger, often in a public place, usually for sexual purposes (*informal*) ○ *picked him up in a pub* **20.** *vt* same as **arrest** (*informal*) ○ *He was picked up on a burglary charge.* **21.** *vi* **BECOME BETTER** to improve after being ill, injured, bad, or unsuccessful (*informal*) ○ *He picked up quickly.*

pick up on *vt* (*informal*) **1.** to notice something, and perhaps mention or question it **2.** to criticize somebody for an action or behaviour, often in a condescending way

pick[2] /pik/ *n* **1. TOOL FOR BREAKING UP HARD SURFACES** a tool used for breaking up hard surfaces, consisting of a long handle and a curved metal head that is pointed at one end and either pointed or like a chisel at the other **2. SMALL TOOL FOR BREAKING INTO PIECES** a small tool used to break up something into smaller pieces (*often used in combination*) **3. SHARP TOOL FOR PICKING** a sharp tool for cleaning something such as the teeth or for getting into small places, as in a lock (*often used in combination*) **4.** *US* MUSIC same as **plectrum** ■ *vi* (**picks, picking, picked**) **WORK WITH PICK** to use a

pick or do labouring work with a pick [14C. Variant of PIKE[2]]

pick[3] *n* another spelling of **pic** (*informal*)

pickaback /píkə bak/ *n, adj, adv* same as **piggyback** (*dated*) [Variant]

pickaninny *n* US spelling of **piccaninny** (*taboo offensive*)

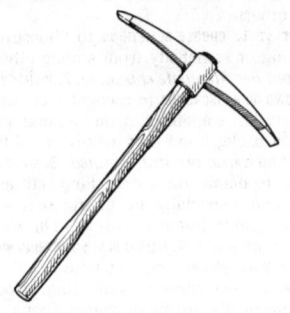
pickaxe

pickaxe /pík aks/ *n* same as **pick**[2] *n* (sense 1) [15C. Alteration (by association with AXE) of obsolete *pikois* < Old French *picois* < Latin *picus* 'woodpecker']

pickerel /píkərəl/ (*plural same* or **-els**) *n* 1. a predatory fish of the pike family, popular as a game fish. Native to: North America. Latin name: *Esox niger*. 2. a young pike [14C. < PIKE[1]; partly after Anglo-Latin *picerellus*]

picket /píkit/ *n* 1. POINTED POST STUCK IN GROUND a post or plank with a pointed end that is hammered into the ground, e.g. as a marker, as a support for a fence, or to tether an animal 2. PROTESTER OR PROTESTERS OUTSIDE BUILDING a person or group of people demonstrating or protesting outside a building, especially a striker or strikers attempting to persuade other people not to enter the workplace during a strike 3. *also* **picket** SOLDIER OR SOLDIERS ON GUARD a soldier or small body of troops used to occupy ground of tactical importance ■ *v* (-ets, -eting, -eted) 1. *vti* HOLD PROTEST OUTSIDE PLACE to hold a demonstration or protest outside a place, especially in order to persuade others not to enter it during a strike 2. *vt* POST GUARDS to post troops as guards 3. *vt* GUARD SOMETHING to patrol or guard a place, especially a military site or position 4. *vt* ENCLOSE OR MARK SOMETHING WITH STAKES to enclose or mark something with wooden stakes driven into the ground, or enclose it with a picket fence 5. *vt* TETHER ANIMAL to tether a horse or other animal [Late 17C. < French *piquet* 'pointed stake' < *piquer* 'prick, pierce' (see PIQUE[1])] —**picketer** *n*

picket fence *n* a fence made of pointed stakes or posts driven into the ground and connected by one or more horizontal bars

picket line *n* a line of people such as striking workers protesting outside a building

AKG London
Mary Pickford

Pickford /píkfərd/, **Mary** (1893–1979) Canadian-born US actor and producer. She starred in films such as *Poor Little Rich Girl* (1917), and cofounded United Artists Studio (1919). Born **Smith, Gladys Marie**. Known as **America's Sweetheart**.

pickings /píkingz/ *npl* things available to be earned or taken ○ *easy pickings*

pickle[1] /pík'l/ *n* 1. SAVOURY PRESERVE a lumpy mixture of chopped vegetables, typically cauliflower, onions,

cucumbers, and gherkins, preserved in vinegar or brine to give it a sharp or spicy flavour and eaten with other foods 2. VEGETABLE PRESERVED IN VINEGAR a small vegetable, e.g. an onion or gherkin, that has acquired a sharp taste by being preserved in vinegar or brine, usually with added spices (*usually used in the plural*) 3. LIQUID FOR PRESERVING FOOD liquid, usually brine or a vinegar solution, used to preserve cold foods such as vegetables or fish 4. CLEANING OR PROCESSING SOLUTION an industrial or commercial solution used to clean or process something 5. AWKWARD SITUATION a difficult or problematic situation (*informal*) 6. TROUBLESOME PERSON a mildly troublesome person, especially a naughty child (*informal*) ■ *vt* (-les, -ling, -led) 1. PRESERVE FOOD to preserve food, especially vegetables or fish, in vinegar, brine, or another solution 2. DIP OR SOAK SOMETHING IN LIQUID to clean or process something by dipping or soaking it in a liquid [14C. < Middle Low German *pekel*] —**pickler** *n*

pickle[2] /pík'l/, **puckle** /púk'l/ *n Scotland* a small amount or quantity (*informal*) [Mid-16C. Origin?]

pickled /pík'ld/ *adj* 1. preserved in vinegar, brine, or another liquid 2. same as **drunk** *adj* (sense 1) (*informal*)

picklock /pík lok/ *n* 1. a tool used to open locks without using a key 2. an opener of locks who does not use a key, especially a burglar

pick-me-up *n* something that lifts the spirits and energizes somebody, especially a stimulating drink (*informal*)

pickney /píkni/ (*plural* **-neys**) *n* same as **child** (senses 1, 4) (*slang; used in Black English*) [Mid-19C. Probably < Portuguese *pequeno* 'small']

~~**picknick**~~ incorrect spelling of **picnic**

pick 'n' mix /píkən míks/ *n* a wide range of items, especially sweets, cheeses, or salads, from which you choose whatever combination you want (*hyphenated when used before a noun*)

pickoff /pík of/ *n* an electronic device that senses movement used, e.g. in the guidance system of an aircraft or as part of a surveillance system

pickpocket /pík pokit/ *n* a thief who steals from people's pockets and bags in public places, usually unnoticed —**pickpocketing** *n*

pick-up *n* 1. LIFTING OR COLLECTING OF SOMETHING the raising, gathering, collection, or removal of something to be taken somewhere else ○ *weekday pick-ups and deliveries* 2. SOMEBODY OR SOMETHING TAKEN SOMEWHERE somebody or something that is moved from one place to another 3. AUTOMOT same as **pick-up truck** 4. *also* **pick-up arm** RECORDING same as **tone arm** 5. RECORDING PART OF TONE ARM a device inside the tone arm of a record player that converts the stylus's vibrations into electrical signals that are converted into sound 6. CONVERTER OF VIBRATIONS ON MUSICAL INSTRUMENT an electromagnetic device that converts the vibrations from the strings of an electric guitar or other amplified instrument into electrical signals that are amplified into sound 7. PART THAT LIFTS SOMETHING a part of a machine or system that lifts or selects something, e.g. the rotating rake on a combine harvester that lifts and gathers straw or hay 8. PROSPECTIVE SEXUAL PARTNER somebody met casually with the aim of developing a sexual relationship (*informal*) 9. HITCHHIKER somebody who hitchhikes (*informal*) 10. IMPROVEMENT an improvement or increase (*informal*) 11. BEVERAGES same as **pick-me-up** (*informal*) 12. ARREST the taking of somebody into custody by a police officer (*informal*) 13. *N Am* POWER TO ACCELERATE the ability of a vehicle to accelerate quickly (*informal*) 14. PHYS RECEIVING OF LIGHT OR SOUND WAVES the receiving and gathering of light or sound waves that are to be converted into electrical impulses 15. PHYS RECEIVER FOR LIGHT OR SOUND WAVES a device used to receive light or sound waves ■ *adj N Am* IMPROMPTU informally organized on the spot and made up of or involving people available at the time

pick-up truck *n* a light truck with a low-sided open back and a tailgate that drops down for easy loading and unloading

Pickwickian /pik wíki ən/ *adj* 1. generous, naive, or benevolent 2. not literal or typical in usage or meaning [Mid-19C. < Mr *Pickwick*, character in Charles Dickens's novel *The Pickwick Papers* (1837)]

picky /píki/ (**-ier, -iest**) *adj* having inflexible likes and dislikes and, therefore, being hard to please or satisfy [Mid-19C. < PICK[1]] —**pickily** *adv* —**pickiness** *n*

pick-your-own *adj* describes crops that can be picked directly by customers, or such a service offered to customers

picky-picky /píkee pikee/ *adj* (*slang; used in Black English*) 1. describes a fabric such as wool or cotton that has small balls of fluff forming on it as a result of wear 2. describes Afro-style hair that is uncombed

picloram /píklə ram/ *n* a herbicide permitted for use on plants other than crops, e.g. the grass of playing fields. Formula: $C_6H_3Cl_3N_2O_2$. [Mid-20C. < PICOLINE + CHLOR- + AMINE]

picnic /píknik/ *n* 1. MEAL TAKEN AND EATEN OUTDOORS an informal meal prepared for eating in the open air or the food that makes up such a meal 2. EASY OR PLEASANT THING something easy to do or pleasant to experience (*informal*) ○ *Moving house was no picnic.* ■ *vi* (-nics, -nicking, -nicked) HAVE PICNIC to eat an informal meal outdoors [Mid-18C. < French *piquenique*] —**picnicker** *n*

CULTURAL NOTE *Picnic at Hanging Rock*, a novel (1967) by Australian author Joan Lindsay. Set in turn-of-the-century Australia, it tells the story of the disappearance of three schoolgirls during a St Valentine's Day picnic at Hanging Rock in Victoria. Although one girl reappears, the mystery is never explained. It was made into a film by Peter Weir in 1976.

picnic day *n Aus* an extra day off work granted by many employers, sometimes used for a picnic for company employees

~~**picnicing**~~ incorrect spelling of **picnicking**

picnic races *npl Aus* horse races for amateur riders, usually local farmers or farmhands, that are major social events in rural areas of Australia

pico- *prefix* 1. one million millionth (10^{-12}) ○ *picofarad* Symbol **p** 2. very small ○ *picornavirus* [Via Spanish *pico* 'beak, small amount' < Latin *beccus* (see BEAK)]

Pico della Mirandola /peékō déllə mi rándōlə/, **Giovanni, Count** (1463–94) Italian humanist philosopher. His 900 philosophical propositions attracted accusations of heresy.

Pico de Teide /peékō day táythə/ highest mountain in Spain, on the island of Tenerife. Height: 3,715 m/12,188 ft.

picofarad /peékō farəd, -farad/ *n* one million millionth of a farad

picogram /peékō gram/ *n* one million millionth of a gram

picoline /píkə leen/ *n* a colourless liquid. Source: coal tar, bone oil. Use: solvent, in organic synthesis. Formula: C_6H_7N. [Mid-19C. < Latin *pic-* 'pitch' + *oleum* 'oil'] —**picolinic** /píkə línnik/ *adj*

picomole /peékōmōl/ *n* one million millionth of a mole

picong /pi kóng/ *n Carib* light-hearted teasing talk [Mid-20C. < Spanish *picón*]

picoplankton /peékō plangktən/ *n* the component of plankton in the size range 0.2–2.0 micrometres

picornavirus /pi káwrnə vírəss/ *n* a small infectious virus, e.g. the virus that causes polio or the common cold. Family: Picornaviridae. [Mid-20C. < PICO- + RNA + VIRUS]

picosecond /peékō sekənd/ *n* one million millionth of a second

picot /peékō/ *n* a loop that forms a pattern with others, e.g. in lace ■ *vt* (-cots /-kōz/, -coting /-kō ing/, -coted /-kō'd/) to embroider small loops on fabric [Early 17C. < French, 'small point' < *pic* 'peak, point' < *piquer* 'to prick' (see PIQUE[1])]

picotee /píkə tee/ *n* a flower, especially a carnation or tulip, that has petals edged with a different, usually darker colour [Early 18C. < French *picotée*, form of past participle of *picoter* 'to prick' < *picot* (see PICOT)]

picowave /peékō wayv/ (**-waves, -waving, -waved**) *vt* to expose food to radiation in order to kill insects, worms, or bacteria

picquet[1] *n* MIL another spelling of **picket** *n* (sense 3)

picquet[2] *n* CARDS another spelling of **piquet**

picr- *prefix* same as **picro-** (*used before vowels*)

picrate /pík rayt/ *n* a salt or ester of picric acid [Mid-19C. < Greek *pikros* 'bitter']

picric acid

picric acid /píkrik-/ *n* a strong toxic yellow crystalline acid. Use: dyes, antiseptics, high explosives. Formula: $C_6H_3N_3O_7$. [< Greek *pikros* 'bitter']

picrite /pík rīt/ *n* a dark-coloured igneous rock made up primarily of coarse grains of olivine and other ferromagnesian minerals [Early 19C. < Greek *pikros* 'bitter']

picro- *prefix* **1.** bitter ○ *picrotoxin* **2.** picric acid ○ *picrate* [< Greek *pikros* 'bitter, sharp' < Indo-European, 'to cut']

picrotoxin /píkrə tóksin/ *n* a bitter crystalline compound. Source: seeds of a South Asian vine. Use: antidote to barbiturate poisoning. Formula: $C_{30}H_{34}O_{13}$.

Pict /pikt/ *n* a member of an ancient people who occupied lands north of the Forth and Clyde rivers in Scotland between the 1st and the 4th centuries AD [Pre-12C. < late Latin *Picti* (plural), probably < Latin *picti* 'painted or tattooed people', form of *pictus* 'painted']

Pictish /píktish/ *adj* relating to the Picts, their culture, or their language ■ *n* an extinct language formerly spoken in Scotland

pictograph /píktō graaf, -graf/, **pictogram** /-gram/ *n* **1.** a graphic symbol or picture representing a word or idea in some writing systems, as opposed to a symbol such as a letter of the alphabet representing an individual sound **2.** a chart or diagram that uses symbols or pictures to represent values [Mid-19C. < Latin *pictus* (see PICTURE)] —**pictographer** /pik tógrəfər/ *n* —**pictographic** /píktə gráffik/ *adj* —**pictographically** *adv* —**pictography** /pik tógrəfi/ *n*

Picton /píktən/ town on the northeastern coast of the South Island, New Zealand. It is a ferry port and tourist centre. Population: 3,990 (2001).

Pictor /píktər/ *n* an inconspicuous constellation of the southern hemisphere between Dorado and Columba. See illustration at **constellation**

pictorial /pik táwri əl/ *adj* **1.** OF PICTURES relating to, composed of, or shown by pictures **2.** ILLUSTRATED containing illustrations or photographs, as opposed to writing or text **3.** DESCRIPTIVE describes language that conjures up vivid images ■ *n* HIGHLY ILLUSTRATED PERIODICAL a newspaper or magazine that has many pictures in it, especially one with far more pictures than text [Mid-17C. < late Latin *pictorius* < Latin *pictor* 'painter' < *pictus* (see PICTURE)] —**pictoriality** /pik táwri álləti/ *n* —**pictorially** *adv* —**pictorialness** *n*

pictorialism /pik táwri əlizəm/ *n* **1.** the use of visual images in the arts, especially those that are representational or realistic **2.** a style of photography, popular at the turn of the 20th century, using soft-focus techniques to imitate academic painting —**pictorialist** *n*

picture /píkchər/ *n* **1.** SOMETHING DRAWN OR PAINTED a shape or set of shapes and lines drawn, painted, or printed on paper, canvas, or some other flat surface, especially shapes that represent a recognizable form or object **2.** PHOTOGRAPHY same as **photograph 3.** TV IMAGE the image on a television screen **4.** FILM a cinema film or motion picture **5.** MENTAL IMAGE a vivid image or impression in the mind of how somebody or something looks **6.** ARTISTIC DESCRIPTION OR REPRESENTATION a description or representation of something in writing, in a film, in music, or some other art form **7.** OBSERVED SITUATION a situation in its context

○ *get the picture* **8.** EMBODIMENT OR EPITOME a typical or perfect example of the way something looks, or somebody or something that embodies a quality or state perfectly ○ *She was the picture of health.* **9.** SOMEBODY WHO CLOSELY RESEMBLES ANOTHER somebody who closely resembles somebody else ○ *She's the absolute picture of her grandmother.* **10.** BEAUTIFUL THING something that is beautiful to look at ■ **pictures** *npl* CINEMA the cinema, as a place of entertainment, or a cinema show (*dated informal*) ○ *go to the pictures* ■ *vt* (**-tures, -turing, -tured**) **1.** IMAGINE SOMETHING to imagine or have an image of somebody or something in mind **2.** DESCRIBE SOMETHING to describe somebody or something in a particular way **3.** FEATURE PICTURE OF SOMEBODY to feature a picture, especially a photograph, of somebody or something in a newspaper, magazine, or book (*often passive*) [15C. < Latin *pictura* < *pictus*, past participle of *pingere* 'to paint'] ◇ **put somebody in the picture** to acquaint somebody with the facts of a situation

CULTURAL NOTE *The Picture of Dorian Gray*, a novel (1890) by Oscar Wilde. In Wilde's update of the Faust legend, the decadent young gentleman Dorian Gray trades his soul for eternal youth and beauty, but is subsequently tormented by a portrait of himself that constantly changes to reflect the ravages of time and of his debauched lifestyle. It was made into a film by Albert Lewin in 1945.

picture book *n* a highly illustrated book, especially one for children, written in a simple style

picture card *n* CARDS same as **court card**

picture hanger *n* HOUSEHOLD same as **picture hook**

picture hat *n* a woman's elaborately decorated hat with a very broad brim, of the kind often featured in informal portraits of women painted in the 18th century

picture hook *n* a hook that is nailed to a wall or suspended from a rail fixed to the wall and used to hang a picture

picture house *n* LEISURE same as **cinema** (sense 3) (*dated*)

picture library *n* a place where photographs and other images are stored, from which they may be borrowed for use in books, magazines, and newspapers

picture messaging *n* the sending of images and photographs from one mobile phone to another

picture moulding *n* **1.** carved or moulded wood used to make picture frames **2.** US BUILDINGS same as **picture rail**

picture palace *n* LEISURE same as **cinema** (sense 3) (*dated*)

picture-perfect *adj* very clean, tidy, ordered, and pleasing, as the subjects of paintings and photographs often are

picture postcard *n* a postcard with a picture, often a photograph of a landmark or landscape, on one side (*dated*)

picture-postcard *adj* very attractive, like the scenes typically photographed for picture postcards

picture rail *n* UK, ANZ, Can a strip of wood or plaster moulding resembling a cornice, fixed high up around the walls of a room, from which you can hang pictures. US term **picture moulding**

picture researcher *n* somebody whose job is finding the photographs, drawings, and other illustrative material for a book or magazine, using picture libraries and other sources

picturesque /píkchə résk/ *adj* **1.** VISUALLY ATTRACTIVE visually very appealing or impressive, often by virtue of quaintness or unusualness or through seeming fit for a painting or photograph **2.** VIVID charmingly or strikingly unusual and often very expressive ○ *a picturesque expression* **3.** OBSCENE containing a lot of swearwords (*informal; used euphemistically*) ○ *picturesque language* ■ *n* VISUALLY ATTRACTIVE OR DISTINCTIVE things that are visually very pleasing or distinctive, considered collectively [Early 18C. Anglicization (after PICTURE) of French *pittoresque* < Italian *pittoresco* < *pittore* 'painter' < Latin *pictor* (see PICTORIAL)] —**picturesquely** *adv* —**picturesqueness** *n*

picture tube *n* ELECTRONICS same as **cathode ray tube**

picture window *n* a large window, usually with a single pane of glass, especially one that has a pleasant view

picture writing *n* **1.** a writing system that uses symbols or pictures to represent whole words or ideas rather than individual sounds, e.g. the writing system of Chinese **2.** the reporting of an event or telling of a story using pictures instead of words, e.g. in ancient cave paintings

picul /pík'l/ *n* a unit of weight used in East and Southeast Asia, especially a Chinese unit equal to 60 kg/133 lb [Late 16C. < Malay, Javanese *pikul* 'load']

piculet /píkyŏŏlət/ *n* (*plural same* or **-lets**) *n* a very small woodpecker with a short tail. Native to: tropics, especially of Americas. Genus: *Picumnus*. [Mid-19C. < Latin *picus* 'woodpecker']

PID *abbr* **1.** MED pelvic inflammatory disease **2.** COMPUT personal identification device

piddle /pídd'l/ *v* (**-dles, -dling, -dled**) **1.** *vi* same as **urinate** (*informal; usually used by children*) **2.** *vti* to do things in a casual, unhurried, or disorganized way, or pass time doing things in this way ○ *wasted a lot of time piddling about in the garden* ■ *n* an act of urinating (*informal; usually used by children*) [Late 18C. Origin ?] —**piddler** *n*

piddling /píddling/ *adj* very small, insignificant, or trivial (*informal*) —**piddlingly** *adv*

piddock /píddək/ *n* a saltwater mollusc that has a hinged shell with serrated edges that it uses to bore into rock and wood. Family: Pholadidae. [Mid-19C. Origin ?]

pidgin /píjjin/ *n* a simplified language made up of parts of two or more languages, used as a communication tool between speakers whose native languages are different. See panel on next page [Early 19C. < Chinese, alteration of BUSINESS] —**pidginization** /píjji nī záysh'n/ *n* —**pidginize** *vt*

pidgin English *n* a pidgin based however loosely on English, especially one formerly used between Chinese people and Europeans, or one currently spoken in West Africa and some Pacific islands

pi-dog *n* ZOOL another spelling of **pye-dog**

PIDS *abbr* MED primary immune deficiency syndrome

pie[1] /pī/ *n* **1.** a baked dish consisting of a filling such as chopped meat or fruit enclosed in or covered with pastry and usually cooked in a container **2.** something regarded as a resource to be shared or divided up ○ *Our competitors are always looking for a larger piece of the overseas pie.* [14C. Origin ?] ◇ **pie in the sky** something described very attractively that is not likely to happen or materialize

pie[2] /pī/ *n* a very small coin formerly used in India, worth one third of a pice [Mid-19C. Via Hindi *paī* < Sanskrit *pādikā* < *pāda* 'quarter']

pie[3] /pī/ *n* PRINTING another spelling of **pi**[2]

pie[4] /pī/ *n* (*plural same* or **pies**) *n* **1.** a bird resembling a magpie, especially one with black and white feathers **2.** same as **magpie** (*archaic*) [14C. Via French < Latin *pica* 'magpie']

piebald /pí bawld/ UK, ANZ, Can *adj* describes a horse whose coat has patches of two or more contrasting colours, especially black and white ■ *n* (*plural same* or **-balds**) a piebald horse ▶ US term (all senses) **pinto** [Late 16C. < PIE[4]; from the resemblance to a magpie's plumage]

piece /peess/ *n* **1.** PART TAKEN FROM LARGER WHOLE a part that has been broken, torn, or cut from a larger whole **2.** PORTION OR SERVING a portion or serving from a larger block or whole **3.** INDIVIDUAL ITEM OR OBJECT an item or object of a particular kind or class ○ *an expensive piece of equipment* **4.** INTERCONNECTING PART one of a set of parts that fit together to form a whole or unit ○ *a 500-piece jigsaw* ○ *took the radio to pieces* **5.** EXAMPLE OF SOMETHING an instance or example of something, often something abstract such as luck ○ *a piece of good fortune* ○ *a useful piece of information* **6.** DECLARATION OF OPINION a statement of opinion on a subject, event, or situation ○ *At least I said my piece.* **7.** ARTS ARTISTIC WORK a single artistic work, e.g. a musical composition, play, or painting ○ *a piano piece* ○ *a piece of music* **8.** MEDIA PUBLISHED ARTICLE an article in a newspaper or magazine ○ *a piece of writing* **9.** COINS COIN a coin of a particular value ○ *a fifty-pence piece* **10.** BOARD GAMES OBJECT MOVED IN BOARD

WORLD ENGLISH A *pidgin* is a simple language that arises from contacts between people with different mother tongues, in situations where relatively uncomplicated ideas are being exchanged. The speech is generally slow and supported by mime and gesture; the vocabulary is basic and taken mostly from the language of the most important group of speakers; and the grammar has much in common with that typically used by native speakers talking to non-native speakers, or by mothers talking to young children.

A simplified pidgin can develop rapidly: if it proves useful, it becomes more complex, and hence flexible. If it becomes a mother tongue, it is expanded to fulfil all its speakers' needs. Such mother tongues are known as *creoles*. Developed pidgins are most likely to be found in multilingual communities, where they are invaluable as lingua francas. They can be found in Papua New Guinea, for example, where there are over 700 languages for an estimated population of five million, and in West Africa, where as many as one-fifth of the world's languages occur.

Pidgins have probably existed for millennia. Evidence suggests that pidginized versions of Latin evolved into the Romance languages, and there was certainly a medieval lingua franca in use during the Crusades. Pidgins with vocabularies from European languages developed extensively in the wake of European expansionism from the 15th century onward.

Each pidgin, like each language, is unique but they share some characteristics: word order is fixed; there is little or no inflection; negation usually involves a 'no' word in front of the verb; nouns and verbs are regular; the small vocabulary is used creatively; and speakers use local idioms, metaphors, and proverbs.

Here is an example of Kamtok, a Cameroon Pidgin English from west-central Africa:

Den i bin lef dat ples, an i bin kam fo i on kontri, an i pipu bin folo i. An i bin di tich di pipu fo insai di Jew dem God haus... (Mark 6: 1–2)

(Then he left that place, and he came into his own country and his people followed him. And he was teaching the people inside the synagogue...). See also *creole*.

GAME in board games, an object that a player moves on the board **11. FIREARM** a gun, especially a handgun (*slang*) **12. OFFENSIVE TERM** an offensive term for a woman (*slang*) **13.** *N Am* **OFFENSIVE TERM** an offensive term for sexual intercourse (*slang*) **14.** *N Am* **ESTIMATE OF DISTANCE** an unspecified distance (*informal*) ○ *You go down the road a piece and then you come to the bridge.* **15.** *regional* **SANDWICH** a sandwich, slice of bread, or snack, especially one taken to be eaten somewhere such as school or work **16.** *ANZ* **FLEECE SCRAP** an inferior scrap of wool from the trimmings of a fleece (*often used in the plural*) ■ *vt* (**pieces, piecing, pieced**) **1. WORK SOMETHING OUT** to put something together gradually, bit by bit ○ *We finally managed to piece together the events of that night.* **2. MEND SOMETHING** to mend something by patching it [12C. < Old French, probably < Gaulish] ◇ **fall** *or* **go to pieces 1.** to become broken into small bits **2.** to become unable to cope ◇ **give somebody a piece of your mind** to rebuke somebody severely and angrily ◇ **of a piece** alike ◇ **pull somebody** *or* **something to pieces 1.** to criticize somebody or something severely **2.** to reduce somebody or something to smaller parts by tugging or tearing forcefully

SPELLCHECK See *peace*.

piece out *vt* to share or dispense something such as food in a makeshift, piecemeal way

pièce de résistance /pi éss de re zís toNss/ (*plural* **pièces de résistance** /*pronunc. same*/) *n* **1.** the most impressive thing or something that brings the greatest pride or satisfaction **2.** the most important dish served at a meal (*formal*) [Late 18C. < French, literally 'piece of resistance']

piece-dyed *adj* dyed after being woven

piece goods *npl* fabrics made and sold in standard lengths

piecemeal /péess meel/ *adv* **1. GRADUALLY** little by little **2. IN PARTS** in separate parts or fragments ■ *adj* **DONE BIT BY BIT** done in a disorganized or fragmentary way ○ *His novel is a ragtag, piecemeal work.* [13C. < PIECE + obsolete *-meal* 'measure' < form of MEAL[1]]

piece of cake *n* something that is very easy to do (*informal*) [< the easiness of eating cake, a soft food]

piece of eight *n* a former Spanish gold coin

piece of piss *n* an offensive term for something that is very easy to do (*slang*)

piece of work *n* **1.** somebody or something remarkable or outstanding **2.** somebody or something unpleasant, troublesome, or strange

piecework /péess wurk/ *n* work paid by the amount done instead of by the time spent doing it

piechart /pí chaart/ *n* a diagrammatic representation of a group shown as a circle divided into sections by straight lines from its centre with areas proportional to the relative size of the quantity represented

pied-à-terre /pi áyd aa taír, peé ed-/ (*plural* **pieds-à-terre** /*pronunc. same*/) *n* a small flat or house used

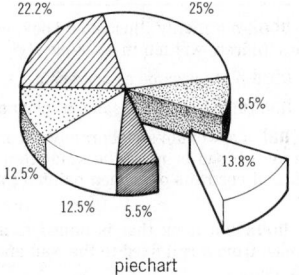

piechart

as a second home for holidays or business purposes [< French, literally 'foot to earth']

piedmont /peéd mont/ *n* a region at the base of a mountain range ■ *adj* lying or formed at the base of a mountain range [Mid-19C. After piedmont]

Piedmont /peéd mont/ region in northwestern Italy, a major commercial and agricultural centre. Capital: Turin. Population: 4,338,262 (1991). Area: 25,399 sq. km/9,807 sq. mi. —**Piedmontese** /peéd mon teéz/ *n, adj*

Piedmont Plateau upland region of the eastern United States, extending from New York State to Alabama between the Appalachian Mountains and the Atlantic Coastal Plain

Pied Piper /píd-/ *n* **1.** in German folklore, a visiting piper whose entrancing music rid the town of Hamelin of its rats. He later lured away its children after town officials refused to pay him for his services. **2.** *also* **pied piper** somebody who attracts supporters and followers, especially by making unrealistic promises

pied wagtail *n* **1.** a small black and white bird with a long black tail. Native to: Europe. Latin name: *Motacilla alba yarrellii.* **2.** a long-tailed black-and-white bird. Native to: Africa. Latin name: *Motacilla aguimp.*

pie-eyed *adj* very drunk (*informal*)

pier /peer/ *n* **1. WALKWAY JUTTING INTO SEA** a platform built on stilts jutting out into a body of water, used as a boat jetty, a place from which to fish, or as an entertainment centre **2.** CONSTR **BREAKWATER** a barrier built out to sea to protect a harbour from heavy waves **3.** CONSTR **VERTICAL STRUCTURAL SUPPORT** a pillar, especially a rectangular one supporting the end of an arch, lintel, or vault **4.** CONSTR **BRIDGE SUPPORT** a vertical structural support between two spans of a bridge **5.** ARCHIT **WALL BETWEEN ADJACENT DOORS** an area of wall between two adjacent doors, windows, or other openings **6.** ARCHIT **COLUMN PROJECTING FROM WALL** a column of masonry projecting from a wall **7.** CONSTR **WALL REINFORCEMENT** a vertical structure, usually of masonry, built against a wall to support it [12C. < Anglo-Latin *pera*]

SPELLCHECK See *peer*[1].

CULTURAL NOTE *The Road to Wigan Pier*, a book (1937) by George Orwell. It combines a first-hand account of the appalling living conditions endured by workers in northern England with a penetrating analysis of class interests and prejudices. Its graphic and moving descriptions, compelling arguments, and restrained anger make it a classic of literary journalism.

pierce /peerss/ (**pierces, piercing, pierced**) *v* **1.** *vti* **BORE INTO SOMETHING** to penetrate through or into something with a sharp pointed object **2.** *vt* **PUT HOLE IN SOMETHING** to make a hole through something ○ *She had her ears pierced.* **3.** *vti* **PENETRATE BARRIER** to break through a barrier of some kind such as a defensive line or security system **4.** *vti* **GAIN SIGHT OR KNOWLEDGE** to perceive something with the eyes or the mind **5.** *vti* **PENETRATE SOMETHING WITH SOUND OR LIGHT** to sound or shine suddenly and sharply through something such as silence or darkness ○ *A dreadful scream pierced the silence.* **6.** *vt* **AFFECT SOMEBODY DEEPLY** to have a sudden, intense, often painful effect on somebody ○ *A stab of fear pierced his heart.* [13C. Via French *percer* < Latin *pertundere* 'bore through' < *tundere* 'to bore'] —**piercer** *n*

Pierce /peerss/, **Franklin** (1804–69) 14th president of the United States (1853–57). A Democrat, he sided with the South on the slavery issue, yet was committed to the Union. See table at **president**

piercing /peérssing/ *adj* **1. PENETRATING** having an unpleasantly intense quality ○ *a piercing cry* **2. PERCEPTIVE** capable of acute perception ○ *her piercing gaze* **3. INTENSELY COLD** having a sharp, deeply chilling coldness ○ *a piercing wind* ■ *n* **1. MAKING OF HOLES IN BODY PARTS** the practice of piercing holes in parts of the body so that rings or studs can be inserted ○ *body piercing* **2. HOLE FOR RING IN BODY** a hole pierced in a part of the body to take a ring or stud ○ *She had piercings on her eyebrow and nose.* —**piercingly** *adv*

pier glass *n* a long narrow mirror, originally designed to fit on a wall between two windows, often above a pier table

Pierian Spring /pī éeri ən-/ *n* in Greek mythology, the spring at Pieria in ancient Macedonia that was sacred to the Muses, who lived there, and gave poetic inspiration to anyone who drank from it

Piero della Francesca /pyáirō déllə fran chéskə/ (1420?–92) Italian painter. One of the leading figures of the early Renaissance, he is noted particularly for his frescoes for the church of San Francesco in Arezzo, Italy.

Pierre /peer/ capital city of South Dakota, on the Missouri River, west of Huron and northeast of Rapid City. Population: 14,012 (2002 estimate).

Pierrot /peérō, pyérrō/ *n* **1.** a character in traditional French pantomime. He is a white-faced clown with a white costume and pointed hat, and is often represented as sad or crying. **2.** *also* **pierrot** a clown with a white face and a baggy white costume [Mid-18C. < French, 'little Peter' < *Pierre* 'Peter']

pier table *n* a small table designed to stand against a narrow section of wall between two large windows

Pietà /peé e taá/, **pietà** *n* a painting or sculpture of the Virgin Mary mourning over Jesus Christ's dead body [Mid-17C. Via Italian < Latin *pietas* (see PIETY)]

Pietermaritzburg /peétər márrits burg/ capital city of KwaZulu-Natal Province, South Africa, situated 72 km/45 mi. northwest of Durban. Population: 156,473 (1991).

Pietersburg /peétərz burg/ former name for **Polokwane**

pietism /pí ətizəm/ *n* **1.** devotion to a deity or deities and observance of religious principles in everyday life **2.** excessive or insincere religious devotion [Early 19C. < PIETISM] —**pietist** *n* —**pietistic** /pī ə tístik/ *adj* —**pietistically** *adv*

Pietism /pí ətizəm/ *n* a German Protestant movement in the 17th and 18th centuries that changed the focus of Lutheranism from ritual and church government to personal piety. It was founded by Philipp Jakob Spener. [Late 17C. < German *Pietismus* < Latin *pietas* (see PIETY)]

piet-my-vrou /peét may frō/ (*plural same*) *n S Africa* BIRDS same as **red-chested cuckoo** [Mid-18C. An imitation of its call, altered as if it meant 'Peter my wife' in Afrikaans]

Pietro da Cortona /pi éttrō də kawr tṓnə/ (1596–1669) Italian architect and painter. His illusionistic frescoes, e.g. the *Allegory of Divine Providence and Baberini Power* (1633–39) and those in Roman churches, had an important influence on the development of baroque art and architecture.

piety /pī́ ə ti/ (*plural* **-ties**) *n* **1. RELIGIOUS DEVOTION** a strong respectful belief in a deity or deities and strict observance of religious principles in everyday life **2. DEVOUT ACT** an action inspired by devout religious principles **3. INSINCERE ATTITUDE** a conventional or hypocritical statement or observance of a belief **4. FAMILY LOYALTY** loyalty to parents and family (*archaic*) [14C. Via French < Latin *pietas* 'dutifulness, piety, compassion' < *pius* 'dutiful, devout']

piezo- *prefix* pressure ○ *piezoelectric crystal* [< Greek *piezein* 'to press' < Indo-European, 'sit']

piezoelectricity /pī éezō i lék tríssəti, peézō éllek-/ *n* the electric current produced by some crystals and ceramic materials when they are subjected to mechanical pressure —**piezoelectric** /peézō i léktrik/ *adj*

piezometer /pīee zómmitər, pee-/ *n* an instrument for measuring the compressibility of a material or fluid under pressure —**piezometric** /pī éezō méttrik, peézo-/ *adj* —**piezometrically** *adv*

piffle /píff'l/ *n* silly talk or ideas (*informal*) ○ *Don't talk piffle!* ■ *vi* (**-fles, -fling, -fled**) to behave in a silly or ineffective way (*dated informal*) [Mid-19C. Origin ?]

piffling /píff'ling/ *adj* of little use, value, or importance (*informal*)

pig /pig/ *n* **1. FARM ANIMAL WITH BROAD SNOUT** a sturdy short-legged hoofed animal with a broad snout, especially a domesticated variety, commonly kept as a farm animal and traditionally represented as fat and pink with a curly tail. Latin name: *Sus scrofa.* **2. PORK** the meat of a pig **3. GREEDY PERSON** somebody who is regarded as slovenly, greedy, or gluttonous (*informal insult*) **4. COARSE PERSON** somebody who is thought to behave in a coarse, discourteous, or brutal manner (*informal insult*) **5. SOMETHING UNPLEASANT** a thing or situation that is difficult or unpleasant (*informal*) ○ *a pig of a job* **6.** METALL **BLOCK OF METAL** a casting of metal in a basic shape suitable for storage or transportation **7.** METALL **METAL MOULD** a basic mould for casting metal, especially iron **8. OFFENSIVE TERM** an offensive term for a member of the police force (*slang*) ■ *v* (**pigs, pigging, pigged**) **1.** *vi* **GIVE BIRTH TO PIGS** to give birth to a litter of pigs **2.** *vt* **EAT GREEDILY** to eat something gluttonously or excessively (*informal*) ○ *Who's pigged all the chocolate biscuits?* [13C. Origin ?] ◇ **make a pig's ear of something** to do something very badly (*informal*) ◇ **a pig in a poke** something that is bought or obtained without being inspected to see whether it is worth having

pig out *vi* to eat greedily or gluttonously (*informal*)

pigeon[1] /píjjən/ *n* **1. HEAVY-BODIED BIRD WITH COOING CALL** a medium-sized bird with a stocky body and short legs, powerful flight and a cooing call, which eats seeds and fruit. There are more than 300 species of pigeon. Native to: found worldwide. Family: Columbidae. **2. MEDIUM-SIZED BIRD LIVING IN CITIES** a variety of rock dove, commonly seen in cities or trained for racing or carrying messages. Latin name: *Columba livia.* **3. GULLIBLE PERSON** somebody who is easily swindled or deceived (*informal*) [14C. Via Old French *pijon* 'young bird' < Vulgar Latin alteration of late Latin *pipion-*, an imitation of cheeping]

pigeon[2] /píjjən/ *n* a matter of concern to or a responsibility of somebody in particular ○ *Matters of this kind are not my pigeon.* [Early 19C. Alteration of PIDGIN]

pigeon breast, pigeon chest *n* a condition in which the sides of the chest are flattened and the centre protrudes like the keel of a boat —**pigeon-breasted** *adj*

pigeonhole /píjjən hōl/ *n* **1. PLACE TO PUT MESSAGES** a small compartment that is part of a set in a desk or wall unit into which papers or messages can be sorted or placed **2. BROAD CATEGORY** a category or label assigned to somebody or something without a great deal of thought ○ *the tendency to put writers into pigeonholes* **3.** BIRDS **PIGEON'S NESTING COMPARTMENT** a small nesting hole in a shelter for domestic pigeons ■ *vt* (**-holes, -holing, -holed**) **1. PUT SOMEBODY IN BROAD CATEGORY** to categorize somebody or something without a great deal of thought **2. POSTPONE SOMETHING** to put something off for a while

pigeonite /píjjə nīt/ *n* a yellow-green aluminosilicate mineral of the pyroxene group, containing iron, magnesium, and calcium. Source: basic igneous rocks. [Early 20C. After *Pigeon* Point, Minnesota, United States]

pigeon pea *n* **1.** a small nutritious seed that is popular in Caribbean cookery **2.** a woody plant of the pea family with three-lobed leaves, cultivated in tropical regions to produce pigeon peas. Flowers: yellow, orange. Native to: Africa. Latin name: *Cajanus cajan.* [< the use of its seeds as pigeon-feed]

pigeon-toed *adj* tending to walk or stand with the toes turned inwards

pigfish /píg fish/ (*plural same* or **-fishes**) *n* a fish of the grunt family. Native to: Atlantic coast of North America. Latin name: *Orthopristis chrysoptera.*

piggery /píggəri/ (*plural* **-ies**) *n* **1.** a farm or a building on a farm where pigs are bred and raised **2.** coarse, greedy, or otherwise distasteful behaviour

piggish /píggish/ *adj* **1. GLUTTONOUS** eating too much too fast **2. COARSE IN BEHAVIOUR** behaving in a coarse, greedy, or otherwise distasteful way **3. OBSTINATE** behaving in a stubborn, uncooperative, or obstructive way —**piggishly** *adv* —**piggishness** *n*

piggy /píggi/ *n* (*plural* **-gies**) (*baby talk*) **1.** a pig or piglet **2.** a toe, especially a toe of a small child ■ *adj* (**-gier, -giest**) same as **piggish**

piggyback /píggi bak/ *n* **1. RIDE ON SOMEBODY'S BACK** a ride on somebody's back or shoulders **2.** TRANSP **HAULING OF ONE VEHICLE BY ANOTHER** the transporting of one vehicle by another, e.g. cars by lorry or lorry trailers by railway wagon ■ *adj, adv* **1. ON SOMEBODY'S BACK** carried on the back or shoulders of another person **2.** TRANSP **ON OTHER VEHICLE** transported on another vehicle **3. AS ADDITION** linked with or added onto something larger or more important ■ *v* (**-backs, -backing, -backed**) **1.** *vt* **CARRY SOMEBODY ON BACK** to carry somebody on the back or shoulders **2.** *vt* TRANSP **TRANSPORT VEHICLE** to transport one vehicle on another **3.** *vti* **ATTACH ONE THING TO ANOTHER** to link or add something to a larger or more important item, or be linked or added in this way [Mid-16C. Origin ?]

piggy bank *n* a child's money box, especially one in the shape of a pig

piggy in the middle *n* **1.** a game played by children, in which two people throw a ball to each other and a third person stands in the middle and tries to intercept it. N Am term **monkey in the middle 2.** somebody who is uncomfortably caught up in a disagreement between two people or groups

piggy-whidden /píggi wíd'n/ *n regional* the smallest or weakest piglet in a litter

REGIONAL NOTE See ***underling***.

pigheaded /píg héddid/ *adj* stubbornly adhering to a belief, decision, or course of action —**pigheadedly** *adv* —**pigheadedness** *n*

pig iron *n* a crude form of iron made in a blast furnace and shaped into rough blocks for storage or transportation. Pig iron is processed further to make steel, wrought iron, and other alloys.

pig Latin *n* a joke dialect coined and used by children, especially one in which first consonants are moved to the end of the words and extra syllables added

piglet /píggləṫ/ *n* a newborn or immature pig

pigment *n* /pígmənt/ **1. COLOURING SUBSTANCE** a substance that is added to give something such as paint or ink its colour. Pigments are often available in the form of dry powders to be added to liquids. **2. NATURAL COLOURING FOR TISSUE** a natural substance in plant or animal tissue that gives it its colour ■ *vt* /pig mént/ (**-ments, -menting, -mented**) **COLOUR SOMETHING** to impart colour to something [Pre-12C. < Latin *pigmentum* < *pingere* 'to paint'] —**pigmentary** /pígməntəri/ *adj*

pigmentation /píg men táysh'n/ *n* **1.** the natural colour of plants and animals **2.** the atypical colouring in plant or animal tissue that occurs as a result of disease

pigmy, etc. another spelling of **pygmy, etc.**

pignut /píg nut/ *n* **1.** the roundish edible tuber of a woodland plant **2.** a plant found in woods and the shaded sides of fields whose underground tubers are eaten as pignuts. Latin name: *Conopodium majus.*

pigpen /píg pen/ *n* **1.** an indoor enclosure in which pigs are kept on a modern pig farm, as distinct from the traditional outdoor pigsty **2.** *N Am* AGRIC same as **pigsty**

Pigs, Bay of ♦ **Bay of Pigs**

pigskin /píg skin/ *n* the skin of a pig, especially when made into leather ■ *adj* made of leather prepared from the skin of a pig

pigsty /píg stī/ (*plural* **-sties**) *n* **1.** a building or enclosure where pigs are kept, especially a traditional outdoor enclosure **2.** a dirty or disorderly place ▶ N Am term **pigpen**

pigswill /píg swil/ *n* waste food and kitchen scraps that are fed to pigs

pigtail /píg tayl/ *n* **1. PLAIT** a plait or bunch of hair, often worn in pairs **2.** HAIR same as **queue** *n* (sense 4) **3. TOBACCO STRAND** a thin twisted piece of tobacco **4.** ELEC **BRAIDED WIRE** a short length of flexible electrical cable or wire, usually braided, connecting two terminals —**pigtailed** *adj*

pigweed /píg weed/ *n* **1.** a hairy-leaved weed of the amaranth family. Flowers: green, in spikes. Native to: North America. Latin name: *Amaranthus retroflexus.* **2.** *US* PLANTS same as **fat hen, goosefoot**

pika /pīkə/ (*plural* **-kas** or *same*) *n* a small short-eared burrowing animal that is related to the rabbit. Native to: rocky mountainous regions of western North America and Asia. Family: Ochotonidae. [Early 19C. < Evenki *piika*]

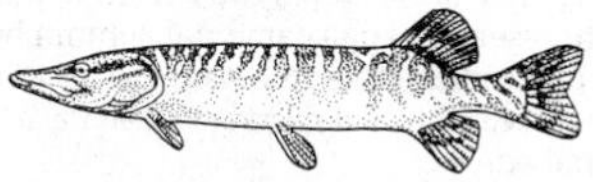

pike

pike[1] /pīk/ (*plural* **pikes** or *same*) *n* **1.** a large predatory freshwater fish with a long body, long broad snout, and sharp teeth, popular as a game fish. Native to: northern waters. Latin name: *Esox lucius.* **2.** a fish that resembles the pike or belongs to the same family, especially the muskellunge or the pickerel [14C. < PIKE[3]; from its long pointed jaws]

pike out *vi Aus* to withdraw from an agreement or commitment (*slang*) [< PIKE[7]]

pike[2] /pīk/ *n* a weapon, formerly used by foot soldiers, consisting of a long pole with a pointed metal head ■ *vt* (**pikes, piking, piked**) to stab or kill somebody with a pike [Early 16C. < French *pique* < *piquer* (see PIQUE[1])]

pike[3] /pīk/ *n* a sharp pointed object of any kind [Old English *pic*, origin ?]

pike[4] /pīk/ *n N England* a pointed rugged summit of a steep hill or mountain [13C. Either < PIKE[3], or < N Germanic]

pike[5] /pīk/ *n* ROADS same as **turnpike** (sense 1) [Early 19C. Shortening]

pike[6] /pīk/ *n* a diving or gymnastic position in which the body is bent at the hips with the head tucked under and the hands touching the toes or behind the knees [Early 20C. Origin ?] —**piked** *adj*

pike[7] /pīk/ (**pikes, piking, piked**) *vi Aus* to let somebody down by breaking an arrangement or commitment (*slang*) ○ *We're playing this evening, but no doubt John will pike on us.* [Late 19C. < slang *pike* 'leave quickly', origin ?]

pikelet /píklət/ *n* **1.** a soft flat yeast cake, traditionally made in northern England, and usually eaten buttered **2.** *ANZ* a small thick pancake made of batter [Late 18C. < Welsh *pyglyd* 'pitchy', in *bara pyglyd* 'pitchy bread']

pikeman /pīkmən/ (*plural* **-men** /-mən/) *n* formerly, a foot soldier armed with a pike

pikeperch /pīk purch/ (*plural* **-perches** or *same*) *n* FISH same as **walleye** (sense 4)

piker /pīkər/ *n* **1.** *US* **CAUTIOUS GAMBLER** somebody who gambles cautiously with little money (*informal*) **2.** *US* **STINGY PERSON** somebody who is stingy with money (*informal*) **3.** *US* **PETTY PERSON** somebody who does things in a small-minded or petty way (*informal*) **4.** *Aus* **UNRELIABLE PERSON** somebody who cannot be depended on to honour an agreement or commitment (*slang*)

pikestaff /pīk staaf/ *n* **1.** the wooden shaft of a pike, which forms the handle **2.** a walking stick with a pointed metal end

pilaf *n* same as **pilau**

Pilar /pi láar/ city and river port on the Paraguay River in southwestern Paraguay. Population: 13,135 (1982).

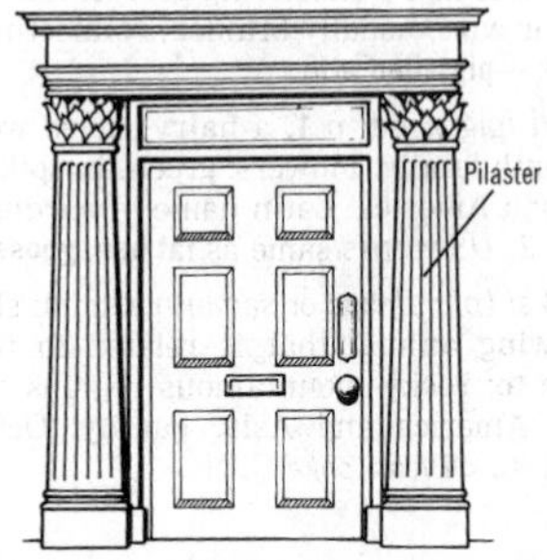

pilaster

pilaster /pi lástər/ *n* a vertical structural part of a building that projects partway from a wall and is made to resemble an ornamental column by adding a base and capital [Late 16C. Via French *pilastre* < Italian *pilastro* or medieval Latin *pilastrum* < Latin *pila* 'pillar'] —**pilastered** *adj*

Pilate /pīlət/, **Pontius** (*fl* 1st century AD) Roman administrator. As procurator of Judaea (AD 26–36) he condemned Jesus Christ to death, albeit reluctantly, according to the Bible.

Pilates /pi láatayz/ *n* a holistic form of exercise and postural therapy that emphasizes the development of the deep abdominal muscles to control body movement and protect the back [Mid-20C. After Joseph H. *Pilates* (1880–1967), German fitness trainer]

pilau /pée low/, **pilaf** /-laf/ *n* a dish of spiced rice, often with chopped vegetables, fish, or meat added [Early 17C. < Turkish *pilâv* 'cooked rice']

Pilbara /pílbrə/ region in western Western Australia, located between the De Grey and Ashburton rivers. Area: 440,000 sq. km/170,000 sq. mi.

pilchard /pílchərd/ (*plural* **-chards** or *same*) *n* **1.** a small sea fish of the herring family with a rounded body and large scales. Native to: Europe. Latin name: *Sardinia pilchardus*. **2.** the flesh of a pilchard used as food [Mid-16C. Origin ?]

Pilcomayo /pilco mī́ō/ river in central South America that rises in the Bolivian Andes and flows southeastwards along the border between Argentina and Paraguay before joining the Paraguay River south of Asunción. Length: 1,125 km/700 mi.

pile[1] /pīl/ *n* **1.** **MOUND OF THINGS** a number of things heaped or stacked one on top of another **2.** **LARGE QUANTITY** a very large amount of something (*informal; often used in the plural*) ○ *I've got piles of work to do.* **3.** **FORTUNE** a very large amount of money, especially one large enough to retire on (*informal*) ○ *He'd already made his pile by the age of 30.* **4.** **BUILDING** a large impressive building **5.** same as **pyre** (*archaic*) **6.** ELEC same as **voltaic pile** **7.** PHYS same as **nuclear reactor** (*dated*) ■ *v* (**piles, piling, piled**) **1.** *vt* **STACK SOMETHING INTO MOUND** to heap or stack things one on top of another **2.** *vt* **PLACE LARGE AMOUNT ON SOMETHING** to heap a large amount of something somewhere ○ *plates piled high with mussels* **3.** *vi* **GO AS CROWD** to move hurriedly in a large disorganized group ○ *We all piled into the car and headed for the seaside.* [15C. Via French < Latin *pila* 'pillar']

pile on *vt* to add more and more of something on a continual basis ○ *Our team piled on the pressure in the second half.* ◇ **pile it on (thick)** to exaggerate something, especially its intensity or severity (*informal*)

pile up *vti* **1.** to accumulate rapidly, or accumulate something rapidly, forming a large amount **2.** to crash vehicles, or collide with other vehicles, starting a chain of collisions

pile[2] /pīl/ *n* **1.** CONSTR **SUNKEN SUPPORT FOR BUILDING** a vertical wood, metal, or concrete support for a building or other structure that is driven into the ground **2.** HERALDRY **HERALDIC SYMBOL** a heraldic figure in the shape of an arrowhead, usually displayed with the point downwards **3.** ARMS **ARROWHEAD** the pointed head of an arrow (*technical*) **4.** ARMS **ANCIENT ROMAN JAVELIN** a javelin used by foot soldiers in ancient Rome ■ *vt* (**piles, piling, piled**) CONSTR **SUPPORT STRUCTURE WITH PILES** to use piles as a support for a building or other structure [Pre-12C. < Latin *pilum* 'javelin']

pile[3] /pīl/ *n* **1.** the surface of a carpet or of a fabric such as velvet that is formed of short, sometimes cut, loops of fibre **2.** the fine soft fur or hair of an animal [Mid-16C. Probably via Anglo-Norman *peile* < Latin *pilus* 'hair']

pilea BIRDS plural of **pileum**

pileate /pīlli ət/, **pileated** /pīl i aytid/ *adj* **1.** describes the condition in which a bird has a crest of feathers on its head **2.** describes a fungus that has a cap-shaped upper part (**pileus**) [Early 18C. < Latin *pileatus* 'wearing a felt cap' < *pileus* 'felt cap']

pile-driver *n* **1.** a large mechanical hammering device that uses steam, compressed air, or gravity to drive construction piles into the ground **2.** a very strong blow or kick (*informal*)

pilei BIOL, CLOTHING plural of **pileus**

piles /pīlz/ *npl* MED same as **haemorrhoids** (*informal*) [15C. Probably < Latin *pila* 'ball'; from their shape]

pileum /pīli əm/ (*plural* **-lea** /-li ə/) *n* the top of a bird's head from the base of the beak to the nape of the neck [Late 19C. < modern Latin, alteration of Latin *pileus* 'felt cap']

pile-up *n* (*informal*) **1.** a collision involving several vehicles **2.** an accumulated number or amount of things such as tasks

pileus /pīli əss/ (*plural* **-lei** /-li ī/) *n* **1.** BOT **CAP OF MUSHROOM** the top cap-shaped part of a mushroom or other fungus **2.** MARINE BIOL **BODY OF JELLYFISH** the part of the body of a jellyfish that resembles an opened umbrella **3.** CLOTHING **ROMAN SKULLCAP** a close-fitting brimless cap worn by ancient Romans [Mid-18C. < Latin *pileus* 'felt cap']

pilewort /pīl wurt/ (*plural* **-worts** or *same*) *n* a flowering plant of the buttercup family, e.g. the lesser celandine. Use: remedy for haemorrhoids. [15C. < singular of PILES]

pilfer /pílfər/ (**-fers, -fering, -fered**) *vti* to steal small items of little value, especially habitually [14C. < Anglo-Norman *pelfrer* 'rob'] —**pilferage** *n* —**pilferer** *n* —**pilfering** *n*

SYNONYMS See ***steal***.

pilgrim /pílgrim/ *n* **1.** somebody who goes on a journey to a holy place for religious reasons **2.** somebody who makes a special journey (*literary*) [12C. Via Provençal *pelegrin* < Latin *peregrinus* (see PEREGRINE)]

CULTURAL NOTE ***The Pilgrim's Progress***, a story (1678, 1684) by John Bunyan. An allegorical account of religious conversion, it describes the journey of a man called Christian from the City of Destruction (the contemporary, corrupt world) to the Celestial City (a state of religious grace). Much of its lasting popularity can be attributed to the author's skill in rendering complex abstract issues immediate, entertaining, and accessible. It is the source of three well-known expressions in use today: *muckraker* (an investigative journalist seeking sensational stories), *slough of despond* (a state of profoundly deep depression), and *vanity fair* (a place or situation of ostentatious empty pride).

Pilgrim *n* any of the English Puritans who founded Plymouth Colony in Massachusetts in 1620

pilgrimage /pílgrimij/ *n* **1.** a journey to a holy place, undertaken for religious reasons **2.** a journey to a place with special significance ○ *Thousands of fans make the pilgrimage to Elvis's birthplace every year.* [13C. < Provençal *pelegrinatge* < *pelegrin* (see PILGRIM)]

~~**pilgrimmage**~~ incorrect spelling of **pilgrimage**

Pilgrims' Way /pílgrimz-/ prehistoric track in southern England, running from Winchester, in Hampshire, to Canterbury, in Kent. Length: 195 km/120 mi.

pili BIOL plural of **pilus**

piling /pīling/ *n* **1.** **SINKING OF PILES** the driving of piles into the ground for structural support **2.** **PILES COLLECTIVELY** piles driven into the ground, considered collectively **3.** CONSTR **STRUCTURE OF PILES** a structure built of piles **4.** CONSTR same as **pile**[2] *n* (sense 1) [15C. < PILE[2]]

Pilipino *n, adj* LANG same as **Filipino**

pill /pil/ *n* **1.** **ROUND TABLET OF MEDICINE** a round solid tablet of medicine to be taken orally **2.** *also* **Pill** **ORAL CONTRACEPTIVE** a contraceptive taken orally **3.** **SOMETHING ROUND** something round, e.g. a ball, bullet, or bomb (*informal*) **4.** **TIRESOME PERSON** an unpleasant or boring person (*dated informal*) ■ **pills** *npl* ANAT **TESTICLES** a man's or boy's testicles (*slang*) ■ *v* (**pills, pilling, pilled**) **1.** *vi* **FORM LITTLE BALLS WHEN RUBBED** to become covered in small balls of matted fibre because of rubbing (*refers to fabrics*) **2.** *vt* **EXCLUDE SOMEBODY** to reject somebody either by vote or consensus (*dated slang*) [15C. < Middle Low German or Middle Dutch *pille*] ◇ **a bitter pill (to swallow)** something that is difficult or painful to accept ◇ **sugar** *or* **sweeten the pill** to make something unpalatable easier to accept or deal with

pillage /píllij/ *vti* (**-lages, -laging, -laged**) **1.** **PLUNDER PLACE** to rob a place using force, especially during a war **2.** **STEAL POSSESSIONS** to steal goods using force, especially during a war ■ *n* **1.** **STEALING OF POSSESSIONS** the theft of goods from a place using force, especially during a war **2.** **STOLEN POSSESSIONS** goods that are stolen using force, especially during a war [14C. < French < *piller* 'to plunder'] —**pillager** *n*

pillar /píllər/ *n* **1.** **COLUMN USED FOR SUPPORT OR DECORATION** a vertical column that is part of a building or other structure and can be either a support or decoration **2.** **SOMETHING TALL AND NARROW** something that is tall and slender like a pillar **3.** **CENTRAL FIGURE** a mainstay of an organization or society ○ *She was a pillar of the community.* ■ *vt* (**-lars, -laring, -lared**) **SUPPORT SOMETHING WITH PILLARS** to support or strengthen something with pillars [13C. Via Anglo-Norman *piler* < Latin *pila*] ◇ **from pillar to post** from one place to another

pillar box *n* a tall round red postbox where letters can be posted for collection

pillar-box red *adj* of a bright red colour, like a British letter box —**pillar-box red** *n*

Pillars of Hercules /píllərz əv húrkyŏŏ leez/ two promontories, the Rock of Gibraltar and Jebel Musa, on either side of the Strait of Gibraltar at the far western end of the Mediterranean. According to legend, the two rocks were separated by Hercules.

Pillars of Islam *npl* same as **Five Pillars of Islam**

pillbox /píl bokss/ *n* **1.** **PILL-CONTAINER** a small container for pills **2.** *also* **pillbox hat** **WOMAN'S BRIMLESS HAT** a woman's shallow brimless hat with a flat top **3.** **FORTIFIED SHELTER** a small fortified shelter with a flat roof

pill bug *n* INSECTS same as **woodlouse** [Because able to roll itself into a ball]

pilled-up /píld-/ *adj* affected by or high on drugs, especially drugs taken in tablet form (*slang*)

pillion /pílli ən/ *n* a seat for a passenger behind the driver of a motorbike or the rider of a horse ■ *adv* seated behind the driver of a motorbike or the rider of a horse [15C. < Gaelic *pillean*, Irish *pillín* 'little couch' < *pell* 'couch' < Latin *pellis* 'skin']

pilliwinks /pílli wingks/ *n* an instrument of torture used on the fingers and thumbs in medieval times (*takes a singular or plural verb*) [15C. Origin ?]

pillock /píllək/ *n* an offensive term that deliberately insults somebody's intelligence or consideration for others (*slang offensive insult*) [Mid-16C. Contraction of archaic *pillicock* 'penis', origin ? + COCK]

pillory /píllәri/ *n* (*plural* **-ries**) **PUNISHMENT DEVICE** a wooden frame with holes into which somebody's head and hands could be locked, formerly used as a means of

public punishment ■ *vt* (**-ries, -rying, -ried**) **1.** **RIDICULE SOMEBODY** to scorn or ridicule somebody or something openly **2.** **PUNISH SOMEBODY IN PILLORY** to put somebody into a pillory as a public punishment [13C. Via Anglo-Latin *pillorium* < Old French *pillorie*]

pillow /píllō/ *n* **1.** **CUSHION FOR HEAD IN BED** a sealed fabric bag stuffed with feathers or a synthetic filling used as a soft support for the head in bed **2.** **SOMETHING LIKE PILLOW** something that is similar to a pillow in appearance or use **3.** HANDICRAFT same as **cushion** *n* (sense 7) ■ *vt* (**-lows, -lowing, -lowed**) **1.** **CUSHION HEAD** to rest the head on a pillow or something else that is soft and comfortable **2.** **ACT AS PILLOW FOR SOMETHING** to provide a soft comfortable surface on which to rest something [Old English *pyle*, via W Germanic < Latin *pulvinus*]

pillowcase /píllō kayss/ *n* a fabric cover for a pillow

pillow lace *n* lace made using bobbins and a firm pad or pillow as a base, as distinct from lace made with a needle and a paper pattern

pillow lava *n* lava that has solidified into pillow-shaped masses, formed from underwater lava flows or from lava flowing into water from land. Each pillow can be up to 2 m/6 ft across and is surrounded by a fine-grained skin.

pillow sham *n N Am* a decorative covering for a pillow on a bed

pillowslip /píllō slip/ *n* HOUSEHOLD same as **pillowcase**

pillow talk *n* the discussion of intimate or private matters in bed with a sexual partner

pilm /pilm/ *n Wales* same as **dust** *n* (senses 1–2) [< Welsh]

pilocarpine /pīlō kaár pīn, -pin/ *n* an organic compound of plant origin. Source: leaves of jaborandi trees. Use: in eye drops to treat glaucoma. [Late 19C. < modern Latin *Pilocarpus*, genus name of the jaborandi tree]

piloerection /pīlō i réksh'n/ *n* the erection of the hairs on the surface of the skin, e.g. to conserve heat [Mid-20C. < Latin *pilus* 'hair']

pilose /pīlōss/, **pilous** /pīləss/ *adj* describes plant parts that are covered with soft hair [Late 18C. < Latin *pilosus* 'hairy' < *pilus* 'hair'] —**pilosity** /pī lóssəti/ *n*

pilot /pīlət/ *n* **1.** **SOMEBODY WHO FLIES PLANE** somebody who pilots an aircraft or spacecraft **2.** **SOMEBODY STEERING SHIPS THROUGH DIFFICULT AREA** somebody with local knowledge whose job is to navigate ships in and out of a harbour or through a difficult stretch of water **3.** **STEERER OF SHIP** somebody who steers a ship or boat **4.** **LEADER** somebody who acts as a leader or guide **5.** BROADCAST **TRIAL TELEVISION PROGRAMME** a television or radio programme made as a prototype for a projected series **6.** **TRIAL RUN** a test of something such as a proposed manufacturing process to discover and solve problems before full implementation **7.** INDUST same as **pilot light** (sense 1) **8.** ENG **MACHINE GUIDE** a guiding part of a tool or machine ■ *vt* (**-lots, -loting, -loted**) **1.** AVIAT **FLY AIRCRAFT** to fly an aircraft or spacecraft **2.** NAUT **NAVIGATE SHIP** to navigate a ship **3.** **BE IN CHARGE OF SOMETHING** to direct the course of something such as a project or a programme of research **4.** **RUN TRIAL OF SOMETHING** to test something such as a proposed manufacturing process to discover and solve problems before full implementation [Early 16C. Via French *pilote* < medieval Latin *pilotus*, alteration of *pedota* < Greek *pēdon* 'oar'] —**pilotless** *adj*

pilotage /pīlətij/ *n* **1.** **PILOTING OF CRAFT** the controlling of a ship, aircraft, or spacecraft **2.** **FEE OF HARBOUR OR RIVER PILOT** the fee paid to a harbour or river pilot **3.** **MANUAL NAVIGATION** the manual navigation of an aircraft, using landmarks and maps

pilot balloon *n* a small balloon launched to study the speed and direction of winds at high altitudes. The balloon is visually tracked by a theodolite.

pilot fish *n* a small striped sea fish, often found swimming with sharks, mantas, and other large fishes, where it finds stray scraps of food. Latin name: *Naucrates ductor*.

pilot house *n* an enclosed control room on or near the bridge of a ship, containing the steering wheel and navigational and communications equipment

pilot lamp *n* a small light in an electric circuit to show whether the power is on or whether an electrical device is operating

pilot light *n* **1.** a small gas flame that remains lit in order to ignite a burner when it is turned on **2.** ELEC same as **pilot lamp**

pilot officer *n* a commissioned officer of the lowest rank in the Royal Air Force

pilot whale *n* a large black toothed whale with a bulbous head, found in warm seas. Genus: *Globicephala*.

pilous *adj* BIOL same as **pilose**

Pils /pilz/ *n* a lager beer similar to Pilsner [Mid-20C. Shortening of PILSNER]

Pilsner /pílznər/, **Pilsener** *n* a lager beer with a strong hops flavour, originally and especially made in Pilsen in the Czech Republic [Late 19C. < German, 'of Pilsen' < *Pilsen* (Czech *Plzeň*), province in the Czech Republic]

Piłsudski /pil sóotski/, **Józef** (1867–1935) Polish nationalist leader. He fought to free Poland from Russian rule. He was Poland's head of state (1918–22) and later its virtual dictator (1926–35). Full name **Piłsudski, Josef Klemens**

Piltdown man /pílt down-/ *n* a supposed primitive form of human being represented by remains of bones found in Sussex in 1912, shown in 1953 to be a hoax [Early 20C. After a village in Sussex]

pilus /pīləss/ (*plural* **-li** /-lī/) *n* a part of a plant or animal organism that looks like a hair [Mid-20C. < Latin, 'hair']

PIM /pim/ *abbr* COMPUT personal information manager

Pima /péemə/ (*plural same or* **-mas**) *n* **1.** a member of a Native North American people who lived in southern and central Arizona and now live mainly in central Arizona **2.** the Uto-Aztecan language of the Pima people. Native speakers: 15,000. [Early 19C. < Spanish, shortening of *Pimahito* < Pima *pimahaitu* 'nothing'] —**Pima** *adj*

Pima-Papago /péemə páppə gō/ *n* the Pima and Papago languages regarded together. They are closely-related members of the Uto-Aztecan family of Native North and Central American languages. Native speakers: 24,000. —**Pima-Papago** *adj*

pimento /pi méntō/ *n* **1.** FOOD same as **pimiento** **2.** COOK same as **allspice** [Late 17C. Via Spanish *pimiento* < Latin *pigmentum* (see PIGMENT)]

pi meson /pī meezon/ *n* PHYS same as **pion**

pimiento /pim yén tō/ (*plural* **-tos**) *n* **1.** a large sweet red pepper. Use: paprika, olive stuffing, garnish. **2.** a plant that produces pimientos. Native to: Europe. Latin name: *Capsicum annuum*. [Mid-17C. < Spanish (see PIMENTO)]

pimp /pimp/ *n* somebody, usually a man, who finds customers for a prostitute in return for a portion of the prostitute's earnings [Late 16C. Origin ?] —**pimp** *vi*

pimpernel /pímpər nel/ (*plural* **-nels** *or same*) *n* a small plant with long trailing stems. Flowers: small, red, white, or purple. Genus: *Anagallis*. [15C. < Old French *pimpernelle* 'burnet', alteration of *piprenelle* < Latin *piper* 'pepper'; because its fruit resemble peppercorns]

pimple /pímp'l/ *n* a small inflamed or pus-filled spot on the skin [14C. Related to Old English *piplian* 'break out in spots'] —**pimpled** *adj* —**pimply** *adj*

pimpmobile /pímp mō beel/ *n N Am* a very showy large car, typical of one that might be used by a pimp (*informal*)

pin /pin/ *n* **1.** **THIN POINTED METAL STICK** a small thin metal stick with a sharp point and a rounded head used for holding pieces of fabric together **2.** **POINTED METAL FASTENER** a fastener with a sharp metal point designed to pierce the things it is fastening **3.** CLOTHING, ARMS same as **safety pin** **4.** JEWELLERY **SOMETHING DECORATIVE ATTACHED TO CLOTHING** a badge, piece of jewellery, or other decorative item that attaches to clothing by means of a sharp metal point or a clasp **5.** HAIR same as **hairpin** (sense 1) **6.** MECH ENG same as **cotter pin** **7.** ELEC **PART OF ELECTRICAL CONNECTOR** a thin metal terminal extending from an electrical or electronic device such as a plug or a valve, used to connect the device by socket to other circuitry ○ *a three-pin plug* **8.** SURG **ROD JOINING BROKEN BONE** a thin metal rod used to hold the ends of a fractured bone together **9.** DENT **ROD ATTACHING TOOTH CAP TO ROOT** a thin metal rod used to attach a crown to the root of a tooth **10.** MECH ENG **KEY PART ENTERING LOCK** the part of a key that inserts into a lock **11.** MUSIC **PEG HOLDING INSTRUMENT STRING** a peg on a stringed instrument such as a piano that holds the strings and can be turned to tighten or loosen them to tune the instrument **12.** BOWLING **SKITTLE** a club-shaped target used in various games of bowling **13.** GOLF **HOLE MARKER** a pole with a flag on it, used to mark each hole on a golf course **14.** WRESTLING **FALL BRINGING WRESTLER'S SHOULDERS ONTO FLOOR** in wrestling, a fall in which an opponent's shoulders are made to touch the mat **15.** BEVERAGES **BEER CASK** a small beer barrel holding 4.5 gallons **16.** COMPUT **GUIDE ON COMPUTER PRINTER** a peg in a set that guides the paper through a computer printer **17.** COMPUT **PART OF PRINTHEAD THAT FORMS LETTERS** a wire in a set on the printhead of a dot matrix printer that forms one dot of a letter or symbol ■ **pins** *npl* ANAT somebody's legs (*informal*) ○ *He's a bit unsteady on his pins.* ■ *vt* (**pins, pinning, pinned**) **1.** **FASTEN SOMETHING WITH PIN** to fasten, attach, or secure something with a pin **2.** **KEEP SOMEBODY FROM MOVING** to hold somebody or something immobile, e.g. on the ground ○ *The beam fell across his back, pinning him to the ground.* **3.** CHESS **STOP CHESS PIECE BEING MOVED** to make it impossible for a chess opponent to move a piece without exposing the king to check or a valuable piece to capture **4.** WRESTLING **HOLD WRESTLER DOWN ON FLOOR** in wrestling, to hold an opponent's shoulders to the mat [12C. < Latin *pinna* 'feather, pointed peak']

pin down *vt* **1.** **IDENTIFY SOMETHING PRECISELY** to determine something with certainty ○ *Can you pin down the time of death?* **2.** **FORCE SOMEBODY TO DECIDE** to force somebody to keep a commitment or come to a decision ○ *I haven't managed to pin him down to a date for our meeting yet.* **3.** **PREVENT SOMEBODY FROM MOVING** to prevent somebody from going anywhere ○ *The platoon was pinned down by enemy fire.*

PIN /pin/ (*plural* **PINs**) *n* a multidigit number that is used by somebody to gain access to an account at a cashpoint machine, a computer, or a telephone system. Full form **personal identification number**

~~**pinacle**~~ incorrect spelling of **pinnacle**

piña colada /peénə kō laádə, peényə-/ *n* a cocktail made from pineapple juice, rum, and coconut [< Spanish, 'strained pineapple']

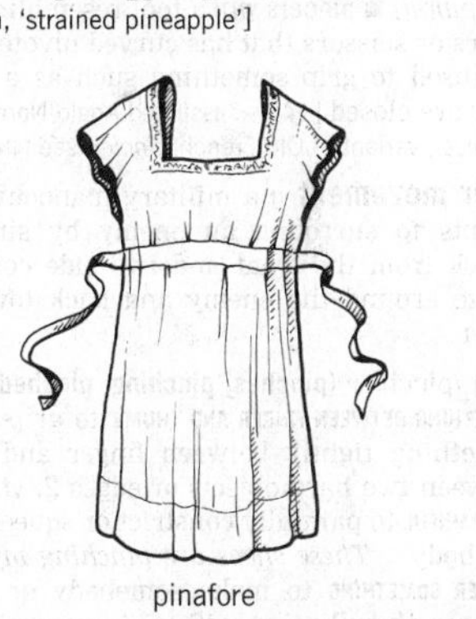

pinafore

pinafore /pínnə fawr/ *n* **1.** *also* **pinafore dress** **DRESS WORN OVER SOMETHING ELSE** a sleeveless dress, usually worn over a blouse or sweater. N Am term **jumper**[2] **2.** **APRON** an apron, usually one with a bib (*dated*) **3.** **GIRL'S OVERGARMENT** a sleeveless collarless garment formerly worn by girls over a dress and fastened at the top of the back [Late 18C. Because originally a garment pinned to the front of a dress]

Pinang ▸ **Penang**

piñata /peen yaá tə/ *n* a decorated papier-mâché container of sweets or small gifts that is hung from the ceiling and is hit and broken by blindfolded people with sticks, traditionally during Latin American festivals. It is often shaped like a donkey or a cartoon character. [Late 19C. < Spanish, 'jug']

Pinatubo, Mount /pinnə tóobō/ active volcano in the Philippines, in the central part of the island of Luzon, north of Manila. It erupted in 1991 and 1992, causing heavy loss of life and widespread destruction of homes and agricultural land. Height: 1,780 m/5,840 ft.

pinball /pínn bawl/ *n* a game played on an electronic

table fitted with obstacles, targets, and pivoted flippers. The player controls the flippers to keep a ball in play, hitting targets to score points. (*often used before a noun*)

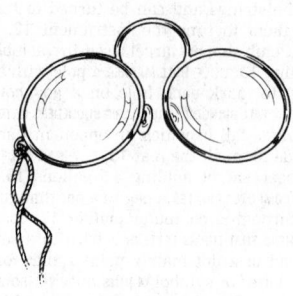

pince-nez

pince-nez /pánss náy/ (*plural* **pince-nez** /-náyz/) *n* a pair of spectacles without side arms, held in place by a clip that fits over the nose [< French, 'pinch the nose']

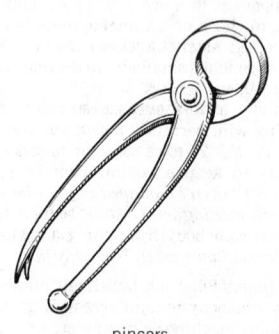

pincers

pincer /pínssər/ *n* a large jointed front claw of some crustaceans and arachnids such as the lobster and scorpion, used for grasping things (*usually used in the plural*) ■ **pincers** *npl* a tool resembling a pair of pliers or scissors that has curved pivoted jaws that are used to grip something such as a nail when they are closed [14C. < assumed Anglo-Norman *pinceour* < *pincer*, variant of Old French *pincier* (see PINCH)]

pincer movement *n* a military manoeuvre that attempts to surround an enemy by simultaneous attack from the front and two side columns that curve around the enemy and back towards each other

pinch /pinch/ *v* (**pinches, pinching, pinched**) **1.** *vti* GRIP SOMETHING BETWEEN FINGER AND THUMB to grip or squeeze something tightly between finger and thumb or between two hard objects or edges **2.** *vti* BE TOO TIGHT AND PAINFUL to painfully constrict or squeeze a part of the body ○ *These shoes are pinching my feet.* **3.** *vt* WITHER SOMETHING to make somebody or something become shrunken or withered, especially through harsh conditions such as cold or hunger ○ *a face pinched with grief and pain* **4.** *vt* IMPOSE FINANCIAL HARDSHIP ON SOMEBODY to put somebody in financial difficulty ○ *Unexpected expenses have really pinched me this month.* **5.** *vti* STEAL SOMETHING to steal something or take something without permission (*informal*) ○ *Who's pinched my pen?* **6.** *vt* ARREST SOMEBODY to arrest somebody for wrongdoing (*informal*) **7.** *vt* GARDENING REMOVE SHOOTS TO ENCOURAGE BUSHY GROWTH to remove new shoots and buds from a plant to make it become more bushy **8.** *vt* SAILING SAIL VESSEL INTO WIND to sail a sailing vessel too close to the wind, so that it loses wind from its sails **9.** *vi* MIN EXTRACT NARROW AND DISAPPEAR to become gradually narrower, eventually disappearing entirely (*refers to a vein of ore*) ■ *n* **1.** PAINFUL SQUEEZE a painful squeeze or nip, especially with the thumb and finger ○ *a pinch on the arm* **2.** VERY SMALL QUANTITY a very small amount of a substance, especially the amount held between the thumb and first finger ○ *Add a pinch of salt.* **3.** CRIME same as **robbery** (*informal*) **4.** ARREST OF SOMEBODY an arrest made by the police (*informal*) **5.** CRITICAL TIME an emergency or critical situation [13C. Via assumed Anglo-Norman *pincher*, variant of Old French

pincier < assumed Vulgar Latin *pinctiare* 'to prick'] ◇ **at a pinch** if absolutely necessary, although preferably not ◇ **feel the pinch** to have financial problems

SYNONYMS See *steal.*

pinch bar *n* a crowbar with a pointed end and a projection that provides a fulcrum, used as a lever, often with a notch, or claw, at the other end

pinchbeck /pínch bek/ *n* **1.** GOLD-COLOURED METAL ALLOY an alloy of copper and zinc used as imitation gold in inexpensive jewellery **2.** CHEAP COPY an inferior imitation ■ *adj* **1.** MADE OF PINCHBECK made from pinchbeck alloy **2.** IMITATION made in imitation of something and usually of inferior quality [Mid-18C. After Christopher *Pinchbeck* (d. 1732), English watchmaker]

pinch effect *n* the narrowing of a beam of charged particles caused by the interaction of each particle with the magnetic field generated by the movement of the beam

pinch hit *n* in baseball, a hit made by a substitute batter —**pinch-hit** *vi* —**pinch hitter** *n*

pinchpenny /pínch peni/ *adj* unwilling to spend or give money ■ *n* (*plural* **-nies**) somebody who is unwilling to spend or give money

pinchpoint /pínch poynt/ *n* **1.** a point in a system or process that is likely to experience or cause delays ○ *a major pinchpoint in the traffic flow* **2.** a narrow area between two surfaces that is likely to trap or catch objects and so is a potential safety hazard

pinch runner *n* in baseball, a runner who replaces a batter who has successfully reached base, usually because the batter is slow or injured

pin curl *n* a flat curl in hair, made by winding strands of hair into a circle and securing it with a clip or hairpin

pincushion /pín kŏosh'n/ *n* a small stuffed pad used for sticking dressmaking pins into when they are not being used

Pindar /píndər/ (518–438 BC) Greek poet. His lyric poetry celebrated victories in the ancient Olympic Games. —**Pindaric** /pin dárrik/ *adj*

Pindaric ode *n* a form of ode with three-stanza sections, the first and second stanzas having one metrical form and the third having a different form

pine

pine[1] /pīn/ *n* **1.** WOOD FROM EVERGREEN TREE the wood from an evergreen tree, varying from soft to hard. Use: furniture-making, construction, finishing material. **2.** EVERGREEN TREE an evergreen coniferous tree with needle-shaped leaves and woody cones, often grown for its wood or resin, or for ornament. Genus: *Pinus.* (*often used before a noun*) **3.** TREE RESEMBLING PINE a coniferous tree or bush that resembles a true pine, e.g. the Norfolk Island pine [Pre-12C. < Latin *pinus*] —**piney** *adj* ◇ **ride the pine** US to be removed from a team during a sports contest ○ *He's been riding the pine all season owing to injuries.*

pine[2] /pīn/ (**pines, pining, pined**) *vi* **1.** to long for somebody or something, especially somebody or something unattainable **2.** to become weak and lose vitality as a result of grief or longing [Old English *pīnian* 'suffer' < *pīne* 'punishment' < Latin *poena* (see PAIN)]

pineal /pínni əl, pī neé əl/ *adj* **1.** relating to or secreted by the pineal gland **2.** shaped like a pine cone [Late 17C. < French *pinéal* < Latin *pinea* 'pine cone' (from its shape) < *pinus* 'pine (tree)']

pineal gland, pineal body *n* a small cone-shaped organ of the brain that secretes the hormone melatonin

into the bloodstream. It is one of the endocrine glands and is situated beneath the back part of the corpus callosum.

pineapple

pineapple /pī nap'l/ *n* **1.** JUICY YELLOW FRUIT a large fruit with juicy yellow flesh, a thick lumpy yellowish-brown skin, and a tuft of tough pointed leaves at the top **2.** (*plural* **pineapples** or *same*) PLANT ON WHICH PINEAPPLES GROW a plant that produces pineapples. Native to: tropical America. Latin name: *Ananas comosus.* **3.** ARMS GRENADE WITH PATTERNED SURFACE a hand grenade with a surface of raised geometric shapes (*slang*) [14C. < the likening of the fruit to a pine cone]

pineapple weed *n* a plant with greenish-yellow flower heads that smell like pineapple when crushed. Native to: Asia. Latin name: *Matricaria matri.*

pine cone *n* the seed case of a pine tree, usually woody, oval, and scaly

pine kernel *n* FOOD same as **pine nut**

pine leaf scale *n* an insect with a tough outer covering that attaches itself to pine needles and seriously inhibits their growth. Latin name: *Chionaspis pinifoliae.*

pine marten *n* a woodland animal, similar in appearance to a weasel, with a dark-brown coat and yellow throat. Native to: Asia, northern Europe, northern North America. Genus: *Martes.*

pinene /pín een/ *n* either of two colourless liquid compounds. Source: turpentine, eucalyptus. Use: manufacture of plastics, solvent. Formula: $C_{10}H_{16}$. [Late 19C. < Latin *pinus* 'pine (tree)']

pine needle *n* the needle-shaped leaf of a pine tree

pine nut *n* a small sweet seed of some pine trees, especially a piñon

pinery /pínəri/ (*plural* **-ies**) *n* **1.** a plantation or heated glasshouse where pineapples are grown commercially **2.** a pine forest, especially one planted for timber production

pinesap /pín sap/ (*plural* **-saps** or *same*) *n* a fleshy red or yellowish plant that resembles the Indian pipe and grows as a parasite on tree roots. Native to: North America. Latin name: *Montropa hypopithys.*

pine snake *n* a large bull snake with black-and-white markings. Native to: pine forests in the eastern United States. Latin name: *Pituophis melanoleucus.*

pine tar *n* a thick sticky brown-to-black substance obtained by the destructive distillation of pine wood. Use: making roofing materials, paints, medicines, shampoos.

pinewood /pín wŏod/ *n* **1.** the wood of a pine tree (*often used before a noun*) **2.** a small forest of pine trees (*often used in the plural*)

piney *adj* BOT another spelling of **piny**

Piney Woods /pīni-/ large forested upland region of the southern and southeastern United States, covering parts of Texas, Oklahoma, Arkansas, Louisiana, Mississippi, Alabama, Georgia, and Florida

pinfeather /pínn fethər/ *n* a feather only recently emerged from a bird's skin and still surrounded by a horny sheath

pinfish /pínn fish/ (*plural* **-fishes** or *same*) *n* a small sea fish of the porgy family with a thin dark-green body and sharp dorsal spines. Native to: southern Atlantic coast of the United States. Latin name: *Lagodon rhomboides.*

a at; aa father; aw all; ay day; ai hair; ə about, item, edible, common, circus; e egg; ee eel; hw when; i it, happy; ī ice; 'l apple; 'm rhythm; 'n fashion; o odd; ō open; ŏo good; oo pool; ow owl; oy oil; th thin; th this; u up; ur urge;

pinfold /pínn fōld/ n 1. an enclosure for stray animals, especially farm animals 2. a place or situation that confines [Pre-12C. < form related to POUND³ 'enclosure' + FOLD²]

ping /ping/ n 1. SOUND a single short ringing sound 2. SONAR PULSE a brief sonic or ultrasonic pulse emitted by a sonar, the reflection or echo of which is used in detecting submarines or shoals of fish 3. N Am AUTOMOT same as **knock** n (sense 5) 4. RESPONSE TIME the length of time, in milliseconds, that it takes to send a message to an intranet, Internet, or web address and receive a reply ○ super-low ping ■ v (pings, pinging, pinged) 1. vti RING to make a single short ringing sound, or make something such as a bell produce a ringing sound 2. vi DETECT UNDERWATER OBJECTS to detect submarines or shoals of fish by emitting and receiving the echo of a brief sonic or ultrasonic pulse 3. vti CHECK FOR RESPONSE FROM WEB ADDRESS to send a packet of data to an intranet, Internet, or web address to check whether it is accessible or is responding [Mid-18C. An imitation of the sound]

pinger /píngər/ n (informal) 1. a device that produces pinging noises, especially one used as part of underwater detection equipment 2. a timer that makes pinging noises as an alarm after a set amount of time

pingo /píng gō/ (plural **-gos**) n a large mound of soil-covered ice forced up by the pressure of water in permafrost [Mid-20C. < Inuit pinguq]

Ping-Pong /píng pong/ tdmk a trademark for table tennis

ping-ponging n the practice of referring a customer or client from one agency or representative to another and vice versa, with no decision being made (slang)

pinguid /píng gwid/ adj containing a lot of fat, oil, or grease [Mid-17C. < Latin pinguis 'fat'] —**pinguidity** /ping gwíddəti/ n

pinhead /pín hed/ n 1. BLUNT END OF PIN the rounded head of a pin 2. SMALL THING something that is very small or trivial 3. OFFENSIVE TERM an offensive term that deliberately insults somebody's intelligence (in-formal insult)

pinhole /pín hōl/ n a tiny hole or puncture of the size made by a pin

pinhole camera n a basic form of camera with a tiny hole for the aperture, and no lens. Light passes through the hole to form an inverted image on the film emulsion

pinion¹ /pínnyən/ vt (-ions, -ioning, -ioned) 1. RESTRAIN SOMEBODY to restrain or immobilize somebody, especially by tying his or her arms 2. KEEP BIRD FROM FLYING to prevent a bird from flying by removing or binding its wing feathers ■ n BIRD'S WING a bird's wing, especially the tip of the wing where the stiff flight feathers are found, containing the carpus, metacarpus, and phalanx bones [15C. < French pignon < Latin pinna 'feather']

pinion² /pínnyən/ n a small gear wheel that engages with a larger gear or with a rack, e.g. in a vehicle steering system [Mid-17C. < French pignon < Latin pinea 'pine cone' < pinus 'pine (tree)']

pinite /pínnīt, pī nīt/ n a grey-green mixture of the minerals mica and chlorite. Source: alteration of cordierite. [Early 19C. < German Pinit, after Pini, mine in Saxony]

pink¹ /pingk/ n 1. PALE REDDISH COLOUR a pale reddish colour that, as a pigment, is formed by mixing red and white 2. PLANT WITH FRAGRANT FLOWERS a plant with narrow greyish-green leaves. Flowers: fragrant, especially pink, white, or red. Genus: Dianthus. 3. FRAGRANT FLOWER the fragrant pink, white, or red flower of a pink plant 4. PLANT SIMILAR TO TRUE PINK a plant that is similar but not related to the pink, e.g. the wild pink or moss pink 5. HIGHEST FORM the highest degree or perfect example of something ○ the pink of perfection 6. RED HUNTING JACKET the scarlet riding coat traditionally worn by fox hunters 7. PINK THING a pink object, especially the pink ball in snooker 8. POL same as **pinko** ■ adj 1. COLOURED PINK of the colour pink 2. SLIGHTLY LEFT-WING relating to or holding political views that tend towards the left (informal disapproving) 3. OF GAYS AND LESBIANS relating to gay and lesbian people (informal; sometimes offensive)

[Late 16C. Origin ?] —**pinkish** adj —**pinkness** n ◇ **in the pink** in excellent physical health (informal dated)

ORIGIN The Dutch phrase pinck oogen meant literally 'small eyes'. It was adopted into English in the partially translated form pink eyes, which may have been used as the name of a plant of the genus Dianthus. The abbreviated form **pink** emerged as a plant name in the 16C. Many of these plants have pale red flowers, and by the 18C **pink** was being used as a colour term.

pink² /pingk/ (pinks, pinking, pinked) vt 1. CUT FABRIC WITH PINKING SHEARS to cut fabric with pinking shears to make a zigzag edge that will not easily fray 2. STAB SOMEBODY to prick somebody's skin with a sword or other pointed weapon 3. DECORATE SOMETHING WITH LITTLE HOLES to make a pattern on leather or other material by punching little holes in the surface [14C. Origin ?]

pink³ /pingk/ n a sailing ship with a narrow over-hanging stern [Late 15C. < Middle Dutch pincke]

pink⁴ /pingk/ (pinks, pinking, pinked) vi AUTOMOT same as **knock** v (sense 8) [Early 20C. An imitation of the sound]

pink bollworm n the pinkish larva of a brown moth that is a common pest in cotton-growing areas. Latin name: Pectinophora gossypiella.

pink-collar adj relating to jobs, especially clerical jobs, traditionally associated with women

pink dollar n ANZ, N Am the collective spending power of gays and lesbians, especially when targeted as consumers. UK term **pink pound**

pink elephants npl hallucinations in any form that are sometimes experienced by somebody who has overindulged in alcohol or drugs (informal humorous)

pinkeye /píngk ī/ n 1. a contagious form of acute conjunctivitis in human beings and some domestic animals marked by inflammation of the eyelid and eyeball 2. a viral or bacterial eye infection of cattle that is characterized by redness of the eye, production of tears that attract flies, and sometimes blindness

pink gin n gin that has Angostura bitters added to it, giving it a pale pinkish colour and an aromatic spicy flavour

pinkie /píngki/, **pinky** (plural **-ies**) n Scotland, N Am the little finger (informal) [Late 16C. Probably < Dutch pinkje < pink 'little finger']

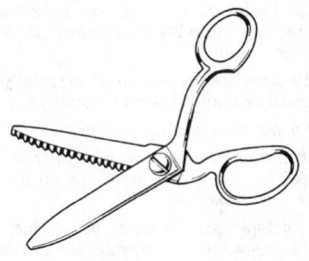

pinking shears

pinking shears /píngking-/, **pinking scissors** npl scissors for cutting cloth that have one blade or both blades serrated, so that whatever they cut has a zigzag edge, either for decoration or to prevent fraying [< PINK²]

pink lady n a cocktail that is made by mixing gin, brandy, lemon or lime juice, egg white, and grenadine

pink money n money belonging to or provided by the gay and lesbian community (informal; sometimes offensive)

pinko /píngkō/ (plural **-os** or **-oes**) n somebody who favours the political left (slang disapproving) [Early 20C. < PINK¹, alluding to RED 'communist']

pink pound n UK the collective spending power of gay and lesbian people, especially when targeted as consumers (sometimes offensive) ANZ, N Am term **pink dollar**

pinkroot /pingk root/ (plural **-roots** or same) n 1. POWDERED ROOT OF TROPICAL PLANT the powdered root of a subtropical plant. Use: formerly, to treat intestinal worms. 2. PLANT WITH RED AND YELLOW FLOWERS a tropical or subtropical perennial plant with pinkish roots. Flowers: red, tinged with yellow on the inside. Native to: southeastern United States. Genus: Spigella. 3. PLANT DISEASE a fungal plant disease that affects bulbous plants, especially onions, causing the roots to become pink and shrivelled and stunting root growth

pink salmon n 1. a small salmon, the male of which has a pinkish body and a distinctive hump on its back at breeding times. Native to: northern Pacific waters. Latin name: Oncorhynchus gorbuscha. 2. the pink flesh of the pink salmon used as food, often tinned

pink slip n N Am a termination of employment notice that an employer gives to an employee in the United States (informal) [< the traditional colour of such notices]

pinky n Scotland, N Am ANAT another spelling of **pinkie**

pin money n 1. MONEY FOR BUYING PERSONAL THINGS money that is earned, put aside, or saved for buying personal, often nonessential things 2. NOT MUCH MONEY a small amount of money 3. MONEY THAT MAN GIVES TO WIFE money that a man gives to his wife, woman partner, or daughter for personal use (dated)

pinna /pínnə/ (plural **-nae** /-nee/ or **-nas**) n 1. ZOOL a feather, wing, fin, or other similarly shaped body part or appendage 2. BOT any one of the several leaflets that make up a pinnate compound leaf 3. ANAT same as **auricle** (sense 1) [Late 18C. < Latin, 'feather'] —**pinnal** adj

pinnace /pínnəss/ n a small boat, e.g. a sailing boat, carried by a larger vessel and used as a gig or a tender [Mid-16C. < French pinace < Latin pinus 'pine (tree)']

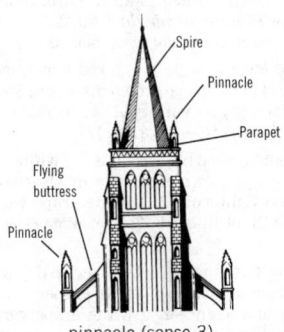

pinnacle (sense 3)

pinnacle /pínnək'l/ n 1. HIGHEST POINT the highest or topmost point or level of something ○ at the pinnacle of her career 2. MOUNTAIN PEAK a natural peak, especially a distinctively pointed one on a mountain or in a mountain range 3. ARCHIT POINTED ORNAMENT a pointed ornament on top of a buttress or parapet ■ vt (-cles, -cling, -cled) 1. ARCHIT ADD PINNACLE TO SOMETHING to provide something with a pinnacle 2. PUT SOMETHING ON PINNACLE to put or set something on a pinnacle or on something resembling a top or peak [13C. Via French < late Latin pinnaculum, literally 'little feather' < Latin pinna 'feather']

pinnae BIOL plural of **pinna**

pinnate /pínnayt/, **pinnated** /-naytid/ adj describes a leaf that has a central axis or stem with parts branching off it [Early 18C. < Latin pinnatus < pinna 'feather'] —**pinnately** adv —**pinnation** /pi náysh'n/ n

pinnati- prefix like a feather ○ pinnatifid [< Latin pinnatus (see PINNATE)]

pinnatifid /pi náttifid/ adj describes leaves that have a central axis with parts branching off it —**pin-natifidly** adv

pinniped /pínni ped/, **pinnipedian** /pínni peédi ən/ n a sea mammal that has a streamlined body and four flippers and eats fish and other meat, e.g. a walrus, sea lion, or seal. Suborder: Pinnipedia. [Mid-19C. < modern Latin Pinnipedia < Latin pinna 'wing, fin' + pes 'foot'] —**pinniped** adj

pinnule /pín yool/, **pinnula** /pínnyoŏlə/ (plural **-lae** /-lee/) n 1. a small fin or fin-shaped part of an organ or organism 2. a small division or lobe of a leaf that

has a central axis with parts branching off it [Late 16C. < Latin *pinnula* 'little feather' < *pinna* 'feather'] —**pinnular** *adj*

PIN number *n* BANKING, COMPUT same as **PIN**

pinny /pínni/ (*plural* **-nies**) *n* same as **apron** (sense 1) (*informal*) [Mid-19C. Shortening of PINAFORE]

Pinochet /peénō shay/, **Augusto** (*b.* 1915) Chilean military dictator. Under his right-wing regime (1973–90) dissidence was suppressed. Full name **Pinochet Ugarte, Augusto**

> 'Don't forget that in the history of the world, there was a plebiscite, in which Christ and Barabbas were being judged, and the people chose Barabbas.'
> [Augusto Pinochet, *Remark*; 1988]

pinochle /peé nuk'l/, **pinocle**, **penuchle**, **penuckle** *n* **1.** a card game for two or four players using two packs of cards that do not include two to eight. Certain combinations of cards score points, as do tricks taken. **2.** a combination of the queen of spades and the jack of diamonds in the game of pinochle [Mid-19C. Origin ?]

pinocytosis /peénō sī tóssiss/ *n* the ingestion of fluid into a cell by turning a portion of the cell membrane inwards to form a sheath that is then pinched off to form an internal vesicle [Late 19C. < Greek *pinein* 'to drink'] —**pinocytotic** /peénō sī tóttik/ *adj* —**pinocytotically** *adv*

pinole /pi nṓli/ *n* flour that is made by mixing lightly roasted cornflour with ground mesquite beans and sometimes other ingredients [Mid-19C. Via American Spanish < Nahuatl *pinolli*]

piñon /pi nyón, pínnyən/ (*plural* **piñons** or **piñones** /pi nyṓ neez/), **pinyon** *n* **1.** *also* **piñon nut** *or* **pinyon nut** a small sweet nut produced by a pine tree **2.** a low-growing pine tree that bears piñons. Native to: southwestern United States. Latin name: *Pinus edulis* or *Pinus monophylla*. [Mid-19C. < Spanish *piñón* < Latin *pineus* 'of pines' < *pinus* 'pine (tree)']

Pinotage /peénə taazh/ *n* **1.** a red wine made from a variety of black grape grown mainly in South Africa **2.** a black grape variety. Use: to make Pinotage. [< French < *Pinot* (see PINOT NOIR)]

Pinot Blanc /peénō blaaN/ *n* **1.** a dry white wine made from a grape grown especially in Alsace but also in Italy and California **2.** a white grape variety. Use: to make Pinot Blanc. [< French, 'white Pinot' (see PINOT NOIR)]

Pinot Grigio /peénō gríjjō/ *n* **1.** a crisp dry white wine made from a variety of white grape grown mainly in Italy and France **2.** a white grape variety. Use: to make Pinot Grigio. [< Italian, 'grey Pinot' (see PINOT NOIR)]

Pinot Noir /peénō nwaár/ *n* **1.** a red wine made from a variety of black grape originally grown in the Burgundy region of France **2.** a black grape variety. Use: to make Pinot Noir. [< French, 'black Pinot' (grape variety) < *pin* 'pine cone'; from the shape of the grape clusters]

pinpoint /pín poynt/ *vt* (**-points, -pointing, -pointed**) IDENTIFY SOMETHING CORRECTLY to identify or locate something accurately ■ *n* **1.** SOMETHING SMALL OR TRIVIAL something small or trivial and with no value or consequence **2.** POINTY TIP OF PIN the sharp end of a pin, or something that resembles it ■ *adj* PRECISELY EXACT reflecting exact meticulous precision

pinprick /pín prik/ *n* **1.** SMALL HOLE MADE BY PIN a small puncture, especially to the skin, made by a pin or something with a similarly sharp end **2.** SLIGHT WOUND a very minor wound **3.** MINOR IRRITANT a minor annoyance, nuisance, or distraction **4.** SMALL MARK a very small dot or mark ■ *vt* (**-pricks, -pricking, -pricked**) PUNCTURE SOMETHING WITH PIN to puncture something, especially the skin, with a pin or something with a similarly sharp end

pins and needles *n* a tingling sensation, especially in the feet or hands, sometimes experienced when a temporarily restricted blood flow to the affected body parts returns to normal (*takes a singular or plural verb*)

Pinsk /pinsk/ city in southwestern Belarus. Population: 133,500 (1999).

pinstripe /pín strīp/ *n* **1.** NARROW LINE any one of many very narrow lines, especially in a fabric **2.** MATERIAL WITH VERY NARROW LINES material that has very narrow lines in it. Use: business suits. (*often used before a noun*) **3.** PINSTRIPE SUIT a suit made of pinstripe fabric (*often used in the plural*) —**pinstriped** *adj*

pint /pīnt/ *n* **1.** UNIT OF LIQUID MEASURE a unit of liquid measure equal to one eighth of a gallon, which is equal to 0.568 litre in the United Kingdom and 0.473 litre in the United States **2.** UNIT OF DRY MEASURE a unit of dry measure equal to one eighth of a gallon, which is equal to 0.568 litre in the United Kingdom and 0.551 litre in the United States **3.** CONTAINER a container or measure that has the capacity of a pint **4.** PINT OF LIQUID a pint of a liquid, especially of beer or milk (*informal*) **5.** *UK* DRINK SERVED IN PUB a drink of beer or some similar alcoholic drink in a pub or bar perhaps, but not necessarily, a single or exact pint (*informal*) [14C. < French *pinte*]

pinta /píntə/ *n* an infectious bacterial skin disease of tropical America that is marked by the formation and eruption of papules, loss of pigmentation, and thickening of the skin [Early 19C. Via Spanish, 'painted spot' < assumed Vulgar Latin *pincta* < past participle of Latin *pingere* 'paint']

pintado petrel /pin taádō-/, **pintado** (*plural* **-dos** or **-does**) *n* BIRDS same as **Cape pigeon** [Via Portuguese *pintado* 'guinea fowl', literally 'painted' (from its black-and-white colouring) < past participle of Latin *pingere* 'paint']

pintail /pín tayl/ (*plural* **-tails** or *same*) *n* a slender duck that has a long pointed tail and brown and white feathers. Native to: northern hemisphere. Latin name: *Anas acuta*. [< the pointed tip of the male bird's tail]

Pinter /píntər/, **Harold** (*b.* 1930) British playwright and director. Many of his numerous plays, which include *The Caretaker* (1960) and *The Homecoming* (1964), explore the alienation and hostility beneath the surface of intimate relationships. His screenplays include *The Handmaid's Tale* (1990). See Cultural note at **birthday** —**Pinteresque** /píntə résk/ *adj*

> 'The earth's about five thousand million years old. Who can afford to live in the past?'
> [Harold Pinter, *The Homecoming*; 1964]

pintle /pínt'l/ *n* a pin or bolt, especially one used as a vertical pivot or hinge, e.g. on a rudder [Old English, 'peg, penis' < Germanic]

pinto /píntō/ *US adj* same as **piebald** ■ *n* (*plural* **-tos**) same as **piebald** [Mid-19C. Via Spanish, 'painted' < past participle of Latin *pingere* 'paint']

pinto bean *n* **1.** a mottled brown and pink kidney-shaped bean, cooked and eaten as a vegetable or used as fodder **2.** a variety of the kidney bean that produces pinto beans [< Spanish *pinto*, 'painted, mottled' (see PINTO)]

pint-size, **pint-sized** *adj* very small, especially smaller than usual or than expected (*informal*)

Pintubi *n, adj* PEOPLES same as **Pintupi**

pin tuck *n* a narrow vertical fold stitched in place and used for decoration, especially on the front of clothes —**pin-tucked** *adj*

Pintupi /píntəpi/ (*plural same* or **-pis**), **Pintubi** /píntəbi/ (*plural same* or **-bis**) *n* a member of an Aboriginal people living in the border regions between Western Australia and Northern Territories [Mid-20C.< Aboriginal] —**Pintupi** *adj*

pin-up *n* **1.** a photograph or poster of a sexually attractive person, especially one in which the person is posing in a seductive way and scantily clothed or naked **2.** somebody considered attractive enough to appear in a pin-up picture

pinwheel /pín weel/ *n N Am* **1.** LEISURE same as **Catherine wheel** (sense 1) **2.** same as **windmill** *n* (sense 4)

pinwork /pín wurk/ *n* the delicate stitches that are raised above the main design in the embroidery of needlepoint lace

pinworm /pín wurm/ *n* **1.** a thread-shaped nematode worm that occurs as a parasite in the intestines of vertebrate animals, including human beings. Family: Oxyuridae. **2.** an infestation of pinworms

piny /pīni/ (**-ier, -iest**), **piney** (**pinier, piniest**) *adj* relating to or resembling pine trees, e.g. in smell

Pinyin /pin yín/ *n* a system for transliterating written Chinese characters into the Roman alphabet, introduced in 1959 and adopted by the People's Republic of China in 1979 [Mid-20C. < Chinese *pīnyīn*, literally 'spell sound']

pinyon *n* TREES another spelling of **piñon**

piolet /peé ə lay/ *n* a double-headed ice axe used by mountaineers [Mid-19C. < French dialect < *piola* 'small axe' < Germanic]

pion /pī on/ *n* an elementary particle of the meson group that has either single positive, negative, or zero charge, a mass approximately 270 times that of the electron, and spin zero [Mid-20C. Contraction of *pi meson*]

pioneer /pī ə neér/ *n* **1.** INVENTOR OR INNOVATOR a person or group that is the first to do something or that leads in developing something new **2.** FIRST PERSON TO EXPLORE TERRITORY a person who is one of the first from another country or region to explore or settle a new area **3.** SOLDIER WHO BUILDS THINGS a foot soldier whose duties include going ahead of the main company to construct things to pave the way for them **4.** FIRST SPECIES TO GROW SOMEWHERE the first species of plant or animal life to begin living in a previously unoccupied site, e.g. a moss beginning to grow on otherwise bare rock ■ *v* (**-neers, -neering, -neered**) **1.** *vt* INVENT NEW THING to experiment with or develop something new **2.** *vti* GO INTO UNEXPLORED TERRITORY to go into previously uncharted or unclaimed territory with the aim of exploring it and possibly settling there **3.** *vi* ACT AS PIONEER to act as a pioneer in a particular field [Early 16C. < French *pionnier* < medieval Latin *pedon-* 'foot soldier' < Latin *ped-* 'foot']

pious /pī əss/ *adj* **1.** RELIGIOUS devoutly religious **2.** RELIGIOUSLY REVERENT characterized by religious reverence **3.** ACTING IN FALSELY MORALIZING WAY talking or acting in a falsely, hypocritically, or affectedly moralizing way **4.** HOLY OR SACRED holy or sacred, especially as distinct from worldly **5.** PRAISEWORTHY deserving to be praised **6.** SHOWING DUE RESPECT showing appropriate respect, especially towards parents (*archaic*) [15C. < Latin *pius* 'dutiful, devout'] —**piously** *adv* —**piousness** *n*

pip[1] /pip/ *n* **1.** SEED OF FRUIT a small hard seed of a fruit such as an apple that usually has several seeds **2.** SECTION OF PINEAPPLE SKIN any one of the many irregular diamond-shaped sections on the outer skin of a pineapple **3.** ROOTSTOCK OR FLOWER a rootstock or flower of some plants, especially the lily of the valley [Late 18C. Shortening of PIPPIN]

pip[2] /pip/ *n* **1.** SPOT ON DIE OR DOMINO a single spot on a die or domino **2.** MARK ON PLAYING CARD a single symbol of a club, diamond, heart, or spade on a playing card **3.** SHORT HIGH-PITCHED SOUND a short, usually high-pitched sound, especially of the kind used in broadcasting as a time signal **4.** SOMETHING INDICATING RANK something that indicates rank, e.g. a diamond-shaped insignia on the shoulder of a British Army officer's uniform (*informal*) **5.** SPECK a very small mark or piece of something ■ *v* (**pips, pipping, pipped**) **1.** *vi* CHEEP to make a cheeping sound, especially when newly hatched (*refers to birds*) **2.** *vti* USE BEAK TO BREAK SHELL to use the beak to break through the shell during hatching (*refers to birds*) **3.** *vi* MAKE SHRILL NOISE to make or emit a short shrill noise [Late 16C. Origin ?]

pip[3] /pip/ *n* **1.** CONTAGIOUS POULTRY DISEASE a contagious disease of birds, especially domestic poultry, characterized by the presence of a thick crust in the mouth and throat, caused by a secretion of mucus **2.** MINOR AILMENT a slight ailment in humans (*archaic*) ■ *vt* (**pips, pipping, pipped**) IRRITATE SOMEBODY to make somebody annoyed or upset (*dated informal*) [14C. Via Middle Dutch *pippe* < Latin *pituita* 'phlegm'] ◇ **give somebody the pip** to annoy or irritate somebody (*dated informal*)

pip[4] /pip/ (**pips, pipping, pipped**) *vt* **1.** to beat somebody in competition, especially when it looked as though the other person was going to stay ahead (*informal*) **2.** to wound or kill a person or animal with a bullet from a gun (*dated*) [Late 19C. Origin ?]

pipa[1] /peépə/ *n* a toad that lives in water, with a flat body, large webbed feet, and no eyelids or tongue. Native to: South America. Genus: *Pipa*. [Early 18C. Probably < Galibi]

pipa[2] /peé paá/ *n* a plucked four-stringed Chinese instrument with a fretted fingerboard like a guitar's [Mid-19C. < Chinese *pípa* 'loquat'; from its shape]

pipal /peé'p'l/, **peepul** n TREES same as **bo tree** [Late 18C. Via Hindi *pīpal* < Sanskrit *pippala*]

pipe[1] /pīp/ n 1. TUBE FOR TRANSPORTING LIQUID OR GAS a long cylindrical tube that water, oil, gas, or other such material passes through 2. TUBE OF ANY KIND an object in tubular form 3. DEVICE FOR SMOKING TOBACCO a small bowl with a hollow stem coming from it, used for smoking tobacco or other substances. Pipes are usually made of wood or clay. The tobacco is burnt in the bowl and the smoke drawn into the mouth through the stem. 4. AMOUNT IN SMOKER'S PIPE the amount of tobacco or other substance that the bowl of a smoker's pipe holds 5. HOLLOW BODY PART a tubular part or organ in a plant or animal, especially one in an animal's respiratory system 6. TUBULAR MUSICAL INSTRUMENT PLAYED BY BLOWING a tubular musical instrument that is played by blowing air into it 7. TUBULAR PART OF MUSICAL ORGAN an upright tubular part of a musical organ that produces sound when air is blown into it 8. WIND INSTRUMENT OF MIDDLE AGES a three-holed wind instrument of the Middle Ages, played with one hand while the other hand beats on a small drum 9. SAILOR'S WHISTLE a small whistle used for signalling orders to a ship's crew, usually by a boatswain 10. HIGH-PITCHED NOISE a high-pitched or shrill noise, e.g. a birdcall 11. GEOL CYLINDER-SHAPED GEOLOGICAL FORMATION a vertical cylinder-shaped geological formation, e.g. a vein of ore 12. GEOL PASSAGE THROUGH WHICH LAVA FLOWS a vertical passage through which molten lava flows 13. METALL HOLE IN CAST METAL a conical cavity in the middle of a piece of metal, produced by gas escaping as the metal cools ■ **pipes** npl 1. MUSIC BAGPIPES a pair of bagpipes 2. N Am VOCAL CORDS the vocal cords or voice, especially when used to sing (*slang*) 3. Aus HUMAN RESPIRATORY PASSAGES the passages of the human respiratory system (*informal*) ■ v (**pipes, piping, piped**) 1. vt CARRY SOMETHING BY PIPE to carry something, especially water, gas, or a semisolid, by means of a pipe, pipeline, or system of pipes ○ *The company pipes crude oil to the refinery.* 2. vti INSTALL OR EQUIP WITH PIPES to equip something with pipes, or install pipes and their connections in something 3. vt PLAY TUNE ON PIPE to play a tune on a musical pipe 4. vt SEND PIPED MUSIC THROUGH PLACE to play prerecorded music in a public place or workplace to create a soothing atmosphere 5. vt SIGNAL SOMETHING USING PIPE to signal the arrival or departure of somebody or something using a pipe 6. vt ORDER CREW USING BOATSWAIN'S PIPE to give orders to a ship's crew using a boatswain's pipe 7. vt DECORATE GARMENT WITH PIPING to add decorative piping to a garment or to soft furnishing 8. vt DECORATE FOOD WITH PIPING to add decorative piping to food, especially by forcing it out of a bag that has a nozzle designed to create the various decorative forms 9. vti MAKE HIGH-PITCHED NOISE to make a high-pitched or shrill noise, or speak or say something in a squeaky voice [Old English *pīpe*, via Germanic < assumed Vulgar Latin *pipa* < Latin *pipare* 'to peep, cheep', an imitation of the sound] — **pipeful** n

pipe down vi to stop talking or become less noisy or boisterous (*informal*)

pipe up vi 1. to say something, often as an interruption or a clarification 2. to begin to sing or play a musical instrument

pipe[2] /pīp/ n 1. LARGE CONTAINER FOR LIQUID a large container for wine, oil, or some other liquid 2. UNIT OF LIQUID CAPACITY a unit of liquid measure for wine, equal to four barrels, two hogsheads, or 105 gallons 3. CASK a cask that has the capacity of four barrels, two hogsheads, or 105 gallons [14C. Via Anglo-Norman < PIPE[1]]

pipe band n a marching or military band with bagpipes, drums, and often a drum major, typically playing traditional Scottish music

pipe bomb n a bomb made of a length of pipe that is filled with explosives and is capped at its ends

pipeclay /pīp klay/ n a very fine white pure clay. Use: pottery, smokers' pipes, whitening leather and other materials. ■ vt (**-clays, -claying, -clayed**) to use pipeclay for whitening leather or some other, usually natural, material

pipe cleaner n a flexible wire covered with fluffy material that is used for cleaning the stems of smokers' pipes and other things that are difficult to access

piped music /pīpt-/ n prerecorded, usually easy-listening music played through speakers in public places and some workplaces to create a soothing atmosphere

pipe dream n an aim, hope, or plan so fanciful that it is very unlikely to be realized [< the dreams caused by smoking opium]

pipefitting /pīp fiting/ n 1. BRANCH OF PLUMBING INVOLVING PIPES the branch of plumbing that involves measuring, cutting, bending, and joining lengths of pipe, either in installation or repairs 2. ACT OR PROCESS OF PIPE INSTALLATION an act or process of installing or connecting pipes 3. SOMETHING USED IN CONNECTING PIPES something that is used in the connection or joining of pipes —**pipefitter** n

pipeline /pīp līn/ n 1. LONG PIPE SYSTEM FOR TRANSPORTING SOMETHING a pipe or system of pipes designed to carry something such as oil, natural gas, or other petroleum-based products over long distances, often underground 2. CHANNEL OF COMMUNICATIONS a channel of communications, especially a private one among several people within a single organization 3. SYSTEM FOR SUPPLYING SOMETHING a system for the supply or transfer of something, especially goods or information ■ vt (**-lines, -lining, -lined**) 1. SEND SOMETHING BY PIPE SYSTEM to send, connect, or carry something by way of a long system of pipes 2. FIT SOMETHING WITH LONG PIPE SYSTEM to fit or supply something with a long system of pipes ◇ **in the pipeline** in preparation but not yet ready

pipe major n a noncommissioned officer in charge of a regiment's pipe band

pip-emma /pīp émmə/ adv in the afternoon (*dated informal*) [Early 20C. < former code names for the letters 'p' and 'm']

pipe of peace n same as **peace pipe**

pipe organ n a musical organ that uses pipes to produce the sound, as opposed to a reed organ or an electric organ. Most church organs are pipe organs.

piper /pīpər/ n 1. somebody who plays the bagpipes 2. somebody who plays a pipe ◇ **he who pays the piper calls the tune** used to say that the person who is paying for something will control what happens

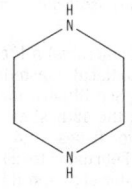

piperazine

piperazine /pi pérrə zeen/ n a colourless crystalline compound. Use: parasiticide, insecticide. Formula: $C_4H_{10}N_2$. [Late 19C. < PIPERIDINE + AZINE]

piperidine

piperidine /pi pérri deen/ n a colourless liquid compound that has a peppery odour resembling ammonia. Use: manufacture of rubber and epoxy resins. Formula: $C_5H_{11}N$. [Mid-19C. < PIPERINE + -IDINE]

piperine /píppə reen/ n a white crystalline alkaloid compound that is the chief active component of pepper. Formula: $C_{17}H_{19}NO_3$. [Early 19C. < Latin *piper* (see PEPPER)]

pipe roll n a collection of accounts dating from between the 12th and the 19th centuries that were submitted annually by sheriffs and other Crown ministers and are kept at the British Exchequer [Probably because rolled up into a tubular shape]

piperonal /píppərō nal/ n a white crystalline compound that has an odour resembling heliotrope. Use: in perfumes and flavourings. Formula: $C_{19}H_{63}$. [Mid-19C. < German *Piperin* 'piperine']

pipe snake n a tropical snake with a fused inflexible skull, vestiges of hind limbs, and two unequally-sized lungs. Family: Anillidae.

pipes of Pan npl MUSIC same as **panpipes**

pipestone /pīp stōn/ n a reddish or pinkish stone resembling clay in consistency that some Native North Americans harden and use for making decorative objects and long, often ornate pipes

pipette /pi pét/ n a small glass tube that liquid is drawn into so that it can be measured, often before it is delivered to another container, e.g. in experiments or in medication doses ■ vt (**-pettes, -petting, -petted**) to measure or deliver an accurate amount of liquid using a pipette [Mid-19C. < French, 'little pipe' < *pipe* 'pipe' < assumed Vulgar Latin *pipa* (see PIPE[1])]

pipi /píppee/ (*plural same* or **-pis**) n ANZ an edible shellfish [Mid-19C. < Maori]

piping /pīping/ n 1. PIPES COLLECTIVELY pipes thought of collectively, especially when they form a connected plumbing system in a house or other building 2. DECORATIVE TWISTED CORD a twisted cord covered with fabric inserted into a seam as a decoration. Use: clothes, soft furnishings. 3. DECORATIVE EFFECT ON FOOD a decorative effect used on food, especially strands or swirls of icing in a contrasting colour 4. SKILL OF PLAYING MUSICAL PIPE the art, technique, or skill of playing the bagpipes or another kind of musical pipe 5. SOUND OF MUSICAL PIPE the sound of bagpipes or some other musical pipe 6. SHRILL NOISE a shrill, high-pitched, or whistling noise ■ adj SHRILLY PITCHED shrill and very high in pitch, as some voices are

piping hot adj describes food or water that is very hot

pipistrelle /píppi strél/, **pipistrel** n a small brown insect-eating bat found throughout the world. Genus: *Pipistrellus*. [Late 18C. Via French < Italian *pipistrello*, alteration of *vipistrello* < Latin *vespertilio* 'bat' < *vesper* 'evening']

pipit /píppit/ n a small songbird of the wagtail family with brown speckled feathers and a long tail. Family: Motacillidae. [Mid-18C. An imitation of its call]

pipkin /pípkin/ n a small cooking pot, usually made of metal or earthenware and with a handle going across the top [Mid-16C. Origin ?]

pippin /píppin/ n 1. VARIETY OF APPLE a variety of cultivated eating or cooking apple 2. PIP OR SEED a pip or seed, especially an apple pip 3. DESIRABLE OR ADMIRABLE PERSON OR THING somebody or something that is particularly desirable or admirable (*dated informal*) [14C. < French *pepin*]

pipsissewa /pip síssəwə/ (*plural* **-was** or *same*) n an evergreen plant with jagged astringent leaves used as a diuretic. Flowers: white or pinkish. Genus: *Chimaphila*. [Late 18C. < Abenaki *kpi-pskwàhsawe* 'flower of the woods']

pipsqueak /píp skweek/ n somebody or something that is small or insignificant, but nevertheless often annoying or troublesome (*informal*)

piquant /peékənt, -kaant/ adj 1. SPICY OR SAVOURY having a flavour, taste, or smell that is spicy or savoury, often with a slightly tart or bitter edge to it 2. SHARPLY STIMULATING OR PROVOCATIVE refreshingly interesting, stimulating, or provocative 3. SHARPLY CRITICAL AND BITING excessively severe or hurtful in tone or content [Early 16C. < French, present participle of *piquer* (see PIQUE[1])] —**piquancy** n —**piquantly** adv —**piquantness** n

pique[1] /peek/ n BAD MOOD a bad mood or feeling of resentment, especially when brought on by an insult, hurt pride, or loss of face ■ v (**piques, piquing,**

piqued) 1. *vt* PUT SOMEBODY IN BAD MOOD to cause somebody to be in a bad mood or to feel resentful 2. *vt* AROUSE SOMEBODY'S INTEREST to cause a feeling of interest, curiosity, or excitement in somebody ○ *piqued my curiosity* 3. *vr* TAKE PRIDE IN SOMETHING to take pride in something, especially a personal attribute or ability [Mid-16C. Via French *piquer* 'prick, irritate' < assumed Vulgar Latin *piccare*]

SPELLCHECK See *peak*[1].

pique[2] /peek/ *n* in the game of piquet, a score of 30 points to an opponent's 0 from the hand as dealt ■ *vti* (**piques, piquing, piqued**) in the game of piquet, to score a pique against an opponent [Mid-17C. < French *pic*]

piqué /peé kay/ *n* a closely woven ribbed fabric produced from natural fibres. Use: shirts and dresses. [Mid-19C. < French, past participle of *piquer* 'prick, stitch' (see PIQUE[1])]

piquet /pi két, -káy/, **picquet** *n* a card game for two players using a deck that does not include two to six [Mid-17C. < French, origin ?]

piracy /pírəssi/ *n* 1. ROBBERY ON HIGH SEAS robbery on the high seas, especially the stealing of a ship's cargo 2. ROBBERY ON ANY FORM OF TRANSPORT robbery committed on board any form of transport, especially an aircraft 3. HIJACKING the hijacking of an aircraft or another form of transport 4. USE OF COPYRIGHT MATERIAL WITHOUT PERMISSION the taking and using of copyright or patented material without authorization or without the legal right to do so 5. ILLEGAL BROADCASTING the unauthorized or illegal broadcasting of TV or radio programmes [Mid-16C. < medieval Latin *piratia* < Latin *pirata* (see PIRATE)]

Piraeus /pī reé əss/ industrial city and seaport serving Athens, Greece. Population: 182,671 (1991).

piragua /pi ra'agwə, pi ràggwə/ *n* CANOEING same as **pirogue** [Early 17C. Via American Spanish < Carib, 'dugout']

piraña *n* FISH another spelling of **piranha**

Pirandello /pírrən déllō/, **Luigi** (1867–1936) Italian playwright. His works, which include *Six Characters in Search of an Author* (1921), explore the human condition with grim humour. He won a Nobel Prize in literature (1934).

'Whoever has the luck to be born a character can laugh even at death. Because a character will never die! A man will die, a writer, the instrument of creation: but what he has created will never die!'
[Luigi Pirandello, *Six Characters in Search of an Author*; 1921]

Piranesi /pírrə náyzi/, **Giovanni Battista** (1720–78) Italian artist. He is noted for his *Imaginary Prisons* (1745) and other engravings and etchings of real or imaginary buildings.

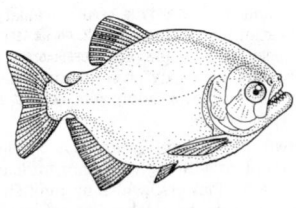

piranha

piranha /pi ra'anə/ (*plural* **-nhas** or *same*), **piraña** (*plural* **-ñas** or *same*) *n* a small freshwater fish that has sharp teeth and strong jaws and is a dangerous predator when attacking in large numbers. Native to: South America. Genus: *Serrasalmo*. [Mid-18C. Via Portuguese < Tupi *piráya*]

pirate /pírət/ *n* 1. ROBBER AT SEA a robber who operates from a ship on the sea 2. SHIP USED BY SEA ROBBERS a ship used by people who rob or otherwise attack shipping on the high seas 3. SOMEBODY USING COPYRIGHT MATERIAL WITHOUT PERMISSION somebody who duplicates or uses copyright or patented material illegally or without authorization 4. SOMEBODY INVOLVED IN ILLEGAL

BROADCASTING somebody who takes part in or manages the unauthorized or illegal broadcasting of TV or radio programmes ■ *v* (**-rates, -rating, -rated**) 1. *vti* ROB SOMETHING ON HIGH SEAS to rob a vessel or commit robbery on the high seas 2. *vt* USE COPYRIGHT MATERIAL WITHOUT PERMISSION to duplicate or use copyright or patented material without authorization or without the legal right to do so [13C. Via Latin *pirata* < Greek *peiratēs* < *peiran* 'to attack'] —**piratic** /pī ráttik/ *adj* —**piratical** *adj* —**piratically** *adv*

pirog /pi rôg/ (*plural* **-rogi** /-rôgi/) *n* a large rectangular pie that has a pastry crust on top and bottom, filled with chopped meat or cabbage, onions, and hard-boiled eggs [Mid-19C. < Russian]

pirogue /pi rôg/ *n* a canoe made from a hollowed-out tree trunk, used especially in southern Louisiana [Early 17C. Via French < Carib *piragua* 'dugout']

piroshki *n* FOOD another spelling of **pirozhki**

pirouette /pírroo ét/ *n* a spin of the body, especially one performed in ballet on tiptoe or on the ball of one foot [Mid-17C. < French] —**pirouette** *vi*

pirozhki /pi róshki/, **piroshki** *n* very small fried or baked pastries, usually filled with finely chopped meat or cabbage and onions (*takes a singular or plural verb*) [Early 20C. < Russian, 'little pirog']

Pisa /peézə/ capital of Pisa Province, Tuscany Region, central Italy. It is known for its leaning bell tower. Population: 89,694 (2001).

pis aller /peéz állay/ (*plural* **pis allers** /*pronunc. same*/) *n* something that is done as a last resort or when no other option is available [< French < *pis* 'worse' + *aller* 'to go']

Pisano /pi za'anō/, **Giovanni** (1250?–1314?) Italian sculptor. The son of Nicola Pisano, he incorporated Gothic style into his sculptures for Siena Cathedral and pulpits for the cathedrals of Pistoia and Pisa, Italy.

Pisano, Nicola (1220?–84?) Italian sculptor. The father of Giovanni Pisano, his fame rests chiefly on his relief sculptures for the Pisa Baptistry, Italy.

piscary /pískəri/ (*plural* **-ries**) *n* 1. a place where people fish or are allowed to fish (*formal*) 2. the legal right to fish in a place even if it belongs to another person [15C. < medieval Latin *piscaria* < Latin *piscis* 'fish']

piscatorial /pískə táwri əl/, **piscatory** /pískətəri/ *adj* relating to fish, fishing, or people who fish (*formal*) [Early 19C. < Latin *piscatorius* < *piscis* 'fish'] —**piscatorially** *adv*

Pisces /pí seez/ (*plural same*) *n* 1. CONSTELLATION IN NORTHERN HEMISPHERE a zodiacal constellation of the northern hemisphere. See illustration at **constellation** 2. 12TH SIGN OF ZODIAC the 12th sign of the zodiac, represented by two fishes and lasting from approximately 19 February to 20 March. Pisces is classified as a water sign and its ruling planets are Jupiter and Neptune. 3. SOMEBODY BORN UNDER PISCES somebody whose birthday falls between 19 February and 20 March [Pre-12C. < Latin, plural of *piscis* 'fish'] —**Piscean** /píssi ən/ *n* —**Pisces** *adj*

pisci- *prefix* fish ○ *piscivorous* [< Latin *piscis* < Indo-European]

pisciculture /píssi kulchər/ *n* the controlled breeding, hatching, and rearing of fish, especially for scientific or commercial purposes —**piscicultural** /píssi kúlchərəl/ *adj* —**pisciculturally** *adv* —**pisciculturist** *n*

piscina /pi seénə/ (*plural* **-nas** or **-nae** /-nee/) *n* 1. in some Christian churches, a sacred container or basin that holds holy water, used to carry it away after ablutions have been completed 2. the place where a priest can wash his hands and the sacred containers used in Mass, located in the sacristy, especially in a Roman Catholic church [Late 16C. < medieval Latin (in classical Latin 'fish pond'), < Latin *piscis* 'fish'] —**piscinal** /píssin'l/ *adj*

piscine /píssīn/ *adj* relating to, characteristic of, or resembling fish (*formal*) [Late 18C. < medieval Latin *piscinus* < Latin *piscis* 'fish']

Piscis Austrinus /píssiss o strínəss, píssiss-/ *n* a small constellation of the southern hemisphere between Grus and Aquarius. See illustration at **constellation**

piscivorous /pi sívvərəss/ *adj* feeding habitually or mainly on fish

pisé /peé zay/, **pisé de terre** /-də táir/ *n* compressed

earth or clay used for making floors or walls [Late 18C. < French *pisé de terre* 'beaten earth']

pish /pish/ *interj* used to express contempt, annoyance, or impatience (*dated*) [Late 16C. Natural exclamation]

pishogue /pi shōg/, **pishoge** *n* Ireland 1. superstition or old-fashioned nonsense 2. a superstitious belief or practice [Early 19C. < Irish *piseog*]

pisiform /píssi fawrm/ *adj* resembling a pea in shape or size ■ *n* same as **pisiform bone** [Mid-18C. < Latin *pisum* 'pea']

pisiform bone *n* the small knobbly bone at the place where the inner bone of the forearm (**ulna**) joins the wrist (**carpus**)

Pisistratus /pīsístrətəs/ (600?–527 BC) Athenian general and tyrant of Athens (560–527 BC). He extended Athenian territory, encouraged the arts, lowered taxes, and improved conditions for the poor.

pismire /píss mīr/ *n* same as **ant** (*archaic or informal*) [14C. < PISS (from the urinous smell of anthills) + obsolete *mire* 'ant']

REGIONAL NOTE See **ant**.

pisolite /píssō līt/ *n* an inorganic limestone consisting of individual spherical concretions (**pisoliths**) [Early 18C. < Greek *pisos* 'pea'] —**pisolitic** /píssō líttik/ *adj*

pisolith /píssəlith/ *n* a spherical concretion with concentric laminations that with others makes up an inorganic limestone. Pisoliths can be up to 10 cm/4 in. in diameter. [Late 18C. < Greek *pisos* 'pea']

piss /piss/ *v* (**pisses, pissing, pissed**) (*slang*) 1. *vi* an offensive term meaning to urinate 2. *vt* an offensive term meaning to discharge a substance such as blood when urinating 3. *vt* an offensive term meaning to urinate on or into something ■ *n* (*slang*) 1. an offensive term for urine 2. an offensive term for an act or instance of urinating 3. ANZ BEVERAGES an offensive term for beer ■ *prefix* an offensive term used to emphasize how bad something is (*informal*) ○ *piss-awful* [13C. Via French *pisser* < assumed Vulgar Latin *pissiare*, an imitation of the sound] ◇ **on the piss** an offensive phrase meaning taking part in a heavy alcohol-drinking session (*slang*) ◇ **piss and vinegar** *US* an offensive term for feisty strength of character and physical vigour (*slang*) ◇ **take the piss** an offensive term meaning to ridicule or mock somebody or something (*slang*)

piss about, piss around *v* (*slang*) 1. *vt* an offensive term meaning to annoy somebody or waste somebody's time, especially deliberately 2. *vi* an offensive term meaning to behave in a silly or childish way, especially by wasting time

piss away *vt* an offensive term meaning to waste something such as money or time (*slang*)

piss down *vi* an offensive term meaning to rain heavily (*slang*)

piss off *v* (*slang*) 1. *vt* an offensive term meaning to annoy, irritate, or upset somebody 2. *vi* an offensive term often used as a command to tell somebody to go away and stop being annoying

piss-annat /píss annət/ *n* regional same as **ant** [Alteration of PISSANT 'ant']

REGIONAL NOTE See **ant**.

pissant /píss ant/, **piss ant** *US* *n* 1. an offensive term for somebody who pays too much attention to small details 2. an offensive term for somebody regarded as being of no importance, significance, or consequence ■ *adj* 1. an offensive term meaning paying too much attention to small details 2. an offensive term meaning regarded as being of no importance, significance, or consequence [Mid-17C. Originally 'ant'; from the urinous smell of anthills]

Pissarro /pi sa'arō/, **Camille** (1830–1903) French painter. He was a major exponent of the impressionist style and is known for his landscapes, river scenes, and street scenes. Full name **Pissarro, Camille Jacob**

piss artist *n* (*slang*) 1. an offensive term for somebody who regularly drinks a lot of alcohol or who regularly gets drunk 2. an offensive term for somebody who is regarded as completely incompetent or who is thought to exaggerate his or her competence

pissed /pist/ *adj* 1. an offensive term meaning ex-

tremely drunk (*slang*) **2.** *N Am* same as **pissed off** (*slang offensive*)

pissed off *adj* an offensive term meaning very annoyed or angry (*slang*) ■ *N Am* term **pissed**

pisser /píssər/ *n* (*slang*) **1.** OFFENSIVE TERM an offensive term for a situation that is extremely annoying or disappointing **2.** *US* SOMEBODY OR SOMETHING SURPRISINGLY GOOD somebody or something that is unexpectedly good or worthwhile (*offensive in some contexts*) **3.** *Aus* OFFENSIVE TERM an offensive term for a public house

pisshead /píss hed/ *n* an offensive term for somebody who frequently or habitually gets very drunk (*slang*)

pissoir /píss waar/ *n* a public urinal, especially one on the streets of some European cities, with a circular screen round it [Early 20C. < French < *pisser* (see PISS)]

pisspot /píss pot/ *n* (*slang*) **1.** *US* an offensive term for somebody regarded as bad-tempered and generally nasty **2.** *ANZ* an offensive term for a habitual drunkard [15C. Originally 'chamber pot']

piss-take *n* an offensive term for a parody, especially one that involves mockery or ridicule (*slang*) — **piss-taker** *n* —**piss-taking** *n*

piss-up *n* (*slang*) **1.** an offensive term for a heavy alcohol-drinking session **2.** an offensive term for a deplorable mess or mix-up

pissy-bed /píssi bed/ *n regional* **1.** same as **ant 2.** same as **dandelion** [< the urinous smell of anthills]

REGIONAL NOTE See **ant.**

pistachio /pi staashi ō, pi stásh-/ (*plural* -os) *n* **1.** a nut with a small green kernel that is eaten fresh and also yields an edible oil **2.** (*plural* **pistachios** or *same*) a tree of the cashew family that produces pistachios. Native to: western Asia. Latin name: *Pistachia vera.* [15C. Directly or via Old French *pistace* < Italian *pistacchio* < Greek *pistakion* < *pistakē* 'pistachio tree']

pistachio green *adj* of a pale whitish-green colour, like a pistachio kernel —**pistachio green** *n*

pistachio nut *n* FOOD same as **pistachio** (sense 1)

piste /peest/ *n* **1.** a downhill track or area of densely packed snow that provides good skiing conditions **2.** a rectangular area, sometimes cordoned off, where a contest, especially a fencing bout, takes place [Early 18C. Via French, 'track' < Latin *pista* < past participle of *pinsere* 'beat']

pistil /pístil/ *n* a carpel or group of fused carpels forming the female reproductive part of a flower and including the ovary, style, and stigma [Early 18C. Directly or via French < Latin *pistillum* 'pestle'; from its shape]

pistillate /písti layt/ *adj* describes a flower that has one or more pistils but usually no stamens

pistol /píst'l/ *n* a small short-barrelled gun designed to be held in one hand ■ *vt* (-tols, -tolling, -tolled) to shoot somebody or something using a pistol [Mid-16C. Via French *pistole* < Czech *pišt'ala* 'pipe' < *pištěti* 'whistle', an imitation of the sound]

pistole /pis tōl/ *n* a gold coin used in some European countries during the 17th and 18th centuries [Late 16C. < French]

pistoleer /písta leér/ *n* somebody, especially a soldier, who carries or uses a pistol (*archaic*)

pistol grip *n* a handle that resembles the butt of a pistol, especially in being shaped to fit the hand

pistol-whip *vt* to hit or beat somebody or something with the butt or barrel of a pistol

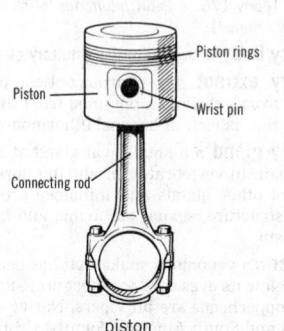

Piston rings
Piston
Wrist pin
Connecting rod
piston

piston /píst'n/ *n* **1.** a metal cylinder that slides up and down inside a tubular housing, receiving pressure from or exerting pressure on a fluid, especially one of several in an internal-combustion engine **2.** the valve mechanism in a brass musical instrument that is used to alter its pitch [Early 18C. Via French < Italian *pestone* 'large pestle' < *pestare* (see PESTO)]

piston ring *n* a metal ring or series of rings fitted round a piston to ensure a tight seal with the cylinder wall and prevent gaseous leakage

piston rod *n* a rod connected to a piston that transmits the motion of the piston to a pump or an engine

pistou /pee too/ *n* a sauce from Provence made of basil, garlic, and olive oil, similar to Italian pesto [Mid-20C. Via French < Provençal, past participle of *pestar* 'crush' < late Latin *pistare* (see PESTO)]

pit¹ /pit/ *n* **1.** BIG HOLE IN GROUND a large hole in the ground **2.** HOLE IN GROUND FOR MINING a deep hole in the ground that gives access to a mining resource, especially coal **3.** MINESHAFT a shaft that gives access to a mine **4.** BLEMISH a blemish or indentation on a surface, especially a small circular scar left by a disease such as chickenpox **5.** LOWEST PART the very bottom of something ○ *in the pit of my stomach* **6.** AREA CONTAINING PARTICULAR SUBSTANCE an area filled with a particular material or substance ○ *a tar pit* **7.** UNTIDY PLACE an extremely untidy or dirty place (*informal*) **8.** same as **bed** *n* (sense 1) (*slang*) **9.** SPORTS ARENA FOR FIGHTING an arena that is cordoned off for bouts of fighting, especially illegal fighting between cocks or dogs **10.** MOTOR SPORTS SERVICING AREA FOR RACING CARS an area, or section of an area, off the side of a motor-racing track where vehicles can get fuel, fresh tyres, and repairs (*often used in the plural*) **11.** AUTOMOT SUNKEN AREA FOR EXAMINING CARS a sunken area, especially in a garage, where the undersides of cars and other motor vehicles can be inspected and repaired **12.** ATHLETICS SANDY AREA WHERE JUMPERS LAND a soft sandy area where a long-jumper, triple-jumper, or pole-vaulter can land safely **13.** ANAT NATURAL HOLLOW a natural hollow, especially on the surface of a body part **14.** BOT CONCAVE SPOT ON PLANT WALL a tiny concavity or thin-walled area in the wall of a plant serving to help transport water and nutrients **15.** THEATRE same as **orchestra pit 16.** FIELD SPORTS same as **pitfall** (sense 2) **17.** GAMBLING AREA IN CASINO the area in a casino where the gambling takes place **18.** *N Am* FIN AREA ON FLOOR OF EXCHANGE the area of the floor of an exchange where commodities trading takes place **19.** CHR same as **hell** *n* (sense 1) (*literary*) ■ **pits** *npl* WORST POSSIBLE THING, PERSON, OR PLACE the worst or most unpleasant thing, person, or place it is possible to find (*informal*) ■ *vt* (**pits, pitting, pitted**) **1.** MAKE SOMEBODY OR SOMETHING OPPONENT to set somebody or something up in opposition to somebody or something else ○ *She was pitted against the three-time world champion.* **2.** MARK SURFACE WITH SMALL HOLES to cause small holes or indentations to form in a surface **3.** BURY SOMEBODY OR SOMETHING to put somebody or something in a deep hole [Old English *pytt*, via Germanic < Latin *puteus* 'pit, well'] ◇ **pit your wits against somebody** to compete with somebody in an intellectual exercise

pit² /pit/ *N Am n* the hard seed of a fruit such as a peach that has only one seed ■ *vt* (**pits, pitting, pitted**) to remove the kernel or stone from a fruit [Mid-19C. Probably < Dutch]

pita¹ /pítta, peéta/ *n* a plant that yields a strong fibre, e.g. agave. Use: paper, cordage. [Late 17C. Via American Spanish < Taino]

pita² *n* FOOD another spelling of **pitta²**

pitapat /pítta pát/ *adv* WITH TAPPING SOUND with quick light tapping noises ■ *n* SERIES OF TAPPING NOISES a series of quick light tapping noises, especially those made by feet running lightly ■ *vi* (-pats, -patting, -patted) MAKE SERIES OF TAPPING NOISES to make a series of quick light tapping noises [Early 16C. An imitation of the sound]

pit bull terrier, **pit bull** *n* a large bull terrier similar to the Staffordshire bull terrier but more muscular and powerful. The breed was first developed in the United States in dog-fighting circles and remains unrecognized by the Kennel Clubs.

Pitcairn Island /pít kairn-/ island in the central South Pacific Ocean. It is the main island of a group forming a dependency of the United Kingdom. It

was first inhabited by mutineers from HMS *Bounty* in 1790. Population: 61 (1991). Area: 36 sq. km/14 sq. mi.

pitch¹ /pich/ *v* (**pitches, pitching, pitched**) **1.** *vti* THROW SOMETHING to throw or hurl something **2.** *vti* BASEBALL THROW BALL TO BATTER in baseball, to throw a baseball from the mound to the batter **3.** *vt* CRICKET BOWL BALL TO BATSMAN in cricket, to bowl a ball so that it hits the ground at a particular spot or distance from the batsman **4.** *vti* GOLF HIT BALL HIGH in golf, to hit a high ball, usually onto the green and often with some backspin so that it does not roll too far on landing **5.** *vt* SET UP TEMPORARY STRUCTURE to set up a camp, tent, marquee, or other temporary structure **6.** *vt* SECURE SOMETHING IN GROUND to secure, embed, or implant something in the ground ○ *pitch tent stakes* **7.** *vti* FALL OR MAKE SOMEBODY FALL DOWN to fall or stumble, especially headfirst, or make somebody or something do this **8.** *vti* SLANT IN PARTICULAR WAY to slope in a particular way or to a particular degree, or make something do this ○ *a steeply pitched roof* **9.** *vi* NAUT WOBBLE UP AND DOWN to move in a rolling alternate front to rear motion, e.g. in rough water or turbulent air currents **10.** *vt* TRY TO SELL OR PROMOTE SOMETHING to try to sell or promote something, often in an aggressive way ○ *pitched his budget proposal to Parliament* **11.** *vt* SET SOMETHING AT LEVEL to put, set, or have something at a particular level, e.g. of intensity or comprehension ○ *a show pitched at an audience in their 20s* **12.** *vt* MUSIC SET INSTRUMENT TO PARTICULAR KEY to set a musical instrument to a particular key **13.** *vt* CARDS LEAD CARD TO ESTABLISH TRUMPS to lead a card of a particular suit in order to establish that suit as trumps for the trick **14.** *vi* *N Am* GIVE ENTHUSIASTIC SUPPORT to provide enthusiastic support for somebody or something ■ *n* **1.** PARTICULAR DEGREE OF SOMETHING a particular degree or level of something ○ *Their anticipation had been at fever pitch for days.* **2.** MUSIC PARTICULAR FREQUENCY OF SINGLE NOTE the level of a sound in a musical scale, according to its frequency **3.** FIELD FOR BALL GAME a playing area for a team ball game **4.** CRICKET AREA BETWEEN CRICKET STUMPS in cricket, the area between the two sets of stumps. The regulation size is 22 yards long and 10 feet wide. **5.** CRICKET PLACE WHERE BALL BOUNCES in cricket, the point that a ball lands on when it is bowled **6.** BASEBALL THROW OF BALL in baseball, the act or an instance of pitching the ball **7.** GOLF HIGH BALL in golf, a shot, especially one from fairway to green, in which the ball lofts high in the air, often with some backspin, so that it does not roll too far on landing **8.** WAY OF THROWING SOMETHING a particular way or manner of throwing something, especially a ball **9.** PLACE WHERE STALL IS ERECTED a place where a stall is erected, especially in a street market **10.** METHOD OF PERSUASION an attempt to persuade somebody to accept or buy something (*informal*) ○ *unwanted telephone sales pitches at inconvenient times* **11.** CONSTR ROOF ANGLE the angle of slope of a roof expressed in degrees **12.** DEGREE OF SLOPE OF SOMETHING the degree, direction, or extent of a slope, especially of a hill, road, or other feature **13.** GEOL TILT OF GEOLOGICAL FORMATION the inclination from the horizontal of a geological formation or structure such as a vein or stratum **14.** ARCHIT VERY TOP OF SOMETHING the highest point of something such as an arch **15.** AVIAT ANGLE OF PROPELLER the angle formed between the plane of a propeller blade and the plane of rotation of the propeller **16.** TOSSING MOTION an act or instance of pitching up and down, e.g. in rough water or air turbulence **17.** MECH ENG DISTANCE BETWEEN THREADS OR GEAR TEETH the distance between corresponding points on adjacent threads on a screw or teeth on a gear **18.** CLIMBING DISTANCE SEPARATING CLIMBERS the distance between climbers making an ascent or descent using the same ropes, equal to one rope length or less [12C. Origin ?] ◇ **queer somebody's pitch** to spoil somebody's plans, or prevent somebody from doing something (*informal*)

pitch in *vi* (*informal*) **1.** to help or cooperate, especially willingly **2.** to begin to do or participate in something, especially with great enthusiasm

pitch into *vt* to begin to attack somebody, either verbally or physically (*informal*)

pitch up *vi* to arrive at a place (*informal*)

pitch² /pich/ *n* **1.** SUBSTANCE OBTAINED FROM TAR a dark sticky substance obtained from tar and used in the building trade, especially for waterproofing roofs **2.** NATURAL TARRY SUBSTANCE a sticky dark substance such as asphalt that is found naturally **3.** RESIN a resin

obtained from the sap of some pine trees ■ *vt* (**pitches, pitching, pitched**) SPREAD PITCH ON SURFACE to coat a surface with pitch [Old English *pic*, via Germanic < Latin *pix*; partly < Anglo-Norman *piche* < Latin *pix*]

pitch-and-putt *n* 1. a game similar to golf, but played on a much shorter course, in which players use only two clubs, an iron and a putter 2. a course for pitch-and-putt, with holes shorter than those for golf

pitch-and-toss *n* a game of skill and luck in which each player throws a coin towards a designated mark. The player whose coin lands closest to the mark takes up then drops all the coins, and any coins that land heads up are won by that player

pitchbend /pích bend/ *n* an instrumental and vocal technique by which the pitch of a note is modified by raising or lowering it slightly

pitch-black *adj* so dark as to make seeing difficult or impossible

pitchblende /pích blend/ *n* a dark-coloured form of the mineral uraninite. Use: source of uranium and radium. [Late 18C. < German *Pechblende* < *Pech* 'pitch' + *Blende* (see BLENDE)]

pitch-dark *adj* same as **pitch-black**

pitched battle /pícht-/ *n* 1. a fierce battle fought by opposing forces who take up prearranged positions in close proximity to each other 2. a bitter conflict or confrontation ○ *a pitched battle between delegates and party leaders*

pitcher[1] /píchər/ *n* 1. a container for liquids with a single handle and a lip or spout for pouring 2. a leaf of the pitcher plant [13C. Via Old French *pichier* < medieval Latin *bicarium*]

pitcher[2] /píchər/ *n* 1. in baseball, the player on the mound who throws the ball to the batter 2. a paving stone, especially one made of granite [Early 18C. < PITCH[1]]

pitcher plant *n* a plant with leaves shaped like a pitcher for attracting, trapping, and digesting insects. Family: Sarraceniaceae.

pitchfork /pích fawrk/ *n* PRONGED FARMING TOOL a farming implement with a long handle and two or three widely spaced, slightly curved prongs, used for lifting and moving hay ■ *vt* (**-forks, -forking, -forked**) 1. USE PITCHFORK TO MOVE HAY to use a pitchfork to lift, turn, or move hay 2. THRUST SOMEBODY INTO DIFFICULT SITUATION to cause somebody to become involved in a situation that is extremely difficult and unwanted [13C. Alteration of *pickfork*, after PITCH[1]]

pitch pine *n* 1. a pine tree that yields pitch or turpentine. Native to: eastern North America. Latin name: *Pinus rigida*. 2. the hard heavy resinous wood of a pine tree

pitchstone /pích stōn/ *n* a dark hydrated volcanic glass similar to obsidian

pitchy /píchi/ (**-ier, -iest**) *adj* 1. covered with or full of pitch 2. resembling pitch, especially in colour, smell, or consistency —**pitchiness** *n*

piteous /píti əss/ *adj* deserving pity, or causing feelings of pity [13C. < Old French *piteus* 'full of pity' < Latin *pietas* (see PIETY)] —**piteously** *adv* —**piteousness** *n*

pitfall /pít fawl/ *n* 1. a potential and usually unanticipated disaster or difficulty 2. a deep concealed hole in the ground intended as a trap

pith /pith/ *n* 1. TISSUE UNDER RIND OF CITRUS FRUITS the soft whitish fibrous tissue that lies under the outer rind of a citrus fruit 2. BOT TISSUE INSIDE STEM OF PLANT the central spongy tissue of the stem of a vascular plant 3. ANAT SPONGY INTERIOR OF BODY PART the soft spongy inner tissue of a part of the body such as a hair shaft or bone 4. CENTRAL PART OF SOMETHING the central and most important part of something such as an argument or discussion 5. VIGOUR strength or stamina ■ *vt* (**piths, pithing, pithed**) 1. BIOL CUT SPINAL CORD OF LABORATORY ANIMAL to cut or destroy the spinal cord of a vertebrate as part of a laboratory experiment 2. AGRIC KILL ANIMAL BY CUTTING SPINAL CORD to kill animals, especially cattle, by cutting through the spinal cord 3. REMOVE PITH FROM PLANT STEM to remove the pith from the centre of a plant stem [Old English *pipa* < Germanic]

pithead /pít hed/ *n* the top part of a mineshaft, including the machinery, equipment, and buildings

Pithecanthropus /píthi kánthrəpəss/ (*plural* **-pi** /-pī/) *n* same as **Java man** (*dated*) [Late 19C. < modern Latin < Greek *pithēkos* 'ape' + *anthrōpos* 'human being'] —**pithecanthropic** /-kan thróppik/ *adj* —**pithecanthropine** /-kánthrə pīn/ *adj* —**pithecanthropoid** /-kánthrə poyd/ *adj*

pith helmet

pith helmet *n* a lightweight hat made from dried pith or some other material, worn in hot climates to protect the head, face, and the back of the neck from strong sunlight

pithos /píth oss, pī́-/ (*plural* **-oi** /-oy/) *n* a large ceramic jar used in ancient Greece for storing oil or grain [Late 19C. < Greek]

pithy /píthi/ (**-ier, -iest**) *adj* 1. brief, yet forceful and to the point, often with an element of wit 2. relating to, containing, or resembling pith —**pithily** *adv* —**pithiness** *n*

pitiable /pítti əb'l/ *adj* 1. arousing or deserving pity or compassion 2. arousing or deserving contempt or derision —**pitiableness** *n* —**pitiably** *adv*

pitiful /píttif'l/ *adj* 1. arousing or deserving pity or compassion 2. arousing or deserving contempt or derision —**pitifully** *adv* —**pitifulness** *n*

SYNONYMS See *moving*.

pitiless /píttiləss/ *adj* 1. lacking in pity, mercy, or sympathy 2. extremely severe ○ *the blazing, pitiless sun* —**pitilessly** *adv* —**pitilessness** *n*

Pitjantjatjara /píchənchə chárrə/ (*plural same* or **-ras**), **Pitjantjara** /píchən járrə/ *n* 1. a member of an Australian Aboriginal people who live in the desert regions in the south of the continent 2. the Pama-Nyungan language of the Pitjantjatjara people. Native speakers: 2,100. [< Pitjantjatjara] —**Pitjantjatjara** *adj*

pitlane /pít layn/ *n* a part of the track of a motor racing circuit that leads into the pits or from the pits back to the main track

Pitlochry /pit lókhri, -lókri/ *town and tourist centre in Perth and Kinross, Scotland, situated on the River Tummel. Population: 2,541 (1991).

pitman /pítmən/ (*plural* **-men** /-mən/) *n* somebody who works in a mine, especially somebody who works at a coalface

piton /pee ton/ *n* a metal spike with an eye at one end driven into ice or a rock crevice and used for securing a rope when climbing [Late 19C. < French, 'eye-bolt']

Pitot-static tube /peetō-/ *n* a device consisting of a Pitot tube and a static tube, used to measure fluid velocity and especially as an air speed indicator in an aircraft [Early 20C. See PITOT TUBE]

Pitot tube *n* 1. an instrument placed in a moving fluid and used along with a manometer to measure fluid velocity 2. PHYS same as **Pitot-static tube** [Late 19C. After Henri *Pitot* (1695–1771), French physicist]

pit stop *n* 1. MOTOR SPORTS REFUELLING STOP FOR CAR DURING RACE a stop in the pits to allow a racing car to be refuelled and serviced during a race 2. BRIEF STOP DURING ROAD JOURNEY a brief stop during a journey by road to rest, refuel, use a toilet, or buy refreshments (*informal*) 3. PLACE TO MAKE PIT STOP a place to make a pit stop during a road journey (*informal*)

Pitt /pit/, **William, 1st Earl of Chatham** (1708–78) British politician. As secretary of state (1756–61), he was the most powerful politician in Great Britain and

effectively prime minister. He headed a new government from 1766 to 1768. Known as **Pitt the Elder**

> 'You cannot conquer America.'
> [William Pitt, *Speech to the House of Lords*; 18 November 1777]

William Pitt (the Younger)

Pitt, William (1759–1806) prime minister of Great Britain (1783–1801 and 1804–06). He was Great Britain's youngest prime minister, at the age of 24. During his first premiership, the Act of Union (1800) incorporated Ireland into the United Kingdom but he resigned following George III's refusal to accept Roman Catholic emancipation. He returned to office for a second administration in 1804. Known as **Pitt the Younger**

pitta[1] /píttə/ *n* a brightly coloured small bird. Native to: Australia, Asia, Africa. Genus: *Pitta*. [Mid-19C. Via modern Latin < Telugu *pitta* 'bird']

pitta[2] /píttə, peétə/, **pita, pitta bread, pita bread** *n* a flat round unleavened bread, originally from Southwest Asia, that can be opened to insert a filling [Mid-20C. < modern Greek *pētta*, *pit(t)a* 'bread, pie']

pittance /pítt'nss/ *n* a very small amount of something, especially money [13C. Via Old French *pietance* < medieval Latin *pietantia* 'pious or charitable gift' < Latin *pietas* (see PIETY)]

pitter-patter /píttər patər/ *n* LIGHT CONTINUOUS TAPPING SOUND a light, rapid, and continuous tapping sound, similar to the sound of raindrops falling on something ■ *vi* (**pitter-patters, pitter-pattering, pitter-pattered**) MAKE LIGHT CONTINUOUS TAPPING SOUND to make or move with a light, rapid, and continuous tapping sound ■ *adv* WITH LIGHT CONTINUOUS TAPPING SOUND with a light, rapid, and continuous tapping sound [15C. An imitation of the sound]

~~**pittiful**~~ incorrect spelling of **pitiful**

pittosporum /pi tóspərəm, píttə spawrəm/ *n* an evergreen bush with leathery leaves, often planted for hedges in warm regions. Flowers: white, purple, or greenish-yellow. Native to: Australasia, Southeast Asia, southern Africa. Genus: *Pittosporum*. [Late 18C. < modern Latin < Greek *pitta* 'pitch' + *sporos* 'seed'; from the resinous pulp around the seeds]

Pittsburgh /píts burg/ *city in southwestern Pennsylvania. It is the second largest city in the state. Population: 327,898 (2002 estimate).

Pitt Street farmer *n Aus* somebody who has money invested in rural properties, often for tax reasons, but who lives and works in the city of Sydney (*informal*) [After a principal street in Sydney]

pituitary /pi tyoó itəri/ *n* (*plural* **-ies**) 1. PHYSIOL same as **pituitary gland** 2. PHARM same as **pituitary extract** ■ *adj* PHYSIOL relating to or produced by the pituitary gland [Early 17C. < Latin *pituitarius* 'of slime or mucus' < *pituita* 'slime']

pituitary body *n* ANAT same as **pituitary gland**

pituitary extract *n* a pharmaceutical preparation made from substances obtained from the pituitary gland that is rich in beneficial hormones

pituitary gland *n* a small oval gland at the base of the brain in vertebrates, producing hormones that control other glands and influence growth of the bone structure, sexual maturing, and general metabolism

pit viper *n* a venomous snake that has heat-sensitive pits below its eyes used to detect prey. Rattlesnakes and copperheads are pit vipers. Native to: Central, North and South America. Family: Crotalidae.

pity /pítti/ *n* **1.** FEELING OF SYMPATHY a feeling of sadness because of another person's trouble or suffering, or the capacity to feel this **2.** REGRETTABLE THING a sad or regrettable thing ○ *It's a pity you couldn't make it.* **3.** MERCY a willingness to help or to forgive somebody ■ *vt* (**-ies, -ying, -ied**) FEEL PITY FOR SOMEBODY to feel pity for somebody ■ *interj* EXPRESSION OF SYMPATHY OR REGRET used to express sympathy or regret about something (*informal*) [13C. Via Old French *pité* < Latin *pietas* 'dutifulness, piety, compassion' (see PIETY)] —**pitying** *adj* —**pityingly** *adv* ◇ **have** *or* **take pity on somebody 1.** to feel pity for somebody **2.** to show mercy to somebody ◇ **(the) more's the pity** used to express regret, disappointment, or annoyance that something is the case (*informal*)

~~pityful~~ incorrect spelling of **pitiful**

pityriasis /pítti rī́ əssiss/ *n* a skin disease affecting humans and animals in which the skin comes off in dry flakes [Late 17C. Via modern Latin < Greek *pituriasis* < *pituron* 'corn husks']

più /pyoo/ *adv* more or increasingly (*used as a musical direction*) [Early 18C. Via Italian < Latin *plus*]

piupiu /pée oo pee oo/ *n* a skirt worn by Maori men and women for traditional ceremonies and dances, made from the leaves of the New Zealand flax [Late 19C. < Maori]

Piura /pee óora/ city in northwestern Peru on the Piura River. The nearby community of San Miguel de Piura, the oldest Spanish settlement in Peru, was founded in 1532 by the conquistador Francisco Pizarro. Population: 324,600 (1990).

Pius IX /pī́ əss/ (1792–1878) pope. (1846–78). His pontificate (1846–78) was marked by the loss of the Papal States, the declaration of papal infallibility, and condemnation of all forms of liberalism. Born **Mastai-Ferretti, Giovanni Maria**

Pius XII (1876–1958) pope (1939–58). He condemned modernism and Communism. He sought to prevent World War II, although his role in the war is the subject of controversy. Born **Pacelli, Eugenio**

Pius V, St (1504–72) pope (1566–72). During his pontificate, he aided French Roman Catholics in their persecution of the Huguenots, excommunicated Elizabeth I of England, and used the Inquisition to punish heretics. Born **Antonio Michele Ghisleri**

Pius X, St (1835–1914) pope (1903–14). During his pontificate he opposed modernism in the Roman Catholic Church, initiated changes to canon law, and introduced a new breviary. Born **Sarto, Giuseppe Melchiorre**

Piute *n, adj* LANG another spelling of **Paiute**

pivot /pívvət/ *n* **1.** MECH ENG POINT ON WHICH SOMETHING TURNS a pin, shaft, or point on which something turns **2.** CRUCIAL PERSON OR THING somebody or something that is essential to the success or effectiveness of an activity or event **3.** TURNING MOVEMENT a turning movement on a pivot or while standing in place **4.** MIL CENTRE POINT OF WHEELING MOVEMENT a person, group of people, or point that acts as the centre around which a military formation carries out a wheeling movement **5.** BASKETBALL OFFENSIVE POSITION OR PLAYER in basketball, an offensive position in which a player faces away from the opposing basket, relays passes, and screens other team members, or a player in this position ■ *v* (**-ots, -oting, -oted**) **1.** *vti* TURN ON PIVOT to turn on a pivot, or make something do this **2.** *vti* WHEEL OR SWING ROUND to wheel or swing round, or make something do this **3.** *vi* DEPEND ON SOMETHING to be dependent on somebody or something, usually a single person, thing, or factor **4.** *vt* PROVIDE SOMETHING WITH PIVOT to provide something with a pivot on which it can turn [15C. < French]

pivotal /pívvət'l/ *adj* **1.** vitally important, especially in determining the outcome, progress, or success of something **2.** relating to or functioning as a pivot

pivotman /pívvət man/ *n* **1.** somebody on whom the success of an organization depends **2.** BASKETBALL same as **pivot** *n* (sense 5)

pix[1] CINEMA, PHOTOGRAPHY, ARTS plural of **pic** (*informal*)

pix[2] *n* CHR another spelling of **pyx**

pixel /píks'l/ *n* a tiny dot of light that is the basic unit from which images on computer or television screens are made [Mid-20C. < PIX[1] + ELEMENT]

pixelated /píksi laytid/, **pixellated** *adj* describes an image on a computer or television screen that is made up of pixels, especially one that is unclear or distorted [Mid-20C. < PIXEL, after PIXILATED]

pixie /píksi/, **pixy** (*plural* **-ies**) *n* a fairy or elf often depicted as having pointed ears, wearing a long pointed hat, and being cheerful and rather mischievous [Mid-17C. Origin ?]

pixilated /píksi laytid/ *adj* **1.** feeling bewildered **2.** intoxicated by alcohol (*informal*) [Mid-19C. < PIXIE, after words such as *elated, titillated*] —**pixilation** /píksi láysh'n/ *n*

pixy *n* another spelling of **pixie**

Pizarro /pi zaárō/, **Francisco** (1476?–1541) Spanish conquistador. He conquered the Inca Empire (1532), founded the city of Lima (1535), and was governor of Peru (1532–41).

pizazz *n* another spelling of **pizzazz** (*informal*)

pizza /péetsə/ *n* a flat round piece of bread dough baked with a variety of toppings, often including tomato sauce and cheese [Late 19C. < Italian, 'pie']

pizzazz /pə záz/, **pizazz, pizzaz, pzazz** *n* an attractive and exciting vitality, especially when combined with style and glamour (*informal*) [Mid-20C. Origin ?]

pizzeria /péetsə reé ə/ *n* a restaurant that specializes in making and serving pizzas [Mid-20C. < Italian < *pizza* 'pizza, pie']

pizzicato /pítsi kaátō/ *adv* by using the fingers to pluck the strings of an instrument that is normally played with a bow, especially a violin (*used as a musical direction*) ■ *n* (*plural* **-tos** or **-ti** /-ti/) a piece of music, or a section of a piece, played pizzicato [Mid-19C. < Italian, past participle of *pizzicare* 'pluck' < *pizzare* 'to prick, sting' < *pizza* 'point'] —**pizzicato** *adj*

pizzle /pízz'l/ *n Aus* the penis of an animal, especially a bull (*sometimes considered offensive*) [Late 15C. < Low German *pēsel* 'little penis' < Middle Low German *pēse* 'penis']

pk *abbr* **1.** pack **2.** ONLINE Pakistan (*used in Internet addresses*) See table at **domain name 3.** park **4.** peak **5.** MEASURE peck

PK *abbr* PARAPSYCHOL psychokinesis

PKI *abbr* E-COMMERCE public key infrastructure

pkt *abbr* packet

PKU *abbr* MED phenylketonuria

Pky, pky, Pkwy *abbr* parkway

pl *abbr* **1.** GRAM plural **2.** Poland (*used in Internet addresses*) See table at **domain name**

PL *abbr* **1.** GRAM plural **2.** LAW public law

Pl. *abbr* Place (*used in addresses*)

PL/1 *abbr* a high level computer programming language specially designed for both business and scientific applications. Full form **programming language 1**

PLA *abbr* Port of London Authority

Plaatje /plaáttki/, **Sol T.** (1876–1932) South African writer, linguist, and politician. He led a campaign against the Natives' Land Act of 1913. Among his works are *Native Life in South Africa* (1916) and *The Boer War Diary of Sol T. Plaatje, an African at Mafeking* (1973) (published posthumously). He was the First Secretary General of the South African National Native Congress, forerunner of the ANC. Full name **Plaatje, Solomon Tshekisho**

placable /plákəb'l/ *adj* easily placated (*formal*) [14C. Directly or via French < Latin *placabilis* < *placare* 'make calm'] —**placability** /pláka bílləti/ *n* —**placably** *adv*

placard /plá kaard/ *n* **1.** NOTICE DISPLAYED IN PUBLIC a large piece of card or board with a notice on it, displayed or carried in public **2.** SMALL CARD OR METAL PLAQUE a small card or metal plaque with a name on it, e.g. a doorplate ■ *vt* (**-ards, -arding, -arded**) **1.** PUT PLACARDS ON SOMETHING to put placards on or in something **2.** PUBLICIZE SOMETHING WITH PLACARDS to advertise or announce something using placards [15C. < French < Old French *plaquier* 'flatten, plaster' < Middle Dutch *placken* 'flatten, patch']

placate /plə káyt/ (**-cates, -cating, -cated**) *vt* to make somebody less angry, upset, or hostile, usually by doing or saying things to please him or her [Late 17C. < Latin *placat-*, past participle of *placare* 'make calm'] —**placation** *n* —**placatory** *adj*

place /playss/ *n* **1.** AREA OR PORTION OF SPACE an area, position, or portion of space that somebody or something can occupy ○ *This is a good place to plant the sapling.* **2.** LOCALITY a geographical locality, e.g. a town, country, or region ○ *People come here to work from lots of different places.* **3.** SQUARE OR STREET a public square or short street with residences on it **4.** DWELLING a house, flat, or other living accommodation ○ *a place of our own* **5.** LOCATION WITH PARTICULAR USE a building or location with a particular purpose ○ *the firm's place of business* ○ *their regular place of worship* **6.** POINT IN SOMETHING a point or position in something such as a book, film, or story ○ *I lost my place when you interrupted me.* **7.** PROPER POSITION the usual or proper position or location for somebody or something ○ *A place for everything, and everything in its place.* **8.** OPPORTUNITY TO STUDY an opportunity to study at a school or university ○ *hoping for a place at Oxford* **9.** STATUS somebody's social position or rank in an organization ○ *know your place* **10.** RESPONSIBILITY somebody's responsibility or right, especially as it relates to the person's role or status ○ *It's not your place to tell me what to do.* **11.** JOB a job or position ○ *was offered a place on the board* **12.** SOMEWHERE TO SIT somewhere for somebody to sit, e.g. at a table or in a theatre ○ *I'll keep a place for you next to me.* **13.** POSITION IN SERIES the position of somebody or something in a sequence or series **14.** HORSERACING WINNING, SECOND, OR THIRD POSITION the winning, second, or third position in a race, especially a horse race **15.** *N Am* HORSERACING SECOND POSITION the second position in a race, especially a horse race **16.** MATHS POSITION OF DIGIT IN NUMBER the relative position of a digit in a number ■ *vt* (**places, placing, placed**) **1.** PUT SOMETHING OR SOMEBODY SOMEWHERE to put something or somebody in a particular location or position ○ *placed the box on the table* **2.** PUT SOMEBODY IN PARTICULAR STATE to cause somebody or something to be in a particular state or condition ○ *Your actions placed all of us in danger.* **3.** SEE SOMEBODY IN PARTICULAR WAY to see or treat somebody or something as having a particular value or character ○ *He placed his family above everything else in his life.* **4.** REMEMBER SOMEBODY OR SOMETHING to recognize or remember somebody or something ○ *I can't place him.* **5.** ASSIGN SOMEBODY to assign somebody to a job, position, home, or the care of somebody else ○ *I'll see if I can place you with the sales team.* **6.** AIM SOMETHING CAREFULLY to aim or calculate something carefully in order to achieve the desired result ○ *Her observations were timely and well placed.* ○ *placed his punches well* **7.** ARRANGE FOR SOMETHING to arrange for something to be dealt with or take place ○ *placed an order for a new car* **8.** HORSERACING WIN OR BE SECOND OR THIRD to finish or cause somebody or something to finish in the winning, second, or third position in a contest, especially a horse race (*usually passive*) ○ *This horse has been placed in its last three outings.* [Pre-12C. Via French < Latin *platea* 'broad way' < Greek *plateia hodos*] ◇ **all over the place** (*informal*) **1.** everywhere **2.** in a state of disorder or confusion ◇ **a place in the sun** a position of success, happiness, or prosperity ◇ **give place (to) 1.** to be succeeded or superseded by somebody or something **2.** to make room for somebody or something ◇ **go places** to become successful (*informal*) ◇ **in place 1.** in position or ready for use **2.** in the position or location in which somebody or something belongs or ought to be ◇ **in place of** instead of or as a replacement for somebody or something ◇ **out of place 1.** not in the position or location in which somebody or something should be **2.** inappropriate or incongruous ◇ **put somebody in his** *or* **her place** to humble somebody who is behaving in an arrogant, presumptuous, or insolent way (*informal*) ◇ **take place** to happen ◇ **take the place of** to be a substitute for or replace somebody or something

SPELLCHECK Do not confuse the spelling of ***place*** and ***plaice*** (the fish), which sound similar.

placebo /plə séebō/ (*plural* **-bos** or **-boes**) *n* **1.** PRESCRIPTION WITHOUT PHYSICAL EFFECT something prescribed for a patient that contains no medicine, but is given for the positive psychological effect it may have because the patient believes that he or she is receiving treatment **2.** PHARM INACTIVE SUBSTANCE

a preparation containing no active ingredients, given to a patient participating in a clinical trial in order to assess the performance of a new drug given to other patients in the trial **3.** SOMETHING DONE TO PLACATE SOMEBODY something of no inherent benefit that is done or said simply to placate or reassure somebody **4.** CHR VESPERS OF OFFICE FOR DEAD in the Roman Catholic Church, the vespers of the office for the dead [13C. < Latin, 'I shall please' (first word in the Vulgate text of Psalm 114:9) < *placere* 'to please']

placebo effect *n* a sense of benefit felt by a patient that arises solely from the knowledge that treatment has been given

place card *n* a small card with somebody's name on it, put on a dining table to show where that person is to sit

placeholder /pláyss hōldər/ *n* a symbol in a mathematical or logical expression used to show a pattern, e.g. by representing a term in an equation or a statement in an argument

place kick *n* a kick used to resume play after a stoppage, especially in rugby or American football, in which the ball is propped or held up on the ground

place-kick *vt* to kick the ball, or score a goal or points by kicking the ball, while it is propped up on the ground —**place-kicker** *n*

placeman /pláyssmən/ (*plural* **-men** /-mən/) *n* somebody appointed to public office as a reward for services to a political party and allowed to use that office to satisfy personal greed or ambition

place mat *n* a protective mat for a place setting at a table

placement /pláyssmənt/ *n* **1.** ACT OF PLACING OR BEING PLACED the act of placing or arranging something in a position or location, or the fact of being placed or arranged in this way **2.** ARRANGING OF JOB OR HOUSING the task of arranging employment or accommodation for somebody, or an instance of this **3.** ARRANGING FOR SUITABLE CLASS the task of helping a student to find a suitable course or class, or an instance of this **4.** *UK* WORK EXPERIENCE AS PART OF STUDY a period of work for practical experience as part of an academic course. ANZ, N Am term **practicum** **5.** SPORTS SKILFUL PLAYING OF BALL in a sport such as tennis or rugby, a player's skill in accurately playing the ball **6.** *US* AMERICAN FOOTBALL PLACE KICK OR PLACING OF BALL in American football, a place kick for a field goal or point after a touchdown, or the positioning of the ball for such a kick

placename /pláyss naym/ *n* the name of a geographical area or feature such as a town, settlement, hill, or body of water

placenta /plə séntə/ (*plural* **-tas** or **-tae** /-tee/) *n* **1.** ANAT ORGAN IN UTERUS OF PREGNANT MAMMAL a vascular organ that develops inside the uterus of most pregnant mammals to supply food and oxygen to the foetus through the umbilical cord. It is expelled after birth. **2.** BOT PART OF OVARY OF PLANT the part of the ovary in a flowering plant that bears ovules **3.** BOT SPORE-BEARING MASS OF TISSUE the tissue in a nonflowering plant where the sporangia or spores develop [Late 17C. < Latin, 'cake' < Greek *plakous* 'flat cake' < *plak-* 'flat surface'] —**placental** *adj, n* —**placentary** *adj*

placentation /plássen táysh'n/ *n* **1.** BIOL FORMATION OR ATTACHMENT OF PLACENTA the process of forming a placenta during pregnancy, or the way in which the placenta is attached to the wall of the uterus **2.** BOT WAY OVULES ARE ATTACHED the way in which ovules are attached to the ovary of a plant **3.** BIOL PLACENTA TYPE the form, structure, or type of a placenta

place of safety order *n* in the United Kingdom, a court order enabling somebody to remove a child or young person temporarily to a place of safety from actual or likely abuse or neglect

placer /pláyssər/ *n Southwest US* a deposit of river sand or gravel containing particles of gold or another valuable mineral [Early 19C. < American Spanish, 'shoal']

place setting *n* a set of items such as cutlery, plates, and glasses arranged on a table to be used by one person at a meal, or the cutlery or plates alone

place value *n* the value of the place that a digit occupies in a numeral

placid /plássid/ *adj* tending or appearing to be calm and not easily excited, upset, or disturbed [Early 17C. Directly or via French < Latin *placidus* 'gentle' < *placere* 'to please'] —**placidity** /plə síddəti/ *n* —**placidly** *adv*

placing /pláyssing/ *n* the issuing of securities to the public through a stockbroker or another intermediary

placket /plákit/ *n* **1.** an opening in a woman's garment such as a skirt or blouse, either where it fastens or at a pocket **2.** a piece of cloth sewn in behind an opening in a woman's garment [Early 17C. Alteration of PLACARD]

placoderm /plákə durm/ *n* an extinct animal resembling a fish that was covered with bony plates and lived in the Palaeozoic era. Class: Placodermi. [Mid-19C. < Greek *plak-* 'flat surface']

placoid /plák oyd/ *adj* describes fish scales that have a flat base and a sharp projecting spine tipped with enamel. The subclass of fish that includes sharks, rays, and skates have placoid scales. [Mid-19C. < Greek *plak-* 'flat surface']

pladdy /pláddi/ (*plural* **-dies**) *n Ireland* a low flat island in Strangford Lough, Northern Ireland [Late 19C. < Old Norse, 'flat island']

plafond /plə fón, pla fóN/ *n* a ceiling, especially one that is highly ornamented [Mid-17C. < French, literally 'flat bottom']

plagal /pláyg'l/ *adj* **1.** describes a musical cadence or harmonic progression in which the subdominant chord is immediately followed by the tonic chord **2.** relating to or being a musical mode beginning on the note a fourth below the keynote of its equivalent authentic mode, but ending on the same final note [Late 16C. < medieval Latin *plagalis* < medieval Greek *plagios hēkhos* 'plagal mode']

plage /plaazh/ *n* a mark on the Sun's surface often associated with sunspots [Late 19C. Via French < Italian *plaggia* < late Latin *plagia* 'plain, shore']

plagiarise *vti* another spelling of **plagiarize**

plagiarism /pláyjərizəm/ *n* **1.** the process of copying another person's idea or written work and claiming it as original **2.** a piece of written work or an idea that somebody has copied and claimed as his or her own —**plagiarist** *n* —**plagiaristic** /pláyjə rístik/ *adj*

plagiarize /pláyjə rīz/ (**-rizes, -rizing, -rized**), **plagiarise** (**-rises, -rising, -rised**) *vti* to copy another person's idea or written work and claim it as original —**plagiarizer** *n*

plagio- *prefix* **1.** oblique, offset ○ *plagiotropism* **2.** disturbance ○ *plagioclimax* [< Greek *plagios* 'sideways' < *plagos* 'side' < Indo-European, 'be flat']

plagioclase /pláyji ə klayz/ *n* a feldspar consisting of sodium and calcium aluminium silicates [Mid-19C. < PLAGIO- + Greek *klasis* 'breaking'] —**plagioclastic** /pláyji ə klástik/ *adj*

plagioclimax /pláyji ō klī maks/ *n* a stable plant community that has arisen as a result of human intervention in the natural succession of communities

plagiotropism /pláyji ō trṓpizəm/ *n* the tendency of a plant's roots, stems, or branches to grow at an angle away from the vertical in response to a stimulus —**plagiotropic** /-trṓpik, -tróppik/ *adj* —**plagiotropically** *adv*

plague /playg/ *n* **1.** MED EPIDEMIC DISEASE a disease that spreads rapidly through a population, killing a great many people, or an outbreak of such a disease **2.** MED same as **bubonic plague** **3.** APPEARANCE OF SOMETHING IN LARGE NUMBERS a sudden appearance or outbreak of something unpleasant in very large numbers or with unusual frequency ○ *a plague of locusts* ○ *a plague of violence* **4.** SOMEBODY OR SOMETHING TROUBLESOME an affliction or extremely troublesome or annoying person or thing ■ *vt* (**plagues, plaguing, plagued**) (*often passive*) **1.** AFFLICT SOMEBODY to cause somebody severe and lasting distress, difficulty, or other affliction ○ *Falling prices and drought plagued the cattle industry.* **2.** ANNOY SOMEBODY CONSTANTLY to persistently harass or annoy somebody ○ *plagued him with requests for autographs* [14C. < Latin *plaga* 'blow, stroke, wound']

plaguy /pláygi/, **plaguey** (**-guier, -guiest**) *adj* causing trouble or irritation (*archaic informal*) —**plaguily** *adv* —**plaguy** *adv*

plaice /playss/ (*plural same*) *n* **1.** a large flat-bodied sea fish with brown skin and red or orange spots. Native to: European waters. Latin name: *Pleuronectes platessa*. **2.** a fish similar to and related to the European plaice. Native to: North American Atlantic. Latin name: *Hippoglossoides platessoides*. [13C. Via Old French *plaïs* < late Latin *platessa* 'flatfish' < Greek *platus* 'broad']

SPELLCHECK See *place*.

plaid /plad/ *n* **1.** TARTAN FABRIC a woollen fabric woven in a tartan or chequered pattern **2.** TARTAN PATTERN a tartan or chequered pattern **3.** TARTAN CLOTH WORN OVER SHOULDER a long rectangular piece of tartan material worn draped over the shoulder as part of traditional Scottish Highland dress [Early 16C. < Gaelic]

Plaid Cymru /plīd kúmri/ *n* the Welsh Nationalist Party [Mid-20C. < Welsh, 'party of Wales']

plain /playn/ *adj* **1.** CLEARLY VISIBLE clearly visible and not blocked or obscured ○ *in plain view* **2.** EASILY UNDERSTOOD clear to the mind or senses ○ *The plain fact is that they lied to us.* **3.** SIMPLE AND ORDINARY simple and ordinary, without ornamentation or frills ○ *plain homely food* ○ *a plain brown envelope* **4.** CANDID truthful and frank ○ *a maverick general known for his plain speaking* **5.** PURE not combined with any other substances ○ *plain water* **6.** UNCOLOURED OR UNPATTERNED lacking any pattern or coloration ○ *plain fabric* **7.** NOT ATTRACTIVE not pretty or good-looking ○ *plain looks* **8.** ADDS EMPHASIS TO NOUN used to emphasize a noun ○ *died of plain neglect* **9.** HANDICRAFT IN SIMPLEST KNITTING STYLE OR STITCH done in the simplest knitting style or stitch ■ *adv* **1.** ADDS EMPHASIS TO ADJECTIVE OR ADVERB used to emphasize an adjective or adverb ○ *just plain wrong* **2.** CLEARLY in a clear or candid way ○ *I'll tell you plain – I've had enough of this.* ■ *n* **1.** GEOG FLAT EXPANSE OF LAND a large expanse of fairly flat dry land, usually with few trees **2.** HANDICRAFT KNITTING STYLE OR STITCH the simplest knitting style or stitch ■ **plains** *npl* GEOG TREELESS LEVEL EXPANSES large expanses of level, almost treeless country in some central states of the United States [13C. Via French < Latin *planus* 'flat'] —**plainly** *adv* —**plainness** *n*

SPELLCHECK **plain** or **plane**? Do not confuse the spelling of *plain* and *plane*, which sound similar. ***Plain*** is more frequently used as an adjective and ***plane*** as a noun. As an adjective, ***plain*** means 'clearly visible', 'simply understood', or 'lacking any pattern or coloration', as in *a plain fabric*, whereas ***plane*** simply means 'flat and level' or 'two-dimensional', as in *a plane surface*. As a noun related to the adjective, ***plane*** denotes (among other things) a flat surface or a level, as in *different planes of existence*, whereas ***plain*** simply denotes a large expanse of flat land, as in *a treeless plain*. There are several other nouns ***plane***, denoting an aircraft, a tool, and a tree.

SYNONYMS See *unattractive*.

plain bread *n Scotland* bread cut from a loaf of white bread that has flat sides and a dark crust on the top and bottom

plainchant /pláyn chaant/ *n* MUSIC same as **plainsong**

plain chocolate *n* **1.** chocolate that is darker and less sweet than milk chocolate, with no milk added **2.** a sweet coated with plain chocolate

plain clothes *npl* ordinary civilian clothes when worn by a police officer on duty —**plain-clothes** *adj*

plain dealing *n* open and honest behaviour or business

plain flour *n* flour that has had no baking powder added to it. N Am term **all-purpose flour**

plain Jane /-jáyn/ *n* a woman who is regarded as not pretty or good-looking (*informal; often considered offensive*)

plain knitting *n* HANDICRAFT same as **garter stitch**

plain loaf *n Scotland* a white loaf baked in a batch, so that the sides are flat and there is a dark crust on its top and bottom only

plain sailing *n* something that is straightforward and easy to do

Plains Indian /pláynz-/ *n* a member of any of the Native American peoples who formerly lived on the Great Plains of North America

plainsman /pláynzmən/ (*plural* **-men** /-mən/) *n* a man who lives on a plain, especially somebody who

settled or lives on the Great Plains of North America

plainsong /pláyn song/ *n* church music that is intended to be sung in unison without instrumental accompaniment [15C. Translation of Latin *cantus planus*]

plain-spoken *adj* speaking or tending to speak truthfully and frankly —**plain-spokenness** *n*

plainswoman /pláynz wŏomən/ (*plural* **-women** /-wimin/) *n* a woman who lives on a plain, especially one who settled or lives on the Great Plains of North America

plaint /playnt/ *n* 1. a statement in writing to a court of law showing the grounds on which a complainant is bringing an action and asking for the grievance to be redressed 2. an expression of grief or sadness (*literary or archaic*) [12C. Via French < Latin *planctus* 'a beating of the breast' < *plangere* 'to beat']

plain text *n* a form of a message that is in ordinary readable language, and not in code

plaintiff /pláyntif/ *n* somebody who begins a lawsuit against somebody else (**defendant**) in a civil court [14C. < French (see PLAINTIVE)]

plaintive /pláyntiv/ *adj* expressing sadness or sounding sad [14C. < French *plaintive, plaintif* < *plaint* (see PLAINT)] —**plaintively** *adv* —**plaintiveness** *n*

plain weave *n* a weave in which the weft passes alternately under and over the warp, the threads forming a simple crisscross pattern

plait /plat/ *n* 1. WOVEN STRANDS something made by weaving three or more strands over and under each other, especially a length of hair with strands woven together like rope or a loaf made by weaving strands of dough together 2. HANDICRAFT same as **pleat** ■ *vt* (**plaits, plaiting, plaited**) 1. WEAVE STRANDS TOGETHER to weave three or more strands of something over and under each other, usually in order to form them either into something that looks like a rope or into a flat band 2. MAKE SOMETHING BY PLAITING to make something by plaiting strands together 3. HANDICRAFT same as **pleat** [15C. < Old French *pleit* < Latin *plicit-*, past participle of *plicare* 'fold']

plan /plan/ *n* 1. SCHEME FOR ACHIEVING OBJECTIVE a method of doing something that is worked out in advance 2. INTENTION something that somebody intends or has arranged to do (*often used in the plural*) ○ *What are your plans for Saturday?* 3. LAYOUT a drawing or diagram on a horizontal plane of the layout or arrangement of something 4. LIST OR OUTLINE a list, summary, or outline of the items to be included in something such as a piece of writing or a meeting 5. ARCHIT PERSPECTIVE DRAWING a scale drawing showing the various perspectives of something, especially a building ■ *v* (**plans, planning, planned**) 1. *vti* WORK OUT HOW TO DO SOMETHING to work out in advance how something is to be done or organized 2. *vt* INTEND TO DO SOMETHING to intend to do something, or make arrangements to do something 3. *vt* ARCHIT MAKE SCALE DRAWING OF SOMETHING to make a scale drawing of something, especially a building [Late 17C. < French, 'ground plan', alteration (after *plan* 'flat') of *plant* < Latin *plantare* (see PLANT)]

plan ahead *vi* to make preparations or arrangements for the future

plan for *vt* to make preparations and arrangements for something on the basis of what is expected to happen

plan on *vt* to intend to do something (*informal*)

plan out *vt* to make a detailed plan for something to be done or organized

plan- *prefix* same as **plano-** (*used before vowels*)

planar /pláynər/ *adj* flat or lying in a single geometric plane —**planarity** /play nárrəti/ *n*

planarian /plə náiri ən/ *n* a small flatworm that lives mainly in fresh water, is not a parasite, and has a three-branched intestine. Order: Tricladida. [Mid-19C. Via modern Latin *Planaria* < Latin *planarius* 'on level ground' < *planus* 'flat' (see PLAIN)]

planation /play náysh'n/ *n* the process of erosion and deposition by which water and wind currents produce a nearly level land surface [Late 19C. < PLANE²]

planchet /pláanchit/ *n* 1. a flat disc of metal ready to be stamped as a coin or medal 2. *US* a small metal container used to measure a radioactive substance

[Early 17C. < obsolete *planch* 'wooden plank, metal plate' < French *planche* (see PLANK)]

planchette /plaan shét/ *n* a small heart-shaped or triangular wooden board on two castors and with a pencil attached that spells out messages supposed to be from the spirit world when people touch it lightly [Mid-19C. < French, 'little plank' < *planche* (see PLANK)]

Planck /plangk/, Max (1858–1947) German physicist. He was the originator and developer of quantum theory and won the Nobel Prize in physics (1918). Full name **Planck, Max Karl Ernst Ludwig**

> 'We have no right to assume that any physical laws exist, or if they have existed up to now, that they will continue to exist in a similar manner in the future.'
> [Max Planck. Quoted in *The Universe in the Light of Modern Physics*, W. H. Johnston (tr.); 1931]

Planck's constant, **Planck constant** *n* a basic physical constant that is equal to the energy of a photon divided by its frequency, with an approximate value of 6.6261×10^{-34} joule-seconds. Symbol *h*

plane[1] /playn/ *n* AVIAT same as **aeroplane** ■ *vi* (**planes, planing, planed**) to travel by aeroplane [Late 20C. Shortening]

SPELLCHECK See *plain*.

plane[2] /playn/ *n* 1. FLAT SURFACE a flat or level surface 2. LEVEL OF REALITY a particular level of existence, mental activity, or achievement ○ *never felt he was on the same intellectual plane as the others* 3. MATHS TWO-DIMENSIONAL SURFACE OR SPACE a two-dimensional surface in which a straight line between any two points will lie wholly on that surface 4. AVIAT WING OR HYDROFOIL a flat surface that provides lift for an aircraft or hydroplane, e.g. a wing or a hydrofoil ■ *adj* 1. FLAT flat or level 2. MATHS TWO-DIMENSIONAL lying within a plane ■ *vi* (**planes, planing, planed**) 1. SKIM OVER SURFACE OF WATER to rise partly out of water and skim along the surface 2. AVIAT, BIRDS GLIDE to glide through the air without propulsion [Early 17C. < Latin *planus* 'flat'] —**planeness** *n*

REGIONAL NOTE See *plain*.

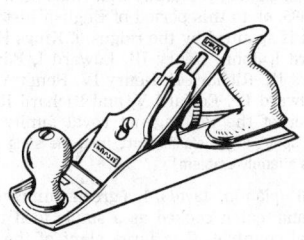

plane

plane[3] /playn/ *n* 1. WOODWORK TOOL FOR SMOOTHING WOOD a tool with an adjustable metal blade at an angle, for smoothing and levelling wood 2. CERAMICS SMOOTHING TROWEL a hand tool with a flat metal blade used for smoothing clay or plaster in a mould ■ *vt* (**planes, planing, planed**) WOODWORK SMOOTH WOOD to smooth or level wood with a plane [14C. Via French < late Latin *plana* < Latin *planare* 'make level' < *planus* 'flat']

plane[4] /playn/ *n* TREES same as **plane tree** [14C. Via French < Latin *platanus* < Greek *platanos* < *platus* 'broad', from the shape of its leaf]

SPELLCHECK See *plain*.

plane angle *n* an angle formed by two straight lines meeting in the same geometric plane

plane geometry *n* the branch of geometry that deals with two-dimensional figures

planer /pláynər/ *n* 1. a person or machine that planes, especially a machine used to plane wood or to cut flat surfaces into metal 2. PRINTING a flat block of wood used to hold type level in a chase [15C. < PLANE²]

plane sailing *n* sailing using a form of navigation that treats the Earth's surface as if it were flat for the purposes of calculating a ship's position and course

planet /plánnit/ *n* 1. ASTRON an astronomical object that orbits a star and does not shine with its own light, especially one of those orbiting the Sun in the solar system 2. ASTROL in astrology, the Sun, the Moon, or any of the planets of the solar system, except Earth, considered to influence events on Earth and the fate or character of individual people 3. same as **Earth** ○ *save the planet* [12C. Via French < Latin *planeta* 'planet, wandering star' < Greek *planētēs* 'wanderer']

CULTURAL NOTE **The Planets**, an orchestral work (1914–16) by British composer Gustav Holst. This suite for orchestra, organ, and chorus is divided into seven movements, each of which represents the astrological character of a planet with appropriate music.

plane table *n* a surveying instrument for use in the field, consisting of a drawing board mounted on adjustable legs with a sighting telescope and ruler

planetar /plánnə taar/ *n* a hypothetical young astronomical object of planetary mass that might have formed in the same way as a star

planetarium /plánnə táiri əm/ (*plural* **-iums** or **-ia** /-i ə/) *n* 1. BUILDING WITH IMAGE OF NIGHT SKY a building with a domed ceiling onto which movable images of the stars, planets, and other objects seen in the night sky are projected for an audience 2. PROJECTOR USED IN PLANETARIUM the special projector used to project images of the night sky for an audience in a planetarium 3. SOLAR SYSTEM MODEL a model of the solar system, often a working model showing how the planets revolve around the Sun (*archaic*) [Mid-18C. < modern Latin < late Latin *planetarius* 'astrologer' < *planeta* (see PLANET)]

planetary /plánnitəri/ *adj* 1. relating to, belonging to, involving, or typical of a planet 2. relating to or involving all of Earth, its people, or countries ■ *n* (*plural* **-ies**) ENG same as **planetary gear**

planetary gear *n* a gearwheel, especially in an epicyclic train, that travels around another, usually central gearwheel

planetary nebula *n* a glowing ring-shaped nebula of expanding gases surrounding a small, very hot white star

planetesimal /plánni téssim'l/ *n* a small rocky astronomical object thought to have orbited the Sun in the early stages of the solar system before coalescing with others to form the planets [Early 20C. < PLANET, after INFINITESIMAL]

planetoid /plánni toyd/ *n* ASTRON same as **asteroid** (sense 1) —**planetoidal** /plánni tóyd'l/ *adj*

planetology /plánni tólləji/ *n* the branch of astronomy that studies the origin and composition of the planets and other solid bodies in the solar system such as comets and meteors —**planetological** /plánnitə lójjik'l/ *adj* —**planetologist** *n*

plane tree *n* a tall deciduous tree that has leaves with pointed lobes, globular fruit clusters, and flaking bark. Native to: temperate northern hemisphere. Genus: *Platanus*. [< PLANE⁴]

planet wheel *n* a wheel in an epicyclic gear system that rotates around the wheel with which it meshes

plangent /plánjənt/ *adj* 1. making a loud and resonant or mournful sound 2. expressing or suggesting grief or sadness (*literary*) [Early 19C. < Latin *plangent-*, present participle of *plangere* 'beat'] —**plangency** *n* —**plangently** *adv*

plani- *prefix* same as **plano-**

planimeter /pla nímmitər/ *n* a mechanical instrument that measures the area of a plane figure as a pointer is moved around the figure's edge [Mid-19C. < French *planimètre* < Latin *planus* 'flat'] —**planimetric** /plánni méttrik/ *adj* —**planimetrically** *adv*

planish /plánnish/ (**-ishes, -ishing, -ished**) *vt* to toughen and smooth the surface of a metal by hammering or rolling it [Late 16C. < Old French *planiss-*, stem of *planir* 'to smooth' < *plain* 'flat' (see PLAIN)] —**planisher** *n*

planisphere /plánni sfeer/ *n* a representation on a flat surface of all or part of a sphere, especially a map of the night sky as seen from one location at a point

in time [< medieval Latin *planisphaerium* < Latin *planus* 'flat' + *sphaera* 'sphere' < Greek *sphaira*] —**planispheric** /plánni sférrik/ *adj*

plank /plangk/ *n* **1.** LONG FLAT PIECE OF WOOD a long flat piece of lumber sawn thicker than a board **2.** POLICY OF POLITICAL PARTY a policy that is part of a political party's platform ■ *vt* (**planks, planking, planked**) PUT PLANKS OVER SOMETHING to cover something with planks [13C. Via Old N French *planke*, variant of Old French *planche* < late Latin *planca* 'slab' < form of Latin *plancus* 'flat']

planking /plángking/ *n* **1.** planks used as building material **2.** the work of covering something with planks or laying planks

plank spanker *n* somebody who plays a guitar (*slang*)

plankter /plángktər/ *n* any of the tiny organisms that make up plankton [Mid-20C. Via German < Greek *plagktēr* 'wanderer' < *plazein* 'wander']

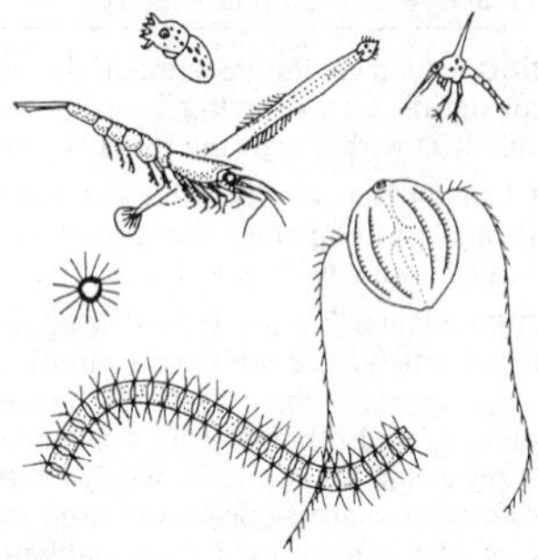

plankton

plankton /plángktən/ *n* a mass of tiny animals and plants floating in the sea or in lakes, usually near the surface, and eaten by fish and other water animals [Late 19C. Via German < Greek, 'wandering thing' < *plazein* 'wander, lead astray'] —**planktonic** /plangk tónnik/ *adj*

planned obsolescence /plánd-/ *n* a policy of designing and making products that quickly become outdated or wear out, so that they must be replaced

planner /plánnər/ *n* **1.** somebody who plans something, especially the development of an area **2.** a chart or notebook in which future events can be noted

planning permission /plánning-/ *n* authorization that must be obtained from a local authority before building a new building or structure or altering an existing one

plano- *prefix* flat ○ *planosol* ○ *plano-concave* [< Latin *planus* 'flat']

plano-concave /pláynō kón kayv/ *adj* flat on one side and concave on the other

plano-convex /pláynō kón veks/ *adj* flat on one side and convex on the other

planogamete /plánnəgə meet, plánnō gámmeet/ *n* a gamete, e.g. a spermatozoon, that is capable of moving

planosol /pláynə sol/ *n* a soil formation found on flat uplands that have high to moderate rainfall, in which a strongly leached upper layer overlies a layer of compacted clay or silt

plant /plaant/ *n* **1.** VEGETABLE ORGANISM a photosynthetic organism that has cellulose cell walls, cannot move of its own accord, grows in soil or water, and usually has green leaves. Kingdom: *Plantae.* **2.** SMALLER VEGETABLE ORGANISM a vegetable organism that does not have a permanent woody stem, e.g. a flower or herb rather than a bush or tree **3.** GARDENING CUTTING OR SEEDLING a cutting or seedling that is ready to be planted out **4.** INDUST FACTORY a factory, power station, or other large industrial complex where something is manufactured or produced **5.** INDUST EQUIPMENT AND MACHINERY the equipment and machinery necessary for carrying on an industrial or engineering activity **6.** LITERAT, THEATRE ACTION OR REMARK THAT BECOMES SIGNIFICANT an action or remark seemingly casually introduced into a narrative or play that turns out later to have great significance (*informal*) **7.** SOMETHING DISHONESTLY HIDDEN TO INCRIMINATE SOMEBODY something secretly put somewhere so that it can be discovered later, e.g. by the police, in order to incriminate somebody (*informal*) **8.** SOMEBODY SECRETLY INTRODUCED INTO GROUP somebody who has been placed secretly in an organization in order to spy on it or to influence its behaviour (*informal*) ■ *v* (**plants, planting, planted**) **1.** *vti* PUT SOMETHING INTO GROUND TO GROW to put something such as a seed, plant, or tuber into the ground to enable it to grow ○ *plant a tree* **2.** *vti* USE AREA FOR GROWING PLANTS to place young plants or sow seeds in an area of ground ○ *wanted to plant that bed with pansies* **3.** *vt* PUT SOMETHING DOWN FIRMLY to put something down or take a position firmly or decisively ○ *planted the stakes about five feet apart* **4.** *vt* PUT IDEA IN SOMEBODY'S MIND to introduce an idea into somebody's mind ○ *She planted the notion in my head that we should move.* **5.** *vt* PLACE SOMETHING IN CONCEALED POSITION to place something such as an explosive or listening device where it will not be easily found by others **6.** *vt* HIDE SOMETHING TO INCRIMINATE SOMEBODY to put something secretly where it can be discovered later, e.g. by the police, in order to incriminate somebody (*informal*) ○ *plant evidence* **7.** *vt* INTRODUCE SPY INTO GROUP to introduce somebody into an organization in order to spy on it or to influence the behaviour of its members (*informal*) ○ *planted an informer in the group* **8.** *vt* STRIKE SOMEBODY to land a blow on somebody (*informal*) **9.** *vt* FISHERIES PUT FISH IN BODY OF WATER to place spawn, young fish, or shellfish into an area of water so that they will develop there ○ *plant oysters* **10.** *vt* ESTABLISH COLONY OR COLONISTS to establish a colony or settlement in a place, or send people to a place as colonists or settlers [Pre-12C. < Latin *plantare* 'plant in the ground' < *planta* 'sole of the foot'] —**plantable** *adj* —**plant-like** *adj*

ORIGIN There did exist a Latin noun *planta* that meant 'shoot, cutting', of uncertain origin, but the meaning of the English noun ***plant*** is not found. It is likely that this sense developed after the classical Latin period and is linked with the action of pressing on a shovel, or some other tool, with the 'sole of the foot' in order to work the soil for planting. Latin *planta* 'sole of the foot' is ultimately from an Indo-European word meaning 'to spread', which is also the ancestor of English *flan, flat*[1], *flounder*[2], and *place.*

plant out *vt* to transplant a seedling that has been grown in a pot or in a sheltered place to open ground

Plantagenet /plan tájjənət/ *adj* relating to or belonging to the English royal family that ruled between 1154 and 1485, or to this period of English history. The period is spanned by the reigns of Kings Henry II, Richard I, John, Henry III, Edward I, Edward II, Edward III, Richard II, Henry IV, Henry V, Henry VI, Edward IV, Edward V, and Richard III. ■ *n* a member of the Plantagenet royal family [< Latin *planta* 'sprig' + *genista* 'broom', from the sprig of broom used as a family emblem]

plantain[1] /plántin, -tayn/ *n* **1.** a green fruit resembling a banana, eaten cooked as a staple food in many tropical countries **2.** a large plant of the banana family that produces plantains. Native to: tropical regions. Latin name: *Musa paradisiaca.* [16C. Via Spanish *plátano* 'plane tree' < Latin *platanus* (see PLANE[4])]

plantain[2] /plántin, -tayn/ *n* a small wild plant with leaves that grow mainly from the plant's base. Flowers: tiny, greenish, in spikes. Native to: northern temperate regions. Family: Plantaginaceae. [14C. Via French < Latin *plantago* < *planta* 'sole of the foot']

plantain lily *n* US same as **hosta**

plantar /plántər/ *adj* relating to, affecting, or occurring on the sole of the foot [Early 18C. < Latin *plantaris* < *planta* 'sole of the foot']

plantar wart *n* MED same as **verruca** (sense 1)

plantation /plaan táysh'n, plan-/ *n* **1.** LARGE ESTATE OR FARM a large estate or farm, especially in a hot climate, where crops such as cotton, coffee, tea, or rubber trees are grown, usually worked by resident labourers **2.** AREA OF PLANTED LAND an area of land on which trees or crops are planted **3.** GROUP OF CULTIVATED PLANTS a large group of cultivated plants, especially trees **4.** *N Am* ESTATE IN S UNITED STATES a large landed estate in the southern United States **5.** COLONY in former times, a colony or settlement **6.** COLONIZATION the act of colonizing a place (*archaic*)

plantcutter /plaánt kutər/ *n* a bird that has a short conical beak with a serrated edge and eats fruit, leaves, and buds. Native to: South America. Family: Phytotomidae.

planter /plaántər/ *n* **1.** LARGE CONTAINER a large decorative container for houseplants or small trees **2.** HEAD OF PLANTATION somebody who owns or manages a plantation **3.** PLANTING MACHINE a machine for planting seeds, tubers, or other plant parts **4.** SETTLER in former times, a settler or colonist **5.** HIST SCOTS OR ENGLISH SETTLER IN ULSTER a Scots or English settler who arrived in Ulster in the 17th century under official patronage

planter's punch *n* a drink made with rum, lime or lemon juice, sugar, water, or soda, and sometimes bitters

plant hormone *n* a hormone produced naturally by plants that activates or regulates their growth, or a synthetic equivalent used to promote growth in cultivated plants

plantigrade /plánti grayd/ *adj* describes an animal such as a bear or a human being that walks on the soles of the feet with the heels touching the ground ■ *n* an animal that walks on the soles of its feet [Mid-19C. Via French < modern Latin *plantigradus* < Latin *planta* 'sole of the foot' + *gradus* 'step']

plantlet /plaántlət/ *n* a young or very small plant

plant louse *n* INSECTS same as **aphid**

plantocracy /plaan tókrəssi/ (*plural* **-cies**) *n* a ruling class made up of the owners and managers of large plantations, or a society ruled by them

plant science *n* the scientific study of plants

plantsman /plaántsmən/ (*plural* **-men** /-mən/) *n* a man who has expert knowledge of garden plants and gardening

plantsperson /plaánts purss'n/ (*plural* **-people** /-peep'l/ or **-persons**) *n* somebody who has expert knowledge of garden plants and gardening

plantswoman /plaánts wŏŏmən/ (*plural* **-women** /-wimin/) *n* a woman who has expert knowledge of garden plants and gardening

planula /plánnyŏŏlə/ (*plural* **-lae** /-lī/) *n* a free-swimming larva of a coelenterate, e.g. a hydra. Planulae have cilia and usually a flattened oval body. [Late 19C. < modern Latin, 'little flat one' < Latin *planus* 'flat'] —**planular** *adj*

plaque /plak, plaak/ *n* **1.** INSCRIBED METAL OR STONE a small flat piece of metal, stone, or other hard material that has an inscription or decoration on it and is fixed to a wall or other surface, often to commemorate somebody or something **2.** DEPOSIT ON SURFACE OF TEETH a film of saliva, mucus, bacteria, and food residues that builds up on the surface of teeth and can cause gum disease **3.** DEPOSIT ON SKIN a small flattened patch or deposit, e.g. on the skin in psoriasis or on the inner wall of an artery in atherosclerosis **4.** CLEAR PATCH IN CULTURE a clear patch in a bacterial or cell culture caused by a virus destroying the cells **5.** SMALL BADGE OR BROOCH a small badge or brooch worn to show membership of or rank in an organization [Mid-19C. Via French < Dutch *plak* 'tablet' < *plakken* 'to stick' < Middle Dutch *placken* 'flatten, patch']

plash[1] /plash/ (*literary*) *n* LIGHT SPLASH a light splash or splashing sound ■ *v* (**plashes, plashing, plashed**) **1.** *vi* SPLASH IN OR THROUGH LIQUID to move in or through something liquid, scattering drops and making light splashing sounds **2.** *vt* SPLASH SOMETHING to splash or spatter a liquid [Early 16C. An imitation of the sound]

plash[2] /plash/ (**plashes, plashing, plashed**) *vt* same as **pleach** [15C. < Old French *pla(i)ssier* (see PLEACH)]

plashy /pláshi/ (**-ier, -iest**) *adj* (*literary*) **1.** liable to splash or be splashed **2.** wet and marshy

-plasia *suffix* growth, formation ○ *hyperplasia* [< modern Latin < Greek *plassein* 'to form, mould']

plasm /plazəm/ *n* **1.** BIOL same as **plasma 2.** protoplasm of a particular type [Early 17C. < late Latin *plasma* 'image, creation' (see PLASMA)] —**plasmic** *adj*

plasm- *prefix* same as **plasmo-** (*used before vowels*)

-plasm *suffix* material that forms or is formed ○ *protoplasm* ○ *neoplasm* [Shortening of PROTOPLASM]

plasma /plázmə/ *n* **1.** FLUID COMPONENT OF BLOOD the clear yellowish fluid component of blood, lymph, or milk,

excluding the suspended corpuscles and cells **2.** BLOOD SUBSTITUTE a blood substitute prepared by removing the cells and corpuscles from donated sterile blood and freezing the resulting fluid until it is needed **3.** IONIZED GAS a hot ionized gas made up of ions and electrons that is found in the Sun, stars, and fusion reactors. Plasma is a good conductor of electricity and reacts to a magnetic field, but otherwise has properties similar to those of a gas. **4.** GREEN CHALCEDONY a green variety of chalcedony. Use: gems, decorative ware. [Early 18C. Via late Latin, 'image, creation' < Greek, 'something moulded' < *plassein* 'to form, mould'] —**plasmatic** /plaz máttik/ *adj*

plasma cell, plasmacyte /plázmə sīt/ *n* a lymphocyte that produces antibodies and is derived from a B cell

plasmagel /plázmə jel/ *n* a form of cytoplasm that resembles jelly and often forms the outer layer of cells

plasmagene /plázmə jeen/ *n* a particle in the cytoplasm of organisms that can replicate itself and is thought to be able to pass on hereditary characteristics in the same way as a chromosomal gene —**plasmagenic** /plázmə jénnik/ *adj*

plasmalemma /plázmə lémmə/ *n* BIOL same as **cell membrane**

plasma membrane *n* BIOL same as **cell membrane**

plasmapheresis /plázmə férrəssiss/ *n* a process in which blood taken from a patient is treated to extract the cells and corpuscles, which are then added to another fluid and returned to the patient's body. An example of its use is the removal of harmful antibodies or immune complexes from the blood in autoimmune diseases such as myasthenia.

plasma screen *n* a very thin, high-definition television or computer display consisting of many pixel-sized gas-filled cells which emit light when an electric current is channelled through them

plasmasol /plázmə sol/ *n* a form of cytoplasm that is more fluid than plasmagel and often forms an inner layer in cells

plasmid /plázmid/ *n* a small circle of DNA that replicates itself independently of chromosomal DNA, especially in the cells of bacteria. Plasmids often contain genes for drug resistance and are used in genetic engineering, since they can be transmitted between bacteria of the same and different species.

plasmin /plázmin/ *n* a plasma enzyme that helps break down fibrin [Mid-19C. < French *plasmine* < *plasma* 'plasma']

plasminogen /plaz mínnəjən/ *n* the inactive precursor of plasmin

plasmo- *prefix* plasma ○ *plasmogamy* [< PLASMA]

plasmodesma /plázmō dézmə/ (*plural* **-mata** /-mətə/) *n* a very fine thread of cytoplasm that in some plants passes through openings in the walls of adjacent cells and forms a living bridge between them [Early 20C. < German *Plasma* 'plasma' + Greek *desma* 'bond']

plasmodium /plaz mṓdi əm/ (*plural* **-dia** /-di ə/) *n* **1.** a mass of protoplasm containing many nuclei that is a stage in the life cycle of some organisms, especially slime moulds **2.** a parasitic protozoan, especially one that causes malaria. Genus: *Plasmodium.* [Late 19C. < PLASMA + modern Latin *-odium* 'resembling' < Greek *-ōdēs* (see -OID)] —**plasmodial** *adj*

plasmogamy /plaz móggəmi/ *n* fusion between cells in some fungi in which the cytoplasm merges but the nuclei remain distinct

plasmolyse /plázmə līz/ (**-lyses, -lysing, -lysed**) *vti* to undergo plasmolysis, or make plasmolysis happen in a cell

plasmolysis /plaz mólləssiss/ *n* the shrinking of the protoplasm in a plant or bacterial cell away from the cell wall, caused by loss of water through osmosis —**plasmolytic** /plázmə líttik/ *adj* —**plasmolytically** *adv*

plasmon /pláz mon/ *n* the sum total of the genetic material in the cytoplasm, as opposed to the nucleus or nuclei, of a cell or an organism

-plast *suffix* living cell, small body ○ *spheroplast* [< Greek *plastos*, past participle of *plassein* 'form, mould']

plaster /plaástər/ *n* **1.** LIME MIXTURE FOR WALLS a mixture of lime, sand, and water that is applied as a liquid paste to the ceilings and internal walls of a building and dries to a hard surface **2.** STICKY BANDAGE a strip of adhesive material, usually with a dressing attached, for sticking over a cut or wound **3.** PIECE OF IMPREGNATED MUSLIN a piece of muslin spread with a curative preparation formerly used for placing over a wound or sore **4.** SCULPTURE, MED same as **plaster of Paris** (*often used before a noun*) ■ *vt* (**-ters, -tering, -tered**) **1.** COVER WALLS WITH PLASTER to apply plaster to the interior walls and ceilings of a building **2.** APPLY SOMETHING THICKLY to apply a thick layer of something to a surface, often in a vigorous or careless way ○ *She didn't bother with fancy brushwork, she just plastered the paint on.* **3.** STICK MASS OF THINGS OVER SURFACE to stick or spread objects in great profusion over a surface ○ *The walls were plastered with election posters.* **4.** MAKE SOMETHING APPEAR IN MANY LOCATIONS to cause a name, story, or image to appear in many conspicuous places ○ *woke up to find her name plastered over every front page* **5.** MAKE SOMETHING STICK TO SOMETHING to make something lie flat and smooth against something or stick to something, e.g. by wetting it ○ *He plastered his hair down with gel.* **6.** APPLY MEDICINAL PLASTER to apply a medicinal plaster to a wound or sore **7.** BOMBARD SOMEBODY to hit somebody or something repeatedly and effectively with blows or weapons (*informal*) [Pre-12C. Directly or via Old French *plastre* 'wall plaster' < medieval Latin *plastrum*, alteration of Latin *emplastrum* < Greek *emplastron* < *emplassein* 'plaster up' < *plassein* 'form, mould'] —**plasterer** *n* —**plastery** *adj*

plasterboard /plaástər bawrd/ *n* reinforced gypsum plaster sandwiched between two layers of strong paper in large sheets, used chiefly for interior walls. N Am term **drywall**

plaster cast *n* **1.** a rigid covering of plaster of Paris moulded round a broken limb to immobilize the fracture site during healing **2.** a copy or mould of an object such as a statue or footprint in plaster of Paris

plastered /plaástərd/ *adj* very drunk (*informal*) [Early 20C. < PLASTER 'hit hard']

plaster of Paris *n* a white powder, calcium sulphate, that when mixed with water forms a quick-hardening paste. It is used in the arts for sculpting and making casts, and in medicine for moulding casts round broken limbs. [Because it originated in Paris]

plaster saint *n* somebody who appears to be or makes a show of being a model of virtue, but often proves a hypocrite ○ *I mean, I'm certainly no plaster saint, but there are things even I wouldn't do.*

plasterwork /plaástər wurk/ *n* objects in plaster, especially the layer of plaster applied to interior wall surfaces or decorative plaster mouldings on ceilings or walls

plastic /plástik/ *n* **1.** SYNTHETIC MATERIAL an extremely versatile synthetic material made from the polymerization of organic compounds. It can be moulded into shapes or fabricated in many different forms for use in commerce and industry. **2.** CREDIT CARDS debit or credit cards as a form of payment as distinct from cash or a cheque (*informal*) ■ *adj* **1.** MADE OF PLASTIC made or consisting of plastic **2.** ABLE TO BE MOULDED able to be shaped or modelled **3.** OF MOULDING, MODELLING, OR SCULPTING relating to or involving moulding, modelling, or sculpting **4.** ARTIFICIAL seeming artificial and unnatural ○ *a plastic smile* **5.** ADAPTING EASILY adapting easily and readily to change **6.** OF PLASTIC SURGERY relating to or involving plastic surgery **7.** PHYS ABLE TO HAVE SHAPE PERMANENTLY CHANGED able to be bent, stretched, squeezed, or pulled out so that the resulting change of shape is permanent **8.** BIOL ADAPTING TO CONDITIONS capable of adapting to conditions during growth or development [Mid-17C. Directly or via French *plastique* < Latin *plasticus* < Greek *plastikos* 'mouldable' < *plastos*, past participle of *plassein* 'form, mould'] —**plastically** *adv*

plastic art *n* **1.** a three-dimensional art, e.g. sculpture, modelling or bas-relief work, pottery, or ceramics **2.** an art that represents subjects for visual appreciation, e.g. painting, sculpture, or architecture

plastic bomb *n* a bomb that employs a plastic explosive for its destructive force

plastic bullet *n* a large bullet made of PVC, sometimes used by the police for riot control in place of metal bullets

plastic explosive *n* an explosive with the consistency of putty that allows it to be easily moulded

Plasticine /plásti seen/ *tdmk* a trademark for a soft coloured modelling material used especially by children

plasticise, etc. *vti* another spelling of **plasticize, etc.**

plasticity /pla stíssəti/ *n* **1.** ABILITY TO BE MOULDED the condition of being soft and capable of being moulded **2.** ABILITY TO KEEP SHAPE AFTER CHANGE the quality that will allow a substance to retain its change in shape after being bent, stretched, or squeezed **3.** THREE-DIMENSIONAL QUALITY the three-dimensional quality of an image

plasticize /plásti sīz/ (**-cizes, -cizing, -cized**), **plasticise** (**-cises, -cising, -cised**) *v* **1.** *vti* to give plastic or mouldable qualities to something, or become plastic or mouldable **2.** *vt* to impregnate or coat something with plastic, usually to make it waterproof —**plasticization** /plásti sī záysh'n/ *n*

plasticizer /plásti sīzər/, **plasticiser** *n* an industrial compound that affects the physical properties of a substance to which it is added, making it more plastic

plastic money *n* debit and credit cards as distinct from cash or cheques

plastic surgeon *n* a physician who performs or specializes in plastic surgery

plastic surgery *n* the branch of surgery that is concerned with repairing especially external damage to the body, remedying impairments, or improving a person's appearance. Cosmetic surgery is a branch of plastic surgery.

plastic wrap *n N Am* a clear plastic film that sticks to itself and to surfaces. Use: to wrap food for storage.

plastid /plástid/ *n* a specialized component (**organelle**) in a photosynthetic plant cell that contains pigment, ribosomes, and DNA, and serves specific physiological purposes such as food synthesis and storage [Late 19C. < Greek *plastid-* < *plastos* 'moulded' (see PLASTIC)]

plastique /pla stéek/ *n* **1.** ARMS same as **plastic explosive** **2.** graceful poses or slow movements in dance [Late 19C. < French (see PLASTIC)]

plastisol /plásti sol/ *n* a suspension of synthetic resin particles convertible by heat into solid plastic [Mid-20C. < PLASTIC + SOL[2]]

plastoquinone /plástō kwínnōn/ *n* a compound found in plants that plays a role in photosynthesis [Mid-20C. < shortening of CHLOROPLAST + QUINONE]

plastron /plástrən/ *n* **1.** UNDER PART OF TORTOISE SHELL the under portion of the shell of a turtle or tortoise that is made up of several, often hinged, bony plates joined to the carapace by bridges located between the animal's legs **2.** WATER-REPELLENT GILL IN WATER INSECTS a tuft of water-repellent hairs on the bodies of some insects that live in water, having the function of trapping air bubbles and acting as an external gill **3.** STEEL BREASTPLATE a steel breastplate worn as part of medieval armour beneath a chain-mail tunic (**hauberk**) **4.** CHEST PAD FOR FENCERS a leather-covered pad for protecting the chest, worn by professional fencers [Early 16C. Via French < Italian *piastrone* 'large breastplate' < *piastra* 'metal plate'] —**plastral** *adj*

-plasty *suffix* surgical repair, plastic surgery ○ *angioplasty* ○ *rhinoplasty* [< Greek *plastos* (see PLASTIC)]

plat[1] /plat/ *n* **1.** *N Am* PLAN OR MAP a plan or map showing property boundaries and geographical features **2.** *Aus, N Am* PLOT OF LAND a small plot or area of land ■ *vt* (**plats, platting, platted**) *N Am* MAP AREA OF LAND to map an area of land to show boundaries and features [Early 16C. Probably alteration of PLOT]

plat[2] /plat/ *n* **1.** same as **plait** *n* (sense 1) (*archaic*) **2.** same as **pleat** ■ *v* (**plats, platting, platted**) **1.** *vt* same as **plait** *v* (senses 1–2) (*archaic*) **2.** same as **pleat** [14C. Alteration of PLAIT]

Plata, Río de la ♦ **Plate, River**

plat du jour /plaá doo zhóor/ (*plural* **plats du jour** /*pronunc. same*/) *n* the featured dish of the day on the menu of a restaurant [Early 20C. < French, 'dish of the day']

plate /playt/ *n* **1.** DISH FROM WHICH FOOD IS EATEN a flat or shallow object, usually round and made of earthenware, china, glass, plastic, or metal, from which food is eaten **2.** CONTENTS OF PLATE a portion of food consisting of the amount served on a plate ○ *a plate of vegetables* **3.** *N Am* SERVED FOOD a particular variety of prepared and served food ○ *a low-calorie plate* **4.** COLLECTION DISH FOR MONEY a shallow metal or wooden container passed round a church for members of the congregation to put money in **5.** DISH FOR GROWING CULTURES a small flat glass or plastic dish with a vertical rim, used in laboratories for growing cultures of microorganisms **6.** THIN SHEET a thin flat rigid sheet or slice of some material, usually of uniform thickness and with a smooth surface **7.** FLAT ANATOMICAL STRUCTURE a thin flat bony or horny anatomical part or formation **8.** THINLY BEATEN METAL metal produced in thin sheets of uniform thickness by beating, rolling, or casting **9.** PIECE OF SHEET METAL a piece, sheet, or slab of flat metal used to join or strengthen things **10.** PIECE OF ARMOUR PLATE a piece or sheet of specially strengthened metal used as part of the cladding of something such as a warship or tank **11.** SECTION OF SUIT OF ARMOUR a thin piece of steel or iron used in making a suit of armour, or armour made from plates **12.** ENGRAVED PLAQUE a metal plaque that bears an engraved or printed legend, name, number, or other inscription (*often used in combination*) **13.** AUTOMOT same as **number plate** **14.** COATING OF METAL a thin coating of metal, typically silver or gold, applied by electrolysis to copper or another base metal **15.** PRECIOUS TABLEWARE tableware and cutlery made out of gold or silver or covered with gold or silver plate **16.** PRIZE OF GOLD OR SILVER CUP a prize, especially in horseracing, consisting of a silver or gold dish or similar trophy **17.** RACE WITH PLATE AS PRIZE a race, especially a horse race, in which the prize is a silver or gold dish or similar trophy **18.** SECTION OF EARTH'S CRUST any segment of the Earth's crust that moves in relation to other segments as defined by the theory of plate tectonics **19.** ARTIFICIAL PALATE FITTED WITH FALSE TEETH a piece of plastic moulded to fit the mouth and holding false teeth or an orthodontic device such as a brace **20.** SENSITIZED SHEET OF GLASS a sheet of glass or other material coated with a light-sensitive film to receive a photographic image **21.** SURFACE FROM WHICH TO PRINT a template for printing, either an engraved metal sheet or a phototypeset page **22.** PRINT TAKEN FROM ENGRAVED SURFACE a print made from a printing plate, especially one inserted into a book on paper different from that on which the text is printed **23.** ILLUSTRATION IN BOOK a full-page illustration or photograph in a book, especially on glossy or coated paper **24.** ELECTRODE a thin flat piece of metal acting as an electrode in a rechargeable battery **25.** BASEBALL same as **home plate** **26.** SHOE WORN BY RACEHORSE a light shoe with which racehorses are shod in preparation for racing **27.** HORIZONTAL SUPPORTING TIMBER a horizontal timber laid along the top of a wall of a building to support the ends of timbers laid at right angles to the wall **28.** *US* CUT OF BEEF a thin cut of beef from the breast or ribs ■ *vt* (**plates, plating, plated**) **1.** COVER SOMETHING WITH METAL to cover metal or metal objects with a thin coating or film of another metal, often a precious or shiny one **2.** COVER SOMETHING WITH METAL SHEETS to cover something, e.g. a ship or tank, with sheets of metal for protection and strength **3.** SET UP TYPE IN PAGE FORM to set up movable type into page form ready for printing **4.** STRENGTHEN BROKEN BONE WITH PLATE to hold a fractured bone in position once it has been set by screwing it, on either side of the fracture, to a metal plate **5.** PUT FOOD ON PLATE to arrange food on a plate [13C. Via French < medieval Latin *plata* 'plate armour' < Greek *platus* 'flat'] —**plateful** *n* ◇ **have something handed to you on a plate** to obtain something without having to put any effort into obtaining it (*informal*) ◇ **on your plate** requiring your attention (*informal*) ○ *I can't do it, I have too much on my plate right now.*

Plate, River estuary of the Paraná and Uruguay rivers, lying between Uruguay and Argentina. Length: 300 km/190 mi. Spanish name **Río de la Plata**

plate armour *n* body armour made up of metal plates, as distinct from the chain mail that it superseded

plateau /pláttō/ *n* (*plural* **-teaus** or **-teaux** /-tōz/) **1.** RAISED AREA WITH LEVEL TOP an area of high ground with a fairly level surface **2.** STABLE PHASE a period or phase in something when there is little increase or decrease **3.** PHASE OF STAGNATION a phase in mental or physical development during which little headway is made ■ *vi* (**-teaus, -teauing, -teaued**) LEVEL OUT to reach a stable phase after a period of movement or development [Late 18C. < French, modern form of Old French *platel* 'small flat thing' < *plate* (see PLATE)]

plate boundary *n* an area on the margins of tectonic plates where seismic, volcanic, and tectonic activity takes place as a consequence of the relative motion of the plates

plated /pláytid/ *adj* **1.** OVERLAID WITH OTHER METAL covered with a thin layer of metal, especially a precious or shiny metal **2.** COVERED WITH PLATES protected and strengthened by a covering of plates **3.** KNITTED WITH TWO YARNS knitted with two kinds of yarn, one appearing on the front and one on the back of the fabric

plate glass *n* strong thick glass in large sheets used for windows and as a construction material for larger buildings (*hyphenated when used before a noun*)

platelayer /pláyt lay ər/ *n* somebody whose job is to lay and maintain railway lines. US term **trackman** [Mid-19C < *plate rail*, early type of rail with a flange along the outer edge]

platelet /pláytlət/ *n* a tiny colourless disc-shaped particle found in large quantities in the blood and playing an important part in the clotting process

platemaker /pláyt maykər/ *n* a person or machine that prepares plates for printing

platen /plátt'n/ *n* **1.** METAL PLATE IN PRINTING PRESS a flat metal plate in a printing press that holds the paper against the inked type **2.** TYPEWRITER ROLLER the cylindrical roller against which the paper is held in a typewriter, and against which the type strikes **3.** WORKTABLE the movable worktable of a machine tool [Mid-16C. < Old French *platine* 'metal plate' < *plat* 'flat' < Greek *platus*]

plater /pláytər/ *n* **1.** SOMEBODY OR SOMETHING THAT PLATES a person or machine that plates things **2.** RACEHORSE IN MINOR RACES a racehorse of average quality that is entered for minor races **3.** BLACKSMITH a blacksmith who specializes in shoeing racehorses

plateresque /pláttə résk/ *adj* relating to a heavily decorated architectural style fashionable in 16th-century Spain, reminiscent of elaborate silverware [Late 19C. < Spanish *plateresco* < *platero* 'silversmith' < *plata* 'silver']

plate tectonics *n* a theory that ascribes continental drift, volcanic and seismic activity, and the formation of mountain belts to moving plates of the Earth's crust supported on less rigid mantle rocks (*takes a singular verb*)

~~**plateu**~~ incorrect spelling of **plateau**

platform /plát fawrm/ *n* **1.** STAGE FOR PERFORMERS OR SPEAKERS a raised level area of flooring for speakers, performers, or participants in a ceremony, making them easily visible to the audience **2.** FLAT RAISED STRUCTURE a simple structure, especially one composed of wooden planks, serving as a base for keeping things clear of the ground **3.** RAISED AREA PROVIDING ACCESS TO TRAINS a raised structure beside the line at a railway station that makes it easier to get on or off and load or unload a train **4.** REAR STEP ON BUS OR TRAM an open step often at the rear of an old-style bus or tram for passengers to stand on as they get into or out of the vehicle **5.** PARTICULAR POLICY OF PARTY SEEKING ELECTION the particular publicly announced policies and promises of a party seeking election, understood as the basis of its actions should it come to power **6.** OPPORTUNITY FOR DOING SOMETHING a position of authority or prominence that provides a good opportunity for doing something **7.** OFFSHORE DRILLING STRUCTURE an anchored offshore structure with living and working accommodation above water level, from which oil or gas wells can be drilled or maintained **8.** STANDARD OPERATING SYSTEM a specific configuration of hardware, a specific operating system, or other software that is a standard for the development and operation of computers and of computerized devices such as personal digital assistants and mobile phones ○ *Some software will only run on a particular platform.* **9.** SHOE WITH DEEP SOLE a shoe or boot with a very thick sole **10.** RAISED AREA OF GROUND a flat raised area of ground [Mid-16C. < French *plateforme* 'diagram' < *plat* 'flat' + *forme* 'form']

platform game *n* a computer game that involves solving largely physical puzzles by finding the right sequence of moves

platform scale *n* a scale with a flat surface that supports the object to be weighed

platform ticket *n* a ticket allowing access to a station platform, formerly purchased by people who were not themselves travelling so that they could meet or see off passengers

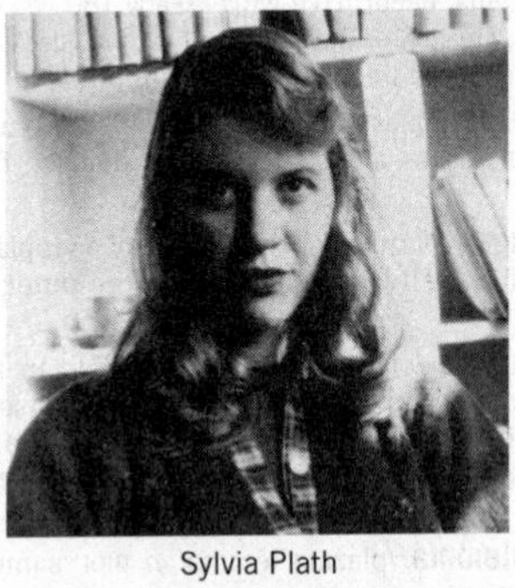

CORBIS/Bettmann

Sylvia Plath

Plath /plath/, **Sylvia** (1932–63) US poet. Her work is best known for its savage imagery and themes of self-destruction, anticipating her own suicide. Her works include the collected poems *The Colossus* (1960) and *Ariel* (1965) and the semiautobiographical novel *The Bell Jar* (1963). She was married to Ted Hughes.

> 'I am no shadow / Though there is a shadow starting from my feet. I am a wife. / The city waits and aches. The little grasses / Crack through stone, and they are green with life.'
> [Sylvia Plath, *Three Women*; 1962]

platin- *prefix* platinum ○ *platinic* [< PLATINUM]

platina /pláttinə, plə téenə/ *n* a naturally occurring platinum alloy [Mid-18C. < Spanish < *plata* 'silver'; because of its colour]

plating /pláyting/ *n* **1.** THIN COVERING OF OTHER METAL a thin covering of another usually more valuable metal applied to a metal surface ○ *gold plating* **2.** COVERING OF METAL PLATES metal plates used to make an exterior covering for something, e.g. a ship's hull **3.** APPLICATION OF COVERING OF METAL the process of applying a covering of metal or metal plates to the surface of something

platinic /plə tínnik/ *adj* relating to, containing, or consisting of platinum, especially in a valency state of four

platinize /plátti nīz/ (**-nizes, -nizing, -nized**), **platinise** (**-nises, -nising, -nised**) *vt* to coat, combine, or treat something with platinum or a platinum compound —**platinization** /plátti nī záysh'n/ *n*

platinoid /plátti noyd/ *adj* RESEMBLING PLATINUM resembling or containing platinum ■ *n* **1.** METAL CHEMICALLY SIMILAR TO PLATINUM a metal that is chemically similar to platinum, specifically iridium, osmium, palladium, rhodium, or ruthenium **2.** ALLOY SIMILAR TO PLATINUM an alloy of copper, zinc, nickel, and tungsten that resembles platinum in not tarnishing readily and in having a strong resistance to the passage of an electric current

platinous /pláttinəss/ *adj* relating to, containing, or consisting of platinum, especially in a valency state of two

platinum /pláttinəm/ *n* a precious silvery-white metallic element, highly malleable and ductile and highly resistant to chemicals and heat. Source: copper, nickel ores. Use: jewellery, catalyst, electroplating. Symbol **Pt**. See table at **element** ■ *adj* having sold 300,000 copies as a single or an album [Early 19C. < PLATINA] ◇ **go platinum** to reach the level of sales designated for platinum status (*refers to musical recordings*)

platinum black *n* platinum in the form of a fine black powder. Use: catalyst in organic synthesis.

platinum blonde, platinum blond *adj* describes hair that is pale silvery-blonde in colour (*hyphenated when used before a noun*)

platinum metal *n* platinum or any of the metals in its group, specifically iridium, osmium, palladium, rhodium, or ruthenium

platitude /plátti tyood/ *n* **1.** a pointless, unoriginal, or empty comment or statement made as though it was significant or helpful **2.** the making of platitudes [Early 19C. < French, 'flatness' < *plat* 'flat'] —**platitudinal** /plátti tyoódinəl/ *adj* —**platitudinous** /plátti tyoódinəss/ *adj*

platitudinize /plátti tyoódi nīz/ (**-nizes, -nizing, -nized**), **platitudinise** (**-nises, -nising, -nised**) *vi* to produce or talk in platitudes —**platitudinizer** *n*

Plato /pláytō/ distinctive dark-floored large crater on the Moon just north of Mare Imbrium, approximately 100 km/60 mi. in diameter

Plato (428?–347 BC) Greek philosopher. A disciple of Socrates and teacher of Aristotle, he founded the Athenian Academy. His works, written in dialogue form, include *Phaedo*, the *Symposium*, and the *Republic*.

> 'The true lover of knowledge naturally strives for truth, and is not content with common opinion, but soars with un-dimmed and unwearied passion till he grasps the essential nature of things.'
> [Plato, *The Republic*; 370? BC]

platonic /plə tónnik/ *adj* **1.** involving friendship, affection, or love without sexual relations between people who might be expected to be sexually attracted to each other **2.** perfect in form or conception but not found in reality [Mid-16C. Via Latin < Greek *Platōnikos* < *Platōn* 'Plato (the philosopher)'] —**platonically** *adv*

Platonic *adj* relating to Plato or his philosophy

Platonism /pláytənizəm/ *n* the philosophy or teachings of Plato, especially the theory that both physical objects and instances of qualities are recognizable because of their common relationship to an abstract form or idea [Late 16C. < modern Latin *Platonismus* < Greek *Platōn* 'Plato (the philosopher)'] —**Platonist** *n*

platoon /plə toón/ *n* **1.** a subdivision of a company of soldiers, usually led by a lieutenant and consisting of two to three sections or squads of ten to twelve people **2.** a body of people or things with a common purpose or goal [Mid-17C. < French *peloton* 'small ball' < *pelote* (see PELLET)]

platoon sergeant *n* a noncommissioned officer in the US army who assists a lieutenant in leading a platoon

Plattdeutsch /plát doych/ *n* LANG same as **Low German** [Mid-19C. Via German < Dutch *Platduitsch* 'low German'; from the flat landscape of N Germany where it is spoken] —**Plattdeutsch** *adj*

platteland /plát land/ *n* remote rural areas in South Africa [Mid-20C. Via Afrikaans < Middle Dutch, 'flat country']

platter /pláttər/ *n* **1.** LARGE FLAT DISH a large flat dish for serving food **2.** SERVED FOOD a variety of prepared and served food (*often used in combination*) *○ a seafood platter* **3.** RECORD a gramophone record (*dated informal*) **4.** COMPUT SURFACE OF HARD DISK the recording surface of a hard disk [14C. < Anglo-Norman *plater* < Old French *plat* < Greek *platus* 'flat']

platy¹ /pláyti/ (**-ier, -iest**) *adj* describes minerals that crystallize in thin sheets and tend to flake along cleavage planes [Mid-16C. < PLATE]

platy² /plátti/ (*plural* **-ys** or **-ies** or *same*) *n* a brightly coloured fish that bears live young, not eggs, often kept as an aquarium fish. Native to: Central America. Genus: *Xiphophorus*. [Early 20C. Shortening of modern Latin *Platypoecilus*, former genus name < Greek *platus* 'flat' + *poikilos* 'spotted']

platyhelminth /plátti hélminth/ *n* ZOOL same as **flatworm** (*technical*) [Late 19C. < modern Latin *Platyhelminthes* < Greek *platus* 'flat' + *helminth-* 'worm'] —**platyhelminthic** /-hel mínthik/ *adj*

platypus /pláttipəss/ (*plural* **-puses** or **-pi** /-pī/) *n* ZOOL same as **duck-billed platypus** [Late 18C. Via modern Latin *Platypus* < Greek *platupous* 'flat-footed' < *platus* 'flat' + *pous* 'foot']

platyrrhine /plátti rīn/ *adj* describes animals, especially New World monkeys, whose nostrils are well separated and point to either side ■ *n* a platyrrhine animal, especially a monkey [Mid-19C. Via modern Latin *Platyrrhini* < Greek *platurrhis* 'broad-nosed' < *platus* 'broad' + *rhis* 'nose']

plaudit /pláwdit/ *n* an expression of praise or approval *○ won plaudits for her skilful handling of the crisis* [Early 17C. < Latin *plaudite* 'applaud!' < *plaudere* 'to clap'; from the customary appeal made by Roman actors at the end of a play]

ORIGIN The Latin word *plaudere* 'to clap, applaud', from which *plaudit* is derived, is also the source of English *applaud* and *explode*.

~~plausable~~ incorrect spelling of **plausible**

plausible /pláwzəb'l/ *adj* **1.** believable and appearing likely to be true, usually in the absence of proof **2.** having a persuasive manner in speech or writing, often combined with an intention to deceive [Mid-16C. < Latin *plausibilis* 'deserving applause' < *plaus-*, past participle of *plaudere* 'clap'] —**plausibility** /pláwzə bílləti/ *n* —**plausibleness** *n* —**plausibly** *adv*

Plautus /pláwtəss/, **Titus Maccius** (254?–184 BC) Roman comic dramatist. His 21 surviving plays, modelled on Greek New Comedy, influenced both Shakespeare and Molière.

> 'He whom the gods love dies young, while he has his strength and senses and wits.'
> [Titus Maccius Plautus, *Bacchides*; 3rd-2nd century BC]

play /play/ *v* (**plays, playing, played**) **1.** *vi* ENGAGE IN ENJOYABLE ACTIVITIES to take part in an enjoyable activity, especially a game, simply for the sake of amusement *○ There were some children my mother wouldn't let me play with.* **2.** *vi* ACT IN FUN to do something for fun, not in earnest *○ He's only playing, he doesn't really mean it.* **3.** *vti* TAKE PART IN GAME OR SPORT to take part in a game or a sporting activity *○ likes to play football* **4.** *vt* COMPETE AGAINST SOMEBODY to compete against somebody in a game or sporting event *○ They play their biggest rival tomorrow.* **5.** *vti* ASSIGN OR HAVE POSITION ON FIELD to assign a player to a particular position on the field, or be assigned such a position **6.** *vt* HIT BALL to hit or kick a ball, puck, or shuttlecock in a particular direction *○ playing the ball straight down the line* **7.** *vt* HIT SHOT to make a shot or stroke in a sporting event **8.** *vt* USE PIECE OR CARD IN GAME to use a card from a hand in a card game or a piece in a board game **9.** *vti* ACT IN PARTICULAR MANNER to deal with a situation in a particular way to achieve a desired result *○ Whether you get what you want depends on how you play it.* *○ We decided to play it safe.* **10.** *vti* ACT PART IN PLAY to portray a character in a theatrical or film production *○'He that plays the king shall be welcome.'* [Shakespeare, *Hamlet*; 1602] **11.** *vt* PRETEND TO HAVE PARTICULAR QUALITY to pretend to be a particular type of person *○ Don't play the innocent with me.* **12.** *vti* PERFORM OR BE PERFORMED SOMEWHERE to perform a play or show a film at a particular theatre or cinema, or be performed or shown there *○ What's playing at the Luxor?* **13.** *vt* PERFORM DRAMATIC WORK BY SOMEBODY to perform the work of a particular dramatist **14.** *vt* PERFORM IN PARTICULAR PLACES to perform in particular places or types of place *○ playing the northern industrial towns* **15.** *vi* MAKE PARTICULAR IMPRESSION ON SOMEBODY to be received in a particular way by somebody, or make a particular impression on that person *○ a policy likely to play well with middle-class voters* **16.** *vti* PERFORM ON MUSICAL INSTRUMENT to use a musical instrument to produce music *○ He plays the trombone.* **17.** *vt* PERFORM MUSICAL WORK to use an instrument to perform a piece of music *○ play a sonata* **18.** *vt* MUSIC PERFORM COMPOSER to perform the music of a particular composer *○ Chopin is notoriously difficult to play well.* **19.** *vti* REPRODUCE RECORDED MUSIC to reproduce recorded music for listening, or be reproduced for listening *○ played my favourite CD* **20.** *vti* MOVE IRREGULARLY OVER SURFACE to move unsteadily or irregularly over a surface, usually in a pleasing way, or cause something to do this *○ sunlight playing on her brown hair* **21.** *vti* DIRECT LIGHT OR WATER to direct light or water over a surface or in a particular direction, or be directed in this manner **22.** *vt* LET FISH PULL ON LINE to tire an already hooked fish by letting it pull on the line as it tries to escape **23.** *vti* GAMBLE to gamble on a game of chance such as roulette or on horse races **24.** *vt* SPECULATE IN MARKET to speculate with securities or

commodities in a market ■ *n* **1.** ENJOYABLE ACTIVITIES activities bringing amusement or enjoyment, especially the spontaneous activity of young children or young animals (*often used before a noun*) *○ young cubs at play* **2.** DRAMATIC COMPOSITION a dramatic work written to be performed by actors on the stage, television, or radio **3.** ACTION DURING GAME the action during a game or series of games *○ Bad light eventually stopped play.* **4.** STATUS OF BALL the position or status of the ball or puck during a game, with regard to whether or not play can, according to the rules, legally continue *○ The ball was ruled to be out of play.* **5.** EFFECTIVE OPERATION a state in which something is effective, operative, or exercises an influence *○ The experts will come into play when the committee resumes its deliberations.* **6.** N Am ACTION OR MOVE IN GAME an action or move in a game *○ drilled the team in several new offensive plays* **7.** TURN IN GAME somebody's turn to move in a game **8.** HANDLING OF SHOT OR MOVE a player's handling of a shot or move or use of a piece or card **9.** GAMBLING participation in betting or gambling **10.** PLOY a ploy or deceptive act *○ The defendant's tears were just a play for your sympathy.* **11.** PUN a pun on a word **12.** FLICKERING MOVEMENT flickering or shimmering movement, especially of light through or on something **13.** ACTIVITY the free-ranging and varied activity of something, e.g. the imagination **14.** LOOSENESS the amount of looseness in something such as a rope, or the room for free movement between parts of a mechanism **15.** SCOPE the freedom to operate given to something or somebody *○ gave free play to his inventiveness* [Old English *pleg(i)an* < Germanic, 'to risk, exercise'] —**playability** /pláyə bílləti/ *n* —**playable** *adj* ◇ **make a play for somebody** *or* **something** to try openly to attract somebody or gain something ◇ **play fair** to act in an honest and reasonable way ◇ **play fast and loose** to act irresponsibly or recklessly without regard to facts or others' feelings ◇ **play hard to get** to avoid agreeing to a suggestion, invitation, or proposal, with the intention of appearing to be desirable or in demand ◇ **play it by ear** to improvise or adapt your response to a situation as it occurs rather than make plans in advance ◇ **play safe** to exercise caution and take few risks

play about *vi* same as **play around** (sense 2)

play along *vi* to pretend to agree with somebody or something in order to gain an advantage or avoid conflict

play around *vi* **1.** to engage in sexual activity with somebody other than a spouse or long-term partner **2.** to behave in an irresponsible or childish way

play at *v* **1.** *vt* to pretend to do or be something, usually without conviction or commitment *○ I was tired of playing at being an entrepreneur.* **2.** *vi* to engage in a game that involves role-playing (*refers typically to children*) *○ playing at doctors and nurses*

play back *vti* to reproduce recorded sound or video material

play down *vt* to represent something as being less important or significant than it is *○ While some patients exaggerate their symptoms, others play them down.* *○ The spin doctors are playing down the significance of the charge.*

play off *v* **1.** *vi* TAKE PART IN DECIDING GAME to take part in a deciding game to find the winner of a tied contest **2.** *vt* BRING PEOPLE INTO CONFLICT to set one person or group against another in order to gain an advantage *○ children playing their parents off each other* **3.** *vt* INTERACT WITH SOMETHING to interact with or react to somebody or something *○ The women are distantly related and the subplot plays off that coincidence.*

play on *v* **1.** *vt* TAKE ADVANTAGE OF SOMEBODY'S NEGATIVE FEELINGS to say or do things that intensify somebody's existing feelings of hope, fear, or insecurity, usually as a way of manipulating that person **2.** *vt* PUN ON SOMETHING to make a pun on a word **3.** *vi* HIT BALL INTO OWN WICKET in cricket, to hit the ball into your own wicket, putting yourself out of the game

play out *v* **1.** *vt* ACT OUT SOMETHING to act out a scene or situation that has been rehearsed or envisaged previously **2.** *vt* FINISH PLAYING SOMETHING to continue to play something to the finish or end *○ We'll play out this hand, then go home.* **3.** *vt* LET SOMETHING OUT GRADUALLY to release something such as a rope bit by bit **4.** *vti* US END to bring something to an end, or come to an end *○ The calamity has yet to play out.*

play up *v* **1.** *vt* EMPHASIZE to emphasize or exaggerate something *○ She played up her commercial know-*

pleura /plooͦrə/ n (plural **-rae** /-ree/ or **-ras**) a thin transparent membrane that lines the chest wall and doubles back to cover the lungs, thereby forming a continuous sac enclosing the narrow pleural cavity. The inner faces of the cavity are lubricated by fluid to ease breathing movements. ■ ZOOL plural of **pleuron** [15C. Via medieval Latin < Greek, 'side, rib'] —**pleural** adj

pleural cavity n the cavity formed between the pleural layer surrounding the lungs and the other layer lining the chest wall

pleurisy /plooͦrəssi/ n inflammation of the membrane (**pleura**) surrounding the lungs, usually involving painful breathing, coughing, and the buildup of fluid in the pleural cavity [14C. Via French < late Latin pleurisis, alteration of Latin pleuritis < Greek < pleura 'side, rib'] —**pleuritic** /plooͦ ríttik/ adj

pleuro- prefix **1.** side, lateral ○ pleurodont **2.** pleura, pleural ○ pleuropneumonia [< Greek pleura 'side, rib']

pleurocentesis /plooͦrə sen teéssiss/ n MED same as **thoracentesis**

pleurodont /plooͦrə dont/ adj **1.** describes teeth that are not rooted in the jawbone, but fused to its inner side, as, e.g. in some reptiles **2.** describes reptiles that have teeth not rooted in the jawbone, but fused to its inner side

pleurodynia /plooͦrə dínni ə/ n **1.** pain in the pleura, between the ribs or in the chest wall area **2.** an illness caused by a Coxsackie virus (not in technical use) [Early 19C. < PLEURO- + Greek odunē 'pain']

pleuron /plooͦr on/ n (plural **-ra** /-rə/) a membrane that encases the lung [Early 18C. Via modern Latin < Greek, 'side, rib']

pleuropneumonia /plooͦrō nyoo móni ə/ n inflammation of the membrane (**pleura**) surrounding the lungs and of the lungs themselves at the same time

pleuston /plooͦstən/ n small animals and plants such as algae that float on the surface of a pool of fresh water [Mid-20C. < Greek pleusis 'sailing', after PLANKTON] —**pleustonic** /ploo stónnik/ adj

Pleven /plév en/ capital city of Pleven Province, northern Bulgaria, situated about 129 km/80 mi. northeast of Sofia. Population: 127,945 (1996).

plexiform /pléksi fawrm/ adj resembling or in the form of a plexus or network [Early 19C. < PLEXUS]

plexor /pléksər/ n a small rubber-headed hammer formerly used to tap the body in a medical examination by percussion and in testing reflexes, e.g. by tapping the knee [Mid-19C. < Greek plēxis 'percussion' < plēssein 'to strike']

plexus /pléksəss/ (plural **-uses** or same) n **1.** a network of nerves, blood vessels, or other vessels in the body **2.** a complex network or interwoven structure [Late 17C. < Latin, past participle of plectere 'plait']

pliable /plíˍəb'l/ adj **1.** FLEXIBLE flexible and easily bent or moulded **2.** EASILY INFLUENCED easily persuaded or influenced **3.** ADAPTABLE adaptable to change [15C. < French < plier 'to fold, bend' (see PLY[2])] —**pliability** /plíˍə bílləti/ n —**pliableness** n —**pliably** adv

SYNONYMS **pliable, ductile, malleable, elastic, pliant**
CORE MEANING: able to be bent or moulded
pliable flexible and easily bent or moulded ○ a young, pliable tree branch **ductile** used to describe metals that can be easily drawn out into a long continuous wire or hammered into thin sheets ○ The alloy possesses a high proportion of tin to copper, giving the metal special ductile qualities. **malleable** used to describe metals or other substances that can be shaped without breaking or cracking ○ Iron possesses a very low carbon content, which makes it tough and malleable. ○ The sculptor used wet, malleable plaster to create a cast of her subject's head. **elastic** used to describe substances or materials that can be stretched without breaking and then return to their original shape ○ An elastic material such as rubber is easily pulled into long strings. ○ Add enough water to form a soft elastic dough and knead until smooth. **pliant** supple and easily bent ○ To execute this move, the wrist must be pliant and completely relaxed. **plastic** easily shaped, moulded, or modelled ○ The clay is plastic and easy to use.

pliant /plíˍənt/ adj **1.** SUPPLE supple and bending easily ○ a pliant tree branch **2.** ADAPTABLE easily adapted

or modified **3.** EASILY INFLUENCED easily persuaded or influenced [14C. < Old French, present participle of plier 'to fold, bend' (see PLY[2])] —**pliancy** n —**pliantly** adv —**pliantness** n

SYNONYMS See **pliable**.

plica /plíˍkə/ (plural **-cae** /-see/) n a fold or folded part, e.g. of skin [Early 18C. < medieval Latin, 'fold' < Latin plicare 'to fold, bend'] —**plical** adj

plicate /plíˍ kayt/, **plicated** /plíˍ kaytid/ adj **1.** arranged in folds like a fan **2.** describes rock with a folded wrinkled texture [Late 17C. < Latin plicat-, past participle of plicare 'fold, bend'] —**plicately** adv —**plicateness** n

plication /plíˍ káysh'n/, **plicature** /plíˍkəchər/ n **1.** PLEATING OF SIDES OF BODY ORGAN the pleating and stitching of the walls of a body organ in order to reduce its size **2.** ACT OF FOLDING the act of folding, or the condition of being folded **3.** FOLD IN SOMETHING a fold or pleat in something

plié /plee ay/ n a ballet movement in which the knees are bent and the back is kept straight [Late 19C. < French, past participle of plier 'fold, bend' (see PLY[2])]

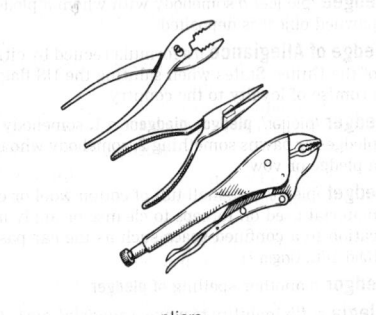

pliers

pliers /plíˍərz/ npl a hand tool with two hinged arms ending in jaws that are closed by hand pressure to grip something [Mid-16C. < PLY[1]]

plight[1] /plíˍt/ n a difficult or dangerous situation, especially a sad or desperate predicament [14C. < Anglo-Norman plit 'wrinkle, situation' (influenced by PLIGHT[2]) < Latin plicitum < past participle of plicare 'fold, bend']

plight[2] /plíˍt/ vt (**plights, plighting, plighted, plighted** or **plight**) to make a formal pledge, especially when promising to marry (dated) ○ plighted her word ■ n a formal promise or pledge (archaic) [Old English plihtan 'endanger' < pliht 'risk, danger' < Germanic, 'risk, pledge yourself'] —**plighter** n ◇ **plight your troth** to promise something solemnly, especially to marry somebody (dated)

plimsoll /plímsˈl/, **plimsole** n UK a light canvas shoe with a rubber sole [Late 19C. Probably < PLIMSOLL LINE, because the line around the shoe resembles it]

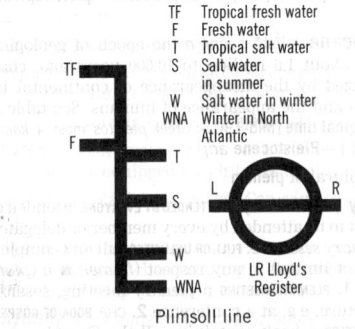

TF	Tropical fresh water
F	Fresh water
T	Tropical salt water
S	Salt water in summer
W	Salt water in winter
WNA	Winter in North Atlantic

LR Lloyd's Register

Plimsoll line

Plimsoll line, **Plimsoll mark** n a mark on the side of a merchant ship indicating the limit to which it can legally be submerged when loaded [After Samuel Plimsoll (1824–98), British politician and reformer]

plink /plíngk/ n HIGH-PITCHED SOUND a short high-pitched metallic sound ■ vti (**plinks, plinking, plinked**) **1.** MAKE HIGH-PITCHED SOUND to make a short high-pitched metallic sound, or cause something to do this **2.** SHOOT AT TARGET to shoot at or hit targets for fun, especially

targets that make a short high-pitched metallic sound when hit [Mid-20C. An imitation of the sound] —**plinker** n

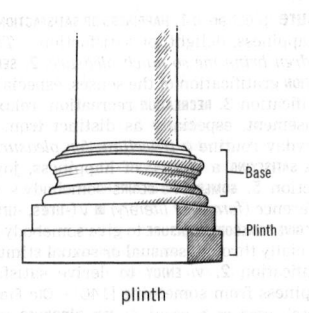

Base

Plinth

plinth

plinth /plinth/ n **1.** SUPPORTING BLOCK a square block beneath a column, pedestal, or statue **2.** SUPPORTING PART OF WALL the part of the wall of a building immediately above the ground, usually a course of stones or bricks **3.** PART OF DOORFRAME the square block at the base on each side of a doorframe **4.** FLAT BASE a flat block used as a base for something, e.g. underneath a heavy machine [Late 16C. Directly or via French < Latin plinthus < Greek plinthos 'tile, squared building stone']

Pliny (the Elder) /plínni-/ (AD 23–79) Roman scholar. His Natural History (AD 77) was a major source of knowledge until the 17th century.

Pliny (the Younger) (AD 62–113) Roman politician and writer. He was the nephew of Pliny the Elder and author of nine books of Letters (AD 100–109).

plio- prefix another spelling of **pleo-**

Pliocene /plíˍ ō seen/, **Pleiocene** n the epoch of geological time, 5 million to 1.6 million years ago, during which a hominid species (**Homo erectus**) first appeared. See table at **geological time** [Mid-19C. < Greek pleiōn 'more' + kainos 'recent', because it is later than the Miocene] —**Pliocene** adj

plissé /plee say/ n **1.** a permanently wrinkled finish given to a fabric by treating it chemically **2.** a fabric with a plissé finish [Late 19C. < French, past participle of plisser 'pleat' < pli 'fold' < plier (see PLY[2])]

PLO abbr POL Palestine Liberation Organization

plod /plod/ vi (**plods, plodding, plodded**) **1.** WALK HEAVILY to walk with a slow heavy tread **2.** WORK SLOWLY BUT STEADILY to work slowly but steadily, especially on something uninteresting or laborious ■ n **1.** SLOW HEAVY STEPS a walk with slow heavy steps **2.** SOUND OF SOMEBODY PLODDING the sound of slow heavy steps **3.** LABORIOUS TASK a task involving long and laborious work **4.** POLICE OFFICER a police officer, especially one of lower rank (informal insult) [Mid-16C. Probably to suggest the motion] —**plodder** n —**plodding** adj —**ploddingly** adv

-ploid suffix having a chromosome number in a particular relationship to the basic number of chromosomes in a group ○ tetraploid [< DIPLOID and HAPLOID]

ploidy /plóydi/ n the multiple of the number of chromosome sets in a cell

Ploieşti /plaw yéshtyə/ city in southeastern Romania. It is the capital of Prahova County and centre of the national oil industry. Population: 253,623 (1997).

plonk[1] /plongk/ v (**plonks, plonking, plonked**). **1.** vi DROP HEAVILY OR SUDDENLY to drop, be dropped, or sit down heavily or suddenly (informal) **2.** vt LAY SOMETHING DOWN HEAVILY OR SUDDENLY to drop or lay something down heavily or suddenly, often with deliberate emphasis (informal) ○ She plonked the book down in front of me. **3.** vi PLAY MUSIC INEXPRESSIVELY to play a musical instrument without much expression or skill ■ n ACTION OR SOUND OF SUDDEN FALL the thudding action or sound of a sudden heavy fall (informal) ■ adv WITH SOUND OF SOMETHING HEAVY FALLING with the sound or action of somebody or something heavy falling suddenly (informal) ○ It landed plonk in my lap. [Late 19C. An imitation of the sound]

plonk[2] /plongk/ n cheap inferior wine (informal) [Mid-20C. Shortening of plink-plonk, origin ?]

plonker /plóngkər/ *n* **1.** an offensive term that deliberately insults somebody's intelligence or common sense (*slang offensive insult*) **2.** an offensive term for a penis (*slang*) [Mid-19C. < PLONK[1]]

plop /plop/ *n* **1.** SOUND OF SOMETHING DROPPING INTO WATER the sound made by something dropping into water without making a large splash **2.** PIECE OF EXCREMENT a piece of human or animal excrement, or an act of excreting faeces (*informal; usually used by or to children*) ■ *v* (**plops, plopping, plopped**) **1.** *vti* FALL OR DROP SOMETHING WITH PLOP to fall into water without making a large splash, or make somebody or something do this **2.** *vi* DROP DOWN QUICKLY AND HEAVILY to drop or sit down quickly and heavily ○ *He plopped down on the nearest chair.* ■ *adv* WITH PLOP with a plopping sound or action ■ *interj* IMITATES SOUND OF DROPPING INTO WATER used to imitate the sound of somebody or something dropping into water without splashing [Early 19C. An imitation of the sound]

plosion /plṓzh'n/ *n* the sound made by a sudden release of breath in pronouncing some sounds, especially a stop consonant [Early 20C. Back-formation < EXPLOSION]

plosive /plṓssiv/ *adj* describes a consonant such as the 'p' in 'pear' that is pronounced by completely closing the breath passage and then releasing air ■ *n* a consonant pronounced with a sudden release of breath [Late 19C. Back-formation < EXPLOSIVE]

plot /plot/ *n* **1.** SECRET HOSTILE PLAN a plan decided on in secret, especially to bring about an illegal or subversive act **2.** STORY LINE the story or sequence of events in something such as a novel, play, or film **3.** PIECE OF GROUND a small piece of ground **4.** *US* ARCHIT PLAN OF BUILDING OR ESTATE an architectural plan of a building or estate **5.** *N Am* CHART a graph, chart, or diagram of something ■ *v* (**plots, plotting, plotted**) **1.** *vti* MAKE SECRET PLAN to make a secret plan, especially to do something illegal or subversive with others **2.** *vt* MARK SOMETHING ON CHART to mark something on a chart, especially the course of a ship or aircraft **3.** *vt US* ARCHIT MAKE PLAN OF BUILDING OR ESTATE to make a plan or map of something such as a building or estate **4.** *vti* MARK POINTS ON GRAPH to mark points on a graph or diagram using coordinates, or be located on a graph by coordinates **5.** *vt* DRAW SOMETHING ON GRAPH to draw a line or curve through points marked on a graph or diagram **6.** *vt* PLAN EVENTS OF STORY to devise the sequence of events in a story or script [< Old English, 'area of ground', origin ?; in 'plan' senses, influenced by obsolete *complot* 'secret scheme' < Old French] ◇ **lose the plot 1.** to lose your self-control, especially in anger **2.** to become muddled or confused, e.g. as a result of dementia in later life **3.** to fail to make sense of something, especially a story

Plotinus /plə tínəss/ (AD 205–270) Egyptian-born philosopher, probably of Roman ancestry. He founded neo-Platonism.

plotter /plóttər/ *n* **1.** somebody who is involved in a secret plan, especially to do something illegal or subversive **2.** a computer output device that draws graphs and other pictorial images on paper, sometimes using attached pens. Large plotters are used in computer-aided design applications to produce more rapidly the engineering drawings and architectural plans once prepared by skilled draughtspeople.

plough back *vt* to invest profits from a business back into the business

plough in *vt* to contribute or devote something, especially money, to a project or place

plough into *vt* (*informal*) **1.** to crash into or hit something with a great deal of force ○ *We lost control and ploughed into the car in front.* **2.** to start a job or undertaking, especially with energy and determination

plough on *vi* to persist determinedly in spite of obstacles, opposition, or warnings (*informal*)

plough under *vt* to bury something by ploughing or digging ○ *Large tracts of forest had been ploughed under by the bulldozers.*

plough /plow/ *n* **1.** FARM IMPLEMENT a heavy farming tool with a sharp blade or series of blades for breaking up soil and making furrows, usually pulled by a tractor or draught animal **2.** HEAVY TOOL a heavy tool or machine used like a plough to cut a cleared route or channel, e.g. a snowplough **3.** WOODWORK NARROW-BLADED PLANE THAT CUTS GROOVES a plane with a narrow blade used to cut grooves in wood **4.** AGRIC PLOUGHED LAND land that has been ploughed ■ *v* (**ploughs, ploughing, ploughed**) **1.** *vti* MAKE FURROWS IN EARTH to break up soil and turn it over into furrows ○ *ploughing a field* **2.** *vti* CUT THROUGH SOMETHING to cut or force a way through something ○ *I ploughed my way through the crowd.* **3.** *vt* MAKE CLEARING IN SOMETHING to make a channel or cleared route in something ○ *ploughed the snow-covered roads* ○ *ploughed the snow from the roads* **4.** *vt* AGRIC PUT UNDER SOIL to put something such as fertilizer or a crop under the surface of the soil, using a plough **5.** *vti* WORK METHODICALLY to work at something and progress slowly and steadily ○ *We ploughed through the backlog of applications.* ○ *ploughing my way through pages of job ads* **6.** *vti* SAIL OVER WATER to sail through a stretch of water (*literary*) ○ *a ship in full sail, ploughing an azure sea* **7.** *vti* FAIL EXAM to fail an examination (*dated informal*) **8.** *vt US* OFFENSIVE TERM an offensive term meaning to have sexual intercourse with somebody (*slang*) [Old English *ploh* < Germanic, < N Italic] —**plougher** *n*

Plough *n* a group of the seven brightest stars in the constellation Ursa Major. N Am term **Big Dipper**

ploughboy /plów boy/ *n* a boy who leads one or more animals while they pull a plough

ploughman /plówmən/ (*plural* **-men** /-mən/) *n* somebody who operates a plough, especially a plough drawn by animals —**ploughmanship** *n*

ploughman's lunch *n* a cold lunch, typically served in a pub, consisting of a plate of bread, cheese, pickle or chutney, and a pickled onion [Probably from the belief that bread and cheese were the staple lunch of the ploughman in former times]

ploughman's spikenard *n* a plant with yellow flowers and purple bracts. Native to: Europe. Latin name: *Inula conyza.* [< the idea that spikenard could heal wounds incurred in working outdoors]

ploughshare /plów shair/ *n* the part of a plough that cuts the soil for the furrow

Plovdiv /plóv dif/ city in southern Bulgaria, the administrative centre of Plovdiv Region. Population: 344,326 (1996).

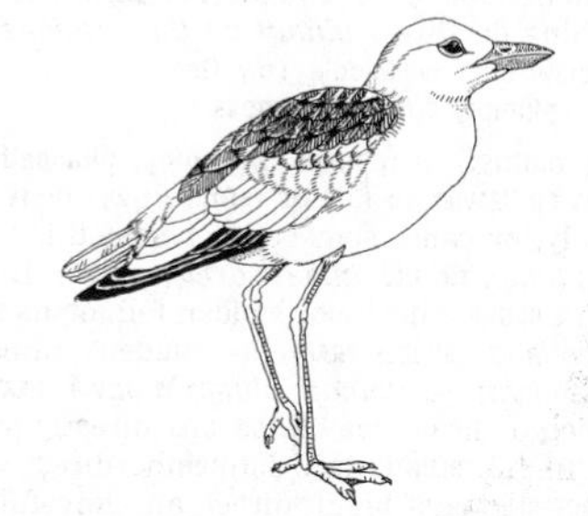

plover

plover /plúvvər/ (*plural* **plovers** or **plover**) *n* **1.** a shorebird that has a short beak and tail and long pointed wings. Family: Charadriidae. **2.** a bird that resembles a plover but is in a different family, e.g. an egyptian plover [14C. Via Anglo-Norman < assumed Vulgar Latin *pluviarius* < Latin *pluvia* 'rain' (see PLUVIAL); because it lives near water]

ploy /ploy/ *n* **1.** DECEPTIVE TACTIC a tactic or manoeuvre, especially one calculated to deceive or frustrate an opponent **2.** ACTIVITY something somebody does as a job, amusement, or pastime **3.** *Scotland* PIECE OF FUN a lighthearted or carefree piece of fun [Late 17C. Origin ?]

PLP *abbr* POL Parliamentary Labour Party

PLR *abbr* LIBRARIES Public Lending Right

PLS *abbr* ONLINE please

PLSS *abbr* MED portable life-support system

pluck /pluk/ *v* (**plucks, plucking, plucked**) **1.** *vt* TAKE SOMETHING AWAY QUICKLY to take something away swiftly, often by means of skill or strength **2.** *vt* QUICKLY REMOVE FEATHERS OR HAIR to pull out by the roots some or all of the feathers or hair from a bird or other animal **3.** *vt* PULL SOMETHING OFF OR OUT to pull something off or out of something else, e.g. fruit from a tree ○ *plucking flowers* **4.** *vt* TAKE SOMETHING CASUALLY to select something randomly or with no obvious reason **5.** *vti* TUG AT SOMETHING to tug quickly at something ○ *felt someone plucking at my sleeve* **6.** *vt* MUSIC PULL AND RELEASE STRINGS to play a stringed musical instrument by quickly pulling and releasing strings with a finger or plectrum ■ *n* **1.** BRAVERY courage and determination in meeting danger or difficulty **2.** ACT OF PLUCKING an act or instance of plucking something **3.** FOOD ANIMAL'S HEART, LIVER, AND LUNGS the heart, liver, and lungs of an animal, used as meat [Old English *pluccian* < Germanic] —**plucker** *n*

SYNONYMS See ***courage***.

pluck up *vt* to muster courage or audacity

plucky /plúki/ (**-ier, -iest**) *adj* showing courage and determination, especially in the face of danger, difficulty, or superior odds —**pluckily** *adv* —**pluckiness** *n*

plug /plug/ *n* **1.** FILLER FOR HOLE something used to fill and tightly close up a hole **2.** STOPPER FOR SINK a rubber or plastic stopper for the drainage hole in a sink or bath **3.** ELECTRICAL CONNECTION the connection at the end of the wire leading from an electrical device, with prongs or pins that allow it to fit into the socket of a power supply **4.** SOCKET an electrical socket, e.g. on a wall (*informal*) **5.** PUBLICIZING MENTION a favourable mention of something to publicize it, e.g. during a broadcast about something else (*informal*) **6.** WEDGE FOR SCREW a hollow piece of plastic pushed inside a hole to act as a holder for a screw that, when inserted, makes the plug expand and completely fill the hole **7.** AUTOMOT same as **spark plug 8.** CAKE OF CHEWING TOBACCO a cake of compressed or twisted tobacco, or a piece of it used for chewing **9.** SEISMOL same as **volcanic plug 10.** OLD HORSE an old and worn-out horse (*slang*) **11.** FISHING WEIGHTED LURE an artificial weighted lure that has hooks attached to it **12.** SMALL PIECE CUT FROM SOMETHING a small wedge cut away from something, especially as a test sample ■ *v* (**plugs, plugging, plugged**) **1.** *vt* CLOSE UP SOMETHING to close up a hole or gap **2.** *vt* GIVE SOMETHING FAVOURABLE PUBLIC MENTION to make a favourable mention of something in order to publicize it, e.g. during a broadcast about something else (*informal*) ○ *a chance to plug her latest novel* **3.** *vt US* SHOOT SOMEBODY to shoot somebody with a gun (*slang*) **4.** *vt* PUNCH SOMEBODY to punch or hit somebody (*slang*) **5.** *vi* WORK STEADILY to work at something steadily and persistently (*informal*) ○ *He is still plugging away in the insurance business.* [Early 17C. < Dutch] —**plugger** *n* ◇ **pull the plug** to discontinue the use of life support systems attached to a terminally ill person (*slang*) ◇ **pull the plug on something** to bring something abruptly to an end, especially by cutting off funds

plug in *vti* to connect an electrical appliance to a power source or to another electrical appliance, or be connected in this way

plug into *vti* to connect something to an electrical power source by means of a plug, or be connected in this way

plug and play *n* a technical standard that allows a peripheral device such as a printer or DVD drive to be connected to a computer and to function immediately without alteration of the system's configuration files

plugged-in /plugd-/ *adj N Am* closely involved with or well-informed about something (*informal*)

plughole /plúg hōl/ *n* an opening in something such as a basin or bath where liquid can drain away when a plug is removed

plug-in *adj* CONNECTIBLE BY MEANS OF PLUG capable of being connected by a plug to an electrical power source ○ *a plug-in hand drill* ■ *n* **1.** SOMETHING CONNECTED BY PLUG a device or appliance that may be connected by a plug to an electrical power source **2.** COMPUT DATA FILE ALTERING APPLICATION a data file that alters or extends the operation of an application

plug-ugly *adj* an offensive term meaning regarded as extremely unattractive (*informal*) ■ *n* (*plural* **plug-uglies**) *N Am* a tough and intimidating person, especially a gangster (*slang*) [*Plug*, origin ?]

plum /plum/ *n* **1.** DARK RED FRUIT a round or oval smooth-skinned fruit, usually red or purple, containing a flattened stone **2.** FRUIT TREE a tree that bears plums. Genus: *Prunus*. **3.** DRIED FRUIT a raisin or other dried fruit used in a cake, pie, or pudding (*archaic*) **4.** DARK REDDISH-PURPLE COLOUR a dark reddish-purple colour **5.**

SOMETHING CHOICE something that is highly desirable or enviable, especially a job or contract (*informal*) ■ *adj* **1.** DESIRABLE highly desirable or profitable (*informal*) ○ *a plum job* **2.** DARK REDDISH-PURPLE of a dark reddish-purple colour [12C. Alteration of Middle Low German, Middle Dutch *prūme*, Old High German *pfrūma* < Latin *prunum* (see PRUNE²)]

SPELLCHECK plum or **plumb**? Do not confuse the spelling of ***plum*** and ***plumb***, which sound similar. ***Plum*** denotes a fruit or, by extension, its dark reddish purple colour, as in a *a plum tree, a gorgeous plum velvet*, or something highly desirable, as in *a plum contract*. ***Plumb*** means 'a weight attached to a line', 'in a vertical position', or 'exactly', as in *a plumb line, plumb in the middle*. ***Plumb*** is the only spelling of the verb: *I had plumbed the depths of despair. Do you know how to plumb in a washing machine?*

plumage /plóomij/ *n* the feathers that cover a bird's body, considered collectively [14C. < French < *plume* (see PLUME)]

plumate /plóo mayt/ *adj* resembling, having, or producing feathers [Early 19C. < Latin *plumatus* 'feathered' < *pluma* 'down, feather']

plumb /plum/ *n* **1.** WEIGHT ATTACHED TO LINE a weight, usually made of lead, attached to a line and used to find the depth of water or to verify a true vertical alignment **2.** TRUE VERTICAL POSITION a true vertical position or alignment ■ *adv* **1.** IN TRUE VERTICAL POSITION in perfect alignment or a true vertical position **2.** EXACTLY precisely or exactly (*informal*) ○ *plumb in the middle* **3.** *N Am* COMPLETELY utterly or totally (*informal*) ○ *plumb lazy* ■ *vt* (**plumbs, plumbing, plumbed**) **1.** FULLY COMPREHEND SOMETHING to succeed in fully understanding something, especially something mysterious **2.** EXPERIENCE SOMETHING TO EXTREME DEGREE to experience something, especially something unpleasant, to an extreme degree ○ *had plumbed the depths of despair* **3.** USE PLUMB TO CHECK SOMETHING to find the depth of water or the vertical alignment of something with a plumb **4.** MAKE SOMETHING VERTICAL to make something properly vertical **5.** CONSTR INSTALL PLUMBING IN SOMETHING to equip something with plumbing [13C. Via Old French *plomb* 'lead weight' < Latin *plumbum* 'lead']

SPELLCHECK See *plum*.

plumb in *vt* to attach a device such as a washing machine to a system of inlet and drainage pipes

plumbago /plum báygō/ (*plural* **-gos**) *n* **1.** an evergreen Mediterranean or tropical plant of the leadwort family. Flowers: blue, white, or red, in clusters. Genus: *Plumbago*. **2.** MINERALS same as **graphite** [Early 17C. < Latin, 'lead ore, plumbago' < *plumbum* 'lead']

plumbate /plúm bayt/ *n* a weakly acidic compound formed by reaction of an lead oxide with an alkali [Mid-19C. < Latin *plumbum* 'lead']

plumb bob *n* the weight, usually a conical metal one, at the end of a plumb line

plumbeous /plúmbi əss/ *adj* relating to, resembling, or made of lead [Late 16C. < Latin *plumbeus* 'of lead' < *plumbum* 'lead']

plumber /plúmmər/ *n* somebody who installs and repairs water, drainage, or heating pipes and fixtures in a building [14C. Via French, 'lead worker' < Latin *plumbarius* < *plumbum* 'lead']

plumber's snake *n* CONSTR same as **snake** *n* (sense 3)

plumbic /plúmbik/ *adj* relating to or containing lead, especially in a valency state of four [Late 18C. < Latin *plumbum* 'lead']

plumbing /plúmming/ *n* **1.** PLUMBER'S WORK the work that a plumber does **2.** PIPES AND FIXTURES the pipes and fixtures that carry or use water or gas in a building **3.** USE OF PLUMB LINE the use of a plumb line to test depth or show a vertical alignment

plumbism /plúmbizəm/ *n* long-term lead poisoning (*technical*) [Late 19C. < Latin *plumbum* 'lead']

plumb line *n* a line with a weight attached, used to find the depth of water or to verify a true vertical alignment

plumbous /plúmbəss/ *adj* relating to or containing lead, especially in a valency state of two [Mid-19C. < Latin *plumbum* 'lead']

plumb rule *n* a plumb line attached to a board, used to check how vertical something is

plume /ploom/ *n* **1.** FEATHER a feather, especially a large or ornamental one **2.** FEATHERS USED AS CREST a feather or bunch of feathers used as a decoration, especially on a hat or helmet **3.** COLUMN OF SOMETHING a rising column of something such as smoke, dust, or water **4.** GEOL MOLTEN ROCK COLUMN a column of molten rock rising through the Earth's mantle **5.** BOT PART RESEMBLING FEATHER a plant part or formation that looks like a feather, e.g. the part of some seeds that allows them to be blown about by the wind **6.** TOKEN OF HONOUR a prize, awarded decoration, or token of honour ■ *v* (**plumes, pluming, plumed**) **1.** *vt* PREEN FEATHERS to preen, smooth, or clean the feathers **2. plume yourself** *vr* BE PROUD OF YOURSELF to take pride in or congratulate yourself on something **3.** *vt* DECORATE SOMETHING WITH FEATHERS to decorate something with a feather or feathers [14C. Via French < Latin *pluma* 'down, feather'] —**plumed** *adj*

plummet /plúmmit/ *vi* (**-mets, -meting, -meted**) **1.** DROP DOWNWARDS FAST to drop steeply and suddenly downwards ○ *plummeted into the ravine* **2.** SUDDENLY DECREASE to experience a sudden unexpected decrease in something such as value or price **3.** SUDDENLY BECOME PESSIMISTIC to decline suddenly, especially from a state of optimism to one of pessimism ■ *n* **1.** SUDDEN DECREASE a sudden unexpected decrease in something such as value or price **2.** CONSTR same as **plumb bob** [14C. < Old French *plomet* 'small lead ball' < Latin *plumbum* 'lead']

plummy /plúmmi/ (**-mier, -miest**) *adj* **1.** RESEMBLING PLUMS resembling, full of, or tasting like plums **2.** RICH AND RESONANT having a voice or tone that is rich, resonant, and mellow, and is thought to be characteristic of the British upper classes **3.** DESIRABLE highly desirable or of superior quality (*informal*)

plumose /plóomōss/ *adj* ZOOL same as **plumate** [Mid-18C. < Latin *plumosus* < *pluma* 'down, feather'] —**plumosely** *adv* —**plumosity** /ploo mróssəti/ *n*

plump¹ /plump/ *adj* **1.** SLIGHTLY OVERWEIGHT rounded and somewhat overweight (*sometimes considered offensive*) **2.** WELL-FLESHED having a pleasing amount of flesh ○ *a plump chicken* **3.** FILLED WITH SOMETHING rounded and filled with something ○ *a plump cushion* ■ *vti* (**plumps, plumping, plumped**) FATTEN OR ROUND to become fatter, rounder, or softer, or make something do this ○ *plump up the cushions* [15C. < Middle Dutch or Middle Low German *plomp* 'blunt, thick'] —**plumply** *adv* —**plumpness** *n*

plump² /plump/ *vti* (**plumps, plumping, plumped**) DROP ABRUPTLY OR HEAVILY to fall or come down heavily or suddenly, or cause somebody or something to do this ○ *plumped down into an armchair* ■ *n* **1.** ABRUPT FALL OR ITS SOUND a heavy or sudden fall, or its sound **2.** *Scotland* SUDDEN RAIN a sudden rainstorm (*nonstandard*) ○ *a thunder plump* ■ *adv* **1.** HEAVILY in a sudden or heavy way **2.** DIRECTLY directly or in a direct line **3.** BLUNTLY in a blunt and direct way ■ *adj* FORCEFULLY DIRECT blunt, direct, and forceful [13C. Probably < Dutch *plompen* or Low German *plumpen* 'to fall into water', an imitation of the sound]

plump for *vt* to suddenly choose or support somebody or something, often after hesitating ○ *The senator has decided to plump for new energy conservation measures.*

plumper /plúmpər/ *n* a pad worn by an actor between the teeth and the inside of the cheeks to make the face seem fatter

plum pudding *n* a rich steamed pudding made from flour, suet, dried fruit, and spices that is often flavoured with brandy or rum [< PLUM 'raisin']

plum tomato *n* an elongated firm-textured tomato. Use: in cooking and for tinned tomatoes. [< its shape]

plumule /plóo myool/ *n* **1.** the rudimentary primary shoot of a plant embryo **2.** a soft down feather of a young bird [Early 18C. < Latin *plumula* 'small feather' < *pluma* 'down, feather']

plumy /plóomi/ (**-ier, -iest**) *adj* **1.** like a feather or plume **2.** made of, covered with, or decorated with feathers or plumes

plunder /plúndər/ *v* (**-ders, -dering, -dered**) **1.** *vti* ROB PLACE OR STEAL GOODS to rob a place or the people living there, or steal goods using violence and often causing damage, especially in wartime or during civil unrest ○ *gangs of looters plundering the electrical shops* **2.** *vt* ROB PLACE BY FRAUD to rob a place or steal goods or money by fraudulent means ○ *a military government that had steadily plundered the country's wealth* **3.** *vt* GET SOMETHING BY SUPERIOR STRENGTH to gain or acquire something by superior strength or skill ○ *They plundered five goals in a one-sided game.* ■ *n* **1.** STOLEN GOODS something stolen by force, especially during wartime or civil unrest **2.** ROBBERY the theft of goods by force or fraud [Mid-17C. Via German *plündern* or Low German *plünderen* < Middle Low German *plunder* 'household goods'] —**plunderable** *adj* —**plunderer** *n*

plunderage /plúndərij/ *n* **1.** the embezzlement of goods aboard a ship **2.** goods embezzled aboard a ship

plunge /plunj/ *v* (**plunges, plunging, plunged**) **1.** *vti* MOVE SUDDENLY DOWNWARDS to move suddenly downwards or forwards, or move something in this way ○ *plunged into the undergrowth and disappeared* **2.** *vt* PUT SOMEBODY OR SOMETHING IN DIFFICULTIES to put somebody or something suddenly into an unpleasant or undesirable situation **3.** *vt* PUT SOMETHING QUICKLY INTO SOMETHING to put something quickly or firmly into something such as a liquid or container ○ *Drain the beans and plunge them into cold water.* **4.** *vi* BECOME INVOLVED ENTHUSIASTICALLY to become involved in something with great enthusiasm ○ *She plunged into student life.* **5.** *vi* EMBARK ON RECKLESS ACTION to begin a course of action suddenly and in a reckless or impetuous way ○ *warned against plunging into hostilities without trying diplomacy first* **6.** *vi* DESCEND PRECIPITOUSLY to descend abruptly or steeply ○ *The mountains plunged to the sea.* **7.** *vi* DROP SUDDENLY IN VALUE to drop suddenly and unexpectedly in value, price, or amount ○ *Prices plunged.* **8.** *vi* GAMBLE RECKLESSLY to gamble, speculate, or take risks in a reckless way (*informal*) ■ *n* **1.** ACT OF LEAPING INTO WATER a dive or leap into water ○ *a headlong plunge into the sea* **2.** SUDDEN DROP IN VALUE a sudden unexpected drop in value, price, or amount ○ *a 38% plunge in PC sales* **3.** SUDDEN RUSH a sudden or violent rush ○ *The dog made a plunge for the open door.* **4.** RECKLESS GAMBLE a reckless gamble or speculation (*informal*) [14C. Via Old French *plongier* < assumed Vulgar Latin *plumbicare* 'heave a sounding lead' < Latin *plumbum* 'lead'] ◇ **take the plunge 1.** to commit suddenly to doing something new, difficult, or irrevocable **2.** to get married or decide to get married (*informal humorous*)

plunge bath *n* a bath large enough for the whole body to be immersed

plunge pool *n* a small deep swimming pool used for cooling the body

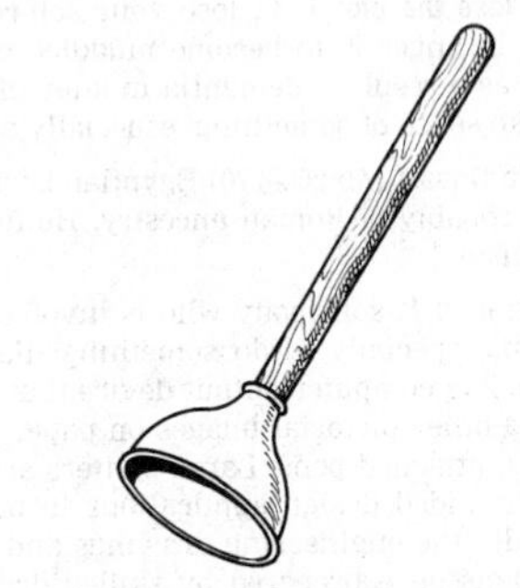

plunger

plunger /plúnjər/ *n* **1.** TOOL FOR CLEARING DRAINS a tool for clearing clogged drains, consisting of a rubber suction cup attached to a long handle **2.** THRUSTING MACHINE PART a part of a machine that thrusts or drops downwards, e.g. a piston **3.** GAMBLER somebody who gambles frequently and recklessly (*informal*)

plunging /plúnjing/ *adj* in a direction or at an angle that plunges downwards

plunk /plungk/ *vti* (**plunks, plunking, plunked**) **1.** TWANG STRINGS to twang the strings of a stringed instrument, especially in an inexpert or inexpressive way, or make a twanging noise **2.** *Aus, N Am* DROP DOWN to drop, or cause something to drop, heavily or suddenly ○ *He plunked down on the nearest chair.* ■ *n* **1.** TWANGING SOUND a twanging sound, e.g. of a string on a stringed instrument being plucked, especially in an inexpert or inexpressive way **2.** *Aus, N Am* SOUND OF HEAVY FALL the action or sound of a sudden heavy fall ○ *A stone hit the tin roof with a plunk.* **3.** *Aus, US* HARD BLOW a hard blow or hit (*informal*) ■

adv **1.** *US* EXACTLY precisely or exactly (*informal*) ○ *plunk in the middle* **2.** *Aus, US* WITH PLUNK with the action or sound of a sudden heavy fall [Early 19C. An imitation of the sound]

Plunket /plúngkit/ *adj NZ* relating to the activities of the Royal New Zealand Plunket Society, an organization devoted to the care of mothers and babies, founded in 1907 ○ *Plunket programmes* [Early 20C. After Victoria *Plunket*, wife of the New Zealand governor general and the society's first president]

Plunket room *n NZ* a mother-and-child health centre run by the Royal New Zealand Plunket Society

pluperfect /ploo púrfikt/ *adj, n* GRAM same as **past perfect** [15C. < Latin *plus quam perfectum* 'more than perfect']

plural /plóorəl/ *adj* **1.** REFERRING TO MORE THAN ONE having a grammatical form that refers to more than one person or thing **2.** CONCERNING MORE THAN ONE concerning, involving, or made up of more than one person or thing ■ *n* **1.** PLURAL CATEGORY the plural number category **2.** GRAM PLURAL FORM OF WORD the plural form of a word ○ *What's the plural of mouse in the computer sense?* [14C. Via French < Latin *pluralis* < *plus* 'more'] —**plurally** *adv*

pluralise *vti* another spelling of **pluralize**

pluralism /plóorəlizəm/ *n* **1.** EXISTENCE OF DIFFERENT GROUPS WITHIN SOCIETY the existence of groups with different ethnic, religious, or political backgrounds within one society **2.** SOCIOL SOCIAL POLICY AND THEORY the policy or theory that minority groups within a society should maintain cultural differences, but share overall political and economic power **3.** CHR HOLDING OF MULTIPLE OFFICES the holding of more than one office or position by somebody, especially in a church **4.** PHILOSOPHY THEORY OF VARIOUS KINDS OF REALITY the philosophical theory that reality is made up of many kinds of being or substance **5.** STATE OF BEING PLURAL the state or condition of being plural —**pluralist** *n* —**pluralistic** /plóorə lístik/ *adj* —**pluralistically** *adv*

plurality /ploor rálləti/ (*plural* **-ties**) *n* **1.** CONDITION OF BEING PLURAL the condition of being plural or numerous **2.** GREAT NUMBER OR PART OF SOMETHING a great number or part of something, particularly when this quantity represents more than half the whole **3.** *N Am* MARGIN GAINED BY ELECTION CANDIDATE the number of votes that an election winner gets, or the number exceeding the nearest rival, when no one has more than 50 per cent of the total votes cast **4.** CHR same as **pluralism** (sense 3)

pluralize /plóorə līz/ (**-izes, -izing, -ized**), **pluralise** (**-ises, -ising, -ised**) *v* **1.** *vti* to make something plural, or become plural **2.** *vi* to hold more than one office, especially ecclesiastical ones, at the same time —**pluralization** /plóorə līz záysh'n/ *n* —**pluralizer** *n*

plural marriage *n* LAW same as **polygamy** (sense 1)

plural voting *n* in former times, a system of voting that permitted some voters to vote more than once in an election or to vote in different constituencies

plus[1] /pluss/ *prep* USED FOR ADDING used to show that one number or amount is added to another ○ *The flight cost £480, plus £20 airport tax.* ■ *adj* **1.** MATHS RELATING TO ADDITION relating to, involving, or showing addition **2.** MATHS WITH FIGURE ON POSITIVE SIDE having a figure or value on the positive side of a scale or axis (*often written as '+'*) **3.** ELEC ENG ON ELECTRICAL POSITIVE SIDE relating to, involving, or on the positive side of an electrical circuit **4.** ADVANTAGEOUS favourable, desirable, or advantageous ○ *On the plus side, there's a big garden.* ○ *one of its plus points* **5.** SOMEWHAT MORE THAN PARTICULAR NUMBER somewhat higher than a particular number or amount ○ *earnings of £100,000 plus* **6.** SOMEWHAT MORE THAN SPECIFIC GRADE somewhat higher than a specific grade for academic work (*often written as '+'*) **7.** FUNGI REPRODUCING ONLY WITH OPPOSITE STRAIN reproducing as an alga or fungus only with an opposite strain ■ *n* (*plural* **pluses** or **plusses**) **1.** MATHS same as **plus sign 2.** POSITIVE QUANTITY a positive quantity or amount ○ *The figures show a plus.* **3.** ADVANTAGE something beneficial or advantageous (*informal*) ○ *Having her in the team is a real plus.* **4.** SURPLUS a surplus or excess ■ *conj* (*informal*) **1.** ⚠ AND and also ○ *Exports have been affected by cheap oil prices plus a strong pound.* **2.** ⚠ FURTHERMORE furthermore or additionally ○ *I'm too busy, plus I'm short of cash.* [Mid-16C. < Latin, 'more']

USAGE Avoid using **plus** to introduce an independent clause: *He is the head of the electrical engineering department, plus he has his own consulting firm.* Use instead: *As well as being the head of the electrical engineering department, he has his own consulting firm.* **Plus which** should not be used to introduce any sentence or clause. Avoid: *She is the head of a large college. Plus which, she is a TV personality.* Use instead: *In addition to being the head of a large college, she is a TV personality.* In formal writing avoid using **plus** in place of *and* as a conjunction joining two subjects in a sentence: *Lack of practice and* [not *plus*] *a knee injury have caused her to drop out.* This use of **plus** as a conjunction is also contested syntactically. Some writers regard it as a preposition, in which case the verb *have caused* in the last sentence would switch from plural to the singular *has caused* with the single subject being *lack*.

plus[2] /pluss/ *suffix* and much more besides (*informal*) ○ *The show is entertainment-plus.*

plus fours *npl* baggy trousers gathered and fastened just below the knee, worn mainly for sports or hunting ○ *golfers in their plus fours* [Because four inches longer in the leg than standard knickerbockers]

plush /plush/ *n* a rich smooth fabric with a long soft nap ■ *adj also* **plushy** /plúshi/ luxurious, expensive, or lavish (*informal*) [Late 16C. < obsolete French *pluche* < Old French *peluchier* 'to pluck' < Latin *pilus* 'hair'] —**plushness** *n*

plus sign *n* the symbol '+', used to show addition or a positive quantity

plus-size *adj* of a size of clothing that is much larger than average ○ *our new range of plus-size fashions* ■ *n* an item of clothing that is much larger than average, especially an item of women's clothing

Plutarch /plóo taark/ (AD 46–120) Greek historian, biographer, and philosopher. His *Parallel Lives* was used by Shakespeare as a source for his history plays.

> 'Caesar said to the soothsayer, "The ides of March are come"; who answered him calmly, "Yes, they are come, but they are not past".'
> [Plutarch, 'Life of Caesar', *Parallel Lives*; 1st-2nd century AD]

Pluto /plóotō/ *n* **1.** the planet in the solar system that is the smallest in diameter and is, on average, the furthest away from the Sun **2.** in Roman mythology, the god of the underworld and husband of Proserpina. He was the god of the dead and also of riches, since precious metals and crops were believed to come from his underground realm. Greek equivalent **Hades** (sense 2) [Via Latin < Greek *Ploutōn* < *ploutos* 'wealth']

plutocracy /ploo tókrəssi/ (*plural* **-cies**) *n* **1.** GOVERNANCE BY WEALTHY the rule of a society by its wealthiest people **2.** SOCIETY RULED BY WEALTHY a society that is ruled by its wealthiest members **3.** WEALTHY RULING CLASS a wealthy social class that controls or greatly influences the government of a society [Mid-17C. < Greek *ploutokratia* < *ploutos* 'wealth'] —**plutocrat** /plóotə krat/ *n* —**plutocratic** /plóotə kráttik/ *adj* —**plutocratically** *adv*

pluton /plóo ton/ *n* a mass of intrusive igneous rock that has solidified underground by the crystallization of magma [Mid-20C. < German, back-formation < *plutonisch* 'plutonic' < Greek *Ploutōn* (see PLUTO)] —**plutonic** /ploo tónnik/ *adj*

Plutonian /ploo tóni ən/ *adj* **1.** relating to or characteristic of the planet Pluto **2.** relating to or characteristic of the Roman god Pluto [Mid-17C. < Greek *Ploutōn* (see PLUTO)]

plutonium /ploo tóni əm/ *n* a highly toxic silvery radioactive metallic element. Source: uranium ore. Use: as plutonium-239, production of atomic energy and weapons. Symbol **Pu**. See table at **element** [Mid-20C. After the planet PLUTO, because it follows uranium and neptunium in the periodic table]

pluvial /plóovi əl/ *adj* **1.** RELATING TO RAIN relating to or caused by rain **2.** RAINY having or affected by much rain ■ *n* WET PERIOD a period of heavy rainfall [Mid-17C. < Latin *pluvialis* < *pluvia* 'rain' < *pluere* 'to rain']

pluvious /plóovi əss/, **pluviose** /plóovi ōss/ *adj* relating to, involving, or typical of rain, especially heavy

rainfall [15C. Via French < Latin *pluviosus* < *pluvia* 'rain' (see PLUVIAL)]

ply[1] /plī/ (**plies, plying, plied**) *v* **1.** *vti* WORK HARD AT SOMETHING to work at a trade or occupation, especially with diligence **2.** *vt* USE SOMETHING DILIGENTLY to use something such as a tool or weapon in a diligent or skilful way ○ *the dexterity with which she plied her needle* **3.** *vt* OFFER SOMETHING FOR SALE to offer goods or services for sale, especially regularly or as an occupation **4.** *vt* KEEP SUPPLYING SOMEBODY WITH SOMETHING to keep supplying somebody with something, especially in an insistent way ○ *kept plying us with offers of food* **5.** *vt* SUBJECT ANOTHER TO SOMETHING INSISTENTLY to keep subjecting somebody to something in an urgent and insistent way ○ *We were plied with questions.* **6.** *vti* TRAVEL ROUTE REGULARLY to travel a route regularly, especially on water **7.** *vi* SAILING ZIGZAG IN BOAT AGAINST WIND to sail a boat on a zigzag course against the wind [14C. Shortening of APPLY]

ply[2] /plī/ *n* (*plural* **plies**) (*often used in combination*) **1.** TWISTED STRAND a twisted single strand, especially of yarn or rope **2.** THIN LAYER OF SOMETHING a layer, sheet, or thickness of something such as wood or a tyre ■ *vt* (**plies, plying, plied**) TWIST OR FOLD SOMETHING TOGETHER to twist strands or fold layers together [14C. < Old French *pli* < *plier* 'to fold, bend' < Latin *plicare*]

Plymouth /plímməth/ **1.** port in Devon, southwestern England. Population: 240,720 (2001). **2.** town in southeastern Massachusetts, on Plymouth Bay, south of Duxbury. It was settled by the Pilgrims in 1620. Population: 53,789 (2002 estimate).

Plymouth Brethren *n* a strict Protestant group founded in the United Kingdom in the late 1820s that has no organized ministry or formal creed and accepts the Bible as its sole guide [After PLYMOUTH, Devon]

Plymouth Rock *n* a domestic hen with white or grey barred plumage, belonging to a US breed. After plymouth, Massachusetts. Kept for: eggs, meat.

plywood /plī wŏŏd/ *n* board made by gluing and compressing thin layers of wood together with the grain of each layer at right angles to the layer next to it [Early 20C. < PLY[2]]

PLZ *abbr* ONLINE same as **PLS**

Plzeň /p'l zénnyə/ capital city of Západočeky Region in the western part of the Czech Republic. Population: 168,422 (1999).

pm *abbr* **1.** TELECOM phase modulation **2.** MED postmortem **3.** premium **4.** ONLINE St-Pierre and Miquelon (*used in Internet addresses*) See table at **domain name**

Pm *symbol* CHEM ELEM promethium

PM *abbr* **1.** Past Master (*of a fraternity*) **2.** Postmaster **3.** MED postmortem **4.** POL Prime Minister **5.** ONLINE private message (*used in e-mails or text messages*) **6.** Provost Marshal

p.m., P.M., pm, PM *adj, adv* between 12 noon and midnight. Full form **post meridiem**

P-mail /peé mayl/, **pmail** *n* mail sent through the postal service

PMG *abbr* **1.** Paymaster General **2.** Postmaster General **3.** Provost Marshal General

PMS *abbr* MED premenstrual syndrome

PMT *abbr* MED premenstrual tension

pn *abbr* ONLINE Pitcairn Island (*used in Internet addresses*) See table at **domain name**

PN, P/N, pn *abbr* FIN promissory note

PNdB *abbr* MEASURE perceived noise decibel

pneum- *prefix* same as **pneumo-** (*used before vowels*)

pneuma /nyóomə/ *n* in Stoicism, the vital spirit or soul [Late 19C. < Greek, 'breath, spirit' < *pnein* 'breathe']

pneumatic /nyoo máttik/ *adj* **1.** USING COMPRESSED AIR operated by compressed air in a tool or machine **2.** FILLED WITH AIR filled with air, especially compressed air **3.** PHYS INVOLVING COMPRESSED GASES relating to, operated by, or typical of the pressure of compressed gases, especially air pressure or compressed air **4.** OF GASES OR WIND relating to or typical of air, gases, or wind **5.** RELIG OF SOUL relating to the soul or spirit **6.** BIRDS HAVING AIR-FILLED CAVITIES describes bird's bones that contain air-filled cavities **7.** FULL-BREASTED having large breasts (*informal; offensive in some contexts*)

[Mid-17C. Via French and Latin < Greek *pneumatikos* < *pneuma* (see PNEUMA)] —**pneumatically** *adv*

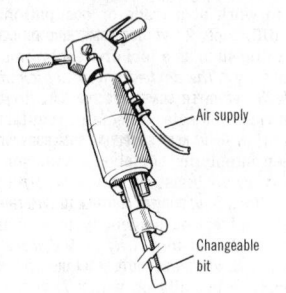

Air supply

Changeable bit

pneumatic drill

pneumatic drill *n* a heavy powerful drill operated by compressed air and used especially for breaking up the surface of roads or pavements

pneumatics /nyoo máttiks/ *n* the branch of physics dealing with the mechanical properties of air and other gases (*takes a singular verb*)

pneumatic tube *n* a tube through which letters and packets are propelled by compressed air

pneumato- *prefix* **1.** air, gas, vapour ○ *pneumatolysis* **2.** respiration, breathing ○ *pneumatophore* **3.** spirits, spiritual ○ *pneumatology* [< Greek *pneumat-*, stem of *pneuma* (see PNEUMA)]

pneumatology /nyoōmə tólləji/ *n* **1.** the branch of Christian theology that deals with the Holy Spirit **2.** the study of spirits or spiritual beings —**pneumatological** /-tə lójjik'l/ *adj* —**pneumatologist** *n*

pneumatolysis /nyoōmə tólləsiss/ *n* the alteration caused in rocks by hot gases escaping from solidifying magma —**pneumatolytic** /nyoō máttō líttik/ *adj*

pneumatophore /nyoo máttō fawr, nyoōməttə fawr/ *n* **1.** a branch in swamp plants such as the mangrove or bald cypress that grows upwards from the roots and carries out respiration **2.** a gas-filled sac that acts as a float in coelenterates such as the Portuguese man-of-war

pneumo- *prefix* **1.** air, gas **2.** lung, pulmonary ○ *pneumocystis* **3.** pneumonia ○ *pneumobacillus* **4.** respiration [< Greek *pneuma* 'breath']

pneumobacillus /nyoōmōbə sílləss/ (*plural* **-li** /-lī/) *n* a Gram-negative bacterium that occurs in the respiratory tract and is one cause of pneumonia. Latin name: *Klebsiella pneumoniae*.

pneumococcus /nyoōmō kókəss/ (*plural* **-cocci** /-kók sī/) *n* a Gram-positive bacterium that occurs in the respiratory tract and is one cause of pneumonia. Latin name: *Streptococcus pneumoniae*. —**pneumococcal** *adj*

pneumoconiosis /nyoōmō kōni ốssiss/, **pneumonoconiosis** /nyoōmənō-/ *n* a disease of the lungs such as silicosis caused by inhaling mineral or metallic dust over a long period [Late 19C. < PNEUMO- + Greek *konis* 'dust']

pneumocystis /nyoōmō sístiss/, **pneumocystis pneumonia** *n* a form of pneumonia that mainly affects people with weakened immune systems. It is caused by the microorganism *Pneumocystis carinii*.

pneumonectomy /nyoōmə néktəmi/ (*plural* **-mies**) *n* the surgical removal of a lung [Late 19C. < Greek *pneumōn* 'lung' (see PNEUMONIA)]

pneumonia /nyoo mốni ə/ *n* an inflammation of one or both lungs, usually caused by infection from a bacterium or virus or, less commonly, by a chemical or physical irritant [Early 17C. < modern Latin < Greek *pneumōn* 'lung', alteration (influenced by *pneuma* 'breath') of *pleumōn*]

pneumonic /nyoo mónnik/ *adj* **1.** relating to or affecting the lungs **2.** relating to, involving, or affected by pneumonia [Late 17C. Via French < Greek *pneumonikos* < *pneumōn* 'lung' (see PNEUMONIA)]

pneumonitis /nyoōmə nítiss/ *n* inflammation of the air sacs in the lungs, usually caused by a virus [Early 19C. < modern Latin < Greek *pneumōn* 'lung' (see PNEUMONIA)]

pneumonoconiosis *n* MED same as **pneumoconiosis**

pneumothorax /nyoōmō tháwr aks/ *n* the presence of air or gas in the pleural cavity surrounding the lungs, causing pain and difficulty in breathing. Pneumothorax can occur spontaneously because of accidental rupture or perforation of the pleura, and in the past it was also a deliberate medical procedure in the treatment of tuberculosis.

~~pnuematic~~ incorrect spelling of **pneumatic**

~~pnuemonia~~ incorrect spelling of **pneumonia**

po /pō/ (*plural* **pos**) *n* HOUSEHOLD same as **chamber pot** (*informal*) [Late 19C. Shortening of French *pot de chambre* 'chamber pot']

Po[1] *symbol* CHEM ELEM polonium

Po[2] /pō/ longest river in Italy. It rises in the Alps near Italy's northwestern border and flows into the Adriatic Sea. Length: 652 km/405 mi.

PO *abbr* **1.** NAVY Petty Officer **2.** AIR FORCE Pilot Officer **3.** postal order **4.** post office

p.o.[1] *abbr* postal order

p.o.[2] *abbr* by mouth (*used on prescriptions*) [Latin *per os*]

POA *abbr* Prison Officers' Association

poach[1] /pōch/ (**poaches, poaching, poached**) *v* **1.** *vti* CATCH GAME ILLEGALLY to catch wild animals or fish illegally on public land or while trespassing on private land **2.** *vti* ENCROACH ON SOMETHING to encroach on somebody's rights, territory, or sphere of operation in order to appropriate or remove another person or thing ○ *A rival company was poaching our customers.* **3.** *vti* SPORTS PLAY SOMEBODY ELSE'S SHOT to play a shot that properly should be handled by a partner in badminton, tennis, squash, or handball **4.** *vti* SOCCER SCORE SNEAK GOAL in football, to score a goal at close range by lingering inside the opposing penalty area while unobserved by defenders ○ *Their striker is an expert at poaching.* **5.** *vti* MAKE GROUND MUDDY to become muddy, or make ground muddy by trampling it **6.** *vi* SINK INTO MUD to sink into soft earth or mud while walking across it [Early 17C. < Old French *pocher* 'trample, trespass', probably < Germanic] —**poachable** *adj*

poach[2] /pōch/ (**poaches, poaching, poached**) *vt* to cook something by simmering it in or over water or another liquid [15C. < Old French *pochier*, originally 'enclose in a bag' < *poche* 'bag']

poached-egg daisy /pōcht-/ *n* a plant with white flowers that have a yellow centre. Latin name: *Polycalymma stuartii*. Native to: dry areas of Australia. [Because its white-and-yellow flower resembles a poached egg]

poacher[1] /pốchər/ *n* **1.** somebody who hunts or fishes illegally, usually while trespassing **2.** in football, a player who scores a goal while lingering around the opposition's penalty area, unobserved by defenders [Mid-17C. < POACH[1]]

poacher[2] /pốchər/ *n* a pan for poaching eggs that has a tightly fitting lid and small metal cups [Mid-19C. < POACH[2]]

PO Box *abbr* Post Office Box

AKG London

Pocahontas: posthumous portrait (1666)

Pocahontas /pókə hóntəss/ (1595?–1617?) Powhatan princess. According to legend, she saved the life of the colonist Captain John Smith (1608). Born **Matoaka**

pochard /póchərd/ *n* a heavy-bodied diving duck with a reddish head and a silver and black beak. Native

to: coastal waters of Europe and Asia. Subfamily: Aythyini. [Mid-16C. Origin ?]

pochette /po shét/ *n* a small handbag shaped like an envelope [Late 19C. < French, 'small pouch' < *poche* 'bag']

pock /pok/ *n* MED same as **pockmark** *n* (sense 1) ■ *vt* (**pocks, pocking, pocked**) to cover something with pockmarks or disfiguring marks (*often passive*) [Old English *poc* < Germanic] —**pocky** *adj*

pocket /pókit/ *n* **1.** SMALL POUCH IN CLOTHES a shaped piece of material forming part of an item of clothing and used to hold small items, e.g. inside trousers or on the outside of a shirt **2.** SMALL FITTED POUCH a small fitted pouch, e.g. a pouch-shaped compartment on the inside of a bag ○ *The suitcase has several inside pockets.* **3.** SMALL POUCH a small pouch, bag, or purse **4.** PERSONAL MONEY somebody's personal financial resources ○ *a holiday paid for out of his own pocket* **5.** SMALL DIFFERENTIATED AREA a small area differentiated from neighbouring areas by a particular feature ○ *pockets of wealth* **6.** CAVITY a type of cavity or opening **7.** ZOOL SAC ON ANIMAL a pouch-shaped sac on an animal's body **8.** GEOL QUANTITY OF ORE IN CAVITY the quantity of petroleum, natural gas, or mineral found in an underground cavity, or a cavity that contains such a substance **9.** SPORTS BOXED-IN POSITION IN RACE a position in a race in which a competitor is blocked by others **10.** CUE GAMES POUCH ON PLAYING TABLE a pouch or net at each corner and side of a billiard, snooker, or pool table ○ *He sank the red in the side pocket.* **11.** Aus FOOTBALL PLAYER IN SIDE POSITION in Australian Rules, a player in one of two side positions at the ends of the ground **12.** AVIAT same as **air pocket 13.** S Africa BAG FOR PRODUCE a long narrow bag in which a particular quantity of fruit or vegetables is sold ■ *vt* (**-ets, -eting, -eted**) **1.** PUT SOMETHING IN POCKET to put something into a pocket ○ *She pocketed the change.* **2.** TAKE SOMETHING DISHONESTLY to appropriate something, often dishonestly ○ *They buy tickets cheaply, sell them for high prices, and pocket the difference.* **3.** CUE GAMES HIT BALL INTO POCKET to hit a ball into one of the pockets on a billiard, snooker, or pool table ○ *pocket the black* **4.** PUT UP WITH SOMETHING to tolerate something unpleasant, especially an insult, without protesting or retaliating **5.** SUPPRESS FEELING to hide or suppress a feeling ○ *Pocket your pride and admit you were wrong.* **6.** ENCLOSE OR SURROUND SOMEBODY OR SOMETHING to enclose or hem in somebody or something **7.** US POL RETAIN PIECE OF LEGISLATION to retain a legislative bill without signing it, especially as a US president, in order to stop it becoming approved by Congress ■ *adj* **1.** SMALL ENOUGH TO CARRY IN POCKET designed for carrying in a pocket ○ *a pocket torch* **2.** SMALL small, especially smaller than something larger of the same type ○ *a pocket trumpet* **3.** CONTAINED isolated and contained in small areas [15C. < Anglo-Norman *pokete* 'small bag' < *poke* 'bag'] —**pocketable** /pókitəb'l/ *adj* ◇ **have deep pockets** to have large financial resources ○ *a price-cutting war which will be won by whoever has the deepest pockets* ◇ **in pocket** making a profit from something ◇ **in somebody's pocket 1.** fully under somebody's control **2.** almost certain to be won by somebody ○ *We thought she had the race in her pocket.* ◇ **line your pocket(s)** to profit at the expense of others ◇ **out of pocket** having lost money on something or spent money without benefit ◇ **pick somebody's pocket** to steal something from somebody's pocket without the person feeling or noticing

pocket battleship *n* a small but powerful and heavily armed battleship, especially one built by Germany in the 1930s to conform to limitations that were placed by treaty on size and armament

pocketbook /pókit boŏk/ *n N Am* **1.** SMALL CASE CARRIED IN POCKET a small case or folder for money and documents, suitable for carrying in a pocket **2.** HANDBAG a purse or handbag **3.** SOMEBODY'S FINANCES somebody's financial resources **4.** PUBL same as **pocket edition**

pocket borough *n* a political constituency in Great Britain before the Reform Act of 1832, whose representative in Parliament was determined by one landowner or landowning family [Because the landowner had the borough 'in his pocket']

pocket edition *n* a book small enough to be carried in a pocket. N Am term **pocketbook**

pocketful /pókitfŏol/ *n* **1.** the amount of something that would fit in a pocket **2.** a large amount of something, especially money (*informal*)

pocket gopher *n* ZOOL same as **gopher** (sense 1)

pocketknife /pókit nīf/ (*plural* **-knives** /-nīvz/) *n US* same as **penknife**

pocket money *n* **1.** a small sum of money paid regularly by parents to a child so that the child can make his or her own purchases. N Am term **allowance 2.** a small amount of personal money, sufficient only for making minor purchases or to cover incidental expenses

pocket mouse *n* a small nocturnal rodent with long hind legs, a long tail, and fur-lined cheek pouches for carrying food. Native to: deserts of western United States and Mexico. Genus: *Perognathus.*

pocket veto *n* in the United States, a failure by the US president to return a bill passed by Congress during its last days in session, in order to prevent its being enacted [< the idea of the executive's holding the bill in a coat pocket]

pocket watch *n* a watch designed to be carried in a pocket, instead of being worn on the wrist

pockmark /pók maark/ *n* (*often used in the plural*) **1. SMALL SCAR LEFT BY SKIN DISEASE** a small permanent circular scar on the skin, especially one left by smallpox, chickenpox, or acne **2. SMALL HOLLOW MARK** a small hollow mark disfiguring a surface ■ *vt* (**-marks, -marking, -marked**) **1. COVER SKIN WITH POCKMARKS** to disfigure the skin with pockmarks **2. MAKE POCKMARKS IN SOMETHING** to make many small indentations or marks in the surface of something

poco /pṓkō/ *adv* a little or slightly (*used in musical directions*) [Early 18C. < Italian, 'little']

poco a poco /pṓkō aa pṓkō/ *adv* little by little (*used in musical directions*) [< Italian, 'little by little']

pococurante /pṓkō kyoo ránti/ (*literary*) *adj* uninterested, indifferent, or nonchalantly detached ■ *n* somebody who is uninterested, indifferent, or nonchalantly detached [Mid-18C. < Italian < *poco* 'little' + *curare* 'to care'] —**pococuranteism** /-ránti izəm/ *n* —**pococurantism** /-rántizəm/ *n*

Pocomania /pṓkō máyni ə/ *n Carib* a religious group in Jamaica whose worship is characterized by singing, dancing, spirit-possession, speaking in tongues, and healing rituals [Mid-20C. Probably an alteration of an African term after Spanish *poco* 'little' + MANIA]

pod[1] /pod/ *n* **1. SEED CASE** the long narrow outer case holding the seeds of a plant such as the pea, bean, or vanilla **2.** AEROSP **DETACHABLE COMPARTMENT OF SPACECRAFT** a specialized detachable compartment on a spacecraft, usually for carrying personnel or instruments **3.** AEROSP, NAVY **STREAMLINED HOUSING FOR EQUIPMENT** a streamlined housing attached to the wing or fuselage of an aircraft, or to the hull of a submarine, to carry fuel, an engine, weaponry, or other equipment **4.** ZOOL **PROTECTIVE EGG CASE** a protective case surrounding the eggs of some fishes and insects such as the grasshopper ■ *v* (**pods, podding, podded**) **1.** *vt* **TAKE PEAS FROM POD** to strip peas out of their pod so that they can be eaten or cooked **2.** *vi* **PRODUCE PODS** to produce fruit in the form of pods [Late 17C. Origin ?]

pod[2] /pod/ *n* a small group of sea animals, especially seals, whales, or dolphins [Mid-19C. Origin ?]

pod[3] /pod/ *n* **1.** a socket holding the bit in a boring tool **2.** a lengthways channel in the barrel of a boring tool [Late 16C. Origin ?]

PO'd /peé ōd/, **p.o.'d** *adj* annoyed or irritated by somebody or something (*informal*) [Abbreviation of *pissed off*]

POD *abbr* COMM pay on delivery

-pod *suffix* foot, part like a foot ◇ *stomatopod* [< Greek *pod-* < Indo-European] —**-podous** *suffix*

podagra /po dággrə/ *n* gout in the foot or the big toe [13C. Via Latin < Greek, 'foot-trap' < *pod-* 'foot' + *agra* 'trap'] —**podagral** *adj* —**podagric** *adj* —**podagrical** *adj* —**podagrous** *adj*

Steve Podborski

Podborski /pod báwrski/, **Steve** (*b.* 1957) Canadian skier. He won eight World Cup events in downhill skiing between 1979 and 1982.

-pode *suffix* another spelling of **-pod**

podesta /pō déstə/ *n* in former times, a chief magistrate or governor of an Italian town, especially during the Middle Ages and Renaissance [Mid-16C. Via Italian < Latin *potestas* 'power' < *potis* 'powerful']

podge /poj/ *n* **1.** an offensive term for a short person who is considered to be carrying more body weight than is desirable or advisable (*insult*) **2.** excess body weight (*informal disapproving; sometimes offensive*) ▶ N Am term **pudge** [Mid-19C. Probably back-formation < PODGY]

Podgorica /pod gáwritsə/ capital city of Montenegro, Federal Republic of Yugoslavia, situated about 19 km/12 mi. north of Lake Shkoder. Population: 163,493 (1998).

podgy /pójji/ (**-ier, -iest**) *adj* short and carrying more body weight than is desirable or advisable (*sometimes offensive*) US term **pudgy** [Mid-19C. Variant of PUDGY] —**podgily** *adv* —**podginess** *n*

podia ARCHIT, FURNITURE plural of **podium**

podiatry /po dī ətri/ *n ANZ, US* the profession concerned with the care of the feet and the treatment of foot disorders. UK, Can term **chiropody** [Early 20C. < Greek *pod-* 'foot'] —**podiatric** /pódi áttrik/ *adj* —**podiatrist** *n*

podium /pṓdi əm/ (*plural* **-diums** or **-dia** /-di ə/) *n* **1. SMALL RAISED PLATFORM** a small raised platform that the conductor of an orchestra, a lecturer, or somebody giving a speech can stand on **2. FOUNDATION WALL** a low wall forming a foundation or base, e.g. for a colonnade **3.** ARCHIT **WALL AROUND ARENA OF AMPHITHEATRE** a low wall encircling the arena of an ancient amphitheatre [Mid-18C. Via Latin < Greek *podion* 'small foot' < *pod-* 'foot']

-podium *suffix* foot, part like a foot ◇ *pseudopodium* [Via modern Latin < Greek *podion* (see PODIUM)]

podophyllin /póddə fíllin/, **podophyllin resin** *n* a greenish or brownish bitter resin. Source: root of the May apple. Use: removal of warts. [Mid-19C. < modern Latin *Podophyllum* < Greek *pod-* 'foot' + *phullon* 'leaf']

podsol, etc. GEOG same as **podzol, etc.**

podzol /pód zol/, **podsol** /pód sol/ *n* an infertile soil that forms in cool moist climates, usually under coniferous or mixed forests. The topsoil consists of leached clay under a layer of organic material. [Early 20C. < Russian < *pod-* 'under' + *zol* 'ash'] —**podzolic** /pod zóllik/ *adj*

podzolization /pód zo lī záysh'n/, **podzolisation**, **podsolization** /pód so lī záysh'n/, **podsolisation** *n* the process whereby minerals are leached from the upper into the lower layers of a soil, leaving the topsoil acidic and infertile and forming a podzol —**podzolize** /pódzə līz/ *vti*

Poe /pō/, **Edgar Allan** (1809–49) US writer and critic. His poems, including 'The Raven' (1845), and short stories, including 'The Pit and the Pendulum' (1842), deal with the mysterious and the macabre. See Cultural note at **morgue, raven**[1]

'Once upon a midnight dreary, while I pondered, weak and weary, / Over many a quaint and curious volume of forgotten lore, / While I nodded, nearly napping, suddenly there came a tapping, / As of some one gently rapping, rapping at my

Edgar Allan Poe

chamber door.'
[Edgar Allan Poe, 'The Raven'; 1845]

POE *abbr* **1.** MIL port of embarkation **2.** port of entry

poem /pṓ im/ *n* **1. PIECE WRITTEN IN VERSE** a complete and self-contained piece of writing in verse that is set out in lines of a set length and uses rhythm, imagery, and often rhyme to achieve its effect **2. WRITING WITH POETIC EFFECT** a piece of writing that is not in verse, but that has the imaginative, rhythmic, or metaphorical qualities usually associated with a poem **3. BEAUTIFUL OR DELIGHTFUL THING** something particularly lovely, beautiful, or delightful [15C. Directly or via French < Latin *poema* < Greek *poiēma* 'making' < *poiein* 'make']

~~poeple~~ incorrect spelling of **people**

poesy /pṓ əzi/ (*plural* **-sies**) *n* poetry or poetic compositions in general, or a single piece of poetry (*archaic or literary*) [14C. Via French *poésie* and Latin *poesis* < Greek *poiēsis* 'making' (see -POIESIS)]

poet /pṓ it/ *n* **1.** somebody who writes poems, especially as a vocation **2.** an imaginative, creative, or artistic person [13C. Via French *poète* and Latin *poeta* < Greek *poiētēs* 'maker, author' < *poiein* 'make']

poet. *abbr* **1.** poetic **2.** poetical **3.** poetry

poetaster /pṓ i tástər/ *n* somebody who writes bad poetry (*literary*) [Late 16C. < modern Latin < Latin *poeta* (see POET)]

poetic /pō éttik/, **poetical** /-ik'l/ *adj* **1. RELATING TO POETRY** relating to, characteristic of, or in the form of poetry **2. RESEMBLING POETRY** having qualities usually associated with poetry, especially in being gracefully expressive, romantically beautiful, or elevated and uplifting **3. SENSITIVE OR INSIGHTFUL** characteristic of a poet, especially in possessing unusual sensitivity or insight, or in being able to express things in a beautiful or romantic way —**poetically** *adv*

Poetic Edda *n* LITERAT same as **Edda** (sense 1)

poeticize /pō étti sīz/ (**-cizes, -cizing, -cized**), **poeticise** (**-cises, -cising, -cised**) *vti* to express or describe something in a poetic style or in poetry

poetic justice *n* a situation in which somebody meets a fate that seems a fitting punishment or, less often, a fitting reward for his or her past actions

poetic licence *n* deliberate misuse of or disregard for the normal rules of fact, style, or grammar by a writer or speaker in order to achieve a special effect

poetics /pō éttiks/ *n* **1. BASIC PRINCIPLES OF POETRY** the literary or philosophical study of the basic principles, forms, and techniques of poetry, or of imaginative writing in general (*takes a singular verb*) **2.** (*plural same*) **TREATISE ON POETRY** a treatise on the nature or principles of poetry **3. WAY OF COMPOSING POEM** the art or technique of writing poetry (*takes a plural verb*)

poetize /pṓ i tīz/ (**-izes, -izing, -ized**), **poetise** (**-ises, -ising, -ised**) *vti* LITERAT same as **poeticize**

poet laureate (*plural* **poets laureate**) *n* **1.** a poet who is appointed a member of the royal household for life by a British monarch and is expected to write poems celebrating great national or royal events **2.** a poet who is specially honoured for his or her work, or who is considered to be the most eminent poet in a particular country, state, or group

poetry /pṓ itri/ *n* **1. LITERATURE IN VERSE** literary works written in verse, in particular verse writing of high quality, great beauty, emotional sincerity or

intensity, or profound insight **2.** **PARTICULAR POEMS CONSIDERED COLLECTIVELY** all the poems written by a particular poet, in a particular language or form, or on a particular subject ○ *a collection of love poetry* **3.** **WRITING OF POEMS** the art or skill of writing poems **4.** **PROSE LIKE POETRY** writing in prose that has a poetic quality **5.** **BEAUTY OR GRACE** something that resembles poetry in its beauty, rhythmic grace, or imaginative, elevated, or decorative style **6.** **POETIC QUALITY** a poetic or particularly beautiful or graceful quality in something [14C. < medieval Latin *poetria* < Latin *poeta* (see POET)]

POEU *abbr* Post Office Engineers Union

po-faced /pō-/ *adj* **1.** inappropriately solemn or disapproving **2.** remaining expressionless or wearing a stern expression, especially when others are laughing or responding in some way [Origin ?]

pogo /pṓgō/ (**-gos, -going, -goed**) *vi* to dance in a punk style of the 1970s by jumping up and down on the spot [Late 20C. < POGO STICK] —**pogo** *n* —**pogoer** *n*

pogonophoran /póggə nóffərən/, **pogonophore** /póggənə fawr/ *n* an animal resembling a worm that has tentacles around the head area, lacks a digestive tract, and lives in vertical tubes in deep water. Phylum: Pogonophora. [Late 20C. < modern Latin *Pogonophora* < Greek *pōgōn* 'beard' + *-phoros* '-bearing'] —**pogonophoran** *adj*

pogo stick *n* a strong metal pole with a spring at the bottom and two footrests to stand on, used to jump up and down or hop along on for play or exercise [Early 20C. Origin ?]

pogrom /póggrəm/ *n* a planned campaign of persecution or extermination sanctioned by a government and directed against an ethnic group, especially against the Jews in tsarist Russia [Early 20C. < Russian, 'devastation' < *gromit* 'wreak havoc' < *grom* 'thunder']

pogue /pōg/ *n* (*slang insult*) **1.** an offensive term for somebody regarded as a coward or sissy **2.** *US* an offensive term for a member of the armed forces employed in a rear echelon support capacity

poi[1] /poy/ *n* a Hawaiian dish made from the root of the taro, cooked, pounded to a paste, and fermented [Early 19C. < Hawaiian]

poi[2] /poy/ *n* a light ball on a string, rhythmically swung to accompany Maori dance and song [Mid-19C. < Maori]

-poiesis *suffix* creation, formation, production ○ *erythropoiesis* [< Greek *poiēsis* < *poiein* 'make']

poignant /póynyənt/ *adj* **1.** **CAUSING SADNESS OR PITY** causing a sharp sense of sadness, pity, or regret **2.** **SHARPLY PERCEPTIVE** particularly penetrating and effective or relevant (*literary*) **3.** **SHARPLY PAINFUL** causing acute physical pain (*literary*) **4.** **STRONG SMELLING OR TASTING** having an often pleasurably strong sharp smell or taste (*archaic*) [14C. < French, present participle of *poindre* 'to prick' < Latin *pungere* 'to prick, sting'] —**poignance** *n* —**poignancy** *n* —**poignantly** *adv*

SYNONYMS See *moving*.

poikilocyte /póykilō sīt/ *n* an unusually shaped red blood cell [Late 19C. < Greek *poikilos* 'spotted, varied, irregular']

poikilotherm /póykilō thurm/ *n* an organism such as a reptile, amphibian, insect, or fish that has a body temperature that varies according to the temperature of the local atmosphere

poikilothermic /póykilō thúrmik/, **poikilothermal** /póykilō thúrm'l/, **poikilothermous** /póykilō thúrməss/ *adj* having a body temperature that varies according to the temperature of the local atmosphere. Reptiles, amphibians, insects, and fish are all poikilothermic. [Late 19C. < Greek *poikilos* 'spotted, varied, irregular'] —**poikilothermism** *n* —**poikilothermy** *n*

poilu /pwaáloo/ *n* a soldier in the French infantry, especially during World War I [Early 20C. < French, 'hairy' < *poil* 'hair' < Latin *pilus*]

poinciana /póynssi aánə/ (*plural* **-as** or *same*) *n* a tree grown for its large reddish-orange flowers. Native to: tropical regions. Genera: *Caesalpinia* or *Delonix*. [Mid-18C. < modern Latin, after M. de *Poinci*, 17C governor of the Antilles]

poind /poynd/ (**poinds, poinding, poinded**) *vt Scotland* **1.** to seize the goods of a debtor so that they can be sold to pay a debt **2.** to impound a stray animal [Old English *gepyndan* 'impound' < POUND[3]]

poinsettia

poinsettia /poyn sétti ə/ (*plural* **-as** or *same*) *n* a bush with bright red bracts resembling petals, popular as a house plant. Native to: Central America. Latin name: *Euphorbia pulcherrima*. [Mid-19C. After Joel R. *Poinsett* (1775–1851), US botanist]

point /poynt/ *n* **1.** **OPINION, IDEA, OR FACT** an opinion, idea, or fact put forward in the course of or forming a main element of a discussion or argument ○ *She made many valid points in her report.* **2.** **UNDERLYING ESSENTIAL IDEA** the essential idea conveyed or intended in something that is said or written ○ *He seems to have missed the point entirely.* **3.** **PURPOSE** the purpose or usefulness of something ○ *Is there really any point in continuing?* **4.** **ITEM IN LIST OR PLAN** an item or detail in something such as a plan, contract, or list ○ *a four-point plan to revive the coal industry* ○ *a point-by-point examination of the contract* **5.** **CONVINCING ARGUMENT OR VIEWPOINT** a cogent or persuasive argument or observation ○ *You have to admit that she has a point there.* **6.** **QUALITY OR FEATURE** a distinguishing quality, feature, or item in the makeup of somebody or something ○ *Generosity is one of her good points.* **7.** **PHYSICAL FEATURE OF LIVESTOCK ANIMAL** an external feature that is assessed when judging the overall shape of a livestock animal, e.g. the face or fetlock **8.** **LOCATION** a specific place or position ○ *a point six miles east of here* **9.** **MOMENT** an individual moment in time ○ *At that point, the door opened and the teacher walked in.* **10.** **PARTICULAR STAGE IN PROCESS** a particular moment or stage in a process, especially one at which a significant change or development occurs or a condition is reached ○ *We have reached the point at which a decision will have to be made.* **11.** **LEVEL OR DEGREE** a level or degree of a quality ○ *He was confident to the point of almost being arrogant.* **12.** **TIME JUST BEFORE SOMETHING HAPPENS** the moment or period of time just before something happens ○ *at the point of death* **13.** **SHARP END OF SOMETHING** the sharp narrowed end of something such as a needle, pencil, or weapon **14.** **END OR TIP** the end or tip of something such as a finger or the projecting angle of something such as the elbow or chin **15.** **SMALL PROJECTION** a small sharp or perceptible projection, e.g. in a piece of writing in Braille **16.** **ACT OF POINTING** the act of pointing, e.g. with a finger **17.** **DOT** a small dot or source of something such as colour or light **18.** **UNIT ON SCALE** a single unit on a scale of measurement ○ *The earthquake measured 6 points on the Richter scale.* ○ *opened up a 10-point lead over her rivals in the polls* **19.** SPORTS, LEISURE **UNIT USED IN SCORING** a unit used in scoring a sport, game, or competition, or as a means of making a quantitative evaluation of something **20.** MUSIC **TIP OF BOW** the tip of the bow of a stringed instrument **21.** ZOOL **ANTLER PRONG** a prong on a deer's antlers **22.** GEOG **HEADLAND** a prominent headland on the coast that juts out into the sea, often the projecting tip of a peninsula (*often used in placenames*) **23.** MATHS **DECIMAL POINT** the dot separating the whole number and fraction in a decimal number. The term 'point' is used particularly when such numbers are spoken aloud. ○ *five point nine* **24.** MATHS **DIMENSIONLESS GEOMETRIC ELEMENT** a dimensionless geometric element whose location in space is defined solely by its coordinates. Geometric figures such as circles, planes, or spheres can be treated as if they are sets of points. **25.** GRAM, PRINTING **PUNCTUATION MARK** in printing or writing, a punctuation mark, especially a full stop **26.** PHON same as **vowel point** **27.** FIN **INVESTMENT PRICE UNIT** a unit used to measure change in the value of an investment, e.g. on a stock exchange ○ *The FTSE index is up 5 points.* **28.** *US* FIN **PERCENTAGE OF LOAN** an amount equivalent to one per cent of the value of a loan, used to calculate the sum that the borrower pays at once to the lender as a service charge **29.** *US* LAW **PENALTY UNIT FOR MOTORIST** a penalty unit given for a driving offence recorded on somebody's driving licence. Receiving a set number of points leads automatically to a penalty. **30.** *US* EDUC **UNIT OF CREDIT FOR STUDENT** a unit of academic credit for a student that is equivalent to one hour of class work per week over a period of one term **31.** CARDS **UNIT OF WINNING POTENTIAL** a unit used in assessing the strength of a hand in bridge **32.** PRINTING, MEASURE **PRINTING UNIT OF MEASUREMENT** a unit of measurement in printing equal to one twelfth of a pica or approximately 0.03515 cm/0.01384 in **33.** MEASURE **DIAMOND WEIGHT UNIT** a unit of weight for a diamond equivalent to one-hundredth of a metric carat **34.** COMPASS **MARK ON COMPASS** one of the 32 direction indicators marked on a compass, e.g. west, west by north, west-northwest, or northwest **35.** COMPASS **ANGLE BETWEEN ADJACENT BEARINGS** the angle between any two adjacent bearings marked on a compass, measuring 11° 15' **36.** MIL **UNIT AHEAD OF FORMATION** a person or unit that moves ahead of a larger formation, acting as a scout and advance guard **37.** MIL **ADVANCE MILITARY POSITION** the position ahead of a larger formation taken by a person or unit acting as point **38.** BASKETBALL **OFFENSIVE POSITION** in basketball, the position in front court taken by the guard who directs the offensive **39.** CRICKET **OFF-SIDE FIELDING POSITION** in cricket, a fielding position on the off side, level with the batsman's wicket and at a distance from it that varies between three or four yards (*silly point*) and about thirty yards (*deep point*) **40.** CRICKET **FIELDER FIELDING AT POINT** in cricket, a fielder fielding at point **41.** HERALDRY **DIVISION OF HERALDIC SHIELD** a position on or division of a heraldic shield in which a charge can be placed ■ **points** *npl* **1.** RAIL **JUNCTION OF TWO CONVERGING RAILWAY TRACKS** the mechanical arrangement by which one railway track diverges or converges with another, allowing trains to change to another line or route **2.** AUTOMOT **ELECTRICAL CONTACTS IN DISTRIBUTOR** the two electrical contacts that act as circuit breakers in the distributor of an internal-combustion engine as current is passed in turn to the cylinders **3.** **TIPS OF TOES OF BALLERINA** the ends of the toes on which a ballerina wearing special shoes raises herself up for some moves and positions while performing **4.** ZOOL **EXTREMITIES OF DOMESTIC ANIMAL** the ears, feet, and tail of a domestic animal ■ *v* (**points, pointing, pointed**) **1.** *vi* **INDICATE WITH EXTENDED FINGER** to extend the finger or a long thin object in the direction of something in order to draw attention to it ○ *I pointed to one of the shrubs and asked its cost.* **2.** *vt* **AIM AT SOMETHING** to hold an object so that its end is aimed at somebody or something ○ *pointed the hose at the flowers* **3.** *vi* **BE TURNED IN PARTICULAR DIRECTION** to be turned towards or aimed in a particular direction ○ *The arrow on the signpost was pointing to the right.* **4.** *vt* **DIRECT SOMEBODY TOWARDS SOMETHING** to indicate the direction in which somebody should go ○ *If you can just point me in the right direction I expect I'll find it.* **5.** *vti* COMPUT **AIM MOUSE OR JOYSTICK** to move a mouse, joystick, or other device so that the cursor on a computer screen is positioned over or touching something ○ *Point at the icon, then double click on it.* **6.** *vi* **SUGGEST SOMETHING IS CASE** to be strong evidence of something or lead the mind to believe or conclude something ○ *It all points to one conclusion.* **7.** *vi* **CALL ATTENTION TO SOMETHING** to call attention to a fact or situation as being important **8.** *vt* **GIVE FORCE TO REMARK** to give additional force, emphasis, or incisiveness to something said or written **9.** *vt* **SHARPEN SOMETHING** to sharpen something so that it has a point at the end **10.** *vt* **STRETCH FOOT DOWNWARDS** especially in ballet, to stretch out the foot or toes so that leg and foot make one comparatively straight line **11.** *vt* CONSTR **REPAIR SOMETHING WITH MORTAR** to repair or finish a wall, chimney, or other structural component by putting mortar or cement between the bricks or stones **12.** *vti* SAILING **SAIL BOAT CLOSE TO WIND** to sail or sail a boat close to the wind **13.** *vti* FIELD SPORTS **POINT MUZZLE AT GAME** to perform the characteristic function of a gun dog by standing still with muzzle and tail outstretched, indicating the whereabouts of game **14.** *vt* MUSIC **MARK PSALM FOR CHANTING** to mark a psalm to indicate how it is to be chanted **15.** *vt* PHON **ADD MARKS OVER**

LETTERS to place diacritics or vowel points over the relevant letters in a text **16.** *vt* GRAM PUNCTUATE TEXT to put punctuation marks into a text **17.** *vi* MED COME TO HEAD to reach the stage of spontaneous rupture or surgical opening, allowing pus to drain (*refers to boils and abscesses*) [13C. Via French < Latin *punctum* 'prick-mark, dot, particle' < past participle of Latin *pungere* 'prick, pierce'] ◇ **a sore point** a cause of annoyance ◇ **be on the point of doing something** to be just about to do something ○ *I was just on the point of leaving.* ◇ **beside the point** irrelevant or unimportant ◇ **in point of fact** used, often when correcting something said before, to emphasize that what is now being stated represents the truth ◇ **make a point of doing something** to be careful to do something and, often, to be seen by others to do it ◇ **not to put too fine a point on it** used to indicate that somebody is being frank or blunt about something ◇ **stretch a point 1.** to make an exception to a rule **2.** to exaggerate ◇ **stretch the point** to exaggerate ◇ **to the point** relevant or worth paying attention to ◇ **(up) to a point** to some extent, but not completely

point out *vt* **1.** to point at or otherwise indicate somebody or something so that somebody will look at that person or thing ○ *Our guide pointed out the most interesting architectural features of the building.* **2.** to tell somebody about or draw somebody's attention to something ○ *She did point out some of the difficulties we might expect to face.*

point up *vt* to emphasize or draw particular attention to something

point-and-click *adj* describes an interface that allows a user to interact with a computer by using a mouse to move a cursor on the computer screen and clicking the mouse button ○ *a point-and-click adventure game*

point-and-shoot *adj* describes a camera that requires no adjustment by the user before taking a photograph, because the focus and exposure are adjusted automatically or are fixed

point bar *n* a sand or gravel ridge formed in a series by the flowing water of a meandering river

point-blank *adv* **1.** AT CLOSE RANGE at or from very close range when firing or shooting **2.** OUTRIGHT directly or bluntly and without further explanation ○ *told them point-blank what I thought of them* ■ *adj* **1.** FIRED AT CLOSE RANGE fired straight and from so close to the target that no adjustment to the aim is necessary for the drop in the bullet's trajectory ○ *point-blank shot* **2.** CLOSE TO TARGET very close to the target when shooting ○ *at point-blank range* **3.** OUTRIGHT direct and blunt ○ *a point-blank refusal* [Origin ?]

point contact *n* contact between a slender wire filament and the surface of a semiconductor so as to form a junction converting alternating current to direct current

point defect *n* an imperfection in the lattice structure of a crystal

point duty *n* the task, usually undertaken by a police officer or traffic warden, of standing at a road junction in order to direct traffic

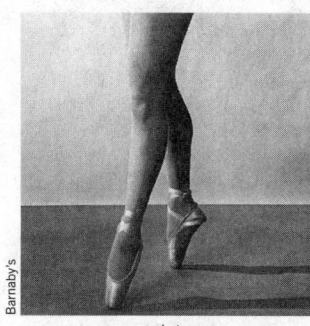

Barnaby's

pointe

pointe /pwaaNt/ *n* the ends of the toes, a position on which a ballerina wearing special shoes raises herself up for some moves and positions while performing [Mid-19C. < French, 'point']

pointed /póyntid/ *adj* **1.** ENDING IN POINT ending in a point or sharp angle **2.** MADE WITH EMPHASIS made with emphasis and carrying an unmistakable message,

often a criticism **3.** CONSPICUOUS made intentionally obvious or noticeable —**pointedness** *n*

pointed arch *n* ARCHIT same as **lancet arch**

pointedly /póyntidli/ *adv* in a deliberate or emphatic way and with no attempt at tact or subtlety ○ *They pointedly ignored me.*

Pointe-Noire /pwaaNt nwaár/ city in the Republic of Congo, and the country's main port. Population: 576,206 (1995).

pointer /póyntər/ *n* **1.** CANE USED FOR POINTING a stick or cane used, especially by a teacher or lecturer, to point something out, e.g. on a chart or large map **2.** INDICATOR ON MEASURING DEVICE a needle that moves around on a measuring instrument to point to part of a dial **3.** HELPFUL HINT a piece of advice or information given to help somebody achieve something or do something the right way ○ *My coach gave me a few pointers on how to hold the racket.* **4.** SIGN INDICATING SITUATION a sign of what is happening or what might happen in the future **5.** GUN DOG a gun dog, usually with a short-haired white coat with coloured patches, belonging to a breed trained to indicate the whereabouts of shot game by standing still with the muzzle and tail outstretched **6.** COMPUT ARROW ON COMPUTER SCREEN an arrow or other symbol on a computer screen that shows the current position of the mouse or other pointing device. The symbol may change shape depending on the task being performed. **7.** COMPUT COMPUTER MEMORY ADDRESS an address, stored as data in a computer's memory, that is the location where specific data is stored ■ **pointers, Pointers** *npl* GUIDE STARS IN PLOUGH CONSTELLATION the two bright stars in the Plough constellation forming the side of the quadrilateral farthest from the handle and used as a guide to find the Pole Star

pointe shoe *n* a woman ballet dancer's slipper made of satin, tied with ribbons, and having a stiff blocked toe, worn for performing or practising on points

pointillism /póyntilizəm/ *n* **1.** a late 19th-century style of painting in which a picture is constructed from dots of pure colour that blend, at a distance, into recognizable shapes and various colour tones. Pointillism developed out of impressionism and its best-known exponent is the French painter Georges Seurat. **2.** a technique of musical composition using sparse isolated notes in widely varying registers [Early 20C. < French *pointillisme*, via *pointiller* 'mark with dots' < Latin *punctum* 'dot'] —**pointillist** *n, adj* —**pointillistic** /póynti lístik/ *adj*

pointing /póynting/ *n* the cement or mortar between the bricks of a wall

pointing device *n* an input device used to manipulate a pointer on a computer display, e.g. a mouse, trackball, or joystick

point lace *n* lace made with a needle instead of bobbins [< POINT in the sense 'prick, stitch']

pointless /póyntləss/ *adj* **1.** having no purpose, use, or sense, or any positive or beneficial effect ○ *It's pointless even attempting to make sense of it.* **2.** in sports, having or scoring no points —**pointlessly** *adv* —**pointlessness** *n*

point man *n* **1.** the lead soldier in a military formation or patrol **2.** *N Am* somebody, especially a man, who is at the forefront of an activity or endeavour

point mutation *n* a mutation that involves a change in a single base or base pair of the nucleotides in a gene, occurring as a result of addition, deletion, or substitution

point of departure *n* a starting point for something

point of honour *n* something that a sense of honour, self-respect, or pride obliges somebody to do

point of inflection *n* a point on a curve at which the arc changes from convex to concave or vice versa. N Am term **inflection point**

point of no return *n* **1.** the time or stage in a process beyond which it becomes impossible to stop or discontinue it **2.** the point in an aircraft's flight after which there will be insufficient fuel left to enable it to return to its starting point

point of order *n* a question raised by one of the participants in a formal debate or meeting that relates to the rules of procedure governing it, in

particular as to whether those rules are being breached

point of presence *n* a location where a user can connect to a network, e.g. a place where subscribers can dial in to an Internet service provider

point of reference *n* something to which somebody can refer in order to check direction or progress, as a guide to action or conduct, or as an aid to understanding or communication

point-of-sale *adj* located, used, or occurring at the place where a product is sold ○ *a point-of-sale display* —**point of sale** *n*

point of view *n* **1.** PERSPECTIVE SOMEBODY BRINGS somebody's way of thinking about or approaching a subject, as shaped by his or her own character, experience, mindset, and history **2.** OPINION somebody's personal opinion on a subject **3.** PARTICULAR PERSPECTIVE ON SUBJECT an aspect from which a subject may be considered or judged **4.** LITERAT ANGLE OF NARRATOR the perspective on events of the narrator or a character in a story **5.** POSITION OF OBSERVER the position or angle from which somebody observes an event or scene

point person *n N Am* somebody who is at the forefront of any activity or endeavour

point source *n* a source of something such as radiant energy or pollution that is or appears to be very small

point-to-point *n* a horse race for amateurs in which horses regularly used in hunting are raced over a marked cross-country course that includes various jumps and obstacles ■ *adj* from one place to another —**point-to-pointer** *n* —**point-to-pointing** *n*

Point-to-Point Protocol *n* a protocol for dial-up access to the Internet using a modem

point woman *n N Am* a woman who is at the forefront of any activity or endeavour

pointy /póynti/ (-ier, -iest) *adj* ending in a point (*informal*)

pointy-headed *adj N Am* regarded as intelligent or intellectual in an arrogant or impractical way (*slang*)

poise[1] /poyz/ *n* **1.** COMPOSURE calm self-assured dignity, especially in dealing with social situations **2.** CONTROLLED GRACE IN MOVEMENT a graceful controlled way of standing, moving, or performing an action **3.** EQUILIBRIUM a stable state of balance **4.** SUSPENDED STATE a state of hovering or being in suspension (*literary*) ■ *vti* (**poises, poising, poised**) BALANCE to be balanced or suspended, or place or hold something in balance or suspension [14C. The noun is via Old French *pois* 'weight, balance'; the verb via *peser* 'weigh', both ultimately < Latin *pensare* (see PENSIVE)]

poise[2] /poyz/ *n* the centimetre-gram-second unit of viscosity equal to one dyne-second per square centimetre [Early 20C. After J. L. M. *Poiseuille* (1799–1868), French physiologist]

poised /poyzd/ *adj* **1.** READY TO ACT fully prepared or in position and about to do something ○ *We are now poised to take over the company.* **2.** READY TO MOVE motionless and balanced or suspended in the air, often just before or in the midst of an action ○ *a bird poised on a branch* **3.** COMPOSED calm, self-assured, and dignified **4.** IN DANGER OF SOMETHING teetering on the edge of a sudden change ○ *stock prices seemingly poised to rise*

~~poisen~~ incorrect spelling of **poison**

poisha /póy shə/ *n* a subunit of currency in Bangladesh. See table at **currency** [Late 20C. < Bangla, alteration of PAISA]

poison /póyz'n/ *n* **1.** TOXIC SUBSTANCE a substance that causes illness, injury, or death if taken into the body or produced within the body **2.** NEGATIVE INFLUENCE something that exercises a powerful destructive or corrupting force, especially in an insidious way **3.** CHEM REACTION-INHIBITING SUBSTANCE a substance that inhibits a chemical reaction or diminishes the activity of a catalyst **4.** PHYS SUBSTANCE SLOWING NUCLEAR REACTION a substance in a nuclear reactor that can absorb neutrons without undergoing fission and therefore slows down the reaction ■ *vt* (**-sons, -soning, -soned**) **1.** GIVE POISON TO SOMEBODY to administer poison to a person or animal, especially with malicious intention **2.** HARM SOMEBODY WITH TOXIC

SUBSTANCE to cause illness, injury, or death to somebody with a poison or other harmful chemical substance **3.** ADD POISON TO SOMETHING to put poison into or onto something in order to harm or kill a person or animal ○ *poisoned bait used to kill rats* **4.** POLLUTE ENVIRONMENT to pollute water, land, or air severely with a harmful substance **5.** CORRUPT OR UNDERMINE SOMEBODY OR SOMETHING to have an evil or corrupting influence on somebody or something, especially by planting hostility or suspicion in somebody's mind against another person **6.** SPOIL SITUATION to spoil something that should be pleasant, enjoyable, or friendly **7.** CHEM INHIBIT CHEMICAL REACTION to inhibit a chemical reaction or activity **8.** PHYS SLOW DOWN NUCLEAR REACTION to slow down or stop a nuclear reaction by the addition of a substance that can absorb neutrons without undergoing fission [13C. Via Old French < Latin *potion-* < *potare* 'to drink'] —**poisoner** *n* ◇ **what's your poison?, name your poison** used to ask what somebody would like to drink (*informal humorous*)

poisoned chalice /póyz'nd-/ *n* a task or decision that will almost inevitably bring harm or unpopularity upon the person who is forced to assume responsibility for it

poison gas *n* a lethal or incapacitating gas used as a weapon in warfare

poison ivy

poison ivy *n* **1.** VINE CAUSING ITCHING RASH a climbing vine of the cashew family that has three-part leaves and white berries. Contact with the plant produces an itching rash. Flowers: small, green. Native to: North America. Genus: *Rhus*. **2.** PLANT RELATED TO POISON IVY a plant related to poison ivy, e.g. poison oak **3.** RASH FROM POISON IVY a rash produced by poison ivy

poison oak *n* **1.** a plant similar or related to poison ivy that produces a rash on contact with the skin. Native to: North America. Genus: *Rhus*. **2.** a rash produced by poison oak

poisonous /póyz'nəss/ *adj* **1.** containing, producing, or acting as a poison **2.** filled with or creating malice, distrust, or hostility —**poisonously** *adv* — **poisonousness** *n*

poison-pen letter *n* a letter containing unpleasant or abusive comments that is sent anonymously to somebody

poison pill *n* a strategic move made by a company in order to make itself seem a less attractive prospect to another company attempting a hostile takeover of it

poison sumac *n* a bush with greenish-white berries that is poisonous to touch. Flowers: greenish. Native to: swamps of southeastern United States. Latin name: *Toxicodendron vernix*.

Poisson /pwáass on, pwáss-/, **Siméon-Denis** (1781–1840) French mathematician and physicist. He is noted for his work on electricity, magnetism, elasticity, and for the Poisson distribution in statistics.

> 'Life is good for only two things, discovering mathematics and teaching mathematics.'
> [Siméon-Denis Poisson. Quoted in *Mathematics Magazine*; February 1991]

Poisson distribution *n* a probability distribution that represents the number of random events occurring over a fixed period of time

Poisson's ratio *n* the ratio of the decrease in width to the increase in length of a material when it is stretched

Poitier /pwáati ay/, **Sidney** (*b.* 1924) US actor and director. He was the first African American Hollywood film star. He won an Academy Award for his role in *Lilies of the Field* (1963).

Poitiers /pwáati ay/ city in west-central France. It is the capital of Vienne Department in Poitou-Charente Region. Population: 83,448 (1999).

poke[1] /pōk/ *v* (**pokes, poking, poked**) **1.** *vti* PROD SOMEBODY OR SOMETHING WITH SOMETHING to push the point of something such as an outstretched finger, elbow, or a stick against somebody or something else **2.** *vt* MAKE HOLE IN SOMETHING to make a hole or opening in something by pushing at it with a finger or a sharp object **3.** *vt* PUSH SOMETHING INTO HOLE to push a finger or a long thin object into a hole, space, or opening **4.** *vti* PROTRUDE FROM SOMETHING to stick out of or through an opening, surface, or covering in such a way that part of the object is visible, or make something stick out in this way ○ *One foot was poking out from under the covers.* **5.** *vi* SEARCH HAPHAZARDLY to search or investigate in a haphazard or aimless manner ○ *poking around in a second-hand bookshop* **6.** *vi* MEDDLE to pry or intrude into something, or meddle with something ○ *Stop poking around in my affairs.* **7.** *vt* STIR FIRE to stir a fire with a poker or similar object in order to make it burn better **8.** *vt* OFFENSIVE TERM an offensive term meaning to have penetrative sex with somebody (*slang*) **9.** *vt* PUNCH SOMEBODY to hit somebody with a fist (*informal*) **10.** *vi* GO SLOWLY to move around or do things in a slow unhurried way ■ *n* **1.** PROD a push or prod with a finger, elbow, stick, or similar pointed object **2.** HAPHAZARD SEARCH a haphazard or aimless search or investigation **3.** PUNCH a blow delivered with the fist (*informal*) **4.** OFFENSIVE TERM an offensive term for an act of penetrative sex (*slang*) [13C. Origin ?]

poke[2] /pōk/ *n* **1.** *regional* a small bag or sack **2.** *Scotland* a paper bag, especially one for holding groceries (*informal*) [13C. < Old N French variant of Old French *poche* 'bag']

poke[3] /pōk/ *n* PLANTS same as **pokeweed** [Mid-17C. < Virginia Algonquian *poughkone*]

pokeberry /pókbəri/ *n* **1.** (*plural* **pokeberries**) the juicy blackish berry that grows on a pokeweed plant **2.** (*plural same* or **pokeberries**) PLANTS same as **pokeweed**

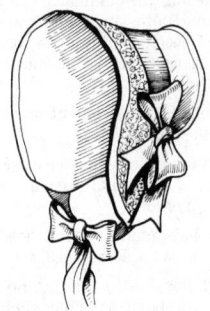
poke bonnet

poke bonnet *n* a woman's bonnet with a deep projecting rim, fashionable in the first half of the 19th century [< POKE[2]]

poker[1] /pókər/ *n* a card game in which players attempt to acquire a winning combination of cards and bet at every deal [Mid-19C. Origin ?]

poker[2] /pókər/ *n* **1.** a metal rod for stirring a fire to make it burn better **2.** somebody or something that pokes, or something used for poking [Mid-16C. < POKE[1]]

poker face *n* a face showing no expression and revealing nothing about what somebody is thinking or feeling [< POKER[1]] —**poker-faced** *adj*

poker machine *n* ANZ GAMBLING same as **fruit machine** [< POKER[1]]

pokerwork /pókər wurk/ *n* HANDICRAFT same as **pyrography** (sense 1) [Early 19C. POKER[2]]

pokeweed /pók weed/ (*plural same* or **-weeds**) *n* a tall plant with blackish berries in elongated clusters, edible shoots, and a poisonous root. Flowers: white. Native to: North America. Latin name: *Phytolacca americana*. [Mid-18C. < POKE[3]]

pokey *adj* another spelling of **poky** (*informal*)

pokie /póki/, **pokey** (*plural* **-eys**) *n* ANZ GAMBLING same as **fruit machine** (*informal*) [Late 20C. Shortening of POKER MACHINE]

poky /póki/ (**-ier, -iest**), **pokey** *adj* (*informal*) **1.** CRAMPED uncomfortably small and cramped **2.** *N Am* SLOW annoyingly slow **3.** *US* SHABBY shabby and old-fashioned [Mid-19C. < POKE[1]] —**pokily** *adv* —**pokiness** *n*

POL *abbr* MIL petroleum, oil, and lubricants

pol. *abbr* **1.** political **2.** politics

Polack /pṓl ak/ *n N Am* a highly offensive term for a Polish person or somebody of Polish descent (*taboo*) [Late 16C. Directly or via French < Polish *Polak*]

Poland

Poland /pṓlənd/ country in eastern Europe, bordering on the Baltic Sea. It became a member of the European Union in 2004. Language: Polish. Currency: zloty. Capital: Warsaw. Population: 38,622,660 (2003). Area: 312,684 sq. km/120,728 sq. mi. Official name **Republic of Poland**

polar /pṓlər/ *adj* **1.** OF OR NEAR EARTH'S POLES relating to, located at, or found in the regions surrounding the North or South Pole **2.** PHYS OF POLE OR POLES relating to a pole or poles of a rotating body, a magnet, or an electrically charged object **3.** AEROSP PASSING OVER POLES OF PLANET passing over, or travelling in an orbit that passes over, a planet's poles ○ *polar orbit* **4.** UTTERLY UNLIKE opposite in tendency, character, or opinions **5.** PIVOTAL of pivotal or central importance **6.** GUIDING serving as a guide or giving direction (*literary*) **7.** CHEM HAVING DIPOLE having a permanent dipole, or having molecules with permanent dipoles ○ *polar molecule* **8.** CRYSTALS HAVING IONIC BOND having an ionic bond, or having crystals with ionic bonds ○ *polar crystal* **9.** MATHS IN POLAR COORDINATE SYSTEM relating to or measured with reference to a system of polar coordinates

polar axis *n* the fixed horizontal line in a system of polar coordinates from which the angle made by the radius vector is measured

polar bear

polar bear *n* a large white mainly meat-eating bear that has wide front feet for swimming. Native to: Arctic coasts and ice floes. Latin name: *Ursus maritimus*.

polar body *n* a cell with a nucleus but little cytoplasm that is produced along with an oocyte, and later discarded, in the process of cell division that leads to an ovum

polar cap *n* **1.** the area around either the North Pole or South Pole that is permanently covered in ice **2.** either of the two polar regions on Mars that are

permanently covered with frozen carbon dioxide and water

polar circle *n* either of the lines of latitude that define the Arctic and Antarctic regions, 66°33' N and 66°33' S

polar coordinates *npl* the two coordinates that locate a point in a plane by specifying the length of a radius vector and the angle it makes with a horizontal line (**polar axis**)

polar front *n* a weather front separating cold polar air and warmer air

polarimeter /pṓlə rímmitər/ *n* an instrument used to measure the rotation of the plane of polarization of light as it passes through a substance, especially a liquid or solution. It is an important tool in the analysis of sugar solutions. [Mid-19C. < modern Latin *polaris* 'polar'] —**polarimetric** /pṓləri méttrik/ *adj* —**polarimetry** *n*

Polaris /pō láariss/ *n* **1.** *N Am* ASTRON same as **Pole Star**. see illustration at **constellation 2.** a US intermediate-range ballistic missile that usually carries a nuclear warhead and is launched from a submarine

polariscope /pō lárriskōp/ *n* an instrument used to study either a substance exposed to polarized light or the effects of a substance on polarized light [Early 19C. < modern Latin *polaris* 'polar']

polarise *vti* another spelling of **polarize**

polarity /pō lárrəti/ (*plural* **-ties**) *n* **1.** a situation in which two people or groups have qualities, ideas, or principles that are diametrically opposed to each other **2.** the condition, in a system, of having opposite characteristics at different points, especially with respect to electric charge or magnetic properties

polarize /pṓlə rīz/ (**-izes, -izing, -ized**), **polarise** (**-ises, -ising, -ised**) *vti* **1.** CAUSE DIVISION OF OPINION to make the differences between groups or ideas ever more clear-cut and extreme, hardening the opposition between them, or become ever more clear-cut and extreme in this way **2.** PHYS ACQUIRE OR MAKE SOMETHING ACQUIRE POLARITY to acquire polarity, or cause something to acquire polarity **3.** PHYS RESTRICT VIBRATION OF LIGHT to cause light to vibrate within particular planes, or vibrate in this way — **polarizable** *adj* —**polarization** /pṓlə rī záysh'n/ *n* —**polarizer** *n*

polarizing microscope /pṓlə rīzing-/ *n* a microscope in which polarized light is used to examine specimens

polar nucleus *n* either of the two nuclei in the centre of the sac of a seed plant embryo that eventually fuse into the endosperm

polarography /pṓlə róggrəfi/ *n* an analytic technique used to study ions in a solution that compares the strength of electric currents passing through the solution during electrolysis and the voltages needed to produce them [Mid-20C. < *polarization*] —**polarographic** /pṓlərə gráffik/ *adj*

Polaroid /pṓlə royd/ *tdmk* **1.** a trademark for a camera that produces pictures that develop within seconds of being taken, or the film used in such a camera **2.** a trademark for a specially treated transparent plastic that allows polarized light through and is used to reduce glare in sunglasses

polar star *n* ASTRON same as **Pole Star**

polder /pṓldər/ *n* an area of land reclaimed from the sea and protected by dykes, especially in the Netherlands [Early 17C. < Dutch] —**polder** *vt*

pole[1] /pōl/ *n* **1.** NORTH OR SOUTH POLE either of the two points on the Earth, the North and South Poles, that are the endpoints of its axis of rotation, are farthest from the equator, and are surrounded by icecaps **2.** ENDPOINT OF SPHERE AXIS either of the two endpoints of the axis of rotation of a sphere, planet, or other astronomical object **3.** ASTRON same as **celestial pole 4.** EITHER OF TWO OPPOSITES either of two completely opposed or contrasted positions, states, or views ○ *They're at opposite poles as far as their taste in music is concerned.* **5.** PHYS END OF MAGNET either of the two ends of a magnet or magnetized body, where the lines of force are most concentrated **6.** ELEC POSITIVE OR NEGATIVE TERMINAL either of two terminals in something such as a battery, generator, or motor that have opposite electric charges **7.** PHYSIOL DISTINCT REGION IN CELL either of two opposite regions that are physiologically or functionally distinct in an organism, cell, or structure, e.g. the opposite ends of the spindle structure formed in the nucleus of a cell during cell division **8.** MATHS ORIGIN OF POLAR COORDINATES the origin in a polar coordinate system **9.** REFERENCE POINT a fixed point of reference (*literary*) [14C. Via Latin < Greek *polos* 'axis'] ◇ **be poles apart** to be as different or as opposed as it is possible to be

SPELLCHECK pole or **poll**? Do not confuse the spelling of ***pole*** and ***poll***, which sound similar. A ***pole*** is a long straight piece of wood, metal, etc. (as in *a ski pole, the pole vault*) or either of two opposite regions of the Earth, a magnet, etc. (as in *the South Pole, be poles apart*). ***Poll*** is a noun or verb referring to an election or survey, as in *going to the polls, an opinion poll.*

pole[2] /pōl/ *n* **1.** LONG STRAIGHT OBJECT a long straight strong piece of wood, metal, or other material, usually with a round cross-section and thin enough to hold in the hands or arms **2.** POLE-VAULTER'S POLE the long flexible shaft made of wood, metal, or fibreglass used by a competitor in the pole vault **3.** SHAFT ON HORSE-DRAWN VEHICLE a single shaft projecting forward from the front of a vehicle between the animals that draw it, to which those animals are attached **4.** MOTOR SPORTS same as **pole position** (sense 1) **5.** MEASURE same as **perch**[1] *n* (senses 4–5) ■ *v* (**poles, poling, poled**) **1.** *vti* PROPEL BOAT WITH POLE to move a boat along by pushing with a pole against a firm surface **2.** *vt* SUPPORT PLANT WITH POLE to use a pole to provide support for a plant **3.** *vti* USE SKI POLES to make forward progress on skis by pushing with ski poles [Old English *pāl*, via Germanic < Latin *palus* 'stake']

SPELLCHECK See ***pole***[1]

Pole /pōl/ *n* **1.** /pōl/ somebody who comes from Poland **2.** somebody who is of Polish descent [Late 16C. Via German < Old Polish *Polanie* 'field-dwellers' < *pole* 'field']

poleax *vt, n* US spelling of **poleaxe**

poleaxe /pṓl aks/ *n* (*plural* **-axes**) **1.** BUTCHER'S AXE a specialized axe with a hammer face opposite the blade, used, especially in former times, for slaughtering animals **2.** BATTLE-AXE a battle-axe with a long or short handle, especially one with a hammer or spike opposite the axe blade **3.** AXE FOR CUTTING RIGGING a short-handled axe used to cut rigging or ropes on sailing ships, especially during combat ■ *vt* (**-axes, -axing, -axed**) **1.** AMAZE AND STUPEFY SOMEBODY to leave somebody stupefied and speechless with astonishment **2.** HIT SOMEBODY VERY HARD to hit somebody hard enough to cause unconsciousness **3.** HIT SOMEBODY OR SOMETHING WITH POLEAXE to hit somebody or something with a poleaxe [14C. Alteration of *pollaxe* 'head-axe' < POLL]

polecat

polecat /pṓl kat/ *n* a woodland animal related to but larger than the weasel that has brown fur and emits a foul smell when disturbed. Native to: Europe, Asia, North Africa. Genus: *Mustela* or *Vormela*. [14C. Origin ?]

pole dancer *n* an entertainer who dances around a pole in an erotic way in a bar or club —**pole dancing** *n*

poleis ANCIENT HIST, POL plural of **polis**[1]

polemic /pə lémmik/ *n* **1.** PASSIONATE ARGUMENT a passionate, strongly worded, and often controversial argument against or, less often, in favour of somebody or something **2.** PASSIONATE CRITIC somebody who engages in a passionate dispute about or argues passionately against somebody or something (*literary*) ■ *adj also* **polemical** /-ik'l/ CONTAINING PASSIONATE ARGUMENT containing or expressing passionate and strongly worded argument against or in favour of somebody or something [Mid-17C. Via medieval Latin < Greek *polemikos* < *polemos* 'war'] —**polemically** *adv* —**polemicist** /pə lémmissist/ *n*

polemics /pə lémmiks/ *n* the art or practice of arguing passionately and strongly for or against something (*takes a singular verb*)

polenta /pō léntə/ *n* in Italian cooking, fine yellow maize meal cooked to a mush with water or stock, sometimes set, sliced, and served baked or fried [Mid-16C. Via Italian < Latin, 'barley meal']

pole piece *n* a shaped piece of ferromagnetic material, usually soft iron, that concentrates and directs the magnetic field of a magnet to maximize the efficiency of devices such as loudspeakers and generators

pole position *n* **1.** the best position on the starting grid of a motor race, usually on the inside of the front row and taken by the driver with the fastest prerace practice time **2.** a very good or advantageous position at the beginning of something

pole star *n* something considered as a guiding light and giver of direction (*literary*)

Pole Star *n* the brightest star in the constellation Ursa Minor, near the celestial north pole. Because it always indicates due north from an observer anywhere on the Earth, it is important for navigation. N Am term **Polaris**. See illustration at **constellation**

Poles'ye /pṓ lez yə/ ➧ **Pripet Marshes**

pole vault *n* **1.** an athletics event in which the competitors use a long flexible pole to swing themselves up and over a very high crossbar **2.** a jump in the pole vault, or any jump made with the help of a pole —**pole-vault** *vti* —**pole-vaulter** *n*

poley /pṓli/ *adj Aus* having no horns ○ *poley cattle* [Mid-19C. < POLL]

police /pə léess/ *n* **1.** ORGANIZATION FOR MAINTAINING LAW AND ORDER a civil organization whose members are given special legal powers by the government and whose task is to maintain public order and to solve and prevent crimes ○ *a police car* **2.** SPECIALIZED FORCE an organized group of people whose job is maintaining order, ensuring that regulations are obeyed, and preventing crime within a particular area or sphere of activity ○ *military police* **3.** POLICE OFFICERS police officers considered as a group (*takes a plural verb*) **4.** PEOPLE ENFORCING CORRECT BEHAVIOUR a group of people who seek to make others' opinions or behaviour conform with their own (*informal*) ○ *fashion police* ■ *vt* (**-lices, -licing, -liced**) **1.** MAINTAIN LAW AND ORDER AT SOMETHING to ensure that law and order are maintained at an event or location, using the police or a military force **2.** ENSURE SOMETHING PROCEEDS ACCORDING TO RULES to ensure that rules and procedures are followed correctly in something, or that something is implemented as agreed [15C. Via French and Latin < Greek *politeia* 'civil organization, the state' < *politēs* 'citizen' (see POLITIC)]

police action *n* a relatively small-scale military action undertaken without a declaration of war, e.g. to prevent violation of an international agreement

police constable *n* POLICE same as **constable**

police dog *n* a dog trained to work with the police in tracking or searching for people, or in detecting illegal substances by smell

police force *n* an organized body of police with jurisdiction within a geographical area or over a group of people

policeman /pə léessmən/ (*plural* **-men** /-mən/) *n* a man who is a police officer, especially a constable

Police Motu /-mō too/ *n* LANG same as **Hiri Motu** —**Police Motu** *adj*

police officer, **policeperson** /pə léess purss'n/ (*plural* **-persons** or **-people** /-peep'l/) *n* a member of a police force

police procedural *n* a crime novel or drama in which the crime is investigated by police officers

police state *n* a country in which the government

uses police, especially secret police, to exercise strict or repressive control over the population

police station *n* the local headquarters of a police force

policewallah /pə leéss wolə/ *n S Asia* same as **policeman**

policewoman /pə leéss wŏŏmən/ (*plural* **-women** /-wimin/) *n* a woman who is a police officer

policy[1] /póllәssi/ *n* (*plural* **-cies**) **1.** COURSE OF ACTION a programme of actions adopted by a person, group, or government, or the set of principles on which they are based **2.** PRUDENCE shrewdness or prudence, especially in the pursuit of a course of action ■ **policies** *npl Scotland* ESTATE GROUNDS the grounds attached to a large country house [14C. Via Old French *policie* 'government, civil organization' < Greek *politeia* (see POLICE)]

policy[2] /póllәssi/ (*plural* **-cies**) *n* a contract that exists between an insurance company and a person or organization buying insurance services, or the document that lists the contract terms [Mid-16C. Via French < Provençal *polissa*, Catalan *police*]

policyholder /póllәssi hōldər/ *n* a named person or organization that has bought an insurance policy

policymaking /póllәssi mayking/ *n* the drawing up of policies, especially the formulating of political policies by members of a government —**policymaker** *n* —**policymaking** *adj*

polio /pṓli ō/ *n* MED same as **poliomyelitis** [Mid-20C. Shortening]

poliomyelitis /pṓli ō mī́ ə lítiss/ *n* a severe infectious viral disease, usually affecting children or young adults, that inflames the brain stem and spinal cord, sometimes leading to loss of voluntary movement and muscular wasting [Late 19C. < modern Latin < Greek *polios* 'grey'; because it affects 'grey matter'] —**poliomyelitic** /-mī́ ə líttik/ *adj*

poliovirus /pṓli ō vīrəss/ *n* one of three forms of a virus that causes poliomyelitis

polis[1] /pólliss/ (*plural* **poleis** /pó līss/) *n* **1.** a city-state in ancient Greece, characteristic of Greek political organization from 800 to 400 BC **2.** the city-state form of government [Late 19C. < Greek, 'city']

polis[2] /pṓliss/ (*plural same*) *n Scotland* the police as a force, or an individual police officer (*nonstandard*) [Late 19C. Alteration of POLICE]

polish /póllish/ *v* (**-ishes, -ishing, -ished**) **1.** *vti* MAKE SMOOTH OR GLOSSY to make something smooth or shiny, or become smooth or shiny, by rubbing with something **2.** *vt* REMOVE OUTER LAYERS OF RICE to remove the outer layers of brown rice to make white rice by rotating the grain in a drum **3.** *vti* IMPROVE to make something more refined, elegant, or complete, or become more refined, elegant, or complete ○ *polish a speech* ■ *n* **1.** SUBSTANCE USED FOR POLISHING a substance used to make something smooth or shiny ○ *furniture polish* **2.** SMOOTHNESS the smoothness or glossiness of something that has been polished ○ *car paintwork with a high polish* **3.** RUB GIVEN TO SOMETHING a rubbing of something designed to make it smooth or glossy **4.** REFINEMENT refinement, especially of style, that is the mark of expertise or experience [13C. < Old French *poliss-*, stem of *polir* < Latin *polire*] —**polisher** *n*

polish off *vt* **1.** to finish something, especially food or a task, quickly and completely **2.** to kill or eliminate somebody (*informal*)

polish up *vt* **1.** to make something smooth or shiny by rubbing it **2.** to improve or refine something such as a prepared speech or knowledge of a foreign language

polish up on *vt* to improve knowledge or skill in a subject

Polish /pṓlish/ *npl* PEOPLE OF POLAND the people of Poland ■ *n* OFFICIAL LANGUAGE OF POLAND the official language of Poland, also spoken in North America and Europe, belonging to the Balto-Slavic branch of Indo-European. Native speakers: 44 million. ■ *adj* OF POLAND relating to Poland, or its people, language, or culture [Early 17C. < POLE]

Polish notation *n* a notation for symbolic logic where the logical operators are placed as prefixes in front of formulas instead of between them, allowing parentheses to be dispensed with. For example, 'p or (q and r)' becomes 'or p and q r'. [Because developed by mathematicians in Poland]

Politburo /póllit byoorō, pə lít-/ *n* the executive and policymaking committee of a governing Communist Party, especially the committee in the former Soviet Union [Early 20C. < Russian *politbyuro* 'political bureau']

polite /pə lī́t/ (**-liter, -litest**) *adj* **1.** showing or possessing good manners or common courtesy **2.** socially superior to ordinary people and considered refined or cultivated [15C. < Latin *politus*, past participle of *polire* 'polish'] —**politely** *adv* —**politeness** *n*

politesse /pólli téss/ *n* politeness of a very formal or genteel kind [Early 18C. < French, 'politeness']

politic /póllətik/ *adj* possessing or displaying shrewdness, tact, or cunning [15C. Via French and Latin < Greek *politikos* 'civic, political' < *politēs* 'citizen' < *polis* 'city'] —**politicly** *adv*

political /pə líttik'l/ *adj* **1.** CONCERNED WITH PARTY POLITICS relating to politics, especially party politics **2.** CONCERNED WITH GOVERNMENT relating to civil administration or government **3.** RESULTING FROM BELIEFS UNACCEPTABLE TO GOVERNMENT arising from somebody's opposition to a government or support for policies and principles regarded by the authorities as unacceptable, or suffering as a result of expressing such opposition or support ○ *a political trial* ○ *a political detainee* **4.** INTERESTED IN POLITICS particularly interested or active in politics ○ *I'm not usually a very political person.* **5.** CONCERNED WITH POWER relating to the balance of power in relationships, especially in a group or organization ○ *a political workplace* **6.** PRAGMATIC carried out for reasons that best serve a desired outcome rather than for other reasons such as being morally justifiable ○ *denies that this was a political decision* —**politically** *adv*

political economy *n* the study of ways in which economics and government policies interact (*dated*) —**political economist** *n*

politically correct *adj* marked by language or conduct that deliberately avoids giving offence, e.g. on the basis of ethnic origin or sexual orientation —**political correctness** *n*

politically incorrect *adj* marked by language or conduct that could give offence, e.g. on the basis of ethnic origin or sexual orientation —**political incorrectness** *n*

political prisoner *n* somebody who is imprisoned because of his or her political actions or beliefs

political science *n* the study of political organizations and institutions, especially governments —**political scientist** *n*

political theatre *n* dramatic performances designed to advance or promote a political cause

politician /póllə tísh'n/ *n* **1.** SOMEBODY ACTIVE IN POLITICS somebody who actively or professionally engages in politics **2.** GOVERNMENT MEMBER a member of a branch of government **3.** SCHEMER somebody who manipulates relationships, especially in a workplace **4.** *US* SOMEBODY SEEKING PERSONAL POWER somebody whose main political motive is self-advancement and whose methods are often unscrupulous (*disapproving*) [Late 16C. < POLITIC]

politicize /pə lítti sīz/ (**-cizes, -cizing, -cized**), **politicise** (**-cises, -cising, -cised**) *v* **1.** *vti* to bring something such as an issue of public interest into the political arena **2.** *vt* to make somebody politically aware or active, or introduce a political element to something —**politicization** /pə lítti sī záysh'n/ *n*

politicking /póllə tiking/ *n* political activity, especially campaigning or speech-making, often when disapproved of as insincere or self-serving

politico /pə líttikō/ (*plural* **-cos**) *n* a politician, especially one whose words are dismissed as trite or whose motives are disapproved of as self-serving (*informal*) [Mid-17C. < Italian or Spanish, 'politician']

politics /póllətiks/ *n* **1.** ACTIVITIES ASSOCIATED WITH GOVERNMENT the theory and practice of government, especially the activities associated with governing, with obtaining legislative or executive power, or with forming and running organizations connected with government (*takes a singular verb*) **2.** POLITICAL LIFE political activity as a profession (*takes a singular verb*) ○ *left the law to enter politics* **3.** POWER RELATIONSHIPS IN SPECIFIC FIELD the interrelationships between the people, groups, or organizations in a particular area of life especially insofar as they involve power and influence or conflict (*takes a singular or plural verb*) ○ *the politics of education* **4.** CALCULATED ADVANCEMENT the use of tactics and strategy to gain power in a group or organization (*takes a singular or plural verb*) **5.** same as **political science** (*takes a singular verb*) ■ *npl* POLITICAL BELIEFS political persuasions or beliefs (*takes a plural verb*)

polity /póllәti/ (*plural* **-ties**) *n* **1.** PARTICULAR FORM OF GOVERNMENT a particular form of government that exists within a state or an institution **2.** POLITICAL ENTITY a state, society, or institution regarded as a political entity **3.** POLITICS AND GOVERNMENT WITHIN SOCIETY the aspect of society that is oriented to politics and government [Mid-16C. Via Latin < Greek *politeia* (see POLICE)]

polje /pṓlyə/ *n* a large low-lying area in a limestone region (**karst**), often surrounded by steep walls and containing a marsh or small lake [Late 19C. < Serbo-Croatian, 'field']

Polk /pōk/, **James Knox** (1795–1849) 11th president of the United States (1845–49). Under his Democratic administration, the United States expanded westwards to the Pacific Ocean. See table at **president**

> 'The people of this continent alone have the right to decide their own destiny.'
> [James Knox Polk, *Speech to the US Congress*; 2 December 1845]

polka /pólkə, pṓl-/ *n* **1.** LIVELY DANCE a lively dance for couples consisting of three quick steps and a hop and originating in Central Europe **2.** MUSIC FOR POLKA the music for a polka ■ *vi* (**-kas, -kaing, -kaed**) DANCE POLKA to dance a polka [Mid-19C. Probably via Czech < Polish, feminine form of *Polak* 'Pole']

polka dot *n* a round spot repeated to form a regular pattern in a contrasting colour on fabric

poll /pōl/ *n* **1.** ELECTION a political election in its entirety, including the casting, recording, and counting of votes **2.** SURVEY OF PUBLIC a questioning of the population or of a representative sample to tally opinions or gather other information ○ *a telephone poll* **3.** NUMBER OF VOTES the total number of votes cast in an election **4.** HEAD the head, or the back part of the head (*archaic*) **5.** STRIKING SURFACE OF HAMMER the broad hitting part of a hammer or axe ■ **polls** *npl* PLACE FOR VOTING a place where votes are recorded during an election ■ *v* (**polls, polling, polled**) **1.** *vt* SAMPLE OPINION METHODICALLY to sample the opinions or attitudes of a group of people systematically **2.** *vt* RECEIVE PARTICULAR NUMBER OF VOTES to receive a particular number of votes in an election **3.** *vti* CAST VOTE IN ELECTION to cast a vote in an election **4.** *vt* CHECK AVAILABILITY OF COMPUTER COMMUNICATION LINES to check communication lines in a computer or computer network to determine if they can receive or transmit data **5.** *vt* SHEAR ANIMAL to clip or shear an animal **6.** *vt* REMOVE HORNS FROM ANIMAL to cut the horns off an animal or shorten its horns [13C. Probably < Middle Dutch or Middle Low German]

SPELLCHECK See *pole*[1].

pollack /póllәk/ (*plural* **-lacks** or *same*), **pollock** (*plural* **-locks** or *same*) *n* **1.** a sea fish of the cod family, with a protruding lower jaw. Native to: North Atlantic. Genus: *Pollachius*. **2.** the flesh of a pollack used as food [Early 16C. Origin ?]

pollard /póllərd, -aard/ *n* **1.** TREE WITH BRANCHES CUT a tree whose branches are cut back extensively to encourage denser growth **2.** ANIMAL WITH HORNS REMOVED OR SHED an animal that has shed its horns or antlers or has had its horns removed ■ *vt* (**-lards, -larding, -larded**) CUT BRANCHES OR HORNS to cut back the branches of a tree, or remove the horns of an animal [Mid-17C. < POLL]

pollen /póllən/ *n* a powdery substance produced by flowering plants that contains male reproductive cells. It is carried by wind and insects to other plants, which it fertilizes. [Mid-18C. < Latin, 'fine flour, dust']

Pollen /póllən/, **Daniel** (1813–96) Irish-born premier of New Zealand (1875–76). He was colonial secretary (1873–77) and took over as premier while Julius Vogel was travelling overseas.

pollen basket *n* the hollow part of a bee's hind leg, used to transport pollen

pollen count *n* a scientific measure of the amount of pollen in a volume of air during a 24-hour period

pollen mother cell *n* a cell in a flowering plant that produces four pollen grains after cell division

pollen sac *n* a cavity in the anther of a flower, where pollen is produced

pollen tube *n* a hollow tube that develops from a pollen grain and conveys male reproductive cells to the egg cell

pollex /pólleks/ (*plural* **-lices** /-seez/) *n* the first digit of the forelimb in birds and animals, or the thumb in humans (*technical*) [Mid-19C. < Latin]

pollie /pólli/, **polly** (*plural* **-lies**) *n Aus* same as **politician** (sense 1) (*informal*) [Shortening]

pollinate /póllə nayt/ (**-nates, -nating, -nated**) *vt* to transfer pollen grains from the male structure of a plant (**anther**) to the female structure of a plant (**stigma**) and fertilize it [Late 19C. < Latin *pollin-*, stem of *pollen* 'fine flour, dust'] —**pollination** /póllə náysh'n/ *n* —**pollinator** *n*

polling booth /pṓling-/ *n UK, ANZ, Can* a booth in which an individual voter marks a ballot paper during an election. US term **voting booth**

polling station *n* a building officially designated for casting votes during an election. N Am term **polling place**

pollinia BOT plural of **pollinium**

polliniferous /póllə níffərəss/ *adj* producing or carrying pollen [Mid-19C. < Latin *pollin-* (see POLLINATE)]

pollinium /pə línni əm/ (*plural* **-ia** /-i ə/) *n* a cohering mass of pollen grains transported as a whole during pollination, typical of orchids and milkweeds [Mid-19C. < modern Latin < Latin *pollin-* (see POLLINATE)]

pollinosis /pólli nṓssiss/ *n* MED same as **hay fever** (*technical*) [Early 20C. < Latin *pollin-* (see POLLINATE)]

polliwog /pólliwog/, **pollywog** *n* ZOOL same as **tadpole** [15C. Alteration of *pollwiggle* < POLL 'head' + WIGGLE]

pollock /póllək/ *n* FISH another spelling of **pollack**

Pollock /póllək/, **Jackson** (1912–56) US artist. A leading abstract expressionist, he used action-painting techniques to create intricate interlaced webs of paint. Full name **Pollock, Paul Jackson**

> 'When I am *in* my painting, I'm not aware of what I am doing. It's only after a sort of "get acquainted" period that I see what I have been about.'
> [Jackson Pollock, 'Winter Possibilities I', *My Painting*; 1947–48]

pollster /pṓlstər/ *n* somebody who conducts public opinion polls

poll tax *n* **1.** a flat-rate tax levied on all members of a population, often as a prerequisite to voting **2.** PUBLIC ADMIN same as **community charge** (*informal*)

pollucite /póllyoo sīt, pə lóoss īt/ *n* a rare colourless feldspathoid mineral that contains caesium [Mid-19C. Alteration of *pollux*, its earlier name, from its association with the mineral CASTOR² (in allusion to CASTOR AND POLLUX)]

pollutant /pə lóot'nt/ *n* a substance that pollutes something, e.g. a chemical or waste product contaminating the air, soil, or water

pollute /pə lóot/ (**-lutes, -luting, -luted**) *vt* **1.** CONTAMINATE SOMETHING to make something impure or unclean, or cause harm to an area of the natural environment, usually by introducing chemicals, waste products, or similarly damaging or poisonous substances **2.** CORRUPT OR DEFILE SOMEBODY to make somebody morally or spiritually impure **3.** DESECRATE SOMETHING to violate the sacred nature of a holy place [14C. < Latin *pollut-*, past participle of *polluere* < Indo-European, 'dirt, make dirty'] —**polluter** *n*

pollution /pə lóosh'n/ *n* **1.** the act of polluting something, especially the natural environment **2.** the state or condition of being polluted, or the presence of pollutants ○ *Pollution in the river will destroy the fish.*

Pollux *n* MYTHOL ➧ **Castor and Pollux**

polly *n Aus* POL another spelling of **pollie** (*informal*)

Pollyanna /pólli ánnə/ *n* an unrealistically optimistic person [Early 20C. After the heroine of children's stories written by Eleanor Hodgman Porter (1868–1920), US author]

pollywog *n* ZOOL another spelling of **polliwog**

polo /pṓlō/ (*plural* **-los**) *n* **1.** a game played by teams on horseback, with players using long-handled mallets to drive a wooden ball into a goal **2.** a game similar to polo, e.g. one in which the participants are mounted on bicycles rather than horses (*usually used in combination*) **3.** SPORTS same as **water polo** **4.** CLOTHING same as **polo shirt** (sense 1) (*informal*) **5.** CLOTHING same as **polo neck** (senses 1–2) (*informal*) [Late 19C. < Tibetan *pholo* 'ball game']

Polo /pṓlō/, **Marco** (1254–1324) Venetian merchant and traveller. His accounts of his travels to China offered Europeans a firsthand view of Asian lands and stimulated interest in Asian trade.

> 'The walls of the halls and chambers are all covered with gold and silver and decorated with pictures of dragons and birds and horsemen and various breeds of beasts and scenes of battle. The ceiling is similarly adorned...nothing to be seen anywhere but gold and pictures.'
> [Marco Polo, 'Kubilai Khan', *The Travels of Marco Polo*; 1298–99]

polo coat *n* a double-breasted overcoat, usually made of camel hair

Polokwane /pṓlō kwaá nay/ capital city of Limpopo Province, South Africa. Population: 39,011 (1991). Former name **Pietersburg**

polonaise /póllə náyz/ *n* **1.** SLOW DANCE a stately formal dance for couples, in 3/4 time **2.** MUSIC FOR POLONAISE the music for a polonaise **3.** DRESS WITH UNDERSKIRT a dress with a tight bodice, cut away at the waist to reveal an inner skirt, worn by European women in the 18th century [Mid-18C. < French, 'Polish']

polo neck *n* **1.** a high rollover collar that fits closely to the neck **2.** a sweater with a high rollover collar that fits closely to the neck ▶ N Am term **turtleneck** —**polo-necked** *adj*

polonium /pə lṓni əm/ *n* a very rare radioactive metallic element. Source: uranium ores. Use: removal of static electricity. Symbol **Po**. See table at **element** [Late 19C. < medieval Latin *Polonia* 'Poland', the home of its discoverer, Marie CURIE]

polony /pə lṓni/ (*plural same or* **-nies**) *n* a large smoked sausage made with a variety of finely ground seasoned meats, usually including beef and pork [Mid-18C. Probably alteration of BOLOGNA]

polo pony *n* a horse ridden in the game of polo

polo shirt *n* **1.** a lightweight casual shirt, usually made of knitted cotton, with a small square collar and a buttoned opening at the neck **2.** a shirt with a polo neck [Because traditionally worn by polo players]

Pol Pot /pól pót/ (1928–98) Cambodian national leader. He led the communist Khmer Rouge to victory, and approximately 1.7 million people died under his rule in Cambodia (1975–79). Born **Saloth Sar**

poltergeist /póltərgīst/ *n* a supposed supernatural spirit that reveals its presence by creating disturbances, e.g. by knocking over objects [Mid-19C. < German, 'noisy ghost']

poltroon /pol tróon/ *n* an offensive term for somebody regarded as a contemptible coward (*archaic*) [Early 16C. Via French < Italian *poltrone* 'coward, lazy person']

~~polution~~ incorrect spelling of **pollution**

poly¹ /pólli/ (*plural* **-ys**) *n* (*informal*) **1.** EDUC same as **polytechnic** **2.** CHEM same as **polythene** **3.** MED same as **polymorph** (sense 3) **4.** *N Am* TEXTILES same as **polyester** (sense 2) [Late 20C. Shortening]

poly² /pólli/ (*plural* **-lies**) *n* an aromatic plant of the mint family. Native to: southern Europe. Latin name: *Teucrium polium*. [Early 16C. Via Latin < Greek *polion*]

poly- *prefix* **1.** more than one ○ *polyandry* **2.** more than normal ○ *polyphagia* **3.** polymer ○ *polyethylene* [< Greek *polus* 'much' < Indo-European, 'fill']

polyA /póli áy/ *n* BIOCHEM same as **polyadenylic acid**

polyacrylamide /pólli ə krílla mīd/ *n* a white solid polymer of acrylamide. Use: thickening, clouding, and absorbent agent.

polyadenylic acid /pólli áddə níllik-/ *n* a segment of RNA made up of multiple units of AMP, found in messenger RNA molecules. It stabilizes RNA during protein synthesis.

polyalcohol /pólli álkə hol/ *n* CHEM same as **polyol**

polyamide /pólli ámmīd, -mid/ *n* a synthetic polymer that has recurring amide groups, e.g. nylon

polyamine /pólli ámm een, -ə meén/ *n* an organic compound containing more than one amino group

polyandry /pólli andri/ *n* **1.** SIMULTANEOUS MARRIAGE TO MULTIPLE HUSBANDS the custom of having more than one husband at a time **2.** FACT OF HAVING MULTIPLE MALE MATES animal mating in which a female mates with more than one male during any single breeding season **3.** FACT OF HAVING MANY STAMENS possession by a plant of a large number of stamens [Late 17C. < Greek *poluandria* 'many husbands' < *andr-* 'man, husband'] —**polyandrous** /pólli ándrəss/ *adj*

polyantha rose /pólli anthə-/ *n* a member of a class of cultivated roses. Flowers: small, mainly scentless, in dense clusters. [< modern Latin, form of *polyanthus* (see POLYANTHUS)]

polyanthus /pólli ánthəss/ *n* a hybrid primrose with bright flowers in a variety of colours. Latin name: *Primula polyantha*. [Early 18C. Via modern Latin < Greek *poluanthos* 'having many flowers' < *anthos* 'flower']

polyanthus narcissus *n* a narcissus with small white or yellow flowers. Native to: Europe, Asia. Latin name: *Narcissus tazetta*.

polyatomic /pólli ə tómmik/ *adj* describes a molecule that has more than two atoms

polybasic /pólli báyssik/ *adj* describes a molecule or compound that has two or more atoms of replaceable hydrogen

polybasite /pólli báy sīt/ *n* a rare grey to black crystalline mineral containing silver, found near silver ores [Mid-19C. < German *Polybasit* < Greek *polus* 'much' + German *Basis* 'base'; from its chemical composition]

polycarbonate /pólli kaárbə nayt, -nət/ *n* a strong synthetic resin. Use: moulded products, unbreakable windows, optical components.

polycarboxylic acid /pólli kaar bok síllik-/ *n* carboxylic acid that contains more than one carboxyl group

polycarpic /pólli kaárpik/, **polycarpous** /-kaárpəss/ *adj* describes a plant that is capable of producing flowers and fruit several times in succession —**polycarpy** /pólli kaarpi/ *n*

polychaete /pólli keet/, **polychete** *n* a sea worm with a segmented body and bristled fleshy appendages used in swimming. Class: Polychaeta. [Late 19C. < modern Latin *Polychaeta* < Greek *polukhaitēs* 'having much hair' < *khaitē* 'long hair'] —**polychaetous** /pólli keétəss/ *adj*

polychlorinated biphenyl /pólli kláwrə naytid bī feén'l/ *n* CHEM full form of **PCB**

polychromatic /pólli krō máttik/ *adj* **1.** having, showing, or consisting of many colours, either at the same time or in sequence **2.** describes electromagnetic radiation that has multiple wavelengths

polychrome /póllikrōm/ *adj* **1.** decorated with many or varied colours **2.** PHYS same as **polychromatic** (sense 1) ■ *n* a polychrome object or artefact

polychromy /pólli krōmi/ *n* the practice of using several different colours in painting, sculpture, or decoration

polyclinic /pólli klínnik/ *n* a clinic, often independent of a hospital, in which medical care is provided by a range of specialists

polyclone /pólliklōn/ *n* a clone derived from groups of cells of different ancestry or genetic constitution —**polyclonal** /pólli klṓn'l/ *adj* —**polyclonally** *adv*

polyconic projection /pólli kónnik-/ *n* a conic map projection in which all meridians, except the central, are curved and the parallels are nonconcentric arcs

polycotton /pólli kot'n/ *n* a fabric that is made from a mixture of polyester and cotton [Late 20C. < POLY¹]

polycotyledon /pólli kotti leéd'n/ *n* a plant with more than two cotyledons —**polycotyledonous** *adj*

polycrystal /pólli kríst'l/ *n* a crystalline structure whose crystals were formed rapidly and randomly

polycrystalline /pólli krístə līn/ *adj* consisting of randomly oriented crystals

polycyclic /pólli síklik/ *adj* 1. describes a shell that has two or more whorls 2. describes a compound having two or more closed rings of atoms —**polycyclic** *n*

polycystic /pólli sístik/ *adj* describes an organ such as a kidney or ovary that has developed multiple cysts

polycystic ovarian syndrome *n* a hormonal disorder in women characterized by enlarged ovaries containing numerous small painless cysts, infertility, excessive hair growth, and acne

polycythaemia /póllisī theémi ə/ *n* an increase in red blood cells, occurring on its own or in conjunction with other diseases, especially of the respiratory or circulatory systems

polycythemia *n* MED US spelling of **polycythaemia**

polydactyl /pólli dáktil/ *adj* describes vertebrates, including human beings, that have more than the normal number of fingers or toes —**polydactyl** *n*

polydipsia /pólli dípsi ə/ *n* excessive thirst [Mid-17C. < POLY- + Greek *dipsa* 'thirst'] —**polydipsic** *adj*

polyelectrolyte /pólli i léktrə līt/ *n* an electrolyte that has a high molecular weight, e.g. a protein

polyembryony /pólli émbri əni/ *n* the production of more than one embryo from a single egg —**polyembryonic** /-émbri ónnik/ *adj*

polyene /pólli een/ *n* a hydrocarbon that has many alternating single and double carbon-carbon bonds

polyester /pólli éstər/ *n* 1. a synthetic polymer in which the monomers are linked together by the chemical group -COO-. Use: resins, plastics, textile fibres. 2. a strong hard-wearing synthetic fabric with low moisture absorbency, made from a polyester

polyethylene /pólli éthə leen/ *n* N Am same as **polythene**

polyethylene glycol *n* a polymer of ethylene compounds. Use: emulsifiers and lubricants in ointments and cosmetics.

Polyfilla /póllifillə/ *tdmk* a trademark for a multipurpose filling plaster

polygamy /pə líggəmi/ *n* 1. the custom of having more than one spouse at the same time 2. animal mating in which an individual mates with more than one animal during any single breeding season [Late 16C. Via French and late Latin < ecclesiastical Greek *polugamia* < *polugamos* 'often married' < Greek *gamos* 'marriage'] —**polygamist** *n* —**polygamous** *adj* —**polygamously** *adv*

polygene /pólli jeen/ *n* one of a group of genes in which the number of those genes present collectively determines the extent of a characteristic such as height —**polygenic** /pólli jénnik/ *adj* —**polygenically** *adv*

polygenesis /pólli jénnəssiss/ *n* origin from more than one species, line of ancestors, or source —**polygenetic** /póllijə néttik/ *adj* —**polygenetically** *adv*

polyglot /pólli glot/ *adj* 1. COMPETENT IN MANY LANGUAGES capable of reading, writing, or speaking many languages 2. IN MANY LANGUAGES written or communicated in many languages ■ *n* 1. MULTILINGUAL PERSON a speaker of many languages 2. BOOK CONTAINING TEXT IN MANY LANGUAGES a book, especially a Bible, that gives the text in several languages 3. MIX OF LANGUAGES a confused mixture of languages [Mid-17C. Via French < Greek *poluglōttos* < *glōtta* 'tongue, language'] —**polyglotism** *n*

polygon /pólligən, -gon/ *n* 1. a two-dimensional geometric figure formed of three or more straight sides 2. a building block of computer graphics ○ *The new character model sports an extremely high number of polygons, with smooth and realistic animations.* [Late 16C. Via late Latin < Greek *polugōnon*, form of *polugōnos* 'many-angled' < *-gōnos* 'angled'] —**polygonal** /pə líggən'l/ *adj* —**polygonally** *adv*

polygonum /pə líggənəm/ *n* a plant with bulbous stem joints and spikes of small flowers. Genus: *Polygonum*. [Early 18C. Via modern Latin < Greek *polu-* *gonon* 'knotgrass', literally 'many-jointed' < *gonu* 'knee, joint']

polygraph /pólli graaf, -graf/ *n* 1. LIE DETECTOR an electrical device that registers involuntary physical processes such as pulse rate and perspiration and that is often used as a lie detector 2. TEST USING POLYGRAPH a test using a polygraph, or a result of this test ■ *vt* (**-graphs, -graphing, -graphed**) GIVE SOMEBODY POLYGRAPH TEST to test somebody, usually somebody suspected of committing a crime, using a polygraph —**polygraphic** /pólli gráffik/ *adj* —**polygraphically** *adv*

polygyny /pə líjjəni/ *n* 1. SIMULTANEOUS MARRIAGE TO MULTIPLE WIVES the custom of being married to more than one wife at the same time 2. FACT OF HAVING MULTIPLE FEMALE MATES animal mating in which a male mates with more than one female during any single breeding season 3. FACT OF HAVING MANY PISTILS OR STYLES the possession by a plant of many pistils or styles [Late 18C. < POLY- + Greek *gunē* 'woman'] —**polygynist** *n* —**polygynous** *adj*

polyhedra MATHS plural of **polyhedron**

polyhedral /pólli heédrəl/ *adj* relating to or in the form of a polyhedron

polyhedral angle *n* a geometric angle formed by the intersection of three or more planes meeting at a point such as the peak of a pyramid

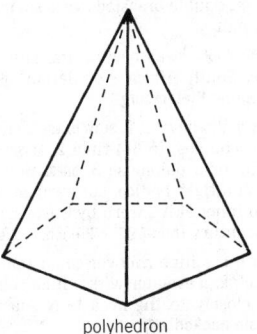

polyhedron

polyhedron /pólli heédrən/ (*plural* **-drons** or **-dra** /-drə/) *n* a three-dimensional geometric figure formed of many faces [Late 16C. < Greek *poluedron* 'many-based figure' < *hedra* 'base']

polyhydroxy /pólli hī dróksi/, **polyhydric** /-hídrik/ *adj* describes a compound that has two or more hydroxyl groups in each molecule

Polyhymnia /pólli hímni ə/ *n* in Greek mythology, the Muse of sacred songs, one of the nine Muses believed to inspire and nurture the arts

polyimide /pólli ímmīd/ *n* a tough durable polymer that contains an imide group. Use: heat-resistant coatings.

polyisoprene /pólli íssə preen/ *n* a polymeric form of isoprene. Source: natural or synthetic rubber.

polymath /pólli math/ *n* somebody with knowledge of many subjects [Early 17C. < Greek *polumathēs* 'somebody with much learning' < *manthanein* 'learn'] —**polymathic** /pólli máthik/ *adj* —**polymathy** /pə límməthi/ *n*

polymer /póllimər/ *n* a natural or synthetic compound that consists of large molecules made of many chemically bonded smaller identical molecules, e.g. starch and nylon [Mid-19C. < Greek *polumerēs* 'having many parts' < *meros* 'part'] —**polymeric** /pólli mérrik/ *adj*

polymerase /póllimə rayz, pə límmə-/ *n* an enzyme that catalyses the elongation of a polymer, especially in DNA or RNA

polymerase chain reaction *n* a technique used to replicate a fragment of DNA and produce a large amount of that sequence

polymerization /pə límmə rī záysh'n, póllimə rī-/, **polymerisation** *n* the chemical reaction in which a compound is made into a polymer by the addition or condensation of smaller molecules —**polymerize** /póllimə rīz, pə límmə rīz/ *vti*

polymerous /pə límmərəss/ *adj* 1. describes an organism that consists of many parts or segments 2. describes a flower that has its petals or sepals arranged in many whorls

polymorph /pólli mawrf/ *n* 1. ANIMAL OR PLANT WITH DIFFERENT FORMS an animal or plant that has several different adult forms 2. CHEMICAL COMPOUND WITH DIFFERENT FORMS a chemical compound that has several crystalline forms 3. WHITE BLOOD CELL WITH SEGMENTED NUCLEUS a white blood cell whose nucleus is segmented into lobes —**polymorphic** /pólli máwrfik/ *adj*

polymorphism /pólli máwrfizəm/ *n* 1. the characteristic of existing in different forms 2. a difference in DNA sequence between individuals

polymorphonuclear leucocyte /pólli máwrfō nyoókli ər-/ *n* BIOL same as **polymorph** (sense 3)

polymyxin /pólli míksin/ *n* a peptide antibiotic. Source: a soil bacterium, [*Bacillus polymyxa*]. Use: treatment of meningitis, inner ear infections. [Mid-20C. < modern Latin *Polymyxa* < Greek *muxa* 'slime']

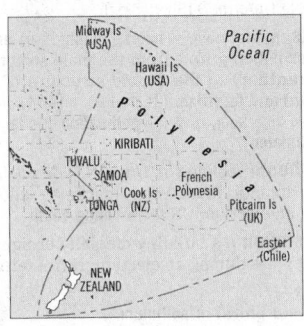

Polynesia

Polynesia /pólli neézi ə/ ethnographic grouping of Pacific islands, encompassing a number of scattered islands in the central and southern Pacific Ocean, including Hawaii, Samoa, Easter Island, the Cook Islands, the Marquesas Islands, French Polynesia, Tonga, Tuvalu, and sometimes New Zealand

Polynesian /pólli neézi ən/ *n* 1. somebody who comes from an island of the central or southern Pacific 2. a group of Austronesian languages, including Fijian, Hawaiian, and Maori, spoken on islands of the central and southern Pacific. Native speakers: 800,000. —**Polynesian** *adj*

polyneuritis /pólli nyoor ŕtíss/ *n* a simultaneous inflammation of several nerves

polynomial /pólli nṓmi əl/ *adj* WITH MORE THAN TWO TERMS describes a mathematical expression that has more than two terms, or a system of taxonomic nomenclature that uses more than two names ■ *n* 1. MULTITERM MATHEMATICAL EXPRESSION a mathematical expression consisting of the sum of a number of terms, each of which contains a constant and variables raised to a positive integral power 2. MULTITERM TAXONOMIC NAME a taxonomic name of a plant or animal that has more than two terms, e.g. one giving a genus, species, and subspecies [Late 17C. After BINOMIAL]

polynucleotide /pólli nyoókli ə tīd/ *n* a chain of chemically bonded nucleotides, as occurs in the structure of DNA and RNA

polyol /pólli ol/ *n* an alcohol that contains more than two hydroxyl groups, e.g. glycerol

polyoma /pólli ṓmə/, **polyoma virus** *n* a virus in rodents that can produce tumours

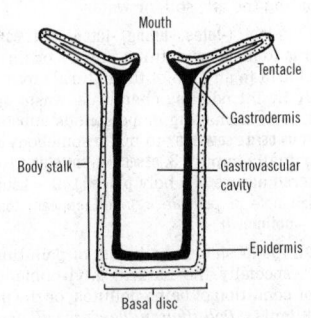

polyp: cross section of a polyp

polyp /póllip/ *n* 1. a single-cavity sea invertebrate (**cnidarian**) in its sedentary stage that attaches to

a rock at one end of its cylindrical body and has a tentacled mouth at the other end **2.** a small stalk-shaped growth sticking out from the skin or from a mucous membrane. Polyps are usually benign, but some become malignant. [14C. Via French *polipe* and Latin *polypus* < Greek *polupous* 'octopus', literally 'many-footed' < *pous* 'foot'] —**polypoid** /pólli poyd/ *adj* —**polypous** *adj*

polypeptide /pólli pép tīd/ *n* a chain of chemically bonded amino acids, as occurs in the structure of protein molecules [Early 20C. < POLY- + PEPTONE]

polypetalous /pólli péttələss/ *adj* describes flowers such as roses and carnations that have many separate petals

polyphagia /pólli fáyjə/ *n* **1.** an insatiable appetite for food **2.** the habit on the part of some animals of feeding on many different types of food — **polyphagous** /pə líffəgəss/ *adj*

polyphase /pólli fayz/ *adj* producing two or more phases of alternating current, or two or more alternating voltages of the same frequency

Polyphemus /pólli féeməss/ *n* in Greek mythology, a cyclops who was blinded by Odysseus after having imprisoned him in a cave

polyphone /pólli fōn/ *n* a letter or character that has more than one way of being pronounced

polyphonic /pólli fónnik/ *adj* **1.** WITH SEVERAL MELODIES describes music consisting of two or more largely independent melodic lines, parts, or voices that sound simultaneously **2.** WITH SEVERAL POSSIBLE PRONUNCIATIONS describes a letter or character that may be pronounced in several different ways **3.** PLAYING SEVERAL NOTES TOGETHER describes a ringtone on a mobile phone that plays several notes or sounds simultaneously, making it sound more musical —**polyphonically** *adv*

polyphonic prose *n* highly rhythmic prose that makes use of poetic devices such as alliteration and assonance

polyphony /pə líffəni/ *n* **1.** musical composition that uses simultaneous, largely independent, melodic parts, lines, or voices **2.** the representation of different sounds by the same letter in a writing system [Early 19C. < Greek *poluphōnia* 'multiplicity of sounds' < *phōnē* 'voice, sound' (see PHONO-)] —**polyphonous** *adj* —**polyphonously** *adv*

polyphyletic /pólli fī léttik/ *adj* derived or descended from several groups of ancestors —**polyphyletically** *adv*

polyphyodont /pólli tī ō dont/ *adj* describes a fish or other vertebrate that grows several sets of teeth in succession

polypi plural of **polypus** (*archaic*)

Polypill /pólli pill/ *n* a proposed drug that would contain substances to lower cholesterol and blood pressure, aspirin to interfere with blood clotting, and folic acid to help prevent atherosclerosis

polyploid /pólli ployd/ *adj* having more than twice the basic number of chromosomes —**polyploid** *n* —**polyploidy** *n*

polypod /pólli pod/ *adj* describes an insect larva such as a caterpillar with a large number of jointed legs on the thorax and unjointed legs on the abdomen, or this stage of larval development [Mid-18C. Via French < Greek *polupod-* 'many-footed' < *pod-* 'foot'] —**polypod** *n*

polypody /póllipōdi/ (*plural* **-dies**) *n* a fern with evergreen pinnate leaves and a creeping rootstock. Genus: *Polypodium*. [15C. Via Latin < Greek *polupodion* 'many-footed one' < *polupod-* (see POLYPOD)]

polyposis /pólli póssiss/ *n* a condition in which numerous polyps develop in a hollow organ such as the bowel

polypropylene /pólli própə leen/, **polypropene** /-prō peen/ *n* a thermoplastic substance that is a synthetic polymer of propylene. Use: pipes, industrial fibres, moulded objects.

polyptych /pólliptik/ *n* an arrangement of three or more panels with a painting or carving on each, usually hinged together and used as an altarpiece in a church [Mid-19C. After DIPTYCH]

polypus /póllipəss/ (*plural* **-pi** /-pī/) *n* same as **polyp** (*archaic*) [14C. < Latin (see POLYP)]

polyrhythm /pólli rith'm/ *n* a technique of musical composition in which several contrasting rhythms are used simultaneously —**polyrhythmic** /pólli rīthmik/ *adj* —**polyrhythmically** *adv*

polyribosome /pólli ríbəsōm/ *n* a cluster of ribosomes linked by a strand of messenger RNA and functioning as a site of protein synthesis

polysaccharide /pólli sákə rīd/, **polysaccharose** /pólli sákəröss/ *n* a complex carbohydrate such as starch or cellulose made up of sugar molecules linked into a branched or chain structure

polysemy /pə líssimi, pólli seemi, pólli seemi/ *n* the existence of several meanings for a single word or phrase [Early 20C. < modern Latin *polysemia* < Greek *polusēmos* 'having many meanings' < *sēma* 'sign, mark'] —**polysemous** /pə líssiməss, pólli seeməss/ *adj*

polysepalous /pólli séppələss/ *adj* describes flowers that have distinctly separate sepals

polysome /póllisōm/ *n* BIOCHEM same as **polyribosome** [Mid-20C. Contraction]

polysomic /pólli sōmik/ *adj* describes a diploid cell or organism in which some of the chromosomes occur more than twice

polysorbate /pólli sáwr bayt/ *n* an emulsifier used in preparing some foods and drugs [Mid-20C. < POLY- + SORBITOL]

polyspermy /pólli spurmi/ *n* the fertilization of an egg by several spermatozoa

polystichous /pə lístikəss, pólli stīkəss/ *adj* describes parts of a plant that are arranged in two or more series of rows [Late 19C. After DISTICHOUS]

polystyrene /pólli stī reen/ *n* a synthetic polymer of styrene that is stable in various physical forms. As a white rigid foam (**expanded polystyrene**) it is used for packing and insulation.

polysulphide /pólli súlfīd/ *n* a sulphide whose molecules have two or more atoms of sulphur

polysyllabic /pólli si lábbik/ *adj* **1.** having more than one or two syllables **2.** using or containing long words, often where shorter words would be adequate or better —**polysyllabically** *adv*

polysyllable /pólli siləb'l, pólli sílləb'l/ *n* a word that has more than one or two syllables

polysynaptic /pólli si náptik/ *adj* describes a reflex in the central nervous system that uses two or more synapses

polysynthetic /pólli sin théttik/ *adj* describes a language in which the syntax is conveyed by means of multiple affixes to single words —**polysynthesis** /pólli sínthəssiss/ *n* —**polysynthetically** *adv*

polytechnic /pólli téknik/ *n* a college offering a range of courses, some of them vocational or technical, at or below the bachelor's degree level. In 1992 all polytechnics in England and Wales became universities. [Early 19C. < French *polytechnique* < Greek *polutekhnos* 'multiskilled' < *tekhnē* 'skill']

polytene /pólli teen/ *adj* describes a giant chromosome with distinct chromosome bands in polyploid cells of some two-winged flies, comprising multiple copies of a chromosome aligned side by side — **polytenic** /pólli teenik/ *adj* —**polyteny** *n*

polytetrafluoroethylene /pólli téttrə floorō éthə leen/ *n* a durable, chemically resistant nonflammable thermoplastic substance. Use: metal coatings, especially for nonstick surfaces of cookware.

polytheism /pólli thi izəm, pólli thee izəm/ *n* the worship of or belief in more than one deity, especially several deities [Early 17C. < French *polythéisme* < Greek *polutheos* 'of many deities' < *theos* 'deity'] — **polytheist** *n* —**polytheistic** /pólli thi ístik/ *adj* —**polytheistically** *adv*

polythene /pólli theen/ *n* a malleable thermoplastic used to make containers, packaging, and electrical insulation materials. It is a polymer of ethylene. N Am term **polyethylene** [Mid-20C. Contraction of POLY-ETHYLENE]

polytonality /pólli tō nálləti/ *n* a technique of musical composition in which several keys are used at once —**polytonal** /pólli tōn'l/ *adj* —**polytonally** *adv*

polytrophic /pólli trófik, -tróffik/ *adj* describes bacteria that derive food from several different sources

polytypic /pólli típpik/, **polytypical** /-típpik'l/ *adj* describes a taxonomic subset, especially a species, that has many subdivisions

polyunsaturated /pólli un sáchə raytid/ *adj* belonging to a class of fats, especially plant oils, that are less likely to be converted into cholesterol in the body. Their molecules have long carbon chains with many double bonds unsaturated by hydrogen atoms.

polyurethane /pólli yóorə thayn/ *n* a thermoplastic polymer that contains an NHCOO chemical group. Use: resins, coatings, insulation, adhesives, foams, fibres.

polyuria /pólli yoóri ə/ *n* the passing of unusually large amounts of urine, e.g. in untreated diabetes

polyvalent /pólli váylənt, pə lívvələnt/ *adj* **1.** describes a chemical element that has more than one valency or a valency of more than two **2.** describes a vaccine that is effective against more than one strain of microorganism, toxin, antigen, or antibody — **polyvalency** /pólli váylənssi/ *n*

polyvinyl /pólli vín'l/ *adj* describes plastics and resins produced by the polymerization of vinyls

polyvinyl acetate *n* INDUST full form of **PVA**

polyvinyl chloride *n* INDUST full form of **PVC**

polyzoan /pólli zō ən/ *n* MARINE BIOL same as **bryozoan** [Mid-19C. < modern Latin *Polyzoa* < *zoon* (see -ZOON)]

pom /pom/ *n* ANZ same as **pommy** (*informal humorous or disapproving*) [Early 20C. Shortening]

POM *abbr* PHARM prescription-only medicine

pomace /púmmiss, pómmiss/ *n* **1.** the pulpy mass that remains after apples or other fruits have been crushed and pressed to extract the juice, e.g. to make cider **2.** the pulpy mass that remains after nuts, fish, or other foods have been crushed and pressed to extract oil or another liquid [Mid-16C. < medieval Latin *pomacium* 'cider' < Latin *pomum* 'apple']

pomaceous /po máyshəss/ *adj* describes a fruit such as an apple or pear that has a large fleshy receptacle with a central seed-bearing core (**pome**) [Early 18C. < Latin *pomum* 'apple']

pomade /pə máyd, -maád/ *n* a perfumed oil or ointment used to make hair look smooth and shiny ■ *vt* (**-mades, -mading, -maded**) to dress hair with pomade [Mid-16C. < French *pommade* < Latin *pomum* 'apple']

pomander /pə mándər/ *n* **1.** AROMATIC MIXTURE a mixture of aromatic substances enclosed in a sachet, ball, or other container, kept near stored clothes or in a room to impart a pleasant smell **2.** POMANDER CONTAINER a container for a pomander, usually a lidded pottery bowl with holes **3.** CLOVE-STUDDED ORANGE an orange or apple studded with cloves, used to scent clothes or a room [15C. < Old French *pome d'ambre* 'apple of amber']

Pomare /po maári/, **Sir Maui** (1876–1930) New Zealand Maori leader and politician. He was New Zealand's minister of health and minister of internal affairs in William Ferguson Massey's government. Full name **Pomare, Sir Maui Wiremu Pita Naera**

pome /pōm/ *n* a fleshy fruit that has a central core typically containing five seeds, e.g. an apple or pear [14C. Via French < Latin *pomum* 'apple']

pomegranate

pomegranate /pómmi granit/ *n* **1.** a round reddish fruit with a tough rind enclosing numerous seeds within a tart juicy red pulp **2.** a tree that produces pomegranates. Native to: tropical Asia. Latin name: *Punica granatum*. [14C. < Old French *pome grenate* 'seedy apple']

~~pomegranite~~ incorrect spelling of **pomegranate**

pomelo /pómmǝlō/ (*plural* **-los**) *n* **1.** a yellow-orange citrus fruit similar to a large grapefruit **2.** a citrus tree that produces pomelos. Native to: Southeast Asia. Latin name: *Citrus maxima*. [Mid-19C. Origin ?]

Pomerania /pómmǝ ráyni ǝ/ historic region in northern Europe on the southern shores of the Baltic Sea in present-day northwestern Poland and northeastern Germany

Pomeranian /pómmǝ ráyni ǝn/ *n* **1. SMALL DOG** a small dog belonging to a breed that has a long silky coat, pointed ears, a pointed muzzle, and a long curling tail **2. SOMEBODY FROM POMERANIA** somebody who comes from Pomerania ■ *adj* **OF POMERANIA** relating to Pomerania, or its people or culture

pomfret[1] /póm frit/ *n* same as **Pontefract cake** [Mid-19C. After *Pomfret* (now *Pontefract*), W Yorkshire]

pomfret[2] /póm frit/ (*plural* **-frets** or same) *n* a tropical sea fish of open seas. Latin name: *Stromateoides argenteus*. [Early 18C. Probably < Portuguese *pampo* + -LET]

pomfret-cake *n* FOOD same as **Pontefract cake**

pomiculture /pómmi kulchǝr/ *n* the cultivation of fruit [Late 19C. < Latin *pomum* 'apple, fruit']

pomiferous /po míffǝrǝss/ *adj* describes fruit plants that bear apples, pears, or any related fleshy fruit with five seeds (**pome**) [Mid-17C. < Latin *pomifer* < *pomum* 'apple, fruit']

pommel /pómm'l, púmm'l/ *n* **1. FRONT OF SADDLE** the front part of a saddle that curves upwards **2. PART OF SWORD HANDLE** the knob at the hilt of a sword **3. HANDLE ON POMMEL HORSE** either of the two curved handles on the top of a pommel horse ■ *vt* (**pommels, pommelling, pommelled**) same as **pummel** [14C. < Old French *pomel* 'little fruit' < Latin *pomum* 'apple, fruit']

pommel horse *n* **1.** a padded oblong piece of gymnastics apparatus that is raised off the floor and has two curved handles on the top **2.** the men's gymnastics event that involves balancing and manoeuvring on a pommel horse

pommy /pómmi/ *ANZ* (*informal humorous or disapproving*) *adj* same as **British** ■ *n* (*plural* **-mies**) a British person [Early 20C. Probably shortening of *pomegranate*, alteration of *Jimmy Grant* or *Pummy Grant*, rhyming slang for IMMIGRANT]

pomo /pṓmō/, **po-mo** *adj* relating to or characteristic of postmodernism (*informal*) ○*beat-generation, counterculture, and pomo literature'* (Hawkeye, *FutureCulture FAQ parts 1 & 2*; 1992) [Late 20C. Contraction and alteration of *post modern*]

Pomo (*plural* same or **-mos**) *n* **1.** a member of a group of Native North American peoples living in northern California **2.** a Native North American language of a group of closely related languages spoken in parts of northern California and belonging to the Hokan branch of Hokan-Siouan languages [Late 19C. < N Pomo *pʰṓ'mo*' 'at the red earth hole'] —**Pomo** *adj*

pomology /po mólləji/ *n* the study or practice of cultivating fruit [Early 19C. < Latin *pomum* 'apple, fruit'] —**pomological** /pómmǝ lójjik'l/ *adj* —**pomologically** *adv* —**pomologist** *n*

Pomona /pǝ mṓnǝ/ *n* in Roman mythology, the goddess of fruit [Mid-17C. < Latin *pomum* 'apple, fruit']

pomp /pomp/ *n* **1.** a display of great splendour and magnificence **2.** an ostentatious and vain display of importance [14C. Via French *pompe* and Latin *pompa* < Greek *pompē* 'solemn procession, sendoff, escort' < *pempein* 'send']

CULTURAL NOTE *Pomp and Circumstance*, an orchestral work (parts 1 to 4: 1901–07; part 5: 1930) by British composer Edward Elgar. The title of this series of five military marches (op. 39) derives from the reference in Shakespeare's *Othello* (Act III, scene iii) to the 'pride, pomp, and circumstance of glorious war'. The first march includes a melody later used for the finale of Elgar's *Coronation Ode*, 'Land of Hope and Glory'.

pompadour

pompadour /pómpǝ door/ *n* a woman's hairstyle, popular in Europe in the 18th century, in which the hair is swept back high off the face over a pad [Mid-18C. After the Marquise de POMPADOUR]

Pompadour /pómpǝ door/, **Marquise de** (1721–64) French noblewoman. She was a mistress of Louis XV and a patron of the arts. She had great influence with Louis in all important political matters. Born **Poisson, Jeanne Antoinette**

pompano /pómpǝnō/ (*plural* **-nos** or same) *n* **1.** a sea fish with a deep flat body and forked tail. Native to: southern Atlantic and Gulf coasts of North America. Latin name: *Trachinotus carolinus*. **2.** FISH same as **butterfish** [Late 18C. < Spanish *pámpano*]

Pompeii: view of the forum, with Vesuvius in the background

Pompeii /pom páy i/ ancient Roman city in southern Italy. It was buried by volcanic ash during the eruption of Mount Vesuvius in AD 79, and has since been partly excavated.

Pompey /pómpi/ (106–48 BC) Roman general and leader. He formed a ruling triumvirate with Caesar and Crassus, but was later defeated by Caesar at Pharsalus (48 BC) and escaped to Egypt, where he was assassinated. Full name **Gnaeus Pompeius Magnus**. Known as **Pompey the Great**

Pompidou /pómpi doo/, **Georges** (1911–74) French politician. He was four times prime minister (1962–68), and followed Charles de Gaulle as president (1969–74).

'A statesman is a politician who places himself at the service of the nation. A politician is a statesman who places the nation at his service.'
[Georges Pompidou, *Observer*; 30 December 1973]

pompom /póm pom/ *n* **1.** a small tufted ball made from wool, silk, or other material, attached as a decoration to hats, shoes, and other articles of clothing **2.** a cheerleader's accessory in the form of a large white or brightly coloured ball-shaped mass of thin paper or plastic strips connected to a handle **3.** BOT same as **pompon** (sense 2) [Mid-18C. < French]

pom-pom /póm pom/ *n* a rapid-firing automatic weapon, especially a cannon used in the Boer War or a double-barrelled antiaircraft gun used in World War II (*slang*) [An imitation of the sound]

pompon /póm pon/ *n* **1.** CLOTHING same as **pompom** (sense 1) **2.** a small round flower of some chrysanthemum or dahlia varieties, or a variety that has this kind of flower [Mid-18C. < French]

pomposity /pom póssǝti/ (*plural* **-ties**) *n* **1.** an excessive sense of self-importance, usually displayed through exaggerated seriousness or stateliness in speech and manner **2.** an act, remark, or gesture that is exaggerated in its seriousness or stateliness and conveys an excessive sense of self-importance

pompous /pómpǝss/ *adj* **1. SELF-IMPORTANT** having an excessive sense of self-importance, usually displayed through exaggerated seriousness or stateliness in speech or manner **2. REVEALING SELF-IMPORTANCE** displaying exaggerated seriousness or stateliness ○ *a pompous gesture* **3. CEREMONIALLY GRAND** full of splendour and magnificence [14C. Via French < Latin *pomposus* < *pompa* (SEE POMP)] —**pompously** *adv* —**pompousness** *n*

'pon /pon/ *prep* same as **upon** (*archaic or literary*) [Mid-16C. Shortening]

Ponca /póngkǝ/ (*plural* same or **-cas**), **Ponka** (*plural* same or **-kas**) *n* **1.** a member of a Native North American people who formerly occupied lands around the Niobrara River in Nebraska and now live mainly in parts of Oklahoma and Nebraska **2.** a Native American language spoken in parts of Oklahoma and Nebraska. It belongs to the Siouan branch of Hokan-Siouan languages and is closely related to Omaha. [Late 18C. < Ponca *ppákka*] —**Ponca** *adj*

ponce /ponss/ *n* **1.** an offensive term for an effeminate or gay man (*insult*) **2.** same as **pimp** (*slang*) [Late 19C. Origin ?] —**poncy** *adj*
ponce about (**ponces about, poncing about, ponced about**), **ponce around** *vi* (*slang*) **1.** to behave in an affected way with the intention of impressing others (*offensive in some contexts*) **2.** to spend time doing or achieving nothing at all

Ponce /pónss ay/ city and port in southern Puerto Rico, on the Caribbean Sea. Population: 187,749 (1990).

Ponce (de León) /pónss dǝ lay ón, pónth ay dǝ lee ón/, **Juan** (1460–1521) Spanish explorer. He was the first European to reach Florida (1513), but failed in his attempt to set up a colony there (1521).

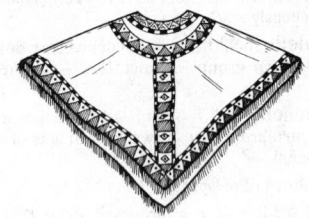
poncho

poncho /pónchō/ (*plural* **-chos**) *n* a simple outer garment for the upper body in the form of a single piece of heavy cloth, often wool, with a slit in it for the head [Early 18C. < American Spanish]

pond /pond/ *n* a small still body of water formed naturally or created artificially, e.g. as a feature in a garden ■ *vi* (**ponds, ponding, ponded**) to collect into shallow pools (*refers to water*) [13C. Alteration of POUND[3] 'enclosure for fish']

ponder /póndǝr/ (**-ders, -dering, -dered**) *vti* to think about something carefully over a period of time [14C. Via French < Latin *ponderare* 'weigh, consider' < *ponder-*, stem of *pondus* 'weight'] —**ponderable** *adj*, *n*

ponderosa pine /póndǝ rṓzǝ-/ *n* a tall pine with yellowish bark and needles grouped in twos or threes, that yields valuable timber. Native to: western North America. Latin name: *Pinus ponderosa*. [< modern Latin < Latin *ponderosus* 'heavy' (SEE PONDEROUS), because of its dense wood]

ponderous /póndǝrǝss/ *adj* **1. MOVING HEAVILY** lumbering and laborious in movement **2. DULL** without liveliness or wit **3. HEAVY-LOOKING** disproportionately thick and heavy [14C. Via French < Latin *ponderosus* < *ponder-*, stem of *pondus* 'weight'] —**ponderously** *adv* —**ponderousness** *n*

Pondicherry /póndi chérri/, **Pondichéry 1.** city and port in southeastern India and capital of the Union Territory of Pondicherry. Population: 203,065 (1991). **2.** Union Territory of India, comprising Pondicherry, Karaikal, and Yanam on the east coast and the enclave of Mahé on the southwest coast. Capital: Pondicherry. Population: 973,829 (2001). Area: 492 sq. km/190 sq. mi.

pond lily *n* PLANTS same as **water lily**

pondokkie /pon dóki/ *n S Africa* a roughly made house or shelter, especially one improvised from available materials (*informal*) [Early 19C. < Afrikaans]

pond scum *n* green freshwater algae that form a layer on the surface of stagnant water

pond-skater *n UK* any of several types of long-legged insect that have slender hairy bodies and travel about on the surface of water. Family: Gerridae. ANZ, N Am term **water strider**

pondweed /pónd weed/ (*plural same* or **-weeds**) *n* **1.** a plant that grows in ponds and slow streams and has jointed stems, floating or submerged leaves, and greenish flowers. Genus: *Potamogeton*. **2.** *UK* a plant that grows in water, e.g. mare's-tail. ANZ, N Am term **waterweed**

pone[1] /pōn/ *n Southern US* FOOD same as **cornpone** [Early 17C. < Virginia Algonquian *poan*, 'thing roasted or baked']

pone[2] /pōn, pṓni/ *n* in card games, the person who does not deal in two-handed games, or the person sitting to the right of the dealer [Early 19C. < Latin 'put!', imperative of *ponere* 'to place']

pong /pong/ (*informal*) *n* an unpleasant smell ■ *vi* (**pongs, ponging, ponged**) to give off an unpleasant smell [Early 20C. Origin ?] —**pongy** *adj*

ponga /póngə/ (*plural* **-gas** or *same*) *n* a tall evergreen tree fern. Native to: New Zealand. Latin name: *Cyathea dealbata*. [Mid-19C. < Maori]

pongal /póng g'l/ *n S Asia* **1.** a Tamil festival. Date: New Year. **2.** a sweet or savoury rice dish popular in South India [Late 18C. < Tamil *ponkal* 'boiling', because the festival involves the cooking of new rice]

pongee /pon jee, pón jee/ *n* a soft, usually unbleached, silk fabric from China or South Asia, or a similar cotton or rayon imitation [Early 18C. < Chinese *běnjī* 'own loom', or *běnzhi* 'home-woven']

pongid /pónjid, póng gid/ *n* an ape of the family that includes the gibbon and the great apes. Family: Pongidae. [Mid-20C. < modern Latin *Pongidae* < Kongo *mpongo* 'ape']

pongo /póng gō/ (*plural* **-gos**) *n* **1.** ZOOL same as **orang-utan 2.** MIL same as **soldier** (*slang; used by navy personnel*) [Early 17C. < Kongo *mpongo* 'ape']

poniard /pónnyərd, -yaard/ (*literary*) *n* a small dagger with a slim blade that is triangular or square in its cross section ■ *vt* (**-iards, -iarding, -iarded**) to stab somebody with a poniard [Mid-16C. < French *poignard* < Latin *pugnus* 'fist']

Ponka *n, adj* LANG, PEOPLES another spelling of **Ponca**

pons /ponz/ (*plural* **pontes** /pón teez/) *n* a whitish band of nerve fibres on the surface of the brain stem between the medulla oblongata and midbrain [Late 17C. < Latin, 'bridge']

pons asinorum /-ássi náwrəm/ *n* a proposition or problem that is especially difficult for an inexperienced person to understand [< Latin, 'bridge of asses']

pons Varolii /-və rṓli í/ *n* ANAT same as **pons** [Late 17C. < Latin, 'bridge of Varolius', after C. *Varoli* (1543–75), Italian anatomist]

pont /pont/ *n S Africa* a flat-bottomed ferryboat [Mid-17C. < Dutch]

Ponta Delgada /póntə del gaádə/ *n* city in Portugal, on São Miguel Island. It is the capital of the autonomous region of the Azores. Population: 21,091 (1991).

Pontchartrain, Lake /póncher trayn/ *n* lake in southeastern Louisiana between the Gulf of Mexico and the Mississippi River. It is spanned by the world's longest causeway. Area: 1,620 sq. km/625 sq. mi.

Ponte ♦ Da Ponte, Lorenzo

Pontefract cake /pónti frakt-/ *n* a small flat round liquorice sweet [After a town in West Yorkshire]

pontes ANAT plural of **pons**

pontifex /pónti feks/ (*plural* **-tifices** /pon tíffi seez/) *n* in ancient Rome, a member of the highest council of priests [Late 16C. < Latin, 'way-maker' < *pont-* 'bridge, way']

Pontifex Maximus /pónti feks máksiməss/ (*plural* **Pontifices Maximi** /pon tíffi seez máksi mī/) *n* in ancient Rome, the chief priest who presided over the highest council of priests

pontiff /póntif/ *n* **1.** the head of the Roman Catholic Church and bishop of Rome **2.** ANCIENT HIST, RELIG same as **pontifex** [Late 16C Via French < Latin *pontifex* (see PONTIFEX)]

pontifical /pon tíffik'l/ *adj* **1.** OF PONTIFF belonging to, befitting, or involving a pope, bishop, or pontifex **2.** POMPOUS displaying an exaggerated sense of self-importance ■ *n* BISHOP'S BOOK a book containing the rites that may be performed only by a bishop ■ **pontificals** *npl* PONTIFF'S VESTMENTS the vestments and insignia of a pope or bishop [15C < Latin *pontificalis* < *pontifex* (see PONTIFEX)] —**pontifically** *adv*

Pontifical Mass *n* especially in the Roman Catholic Church, a High Mass that is celebrated by a bishop

pontificate *vi* /pon tíffi kayt/ (**-cates, -cating, -cated**) **1.** SPEAK POMPOUSLY to speak about something in a knowing and self-important way, especially when not qualified to do so **2.** SERVE AS BISHOP to officiate as a bishop, especially in celebrating Mass ■ *n* /pon tíffikat, -kayt/ TERM OF OFFICE the office or term of office of a pope or bishop [Early 19C. < medieval Latin *pontificat-*, past participle of *pontificare* < Latin *pontifex* (see PONTIFEX)] —**pontification** /pon tíffi káysh'n/ *n* —**pontificator** *n*

pontil /póntil/ *n* GLASS same as **punty** [Mid-19C. < French]

pontine /pón tīn/ *adj* relating to or situated in the whitish band of nerve fibres (**pons**) on the surface of the brain stem between the medulla oblongata and midbrain [Late 19C. < Latin *pont-* 'bridge, way']

pontoon[1] /pon toón/ *n* **1.** FLOATING SUPPORT FOR BRIDGE a floating structure used as a support for a bridge across a river, especially one put in place temporarily **2.** FLOAT ON AIRCRAFT a float on an aircraft that provides buoyancy or stability when the aircraft is on water **3.** FLOATING DOCK a floating structure used as a dock [Late 17C. Via French < Latin *ponton-* 'floating bridge' < *pont-* 'bridge']

pontoon[2] /pon toón/ *n* **1.** CARD GAME a gambling card game in which the aim is to accumulate cards that add up to an exact value of 21 **2.** HAND WITH 21 POINTS a hand that contains exactly 21 points in the first deal in pontoon ■ *interj* SHOUT OF PONTOON a shout of pontoon made by a player with a winning hand ▶ N Am term (all senses) **blackjack** [Early 20C. Probably alteration of French *vingt-et-un* 'twenty-one']

pontoon bridge *n* a temporary bridge built across a river, supported by floating structures

Pontormo /pon tórmō/, **Jacopo da** (1494–1557) Italian painter. The exaggerated forms and bright colours of paintings such as *Deposition* (1526) influenced early mannerists.

Pontypool /póntə poól/ *n* town in Monmouthshire, Wales. Population: 35,564 (1991).

Pontypridd /póntə preéth/ *n* town near Cardiff, Wales. Population: 28,487 (1991).

pony /póni/ (*plural* **-nies**) *n* **1.** SMALL HORSE any breed of small horse **2.** POLO HORSE a horse used in polo **3.** ANY HORSE a horse of any kind, especially a racehorse (*informal*) **4.** SMALL GLASS a small drinking glass, especially one used for liqueurs **5.** *Aus* BEER GLASS a small beer glass, containing 200 ml/7 oz in New South Wales and 114 ml/4 oz in Victoria and Western Australia **6.** £25 the sum of £25 (*slang*) [Mid-17C. Origin ?]

pony up (**ponies up, ponying up, ponied up**) *vti N Am* to pay somebody the money that is owed to him or her (*informal*)

pony express *n* a system of carrying mail using relays of horses and riders that operated in the American West from St Joseph, Missouri, to Sacramento, California, from 1860 to 1861

ponytail /póni tayl/ *n* a hairstyle in which long hair is pulled back and tied behind the head so that it hangs down like a pony's tail —**ponytailed** *adj*

pony-trekking *n* a leisure activity that involves riding across open countryside on a pony, usually in organized groups

Ponzi scheme /pónzi-/ *n US* a pyramid investment swindle in which supposed profits are paid to early investors from money actually invested by later participants [Early 20C. After Charles *Ponzi* (d. 1949)]

poo /poo/ (*informal; usually used by children*) *n* excrement, or an act of defecating ■ *vi* (**poos, pooing, pooed**) to excrete faeces. Same as **defecate** [Variant of POOH]

pooch /pooch/ *n* same as **dog** (sense 1) (*informal*) [Early 20C. Origin ?]

poodle

poodle /poód'l/ *n* a dog with a thick curly coat, usually clipped short, belonging to either a small breed (**toy poodle**), or a large breed (**standard poodle**) originally developed in Europe for hunting [Early 19C. < German *Pudel*, shortening of *Pudelhund* < Low German *pudeln* 'splash in water' + German *Hund* 'dog']

poodle-faker *n* a man who seeks out the company of women, especially a genteel young man who flatters older women, often for selfish reasons (*dated informal disapproving*) [< the idea that the man resembles a fawning lap dog]

poof[1] /poof, poof/, **pouf, pouffe, poove** /poov/ *n* an offensive term for an effeminate or gay man (*insult*) [Mid-19C. Probably alteration (after POUF[1] 'puffed-out hairstyle') of PUFF 'powder puff']

poof[2] /poof, poof/ *interj* (*informal*) **1.** used to indicate that something happens suddenly **2.** used to express disdain for or dismissal of something [Early 19C. An imitation of the sound of a rush of air or breath]

poofter /poófter, poóftər/ *n* same as **poof**[1] (*slang offensive*) [Early 20C. Alteration of POOF[1]]

poofy /poófi, poóffi/ (**-ier, -iest**) *adj* an offensive term meaning effeminate or gay (*insult*) [Mid-20C. < POOF[1]]

pooh /poo/ *interj* (*informal*) **1.** used to indicate that there is an unpleasant smell **2.** used to express disdain or dismissal [Late 16C. An imitation of the sound of blowing something away with the lips]

Pooh-Bah /poó baá/, **pooh-bah** *n* **1.** a pompous self-important official, especially one who holds more than one office but is ineffectual in all of them **2.** a leader, high official, or important person [Late 19C. After a character in *The Mikado*, operetta by W. S. Gilbert and Sir Arthur Sullivan]

pooh-pooh (**pooh-poohs, pooh-poohing, pooh-poohed**) *vt* to dismiss or express disdain for something [Late 18C. Doubled form of POOH]

pooja *n Carib* another spelling of **puja**

pooka /poókə/ *n Ireland* in Irish folklore, a mischievous spirit, especially one that takes on the form of an animal [Early 19C. < Irish *púca*]

pool[1] /pool/ *n* **1.** WATER a small body of still water, usually one that occurs naturally **2.** PUDDLE a small amount of any liquid lying on a surface **3.** SWIMMING POOL a swimming pool or paddling pool **4.** DEEP PART OF WATER a deep place in a river or stream where the water runs more slowly **5.** WATER BEHIND DAM a body of water collected behind a dam **6.** PATTERN RESEMBLING POOL a pattern or arrangement of something such as light that resembles a pool of liquid ○ *The floodlights bathed her in a pool of light.* **7.** UNDERGROUND OIL OR GAS an accumulation of oil or gas in a region of porous sedimentary rock ■ *vi* (**pools, pooling, pooled**) **1.** FORM POOL to collect in or form a pool **2.** ACCUMULATE IN BODY

PART to collect in a body part or organ (*refers to blood*) [Old English *pōl* < Germanic]

pool[2] /pool/ *n* **1.** BALL AND CUE GAME a game played with a cue stick, cue ball and 15 balls on a felt-covered table with six pockets **2.** FORM OF GAMBLING a form of gambling in which the participants contribute an amount to a common fund that is divided among the winners **3.** TOTAL AMOUNT STAKED the collective amount that the players in a gambling game have staked **4.** COLLECTIVE RESOURCE a joint supply of vehicles, commodities, or workers that is shared and used by members of a group **5.** GROUP OF REPORTERS a selected group of reporters who cover an event and make their reports available to all participating news organizations **6.** FIN INVESTMENT FUND a collection of investments such as stocks in properties in an investment trust that are managed as a group for a common purpose or group of owners **7.** COMM BUSINESS TRUST an agreement between competing businesses to control production and sales in order to guarantee profits ■ *vt* (**pools, pooling, pooled**) SHARE RESOURCES to combine something to form a supply that can be shared by a group of people or companies [Late 17C. Via French *poule* 'hen, gambling stakes' (hens were used as game prizes) < Latin *pullus* 'young animal']

Poole /pool/ port in Dorset, southern England. It is a resort and sailing centre. Population: 138,288 (2001).

pool hall *n US* a commercial establishment where pool is played

pool noodle *n Aus* same as **noodle**[1] (sense 2)

poolroom /pool room, -ro͝om/ *n* a room or commercial establishment where pool or billiards is played

pools /poolz/ *npl* an organized form of gambling, conducted mainly by post, that involves predicting the outcome of football matches [Mid-20C. < POOL[2] *n* (sense 2)]

poolside /pool sīd/ *n* the area around the sides of a swimming pool (*often used before a noun*)

poon /poon/ (*plural* **poons** or *same*) *n* a tree with leathery leaves and strong light wood. Native to: southern Asia. Genus: *Calophyllum*. [Late 17C. Via Sinhalese < Malayalam *punna* or Tamil *punnai*]

Poona former name for **Pune**

Poons /poonz/, **Larry** (*b.* 1937) US painter. An influential figure in the op art movement in the 1960s, he later abandoned geometric patterns for more painterly compositions.

poop[1] /poop/ *n* NAUT **1.** RAISED AREA AT REAR OF SHIP the raised cabins at the stern of an old sailing ship, or the raised area at the stern of a modern ship, lying above the level of the main deck **2.** same as **poop deck** ■ *v* (**poops, pooping, pooped**) **1.** *vt* BREAK OVER STERN to break over a ship at the stern (*refers to waves*) **2.** *vi* HAVE WAVES BREAKING OVER STERN to have waves break over its stern, especially repeatedly (*refers to boats*) [15C. Via French < Latin *puppis*]

poop[2] /poop/ (**poops, pooping, pooped**) *vt* to make somebody feel exhausted (*informal; usually passive*) ○ *were pooped by the long hike* [Mid-20C. Origin ?] —**pooped** *adj*

poop out *vi* (*dated slang*) **1.** to stop doing something, usually because of exhaustion or fear **2.** to stop operating, e.g. because of mechanical failure

poop[3] /poop/ *n N Am* facts or information about something (*slang*) [Mid-20C. Origin ?]

poop[4] /poop/ (*informal; often used by or to children*) *n* excrement, a stool, or an act of defecating ■ *vi* (**poops, pooping, pooped**) same as **defecate** (sense 1) [Mid-16C. An imitation of a short blast of sound (part of the original meaning)]

poop deck *n* a raised open deck at the stern of a ship, with cabins below it

pooper-scooper /poopər skoopər/ *n* a small shovel used to clean up dog excrement, used especially by a dog owner whose dog defecates in a public place (*informal*) [< POOP[4]]

poo-poo (*baby talk*) *n* excrement, or an act of defecating ■ *vi* (**poo-poos, poo-pooing, poo-pooed**) same as **defecate** (sense 1) [Doubled form of POO]

poor /pawr, poor/ *adj* **1.** NOT RICH lacking money or material possessions **2.** AFFECTED BY POVERTY characterized by widespread or evident poverty ○ *a poor part of town* **3.** INFERIOR not of good quality or not in good condition ○ *We received a very poor education.* **4.** LACKING SKILL having little skill or ability ○ *I had always been a poor athlete at school.* **5.** LOW OR INADEQUATE lower than expected or needed in quantity, number, or amount ○ *poor wages* **6.** WEAK lacking strength, power, stamina, or resilience ○ *in poor health* **7.** DEFICIENT lacking or deficient in something (*often used in combination*) ○ *cash-rich but time-poor* **8.** LACKING PRODUCTIVE POTENTIAL lacking fertility or nutrients **9.** LOW IN VALUATION low in a scale of value ○ *has a poor opinion of himself* **10.** DESERVING PITY deserving pity or compassion, especially because of something that has just happened ■ *npl* PEOPLE WHO ARE POOR people who lack money or material possessions ○ *The poor are always with us.* [12C. Via Old French *povre* < Latin *pauper* (see PAUPER)] —**poorness** *n*

poor box *n* a box, especially one kept in a church, that is used to collect money for the poor

poor boy *n Can, US regional* a sandwich made from a long roll cut horizontally [Because originally made from discarded scraps and ends, and given to poor people]

poorhouse /páwr howss, po͝or-/ (*plural* **-houses** /-howziz/) *n* a publicly funded institution that formerly existed to house people who were too poor to provide for themselves

poori *n* another spelling of **puri**

Poor Knights Islands /páwr nīts-/ group of uninhabited islands in the southwestern Pacific Ocean, 24 km/15 mi. off the northeastern coast of the North Island, New Zealand. Area: 3 sq. km/1 sq. mi.

poor law *n* a law or system of laws relating to the provision of support for poor people

poorly /páwrli, po͝orli/ *adv* **1.** INADEQUATELY in an inferior or inadequate way ○ *He did poorly in the exam.* **2.** UNFAVOURABLY with an unfavourable opinion or attitude ○ *They looked poorly on any suggestion of spending money.* ■ *adj* PHYSICALLY UNWELL feeling physically unwell or in poor physical health (*informal*)

poor mouth *n Ireland, N Am* complaints about being poor, regarded as made to win sympathy, sometimes when the complainer is not truly poor (*informal disapproving*)

poor-mouth *vi Ireland, N Am* to complain of a lack of money, especially when feigning or exaggerating poverty, often in order to win sympathy (*informal disapproving*)

poor rate *n* a tax formerly levied from parishes to raise money for housing and feeding people in need of financial support

poor relation *n* somebody or something that is inferior compared to another

poor white *n US* an offensive term for an uneducated lower-class white person who has an income considerably lower than average (*informal*)

Pooterish /po͝otərish/ *adj* self-importantly genteel or middle-class, especially amusingly so [Mid-20C. After Charles *Pooter*, character in *Diary of a Nobody* (1892), by George and Weedon Grossmith]

pootle /po͝ot'l/ (**-tles, -tling, -tled**) *vi* to move at a leisurely pace (*informal*) [Late 20C. Blend of *poodle* 'move at a leisurely pace' + TOOTLE]

poove *n* same as **poof**[1] (*slang offensive*)

pop[1] /pop/ *n* **1.** SUDDEN BURSTING SOUND a sudden explosive sound, like the sound produced when a balloon bursts or a cork comes out of a bottle **2.** FIZZY DRINK a carbonated drink, usually sweet and flavoured with fruit (*informal*) **3.** GUNSHOT a shot with a firearm **4.** ATTEMPT a try at doing something (*informal*) ■ *v* (**pops, popping, popped**) **1.** *vti* MAKE BURSTING SOUND to make a sudden explosive sound, like the sound of a cork coming out of a bottle or a balloon bursting, or cause something to make this sound **2.** *vti* BURST to burst with a sudden explosive sound, or make something do this **3.** *vi* BULGE to become wide open and seem to bulge out of the sockets (*refers to somebody's eyes*) **4.** *vi* GO BRIEFLY to go, come, or visit for a brief time (*informal*) ○ *I might pop in later for a chat.* **5.** *vt* OPEN OR CLOSE SOMETHING to move something quickly and suddenly into an open or closed position (*informal*) ○ *He popped the lid up.* **6.** *vt* PUT QUICKLY to put or place something somewhere with a sudden rapid movement (*informal*) ○ *Before I could speak he had popped the cake into my mouth.* **7.** *vt* TAKE BY SWALLOWING to take a drug orally (*informal*) ○ *pop pills* **8.** *vt* PAWN SOMETHING to pawn something (*informal*) ■ *adv* **1.** WITH BURSTING NOISE with a sudden bursting sound **2.** UNEXPECTEDLY suddenly or abruptly ■ *interj* INDICATING BURSTING NOISE used to indicate a sudden bursting noise [14C. An imitation of the sound] ◇ **a pop** for each one (*slang*) ○ *It'll cost you £10 a pop.*

pop off *vi* to die suddenly (*informal*)

pop up *vi* to appear suddenly and unexpectedly

pop[2] /pop/ *n* **1.** *also* **Pop** used for referring to or addressing your father (*informal*) **2.** used, either affectionately or patronizingly, to address a much older man (*dated slang*) [Mid-19C. Shortening of POPPA]

pop[3] /pop/ *n* **1.** MUSIC same as **pop music** **2.** ARTS same as **pop art** ■ *adj* **1.** musically commercial, especially by being tuneful, uptempo, and repetitive, and targeted at the general public and the youth market in particular ○ *a pop song* **2.** intended for or appreciated by a wide public, and often regarded as oversimplified for the sake of greater accessibility (*informal*) ○ *magazines full of pop psychology* [Late 19C. Shortening of POPULAR]

POP *abbr* **1.** ENVIRON persistent organic pollutant **2.** COMM point of presence **3.** Post Office Preferred (*used to describe the size of envelopes and packages*) **4.** COMM proof of purchase

pop. *abbr* **1.** popular **2.** population

pop art *n* an art movement of the 1950s to 1970s that incorporated modern popular culture and the mass media. It included such artists as Andy Warhol and Roy Lichtenstein.

popcorn /póp kawrn/ *n* **1.** the kernels of a variety of maize, heated until they become puffy, then usually flavoured with butter and sugar and eaten as a snack **2.** a variety of maize with hard kernels that pop open to form white puffs when heated. Latin name: *Zea mays praecox*.

popcorn movie *n* a popular and highly entertaining film (*informal*)

pope /pōp/ *n* **1.** *also* **Pope** ROMAN CATHOLIC CHURCH HEAD the head of the Roman Catholic Church and bishop of Rome **2.** *also* **Pope** COPTIC CHURCH HEAD the head of the Coptic Church **3.** *also* **Pope** ORTHODOX PRIEST a priest in the Eastern Orthodox Church **4.** POWERFUL PERSON somebody who has great authority or status **5.** (*plural* **popes** or *same*) FISH same as **ruffe** [Pre-12C. Via Latin *papa* < Greek *pappas* 'father'] —**popedom** *n*

Pope /pōp/, **Alexander** (1688–1744) English poet. He wrote the mock-heroic poem *The Rape of the Lock* (1712) and *An Essay on Man* (1733–34).

> 'To err is human; to forgive, divine.'
> [Alexander Pope, *An Essay on Criticism*; 1711]

> 'All nature is but art, unknown to thee; / All chance, direction, which thou canst not see; / All discord, harmony, not understood; / All partial evil, universal good; / And spite of Pride, in erring Reason's spite, / One truth is clear, "Whatever IS, is RIGHT".'
> [Alexander Pope, *An Essay on Man*; 1733–34]

> 'Expression is the dress of thought.'
> [Alexander Pope, *An Essay on Criticism*; 1711]

popery /pṓpəri/ *n* an offensive term for the Roman Catholic Church, its doctrines, or its practices

pope's nose *n N Am* same as **parson's nose**

popeyed /póp īd/ *adj* **1.** with the eyes bulging out **2.** with the eyes wide open in surprise or disbelief

pop group *n* a small number of musicians who play pop music together as a unit

popgun /póp gun/ *n* **1.** a toy gun that uses compressed air to shoot pellets, balls, or a cork tied to a string. It makes a popping sound. **2.** a useless or unimpressive firearm (*informal*)

popinjay /póppin jay/ *n* a vain and conceited person (*dated*) [13C. Via Old French *papegay* 'parrot' < Arabic *babbaġā*]

popish /pṓpish/ *adj* an offensive term meaning associated with the Roman Catholic Church, its doctrines, or its practices —**popishly** *adv*

poplar /pópplər/ n 1. a slender tree of the willow family with triangular leaves, flowers in catkins, and soft wood. Native to: northern temperate regions. Genus: *Populus*. 2. the light-coloured wood of a poplar (*often used before a noun*) 3. TREES same as **tulip tree** [14C. Via Anglo-Norman *popler* < Latin *populus*]

poplin /pópplin/ n a plain strong cotton fabric with fine ribbing. Use: clothes, upholstery. (*often used before a noun*) [Early 18C. < obsolete French *papeline* < medieval Latin *papalis* 'papal' (because made at the papal town of Avignon) < Latin *papa* (see POPE)]

popliteal /póppli teé əl, po plítti əl/ adj relating to or located in the part of the leg behind the knee joint [Late 18C. < modern Latin *popliteus* < Latin *poples* 'ham, back of the knee']

pop music n modern commercial music, usually tuneful, uptempo and repetitive, that is aimed at the general public and the youth market in particular

Popocatépetl /póppə káttə pet'l/ volcano in southern-central Mexico. Height: 5,452 m/17,887 ft.

Popova /pop óvər/, Liubov (1889–1924) Russian painter and designer. Influenced by futurism and constructivism, she designed stage sets and textiles for Moscow's First State Textile Printing Factory.

popover /póp óvər/ n 1. a simple garment for women or girls that can be slipped over the head 2. *N Am* a light hollow muffin-shaped quick bread made from eggs, flour, and milk

poppa /póppə/ n *N Am* same as **father** (*informal*) [Late 19C. Alteration of PAPA[1]]

poppadom /póppədəm, -dom/, **poppadum**, **papadum** n in South Asian cooking, a fried or roasted plate-sized wafer made from gram flour or flour from pulses, eaten as an appetizer or accompaniment to a meal [Early 19C. < Tamil *pappaṭam*]

popper /póppər/ n CLOTHING same as **press stud** ■ **poppers** npl small vials of amyl nitrate or butyl nitrate for inhaling as an illicit drug (*slang*)

poppet /póppit/ n 1. used to address a sweet and dear person, especially a child (*informal*) 2. ENG same as **poppet valve** 3. a steel beam or timber that is used to support the front and back ends of a ship when it is being launched [14C. Origin ?]

poppet head n the framework at the top of a mineshaft that supports the pulleys for the winding mechanism

poppet valve n a valve that is raised and lowered by a vertical guide, e.g. the intake and exhaust valves of the cylinders in an internal-combustion engine

popping crease /pópping-/ n the line at which a cricket batsman stands when facing the bowler. It runs parallel to the wicket and lies 1.2 m/4 ft in front of it. [Probably because it originally marked the line that the ball had to cross before it could be struck]

popple[1] /pópp'l/ (**-ples, -pling, -pled**) vi to move in an irregular tumbling or bubbling manner, like water does when it boils [14C. Probably < Middle Dutch *popelen* 'to babble, murmur', an imitation of the sound]

popple[2] /pópp'l/ n TREES same as **poplar** (sense 1) (*informal*) [14C. < Latin *populus*]

poppy

poppy /póppi/ (*plural* **-pies**) n 1. PLANT WITH RED FLOWERS an annual or perennial plant that has cup-shaped seed pods and milky sap. Flowers: large, red, orange, or white. Genus: *Papaver*. 2. FLOWER COMMEMORATING WAR DEAD a real or artificial poppy worn in commemoration of the war dead around the time

of Remembrance Sunday 3. PLANT LIKE TRUE POPPY any flowering plant that is similar or related to a poppy, e.g. a California poppy or Welsh poppy 4. ORANGE-RED COLOUR a bright red colour tinged with orange [Pre-12C. < Vulgar Latin alteration of Latin *papaver*]

poppycock /póppi kok/ n absurd speech or writing (*dated informal*) [Mid-19C. < Dutch dialect *pappekak* < *pap* 'soft, pap' + *kak* 'dung']

Poppy Day n CALENDAR same as **Remembrance Sunday**

poppyhead /póppi hed/ n an ornamental carved top on the end of a pew in a Gothic church

poppy seed n the small black seed of the poppy, used in cooking and in baking

poppyshow /póppi shō/ n same as **pappyshow** (*slang; used in Black English*)

pop shop n COMM same as **pawnshop** (*informal*) [< POP[1] 'to pawn']

Popsicle /pópsik'l/ tdmk *N Am* a trademark for a coloured fruit-flavoured ice on one or two sticks

popsock /póp sok/ n a woman's short stocking, reaching up to the knee. Popsocks are usually sheer and are often worn under trousers. (*usually used in the plural*)

pop-top n 1. *N Am* CAN TOP the top or portion of the top of a can that can be removed by pulling an attached ring or tab 2. *N Am* CAN a can whose top is opened by pulling an attached ring or tab 3. VAN ROOF a van roof that can be raised to create extra headroom while the van is stationary 4. VAN a van with a pop-top

populace /póppyōoləss/ n 1. the inhabitants of a town, region, or other area 2. ordinary people, as distinct from the political elite or the aristocracy [Late 16C. Via French < Italian *popolaccio* 'rabble' < *popolo* 'people' < Latin *populus*]

SPELLCHECK Do not confuse the spelling of **populace** and **populous**, which sound similar. **Populace** is a noun meaning 'the inhabitants or ordinary people of a place', whereas **populous** is an adjective meaning 'densely populated'.

popular /póppyōolər/ adj 1. APPEALING TO GENERAL PUBLIC appealing to or appreciated by a wide range of people ○ *the most popular name for babies this year* 2. WELL-LIKED liked by a person or group of people ○ *popular with young audiences* 3. OF GENERAL PUBLIC relating to the general public ○ *popular appeal* 4. AIMED AT NONSPECIALISTS designed to appeal to or be comprehensible to the nonspecialist ○ *popular science* 5. BELIEVED BY PEOPLE IN GENERAL believed, embraced, or perpetuated by ordinary people ○ *popular myths* 6. INEXPENSIVE designed to be affordable to people on average incomes ○ *a new popular car* [15C. Via Anglo-Norman < Latin *popularis* 'of the people' < *populus* 'people']

popular etymology n LING same as **folk etymology** (sense 2)

popular front n a broad-based coalition of left-wing political parties, formed to oppose fascism or institute social reforms, especially in Europe in the mid-1930s

popularise vt another spelling of **popularize**

popularity /póppyōo lárrəti/ n 1. admiration, approval, or acceptance of somebody or something by people in general or by a group of people 2. the desire or demand for something such as a manufactured product

popularize /póppyōolə rīz/ (**-izes, -izing, -ized**), **popularise** (**-ises, -ising, -ised**) vt 1. to make something widely liked or appreciated 2. to make something accessible and comprehensible to a wide audience —**popularization** /póppyōolə rī záysh'n/ n —**popularizer** n

popularly /póppyōolərli/ adv 1. by most people or in most situations 2. by the general public, as distinct from specialists

popular music n MUSIC same as **pop music**

popular sovereignty n in the United States, the doctrine that the people are sovereign and a government is subject to the will of the people

populate /póppyōo layt/ (**-lates, -lating, -lated**) vt 1. to live in an area, region, or country (*often passive*) 2. to supply an area with inhabitants [Late 16C.

< medieval Latin *populat-*, past participle of *populare* < Latin *populus* 'people'] —**populated** adj

population /póppyōo láysh'n/ n 1. PEOPLE IN PLACE all of the people who inhabit an area, region, or country 2. ALL PEOPLE OF GROUP all of the people of a particular nationality, ethnic group, religion, or class who live in an area 3. NUMBER OF PEOPLE the total number of people who inhabit an area, region, or country, or the number of people in a particular group who inhabit an area 4. ACT OF SUPPLYING INHABITANTS the populating of an area with inhabitants 5. ECOL INDIVIDUALS OF SAME SPECIES all the plants or animals of a particular species present in a place 6. STATS GROUP STATISTICALLY SAMPLED the entire group of individuals or items from which a sample may be selected for statistical measurement

population revolution n the huge growth in population in western Europe that began about 1730. It was a prelude to the Industrial Revolution.

populism /póppyōolizəm/ n 1. politics or political ideology based on the perceived interests of ordinary people, as opposed to those of a privileged elite 2. focus or emphasis on the lives of ordinary people, e.g. in the arts and in politics [Late 19C. < Latin *populus* 'people']

populist /póppyōolist/ n an advocate of the rights and interests of ordinary people, e.g. in politics or the arts ■ adj emphasizing or promoting ordinary people, their lives, or their interests [Late 19C. < Latin *populus* 'people']

populous /póppyōoləss/ adj with a large number of inhabitants [15C. < late Latin *populosus* < Latin *populus* 'people'] —**populously** adv —**populousness** n

SPELLCHECK See **populace**.

pop-up adj 1. UPWARD-LIFTING having a mechanism that makes something move quickly upwards ○ *pop-up headlines* 2. PRESENTED ON COMPUTER SCREEN TEMPORARILY appearing quickly and temporarily on a computer screen when a special key is pressed or a button is clicked with a mouse ○ *a pop-up menu* 3. WITH RISING CUT-OUT FIGURES containing cut-out figures that rise up as a page is opened ○ *a pop-up book* ■ ITEM WITH POP-UP FIGURES a book or card that contains pop-up figures, or a pop-up figure

porbeagle /páwr beeg'l/ (*plural* **-gles** or *same*) n a large and voracious shark with a crescent-shaped tail. Native to: North Atlantic. Latin name: *Lamna nasus*. [Mid-18C. < Cornish *porbugel*]

porcelain /páwrssəlin, -layn/ n 1. CERAMIC MATERIAL a hard translucent ceramic material used for making plates, cups, and other items (*often used before a noun*) 2. ITEMS MADE OF PORCELAIN objects made of porcelain, e.g. expensive crockery or decorative figurines 3. DECORATIVE OBJECT a single object made from porcelain, especially a decorative object [Mid-16C. Via French < Italian *porcellana* 'cowrie shell', (from its texture) 'porcelain', literally 'like a young sow' (because of the shell's shape) < *porca* 'sow' < form of Latin *porcus* 'pig'] —**porcellaneous** /páwrssə láyni əss/ adj

porcelain clay n GEOL same as **kaolin**

porcelain enamel n a glass coating that is fused to a metal by firing

porch /pawrch/ n 1. a covered shelter at the entrance to a building 2. *N Am* a raised platform with a roof that runs along the side of a house, partly enclosed with low walls or fully enclosed with screens or windows [13C. Via French < Latin *porticus* 'covered entry' < *porta* 'gate']

porcine /páwr sīn/ adj relating to or resembling pigs [Mid-17C. Via French < Latin *porcinus* < *porcus* 'pig']

porcino /pawr chéenō/ (*plural* **-ni** /-ni/), **porcini mushroom** n FOOD same as **cep** [Late 20C. < Italian, shortening of *fungo porcino* 'porcine mushroom']

porcupine /páwrkyōo pīn/ n a large rodent whose body is covered with long protective quills that it can erect in defence against predators. Families: Hystricidae or Erethizontidae. [14C. < Old French *porc espin* 'spiny pig']

ORIGIN When French *porc espin* was adopted by English as **porcupine** it underwent a range of odd transformations, including *portpen, porpoynt, porpentine* (the form used by Shakespeare: the ghost of Hamlet's father speaks of the 'quills upon the fretful porpentine'), *por-*

porcupine

kenpick, and *porpin* before finally settling down in the 17th century to ***porcupine***. Around 1700 the fanciful variant *porcupig* was coined.

Porcupine /páwrkyoŏ pīn/ river in North America that originates in northern Yukon Territory, Canada, joining the Yukon River in northeastern Alaska. Length: 916 km/569 mi.

porcupine fish *n* a sea fish that has strong sharp spines covering its body. Native to: tropics. Family: Diodontidae.

porcupine provisions *npl* measures taken by a company to discourage an unwanted takeover

pore[1] /pawr/ *n* **1. TINY OPENING IN SKIN** a tiny opening in human skin, or in the skin or other outer covering of an animal, through which substances can pass. Perspiration is released through the pores. **2. TINY OPENING IN PLANT** a tiny opening in a leaf or stem of a plant used to absorb or release substances, e.g. in photosynthesis or respiration **3.** GEOL **SMALL SPACE IN ROCK** a small space that is surrounded by rock or soil. It may be filled with water, crude oil, or natural gas. [14C. Via French and Latin < Greek *poros* 'passage']

USAGE See ***pour.***

pore[2] /pawr/ (**pores, poring, pored**) *vi* **1.** to study something carefully and thoughtfully ○ *poring over a book* **2.** to meditate on or think carefully about something [13C. Origin ?]

USAGE See ***pour.***

pore fungus *n* any fungus that has spores in tiny tubules that lead to outside pores. Families: Boletaceae or Polyporaceae.

porgy /páwrgi/ (*plural same or* **-gies**) *n* **1. SEA FOOD FISH** a sea food fish that has a deep flat body with large scales. Native to: Mediterranean Sea, Atlantic Ocean. Latin name: *Pagrus pagrus*. **2. FISH RELATED TO PORGY** a sea fish related to the porgy, with a similarly deep flat body. Family: Sparidae. **3. UNRELATED FISH LIKE PORGY** a fish that is similar to the porgy but unrelated, e.g. the menhaden [Mid-17C. Via Spanish, Portuguese *pargo* < Greek *phagros* 'sea bream']

poriferan /paw ríffərən/ *n* MARINE BIOL same as **sponge** *n* (sense 1) (*technical*) ■ *adj* belonging or relating to the sponges [Mid-19C. < modern Latin *Porifera* 'passage-bearing' < Latin *porus* 'pore (of the skin)']

porin /páwrin/ *n* a ring-shaped protein that spans a membrane in living cells to create a channel for the passage of small molecules [Late 20C. < PORE[1]]

pork /pawrk/ *n* **1.** the flesh of a pig eaten as food, usually cooked fresh. Cured pig flesh is usually referred to as bacon or ham. (*often used before a noun*) **2.** *US* government money and jobs awarded by politicians to their supporters or constituents to win their favour, especially when awarded wastefully (*informal*) [13C. Via French < Latin *porcus* 'pig']

pork barrel *n N Am* government-funded projects that bring jobs and other benefits to an area and give its political representative the opportunity to award favours and reap the ensuing prestige (*informal; hyphenated before a noun*)

pork belly *n* a side of fresh pork, or a cut of meat from this

porkbush /páwrk boŏsh/ *n S Africa* PLANTS same as **spekboom**

porker /páwrkər/ *n* **1.** a young fattened pig, especially one raised for its meat **2.** person or animal regarded as overweight (*informal insult*)

pork pie *n* a round raised pie filled with minced pork and usually eaten cold

porkpie hat /páwrk pī-/, **porkpie** *n* **1.** a man's hat with a flat crown and small brim that can be turned up, first popular in the 1850s **2.** a woman's round hat without a brim, first popular in the 1860s [< its shape]

pork rinds *npl ANZ, N Am* same as **pork scratchings**

pork scratchings *npl UK* small pieces of fried pork rind and fat that are eaten as a snack. ANZ, N Am term **pork rinds**

porky /páwrki/ *adj* (**-kier, -kiest**) **1.** relating to or resembling pork **2.** regarded as overweight (*informal insult*) ■ *n* (*plural* **-kies**) same as **lie**[2] *n* (sense 1) (*slang; often used in the plural*) ○ *Who's been telling porkies, then?* [In noun sense < rhyming slang *pork pie*]

porn /pawrn/, **porno** /páwrnō/ *n* same as **pornography** (*informal; often used before a noun*) [Mid-20C. Shortening]

pornographic /páwrnə gráffik/ *adj* **1.** sexually explicit and intended to cause sexual arousal **2.** producing or selling sexually explicit magazines, films, or other materials —**pornographically** *adv*

pornography /pawr nóggrəfi/ *n* **1.** films, magazines, writings, photographs, or other materials that are sexually explicit and intended to cause sexual arousal **2.** the production or sale of sexually explicit films, magazines, or other materials [Mid-19C. Via French < Greek *pornographos* 'writing about prostitutes' < *pornē* 'prostitute'] —**pornographer** *n*

porosity /paw róssəti/ (*plural* **-ties**) *n* **1. POROUS QUALITY** the porous nature of something, or the extent to which something is porous **2.** GEOL, ENG **PERCENTAGE OF PORE SPACE** the ratio of the space taken up by the pores in a soil, rock, or other material to its total volume. It is expressed as a percentage. **3.** GEOL, ENG **PORE** a pore in soil, rock, or other material (*technical*) [14C. Via French < medieval Latin *porositas* < *porosus* (see POROUS)]

porous /páwrəss/ *adj* **1. WITH PORES** having a surface that contains pores or a body that contains cavities **2. PERMEABLE** permitting the movement of fluids or gases through it by way of pores or other passages **3. BREACHABLE** easy to cross, infiltrate, or penetrate [14C. Via French < medieval Latin *porosus* < Latin *porus* 'passage, pore'] —**porously** *adv* —**porousness** *n*

porphyria /pawr fírri ə/ *n* a medical condition caused by the body's failure to metabolize porphyrins. Symptoms of the hereditary form include abdominal pain, sensitivity to sunlight, confusion, and excretion of porphyrins in the urine. [Early 20C. < PORPHYRIN]

porphyrin /páwrfərin/ *n* a metal-containing pigment in animal and plant tissue, consisting of four pyrrole rings linked by methylene groups, e.g. haemoglobin [Early 20C. < Greek *porphura* 'purple', from the colour of the pigments]

porphyritic /páwrfə ríttik/ *adj* **1.** relating to or containing porphyry **2.** containing isolated large and distinct crystals in a mainly fine-grained rock

porphyry /páwrfəri/ *n* **1.** a reddish-purple rock containing large distinct feldspar crystals embedded in a fine-grained groundmass **2.** any predominantly fine-grained igneous rock that contains isolated large crystals [14C. Via Old French *porfire* < Greek *porphuritēs* < *porphura* 'purple', from its colour]

porpoise /páwrpəss/ (*plural same or* **-poises**) *n* **1.** a toothed sea mammal, related to the whales and dolphins, that has a blunt snout and a triangular dorsal fin. Family: Phocaenidae. **2.** a popular but technically inaccurate term for a dolphin [14C. < Old French *porpeis* < Latin *porcus* 'pig' + *piscis* 'fish']

porridge /pórrij/ *n* **1.** a dish made from oatmeal or another cereal cooked with milk or water to form a thick liquid, often eaten at breakfast. N Am term **oatmeal 2.** a term of imprisonment (*slang*) [Mid-16C. Alteration of POTTAGE. In the meaning 'imprisonment', from the idea that porridge is a common prison food]

porringer /pórrinjər/ *n* a small bowl, usually with a handle, used for soup, stew, or porridge [Early 16C. Alteration of *pottinger* < French *potager* < *potage* (see POTTAGE)]

port[1] /pawrt/ *n* **1. HARBOUR** a place by the sea, or by a river or other waterway, where ships and boats can dock, load, and unload **2. TOWN WITH HARBOUR** a town or city built around a port **3. WATERFRONT** the waterfront area of a port **4. COVE** a sheltered place along a coast, where boats are protected from storms and rough seas **5.** GEOG same as **port of entry** [Pre-12C. < Latin *portus*] ◇ **any port in a storm** any source of help or refuge is welcome in desperate circumstances

port[2] /pawrt/ *n* **1.** COMPUT **EXTERNAL COMPUTER CONNECTION** an external socket on a computer's main unit (**CPU**) where a peripheral device such as a printer, keyboard, or network cable is plugged in **2.** COMPUT **ADAPTATION OF SOFTWARE** the act of converting software so that it can run on a different operating system **3.** NAUT **OPENING IN BOAT** a watertight opening in the side of a boat, used for loading and unloading and as a means of general access to the holds **4.** NAUT same as **porthole** (sense 1) **5.** MIL **GUN HOLE** a small opening in an armoured vehicle, military aircraft, naval vessel, or fortification through which a gun can be fired **6.** ENG **VALVE-OPERATED OPENING** an opening controlled by a valve, e.g. any of the openings in the cylinder of an internal combustion engine **7.** *Scotland* **CITY GATE** a city gate, or the original site of a gate that is no longer there (*often used in placenames*) ■ *vt* (**ports, porting, ported**) COMPUT **CONVERT SOFTWARE FOR DIFFERENT SYSTEM** to convert software to run on a different operating system [13C. Via French, 'gate' < Latin *porta*]

port[3] /pawrt/ *n* **LEFT SIDE ON SHIP OR PLANE** the left-hand side of a boat or aeroplane when facing forwards ■ *adj, adv* **ON LEFT** on or to the left-hand side of boat or aeroplane when facing forwards ■ *vti* (**ports, porting, ported**) **TURN TO PORT** to turn towards the port side, or make a ship do this [Mid-16C. Shortening of *port side* < PORT[1], because the side that faced the pier and over which cargo was loaded]

port[4] /pawrt/ *n* a strong sweet fortified wine usually drunk after dinner. It is usually a deep red colour, but some kinds are brownish (**tawny port**) and some white. Originally from Portugal, port-style wine is now made in other countries. [Late 17C. After PORTO]

port[5] /pawrt/ *vt* (**ports, porting, ported**) to carry a weapon positioned diagonally across the body with the muzzle or blade in front of the left shoulder ■ *n* the position of a rifle or sword when ported [Mid-16C. Via French < Latin *portare* 'carry']

portable /páwrtəb'l/ *adj* **1. EASILY MOVED ABOUT** designed to be light or compact enough to carry or move easily from place to place **2.** COMPUT **EASY TO CONVERT** describes software that can be easily converted to run on different computer operating systems ■ *n* **EASILY TRANSPORTED OBJECT** a device or an appliance that is designed to be easily carried or moved from place to place [14C. Via French < late Latin *portabilis* < Latin *portare* 'carry'] —**portability** /páwrtə bíllәti/ *n* —**portably** *adv*

portable document format *n* COMPUT full form of **pdf**

Portadown /páwrtə dówn/ town in the Craigavon District of County Armagh, Northern Ireland. Population: 21,299 (1991).

portage /páwrtij, pawr taazh/ *n* **1. ACT OF CARRYING** the carrying or transporting of something **2. CHARGE FOR CARRYING** a charge made for carrying or transporting something **3. CARRYING OF BOATS OVERLAND** the carrying of boats or cargo across land from one waterway to another or around an unnavigable section of a waterway **4. OVERLAND ROUTE TO WATERWAY** an overland route used when transporting a boat or its cargo from one waterway to another ■ *vti* (**-ages, -aging, -aged**) **CARRY SOMETHING OVERLAND TO WATERWAY** to carry boats or cargo across land from one waterway to another or around an unnavigable portion of a waterway [13C. < French < Latin *portare* 'carry']

Portakabin /páwrtə kabin/ *tdmk* a trademark for a portable building that can be assembled quickly and used for a variety of purposes, e.g. as an office or a schoolroom

portal /páwrt'l/ *n* **1. LARGE GATE** a large or elaborate gate or entrance (*literary*) **2. ENTRANCE** any entrance to a place, or any means of access to something (*literary*) **3.** *also* **portal site** ONLINE **HOME SITE FOR WEB BROWSER** a website that provides links to information and other websites **4.** CONSTR **TUNNEL ENTRANCE** the entrance

to a tunnel ■ *adj* ANAT OF PORTAL VEIN OR SYSTEM relating to the portal vein, portal system, or the opening in the liver through which the portal vein passes [14C. Via French < medieval Latin *portale* < Latin *porta* 'gate']

portal bridge *n* a bridge that is supported from beneath by an angled member at each end, often used for road bridges

portal site *n* ONLINE same as **portal** *n* (sense 3)

portal system *n* a network of blood vessels that begin in the capillaries of one organ and end in the capillaries of another, especially the portal veins connecting the liver and intestines

portal vein *n* a vein that carries blood from the digestive organs, gall bladder, and spleen to the liver, especially the vein from the intestines carrying nutrient-rich blood

portamento /páwrtə méntō/ (*plural* -**ti** /-ti/) *n* a smooth glide from one note to another when singing or playing a stringed instrument [Late 18C. < Italian, 'carrying', because the finger slides from one note to the next]

Port Arthur /páwrt aárthər/ 1. town in Australia, in southern Tasmania. It was the site of a major penal settlement between 1830 and 1837. Population: 190 (1994). 2. former name for **Lushun**

portative organ /páwrtətiv-/ *n* a small portable organ operated by bellows, used in medieval and Renaissance music

Port Augusta city in South Australia, at the head of the Spencer Gulf. The city is a railway junction and industrial centre. Population: 13,593 (2002 estimate).

Port-au-Prince /páwrt ō prínss/ capital city and chief port of Haiti, on Gonáve Gulf. Population: 990,558 (1999).

Port Blair port on South Andaman Island in the Bay of Bengal, and capital of the Indian Union Territory of Andaman and Nicobar Islands. Population: 49,634 (1981).

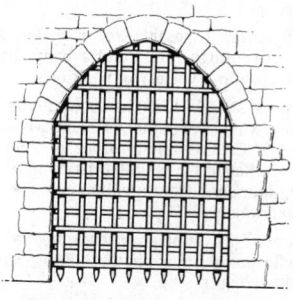
portcullis

portcullis /pawrt kúlliss/ *n* a heavy iron or wooden grating that is set in vertical grooves and lowered to block the gateway to a castle or fortification [14C. < Old French *porte coleïce* 'sliding door']

port de bras /páwr də braá/ *n* the proper movement of the arms in ballet, or exercises for developing this [< French, 'carriage of the arms']

Port du Salut *n* FOOD same as **Port-Salut**

Porte /pawrt/ *n* the court or government of the Ottoman Empire. It was situated in Constantinople. [Early 17C. < French (*la Sublime*) *Porte* '(the exalted) Gate', translation of the Turkish title of the central office; from the palace gate where justice was administered]

porte-cochere *n* 1. a large covered entrance for vehicles in a wall or building leading to a courtyard 2. a large roof or awning extending from the entrance of a building to the driveway [Late 17C. < French *porte cochère* 'door for coaches']

Port Elizabeth /-i lízzəbəth/ city in Eastern Cape Province, southeastern South Africa, situated on Algoa Bay, on the Indian Ocean. Population: 1,035,000 (1995).

portend /pawr ténd/ (-**tends**, -**tending**, -**tended**) *vt* 1. to be an indication that something, especially something unpleasant, is going to happen 2. to indicate or signify something [15C. < Latin *portendere* 'stretch forward' < *tendere* 'hold out, stretch']

portent /páwr tent/ *n* 1. OMEN an indication that some-

thing, often something unpleasant, is going to happen 2. SIGNIFICANCE ominous or prophetic significance 3. MARVEL a wonderful or marvellous thing (*formal*) [Late 16C. < Latin *portentum* < *portendere* (see PORTEND)]

portentous /pawr téntəss/ *adj* 1. SIGNIFICANT very serious and significant, especially with regard to future events 2. POMPOUS excessively serious or pompous 3. AMAZING inspiring wonder and amazement — **portentously** *adv* —**portentousness** *n*

porter[1] /páwrtər/ *n* 1. LUGGAGE CARRIER a worker who carries people's luggage, e.g. at an airport or railway station, or in a hotel 2. HOSPITAL EMPLOYEE an employee who moves patients between departments or wards in a hospital 3. *N Am* TRAIN ATTENDANT an attendant in a train [14C. Via French *porteur* < medieval Latin *portator* 'carrier' < Latin *portat-*, past participle of *portare* 'carry']

porter[2] /páwrtər/ *n* 1. GATEKEEPER somebody who is in charge of the door or gate of a building or institution 2. COLLEGE RECEPTION PERSON an employee who supervises the main entrance at a university or college, answering enquiries and doing other tasks 3. *UK* CARETAKER the caretaker of a building, especially a block of flats, who is responsible for the general maintenance of the building. N Am term **superintendent** [13C. Via French < late Latin *portarius* < Latin *porta* 'gate']

porter[3] /páwrtər/ *n* a dark sweet beer, similar to light stout, made from malt that has been browned or charred [Early 18C. Shortening of *porter's ale* < PORTER[1]]

Porter /páwrtər/, **Cole** (1893–1964) US composer and lyricist. He is known for his witty sophisticated songs, and for musicals such as *Kiss Me Kate* (1949). Full name **Porter, Cole Albert**

'In olden days, a glimpse of stocking / Was looked on as something shocking, / But now, Heaven knows, / Anything goes.'
[Cole Porter, 'Anything Goes', *Anything Goes*; 1934]

Porter, Katherine Anne (1890–1980) US writer. Regarded as one of the leading modern writers of short stories, she received the 1966 Pulitzer Prize for *Collected Short Stories* (1965).

'Miracles are instantaneous, they cannot be summoned, but come of themselves, usually at unlikely moments and to those who least expect them.'
[Katherine Anne Porter, *Ship of Fools*; 1962]

Porter, Peter (b. 1929) Australian-born British poet and critic. His many collections of formally elegant verse include *The Automatic Oracle* (1987). Full name **Porter, Peter Neville Frederick**

'Language of the liberal dead speaks / From the soil of Highgate, tears / Show a great water table is intact. / You cannot leave England, it turns / A planet majestically in the mind.'
[Peter Porter, 'The Last of England', *The Last of England*; 1970]

Porter, Rodney (1917–85) British biochemist. He is noted for his work on the chemical structure of antibodies, for which he shared a Nobel Prize in physiology or medicine (1972). Full name **Porter, Rodney Robert**

Porter, William Sydney ♦ Henry, O.

porterage /páwrtərij/ *n* 1. the work of carrying that is performed by porters 2. a fee charged by porters for carrying things

porterhouse /páwrtər howss/ (*plural* -**houses** /-howziz/) *n* an establishment that sold porter and sometimes also served meals (*archaic*)

porterhouse steak *n* a beef steak from the thick end of the sirloin

portfire /páwrt fīr/ *n* a slow fuse. Use: formerly, explosives in mining and for rockets and fireworks. [Mid-17C. Anglicization of French *porte-feu* 'fire-carrier']

portfolio /pawrt fóli ō/ (*plural* -**os**) *n* 1. FLAT CASE FOR DOCUMENTS a large flat case for carrying documents such as maps, photographs, or drawings 2. PORTFOLIO CONTENTS the contents of a portfolio, especially when they represent somebody's creative work 3. MINISTERIAL RESPONSIBILITIES the post or responsibilities

of a cabinet minister or minister of state 4. GROUP OF INVESTMENTS all the investments held by a person or organization 5. RANGE OF PRODUCTS the complete range of products or designs offered by a company (*formal*) [Early 18C. < Italian *portafoglio* < *portare* 'carry' + *foglio* 'sheet, page']

portfolio worker *n* somebody who offers skills and experience in a number of different areas, often working on a short-term or part-time basis

Port-Gentil /pawr zhaaN teé/ city and seaport in western Gabon. It is the capital of Ogooué-Maritime Province. Population: 125,000 (1993).

Port Harcourt /-haárkərt/ major port and capital city of Rivers State, southern Nigeria. Population: 399,700 (1995).

Porthcawl /pawrth káwl/ town near Bridgend in southern Wales. Population: 15,922 (1991).

Port Hedland /-hédlənd/ town in northwestern Western Australia. It is a mining centre and port. Population: 12,846 (1996).

porthole /páwrt hōl/ *n* 1. a small round window with a metal frame in the side of a ship 2. a small opening in a fortified wall through which weapons can be fired

Portia /páwrshə/ *n* a small inner natural satellite of Uranus, discovered in 1986 by the Voyager 2 planetary probe. It is approximately 110 km/68 mi. in diameter.

portico

portico /páwrtikō/ (*plural* -**coes** or -**cos**) *n* 1. a covered entrance to a large building 2. a covered walkway, often leading to the main entrance of a building, that consists of a roof supported by pillars [Early 17C. Via Italian < Latin *porticus* < *porta* 'gate']

portière /páwrti áir/ *n* a heavy curtain hung across a doorway [Mid-19C. < French < *porte* 'door' < Latin *porta* 'gate']

portion /páwrsh'n/ *n* 1. FRACTION a part or section of a larger whole 2. HELPING OF FOOD an amount of food for one person 3. INHERITANCE a part of an estate that has been bequeathed to an heir 4. LAW same as **dowry** (sense 1) 5. FATE an unavoidable event or part of somebody's life (*literary*) ○ *It was her portion in life to teach reading only.* ■ *vt* (-**tions**, -**tioning**, -**tioned**) 1. DIVIDE SOMETHING to divide something into parts for use 2. ENDOW WOMAN to give a dowry to a woman (*archaic*) [14C. Via French < Latin *portion-*] —**portionable** *adj* —**portioner** *n*

Port Jackson /-jáks'n/ coastal inlet in eastern New South Wales, Australia. The site of the city of Sydney, it is more commonly known as Sydney Harbour. Area: 54 sq. km/20 sq. mi.

Portland /páwrtlənd/ 1. city in Oregon, situated in the northwestern part of the state on the Willamette River. It is the state's largest city and its economic and cultural centre. Population: 539,438 (2002 estimate). 2. city in southwestern Maine, on the southern shore of Casco Bay, northeast of Saco. Population: 63,882 (2002 estimate).

Portland, Isle of peninsula on the coast of Dorset, southern England, connected to the mainland by Chesil Bank, a shingle ridge. Area: 12 sq. km/5 sq. mi.

Portland cement *n* a cement that hardens under water, made by burning limestone and clay [Because a similar colour to stone, quarried on the Isle of PORTLAND]

Port Laoise /-leésh/ county town of Laois, central Republic of Ireland. Population: 8,360 (1991).

Port Lincoln town on Boston Bay in South Australia. It is a fishing port and tourist resort. Population: 14,049 (2002 estimate).

Port Louis /-lŏŏ iss, -lŏŏ i/ capital city and chief port of Mauritius, on the northeastern coast of the island. Population: 147,131 (1998).

portly /páwrtli/ (**-lier, -liest**) adj 1. slightly overweight but dignified 2. having an air of grandeur (archaic) [15C. < PORT⁵ in the old sense 'bearing, manner'] —**portliness** n

Port Macquarie /-mə kwórri/ coastal town in southeastern New South Wales, Australia. It is a residential and tourist centre. Population: 26,797 (1991).

portmanteau /páwrt mántō/ n (plural **-teaus** or **-teaux** /-tōz/) an old type of large leather suitcase, especially one that opened out into two compartments ■ adj combining several uses or qualities [Mid-16C. < French portemanteau < porter 'carry' + manteau 'cloak']

portmanteau word n a word that combines the sound and meaning of two words, e.g. 'smog', a combination of 'smoke' and 'fog' [< the description (in Lewis Carroll's Through the Looking Glass) of the word slithy as a 'portmanteau' because 'there are two meanings packed up into one word']

Port Moresby /-máwrzbi/ capital city of Papua New Guinea, situated on the southern coast of the island of New Guinea. Population: 259,000 (2001).

Porto /páwrtō/, **Oporto** /ō-/ city and port in northwestern Portugal, situated about 274 km/170 mi. north of Lisbon. Population: 285,320 (1995).

Porto Alegre /-ə léggri/ capital city of Rio Grande do Sul State, southeastern Brazil, and the country's leading river port. It lies at the junction of five rivers. Population: 1,288,879 (1996).

portobello /páwrtə béllō/ (plural **-los**), **portobello mushroom** n a very large dark mushroom known for its meaty texture

port of call n 1. any port, other than the home port, that a vessel visits on a journey 2. a place visited during a holiday, trip, or excursion (informal)

port of entry n a place where passengers and goods may enter a country under the supervision of customs officials, e.g. a port or an airport

Port-of-Spain, Port of Spain capital city and main port of Trinidad and Tobago. It is situated in the northwestern part of the island of Trinidad. Population: 53,000 (2000).

Porto-Novo /-nōvō/ capital city of Benin, and its main seaport, situated on a lagoon that extends along the Gulf of Guinea. Population: 232,756 (2000).

Port Phillip Bay /-fíllip-/ bay in southern Victoria, Australia. The city of Melbourne lies on its southern shore. Area: 2,000 sq. km/800 sq. mi.

Port Pirie /-peéri/ city in South Australia, on the Spencer Gulf. It is a port and industrial centre. Population: 17,587 (2002 estimate).

portrait /páwrtrit, -trayt/ n 1. PICTURE OF PERSON a painting, photograph, or drawing of somebody, somebody's face, or a related group 2. DESCRIPTION a description of something such as a person, place, or period ■ adj TALLER THAN WIDE describes a piece of paper, illustration, book, or page that is taller than it is wide [Mid-16C. < French < past participle of Old French portraire (see PORTRAY)]

CULTURAL NOTE *Portrait of a Lady*, a novel (1881) by US writer Henry James. Through the story of Isabel Archer, a young American woman who travels to Europe and is duped into marrying an urbane but materialistic fellow expatriate, the author explores the contrasting characteristics of the Old World (sophisticated but corrupt) and the New (idealistic but naive). It was made into a film by Jane Campion in 1997.

portraitist /páwrtrətist, páwrtritist/ n somebody who specializes in portraits, e.g. a photographer or painter

portraiture /páwrtrichər/ n 1. MAKING OF PORTRAITS the art or practice of making portraits 2. PORTRAITS portraits considered collectively 3. PORTRAIT a portrait painting, drawing, or photography (formal)

portray /pawr tráy/ (**-trays, -traying, -trayed**) vt 1. DEPICT

SOMETHING OR SOMEBODY VISUALLY to depict something such as a person or a scene in a painting, photograph, drawing, or sculpture 2. DEPICT SOMETHING OR SOMEBODY VERBALLY to represent somebody or something in words 3. PLAY ROLE IN DRAMA to play a character in drama [13C. < Old French portraire 'draw out' < traire 'draw' < Latin trahere] —**portrayable** adj —**portrayal** n —**portrayer** n

Port Said /-síd/ city and port in northeastern Egypt, at the Mediterranean end of the Suez Canal. Population: 469,000 (1998).

Port-Salut /páwr sa lŏŏ/, **Port du Salut** /páwr doo sa lŏŏ/ n a flat round mild French cheese with an orange rind, made from whole milk [Late 19C. After Notre Dame de Port-du-Salut, Trappist monastery in NW France]

Portsmouth /páwrtsməth/ city and naval base in Hampshire, southern England. Population: 186,701 (2001).

Port Stanley ♦ **Stanley²**

Port Sudan city in northeastern Sudan, and the country's only seaport, situated on the Red Sea 322 km/200 mi. northeast of Khartoum. Population: 305,385 (1993).

Port Sunlight /-sún līt/ village in Merseyside, northwestern England. It was created in 1888 to provide accommodation for the workers of the Sunlight soap factory.

Port Talbot /pawrt táwlbət, pawr táwlbət/ town in southern Wales. It is the administrative centre of Neath and Port Talbot unitary authority and was a major steel-making centre. Population: 37,647 (1991).

Portugal

Portugal /páwrchŏŏg'l/ country in southwestern Europe, in the southwestern part of the Iberian Peninsula. Language: Portuguese. Currency: euro. Capital: Lisbon. Population: 10,102,022 (2003). Area: 92,345 sq. km/35,655 sq. mi. Official name **Portuguese Republic**

~~Portugese~~ incorrect spelling of **Portuguese**

Portuguese /páwrchŏŏ geéz/ n 1. the Romance official language of Portugal and Brazil, also an official language in some African countries. Native speakers: 150 million. Other speakers: 30 million. 2. somebody who comes from Portugal [Late 16C. < Portuguese português < medieval Latin Portus Cale, the port of Gaya (Porto)] —**Portuguese** adj

Portuguese India territories in India formerly ruled by Portugal, considered as a group. They included Goa, Daman, Diu, Dadra, and Nagar Haveli. They were taken over by India between 1954 and 1961.

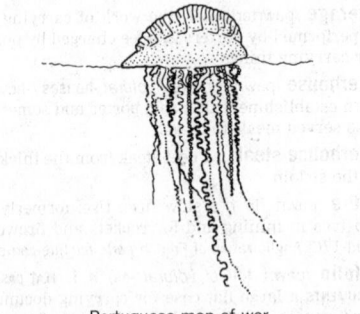

Portuguese man-of-war

Portuguese man-of-war (plural **Portuguese man-of-wars** or **Portuguese men-of-war**) n a sea organism

(hydrozoan) that resembles a jellyfish and lives in warm waters. It has a transparent gas-filled float and long stinging, often poisonous tentacles. Genus: *Physalia*. [< its crest, resembling a sail]

portulaca /páwrtyŏŏ lákə/ n a widely cultivated fleshy-leaved plant. Flowers: brightly coloured. Native to: tropical and subtropical America. Genus: *Portulaca*. [Mid-16C. < Latin, 'purslane' < portula 'little gate' < porta 'gate'; because the covering of the seed capsule resembles a gate]

port-wine stain n a conspicuous purplish birthmark, especially on the face or neck

POS abbr COMM point of sale

posable adj another spelling of **poseable**

posada /pō saádə/ n in a Spanish-speaking country, a hotel, pension, or hostel [Mid-18C. < Spanish < posar 'stay, lodge' < late Latin pausare (see POSE¹)]

pose¹ /pōz/ v (**poses, posing, posed**) 1. vti ADOPT POSTURE to adopt a physical posture for a photograph or painting, or position somebody or something for this purpose 2. vi IMPERSONATE SOMEBODY OR SOMETHING to pretend to be somebody or something else ○ got past the security guards by posing as a journalist 3. vt PRESENT SOMETHING to be the cause of something such as a problem, threat, danger, or challenge ○ a breakdown of negotiations that poses a threat to peace 4. vt ASK QUESTION to ask a question, often one that requires some consideration 5. vi BE PRETENTIOUS to behave, dress, or assume a mental attitude intended to impress others (disapproving) ■ n 1. POSTURE a physical posture, e.g. one adopted for a painting or photograph 2. PRETENCE a way of behaving or dressing intended to impress others (disapproving) ○ His sudden interest in opera is just a pose. [14C. Via French poser < late Latin pausare 'rest, cease' < Latin pausa (see PAUSE)]

pose² /pōz/ (**poses, posing, posed**) vt to confuse or baffle somebody (archaic) [Early 16C. Partly shortening of obsolete appose 'examine, interrogate' < Old French aposer, variant of opposer (see OPPOSE); partly < Old French poser 'assume']

poseable /pōzəb'l/, **posable** adj describes a doll or figure with jointed limbs and a body that can be made to pose in a variety of positions

Poseidon /pə síd'n/ n 1. in Greek mythology, the god of the sea, water, earthquakes, and horses, who was the son of Cronus and brother of Zeus. Roman equivalent **Neptune** 2. a US ballistic missile capable of being launched from a submarine and carrying a nuclear warhead

poser¹ /pōzər/ n 1. same as **poseur** (informal) 2. somebody who poses for a photograph or work of art [Late 19C. < POSE¹]

poser² /pōzər/ n a difficult question or problem [Late 16C. < POSE²]

~~posess~~ incorrect spelling of **possess**

~~posession~~ incorrect spelling of **possession**

poseur /pō zúr/ n somebody who tries to impress others by behaving in an affected way [Late 19C. < French < poser (see POSE¹)]

posey /pōzi/ (**-ier, -iest**) adj trying to impress others by behaving in an affected way (informal)

posh /posh/ (informal) adj 1. FOR WELL-OFF PEOPLE elegant, fashionable, and expensive 2. UPPER-CLASS from, imitating, or characteristic of the upper classes ■ adv LIKE UPPER CLASS PERSON like somebody from the upper classes ○ She talks posh to try and impress people. [Early 20C. Origin ?] —**poshly** adv —**poshness** n

ORIGIN The legend has become widely circulated that *posh* is an acronym formed from the initial letters of *port out, starboard home*, an allusion to the fact that wealthy passengers could afford the more expensive cabins on the port side of the ships going out to India, and on the starboard side returning to the United Kingdom, which kept them out of the heat of the sun. Pleasant as this story is, it has never been substantiated. Another possibility is that *posh* may be the same word as the now obsolete *posh* 'dandy, swell', a slang term current around the end of the 19th century. This too is of unknown origin, but it has been linked with the still earlier 19th-century slang term *posh* 'halfpenny', hence broadly 'money', which may have come ultimately from Romany *posh* 'half'.

posit /pózzit/ (*formal*) *vt* (**-its, -iting, -ited**) **1.** PUT SOMETHING FORWARD to put forward for consideration something such as a suggestion, assumption, or fact **2.** POSITION SOMETHING to place something firmly in position ■ *n* SOMETHING PUT FORWARD a suggestion, assumption, or fact put forward for consideration [Mid-17C. < Latin *posit-*, past participle of *ponere* 'place']

positif /póssitif/ *n* a manual that controls the softer stops on a church organ [< Old French, 'movable church organ' < Latin *positivus* (see POSITIVE)]

position /pə zísh'n/ *n* **1.** LOCATION the place where somebody or something is, especially in relation to other things ○ *confirm their position and direction by radio* **2.** POSTURE the posture that somebody's body is in ○ *The accident victim had been placed in the recovery position.* **3.** ARRANGEMENT the way or direction in which an object is placed or arranged ○ *the position of the hour hand* **4.** SITUATION a particular set of circumstances ○ *I wouldn't sell just yet if I were in your position.* **5.** RANK somebody's standing or level of importance in society or an organization ○ *In her position she should set an example for others.* **6.** POST a job or post in a company or organization ○ *the position of marketing manager* **7.** VIEW a policy, view, or opinion, especially an official one ○ *What's your position on the euro?* **8.** PLACE IN ORDER the place that a person, team, or organization occupies in a race, contest, or list ○ *The liberals were squeezed into third position by the two main parties.* **9.** CORRECT PLACE the correct or usual place or arrangement of an object or person ○ *Once the dignitaries are in position, the ceremony can start.* **10.** SEXUAL POSTURE the posture used by a couple in sexual intercourse **11.** MIL STRATEGIC PLACE a strategic area or point that is occupied by military personnel or where weapons are placed ○ *The enemy took up positions on a hill overlooking the fort.* **12.** ROLE IN TEAM the part of a playing area where a player is based and usually plays ○ *The substitute took up a midfield position.* **13.** BOARD GAMES ARRANGEMENT OF PIECES the arrangement of the pieces or counters in a board game such as chess or backgammon at a specific time **14.** FIN DEALER'S RESPONSIBILITY a dealer's commitment to buy or sell a specific number of securities or commodities **15.** FIN INVESTOR'S STATUS an investor's status based on holdings with regard to market trends **16.** MUSIC FINGERING ON INSTRUMENT the placement of the fingers on a keyboard or string instrument **17.** MUSIC EXTENSION OF TROMBONE SLIDE the extent to which a trombone slide is pushed out **18.** MUSIC ARRANGEMENT OF NOTES the arrangement of individual notes within a chord. Root position is the most fundamental position. **19.** LITERAT VOWEL LENGTH AFFECTED BY LOCATION in classical poetry, a short vowel counting as a long vowel because it comes before two or more consonants ■ *vt* (**-tions, -tioning, -tioned**) **1.** PUT SOMETHING IN PLACE to put something in a particular or suitable place ○ *Position the two pieces so that they are at right angles.* **2.** PLACE SOMEBODY to place somebody or yourself in a particular or suitable area, place, or situation ○ *This strategy will position us advantageously in the market.* **3.** LOCATE SOMETHING to determine the site or location of something ○ *Air traffic controllers have positioned the unknown aircraft at 50 miles north of the airport.* [14C. Directly or via French < Latin *position-* < *posit-*, past participle of *ponere* 'place'] —**positional** *adj* —**positionally** *adv* —**positioner** *n*

ORIGIN The Latin word *ponere* 'to place', from which ***position*** is derived, is also the source of English *component, compost, compound*[1], *deposit, dispose, expose, impose, opponent, positive, post* ('place or position' and 'letters and parcels'), *postpone, posture, repose* ('place, trust'), *suppose*, and *transpose*.

position audit *n* an assessment of a company's or organization's commercial standing carried out to help future planning

position effect *n* a change in a gene's expression depending on its location on the chromosome in relation to other genes

position paper *n* an in-depth report on a matter that gives the official view and recommendations of a government or organization

positive /pózzətiv/ *adj* **1.** OPTIMISTIC confident, optimistic, and focusing on good things rather than bad ○ *a positive attitude about work* **2.** SURE certain and not in doubt ○ *'Are you sure that's what you want to do?' 'Yes, I'm positive'.* **3.** BENEFICIAL producing good results because of having an innately beneficial character ○ *a very positive experience* **4.** ENCOURAGING GOOD BEHAVIOUR encouraging behaviour, especially in the young, that is considered morally good ○ *a positive role model* **5.** AFFIRMATIVE indicating agreement or affirmation ○ *positive feedback* **6.** ADDS EMPHASIS used to emphasize the degree to which something is true, striking, or impressive (*informal*) ○ *Hiring her is a positive triumph for the department.* **7.** LAW IRREFUTABLE conclusive and beyond doubt or question ○ *positive identification of the suspect* **8.** SCI, MATHS QUANTIFIABLE capable of being measured, detected, or perceived ○ *a positive correlation between investment in telecommunications and economic development* **9.** MED INDICATING PRESENCE OF SOMETHING indicating the presence of a particular organism or component in the results of a test or examination ○ *a positive test for diabetes* **10.** MED same as **Rh positive** **11.** MATHS MORE THAN ZERO having a value higher than zero. Symbol **+** **12.** MATHS NOT NEGATIVE measured in a direction or designated as a quantity equal in magnitude, but opposite to that regarded as negative **13.** PHILOSOPHY EMPIRICAL relating to the theory that knowledge can be acquired only through direct observation and experimentation, and not through metaphysics or theology **14.** BIOL SHOWING RESPONSE indicating growth, response, or movement towards a stimulus such as light **15.** PHYS WITH ELECTRICAL CHARGE LIKE PROTON having an electrical charge of an opposite polarity to that of an electron and the same polarity as that of a proton **16.** PHYS WITH POSITIVE CHARGE having an overall positive electrical charge, sometimes caused by the loss of one or more electrons **17.** PHYS WITH HIGHER ELECTRICAL POTENTIAL having a higher electrical potential than the ground or the defined neutral point ○ *a positive electrode* **18.** ELEC same as **electropositive** (sense 1) **19.** PHOTOGRAPHY LIKE SUBJECT describes photographic images that have colours or values of dark and light corresponding to the subject **20.** OPTICS MAKING LIGHT CONVERGE making a parallel beam of light converge **21.** GRAM NOT COMPARATIVE OR SUPERLATIVE relating to the basic form of an adjective or adverb, and not to its comparative or superlative forms **22.** ENG WITH NO SLACK describes a mechanical action or device having little or no play **23.** ASTROL OF ZODIAC SIGNS relating to the air or fire signs of the zodiac ■ *n* **1.** POSITIVE THING something that shows agreement, support, or affirmation (*informal*) ○ *Not a bad situation when we weigh up all the positives.* **2.** MATHS SOMETHING GREATER THAN ZERO a value or number higher than zero **3.** PHOTOGRAPHY IMAGE LIKE SUBJECT a photographic image in which the light and dark tones and colours correspond to those of the original subject **4.** PHYS SOMETHING WITH POSITIVE CHARGE something that carries a positive electrical charge **5.** PHYS CELL PLATE OR TERMINAL a positively charged plate or terminal in a cell **6.** GRAM BASIC FORM OF MODIFIER an adjective or adverb in its basic form, and not in the comparative or superlative **7.** MUSIC MEDIEVAL ORGAN a small medieval organ with just one manual and no pedals **8.** MUSIC another spelling of **positif** [14C. Via French < Latin *positivus* < *posit-* (see POSITION)] —**positiveness** *n* —**positivity** /pózzə tívvəti/ *n*

positive discrimination *n* the practice of setting aside training or employment resources or positions for members of disadvantaged groups such as members of ethnic minorities, people with disabilities, or women. N Am term **affirmative action**

positive gloss *n* an interpretation of something unpleasant or unfavourable that is intended to make people see it in a good, rather than a bad, light ○ *sought to put a positive gloss on an increasingly difficult situation*

positively /pózzətivli/ *adv* **1.** ENCOURAGINGLY in an encouraging, supportive, or optimistic way **2.** ADDS EMPHASIS used to emphasize an often already emphatic quality, characteristic, or action ○ *looking positively radiant* **3.** DEFINITELY used to emphasize that the truth of a statement or response is beyond any doubt ○ *This is positively the last chance you're going to get.*

positive prescription *n* LAW same as **prescription** (sense 7)

positive vetting *n* the practice of investigating somebody's background and personal life in order to determine suitability for sensitive or confidential work, especially work involving matters of national security

positivism /pózzətivizəm/ *n* **1.** the theory that knowledge can be acquired only through direct observation and experimentation, and not through metaphysics or theology **2.** the state or quality of being positive —**positivist** *n, adj* —**positivistic** /pózzəti vístik/ *adj* —**positivistically** *adv*

positron /pózzi tron/ *n* an elementary particle of antimatter that has the same mass as an electron, but the opposite electrical charge [Mid-20C. Blend of POSITIVE + ELECTRON]

positron emission tomography *n* a method of medical imaging capable of displaying the metabolic activity of organs in the body that is useful in diagnosing cancer, locating brain tumours, and investigating other brain disorders

positronium /pózzi trṓni əm/ *n* a combination of a positron and an electron that rapidly decays to produce two or three photons

posology /pə sólləji/ *n* the study of the dosage of medicines [Early 19C. < French *posologie* < Greek *posos* 'how much'] —**posological** /póssə lójjik'l/ *adj*

posse /póssi/ *n* **1.** SHERIFF'S HELPERS especially in the western United States in the 19th-century, a group of citizens assembled by a sheriff to assist in maintaining law and order **2.** ASSEMBLED GROUP a group of people assembled for a common purpose (*informal*) **3.** GROUP OF FRIENDS a group of young people who spend time together socially or share a common interest (*slang; originally used in Black English*) [Mid-17C. Shortening of *posse comitatus* < medieval Latin, 'force of the county']

possee /póssee/ *n* same as **posse** (sense 3) (*informal*)

possess /pə zéss/ (**-sesses, -sessing, -sessed**) *vt* **1.** OWN SOMETHING to have or own something **2.** HAVE SOMETHING AS ABILITY to have something as an ability, quality, or characteristic **3.** HAVE KNOWLEDGE OF SOMETHING to have or acquire skill or knowledge of something **4.** TAKE CONTROL OF SOMEBODY to take control of somebody so that the person's behaviour or thinking is affected ○ *possessed by fear and unable to speak* **5.** FILL SOMEBODY WITH AN EMOTION to cause somebody to be influenced by something, especially an emotion ○ *The news possessed us with foreboding.* **6.** CONTROL FEELING to control yourself or a feeling (*formal*) **7.** HAVE SEX WITH SOMEBODY to have sexual intercourse with somebody (*dated; sometimes considered offensive*) **8.** SEIZE SOMETHING to gain or seize something (*archaic*) [14C. Via Old French *possesser* < Latin *possess-*, past participle of *possidere* 'sit on as head' < *sedere* 'sit'] —**possessor** *n*

possessed /pə zést/ *adj* **1.** CONTROLLED controlled or strongly influenced, especially by a supposed evil supernatural force or a strong emotion ○ *screaming and shouting like a man possessed* **2.** HAVING QUALITY having something as a quality, characteristic, or belief (*literary*) ○ *He was possessed of a sharp wit.* **3.** OWNING having or owning something ○ *an only child possessed of a great fortune* **4.** same as **self-possessed**

possession /pə zésh'n/ *n* **1.** OWNERSHIP the act or state of owning or holding something ○ *You can take possession of the house on Friday.* **2.** SOMETHING OWNED something owned or held **3.** POL COLONY a country or region controlled or governed by another country (*often used in the plural*) **4.** STATE OF BEING CONTROLLED the condition of being controlled by or appearing to be controlled by a supposed supernatural force or a strong emotion **5.** LAW OCCUPANCY the physical occupancy of something such as a house, whether or not as its owner **6.** CRIME ILLEGAL OWNERSHIP OF SOMETHING the crime of having or owning something illegal such as a weapon, contraband, stolen property, or illegal drugs **7.** CONTROL OF BALL in various sports, control of the ball or puck by a player or team ■ **possessions** *npl* PROPERTY personal property —**possessional** *adj*

possession order *n* a court order authorizing somebody to take possession of or recover property

possessive /pə zéssiv/ *adj* **1.** DEMANDING EXCLUSIVITY wishing to control somebody exclusively or to be the sole object of somebody's love **2.** SELFISH tending not to share possessions with others **3.** OF OWNERSHIP relating to ownership ○ *possessive pride* **4.** GRAM SHOWING OWNERSHIP IN GRAMMATICAL TERMS indicating grammatical ownership, e.g. in pronouns such as 'his'

or 'her' ■ *n* GRAM **1. WORD SHOWING OWNERSHIP** a noun, pronoun, determiner, or form of a word that indicates ownership or association **2. POSSESSIVE CASE** the possessive or genitive case —**possessively** *adv* —**possessiveness** *n*

USAGE See ***apostrophe***[1].

possessory /pə zéssəri/ *adj* **1.** relating to possession or a possessor (*formal*) **2.** arising from or depending on legal possession

posset /póssit/ *n* a drink made from hot milk curdled with beer or wine and flavoured with spices, formerly drunk as a remedy for colds ■ *vi* (**-sets, -seting, -seted**) to regurgitate milk (*refers to babies*) [15C. Origin ?]

possibility /póssə bílləti/ *n* (*plural* **-ties**) **1. SOMETHING POSSIBLE** something that is possible **2. STATE OF BEING POSSIBLE** the condition or quality of being possible **3. CONTENDER** somebody who is considered a possible winner, choice, or candidate ■ **possibilities** *npl* **POTENTIAL** the potential for successful future development ○ *The house needs a lot of work, but it's got possibilities.*

possible /póssəb'l/ *adj* **1. LIKELY TO HAPPEN** capable of happening or likely to happen in the future **2. MAYBE REAL OR TRUE** capable of being real, present, or true **3. CAPABLE OF HAPPENING BUT UNLIKELY** theoretically capable of happening or existing, although unlikely in practice **4. POTENTIAL** having potential as a particular thing or for a particular purpose **5. PROPER** in keeping with convention, decorum, or tradition ■ *n* **POSSIBILITY** somebody or something that is a possibility [14C. Via French < Latin *possibilis* < *posse* 'be able' (see POTENT[1])]

possibly /póssəbli/ *adv* **1. PERHAPS** likely, or maybe so, but not definitely so **2. AS POSSIBILITY** as something that is possible or may be realized **3. SUGGESTS EFFORT** used to indicate the magnitude of effort or difficulty ○ *They've done everything they possibly could.* **4. ADDS EMPHASIS** used to express shock, disbelief, or amazement ○ *How could you possibly have believed that?* **5. SUGGESTS IMPOSSIBILITY** used in negative sentences and phrases to emphasize that something cannot be done or cannot happen ○ *I couldn't possibly tell you.* **6. USED AS REQUEST MODIFIER** used with requests to suggest the speaker's awareness of an imposition ○ *Could you possibly post this letter for me on your way to the station?*

possie /pózzi/, **pozzie** *n ANZ* a position or location (*informal*) [Early 20C. Shortening]

POSSLQ *abbr* person of the opposite sex sharing living quarters (*informal*)

possum /póssəm/ *n* ZOOL **1.** *N Am* same as **opossum** (*informal*) **2.** *ANZ* same as **phalanger** [Early 17C. Shortening] ◇ **play possum** to feign death, illness, or sleep, or pretend to be uninvolved in something, in order to protect yourself

post[1] /pōst/ *n* **1. UPRIGHT POLE** a pole of wood or metal fixed in the ground in an upright position, serving as a support, marker, or place for attaching things **2.** CONSTR **UPRIGHT FRAME PART** a vertical piece in a building frame that supports a beam **3.** HORSERACING **RACECOURSE INDICATOR** either of two upright poles marking the starting point and finishing line on a racecourse **4. FURNITURE SUPPORT** one of the upright supports of a piece of furniture such as a chair or a four-poster bed **5.** SPORTS same as **goalpost** (*informal*) **6.** JEWELLERY **EARRING PART** a metal stem on a pierced earring that passes through the ear and fits into a cap at the back **7.** ONLINE same as **posting**[1] *n* (sense 1) ■ *vt* (**posts, posting, posted**) **1. DISPLAY SOMETHING** to display something such as an announcement, name, or result in a public place **2. PUBLISH SOMETHING ELECTRONICALLY** to make text appear online or at an Internet location **3.** LEISURE **SCORE POINTS** to score something, e.g. points, in a game or sport ○ *posted his first century on his home ground* **4. GIVE NOTICE OF MARRIAGE** to announce a forthcoming marriage in a church ○ *post the banns* **5.** NAUT **NAME SHIP** to publish the name of a ship presumed lost or sunk [Pre-12C. < Latin *postis* 'something that stands in front' < Indo-European, 'to stand'] ◇ **pip somebody at the post** to beat somebody in the very final stages of something

post[2] /pōst/ *n* **1. POSTAL SERVICE** the official system for collecting, conveying, and delivering letters and parcels to another place ○ *I'll send the contract to you by post.* **2.** MAIL **LETTERS AND PARCELS** letters and parcels that have been sent or are to be sent through the postal system ○ *Is there any post for me today?* **3. LETTER COLLECTION TIME** the time when letters and parcels are collected from a post box or delivered ○ *If you rush you'll catch the last post.* **4.** HIST **STATION ON ROUTE** formerly, a station along a route where mounted messengers or couriers rested and changed horses **5.** HIST **MAIL DELIVERER** formerly, a rider who covered the distance from one post to the next in a delivery system ■ *v* (**posts, posting, posted**) **1.** *vt* MAIL **SEND LETTER OR PARCEL** to send a letter or parcel through the postal system **2.** *vt* ACCT **WRITE SOMETHING IN LEDGER** to enter a transaction in a ledger **3.** *vt* ONLINE **UPDATE DATABASE** to update a database record by entering or transferring information **4.** *vti* **SEND MESSAGE ELECTRONICALLY** to place or send a message on a newsgroup or bulletin board on the Internet or some other electronic network **5.** *vi* HIST **TRAVEL BY POST** to travel using relays of horses **6.** *vi* **TRAVEL FAST** to travel at speed (*archaic*) **7.** *vi* RIDING **KEEP RHYTHM WITH HORSE** to bob up and down in the saddle in time with a horse's trot ■ *adv* **QUICKLY** quickly (*archaic*) [Early 16C. Via French, 'relay station' < Latin *posita*, form of past participle of *ponere* 'place'] ◇ **keep somebody posted** to keep somebody informed by supplying new information regularly

post[3] /pōst/ *n* **1. EMPLOYMENT SITUATION** a position of employment **2. WORKPLACE OR STATION** a place where somebody has been assigned a duty or responsibility **3.** *Aus, N Am* MIL **MILITARY BASE** a place such as a military base, camp, or garrison where troops are stationed **4.** MIL **BUGLE CALL** either of two evening bugle calls given as a signal for army personnel to retire to their quarters **5.** COMM same as **trading post** (sense 1) ■ *vt* (**posts, posting, posted**) **1. ASSIGN SOMEBODY TO DUTY** to assign somebody to a particular place or station for a period of duty ○ *post a security guard at the exit* **2.** *UK, Can* **SEND SOMEBODY AWAY TO WORK** to send somebody somewhere, often abroad, to take up an appointment ○ *After she qualified, she was posted to South America for two years.* **3.** *Aus, N Am* MIL **TRANSFER SOLDIER** to assign or transfer somebody to a military unit or command **4.** *US* LAW **PAY MONEY TO SET SOMEBODY FREE** to pay somebody's bond or bail [Mid-16C. Via French *poste* < Latin *positum* < past participle of *ponere* 'place']

post[4] /pōst/ *n* a postmortem examination of a corpse (*informal*) [Mid-20C. Shortening]

POST /pōst/ *abbr* **1.** COMM point-of-sale terminal **2.** COMPUT Power On Self-Test

post- *prefix* **1.** after, later ○ *postwar* ○ *postdate* **2.** behind ○ *postorbital* [< Latin *post* < Indo-European, 'off, away']

postapocalyptic *adj*
postapostolic *adj*
postatomic *adj*
postbaptismal *adj*
postbiblical *adj*
post-Cartesian *adj*
postclassical *adj*
postcoital *adj*
postcolonial *adj*
postconception *adj*
postconcert *adj*
postconquest *adj*
postconsonantal *adj*
postcoup *adj*
postcrash *adj*
post-Darwinian *adj*
postdepression *adj*
postdivorce *adj*
postelection *adj*
postexercise *adj*
postflight *adj*
post-Freudian *adj*
postglacial *adj*
postgraduation *adj*
postindependence *adj*
postindustrial *adj*
postinfective *adj*
postinoculation *adj*
post-Keynesian *adj*
postliberation *adj*
postmedieval *adj*
postmenopausal *adj*
postmidnight *adj*
postnuptial *adj*
postpuberty *adj*
postpunk *adj*
postrecession *adj*
post-Reformation *adj*
post-Renaissance *adj*
postretirement *adj*
postrevolutionary *adj*
postromantic *adj*
postseason *n, adj*
postshow *adj*
poststrike *adj*
postsurgical *adj*
post-Talmudic *adj*
post-theatre *adj*
post-transfusion *adj*
post-traumatic *adj*
post-treatment *adj*
postvaccinal *adj*
postverbal *adj*
post-Victorian *adj*

postage /pōstij/ *n* the amount of money paid for the delivery of a piece of mail

postage due stamp *n* a stamp on a letter indicating that the postage charge has not been fully paid

postage meter *n N Am* MAIL same as **franking machine**

postage stamp *n* **1. GUMMED POSTAGE MARKER** an illustrated paper stamp affixed to letters and parcels to show payment of postage **2. PRINTED MARK** a printed mark or impression on an envelope indicating that the postage charge has been paid ■ *adj* **TINY** extremely small (*hyphenated before a noun*) ○ *a postage-stamp bikini*

postal /pōst'l/ *adj* relating to a post office or the delivery of post —**postally** *adv* ◇ **go postal** *US* to become extremely angry, often in a way that leads to violence (*slang*)

postal card *n US* a plain postcard with prepaid postage, sold in post offices

postal code *n Can* same as **postcode**

postal money order *n N Am* MAIL same as **postal order**

postal note *n ANZ* same as **postal order**

postal order *n UK* a voucher for a sum of money, payable to a named person, that can be bought at a post office. N Am term **postal money order**

postal vote *n* a vote that is posted instead of being made in person, usually because the voter cannot get to the polling station. N Am term **absentee ballot**

post-and-rail fence *n* a fence of horizontal timbers threaded between upright posts

postbag /pōst bag/ *n* **1.** *UK* a bag or satchel used to carry letters and parcels by the person delivering them. ANZ term **mailbag 2.** the letters and messages received by an MP, famous person, or television or radio programme ► N Am term **mailbag**

post-bellum /pōst bélləm/, **postbellum** *adj* relating to or occurring in the period after a war, especially the American Civil War [< Latin *post bellum* 'after the war']

post-boost phase *n* the last phase of the flight of a multistage missile, when it releases its payload

postbox /pōst boks/ *n* a box in a public place where letters can be posted for collection. N Am term **mailbox**

postcard /pōst kaard/ *n* a card used to carry a message, usually with a picture or a photograph on one side, that can be sent through the postal system without an envelope

post chaise *n* a closed horse-drawn carriage with four wheels that was used in the 18th and 19th centuries as a fast means of transporting letters, parcels, and passengers [< POST[2]]

postcode /pōst kōd/ *n* a group of letters and numbers added at the end of an address to facilitate the sorting of letters and parcels and speed up the process of delivery. US term **ZIP Code**

postcode lottery /pōst kōd-/ *n* the unequal or inconsistent distribution of a public service such as health care across different areas of the United Kingdom

Postcomm /pōst kom/ *n* in the United Kingdom, the independent regulatory body for postal services. Full form **Postal Services Commission**

post-Communist *adj*

postdate /pōst dáyt/ (**-dates, -dating, -dated**) *vt* **1. DATE CHEQUE LATER** to put a date on a cheque later than the current day's date in order to delay payment **2. HAPPEN LATER THAN SOMETHING** to happen or be at a later date than something **3. ASSIGN LATER DATE TO EVENT** to assign a date to something such as an event in history that is later than the one previously assigned

postdoc /pōst dok/ (*informal*) *n* a postdoctoral grant, fellowship, or scholar ■ *adj* EDUC same as **postdoctoral** [Late 20C. Shortening]

postdoctoral /pōst dóktərəl/ *adj* relating to academic work or research done after a doctorate has been awarded

poster /pōstər/ *n* **1. PRINTED PICTURE** a printed picture, often a reproduction of a photograph or artwork, used for decoration **2. ADVERTISEMENT** a bill or placard in a public place advertising something **3. SENDER** somebody who posts a message to an online or Internet address

poster child *n* **1.** *N Am* somebody, especially a child, chosen to represent a charitable or other cause by appearing in promotional material **2.** somebody or something appearing as a representative or

illustrative example of something (sometimes offensive)

poster colour n Aus, US ART same as **poster paint**

poste restante /pōst rést ont/ n 1. a department of a post office where letters and parcels are held for people until they collect them 2. an address on a letter or parcel indicating that it should be held at a post office until collection by the addressee ▶ N Am term **general delivery** [< French, 'mail remaining' (at the post office)]

posterior /po steéri ər/ adj 1. BEHIND situated at the rear or behind something 2. NEAR BACK situated near or towards the back of the body of a person or animal 3. FOLLOWING IN SERIES coming after something in an order or series (formal) 4. SUBSEQUENT following something in time (formal) 5. BOT NEAREST STEM nearest the main stem or axis of a plant ○ the posterior flower ■ n BOTTOM the buttocks (humorous) [Early 16C. < Latin, 'coming farther after' < posterus 'coming after' < post 'after, behind'] —**posteriorly** adv

posterity /po stérrəti/ n (formal) 1. all future generations 2. all of somebody's descendants [14C. Via French < Latin posteritas < posterus (see POSTERIOR)]

postern /póstərn/ n a small gate or entrance at the back of a building, especially a castle or a fort [13C. Via Old French pasterne < late Latin posterula 'small back door' < Latin posterus (see POSTERIOR)]

poster paint n a paint made from pigment mixed with water-soluble gum that is often used for painting posters and by children. N Am term **tempera**

post exchange n US MIL full form of **PX**

postexilian /pōst ek sílli ən, pōst ig zílli ən/, **postexilic** /-ek síllik, -ig zíllik/ adj occurring or in existence after the period of Babylonian captivity of the Jewish people, 587–539 BC

postfeminist /pōst fémminist/ adj 1. REFLECTING FEMINISM developing out of or including the principles of feminism 2. GOING BEYOND FEMINISM differing from or showing a re-evaluation of the principles of feminism 3. AFTER FEMINISM occurring or having developed after the feminist movement of the 1970s (sometimes considered offensive) ■ n SUPPORTER OF POSTFEMINIST IDEAS somebody who supports or believes in postfeminist ideas —**postfeminism** n

postfix vt /pōst fíks/ (-fixes, -fixing, -fixed) to add a letter or group of letters to the end of a word (formal) ■ n /pōst fiks/ same as **suffix** [Late 20C. After PREFIX[1]] —**postfixal** /pōst fíks'l/ adj

post-free adj MAIL same as **postpaid**

post-genitive /pōst jénnətiv/ n a double possessive construction in which 'of' and an apostrophe + 's' are both used, e.g. a letter of Sam's

postgrad /pōst grád/ EDUC n same as **postgraduate** (informal) ■ adj same as **postgraduate**

postgraduate /pōst gráddyoŏ ət/ adj relating to academic study after graduation from a university or college or to a student who is studying for a higher degree after graduating with a first degree. N Am term **graduate** ■ n somebody who has graduated from a university or college with a first degree and is studying for a higher degree

Postgraduate Certificate of Education n EDUC full form of **PGCE**

post-haste /pōst háyst/ adv as quickly as possible [Mid-16C. < Haste, post, haste, an instruction on letters]

post hoc /pōst hók/ n the fallacy of arguing that since one event happened before a second, the first caused the second [Mid-19C. < Latin, 'after this', referring to the fallacy post hoc, ergo propter hoc 'after this, therefore because of this']

postholder /pōst hōldər/ n somebody who occupies a specific position of employment in a company, organization, or institution

post horn n a simple, usually valveless horn, formerly used to announce the arrival of a coach carrying letters and parcels [< POST[2]]

post horse n formerly, a horse kept at an inn or post house for use by postriders or for hire by travellers

post house n formerly, an inn where post horses were kept

posthumous /póstyoŏmǝss/ adj 1. AFTER SOMEBODY'S DEATH occurring after somebody's death 2. PUBLISHED AFTER DEATH published or printed after the author's death 3. BORN AFTER FATHER'S DEATH born after the death of the father ○ a posthumous heir [Early 17C. < late Latin posthumus, alteration (after medieval Latin humare 'bury') of Latin postumus 'last' < posterus (see POSTERIOR)] —**posthumously** adv

posthypnotic suggestion /pōst hip nóttik-/ n a suggestion made to somebody under hypnosis that is to be acted upon at a later time after the period of hypnosis is over

postie /pósti/ n a postman or postwoman (informal) [Late 19C. < POST[2]]

postil /póstil/ n a note or commentary on a text in the margin (archaic) [14C. Via French < medieval Latin postilla] —**postil** vti

postilion /po stílli ən/, **postillion** n somebody riding the near front horse in a team of horses drawing a carriage [Early 17C. Via French postillon 'relay rider' < Italian postiglione < posta < Latin posita (see POST[2])]

postimpressionism /pōst im présh'nizəm/ n a school of painting in late 19th-century France that rejected the naturalism of impressionism, but adapted its use of colour and form to a more subjective style —**postimpressionist** n, adj —**postimpressionistic** /-im preshə nístik/ adj

posting[1] /pósting/ n 1. ONLINE MESSAGE a message sent to and displayed on an online facility such as an Internet newsgroup or bulletin board 2. ACCT BOOK-KEEPING ACTIVITY the activity of making entries in a ledger 3. ACCT LEDGER ENTRY an entry made in a ledger ■ adj RELATING TO POST relating to the sending and collecting of post [Late 16C. < POST[3]]

posting[2] /pósting/ n an appointment to a job, position, or unit, usually overseas [Mid-19C. < POST[2]]

Post-it tdmk a trademark for self-sticking slips of paper sold in pad form

postlude /pōst lood/ n 1. a piece of organ music played at the end of a church service 2. a final or concluding phase, chapter, or development (literary) [Mid-19C. After PRELUDE]

postman /pōstmən/ n (plural -men /-mən/) a man whose job it is to collect and deliver letters and parcels that have been sent by post. N Am term **mailman**

postman's knock n a children's game in which one player gives another a pretend letter and is given a kiss in return. N Am term **post office**

postmark /pōst maark/ n an official mark, usually covering a postage stamp, that indicates when and where a letter or parcel was posted ■ vt (-marks, -marking, -marked) to stamp a postmark on a letter or parcel

postmaster /pōst maastər/ n 1. POST OFFICE OFFICIAL the person in charge of a post office or postal district 2. WEBSITE MANAGER the person responsible for the maintenance of a website and for being the contact point for information and complaints 3. E-MAIL PROGRAM a computer program that distributes, forwards, and receives electronic mail

postmaster general (plural **postmasters general**) n the executive head of the postal service in some countries such as the United Kingdom

post meridiem /-mə ríddi əm/ adv TIME full form of **p.m.** [< Latin, 'after midday']

post mill n a windmill with its machinery assembled around an upright spindle and with a blade at the back that makes the sails turn to face the direction of the wind

postmillennial /pōst mi lénni əl/ adj occurring or existing after a millennium

postmistress /pōst mistrəss/ n a woman in charge of a post office (dated)

postmodernism /pōst móddərnizəm/ n a style in architecture, art, literature, and criticism developed after and often in reaction to modernism, characterized by reference to other periods or styles in a self-conscious way and a rejection of the notion of high art —**postmodern** n, adj —**postmodernist** n, adj

postmortem /pōst máwrtəm/ n 1. also **postmortem examination** same as **autopsy** (sense 1) 2. an analysis carried out shortly after the conclusion of an event, especially an unsuccessful one ○ the usual media postmortems the day after the election ■ adj occurring after death [Mid-18C. < Latin post mortem 'after death']

postnasal drip /pōst náyz'l-/ n a continual dripping of mucus from the rear of the nose into the throat, often caused by an allergy or a cold

postnatal /pōst náyt'l/ adj 1. occurring immediately or soon after childbirth 2. relating to an infant immediately after birth ○ postnatal development —**postnatally** adv

postnatal depression n a state of severe, even suicidal, depression that can affect a woman soon after giving birth to a baby. N Am term **postpartum depression**

post-obit n a bond that pays after the death of somebody from whom the issuer of the bond expects to inherit (dated) ■ adj coming into effect after somebody's death (formal) ○ post-obit payments [Mid-18C. < Latin post obitum 'after death']

post office n 1. an office or building where the public has access to services of the postal system 2. the national organization or government department that is responsible for a country's postal service 3. N Am LEISURE same as **postman's knock**

post office box n a private numbered box in a post office where letters are held until collected by the addressee

postop /pōst óp/, **post-op** adj MED same as **postoperative** (informal) [Late 20C. Shortening]

postoperative /pōst ópprətiv/ adj occurring after a surgical operation —**postoperatively** adv

postorbital /pōst áwrbit'l/ adj situated behind the eye or the eye socket

postpaid /pōst páyd/ adj with the postage paid in advance

postpartum /pōst paártəm/ adj relating to or occurring in the period immediately after childbirth [Mid-19C. < Latin post partum 'after childbirth']

postpartum depression n N Am MED same as **postnatal depression**

postperson /pōst purss'n/ (plural -**persons** or -**people** /-peep'l/) n somebody whose job is to collect and deliver letters and parcels that have been sent by post. US term **mailperson**

postpone /pōst pōn/ (-pones, -poning, -poned) vt 1. to put something off until a later time or date 2. to ascribe less importance to something (formal) [15C. < Latin postponere 'place later' < ponere 'place'] —**postponable** adj —**postponement** n —**postponer** n

postpose /pōst pōz/ (-poses, -posing, -posed) vti to place a word or phrase after another or at the end of a sentence or construction [Late 19C. Back-formation < POSTPOSITION]

postposition /póstpə zísh'n/ n 1. the placement of a word or phrase after the word or phrase it qualifies, e.g. the placement of 'bold and free' in the phrase 'poets bold and free' 2. GRAM same as **postpositive** [Mid-17C. After PREPOSITION] —**postpositional** adj —**postpositionally** adv

postpositive /pōst pózzətiv/ adj describes an adjective or modifier that is placed after the word or phrase it qualifies ■ n an adjective or modifier that is placed after the word or phrase it qualifies [Late 18C. < late Latin postpositivus < Latin postponere (see POSTPONE)] —**postpositively** adv

postprandial /pōst prándi əl/ adj occurring after a meal (formal or humorous) —**postprandially** adv

post-print adj belonging to the era of electronic communication ○ the post-print revolution

postproduction /pōst prə dúksh'n/ n the final stage in the making of a recording, film, or television programme that includes editing, sound dubbing, and adding special effects

postrider /pōst rídər/ n formerly, somebody who delivered or relayed mail on horseback

postscript /pōst skript/ n 1. a short message added on to the end of a letter, after the signature 2. an addition to the end of something such as a book, story, or document [Mid-16C. < Latin postscriptum < past participle of postscribere 'write after' < scribere 'write']

post-structuralism n an intellectual movement derived from structuralism but questioning the

basis upon which the structures of society, language, and mores have been conceptualized —**poststructuralist** *adj, n*

postsynaptic /pṓst si náptik/ *adj* describes a nerve cell, muscle cell, or region of cell membrane that receives signals transmitted across a synapse from another nerve cell

postsynch /pṓst síngk/ (**-synchs, -synching, -synched**) *vt* to add sound or music to a film at a later time

post transaction *n* submission by a retailer of a previously authorized transaction to the acquirer for payment

posttranscriptional /pṓst tran skrípsh'nəl/ *adj* describes processes or components that become involved in carrying out the genetic instructions of a living cell only after the stage of transcription of a gene or genes

posttranslational /pṓst trans láysh'nəl/ *adj* describes processes or components that become involved in carrying out the genetic instructions of living cells only after translation of RNA to protein

post-traumatic stress disorder *n* a psychological condition affecting people who have suffered severe emotional trauma as a result of an experience such as combat, crime, or natural disaster, and causing sleep disturbances, flashbacks, anxiety, tiredness, and depression

postulant /póstyŏŏlənt/ *n* somebody who applies to join a religious order (*formal*) [Mid-18C. Directly or via French < Latin *postulant-*, present participle of *postulare* 'nominate, demand'] —**postulancy** *n*

postulate *vt* /póstyŏŏ layt/ (**-lates, -lating, -lated**) **1.** ASSUME SOMETHING to assume or suggest that something is true or exists, especially as the basis of an argument or theory **2.** CLAIM SOMETHING to demand or claim something **3.** NOMINATE SOMEBODY to put forward a candidate for a post or office pending approval from a higher authority (*formal*) ■ *n* /póstyŏŏlət/ **1.** SOMETHING ASSUMED TRUE something that is assumed or believed to be true and that is used as the basis of an argument or theory **2.** PRINCIPLE a basic principle **3.** PRECONDITION an essential precondition or requirement **4.** MATHS, LOGIC STATEMENT UNDERPINNING THEORY a statement that is assumed to be true but has not been proved and that is taken as the basis for a theory, line of reasoning, or hypothesis [Mid-16C. < Latin *postulat-*, past participle of *postulare* 'nominate, demand'] —**postulation** /póstyŏŏ láysh'n/ *n* —**postulational** *adj*

postulator /póstyŏŏ laytər/ *n* **1.** in the Roman Catholic Church, an official, usually a priest, who presents a request for a deceased person to be beatified or canonized **2.** somebody who postulates something

posture /póschər/ *n* **1.** BODY POSITION a position that the body can assume, e.g. standing, sitting, kneeling, or lying down **2.** PHYSICAL CARRIAGE the way in which somebody holds his or her body, especially when standing ○ *had poor posture as a child* **3.** POSE CONVEYING ATTITUDE a physical pose that conveys a mental or emotional attitude ○ *a posture of defiance* **4.** DECEPTIVE STANCE a position, attitude, or stance that is intended to deceive **5.** CULTIVATED POSITION a practised or cultivated arrangement of the body, e.g. a position used in yoga **6.** ATTITUDE a frame of mind or attitude ○ *a conciliatory posture* **7.** ARRANGEMENT OF PARTS the way that components of an object or situation are arranged in relation to one another ■ *v* (**-tures, -turing, -tured**) **1.** *vi* ASSUME STANCE to assume an affected or exaggerated pose or attitude **2.** *vti* ADOPT POSTURE to adopt a particular posture, or make somebody do this [Late 16C. Via French < Latin *positura* < *posit-* (see POSITION)] —**postural** *adj* —**posturer** *n*

postviral syndrome /pṓst vírəl-/ *n* MED same as **chronic fatigue syndrome**

postvocalic /pṓst vō kállik/ *adj* coming after a vowel

postwar /pṓst wáwr/ *adj* occurring or existing after a war, especially World War II

postwoman /pṓst wŏŏmən/ (*plural* **-women** /-wimin/) *n* a woman whose job it is to collect and deliver letters and parcels that have been sent by post. N Am term **mailwoman**

posy /pṓzi/ (*plural* **-sies**) *n* **1.** a small bunch of flowers **2.** a short verse or inscription, especially on a trinket or ring (*archaic*) [Mid-16C. Alteration of POESY]

pot[1] /pot/ *n* **1.** CONTAINER FOR COOKING a container made of metal, pottery, or glass that is usually cylindrical and watertight with an open top and sometimes a lid, used especially for cooking or storage **2.** SOMETHING RESEMBLING POT something similar to a pot in shape or function, e.g. a flowerpot or teapot **3.** CONTENTS OF POT the contents of a pot, or the amount that it will hold ○ *made a pot of coffee* **4.** CLAY OBJECT a dish or container made from clay, especially one of artistic or historical interest **5.** N Am COMMON FUND a common fund of money for an activity such as a party or trip that is contributed to by all the members of a group (*informal*) **6.** same as **potty**[2] **7.** LARGE AMOUNT OF MONEY a large amount of money (*informal*) ○ *made pots of money* **8.** DRINKING VESSEL a large drinking vessel, usually glass or pewter, for beer **9.** CARDS MONEY BET IN CARD GAME all the money that is bet in a game of cards, especially poker, and that is taken by the winning player **10.** CUE GAMES HIT OF BALL INTO POCKET in billiards or snooker, a hit of a ball that sends it into any of the pockets at the edge of the table **11.** CUP WON IN COMPETITION a vessel, especially a silver cup, that is won in a competition, especially a sports contest (*informal*) **12.** FISHERIES FISH OR LOBSTER TRAP a basket or cage used for catching lobsters, eels, or fish **13.** ANAT same as **potbelly** (*informal*) **14.** SPORTS same as **potshot** (sense 2) **15.** Aus BEER GLASS in Queensland and Victoria, a medium-sized beer glass containing 285 ml/10 oz ■ *v* (**pots, potting, potted**) **1.** *vt* PUT PLANT IN POT to put a plant into a pot with soil or compost **2.** *vti* SHOOT ANIMAL FOR FOOD to shoot or shoot at a bird or animal, especially for food **3.** *vti* SHOOT AT SOMETHING NEARBY to shoot or shoot at an easy target, especially casually **4.** *vt* COOK PRESERVE FOOD to preserve food in a pot **5.** *vti* CUE GAMES HIT BALL INTO POCKET in billiards or snooker, to hit a ball into any of the pockets at the edge of the table **6.** *vti* CERAMICS SHAPE CLAY to shape a pot or other item from clay **7.** *vt* ELECTRONICS PROTECT ELECTRONIC COMPONENTS to encapsulate electronic components in an insulating resin in order to protect them and hold them in place. The technique is used in high technology industries such as avionics as well as in automotive, medical, and consumer electronics. **8.** *vt* PUT CHILD ON POTTY to put a young child on a potty [Pre-12C. Directly or (later) via French < assumed Vulgar Latin *pottus*] —**potful** *n* ◇ **go to pot** to get much worse or become useless, worthless, or extremely unsatisfactory (*informal*)

pot on *vt* to transfer a growing plant from a smaller to a larger pot

pot up *vt* to plant a seedling or cutting in a pot, separating it from others with which it originally grew

pot[2] /pot/ *n* DRUGS same as **cannabis** (*slang*) [Mid-20C. Probably shortening of Mexican Spanish *potiguaya* 'marijuana leaves']

pot[3] /pot/ *n* PHYS same as **potentiometer** (*informal*) [Mid-20C. Shortening]

potable /pṓtəb'l/ *adj* suitable for drinking because clean and uncontaminated ■ *n* a liquid that is suitable for drinking, especially an alcoholic drink [15C. Directly or via French < late Latin *potabilis* < Latin *potare* 'to drink' (see POTION)] —**potability** /pṓtə bílləti/ *n* —**potableness** *n*

potage /po taázh, pó taazh/ *n* a thick soup [12C. < French 'what is put in a pot' < *pot* (see POT[1])]

potash /pót ash/ *n* **1.** a potassium compound, especially potassium chloride, sulphate, or oxide. Use: in fertilizers. **2.** CHEM same as **potassium carbonate 3.** CHEM same as **potassium hydroxide** [Early 17C. < obsolete Dutch *potasschen* (plural) now *potasch*]

potash alum *n* CHEM same as **alum**

potassium /pə tássi əm/ *n* a soft silvery-white highly reactive element of the alkali metal group. Source: carnallite, sylvite. Use: coolant in nuclear reactors, in fertilizers. Symbol **K**. See table at **element** [Early 19C. < modern Latin < *potassa* 'potash']

potassium-argon dating *n* a technique for estimating the age of rocks older than 250,000 years, based on the time taken for the radioactive decay of the potassium-40 isotope into a stable argon isotope. The half-life of potassium-40 is about 1.28×10^9 years, and the ratio of potassium to argon in the specimen gives an indication of its age.

potassium bitartrate /-bī taár trayt/ *n* a white powder or crystalline compound. Use: in baking powder, medicine, food preparation. Formula: $KHC_4H_4O_6$.

potassium bromide *n* a white crystalline compound. Use: in lithography, medicine, photography, soap. Formula: KBr.

potassium carbonate *n* a white salt. Use: in brewing, ceramics, explosives, fertilizers, glass, soap. Formula: K_2CO_3.

potassium chlorate *n* a white salt that detonates with heat. Use: fireworks, matches, explosives, textile printing, paper manufacture, as bleach and disinfectant. Formula: $KClO_3$.

potassium chloride *n* a colourless crystalline salt. Use: as fertilizer, in photography, medicine. Formula: KCl.

potassium cyanide *n* a very poisonous white crystalline chemical salt. Use: extraction of gold and silver from their ores, electroplating, photography, insecticide. Formula: KCN.

potassium dichromate *n* a yellow-red poisonous crystalline compound. Use: manufacture of explosives, safety matches, dyes. Formula: $K_2Cr_2O_7$.

potassium ferricyanide *n* a bright red poisonous crystalline compound that decomposes when heated. Use: textile printing, wool dyeing, blueprint paper, fertilizer. Formula: $K_3Fe(CN)_6$.

potassium ferrocyanide *n* a yellow crystalline compound. Use: in medicine, explosives. Formula: $K_4Fe(CN)_6$.

potassium hydrogen carbonate *n* a white powder or granular compound. Use: in baking powder, as antacid. Formula: $KHCO_3$.

potassium hydrogen tartrate *n* CHEM same as **potassium bitartrate**

potassium hydroxide *n* a caustic toxic white solid. Use: manufacture of soap, detergents, liquid shampoos, matches. Formula: KOH.

potassium iodide *n* a white crystalline compound with a salty taste. Use: in medicine and photography, additive in table salt. Formula: KI.

potassium nitrate *n* a white crystalline salt. Use: in fireworks, explosives, matches, as fertilizer, meat preservative. Formula: KNO_3.

potassium permanganate *n* a dark purple toxic odourless crystalline compound. Use: bleach, disinfectant, antiseptic, in deodorizers and dyes. Formula: $KMnO_4$.

potassium sodium tartrate *n* a colourless crystalline salt. Use: mild laxative, food preservative, in electronics.

potassium sulphate *n* a colourless crystalline compound. Use: in aluminium, glass, cement, fertilizers, medicine. Formula: K_2SO_4.

potation /pō táysh'n/ *n* (*literary*) **1.** the act or an instance of drinking **2.** a drink, especially an alcoholic drink [15C. Directly or via French < Latin *potation-* < *potare* 'to drink' (see POTION)]

potato

potato /pə táytō/ (*plural* **-toes**) *n* **1.** a rounded white tuber cooked in a variety of ways as a vegetable. Use: industrial source of starch. **2.** a perennial plant that produces potatoes underground. Native to: South America. Latin name: *Solanum tuberosum*. **3.** FOOD, PLANTS same as **sweet potato** [Mid-16C. < Spanish *patata*, alteration of Taino *batata* 'sweet potato']

potato beetle *n* INSECTS same as **Colorado beetle**

potato blight *n* a highly destructive disease of the potato caused by the fungus *Phytophthora infestans*. It was the cause of the loss of the potato crop in Ireland in the 19th century.

potato cake *n* a flat round mass of seasoned potato, either cooked and mashed or raw and grated, that has been fried or sautéed

potato chip *n ANZ, N Am* a very thin slice of potato that has usually been deep-fried in oil, salted, sometimes flavoured, and packaged and sold to be eaten cold as a snack. UK term **crisp**

potato crisp *n UK* FOOD same as **crisp** *n* (sense 1)

~~potatoe~~ incorrect spelling of **potato**

potato pancake *n* a pancake made from a mixture of coarsely grated potato with egg, flour, and seasonings

potato scone *n* a pancake of dough containing mashed potato and flour, fried and served hot

potato skin *n* a piece of skin from a hollowed-out baked potato that is then baked further, or a piece of deep-fried skin of a raw potato, served as an appetizer (*often used in the plural*)

pot-au-feu /pót ō fő/ (*plural* **pots-au-feu** /*pronunc. same*/) *n* **1.** a French stew of slowly boiled meat and vegetables, the meat usually being eaten separately from the vegetables and stock, which are served first as a soup **2.** a large earthenware pot in which pot-au-feu is traditionally cooked [< French, 'pot on the fire']

Potawatomi /pótta wóttəmi/ (*plural same* or **-mis**) *n* **1.** a member of a Native North American people who lived in the north-central states, and who now live mainly in Kansas, Oklahoma, Michigan, and Ontario **2.** the Algonquian language of the Potawatomi people. Native speakers: 50. —**Potawatomi** *adj*

potbellied /pót belid/ *adj* having a round bulging stomach or abdomen

potbellied pig *n* a small domesticated pig with a rounded shape and a dark skin with a lighter band running around its middle, sometimes kept as a pet. Native to: Vietnam.

potbellied stove *n N Am* HOUSEHOLD same as **potbelly stove**

potbelly /pót beli/ (*plural* **-lies**) *n* **1.** a round bulging stomach or abdomen **2.** somebody with a potbelly

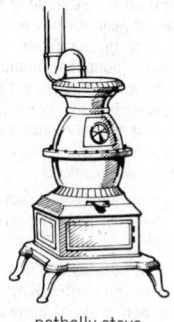
potbelly stove

potbelly stove *n N Am* a wood- or coal-burning stove that has a rounded bulbous body

potboiler /pót boylər/ *n* a book, film, or other work that is produced quickly to make money and has little literary or artistic quality (*informal*) [< its purpose of 'boiling the pot', providing money for food]

pot-bound /pót bownd/ *adj* describes a pot plant whose roots have grown very dense and have filled its pot so that its growth is restricted. Some plants thrive in this condition.

poteen /po teén, -cheén/ *n* in Ireland, a spirit that has been distilled illegally, especially from potatoes [Early 19C. < Irish (*fuisce*) *poitín* 'small pot (whiskey)' < *pota* 'pot']

potency /pót'nssi/ (*plural* **-cies**) *n* **1.** STRENGTH OF MEDICINE the strength of something such as a drug, medicine, or alcoholic drink **2.** STATE OF BEING POTENT the state or quality of being potent **3.** ABILITY TO DEVELOP a capacity for growth or development

potent[1] /pót'nt/ *adj* **1.** STRONG AND EFFECTIVE possessing great physical, political, or military strength and power ○ *a potent force* **2.** POWERFULLY PERSUASIVE exerting or capable of exerting great powers of persuasion or influence ○ *a potent symbol* **3.** WITH STRONG PHYSIOLOGICAL EFFECT producing a powerful effect on the body or mind when taken, eaten, or drunk ○ *The local brew is said to be particularly potent.* **4.** CAPABLE OF SEXUAL INTERCOURSE used to describe a man who is capable of achieving an erection or ejaculation [15C. < Latin *potent-*, present participle of *posse* 'be powerful', contraction of *potis esse* < *potis* 'able' + *esse* 'be'] —**potently** *adv*

potent[2] /pót'nt/ *adj* describes a heraldic cross that has four arms with a bar across the end of each arm [14C. Alteration of obsolete *potence* 'crutch', or via its French source < Latin *potentia* 'power' < *potent-* (see POTENT[1])]

potentate /pót'n tayt/ *n* somebody with great power or influence, especially a ruler

potential /pə ténsh'l/ *adj* **1.** POSSIBLE BUT AS YET NOT ACTUAL having a latent possibility or likelihood of occurring, or of doing or becoming something ○ *posed a potential danger* ○ *a potential investor* **2.** EXPRESSING POSSIBILITY describes a verb or verb form that expresses possibility, e.g. 'may' or 'might' in English ■ *n* **1.** CAPACITY FOR DEVELOPMENT a capacity to develop, succeed, or become something ○ *has the potential to be profitable* ○ *unable to use her expertise to its full potential* **2.** POTENTIAL VERB FORM a verb or verb form that expresses possibility, e.g. 'may' or 'might' in English **3.** PHYS same as **electric potential** [14C. Directly or via French < late Latin *potentialis* < Latin *potent-* (see POTENT[1])] —**potentially** *adv*

potential difference *n* the work done in moving a unit electric charge between two points in an electric field. Symbol Δ*V*, Δ*U*

potential divider *n* ELEC ENG same as **voltage divider**

potential energy *n* the energy that a body or system has stored because of its position in an electric, magnetic, or gravitational field, or because of its configuration. Symbol *V*, E_p

potentiality /pə ténshi álləti/ (*plural* **-ties**) *n* **1.** a capacity to grow, develop, or become something **2.** somebody or something capable of growing, developing, or becoming something

potential well *n* a region in an electric, magnetic, or gravitational field in which an object has a lower potential energy than it would have in all adjacent regions

potentiate /pə ténshi ayt/ (**-ates**, **-ating**, **-ated**) *vt* to improve the effectiveness of a drug or treatment, especially by adding another drug or agent —**potentiator** *n*

potentilla /pót'n tíllə/ (*plural* **-las** or *same*) *n* a cultivated flowering plant or small bush. Flowers: small, yellow, white, or red, five-petalled. Genus: *Potentilla*. [Mid-16C. < medieval Latin, 'powerful little (plant)' (from its use in medicine) < Latin *potent-* (see POTENT[1])]

potentiometer /pə ténshi ómmitər/ *n* **1.** a device for measuring an unknown potential difference or electromotive force by comparing it against a known standard **2.** a three-terminal component, typically used as a volume or brightness control, that gives a variable electric potential by rotating a shaft or moving a slider [Late 19C. < POTENTIAL] —**potentiometry** *n*

potentiometric /pə ténshi ə méttrik/ *adj* indicating the completion of a chemical reaction by a change in potential at an electrode immersed in the solution where the reaction is taking place [Early 20C. < POTENTIAL]

pothead /pót hed/ *n* a regular or heavy smoker of cannabis (*slang disapproving*)

pothecary /póthəkəri/ (*plural* **-ies**) *n* (*archaic or regional*) **1.** OCCUPATIONS same as **pharmacist 2.** COMM same as **pharmacy** [14C. Shortening of APOTHECARY]

pother /póthər/ *n* **1.** NERVOUS STATE a state of emotional agitation, especially over something trivial **2.** COMMOTION a great deal of frenzied activity or conversation, especially over something trivial **3.** CHOKING CLOUD a suffocating cloud of smoke or dust ■ *vti* (**-ers**, **-ering**, **-ered**) CONFUSE SOMEBODY OR BE CONFUSED to confuse or worry somebody, or become confused or worried [Late 16C. Origin ?]

potherb /pót hurb/ *n* a herb or vegetable used to add flavour in cooking

potholder /pót hōldər/ *n* a pad of fabric used to protect the hands from hot pots and cooking utensils

pothole /pót hōl/ *n* **1.** HOLE IN ROAD a hole in the surface of a road **2.** VERTICAL HOLE IN LIMESTONE AREA a vertical deep hole or shaft formed naturally in limestone regions by the erosive action of running water **3.** HOLE IN RIVER BED a bowl-shaped hole in the bed of a river or stream, formed by the abrasive action of stone, gravel, or ice being churned in an eddy

pothole lake *n* a small lake formed in a limestone pothole depression

potholing /pót hōling/ *n* the activity of exploring potholes and underground caves connected by them, especially as a hobby or sport —**potholer** *n*

pothook /pót hŏŏk/ *n* **1.** an S-shaped hook fixed above an open fire, from which a pot or kettle is hung **2.** a handwriting mark beginning or ending in a curve

pothouse /pót howss/ (*plural* **-houses** /-howziz/) *n* same as **pub** (sense 1) (*dated*)

pothunter /pót huntər/ *n* **1.** HUNTER VIOLATING RULES somebody who hunts game, often indiscriminately and disregardful of rules **2.** PRIZE-SEEKER a participant in competitions and races with more interest in the prizes than the sport (*informal disapproving*) **3.** AMATEUR ARCHAEOLOGIST somebody who digs for ancient pots and other objects but who is not a professional archaeologist —**pothunting** *n*

potion /pósh'n/ *n* a liquid to be drunk that is medicinal, supposedly magical, or poisonous [13C. Via French < Latin *potion-* < *potare* 'to drink' < *potus* 'drink']

Potiphar /póttifər/ *n* in the Bible, the Egyptian who bought Joseph as a slave and later imprisoned him when he was falsely accused of attempting to have sexual relations with his wife. (Genesis 37).

potjie /póyki/ *n S Africa* a rounded three-legged cast-iron pot in which food is cooked over an open fire [Late 20C. < Afrikaans, 'little pot']

potlatch /pót lach/ *n* among Native American peoples of the coast of northwestern North America, a ceremony of feasting in which the host gains prestige by giving gifts or, sometimes, destroying wealth [Mid-19C. < Chinook Jargon *patlá* < Nootka *p'achitl* 'giving or gift']

potluck /pot lúk/ *n* **1.** CHOICE FROM WHAT IS AVAILABLE a choice from whatever happens to be available in a particular situation ○ *take potluck* **2.** FOOD AVAILABLE FOR UNEXPECTED GUEST whatever food happens to be available to serve an unexpected guest **3.** *N Am* MEAL TO WHICH EVERYONE BRINGS SOMETHING a meal to which each participant brings one dish that is shared by everyone (*often used before a noun*) ○ *a potluck dinner* [Late 16C. < POT[1]]

potman /pótmən/ (*plural* **-men** /-mən/) *n* a man employed in a public house, especially to collect empty glasses (*dated*)

pot marigold *n* a garden plant of the daisy family. Flowers: large, bright yellow or orange. Native to: Europe. Latin name: *Calendula officinalis*.

Potomac /pə tŏm ak/ river of the eastern United States, formed by the confluence of its north and south branches near Cumberland, Maryland, and emptying into Chesapeake Bay. It flows through Washington, DC. Length: 616 km/383 mi.

potometer /pə tómmitər/ *n* an instrument used to determine the rate of a plant's transpiration by measuring water uptake [Late 19C. < Greek *poton* 'drink']

potoo /pə tóó/ (*plural same*) *n* a nocturnal bird that eats insects. Native to: Mexico, Central and South America. Genus: *Nyctibius*. [Mid-19C. Via Jamaican Creole < Twi, an imitation of the bird's call]

potoroo /pótta róó/ (*plural* **-roos**) *n* a rabbit-sized member of the kangaroo family that looks like a rat and has powerful hind legs that it uses for jumping. Latin name: *Potorous tridactylus*. [Late 18C. < Aboriginal]

pot plant *n* a plant that is growing in a flowerpot and is kept in a house or office for display and decoration. N Am term **potted plant**

potpourri /pō póŏri, pŏpə reé/ (*plural* **-ris**) *n* **1.** a collection of dried flower petals, leaves, herbs, and

spices that is used to scent the air **2.** a mixture of miscellaneous things [Early 17C. < French, 'mixed stew', literally 'rotten pot', translation of Spanish *olla podrida*]

~~**potray**~~ incorrect spelling of **portray**

pot roast *n* a dish consisting of a piece of beef cooked slowly in the oven in a closed pot in its own juices, often on a bed of vegetables —**pot-roast** *vti*

Potsdam /póts dam/ city in northeastern Germany approximately 29 km/18 mi. southwest of Berlin. It was the site of the Potsdam Conference (July–August 1945), at which US, British, and Soviet leaders discussed the postwar administration of Germany. Population: 138,268 (1997).

potsherd /pót shurd/, **potshard** /-shard/ *n* a fragment of pottery, especially one found at an archaeological site [14C. < POT^1]

potshot /pót shot/ *n* **1.** a criticism made without careful consideration and aimed at an easy target ○ *journalists taking potshots at the government* **2.** a quick careless, and usually easy, shot taken at something such as game [Mid-19C. Because originally a shot to get food for the cooking 'pot']

pot still *n* an apparatus for distilling whisky that applies heat directly to the container holding the wash

potstone /pót stōn/ *n* an impure variety of talc, used in the past to make cooking vessels

pottage /póttij/ *n* a thick vegetable, or meat and vegetable, soup [Mid-16C. Anglicization of POTAGE]

potted /póttid/ *adj* **1.** GROWING IN POT planted in a pot **2.** PRESERVED IN POT cooked or preserved in a vessel such as a pot or jar ○ *potted beef* **3.** SUPERFICIALLY SUMMARIZED reproduced in a brief and often superficial form (*informal*) ○ *a potted biography*

potted plant *n* N Am same as **pot plant**

potter^1 /póttər/ *n* a maker of pottery [Pre-12C. < POT^1]

potter^2 /póttər/ (**-ters, -tering, -tered**) *vi* **1.** to do relatively unimportant things in a relaxed and unhurried way ○ *pottering about in the greenhouse* N Am term **putter**^{2} **2.** to move about slowly and without any particular goal [Mid-16C. < obsolete *pote* 'push', origin ?] —**potterer** *n*

Beatrix Potter

Potter /póttər/, **Beatrix** (1866–1943) British children's writer and illustrator. Her illustrated animal stories, including *The Tale of Peter Rabbit* (1900) and *The Tailor of Gloucester* (1902), became children's classics. Full name **Potter, Helen Beatrix**

> 'Don't go into Mr McGregor's garden: your Father had an accident there; he was put in a pie by Mrs McGregor.'
> [Beatrix Potter, *The Tale of Peter Rabbit*; 1900]

Potteries /póteriz/ a region in Staffordshire, west-central England, famous for its ceramics factories

potter's clay *n* clay that does not contain any iron and is suitable for making pottery

potter's field *n* in the Bible, an area of land near Jerusalem bought as a burial ground for strangers with the money that was given to Judas for betraying Jesus Christ

potter's wheel *n* a device for moulding clay into pottery by hand, consisting of a rotating horizontal disc that holds and turns the clay between the potter's hands

potter wasp *n* a small solitary wasp that constructs elaborate clay pots in which it lays its eggs and puts caterpillars to serve as food for the young. Genus: *Eumenes*.

pottery /póttəri/ (*plural* **-ies**) *n* **1.** OBJECTS MADE OF BAKED CLAY objects that are made by moulding or shaping moist clay and hardening it by heating in a kiln, e.g. vases, pots, plates, or sculptured articles **2.** MAKING OF POTTERY the art, craft, or occupation of making pottery **3.** PLACE WHERE POTTERY IS MADE a workshop, factory, or other place where pottery is made

potting compost /pótting-/ *n* a mixture with a soil, peat, or fibre base and a balanced nutrient content that is used for growing plants in pots

potting shed *n* a small shed in a garden for storing flowerpots, compost, and other gardening materials

potto /póttō/ (*plural* **-tos**) *n* a small primate that has small ears, large eyes, and a short bushy tail and lives in the lower branches of trees. Native to: rainforests of West and Central Africa. Latin name: *Perodicticus potto*. [Early 18C. Probably < a West African language]

Pott's disease /póts-/ *n* a tubercular disease of the spine, marked by the destruction of the bone and discs and curvature of the spine [Mid-19C. After Sir Percivall *Pott* (1713–88), English surgeon]

potty^1 /pótti/ (**-tier, -tiest**) *adj* (*informal*) **1.** IRRATIONAL slightly irrational **2.** KEEN OR ENTHUSIASTIC very enthusiastic about or obsessed by somebody or something **3.** TRIVIAL trivial and unimportant [Mid-19C. Origin ?] —**pottiness** *n*

potty^2 /pótti/ (*plural* **-ties**) *n* a bowl, used especially by young children who cannot yet use a toilet, to eliminate body waste [Mid-20C. < POT^1]

potty-chair *n* a small chair with a pot in the seat, used by young children who are being trained to use a toilet

potty-train *vti* to train a young child to use a potty instead of a nappy (*informal*)

POTUS /pṓtəss/ *n US* used as shorthand by White House staff in memos and internal documents to refer to the US president. Full form **President of the United States**

pot-walloper *n* in some English boroughs before 1832, a man entitled to vote because he had his own fireplace as a homeowner, tenant, or lodger [Early 18C. Alteration (after WALLOP) of *potwaller* 'potboiler' < POT^1 + obsolete *wall* 'boil' < Germanic]

pouch /powch/ *n* **1.** SMALL SOFT BAG a small bag or container made of a soft material such as fabric or leather **2.** SOMETHING RESEMBLING POUCH something that looks like a pouch, especially a small baggy fold of skin **3.** POCKET OF SKIN IN ANIMAL a structure in an animal resembling a pouch, especially one on the abdomen of a marsupial for carrying young, or in the cheek of a rodent for carrying food **4.** BODY CAVITY RESEMBLING POCKET a pocket-shaped space or structure in the body **5.** PLANT CAVITY a cavity in a plant shaped like a pocket **6.** BAG FOR MAIL a lockable bag or sack for carrying mail, especially diplomatic correspondence **7.** *Scotland* CLOTHING same as **pocket** *n* (sense 1) ■ *v* (**pouches, pouching, pouched**) **1.** *vt* PUT SOMETHING IN POUCH to put something into a pouch **2.** *vti* FORM POUCH to make something, or be made, into a shape resembling a pouch **3.** *vt* GAIN SOMETHING to take, gain, or win something (*informal*) **4.** *vt* CATCH BALL to catch the ball in a ball game, especially cricket (*informal*) [13C. < Anglo-Norman *puche*, Old N French *pouche*, Old French *poche* 'bag' < Germanic] —**pouchy** *adj*

pouf^1 /poof/, **pouffe** *n* **1.** PADDED STOOL a round or square piece of padded furniture with an upholstered cover, used as a seat or footrest. N Am term **hassock** **2.** PUFFED-OUT HAIRSTYLE a puffed-out hairstyle, similar to a bouffant, fashionable especially in the 18th century **3.** PAD IN HAIR a pad worn in the hair to help shape a pouf **4.** BUNCHED-UP PART OF DRESS a part of a dress or skirt gathered up to form a soft projecting shape [Early 19C. < French, an imitation of the sound of a puff]

pouf^2 /pŏof, poof/, **pouffe** *n* another spelling of **poof**^{1} (*slang offensive*)

Pouilly-Fuissé /pŏo yee fwée say/ *n* a dry white wine from east-central France [After two villages in the Burgundy region of France]

Pouilly-Fumé /pŏo yee fyŏo may/ *n* a dry white wine from west-central France [Mid-20C. < French, 'smoked Pouilly']

Poujadism /pŏo zhaadizəm/ *n* a right-wing political movement in France in the 1950s, with mainly middle-class support [Mid-20C. < French *Poujadisme*, after Pierre *Poujade* (1920–), French publisher and politician] —**Poujadist** *n, adj*

poulard /pŏo laard/, **poularde** *n* a young domestic hen (**pullet**) that has been spayed to encourage fattening [Mid-18C. < French *poularde* < *poule* 'hen' (see PULLET)]

Poulenc /pŏol angk, pŏol aNk/, **Francis** (1899–1963) French composer and pianist. He was a member of the Paris-based group of composers known as 'Les Six'. His music, tuneful and satirical, includes ballets, operas, chamber music, and songs.

poult /pōlt/ *n* a young fowl, especially a turkey or pheasant [15C. Contraction of PULLET]

poulterer /pṓltərər/ *n* a buyer, preparer, and seller of poultry [Late 16C. Alteration of archaic *poulter* < Old French *pouletier* < *poulet* (see PULLET)]

poultice /pṓltiss/ *n* a warm moist preparation placed on an aching or inflamed part of the body to ease pain, improve circulation, or hasten the expression of pus [14C. < Latin *pultes*, plural of *puls* 'pottage, thick gruel']

poultry /pṓltri/ *n* **1.** domestic fowl in general, e.g. chickens, turkeys, ducks, or geese, raised for meat or eggs (*takes a singular or plural verb*) **2.** the meat of domestic fowl [14C. < Old French *pouletrie* < *pouletier* 'poulterer' < *poulet* (see PULLET)]

pounce^1 /pownss/ *vi* (**pounces, pouncing, pounced**) **1.** JUMP SUDDENLY ON to jump or swoop suddenly towards or onto somebody or something, especially onto prey **2.** ATTACK OR TAKE QUICKLY to move very quickly and suddenly in attacking somebody or obtaining something ○ *He pounced on the book and carried it off to his room.* **3.** REACT SWIFTLY TO SOMETHING to be quick to notice and make use of something ○ *She immediately pounced on his admission that he'd known all about it.* ■ *n* ACT OF SUDDENLY JUMPING ON an act of suddenly jumping or swooping towards or onto somebody or something, especially onto prey [14C. Either shortening of PUNCHEON^2, or < Old French *poinson* 'pointed tool' < Latin *punct-* (see PUNCTURE)] —**pouncer** *n*

pounce^2 /pownss/ *n* **1.** POWDER USED FOR PRODUCING IMAGE powdered charcoal or other fine powder sprinkled over a stencil to reproduce the main lines of a pattern or design on the surface beneath the stencil **2.** POWDER TO STOP INK FROM RUNNING a very fine powder formerly used to stop ink from spreading on unglazed paper ■ *vt* (**pounces, pouncing, pounced**) **1.** REPRODUCE SOMETHING WITH POUNCE to reproduce a pattern or design on something by sprinkling pounce over a stencil **2.** BLOT PAPER WITH POUNCE to sprinkle paper with pounce to prevent ink from running [Late 16C. < French < Latin *pumic-* 'pumice']

pouncet box /pównssət-/ *n* a small box with a perforated lid, used to hold a perfumed substance [Late 16C. Origin ?]

pound^1 /pownd/ *n* **1.** COMMON UNIT OF CURRENCY the main unit of currency in the United Kingdom and several other countries. See table at **currency** **2.** FORMER IRISH CURRENCY the main unit of the former currency of the Republic of Ireland **3.** same as **pound scots** **4.** AVOIRDUPOIS UNIT OF WEIGHT a unit of weight in the avoirdupois system, divided into 16 oz and equivalent to 0.45 kg **5.** TROY UNIT OF WEIGHT a unit of weight in the troy system that is divided into 12 oz and is equivalent to 0.37 kg **6.** UNIT OF FORCE a unit of force, equal to the gravitational force experienced by a pound mass accelerating at 9.80665 m/32.174 ft per second per second [Old English *pund*, via Germanic < Latin *pondo* 'weight of a pound' < (*libra*) *pondo* '(pound) by weight'] ◇ **get** *or* **have your pound of flesh** to get what is due to you, even if it causes difficulties or hardship to others

pound^2 /pownd/ *v* (**pounds, pounding, pounded**) **1.** *vti* STRIKE SOMETHING HARD AND REPEATEDLY to strike somebody or something with repeated heavy blows **2.** *vt* BEAT SOMETHING TO PULP OR POWDER to beat something into a pulp or powder with repeated heavy blows **3.** *vi* THROB to beat or throb heavily ○ *My heart was pounding.* **4.** *vt* BOMBARD SOMETHING to attack a place continuously with bombs or large guns ○ *pounding the city for a*

few weeks **5.** vi **RUN HEAVILY** to move, especially to run, fast or energetically and with heavy, noisy steps **6.** vt **WALK ALONG SOMETHING** to spend a long time walking along a regular route or walking to and fro in an area ○ *pounding the streets of Manhattan and taking in the sights* **7.** vt **TEACH BY REPETITION** to teach something, or make sure somebody understands something, by using constant repetition and drilling ■ n **ACT OF POUNDING** the act or sound of pounding [Old English *pūnian* < Germanic] —**pounder** n

pound out vt **1.** to produce something by working in a diligent continuous way ○ *pound out an essay* **2.** to produce something with heavy blows or loud thumping noises ○ *pound out a tune on the piano*

pound³ /pownd/ n **1.** **ENCLOSURE FOR STRAY ANIMALS** a fenced-off area where stray animals, especially dogs, are kept **2.** **ENCLOSURE FOR VEHICLES OR OTHER GOODS** a fenced-off area where vehicles or other goods that have been taken by the police or another authority are kept until a debt or fine has been paid **3.** **PLACE FOR ANIMALS OR FISH** an area in which animals or fish are trapped or kept **4.** **PRISON AREA** a place where people are held prisoner ■ vt **(pounds, pounding, pounded)** **PUT SOMETHING IN POUND** to confine an animal or person in a pound [Old English *pund-*, origin ?]

US Office of War Information

Ezra Pound

Pound /pownd/, **Ezra** (1885–1972) US writer. He was an influential poet, critic, translator, and mentor of other poets, and a founder of imagism. His major work is the *Cantos* (1915–70). Full name **Pound, Ezra Loomis**

> 'The apparition of these faces in the crowd; / Petals on a wet black bough.'
> [Ezra Pound, 'In a Station of the Metro', *Dramatis Personae*; 1926]

> 'Great literature is simply language charged with meaning to the utmost possible degree.'
> [Ezra Pound, *How to Read*; 1931]

poundage¹ /pówndij/ n **1.** **WEIGHT IN POUNDS** the weight of somebody or something expressed in pounds **2.** **PAYMENT PER POUND OF WEIGHT** a tax, charge, commission, or other payment for something calculated per pound of weight **3.** **PAYMENT PER POUND STERLING** a tax, charge, commission, or other payment for something calculated per pound sterling [14C. < POUND¹]

poundage² /pówndij/ n **1.** the confinement of animals in an enclosed area or pound **2.** the fee that must be paid for the return of an impounded vehicle, animal, or other goods [Mid-16C. < POUND³]

poundal /pównd'l/ n a British unit of force, equal to the force that will impart an acceleration of one foot per second per second to a mass of one pound [Late 19C. < POUND¹]

pound cake n N Am a rich dense yellow cake that is traditionally made with a pound each of butter, sugar, flour, and eggs, or with equal weights of each of these ingredients

pound cost averaging n the periodic purchase of the same amount in pounds sterling of the same security at regular time intervals regardless of the price of the security

pound-foolish adj unwise when dealing with large sums of money

pound scots (*plural* **pounds scots**) n a former unit of currency in Scotland

pound sign n **1.** the symbol (£) which indicates pound sterling **2.** US same as **hash**¹ n (sense 1)

pound sterling (*plural* **pounds sterling**) n the official name for the unit of currency used in the United Kingdom

pour /pawr/ (**pours, pouring, poured**) v **1.** vt **MAKE SOMETHING FLOW** to make a substance flow out or down in a stream ○ *poured the sugar into the bowl* **2.** vti **SERVE DRINK** to serve a drink from a container such as a pot or jug into a cup, mug, or glass ○ *Let me pour you some tea.* **3.** vi **FUNCTION AS CONTAINER FOR POURING** to function as a container from which liquid is poured ○ *This teapot doesn't pour very well.* **4.** vi **FLOW IN LARGE QUANTITIES** to flow down or out, especially in large quantities ○ *Smoke poured from the burning building.* **5.** vi **RAIN HEAVILY** to rain very heavily ○ *It poured for hours.* **6.** vi **COME IN LARGE QUANTITIES** to come or go quickly and in large quantities ○ *Letters of complaint came pouring in.* **7.** vt **EXPRESS FEELING** to express a feeling at length and without restraint ○ *poured his heart out to me* **8.** vt **GIVE SOMETHING IN LARGE AMOUNT** to expend a large amount of something, e.g. time, money, or effort ○ *poured a lot of blood, sweat, and tears into that project* [13C. Probably via Old French dialect *purer* 'sift, pour out' < Latin *purare* 'purify' < *purus* 'pure']

USAGE pour or **pore**? 'To study something carefully and thoughtfully' (**pore**) might seem to have more in common with 'to make a substance flow' (**pour**) than with 'a tiny opening' (**pore**). Perhaps it has, but all three words have been derived separately, despite the fact that one of the verbs has the same spelling as the noun. You **pour** from the pot into a teacup, **pore** over a text, and have **pores** in your skin.

pourboire /poor bwaar/ n a sum of money given for services rendered or anticipated [Early 19C. < French, literally 'for drinking']

pour point n the lowest temperature at which a liquid will continue to flow

pousse-café /poss ka fáy/ n **1.** a drink consisting of different-coloured liqueurs poured in one glass and forming layers because each liqueur has a different density **2.** a liqueur served after dinner, with or after coffee [< French, literally 'push coffee']

pousse-pousse /poss pooss/ n in Madagascar, a small vehicle with two wheels and a seat for passengers, pulled along by somebody walking in front of it [Reduplication of French *pousse*, 'to push'.]

poussin /poo saN/ n a chicken reared to be eaten when very young and tender [Mid-20C. Via French < late Latin *pullicenus* 'small young fowl' < Latin *pullus* 'young fowl']

Poussin /poo saN/, **Nicolas** (1594–1665) French painter. He was a master of French classicism, and was influenced by Raphael.

> 'The idea of beauty does not descend into matter unless this is prepared as carefully as possible.'
> [Nicolas Poussin. Quoted in *Lives of the Modern Painters, Sculptors and Architects*, Giovanni Pietro Bellori; 1672]

pout¹ /powt/ v (**pouts, pouting, pouted**) **1.** vti **PUSH LIPS OUTWARDS** to push the lower lip or both lips outwards in an expression of bad temper or sulkiness **2.** vti **ADOPT SEXY EXPRESSION** to push the lips outwards in order to look sexually attractive **3.** vi **SULK** to show disappointment, anger, or resentment, usually in silence ○ *still pouting because he missed the game* **4.** vt **SAY SOMETHING SULKILY** to say something with a pout ○ *pouted that the whole thing wasn't fair* ■ n **1.** **EXPRESSION WITH LIPS PUSHED OUT** an expression of the face with the lower lip or both lips pushed out **2.** **SULKY MOOD** a period or display of sulkiness [14C. Origin ?] —**poutingly** adv —**pouty** adj

pout² /powt/ (*plural same* or **pouts**) n FISH **1.** same as **bib** (sense 3) **2.** same as **hornpout** [Old English *-pūte*, origin ?]

pouter /pówtər/ n **1.** somebody who pouts **2.** *also* **pouter pigeon** a domesticated pigeon belonging to a breed with a pouch in its throat that can be greatly inflated

poutine /poo teen/ n a dish originating in Quebec that consists of chips and curd cheese, covered with tomato sauce or gravy

POV abbr point of view (*used in e-mails or text messages*)

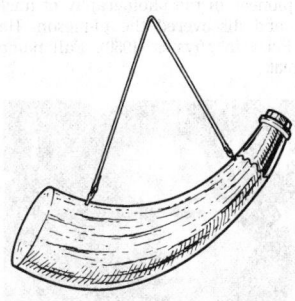

powder horn

poverty /póvvərti/ n **1.** **STATE OF BEING POOR** the state of not having enough money to take care of basic needs such as food, clothing, and housing **2.** **LACK** a deficiency or lack of something ○ *poverty of emotion* **3.** **INFERTILITY OF SOIL** lack of soil fertility or nutrients [12C. Via Old French *poverte* < Latin *paupertas* < *pauper* 'poor' (see PAUPER)]

Poverty Bay /póvvərti-/ bay on the eastern coast of the North Island, New Zealand. The city of Gisborne lies on its northern shore.

poverty line, **poverty level** n a level of income below which somebody is considered to be living in poverty. It is based on the price of basic necessities and is usually determined by a government.

poverty-stricken adj in a state of extreme poverty

poverty trap n a situation in which an unemployed person will lose money by working because more will be lost in state benefits than is gained in income

pow /pow/ interj used to imitate the sound of an explosion or gun, or of a sudden impact, e.g. of somebody being hit (*informal*) [Late 19C. An imitation of the sound]

POW abbr prisoner of war

powder /pówdər/ n **1.** **LOOSE DRY PARTICLES** a substance in the form of a mass of very small, loose dry grains **2.** **PARTICULAR KIND OF POWDER** powder that is produced for a particular purpose ○ *face powder* **3.** **ARMS** same as **gunpowder 4.** **DRY SNOW** light dry snow ■ v (**-ders, -dering, -dered**) **1.** vt **PUT POWDER ON SOMETHING** to cover something with powder, or sprinkle powder on something **2.** vti **TURN SOMETHING INTO POWDER** to turn a solid into powder by crushing it, or become a powder [13C. < French *poudre*, alteration of *poldre* < Latin *pulver-* 'dust'] —**powderer** n —**powdery** adj

powder blue adj of a very pale purplish-blue colour (*hyphenated before a noun*) —**powder blue** n

powder burn n a minor skin burn caused by being very close to a brief intense explosion, especially the firing of a gun, sometimes used as evidence in a court of law

powder compact n COSMETICS same as **compact**¹ n (sense 1)

powder flask n a small flask used for keeping gunpowder for loading a firearm

powder horn n a small container consisting of the hollow horn of an ox or cow, used for keeping gunpowder for loading a firearm

powder keg n **1.** a small barrel used to hold gunpowder or blasting powder **2.** a tense situation that may easily erupt into violence

powder metallurgy n the technology used in producing solid objects, e.g. self-lubricating bearings, from powdered metals or carbides by compressing or heating them without melting them

powder monkey n **1.** somebody who deals with explosives, e.g. in mining or construction (*slang*) **2.** a boy formerly employed on a warship to carry gunpowder from the store to the guns

powder puff n a soft or fluffy pad used for putting powder on the face or skin

powder room n a toilet for women

powdery mildew n a fungal disease that produces a white powdery covering on plant leaves

Powell /pô əl/, **Sir Anthony** (1906–2000) British novelist. His major work is the series of 12 novels, *A Dance to the Music of Time* (1951–75), which examines English upper-middle-class life in the mid-20th century. Full name **Powell, Sir Anthony Dymoke**

Powell /pów əl/, **Cecil** (1903–69) British physicist. He

was a pioneer in the photography of nuclear processes, and discovered the pi-meson. He won a Nobel Prize in physics (1950). Full name **Powell, Cecil Frank**

Department of Defense, Washington, D.C.

Colin Powell

Powell, Colin (*b.* 1937) US general and secretary of state (2001–). He was chairman of the Joint Chiefs of Staff during the Gulf War (1991) and became secretary of state under President George W Bush. Full name **Powell, Colin Luther**

'One of the fondest expressions around is that we can't be the world's policeman. But guess who gets called when suddenly someone needs a cop.'
[Colin Powell, *Life*; March 1991]

'Avoid having your ego so close to your position that when your position falls, your ego goes with it.'
[Colin Powell, 'Colin Powell's Rules', *Parade*; August 1989]

Powell, Michael (1905–90) British film director. In partnership with Emeric Pressburger, he made a number of films noted for their imagery and technical virtuosity, including *The Red Shoes* (1948).

'The real reason why *The Red Shoes* was such a success, was that we had all been told for ten years to go out and die...now that the war was over *The Red Shoes* told us to go and die for art.'
[Michael Powell, *A Life in Movies*; 1986]

power /pów ər/ *n* **1.** CAPACITY TO DO SOMETHING the ability, strength, and capacity to do something ○ *The pilot did everything in his power to avoid the disaster.* **2.** STRENGTH physical force or strength **3.** CONTROL AND INFLUENCE control and influence over other people and their actions ○ *She made you stay behind just to show how much power she has over you.* **4.** AUTHORITY TO ACT the authority to act or do something according to a law or rule **5.** POLITICAL CONTROL the political control of a country, exercised by its government or leader **6.** SOMEBODY WITH POWER a politically, financially, or socially powerful person **7.** IMPORTANT COUNTRY a country that has military or economic resources and is considered to have political influence over other countries **8.** PERSUASIVENESS the ability to influence people's judgment or emotions **9.** SKILL a faculty, skill, or ability ○ *musical powers* **10.** ENERGY TO DRIVE MACHINERY energy or force used to drive machinery or produce electricity **11.** ELECTRICITY electricity made available for use **12.** MEASURE OF RATE OF DOING WORK a measure of the rate of doing work or transferring energy, usually expressed in terms of wattage or horsepower. Symbol *P* **13.** MATHS NUMBER OF MULTIPLICATION OPERATIONS the number of times a quantity is to be successively multiplied by itself, usually written as a small number to the right of and above the quantity **14.** OPTICS MAGNIFYING ABILITY a measure of the ability of a lens, mirror, or prism to magnify an image **15.** STATS PROBABILITY OF REJECTING NULL HYPOTHESIS the probability of rejecting the null hypothesis as false when an alternative hypothesis is true **16.** CHR ANGEL OF FOURTH-HIGHEST ORDER an angel of the fourth of the nine orders of angels in the traditional Christian hierarchy ■ *v* (**-ers, -ering, -ered**) **1.** *vt* PROVIDE ENERGY TO OPERATE SOMETHING to supply a machine or tool with the energy it needs to operate ○ *electrically powered* **2.** *vi* MOVE ENERGETICALLY to move fast and with great determination and energy ○ *He came powering down the home straight.* ■ *adj* **1.** RUN BY ELECTRICITY OR FUEL receiving power from a motor using electrical energy or fuel such as petrol, instead of relying on manual labour ○ *power tools* **2.** INTENDED FOR BUSINESS SUCCESS designed or believed to improve somebody's status, influence, or effectiveness in business ○ *power dressing* [13C. < Anglo-Norman *poer*, Old French *poeir* < assumed Vulgar Latin *potere* 'be powerful' < Latin *potis* 'able'] ◇ **do somebody** *or* **something the power of good** to benefit somebody or something greatly (*informal*) ◇ **the powers that be** the people in authority

power down *vti* to switch a computer off in the correct way, bringing an orderly end to system operation

power up *v* **1.** *vti* to switch on a computer, printer, or other peripheral device **2.** *vt* to give somebody or something increased energy or capability

power base *n* a position, region, or group of voters providing the foundation of somebody's political power or support

powerboat /pów ər bōt/ *n* SPORTS same as **motorboat** — **powerboating** *n*

power brake *n* an automotive brake in which the pressure on a piston operates the brake cylinder

power broker *n* a person or country that has great influence, especially in politics or commerce, and is able to use this influence to affect the policies and decisions of others

power centre *n* Can a shopping centre containing several large superstores or discount stores

power cut *n* a temporary loss of electricity supply to a building or to an area of a town. N Am term **power outage**

power dive *n* a steep dive made by an aircraft with its engines at high power to increase the speed — **power-dive** *vti*

power forward *n* **1.** TALL FORWARD WHO EXCELS UNDER BASKET in basketball, a tall forward who plays the low-post position because his or her height provides an advantage for blocking shots and rebounding **2.** POWER FORWARD'S POSITION in basketball, the position in which a power forward plays **3.** FORWARD KNOWN FOR STRENGTH AND AGGRESSIVENESS in ice hockey, a forward who is valued as much for strength and aggressiveness as for playing skills

powerful /pów ərf'l/ *adj* **1.** INFLUENTIAL able to exert a lot of influence and control over people and events ○ *a powerful nation* **2.** STRONG having or exerting great physical or mental strength **3.** EFFECTIVE possessing the strength or qualities to produce a fast and effective result ○ *a powerful antibiotic* **4.** PERSUASIVE able to produce a strong effect on people's ideas or emotions ○ *a powerful film* ■ *adv* Southern US same as **extremely** ○ *He was powerful thirsty.* —**powerfully** *adv* —**powerfulness** *n*

powerhouse /pów ər howss/ (*plural* **-houses** /-howziz/) *n* somebody or something that is full of energy and very productive (*informal*) ○ *a publishing powerhouse*

powerless /pówərləss/ *adj* lacking power, strength, or effectiveness —**powerlessly** *adv* —**powerlessness** *n*

powerlifting /pów ər lifting/ *n* weightlifting that emphasizes strength, in which the lifter competes against others in performing a bench press, a squat, and a two-handed dead lift

power line *n* a cable that carries electricity from a power station to the users of the electricity or between electric utilities in a network

power nap *n* a short sleep taken by a businessperson in the office in order to feel revitalized

power of appointment *n* the authority given to somebody to select beneficiaries and to allocate money and other property from a person's estate to those beneficiaries

power of attorney *n* the legal authority to act for another person in legal and business matters

power outage *n* N Am same as **power cut**

power pack *n* a device for converting a supply of electricity to direct or alternating current at the correct voltage for a piece of electrical or electronic equipment

power plant *n* **1.** N Am same as **power station 2.** a unit that supplies the power to move a self-propelled object, e.g. a diesel-electric engine in a locomotive or an internal-combustion engine in an automobile

power play *n* **1.** BID FOR ADVANTAGE an attempt to gain an advantage by a display of strength or superiority, e.g. in a negotiation or relationship **2.** TACTIC OF CONCENTRATING PLAYERS a tactic used in sport consisting of concentrating players in one area **3.** TACTIC OF CONCENTRATING RESOURCES a tactic in business, commerce, or politics that involves concentrating resources and effort in one area **4.** NUMERICAL ADVANTAGE IN ICE HOCKEY a situation or period of time in ice hockey during which one team has a numerical advantage because the other team has one or more players in the penalty box

power point *n* ELEC same as **socket** *n* (sense 2)

power politics *n* political relations and actions based on an implied threat of the use of political, economic, or military power by a participant (*takes a singular verb*)

power series *n* an infinite series in which the terms contain regularly increasing integral powers of a variable. A typical series would be $Sn = 1 + 2x + 3x^2 + 4x^3 + ... + nxn^{-1}$.

power shovel *n* a mobile machine for excavating and removing debris, with a movable lever arm ending in a hinged digging bucket

power station *n* an industrial complex where power, especially electricity, is generated from another source of energy such as burning coal, nuclear reactions, or flowing water. N Am term **power plant**

power steering *n* a system of steering for a motor vehicle in which turning the steering wheel is made easier by supplementary power from the vehicle's engine

power takeoff *n* **1.** the transfer of power from a vehicle's engine to another piece of machinery such as a winch or hydraulic pump **2.** a device for transferring power from a vehicle's engine to another piece of machinery

power train *n* the portion of a vehicle's drive mechanism that transmits power from the engine to the wheels, tracks, or propellers. A car's power train includes the clutch, transmission, drive shaft, and differential.

power-up *n* **1.** an act of switching on a computer system **2.** an icon in a computer game, typically appearing upon the destruction of an enemy, that gives the player a greater advantage

power user *n* a computer user who is expert in one or more software applications (*informal*)

power walking *n* a form of exercise involving energetic walking in which the arms are swung backwards and forwards, sometimes using weights, in order to increase the heart rate —**power walker** *n*

Powhatan /pów ə tan, pow hátt'n/ (1550?–1618) Algonquian leader. He led the Powhatan confederacy of Algonquian peoples in Virginia, and was the father of Pocahontas. Born **Wahunsonacook**

powwow /pów wow/ *n* **1.** NATIVE AMERICAN CEREMONY a traditional Native American ceremony featuring dance, feasting, and a blessing by a shaman for an event such as a marriage, a major hunt, or a gathering of nations **2.** MEETING a meeting or gathering to discuss something (*informal*) ■ *vi* (**-wows, -wowing, -wowed**) HAVE POWWOW to hold a powwow (*informal*) [Early 19C. < Narraganset *powwaw* 'shaman']

Powys /pów iss/ county in central Wales. Llandrindod Wells is its administrative centre. Population: 126,354 (2001). Area: 5,205 sq. km/2,009 sq. mi.

pox /poks/ *n* **1.** a venereal disease, especially syphilis (*informal*) **2.** a viral disease that causes pus-filled blisters (**pustules**) to form on the skin, and often leaves scars (**pockmarks**), e.g. smallpox or chickenpox [Alteration of *pocks*, plural of POCK] ◇ **a pox on somebody** *or* **something** used to express a wish that misfortune will come to somebody or something (*archaic*)

poxvirus /póks vírəss/ *n* an oval-shaped DNA-containing virus responsible for diseases that cause pus-filled blisters (**pustules**) to form on the skin

poxy /póksi/ (**-ier, -iest**) *adj* bad, unpleasant, annoying, or generally worthless (*informal*)

Poynting theorem /póynting-/ *n* the theorem stating that the rate of flow of electromagnetic energy per unit area equals the cross product of the electric

and magnetic vectors [Late 19C. After J. H. *Poynting* (1852–1914), English physicist]

Poznań /pṓz nan/ city in western Poland. It is the capital of Poznań Province. Population: 580,000 (1997).

pozzie *n ANZ* another spelling of **possie** (*informal*)

pozzuolana /pótswə láanə/, **pozzolana** /pótsə-/ *n* a porous volcanic ash that when mixed with cement hardens either in air or under water [Early 18C. < Italian *pozz(u)olana (terra)* '(earth) of Pozzuoli' (town near Naples, S Italy)]

Pozzuoli /pot swáwli/ town in Campania Region, southern Italy. Population: 78,754 (2001).

pp[1] *abbr* **1.** GRAM past participle **2.** MUSIC pianissimo **3.** PRINTING privately printed

pp[2], **pp.** *abbr* pages

pp[3] *abbr* BUSINESS by proxy (*used when signing documents on behalf of somebody else*) [Latin *per procurationem*]

PP *abbr* **1.** PHARM after a meal (*used in prescriptions*) **2.** MAIL parcel post **3.** CHR parish priest **4.** past president **5.** MAIL postpaid **6.** MAIL prepaid **7.** GRAM prepositional phrase

ppb *abbr* MEASURE parts per billion

PPP *abbr* BUSINESS, GOV public private partnership

PPV *abbr* **1.** MEDIA pay-per-view **2.** *Aus* Permanent Protection Visa

pr *abbr* ONLINE Puerto Rico (*used in Internet addresses*) See table at **domain name**

Pr *symbol* CHEM ELEM praseodymium

PR *abbr* **1.** Puerto Rico **2.** BUSINESS public relations

pr. *abbr* GRAM pronoun

praam *n* NAUT another spelling of **pram**[2]

practicable /práktikəb'l/ *adj* **1.** capable of being carried out or put into effect **2.** capable of being used successfully [Mid-17C. < French < *practiquer* 'put into practice' < medieval Latin *practica* < form of Greek *praktikos* 'practical' (see PRACTISE)]

USAGE practicable or **practical**? These two adjectives have overlapping meanings. Both indicate that something can be done, but ***practical*** also implies that it is appropriate, sensible, or useful: *It is practicable to do the calculation in the traditional way, but far more practical to use a computer.* The difference between ***impracticable*** and ***impractical*** is rather more clear-cut: ***impracticable*** means 'impossible' and ***impractical*** means 'not workable when put into practice'.

practical /práktik'l/ *adj* **1.** CONCERNED WITH MATTERS OF FACT concerned with actual facts and real life and experience, not theory ○ *the practical applications of this research* **2.** USEFUL appropriate, sensible, and likely to be effective ○ *practical advice* **3.** GOOD AT SOLVING PROBLEMS good at managing matters and dealing with problems and difficulties ○ *He's terribly clever, but not very practical.* **4.** SUITABLE FOR EVERYDAY USE plain, functional, and suitable for everyday use **5.** VIRTUAL resembling a particular thing in almost every way (*informal*) ○ *The campaign was a practical disaster.* **6.** *N Am* PRACTISING involved in the actual work of a profession or activity ○ *practical physician* ■ *n* EDUC LESSON WITH HANDS-ON ACTIVITIES a lesson or examination that requires participation in an activity such as an experiment or a medical procedure ○ *a physics practical* [Mid-16C. < late Latin *practicus* < Greek *praktikos* (see PRACTICE)]

USAGE See ***practicable.***

practicality /prákti kálləti/ (*plural* **-ties**) *n* **1.** the quality or state of being practical **2.** a practical aspect or requirement of a situation (*usually used in the plural*)

practical joke *n* a trick that is carried out on somebody to make him or her look silly and to amuse others —**practical joker** *n*

practically /práktikli/ *adv* **1.** very nearly but not quite ○ *It was practically impossible to hear what was going on because of the noise.* **2.** in a way that is useful, sensible, or practical ○ *We've got to look at this thing practically.*

practical nurse *n N Am* **1.** a nurse who has completed a level of training lower than that of a registered nurse **2.** somebody who has considerable experience of caring for people but who does not have a college degree in nursing

practical reconciliation *n Aus* the Australian Liberal federal government's approach to reconciliation with indigenous peoples, characterized by the provision of improved basic services to indigenous communities

practice /práktiss/ *n* **1.** REPETITION IN ORDER TO IMPROVE the process of repeating something many times in order to improve performance **2.** PROCESS OF CARRYING OUT AN IDEA the process of carrying out an idea, plan, or theory ○ *It's more difficult to put these ideas into practice.* **3.** WORK OF PROFESSIONAL PERSON the business of a lawyer, doctor, dentist, or other professional **4.** USUAL PATTERN OF ACTION an established way of doing something, especially one that has developed through experience and knowledge ○ *good business practices* **5.** PERFORMANCE OF RELIGION, PROFESSION, OR CUSTOMS the performance of a religion, profession, set of customs, or established habit ■ *vti* US spelling of **practise** [15C. < PRACTISE] ◇ **in practice 1.** in the real world and under everyday conditions, as opposed to in theory **2.** having recently practised or exercised a skill so as to be currently proficient ◇ **out of practice** not having recently practised or exercised a skill so as to be currently less proficient than usual

SPELLCHECK practice or **practise**? Do not confuse the spelling of ***practice*** and ***practise***, which sound similar. In British English, ***practice*** is the spelling of the noun and ***practise*** is the spelling of the verb: *Practice makes perfect. Practise what you preach.* (Note also the spelling of words derived from the verb, as in *a practising lawyer* and *a practised liar.*) In US English, ***practice*** is the usual spelling for both noun and verb.

SYNONYMS See ***habit.***

practice teaching *n N Am* same as **teaching practice**

~~practicle~~ incorrect spelling of **practical**

~~practicly~~ incorrect spelling of **practically**

practicum /práktikəm/ *n ANZ, N Am* a period of work for practical experience as part of an academic course. UK term **placement** [Early 20C. < late Latin, form of *practicus* 'active, practical' < Greek *praktikos* (see PRACTISE)]

practise /práktiss/ (**-tises, -tising, -tised**) *v* **1.** *vti* REPEAT IN ORDER TO IMPROVE to do something, especially exercises, repeatedly in order to improve performance **2.** *vt* DO SOMETHING AS CUSTOM to do something as an established custom or habit **3.** *vti* WORK IN LAW OR MEDICINE to work in a job or profession, especially law or medicine **4.** *vt* FOLLOW RELIGION to act according to the beliefs and customs of a particular religion **5.** *vt* PERPETRATE to perpetrate something morally bad such as deceit or cruelty **6.** *vi* TAKE ADVANTAGE OF SOMEBODY to take advantage of somebody, especially somebody who is gullible [14C. Directly or via French < medieval Latin *practizare*, alteration of *practicare* < Greek *praktikos* 'practical' < *prattein* 'do'] —**practiser** *n* ◇ **practise what you preach** to behave in the same way that you advise or instruct others to behave

SPELLCHECK See ***practice.***

practised /práktist/ *adj* expert in doing something because of long experience

practising /práktising/ *adj* actively involved in a particular activity such as a profession, religion, or way of life

practitioner /prak tísh'nər/ *n* **1.** somebody who practises a profession, especially medicine **2.** in Christian Science, somebody who carries out ministry and spiritual healing [Mid-16C. < obsolete *practician* < Old French *practicien* < *practiser* < medieval Latin *practizare* (see PRACTISE)]

Prado /praádō/ *n* a museum in Madrid that contains the Spanish national collection of paintings, sculptures, and drawings. It was founded by Fernando VII in 1810.

praemunire /preé myoo nī́ri, -neéri/ *n* the offence under English law of accepting the authority of some other power over that of the English crown, or an accusation to that effect [< medieval Latin *praemunire facias* 'that you warn' (words in the writ)]

praenomen /pree nṓmən/ (*plural* **-nomens** or **-nomina** /-nómminə/) *n* in ancient Rome, somebody's first name [Early 17C. < Latin, 'forename' < *nomen* 'name'] —**praenominal** /pree nómmin'l/ *adj* —**praenominally** *adv*

praesidium *n* POL another spelling of **presidium**

praetor /preétər, -tawr/, **pretor** *n* in ancient Rome, any of several magistrates ranking immediately below the consuls and acting as the chief law officers of the state [15C. < Latin] —**praetorial** /pree táwri əl/ *adj* —**praetorship** *n*

praetorian /pree táwri ən/, **pretorian** *adj* **1.** RELATING TO PRAETORS relating to praetors or to the office of praetor **2.** CORRUPT corrupt and venal (*formal*) ■ *n* ANCIENT ROMAN OF PRAETOR RANK in ancient Rome, a holder or former holder of the office of praetor

Praetorian, Pretorian *adj* belonging or relating to the Praetorian Guard ■ *n* a member of the Praetorian Guard

Praetorian Guard *n* **1.** in ancient Rome, the emperor's bodyguard **2.** a soldier of the emperor's bodyguard in ancient Rome

pragmatic /prag máttik/ *adj* **1.** CONCERNED WITH PRACTICAL RESULTS more concerned with practical results than with theories and principles **2.** PHILOSOPHY RELATING TO PHILOSOPHICAL PRAGMATISM relating to or characteristic of philosophical pragmatism **3.** LING RELATING TO PRAGMATICS relating or belonging to pragmatics **4.** POL POLITICAL relating to affairs of state (*formal*) [Late 16C. Via late Latin < Greek *pragmatikos* < *pragma* 'deed, action'] —**pragmaticality** /prag mátti kálləti/ *n* —**pragmatically** /prag máttikli/ *adv*

pragmatics /prag máttiks/ *n* the branch of linguistics that studies language use rather than language structure (*takes a singular verb*)

pragmatic sanction *n* a special decree issued by a sovereign that has the force of law

pragmatism /prágmətizəm/ *n* **1.** a straightforward practical way of thinking about things or dealing with problems, concerned with results rather than with theories and principles **2.** a philosophical view that a theory or concept should be evaluated in terms of how it works and its consequences as the standard for action and thought —**pragmatist** *n* —**pragmatistic** /prágmə tístik/ *adj*

Prague /praag/ capital city of the Czech Republic, located in the west of the country. Population: 1,178,576 (2001).

prahu *n* same as **proa**

Praia /prī́ ə/ capital city of the Republic of Cape Verde, in southeastern São Tiago Island. Population: 94,757 (1999).

prairie /práiri/ *n* a treeless grass-covered plain in the United States and Canada, especially in the Midwest and the West ■ **prairies** *npl Can* the Prairie Provinces of Manitoba, Alberta, and Saskatchewan in Canada [Late 18C. Via French < assumed Vulgar Latin *prataria* < Latin *pratum* 'meadow']

prairie chicken *n* a game bird of the grouse family that has mottled brownish feathers, the male of which has inflatable air sacs on its throat that it uses in courtship. Native to: grasslands of North America. Genus: *Tympanuchus*.

prairie dog *n* a burrowing rodent of the squirrel family with light brown fur that lives in large underground colonies. Native to: grasslands of North America. Genus: *Cynomys*.

prairie oyster *n* **1.** a drink consisting of a raw egg, Worcestershire sauce, salt, and pepper, taken as a cure for a hangover or hiccups **2.** *N Am* the fried testicle of a calf or pig, eaten as a delicacy in the Midwestern United States (*usually used in the plural*)

prairie schooner *n* a large covered wagon pulled by horses or oxen that was used by pioneers crossing the North American prairies in the 19th century

praise /prayz/ *n* **1.** EXPRESSION OF ADMIRATION words that express approval or admiration, e.g. for somebody's achievements or for something's good qualities **2.** WORSHIP worship and thanks to God or a deity (*often used in the plural*) ■ *vt* (**praises, praising, praised**) **1.** EXPRESS ADMIRATION FOR SOMEBODY OR SOMETHING to express approval or admiration for somebody or something **2.** WORSHIP GOD to give worship and thanks to God or a deity [13C. Via French < late Latin *pretiare* 'to prize' < *pretium* 'price'] —**praiser** *n* ◇ **sing somebody's** *or* **something's praises** to praise somebody or something enthusiastically ○ *She's not one to sing her own praises.*

praiseworthy /práyz wurthi/ *adj* deserving praise — **praiseworthily** *adv* — **praiseworthiness** *n*

prajna /prújnə, prúzhnə/ *n* in Buddhist teaching, direct awareness and understanding of truth not achieved by intellectual or rational means [Early 19C. < Sanskrit *prajñā* 'know directly']

Prakrit /praákrit/ *n* an Indic language belonging to a group spoken in northern India from approximately 400 BC to AD 1000. Prakrits are Indic languages that developed from Sanskrit, the most well-known being Pali. [Mid-18C. < Sanskrit *prākṛta* 'natural, vernacular' < *pra-* 'forward' + *kṛta-* 'made'] —**Prakrit** *adj*

praline /práa leen/ *n* 1. a sweet or dessert topping made of nuts caramelized in boiling sugar syrup 2. a chocolate with a soft filling made from crushed caramelized nuts, usually almonds [Early 18C. After Marshal de Plessis-*Praslin* (1598–1675), French officer]

pralltriller /práal trilər/ *n* a musical embellishment made by the quick alternation of a note with the note immediately above it [Mid-19C. < German, 'bouncing trill']

pram[1] /pram/ *n* a cot on four wheels with a handle at one end and a hood at the other, in which a baby can be transported out of doors. N Am term **baby carriage** [Late 19C. Contraction of PERAMBULATOR]

pram[2] /praam/, **praam** *n* 1. a small fishing boat with a flat bottom and a square front 2. a flat-bottomed barge used in Baltic ports [Mid-16C. Via Dutch < Czech *prám* 'raft']

prana /práanə/ *n* 1. in yoga, the practice of inhaling, holding the breath, and exhaling according to fixed patterns 2. in Hinduism, breath or breathing [Mid-19C. < Sanskrit *prāṇa* 'breathing out']

pranam /prə naám/ *n S Asia* a respectful gesture of greeting made by pressing the palms together and often followed by bending to touch the other person's feet [Mid-19C. < Hindi]

prance /praanss/ *v* (**prances, prancing, pranced**) 1. *vi* MOVE IN SPRIGHTLY MANNER to walk or move in a lively, but often exaggerated way that suggests arrogance 2. *vti* SHOW JUMPING JUMP FORWARD ON BACK LEGS to jump, or make a horse jump, forwards on its hind legs with its front legs raised 3. *vti* SHOW JUMPING WALK WITH LIVELY STEPS to walk, or make a horse walk, with lively springing steps ■ *n* PRANCING MOVEMENT a lively, springing, or carefree movement [14C. Origin ?] —**prancer** *n* —**prancing** *adj* —**prancingly** *adv*

prandial /prándi əl/ *adj* relating to a meal, especially lunch or dinner (*formal or humorous*) [Early 19C. < Latin *prandium* 'late breakfast'] —**prandially** *adv*

prang /prang/ *vt* (**prangs, pranging, pranged**) 1. CRASH SOMETHING to crash or damage a vehicle or aircraft (*informal*) 2. BOMB SOMETHING to bomb a target (*dated slang*) ■ *n* 1. CRASH a crash in a vehicle or aircraft (*informal*) 2. BOMBING RAID a bombing raid (*dated slang*) [Mid-20C. Origin ?]

prank[1] /prangk/ *n* a mischievous trick or silly stunt done for amusement [Late 16C. Origin ?] —**prankish** *adj*

prank[2] /prangk/ *vti* to embellish something or dress in an ostentatious manner (*archaic*) [Mid-16C. Probably < Middle Dutch *pronken* or Middle Low German *prunken* 'show off']

prank call *n* a digitized trick phone call or image that can be downloaded and sent to somebody's phone as a practical joke

prankster /prángkstər/ *n* somebody who enjoys playing mischievous tricks on people

~~**prarie**~~ incorrect spelling of **prairie**

prasad /prə saád/, **prasada** /prə saádə/ *n* food or other items given in offering to a Hindu deity. The food is later shared among those making the offerings. [Early 19C. < Sanskrit *prasāda* 'kindness, grace']

Prasad /prə saád/, **Rajendra** (1884–1963) first president of India (1950–62). A member of the Indian National Congress, he presided over the Constituent Assembly (1946–49) before becoming president.

prase /práyz/ *n* a green form of quartz [Late 18C. Via French < Greek *prasios* 'leek-coloured' < *prason* 'leek']

praseodymium /práyzi ō dímmi əm/ *n* a soft ductile silvery metallic element belonging to the rare-earth group. Use: alloys, colouring for glass. Symbol **Pr**.

See table at **element** [Late 19C. < Greek *prasios* 'leek-coloured' (see PRASE)]

prat /prat/ *n* 1. FOOL somebody regarded as unintelligent (*slang insult*) 2. BOTTOM the buttocks (*slang*) ■ *vi* (**prats, pratting, pratted**) BEHAVE THOUGHTLESSLY OR EXASPERATINGLY to behave in an unintelligent way, especially when this causes exasperation or leads to time-wasting (*insult*) [Mid-16C. Origin ?]

prate /prayt/ *vi* (**prates, prating, prated**) to talk in a silly way and at length about nothing important ■ *n* silly or idle talk [15C. < Middle Dutch *praten*] —**prater** *n* —**pratingly** *adv*

pratfall /prát fawl/ *n N Am* (*slang*) 1. a backward fall onto the buttocks, especially one executed deliberately for comic effect 2. an embarrassing or humiliating mistake or failure

pratie /práyti/ *n Ireland* FOOD same as **potato** (*informal*) [Late 18C. < Irish *prátai*, plural of *práta*]

pratincole /prátting kōl/ *n* a brown or grey bird with long pointed wings, a forked tail, and a short beak. Native to: Europe, Africa, Asia. Family: Glareolidae. [Late 18C. < modern Latin *pratincola* < Latin *pratum* 'meadow' + *incola* 'dweller']

pratique /pra teék/ *n* permission granted to a ship or boat to use a port on satisfying the local quarantine regulations or on producing a clean bill of health [Early 17C. < French, 'practice']

prattle /prátt'l/ *vi* (**-tles, -tling, -tled**) to talk in a silly, idle, or childish way ■ *n* silly, idle, or childish talk [Mid-16C. Origin ?] —**prattler** *n* —**prattlingly** *adv*

prau *n* SAILING same as **proa**

pravastatin /právvə státtin/ *n* a drug used to reduce unusually high levels of blood cholesterol [Mid-20C. < *pra-* + *vastatin*, INN stem]

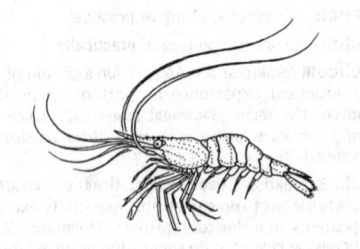

prawn

prawn /prawn/ *n* an edible sea animal resembling a shrimp, with a slender body, a long tail, five pairs of legs, and two pairs of pincers. Genera: *Palaemon* or *Penaeus*. ■ *vi* (**prawning, prawned**) to fish for prawns [15C. Origin ?] —**prawner** *n* ◇ **come the raw prawn** *Aus* to try to deceive or mislead someone, usually by acting or pleading innocent (*informal*)

prawn cocktail *n* cooked and shelled prawns in a seafood dressing, usually served in a small bowl or glass with salad garnish and eaten cold as a starter

prawn cracker *n* a light and puffy prawn-flavoured snack food resembling a crisp, made from rice flour and often served with a Chinese meal as an appetizer

praxis /práksiss/ *n* (*formal*) 1. the practical side and application of something such as a professional skill, as opposed to its theory 2. established custom or habitual practice [Late 16C. Via medieval Latin < Greek, 'action, custom, behaviour' < *prattein* 'do']

Praxiteles /prak síttə leez/ (390?–330? BC) Greek sculptor. Apart from *Hermes with the Infant Dionysus*, his work is known only in the form of Roman copies.

pray /pray/ *v* (**prays, praying, prayed**) 1. *vti* RELIG SPEAK TO GOD to speak to God, a deity, or a saint, e.g. in order to give thanks, express regret, or ask for help 2. *vti* HOPE STRONGLY to hope strongly for something ○ *I'm just praying that it won't rain on Saturday.* 3. *vti* ADDRESS EARNEST REQUEST TO SOMEBODY to ask somebody for something, especially earnestly or with passion ○ *He prayed to be allowed to go back home to his family.* 4. *vt* ATTEMPT TO GET SOMETHING ACHIEVED to attempt to achieve something by prayer or by wishing very

hard ○ *The villagers tried to pray the drought away.* ■ *interj* EMPHASIZING QUESTION OR COMMAND used to emphasize a question or a command, either politely or sarcastically (*dated or humorous*) ○ *And what, pray, do you think you're doing?* [13C. Via Old French *preier* < Latin *precari* 'entreat' < *prec-* 'prayer']

prayer /prair/ *n* 1. ADDRESS TO GOD a spoken or unspoken address to God, a deity, or a saint. It may express praise, thanksgiving, confession, or a request for something such as help or somebody's wellbeing. 2. ADDRESSING OF GOD the act or practice of making spoken or unspoken addresses to God, a deity, or a saint ○ *kneeling in prayer* 3. RELIG same as **prayers** 4. SOMETHING WISHED FOR something that is wanted or hoped for very much ○ *My only prayer is that it doesn't last too long.* ■ *prayers npl* RELIGIOUS SERVICE a religious service at which prayers are said ○ *attended evening prayers at seven* [13C. Via Old French *preiere* < Latin *precarius* 'obtained by entreaty' < *precari* (see PRAY)] ◇ **not have a prayer** to have not even a slight chance of achieving something ○ *I don't have a prayer of getting the manager's job.*

prayer beads *npl* a string of beads used to keep count of prayers being recited, e.g. a rosary

prayer book *n* a book containing the prayers regularly used in religious services

prayerful /práirf'l/ *adj* 1. RELIG PRAYING FREQUENTLY liking to pray or praying frequently 2. RELIG INFLUENCED BY PRAYER strongly influenced by or involving prayer 3. EARNEST earnest or sincere —**prayerfully** *adv* —**prayerfulness** *n*

prayer mat *n* ISLAM same as **prayer rug**

Prayer over the Gifts *n* in the Roman Catholic Mass, a variable prayer said at the conclusion of the Preparation of the Gifts and before the Preface. Former name **the Secret**

prayer rug, **prayer mat** *n* a rug on which a Muslim kneels to pray

prayer shawl *n* JUDAISM same as **tallith**

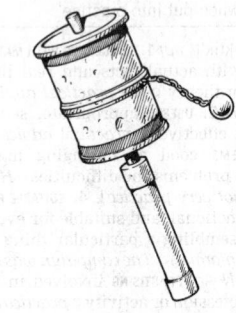

prayer wheel

prayer wheel *n* in Tibetan Buddhism and some other religions, a hollow cylinder containing prayers written on a scroll. It that must be turned, by hand or machinery, to make the prayers effective.

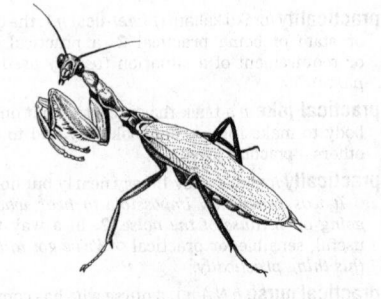

praying mantis

praying mantis /práying-/ *n* a large greenish-brown predatory insect with long forelegs that are raised and folded at rest, as if in prayer. Native to: Europe. Latin name: *Mantis religiosis.* See illustration on previous page

PRB *abbr* Pre-Raphaelite Brotherhood (*used after the name of a painter*)

PRC *abbr* People's Republic of China

Pré ➧ **du Pré, Jacqueline**

pre- *prefix* **1.** before, earlier ○ *preschool* ○ *predate* **2.** in advance, preparatory ○ *presell* ○ *prerelease* **3.** in front of ○ *premolar* [< Latin *prae* 'in front, before' < Indo-European]

preadolescence *n*
preadolescent *n, adj*
preagricultural *adj*
preannounce *vt*
preapprove *vt*
prearrange *vt*
prearrangement *n*
preassemble *vt*
preassign *vt*
preauthorized *adj*
prebake *vt*
prebiblical *adj*
preblended *adj*
prebreakfast *adj*
pre-Buddhist *adj*
pre-Celtic *adj*
pre-Christian *adj*
pre-Christmas *adj*
pre-Civil War *adj*
preclassical *adj*
precollege *adj*
precolonial *adj*
preconsonantal *adj*
preconstructed *adj*
preconvention *adj*
precook *vt*
precooked *adj*
precool *vt*
precrash *adj*
precreation *n*
precut *adj*
predawn *adj*
predecimal *adj*
predefine *vt*
predefined *adj*
predesignate *vt*
predesignation *n*
predinner *adj*
predyed *adj*
pre-election *adj*
pre-erect *vt*
pre-establish *vt*
pre-exist *vti*
pre-existence *n*
prefight *adj*
prefilled *adj*
preflight *adj, vt, n*
prefocused *adj*
prefrozen *adj*
pregame *adj*
preganglionic *adj*
preglacial *adj*
preheat *vt*
preheater *n*
prehominid *adj, n*
prehuman *adj*
preimpressionism *n*
preimpressionist *n*
pre-Inca *adj*
pre-Incan *adj*
preindependence *adj, adv*
preindustrial *adj*
preinterview *adj*
preinvasion *adj*
prekindergarten *adj*
prelaunch *adj*
prelogical *adj*
prelunch *adj*
premade *adj*
premanufacture *vt*
prematch *adj*
premating *adj*
premeal *adj*
premigration *n*
premix *n, vt*
premodern *adj*
prenotification *n*
prenotify *vt*
pre-Olympian *adj*
preorder *vt*
preorganization *n*
preowned *adj*
prepacked *adj*
preperformance *adj*
prepill *adj*
preplan *vt*
preprepared *adj*
prepubertal *adj*
prepuberty *n*
prepublication *adj*
prepurchase *vt*
prequalification *n*
prequalify *vi*
prerace *adj*
prereading *adj*
pre-Reformation *adj*
preregister *vti*
preregistration *n*
prerelease *n, adj*
pre-Renaissance *adj*
preretirement *n*
prerevolutionary *adj*
pre-Roman *adj*
preromantic *n*
prescientific *adj*
prescore *vti*
prescreen *vt*
preseason *n*
preselect *vt*
preselection *n*
preshow *adj*
preshrink *vt*
presignify *vt*
presoak *vt, n*
pre-Socratic *adj*
presort *vt*
presurgery *adj*
pretape *vt*
pretax *adj*
pretheatre *adj*
pretournament *adj*
pretreat *vt*
pretreatment *n*
pretrial *adj*
pre-university *adj*
prewarn *vt*
prewire *vt*
prewrap *vt*

preach /preech/ (**preaches, preaching, preached**) *v* **1.** *vti* RELIG **GIVE SERMON** to give a talk on a religious or moral subject, especially in church **2.** *vi* **GIVE ADVICE IN IRRITATING WAY** to give advice on morality or behaviour in an irritatingly tedious or overbearing way **3.** *vt* **URGE PEOPLE TO ACCEPT IDEA** to make an opinion or attitude known to others and urge others to share it ○ *preached restraint in the midst of chaos* [13C. Via Old French *prechier* < Latin *praedicare* (see PREDICATE)] —**preachable** *adj*

preacher /préechər/ *n* (*informal*) **1. MINISTER** somebody whose occupation is to give sermons, preach the gospel, or conduct religious services, especially a minister of a Protestant church **2. SOMEBODY GIVING ADVICE ON MORALS** somebody who gives advice on morality or behaviour in an irritatingly tedious or overbearing way **3. SOMEBODY URGING ACCEPTANCE OF IDEA** somebody who makes an opinion or attitude known to others and urges them to share it

preachify /préechi fī/ *vi* to preach or give advice on morality or behaviour in an irritatingly tedious or overbearing way (*informal*) —**preachifying** *n*

preachment /préechmənt/ *n* (*informal*) **1.** a sermon or talk on a moral or religious subject **2.** tedious or overbearing advice on morals or behaviour

preachy /préechi/ *adj* giving, or in the habit of giving, advice on morality or behaviour in an irritatingly tedious or overbearing way (*informal*) —**preachiness** *n*

preadaptation /pree áddap táysh'n/ *n* an anatomical or behavioural feature of an organism that is highly suited to an adjacent habitat, thus allowing for migration and increased survival rate in response to environmental change. The lungs that have developed in some fish were probably originally buoyancy aids, but became used for breathing air. —**preadapt** /-ə dápt/ *vti* —**preadapted** *adj* —**preadaptive** /-ə dáptiv/ *adj*

preamble /pree ámb'l/ *n* **1.** a section at the beginning of a speech, report, or formal document that introduces what follows **2.** something that precedes, introduces, or leads up to something else ○ *high winds as a preamble to a winter storm* [14C. < French *préambule* < late Latin *praeambulus* 'going in front' < Latin *ambulare* 'to walk']

preamplifier /pree ámpli fīər/ *n* an amplifying circuit, e.g. in a radio or television, that is designed to strengthen very weak signals and then transmit them to a more powerful amplifier

prebend /prébbənd/ *n* **1.** an allowance paid by a cathedral or collegiate church to a member of its clergy, or the property or tithe that is the source of this allowance **2.** CHR same as **prebendary 3.** the position of prebendary in the Church of England [15C. Via French < late Latin *praebenda* 'things to be supplied' < Latin *praebere* 'offer', literally 'hold in front'] —**prebendal** *adj*

prebendary /prébbəndəri/ (*plural* **-ies**) *n* a member of the clergy of a cathedral or collegiate church, either one who receives an allowance from it or an honorary member who receives no payment —**prebendaryship** *n*

prebiotic /prée bī óttik/ *n* a dietary supplement in the form of nondigestible carbohydrate that favours the growth of desirable microflora in the large bowel

Precambrian /pree kámbri ən/ *n* the period of geological time, 4,650 to 700 million years ago, during which the Earth's crust consolidated and primitive life first appeared —**Precambrian** *adj*

precancel /pree kánss'l/ *vt* (**-cels, -celling, -celled**) to cancel the postage stamp on an envelope before posting it ■ *n* a stamp that has been cancelled before posting, or an item bearing such a stamp —**precancellation** /pree kánssə láysh'n/ *n*

precancerous /pree kánssərəss/ *adj* describes conditions or tissue anomalies that are capable of becoming cancerous if left untreated

precarious /pri káiri əss/ *adj* **1.** dangerously unstable, unsteady, uncertain, or insecure **2.** based on uncertain premises or unwarranted assumptions (*formal*) [Mid-17C. < Latin *precarius* 'depending on entreaty, uncertain'] —**precariously** *adv* —**precariousness** *n*

precast /prée kaast/ *adj* poured into a cast of the required shape and allowed to harden before being taken out and put into position ○ *buildings made entirely of precast concrete* —**precast** *vt*

precatory /prékətəri/ *adj* expressing a wish, request, entreaty, or recommendation (*formal*) [Mid-17C. < late Latin *precatorius* < Latin *precari* 'entreat' (see PRAY)]

precaution /pri káwsh'n/ *n* **1.** an action taken to protect against possible harm or trouble or to limit the damage if something goes wrong ○ *wearing a hat as a precaution against sunstroke* **2.** the foresight to protect against possible harm or trouble or to limit the damage if something goes wrong [Late 16C. Via French < late Latin *precaution-* < Latin *precaut-*, past participle of *praecavere*, literally 'take care before' < *cavere* 'take heed'] —**precautional** *adj* —**precautionary** *adj* —**precautious** *adj*

precede /pri séed/ (**-cedes, -ceding, -ceded**) *vt* **1.** to come, go, be, or happen before somebody or something else in time, position, or importance **2.** to say or do something before something else [14C. Via French < Latin *praecedere* 'go before' < *cedere* 'give way']

SPELLCHECK precede or **proceed**? Do not confuse the spelling of ***precede*** and ***proceed***, which sound similar. The verb ***precede*** has the prefix *pre-* ('before') and means 'come or go before': *March precedes April.* The verb ***proceed*** has the prefix *pro-* ('forward') and means 'begin or continue with an action' or 'progress': *She proceeded to explain what had gone wrong.*

---

precedence /préssidənss/, **precedency** /-dənssi/ *n* **1. PRIORITY** the right or need to be dealt with before somebody or something else or to be treated as more important than somebody or something else ○ *The interests of the rest of the group take precedence over any personal wishes.* **2. RELATIVE IMPORTANCE** a relative importance in rank and status that determines something such as the order in which participants are placed in a formal situation **3. GREATER IMPORTANCE** the fact of being more important than others (*formal*)

precedent *n* /préssidənt/ **1. EXAMPLE FOR LATER ACTION OR DECISION** an action or decision that can be used subsequently as an example for a similar decision or to justify a similar action **2. ESTABLISHED PRACTICE** an established custom or practice **3.** LAW **REQUIREMENT TO FOLLOW EARLIER COURT DECISIONS** the doctrine that requires a court to follow decisions of superior or previous courts ■ *adj* /préssidənt, pri séed'nt/ **PRECEDING** coming, going, existing, or happening before somebody or something else (*formal*) —**precedently** *adv*

preceding /pri seeding/ *adj* coming, going, existing, or happening immediately before somebody or something else

~~**preceed**~~ incorrect spelling of **precede**

~~**precence**~~ incorrect spelling of **presence**

precentor /pri séntər/ *n* **1. LEADER OF CHURCH SINGING** a leader of the congregation or choir in a church **2.** CHR **LEADER OF CATHEDRAL MUSIC** a member of the clergy of a cathedral who is nominally in charge of the music in the cathedral **3.** *Scotland* **OFFICIAL SINGER IN SOME PRESBYTERIAN CHURCHES** in small Presbyterian denominations that disapprove of instrumental music in church, an official appointed by the Kirk Session to lead the singing by singing lines for the congregation to repeat [Early 17C. < Latin *praecentor* < *praecinere*, literally 'sing before' < *canere* 'sing'] —**precentorship** *n*

precept /prée sept/ *n* **1. PRINCIPLE** a rule, instruction, or principle that guides somebody's actions, especially one that guides moral behaviour (*formal*) **2. WARRANT OR WRIT** a warrant or writ that is issued by a legal authority **3. ORDER FOR PAYMENT** an order for the payment of money [14C. < Latin *praeceptum* 'something taught', < past participle of *praecipere* 'teach', literally 'take before' < *capere* 'take']

preceptive /pri séptiv/ *adj* giving instructions or orders, or setting out rules or principles (*formal*) —**preceptively** *adv*

preceptor /pri séptər/ *n* **1.** EDUC **TEACHER** a teacher or instructor (*formal*) **2.** MED **SPECIALIZED TUTOR** a specialist in a profession, especially medicine, who gives practical training to a student **3.** HIST **HEAD OF PRECEPTORY** the head of a community of Knights Templars —**preceptoral** *adj* —**preceptorate** *n* —**preceptorship** *n*

preceptory /pri séptəri/ (*plural* **-ries**) *n* a community of Knights Templars

precess /pri séss/ (**-cesses, -cessing, -cessed**) *vti* to spin with a motion in which the axis of rotation describes a cone, or make something spin in this way [Late 19C. Back-formation < PRECESSION]

precession /pri sésh'n/ *n* the regular motion of a spinning body such as a spinning top or a planet, in which the axis of rotation describes a cone [Late 16C. < late Latin *praecession-* < Latin *praecess-*, past

participle of *praecedere* 'go before' (see PRECEDE)] —**precessional** *adj*

precession of the equinoxes *n* the slow westward movement of the equinoxes, resulting from the Earth's precessional motion, making them occur slightly earlier each year

precinct /préé singkt/ *n* **1.** SPECIAL PART OF TOWN a part of a town designated for a particular use, especially an area accessible only to pedestrians or a purpose-built area containing many shops ○ *a shopping precinct* **2.** *US* PUBLIC ADMIN CITY AREA PATROLLED BY POLICE UNIT a district of a city or town under a particular unit of the police force **3.** *US* PUBLIC ADMIN POLICE UNIT OR STATION the police unit or police station of a city or town district **4.** *N Am* POL ELECTORAL DISTRICT a small electoral district of a city or town, forming part of a ward **5.** BOUNDARY a boundary marking out an area ■ **precincts** *npl* AREA AROUND SOMETHING the area surrounding a building or institution such as a cathedral or college [15C. < medieval Latin *praecinctum* 'something encircled', < past participle of Latin *praecingere* 'gird about' < *cingere* 'gird']

preciosity /préshi óssəti/ (*plural* **-ties**) *n* ridiculous overrefinement in language or manners, or an example of this ○ *It might be quite a good poem if all the preciosities were removed.* [14C. Via French < Latin *pretiositas* < *pretiosus* 'precious' (see PRECIOUS)]

precious /préshəss/ *adj* **1.** VALUABLE worth a great deal of money **2.** VALUED highly valued, much loved, or considered to be of great importance ○ *Your friendship is very precious to me.* **3.** NOT TO BE WASTED rare or unique and therefore to be used wisely or sparingly or treated with care **4.** USED FOR EMPHASIS used for emphasis to express irritation, dislike, contempt, bemusement, or some other strong emotion (*informal*) ○ *I'm tempted to tell them what they can do with their precious training course!* **5.** FASTIDIOUS OR AFFECTED too carefully refined in language, dress, or manners ■ *adv* VERY very ○ *And precious little thanks I got!* ■ *n* TERM OF ENDEARMENT used as term of affection in talking to somebody ○ *Good morning, my precious.* [13C. Via French < Latin *pretiosus* < *pretium* 'price'] —**preciously** *adv* —**preciousness** *n*

precious coral *n* MARINE BIOL same as **red coral**

precious metal *n* gold, silver, or platinum, usually when found in the natural state

precious stone *n* a relatively rare and valuable mineral used in jewellery, e.g. a diamond or ruby

precipice /préssəpiss/ *n* **1.** a high, vertical, or very steep rock face **2.** a very dangerous situation [Late 16C. Directly or via French < Latin *praecipitium* < *praecipit-* 'headlong' (see PRECIPITATE)] —**precipiced** *adj*

precipitant /pri síppitənt/ *adj* **1.** TOO HASTY done too quickly and impulsively, often resulting in mistakes **2.** SUDDEN OR UNEXPECTED happening suddenly or unexpectedly ■ *n* CHEM SOMETHING CAUSING PRECIPITATION a substance that causes precipitation [Early 17C. < French *précipitant*, present participle of *précipiter* < Latin *praecipitare* (see PRECIPITATE)] —**precipitancy** *n* —**precipitantly** *adv*

precipitate *adj* /pri síppi tayt, -tət/ **1.** DONE OR ACTING RASHLY done or acting too quickly and without enough thought ○ *I may have been precipitate in accepting their offer.* **2.** HURRIED very hurried ○ *made a precipitate departure* **3.** SUDDEN sudden and unexpected ■ *v* /pri síppi tayt/ (**-tates, -tating, -tated**) **1.** *vt* MAKE SOMETHING HAPPEN QUICKLY to make something happen suddenly and quickly **2.** *vt* SEND SOMEBODY OR SOMETHING RAPIDLY to send somebody or something suddenly and rapidly into a particular state or condition ○ *A minor border skirmish precipitated the two countries into war.* **3.** *vti* THROW OR FALL FROM ABOVE to throw somebody or something from a great height, or fall from a great height (*formal*) **4.** *vti* METEOROL MAKE RAIN OR SNOW FALL to cause liquid or solid forms of water, condensed in the atmosphere, to fall to the ground as rain, snow, or hail, or fall in such a form **5.** *vti* CHEM SEPARATE SOLID OUT OF SOLUTION to cause a solid to separate out from a solution as a result of a chemical reaction, or separate out in this way ■ *n* /pri síppi tət, -tayt/ CHEM SUSPENSION OF SMALL PARTICLES a suspension of small solid particles that are formed in a solution as a result of a chemical reaction and usually settle out of the solution [Early 16C. < Latin *praecipitat-*, past participle of *praecipitare* 'throw down' < *praeceps* 'headlong' < *caput* 'head'] —**precipitable** *adj* —**precipitately** *adv* —**precipitateness** *n* —**precipitative** *adj* —**precipitator** *n*

precipitation /pri síppi táysh'n/ *n* **1.** RAIN, SNOW, OR HAIL rain, snow, or hail, all of which are formed by condensation of moisture in the atmosphere and fall to the ground **2.** FORMATION OF RAIN, SNOW, OR HAIL the formation of rain, snow, or hail from moisture in the air **3.** FORMATION OF SUSPENSION IN SOLUTION the formation of a suspension of an insoluble compound by mixing two solutions **4.** HASTE great or excessive haste (*formal*) ○ *He deeply regretted the precipitation of his resignation from the position.* **5.** HASTENING OF SOMETHING the act of making something happen earlier or more suddenly than expected (*formal*) ○ *circumstances that led to the precipitation of my decision to resign* **6.** THROWING DOWN OF SOMEBODY OR SOMETHING the throwing of somebody or something from a great height (*formal*)

precipitin /pri síppitin/ *n* an antibody that, when combined with its antigen, forms a substance that separates out of solution and can be detected visually [Early 20C. < PRECIPITATE]

precipitinogen /pri síppi tinnəjən/ *n* an antigen that causes the formation of a specific precipitin. This reaction can be used to identify an unknown antigen.

precipitous /pri síppitəss/ *adj* **1.** DONE RASHLY done or acting too quickly and without enough thought **2.** GEOG LIKE PRECIPICE very high and steep ○ *precipitous mountain slopes* **3.** GEOG WITH PRECIPICES having a number of precipices ○ *precipitous terrain* [Mid-17C. < French *précipiteux* < Latin *praecipitium* < *praecipit-* 'headlong' (see PRECIPITATE)] —**precipitously** *adv* —**precipitousness** *n*

précis /práy see/ *n* (*plural* **précis**) a shortened version of a speech or written text, containing the main points and omitting minor details ■ *vt* (**précis, précising** /-seeing/, **précised** /-seed/) to make a précis of something [Mid-18C. < French, 'abridged']

precise /pri síss/ *adj* **1.** EXACT OR DETAILED exact and accurate, or detailed and specific ○ *The train leaves an hour from now, or 57 minutes, to be precise.* **2.** HANDLING SMALL DETAILS able to assimilate details or wanting to be given details **3.** INDICATING SOMETHING SPECIFIC indicating that something is the exact one that is being referred to ○ *At that precise moment, in he came.* **4.** CAREFUL ABOUT DETAILS very careful about small details, especially of correct behaviour **5.** CLEAR distinct and correct ○ *a very precise speaker* [Early 16C. Via French < Latin *praecisus*, past participle of *praecidere* 'cut off in front' < *caedere* 'cut'] —**preciseness** *n*

precisely /pri síssli/ *adv* **1.** EXACTLY used to indicate that something is stated exactly ○ *That is precisely what I mean.* **2.** IN DETAIL in complete and accurate detail ○ *Tell me precisely what happened.* **3.** ACCURATELY with absolute accuracy ○ *instruments that must be adjusted precisely before use* **4.** CLEARLY clearly and distinctly ○ *She speaks very precisely.* **5.** USED FOR EMPHASIS used to add emphasis when specifying something ○ *It was precisely because you didn't ask that she thought you didn't need her help.* **6.** EXPRESSING AGREEMENT used to indicate complete agreement with what has been said ○ *'But I don't think they can be relied on'. 'Precisely'.*

precisian /pri sízh'n/ *n* somebody who is concerned about correct rules and behaviour, especially in moral and religious matters (*formal*) —**precisianism** *n*

precision /pri sízh'n/ *n* **1.** EXACTNESS exactness or accuracy **2.** MATHS ACCURACY IN CALCULATION the accuracy to which a calculation is performed, specifying the number of significant digits with which the result is expressed ■ *adj* RELATING TO EXACTNESS OR ACCURACY allowing for, made with, or requiring great exactness or accuracy ○ *precision instruments* [Late 16C. Via French < Latin *praecision-* < *praecis-*, past participle of *praecidere* (see PRECISE)]

preclinical /pree klínnik'l/ *adj* relating to or characteristic of a disease before the symptoms become evident —**preclinically** *adv*

preclude /pri klóod/ (**-cludes, -cluding, -cluded**) *vt* **1.** to prevent something from happening or somebody from doing something ○ *That shouldn't preclude a satisfactory outcome.* **2.** to exclude somebody or something, especially in advance ○ *Having a relative in the company precludes me from entering the contest.* [Early 17C. < Latin *praecludere* 'close off ahead' < *claudere* 'close'] —**preclusion** /-klóozh'n/ *n* —**preclusive** /-klóossiv/ *adj* —**preclusively** *adv*

precocial /pri kósh'l/ *adj* describes some animals that display independent activity at birth, especially young birds that are hatched covered with down and with open eyes [Late 19C. < modern Latin *Praecoces* 'precocial birds' < plural of Latin *praecoc-* 'precocious' (see PRECOCIOUS)]

precocious /pri kóshəss/ *adj* **1.** developed or mature, especially mentally, at an unusually early age, or showing such advanced development **2.** describes a plant or tree that blossoms before its leaves appear or that produces fruits only a few years after planting [Mid-17C. < Latin *praecoc-* 'ripening early', literally 'cooked ahead' < *coquere* 'to cook'] —**precociously** *adv* —**precociousness** *n* —**precocity** /pri kóssəti/ *n*

precognition /préé kog nísh'n/ *n* **1.** the ability to know what is going to happen in the future, especially if based on extrasensory perception **2.** in Scotland, an official investigation of the facts of a case by interrogating witnesses in preparation for a trial, to make it possible to prepare a relevant charge in defence. This is done by the procurator fiscal. —**precognitive** /pree kógnitiv/ *adj*

pre-Columbian *adj* relating to North, Central, or South America before the arrival of Christopher Columbus in 1492

preconceived /préé kən séévd/ *adj* formed in the mind in advance, especially if based on little or no information or experience and reflecting personal prejudices —**preconceive** *vt*

preconception /préé kən sépsh'n/ *n* an idea or opinion formed in advance, especially if it is based on little or no information or experience and reflects personal prejudices

preconcert /pree kónssərt/ (**-certs, -certing, -certed**) *vt* to agree, arrange, or organize something beforehand (*archaic*)

precondition /préé kən dísh'n/ *n* something that must be done or agreed before something else can happen ○ *They made a total ceasefire a precondition of the talks.* ■ *vt* (**-tions, -tioning, -tioned**) to prepare somebody or something for a process, or put somebody into a desired mental state

preconize /préékə nīz/ (**-izes, -izing, -ized**), **preconise** (**-ises, -ising, -ised**) *vt* **1.** PROCLAIM SOMETHING to proclaim or announce something (*formal*) **2.** SUMMON SOMEBODY to summon somebody publicly (*formal*) **3.** CHR GIVE PAPAL APPROVAL TO BISHOP in the Roman Catholic Church, to make a public announcement of papal approval of the appointment of a bishop [15C. < medieval Latin *praeconizare* < Latin *praecon-* 'public crier'] —**preconization** /préékə nī záysh'n/ *n*

preconscious /pree kónshəss/ *n* in Freudian theory, the part of the mind lying between the conscious and the unconscious. It contains information, thoughts, and feelings that are not present in conscious awareness but can readily be brought into the conscious mind. ■ *adj* relating to or contained in the preconscious —**preconsciously** *adv* —**preconsciousness** *n*

precontract *n* /pree kón trakt/ CONTRACT MADE IN ADVANCE a contract made in advance to prevent a subsequent contract, especially a betrothal ■ *vti* /pree kən trákt/ (**-tracts, -tracted, -tracting**) **1.** MAKE CONTRACT IN ADVANCE to make a contract or enter into an agreement in advance **2.** PLEDGE SOMEBODY IN MARRIAGE in former times, to pledge somebody to marriage by an earlier agreement, or be pledged in this way

precritical /pree kríttik'l/ *adj* relating to the time or state before a crisis or before something such as a disease reaches a critical condition

precursor /pri kúrssər/ *n* **1.** SOMEBODY OR SOMETHING THAT COMES EARLIER somebody or something that comes before, and is often considered to lead to the development of, another person or thing **2.** PREVIOUS HOLDER OF JOB somebody who held a position or job before somebody else **3.** CHEM CHEMICAL COMPOUND PRECEDING ANOTHER a chemical compound that leads to another, usually more stable, product in a series of connected reactions [Early 16C. < Latin *praecursor* < *praecurs-*, stem of *praecurrere* 'run before' < *currere* 'run']

precursory /pree kúrssri, pri-/, **precursive** /-kúrssiv/ *adj* **1.** at an initial or preparatory stage **2.** serving as an indication of something to come (*formal*)

predacious /pri dáyshəss/, **predaceous** *adj* **1.** describes animals that hunt, kill, and eat other animals (*technical*) **2.** attacking and stealing from other people (*formal*) [Early 18C. < Latin *praedari* 'seize as plunder' (see PREDATORY)] —**predaciousness** *n* —**predacity** /pri dássəti/ *n*

predate /prée dáyt/ (**-dates, -dating, -dated**) *vt* **1.** to come before somebody or something else in time **2.** to put a date on something that is earlier than the actual date, or say that something occurred at an earlier date than it actually did

predation /pri dáysh'n/ *n* **1.** the relationship between two groups of animals in which one species hunts, kills, and eats the other **2.** the act of plundering, stealing, or destroying [15C. < Latin *praedation-* < *praedari* 'seize as plunder' (see PREDATORY)]

predator /préddətər/ *n* **1. CARNIVOROUS ANIMAL OR DESTRUCTIVE ORGANISM** a carnivorous animal that hunts, kills, and eats other animals in order to survive, or any other organism that behaves in a similar manner **2. SOMEBODY WHO PLUNDERS OR DESTROYS** a person, group, company, or state that steals from others or destroys others for gain **3. RUTHLESSLY AGGRESSIVE PERSON** an aggressive, determined, or persistent person [Early 20C. < Latin *praedator* < *praedari* 'seize as plunder' (see PREDATORY)]

predatory /préddətəri/ *adj* **1. RELATING TO PREDATORS** relating to or characteristic of animals that survive by preying on others **2. GREEDILY DESTRUCTIVE** greedily eager to steal from or destroy others for gain **3. RUTHLESSLY AGGRESSIVE** extremely aggressive, determined, or persistent [Late 16C. < Latin *praedatorius* < *praedari* 'seize as plunder' < *praeda* 'booty'] —**predatorily** *adv* —**predatoriness** *n*

predatory pricing *n* the act of setting prices at very low levels in order to force other companies out of the market

predecease /préedi seéss/ (**-ceases, -ceasing, -ceased**) *vt* to die before somebody else ○ *His eldest son predeceased him.* —**predecease** *n*

predecessor /préedi sessər/ *n* **1.** somebody who held a position or job before somebody else **2.** a thing previously in use or existence that has been replaced or succeeded by another ○ *I hope my new car will be more reliable than its predecessor.* **3.** same as **ancestor** (*archaic*) [14C. Via French < late Latin *praedecessor* 'somebody who has departed before' < Latin *decedere* 'depart']

predella /pri déllə/ *n* **1.** the platform for an altar, or the step on which an altar rests **2.** the decorative base of an altarpiece, embellished with small paintings or sculptures [Mid-19C. < Italian, 'stool']

predestinarian /prée desti náiri ən/ *n* somebody who believes in predestination ■ *adj* relating to predestination or to people who believe in it —**predestinarianism** *n*

predestinate /pree désti nayt/ *vt* (**-nates, -nating, -nated**) RELIG same as **predestine** ■ *adj* **1.** decided in advance **2.** in some religious beliefs, decided and decreed in advance by God, a deity, or fate [14C. < ecclesiastical Latin *praedestinat-*, past participle of *praedestinare* (see PREDESTINE)]

predestination /pree désti náysh'n/ *n* **1. ADVANCE DECISION BY GOD ABOUT EVENTS** in some religious beliefs, the doctrine that God, a deity, or fate has established in advance everything that is going to happen and that nothing can change this **2. GOD'S DECISION WHO GOES TO HEAVEN** in some religious beliefs, the doctrine that God decided at the beginning of time who would go to heaven after death and who would not **3. ACT OF FOREORDAINING** the human or supposedly divine act of deciding the fate of people or things beforehand

predestine /pree déstin/ (**-tines, -tining, -tined**) *vt* **1.** to decide in advance what is going to happen **2.** in some religious beliefs, to select in advance who will go to heaven after death and who will not [14C. Directly or via French < ecclesiastical Latin *praedestinare* 'foreordain' < Latin *destinare* 'decree'] —**predestinable** *adj*

predetermine /prée di túrmin/ (**-mines, -mining, -mined**) *vt* **1.** to decide, agree, or arrange something in advance ○ *at a predetermined place* **2.** to ordain something in advance (*usually used in the passive*) ○ *Are our lives predetermined?* —**predeterminate** *adj* —**predetermination** /prée di túrmi náysh'n/ *n* —**predeterminative** *adj*

predeterminer /prée di túrminər/ *n* a word that precedes and qualifies another determiner, as 'both' does in 'both my hands'

predicable /préddikəb'l/ (*formal*) *adj* able to be stated, or able to be said about somebody or something ■ *n* a quality or attribute by which somebody or something can be described [Mid-16C. < medieval Latin *praedicabilis* < Latin *praedicare* (see PREDICATE)] —**predicability** /préddikə bílləti/ *n*

predicament /pri díkəmənt/ *n* **1.** a difficult, unpleasant, or embarrassing situation from which there is no clear or easy way out **2.** in logic, a category or class that can be assigned to something [14C. < late Latin *praedicamentum* 'class, category' (translation of Greek *katēgoria*) < Latin *praedicare* 'proclaim' (see PREDICATE)]

predicant /préddikənt/ *adj* relating to or involved in preaching (*formal*) ■ *n* **1.** a member of a religious order, especially the Dominicans, that has a commitment to preaching **2.** *S Africa* CHR same as **predikant** [Late 16C. < Latin *praedicant-*, present participle of *praedicare* 'declare publicly', (in ecclesiastical Latin) 'preach' (see PREDICATE)]

predicate *n* /préddikət/ **1.** GRAM **PART OF SENTENCE EXCLUDING SUBJECT** a word or combination of words, including the verb, objects, or phrases governed by the verb that make up one of the two main parts of a sentence **2.** LOGIC **EVERYTHING IN SENTENCE EXCLUDING NAMES** everything in a simple sentence other than names, e.g. 'runs' in 'Lee runs' and 'is taller than' in 'Lee is taller than Glen' **3.** LOGIC **SOMETHING AFFIRMED OR DENIED** something that is affirmed or denied about something else ■ *vt* /préddi kayt/ (**-cates, -cating, -cated**) **1. BASE SOMETHING ON SOMETHING** to base an opinion, an action, or a result on something (*formal*) ○ *predicated on reason* **2. STATE SOMETHING** to state or assert something (*formal*) **3. IMPLY SOMETHING** to imply or suggest something (*formal*) **4.** LOGIC **ASSERT SOMETHING ABOUT SUBJECT OF STATEMENT** to assert or affirm something about the subject of a statement **5.** LOGIC **MAKE EXPRESSION PREDICATE OF STATEMENT** to make an expression or term the predicate of a statement [Mid-16C. < late Latin *praedicatum* < past participle of Latin *praedicare* 'declare publicly', literally 'declare before' < *dicare* 'declare, state'] —**predication** /préddi káysh'n/ *n*

predicate calculus *n* the branch of symbolic logic that uses symbols to explore relationships between and within propositions

predicative /pri díkətiv/ *adj* **1. FORMING PREDICATE** describes an adjective or noun that forms all or part of the predicate of a sentence. In 'I am happy', 'happy' is predicative, whereas in 'a happy face' it is 'attributive'. **2.** GRAM **STATING SOMETHING** describes a use of the verb 'to be' that makes a statement about the subject of the sentence **3.** LOGIC **ACTING AS PREDICATE** acting as a logical predicate [Mid-19C. < Latin *praedicativus* < past participle of *praedicare* (see PREDICATE)] —**predicatively** *adv*

predict /pri díkt/ (**-dicts, -dicting, -dicted**) *vti* to say what is going to happen in the future, often on the basis of present indications or past experience [Mid-16C. < Latin *praedict-*, past participle of *praedicere* 'say in advance' < *dicere* 'say'] —**predictor** *n*

predictable /pri díktəb'l/ *adj* **1.** happening or turning out in the way that might have been expected or predicted **2.** rarely or never behaving or happening in an unusual or unexpected way —**predictability** /pri díktə bílləti/ *n* —**predictably** *adv*

prediction /pri díksh'n/ *n* **1.** a statement of what somebody thinks will happen in the future **2.** the making of a statement or forming of an opinion about what will happen in the future

predictive /prə díktiv/ *adj* relating to the forecasting of a likely result or outcome ○ *a predictive medical test* —**predictively** *adv* —**predictiveness** *n*

predictive text entry *n* digital technology that anticipates the word a computer or mobile phone user is in the process of keying

predigest /prée dī jést, -di-/ (**-gests, -gesting, -gested**) *vt* **1.** to treat food with chemicals or enzymes so that it is more easily digested, especially for people with digestion problems **2.** to produce information in a simplified form so that it is easy to understand —**predigestion** /-jésch'n/ *n*

predikant /préddikənt/ (*plural* **-kants** or **-cants**) *n S Africa* a minister of the Dutch Reformed Church [Early 19C. < Dutch < Latin *praedicant-* (see PREDICANT)]

predilection /préedi léksh'n/ *n* a special liking or preference for something [Mid-18C. < French *prédilection* < medieval Latin *praediligere* 'love above others' < Latin *diligere* 'to love']

predispose /préedi spṓz/ (**-poses, -posing, -posed**) *vt* (*formal*) **1.** to make somebody feel favourably about somebody or something else in advance **2.** to make somebody liable or inclined to do something such as catch an illness or behave in a particular way ○ *Her fair skin predisposes her to sunburn.* —**predisposal** *n*

predisposition /prée dispə zísh'n/ *n* **1. FAVOURABLE ATTITUDE OR INCLINATION** a favourable attitude towards somebody or something, or an inclination to do something **2. LIABILITY TO SOMETHING** a liability or tendency to do something such as behave in a particular way **3.** MED **TENDENCY TO DEVELOP DISEASE** a susceptibility to a disease, arising from a hereditary or other factor

prednisolone /pred níssə lōn/ *n* a synthetic steroid hormone, similar to cortisone. Use: treatment of allergies, suppression of inflammatory diseases. [Mid-20C. < PREDNISONE, by insertion of -OL[1]]

prednisone /préddni sōn/ *n* a synthetic steroid hormone produced from cortisone. Use: treatment of allergies and autoimmune diseases. [Mid-20C. Blend of *pregnane*, a synthetic hydrocarbon + DIENE + CORTISONE]

predoctoral /pree dóktərəl/ *adj* relating to or involving research or studies that will lead to a doctorate

predominant /pri dómminənt/ *adj* **1.** commonest or greatest in number or amount ○ *a predominant shellfish species in the estuary* **2.** most important, powerful, or influential ○ *gave the predominant reason for instituting an embargo* —**predominance** *n*

predominantly /pri dómminəntli/ *adv* in the greatest number or amount

predominate /pri dómmi nayt/ (**-nating, -nated**) *v* **1.** *vi* **BE IN MAJORITY** to be the most common or greatest in number or amount **2.** *vi* **BE MORE IMPORTANT** to have greater importance, power, or influence than others **3.** *vt* **DOMINATE SOMEBODY OR SOMETHING** to dominate or control somebody or something [Late 16C. < medieval Latin *predominat-*, past participle of *predominari* 'rule over' < Latin *dominari* 'rule'] —**predominately** /-dóminətli/ *adv* —**predomination** /-dommi náysh'n/ *n* —**predominator** *n*

~~**predominately**~~ incorrect spelling of **predominantly**

pre-eclampsia /prée i klámpsi ə/ *n* a potentially dangerous condition that may develop in late pregnancy and may lead to convulsions if not treated. Symptoms are high blood pressure, fluid retention, excessive weight gain, and the presence of protein in the urine.

pre-embryo /pree émbri ō/ *n* a fertilized ovum before implantation in the womb and before differentiation of embryonic tissue —**pre-embryonic** /prée embri ónnik/ *adj*

preemie /préemi/, **premie** *n N Am* a premature baby born before it is fully developed, usually before 35 weeks of gestation (*informal*) [Early 20C. < shortening of PREMATURE]

pre-eminent /pri émminənt/ *adj* standing out among all others because of superiority in a field or activity [15C. < Latin *praeeminent-*, present participle of *praeeminere* 'stand out in front' < *eminere* 'stand out'] —**pre-eminence** *n* —**pre-eminently** *adv*

pre-empt /pri émpt/ (**-empts, -empting, -empted**) *v* **1.** *vt* **ACT TO PREVENT SOMETHING** to do something that makes it pointless or impossible for somebody else to do what he or she intended **2.** *vt N Am* **OCCUPY SOMETHING** to occupy public land in order to have the right to buy it later **3.** *vt* **REPLACE SOMETHING** to take the place of something, especially of something less important **4.** *vi* CARDS **MAKE BID THAT BLOCKS OTHERS** in bridge, to make a bid intended to prevent further

bidding [Mid-19C. Back-formation < PRE-EMPTION] —**pre-emptor** *n* —**pre-emptory** *adj*

pre-emption /pri émpsh'n/ *n* **1.** ACTION PREVENTING SOMETHING action that makes it pointless or impossible for somebody else to do what he or she intended **2.** *N Am* OCCUPATION OF PUBLIC LAND the occupation of public land in order to have the right to buy it later, or the right to buy that is gained in this way **3.** OPTION TO BUY PROPERTY an option to purchase property if and when it is put up for sale **4.** MIL STRATEGY OF FIRST ATTACK the strategy of attacking an enemy in order to prevent that enemy from attacking first [Early 17C. < medieval Latin *praeemption-* < *praeempt-*, past participle of *praeemere* 'buy first' < Latin *emere* 'buy']

pre-emptive /pri émptiv/ *adj* **1.** DONE BEFORE OTHERS CAN ACT done before somebody else has had an opportunity to act so as to make his or her planned action pointless or impossible **2.** MIL INTENDED TO PREVENT ATTACK intended to eliminate or lessen an enemy's capacity to attack ○ *a pre-emptive strike* **3.** CARDS PREVENTING FURTHER BIDDING in bridge, intended to prevent further bidding [Late 18C. < medieval Latin *praeempt-* (see PRE-EMPTION)] —**pre-emptively** *adv*

pre-emptive right *n* a right to be offered first refusal in selling or buying an asset

~~preemptory~~ incorrect spelling of **peremptory**

preen[1] /preen/ (**preens, preening, preened**) *vti* **1.** GROOM FEATHERS WITH BEAK to clean, smooth, or arrange the feathers with the beak (*refers to birds*) **2.** GROOM FUR WITH TONGUE to clean and smooth the fur by licking it (*refers to a furred mammal*) **3.** CARE EXCESSIVELY FOR PERSONAL APPEARANCE to spend a long or excessive time attending to personal appearance, especially making small finishing touches to the hair, the face, or clothes ○ *busy preening in front of the mirror* **4.** SHOW SELF-SATISFACTION to feel excessively self-satisfied and display that feeling by gloating [15C. Probably < Old French *proignier* 'to prune'] —**preener** *n*

preen[2] /preen/ *n* **1.** a decorative pin or brooch **2.** *Scotland* a pin for holding or securing fabric [Old English *prēon* < Germanic]

pre-engineered /prée enji neérd/ *adj* constructed using prefabricated parts

pre-enjoyed *adj US* previously owned or used (*often used euphemistically*)

pre-exilian /prée ig zílli ən, -ik zílli ən/ *adj* relating to or occurring in the period before the exile of the Jews to Babylon in the 6th century BC

pref. *abbr* **1.** preface **2.** prefatory **3.** preference **4.** preferred **5.** GRAM prefix

prefab /prée fab/ (*informal*) *n* a prefabricated house or building ■ *adj* relating to or constructed from prefabricated parts [Mid-20C. Shortening]

prefabricate /pree fábbri kayt/ (**-cates, -cating, -cated**) *vt* **1.** to manufacture sections of something, especially a building, that can be transported to a site and easily assembled there **2.** to produce something in an unoriginal or standardized way —**prefabrication** /pree fábbri káysh'n/ *n* —**prefabricator** *n*

preface /préffəss/ *n* **1.** INTRODUCTORY PART OF TEXT an introductory section at the beginning of a book or speech that comments on aspects of the text such as the writer's intentions ○ *in the preface to the second edition* **2.** PRELIMINARY ACTION an action or event that precedes something more important **3.** *also* **Preface** CHR PRAYER DURING MASS a prayer said by a priest during Mass, especially the prayer that begins 'Lift up your hearts' **4.** *also* **Preface** CHR PRAYER FOR PARTICULAR PURPOSE in the Roman Catholic Church, a prayer used for a particular purpose ■ *vt* (**-aces, -acing, -aced**) **1.** INTRODUCE SOMETHING WITH PREFACE to introduce an action, speech, or piece of writing with something ○ *He prefaced his remarks with an apology.* **2.** SERVE AS INTRODUCTION TO SOMETHING to act as a preface to an action, speech, or piece of writing [14C. Via French < medieval Latin *praefatia* < Latin *praefat-*, past participle of *praefari* 'say before' < *fari* 'speak']

prefaded /pree fáydid/ *adj* given an artificially faded, worn, or old appearance ○ *prefaded denim* —**prefade** *vt*

prefatory /préffətəri/ *adj* serving to introduce something such as a main body of text or a speech ○ *prefatory remarks introducing the Prime Minister* [Late 17C. < Latin *praefat-* (see PREFACE)] —**prefatorily** *adv*

prefect /prée fekt/ *n* **1.** EDUC PUPIL ASSISTING WITH DISCIPLINE a senior pupil who is given some authority over other pupils in matters of discipline **2.** PUBLIC ADMIN HIGH-RANKING ADMINISTRATIVE OFFICIAL the highest official in an administrative district (**department**) or former territorial possession of France or in an administrative region of Italy **3.** POLICE FRENCH CHIEF OF POLICE the head of a French police force, especially in Paris **4.** ANCIENT HIST ROMAN MAGISTRATE OR COMMANDER a senior administrative or military official in ancient Rome **5.** CHR SENIOR MASTER AT JESUIT SCHOOL a senior master or administrator with special responsibilities at a Jesuit school or college [14C. Via French < Latin *praefectus* 'overseer' < past participle of *praeficere* 'set over' < *facere* 'make'] —**prefectorial** /prée fek táwri əl/ *adj*

prefecture /prée fekchər/ *n* **1.** DISTRICT UNDER PREFECT'S JURISDICTION the district over which a prefect has jurisdiction **2.** OFFICE OF PREFECT the office or authority of a prefect **3.** PREFECT'S RESIDENCE the official residence of a prefect in countries such as France or Italy —**prefectural** /pree fékchərəl/ *adj*

prefer /pri fúr/ (**-fers, -ferring, -ferred**) *vt* **1.** LIKE SOMEBODY OR SOMETHING BETTER to like or want somebody or something more than somebody or something else ○ *I prefer tea to coffee.* **2.** LAW LAY CHARGE BEFORE COURT to make a charge against somebody by submitting details of the alleged offence to a court, magistrate, or judge for examination, or prosecute such a charge ○ *preferred charges against the accused* **3.** LAW GIVE PRIORITY TO SOMEBODY to give priority to one person, especially a creditor, over others **4.** PROMOTE SOMEBODY to promote somebody to a higher position or rank (*archaic*) [14C. Via French *préferer* < Latin *praeferre* 'put before' < *ferre* 'carry, bear']

preferable /préffərəb'l/ *adj* more likely to be enjoyable, useful, or desired than somebody or something else —**preferability** /préffərə bílləti/ *n*

preferably /préffərəb'li/ *adv* used to specify more exactly what is required or desired ○ *Plan to arrive early, preferably before the rush hour.*

~~preferance~~ incorrect spelling of **preference**

~~prefered~~ incorrect spelling of **preferred**

preference /préffərənss/ *n* **1.** SELECTION OF SOMEBODY OR SOMETHING the view that one person, object, or course of action is more desirable than another, or a choice based on such a view ○ *The judges showed a marked preference for representational art.* **2.** SOMEBODY OR SOMETHING PREFERRED a person, object, or course of action that is more desirable than another, or the state of being that desirable choice ○ *State your preferences clearly.* **3.** RIGHT TO EXPRESS CHOICE the right or opportunity to choose a person, object, or course of action that is considered more desirable than another ○ *We exercised our preference.* **4.** LAW PRIORITY OF ONE CREDITOR OVER OTHERS priority given to a creditor, e.g. when a debtor goes bankrupt, or the right of one creditor to receive payment before others **5.** COMM FAVOURITISM IN INTERNATIONAL TRADE priority given to a particular country or group of countries in international trade ■ **preferences** *npl* POL VOTES UNDER PREFERENTIAL VOTING SYSTEM votes assigned to second or third choice candidates, and so on, under the preferential voting system, e.g. in Australia ■ *v Aus* ALLOCATE VOTES in an election run under the preferential voting system, to allocate your preferential votes to a particular party

preference shares *npl* shares whose holders are the first to receive dividends from available profit. Preference shares are redeemed before ordinary shares when a company is liquidated. N Am term **preferred stock**

preferential /préffə rénsh'l/ *adj* **1.** giving advantage or priority to a person or group ○ *preferential treatment* **2.** giving advantage or priority to a country or group of countries in international trade —**preferentialism** *n* —**preferentialist** *adj* —**preferentiality** /préffə rénshi álləti/ *n* —**preferentially** *adv*

preferential voting *n* an electoral system used in some countries such as Australia, in which voters indicate their chosen candidates in order of preference

preferment /pri fúrmənt/ *n* (*formal*) **1.** appointment to a higher position or rank, especially in the church **2.** an office, appointment, or position of high rank or honour, especially one that brings social advancement or financial reward

preferred stock /pri fúrd-/ *n N Am* FIN same as **preference shares**

prefiguration /prée figə ráysh'n/ *n* (*formal*) **1.** a representation, often in form or likeness, of a person, thing, or event that is to come **2.** somebody or something that represents, often in form or likeness, a person, thing, or event that is to come

prefigure /pree fíggər/ (**-ures, -uring, -ured**) *vt* **1.** to represent, often in form or likeness, a person, thing, or event that is to come ○ *designs that prefigured modern architecture* **2.** to think about or imagine a person, thing, or event in advance [15C. < ecclesiastical Latin *praefigurare* 'depict beforehand' < Latin *figura* 'figure'] —**prefigurative** *adj* —**prefiguratively** *adv* —**prefigurement** *n*

prefix[1] /prée fiks/ *n* **1.** WORD ELEMENT BEGINNING VARIOUS WORDS a linguistic element that is not an independent word, but is attached to the beginning of a word to modify its meaning. For example, 'un-' is a prefix meaning 'not'. **2.** TITLE BEFORE SOMEBODY'S NAME a title before somebody's name, e.g. the prefix 'The Honourable' before an MP's full name **3.** SOMETHING PRECEDING SOMETHING ELSE something that comes before something else, e.g. a fixed group of digits at the beginning of a telephone number ■ *vt* (**-fixes, -fixing, -fixed**) **1.** PUT SOMETHING BEFORE SOMETHING ELSE to place something in front of something else ○ *You must prefix the number with the area code.* **2.** INTRODUCE SOMETHING WITH SOMETHING ELSE to say or do something by way of introduction to something else ○ *His requests for money were usually prefixed by an apology.* **3.** ADD PREFIX TO WORD to attach a prefix at the beginning of a word in order to alter its meaning [Mid-17C. Via French < Latin *praefixum* < past participle of *praefigere* 'fix in front' < *figere* 'fasten'] —**prefixal** /prée fiks'l, prée fíks'l/ *adj* —**prefixally** *adv* —**prefixation** /prée fik sáysh'n/ *n* —**prefixion** /pree fíksh'n/ *n*

prefix[2] /pree fíks/ (**-fixes, -fixing, -fixed**) *vt* to decide on something such as a price, date, or meeting place beforehand ○ *They duly arrived at the prefixed hour.* [15C. < French *préfixer* < Latin *praefix-*, past participle of *praefigere* (see PREFIX[1])]

preform /pree fáwm/ (**-forms, -forming, -formed**) *vt* **1.** to shape or form something beforehand **2.** to give something a preliminary shape —**preformation** /prée fawr máysh'n/ *n*

prefrontal /pree frúnt'l/ *adj* **1.** relating to or situated in the foremost part of the brain **2.** located in front of the frontal bone

prefrontal lobotomy *n* a surgical operation in which the nerves connecting the front part of the brain (**prefrontal lobe**) to the thalamus are severed. Prefrontal lobotomy was formerly a method of reducing severe emotional disturbances, but the operation had serious side effects.

preggers /préggərz/ *adj* BIOL same as **pregnant** (*informal*) [Mid-20C. Alteration]

pregnable /prégnəb'l/ *adj* able to be captured or attacked [15C. < Old French < stem of *prendre* 'take' < Latin *prehendere* 'seize'] —**pregnability** /prégnə bílləti/ *n*

pregnancy /prégnənssi/ (*plural* **-cies**) *n* **1.** CONDITION OF BEING PREGNANT the physical condition of a woman or female animal carrying unborn offspring inside her body, from fertilization to birth **2.** INSTANCE OF BEING PREGNANT an individual occurrence or experience of being pregnant **3.** TIME OF CARRYING UNBORN OFFSPRING the period during which a woman or female animal carries unborn offspring inside her body, from fertilization to birth **4.** SIGNIFICANCE importance or fullness of meaning ○ *the pregnancy of his words*

pregnant /prégnənt/ *adj* **1.** CARRYING OFFSPRING WITHIN BODY carrying unborn offspring inside the body **2.** SIGNIFICANT full of meaning or importance ○ *After a pregnant pause, the general began briefing the media on the surprise attack.* **3.** FULL OF SOMETHING pervaded by something, usually something intangible **4.** CREATIVE full of creative power ○ *the child's pregnant imagination* **5.** PRODUCTIVE producing a lot of useful results ○ *It was a pregnant endeavour, yielding much experience, information, and help.* [15C. Directly or via French *preignant* < Latin *praegnant-*, alteration of *praegnat-*, probably < *prae-* 'before' + *gnatus* 'born'] —**pregnantly** *adv*

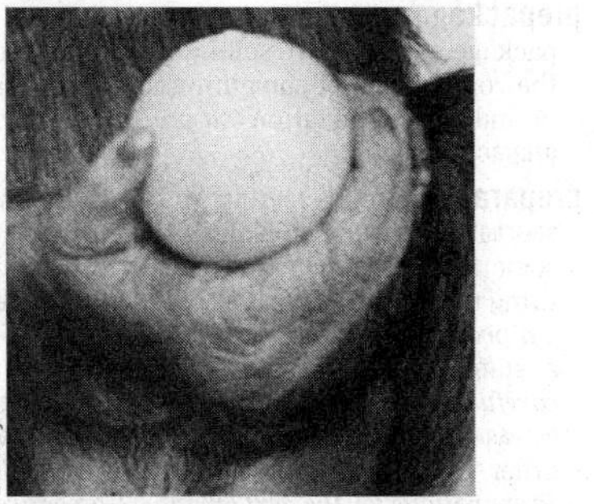
Barnaby's

prehensile: chimpanzee grasping a ball

prehensile /pri hén sīl/ *adj* **1. ABLE TO GRASP SOMETHING** able to take hold of things, especially by wrapping around them ○ *The monkey has a prehensile tail.* **2. QUICK TO UNDERSTAND** skilled at grasping ideas and concepts **3. AGGRESSIVELY EAGER** excessively eager for gain or profit [Late 18C. < French *préhensile* < Latin *prehens-*, past participle of *prehendere* 'seize'] —**prehensility** /prée hen sílləti/ *n*

ORIGIN The Latin word *prehendere* 'to seize', from which ***prehensile*** is derived, is also the source of English *apprehend, apprentice, comprehend, comprise, impregnable, prey, prison, reprehend, reprieve,* and *surprise.*

prehension /pri hénsh'n/ *n* (*formal*) **1. ACT OF FIRMLY GRASPING** the act of firmly taking hold of something **2. PERCEIVING OF SOMETHING THROUGH SENSES** the perception by the senses of a sight, sound, smell, taste, or texture **3. COMPREHENSION** the process of understanding [Mid-16C. < Latin *prehension-* < *prehens-* (see PREHENSILE)]

prehistoric /prée hi stórrik/, **prehistorical** /-stórrik'l/ *adj* **1. BEFORE RECORDED HISTORY** relating to the period before history was first recorded in writing **2.** LING **RELATING TO LANGUAGE BEFORE WRITING** relating or belonging to a language before it was recorded in writing **3. VERY OLD OR OLD-FASHIONED** very old, old-fashioned, or out of date ○ *prehistoric views about nutrition* —**prehistorically** *adv*

prehistory /pree hístəri/ *n* **1. HISTORY BEFORE WRITTEN WORD** the period before history was first recorded in writing **2. STUDY OF PREHISTORIC PERIOD** the study of the prehistoric period using archaeological evidence **3. EVENTS LEADING UP TO SOMETHING** the events and circumstances preceding an event or situation —**prehistorian** /prée hi stáwri ən/ *n*

preignition /prée ig nísh'n/ *n* ignition of fuel in an internal-combustion engine before the spark has been generated, causing inefficient operation. Preignition may be caused by a hot spot in the cylinder. —**preignite** *vti*

prejudge /pree júj/ (**-judges, -judging, -judged**) *vt* to judge a person, issue, or case before sufficient evidence is available [Late 16C. Via French *préjuger* < Latin *praejudicare* < *judicare* 'to judge'] —**prejudger** *n* —**prejudgment** *n*

prejudice /préjjōōdiss/ *n* **1. OPINION FORMED BEFOREHAND** a preformed opinion, usually an unfavourable one, based on insufficient knowledge, irrational feelings, or inaccurate stereotypes **2. HOLDING OF ILL-INFORMED OPINIONS** the holding of preformed opinions based on insufficient knowledge, irrational feelings, or inaccurate stereotypes **3. IRRATIONAL DISLIKE OF SOMEBODY** an unfounded hatred, fear, or mistrust of a person or group, especially one of a particular religion, ethnicity, nationality, sexual preference, or social status **4.** LAW **DISADVANTAGE OR HARM** disadvantage or harm caused to somebody or something ■ *vt* (**-dices, -dicing, -diced**) **1. MAKE SOMEBODY PREJUDGE SOMEBODY OR SOMETHING** to make somebody form an opinion about somebody or something in advance, especially an irrational one, based on insufficient knowledge **2. AFFECT SOMEBODY OR SOMETHING ADVERSELY** to cause harm or disadvantage to somebody or something [13C. Via French < Latin *praejudicium* 'judgment in advance' < *judicium* 'judgment'] —**prejudiced** *adj* ◇ **without prejudice** without doing any harm to any legal right or claim that somebody has (*formal*)

prejudicial /préjjōō dísh'l/ *adj* **1.** causing disadvantage or harm to somebody or something **2.** leading to the formation of prejudiced ideas or opinions —**prejudicially** *adv*

prelacy /préləssi/ (*plural* **-cies**) *n* **1.** the office or position of a prelate in the Christian church **2.** prelates considered as a group [14C. Via Anglo-Norman < medieval Latin *prelatia* < *praelatus* (see PRELATE)]

prelapsarian /prée lap sáiri ən/ *adj* relating to or belonging to the biblical time before Adam and Eve lost their innocence in the Garden of Eden [Late 19C. < PRE- + Latin *lapsus* 'sin, fall']

prelate /préllət/ *n* a high-ranking member of the Christian clergy, e.g. an abbot, bishop, or cardinal [13C. Via French < medieval Latin *praelatus*, < past participle of Latin *praeferre* (see PREFER)] —**prelatic** /pri láttik/ *adj*

prelature /prélləchər/ *n* CHR same as **prelacy**

prelibation /prée lī báysh'n/ *n* same as **foretaste** (*archaic*) [Early 16C. < Latin *praelibation-* < *praelibare* 'taste beforehand' < *libare* 'pour out']

prelim /prée lim/ *n* **1. PRELIMINARY CONTEST** a preliminary contest or event (*informal*) **2.** *Scotland* **SCOTTISH SCHOOL EXAMINATION** in Scotland, a school examination taken to prepare students for a public examination (*informal*) **3. UNIVERSITY EXAM** the first public examination in some universities ■ **prelims** *npl* **BOOK FRONT MATTER** the initial pages of a book, including the title page and table of contents, that precede the main text (*informal*) [Late 19C. Shortening of PRELIMINARY]

preliminary /pri límminəri/ *adj* **COMING BEFORE SOMETHING** occurring before and leading up to something, especially an event of greater size and importance ■ *n* (*plural* **-ies**) **1. INTRODUCTORY OR PREPARATORY ACTIVITY** something said or done before something else, often by way of introduction to or preparation for something of greater size and importance (*often used in the plural*) **2. INTRODUCTORY CONTEST** a sporting contest held before the main event, especially in boxing or wrestling **3. ELIMINATORY CONTEST** an eliminatory contest to select the finalists in a sporting competition **4.** EDUC **PREPARATORY EXAMINATION** a test that prepares students for a subsequent examination of greater difficulty and importance [Mid-17C. Directly or via French < modern Latin *praeliminaris* < Latin *limen* 'threshold'] —**preliminarily** *adv*

preliterate /pree líttərət/ *adj* describes a society that has not yet developed a written language ■ *n* a member of a society with no written language —**preliteracy** /pree líttərəssi/ *n*

preloved /pree lúvd/ *adj NZ* previously owned or used (*informal; euphemistic*) ○ *a preloved car*

prelude /préllyood/ *n* **1.** MUSIC **INTRODUCTORY PIECE OF MUSIC** a piece of music that introduces or precedes another one **2.** MUSIC **FREE-STANDING PIECE OF MUSIC** a short musical composition, often one for piano, and often forming part of a set of such works **3. INTRODUCTORY EVENT OR OCCURRENCE** an event or action that introduces or precedes something else, especially something longer and more important ■ *v* (**-udes, -uding, -uded**) **1.** *vti* **ACT AS PRELUDE TO SOMETHING** to act as an introduction to something else, especially something that is longer and more important **2.** *vt* **INTRODUCE SOMETHING WITH PRELUDE** to precede something, especially a piece of music, with a prelude [Mid-16C. Directly or via French *prélude* < medieval Latin *praeludium* < Latin *praeludere* 'play before' < *ludere* 'play'] —**prelusive** /pri lóossiv/ *adj* —**prelusively** *adv* —**prelusorily** /-lóossərəli/ *adv* —**prelusory** /-lóossəri/ *adj*

CULTURAL NOTE ***The Prelude***, a poem (1805) by William Wordsworth. Planned as a preface to a never-completed philosophical poem called *The Recluse*, this autobiographical account of the poet's intellectual and spiritual development was published posthumously (1850) in a revised form. Rejecting contemporary rationalist philosophies, it proclaims Wordsworth's faith in the redeeming power of poetry and the imagination.

prem /prem/ *n* a premature baby (*informal*) [Mid-20C. Shortening of PREMATURE]

premarital /pree márrit'l/ *adj* occurring or existing before marriage

premature /prémməchər/ *adj* **1.** occurring, existing, or developing earlier than is expected, normal, or advisable ○ *It would be premature to suggest that there is a link between these events.* **2.** born before completing the normal gestation period, or, for a human infant, weighing less than 2.5 kg/5 lb 8 oz at birth [Early 16C. < Latin *praematurus* 'ripening too early' < *maturus* 'ripe'] —**prematurely** *adv* —**prematurity** /prémmə chóorəti/ *n*

premaxilla /prée mak síllə/ (*plural* **-lae** /-lee/) *n* either of two bones that form the front part of the upper jaw in vertebrates and that bear the incisors. In humans, it merges with the rest of the maxilla during embryonic development. —**premaxillary** *adj*

premed /pree méd/ (*informal*) *n* **1.** MED same as **premedication 2.** *N Am* a student in a premedical programme **3.** *Aus, N Am* a premedical course of study ○ *majoring in premed* ■ *adj* same as **premedical** [Mid-20C. Shortening]

premedical /pree méddik'l/ *adj* relating to or engaged in the course of studies that somebody must complete before entering medical school —**premedically** *adv*

premedication /prée medi káysh'n/ *n* **1.** the practice of giving drugs to a patient before a general anaesthetic to relieve anxiety, diminish body reactions to pain, or improve postoperative comfort **2.** the drugs given to a patient in premedication

premeditate /pri méddi tayt/ (**-tates, -tating, -tated**) *v* **1.** *vt* to plan or devise something, especially a crime, in advance **2.** *vti* to consider or think carefully about something beforehand [Mid-16C. < Latin *praemeditat-*, past participle of *praemeditari* 'think about beforehand' < *meditare* (see MEDITATE)] —**premeditated** *adj* —**premeditative** *adj* —**premeditator** *n*

premeditation /pri méddi táysh'n/ *n* **1.** the act of thinking about and planning a crime beforehand, rather than acting on impulse in a moment of passion or mindlessness **2.** the act of thinking about something before doing it [15C. Directly or via French < Latin *praemeditation-* < *praemeditat-* (see PREMEDITATE)]

premenopausal /prée menō páwz'l/ *adj* describes the stage in a woman's life just before the onset of the menopause, or a woman at this stage. Such a woman is still menstruating, but may show some signs of the menopause, e.g. irregular menstrual periods.

premenstrual /pree ménstruəl/ *adj* relating to, or occurring in, the days immediately before the start of a woman's menstrual period

premenstrual syndrome *n* a group of symptoms such as nervous tension, irritability, tenderness of the breasts, and headache, experienced by some women in the days preceding menstruation and caused by hormonal changes

premie *n N Am* MED another spelling of **preemie** (*informal*)

premier /prémmi ər/ *adj* **1. BEST OR MOST IMPORTANT** first in importance, size, or quality **2. COMING FIRST** happening or existing first ■ *n* **1. PRIME MINISTER** a prime minister or head of government **2. LEADER OF AUSTRALIAN STATE GOVERNMENT** the head of government of an Australian state or territory **3. LEADER OF CANADIAN PROVINCE** the governmental head of a Canadian province ■ **premiers** *npl Aus* **WINNERS OF SPORTING CHAMPIONSHIP** in Australian Rules football, rugby league, and some other sports, the winners of the premiership [15C. Via French < Latin *primarius* 'foremost' (see PRIMARY)]

premier danseur /prémm yay daaN súr/ (*plural* **premiers danseurs** /*pronunc. same*/) *n* the principal man dancer in a ballet company [Early 19C. < French, 'first (male) dancer']

premiere /prémmi air/ *n* **1. FIRST PUBLIC PERFORMANCE** the first public performance or showing of something such as a play or film **2. LEADING WOMAN ACTOR** the principal woman performer in a theatre company ■ *v* (**-mieres, -miering, -miered**) **1.** *vti* **PRESENT OR BE PRESENTED AS PREMIERE** to perform, show, or broadcast a play, film, or similar piece of work publicly for the first time, or be publicly performed for the first time ○ *The film premiered in Britain.* **2.** *vi* **GIVE FIRST PUBLIC PERFORMANCE** to appear on stage or screen for the first time, especially in a leading role ○ *Not many young performers get to premiere on Broadway.* ■ *adj* **BEST OR MOST IMPORTANT** first in importance, quality, or size [Mid-20C. < French, feminine form of *premier* 'foremost' (see PREMIER)]

première danseuse /prémm yair daaN sőz/ (*plural* **premières danseuses** /*pronunc. same*/) *n* the principal

woman dancer in a ballet company [Early 19C. < French, 'first (female) dancer']

premiership /prémmi ərship/ *n* **1.** the office or position of a premier **2.** a championship in some sports such as football and rugby, or the competition to decide this

premillennial /prée mi lénni əl/ *adj* relating to or occurring in the period immediately before a millennium —**premillennially** *adv*

premillennialism /prée mi lénni əlizəm/ *n* the belief that Jesus Christ will return for the Last Judgment just before the one-thousand-year reign of peace (**millennium**) mentioned in the Bible —**premillenarian** /prée milə náiri ən/ *adj, n* —**premillennialist** *n*

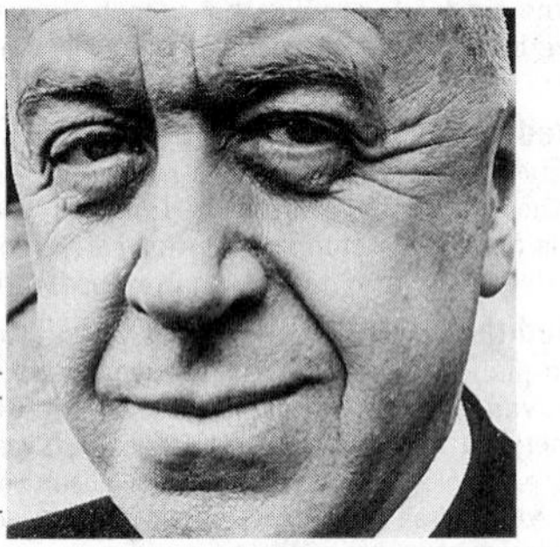

Express Newspapers

Otto Preminger

Preminger /prémminjər/, **Otto** (1906–86) Austrian-born US film director, producer, and actor. His films include *Laura* (1944), *Carmen Jones* (1954), and *Exodus* (1960). Full name **Preminger, Otto Ludwig**

premise /prémmiss/, **premiss** *n* **BASIS OF ARGUMENT** a proposition that forms the basis of an argument or from which a conclusion is drawn ○ *I question the premise on which your whole theory is based.* ■ *v* (**-ises, -ising, -ised**) **1.** *vt* **BASE SOMETHING ON SOMETHING** to base something on the foundation of a proposition or idea, stated or assumed to be true ○ *a budget premised on growth not stability* **2.** *vti* **PROPOSE AS PREMISE** to put forward a proposition as a premise in an argument **3.** *vt* **SAY SOMETHING BY WAY OF INTRODUCTION** to state something in advance to introduce or explain what follows (*formal*) [14C. Via French < medieval Latin *praemissa (propositio)* '(the proposition) set before' < past participle of *praemittere* 'set in front' < *mittere* 'send']

premises /prémmissiz/ *npl* **1. LAND AND BUILDINGS** a piece of land and the buildings on it **2. PART OR ALL OF BUILDING** a building or part of a building, especially when used for commercial purposes **3.** LAW **MATTERS PREVIOUSLY MENTIONED** matters previously stated or referred to in a legal document such as a deed [15C. < medieval Latin *praemissa* 'things stated at the beginning' (see PREMISE)]

premiss *n* LOGIC another spelling of **premise**

premium /préemi əm/ *n* **1. COST OF INSURANCE** the sum of money paid, usually at regular intervals, for an insurance policy ○ *My insurance premium went up as a result of the accident.* **2. ADDITIONAL SUM** a sum of money paid in addition to a normal wage, rate, price, or other amount **3. PRIZE** an award or prize given, e.g. to the winner of a competition **4. INDUCEMENT TO BUY** a gift or reduced price offered as an incentive to purchase another product or service ○ *The manufacturer offered premiums, in the form of free merchandise, for every purchase of a new car.* **5. AMOUNT ABOVE PAR VALUE** the amount above its nominal value at which something, especially a security, sells **6. COST OF SECURITIES OPTION** the sum or cost at which a securities option is bought or sold **7. FEE FOR INSTRUCTION** a fee paid for training or apprenticeship in a profession or trade **8.** *US* **EXTRA CHARGE FOR BORROWING MONEY** an amount charged in addition to interest on a loan ■ *adj* **1. HIGH-QUALITY** of very high quality **2. UNUSUALLY HIGH** higher than normal, especially in price ○ *premium petrol prices* [Early 17C. < Latin *praemium* 'reward' < *prae-* 'before' + *emere* 'take, buy'] ◇ **at a premium 1.** much in demand and therefore difficult to obtain **2.** selling for a high price, or for a higher price than usual, because of scarcity ◇ **put a premium on** to place a high value on somebody or something

Premium Bond, **Premium Savings Bond** *n* a savings bond issued by the Treasury and purchased by the public, on which no interest is paid. Instead, there are monthly draws for cash prizes.

premolar /pree mṓlər/ *n* either of two teeth on each side of both jaws that lie immediately behind the canines and in front of the molars and are used for grinding and chewing —**premolar** *adj*

premonition /prémmə nísh'n/ *n* **1.** a strong feeling, without a rational basis, that something is going to happen **2.** an advance warning about a future event [Mid-16C. Directly or via French < late Latin *praemonition-* < Latin *praemonere* 'forewarn' < *monere* 'warn'] —**premonitorily** /pri mónnitərəli/ *adv* —**premonitory** *adj*

premumble /prée mumb'l/ *n* a series of opening remarks, often gratuitous, made by a speaker prior to the beginning of his or her real presentation (*slang*) [Late 20C. After PREAMBLE]

prenatal /prée náyt'l/ *adj N Am* same as **antenatal** —**prenatally** *adv*

prenominal /pree nómmin'l/ *adj* **1.** occurring before a noun, or used only before a noun **2.** relating to an ancient Roman's first name (**praenomen**)

prenotion /prée nōsh'n/ *n* **1.** a preconceived idea about somebody or something **2.** a feeling that something is about to occur or may occur [Early 17C. < Latin *praenotion-* < *notion-* 'concept' (see NOTION)]

prenuptial /pree núpsh'l/ *adj* occurring or existing before a marriage

prenuptial agreement *n* an agreement made between a couple before marriage relating to the arrangement of financial matters and division of property in the event of their divorce

preoccupation /pri ókyoo páysh'n/, **preoccupancy** /pri ókyoopənssi/ (*plural* **-cies**) *n* **1.** constant thought about or persistent interest in something ○ *a preoccupation with fame and fortune* **2.** a subject or activity that constantly occupies somebody's thoughts ○ *His children are his main preoccupation at the moment.* [Early 17C. Directly or via French < Latin *praeoccupation-*, literally 'seizing in advance' < *praeoccupare* < *occupare* (see OCCUPY)]

preoccupied /pri ókyoo pīd/ *adj* **1. HAVING ATTENTION TAKEN UP WITH SOMETHING** completely absorbed in thinking about something or doing something, sometimes to the extent of neglecting other things ○ *She was too preoccupied to notice what was going on.* **2. OCCUPIED** already occupied by somebody or something else ○ *a preoccupied airline seat* **3.** BIOL **ALREADY IN USE** describes a scientific name that has already been used to designate a species, genus, or other taxonomic group and therefore cannot be used again

preoccupy /pri ókyoo pī/ (**-pies, -pying, -pied**) *vt* **1.** to fill somebody's thoughts completely, sometimes in a way that blunts his or her response to other things **2.** to occupy something in advance, or before somebody else

preop /pree óp/ *adj* same as **preoperative** (*informal*) [Mid-20C. Shortening]

preoperative /pree óppərətiv/ *adj* occurring or done before a surgical operation

preordain /prée awr dáyn/ (**-dains, -daining, -dained**) *vt* **1.** to decide in advance that something will happen, or determine somebody's future, usually by fate or divine decree **2.** to decide, determine, or arrange something beforehand —**preordainment** *n* —**preordination** /prée awrdi náysh'n/ *n*

preovulatory /prée ovyoo laytəri/ *adj* relating to the stage of the menstrual cycle between menstruation and ovulation that lasts from 6 to 13 days

prep /prep/ *n* (*informal*) **1.** EDUC same as **preparation** (senses 5–6) **2. PREPARATION** preparation for an activity **3.** *US* EDUC same as **preparatory school** (sense 2) **4.** *US* EDUC same as **preppy** *n* (sense 2) ■ *v* (**preps, prepping, prepped**) **1.** *vt* MED **PREPARE SOMEBODY FOR SURGERY** to make a patient ready for an operation or other hospital procedure (*informal*) **2.** *vt* ART **PREPARE SOMETHING FOR PAINTING** to prime a surface for painting **3.** *vi N Am* **PREPARE FOR SOMETHING** to study or train for an examination, sporting event, or other activity (*informal*) ■ *adj* **PREPARATORY** serving as preparation (*informal*) [Mid-19C. Shortening of PREPARATION]

prep. *abbr* **1.** preparation **2.** preparatory **3.** GRAM preposition

prepackage /pree pákij/ (**-ages, -aging, -aged**) *vt* **1.** to package goods before selling them **2.** to arrange all the components of something in advance, allowing no individual variation ○ *a prepackaged holiday* —**prepackaged** *adj*

preparation /préppə ráysh'n/ *n* **1. PREPARING SOMETHING OR SOMEBODY** the work or planning involved in making something or somebody ready or in putting something together in advance (*often used before a noun*) ○ *a preparation time of about 45 minutes* **2. READINESS** a state of readiness ○ *Twenty place settings lay carefully arranged in preparation for the guests.* **3. PREPARATORY MEASURE** something done in advance in order to be ready for a future event (*often pl*) ○ *Preparations for the next Olympic Games are already under way.* **4. MIXTURE** a substance, e.g. a medicine, that is made by combining various ingredients ○ *a cough preparation* **5. HOMEWORK** at a boarding school or private school, work to be done by pupils outside normal school hours **6. STUDY TIME** at a boarding school, the time during which pupils do homework or prepare for lessons **7.** MUSIC **SOFTENING APPROACH TO DISSONANCE** in traditional composition, a lessening of the effect of a dissonant chord by using the discordant note harmonically in a preceding chord [14C. Via French < Latin *praeparation-* < *praeparare* (see PREPARE)]

Preparation of the Gifts *n* the offertory in the Roman Catholic Mass

preparative /pri párrətiv/ *adj* same as **preparatory** (senses 1–2) ○ *a series of preparative lectures* ■ *n* something that prepares for or introduces a more important event or action (*formal*) ○ *Her preparative was excellent and we felt ready to perform the procedure.* [15C. Via French < medieval Latin *praeparativus* < Latin *praeparare* (see PREPARE)] —**preparatively** *adv*

preparatory /pri párrətəri/ *adj* **1.** done in preparation for something else, as a preparation for something, or to make something ready ○ *preparatory design work* **2.** acting as an introduction to something ○ *preparatory remarks before a news conference* [15C. < medieval Latin *praeparatorius* < *praeparator* 'preparer' < Latin *praeparari* (see PREPARE)] —**preparatorily** *adv* ◇ **preparatory to** before or in preparation for something

preparatory school *n* **1.** in the United Kingdom, a private, usually single-sex, school that prepares students between the ages of 6 and 13 for entrance into a private boarding school **2.** *US* in the United States, a private secondary school that prepares students for college, often with academic requirements for entry

prepare /pri páir/ (**-pares, -paring, -pared**) *v* **1.** *vti* **MAKE SOMETHING READY** to take the necessary action to put something into a state where it is fit for use or action, or for a particular event or purpose ○ *preparing the aircraft for takeoff* **2.** *vti* **MAKE SOMEBODY READY** to put somebody or yourself into a suitable physical or mental state to do or experience something ○ *They prepared to go.* ○ *Prepare yourselves for a shock.* **3.** *vt* **MAKE SOMETHING BY PUTTING THINGS TOGETHER** to make something by combining various ingredients ○ *meals that can be prepared in less than half an hour* **4.** *vt* **EQUIP SOMEBODY** to provide somebody or something with the necessary equipment for an activity ○ *The expedition had not been properly prepared for arctic conditions.* **5.** *vt* MUSIC **LESSEN EFFECT OF DISSONANCE** to lessen the effect of a dissonant chord by using the discordant note harmonically in a preceding chord [15C. Directly or via French < Latin *praeparare* 'make ready beforehand' < *parare* 'make ready'] —**preparer** *n*

prepared /pri páird/ *adj* **1. WILLING** willing and able to do something ○ *Are you prepared to testify in court?* **2. READY TO DEAL WITH SOMETHING** in a suitable physical or mental state to be able to cope with something, often something hard or bad ○ *We had taken the necessary defensive measures and were prepared for the attack when it came.* **3. MADE, OR MADE READY, BEFOREHAND** made ready or put together in advance ○ *a specially prepared surface* ○ *a prepared statement*

preparedness /pri páiridnəss/ *n* readiness for action, especially military action

prepared piano *n* a piano that has been modified to produce special effects, usually by placing objects on or between its strings

prepay /pree páy/ (**-pays, -paying, -paid** /-páyd/) *vt* to

pay in advance for something such as the postage on a letter or parcel —**prepaid** *adj* —**prepayable** *adj* —**prepayment** *n*

prepense /pri pénss/ *adj* planned or contemplated in advance (*archaic*) ○ *acted with malice prepense* [Early 18C. Shortening of *prepensed*, past participle of *prepense* 'premeditate', alteration of obsolete *purpense* < Anglo-Norman *purpenser* < Latin *pensare* 'think']

~~**preperation**~~ incorrect spelling of **preparation**

preponderance /pri póndərənss/, **preponderancy** /-rənssi/ *n* (*formal*) **1.** a large number or the majority (*takes a singular or plural verb*) ○ *A preponderance of the settlers in this area were French.* **2.** dominance or superiority in force, importance, or influence ○ *The preponderance of the evidence is in support of this theory.*

preponderant /pri póndərənt/ *adj* greater in number, power, or importance than something else of the same nature or class [Mid-17C. < Latin *praeponderant-*, present participle of *praeponderare* 'outweigh' < *ponderare* 'weigh' (see PONDER)] —**preponderantly** *adv*

preponderate /pri póndə rayt/ (**-ates, -ating, -ated**) *vi* to be greater in weight, strength, number, or importance than something else [Early 17C. < Latin *praeponderat-*, past participle of *praeponderare* (see PREPONDERANT)] —**preponderately** *adv* —**preponderation** /-póndə ráysh'n/ *n*

prepone /pree pṓn/ (**-pones, -poning, -poned**) *v S Asia* to reschedule something for an earlier time or date [Late 20C. After POSTPONE]

preposition /préppə zísh'n/ *n* a member of a set of words used in close connection with, and usually before, nouns and pronouns to show their relation to another part of a clause. An example is 'off' in 'He fell off his bike' and 'What did he fall off?' [14C. < Latin *praeposition-* 'putting before, preposition' < *praeponere* 'put before' < *ponere* 'put'] —**prepositional** *adj*

pre-position *vt* to put somebody or something in position beforehand, especially to deploy ships and troops to an area of possible future conflict

prepositional phrase *n* a phrase made up of a preposition followed by a noun or pronoun, e.g. 'over the hill'. Prepositional phrases can be used adverbially or adjectivally.

prepositive /pree pózzətiv/ *adj* describes a word that is placed before the word it modifies ■ *n* a prepositive word or element [Late 16C. < late Latin *praepositivus* < past participle of Latin *praeponere* (see PREPOSITION)] —**prepositively** *adv*

prepossessing /prée pə zéssing/ *adj* creating a pleasing impression —**prepossessingly** *adv*

prepossession /prée pə zésh'n/ *n* **1.** prejudice or bias concerning somebody or something **2.** the occupation of the mind by thoughts or feelings

preposterous /pri póstərəss/ *adj* going very much against what is thought to be sensible or reasonable [Mid-16C. < Latin *praeposterus* 'inverted', literally 'having the first thing last'] —**preposterously** *adv* —**preposterousness** *n*

prepotent /pri pṓt'nt/ *adj* **1.** greater in power, force, or influence **2.** showing great effectiveness in conferring genetic traits or in fertilization [15C. < Latin *praepotent-* 'more powerful' < *potent-* (see POTENT[1])] —**prepotency** *n* —**prepotently** *adv*

preppy /préppi/, **preppie** *N Am* (*informal*) *adj* RELATING TO YOUNG WELL-EDUCATED AFFLUENT PEOPLE relating to or characteristic of well-educated, fairly affluent young people who are known for their neat, traditional, often expensive style of dress ■ *n* (*plural* **-pies**; *plural* **-pies**) **1.** WELL-EDUCATED AFFLUENT YOUNG PERSON a young person who dresses with preppy style or behaves in a way that suggests a traditional training in good manners **2.** PREPARATORY SCHOOL STUDENT a young person who is studying or has studied at a preparatory school —**preppily** *adv* —**preppiness** *n*

preprandial /pree prándi əl/ *adj* taking place before a meal, especially an evening meal (*formal or humorous*)

preprint /pree prínt/ *n* **1.** DRAFT CIRCULATED BEFORE PUBLICATION a piece of writing, especially a contribution to an academic journal, that is printed and often distributed in a preliminary form before official publication **2.** SOMETHING PRINTED IN ADVANCE something that is printed in advance, especially before publication in full ○ *There was so much interest in the work that the publishers issued a preprint of the Introduction.* ■ *v* (**-prints, -printing, -printed**) **1.** *vt* PRINT SOMETHING BEFORE OFFICIAL PUBLICATION to issue something, especially an article or other piece of writing, in draft form before its official publication **2.** *vti* PRINT SOMETHING IN ADVANCE to print something in advance of its being used or prior to full printing

preprocess /pree prṓssess/ (**-esses, -essing, -essed**) *vt* to analyse computer data such as control statements embedded in a program, and take appropriate action before processing the data —**preprocessor** *n*

preproduction /prée prə dúksh'n/ *n* PRELIMINARY WORK the plans and activities, e.g. those relating to finance, equipment, and personnel, that precede the production phase of a project, especially in the entertainment and manufacturing industries ■ *adj* **1.** HAPPENING BEFORE PRODUCTION preceding a production phase **2.** PROTOTYPIC produced as a trial or prototype

preprogram /pree prṓ gram/ (**-grams, -gramming, -grammed**) *vt* to program a computer or other device in advance

preprogramme /pree prṓ gram/ (**-grammes, -gramming, -grammed**) *vt* to prepare somebody in such a way that a later response in a desired manner is assured

prep school *n* EDUC same as **preparatory school** (*informal*)

prepubescent /préepyoo béss'nt/ *adj* at or characteristic of the stage of life just before puberty ■ *n* a child at the stage of development just before puberty —**prepubescence** *n*

prepuce /prée pyooss/ *n* (*technical*) **1.** same as **foreskin 2.** the loose fold of skin that covers the tip of the clitoris [14C. Via French < Latin *praeputium*] —**preputial** /pri pyoosh'l/ *adj*

prequel /préekwəl/ *n* a film or novel set at a time preceding the action of an existing work, especially one that has achieved commercial success [Late 20C. Blend of PRE- + SEQUEL]

Pre-Raphaelite /prée ráffə līt, -ráffi ə-/ *n* a member of a group of painters and writers (**the Pre-Raphaelite Brotherhood**) founded in 1848 with the aim of reviving the simpler and more direct style of Italian painting before Raphael. The group included Rossetti and Millais. ■ *adj* relating or belonging to the Pre-Raphaelites, or characteristic of their style of painting or writing —**Pre-Raphaelitism** *n*

prerecord /prée ri káwrd/ (**-cords, -cording, -corded**) *vt* to record something, e.g. a message or television or radio programme, for later use or broadcasting —**prerecorded** *adj* —**prerecording** *n*

prerequisite /pree rékwəzit/ *n* an object, quality, or condition that is required in order for something else to happen ○ *A degree is a prerequisite for entry into this profession.* ■ *adj* required in order for something else to happen ○ *A good command of Spanish is prerequisite for the Spanish literature course.*

prerogative /pri róggətiv/ *n* **1.** PRIVILEGE RESTRICTED TO PEOPLE OF RANK an exclusive privilege or right enjoyed by a person or group occupying a particular rank or position ○ *It was her prerogative as leader to choose a successor.* **2.** INDIVIDUAL RIGHT OR PRIVILEGE a privilege or right that allows a particular person or group to give orders or make decisions or judgments ○ *It's not his prerogative to say who can come.* **3.** PRIVILEGE RESULTING FROM NATURAL ADVANTAGE the right conferred by a natural advantage that places somebody in a position of superiority ○ *the prerogatives conferred by age* **4.** SOVEREIGN POWER, PRIVILEGE, OR IMMUNITY the power or right of a monarch or government to do something or be exempt from something **5.** SUPERIORITY superiority in rank or nature [14C. Via French < Latin *praerogativa* < *praerogare* 'ask first' < *rogare* 'ask']

pres. *abbr* **1.** GRAM present **2.** presidential

Pres. *abbr* President

presage /préssij/ *n* **1.** PORTENT OR OMEN a sign or warning of a future event **2.** SENSE OF SOMETHING TO COME a feeling that a particular thing, often something unpleasant, is about to happen **3.** FUTURE IMPORT significance with regard to future events ○ *a moment of great presage* ■ *v* (**presages, presaging, presaged**) **1.** *vt* FORETELL SOMETHING to be or give a sign or warning of a future event ○ *Clear skies that night presaged fine weather for the picnic.* **2.** *vt* HAVE PRESENTIMENT OF SOMETHING to know intuitively that a particular thing is going to happen **3.** *vti* PREDICT to predict a future event [14C. Directly or via French < Latin *praesagire* 'forebode' < *sagire* 'perceive'] —**presager** *n*

presale /pree sáyl/ *n* a private sale of products, objects, or works of art that takes place before a public sale

presbyopia /-ṓpi ə/ *n* progressive reduction in the eye's ability to focus, with consequent difficulty in reading at the normal distance, associated with ageing. It typically starts at middle age, and is due to age-related loss of elasticity of the lens. [Late 18C. < Greek *presbus* 'man of advanced years'] —**presbyope** /prézbi ōp/ *n* —**presbyopic** /prézbi óppik/ *adj*

presbyter /prézbitər/ *n* **1.** MEMBER OF EARLY CHURCH ADMINISTRATION in early Christianity, an administrative official of a local church **2.** MEMBER OF CLERGY an ordained member of the clergy in many Christian churches **3.** LAY OFFICIAL IN PRESBYTERIAN CHURCH any lay person chosen by the congregation to govern a Presbyterian or other Reformed church [Late 16C. Via ecclesiastical Latin < Greek *presbuteros* 'elder of the church' < *presbus* 'man of advanced years']

presbyterate /prez bíttərət/ *n* **1.** the office or position of a presbyter **2.** an order or group of presbyters

presbyterial /prézbi téeri əl/ *adj* relating to a presbyter or presbytery

presbyterian /prézbi téeri ən/ *adj* characterized by or relating to the government of a church by democratically elected lay officials ■ *n* a supporter and advocate of church government by democratically elected lay officials

Presbyterian *adj* relating or belonging to any Protestant church governed by the presbyterian system ■ *n* a member of a presbyterian church —**Presbyterianism** *n*

presbytery /prézbitəri/ (*plural* **-ies**) *n* **1.** GROUP OF PRESBYTERS a group of presbyters in the early Christian church or in a modern Presbyterian church **2.** COURT OF PRESBYTERIAN CHURCH a court composed of ministers and lay officials in a Presbyterian Church, or the churches under the jurisdiction of such a court **3.** GOVERNMENT BY PRESBYTERS the government of a church by democratically elected lay officials **4.** PART OF CHURCH FOR CLERGY part of a church or cathedral, or a separate building, for the use of clergy only **5.** HOME OF ROMAN CATHOLIC PARISH PRIEST the home of a Roman Catholic parish priest

preschool /prée skool/ *adj* **1.** UNDER SCHOOL AGE below the age at which compulsory schooling begins **2.** FOR PRESCHOOL CHILDREN relating to or provided for children below the age at which compulsory schooling begins ■ *n ANZ, N Am* EDUC a school for preschool children. UK term **nursery school** —**preschooler** *n* —**preschooling** *n*

prescience /préssi ənss/ *n* knowledge of actions or events before they happen [14C. Via French < late Latin *praescientia* 'foreknowledge' < Latin *praescient-* (see PRESCIENT)]

prescient /préssi ənt/ *adj* having or showing knowledge of actions or events before they take place [Early 17C. < Latin *praescient-*, present participle of *praescire* 'know beforehand' < *scire* 'know'] —**presciently** *adv*

prescind /pri sínd/ (**-scinds, -scinding, -scinded**) *vi* to detach the mind from something, typically a concept, notion, or fixed idea (*formal*) [Mid-17C. < Latin *praescindere* 'cut off in front' < *scindere* 'cut off']

prescribe /pri skrī́b/ (**-scribes, -scribing, -scribed**) *v* **1.** *vti* ORDER USE OF MEDICATION to order a course of treatment for a patient, usually the use of a particular drug at set times and dosages ○ *Most doctors are wary of prescribing antibiotics for relatively minor infections.* **2.** *vt* RECOMMEND REMEDY to recommend a particular course of action or treatment as a remedy for something ○ *I prescribe lots of tender loving care.* **3.** *vt* LAY DOWN RULE to say with authority that a course of action should be taken ○ *the penalties prescribed by law* **4.** *vi* SET DOWN REGULATIONS to lay down rules or laws **5.** *vti* LAW CLAIM PROPERTY RIGHT to claim a right to something on the grounds of possession over a long period of time

[15C. < Latin *praescribere* 'write before' < *scribere* 'write'] —**prescribable** *adj* —**prescriber** *n*

prescribed illness /pri skrĭbd-/ *n* an illness arising from chemical hazards in the workplace, e.g. mercury poisoning, or from dangerous circumstances, e.g. decompression sickness

prescript /préeskript/ (*formal*) *n* a rule or regulation that has been laid down ■ *adj* laid down as a rule or regulation [Mid-16C. < Latin *praescriptum* 'something prescribed' < past participle of *praescribere* (see PRESCRIBE)]

prescription /pri skrípsh'n/ *n* **1. WRITTEN ORDER FOR MEDICINE** a written order issued by a doctor or other qualified practitioner that authorizes a chemist to supply a specific medication for a patient, with instructions on its use (*often used before a noun*) **2. PRESCRIBED MEDICINE** a drug or other medication prescribed by a doctor or other qualified practitioner ○ *I've got to pick up my son's prescription.* **3. ORDER FOR LENS TO CORRECT EYESIGHT** a written order from an optometrist or ophthalmologist for glasses or contact lenses of a particular type and strength to correct the eyesight of a particular person (*often used before a noun*) ○ *prescription sunglasses* **4. PROVEN FORMULA FOR SOMETHING** a proven formula for causing something else to happen ○ *Caring about others' feelings is a prescription for a fulfilling life.* **5. AUTHORITATIVE RECOMMENDATION** the act of ordering or recommending a particular course of action authoritatively **6. SOMETHING ORDERED OR RECOMMENDED** a practice or course of action that is authoritatively ordered or recommended **7.** LAW **PRESUMPTION OF RIGHT OF POSSESSION** a presumption of the right of possession of property, based on long-term exercise of property rights [14C. Via French < Latin *praescription-* < *praescribere* (see PRESCRIBE)]

prescription drug *n* a drug that can be dispensed only upon presentation of a legally valid prescription

prescriptive /pri skríptiv/ *adj* **1. MAKING OR ADHERING TO REGULATIONS** establishing or adhering to rules and regulations ○ *prescriptive grammarians* **2. CUSTOMARY** based on or authorized by long-standing custom (*dated*) **3.** LAW **GROUNDED IN LEGAL PRESCRIPTION** based on legal prescription —**prescriptively** *adv* —**prescriptiveness** *n*

presell /pree sél/ (**-sells, -selling, -sold** /-sōld/) *vt* **1. POPULARIZE SOMETHING BEFOREHAND** to promote a product or entertainment before it is generally available to the public, by means of advertising and publicity **2. SELL BOOK EARLY** to sell a book before its official publication date **3. ARRANGE SALE OF SOMETHING BEFOREHAND** to agree to sell a house, car, or other item before it is actually available

presence /prézz'nss/ *n* **1. EXISTENCE IN PLACE** the physical existence or detectability of something in a place at a particular time ○ *the presence of contaminants in the water supply* **2. ATTENDANCE** somebody's attendance at an event or physical existence in a place with other people ○ *Our presence is requested at the board meeting.* **3. AREA WITHIN SIGHT OR EARSHOT** the immediate vicinity of somebody or something ○ *How dare you use that kind of language in my presence!* **4. IMPRESSIVE QUALITY** an impressive appearance or bearing ○ *has a certain presence about her that garners respect* **5. INVISIBLE SUPPOSED SUPERNATURAL BEING** a supernatural spirit that is felt to be nearby ○ *A malevolent presence filled the room.* **6. PERSON PRESENT** somebody who is notably present ○ *the venerable scholar, a dignified presence in the academic procession* **7. GROUP OF OFFICIAL PERSONNEL** a group of official personnel, especially police, military forces, or diplomats, present or stationed in a place to represent their country and maintain its interest ○ *maintained a heavy military presence in the capital* [14C. Via French < Latin *praesentia* < *praesent-* (see PRESENT²)] ◇ **make your** *or* **its presence felt** to influence what is going on

presence chamber *n* the room in which a monarch or ruler or other important person receives guests and holds assemblies

presence of mind *n* the ability to remain calm and act decisively and effectively in a crisis ○ *At least she had the presence of mind to call the fire brigade.*

present¹ *v* /pri zént/ (**-sents, -senting, -sented**) **1.** *vt* **GIVE SOMETHING** to give or hand something to somebody, often in a humorously formal manner ○ *Then she presented me with the bill!* **2.** *vt* **AWARD SOMETHING TO SOMEBODY** to give or award something to somebody in a formal or ceremonial manner or at a ceremonial occasion ○ *The mayor came in person to present the prizes.* **3.** *vt* **OFFER SOMETHING FORMALLY** to offer or convey something such as your compliments or apologies to somebody formally ○ *May I present my warmest congratulations?* **4.** *vt* **HAND SOMETHING OVER OFFICIALLY** to put something forward for inspection or consideration, typically in a formal or official manner or capacity ○ *proposals to be presented at the next meeting* **5.** *vt* **MAKE SOMETHING EVIDENT** to show or display something ○ *taking care to present his best side to the camera* **6.** *vt* **POSE PROBLEM** to pose a problem or difficulty to somebody ○ *presenting a direct threat to national security* **7.** *vt* LAW **BRING CHARGE** to put a charge before a court of law so that it can be considered or tried **8.** *vt* **INTRODUCE SOMEBODY FORMALLY** to introduce somebody formally, especially to somebody of higher rank ○ *They were presented to the Queen.* **9.** *vt* **INTRODUCE WOMAN INTO SOCIETY** to introduce a young woman formally into fashionable society ○ *Her family planned to present her at the Christmas debutante ball in New York.* **10.** *vt* **HOST PROGRAMME** to introduce, or act as the host of, a television or radio programme or an infomercial ○ *He used to present a game show on ITV.* **11.** *vt* **OFFER PUBLIC ENTERTAINMENT** to bring a film, play, or other form of entertainment to the public **12.** *vt* **PORTRAY SOMETHING ARTISTICALLY** to represent something or somebody in a particular way in the arts ○ *In the film, Romeo and Juliet are presented as modern teenagers.* **13.** *vr* **BE IN APPOINTED PLACE** to appear, especially at an appointed time and place ○ *Present yourselves at the gate at eight o'clock.* **14.** *vr* **ARISE** to come into being or happen ○ *when an opportunity presents itself* **15.** *vi* **PRODUCE SPECIFIC IMPRESSION** to produce a particular impression, especially a favourable one (*formal*) ○ *She presents as a pleasant young woman.* **16.** *vi* MED **HAVE PARTICULAR SYMPTOMS** to exhibit a particular symptom or symptoms on examination **17.** *vi* MED **EXIT BIRTH CANAL IN POSITION** to appear during the process of being born (*refers to foetuses*) ■ *n* /prézz'nt/ **GIFT** something that is given to somebody out of kindness or to celebrate an occasion such as a birthday [13C. Via French < Latin *praesentare* 'make present' < *praesent-* (see PRESENT²)] —**presentee** /prézz'n tée/ *n* —**presenter** *n*

SYNONYMS See *give*.

present² /prézz'nt/ *adj* **1. CURRENTLY HAPPENING** taking place or existing now ○ *in our present circumstances* ○ *up to the present day* **2. IN PLACE** existing, detectable, or in attendance in a place ○ *There were over a hundred people present at the reception.* **3. NOW UNDER DISCUSSION** being considered or talked about at this time **4.** GRAM **RELATING TO CURRENT TIME** describes a verb form or tense that expresses the current time ■ *n* **1. THE HERE AND NOW** the current time or moment ○ *The story takes place in the present.* **2.** GRAM **CURRENT-TIME VERB TENSE** a grammatical tense that expresses current time **3.** GRAM **CURRENT-TIME VERB** a form of a verb used to express the present tense, indicating that the action is happening now ■ **presents** *npl* **LEGAL OR FORMAL DOCUMENT** this legal or formal document (*formal*) ○ *terms discussed in these presents* [13C. Via French < Latin *praesent-*, present participle of *praeesse* 'be in front of' < *esse* 'be'] ◇ **at present** just now ◇ **for the present** as far as the present time is concerned

presentable /pri zéntəb'l/ *adj* **1.** looking or being good enough to be introduced to other people ○ *Make sure you look presentable.* **2.** good enough to be offered, shown, or given to other people ○ *still a presentable gift* —**presentability** /pri zéntə bíllәti/ *n* —**presentably** *adv*

present arms /pri zént-/ *n* a drill movement in which a salute is given by bringing a rifle vertically in front of the body, or the command to give such a salute —**present arms** *vi*

presentation /prézz'n táysh'n/ *n* **1. ACT OF PRESENTING SOMETHING** an act of presenting something or the state of being presented **2. WAY SOMETHING APPEARS WHEN OFFERED** the manner in which something is shown, expressed, or laid out for other people to see ○ *Presentation is an important part of the chef's job.* **3. FORMAL HANDING-OVER OF GIFT** the action of presenting somebody with an award or a token of appreciation in front of other people, or an occasion when this is done ○ *the presentation of the trophy* **4. PREPARED REPORT READ BEFORE AUDIENCE** a formal talk made to a group of people, e.g. on somebody's recent work or some aspect of business, often with handouts, diagrams, or other visual aids ○ *He gave a presentation on modern irrigation methods.* **5. PREPARED PERFORMANCE FOR AUDIENCE** a performance, exhibition, or demonstration put on before an audience **6. SOMEBODY'S INTRODUCTION INTO SPECIAL SOCIAL GROUP** an occasion when somebody is first presented at court or into society, or the official or recognized process of first presenting somebody in this way **7.** MED **PART OF BABY APPEARING FIRST** the part of a baby that appears first at birth, normally the crown of the head ○ *a breech presentation* **8.** CHR **ACT OF NOMINATING CLERGY MEMBER** the act or power of nominating a member of the clergy to a paid office in a church **9.** PHILOSOPHY, PSYCHOL **OBJECT OF PERCEPTION** something that is perceived, remembered, or acquired as knowledge **10.** COMM same as **presentment** (sense 3) —**presentational** *adj*

Presentation of the Virgin Mary *n* a festival celebrated by the Roman Catholic and Eastern Orthodox churches marking the Virgin Mary's presentation at the temple. Date: 21 November.

presentative /pri zéntətiv/ *adj* able to be known directly without any reflective or cognitive process being necessary

present-day *adj* found or existing in modern times ○ *out of touch with present-day society and the Internet culture*

presenteeism /prézz'n tée izəm/ *n* the practice of spending longer hours at work than are contractually required

Present Era *n* the period after the birth of Jesus Christ (*used in dates*)

USAGE See ***AD*¹**.

presentiment /pri zéntimənt/ *n* an awareness of some event, especially an unpleasant event, before it takes place and before there is any reason to suspect it or know about it ○ *a presentiment of doom* [Early 18C. < obsolete French *présentiment* < Latin *praesentire* 'perceive beforehand' < *sentire* 'feel'] —**presentimental** /pri zénti mént'l/ *adj*

presently /prézz'ntli/ *adv* **1.** not at this exact moment but in a short while ○ *I'll be there presently.* **2.** now, or during the current period (*some people object to this usage*) ○ *Yes, he's presently engaged in a research job for the company.*

presentment /pri zéntmənt/ *n* **1. PRESENTATION** the act of presenting something, or the way in which something is presented **2. STATEMENT BY JURY** formerly, a formal statement made on oath by a jury to a court concerning facts and matters within their own knowledge **3.** COMM **PRESENTING OF NEGOTIABLE DOCUMENT** the presenting of a negotiable document for payment

present participle *n* the form of a verb that suggests a progressive or active sense and that ends in '-ing' in English, e.g. 'flying'

present perfect *n* the form of a verb that suggests that an action has been completed, formed in English by preceding the verb with 'have' or 'has' and usually ending the verb with '-ed', e.g. 'have departed' —**present perfect** *adj*

present tense *n* the tense of a verb that suggests actions or the situation at the time of speaking or writing

present value *n* the value now of a sum of money expected to be received in the future, calculated by subtracting the interest and other value that will accrue in the intervening period

preservation /prézzər váysh'n/ *n* **1. PROTECTION FROM HARM** the guarding of something from danger, harm, or injury **2. MAINTENANCE UNCHANGED** the maintenance of something, especially something of historic value, in an unchanged condition **3. UPHOLDING OF SOMETHING** the keeping of something intangible intact ○ *preservation of freedom of speech*

preservationist /prézzər váysh'nist/ *n* somebody who tries to prevent things from being damaged, destroyed, or altered, particularly things of natural or historical interest —**preservationism** *n*

preservative /pri zúrvətiv/ *adj* having the ability to protect something from decay or spoilage ■ *n* some-

thing that provides protection from decay or spoilage, e.g. a food additive

preserve /pri zúrv/ *vt* (**-serves, -serving, -served**) **1. MAKE SURE SOMETHING LASTS** to keep something protected from anything that would cause its current quality or condition to change or deteriorate or cause it to fall out of use ○ *They are anxious to preserve the area's rural character.* ○ *We need to preserve professional standards of conduct.* **2. MAINTAIN SOMETHING** to keep up or maintain something ○ *She preserved a cool and composed manner throughout the interrogation.* **3. TREAT FOOD FOR STORAGE** to treat or store food in such a way as to protect it from decay, e.g. by pickling, drying, salting, freezing, or canning **4. MAKE JAM FROM SOMETHING** to make jam or marmalade out of a fruit **5. KEEP ANIMALS IN SECURE AREA** to rear wild animals, especially fish and birds, in a protected area of water or land, so that they can be fished or shot for sport in the hunting season **6. PROTECT SOMEBODY OR SOMETHING** to protect somebody or something from danger, especially the danger of being killed or damaged (*formal or literary*) ○ '*The Lord shall preserve thee from all evil*' (*Psalm 121*) ■ *n* **1. EXCLUSIVE AREA OF ACTIVITY** something that one particular person or group regards as being his, her, or its exclusive concern, or a place kept for one person or group to enjoy exclusively ○ *The children considered the tree house their own preserve.* **2. FRUIT JAM** a sweet thick foodstuff made by boiling fruit in sugar and water, eaten on bread or in desserts and cakes. Preserves can be kept for several years in airtight jars, bottles, or cans. (*often used in the plural*) **3. AREA FOR PRIVATE HUNTING** an area where game is kept for private hunting **4.** *N Am* ENVIRON same as **reserve** *n* (sense 2) [14C. Via French < medieval Latin *praeservare* 'guard beforehand' < Latin *servare* 'keep'] —**preservable** *adj*

preserver /pri zúrvər/ *n* something used to keep somebody or something safe, undamaged, or unchanged

preset /pree sét/ *vt* (**-sets, -setting, -set**) to arrange the settings of a timing device controlling an electrical appliance so that the appliance is automatically switched on at a specific time ○ *The central heating is preset to come on in the morning and evening.* ■ *n* an electronic timing device or system that is used to make an appliance operate at a later time

preshrunk /pree shrúngk/ *adj* with the fabric already shrunk before being sold, so that it will not shrink when washed

preside /pri zíd/ (**-sides, -siding, -sided**) *vi* **1. BE OFFICIALLY IN CHARGE** to be the chairperson or hold a similar position of authority at a formal gathering of people **2. HAVE CONTROL** to be the most powerful person or the one everyone else obeys, usually in a specific place or situation ○ *the question of who will preside over the business once their mother retires* **3. PERFORM AS INSTRUMENTALIST** to be the featured instrumentalist in a musical performance ○ *preside at the organ* [Early 17C. Via French < Latin *praesidere* 'sit in front of' < *sedere* 'sit'] —**presider** *n*

presidency /prézzidənssi/ (*plural* **-cies**) *n* **1.** *also* **Presidency POSITION OF PRESIDENT OF NATION** the job or function of president of a republic, or a president's term of office **2. JOB OF PRESIDENT** the status, post, or function of being president of a company, society, institution, or similar body ○ *The presidency of the club turned out to be a thankless task.* **3. LATTER-DAY SAINTS COUNCIL** a three-person executive council in the Church of Jesus Christ of Latter-Day Saints **4. LATTER-DAY SAINTS GOVERNING COUNCIL** the governing body of the Church of Jesus Christ of Latter-Day Saints

president /prézzidənt/, **President** *n* **1. HEAD OF STATE OF REPUBLIC** the head of state, or head of state and chief political executive, of a republic **2. HIGHEST-RANKING MEMBER OF ASSOCIATION** the highest-ranking member of an organization or institution **3. SOMEBODY IN CHARGE OF MEETING** somebody who is appointed or elected to oversee a meeting **4. HEAD OF EDUCATIONAL ESTABLISHMENT** the highest-ranking executive officer of some universities and colleges **5.** *N Am* **HEAD OF COMPANY** the highest-ranking executive officer of a business or corporation **6. LATTER-DAY SAINTS LEADER** in the Church of Jesus Christ of Latter-Day Saints, a man who is a member of the church's governing board. Together with counsellors and the Council of the Twelve Apostles, he makes major church policy and decisions. [14C. Via French < Latin *praesident-* < present participle of *praesidere* (see PRESIDE)] —**presidentship** *n*

PRESIDENTS OF THE UNITED STATES

Term of office	President	Political party
1789–1797	George Washington	
1797–1801	John Adams	*Federalist*
1801–1809	Thomas Jefferson	*Democratic-Republican*
1809–1817	James Madison	*Democratic-Republican*
1817–1825	James Monroe	*Democratic-Republican*
1825–1829	John Quincy Adams	*Democratic-Republican*
1829–1837	Andrew Jackson	*Democrat*
1837–1841	Martin Van Buren	*Democrat*
1841	William Henry Harrison	*Whig*
1841–1845	John Tyler	*Whig*
1845–1849	James Polk	*Democrat*
1849–1850	Zachary Taylor	*Whig*
1850–1853	Millard Fillmore	*Whig*
1853–1857	Franklin Pierce	*Democrat*
1857–1861	James Buchanan	*Democrat*
1861–1865	Abraham Lincoln	*Republican*
1865–1869	Andrew Johnson	*Democrat*
1869–1877	Ulysses S. Grant	*Republican*
1877–1881	Rutherford B. Hayes	*Republican*
1881	James Garfield	*Republican*
1881–1885	Chester A. Arthur	*Republican*
1885–1889	Grover Cleveland	*Democrat*
1889–1893	Benjamin Harrison	*Republican*
1893–1897	Grover Cleveland	*Democrat*
1897–1901	William McKinley	*Republican*
1901–1909	Theodore Roosevelt	*Republican*
1909–1913	William Howard Taft	*Republican*
1913–1921	Woodrow Wilson	*Democrat*
1921–1923	Warren G. Harding	*Republican*
1923–1929	Calvin Coolidge	*Republican*
1929–1933	Herbert Hoover	*Republican*
1933–1945	Franklin Delano Roosevelt	*Democrat*
1945–1953	Harry S. Truman	*Democrat*
1953–1961	Dwight D. Eisenhower	*Republican*
1961–1963	John F. Kennedy	*Democrat*
1963–1969	Lyndon Johnson	*Democrat*
1969–1974	Richard Nixon	*Republican*
1974–1977	Gerald Ford	*Republican*
1977–1981	Jimmy Carter	*Democrat*
1981–1989	Ronald Reagan	*Republican*
1989–1993	George Bush	*Republican*
1993–2001	Bill Clinton	*Democrat*
2001–	George W. Bush	*Republican*

president-elect (*plural* **presidents-elect**) *n* an elected or appointed president who has not yet been officially installed

presidential /prézzi dénsh'l/ *adj* **1.** relating to the post of president, or used or owned by a president ○ *The presidential elections dominated the news.* **2.** presided over by a president, or presiding like one —**presidentially** *adv*

Presidents' Day *n* an official holiday in the United States commemorating the birthdays of George Washington and Abraham Lincoln. Date: third Monday in February.

presidio /pri síddi ō, pri zíddi ō/ (*plural* **-os**) *n* Southwest US a fortified settlement, especially of the type established by Spanish colonizers in the southwestern part of what is now the United States [Mid-18C. Via Spanish < Latin *praesidium* 'garrison, fortification' < *praesidere* (see PRESIDE)]

presidium /pri síddi əm, -zíddi-/ (*plural* **-iums** or **-ia** /-i ə/), **praesidium** *n* a permanent executive committee that acted for a larger legislature in the former Soviet Union and other Communist countries [Early 20C. Via Russian < Latin *praesidium* (see PRESIDIO)]

Elvis Presley

Presley /prézzli/, **Elvis** (1935–77) US singer and actor. Renowned as a pioneer of rock and roll, he also acted in several Hollywood films. Full name **Presley, Elvis Aron.** Known as **The King**

'I learned very early in life that: "Without a song, the day would never end; without a song, a man ain't got a friend; without a song, the road would never bend—without a song". So I keep singing a song. Goodnight. Thank you.'
[Elvis Presley, *Acceptance speech, Ten Outstanding Young Men of the Year Awards*; 16 January 1971]

press[1] /press/ *v* (**presses, pressing, pressed**) **1.** *vti* **PUSH AGAINST SOMETHING** to use a steady and significant force to put weight on something, sometimes to make it move or start working ○ *press the button* **2.** *vt* **SQUEEZE JUICE OUT OF SOMETHING** to squeeze the juice or oil out of something using force to compress it ○ *pressing grapes* **3.** *vt* **SMOOTH SOMETHING WITH HOT IRON** to remove unwanted creases from a garment or piece of cloth, or make a deliberate crease in a garment or piece of cloth, using a hot iron or other device ○ *pressed a shirt* **4.** *vt* **CHANGE OBJECT'S SHAPE BY SQUEEZING** to change the shape of something by squeezing it or putting a steady weight on it, especially in order to make it more compact ○ *pressed the clay into a ball* **5.** *vt* **FLATTEN SOMETHING TO PRESERVE IT** to flatten and dry a natural object such as a flower so that it does not decompose and can be kept or used decoratively ○ *pressed flowers as a hobby* **6.** *vt* **MAKE SOMETHING USING MOULD** to form something in a mould, especially to make gramophone records **7.** *vt* **HOLD SOMETHING TIGHTLY** to grip or clasp somebody or something firmly but not roughly with the hands or arms, especially to show affection or moral support ○ *She pressed his hand in sympathy.* **8.** *vi* **TRY HARD** to make great or greater efforts in order to achieve something, but not necessarily succeed **9.** *vt* **FORCE SOMEBODY** to force somebody into doing something he or she did not want or intend to do ○ *They pressed her into standing for the election.* **10.** *vt* **TRY TO OBTAIN SOMETHING FROM SOMEBODY** to ask somebody persistently or forcefully to supply, accept, or do something ○ *They pressed him for an immediate response.* **11.** *vt* **EMPHASIZE SOMETHING** to make sure that something is fully recognized and understood or stress its importance ○ *pressed his point* **12.** *vt* **DEMAND SOMETHING** to plead or demand something insistently **13.** *vi* **MOVE AS CROWD** to move together as a body, especially in a forceful way or

so as to crowd somebody or something ○ *The crowd pressed forward as the gates opened.* **14.** *vi* **REQUIRE ATTENTION** to need to be dealt with urgently (*dated or formal*) ○ *I'd like to help now, but business presses.* **15.** *vti* BASKETBALL **HARASS OPPONENT** to use a harassing and aggressive defence against an opponent in basketball ■ *n* **1. ACT OF PRESSING** an act of pressing something ○ *I gave the doorbell a few presses but nobody answered.* **2. FOOD PREPARATION DEVICE** a piece of equipment designed to crush something to release the juices or create a pulp ○ *a garlic press* **3. DEVICE FOR FLATTENING SOMETHING** a piece of equipment used to keep or make something smooth and uncreased ○ *a trouser press* **4. LINEN CUPBOARD** a shelved cupboard, usually of a large size, for storing bed or table linens or clothes **5.** RACKET GAMES **CLAMP FOR RACKETS** a clamp for holding a tennis or other racket to prevent it from warping when it is not in use **6. MACHINE FOR SHAPING MATERIALS BY MECHANICAL PRESSURE** a machine that, by applying pressure to a piece of metal or other material, can shape, form, cut, stamp, or otherwise cause a physical change to occur **7. NEWSPAPERS OR REPORTERS** the news-gathering business generally, or all the people involved in gathering and reporting on the news, especially journalists working on newspapers ○ *refused to talk to the press* **8. COMMENTS BY JOURNALISTS** the opinions expressed in articles or reviews in the newspapers or magazines ○ *His new musical had a lot of good press.* **9.** PRINTING same as **printing press** **10.** PUBL **PUBLISHING COMPANY** a company that publishes books (*used especially in names*) **11.** PRINTING **PROCESS OR SKILL OF PRINTING** the technical or physical process used by a printer and the skills a printer requires ○ *about to go to press* **12. CROWD** a tightly-packed crowd of people **13. POWERFUL MOVEMENT** the crowding and pressing together of a lot of people or things at the same time (*literary*) ○ *He could not move because of the press of people.* **14. DEFENCE IN SPORT** an aggressive defence, especially in basketball **15. LIFTING OF WEIGHT ABOVE HEAD** in weightlifting, a lift in which the weight is raised to shoulder height and then to above the head without moving the legs [14C. Via French < Latin *pressare* 'keep on pressing' < *press-*, past participle of *premere* 'press'] —**presser** *n* ◇ **be pressed for something** to be short of something, usually time

ORIGIN The Latin word *premere* 'to press', from which *press* is derived, is also the source of English *compress, depress, express, impress*[1], *oppress, repress,* and *suppress.*

press for *vt* to seek or demand something with great urgency ○ *They pressed for an immediate review of the situation.*
press on *vi* to continue in an urgent or persistent manner ○ *Night was falling but they pressed on despite their weariness.*

press[2] /press/ *vt* (**presses, pressing, pressed**) **1. FORCE SOMEBODY INTO MILITARY SERVICE** to forcibly recruit somebody into military service **2. USE SOMEBODY OR SOMETHING FOR NEW PURPOSE** to take somebody or something out of its intended place or function and put it to a different use (*literary*) ■ *n* **FORCING OF SOMEBODY INTO MILITARY SERVICE** the act of recruiting people into military service by force [Late 16C. Alteration (influenced by PRESS[1]) of obsolete *prest* 'enlist by paying in advance', via French < Latin *praestare* < *stare* 'to stand']

press agent *n* a promoter who contacts, liaises with, and gives information to the press on behalf of a client

Press Association *n* the national news agency for the United Kingdom and Ireland

pressboard /préss bawrd/ *n US* **1.** a heavy cardboard or pasteboard with a glazed finish **2.** a small ironing board used especially for pressing the sleeves of garments

press box *n* a section in a sports stadium or similar venue kept exclusively for journalists to work in

Pressburger /préss burgər/, **Emeric** (1902–88) Hungarian-born British film director. In partnership with Michael Powell, he made a number of films exploring complex moral themes, including *Black Narcissus* (1947). Born **Pressburger, Imre**

press conference *n* a meeting to which members of the press are invited to hear a prepared statement and usually to ask questions about that statement

pressed /prest/ *adj* **1.** made compact and firm by being forced mechanically into cans or containers ○ *pressed meat* **2.** having urgent or worrying things to deal with ○ *She is particularly pressed today, so I won't ask her to help if I can avoid it.*

press gallery *n* a raised gallery with seating at the back of a courtroom or legislative assembly room, where newspaper reporters and other members of the press can sit

press gang *n* formerly, a group of military personnel whose job was to find people to force into military service

press-gang *vti* to force people into military service or into doing anything that they are reluctant to do ○ *I never wanted to go to camp – my parents press-ganged me into it.*

pressie *n* another spelling of **prezzie** (*informal*)

pressing /préssing/ *adj* **1. URGENT** needing to be attended to without delay ○ *a pressing engagement* **2. VERY PERSISTENT** persistent and demanding, and therefore difficult to ignore or refuse ○ *Her invitations were so pressing that we eventually had to accept.* ■ *n* **GRAMOPHONE RECORDS MADE AT ONE TIME** all the gramophone records produced at one time from a master mould —**pressingly** *adv* —**pressingness** *n*

press kit *n* a package of background and promotional material relating to a product, distributed to the media by a press agent or publicity department

pressman /préss man, -mən/ (*plural* **-men** /-men, -mən/) *n* **1.** somebody, especially a man, who operates a printing press **2.** a man working as a newspaper reporter (*dated*)

pressmark /préss maark/ *n* same as **shelf mark**

press of canvas *n* SAILING same as **press of sail**

press officer *n* somebody employed by an organization or government department to provide the news media with information about the organization or department

press of sail *n* the largest amount of sail that a ship can safely carry

pressor /préssər/ *adj* relating to or bringing about an increase in blood pressure

pressperson /préss purss'n/ (*plural* **-persons** or **-people** /-peep'l/) *n* **1.** somebody who operates a printing press **2.** *S Asia* a newspaper reporter

press release *n* an official statement or account of a news story that is specially prepared and issued to newspapers and other news media for them to make known to the public

pressrun /préss run/ *n* **1.** the continuous running of a printing press until a set number of copies is printed **2.** the number of copies run off in a continuous printing operation

press stud *n* a manufactured device with two halves that push tightly into each other, generally used instead of a button to keep a piece of clothing fastened. N Am term **snap**

press-up *n UK* a physical exercise in which, from a position of lying flat on the front with the hands under the shoulders, the body is pushed off the floor until the arms are straight. ANZ, N Am term **push-up**

pressure /préshər/ *n* **1. PROCESS OF PRESSING STEADILY** the applying of a firm regular weight or force against somebody or something ○ *The pressure of her hand on his was comforting.* **2. CONSTANT STATE OF WORRY AND URGENCY** powerful and stressful demands on somebody's time, attention, and energy, or a demand of this sort ○ *They were under constant pressure to achieve near impossible output targets.* **3. FORCE THAT PUSHES OR URGES** something that affects thoughts and behaviour in a powerful way, usually in the form of several outside influences working together persuasively **4.** PHYS **FORCE PER UNIT AREA** the force acting on a surface divided by the area over which it acts. Symbol *p* **5.** METEOROL same as **atmospheric pressure** ■ *vt* (**-sures, -suring, -sured**) **MAKE SOMEBODY DO SOMETHING** to apply great persuasion or a strong influence on somebody in order to force him or her to do something [14C. < Latin *pressura* < *press-* (see PRESS[1])] —**pressureless** *adj*

pressure cooker *n* a specially-designed pan used to steam food at high pressure, at a higher temperature and in a shorter time than by boiling —**pressure-cook** *vt*

pressure group *n* a number of people who work together to make their concerns known to those in government and to influence the passage of legislation

pressure point *n* a point at which an artery can be compressed against a bone using a finger, so stemming blood flow to the part of the body that the artery supplies

pressure sore *n* MED same as **bedsore**

pressure suit *n* an inflatable airtight suit, similar to that worn by deep-sea divers, used to protect against the effects of low pressure at very high altitude or in space

pressure vessel *n* a cylindrical or spherically shaped container designed to withstand bursting pressures

pressurize /préshə rīz/ (**-izes, -izing, -ized**), **pressurise** (**-ises, -ising, -ised**) *vt* **1. INCREASE AIR PRESSURE IN ENCLOSED SPACE** to increase the air pressure in an enclosed space, e.g. inside an aircraft, in order to maintain air at close to normal atmospheric pressure when the external air pressure falls **2. INCREASE AIR PRESSURE IN CONTAINER** to increase the pressure of a gas or liquid in a container beyond normal levels **3. MAKE SOMEBODY DO SOMETHING** to apply great persuasion or a strong influence on somebody in order to force him or her to do something ○ *colleagues who had pressurized me to apply for membership* —**pressurization** /préshə rī záysh'n/ *n* —**pressurizer** *n*

presswoman /préss wŏŏmən/ *n* a woman working as a newspaper reporter (*dated*)

presswork /préss wurk/ *n* the operation or management of a printing press, or the work done by it

Prester John /préstər jón/ *n* a legendary Christian priest-king who was believed to rule over a vast kingdom of great wealth in Asia or Africa during the Middle Ages [< Old French *prestre Jehan*, medieval Latin *presbyter Johannes* 'John the priest']

prestidigitation /présti díjji táysh'n/ *n* sleight of hand used in performing magic tricks (*formal or humorous*) [Mid-19C. < French < *prestidigitateur* 'person practising sleight of hand' < *preste* 'nimble' + Latin *digitus* 'finger'] —**prestidigitator** /présti díjji taytər/ *n*

prestige /pre stéezh, -stéej/ *n* **1.** honour, awe, or high opinion inspired by or derived from a high-ranking, influential, or successful person or product **2.** attractiveness and importance that is very obvious or enviable, associated with wealthy or successful people ○ *It's a prestige car and its price reflects that.* [Mid-17C. Via French < Latin *praestigiae* 'illusions, juggler's tricks'] —**prestigious** /pre stíjjəss/ *adj*

prestissimo /pre stíssi mō/ *adv* played or to be played as fast as possible (*used as a musical direction*) ■ *n* (*plural* **-mos**) a musical composition or passage that is to be played as fast as possible [Early 18C. < Italian, superlative of *presto* (see PRESTO)] —**prestissimo** *adj*

presto /préstō/ *adv* **1. VERY FAST** played or to be played very fast (*used as a musical direction*) **2. IMMEDIATELY** instantly, as if magically (*informal*) ■ *n* (*plural* **-tos**) **VERY FAST MUSICAL PIECE** a musical composition or passage that is to be played very fast [Late 16C. Via Italian, 'quick' < Latin *praesto* 'at hand'] —**presto** *adj*

Preston /préstən/ city and port in Lancashire, northwestern England. It is the county's administrative centre. Population: 129,633 (2001).

Preston /prést'n/, **Margaret** (1875–1963) Australian artist. Sometimes influenced by Aboriginal art, her paintings, engravings, and woodcuts are executed in a bold, decorative style. Born **Macpherson, Margaret Rose**

prestress /pree stréss/ (**-stresses, -stressing, -stressed**) *vt* to apply stress to something such as a cable or beam so that it will bear a load better when in use

prestressed concrete /prée strest-/ *n* concrete that is cast over cables that are under tension, so as to increase its strength

Prestwich /préstwich/ industrial town 8 km/5 mi. northwest of Manchester, England. Population: 31,801 (1991).

Prestwick /préstwik/ town near Ayr, southwestern

Scotland, on the Firth of Clyde. It is home to an international airport. Population: 13,705 (1991).

presumably /pri zyóːməbli/ *adv* used to show that you expect that something is the case or will happen or has happened ○ *Presumably that man is her father.*

presume /pri zyóːm/ (**-sumes, -suming, -sumed**) *v* **1.** *vti* **BELIEVE SOMETHING TO BE TRUE** to accept that something is almost certain to be correct even though there is no proof of it, on the grounds that it is extremely likely ○ *After several days of searching, they presumed that there were no survivors.* **2.** *vt* **CONSIDER SOMETHING TRUE WITHOUT LEGAL PROOF** to assume that something is true in the absence of legal proof that will confirm or contradict it **3.** *vt* **SEEM TO PROVE SOMETHING** to indicate the existence or truth of something (*formal*) ○ *Your line of reasoning presumes his being at home the whole evening.* **4.** *vi* **BEHAVE ARROGANTLY OR OVERCONFIDENTLY** to behave so inconsiderately, disrespectfully, or overconfidently as to do something without being entitled or qualified to do it (*usually used in negative statements*) ○ *I would never presume to tell you how to run your business.* **5.** *vi* **TAKE ADVANTAGE** to exploit or take advantage of somebody unscrupulously ○ *would not want to presume on the generosity of a stranger* [14C. Via French < Latin *praesumere* 'take before, anticipate' < *sumere* 'take'] —**presumable** *adj* —**presumer** *n* —**presuming** *adj* —**presumingly** *adv*

presumption /pri zúmpsh'n/ *n* **1. SOMETHING BELIEVED WITHOUT ACTUAL EVIDENCE** a belief based on the fact that something is considered to be extremely reasonable or likely ○ *I acted on the presumption that their IDs were genuine.* **2.** LAW **LEGAL INFERENCE** an inference that something is the case, in the absence of evidence rebutting that assumption and on the basis of other known facts ○ *a presumption of innocence* **3. SOMETHING THAT COULD BE PROOF** an indication that something exists or is true (*formal*) **4. RUDENESS OR ARROGANCE** behaviour that is inconsiderate, disrespectful, or overconfident [12C. Via French < Latin *praesumption-* < *praesumere* (see PRESUME)]

~~**presumptious**~~ incorrect spelling of **presumptuous**

presumptive /pri zúmptiv/ *adj* **1. PROBABLE** based on what is thought most likely or reasonable (*formal*) **2. CAUSING PEOPLE TO PRESUME SOMETHING** forming a reasonable basis for the acceptance that something exists or is true (*formal*) **3. EXPECTED TO BECOME SOMETHING** expected or thought likely to become something (*archaic or formal*) ○ *heir presumptive* **4.** BIOL **POTENTIALLY ABLE TO DIFFERENTIATE** describes cells or tissue of an early embryo that, in the normal course of development, will differentiate to form a particular organ or tissue in the mature embryo [15C. Via French < late Latin *praesumptivus* < Latin *praesumere* (see PRESUME)] —**presumptively** *adv* —**presumptiveness** *n*

presumptuous /pri zúmptyoo əss, -zúmpshəss/ *adj* inconsiderate, disrespectful, or overconfident, especially in doing something when not entitled or qualified to do it [14C. Via French < late Latin *praesumptuosus* < Latin *praesumere* (see PRESUME)] —**presumptuously** *adv* —**presumptuousness** *n*

presuppose /prée sə póz/ (**-poses, -posing, -posed**) *vt* **1.** to make something necessary if a particular thing is to be shown to be true or false. The sentence 'Fred loves his daughter' presupposes that Fred has a daughter. **2.** to believe that a particular thing is true before there is any proof of it ○ *the tendency to presuppose that everybody will understand English* —**presupposition** /prée supə zísh'n/ *n*

prêt-à-porter /prét aa páwr tay/ *adj* manufactured in standard sizes ready to be bought off the peg in shops ■ *n* clothing that is manufactured in standard sizes ready to be bought off the peg [Mid-20C. < French, 'ready-to-wear']

preteen /prée téen/, **preteenager** /-téen ayjər/ *adj* **1. FOR CHILDREN BETWEEN 9 AND 12** relating to, made for, or directed at children in the few years immediately before they become teenagers ○ *preteen clothing* **2. BETWEEN 9 AND 12 YEARS OLD** describes somebody during the few years immediately before the person becomes a teenager ○ *my preteen daughter* ■ *n* **CHILD BETWEEN 9 AND 12** a girl or boy in the few years before becoming a teenager

pretence /pri ténss/ *n* **1. INSINCERE OR FEIGNED BEHAVIOUR** something done or a way of behaving that is not genuine, but is intended to deceive somebody ○ *His display of affection was certainly a pretence.* **2. UNWARRANTED CLAIM** a claim, especially one with few facts to support it (*often used in the negative*) ○ *makes no pretence of expertise* **3. MAKE-BELIEVE** make-believe or things imagined **4.** same as **pretension**[1] (sense 1) [14C. < Anglo-Norman < medieval Latin *pretensus* 'alleged' < past participle of Latin *praetendere* (see PRETEND)]

USAGE pretence or **pretext**? A ***pretext*** is a misleading or untrue reason given to mask a real reason (*came here on the pretext of offering condolences*). ***Pretence*** means: 'insincere behaviour' (*lived a life of pretence*); 'an unwarranted claim' (*made no pretence of being an expert*); and 'pretension' (*resisted conformity and pretence*).

pretend /pri ténd/ *v* (**-tends, -tending, -tended**) **1.** *vti* **ACT AS IF SOMETHING WERE TRUE** to make believe that something is the case or that you are doing something by using your imagination or acting skills ○ *The little girl liked to pretend that she was an astronaut.* ○ *We pretended to be interested in what she was saying.* **2.** *vt* **MAKE INSINCERE CLAIM ABOUT SOMETHING** to claim untruthfully or exaggeratedly to be or to have a particular thing, or imply something in this way ○ *I don't pretend to be an authority on this.* **3.** *vt* **MAKE SOMETHING SEEM TO BE TRUE** to act in a way intended to make somebody believe something untrue or misleading ○ *pretending to be ill* **4.** *vi* **CLAIM TO OWN SOMETHING** to make an untruthful or dubious claim of ownership or the right to something, especially something valuable, admirable, or prestigious (*formal*) ○ *pretends to the throne* ■ *adj* **IMAGINARY** existing only in the imagination, not real (*informal; usually used by children*) ○ *I made a pretend house where my pretend horse lives.* [14C. Directly or via French < Latin *praetendere* 'extend in front' < *tendere* 'to stretch'] —**pretended** *adj*

pretender /pri téndər/ *n* **1.** somebody who claims a disputed right to a special rank, title, or privilege, especially a royal title. Both the son and the grandson of James II of Great Britain claimed the throne and were known as the Old Pretender and the Young Pretender. **2.** somebody who intentionally gives a false impression to somebody else

pretense *n* US spelling of **pretence**

pretension[1] /pree ténsh'n/ *n* **1. AFFECTED BEHAVIOUR** affected behaviour intended to give an appearance of greater importance, status, or knowledge than is warranted **2. QUESTIONABLE CLAIM TO SOMETHING** an untruthful or dubious assertion of a right to something, especially something valuable, admirable, or prestigious (*often used in the plural and with negatives*) ○ *His pretensions to aristocratic birth were unconvincing.* **3. MAKING OF CLAIM TO SOMETHING** the act of formally putting forward a claim (*formal*) [15C. < medieval Latin *praetension-* < past participle of Latin *praetendere* (see PRETEND)]

pretension[2] /pree ténsh'n/ (**-sions, -sioning, -sioned**) *vt* to strengthen reinforced concrete by applying tension to the reinforcing steel before the concrete has set [Mid-20C. < PRE- + TENSION]

pretentious /pri ténshəss/ *adj* **1. SELF-IMPORTANT AND AFFECTED** acting as though more important or special than is warranted, or appearing to have an unrealistically high self-image **2. MADE TO LOOK OR SOUND IMPORTANT** intended to seem to have a special quality or significance, but often seeming forced or too clever ○ *dismissed it as yet another pretentious film* **3. OSTENTATIOUS** extravagantly and consciously showy or glamourous [Mid-19C. < French *prétentieux* < *prétention* < medieval Latin *praetension-* (see PRETENSION[1])] —**pretentiously** *adv* —**pretentiousness** *n*

preter- *prefix* beyond ○ *preternatural* [< Latin *praeter* < *prae* 'before']

preterite /préttərit/ *n* GRAM same as **past tense** [14C. Via French < Latin *(tempus) praeteritum* 'past (tense)' < past participle of *praeterire* (see PRETERITION)] —**preterite** *adj*

preterition /préttə rísh'n/ *n* **1.** the act of passing over something or leaving something out (*formal*) **2.** the Calvinist doctrine that those people who were not predestined to be saved were passed over by God [Late 16C. < late Latin *praeterition-* 'a passing by' < Latin *praeterire* 'go by' < *ire* 'go']

preterm /prée túrm/ *adj* born before completion of a pregnancy of normal length

pretermit /préetər mít/ (**-mits, -mitting, -mitted**) *vt* (*formal*) **1.** to overlook or ignore something deliberately **2.** to leave something out or undone [15C. < Latin *praetermittere* 'let go by' < *mittere* 'send off'] —**pretermission** /-mísh'n/ *n* —**pretermitter** *n*

preternatural /préetər náchərəl/ *adj* **1.** exceeding what is normal in nature (*formal or literary*) **2.** supernatural or uncanny (*literary*) [Late 16C. < medieval Latin *praeternaturalis* < Latin *praeter naturam* 'beyond nature'] —**preternaturalism** *n* —**preternaturality** /préetər náchə rálləti/ *n* —**preternaturally** *adv*

pretext /prée tekst/ *n* a misleading or untrue reason given for doing something in an attempt to conceal the real reason [Early 16C. < Latin *praetextus* 'show, display' < past participle of *praetexere* 'weave before, adorn' < *texere* 'weave']

USAGE See ***pretence***.

pretor *n* ANCIENT HIST another spelling of **praetor**

Pretoria /pri táwri ə/ administrative capital of South Africa, in the northeast of the country. Population: 1,985,995 (2001).

pretorian, etc. ANCIENT HIST another spelling of **praetorian, etc.**

Pretorius /pri táwri əss/, **Andries** (1798–1853) Boer general and political leader. The father of Marthinus Pretorius, he was a leader of the Great Trek, and fought the Zulus and the British. Full name **Pretorius, Andries Wilhemus Jacobus**

Pretorius, Marthinus (1819–1901) Boer general and political leader. The son of Andries Pretorius, he was president of the Transvaal (1857–71) and of the Orange Free State (1859–63). Full name **Pretorius, Marthinus Wessels**

prettify /prítti fī/ (**-fies, -fying, -fied**) *vt* to give a person, place, or thing some added decoration, especially of a rather superficial or fussy kind —**prettification** /príttifi káysh'n/ *n* —**prettifier** *n*

pretty /prítti/ *adj* (**-tier, -tiest**) **1. WITH PLEASANT FACE** having an attractive pleasant face that is graceful and appealing rather than outstandingly beautiful **2. NICE TO LOOK AT** pleasing or charming in a delicate, gentle, or decorative way ○ *The garden looks so pretty at this time of year.* ○ *a pretty tune* **3. GRACEFUL** used to describe a boy or man who has the pleasing looks and graceful manner often associated with a woman (*sometimes offensive*) **4. UNSATISFACTORY** very bad or unsatisfactory (*informal*) ○ *got into a pretty mess* **5. WEAK AND SUPERFICIAL** appealing or charming to hear or look at, but without any deep meaning or sincerity ○ *pretty words* **6. LARGE** large in size, extent, or value (*informal*) ○ *cost a pretty penny* ■ *adv* **FAIRLY** to a fairly large, noticeable, or reasonable extent (*informal*) ○ *I'm pretty sure I lost my keys.* ■ *n* (*plural* **-ties**) **SOMEBODY WHO IS PRETTY** a pretty person, thing, or animal (*archaic informal*) ■ *vt* (**-ties, -tying, -tied**) **MAKE SOMEBODY OR SOMETHING PRETTY** to make somebody or something pretty to look at [Old English *prættig* < Germanic, 'trick'] —**prettily** *adv* —**prettiness** *n* ◇ **pretty well** nearly completely (*informal*) ○ *I've pretty well finished reading it.*

SYNONYMS See ***good-looking***.

pretty up *vt* same as **pretty**

Pretty Good Privacy E-COMMERCE full form of **PGP**

pretty-pretty *adj* pretty in a way that looks contrived or ridiculous (*informal*) ○ *a pretty-pretty hat covered in flowers and ribbons*

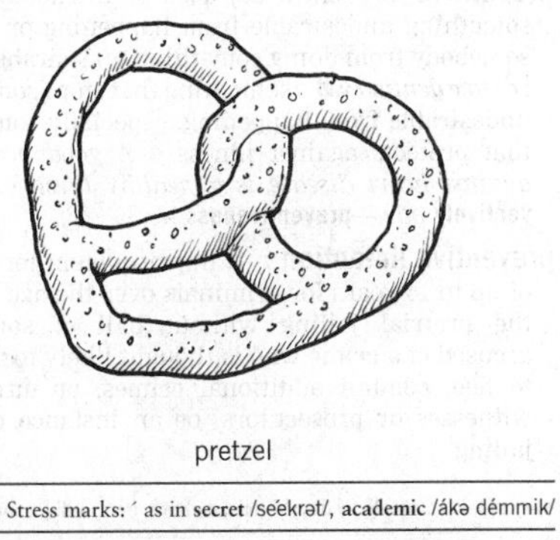

pretzel

pretzel /préts'l/ *n* a crisp salted knot-shaped or stick-shaped biscuit with a golden-brown glaze. See illustration on previous page (*often used in the plural*) [Mid-19C. < German]

prevail /pri váyl/ (**-vails, -vailing, -vailed**) *vi* **1. BE STRONGER** to prove to be stronger and in the position of greater influence and power ○ *He prevailed over his enemies.* **2. WIN THROUGH** to prove to be effective ○ *Justice will prevail.* **3. PREDOMINATE** to predominate or be the most common or frequent ○ *Sunny skies prevail across the northeast.* **4. BE CURRENT** to remain in general use or effect (*formal*) ○ *The old customs still prevail in some parts of the country.* [14C. < Latin *praevalere* 'be stronger' < *valere* 'be strong'] —**prevailer** *n*

prevail on, prevail upon *vt* to persuade somebody to do something ○ *They prevailed on her to take part.*

prevailing /pri váyling/ *adj* **1.** found most commonly or having the most power or effect in an area ○ *prevailing winds* **2.** found, existing, or in force at a particular time ○ *the prevailing view among modern scientists* —**prevailingly** *adv*

prevalent /prévvələnt/ *adj* occurring, accepted or practised commonly or widely ○ *reported a prevalent belief that the economy is structurally sound* [Late 16C. < Latin *praevalent-*, present participle of *praevalere* (see PREVAIL)] —**prevalence** *n* —**prevalently** *adv*

SYNONYMS See ***widespread***.

prevaricate /pri várri kayt/ (**-cates, -cating, -cated**) *vi* to avoid giving a direct and honest answer or opinion, or a clear and truthful account of a situation, especially by quibbling or being deliberately ambiguous or misleading [Mid-16C. < Latin *praevaricat-*, past participle stem of *praevaricari* 'walk crookedly' < *varus* 'crooked, knock-kneed'] —**prevarication** /pri várri káysh'n/ *n* —**prevaricator** *n*

USAGE prevaricate or **procrastinate**? These two verbs are sometimes confused. ***Prevaricate*** means 'to avoid giving a direct answer or a truthful account' whereas ***procrastinate*** means 'to postpone something': *Don't prevaricate – tell me exactly what happened. Don't procrastinate – the sooner you make a start, the sooner it will be finished.*

~~prevelant~~, ~~prevelent~~ incorrect spelling of **prevalent**

prevenient /pri véeni ənt/ *adj* (*formal*) **1.** coming or occurring in advance of another thing **2.** producing a sense of anticipation [Early 17C. < Latin *praevenient-*, present participle of *praevenire* 'come before' (see PREVENT)]

prevent /pri vént/ (**-vents, -venting, -vented**) *vt* **1. STOP SOMETHING FROM HAPPENING** to cause something not to happen or not to be done ○ *Rain prevented them from playing the match.* **2. STOP SOMEBODY FROM DOING SOMETHING** to be the reason why somebody does not or cannot do something ○ *a sense of duty that prevented him from abandoning the project* **3. STAND IN WAY OF SOMETHING** to be the reason why something is impossible or very difficult ○ *Modesty prevents that I reveal the true reason.* [15C. < Latin *prevent-*, past participle of *praevenire* 'come before, prevent' < *venire* 'come'] —**preventability** /pri véntə bíllәti/ *n* —**preventable** *adj* —**preventably** *adv* —**preventer** *n*

preventative /pri véntətiv/ *adj, n* same as **preventive**

prevention /pri vénsh'n/ *n* **1.** an action or actions taken to stop somebody from doing something or to stop something from happening ○ *the prevention of crime* **2.** an action that makes it impossible or very difficult for somebody to do something or for something to happen ○ *taking aspirin as a prevention against heart attacks*

preventive /pri véntiv/ *adj* used or intended to stop something undesirable from happening or to stop somebody from doing something undesirable ○ *preventive dentistry* ■ *n* something that stops something undesirable from happening, especially something that protects against illness ○ *A good preventive against heart disease is a healthy lifestyle.* —**preventively** *adv* —**preventiveness** *n*

preventive detention *n* **1.** imprisonment for a term of up to 14 years for criminals over the age of 30 **2.** the pretrial jailing without bail of somebody accused of a crime who is thought likely to attempt to flee, commit additional crimes, or intimidate witnesses or prosecutors, or an instance of such jailing

preverbal /pree vúrbəl/ *adj* **1.** at the stage of development when a child is not yet able to use speech **2.** coming before a verb

preview /prée vyoo/ *n* **1. OPPORTUNITY TO SEE SOMETHING IN ADVANCE** a showing of something, especially a film, play, or exhibition, to a select audience before the general public sees it **2. DESCRIPTION OF FORTHCOMING SHOW** a piece printed in a paper or magazine or broadcast on radio or TV describing and commenting on something that is soon to be broadcast or presented to the public **3. PROMOTIONAL FILM** a short film shown on TV or at the cinema promoting an forthcoming film or programme **4. INDICATION OF FUTURE EVENT** a sample or foretaste of something likely to occur in the future ○ *polls that could provide a preview of actual election results* ■ *vt* (**-views, -viewing, -viewed**) **1. SHOW SOMETHING IN ADVANCE** to put on a performance or showing of something for a select audience before the general public has the opportunity to see it **2. DESCRIBE SHOW IN ADVANCE** to write, print, or broadcast a short piece that describes and comments on something that is soon to be broadcast or presented to the public

previous /préevi əss/ *adj* **1. COMING BEFORE SOMEBODY OR SOMETHING** occurring before somebody or something of the same kind ○ *his previous girlfriend* ○ *the previous edition* **2. ALREADY ARRANGED** existing, made, or settled before the one being referred to now ○ *a previous engagement* **3. ACTING TOO HASTILY** saying or doing something earlier than is appropriate (*informal*) ■ *n* CRIME **CRIMINAL RECORD** previous convictions for a criminal offence (*slang*) [Early 17C. < Latin *praevius* 'going before' < *via* 'way'] —**previousness** *n* ◇ **previous to something** before a particular thing took place

previously /préevi əsli/ *adv* at an earlier time or on an earlier occasion

previous question *n* **1.** in the House of Commons, a motion to stop a question being debated, so that a vote cannot be held on it **2.** in the House of Lords and US legislative bodies, a motion to put a question that will end a debate so that a vote on a bill can be taken without delay

prevision /pri vízh'n/ *n* (*formal or literary*) **1.** the ability to predict or foresee things **2.** a prediction or premonition

prevocalic /prée vō kállik/ *adj* describes a consonant that comes immediately before a vowel —**prevocalically** *adv*

prewar /prée wáwr/ *adj* dating from or belonging to the period before a war, especially World War I or World War II ○ *prewar fashions*

prewashed /prée wósht/ *adj* washed before being packaged and sold in the shops —**prewash** *n, vt*

prey /pray/ (*plural* **preys**) *n* **1. ANIMAL HUNTED BY OTHER ANIMALS** an animal or animals caught, killed, and eaten by another animal as food ○ *The common shrew's prey consists largely of earthworms and woodlice.* **2. SOMEBODY TREATED UNKINDLY BY OTHERS** somebody who is attacked by or receives cruel or unfair treatment from somebody else ○ *a young heiress who was the prey of fortune hunters* **3. KILLING OF OTHER ANIMALS AS FOOD** the natural practice or habit of predatory animals of hunting, killing, and eating other animals ○ *a bird of prey* **4. PLUNDER** items stolen or plundered (*archaic or literary*) [13C. Via Old French *preie* < Latin *praeda* 'booty'] —**preyer** *n* ◇ **be (a) prey to something** to experience something unpleasant regularly or be at risk of something unpleasant

SPELLCHECK See *pray*.

prey on, prey upon *vt* **1.** to hunt and kill other animals for food ○ *Owls prey on mice and rabbits.* **2.** to victimize or exploit somebody

prezzie /prézzi/, **pressie** *n* a gift or present (*informal*) ○ *Did you get lots of prezzies on your birthday?* [Mid-20C. Shortening and alteration of PRESENT[1]]

Priam /prī əm/ *n* in Greek mythology, the king of Troy, husband of Hecuba, and father of Hector, Paris, and Cassandra

priapic /prī áppik/ *adj* **1. OF MALE SEXUAL ACTIVITY** relating to or showing a preoccupation with male sexual activity **2. RELATING TO PHALLUS** relating to or resembling a phallus (*dated or literary*) **3.** MED **WITH PENIS PERMANENTLY ERECT** having a permanently erect penis [Late 18C. < Latin *Priapus*, Greek *Priapos* 'Priapus', symbolized by the erect phallus]

priapism /prí əpizəm/ *n* a medical disorder in which there is persistent, often painful erection of the penis in the absence of sexual interest [Early 17C. < Latin *Priapus* (see PRIAPIC)]

Priapus /prī áypəss/ *n* in Greek mythology, the god of fertility

Pribilof Islands /príbbi lof-/ group of islands off southwestern Alaska, in the southeastern Bering Sea. Population: 901 (1990). Area: 161 sq. km/62 sq. mi.

price /prīss/ *n* **1. COST OF SOMETHING BOUGHT OR SOLD** the amount, usually of money, that is offered or asked for when something is bought or sold **2. SOMETHING SACRIFICED TO GET SOMETHING ELSE** something lost or given in order to achieve a particular position or condition ○ *Unwanted media attention is the price of fame.* **3. SUFFICIENT BRIBE** the sum of money or other recompense in return for which somebody agrees to do something ○ *The price of her cooperation was an invitation to the gala dinner.* **4. REWARD MONEY** a sum of money offered as a reward for the capture or killing of a criminal or outlaw (*dated or literary*) ○ *an outlaw with a price on his head* **5. MEASURE OF VALUE OF SOMETHING** an estimate of what somebody or something is worth, e.g. how important, useful, or irreplaceable he, she, or it is (*dated or literary*) **6. BETTING ODDS** betting or gambling odds ■ *vt* (**prices, pricing, priced**) **1. DECIDE HOW MUCH SOMETHING COSTS** to state or fix the exact amount that a customer or consumer must pay for something ○ *He priced the antique clock at £500.* **2. MARK SOMETHING WITH PRICE** to show how much something costs, especially by writing on the item itself or by attaching a label or price tag ○ *spent the morning pricing merchandise* **3. FIND OUT WHAT SOMETHING COSTS** to check the price that has been set for a product, or compare the different prices charged at a variety of shops or from different companies ○ *priced a few computers before deciding which one to buy* [13C. Via Old French *pris* < Latin *pretium* 'price, money'] —**pricer** *n* ◇ **at any price** no matter how great the cost may be (*often used with a negative*) ◇ **at a price** at a considerable cost ◇ **beyond price** priceless ◇ **pay the price (for something)** to suffer the unpleasant consequences of something that you have done ◇ **what price something?** used to suggest that something such as an ideal or a promise has no value ○ *'What Price Glory?'* (Maxwell Anderson, *What Price Glory?*, 1924)

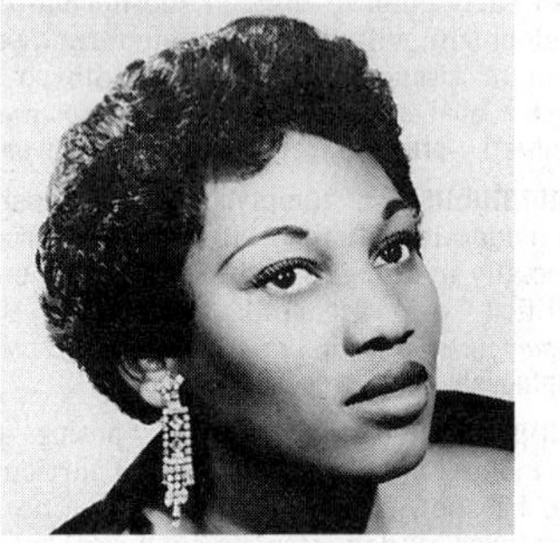

US Information Agency

Leontyne Price

Price /prīss/, **Leontyne** (*b.* 1927) US operatic soprano. During a long career as a major international opera star (1952–85), she was especially associated with Italian opera. Full name **Price, Mary Violet Leontyne**

> 'Once you get on stage, everything is right. I feel the most beautiful, complete, fulfilled. I think that's why, in the case of noncompromising career women, parts of our personal lives don't work out. One person can't give you the feeling that thousands of people give you.'
> [Leontyne Price. Quoted in *I Dream a World: Portraits of Black Women Who Changed America*, Brian Lanker; 1989]

price control *n* government control over prices of goods and services, usually introduced as an emergency measure

price-cutting *n* the reduction of prices below their usual level in order to sell more than competitors

price discrimination *n* the charging of different prices for the same product or service in different markets

price-dividend ratio *n* the ratio of a share's price to the dividends paid in the previous year

price-earnings ratio *n* the ratio of a share's price to its earnings, which provides an indication of its value

price fixing *n* the setting of prices by government or by agreement between producers, instead of by free market operation

price index *n* a mathematical quantity that is used to measure movements in price levels over different periods of time

price leadership *n* the setting of a price by the market leader at a level that competitors can match in order to avoid price-cutting

priceless /prīssləss/ *adj* **1.** worth more than can be calculated in terms of money ○ *the priceless treasures of the pharaohs' tombs* **2.** extremely comical and amusing (*informal*) ○ *a priceless comment* —**pricelessly** *adv* —**pricelessness** *n*

price point *n* the retail price of a product, especially within a range of prices of similar goods

price ring *n* a group of traders who cooperate, usually illegally, to maintain the price of the goods that they sell in order to prevent competition

price support *n* government maintenance of price levels, e.g. by subsidies to producers

price tag *n* **1.** a small label attached to an item that is for sale, with the price written or printed on it **2.** the amount that something costs, whether in money or in something else such as emotional outlay or loss of life or health (*informal*)

pricey /prīssi/ (**-ier, -iest**), **pricy** *adj* charging high prices or costing a great deal (*informal*) ○ *a pricey restaurant* —**priceyness** *n*

Prichard /prich aard/, **Katherine Susannah** (1883–1969) Australian writer. Her fiction, including *Working Bullocks* (1926) and *Coonardoo* (1929), interprets Australian life in terms of class struggle.

prick /prik/ *v* (**pricks, pricking, pricked**) **1.** *vt* **PIERCE SMALL HOLE IN SOMETHING** to puncture the surface of something, especially the skin, by piercing it lightly with something sharp and finely pointed ○ *pricked her finger on a cactus needle* **2.** *vti* **HURT IN STINGING WAY** to feel a slight stinging sensation, or cause something such as the eyes or the skin to hurt in this way ○ *felt his eyes prick with tears* **3.** *vt* **SUDDENLY CAUSE DISCOMFORT TO SOMEBODY** to make somebody feel a sudden strong unease, e.g. because of guilt or shame ○ *His conscience began to prick him.* **4.** *vt* **OUTLINE SOMETHING USING TINY HOLES** to make a number of small holes in or through the surface of a board, piece of card, or fabric so as to form the outline of something **5.** *vti* **RAISE EARS** to cause an animal's ears to stick up straight on hearing something, or stick up straight for this reason ○ *The dog pricked its ears at the sound of its master's voice.* **6.** *vt* **PUSH SOMEBODY INTO ACTIVITY** to force or encourage somebody to start or continue with greater speed an activity or course of action ○ *If only we could prick him into action.* **7.** *vt* **MAKE ANIMAL MOVE FASTER** to urge an animal, especially a horse, to gallop or move more quickly by digging the spurs or heels into its flank (*archaic or literary*) ■ *n* **1. QUICK SHARP PAIN** a sudden twinge of pain such as that caused by a fine point being pushed into the skin **2. SMALL PUNCTURE** a small puncture, hole, or indented mark, or an act of piercing that causes such a puncture **3. TABOO TERM** a highly offensive term for a penis (*taboo*) **4. TABOO TERM** a highly offensive term for a man regarded as inadequate or unpleasant (*taboo*) **5. PAINFUL THOUGHT** a sudden unpleasant thought or feeling, often one related to a past action or event **6. HARE'S FOOTPRINT** the footprint of an animal such as a hare **7. POINTED IMPLEMENT** a pointed implement or weapon, e.g. a goad (*archaic*) [Old English *prica* < W Germanic] ◇ **kick against the pricks** to show opposition to authority, rules, or circumstances that you have no power to influence

prick out *vt* to make a series of small holes in an area of soil and put young seedlings into these holes to grow

pricker /príkər/ *n* a tool used to prick or pierce small holes in something

pricket /príkit/ *n* **1.** a male deer in its second year, usually one with unbranched antlers **2.** a metal spike for sticking a candle on

prickle /prík'l/ *n* **1. TINGLING FEELING** a tingling or stinging sensation **2. PROJECTION ON PLANT** a sharp pointed projection on the outer surface of a leaf or plant ■ *vti* (**-les, -ling, -led**) **HURT IN STINGING WAY** to feel a sharp stinging pain, or cause something such as the eyes or the skin to hurt in this way ■ *n* ZOOL **ANIMAL'S SPINE** a spine on an animal such as a hedgehog [Old English *pricel* 'small prick' < W Germanic, 'prick']

prickly /príkli/ (**-lier, -liest**) *adj* **1. WITH SMALL SHARP SPIKES** having a surface or skin with prickles on it **2. UNCOMFORTABLE** irritating to the skin, especially because of fibres or prickles that are rough to the touch **3. OVERSENSITIVE** easily angered, offended, or upset (*informal*) ○ *He's very prickly on that subject.* **4. PROBLEMATIC OR UPSETTING** especially difficult and likely to upset people (*informal*) ○ *They tried to keep off prickly subjects like politics and religion.* —**prickliness** *n*

prickly ash *n* **1.** an aromatic bush or small tree with prickly branches. Flowers: small, greenish, in clusters. Native to: eastern North America. Latin name: *Zanthoxylum americanum*. **2.** a spiny bush or tree with pinnately compound leaves. Native to: southern United States. Latin name: *Zanthoxylum clavaherculis*.

prickly-backed urchin *n regional* same as **hedgehog**

REGIONAL NOTE See ***hedgehog***.

prickly heat *n* a rash of tiny raised spots, accompanied by redness and itching, appearing on the skin in hot or humid conditions. Technical name **miliaria**

prickly pear *n* a cactus with flattened, jointed, spiny stems and pear-shaped fruits that are edible in some species. Flowers: large, yellow or orange. Native to: North, Central, and South America. Genus: *Opuntia*.

prickly poppy *n* a poppy plant with bristly stems and leaves. Flowers: yellow, lavender, or white. Use: formerly, in herbal medicine. Genus: *Argemone*.

prick-teaser, **prick-tease** *n* a highly offensive term for somebody who makes sexual advances towards a man without intending to have sex with him (*taboo*)

pricy *adj* COMM another spelling of **pricey** (*informal*)

pride /prīd/ *n* **1. SATISFACTION WITH SELF** the happy satisfied feeling somebody experiences when having or achieving something special that other people admire ○ *took great pride in his work* **2. PROPER SENSE OF OWN VALUE** the correct level of respect for the importance and value of your personal character, life, efforts, or achievements ○ *He had lost all his confidence and pride.* **3. FEELING OF SUPERIORITY** a haughty attitude shown by somebody who believes, often unjustifiably, that he or she is better than others ○ *Her pride prevented her from mixing with those she considered her social inferiors.* **4. SOURCE OF PERSONAL SATISFACTION** something such as an achievement or possession that somebody feels especially pleased and satisfied with ○ *His grandchildren were his pride and joy.* **5. BEST TIME** the best condition or period of something (*literary*) **6. GROUP OF LIONS** a group of lions, usually consisting of up to a dozen related adult females, their cubs and juveniles, plus from one to six adult males ■ *vr* (**prides, priding, prided**) **pride yourself BE PROUD OF SOMETHING** to obtain personal satisfaction and pleasure from a particular source, especially something accomplished or a quality possessed ○ *He prides himself on his meticulous timekeeping.* [Pre-12C. < PROUD] —**prideful** *adj* —**pridefully** *adv* ◇ **pride of place** the most important or prominent position

CULTURAL NOTE ***Pride and Prejudice***, a novel (1813) by Jane Austen. Through the story of the relationship between Elizabeth Bennet, the fiercely independent daughter of minor gentry, and Mr Darcy, a wealthy and haughty nobleman, Austen reveals how both pride and prejudice create barriers to mutual understanding.

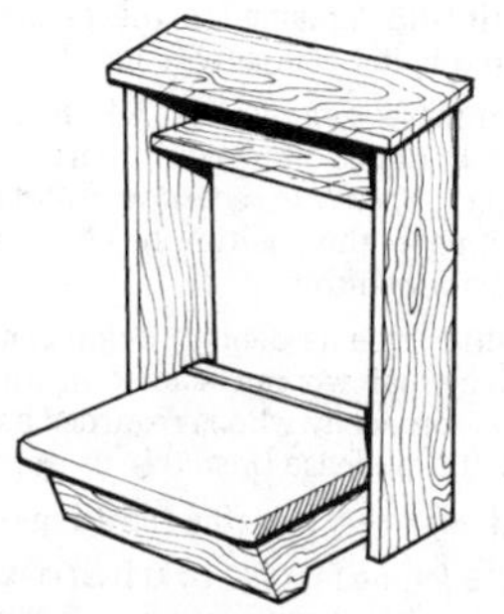

prie-dieu

prie-dieu /preé dyő/ (*plural* **prie-dieux** /-dyő/) *n* a shelved wooden desk for use when praying, usually with a low surface for kneeling on and a higher surface for resting the elbows or a book on [Mid-18C. < French, 'pray God']

prier /prī ər/, **pryer** *n* somebody who pries

priest /preest/ *n* **1. ORDAINED CHRISTIAN MINISTER** an ordained minister, especially in the Roman Catholic, Anglican, or Eastern Orthodox churches, responsible for administering the sacraments, preaching, and ministering to the needs of the congregation **2. MINISTER OF NON-CHRISTIAN RELIGION** a spiritual leader or teacher of a non-Christian religion **3. DESCENDANT OF FAMILY OF AARON** somebody descended from the family of Aaron of the house of Levi, appointed as priests in the Hebrew Scriptures [Old English *prēost*, via Germanic < ecclesiastical Latin *presbyter* (see PRESBYTER)]

priestess /pree stéss, preést ess, preéstiss/ *n* a woman who is a spiritual leader in a pagan religion

priesthood /preést hood/ *n* **1.** the official role, position, or office of a priest **2.** the priests of a particular religion, considered as a group

Priestley /preéstli/, **J. B.** (1894–1984) British novelist, playwright, and broadcaster. Among his works are *The Good Companions* (1929), *English Journey* (1934), and *An Inspector Calls* (1947). Full name **Priestley, John Boynton**

Priestley, Joseph (1733–1804) British chemist and political radical. He isolated and described the properties of oxygen and other gases, and is considered one of the founders of modern chemistry.

> 'More is owing to what we call *chance*, that is, philosophically speaking, to the observation of events arising from *unknown causes*, than to any proper *design*, or pre-conceived theory of the business.'
> [Joseph Priestley, *Experiments and Observations of Different Types of Air*; 1775]

priestly /preéstli/ *adj* **1.** used, worn, or performed exclusively by priests ○ *priestly garments* **2.** characteristic of or suitable for a priest —**priestliness** *n*

priest-ridden *adj* influenced or controlled by priests or religious dogma to what is regarded as an unacceptable degree (*literary*)

priest's hole, **priest-hole** *n* a small hidden room or space in an English house, created as a hiding-place for Roman Catholic priests and others trying to escape persecution after the English Reformation

prig /prig/ *n* somebody who is regarded as taking pride in behaving in a very correct and proper way, and in feeling morally superior to others [Late 17C. Origin ?] —**priggery** *n* —**priggish** *adj* —**priggishly** *adv* —**priggishness** *n* —**priggism** *n*

prill /pril/ *vt* (**prills, prilling, prilled**) to make a solid into granules or pellets that flow freely and do not clump together ■ *n* a granule or pellet made by prilling [Late 18C. Origin ?]

prim /prim/ *adj* (**primmer, primmest**) **1. PRUDISH** easily shocked by vulgar or obscene language or behaviour **2. FORMAL AND PROPER** excessively formal and proper in manner or appearance ■ *v* (**prims, primming, primmed**) **1.** *vti* **ASSUME PROPER EXPRESSION** to take on an affectedly proper expression **2.** *vt* **MAKE SOMEBODY LOOK VERY PROPER** to make somebody look excessively proper [Early 18C. Origin ?] —**primly** *adv* —**primness** *n*

prima ballerina /preémə-/ *n* the principal woman dancer in a ballet company [< Italian, 'first ballerina']

primacy /prímassi/ (*plural* **-cies**) *n* **1.** the state of being the first or most important part or aspect of something ○ *Speech is regarded as having primacy over writing.* **2.** the position or office of a primate in a Christian church

prima donna /preémə dónnə/ (*plural* **prima donnas**) *n* **1.** the principal woman soloist in an opera production **2.** somebody who is regarded as demanding and difficult to please (*insult*) [< Italian, 'first lady']

primaeval *adj* PREHIST another spelling of **primeval**

prima facie /prímə fáyshi/ *adv* **AT FIRST GLANCE** on initial examination or consideration ○ *Prima facie, this lawsuit seems spurious.* ■ *adj* **1. APPARENT** clear from a first impression ○ *a prima facie counterexample to your hypothesis* **2. LEGALLY SUFFICIENT** sufficient in law to establish a case or fact, unless disproved [< Latin, 'at first appearance']

primage /prímij/ *n NZ* a tax payable in addition to customs duty [15C. < Anglo-Latin *primagium*]

primal /prím'l/ *adj* **1.** first or earliest, and often basic ○ *the primal instinct for survival* **2.** most significant and primary ○ *our primal need for a new fuel source* [Mid-16C. < medieval Latin *primalis* < Latin *primus* 'first'] —**primality** /prī mállәti/ *n*

primal scream *n* a cry of extreme anger that somebody undergoing primal therapy is encouraged to utter

primal therapy *n* a style of psychotherapy in which somebody relives past traumas and unleashes repressed anger and frustration through screams, tantrums, or beating inanimate objects

primaquine /prímə kween/, **primaquine phosphate** *n* a synthetic drug derived from quinoline. Use: treatment of malaria. Formula: $C_{15}H_{21}N_3O$. [Mid-20C. < 1st element probably < form of Latin *primus* 'first' + *-quine*, INN stem]

primarily /prímərəli, prī márrəli/ *adv* **1.** mainly or mostly ○ *Baldness is primarily found among adult men.* **2.** originally or at first

primary /prímәri/ *adj* **1. FIRST IN SEQUENCE** first or earliest in a sequence ○ *the primary stage of development* **2. MOST IMPORTANT** ranked as most important **3. BASIC** essential or basic to something **4. FIRST-HAND** obtained directly from or due directly to something ○ *seeking out primary sources of information* **5. ORIGINAL** existing first, from the beginning, or before all others **6. RELATING TO EARLY EDUCATION** relating to the early years of formal education, usually for children between the ages of 5 and 12 **7. RELATING TO NATURAL RESOURCE INDUSTRY** relating to or produced by an industry such as forestry, mining, or agriculture, that collects and processes a natural resource **8.** ELEC **OF CURRENT-INDUCING COMPONENT** describes a circuit component such as a coil that induces a current in a neighbouring circuit **9.** CHEM **SUBSTITUTING ATOMS** relating to or resulting from the replacement of one or more atoms in a molecule **10.** CHEM **OF ATTACHED CARBON ATOM** describes a carbon atom in a molecule that is bonded to one other carbon atom only **11.** BIOCHEM **OF AMINO ACID SEQUENCE** describes the basic type, number, or sequence of amino acids in a polypeptide **12.** BOT **GROWN FROM EMBRYONIC TISSUE** describes growth from embryonic tissue in the tip of a root or shoot ■ *n* (*plural* **-ies**) **1. FIRST THING** something that is first in time or order **2. MOST IMPORTANT THING** a part or aspect of something that is the most important **3. BASIC PART OR ASPECT** something that is essential or basic to something **4. ORIGINAL FORM** the earliest form of something **5.** EDUC same as **primary school** (*used in school names*) **6.** POL **ELECTION OF CANDIDATES FOR GOVERNMENTAL POSITION** in the United States, an election in which members of a party choose candidates for a governmental position **7.** POL **ELECTION OF DELEGATES TO CHOOSE CANDIDATES** in the United States, an election to choose delegates who will choose the party's candidates at a political convention **8.** COLOURS same as **primary colour** **9.** ELEC same as **primary coil** **10.** ASTRON **BRIGHTER STAR OF BINARY STAR** the brighter or larger of two stars in a binary star **11.** ASTRON same as **primary planet** **12.** BIRDS same as **primary feather** [15C. < Latin *primarius* < *primus* 'first']

primary accent *n US* same as **primary stress**

primary care *n* the level of health care at which a patient is assessed and treated by a general practitioner or nurse, or, if necessary, is referred to a specialist

primary cell *n* an electrical cell that uses an irreversible chemical reaction to generate electricity and, as a result, cannot be recharged

primary coil *n* a coil forming part of a machine or circuit in which the current flow sets up the magnetic flux necessary for the operation of the machine or circuit

primary colour *n* **1.** each of the three basic colours of the spectrum, red, yellow, or blue (**primary additive colours**), from which all other colours can be blended **2.** each of the three basic colours, cyan, magenta, or yellow (**primary subtractive colours**), which, when subtracted from white, can produce all other colours

primary consumer *n* an animal that eats plants, considered in terms of its position in a food chain

primary feather *n* a main flight feather on the outer half of a bird's wing

primary planet *n* a planet in direct orbit around a sun

primary process *n* in Freudian psychoanalysis, a basic process that is involved in the functioning of the id and is ruled by the pleasure principle

primary production *n* the total chemical energy produced by photosynthesis

primary qualities *npl* properties, e.g. spatial location, that are independent of the mind and are inseparable from the objects studied by sciences such as physics

primary school *n* **1.** in the United Kingdom, a school in which children usually aged between 5 and 11 or 12 are taught **2.** in the United States, a school in which the first four to eight grades are taught, often including kindergarten as well

primary storage *n* the main memory in a computer, including the random-access memory and the read-only memory, directly accessible by the processor

primary stress *n UK, ANZ, Can* the strongest force used in pronouncing one of the syllables of a word with more than one syllable or the mark, usually ', used to indicate this. For example, in the word 'secondary', the primary stress falls on the first syllable. US term **primary accent**

primary syphilis *n* the first of the three stages of syphilis, in which a painless growth (**chancre**) grows at the site of infection and the infecting bacterium (**spirochaete**) spreads throughout the body

primary wave *n* a seismic wave that creates vibrations parallel to its direction

primate /prí mayt/ *n* **1.** a member of an order of mammals with a large brain and complex hands and feet, including humans, apes, and monkeys. Order: Primates. **2.** *also* **Primate** an archbishop or high-ranking bishop [12C. < Latin *primat-* 'of the first rank' < *primus* 'first'] —**primatial** /prī máysh'l/ *adj*

~~**primative**~~ incorrect spelling of **primitive**

primatology /prímə tólləji/ *n* the scientific study of primates, especially nonhuman primates —**primatological** /prímətə lójjik'l/ *adj* —**primatologist** *n*

primavera[1] /preémə váirə/ (*plural* **-ras** or *same*) *n* **1.** the light coloured wood of a Central American tree. Use: furniture-making. **2.** a tree that has yellow flowers and palmate leaves and yields primavera. Native to: Central America. Latin name: *Cybistax donnellsmithii*. [Late 19C. Via Spanish, 'springtime' (because the tree flowers in spring) < late Latin *prima vera* (see PRIMAVERA[2])]

primavera[2] /preémə váirə/ *adj* made with an assortment of fresh spring vegetables, especially sliced as an accompaniment to pasta, meat, or seafood [Late 20C. < Italian *(alla) primavera* '(in the) spring (style)' < late Latin *prima vera* 'early spring' < Latin *primum ver* 'first spring']

prime[1] /prīm/ *adj* **1. BEST** of the highest quality ○ *prime grade beef* **2. FIRST IN IMPORTANCE** of the greatest importance or the highest rank **3. EARLIEST** earliest in time or sequence **4.** MATHS **NOT DIVISIBLE WITHOUT REMAINDER** describes a number that can be divided without a remainder only by one and itself **5.** MATHS **LACKING COMMON FACTORS** describes a number that has no common factors with another number ○ *15 is prime to 8.* ■ *n* **1. BEST STAGE OF SOMETHING** the best state or stage of something, especially the most active and enjoyable period in adult life ○ *in the prime of life* **2. EARLIEST PERIOD OF SOMETHING** the earliest part of something, e.g. the early hours of daylight or the first season of the year **3. DISTINGUISHING MARK** a mark (') added to a number, character, or expression in order to distinguish it from another, or as the symbol for measurement in feet or the minutes of an arc **4.** MUSIC **FIRST NOTE IN MUSICAL SCALE** the first note of a musical scale **5.** CHR **SECOND CANONICAL HOUR** in the Roman Catholic Church, the second of the seven separate hours (**canonical hours**) that are set aside for prayer each day **6.** FENCING **FIRST PARRYING POSITION** the first of the eight parrying positions in fencing **7.** MATHS same as **prime number** **8.** FIN same as **prime rate** [Pre-12C. Via French < Latin *primus* 'first'] —**primely** *adv* —**primeness** *n*

CULTURAL NOTE ***The Prime of Miss Jean Brodie***, a novel (1961) by Muriel Spark. The best known of Spark's novels, it is set in an Edinburgh girls' school and describes the powerful and lasting influence of an unconventional schoolteacher, Miss Jean Brodie, on a group of promising but impressionable pupils. It was adapted for the theatre in 1966 and made into a film by Ronald Neame in 1968.

---

prime[2] /prīm/ *v* **1.** *vt* **BRIEF SOMEBODY** to give somebody, especially a witness in a court case, information or instructions on how to behave or answer questions **2.** *vti* **MAKE OR BECOME READY** to make something ready for use, or become ready for use **3.** *vt* **PREPARE SURFACE FOR PAINTING** to prepare a surface for painting or a similar process by treating it with a sealant or an undercoat of paint **4.** *vt* **PUT CHARGE IN GUN** to make a firearm ready for use by putting a charge in it **5.** *vt* **PROVIDE EXPLOSIVE WITH FUSE** to make an explosive ready for use by inserting a fuse **6.** *vt* **PREPARE SOMETHING FOR OPERATION** to put liquid in something such as a pump or carburettor in order to get it started **7.** *vt* **PLY SOMEBODY WITH DRINK** to provide somebody with large quantities of alcohol in order to prepare him or her for doing something [Early 16C. Origin ?]

prime cost *n* the cost of the material and labour necessary to make a product

prime interest rate *n* FIN same as **prime rate**

prime meridian *n* the 0° longitude meridian passing through Greenwich, England, from which other longitudes are calculated

prime minister, Prime Minister *n* **1.** in a parliamentary system, the head of the cabinet and, usually, chief executive. See table on next page **2.** the chief minister appointed by the ruler of a country —**prime ministerial** *adj* —**prime ministership** *n*

prime mover *n* **1. MOST IMPORTANT CAUSE OF SOMETHING** somebody or something that initiates a process or activity and is usually the most important factor in its continuation **2.** RELIG **GOD** God, considered to be the first cause or origin of everything **3.** PHILOSOPHY **SOURCE OF ALL MOTION** in Aristotelian philosophy, the initial source of all movement **4. NATURAL OR PHYSICAL ENERGY SOURCE** a natural or physical source of energy such as wind or electricity that can be harnessed to power a machine **5. ENERGY CONVERTER** a machine that converts energy from a natural or physical source in order to power equipment such as a windmill or turbine

prime number *n* a whole number that can only be divided without a remainder by itself and one

primer[1] /prímər/ *n* **1.** a book used to teach young children to read, usually containing simple stories **2.** a book that provides an introduction to a topic [14C. < Anglo-Norman < Latin *primarius* (see PRIMARY)]

primer[2] /prímər/ *n* **1. UNDERCOAT** a paint or sealant used to prepare a surface for painting or a similar process, or a coat of this material **2. PRIMING AGENT** a person or device that primes something **3. EXPLOSIVE IGNITER** a small container or wafer of explosive material such as gunpowder, used to ignite the main explosive charge of a firearm or explosive **4.** BIOCHEM **GENETIC MATERIAL** a short sequence of RNA that is made before DNA formation can proceed [15C. < PRIME[2]]

prime rate *n* the lowest rate of interest on loans that is available from a bank at a given time

PRIME MINISTERS OF AUSTRALIA, CANADA, NEW ZEALAND, AND THE UNITED KINGDOM AFTER 1900

Prime Ministers of Australia

Term of Office	Prime Minister
1901–1903	Edmund Barton
1903–1904	Alfred Deakin
1904	John Christian Watson
1904–1905	George Houston Reid
1905–1908	Alfred Deakin
1908–1909	Andrew Fisher
1909–1910	Alfred Deakin
1910–1913	Andrew Fisher
1913–1914	Joseph Cook
1914–1915	Andrew Fisher
1915–1923	William Morris Hughes
1923–1929	Stanley Melbourne Bruce
1929–1932	James Henry Scullin
1932–1939	Joseph Aloysius Lyons
1939	Earle Page
1939–1941	Robert Menzies
1941	Arthur William Fadden
1941–1945	John Curtin
1945	Francis Michael Forde
1945–1949	Joseph Benedict Chifley
1949–1966	Robert Menzies
1966–1967	Harold Holt
1967–1968	John McEwen
1968–1971	John Gorton
1971–1972	William McMahon

Australia . . .

Term of Office	Prime Minister
1972–1975	Gough Whitlam
1975–1983	Malcolm Fraser
1983–1991	Bob Hawke
1991–1996	Paul Keating
1996–	John Howard

Prime Ministers of Canada

Term of Office	Prime Minister
1896–1911	Wilfred Laurier
1911–1920	Robert Laird Borden
1920–1921	Arthur Meighen
1921–1926	W.L. Mackenzie King
1926	Arthur Meighen
1926–1930	W.L. Mackenzie King
1930–1935	Richard Bedford Bennett
1935–1948	W.L. Mackenzie King
1948–1957	Louis St. Laurent
1957–1963	John G. Diefenbaker
1963–1968	Lester B. Pearson
1968–1979	Pierre Trudeau
1979–1980	Joseph Clark
1980–1984	Pierre Trudeau
1984	John M. Turner
1984–1993	Brian Mulroney
1993	Kim Campbell
1993–2003	Jean Chrétien
2003–	Paul Martin

Prime Ministers of New Zealand

Term of Office	Prime Minister
1893–1906	Richard John Seddon
1906	William Hall-Jones
1906–1912	Joseph George Ward
1912	Thomas Mackenzie
1912–1925	William Ferguson Masey
1925	Francis Henry Dillon Bell
1925–1928	Joseph Gordon Coates
1928–1930	Joseph George Ward
1930–1935	George William Forbes
1935–1940	Michael Joseph Savage
1940–1949	Peter Fraser
1949–1957	Sydney George Holland
1957	Keith Jacka Holyoake
1957–1960	Walter Nash
1960–1972	Keith Jacka Holyoake
1972	John Ross Marshall
1972–1974	Norman Eric Kirk
1974–1975	Wallace Edward Rowling
1975–1984	Robert David Muldoon
1984–1989	David Russell Lange
1989–1990	Geoffrey Palmer
1990	Michael Moore
1990–1997	James Bolger
1997–1999	Jenny Shipley
1999–	Helen Clark

Prime Ministers of the United Kingdom

Term of Office	Prime Minister
1902–1905	Arthur James Balfour
1905–1908	Henry Campbell-Bannerman
1908–1916	Herbert Henry Asquith
1916–1922	David Lloyd George
1922–1923	Andrew Bonar Law
1923–1924	Stanley Baldwin
1924	Ramsay MacDonald
1924–1935	Stanley Baldwin
1929–1935	Ramsay MacDonald
1935–1937	Stanley Baldwin
1937–1940	Neville Chamberlain
1940–1945	Winston Churchill
1945–1951	Clement Attlee
1951–1955	Winston Churchill
1955–1957	Anthony Eden
1957–1963	Harold Macmillan
1963–1964	Alec Douglas-Home
1964–1970	Harold Wilson
1970–1974	Edward Heath
1974–1976	Harold Wilson
1976–1979	James Callaghan
1979–1990	Margaret Thatcher
1990–1997	John Major
1997–	Tony Blair

---

primero /pri máirō/ *n* a card game played for money in the 16th and 17th centuries [Mid-16C. Alteration of Spanish *primera*, form of *primero* 'first' < Latin *primarius* (see PRIMARY)]

primers /prímərz/ *n NZ* the first classes of primary school (*informal; takes a singular verb*) [Early 20C. < shortening of PRIMARY]

prime time *n* the hours when television audiences are usually largest, typically from 7.00 pm to 11.00 pm —**primetime** *adj*

primeval /prī meev'l/, **primaeval** *adj* at or from the ancient original stages in the development of something [Mid-17C. < Latin *primaevus* < *primus* 'first' + *aevum* 'age'] —**primevally** *adv*

prime vertical *n* the imaginary circle around Earth that goes through the highest point of the celestial sphere directly above an observer and meets the horizon at east and west

primi MUSIC plural of **primo**

primigravida /prími grávvidə/ (*plural* **-das** or **-dae** /-dee/) *n* a woman experiencing her first pregnancy [Late 19C. < modern Latin < *gravida* 'pregnant', after PRIMIPARA]

priming /príming/ *n* ARMS same as **primer²** (sense 3)

primipara /prī míppərə/ (*plural* **-ras** or **-rae** /-ree/) *n* a woman who has given birth only once, whether it was a single or a multiple birth, and whether the baby was alive or stillborn [Mid-19C. < modern Latin < Latin *primus* 'first' + *-para* 'bearing', form of *-parus* (see -PAROUS)] —**primiparity** /prími párrəti/ *n* —**primiparous** /prī míppərəss/ *adj*

primitive /prímmətiv/ *adj* **1.** FIRST relating to or occurring at the first stages or form of something **2.** BIOL DEVELOPMENTALLY EARLY relating to or appearing in an earlier stage of biological development, particularly of an embryo or species **3.** VERY SIMPLE IN DESIGN crudely simple in design or construction (*offensive in some contexts*) ○ *built a primitive shelter from palm leaves* **4.** ORIGINAL not derived from other things **5.** WITH SIMPLE TECHNOLOGICAL DEVELOPMENT not using or relying on complex modern technologies to provide comfort and efficiency (*sometimes considered offensive*) ○ *primitive camping facilities* **6.** MATHS FORMING BASIS OF SOMETHING acting as a basis from which something else is derived **7.** NATURAL arising from an inherent characteristic **8.** ARTS ARTISTICALLY UNTRAINED created by an artist with no formal training, especially using a simple style **9.** ARTS EARLY MEDIEVAL created by an early medieval European artist or a folk artist **10.** LING USED FOR DERIVING OTHER WORD having a word form from which another word is derived ○ *The primitive root in 'children' is 'child'.* **11.** LING EARLIER IN LINGUISTIC DEVELOPMENT belonging to or constituting an earlier form of a language ■ *n* **1.** SOMEBODY OR SOMETHING FROM ORIGINAL STAGE somebody or something from the first stage or form of something **2.** SOMEBODY FROM CULTURE WITH SIMPLE TECHNOLOGIES a member of a people who do not use or rely on complex modern technologies (*often considered offensive*) **3.** ARTS UNTRAINED ARTIST an artist without formal training, especially one using a simple style **4.** ARTS EARLY MEDIEVAL ARTIST an artist or folk artist,

especially a painter, whose work was characteristic of the style of early medieval Europe **5.** ARTS **WORK BY EARLY MEDIEVAL ARTIST** a painting or other work by an early medieval artist or a folk artist **6.** DERIVATION something such as a concept, feature, or formula from which something else is derived **7.** MATHS **BASIC GEOMETRIC FORM OR FUNCTION** a geometric form or function from which another is derived **8.** COMPUT **BASIC ELEMENT OF COMPUTER PROGRAM** a simple element of a computer program or graphic design from which larger programs or images can be constructed **9.** LING same as **root**[1] (senses 12–13) (*dated technical*) [14C. Directly or via French < Latin *primitivus* < *primitus* 'in the first place' < *primus* 'first'] —**primitively** *adv* —**primitiveness** *n*

primitivism /prímməti vìzəm/ *n* **1.** STATE OF BEING PRIMITIVE the state of being primitive, or the qualities associated with being primitive **2.** ARTS **SIMPLICITY OF STYLE** simplicity or naivety of artistic style **3.** OPPOSITION TO MODERN LIFE the belief that less technologically dependent cultures and ways of living are inherently better than more technologically dependent ones —**primitivist** *n, adj* —**primitivistic** /prímməti vístik/ *adj*

primo /préemō/ *n* (*plural* **-mos** or **-mi** /-mi/) LEAD MUSICAL PART the lead musical part in a duet, trio, or ensemble composition ■ *adj* **1.** US FIRST first in a sequence or series (*formal*) **2.** N Am EXCELLENT of the finest quality or greatest value (*slang*) ○ *This pizza is primo!* [Mid-18C. Via Italian and Spanish, 'first, prime' < Latin *primus*]

primogenitor /prímō jénnitər, preémō-/ *n* (*formal*) **1.** the first ancestor of a people or other group **2.** an ancestor or forebear [Mid-17C. Alteration of PROGENITOR, after PRIMOGENITURE]

primogeniture /prímō jénnichər, preémō-/ *n* (*formal*) **1.** the state of being the first-born child of a set of parents **2.** the right of the first-born child, usually the eldest son, to inherit the parents' entire estate [Early 17C. < medieval Latin *primogenitura* < Latin *primus* 'first' + *genitura* 'birth'] —**primogenital** *adj* —**primogenitary** *adj*

primordia BIOL plural of **primordium**

primordial /prī máwrdi əl/ *adj* **1.** EXISTING FIRST existing at the beginning of time or of the development of something **2.** BASIC essential or basic to something **3.** BIOL OF EARLIEST STAGE OF DEVELOPMENT relating to cells, tissues, organs, or organisms at the earliest stage of development [14C. < late Latin *primordialis* < Latin *primordium* 'origin' < *primus* 'first' + *ordiri* 'begin'] —**primordiality** /prī máwrdi álləti/ *n* —**primordially** *adv*

primordium /prī máwrdi əm/ *n* (*plural* **-dia** /-di ə/) a tissue or organ in the earliest stage of embryonic development, found when the dividing cells in the fertilized ovum first differentiate [Late 16C. < Latin (see PRIMORDIAL)]

primp /primp/ *vti* (**primps, primping, primped**) to groom yourself, somebody, or something in a fussy way ○ *spending all day primping in front of the mirror* [Late 16C. Origin ?]

primrose

primrose /prím rōz/ *n* **1.** a small perennial plant with pale yellow flowers that appear in early spring in northern temperate regions. Native to: Europe. Latin name: *Primula vulgaris*. **2.** ANZ, US same as **primula** [14C. Via French < medieval Latin *prima rosa* 'first rose', from its early flowering]

primrose path *n* an easy or pleasurable way of life, especially one that leads to disaster (*literary*) [< 'the primrose path of dalliance' in Shakespeare's *Hamlet*]

primula /prímmyōōlə/ (*plural* **-las** or *same*) *n* UK, Can a small perennial plant with colourful flowers. Genus: *Primula*. ANZ, US term **primrose** [Mid-18C. Via modern Latin < medieval Latin *primula (veris)* 'first fruit (of spring)' < Latin *primulus* < *primus* 'first'] —**primulaceous** /prímmyōō láyshəss/ *adj*

primum mobile /príməm mōbíli/ *n* **1.** in Ptolemaic astronomy, the outermost sphere of the universe, thought to revolve every 24 hours, moving the inner spheres with it **2.** PHILOSOPHY same as **prime mover** (sense 3) [15C. < medieval Latin, 'first moving thing']

primus /príməss/ (*plural* **-muses**), **Primus** *n Scotland* the highest ranking bishop in the Scottish Episcopal Church [Late 16C. < Latin, 'first']

primus inter pares /príməss intər páá reez, preé-/ *n* the representative or leader of a group of equals [< Latin, 'first among equals']

Primus stove /príməss-/ *tdmk* a trademark for a portable paraffin cooking stove

prince /prinss/ *n* **1.** ROYAL MAN OR BOY a man or boy in a royal family, especially a son of a reigning king or queen **2.** MALE RULER a man who rules a principality **3.** EUROPEAN NOBLEMAN a nobleman in some European countries, usually of a rank below duke **4.** HIGHLY REGARDED MAN a man or boy who is ranked highly in his field ○ *Robin Hood was the prince of thieves.* **5.** N Am GOOD MAN a man who is outstanding, especially because of his generous or chivalrous nature (*informal*) [12C. Via French < Latin *princeps* 'somebody who takes first place'] —**princedom** *n*

CULTURAL NOTE *The Prince*, a political treatise (1513) by Italian writer Niccolò Machiavelli. Machiavelli based this guide to gaining and maintaining political power on his study of history and his experience of politics. The first work of its kind to present a political philosophy derived from a study of human behaviour rather than traditional ethics, it gained lasting notoriety by justifying the judicious use of ruthlessness and deceit.

Prince Albert *n* in body piercing, a ring put through the tip of the penis [Late 19C. After Prince ALBERT, who gave his name to the ALBERT, watch chain]

Prince Charles Island /prinss cháarlz-/ *n* largest island in Foxe Basin, west of Baffin Island, in Nunavut, Canada. Area: 9,521 sq. km/3,676 sq. mi.

prince charming, **Prince Charming** *n* **1.** a man who fulfils the romantic ideal of the perfect lover (*informal*) **2.** a man who actively seeks to charm people, especially women, and gain their liking [Mid-19C. After the hero of the fairy tale *Cinderella*]

prince consort *n* a prince who is married to a reigning queen

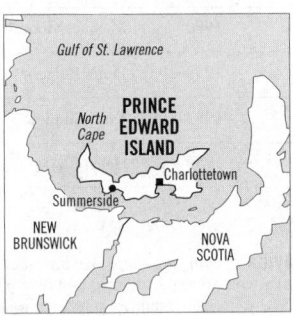

Prince Edward Island

Prince Edward Island /-éddwərd-/ smallest province in Canada, in the east of the country, in the Gulf of St Lawrence, opposite New Brunswick and Nova Scotia. Capital: Charlottetown. Population: 139,900 (2002). Area: 5,660 sq. km/2,185 sq. mi. —**Prince Edward Islander** *n*

Prince Edward Island National Park national park in eastern Canada, on the Northern shore of Prince Edward Island. Area: 22 sq. km/9 sq. mi.

princeling /prínssling/, **princelet** /prínsslət/ *n* a prince of low rank, age, or importance

princely /prínssli/ (**-lier, -liest**) *adj* **1.** relating to, belonging to, or suitable for a prince **2.** generous as an amount of money, or requiring the expenditure of large sums of money ○ *a princely manor in the country* —**princeliness** *n*

Prince of Wales Island 1. island in southeastern Alaska. It is the largest island in the Alexander Archipelago. Population: 5,771 (2002 estimate). Area: 5,778 sq. km/2,231 sq. mi. **2.** island in northern Canada, in Nunavut, between Victoria and Somerset islands. Area: 33,339 sq. km/12,872 sq. mi. **3.** island in northern Australia, in Queensland. Population: 90 (1971). Area: 180 sq. km/69 sq. mi.

prince regent (*plural* **prince regents** or **princes regent**) *n* a prince who rules in the monarch's place, e.g. when the monarch is abroad, ill, or still a child

prince royal (*plural* **princes royal**) *n* the eldest son of a reigning monarch

prince's-feather (*plural* **prince's-feathers** or *same*) *n* a tall annual plant with reddish leaves. Flowers: red, in spikes. Native to: North America. Family: Amaranthus.

princess /prin séss, prínsess/ *n* (*plural* **-cesses**) **1.** ROYAL WOMAN OR GIRL a woman or girl in a royal family, especially a daughter of the reigning king or queen **2.** PRINCE'S WIFE the wife or widow of a prince **3.** DAUGHTER OF MONARCH'S SON a daughter of a son of the sovereign **4.** FEMALE RULER a woman who rules a principality **5.** EUROPEAN NOBLEWOMAN a noblewoman in some European countries, usually of a rank below duchess **6.** SPOILED YOUNG WOMAN a rich young woman considered to be spoiled or arrogant **7.** HIGHLY REGARDED WOMAN a woman who is ranked highly in her field, or who has other outstanding qualities (*dated*) ■ *adj* FITTED AT TOP WITH FLARED SKIRT describes a woman's or girl's garment made with long triangular pieces of fabric that reach from neck to hem, fitted at the bodice with a flared skirt [14C. < French *princesse* < *prince* (see PRINCE)]

princess royal (*plural* **princesses royal**) *n* the eldest daughter of a reigning monarch, especially of a British monarch, who confers the title on her as a special honour

Princeton /prínstən/ town in west-central New Jersey. It is home to Princeton University, founded in 1746. Population: 16,590 (2002 estimate).

principal /prínssip'l/ *adj* **1.** PRIMARY first or among the first in importance or rank **2.** FIN INITIALLY INVESTED relating to the initial amount of money that was invested or borrowed ■ *n* **1.** HEAD OF SCHOOL the head administrator of a school, college, or university **2.** MOST IMPORTANT PERSON the leading or most highly ranked person **3.** SIGNIFICANT PARTICIPANT any one of the most significant participants in an event or a situation ○ *the principals in the property transaction* **4.** FIN ORIGINAL AMOUNT INVESTED the initial sum of money invested or borrowed, before interest or other revenue is added, or the remainder of that sum after payments have been made **5.** EDUC HEAD OF SCHOOL DEPARTMENT the head of a department in a Scottish school ○ *She was promoted to principal of English.* **6.** POL SENIOR CIVIL SERVANT a civil servant of a rank below a Secretary **7.** THEATRE, ARTS LEAD PERFORMER a lead actor, singer, or dancer in a theatrical or musical performance **8.** MUSIC LEAD MUSICIAN the lead musician in a section of an orchestra, or the part played by that musician **9.** LAW REPRESENTED PERSON somebody for whom a representative or proxy acts in a legal matter **10.** LAW RESPONSIBLE PARTY somebody who is directly responsible for something **11.** LAW CRIMINAL the perpetrator of a crime **12.** CONSTR MAIN SUPPORT BEAM the main support beam, girder, or truss in a roof, bridge, or other construction [13C. Via French < Latin *principalis* < *princip-* 'somebody who takes first place'] —**principally** *adv* —**principalship** *n*

USAGE **principal** or **principle**? These two words, though they have the same pronunciation, have different meanings and functions. *Principle* is a noun only, meaning 'a basic assumption', 'an ethical standard', and 'a way of working', as in *the principles of a democratic system; a woman of principle; studied the principles of the internal-combustion engine*. By contrast, *principal*, as a noun, means 'the head of a school or college', 'an important participant', 'a lead performer', and 'a monetary amount invested', as in *was sent to the principal's office; a principal in an accounting firm; a principal of £500,000*. As an adjective it means 'primary': *our principal* [not *principle*] *reason for an appeal*.

principal axis *n* the line that passes through the centre of curvature of a lens

principal boy *n* a woman who plays the leading man's part in a pantomime

principal diagonal *n* in a square matrix, the diagonal line that extends from the upper left corner to the lower right corner

principality /prínssə pálləti/ (*plural* **-ties**) *n* **1.** COUNTRY OR TERRITORY a territory ruled by a prince or princess **2.** POSITION OF PRINCE the position or jurisdiction of a prince **3.** CHR ANGEL OF THIRD-HIGHEST ORDER an angel of the third of the nine orders of angels in the traditional Christian hierarchy

principal parts *npl* **1.** the basic forms of a verb, from which other forms are derived, in an inflected language such as Latin **2.** the infinitive, past tense, and participial forms of an English verb

principal teacher *n* Scotland EDUC same as **principal** *n* (sense 5)

Príncipe /prínssi pay/ second largest island in São Tomé and Príncipe. Population: 5,900 (1995). Area: 306 sq. km/118 sq. mi.

principle /prínssip'l/ *n* **1.** BASIC ASSUMPTION an important underlying law or assumption required in a system of thought **2.** ETHICAL STANDARD a standard of moral or ethical decision-making ○ *I buy recyclable products as a matter of principle.* **3.** WAY OF WORKING the basic way in which something works **4.** SOURCE the primary source of something **5.** CHEM CHARACTERISTIC INGREDIENT an ingredient of a substance that gives the substance a special quality [14C. < Anglo-Norman, alteration of French *principe* < Latin *principium* < *princip-* 'somebody who takes first place'] —**principled** *adj* ◇ **in principle** in theory or in the essentials ◇ **on principle** because of a particular ethical standard that somebody believes in

USAGE See *principal*.

Principle *n* used in Christian Science to refer to God

prink /pringk/ (**prinks, prinking, prinked**) *vti* to dress or groom somebody or yourself in a fancy or fussy way [Late 16C. Origin ?] —**prinker** *n*

print /print/ *n* **1.** PRESSED MARK a mark made by pressing something onto a surface ○ *left dirty paw prints on the carpet* **2.** WRITING ON SURFACE words, figures, or symbols on a surface, especially when produced by a machine ○ *books available in large print* **3.** PUBLISHED STATUS the state of being in a printed form or being published ○ *We don't want these typographical errors to make it into print.* **4.** ARTWORK a work of art made by inking a surface with a raised design and pressing it onto paper or another surface **5.** FABRIC WITH DESIGN a fabric with an ink or paint design on its surface, or the design itself (*often used before a noun*) ○ *She was wearing a new print dress.* **6.** PHOTOGRAPH a photograph, usually on paper, made from a negative **7.** CINEMA FILM COPY a copy of a film **8.** ART STAMP OR DIE a stamp or die used to make marks on a surface **9.** CRIME same as **fingerprint** (*informal*) ■ *v* (**prints, printing, printed**) **1.** *vti* MAKE SOMETHING WITH PRINTING MACHINE to make a copy, document, or publication using a printing press or a computer printer ○ *These books were printed in Canada.* **2.** *vti* PUBLISH SOMETHING to publish information or a publication ○ *The company prints several news magazines in addition to books.* **3.** *vti* MARK SOMETHING USING PRESSURE to produce a mark, design, or lettering on a surface by pressing something on it ○ *A machine prints the corporate logo onto pencils.* **4.** *vti* PRESS DESIGNS ONTO SOMETHING to press a mark, design, or lettering onto something ○ *We printed enough T-shirts for the whole team.* **5.** *vti* WRITE SEPARATED LETTERS to write something by hand, using separated letters rather than script ○ *Print your name under your signature.* **6.** *vti* PHOTOGRAPHY, CINEMA MAKE COPY FROM NEGATIVE to make a positive image or copy of a photograph or film from a negative **7.** *vi* PRINTING WORK AS PRINTER to do the work of a printer ■ *adj* RELATING TO PUBLISHED MEDIA produced by or relating to the published media [13C. < Old French *preinte*, form of past participle of *preindre* 'press' < Latin *premere*] ◇ **in print 1.** currently available from a publisher **2.** printed in a book, newspaper, or magazine ◇ **out of print** not currently available from a publisher

print out *vt* to produce a printed copy of data from a computer

printable /príntəb'l/ *adj* **1.** sufficiently inoffensive, correct, or well-written as to be fit to be printed in a

publication ○ *Some of the player's comments weren't printable.* **2.** capable of being printed or printed on ○ *This paper's too glossy to be printable.* —**printability** /príntə bílləti/ *n*

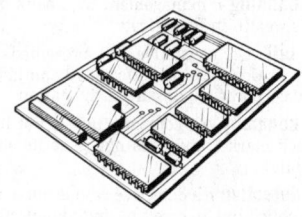

printed circuit

printed circuit /príntid-/ *n* an electronic circuit in which some components and the connections between them are formed by etching a metallic coating on one or both sides of an insulating board

printed matter *n* published material, e.g. books, newspapers, magazines, or catalogues

printer /príntər/ *n* **1.** PERSON OR COMPANY IN PRINTING TRADE a person or company in the business of printing books, newspapers, or magazines **2.** MACHINE FOR PRINTING a machine that prints books, newspapers, or magazines **3.** MACHINE FOR PRINTING COMPUTER DATA a device that produces computer-generated text or graphics on paper, transparencies, or similar media **4.** MACHINE FOR COPYING FILM a machine that makes duplicates of film, normally a positive from a negative

printer driver *n* a software routine that formats an application's data to print properly on a particular printer

printer's devil *n* an apprentice or young assistant to a printer [< DEVIL 'apprentice']

printhead /print hed/ *n* a part of a computer printer that transfers the characters to paper

printing /prínting/ *n* **1.** PRODUCTION OF COPIES the process or business of producing copies of documents, publications, or images **2.** PRINTED CHARACTERS typographical characters as they appear on paper or another surface ○ *The printing has washed off this bottle.* **3.** LETTERS WRITTEN SEPARATELY letters written separately or the act of writing letters separately, in contrast to script characters ○ *Her printing is easier to read than her handwriting.* **4.** PRINT RUN the process or output of one print run of a publication ○ *This book is in its eighth printing.*

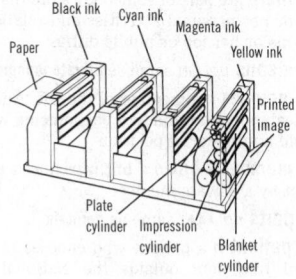

printing press

printing press *n* a machine that presses inked set type or etched plates onto paper or textiles that are fed through it

printmaker /print maykər/ *n* an artist who designs and makes prints —**printmaking** *n*

printout /print owt/ *n* a paper copy of data from a computer

print run *n* the number of copies of a publication, document, or artwork that are printed in a single batch ○ *an initial print run of 30,000 copies*

prion[1] /prí ən, prée ən/ *n* an infectious particle of protein that, unlike a virus, contains no nucleic acid, does not trigger an immune response, and is not destroyed by extreme heat or cold. These par-

ticles are considered responsible for such diseases as scrapie, BSE, kuru, and Creutzfeldt-Jakob disease. [Late 20C. < *proteinaceous* + INFECTIOUS + -ON[1]]

prion[2] /prí ən/ *n* a small seabird with a serrated beak and soft blue-grey markings like a pigeon's. Native to: southern oceans. Genus: *Pachyptila*. [Mid-19C. Via modern Latin < Greek *priōn* 'saw']

prior[1] /prí ər/ *adj* **1.** EARLIER earlier in time or sequence ○ *a prior engagement* **2.** MORE IMPORTANT more important or basic ■ *n Am* EARLIER CRIMINAL CONVICTION an earlier conviction for a criminal act (*informal*) ○ *Check to see whether the suspect has any priors.* [Early 18C. < Latin, 'former, elder, superior', literally 'more before'] ◇ **prior to somebody** *or* **something** before somebody or something in time

prior[2] /prí ər/ *n* **1.** ABBOT'S DEPUTY an officer in a monastery of a rank below abbot **2.** MALE RELIGIOUS SUPERIOR a man who is superior in some religious communities **3.** SENIOR MEDIEVAL MAGISTRATE a senior magistrate in some medieval Italian republics, especially Florence [Pre-12C. < medieval Latin < Latin (see PRIOR[1])]

priorate /prí ərət/ *n* the position or term of office of a prior or prioress

prioress /prí ə réss/ *n* **1.** a woman officer in a convent of a rank below abbess **2.** a woman superior in some religious communities

prioritize /prī órri tīz/ (**-tizes, -tizing, -tized**), **prioritise** (**-tises, -tising, -tised**) *vti* **1.** to order things according to their importance or urgency ○ *I must prioritize my list of things to do.* **2.** to regard something as most important or urgent ○ *I have to prioritize finding a job.* —**prioritization** /prī órri tī záysh'n/ *n*

priority /prī órriti/ (*plural* **-ties**) *n* **1.** GREATEST IMPORTANCE the state of having most importance or urgency ○ *Give this case priority treatment.* **2.** SOMEBODY OR SOMETHING IMPORTANT somebody or something that is ranked highly in terms of importance or urgency ○ *You've got to get your priorities right.* **3.** RIGHT OF PRECEDENCE the right to be ranked above others **4.** EARLIER OCCURRENCE the state of having preceded something else

priory /prí əri/ (*plural* **-ies**) *n* a religious community or home headed by a prior or prioress, e.g. a monastery or convent

Pripet Marshes /príp ət-/, **Pripyat' Marshes** /preépyət-/, **Poles'ye** /pŏ les yə/ swamp region in southern Belarus and northwestern Ukraine, along the River Pripet. Area: 270,000 sq. km/104,000 sq. mi.

prise /prīz/ (**prises, prising, prised**) *vt* **1.** to open or part something by levering ○ *I used a screwdriver to prise the lid off the paint.* **2.** to get something, especially information, from somebody or something with difficulty [14C. Probably < Old French *prise* (see PRIZE[2])]

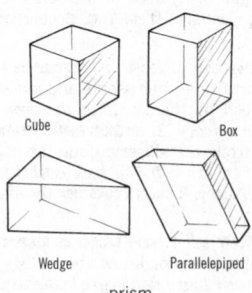

Cube   Box

Wedge   Parallelepiped

prism

prism /prízzəm/ *n* **1.** SOLID FOR DISPERSING LIGHT a transparent polygonal solid object with flat faces and a usually triangular cross-section, used for separating white light into a spectrum of colours **2.** SOMETHING MADE OF CUT GLASS a cut-glass object, especially one that can separate white light into a spectrum **3.** CRYSTALS CRYSTAL TYPE a crystal form with faces that are parallel to a single axis **4.** MATHS PARALLELOGRAM-SIDED SOLID a three-dimensional geometric figure with ends that are identical polygons and with sides that are parallelograms [Late 16C. Via late Latin < Greek *prisma* 'something sawn' (because of its shape) < *prizein* 'to saw']

prismatic /priz máttik/ *adj* **1.** RELATING TO PRISM resembling or relating to a prism **2.** SEPARATED BY PRISM

describes light that shows the colours of the spectrum, as refracted by a prism **3.** COLOURFUL brightly coloured, like a rainbow [Early 18C. < French *prismatique* < Greek *prismat-*, stem of *prisma* (see PRISM)] —**prismatically** *adv*

prismoid /príz moyd/ *n* a body like a prism with sides that are parallelograms or trapezoids and equal-sided polygons as bases [Early 18C. < PRISM, after *rhomboid*] —**prismoidal** /priz móyd'l/ *adj*

prison /prízz'n/ *n* **1.** a secure place where somebody is confined as punishment for a crime or while waiting to stand trial **2.** a place or condition of captivity or unwanted restraint ○ *His fears are a prison that he cannot escape.* ■ *vt* **(-ons, -oning, -oned)** same as **imprison** (*archaic or literary*) [12C. Via French < Latin *prension-* 'seizing' < *prehendere* 'seize']

prison camp *n* a camp where prisoners of war are confined

prisoner /prízz'nər/ *n* **1.** SOMEBODY HELD IN PRISON somebody confined in a prison as a punishment for a crime or while waiting to stand trial **2.** SOMEBODY HELD AGAINST WILL somebody who is confined in a place ○ *He's been taken prisoner by a group of rebel soldiers.* **3.** SOMEBODY WHO IS OR FEELS TRAPPED somebody who cannot escape a situation or condition

prisoner of conscience *n* somebody held in a prison by a state, especially an oppressive regime, because of his or her political or religious beliefs

prisoner of war *n* somebody who has been captured and imprisoned by an enemy during a war

prisoner's base *n* a children's game in which two teams try to tag each other's members, thereby adding them to their team at their base [Alteration of *prison bars*]

~~**prisonner**~~ incorrect spelling of **prisoner**

prissy /príssi/ **(-sier, -siest)** *adj* behaving in a very prudish and proper way, or reflecting prudishness and properness [Late 19C. Probably blend of PRIM + SISSY] —**prissily** *adv* —**prissiness** *n*

Priština /préeshtinə/ the largest city in the province of Kosovo in the Federal Republic of Yugoslavia. Population: 241,565 (1997).

pristine /prís teen/ *adj* **1.** IMMACULATE so clean and neat as to look as good as new ○ *The house is in pristine condition.* **2.** UNSPOILED not yet ruined by human encroachment ○ *acres of pristine forest* **3.** IN OR OF ORIGINAL STATE in or belonging to an original state or condition [Mid-16C. < Latin *pristinus* 'former']

Pritchett /príchit/, **Sir V. S.** (1900–97) British writer. An acclaimed novelist, critic, biographer, and travel writer, he is best known for his short stories, the first collection of which was *The Spanish Virgin and Other Stories* (1930). Full name **Pritchett, Sir Victor Sawdon**

prithee /príthi/ *interj* used to introduce a request to somebody (*archaic*) [Late 16C. Contraction of *(I) pray thee*]

privacy /prívvəssi, prívəssi/ *n* **1.** SECLUSION the state of being apart from other people and not seen, heard, or disturbed by them ○ *Shut the door so we can have some privacy.* **2.** FREEDOM FROM ATTENTION OF OTHERS freedom from the observation, intrusion, or attention of others ○ *If you seek celebrity, you must sacrifice privacy.* **3.** HIDDEN CONDITION the state of being kept secret

private /prívət/ *adj* **1.** KEPT SECRET OR RESTRICTED not for other people to see or know about ○ *My salary is a private matter that I don't care to discuss.* **2.** SECLUDED sufficiently secluded for people to be alone and not watched, heard, or disturbed by others ○ *Let's find a private corner where we can talk.* **3.** PERSONAL belonging to, restricted to, or intended for an individual person ○ *The master bedroom has a private bathroom.* **4.** NOT PUBLIC not open to the public **5.** ACTING IN PERSONAL CAPACITY holding no official position in government ○ *a private citizen* **6.** NONGOVERNMENTAL not supported by government funding **7.** RESERVED AND SECRETIVE preferring not to disclose personal information or to discuss personal feelings with others ○ *She's a very private person.* **8.** NOT UNDERSTANDABLE BY EVERYONE excluding people who do not share the knowledge required to understand ○ *a private joke* **9.** MIL LOWEST-RANKING relating to the lowest rank of soldier ■ *n* MIL LOWEST-RANKING SOLDIER a soldier of the lowest rank ■ **privates** *npl* ANAT same as **genitals** (*informal*) [14C. < Latin *privatus* 'isolated, not in public life', past participle of *privare* (see PRIVATION)] —**privately** *adv* —**privateness** *n*

private bank *n* a bank that offers individualized financial and investment advice and services to wealthy clients

private banking *n* management by a bank of a customer's wealth in its entirety

private bill *n* a legislative bill presented in Parliament or Congress that affects only an individual person, corporation, or part of the nation

private company *n* a company that is not listed on the stock market and does not issue its shares to the public

private detective *n* a detective who is not a member of the police but is hired by individual clients or companies

private enterprise *n* **1.** business activities that are not regulated or owned by the government **2.** a company that is owned by a private individual or individuals and not by the government

privateer /prívə teér/ *n* **1.** a ship that belongs to and is run by a person or company but is authorized by the government to engage in battle during war **2.** the commander or a crew member of a privateer [Mid-17C. After VOLUNTEER]

private eye *n* CRIME same as **private detective** (*informal*) [*Eye*, spelling of *I.*, abbreviation of *investigator*]

Private Finance Initiative *n* full form of **PFI**

private first class (*plural* **privates first class**) *n* US an enlisted person in the US Army or Marine Corps of a rank above private

private hotel *n* **1.** a privately run hotel that has the right to refuse potential guests **2.** ANZ a small residential hotel that does not have a licence to sell alcoholic beverages

private income *n* income from sources other than employment, e.g. from investments or allowances

private investigator *n* CRIME same as **private detective**

private key cryptography *n* an encryption method using a single key known to both the sender and receiver for encoding and decoding an Internet message

private label card *n* a credit card for use at only one retailer that is issued and managed by a third party

private language *n* an exclusive language devised and spoken by a restricted group of people, especially twins

private law *n* the branch of law concerned with the rights and responsibilities of individual people

private life *n* the part of somebody's life that relates to his or her personal activities and relationships, not to his or her job or public duties

private means *npl* FIN same as **private income**

private member *n* a member of the UK, Australian, New Zealand, and Canadian parliaments who does not hold a ministerial position

private member's bill *n* a bill introduced in a parliament by a private member

private parts *npl* ANAT same as **genitals**

private patient *n* a patient who chooses to pay for medical treatment outside the National Health Service, usually to obtain advantages such as the avoidance of a long wait for surgery

private pay bed *n* a hospital bed reserved for a paying patient rather than a National Health Service patient

private practice *n* **1.** a professional business owned and managed by an individual professional such as a lawyer, rather than by an organization **2.** a doctor's practice that is not part of the National Health Service. Few doctors engage in full-time private practice, but many NHS consultants pursue part-time private practice.

private school *n* a primary or secondary school that is not run by the government and therefore charges fees for tuition

private secretary *n* a secretary employed to manage somebody's personal or confidential affairs, especially those of a business executive or public figure

private sector *n* the part of a free market economy that is made up of companies and organizations that are not owned or controlled by the government

private treaty *n* the sale of property according to terms negotiated by the buyer and seller

private view, private viewing *n* a preview of a film or an exhibition that is open only to invited guests

privation /prī váysh'n/ *n* **1.** lack of the basic necessities of life such as food, housing, and heating **2.** the act of depriving somebody of something [14C. < Latin *privation-* < *privare* 'deprive, isolate' < *privus* 'single, isolated']

privatise *vt* SOC SCI another spelling of **privatize**

privatism /prívətizəm/ *n* an attitude or lifestyle in which somebody ignores all but his or her own interests —**privatist** *n, adj* —**privatistic** /prívə tístik/ *adj*

privative /prívvətiv/ *adj* **1.** RELATING TO LACK OR NEGATION indicating the absence or negation of some quality ○ *a privative term* **2.** CAUSING DEPRIVATION causing or experiencing deprivation ■ *n* AFFIX DENOTING LACK OR NEGATION an affix, word, or expression that denotes the absence or negation of some quality, e.g. English 'non-' or Greek 'a-' [Late 16C. Directly or via French < Latin *privativus* < *privare* (see PRIVATION)] —**privatively** *adv*

privatize /prívə tīz/ **(-tizes, -tizing, -tized)**, **privatise** **(-tises, -tising, -tised)** *vt* to transfer to private ownership an economic enterprise or public utility that has been under state ownership —**privatization** /prívə tī záysh'n/ *n*

~~**privelage**~~ incorrect spelling of **privilege**

privet /prívvit/ *n* an evergreen bush commonly used for hedging. Flowers: white, in clusters. Native to: Europe, North Africa, Asia. Latin name: *Ligustrum vulgare* or *Ligustrum ovalifolium.* [Mid-16C. Origin ?]

privilege /prívvəlij/ *n* **1.** RESTRICTED RIGHT OR BENEFIT an advantage, right, or benefit that is not available to everyone **2.** RIGHTS AND ADVANTAGES ENJOYED BY ELITE the rights and advantages enjoyed by a relatively small group of people, usually as a result of wealth or social status ○ *a system founded on privilege* **3.** SPECIAL HONOUR a special treat or honour ○ *It was a privilege to work with you.* **4.** LAWMAKER'S RIGHT TO SPECIAL TREATMENT the right to or granting of special treatment or benefits such as freedom from prosecution to members of a legislative body ■ *vt* **(-leges, -leging, -leged)** **1.** GIVE SOMEBODY SPECIAL RIGHTS to grant special rights or benefits to somebody or something **2.** GRANT EXEMPTION TO SOMEBODY to exempt or release somebody or something from something [12C. Via French < Latin *privilegium* 'private law' < *privus* 'single, isolated' + *leg-* 'law']

privileged /prívvəlijd/ *adj* **1.** ENJOYING SPECIAL ADVANTAGES enjoying privileges, especially the resources and advantages associated with the upper classes or the rich **2.** HONOURED OR FORTUNATE fortunate in having a special advantage or opportunity to do something ○ *I feel privileged to be here today.* ■ *npl* PEOPLE ENJOYING SPECIAL ADVANTAGES a class of people, especially the rich or the upper classes, that benefits from special rights or resources (*takes a plural verb*)

privileged communication *n* **1.** a confidential conversation or correspondence that does not have to be disclosed in a court of law **2.** speech or writing that is not subject to libel or slander laws

privity /prívvəti/ (*plural* **-ties**) *n* **1.** SHARED KNOWLEDGE OF SECRET the state of sharing knowledge of or colluding in something secret **2.** LAW LEGALLY RECOGNIZED RELATIONSHIP a legally recognized relationship between two parties, e.g. between members of a family, between an employer and employees, or between others who have entered into a contract together **3.** LAW RELATIONSHIP TO PROPERTY a successive or mutual relationship to some property [12C. Via French < medieval Latin *privitas* < Latin *privus* 'single, isolated']

privy /prívvi/ *adj* **1.** SHARING SECRET KNOWLEDGE sharing knowledge of something secret or private ○ *I was privy to their plans to elope.* **2.** RELATING TO SOMEBODY IN PRIVATE CAPACITY relating to somebody, especially a British monarch, as a private person, not as an official personage **3.** SECRET done or spoken secretly

or privately (*archaic*) ■ *n* (*plural* **-ies**) **1.** TOILET an outside toilet **2.** LAW SOMEBODY ELSE INVOLVED IN SOMETHING somebody who has an interest or agency in something that involves another party [12C. Via French *privé* < Latin *privatus* (see PRIVATE)]

privy chamber *n* an apartment reserved for private use in a royal residence

privy council *n* a committee that advises a ruler — **privy counsellor** *n*

Privy Council *n* the committee that advises a British king or queen. It consists mainly of present and former members of the Cabinet. —**Privy Counsellor** *n*

Privy Purse *n* **1.** the allowance from public funds given to the British monarch to cover personal expenses **2.** the official who manages the personal finances of the British monarch

Privy Seal *n* **1.** a seal that used to be attached to documents authorized by the British king or queen **2.** POL same as **Lord Privy Seal**

prix fixe /prée féeks/ (*plural* **prix fixes**) *n* **1.** a meal with several courses that is offered by a restaurant at a set price **2.** a set price for a restaurant meal with several courses [< French, 'fixed price']

prize[1] /prīz/ *n* **1.** AWARD FOR WINNER something that is given to the winner of a contest or competition **2.** SOMETHING HIGHLY VALUED something that somebody values highly, especially because it takes great skill, effort, or luck to get ■ *vt* (**prizes, prizing, prized**) TREASURE SOMETHING to value something highly ○ *This award is something I'll always prize.* ■ *adj* COMPLETE perfect as an example of something, especially something undesirable ○ *I made a prize fool of myself.* [Late 16C. Variant of PRICE]

prize[2] /prīz/ *n* something captured and kept, especially a ship or its contents taken by another ship in wartime [13C. < Old French *prise* 'something seized', form of past participle of *prendre* 'take, seize' < Latin *prehendere*]

prize[3] *vt* US spelling of **prise**

prizefight /prīz fīt/ *n* a boxing match in which the winner receives a cash prize —**prizefighter** *n* —**prizefighting** *n*

prize-giving *n* a ceremony at which prizes are awarded, especially for schoolwork

prize ring *n* **1.** a boxing ring where prizefights are held **2.** the sport or business of professional boxing

prizewinner /prīz winər/ *n* somebody or something that wins a prize in a competition —**prizewinning** *adj*

prn *abbr* MED as required (*used on medical prescriptions*) [< Latin *pro re nata*]

pro[1] /prō/ *n* (*plural* **pros**) **1.** SUPPORTING ARGUMENT an argument in favour of a proposal or position **2.** SIDE ARGUING FOR SOMETHING a person or side in a debate, argument, or campaign that is in favour of a proposal or proposition ■ *prep* FOR in favour of ■ *adv* IN SUPPORT OF SOMETHING on the side that favours one side of an issue [14C. < Latin, 'for' (see PRO-[1])]

pro[2] /prō/ *n* (*plural* **pros**) **1.** PROFESSIONAL PERSON a professional, especially in sports (*informal*) **2.** SKILLED PERSON an experienced and skilled person (*informal*) **3.** CRIME same as **prostitute** *n* (sense 1) (*slang*) ■ *adj* PROFESSIONAL relating to or typical of an activity, especially a sport, from which somebody earns a living ■ *adv* PROFESSIONALLY as a professional [Mid-20C. Shortening]

pro[3] /prō/ *abbr* professional practice (*used in Internet addresses*) See table at **domain name**

PRO *abbr* **1.** Public Record Office **2.** public relations officer

pro-[1] *prefix* **1.** substituting for, acting in place of ○ *proconsul* **2.** in favour of ○ *pronuclear* [Via French < Latin *pro* 'for' < Indo-European, 'forward, before']

pro-American *adj, n*
pro-British *adj*
probusiness *adj*
procapitalist *adj, n*
pro-Catholic *adj, n*
pro-China *adj*
pro-Chinese *adj*
pro-Communist *adj*
prodemocracy *adj*
prodemocratic *adj*
prodevolution *adj*
proenvironment *adj*
proestablishment *adj*
pro-European *adj, n*
profamily *adj*
profeminist *adj, n*
pro-German *adj*
progovernment *adj*
proimperial *adj*
proindependence *adj*
prointellectual *adj, n*
pro-Islamic *adj*
prolabour *adj*
promanagement *adj*
promilitary *adj*
promonarchist *adj, n*
promonarchy *adj*
pro-Muslim *adj, n*
propeace *adj*
pro-Protestant *adj, n*
prorebel *adj*
proreform *adj*
prorestoration *adj*
prorevision *adj*
prorevolutionary *adj*
proseparatist *adj, n*
pro-Soviet *adj, n*
prosupervision *adj*
prosurrender *adj*
prosyndicalism *n*
prounion *adj*
prowar *adj*
pro-Western *adj*
proworker *adj*

pro-[2] *prefix* **1.** rudimentary, precursor ○ *prothrombin* **2.** before, earlier than ○ *procambium* **3.** in front of ○ *prothoracic* [Via French < Greek *pro* 'in front, before' < Indo-European 'forward, before']

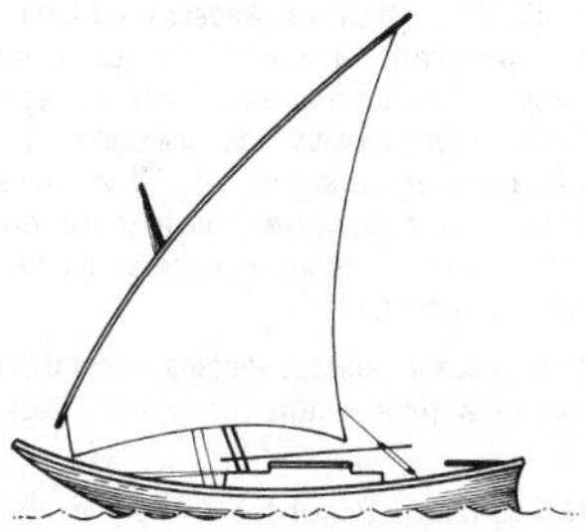

proa

proa /prṓ ə/ (*plural* **-as**), **prau** /prow/ (*plural* **praus**), **prahu** /praá oo/ (*plural* **-us**) *n* a Malayan boat with a triangular sail and a single outrigger [Late 16C. < Malay *pārāhū* 'boat']

proactive /prō áktiv/ *adj* taking the initiative by acting rather than reacting to events [Mid-20C. After RETROACTIVE] —**proactively** *adv*

USAGE When people name words they dislike as jargon, ***proactive*** is often on the list. ***Proactive*** does meet a need, serving as the opposite of *reactive* more naturally than, for example, *anticipatory* or *assertive* is able to. Nonetheless, it should be used sparingly.

pro-am /prṓ ám/ *adj* involving or composed of professional and amateur sports players ■ *n* a competition in which professional players compete against amateurs, or in which professionals and amateurs compete together [Mid-20C. < PRO[2] + *am*, shortening of AMATEUR]

probabilism /próbbəbəlizəm/ *n* **1.** the belief that certainty is impossible, and that therefore decisions must be based on probabilities **2.** the principle whereby, in moral questions in which nothing is certain, somebody may follow the probability favourable to him or her rather than a more probable, but less favourable view —**probabilist** *n, adj* —**probabilistic** /próbbəbə lístik/ *adj* —**probabilistically** *adv*

probability /próbbə bílləti/ (*plural* **-ties**) *n* **1.** STATE OF BEING PROBABLE the state of being probable, or the extent to which something is probable ○ *We must take into account the probability of another earthquake.* **2.** SOMETHING LIKELY TO HAPPEN something that is likely to happen or exist ○ *We must prepare for all probabilities.* **3.** STATS MATHEMATICAL LIKELIHOOD OF EVENT the likelihood that an event will occur, expressed as the ratio of the number of favourable outcomes in the set of outcomes divided by the total number of possible outcomes ◇ **in all probability** used to suggest that something is highly probable

probability density function *n* **1.** STATS same as **probability function 2.** a function of a continuous variable such that the integral of the function over a specific region yields the probability that its value will fall within the region

probability function *n* a function of a discrete random variable that yields the probability of occurrence of distinct outcomes

probability theory *n* the branch of mathematics that deals with quantities with random distributions, with the aim of predicting how defined systems will behave

probable /próbbəb'l/ *adj* likely to exist, occur, or be true, although evidence is insufficient to prove or predict it ■ *n* somebody or something that is likely to be chosen for something or is likely to do something ○ *a probable for the team* [14C. Directly or via French < Latin *probabilis* 'provable, plausible' < *probare* (see PROVE)]

probable cause *n* sufficient reason to believe that an arrest or search of a suspect is warranted

probable error *n* the amount by which a statistic may vary from fact, based on chance factors

probably /próbbəbli/ *adv* as is likely or to be expected ○ *I'll probably come tonight.*

proband /prṓ band/ *n* GENETICS same as **propositus** (sense 3) [Early 20C. < Latin *probandus-* 'for testing, to be tested' < *probare* (see PROVE)]

probate /prṓ bayt/ *n* **1.** the legal certification of the validity of a will **2.** an official copy of a will that is legally certified as genuine and given to the executors [14C. < Latin *probatum* 'thing proved' < *probare* (see PROVE)]

probate court *n* a court that deals with the legal certification of wills and the administration of estates of the deceased

probation /prə báysh'n/ *n* **1.** SUPERVISION BY PROBATION OFFICER the supervision of the behaviour of a young or first-time criminal offender by a probation officer. During the period of supervision, the offender must regularly report to the probation officer and must not commit any further offences. **2.** PERIOD OF TESTING SOMEBODY'S SUITABILITY a period during which somebody's suitability for a job or other role is being tested **3.** TESTING OF SOMETHING the testing or proving of something (*formal*) —**probational** *adj* —**probationally** *adv* —**probationary** *adj*

probationary assistant *n NZ* a teacher undergoing a probation period

probationer /prə báysh'nər/ *n* **1.** somebody on probation, especially somebody under supervision because he or she is new to a job or has just been released from prison **2.** a student Scottish Presbyterian minister who has received a licence but has not yet been ordained

probation officer *n* an official who supervises criminal offenders on probation

probative /prṓbətiv/, **probatory** /prṓbətəri/ *adj* **1.** supplying proof or evidence **2.** designed to test or prove somebody or something [15C. < Old French *probatif* < Latin *probare* (see PROVE)]

probe /prōb/ *n* **1.** INVESTIGATION a thorough investigation, often into illegal or suspicious activities **2.** CIRCUIT-TESTING DEVICE a device with a metal tip used to test the behaviour of electrical circuits, e.g. the probe on a voltmeter or ammeter **3.** SURGICAL INSTRUMENT FOR EXPLORING a long thin instrument used by doctors and dentists for exploring or examining **4.** AEROSP same as **space probe** ■ *vti* (**probes, probing, probed**) **1.** INVESTIGATE SOMETHING COMPLETELY to conduct a thorough investigation into something **2.** CHECK SOMETHING USING PROBE to examine something with a probe **3.** EXAMINE AREA to search or explore a place [Mid-16C. < medieval Latin *proba* 'examination' < Latin *probare* (see PROVE)] — **probeable** *adj* —**prober** *n* —**probingly** *adv*

probenecid /prō bénnəssid/ *n* a drug that promotes the excretion of uric acid. Use: treatment of gout. [Mid-20C. Blend of PROPYL + BENZENE + ACID]

probiotic /prṓ bī óttik/ *n* a substance containing live microorganisms that claims to be beneficial to humans and animals, e.g. by restoring the balance of microflora in the digestive tract

probity /prṓbəti/ *n* absolute moral correctness [Early 16C. Via French < Latin *probitas* < *probus* 'good']

problem /próbbləm/ *n* **1.** DIFFICULTY a difficult situation, matter, or person **2.** PUZZLE TO BE SOLVED a question or puzzle that needs to be solved **3.** MATHS STATEMENT REQUIRING MATHEMATICAL SOLUTION a statement or proposition requiring an algebraic, geometric, or other mathematical solution ■ *adj* HARD TO DEAL WITH difficult to discipline or deal with ○ *a problem child* [14C. Via French and Latin < Greek *problēma* 'projection, obstacle', literally 'thing thrown in front' < *ballein* 'to throw'] ◇ **no problem** used to indicate that something will not cause any difficulty or inconvenience (*informal*)

SYNONYMS ***problem, mystery, puzzle, riddle, conundrum, enigma***

CORE MEANING: something difficult to solve or understand

problem a difficult situation, matter, or person ○ *an*

ongoing problem ○ *problems with the staff* **mystery** an event or situation that is difficult to fully understand or explain, or a person about whom little is known ○ *the key to understanding the mysteries of the universe* ○ *The question of who Barry really was remains a mystery.* **puzzle** a problem or situation that is difficult or impossible to resolve, or somebody whose behaviour or motives are difficult to understand ○ *The puzzle of the missing letters remained.* **riddle** something that is puzzling or confusing ○ *The DNA team announced they had solved the riddle of the unidentified human remains.* **conundrum** something that is puzzling or confusing ○ *Here's the conundrum: if advances in productivity result in more workers losing their jobs, who will be able to buy the products and services being produced?* **enigma** somebody or something that is not easily explained or understood ○ *After 20 years of marriage, Madeleine was still very much an enigma to him.*

problematic /próbblə máttik/, **problematical** /-máttik'l/ *adj* involving difficulties or problems ■ *n* a matter or issue that is problematic —**problematically** *adv*

~~**probly**~~ incorrect spelling of **probably**

pro bono /prō bṓnō/ *adj, adv* done or undertaken for the public good without any payment or compensation [Shortening of Latin *pro bono publico* 'for the public good']

proboscidean /próbbə síddi ən/, **proboscidian** *n* a very large mammal that has a trunk and tusks, e.g. an elephant, mammoth, or mastodon. Order: Proboscidea. [Mid-19C. < modern Latin *Proboscidea* < Latin *proboscid-*, stem of *proboscis* (see PROBOSCIS)] —**proboscidean** *adj*

proboscis /prō bóssiss/ (*plural* **-boscises** or **-bosces** /-bós seez/ or **-boscides** /-si deez/) *n* **1.** LONG FLEXIBLE SNOUT the long flexible snout of some mammals such as the tapir, the elephant seal, or the proboscis monkey **2.** ELEPHANT'S TRUNK the trunk of an elephant or related extinct mammal **3.** LONG MOUTHPARTS OF INVERTEBRATE the long or tubular mouthparts of some insects, worms, and spiders, used for feeding, sucking, and other purposes **4.** LARGE NOSE a human nose, especially a large one (*humorous*) [Late 16C. Via Latin < Greek *proboskis* 'elephant's trunk' < *boskein* 'to feed']

proboscis monkey *n* a large monkey with reddish fur and a protruding bulbous nose that in older males becomes pendulous. Native to: Borneo. Latin name: *Nasalis larvatus*.

procaine /prṓ kayn, -káyn/, **procain** *n* a white or colourless crystalline ester. Use: local anaesthetic, in the form of its hydrochloride. Formula: $C_{13}H_{20}N_2O_2$.

procambium /prō kámbi əm/ *n* undifferentiated plant tissue that develops into cambium and vascular tissue —**procambial** *adj*

procaryote *n* BIOL another spelling of **prokaryote**

~~**procede**~~ incorrect spelling of **proceed**

procedure /prə séejər/ *n* **1.** an established or correct method of doing something **2.** any means of doing or accomplishing something ○ *an extremely unorthodox procedure* **3.** COMPUT same as **routine** *n* (sense 5) **4.** COMPUT same as **subroutine** [Early 17C. < French *procédure* < *procéder* (see PROCEED)] —**procedural** *adj, n*

proceed /prə séed/ (**-ceeds, -ceeding, -ceeded**) *vi* **1.** BEGIN ACTION to go on to do something **2.** CONTINUE WITH ACTION to continue with a course of action **3.** PROGRESS to progress in a steady or particular manner **4.** GO IN PARTICULAR DIRECTION to go in a particular direction, especially forward **5.** DEVELOP to come from or arise from something **6.** LAW SUE to bring legal action against somebody [14C. Via French *procéder* < Latin *procedere* 'go forward' < *cedere* 'go'] —**proceeder** *n*

SPELLCHECK See *precede*.

proceeding /prə séeding/ *n* PROCEDURE an action or course of action ■ **proceedings** *npl* **1.** LEGAL ACTION legal action brought against somebody **2.** SERIES OF EVENTS a series of related events occurring at one time or in one place **3.** PUBLISHED RECORDS published records of a meeting or conference

proceeds /prṓ seedz/ *npl* the money derived from a sale or other commercial transaction

process[1] /prṓ sess/ *n* **1.** SERIES OF ACTIONS a series of actions directed towards a specific aim **2.** SERIES OF NATURAL OCCURRENCES a series of natural occurrences that produce change or development **3.** LAW SUMMONS TO APPEAR IN COURT a summons or writ ordering somebody to appear in court **4.** LAW LEGAL PROCEEDINGS the entire proceedings in a lawsuit **5.** BIOL NATURAL OUTGROWTH a part that naturally grows on or sticks out on an organism ■ *v* (**-esses, -essing, -essed**) **1.** *vt* PREPARE SOMETHING USING A PROCESS to treat or prepare something in a series of steps or actions, e.g. using chemicals or industrial machinery **2.** *vt* TREAT FILM WITH CHEMICALS to treat light-sensitive film or paper with chemicals in order to make a latent image visible **3.** *vt* FOLLOW PROCEDURES to deal with somebody or something according to an established procedure **4.** *vti* PREPARE FOOD IN FOOD PROCESSOR to chop, mix, or otherwise prepare food in a food processor or blender **5.** *vt* COMPUT USE PROGRAM ON DATA to use a computer program to work on data in some way, e.g. to sort a database or recalculate a spreadsheet **6.** *vt* LAW SERVE SUMMONS ON SOMEBODY to serve a summons or writ on somebody **7.** *vt* LAW BRING LEGAL ACTION to bring a legal action against somebody [14C. Via French < Latin *processus* < *process-*, past participle of *procedere* (see PROCEED)]

process[2] /prə séss/ (**-esses, -essing, -essed**) *vi* to move forwards in a procession [Early 19C. Back-formation < PROCESSION]

processed /prṓss est/ *adj* treated by a chemical or industrial process

processed cheese *n* a blend of several types of cheese with emulsifiers added, sometimes sold in individually wrapped thin slices

process engineering *n* the branch of engineering that determines the sequence of operations and the selection of tools required to manufacture a product

process industry *n* an industry in which raw materials are treated or prepared in a series of stages, e.g. using chemical processes. Process industries include oil refining, petrochemicals, water and sewage treatment, food manufacture, and pharmaceuticals.

procession /prə sésh'n/ *n* **1.** GROUP OF PEOPLE MOVING FORWARDS a group of people or vehicles moving forwards in a line as part of a celebration, commemoration, or demonstration **2.** FORWARD MOVEMENT the movement forwards of a group of people or vehicles as part of a celebration, commemoration, or demonstration **3.** SUCCESSION a series of people or things coming one after the other [12C. Directly or via French < Latin *procession-* < *process-* (see PROCESS[1])]

processional /prə sésh'nəl/ *adj* **1.** FOR PROCESSION used for or in a procession **2.** FORMING PROCESSION taking the form of a procession ■ *n* **1.** MUSIC FOR PROCESSION a piece of music suitable for accompanying a procession **2.** CHURCH MUSIC FOR ENTRY OF CLERGY a hymn or other piece of music that accompanies the entry of the clergy into a church **3.** BOOK OF HYMNS AND PRAYERS a book of hymns and prayers for use during a religious procession —**processionally** *adv*

processor /prṓ sessər/, **processer** *n* **1.** somebody or something that processes things **2.** the central processing unit of a computer **3.** COMPUT same as **microprocessor** **4.** HOUSEHOLD same as **food processor**

process-server *n* somebody who serves a writ or summons ordering somebody to appear in court

procès-verbal /próssay vur baál/ (*plural* **procès-verbaux** /próssay vur bṓ/) *n* a written account of official proceedings [Mid-17C. < French, 'oral proceedings', originally evidence from police officers who could not write]

prochlorperazine /prṓ klawr pérrə zeen/ *n* a phenothiazine drug. Use: control of nausea and vomiting, to relieve symptoms of Ménière's disease, migraine, and anxiety. [Mid-20C. Blend of PROPYL + CHLOR- + PIPERAZINE]

pro-choice *adj* advocating open legal access to voluntary abortion

proclaim /prə kláym/ (**-claims, -claiming, -claimed**) *vt* **1.** DECLARE SOMETHING PUBLICLY to announce something publicly or formally **2.** DECLARE SOMEBODY TO BE SOMETHING to declare publicly that somebody is something **3.** SHOW WHAT SOMETHING IS to show or reveal clearly what something is **4.** MAKE SOMETHING CLEAR to state something emphatically or openly [14C. Via French < Latin *proclamare* 'cry out' < *clamare* 'to cry'] —**proclaimer** *n* —**proclamatory** /prə klámmətəri/ *adj*

proclamation /próklə máysh'n/ *n* **1.** a public or formal announcement **2.** the act of announcing something publicly or formally [14C. Directly or via French < Latin *proclamation-* < *proclamare* (see PROCLAIM)]

proclitic /prō klíttik/ *adj* describes a reduced form of a word that is closely attached in pronunciation to the word following it and has no accent of its own, e.g. 'd'' in 'd'you' [Mid-19C. < modern Latin *procliticus*, after late Latin *encliticus* 'enclitic'] —**proclitic** *n*

proclivity /prə klívvəti/ (*plural* **-ties**) *n* a natural tendency to behave in a particular way [Late 16C. < Latin *proclivitas* < *proclivis* 'inclined' < *clivus* 'slope']

~~**proclomation**~~ incorrect spelling of **proclamation**

Procne /prókni/ *n* in Greek mythology, an Athenian princess whose husband, Tereus, raped her sister, Philomela. She avenged this act by killing their own son and feeding him to Tereus.

proconsul /prō kónss'l/ *n* **1.** GOVERNOR OF ANCIENT ROMAN PROVINCE a governor of an ancient Roman province, usually a former consul **2.** GOVERNOR OF COLONY a governor or administrator of a colony or other dependency **3.** GOV, INTERNAT REL ADMINISTRATOR OF MILITARY-GOVERNED NATION a senior administrator with broad powers in a nation recently invaded and under the control of the invader's armed forces, charged with pacifying the population, restoring vital services, and establishing new governance [14C. < Latin, '(person acting) for the consul'] —**proconsular** /-kónssyoǒlər/ *adj* —**proconsulate** /-kónssyoǒlət/ *n* —**proconsulship** *n*

Procopius /prə kṓpi əss/ (500?–565?) Byzantine historian. He wrote *The Books About the Wars* and other texts that document the reign of Justinian I and the Byzantine court.

procrastinate /prō krásti nayt/ (**-nates, -nating, -nated**) *vti* to postpone doing something, especially as a regular practice [Late 16C. < Latin *procrastinat-*, past participle of *procrastinare* 'put off until tomorrow' < *cras* 'tomorrow'] —**procrastination** /prō krásti náysh'n/ *n* —**procrastinator** *n*

USAGE See *prevaricate*.

procreate /prṓkri ayt, prṓkri áyt/ (**-ates, -ating, -ated**) *v* **1.** *vti* to produce offspring by reproduction **2.** *vt* to create or produce something [Mid-16C. < Latin *procreat-*, past participle of *procreare* 'bring forth' < *creare* 'bring forth, produce'] —**procreant** /prṓkri ənt/ *adj* —**procreation** /prṓkri áysh'n/ *n* —**procreative** *adj* —**procreator** *n*

Procrustean /prō krústi ən/ *adj* trying to establish conformity by using any and all means, including violence [Mid-19C. < PROCRUSTES]

Procrustes /prō krús teez/ *n* in Greek mythology, a robber who abducted strangers and forced them to fit perfectly into a bed by either cutting off or stretching their limbs

procryptic /prō kríptik/ *adj* describes an animal that has a coloration or pattern of shading that acts as camouflage [Late 19C. < PRO-[1] + Greek *kruptikos* (see CRYPTIC), probably after PROTECTIVE] —**procryptically** *adv*

proct- *prefix* same as **procto-** (*used before vowels*)

proctitis /prok títiss/ *n* inflammation of the rectum [Early 19C. < Greek *prōktos* 'anus']

procto- *prefix* anus, anal, rectum, rectal ○ *proctoscope* [< Greek *prōktos*]

proctodaeum /proktə dée əm/ (*plural* **-daea** /-dée ə/ or **-daeums**) *n* the exterior section of an embryo that develops into part of the anal canal [Late 19C. < modern Latin < Greek *prōktos* 'anus' + *hodaios* 'on the way' < *hodos* 'way']

proctology /prok tólləji/ *n* the branch of medicine concerned with disorders of the colon, rectum, and anus —**proctological** /próktə lójjik'l/ *adj* —**proctologist** *n*

proctor /próktər/ *n* **1.** UNIVERSITY OFFICER IN CHARGE OF DISCIPLINE either of two officers at some universities elected annually and assigned to supervise undergraduate discipline **2.** *N Am* EDUC same as **invigilator** **3.** LEGAL REPRESENTATIVE somebody who conducts somebody else's case in court (*dated*) **4.** CLERGY REPRESENTATIVE any one of the representatives of the clergy in the Church of England convocation ■ *vt*

(-tors, -toring, -tored) *N Am* EDUC same as **invigilate** [14C. Contraction of PROCURATOR] —**proctorial** /prok táwri əl/ *adj* —**proctorship** *n*

proctoscope /próktə skōp/ *n* a tubular medical instrument with an integral light source, used for examining the anal canal and rectum —**proctoscopic** /próktə skóppik/ *adj* —**proctoscopy** /prok tóskəpi/ *n*

procumbent /prō kúmbənt/ *adj* **1.** lying down with the face to the ground **2.** describes a plant stem that grows along the ground without taking root [Mid-17C. < Latin *procumbent-*, present participle of *procumbere* 'fall forward' < *cumbere* 'lie down']

procuration /prókyoŏ ráysh'n/ *n* **1.** ACQUIRING OF SOMETHING the obtaining of something, especially by effort (*formal*) **2.** CRIME PROVIDING OF PROSTITUTE the crime of providing somebody for prostitution **3.** LAW ENGAGING OF PROCURATOR the engaging of an agent to manage somebody's affairs **4.** LAW AUTHORIZING OF PROCURATOR the authorization given to somebody who acts as an agent to manage somebody else's affairs [15C. Directly or via French < Latin *procuration-* < *procurat-* (see PROCURATOR)]

procurator /prókyoŏ raytər/ *n* **1.** an agent engaged to manage somebody else's affairs **2.** in ancient Rome, an administrative official with legal or fiscal powers [13C. Directly or via French < Latin, 'agent, manager, tax-collector' < *procurat-*, past participle of *procurare* (see PROCURE)] —**procuratorial** /prókyoŏrə táwri əl/ *adj* —**procuratorship** *n*

procurator fiscal /prókyoŏ raytər físk'l/ (*plural* **procurators fiscal** or **procurator fiscals**) *n* in Scotland, a public prosecutor and coroner

procure /prə kyóor/ (**-cures, -curing, -cured**) *v* **1.** *vt* to obtain something, especially by effort **2.** *vti* to provide somebody for prostitution [13C. Via French < Latin *procurare* 'take care of, manage' < *curare* 'care for'] —**procurable** *adj* —**procural** *n* —**procurance** *n* —**procurement** *n* —**procurer** *n*

SYNONYMS See ***get***[1].

procuress /prə kyóor ess/ (*plural* **-esses**) *n* a woman who provides people for prostitution

Procyon /prṓsi ən/ *n* a binary star in the constellation Canis Minor and one of the brightest stars in the sky [< Greek, literally 'before the dog', because it rises before the Dog Star, Sirius]

prod /prod/ *vti* (**prods, prodding, prodded**) **1.** POKE SOMEBODY OR SOMETHING to poke somebody or something with a finger, elbow, or pointed object **2.** INCITE SOMEBODY TO ACTION to incite or encourage somebody to take action ■ *n* **1.** A POKE a poke with a finger, elbow, or pointed object **2.** INCITEMENT TO ACTION an incitement or encouragement to do something **3.** POKING INSTRUMENT an instrument used for poking a person or animal [Mid-16C. Origin ?] —**prodder** *n*

Prod /pród/, **Proddie** /próddi/ *n Ireland, Scotland* an offensive term for a Protestant (*slang*) [Mid-20C. Shortening, after a pronunciation]

prodigal /próddig'l/ *adj* **1.** WASTEFUL tending to spend money wastefully **2.** PRODUCING GENEROUS AMOUNTS giving or producing something in large amounts ■ *n* **1.** SPENDTHRIFT somebody who spends money wastefully **2.** REPENTANT WASTREL somebody who, after leaving home, behaves wastefully and disgracefully, but repents and is forgiven and warmly welcomed on returning [Early 16C. Via French < late Latin *prodigalis* < Latin *prodigus* 'wasteful' < *prodigere* 'drive away, squander' < *agere* 'to drive'] —**prodigality** /próddi gálləti/ *n* —**prodigally** *adv*

prodigal son *n* a man or youth who is a prodigal

prodigious /prə díjjəss/ *adj* **1.** great in amount, size, or extent **2.** very impressive or amazing [Mid-16C. < Latin *prodigiosus* 'marvellous' < *prodigium* 'prophetic sign, portent'] —**prodigiously** *adv* —**prodigiousness** *n*

prodigy /próddiji/ (*plural* **-gies**) *n* **1.** somebody who shows an exceptional talent at an early age **2.** something very impressive or amazing [15C. < Latin *prodigium* 'prophetic sign, portent']

prodrome /prṓdrōm/ *n* a symptom indicating the start of a disease [Mid-17C. Via French < Greek *prodromos* 'a running before' < *dromos* 'running'] —**prodromal** /prō drṓm'l/ *adj* —**prodromic** /prō drómmik/ *adj*

prodrug /prṓ drug/ *n* an inactive form of a drug that is converted into an active form in the body by a chemical reaction in the digestive tract. Use: chemotherapeutic agent targeting cancer cells.

produce *v* /prə dyóoss/ (**-duces, -ducing, -duced**) **1.** *vti* MAKE SOMETHING to make or create something ○ *able to produce a tasty meal from the most unpromising ingredients* **2.** *vti* MANUFACTURE SOMETHING to manufacture goods for sale ○ *They produce electrical goods mainly for export.* **3.** *vt* CAUSE SOMETHING to cause something to happen or arise ○ *Marjorie's calls for silence failed to produce the desired effect.* **4.** *vti* YIELD SOMETHING to grow, bring forth, or bear something ○ *produce seeds* **5.** *vt* TAKE SOMETHING OUT to pull something out and show it ○ *He produced a pistol from his pocket and started waving it around.* **6.** *vt* PRESENT SOMETHING to put something forward for inspection or consideration ○ *produced no evidence to support her claim* **7.** *vt* ARTS ORGANIZE THE MAKING OF SOMETHING to organize and supervise the making or staging of something ○ *produce a new album* **8.** *vt* MATHS EXTEND SOMETHING IN SPACE to extend the length of a line ■ *n* /próddyooss/ FARM OR GARDEN PRODUCTS products of farms or gardens, especially fruits and vegetables [15C. < Latin *producere* 'lead or bring out' < *ducere* 'to lead'] —**producibility** /prə dyóossə bílləti/ *n* —**producible** *adj*

producer /prə dyóossər/ *n* **1.** SOMETHING GENERATING ITEMS FOR SALE a person, company, or country that produces goods or services for sale **2.** ORGANIZER OF FILM OR RECORDING an organizer and administrator of the making of a film, broadcast, or recording, or the staging of a play **3.** SOMETHING THAT PRODUCES somebody or something that produces something **4.** INDUST APPARATUS FOR PRODUCER GAS a furnace used for making producer gas **5.** ECOL ORGANISM THAT MAKES ITS FOOD an organism that manufactures its own food from simple inorganic substances, e.g. a green plant

producer gas *n* a fuel consisting of carbon monoxide, nitrogen, and hydrogen, made by passing air and steam over hot coke in a furnace

producer goods, producer's goods *npl* raw materials, equipment, and other goods that are used to manufacture consumer goods

product /próddukt/ *n* **1.** COMMODITY PRODUCED FOR SALE a commodity that is produced by manufacture or by a natural process and is offered for sale **2.** COMPANY'S GOODS OR SERVICES the goods or services produced by a company **3.** RESULT something that arises as a consequence of something else **4.** MATHS RESULT OF MULTIPLYING the result of the multiplication of two or more quantities **5.** CHEM CHEMICAL SUBSTANCE a substance produced in a chemical reaction [15C. < Latin *productus*, past participle of *producere* (see PRODUCE)]

production /prə dúksh'n/ *n* **1.** MAKING OF SOMETHING the making or creation of something **2.** SOMETHING PRODUCED something that has been made or created **3.** PRODUCING OF GOODS the process of manufacturing a product for sale **4.** COMPANY'S PRODUCT the goods or services produced by a company **5.** SUPERVISION OF RECORDING OR FILMING the organization and supervision of the making of a film, broadcast, or recording, or the staging of a play **6.** FILM OR RECORDING a film, play, broadcast, or recording that has been produced for the public **7.** PRESENTATION OF SOMETHING the showing or presenting of something such as evidence or proof —**productional** *adj*

production line *n* a sequence of machines or processes in a factory through which the products pass until they are fully assembled

production number *n* a piece of music in a musical that is sung and danced by featured actors supported by the chorus ◇ **make a (great) production number out of something** to exaggerate the seriousness or importance of something (*informal*)

productise *v* COMM another spelling of **productize**

productive /prə dúktiv/ *adj* **1.** PRODUCING MUCH producing something abundantly and efficiently **2.** WORTHWHILE producing satisfactory or useful results **3.** PRODUCING SOMETHING producing or able to produce something **4.** ECON PRODUCING GOODS producing goods and services of exchangeable value **5.** MED PRODUCING MUCUS describes a cough that produces mucus **6.** GRAM USED TO FORM WORDS describes a prefix or suffix that is used in forming new words —**productively** *adv* —**productiveness** *n*

productivity /próddukˈ tívvəti/ *n* **1.** the rate at which a company produces goods or services, in relation to the amount of materials and number of employees needed **2.** the ability to be productive

productize /próddək tīz/ (**-izes, -izing, -ized**), **productise** (**-ises, -ising, -ised**) *vti* to convert something such as an idea, a process, a prototype, or an area of expertise into a marketable and salable product

product liability *n* the liability of manufacturers and traders for damage or injury caused to purchasers or bystanders by their products

product line *n* **1.** the whole range of products marketed by a company **2.** a group of related products marketed by the same company that differ only in size or style

product placement *n* the practice of placing brand-name items as props in, e.g. films, television shows, or music videos as a form of advertising

product recall *n* the act of requesting the return of a commercial product to the retailer or manufacturer because of a defect or a safety or efficiency problem

proem /prṓ em/ *n* an introduction to a literary work or a speech [14C. Via Old French *pro(h)eme* < Greek *prooimion*, literally 'song before' < *oimē* 'song'] —**proemial** /prō émmi əl/ *adj*

proenzyme /prō én zīm/ *n* the inactive precursor of an enzyme, especially one secreted by living cells and activated by an acid, another enzyme, or other catalytic means

proestrus *n* PHYSIOL US spelling of **pro-oestrus**

prof /prof/ *n* a college or university professor (*informal*) [Mid-19C. Shortening]

Prof. *abbr* EDUC Professor

profane /prə fáyn/ *adj* **1.** IRREVERENT showing disrespect for God, any deity, or religion **2.** SECULAR not connected with or used for religious matters **3.** UNINITIATED not initiated into sacred or secret rites ■ *vt* (**-fanes, -faning, -faned**) TREAT SOMETHING IRREVERENTLY to treat something sacred with disrespect [14C. Via French < Latin *profanus* 'outside the temple, not sacred' < *fanum* 'temple'] —**profanation** /próffə náysh'n/ *n* —**profanatory** /prə fánnətəri/ *adj* —**profanely** *adv* —**profaneness** *n* —**profaner** *n*

profanity /prə fánnəti/ (*plural* **-ties**) *n* **1.** language or behaviour that shows disrespect for God, any deity, or religion **2.** a word or phrase that shows disrespect for God, any deity, or religion

profess /prə féss/ (**-fesses, -fessing, -fessed**) *v* **1.** *vti* DECLARE SOMETHING OPENLY to make a statement acknowledging something openly or publicly ○ *Having professed his belief in the remedy, he had little choice but to try it.* ○ *They professed themselves delighted with the results.* **2.** *vt* DECLARE SOMETHING FALSELY to make a statement falsely claiming that something is the case ○ *Many profess to despise what secretly they hunger after.* **3.** *vt* RELIG EXPRESS FAITH IN PARTICULAR BELIEF to follow a particular religion **4.** *vti* RELIG BECOME PRIEST OR NUN to admit somebody into a religious order, or be admitted into a religious order [15C. < Old French *profes* 'having taken religious vows' < Latin *profess-*, past participle of *profiteri* 'declare publicly' < *fateri* 'acknowledge'] —**professed** *adj* —**professedly** /prə féssidli/ *adv*

profession /prə fésh'n/ *n* **1.** OCCUPATION REQUIRING EXTENSIVE EDUCATION an occupation that requires extensive education or specialized training **2.** PEOPLE IN PROFESSION the people who practise a particular profession ○ *the legal profession* **3.** DECLARATION a public acknowledgment or declaration of something ○ *a profession of support* **4.** DECLARATION OF FAITH a declaration of belief in a religion or faith [13C. Directly or via French < Latin *profession-* < *profess-* (see PROFESS)]

professional /prə fésh'nəl/ *adj* **1.** OF PROFESSION relating to or belonging to a profession ○ *professional people* **2.** FOLLOWING OCCUPATION AS PAID JOB engaged in an occupation as a paid job rather than as a hobby ○ *professional tennis player* **3.** BUSINESSLIKE conforming to the standards of skill, competence, or character normally expected of a properly qualified and experienced person in a work environment ○ *professional attitude* **4.** VERY COMPETENT showing a high degree of skill or competence ○ *did a very professional job* **5.** DOING SOMETHING HABITUALLY habitually, and usually annoyingly, indulging in a particular activity ○ *a professional complainer* ■ *n* **1.** MEMBER OF PROFESSION somebody whose occupation requires extensive education or specialized training **2.** SOME-

BODY IN SKILLED JOB a worker in a paid occupation that usually requires a high degree of training and skill 3. SOMEBODY VERY COMPETENT somebody with a high degree of skill or competence 4. TEACHER AT SPORTS CLUB an expert player of a sport who is paid to teach other players in a club —**professionally** adv

professional association n an organization composed of members of a particular profession that regulates entry to and sets and maintains standards for that profession

professional foul n a deliberate foul in football, usually committed in order to prevent the opposing team gaining a potentially crucial advantage in field position or goal-scoring opportunity

professionalise vt HR another spelling of **professionalize**

professionalism /prə fésh'nəlizəm/ n 1. the skill, competence, or character expected of a member of a highly trained profession 2. the following of an activity for financial gain rather than as an amateur

professionalize /prə fésh'nə līz/ (-izes, -izing, -ized), **professionalise** (-ises, -ising, -ised) vti to become professional or proceed with something in a professional way, e.g. make an activity professional by paying participants or by setting high standards that must be met —**professionalization** /prə fésh'nə lī záysh'n/ n

professor /prə féssər/ n 1. HIGHEST RANKING UNIVERSITY TEACHER a teacher of the highest academic rank in a college or university, often the head of a particular academic department 2. N Am UNIVERSITY TEACHER a teacher in a university or college 3. SENIOR NONACADEMIC TEACHER a senior teacher of a nonacademic discipline in an institution other than a university, e.g. a music or drama school 4. SOMEBODY PROFESSING BELIEF somebody who professes a religious or other belief (formal) [14C. Directly or via French < Latin profess- (see PROFESS)] —**professorial** /próffə sáwri əl/ adj —**professorially** adv —**professorship** n

professoriate /próffə sáwri ət/, **professorate** /prə féssərət/ n 1. professors as a group 2. the status or position of professor

proffer /próffər/ (-fers, -fering, -fered) vt 1. to hold something out to somebody so that he or she can take or grasp it 2. to offer something for consideration to somebody ○ proffer a suggestion [13C. < Old French proffrir 'offer forth' < offrir 'to offer'] —**profferer** n

~~**proffesor**~~ incorrect spelling of **professor**

proficient /prə físh'nt/ adj having a high degree of skill in something [Late 16C. Via French < Latin proficient-, present participle of proficere 'make progress' < facere 'make'] —**proficiency** n —**proficiently** adv

profile /pró fīl/ n 1. VISIBILITY a level or degree of noticeability ○ kept a low profile 2. SIDE VIEW OF FACE the outline of somebody's face as seen from the side 3. ARTWORK OF SOMEBODY'S PROFILE a visual representation of the outline of somebody's face as seen from the side 4. SHORT BIOGRAPHY a short biographical account of somebody 5. BRIEF DESCRIPTION a brief description that summarizes the characteristics of somebody or something ○ a profile of her past philanthropy 6. PUPIL ASSESSMENT an assessment of the range of qualities, attitudes, and behaviour of a pupil, providing a fuller picture of the pupil than that given by traditional school reports 7. STATS DESCRIPTIVE DATA a set of data, usually in graph or table form, that indicates the extent to which something matches tested or standard characteristics 8. GEOG VERTICAL SECTION OF PHYSICAL FEATURE a vertical section through a physical feature, e.g. through soil, showing its development from bedrock ■ vt (-files, -filing, -filed) 1. WRITE SHORT ACCOUNT OF SOMEBODY to write or present a short biographical account or description of somebody or something 2. SHOW SOMEBODY'S FACIAL PROFILE to represent the outline of somebody's face as seen from the side 3. ANALYSE AND CLASSIFY SOMEBODY to subject somebody to profiling, e.g. in a criminal investigation [Mid-17C. < Italian profilo < profilare 'draw in outline' < filo 'thread' < Latin filum] —**profiler** n

profiling /pró fīling/ n the analysis and classification of somebody based on personal information such as ethnicity, shopping habits, or behavioural patterns, used e.g. in criminal investigations or product advertising ○ racial profiling ○ consumer profiling

profit /próffit/ n 1. EXCESS OF INCOME OVER EXPENDITURE the excess of income over expenditure, especially in business 2. INCOME FROM SOMETHING income from an investment or transaction 3. ADVANTAGE an advantage or benefit derived from an activity ■ v (-its, -iting, -ited) 1. vi MAKE MONEY ON SOMETHING to gain financial profit from something 2. vti BENEFIT FROM SOMETHING to gain an advantage or benefit from something, or provide an advantage or benefit [13C. Via French < Latin profectus 'progress, profit' < past participle of proficere (see PROFICIENT)] —**profiter** n —**profitless** adj —**profitlessly** adv

SPELLCHECK **profit** or **prophet**? Do not confuse the spelling of **profit** and **prophet**, which sound similar. **Profit** is a noun and verb referring to financial gain, benefit, or advantage: We made a profit of £100 on the transaction. They profited from the umpire's decision. The word **prophet** is only used as a noun, denoting somebody who foretells the future, as in an Old Testament prophet, prophets of doom.

profitable /próffitəb'l/ adj 1. yielding a financial profit 2. of some use, benefit, or advantage to somebody —**profitability** /próffitə billəti/ n —**profitably** adv

profit and loss n an account showing income and expenditure over a given period and indicating net profit or loss

profit centre n a section or activity of a company that is independently profitable

profiteer /próffi teér/ (-eers, -eering, -eered) vi to make excessive profits by charging high prices for scarce, necessary, or rationed goods —**profiteer** n —**profiteering** n

profiterole /prə fíttərōl/ n a small ball of choux pastry filled with cream and usually served with chocolate sauce [Early 16C. < French, 'small gain' < profit (see PROFIT)]

profitmaking /próffit mayking/ adj operated with the primary aim of making a profit

profit margin n a measure of profitability determined by dividing income after subtracting related expenses by sales, expressed as a percentage

profit sharing n a system by which the employees of a company receive a prearranged share of the company's profits (hyphenated when used before a noun)

profits warning n an announcement by a company of lower than expected profits for a particular period

profit taking n the selling of commodities, securities, or shares at a time when their current market value is greater than the price at which they were purchased

profligate /próffligət/ adj 1. WASTEFUL extremely extravagant or wasteful 2. WITH LOW MORALS having or showing extremely low moral standards ■ n 1. SOMEBODY WASTEFUL an extremely extravagant or wasteful person 2. SOMEBODY WITH LOW MORALS somebody with extremely low moral standards [Mid-16C. < Latin profligatus, past participle of profligare 'strike down, ruin' < fligere 'to strike'] —**profligacy** n —**profligately** adv

pro-form n UK a word that replaces a previously mentioned word or phrase and assumes its meaning, e.g. 'does' in the sentence 'You look tired and so does John'. ANZ, N Am term **substitute**

pro forma /pró fáwrmə/ adj 1. FORMAL OR CONVENTIONAL done or existing only as a formality 2. PROVIDED IN ADVANCE provided in advance in order to supply descriptions of something or to serve as a model, e.g. of a later version of a document ■ adv FOR CONVENTION'S SAKE for the sake of or in accordance with convention [< Latin, 'for form's sake']

profound /prə fównd/ adj 1. GREAT very great, strong, or intense ○ profound effect ○ profound regret 2. SHOWING GREAT UNDERSTANDING showing great perception, understanding, or knowledge ○ profound insight 3. REQUIRING THOUGHTFUL STUDY containing far-reaching ideas or essential wisdom and experience that usually require serious thought to be fully appreciated ○ a profound meditation on the human condition 4. VERY DEEP extending to or situated at a great depth (literary) [13C. Via French < Latin profundus 'bottom forwards or downwards' < fundus 'bottom'] —**profoundly** adv —**profoundness** n

profundity /prə fúndəti/ (plural -ties) n 1. INTENSE INSIGHT intense intellectual or human insight that deals

seriously with the most vital aspects of any question 2. SOMETHING SHOWING INSIGHT something that shows great perceptiveness or knowledge or requires great perceptiveness or knowledge to be properly understood 3. INTELLECTUAL COMPLEXITY the intellectual complexity or abstruseness of something 4. GREATNESS the greatness, strength, or intensity of something 5. GREAT DEPTH extension to or location at a great depth (literary) [15C. Via French < late Latin profunditas < profundus (see PROFOUND)]

profuse /prə fyóoss/ adj 1. VOLUBLY EXPRESSED expressed at length, many times, and in many words ○ profuse apologies 2. GENEROUS IN GIVING giving something freely and lavishly or extravagantly 3. COPIOUS occurring or appearing in large amounts [15C. < Latin profusus, past participle of profundere 'pour out' < fundere 'pour'] —**profusely** adv —**profuseness** n

profusion /prə fyóozh'n/ n 1. a large quantity of something 2. the quality of being profuse

prog /prog/ n a television or radio programme (informal) [Late 20C. Shortening]

prog. abbr 1. program 2. programme 3. progress 4. EDUC progressive

Prog. abbr HIST Progressive

progenitor /prō jénnitər/ n 1. a direct ancestor of somebody or something 2. the originator of an original model for something [14C. < Latin, 'begetter' < progenit-, past participle of progignere < gignere 'beget']

progeny /prójjəni/ (plural -nies) n 1. the offspring of a person, animal, or plant 2. things that develop or result from something [13C. Via Old French progenie < Latin progenies 'offspring' < progignere (see PROGENITOR)]

progeria /prō jeéri ə/ n a rare condition of premature ageing that begins in childhood or early adult life and leads to death within a few years [Early 20C. < modern Latin < Greek progēros, literally 'aged forwards' < gēras 'old age']

progestational /prō je stáysh'nəl/ adj 1. relating to the stage of the menstrual cycle after ovulation when progesterone is produced 2. relating to or resembling progesterone or its effects

progesterone

progesterone /prō jéstərōn/ n a sex hormone produced in women, first by the corpus luteum of the ovary to prepare the womb for the fertilized ovum, and later by the placenta to maintain pregnancy. Formula: $C_{21}H_{30}O_2$. [Mid-20C. < PRO-[1] + GESTATION + STEROL + -ONE]

progestin /prə jéstin/ n a progestogen, especially progesterone [Early 20C. < PRO-[1] + GESTATION + -IN]

progestogen /prə jéstəjən/ n a steroid hormone or agent having effects similar to those of progesterone, or progesterone itself [Mid-20C. < PRO-[1] + GESTATION + -GEN]

proglottid /prō glóttid/, **proglottis** /-glóttiss/ (plural -tides /-tideez/) n a segment of a tapeworm's body [Late 19C. < Greek proglōttid 'tip of the tongue'] —**proglottic** adj

prognathous /prógnəthəss, prog náythəss/, **prognathic** /prog náthik/ adj describes an animal with a jaw that sticks out markedly [Mid-19C. < PRO-[2] + Greek gnathos 'jaw'] —**prognathism** /prógnəthizəm/ n

prognosis /prog nóssiss/ (plural -noses /-nōs seez/) n 1. a medical opinion as to the likely course and outcome of a disease 2. a prediction about how a given situation will develop [Mid-17C. Via late Latin < Greek prognōsis 'knowledge beforehand' < gignōskein 'know']

prognostic /prog nóstik/ *adj* **1. OF DISEASE PROGNOSIS** relating to or acting as a prognosis of a disease **2. OF PREDICTION** relating to or acting as a prediction ■ *n* **1. INDICATION OF COURSE OF DISEASE** an indicator used in making a prognosis concerning a disease **2. PREDICTION** a prediction as to how a given situation will develop [15C. Via French and Latin < Greek *prognōstikos* 'of knowledge beforehand' < *prognōsis* (see PROGNOSIS)]

prognosticate /prog nósti kayt/ (**-cates, -cating, -cated**) *v* **1.** *vti* to predict or foretell future events **2.** *vt* to be an indication of the likely future course of something —**prognostication** /prog nósti káysh'n/ *n* —**prognosticative** *adj* —**prognosticator** *n*

prograde /prṓ grayd/ *adj* moving in the same orbital or rotational direction as another astronomical body

program /prṓ gram/ *n* **1. INSTRUCTIONS OBEYED BY COMPUTER** a list of instructions in a programming language that tells a computer to perform a task **2. OPERATING INSTRUCTIONS FOR MACHINE** a set of coded operating instructions used to run a machine automatically **3.** US spelling of **programme** ■ *v* (**-grams, -gramming** or **-graming, -grammed** or **-gramed**) **1.** *vti* **WRITE COMPUTER PROGRAM** to write a program for a computer, or load a program into a computer **2.** *vt* **INSERT OPERATING INSTRUCTIONS INTO MACHINE** to insert coded operating instructions into a machine **3.** *vt* US spelling of **programme** [Mid-17C. Via French < Greek *programma* 'public notice', literally 'something written publicly' < *graphein* 'write']

program director *n ANZ, N Am* an executive who is responsible for the selection and scheduling of television or radio programmes for broadcast. UK term **head of programming**

programer *n US* COMPUT another spelling of **programmer**

program evaluation and review technique *n* MANAGEMT full form of **PERT**

programing *n US* COMPUT, BROADCAST US spelling of **programming**

programmable /prō grámməb'l, prṓ gram-/ *adj* **1.** able to receive coded operating instructions **2.** able to be trained to do something automatically, especially to react to a stimulus —**programmability** /prṓ gramə bíllәti/ *n*

programmatic /prṓgrə máttik/ *adj* **1. RELATING TO PROGRAMME** relating to or consisting of a programme **2. SYSTEMATIC** following a plan or programme **3. OF PROGRAMME MUSIC** relating to or composed as programme music —**programmatically** *adv*

programme /prṓ gram/ *n* **1. PLAN** a planned sequence of events or activities over a period of time, or a plan of such a sequence ○ *a programme of concerts* **2. SERIES OF MEASURES TO ACHIEVE AIM** a planned series of measures or events intended to achieve a particular purpose ○ *a programme to rehouse council tenants* **3. BROADCAST** a television or radio broadcast **4. BOOKLET GIVING DETAILS OF PERFORMANCE** a booklet or leaflet giving details of a theatrical or musical performance **5. SERIES OF CLASSES** a series of classes or lectures ■ *vt* (**-grammes, -gramming, -grammed**) **1. SCHEDULE SOMETHING** to schedule something as part of a programme **2. TRAIN SOMEBODY TO ACT AUTOMATICALLY** to train a person or animal to do something automatically, especially to react automatically to a stimulus ▶ US spelling (all senses) **program** [Mid-17C. Via French < Greek *programma* 'written public notice' < *graphein* 'write']

programmed learning /prṓ gramd-/, **programmed instruction** *n* a learning method based on self-instructional materials that are designed to allow pupils to progress at their own pace, step by step, through structured sequences

programme music *n* music that depicts or is inspired by a story, object, or scene

programme of study *n* the subjects and skills taught to pupils of different abilities and degrees of maturity during each key stage of the National Curriculum in England and Wales

programmer /prṓ gramər/ *n* a writer of computer programs

programming /prṓ graming/ *n* **1.** the designing or writing of computer programs **2.** the selection and scheduling of television or radio programmes, or the programmes themselves

programming language *n* a unique vocabulary and set of rules for writing computer programs

program trading *n* the automatic buying and selling of large quantities of shares using computer programs that monitor price changes —**program trade** *n* —**program trader** *n*

progress *n* /prṓ gress/ **1. POSITIVE DEVELOPMENT** development, usually of a gradual kind, towards achieving a goal or reaching a higher standard ○ *making progress in the talks* **2. ADVANCE OF HUMAN SOCIETY** the general advance of human society and industry over time towards a state of greater civilization ○ *Most Victorians believed in progress.* **3. MOTION TOWARDS SOMETHING** movement forwards or onwards **4. ROYAL TOUR** an official tour by a reigning king or queen through his or her kingdom (*archaic*) ■ *v* /prə gréss/ (**-gresses, -gressing, -gressed**) **1.** *vi* **IMPROVE** to develop or advance continuously **2.** *vi* **MOVE ALONG** to move forwards or onwards **3.** *vt* **HELP COMPLETE SOMETHING** to bring something closer to completion [15C. < Latin *progressus*, past participle of *progredi* 'go forwards' < *gradi* 'to walk'] ◇ **in progress** currently happening or being done

progress chaser *n* somebody employed to check the progress of a piece of manufacturing or other work and ensure its prompt delivery

progression /prə grésh'n/ *n* **1. GRADUAL ADVANCEMENT** a gradual change or advancement from one state to another **2. FORWARD MOVEMENT** movement forwards or onwards **3. SERIES OF RELATED THINGS** a series or succession of related things **4.** MATHS **SEQUENCE OF RELATED NUMBERS** a sequence of numbers or terms in which each can be derived from its predecessor using a constant formula **5.** MUSIC **SERIES OF NOTES OR CHORDS** a movement from one musical note or chord to another [14C. Directly or via French < Latin *progression-* < *progressus* (see PROGRESS)] —**progressional** *adj* —**progressionally** *adv*

progressive /prə gréssiv/ *adj* **1. PROGRESSING GRADUALLY** developing gradually over a period of time ○ *a progressive decline in popularity* **2. FAVOURING REFORM** advocating social, economic, or political reform **3. BECOMING MORE SEVERE** describes a disease that becomes more widespread or severe over time **4. INFORMAL AND LESS STRUCTURED EDUCATIONALLY** relating to or using a more informal, less structured approach to the education of children **5. WITH HIGHER RATES FOR HIGHER INCOMES** describes a form of taxation in which the tax rate increases in proportion to the taxable income **6.** GRAM **EXPRESSING CONTINUOUS ACTION** describes an aspect or form of a verb, expressing continuous action **7.** CARDS, DANCE **HAVING CHANGES OF PARTNER** involving a change of partner at various stages of the game or dance ■ *n* **1. ADVOCATE OF REFORM** a supporter or advocate of social, political, or economic reforms **2.** GRAM **PROGRESSIVE FORM OF VERB** the progressive aspect of a verb, or a verb in the progressive aspect [Early 17C. Directly or via French < medieval Latin *progressivus* < Latin *progressus* (see PROGRESS)] —**progressively** *adv* —**progressiveness** *n*

Progressive *adj* **1. OF PROGRESSIVE POLITICAL PARTY** belonging to or associated with a political party that calls itself progressive or advocates social reform **2. OF NONORTHODOX JEWISH RELIGIOUS MOVEMENT** relating to a Jewish religious movement whose members do not believe that the Torah was given literally and directly by God to Moses ■ *n* **MEMBER OF PROGRESSIVE PARTY** a member of a progressive political party

Progressive Conservative *n* in Canada, a member or supporter of the Progressive Conservative Party

Progressive Conservative Party *n* a Canadian federal and provincial political party that became part of the Conservative Party of Canada. It originally derived its political principles from British Toryism.

Progressive Democrat *n* in the Republic of Ireland, a member of the Progressive Democrats

Progressive Democrats *npl* a political party in the Republic of Ireland, founded in 1985 and advocating fiscal prudence, reduced taxes, and individual responsibility

progressive education *n* a 20th-century theory of education that stresses children's self-expression, an informal classroom atmosphere, and individual attention

Progressive Federal Party *n* a South African political party formed in 1977 by a merger between the Progressive Party and members of the United Party. In 1989 it disbanded and joined two other parties to form the Democratic Party.

progressive jazz *n* a form of experimental, free-flowing, and improvisational jazz that uses dissonance and complex rhythms

Progressive Party *n* **1. US POLITICAL PARTY** in the United States, one of three related political parties that favoured social reform and were active in the presidential elections of 1912, 1924, and 1948 **2. CANADIAN POLITICAL PARTY** a Canadian national political party formed in 1920 from members of farmers' movements and dissident Liberals that was dissolved in 1942 **3. S AFRICAN POLITICAL PARTY** a South African national political party that was formed in 1959 by members of the United Party and merged again with part of the United Party in 1977 to form the Progressive Federal Party

Progressive Rock *n* rock music originating in the early 1970s and characterized by technically elaborate and sometimes experimental arrangements

progressivism /prə gréssivizəm/ *n* **1.** the beliefs and practices of progressives **2.** the theories and practices of progressive education —**progressivist** *n*

progress payment *n* a partial payment made to a contractor when a stage of a job is completed

prohibit /prə híbbit/ (**-its, -iting, -ited**) *vt* **1.** to stop somebody doing something by passing a law or rule that forbids it **2.** to prevent somebody from doing something [15C. < Latin *prohibit-*, past participle of *prohibere* 'hold back' < *hibere* 'to hold'] —**prohibiter** *n*

prohibition /prṓ i bísh'n/ *n* **1. FORBIDDING OF SOMETHING** the act or process of forbidding something **2. ORDER THAT FORBIDS** an act or order that forbids something **3. COURT ORDER** an order from a superior court that forbids an inferior court to decide on a matter beyond its jurisdiction **4. OUTLAWING OF TRADE IN ALCOHOLIC BEVERAGES** a policy that forbids by law the manufacture, sale, and transport of alcoholic beverages [14C. Directly or via French < Latin *prohibition-* < *prohibit-* (see PROHIBIT)] —**prohibitionary** *adj*

Prohibition *n* in the United States, the period between 1919 and 1933 during which the manufacture, sale, and transport of alcoholic beverages was forbidden

prohibitionist /prṓ i bísh'nist/ *n* **1.** somebody who supports a legal ban on the manufacture and sale of alcoholic beverages **2.** in the United States during Prohibition, a supporter of the legal ban on the manufacture, sale, and transport of alcoholic beverages —**prohibitionism** *n* —**Prohibitionism** *n*

Prohibition Party *n* a political party in the United States founded in 1869 that advocated the banning of alcoholic beverages

prohibitive /prə híbbitiv/ *adj* **1.** too expensive or costly for most people to buy **2.** prohibiting or forbidding something —**prohibitively** *adv* —**prohibitiveness** *n*

prohibitory /prə híbbitəri/ *adj* **1.** preventing or forbidding something **2.** likely to prevent or forbid something (*formal*)

proinsulin /prō ínssyoolin/ *n* the inactive precursor of insulin produced in the pancreas

project *n* /prójjekt/ **1. TASK OR SCHEME** a task or scheme that requires a large amount of time, effort, and planning to complete (*often used before a noun*) ○ *a project to develop a faster delivery service* ○ *project management* **2. UNIT OF WORK** an organized unit of work ○ *a class project* **3. PUBLIC WORK** an extensive organized public undertaking ○ *a construction project* **4.** *N Am* PUBLIC ADMIN same as **housing project** (*often used in the plural*) ■ *v* /prə jékt/ (**-jects, -jecting, -jected**) **1.** *vti* **STICK OUT** to jut out beyond or farther than something, or make something jut out beyond or farther than something ○ *The balcony projected several metres.* **2.** *vt* **ESTIMATE SOMETHING** to estimate something by extrapolating data ○ *project a 3% growth rate* **3.** *vt* **DIRECT IMAGE ONTO SURFACE** to make an image appear on a surface ○ *projected the photograph onto the screen* **4.** *vt* **COMMUNICATE SOMETHING** to communicate something effectively ○ *projects himself as a confident speaker* **5.** *vti* **MAKE VOICE AUDIBLE** to make the voice heard clearly and at a distance, or be effective in making the voice heard ○

projecting her voice to the back of the auditorium **6.**
vt **PROPOSE PLAN** to propose a plan of action (*often passive*) ○ *projects an extended tour next year* **7.** *vt* **IMAGINE SOMETHING** to use the imagination to see or remember something ○ *She projected herself back into the past.* **8.** *vt* **THROW SOMETHING** to throw or cast something (*formal*; *usually passive*) **9.** *vt* **PSYCHOL BELIEVE OTHERS SHARE FEELING** to make a thought or feeling seem to have an external and objective reality, especially to ascribe a disturbing personal thought or feeling to others ○ *He had projected his fear of heights onto her.* **10.** *vt* **MATHS DRAW PROJECTION OF FIGURE** to transform a geometric figure into another by drawing straight lines through every point of the figure to another plane [14C. < Latin *projectum* 'something thrown forwards' < *proicere* 'throw forwards' < *jacere* 'to throw']

projectile /prō jék tīl/ *n* **MISSILE OR SHELL** an object that can be fired or launched, e.g. an artillery shell or a rocket ■ *adj* **1.** **IMPELLED FORWARDS** hurled or impelled forwards **2.** **ZOOL CAPABLE OF BEING THRUST FORWARDS** describes a part of an animal's body that can be thrust forwards, e.g. the jaws in some types of fish

projection /prə jéksh'n/ *n* **1.** **SOMETHING THAT STICKS OUT** something that juts out or overhangs **2.** **ESTIMATE** an estimate of the rate or amount of something **3.** **CASTING OF SOMETHING ON SURFACE** the projecting of an image or picture on a surface **4.** **SOMETHING CAST ON SURFACE** an image or picture projected on a surface **5.** **PROTRUSION** the act or process of projecting something or the fact of projecting **6.** **PSYCHOL UNCONSCIOUS TRANSFER OF FEELING** the unconscious ascription of a personal thought, feeling, or impulse, especially one considered undesirable, to somebody else **7.** **MAPS REPRESENTATION ON SURFACE** a means of representing lines, figures, or solids on a flat surface such as a map that conforms to the viewing direction or follows particular rules **8.** **MATHS DRAWN REPRESENTATION** the representation of a line, figure, or solid on a flat surface **9.** **HIST MIXING BY ALCHEMIST** in alchemy, the mixing of powdered philosopher's stone with base metals in order, supposedly, to transmute them into gold or silver —**projectional** *adj*

projection booth *n* N Am **CINEMA, THEATRE** same as **projection room**

projectionist /prə jéksh'nist/ *n* somebody whose job is to operate the projector and screen the film in a cinema and take responsibility for the quality of the image and sound

projection room *n* an enclosed compartment in a cinema or theatre from where films, slides, or lights are projected onto a screen or stage. N Am term **projection booth**

projection television, **projection TV** *n* a television picture display system in which an enlarged picture is projected onto a screen

projective /prə jéktiv/ *adj* **1.** relating to or made by projection **2.** relating to or involving a psychological test in which something in the subject's unconscious is revealed by his or her response to specific images —**projectively** *adv*

projective geometry *n* the study of those properties of plane geometric figures that do not vary when they are projected onto another plane and of the transformations of size and perspective that accompany this

projective test *n* a psychological test that uses images in order to evoke responses from a subject and reveal hidden aspects of the subject's mental life

projector /prə jéktər/ *n* a piece of equipment for projecting the image from film onto a screen and for playing back recorded sound from tracks on the film

projet /prózhay/ *n* a plan or outline, especially of a draft law or treaty [Early 19C. Via French < Latin *projectum* (SEE PROJECT)]

prokaryon /prō kárri on/ *n* the nucleus of a cell or organism with no membrane separating the area containing DNA from the rest of it [Mid-20C. < Greek *pro-* 'before' + *karuon* 'nut']

prokaryote /prō kárri ot/, **procaryote** *n* an organism whose DNA is not contained within a nucleus, e.g. a bacterium [Mid-20C. < French < Greek *pro-* 'before' +

karuōtos 'having nuts' < *karuon* 'nut'] —**prokaryotic** /prō kárri óttik/ *adj*

Sergey Prokofiev

Prokofiev /prə kóffi ef/, **Sergey** (1891–1953) Russian composer. His symphonies, concertos, ballets, and operas include *The Love of Three Oranges* (1921), *Peter and the Wolf* (1934), and *Romeo and Juliet* (1936). Full name **Prokofiev, Sergey Sergeyevich**

prolactin /prō láktin/ *n* a pituitary hormone that stimulates lactation after childbirth

prolamine /prólə meen, -min/ *n* a simple protein found in grains [Early 20C. < PROLINE + AMMONIA + -INE]

prolapse /pró laps, prō láps/ *n* also **prolapsus** /prō lápsəss/ a slippage or sinking of a body organ or part such as a valve of the heart from its usual position ■ *vi* (-**lapses**, -**lapsing**, -**lapsed**) to slip or fall out of its proper place in the body [Late 16C. < Latin *prolaps-*, past participle of *prolabi* 'fall forwards' < *labi* 'to fall'] —**prolapsed** *adj*

prolate /pró layt/ *adj* describes rock fragments that are elongated in the direction of the polar diameter [Late 17C. < Latin *prolatus*, past participle of *proferre* 'carry forwards' < *ferre* 'carry'] —**prolately** *adv* —**prolateness** *n*

prole /prōl/ *n* **SOC SCI** same as **proletarian** *n* (sense 1) (*informal insult*) ■ *adj* same as **proletarian** (*informal*) [Late 19C. Shortening.]

proleg /pró leg/ *n* a leg on the abdomen of a caterpillar or other insect larva

prolegomenon /pró le gómminən/ (*plural* -**ena** /-inə/) *n* a preliminary discussion or introductory essay, especially to a book or treatise [Mid-17C. < Greek < *prolegein* 'say before' < *legein* 'to say'] —**prolegomenal** *adj*

prolepsis /prō lépsiss/ (*plural* -**lepses** /-lép seez/) *n* **1.** **INTRODUCTORY ANTICIPATION OF OBJECTION** a preface intended to anticipate and answer an objection to an argument **2.** **ANTICIPATORY ADJECTIVE** the use after a verb of an adjective that anticipates the result of the verb's action, e.g. 'to iron a shirt smooth' **3.** **ANACHRONISTIC ASSUMPTION** the anachronistic assumption that a future event or condition has already happened, e.g. in the phrase 'precolonial United States' [Late 16C. Via Latin < Greek *prolēpsis* < *prolambanein* 'take before' < *lambanein* 'take'] —**proleptic** *adj* —**proleptically** *adv*

proletarian /prōlə táiri ən/ *adj* **OF WORKING CLASS** relating to the working class ■ *n* **1.** **WORKER** a member of the working class **2.** **INDUSTRIAL WAGE-EARNER** in Marxist theory, a member of the industrial working class whose only asset is labour sold to an employer **3.** **IMPOVERISHED ANCIENT ROMAN** a member of an impoverished social class of ancient Rome that had the lowest status and possessed no property [Mid-17C. < Latin *proletarius* 'low-status Roman who serves the state only by producing offspring' < *proles* 'offspring'] —**proletarianism** *n*

proletariat /prōlə táiri ət/ *n* **1.** **WORKING CLASS** the class of wage-earning workers in society (*takes a singular or plural verb*) **2.** **CLASS OF INDUSTRIAL WAGE-EARNERS** in Marxist theory, the class of industrial workers whose only asset is the labour they sell to an employer **3.** **ANCIENT ROMAN SOCIAL CLASS** a social class of ancient Rome that had the lowest status and possessed no property [Mid-19C. < French *prolétariat* < Latin *proletarius* (SEE PROLETARIAN)]

pro-life *adj* in favour of bringing the human foetus to full term, especially, involved in campaigning

against abortion and experimentation on embryos —**pro-lifer** *n*

proliferate /prə líffə rayt/ (-**ates**, -**ating**, -**ated**) *v* **1.** *vi* to increase greatly in number **2.** *vti* to multiply cells in the process of reproducing new cells, offspring, or parts, as in the budding of plants, or be multiplied in this way [Late 19C. Back-formation < *proliferation* < French *prolifération* < medieval Latin *prolifer* (see PROLIFEROUS)] —**proliferation** /prə líffə ráysh'n/ *n* —**proliferative** *adj* —**proliferator** *n*

proliferous /prə lífferəss/ *adj* producing or growing many cells, buds, or shoots [Mid-17C. < medieval Latin *prolifer* 'bearing offspring' < *proles* 'offspring']

prolific /prə líffik/ *adj* **1.** **HIGHLY PRODUCTIVE** producing ideas or works frequently and in large quantities **2.** **FRUITFUL** producing a lot of fruit or many offspring **3.** **ABUNDANT OR ABOUNDING** present in large numbers, or containing large numbers of quantities of something, especially animal life ○ *a period prolific of creative achievement* [Mid-17C. < medieval Latin *prolificus* < Latin *proles* 'offspring'] —**prolificacy** *n* —**prolifically** *adv*

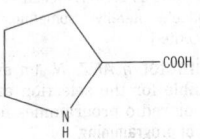

proline

proline /pró leen/ *n* an amino acid found in many proteins, particularly in collagen. Formula: $C_5H_9NO_2$. [Early 20C. Contraction of *pyrrolidine-2-carboxylic acid*]

prolix /próliks, prō líks/ *adj* tiresomely wordy [15C. Directly or via French < Latin *prolixus* 'that has flowed out' < past participle of *liquere* 'flow'] —**prolixity** /prō líksəti/ *n* —**prolixly** *adv*

SYNONYMS See *wordy*.

prolocutor /prō lókyōōtər/ *n* **1.** somebody who chairs an ecclesiastical convocation in the Anglican Church **2.** same as **spokesperson** (*archaic or formal*) [15C. Latin, 'pleader, advocate' < *proloqui* 'speak out' < *loqui* 'speak'] —**prolocutorship** *n*

prolog *n* THEATRE US spelling of **prologue**

Prolog /pró log/, **PROLOG** *n* a high-level programming language based on logical rather than mathematical relationships [Late 20C. < PROGRAMMING + LOGIC]

prologue /pró log/ *n* **1.** **INTRODUCTORY STATEMENT** an introductory passage or speech before the main action of a novel, play, or long poem **2.** **ACTOR INTRODUCING ACTION OF PLAY** an actor who speaks introductory lines to a dramatic performance before the main action begins **3.** **PRELIMINARY EVENT** an event or act that leads to something more important ○ *The affair was a prologue to the complete breakdown of their marriage.* ■ *vt* (-**logues**, -**loguing**, -**logued**) **PREFACE SOMETHING WITH PROLOGUE** to preface something such as a novel or play with a prologue [14C. Via French and Latin < Greek *prologos*, literally 'speech before' < *logos* 'speech']

prolong /prə lóng/ (-**longs**, -**longing**, -**longed**) *vt* to make something go on longer [15C. Directly or via French *prolonger* < late Latin *prolongare* 'lengthen out' < Latin *longus* 'long'] —**prolongation** /pró long gáysh'n/ *n* —**prolonger** *n* —**prolongment** *n*

prolonge /prə lónj/ *n* a rope with a hook and a toggle used to tow something heavy, especially a gun carriage [Mid-19C. < French *prolonger* (see PROLONG)]

prom /prom/ *n* **1.** **ROADS** same as **promenade** *n* (sense 1) (*informal*) **2.** **MUSIC** same as **promenade concert** (*informal*) **3.** N Am a formal dance for high-school or college students, usually held at the end of the school year [Late 19C. Shortening of PROMENADE]

PROM /prom/ *abbr* COMPUT programmable read-only memory

prom. *abbr* GEOG promontory

promenade /prómmə naád/ *n* **1. SEAFRONT PATH** a paved path or terrace along a seafront **2. WALK FOR PLEASURE** a leisurely walk or stroll, usually in a public place, that is taken for pleasure or to be seen (*formal*) **3. MARCHING DANCE MOVEMENT** a marching movement in country dancing ■ *v* (**-nades, -nading, -naded**) **1.** *vi* **STROLL FOR PLEASURE** to walk in a slow and leisurely way, especially up and down a street or in a public place **2.** *vi* **MARCH DURING DANCE** to perform a marching movement in country dancing **3.** *vt* **PROMENADE IN PLACE** to be in a particular public place promenading [Mid-16C. < French < *se promener* 'go for a walk' < late Latin *prominare* 'drive forwards' < *minare* 'to drive']

promenade concert *n* a concert, usually of classical music, at which part of the audience stands in an area without seating

promenade deck *n* a covered upper deck on a passenger ship on which passengers can walk

promethazine /prō méthə zeen/ *n* an antihistamine drug. Use: treatment of allergies, motion sickness. [Mid-20C. < PROPYL + METHYL + AZINE]

Promethean /prə meéthi ən/ *adj* **1.** relating to the Titan Prometheus **2.** creative and imaginatively original

Prometheus /prə meéthi əss/ *n* **1.** in Greek mythology, a Titan who became a hero to humankind because he stole fire from the gods and gave it to them **2.** a small inner natural satellite of Saturn, discovered in 1980 by Voyager 2. It is irregular in shape having a maximum dimension of 150 km/9.3 mi. [Late 16C. Via Latin < Greek *Promētheus*]

promethium /prə meéthi əm/ *n* a radioactive metallic element. Source: fission of uranium, thorium, or plutonium. Use: phosphorescent paints, X-ray source. Symbol **Pm**. See table at **element** [Mid-20C. After PROMETHEUS]

prominence /prómminənss/, **prominency** /-nənssi/ (*plural* **-cies**) *n* **1. CONSPICUOUS IMPORTANCE** the condition or quality of being significantly important or well-known **2. SOMETHING THAT STICKS OUT** something that projects or protrudes, especially a geographical feature or a body part **3. GAS STREAM FROM SUN** a visible stream of glowing gas that shoots out from the Sun, seen in the upper chromosphere and lower corona

prominent /prómminənt/ *adj* **1. STICKING OUT** large and projecting ○ *prominent chin* **2. NOTICEABLE** noticeable or conspicuous ○ *prominent position* **3. WELL-KNOWN** distinguished, eminent, or well-known ○ *a prominent figure in the arts* [15C. < Latin *prominent-*, present participle of *prominere* 'project forwards' < *minere* 'to project'] —**prominently** *adv*

~~**promiscous**~~ incorrect spelling of **promiscuous**

promiscuity /prómmi skyoó əti/ *n* **1.** behaviour characterized by casual and indiscriminate sexual intercourse, often with many people **2.** confused or indiscriminate mixing (*formal*)

promiscuous /prə mískyoo əss/ *adj* **1. SEXUALLY INDISCRIMINATE** having many indiscriminate or casual sexual relationships **2. CHOOSING WITHOUT DISCRIMINATING** choosing carelessly or without discrimination **3. CONFUSEDLY MIXED** mixed in an indiscriminate or disorderly way (*formal*) **4. RANDOM** occurring without any set or specific pattern or time (*literary*) ○ *a sail caught by a promiscuous wind* [Early 17C. < Latin *promiscuus*, literally 'mixed forwards' < *miscere* 'to mix'] —**promiscuously** *adv* —**promiscuousness** *n*

promise /prómmiss/ *v* (**-ises, -ising, -ised**) **1.** *vti* **VOW** to assure somebody that something will certainly happen or be done ○ *promised to come* ○ *promised that the patient would recover* **2.** *vt* **PLEDGE SOMETHING** to pledge to somebody to provide or do something ○ *promised them a kitten* **3.** *vti* **MAKE SOMEBODY EXPECT SOMETHING** to cause somebody to expect something ○ *The sky promised rain.* **4.** *vt* **ASSURE OR WARN SOMEBODY** to assure or warn somebody that something is true or inevitable ○ *Things will be fine, I promise you.* **5.** *vt* **AFFIANCE SOMEBODY** to engage somebody to be married (*dated*) ○ *She told him that she was promised to someone else.* ■ *n* **1. ASSURANCE OR UNDERTAKING** an assurance that something will be done or not done ○ *He never keeps his promises.* **2. INDICATION OF SUCCESS** an indication that somebody or something will turn out well or successfully ○ *showed great promise* **3. SIGNAL OF SOMETHING** an indication that something is likely to happen [14C. Directly or via French < Latin *promissum* < *promiss-*, past participle of *promittere* 'send forwards' < *mittere* 'send'] —**promisee** /prómmi seé/ *n* —**promiser** *n* —**promisor** /prómmi sáwr/ *n*

Promised Land /prómmist-/ *n* **1.** the land of Canaan, according to the Bible promised by God to the descendants of Abraham **2.** *also* **promised land** heaven, or a place or situation of great happiness or success

promising /prómmissing/ *adj* likely to be successful or to turn out well —**promisingly** *adv*

promissory /prómmissəri/ *adj* **1.** concerning, containing, or implying a promise **2.** stating how the terms of an insurance contract will be fulfilled [15C. < medieval Latin *promissorius* < Latin *promiss-* (see PROMISE)]

promissory note *n* a signed agreement promising payment of a sum of money on demand or at a specific time

promo /prṓmō/ (*informal*) *n* (*plural* **-mos**) something that promotes or advertises a product, e.g. a recorded announcement, commercial, or video ■ *adj* involved or engaged in the promotion or advertising of something [Mid-20C. Shortening of PROMOTION or *promotional*]

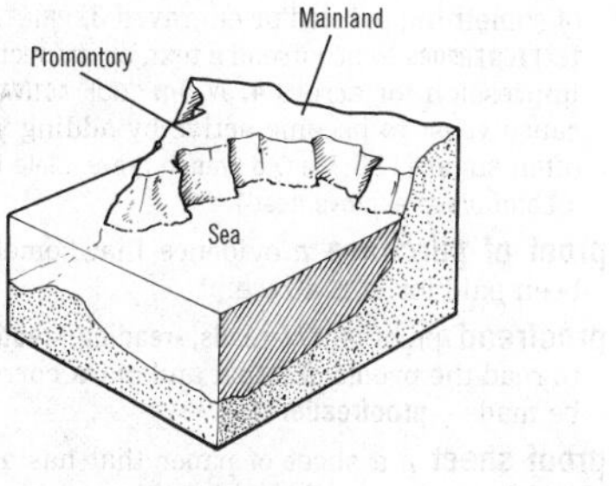

promontory

promontory /prómməntəri/ (*plural* **-ries**) *n* **1.** a point of land that juts out into the sea **2.** a prominent or protruding part of an organ or structure in the body [Mid-16C. < medieval Latin *promontorium*, alteration of Latin *promunturium*]

promote /prə mṓt/ (**-motes, -moting, -moted**) *vt* **1. ADVANCE SOMEBODY IN POSITION** to raise somebody to a more senior job or a higher position or rank **2. SUPPORT OR ENCOURAGE SOMETHING** to encourage the growth and development of something **3. ADVERTISE SOMETHING** to publicize a product so that people will buy or hire it **4. ADVANCE SOMETHING** to further something by helping to arrange or introduce it **5. RAISE TEAM TO HIGHER DIVISION** to move a sports team or player from a lower to a higher division of a league **6.** CHESS **EXCHANGE PAWN FOR MORE POWERFUL PIECE** in chess, to exchange a pawn for a more powerful piece, especially a queen, when it reaches an opponent's end of the board **7.** *US* **MOVE SOMEBODY TO NEXT GRADE** to move a student to the next higher grade at the end of the school year [14C. < Latin *promot-*, past participle of *promovere* 'move forwards' < *movere* 'to move'] —**promotable** *adj*

promoter /prə mṓtər/ *n* **1. ARRANGER OF PUBLIC EVENT** a person or organization that stages an entertainment, a sporting contest, or other public event ○ *boxing promoter* **2. ADVOCATE** a supporter or advocate of something **3. ACQUIRER OF CAPITAL FOR VENTURE** somebody who raises money for a financial or commercial undertaking **4. PUBLICIST FOR PRODUCT** somebody who tries to make a product or service more widely known or more successful **5.** GENETICS **BINDING SITE IN DNA CHAIN** in a DNA chain, a sequence to which the enzyme RNA polymerase binds so as to start transcription **6.** CHEM **SUBSTANCE ADDED TO CATALYST** a chemical additive that increases the efficiency of a catalyst **7.** MED **SOMETHING THAT ENCOURAGES TUMOUR CELLS** a substance that when given after a carcinogen encourages tumour cells to form or grow

promoter gene *n* GENETICS same as **promoter** (sense 5)

promotion /prə mṓsh'n/ *n* **1. ADVANCEMENT IN POSITION** an advancement to a more senior job or a higher rank, grade, or position **2. ENCOURAGEMENT FOR ACTIVITY** encouragement of the growth or development of something **3. SOMETHING THAT PROMOTES** something such as an advertising campaign that is designed to promote a product, cause, or organization **4.** MARKETING **PROCESS OF PROMOTING** the act or process of making a product, cause, or organization more widely known or more successful **5. ADVANCE INTO HIGHER DIVISION** advance by a sports team or player into a higher division of a league **6.** CHESS **EXCHANGE OF PAWN FOR SUPERIOR PIECE** in chess, the act of exchanging a pawn for a more powerful piece, usually a queen, when it reaches an opponent's end of the board —**promotional** *adj*

promotive /prə mṓtiv/ *adj* tending to further or encourage something

prompt /prompt/ *adj* **1. DONE IMMEDIATELY** done at once and without delay **2. QUICK TO ACT** ready, punctual, or quick to act ■ *adv* **PUNCTUALLY** in a punctual way (*informal*) ■ *v* (**prompts, prompting, prompted**) **1.** *vt* **CAUSE SOMEBODY TO ACT** to make somebody decide to do something ○ *What prompted him to change his mind, we don't yet know.* **2.** *vt* **BRING ABOUT SOMETHING** to cause something to happen ○ *Fears of inflation prompted an immediate rise in interest rates.* **3.** *vti* **PROVIDE ACTOR WITH LINES** to provide actors during a performance with words or lines they have forgotten ○ *She had to be prompted three times in the first scene.* **4.** *vt* **REMIND SOMEBODY** to suggest something that somebody ought to say, or give a reminder to a speaker ○ *His wife had to prompt him to mention the cleaning staff.* ■ *n* **1. WORDS SUPPLIED TO PERFORMER** a reminder to a performer of the words or lines he or she has forgotten **2. OCCURRENCE OF PROMPT** the act or occasion of reminding a performer of forgotten words or lines **3. SOMETHING CUEING RESPONSE** a symbol or message displayed on a computer monitor or an audio signal informing a computer user that some input is required **4.** COMM **TIME LIMIT FOR PAYMENT** the time limit of payment for goods or services, as indicated on a prompt note [14C. < Latin *promptus* 'ready', past participle of *promere*, literally 'take forwards' < *emere* 'take'] —**promptly** *adv* —**promptness** *n*

promptbook /prómpt book/ *n* a copy of a script for a prompter to use

prompt box *n* a box situated beneath the stage in a theatre in which the prompter sits

prompter /prómptər/ *n* somebody in a theatre whose job is to prompt actors who have forgotten their words or lines

promptitude /prómpti tyood/ *n* punctuality or quickness to act

prompt note *n* a written reminder sent to the purchaser of something, stating when payment is due

prompt side *n* the side of the stage in a theatre where the prompter sits

promulgate /prómm'l gayt/ (**-gates, -gating, -gated**) *vt* (*formal*) **1.** to proclaim or declare something officially, especially to publicize formally that a law or decree is in effect **2.** to make something widely known [Mid-16C. < Latin *promulgat-*, past participle of *promulgare* 'bring to public notice', literally 'milk forwards' < *mulgere* 'to milk'] —**promulgation** /prómm'l gáysh'n/ *n* —**promulgator** *n*

pron, pron. *abbr* GRAM **1.** pronominal **2.** pronoun

pron. *abbr* **1.** GRAM pronominal **2.** LANGUAGE pronounced **3.** LANGUAGE pronunciation

pronate /prō nayt/ (**-nates, -nating, -nated**) *vt* (*technical*) **1.** to turn the hand or forearm so that the palm faces downwards **2.** to rotate the bones of the foot so that the weight is borne mainly on the inside of the foot [Mid-19C. Back-formation < *pronation* < PRONE or its source Latin *pronus*] —**pronation** /prō náysh'n/ *n*

pronator /prṓ naytər/ *n* a muscle that turns a part of the body so that it faces downwards, e.g. one of the muscles in the forearm that rotates the hand into the palm-down position [Early 18C. < modern Latin < Latin *pronus* (see PRONE), after SUPINATOR]

prone /prōn/ *adj* **1. DISPOSED TO SOMETHING** inclined to do or be affected by something ○ *prone to exaggerate* **2. FACE DOWN** lying face down ○ *prone position* **3. IN DOWNWARD DIRECTION** sloping, leaning, or moving down-

wards [15C. < Latin *pronus* 'bent forwards' < *pro* 'forwards'] —**pronely** *adv* —**proneness** *n*

pronephros /prō néff ross/ (*plural* **-roi** /-roy/ or **-ra** /-rə/) *n* the first of three segments of the kidney, functional in some vertebrate embryos but not in adults [Late 19C. < PRO-² + Greek *nephros* 'kidney'] —**pronephric** *adj*

prong /prong/ *n* a thin sharp point at the end of something such as a fork ■ *vt* (**prongs, pronging, pronged**) to prick or stab something with a sharp pointed end [15C. < Anglo-Latin *pronga*] —**pronged** *adj*

pronghorn /próng hawrn/, **pronghorn antelope** *n* an animal similar to an antelope that is the fastest North American mammal. Native to: Mexico, western United States. Latin name: *Antilocapra americana*.

pronominal /prō nómmin'l/ *adj* like or functioning as a pronoun ■ *n* a word that functions like a pronoun [Late 17C. < late Latin *pronominalis* < Latin *pronomen* (see PRONOUN)] —**pronominally** *adv*

pronominalize /prō nómminə līz/ (**-izes, -izing, -ized**), **pronominalise** (**-ises, -ising, -ised**) *vt* in transformational grammars, to replace a noun or noun phrase in a sentence with a pronoun —**pronominalization** /prō nómminə līz záysh'n/ *n*

pronoun /prō nown/ *n* a word that substitutes for a noun or a noun phrase, e.g. 'I', 'you', 'them', 'it', 'ours', 'who', 'which', 'myself', and 'anybody'. English pronouns differ from nouns in sometimes having an objective form, e.g. 'her' for 'she' and 'me' for 'I'. [15C. < PRO-¹ + NOUN, after French *pronom*, Latin *pronomen* 'something in place of a name' < *nomen* 'name']

pronounce /prə nównss/ (**-nounces, -nouncing, -nounced**) *v* **1.** *vti* UTTER SOUNDS OR WORDS to articulate sounds or words, especially in a way acceptable to the person to whom they are spoken or by most speakers of a language **2.** *vti* FORMALLY DECLARE SOMETHING to declare something officially to be the case **3.** *vt* GIVE JUDGMENT to render an opinion or judgment **4.** *vt* PHON SYMBOLIZE SOUND OF WORD to indicate with symbols how a word should be spoken [14C. Via Old French *pronuncier* < Latin *pronuntiare* 'announce before' < *nuntiare* 'announce'] —**pronounceable** *adj* —**pronouncement** *n* —**pronouncer** *n*

pronounced /prə nównst/ *adj* **1.** noticeable or obvious **2.** voiced or spoken —**pronouncedly** /-sidli/ *adv*

~~pronounciation~~ incorrect spelling of **pronunciation**

pronto /próntō/ *adv* in a prompt or rapid way (*informal*) [Mid-19C. Via Spanish < Latin *promptus* (see PROMPT)]

pronuclear /prō nyóokli ər/ *adj* **1.** in favour of using nuclear power as a source of energy, or supporting the use of nuclear weapons **2.** relating to a pronucleus —**pronuclearist** *n, adj*

pronucleus /prō nyóokli əss/ (*plural* **-clei** /-kli ī/ or **-cleuses**) *n* the nucleus of a fully matured ovum or spermatozoan before the nuclei are fused during fertilization

pronunc. *abbr* pronunciation

pronunciamento /prə núnssi ə méntō/ (*plural* **-tos**) *n* an announcement, proclamation, or manifesto, especially one issued by a revolutionary group [Mid-19C. < Spanish < *pronunciar* 'announce' < Latin *pronuntiare* (see PRONOUNCE)]

pronunciation /prə núnssi áysh'n/ *n* **1.** MAKING OF SOUNDS OF SPEECH the way in which a sound, word, or language is articulated, especially in conforming to an accepted standard **2.** ACT OF SPEECH the act of articulating a sound or word **3.** PHON TRANSCRIPTION OF SOUNDS a phonetic transcription of sounds [15C. Directly or via French < Latin *pronuntiation-* < *pronuntiare* (see PRONOUNCE)]

pro-oestrus /prō éestrəss/ *n* the period in the oestrus cycle immediately preceding oestrus

proof /proof/ *n* **1.** CONCLUSIVE EVIDENCE evidence or an argument that serves to establish a fact or the truth of something **2.** TEST OF SOMETHING a test or trial of something to establish whether it is true **3.** STATE OF HAVING BEEN PROVED the quality or condition of having been proved **4.** LAW TRIAL EVIDENCE evidence presented in a trial for consideration by the court **5.** LAW SCOTTISH LEGAL PROCESS OR TRIAL in Scottish law, a process

by which evidence in a civil case is heard prior to a trial, or a civil trial before a judge and without a jury to determine the issues on which the trial will take place **6.** MATHS, LOGIC SEQUENCE OF STEPS TO VALIDATE SOLUTION the sequence of steps or stages used in establishing the validity of a mathematical or philosophical proposition. These steps are a logical derivation of the proposition from axioms, or explicit assumptions, and previously proved propositions. **7.** STRENGTH OF ALCOHOLIC CONTENT the relative strength of an alcoholic beverage expressed by a number that is twice the percentage of the alcohol present in the liquid **8.** PRINTING COPY USED FOR CHECKING ERRORS a printed copy used for checking corrections before the final printing of a text or image **9.** ARTS IMPRESSION FROM ENGRAVED PLATE an impression taken from an engraved plate before it is printed **10.** PHOTOGRAPHY PRINT FROM NEGATIVE a photographic print made from a negative and checked for quality prior to further reproduction **11.** COINS COIN IMPRESSION a preliminary impression of a coin, intended as a specimen for display ■ *adj* **1.** IMPERVIOUS TO SOMETHING capable of resisting something that may have a harmful or unwanted effect **2.** HAVING RELATIVE ALCOHOLIC STRENGTH having a particular alcoholic strength that is expressed by a number that is twice the percentage of alcohol present in the liquid (*often used in combination*) **3.** RESISTANT capable of resisting or withstanding something ■ *vt* (**proofs, proofing, proofed**) **1.** MAKE SOMETHING RESISTANT to make something capable of resisting harm, injury, or damage **2.** PRINTING, ARTS PRINT PROOF OF SOMETHING to make a trial impression of something printed or engraved **3.** PRINTING INSPECT TEXT FOR ERRORS to proofread a text, or inspect a printed impression for errors **4.** *N Am* COOK ACTIVATE YEAST to cause yeast to become active by adding water and often sugar [13C. Via Old French *preve* < late Latin *proba* < Latin *probare* 'prove, test']

proof of purchase *n* evidence that something has been paid for, e.g. a receipt

proofread /proof reed/ (**-reads, -reading, -read** /-red/) *vti* to read the proofs of a text and mark corrections to be made —**proofreader** *n*

proof sheet *n* a sheet of paper that has a printer's proof on it, usually with wide margins so that corrections can be marked up easily

proof spirit *n* an alcoholic beverage or a mixture of alcohol and water. In the United Kingdom and Canada proof spirit is 57.1 per cent alcohol by volume at 10.6°C51°F, while in the United States, it is 50 per cent alcohol at 15.6°C60°F. Use: formerly, as a standard for measuring alcoholic strength.

proof theory *n* the part of the theory of logic concerned with the exact nature of deriving propositions and conclusions

prop¹ /prop/ *n* **1.** RIGID SUPPORT a rigid object, e.g. a beam, stake, or pole, that supports something or holds it in place **2.** COMFORTING PERSON OR THING somebody or something that provides comfort or assistance **3.** RUGBY PLAYER AT EITHER END OF FRONT ROW in rugby, a forward at either end of the front row of a scrum **4.** *Aus* SUDDEN STOP a sudden or unexpected stop, especially of a horse ■ *v* (**props, propping, propped**) **1.** *vt* SUPPORT SOMETHING WITH PROP to use a rigid object to support something or hold it in place **2.** *vi Aus* STOP ABRUPTLY to come to a sudden and unexpected stop (*refers to horses*) [15C. < Middle Dutch *proppe* 'vine prop, support']

prop up *vt* to give support or help to somebody or something

prop² /prop/ *n* an object used during the performance of a play or film [Mid-19C. Shortening of PROPERTY]

prop³ /prop/ *n* an aircraft propeller (*informal*) [Early 20C. Shortening]

prop. *abbr* **1.** GRAM proper **2.** properly **3.** property **4.** PHILOSOPHY, MATHS proposition **5.** COMM proprietor

propaedeutic /prō pee dyóotik/ *adj* providing preparatory instruction (*formal*) ■ *n* a preliminary course of study that precedes more advanced instruction (*often used in the plural*) [Late 18C. < PRO-² + Greek *paideutikē* 'education', after Greek *propaideuein* 'teach beforehand']

propaganda /próppə gándə/ *n* **1.** information put out by an organization or government to promote a policy, idea, or cause **2.** deceptive or distorted in-

formation that is systematically spread [Early 18C. < modern Latin, in *Congregatio de propaganda fide* 'Congregation for the Propagation of the Faith'] —**propagandism** *n* —**propagandist** *n, adj*

Propaganda *n* a committee of Roman Catholic cardinals, the Congregation for the Propagation of the Faith, in charge of supervising foreign missions and educating priests to serve in them

propagandize /próppə gán dīz/ (**-dizes, -dizing, -dized**), **propagandise** (**-dises, -dising, -dised**) *vti* to organize or spread propaganda

propagate /próppə gayt/ (**-gates, -gating, -gated**) *v* **1.** *vti* BIOL REPRODUCE ORGANISM to reproduce a plant or animal, or cause one to reproduce **2.** *vti* GARDENING CREATE NEW PLANTS to multiply plants by the use of seeds or cuttings **3.** *vt* SPREAD SOMETHING WIDELY to spread an idea or custom to many people **4.** *vti* PHYS IMPEL SOMETHING FORWARDS to move or transmit something such as a sound or light wave forwards through a medium such as air [Late 16C. < Latin *propagat-*, past participle of *propagare* 'breed plants from shoots or layers' < *propago* 'layer'] —**propagable** *adj* —**propagation** /próppə gáysh'n/ *n* —**propagational** *adj* —**propagative** *adj*

propagator /próppə gaytər/ *n* **1.** somebody who spreads ideas or beliefs widely **2.** a shallow box with a transparent cover used for germinating seeds or allowing cuttings to take root, especially one that can be heated

propagule /próppə gyool/, **propagulum** /prō pággyōoləm/ (*plural* **-lums** or **-la** /-lə/) *n* a part of a plant or fungus, e.g. a bud or a spore, that becomes detached from the rest and forms a new organism [Mid-19C. < modern Latin *propagulum* 'little shoot' < *propago* 'layer']

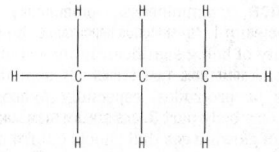

propane

propane /prō payn/ *n* a flammable colourless hydrocarbon gas. Use: fuel, propellant, refrigerant. Formula: C_3H_8. [Mid-19C. < PROPIONIC]

propanoic acid /prōpə nō ik-/ *n* CHEM same as **propionic acid**

propanol /prōpə no/ *n* CHEM same as **propyl alcohol**

propanone /prōpə nōn/ *n* CHEM same as **acetone** (*technical*)

proparoxytone /prōpə róksitōn/ *n* in classical Greek grammar, a word that has an acute accent on the third syllable from the end ■ *adj* describes a word that has an acute accent on the third syllable from the end [Mid-18C. < Greek *proparoxutonos* < *oxutonos* 'having an acute accent']

propel /prə pél/ (**-pels, -pelling, -pelled**) *vt* **1.** to move or push somebody or something forwards **2.** to impel somebody to do something or cause something to happen [15C. < Latin *propellere* 'drive forwards' < *pellere* 'to drive']

propellant /prə péllənt/ *n* **1.** SUBSTANCE GIVING THRUST TO ROCKET a substance that is burned to give upward thrust to a rocket **2.** EXPLOSIVE CHARGE FOR GUN an explosive charge that projects a bullet from a gun **3.** GAS IN AEROSOL a compressed inert gas used to dispense the contents of an aerosol container when pressure is applied and released

propellent /prə péllənt/ *adj* tending to drive or move something forwards ■ *n* same as **propellant**

propeller

propeller /prə péllər/ *n* a revolving shaft with spiral blades that causes a ship or an aircraft to move by the backward thrust of water or air

propeller shaft *n* **1.** the shaft in a ship or aircraft that transmits power from the engine to the propeller **2.** MECH ENG same as **drive shaft** (sense 1)

propelling pencil *n* a pencil with a replaceable lead that can be extended as it gets worn down. N Am term **mechanical pencil**

propellor incorrect spelling of **propeller**

propene /prō peen/ *n* CHEM same as **propylene** [Mid-19C. < PROPYL]

propenoic acid /prōpə nō ik-/ *n* CHEM same as **acrylic acid**

propensity /prə pénssəti/ (*plural* **-ties**) *n* a tendency to demonstrate particular behaviour [Late 16C. < obsolete *propense* 'inclined, prone' < Latin *propensus*, past participle of *propendere* 'hang forwards' < *pendere* 'hang']

proper /próppər/ *adj* **1.** CORRECT appropriate or correct ○ *need to put the issue in its proper perspective* **2.** NEEDED AND APPROPRIATE fulfilling all expectations or criteria ○ *He needs proper medical care.* **3.** WITH CORRECT MANNERS behaving in a respectable or socially acceptable way **4.** CHARACTERISTIC OF SOMEBODY characteristic of or belonging exclusively to somebody or something **5.** NARROWLY IDENTIFIED strictly identified and distinguished from something else ○ *stayed in the suburbs, not the city proper* **6.** COMPLETE thorough and complete ○ *regards him as a proper nuisance* **7.** HERALDRY SHOWING NATURAL COLOURS showing the natural colours in the design or device of a heraldic object **8.** CHR USED ON HOLY OCCASION reserved as a prayer, lesson, or rite for a holy day or festival **9.** GOOD-LOOKING physically handsome and admirable (*archaic*) **10.** MATHS INCLUDED IN SECOND SET included as a mathematical set in a second set but not the same as it ■ *adv* **1.** *regional* TOTALLY exceedingly or completely **2.** PROPERLY in a correct or proper way (*nonstandard*) ■ *n also* **Proper** CHR SERVICE FOR HOLY OCCASION a Christian church service designated for use on a holy day or festival ■ *adj US* EXCESSIVELY POLITE rigidly polite, or exhibiting excessive formality ○ *She's very proper, and never wears slacks in public.* [13C. Directly or via French < Latin *proprius* 'your own, particular, special'] —**properness** *n*

proper adjective *n* an adjective that is formed from a proper noun, as 'Canadian' is from 'Canada'

proper fraction *n* a fraction in which the value of the numerator is less than the value of the denominator, e.g. $\frac{5}{8}$

properly /próppərli/ *adv* **1.** APPROPRIATELY in a suitable or appropriate way ○ *properly dressed for the occasion* **2.** CORRECTLY in a correct or well-mannered way ○ *If you can't behave properly, we'll have to go home.* **3.** IN REALITY in a correct and appropriate situation ○ *The chair properly belongs in the corner.* **4.** TOTALLY to the fullest degree or extent ○ *By the end of the day she was properly tired.*

proper noun, proper name *n* the name of a specific person or thing, normally beginning with a capital letter and not used with the indefinite article or a modifier, e.g. 'York', 'Sally', or 'Henderson'

property /próppərti/ (*plural* **-ties**) *n* **1.** SOMETHING OWNED something of value that is owned, e.g. land or a patent **2.** OWNED BUILDING OR PIECE OF LAND a piece of land or a building or part of a building that is owned by somebody ○ *a property owner* **3.** LAW RIGHT TO OWN SOMETHING the right to own, possess, or use something **4.** TRAIT OR ATTRIBUTE a characteristic quality or distinctive feature of something (*often used in the plural*) **5.** SOMETHING AT SOMEBODY'S DISPOSAL something at the disposal of a person, a group, or the public ○ *community property* **6.** ARTS PROP a stage prop (*formal*) **7.** PHILOSOPHY DISTINCTIVE BUT NOT ESSENTIAL QUALITY in Aristotelian philosophy, an attribute or quality that is peculiar to a whole class or species, but not essential to it **8.** *Aus* LAND IN COUNTRY a piece of rural land, usually a farm, ranch, or estate [13C. < Anglo-Norman *proprete*, variant of Old French *propriété* < Latin *proprietas* 'ownership, appropriateness' < *proprius* 'your own, particular, special']

property centre *n* a place where property is advertised for sale or purchase and where conveyancing is offered by a group of solicitors

property tax *n* a tax based on the value of a house or other property

prop forward *n* RUGBY same as **prop**[1] *n* (sense 3)

prophage /prō fayj/ *n* a stable form of virus (**bacteriophage**) that infects a bacterium with genetic material that is integrated into and replicated as part of the host bacterium's chromosome without harming the bacterium

prophase /prō fayz/ *n* the first phase in cell division, when chromosomes condense and can be seen as two chromatids

prophecy /próffəssi/ (*plural* **-cies**) *n* **1.** DIVINE PREDICTION a prediction of a future event that is believed to reveal the will of a deity **2.** PREDICTION a prediction that something will occur in the future **3.** SUPPOSED ABILITY TO PREDICT FUTURE the supposed ability to predict the future when inspired by a deity [13C. Via French *prophecie* and late Latin *prophetia* < Greek *prophēteia* < *prophētēs* (see PROPHET)]

USAGE prophecy or **prophesy**? Though spelt almost alike, these two words are pronounced differently and have different grammatical functions. ***Prophecy***, a noun only, means 'a prediction' or 'the supposed ability to predict the future', as in *a dire economic prophecy.* ***Prophesy***, a verb, means 'to predict', as in *would not go so far as to prophesy a recession just yet.*

prophesy /próffə sī/ (**-sies, -sying, -sied**) *v* **1.** *vti* to predict what is going to happen **2.** *vi* to supposedly reveal the will of a deity in predicting a future event [14C. < Old French *prophecier* < *prophecie* (see PROPHECY)] —**prophesiable** *adj* —**prophesier** *n*

USAGE See ***prophecy.***

prophet *n* **1.** SOMEBODY WHO INTERPRETS DIVINE WILL somebody who claims to interpret or transmit the commands of a deity **2.** SOMEBODY PREDICTING THE FUTURE somebody who predicts the future ○ *prophets of economic doom* **3.** ADVOCATE OF SOMETHING somebody who advocates a cause or idea **4.** INSPIRED LEADER somebody considered to be an inspired leader or teacher [12C. Via French and Latin < Greek *prophētēs* 'somebody who speaks beforehand' < *phētēs* 'speaker']

SPELLCHECK See ***profit.***

Prophet *n* **1.** Muhammad, the founder of Islam **2.** Joseph Smith, the founder of the Church of Jesus Christ of Latter-Day Saints ■ **Prophets** *npl* the prophetic books of the Bible. See table at **Bible**

prophetess /próffi téss/ *n* a female prophet

prophetic /prə féttik/ *adj* **1.** predicting or foreshadowing something that does eventually happen **2.** relating to a prophet [15C. Via French or late Latin < Greek *prophētikos* < *prophētes* (see PROPHET)] —**prophetical** *adj* —**prophetically** *adv*

Prophet's Birthday *n* ISLAM same as **Mawlid al-Nabi**

prophylactic /próffi láktik/ *adj* protecting against infection or disease ■ *n* **1.** *N Am* HEALTH same as **condom** **2.** a drug or agent that prevents the development of disease [Late 16C. Via French *prophylactique* < Greek *prophulaktikos prophulassein*, literally 'keep guard in front of' < *phulassein* 'to guard'] —**prophylactically** *adv*

prophylaxis /próffi lákssiss/ (*plural* **-laxes** /-lák seez/) *n* **1.** a treatment that prevents disease or stops it spreading, e.g. vaccination **2.** a dental treatment to remove plaque and tartar from the teeth [Mid-19C. < modern Latin, 'guarding in front of' < Greek *pro* 'in front of' + *phulaxis* 'guarding']

propinquity /prə píngkwəti/ *n* nearness in space, time, or relationship (*formal*) [14C. Directly or via French < Latin *propinquitas* < *prope* 'near']

propionate /prōpi ə nayt/ *n* a chemical compound that is a salt or ester of propionic acid [Late 19C. < PROPIONIC]

propionic /prōpi ónnik/ *adj* derived from propionic acid [Mid-19C. < Greek *pro* 'in front' + *piōn* 'fat', because it is first in order of the fatty acids]

propionic acid *n* a colourless liquid fatty acid. Use: manufacture of artificial flavours, perfumes, and preservatives. Formula: $C_3H_6O_2$.

propitiate /prə píshi ayt/ (**-ates, -ating, -ated**) *vt* to appease or conciliate somebody or something [Late 16C. < Latin *propitiat-*, past participle of *propitiare* 'make favourable' < *propitius* 'favourable'] —**propitiable** *adj* —**propitiation** /prə píshi áysh'n/ *n* —**propitiative** /-ətiv/ *adj* —**propitiator** *n* —**propitiatory** *adj*

propitious /prə píshəss/ *adj* **1.** favourable and likely to lead to success **2.** kindly disposed or gracious (*formal*) [15C. Directly or via French < Latin *propitius* 'favourable'] —**propitiously** *adv* —**propitiousness** *n*

propjet /próp jet/ *n* AVIAT, MECH ENG same as **turboprop** [Mid-20C. < PROP[3]]

proplyd /próplid, própplid/ *n* the disc of gases and dust that comprises a protoplanet [Late 20C. Contraction of *protoplanetary disc*]

propoganda incorrect spelling of **propaganda**

propolis /próppəliss/ *n* a waxy resinous substance that comes from buds, used by bees as a cement and caulking in making their hives [Early 17C. Via Latin < Greek, literally 'before a city' < *polis* 'city' (originally a structure around the opening of a hive)]

proponent /prə pōnənt/ *n* **1.** ADVOCATE somebody who advocates something **2.** LAW PRESENTER OF WILL somebody who presents a will for probate **3.** PROPOSER somebody who proposes something [Late 16C. < Latin *proponent-*, present participle of *proponere* (see PROPOSITION)]

proportion /prə páwrsh'n/ *n* **1.** PART OF WHOLE a quantity of something that is part of the whole amount or number ○ *What proportion of their time is spent on administration?* **2.** RELATIONSHIP BETWEEN QUANTITIES the relationship between two or more amounts or numbers, or between the parts of a whole ○ *The proportion of lorries to cars on the road has remained the same.* **3.** RELATIVE SIZE the correct or desirable relationship of size, quantity, or degree between two or more things or parts of something ○ *An understanding of proportion is essential for an architect.* **4.** RELATIVE IMPORTANCE the importance of different aspects of a situation when compared with each other ○ *The media blew the incident all out of proportion.* **5.** MATHS RATIO a relationship between two variables that remains fixed **6.** MATHS EQUALITY OF TWO RATIOS a relationship of equality between two ratios, in which the first term divided by the second equals the third divided by the fourth, as in $\frac{1}{2} = \frac{3}{6}$ ■ **proportions** *npl* **1.** SIZE OF SOMETHING the size or shape of something **2.** IMPORTANCE OF SOMETHING the importance or seriousness of something ■ *vt* (**-tions, -tioning, -tioned**) **1.** MAINTAIN RELATIONSHIP BETWEEN THINGS to create or maintain a relationship of size, quantity, or degree between two or more things **2.** BALANCE SOMETHING to give something a pleasing shape, appropriate dimensions, or a harmonious arrangement of parts (*usually passive*) ○ *a beautifully proportioned design* [14C. Directly or via French < Latin *proportion-* < *pro portione* 'according to (each) part' < *portion-* 'part, portion'] —**proportionability** /prə páwsh'nə bílləti/ *n* —**proportionable** *adj* —**proportionably** *adv* —**proportionment** *n*

USAGE See ***percentage.***

proportional /prə páwrsh'nəl/ *adj* **1.** IN PROPORTION having the correct relationship of size, quantity, or degree to something else, or remaining in the same relationship when things change ○ *The rate of pay is proportional to the complexity of the task.* **2.** MATHS RELATED BY RATIO related by or possessing a constant ratio ■ *n* MATHS TERM IN PAIR OF EQUIVALENT RATIOS one of the four terms in a relationship of proportion

between two ratios, where the first term divided by the second equals the third divided by the fourth [14C. < late Latin *proportionalis* < Latin *proportion-* (see PROPORTION)] —**proportionality** /prə páwrsh'n állәti/ *n* —**proportionally** *adv*

proportional representation *n* an electoral system in which each party's share of the seats in government is the same as its share of all the votes cast

proportional tax *n* a tax in which the proportion of income paid in tax is constant when income rises

proportionate *adj* /prə páwrsh'nət/ having the correct relationship of size, quantity, or degree to something else, or remaining in the same relationship when things change ○ *The fall in price led to a proportionate rise in sales.* ■ *vt* /prə páwrsh'n ayt/ (**-ates, -ating, -ated**) to give two or more things the correct relationship of size, quantity, or degree [14C. < late Latin *proportionatus* < Latin *proportion-* (see PROPORTION)] —**proportionately** /-ətli/ *adv*

proposal /prə pṓz'l/ *n* **1. SUGGESTED IDEA OR PLAN** a suggestion or intention, especially one put forward formally or officially **2. ACT OF PROPOSING** the act of making a suggestion or stating an intention **3. REQUEST TO MARRY SOMEBODY** a request for somebody to enter into marriage **4.** POL, LAW **DRAFT LAW FROM EC** a draft law proposed by the European Commission to the Council of Ministers

propose /prə pṓz/ (**-poses, -posing, -posed**) *v* **1.** *vt* **MAKE SUGGESTION** to put forward something such as an idea or suggested course of action formally or officially ○ *Harsher penalties have been proposed.* **2.** *vt* **STATE INTENTION** to announce a plan or intended course of action ○ *What do you propose to do about it?* **3.** *vt* **NOMINATE SOMEBODY** to put forward somebody's name for an elected position or a promotion ○ *propose her for the new position* **4.** *vti* **OFFER MARRIAGE** to make an offer of marriage to somebody ○ *He proposed while we were on holiday.* **5.** *vt* **SUGGEST TOAST OR VOTE OF THANKS** to ask others to join in something such as a toast or a vote of thanks ○ *I propose a toast to Chris and Sarah.* [14C. < French *proposer* 'put forward' < *poser* (see POSE[1]), after Latin *proponere*] —**proposable** *adj* —**proposer** *n*

proposita /prō pózzitə/ (*plural* **-tae** /-tee/) *n* a woman who is involved in legal proceedings [Late 20C. < Latin, form of *propositus* (see PROPOSITUS)]

propositi LAW, GENETICS plural of **propositus**

proposition /próppə zísh'n/ *n* **1. PROPOSAL** an idea, offer, or plan put forward for consideration or discussion **2. STATEMENT** a statement of opinion or judgment **3. OFFER OF SEXUAL INTERCOURSE** an invitation to have sexual intercourse **4. PRIVATE AGREEMENT** a private deal or agreement **5. SOMEBODY OR SOMETHING TO BE FACED** somebody or something to be dealt with (*informal*) ○ *The news that he would be there certainly made the party a more attractive proposition.* **6.** MATHS **THEOREM** a statement or theorem to be demonstrated **7.** PHILOSOPHY **MEANING OF DECLARATIVE SENTENCE** the meaning of a declarative sentence that expresses something that can be true or false ■ *vt* (**-tions, -tioning, -tioned**) **1. OFFER SEX TO SOMEBODY** to invite somebody to have sexual intercourse **2. OFFER DEAL TO SOMEBODY** to offer to make a private deal or agreement with somebody [14C. Directly or via French < Latin *proposition-* < *proposit-*, past participle of *proponere* 'put forth' < *ponere* 'to place'] —**propositional** *adj* —**propositionally** *adv*

propositional attitude *n* in philosophy, an attitude taken by somebody towards a proposition, e.g. in believing it, knowing it, or desiring it

propositional calculus *n* the branch of deductive logic that deals with the relationships formed between propositions linked by connectives such as 'and', 'but', 'if', or 'or'

propositional function *n* LOGIC same as **open sentence**

propositus /prō pózzitəss/ (*plural* **-ti** /-tī/) *n* **1. ORIGINAL ANCESTOR** the original ancestor of a line of descent **2. MAN LITIGANT** a man who is involved in legal proceedings **3. FIRST PERSON INVESTIGATED IN FAMILY STUDY** the first person to be investigated in the genetic study of a family [Mid-18C. < Latin, past participle of *proponere* (see PROPOSITION)]

propound /prə pównd/ (**-pounds, -pounding, -pounded**) *vt* **1.** to put forward a suggestion or theory for others to consider **2.** to present a document to a court or other authority in order that its validity can be established [Mid-16C. Alteration of obsolete *propone* < Latin *proponere* (see PROPOSITION)] —**propounder** *n*

propr. *abbr* COMM proprietor

propraetor /prō préetər/, **propretor** *n* in ancient times, a Roman citizen sent to govern a province, usually after serving as a senior magistrate (**praetor**) in Rome [Late 16C. < Latin < *pro praetore* 'for the praetor']

propranolol /prō práannə lol/ *n* a drug that slows heart rate and heart output. Use: treatment of angina pectoris, irregular heart rhythms, migraine, high blood pressure. [Mid-20C. < PROPYL + *-r-* + *-olol*, INN stem]

proprietary /prə prī́ ətəri/ *adj* **1. USED WITH EXCLUSIVE LEGAL RIGHT** used, manufactured, or sold by a person or company with an exclusive property right such as a patent or trademark ○ *a proprietary drug* **2. EXHIBITING CHARACTERISTICS OF OWNERSHIP** exhibiting characteristics that indicate ownership of somebody or something ○ *The child kept a proprietary hold on the toy.* **3. RELATING TO OWNERS OR OWNERSHIP** relating to an owner, ownership, or something owned **4. PRIVATELY OWNED** privately owned and run ■ *n* (*plural* **-ies**) **1.** PHARM **PROPRIETARY AGENT** a drug or other substance made and sold under the legal protection of a trademark or patent **2. OWNER** an owner or a group of owners **3. OWNERSHIP** the right of ownership, or something exclusively owned [15C. Directly or via French < late Latin *proprietarius* 'of a property holder' < Latin *proprietas* (see PROPERTY)] —**proprietarily** *adv*

proprietary name *n* a product name that is registered as a trademark

proprietor /prə prī́ ətər/ *n* **1. OWNER OF BUSINESS** the owner of a commercial enterprise or establishment such as a shop, hotel, or restaurant **2. LEGAL OWNER** the legal owner of something **3. FREEHOLDER OF PROPERTY** somebody identified on the Land Registry as the freeholder of a property [15C. Alteration of PROPRIETARY] —**proprietorial** /prə prī́ ə táwri əl/ *adj* —**proprietorially** *adv* —**proprietorship** *n*

propriety /prə prī́ əti/ *n* **1. SOCIALLY CORRECT OR APPROPRIATE BEHAVIOUR** conformity to the standards of politeness, respect, decency, or morality conventionally accepted by a society **2. QUALITY OF BEING SOCIALLY APPROPRIATE** the quality of displaying behaviour thought to be correct or appropriate ■ **proprieties** *npl* **RULES OF ETIQUETTE** the accepted standards of correct or appropriate social behaviour [15C. < French *propriété* (see PROPERTY)]

proprioceptor /prṓpri ə séptər/ *n* a sensory nerve ending in muscles, tendons, and joints that provides a sense of the body's position by responding to stimuli from within the body [Early 20C. < Latin *proprius* 'your own' + RECEPTOR] —**proprioception** /prṓpri ə sépsh'n/ *n* —**proprioceptive** *adj*

prop root *n* a root that grows from the stem of a plant above the ground and helps to support it. The mangrove and maize are examples of plants with prop roots.

props master *n* somebody in charge of stage props

proptosis /prop tṓssiss/ *n* the forward displacement or protrusion of an organ of the body, especially an eyeball [Late 17C. Via late Latin < Greek *proptōsis* 'a falling forwards' < *propiptein* 'fall forwards']

propulsion /prə púlsh'n/ *n* **1.** the process by which an object such as a motor vehicle, ship, aircraft, or missile is moved forwards **2.** the force by which an object such as a motor vehicle, ship, aircraft, or missile is moved forwards [Early 17C. < obsolete *propulse* 'drive away' < Latin *propulsare* < *propuls-*, past participle of *propellere* (see PROPEL)] —**propulsive** *adj* —**propulsory** *adj*

propyl /prṓp il/ *adj* relating to the group of atoms derived from propane after the loss of a hydrogen atom. Formula: C_3H_7. [Mid-19C. < PROPIONIC]

propylaeum /próppi lée əm/ (*plural* **-laea** /-lée ə/) *n* a colonnaded gate or entrance to a building or group of buildings, especially to a temple [Early 18C. Via Latin < Greek *propulaion* < form of *propulaios* 'before the gate' < *pulē* 'gate']

propyl alcohol *n* a colourless alcohol. Use: solvent, antiseptic. Formula: C_3H_8O.

propylene /prṓpi leen/ *n* a flammable gaseous hydrocarbon. Source: petroleum. Use: organic synthesis. Formula: C_3H_6.

propylene glycol *n* a colourless thick sweet-tasting liquid. Source: propylene. Use: antifreeze in brake fluid, solvent, lubricant. Formula: $C_3H_8O_2$.

propylon /prṓpi lon/ (*plural* **-lons** or **-la** /-lə/) *n* BUILDINGS same as **propylaeum** [Mid-19C. Via Latin < Greek *propulon*, literally 'before the gate' < *pulē* 'gate']

pro rata /-ráatə/ *adv, adj* in accordance with a fixed proportion [< Latin, 'according to the rate']

prorate /prō ráyt/ (**-rates, -rating, -rated**) *vti* to calculate, divide, or distribute something on a pro rata basis [Mid-19C. < PRO RATA] —**proratable** *adj* —**proration** /-ráysh'n/ *n*

prorogue /prō rṓg/ (**-rogues, -roguing, -rogued**) *v* **1.** *vti* to discontinue the meetings of a parliament or other body without formally ending the session, or be discontinued in this way **2.** *vt* to defer something to a later date or to a subsequent meeting [15C. Via French < Latin *prorogare* 'prolong' *rogare* 'ask'] —**prorogation** /prṓrō gáysh'n/ *n*

pros. *abbr* LITERAT prosody

prosaic /prō záy ik/ *adj* **1.** not having any features that are interesting or imaginative **2.** characteristic of, resembling, or consisting of prose [Late 16C. Directly or via French < late Latin *prosaicus* < Latin *prosa* (see PROSE)] —**prosaically** *adv* —**prosaicness** *n*

prosaism /prō záy izəm/, **prosaicism** /prō záy i sizəm/ *n* **1.** a dull or unimaginative expression or style of writing **2.** a word, phrase, or style of writing used in prose —**prosaist** *n*

pros and cons *npl* the arguments for and against something

Pros. Atty *abbr US* LAW prosecuting attorney

proscenium /prə séeni əm/ (*plural* **-nia** /-ni ə/ or **-niums**) *n* **1.** the part of a theatre stage that is in front of the curtain **2.** the stage of a theatre in ancient Greece or Rome [Early 17C. Via Latin < Greek *proskēnion* 'front stage' < *skēnē* 'stage, scenes']

prosciutto /prō shóotō/ *n* Italian cured ham, usually served cold and uncooked in thin slices [Mid-20C. < Italian]

proscribe /prō skrīb/ (**-scribes, -scribing, -scribed**) *vt* **1. BAN SOMETHING** to prohibit something that is considered undesirable by those in authority **2. CONDEMN SOMETHING** to denounce or condemn something **3. BANISH SOMEBODY** to banish or exile somebody **4. OUTLAW SOMEBODY PUBLICLY** especially in ancient Rome, to state publicly that somebody is no longer protected by the law [15C. < Latin *proscribere* 'publish in writing, publish somebody's name as outlawed' < *scribere* 'write'] —**proscriber** *n*

proscription /prō skrípsh'n/ *n* **1. BANNING OF SOMETHING** the prohibition of something considered undesirable by those in authority **2. CONDEMNATION OF SOMETHING** the denunciation or condemnation of something **3. BANISHING OF SOMEBODY** the banishment or exiling of somebody **4. PUBLIC OUTLAWING OF SOMEBODY** especially in ancient Rome, a public statement by which somebody is no longer granted the protection of the law [14C. < Latin *proscription-* < past participle of *proscribere* (see PROSCRIBE)] —**proscriptive** *adj* —**proscriptively** /-skríptivli/ *adv* —**proscriptiveness** *n*

prose /prōz/ *n* **1. LANGUAGE THAT IS NOT POETRY** writing or speech in its normal continuous form, without the rhythmic or visual line structure of poetry **2. ORDINARY STYLE OF EXPRESSION** writing or speech that is ordinary or matter-of-fact, without embellishment **3. PASSAGE FOR TRANSLATION** a piece of text to be translated into another language as an exercise for students **4.** CHR same as **sequence** *n* (sense 6) ■ *v* (**proses, prosing, prosed**) **1.** *vti* **WRITE SOMETHING IN PROSE** to write something in prose **2.** *vt* **REWRITE SOMETHING AS PROSE** to turn poetry into prose **3.** *vi* **SPEAK OR WRITE PROSAICALLY** to speak or write in an ordinary, matter-of-fact, or unimaginative style [13C. Via French < Latin *prosa (oratio)* 'straightforward (discourse)' < *provertere* 'turn forward' < *vertere* 'to turn']

prosector /prō séktər/ *n* somebody who prepares or dissects cadavers for anatomy demonstrations [Mid-19C. Directly or via French < late Latin, 'in place of the cutter' < Latin *sector* (see SECTOR)]

prosecute /próssi kyoot/ (**-cutes, -cuting, -cuted**) v **1.** vti TAKE LEGAL ACTION AGAINST SOMEBODY to have somebody tried in a court of law for a civil or criminal offence ○ *Trespassers will be prosecuted.* **2.** vti PURSUE CASE IN COURT to pursue a claim or action in a court of law as the representative of the person or people bringing the action **3.** vt PERFORM ACTIVITY OR OCCUPATION to engage in or carry on an activity or occupation (*formal*) ○ *prosecute a trade* **4.** vt TAKE SOMETHING TO COMPLETION to carry on doing something, usually until it is finished or accomplished (*formal*) ○ *prosecute an investigation* [15C. < Latin *prosecut-*, past participle of *prosequi* 'follow forward' < *sequi* 'follow']—**prosecutable** *adj*

~~prosecuter~~ incorrect spelling of **prosecutor**

prosecuting attorney /próssi kyooting-/ n US a lawyer representing the state or the people in a criminal trial

prosecution /próssi kyóosh'n/ n **1.** PURSUIT OF LEGAL ACTION the trial of somebody in a court of law for a criminal offence **2.** LAWYERS TRYING TO PROVE SOMEBODY'S GUILT the lawyers representing the person or people who are taking legal action against somebody in a court of law, especially the Crown or the people in a criminal trial ○ *a witness for the prosecution* **3.** PERFORMANCE OF ACTIVITY OR OCCUPATION the carrying on of an activity or occupation (*formal*) ○ *the prosecution of your duty* **4.** CONTINUATION TO COMPLETION the continuation of or perseverance in a task or activity, usually until it is finished or accomplished (*formal*)

prosecutor /próssi kyootər/ n **1.** somebody who initiates a legal prosecution **2.** US LAW same as **prosecuting attorney**

Prose Edda n LITERAT same as **Edda** (sense 2)

proselyte /próssə līt/ n a new convert to a religious faith or political doctrine [14C. Via late Latin < Greek *proseluthos* 'somebody who comes to a place' < *proserkhesthai* 'come to']—**proselytic** /-líttik/ *adj*—**proselytism** /-lə tizəm/ n

proselytize /próssələ tīz/ (**-tizes, -tizing, -tized**), **proselytise** (**-tises, -tising, -tised**) vti to try to convert somebody to a religious faith or political doctrine—**proselytization** /próssələ tī záysh'n/ n—**proselytizer** n

prose poem n a piece of creative writing that has the structure of prose but the style and language of poetry

Proserpina /prə súrpinə/, **Proserpine** /próssər pīn/ n in Roman mythology, the goddess of the Earth. Greek equivalent **Persephone**

prosimian /prō símmi ən/ n a nocturnal lower primate with large eyes and ears, e.g. a lemur or bush baby. Suborder: Prosimii.

prosit /prózit/ interj used as a drinking toast, to wish somebody good health or good fortune [Mid-19C. Via German < Latin, 'may it benefit', 3rd person present subjunctive singular of *prodesse* (see PROUD)]

prosody /próssədi/ (*plural* **-dies**) n **1.** STUDY OF POETIC STRUCTURE the study of the structure of poetry and the conventions or techniques involved in writing it, including rhyme, metre, and the patterns of verse forms **2.** SYSTEM OR THEORY OF WRITING VERSE a particular system or theory of writing poetry **3.** RHYTHM OF SPEECH the rhythm of spoken language, including stress and intonation, or the study of these patterns [15C. Via Latin < Greek *prosōidia* 'song with an instrumental accompaniment' < *pros* 'in addition to' + *ōidē* 'song']—**prosodic** /prə sóddik/ *adj*—**prosodically** *adv*—**prosodist** n

prosoma /prō sṓmə/ (*plural* **-mas** or **-mata** /-mətə/) n the region near the head of spiders and some related arthropods, composed of fused segments of head and thorax [Late 19C. < PRO-² + Greek *sōma* 'body']

prosopography /próssə póggrəfi/ n a collection of biographical sketches used by social and political historians studying a particular historical period [Mid-16C. < modern Latin *prosopographia* 'writing about somebody' < Greek *prosōpon* 'face, person']—**prosopographer** n—**prosopographical** /próssəpə gráffik'l/ *adj*

prosopopoeia /próssəpə pēē ə/, **prosopopeia** n **1.** a figure of speech that presents an imaginary or dead person as speaking **2.** a figure of speech in which human qualities are attributed to objects or abstract notions [Mid-16C. Via Latin < Greek *prosōpopoiia* 'representation in human form' < *prosōpon* 'face, person' + *poiein* 'make']

prospect n /próss pekt/ **1.** POSSIBILITY OF SOMETHING HAPPENING SOON a chance or the likelihood that something will happen in the near future, especially something desirable **2.** VISION OF FUTURE something that is expected or certain to happen in the future, or a mental picture of this ○ *I don't relish the prospect of spending five months at sea.* **3.** EXTENSIVE OUTLOOK OR SCENE a view, especially one from a high position over a large expanse of land or water ○ *a pleasant prospect* **4.** DIRECTION FACED the direction in which something faces ○ *a northerly prospect* **5.** LIKELY CUSTOMER a customer who may be interested in buying something **6.** SOMEBODY OR SOMETHING WITH POTENTIAL somebody or something that is likely to succeed ○ *She's our brightest prospect.* **7.** SURVEY an act of making a survey, examination, or observation **8.** MINERAL LOCATION the location of a mineral deposit, or an area believed to have mineral deposits **9.** MINERAL DEPOSIT a probable mineral deposit or one that definitely exists **10.** MINERAL SAMPLE TO BE ANALYSED a sample of a mineral to be analysed for its components **11.** MINERAL YIELD the yield that can be obtained by mining a mineral ■ **prospects** npl EXPECTATIONS OF SUCCESS the likelihood of being successful or prosperous in the future, especially in a job or career ○ *Young people who leave school early certainly limit their prospects.* ○ *eager to improve her career prospects* ■ v /prə spékt, próss pekt/ (**-pects, -pecting, -pected**) **1.** vti SEARCH FOR MINERAL DEPOSITS IN AREA to explore an area in search of oil or valuable minerals, especially gold **2.** vt WORK MINE to work a mine to see how profitable it is **3.** vi LOOK FOR SOMETHING to search or watch for something ○ *prospect for business* [15C. < Latin *prospectus* 'view' < past participle of *prospicere* 'look forward' < *specere* 'look at']—**prospectless** /próss pektləss/ *adj*

prospective /prə spéktiv/ *adj* **1.** expected or hoping to do or become something ○ *his prospective mother-in-law* **2.** likely or expected to happen ○ *prospective changes*—**prospectively** *adv*

prospector /prə spéktər, próss pektər/ n somebody who explores an area in search of oil, gold, or other mineral deposits

prospectus /prə spéktəss/ n **1.** UK, ANZ, Can a brochure or pamphlet that advertises or describes the activities, staff, and facilities of an organization or an institution such as a school, college, or university. US term **catalogue** **2.** an official document giving details about something that is going to happen such as an issue of shares, a forthcoming publication, a new business, or a proposed project [Mid-18C. < Latin (see PROSPECT)]

prosper /próspər/ (**-pers, -pering, -pered**) v **1.** vi to be successful, especially in financial or economic terms **2.** vt to make somebody or something successful or profitable (*archaic*) [14C. Directly or via French < Latin *prosperare* < *prosperus* 'doing well']

prosperity /pro spérrəti/ n the condition of enjoying wealth, success, or good fortune [13C. Via French < Latin *prosperitas* < *prosperus* 'doing well']

prosperous /próspərəss/ *adj* **1.** FINANCIALLY SUCCESSFUL successful and flourishing, especially earning or producing great wealth **2.** WEALTHY having wealth, or associated with wealthy people **3.** FULL OF GOOD FORTUNE characterized by success or good fortune ○ *wishing you a prosperous New Year* **4.** PROMISING likely to be successful or bring a good result—**prosperously** *adv*—**prosperousness** n

pross /pross/, **prossie** /próssi/ n CRIME same as **prostitute** n (sense 1) (*slang*) [Early 20C. Shortening]

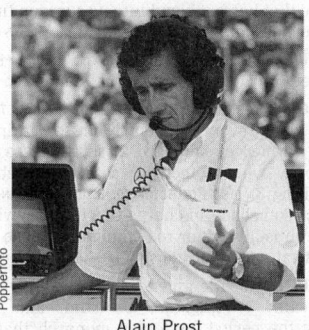
Alain Prost

Popperfoto

Prost /prost/, **Alain** (*b.* 1955) French racing driver. He was Formula One world champion (1985, 1986, 1989, and 1993) and four times runner-up.

> 'When you start off as a driver, it is a sport; but when you get into Formula One, it suddenly becomes a job.'
> [Alain Prost, *Sunday Telegraph*; 18 June 1989]

prostacyclin /próstə síklin/ n a prostaglandin that dilates blood vessels and inhibits the formation of blood clots [Late 20C. < PROSTATE + CYCLIC]

prostaglandin /próstə glándin/ n an unsaturated fatty acid found in all mammals that performs a similar function to that of hormones in controlling smooth muscle contraction, blood pressure, inflammation, and body temperature [Mid-20C. < PROSTATE + GLAND¹]

prostate /pró stayt/ n ANAT same as **prostate gland** [Mid-17C. Via modern Latin *prostata* < Greek *prostatēs* 'guardian' (of the bladder) < *proïstanai* 'set before' < *histanai* 'cause to stand']—**prostatic** /pro státtik/ *adj*

prostatectomy /próstə téktəmi/ (*plural* **-mies**) n the surgical removal of the whole or part of the prostate gland

prostate gland n an 'O'-shaped gland in males that surrounds the urethra below the bladder, secreting a fluid into the semen that acts to improve the movement and viability of sperm

prostate-specific antigen n a protein and sugar complex (**glycoprotein**) found in the cells of the prostate of all men that is present in increased amounts when various prostate diseases, especially cancer, occur

prostatism /próstə tizəm/ n a disorder of the prostate gland, especially enlargement that blocks or inhibits urine flow

prostatitis /próstə títiss/ n inflammation of the prostate gland

prosthesis /pross theéssiss/ (*plural* **-theses** /-theés seez/) n **1.** an artificial body part, e.g. an artificial limb or eye **2.** the branch of surgery concerned with replacing missing body parts with artificial devices **3.** LING same as **prothesis** (sense 1) [Mid-16C. Via late Latin < Greek, 'addition' < *prostithenai* 'add to' < *tithenai* 'to place']—**prosthetic** /pross théttik/ *adj*—**prosthetically** *adv*

prosthetic group n the part of a conjugated protein that is not an amino acid, e.g. the lipid group in lipoprotein

prosthetics /pros théttiks/ n the branch of medicine dealing with the design, production, and use of artificial body parts (*takes a singular verb*)—**prosthetist** /prósthətist/ n

prosthodontics /próssthə dóntiks/ n the branch of dentistry that deals with the replacement of teeth and parts of the jaw (*takes a singular verb*) [Mid-20C. < PROSTHESIS, after ORTHODONTICS]—**prosthodontic** *adj*—**prosthodontist** n

prostitute /prósti tyoot/ n **1.** SOMEBODY PAID FOR SEXUAL INTERCOURSE somebody who is paid to provide sexual intercourse or other sex acts **2.** SOMEBODY WHO DEGRADES TALENT FOR MONEY somebody who uses a skill or ability in a way that is considered unworthy, usually for financial gain ■ vt (**-tutes, -tuting, -tuted**) **1.** MISUSE SOMETHING FOR GAIN to use a skill or ability in a way that is considered unworthy, usually for financial gain ○ *He has been accused of prostituting his talent by appearing in TV commercials.* **2.** WORK OR OFFER SOMEBODY AS PROSTITUTE to offer somebody or yourself for sexual intercourse or other sex acts in exchange for money [Mid-16C. < Latin *prostitut-*, past participle of *prostituere* 'expose publicly, offer for sale' < *statuere* 'to set, place']—**prostitutor** n

prostitution /prósti tyoósh'n/ n **1.** the act of engaging in sexual intercourse or performing other sex acts in exchange for money, or of offering another person for such purposes **2.** the use of a skill or ability in a way that is considered unworthy, usually for financial gain

prostomium /prō stṓmi əm/ (*plural* **-mia** /-mi ə/) n the part of the head of some worms such as the earthworm that is in front of the mouth [Late 19C. Via modern Latin < Greek *prostomion* 'something in front of the mouth' < *stoma* 'mouth']—**prostomial** *adj*

prostrate *v* /pro stráyt/ (**-trates, -trating, -trated**) 1. **prostrate yourself** *vr* LIE FACE DOWNWARDS to lie prone or stretched out with the face downwards or bow very low, e.g. in worship or submission ○ *He prostrated himself before the emperor.* 2. *vt* LAY SOMEBODY OR SOMETHING ON GROUND to lay or throw somebody or something flat on the ground ○ *was prostrated by a blow on the head* 3. *vt* INCAPACITATE SOMEBODY to make somebody physically or emotionally weak or helpless ○ *was prostrated by illness* ■ *adj* /pró strayt/ 1. LYING FLAT ON FACE lying prone or stretched out with the face downwards, e.g. in worship or submission 2. LYING DOWN stretched out in a horizontal position, often because of illness or injury 3. DRAINED OF ENERGY drained of physical strength or incapacitated by overexertion or powerful emotion ○ *prostrate with grief* 4. BOT GROWING ALONG GROUND describes a plant that grows or trails along the ground ○ *a prostrate shrub* [14C. < Latin *prostratus*, past participle of *prosternere* 'throw in front of' < *sternere* 'spread out, lay down'] —**prostration** *n*

prostyle /pró stīl/ *adj* describes a building such as a Greek temple that has a row of columns at the front [Late 17C. < Latin *prostylos* 'having pillars in front' < *stilus* 'pointed writing instrument, stake']

prosy /prózi/ (**-ier, -iest**) *adj* dull and commonplace, with no interesting, imaginative, or eloquent features —**prosily** *adv* —**prosiness** *n*

Prot. *abbr* 1. HIST Protectorate 2. CHR Protestant

prot- *prefix* same as **proto-** (*used before vowels*)

protactinium /prō tak tínni əm/ *n* a toxic radioactive metallic element. Source: uranium ores. Symbol **Pa**. See table at **element** [Early 20C. < PROTO- + ACTINIUM, because the most common isotope decays to give actinium]

protagonist /prō tággənist/ *n* 1. MAIN CHARACTER the most important character in a novel, play, story, or other literary work 2. MAIN CHARACTER IN ANCIENT GREEK DRAMA in ancient Greek drama, the first actor who interacted with the chorus 3. LEADING FIGURE a main participant in an event such as a contest or dispute ○ *two protagonists in a long-running dispute* 4. SUPPORTER an important or influential supporter or advocate of something such as a political or social issue ○ *an early protagonist of educational reform* [Late 17C. < Greek *prōtagōnistēs* 'actor who plays the chief part' < *agōnistēs* 'actor, competitor' < *agōn* 'contest'] —**protagonism** *n*

Protagoras /prōtágərəs/ (480?–411? BC) Greek philosopher. The first of the sophists, he taught that nothing is absolutely good or bad, true or false.

> 'Man is the measure of all things: of those which are, that they are; of those which are not, that they are not.'
> [Protagoras, 'On the Gods'; 5th century BC]

protamine /prótə meen/ *n* 1. an arginine-rich peptide found in chromosomes that has the property of being able to condense DNA 2. a therapeutic drug derived from protamine. Use: controlling bleeding, slow-release insulin application in diabetes treatment.

protanopia /prótə nópi ə/ *n* a form of colour blindness in which the retina fails to distinguish between red and green [Early 20C. < PROTO- (red being regarded as the first of the primary colours) + AN-] —**protanopic** /prótə nóppik/ *adj*

protasis /próttəsiss/ (*plural* **-tases** /-tə seez/) *n* the part of a conditional sentence that contains the condition, e.g. 'if he asks' in 'if he asks, I'll tell him' [Mid-16C. Via Latin < Greek < *proteinein* 'put forward, propose' < *teinein* 'to stretch'] —**protatic** /pro táttik/ *adj*

prote- *prefix* same as **proteo-** (*used before vowels*)

protea /próti ə/ (*plural* **-as** or *same*) *n* an evergreen bush or tree, grown for its colourful bracts and dense flower heads. Native to: southern Africa. Genus: *Protea*. [Mid-18C. < modern Latin, after PROTEUS, from the variety of form in the genus]

protean /próti ən, prō tée ən/ *adj* 1. variable or continually changing in nature, appearance, or behaviour 2. showing great variety, diversity, or versatility [Late 16C. < PROTEUS]

protease /próti ayz, -ayss/ *n* an enzyme that breaks down proteins and peptides by catalysing the hydrolysis of peptide bonds [Early 20C. < PROTEIN]

protease inhibitor *n* a compound that breaks down protease, inhibiting the replication of viruses and development of some cancers. Use: treatment of Aids.

proteasome /próti ə sōm/ *n* a cluster of proteins found in the cytoplasm of living cells that degrades damaged or redundant proteins

protect /prə tékt/ (**-tects, -tecting, -tected**) *vt* 1. KEEP SOMEBODY OR SOMETHING SAFE to prevent somebody or something from being harmed or damaged 2. HELP HOME INDUSTRIES BY TAXING IMPORTS to help the industries in a country by imposing customs duties on imports from other countries 3. GUARANTEE PAYMENT OF DRAFT to put up money in advance to guarantee that a draft or note is paid [15C. < Latin *protect-*, past participle of *protegere* 'cover in front' < *tegere* 'to cover']

SYNONYMS See ***safeguard***.

---

protectant /prə téktənt/ *n* a substance that prevents something from being damaged, e.g. a coating used to stop metal going rusty

protected /prə téktid/ *adj* 1. ENDANGERED legally classified as a species in danger of extinction 2. SHELTERED sheltered from the elements 3. COMPUT LOCKED AGAINST UNAUTHORIZED CHANGES locked against changes by unauthorized users of a computer program

protection /prə téksh'n/ *n* 1. SAFEGUARDING OF SOMEBODY OR SOMETHING the act of preventing somebody or something from being harmed or damaged, or the state of being kept safe 2. SOMETHING THAT PROTECTS SOMEBODY OR SOMETHING something that prevents somebody or something from being harmed or damaged 3. INSURANCE COVER an agreement by an insurance company to pay compensation or costs if a specific undesirable event occurs 4. PROMISE OF SAFETY FROM CRIMINAL ATTACK a promise made by a gangster or other person that somebody or something will not be harmed or damaged if money is paid, or the payment extorted in return for such a promise (*informal*) 5. CONDOM a form of contraception, usually a condom, used during sexual intercourse to prevent sperm or disease-causing organisms from entering the body 6. GUARANTEE OF FREEDOM AND SAFETY a document that enables somebody to travel around in freedom and safety, especially in another country or in enemy territory 7. ECON same as **protectionism** 8. CLIMBING SAFETY EQUIPMENT FOR CLIMBER the safety equipment used by mountain climbers to keep them from falling, e.g. pitons, harnesses, and ropes

protectionism /prə téksh'nizəm/ *n* the system of imposing duties on imports into a country in order to protect domestic industries —**protectionist** *n, adj*

protection money *n* money paid to a gangster or other person who threatens to harm somebody or damage something unless the money is paid

protective /prə téktiv/ *adj* 1. GIVING PROTECTION preventing somebody or something from being harmed or damaged, or designed or intended for this purpose ○ *a protective covering* 2. TAKING GREAT CARE OF SOMEBODY anxious to protect or defend somebody or something, often excessively so ○ *She had always felt protective towards her younger brother.* 3. INTENDED TO HELP DOMESTIC INDUSTRIES intended to give an advantage to a country's domestic industries ○ *a protective tariff* ■ *n* 1. SOMETHING THAT PROTECTS something that prevents somebody or something from being harmed or damaged 2. HEALTH same as **condom** (*formal*) —**protectively** *adv* —**protectiveness** *n*

protective coloration, **protective colouring** *n* the combination of surface colours and patterns on an animal that helps it blend into its surroundings and so evade predators

protective custody *n* detention by the police in order to give protection from harm by somebody

protector /prə téktər/ *n* 1. SOMETHING THAT PROTECTS something that prevents somebody or something from being harmed or damaged 2. SOMEBODY WHO PROTECTS somebody who protects or defends somebody or something 3. *also* **Protector** SOMEBODY RULING IN PLACE OF MONARCH somebody in charge of a country while the monarch is absent, or too young or unfit to rule —**protectoral** *adj* —**protectorship** *n*

Protector *n* the title given to the head of the Commonwealth of England, Scotland, and Ireland during the period without a monarch that lasted from 1653 to 1659. The title was held by Oliver Cromwell from 1653 to 1658 and by Richard Cromwell from 1658 to 1659.

protectorate /prə téktərət/ *n* 1. STATE DEFENDED BY ANOTHER a country or region that is defended and controlled by a more powerful state, or the relationship between the two 2. PLACE DEPENDENT ON ANOTHER an area or country that is dependent on another more powerful nation 3. OFFICE OF PROTECTOR the position or term of office of a protector

protégé /prótti zhay, próti-/ *n* a young person who receives help, guidance, training, and support from somebody who is older and has more experience or influence [Late 18C. < French < past participle of *protéger* 'protect' < Latin *protegere* (see PROTECT)]

protégée /prótti zhay, próti-/ *n* a young woman who receives help, guidance, training, and support from somebody who is older and has more experience or influence [Late 18C. < French, feminine of *protégé* (see PROTÉGÉ)]

protei MICROBIOL plural of **proteus**

proteid /próti id/ *n* a salamander that retains its larval form as an adult, e.g. an olm or a mud puppy. Family: Proteidae. [Late 19C. < modern Latin *Proteus*, after PROTEUS]

protein /prō teen/ *n* 1. a complex natural substance that has a globular or fibrous structure composed of linked amino acids. Proteins are essential to the structure and function of all living cells and viruses. 2. a food source that is rich in protein molecules ○ *a balanced diet of fresh vegetables, fruit, and protein* [Mid-19C. < French < Greek *prōteios* 'primary' < *prōtos* 'first'; from its importance to the proper functioning of the body] —**proteinaceous** /próti náyshəss/ *adj* —**proteinic** /prō téenik/ *adj* —**proteinous** /prō téenəss/ *adj*

proteinase /próti nayz, -nayss/ *n* an enzyme that splits the peptide bonds of proteins

protein engineering *n* the process of making changes in the sequence of a gene coding for a protein in order to bring about desirable changes in function

proteinoid /próti noyd/ *n* a polypeptide that is obtained by polymerization of mixtures of amino acids and that has properties thought to be similar to those of early forms of protein

proteinuria /próti nyóori ə/ *n* the presence of protein in the urine, which is usually an indication of disease

pro tem /prō tém/ *adv, adj* at the present time, but not permanently [Shortening of Latin *pro tempore* 'for the time being']

proteo- *prefix* protein ○ *proteolysis* [< PROTEIN]

proteolysis /próti óllәssiss/ *n* the breakdown of proteins or peptides into amino acids —**proteolytic** /-ə líttik/ *adj* —**proteolytically** *adv*

proteome /próti ōm/ *n* the set of proteins specified by genes within an organism [Late 20C. Blend of PROTEIN + GENOME] —**proteomic** /próti ómik, -ómmik/ *adj*

proteomics /prōtee ómiks/ *n* the study of proteins expressed by genes within an organism, with applications in the understanding of disease and in drug development (*takes a singular verb*) [Late 20C. Blend of PROTEIN + GENOMICS]

proteose /próti ōz/ *n* a water-soluble protein derivative formed during hydrolytic processes such as digestion that does not coagulate when heated and precipitates if mixed with some sulphur-containing compounds

Proterozoic /prōtərō zó ik/ *n* the aeon of geological time, 2.5 billion to 570 million years ago, during which sea plants and animals first appeared. See table at **geological time** [Early 20C. < Greek *proteros* 'former' + *zōē* 'life'] —**Proterozoic** *adj*

protest *v* /prə tést/ (**-tests, -testing, -tested**) 1. *vi* COMPLAIN OR OBJECT STRONGLY to express strong disapproval of or disagreement with something 2. *vi* COMPLAIN OR OBJECT PUBLICLY to express strong opposition or disapproval in the form of a public demonstration or other action 3. *vti* SAY FIRMLY THAT SOMETHING IS TRUE to state or affirm something in strong or formal terms ○ *He continued to protest his innocence.* 4. *vt N Am* PROTEST AGAINST SOMETHING to complain about or protest against something ○ *protested the outcome* 5. *vt* FIN DECLARE

FINANCIAL NOTE DISHONOURED to state formally that a note or bill has been dishonoured **6.** *vt* ANNOUNCE SOMETHING to declare or proclaim something (*archaic*) ■ *n* /prṓ test/ **1.** STRONG COMPLAINT OR OBJECTION an expression or display of strong disapproval of or disagreement with something **2.** DEMONSTRATION OF PUBLIC OPPOSITION OR DISAPPROVAL an expression of strong opposition to or disapproval of something in the form of a public demonstration or other action ○ *student protests* ○ *went on a protest march* **3.** LAW CREDITOR'S FORMAL STATEMENT a formal statement drawn up by a notary on behalf of a creditor, declaring that somebody has refused to honour a bill **4.** CAPTAIN'S STATEMENT ABOUT DAMAGE TO SHIP a statement made by the master of a damaged vessel, declaring when and how a ship was damaged [14C. Via French < Latin *protestari* 'declare publicly' < *testari* 'declare'] —**protestant** /próttistənt/ *n* —**protester** *n* —**protestingly** *adv*

SYNONYMS See ***complain*** and ***object.***

Protestant *n* **1.** a member or adherent of any denomination of the Western Christian church that rejects papal authority and some fundamental Roman Catholic doctrines, and believes in justification by faith. The formulation of Protestants' beliefs began with the Reformation in the 16th century. **2.** somebody who makes a protest against an action —**Protestant** *adj*

Protestant ethic *n* CHR same as **Protestant work ethic**

Protestantism /prótistəntizəm/ *n* **1.** BELIEF IN PROTESTANT DOCTRINES adherence to the principles of the Protestant religion **2.** RELIGIOUS MOVEMENT OPPOSING ROMAN CATHOLICISM a Christian religious movement originating in the 16th century from Martin Luther's attack on Roman Catholic doctrine. It grew to encompass many churches and denominations denying papal authority and believing in justification by faith. **3.** ALL PROTESTANT CHURCHES the Protestant churches considered as a whole

Protestant work ethic *n* a belief in the moral value of work, thrift, and the responsibility of each person for his or her actions

protestation /prótti stáysh'n/ *n* **1.** FORMAL AFFIRMATION a strong or firm declaration that something is true (*often used in the plural*) ○ *protestations of loyalty* **2.** ACT OF COMPLAINING OR OBJECTING the act of expressing strong disapproval of or disagreement with something **3.** COMPLAINT OR OBJECTION a statement expressing strong disapproval of or disagreement with something

protest vote *n* the casting of a vote for a candidate or party as a means of showing dissatisfaction with another candidate or party

proteus /prṓti əss/ (*plural* **-tei** /-ti ī/) *n* a rod-shaped bacterium associated with enteritis and urinary tract infections. Genus: *Proteus.* [Early 19C. < modern Latin, after PROTEUS]

Proteus /prṓti əss/ *n* **1.** in Greek mythology, a prophetic sea god who could change his shape at will **2.** the second-largest natural satellite of Neptune, discovered in 1989 by Voyager 2. It is irregular in shape, having a maximum dimension of approximately 440 km/275 mi.

prothalamion /prṓthə láymi ən/ (*plural* **-mia** /-mi ə/), **prothalamium** /-əm/ *n* a song or poem celebrating a future marriage (*literary*) [Late 16C. After *epithalamion*, variant of EPITHALAMIUM]

prothallus /prō thálləss/ (*plural* **-li** /-lī/), **prothallium** /prō thálli əm/ (*plural* **-lia** /-li ə/) *n* a flat green organ bearing the reproductive organs (**gametophytes**) of ferns and related plants [Mid-19C. < modern Latin Greek *thallos* 'green shoot'] —**prothallial** /prō thálli əl/ *adj* —**prothallic** *adj*

prothesis /próthəssiss/ (*plural* **-eses** /-əs seez/) *n* **1.** the addition of a sound or sounds at the beginning of a word to make the word easier to pronounce **2.** in the Eastern Orthodox Church, the preparations for the offering of Communion [Late 16C. < Greek, 'a placing before or in public' < *thesis* 'placing'] —**prothetic** /prō théttik/ *adj* —**prothetically** *adv*

prothonotary /prṓthə nṓtəri, prō thónnətəri/ (*plural* **-ies**), **protonotary** /prṓtə nṓtəri, prō tónnətəri/ *n* **1.** the chief clerk in some courts of law **2.** *also* **prothonotary apostolic** (*plural* **prothonotaries apostolic**) *or* **protonotary apostolic** (*plural* **protonotaries apostolic**) in the Roman Catholic Church, one of twelve officials who can act as a notary to authenticate papal proceedings, documents, and acts [15C. < medieval Latin *protonotarius* < Greek *prōtos* 'first' + Latin *notarius* 'notary'] —**prothonotarial** /prō thónnə táiri əl/ *adj*

prothoracic gland /prōthə rássik-/ *n* a gland in insects that secretes the steroid hormone ecdysone, responsible for controlling moulting and metamorphosis

prothrombin /prō thrómbin/ *n* a plasma protein that is converted to thrombin during blood clotting

protist /prṓtist/ *n* an organism belonging, in an older classification system, to the kingdom that includes protozoans, bacteria, and single-celled algae and fungi. Kingdom: *Protista.* [Late 19C. < modern Latin *Protista* < Greek *prōtistos* 'very first' < *prōtos* 'first'] —**protistan** /prō tístən/ *adj* —**protistology** /prṓti stólləji/ *n*

protium /prṓti əm/ *n* the most common and lightest isotope of hydrogen, with atomic mass 1 [Mid-20C. < Greek *prōtos* 'first']

proto- *prefix* **1.** first in time, earliest ○ *protolithic* ○ *protomartyr* **2.** original, ancestral ○ *protostar* ○ *Proto-Norse* **3.** first in a series, having the least amount of a particular element or radical ○ *protactinium* [< Greek *prōtos*]

protocol /prṓtə kol/ *n* **1.** ETIQUETTE OF FORMAL OCCASIONS the rules or conventions of correct behaviour on official or ceremonial occasions **2.** CODE OF CONDUCT the rules of correct or appropriate behaviour of a group, organization, or profession **3.** INTERNAT REL INTERNATIONAL AGREEMENT a formal agreement between states or nations **4.** AMENDMENT something that amends a treaty or other formal document **5.** INTERNAT REL SOMETHING ADDED TO TREATY something added to a treaty that deals with minor details or makes it easier to understand **6.** RECORD OR DRAFT OF AGREEMENT a written record or preliminary draft of a treaty or other agreement **7.** COMPUT RULES FOR NETWORKING COMPUTERS a set of technical rules for the transmission and receipt of information between computers **8.** PHILOSOPHY same as **protocol statement** **9.** MED, SCI RESEARCH PLAN a detailed plan for a scientific experiment, medical trial, or other piece of research [15C. Via French and medieval Latin < Greek *prōtokollon* 'first leaf of a book']

protocol statement *n* a statement that can be immediately verified by experience

protocontinent /prṓtō kóntinənt/ *n* **1.** a large unbroken mass of land capable of becoming a major continent **2.** GEOL same as **supercontinent**

protogalaxy /prṓtō gálləksi/ (*plural* **-ies**) *n* a hypothetical cloud of gas believed to have been formed about 14 billion years ago from dark matter, neutral hydrogen, and helium, from which all the galaxies and stars evolved

Proto-Germanic /prṓtō-/ *n* a reconstructed hypothetical language that is believed to be the ancestor of the Germanic branch of the Indo-European family of languages —**Proto-Germanic** *adj*

protohuman /prṓtō hyóomən/ *n* an extinct hominid or primate that has some of the characteristics of modern people —**protohuman** *adj*

Proto-Indo-European *n* a reconstructed hypothetical language that is believed to be the ancestor of all the Indo-European languages —**Proto-Indo-European** *adj*

protoindustrialization /prṓtō in dústri ə lī záysh'n/, **protoindustrialisation** *n* the preliminary shift from an agricultural to an industrial economy, marked by the rapid spread of home-based manufacturing

protolanguage /prṓtō lang gwij/ *n* a recorded or reconstructed language that is the ancestor of another language or family of languages

protolithic /prṓtō líthik/ *adj* relating to the earliest part of the Stone Age [Late 19C. After NEOLITHIC]

protomartyr /prṓtō maártər/ *n* **1.** St Stephen, the first Christian martyr **2.** the first person to die for a cause

protomorphic /prṓtō máwrfik/ *adj* having a primitive structure

proton /prṓ ton/ *n* a stable elementary particle of the baryon family that is a component of all atomic nuclei and carries a positive charge equal to that of the electron's negative charge. Symbol **p** [Late 19C. < Greek *prōton*, form of *prōtos* 'first, elementary'] —**protonic** /prō tónnik/ *adj* —**protonically** *adv*

protonema /prṓtə neémə/ (*plural* **-mata** /-mətə/) *n* the primary thread-shaped structure of mosses and some liverworts that results from the germination of a spore and gives rise to a new plant [Mid-19C. < PROTO- + Greek *nēma* 'thread'] —**protonemal** *adj*

protonics /prō tónniks/ *n* the scientific study and technological application of protons in motion in conducting materials such as electrolytes (*takes a singular verb*)

proton number *n* PHYS same as **atomic number**

Proto-Norse *n* the form of the North Germanic language used in parts of Scandinavia, especially Norway and Iceland, until about the 8th century AD —**Proto-Norse** *adj*

protonotary *n* LAW, CHR same as **prothonotary**

proton synchrotron *n* a circular, very high-energy particle accelerator that accelerates protons through the action of magnetic fields and a high-frequency electric field

proto-oncogene /prṓtō óngkə jeen/ *n* a normal gene that can mutate or be activated by a cancer-causing virus to form a cancer-producing gene

protoplanet /prṓtō planit/ *n* a theoretical mass of gas in the clouds of gas and dust around a star that is believed to develop into a planet —**protoplanetary** /prṓtō plánitəri/ *adj*

protoplasm /prṓtō plazəm/ *n* the colourless liquid or colloidal contents of a living cell, composed of proteins, fats, and other organic substances in water, and including the nucleus and cytoplasm [Mid-19C. < German *Protoplasma* 'first created thing' < Greek *plasma* (see PLASMA)] —**protoplasmic** /prṓtō plázmik/ *adj*

protoplast /prṓtō plast/ *n* the living substance of a plant or bacterial cell, excluding the cell wall [Mid-16C. Via French and late Latin, 'first created being' < Greek *prōtoplastos* < *plastos* 'formed' < *plassein* 'to form'] —**protoplastic** /prṓtō plástik/ *adj*

protoporphyrin /prṓtō páwrfirin/ *n* a purple porphyrin acid that combines with iron to form the deep red of iron-containing proteins such as haemoglobin and cytochrome

Proto-Romance *n* the language that developed from Vulgar Latin and gave rise to the Romance languages. Some Proto-Romance forms are hypothetical and reconstructed; for others there is written evidence. —**Proto-Romance** *adj*

Proto-Semitic /prṓtō si míttik/ *n* a hypothetical reconstructed language that is believed to be the ancestor of the Semitic branch of the Afro-Asiatic family of languages —**Proto-Semitic** *adj*

protostar /prṓtō staar/ *n* an interstellar cloud of gas and dust thought to develop into a star when it has collapsed sufficiently for nuclear reactions to begin

protostome /prṓtə stōm/ *n* an invertebrate animal, e.g. a mollusc or arthropod, in which the mouth forms directly from the blastopore

prototherian /prṓtō theéri ən/ *n* an echidna, platypus, or one of many extinct related mammals. Subclass: Prototheria. [Late 19C. < PROTO- + Greek *therion* 'wild animal']

prototrophic /prṓtə trṓfik, -trófik/ *adj* describes a microorganism that has the same nutritional needs and metabolic characteristics as the wild parent strain —**prototroph** /prṓtə trōf/ *n*

prototype /prṓtə tīp/ *n* **1.** ORIGINAL USED AS MODEL the original form of something, which has the essential features and is the model for subsequent forms **2.** FULL-SIZE FUNCTIONAL MODEL a first full-size functional model to be manufactured, e.g. of a car or a machine ○ *A prototype of the solar-powered car will be on display next month.* **3.** STANDARD EXAMPLE a standard example of a particular kind, class, or group **4.** BIOL PRIMITIVE FORM a primitive form believed to be the original type of a species or group, exhibiting the essential features of the later type ■ *vti* (**-types, -typing, -typed**) CREATE PROTOTYPE to develop a prototype of something [Early 17C. Via French and late Latin < Greek *prōtotypon* 'primitive form' < *typos* 'impression'] —**pro-**

totypal /prõtə típ'l/ *adj*—**prototypic** /-típpik/ *adj*—**prototypical** *adj*—**prototypically** *adv*

protoxide /prõ tók sīd/ *n* an oxide of an element that has the lowest proportion of oxygen of all the oxides of that element

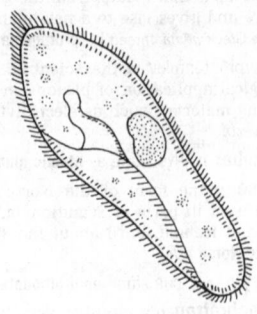

protozoan

protozoan /prõtə zṓ ən/, **protozoon** /-on/ (*plural* **-zoons** or **-zoa** /-zṓ ə/) *n* a single-celled organism that can move and feeds on organic compounds of nitrogen and carbon, e.g. an amoeba. Kingdom: *Protoctista*. [Mid-19C. < modern Latin *Protozoa* 'first animals' < Greek *zōia*, plural of *zōion* 'animal'] —**protozoal** *adj*—**protozoan** *adj*—**protozoic** *adj*

protozoology /prõtõ zõ ólləji, -zoo-/ *n* the branch of zoology that studies protozoans [Early 20C. < PROTOZOAN] —**protozoological** /prõtõ zṓ ə lójjik'l, -zoo-/ *adj*—**protozoologist** *n*

protozoon *n* MICROBIOL another spelling of **protozoan**

protract /prə trákt/ (**-tracts, -tracting, -tracted**) *vt* 1. MAKE SOMETHING LAST to make something last longer 2. PHYSIOL EXTEND BODY PART to extend or lengthen a body part 3. MATHS PLOT AND DRAW LINES to plot lines and draw them using a scale and protractor [Mid-16C. < Latin *protract-*, past participle of *protrahere* < *trahere* 'draw'] —**protractive** *adj*

protracted /prə tráktid/ *adj* lasting or drawn out for a long time —**protractedly** *adv*—**protractedness** *n*

protractile /prə trák tīl/ *adj* 1. capable of being thrust out 2. ZOOL same as **protrusile**

protraction /prə tráksh'n/ *n* 1. the act of protracting something 2. the act of drawing something such as a building or an area of land to scale, or a drawing of this kind

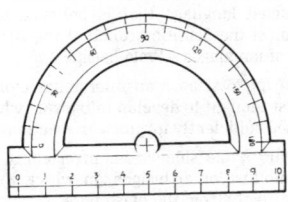

protractor

protractor /prə tráktər/ *n* 1. INSTRUMENT FOR MEASURING ANGLES an instrument shaped like a semicircle marked with the degrees of a circle, used to measure or mark out angles 2. SOMEBODY OR SOMETHING THAT LENGTHENS SOMETHING somebody or something that extends or lengthens something 3. ANAT MUSCLE THAT EXTENDS BODY PART a muscle with the function of extending a body part

~~protray~~ incorrect spelling of **portray**

protrude /prə troód/ (**-trudes, -truding, -truded**) *vti* to stick out from the surroundings, or make something do this [Early 17C. < Latin *protrudere* 'thrust forwards' < *trudere* 'thrust'] —**protrudable** *adj*—**protrudent** *adj*

protrusile /prə troó sīl/, **protrusible** /prə troózəb'l/ *adj* used to describe an organ or appendage that can be quickly extended, e.g. the mouth of many fishes or

the proboscis of nemertine worms [Mid-19C. < Latin *protrus-* (see PROTRUSION)]

protrusion /prə troózh'n/ *n* 1. something that sticks out from its surroundings 2. the act of protruding, or the state of being protruded [Mid-17C. < medieval Latin *protrusion-* < Latin *protrus-*, past participle of *protrudere* (see PROTRUDE)]

protrusive /prə troóssiv/ *adj* 1. jutting or sticking out 2. having a brash forward manner [Late 17C. < Latin *protrus-* (see PROTRUSION)] —**protrusively** *adv*

protuberance /prə tyoóbərənss/, **protuberancy** /-rənssi/ (*plural* **-cies**) *n* 1. something that sticks out from its surroundings ○ *the small fleshy protuberance that dangles down from the soft palate* 2. the fact or condition of sticking out, being swollen, or bulging [Mid-17C. < PROTUBERANT]

protuberant /prə tyoóbərənt/ *adj* sticking out from the surroundings in a bulging rounded manner [Mid-17C. < late Latin *protuberant-*, present participle of *protuberare* 'swell forwards' < Latin *tuber* 'lump'] —**protuberantly** *adv*

protuberate /prə tyoóbə rayt/ (**-ates, -ating, -ated**) *vi* to stick out from the surroundings in a bulging rounded manner [Late 16C. < Latin *protuberat-*, past participle of *protuberare* (see PROTUBERANT)]

protyle /prṓ tīl/ *n* an imaginary substance from which the chemical elements were supposed to have been formed [Late 19C. < PROTO- + Greek *hulē* 'matter']

proud /prowd/ *adj* 1. PLEASED AND SATISFIED feeling pleased and satisfied, e.g. about having done something or about owning something ○ *I am very proud to be here today to give you this award.* 2. HAVING SELF-RESPECT having a proper amount of self-respect 3. FOSTERING FEELINGS OF PRIDE characterized by feelings of pride ○ *the proudest moment in your life* 4. ARROGANT having an exaggerated opinion of personal worth or abilities 5. IMPRESSIVE looking magnificent and impressive, or behaving in an impressive way ○ *the proud spires of Oxford* 6. HIGH-SPIRITED high-spirited and strong ○ *a proud horse* 7. PROJECTING projecting slightly from a surrounding surface [Pre-12C. < Old French *prud* < Latin *prodesse* 'be beneficial', literally 'be for' < *esse* 'be'] —**proudly** *adv*—**proudness** *n* ◇ **do somebody proud** 1. to treat somebody well and generously 2. to bring honour or distinction to somebody

SYNONYMS *proud, arrogant, conceited, egotistical, vain*
CORE MEANING: describing somebody who is pleased with himself or herself

proud feeling pleased and satisfied about having done something or about owning something ○ *We were very proud of our DIY project.* **arrogant** feeling or showing self-importance and contempt for others ○ *What makes this arrogant man think that I would be interested in him?* ○ *Sometimes the chairman displays not just cockiness, but an almost arrogant attitude.* **conceited** having or showing an excessively high opinion of your own qualities or abilities ○ *She was less brilliant than her sister and also, perhaps as a consequence, less conceited.* ○ *I don't know how to say this without sounding conceited, but my son is really something special.* **egotistical** having an exaggerated sense of self-importance, especially tending to speak or write about yourself excessively ○ *a documentary that portrays her as egotistical and publicity-hungry* ○ *an intensely egotistical and unfeeling man* **vain** excessively proud, especially of personal appearance ○ *He was vain about his looks, and even more vain about the state of his physique.* ○ *Being vain, she did not want to admit that her German was insufficient for a diplomatic conversation.*

Proudhon /proódon/, **Pierre Joseph** (1809–65) French writer and revolutionary leader who condemned the abuses of wealth and power. His radical theories had an important influence on the development of socialism and anarchism.

> 'Property is theft.'
> [Pierre Joseph Proudhon, *Qu'est-ce que la propriété* (*What is Property?*); 1840]

Proulx /proó/, **E. Annie** (*b.* 1935) US writer best known for her novel *The Shipping News* (1993) which was awarded the 1994 Pulitzer Prize for fiction

Marcel Proust

Proust /proost/, **Marcel** (1871–1922) French novelist. He wrote a series of partly autobiographical novels, *À la recherche du temps perdu* (*Remembrance of Things Past*) (1913–27). See Cultural note at **remembrance** —**Proustian** *adj*

> 'It is in moments of illness that we are compelled to recognize that we live not alone but chained to a creature of a different kingdom, whole worlds apart, who has no knowledge of us and by whom it is impossible to make ourselves understood: our body.'
> [Marcel Proust, 'Le Côté de Guermantes' ('The Guermantes Way)', *À la recherche du temps perdu* (*Remembrance of Things Past*); 1913–27]

proustite /proóst īt/ *n* a deep red mineral consisting of silver arsenic sulphide. Use: source of silver. [Mid-19C. After Joseph L. *Proust* (1754–1826), French chemist]

prov. *abbr* 1. province 2. provincial 3. provisional

Prov. *abbr* 1. Provençal 2. BIBLE Proverbs 3. EDUC, RELIG Provost

prove /proov/ (**proves, proving, proved, proved** or **proven** /prṓv'n, proov'n/) *v* 1. *vt* ESTABLISH TRUTH OF SOMETHING to establish the truth or existence of something by providing evidence or argument 2. *vti* TURN OUT TO BE SOMETHING to turn out to be a particular thing or a thing of a particular character after time or testing ○ *It proved impossible to dislodge the rock.* 3. **prove yourself** *vr* DEMONSTRATE COMPETENCE to show yourself to be competent and worthy ○ *eager to prove himself in his new job* ○ *proved herself more than capable of achieving excellent results* 4. *vt* CHEM, MINERALS TEST SOMETHING TO DETERMINE CHARACTERISTICS to subject something to scientific analysis to determine its worth or characteristics 5. *vt* MATHS CHECK RESULT OF CALCULATION to verify that a mathematical result is correct 6. *vt* MATHS DEMONSTRATE TRUTH OF HYPOTHESIS to demonstrate that a hypothesis or proposition is true 7. *vt* LAW DEMONSTRATE THAT WILL IS GENUINE to establish that a will is genuine or valid 8. *vt* PRINTING, ARTS MAKE IMPRESSION OF SOMETHING to make a test impression of a negative, etching, or type 9. *vi* FOOD RISE IN WARM PLACE to rise in a warm place before being baked (*refers to dough*) [12C. Via Old French *prover* < Latin *probare* 'test, prove to be good' < *probus* 'good'] —**provability** /proóvə bílləti/ *n* —**provable** *adj*—**provably** *adv*

USAGE proved or proven? The past participles *proved* and *proven* are both often used as verbs, with auxiliaries, and also as predicative adjectives (after *be*). Whether to say, for example, *We have proved our case* or *We have proven our case*, and *The case is proved* or *The case is proven* is a matter of choice. *Proved* is more common in British English. It is not, however, ordinarily employed as an adjective preceding a noun: *proven case* is the standard form.

ORIGIN The Latin word *probus* 'good', from which *prove* is derived, is also the source of English *approve, probable, probe, probity, proof, reprobate,* and *reprove.*

proven /prṓv'n, proov'n/ *adj* 1. done or used before and known to work or be satisfactory 2. shown to be true beyond any doubt —**provenly** *adv*

provenance /próvənənss/ *n* 1. the place of origin of something 2. the source and ownership history of a work of art or literature or of an archaeological

find [Late 18C. Via French < Latin *provenire* 'arise', literally 'come forth' < *venire* 'come']

SYNONYMS See ***origin.***

Provençal /próvvon saál/ *n* **1.** **LANGUAGE OF SE FRANCE** a Romance language spoken in southeastern France, closely related to French, Italian, and Catalan. Native speakers: 4 million. **2.** **SOMEBODY FROM PROVENCE** somebody who comes from Provence ■ *adj* **1.** **OF PROVENCE** relating to Provence, or its people or culture **2.** **OF LANGUAGE OF PROVENCE** relating to the Provençal language [Late 16C. Via French < Latin *provincialis* 'provincial' < *provincia* (see PROVINCE), colloquial name for S Gaul during Roman rule]

Provençale /próvvon saál/ *adj* prepared with olive oil, garlic, herbs, and tomatoes [Mid-19C. < French *à la provençale* 'in the Provençal manner']

Provence /pro vóNss/ region in southeastern France, bordering the Mediterranean Sea. It was an ancient Roman province.

provender /próvvindər/ *n* **1.** food for livestock, especially hay or other dry fodder (*archaic*) **2.** food (*literary or humorous*) [14C. < Old French *provendre*, variant of *provende*, alteration (influenced by Latin *providere* 'to supply') of *praebenda* 'things to be given']

provenience /prō véeni ənss/ *n US* HIST same as **provenance** [Late 19C. < Latin *provenient-*, present participle of *provenire* (see PROVENANCE)]

proventriculus /prō ven tríkyŏoləss/ (*plural* **-li** /-lī/) *n* **1.** **PART OF BIRD'S STOMACH** the first part of a bird's stomach, where digestive enzymes are mixed with food before it goes to the gizzard. It is analogous to the gizzard in insects and crustaceans. **2.** **PART OF INVERTEBRATE'S STOMACH** the thin-walled section of the stomach of some invertebrates **3.** **PART OF INSECT'S STOMACH** the part of the foregut in some insects that has teeth or plates for grinding food —**proventricular** *adj*

proverb /próvvurb/ *n* a short well-known saying that expresses an obvious truth and often offers advice [14C. Via French < Latin *proverbium* 'saying, saw' < *verbum* 'word']

proverbial /prə vúrbi əl/ *adj* **1.** **EXPRESSED AS PROVERB** expressed as a proverb, or resembling a proverb either in form or because of being widely known or referred to **2.** **USED IN PROVERB** used to refer to a particular proverb or similar well-known phrase ○ *She was behaving like the proverbial cat on hot bricks.* **3.** **WELL-KNOWN** widely known and recognized, and often viewed as stereotypical ○ *their proverbial hospitality* ■ *n* **WORD SUBSTITUTE** used to refer to something in an expression or saying that is not being explicitly stated (*informal; often used euphemistically*) ○ *You'll find they've got you by the proverbials.* —**proverbially** *adv*

Proverbs /próvvurbz/ *n* a book of the Bible that consists of the proverbs of wise men, including Solomon (*takes a singular verb*) See table at **Bible**

provide /prə vīd/ (**-vides, -viding, -vided**) *v* **1.** *vt* **SUPPLY SOMEBODY WITH SOMETHING** to supply somebody with something, or be a source of something needed or wanted by somebody **2.** *vt* **MAKE SOMETHING AVAILABLE** to make something available to somebody **3.** *vt* LAW **REQUIRE SOMETHING AS CONDITION** to require something in advance as a condition or as part of a contract (*formal*) **4.** *vi* **TAKE PRECAUTIONS** to take precautions to prevent harm or bring about good ○ *provide against disaster* **5.** *vi* **SUPPLY MEANS OF SUPPORT** to supply the material means of support for somebody ○ *provides for his children* [15C. < Latin *providere* 'prepare in advance, supply', literally 'see ahead' < *videre* 'see']

provided /prə vídid/, **provided that** *conj* same as **providing** ○ *He can play provided that he has no injuries.*

providence /próvvid'nss/ *n* **1.** *also* **Providence** **GOD'S GUIDANCE** the wisdom, care, and guidance believed to be provided by God **2.** *also* **Providence** **GOD** God perceived as a caring force guiding humankind **3.** **GOOD JUDGMENT AND MANAGEMENT** good judgment and foresight in the management of affairs or resources [14C. Directly or via French < Latin *providentia* 'foresight' < *provident-*, present participle of *providere* (see PROVIDE)]

Providence /próvvid'nss/ capital of Rhode Island and its largest city, located in the northeastern part of the state. Population: 175,901 (2002 estimate).

provident /próvvid'nt/ *adj* **1.** carefully preparing for future needs **2.** economical in the use of resources [15C. < Latin *provident-*, present participle of *providere* (see PROVIDE)]

providential /próvvi dénsh'l/ *adj* **1.** relating to or believed to be determined by providence **2.** so favourable that it seems determined by providence

provident society *n* FIN same as **friendly society**

provider /prə vídər/ *n* **1.** an organization or company that provides access to a service or system such as a mobile phone, cable, or computer network ○ *an Internet provider* ○ *a health care provider* **2.** somebody who provides material support for somebody or something, especially a family

providing /prə víding/, **providing that** *conj* on the understanding that another thing will also occur or be done ○ *We can save these people providing we get the equipment we need.*

province /próvvinss/ *n* **1.** POL **ADMINISTRATIVE DIVISION OF NATION** an administrative region or division of a country **2.** **AREA OF KNOWLEDGE** a sphere of knowledge or activity **3.** CHR **ECCLESIASTICAL TERRITORY** an ecclesiastical territory of more than two dioceses, under the jurisdiction of an archbishop or metropolitan **4.** ANCIENT HIST **REGION OF ROMAN EMPIRE** a country or region controlled by the ancient Roman Empire through an appointed governor **5.** ECOL **AREA CHARACTERIZED BY PLANTS AND ANIMALS** a biogeographical area within a region that is defined by the plants and animals that inhabit it ■ **provinces** *npl* **NONMETROPOLITAN PARTS OF NATION** the parts of a country exclusive of the capital and larger cities [14C. Directly or via French < Latin *provincia* 'territory conquered by Rome' < *vincere* 'conquer']

Provincetown /próvvinss town/ town in southeastern Massachusetts, at the tip of Cape Cod. It is an artists' colony, and the site of the Pilgrims' first landing in 1620. Population: 3,484 (2002 estimate).

provincial /prə vínsh'l/ *adj* **1.** **OF PROVINCE** belonging to or coming from a province **2.** **UNSOPHISTICATED AND NARROW-MINDED** unsophisticated and unwilling to accept new ideas or ways of thinking **3.** ARCHIT, FURNITURE **SIMPLE AND PLAIN** in a simple and plain decorative style ■ *n* **1.** **SOMEBODY FROM PROVINCES** somebody who comes from or lives in the provinces **2.** **SOMEBODY UNSOPHISTICATED** an unsophisticated or narrow-minded person **3.** CHR **HEAD OF PROVINCE** the head of an ecclesiastical province or of a religious order in a province [14C. Directly or via French < Latin *provincialis* < *provincia* (see PROVINCE)] —**provinciality** /prə vínshi állәti/ *n* —**provincially** *adv*

Provincial Council *n* a council that formerly administered a New Zealand province

provincial court *n* a Canadian court that deals with less serious offences and whose judges are appointed and paid by the province

provincialism /prə vínshə'lizəm/ *n* **1.** narrow-mindedness and lack of sophistication **2.** something that originates in a province, e.g. a word, phrase, trait, or custom

provincial police *n* a Canadian police force that has jurisdiction within a province, but not in urban areas, which have their own municipal police

proving ground /próoving-/ *n* a place or situation in which somebody or something new is tried out or tested

provirus /prō vīrəss/ *n* a form of a virus that is integrated into the genetic material of the host and passed on from one cell generation to the next

provision /prə vízh'n/ *n* **1.** **SUPPLYING OF SOMETHING** the act of providing or supplying something ○ *the provision of after-school clubs* **2.** **ACTION TAKEN TO PREPARE FOR SOMETHING** a preparatory step taken to meet a possible or expected need ○ *No provision has been made for people with disabilities.* **3.** **SOMETHING PROVIDED** something provided or supplied **4.** LAW **LEGAL CLAUSE STATING CONDITION** a clause in a law or contract stating that a condition must be met **5.** ACCT **ESTIMATE OF LIABILITY** an estimate of a known liability such as depreciation, the value of which cannot be explicitly determined ■ *npl* **1.** **provisions** **FOOD AND OTHER SUPPLIES** supplies of food and other necessities, especially for a journey **2.** *Carib* **STARCHY FRUIT AND VEGETABLES** edible tubers such as eddoes, dasheen, cassava (**ground provisions**) or starchy fruit and vegetables such as breadfruit ■ *vt* (**-sions, -sioning, -sioned**) **PROVIDE SOMEBODY WITH SUPPLIES** to provide somebody with supplies, especially for a journey [14C. Via French < Latin *provision-* 'foresight, preparation' < *provis-*, past participle of *providere* (see PROVIDE)] —**provisioner** *n*

provisional /prə vízh'nəl/ *adj* **TEMPORARY OR CONDITIONAL** temporary or conditional, pending confirmation or validation ○ *a provisional government* ■ *n* **1.** *US* HR **SOMEBODY HIRED TEMPORARILY** somebody hired temporarily for a job, especially before being qualified to do it permanently **2.** STAMPS **TEMPORARY POSTAGE STAMP** a postage stamp used temporarily until an official permanent stamp is issued —**provisionally** *adv*

Provisional *n* a member of an unofficial faction of the Irish Republican Army that was originally set up to strive for an independent Ireland by force of arms —**Provisional** *adj*

provisional licence *n* a driving licence for people who have not yet passed a driving test and are subject to various restrictions. Aus term **learner's licence.** N Am term **learner's permit**

proviso /prə vízō/ (*plural* **-sos** or **-soes**) *n* **1.** a condition asked as part of an agreement **2.** a clause introducing a condition in a contract [15C. < medieval Latin *proviso quod* 'provided that' < Latin *proviso*, form of past participle of *providere* (see PROVIDE)]

provisory /prə vízəri/ *adj* **1.** stating a condition **2.** same as **provisional** [Early 17C. < medieval Latin *provisorius* 'of papal provision' < Latin *provisus*, past participle of *providere* (see PROVIDE)] —**provisorily** *adv*

provitamin /prō víttəmin/ *n* a chemical compound (**precursor**) that is converted to a vitamin during normal biochemical processes

Provo /prṓvō/ (*plural* **-vos**) *n* POL same as **Provisional** (*informal*) [Late 20C. Shortening]

provocation /próvvə káysh'n/ *n* **1.** **ACT OF PROVOKING** the act of provoking somebody or something **2.** **CAUSE OF ANGER** something that makes somebody angry or indignant **3.** LAW **REASON FOR ATTACKING SOMEBODY** something that incites somebody to attack somebody else [14C. Directly or via French < Latin *provocation-* < *provocare* (see PROVOKE)]

provocative /prə vókətiv/ *adj* **1.** deliberately aimed at exciting or annoying people ○ *a provocative remark* **2.** intended to arouse somebody sexually [15C. Directly or via French < late Latin *provocativus* < *provocare* (see PROVOKE)] —**provocatively** *adv* —**provocativeness** *n*

provoke /prə vṓk/ (**-vokes, -voking, -voked**) *vt* **1.** **MAKE SOMEBODY FEEL ANGRY** to make somebody feel angry or indignant **2.** **ELICIT RESPONSE** to be the cause or occasion of an emotion or response ○ *Her bravery provoked a lot of sympathy.* **3.** **STIR SOMEBODY TO EMOTION** to stir somebody to an emotion or response ○ *The article provoked me to write a letter to the editor.* **4.** **INCITE SOMETHING** to bring something about intentionally ○ *provoke an argument* **5.** **CAUSE ACTIVITY** to serve as the stimulus for an activity ○ *Her new novel should provoke a lot of discussion.* [14C. Directly or via French < Latin *provocare* 'summon' < *vocare* 'to call' < *vox* 'voice'] —**provoker** *n* —**provokingly** *adv*

provolone /prṓvə lṓni/ *n* a semisoft Italian cheese originally made from water buffalo's milk and now from cow's milk, often smoked and used widely in cooking [Mid-20C. < Italian < *provola* 'buffalo's milk cheese']

provost /próvvəst/ *n* **1.** **HEAD OF EDUCATIONAL ESTABLISHMENT** the head of some educational establishments, especially some Oxford and Cambridge colleges **2.** **SENIOR DIGNITARY OF CATHEDRAL** the senior dignitary of a cathedral or collegiate church **3.** **HEAD OF SCOTTISH CITY GOVERNMENT** until 1975, somebody elected to be head of government in a city, town, or borough in Scotland. Provost is still used as a courtesy title by some Scottish local authorities. [Pre-12C. < medieval Latin *propositus*, alteration of Latin *praepositus* 'somebody placed in front' < *ponere* 'to place']

provost court /próvvəst-, prə vṓ-/ *n* a military court set up in an occupied hostile territory for the trial of minor offences

provost guard /próvvəst-, prə vṓ-/ *n US* a detail of soldiers performing police duties under the authority of the provost marshal

provost marshal /próvvəst-, prə vṓ-/ *n* the army officer in charge of a unit of military police

prow /prow/ *n* **1.** the forward part of a ship **2.** the projecting front part of something [Mid-16C. Via French *proue* and Latin *prora* < Greek *prōra* 'front of a ship' < *pro* 'forward']

prowess /prów ess/ *n* **1.** exceptional ability or skill **2.** extraordinary valour and ability in combat [13C. < Old French *proesce* 'bravery' < *prou* 'brave', variant of *prud* (see PROUD)]

prowl /prowl/ *vti* (**prowls, prowling, prowled**) to roam around an area stealthily in search of prey, food, or opportunity ■ *n* the act of roaming stealthily for prey, food, or opportunity [14C. Origin ?] ◇ **on the prowl** moving around stealthily looking for somebody or something

prowl car *n US* POLICE same as **squad car**

prowler /prówlər/ *n* **1.** somebody who moves stealthily around an area looking for an opportunity to commit a criminal act **2.** a person or animal that prowls

prox. *abbr* proximo

proxemics /prok séemiks/ *n* the study of the distance individuals maintain between each other in social interaction and its significance (*takes a singular verb*) [Mid-20C. < PROXIMITY, after PHONEMICS]

proximal /próksim'l/ *adj* **1.** nearer to the point of reference or to the centre of the body than something else is. For example, the elbow is proximal to the hand. **2.** describes the surface of a tooth nearest to either the one behind it or the one in front of it **3.** same as **proximate** [Early 18C. < Latin *proximus* (see PROXIMITY)] —**proximally** *adv*

proximate /próksimət/ *adj* **1.** PROBABLE most likely ○ *The proximate cause of the damage must be established.* **2.** NEAREST nearest in order, time, or place **3.** VERY CLOSE very close in space or time **4.** ABOUT TO HAPPEN soon to appear or take place **5.** APPROXIMATE almost accurate [Late 16C. < Latin *proximat-*, past participle of *proximare* 'come near' < *proximus* (see PROXIMITY)] —**proximately** *adv* —**proximation** /próksi máysh'n/ *n*

proxime accessit /próksimi ak séssit, próksi may ək-/ *n* somebody who comes immediately after the winner in a competitive examination (*formal*) [< Latin, 'he or she came very close']

proximity /prok símməti/ *n* closeness in space or time [15C. < Latin *proximitas* 'nearness' < *proximus* 'nearest', superlative of *prope* 'near']

proximity card *n* a plastic card carrying electronically coded information accessed by holding the card near a reading device. Proximity cards are often used to open doors as part of a security system.

proximity fuse *n* a fuse, usually part of a warhead, that will activate and cause detonation when the warhead is at a specific distance from the target

proximity operator *n* a Boolean operator separating words or phrases in a text search that directs the search engine to locate pages in which the words are near one another in any direction, the acceptable distance varying among search engines

proximo /próksimō/ *adv* occurring during the next month (*archaic*) ○ *proposed a meeting for the fifth proximo* [Mid-19C. < Latin *proximo (mense)* 'in the next (month)']

proxy /próksi/ (*plural* **-ies**) *n* **1.** AUTHORIZED CAPACITY OF SUBSTITUTE the function or power of somebody authorized to act for another person **2.** SUBSTITUTE somebody authorized to act for another person **3.** AUTHORIZATION DOCUMENT FOR STAND-IN a document authorizing somebody to act for another person **4.** LAW, FIN DOCUMENT AUTHORIZING VOTE ON ANOTHER'S STOCK a document authorizing somebody to vote on matters of corporate stock on behalf of somebody else [15C. < medieval Latin *procuratia*, alteration of Latin *procuratio* 'care, management' < *procurare* (see PROCURE)]

proxy server *n* a computer system that gives users more rapid access to popular websites by storing frequently requested and recently used items

Prozac /prō zak/ *tdmk* a trademark for the antidepressant drug fluoxetine

PRP *abbr* **1.** performance-related pay **2.** profit-related pay

prs *abbr* pairs

prude /prood/ *n* somebody who is easily offended by matters relating to sex or nudity [Early 18C. < French, back-formation < Old French *prudefemme* (misunderstood as 'virtuous woman'), feminine of *prud'homme* < assumed *pro de ome* 'fine (thing) of a man'] —**prudery** /próodəri/ *n* —**prudish** *adj* —**prudishly** *adv* —**prudishness** *n*

prudent /próod'nt/ *adj* **1.** HAVING GOOD SENSE having good sense in dealing with practical matters **2.** CAREFULLY CONSIDERING CONSEQUENCES using good judgment to consider likely consequences and act accordingly **3.** CAREFUL IN MANAGING RESOURCES careful in managing resources so as to provide for the future [14C. Directly or via French < Latin *prudent-*, contraction of *provident-* (see PROVIDENT)] —**prudence** *n* —**prudently** *adv*

SYNONYMS See *cautious.*

prudential /proo dénsh'l/ *adj* **1.** resulting from, depending on, or marked by prudence **2.** using prudence, especially in business matters —**prudentially** *adv*

pruinose /próo i nōss, -nōz/ *adj* describes something such as a fruit or a leaf that has a white powdery coating [Early 19C. < Latin *pruinosus* < *pruina* 'hoar frost']

prune[1] /proon/ *v* (**prunes, pruning, pruned**) **1.** *vti* CUT BRANCHES OF PLANT to cut branches away from a plant to encourage fuller growth **2.** *vt* REDUCE SOMETHING BY REMOVING UNWANTED MATERIAL to reduce something by removing whatever is unnecessary or unwanted **3.** *vt* REMOVE SOMETHING UNNECESSARY to remove something considered unnecessary or unwanted ■ *n* PRUNING OF SOMETHING an act of pruning a plant or something with unnecessary or unwanted parts [14C. < Old French *proignier* 'cut in a rounded shape in front' < Latin *rotundus* 'round'] —**prunable** *adj* —**pruner** *n*

prune[2] /proon/ *n* **1.** DRIED PLUM a plum that has been preserved by drying **2.** *N Am* PLUM TO BE DRIED a plum suitable for drying (*informal*) **3.** OFFENSIVE TERM an offensive term that deliberately insults somebody's intelligence, competence, or ability to interest others (*insult*) [14C. Via French and Latin < Greek *prounon*, variant of *proumnon* 'plum']

prunella[1] /proo néllə/ *n* a wool fabric with a twill weave. Use: academic gowns, clerical robes, shoe uppers. [Mid-17C. Alteration of French *prunelle* 'sloe', diminutive of *prune* 'plum' (see PRUNE[2])]

prunella[2] /proo néllə/ (*plural* **-las** or *same*) *n* PLANTS same as **selfheal** [Late 16C. < modern Latin *Prunella* < *prunella*, alteration of medieval Latin *brunella*, a disease in which the tongue develops a brown coating, which selfheal was thought to cure]

prunelle /proo nél/ *n* **1.** a sweet French liqueur flavoured with sloes **2.** TEXTILES same as **prunella**[1] [15C. < French (see PRUNELLA[1])]

pruning hook /próoning-/ *n* a tool with a hooked blade and sometimes a long handle, used to prune trees and bushes

prurient /próori ənt/ *adj* having or intended to arouse an unwholesome interest in sexual matters [Mid-17C. < Latin *prurient-*, present participle of *prurire* 'itch, long for'] —**prurience** *n* —**pruriently** *adv*

prurigo /proor rígō/ *n* a chronic inflammatory skin disease causing small itchy swellings [Mid-17C. < Latin, 'itching' < *prurire* 'itch, long for'] —**pruriginous** /proor ríjjinəss/ *adj*

pruritus /proor rítəss/ *n* an intense feeling of itchiness [Mid-17C. < Latin < 'itch, long for']

prusik /prússik/ *n* **1.** *also* **Prusik knot** KNOT ATTACHING SLING TO ROPE a knot used to tie a small sling to a climbing rope, forming a loop that holds fast when weighted but can be slid along the rope when unweighted **2.** *also* **Prusik** SLING ATTACHED TO ROPE a small sling attached to a climbing rope using a prusik knot ■ *vi* (**-iks, -iking, -iked**) ASCEND OR DESCEND ROPE to ascend or descend a climbing rope using a prusik sling [Mid-20C. After Karl *Prusik* (1897–1961), Austrian mountaineer]

Prussia /prúshə/ former state and kingdom in Germany. Its capital was Berlin. —**Prussian** *adj, n*

Prussian blue *n* **1.** *also* **prussian blue** a water-insoluble blue iron pigment **2.** a rich dark blue colour tinged with green [Because discovered in 1704 by a Prussian dyer called Diesbach] —**Prussian-blue** *adj*

prussiate /prúshi ət/ *n* **1.** a chemical compound that is a ferrocyanide or ferricyanide **2.** a chemical compound that is a salt of hydrocyanic acid [Late 18C. < *prussic* (see PRUSSIC ACID)]

prussic acid /prússik-/ *n* CHEM same as **hydrocyanic acid** [< *Prussian*, because first obtained from Prussian blue]

pry[1] /prī/ *vi* (**pries, prying, pried**) BE INQUISITIVE to enquire nosily or excessively about somebody's private affairs ■ *n* (*plural* **pries**) **1.** ACT OF PRYING the act of prying into somebody's private affairs **2.** INQUISITIVE PERSON somebody who pries into other people's private affairs [14C. Origin ?] —**pryingly** *adv*

pry[2] /prī/ (**pries, prying, pried**) *vt N Am* to open or part something by using leverage [Early 19C. Back-formation < PRISE, misunderstood as 3rd person present singular]

pryer *n* another spelling of **prier**

prytaneum /príttə née əm/ (*plural* **-nea** /-née ə/) *n* in ancient Greece, a public building used as a meeting place [Early 17C. Via Latin < Greek *prutaneion* < *prutanis* 'prince, ruler']

Przewalski's horse /pəzhə válskiz-, shə-/ *n* a wild horse with a stocky body, a chestnut coat, and an erect dark mane. Native to: Asia. Latin name: *Equus caballus przevalskii*. [Late 19C. After N. M. *Przhevalskiĭ* (1839–88), Russian explorer]

ps *abbr* postscript

PS *abbr* **1.** Passenger Steamer **2.** POL Permanent Secretary **3.** GRAM phrase structure **4.** Police Sergeant **5.** postscript **6.** private secretary **7.** THEATRE prompt side

Ps. *abbr* BIBLE (Book of) Psalms

PSA *abbr* **1.** MED prostate-specific antigen **2.** *NZ* Public Service Association

Psa. *abbr* BIBLE (Book of) Psalms

psalm /saam/, **Psalm** *n* a sacred song or poem of praise, especially one in the Book of Psalms in the Bible [12C. Via late Latin < Greek *psalmos* 'harp song' < *psallein* 'to pluck'] —**psalmic** *adj*

psalmist /sáamist/ *n* the author of a psalm

psalmody /sáamədi, sálm-/ (*plural* **-dies**) *n* **1.** PSALM SINGING the singing of psalms in divine worship **2.** MUSIC MUSICAL ARRANGEMENTS FOR PSALMS the prescribed arrangements for singing individual psalms from the Book of Psalms **3.** SET OF PSALMS a collection of psalms [14C. Via late Latin < Greek *psalmōidia* < *psalmos* (see PSALM) + *ōidē* 'song'] —**psalmodic** /saa móddik, sal-/ *adj* —**psalmodist** *n*

Psalms /saamz/ *n* a book of the Bible that consists of 150 poems and hymns to God, traditionally attributed to King David (*takes a singular verb*) See table at **Bible**

Psalter /sáwltər, sóltər/, **psalter** *n* a book containing psalms, or the Book of Psalms, used in worship [Pre-12C. < ecclesiastical Latin *psalterium* 'Book of Psalms' < Latin (see PSALTERY)]

psalterium /sawl téeri əm, sol-/ (*plural* **-ria** /-ri ə/) *n* ZOOL same as **omasum** [Mid-19C. < Latin, 'stringed instrument' (see PSALTERY)]

psaltery /sáwltəri, sóltəri/ (*plural* **-ies**) *n* an ancient musical instrument with numerous strings, plucked with the fingers or with a plectrum [13C. Via French < Latin *psalterium* 'stringed instrument' < Greek *psaltērion* 'stringed instrument played by plucking' < *psallein* 'to pluck']

psammite /sámmīt/ *n* **1.** a rock formed principally of sand **2.** a metamorphosed sandstone containing large amounts of quartz [Mid-19C. < Greek *psammos* 'sand'] —**psammitic** /sa míttik/ *adj*

p's and q's /péez ən kyóoz/ *npl* the polite manners and behaviour that somebody adopts when eager to make a good impression ○ *We'd better mind our p's and q's.* [Origin ?]

PSA test *n* a test for prostate cancer that detects the presence in the blood of a protein produced by prostate cells. Full form **prostate-specific antigen test**

PSBR *abbr* public sector borrowing requirement

PSE *n* the study of social, especially health-related issues as a school subject. Full form **Personal and Social Education**

psephology /si fólləji/ *n* the statistical study of elections [Mid-20C. < Greek *psēphos* 'pebble, vote'; from the Greek practice of using pebbles to vote] —**psephological**

/séffə lójjik'l/ *adj* —**psephologically** *adv* —**psephologist** *n*

pseud /syood/ *n* somebody who pretends to know much about art and culture [Mid-20C. Shortening of PSEUDO]

pseud. *abbr* pseudonym

pseud- *prefix* same as **pseudo-** (*sometimes used before vowels*)

pseudaxis /syoo dáksiss/ (*plural* -**axes** /-ák seez/) *n* BOT same as **sympodium**

pseudepigrapha /syoódi píggrəfə/ *npl* anonymous or pseudonymous writings professing to be biblical, but not included in any biblical canon [Late 17C. < Greek, form of *pseudepigraphos* 'with false title' < *epigraphein* 'write on' (see EPIGRAPH)] —**pseudepigraphic** /syoód epi gráffik/ *adj* —**pseudepigraphical** *adj* —**pseudepigraphous** *adj*

pseudo /syoódō/ *adj* not authentic or sincere, in spite of appearances [14C. < Greek *pseudo-* < *pseudēs* (see PSEUDO-)]

pseudo- *prefix* **1.** similar ○ *pseudobulb* **2.** false, spurious ○ *pseudoscience* [< Greek *pseudēs* < *pseudein* 'to lie']

pseudoarchaic *adj*	**pseudoknowledge** *n*
pseudoboycott *n*	**pseudoliberation** *n*
pseudo-Christian *n, adj*	**pseudomedical** *adj*
pseudocode *n*	**pseudomembrane** *n*
pseudoconcept *n*	**pseudo-obstruction** *n*
pseudodemocracy *n*	**pseudoproblem** *n*
pseudodemocratic *adj*	**pseudoprophet** *n*
pseudoenquiry *n*	**pseudoquestion** *n*
pseudoequality *n*	**pseudorabies** *n*
pseudoevent *n*	**pseudorational** *adj*
pseudoextinction *n*	**pseudorationalism** *n*
pseudo-Gothic *n, adj*	**pseudoreligion** *n*
pseudogovernment *n*	**pseudoreligious** *adj*
pseudohermaphrodite *n*	**pseudo-Renaissance** *adj, n*
pseudohistory *n*	
pseudoideal *adj*	**pseudostatement** *n*
pseudointellectual *adj, n*	**pseudo-Tudor** *adj, n*

pseudobulb /syoódō bulb/ *n* a thickened part of a stem that lies above the ground, e.g. in many orchids

pseudocarp /syoódō kaarp/ *n* a fruit formed by combining the ripened ovary with another structure, often the receptacle, e.g. a strawberry [Mid-19C. < PSEUDO- + Greek *karpos* 'fruit'] —**pseudocarpous** /syoódō kaárpəss/ *adj*

pseudoclassic /syoódō klássik/ *adj* posing as or mistakenly believed to be classic

pseudoclassicism /syoódō klássisizəm/ *n* the use in art and literature of ancient Greek and Roman styles —**pseudoclassical** *adj*

pseudocoelomate /syoódō seeləmət, -mayt/ *n* an invertebrate that has a fluid-filled body cavity not lined with mesoderm tissue, e.g. a nematode or rotifer —**pseudocoelomate** *adj*

pseudocyesis /syoódō sī éessiss/ (*plural* -**eses** /-eés seez/) *n* MED same as **phantom pregnancy** (*technical*) [Mid-19C. < PSEUDO- + Greek *kuēsis* 'conception']

pseudogene /syoódō jeen/ *n* a nonfunctional DNA sequence that is very similar to the sequence of a functional gene

pseudohermaphroditism /syoódō hur máffrə dītizəm/ *n* a condition in which somebody has either ovaries (**female pseudohermaphroditism**) or testes (**male pseudohermaphroditism**) but has external genitalia of ambiguous appearance

pseudo-intransitive *adj* used to describe a normally transitive verb employed when its direct object is not explicitly stated or when its direct object becomes the subject of the sentence

pseudomonad /syoódō mó nad/ *n* a rod-shaped bacterium that lives in soil or decomposing organic material. Some pseudomonads are pathogenic to plants and animals. Genus: *Pseudomonas*. [Early 20C. < modern Latin *Pseudomonad-* 'false monad' < late Latin *monad-* (see MONAD)]

pseudomorph /syoódō mawrf/ *n* **1.** a mineral that has replaced another and taken its shape **2.** an irregular or deceptive form —**pseudomorphic** /syoódō máwrfik/ *adj* —**pseudomorphism** *n* —**pseudomorphous** /syoódō máwrfəss/ *adj*

pseudonym /syoódənim/ *n* a name that is not somebody's original name, especially one used by an author in publications [Mid-19C. Via French *pseudonyme* < Greek *pseudōnumon* 'false name' < *onuma* 'name'] —**pseudonymity** /syoódə nímməti/ *n* —**pseudonymous** /syoo dónniməss/ *adj*

pseudopodium /syoódō pṓdi əm/ (*plural* -**dia** /-di ə/), **pseudopod** /syoódō pod/ *n* a temporary cytoplasmic protrusion in amoebae and other protozoans, used for locomotion and to take up food

pseudopregnancy /syoódō prégnənssi/ (*plural* -**cies**) *n* MED same as **phantom pregnancy**

pseudorandom /syoódō rándəm/ *adj* relating to random numbers generated by a computational process

pseudoscience /syoódō sī ənss/ *n* a theory or method doubtfully or mistakenly held to be scientific —**pseudoscientific** /soódō sī ən tíffik/ *adj* —**pseudoscientist** /-sī əntist/ *n*

pseudosophistication /syoódō sə físti káysh'n/ *n* false or pretended sophistication

pseudotuberculosis /syoódō tyōo búrkyōo lóssiss/ *n* a disease marked by the formation of nodules of inflamed tissue similar to those in tuberculosis, but not caused by the tubercle bacillus

pseudovector /syoódō véktər/ *n* a quantity, e.g. area or torque, that has magnitude and direction but whose component signs are unchanged if the signs of a set of coordinate axes are reversed

psf, **p.s.f.** *abbr* MEASURE pounds per square foot

Psge *abbr* Passage (*used in addresses*)

pshaw /pshaw/ *interj* used to express disbelief, impatience, or contempt (*dated*) [Late 17C. Natural exclamation]

PSHE *n* the study of social, especially health-related issues as a school subject. Full form **Personal, Social, and Health Education**

psi[1] /psī/ *n* the 23rd letter of the Greek alphabet, represented in the English alphabet as 'ps'. See table at **alphabet** [15C. < Greek *psei*]

psi[2], **p.s.i.** *abbr* MEASURE pounds per square inch

psia, **p.s.i.a.** *abbr* MEASURE pounds per square inch, absolute

psid, **p.s.i.d.** *abbr* MEASURE pounds per square inch, differential

psig, **p.s.i.g.** *abbr* MEASURE pounds per square inch, gauge

psilocin /síləssin, síll-/ *n* a hallucinogenic compound produced in the body after eating a specific mushroom. Formula: $C_{12}H_{16}N_2O$. [Mid-20C. < Greek *psilos* 'smooth']

psilocybin /sílə síbin, síllə-/ *n* a crystalline hallucinogen obtained from a specific mushroom. Formula: $C_{19}HN_2O_3P_2$. [Mid-20C. < Greek *psilos* 'smooth' + *kubē* 'head']

psilomelane /si lómmi layn/ *n* a mixed hydrated manganese oxide mineral occurring in dark-coloured rounded masses [Mid-19C. < Greek *psilos* 'smooth' + *melas* 'black']

psi particle *n* SCI same as **J/psi particle**

psittacine /síttə sīn, -ssin/ *adj* belonging to the parrot family, or relating to, affecting, or resembling parrots or related birds ■ *n* a bird that belongs to the parrot family [Late 19C. < Latin *psittacinus* < *psittacus* 'parrot' (see PSITTACOSIS)]

psittacosis /síttə kṓssiss/ *n* a contagious disease of parrots and related birds that can be transmitted to humans, sometimes causing serious lung infection. It is caused by the bacterium *Chlamydia psittaci*. [Late 19C. < Latin *psittacus* < Greek *psittakos* 'parrot']

PSL *abbr* private sector liquidity

PSNI *abbr* Police Service of Northern Ireland

psoas /sṓ əss/ (*plural* **psoai** /sṓ ī/ or **psoae** /sṓ ee/) *n* either of two pairs of muscles that are located in the groin and help to flex the hip joint [Late 17C. < Greek, accusative plural of *psoa* 'muscle of the loins']

psocid /sṓkid, sṓssid/ (*plural* -**cids** or *same*) *n* a tiny winged insect with reduced veins in the wings and unusual rasping mouthparts. Family: Psocidae.

[Late 19C. < modern Latin *Psocus* < Greek *psōkhein* 'grind']

psoralen /sáwrələn/ *n* a chemical that reacts with DNA in the presence of light and can cause mutations. Source: umbelliferous plants such as celery, carrots, parsley. Use: with ultraviolet light in treatment of severe acne and psoriasis. [Mid-20C. < modern Latin *Psoralea* < Greek *psōraleos* 'itchy' < *psōra* 'itch, mange']

psoriasis /sə rí əssiss/ *n* a skin disease usually marked by red scaly patches [Late 17C. Via Latin, 'scurvy, mange' < Greek *psōriasis* 'itching' < *psōra* 'itch, mange'] —**psoriatic** /sáwri áttik/ *adj*

PSS, **pss** *abbr* postscripts

psst /pst/ *interj* used to get the attention of somebody without alerting somebody else [Early 20C. An imitation of the sound]

PST *abbr* **1.** TIME Pacific Standard Time **2.** *Can* FIN provincial sales tax

PSTN *abbr* Public Switched Telephone Network

~~psuedonym~~ incorrect spelling of **pseudonym**

PSV *abbr* public service vehicle

psych /sīk/ (**psychs**, **psyching**, **psyched**) *vt US* (*slang*) **1.** PSYCHOL same as **psych out** (sense 1) **2.** same as **psych up** [Early 20C. Origin ?]

psych out *v* (*slang*) **1.** *vt* INTIMIDATE SOMEBODY to intimidate somebody or undermine the confidence of somebody **2.** *vt* PUZZLE SOMETHING OUT to analyse, solve, or understand something such as a problem **3.** *vt* GUESS SOMEBODY'S THOUGHT PROCESSES to guess or anticipate correctly the intentions or thoughts of another person **4.** *vi* COLLAPSE EMOTIONALLY to break down psychologically ○ *The prisoner psyched out completely.*

psych up *vr* **psych yourself up** to prepare yourself or somebody else mentally for a task or action (*informal*) ○ *She's been psyching herself up for this interview all week.*

psych. *abbr* **1.** psychological **2.** psychology

psych- *prefix* same as **psycho-** (*used before vowels*)

psyche /sī́ki/ *n* **1.** the human spirit or soul **2.** the human mind as the centre of thought and behaviour [Mid-17C. Via Latin < Greek *psukhē* 'breath, soul, mind' < *psukhein* 'breathe']

Psyche /sī́ki/ *n* in Roman mythology, a beautiful young woman who was loved by Cupid and ultimately made immortal by Jupiter. Cupid visited her secretly at night, forbidding her ever to look at him. When she did, he abandoned her, but they were eventually reunited.

psyched /sīkt/ *adj N Am* extremely excited about and psychologically prepared for something (*slang*)

psychedelia /sī́kə deéli ə/ *n* the subculture of artefacts, phenomena, writings, or art associated with psychedelic drugs [Mid-20C. Back-formation < PSYCHEDELIC]

psychedelic /sī́kə déllik/ *adj* **1.** RELATING TO HALLUCINOGENIC DRUGS relating to, caused by, or describing drugs that generate hallucinations, atypical psychic states, or states that resemble psychiatric disorders **2.** WILDLY DISTORTED weird, distorted, wildly colourful, or otherwise resembling images or sounds experienced by somebody under the influence of a psychedelic drug ■ *n* DRUG a psychedelic drug [Mid-20C. < Greek *psukhē* 'mind' + *dēloun* 'reveal, make visible' < *dēlos* 'clear'] —**psychedelically** *adv*

psychiatric /sī́ki áttrik/ *adj* relating to psychiatry or its patients —**psychiatrically** *adv*

psychiatric hospital *n* a hospital dedicated to the treatment, care, and protection of people with serious psychiatric disorders who are judged to be unfit or unsafe to live unsupervised and untreated in society

psychiatric social worker *n* a social worker specializing in psychiatric cases

psychiatrist /sī kí́ ətrist/ *n* a doctor trained in the treatment of people with mental illnesses

psychiatry /sī kí́ ətri/ *n* a medical specialization concerned with the diagnosis and treatment of disorders that have primarily mental or behavioural symptoms and with the care of people having such disorders [Mid-19C. < French *psychiatrie* < Greek *psukhē* 'mind' + *iatreia* 'cure']

psychic /sīkik/ *adj* **1. OF HUMAN MIND** relating to the human mind **2. OUTSIDE SCIENTIFIC KNOWLEDGE** outside the sphere of scientific knowledge **3. SUPPOSEDLY SENSITIVE TO SUPERNATURAL FORCES** claiming, or believed to have, extraordinary sensitivity to nonphysical or supernatural forces **4. CLAIRVOYANT** able, or considered able, to perceive people's unexpressed thoughts or foresee the future (*informal*) ○ *I knew you were going to say that! I must be psychic.* ■ *n* **SOMEBODY SUPPOSEDLY SENSITIVE TO SUPERNATURAL** somebody who is, or is believed to be, sensitive to nonphysical or supernatural forces [Late 18C. < Greek *psukhikos* 'of the soul or spirit' < *psukhē* (see PSYCHE)] —**psychical** *adj* —**psychically** *adv*

psycho /sīkō/ (*slang insult*) *n* (*plural* **-chos**) an offensive term for somebody who has a psychiatric or personality disorder ■ *adj* an offensive term for behaving in an uncontrolled and unpredictable way [Mid-20C. Shortening of PSYCHOPATH]

CULTURAL NOTE ***Psycho***, a film (1960) by British director Alfred Hitchcock. A disturbing horror film with a rich vein of black comedy, it tells the story of a woman who flees her home after stealing money from her boss. Stopping at a motel run by the sinister Norman Bates and his apparently domineering mother, she is brutally murdered while taking a shower. Members of her family subsequently investigate the death.

psycho- *prefix* **1.** mind, mental ○ *psychoactive* **2.** psychology, psychological ○ *psychobabble* [< Greek *psukhē* (see PSYCHE)]

psychoacoustics /sīkō ə ko͞ostiks/ *n* the scientific study of the psychological and physiological principles of sound perception (*takes a singular verb*)

psychoactive /sīkō áktiv/ *adj* describes drugs or medication having a significant effect on mood or behaviour

psychoanal. *abbr* PSYCHOANAL psychoanalysis

psychoanalyse /sīkō ánnə līz/ (**-lyses, -lysing, -lysed**) *vt* to treat a patient by applying the methods of psychoanalysis in a psychotherapeutic setting —**psychoanalyser** *n*

psychoanalysis /sīkō ə nálləsiss/ *n* **1.** a psychological theory and therapeutic method developed by Sigmund Freud, based on the ideas that mental life functions on both conscious and unconscious levels and that childhood events have a powerful psychological influence throughout life **2.** treatment by psychoanalysis, interpreting material presented by a patient in order to bring the processes of the unconscious into conscious awareness —**psychoanalyst** /-ánnəlist/ *n* —**psychoanalytic** /-ánnə líttik/ *adj* —**psychoanalytical** *adj* —**psychoanalytically** *adv*

psychoanalyze *vt* MED US spelling of **psychoanalyse**

psychobabble /sīkō babb'l/ *n* psychological jargon used inaccurately to talk about personal problems

psychobiography /sīkō bī óggrəfi/ (*plural* **-phies**) *n* a biography that focuses on the psychological profile of the subject

psychobiology /sīkō bī ólləji/ *n* the study of the biological bases of behaviour —**psychobiological** /sīkō bī ə lójjik'l/ *adj* —**psychobiologically** *adv* —**psychobiologist** *n*

psychochemical /sīkō kémmik'l/ *n* a drug that affects mood or behaviour ■ *adj* relating to or acting like a psychoactive drug

~~psychodelic~~ incorrect spelling of **psychedelic**

psychodrama /sīkō draamə/ *n* a form of psychotherapy in which patients are required to perform roles in dramas illustrating their problems before an audience of other patients —**psychodramatic** /sīkō drə máttik/ *adj*

psychodynamics /sīkō dī námmiks/ *n* **1.** the interaction of the emotional and motivational forces that affect behaviour and mental states, especially on a subconscious level (*takes a singular or plural verb*) **2.** the study of the emotional and motivational forces that affect behaviour and mental states (*takes a singular verb*) —**psychodynamic** *adj* —**psychodynamically** *adv*

psychogenesis /sīkō jénnəsiss/ *n* the psychological rather than physical cause of a disorder —**psychogenetic** /-jə néttik/ *adj* —**psychogenetically** *adv*

psychogenic /sīkō jénnik/ *adj* originating in mental or emotional rather than in physiological processes —**psychogenically** *adv*

psychogeriatric /sīkō jérri áttrik/ *adj* relating to psychiatric disorders experienced by elderly people, or to elderly people with such disorders

psychogeriatrics /sīkō jérri áttriks/ *n* the branch of medicine concerned with the psychology and psychiatric disorders experienced by elderly people (*takes a singular verb*)

psychohistory /sīkō hístəri/ (*plural* **-ries**) *n* the psychological analysis of somebody's life or of historical events —**psychohistorian** /-hi stáwri ən/ *n* —**psychohistorical** /-stórrik'l/ *adj*

psychokinesis /sīkō ki née̅siss, -kī-/ *n* the supposed ability to use mental powers to make objects move or to otherwise affect them —**psychokinetic** /-ki néttik, -kī-/ *adj*

psychol. *abbr* PSYCHOL **1.** psychological **2.** psychologist **3.** psychology

psycholinguistics /sīkō ling gwístiks/ *n* the study of language acquisition and use in relation to the psychological factors controlling its use and recognition (*takes a singular verb*) —**psycholinguist** /sīkō líng gwist/ *n* —**psycholinguistic** *adj*

psychological /sīkə lójjik'l/ *adj* **1. OF PSYCHOLOGY** relating to psychology **2. OF HUMAN MIND** relating to the mind or mental processes **3. AFFECTING HUMAN MIND** affecting or intended to affect the mind or mental processes **4. EXISTING ONLY IN HUMAN MIND** existing only in the mind, without having a physical basis ○ *His health problem is psychological.* —**psychologically** *adv*

psychological dependence *n* a strong desire for something without being physically addicted to it

psychological moment *n* the time at which the mental state of a person or group of people is most receptive or appropriate

psychological profiling *n* the analysis of somebody's behaviour and psychological characteristics, used especially to identify and target a potential terrorist or a suspect in a criminal investigation

psychological warfare *n* **1.** tactics that use propaganda to try to demoralize an enemy in war, usually including the civilian population **2.** the use of psychological tactics to disconcert and disadvantage an opponent in an everyday or a business context, e.g. by causing the opponent to feel fear or anxiety

psychologise *vti* MED another spelling of **psychologize**

psychologism /sī kólləjizəm/ *n* a belief in or emphasis on the importance of psychology in other fields such as history or philosophy —**psychologistic** /sī kóllə jístik/ *adj*

psychologist /sī kólləjist/ *n* **1.** a professional who studies behaviour and experience, and who is licensed to provide therapeutic services or to work in an academic setting **2.** a student of psychology, especially as a main subject at university or college

psychologize /sī kóllə jīz/ (**-gizes, -gizing, -gized**), **psychologise** (**-gises, -gising, -gised**) *v* **1.** *vt* to interpret behaviour in psychological terms or concepts **2.** *vi* to think, analyse, or reason psychologically

psychology /sī kólləji/ (*plural* **-gies**) *n* **1. STUDY OF HUMAN MIND** the scientific study of the human mind and mental states, and of human and animal behaviour **2. CHARACTERISTIC MENTAL MAKEUP** the characteristic temperament and associated behaviour of a person or group, or that exhibited by those engaged in an activity **3. SUBTLE MANIPULATIVE BEHAVIOUR** subtle clever actions and words used to influence a person or group

psychomachia /sīkō máki ə/, **psychomachy** /sī kómaki/ *n* conflict of the soul between the spirit and the flesh (*literary*) [Early 17C. < late Latin < Greek *psukhē* 'soul' + *makhē* 'battle']

psychometrics /sīkō méttriks/ *n* a branch of psychology dealing with the measurement of mental traits, capacities, and processes (*takes a singular verb*) —**psychometric** *adj* —**psychometrical** *adj* —**psychometrically** *adv* —**psychometrician** /sīkō mə trísh'n/ *n*

psychometry /sī kómmətri/ *n* **1.** PSYCHOL same as **psychometrics 2.** the alleged ability to obtain information about a person or event by touching an object related to that person or event —**psychometrist** *n*

psychomotor /sīkō mṓtər/ *adj* relating to bodily movement triggered by mental activity, especially voluntary muscle action

psychoneuroimmunology /sīkō nyo͞orō ímmyo͞o nólləji/ *n* a branch of medicine concerned with how emotions affect the immune system

psychoneurosis /sīkō nyo͞o rṓssiss/ (*plural* **-roses** /-rṓs seez/) *n* PSYCHIAT same as **neurosis** —**psychoneurotic** /-róttik/ *adj*

psychopath /sīkō path/ *n* **1.** somebody affected with a personality disorder marked by aggressive, violent, antisocial thought and behaviour and a lack of remorse or empathy (*technical*) **2.** an offensive term for somebody who is regarded as highly antisocial, aggressive, and lacking in empathy (*insult*) —**psychopathic** /sīkō páthik/ *adj* —**psychopathically** *adv*

psychopathology /sīkō pə thólləji/ *n* the study of the causes and development of psychiatric disorders —**psychopathological** /sīkō páthə lójjik'l/ *adj* —**psychopathologist** *n*

psychopathy /sī kóppəthi/ (*plural* **-thies**) *n* **1.** a severe personality disorder marked by antisocial thought and behaviour (*not used technically*) **2.** any psychiatric illness (*dated*)

psychopharmacology /sīkō faarmə kólləji/ *n* the scientific study of the effects of drugs on thought and behaviour —**psychopharmacological** /-kə lójjik'l/ *adj* —**psychopharmacologist** *n*

psychophysics /sīkō fízziks/ *n* a branch of psychology dealing with the effects of physical stimuli on sensory perceptions and mental states (*takes a singular verb*) —**psychophysical** *adj*

psychophysiology /sīkō fízzi ólləji/ *n* the study of the effects of physical processes on mental states and behaviour

psychoses plural of **psychosis**

psychosexual /sīkō sékshoo əl/ *adj* relating to the mental and emotional aspects of sexuality and sexual development —**psychosexuality** /-sékshoo álləti/ *n* —**psychosexually** *adv*

psychosis /sī kṓssiss/ (*plural* **-choses** /-kṓseez/) *n* a psychiatric disorder such as schizophrenia or mania that is marked by delusions, hallucinations, incoherence, and distorted perceptions of reality

psychosocial /sīkō sṓsh'l/ *adj* relating to both the psychological and the social aspects of something, or relating to something that has both of these aspects

psychosomatic /sīkō sə máttik/ *adj* **1.** describes a physical illness that is caused by mental factors such as stress, or the effects related to such illnesses **2.** involving both the mind and body —**psychosomatically** *adv*

psychosurgery /sīkō súrjəri/ (*plural* **-ies**) *n* surgery now performed only in rare cases to relieve severe psychotic disorder or to prevent some forms of epileptic seizure

psychosynthesis /sīkō sínthəsiss/ *n* **1.** a psychotherapeutic movement, opposed to psychoanalysis, that attempts to restore useful inhibitions and control **2.** a holistic form of psychotherapy involving clients in an exploration of the emotional, intellectual, physical, and spiritual aspects of the self

psychotherapy /sīkō thérrəpi/ *n* the treatment of mental disorders by psychological methods —**psychotherapeutic** /-therrə pyo͞otik/ *adj* —**psychotherapeutically** *adv* —**psychotherapist** *n*

psychothriller /sīkō thrilər/ *n* an exciting book or film in which tension is generated by the psychological pressures on the characters rather than by action

psychotic /sī kóttik/ *adj* relating to, characteristic of, or affected by psychosis [Late 19C. < PSYCHOSIS] —**psychotically** *adv*

psychotomimetic /sī kóttō mi méttik/ *adj* describes a drug or other factor that produces a condition resembling psychosis ■ *n* a drug or other factor

psychotropic /síkō trŏpik, -tróppik/ *adj* describes drugs that are capable of affecting the mind, e.g. those used to treat psychiatric disorders —**psychotropic** *n*

psychro- *prefix* cold ○ *psychrophilic* [< Greek *psukhros*]

psychrometer /sī krómmitər/ *n* an instrument consisting of two thermometers, used to measure atmospheric humidity. The bulb of one thermometer is kept moist and the effect of evaporative cooling on it is compared to the other, which is kept dry.

psychrophilic /sîkrō fíllik/ *adj* thriving at low temperatures ○ *psychrophilic bacteria*

~~psycology~~ incorrect spelling of **psychology**

psyllium /síli əm/ *n* an annual plant of the plantain family with edible seeds. Use: dietary source of fibre, mild laxative. Native to: Europe, Asia. Latin name: *Plantago psyllium*. [Mid-16C. Via Latin < Greek *psullion* 'little flea' < *psulla* 'flea'; because the seeds resemble fleas]

pt[1] *abbr* 1. part 2. MED patient 3. FIN payment 4. MEASURE pint 5. point 6. port

pt[2] *abbr* ONLINE Portugal (*used in Internet addresses*) See table at **domain name**

Pt[1] *abbr* (*used in placenames*) 1. Point 2. Port

Pt[2] *symbol* CHEM ELEM platinum

PT[1] *abbr* 1. TIME Pacific Time 2. *US* physical therapy 3. postal telegraph

PT[2] *n* gymnastics, athletics, team sports, and other forms of physical exercise taught to children at school. Full form **physical training**

pt. *abbr* GRAM preterite

p.t. *abbr* 1. part-time 2. GRAM past tense 3. pro tem

pta *symbol* MONEY, HIST peseta

PTA *abbr* 1. EDUC Parent-Teacher Association 2. TRANSP Passenger Transport Authority

ptarmigan

ptarmigan /taármigən/ (*plural same* or **-gans**) *n* a wild bird of the grouse family, that has feet covered with feathers and white plumage in the winter. Native to: mountainous regions. Genus: *Lagopus*. [Late 16C. Alteration (influenced by Greek *pt-* as in *pteron* 'wing') of Gaelic *tarmachan*, literally 'little ptarmigan' < *tarmach* 'ptarmigan']

PT boat *n ANZ, N Am* NAVY same as **motor torpedo boat**

PTC *abbr* CHEM phenylthiocarbamide

Pte *abbr* MIL, COMM Private

PTE *abbr* TRANSP Passenger Transport Executive

pteranodon /tə ránnə don/ *n* an extinct toothless flying reptile with a bony crest. Genus: *Pteranodon*. [Late 19C. < modern Latin < Greek *pteron* 'wing']

pteridology /térri dólləji/ *n* the branch of botany that is concerned with the study of ferns [Mid-19C. < Greek *pterid-* 'fern'] —**pteridological** /térridə lójjik l/ *adj* —**pteridologist** *n*

pteridophyte /térridə fīt/ *n* a plant that has no flowers or seeds and reproduces by means of spores. Ferns and some mosses are pteridophytes. Division: *Pteridophyta*. [Late 19C. < Greek *pterid-* 'fern'] —**pteridophytic** /térridə fíttik/ *adj* —**pteridophytous** /térri dóffitəss/ *adj*

pteridosperm /térridə spurm/ *n* an extinct plant that bore seeds and resembled a fern [Early 20C. < Greek *pterid-* 'fern']

pterodactyl /térrə dáktil/ *n* an extinct flying reptile (**pterosaur**) of the Jurassic and Cretaceous periods with membranous wings and a rudimentary tail and beak. Genus: *Pterodactylus*. [Early 19C. < modern Latin *Pterodactylus* < Greek *pteron* 'wing' + *daktulos* 'finger']

pteropod /térrə pod/ *n* a sea gastropod mollusc that has a foot with wing-shaped lobes that are used as swimming organs. Order: Thecosomata or Gymnosomata. [Mid-19C. < modern Latin *Pteropoda* < Greek *pteron* 'wing' + modern Latin *-poda* 'foot']

pterosaur /térrə sawr/ *n* an extinct flying reptile of the Triassic, Jurassic, and Cretaceous periods that had membranous wings supported by an elongated fourth digit. Order: Pterosauria. [Mid-19C. < modern Latin *Pterosauria* < Greek *pteron* 'wing' + *sauros* 'lizard']

-pterous *suffix* having wings of a particular kind or number ○ *orthopterous* ○ *dipterous* [< Greek *pteron* 'wing, feather' < Indo-European, 'to fly']

pteroylglutamic acid /térrō īl gloo támmik-/ *n* CHEM same as **folic acid** (*technical*) [< Greek *pteron* 'wing' (referring to compounds occurring in insect wings) + ACYL]

pterygium /tə ríjji əm/ (*plural* **-iums** or **-ia** /-i ə/) *n* a triangular patch of tissue that obstructs vision by growing over usually the inner side of the eye. It results from degeneration of the cornea and is associated with prolonged exposure to sun and wind. [Mid-17C. Via modern Latin < Greek *pterugion* 'little wing' < *pterux* 'wing']

pterygoid process /térri goyd-/ *n* either of two bony plates extending downwards from the sphenoid bone of the skull [< modern Latin *pterygoides* 'like a wing' < Greek *pterux* 'wing']

pteryla /térrilə/ (*plural* **-lae** /-lī/) *n* a defined area on the skin of a bird from which feathers grow [Mid-19C. < modern Latin < Greek *pteron* 'feather' + *hulē* 'forest']

PTFE *abbr* CHEM polytetrafluoroethylene

ptg *abbr* printing

PTH *abbr* BIOCHEM parathyroid hormone

PTN *abbr* public telephone network

PTO *abbr* 1. Patent and Trademark Office 2. **pto** please turn over

Ptolemaeus /tóllə máyəss/ large walled plain on the Moon that is noticeably hexagonal in shape and has a highly cratered floor. Located northeast of Mare Imbrium, it is approximately 140 km/85 mi. across.

Ptolemaic /tóllə máy ik/ *adj* 1. relating to the geographer and astronomer Ptolemy or to his system of planetary motion 2. relating to the dynasty of pharaohs of ancient Egypt founded by Ptolemy I, or to Egypt during their rule

Ptolemaic system *n* a theory of planetary motion developed by Ptolemy that held that Earth was at the centre of the universe with the Sun, Moon, and planets revolving around it. The most influential of the geocentric theories, it dominated thinking for 14 centuries until the Copernican system was accepted.

Ptolemaist /tóllə máy ist/ *n* a believer in the Ptolemaic system of planetary motion

Ptolemy /tólləmi/ (AD 100?–170?) Greek astronomer, mathematician, and geographer. His Earth-centred model of the universe prevailed until the 16th century. His writings are collected in the *Almagest*. Full name **Ptolemaeus, Claudius**

Ptolemy I (367?–283? BC) king of Egypt. A Macedonian by birth and general in Alexander the Great's army, he became king of Egypt in 305 BC, thereby founding the Ptolemaic dynasty. Known as **Ptolemy Soter**

Ptolemy XV (47–30 BC) king of Egypt. He was the son of Cleopatra and the last of the Ptolemaic dynasty. His reign (44–30 BC) ended when he was killed by Roman forces after the defeat of his mother and Mark Antony. Known as **Caesarion**

ptomaine /tố mayn/ *n* one of a foul-smelling group of organic bases containing nitrogen. Source: bacteria during the decay of proteins. [Late 19C. Via French < Italian *ptomaina* < Greek *ptōma* 'fallen body, corpse' < *piptein* 'to fall']

ptomaine poisoning *n* food poisoning caused by bacteria, but formerly believed to be caused by ptomaines

ptosis /tốssiss/ (*plural* **ptoses** /tốseez/) *n* a drooping of the upper eyelid, resulting from muscle weakness or an inability to move muscles [Mid-18C. < Greek *ptōsis* 'a falling' < *piptein* 'to fall']

pts *abbr* 1. parts 2. FIN payments 3. MEASURE pints 4. points 5. ports

PTSD *abbr* PSYCHOL post-traumatic stress disorder

PTV *abbr* MEDIA pay television

Pty *abbr* BUSINESS proprietary (*used in 'Pty Ltd' to indicate a private limited company*)

ptyalin /tī əlin/ *n* an enzyme in saliva that catalyses the digestion of starches [Mid-19C. < Greek *ptualon* 'saliva']

ptyalism /tī əlizəm/ *n* excessive production of saliva [Late 17C. < Greek *ptualismos* 'salivation' < *ptualon* 'saliva' < *ptuein* 'to spit']

Pu *symbol* CHEM ELEM plutonium

pub /pub/ *n* 1. a building where drinks, especially alcoholic ones, can be bought and consumed on the premises. Pubs frequently offer food, and sometimes accommodation, as well. 2. *Aus* same as **hotel** (*informal*) [Mid-19C. Shortening of PUBLIC HOUSE]

pub. *abbr* 1. public 2. publication 3. published 4. publisher 5. publishing

pubbing /púbbing/ *n* the social activity of going to a pub or pubs (*informal*)

pub-crawl (*informal*) *n* a tour in which somebody visits and drinks at several pubs in succession ■ *vi* to go drinking at several pubs in succession

puberty /pyoobərti/ *n* the stage in human physiological development when somebody becomes capable of sexual reproduction. It is marked by genital maturation, development of secondary sex characteristics, and, in girls, the first occurrence of menstruation. [14C. Directly or via French < Latin *pubertas* < *pubes* 'adult'] —**pubertal** *adj*

pubes[1] *n* /pyoó beez/ (*plural* **-bes** /pyoó beez/) the part of the abdomen immediately above the external genitalia that is covered with hair from puberty onwards (*takes a singular verb*) ■ *npl* /pyoobz/ the hair growing on the lower abdomen from puberty onwards (*informal; takes a plural verb*) [Late 16C. < Latin *pubes* 'pubic hair, genital region']

pubes[2] ANAT *plural of* **pubis**

pubescent /pyoo béss'nt/ *adj* 1. reaching or having attained puberty 2. covered with down or fine hair [Mid-17C. Directly or via French < Latin *pubescent-*, present participle of *pubescere* 'reach puberty' < *pubes* 'adult'] —**pubescence** *n*

pub grub *n* food, usually of a relatively simple and inexpensive type, served in a pub (*informal*)

pubic /pyoóbik/ *adj* relating to or located near or on the pubes or pubis ○ *pubic hair*

pubic bone *n* ANAT same as **pubis**

pubic louse *n* INSECTS same as **crab**[1] (sense 4)

pubis /pyoóbiss/ (*plural* **pubes** /pyoó beez/) *n* the bone that forms the lower front section of the hipbone in humans and is one of a pair joined at the front of the pelvis. Although a separate bone in infants, it later fuses with the ilium and the ischium to form the hipbone. [Late 16C. Shortening of Latin *os pubis* 'bone of the genital region']

publ. *abbr* 1. publication 2. published 3. publisher

public /púbblik/ *adj* 1. CONCERNING ALL THE PEOPLE relating to or concerning the people at large or all members of a community ○ *public support for the policy* 2. FOR COMMUNITY USE provided for the use of a community ○ *public library* 3. OPEN TO ALL open to everyone, and typically frequented by large numbers of people ○ *public spaces* 4. WELL KNOWN known to large numbers of the community through being involved in activities such as politics or entertainment ○ *maintained a very public persona* 5. DONE OPENLY made, done, or happening openly, for all to see ○ *a public debate* 6. KNOWN BY ALL MEMBERS OF COMMUNITY known or potentially known by all members of a community ○ *make the information public* ○ *a public disgrace* 7. OF STATE relating to or involving the state and governmental agencies rather than private cor-

porations or industry ○ *working in the public sector* **8. BELONGING TO COMMUNITY** belonging to the community as a whole and administered through its representatives in government ○ *public land* **9. HAVING OPENLY PURCHASABLE SHARES** describes companies whose shares are available, or are made available, for anyone to buy ■ *n* **1. EVERYONE** the community as a whole (*takes a singular or plural verb*) ○ *The government has been misleading the public.* **2. PARTICULAR PART OF COMMUNITY** a section of the community, united by a common interest ○ *the reading public* **3. FANS OR FOLLOWERS** the fans or followers of a performer or author ○ *went to meet her adoring public* **4.** LEISURE same as **public bar** [15C. Directly or via French < Latin *publicus*, alteration of *poplicus* < *populus* 'people'] **—publicness** *n*

public access *n* in US law, the availability of cable broadcasting facilities for the transmission of programmes produced by members of the public (*hyphenated before a noun*)

public-address system *n* full form of **PA**²

public affairs *npl* issues that affect people generally, especially political issues, or issues arising from the relationship of the public to an organization such as a government body or a financial institution (*takes a plural verb*) ■ *n* the study of issues involving the interrelationships between the public and major institutions such as government (*takes a singular verb*)

~~publically~~ incorrect spelling of **publicly**

publican /púbblikən/ *n* **1.** the owner or manager of a pub **2.** in ancient Rome, a collector of taxes [12C. Via French < Latin *publicanus* < *publicus* (see PUBLIC)]

public assistance *n* N Am aid consisting of money, food, food stamps, or other benefits, given by government agencies to people on low incomes, dependent children, and others in financial distress

publication /púbbli káysh'n/ *n* **1. ACT OF PUBLISHING** the act of making printed material, especially books, available for sale to the public (*often used before a noun*) **2. PUBLISHED ITEM** an item that has been published, especially in printed form **3. PUBLIC COMMUNICATION OF SOMETHING** the communication of information to the public [14C. Via French < Latin *publication-* < *publicare* (see PUBLISH)]

public bar *n* a bar in a pub that, typically, has less luxurious furnishings and where drinks are sold more cheaply than in a saloon or lounge bar

public bill *n* a bill presented in a parliament or other legislative body by a government, dealing with public policy

public company *n* a limited company whose shares can be bought and sold on the stock market. N Am term **public corporation**

public convenience *n* a toilet in a public place such as a town centre, for use by members of the public

public corporation *n* **1.** in the United Kingdom, an organization set up by the government to run a state-owned enterprise, e.g. the BBC. Its chairman and governors are appointed by a government minister. **2.** *N Am* same as **public company**

public defender *n* in the United States, an attorney who represents defendants who cannot afford their own lawyers

public domain *n* **1. REVEALED CONDITION** the condition of being openly known or revealed as opposed to being kept a secret ○ *The information is now in the public domain.* **2. NOT IN COPYRIGHT** in US law, the condition of not being protected by patent or copyright and so freely available for use ○ *public domain software* **3.** *US* **GOVERNMENT LAND** land that is owned and administered by a government

public enemy *n* a threat to the public, especially a violent criminal

public enterprise *n* economic activity by government departments and quangos

public expenditure *n* spending by the government or government-owned bodies

public eye *n* intense scrutiny by the public ○ *The lens of the public eye is focused on the sensational trial.* ◇ **in the public eye** regularly receiving attention from the media

public figure *n* somebody who is widely known to the public and whose lifestyle is the subject of great scrutiny

public health *n* the general health of a community and the practice and study of ways to preserve and improve it. Public health includes health education, sanitation, control of diseases, and regulation of pollution.

public house *n* LEISURE same as **pub** (sense 1) (*formal*)

public intellectual *n* US an expert within a particular field whose opinions and published works are well known, and who frequently appears in the media to comment on newsworthy issues

public interest *n* **1.** the general benefit of the public ○ *a law that would be contrary to the public interest* **2.** the general level of interest shown by people towards an issue or event ○ *Public interest in the earnings of corporate executives is at an all-time high.*

publicise *vt* another spelling of **publicize**

publicist /púbblissist/ *n* **1.** a promoter who seeks to obtain media publicity for a client **2.** MEDIA same as **journalist** (*archaic*) [Late 18C. < French *publiciste* < Latin *publicus* (see PUBLIC), after *canoniste* 'canon lawyer']

publicity /pu blíssəti/ *n* **1. ACTIVITY STIMULATING PUBLIC INTEREST** activity, especially advertising and the dissemination of information, designed to increase public interest in or awareness of something or somebody (*often used before a noun*) ○ *The event was dismissed as a mere publicity stunt.* **2. INTEREST CREATED BY PUBLICITY** public or media interest gained as a result of publicizing something ○ *We got more publicity from that one newspaper photograph than from a hundred advertisements.* **3. ATTENTION-GETTING INFORMATION** information, material, or other means used to publicize something or somebody ○ *The lawsuit that turned out to be great publicity.* **4. CONDITION OF BEING PUBLIC** the condition of being known or available to the public (*formal*) [Late 18C. < French *publicité* < *public* < Latin *publicus* (see PUBLIC)]

publicize /púbbli sīz/ (**-cizes, -cizing, -cized**), **publicise** (**-cises, -cising, -cised**) *vt* to make something generally known or known to a group, typically by advertising

public key cryptography *n* in computing, an encryption method that uses two mathematically related keys for encrypting and decrypting a message

public key encryption *n* in computing, a message encryption technique in which encoding is done using a generally available public key but decoding is done using a private key available only to the receiver

public law *n* **1.** the branch of law that deals with a state and its relationships with its citizens **2.** a law that applies to the public

Public Lending Right *n* the right of authors to receive a small fee every time their books are borrowed from public libraries in the United Kingdom

public-liability insurance *n* insurance that compensates people if they experience injury or damage resulting from lack of reasonable care by an insured business or organization

public life *n* **1.** employment as an appointed or elected official accountable to the public **2.** the part of somebody's life that is known or is of interest to the public and the media

public limited company *n* a company whose shares can be bought and sold on the stock market and whose shareholders are subject to restricted liability for any debts or losses

publicly /públikli/ *adv* **1.** in a public or open manner **2.** by or in the name of the public

public nuisance *n* **1.** an action or a thing that harms the community in general **2.** somebody regarded as irritating or offensive (*insult*)

public opinion *n* the general attitude or feeling of the public concerning an issue, especially when this has an effect on political decision-making

public ownership *n* ownership by the state of some-

thing regarded as a national asset such as coal, water, or the telecommunications industry

public private partnership *n* a partnership between government and the private sector for the purpose of more effectively providing services and infrastructure traditionally provided by the public sector

public prosecutor *n* a government law official prosecuting criminal offences on behalf of the community or the state

Public Record Office *n* a UK institution in which official documents, historical and modern, are stored after they are released under the thirty-year rule. They may be consulted by the public.

public relations *n* **1. PROMOTION OF FAVOURABLE IMAGE** the practice or profession of establishing, maintaining, or improving a favourable relationship between an institution or person and the public (*takes a singular verb*) **2. PUBLIC IMAGE** the relationship between an institution or person and the public, with respect to whether that institution or person is seen in a positive or negative light (*takes a singular or plural verb*) ○ *The project was a public relations disaster.* **3. DEPARTMENT MANAGING PUBLIC RELATIONS** the department in an organization that is responsible for public relations (*takes a singular verb*)

public room *n* **1.** *US* a room into which the public is admitted without discrimination, e.g. the lobby in a hotel **2.** *Scotland* any room in a private house into which strangers may traditionally be invited, e.g. a sitting room or dining room. It is often contrasted with a private room such as a bedroom.

public school *n* **1.** in England and Wales, an independent fee-paying secondary school, typically a single-sex boarding school **2.** in the United States, a state-funded elementary or secondary school providing education free for all local children and young people

public sector *n* the part of the economy that is controlled by government spending and employment (*hyphenated before a noun*)

public-sector borrowing requirement *n* the amount that the government needs to borrow in any fiscal year in order to be able to meet its budgeted costs

public servant *n* **1.** an appointed or elected holder of a government position or office **2.** *ANZ* GOV same as **civil servant**

public service *n* **1. GOVERNMENT EMPLOYMENT** government employment, especially within the civil service **2. PROVISION OF ESSENTIAL SERVICES** the business or activity of providing the public with essential goods or services such as electric power **3. SERVICE BENEFITING GENERAL PUBLIC** a service that is run for the benefit of the general public, e.g. the utilities, the emergency services, transport, and broadcasting (*hyphenated before a noun*) **4.** *ANZ* POL **DEPARTMENTS IMPLEMENTING GOVERNMENT POLICY** the range of departments and organizations responsible for implementing government policy

public-service broadcasting *n* noncommercial broadcasting sponsored by the state, e.g. programmes broadcast in the United Kingdom by the BBC

public speaking *n* the skill, practice, or process of making speeches to large groups of people **—public speaker** *n*

public spending *n* the spending of money by government and governmental bodies (*hyphenated before a noun*)

public-spirited *adj* motivated by or showing genuine concern for others in the community

public transport *n* a network of passenger vehicles for use by the public running on set routes, usually at set times and charging set fares (*hyphenated before a noun*)

public utility *n* a government-regulated company that provides an essential public service such as water, gas, or electricity (*hyphenated before a noun*)

public works *npl* civil-engineering projects that are government owned or financed, and undertaken specifically for the benefit of the public

publish /púbblish/ (-lishes, -lishing, -lished) v 1. *vti* PREPARE AND PRODUCE TEXT OR SOFTWARE to prepare and produce material in printed or electronic form for distribution and, usually, sale 2. *vt* DISTRIBUTE WORK OF AUTHOR to make the work of a particular author available in printed or other form 3. *vt* MAKE SOMETHING PUBLIC KNOWLEDGE to announce something publicly [14C. < Old French *publiss-*, stem of *publier* < Latin *publicare* 'make public' < *publicus* (see PUBLIC)] —**publishable** adj

publisher /púbblishər/ n 1. a company or person that publishes products such as books, journals, or software 2. the owner or representative of the owner of a newspaper, periodical, or publishing house

publishing /púbblishing/ n the trade, profession, or activity of preparing and producing material in printed or electronic form for distribution to the public

publishing house n an established publishing company that prepares and produces material in printed or electronic form for distribution and, usually, sale

PUC n S Asia a pre-university junior college

Puccini /poo chéeni/, **Giacomo** (1858–1924) Italian composer. His lyrical theatrical operas include *La Bohème* (1896), *Tosca* (1900), *Madame Butterfly* (1904), and *Turandot* (1926), left uncompleted at his death.

puccoon /pə kóon/ (*plural* **-coons** or *same*) n 1. a plant whose roots yield a reddish dye, e.g. gromwell or bloodroot. Native to: North America. Latin name: *Lithospermum canescens* or *Sanguinaria canadensis*. 2. a dye made from puccoon [Early 17C. < Virginia Algonquian *poughkone*]

puce /pyooss/ adj of a brilliant purplish-red colour [Late 18C. Via French, 'flea' (in *couleur puce* 'flea-coloured') < Latin *pulex*] —**puce** n

Pucelle /poo sél/, **Jean** (1300–55) French manuscript illuminator. His use of perspective in *Belleville Breviary* (1325) shows the influence of the beginnings of the Italian Renaissance.

puck /puk/ n 1. DISC IN ICE HOCKEY a small disc of hard rubber that the players hit in ice hockey 2. STROKE AT BALL in the Irish sport of hurling, a player's stroke at the ball ■ *vt* (**pucks, pucking, pucked**) 1. STRIKE BALL in the Irish sport of hurling, to strike the ball 2. *Ireland* HIT SOMETHING HARD to hit something with great force (*slang*) [Late 19C. Origin ?]

Puck n 1. *also* **puck** in English folklore, a mischievous or malevolent spirit 2. a small natural satellite of Uranus, discovered in 1985 by the Voyager 2 planetary probe. It is approximately 154 km in diameter. [Old English *pūca*, origin ?]

pucka adj another spelling of **pukka**

pucker /púkər/ *vti* (**-ers, -ering, -ered**) to gather something such as cloth or the skin around the lips, or be gathered, in such a way that wrinkles or small creases are formed ■ n a small wrinkle, fold, or crease [Late 16C. Probably < POCKET]

puckeroo /púkə roo/ adj NZ broken, destroyed, or not working (*informal*) [Late 19C. < Maori *pakaru* 'broken']

puckish /púkish/ adj mischievous or naughty in a playful way [Late 19C. < PUCK] —**puckishly** adv —**puckishness** n

puckle n Scotland FOOD same as **pickle²** (*informal*)

pud /pood/ n same as **pudding** (senses 1–2) (*informal*)

pudding /póodding/ n 1. SWEET COOKED DESSERT a sweet cooked dessert containing flour or a cereal product and other ingredients such as sugar, fruit, or eggs (*often used in combination*) 2. DESSERT the dessert course of a meal ○ *What's for pudding?* 3. COOKED SAVOURY DISH a substantial savoury cooked dish usually covered with, or encased in, suet pastry or sometimes breadcrumbs (*often used in combination*) 4. TYPE OF SAUSAGE a sausage made with ingredients such as minced meat, seasonings, and oatmeal packed into a skin or bag and usually boiled (*usually used in combination*) ○ *black pudding* [13C. Via French *boudin* 'black pudding' < Latin *botellus* 'sausage'] —**puddingy** adj

pudding basin n a deep bowl used for making puddings, especially steamed puddings (*hyphenated before a noun*)

pudding-basin haircut n a haircut with the hair cut in a continuous straight line all the way round the head

pudding stone n a conglomerate rock in which the pebbles have a different colour and texture from the material binding them together (**matrix**)

puddle /púdd'l/ n 1. SHALLOW POOL OF WATER a shallow pool of water, e.g. one formed by rainwater in a hollow on a road 2. POOL OF LIQUID a small pool of liquid 3. CIV ENG WATERPROOF LINING MATERIAL nonporous material made from thoroughly mixed wet clay and sand and used as a waterproof lining, e.g. in constructing a canal 4. ROWING EDDY FROM OAR STROKE the swirling surface of the water after the blade of an oar has completed a stroke ■ v (**-dles, -dling, -dled**) 1. *vi* MESS ABOUT to potter or mess about 2. *vi* SPLASH ABOUT IN SHALLOW WATER to wade, dabble, or splash in shallow water or puddles 3. *vt* CIV ENG WATERPROOF SOMETHING WITH PUDDLE to make a canal or pool waterproof by lining it with puddle 4. *vt* CIV ENG MIX CLAY AND SAND to work clay and sand to make puddle 5. *vt* METALL PROCESS PIG IRON to convert pig iron to wrought iron by heating it in a furnace in the presence of an oxidizing agent such as ferric oxide to remove carbon [14C. < Old English *pudd* 'ditch'] —**puddler** n —**puddly** adj

pudendum /pyoo déndəm/ (*plural* **-da** /-də/) n the human external genital organs [Mid-17C. < Latin < *pudere* 'make or feel ashamed'] —**pudendal** adj

pudge /puj/ n N Am 1. same as **podge** (sense 2) (*informal insult*) 2. same as **podge** (sense 1) (*insult*) [Mid-19C. Origin ?]

pudgy /púji/ (**-ier, -iest**) adj N Am same as **podgy** (*informal*) —**pudgily** adv —**pudginess** n

Pudsey /púdsi/ town in West Yorkshire, northern England, 10 km/6 mi. west of Leeds. Population: 31,636 (1991).

Puebla /pwébblə/ 1. state in east-central Mexico. Capital: Puebla. Population: 5,076,686 (2000). Area: 33,995 sq. km/13,126 sq. mi. 2. capital city of Puebla State in east-central Mexico. It has one of the oldest cathedrals in Latin America. Population: 1,346,916 (2000).

pueblo /pwébblō/ (*plural* **-los**) n 1. a village built by Native North or Central Americans in the southwestern United States and Central America, containing at least one, but typically a cluster of multistorey stone or adobe houses 2. a town or village in a Spanish-speaking country [Early 19C. Via Spanish < Latin *populus* 'people']

Pueblo (*plural same* or **-los**) n a member of a Native North or Central American people who live or lived in pueblos. The Hopi, Taos, and Zuñi are all Pueblo peoples. —**Pueblo** adj

puerile /pyóor īl/ adj 1. regarded as childishly silly or immature 2. relating to or characteristic of childhood (*formal*) [Late 16C. Directly or via French < Latin *puerilis* < *puer* 'child, boy'] —**puerilely** adv —**puerility** /pyoor rílləti/ n

puerilism /pyoórilizəm/ n childish or immature behaviour by an adult

puerperal /pyoo úrpərəl/ adj relating to childbirth or the time immediately following childbirth [Mid-18C. < Latin *puerperus* 'bearing children' < *puer* 'child' + *-parus* 'bearing']

puerperal fever n MED same as **puerperal sepsis**

puerperal psychosis n a psychiatric disorder that may affect women in the first two weeks after giving birth. It may be depressive or schizophrenic and may involve false ideas concerning the baby.

puerperal sepsis n blood poisoning following childbirth, caused by infection of the placental site

puerperium /pyoor péeri əm/ n the period immediately after childbirth when the womb is returning to its normal size, lasting approximately six weeks [Early 17C. < Latin *puerperus* (see PUERPERAL)]

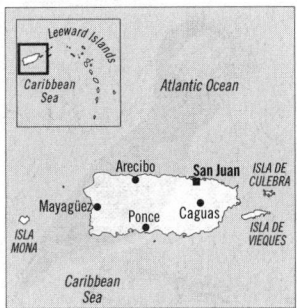

Puerto Rico

Puerto Rico /pwúrtō réekō/ commonwealth of the United States, occupying one large island and several small ones in the northern Caribbean, east of the Dominican Republic. Language: Spanish, English. Currency: US dollar. Capital: San Juan. Population: 3,937,316 (2001). Area: 8,959 sq. km/3,459 sq. mi. —**Puerto Rican** n, adj

puff /puf/ n 1. SHORT SUDDEN RUSH OF AIR a short sudden rush of air, wind, gas, or smoke 2. SOUND OF PUFF the short sound made by a rush of air or gas 3. AMOUNT IN PUFF the amount of substance contained in a puff 4. SHORT EXHALATION a short blowing out of breath 5. INHALATION FOLLOWED BY EXHALATION an inhalation followed by an exhalation, especially when smoking 6. LIGHT PASTRY SNACK a snack or cake consisting of puff pastry with a sweet or sometimes savoury filling (*often used in combination*) ○ *a cream puff* 7. EXAGGERATED PRAISE OR PUBLICITY an exaggerated or flattering expression of praise, especially in publicizing something or somebody 8. COSMETICS same as **powder puff** 9. SWELLING a rounded swelling or projection on something 10. GATHERED SECTION OF FABRIC a piece of fabric gathered around the edges and bulging in the middle 11. VOLUMINOUS HAIRSTYLE hair arranged in an enlarged mass by combing, rolling, or padding it 12. US QUILTED BEDSPREAD a quilted and padded covering for a bed (*dated*) 13. GENETICS ENLARGED REGION ON CHROMOSOME an enlarged region on a chromosome resulting from active RNA synthesis ■ v (**puffs, puffing, puffed**) 1. *vi* BREATHE QUICKLY to breathe quickly in short blasts 2. *vti* EMIT GAS IN SHORT BLASTS to emit or blow steam, gas, or smoke in short blasts 3. *vti* INHALE AND EXHALE SMOKE to inhale and exhale smoke from a cigarette, cigar, or pipe 4. *vi* MOVE WHILE EMITTING SMOKE PUFFS to move in a particular direction or way emitting puffs of smoke or steam 5. *vi* MOVE WHILE PANTING to move in a particular direction or way while panting ○ *He puffed up the hill.* 6. *vti* SWELL UP to swell, or make something swell, e.g. with air or pride ○ *puffed out his cheeks* ○ *puffing up balloons* 7. *vt* SPEAK HIGHLY OF SOMEBODY OR SOMETHING to praise somebody or something extravagantly, especially in publicity material 8. *vt* MAKE SOMEBODY BREATHLESS to make somebody breathless, e.g. after heavy exercise (*informal*) ○ *Phew! I'm puffed!* [12C. Origin ?] ◇ **out of puff** out of breath (*informal*)

puff adder n 1. a viper that inflates its body and hisses when alarmed. Genus: *Bitis*. Native to: Africa. 2. REPT same as **hognose snake**

puffball /púf bawl/ n a round fungus that produces a cloud of dark spores when disturbed. Many species are edible when immature. Genus: *Lycoperdon* or *Calvatia*.

puffed out /puft-/ adj out of breath because of exertion (*informal*)

puffed-up adj self-important or pompous

puffer /púffər/ n 1. something or somebody that puffs, especially a steam-driven train or cargo vessel 2. *also* **pufferfish** /púffər fish/ (*plural same* or **-fishes**) a tropical sea fish, poisonous in some species, that can inflate its body with water to appear larger to predators. Although poisonous, some varieties can be eaten as food after special preparation. Family: Tetraodontidae.

puffery /púffəri/ n exaggerated or excessively flattering praise, especially in publicity (*informal*)

puffin

puffin /púffin/ (*plural* **-fins** or *same*) *n* a black and white diving seabird of the auk family with a short neck and a triangular, brightly coloured beak. Genus: *Fratercula*. [14C. Origin ?]

puff pastry *n* a light flaky multilayered pastry made by repeated rolling and folding of extremely rich buttery pastry dough, which then rises during baking

puffy /púffi/ (**-ier**, **-iest**) *adj* **1.** SWOLLEN swollen, especially because of tiredness, injury, crying, or poor health **2.** SHORT OF BREATH with a tendency to puff and pant **3.** POMPOUS pompous or self-important — **puffily** *adv* —**puffiness** *n*

pug

pug[1] /pug/ *n* a short compact dog with a wrinkled face, short coat, and curled tail, belonging to a breed of Asian origin [Mid-18C. Origin ?]

pug[2] /pug/ *vt* (**pugs**, **pugging**, **pugged**) **1.** KNEAD CLAY WITH WATER to mix clay with water to make it pliable enough to form bricks or pottery **2.** FILL GAP WITH CLAY to fill in a gap with clay or mortar ■ *n* CLAY SUITABLE FOR MOULDING clay mixed with water until it is pliable enough to form bricks or pottery [Early 19C. Origin ?] —**puggy** *adj*

pug[3] /pug/ *n* BOXING same as **boxer**[1] (*slang*) [Mid-19C. Shortening of *pugilist*]

pugaree *n* S Asia CLOTHING same as **puggree**

Puget Sound /pyoójit-/ deep inlet of the Pacific Ocean, in northwestern Washington State. Area: 561 sq. km/217 sq. mi.

puggled /púgg'ld/, **puggled out** *adj* Scotland in a state of extreme tiredness, usually from working hard at something (*informal*) [Early 20C. Alteration of slang *puggle* 'psychiatrically disordered' < Hindi *pāgal*, *paglā* 'person with a psychiatric disorder']

puggree /púggri/, **pugree**, **pugaree** /púggəri/ *n* S Asia same as **turban** (sense 1) [Mid-17C. < Hindi *pagřī*]

pugilism /pyoójilizəm/ *n* the practice, sport, or profession of boxing [Late 18C. < Latin *pugil* 'boxer'] —**pugilist** *n*—**pugilistic** /pyoóji lístik/ *adj*—**pugilistically** *adv*

pugil-stick /pyoójil-/ *n* a long stick with padded ends used in game shows involving mock combats [Probably < shortening of PUGILISM]

Pugin /pyoójin/, **Augustus** (1812–52) British architect and designer. He was leader of the Gothic revival, and his most influential work was the interior and exterior decoration of the Houses of Parliament in London, begun in 1836. Full name **Pugin, Augustus Welby Northmore**

'The two great rules for design are these: first, that there should be no features about a building which are not necessary for convenience, construction or propriety; second, that all ornament should consist of enrichment of the essential construction of the building.'
[Augustus Pugin, *The True Principles of Pointed or Christian Architecture*; 1841]

pug mill *n* a machine in which materials are ground and mixed, e.g. clay with water for building or pottery-making, or cement for building [< PUG[2]]

pugnacious /pug náyshəss/ *adj* inclined to fight or be aggressive [Mid-17C. < Latin *pugnac-* < *pugnus* 'fist'] — **pugnaciously** *adv*—**pugnacity** /pug nássəti/ *n*

pug nose *n* a short stubby nose with a turned-up or flattened end [< PUG[1]] —**pug-nosed** *adj*

puh-leeze /pə leéz/, **puh-lease** *interj* used facetiously to express astonishment, disbelief, or indignation (*informal*) [Late 20C. Alteration of PLEASE]

puisne /pyoóni/ *adj* LAW **1.** OF HIGH COURT describes a justice of the High Court of England and Wales **2.** US OF YOUNGER OR JUNIOR STATUS junior or younger in status or rank or in age **3.** US OF JUDGE'S RANK describes an associate justice of a higher court [Late 16C. < Old French, 'born after' < *puis* 'after' + *né* 'born']

puissance /pweé soNs, pyoó iss'nss/ *n* **1.** a competition in showjumping in which horses attempt to clear an obstacle that is raised higher for each round, until all but the winner are eliminated **2.** power or might (*literary*) [15C. < French < *puissant* (see PUISSANT)]

puissant /pyoó iss'nt/ *adj* powerful or mighty (*literary*) [15C. < French < Latin *posse* 'be able', after *potent-* 'powerful'] —**puissantly** *adv*

puja /poójə/, **pooja** *n* **1.** in Hinduism, daily devotion consisting of a ritual offering of food, drink, and ritual actions and prayers, most commonly to an image of a deity **2.** Carib a Hindu prayer ceremony [Late 17C. < Sanskrit *pūjā* 'worship']

puke /pyook/ (*slang*) *vti* (**pukes**, **puking**, **puked**) BE SICK to vomit, or vomit something up ■ *n* **1.** SOMETHING VOMITED vomited food or other matter **2.** ACT OF VOMITING the vomiting up of something **3.** SOMEBODY DESPICABLE somebody regarded as contemptible or annoying [Late 16C. Probably an imitation of the sound of vomiting]

pukeko /poókəkō/ (*plural* **-kos** or *same*) *n* NZ same as **purple gallinule** [Mid-19C. < Maori]

pukka /púkə/, **pucka** *adj* **1.** GENUINE genuine or authentic (*informal*) **2.** RESPECTABLE of high social status (*informal*) **3.** EXCELLENT of the highest quality or standard (*informal*) **4.** S Asia WELL DONE OR MADE properly done or made [Late 17C. < Hindi *pakkā* 'cooked, ripe']

pul /pool/ (*plural* **puls** or **puli** /poóli/) *n* a subunit of Afghan currency. See table at **currency** [Mid-19C. < Pashto]

pula /poólə/ (*plural same*) *n* the main unit of Botswanan currency. See table at **currency** [Late 20C. < Setswana, literally 'rain']

pulchritude /púlkri tyood/ *n* physical beauty (*literary or humorous*) [14C. < Latin *pulchritudo* < *pulcher* 'beautiful'] —**pulchritudinous** /púlkri tyoódinəss/ *adj*

pule /pyool/ (**pules**, **puling**, **puled**) *vi* to whine, whimper, or cry plaintively (*archaic*) [Early 16C. Probably an imitation of the sound of whimpering] —**puler** *n*—**pulingly** *adv*

puli[1] /poóli/ (*plural* **-lik** /-lik/ or **-lis**) *n* a medium-sized Hungarian sheepdog with long hair that can be combed out or left corded [Mid-20C. < Hungarian]

puli[2] /poóli/ MONEY plural of **pul**

Pulitzer /poólitsər/, **Joseph** (1847–1911) Hungarian-born US journalist and patron of the arts. He established the Pulitzer Prizes in literature and journalism.

Pulitzer prize /poólitsər-/ *n* a prize awarded annually for excellence in American journalism, literature, or music [Early 20C. After Joseph *Pulitzer*]

pull /pool/ *v* (**pulls**, **pulling**, **pulled**) **1.** *vti* DRAW SOMEBODY OR SOMETHING NEARER to apply force to somebody or something so as to draw or tend to draw that person or thing towards the origin of the force **2.** *vt* REMOVE SOMETHING FORCIBLY to remove or extract something by exerting force **3.** *vt* DRAW LOAD to draw a load such as

a trailer or plough **4.** *vti* TUG AT SOMEBODY OR SOMETHING to tug at or jerk somebody or something **5.** *vt* MED STRAIN MUSCLE to strain and damage a muscle, ligament, or tendon **6.** *vt* PRESS SOMETHING TO OPERATE IT to apply force to a trigger, lever, or switch so as to operate a weapon or machine **7.** *vt* OPEN OR CLOSE CURTAINS to open or close curtains or window coverings **8.** *vti* TEAR SOMETHING to tear or rip something apart or into pieces **9.** *vt* STRETCH SOMETHING to stretch something elastic **10.** *vt* TAKE OUT WEAPON to take out a weapon in readiness to attack somebody (*informal*) **11.** *vt* ATTRACT PEOPLE to draw a large number of people, e.g. as audience members or voters (*informal*) **12.** *vt* DO SOMETHING UNDERHANDEDLY to do something undesirable or despicable in an underhand way (*informal*) ○ *How could you pull such a sneaky trick?* **13.** *vti* AUTOMOT MANOEUVRE VEHICLE to manoeuvre a vehicle in a particular direction **14.** *vi* AUTOMOT DRIFT TO ONE SIDE BECAUSE FAULTY to drift to one side or the other, usually because of a fault (*refers to motor vehicles or their steering*) ○ *My car pulls to the left.* **15.** *vi* AUTOMOT PRODUCE SUFFICIENT DRIVING POWER to produce sufficient driving power to move a vehicle **16.** *vi* INHALE DEEPLY to inhale deeply when smoking, or take a deep gulp at a drink **17.** *vt* BEVERAGES POUR DRINK FROM CASK to extract beer or a similar drink from a cask by operating a handle attached to a pump **18.** *vt* COMM, PUBL REMOVE SOMETHING FROM CIRCULATION to remove something from circulation, or prevent it from ever getting into circulation (*informal*) ○ *The manufacturer pulled the product after safety questions were raised.* **19.** *vti* ATTRACT SEXUAL PARTNER to meet and succeed in attracting somebody, often so as to have a casual and usually brief sexual relationship (*slang*) ○ *Did you pull at the party?* **20.** *vt* PRINTING MAKE PROOF FOR CORRECTION to make a printing proof **21.** *vt* HORSERACING REIN HORSE BACK to rein in a horse, especially so as to prevent it from winning a race **22.** *vt* HIT BALL TOO FAR TO SIDE to hit a ball farther left for a right-handed player or farther right for a left-handed player than intended ■ *n* **1.** ACT OF PULLING the act of pulling somebody or something, or an instance of being pulled **2.** PULLING FORCE the physical force involved in the action of pulling **3.** SUSTAINED EFFORT a sustained effort, especially under difficult circumstances **4.** SOMETHING USED FOR PULLING something used for pulling, e.g. a knob, handle, or tab (*often used in combination*) **5.** DEEP INHALATION OR GULP the inhaling or drinking of something deeply **6.** INFLUENCE special influence, usually because of personal position within an organization or society, or personal connection with somebody (*informal*) ○ *used his pull to get tickets for the final* **7.** POWER TO ATTRACT the ability or power to attract an audience or supporters (*informal*) **8.** PRINTING PROOF COPY FOR CORRECTION a printing proof made for correction **9.** HORSERACING RESTRAINT OF HORSE the restraining of a horse by its rider, especially to keep it from winning **10.** PULLING OF BALL TO SIDE the hitting of a ball farther left for a right-handed player or farther right for a left-handed player than intended, or a ball that is pulled in this way **11.** ARMS RESISTANCE IN FIRING MECHANISM the amount of resistance in a firing mechanism such as a trigger or bowstring [Old English *pullian*, originally 'pluck', probably < W Germanic] —**puller** *n*

SYNONYMS **pull, drag, draw, haul, tow, tug, yank**
CORE MEANING: to move something towards you or in the same direction as you

pull to apply force to somebody or something so as to draw or tend to draw that person or thing towards the origin of the force ○ *They pulled their sledge twenty-four kilometres without skis.* ○ *If you pull the cord, your light'll come on.* **drag** to move something, especially something that is too large, heavy, or cumbersome to carry, by pulling it along the ground or across a surface ○ *dragging the dog over to the car* ○ *a scraping sound as of something being dragged along the ground* **draw** to pull something, or lead or pull somebody, in a particular direction, especially towards or away from something ○ *We reached out and drew her into the circle.* ○ *He drew a silk handkerchief from his pocket.* **haul** to pull something with continuous and laborious movements ○ *He hauled the box up the stairs.* **tow** to pull something such as a barge or a broken-down car along by a rope or chain attached to it ○ *The two boats were towed into the port.* ○ *We had to tow the damaged car back to the pits.* **tug** to pull at or drag somebody or something with a

sharp forceful movement ○ *Frantically, I tried to tug my finger free.* ○ *The child approached and tugged at his arm, whining, 'I want to go home, Daddy'.* **yank** to pull somebody or something suddenly and sharply ○ *He yanked the cable from the socket.* ○ *When the lift stopped, she yanked the gate back and stepped out.*

pull about *vt* to treat somebody or something roughly or brutally

pull ahead *vi* to move in front of or gain a lead over somebody or something moving in the same direction

pull away *vi* **1.** MOVE AWAY to move away from somebody or something **2.** DRAW BACK to draw back from somebody or something, either physically or emotionally **3.** START TO WIN to start to win something such as a competition or race by widening the margin over an opponent

pull back *v* **1.** *vti* to withdraw, or make people, especially troops, withdraw **2.** *vi* to decide not to do something, especially in order to avoid a bad outcome

pull down *vt* **1.** DEMOLISH SOMETHING to destroy or demolish something, especially a building **2.** REDUCE SOMETHING TO LOWER LEVEL to reduce something such as a price to a lower level or value **3.** DECREASE WELLBEING OF SOMEBODY to have a detrimental effect on the health or mental wellbeing of somebody **4.** COMPUT MAKE MENU APPEAR to make a menu appear on a computer screen by clicking on its heading **5.** *N Am* EARN AMOUNT to earn a particular amount of money (*slang*)

pull for *vt N Am* to hope that somebody or something will succeed in an endeavour

pull in *v* **1.** *vi* TRANSP ARRIVE to arrive and stop, usually at a station **2.** *vti* AUTOMOT same as **pull over 3.** *vt* ARREST SOMEBODY to arrest somebody, or take somebody into a police station for questioning (*informal*) **4.** *vt* EARN AMOUNT to earn a particular amount of money (*informal*)

pull off *vt* to achieve something impressive, particularly through a combination of skill and luck (*informal*)

SYNONYMS See **accomplish**.

pull on *vt* to put on clothing or an item of clothing, especially in haste

pull out *v* **1.** *vi* WITHDRAW to withdraw from an obligation or commitment ○ *They are threatening to pull out of the deal.* **2.** *vti* RETREAT to retreat, or cause somebody to retreat ○ *The army is pulling out.* **3.** *vi* TRANSP MANOEUVRE INTO TRAFFIC FLOW to drive a vehicle away from the side of a road, e.g. so as to join a flow of traffic **4.** *vi* TRANSP MANOEUVRE VEHICLE BEFORE OVERTAKING to drive a vehicle out from behind another vehicle so as to overtake **5.** *vi* TRANSP DEPART to depart from a station or stopping place **6.** *vti* AVIAT LEVEL OUT AIRCRAFT FROM DIVE to level out, or make an aircraft level out from a dive

pull over *vti* to drive a vehicle to the side of a road and stop, or make the driver of a vehicle do this

pull through *vti* to recover from a period of illness or difficulties, or help somebody to do this

pull together *v* **1.** *vi* to cooperate, collaborate, or work together **2.** **pull yourself together** *vr* to recover your composure or self-control (*informal*)

pull up *v* **1.** *vti* TRANSP ARRIVE SOMEWHERE to arrive and stop at a place, or make a person, animal, or vehicle do this **2.** *vt* SCOLD SOMEBODY to scold or reprimand somebody sharply **3.** *vi* CATCH UP IN RACE to move into a closer or level position with somebody, e.g. in a race

pullback /póol bak/ *n* **1.** an act of pulling back, especially a withdrawal of troops **2.** a device for holding, restraining, or drawing something back

pull-down *adj* describes a software menu or another item that can be made to appear on a computer screen by clicking on its heading ■ *n* a pull-down feature on a computer screen

pulled threadwork /póold-/ *n* an embroidery technique in which tight stitches are used to draw some threads together and separate others, thereby forming lacy patterns

pullet /póollit/ *n* a young female chicken, especially one that has not started to lay eggs [14C. < French *poulet* 'little hen' < *poule* 'hen' < Latin *pulla*, feminine of *pullus* 'chicken, young animal']

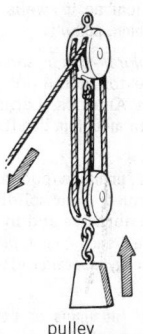

pulley

pulley /póolli/ (*plural* **-leys**) *n* **1.** WHEEL WITH GROOVED RIM a mounted rotating wheel with a grooved rim over which a belt or chain can move to change the direction of a pulling force **2.** SYSTEM OF PULLEYS a system of pulleys together with a mounting block and tackle, used to improve leverage in lifting heavy weights **3.** *Scotland* FRAME ON PULLEYS FOR DRYING CLOTHES in Scotland, a frame on which clothes are dried that is raised to the ceiling by means of pulleys [14C. < French *polie*, probably < Greek *polos* 'pole']

pull factor *n* **1.** a measure of the strength of the retail trade in an area, based on a comparison of local spending in relation to that of a wider geographical area, e.g. a state ○ *The pull factor equates sales per person in the town with sales per person in the state.* **2.** a social or environmental benefit that draws people from one region or country to another

pull-in *n* (*dated*) **1.** an area at the side of a road where drivers can pull over and stop their vehicles **2.** a café catering for drivers, situated beside a road

pulling power /póoling-/ *n* the ability to attract the interest of people, either commercially or sexually ○ *Five ways to increase the pulling power of your ads.* ○ *great clothes with pulling power*

Pullman /póolmən/ *n* **1.** a comfortable train-carriage for sitting or sleeping in **2.** *US* a large suitcase [Mid-19C. After George PULLMAN]

Pullman /póolmən/, **George** (1831–97) US inventor and manufacturer. He designed the first railway sleeping car (1863). Full name **Pullman, George Mortimer**

pull-ons *npl* women's trousers with an elasticated waist and no fastening, usually made in a plain style in comfortable stretchy fabric

pullorum disease /póo láwrəm-/ *n* a highly infectious disease of young poultry caused by the bacterium *Salmonella pullorum*, and marked by diarrhoea [< modern Latin *pullorum*, 'of chickens']

pullout /póol owt/ *n* **1.** PUBL REMOVABLE SECTION OF PUBLICATION an object intended to be pulled out of a publication, e.g. a removable section of a magazine or a part of a book that folds out **2.** WITHDRAWAL a withdrawal from an obligation or other demanding situation **3.** RETREAT a retreat from a place or military involvement **4.** OBJECT FOR PULLING OUT an object intended to be pulled out, especially a piece of furniture that can be pulled out from a wall or opened out ○ *a pullout couch* **5.** AVIAT LEVELLING-OUT MANOEUVRE OF AIRCRAFT an aircraft manoeuvre in which a dive changes to level flight

pullover /póol ōvər/ *n* a garment, especially a jumper, put on by being pulled over the head

pull-tab *n N Am* BEVERAGES same as **ring-pull**

pull technology *n* Internet technology that provides data or other material when a user requests an update or chooses to retrieve content from a supplier. Web browsing is an example of pull technology.

pull-through *n* a weighted cord with a rag at one end, pulled through a wind instrument or the barrel of a rifle to clean the inside of it

pullulate /púllyoo layt/ (**-lates, -lating, -lated**) *vi* **1.** TEEM to teem or swarm with something (*literary*) **2.** BOT GERMINATE to germinate or sprout (*technical*) **3.** ZOOL BREED to breed freely or rapidly (*technical*) [Early 17C. < Latin *pullulat-*, past participle of *pullulare* 'grow, sprout' < *pullus* 'chicken, young animal'] —**pullulation** /púllyoo láysh'n/ *n*

pull-up *n* **1.** *UK* a physical exercise in which the hands are placed on an overhead horizontal bar, and the body is lifted by pulling upwards with the arms. ANZ, N Am term **chin-up 2.** ROADS, COMM same as **pull-in** (*dated*)

pulmonary /púlmənəri, pool-/ *adj* **1.** relating to or affecting the lungs **2.** ZOOL same as **pulmonate** *adj* (sense 1) [Early 18C. < Latin *pulmonarius* < *pulmo* 'lung']

pulmonary anthrax *n* a form of pneumonia caused by inhaling anthrax bacteria

pulmonary artery *n* either of two arteries that carry blood in need of oxygen from the right side of the heart to the lungs

pulmonary vein *n* one of the four veins that carry oxygen-rich blood from the lungs to the left side of the heart

pulmonate /púlmənət, pool-/ ZOOL *adj* **1.** WITH LUNGS having lungs or organs that function as lungs **2.** WITH SAC LIKE LUNG describes a mollusc that has a sac functioning as a lung ■ *n* MOLLUSC WITH LUNG SAC a mollusc with a sac functioning as a lung, e.g. land snails, slugs, and many freshwater snails. Subclass: Pulmonata. [Mid-19C. < modern Latin *pulmonatus* < Latin *pulmo* 'lung']

pulmonic /pul mónnik, pool-/ *adj* ANAT same as **pulmonary** (sense 1) [Mid-17C. Directly or via French < modern Latin *pulmonicus* < Latin *pulmo* 'lung']

pulmonology /póolmə nólləji/ *n* the branch of medicine that deals with the structure, physiology, and diseases of the lungs —**pulmonologic** /póolmənə lójjik/ *adj* —**pulmonological** *adj* —**pulmonologist** *n*

pulp /pulp/ *n* **1.** SOFT MATERIAL a soft or soggy mass **2.** CRUSHED WOOD FOR PAPER crushed wood or other materials that are used to make paper **3.** CHEAP BOOKS OR MAGAZINES novels or magazines produced on cheap paper, especially crime, horror, or science fiction stories (*often used before a noun*) ○ *a prize collection of classic pulp fiction* **4.** SOFT FLESHY PLANT TISSUE soft fleshy plant tissue, e.g. the inner part of a fruit or vegetable **5.** STEM PITH the pith inside a plant stem **6.** DENT INSIDE OF TOOTH the sensitive tissue at the centre of a tooth, consisting of nerves and blood vessels **7.** PULVERIZED ORE ore that has been mined and pulverized, especially when mixed with water ■ *v* (**pulps, pulping, pulped**) **1.** *vti* CRUSH SOMETHING to crush something into pulp, or be crushed into pulp **2.** *vt* REMOVE PULP FROM SOMETHING to remove the pulp from something, especially the soft fleshy tissue from fruit or vegetables [14C. < Latin *pulpa*] —**pulpy** *adj*

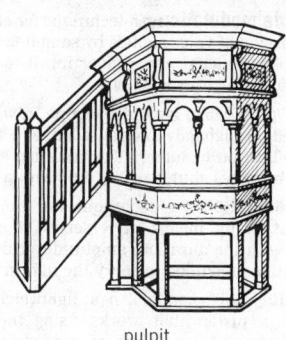

pulpit

pulpit /póolpit/ *n* **1.** PLATFORM IN CHURCH a raised platform or stand in a Christian church that is used by the priest or minister for preaching or leading a service **2.** CHRISTIAN CLERGY the Christian clergy considered as a group **3.** GUARDRAIL ON BOAT a metal guardrail on the bow or stern of a small boat [14C. < Latin *pulpitum* 'platform, scaffold', (in late Latin) 'pulpit']

pulpwood /púlp wood/ *n* a soft wood that is used to make paper, e.g. aspen, pine, or spruce

pulque /póolki, pool kay/ *n* a thick alcoholic drink made in Mexico from the sap of the agave plant [Late 17C. Via Mexican Spanish < Nahuatl *puliuhki* 'decomposed']

pulsar /púl saar/ *n* a small dense star that emits brief intense bursts of visible radiation, radio waves, and X-rays, and is generally believed to be a rapidly rotating neutron star [Mid-20C. Contraction of *pulsating star*, after QUASAR]

pulsate /pul sáyt/ (**-sates, -sating, -sated**) *vi* **1.** THROB to vibrate or throb **2.** BE FULL OF ENERGY to be full of energy, bustling activity, or excitement ○ *The whole city is pulsating with excitement at this time of year.* **3.** PHYSIOL EXPAND AND CONTRACT to expand and contract with a strong regular beat (*refers to blood vessels*) **4.** PHYSIOL VARY REPEATEDLY IN INTENSITY OR MAGNITUDE to vary in intensity or magnitude, especially in a repeated way [Late 18C. < Latin *pulsat-*, past participle of *pulsare* 'beat repeatedly' < *pellere* 'to beat'] —**pulsatory** /púlssətəri, pul sáytəri/ *adj*

pulsatile /púlssə tīl/ *adj* pulsating or vibrating rhythmically —**pulsatility** /púlssə tílləti/ *n*

pulsation /pul sáysh'n/ *n* PHYSIOL **1.** PULSATING the act of pulsating **2.** BEATING OF HEART the rhythmic change in volume that takes place in the heart or an artery **3.** BEAT a single beat or pulse

pulsative /púlssə tiv/ *adj* same as **pulsatile**

pulsator /pul sáytər/ *n* **1.** a device or machine that pulsates while operating **2.** a device that stimulates or maintains a rhythmic motion such as respiration

pulse[1] /pulss/ *n* **1.** REGULAR BEAT OF BLOOD FLOW the regular expansion and contraction of an artery, caused by the heart pumping blood through the body. It can be felt through an artery that is near the surface such as the one in the wrist on the same side as the thumb. **2.** SINGLE BEAT OF BLOOD FLOW a single expansion and contraction of an artery, caused by a beat of the heart **3.** RHYTHMIC BEAT a beat or throb, e.g. of a drum, or a series of rhythmic beats or throbs **4.** CHANGE OR REPEATING CHANGE IN MAGNITUDE a brief temporary change in a normally constant quantity, e.g. in a voltage, or a series of intermittent disturbances that are regular in form and frequency of occurrence **5.** CURRENT ATTITUDES the sentiments, opinions, or attitudes current in a society or group ○ *a journalist who really has a finger on the pulse of society* **6.** VITALITY energy and excitement ○ *I love the pulse of city life.* ■ *vi* (**pulses, pulsing, pulsed**) **1.** BEAT RHYTHMICALLY to move or throb with a strong regular rhythm **2.** PHYS UNDERGO BRIEF SUDDEN CHANGES to undergo a series of brief sudden changes in quantity, e.g. in voltage **3.** BE ENERGETIC to be full of energy and excitement ○ *an area pulsing with creative energy* [14C. Via French < Latin *puls-*, past participle of *pellere* 'to beat']

pulse[2] /pulss/ *n* **1.** an edible seed from a pod, e.g. a pea or bean, eaten fresh or dried **2.** a plant that has pods as fruits and roots that bear nodules containing nitrogen-fixing bacteria, e.g. the pea, bean, alfalfa, or clover [13C. Via French < Latin *puls* 'porridge']

pulse code modulation *n* a technique for electronic transmission of voice signals by sampling the amplitude of the signal and converting it to a coded digital form for transmission

pulsejet /púlss jet/ *n* a ramjet engine in which air, admitted through movable vanes, mixes with fuel in the combustion chamber. The resulting explosion forces the vanes shut, causing a pulsating thrust.

pulse modulation *n* a technique for transmitting information by means of a series of electrical pulses, with the duration, amplitude, or frequency of the pulses modified to carry the information

pulsometer /pul sómmitər/ *n* a lightweight pump without a piston that works using the partial vacuum created by pulses of condensing steam being forced between two chambers [Mid-19C. < PULSE[1]]

pulverize /púlvə rīz/ (**-izes, -izing, -ized**), **pulverise** (**-ises, -ising, -ised**) *v* **1.** *vti* CRUSH SOMETHING TO POWDER to crush or grind something into a powder or dust, or be crushed or ground into a powder or dust **2.** *vt* DESTROY SOMETHING to demolish something completely (*informal*) ○ *The storm pulverized the town.* **3.** *vt* DEFEAT SOMEBODY to subject an opponent to a crushing defeat (*informal*) ○ *We completely pulverized the other team.* [15C. < late Latin *pulverizare* < Latin *pulver-* 'powder, dust'] —**pulverizable** *adj* —**pulverization** /púlvə rī záysh'n/ *n* —**pulverizer** *n*

pulvinate /púlvi nayt/ *adj* **1.** shaped like a cushion **2.** describes a leafstalk that has a swelling at its base [Early 19C. < Latin *pulvinatus* < *pulvinus* 'cushion, pillow']

pulvinus /pul vínəss/ (*plural* **-ni** /-nī/) *n* a swelling at the base of a leafstalk that causes changes in the

position of the leaf as it swells and shrinks [Mid-19C. < Latin, 'cushion, pillow']

puma /pyóomə/ (*plural* **-mas** or *same*) *n* a large tawny wild cat. Native to: mountains of Canada to the forests of South America. Latin name: *Felis concolor*. N Am term **mountain lion** [Late 18C. Via Spanish < Quechua *púma*]

pumice /púmmiss/, **pumicite** /púmmi sīt/ *n* a very light porous rock formed from solidified lava, used in solid form as an abrasive and in powdered form as a polish [15C. Via French < Latin *pumic-* 'foam', because of the stone's spongy appearance] —**pumiceous** /pyoo míshəss/ *adj*

pummel /púmm'l/ (**pummels** or **pommels, pummelling** or **pommelling, pummelled** or **pommelled**) *vt* **1.** to hit somebody or something with repeated blows, especially using the fists **2.** to cause serious damage to something [Mid-16C. Alteration of POMMEL]

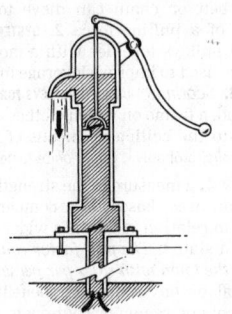

pump: cross section of a water pump

pump[1] /pump/ *v* (**pumps, pumping, pumped**) **1.** *vti* MAKE LIQUID OR GAS FLOW to force a liquid or gas to flow **2.** *vt* MAKE SOMETHING MOVE UP AND DOWN to move a handle, lever, or other device up and down energetically ○ *frantically pumping the brakes* **3.** *vt* ASK SOMEBODY QUESTIONS to try to get information from somebody by asking questions repeatedly and forcefully **4.** *vt* MED FLUSH OUT SOMEBODY'S STOMACH to flush out the contents of somebody's stomach, usually to remove poison, drugs, or alcohol. A tube and a funnel are used to pour in water and allow the diluted stomach contents to run out. ■ *n* **1.** MECH ENG DEVICE FOR MOVING LIQUID OR GAS a device that is used to raise, compress, or transfer liquids or gases and is operated by a piston or similar mechanism **2.** PHYSIOL WAY OF MOVING IONS OR MOLECULES a mechanism for the active movement of ions or molecules across a cell membrane [15C. Probably ultimately an imitation of the sound of pumping]

pump into *vt* to supply a large quantity of something, especially money, for something ○ *pumping money into the local economy*

pump out *vt* **1.** to produce something continually and in large quantities ○ *a new radio station pumping out dance music 24 hours a day* **2.** to remove fluid from something using a pump ○ *We had to pump out the boat again because it was leaking so badly.*

pump up *vt* **1.** INFLATE SOMETHING to inflate something such as a tyre or ball using a pump **2.** TURN SOMETHING UP to increase the volume of sound, especially of music, produced by amplifiers or speakers (*informal*) **3.** MAKE SOMEBODY EXCITED to make somebody excited or enthusiastic (*informal*) ○ *pumped them up for the game* **4.** GYM BUILD MUSCLE to increase the mass of a muscle by body-building techniques (*informal*)

pump[2] /pump/ *n* **1.** CANVAS SHOE WITH RUBBER SOLE a low flat canvas shoe with a rubber sole, worn especially by children for physical education **2.** SOFT SHOE FOR DANCING a light soft shoe for dancing **3.** *N Am* CLOTHING same as **court shoe 4.** *US* MAN'S FORMAL SHOE a man's patent leather slip-on shoe worn with formal attire [Mid-16C. Origin ?]

pump-and-dump, pump-'n-dump *adj* describes a fraudulent scheme in which unscrupulous stockbrokers, commentators, or shareholders highly recommend their own shares in order to drive up the price before selling for a quick profit (*slang*)

pumped storage /púmpt-/ *n* a way of generating hydroelectric power during peak periods that involves pumping water up to a reservoir during

periods of low demand and releasing it during peak periods

pumpernickel /púmpər nik'l, póom-/ *n* a dark dense, slightly sour bread that is made from coarse rye flour [Mid-18C. < German dialect, earlier 'person regarded as loutish' < *pumpern* 'break wind' + *Nickel* 'goblin']

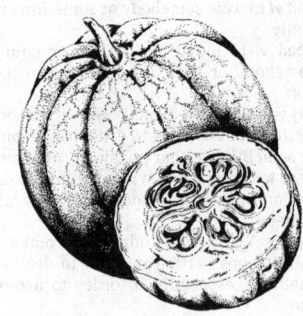

pumpkin

pumpkin /púmpkin/ *n* **1.** a round large fruit with a thick orange-skinned rind, pulpy flesh, and many seeds, cooked and eaten as a vegetable or in sweet dishes **2.** the trailing or climbing plant that produces pumpkins. Genus: *Cucurbita*. [Late 17C. Alteration of obsolete *pumpion*, via obsolete French *pompon, popon* < Latin *pepon-, pepo* 'pumpkin, large melon' < Greek *pepōn*, literally 'ripe']

pumpkinseed /púmpkin seed/ *n* **1.** a seed of a pumpkin **2.** a common freshwater sunfish that has an olive-coloured upper body shading to yellow or orange on its belly, with one red spot on each gill cover. Native to: North America. Latin name: *Lepomis gibbosus*. [Early 19C. In sense 2 < its shape and orange colour]

pump priming *n* **1.** the use of investment to stimulate the economy in depressed regions and bring about self-sustaining growth **2.** the process or act of making a pump work more effectively by pouring fluid into it as it starts up

pump room *n* a building or room at a spa where mineral water can be drunk

pum pum /púm pum/ *n* a highly offensive term for a woman's genitals (*taboo; used in Black English*) [Origin ?]

pun /pun/ *n* a humorous use of words that involves a word or phrase that has more than one possible meaning ■ *vi* (**puns, punning, punned**) to make, or use puns [Mid-17C. Origin ?] —**punner** *n* —**punny** *adj*

puna /póonə/ *n* **1.** MED same as **altitude sickness 2.** a cold dry flat treeless area at a high altitude in the Andes [Early 17C. Via American Spanish < Quechua]

punani /poo naáni/ (*plural* **-nis**) *n* a highly offensive term for a woman's genitals (*taboo; used in Black English*) [< Hawaiian, literally 'heavenly flower']

Puncak Jaya /póon chaak jaá yaa/ highest mountain in Indonesia, in the Surdiman Range, in western New Guinea. Height: 5,030 m/16,502 ft.

punch[1] /punch/ *vt* **1.** HIT SOMEBODY OR SOMETHING to hit somebody or something with the fist **2.** PRESS BUTTON to press a key or button on a computer keyboard or other device with a quick thrusting movement of the finger ○ *Punch the return key.* **3.** HIT BALL USING SHORT SWING in some sports, to hit a ball using a short sharp swing **4.** *US* POKE SOMETHING to poke or prod something **5.** *N Am* AGRIC HERD CATTLE to herd cattle on horseback **6.** *Aus* FOOTBALL PASS BALL in Australian Rules, to pass the ball by punching it to another player ■ *n* **1.** BLOW WITH FIST a blow to somebody or something with a fist **2.** VIGOUR drive, energy, or power that enlivens or invigorates something ○ *a performance that lacked punch.* **3.** *Aus* FOOTBALL FOOTBALL PASS in Australian Rules, a pass made by punching the ball to another player [14C. < Old French *poinsonner* 'to prick' < *poinson, poinchon* (see PUNCHEON[2])] ◇ **not pull any** or **your punches, pull no punches** to use as much force and energy as necessary or possible in order to attain a goal or convey a message ◇ **pack a punch** to be very powerful or strong (*informal*) ◇ **roll with the punches** to adapt easily to a difficult situation (*informal*)

punch in *v* **1.** *vi N Am* to arrive for work, or record the

time of arrival for work, by inserting a personalized card into a time clock **2.** *vt* to enter information into a computer using the keyboard

punch out *v* **1.** *vi N Am* to leave work, or record the time of departure from work, by inserting a personalized card into a time clock **2.** *vt US* to knock somebody unconscious with a hard punch

punch[2] /punch/ *n* **1.** TOOL FOR MAKING HOLES a tool used to make holes in a material or an object **2.** TOOL FOR STAMPING OR CUTTING DESIGNS a tool that is hit to stamp a design on something or to cut something to a shape **3.** STAMPING OR CUTTING PART OF PUNCH the die or solid part of a punch, containing the stamping or cutting tool **4.** TOOL FOR DRIVING BOLTS OUT a tool used to knock a bolt or rivet out of a hole ■ *vt* **(punches, punching, punched) 1.** MAKE HOLE USING PUNCH to make a hole using a punch **2.** STAMP SOMETHING USING PUNCH to stamp or cut something using a punch [Early 16C. Origin ?]

punch[3] /punch/ *n* a drink made with a mixture of fruit juice, spices, and often wine or spirits, usually served hot [Mid-17C. Origin ?]

Punch /punch/ *n* a character from traditional children's puppet shows. He is a red-cheeked hook-nosed clown who behaves in an argumentative or aggressive manner. [Late 17C. Shortening of PUNCHINELLO] ◇ **pleased as Punch** extremely pleased (*informal*)

Punch and Judy, Punch-and-Judy show *n* a comic children's puppet show featuring Punch and Judy, a quarrelsome couple, together with a number of other standard characters

punchbag /púnch bag/ *n* **1.** *UK* a large heavy bag, usually suspended from a rope, used by boxers to improve their punching skills **2.** somebody who is regularly abused or treated with disrespect (*informal*) ▶ ANZ, N Am term **punching bag**

punchball /púnch bawl/ *n* a large heavy ball on a stand, used for training or exercise, especially by boxers

punchboard /púnch bawrd/ *n* a board with small holes, each containing a slip of paper. Players buy a chance to punch out a slip to see if they have won a prize.

punchbowl /púnch bōl/ *n* **1.** a large bowl for serving punch, often with a matching ladle and cups **2.** a bowl-shaped hollow found on hills or mountains

punch card *n* a card with patterns of holes punched in it, used to store information in early computers and telex machines

punch-drunk *adj* **1.** dazed or confused by something such as a bad experience (*informal*) **2.** showing signs of confusion and disorientation as a result of brain damage caused by blows to the head during boxing bouts

punched card /púncht-/ *n* COMPUT same as **punch card**

punched tape *n* a strip of paper tape with patterns of holes punched in it, used to store information in early computers and telex machines

puncheon[1] /púnchən, púnshən/ *n* **1.** a large cask containing between 70 and 100 gallons **2.** a unit of capacity, equal to between 70 and 100 gallons [15C. < Old French *poinçon, poinchon*]

puncheon[2] /púnchən, púnshən/ *n* a short upright piece of wood used for structural framing [15C. < Old French *poinchon* < Latin *punct-*, past participle of *pungere* 'prick, sting']

Punchinello /púnchi néllō/ (*plural* **-los**) *n* **1.** a comic character who appears in Italian puppet and clown shows and is probably the source of Punch **2.** somebody who is considered silly or unintelligent (*archaic*) [Mid-17C. < Italian dialect *Pollecinella*]

punching bag /púnching-/ *n ANZ, N Am* BOXING same as **punchbag** (sense 1)

punchline /púnch līn/ *n* the last part of a joke or funny story that delivers the meaning and the bulk of the humour [< PUNCH[1]]

punch pass *n* FOOTBALL same as **handpass** —**punch-pass** *vi*

punch-up *n UK, Aus, Can* a fistfight or brawl (*informal*)

punchy /púnchi/ **(-ier, -iest)** *adj* (*informal*) **1.** forceful and concise ○ *a good punchy slogan* **2.** same as **punch-drunk** [Early 20C. < PUNCH[1]] —**punchily** *adv* —**punchiness** *n*

punctate /púngk tayt/ *adj* having tiny spots, holes, or dents ○ *a punctate leaf* [Mid-17C. < Latin *punctum* (see POINT)] —**punctation** /pungk táysh'n/ *n*

punctilio /pungk tílli ō/ (*plural* **-os**) *n* (*formal*) **1.** strict adherence to even the finest points of etiquette **2.** a very fine point of etiquette [Late 16C. Via obsolete Italian *puntiglio* and Spanish *puntillo* 'small point' < Latin *punctum* (see POINT)]

punctilious /pungk tílli əss/ *adj* **1.** very careful about the conventions of correct behaviour and etiquette ○ *always punctilious in his manners* **2.** showing great care in small details ○ *a punctilious execution of a complex design* [Mid-17C. < French *pointilleux* < *pointille* 'small point' < *pointe* < Latin *punctum* (see POINT)] —**punctiliously** *adv* —**punctiliousness** *n*

SYNONYMS See ***careful***.

punctual /púngkchoo əl/ *adj* **1.** arriving or taking place at the arranged time ○ *a punctual start to a meeting* **2.** MATHS relating to or possessing the properties of a point in space [14C. < medieval Latin *punctualis* < Latin *punctum* (see POINT)] —**punctuality** /púngkchoo állәti/ *n* —**punctually** *adv*

punctuate /púngktyoo ayt/ **(-ates, -ating, -ated)** *v* **1.** *vti* ADD PUNCTUATION TO TEXT to put punctuation marks in written work **2.** *vt* INTERRUPT SOMETHING OFTEN to interrupt a situation or activity frequently (*often passive*) ○ *a talk punctuated by humorous anecdotes* **3.** *vt* EMPHASIZE SOMETHING to do or say something in order to add emphasis [Mid-17C. < medieval Latin *punctuat-*, past participle of *punctuare* 'mark with points' < Latin *punctum* (see POINT)] —**punctuator** *n*

punctuated equilibrium /púngkchoo aytid-/ *n* a theory of evolution holding that evolutionary change tends to be characterized by long periods of stability, or equilibrium, punctuated by episodes of very fast development

punctuation /púngkchoo áysh'n/ *n* **1.** MARKS USED TO ORGANIZE WRITING the standardized nonalphabetical symbols or marks that are used to organize writing into clauses, phrases, and sentences, and in this way make its meaning clear **2.** USE OF PUNCTUATION the use of punctuation marks **3.** ACT OF PUNCTUATING WRITING the act of punctuating writing, or an occasion during which writing is punctuated

punctuation mark *n* a symbol that is used to organize and clarify the meaning of writing, e.g. a comma, full stop, or question mark

puncture /púngkchər/ *n* SMALL HOLE a small hole or wound made by a sharp object ■ *v* **(-tures, -turing, -tured) 1.** *vti* MAKE OR GET HOLE to sustain a small hole or wound in something such as a tyre or the skin, or cause such a hole **2.** *vt* RUIN SOMEBODY'S CONFIDENCE to suddenly reduce or destroy somebody's confidence, arrogance, or conviction ○ *The interview punctured his self-esteem.* [14C. < Latin *punctura* < *punct-*, past participle of *pungere* 'prick, sting'] —**puncturable** *adj* —**puncturer** *n*

pundit /púndit/ *n* **1.** a critic or authority on a subject, especially in the media ○ *The election results surprised the political pundits.* **2.** somebody with knowledge and wisdom **3.** RELIG same as **pandit** [Late 17C. Via Hindi *paṇḍit* < Sanskrit *paṇḍita-* 'learned']

Pune /po͞onə/ city in Maharashtra State, west-central India. Population: 3,755,525 (2001).

pungent /púnjənt/ *adj* **1.** STRONG SMELLING OR STRONG TASTING having a strong smell or a powerfully sharp or bitter taste **2.** CAUSTIC expressed in or showing a witty and biting manner ○ *pungent observations about government corruption* **3.** BIOL SHARP AND POINTED describes a plant or animal part that ends in a sharp point ○ *a plant with elongated pungent leaves* [Late 16C. < Latin *pungent-*, present participle of *pungere* 'prick, sting'] —**pungency** *n* —**pungently** *adv*

Punic /pyo͞onik/ *adj* relating to the ancient Carthaginians, Carthage, or the Carthaginian language ■ *n* a Semitic language of ancient Carthage, related to Phoenician [15C. < Latin *Punicus* < *Poenus* < Greek *Phoinix* 'Phoenician']

punish /púnnish/ **(-ishes, -ishing, -ished)** *v* **1.** *vti* MAKE SOMEBODY UNDERGO PENALTY to subject somebody to a penalty for wrongdoing **2.** *vt* IMPOSE PENALTY ON CRIME to respond to a crime or other wrong act by imposing a penalty (*often passive*) ○ *crimes formerly punished by death* **3.** *vt* TREAT SOMEBODY OR SOMETHING ROUGHLY to treat somebody or something harshly, causing damage or pain ○ *punished the champ with some powerful body blows* **4.** *vt* TREAT SOMEBODY UNFAIRLY to treat somebody unfairly or discriminate against somebody **5.** *vt* EAT OR DRINK SOMETHING to eat or drink something quickly and enthusiastically (*informal*) ○ *The guests were really punishing the hors d'oeuvres.* [14C. < Old French *puniss-*, stem of *punir* < Latin *punire* < *poena* 'penalty'] —**punishable** *adj* —**punisher** *n*

punishing /púnnishing/ *adj* very demanding, either physically or mentally ○ *a punishing schedule* —**punishingly** *adv*

punishment /púnnishmənt/ *n* **1.** ACT OF PUNISHING the act or an instance of punishing **2.** PENALTY FOR DOING SOMETHING WRONG a penalty that is imposed on somebody for wrongdoing **3.** ROUGH USE rough treatment or heavy use ○ *a sturdy car that can take a lot of punishment*

punitive /pyo͞onətiv/, **punitory** /pyo͞onitəri/ *adj* **1.** relating to, done as, or imposed as a punishment ○ *punitive air strikes* **2.** causing great difficulty or hardship ○ *punitive taxation* [Early 17C. < medieval Latin *punitivus* < Latin *punit-*, past participle of *punire* (see PUNISH)] —**punitively** *adv* —**punitiveness** *n*

punitive damages *npl* damages that are awarded by a court to punish the defendant rather than to compensate the victim

punitory *adj* same as **punitive**

Punjab /punjaáb/ **1.** former province in the northwest of British India, divided in 1947, when the eastern part became the Indian state of Punjab (divided in 1966 into three on linguistic grounds) and the western part became the Pakistan province of Punjab **2.** state in northwestern India, bordering the province of Punjab in Pakistan. Capital: Chandigarh. Population: 24,289,296 (2001). Area: 50,362 sq. km/19,445 sq. mi. **3.** province of northeastern Pakistan, bordering the Indian state of Punjab. Capital: Lahore. Population: 72,585,000 (1998). Area: 205,344 sq. km/79,284 sq. mi.

Punjabi /pun jaábi/, **Panjabi** *adj* OF PUNJAB relating to the states or the former province of Punjab, or their people or culture ■ *n* (*plural* **-bis**) **1.** SOMEBODY FROM PUNJAB somebody who comes from Punjab **2.** LANGUAGE OF PUNJAB a language that is the official language of Punjab, India, belonging to the Indo-Iranian language family. Native speakers: 70 million. [Early 19C. < Urdu *Panjābī* < *Panjāb* 'Punjab' < Sanskrit *pañca āpas* 'five rivers']

punk /pungk/ *n* **1.** YOUTH MOVEMENT a youth movement of the late 1970s, characterized by loud aggressive rock music, confrontational attitudes, body piercing, and unconventional hairstyles, makeup, and clothing **2.** SOMEBODY BELONGING TO PUNK MOVEMENT a member of the punk movement of the late 1970s **3.** MUSIC same as **punk rock 4.** OFFENSIVE TERM an offensive term for a young man regarded as worthless, lazy, or arrogant (*informal*) **5.** *US* DRIED WOOD dried or decayed wood used as tinder ■ *adj* NO GOOD inferior in quality or condition (*informal*) [Late 17C. Origin ?]

punka /púngkə/, **punkah** *n S Asia* a hand-held fan for cooling or ventilation, or, formerly, a ceiling fan operated by an attendant [Early 17C. Via Hindi *paṅkhā* < Sanskrit *pakṣakaḥ* < *pakṣaḥ* 'wing']

punk rock *n* fast loud rock music often with confrontational lyrics that characterized the punk movement —**punk rocker** *n*

punnet /púnnit/ *n* a small light rectangular basket or container in which fruits such as strawberries or raspberries are sold [Early 19C. Origin ?]

punny /púnni/ *n* a highly offensive term for a woman's genitals (*taboo; used in Black English*)

punster /púnstər/ *n* somebody who frequently makes puns

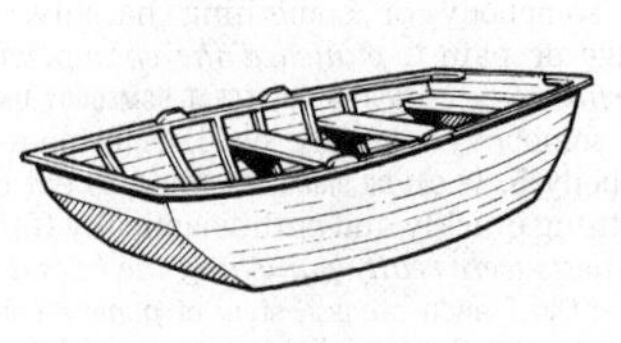

punt

punt[1] /punt/ *n* **FLAT-BOTTOMED BOAT** a narrow open boat with square ends that has a flat bottom and is propelled by means of a long pole ■ *v* (**punts, punting, punted**) **1.** *vi* **GO IN PUNT** to travel in a punt **2.** *vti* **PROPEL PUNT** to propel a punt using a long pole [Pre-12C. < Latin *ponto*] —**punter** *n*

punt[2] /punt/ *n* **KICK** a kick in which somebody drops a ball and kicks it before it hits the ground ■ *v* **1.** *vti* **KICK BALL** to drop a ball and then kick it before it hits the ground **2.** *vi US* **GIVE UP SOMETHING** to stop doing something, especially something regarded as tedious or difficult (*informal*) ○ *I did sit down to study, but decided to punt.* [Mid-19C. Origin ?] —**punter** *n*

punt[3] /punt/ *n* a bet or gamble, especially one placed with a bookmaker (*informal*) ■ *vi* (**punts, punting, punted**) to bet or gamble, especially with a bookmaker [Early 18C. < French *ponter*]

punt[4] /punt/ *n* the main unit of the former Irish currency [Late 20C. < Irish *púnt*]

punt[5] /punt/ *n* the indentation in the bottom of a champagne or wine bottle [Mid-19C. Origin ?]

Punta Arenas /poŏntə ə ráynəss/ city in southern Chile, on the Strait of Magellan, the southernmost city in the world. Population: 125,631 (1998).

punter /púntər/ *n* **1. CUSTOMER** an ordinary member of the public, especially a customer or a member of an audience (*slang*) ○ *Give the punters what they want: that's my motto.* **2. GAMBLER** somebody who takes part in gambling (*informal*) **3. PROSTITUTE'S CLIENT** a client of a prostitute (*informal*) [Early 18C. < PUNT[3]]

Puntland /poŏntlənd/ autonomous region of north-eastern Somalia, which is seeking independent nation status

punty /púnti/ (*plural* **-ties**) *n* a long metal rod on which molten glass is turned and worked during the glass-blowing process [Mid-17C. < French *pontil* 'pontil']

puny /pyoóni/ *adj* **1.** very small or thin and weak **2.** less than is required to be effective ○ *a puny attempt at an apology* [Late 16C. Anglicization of PUISNE] —**punily** *adv* —**puniness** *n*

pup /pup/ *n* **1. YOUNG DOG** a dog under a year old **2. YOUNG ANIMAL** a young animal of various species such as mice, rats, and seals **3. IMPUDENT YOUTH** an inexperienced or arrogant young person, especially a boy or young man (*dated informal*) ■ *vi* (**pups, pupping, pupped**) **BEAR PUPS** to give birth to pups [Late 16C. Shortening of PUPPY] ◇ **be sold a pup** to buy something worthless or useless (*informal*)

pupa /pyoópə/ (*plural* **-pae** /-pee/ or **-pas**) *n* an insect at the stage between a larva and an adult in complete metamorphosis, during which the insect is in a cocoon or case, stops feeding, and undergoes internal changes [Late 18C. < Latin, 'girl, doll'] —**pupal** *adj*

pupate /pyoo páyt/ (**-pates, -pating, -pated**) *vi* to develop from a larva into a pupa —**pupation** /pyoo páysh'n/ *n*

pupfish /púp fish/ (*plural same* or **-fishes**) *n* a tiny killifish. Native to: streams and springs in southwestern United States and Mexico. Genus: *Cyprinodon.*

pupil[1] /pyoóp'l/ *n* **1. STUDENT** a young student, taught at school or by a private teacher **2. FOLLOWER OR STUDENT OF SOMEBODY** a student who learns from a mentor or other person who is skilled, knowledgeable, or experienced ○ *a pupil of Jung* **3.** LAW **TRAINEE BARRISTER** somebody who trains to become a barrister **4.** LAW **CHILD IN CARE OF LEGAL GUARDIAN** in Scottish law, a girl under 12 or a boy under 14 who is in the care of a legal guardian [14C. < Latin *pupillus* 'little boy' < *pupus* 'boy']

pupil[2] /pyoóp'l/ *n* the dark circular opening at the centre of the iris in the eye, where light enters the eye [14C. Via French < Latin *pupilla* 'little doll' < *pupa* 'girl, doll'; from the tiny image that you see when looking into another person's eye]

pupillage /pyoópəlij/ *n* **1.** the state of being a pupil, or the period during which somebody is a pupil **2.** in English law, the period of time that a trainee barrister spends working in the chambers of a member of the bar immediately before qualifying

pupillary[1] /pyoópələri/ *adj* relating to a pupil or a legal ward of a guardian [Early 17C. Directly or via French < Latin *pupillaris* < *pupillus* (see PUPIL[1])]

pupillary[2] /pyoópələri/ *adj* relating to or affecting the pupil of the eye [Late 18C. < Latin *pupilla* (see PUPIL[2])]

puppa /púppə/ *n* same as **father** (*slang; used in Black English*) [Late 20C. Probably variant of POPPA]

puppet /púppit/ *n* **1.** a doll or figure representing a person or animal that is moved using the hands inside the figure or by moving rods, strings, or wires attached to it **2.** a person, government, or organization whose actions are controlled by others [Mid-16C. Variant of POPPET]

puppeteer /púppi teér/ *n* somebody who operates puppets or gives puppet shows

puppetry /púppitri/ *n* the art of making or operating puppets

Puppis /púppiss/ *n* a constellation of the southern hemisphere lying partly in the Milky Way, located between Vela and Canis Major. See illustration at **constellation**

puppy /púppi/ (*plural* **-pies**) *n* **1.** a dog under a year old **2.** an inexperienced or arrogant young person, especially a boy or young man (*dated informal*) [15C. Origin ?] —**puppyhood** *n* —**puppyish** *adj*

puppy fat *n* the plumpness that some children develop when they are young, which disappears as they mature (*informal*) N Am term **baby fat**

puppy love *n* the love or infatuation felt by adolescents

pup tent *n* CAMPING same as **shelter tent**

Purana /poo raánə/ (*plural* **-nas**) *n* any of a group of sacred Hindu texts written in Sanskrit that recount the lives of deities and the creation, destruction, and recreation of the universe [Late 17C. < Sanskrit *purāṇah* < *purāṇa-* 'belonging to former times' < *purā* 'formerly'] —**Puranic** /poo raánik/ *adj*

Purbach /púr bak/ hexagonal lunar crater visible in the southwestern quadrant of the Moon, approximately 120 km/75 mi. in diameter

purblind /púr blīnd/ *adj* **1.** an offensive term meaning visually impaired **2.** slow or unwilling to understand (*formal*) [13C. < PURE]

Purcell /pur sél/, **Henry** (1659–95) English composer. He wrote numerous instrumental and vocal pieces, including the opera *Dido and Aeneas* (1689) and incidental music for *The Tempest* (1695).

purchase /púrchəss/ *v* (**-chases, -chasing, -chased**) **1.** *vti* **GET SOMETHING BY PAYING MONEY** to buy something using money or its equivalent **2.** *vt* **OBTAIN SOMETHING THROUGH HARD WORK** to obtain something by hard work or sacrifice ○ *a victory purchased with great effort* **3.** *vt* **MOVE SOMETHING USING LEVER** to move, lift, or hold on to something using a device such as a lever ■ *n* **1. ACT OF BUYING** the act of buying something using money or its equivalent **2. SOMETHING BOUGHT** an item that somebody has bought **3. HOLD** a firm grip or hold on something ○ *hands too slippery to get a purchase on the rock* **4. ADVANTAGE** influence, power, or another advantage that can be exercised ○ *an attempt to gain some purchase over his rivals* **5. POWER GIVEN BY LEVER** a measure of the mechanical advantage given by a pulley or lever [13C. < Anglo-Norman *purchacer* 'pursue', literally 'chase eagerly' < Old French *chacier* (see CHASE[1])] —**purchasable** *adj* —**purchaser** *n*

purchase ledger *n* a record kept by a business of its accounts with other businesses from which it buys goods on credit

purchase tax *n* a former UK tax on nonessential consumer goods. It was replaced by value-added tax or VAT.

purchasing power /púrchəssing-/ *n* **1.** the ability to make purchases according to income and savings **2.** the value of a currency measured in terms of the goods and services it can buy ○ *the purchasing power of the yen*

purdah /púrdə/ *n* **1. KEEPING OF WOMEN FROM PUBLIC VIEW** the Hindu and Islamic custom of keeping women fully covered with clothing and apart from the rest of society **2. SCREEN** a screen or curtain used in some Hindu communities to keep women out of view **3. VEIL** a veil worn by some Hindu and Muslim women as part of purdah [Early 19C. Via Urdu *pardah* 'veil' < Middle Persian *pardak*]

pure /pyoor, pyawr/ (**purer, purest**) *adj* **1. NOT MIXED** not mixed with any other substance ○ *This jacket is pure wool.* **2. FREE FROM CONTAMINATION** clean and free from impurities ○ *The water from the spring is completely pure.* **3. COMPLETE** sheer or complete ○ *a look of pure terror* **4. CLEAR** describes colour, sound, or light that is pleasingly clear and vivid **5. RELATING TO THEORY** relating to theory rather than practical applications ○ *pure science* **6. CHASTE** virtuous and chaste (*literary*) **7. OF UNMIXED ANCESTRY** having unmixed parentage or ancestry **8.** BIOL **PRODUCED BY CONSTANT INBREEDING** produced by continual inbreeding or self-fertilization and producing offspring with the same hereditary characteristics **9.** MUSIC, PHYS **COMPOSED OF SINGLE FREQUENCY** describes sound composed of a single frequency **10.** MUSIC **WITHOUT DISCORD** describes a musical tone without discord **11.** PHON **PRONOUNCED WITH ONE UNCHANGING SOUND** describes a vowel that is pronounced with a single unchanging sound **12.** PHON **PRONOUNCED WITHOUT ANOTHER CONSONANT** describes a consonant that is pronounced unaccompanied by any other consonant [13C. Via French < Latin *purus*] —**pureness** *n*

pureblood /pyoŏr blud, pyáwr-/, **pureblooded** /pyoŏr bludid, pyáwr-/ *adj* having an ancestry that is exclusively of one type —**pureblood** *n*

purebred /pyoŏr bred, pyáwr-/ *adj* having ancestors that belong to the same breed or variety as a result of controlled breeding ○ *a purebred Arabian stallion* ■ *n* a purebred plant or animal

pure democracy *n* a form of democracy in which the people exercise direct power instead of electing representatives to govern on their behalf

purée /pyoŏr ay, pyáwr-/, **puree** *n* a food that has been made into a thick moist paste by rubbing it through a sieve, mashing it, or blending it ■ *vti* (**-rées, -réeing, -réed; -rees, -reeing, -reed**) to become a purée, or sieve, mash, or blend food into a purée ○ *Purée the vegetables and add them to the stock.* [Early 18C. < French < form of past participle of *purer* 'squeeze out', literally 'make pure' < Latin *purare* < *purus* 'pure']

Pure Land Buddhism *n* a form of Mahayana Buddhism that worships the Buddha Amitabha as a compassionate saviour and promises rebirth in paradise, known as the Pure Land, as a reward for faith [*Pure Land* is a translation of Chinese *Qingtu*]

purely /pyoŏrli, pyáwrli/ *adv* **1. ENTIRELY** in a complete, entire, or total way ○ *a purely financial decision* **2. MERELY** solely or simply ○ *surgery for purely cosmetic purposes* **3. WITH NOTHING ADDED** in a way that is free of any added substances or of any contaminants ○ *sheep that have been purely bred from the original stock* **4. INNOCENTLY** in a way that is innocent, pure, or chaste

purfle /púrf'l/ *n* an ornamental border on clothing or furniture, consisting of a ruffled or curved band ■ *vt* (**-fles, -fling, -fled**) to decorate clothing or furniture with a purfle [14C. < Old French *porfil* < *porfiler* < assumed Vulgar Latin *profilare* 'spin forward' < Latin *filum* 'thread'] —**purfling** *n*

purgation /pur gáysh'n/ *n* the act of purging or being purged, especially from guilt or sin (*formal*)

purgative /púrgətiv/ (*formal*) *n* a drug or other substance that causes evacuation of the bowels ■ *adj* acting as a purgative —**purgatively** *adv*

purgatorial /púrgə táwri əl/ *adj* (*literary*) **1.** relating to or similar to purgatory **2.** serving to rid somebody of sin —**purgatorially** *adv*

purgatory /púrgətəri/ *n* **1.** *also* **Purgatory** in Roman Catholic doctrine, the place where souls remain until they have expiated their sins and can go to heaven **2.** an extremely uncomfortable, painful, or unpleasant situation or experience ○ *the purgatory of lost love* [12C. Via French < medieval Latin *purgatorium* < Latin *purgare* 'purify' (see PURGE)]

purge /purj/ *v* (**purges, purging, purged**) **1.** *vt* **GET RID OF OPPONENTS** to remove opponents or people considered undesirable from a state or organization **2.** *vt* **REMOVE SOMETHING UNDESIRABLE** to get rid of something undesirable, impure, or imperfect **3.** *vt* RELIG **FREE SOMEBODY FROM GUILT OR SIN** to make somebody or something pure and free from guilt, sin, or defilement (*formal*) ○ *purge a soul of its sins* **4.** *vt* COMPUT **DELETE DATA** to delete unwanted or unneeded data from disk storage in a systematic fashion so as to remove all references to the data **5.** *vi* PSYCHOL, MED **VOMIT OR USE LAXATIVES** to rid the body of food by using laxatives or inducing vomiting **6.** *vti* MED **EMPTY BOWELS** to empty the bowels, or cause somebody to empty the bowels ■ *n* **1. GETTING RID OF OPPONENTS** the removal of opponents or people considered undesirable from a state or organization **2. GETTING RID OF SOMETHING UNDESIRABLE** the removal of something undesirable, impure, or imperfect **3.** MED **LAXATIVE** something that acts as a laxative (*archaic*) [13C. Via French < Latin *purgare* 'purify' < *purus* 'pure'] —**purger** *n*

puri /pŏŏri/ (*plural same* or **-ris**), **poori** *n* a small piece of light flat unleavened South Asian bread that is fried and served hot [Mid-20C. Via Hindi *pūrī* < Sanskrit *pūrikā*]

purificator /pyŏŏrifi kaytər, pyáwr-/ *n* a linen cloth used in some Christian churches to wipe the chalice after the celebration of Communion

purify /pyŏŏri fī, pyáwr-/ (**-fies, -fying, -fied**) *v* **1.** *vti* to rid something of harmful, inferior, or unwanted contaminants, or get rid of harmful, inferior, or unwanted contaminants ○ *We use special filters to purify the water.* **2.** *vt* to free somebody of sin, guilt, or defilement, e.g. in a ceremony or a ritual cleansing —**purification** /pyŏŏrifi káysh'n/ *n* —**purificatory** /pyŏŏrifi kaytəri, pyáwr-/ *adj* —**purifier** *n*

Purim /pŏŏrim, pyŏŏrim, poo reém/ *n* a Jewish festival marking the Jewish people's deliverance from a plot to massacre them. Date: 14th day of Adar. [14C. < Hebrew *pūrīm* 'lots (cast)']

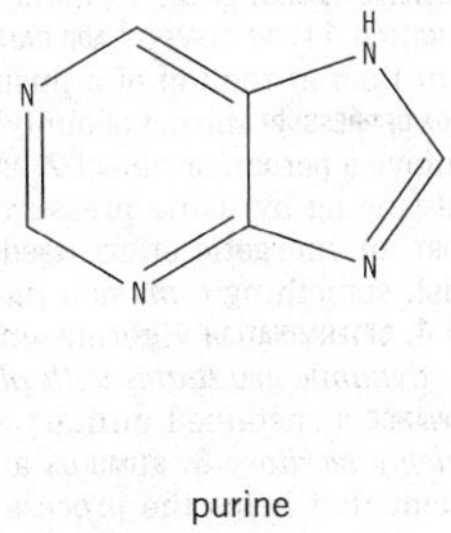

purine

purine /pyŏŏr een, pyáwr-/ *n* **1.** a nitrogen-containing substance derived from uric acid that is the precursor of several biologically important compounds. Formula: $C_5H_4N_4$. **2.** a derivative of purine, especially either of the bases adenine and guanine, which are found in RNA and DNA [Late 19C. < German *Purin* < blend of Latin *purus* 'pure' + modern Latin *uricum* 'uric acid']

purism /pyŏŏrizəm, pyáwr-/ *n* insistence on the maintenance or observance of traditional standards in a field, especially in the use of language

purist /pyŏŏrist, pyáwr-/ *n* somebody who seeks to maintain the pure or traditional form of something —**puristic** /pyoor ístik, pyawr-/ *adj* —**puristically** *adv*

puritan /pyŏŏrit'n, pyáwrit'n/ *n* somebody who lives by a strict moral or religious code, especially somebody who is suspicious of pleasure ■ *adj* RELIG **1.** same as **puritanical 2.** same as **puritanical** [Late 16C. < PURITAN] —**puritanism** *n*

Puritan /pyŏŏrit'n, pyáwr-/ *n* a member of a group of Protestants in 16th- and 17th-century England and 17th-century America who believed in strict religious discipline and called for the simplification of acts of worship ■ *adj* relating to Puritans or their beliefs or religious movement ○ *a Puritan form of worship* [Late 16C. < Latin *puritas* 'purity' < *purus* 'pure'] —**Puritanism** *n*

puritanical /pyŏŏri tánnik'l, pyáwr-/, **puritanic** /pyŏŏr itánnik/ *adj* adhering to strict moral or religious principles —**puritanically** *adv* —**puritanicalness** *n*

purity /pyŏŏrəti, pyáwrəti/ (*plural* **-ties**) *n* **1. FREEDOM FROM CONTAMINANTS** the absence, or degree of absence, of anything harmful, inferior, unwanted, or of a different type ○ *tests to establish the purity of the water* **2. INNOCENCE** virtue and innocence ○ *the purity of young children* **3. CLARITY** clarity of tone or sound **4. COLOUR SATURATION** the degree of saturation or lack of white in a colour **5.** LING **CORRECTNESS** the observance of traditional standards of correctness in speech and writing

Purkinje cell /pur kínjee-/ *n* one of the many densely branching neurons found in the middle layer of the brain's cerebellar cortex [Late 19C. After J. E. *Purkinje* (1787–1869), Bohemian physiologist]

purl[1] /purl/ HANDICRAFT *n* **1. STITCH IN KNITTING** a reverse plain knitting stitch, often combined with a plain stitch to create a ribbed effect **2.** *also* **pearl GOLD OR SILVER THREAD** sewing thread that is made from gold or silver wire **3.** *also* **pearl BORDER ON LACE OR BRAID** a decorative looped border sewn on lace or braid ■ *vti* (**purls, purling, purled**) **KNIT WITH PURL** to knit something using a purl stitch [14C. Origin ?]

purl[2] /purl/ (*literary*) *vi* (**purls, purling, purled**) to flow with a soft murmuring sound, producing gentle ripples (*refers to rivers and streams*) ■ *n* the soft murmuring sound and gentle rippling movement of a river or stream [15C. Probably < N Germanic]

purler /púrlər/ *n* **1.** a headlong fall (*informal*) **2.** *ANZ* another spelling of **pearler** (sense 3) (*dated informal*) [Mid-20C. Origin ?]

purlieu /púrlyoo/ *n* **1. OUTLYING DISTRICT** a district on the outskirts of a city or town **2. SHABBY AREA** an area or district, especially one that is old and poor (*formal*) ○ *the lowest slums and purlieus of our great towns* **3. FREQUENTED PLACE** a place that somebody often visits (*formal*) **4. LAND ON EDGE OF ROYAL FOREST** land that once lay within the boundary of a royal forest and was later separated from it, but remained subject to royal laws on hunting ■ **purlieus** *npl* **ENVIRONS** the outer regions or boundaries of a place (*formal*) [15C. Probably alteration (influenced by LIEU) of Anglo-Norman *puralee* 'king's trip around the borders' < *pur-* 'forth' + *aller* 'go']

purlin /púrlin/ *n* a horizontal roof beam that supports the rafters [15C. Origin ?]

purloin /pur lóyn/ (**-loins, -loining, -loined**) *vt* same as **steal** (*formal or humorous*) ○ *He purloined several small items, including a silk scarf.* [14C. < Anglo-Norman *purloigner* 'move far away' < Old French *loing* 'far' < Latin *longus* 'long'] —**purloiner** *n*

SYNONYMS See ***steal***.

purple /púrp'l/ *n* **1. COLOUR COMBINING RED AND BLUE** a dark colour that is formed as a pigment by combining red and blue **2. PURPLE OBJECT** an object, substance, or fabric that is purple in colour **3.** CLOTHING **ROBE IN COLOUR PURPLE** a cloth or robe in the colour purple that was formerly worn as a symbol of imperial, royal, or other high rank **4. IMPERIAL RANK** imperial power or high rank **5.** CHR **RANK OF CARDINAL OR BISHOP** the rank or office of a cardinal or a bishop **6.** CHR **BISHOPS** bishops regarded as a group ■ *adj* **1. OF DARK RED-BLUE** of a dark red-blue colour **2.** LITERAT **ELABORATE OR EXAGGERATED** elaborate in style and containing too many literary effects ○ *purple prose* ■ *vti* (**-ples, -pling, -pled**) **TURN SOMETHING PURPLE** to become purple, or make something become purple ○ *His eyes narrowed and his cheeks purpled.* [Pre-12C. Alteration of Latin *purpura* < Greek *porphura* 'shellfish yielding purple dye'] —**purpleness** *n* —**purplish** *adj* —**purply** *adj*

CULTURAL NOTE ***The Color Purple***, a novel (1982) by US writer Alice Walker. In it, Celie, an uneducated young African American woman growing up in the American South after the Civil War, confides the story of her life in a series of letters to her sister, a missionary in Africa, and to God. She tells of abuse and suffering, and her gradual empowerment through friendship and love. The novel is celebrated for the emotional power of its Black vernacular language. In 1985 Steven Spielberg made it into a film starring Whoopi Goldberg.

purple finch *n* a finch, similar to the house finch, with a raspberry-red head and breast. Native to: North America. Latin name: *Carpodacus purpureus.*

purple gallinule *n* **1.** a water bird with dark bluish-purple feathers and red legs. Native to: Mediterranean, Africa, Asia, North and South America, New Zealand, Pacific. Genus: *Porphyrio.* **2. American purple gallinule** a large water bird with purplish feathers. Native to: North, Central and South America. Latin name: *Porphyrula martinica.*

purple heart *n* a purple heart-shaped amphetamine tablet (*dated slang*)

purpleheart /púrp'l haart/ (*plural* **-hearts** or *same*) *n* a tree with hard brownish wood that turns purple when exposed to air. Native to: tropical South America. Genus: *Peltogyne.*

Purple Heart *n* a decoration awarded to members of the US armed forces who have been wounded in action [< the silver heart and the purple ribbon from which it is suspended]

purple loosestrife *n* a marsh plant with lance-shaped leaves. Flowers: purple, in spikes. Latin name: *Lystrum salicaria.*

purple martin *n* a large bird of the swallow family with shiny blue-black feathers, a notched tail, and, in the female, a greyish breast. Native to: North America. Latin name: *Progne subis.*

purple passage *n* a section in a piece of writing that is very elaborate or contains too much imagery [Translation of Latin *purpureus pannus*, coined by the poet HORACE in his *Ars Poetica* ('The Art of Poetry'); from the qualities of brilliance and ornateness ascribed to the colour purple]

purple patch *n* **1.** a period of good luck or success (*informal*) **2.** LITERAT same as **purple passage**

purport *vti* /pər páwrt/ (**-ports, -porting, -ported**) **1. CLAIM TO BE SOMETHING** to claim or seem to be something or somebody ○ *The book purports to be a series of predictions.* **2. INTEND SOMETHING** to intend to do something (*formal*) ○ *While this new measure provided money for research, it also purported to cut spending overall.* ■ *n* /pər páwrt, púr pawrt/ (*formal*) **1. SENSE** the meaning or significance of something ○ *The purport of the remarks was difficult to discern.* **2. INTENT** intention or purpose of something ○ *The principal purport of his letter was to inform them that he would soon be leaving the country.* [15C. Via Anglo-Norman *purporter* 'carry forward' < Latin *portare* 'carry'] —**purported** *adj*

USAGE The passive form of the verb ***purport*** is often used in place of the active form with the same meaning: *The novel purports* [or *is purported*] *to be autobiographical.* Some people regard any passive use of the verb as incorrect, and it is often better to use *alleged, supposed,* or some other synonym in place of *purported*: *The president is alleged* [not *purported*] *to have vetoed the proposal.*

purpose /púrpəss/ *n* **1. REASON FOR EXISTENCE** the reason for which something exists or for which it has been done or made ○ *the purpose of life* **2. DESIRED EFFECT** the goal or intended outcome of something ○ *The purpose of the law is to control pollution.* **3. DETERMINATION** the desire or the resolve necessary to accomplish a goal ○ *You need to act with purpose.* ■ *vt* (**-poses, -posing, -posed**) **SET SOMETHING AS GOAL** to intend or determine to do something [13C. < Old French *purpos* < *purposer* 'intend', alteration (influenced by *poser* 'put') of Latin *proponere* 'put forward'] —**purposeless** *adj* —**purposelessly** *adv* —**purposelessness** *n* ◇ **be at cross purposes 1.** to be talking about different things and so be involved in a misunderstanding **2.** to have intentions that conflict with somebody else's, when you should both be working together ◇ **on purpose**

deliberately ◇ **to good purpose** successfully, or with good results (*formal*) ◇ **to no purpose** without success or achieving useful results (*formal*) ◇ **to the purpose** relevant

purpose-built *adj* designed for a specific use or to meet specific needs ○ *a purpose-built swimming pool*

purposeful /púrpəssf'l/ *adj* **1.** showing a clear determination ○ *She set off with a purposeful stride.* **2.** having a definite purpose or aim ○ *purposeful activity* —**purposefully** *adv* —**purposefulness** *n*

USAGE See ***purposely.***

purposely /púrpəssli/ *adv* deliberately or with an express purpose in mind ○ *They purposely left our names off the list.*

USAGE purposely or **purposefully**? These two adverbs are sometimes confused. Although both imply that somebody has a specific purpose in mind, they are used in different contexts and are not interchangeable. ***Purposely*** means 'deliberately or with an express purpose in mind': *I purposely left the door unlocked.* ***Purposefully*** means 'in a determined way' or 'with a definite aim': *She strode purposefully across the yard.*

purposive /púrpəssiv/ *adj* **1.** having a use or purpose ○ *Most human activity is purposive.* **2.** showing determination ○ *She had a purposive air about her that morning.* —**purposively** *adv* —**purposiveness** *n*

purpura /púrpyŏŏrə/ *n* a condition in which bleeding under the skin causes purplish blotches to appear on the skin [Mid-18C. < Latin (see PURPLE)] —**purpuric** /pur pyŏŏrik/ *adj*

purpure /púrpyoor/ *n* in heraldry, the colour purple [Pre-12C. < Latin *purpura* (see PURPLE)]

purpurin /púrpyŏŏrin/ *n* a reddish-orange crystalline compound. Use: manufacture of dyes, biological stain, reagent for the detection of boron. Formula: $C_{14}H_8O_5$.

purr /pur/ *n* **1.** CAT'S LOW MURMURING NOISE the characteristic soft low murmuring noise that a cat makes when it seems to be contented **2.** PURRING SOUND a sound similar to the purr of a cat ○ *the purr of the engine* ■ *v* (**purrs, purring, purred**) **1.** *vi* EMIT PURR to make the characteristic soft low murmuring noise that a cat makes when it seems to be contented **2.** *vti* SAY SOMETHING IN SOFT THROATY VOICE to speak, or say something, in a soft throaty voice that suggests pleasure, contentment, or sensuality **3.** *vi* MAKE LOW REGULAR MECHANICAL SOUND to make the soft low vibrating noise that a machine, especially an engine, makes when it is perfectly tuned and is running well [Early 17C. An imitation of the sound] —**purringly** *adv*

purse /purss/ *n* **1.** SMALL BAG FOR CARRYING PERSONAL MONEY a small bag holding personal money, often with separate compartments for coins and notes, carried in the pocket or kept inside a handbag or other bag. N Am term **change purse 2.** *N Am* same as **handbag** *n* (sense 1) **3.** PRIZE MONEY a sum of money offered as a prize, especially the total sum of money offered in prizes ○ *with a purse of over £20,000* **4.** AVAILABLE FUNDS an amount of money available to spend ○ *The legislators overestimated the size of the public purse.* ■ *vt* (**purses, pursing, pursed**) DRAW LIPS TOGETHER AT SIDES to draw the lips together at the sides so that they wrinkle and form a circle, usually when deep in thought or to express disapproval [13C. Alteration of late Latin *bursa* < Greek, 'hide, leather'] ◇ **you can't make a silk purse out of a sow's ear** used to emphasize the impossibility of making something of superior quality from inferior materials or beginnings

purser /púrssər/ *n* the officer on a merchant ship or commercial aircraft who is responsible for managing the money and who, on a passenger ship, is responsible for the wellbeing of the passengers

purse seine *n* a large commercial fishing net pulled by two boats, with ends that are pulled together round a shoal of fish so that the net forms a pouch

purse strings *npl* control over the money that is available to spend

purslane /púrsslən/ (*plural* **-lanes** or *same*) *n* a trailing weed sometimes used in salad or cooked and served as a vegetable. Native to: Asia. Genus: *Portulaca.*

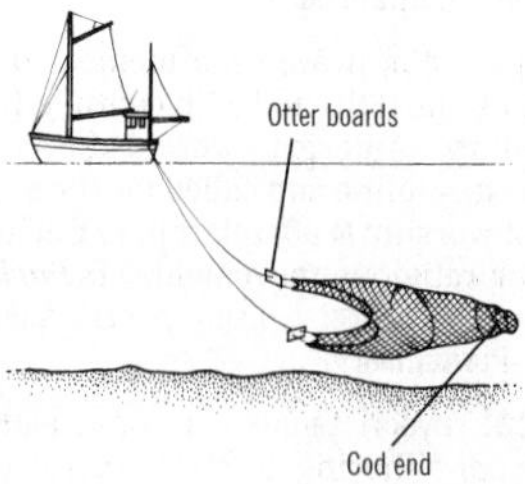

purse seine

[14C. < Old French *porcelaine*, alteration (influenced by *porcelaine* 'porcelain') of Latin *porcilaca* < *portulaca*]

pursuance /pər syŏŏ ənss/ *n* the process of doing something or carrying it out in the way that is expected or required (*formal*) ○ *in pursuance of our agreement*

pursuant /pər syŏŏ ənt/ *adj* following in order to catch [Mid-16C. < Old French *poursuiant*, present participle of *poursuir* (see PURSUE)] —**pursuantly** *adv* ◇ **pursuant to** something in accordance with something (*formal*)

pursue /pər syŏŏ/ (**-sues, -suing, -sued**) *v* **1.** *vti* CHASE SOMEBODY to follow somebody, sometimes for a long time, in order to catch or capture him or her **2.** *vt* CARRY SOMETHING OUT to work at something or carry it out ○ *pursuing his studies* **3.** *vt* CONTINUE WITH SOMETHING to continue with something or follow it up ○ *pursuing a number of lines of enquiry* **4.** *vt* STRIVE FOR SOMETHING to try hard to achieve or obtain something over a period of time **5.** *vt* SEEK SOMEBODY PERSISTENTLY FOR SEXUAL PARTNER to make persistent attempts to start a sexual relationship with somebody **6.** *vt* BE EVER-PRESENT PROBLEM FOR SOMEBODY to be an ongoing persistent problem for a person or organization ○ *Poor investment decisions pursued the company.* **7.** *vt* FOLLOW ROUTE to go along a route or direction [14C. < Anglo-Norman *pursuer*, variant of Old French *poursuir*, *pursivre* < Latin *prosequi* 'follow forward' (see PROSECUTE)] —**pursuable** *adj* —**pursuer** *n*

SYNONYMS See ***follow.***

pursuit /pər syŏŏt/ *n* **1.** ACT OF CHASING AFTER SOMETHING the act of chasing after somebody or something in order to catch, attack, or overtake that person or thing ○ *in pursuit of the stolen car* **2.** ACT OF STRIVING FOR SOMETHING the effort made to try to achieve or obtain something over a period of time ○ *the pursuit of happiness* **3.** HOBBY a pastime, hobby, or leisure activity **4.** CYCLE RACE WITH OBJECT OF OVERTAKING a cycle race in which the riders start from points on opposite sides of a circular track and race to overtake each other rather than to reach a set finishing line first [14C. < Anglo-Norse *purseute*, variant of Old French *poursuite* < *poursuir* (see PURSUE)]

pursuit plane *n* a fighter plane before World War II

pursuivant /púrssivənt/ *n* **1.** JUNIOR OFFICER IN COLLEGE OF ARMS an officer of the lowest rank in a college of arms **2.** ROYAL OR STATE MESSENGER a messenger employed by the British government or the monarch to deliver warrants **3.** FOLLOWER a follower or attendant (*archaic*) [14C. < Old French *pursivant*, present participle of *pursivre* (see PURSUE)]

pursy /púrssi/ (**-sier, -siest**) *adj* (*archaic*) **1.** getting out of breath easily **2.** weighing more than is healthy [15C. < Anglo-Norman *porsif*, variant of Old French *polsif* < *polser* 'pant' < Latin *pulsare* 'drive repeatedly' (see PUSH)] —**pursiness** *n*

purulent /pyŏŏrŏŏlənt/ *adj* relating to, containing, or consisting of pus [15C. Via French < Latin *purulentus* 'full of pus' < *pur-* 'pus'] —**purulence** *n* —**purulently** *adv*

purvey *vt* /pər váy/ (**-veys, -veying, -veyed**) **1.** CIRCULATE GOSSIP to publish or pass on news or information, especially gossip, scandal, or other kinds of information that people generally feel should not be circulated **2.** SELL GOODS to supply goods, especially foods, commercially (*formal*) ■ *n* /púrvay/ *Scotland* FOOD LAID ON the food and drink that is provided at a party or other gathering (*dated*) [12C. Via Anglo-Norman *purveier*, Old French *porveeir* < Latin *providere* (see PROVIDE)]

purveyance /pər váyənss/ *n* the supplying of something, especially food (*formal*)

purveyor /pər váyər/ *n* **1.** a supplier, seller, or circulator of something, especially something that is disapproved of or ridiculed ○ *a purveyor of cheap gossip* **2.** a person or company supplying goods, especially foods (*formal*)

purview /púr vyoo/ *n* **1.** the scope or range of something such as a court's jurisdiction or somebody's knowledge **2.** the main body of a written piece of legislation that follows the introductory section or preamble and contains the clauses that state what the law requires [15C. < Anglo-Norman *purveii*, Old French *porveii*, past participle of *porveeir* (see PURVEY)]

pus /puss/ *n* the yellowish or greenish fluid that forms at sites of infection, consisting of dead white blood cells, dead tissue, bacteria, and blood serum [14C. < Latin]

Pusan /poo sán/ city and port on Korea Strait in southeastern South Korea. It is the second largest city in the country. Population: 3,813,814 (1995).

Pusey /pyŏŏzi/, **Edward** (1800–82) British clergyman and theologian. He became a leader of the Oxford Movement in 1841 after John Henry Newman converted to Roman Catholicism. Full name **Pusey, Edward Bouverie**

Puseyism /pyŏŏzi izəm/ *n* the teachings of Edward Pusey, leader of the Oxford Movement, who advocated a renewal of Catholic practices in the Church of England

push /pŏŏsh/ *v* (**pushes, pushing, pushed**) **1.** *vti* PRESS AGAINST SOMETHING TO MOVE IT to press against somebody or something in order to move that person or object **2.** *vti* CAUSE SOMETHING TO ADVANCE BY FORCE to advance by using pressure or force, or make somebody or something advance in this way ○ *She pushed to the front.* **3.** *vt* ENCOURAGE SOMEBODY STRONGLY to urge somebody strongly to take an action or move in a particular direction ○ *pushed their children to succeed* **4.** *vt* DEPEND ON OR EXPLOIT SOMETHING to depend on or exploit something to the limits of what is wise or acceptable ○ *Don't push your luck.* **5.** *vt* USE ENERGY TO ACCOMPLISH SOMETHING to use effort or energy to promote or accomplish something ○ *push a bill through the legislative process* **6.** *vti* EXTEND SOMETHING BEYOND LIMITS to extend something or go beyond the usual limits ○ *pushing the boundaries of knowledge in this field* **7.** *vt* FORCE SOMETHING TO CHANGE to force something, especially a financial system, to change in some way ○ *a fear that increased competition will push prices down* **8.** *vt* TRY TO SELL SOMETHING to promote the sale or use of something, or the acceptance of an idea **9.** *vt* SELL DRUGS to sell drugs illegally (*slang*) **10.** *vi* MIL ADVANCE AGAINST ENEMY to make a sustained military advance **11.** *vt* COMPUT ADD DATA TO PUSHDOWN LIST to add an item at the top of a pushdown list ■ *n* **1.** APPLICATION OF PRESSURE the act of applying pressure in order to move a person or object **2.** ACT OF ADVANCING an act of advancing by using pressure or force **3.** ENERGETIC EFFORT an energetic effort used to promote or accomplish something ○ *make a push to reform the tax code* **4.** DETERMINATION vigorous energy or will to succeed ○ *dynamic graduates with plenty of push* **5.** MILITARY ADVANCE a sustained military advance ○ *a push into enemy territory* **6.** STIMULUS a stimulus or encouragement that helps the process of starting, finishing, or changing something **7.** HOCKEY CONTINUOUS NUDGING SHOT WITH STICK in hockey, a shot in which the ball is moved forwards along the ground to another player by the application of continuous pressure with the stick, instead of being hit **8.** COMPUT NETWORK SERVICE TRANSMITTING DATA a network service in which the source of the data initiates the transmission [14C. Via French *pousser* < Latin *pulsare* 'drive repeatedly' < *pellere* 'to drive, thrust'] ◇ **at a push** if really necessary (*informal*) ◇ **be pushing...** to be approaching a particular age (*informal*) ○ *He must be pushing 40.* ◇ **give somebody the push** to dismiss somebody (*informal*) ◇ **when** *or* **if push comes to shove** at the point when something must be done or a decision must be made

push about, push around *vt* to treat somebody in a domineering way, especially by making unfair demands or giving repeated orders, and generally showing no respect (*informal*)

push ahead *vti* to carry on with, or cause the ad-

vancement of, a process or project with renewed determination or effort ○ *a pledge to push ahead with plans for closer economic and political ties*
push along *vi* to leave or go away (*informal*) ○ *It's time I was pushing along.*
push back *vt* **1.** to set the time at which something is to happen to a later time ○ *agreed to push back the deadline by 10 days* **2.** to force an aggressive group of people to retreat ○ *Police pushed back protesters amid a hail of rocks and bottles.*
push forward *vti* same as **push ahead**
push in *vi* to force yourself unfairly into a queue of people, ahead of others who arrived before you
push off *v* **1.** *vti* to move a boat out into open water, away from the place where it has been tied up **2.** *vi* to leave or go away (*informal*)
push on *vi* to continue on a journey, or carry on with an activity with renewed determination or effort
push through *vt* to get something accepted or agreed quickly, especially by using persuasion or force

pushback /pŏosh bak/ *n* **1.** a mechanism that forces something backwards, e.g. a device fitted to a door that forces it back into its closed position after somebody has opened it **2.** in hockey, a stick stroke used to start a game or to restart it after a goal has been scored

push-bike *n* a bicycle that is propelled by being pedalled (*informal*)

push broom *n* a very wide brush designed to sweep large areas by being pushed

push button *n* a button that, when pushed, mechanically opens or closes an electrical circuit, e.g. a doorbell ○ *a row of levers and push buttons*

push-button *adj* **1.** OPERATED BY PUSHING BUTTON operated by pushing a button or buttons to open or close an electrical circuit **2.** EQUIPPED WITH AUTOMATIC DEVICES equipped with modern devices that perform tasks more or less automatically ○ *the push-button kitchen* **3.** INSTANTLY PROVIDED obtained, provided, or produced easily and instantly

pushcart /pŏosh kaart/ *n N Am* same as **barrow**[1] (sense 1)

pushchair /pŏosh chair/ *n* same as **buggy**[1] (sense 3)

pushdown /pŏosh down/ *n* a method of organizing computer data in which the item most recently added to a list becomes the first item to be retrieved or removed (*often used before a noun*) ○ *a pushdown stack*

pushed /pŏosht/ *adj* (*informal*) **1.** lacking something, usually time or money ○ *We're pushed for time now.* **2.** able to do something only with difficulty or effort ○ *I'd be hard pushed to remember the last time I saw a good film.*

pusher /pŏoshər/ *n* (*informal*) **1.** a dealer in illegal drugs **2.** somebody ambitious who is always trying aggressively to outdo other people

push fit *n* a join that enables two pieces to be pushed together rather than fixed in some other way

pushing /pŏoshing/ *adj* **1.** showing energy, initiative, and ambition **2.** aggressively self-confident or assertive —**pushingly** *adv*

Pushkin /pŏoshkin/, **Aleksandr** (1799–1837) Russian writer. He was an author of plays, novels, and short stories, and his best-known works include the verse novel *Eugene Onegin* (1831) and the tragic play *Boris Godunov* (1825). Full name **Pushkin, Aleksandr Sergeyevich**

> 'With a sharp epigram it's pleasant / to infuriate a clumsy foe.'
> [Aleksandr Pushkin, *Eugene Onegin*; 1831]

push money *n* a cash reward that a manufacturing company pays to a retailer who sells large quantities of its products or sells off old or unwanted stock

pushover /pŏosh ōvər/ *n* (*informal*) **1.** something that is very easy to do, deal with, or accomplish with success **2.** somebody who is easily persuaded, deceived, or defeated

pushpin /pŏosh pin/ *n N Am* a drawing pin with a cylindrical head, used to fix paper or other lightweight materials to a wall or bulletin board

push-pull *adj* describes an electronic circuit in which two components are arranged so that an alternating input makes them transmit a current alternately. This type of circuit is commonly used in audio amplifiers to reduce harmonic distortion.

push rod *n* a metal rod operated by a cam to open and close a valve in an internal combustion engine

push-start *vt* to start a motor vehicle's engine by pushing the vehicle with the gear engaged and the clutch pressed down until it picks up speed, then releasing the clutch ■ *n* an act of push-starting a vehicle's engine

push technology *n* Internet technology that provides data or other material from a supplier to a subscriber at regular intervals or whenever a new version is available, without the user needing to ask for it

Pushto, **Pushtu** *n, adj* PEOPLES, LANG same as **Pashto**

push-up *n* **1.** *ANZ, N Am* same as **press-up** **2.** a method of organizing computer data in which the first item added to a list becomes the first item to be retrieved or removed

pushy /pŏoshi/ (**-ier, -iest**) *adj* excessively aggressive or forceful in competing or dealing with others (*informal*) ○ *pushy sales techniques* —**pushily** *adv* —**pushiness** *n*

pusillanimous /pyŏossi lánnimәss/ *adj* showing a contemptible lack of boldness and resolve (*formal*) [15C. < late Latin *pusillanimis* < Latin *pusillis* 'very small' + *animus* 'mind'] —**pusillanimity** /pyŏossilә nímmәti/ *n* —**pusillanimously** *adv*

SYNONYMS See *cowardly*.

puss[1] /pŏoss/ *n* an affectionate word used for or to address a cat (*informal; often used by or to children*) [Early 16C. Probably < Middle Low German *pūs*]

puss[2] /pŏoss/ *n* somebody's face or mouth (*slang*) ○ *a familiar puss* [Late 19C. < Irish *pus* 'lip, mouth']

pussy /pŏossi/ (*plural* **-ies**) *n* **1.** CAT an affectionate word used for or to address a cat (*informal; often used by or to children*) **2.** FURRY FLOWER a furry hanging flower (**catkin**) of the pussy willow or other tree **3.** TABOO TERM a highly offensive term for the vulva (*taboo*) **4.** OFFENSIVE TERM an offensive term for sexual intercourse with a woman (*slang*) **5.** OFFENSIVE TERM an offensive term for women regarded as a source of sexual pleasure (*slang*) [Late 16C. < PUSS[1]]

pussycat /pŏossi kat/ *n* **1.** an affectionate word for a cat (*often used by or to children*) **2.** a gentle and easygoing person (*informal*)

pussyfoot /pŏossi fŏot/ (**-foots, -footing, -footed**) *vi* (*informal*) **1.** to behave hesitantly or indecisively, or avoid speaking frankly or openly **2.** to move quietly and usually secretively

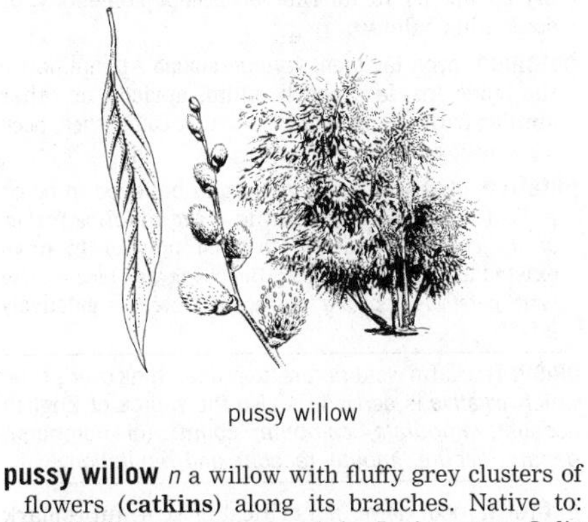

pussy willow

pussy willow *n* a willow with fluffy grey clusters of flowers (**catkins**) along its branches. Native to: North America, Europe, Asia. Latin name: *Salix discolor* or *Salix caprea* or *Salix cinerea*.

pustulant /pústyŏolәnt/ *adj* causing pustules to form on the skin ■ *n* a substance that causes pustules to form on the skin

pustulate *vti* /pústyŏo layt/ (**-lates, -lating, -lated**) to become covered with pustules, or cause pustules to form on the skin ■ *adj* /pústyŏolәt/ covered with pustules —**pustulation** /pústyŏo láysh'n/ *n*

pustule /púss tyool/ *n* **1.** a small round raised area of inflamed skin filled with pus **2.** a small raised discoloured area, especially on a plant [14C. < Latin *pustula*] —**pustular** /pústyŏolәr/ *adj*

put /pŏot/ *v* (**puts, putting, put**) **1.** *vt* PLACE SOMETHING to move something into a particular place or position ○ *I put my arms around her.* ○ *They put the child's money into a trust fund.* **2.** *vt* CAUSE SOMEBODY TO GO to cause somebody to go to a place and stay there for a period of time ○ *put him in prison* **3.** *vt* PLACE SOMEBODY IN SITUATION to place somebody or something in a particular state or situation ○ *It put me in mind of my last visit.* **4.** *vt* SET SOMEBODY TO SOMETHING to make somebody do something ○ *She was put to work in the garden.* **5.** *vt* MAKE SOMEBODY HAVE SOMETHING to make somebody or something have or be affected by something ○ *They put pressure on him to accept the offer.* **6.** *vt* EXPRESS JUDGMENT OF SOMETHING to have a particular attitude towards somebody or something ○ *Most people put a high value on educational qualifications.* **7.** *vt* USE SOMETHING to use or apply something ○ *Put your mind to it.* **8.** *vt* INVEST SOMETHING to invest money, time, or effort in something ○ *We offered to put some money into the scheme.* **9.** *vt* EXPRESS SOMETHING to express or state something in a particular way ○ *How can I put this without offending you?* ○ *put your thoughts into words* **10.** *vt* CREATE DISTANCE to create a particular distance of time or space between yourself and something or somebody else **11.** *vt* BRING SOMETHING UP FOR SOMEBODY to bring something up as a question, vote, or proposal for somebody **12.** *vt* SET WORDS TO MUSIC to provide words with a musical form ○ *put the words to music* **13.** *vt* ESTIMATE SOMETHING to make an estimate of something such as the time ○ *I put the time at about 11 o'clock.* **14.** *vt* SET RESTRICTION to set a limit or a restriction ○ *We must put a stop to this at once!* **15.** *vt* WRITE OR PRINT SOMETHING to change or translate information from one kind of language to another **16.** *vt* GAMBLING PLACE BET to bet an amount of money on a race or contest **17.** *vt* ATHLETICS THROW HEAVY METAL BALL to throw the heavy metal ball in the shot put **18.** *vi* NAUT SET COURSE to take a particular course ○ *lifted anchor and put to sea* ■ *n* **1.** ATHLETICS THROW OF HEAVY METAL BALL in the shot put, a throw of the heavy metal ball **2.** FIN OPTION TO SELL an option giving the owner of an underlying asset the right to sell a set quantity at a set price during a limited time period [Assumed Old English *putian*, origin ?]
put about *v* **1.** *vt* CIRCULATE INFORMATION to circulate something such as news or gossip **2.** *vti* CHANGE SHIP'S COURSE to make a ship change course, or change course **3.** **put yourself about** *vr* MAKE YOURSELF KNOWN TO MANY PEOPLE to make yourself known to many different people, e.g. in order to start friendships or establish business contacts (*informal*)
put across *vt* to make something understood or accepted by expressing it clearly ◇ **put one across (on) somebody** to deceive or trick somebody (*informal*)
put aside *vt* **1.** SEPARATE SOMETHING FOR DISCARDING OR SAVING to separate something from something else and discard it or save it for later use **2.** IGNORE SOMETHING to disregard something ○ *They agreed to put aside their differences.* **3.** SET SOMETHING DOWN to stop holding, looking at, or concentrating on something and set it to one side
put away *vt* **1.** PUT SOMETHING IN USUAL STORAGE PLACE to put something in the place where it is normally stored or kept ready for use **2.** SAVE SOMETHING FOR FUTURE to save something, especially money, for future use **3.** VET same as **put down** (sense 7) **4.** EAT FOOD QUICKLY to eat food, especially quickly, greedily, or in large quantities (*informal*) **5.** CONFINE SOMEBODY to put somebody in prison or another form of confinement (*informal*)
put back *vt* **1.** RETURN SOMETHING TO WHERE IT BELONGS to return something to the place it was taken from or to the place where it is normally kept **2.** PAY SOMETHING BACK to give something back to a person or group in exchange for help or benefits received **3.** RESTORE SOMETHING TO OPERATION to restore a machine to operation **4.** RESTORE PIECES TO WHOLE to restore pieces or fragments to a unified whole ○ *putting the engine back together again* **5.** DELAY SOMETHING to delay somebody or something, or postpone something **6.** DRINK ALCOHOL to drink alcoholic drinks, especially quickly
put by *vt* to save something, especially money, for future use
put down *v* **1.** *vt* RELEASE HOLD ON SOMETHING to release a

hold or grip on something and put it on a lower surface, or restore to the ground somebody who has been lifted up **2.** *vt* WRITE SOMETHING to write something on paper **3.** *vt* SUPPRESS REBELLION to use force to bring a rebellion to an end **4.** *vt* SUBMIT FOR FORMAL DISCUSSION to submit something formally so that it can be discussed or debated **5.** *vt* PAY DEPOSIT ON SOMETHING to pay part of the cost of a purchase as a deposit **6.** *vt* ATTRIBUTE SOMETHING TO SOMETHING to give something as or understand something to be a cause or reason for something else ○ *I put his unfriendliness down to shyness.* **7.** *vt* KILL ANIMAL HUMANELY to kill an animal in a humane way, especially because it is ill, injured, or in pain **8.** *vt* DEPOSIT PASSENGER to let a passenger get off or get out of a commercial transport vessel, aircraft, or vehicle **9.** *vti* LAND AEROPLANE to land an aircraft somewhere **10.** *vt* PUT CHILD TO BED to put a baby or small child to bed **11.** *vt* DISPARAGE OR BELITTLE SOMEBODY to make somebody or something appear ridiculous or unimportant by being critical or scornful (*informal*)

put forth *v* (*formal*) **1.** *vt* MAKE SOMETHING KNOWN to make something known, e.g. by stating it, publishing it, or formally submitting it for discussion **2.** *vt* GROW LEAVES OR OTHER PARTS to send out new leaves or new growth **3.** *vt* EXERT EFFORT to exert strength or make an effort in an attempt to accomplish something **4.** *vi* START JOURNEY to begin a journey or voyage

put forward *vt* **1.** MAKE SOMETHING KNOWN to make something known, e.g. by stating it, publishing it, or formally submitting it for discussion **2.** OFFER SOMEBODY AS CANDIDATE to suggest somebody as a candidate for something **3.** MAKE CLOCK SHOW LATER TIME to change the time on a clock so that it shows a later time

put in *v* **1.** *vt* GIVE TIME OR ENERGY to devote time or effort **2.** *vt* INSTALL SOMETHING to install something, especially equipment or fittings in a house **3.** *vt* MAKE CLAIM to make a claim or application for something **4.** *vt* SAY SOMETHING to make a remark, especially to add something to a conversation **5.** *vt* MAKE OPPOSING CRICKET TEAM BAT in cricket, to decide that the opposing team should bat first **6.** *vi* NAUT BRING SHIP INTO PORT to bring a ship or boat into a port, especially for a short stay

put off *v* **1.** *vt* POSTPONE SOMETHING to delay or postpone something **2.** *vt* DELAY OR HINDER SOMEBODY to delay somebody or stop somebody from acting or proceeding **3.** *vt* MAKE SOMEBODY DISGUSTED to disgust or repel somebody **4.** *vt* DISCOURAGE SOMEBODY to make somebody lose interest in or enthusiasm for something **5.** *vt* DISTRACT SOMEBODY to disturb somebody's concentration or divert somebody's attention **6.** *vi* START BOAT JOURNEY to start a journey in a boat or ship ◇ **put somebody off his** *or* **her stride** *or* **stroke** to distract somebody from what he or she is doing and make that person do it less well

put on *vt* **1.** START SOMETHING OPERATING to make something electrical or mechanical start operating, e.g. by turning a knob or pressing a switch **2.** COVER SOMETHING WITH CLOTHING to cover the body or a part of the body with clothing, headgear, footwear, or other accessories **3.** APPLY SOMETHING TO SKIN to apply something such as makeup or lotion to the skin **4.** ORGANIZE SOMETHING to organize and present an event such as a theatrical entertainment **5.** GAIN OR ADD SOMETHING to gain something that is additional or extra ○ *He's been putting on weight.* **6.** PRESCRIBE SOMETHING FOR SOMEBODY to prescribe something for somebody such as medication or a special diet ○ *put her on a low-salt diet* **7.** ADD SOMETHING to add something to a cost or value **8.** ADOPT FALSE BEHAVIOUR to adopt an attitude or way of behaving that is false or insincere **9.** PROVIDE SOMETHING to provide something as a service or facility **10.** MAKE SOMETHING SUBJECT TO IMPOSITION to impose something such as a tax or a restriction **11.** PLACE BET to make a bet, or offer money as a stake for a bet **12.** HAND TELEPHONE TO SOMEBODY to hand a telephone to somebody so that he or she can speak to somebody on the other end ○ *I'll put her on.* **13.** TEASE SOMEBODY to make fun of somebody, especially by pretending something (*informal*) ○ *You're putting me on.*

put on to *vt* **1.** INFORM SOMEBODY ABOUT SOMETHING OR SOMEBODY to tell somebody about something or somebody previously unknown to him or her **2.** ALLOW PEOPLE TO SPEAK BY TELEPHONE to allow somebody to speak to somebody else by telephone, e.g. by handing over the telephone or making a connection via a switchboard **3.** REVEAL TRUTH ABOUT SOMEBODY to make somebody suspect, or realize the truth about, somebody else (*informal*)

put out *v* **1.** *vt* EXTINGUISH LIGHT OR FIRE to switch off a light or extinguish a fire **2.** *vt* ANNOY SOMEBODY to annoy, upset, or offend somebody ○ *Don't worry if they are put out by your reaction; the truth is best.* **3.** *vt* MAKE SOMETHING KNOWN to make something widely known, e.g. by announcing or broadcasting it **4.** *vt* CAUSE INCONVENIENCE to cause somebody inconvenience **5.** *vt* CAUSE INJURY TO SOMETHING to cause injury to a part of the body ○ *I put my back out.* **6.** *vt* PRODUCE SOMETHING to manufacture or produce something **7.** *vt* ELIMINATE PLAYER to eliminate a player from a game or competition **8.** *vi* SET OFF IN BOAT to start sailing in a boat after a period spent at rest in harbour or on shore **9.** *vt* ANAESTHETIZE SOMEBODY to make somebody unconscious by means of an anaesthetic **10.** *vi N Am* AGREE TO SEX to agree to have sex (*slang; refers to women; often offensive*)

put over *vt* to make something understood by expressing it clearly ◇ **put one over (on somebody)** to make somebody believe or accept something by using deceit (*informal*)

put through *vt* **1.** MAKE SOMEBODY UNDERGO SOMETHING to make somebody experience something difficult or unpleasant **2.** CARRY SOMETHING OUT to process something or take it to a successful conclusion **3.** CONNECT SOMEBODY BY TELEPHONE to connect somebody by telephone to somebody else **4.** MAKE TELEPHONE CALL to make a telephone call to somebody

put to *vi* to tie up a boat in a sheltered spot or harbour

put under *vt* to give somebody an anaesthetic to cause unconsciousness

put up *v* **1.** *vt* INCREASE SOMETHING to raise or increase something **2.** *vt* BUILD SOMETHING to build or erect something **3.** *vt* FASTEN SOMETHING TO WALL to fasten something to a wall, fence, or other upright surface **4.** *vti* ACCOMMODATE SOMEBODY to give somebody accommodation, or find accommodation somewhere ○ *put us up for the night* **5.** *vt* ENGAGE IN SOMETHING to engage in or carry on something ○ *put up a fight* **6.** *vt* PROVIDE SOMETHING to offer or provide something, especially money **7.** *vt* PUT SOMETHING ON MARKET to offer something for sale ○ *The house contents were put up for auction.* **8.** *vt* PILE HAIR ON TOP OF HEAD to fix long hair in a style that is coiled or piled on the top of the head and then secured, usually with hairpins **9.** *vti* OFFER SOMEBODY AS CANDIDATE to propose somebody as a candidate **10.** *vt* SCARE GAME BIRD INTO AIR to scare a game bird out from its hiding place and up into the air **11.** *vt* RETURN WEAPON TO HOLDER to return a weapon taken out for use to its holder (*archaic*) ◇ **put up or shut up** used to indicate that somebody should either do something about something or else stop talking about it (*informal*)

put upon *vt* to treat somebody badly or take advantage of somebody

put up to *vt* to encourage or persuade somebody to do something unpleasant or destructive

put up with *vt* to tolerate or accept somebody or something calmly

putamen /pyoo táy men/ (*plural* **-tamina** /-támminə/) *n* the stone inside a peach, plum, apricot, or other similar fruit (*technical*) [Mid-19C. < Latin, 'shell, peel' < *putare* 'to prune']

putative /pyŏŏtətiv/ *adj* **1.** generally believed to be or regarded as being something ○ *the putative father of the child* **2.** believed to exist now or to have existed at some time [15C. Directly or via French < late Latin *putativus* < *putare* 'prune, think over'] —**putatively** *adv*

ORIGIN The Latin word *putare* 'to prune, think over', from which ***putative*** is derived, is also the source of English *account, amputate, compute, count*[1] (of numbers), *deputy, dispute, impute, recount,* and *reputation.*

---

putdown /pŏŏt down/ *n* a critical or scornful remark intended to make somebody appear ridiculous or unimportant (*informal*)

Putin /pŏŏtin/, **Vladimir** (*b.* 1952) Russian politician. He worked in the KGB and local government before becoming prime minister of the Russian Federation in 1999 and president in 2000. Full name **Putin, Vladimir Vladimirovich**

put-in *n* in rugby, an act of using the hands to send the ball into a scrum to restart play

putlog /pŏŏt log/ *n* a short horizontal beam that helps to support the planks forming the floor of a scaffold [Mid-17C. Origin ?]

put-on *adj* FALSE assumed or adopted for effect or in order to deceive ○ *a put-on accent* ■ *n* (*informal*) **1.** ACT OF TEASING SOMEBODY the act of intentionally deceiving or giving somebody the wrong impression, especially for humorous effect **2.** PRANK an instance of teasing somebody, especially as a joke

Putonghua /pŏŏ tŏŏng hwaá/ *n* LANG same as **Chinese** (sense 3) [Mid-20C. < Chinese *pǔtōnghuà* < *pǔtōng* 'common' + *huà* 'spoken language'] —**Putonghua** *adj*

put option *n* FIN same as **put** *n* (sense 2)

put out *adj* having been inconvenienced, upset, annoyed, or offended by somebody or something ○ *I do feel a little put out not to have been invited.*

putout /pŏŏt owt/ *n* in baseball, a play in which a batter or base runner is retired ■ *vt* to cause somebody to become unconscious, especially by anaesthetizing him or her

put-put /pút put/ (*informal*) *n* **1.** SOUND OF SMALL ENGINE the sound made by a small petrol engine, especially an old or broken one **2.** PETROL ENGINE a small petrol engine **3.** VEHICLE WITH PETROL ENGINE a vehicle, especially a boat, fitted with a small petrol engine ■ *vi* (**put-puts, put-putting, put-putted**) MOVE SLOWLY UNDER LITTLE POWER to move slowly or hesitantly under the power of a small petrol engine [An imitation of the sound]

putrefy /pyŏŏtri fī/ (**-fies, -fying, -fied**) *vti* to decay with a foul smell, or make something decay with a foul smell [15C. < Latin *putrefacere* < *putr-* 'rotten' + *facere* 'make'] —**putrefaction** /pyŏŏtri fáksh'n/ *n* —**putrefactive** /pyŏŏtri fáktiv/ *adj* —**putrefiable** *adj* —**putrefier** *n*

putrescent /pyoo tréss'nt/ *adj* **1.** rotting **2.** relating to the process of decay [Mid-18C. < Latin *putrescent-*, present participle of *putrescere* 'begin to rot' < *putr-* 'rotten'] —**putrescence** *n*

putrescible /pyoo tréssəb'l/ *adj* capable of decaying or rotting [Late 18C. < Latin *putrescere* (see PUTRESCENT)]

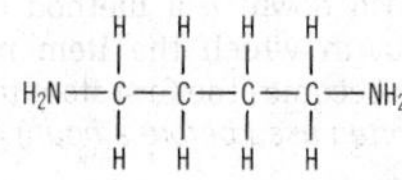

putrescine

putrescine /pyoo trésseen, -tréssin/ *n* a colourless crystalline compound (**ptomaine**). Source: decaying animal tissue. Formula: $C_4H_{12}N_2$. [Late 19C. < Latin *putrescere* (see PUTRESCENT)]

putrid /pyŏŏtrid/ *adj* **1.** DECAYING WITH DISGUSTING SMELL rotting and giving off a foul smell **2.** DISGUSTING physically or morally disgusting **3.** WORTHLESS worthless or contemptible (*informal*) [15C. < Latin *putridus* 'rotten' < *putr-*] —**putridity** /pyoo tríddəti/ *n* —**putridly** *adv* —**putridness** *n*

putsch /pŏŏch/ *n* a sudden planned attempt to overthrow a government using military force [Early 20C. < Swiss German, 'thrust, blow'] —**putschist** *n*

putt /put/ *vti* (**putts, putting, putted**) to hit a golf ball with a gentle tapping stroke along the ground on a green, aiming for the hole ■ *n* a gentle tapping stroke that rolls a golf ball along the ground on a green, aiming for the hole [Mid-18C. Variant of PUT]

puttee /pútti/ *n* **1.** a strip of cloth wrapped round the lower leg from the ankle to the knee, especially one worn as part of a military uniform. See illustration on next page **2.** a leather legging or gaiter that covers the lower leg [Late 19C. Via Hindi *paṭṭī* < Sanskrit *paṭṭikā* 'bandage, strip of cloth']

putter[1] /púttər/ *n* **1.** a golf club with a flat-faced metal head, for hitting a golf ball with a gentle tapping stroke on a green **2.** a golfer who is in the process of putting [Mid-18C. < PUTT]

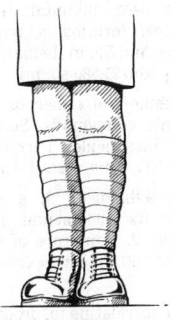

puttee

putter[2] /púttər/ (**-ters, -tering, -tered**) *vi N Am* same as **potter**[2] (sense 1) [Late 19C. Variant]

putti ARTS plural of **putto**

putting green /pútting-/ *n* **1.** GOLF same as **green** *n* (sense 7) **2.** a lawn with holes for practising putting strokes

Puttnam /pútnəm/, **David, Baron Puttnam of Queensgate** (*b.* 1941) British film producer. He helped revive the British film industry with *Chariots of Fire* (1981) and *The Killing Fields* (1984).

> 'The medium is too powerful and important an influence on the way we live—the way we see ourselves—to be left solely to the tyranny of the box-office or reduced to the sum of the lowest common denominator of public taste.'
> [Attributed to David Puttnam]

putto /poóttō/ (*plural* **-ti** /-ti/) *n* in art especially of the baroque period, an infant boy or cherub, often portrayed with wings [Mid-17C. Via Italian < Latin *putus* 'boy']

putty /pútti/ *n* **1.** PASTE USED IN GLAZING WINDOWS a paste with the consistency of dough made from linseed oil and powdered chalk, used to fix glass into wooden window frames and to fill holes in wood **2.** PASTE FORMING TOP COAT ON PLASTER a thin paste of lime, water, and sand or plaster of Paris, used as a finishing coat on plaster **3.** COLOURS LIGHT GREY COLOUR a light yellowish-grey colour ■ *adj* COLOURS LIGHT GREY of a light yellowish-grey colour ■ *vt* (**-ties, -tying, -tied**) FIX OR REPAIR SOMETHING WITH PUTTY to fix windows into wooden frames, or fill holes in wood, using putty [Mid-17C. < French *potée*, originally 'potful' < *pot* 'pot'] ◇ **be putty in somebody's hands** to be easily influenced and controlled by somebody else

putty knife *n* a tool similar to a knife with a blunt wide flexible blade, especially one used by glaziers to spread putty onto wooden window frames

putty powder *n* a powder consisting of tin oxide or a mixture of tin and lead oxides. Use: polishing metal and glass.

puttyroot /pútti root/ *n* an orchid with only one leaf. Flowers: brown or purplish-brown. Native to: North America. Latin name: *Aplectrum hyemale*. [Mid-19C. Because the substance found in the plant's corm resembles putty]

Putumayo /poótə mĩyo/ *river* that rises in the Colombian Andes and flows southeastwards along the border between Colombia and Peru before joining the Amazon in Brazil. Length: 1,610 km/1,000 mi.

put-up *adj* fraudulently or dishonestly planned or done (*informal*) ◇ *Was the fire a put-up job?*

put-upon *adj* treated badly, especially by being taken advantage of or being asked to do an excessive amount of work

putz /puts/ *n N Am* **1.** somebody regarded as very unintelligent and unpleasant (*informal insult*) **2.** an offensive term for a penis (*slang*) [Early 20C. < Yiddish *potz* 'fool, penis']

Puvis de Chavannes /poo veé də sha ván/, **Pierre** (1824–98) French painter best known for his murals. His paintings were often based on allegorical or classical subjects.

Puy de Sancy /pwee də saáN see/ *mountain* in central France. It is the highest peak in the Massif Central. Height: 1,886 m/6,188 ft.

---

puy lentil /pwee-/ *n* a small dark blue-green lentil with a distinctive flavour [After Le *Puy*, town in the Haute-Loire region, France]

puzzle /púzz'l/ *vt* (**-zles, -zling, -zled**) CONFUSE SOMEBODY to confuse somebody by being difficult or impossible to understand ■ *n* **1.** GAME OF SKILL OR INTELLIGENCE a game or toy designed to test skill or intelligence **2.** DIFFICULT PROBLEM OR SITUATION a problem or situation that is difficult or impossible to resolve **3.** SOMEBODY MYSTERIOUS somebody whose behaviour or motives are difficult to understand [Late 16C. Origin ?] —**puzzlement** *n* —**puzzling** *adj* —**puzzlingly** *adv*

SYNONYMS See *problem*.

puzzle out *vt* to use logic or reasoning to reach an understanding of something confusing or complicated

puzzle over *vt* to spend time thinking about and trying to understand something confusing or complicated

puzzle game *n* a computer game that involves solving puzzles

puzzler /púzzlər/ *n* **1.** something confusing, mystifying, or testing skill or intelligence **2.** somebody who likes to solve puzzles **3.** COMPUT GAMES same as **puzzle game**

PVA *n* a colourless resin used in adhesives and paints. Full form **polyvinyl acetate**

PVC *n* a hard-wearing synthetic resin made by polymerizing vinyl chloride. Use: flooring, piping, clothing. Full form **polyvinyl chloride**

PVS *abbr* MED **1.** persistent vegetative state **2.** post-viral syndrome

Pvt., PVT *abbr* MIL Private

pw *abbr* ONLINE Palau (*used in Internet addresses*) See table at **domain name**

PW *abbr* **1.** MAIL Palau **2.** POLICE Policewoman

p.w. *abbr* per week

PWA *n* somebody affected by Aids. Full form **person with Aids**

PWC *abbr* US SPORTS personal watercraft

PWR *abbr* INDUST pressurized-water reactor

pwt *abbr* MEASURE pennyweight

PX *n* a store in a US military base selling goods to military personnel and their families, as well as to some authorized civilians. Full form **Post Exchange**

py *abbr* ONLINE Paraguay (*used in Internet addresses*) See table at **domain name**

py- *prefix* same as **pyo-** (*used before vowels*)

pya /pyaa/ *n* a subunit of currency in Myanmar. See table at **currency** [Mid-20C. < Burmese]

pyaemia /pī eémiə/ *n* a disease caused by pus-forming microorganisms in the bloodstream [Mid-19C. < Greek *puon* 'pus']

pycnidium /pik níddi əm/ (*plural* **-nidia** /-níddi ə/) *n* an asexual flask-shaped structure in some fungi [Mid-19C. < modern Latin < Greek *puknos* 'thick, dense']

pycno- *prefix* dense, density ◇ *pycnometer* [< Greek *puknos* 'strong, thick, dense']

pycnogonid /pik nóggənid/ *n* MARINE BIOL same as **sea spider** [Late 19C. < modern Latin *Pycnogonida* < *pycnogonum* < Greek *gonu* 'knee']

pycnometer /pik nómmitər/ *n* a standard container of accurately defined volume used to determine the relative density of liquids and solids —**pycnometric** /píknō méttrik/ *adj*

pye-dog /pī-/ *n* a stray half-wild dog found in villages in Asia [Mid-19C. *Pye*, origin ?]

pyel- *prefix* same as **pyelo-** (*used before vowels*)

pyelitis /pī ə lítiss/ *n* inflammation of the part of the kidney (**pelvis**) from which urine drains into the tube leading to the bladder, sometimes caused by a bacterial infection that may occur during pregnancy —**pyelitic** /pī ə líttik/ *adj*

pyelo- *prefix* kidney, pelvis of the kidney ◇ *pyelonephritis* [< Greek *puelos* 'basin, trough']

pyelogram /pī əlō gram/ *n* an X-ray of the urine-collecting part of the kidney. The X-ray is taken after the introduction of a contrast medium either

---

into the bloodstream or directly into the kidney in order to highlight the internal structures.

pyelography /pī ə lóggrəfi/ *n* the branch of radiography dealing with the kidneys and surrounding tissue, usually involving introduction of a contrast medium in order to highlight the internal structures —**pyelographic** /-əlō gráffik/ *adj*

pyelonephritis /pī əlō ni frítiss/ *n* inflammation of the kidney, including both the urine-forming and urine-collecting parts

pyemia *n* MED US spelling of **pyaemia**

pygidium /pī jíddiəm/ (*plural* **-gidia** /-jíddi ə/) *n* **1.** the hindmost part of the body in some insects, worms, and other invertebrates **2.** a protective covering of the anal portion of the abdomen of some invertebrates [Mid-19C. < Greek *puge* 'rump'] —**pygidial** *adj*

Pygmalion /pig máyli ən/ *n* in Greek mythology, a king of Cyprus who fell in love with the goddess Aphrodite and made a statue of her that she brought to life as Galatea

pygmy /pígmi/, **pigmy** *n* (*plural* **-mies**) **1.** OFFENSIVE TERM an offensive term for somebody who is of shorter than average height **2.** OFFENSIVE TERM an offensive term that insults somebody's importance, knowledge, or ability ■ *adj* OF SMALL BREED belonging to a small breed (*sometimes offensive*) ◇ *a pygmy hippopotamus* [14C. Via Latin *pygmaei* (plural) < Greek *pugmaios* (singular) 'dwarfish' < *pugmē* 'distance from the elbow to the knuckles']

Pygmy (*plural* **-mies**), **Pigmy** *n* ANTHROP **1.** same as **Negrillo 2.** same as **Negrito**

pygmy chimpanzee *n* VERTEB same as **bonobo**

pyinkado /pyíngkə dō/ (*plural* **-dos**) *n* a tree that yields a valuable reddish-brown hardwood. Use: construction, flooring. Native to: Southeast Asia. Latin name: *Xylia xylocarpa*. [Mid-19C. < Burmese]

pyjama party *n* a party at which the guests wear pyjamas for fun or, especially in the case of children, bring their pyjamas so that they can stay the night

pyjamas /pə jaáməz/ *npl* **1.** SLEEPING CLOTHES a light loose pair of trousers and a matching loose-fitting shirt or top for wearing in bed **2.** LOOSE TROUSERS WORN IN EASTERN COUNTRIES loose-fitting trousers made of silk or lightweight cotton tied at the waist, worn by both men and women in parts of Asia, particularly Turkey and South Asia **3.** WOMAN'S LOOSE-FITTING TROUSER SUIT a woman's suit consisting of a loose blouse and flared trousers [Early 19C. < Persian, Urdu *pāy-jāmah* 'leg garment']

pylon (sense 4)

pylon /pílən/ *n* **1.** METAL TOWER SUPPORTING HIGH-VOLTAGE CABLES a tall metal tower typically made of crisscrossing steel bars that supports high-voltage cables across a long span **2.** AIRFIELD TOWER TO GUIDE PILOT a tower erected at an airfield to mark a course for pilots, e.g. in a race **3.** BRACKET FIXING SOMETHING TO AIRCRAFT BODY a rigid metal bracket that attaches an external aircraft part such as an engine, fuel tank, or armament to the main body of the aircraft **4.** TALL VERTICAL PART OF STRUCTURE a tall vertical structure on or forming part of a building or other construction, especially an ancient structure, e.g. a decorative gateway or a monumental pillar [Mid-19C. < Greek *pulōn* 'gateway' < *pulē* 'gate']

pylorectomy /pílaw réktəmi/ (*plural* **-mies**) *n* the surgical removal of all or part of the pylorus,

sometimes including the removal of part of the stomach [Late 19C. < PYLORUS]

pylorus /pī láwrəss/ (plural **-ri** /-rī/) n the thick muscular ring (**sphincter**) surrounding the outlet of the stomach into the duodenum. It closes to prevent unduly large pieces of food from leaving, thus enabling stomach acid and enzymes to break them down further. [Early 17C. Via late Latin < Greek puloros 'gatekeeper' < pulē 'gate']—**pyloric** /pī lórrik/ adj

Pym /pim/, **Barbara** (1913–80) British novelist. Many of her novels e.g. A Glass of Blessings (1958), are satirical comedies, focusing on the ironies and intrigues of village life. Full name **Pym, Barbara Mary Crampton**

Pym, John (1583?–1643) English Parliamentary leader. He was one of the five MPs whom Charles I tried to arrest (1642), and was active in events leading up to the Civil War.

Pynchon /pínchən/, **Thomas** (b. 1937) US novelist. His works, known for their intricate plots and experimental techniques, include V (1963) and Gravity's Rainbow (1973).

> 'Now there grows among all the rooms, replacing the night's old smoke, alcohol and sweat, the fragile, musaceous odor of Breakfast…Is there any reason not to open every window, and let the kind scent blanket all Chelsea?'
> [Thomas Pynchon, Gravity's Rainbow; 1973]

PYO abbr pick your own

pyo- prefix pus ○ pyoderma [< Greek puon < Indo-European, 'to rot']

pyoderma /pī ō dúrmə/ n a skin infection causing the development of pus or pustules

pyogenesis /pī ō jénnəssiss/ n the formation or production of pus —**pyogenic** adj

Pyongyang /pyóng yáng/, **P'yŏngyang** capital city of North Korea, situated on the Taedong River in the western part of the country. It is thought to be the oldest city on the Korean Peninsula. Population: 2,500,000 (1995).

pyorrhea n MED US spelling of **pyorrhoea**

pyorrhoea /pī ə reé ə/ n inflammation of the gums with a loosening of the teeth and a discharge of pus from the tooth sockets [Early 19C. < modern Latin, 'flowing of pus' < Greek puon 'pus']—**pyorrhoeal** adj —**pyorrhoeic** adj

pyr- prefix same as **pyro-** (used before vowels or h)

pyracantha /pīrə kánthə/ n UK, Can an evergreen bush of the rose family with spiky branches and leaves, and red or yellow berries. Flowers: white in clusters. Native to: Europe, Asia. Latin name: Pyracantha coccinea. ANZ, US term **firethorn** [Early 17C. Via modern Latin < Greek purakantha, an unidentified plant < pur 'fire' + akantha 'thorn']

pyralid /pírrəlid/ n a small or medium-sized, slender moth with long triangular forewings. Family: Pyralidae. [Late 19C. < modern Latin Pyralidae < Greek puralis 'mythical fly said to live in fire' < pur 'fire']—**pyralid** adj

pyramid: Chephren pyramid, Giza, Egypt

AKG London

pyramid /pírrəmid/ n **1. EGYPTIAN TOMB** a huge stone tomb of ancient Egyptian royalty with a square base and triangular walls that slope to meet in a point at the top **2. SOLID TRIANGULAR SHAPE** a solid shape or structure that has triangular sides that slope to meet in a point and a base that is often, but not necessarily,

a square. The volume of a pyramid is one-third of the product of the area of the base and the height of the vertex. **3. SYSTEM WITH EXPANDING STRUCTURE** an arrangement or system that has a small number of items at one point and expands gradually to have a large number at the opposite point **4. POINTED BODY PART** a pointed or cone-shaped body part, e.g. either of two bundles of fibres located in the brain **5. FIN INVESTMENT METHOD** a financial risk structure that spreads investments between high, medium, and low risk **6. CRYSTALS CRYSTALLINE FORM** a crystalline form in which three or more nonparallel faces intersect all three axes of the crystal ■ vi (**-mids, -miding, -mided**) **TAKE ON PYRAMID SHAPE** to take on the shape of a pyramid, with few items at one point or level and gradually increasing numbers towards the opposite point or level [Mid-16C. Via Latin < Greek puramid-] —**pyramidal** /pī rámmid'l/ adj —**pyramidally** adv —**pyramidic** /pírrə míddik/ adj —**pyramidical** adj —**pyramidically** adv

pyramidal peak n a high mountain peak formed by the walls of three or more adjacent steep-sided glacial basins, e.g. the Matterhorn

pyramidal tract n either of two bundles of nerve fibres, shaped like inverted pyramids, running from each hemisphere of the cerebral cortex down the spinal cord to all voluntary muscles of the body. In the brain, they are susceptible to stroke damage that can lead to inability to move one side of the body.

pyramid scheme n a fraudulent scheme in which the perpetrators recruit people to pay money to those above them in a hierarchy on the expectation that they will get payments from those below. When the number of newly recruited people eventually dwindles, the payment structure collapses.

pyramid selling n a method of distributing goods in bulk to a number of distributors, who in turn sell the goods in batches to a number of other distributors, and so on

Pyramus and Thisbe /pírəməs ənd thízbi/ n in an ancient story, two young Babylonian lovers who were forbidden to marry and committed suicide in tragic circumstances. Pyramus, thinking Thisbe has been killed by a lion, kills himself, and Thisbe, on finding his body, kills herself.

pyran /pī ran/ n either of two isomers of a crystalline cyclic compound with a ring consisting of five carbon atoms and an oxygen atom with two double bonds. It is best known for its benzene derivatives, which are naturally occurring dyes that produce the colours of flowers. Formula: C_5H_6O. [Early 20C. < PYRONE]

pyrargyrite /pī ra'arjə rīt/ n a deep red to black lustrous mineral that consists of silver antimony sulphide and is a source of silver. It is commonly found associated with other silver ores. [Mid-19C. < PYRO- + Greek arguros 'silver']

pyrazole /pī'rəzōl/ n a crystalline cyclic compound with a ring consisting of three carbon atoms and two nitrogen atoms with two double bonds. The ring system does not occur naturally, and pyrazole and its derivatives are exclusively synthetic compounds. Formula: $C_3H_4N_2$. [Late 19C. < PYRROLE + AZO-]

pyre /pīr/ n a pile of burning material, especially a pile of wood on which a dead body is ceremonially cremated [Mid-17C. Via Latin pyra < Greek pura < pur 'fire']

pyrene[1] /pī reen/ n the stone inside some types of fruit such as cherries (technical) [Mid-19C. Via modern Latin < Greek purēn]

pyrene[2] /pī reen/ n a solid, crystalline, colourless to yellow, multiple-ringed hydrocarbon compound that has been shown to be carcinogenic. Source: coal tar. Formula: $C_{16}H_{10}$. [Mid-19C. < Greek pur 'fire']

Pyrenean /pírrəneeən/ adj relating to, characteristic of, or coming from the Pyrenees

Pyrenean mountain dog n a large bulky dog with a thick shaggy white coat, belonging to a breed originally developed to protect sheep from wild animals in mountain areas

Pyrenees /pírrə neéz/ mountain range in southwestern Europe, forming a natural boundary between France and Spain. Length: 435 km/270 mi. Area: 55,374 sq. km/21,380 sq. mi.

pyrethrin /pī reéthrin/ n either of two oily liquid complex organic compounds. Source: pyrethrum flowers. Use: insecticide. Formula: $C_{21}H_{28}O_3$ or $C_{22}H_{28}O_5$. [Early 20C. < PYRETHRUM] —**pyrethroid** adj, n

pyrethrum /pī reéthrəm/ n **1.** a chrysanthemum cultivated for its ornamental flowers. Genus: Chrysanthemum. **2.** a mixture of pyrethrins. Use: insecticide. [Mid-16C. Via Latin < Greek purethron 'fever-few']

pyretic /pī réttik/ adj relating to, producing, or having a fever ■ n an agent that causes fever [Mid-19C. < modern Latin pyreticos < Greek puretos 'fever' < pur 'fire']

Pyrex /pī'r eks/ tdmk a trademark for a type of borosilicate glass that is resistant to heat and chemicals and is used in household kitchenware and laboratory apparatus

pyrexia /pī réksi ə/ n same as **fever** n (sense 1) (technical) [Mid-18C. < modern Latin < Greek purexis < puressein 'be feverish' < pur 'fire']—**pyrexial** adj —**pyrexic** adj

pyrheliometer /pīr heéli ómmitər/ n an instrument that measures the intensity of the Sun's radiation received at the Earth's surface [Mid-19C. < Greek pur 'fire' + helios 'sun']—**pyrheliometric** /pīr heéli ə méttrik/ adj

pyric /pī'rik/ adj relating to burning, or produced as a result of burning [Mid-20C. < French pyrique < Greek pur 'fire']

pyridine

pyridine /pírri deen/ n a toxic flammable liquid with a noxious smell. Source: bone oil, coal tar. Use: manufacture of chemicals, pharmaceuticals, and paints, textile dyeing. Formula: C_5H_5N. [Mid-19C. < Greek pur 'fire']

pyridoxal /pírri dóks'l/ n a coenzyme derived from vitamin B_6 that is involved in the synthesis of amino acids [Mid-20C. < PYRIDOXINE]

pyridoxamine /pírri dóksə meen/ n an amine form of vitamin B_6 derived from pyridoxine that acts as a coenzyme in protein metabolism [Mid-20C. < PYRIDINE + OXY-]

pyridoxine /pírri dók seen/ n a form of vitamin B_6 derived from pyrimidine, found in cereals, yeast, liver, and fish. In an organism, pyridoxine is metabolically changed to pyridoxal and pyridoxamine. Formula: $C_{18}H_{11}NO_3$. [Mid-20C. < PYRIDINE + OXY-]

pyriform /pírri fawrm/ adj shaped like a pear [Mid-18C. < modern Latin pyriformis < Latin pyrum 'pear']

pyrimethamine /pīrə méthə meen/ n a synthetic drug derived from pyrimidine. Use: treatment of malaria and toxoplasmosis. [Mid-20C. < PYRIMIDINE + ETHYL-AMINE]

pyrimidine /pī rímmi deen/ n **1.** a nitrogenous base with a six-sided ring structure **2.** a biologically significant derivative of pyrimidine, especially the bases cytosine, thymine, and uracil found in RNA and DNA [Late 19C. < PYRIDINE + IMIDE]

pyrite /pī'r īt/, **pyrites** /pī rī teez/ n a common iron sulphide mineral with a brassy metallic lustre. Use: source of iron and sulphur. [Mid-19C. < French, or Latin pyrites < Greek purites (lithos) 'fire (stone)'] —**pyritic** /pī ríttik/ adj

pyro- *prefix* **1.** fire, heat ○ *pyromania* **2.** produced by fire or heat ○ *pyrography* **3.** fever ○ *pyrogenic* **4.** derived from an acid by loss of a molecule of water ○ *pyrophosphate* [< Greek *pur* 'fire' < Indo-European]

pyrocatechol /pírō kátti chol, -kol/ *n* same as **catechol**

pyrocellulose /pírō séllyŏolŏss/ *n* a highly nitrated cellulose. Use: manufacture of explosives, particularly smokeless powder.

pyrochemical /pírō kémmik'l/ *adj* relating to or resulting from chemical changes that take place at very high temperatures —**pyrochemically** *adv*

pyroclastic /pírō klástik/ *adj* describes sedimentary rock that is composed of fragments of volcanic rock produced by the explosion of a volcanic eruption (*pyroclastic flow*)

pyroconductivity /pírō kon duk tívvəti/ *n* the capacity to conduct electricity created in a solid substance by heating it to a high temperature

pyroelectricity /pírō i lek tríssəti, -əllek-/ *n* the production of electric charges on opposite faces of some crystals by a change in temperature — **pyroelectric** /pírō i lék trik/ *adj*

pyrogallol /pírō gállol/ *n* a lustrous white crystalline organic compound that is bitter and toxic. Use: photographic developer, absorbent for oxygen in gas analysis. Formula: $C_6H_6H_3$. [PYRO- + Latin *galla* 'oak apple'] —**pyrogallic** *adj*

pyrogen /pírō jen/ *n* a substance that causes fever, especially a substance introduced into somebody's bloodstream

pyrogenic /pírō jénnik/ *adj* **1.** causing fever or produced as a result of fever **2.** produced by igneous activity

pyrography /pī róggrəfi/ *n* (*plural* **-phies**) **1.** the art or technique of creating designs on wood and leather using heated tools that burn away some of the surface **2.** a design burned into wood or leather using a heated tool —**pyrographer** *n* —**pyrographic** /pírō gráffik/ *adj*

pyroligneous acid /pírō lígni əss-/ *n* a reddish-brown liquid of which the primary constituent is acetic acid, produced by the destructive distillation of wood. Among its impurities may be acetone, methanol, wood oils, and tars.

pyrolusite /pírō loŏ sīt/ *n* a black or grey powdery metallic manganese oxide mineral. Source: deep-sea nodules. Use: source of manganese. [Early 19C. < PYRO- + Greek *lousis* 'washing'; from its use in decolorizing glass]

pyrolysate /pírō lí sayt/ *n* a product of a chemical change caused by heating

pyrolyse /pírō līz/ (**-yses, -ysing, -ysed**) *vt* to make a complex chemical substance decompose into simpler substances by heating it [Early 20C. < PYROLYSIS, after ANALYSE] —**pyrolyser** *n*

pyrolysis /pī rólləssiss/ *n* the use of heat to break down complex chemical substances into simpler substances —**pyrolytic** /pírō líttik/ *adj*

pyrolyze *vt* CHEM US spelling of **pyrolyse**

pyromancy /pírō manssi/ *n* attempting to tell the future by using fire or flames [14C. Via French and late Latin < Greek *puromanteia* < *pur* 'fire'] —**pyromancer** *n* —**pyromantic** /pírō mántik/ *adj*

pyromania /pírō máyni ə/ *n* the uncontrollable urge to set fire to things —**pyromaniac** *n* —**pyromaniacal** /-mə nī ək'l/ *adj*

pyrometallurgy /pírō me tállərji/ *n* the treatment of ores and metals using high-temperature processes, or the study of these processes, which include alloying, casting, distilling, roasting, refining, sintering, smelting, and heat treating

pyrometer /pī rómmitər/ *n* an instrument that measures high temperatures, typically by converting brightness, radiation, or electric current measurements into temperature readings —**pyrometric** /pírō méttrik/ *adj* —**pyrometrical** *adj* —**pyrometrically** *adv* —**pyrometry** *n*

pyromorphite /pírō máwr fīt/ *n* a rare green, or sometimes brownish-grey, white, or yellow mineral occurring as crystals in lead deposits

pyrone /pírōn/ *n* either of two six-membered organic ring compounds containing five carbon atoms and an oxygen atom, with a second oxygen atom attached to one of the carbon atoms. The benzene derivative is used as a pharmaceutical. Formula: $C_5H_4O_2$.

pyronine /pírə neen/ *n* a red dye used in biological tests, especially a test to detect the presence of RNA [Late 19C. < German]

pyrope /pírōp/ *n* a deep red garnet containing magnesium and aluminium. Use: gems. [Early 19C. Via French and Latin < Greek *puropos* 'fiery-eyed' < *pur* 'fire']

pyrophobia /pírō fóbi ə/ *n* an irrational fear of fire

pyrophoric /pírō fórrik/ *adj* **1.** bursting into flames spontaneously when exposed to air **2.** giving off sparks when struck or scraped [Mid-19C. < Greek *purophoros* 'fire-bearing' < *pur* 'fire']

pyrophosphate /pírō fós fayt/ *n* a salt or ester produced when pyrophosphoric acid reacts with some metals or metallic compounds

pyrophosphoric acid /pírō fosfórrik-/ *n* a viscous liquid formed when phosphoric acid is heated and loses a water molecule. Use: catalyst. Formula: $H_4P_2O_7$.

pyrophotometer /pírō fō tómmitər/ *n* an instrument that determines the temperature of an incandescent body as a function of the light it emits

pyrophyllite /pírō fíllīt/ *n* a silvery-white or greenish mineral that is similar to talc in structure but contains hydrous aluminium silicate. Source: metamorphic rocks. [Early 19C. < German *Pyrophyllit* < Greek *pur* 'fire' + *phullon* 'leaf'; because it exfoliates when exposed to flame]

pyrosis /pī róssiss/ *n* same as **heartburn** (*technical*) [Late 18C. < Greek *purōsis* 'burning' < *pur* 'fire']

pyrostat /pírō stat/ *n* a thermostat that is suitable for use at very high temperatures [After THERMOSTAT] —**pyrostatic** /pírō státtik/ *adj*

pyrotechnic /pírō téknik/, **pyrotechnical** /-téknik'l/ *adj* **1.** relating to, used in, or involving fireworks **2.** showing brilliance, e.g. in style or technique [Early 19C. < modern Latin *pyrotechnia* < Greek *pur* 'fire' + *tekhnē* 'craft'] —**pyrotechnically** *adv* —**pyrotechnist** *n*

pyrotechnics /pírō tékniks/ *n* **1.** CRAFT OF MAKING FIREWORKS the craft or skill of making and using fireworks (*takes a singular verb*) **2.** FIREWORK DISPLAY a display of fireworks (*takes a singular or plural verb*) **3.** SHOWY DISPLAY an extravagant display of brilliance, virtuosity, or strong emotion (*takes a singular or plural verb*)

pyroxene /pī rók seen/ *n* a mineral belonging to a group of dark green, brown, or black silicate minerals containing varying amounts of calcium, aluminium, iron, magnesium, and sodium. Source: igneous and metamorphic rocks. [Early 19C. < French *pyroxène* < Greek *pur* 'fire' + *xenos* 'stranger'; because originally thought to be a foreign substance in igneous rock] —**pyroxenic** /pī rok sénnik/ *adj*

pyroxenite /pī róksə nīt/ *n* an igneous rock consisting mainly of pyroxene and olivine

pyroxylin /pī róksəlin/ *n* a form of cellulose nitrate. Use: manufacture of plastics and lacquers. [Mid-19C. < PYRO- + XYLO-]

pyrrhic /pírrik/ *n* a metrical foot of two short or unaccented syllables ■ *adj* relating to or written in pyrrhics [Early 17C. Via Latin < Greek *purríkhē*, after *Pyrrhikhos*, its supposed inventor]

Pyrrhic victory *n* a victory won at such great cost to the victor that it is tantamount to a defeat [Late 19C. < PYRRHUS]

Pyrrhonism /pírrōnizəm/ *n* **1.** the doctrine of the ancient Greek philosopher Pyrrho, who believed that it was impossible to be certain about anything and therefore suspended judgment on everything **2.** scepticism to an extreme or excessive degree [Late 17C. < Greek *Purrhōn* 'Pyrrho' (360?–272? BC), Greek philosopher] —**Pyrrhonist** *n*, *adj*

pyrrhotite /pírrō tīt/, **pyrrhotine** /-teen/ *n* a common yellow-brown lustrous iron sulphide mineral. Source: igneous rocks. Use: source of iron. [Mid-19C. Alteration of German *Pyrrhotin* < Greek *purrotēs* 'fiery redness' < *pur* 'fire']

Pyrrhus /pírrəss/ (318?–272 BC) king of Epirus. The king of a Greek province (307–302, 297–272 BC), he invaded Italy and defeated the Roman army at Heraclea (280 BC) and Asculum (279 BC), but sustained huge losses to his troops.

'Such another victory and we are ruined.'
[Pyrrhus, on defeat of the Romans at Asculum; 279 BC. Quoted in 'Pyrrhus', *Plutarch Parallel Lives*]

pyrrole

pyrrole /pírrōl/ *n* a colourless toxic liquid compound containing carbon, hydrogen, and nitrogen. Source: biological substances such as chlorophyll, haemoglobin, and bile pigments. Formula: C_4H_5N. [Mid-19C. < Greek *purros* 'fiery red' < *pur* 'fire'] —**pyrrolic** /pi róllik/ *adj*

pyruvate /pī roŏ vayt/ *n* a chemical compound derived from pyruvic acid. It is a salt or ester of this acid. [Mid-19C. < PYRUVIC ACID]

pyruvic acid /pī roŏvik-/ *n* a colourless acid that is formed as an intermediate compound during the metabolism of carbohydrates and proteins. Formula: $C_3H_4O_3$. [Mid-19C. < PYRO- + Latin *uva* 'grape'; because obtained by dry distillation from racemic acid]

Pythagoras /pī thággərəss/ (582?–500? BC) Greek philosopher and mathematician. He and his followers made important discoveries about number and proportion, including Pythagoras' theorem, which they believed underlay everything in the universe. They also proposed that Earth is a globe, and that the planets orbit the Sun. —**Pythagorean** /pī thággə reé ən/ *adj*, *n*

Pythagoras' theorem *n* a proved geometric proposition stating that the square of the longest side (**hypotenuse**) of a right-angled triangle is equal to the sum of the squares of the other two sides

Pythagoreanism /pī thággə reé ənizəm/ *n* the theories and teachings of Pythagoras, especially those that apply mathematics to the workings of the universe

Pytheas /píthi əss/ (*fl* 300 BC) Greek mathematician, astronomer, and explorer. He explored the Atlantic coast of Europe, possibly reaching Norway, and sailed around Britain.

Pythian Games /píthi ən-/ *npl* a series of athletic contests held every four years in Delphi in ancient Greece in honour of the god Apollo [< Latin *Pythius* < Greek *Puthios* < *Puthō* 'Delphi']

python

python /píth'n/ *n* a nonvenomous constricting snake that kills its prey through suffocation and can reach

lengths of over 6 m/19 ft. Native to: Asia, Africa, Australia. Family: Pythonidae. [Mid-19C. Directly or via French < Latin < Greek *Puthōn*, mythical serpent killed by Apollo]

Pythonesque /pītha nésk/ *adj* absurdly or surreally comical in a way that is reminiscent of the 1970s British TV comedy show *Monty Python's Flying Circus*

pythoness /pītha ness/ *n* in ancient Greek religion, a woman believed to be possessed by the spirit of an oracle, especially Apollo's priestess at Delphi [14C. < late Latin *pythonissa*, feminine of *python* (see PYTHON)]

pyuria /pī yŏŏri ə/ *n* the presence of pus in the urine

pyx /piks/, **pix** *n* **1.** a container in which the consecrated wafers for Communion are placed so that they can be taken to those who cannot leave home **2.** a chest in which newly minted coins are placed before being tested [14C. Via Latin < Greek *puxis* 'box' (see PYXIS)]

pyxis /píksiss/ (*plural* **-ides** /-i deez/), **pyxidium** /pik síddi əm/ (*plural* **-dia** /-di ə/) *n* a seed capsule with a cap that falls off to release the seeds [Late 17C. Via Latin < Greek *puxis* 'box' < *puxos* 'boxwood']

Pyxis /píksiss/ *n* a small constellation of the southern hemisphere. See illustration at **constellation**

pzazz *n* same as **pizzazz**

Qq

q¹ /kyoo/ (*plural* **q's**), **Q** (*plural* **Q's** *or* **Qs**) *n* **1.** the 17th letter of the English alphabet, representing a consonant sound **2.** a written representation of the letter 'q'

q² *abbr* **1.** MEASURE quart **2.** quarter **3.** quarterly **4.** PRINTING quarto **5.** query **6.** question **7.** MEASURE quintal **8.** PRINTING quire

Q¹ /kyoo/ (*plural* **Q's** *or* **Qs**) *n* something shaped like a letter 'Q'

Q² /kyoo/ *abbr* **1.** MIL quartermaster **2.** PRINTING quarto **3.** Quebec **4.** CHESS queen **5.** MONEY quetzal

Q³ *symbol* PHYS heat

Q. *abbr* FIN quarter (of a year)

qa *abbr* Qatar (*used in Internet addresses*) See table at **domain name**

Qabalah *n* JUDAISM another spelling of **Kabbalah**

Qaddafi /gə daáfee, kə-/, **Gaddafi, Gadaffi, Muammar al-** (*b.* 1942) Libyan soldier and national leader. He seized power in a coup against the Libyan monarchy (1969). He imposed Islamic and socialist policies and supported revolutionary and terrorist movements abroad.

qadi *n* ISLAM another spelling of **cadi**

Q & A *abbr* question and answer

Qaro another spelling of **Caro**

qat *n* DRUGS another spelling of **khat**

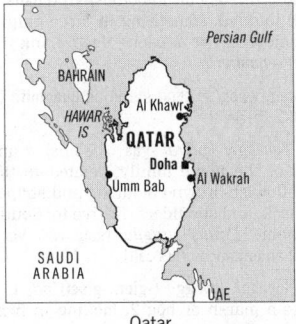
Qatar

Qatar /ka taár, káttaar, kúttər/ country in eastern Arabia, on a peninsula in the Persian Gulf, north of Saudi Arabia and the United Arab Emirates. Language: Arabic. Currency: Qatar riyal. Capital: Doha. Population: 817,052 (2003). Area: 11,427 sq. km/4,412 sq. mi. Official name **State of Qatar** —**Qatari** /kə taári/ *adj, n*

Qattara Depression /kə taárə-/ desert basin in northwestern Egypt. Its lowest point is 133 m/435 ft below sea level. Area: 18,000 sq. km/6,950 sq. mi.

Qayrawan, Al- /kírə waán/, ♦ **Kairouan**

QB *abbr* **1.** LAW Queen's Bench **2.** CHESS queen's bishop

Q-boat *n* same as **Q-ship**

QBP *abbr* CHESS queen's bishop's pawn

QC *abbr* **1.** Quebec **2.** Queen's Counsel

QCD *abbr* quantum chromodynamics

q.e. *abbr* which is (*used in doctors' prescriptions*) [Latin *quod est*]

QED *abbr* **1.** PHYS quantum electrodynamics **2.** quod erat demonstrandum

QEF *abbr* which was to be done [Latin *quod erat faciendum*]

QF *abbr* ARMS quick-firing

Q fever *n* an infectious disease caused by rickettsial bacteria and characterized by fever, chills, and muscle pain [Mid-20C. Probably abbreviation of QUEENSLAND]

qi, Qi *n* PHILOSOPHY another spelling of **chi²**

qibla *n* ISLAM another spelling of **kiblah**

q.i.d. *abbr* four times per day (*used in doctors' prescriptions*) [Latin *quater in die*]

qigong /chee góng/ *n* a Chinese practice that incorporates physical postures, breathing techniques, and mental focus, intended to improve physical and emotional health [Mid-20C. < Chinese *qi* 'energy' and *gong* 'skill']

Qin /chin/, **Ch'in** *n* a dynasty in ancient China that ruled from 221 until 206 BC, during which the first unified Chinese empire emerged and much of the Great Wall of China was built [Late 18C. < Chinese *Qín*]

qindar /kín daar/, **qindarke** /kin daárkə/ (*plural* **-ka** /*pronunc. same*/), **qintar** /kín taar/ *n* a subunit of Albanian currency. See table at **currency** [< Albanian < *qind, qint* 'hundred' < Latin *centum*]

Qing /ching/, **Ch'ing** *n* the last of the Chinese dynasties, founded by the conquering Manchu who ruled from 1644 until 1912, when the nationalist revolutionaries overthrew it [Late 18C. < Chinese *Qīng*]

Qingdao /ching dów/ city on the Yellow Sea, in Shandong Province, eastern China, between Beijing and Shanghai. Population: 3,140,000 (1995).

Qinghai /chíng hí/ province in western China bounded by Xinjiang Uygur, Gansu, Sichuan, and Tibet. Capital: Xining. Population: 4,880,000 (1997). Area: 720,999 sq. km/278,379 sq. mi.

Qinghai Hu /chíng hí hoo/ saline lake in west-central China, the largest lake in the country

qintar *n* MONEY same as **qindar**

Qiqihar /chee chee haár/ city and port in Heilongjiang Province, China, situated on the left bank of the River Nen 274 km/170 mi. northwest of Harbin. Population: 1,520,000 (1995).

qiviut /keévi ət/ *n* the soft wool that grows beneath the long outer coat of a musk ox. Use: yarn. [Mid-20C. < Inuit]

QKt *abbr* CHESS queen's knight

QKtP *abbr* CHESS queen's knight's pawn

ql *abbr* MEASURE quintal

QL *abbr* COMPUT query language

q.l. *abbr* as much as you like (*used in doctors' prescriptions*) [Latin *quantum libet*]

Qld *abbr* Queensland

qlty *abbr* quality

qm *abbr* every morning (*used in doctors' prescriptions*) [Latin *quaque mane*]

QM *abbr* MIL quartermaster

QMC *abbr* MIL quartermaster corps

QMG *abbr* MIL Quartermaster General

QMS *abbr* MIL Quartermaster Sergeant

qn *abbr* question

q.n. *abbr* every night (*used in doctors' prescriptions*) [Latin *quaque nocte*]

qof *n* another spelling of **qoph**

Qom /koóm/, **Qum** city in central Iran, on the River Qom. It is one of the sacred cities of Iran and a centre of pilgrimage for Shiite Muslims. Population: 777,677 (1996).

qoph /kof/, **qof, kof, koph** *n* the 19th letter of the Hebrew alphabet, represented in the English alphabet as 'q'. See table at **alphabet** [< Hebrew *qōph* < Semitic, 'eye of a needle']

qorma *n* FOOD another spelling of **korma**

QP *abbr* CHESS queen's pawn

qq. *abbr* questions

qqv *abbr* which (things) see (*used as a cross reference to more than one item*) [Latin *quae vide*]

QR *abbr* CHESS queen's rook

qr. *abbr* **1.** quarter **2.** quarterly **3.** PRINTING quire

QRP *abbr* CHESS queen's rook's pawn

QS *abbr* LAW quarter sessions

q.s.¹ *abbr* quarter section (*used of land*)

q.s.² *abbr* as much as suffices (*used in doctors' prescriptions*) [Latin *quantum sufficit*]

Q-ship *n* an armed ship disguised as a merchant ship, used to decoy or destroy enemy vessels [< the naval designation for this type of vessel]

QSO *abbr* ASTRON quasi-stellar object

qt *abbr* **1.** quantity **2.** MEASURE quart

q.t. *abbr* quiet (*informal*) ◇ **on the q.t.** quietly and secretly

qto *abbr* PRINTING quarto

qty *abbr* quantity

qu. *abbr* **1.** queen **2.** query **3.** question

qua /kway, kwaa/ *prep* in the capacity or function of (*formal*) ◦'*Restrictions on trade, or on production for purposes of trade, are indeed restraints; and all restraint, qua restraint, is an evil.*' (John Stuart Mill, *On Liberty*; 1859) [Mid-17C. < Latin, form of *qui* 'who']

quack¹ /kwak/ *n* SOUND MADE BY DUCK the harsh sound typically made by a duck ■ *vi* (**quacks, quacking, quacked**) **1.** MAKE SOUND OF DUCK to make the harsh sound that is characteristic of a duck **2.** SPEAK IRRITATINGLY to speak loudly and endlessly in an irritating manner (*slang*) [Early 17C. An imitation of the sound]

quack² /kwak/ *n* **1.** FAKE DOCTOR somebody who practises medicine without training or qualifications (*often used before nouns*) **2.** same as **doctor** *n* (sense 1) (*dated informal*) **3.** A FRAUD anyone who falsely claims skills and qualifications ■ *vi* (**quacks, quacking, quacked**) BE QUACK to practise medicine without training or qualifications, or to make false claims of expertise in any field [Early 17C. Shortening of QUACKSALVER] —**quackery** *n* —**quackish** *adj*

quack grass *n* PLANTS same as **couch grass**

quacksalver /kwák salvər/ *n* somebody who falsely claims to have medical or other skills or qualifications (*archaic*) [Late 16C. < obsolete Dutch, 'salvehawker' < Dutch *kwaken* 'quack, prattle' + *zalf* 'salve']

quad¹ /kwod/ *n* same as **quadruplet** (*informal*) [Late 19C. Shortening]

quad[2] /kwod/ *n* same as **quadriceps** (*informal*) [Mid-20C. Shortening]

quad[3] /kwod/ *n* in traditional hot-metal printing, a piece of blank type metal used for spacing [Late 19C. Shortening of QUADRAT]

quad[4] /kwod/ *n* same as **quadrangle** (*informal*) [Early 19C. Shortening]

quad[5] /kwod/ *adj* same as **quadraphonic** (*informal*) [Late 20C. Shortening]

quad[6] *abbr* MATHS **1.** quadrangle **2.** quadrant **3.** quadrilateral

quad bike *n* a four-wheeled all-terrain motor vehicle seating one person and having four oversized tyres [< QUADRI-]

quadr- *prefix* same as **quadri-** (*used before vowels*)

quadra- *prefix* same as **quadri-**

quadragenarian /kwóddrəjə náiri ən/ (*formal*) *n* somebody between the ages of 40 and 49 ■ *adj* between the ages of 40 and 49 [Mid-19C. < late Latin *quadragenarius* < *quadraginta* 'forty']

Quadragesima /kwóddrə jéssimə/ *n* in the Christian liturgical calendar, the first Sunday in Lent [14C. < late Latin *quadragesima (dies)* 'fortieth (day)' (before Easter) < *quadraginta* 'forty']

quadragesimal /kwóddrə jéssim'l/ *adj* relating to Lent

quadrangle /kwód rang g'l/ *n* **1.** FOUR-SIDED SHAPE a two-dimensional figure that consists of four points connected by straight lines, especially a rectangle **2.** OPEN AREA SURROUNDED BY BUILDINGS an open rectangular yard that is surrounded on all four sides by buildings **3.** BUILDINGS SURROUNDING YARD the buildings that surround an open rectangular yard [15C. Directly or via French < late Latin *quadrangulum* < Latin *quadrangulus* 'having four corners'] —**quadrangular** /kwod ráng gyŏŏlər/ *adj*

quadrant /kwóddrənt/ *n* **1.** MATHS QUARTER OF CIRCUMFERENCE OF CIRCLE a 90° arc representing one fourth of the circumference of a circle **2.** MATHS QUARTER OF AREA OF CIRCLE the area bounded by a quadrant and the two perpendicular lines that connect it to the centre of the circle **3.** MATHS QUARTER OF PLANE SURFACE any of the four sections into which the perpendicular axes of a coordinate system divide a two-dimensional surface **4.** MATHS QUARTER OF AREA OR SURFACE any of the four approximately equal parts into which an area or a surface is divided by two real or imaginary perpendicular lines **5.** ASTRON DEVICE FOR MEASURING ANGLE OF STAR an instrument with a movable sighting mechanism attached to a 90-degree arc, formerly used in astronomy and navigation to measure the angles and altitudes of stars **6.** MECH ENG DEVICE SHAPED LIKE QUARTER CIRCLE a mechanical device or machine part in the shape of a quarter of a circle [14C. < Latin *quadrant-*, stem of *quadrans* 'fourth part, quarter']

quadraphonic /kwóddrə fónnik/, **quadrophonic** *adj* using a four-channel system to record and reproduce sound. The four separate signals may be fed to individual loudspeakers placed in the corners of a room. —**quadraphonics** *n* —**quadraphony** /kwo dróffəni/ *n*

quadrat /kwódrət/ *n* **1.** PRINTING same as **quad**[3] **2.** a small plot of land set aside for plant and animal population studies [Late 17C. Variant of QUADRATE]

quadrate *n* /kwód rayt/ **1.** SQUARE OR CUBE a square or cube, or a square or cubic area, space, or thing **2.** JAW JOINT in birds, fish, reptiles, and amphibians, a bony or cartilaginous part of the upper jaw that articulates with the lower jaw at the side of the skull. In mammals, this structure has evolved into the incus, a small bone of the middle ear. ■ *adj* **1.** OF VERTEBRATE QUADRATE relating to the quadrate in vertebrates **2.** SQUARE OR RECTANGULAR with four sides and four right angles ■ *v* /kwo dráyt/ (**-rates, -rating, -rated**) **1.** *vt* MAKE SOMETHING SQUARE to make something square or rectangular **2.** *vti* CONFORM OR CORRESPOND to conform or correspond with something, or make one thing conform or correspond with another [14C. < Latin *quadratum* < *quadrum* 'square']

quadratic /kwo dráttik/ *adj* relating to or containing terms with powers no higher than the power of two ■ *n* MATHS same as **quadratic equation** [Mid-17C. < QUADRATE] —**quadratically** *adv*

quadratic equation *n* an equation containing one or more terms raised to the power of two but no higher

quadratics /kwo dráttiks/ *n* the branch of algebra that deals with quadratic equations (*takes a singular verb*)

quadrature /kwódrəchər/ *n* **1.** MAKING SOMETHING SQUARE the process of making something square or dividing something into squares **2.** MATHS TECHNIQUE FOR EQUATING AREAS the construction of a square with an area equal to that of a specified surface **3.** ASTRON 90° SEPARATION OF OBJECTS the relative position of two astronomical objects with a separation of 90° as seen from a third, especially the Sun and Moon as seen from Earth

quadrennia TIME plural of **quadrennium**

quadrennial /kwo drénni əl/ *adj* **1.** HAPPENING EVERY FOUR YEARS occurring every fourth year **2.** LASTING FOUR YEARS lasting for four years ■ *n* FOUR-YEAR PERIOD a period of four years —**quadrennially** *adv*

quadrennium /kwo drénni əm/ (*plural* **-niums** or **-nia** /-ni ə/) *n* a period of four years [Early 19C. < Latin *quadriennium* < *quadri-* 'four' + *annus* 'year']

quadri- *prefix* **1.** four, fourth ○ *quadripartite* ○ *quadricentennial* **2.** square ○ *quadric* [< Latin < Indo-European, 'four']

quadric /kwóddrik/ *adj* MATHS same as **quadratic** ■ *n* a surface or curve specified by a second degree equation [Mid-19C. < Latin *quadra*, form of *quadrum* 'square']

quadricentennial /kwóddri sen ténni əl/ *n* a 400th anniversary, or a celebration of it ■ *adj* marking or relating to a 400th anniversary

quadriceps /kwóddri seps/ (*plural same* or **-cepses**) *n* a large four-part muscle at the front of the thigh that acts to extend the leg [Mid-19C. < Latin, 'four-headed'] —**quadricipital** /kwóddri síppit'l/ *adj*

quadriga /kwo dreégə/ (*plural* **-gae** /-dreéjee/) *n* in ancient Greece or Rome, a two-wheeled chariot that was drawn by four horses harnessed alongside each other [Early 18C. < Latin < *quadrijuga* 'team of four' < *quadri-* 'four' + *jugum* 'yoke']

quadrilateral /kwóddri láttərəl/ *n* a two-dimensional geometric figure with four sides ■ *adj* with four sides

quadrille[1] /kwə dríl/ *n* **1.** a French square dance in a lively duple time, popular in the 18th and 19th centuries, danced by four or more couples **2.** the music for a quadrille, often taken from a popular source and usually in a lively duple time [Mid-18C. Via French < Spanish *cuadrilla* 'troop, company' < *cuadro* 'square' < Latin *quadrum*]

quadrille[2] /kwə dríl/ *n* a card game for four players that uses a deck of 40 cards. It was popular in the 18th century. [Early 18C. < French]

quadrillion /kwo drílli ən/ (*plural* **-lions** or *same*) *n* **1.** the number equal to 10^{15}, written as 1 followed by 15 zeros **2.** the number equal to 10^{24}, written as 1 followed by 24 zeros (*dated*) [Late 17C. < QUADRI-, after BILLION] —**quadrillion** *adj, pron* —**quadrillionth** *adj, n*

quadripartite /kwóddri paár tīt/ *adj* **1.** made up of four parts, or divided into four **2.** involving the participation of four people or groups

quadriplegia /kwóddri pleéji ə/ *n* the inability to move all four limbs or the entire body below the neck —**quadriplegic** *n, adj*

quadrivalent /kwóddri váylənt/ *adj* **1.** CHEM same as **tetravalent** **2.** with four different valencies —**quadrivalency** *n*

quadrivial /kwo drívvi əl/ *adj* **1.** with four roads or ways going in different directions and meeting at the same point **2.** relating to the quadrivium

quadrivium /kwo drívvi əm/ *n* a set of four of the seven liberal arts taught in medieval universities, consisting of arithmetic, geometry, music, and astronomy. The three lower arts (**trivium**) were grammar, rhetoric, and logic. [Early 19C. < Latin, 'crossroads' < *quadri-* 'four' + *via* 'road']

quadroon /kwo dróon/ *n* an offensive term for somebody with one Black and three white grandparents [Mid-17C. < Spanish *cuarterón* < Latin *quartus* 'fourth']

quadrophonic *adj* RECORDING same as **quadraphonic**

quadru- *prefix* same as **quadri-**

quadrumanous /kwo dróomənəss/ *adj* with four feet that can also be used as hands, each having an opposable first digit. Most primates, apart from human beings, are quadrumanous. (*dated*) [Late 17C. < Latin *quadru-*, variant of *quadri-* 'four' + *manus* 'hand']

quadrumvirate /kwo drúmvərət/ *n* a group of four people sharing power, especially forming a government [Mid-18C. < QUADRI-, after TRIUMVIRATE]

quadruped /kwóddroo ped/ *n* an animal with four limbs and feet, all of which are used for walking, e.g. a lion or lizard ■ *adj* with four feet —**quadrupedal** /kwo dróopid'l, kwóddroo pédd'l/ *adj*

quadruple /kwóddroop'l, kwo dróop'l/ *vti* (**-ples, -pling, -pled**) INCREASE FOURFOLD to multiply something by four, or become four times as great ■ *adj* **1.** MULTIPLIED BY FOUR four times as great **2.** WITH FOUR PARTS made up of four parts **3.** MUSIC WITH FOUR BEATS PER BAR describes a time or metre consisting of four beats to a bar ■ *n* QUANTITY FOUR TIMES AS GREAT a number or amount that is four times as great as another [14C. Via French < Latin *quadruplus* 'fourfold' < *quadri-* 'four'] —**quadruply** *adv*

quadruplet /kwóddrooplət/ *n* **1.** ONE OF FOUR BABIES any of four babies born to the same mother from one pregnancy **2.** FOUR SIMILAR THINGS a set of four identical or very similar things **3.** MUSIC FOUR QUICK NOTES a group of four notes performed in the time usually occupied by three

quadruplex /kwóddroo pleks/ *n N Am* a building, especially a house, that is divided into four separate living units [Late 20C. < alteration of QUADRI-, after DUPLEX]

quadruplicate *vti* /kwo dróopli kayt/ (**-cates, -cating, -cated**) INCREASE FOURFOLD to multiply something by four, or be multiplied by four ■ *adj* /kwo dróoplikət/ WITH FOUR PARTS consisting of four identical or corresponding parts ■ *n* /kwo dróoplikət/ ONE OF FOUR any of a set of four identical things or copies [Mid-17C. < QUADRI-, after DUPLICATE] —**quadruplication** /kwo dróopli káysh'n/ *n*

quaere /kweéri/ *interj* used to introduce a query (*formal*) [Mid-16C. < Latin (see QUERY)]

quaestor /kweéstər/ *n* in ancient Rome, a magistrate responsible chiefly for financial administration [14C. < Latin < *quaest-* past participle of *quaerere* 'enquire'] —**quaestorial** /kwee stáwri əl/ *adj* —**quaestorship** *n*

quaff /kwof/ (*literary or humorous*) *vti* (**quaffs, quaffing, quaffed**) to drink something in large gulps or with great enjoyment ■ *n* a long deep drink [Early 16C. Origin ?] —**quaffer** *n*

quag /kwag, kwog/ *n* GEOG same as **quagmire** (sense 1) [Late 16C. Origin ?]

quagga /kwággə/ (*plural* **-gas** or *same*) *n* an extinct animal of the horse family, related to the zebra, with yellowish-brown colouring and stripes on the head, neck, and shoulders. Native to: South Africa. Latin name: *Equus quagga.* [Late 18C. Via Afrikaans < Nguni, an imitation of its call]

quaggy /kwággi, kwóggi/ (**-gier, -giest**) *adj* **1.** soft and wet like a marsh or bog **2.** lacking in firmness —**quagginess** *n*

quagmire /kwág mīr, kwóg-/ *n* **1.** a soft marshy area of land that gives way when walked on **2.** an awkward, complicated, or dangerous situation from which it is difficult to escape

quahog /kwaá hog/, **quahaug** *n* a thick-shelled edible clam, the shells of which were formerly used as money by Native North Americans. Native to: North Atlantic coast of the United States. Latin name: *Mercenaria mercenaria.* [Mid-18C. < Narraganset *poquaû hock*]

quaich /kwaykh/, **quaigh** *n Scotland* a shallow drinking vessel with two handles, usually made from wood or metal [Mid-17C. Via Scottish Gaelic < Old Irish *cúach* < medieval Latin *caucus* 'drinking cup']

Quai d'Orsay /káy dáw say/ *n* **1.** the street along the south bank of the Seine in Paris on which the French foreign office is located **2.** the French foreign office itself ○ *The Quai d'Orsay chose to make no immediate comment on the crisis.*

quaigh *n Scotland* HOUSEHOLD another spelling of **quaich**

quail

quail[1] /kwayl/ (*plural* **quails** or *same*) *n* **1.** a small migratory game bird with mottled brown feathers and a short tail. Native to: Europe, Asia, Africa. Genus: *Coturnix*. **2.** a small game bird related to quail, e.g. a bobwhite. Native to: North America. Family: Odontophoridae. [14C. Via French < medieval Latin *coacula* < Germanic, an imitation of its call]

quail[2] /kwayl/ (**quails, quailing, quailed**) *vi* to tremble with or feel fear or apprehension [Early 19C. Probably < Middle Dutch *qualen* 'suffer']

SYNONYMS See *recoil*.

---

quaint /kwaynt/ *adj* **1. ATTRACTIVELY OLD-FASHIONED** with a charming old-fashioned quality ○ *a quaint little shop* **2. PLEASANTLY STRANGE** strange or unusual in a pleasing or interesting way **3. ECCENTRICALLY OUTDATED** amusingly or irritatingly inappropriate to modern circumstances [12C. Via Old French *cointe, queinte* 'clever' < Latin *cognit-*, past participle of *cognoscere* 'get to know' (see COGNITION)] —**quaintly** *adv* —**quaintness** *n*

quake /kwayk/ *vi* (**quakes, quaking, quaked**) **1. TREMBLE WITH FEAR** to shake or tremble, especially with fear **2. SHAKE** to shake or rock, e.g. from instability or a geological disturbance ■ *n* **1.** same as **earthquake** (*informal*) **2. SHAKING** a tremor or shake [Old English *cwacian*, origin ?] —**quaky** *adj*

Quaker /kwáykər/ *n* a member of the Society of Friends, a Christian denomination founded in England in the 17th century that rejects formal sacraments, ministry, and creed, and is committed to pacifism. At meetings members are encouraged to speak when they feel moved to do so. [Late 17C. Probably because founder George FOX admonished that they should 'tremble at the word of the Lord'] —**Quakerism** *n* —**Quakerly** *adj*

Quaker gun *n* a dummy gun or cannon, usually made of wood, used in military training or to deceive an enemy [< Quakers' refusal to fight in wars]

quaking aspen /kwáyking-/ *n* an aspen tree whose rounded flat leaves tremble in the wind. Native to: northern United States, Canada. Latin name: *Populus tremuloides*.

quale /kwáyli/ (*plural* **-lia** /-li ə/) *n* a property of something, e.g. its feel or appearance, rather than the thing itself [Mid-17C. < Latin, form of *qualis* 'of what kind']

qualification /kwóllifi káysh'n/ *n* **1. ESSENTIAL ATTRIBUTE** a skill, quality, or attribute that makes somebody suitable for a job, activity, or task **2. OFFICIAL REQUIREMENT** a condition or requirement, e.g. passing an examination, that must be met by somebody who is to be eligible for a position or privilege (*often used in the plural*) **3. MEETING OF REQUIREMENTS** the meeting of a condition or requirement to become eligible for a position or privilege **4. SOMETHING RESTRICTIVE** something that modifies, limits, or restricts **5. RESTRICTING OF SOMETHING** the modification or limitation of something, e.g. in meaning, scope, or strength

qualifier /kwólli fī ər/ *n* **1. QUALIFYING PERSON OR TEAM** a person or team that is successful in the preliminary part of a competition and earns the right to take part in the next round of a competition **2. EARLY ROUND** a preliminary round of a competition **3. SOMEBODY WITH RIGHT OR SKILLS** somebody who has the appropriate qualifications for something **4. GRAM WORD MODIFYING ANOTHER** a word or phrase that restricts or modifies the meaning of another word or phrase, e.g. the word 'fairly'

qualify /kwólli fī/ (**-fies, -fying, -fied**) *v* **1.** *vti* **BE OR MAKE SOMEBODY SUITABLE** to have a skill or attribute necessary for an activity, or give somebody such a skill or attribute **2.** *vti* **HAVE OR GIVE SOMEBODY ELIGIBILITY** to become legally eligible for a position or privilege, or make somebody legally eligible ○ *Did your exam results qualify you for the job?* **3.** *vt* **MODIFY SOMETHING** to modify or limit something in meaning, scope, or strength **4.** *vt* **MODERATE SOMETHING** to make something less strong or extreme **5.** *vt* **DESCRIBE SOMETHING AS SOMETHING** to attribute a quality or characteristic to something **6.** *vt* **GRAM MODIFY MEANING OF WORD** to modify or restrict the meaning of a word **7.** *vi* **WIN FIRST ROUND OF COMPETITION** to complete the preliminary part of a competition successfully and earn the right to go on to the next stage [Mid-16C. Via French *qualifier* < medieval Latin *qualificare* 'attribute a quality to' < Latin *qualis* 'of what kind'] —**qualifiable** *adj* —**qualificatory** /kwóllifi kaytəri/ *adj* —**qualified** *adj*

qualitative /kwóllitətiv/ *adj* relating to or based on the quality or character of something, often as opposed to its size or quantity [Early 17C. < late Latin *qualitativus* < Latin *qualitat-* (see QUALITY)] —**qualitatively** *adv*

qualitative analysis *n* identification of the chemical components of a substance

quality /kwólləti/ (*plural* **-ties**) *n* **1. STANDARD** the general standard or grade of something ○ *the poor quality of the air* ○ *poor-quality work* ○ *goods of the highest quality* **2. CHARACTERISTIC** a characteristic of somebody or something ○ *Honesty is one of her best qualities.* **3. ESSENTIAL PROPERTY** an essential identifying nature or character of somebody or something ○ *the soothing quality of the music* **4. EXCELLENCE** the highest or finest standard (*often used before a noun*) ○ *quality products* **5. UPPER SOCIAL CLASS** high social position or aristocratic breeding (*dated informal*) ○ *a family of quality* **6. PEOPLE OF UPPER SOCIAL CLASS** people of high social position or aristocratic breeding (*archaic*) ○ *mixing with the quality* **7. PHON CHARACTER OF VOWEL SOUND** the character of a vowel sound that depends on such factors as the shape of the mouth and position of the tongue when it is uttered **8. MUSIC TONE OF NOTE** the distinctive tone of a musical note **9. LOGIC AFFIRMATIVE OR NEGATIVE CHARACTERISTIC** the positive or negative nature of a logical proposition [13C. Via French *qualité* < Latin *qualitat-* < *qualis* 'of what kind']

quality circle *n* a group of employees from different levels of a company who meet regularly to discuss ways of improving quality and to resolve any problems related to production

quality control *n* a system for achieving or maintaining the desired level of quality in a manufactured product by inspecting samples and assessing what changes may be needed in the manufacturing process

quality factor *n* a number by which a given dose of absorbed radiation is multiplied to determine the radiation's biological effect

quality of life *n* the degree of enjoyment and satisfaction experienced in everyday life as opposed to financial or material well-being

quality time *n* time spent with friends or family in enjoyable activities that enhance the relationship ○ *working parents determined to spend quality time with their kids*

qualm /kwaam/ *n* **1.** a sudden feeling of uncertainty or apprehension, especially a misgiving about an action or conduct **2.** a sudden pang of nausea [Early 16C. Origin ?] —**qualmish** *adj*

quamash /kwaʼa mash, kwə másh/ (*plural* **-ashes** or *same*) *n* PLANTS same as **camas** [Variant]

Quanah /kwáanə/ (1845?–1911) Comanche leader. He led many raids against white settlers in the southwest during the early 1870s, but after surrendering in 1875, he encouraged his people to accept assimilation. Known as **Chief Quanah**. Full name **Parker, Quanah**

quandary /kwóndəri/ (*plural* **-ries**) *n* a state of uncertainty or indecision as to what to do in a difficult situation [Late 16C. < ?]

quandong /kwón dong/ (*plural* **-dongs** or *same*) *n* **1. RED FRUIT** a large red fruit, or its edible kernel. Use: jam. **2. SMALL AUSTRALIAN TREE** a small tree that produces quandongs. Native to: Australia. Latin name: *Santalum acuminatum*. **3. LARGE AUSTRALIAN TREE** a large

timber tree with a buttressed trunk and shiny blue fruits containing edible seeds. Native to: Australia. Latin name: *Elaeocarpus grandis*. [Mid-19C. < Wiradhuri *guwandhang*]

quandry incorrect spelling of **quandary**

quango /kwáng gō/ (*plural* **-gos**) *n* an organization that is able to act independently of the government that finances it [Late 20C. Acronym < *quasiautonomous nongovernmental organization*]

quant[1] /kwont/ *n* a long pole for pushing against the bottom of a river or lake to propel a boat ■ *vti* (**quants, quanting, quanted**) to move a punt or other boat along with a quant [15C. < ?]

quant[2] /kwont/ *n* somebody skilled in computing and the analysis of quantitative data, employed by a company to make financial predictions (*slang*) [Late 20C. Shortening of QUANTITATIVE]

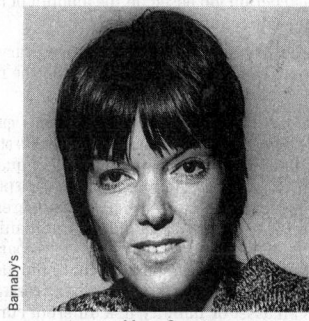

Mary Quant

Quant /kwont/, **Mary** (*b.* 1934) British fashion designer. A leader of 1960s London style, she created the miniskirt and hot pants, and later expanded her business into cosmetics and textiles.

> 'Legs stay throughout a woman's life.'
> [Mary Quant. Quoted in *The Beautiful People*, Marilyn Bender; 1967]

quant. *abbr* quantitative

quanta PHYS, FIN plural of **quantum**

quantic /kwóntik/ *n* a mathematical expression with more than one variable that contains terms raised to the same power with respect to all the variables [Mid-19C. < Latin *quantus* 'how much']

quantifier /kwónti fī ər/ *n* a word that indicates the range of individuals or items referred to, e.g. 'all', 'some', or 'most', or a logical symbol with this meaning

quantify /kwónti fī/ (**-fies, -fying, -fied**) *vt* **1.** to calculate or express the number, degree, or amount of something **2.** to use a quantifier to limit the range of individuals or items referred to in a sentence or proposition [Mid-19C. < medieval Latin *quantificare* < Latin *quantus* 'how much'] —**quantifiable** /kwónti fī əb'l/ *adj* —**quantification** /kwóntifi káysh'n/ *n*

quantise *vt* PHYS another spelling of **quantize**

quantitate /kwónti tayt/ (**-tates, -tating, -tated**) *vt* to estimate or determine precisely the number, degree, or amount of something [Mid-20C. Back-formation < QUANTITATIVE] —**quantitation** /kwónti táysh'n/ *n*

quantitative /kwóntitətiv/ *adj* **1. RELATING TO QUANTITY** relating to, concerning, or based on the amount or number of something **2. MEASURABLE** capable of being measured or expressed in numerical terms **3. LITERAT BASED ON LENGTH OF SYLLABLES** relating or belonging to a system of poetic metre based on the length of syllables rather than on stress. Classical Latin and Greek verse uses a quantitative system. [Late 16C. < medieval Latin *quantitativus* < Latin *quantit-* (see QUANTITY)] —**quantitatively** *adv* —**quantitativeness** *n*

quantitative analysis *n* determination of the relative amounts of the components of a substance

quantitative digital radiography *n* a method of detecting thinning of the bones (**osteoporosis**) by assessing the levels of calcium present, usually in the spine and hip

quantity /kwóntəti/ (*plural* **-ties**) *n* **1. AMOUNT** an amount or number of something **2. MEASURABLE PROPERTY** the measurable property of something ○ *a question of quantity not quality* **3. LARGE AMOUNTS** a large amount

or number ○ *Foodstuffs were imported in quantity.* **4.** MATHS **ENTITY WITH NUMERICAL VALUE** a mathematical entity that has a numerical value or magnitude **5.** PHYS **PARTICULAR MAGNITUDE OF SOMETHING** the product of a measurable phenomenon such as electric current or radiation intensity and the time during which the phenomenon is measured **6.** LOGIC **UNIVERSAL OR PARTICULAR NATURE OF PROPOSITION** the characteristic of a logical proposition that distinguishes it as universal or particular **7.** PHON **DURATION OF SPEECH SOUND** the length of a vowel sound or syllable [13C. Via French *quantité* < Latin *quantitat-* < *quantus* 'how much'] ◇ **be an unknown quantity** to have characteristics or qualities that are not yet known and that may affect the outcome of something

USAGE See *number.*

quantity surveyor *n* somebody who assesses the cost of a construction job based on the amount of labour and materials required to complete it

quantity theory *n* the theory that prices vary with the amount of money in circulation and the rate at which it circulates

quantize /kwón tīz/ (-tizes, -tizing, -tized), **quantise** (-tises, -tising, -tised) *vt* **1. EXPRESS SOMETHING IN QUANTUM NUMBERS** to express something in terms of quantum numbers **2. APPLY QUANTUM MECHANICS TO SOMETHING** to divide something into tiny discrete increments applying the rules of quantum mechanics **3.** ACOUSTICS **SEPARATE SIGNAL INTO LEVELS** to separate a continuously variable sound signal into defined levels **4.** FIN **QUOTE SOMETHING IN DIFFERENT CURRENCY** to express an asset or liability in a different currency from that normally used [Early 20C. < QUANTUM] —**quantization** /kwón tī záysh'n/ *n*

quant jock *n US* COMM same as **quant**[2] (*slang*)

Quantock Hills /kwóntək-/ ridge of hills in Somerset, southwestern England, an Area of Outstanding Natural Beauty. Its highest peak is Will's Neck, 385 m/1,262 ft.

quantum /kwóntəm/ *n* (*plural* **-ta** /-tə/) **1. SMALLEST QUANTITY OF ENERGY** the smallest discrete quantity of a physical property such as electromagnetic radiation or angular momentum **2. QUANTITY** a required quantity or amount, especially an amount of money paid in recompense **3. PARTICULAR AMOUNT** a portion or allotment ■ *adj* **MAJOR** sudden, dramatic, and significant [Early 17C. < Latin, form of *quantus* 'how much'] —**quantal** *adj*

quantum bit *n* PHYS full form of **qubit**

quantum chromodynamics *n* a quantum field theory of elementary particles that states that the colour properties of quarks are bound together by gluons (*takes a singular verb*)

quantum computer *n* a computer that uses the quantum mechanical properties of elementary particles such as photons for transferring, processing, and storing information —**quantum computing** *n*

quantum cosmology *n* the cosmology of the universe during and immediately after the big bang as described through the laws of quantum mechanics —**quantum cosmological** *adj*

quantum dot *n* a small crystal containing a few hundred to several million atoms that has specific quantum-mechanical characteristics

quantum electrodynamics *n* a quantum field theory that describes the properties of electromagnetic radiation and its interaction with electrically charged particles

quantum field theory *n* a theory developed from quantum mechanics based on the assumption that elementary particles interact through the influence of fields around them and the exchange of energy

quantum foam *n* an extremely tiny hypothetical region of space-time in which numerous particles are formed and destroyed

quantum gravity *n* the gravitational field of subatomic physics expressed through quantum mechanics —**quantum gravitational** *adj*

quantum jump *n* **1.** the sudden transition of an atom or particle from one energy state to another **2.** same as **quantum leap**

quantum leap *n* a sudden, dramatic, and significant change or advance ○ *a quantum leap in our understanding of molecular science*

quantum mechanics *n* the study and analysis of the interactions of atoms and elementary particles based on quantum theory. The study evolved in an effort to explain the behaviour of atoms and subatomic particles, which do not obey the laws of classical Newtonian mechanics. (*takes a singular verb*) —**quantum mechanical** *adj*

quantum number *n* any of the set of integers or half integers that characterize the properties and energy states of an elementary particle or system

quantum physics *n* the branch of physics that uses quantum theory

quantum statistics *n* the statistical description of systems of particles that are subject to the laws of quantum physics rather than classical physics (*takes a singular verb*)

quantum theory *n* a theory describing the behaviour and interactions of elementary particles or energy states based on the assumptions that energy is subdivided into discrete amounts and that matter possesses wave properties

quantum well *n* a thin layer of material with a high density of electrons whose potential energy is less than the surrounding layers and whose motion is restricted to one dimension, often used in laser and semiconducting applications

Qu'Appelle /kwə pél, kə pél/ river in southern Saskatchewan, which joins the Assiniboine River east of the Manitoba border. Length: 435 km/270 mi.

quar. *abbr* **1.** quarter **2.** quarterly

quarantine /kwórrən teen/ *n* **1. ISOLATION BECAUSE OF DISEASE** enforced isolation of people or animals that may have been exposed to a contagious or infectious disease, e.g. when entering a country (*often used before nouns*) **2. PLACE OF ISOLATION** a place in which people or animals spend a period of isolation to prevent the spread of disease **3. TIME OF ISOLATION** the period of time during which people or animals are kept in isolation to prevent the spread of disease **4. CONDITION OR PERIOD OF ISOLATION** enforced isolation, e.g. for social or political reasons, or a period of such isolation ■ *vt* (**-tines, -tining, -tined**) **1. ISOLATE SOMEBODY** to isolate a person or animal that may have been exposed to a contagious or infectious disease in order to prevent the possible spread of that disease **2. DETAIN SOMEBODY** to isolate or detain somebody, e.g. for social or political reasons [Early 17C. Via Italian *quarantina* < Latin *quadraginta* 'forty'; because ships suspected of carrying disease were refused entrance to port for 40 days] —**quarantinable** *adj*

quarantine flag *n* a yellow flag flown by a ship or boat arriving from abroad to indicate that there is no disease aboard. A second flag is flown if the vessel is not free of disease.

~~quarentine~~ incorrect spelling of **quarantine**

quark[1] /kwaark/ *n* an elementary particle with an electric charge equal to one-third or two-thirds that of the electron. Quarks are believed to be the constituents of baryons and mesons. [Mid-20C. Alluding to 'three quarks for Mr. Mark' in James Joyce's *Finnegans Wake*; because originally there were thought to be three quarks]

quark[2] /kwaark/ *n* a soft cheese of German origin made from skimmed milk [Mid-20C. Via German < Slavic]

quarrel[1] /kwórrəl/ *n* **1. ARGUMENT BETWEEN PEOPLE** an angry dispute between two or more people **2. REASON TO ARGUE** a reason for a disagreement or dispute between people ○ *I have no quarrel with their proposals.* ■ *vi* (**-rels, -relling, -relled**) **1. ARGUE VEHEMENTLY** to engage in an angry dispute **2. DISAGREE WITH SOMETHING** to dispute or disagree with something such as a decision **3. FIND FAULT** to complain about something [14C. Via French < Latin *querela* 'complaint' < *queri* 'complain'] —**quarreller** *n*

quarrel[2] /kwórrəl/ *n* **1.** a small square or diamond-shaped pane of glass in a window **2.** a short square-headed bolt or arrow used in a crossbow [12C. Via French < assumed Vulgar Latin *quadrellus* 'small square' < Latin *quadrum* 'square']

quarrelsome /kwórrəlsəm/ *adj* having a tendency to argue with people —**quarrelsomely** *adv* —**quarrelsomeness** *n*

quarrier /kwórri ər/ *n* a worker in a stone quarry

quarry[1] /kwórri/ *n* (*plural* **-ries**) **1. OPEN AREA FOR MINING** an open excavation from which stone or other material is extracted by blasting, cutting, or drilling **2. SOURCE** a rich source of something ■ *v* (**-ries, -rying, -ried**) **1.** *vti* **OBTAIN SOMETHING FROM QUARRY** to extract stone or other material from a quarry **2.** *vt* **USE PLACE FOR EXTRACTING STONE** to make a quarry in a place such as a hillside and remove material from it ○ *The area was extensively quarried last century.* **3.** *vti* **EXTRACT SOMETHING LABORIOUSLY** to obtain something such as facts or information by searching laboriously and carefully [14C. < medieval Latin *quarreia* < Old French *quarriere* < *quarre* 'square-cut stone' < Latin *quadrum* 'square']

quarry[2] /kwórri/ (*plural* **-ries**) *n* **1.** an animal or bird that is hunted **2.** somebody or something that is chased or hunted by another [15C. Via Anglo-Norman *couree* 'entrails of an animal given to the hounds' < assumed Vulgar Latin *corata* < Latin *cor* 'heart']

quarry[3] /kwórri/ (*plural* **-ries**) *n* **1.** a square or diamond shape **2.** something with a square or diamond shape, e.g. a pane of glass in a latticed window [Mid-16C. Alteration of QUARREL[2]]

quarry tile *n* a tile with a square or diamond shape, especially a hard-wearing unglazed clay tile used for flooring [< QUARRY[3]]

quart[1] /kwawrt/ *n* **1. ONE-QUARTER OF GALLON** a unit of measurement for liquids equal to two pints **2. ONE-EIGHTH OF PECK** a unit of measurement for dry substances equal to two pints **3. CONTAINER OR CONTENTS** a container that holds one quart, or the contents of such a container [13C. Via French < Latin *quartus* 'fourth']

quart[2] /kwawrt/ *n* **1.** a sequence of four cards in piquet and some other card games **2.** FENCING same as **quarte** [Mid-17C. Via French, 'fourth' < Latin *quartus*]

quartan /kwáwrt'n/ *adj* describes a fever that recurs every fourth day, e.g. in some types of malaria [13C. < Old French *quartaine* < Latin *quartus* 'fourth']

quarte /kaart/, **carte** *n* in fencing, the fourth of the eight parrying or attacking positions [Late 17C. Variant of QUART[2]]

quarter /kwáwrtər/ *n* **1. ONE OF FOUR PARTS** one of four equal or approximately equal parts into which something is or may be divided **2.** MATHS **ONE-FOURTH** a number that is equal to one divided by four, represented by the symbol $\frac{1}{4}$ **3.** TIME **15 MINUTES BEFORE OR AFTER HOUR** a point in time 15 minutes before or after the hour, marked on a traditional clock face at 3 and 9 **4.** CALENDAR **PERIOD OF THREE MONTHS** a three-month period regarded as one of four parts of a year, especially for accounting purposes **5.** SPORTS **PART OF SPORTING CONTEST** in some sports, one of the four equal parts into which a game is divided **6.** ASTRON **MOON PHASE** either of the two phases of the Moon in which half of its illuminated surface can be seen from the Earth **7.** ASTRON **QUARTER OF MOON'S ORBIT** one-fourth of the Moon's orbital period around the Earth **8.** *also* **Quarter DISTRICT OF TOWN** an area in a town of a particular type or inhabited by a particular group of people ○ *the French Quarter* **9. UNSPECIFIED SOURCE** an unspecified person or group of people ○ *help from any quarter* **10.** COMPASS **NORTHEAST, SOUTHEAST, SOUTHWEST, OR NORTHWEST** each of the four compass points that lie midway between north, east, south, and west **11. MERCY** mercy offered to a defeated enemy **12.** MEASURE **4 OZ OF SOMETHING** an amount of something weighing 113.4 g/4 oz or a quarter of a pound (*informal*) **13.** MEASURE **28 LB IN WEIGHT** in the United Kingdom, a unit of weight equal to 12.71 kg/28 lb or one quarter of a hundredweight **14.** MEASURE **8 BUSHELS** a unit of capacity for grain and similar substances equal to approximately 8 bushels **15.** MONEY **25 CENTS** in the United States and Canada, the sum of 25 cents **16.** COINS **COIN WORTH 25 CENTS** in the United States and Canada, a coin worth 25 cents or one quarter of a dollar **17.** AGRIC, MEASURE **QUARTER OF SQUARE MILE** one quarter of a square mile of rural land **18.** NAUT **SIDE OF REAR HALF OF VESSEL** either side of the rear half of a boat or ship, usually behind the rearmost mast **19.** HERALDRY **SECTION OF HERALDIC SHIELD** one of the four sections into which a heraldic shield may be divided **20. PART OF ANIMAL OR BIRD** one of the four parts into which the body of an animal or bird may be divided, with a leg or wing forming part of each quarter **21. PART OF HOOF** the side of a

horse's hoof **22.** SHOE PART the part of a shoe between the heel and the front part of the upper ■ **quarters** *npl* **1.** ACCOMMODATION living or sleeping accommodation provided for somebody such as military personnel and their families, household employees, or members of a ship's crew **2.** HINDQUARTERS the hindquarters or haunches of a horse ■ *adj* BEING ONE OF FOUR being one of four parts into which something is or may be divided ■ *v* (**-ters, -tering, -tered**) **1.** *vt* DIVIDE SOMETHING INTO FOUR to divide something into four equal or approximately equal parts **2.** *vt* GIVE SOMEBODY LODGINGS to assign accommodation to somebody ○ *The soldiers were quartered in an old barn.* **3.** *vt* HIST CUT BODY INTO FOUR to cut a human body into four parts following an execution **4.** *vt* HERALDRY DIVIDE SHIELD INTO FOUR to divide a heraldic shield into four sections **5.** *vi* CROSS IN ZIGZAG COURSE to cover all parts of an area of land, sea, or air by ranging from side to side while moving forwards, e.g. while searching for somebody or something **6.** *vi* NAUT COME FROM REAR PART OF SIDE to come from a direction at approximately 45 degrees to the stern of a boat or ship **7.** *vt* POSITION SOMETHING AT 90 DEGREES to locate or position a machine part at right angles to another [13C. Via French < Latin *quartarius* 'fourth part' < Latin *quartus* 'fourth'] ◇ **at close quarters** from very near

quarterage /kwáwtərij/ *n* a sum of money paid or received every three months

quarterback /kwáwrtər bak/ *n* in American football, a player positioned behind the centre who directs the play by calling signals

quarter-bound *adj* describes a book that is bound in one material, usually leather, on the spine and in another on the covers

quarter day *n* each of four days in a year regarded as the beginning or end of a quarter, when payments are due

quarterdeck /kwáwrtər dek/ *n* the rear part of the upper deck of a ship, where official ceremonies traditionally take place on a vessel

quarterfinal /kwáwrtər fīn'l/ *n* each of four contests in a tournament or competition, the winners of which go on to play each other in the semifinals [Early 20C. After SEMIFINAL] —**quarterfinalist** *n*

quarter horse *n* a strong horse formerly bred in the United States to run short races [< *quarter-race*, a race over a quarter of a mile]

quarter hour *n* **1.** a period of 15 minutes **2.** either of the points on a clock face that indicate a time 15 minutes before or after the hour, or one of these times ○ *The clock chimes on the quarter hour.*

quarterlife crisis /kwáwrtər līf-/ *n* feelings of doubt and confusion about identity and the future experienced by some people in their twenties

quarterlight /kwáwrtər līt/ *n* a small triangular window in the side of some cars and other vehicles that can be pivoted open for ventilation

quarterly /kwáwrtərli/ *adj* **1.** HAPPENING EVERY THREE MONTHS happening, produced, or published four times a year, at three-month intervals **2.** HERALDRY DIVIDED INTO FOUR describes a heraldic shield that is divided into four sections ■ *adv* EVERY THREE MONTHS four times a year, at three-month intervals ■ *n* (*plural* **-lies**) JOURNAL PUBLISHED EVERY THREE MONTHS a magazine or journal published four times a year, at three-month intervals

quartermaster /kwáwrtər maastər/ *n* **1.** an army officer responsible for providing soldiers with food, clothing, equipment, and living quarters **2.** in the navy, a petty officer or ship's mate with some responsibilities for navigation and signals

quartern /kwáwrtərn/ *n* **1.** ONE FOURTH a fourth part of something, especially of some old weights and measures **2.** *also* **quartern loaf** SMALL LOAF a loaf of bread 10 cm/4 in square, used especially for making sandwiches **3.** *also* **quartern loaf** LARGE LOAF a loaf of bread weighing 1.6 kg/4 lb [13C. < Anglo-Norman *quartrun*]

quarter note *n N Am* MUSIC same as **crotchet** (sense 1)

quarter-phase *adj* ELEC ENG same as **two-phase** [Because the two currents are 90° out of phase]

quarterpipe /kwáwrtər pīp/ *n* in snowboarding, a snow structure resembling a 'U'-shaped structure (**halfpipe**) with one wall removed, used as a jumping-off place

quarter rest *n N Am* same as **crotchet rest**

quarter round *n* an architectural moulding that, in cross section, is the shape of a quarter of a circle

quartersawn /kwáwrtər sawn/ *adj* describes wooden boards sawn from a log cut into quarters lengthways so as to show off the grain of the wood

quarter section *n N Am* a tract of land measuring 800 m/0.5 mi. on each side, equal to 65 hectares/160 acres or one-fourth of a section

quarter sessions *npl* formerly in England and Wales, a local court sitting quarterly with limited authority to try civil and criminal cases

quarterstaff /kwáwrtər staaf/ (*plural* **-staves** /-stayvz/ or **-staffs**) *n* a long heavy wooden stick tipped with iron, formerly used in hand-to-hand fighting [Mid-16C. Origin ?]

quarter step *n US* MUSIC same as **quarter tone**

quarter tone *n UK, ANZ, Can* a musical interval that is equal to half a semitone. US term **quarter step**

quartet /kwawr tét/, **quartette** *n* **1.** MUSICAL GROUP a group of four singers or musicians (*takes a singular or plural verb*) **2.** PIECE OF MUSIC a piece of music written for four voices or instruments **3.** GROUP OF FOUR a group or set of four people, organizations, or things (*takes a singular or plural verb*) [Late 18C. Via French *quartette* < Italian *quartetto* < *quarto* 'fourth' < Latin *quartus*]

Quartet *n* an international group of representatives from the United States, the European Union, the Russian Federation, and the United Nations that meets regularly to promote peace between Israel and the Palestinian Authority

quartic /kwáwrtik/ *adj* relating to or involving the fourth degree of power of an unknown quantity or variable. A quartic equation has the general form $ax^4 + bx^3 + cx^2 + dx + e = 0$. [Mid-19C. < Latin *quartus* 'fourth']

quartier /kaárti ay/ (*plural* **-ers** /*pronunc. same*/) *n* a district of a city or town in France [Early 19C. < French, 'quarter']

quartile /kwáwr tīl/ *n* **1.** STATISTICAL DIVISION each of four equal groups into which a statistical sample may be divided **2.** STATISTICAL VALUE in statistics, each of the three values that divide a frequency distribution into four parts that each contain a quarter of the sample population **3.** DISTANCE BETWEEN PLANETS the astrological aspect of planets that are distant from each other by 90° or one-fourth of the zodiac [Early 16C. < Old French *quartil* < Latin *quartus* 'fourth']

quarto /kwáwrtō/ (*plural* **-tos**) *n* **1.** a book with pages of a size traditionally created by folding a single sheet of standard-sized printing paper in half twice, giving four leaves or eight pages **2.** the page size of a quarto book [Late 16C. < Latin *(in) quarto* 'in a fourth' < *quartus* 'fourth']

quartz /kwawrts/ *n* a common, hard, usually colourless, transparent crystalline mineral with coloured varieties. Use: electronics, gems. [Mid-18C. < German *Quarz* < W Slavic, 'hard']

quartz clock *n* a clock in which the time-keeping mechanism is accurately controlled by a quartz crystal that vibrates at a fixed frequency in an oscillating electric circuit

quartz crystal *n* a small piece of quartz cut so that it vibrates at a known frequency

quartz glass *n* a clear glass made from melted silica that can withstand high or rapidly changing temperatures and is unusually transparent to ultraviolet radiation

quartz heater *n* a portable electric heater with heating elements sealed in quartz glass tubes

quartziferous /kwawrt síffərəss/ *adj* containing or consisting of quartz

quartz-iodine lamp *n* a very bright lamp with a bulb made of quartz glass that has a tungsten filament and usually contains iodine vapour. Use: car headlights, film projectors.

quartzite /kwáwrts īt/ *n* a pale metamorphic rock composed mainly of quartz, formed by the action of heat and pressure on sandstone. Use: building materials. —**quartzitic** /kwawrt síttik/ *adj*

quartz lamp *n* a mercury-vapour lamp with a bulb made from quartz glass that produces light rich in ultraviolet radiation and is used for street lighting and sun lamps

quartz watch *n* a watch in which the time-keeping mechanism is accurately controlled by a quartz crystal that vibrates at a fixed frequency in an oscillating electric circuit

quasar /kwáy zaar, -saar/ *n* a compact object in space, usually with a large red shift indicating extreme remoteness, that emits huge amounts of energy, sometimes equal to the energy output of an entire galaxy [Mid-20C. Contraction of QUASI-STELLAR OBJECT]

quash[1] /kwosh/ (**quashes, quashing, quashed**) *vt* **1.** to suppress something such as a rebellion or political protest completely by means of force **2.** to prevent feelings from developing or being expressed [14C. Via French < medieval Latin *quassare* 'shake to pieces' < *quatere* 'shake']

quash[2] /kwosh/ (**quashes, quashing, quashed**) *vt* to declare formally that something such as a law or a court's verdict is not valid [13C. Via French < Latin *cassare* < *cassus* 'empty, void']

quasi /kwáy zī, kwáy sī, kwaázi/ *adj* resembling somebody or something in some ways, but not exactly the same ○ *a quasi support group* [15C. Via French < Latin, 'as if' < *quam* 'as' + *si* 'if']

quasi- *prefix* as if, resembling ○ *quasi-judicial* [Via French < Latin *quasi* (see QUASI)]

quasi-abstract *adj*
quasi-chemical *adj*
quasi-contractual *adj*
quasi-crystalline *adj*
quasi-diplomatic *adj*
quasi-domestic *adj*
quasi-fascist *adj*
quasi-governmental *adj*
quasi-legal *adj*
quasi-legendary *adj*
quasi-legitimate *adj*
quasi-Marxist *adj*
quasi-military *adj*
quasi-modern *adj*
quasi-mystical *adj*
quasi-nominal *adj*
quasi-official *adj*
quasi-periodic *adj*
quasi-private *adj*
quasi-privatization *n*
quasi-privatize *vt*
quasi-public *adj*
quasi-regal *adj*
quasi-religious *adj*
quasi-scientific *adj*
quasi-theatrical *adj*

quasi-judicial *adj* **1.** describes decision-making powers that are similar to those of a court judge **2.** describes an arbitrator or enquiry with powers that are similar to those of a court judge —**quasi-judicially** *adv*

quasi-legislative *adj* **1.** describes bodies that are empowered to make regulations having the force of law **2.** describes regulations that are not regarded as laws proper but have the force of law

quasi-private *adj*

quasi-stellar object *n* ASTRON same as **quasar**

quass *n* BEVERAGES another spelling of **kvass**

quassia /kwóshə/ *n* **1.** PALE WOOD a fine-grained pale wood. Use: furniture-making. **2.** INSECTICIDE a bitter substance obtained from the bark and wood of a tropical tree. Use: insecticide. **3.** TREE YIELDING QUASSIA a bush or small tree with scarlet flowers that yields quassia. Native to: tropical America. Genus: *Quassia*. [Mid-18C. < ?]

quatercentenary /kwáttər sen teénəri/ (*plural* **-ries**) *n* a four-hundredth anniversary [Late 19C. < Latin *quater* 'four times']

quaternary /kwə túrnəri/ *adj* **1.** OCCURRING IN FOURS consisting of four parts, or occurring in sets of four **2.** HAVING FOUR-ATOM BONDS bonded to four other non-hydrogen atoms or groups of atoms, or containing atoms bonded in this way ■ *n* (*plural* **-ies**) FOURTH MEMBER the fourth member of a set [15C. < Latin *quaternarius* < *quaterni* 'by fours' < *quater* 'four times']

Quaternary *n* the current period of geological time, beginning 1.6 million years ago and characterized by the appearance and dominance of humans. See table at **geological time** —**Quaternary** *adj*

quaternary ammonium compound *n* a nitrogen compound regarded as a derivative of ammonium. Use: solvents, disinfectants.

quaternion /kwə túrni ən/ *n* a generalized complex number that contains four terms, one real and three imaginary, and is the sum of a real number and a

vector [14C. < late Latin *quaternion-* < Latin *quaterni* (see QUATERNARY)]

quaternity /kwə túrnəti/ (*plural* **-ties**) *n* a set of four, especially the four beings that, in some religions, are unified in God [Early 16C. < late Latin *quaternitas* < Latin *quaterni* (see QUATERNARY)]

quatrain /kwó trayn/ *n* a verse of poetry consisting of four lines, especially one with lines that rhyme alternately [Late 16C. < French < *quatre* 'four' < Latin *quattuor*]

quatrefoil (sense 2)

quatrefoil /káttrə foyl/ *n* **1.** a design or symbol in the shape of a flower with four petals or a leaf with four parts, often used in heraldry **2.** an architectural decoration consisting of four arcs radiating from a centre like flower petals [15C. < Anglo-Norman, 'four-leaf']

quattrocento /kwáttrō chéntō/ *n* the 15th century in Italy, especially with reference to art and literature [Late 19C. < Italian, shortening of *mil quattrocento* 'one thousand four hundred']

quaver /kwáyvər/ *v* (**-vers, -vering, -vered**) **1.** *vi* TREMBLE SLIGHTLY to tremble because of nervousness or fear **2.** *vti* SAY TREMBLINGLY to say something or speak in a trembling voice because of nervousness or fear **3.** *vi* SING WITH TRILL to sing in a trilling voice ■ *n* **1.** TREMBLING SOUND a tremble in the voice caused by nervousness or fear **2.** LENGTH OF NOTE a musical note with the time value of one eighth of a semibreve. It is written as a filled note head with a stem and one tail. N Am term **eighth note 3.** TRILL an alternation of a musical tone with the tone just above it [15C. < obsolete *quave* 'tremble' < Germanic] —**quaveringly** *adv* —**quavery** *adj*

quaver rest *n* a musical rest equal in length to a quaver. N Am term **eighth rest**

quay /kee/ *n* a platform that runs along the edge of a port or harbour, where boats are loaded and unloaded [14C. Via Old N French *cai* < Gaulish *caio* 'rampart']

quayage /kee ij/ *n* **1.** FEE FOR USING QUAY a charge that ship owners must pay to dock at a quay in order to load and unload there **2.** QUAY SPACE the space available on a quay for ships to load and unload **3.** QUAY SYSTEM a system of quays

Quayle /kwayl/, **Sir Anthony** (1913–89) British actor and director. He was cofounder of the Royal Shakespeare Memorial Theatre Company, and set up his own touring company in 1982.

quayside /kee sīd/ *n* the edge of a quay, where it meets the water

qubit /kyoóbit/ *n* an elementary particle such as an electron or photon that can store data and perform computational tasks within a quantum computer's processor and memory [Late 20C. < QUANTUM + BIT³]

Que. *abbr* Quebec

quean /kween/ *n* (*archaic*) **1.** an offensive term that deliberately insults a woman's morality **2.** *Scotland* same as **quine** [Old English *cwene* 'woman', related to QUEEN]

queasy /kweézi/ (**-sier, -siest**) *adj* **1.** NAUSEOUS feeling ill in the stomach, as if on the point of vomiting **2.** EASILY NAUSEATED easily made to feel nauseous **3.** CAUSING NAUSEA causing a feeling of nausea **4.** CAUSING UNEASINESS causing a feeling of uneasiness [15C. < ?] —**queasily** *adv* —**queasiness** *n*

Quebec¹ /kwi bék, ki-/, **Québec** /kay-/ **1.** *also* **Quebec City** *or* **Québec City** capital of Quebec Province, Canada, on the St Lawrence River. Population:

169,076 (2001). **2.** province in eastern Canada, situated between Ontario and Newfoundland, with French-based social institutions, language, and culture. Capital: Quebec. Population: 7,455,200 (2002). Area: 1,542,056 sq. km/595,391 sq. mi. Former name **Canada East** (1841–67) —**Quebecer** *n*

Quebec² /kwi bék, ki-/ *n* a code word for the letter 'Q', used in international radio communications

Québécois /kwi bé kwaa, kay-/, **Québecois**, **Quebecois** *adj* relating to Quebec, especially its French-speaking inhabitants or their culture ■ *n* (*plural same*) somebody who comes from Quebec, especially somebody who is French-speaking [Late 19C. < French, 'from Quebec']

quebracho /kay braáchō/ (*plural* **-chos**) *n* a tree with hard tannin-rich wood. Native to: southern South America. Genus: *Schinopsis*. [Late 19C. < Spanish, alteration of *quiebrahacha* 'axe-breaker' < *quebrar* 'to break' + *hacha* 'axe']

Quechua /kéchwə/ (*plural same* or **-uas**), **Kechua**, **Quichua** /kíchwə/ *n* **1.** a member of a Native South American people living in the Andes **2.** the language of the Quechua people. Native speakers: 11 million. [Mid-19C. < Spanish] —**Quechua** *adj* —**Quechuan** *adj, n*

queen /kween/ *n* **1.** FEMALE RULER a woman who rules over a country, usually by right of birth **2.** KING'S WIFE the wife or widow of a king **3.** ADMIRED WOMAN a greatly admired woman who stands over all others ○ *the queen of blues* **4.** BEST PLACE OR THING a place or thing considered the best of its kind and personified as a woman **5.** CHESS MOST POWERFUL CHESS PIECE the most powerful piece in chess, able to move over any number of squares forwards, backwards, sideways, and diagonally **6.** CARDS FACE CARD a playing card with a picture of a queen on it, ranking above a jack and below a king **7.** INSECTS EGG-LAYING INSECT a large, fully developed female that lays eggs in a colony of social insects, e.g. bees or ants **8.** VERTEB FEMALE CAT an adult female cat, especially one used for breeding **9.** OFFENSIVE TERM an offensive term for a gay man, especially one regarded as behaving in a flamboyant and stereotypically effeminate way (*insult*) ■ *vti* (**queens, queening, queened**) CHESS MAKE PAWN INTO QUEEN in chess, to promote a pawn to the rank of queen by managing to take it to the opponent's end of the board, or become promoted from pawn to queen [Old English *cwēn* < Indo-European] —**queenship** *n* ◇ **queen it** to behave in a domineering, arrogant way (*informal*)

Queen Anne *n* a style of furniture popular in the United Kingdom in the early 18th century, characterized by the use of simple curves and cabriole legs [Early 19C. After Queen ANNE]

Queen Anne's lace *n* PLANTS same as **cow parsley** [Late 19C. After Queen ANNE]

queen bee *n* **1.** a large, fully developed female bee that lays eggs continually **2.** a woman or girl who is treated as the most important member of her group, or who behaves as if she is (*informal*)

queencake /kween kayk/ *n* a small currant cake, usually heart-shaped

Queen Charlotte Islands /kween shaárlət-/ island group in British Columbia, Canada, northwest of Vancouver Island in the Pacific Ocean. Population: 3,368 (1986). Area: 9,596 sq. km/3,705 sq. mi.

queen consort (*plural* **queens consort**) *n* a woman married to a reigning king

queen cup *n* a stemless plant that produces a single white flower and a blue berry. Native to: western North America. Latin name: *Clintonia uniflora*.

queen dowager *n* a widow of a king

Queen Elizabeth Islands island group in the Arctic Archipelago, northern Canada, in the Arctic Ocean, west of Greenland. Area: 425,000 sq. km/164,000 sq. mi.

queenly /kween li/ *adj* **1.** REGAL having the qualities traditionally associated with a queen, especially grace and dignity **2.** RELATING TO QUEEN relating to or suitable for a queen ■ *adv* REGALLY in a way thought fitting for or typical of a queen, especially with grace and dignity —**queenliness** *n*

Queen Maud Gulf /-máwd-/ gulf in the Arctic Ocean, between southeastern Victoria Island and the mainland of Nunavut, Canada

queen mother *n* the mother of a reigning king or queen and the widow of a former king

queen of puddings *n* a pudding made of breadcrumbs and milk, often with a layer of meringue on top

Queen of the May *n* same as **May queen**

queen-of-the-prairie *n* a plant that grows in grasslands. Flowers: small, pink. Native to: central and eastern United States. Latin name: *Filipendula rubra*.

queen olive *n* a large edible olive with a long flat stone

queen post *n* either of two vertical posts forming part of the triangular framework that supports a roof [After KING POST]

queen regent (*plural* **queens regent**) *n* a queen reigning on behalf of another person, especially one too young to take the throne

queen regnant (*plural* **queens regnant**) *n* a queen who reigns in her own right, as distinct from the wife of a king

Queens /kweenz/ borough of New York City, on western Long Island. Population: 2,237,815 (2002 estimate). Area: 282 sq. km/109 sq. mi.

Queen's Bench *n* a division of the High Court of Justice in England (*used when the reigning monarch is a woman or girl*)

Queensberry rules /kweénzbəri-/ *npl* **1.** the rules that govern boxing **2.** accepted standards of fairness or courtesy in any situation (*informal*) [Late 19C. After John Sholto Douglas (1844–1900), 9th Marquess of Queensberry, who supervised their preparation in 1867]

Queen's Counsel *n* a senior barrister in England, entitled to wear a silk gown and sit inside the bar of the court (*used when the reigning monarch is a woman or girl*)

Queen's English *n* standard written or spoken British English, regarded as the most correct form of the language (*used when the reigning monarch is a woman or girl*)

Queen's evidence *n* in English law, evidence for the prosecution given by somebody who took part in a crime, usually in exchange for leniency (*used when the reigning monarch is a woman or girl*)

Queen's Highway *n* a public road, regarded as belonging ultimately to the monarch (*formal*; *used when the reigning monarch is a woman or girl*)

queenside /kweén sīd/ *n* the side of a chessboard on which the queen is located at the beginning of a game

queen-size *adj* N Am describes beds and bedclothes that are larger than the standard size but smaller than king-size ○ *a queen-size bed* [After KING-SIZE]

Queensland /kweénzland, -land/ state in northeastern Australia. Capital: Brisbane. Population: 3,796,800 (2003). Area: 1,727,200 sq. km/666,880 sq. mi.

Queenslander /kweénzləndər/ *n* **1.** somebody who comes from or lives in Queensland **2.** *Aus* a style of house, common in Queensland, that is typically made of wood, built on a raised platform, and has a wide veranda

Queen's proctor *n* in the United Kingdom, an official of the High Court of Justice who has rights to intervene when there are charges of collusion or suppression of facts. The cases in which the Queen's Proctor may act include those involving divorces and wills. (*used when the reigning monarch is a woman or girl*)

Queen's Regulations *n* regulations that govern the armed forces of the United Kingdom and some Commonwealth countries (*used when the reigning monarch is a woman or girl*)

queen's shilling *n* in former times, a coin given to new military recruits as a symbol of enlistment into the British army (*used when the reigning monarch is a woman or girl*)

Queen's speech *n* (*used when the reigning monarch is a woman or girl*) **1.** in the United Kingdom, a speech given by the monarch at the opening of Parliament each year, setting out the government's proposed legislation **2.** in the United Kingdom, a

speech by the monarch to the nation and the Commonwealth broadcast on Christmas Day

Queenstown /kweénz town/ resort town in the southwestern part of the South Island, New Zealand, situated on the shore of Lake Wakatipu. Population: 8,538 (2001).

queen substance *n* a pheromone secreted by a queen bee and consumed by worker bees in the same hive that prevents the worker bees from becoming fully developed and reproducing

queer /kweer/ *adj* **1. NOT USUAL** not usual or expected **2. ECCENTRIC** eccentric or unconventional (*informal*) **3. SUSPICIOUS** arousing suspicion (*informal*) **4. NAUSEOUS** slightly unwell, especially nauseous or faint (*dated*) **5. OFFENSIVE TERM** an offensive term meaning gay ■ *n* **OFFENSIVE TERM** an offensive term for a gay man (*insult*) ■ *vt* (**queers, queering, queered**) (*dated*) **1. THWART SOMETHING** to spoil or thwart something, especially somebody's plans **2. COMPROMISE SOMEBODY** to put somebody in an awkward situation [Early 16C. Probably < Low German *quer* 'oblique, crooked'] —**queerish** *adj* —**queerly** *adv* —**queerness** *n*

USAGE See *insult.*

queer bashing *n* an offensive term for the practice or an instance of committing unprovoked acts of violence against gay and lesbian people (*slang*) —**queer basher** *n*

queercore /kweér kawr/ *n* (*slang*) **1.** a gay youth movement that rejects the stereotype of a gay person as a persecuted victim by confidently and assertively proclaiming homosexuality, especially in punk-style music **2.** a style of music similar to punk rock with lyrics that proclaim homosexuality confidently and assertively [Late 20C. < QUEER + HARD CORE]

queer fish *n* somebody considered to have unusual habits or beliefs (*dated informal*)

quelea /kwéliə/ (*plural* **-as** or *same*) *n* a brownish bird of the weaverbird family, the male of which has either a black face or a red head. Native to: Africa. Genus: *Quelea*.

quell /kwel/ (**quells, quelling, quelled**) *vt* **1.** to bring something to an end, usually by means of force ○ *using tear gas to quell the riot* **2.** to allay a disturbing feeling or thought in a reassuring way [Old English *cwellan* 'kill' < Indo-European, 'stab, kill']

quench /kwench/ (**quenches, quenching, quenched**) *vt* **1. SATISFY THIRST** to satisfy a thirst by drinking something **2. EXTINGUISH FIRE** to put out a fire or light **3. SUPPRESS FEELING** to suppress a feeling completely, especially enthusiasm or desire **4. COOL METAL** to cool hot metal by plunging it into cold water or other liquid [Old English *ācwencan* < Germanic] —**quenchable** *adj* —**quencher** *n* —**quenchless** *adj*

quenelle /kə nél/ *n* a seasoned meat or fish dumpling poached in water and served with a sauce [Mid-19C. Via French < German *Knödel* 'dumpling']

quercetin /kwúrssitin/ *n* a yellow compound. Source: rind and bark of oak, Douglas fir, and many other plants. Use: treatment of fragile capillaries. Formula: $C_{15}H_{10}O_7$. [Mid-19C. < Latin *quercetum* 'oak forest' < *quercus* 'oak']

quercitron /kwúrssitrən/ *n* **1.** the bright orange inner bark of the black oak tree. Use: tanning, dyeing. **2.** yellow dye made from quercitron [Late 18C. < Latin *quercus* 'oak' + CITRON, from the colour of its bark]

querida /ke reédə/ (*plural* **-das**) *n Philippines* a man's mistress [Mid-19C. < Spanish, 'darling, beloved' < *querer* 'desire' < Latin *quaerere* 'seek']

querist /kweérist/ *n* a questioner (*archaic*) [Mid-17C. < *quere* (see QUERY)]

quern /kwurn/ *n* a simple stone mill used for grinding grain by hand [Old English *cweorn* < Indo-European, 'heavy']

querulous /kwérrooləss, -ryoo-/ *adj* **1.** inclined to complain or find fault **2.** whining or complaining in tone [15C. < late Latin *querulosus* < Latin *queri* 'complain'] —**querulously** *adv* —**querulousness** *n*

query /kweéri/ *n* (*plural* **-ries**) **1. QUESTION** a request for information **2. DOUBT** a doubt or criticism **3.** GRAM same as **question mark** ■ *vt* (**-ries, -rying, -ried**) **1. QUESTION SOMETHING** to express doubts about, or objections to, something **2. ASK SOMETHING** to ask something as a question [Mid-17C. < obsolete *quere* 'ask' (imperative), 'query' < Latin *quaere* 'ask' < *quaerere* 'seek'] —**querier** *n*

ques. *abbr* question

quesadilla /káy sə deéyə/ *n* a tortilla filled with cheese and other ingredients and grilled [Mid-20C. < Mexican Spanish < Spanish *queso* 'cheese']

quest /kwest/ *n* **1. SEARCH** a search for something, especially a long or difficult one **2. ADVENTUROUS EXPEDITION** a journey in search of something, especially one made by knights in medieval tales (*literary*) **3. SOMETHING SOUGHT** the object or goal of a quest (*literary*) ○ *Peace is still our quest.* **4.** COMPUT GAMES **GAME OBJECTIVE** an objective to be achieved in a computer game ○ *Strange things will happen if you perform quests out of sequence.* ■ *v* (**quests, questing, quested**) **1.** *vti* **SEEK SOMETHING** to seek or go in search of something (*literary*) **2.** *vi* FIELD SPORTS **TRACK ANIMALS** to follow the track of a bird or animal that is being hunted (*refers to hunting dogs*) [14C. Via French < Latin *quaesita* < form of past participle of *quaerere* 'seek'] —**quester** *n* —**questingly** *adv*

question /kwéschən/ *n* **1. WRITTEN OR SPOKEN ENQUIRY** a request for information or for a reply, which usually ends with a question mark if written or on a rising intonation if spoken ○ *Does anyone have any questions?* **2. DOUBT** a doubt or uncertainty about somebody or something **3. ISSUE** a matter that is the subject of discussion, debate, or negotiation **4.** EDUC **EXAMINATION PROBLEM** a problem to be discussed or solved in an examination ■ *v* (**-tions, -tioning, -tioned**) **1.** *vti* **INTERROGATE SOMEBODY** to ask somebody for information, especially formally or officially and on a specific topic **2.** *vt* **DOUBT SOMETHING** to raise doubts about something, especially about its truth, genuineness, or usefulness [13C. Via French < Latin *quaestion-* 'enquiry' < past participle of *quaerere* 'seek'] —**questioner** *n* ◇ **beg the question 1.** to take for granted the very point that needs to be proved, and so fail to address an issue properly **2.** to give rise to something else that should be answered or explained ◇ **be out of the question** to be impossible or unacceptable ◇ **call something into question** to raise doubts about something ◇ **in question** used to indicate the person or thing under discussion ◇ **pop the question** to propose marriage to somebody (*informal*)

USAGE To ***beg the question*** is often used to mean 'to raise the question' or 'to avoid a direct answer', since both meanings are consistent with the form of the idiom. The basic meaning of this idiom relates to the validity of a proposition that is used as a basis of argument. For example, in an argument about the effect on the environment of gas emissions from road traffic, the proposition that a higher tax on vehicles would contribute to cleaner air ***begs the question*** because it needs to be proved that raising taxes would result in fewer road users. The fallacy implied by the notion of ***begging the question*** usually involves the omission of one stage in an argument or a questionable assumption of its validity.

SYNONYMS ***question, quiz, interrogate, cross-examine, grill, give the third degree***

CORE MEANING: to ask for information

question to ask somebody for information, especially formally or officially and on a specific topic ○ *Patients were questioned in detail about their symptoms.* **quiz** to subject somebody to sustained close questioning ○ *Anne was being quizzed by her aunt about her many boyfriends.* **interrogate** to question somebody thoroughly, often in an aggressive or threatening manner and especially as part of a formal enquiry, for example in a police station or courtroom ○ *Police are interrogating two men and a woman arrested on Thursday.* **cross-examine** (*informal*) to ask somebody a lot of detailed questions in a persistent or aggressive way ○ *We were cross-examined about who we'd spoken to and why it had taken us so long to get home.* **grill** (*informal*) to question somebody in a persistent manner ○ *Lawyers on both sides grilled a DNA expert about his analysis of the blood found in the vehicle.* **give the third degree** (*informal*) to subject somebody to intensive interrogation, especially when accompanied by rough physical treatment ○ *Then they brought in a couple of other supporting interrogators and gave me the third degree.* ○ *My mother gave me the third degree whenever I was out late.*

questionable /kwéschənəb'l/ *adj* **1.** open to doubt or disagreement **2.** not respectable or morally acceptable ○ *questionable motives* —**questionability** /kwéschənə bílləti/ *n* —**questionably** *adv*

~~**questionaire**~~ incorrect spelling of **questionnaire**

questioning /kwéschəning/ *n* a situation in which somebody is asked a lot of questions, especially formally or officially, or an instance of this ■ *adj* expressing a question without using words ○ *a questioning glance* —**questioningly** *adv*

questionless /kwéschənləss/ *adj* **1.** same as **unquestionable 2.** same as **unquestioning**

question mark *n* the punctuation mark (?) placed at the end of a sentence or phrase intended as a direct question. It is also used after a word or phrase whose appropriateness is in doubt, or after a number or date whose accuracy is in doubt. ◇ **a question mark over something** an area of doubt and uncertainty concerning something

USAGE The ***question mark*** is used after a direct question: *'Where are you going?' 'What for?'* It is not used in indirect questions: *He asked her where she was going.* It may also be used in other contexts, e.g. in creative writing, to indicate that somebody is wondering about something (*He assumed she had gone to visit her mother. But why had she taken her passport?*) or in journalism to anticipate a reader's question (*How is the tax calculated? It is based on the current market value of the property*). The question mark may also indicate uncertainty, especially when placed before or after a date: *François Rabelais (1493?–1553).* The question mark may mark a sentence that has the function but not the structure of a question: *You're from Liverpool then?* It may be omitted from a sentence that has the structure of a question, but is not intended as such: *Will you keep quiet for a minute.*

question master *n* somebody who asks questions on a broadcast quiz show

questionnaire /kwéschə náir, késchə-/ *n* **1.** a set of questions used to gather information in a survey **2.** a printed paper or form that contains a questionnaire [Late 19C. < French < *questionner* 'ask' < *question* (see QUESTION)]

question tag *n* a short phrase at the end of a statement that changes it into a question. In English, examples are the phrases 'isn't it?' and 'have you?'

question time *n* in Parliament, a period of time every day during which members of parliament may address questions to government ministers

Quetta /kwéttə/ capital of Baluchistan Province, west-central Pakistan. Population: 560,307 (1998).

quetzal

quetzal /kéts'l, kwéts'l/ (*plural* **-zals** or **-zales** /ket saá layss/) *n* **1.** a bird with brilliant green and red feathers. The male of one species, resplendent quetzal, has long streaming tail feathers. Native to: Central and South America. Genus: *Pharomachrus*. **2.** the main unit of Guatemalan currency. See table at **currency** [Early 19C. Via American Spanish < Nahuatl *quetzalli* 'brilliantly coloured tail feather']

Quetzalcoatl /kéts'l kō átt'l/ *n* in Toltec and Aztec mythology, a god and the legendary ruler of Mexico, represented as a feathered serpent [Via Spanish < Nahuatl *Quetzalcōātl* < *quetzalli* 'brilliantly coloured tail feather' + *cōātl* 'snake']

queue /kyoo/ *n* **1. LINE OF WAITING PEOPLE** a line of people or vehicles waiting for something. N Am term **line**[1] **2.** COMPUT **SET OF COMPUTER TASKS** a series of messages

or jobs waiting to be processed automatically one after the other by a computer system **3.** COMPUT **LIST OF DATA** a list of computer data constructed and maintained on a first in, first out basis **4.** HIST **MAN'S PIGTAIL** a short plait of hair worn at the back of the neck by soldiers and sailors in the late 18th and early 19th centuries ■ *v* (**queues, queueing** or **queuing, queued**) **1.** *vi* **FORM WAITING LINE** to form a line while waiting for something **2.** *vi* **WAIT IN LARGE NUMBERS** to be waiting for or eagerly anticipating something along with a lot of other people (*informal*) ○ *the most eminent critics queueing up to review her latest book* **3.** *vt* COMPUT **ADD SOMETHING TO COMPUTER'S TASKS** to add a job or message to the list of tasks being held in storage by a computer, awaiting automatic dispatching [Late 16C. Via French < Latin *cauda* 'tail'] ◇ **jump the queue** to push in or move ahead of others unfairly in a queue

SPELLCHECK See *cue*[1].

queue-jump *vt* to push in or move ahead of others unfairly in a queue or in a situation where people should wait their turn —**queue-jumper** *n*

Quezon City /káy son-/ city in central Luzon, Philippines. It was the national capital from 1948 to 1976. Population: 2,112,722 (1999).

Quezon y Molina /káyz on ee mo léenə, ke thón-/, **Manuel** (1878–1944) Philippine politician. He worked for Philippine independence, and was elected the first president of the Commonwealth of the Philippines (1935–44). Full name **Quezon y Molina, Manuel Luis**

quibble /kwíbb'l/ *vi* (**-bles, -bling, -bled**) to argue over unimportant things and make petty objections ■ *n* **1.** an unimportant distinction or petty objection **2.** same as **pun** (*archaic*) [Early 17C. Probably < obsolete *quib* 'pun, equivocation' < Latin *quibus* 'whom, for whom', often used in legal documents] —**quibbler** *n* —**quibblingly** *adv*

quiche /keesh/ *n* a savoury flan filled with an egg-and-cream mixture and various meat or vegetable ingredients [Mid-20C. Via French < German dialect *Küche* 'small cake' < German *Kuchen* 'cake']

quiche Lorraine /-lə ráyn/ *n* a quiche made with cheese and bacon [Mid-20C. After LORRAINE, France]

Quichua *n, adj* PEOPLES, LANG same as **Quechua**

quick /kwik/ *adj* **1. DOING SOMETHING FAST** moving or doing something fast **2. ALERT** demonstrating alertness or sharp perception ○ *She has a very quick mind.* **3. NIMBLE** moving swiftly and with skill ○ *quick fingers* **4. DONE WITHOUT DELAY** done or doing something without delay ○ *They promised a quick delivery.* **5. EASILY ANGERED** describes a temper that is easily roused **6. BRIEF** taking or lasting only a short time ○ *We stopped to have a quick chat.* **7. HASTY** tending to be hasty ○ *Don't be too quick to blame others.* **8.** same as **alive** (sense 1) (*archaic*) ■ *n* **1. FLESH UNDER NAIL** the sensitive flesh under a fingernail or toenail **2. SOMEBODY'S SENSITIVITIES** somebody's deepest feelings or most private emotions ○ *criticisms that cut him to the quick* ■ *npl* **THE LIVING** those people who are alive (*archaic*) ○ *the quick and the dead* ■ *adv* **FAST** in a speedy manner (*informal*) ○ *Come quick!* [Old English *cwic(u)* 'alive, lively' < Indo-European, 'to live'] —**quickly** *adv* —**quickness** *n* ◇ **quick and dirty** produced to meet an immediate or pressing need, rather than in accordance with high standards of research or design (*informal*)

SYNONYMS See *intelligent*.

quick assets *npl* cash along with other assets that can readily be converted into cash

quick bread *n* bread leavened with baking powder or soda, as opposed to yeast, and ready to bake as soon as it is mixed

quick-change artist *n* a performer or other person who is skilled at changing quickly from one costume or character to the next

quicken /kwíkən/ (**-ens, -ening, -ened**) *v* **1.** *vti* **INCREASE IN SPEED** to become faster, or make something faster **2.** *vti* **STIMULATE SOMETHING** to stimulate something such as interest or enthusiasm, or be stimulated **3.** *vi* **COME TO LIFE** to begin a period of development **4.** *vi* **MOVE IN WOMB** to begin to move and be felt moving in the womb (*refers to foetuses*)

quick-fire /kwík fīr/ *adj UK, Can* **1.** designed to fire shots in quick succession **2.** coming one after another in rapid succession (*informal*) ○ *a round of quick-fire questions* ► ANZ, US term **rapid-fire**

quick fix *n* a speedily or hastily contrived solution to a problem, often one that fails to resolve long-term issues (*informal*)

quick-freeze *vt* to freeze food rapidly in an effort to keep its full flavour and nutritional value

quickie /kwíki/ *n* something that is done hurriedly, especially a hurried act of sex or a speedily consumed alcoholic drink (*informal*)

quicklime /kwík līm/ *n* CHEM same as **calcium oxide** [14C. Translation of Latin *calx viva* 'living lime']

quick march *n* a march at the fastest military pace (**quick time**) ■ *interj* used to order troops or a band to march in quick time

quicksand /kwík sand/ *n* **1.** a deep mass of loose wet sand that sucks down any heavy object falling onto its surface **2.** a hidden trap from which escape is difficult or impossible

quickset /kwík set/ *n* **1.** a plant cutting, especially a cutting of hawthorn, planted with others to make a hedge **2.** a hedge, especially of hawthorn, grown from cuttings

quicksilver /kwík silvər/ *adj* tending to change rapidly and unpredictably ■ *n* CHEM ELEM same as **mercury** (sense 1) (*archaic or literary*) [Pre-12C. Translation of Latin *argentum vivum* 'living silver', from the way it moves in its fluid state]

quickstep /kwík step/ *n* **1. FAST BALLROOM DANCE** a ballroom dance with fast steps **2. DANCE MUSIC** the music for a quickstep **3.** MIL **MARCHING STEP** the marching step used in the fastest marching pace (**quick time**)

quick study *n N Am* a fast learner of something

quick-tempered *adj* same as **short-tempered** —**quick-temperedness** *n*

quickthorn /kwík thawrn/ *n* a thorny plant, especially hawthorn, planted and cut to form a hedge [Early 17C. < its rapid growth]

quick time *n* a fast military marching pace, approximately 120 paces per minute

quick trick *n* in bridge, a high-ranking card, or a combination of high-ranking cards, that makes it possible to win a trick on the first or second round of the suit

quick-witted *adj* able to think quickly and inventively —**quick-wittedly** *adv* —**quick-wittedness** *n*

quid[1] /kwid/ (*plural same*) *n* a pound sterling (*informal*) [Late 17C. Origin ?] ◇ **be quids in** to have made a profit or be in a financially advantageous position (*informal*) ◇ **not the full quid** *Aus* an offensive term meaning unintelligent (*slang insult*)

quid[2] /kwid/ *n* a piece of chewing tobacco [Early 18C. Alteration of CUD]

Quidditch /kwíddich/ *n* in the Harry Potter novels by J. K. Rowling, a fictional game played on broomsticks. [Late 20C. Coined by J. K. ROWLING, origin ?]

quiddity /kwíddəti/ (*plural* **-ties**) *n* **1.** the real nature or essential character of something **2.** an unimportant or trifling distinction [Mid-16C. < medieval Latin *quidditas* < Latin *quid* 'what']

quidnunc /kwíd nungk/ *n* a nosy or gossipy person (*formal*) [Early 18C. < Latin, 'what now']

quid pro quo /kwíd prō kwṓ/ (*plural* **quid pro quos**) *n* **1.** something given or done in exchange for something else **2.** the giving of something in return for something else, often in a spirit of cooperation [Mid-16C. < Latin, 'something for something']

quiescent /kwi éss'nt/ *adj* inactive or at rest [Early 17C. < Latin *quiescent-*, present participle of *quiescere* 'come to rest' (see QUIET)] —**quiescence** *n* —**quiescently** *adv*

quiet /kwī ət/ *adj* **1. NOT NOISY** making little or no noise **2. STILL** free from noise or commotion ○ *in a quiet corner of the room* **3. DONE IN PRIVATE** carried out in private, with voices not raised, in order not to be overheard ○ *I'd like a quiet word with you.* **4. UNDISTURBED** free from trouble or disturbance ○ *a quiet life* **5. RELAXING** relaxing, peaceful, and free from excitement ○ *a quiet evening at home* **6. NOT SHOWY** not grand, showy, or pretentious ○ *a quiet wedding* **7. RESTRAINED** displaying calmness and self-control and not inclined to speak much ○ *the doctor's quiet manner* **8. UNSPOKEN** not expressed in words ○ *a sense of quiet optimism* **9. NOT FLOURISHING** not busy, active, or flourishing ○ *Business is a little too quiet.* **10. CALM OR MOTIONLESS** marked by very little motion ○ *a quiet sea* ■ *n* **ABSENCE OF NOISE** the absence of noise or disturbance ○ *the quiet of the forest* ■ *v* (**-ets, -eting, -eted**) **1.** *vti N Am* same as **quieten** (sense 1) **2.** *vt N Am* same as **quieten** (sense 2) **3.** *vt US* LAW **SECURE LEGAL CLAIM** to make a legal claim secure by resolving all possible challenges to it [14C. Via French < Latin *quiet-*, past participle of *quiescere* 'come to rest' < *quies* 'rest, quiet'] —**quietly** *adv* —**quietness** *n* ◇ **on the quiet** secretly

SPELLCHECK quiet or **quite**? Do not confuse the spelling of ***quiet*** and ***quite***, which sound similar. ***Quiet*** is an adjective and noun referring to lack of noise, as in *be quiet and listen, in the quiet of the evening.* ***Quite*** is an adverb meaning 'entirely' or 'somewhat': *That's quite acceptable. It's quite expensive.*

SYNONYMS See *silent*.

quieten /kwī ət'n/ (**-ens, -ening, -ened**) *v* **1.** *vti* to become calm and quiet, or make somebody calm and quiet ○ *Will you all just quieten down, please?* **2.** *vt* to calm somebody's negative feelings ► N Am term **quiet**

quietism /kwī ətizəm/ *n* **1.** a system of Christian mysticism that requires a withdrawal from the world, a renunciation of the individual will, and passive contemplation of God and divine things **2.** a state of calmness, especially one arising from noninvolvement in something (*literary*) [Late 17C. < Italian *quietismo* < *quieto* < Latin *quiet-* (see QUIET)] —**quietist** *adj, n* —**quietistic** /kwī ə tístik/ *adj*

quietude /kwī ə tyood/ *n* the state of being quiet, peaceful, or tranquil (*literary*) [Late 16C. Directly or via French < medieval Latin *quietudo* < Latin *quiet-* (see QUIET)]

quietus /kwī éetəss, -áy-/ *n* (*literary*) **1. DEATH** death, especially when viewed as a welcome release from life **2. RELEASE** a release from a debt or duty **3. CHECK** something that brings an activity to an end [Mid-16C. < medieval Latin *quietus (est)* '(it is) at rest', acknowledging receipt or discharge of an obligation]

quiff /kwif/ *n* a part of a man's hairstyle in which the hair at the front is brushed upwards and backwards [Late 19C. < ?]

QuikClot /kwík clot/ *tdmk* a trademark for a granular material that, when poured directly into a wound, absorbs water from the blood, thereby concentrating blood-clotting protein factors

quill /kwil/ *n* **1. LARGE FEATHER** a large stiff feather from a bird's wing or tail, or the hollow shaft of such a feather **2. PEN MADE FROM FEATHER SHAFT** an old-fashioned pen made from the shaft of a feather **3. SPINE** a sharp hollow spine on the body of a porcupine or hedgehog **4.** TEXTILES **SPINDLE OR BOBBIN** a spindle or bobbin onto which thread or yarn is wound **5.** MECH ENG **HOLLOW SHAFT** in a mechanical device, a hollow shaft in which a second independently rotating shaft is enclosed ■ *vt* (**quills, quilling, quilled**) **1.** TEXTILES **WIND THREAD** to wind thread or yarn onto a spindle or bobbin **2.** HANDICRAFT **MAKE FOLDS IN SOMETHING** to make small rounded folds in fabric, e.g. to make a ruff [15C. Origin ?]

quillai bark /kée lay-/ *n* INDUST same as **soapbark** (sense 1) [Via modern Latin and Spanish < Araucanian, 'soapbark tree' < *quillcan* 'to wash']

quillback /kwíl bak/ (*plural* **-backs** or *same*), **quillback carpsucker** /-kaárp sukər/ *n* a freshwater fish of the sucker family with a long ray projecting from its dorsal fin. Native to: North America. Latin name: *Carpiodes cyprinus*.

Quiller-Couch /kwíllər kóoch/, **Sir Arthur** (1863–1944) British author. The editor of the *Oxford Book of English Verse* (1900) and other anthologies, he also wrote novels under the pseudonym 'Q'. Full name **Quiller-Couch, Sir Arthur Thomas**

quill pen *n* ART same as **quill** *n* (sense 2)

quillwort /kwíl wurt/ *n* a nonflowering water plant that produces a rosette of tubular leaves, at the bases of which are spore-forming organs. Genus: *Isoetes*.

quilt /kwilt/ *n* **1. BED COVER** a bed cover made of two layers of fabric stitched together with padding held in place by decorative intersecting seams **2.** same

as **duvet** (sense 1) (*informal*) **3.** SOMETHING SIMILAR TO QUILT something that resembles a quilt or is quilted ■ *vt* (**quilts, quilting, quilted**) SEW FABRIC LIKE QUILT to sew two layers of fabric together with a filling, especially using decorative stitching [13C. Via Anglo-Norman < Latin *culcita* 'cushion, mattress'] —**quilter** *n*

quilting /kwílting/ *n* **1.** the sewing of quilted bed covers or other quilted work **2.** material that has been quilted or that is used to make quilts

Quimper /kaN pér/ *n* city in northwestern France. Population: 63,238 (1999).

quin /kwin/ *n* same as **quintuplet** (*informal*) [Mid-20C. Shortening]

quin- *prefix* same as **quino-** (*used before vowels*)

quinacrine hydrochloride /kwínnə kreen-/ *n* same as **mepacrine** [< blend of QUINOLINE + ACRIDINE]

quinalizarin /kwínnə lízzərin/ *n* a red crystalline organic compound with a green metallic lustre. Use: cotton dye. Formula: $C_{14}H_8O_6$.

quinary /kwínəri/ (*formal*) *adj* consisting of five parts, or occurring in sets of five ■ *n* (*plural* **-ries**) a set of five, or the fifth member of a set [Early 17C. < Latin *quinarius* < *quini* 'five each' < *quinque* 'five']

quinate /kwí nayt/ *adj* describes leaves that occur in clusters of five [Early 19C. < modern Latin *quinatus* < Latin *quini* (see QUINARY)]

quince

quince /kwinss/ *n* **1.** an aromatic apple-shaped or pear-shaped yellow or orange fruit that is edible only when cooked. Use: preserves. **2.** a small tree that produces quinces. Native to: western Asia. Latin name: *Cydonia oblonga*. [14C. Via Old French *cooin* < Latin (*malum*) *cotoneum* < Greek (*mēlon*) *kudōnion*, literally 'apple of Cydonia' (now Canea, Crete)]

quincentenary /kwín sen téenəri, -ténnəri/ (*plural* **-ries**), **quincentennial** /-ténni əl/ *n* a 500th anniversary [Late 19C. < Latin *quinque* 'five'] —**quincentary** *adj*

Quincey ♦ de Quincey, Thomas

quincunx /kwín kungks/ *n* an arrangement of five objects in a square, with four at the corners and one in the centre [Mid-17C. < Latin, 'five-twelfths' (from the use of this pattern on a Roman coin worth five-twelfths of a standard unit of currency) < *quinque* 'five' + *uncia* 'twelfth part' (see OUNCE[1])] —**quincuncial** /kwin kúnsh'l/ *adj*

quindecagon /kwin dékəgən/ *n* a two-dimensional geometric figure formed of 15 angles and 15 sides [Late 16C. < Latin *quindecim* 'fifteen']

quindecennial /kwíndi sénni əl/ *adj* **1.** AT 15-YEAR INTERVALS happening once every 15 years **2.** WITH 15-YEAR DURATION lasting for 15 years ■ *n* ANNIVERSARY a 15th anniversary [Late 20C. < Latin *quindecim* 'fifteen', after CENTENNIAL]

quine /kwīn/ *n* Scotland a young woman or girl [Variant of QUEAN]

Quine /kwīn/, **W. V.** (1908–2000) US philosopher. He contributed to the theory of pragmatism and to mathematical set theory. Full name **Quine, Willard Van Orman**

'We know what it is like to be conscious, but not how to put it into satisfactory scientific terms. Whatever it may precisely be, consciousness is a state of the body, a state of nerves.'
[W. V. Quine, *Quiddities: An Intermittently Philosophical Dictionary*; 1987]

quinella /kwi néllə/ *n* a bet in which the punter picks the first two finishers in a race but does not have to place them [Early 20C. < American Spanish *quiniela* < Spanish *quina* 'keno' < French *quine* (see KENO)]

quinic acid /kwínnik-/ *n* a white crystalline organic compound. Source: cinchona bark, coffee beans, leaves of many plants. Use: in medicine. Formula: $C_6H_7(OH)_4COOH$. [< Spanish *quina* 'cinchona bark' (see QUINO-)]

quinidine /kwínni deen/ *n* a colourless crystalline organic compound related to quinine. Source: cinchona bark. Use: treatment of malaria, heart disorders. Formula: $C_{20}H_{24}N_2O_2$.

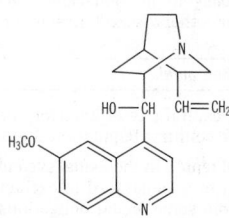

quinine

quinine /kwi néen, kwínneen/ *n* a bitter-tasting drug made from cinchona bark. Use: treatment of malaria. Formula: $C_{20}H_{24}N_2O_2$. [Early 19C. < Spanish *quina* 'cinchona bark' (see QUINO-)]

quinnat salmon /kwínnat-/ *n* FISH same as **Chinook salmon** [< Chinook *ikwanat*]

quino- *prefix* **1.** cinchona, cinchona bark ○ *quinone* **2.** quinone ○ *quinoline* [Via Spanish *quina* 'cinchona bark' < Quechua *kina*]

quinoa /kwi nó ə/ *n* a plant of the goosefoot family that is cultivated for its seeds, which are ground and eaten. Native to: Andes. Latin name: *Chenopodium quinoa*. [Early 17C. Via Spanish < Quechua *kinoa*]

quinoline /kwínnə leen, -lin/ *n* an oily colourless substance. Source: coal tar. Use: manufacture of antiseptics and dyes. Formula: C_9H_7N.

quinone /kwi nón, kwínnōn/ *n* **1.** CHEM same as **benzoquinone** **2.** an organic yellow, orange, or red compound. Source: pigments in plants, fungi, and bacteria, vitamins in animals. —**quinonoid** /kwínnə noyd, kwi nó noyd/ *adj, n*

quinquagenarian /kwíngkwəjə náiri ən/ (*formal*) *adj* 50 years old, or between the ages of 50 and 59 ■ *n* somebody between 50 and 59 years of age [Early 19C. < Latin *quinquagenarius* < *quinquaginta* 'fifty']

Quinquagesima /kwíngkwə jéssimə/ *n* in the Christian liturgical calendar, the Sunday before Lent, seven weeks or the fiftieth day before Easter [14C. Via medieval Latin, 'fiftieth (day)' < Latin *quinquagesimus* < *quinquaginta* 'fifty']

quinque- *prefix* five ○ *quinquennial* [< Latin *quinque* < Indo-European]

quinquennium /kwing kwénni əm/ (*plural* **-nia** /-ni ə/) *n* a period of five years [Early 17C. < Latin, < *quinque* 'five' + *annus* 'year'] —**quinquennial** *adj* —**quinquennially** *adv*

quinquereme /kwíngkwi reem/ *n* an ancient Greek or Roman galley ship propelled by five banks of oars on each side [Mid-16C. < Latin *quinqueremis* < *quinque* 'five' + *remus* 'oar']

quinquevalent /kwíngkwi váylənt/ *adj* CHEM same as **pentavalent**

quinsy /kwínzi/ *n* a severe inflammation of the throat near a tonsil that sometimes leads to the formation of an abscess that may require surgery [14C. Directly or via French < medieval Latin *quinancia* < Greek *kunagkhē*, literally 'dog-strangling' < *kuōn* 'dog' + *ankhein* 'to squeeze']

quint /kwint/ *n* **1.** in the card game piquet, a sequence of five cards of the same suit **2.** *N Am* same as **quintuplet** (*informal*) [Late 17C. Via French, 'fifth' < Latin *quintus*]

quintain /kwíntin/ *n* a target used by a medieval knight for jousting practice [15C. Via French < medieval

Latin *quintana* (*via*) 'fifth (street)' (in a Roman camp) < Latin *quintus* 'fifth']

quintal /kwínt'l/ *n* **1.** in the metric system, a unit of weight equal to 100 kg **2.** MEASURE same as **cental, hundredweight** (sense 1) [15C. Directly or via French < medieval Latin *quintale* < Arabic *kintār* < Latin *centenarius* 'containing a hundred' (see CENTENARY)]

quintan /kwíntən/ *adj* describes a fever that flares up every fifth day [Mid-17C. Via medieval Latin *quintana* from Latin *quintus* 'fifth'] —**quintan** *n*

quinte /kwint, kaNt/ *n* in fencing, the fifth in the eight parrying or attacking positions [Early 18C. From French, feminine of *quint* (see QUINT)]

quintessence /kwin téss'nss/ *n* **1.** EMBODIMENT the purest or most perfect example of something **2.** CHEM EXTRACT the purest extract or essence of a substance, containing the substance's properties in their most concentrated form **3.** PHILOSOPHY FIFTH ELEMENT in ancient and medieval philosophy, the fifth element after earth, air, fire, and water. Heavenly bodies were said to be made of it. **4.** ASTRON HYPOTHETICAL REPULSIVE FORCE a hypothetical repulsive force in cosmology that permeates the whole of space and counteracts the force of gravity [15C. Via French < medieval Latin *quinta essentia* 'fifth essence'] —**quintessential** /kwínti sénsh'l/ *adj* —**quintessentially** *adv*

quintet /kwin tét/, **quintette** *n* **1.** MUSICIANS a group of five singers or musicians (*takes a singular or plural verb*) **2.** MUSIC a piece of music written for five voices or instruments **3.** GROUP OF FIVE a group or set of five people or things [Late 18C. Via French < Italian *quintetto* < *quinto* 'fifth' < Latin *quintus*]

quintic /kwíntik/ *adj* relating to the fifth power in a mathematical expression or equation [Mid-19C. < Latin *quintus* 'fifth']

quintile /kwín tīl/ *n* **1.** STATISTICAL DIVISION one of the five equal populations into which a statistical sample can be divided **2.** STATISTICAL VALUE in statistics, one of the values that divide a frequency distribution into five parts, each containing a fifth of the sample population **3.** DISTANCE BETWEEN PLANETS the astrological aspect of planets that are distant from each other by 72 degrees or one fifth of the zodiac [Early 17C. Latin *quintilis* < *quintus* 'fifth']

Quintilian /kwin tílyən/ (AD 35?–95?) Roman rhetorician. His 12-volume *Institutio Oratoria* (*Training of an Orator*) had an important influence on Renaissance theories of education. Full name **Marcus Fabius Quintilianus**

'A liar should have a good memory.'
[Quintilian, *Institutio Oratoria* (*Training of an Orator*); 90?]

quintillion /kwin tíllyən/ *n* **1.** the number equal to 10^{18}, written as 1 followed by 18 zeros **2.** the number equal to 10^{30}, written as 1 followed by 30 zeros (*dated*) —**quintillion** *adj, pron* —**quintillionth** *adj, n, pron*

quintuple /kwíntyoŏp'l, kwin tyoŏp'l/ *adj* **1.** FIVE TIMES AS MUCH five times as much or as many **2.** CONSISTING OF FIVE PARTS made up of five parts **3.** MUSIC HAVING FIVE BEATS TO BAR having five musical beats to the bar ■ *vti* (**-ples, -pling, -pled**) MULTIPLY BY FIVE to multiply something by five, or be multiplied by five [Late 16C. Via French < medieval Latin *quintuplus* 'fivefold' < Latin *quintus* 'fifth']

quintuplet /kwín tyoŏplət, kwin tyoŏp-/ *n* **1.** ONE OF FIVE OFFSPRING one of five offspring born to one mother from a single pregnancy **2.** GROUP OF FIVE a group of five things, especially five of the same kind **3.** MUSIC GROUP OF FIVE MUSICAL NOTES a group of five musical notes to be played in the time usually occupied by three or four notes

quintuplicate *adj* /kwin tyoŏplikit/ MULTIPLIED BY FIVE multiplied by five ■ *n* /kwin tyoŏplikit/ **1.** ONE OF FIVE one of a set of five identical things **2.** GROUP OF FIVE a group of five usually identical things ■ *vt* /kwin tyoŏpli kayt/ (**-cates, -cating, -cated**) MAKE FIVE COPIES OF SOMETHING to make five copies of something [Mid-17C. < Latin *quintus* 'fifth', after DUPLICATE] —**quintuplication** /kwin tyoŏpli káysh'n/ *n*

quip /kwip/ *n* **1.** WITTICISM a witty remark, especially one made on the spur of the moment **2.** PETTY DISTINCTION a small and unimportant distinction (*archaic*) ■ *vti* (**quips, quipping, quipped**) SAY SOMETHING WITTILY to make

a witty remark, especially on the spur of the moment [Mid-16C. Origin ?]

quipster /kwípstər/ n somebody who makes witty remarks

quipu /kée poo/ (plural **-pus**) n a device consisting of a set of coloured and knotted cords used by the Incas for conveying messages and for record-keeping [Early 18C. Via Spanish < Quechua kipu 'knot']

quire /kwīr/ n 1. a set of 24 or 25 sheets of paper of the same size and quality, equalling one twentieth of a ream 2. a bundle of sheets of paper folded together for binding into a book, especially a four-sheet bundle, folded once to make eight leaves or sixteen pages [15C. < Old French qua(i)er 'copybook', literally 'set of four (sheets)' < Latin quaterni (see QUATERNARY)]

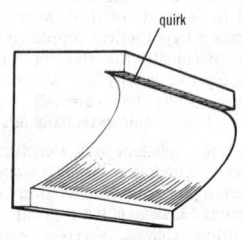
quirk (sense 4)

quirk /kwurk/ n 1. ODD EVENT a strange and unexpected turn of events ○ a strange quirk of fate 2. ODD MANNERISM a peculiar habit, mannerism, or aspect of somebody's character 3. CURVED SHAPE a curved shape, pattern, or decoration, e.g. a flourish in handwriting 4. ARCHIT GROOVE a continuous groove running along a moulding or separating a moulding from adjoining members [Mid-16C. < ?] —**quirkily** adv —**quirkiness** n —**quirky** adj

quirt /kwurt/ n Southwest US a riding whip with a short handle and a braided leather lash [Mid-19C. < Mexican Spanish cuarta 'whip']

quisling /kwízzling/ n a traitor, especially somebody who collaborates with an occupying force [Mid-20C. After Vidkun Quisling, puppet premier of Norway during Nazi occupation] —**quislingism** n

ORIGIN Vidkun Quisling was a Norwegian politician who from 1933 led the National Union Party, the Norwegian fascist party. (Quisling was not his real name – he was originally Abraham Lauritz Jonsson.) When the Germans invaded Norway in 1940, he gave them active support, urging his fellow Norwegians not to resist them, and in 1942 he was installed by Hitler as a puppet premier. In 1945 he was shot for treason.

quit /kwit/ v (**quits, quitting, quitted** or **quit**) 1. vti RESIGN FROM POSITION to give up, leave, or resign from a position or organization 2. vti STOP DOING SOMETHING to stop doing something, especially something bad or irritating ○ Quit moaning. 3. vt LEAVE PLACE to depart from a place (archaic) ○'No, he would sooner quit Kellynch Hall at once, than remain in it on such disgraceful terms.' (Jane Austen, Persuasion; 1818) 4. vti COMPUT EXIT FROM PROGRAM to exit from a computer program using the required exit procedure, so that the data and program configuration are saved 5. vti MOVE OUT to move out of rented property ○ He gave his tenants notice to quit. ■ adj UNBURDENED no longer troubled with a problem or difficult situation (formal) ○'it would be easier to die than to live, and so be quit of all the trouble' (Bram Stoker, Dracula; 1897) [13C. < Old French quiter 'release, set free' < Latin quiet- (see QUIET)]

quitch grass /kwítch-/, **quitch** n PLANTS same as **couch grass** [Old English cwice]

quitclaim /kwít klaym/ n RENUNCIATION OF CLAIM a formal statement renouncing a legal claim previously made ■ vt (**-claims, -claiming, -claimed**) 1. RENOUNCE CLAIM to formally withdraw a legal claim previously made 2. FREE SOMEBODY FROM LIABILITY to formally declare somebody to be no longer legally liable for something [13C. < Anglo-Norman quiteclamer 'proclaim somebody free' < quite 'free' + clamer 'proclaim']

quite /kwīt/ adv 1. SOMEWHAT to some degree, but not to a great degree ○ The film was quite good, but I wouldn't bother seeing it again. 2. ENTIRELY in the highest degree or to the fullest extent ○ not quite as bad as all that 3. NEARLY used with a negative to indicate that something has almost reached a state or condition ○ The dress is not quite finished. 4. EMPHASIZING EXTENT used with expressions of quantity to emphasize the great extent of something ○ quite some time ago 5. EMPHASIZING EXCEPTIONAL QUALITY used to emphasize the exceptional or impressive nature of somebody or something ○ That was quite a celebration we had yesterday. 6. EXPRESSING AGREEMENT used on its own or before 'so' to express agreement or understanding ○ 'I didn't think it was up to me to say anything.' 'Quite.' [14C. Variant of QUIT (adj)] ◇ **be quite something** to be remarkably good, fine, attractive, or otherwise admirable or impressive (informal)

SPELLCHECK See **quiet**.

Quito /kée̅tō̅/ capital city of Ecuador, situated in the north of the country. Population: 1,615,809 (2000).

quitrent /kwít rent/ n in the feudal system, a rent paid by a tenant to a feudal lord in exchange for being released from some feudal obligations [15C. < QUIT (adj)]

quits /kwits/ adj on even terms, especially following the repayment of a debt (informal) [Mid-17C. Probably < QUIT (adj), influenced by medieval Latin quittus 'freed'] ◇ **call it quits** 1. to agree with somebody that neither owes the other money, a favour, or an act of vengeance 2. to agree or decide to stop doing work or an activity (informal) 3. to agree that an argument or dispute is over (informal)

quittance /kwítt'nss/ n 1. release from a debt or obligation 2. a document or statement that releases somebody from a debt or obligation [13C. < Old French quitance < quiter (see QUIT)]

quitter /kwíttər/ n somebody who gives up easily (informal)

quittor /kwíttər/ n an infectious disease that causes inflammation in the feet of horses and donkeys [13C. Origin ?]

quiver[1] /kwívvər/ vi (**-ers, -ering, -ered**) to shake rapidly with small movements ■ n a repeated small rapid shaking movement [15C. Probably < assumed Old English cwifer 'active, nimble', suggestive of the movement] —**quiverer** n —**quivery** adj

quiver[2] /kwívvər/ n 1. a long narrow case for holding arrows 2. the arrows contained in a quiver [14C. Via Anglo-Norman quiveir < medieval Latin cucurum]

quiverful /kwívvərfŏŏl/ (plural **-erfuls** or **-ersful**) n 1. the full number of arrows held in a quiver 2. a large number of people or things, especially the full number of children in a large family (literary)

qui vive /kée veev/ [< French, 'long live who?' (i.e. 'whose side are you on?'), used by sentries to challenge somebody approaching their post] ◇ **on the qui vive** alert and vigilant

quixotic /kwik sóttik/ adj 1. EXCESSIVELY ROMANTIC tending to take a romanticized view of life 2. IMPRACTICAL motivated by an idealism that overlooks practical considerations 3. IMPULSIVE tending to act on impulse [Late 18C. < Don Quixote, hero of a novel by Miguel de CERVANTES] —**quixotically** adv —**quixotism** /kwíksətizəm/ n

quiz /kwiz/ n (plural **quizzes**) 1. TEST OF KNOWLEDGE a test of knowledge in the form of a short or rapid series of questions 2. TRICK a hoax, joke, or other trick (archaic) 3. ECCENTRIC somebody considered to be eccentric (archaic) ○'I could make out that he was at once the quiz of the ward-room' (Robert Louis Stevenson, The Wrecker; 1896) ■ vt (**quizzes, quizzing, quizzed**) 1. INTERROGATE SOMEBODY to subject somebody to sustained close questioning ○ She was quizzed about the disappearance of the money. 2. N Am TEST STUDENT OR CLASS to give a short test to a class of pupils or students 3. RIDICULE SOMEBODY to make fun of somebody (archaic) 4. PEER AT SOMEBODY to look intently at somebody (archaic) [Late 18C. Origin ?] —**quizzer** n

SYNONYMS See **question**.

~~quizes~~ incorrect spelling of **quizzes**

quizmaster /kwíz maastər/ n somebody who presents a quiz show and puts the questions to the contestants

quiz show n a television or radio programme in the form of a game in which contestants compete against each other for prizes by answering questions that test their general or specialist knowledge

quizzical /kwízzik'l/ adj expressing a question, puzzlement, or doubt in a mocking or amused way ○ a quizzical glance —**quizzically** adv

Qum another spelling of **Qom**

quod /kwod/ n CRIME same as **jail** n (sense 1) (slang) [Late 17C. < ?]

quod erat demonstrandum /kwód érrat démmən strándəm/ adv used in a formal conclusion to indicate that something such as a fact is proof of the theory that has just been been advanced [< Latin, 'which was to be proved']

quodlibet /kwóddli bet/ n 1. a theological question put forward as an exercise for discussion 2. a musical performance composed largely of familiar tunes [14C. < medieval Latin quodlibetum < Latin quodlibet 'whatever pleases']

quo-he /kwő hee/ npl Ireland an offensive term that disparages country people as unintelligent or uninformed (insult) [< Irish ceogh 'foggy']

quoin

quoin /koyn, kwoyn/, **coign** /koyn/, **coigne** n 1. OUTER CORNER the outer corner of a wall 2. BLOCK FORMING CORNER a stone block used to form a quoin, especially when it is different, e.g. in size or material, from the other blocks or bricks in the wall 3. ARCHIT same as **keystone** (sense 1) ■ vt (**quoins, quoining, quoined; coigns, coigning, coigned; coignes, coigning, coigned**) BUILD CORNER WITH DISTINCTIVE BLOCKS to build an outer corner of a wall using blocks that are different, e.g. in size or texture, from the other blocks or bricks used to build the wall [Mid-16C. Variant of COIN]

quoit

quoit /koyt, kwoyt/ n a ring used in the game of quoits [14C. Probably via Old French coite 'flat stone, quoit' < Latin culcita 'cushion']

quoits /koyts, kwoyts/ n a game in which players attempt to throw rings over or near a small post (takes a singular verb)

quokka /kwókə/ n a small short-tailed wallaby that lives in large colonies. Native to: islands off the coast of Western Australia. Latin name: Setonix brachyurus. [Mid-19C. < Nyungar kwaka]

quondam /kwón dam, -dəm/ adj of an earlier time (archaic or literary) ○'... now torn and rent by their quondam allies' (Jack London, The Iron Heel; 1907) [Mid-16C. < Latin, < quom 'when']

quorate /kwáw rayt, -rət/ *adj* describes a meeting attended by at least the minimum number of members that the rules state are needed in order for business to be conducted

Quorn /kwawrn/ *tdmk* a trademark for a vegetable protein used in cooking as a meat substitute

quorum /kwáwrəm/ *n* a fixed minimum number of members of a legislative assembly, committee, or other organization who must be present before the members can conduct valid business [15C. < Latin, 'of whom', used in requests for people to serve on committees]

quot. *abbr* quotation

quota /kwótə/ *n* 1. a proportional share of something that somebody should contribute or receive ○ *You haven't done your quota of night shifts.* 2. a maximum number or quantity that is permitted or needed ○ *European fishing quotas* [Early 17C. Via medieval Latin *quota (pars)* 'how large (a part)?', feminine of *quotus* (see QUOTE)]

quotable /kwótəb'l/ *adj* 1. worthy of being quoted 2. able to be quoted in a publication such as a newspaper because the person speaking or writing has given permission —**quotability** /kwótə bílləti/ *n*

quotation /kwō táysh'n/ *n* 1. SOMETHING QUOTED a piece of speech or writing quoted somewhere, e.g. in a book or magazine ○ *a quotation from Henry James* 2. QUOTING OF SOMEBODY'S WORDS the quoting of what somebody has said or written 3. *UK* BUSINESS ESTIMATE FOR WORK an estimated price for a job or service. ANZ, N Am term **quote** 4. FIN SHARE PRICE the prevailing price at which a stock, bond, or commodity may be purchased or sold 5. FIN QUOTING OF PRICES the quoting of prevailing stock, bond, or commodity market prices 6. ARTS REUSE OF ARTISTIC MATERIAL the use in an artistic work, especially music, of material taken from or alluding to somebody else's work

quotation mark *n N Am* same as **inverted comma**

quote /kwōt/ *v* (**quotes, quoting, quoted**) 1. *vti* REPEAT SOMEBODY'S EXACT WORDS to repeat or copy the exact words spoken or written by somebody 2. *vti* REFER TO SOMETHING FOR PROOF to refer to something as an example in support of an argument ○ *He quoted some recently published statistics.* 3. *vti* BUSINESS GIVE ESTIMATE FOR COST to give an estimate of the price of providing somebody with a product or service 4. *vt* FIN GIVE CURRENT MARKET PRICE OF SOMETHING to state the current market price of a share, bond, or commodity 5. *vt* GAMBLING GIVE BETTING ODDS FOR SOMETHING to give somebody or something such as a racehorse particular betting odds (*usually passive*) 6. *vt* ARTS REPEAT PART OF ARTISTIC WORK to repeat an excerpt from an artistic work created by somebody else, especially a piece of music 7. *vti* PRINTING PUT PUNCTUATION AROUND QUOTATION to place quotation marks around a passage of speech or writing that is being quoted ■ *n* 1. LITERAT (*informal*) 2. PRINTING same as **inverted comma** (*often used in the plural*) 3. *ANZ, N Am* BUSINESS same as **quotation** (sense 3) ■ *interj* INTRODUCING QUOTATION used to show that the following words are a quotation (*often followed by 'unquote'*) ○ *She told me she is, quote, 'too good for him', unquote.* [14C. Via medieval Latin *quotare* 'number chapters' < Latin *quotus* 'of what number or amount' < *quot* 'how many?'] —**quoter** *n*

quotee /kwō teé/ *n* a person whose words are quoted by another person

quoth /kwōth/ *vt* said (*archaic or literary; 1st and 3rd person singular, before the subject*) ○ *'I swoon', quoth he.* [Old English *cwað*, the past tense of *cwepan* 'to say' (source of English *bequeath*)]

quotidian /kwō tíddi ən/ *adj* 1. COMMONPLACE of the most ordinary everyday kind (*formal*) 2. DONE DAILY done or experienced on a daily basis (*formal*) 3. MED RECURRING DAILY describes a fever that recurs or flares up every day ■ *n* MED FEVER RECURRING DAILY a fever, especially malaria, in which attacks of the illness recur daily [14C. Via French < Latin *quotidianus* < *cotidie* 'every day']

quotient /kwósh'nt/ *n* 1. MATHS RESULT OF DIVISION the number that results from the division of one number by another 2. MATHS RATIO a ratio of two numbers or quantities 3. MATHS WHOLE NUMBER RESULT OF DIVISION the whole number element of the result of dividing one number by another 4. AMOUNT OF QUALITY a scale, or a point on a scale, indicating the amount, degree, or level of something (*informal*) [15C. < Latin *quotient-* 'how many times?' < *quot* 'how many']

quo warranto /kwó wə rántō/ (*plural* **quo warrantos**) *n* a document issued by a court of law formally requiring somebody to state by what authority he or she has acted or has held a position [From Law Latin, literally 'by what warrant?', words in the writ]

Qŭqon /koŏ kón/ city in eastern Uzbekistan, in the Fergana Province. Population: 175,000 (1991).

Qur'an *n* ISLAM another spelling of **Koran**

Quttinirpaaq National Park /khoŏt tee neelk paak-/ national park, established in 1988, in the northern part of Ellesmere Island situated in the Arctic Ocean, Nunavut, northeastern Canada. Area: 37,775 sq. km/14,585 sq. mi. Former name **Ellesmere Island National Park Reserve**

qv *abbr* which see (*used to indicate a cross reference to something within the same book or article*) [Latin, *quod vide*]

Q value *n* the energy released or absorbed during a particle or nuclear reaction

Qwaqwa /kwaʼakwə/ former homeland in South Africa, now part of Free State Province

qwerty /kwúrti/, **QWERTY** *adj* describes an English-language typewriter or computer keyboard with keys for the Roman alphabet, the top row of alphabetical characters being the letters Q, W, E, R, T and Y. ◊ **azerty**

qy *abbr* query

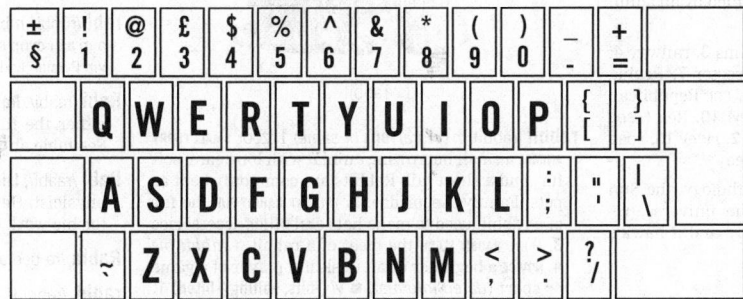

qwerty

r[1] /aar/ (*plural* **r's**), **R** (*plural* **R's** or **Rs**) *n* **1.** 18TH LETTER OF ENGLISH ALPHABET the 18th letter of the English alphabet, representing a consonant sound **2.** LETTER 'R' WRITTEN a written representation of the letter 'r' **3.** 'R'-SHAPED OBJECT something shaped like a letter 'R' ◇ **the three R's** the basic skills of reading, writing, and arithmetic

r[2] *symbol* **1.** MATHS radius **2.** ELEC ENG resistance

r[3] *abbr* **1.** TRANSP railway **2.** rare **3.** recto **4.** right **5.** GEOG river **6.** road **7.** MEASURE rod **8.** MONEY rouble **9.** BASEBALL, CRICKET run(s) **10.** MONEY rupee

R[1] *symbol* **1.** PHYS gas constant **2.** CHEM radical **3.** PHYS, MEASURE Réaumur scale **4.** ELEC ENG resistance

R[2] /aar/, **r** *v* a written form of 'are' (*informal; used in e-mails or text messages*) [Because the letter R and *are* are pronounced the same]

R[3] *n* in Australia, a rating indicating that a film may not be seen by anyone under 18. Full form **restricted**

R[4] /aar/ *tdmk* in the United States, a trademark for a rating indicating that a film can be seen by children under the age of 17 only if accompanied by an adult. Full form **restricted**

R[5] *abbr* **1.** JUDAISM rabbi **2.** MATHS radius **3.** railway **4.** MONEY rand **5.** GEOG range **6.** CHR rector **7.** Regina (*used after the name of a queen*) **8.** POL Republican **9.** CHR response (*in Christian liturgy*) **10.** Rex (*used after the name of a king*) **11.** right **12.** river **13.** road **14.** royal **15.** rouble **16.** MONEY rupee

Ra[1] /raa/, **Re** /ray/ *n* in Egyptian mythology, the Sun god, creator and controller of the universe, represented as having a human body and a hawk's head [From Egyptian *rˁ*]

Ra[2] *symbol* CHEM ELEM radium

RA *abbr* **1.** NAVY Rear Admiral **2.** ASTRON right ascension **3.** Royal Academician **4.** Royal Academy **5.** Royal Artillery

R.A. *abbr* ASTRON right ascension

RAA *abbr* Royal Academy of Arts

RAAF /raf/ *abbr* Royal Australian Air Force

raag *n* MUSIC same as **raga**

raahtid *interj* another spelling of **raatid** (*taboo offensive; used in Black English*)

raas /raass/ *adj* (*slang; used in Black English*) **1.** an offensive term meaning bad **2.** an offensive term meaning lacking in intelligence [Origin ?]

raas-claat /-klaat/ *interj* a highly offensive term used as a swearword (*taboo; used in Black English*) [< *claat*, form of CLOTH 'sanitary towel']

raatid /raˊatid/, **raahtid** *interj* a highly offensive term used as a swearword (*taboo; used in Black English*)

Rabat /rə baˊat/ capital city of Morocco, situated in the northwest of the country, at the mouth of the River Bou Regreg, on the Atlantic coast. Population: 1,385,872 (1994).

rabbet /rábbit/ *N Am* CONSTR *n* same as **rebate**[2] ■ *vt* (**-bets, -beting, -beted**) same as **rebate**[2] [15C. < Old French *rab(b)at* 'recess' < *rabattre* (see REBATE[1])]

rabbi /rábbī/ *n* **1.** the leader of a Jewish congregation, or the chief religious official of a synagogue **2.** a scholar qualified to teach or interpret Jewish law [Pre-12C. Via late Latin and Greek < Hebrew *rabbī* 'my teacher']

rabbinate /rábbinət/ *n* **1.** the post or term of office of a rabbi **2.** rabbis considered as a group

rabbinic /rə bínnik/, **rabbinical** /-nik'l/ *adj* relating to rabbis or to their beliefs, language, teachings, or writings —**rabbinically** *adv*

Rabbinic Hebrew *n* the form of Hebrew used by rabbis between the 5th and 16th centuries

rabbinism /rábbinizəm/ *n* the teachings of Jewish scholars, especially the scholars of the Talmudic period —**rabbinist** *n, adj*—**rabbinistic** /rábbi nístik/ *adj*

rabbit

rabbit /rábbit/ *n* (*plural* **-bits** or *same*) **1.** ZOOL SMALL FURRY ANIMAL a small burrowing animal with long ears, soft fur, and a short tail. Rabbits are commonly kept as pets. Family: Leporidae. **2.** INDUST RABBIT FUR the fur of a rabbit, used to make hats and other accessories **3.** FOOD RABBIT FLESH the meat of a rabbit ○ *rabbit pie* **4.** NOVICE a beginner or an unskilful player of a game or sport (*dated informal*) ■ *vi* (**-bits, -biting, -bited**) **1.** HUNT RABBITS to go hunting for wild rabbits **2.** CHATTER to talk for a long time about unimportant things (*informal*) ○ *He spent over an hour rabbiting to his mother on the phone.* [14C. Probably < Old French < Middle Dutch or Low German *robbe*] —**rabbiter** *n*

rabbit ears *npl N Am* a V-shaped aerial made up of two metal rods on a base, designed to sit on top of a television set

rabbit fever *n* VET same as **tularaemia**

rabbit food *n* a vegetarian diet regarded as providing insufficient nutrition for a human being (*informal disapproving*)

rabbiting /rábbiting/ *n* the activity of hunting for wild rabbits

rabbit-proof fence *n Aus* a boundary between Australian states (*informal*) ○ *the daftest scheme hatched this side of the rabbit-proof fence* [Because fences were formerly erected along state boundaries to limit the spread of rabbits]

rabbit punch *n* a short sharp blow to the back of the neck —**rabbit-punch** *vt*

rabbit warren *n* ZOOL same as **warren** (sense 1)

rabble[1] /rább'l/ *n* **1.** UNRULY CROWD a noisy and unruly crowd of people **2.** OFFENSIVE TERM an offensive term that deliberately insults people lacking in wealth and status (*insult; takes a singular or plural verb*) **3.** OFFENSIVE TERM an offensive term that deliberately insults the abilities or significance of a group of people (*insult*) [14C. Origin ?]

rabble[2] /rább'l/ *n* a device for stirring or skimming molten metal in a furnace ■ *vt* (**-bles, -bling, -bled**) to stir or skim molten metal with a rabble [Mid-19C. Via French *râble* 'fire rake' < Latin *rutabulum* < *ruere* 'rake up'] —**rabbler** *n*

rabble-rouser *n* somebody who stirs up anger, violence, or other strong feelings in a crowd, especially for political reasons —**rabble-rousing** *n, adj*

Rabelais /rábbə lay/, **François** (1493?–1553) French humanist and writer. His greatest works, *Pantagruel* (1532) and *Gargantua* (1534), satirized medieval scholasticism and are notable for their exuberance and earthy humour. —**Rabelaisian** /rábbə láyziən, rábbə láyzh'n/ *adj, n*

'Be still indebted to somebody or other, that there may be somebody always to pray for you.'
[François Rabelais, 'Le Tiers Livre des faicts et dicts héroïques du bon Pantagruel (The Third Book of the Heroic Deeds and Words of Good Pantagruel)'; 1546]

rabi /rúbbi/ *n* in South Asia, the spring harvesting of a grain crop sown the previous September [Mid-19C. Via Persian and Urdu < Arabic *rabīˁ* 'spring']

Rabi /raˊabi/, **Rabia** /rə beé ə/ *n* in the Islamic calendar, either the third or the fourth month of the year. See table at **calendar** [Mid-18C. < Arabic *rabīˁ*]

Rabi /raˊabi/, **Isidor Isaac** (1898–1988) Austrian-born US physicist. He won the Nobel Prize in physics (1944) for his work on the atom.

Rabia /rə beé ə/ *n* CALENDAR, ISLAM same as **Rabi**

rabid /rábbid/ *adj* **1.** INTENSE feeling or showing an emotion or need extremely intensely ○ *a rabid lust for power* **2.** MED, VET HAVING RABIES infected with rabies **3.** FANATICAL having extremist attitudes or views, especially in politics **4.** FURIOUS extremely angry or violent [Early 17C. < Latin *rabidus* < *rabere* 'rave, be mad'] —**rabidity** /rə bíddəti/ *n* —**rabidly** *adv* —**rabidness** *n*

rabies /ráy beez/ *n* an often fatal viral disease that affects the central nervous systems of most warm-blooded animals and is transmitted in the saliva of an infected animal. It causes convulsions, inability to move, and untypical behaviour. [Late 16C. < Latin, 'fury' < *rabere* 'rave, be mad'] —**rabic** *adj* —**rabietic** /ráybi éttik/ *adj*

Rabin /ra beén/, **Yitzhak** (1922–95) Israeli soldier and prime minister (1974–77 and 1992–95). He was awarded the Nobel Peace Prize during his second premiership (1994), but was assassinated a year later.

'We say to you today in a loud and clear voice: enough of blood and tears. Enough.'
[Yitzhak Rabin, *Remarks to the Palestinians, upon the signing of the Israel-Palestine Declaration, Washington, DC*; 13 September 1993]

RAC[1] *abbr* Royal Armoured Corps

RAC[2] *n* a UK company that provides breakdown and other services to motorists and travellers [Abbreviation of *Royal Automobile Club*]

raccoon

raccoon /rə koͦn, ra-/ (*plural* **-coons** or *same*), **racoon** *n* **1.** a small animal with greyish-black fur, black patches around the eyes, and a long bushy ringed tail. Native to: forests of North and Central America. Genus: *Procyon*. **2.** the fur of a raccoon [Early 17C. < Virginia Algonquian *aroughcun*]

raccoon dog *n* a small wild dog with facial markings similar to a raccoon's and a thick yellow-brown coat. Native to: woodland areas of East Asia. Latin name: *Nyctereutes procyonoides*.

race[1] /rayss/ *n* **1. CONTEST OF SPEED** a contest to decide who is the fastest, e.g. between runners or horse riders **2. CONTEST BETWEEN RIVALS** a contest between two or more people seeking to do or reach the same thing, or do or reach something first **3. OCEANOG, GEOG WATER CURRENT** a strong localized current in the sea or a river **4. CIV ENG WATER CHANNEL** a channel that carries water from one place to another, especially from a stream to a water wheel **5. MECH ENG GROOVE GUIDING SLIDING OBJECT** a groove along which something such as a ball bearing slides **6. NARROW PASSAGE** a narrow track or passage, e.g. one leading sheep from their enclosure to a dip **7. REGULAR COURSE** the fixed course regularly followed or travelled by something, especially the Sun or the Moon (*archaic or literary*) **8. JOURNEY** a single passage along a fixed course, especially the course that somebody's life follows (*archaic or literary*) ■ **races** *npl* **HORSERACING HORSE RACES OR HORSERACING** horse races, the racetrack at which they are run, or horseracing as a spectator sport ○ *We spent the day at the races.* ■ *v* (**races, racing, raced**) **1.** *vti* **COMPETE AGAINST SOMEBODY IN RACE** to compete with somebody in a contest of speed **2.** *vt* **ENTER SOMETHING IN RACE** to enter, ride, or drive something such as a horse or car in a race **3.** *vti* **MOVE VERY FAST** to move somewhere with great speed or haste, or make somebody or something move in this way **4.** *vi* **BEAT FAST** to beat much faster than usual, e.g. because of nervousness or excitement (*refers to the heart*) **5.** *vti* **AUTOMOT IDLE FAST** to run at a high speed, or make an engine or motor run at a high speed [13C. < Old Norse *rás* 'rush, running' < Indo-European, 'be in motion']

race off *vt Aus* an offensive term meaning to take somebody away with the intention of having sex with him or her (*slang*)

race[2] /rayss/ *n* **1. GROUP OF HUMANS** one of the groups into which the world's population can be divided on the basis of physical characteristics such as skin or hair colour **2. FACT OF BELONGING TO GROUP** the fact of belonging to a group of humans who share the same physical features such as skin colour ○ *an attempt to end discrimination on grounds of race* **3. HUMANKIND** humanity considered as a whole ○ *the fate of the race* **4.** BIOL **STRAIN OF ORGANISM** a genetically distinct population within a species that may also be geographically isolated **5.** WINE **DISTINCTIVE TASTE OF WINE** the distinctive taste of a wine, by which its grape variety or region of origin can be identified [Early 16C. Via French < Italian *razza*]

racecar /rayss kaar/ *n N Am* same as **racing car**

race card ◇ **play the race card** to use the issue of race, e.g. in legal argumentation or in a debate, to win an advantage or make a point (*informal*)

racecard /rayss kaard/ *n* the programme of events at a race meeting

racecourse /rayss kawrss/ *n* a track around which

horses race, or the grounds in which the track is sited

racegoer /rayss gō ər/ *n* somebody attending a race meeting or who regularly goes to race meetings

racehorse /rayss hawrss/ *n* a horse bred and trained to run in races

racemate /rayssə mayt/ *n* a chemical compound that does not deflect or absorb any of the light passing through it [Mid-19C. < RACEMIC]

raceme /rásseem/ *n* a flower cluster (**inflorescence**) in which the flowers are borne on short stalks along a long main stem, as they are in the lily of the valley [Late 18C. < Latin *racemus* 'bunch of grapes']

race meeting *n* a series of horse races held on the same course on a single day or over consecutive days

racemic /rə seemik, -semmik/ *adj* describes a chemical compound that does not deflect or absorb any of the light passing through it. This is because it consists of a precise mixture of dextrorotatory and laevorotatory isomers. [Late 19C. < Latin *racemus* 'bunch of grapes', because the compound was originally derived from grapes]

racemic acid *n* a form of tartaric acid that does not deflect or absorb any of the light passing through it. Source: grape juice.

racemization /rássi mī záysh'n/, **racemisation** *n* the process of converting from an optically active compound or mixture to one that is racemic —**racemize** /rássə mīz/ *vt*

racemose /rássimōss, -mōz/ *adj* **1.** describes a flower cluster (**inflorescence**) in which the flowers are borne on short stalks on a long main stem, as they are in the lily of the valley **2.** describes glands that resemble a bunch of grapes in their structure —**racemosely** *adv*

racer /ráyssər/ *n* **1. SOMEBODY OR SOMETHING THAT RACES** a person, animal, or vehicle competing in a race **2. COMPUTER RACING GAME** a computer game that involves racing vehicles **3. THIN FAST-MOVING SNAKE** a slender fast-moving nonvenomous snake. Native to: North America. Genus: *Coluber*. **4. TRACK FOR MOVABLE ARTILLERY GUN** a circular rail on which the travelling platform of a heavy artillery gun is mounted

racerunner /rayss runnər/ *n* a fast-moving lizard. Native to: North and Central America. Genus: *Cnemidophurus*.

racetrack /rayss trak/ *n* a track around which cars or runners race, or the grounds in which such a track is sited

race-walk *vi* to compete in the sport of race walking

race walking *n* the sport of racing at a fast walking pace, with rules that require walkers to keep at least one foot on the ground at all times —**race walker** *n*

raceway /rayss way/ *n N Am* **1.** CIV ENG same as **race**[1] (sense 4) **2.** a track on which races, especially harness races, are held, or the grounds in which the track is sited

Rachel /ráchəl/ *n* in the Bible, the daughter of Laban, wife of Jacob, and mother of Joseph and Benjamin (Genesis 29–35)

rachilla /rə killə/ (*plural* **-lae** /-lee/), **rhachilla** (*plural* **-lae**) *n* a side branch of a compound leaf that bears the individual leaflets, e.g. on a fern [Mid-19C. < modern Latin, 'little rachis' < *rachis* (see RACHIS)]

rachis /ráykiss/ (*plural* **rachises** or **rachides** /ráyki deez/), **rhachis** (*plural* **rhachises** or **rhachides**) *n* **1.** BOT **PLANT STEM** the main stem of a flower cluster or a compound leaf **2.** BIRDS **FEATHER SHAFT** the main shaft of a feather **3.** ANAT **SPINE** the spine of a vertebrate animal (*technical*) [Late 18C. Via modern Latin < Greek *rhakhis* 'spine, ridge'] —**rachial** *adj* —**rachidial** /rə kiddi əl/ *adj*

rachitis /rə kítiss/ *n* MED same as **rickets** (*technical*) [Early 18C. < Greek *rhakhitis* 'disease of the spine' < *rhakhis* 'spine'] —**rachitic** /rə kíttik/ *adj*

Sergei Rachmaninov

Rachmaninov /rak mánni nof/, **Sergei** (1873–1943) Russian-born composer and pianist. His symphonies and compositions for piano are considered the last major musical expression of the Romantic era. Full name **Rachmaninov, Sergei Vasilyevich**

Rachmanism /rákmənizəm/, **rachmanism** *n* exploitation or intimidation by a landlord of tenants living in slum property [Mid-20C. After Peter *Rachman* (1919–62), notoriously unscrupulous London landlord in the 1950s]

racial /ráysh'l/ *adj* **1.** existing or taking place between different races ○ *racial harmony* **2.** relating to or characteristic of races or a race of people —**racially** *adv*

racialism /ráysh'lizəm/ *n* SOCIOL same as **racism** (*dated*) —**racialist** *n, adj* —**racialistic** /ráyshə lístik/ *adj*

racialize /ráysh'līz/ (**-izes, -izing, -ized, -ized** /ráysh'l īz/), **racialise** (**-cialises, -cialising, -cialised**) *vti* **1. DISTINGUISH BY RACE** to make distinctions or classify people according to race **2. MAKE SOMETHING SEEM RACIAL** to put something into a racial context **3. SEE SOMETHING FROM RACIAL PERSPECTIVE** to view or experience something from a racial perspective

racial profiling *n* the alleged policy of some police to attribute criminal intentions to members of some ethnic groups and to stop and question them in disproportionate numbers without proper cause

Racine /ra seen/, **Jean Baptiste** (1639–99) French playwright. Considered to be the greatest French classical tragedian, he adapted Greek and Roman subjects in works such as *Andromaque* (1667) and *Phèdre* (1677). —**Racinian** /ra síni ən/ *adj*

'Innocence has nothing to dread.'
[Jean Baptiste Racine, *Phèdre*; 1677]

racing /ráyssing/ *n* the sport of taking part in races, e.g. as a runner, on a horse, or in a sports car

racing bike *n* a bicycle or motorcycle used, designed, or adapted for racing (*informal*)

racing car *n* a car used, designed, or adapted for racing. N Am term **racecar**

racism /ráyssizəm/ *n* **1.** prejudice or animosity against people who belong to other races ○ *I am a Muslim and … my religion makes me against all forms of racism.* (Malcolm X, *Speech, Prospects for Freedom*; 1965) **2.** the belief that people of different races have different qualities and abilities, and that some races are inherently superior or inferior

racist /ráyssist/ *adj* **1. BASED ON RACISM** based on prejudices and stereotypes related to race **2. PREJUDICED AGAINST OTHER RACES** prejudiced against all people who belong to other races ○ *Black power … a call to reject the racist institutions and values of this society* (Stokely Carmichael [Kwame Tore] and Charles Vernon Hamilton, *Black Power!*; 1967) ■ *n* **RACIST PERSON** somebody who hates others who are not of his or her own race

rack[1] /rak/ *n* **1. FRAMEWORK FOR HOLDING THINGS** a framework or stand for carrying, holding, or storing things ○ *a wine rack* **2.** AGRIC **FEED-HOLDING FRAMEWORK** a framework containing hay or other fodder for livestock **3.** AIR FORCE **BOMB-HOLDING FRAMEWORK** a framework holding bombs or rockets that is attached to an aircraft **4.** MECH ENG **TOOTHED BAR** a bar with notches, designed to engage the teeth of a pinion or worm gear and

convert rotary motion to linear motion, e.g. in a vehicle's steering system **5.** INSTRUMENT OF TORTURE a torture device used to stretch the body of somebody strapped horizontally onto it **6.** *N Am* CUE GAMES same as **frame** (senses 15–17) ■ *vt* (**racks, racking, racked**) **1.** CAUSE SOMEBODY PAIN to cause somebody great pain or stress ○ *the coughing spasms that racked his body* **2.** SHAKE SOMETHING VIOLENTLY to shake or strain something with violent force ○ *The high winds racked villages all along the coast.* **3.** TRY TO USE SOMETHING TO MAXIMUM to make a great effort to use all the resources of something such as the brain or the memory to the fullest extent ○ *I racked my memory trying to think where I'd seen him before.* **4.** TORTURE SOMEBODY ON RACK to stretch the body of somebody strapped horizontally on a rack as a means of torture **5.** PUT SOMETHING IN RACK to place something in or on a rack **6.** MECH ENG MOVE SOMETHING WITH RACK to move a device or part using a rack-and-pinion system [14C. < Dutch *rak* 'framework'] —**racker** *n* ◇ **on the rack** experiencing great mental anguish (*informal*)

SPELLCHECK rack or **wrack?** Do not confuse the spelling of **rack** and **wrack**, which sound similar. **Rack** is the more common word, and the only spelling you should use for the meanings 'framework for holding things' (as in *wine rack*), 'toothed bar' (as in *rack and pinion*), 'joint of meat' (as in *rack of lamb*), 'instrument of torture' (as in *stretched on the rack*), and 'accumulate' (as in *racked up 100 points*). **Rack** is also the usual spelling of the verb meaning 'subject to great stress, pain, torture, etc'., as in *racked with guilt, rack your brains.* The noun in the phrase *rack and ruin* can be spelt **rack** or **wrack**, but **rack** is the more common spelling. The noun **wrack** is chiefly used to denote a type of seaweed.

rack off *vi Aus* an offensive term often used as a command to tell somebody to go away (*slang*)
rack up *vt* to accumulate something such as points (*informal*) ○ *The company racked up sales of $8 million in its first year of trading.*

rack² /rak/ *n* a joint of meat, usually lamb, consisting of one or both sides of the front ribs, prepared for roasting, often joined end to end in a circle [Late 16C. Origin ?]

rack³ /rak/ (**racks, racking, racked**) *vt* to siphon clear wine or beer out of a barrel, leaving the sediment behind [15C. < Provençal *arracar* < *raca* 'dregs']

rack⁴ /rak/ *n* in dressage, a fast walking pace for a horse in which each foot is lifted off the ground in turn ■ *vi* to walk at a fast pace, lifting each foot off the ground in turn (*refers to horses*) [Late 16C. Origin ?]

rack⁵ /rak/ *n* a mass of broken cloud blown fast by the wind ■ *vi* (**racks, racking, racked**) to be blown fast by the wind (*archaic; refers to clouds*) [14C. Origin ?]

rack⁶ /rak/ *n* a state of ruin or destruction (*archaic*) [Late 16C. Variant of WRACK²] ◇ **go to rack and ruin** to deteriorate into a state of neglect or ruin

SPELLCHECK See *rack¹*.

rack-and-pinion *adj* relating to or using a mechanical system in which a toothed wheel (**pinion**) engages a notched bar (**rack**) to convert rotary motion into linear motion

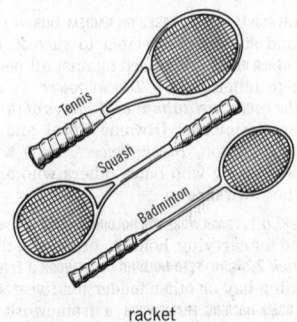

racket

racket¹ /rákit/, **racquet** *n* **1.** a lightweight bat with a network of strings, used in tennis, badminton,

squash, and similar games. The frame is usually made of a substance such as wood, aluminium, or graphite, and the strings of gut or nylon. **2.** a snowshoe in the shape of a racket [Early 16C. Via French *raquette* < Arabic *ráhat* 'palm of the hand']

racket² /rákit/ *n* **1.** NOISE a loud noise, especially when it disturbs people (*informal*) **2.** ILLEGAL SCHEME an illegal or dishonest money-making scheme, involving activities such as bribery, fraud, or intimidation (*informal*) **3.** BUSINESS a business, job, or activity of any kind (*informal*) ○ *He's in the advertising racket* **4.** EASY LIVING an easy and very profitable way of earning a living (*informal*) **5.** PARTY an uproarious party (*dated*) ○ *'We had a fine old racket in the commandant's office.'* (John Buchan, *Greenmantle*; 1916) **6.** MUSIC OLD WOODWIND INSTRUMENT a woodwind instrument of the Renaissance and Baroque periods, consisting of a long tube coiled and enclosed in a cylinder **7.** MUSIC ORGAN STOP an organ stop that imitates the sound of the racket ■ *vi* (**-ets, -eting, -eted**) **1.** MOVE AROUND NOISILY to make a lot of noise while moving around (*informal*) ○ *We could still hear them racketing around downstairs.* **2.** LIVE DEBAUCHED LIFE to lead a riotous life devoted to pleasure (*dated*) [Mid-16C. Origin ?]

racketball *n* RACKET GAMES another spelling of **racquetball**

racketeer /ráki teér/ *n* somebody who profits from illegal activities such as bribery, fraud, or intimidation ■ *vi* (**-eers, -eering, -eered**) to make money from illegal activities, or operate a racket —**racketeering** *n*

rackets *n* RACKET GAMES another spelling of **racquets**

racket-tail, racquet-tail *n* a bird of the hummingbird family that has racket-shaped tail feathers —**racket-tailed** *adj*

rackety /rákiti/ *adj* **1.** noisy and boisterous (*dated*) **2.** leading a lively but sometimes rather dissipated social life

Rackham /rákəm/, **Arthur** (1867–1939) British illustrator and watercolour painter. He created fanciful illustrations for editions of literary classics, as well as for children's books.

rackling /rákling/ *n regional* the smallest or weakest piglet in a litter [Origin uncertain: perhaps from *rack of bones* 'thin person or animal']

REGIONAL NOTE See *underling*.

rack railway *n UK, ANZ, Can* a mountain railway that has locomotives with a central cogwheel that engages with a toothed rack between the rails in order to pull the train up steep slopes. US term **cog railway**

rack-rent *n* an unreasonably high rent ■ *vti* to charge a tenant an unreasonably high rent [RACK¹ to torture'] —**rack-renter** *n*

raclette /ra klét/ *n* **1.** a Swiss dish consisting of slices of melted cheese served on boiled potatoes or bread **2.** a hard-crusted type of Swiss cheese that melts easily, traditionally used for raclette [Mid-20C. < French < *racler* 'scrape', because the cheese is melted and scraped onto a plate]

racon /ráy kon/ *n* NAVIG same as **radar beacon** [Mid-20C. Blend of RADAR + BEACON]

raconteur /rá kon túr/ *n* somebody who tells stories or anecdotes in an interesting or entertaining way [Early 19C. < French < Old French *raconter* 'recount, retell']

racoon *n* ZOOL another spelling of **raccoon**

racquet *n* RACKET GAMES, CLOTHING another spelling of **racket¹**

racquetball /rákit bawl/, **racketball** *n* a game played on a four-walled indoor court by two, three, or four players using short-handled rackets and a ball larger than the ball used in squash or racquets

racquets /rákits/, **rackets** *n* a fast game similar to squash played by two or four people on a four-walled indoor court using long-handled rackets and a small hard ball. It is derived from the old game of real tennis. (*takes a singular verb*) [Early 19C. Plural of *racquet*, variant of RACKET¹]

racquet-tail *n* BIRDS another spelling of **racket-tail**

racy /ráyssi/ (**-ier, -iest**) *adj* **1.** MILDLY INDECENT mildly shocking because of references to or descriptions of sex **2.** LIVELY full of energy or spirit ○ *'the peculiar mixture of accurate knowledge and of racy imagination which gave them their fascination'* (Arthur Conan Doyle, *The Lost World*; 1912) **3.** DISTINCTIVE having a distinctive quality or flavour **4.** PUNGENT sharp or piquant in taste or smell [Mid-17C. < RACE¹] —**racily** *adv* —**raciness** *n*

rad¹ /rad/ *n* the unit formerly used to measure the level of ionizing radiation absorbed by something, equal to 0.01 joule per kilogram of irradiated material [Early 20C. Acronym < *radiation absorbed dose*]

rad² /rad/ (**radder, raddest**) *adj N Am* very good, desirable, admirable, or fashionable (*slang*) ○ *a totally rad idea* [Early 19C. Shortening of RADICAL]

rad³ *symbol* MATHS radian

rad. *abbr* **1.** radiator **2.** MATHS radical **3.** radio **4.** MATHS radius **5.** MATHS radix

RADA /ráadə/ *abbr* Royal Academy of Dramatic Art

radar /ráy daar/ *n* **1.** a system that uses reflected radio waves to determine the presence, location, and speed of distant objects. The system has military, policing, and navigational applications. Examples of its uses include the locating of enemy aircraft or ships and the monitoring of vehicle speeds. **2.** the electronic equipment that transmits and receives high-frequency radio waves to detect, locate, and track distant objects [Mid-20C. Acronym < *radio detection and ranging*]

radar astronomy *n* the use of radar techniques to study and map astronomical objects in the solar system

radar beacon *n* a ground-based, fixed-position radar receiver-transmitter whose signals can be received by an aircraft or ship's navigator to determine bearing and range

radar gun *n* a small hand-held radar device used to determine the speed of nearby objects

radarscope /ráy daar skōp/ *n* the screen on radar equipment that displays the reflected radio signal as a dot of light. In sophisticated screens, data such as speed, direction, and altitude are also shown.

radar screen ◇ **be on** *or* **off somebody's radar screen** to be of interest to somebody and receive his or her attention (*informal*)

radar trap *n* ROADS same as **speed trap**

raddle¹ /rádd'l/ (**-dles, -dling, -dled**) *vt* to twist or weave things together [Late 17C. < Anglo-Norman *reidele* 'wooden pole', Old French *reddalle*]

raddle² /rádd'l/ *n, vt* MINERALS, AGRIC same as **ruddle** [Early 16C. < form of RED]

raddled /rádd'ld/ *adj* having a worn-out appearance that suggests long life or a life of indulgence [Late 17C. < ?]

radial /ráydi əl/ *adj* **1.** SPREADING FROM CENTRE OUTWARDS spreading out from a common centre like the spokes of a wheel ○ *petals in a radial arrangement* **2.** OF RADIUS relating to a radius, especially moving along a radius **3.** ZOOL WITH BODY PARTS IN CIRCULAR ARRANGEMENT used to describe the arrangement of the bodies of invertebrate sea animals such as the starfish and sea anemone in which parts spread out from a single centre **4.** ANAT OF FOREARM BONE relating to the radius bone of the forearm ■ *n* AUTOMOT same as **radial tyre** —**radially** *adv*

radial drilling machine *n* a machine with a drilling head mounted on an arm that can be freely rotated to allow a workpiece to be drilled at any point

radial engine *n* an internal-combustion engine that has its cylinders arranged around a central crankshaft like the spokes of a wheel, instead of in one or two straight rows

radial keratotomy *n* a surgical operation for correcting short-sightedness, using a series of small radial incisions to change the shape of the cornea

radial-ply *adj* describes a tyre in which the fabric cords that make up the foundation of the tyre run at right angles to the circumference of the tyre

radial symmetry *n* symmetry in which something can be divided into two identical halves by a line

or plane passing through a central point or axis at any angle —**radially symmetrical** *adj*

radial tyre *n* a tyre in which the fabric cords that make up the foundation of the tyre run at right angles to the circumference of the tyre

radial velocity *n* the velocity of a star or other astronomical object measured along the observer's line of sight

radian /ráydi ən/ *n* a unit of angular measurement equivalent to the angle between two radii that enclose a section of a circle's circumference (**arc**) equal in length to the length of a radius. There are 2π radians in a circle. Symbol **rad** [Late 19C. < RADIUS]

radiance /ráydi ənss/ *n* **1.** HAPPINESS OR ENERGY joy, energy, or good health discernible in somebody's face or demeanour **2.** LIGHT bright or glowing light **3.** PHYS MEASURE OF RADIANT ENERGY a measure of the amount of radiant energy emitted or received per unit area of a surface over a specific time. Symbol L_e

radiant /ráydi ənt/ *adj* **1.** SHOWING HAPPINESS expressing joy, energy, or good health in a pleasing way **2.** SHINING lit with a bright or glowing light **3.** PHYS IN RAY FORM describes light, heat, or other energy emitted in the form of rays or waves ○ *radiant heat* **4.** PHYS EMITTING RADIANT ENERGY emitting light, heat, or other energy in the form of rays or waves ■ *n* **1.** ELEC ENG HEATING ELEMENT an element in a heater that gives out radiant heat **2.** ASTRON POINT OF ORIGIN OF METEOR SHOWER a point in space from which a meteor shower appears to originate [15C. < Latin *radiant-*, present participle of *radiare* (see RADIATE)] —**radiantly** *adv*

radiant energy *n* energy emitted as waves, usually electromagnetic waves, through space or some other medium. Symbol Q_e

radiant flux *n* the rate of flow of radiant energy. Symbol Φ_e

radiant heat *n* heat transmitted by infrared radiation from a heat source, and not by conduction or convection

radiant heating *n* heating by means of heaters such as radiators, not by forced hot air

radiata /ráydi áatə/, **radiata pine** *n* ANZ a Monterey pine tree [Mid-20C. < modern Latin, < Latin *radiare* (see RADIATE), because its cones grow in rings]

radiate *v* /ráydi ayt/ (**-ates, -ating, -ated**) **1.** *vti* PHYS EMIT ENERGY AS RAYS OR WAVES to send out energy such as heat or light, in the form of rays or waves, or be sent out in this form **2.** *vti* SHOW FEELING OR QUALITY to show a feeling or quality clearly through looks, speech, behaviour, or content, or be shown in this way ○ *a popular speech that radiated goodwill and commitment* **3.** *vti* SPREAD FROM CENTRE to spread out from a central point like rays, or cause something to spread out in this way **4.** *vi* BIOL DEVELOP AND SPREAD to develop into several different forms capable of exploiting different resources or of living in different environments (*refers to animal and plant species*) ■ *adj* /ráydi ət, -ayt/ **1.** WITH RADIATING PARTS with, or in the form of, parts spreading out from a common centre **2.** BOT WITH PETALS RADIATING FROM CENTRE describes a flower head that has petals radiating from a centre, e.g. that of a daisy **3.** ZOOL WITH RADIALLY SYMMETRICAL BODY used to describe the bodies of starfish and other vertebrate sea organisms with body parts radiating from a common centre **4.** WITH RAYS surrounded or decorated with rays [Early 17C. < Latin *radiat-*, past participle of *radiare* 'emit rays' < *radius* 'ray'] —**radiately** *adv* —**radiative** *adj*

radiation /ráydi áysh'n/ *n* **1.** PARTICLES EMITTED BY RADIOACTIVE SUBSTANCES energy emitted in the form of particles by substances such as uranium and plutonium, whose atoms are not stable and are spontaneously decaying. This energy can be converted into electrical power, but it can also cause severe or fatal health problems to people who are exposed to it. **2.** PHYS ENERGY EMITTED IN RAYS OR WAVES energy emitted from a source in the form of rays or waves, e.g. heat, light, or sound **3.** PHYS RADIATING OF ENERGY the emission of energy in the form of rays or waves **4.** EFFECT OF RADIATING the feeling of something being radiated, e.g. heat from a hot oven **5.** MED same

as **radiotherapy 6.** ECOL same as **adaptive radiation** — **radiational** *adj*

radiational cooling *n* loss of heat from the Earth's surface and from air near the Earth's surface, occurring mainly at night

radiation biology *n* BIOL same as **radiobiology**

radiation sickness *n* a medical condition caused by overexposure to X-rays or to emissions from radioactive material. Symptoms include fatigue, headache, vomiting, diarrhoea, loss of hair and teeth, and in severe cases, haemorrhaging and death.

radiation therapy *n* PHYSIOL same as **radiotherapy**

radiator /ráydi aytər/ *n* **1.** ROOM HEATER WITH PIPES a room-heating device that emits heat from pipes through which hot water, steam, or hot oil circulates, especially one connected to a central boiler-fed system **2.** AUTOMOT ENGINE-COOLING DEVICE a device that prevents a vehicle's engine from overheating, consisting of tubes through which heated water from the engine circulates to be cooled. Cool air is usually circulated around the tubes by means of a fan. A fan **3.** ANZ ELECTRIC HEATER an electric fire or heater **4.** PHYS DEVICE EMITTING RADIANT ENERGY a device that emits radiant energy, e.g. a light bulb or a television transmitter

radical /ráddik'l/ *adj* **1.** BASIC relating to or affecting the basic nature or most important features of something ○ *a radical difference between the two* **2.** PERVASIVE far-reaching, searching, or thoroughgoing ○ *a radical reorganization of the company* **3.** FAVOURING MAJOR CHANGES favouring or making economic, political, or social changes of a sweeping or extreme nature **4.** *US* EXCELLENT very good, desirable, admirable, or fashionable (*slang*) **5.** MED REMOVING DISEASE SOURCE describes medical treatment that is intended to remove the source of a disease, rather than simply treat the symptoms ○ *a radical mastectomy* **6.** BOT GROWING FROM ROOT growing from a root of a plant or from the base of a stem **7.** MATHS OF MATHEMATICAL ROOT relating to the roots of numbers **8.** LING OF WORD ROOTS relating to the roots of words ■ *n* **1.** SOMEBODY WITH RADICAL VIEWS somebody with radical views on political, economic, or social issues ○ *the radicals in the party* **2.** MATHS MATHEMATICAL ROOT a mathematical root of another number or quantity **3.** CHEM same as **free radical 4.** CHEM CHEMICAL GROUP a chemical group that behaves as a single entity in reactions (*dated*) **5.** LING same as **root**[1] (sense 10) [14C. < late Latin *radicalis* 'of roots' < *radic-* 'root'] —**radically** *adv* —**radicalness** *n*

radical chic *n* the fashionable adoption of radical left-wing views by rich or famous people ○*'Radical chic invariably favors radicals who seem primitive, exotic, and romantic.'* (Tom Wolfe, *Radical Chic*; 1970)

radicalise *vti* POL another spelling of **radicalize**

radicalism /ráddik'lizəm/ *n* **1.** POLITICS ADVOCATING MAJOR CHANGES political policies that advocate more sweeping political, economic, or social change than that traditionally supported by the mainstream political parties **2.** POLITICALLY RADICAL ATTITUDES support for radical political policies **3.** SIGNIFICANT CHANGE sweeping change in a context, or the attitudes of people who favour sweeping change —**radicalistic** /ráddikə lístik/ *adj* —**radicalistically** *adv*

radicalize /ráddikə līz/ (**-izes, -izing, -ized**), **radicalise** (**-ises, -ising, -ised**) *vti* **1.** to undergo fundamental change, or introduce sweeping change in something **2.** to adopt politically radical views, or cause somebody to do this ○ *The experience of war radicalized the younger generation.* —**radicalization** /ráddikə līzáysh'n/ *n*

radical sign *n* the sign $\sqrt{\ }$ placed before a mathematical expression to denote the extraction of a square root or higher root. Roots higher than a square root are indicated by a superscript number preceding the sign.

radicand /ráddi kand/ *n* a mathematical quantity from which a square root or higher root is to be extracted [Late 19C. < Latin *radicandus* < *radicare* 'take root' < *radic-* 'root']

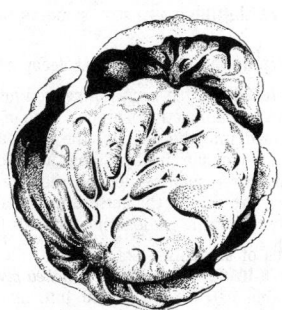

radicchio

radicchio /ra díki ō/ (*plural* **-os**), **radichio** *n* a variety of chicory with reddish-purple and white leaves, usually eaten raw in salads. Native to: Italy. [Late 20C. Via Italian, 'chicory' < Latin *radicula* (see RADICLE)]

radices MATHS, BIOL plural of **radix**

radichio *n* FOOD, PLANTS another spelling of **radicchio**

radicle /ráddik'l/ *n* **1.** the part of a plant embryo that forms the root of the young plant **2.** a small body part that superficially resembles the root of a plant, e.g. a branch of a nerve [Late 17C. < Latin *radicula* 'little root' < *radic-* 'root'] —**radicular** /ra díkyōōlər/ *adj*

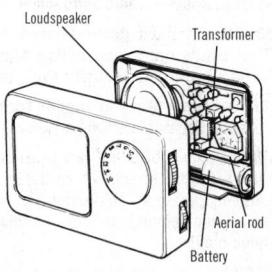

radio

radio /ráydi ō/ *n* (*plural* **-os**) **1.** USE OF ELECTROMAGNETIC WAVES FOR COMMUNICATION the use of electromagnetic waves to transmit and receive information, as in sound broadcasts or two-way communication, without the need for connecting wires **2.** COMMUNICATION USING RADIO WAVES communication that takes place by means of radio waves **3.** DEVICE RECEIVING SOUND BROADCASTS an electronic device for receiving sound broadcasts transmitted via radio signals **4.** TWO-WAY COMMUNICATION DEVICE an electronic device used to send and receive radio signals, used for two-way communication **5.** RADIO BROADCASTS sound broadcasts transmitted by means of radio waves **6.** BROADCASTING OF PROGRAMMES BY RADIO the broadcasting by radio of programmes for the public **7.** RADIO BROADCASTING STATION OR ORGANIZATION a station for transmitting radio broadcasts, or an organization involved in radio broadcasting ○ *Radio 1* **8.** SOUND BROADCASTING radio broadcasting as an industry or profession ○ *She works in radio.* ■ *vti* (**-os, -oing, -oed**) CONTACT SOMEBODY BY RADIO to communicate by radio or send somebody a message by radio ■ *adj* PHYS OF ELECTROMAGNETIC WAVES relating to electromagnetic waves or electromagnetic phenomena with frequencies between 10 kHz and 300,000 MHz [Early 20C. Shortening of *radiotelegraph*]

radio- *prefix* **1.** radiation ○ *radiocarbon* **2.** radio ○ *radiolocation* [In sense 1 < shortening of words such as RADIATION, RADIOLOCATION; in sense 2 < RADIO]

radioactive /ráydi ō áktiv/ *adj* **1.** EMITTING RADIATION describes a substance such as uranium or plutonium that emits energy in the form of streams of particles, owing to the decaying of its unstable atoms. This energy can be damaging or fatal to the health of people exposed to it. **2.** PHYS OF OR USING RADIOACTIVE SUBSTANCES relating to or making use of radioactive substances or the radiation they emit **3.** *US* HIGHLY CONTROVERSIAL so highly controversial that people tend to avoid the person or issue in question ○ *The topic of campaign finance reform is radioactive in many constituencies.* —**radioactively** *adv*

Loudspeaker / Transformer / Aerial rod / Battery

radioactive dating *n* ARCHAEOL same as **radiometric dating**

radioactive decay *n* PHYS same as **decay** *n* (sense 4)

radioactive series *n* a series of related atom types (**nuclides**) of radioactive isotopes, each of which is transformed into the next by the emission of an elementary particle until a stable nuclide results. There are three such sequences, the thorium, the uranium-radium, and the actinium, and almost all naturally occurring radioactive isotopes belong to one of them.

radioactive tracer *n* a substance with a radioactive isotope that can be introduced into and tracked within the body to study disease and biochemical processes

radioactive waste *n* waste material that is radioactive, particularly the waste from nuclear reactors and medical treatment and research

radioactivity /ráydi ō ak tívvəti/ *n* **1.** the radioactive nature of a substance such as uranium or plutonium **2.** the high-energy particles emitted by radioactive substances

radio alarm *n* an electronic device that combines a radio with the functions of an alarm clock. It can be set not only to sound an alarm, but also to turn on the radio at a preset time.

radio astronomy *n* a branch of astronomy that deals with the detection and analysis of radio waves received from space —**radio astronomer** *n*

radio beacon *n* a fixed ground-based radio transmitter that sends out a distinctive signal to help aircraft and shipping to identify their position

radio beam *n* a beam of radio signals transmitted by a radio beacon for navigation purposes

radiobiology /ráydi ō bī óllǝji/ *n* a branch of biology that deals with the effects of radiation on living tissues and organisms —**radiobiologic** /ráydi ō bī ə lójjik/ *adj* —**radiobiological** *adj* —**radiobiologically** *adv* —**radiobiologist** *n*

radio button *n* in a computer dialogue box, any of several circles or rectangles, each with text next to it, representing a fixed set of choices, one of which must be selected

radio car *n* **1.** a car, especially a police car, equipped with a two-way radio **2.** a vehicle from which radio broadcasts are made, especially interviews

radiocarbon /ráydi ō kaárbən/ *n* a radioactive form of carbon, especially the isotope of carbon that has a mass number of 14

radiocarbon dating *n* GEOL same as **carbon dating**

radio cassette, **radio-cassette player** *n* a radio and a cassette player combined in a single, usually portable machine

radiochemistry /ráydi ō kémmistri/ *n* a branch of chemistry that deals with radioactive elements and their applications —**radiochemical** *adj* —**radiochemically** *adv* —**radiochemist** *n*

radio compass *n* a navigation device that uses incoming radio signals from radio beacons to determine the position of a ship or an aircraft

radio-controlled *adj* describes a device whose operation or movement is controlled from a distance using a transmitter, often hand-held, that sends radio signals to the device

radioelement /ráydi ō éllimənt/ *n* a chemical element that is radioactive

radio frequency *n* **1.** any of the frequencies of electromagnetic radiation in the range between 10 kHz and 300 MHz, including those used for radio and television transmission **2.** a frequency on which a radio station broadcasts its programmes

radio galaxy *n* a galaxy that is a strong source of radio-frequency waves

radiogenic /ráydi ō jénnik/ *adj* **1.** describes a substance created as a result of the spontaneous decaying of the unstable atoms of another substance ○ *a radiogenic isotope* **2.** emitted as a result of radioactive decay ○ *radiogenic heat*

radiogram /ráydi ō gram/ *n* **1.** a telegram sent by radio

2. MED same as **radiograph 3.** a radio and a record player combined in a single cabinet

radiograph /ráydi ō graaf, -graf/ *n* an image produced on film or another sensitive surface by radiation such as X-rays or gamma rays passing through an object ■ *vt* (**-graphs, -graphing, -graphed**) to make a radiograph of something, especially a part of the body —**radiographer** /ráydi óggrəfər/ *n* —**radiographic** /ráydi ō gráffik/ *adj* —**radiographically** *adv* —**radiography** /ráydi óggrəfi/ *n*

radioimmunoassay /ráydi ō immyǒōnō ássay, -ə sáy/ *n* the technique of measuring the levels of antibodies in the blood by introducing into the bloodstream a substance that has a radioactive tracer attached to it —**radioimmunoassayable** /-ə sáy əb'l/ *adj*

radioiodine /ráydi ō í ə deen/ *n* a radioactive form of iodine. Use: in medicine as a tracer.

radioisotope /ráydi ō íssətōp/ *n* a form of a chemical element (**isotope**) that is radioactive —**radioisotopic** /-īssə tóppik/ *adj*

radio jet *n* a stream of rapidly moving gas associated with a revolving band of matter (**accretion disc**) that emits radio waves as it traverses a magnetic field

radiolabel /ráydi ō láyb'l/ *n* a radioactive substance attached to another substance as a means of tracing the location or tracking the movement of that substance. The technique is used in medicine, e.g. to monitor the distribution of a drug throughout the body. ■ *vt* (**-labels, -labelling, -labelled**) to attach a radiolabel to a substance —**radiolabelled** *adj* —**radiolabelling** *n*

radiolarian /ráydi ō láiri ən/ *n* a single-celled sea organism with a round silica-containing shell that has the organs of movement radiating around it. Amoebas are radiolarians. [Late 19C. < modern Latin *Radiolaria* < *radiolus* 'little staff, stick' < *radius* 'staff, spoke, ray']

radiolocation /ráydi ō lō káysh'n/ *n* the use of radar to detect distant objects

radiology /ráydi ólləji/ *n* **1.** the branch of medicine that deals with the use of X-rays and radioactive substances such as radium in the diagnosis and treatment of diseases **2.** the science of radiation and radioactive substances and their applications, e.g. in structural analysis —**radiologic** /ráydi ə lójjik/ *adj* —**radiological** *adj* —**radiologically** *adv* —**radiologist** *n*

radiolucent /ráydi ō lóoss'nt/ *adj* interfering very little or not at all with the passage of X-rays and other forms of electromagnetic radiation —**radiolucency** *n*

radiolysis /ráydi óllississ/ *n* the breakdown of something into its chemical components by means of X-rays or other radiation —**radiolytic** /-ō líttik/ *adj*

radiometer /ráydi ómmitər/ *n* a device used to detect and measure radiant energy, especially an instrument used to demonstrate the conversion of such energy into mechanical work —**radiometric** /-ə méttrik/ *adj* —**radiometrically** *adv* —**radiometry** *n*

radiometric dating *n* a method of determining the age of objects or material using the decay rates of radioactive components such as potassium-argon

radiomimetic /rádi əmi méttik/ *adj* exerting effects similar to those of ionizing radiation ○ *the radiomimetic effects of some chemicals such as urethane*

radionics /ráydi ónniks/ *n* the use in alternative medicine of an electronic device that can detect vitamin and mineral deficiencies from a hair sample or can detect subtle energy changes in the body. Its results are used to determine appropriate herbal or homeopathic treatments (*takes a singular verb*) [Mid-20C. Blend of RADIATION + ELECTRONICS]

radionuclide /ráydi ə nyóōklīd/ *n* a radioactive nuclide

radiopaque /ráydi ō páyk/ *adj* blocking the passage of X-rays and other forms of electromagnetic radiation —**radiopacity** /-ō pássəti/ *n*

radiopharmaceutical /ráydi ō faarmə syóōtik'l/ *n* a radioactive drug or substance. Use: diagnosis and treatment of disease. —**radiopharmaceutical** *adj*

radiophone /ráydi ō fōn/ *n* TELECOM same as **radiotelephone**

radiophotograph /ráydi ō fōtə graaf, -graf/, **radiophoto** /ráydi ō fō tō/ (*plural* **-tos**) *n* a photograph or another image that is sent from one location to another by means of radio waves

radioprotective /ráydi ō prə téktiv/ *adj* protecting or helping to protect against the harmful effects of X-rays and other radiation —**radioprotection** *n*

radioresistant /ráydi ō ri zístənt/ *adj* resistant to the effects of radiant energy ○ *radioresistant tumours* —**radioresistance** *n*

radioscopy /ráydi ō óskəpi/ *n* the use of X-rays or another form of electromagnetic radiation to study the internal structure of something —**radioscopic** /ráydi ə skóppik/ *adj* —**radioscopical** *adj*

radiosensitive /ráydi ō sénsitiv/ *adj* sensitive to the biological effects of radiant energy such as X-rays —**radiosensitivity** /-senssə tívvəti/ *n*

radiosonde /ráydi ō sond/ *n* an instrument carried aloft by a balloon and used to measure and transmit meteorological data by radio

radio spectrum *n* the range of radio frequencies used for radio, television, and other electromagnetic communications, between 10 Khz and 300 MHz

radiotelephone /ráydi ō téllə fōn/ *n* a telephone that transmits sound signals by radio waves rather than through wires

radio telescope *n* an astronomical instrument used to detect and analyse radio waves from astronomical objects. It consists of an antenna, often in the form of a large dish, a detector, and an amplifier.

radioteletype /ráydi ō téllitīp/ *n* **1.** a teleprinter that transmits and receives by radio rather than along a cable **2.** a receiving and transmitting system that uses radioteletypes

radiotherapy /ráydi ō thérrəpi/ *n* the treatment of disease using radiation X-rays or beta rays directed at the body from an external source or emitted by radioactive materials placed within the body —**radiotherapeutic** /-therə pyóōtik/ *adj* —**radiotherapist** *n*

radiothorium /ráydi ō tháwri əm/ *n* a radioactive isotope of the element thorium, with a mass number of 228

radiotoxic /ráydi ō tóksik/ *adj* relating to the toxic effects of radiation or radioactive substances

radiotracer /ráydi ō tráyssər/ *n* a radioactive substance introduced into the body as a tracer, e.g. to observe the steps in a chemical or biochemical process or locate diseased cells or tissue

radio wave *n* an electromagnetic wave whose frequency falls within the radio spectrum

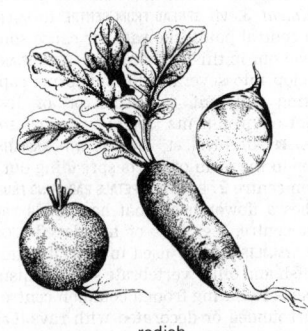

radish

radish /ráddish/ *n* **1.** a crisp pungent round or bloated root, with a red or white skin, eaten raw **2.** a plant of the mustard family that produces radishes. Native to: Europe, Asia. Latin name: *Raphanus sativus*. [Pre-12C. < Latin *radic-* 'root']

radium /ráydi əm/ *n* a white highly radioactive metallic element. Source: pitchblende, carnotite. Use: luminous coatings, treatment of cancer. Symbol **Ra**. See table at **element** [Late 19C. < Latin *radius* 'staff, spoke, ray, beam of light'; from the rays emitted by radium, which penetrate specific opaque materials]

radium therapy *n* the medical use of radium to treat cancer and other diseases with radiation

radius /ráydi əss/ (*plural* **-dii** /-di ī/ or **-diuses**) *n* **1.** MATHS **LINE FROM CENTRE** a straight line extending from the centre of a circle to its edge or from the centre of a sphere to its surface. Symbol **r 2.** MATHS **LENGTH OF RADIUS** the length of a radius. Symbol **r 3. CIRCULAR AREA** an area enclosed by a circle that has a radius of a particular length ○ *all the houses within a radius of 2 miles of the explosion* **4. RANGE OF EFFECTIVENESS OR INFLUENCE** the area or range within which somebody or something can act, work, or exert influence effectively ○ *beyond the radius of the UN's influence* **5.** ANAT **BONE IN ARM OR FORELIMB** the shorter and thicker of the two bones in the human forearm, the one on the thumb side, or the equivalent bone in the lower forelimbs of animals **6. RADIATING PART** a radiating line, part, or structure [Late 16C. < Latin, 'staff, spoke, ray, beam of light']

radius of action *n* **1.** a broadly circular area in which a military unit can operate or bring force to bear on an enemy **2.** the distance a vehicle, ship, or aircraft can travel and return safely to base without refuelling

radius of curvature *n* the radius of the circle whose curvature matches that of a curve at a given point

radius vector *n* **1.** a line connecting a fixed point or origin and a variable point, or the length of such a line **2.** a line connecting the centre of an astronomical object and the centre of another in orbit around it

radix /ráydiks/ (*plural* **radices** /ráydi seez/ or **radixes**) *n* **1.** the base of a number system or system of logarithms **2.** a root part or point where a plant or animal part begins [Late 16C. < Latin, 'root, radish, foundation' < Indo-European]

RADM, RAdm *abbr* NAVY rear admiral

radome /ráy dōm/ *n* a dome-shaped protective enclosure for a radar antenna, made from materials that do not interfere with the transmission and reception of radio waves [Mid-20C. Blend of RADAR + DOME]

radon /ráy don/ *n* a heavy gaseous radioactive element. Source: radioactive decay of radium, in small quantities in rock and soil. Use: radiotherapy. Symbol **Rn**. See table at **element** [Early 20C. < RADIUM]

radula /ráddyŏŏlə/ (*plural* **-lae** /-lee/) *n* a band of tissue in the mouth of some molluscs **(gastropods)** containing rows of small teeth, used in scraping off particles of food and bringing them into the mouth [Mid-18C. < Latin, 'scraper' < *radere* 'scrape'] —**radular** *adj*

radwaste /rád wayst/ *n* same as **radioactive waste** (*informal*) [Late 20C. Contraction]

Raeburn /ráybərn/, **Sir Henry** (1756–1823) Scottish painter. A portraitist, especially of the Scottish upper classes, he is best known for *The Rev. Robert Walker Skating* (1784).

RAEC *abbr* Royal Army Educational Corps

RAF *abbr* Royal Air Force

RAFDS *abbr* Royal Australian Flying Doctor Service

Raffarin /ráffə raN/, **Jean-Pierre** (*b.* 1948) prime minister of France (2002–). A public relations expert, he became vice president of the newly-formed free-market Liberal Democracy Party (1997) and prime minister of the centre-right coalition government (2002).

Rafferty /ráffərti/, **Chips** (1909–71) Australian actor. His films include *The Sundowners* (1960) and *Wake in Fright* (1971). Born **Goffage, John William Pilbean**

Rafferty's Rules /ráffərtiz-/, **Rafferty Rules** *n ANZ* a disorganized shambles with no rules, guidelines, or system whatsoever [Early 20C. < ?]

raffia /ráffi ə/, **raphia** *n* **1.** fibre in the form of flexible straw-coloured ribbons. Source: leaves of the raffia palm. Use: mats, baskets. **2.** TREES same as **raffia palm** [Late 19C. < Malagasy *rafia*]

raffia palm *n* a palm tree with large leaves that yield a strong fibre. Native to: Madagascar. Latin name: *Raphia ruffia.*

raffinate /ráffi nayt/ *n* the remaining or refined part of a liquid mixture, left after other substances dissolved in it have been extracted [Early 20C. < French *raffinat* < *raffiner* 'refine']

raffinose /ráffi nōz, -nōss/ *n* a white crystalline slightly sweet sugar. Source: cottonseed meal, sugar beet, molasses. Formula: $C_{18}H_{32}O_{16}$. [Late 19C. < French *raffiner* 'refine']

raffish /ráffish/ *adj* **1.** displaying a charming free-spirited disregard for the conventions of society or for approved behaviour ○ *a raffish politician whose engaging antics never alienated the voters* **2.** displaying an exaggerated or obtrusive showiness ○ *a raffish hotel* [Early 19C. < 2nd element of RIFFRAFF] —**raffishly** *adv* —**raffishness** *n*

raffle[1] /ráff'l/ *n* an event in which numbered tickets are sold, some of which are drawn at random to win prizes. The prizes in a raffle are often objects rather than money and raffles are usually held in order to raise money for some cause or organization. ○ *I won this vase in a raffle.* ■ *vt* (**-fles, -fling, -fled**) to offer or give away something as a prize in a raffle [14C. < Old French, 'act of plundering'] —**raffler** *n*

raffle[2] /ráff'l/ *n* **1.** unwanted items or debris **2.** tangled ropes or other bits and pieces on a ship [Late 18C. < ?]

Raffles /ráff'lz/, **Sir Stamford** (1781–1826) British colonial administrator. He was lieutenant governor of Java (1811–16) and Bengkulu (1818–24), and founder of the city of Singapore (1819). Full name **Raffles, Sir Thomas Stamford**

rafflesia /ra fleézi ə/ *n* a leafless tropical plant that is a parasite of other plants and has large foul-smelling flowers that are pollinated by carrion flies. Native to: Asia. Genus: *Rafflesia.* [Early 19C. < modern Latin, after Sir Stamford RAFFLES]

raft[1] /raaft/ *n* **1. FLAT BOAT** a flat floating structure made of wooden planks, logs, barrels, or similar materials, used as a boat or anchored in the water as a dock or diving platform **2. INFLATABLE BOAT OR MAT** an inflatable flat-bottomed rubber or plastic boat used for drifting along on a river, or an inflatable rectangular mat used for surfing or lounging in the water **3. BASE SLAB FOR BUILDING** a thick concrete slab laid down as a foundation for a building that is being constructed on soft ground **4.** *N Am* **COLLECTION OF FLOATING OBJECTS** a group of animals, especially wildfowl, or a mass of things floating or travelling together on water ○ *a raft of ducks* ■ *v* (**rafts, rafting, rafted**) **1.** *vt* **MOVE SOMETHING BY RAFT** to transport something by raft **2.** *vi* **SAIL ON RAFT** to travel on a raft **3.** *vt* **FORM RAFT** to form something into a raft, or make something gather together into a raft ○ *The lumberjacks rafted the logs together before sending them downstream.* [13C. < Old Norse *raptr* 'log, beam']

CULTURAL NOTE ***The Raft of the Medusa***, a painting (1819) by French artist Théodore Géricault. This monumental work is a harrowing depiction of the suffering of the survivors of an infamous 1816 shipwreck. Géricault's treatment of a contemporary subject in an epic style more traditionally associated with classical or historical themes was seen as a significant development in European art.

---

raft[2] /raaft/ *n* a very large number or amount of something (*informal*) ○ *a whole raft of proposals* [Mid-19C. Alteration of 2nd element of RIFFRAFF, probably after RAFT[1]]

rafter[1] /raáftər/ *n* a sloping supporting timber, beam, or board that runs from the ridge beam of a roof to its edge [Old English *ræfter* < Germanic] —**raftered** *adj* —**raftering** *n*

rafter[2] /raáftər/ *n* **1.** a traveller on a raft **2.** a lumberjack who ties logs into a raft to transport them downstream [Early 19C. < RAFT[1]]

Rafter /raáftər/, **Pat** (*b.* 1972) Australian tennis player. He was the US Open singles champion in 1997 and 1998, and twice runner-up at Wimbledon. Full name **Rafter, Patrick**

rafting /raáfting/ *n* the outdoor leisure pursuit of floating on a lake or river in a raft

rafty /raáfti/ (**-ier, -iest**) *adj N England* rancid in taste or smell (*informal*) [Mid-17C. Origin ?]

RAFVR *abbr* Royal Air Force Volunteer Reserve

rag[1] /rag/ *n* **1. SMALL PIECE OF CLOTH** a small piece or scrap of usually old or unwanted cloth used for cleaning, polishing, or applying liquid substances **2. SMALL TATTERED PIECE** a small, irregular, or tattered scrap or piece of material **3. PIECE OF CLOTHING** an item of clothing, thought of as being worn or tattered and not really fit to wear (*informal; often ironic*) **4. INFERIOR NEWSPAPER** a newspaper with low journalistic standards, or any newspaper regarded with contempt (*informal*) **5.** PAPER **CLOTH FOR MAKING PAPER** cloth or cloth fibres that are used in making paper ■ **rags** *npl* **WORN-OUT CLOTHES** clothes that are tattered, frayed, or torn [14C. Probably < Old Norse *rogg* 'shaggy tuft'] ◇ **be (like) a red rag to a bull (to somebody)** to be certain to make somebody angry ◇ **go from rags to riches** to start off in poverty and then become very wealthy ◇ **in rags** in a worn-out, tattered, and torn condition ◇ **lose your rag** to lose your temper (*informal*)

rag[2] /rag/ *v* (**rags, ragging, ragged**) **1.** *vti* **TEASE OR TAUNT SOMEBODY** to subject somebody to persistent teasing or taunting (*informal*) ○ *His friends ragged him about his new haircut.* **2.** *vt* **PLAY PRANKS ON SOMEBODY** to play pranks or jokes on somebody, often to the point of tormenting him or her (*dated informal*) **3.** *vi* **BEHAVE BOISTEROUSLY** to take part in good-humoured, boisterous activity (*dated informal*) **4.** *vt* **SCOLD SOMEBODY** to scold somebody persistently or vehemently (*slang*) ■ *n* **1. CHARITY FUND-RAISING AT UNIVERSITY** an activity or a set of activities conducted by university students in order to raise money for charity while having a good time **2. PRACTICAL JOKE** a prank or practical joke, especially by a student on a fellow student (*dated informal*) [Mid-18C. Origin ?] —**ragging** *n*

rag[3] /rag/ *n* jazz in which a syncopated rhythm in the melody is accompanied by a steady beat, or a piece of music in this style ■ *vt* (**rags, ragging, ragged**) to compose or perform ragtime music [Late 19C. Origin ?]

rag[4] /rag/ *n* **1.** GEOL, INDUST same as **ragstone 2.** a roofing slate that has a rough surface on one side [13C. Origin ?]

rag[5] /raag/ *n* MUSIC same as **raga**

raga /raágə/, **rag** /raag/, **raag** *n* a scale, melody, or rhythmic pattern that forms the basis of the classical music of South Asia. Particular ragas are associated with different times of the day, and are intended to create different moods. Performances may be partly or completely improvised. [Late 18C. < Sanskrit *rāga* 'colour, harmony']

ragamuffin /rággə mufin/ *n* **1.** MUSIC same as **ragga 2.** a child dressed in worn or tattered clothes, often one allowed to roam the streets (*dated*) [14C. Origin ?]

rag-and-bone man *n* somebody who travels the streets buying and selling unwanted clothes and household items, and other discarded things [< RAG[1]]

ragbag /rág bag/ *n* **1.** a bag in which unwanted clothes and bits of cloth are kept for use as rags **2.** a collection of miscellaneous things (*informal*) [Early 19C. < RAG[1]]

rag doll *n* a floppy stuffed cloth doll [< RAG[1]]

rage /rayj/ *n* **1. EXTREME ANGER** sudden and extreme anger ○ *tears of rage* **2. ANGRY OUTBURST** an outburst of strong anger ○ *flew into a rage* **3. OBJECT OF FAD** something that is the object of a short-lived fascination, fashion, or enthusiasm shared by many people ○ *Those toys are all the rage for kids at the moment.* **4. FORCE OR INTENSITY** extreme or unrelenting intensity **5. STRONG PASSION OR ENTHUSIASM** a strong and sometimes overpowering desire or enthusiasm **6.** *ANZ* **PARTY** a party or celebration ○ *The kids are planning a bit of a rage this weekend to celebrate the end of term.* ■ *vi* (**rages, raging, raged**) **1. ACT WITH OR FEEL RAGE** to speak or do something with sudden, extreme anger, or feel such strong anger ○ *She was raging against the injustice of the situation.* **2. OCCUR WITH VIOLENCE** to occur, continue, move, or spread with great force and violence ○ *The storm raged for three days.* **3.** *ANZ* **HOLD PARTY** to have a party to celebrate something or to socialize ○ *We were out raging all weekend.* [13C. Via French < Vulgar Latin *rabia*, alteration of Latin *rabies* (see RABIES)]

SYNONYMS See *anger*.

ragee *n* FOOD, PLANTS another spelling of **ragi**

~~rageing~~ incorrect spelling of **raging**

ragga /rággə/ *n* a style of reggae characterized by long rap monologues and repetitive beats [Late 20C. Shortening of RAGAMUFFIN]

ragged /rággid/ *adj* **1.** TATTERED frayed or torn into irregular shapes or pieces, especially along the edge **2.** WEARING RAGS dressed in torn, tattered, or frayed clothes **3.** HAVING UNEVEN EDGE OR SURFACE having a surface, edge, or outline that is rough, uneven, or jagged **4.** UNKEMPT rough and irregular in appearance and suggesting neglect and a lack of grooming ○ *a ragged beard* **5.** OF VARYING QUALITY of unequal quality, some parts being less good than others ○ *He gave a rather ragged performance as Othello.* **6.** NOT FIRM OR REGULAR done in an uncoordinated, hesitant, or irregular way, especially by a group who do not manage to do something all together or in unison **7.** EXHAUSTED extremely tired or anxious ○ *speaking with a ragged voice* [13C. < RAG[1]] —**raggedly** *adv* —**raggedness** *n*

ragged robin *n* a perennial plant of the pink family. Flowers: pink or white, with ragged petals. Latin name: *Lychnis floscuculi.*

raggedy /rággidi/ *adj* (*informal*) **1.** TATTERED having been torn and worn excessively **2.** BADLY DRESSED wearing worn-out torn clothes **3.** ROUGH OR UNEVEN having rough untidy ends or edges

raggee *n* FOOD, PLANTS another spelling of **ragi**

raggle-taggle /rágg'l tágg'l/ *adj* consisting of a mixture of strange or very different things, often with an element of untidiness or scruffiness ○ *a raggle-taggle collection of animals in a small zoo* [Early 20C. Alteration of RAGTAG]

ragi /rággi/, **ragee, raggee** *n* **1.** the grain of a cereal grass used as food in South Asia and parts of Africa **2.** a cereal grass cultivated for ragi. Latin name: *Eleusine coracana.* [Late 18C. < Hindi *rāgī*]

raging /ráyjing/ *adj* **1.** VERY ANGRY out of control or angry **2.** VERY STRONG done or happening with great force or intensity **3.** VERY SEVERE OR PAINFUL very severe and causing great pain or distress ○ *a raging toothache* **4.** CONSIDERABLE very good or great ○ *The play was a raging success.*

raglan /rágglən/ *adj* **1.** EXTENDING TO COLLAR describes a sleeve extending to the collar of a garment instead of ending at the shoulder, attached with slanting seams running from under the arm to the neck **2.** HAVING RAGLAN SLEEVES made with raglan sleeves ■ *n* GARMENT WITH RAGLAN SLEEVES an overcoat, jumper, or other garment that has raglan sleeves [Mid-19C. After Lord *Raglan* (1788–1855), British field marshal]

ragman /rág man/ (*plural* **-men** /-men/) *n* a dealer in old cloth and clothes [14C. < RAG[1]]

ragnail /rág nayl/ *n Scotland* same as **hangnail** [< RAG[1]; from its being ragged]

Ragnarök /raágnə rok/ *n* in Norse mythology, the final destruction of the gods in a great battle against the forces of evil, after which a new world will arise [Mid-18C. < Old Norse *ragnarök* 'fate of the gods' < *regin* 'gods' + *rok* 'fate']

ragout /ra góo/ *n* a rich slow-cooked stew of meat and vegetables [Mid-17C. < French < *ragoûter* 'renew the appetite' < *goût* 'taste' < Latin *gustus*]

ragpicker /rág pikər/ *n* a gatherer and seller of old clothes and other discarded items [Mid-19C. < RAG[1]]

rag-rolling *n* the decorative technique of using a crumpled cloth to dab paint that has been applied to a wall or other surface, in order to produce an irregularly patterned effect [< RAG[1]]

rag rug *n* a rug made by knotting or hooking short strips of waste fabric through a base to form a shaggy pile [< RAG[1]]

ragstone /rág stōn/ *n* a hard sandstone or limestone that tends to break up into slabs and is used as a building material [14C. < RAG[4]]

ragtag /rág tag/ *adj* **1.** made up of a wide-ranging mix of people or things, often ones that are of questionable quality ○ *a ragtag team made up of friends and acquaintances* **2.** untidy, unkempt, or ragged in appearance [Late 19C. < RAG[1]]

ragtag and bobtail *n* people who are considered members of the lowest social classes, especially when regarded as dissatisfied with their lives and likely to be disorderly or rebellious (*dated insult*)

ragtime /rág tīm/ *n* a style of US popular music of the late 19th and early 20th centuries characterized by distinctive syncopated right-hand rhythms against a regularly accented left-hand beat. Ragtime was widely popularized by the pianist and composer Scott Joplin. [Late 19C. < RAG[3]]

ragtop /rág top/ *n N Am* CARS same as **soft top** (*slang*) [Mid-20C. < RAG[1]]

rag trade *n* the clothing industry and the various professions involved in the design, manufacture, and sale of clothing (*informal*) [< RAG[1]]

ragweed /rág weed/ *n* **1.** PLANTS same as **ragwort 2.** a weedy plant with small green flower heads producing large amounts of pollen that causes hay fever in many people. Native to: North America. Genus: *Ambrosia.* [Mid-17C. < RAG[1]; from the raggedness of the leaves]

ragworm /rág wurm/ *n UK, Can* a sea worm often used as fishing bait. Genus: *Nereis.* US term **clamworm** [Mid-19C. < RAG[1]; from the ragged appearance of its appendages]

ragwort /rág wurt/ *n* a plant that has clusters of small yellow flowers with radiating petals like those of daisies. Genus: *Senecio.* [15C. < RAG[1]; from the raggedness of the leaves]

rah /raa/ *interj* used to express approval or encouragement (*informal*) [Mid-19C. Shortening of HURRAH]

Rahman /rə maán/, **Mujibur** (1920–75) Bangladeshi politician. The founding father of Bangladesh, he served as the country's first prime minister (1972–75). He was assassinated in a military coup soon after becoming president in 1975.

Rahman, Ziaur (1935–81) president of Bangladesh (1977–81). During his presidency, he ended martial law but was assassinated in an attempted military coup.

rah-rah /raá raa/ *adj N Am* spiritedly and often unthinkingly enthusiastic (*slang*) ○ *the rah-rah attitude of the project's supporters* [Early 20C. Doubling of RAH]

rah-rah skirt, ra-ra skirt *n* a short full skirt usually layered or with rows of frills, popular in the 1980s [Because in a style originally worn by cheerleaders]

rahui /raá hoo i/ (*plural* **-huis**) *n NZ* a sign warning against trespass [Mid-19C. < Maori]

rai /rī/ *n* a form of music popular in Algeria that combines Algerian traditional music with Western rock [Late 20C. < Arabic]

raid /rayd/ *n* **1.** SUDDEN ATTACK a sudden attack made by soldiers, aircraft, police, bandits, or any other force in an attempt to seize or destroy something **2.** FIN PURCHASE OF SHARES TO CONTROL the buying of a large number of shares in a company in an attempt to gain control of it ○ *The company beat off the raid but took on debt to buy its own shares.* **3.** FIN ILLEGAL ATTEMPT TO LOWER STOCK PRICE the illegal coordinated selling of shares in a company's stock by a group of speculators in an attempt to make the stock price fall **4.** *N Am* BUSINESS ENTICEMENT OF VALUED PEOPLE in the business world, an attempt by an organization to lure away a competitor's employees, members, or clients ○ *a raid by one advertising agency on another's clients* ■ *v* (**raids, raiding, raided**) **1.** *vti* MAKE SURPRISE ATTACK to make or participate in a raid on somebody or something **2.** *vt* STEAL SOMETHING FROM SOMEWHERE to take something secretly or stealthily because it is illegal or forbidden ○ *The bank's funds had been raided by its former president.* **3.** *vt N Am* BUSINESS LURE SOMEBODY AWAY to lure somebody away from another organization, usually from a competitor ○ *The new hockey league began to raid players from its rival.* [15C. Scots dialect form of ROAD] —**raider** *n*

rail[1] /rayl/ *n* **1.** LONG PIECE OF WOOD OR METAL a long horizontal or sloping piece of wood, metal, or other material that is used as a barrier, support, or place to hang things **2.** FENCE OR RAILING a structure made of a rail or rails and their supports, e.g. a fence or railing (*often used in the plural*) **3.** RAIL STEEL BAR OF RAILWAY TRACK a narrow steel bar, or a series of connected bars laid in two parallel lines, supporting and guiding the wheels of railway engines and carriages or anything similar **4.** TRANSP RAILWAY the railway as a means or form of transport ○ *rail travel* ■ *vt* (**rails, railing, railed**) PUT RAIL ON OR ROUND SOMETHING to put a rail or railing on or around something to provide a guard, barrier, or support ○ *They ought to rail off the children's play area.* [13C. Via Old French *reille* 'bar' < Latin *regula* 'straight stick, rod'] —**railless** *adj* ◇ **go off the rails 1.** to begin to behave in an unacceptable, irresponsible, or illegal way **2.** to begin to go wrong and lose direction

rail[2] /rayl/ (**rails, railing, railed**) *vi* to denounce, protest against, or attack somebody or something in bitter or harsh language ○ *Some people rail against the injustice of the system.* [15C. Via French *railler* 'mock, tease' < Old Provençal *ralhar* 'chat, joke' < late Latin *ragere* 'neigh, roar'] —**railer** *n*

rail[3] /rayl/ (*plural* **rails** or *same*) *n* a small or medium-sized wading bird with a short tail, short wings, and long toes. Family: Rallidae. [15C. < Old French *raale* < Latin *ras-*, past participle of *radere* 'scrape']

railcar /ráyl kaar/ *n* **1.** a self-propelled, usually diesel-powered passenger railway coach for use on branch lines **2.** *N Am* a railway carriage [Mid-19C. < RAIL[1]]

railcard /ráyl kaard/ *n* an identity card allowing the holder, e.g. a student, senior citizen, or family group, to buy rail tickets at reduced rates, usually restricted to off-peak travel times [Late 20C. < RAIL[1]]

railhead /ráyl hed/ *n* **1.** the farthest point to which the track of a railway line runs **2.** a place where supplies, often military materials, are unloaded from railway wagons for distribution to other points [Early 20C. < RAIL[1]]

railing /ráyling/ *n* **1.** STRUCTURE WITH RAILS AND POSTS a structure consisting of one or more rails and their supports, used to provide a barrier or support in walking or climbing, or the upper rail of such a structure **2.** METAL FENCE an often ornamental fence of vertical metal poles held in position by one or more narrow horizontal bars, providing a barrier round something such as a park (*usually used in the plural*) ○ *ivy growing up the railings* **3.** RAILS long horizontal pieces of sturdy material for making a railing [14C. < RAIL[1]]

raillery /ráyləri/ (*plural* **-ies**) *n* **1.** humorous, playful, or friendly ridiculing of somebody or something **2.** a remark that ridicules somebody or something jokingly and with good humour [Mid-17C. < French *raillerie* < *railler*]

raillink /ráyl lingk/ *n* a short connecting railway line, usually between a city centre and an airport [Late 20C. < RAIL[1]]

railroad /ráyl rōd/ *n N Am* same as **railway** (senses 1–2) ■ *v* (**-roads, -roading, -roaded**) **1.** *vt* FORCE SOMETHING THROUGH QUICKLY WITHOUT DISCUSSION to push something through a legislature, committee, or other decision-making body quickly so that there is not enough time for objections to be considered (*informal*) ○ *The changes to the proposal were railroaded through the subcommittee.* **2.** *vt* FORCE SOMEBODY TO ACT HASTILY to force a person or group to make a decision or take action quickly, without time for consideration or discussion (*informal*) **3.** *vt* CONVICT SOMEBODY TOO QUICKLY to convict somebody on the basis of flimsy or false evidence (*informal*) **4.** *vt US* RAIL TRANSPORT SOMETHING BY RAIL to transport or send something by rail **5.** *vi US* BE RAILWAY WORKER to work on a railway ○ *She used to railroad for the Southern Pacific.* [Mid-18C. < RAIL[1]]

railslide /ráyl slīd/ (**-slides, -sliding, -slid** /-slid/) *vi* in skateboarding, to slide along the top or upper edge of a ramp or obstacle using the bottom of the board rather than the wheels [Late 20C. < RAIL[1]]

railtour /ráyl toor/ *n* an excursion on a chartered or special train intended for railway enthusiasts [Mid-20C. < RAIL[1]]

Railtrack /ráyl trak/ *n* a company that operated the UK railway infrastructure before its shares were

suspended towards the end of 2001 and its functions were assumed by Network Rail [Late 20C. < RAIL¹]

railway /ráyl way/ n UK, ANZ, Can 1. a track consisting of steel rails usually fastened to wood or concrete sleepers, designed to carry the engine and carriages of a train or anything similar 2. a network of railway lines, together with the trains, buildings, equipment, and staff needed to operate a rail transport system, or the organization or company that owns or runs this ▶ US term **railroad** [Late 17C. < RAIL¹] —**railwayman** n

raiment /ráymənt/ n CLOTHING same as **clothing** (sense 1) (archaic or literary) [14C. Shortening of arrayment]

rain /rayn/ n 1. WATER FALLING FROM CLOUDS water condensed from vapour in the atmosphere and falling in drops from clouds 2. PERIOD OF WET WEATHER any storm, shower, or other quantity of water falling from the sky 3. RAINY WEATHER weather marked by heavy or persistent rainfall 4. GREAT NUMBER OR FLOW a great number of small individual things coming in a steady flow or anything else flowing or falling like rain ○ A rain of dust fell from the crumbling ceiling. ■ **rains** npl RAINY SEASON in some countries, a season of the year when a lot of rain falls ■ v (**rains, raining, rained**) 1. vi DROP RAIN to fall from the sky or release water in the form of rain ○ It's raining again. 2. vti COME IN GREAT NUMBER to come or fall in the form of a great number of units arriving separately but in very quick succession or in a continuous stream, or drop or deliver something in this way ○ Missiles rained down on us from the defenders on the battlements. ○ Reporters rained questions on the beleaguered police chief. 3. vt GIVE SOMETHING GENEROUSLY to give somebody something in large quantities, continuously, and over a considerable period of time ○ Generous to a fault, they positively rained gifts on all their friends. [Old English regn, rēn < Germanic] —**rainless** adj ◇ **(as) right as rain** perfectly all right (informal) ◇ **(come) rain or shine** whatever the weather or the circumstances ○ The picnic will be held, rain or shine.

SPELLCHECK rain, reign, or rein? Do not confuse the spelling of **rain**, **reign**, and **rein**, which sound similar. **Rain** refers to water falling from the sky: The crops need rain. It rained all afternoon. **Reign** refers to the rule of a monarch, or to the dominant factor in a situation: The castle was built during the reign of King Henry VIII. Confusion reigned in the town. **Rein** refers to a strap for controlling a horse, or to any other similar means of restraint: He pulled on the reins to stop the horse. They kept a tight rein on expenditure. She reined back her mount.

rain off vt UK to cause an event such as a sporting fixture to be cancelled or postponed because of rain (usually passive) ANZ, N Am term **rain out**
rain out vt ANZ, N Am same as **rain off**

rainbird /ráyn burd/ n a bird thought to call before rainstorms, e.g. a green woodpecker or some members of the cuckoo family

rainbow /ráyn bō/ n 1. MULTICOLOURED ARC IN SKY an arc of light separated into bands of colour that appears when the Sun's rays are refracted and reflected by drops of mist or rain. The colours of the rainbow are conventionally said to be red, orange, yellow, green, blue, indigo, and violet. 2. ARC OF BANDS OF COLOUR a multicoloured arc similar to a rainbow 3. BRIGHT MULTICOLOURED SIGHT an arrangement, display, or sight containing many bright colours or bright multicoloured objects ○ Her makeup box was a rainbow of colours. 4. FALSE HOPE a goal, hope, or ideal that is unlikely to be achieved or realized 5. VARIED ASSORTMENT a wide range or varied assortment of things, usually coexisting without clashing ■ adj 1. HAVING VARIED COLOURS having the colours of the rainbow or colours as varied as those of a rainbow 2. MADE OF MANY DIFFERENT THINGS comprising a wide variety of types or elements, especially made up of people of different ethnic groups or from a variety of minority groups ○ a rainbow coalition

CULTURAL NOTE The Rainbow, a novel (1915) by D. H. Lawrence. Set in the English Midlands between 1840 and 1905, it describes the impact of contemporary social developments on the lifestyles and attitudes of succeeding generations of a provincial family, the Brangwens. The latter part of the book focuses on Ursula, the family's first independent woman, whose story is continued in a subsequent novel Women in Love (1920).

rainbow lorikeet n a colourful bird of the parrot family with a blue head, orange breast, and green wings and back that feeds on nectar, fruit, and seeds. Native to: northern and eastern forests of Australia. Latin name: Trichoglossus haematodus.

rainbow trout n a freshwater game fish with a reddish or pinkish band along either side of its body and numerous black spots. Native to: North America, but widely introduced elsewhere. Latin name: Salmo gairdneri.

rain check n N Am 1. a ticket or ticket stub entitling somebody to attend an event cancelled because of rain at a later rescheduled time 2. a promise or voucher guaranteeing that an offer that cannot be fulfilled or accepted at present will be fulfilled or accepted at a later time ◇ **take a rain check (on something)** N Am to delay doing something until a later date or time (informal)

raincoat /ráyn kōt/ n a coat designed to keep the wearer dry when worn in the rain, with a water-resistant or waterproof surface or coating

rain date n N Am a date that an event will be rescheduled to if rainy weather forces cancellation on the intended date

raindrop /ráyn drop/ n a drop of water that falls from a cloud in the sky

rainfall /ráyn fawl/ n 1. the amount of rain that falls in a location over a period of time ○ the annual rainfall in a city 2. a rain shower or rainstorm

rainforest /ráyn forist/ n a thick evergreen tropical forest found in areas of heavy rainfall and containing trees with broad leaves that form a continuous canopy

rain gauge n a device used to measure the amount of rain that falls in a location

rain hat n a hat that provides protection from rain for the wearer's head

Rainier III /ráyni ay/ (b. 1923) prince of Monaco. He acceded to the throne in 1949, and in 1962 agreed to a new constitution reducing the power of the monarchy. Born **Grimaldi, Rainier Louis Henri Maxence Bertrand de**

Rainier, Mount /ráyni ər, rə neér, ray neér/ highest peak in Washington State. It is a dormant volcano, with a permanently snow-covered summit. Height: 4,392 m/14,410 ft.

rainmaker /ráyn maykər/ n 1. SOMEBODY MAGICALLY CAUSING RAIN somebody who is believed to have the magic powers to make rain fall 2. SOMEBODY WHO CAUSES RAIN somebody whose job is cloud-seeding especially in times of severe drought (informal) 3. N Am HIGH ACHIEVER an achiever of outstanding results in a profession or politics (informal) ○ a rainmaker in the law firm who accrued thousands of billing hours on big clients —**rainmaking** n

rainout /ráyn owt/ n 1. atmospheric pollution that is carried down to the ground in rain, e.g. radioactive fallout 2. N Am an event that is cancelled or postponed because of rainy weather, or the cancellation or postponement of an event because of rain ○ There was a rainout at the ballpark today.

rainproof /ráyn proof/ adj designed or treated to prevent rain from soaking in or passing through ■ vt (**-proofs, -proofing, -proofed**) to treat something such as an item of clothing so that it becomes rainproof

rain shadow n an area on the side of a mountain barrier that is sheltered from prevailing winds and rain-bearing clouds, resulting in relatively dry conditions

rainstorm /ráyn stawrm/ n a storm with heavy or steady rain

rain tree n a tree with pale pink flowers and long horizontal branches, whose wood is used in the manufacture of furniture. Native to: tropical America. Latin name: Albizia saman. [Because its leaves close up when it rains]

rainwash /ráyn wosh/ n rock and soil washed away and deposited elsewhere by rainwater, or the process of erosion by rainwater

rainwater /ráyn wawtər/ n water that has fallen as rain, which usually has relatively small amounts of minerals dissolved in it

rainwear /ráyn wair/ n clothing, mainly outerwear, that is waterproof and is designed to keep the wearer dry in rainy weather

rainy /ráyni/ (**-ier, -iest**) adj characterized by or bringing rain, especially long or frequently recurring periods of rainfall —**rainily** adv —**raininess** n

rainy day n a possible time of need in the future

Raipur /rī poor/ capital city of Chhattisgarh State in eastern India. Population: 438,639 (1991).

Rais /rayss/, **Gilles de, Baron** (1404–40) French politician and marshal of France. In his pursuit of riches he turned to alchemy and Satanism, and was executed for heresy and child murder.

raise /rayz/ v (**raises, raising, raised**) 1. vt MOVE SOMETHING HIGHER to cause somebody or something to move to a higher level or position ○ She was too weak to raise her head from the pillow. 2. vt MAKE SOMEBODY STAND OR SIT UP to move yourself or somebody else to a standing or sitting position ○ I raised myself with difficulty and staggered to the door. 3. vt DIRECT SOMETHING AT HIGHER ANGLE to direct something upwards, or make something point at a higher angle ○ She answered without raising her eyes from the book. 4. vt PUT SOMETHING UP to set up, erect, or build something ○ Neighbours helped us raise a new barn on the weekend. 5. vt STRETCH SOMETHING OUT to make something such as a crest or frill stretch out and become more visible 6. vt CAUSE SOMETHING TO SWELL UP to make something rise up or swell up, e.g. on somebody's skin 7. vt MAKE SOMETHING LARGER OR GREATER to increase something in size, amount, value, or scope ○ They've raised the ticket prices yet again. 8. vt INTENSIFY SOMETHING to increase something in degree, strength, or pitch ○ raised their voices 9. vt IMPROVE SOMEBODY'S CONDITION to improve somebody's situation or condition, or move somebody to a higher rank or status ○ helping the downtrodden to raise themselves 10. vt IMPROVE SOMETHING to make something better in some way ○ Their visit raised his spirits. ○ You can't raise educational standards unless you train and motivate the teachers better. 11. vt GROW OR BREED SOMETHING to grow vegetables or breed and care for animals, usually for profit or personal satisfaction 12. vt ACT AS PARENT OR GUARDIAN TO SOMEBODY to look after somebody as or like a parent, while he or she is growing up (often passive) ○ After my parents died, I was raised by my grandfather. 13. vt OFFER SOMETHING FOR CONSIDERATION to put something forward for consideration or discussion ○ I'd like to raise a number of points that I think need clarification. 14. vt COLLECT SOMETHING TOGETHER to gather something together, collect something, or ask for something and be given it ○ raising money for the local orphanage 15. vt CAUSE SOMETHING to cause something to appear, arise, form, or occur ○ The strict new rules raised a storm of protest. 16. vt GIVE SIGN OF FEELING to produce a response such as a smile or cheer, or cause somebody else to produce one ○ She obviously felt awful, but still managed to raise a faint smile. 17. vt START SOMETHING NOISY to start something that involves a lot of loud noise or boisterous activity ○ Raise the alarm! 18. vt ROUSE SOMEBODY to rouse somebody from sleep, or bring a dead person back to life ○ They were shouting loud enough to raise the dead. 19. vt CALL SOMETHING UP to attempt to cause a supernatural being to appear, e.g. by special ceremonies or magic 20. vt PUT SOMEBODY IN AUTHORITY to place somebody in a position of power or authority (literary) 21. vt COMMUNICATION CONTACT SOMEBODY BY RADIO to get into contact with somebody by radio ○ Air traffic control was still trying to raise the missing plane. 22. vt MATHS MULTIPLY NUMBER to multiply a term or number by itself a particular number of times ○ 2 raised to the power of 4 is 16. 23. vti CARDS INCREASE BET OR BID in poker and other games, to increase a bet, or bet more than another player, often specifying the amount of the increase 24. vt CARDS INCREASE PARTNER'S BID in bridge, to make a higher bid in the suit bid

by your partner **25.** *vt* MIL **END SIEGE** to end a siege by withdrawing the besieging force or forcing it to withdraw **26.** *vt* POL, COMM **END SOMETHING** to bring a ban or restriction imposed on somebody to an end ○ *finally raised the arms embargo* **27.** *vt* NAUT **SEE LAND APPEAR ON HORIZON** to sight land on the horizon after a sea voyage ○ *The ship raised Bermuda two days after leaving New York.* **28.** *vt* COOK **MAKE DOUGH RISE** to make dough rise and swell by using yeast or a similar agent **29.** *vt* PHON **REPLACE VOWEL BY HIGHER VOWEL** to replace a vowel by one formed with the tongue higher in the mouth **30.** *vt* US FIN **FRAUDULENTLY INCREASE SOMETHING'S VALUE** to increase the face value of something, especially a cheque, in an attempt to defraud somebody ○ *The embezzler was caught raising cheques.* **31.** *vi* US same as **rise** (nonstandard) ○ *'Jimmy gazed at her in such consternation that he felt his hair begin to raise!'* (George Randolph Chester, *The Jingo*; 1912) ■ *n* **1.** *Aus, N Am* PAY INCREASE an increase in somebody's rate of pay **2.** ACT OF INCREASING the raising of somebody or something, or the amount by which somebody or something is raised, e.g. in cards [12C. < Old Norse *reisa* < Germanic] —**raisable** *adj* —**raiser** *n*

SYNONYMS *raise, elevate, lift, hoist*
CORE MEANING: to move something to a higher position
raise to cause something to move to a higher level or position ○ *Merrill raised her wrist to peer at her watch.* ○ *He raised his eyebrows and gave her a cool stare.* **elevate** to raise something to a higher level or position (less commonly used than 'raise') ○ *You might want to elevate the head of the bed at night.* **lift** to move something from one position to another, higher position ○ *She felt too exhausted even to lift the remote control off the sofa.* ○ *His colleagues had tried to lift him out with a rope and safety harness.* **hoist** to raise something, especially using a mechanical device such as a winch ○ *They made ready to hoist the sail.* ○ *An enormous crane hoisted the steel beams to the roof.*

raised beach /ráyzd-/ *n* a former beach found above the present shoreline of a sea or lake following a fall in water level or a rise in land level. Raised beaches are common in areas once glaciated, which rise as the land surface readjusts to the removal of the weight of a former icecap.

raised point *n* US HANDICRAFT same as **gros point**

raised work *n* embroidery stitches that produce a raised surface on the fabric or that are worked over a piece of padding

raisin /ráyz'n/ *n* a sweet grape that has been dried in the sun or by being processed with heat, usually to prevent spoiling and permit long-term storage [14C. Via French, 'grape' < Latin *racemus* 'bunch, cluster']

raisin bread *n* ANZ, US bread containing raisins, currants, or sultanas

raisin toast *n* ANZ bread containing raisins, currants, or sultanas, toasted

raison d'état /ráy zoN day taá/ (plural **raisons d'état** /pronunc. same/) *n* an overriding concern, usually the interests of the country concerned, that justifies political or diplomatic action that might otherwise be considered reprehensible [< French, 'reason of state']

raison d'être /ráy zoN déttrə/ (plural **raisons d'être** /pronunc. same/) *n* something that gives meaning or purpose to somebody's life, or the justification for something's existence [< French, 'reason for being']

raita /rítə/ *n* a South Asian dish served with curries, consisting of yoghurt usually mixed with finely chopped cucumber, mint, or garlic [Mid-20C. < Hindi *rāytā*]

Raj /raaj/ *n* in South Asia, the period of British rule up to 1947 of what are now the countries of India, Pakistan, Bangladesh, Nepal, Bhutan, and Sri Lanka [Late 18C. Via Hindi *rāj* < Sanskrit *rājya* 'kingdom, rule']

raja *n* POL another spelling of **rajah**

Rajab /rə jáb/ *n* in the Islamic calendar, the seventh month of the year. See table at **calendar** [Late 18C. < Arabic]

rajah /raájə/, **raja** *n* a prince or ruler in South Asia or

parts of Southeast Asia [Mid-16C. Via Hindi *rājā* < Sanskrit *rajan* 'king']

Rajasthan /raájə staan/, **Rājasthān** state in northwestern India, bordering Pakistan. Capital: Jaipur. Population: 56,473,122 (2001). Area: 342,239 sq. km/132,139 sq. mi.

Rajasthani /raájə staáni/ *n* **1.** an Indic group of languages spoken in northwestern India and neighbouring parts of Pakistan. Native speakers: 25 million. **2.** somebody who comes from Rajasthan [Early 20C. < Hindi *Rājasthāni* < *Rājasthān* 'Rajasthan'] —**Rajasthani** *adj*

Rajkot /raáj kót/ city and administrative headquarters of Rajkot District, in Gujarat State, west-central India. Population: 559,407 (1991).

Rajneesh /raaj neésh/, **Bhaghwan Shree** (1931–90) Indian spiritual teacher. As founder of the Neo-Sannyas Movement in the late 1960s, he established meditation centres in India, Europe, and the United States. Born **Mohan, Rajneesh Chandra**

Rajput /raáj pŏot/ *n* a member of one group of the Kshatriya caste, the second of the four Hindu castes [Late 16C. < Hindi *rājpūt* 'king's son' < Sanskrit *rajan* 'king' + *putra* 'son']

Rajya Sabha /raáajyə súbbə/ *n* the upper house of India's national parliament [< Sanskrit, 'state assembly']

Rakaia /rə kí ə/ river in the South Island, New Zealand. It rises in the Southern Alps and flows into the Pacific Ocean west of the Banks Peninsula. Length: 145 km/90 mi.

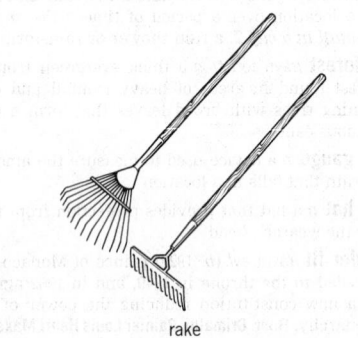

rake

rake[1] /rayk/ *n* **1.** LONG-HANDLED TOOTHED GARDENING TOOL a tool with a long handle and a head with long teeth, used for gathering leaves or cut grass, or for smoothing or loosening the surface of the soil in a garden **2.** TOOL RESEMBLING GARDEN RAKE a tool that is broadly similar to a garden rake but is used for a different purpose, e.g. digging clams or gathering money at a gambling table **3.** CLEARING, GATHERING, OR SMOOTHING an act of clearing, gathering, or smoothing something with a rake or similar implement **4.** ACT OF SEARCHING a search through something ■ *v* (**rakes, raking, raked**) **1.** *vti* MOVE SOMETHING WITH RAKE to gather something together, or remove or clear something, using a rake or similar implement ○ *raked up the dead leaves* **2.** *vti* WORK WITH RAKE to make something neat, smooth something out, or loosen something using a rake or similar tool **3.** *vti* SEARCH THROUGH SOMETHING to search through or examine something thoroughly, or make a search for something **4.** *vt* USE SOMETHING LIKE RAKE to draw or move something through or across something else like a rake ○ *She raked her fingers through her hair.* **5.** *vt* SCRAPE OR SCRATCH SOMETHING to claw, scrape, or scratch somebody or something with a dragging movement like the action of somebody using a rake **6.** *vti* PASS ACROSS SOMETHING to pass across the whole length or extent of something in a continuous sweeping movement, or cause something to do this ○ *The spotlight raked around the perimeter fence.* **7.** *vti* SHOOT ALONG LENGTH OF SOMETHING to aim shots from a gun or guns in quick succession over the whole length or extent of something ○ *The ship's cannon raked the land battery.* [Old English *raca, racu* < Germanic]

rake in *vt* to take in large quantities of something, especially money gained or earned with relatively little effort (informal)

rake over *vt* same as **rake up** (sense 1) (informal)

rake together *vt* to gather people or things together with difficulty (informal)

rake up *vt* (informal) **1.** to mention or bring up for discussion something unfortunate or undesirable that happened in the past **2.** same as **rake together**

rake[2] /rayk/ *n* **1.** SLANT OR SLOPE a slant away from an upright or perpendicular position, or an incline upwards from a flat or horizontal position such as that on a ship or a stage **2.** AVIAT ANGLE OF WING OR PROPELLER the angle that a wing or propeller blade of an aircraft makes with a perpendicular or line of symmetry ■ *vti* (**rakes, raking, raked**) ANGLE to design or build something with a slant or slope away from the vertical or horizontal, or be designed or built in this way ○ *a jet with wings that rake sharply back* [Early 17C. < ?]

rake[3] /rayk/ *n* an unrestrained indulger in pleasures and vices, e.g. drinking and gambling [Mid-17C. Shortening of *rakehell*, by folk etymology < obsolete *rakel* 'hasty, rash' Origin ?]

CULTURAL NOTE *The Rake's Progress*, a series of paintings (1735?) by British artist William Hogarth. These eight satirical scenes, which were much influenced by contemporary theatre, depict the moral decline of a young city gentleman who inherits a fortune and squanders it on vice. Hogarth created engravings of the same images, which were immensely popular. In 1951, Igor Stravinsky turned the story into an opera with a libretto by W. H. Auden.

rake[4] /rayk/ *n* a distinct break or shallow gully that slants obliquely across a rock face [14C. < Old Norse *rák* 'stripe, streak']

rake-and-scrape *vi* Carib to save money little by little, with great difficulty, usually for a specific purpose

rake-and-scrape band *n* Carib a rural folk-band consisting of skin drum, accordion, rattle, and bottle or piece of iron

rakee *n* BEVERAGES another spelling of **raki**

rake-off *n* a portion or share of a profit, fee, or something similar, especially as a bribe or other illegal or morally dubious payment (informal) [< RAKE[1]]

rakhi *n* HINDUISM same as **Raksha Bandhan**

raki /ráki, raa keé/, **rakee** *n* an aniseed-flavoured alcoholic drink from the eastern Mediterranean, especially a brandy made in Turkey and the Balkans from grapes, plums, or grain [Late 17C. Via Turkish *rāqī* < Arabic *arakī*]

rakish[1] /ráykish/ *adj* **1.** stylish in a dashing or sporty way ○ *a hat worn at a rakish angle* **2.** having a streamlined look that suggests rapid movement through the water ○ *a rakish yacht* [Early 19C. < RAKE[2]] —**rakishly** *adv* —**rakishness** *n*

rakish[2] /ráykish/ *adj* having or showing a strong concern for presenting a stylish self-confident appearance [Early 18C. < RAKE[3]] —**rakishly** *adv* —**rakishness** *adv*

Raksha Bandhan /rúk shaa búndən/, **Rakhi** *n* a Hindu festival celebrating the bond between brother and sister. Date: middle of Sravana. [< Sanskrit, 'knot of protection']

raku /raákoo/ *n* a pottery technique in which pots are raw-glazed at a low temperature then taken red-hot from the kiln and plunged in water or sawdust for reduction or carbonizing [Late 19C. < Japanese, 'ease, enjoyment']

rale /raal/, **râle** *n* an intermittent crackling or bubbling sound produced by fluid in the air passages and air sacs of the lungs and heard through a stethoscope [Early 19C. < French *râle* < *râler* 'make a rattling sound in the throat']

Raleigh /raáli, ráwli/ capital city of North Carolina, located in the centre of the state. Population: 306,944 (2002 estimate).

Raleigh, Sir Walter (1554–1618) English navigator and writer. A favourite of Queen Elizabeth I, he led three expeditions to the Americas, and made the first attempt to found an English colony at Roanoke Island, North Carolina (1585). He wrote his *History*

of the World (1614) while imprisoned for treason (1603–16?).

> '[History] hath triumphed over time, which besides it, nothing but eternity hath triumphed over.'
> [Sir Walter Raleigh, Preface, *The History of the World*; 1614]

rall. *abbr* MUSIC rallentando

rallentando /rállən tándō/ *adv* with a gradual slowing of pace (*used as a musical direction*) [Early 19C. < Italian, present participle of *rallentare* 'slow down'] —**rallentando** *adj*

rally[1] /rálli/ *n* (*plural* **-lies**) **1.** GATHERING a large meeting or gathering of people, usually organized by a movement or political party and intended to inspire and generate enthusiasm among those present **2.** MOTOR SPORTS CAR RACE a car race that is held on public roads using a route not known in advance by the drivers, with special rules for speed or time **3.** RACKET GAMES EXCHANGE OF SHOTS in tennis and other racket sports, an exchange of several shots between two opponents or sides before a point is scored **4.** RECOVERY OR IMPROVEMENT a sudden recovery or improvement after a setback, crisis, or period of illness, inactivity, or deterioration **5.** MIL REASSEMBLY OF TROOPS a regrouping of a disorganized military force and the re-establishment of command over it, or the signal calling for this ○ *The retreating hussars made a rally and drove the attackers back.* **6.** FIN RENEWED BUYING OF STOCKS a renewed buying of stocks after a period of selling, with a resultant rise in stock prices ○ *a rally in the industrial sector of the stock market* ■ *v* (**-lies, -lying, -lied**) **1.** *vti* GATHER TOGETHER FOR SOMETHING to come together, uniting for a common purpose or in a common cause, or call on people to do this ○ *The instinct of the party faithful was to rally behind the leader in a crisis.* **2.** *vti* MIL FORM TOGETHER AGAIN to reorganize after a setback and restore order and morale, or make people do this, especially by stopping troops retreating further ○ *The captain rallied his troops and formed a defensive line.* **3.** *vti* REVIVE OR RECOVER to recover or improve after a setback, crisis, or period of illness, inactivity, or deterioration, or make somebody or something do this ○ *Our spirits rallied once we had our first success.* **4.** *vi* FIN INCREASE IN VALUE to increase sharply in value or price owing to renewed buying by investors **5.** *vi* FIN BEGIN BUYING STOCKS AGAIN to be involved in renewed buying of stocks after a period of selling ○ *The market rallied in the afternoon.* **6.** *vi* RACKET GAMES EXCHANGE SHOTS in tennis and other racket sports, to exchange a series of shots before a point is scored [Late 16C. < French *rallier* 'reunite' < *alier* 'join, ally'] —**rallier** *n*

rally round *vi* to come to the aid of somebody in difficulty or need, offering either practical or moral support

rally[2] /rálli/ (**-lies, -lying, -lied**) *vt* to tease or ridicule somebody in a friendly or good-humoured way ○ *She rallied him about his cooking skills.* [Mid-17C. < French *railler* (see RAIL[2])]

rallycross /rálli kross/ *n* motor racing on a circuit partly on roads and partly across country [Mid-20C. < RALLY[1] + AUTOCROSS]

rallying /rálli ing/ *n* car racing on public roads using a route not known in advance by the drivers and with special rules for speed or time

ralph /ralf/ (**ralphs, ralphing, ralphed**) *vi* US same as **vomit** (*slang*) [Late 20C. Probably < the man's first name *Ralph*, as supposedly resembling the sound of vomiting]

ram /ram/ *n* **1.** MALE SHEEP a male sheep **2.** BATTERING OR CRUSHING DEVICE a device designed to batter, crush, press, or push something, e.g. a projecting underwater part of a boat's prow or the weight dropped by a pile driver **3.** ENG same as **hydraulic ram 4.** WARSHIP WITH RAM formerly, a warship equipped with a projecting underwater part on the prow that was designed to make a hole in the hull of an enemy warship ■ *v* (**rams, ramming, rammed**) **1.** *vti* STRIKE SOMETHING WITH GREAT FORCE to hit or collide with something, with great force or violence, or make something do this ○ *She swerved, almost ramming into a wall.* **2.** *vt* COLLIDE WITH SOMETHING DELIBERATELY to collide with another ship or vehicle deliberately in order

to sink, disable, or damage it ○ *The police car rammed the getaway vehicle and pushed it off the road.* **3.** *vt* FORCE SOMETHING INTO PLACE to press, force, or push something into place ○ *He quickly rammed another charge down the barrel and took aim.* **4.** *vt* US POL FORCE ACCEPTANCE OF SOMETHING to force the passage of a bill or acceptance of a suggestion, usually despite strong objection ○ *rammed the legislation through Congress* **5.** *vt* PRESENT SOMETHING VERY FORCEFULLY to present something forcefully in order to impress and convince people ○ *In a series of high-profile interviews she rammed home her message.* ■ *adj* Carib same as **boar** [Old English *ram(m)*] —**rammer** *n*

Ram /ram/ *n* ZODIAC same as **Aries** (sense 2)

RAM *abbr* **1.** /ram/ COMPUT random-access memory **2.** PHYS relative atomic mass **3.** ENG rocket-assisted motor **4.** MUSIC Royal Academy of Music

r.a.m. *abbr* relative atomic mass

Rama /raáma/ *n* in Hinduism, an incarnation (**avatar**) of the god Vishnu

Rama IX /raáma/ (b. 1927) king of Thailand. He ascended the throne in 1950. Born **Bhumibol Adulyadej**

Ramadan /rámmə daán, -dan/ *n* **1.** in the Islamic calendar, the ninth month of the year. During Ramadan, Muslims fast between dawn and dusk. See table at **calendar 2.** the daily fast between sunrise and sunset practised during Ramadan [Late 16C. < Arabic, 'the hot month' < *ramaḍ* 'dryness']

Ramakrishna /raamə kríshnə/, **Sri** (1834–86) Indian religious teacher. He taught that all mystical religious experiences are equally valid and was instrumental in bringing about the 19th-century Hindu revival in India. His followers founded the Ramakrishna Mission. Born **Chatterji, Gadadhar**

Raman /raámən/, **Sir Chandrasekhara** (1888–1970) Indian physicist. His work on molecular diffraction of light won him the Nobel Prize in physics (1930). Full name **Raman, Sir Chandrasekhara Venkata**

Raman effect *n* the change in wavelength and phase exhibited by monochromatic light passing through a transparent medium. The scattering that results is used in Raman spectroscopy to obtain information about the structure of molecules. [Early 20C. After Sir Chandrasekhara Venkata RAMAN]

ramate *adj* BIOL same as **ramose**

Ramayana /raa mí ənə/ *n* a great epic of the Hindu religion and of classical Sanskrit literature that tells of the adventures of Rama, an incarnation (**avatar**) of the god Vishnu

Dame Marie Rambert

Rambert /raam báir/, **Dame Marie** (1888–1982) Polish-born British ballet dancer and teacher. She founded the Ballet Rambert (1926), later called the Rambert Dance Company, which promoted the work of British choreographers. Born **Rambach, Miriam**

> 'That scene began with the Chosen Virgin...her folded hands under her right cheek, her feet turned in, in a truly prehistoric and beautiful pose. But to the audience of the time it appeared ugly and comical...and yet now there is no doubt that a masterpiece had been created that night.'
> [Dame Marie Rambert, *Quicksilver*; 1913]

ramble /rámb'l/ *vi* (**-bles, -bling, -bled**) **1.** TALK OR WRITE

AIMLESSLY to talk or write for a long time, not always keeping to the intended subject or tending to change the subject ○ *The speaker rambled on for over an hour.* **2.** WALK FOR PLEASURE to go for a walk for pleasure, usually in the countryside and sometimes without a fixed route in mind ○ *He had spent a week rambling about among the villages of the Apennines.* **3.** FOLLOW CHANGING COURSE to have, follow, or proceed along a winding or often changing course ○ *The path rambled though the fields down to the river.* **4.** GROW IN RANDOM WAY to grow in random directions, usually covering a sizable area in the process ○ *Vines rambled all over the low stone wall.* ■ *n* WALK TAKEN FOR PLEASURE a walk for pleasure, usually in the countryside and sometimes without a fixed route in mind ○ *a ramble through the woods* [15C. Origin ?]

rambler /rámblər/ *n* **1.** WALKER somebody who walks in the countryside for pleasure **2.** SOMEBODY WHO TALKS TOO MUCH somebody who talks or writes for a long time, not always keeping to the intended subject or tending to change the subject **3.** CLIMBING ROSE a hybrid climbing rose with long flexible canes and clusters of small double flowers

rambling /rámbling/ *adj* **1.** NOT TO POINT continuing for too long and with many changes of subject ○ *a long, rambling story* **2.** SPREAD OUT built or spread over a large area and not clearly organized or regular in shape ○ *a rambling old house* **3.** GROWING AS RAMBLER growing with long straggling shoots **4.** MEANDERING not following a direct course ○ *a narrow rambling path through the hills* **5.** PREFERRING TO ROAM preferring to move from place to place rather than stay in one place or settle down —**ramblingly** *adv*

SYNONYMS See *wordy*.

Rambo /rámbō/ (*plural* **-bos**) *n* an aggressive or violent person who breaks rules or laws to achieve what he or she believes to be right (*slang*) [Late 20C. After John *Rambo*, aggressive protagonist in the film *First Blood* (1982)]

Rambouillet /rámboōyay/ town in Yvelines Department, north-central France, southwest of Paris. The town's chateau is the French president's summer residence and is used for international conferences. Population: 24,758 (1999).

rambunctious /ram búngkshəss/ *adj* noisy, very active, and hard to control, usually as a result of excitement or youthful energy (*informal*) [Mid-19C. Origin ?] —**rambunctiously** *adv* —**rambunctiousness** *n*

rambutan /ram boót'n/ *n* **1.** an oval red spiny fruit with a mildly acidic taste **2.** a tree that produces rambutans. Native to: Malaysia. Latin name: *Nephelium lappaceum.* [Early 18C. < Malay, < *rambut* 'hair'; from the hairy skin of the fruit]

RAMC *abbr* Royal Army Medical Corps

ramekin /rámmikin/, **ramequin** *n* **1.** a small ovenproof dish with vertical fluted sides designed to hold a single serving of a prepared food, especially one that is baked **2.** a portion of food cooked and served in a ramekin [Early 18C. Via French < Middle Dutch *rameken*, literally 'little cream' < *ram* 'cream']

ramen /ráymən/ *n* a Japanese dish of thin white noodles in small dried cakes, served in a thin well-flavoured soup or stock [Late 20C. Via Japanese *rāmen* < Chinese *lāmiàn* 'pulled noodles']

ramequin *n* HOUSEHOLD, FOOD another spelling of **ramekin**

Rameses II /rámmə seez/, **Ramses II** /rámseez/ (*fl* 13th century BC) Egyptian pharaoh. His long and prosperous reign (1279–13 BC), which marked the pinnacle of Egypt's power, saw the building of numerous monuments, including the sandstone temples at Abu Simbel. The Exodus of the Israelites from Egypt is thought to have occurred during his rule. Known as **Rameses the Great**

Rameses III, **Ramses III** (*fl* 12th century BC) Egyptian pharaoh. As pharaoh (1184–53 BC), he was a great military leader, repeatedly saving the country from invasion, notably by the Libyans.

ramet /ráymət/ *n* a member of a collection of organisms, cells, or molecular segments (**clone**) that are genetically identical direct descendants of a

single parent by asexual reproduction [Early 20C. < Latin *ramus* 'branch']

rami BIOL plural of **ramus**

ramie /rámmi/ *n* **1.** STRONG FIBRE a lustrous soft durable fibre obtained from the bark of a bush. Use: fabric, rope. **2.** CLOTH fabric made from ramie fibre **3.** ASIAN BUSH a perennial bush whose bark yields ramie. Native to: Asia. Latin name: *Boehmeria nivea*. [Early 19C. < Malay *rami*]

ramification /rámmifi káysh'n/ *n* **1.** COMPLICATING RESULT a usually unintended consequence of an action, decision, or judgment that may complicate a situation or make the desired result more difficult to achieve ○ *an unexpected ramification of a new law* **2.** BRANCHING the process of dividing or spreading out into branches **3.** BRANCH a branch or arrangement of branches

ramiform /rámmi fawrm/ *adj* spreading out like branches or having the form of a branch or branches [Mid-19C. < Latin *ramus* 'branch']

ramify /rámmi fī/ (**-fies, -fying, -fied**) *vi* **1.** to divide into branches or similar parts **2.** to have usually unintended consequences that may complicate a situation or make the desired result more difficult to achieve ○ *Their difficulties ramified after they made the suggested changes.* [Mid-16C. Via Old French *ramifier* < medieval Latin *ramificare* < Latin *ramus* 'branch']

ramjet /rám jet/ *n* a jet engine in which fuel is burned in a duct with air compressed by the forward motion of the aircraft

rammy /rámmi/ (*plural* **-mies**) *n Scotland* a noisy argument or fight (*informal*) [Mid-20C. < ?]

ramose /ráy mōss, ra móss/, **ramous** /ráy məss/, **ramate** /ráy mayt/ *adj* having many branches or divided into many branches [Late 17C. < Latin *ramosus* 'having many branches' < *ramus* 'branch'] —**ramosely** *adv*

ramp[1] /ramp/ *n* **1.** SLOPING PATH OR ACCESS a sloping surface that allows access from one level to a higher or lower level, or raises something up above floor or ground level ○ *The ship slid slowly down the ramp into the water.* **2.** MOVABLE STAIRS a movable set of stairs used for boarding or disembarking from an aircraft **3.** CURVED BEND IN HANDRAIL a curved bend or slope in a handrail or coping where it changes direction, e.g. on a stair landing **4.** ROAD RIDGE a raised part of a road constructed to make traffic slow down ■ *vt* (**ramps, ramping, ramped**) BUILD SOMETHING WITH SLOPE to build something with a sloped surface, or provide something with a ramp ○ *The entrance must be ramped for wheelchair access.* [Late 18C. < French *rampe* < *ramper* 'crawl, creep, rear up'] —**ramped** *adj*

ramp up *vti* to cause the level or intensity of something to increase sharply, or increase in this way ○*As business ramps up to manage greater responsibility for its social and environmental impacts...'* (*Marketing Week*; December 1998)

ramp[2] /ramp/ (**ramps, ramping, ramped**) *vi* **1.** ACT THREATENINGLY to act in a threatening manner or assume a threatening stance, e.g. rearing with the forelegs ready to strike **2.** MOVE VIOLENTLY OR THREATENINGLY to move or rush violently, threateningly, or furiously **3.** HERALDRY BE SHOWN REARING UP IN PROFILE to be in the rampant position ○ *an old seal marked with a ramping lion on a shield* [14C. < French *ramper* 'crawl, creep, rear up']

rampage *vi* /ram páyj/ (**-pages, -paging, -paged**) to engage in uncontrolled violent or riotous behaviour, or commit a series of violent or riotous acts ○ *This weather system has rampaged up the coast, with blizzards and howling winds causing severe damage.* ■ *n* /rám payj, ram páyj/ an outburst of uncontrolled violent or riotous behaviour, or a series of violent or riotous actions [Early 18C. Probably < RAMP[2]] —**rampageous** /ram páyjəss/ *adj* —**rampageously** *adv* —**rampager** *n* —**rampaging** *adj* ◇ **on the rampage** behaving in a wild and uncontrolled manner

rampant /rámpənt/ *adj* **1.** OCCURRING UNCHECKED happening in an unrestrained manner, usually so as to be regarded as a menace ○ *rampant inflation* **2.** BOT GROWING WILDLY growing strongly and to a very large size, or spreading uncontrollably **3.** FIERCE exhibiting ferocious behaviour or fierceness of spirit **4.** HER-

ALDRY ON HIND LEGS describes a heraldic beast depicted rearing up, in profile, and with its forelegs raised, the right one above the left **5.** CONSTR WITH UNEQUAL SUPPORTS having a support or an abutment that is higher on one side than the other [14C. < French, present participle of *ramper* 'rear up'] —**rampancy** *n* —**rampantly** *adv*

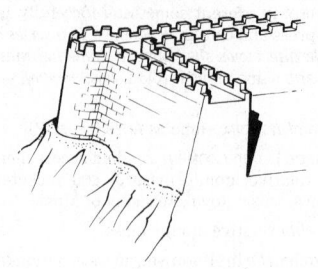

rampart

rampart /rám paart/ *n* a defensive fortification made of an earthen embankment, often topped by a low protective wall ■ *vt* (**-parts, -parting, -parted**) to protect somebody or something with ramparts or something similar ○ *walls ramparting a town* [Late 16C. < French *rempart* < *remparer* 'defend again' < Old French *emparer* 'defend']

rampike /rám pīk/ *n* a dead tree that is still standing, especially one reduced by fire to little more than a trunk [Late 16C. < ?]

rampion /rámpi ən/ *n* **1.** a plant with a white edible root used in salads. Flowers: bluish, in clusters. Native to: Europe, Asia. Latin name: *Campanula rapunculus*. **2.** a plant related to the rampion. Flowers: usually blue. Genus: *Phyteuma*. [Late 16C. Probably alteration of Old French *raiponce* < Old Italian *raponzo* < Latin *rapum* 'turnip']

Rampur /rám pŏŏr/ city and administrative headquarters of Rampur District, Uttar Pradesh State, northern India. Population: 243,742 (1991).

ram-raid *n* a theft carried out by driving a stolen car through a shop window and stealing the goods inside ■ *vti* to carry out a ram-raid on a shop — **ram-raider** *n* —**ram-raiding** *n*

ramrod /rám rod/ *n* **1.** ARMS ROD FOR LOADING GUN a rod for loading a charge into a muzzle-loading musket, cannon, or other gun **2.** ARMS ROD FOR CLEANING GUN a rod for cleaning the barrel of a firearm **3.** *US* STERN OR STRICT OVERSEER a stern or strict boss, commander, or other person in a position of authority ■ *adv* RIGIDLY rigidly or stiffly ○ *ramrod straight* ■ *vt* (**-rods, -rodding, -rodded**) *US* **1.** PUSH SOMETHING THROUGH BY FORCE to push through or achieve something by force or threat ○ *tried to ramrod the bill through the legislature* **2.** CONTROL SOMEBODY STRICTLY to exert strict control over somebody or enforce strict discipline on somebody

Ramsay /rámzi/, **Sir William** (1852–1916) British chemist. He was the first to isolate helium from terrestrial sources (1895), and discovered argon (in collaboration with Lord Rayleigh), neon, krypton, and xenon. He was awarded the Nobel Prize in chemistry (1904).

Ramses ♦ **Rameses II, Rameses III**

Ramsey /rámzi/, **Sir Alf** (1922–99) British footballer and manager. He was manager of the England team (1963–74), which he led to a World Cup victory (1966). Full name **Ramsey, Sir Alfred Ernest**

Ramsey Island islet off the coast of Pembrokeshire, Wales. Area: 3 sq. km/1 sq. mi.

Ramsgate /rámz gayt, rámzgit/ town on the eastern coast of Kent, southeastern England. Population: 37,895 (1991).

ramshackle /rám shak'l/ *adj* poorly maintained or constructed and seeming likely to fall apart or collapse [Mid-19C. Back-formation < *ramshackled*, alteration of obsolete *ransackled* < RANSACK]

ram's horn *n* JUDAISM same as **shofar**

ramsons /rámzə'nz/ *n* a wild garlic with round heads of white flowers and a bulbous root. Native to: Europe, Asia. Latin name: *Allium ursinum*. (*takes a singular verb*) [Mid-16C. < Old English *hram(e)san*, plural of *hramsa* < Germanic, later misinterpreted as singular]

ramulose /rámmyŏŏ lōss/ *adj* having many small branches [Mid-18C. < Latin *ramulosus* 'full of branching veins' < *ramus* 'branch']

ramus /ráyməss/ (*plural* **-mi** /-mī/) *n* a small branching body part, e.g. a stem, bone, or nerve [Early 18C. < Latin, 'branch']

ran past tense of **run**

Ran /ran/ *n* in Norse mythology, the goddess of the sea

RAN *abbr* **1.** request for authority to negotiate **2.** *Aus* Royal Australian Navy

Rance /raaNss/ river in Brittany, in northwestern France. Length: 100 km/62 mi.

ranch /raanch/ *n* **1.** LIVESTOCK FARM ON OPEN LAND a farm where cattle, sheep, horses, or other livestock are raised on large tracts of open land, especially in North and South America and Australia **2.** SPECIALIZED FARM a large farm devoted to keeping a particular type of animal or growing a particular type of crop **3.** *N Am* BUILDINGS same as **ranch house 4.** *N Am* FOOD same as **ranch dressing** ■ *v* (**ranches, ranching, ranched**) **1.** *vi* WORK ON RANCH to own, manage, or work on a ranch **2.** *vt* RAISE ANIMALS ON RANCH to breed, raise, or tend animals on a ranch ○ *ranching cattle in western Texas* [Early 19C. Via American Spanish *rancho* < Spanish, 'group of people who eat together' < French *ranger* 'arrange in position' < *rang* 'row, line'] —**ranching** *n*

ranch dressing *n N Am* a creamy salad dressing that has a mixture of mayonnaise and buttermilk or milk as its base

rancher /ráanchər/ *n* **1.** somebody who owns or manages a ranch **2.** *N Am* BUILDINGS same as **ranch house** (sense 2)

ranchera /ran cháirə/ *n* a traditional Mexican ballad, often a love song, accompanied by a mariachi band [< American Spanish, literally 'woman who runs a ranch', form of RANCHERO]

ranchero /raan cháirō/ (*plural* **-ros**) *n Southwest US* somebody who owns or manages a ranch, especially a Hispanic rancher in the southwestern United States and in Latin America [Early 19C. < American Spanish < *rancho* (see RANCH)]

ranch house *n N Am* **1.** the building on a ranch where the owner or manager lives that usually has one storey, a spread-out floor plan, and a roof that is not steeply pitched **2.** a single-storey house built in a style similar to a traditional ranch house, especially one located in a suburban housing development

Ranchi /ránchi/ capital city of Bihar State, northeastern India. Population: 862,850 (2001).

rancho /ráanchō/ (*plural* **-chos**) *n Southwest US* **1.** AGRIC same as **ranch** *n* (senses 1–2), **ranch house** (sense 1) **2.** a hut where a ranch worker lives, or a group of such huts [Early 19C. < American Spanish (see RANCH)]

rancid /ránssid/ *adj* **1.** having the strong disagreeable smell or taste of decomposing fats or oils **2.** causing disgust or offence [Mid-17C. < Latin *rancidus* 'stinking, rank' < *rancere* 'to stink'] —**rancidity** /ran síddəti/ *n* —**rancidness** *n*

rancor *n US* spelling of **rancour**

rancour /rángkər/ *n* a bitter, deeply held, and long-lasting ill will or resentment [12C. Via French < Latin *rancor* 'stinking smell or offensive flavour, bitterness' < *rancere* 'to stink'] —**rancorous** *adj* —**rancorously** *adv* —**rancorousness** *n*

rand /rand/ (*plural same*) *n* the main unit of South African currency. See table at **currency** [Mid-20C. After the *Rand*, gold-mining district in Transvaal, South Africa < Afrikaans *rand* 'ridge of ground' < Dutch, 'edge']

randan[1] /ran dán, rán dan/ *n* a noisy and boisterous celebration (*dated informal*) [Early 18C. < ?]

randan[2] /ran dán, rán dan/ *n* **1.** a boat designed to be rowed by three people **2.** the method of rowing a

randan, with one person using two oars and the other two using one oar each [Early 19C. Origin ?]

R & B *abbr* rhythm and blues

R & D *abbr* research and development

randem /rándəm/ *adv* with a team of three horses harnessed one behind another ■ *n* a team of three horses harnessed one behind another, or a carriage pulled by such a team [Late 19C. Probably alteration of RANDOM, after TANDEM]

random /rándəm/ *adj* **1. WITHOUT PATTERN** done, chosen, or occurring without an identifiable pattern, plan, system, or connection ○ *random checks* **2. LACKING REGULARITY** with a pattern or in sizes that are not uniform or regular ○ *a wall constructed of random stones* **3.** STATS **EQUALLY LIKELY** relating or belonging to a set in which all the members have the same probability of occurrence ○ *a random sampling* **4.** STATS **HAVING DEFINITE PROBABILITY** relating to or involving variables that have undetermined value but definite probability [Mid-17C. < Old French *randon* 'impetuosity, rush' < *randir* 'run' < Germanic] —**randomly** *adv* —**randomness** *n* ◇ **at random** without an identifiable pattern, plan, system, or connection

random-access *adj* relating to the capability of a computer to obtain information from any memory location without having to begin its search at the memory's starting-point and work through it in sequence ○ *random-access input/output*

random-access memory *n* the primary working memory in a computer, used for the temporary storage of programs and data and in which the data can be accessed directly and modified

randomize /rándə mīz/ (**-izes, -izing, -ized**), **randomise** (**-ises, -ising, -ised**) *vti* to arrange or select items so that no identifiable pattern or order determines the resulting arrangement or the selection process —**randomization** /rándə mī záysh'n/ *n* —**randomizer** *n*

random number *n* a number in a series of numbers that have no pattern in their progression

random sample *n* a sample of subjects that is randomly selected from a group and is therefore assumed to be representative of that group

random segregation *n* a principle in genetics holding that during meiosis the two separated partners of a chromosome pair are distributed randomly to the reproductive cells (**gametes**), each gamete having an equal chance of receiving either chromosome

random variable *n* a variable that can have any of a range of values that occur randomly but can be described probabilistically

random walk *n* a mathematical model applicable to various processes such as diffusion in which the direction and sometimes the magnitude of successive steps are determined by chance

R and R, R & R *abbr* **1.** MIL rest and recreation **2.** rest and relaxation

randy /rándi/ (**-dier, -diest**) *adj* having a strong desire for sex (*informal*) [Late 17C. < *rand*, Scots variant of RANT] —**randily** *adv* —**randiness** *n*

ranee *n* POL another spelling of **rani**

rang past tense of **ring**[2]

rangatira /rángə tèerə/ *n NZ* a Maori chief or noble [Early 19C. < Maori]

range /raynj/ *n* **1. VARIETY** the number and variety of different things that something includes or can deal with ○ *dealing with a wide range of people* **2. NUMBER OF SIMILAR THINGS** a number or set of different things belonging to the same general category **3. SET OF PRODUCTS PRODUCED OR SOLD** all the products produced or sold by somebody considered as a set, often ranked according to price and degree of sophistication ○ *the best-selling product in its range* **4. CATEGORY DEFINED BY LIMITS** a category defined by an upper and a lower limit ○ *the age range 25 to 45* **5. AREA OF EFFECTIVE OPERATION** the area within which, or the distance over which, something can operate effectively ○ *out of range of the radar* **6.** MIL **FARTHEST DISTANCE FOR EFFECTIVE OPERATION** the farthest distance at which something can operate effectively, e.g. the farthest distance to which a gun can shoot a bullet or shell **7.** ARMS **DISTANCE BETWEEN WEAPON AND TARGET** the distance between two things, especially a gun or a tracking device and the object it is aimed at **8. PRACTICE AREA** a place where an activity is practised or performed ○ *a shooting range* **9.** TRANSP **DISTANCE TRAVELLED WITHOUT REFUELLING** the farthest distance that a vehicle or aircraft can travel without needing to refuel **10.** MUSIC **NOTES PRODUCED BY VOICE OR INSTRUMENT** the notes, from highest to lowest, that somebody's voice or a musical instrument can produce **11.** MUSIC **REGISTER OF MUSICAL PASSAGE** the register of a musical passage, from its highest to lowest note **12.** GEOG **ROW OF MOUNTAINS** a number of mountains or hills forming a connected row or group **13. MOVEMENT OVER AREA** movement over or within an area **14.** *N Am* AGRIC **OPEN LAND FOR GRAZING FARM ANIMALS** a large area of open land on which farm animals can graze **15.** ECOL **AREA WHERE ORGANISM IS NORMALLY FOUND** a geographical area in which a species of organism normally lives or grows **16.** HOUSEHOLD **STOVE** a cooking stove with one or more ovens and with hot plates or burners on top, especially a large old-fashioned one heated with solid fuel and often kept constantly burning **17.** MATHS **SET OF VALUES** the set of values that can be taken by a function or a variable **18.** STATS **EXTENT OF FREQUENCY DISTRIBUTION** the difference between the smallest and the largest value in a frequency distribution **19. TWO-SIDED BOOKCASE** a large free-standing bookcase in a library that is built to hold books on both sides **20.** *Can, Western US* CONSTR **NORTH-SOUTH STRIP OF TOWNSHIPS** a north-south strip of townships six miles square and numbered east and west from a meridian in a public land survey ■ *v* (**ranges, ranging, ranged**) **1.** *vi* **VARY BETWEEN LIMITS** to vary between a particular upper and lower limit ○ *prices ranging from £1.50 to £10.00* **2.** *vi* **DEAL WITH NUMBER OF THINGS** to include, cover, or deal with a number of different things, usually within the same context ○ *Her interests range from tennis to parachuting.* **3.** *vt* **ARRANGE THINGS IN LINE** to arrange things in a particular way, especially in a line or row (*usually passive*) ○ *Jars of pickles were ranged along the kitchen shelf.* **4.** *vt* **ALIGN OR CLASSIFY SOMEBODY OR SOMETHING** to put something or somebody into a particular group or category ○ *The cadets were ranged into platoons by height.* **5. range yourself** *vr* **GIVE PERSONAL SUPPORT** to support or side with somebody **6.** *vti* **TRAVEL FREELY AND EXTENSIVELY** to move freely across, through, or back and forth within a particular area ○ *She allowed her thoughts to range freely over the events of the previous week.* **7.** *vti* **POINT OR AIM SOMETHING** to point or aim something such as a gun, missile, or telescope at an object, or be pointed at an object **8.** *vi* ARMS **TRAVEL PARTICULAR DISTANCE** to be able to travel a particular distance (*refers to bullets or missiles*) **9.** *vi* ECOL **LIVE OR GROW** to live or grow in a particular geographical area (*refers to animals or plants*) ○ *Buffalo once ranged over the plains.* **10.** *vt* AGRIC **PUT LIVESTOCK OUT TO GRAZE** to put livestock out to graze on a large open area [13C. < Old French *rangier* 'put in order' < *ranc* 'row']

rangefinder /ráynj fīndər/ *n* an instrument used to estimate the distance between the user and an object, especially one that is to be shot at or photographed

rangeland /ráynj land/ *n* AGRIC same as **range** *n* (sense 14)

range pole *n* CONSTR same as **ranging pole**

ranger /ráynjər/ *n* **1. OFFICIAL OVERSEEING COUNTRYSIDE AREA** somebody whose job is to oversee, protect, and patrol a forest or an area of natural beauty **2.** *US* **MEMBER OF RURAL POLICE UNIT** a member of an armed law-enforcement unit in parts of the United States, especially Texas **3. WANDERER** somebody who wanders

Ranger *n* **1.** a member of the senior branch of the Guides for girls between 14 and 19 years of age **2.** a member of a military unit of the United States Army specially trained for commando raids

ranging pole /ráynjing-/, **ranging rod** *n* a pole, usually held vertically, used to mark a specific position when surveying a plot of land

rangiora /rúngi awrə/ *n* an evergreen tree with large oval leaves. Flowers: small, greenish-white. Native to: New Zealand. Latin name: *Brachyglottis repanda*. [Mid-19C. < Maori]

Rangitaiki /rúngi tī ki/ river in the centre of the North Island, New Zealand. It flows northwards into the Bay of Plenty. Length: 193 km/120 mi.

Rangitata /rúngi taa taa/ river in the east of the South Island, New Zealand, formed by the confluence of the rivers Clyde and Havelock, and emptying into Canterbury Bight. Length: 121 km/75 mi.

Rangitikei /rúngi tī kay/ river in the centre of the North Island, New Zealand. It rises in the Kaimanawa Mountains and flows southwards into South Taranaki Bight. Length: 241 km/150 mi.

Rangitoto Island /ráng gə tṓtō-/ uninhabited volcanic island in Hauraki Gulf, off the northeastern coast of the North Island, New Zealand. Area: 23 sq. km/9 sq. mi.

Rangoon /rang gṓon/ former name for **Yangon** (*until 1989*)

rangy /ráynji/ (**-ier, -iest**) *adj* tall and lean, with long legs —**ranginess** *n*

rani /raáni, raa neé/, **ranee** *n* a Hindu queen or princess, or the wife or widow of a rajah in South Asia or parts of Southeast Asia [Late 17C. Via Hindi < Sanskrit *rājñī* < *rājan* 'king']

ranitidine /ra nítti deen/ *n* a drug that reduces the secretion of stomach acid. Use: to treat peptic ulcers.

Ranjit Singh /ránjit síng/ (1780–1839) Indian warrior. He founded the Sikh kingdom in the Punjab, India, which he built up from a small confederacy. It was annexed by the British in 1849.

rank[1] /rangk/ *n* **1. OFFICIAL STATUS WITHIN ORGANIZATION** an official title or category that shows the holder's relative importance or seniority within an organization, especially a military force ○ *attained the rank of colonel* **2. STATUS IN RELATION TO OTHERS** the degree of importance or excellence of somebody or something in relation to other members of a group ○ *a political journalist of the first rank* **3. HIGH STATUS** high status or importance, especially in the armed forces or among the wealthy **4. LINE OF PEOPLE OR THINGS** a line of people, especially soldiers, or things standing or placed side by side **5.** TRANSP **PLACE FOR TAXIS TO WAIT** a place where taxis wait for passengers **6.** CHESS **HORIZONTAL LINE OF SQUARES ON CHESSBOARD** a horizontal line of squares on a chessboard **7.** MATHS **LINEARLY INDEPENDENT ROWS** in mathematics, the largest number of linearly independent rows in a matrix **8.** MUSIC **SET OF ORGAN PIPES** a set of organ pipes linked to a particular stop ■ **ranks** *npl* **1. ORDINARY SOLDIERS** members of the armed forces who are not officers, or the ordinary members of any organization who do not hold high office **2. PEOPLE IN GROUP OR CATEGORY** people belonging to a particular group or category, considered collectively and usually with the understanding that there are large numbers of them ○ *among the ranks of her supporters* ■ *v* (**ranks, ranking, ranked**) **1.** *vti* **HAVE OR GIVE SOMETHING RATING** to have a particular rating, position, or importance in relation to other people or things in a group, or give somebody or something such a rating ○ *This ranks fairly high on my list of desirable improvements.* **2.** *vti* **POSITION THINGS OR STAND IN ROWS** to place people or things in a row or rows, or stand or be placed in rows (*usually passive*) **3.** *vt N Am* **OUTRANK SOMEBODY OR SOMETHING** to have a higher rank than and take precedence over somebody or something else in a group, especially in a hierarchy ○ *A colonel ranks a major.* [14C. < Old French *ranc* 'row' < Germanic] ◇ **break ranks 1.** to leave an ordered line of soldiers, especially when being attacked **2.** to stop supporting the policy of a group of which you are a member ◇ **close ranks 1.** to form into tight disciplined lines in preparation for an expected attack (*refers to soldiers*) **2.** to unite closely, especially when taking defensive action ◇ **pull rank (on somebody)** to assert authority over somebody in a hierarchy, especially in order to obtain personal advantage ◇ **rise (up) through the ranks** to reach a senior position in an organization by gradual promotions from an originally low position

rank[2] /rangk/ *adj* **1. UTTER** of the most extreme and obvious kind ○ *a rank amateur* **2. FOUL** foul-smelling or foul-tasting ○ *the rank odour of rotten eggs* **3. TOO VIGOROUS** describes vegetation that is growing too

vigorously ○*'the rank ailanthus'* (T.S. Eliot, *The Dry Salvages*; 1941) **4.** same as **impudent** (*slang; used in Black English*) [Old English *ranc* 'haughty, full-grown', of uncertain origin: perhaps ultimately from an Indo-European word meaning 'to move straight ahead' that is also the ancestor of English *right*] —**rankly** *adv* —**rankness** *n*

Rank /rangk/, **J. Arthur, 1st Baron** (1888–1972) British film magnate. The head of several British film companies, he was a leading figure in the industry, especially in the 1940s and 1950s. Full name **Rank, Joseph Arthur**

Rank, Otto (1884–1939) Austrian psychologist and psychotherapist. An early associate of Freud, he applied Freudian techniques to the interpretation of myths in *Myth of the Birth of the Hero* (1909), but later differed from Freud in ascribing neurosis to birth trauma.

rank and file *n* **1.** the majority of a group or organization, especially all of the members who have no power or influence ○ *the union's rank and file* **2.** the ordinary troops in a military organization, excluding officers —**rank-and-file** *adj* —**rank and filer** *n*

rank correlation *n* an assessment of the extent to which different ways of ranking the members of a set correlate with one another

ranker /rángkər/ *n* **1.** a private in the army **2.** a commissioned army officer who has previously served as a private

rankin' /rángkin/ *adj* of the best quality or the highest standard (*slang; used in Black English*)

Rankine scale /rángkin-/ *n* an absolute temperature scale in which each degree equals one degree on the Fahrenheit scale, with the freezing point of water being 491.67° and its boiling point 671.67° [Mid-19C. After the W. J. M. *Rankine* (1820–72), British physicist and engineer]

ranking /rángking/ *n* POSITION IN RELATION TO OTHERS the position or status held by or allocated to somebody or something in relation to others in a group ■ *adj* *N Am* **1.** FOREMOST considered to be the most eminent or important of the members of a particular group ○ *the ranking diplomat at the reception* **2.** HOLDING HIGH RANK holding a high rank in a military or other organization

rankle /rángk'l/ (**-kles, -kling, -kled**) *vi* to cause persistent feelings of bitterness, resentment, or anger ○ *It still rankles after all these years.* [14C. < Old French *raoncler* < *raoncle* 'festering sore', literally 'little snake (bite)' < Latin *dracunculus* < *draco* (see DRAGON)]

Rann of Kutch /rán əv kúch, -kŏŏch/ region of mud flats and salt marshes in western India and southern Pakistan. Area: 21,000 sq. km/8,100 sq. mi.

ransack /rán sak/ (**-sacks, -sacking, -sacked**) *vt* **1.** to go through a place stealing some things and usually destroying or spoiling everything else **2.** to search something very thoroughly but handling things carelessly ○ *I ransacked the drawers but couldn't find my keys.* [13C. < Old Norse *rannsaka* < *rann* 'house' + *-saka* 'search'] —**ransacker** *n*

ransom /ránsəm/ *n* **1.** MONEY DEMANDED FOR RELEASING CAPTIVE a sum of money demanded or paid for the release of somebody who is being held prisoner **2.** RELEASE OF PRISONER the release of a prisoner in return for the payment of money **3.** DELIVERANCE the act of saving somebody from an oppressed condition or dangerous situation through self-sacrifice (*literary*) ■ *vt* (**-soms, -soming, -somed**) **1.** PAY MONEY FOR SOMEBODY'S RELEASE to obtain the release of somebody from captivity by paying money to the captor **2.** RELEASE CAPTIVE ON RECEIPT OF MONEY to set a captive free or release something being held on the receipt of money **3.** RESCUE OR REDEEM SOMEBODY to rescue or redeem somebody, especially by a self-sacrificing act, and especially from sin or its punishment (*literary*) [13C. Via Old French *ransoun* < Latin *redemption-* (see REDEMPTION)] —**ransomer** *n* ◇ **a king's** *or* **queen's ransom** a very large amount of money ◇ **hold somebody to ransom 1.** to use threats to try to make somebody do what you want **2.** to hold somebody captive until a sum of money is paid for his or her release

rant /rant/ *vti* (**rants, ranting, ranted**) to speak or say something in a very loud, aggressive, or bombastic way, usually at length and repetitively ○ *He ranted for hours about how ungrateful we were.* ■ *n* a very loud, aggressive, or bombastic speech that is usually long and repetitive [Late 16C. < Dutch *ranten*] —**ranter** *n* —**ranting** *adj, n* —**rantingly** *adv*

ranula /ránnyŏŏlə/ *n* a cyst that forms on the underside of the tongue when the duct of a salivary or mucous gland is blocked [Mid-17C. < Latin, 'little frog' < *rana* 'frog']

ranunculus /rə núngkyŏŏləss/ (*plural* **-luses** *or* **-li** /-lī/) *n* a plant that has divided leaves and flowers with five petals, e.g. the buttercup, clematis, and columbine. Genus: *Ranunculus*. [Late 16C. < modern Latin, < Latin, 'little frog' < *rana* 'frog'] —**ranunculaceous** /rə núngkyŏŏ láyshəss/ *adj*

RAOC *abbr* Royal Army Ordnance Corps

rap[1] /rap/ *v* (**raps, rapping, rapped**) **1.** *vti* HIT SOMEBODY OR SOMETHING SHARPLY to strike somebody or something with a quick sharp blow ○ *The teacher rapped on the desk to get the students' attention.* **2.** *vt* SAY SOMETHING QUICKLY to say something in a quick sharp way ○ *The sergeant rapped out an order.* **3.** *vt* REBUKE SOMEBODY to criticize or rebuke somebody harshly **4.** *vi* PERFORM MUSIC WITH SPOKEN RHYTHMIC VOCALS to speak in verse using rhythm and rhyme over music with a strong beat, usually hip hop **5.** *vi* US TALK INFORMALLY to have an informal talk or discussion (*slang*) ○ *We rapped till dawn.* ■ *n* **1.** SHARP BLOW a quick sharp blow **2.** SOUND OF KNOCKING a quick sharp knocking sound **3.** POPULAR MUSIC WITH SPOKEN RHYTHMIC VOCALS a vocal style in which performers use rhythm and rhyme to speak in verse over music with a strong beat, usually hip hop. Rap developed from African American hip hop music and culture in the 1970s. **4.** REBUKE a harsh criticism or rebuke (*informal*) **5.** *N Am* CRIMINAL CHARGE a criminal charge brought against somebody (*informal*) **6.** *N Am* JAIL SENTENCE a jail sentence given to somebody found guilty of a crime (*informal*) **7.** *US* SOMEBODY OR SOMETHING NEGATIVE somebody or something thought of as negative or unfortunate (*informal*) ○ *You got a bum rap this time.* **8.** *US* INFORMAL TALK an informal talk or discussion (*slang*) [13C. < ?] ◇ **beat the rap** *N Am* to avoid conviction on a charge (*informal*) ◇ **not give a rap** *US* to not care at all (*informal*) ◇ **take the rap (for something)** to take the blame or punishment for something, whether or not it was your fault (*slang*)

SPELLCHECK rap or **wrap**? Do not confuse the spelling of *rap* and *wrap*, which sound similar. *Rap* is a verb or noun referring to a sharp blow or sound or a type of popular music with spoken rhyming vocals, as in *to rap on the door, a rap singer*. *Rap* is also used in some fixed phrases: *I don't give a rap. She took the rap for his mistake.* *Wrap* is a verb meaning 'cover, wind, envelop, engross' (as in *to wrap up a parcel, wrapped in thought*) or a noun meaning 'shawl, cloak, or similar garment', 'filled tortilla sandwich', or 'completion of filming'. *Wrap* is also used in the fixed phrase *keep under wraps*, meaning 'keep secret'.

rap[2] /rap/ *vt* *Aus* another spelling of **wrap** *v* (sense 10)

rapacious /rə páyshəss/ *adj* **1.** GRASPING greedy and grasping, especially for money, and sometimes willing to use unscrupulous means to obtain what is desired **2.** DESTRUCTIVE AND VICIOUS engaging in violent pillaging and likely to harm or destroy things **3.** ZOOL PREDATORY living by eating live prey [Mid-17C. < Latin *rapac-* 'tearing, grasping' < *rapere* 'seize'] —**rapaciously** *adv* —**rapaciousness** *n*

rape[1] /rayp/ *n* **1.** FORCING OF SOMEBODY INTO SEX the crime of using force somebody to have sexual intercourse with somebody **2.** INSTANCE OF RAPE an instance of the crime of rape **3.** VIOLENT DESTRUCTIVE TREATMENT the violent, destructive, or abusive treatment of something ○ *the rape of a beautiful stretch of countryside* **4.** ABDUCTION an act of seizing somebody and carrying him or her away by force (*archaic*) ■ *vt* (**rapes, raping, raped**) **1.** FORCE SOMEBODY TO HAVE SEX to force somebody to have sexual intercourse **2.** VIOLATE SOMETHING to treat something in a violent, destructive, or abusive way ○ *rape the land for its resources* [14C. Via Anglo-Norman < Latin *rapere* 'seize']

ORIGIN The Latin word *rapere* 'to seize', from which **rape** is derived, is also the source of English *rapacious, rapid, rapine, rapture, ravage, raven*[1], *ravine, ravish, surreptitious*, and *usurp*.

rape[2] /rayp/ *n* a commercially grown annual plant of the cabbage family. Flowers: bright yellow. Use: oil, fodder. Latin name: *Brassica napus*. [14C. < Latin *rapa* 'turnip']

rape[3] /rayp/ *n* the skins and stalks of grapes after their juice has been extracted for use in winemaking [Early 17C. < French *râpe* 'grape stalk' < Old French *rasper* 'scrape']

rape oil *n* an oil extracted from the seeds of the rape plant. Use: lubricant, making soap, cooking.

rapeseed /rayp seed/ *n* the seeds of the rape plant

rapeseed oil *n* INDUST, FOOD same as **rape oil**

rape shield law *n* a law that prohibits the defence in a rape trial from questioning the victim about her or his previous sexual experiences

raphae ANAT, BOT plural of **raphe**

Raphael /ráffay əl/ *n* in Hebrew tradition, one of the seven archangels, and the angel of healing

Raphael /ráffi el/ (1483–1520) Italian artist. A master of the Italian High Renaissance, he is best known for his religious paintings. Born **Sanzio, Raffaello**

raphe /ráyfi/ (*plural* **-phae** /-fee/) *n* **1.** CONNECTING RIDGE a connecting ridge or seam between two similar parts of an organ of the body, e.g. between the two halves of the medulla oblongata or along the scrotum **2.** BOT RIDGE ALONG SOME SEED COATS a ridge along the coat of some seeds formed by fusion of the connecting stalk (**funiculus**) with the outer layer of the developing ovule **3.** BOT LONGITUDINAL GROOVE a longitudinal groove on the valve of a diatom [Mid-18C. Via modern Latin < Greek *rhaphē* 'seam' < *rhaptein* 'sew']

raphia *n* INDUST, TREES another spelling of **raffia**

raphide /ráy fīd/, **raphis** /ráyfiss/ (*plural* **raphides** /ráffi deez/) *n* a crystal of calcium oxalate found in some plant cells as a by-product of their metabolism [Mid-19C. Via French < Greek *rhaphid-* 'needle' < *rhaptein* 'sew']

rapid /ráppid/ *adj* acting, moving, or happening very quickly ○ *a rapid increase in turnover* ■ **rapids** *npl* a part of a riverbed where the water moves very fast, usually over rocks or round boulders ○ *crossed the rapids in a small canoe* [Mid-17C. < Latin *rapidus* 'seizing' < *rapere* 'seize'] —**rapidly** *adv* —**rapidness** *n*

rapid eye movement *n* jerky movements of the eyeballs while the eyes are closed, characteristic of somebody who is dreaming while asleep, especially during REM sleep

rapid eye movement sleep *n* PHYSIOL full form of **REM sleep**

rapid-fire *adj* ANZ, US same as **quick-fire**

rapid prototyping *n* a method of quickly creating mechanical components, especially those with complex shapes, from a computer-based drawing that can be used to check the validity of a design

rapid transit *n* *N Am* a high-speed urban public-transport system using underground or elevated railways or a combination of both

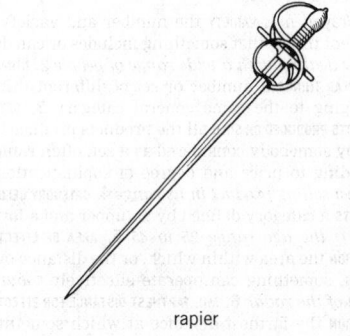

rapier

rapier /ráypi ər/ *n* a sword with a cup-shaped hilt and a long slender blade that can have two cutting

edges, or only a sharply pointed tip for thrusting [Early 16C. Probably via Dutch or Low German *rappir* < French *rapière* in obsolete *espee rapière* 'rapier sword']

rapine /ráppīn, -ppin/ *n* the use of force to seize somebody else's property (*literary*) [14C. Directly or via French < Latin *rapina* < *rapere* 'seize']

rapini /ra péeni/ *npl* the leaves of immature turnip plants, used especially in Italian and Chinese cooking [Late 20C. < Italian]

rapist /ráypist/ *n* somebody who uses force to have sexual intercourse with somebody else

rappee /ra pée/ *n* a moist, strongly flavoured snuff made from dark coarse tobacco [Mid-18C. < French *tabac râpé* 'rasped tobacco' < *râper* 'rasp' < Germanic]

rappel /ra pél/ *N Am* CLIMBING *vi* (**-pels, -pelling, -pelled**) same as **abseil** ■ *n* same as **abseil** [Mid-20C. < French, < Old French *rapeler* 'to recall' < *apeler* 'to call']

rappen /rápp'n/ (*plural same*) *n* a Swiss centime [Mid-19C. < German, < Middle High German *rappe* 'raven', referring to the depiction of a bird on a coin of the Middle Ages]

rapper /ráppər/ *n* somebody who performs rap music

rapport /ra páwr/ *n* an emotional bond or friendly relationship between people based on mutual liking, trust, and a sense that they understand and share each other's concerns ○ *She manages to strike up a rapport with audiences as soon as she steps onto the platform.* [Mid-17C. < French, < *rapporter* 'bring back' < *aporter* 'bring' < Latin *portare* 'carry']

rapporteur /ráppawr túr/ *n* somebody who is appointed to investigate a subject and deliver a report on it [Late 15C. < French, < *rapporter* (see RAPPORT)]

rapprochement /ra próshmoN/ *n* the establishment or renewal of friendly relations between people or nations that were previously hostile or unsympathetic towards each other [Early 19C. < French, < *rapprocher* 'bring together' < *approcher* (see APPROACH)]

rapscallion /rap skálli ən/ *n* (*archaic or humorous*) **1.** a mischievous and annoying child **2.** a disreputable and dishonest person [Late 17C. Alteration of *rascallion*, probably < RASCAL]

rap sheet *n N Am* a list of somebody's past arrests and convictions (*slang*)

rapt /rapt/ *adj* **1.** COMPLETELY ENGROSSED involved in, fascinated by, or concentrating on something to the exclusion of everything else ○ *staring with rapt attention at the speaker* **2.** BLISSFULLY HAPPY showing or suggesting deep emotions of joy or ecstasy **3.** *Aus* PLEASED extremely pleased (*informal*) [14C. < Latin *raptus*, past participle of *rapere* 'seize'] —**raptly** *adv* —**raptness** *n*

raptor /ráptər/ *n* BIRDS same as **bird of prey** [14C. < Latin, 'robber' < *rapere* 'seize']

raptorial /rap táwri əl/ *adj* **1.** USING OTHER ANIMALS AS PREY able to live by catching prey **2.** ADAPTED FOR CATCHING PREY specially adapted for seizing prey, as are the feet of birds of prey with their sharp talons **3.** OF PREDATORY BIRDS relating to or typical of birds of prey

rapture /rápchər/ *n* **1.** OVERWHELMING HAPPINESS a euphoric transcendent state in which somebody is overwhelmed by happiness or delight and unaware of anything else **2.** CHR MYSTICAL TRANSPORTATION a mystical experience in which somebody believes he or she is transported into the spiritual realm, sometimes applied to the second coming of Jesus Christ, when true believers are expected to rise up to join him in heaven ■ **raptures** *npl* STATE OF GREAT HAPPINESS OR ENTHUSIASM a state of great happiness or enthusiasm about something, or words and gestures that express this ○ *went into raptures about the meal they'd had* [Late 16C. Directly or via French < medieval Latin *raptura* 'seizure' < Latin *raptus* (see RAPT)] —**rapturous** *adj*

rapture of the deep *n* MED same as **nitrogen narcosis**

rara avis /ráirə áyviss/ (*plural* **rarae aves** /ráir ee áy veez/) *n* somebody or something that is rarely encountered [From Latin, literally 'rare bird']

ra-ra skirt *n* CLOTHING another spelling of **rah-rah skirt**

rare[1] /rair/ (**rarer, rarest**) *adj* **1.** INFREQUENT OR UNUSUAL not happening or found often ○ *It's rare for them to miss a meeting.* **2.** VALUABLE particularly interesting or valuable, especially to collectors or scholars, because only a few exist ○ *a collection of rare 18th-century porcelain* **3.** GREAT unusually great or excellent ○ *a rare gift for languages* **4.** CONTAINING LITTLE OXYGEN thin in density and containing so little oxygen that breathing is difficult [15C. < Latin *rarus* 'having a loose texture, scarce'] —**rareness** *n*

rare[2] /rair/ (**rarer, rarest**) *adj* describes meat that is cooked quickly and lightly so as to remain raw and juicy inside [Mid-17C. Alteration of dialect *rear* 'underdone' (describing eggs), origin ?]

rarebit /ráir bit/ (*plural same* or **-bits**) *n* FOOD same as **Welsh rarebit** [Late 18C. Alteration of RABBIT in *Welsh rabbit*, earlier form of WELSH RAREBIT]

rare earth *n* an oxide of a rare-earth element

rare-earth element *n* a member of the lanthanide series, which contains 15 elements that have atomic numbers from 57 to 71 and share closely related chemical properties

raree show /ráiri-/ *n* (*archaic*) **1.** same as **peepshow** (sense 2) **2.** a street show or spectacle with unusual or outlandish items on view [Alteration of *rare show*]

rarefaction /ráiri fáksh'n/, **rarefication** /ráirifi káysh'n/ *n* the process of becoming or of making something such as a gas less dense [Early 17C. < medieval Latin *rarefaction-* < past participle of Latin *rarefacere* (see RAREFY)] —**rarefactional** *adj*

rarefied /ráiri fīd/ *adj* **1.** WITH LOW DENSITY describes an atmosphere that has a low density, especially owing to a low oxygen content **2.** ESOTERIC OR ELITE seemingly distinct or remote from ordinary reality and common people, and often purged of anything perceived as coarse or tasteless **3.** OF HIGH STANDARD showing very high quality in character or style (*literary*) ○ *Milton's rarefied prose*

rarefy /ráiri fī/ (**-fies, -fying, -fied**) *v* **1.** *vti* to make something, especially a gas, less dense, or become less dense **2.** *vt* to make something less connected with or typical of the ordinary [14C. Directly or via French *raréfier* < medieval Latin *rareficare* < Latin *rarefacere* 'make rare' < *rarus* 'scarce' + *facere* 'do'] —**rarefiable** *adj*

rare gas *n* CHEM same as **noble gas**

rarely /ráirli/ *adv* **1.** almost never or not very often **2.** exceptionally well

rareripe /ráir rīp/ *US adj* ripening early ■ *n* a fruit or vegetable that ripens early [Early 18C. < *rare* 'early', variant of *rathe* < Old English *hræþ* 'quick' < Germanic]

raring /ráiring/ *adj* very enthusiastic and eager to start doing something (*informal*) ○ *They were raring to go.* [Early 20C. Present participle of *rare*, variant of REAR[1]]

rarity /ráirəti/ (*plural* **-ties**) *n* **1.** something that happens rarely or is particularly interesting or valuable because it is so unusual **2.** the fact of happening very seldom or of being very unusual

RAS *abbr* **1.** Royal Agricultural Society **2.** Royal Astronomical Society

Ras al-Am /ráass al áam/ *n* an Islamic festival, the first day of the first month of the Hegira calendar, marking the withdrawal of Muhammad from Mecca to Medina in 622 AD. Date: 1st of Muharram.

rasam /rússəm/ *n* in South Indian cooking, a thin spicy drink or thin lentil soup, either mixed with rice or drunk by itself [Via Tamil < Sanskrit *rasa* 'flavour']

~~**rasberry**~~ incorrect spelling of **raspberry**

rasbora /raz báwrə/ *n* a tropical freshwater fish, several species of which are brightly coloured and often kept in aquariums. Native to: East Africa, Asia. Genus: *Rasbora*. [Mid-20C. < modern Latin, origin ?]

rascal /ráask'l/ *n* **1.** somebody who behaves in a mischievous teasing way, especially a child (*humorous*) **2.** somebody, especially a man, who is dishonest or otherwise unethical [14C. < Old French *rascaille* 'mob, rabble'] —**rascally** *adj*

rase *vt* another spelling of **raze** (*literary*)

rasgulla /russ góollə/ *n* in South Asian cooking, a dessert consisting of a ball of curd cheese (**paneer**) cooked in syrup [Mid-20C. < Hindi *rasgullā* 'juice ball']

rash[1] /rash/ *adj* acting with, resulting from, or characteristic of thoughtless, impetuous behaviour [14C. Probably < Germanic, 'quick'] —**rashly** *adv* —**rashness** *n*

rash[2] /rash/ *n* **1.** an outbreak on the surface of the skin that is often reddish and itchy **2.** a series of events that happen in a brief period and are considered to be unusual or rare ○ *a rash of burglaries* [Early 18C. Origin ?]

rasher /ráshər/ *n* **1.** a slice of bacon or ham, cooked or uncooked **2.** *N Am* an order or portion of slices of cooked bacon or ham [Late 16C. Origin ?]

Rashîd /ra sheéd/ town in Egypt, on the Mediterranean coast. Population: 52,014 (1986).

rash vest *n Aus* a thin, synthetic, elasticated, short- or long-sleeved shirt worn by surfers under a wet suit to prevent skin irritation or by swimmers on its own to provide sun protection

ras malai /rúss mə lī/ *n* in South Asian cooking, a dessert consisting of small balls or squares of curd cheese (**paneer**) served cold in thickened and sweetened milk [From Hindi *ras* 'juice' + *malāī* 'cream']

Rasmussen /rássməss'n/, **Anders Fogh** (*b.* 1953) prime minister of Denmark (2001–). A Liberal Party politician, he formed a right-wing coalition of Liberals and Conservatives in 2001 to win an election that was dominated by asylum issues.

rasorial /rə sáwri əl/ *adj* describes a bird that is capable of or adapted for scratching the ground to look for food [Mid-19C. < late Latin *rasor* 'scraper' < Latin *ras-* past participle of *radere* 'scrape']

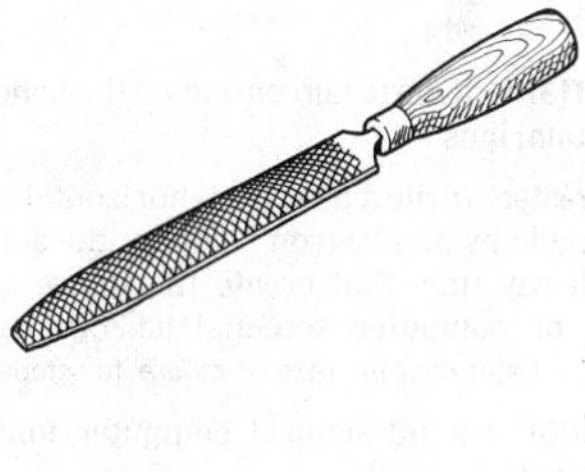

rasp (sense 2)

rasp[1] /raasp/ *n* **1.** HARSH GRATING SOUND a harsh grating sound, similar to that of a rasp or saw cutting into wood **2.** LARGE-TOOTHED FILE a tool used for scraping or smoothing wood or metal, similar to a file, but with larger teeth on its cutting surface **3.** ACT OF SMOOTHING SOMETHING the act of smoothing the surface of something such as wood or metal with a rasp ■ *v* (**rasps, rasping, rasped**) **1.** *vt* SAY SOMETHING IN HARSH VOICE to utter something, especially an order, in a harsh voice **2.** *vti* FILE OR SCRAPE SOMETHING to use a rasp to file or scrape a surface in order to remove unevenness **3.** *vt* IRRITATE SOMEBODY to irritate or annoy somebody [13C. < Old French *rasper* 'scrape' < Germanic] —**rasper** *n* —**rasping** *adj* —**raspingly** *adv* —**raspy** *adj*

rasp[2] /raasp/ *n Scotland* same as **raspberry** (senses 1–2) (*informal*) [Mid-16C. Shortening of obsolete *raspis* 'raspberry', origin ?]

raspatory /ráaspətəri/ (*plural* **-ries**) *n* a surgical instrument similar to a rasp, used to smooth the ends of a bone [15C. < medieval Latin *raspatorium* < *raspare* 'to scrape' < Germanic]

raspberry /ráazbəri/ (*plural* **-ries**) *n* **1.** SMALL CUP-SHAPED FRUIT a small red cup-shaped fruit with a sweet taste that grows round a pithy stalk and is made up of many tiny juicy globes (**drupelets**) **2.** RASPBERRY BUSH a shrubby plant that produces raspberries. Genus: *Rubus*. **3.** RUDE NOISE a rude noise meant to imitate the sound of breaking wind, made by blowing air through pursed lips and intended as an insult or a gesture of disapproval or defiance (*informal*) N Am term **Bronx cheer 4.** RED COLOUR a deep purplish-pink colour [Early 17C. < RASP[2]] —**raspberry** *adj*

raspings /ráaspingz/ *npl* fine breadcrumbs, often toasted, used to coat fish or other foods before frying or baking

Grigory Rasputin

Rasputin /ra spyoótin/, **Grigory** (1869?–1916) Russian peasant and self-proclaimed holy man. His friendship with Russia's last tsar and tsarina wrecked the Romanov dynasty's prestige and contributed to the coming of the Russian Revolution (1917). Full name **Rasputin, Grigory Yetimovich**

Rasta /rásta/ (*informal*) *n* **1.** PEOPLES same as **Rastafarian 2.** RELIG same as **Rastafarianism** (*used in Black English*) ■ *adj* relating to Rastafarians or Rastafarianism [Mid-20C. Shortening]

Rastafari /rásta faári/ *interj* used as a greeting to another Rastafarian (*used in Black English*)

Rastafarian /rásta fáiri ən/ *n* a member of an Afro-Caribbean religious group that venerates the former emperor of Ethiopia, Haile Selassie, forbids the cutting of hair, and stresses Black culture and identity [Mid-20C. < Amharic *Ras Tafari* 'prince to be feared', name given to HAILE SELASSIE I before he came to power]

Rastafarianism /rásta fáiri ənizəm/ *n* the belief system of Rastafarians

raster /rástər/ *n* the pattern of horizontal scanning lines made by an electron beam on the surface of a cathode-ray tube that create the image on a television or computer screen [Mid-20C. Via German, 'screen' < Latin *rastrum* 'rake' < *radere* 'to scrape']

raster font *n* a bit-mapped computer font formed from pixels

rasterize /rásta rīz/ (**-izes, -izing, -ized**), **rasterise** (**-ises, -ising, -ised**) *vt* to convert a digitized image into a format suitable for display on a computer monitor or printout

rat

rat /rat/ *n* **1.** LONG-TAILED RODENT a long-tailed rodent, larger than a mouse. Genus: *Rattus.* **2.** ANIMAL LIKE RAT an animal that resembles a rat **3.** SOMEBODY UNTRUSTWORTHY somebody regarded as malicious, underhanded, and deceitful, especially somebody who betrays friends or confidences (*informal insult*) ■ *v* (**rats, ratting, ratted**) **1.** *vi* HUNT RATS to hunt and kill rats **2.** *vt US* MAKE HAIR STAND HIGH ON HEAD to use a comb to tease hair into knots with quick repeated movements, which makes it stand up high from the scalp [Old English *ræt*] ◇ **smell a rat** be suspicious that something is not right (*informal*)

rat on *vt* (*informal*) **1.** to betray somebody's trust, especially by revealing something told in confidence **2.** to abandon somebody or something, or fail to do something

rata /ráatə/ *n* a tree of the myrtle family with hard red wood and crimson flowers. Native to: New Zealand. Genus: *Metrosideros.* [Late 18C. < Maori]

ratable /ráytəb'l/, **rateable** *adj* **1.** able to be estimated or have a value placed on it **2.** liable for tax — **ratability** /ráytə bílləti/ *n* —**ratably** *adv*

ratables /ráytəb'lz/, **rateables** *npl US* **1.** government income derived from taxes on property **2.** buildings or other property, especially those in commercial use, that supply local government with tax income

ratafia /rátta feé ə/ *n* **1.** a liqueur made from fruit juices or softened fruit in liquor, especially brandy, and often flavoured with almonds or with peach or apricot kernels **2.** *also* **ratafia biscuit** a small biscuit similar to a macaroon, flavoured with almond or ratafia [Late 17C. Via French < Caribbean Creole]

Ratana /raáatənə/, **Tahupotiki Wiremu** (1873?–1939) New Zealand religious leader. He founded the Ratana Church (1925), a Maori revivalist movement that formed a lasting political alliance with New Zealand's Labour Party.

rataplan /rátta plan/ *n* a noise like the rapid beating of a drum, the sound of horses' hooves striking the ground, or machine-gun fire, made up of a series of short repeated sounds [Mid-19C. < French, an imitation of the sound]

rat-arsed /-aarst/ *adj* an offensive term meaning extremely drunk (*slang*)

ratatat-tat /rátta tat tát/, **rat-a-tat** /rátta tát/, **rat-tat** /rát tát/, **rat-tat-tat** /rát tat tát/ *n* the distinctive rhythmic pattern of short loud sounds made by somebody knocking at a door ■ *interj* an imitation of the sound of somebody knocking on a door [Late 17C. An imitation of the sound]

ratatouille /rátta too i/ (*plural same* or **-illes**) *n* a dish of stewed vegetables, originally from southern France, usually consisting of tomatoes, onions, peppers, aubergines, and courgettes cooked slowly in olive oil [Late 19C. < French, alteration of *touiller* 'stir' < Old French *tooiller* 'drag around']

ratbag /rát bag/ *n* (*slang insult*) **1.** an offensive term that deliberately insults somebody's character **2.** ANZ an offensive term that deliberately insults somebody's intelligence or common sense

ratbite fever /rát bīt-/ *n* an infectious disease in humans caused by the bite of a rat infected with either of two bacteria, *Streptobacillus moniliformis* or *Spirillum minus*

rat-catcher *n* somebody whose job is to rid buildings of rats and other vermin

rat cheese *n US* Cheddar cheese (*informal humorous*)

ratchet /ráchit/ *n* **1.** TURNING DEVICE MOVING IN ONE DIRECTION a mechanism, used especially in lifting devices and some hand tools, consisting of a metal wheel operating with a catch that permits motion in only one direction **2.** RATCHET WHEEL OR PAWL either of the main parts of a ratchet device, the toothed wheel or bar, or the pawl ■ *v* (**-ets, -eting** or **-etting, -eted** or **-etted**) **1.** *vt US* FORCE SOMETHING UP OR DOWN to force something such as prices or political rhetoric to rise or fall in level or intensity by deliberately applying pressure in successive and irreversible stages **2.** *vti* MOVE WITH RATCHET to move gradually up or down by means of a ratchet, or to move something in this way [Mid-17C. < French *rochet* 'spool' < Germanic]

ratchet effect *n* the failure of wages or prices that have risen or fallen because of temporary market pressure to return to their previous level once that pressure is removed

ratchet wheel *n* a toothed wheel in a ratchet mechanism

rate /rayt/ *n* **1.** SPEED the speed at which one measured quantity happens in relation to another measured amount such as time ○ *We'll have to step up our work rate if we're going to finish on schedule.* **2.** AMOUNT IN RELATION TO STANDARD FIGURE the amount, frequency, or speed of something expressed as a proportion of a larger figure or in relation to a whole ○ *The drop-out rate at the end of the first year is around one in three.* **3.** COMM CHARGE the amount of money charged per unit, e.g. per hour, per page, or per thousand, for a job, service, or commodity ○ *I'm* charging you the going rate for the job. **4.** NAVY RANK OF RATING the rank of rating in a navy, especially the Royal Navy ■ **rates** *npl* FORMER LOCAL TAX formerly in the United Kingdom, a tax levied by local authorities on all properties in their areas of jurisdiction, based on a fixed ratable value for each property ■ *v* (**rates, rating, rated**) **1.** *vt* SET VALUE ON SOMETHING to calculate or appraise the value of something ○ *How would you rate this gem collection?* **2.** *vti* ASSESS SOMETHING OR BE ASSESSED to have a particular value, position, or importance relative to other people or things, or be regarded as having this ○ *This rates as undoubtedly the worst film I have ever seen.* **3.** *vt* DESERVE SOMETHING to deserve or be worthy of something ○ *Her latest book didn't even rate a review.* **4.** *vt* CLASSIFY SOMETHING to give a particular classification or rating to something such as a machine, identifying its performance capabilities and limits **5.** *vt* FIN VALUE SOMETHING FOR TAX PURPOSES to value something, especially a property, for tax purposes **6.** *vt* THINK HIGHLY OF SOMEBODY OR SOMETHING to like, approve of, or regard somebody or something as good or excellent (*informal*) ○ *My friends really rate him, but I think his work is amateur.* [15C. Via French < medieval Latin (*pro*) *rata* (*parte*) '(according to a) fixed (part)' < Latin *ratus*, past participle of *reri* 'calculate'] ◇ **at any rate** used to indicate that an important point is true, whatever other considerations there may be ◇ **at a rate of knots** very quickly

ORIGIN The Latin word *reri* 'to calculate', from which *rate* is derived, is also the source of English *ratify*, *ration*, and *reason*.

rateable *adj* FIN another spelling of **ratable**

rate-cap *vt* formerly, to set an upper limit on the amount of money that a local authority could raise by means of rates —**rate-capping** *n*

rate constant *n* the constant in a mathematical expression relating the concentrations of the reactants and the products for a particular chemical reaction

ratel /ráyt'l/ (*plural same* or **-tels**) *n* an aggressive carnivorous animal with short thick legs, a strong body with a thick furry coat, dark underneath and whitish on top, and a head similar to a badger's. Native to: Asia, Africa. Latin name: *Mellivora capensis.* [Late 18C. < Afrikaans]

ratemaking /ráyt mayking/ *n US* the process or business of establishing rates of payment for such things as public transport or utilities

rate of change *n* the ratio of the difference in values of a variable during a time period to the length of that time period

rate of exchange *n* FIN same as **exchange rate**

rate of return *n* the amount of income generated in a year by capital invested, expressed as a percentage of the total sum invested

ratepayer /ráyt payər/ *n* formerly, somebody who paid a tax to a local authority, based on the value of his or her dwelling

rater /ráytər/ *n US* **1.** somebody who establishes rates or ratings **2.** somebody with a particular rank or level of ability (*often used in combination*) ○ *All of them are second-raters with delusions of grandeur.*

ratfink /rát fingk/ *n N Am* an offensive term that deliberately insults somebody's character or behaviour (*insult*)

ratfish /rát fish/ (*plural same* or **-fishes**) *n* a cartilaginous deep-sea fish with a long narrow tail, found worldwide. Family: Chimaeridae.

rath[1] /rath/ *n* a circular enclosure built in ancient Ireland, surrounded by an earth wall and used as a fort or dwelling place [14C. < Irish]

rath[2] /ruth/, **ratha** /rúthə/ *n S Asia* a four-wheeled chariot, especially an elaborate, carved ceremonial chariot pulled by devotees in which a representation of a deity is taken out in procession on festival days [From Sanskrit, 'wagon, chariot']

Rathenau /ráatə now/, **Walther** (1867–1922) German political economist and public servant. As foreign minister, he represented Germany at reparations conferences after World War I. He was assassinated by German nationalists.

'There comes a painful moment in the life of every young German Jew...when he fully realizes for the first time that he has come into the world as a second-class citizen, and that no virtue and no merit can free him from this situation.'
[Walther Rathenau. Quoted in *Europe Since 1870*, James Joll; 1973]

rather /raáthər/ *adv* **1.** SOMEWHAT to some extent or degree ○ *rather disappointing* **2.** CONSIDERABLY to a great extent or degree ○ *I think the irises are rather lovely.* **3.** MORE WILLINGLY more readily or willingly ○ *You go to the cinema; I'd rather stay in tonight.* **4.** WITH MORE JUSTIFICATION with more logic, evidence, precision, or justification ○ *You should praise rather than blame them.* **5.** ON CONTRARY in contrast or opposition to what has been claimed or expected ○ *You think she's snobbish? Rather, I'd say she's shy.* ■ *interj UK* MOST CERTAINLY used to express complete or enthusiastic agreement with what has just been said (*dated*) [Old English *hræþor*, originally comparative form of *hraeþ* 'quick' < Germanic]

Rathlin Island /ráthlin-/ island in Northern Ireland, off the northern coast of County Antrim. It is home to three lighthouses. Length: 10 km/6 mi.

rat hole *n* the entrance to a rat's nest

rathskeller /raát skelər/ *n N Am* a beer hall or restaurant that serves German dishes, usually located below street level [Early 20C. < obsolete German, 'council cellar' (cellar of the town hall) < *Rat* 'council' + *Keller* 'cellar']

rath yatra /rúth yaatrə/ *n S Asia* a procession in which a representation of a Hindu deity is carried in a ceremonial chariot, especially the annual procession of Juggernaut in Puri [*Yatra* from Sanskrit *yātrā*, from *yā* 'to travel']

ratify /rátti fī/ (**-fies, -fying, -fied**) *vt* to give formal approval to something, usually an agreement negotiated by somebody else, in order that it can become valid or operative [14C. Via French *ratifier* < medieval Latin *ratificare* 'make fixed' < Latin *ratus* (see RATE)] —**ratifiable** *adj* —**ratification** /rāttifi káysh'n/ *n* —**ratifier** *n*

ratiné /rátti nay/, **ratine** /ra téen/ *n* a loosely woven cloth with a coarse knobbly texture [Early 20C. < French, past participle of *ratiner* 'raise a nap' < *ratine* 'nap, twilled fabric']

rating /ráyting/ *n* **1.** ASSESSMENT an assessment or classification of somebody or something on a scale according to how much or how little of a quality he, she, or it possesses ○ *On a scale of one to ten, their rating would be about six* **2.** COMM CREDIT STANDING an assessment of the financial status and creditworthiness of a person or company ○ *a credit rating* **3.** NAVY ORDINARY SAILOR a serving member of a navy, especially the Royal Navy, who is not an officer **4.** SAILING RACING YACHT CLASSIFICATION a classification of a racing yacht, based on factors such as its size, weight, and area of sail **5.** MECH ENG PERFORMANCE LIMIT OF MACHINE the performance limit of a machine or system, expressed as capacity, range, or working capability, e.g. the voltage rating on a household appliance ■ **ratings** *npl* MEDIA ESTIMATE OF AUDIENCE SIZE the estimated number of people who tuned in to a TV or radio programme, used as an indication of its relative popularity

ratio /ráyshi ō/ (*plural* **-tios**) *n* **1.** PROPORTIONAL RELATIONSHIP a proportional relationship between two different numbers or quantities **2.** MATHS ONE NUMBER DIVIDED BY ANOTHER a quotient of two numbers or expressions arrived at by dividing one by the other **3.** *US* FIN RELATIVE VALUE OF GOLD AND SILVER the value of gold and silver relative to each other in a monetary system based on these two metals [Mid-17C. < Latin, 'calculation' (see REASON)]

ratiocinate /rátti óssi nayt/ (**-nates, -nating, -nated**) *vi* to think or put forward an argument about something in a strictly logical way (*formal*) [Mid-17C. < Latin *ratiocinat-*, past participle of *ratiocinari* 'compute' < *ratio* (see RATIO)] —**ratiocination** /rátti ossi náysh'n/ *n* —**ratiocinative** /-nətiv/ *adj* —**ratiocinator** *n*

ration /rásh'n/ *n* **1.** FIXED AMOUNT ALLOCATED TO SOMEBODY a fixed and limited amount of something, especially food, given or allocated to a person or group from the stocks available, especially during a time of shortage or a war **2.** ADEQUATE AMOUNT the amount of something that it seems fair or desirable for somebody to have ○ *rather more than your ration of good luck* ■ **rations** *npl* AMOUNT OF FOOD OFFICIALLY ALLOCATED food, especially an amount of food from a limited stock allocated to somebody such as a soldier or hiker ○ *The campers had to carry their own rations.* ■ *vt* (**-tions, -tioning, -tioned**) **1.** RESTRICT AVAILABLE AMOUNT OF SOMETHING to restrict the amount of something, usually a commodity in short supply, that somebody is allowed to buy, consume, or use ○ *Petrol was rationed, so long journeys were out of the question.* **2.** LIMIT QUANTITY AVAILABLE TO SOMEBODY to allow somebody only a limited quantity of something ○ *rationed herself to one cup of coffee a day* [Early 18C. Via French < Spanish *ración* < Latin *ratio* (see RATIO)]

ration out *vt* to distribute something, especially something that is in short supply, in fixed or strictly limited quantities

rational /rásh'nəl/ *adj* **1.** REASONABLE AND SENSIBLE governed by, or showing evidence of, clear and sensible thinking and judgment, based on reason rather than emotion or prejudice **2.** IN ACCORDANCE WITH REASON AND LOGIC presented or understandable in terms that accord with reason and logic or with scientific knowledge ○ *a rational explanation* **3.** ABLE TO REASON endowed with the ability to reason, as opposed to being governed solely by instinct and appetite **4.** MATHS EXPRESSIBLE AS RATIO OF POLYNOMIALS in mathematics, able to be expressed exactly as the quotient of two whole numbers or polynomials ○ *a rational function* ■ *n* MATHS same as **rational number** [14C. < Latin *rationalis* < *ratio* (see RATIO)] —**rationally** *adv*

USAGE Do not confuse ***rational*** and ***rationale***, which are linked by the idea of 'reason' but otherwise differ in meaning, spelling, and pronunciation. ***Rational*** is an adjective meaning 'reasonable and sensible' (*a perfectly rational argument*), whereas ***rationale*** is a noun meaning 'the reasoning that underlies something' (*explained the rationale behind the new guidelines*).

rational choice theory *n* the hypothesis, derived from game theory, that there is a rational, definable, and calculable basis to human decision-making

rationale /ráshə naál/ *n* the reasoning or principle that underlies or explains something, or a statement setting out this reasoning or principle [Mid-17C. < modern Latin, < Latin *rationalis* (see RATIONAL)]

USAGE See ***rational***.

rational-emotive behaviour therapy, **rational-emotive therapy** *n* a form of cognitive-behavioural therapy in which somebody is encouraged to examine and change irrational thought patterns and beliefs in order to reduce dysfunctional behaviour

rationalisation, **etc.** *n* another spelling of **rationalization, etc.**

rationalism /rásh'nəlizəm/ *n* **1.** the belief that thought and action should be governed by reason **2.** the belief that reason and logic are the primary sources of knowledge and truth and should be relied on in searching for and testing the truth of things —**rationalist** *n* —**rationalistic** /rásh'nə lístik/ *adj* —**rationalistically** *adv*

rationality /ráshə nálləti/ (*plural* **-ties**) *n* **1.** rational thought or behaviour, or the ability to think rationally **2.** a rational belief, opinion, or action (*often used in the plural*)

rationalization /rásh'nə lī záysh'n/, **rationalisation** *n* **1.** the process of rationalizing something, or an instance of rationalizing something **2.** in psychoanalytic theory, a defence mechanism whereby people attempt to hide their true motivations and emotions by providing reasonable or self-justifying explanations for irrational or unacceptable behaviour

rationalize /rásh'nə līz/ (**-izes, -izing, -ized**), **rationalise** (**-ises, -ising, -ised**) *v* **1.** *vti* OFFER REASONABLE EXPLANATION FOR SOMETHING to attempt to justify behaviour normally considered irrational or unacceptable by offering an apparently reasonable explanation **2.** *vti* MAKE SOMETHING MORE EFFICIENT AND PROFITABLE to make a business or operation more efficient and profitable, e.g. by reducing the workforce **3.** *vt* MAKE SOMETHING RATIONAL to make something rational, logical, or consistent **4.** *vt* INTERPRET SOMETHING RATIONALLY to interpret something from a rational or logical perspective **5.** *vt* MATHS ELIMINATE IRRATIONAL NUMBERS FROM SOMETHING to eliminate irrational numbers from an expression or an equation —**rationalizable** *adj* —**rationalizer** *n*

rational number *n* a whole number or the quotient of any whole numbers, excluding zero as a denominator

ratio scale *n* a scale for measuring data that makes it possible to compare different values and to state the difference between them in the form of a ratio

ratite /ráttīt/ (*plural same* or **-ites**) *n* a flightless bird such as an ostrich or emu that has a flat breastbone without the ridge-shaped part (**keel**) to which the flight muscles are attached in a flying bird [Late 19C. < Latin *ratitus* 'having the figure of a raft' < *ratis* 'raft']

rat kangaroo *n* a small kangaroo resembling a rat, with long hind legs for jumping. Native to: Australia, Tasmania. Genera: *Potorus* or *Bettongia*.

ratline /ráttlin/, **ratlin** *n* a small rope fastened horizontally between the shrouds in the rigging of a sailing ship to form a rung of a ladder for the crew going aloft [15C. Origin ?]

RATO /ráytō/ *abbr* ENG rocket-assisted takeoff

ratoon /ra tóon/, **rattoon** *n* **1.** SHOOT AT BASE OF CROP PLANT a shoot growing up from the base of a crop plant such as sugar cane or bananas after the previous growth has been cut back **2.** CROP PRODUCED ON RATOONS a crop that is produced on ratoons, e.g. sugar cane, bananas, or pineapples ■ *vti* (**-toons, -tooning, -tooned**) PROPAGATE SOMETHING WITH RATOONS to propagate a crop by inducing the formation of ratoons, or send up ratoons [Mid-17C. < Spanish *retoño* 'new shoot']

rat pack *n* a group of people with close ties or common interests and aims, whose activities are sometimes regarded with suspicion or disapproval (*slang insult*)

rat race *n* the struggle to survive and make progress in the competitive environment of modern life, seen as a dehumanizing and ultimately futile activity (*informal*) ○ *I'd like to get out of this rat race and retire to an isolated farm.*

rat run *n* a narrow road, usually a residential street, used by drivers at busy times to avoid the heavier traffic on nearby main roads (*informal*)

rats /rats/ *interj* used to express annoyance or contempt (*informal*) [Late 19C. Plural of RAT]

ratshit /rátshit/ *adj Aus* a highly offensive term meaning lacking in quality or excellence (*taboo*)

rat snake *n* a large nonvenomous snake that eats rodents. Native to: North America, Asia. Genera: *Elaphe* or *Ptyas*.

rat's tails *npl* long thin hanging strands of greasy or wet hair (*informal disapproving*)

rattail /rát tayl/ *n* a hairless tail on a horse ■ *adj* looking like or having a part that resembles a rat's tail ○ *a rattail comb*

rattan /ra tán/ *n* **1.** STEMS OF TROPICAL PLANT the stems of a tropical plant. Use: wickerwork, furniture, canes. **2.** TROPICAL ASIAN CLIMBING PALM a climbing palm that is the source of rattan. Native to: tropical Asia. Genera: *Calamus* or *Daemonorops* or *Plectomia*. **3.** WALKING STICK a walking stick or cane made from rattan [Mid-17C. < Malay *rotan*]

rat-tat, **rat-tat-tat** *n, interj* same as **ratatat-tat**

ratted /ráttid/ *adj* **1.** very drunk (*slang*) **2.** *US* describes hair with tangles combed into it in order to make it look fuller [Late 20C. In sense 1 probably after RATARSED]

ratter /ráttər/ *n* an animal, especially a cat or dog, that is good at catching rats

rattle[1] /rátt'l/ *v* (**-tles, -tling, -tled**) **1.** *vti* MAKE SHORT SHARP KNOCKING SOUNDS to make short sharp knocking sounds in quick succession, especially as a result of being moved or shaken, or make something do this ○ *He picked up the box and rattled it.* ○ *The windows and doors rattled in the wind.* **2.** *vi* MOVE WITH RATTLING SOUND

to move while making a rattling sound ○ *The old car rattled noisily down the street.* **3.** *vt* **DISCONCERT SOMEBODY** to make somebody lose composure and feel frightened, worried, confused, or annoyed ■ *n* **1.** **SHORT SHARP KNOCKING SOUNDS** a quick succession of short sharp knocking sounds, usually caused by something being moved or shaken **2.** **BABY'S TOY** a baby's toy consisting of a hollow shape with small objects inside, that rattles when it is shaken **3.** **NOISEMAKER** an object that produces a rattling sound, e.g. a musical instrument or a tool used by a shaman **4.** **MED** **RATTLING NOISE IN THROAT** a rattling or rasping noise made in the throat, caused by obstructed breathing and heard especially near death **5.** **REPT** **TIP OF RATTLESNAKE'S TAIL** a set of loosely attached horny segments at the end of a rattlesnake's tail that produce a rattling or buzzing sound when shaken **6.** **PLANTS** **PLANT WITH RATTLING SEEDS** a plant whose seeds rattle inside the seed capsule [14C. Probably < Middle Low German *ratelen*, an imitation of the sound]

rattle around *vi* to be in a room, house, or building that is much bigger than is required (*informal*) ○ *There's just the two of us rattling around in this place.*

rattle off *vt* to say, read aloud, or perform something very rapidly or with no apparent effort

rattle on *vi* to talk rapidly and at length about something of little interest or importance to the listener

rattle through *vt* to do something very quickly and often in a perfunctory way ○ *He rattled through the agenda, scarcely pausing for breath.*

rattle[2] /rátt'l/ (**-tles, -tling, -tled**) *vt* to attach ratlines to the shrouds in the rigging of a ship [Early 18C. Back-formation < *ratling*, variant of RATLINE]

Rattle /rátt'l/, **Sir Simon** (*b.* 1955) British conductor. A leading interpreter of 20th-century music, he was principal conductor of the City of Birmingham Symphony Orchestra (1980–97), and in 2002 succeeded Claudio Abbado as conductor of the Berlin Philharmonic. Full name **Rattle, Sir Simon Denis**

rattlebrained /rátt'l braynd/ *adj US* an offensive term meaning regarded as silly and excessively talkative (*informal insult*)

rattler /rátt'lər/ (*plural same* or **-tlers**) *n* **1.** somebody or something that rattles **2.** *US* **REPT** same as **rattlesnake** (*informal*) **3.** *US* **RAIL** same as **freight train** (*informal*)

rattlesnake

rattlesnake /rátt'l snayk/ (*plural same* or **-snakes**) *n* a large venomous snake of the pit viper family, whose tail has loosely attached horny segments that rattle or buzz when vibrated. Native to: North and South America. Genus: *Crotalis* or *Sistrurus*.

rattlesnake plantain *n* an orchid with striped or mottled leaves resembling a rattlesnake's skin. Flowers: white or yellow, in spikes. Genus: *Goodyera*.

rattletrap /rátt'l trap/ *n* an old noisy worn-out car or other vehicle (*informal*)

rattling /rátt'ling/ *adj* moving or talking at a quick or lively pace ○ *a rattling TV debate* ■ *adv* extremely (*dated informal*) ○ *tells a rattling good story* —**rattlingly** *adv*

rattly /rátt'li/ (**-tlier, -tliest**) *adj* making a loud rattling noise ○ *a rattly air conditioner*

rattoon *n* **PLANTS** another spelling of **ratoon**

rat-trap *n* **1.** **TRAP FOR RATS** a trap designed to catch rats **2.** **SQUALID DWELLING** a dilapidated dirty unsafe dwelling (*informal*) **3.** **BICYCLE PEDAL** a bicycle pedal with an all-

metal footrest with serrated edges and a toe clip on the front (*informal*)

ratty /rátti/ (**-tier, -tiest**) *adj* **1.** **IRRITABLE** irritable or annoyed (*informal*) ○ *Don't get ratty: it won't take very long.* **2.** **OF RATS** relating to or believed to be characteristic of rats **3.** **INFESTED WITH RATS** full of or overrun with rats **4.** **MESSY** having a messy and generally unkempt appearance (*informal*) **5.** *N Am* **DILAPIDATED** in an unsafe, rundown condition and unfit for human habitation (*informal*) **6.** *Aus* **OFFENSIVE TERM** an offensive term meaning appearing to be or behaving as if mentally ill (*slang*) —**rattily** *adv* —**rattiness** *n*

raucous /ráwkəss/ *adj* **1.** loud and harsh-sounding **2.** characterized by loud noise, shouting, and ribald laughter [Mid-18C. < Latin *raucus* 'hoarse'] —**raucity** /ráwssəti/ *n* —**raucously** *adv* —**raucousness** *n*

raunch /rawnch/ *n* (*informal*) **1.** **SEXUAL EXPLICITNESS** sexual explicitness or suggestiveness of an earthy or vulgar kind, especially as part of a performer's material or act **2.** **SEXUALLY EXPLICIT MATERIAL** sexually explicit or lewd material or language **3.** *US* **MESSINESS** lack of cleanliness or neatness [Mid-20C. Back-formation < RAUNCHY]

raunchy /ráwnchi/ (**-chier, -chiest**) *adj* (*informal*) **1.** sexually explicit or suggestive in an earthy or vulgar way **2.** *N Am* lacking cleanliness or neatness [Mid-20C. Origin ?] —**raunchily** *adv* —**raunchiness** *n*

AKG London
Robert Rauschenberg

Rauschenberg /rówsh'n burg/, **Robert** (*b.* 1925) US artist. His hybrid three-dimensional works such as *Monogram* (1955–59) had a strong influence on the pop art movement of the 1960s.

> 'Painting is always strongest when in spite of composition, color, etc., it appears as a fact, or an inevitability, as opposed to a souvenir or arrangement.'
> [Robert Rauschenberg. Quoted in *Sixteen Americans*, Dorothy C. Miller (ed.); 1959]

rauwolfia /raw woolfi ə, row-/ (*plural same* or **-as**) *n* **1.** a dried root with medicinal properties. Use: sedatives. **2.** the tropical tree or bush whose root has medicinal properties. Native to: Southeast Asia. Latin name: *Rauwolfia serpentina.* [Mid-18C. < modern Latin, after Leonhard *Rauwolf* (?-1596), German botanist and physician]

ravage /rávvij/ *v* (**-ages, -aging, -aged**) **1.** *vti* **COMPLETELY WRECK OR DAMAGE SOMETHING** to cause overwhelming damage or destruction to something (*often passive*) ○ *a war-ravaged country* **2.** *vt* **WRECK AND PLUNDER PLACE** to plunder or sack a place or area ○ *a village ravaged of all its valuables by army deserters* ■ *n* **ACT OF DESTROYING OR PLUNDERING** the destruction, damaging, or plundering of something ■ **ravages** *npl* **DAMAGING EFFECTS** the damaging or disfiguring effects of something ○ *the ravages of time* [Early 17C. < French *ravager*, alteration of *ravine* 'rushing of water' < Latin *rapere* 'seize'] —**ravagement** *n* —**ravager** *n*

RAVC *abbr* Royal Army Veterinary Corps

rave /rayv/ *v* (**raves, raving, raved**) **1.** *vi* **GIVE HIGH PRAISE TO** give praise in a very enthusiastic way ○ *All the critics raved about her performance.* **2.** *vti* **SPEAK WILDLY AND INCOHERENTLY** to speak or say something in a loud, irrational, or incoherent way **3.** *vi* **STORM** to storm and rage with intensity (*literary*) **4.** *vi* **HAVE GOOD TIME** to have a good time, especially at a party, in a wild uninhibited way (*dated slang*) ■ *n* **1.** **LARGE-SCALE PARTY** a large party or club event at which pop music is

played, lasting sometimes all night **2.** **ENTHUSIASTIC PRAISE** an expression of very enthusiastic praise (*informal*) ○ *Her performance received raves from the audience.* **3.** **ACT OF RAVING** an act or instance of raving **4.** **CRAZE** a craze or fad (*dated slang*) ■ *adj* **VERY ENTHUSIASTIC** expressing very enthusiastic praise (*informal*) ○ *rave reviews* [14C. < Old French *raver*] ◇ **rave it up** same as **rave** *n* (sense 1) (*slang dated*)

ravel /rávv'l/ *v* (**-els, -elling, -elled**) **1.** *vti* **FRAY** to come loose from a knitted or woven fabric, or cause threads to do this **2.** *vti* **TANGLE** to become tangled, or cause threads or fibres to tangle **3.** *vt* **UNRAVEL SOMETHING COMPLICATED** to clarify or resolve something complicated **4.** *vti* **COMPLICATE SOMETHING** to make something complicated or involved, or become complicated or involved **5.** *vti* **BREAK UP ROAD SURFACE** to break up a road surface, or begin to break into fragments ■ *n* **LOOSE THREAD OR FIBRE** an unravelled thread or fibre [Late 16C. Probably < Dutch *ravelen*] —**ravelment** *n*

AKG London
Maurice Ravel

Ravel /rə vél/, **Maurice** (1875–1937) French composer. A master of orchestration, he wrote impressionistic pieces that are classics of the 20th-century repertoire. His works include *Boléro* (1928) and *Daphnis et Chloé* (1912). Full name **Ravel, Maurice Joseph**

ravelin /rávvlin/ *n* a small outwork in fortifications consisting of two embankments shaped like an arrowhead that point outwards in front of a larger defence work [Late 16C. Via French < Italian *ravellina*]

raven

raven[1] /ráyv'n/ *n* a large bird belonging to the crow family with glossy black feathers, a wedge-shaped tail, and a large beak. Native to: northern hemisphere. Latin name: *Corvus corax.* ■ *adj* of a deep lustrous black (*literary*) [Old English *hræfn*. Ultimately from a prehistoric Germanic word, thought to be an imitation of its croaking]

CULTURAL NOTE *The Raven*, a poem (1845) by US writer Edgar Allen Poe. This melancholy tale of lost love gained Poe national fame. As a young student mourns the death of his lover, a raven – a traditional symbol of doom – appears at his window. To every question that the student poses about his future and his lover, the bird responds 'Nevermore'.

raven[2] /rávv'n/ (**-ens, -ening, -ened**) *vti* **1.** to eat something voraciously or greedily **2.** to take something away by force, especially prey or plunder (*archaic*) [15C. Via Old French *raviner* 'seize' < Latin *rapere* 'seize'] —**ravener** *n*

ravening /rávv'ning/ *adj* living by hunting prey, es-

pecially in a greedy voracious way —**raveningly** adv

Ravenna /rə vénnə/ capital city of Ravenna Province, Emilia-Romagna Region, northeastern Italy. An ancient Roman city, it contains several early Christian churches. Population: 138,122 (1999).

ravenous /rávv'nəss/ adj 1. extremely hungry 2. greedy for something, especially for the gratification of wants or desires —**ravenously** adv **ravenousness** n

raver /ráyvər/ n 1. somebody who goes to raves (informal) 2. somebody who has an active and uninhibited social life (dated informal)

rave-up n a wild noisy party with music, drinking, and dancing (dated informal)

ravin /rávvin/ n the act of violently seizing something (archaic or literary) [14C. < Old French ravine (see RAVINE)]

ravine /rə veen/ n a deep narrow valley, especially one formed by running water [15C. < Old French ravine 'rapine, violent rush' < Latin rapere 'seize']

raving /ráyving/ adj 1. IRRATIONAL wildly irrational, angry, or insulting 2. ADDS EMPHASIS used to emphasize the sense of admiration and excitement felt for something (informal) ○ a raving review of the play ■ adv COMPLETELY in the fullest degree (informal) ○ raving mad ■ **ravings** npl WILDLY IRRATIONAL SPEECH wildly irrational, angry, or insulting utterances ○ the ravings of a person cheated —**ravingly** adv

ravioli /rávvi ṓli/ n a food made from small squares of pasta sealed around a meat, cheese, or vegetable filling [Mid-19C. < Italian, plural of dialectal raviolo 'small turnip']

ravish /rávvish/ (-ishes, -ishing, -ished) vt 1. RAPE SOMEBODY to force somebody to engage in sexual intercourse (literary) 2. CARRY SOMETHING OFF to capture and carry off something by force (archaic or literary) 3. OVERWHELM SOMEBODY EMOTIONALLY to overwhelm somebody with deep and pleasurable feelings or emotions (usually passive) [13C. < French raviss- 'seize' < Latin rapere] —**ravisher** n —**ravishment** n

ravishing /rávvishing/ adj extremely delightful or beautiful —**ravishingly** adv

raw /raw/ adj 1. UNCOOKED not cooked 2. UNPROCESSED not processed, refined, or treated in any way ○ raw sewage 3. HURT AND SORE cut, scraped, or inflamed, often painfully so 4. INEXPERIENCED lacking training or experience ○ raw army recruits ○ raw talent 5. COLD extremely cold and harsh ○ a raw wind 6. NOT SUBTLE not subtle, restrained, or refined ○ the raw power of the music 7. BRUTALLY REALISTIC factual and realistic, especially concerning unpleasant matters ○ the raw facts 8. NOT CHANGED OR INTERPRETED in an original state and not yet subjected to correction or analysis ○ raw data 9. TEXTILES same as **raw-edged** (sense 1) [Old English hrēaw. Ultimately from an Indo-European word that also produced Latin crudus 'raw' (source of English crude and cruel)] —**rawly** adv —**rawness** n ◇ **in the raw** 1. not wearing clothes (informal) 2. in a natural state, without embellishment or refinement

Rawalpindi /ráwl píndi/, **Rāwalpindi** city of Punjab Province, northern Pakistan. Population: 1,406,214 (1998).

rawboned /ráw bṓnd/ adj having a lean body with prominent bones

raw deal n an arrangement, situation, or treatment that is unfair

raw-edged adj 1. with an unhemmed, sometimes frayed or untidily cut edge 2. brutally realistic in depicting unpleasant situations

rawhide /ráw hīd/ n 1. untanned animal hide 2. a whip or rope made of rawhide

rawhide hammer n a hammer designed to avoid damage to finished surfaces, with a head made from a tight roll of hide held in a metal tube

rawinsonde /ráywin sond/ n a balloon carrying meteorological instruments that has a trackable radar target and is used to observe the velocity and direction of upper-air winds [Mid-20C. < blend of RADAR + WIND[1]]

Rawlings /ráwlingz/, **Jerry** (b. 1947) president of Ghana (1992–2000). He led two military coups in 1979 and 1981 before being elected president in 1992. He also served as chair of the Economic Community of West African States (1994–96). Full name **Rawlings, Jerry John**

raw material n 1. a natural unprocessed material that is used in a manufacturing process 2. somebody or something considered to have potential for use or development

raw sienna n 1. a yellowish-brown colour 2. a natural brownish-yellow substance that is used as a pigment

raw silk n 1. silk fibres reeled from silkworm cocoons and left untreated 2. a fabric or yarn made from raw silk

Rawsthorne /ráwss thawrn/, **Alan** (1905–71) British composer. His symphonies, concertos, and chamber and orchestral works follow traditional principles of tonality.

rax /raks/ (raxes, raxing, raxed) v Scotland 1. vti to stretch something out, or be stretched out 2. vt to pass something with an outstretched hand [Old English raxan. Ultimately from a prehistoric Germanic word that also produced German recken 'to stretch']

ray[1] /ray/ n 1. NARROW BEAM OF LIGHT a narrow beam of light from the Sun or an artificial light source 2. TRACE OF SOMETHING POSITIVE a slight indication of something positive in a difficult or worrying situation ○ a ray of hope 3. PHYS BEAM OF ENERGY a thin beam of radiant energy or particles 4. MATHS LINE EXTENDING FROM POINT a straight line that extends from a point infinitely in one direction 5. ZOOL ARM OF STARFISH an arm of a starfish or other animal with body parts radiating from the centre 6. ASTRON BRIGHT STREAK FROM LUNAR CRATER a bright streak on the lunar surface that radiates from a crater 7. BOT RADIAL STRAND OF PLANT PITH a distinct strand of tissue running radially through the conducting tissues in the stem of a plant ■ **rays** npl SUNSHINE hot or warm sunshine (informal) ○ catch some rays ■ v (rays, raying, rayed) 1. vti EMIT LIGHT to shine or emit rays, e.g. of light or electromagnetic particles 2. vi EXTEND IN LINES to extend in radiating lines from a point [14C. Via French rai < Latin radius 'staff, spoke, ray, beam of light'] —**rayed** adj ◇ **catch some rays** to go sunbathing (slang)

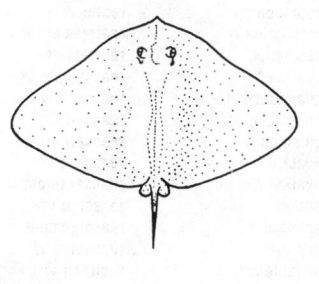

ray

ray[2] /ray/ n a fish with a cartilaginous skeleton, a horizontally flat head and body, broad pectoral fins, and a tapering tail. Order: Rajiformes. [14C. Via French < Latin raia]

ray[3] /ray/ n a syllable that represents the second note in a scale when singing solfeggio. In fixed solfeggio it represents the note D. N Am term **re**[2] [15C. Alteration of RE[2]]

Man Ray

Ray /ray/, **Man** (1890–1976) US artist. Founder of the New York Dada movement, he is known for his avant-garde photographs and paintings. Born **Rudnitsky, Emanuel**

Satyajit Ray

Ray, Satyajit (1921–92) Indian film director. His Apu (1955–59) and Calcutta (1970–75) film trilogies won him international acclaim.

'You may suffer bereavement but life does not stop. It goes on.'
[Satyajit Ray, Deliverance; 1981]

Ray-Bans tdmk a trademark for a brand of sunglasses

ray flower, **ray floret** n a radiating part of the flower of a composite plant such as the dandelion or daisy, comprising either the whole flower head, as in a dandelion, or only its margin, as in a daisy

ray gun n in science fiction, a gun capable of firing rays of energy that stun or destroy

Rayleigh /ráyli/, **John William Strutt, 3rd Baron** (1842–1919) British physicist. He performed research into resonance and vibration, and, with Sir William Ramsay, discovered argon (1894).

Rayleigh scattering n the scattering of electromagnetic radiation into different wavelengths by very small particles of matter, responsible for red sunrises and sunsets as well as the blue of the daytime sky [Mid-20C. After John William Strutt RAYLEIGH]

rayless /ráyləss/ adj 1. dark, gloomy, or lacking light (literary) 2. lacking the ray flowers that typically form part of the flower heads of composite plants such as the daisy —**raylessly** adv —**raylessness** n

Raymond Terrace /ráymənd-/ town in eastern New South Wales, Australia, located at the junction of the Hunter and Williams rivers. Population: 11,151 (1991).

Raynaud's disease /ráy nōz-/ n a disorder of the blood vessels in which somebody is affected by Raynaud's phenomenon without any identifiable underlying cause [Late 19C. After Maurice Raynaud (1834–81), French physician]

Raynaud's phenomenon n spasms of the arteries of the fingers and toes, usually brought on by cold, causing the hands and feet to become pale, cold, numb, and sometimes painful. Causes include diseases of the arteries, rheumatoid arthritis, and repeated trauma to the fingers. [Mid-20C. See RAYNAUD'S DISEASE]

rayon /ráy on/ n 1. a synthetic textile fibre made from cellulose 2. a synthetic fabric or yarn made from rayon fibres [Early 20C. < RAY[1]]

raze /rayz/ (razes, razing, razed), **rase** (rases, rasing, rased) vt 1. to destroy or level a building or settlement completely 2. US to scrape or shave something off something else [Mid-16C. Via French raser 'shave off' < Latin radere 'scrape'] —**razer** n

Raznatovic /raaz náatə vich/, **Zeljko** (1952–2000) Yugoslavian paramilitary commander. An escaped bank robber, he formed the 'Tigers' militia (1990), which was linked by the International War Crimes Tribunal to several massacres in Bosnia and Croatia. He was assassinated in Belgrade before he could stand trial. Known as **Arkan**

razoo /raa zóo, rə zóo/ (plural -zoos) n Aus a gambling chip (informal) [Mid-20C. < ?] ◇ **not have a brass razoo** ANZ to have no money at all ◇ **not worth a brass razoo** ANZ having no worth at all

razor /ráyzər/ *n* an instrument with a blade or powered cutting head that is used for shaving hair off the face or body ■ *vt* (**-zors, -zoring, -zored**) to shave or cut hair using a razor [13C. < Old French *rasor* < *raser* 'shave off' (see RAZE)]

razorback /ráyzər bak/ *n* **1.** MARINE BIOL same as **finback 2.** a feral pig that has a narrow body, ridged back, and long legs. Native to: southeastern United States. **3.** *N Am* GEOG a hill that has a sharp ridge

razorbill

razorbill /ráyzər bil/, **razor-billed auk** /ráyzər bild áwk/ *n* a seabird of the auk family, with black and white feathers and a sharp thick beak. Native to: North Atlantic coasts. Latin name: *Alca torda*.

razor blade *n* a flat blade designed to be used in a safety razor

razor clam *n* *N Am* ZOOL same as **razor-shell**

razor cut *n* a haircut that is done using a razor instead of scissors ■ *vt* to cut or style hair with a razor

razor-shell *n* a bivalve mollusc that has a long narrow tubular shell with squared ends. Native to: Atlantic and Pacific coasts. Family: Solenidae. N Am term **razor clam**

razor wire *n* wire with sharp pieces of metal fixed along its length, used for fences and barriers

razz /raz/ *N Am* (*informal*) *vt* (**razzes, razzing, razzed**) to tease or make fun of somebody ■ *n* a raspberry noise [Early 20C. Shortening and alteration of RASPBERRY]

razzle /rázz'l/ [Early 20C. Shortening] ◇ **on the razzle** enjoying a spell of unrestrained partying or heavy drinking (*dated informal*)

razzle-dazzle *n* **1.** an often gaudy showiness that is designed to be impressive and exciting (*informal*) ○ *a razzle-dazzle of pairs figure skating* **2.** same as **razzle** [Late 19C. Rhyming compound < DAZZLE] ◇ **on the razzle-dazzle** same as **on the razzle** (*dated informal*)

razzmatazz /rázmə táz/ *n* showiness that is designed to be impressive and exciting, especially in the context of a stage show or other spectacle [Late 19C. Origin ?]

Rb *symbol* CHEM ELEM rubidium

rbc, RBC *abbr* MED red blood (cell) count

RBE *abbr* BIOL relative biological effectiveness

rc *abbr* reinforced concrete

RC *abbr* **1.** MED Red Cross **2.** MIL Reserve Corps **3.** CHR Roman Catholic

R.C. *abbr* CHR Roman Catholic

RCA *abbr* Royal College of Art

rcd *abbr* received

RCM *abbr* Royal College of Music

RCMP *abbr* Royal Canadian Mounted Police

RCN *abbr* **1.** Royal Canadian Navy **2.** Royal College of Nursing

r-colour *n* in phonetics, the effect of an 'r' sound uttered simultaneously with a vowel by constricting the oral cavity with the tongue

RCP *abbr* MED Royal College of Physicians

rcpt *abbr* COMM receipt

RCS *abbr* **1.** Royal College of Science **2.** MED Royal College of Surgeons **3.** Royal Corps of Signals

rct *abbr* recruit

RCT *abbr* Royal Corps of Transport

RCVS *abbr* Royal College of Veterinary Surgeons

rd *abbr* **1.** COMM rendered **2.** road **3.** MEASURE rod **4.** round

Rd *abbr* Road (used in addresses)

RD *abbr* **1.** BANKING refer to drawer (*used on cheques*) **2.** MAIL Rural Delivery

R/D *abbr* BANKING refer to drawer (*used on cheques*)

RDA *abbr* HEALTH recommended daily allowance

RDF *abbr* MEDIA radio direction finder

RDO *n Aus* a day off given by some employers in lieu of extra hours worked, sometimes on a regular basis (*informal*) Full form **rostered day off**

RDS[1] *n* a system for tuning radio receivers automatically by sending digital signals with normal radio programmes [Shortening of *radio data system*]

RDS[2] *abbr* MED respiratory distress syndrome

re[1] /ree, ray/ *prep* with reference to [Early 18C. < Latin, 'on the matter of', form of *res* 'thing, matter']

USAGE The use of **re** meaning 'with reference to' is largely restricted to the language of business, but it is also used informally as a convenient short form: *Re your recent proposal – I fully agree.*

re[2] /ray/ *n N Am* MUSIC same as **ray**[3] [15C. Shortening of medieval Latin *resonare* 'resound' in a Latin hymn to St John the Baptist, from which names of hexachords were taken]

re[3] *abbr* Réunion (*used in Internet addresses*) See table at **domain name**

're *contr* are ○ *They're planning to come.*

Re[1] /ray/ *n* MYTHOL same as **Ra**[1]

Re[2] *abbr* MONEY rupee ■ *symbol* **1.** PHYS Reynold's number **2.** CHEM ELEM rhenium

RE *abbr* **1.** Reformed Episcopal **2.** Religious Education **3.** Right Excellent **4.** Royal Engineers

re- *prefix* **1.** again, anew ○ *rebuild* **2.** back, backward ○ *recall* [Via Old French from Latin]

reabsorb *vt*	**reapportionment** *n*
reabsorption *n*	**reappraisal** *n*
reaccept *vt*	**reappraise** *vt*
reacceptance *n*	**rearm** *vti*
reaccreditation *n*	**rearmament** *n*
reaccustom *vt*	**rearrest** *vt*
reacquaint *vt*	**reassemble** *vti*
reacquaintance *n*	**reassembly** *n*
reacquire *vt*	**reassert** *v*
reacquisition *n*	**reassertion** *n*
reactivate *vti*	**reassess** *vt*
reactivation *n*	**reassessment** *n*
readapt *vti*	**reassign** *vt*
readaptation *n*	**reassignment** *n*
readjust *vti*	**reassume** *vt*
readjustable *adj*	**reattach** *vt*
readjuster *n*	**reattachment** *n*
readjustment *n*	**reattain** *vt*
readmit *vt*	**reattainment** *n*
readmittance *n*	**reattempt** *vt*
readopt *vt*	**reauthorization** *n*
readoption *n*	**reauthorize** *vt*
readvertise *vti*	**reawaken** *vti*
readvertisement *n*	**rebadge** *vt*
reaffirm *vti*	**rebaptism** *n*
reaffirmation *n*	**rebaptize** *vt*
reallocate *vt*	**rebind** *vt, n*
reallocation *n*	**reboil** *vti*
reallot *vt*	**rebook** *vti*
reallotment *n*	**reborrow** *vt*
realter *vt*	**rebroadcast** *vti, n*
reanalyse *vt*	**reburial** *n*
reanalysis *n*	**rebury** *vt*
reanimate *vt*	**rebuy** *vti*
reanimation *n*	**recalculate** *vti*
reannex *vt*	**recalculation** *n*
reannexation *n*	**recalibrate** *vt*
reappear *vi*	**recapitalization** *n*
reappearance *n*	**recapitalize** *vt*
reapplication *n*	**recaution** *vt*
reapply *vti*	**recentralization** *n*
reappoint *vt*	**recentralize** *vti*
reappointment *n*	**recertification** *n*
reapportion *vt*	**recertify** *vt*

recharter *vt*	**re-enlist** *vti*
recheck *vti*	**re-enlistment** *n*
rechristen *vt*	**re-equip** *vt*
recirculate *vti*	**re-equipment** *n*
recirculation *n*	**re-erect** *vt*
reclassification *n*	**re-erection** *n*
reclassify *vt*	**re-escalate** *vti*
recolonization *n*	**re-escalation** *n*
recolonize *vt*	**re-establish** *vt*
recolour *vt*	**re-establishment** *n*
recombine *vti*	**re-evaluate** *vt*
recommission *vt*	**re-evaluation** *n*
recommit *vt*	**re-evaporate** *vti*
recommitment *n*	**re-evaporation** *n*
recommittal *n*	**re-examination** *n*
recompile *vt*	**re-examine** *vt*
recompose *vt*	**re-experience** *vt*
recomposition *n*	**re-exploration** *n*
reconduct *vt*	**re-explore** *vt*
reconfiguration *n*	**refashion** *vt*
reconfigure *vt*	**refight** *vti*
reconfirm *vt*	**refile** *vt*
reconfirmation *n*	**refinish** *vt*
reconnect *vt*	**refinisher** *n*
reconnection *n*	**refire** *vti*
reconquer *vt*	**refloat** *vt*
reconquest *n*	**refold** *vt*
reconsecrate *vt*	**reformat** *vt*
reconsecration *n*	**reformulate** *vt*
reconsider *vti*	**reformulation** *n*
reconsideration *n*	**refortification** *n*
reconsolidate *vt*	**refortify** *vt*
reconsolidation *n*	**reframe** *vt*
recontaminate *vt*	**refreeze** *vti*
recontamination *n*	**refry** *vt*
reconvene *vti*	**regather** *vt*
reconversion *n*	**regift** *vti*
reconvert *vti*	**regild** *vt*
recook *vt*	**reglaze** *vt*
recopy *vti*	**regrant** *vt*
recross *vti*	**regrind** *vt*
recrystallization *n*	**regrow** *vti*
recrystallize *vti*	**regrowth** *n*
recut *vt*	**rehang** *vt*
rededicate *v*	**reharden** *vti*
rededication *n*	**rehear** *vt*
redeliver *vti*	**rehearing** *n*
redesign *vt, n*	**reheat** *vti*
redetermination *n*	**reheater** *n*
redetermine *vti*	**reignite** *vt*
redifferentiate *vti*	**reignition** *n*
redifferentiation *n*	**reimport** *vt, n*
redigest *vt*	**reimportation** *n*
rediscount *vt*	**reimpose** *vt*
rediscover *vt*	**reimposition** *n*
rediscovery *n*	**reimpress** *vt*
redissolution *n*	**reimprison** *vt*
redissolve *vti*	**reincorporate** *vt*
redistil *vt*	**reincorporation** *n*
redistillation *n*	**reinfect** *vt*
redivide *vti*	**reinfection** *n*
redivision *n*	**reinflate** *vt*
redraw *vt*	**reinflation** *n*
re-edit *vti*	**reinject** *vt*
re-educate *vt*	**reinjection** *n*
re-education *n*	**reinsert** *vt*
re-educative *adj*	**reinsertion** *n*
re-elect *vt*	**reinspect** *vt*
re-election *n*	**reinspection** *n*
re-eligibility *n*	**reinstall** *vt*
re-eligible *adj*	**reinstallation** *n*
re-embark *vti*	**reintegrate** *vt*
re-embarkation *n*	**reintegration** *n*
re-embrace *vt*	**reinter** *vt*
re-emerge *vi*	**reinterment** *n*
re-emergence *n*	**reinterpret** *vt*
re-emergent *adj*	**reinterpretation** *n*
re-emission *n*	**reinterview** *n*
re-emit *vt*	**reintroduce** *vt*
re-emphasis *n*	**reintroduction** *n*
re-emphasize *vt*	**reinvade** *vt*
re-employ *vt*	**reinvasion** *n*
re-employment *n*	**reinvestigate** *vti*
re-enact *vt*	**reinvestigation** *n*
re-enactment *n*	**reinvigorate** *vt*
re-engage *vti*	**reinvigoration** *n*
re-engagement *n*	**reinvigorator** *n*

reissue *vt, n*
rejudge *vt*
relabel *vt*
relaunch *vt, n*
relearn *vt*
relet *vt*
relicense *vt*
relight *vt*
reline *vt*
reload *vti*
remail *vt*
remarket *vt*
remarriage *n*
remarry *vti*
remeasure *vti*
remeasurement *n*
remelt *vti*
remend *vt*
remilitarization *n*
remilitarize *vt*
remodification *n*
remodify *vt*
remonetization *n*
remonetize *vt*
rename *vt*
renationalization *n*
renationalize *vt*
renegotiate *vti*
renegotiation *n*
renominate *v*
renomination *n*
renumber *vt*
reoccupation *n*
reoccupy *vti*
reoccur *vi*
reoccurrence *n*
reorchestrate *vt*
reorchestration *n*
reorder *vti, n*
repack *vti*
repackage *vt*
repaginate *vt*
repagination *n*
repaint *vti, n*
repaper *vti*
repass *vti*
repave *vt*
repeople *vt*
rephotograph *vt*
rephrase *vt*
repin *vt*
replan *vt*
repolish *vt, n*
repopulate *vt*
repopulation *n*
reposition *vt*
repot *vt*
repotting *n*
reprice *vt*
reprivatization *n*
reprivatize *vt*
reprocess *vt*
reprogram *vt*
reprogrammability *n*
reprogrammable *adj*
republication *n*
republish *vt*
republisher *n*
repurchase *n, vt*
reread *vt*
rerecord *vti*
rerecording *n*
reregister *vti*
reregistration *n*
reregulate *vti*
reregulation *n*
reroof *vt*
reroute *vt*
reseal *vt*
resealable *adj*
resegregate *vt*
resegregation *n*
reselect *vt*
reselection *n*
resell *vti*
reseller *n*
resend *vt*
reship *vt*
reshow *vti*
resite *vt*
resize *vt*
resold
resole *vt*
respray *vt, n*
restage *vt*
restart *n, vti*
restartable *adj*
restring *n, vt*
restrung *adj*
restudy *vt*
resubmit *vt*
resupply *vt, n*
resurvey *vti, n*
resynthesization *n*
resynthesize *vt*
reteach *vt*
retie *vt*
retime *vt*
retitle *vt*
retransfusion *n*
retranslate *vt*
retranslation *n*
retransmission *n*
retransmit *vt*
retune *vt*
retype *vt*
reupholster *vt*
reutilization *n*
reutilize *vt*
revaccinate *vt*
revaccination *n*
revalidate *vt*
revalidation *n*
revalorization *n*
revalorize *vt*
revaluate *vt*
revaluation *n*
revalue *vt*
revarnish *vt*
revisitation *n*
rewash *vt*
reweave *vt*
reweigh *vt*
rewrap *vt*

reach /reech/ *v* (**reaches, reaching, reached**) **1.** *vt* ARRIVE AT PLACE to arrive or come to a particular place or point **2.** *vt* ARRIVE AT STATE to get into a particular state or condition ○ *I had reached desperation point.* **3.** *vti* EXTEND AS FAR AS SOMETHING to stretch out physically or extend as far as a particular place or point ○ *I can't reach the top shelf without a chair.* **4.** *vi* MOVE TOWARDS SOMETHING TO TOUCH IT to move towards something in order to touch or grasp it ○ *She reached for her coat.* **5.** *vti* INFLUENCE PEOPLE to have an influence or impact on people or on a group ○ *This campaign will reach millions of people.* **6.** *vt* CONTACT SOMEBODY to communicate with somebody ○ *I'll try to reach you at home.* **7.** *vt* PASS SOMEBODY SOMETHING to pass or hand somebody something (*informal*) ○ *Just reach me down that file, would you.* **8.** *vi* STRIVE FOR SOMETHING to strive too much to achieve or acquire something, especially without success **9.** *vi* SAILING SAIL WITH WIND TO SIDE to sail on a tack with the wind blowing from the side **10.** *vi Carib* ARRIVE to arrive at a destination ○ *We reach early in the morning.* **11.** *vi Carib* GO to go as far as ○ *How far yuh reachin?* **12.** *vt Carib* BECOME to become ■ *n* **1.** EXTENT OF REACHING the extent or range that somebody or something is able to reach ○ *The top shelf is just beyond his reach.* **2.** ACT OF STRETCHING OUT the act of stretching out or extending **3.** RANGE OF POWER the extent of the power or influence exercised by somebody or something ○ *beyond the reach of the law* **4.** STRETCH OF WATER a stretch of open water, e.g. on a river **5.** NUMBER OF VIEWERS the number of viewers who visit a website or watch a television programme (*informal*) ○ *Reach is one factor determining whether companies invest in the Web.* **6.** SAILING TACK SAILED BY VESSEL a tack sailed by a vessel with the wind blowing from the side ■ **reaches** *npl* AREA OR LEVEL an area or level of something ○ *the upper reaches of the Amazon* [Old English *rǣcan*. Ultimately from a prehistoric Germanic word that also produced German *reichen* 'to reach'] —**reachable** *adj* —**reacher** *n* ◇ **out of reach 1.** beyond the grasp of somebody's outstretched hand **2.** not able to be achieved or attained by somebody ◇ **within** *or* **in reach 1.** able to be grasped by somebody with an outstretched hand **2.** achievable or attainable

react /ri ákt/ (**-acts, -acting, -acted**) *vi* **1.** RESPOND EMOTIONALLY to respond to something by showing the feelings or thoughts it arouses ○ *Officials reacted with guarded optimism.* **2.** RESPOND BY TAKING ACTION to respond to something by taking action ○ *The government reacted by sending in troops.* **3.** BE IN OPPOSITION to act in opposition to somebody or something ○ *children reacting against their parents* **4.** UNDERGO PHYSICAL RESPONSE to respond to the physical effects of something such as a medication or air pollutants **5.** CHEM CHANGE CHEMICALLY to undergo a chemical reaction

reactance /ri áktənss/ *n* opposition to the flow of alternating current caused by the inductance and capacitance in a circuit, measured in ohms. Symbol ***X***

reactant /ri áktənt/ *n* a substance that reacts with another in a chemical reaction

reaction /ri áksh'n/ *n* **1.** EMOTIONAL RESPONSE an emotional or intellectual response that something arouses ○ *My initial reaction was to laugh.* **2.** ACTIVE RESPONSE a response to something that involves taking action, or an action taken in response to something ○ *Prices jumped in reaction to rumours of a shortage.* **3.** OPPOSING ACTION an act in opposition to somebody or something ○ *a reaction against consumerism* **4.** PHYSICAL RESPONSE a response to the physical effects of something such as heat, cold, or pollution **5.** MED BODILY RESPONSE TO SUBSTANCE a bodily response to a foreign substance such as an infectious agent, medication, or allergen **6.** POL STRONG CONSERVATISM opposition to progressive social or political change **7.** PHYS FORCES ACTING ON BODY an equal but opposite force exerted by a body when a force acts upon it **8.** INDUST NUCLEAR PROCESS a nuclear process resulting in a change in the structure of atomic nuclei ■ **reactions** *npl* SOMEBODY'S ABILITY TO REACT QUICKLY somebody's ability to respond quickly to an unexpected situation, especially one of danger ○ *His quick reactions saved us from certain death.* —**reactional** *adj*

reactionary /ri áksh'nəri/ *adj* opposed to progressive social or political change ■ *n* (*plural* **-ies**) somebody who is reactionary

reaction engine *n* an engine such as a jet or rocket engine that produces thrust by ejecting a stream of gas at high velocity

reaction formation *n* in psychoanalysis, a defence mechanism in which somebody condemns something that has an unconscious appeal

reaction time *n* **1.** the interval of time between the application of a stimulus and the first indication of a response **2.** COMPUT same as **access time**

reactive /ri áktiv/ *adj* **1.** REACTING tending to react to events and situations rather than initiating or instigating them **2.** CHEM REACTING CHEMICALLY taking part in a chemical reaction **3.** PSYCHIAT CAUSED BY STIMULI OR EVENTS describes a psychiatric condition caused by situations or stimuli such as the behaviour of other people or the death of a loved one —**reactively** *adv* —**reactiveness** *n* —**reactivity** /reé ak tívvəti/ *n*

reactor /ri áktər/ *n* **1.** SOMEBODY OR SOMETHING THAT REACTS somebody or something that reacts or takes part in a reaction **2.** INDUST same as **nuclear reactor 3.** INDUST CONTAINER IN WHICH CHEMICAL REACTION OCCURS a vessel or other equipment in which an industrial chemical reaction takes place **4.** ELEC COMPONENT IN ELECTRICAL CIRCUIT a component in an electrical circuit used to create reactance, e.g. a capacitor or an inductor **5.** MED SOMEBODY SENSITIVE TO MEDICATION a person or animal that displays a reaction to a medication, vaccine, or other substance, especially one that shows a positive reaction to a skin test for latent infection

read *v* /reed/ (**reads, reading, read** /red/) **1.** *vti* INTERPRET WRITTEN MATERIAL to identify and understand the meaning of the characters and words in written or printed material **2.** *vti* UTTER WRITTEN WORDS to say the words of written or printed material aloud **3.** *vti* LEARN SOMETHING BY READING to find something out by studying written or printed material ○ *I read it in a book.* **4.** *vt* INTERPRET NONWRITTEN MATERIAL to interpret the information conveyed by movements, signs, or signals ○ *We could no longer read the trail.* **5.** *vti* INTERPRET PRINTED SIGNS to be able to identify and understand printed or written signs or symbols ○ *to learn to read music* **6.** *vt* BE ABLE TO READ FOREIGN LANGUAGE to know another language well enough to be able to read in it ○ *Can you read French?* **7.** *vt* UNDERSTAND SOMETHING INTUITIVELY to have an understanding of something by experience or intuitive means ○ *claiming to be able to read the future* **8.** *vti* PUBL same as **proofread 9.** *vti* GIVE PARTICULAR INTERPRETATION TO SOMETHING to interpret something, or be interpreted, in a particular way ○ *I read this passage as being extremely optimistic.* **10.** *vi* HAVE QUALITIES THAT AFFECT UNDERSTANDING to have particular characteristics that affect the way something is understood ○ *In the original it reads as poetry rather than prose.* **11.** *vi* HAVE PARTICULAR WORDS to have a particular wording ○ *a sign that reads DANGER* **12.** *vt* EDUC TAKE UNIVERSITY COURSE to pursue a particular course of study at a university **13.** *vti* MEDIA HEAR SOMETHING ON TWO-WAY RADIO to receive and understand a message sent by somebody on a two-way radio **14.** *vt* INDICATE DATA to indicate or display data such as a temperature ○ *What does the thermometer read?* **15.** *vt* PUBL SUBSTITUTE WORD to substitute a word or words for others that were printed incorrectly ○ *For 'peasant' read 'pheasant'.* **16.** *vti* COMPUT TRANSFER DATA INTO COMPUTER MEMORY to transfer program instructions or data from a storage device into a computer's main memory **17.** GENETICS DECODE RNA to recognize sections of RNA (**codons**) that are responsible for different amino acid sequences and assemble them into a protein chain (*refers to enzymes*) ■ *n* /reed/ **1.** READING MATERIAL something that produces a particular reaction in the reader when read (*informal*) ○ *a thrilling read* **2.** TIME SPENT READING a period devoted to reading ○ *She settled down for a long read.* ■ *adj* /red/ KNOWLEDGEABLE informed or provided with knowledge through reading ○ *He was without formal education but was literate, well read, and articulate.* [Old English *rǣdan* < Indo-European] ◇ **take something as read** to assume something to be the case

SPELLCHECK read or **reed**? Do not confuse the spelling of ***read*** and ***reed***, which sound similar. ***Read*** is chiefly used as a verb, meaning 'interpret written material': *I never read the sports pages of the newspaper.* It is occasionally used as a noun, meaning 'something read' or 'a session of reading': *Her new novel is a good read.* ***Reed*** is only used as a noun, denoting a tall plant that grows near water, or the vibrating part of musical instruments such as the clarinet or oboe.

USAGE read or **red**? The verb ***read*** has two pronunciations. In the infinitive or present tense it rhymes with ***weed*** and as the past tense or past participle it rhymes with ***wed***. The word ***red*** denotes the colour of blood and is not an alternative spelling of ***read*** as a past form, which sounds similar: *I read* [not *red*] *the letter aloud. Have you read* [not *red*] *this book?* Confusion may arise because the past tense and past participle of the verb *lead* is *led*.

read into *vt* to detect meanings in speech or written text that were not necessarily intended by the speaker or writer

read out *vt* **1.** READ SOMETHING ALOUD to read written or printed material aloud **2.** COMPUT RETRIEVE INFORMATION

FROM COMPUTER to retrieve data from the memory or a disk or other storage device of a computer **3.** US EXPEL SOMEBODY FROM ORGANIZATION to expel somebody formally from a political party, organization, or other group

read up *vti* to learn a lot about a subject by reading about it or researching it

Read /reed/, **Sir Herbert** (1893–1968) British art historian. A prominent advocate in his day of contemporary British art, he founded the Institute of Contemporary Arts in London (1947). Full name **Read, Sir Herbert Edward**

readable /reédəb'l/ *adj* **1.** able to be read **2.** written in a style that is enjoyable and interesting to read — **readability** /reédə bílləti/ *n* — **readably** *adv*

readdress /reé ə dréss/ (-dresses, -dressing, -dressed) *vt* **1.** to put a new address on a letter or parcel **2.** to return to a problem or issue with the intention of resolving it

reader /reédər/ *n* **1.** SOMEBODY WHO READS somebody who reads something ○ *He was never much of a reader.* ○ *a reader of mysteries* **2.** READING DEVICE a device that reads, especially one connected to a computer for reading media **3.** EDUC EDUCATIONAL BOOK a textbook used in learning to read **4.** LITERAT ANTHOLOGY an anthology of literary works **5.** PUBL SOMEBODY WHO READS FOR PUBLISHER somebody who reads manuscripts for a publisher to assess whether they are publishable **6.** CHR same as **lay reader 7.** JUDAISM same as **cantor** (sense 1) **8.** EDUC LECTURER AT UNIVERSITY a lecturer at university who ranks above a senior lecturer and below a professor

readership /reédər ship/ *n* **1.** the group or number of people who read a particular publication **2.** the position of reader in a British university, of a rank above senior lectureship

readily /réddili/ *adv* **1.** with little difficulty **2.** promptly and without any hesitation

reading /reéding/ *n* **1.** IDENTIFYING OF WRITTEN OR PRINTED WORDS the process of identifying and understanding the meaning of the characters and words in written or printed material **2.** MATERIAL THAT IS READ written or printed material that can be read **3.** OCCASION OF READING SOMETHING an occasion during which somebody reads something to an audience or congregation ○ *a poetry reading* **4.** TEXT READ TO AUDIENCE OR CONGREGATION a piece of literature that is read to an audience, or a passage from a sacred text that is read to a congregation **5.** INTERPRETATION OF SOMETHING an interpretation or understanding of a situation or of something that has been written or said **6.** TECH INFORMATION TAKEN FROM EQUIPMENT a piece of information or a measurement taken from a piece of equipment or with the help of equipment **7.** POL RECITAL OF PARLIAMENTARY BILL the process of formally reciting the text of a bill as part of the procedure in Parliament, after which it has to pass through three other stages before it can become law **8.** POL ONE OF BILL'S PARLIAMENTARY STAGES one of the three stages that a bill passes through in Parliament before it becomes law

Reading /rédding/ town in central southern England. It is home to the University of Reading, founded in 1892. Population: 143,096 (2001).

reading age *n* a child's competence in reading, measured against the average competence of children of the same age

reading frame *n* a sequence of three nucleotides on DNA or messenger RNA that indicates the starting point for translation to produce a polypeptide

README file /reéd meé-/ *n* a computer text file that contains information a user may need in order to install or operate a program

read-only *adj* describes computer files that can be retrieved and displayed but cannot be changed or deleted

read-only memory *n* a small computer memory for the permanent storage of data that cannot subsequently be altered or added to

read-out *n* **1.** DATA RETRIEVAL the retrieving of data from a computer's memory, disk, or other storage device **2.** DATA RETRIEVED BY COMPUTER the data retrieved from a computer's memory, disk, or other storage system

3. DEVICE DISPLAYING INFORMATION a part of a piece of equipment that displays information

readthrough /reéd throo/ *n* a reading of a play without acting, allowing actors to familiarize themselves with the dialogue before full rehearsals begin

read-write head *n* a magnetic device that can both read data from and write data to a magnetic medium such as a computer floppy or hard disk

ready /réddi/ *adj* (-ier, -iest) **1.** PREPARED FOR SOMETHING prepared for something that is going to happen ○ *Are you ready to leave?* **2.** FINISHED AND AVAILABLE FOR USE finished or completed and so able to be used immediately ○ *When will dinner be ready?* **3.** ON POINT OF DOING SOMETHING on the point of doing something or liable to do something ○ *This old roof is ready to cave in.* **4.** WILLING TO DO SOMETHING eager, willing, or prepared to do something ○ *Don't be so ready to give in!* **5.** QUICKLY PRODUCED quickly and easily given, provided, or available ○ *a ready response to questions about wrongdoing* **6.** PREPARED IN ADVANCE prepared or blended in advance, and able to be used with very little additional preparation (*often used in combination*) ○ *available ready-sliced in small packets* **7.** INTELLIGENT intelligent, alert, and quick-witted ○ *a ready wit* ■ *vt* (-ies, -ying, -ied) PREPARE SOMETHING to prepare something, especially so that it is in a condition for something to happen to it ■ *n* CASH ready money (*informal*) [12C. < Old English *ræde* 'prompt' < Germanic] — **readiness** *n* ◇ **at the ready** prepared for immediate use or action

ready cash *n* N Am same as **ready money**

ready-made *adj* **1.** already prepared or made for convenience **2.** thought out in advance ○ *ready-made excuses* ■ *n* N Am CLOTHING same as **ready-to-wear**

ready-mix *n* a correct mixture of ingredients that is preblended and able to be used with very little additional preparation — **ready-mixed** *adj*

ready money *n* money that is available to be spent immediately, usually as notes and coins. N Am term **ready cash**

ready reckoner *n* a table that shows frequently used arithmetic calculations for easy reference

ready-to-wear *adj* describes clothing offered for sale in a standard size and completely finished, as opposed to clothing made to the customer's specifications or requirements ■ *n* a ready-to-wear item of clothing. N Am term **ready-made**

reafforest /reé ə fórrist/ *vti* FORESTRY same as **reforest** — **reafforestation** /reé ə fórri stáysh'n/ *n*

The White House

Ronald Reagan

Reagan /ráygən/, **Ronald** (1911–2004) 40th president of the United States (1981–89). After a career as a film actor and then as governor of California (1967–75), he served as a Republican president for two terms. His administration was marked by improved relations with the former Soviet Union during the closing years of the Cold War. Full name **Reagan, Ronald Wilson**. See table at **president**

'We will never forget them, nor the last time we saw them this morning, as they prepared for the journey and waved goodbye and "slipped the surly bonds of earth" to "touch the face of God".'
[Ronald Reagan, *Broadcast from the Oval Office after the loss of space shuttle* Challenger *and all its crew, Washington, DC*; 28 January 1986]

Reaganomics /ráygə nómmiks/ *n* the free-market economic approach espoused by US president Ronald Reagan, involving cuts in taxes and social spending together with deregulation of domestic markets (*takes a singular verb*) [Late 20C. Blend of REAGAN + ECONOMICS]

reagent /ri áyjənt/ *n* a substance taking part in a chemical reaction, especially one used to detect, measure, or prepare another substance

reagin /reé əjin/ *n* an antibody involved in allergic reactions such as hay fever. Reagins are produced following an initial exposure to an allergenic substance and they interact with allergenic substances to trigger the release of histamines, causing inflammation, swelling, and other symptoms. [Early 20C. < German, < *reagieren* 'react'] — **reaginic** /reé ə jínnik/ *adj*

real[1] /reé əl, reel/ *adj* **1.** PHYSICALLY EXISTING having actual physical existence ○ *practise medicine with real patients* **2.** VERIFIABLE verifiable as actual fact, e.g. legally or scientifically ○ *What is his real name?* **3.** NOT IMAGINARY existing as fact, rather than as a product of dreams or the imagination ○ *In the real world things are somewhat different.* **4.** NOT ARTIFICIAL genuine and original, not artificial or synthetic ○ *real leather* **5.** TRADITIONAL AND AUTHENTIC prepared or made in a traditional or authentic way, rather than being mass-produced or artificial ○ *looking for some real food* **6.** UNDISPUTED based on fact, observation, or experience and so undisputed ○ *The real success of the evening was the comedy act.* **7.** ESSENTIAL of basic, essential, or critical importance ○ *And the real question for America is: why take the risk?* **8.** EMPHASIZING TRUTH used to emphasize the accuracy or appropriateness of a particular thing ○ *He's a real professional.* **9.** SINCERE honest or sincere, not feigned or affected ○ *express your real feelings* **10.** ECON IN TERMS OF PURCHASING POWER regarded in terms of purchasing power rather than the actual amount **11.** LAW RELATING TO FIXED PROPERTY relating to land and the fixed property associated with it **12.** PHILOSOPHY ABOUT EXISTENCE concerned with independent objective existence **13.** MATHS INVOLVING ONLY RATIONAL OR IRRATIONAL NUMBERS involving, relating to, or having elements of the set of rational or irrational numbers only ■ *adv* N Am VERY very or extremely (*informal*) ○ *I'm real tired.* ■ *n* **1.** REALITY everything that exists in the actual world **2.** MATHS same as **real number** [15C. Directly or via French < late Latin *realis* 'relating to things (in law)' < Latin *res* 'thing, fact'] — **realness** *n* ◇ **for real** N Am seriously, not as a joke or as a practice (*informal*) ◇ **get real 1.** used to indicate strongly that what somebody said or thought is unrealistic or out of touch with the facts (*slang*) **2.** to begin to take a realistic view of a situation ○ *He needs to get real.* ◇ **(in) real life** in the course of normal life as opposed to imagined or fictional representations of life, e.g. in books and films

real[2] /ray aál/ (*plural* **-als** or **-ales** /-aáles/) *n* **1.** the main unit of Brazilian currency. See table at **currency 2.** a former coin used in several Spanish-speaking countries [Late 16C. Via Spanish < Latin *regalis* (see ROYAL)]

real[3] /ray aál/ (*plural* **reals** or **reis** /rayss/) *n* a former unit of Portuguese currency [Mid-20C. Via Portuguese < Latin *regalis* (see ROYAL)]

real ale *n* a beer that is allowed to ferment in the cask and does not have carbon dioxide added to it when it is served

real estate *n* ANZ, N Am land including all the property on it that cannot be moved and any attached rights

real-estate agent *n* ANZ, N Am somebody who buys,

sells, and leases property on behalf of somebody else

real focus *n* a point from which light diverges or at which it converges

realgar /ri álgər/ *n* a soft orange-red arsenic sulphide mineral. Use: tanning, paints, fireworks. [14C. Via medieval Latin *realger* < Arabic *rahj al-ḡār* 'powder of the cave']

realign /reé ə līn/ (**-ligns**, **-ligning**, **-ligned**) *v* **1.** *vt* STRAIGHTEN SOMETHING AGAIN to readjust or manipulate something so that it is in a straight line or is correctly oriented **2.** *vti* CHANGE SOMETHING TO FIT SITUATION to alter or change something to fit different circumstances **3.** *vti* MAKE NEW ALLIANCES to form new alliances or associations, or cause people or groups to do this ○ *The party has realigned itself with several former ideological opponents.* —**realignment** *n*

real image *n* an optical image of something that is produced by reflection or refraction and can be transferred onto a surface such as the film inside a camera

realise *vti* another spelling of **realize**

realism /reé əlizəm/ *n* **1.** PRACTICAL UNDERSTANDING OF LIFE a practical understanding and acceptance of the actual nature of the world, rather than an idealized or romantic view of it **2.** ACCURACY OF SIMULATION the simulation of something in a way that accurately resembles real things ○ *the increasing realism of computer graphics* **3.** LIFELIKE ARTISTIC REPRESENTATION in artistic and literary works, lifelike representation of people and the world, without any idealization **4.** PHILOSOPHY THEORY THAT THINGS EXIST OBJECTIVELY the theory that things such as universals, moral facts, and theoretical scientific entities exist independently of people's thoughts and perceptions **5.** PHILOSOPHY THEORY OF OBJECTIVELY EXISTING WORLD the theory that there is an objectively existing world, not dependent on our minds, and that people are able to understand aspects of that world through perception **6.** PHILOSOPHY THEORY THAT STATEMENTS HAVE TRUTH VALUES the theory that every declarative statement is either true or false, regardless of whether this can be verified

realist /reé əlist/ *n* **1.** somebody who only considers things as they are or appear to be, and avoids ideals and abstractions **2.** somebody who practises realism in the arts or believes in philosophical theories of realism

realistic /reé ə lístik/ *adj* **1.** PRACTICAL seeking what is achievable or possible, based on known facts ○ *Set realistic goals when looking for a new job.* **2.** SIMULATING REALITY simulating real things or imaginary things in a way that seems real ○ *computer games with realistic graphics* **3.** REASONABLE not priced or valued too low or high ○ *a realistic price* **4.** REPRESENTING LIFE ACCURATELY in the arts and literature, representing life as it really is, rather than an idealized picture of it **5.** PHILOSOPHY RELATING TO REALISM relating to philosophical theories of realism —**realistically** *adv*

~~realisticly~~ incorrect spelling of **realistically**

reality /ri álləti/ (*plural* **-ties**) *n* **1.** REAL EXISTENCE actual being or existence, as opposed to an imaginary, idealized, or false nature **2.** ALL THAT EXISTS OR HAPPENS everything that actually does or could exist or happen in real life **3.** SOMETHING THAT EXISTS OR HAPPENS something that has real existence and must be dealt with in real life ○ *a vision that ignores the realities of the business world* **4.** TYPE OF EXISTENCE an existence or universe, either connected with or independent from other kinds ○ *fantastic notions of alternative realities* **5.** PHILOSOPHY TOTALITY OF REAL THINGS the totality of real things in the world, independent of people's knowledge or perception of them ◇ **in reality** in actual fact

reality check *n N Am* something said or done to demonstrate the unrealistic nature of somebody's ideas or desires (*informal*)

reality principle *n* in Freudian psychoanalysis, the ego's ability to postpone gratification to avoid unpleasant consequences or to gain greater reward

reality show *n* a television or radio programme that

deals with real people in real situations. Reality shows range from those depicting police operations and emergency rescues to those in which people divorce, choose marriage partners, or actively deal with their personal problems on air.

reality tourism *n* travel to areas of the world deemed politically unstable or less developed, in order to experience at first hand economic disadvantage, conflict, repression, etc.

reality TV *n* television programmes that present real people in live, though often deliberately manufactured, situations and monitor their emotions and behaviour

realize /reé ə līz/ (**-izes**, **-izing**, **-ized**), **realise** (**-ises**, **-ising**, **-ised**) *v* **1.** *vti* KNOW AND UNDERSTAND SOMETHING to know, understand, and accept something ○ *doesn't realize how lucky he is* **2.** *vti* BE OR BECOME AWARE OF SOMETHING to be aware or conscious of something, or to become aware of something ○ *Do you realize the problems you've caused?* **3.** *vt* ACHIEVE SOMETHING to fulfil a specific vision, plan, or potential **4.** *vt* TRANSLATE SOMETHING INTO MONEY to translate something into a particular amount of money, usually by selling it **5.** *vt* FIN CONVERT GAIN OR LOSS INTO CASH to convert a paper gain or loss into a cash gain or loss by closing out the original transaction ○ *realize our assets* **6.** *vt* TURN WORK INTO PERFORMANCE to turn something such as a play or novel into a stage or film performance **7.** *vt* MUSIC INTERPRET PIECE OF MUSIC to interpret a musical composition, especially the figured bass of a baroque composition [Early 17C. < REAL[1] after French *réaliser*] —**realizable** *adj* —**realization** /reé ə līˈzáysh'n/ *n* —**realizer** *n*

SYNONYMS See *accomplish.*

real-life *adj* actual or true, as opposed to fictional or imaginary ○ *The part of the child was played by the actor's real-life daughter.*

real-live *adj* not artificial, imagined, or invented ○ *face-to-face with a real-live gangster*

really /reé əli, reéli/ *adv* **1.** IN FACT in fact or in reality, especially as distinct from what has been believed until now ○ *She's really going to Paris, not Bangkok.* **2.** GENUINELY used to emphasize the truthfulness or accuracy of what is being said ○ *She really is going to Paris next year.* **3.** VERY used to emphasize the extent to which something is true ○ *That's really interesting.* **4.** PROPERLY in order to act in the correct or proper manner ○ *You should really apply in writing.* ■ *interj* EXCLAMATION OF SURPRISE used to express surprise, doubt, or exasperation ○ *You're getting married? Really!* ○ *Well really, how rude!*

realm /relm/ *n* **1.** SCOPE OF SOMETHING an area or domain, e.g. of thought or knowledge ○ *Here the scenario enters the realms of fantasy.* **2.** AREA OF INTEREST a defined area of interest or study ○ *the realm of pure mathematics* **3.** KINGDOM a country ruled by a monarch [13C. Via Old French *realme* < Latin *regimen* 'government' (see REGIMEN)]

real number *n* a number that is either rational or irrational rather than imaginary

realo /reé əlō, ray aálō/ (*plural* **-os**) *n* a member of the Green movement who believes in working within the existing social system to effect change [Late 20C. < German < *Realist* 'realist']

real part *n* the part of a complex number that does not have an imaginary factor, e.g. the number 3 in the complex number 3 + 5i

realpolitik /ray aál poli teek/ *n* politics based on pragmatism or practicality rather than on ethical or theoretical considerations [Early 20C. < German, 'real politics'] —**realpolitiker** /-polittikər/ *n*

real presence *n* in Christianity, the doctrine that the body and blood of Jesus Christ are actually present in the ritual of Communion

real property *n* land together with all the property on it that cannot be moved, together with any attached rights

real tennis *n* a form of tennis played on an indoor court with a sloping roof against which the ball can be hit. N Am term **court tennis** [*Real* because it was the original game of tennis]

real time *n* **1.** the actual time during which something happens **2.** the time in which a computer system processes and updates data as soon as it is received from some external source such as an air-traffic control or antilock brake system. The time available to receive the data, process it, and respond to the external process is dictated by the time constraints imposed by the process. —**real-time** *adj*

realty /reé əlti/ *n* LAW same as **real property**

real-world *adj* relevant or practical in terms of everyday life

~~realy~~ incorrect spelling of **really**

ream[1] /reem/ *n* a quantity of paper, formerly 480 sheets but now usually 500 sheets ■ **reams** *npl* a large quantity of material, especially written material [14C. Via Old French *raime* < Arabic *rizma* 'bundle']

ream[2] /reem/ (**reams**, **reaming**, **reamed**) *vt* **1.** FORM HOLE WITH REAMER to form, enlarge, or shape a hole with a reamer **2.** N Am SQUEEZE CITRUS JUICE to squeeze the juice from a citrus fruit with a reamer **3.** US CHEAT SOMEBODY to cheat or swindle somebody (*slang*) **4.** N Am REPRIMAND SOMEBODY to reprimand somebody severely (*slang*) **5.** US TABOO TERM a highly offensive term meaning to have anal intercourse with somebody (*taboo*) [Mid-18C. Origin ?]

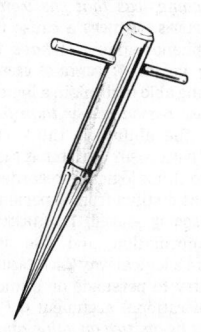

reamer

reamer /reémər/ *n* **1.** a tool that is used to form, enlarge, or shape holes **2.** N Am same as **lemon-squeezer**

reap /reep/ (**reaps**, **reaping**, **reaped**) *vt* **1.** to obtain something, especially as a consequence of previous effort or action **2.** to cut and gather a crop, especially a grain crop, from the land where it is growing [Old English *rīpan*. Origin uncertain: perhaps ultimately from an Indo-European word meaning 'to tear'] —**reapable** *adj*

reaper /reépər/ *n* somebody or something that reaps, especially, formerly, a machine for harvesting grain crops

Reaper *n* same as **Grim Reaper**

rear[1] /reer/ (**rears**, **rearing**, **reared**) *v* **1.** *vt* RAISE YOUNG ANIMALS OR CHILDREN to bring up and care for young animals or children until they are fully grown **2.** *vt* GROW PLANT to raise a plant to full growth **3.** *vi* RISE ON HIND LEGS to rise up on the hind legs (*refers to animals*) **4.** *vi* RISE HIGH to rise high into the air ○ *tall office buildings rearing into the night sky* [Old English *rǣran*. Ultimately from an Indo-European word that is also the ancestor of English *raise* and *rise*] —**rearer** *n*

rear[2] /reer/ *n* **1.** BACK OF SOMETHING the back of something, or the area near the back of something **2.** PART OF ARMY FARTHEST FROM FRONT the part of an army or a procession that is farthest from the front **3.** BUTTOCKS somebody's buttocks, or the similar part of an animal (*informal*) ■ *adj* BACK situated at the back ○ *Do not join the rear four carriages.* [Late 16C. Via Old French *rere* < Latin *retro* 'back, behind'] ◇ **bring up the rear** to be at the back, particularly in a race or procession

rear admiral *n* an officer in the British or Canadian navies of a rank above commodore, or above captain in the US Navy or Coast Guard

rear end *n* same as **rear**[2] *n* (senses **1**, **3**)

rear-end *vt N Am* to collide with the back of another vehicle

rear-ender *n N Am* an accident in which one vehicle collides with the back of another (*informal*)

rearguard /reér gaard/ *n* **1.** a body of troops designated to delay the enemy during a retreat or withdrawal **2.** members of a political party or other organization who are strongly conservative and opposed to change and progress (*disapproving*)

rear light, rear lamp *n UK* a red light that is usually one of a pair at the back of a vehicle. ANZ, N Am term **tail light**

rearmost /reér mōst/ *adj* farthest towards the back

rearrange /reé ə ráynj/ (**-ranges, -ranging, -ranged**) *vt* **1.** to change the order or position of something **2.** to reschedule the time of something such as an event —**rearrangement** *n*

rearview mirror /reér vyoo-/ *n* a mirror attached to the inside of the windscreen of a vehicle, allowing the driver to see behind the vehicle

rearward /reérwərd/ *adj* located in or near the rear or back ■ *adv* same as **rearwards**

rearwards /rírwərdz/ *adv* towards or in the rear or back

reason /reéz'n/ *n* **1. JUSTIFICATION** an explanation or justification for something ○ *refused to give a reason for her behaviour* **2. MOTIVE** a motive or cause for acting or thinking in a particular way ○ *His only reason for going was that she would be there.* **3. CAUSE THAT EXPLAINS SOMETHING** a cause that explains a particular phenomenon ○ *What's the reason for grass being green?* **4. POWER OF ORDERLY THOUGHT** the power of being able to think in a logical and rational manner ○ *use reason rather than force* **5. ABILITY TO THINK CLEARLY** the ability to think clearly and coherently **6.** PHILOSOPHY **INTELLECT AS BASIS FOR KNOWLEDGE** the ability to think logically regarded as a basis for knowledge, as distinct from experience or emotions ■ *v* (**-sons, -soning, -soned**) **1.** *vi* **THINK IN LOGICAL WAY** to consider information and use it to reach a conclusion in a logical way **2.** *vi* **PERSUADE USING RATIONAL ARGUMENT** to try to persuade or influence somebody by means of rational argument ○ *I tried to reason with him but he insisted on going ahead.* **3.** *vt* **RESOLVE USING RATIONAL THOUGHT** to formulate or resolve something using rational means ○ *reason out a maths problem* [13C. Via Old French *reisun* < Latin *ratio* 'calculation, thought' < past participle of *reri* 'calculate, think'] —**reasoned** *adj* —**reasoner** *n* ◇ **by reason of** because of ◇ **it stands to reason** used to emphasize that something seems obvious or logical ◇ **listen to reason** to take note of sensible advice ◇ **within reason** within reasonable limits

USAGE the reason is that... or the reason is because...? Particularly in writing, ***reason*** is more correctly followed by *that* than by *because* in sentences of the type *The reason I left is that* [not *because*] *I was bored.* Alternatively, simply use: *I left because I was bored.* Informally, however, and especially in conversation, *the reason is because* does occur and *that* is sometimes omitted altogether: *The reason I left is because I was bored. The reason I left is I was bored.*

USAGE See ***why.***

SYNONYMS See ***deduce.***

reasonable /reéz'nəb'l/ *adj* **1. RATIONAL** sensible and capable of making rational judgments ○ *He did what any reasonable person would have done in that situation.* **2. IN ACCORD WITH COMMON SENSE** acceptable and according to common sense or normal practice ○ *hoping to arrive at a reasonable time* **3. NOT EXPECTING MORE THAN IS POSSIBLE** not expecting or demanding more than is possible or achievable ○ *Come on, be reasonable!* **4. NOT EXORBITANT** fairly priced and not too expensive ○ *Three bottles for £7.50 is very reasonable.* **5. FAIRLY GOOD** fairly good but not excellent ○ *The food was reasonable.* **6. FAIRLY LARGE** large enough but not excessive ○ *He earns a reasonable amount of money.* —**reasonableness** *n* —**reasonably** *adv*

SYNONYMS See ***valid.***

reasoning /reéz'ning/ *n* **1.** the use of logical thinking in order to find results or draw conclusions **2.** an argument or other example of logical thinking ○ *Her reasoning was based on the available facts.*

reassure /reé ə shoór, -sháwr/ (**-sures, -suring, -sured**) *vt* **1.** to make somebody feel less anxious or worried **2.** INSUR same as **reinsure** —**reassurance** *n* —**reassurer** *n*

reassuring /reé ə shoóring, -sháwring/ *adj* having the effect of making people feel less anxious or worried —**reassuringly** *adv*

Réaumur /ráy ə myoor/ *adj* using or measured on the Réaumur scale [Early 19C. After René Antoine Ferchault de *Réaumur* (1683–1757), French physicist]

Réaumur scale *n* an obsolete temperature scale on which water freezes at 0 degrees and boils at 80 degrees under normal atmospheric conditions

reave /reev/ (**reaves, reaving, reaved** or **reft** /reft/) *vt* (*archaic*) **1.** to plunder something or carry something off by force **2.** to rob somebody or deprive somebody of something [Old English *rēafian*. Ultimately from a prehistoric Germanic word that is also the ancestor of English *rob*] —**reaver** *n*

reb /reb/, **Reb** *n US* same as **Johnny Reb** (*informal*) [Mid-19C. Shortening of REBEL]

Reb /reb/ *n* in Jewish culture, a title of respect that is roughly equivalent to 'Mister' (*used with a man's first name*) [Late 19C. < Yiddish, shortening of *rebbe* (see REBBE)]

rebarbative /ri baárbətiv/ *adj* unpleasant, annoying, or forbidding (*formal*) [Late 19C. < French *rébarbatif* < *rebarber*, literally 'face beard to beard' < *barbe* 'beard'] —**rebarbatively** *adv*

rebate[1] *n* /reé bayt/ money that is paid back, e.g. because somebody has overpaid tax or is entitled to a refund ■ *vt* /ri báyt/ (**-bates, -bating, -bated**) to give somebody an amount of money as a rebate [15C. < French *rabattre* 'beat down again' < *abattre* 'beat down' < Latin *battuere* 'beat'] —**rebatable** /ri báytəb'l/ *adj* —**rebater** *n*

rebate[2] *n* /reé bayt/ **GROOVE CUT FOR WOOD JOINT** a groove or step cut along the length of the edge of a piece of wood that is to be joined to another with a corresponding tongue or ledge cut into it ■ *vt* /ri báyt/ (**-bates, -bating, -bated**) **1. CUT REBATE IN SOMETHING** to cut a rebate in a piece of wood **2. JOIN PIECES WITH REBATE** to join two pieces of wood at their edges by means of a rebate ▶ N Am term (all senses) **rabbet** [Late 17C. Alteration of RABBET]

rebbe /rébbə/, **Rebbe** *n* a rabbi or spiritual leader of a Hasidic Jewish community [Late 19C. Via Yiddish < Hebrew *rabbī* 'my teacher']

rebbetzin /rébbətsən/, **rebbitzin** *n* the wife of a rabbi [Late 19C. < Yiddish < *rebbe* (see REBBE)]

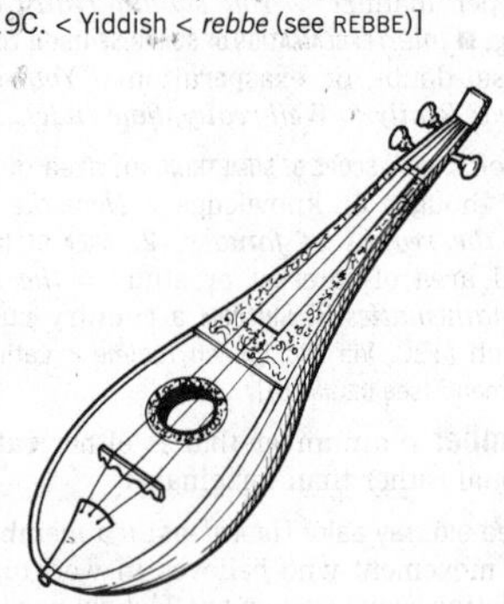

rebec

rebec /reé bek/, **rebeck** *n* a two- or three-stringed medieval instrument that looks like a lute and is played with a bow. It is one of the earliest bowed stringed instruments. [Early 16C. Via French < Arabic *rabāb*]

Rebecca /ri békə/, **Rebekah** *n* in the Bible, the wife of Isaac, and mother of Jacob and Esau

rebeck *n* MUSIC another spelling of **rebec**

Rebekah *n* BIBLE another spelling of **Rebecca**

rebel *n* /rébb'l/ **1. SOMEBODY UNCONVENTIONAL** somebody who rejects the codes and conventions of society **2. SOLDIER WHO OPPOSES GOVERNMENT** a soldier who belongs to a force seeking to overthrow a government or ruling power **3. PROTESTER** somebody who defiantly protests against authority ■ *vi* /ri bél/ (**rebels, rebelling, rebelled**) **1. REVOLT AGAINST GOVERNMENT** to fight to overthrow a government or ruling power **2. REFUSE TO CONFORM** to refuse to conform to the usual codes and conventions of society **3. PROTEST BY DEFYING AUTHORITY** to protest by defying a government or other form of authority ○ *students rebelling against education funding cuts* **4. HAVE DISLIKE FOR SOMETHING** to experience or express an intense dislike or distaste for something ○ *When mama went to work, grandma rebelled at the idea of taking care of the children.* [13C. Via French < Latin *rebellis* < *bellum* 'war']

~~**rebelion**~~ incorrect spelling of **rebellion**

rebellion /ri béllyən/ *n* **1.** an organized attempt to overthrow a government or other authority by the use of violence **2.** opposition to or defiance of authority, accepted moral codes, or social conventions

rebellious /ri béllyəss/ *adj* **1.** opposing or defying authority, accepted moral codes, or social conventions **2.** fighting to overthrow a government or other authority —**rebelliously** *adv* —**rebelliousness** *n*

rebel yell *n US* an exuberant high-pitched yell, e.g. that used in battle by soldiers of the Confederacy during the American Civil War

rebid *n* /reé bid/ a further bid in an auction at bridge, especially one of the same suit as a previous one ■ *vi* /ri bíd/ (**-bids, -bidding, -bid**) to make a bid in an auction at bridge after previously bidding no trump or a suit, especially one in the same suit

rebirth /ree búrth/ *n* **1. REGENERATION OF SOMETHING DESTROYED** the regeneration of something that has died or has been destroyed **2. REVIVAL OF IDEAS OR FORCES** the revival of important ideas or forces, usually as part of broad and significant change **3.** RELIG **REINCARNATION** the act or process of reincarnation

rebirthing /ree búrthing/ *n* therapy involving breathing in a way considered to reproduce the trauma of being born —**rebirther** *n*

reblochon /rə blóshoN/ *n* a soft delicately flavoured washed-rind cheese with a pale pinkish skin, made in the Savoy region of France [Early 20C. < French, < *reblocher* 'milk for a second time']

reboot *v* /ree boót/ (**-boots, -booting, -booted**) **1.** *vti* to restart a computer or an operating system, or be restarted **2.** *vt* COMPUT same as **warmboot** ■ *n* /reé boot/ a restart of a computer or an operating system

rebore *vt* /ree báwr/ (**-bores, -boring, -bored**) to enlarge the bore hole of a cylinder in a car's engine and fit it with new pistons ■ *n* /reé bawr/ the process of reboring a cylinder or all the cylinders in an engine

reborn /ree báwrn/ *adj* recreated or regenerated, especially in order to be more effective or modern, or renewed spiritually

rebound *vi* /ri bównd/ (**-bounds, -bounding, -bounded**) **1. SPRING BACK** to spring back or recoil **2. MOVE BACK TO PREVIOUS LEVEL** to recover from a setback and move back to a previous or higher level or position **3. HAVE UNDESIRABLE EFFECT** to affect the person who does or creates something directly, especially in an unpleasant or unwelcome way ■ *n* /reé bownd/ **1. UPWARD MOVEMENT** an upward movement or a recovery, especially after a setback **2.** SPORTS **BALL THAT BOUNCES** a ball that bounces back, particularly off a backboard or rim of the basket in basketball or off the goalkeeper or goalpost in hockey, football, or a similar sport —**rebounder** *n* ◇ **on the rebound** starting something new in the wake of a disappointment or setback, often the ending of a relationship, and therefore feeling uneasy or vulnerable

USAGE rebound or redound? In its figurative use, ***rebound*** is a metaphor based on the image of an object bouncing and returning. Just as a ball that ***rebounds*** affects the person who threw it, so an action or statement ***rebounds*** on its creator when it affects him or her directly, usually in an unpleasant or unwelcome way: *His tactic of implementing the changes without consultation rebounded on him when his team walked out in protest.* ***Redound***, a much rarer word, is sometimes used in the same way as ***rebound***, but in its primary meaning it is followed by *to* and means 'to have a particular consequence', with something good or positive as the object (the opposite connotation to ***rebound***): *The individual performances redounded to the benefit of the team as a whole.* Note that only ***rebound*** can be used as a noun.

rebozo /ri bṓzō/ (*plural* **-zos**) *n* a long woollen or linen

scarf worn over the head and shoulders, mainly by women in Mexico [Early 19C. < Spanish < *rebozar* 'to muffle']

rebuff /ri búf/ *vt* (**-buffs, -buffing, -buffed**) **1. REJECT OR SNUB SOMETHING** to reject or snub an offer, advance, or approach made by somebody **2. REPEL ATTACK** to beat back or repel an attack or an attacking force ■ *n* **1. REJECTION** a blunt rejection or snub of an offer, advance, or approach made by somebody else **2. SETBACK** a sudden severe setback to progress [Late 16C. Via French < Italian *ribuffare* 'scold' < *buffo* 'puff', an imitation of the sound]

USAGE See *refute.*

rebuild /ree bíld/ (**-builds, -building, -built** /-bílt/) *vt* **1. BUILD STRUCTURE AGAIN** to construct a building or other structure again because it has been damaged or destroyed **2. RESTORE SOMETHING** to work to restore something that has been weakened, damaged, or ruined ○ *rebuilt her confidence* **3. MAKE MAJOR CHANGES TO SOMETHING** to make major alterations or improvements to something ○ *to rebuild society for the information age* —**rebuilder** *n*

rebuke /ri byóok/ *vt* (**-bukes, -buking, -buked**) to criticize or reprimand somebody, usually sharply ■ *n* a reprimand or expression of criticism or disapproval [14C. < Anglo-Norman, Old N French *rebuker* 'chop wood' < Old French *busche* 'log' < Germanic] —**rebuker** *n*

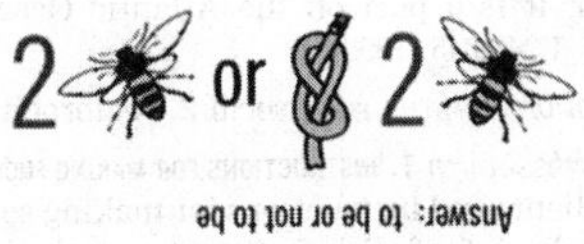

rebus

rebus /réebəss/ (*plural* **-buses**) *n* **1.** a puzzle in which the syllables of words and names are represented either by pictures of things that sound the same or by letters **2.** a heraldic emblem showing a picture that represents the name of the bearer, e.g. a picture of a lion for somebody named Lyon [Early 17C. Via French < Latin, literally 'by things', form of *res* 'thing']

rebut /ri bút/ (**-buts, -butting, -butted**) *vti* to deny the truth of something, especially by presenting arguments that disprove it [13C. < Anglo-Norman *rebuter*, Old French *reboter* < *boter* 'butt, ram'] —**rebuttable** *adj* —**rebuttal** *n*

USAGE See *refute.*

rebutter /ri búttər/ *n* **1.** somebody who rebuts something **2.** the defendant's answer in the third round of pleading in a legal action (*archaic*)

rec /rek/ *n* LEISURE (*informal*) **1.** same as **recreation** (sense 1) (*often used before a noun*) ○ *rec room* **2.** same as **recreation ground** [Early 20C. Shortening]

rec. *abbr* **1.** COMM receipt **2.** COMM received **3.** COOK recipe **4.** recommended **5.** MAIL recorded **6.** recorder **7.** recording **8.** recreation

recalcitrant /ri kálssitrənt/ *adj* **1. RESISTING AUTHORITY** stubbornly resisting the authority of another person or group **2. HARD TO DO OR HANDLE** difficult to deal with or operate ○ *struggling in front of the mirror with a recalcitrant tie* ■ *n* **STUBBORN OPPONENT** somebody who stubbornly resists authority or control ○ *A few recalcitrants refused to submit.* [Mid-19C. Directly or via French < Latin *recalcitrant-* present participle of *recalcitrare* 'kick back' (used of horses) < *calcitrare* 'kick (with the heels)' < *calc-* 'heel'] —**recalcitrance** *n* —**recalcitrantly** *adv*

SYNONYMS See *unruly.*

recalesce /réekə léss/ (**-lesces, -lescing, -lesced**) *vi* to exhibit or undergo a sudden increase in temperature and brightness (*refers to cooling metals*) [Late 19C. Back-formation < RECALESCENCE]

recalescence /réekə léss'nss/ *n* a sudden increase in the temperature and brightness of a cooling metal, caused by the release of latent heat as the metal undergoes a change in crystalline structure [Late 19C. < RE- + Latin *calescere* 'grow warm' < *calere* 'be warm'] —**recalescent** *adj*

recall *v* /ri káwl/ (**-calls, -calling, -called**) **1.** *vti* **REMEMBER SOMETHING** to remember something or bring something back to mind ○ *I don't recall what she was wearing.* **2.** *vt* **ORDER SOMEBODY OR SOMETHING BACK** to order something or somebody to come back or be sent back ○ *recalled the ambassador to Washington* **3.** *vt* **REVOKE SOMETHING** to revoke or cancel a previous decision or instruction ○ *The manufacturer has recalled all models built in 2003.* **4.** *vt* **BRING ATTENTION BACK** to bring somebody's attention or thoughts back to an ongoing matter **5.** *vt* **RESEMBLE SOMEBODY OR SOMETHING** to remind another person of somebody or something familiar or previously seen ○ *Her face recalls that of her grandmother.* ■ *n* /ri káwl, rée kawl/ **1. REMEMBERING** the remembering of something or the calling back of somebody or something **2. MEMORY** somebody's memory or ability to remember ○ *a vague recall of the actual events* **3. REQUEST TO RETURN PRODUCT** a request by a manufacturer to return a product because of a fault or contamination **4. REVOCATION** a revocation or cancellation of a previous decision or instruction **5.** MIL **SIGNAL TO RETURN** a signal, especially a bugle call, ordering troops to return to their positions or to a rallying point **6.** *N Am* POL **DISMISSAL FROM OFFICE BY VOTE** the dismissal from office of an elected official by a popular vote, or the right of the electors to do this [Late 16C. After French *rappeler* or Latin *revocare*] —**recallability** /ri káwlə bílləti/ *n* —**recallable** *adj* —**recaller** *n*

recamier /ray kámmi ay/ *n* a couch with a high headrest and low footrest, often without a back [Early 20C. After Jeanne *Récamier* (1777–1849), French hostess, portrayed reclining on a couch in a painting]

recanalization /ree kánnə lī záysh'n/, **recanalisation** *n* the surgical unblocking of an obstructed vessel within the body or the reconnection of a tube or duct

recant /ri kánt/ (**-cants, -canting, -canted**) *vti* to deny believing in something or withdraw something previously said ○ *She stands by what she said and refuses to recant.* [Mid-16C. < Latin *recantare* 'sing back' < *cantare* 'sing'] —**recantation** /rée kan táysh'n/ *n* —**recanter** *n*

recap[1] /rée kap/ *vti* (**-caps, -capping, -capped**) to go over the main points of something such as an argument or a proposal again ■ *n* a summing-up of the main points of something previously put forward [Mid-20C. Shortening of RECAPITULATE]

recap[2] *ANZ, US n* /rée kap/ same as **remould** ■ *vt* /ree káp/ (**-caps, -capping, -capped**) to retread a tyre [Mid-20C. Formed from CAP[1]. Originally in the sense 'to put a cap on something again'] —**recappable** /ree káppəb'l/ *adj*

recapitulate /réekə píchoo layt/ (**-lates, -lating, -lated**) *v* **1.** *vti* same as **recap**[1] (*formal*) **2.** *vt* to repeat stages from the evolution of the species during the embryonic period of an animal's life [Late 16C. Partly < Latin *recapitulat-*, past participle of *recapitulare* 'restate by chapters' < *capitulum* 'chapter'; partly back-formation < RECAPITULATION] —**recapitulative** /-lətiv/ *adj* —**recapitulatory** /-ətəri/ *adj*

recapitulation /réekə píchoo láysh'n/ *n* **1.** same as **recap**[1] (*formal*) **2.** BIOL the theoretical process of going through successive stages during the embryonic period of an animal's life that duplicate the evolutionary stages the species experienced **3.** MUSIC the repetition of earlier themes in a piece of music, especially in sonata form at the end of a movement [14C. Directly or via French < late Latin *recapitulation-* < Latin *recapitulat-* (see RECAPITULATE)]

recaption /ree kápsh'n/ *n* the taking back, by peaceful means, of property from somebody who has unlawfully taken it, or of a spouse or child from somebody who has unlawfully detained him or her [Early 17C. < Anglo-Latin *recaption-* 'capturing back' < Latin *caption-* 'capturing' < *capere* 'take']

recapture /ree kápchər/ (**-tures, -turing, -tured**) *vt* **1.** to take back somebody or something that has escaped or has been taken away **2.** to have, show, or experience again something that existed in the past or has been lost ○ *a failed attempt to recapture their youth* —**recapture** *n*

recast /ree káast/ (**-casts, -casting, -cast**) *vt* **1. CAST OBJECT AGAIN** to repeat the casting process for an object formed in a mould **2. CHANGE SOMETHING** to change the form of something ○ *The experience led him to recast his philosophy of life.* **3. GIVE ROLES TO DIFFERENT ACTORS** to assign roles in something such as a play or film to different actors ○ *recast the play for a road tour*

recce /réki/ (*slang*) *n* same as **reconnaissance** (sense 1) ○ *He's gone for a recce along the beach.* ■ *vt* (**-ces, -ceing, -ced**) same as **reconnoitre** [Mid-20C. Shortening and alteration]

~~**reccommend**~~ incorrect spelling of **recommend**

recd, rec'd *abbr* received

recede /ri séed/ (**-cedes, -ceding, -ceded**) *vi* **1. GO BACK** to go back or down from a point or level ○ *waiting for the flood waters to recede* **2. GET FURTHER AWAY** to become more distant or unlikely ○ *As the ship gathered speed, the island receded in the distance.* **3. SLOPE** to slope backwards **4. GO BALD** to gradually go bald from the front of the head backwards (*refers to hair or a person*) **5. BECOME LESS** to become less in value or quality ○ *The value of her shares receded sharply.* **6. WITHDRAW** to engage in a retreat [15C. Directly or via French < Latin *recedere* 'go back' < *cedere* 'give away']

receipt /ri séet/ *n* **1. ACKNOWLEDGMENT OF RECEIVING** a written or printed acknowledgment that something such as money or goods has been given to the person who issues the acknowledgment ○ *The shop will exchange goods if you have a receipt.* **2. ACT OF RECEIVING** the fact or time of receiving something ○ *The balance is payable on receipt of the goods.* **3.** COOK same as **recipe** (sense 1) (*archaic*) ■ **receipts** *npl* **AMOUNT RECEIVED** the amount of money or goods received, especially in business ○ *Receipts are down on last month.* ■ *v* (**-ceipts, -ceipting, -ceipted**) **1.** *vt* **ACKNOWLEDGE PAYMENT** to sign a bill to acknowledge that it has been paid **2.** *vti* **GIVE RECEIPT** to give a receipt for money or goods [14C. < Anglo-Norman or Old N French *receite* '(medicinal) recipe, receipt' < Latin *recipere* (see RECEIVE)]

receivable /ri séevəb'l/ *adj* **1. SUITABLE TO BE RECEIVED** suitable to be received, especially as payment ○ *receivable notes* **2. AWAITING PAYMENT** describes a bill or account that is due to be paid ■ **receivables** *npl* **MONEY OWED** business assets consisting of amounts of money that a company is owed

receive /ri séev/ (**-ceives, -ceiving, -ceived**) *v* **1.** *vti* **GET SOMETHING** to take or accept something given ○ *It is better to give than to receive.* **2.** *vti* **ACCEPT ELECTRONIC SIGNALS** to pick up electronic signals and convert them into sound or pictures ○ *This radio is able to transmit and receive.* **3.** *vt* **TAKE DELIVERY OF MESSAGE** to take delivery of a message such as a letter or telephone call ○ *We've received a few complaints.* **4.** *vt* **LEARN INFORMATION** to learn of something such as news or information **5.** *vt* **MEET WITH SOMETHING** to meet with or experience something ○ *We received a warm reception from the crowd.* **6.** *vt* **ACQUIRE SOMETHING** to come to have something, e.g. through effort ○ *the medical training students receive* **7.** *vt* **REACT TO SOMETHING** to react to something in a particular way ○ *The proposals were not well received by the members.* **8.** *vt* **BE HURT BY SOMETHING** to be subjected to something such as an injury, blow, or pressure ○ *She received the full force of the blow on her face.* **9.** *vti* **ENTERTAIN VISITORS** to be free to see or admit visitors ○ *Find out the hours during which patients can receive visitors.* **10.** *vt* **CATCH SOMETHING** to hold or take something ○ *A water butt receives the overflow from the guttering.* **11.** *vt* **BEAR SOMETHING** to bear or sustain something such as a burden ○ *The bridge is reinforced to receive the weight of heavy traffic.* **12.** *vt* **GREET GUESTS** to greet and admit guests ○ *We were received by the duke himself.* **13.** *vt* **HEAR AND ACKNOWLEDGE SOMETHING** to hear and acknowledge something formally ○ *The priest received her confession.* **14.** *vt* **ADMIT SOMEBODY** to allow a person entry ○ *A knight had to prove himself worthy before being received into their fellowship.* **15.** *vti* LAW **ACCEPT**

STOLEN GOODS to accept or deal in stolen goods **16.** *vti* **CATCH BALL** to catch, hit, or kick a ball played by an opponent **17.** *vi* CHR **TAKE COMMUNION** in the Christian church, to take Communion [14C. Via Old French *receivre* < Latin *recipere* 'take back' < *capere* 'take']

received /ri séevd/ *adj* generally accepted as true ○ *The received wisdom in these matters is seldom wrong.*

Received Pronunciation *n* the accent of British English that educated people from the southern part of England traditionally use, widely regarded as the least regionally modified of all British accents

receiver /ri séevər/ *n* **1. PART OF PHONE** the part of a telephone that contains the earpiece and mouthpiece and receives and converts electronic signals into sound **2. DEVICE FOR PICKING UP SIGNALS** an electrical device that receives and converts electronic signals into sound or pictures **3.** LAW, FIN **SOMEBODY APPOINTED TO RUN BUSINESS** somebody appointed by a court to manage a business or property that is involved in a legal process such as bankruptcy **4.** LAW **SOMEBODY DEALING IN STOLEN GOODS** a dealer in stolen goods **5. SOMEBODY WHO RECEIVES SOMETHING** somebody who receives or takes delivery of something **6.** AMERICAN FOOTBALL **PLAYER CATCHING FORWARD PASS** an American football player on the attacking side who is eligible to catch a forward pass **7.** BASEBALL same as **catcher** (sense 2) **8.** CHEM **CONTAINER USED IN DISTILLING** a container used during distillation to collect the distillate

receivership /ri séevərship/ *n* **1.** management by a receiver of a business or property that is involved in a legal process such as bankruptcy ○ *The company is now in receivership.* **2.** the office or duties of somebody appointed by a court to manage a business or property that is involved in a legal process such as bankruptcy

receiving end /ri séeving-/ *n* the position of having to endure something ○ *We were on the receiving end of some harsh criticism.*

receiving line *n* a group of people who stand in a line to greet individually the guests at a formal occasion such as a wedding reception

receiving order *n* a court order that appoints a receiver to take charge of a business involved in a legal proceeding such as bankruptcy

recension /ri sénsh'n/ *n* **1.** a critical revision carried out on a literary text **2.** a literary text that has been given a critical revision [Mid-17C. < Latin *recension-* 'review' < *recensere* 'reassess' < *censere* 'appraise, assess']

recent /réess'nt/ *adj* **1.** having happened or appeared not long ago ○ *the recent birth of her child* **2.** from current times or the very near past ○ *recent political trends* [15C. Directly or via French < Latin *recent-*] —**recency** *n* —**recently** *adv* —**recentness** *n*

Recent *n* GEOL same as **Holocene** —**Recent** *adj*

receptacle /ri séptək'l/ *n* **1. CONTAINER** a container that holds, contains, or receives a liquid or solid **2. FLOWER-BEARING PART** the end of a flower stalk, bearing the parts of a flower or the florets of a composite flower **3. PLANT PART FOR REPRODUCTION** in a plant that reproduces through spores, e.g. an alga or liverwort, the part that bears the reproductive organs [14C. Directly or via French < Latin *receptaculum* 'place in which to store something received' < *recipere* (see RECEIVE)]

reception /ri sépsh'n/ *n* **1. PLACE WHERE VISITORS ARE RECEIVED** a place in a hotel, office, or public building where visitors are first received ○ *I'll be waiting for you in reception.* **2. FORMAL PARTY** a formal party to welcome somebody or celebrate an event such as a wedding **3. WAY SOMEBODY OR SOMETHING IS RECEIVED** the way in which somebody or something is received or greeted ○ *The audience gave her a warm reception.* **4. ACT OF RECEIVING** the act of receiving something given or sent **5. QUALITY OF SIGNAL** the quality of the signal received by a radio or television set ○ *We don't get very good reception on this channel.* **6.** ELECTRONICS **CONVERSION OF ELECTRONIC SIGNALS** the process of receiving and converting electronic signals **7.** BUILDINGS same as **reception room 8.** AMERICAN FOOTBALL **CATCHING OF FORWARD PASS** in American football, the catching of a pass made towards the opponent's goal **9.** EDUC **FIRST CLASS AT INFANT SCHOOL** the class of children beginning their first year of full-time education [14C. Directly or via French < Latin *reception-* < *recipere* (see RECEIVE)]

reception centre *n* **1.** a place that accommodates people in need of shelter, e.g. homeless people, refugees, or survivors of natural disasters, until more permanent accommodation can be found **2.** a children's home run by a local authority to house children whose families cannot look after them, either temporarily or for a longer period

receptionist /ri sépsh'nist/ *n* an employee who greets visitors, customers, or patients, answers the telephone, and makes appointments

reception room *n* **1.** a room used for entertaining guests in a house ○ *The house has four bedrooms and two reception rooms.* **2.** a room used for a party or reception in a hotel

receptive /ri séptiv/ *adj* **1. WILLING TO ACCEPT** ready and willing to accept something such as new ideas ○ *The city's art collectors were highly receptive to the new wave in painting.* **2. QUICK TO LEARN** quick to take in new information **3.** PHYSIOL **RECEIVING AND TRANSMITTING STIMULI** describes a sensory organ that is capable of transmitting and receiving stimuli [15C. Directly or via French < medieval Latin *receptivus* < Latin *recipere* (see RECEIVE)] —**receptively** *adv* —**receptiveness** *n* —**receptivity** /rée sep tívvəti/ *n*

receptor /ri séptər/ *n* **1.** PHYSIOL **SENSITIVE NERVE ENDING** a nerve ending that is sensitive to stimuli and can convert them into nerve impulses **2.** ELECTRONICS **RECEIVING DEVICE** a device designed to receive electronic signals **3.** CHEM **SPECIFIC CELL BINDING SITE OR MOLECULE** a molecule, group, or site that is in a cell or on a cell surface and binds with a specific molecule, antigen, hormone, or antibody **4.** ENVIRON **RECEIVER OF POLLUTION** somebody or something adversely affected by a pollutant [15C. Directly or via Old French *receptour* 'person who harbours criminals or stolen goods' < Latin *receptor* < *recipere* (see RECEIVE)]

recess /ri séss, rée sess/ *n* **1. BREAK FROM BUSINESS** a time during which no work or business is done, specifically a long period in which a legislative body is not sitting or a short break during court proceedings **2.** *N Am* EDUC same as **break**[1] *n* (sense 4) **3. INDENTED OR HOLLOWED-OUT SPACE** an area set into a wall or other flat surface, e.g. an alcove or niche ○ *a recess large enough to take a bed* **4. REMOTE PLACE** a remote or secluded place (*often used in the plural*) ○ *A distant memory haunted the recesses of her mind.* **5.** ANAT **BODY CAVITY** a concave area or cavity in a part of the body ■ *vt* (**-cesses, -cessing, -cessed**) **1. PUT SOMETHING IN ALCOVE** to put something in a recess, especially in a wall ○ *a chapel recessed in a transept of the cathedral* **2. MAKE INDENTATION IN SOMETHING** to make a recess in something, especially a wall ○ *The north wall of the chamber has been recessed to form an alcove.* [Mid-16C. Directly or via French < Latin *recessus* 'going back' < *recedere* 'go back']

recession /ri sésh'n/ *n* **1. DEPRESSION IN ECONOMIC ACTIVITY** a period, shorter than a depression, during which there is a decline in economic trade and prosperity **2. WITHDRAWAL OF SOMEBODY IN CEREMONY** the withdrawal of the participants in a ceremony, e.g. the clergy and choir after a church service **3. RECEDING** the process of going back or becoming more distant

recessional /ri sésh'nəl/ *adj* involving or typical of a recession ■ *n* in Christianity, a hymn sung as the clergy and choir withdraw from a church after a service

recessive /ri séssiv/ *adj* **1. PRODUCING EFFECT IN SPECIFIC CONDITIONS** used to describe a gene that produces an effect in an organism only when its matching allele is identical. The effect is masked when the matching allele is nonidentical. **2. CONTROLLED BY RECESSIVE GENE** describes a characteristic or trait determined by a recessive gene **3. RECEDING** tending to go backwards or to recede ○ *recessive flood waters* **4.** PHON **AT BEGINNING OF WORD** describes stress that is placed at or near the beginning of a word ■ *n* GENETICS **1. RECESSIVE CHARACTERISTIC** a recessive gene or trait **2. ORGANISM WITH RECESSIVE CHARACTERISTIC** an organism that has a recessive gene or trait —**recessively** *adv* —**recessiveness** *n*

Rechabite /rékə bīt/ *n* somebody who abstains from alcoholic beverages, especially a member of the Independent Order of Rechabites, a benefit society founded in 1835 [14C. < ecclesiastical Latin *Rechabita* 'descendants of Rechab', translation of Hebrew *rēkābīm* < *rēkāb* 'Rechab', in the Bible, ancestor of an Israelite family who refused to drink wine (Jeremiah 35:6)]

recharge /ree chaárj/ (**-charges, -charging, -charged**) *vt* **1.** to replenish the amount of electric power in something, especially a battery **2.** to renew something such as somebody's energy ○ *We felt recharged after the weekend.* —**rechargeable** *adj* —**recharger** *n*

réchauffé /ray shō fay/ *n* **1.** a dish of reheated leftovers **2.** a piece of work, e.g. a piece of writing, that is merely a reuse of old material [Early 19C. < French, past participle of *réchauffer* 'reheat' < Latin *calere* 'make or be warm']

recherché /rə sháir shay/ *adj* **1. RARE AND EXQUISITE** marked by such rare and exquisite quality that it is known only to connoisseurs **2. APPRECIATING FINE THINGS** having a deep appreciation of unusual or choice things ○ *a recherché taste in sculpture* **3. AFFECTED** marked by excessive refinement or exaggerated importance ○ *Some of his ideas are a little recherché for my taste.* [Late 17C. < French, past participle of *rechercher* 'seek thoroughly' < *chercher* 'seek']

recidivism /ri síddivizəm/ *n* the tendency to relapse into a previous undesirable type of behaviour, especially crime [Late 19C. < *recidivist*, < French *récidiviste* < Latin *recidivus* 'falling back' < *recidere* 'fall back' < *cadere* 'fall'] —**recidivist** *n, adj* —**recidivistic** /ri síddi vístik/ *adj*

~~**reciept**~~ incorrect spelling of **receipt**

~~**recieve**~~ incorrect spelling of **receive**

Recife /re séefə/ capital city of Pernambuco State, northeastern Brazil, and the major city of the region. It is a port on the Atlantic Ocean. Population: 1,346,045 (1996).

recip. *abbr* **1.** MATHS reciprocal **2.** reciprocity

recipe /réssəpi/ *n* **1. INSTRUCTIONS FOR MAKING FOOD** a list of ingredients and instructions for making something, especially a food dish **2. METHOD** a method of doing something or a combination of circumstances likely to bring something about ○ *Hard work is the recipe for success.* **3.** MED **PRESCRIPTION** a prescription for a therapeutic preparation (*archaic*) [14C. Directly or via French < Latin, 'take!', form of *recipere* (see RECEIVE)]

recipient /ri síppi ənt/ *n* somebody or something that receives something ■ *adj* tending or able to receive [Mid-16C. Directly or via French < Latin *recipient-*, present participle of *recipere* (see RECEIVE)] —**recipience** *n*

reciprocal /ri síppərk'l/ *adj* **1. GIVEN BY EACH SIDE** given or shown by each of two sides or people to the other ○ *reciprocal compliments* **2. IN RETURN** given or done in return for something else ○ *a reciprocal attack on the aggressor* **3.** MATHS **MULTIPLIED TO GIVE ONE** describes a number or quality that is related to another by the fact that when multiplied together the product is one **4.** MATHS **COMPLEMENTING** serving to complement one another ○ *reciprocal angles* ■ *n* **1. SOMETHING MUTUAL** something that is mutual or done in return **2.** MATHS **NUMBER MULTIPLIED TO GIVE ONE** a number or quantity that is related to another by the fact that when multiplied together the product is one ○ *4 and $\frac{1}{4}$ are reciprocals.* [Late 16C. < Latin *reciprocus* 'going backwards and forwards' < *re-* 'backwards' + *pro-* 'forwards'] —**reciprocality** /ri síppra kálləti/ *n* —**reciprocally** *adv*

reciprocal link *n* a link in both directions from one website to another as a form of bartering for advertising space

reciprocal pronoun *n* a word or phrase representing two or more things that mutually correspond to one another, e.g. 'each other'

reciprocate /ri síppra kayt/ (**-cates, -cating, -cated**) *v* **1.** *vti* **GIVE MUTUALLY** to give or feel something mutually or in return ○ *I couldn't accept such a generous gift without reciprocating.* **2.** *vti* ENG **MOVE BACKWARDS AND FORWARDS** to move backwards and forwards in an alternating motion, or move something in this way **3.** *vi* **BE COMPLEMENTARY** to be the same or complementary [Late 16C. < Latin *reciprocat-*, past participle of *reciprocare* 'move backwards and forwards, reciprocate' < *reciprocus* (see RECIPROCAL)] —**reciprocation** /ri síppra káysh'n/ *n* —**reciprocative** *adj* —**reciprocator** *n*

reciprocating engine /ri síppra kayting-/ *n* an engine

with one or more cylinders in which pistons move backwards and forwards

reciprocity /réssi prόssəti/ (*plural* **-ties**) *n* **1.** a relationship between people involving the exchange of goods, services, favours, or obligations, especially a mutual exchange of privileges between trading nations ○ *the long-standing tariff reciprocity between our two countries* **2.** something done mutually or in return [Mid-18C. < French *réciprocité* < Latin *reciprocus* (see RECIPROCAL)]

reciprocity failure *n* in photography, the failure of light intensity and exposure time to act reciprocally when their values are extremely high or low, sometimes affecting the colour characteristics of the resulting photograph

recision /ri sízh'n/ *n* the cancellation or rescinding of something [Early 17C. < Latin *recision-* 'cutting back' < *recidere* 'cut back' < *caedere* 'cut']

recit. *abbr* MUSIC recitative

recital /ri sīt'l/ *n* **1.** SOLO PERFORMANCE a musical or dance performance given by a soloist or small group **2.** PERFORMANCE BY STUDENTS a performance given by music or dance students to demonstrate the progress they have made **3.** RECITING the reading aloud or reciting from memory of something such as a poem **4.** DETAILED ACCOUNT a detailed account or report of something ○ *his recital of the events of the day* **5.** LAW DETAILED PRESENTATION OF FACT a statement in a judgment laying out jurisdictional facts, or a deed's preliminary part laying out the circumstances leading to its existence (*often used in the plural*) —**recitalist** *n*

recitation /réssi táysh'n/ *n* **1.** READING ALOUD the public reading aloud of something or reciting of something from memory, especially poetry **2.** MATTER READ ALOUD material read aloud or recited from memory in public, especially poetry **3.** ACT OF REPORTING SOMETHING the act of listing or reporting something

recitative[1] /réssitə téev/, **recitativo** /-téevō/ (*plural* **-vos**) *n* **1.** a style of singing that is close to the rhythm of natural speech, used in opera for dialogue and narration **2.** a passage in a musical composition that is sung in the form of recitative [Mid-17C. < Italian *recitativo* < Latin *recitat-*, past participle of *recitare* (see RECITE)]

recitative[2] /ri sītətiv/ *adj* relating to recital or recitation [Mid-17C. < Italian *recitativo* (see RECITATIVE[1])]

recitativo *n* MUSIC same as **recitative**[1]

recite /ri sīt/ (**-cites, -citing, -cited**) *v* **1.** *vti* REPEAT OR READ ALOUD to read something aloud or repeat something from memory, either for an audience or in a class **2.** *vt* GIVE DETAILED ACCOUNT OF SOMETHING to give a detailed account of an occurrence or event ○ *There's no need to recite every detail of your weekend.* **3.** *vt* LIST SOMETHING to give a list of things ○ *He then recited all my faults.* [15C. Directly or via French *réciter* < Latin *recitare* 'summon again' < *citare* 'summon repeatedly'] —**reciter** *n*

reck /rek/ (**recks, recking, recked**) *vti* (*archaic*) **1.** to care or mind about something **2.** to matter, or matter to somebody [Old English *rēcan* < Germanic]

reckless /rékləss/ *adj* marked by a lack of thought about danger or other possible undesirable consequences ○ *with a reckless disregard for the established safety procedures* [Old English *rec(c)elēas* < Germanic] —**recklessly** *adv* —**recklessness** *n*

reckon /rékən/ (**-ons, -oning, -oned**) *v* **1.** *vt* REGARD SOMEBODY OR SOMETHING AS SOMETHING to consider somebody or something to be something (*often passive*) ○ *She's reckoned the best in her field.* **2.** *vti* COUNT to count or calculate something ○ *We reckoned its speed at approximately 350 mph.* **3.** *vt* INCLUDE SOMEBODY OR SOMETHING to include or class a person or thing as being part of a particular group ○ *I reckon him among my friends.* **4.** *vti* THINK OR BELIEVE SOMETHING to suppose something to be true (*informal*) ○ *I reckon we're finished now.* **5.** *vt* THINK HIGHLY OF SOMETHING to rate something or somebody highly (*informal*) ○ *This kid really reckons his chances of winning.* [Old English *gerecenian* < Germanic] —**reckonable** *adj*

reckon on *vt* to expect with confident assurance (*informal*) ○ *You can reckon on my support.*

reckon with *vt* **1.** to deal or come to terms with somebody powerful ○ *If he lets you down, he'll have me to reckon with.* **2.** to take somebody or something into account ○ *We didn't reckon with the strength of the tide.*

reckon without *vt* to fail to take something into account ○ *The government reckoned without the strength of public feeling against the new measure.*

reckoner /rékənər/ *n* a book of tables of calculations that are already worked out and are used as an aid in calculation

reckoning /rékəning/ *n* **1.** CALCULATION the act or a system of calculating something ○ *By my reckoning, it shouldn't have taken them more than three hours to get there.* **2.** DETERMINATION OF POSITION calculation of an aircraft's, a spacecraft's, or a vessel's position in the air, in space, or on the sea **3.** SETTLEMENT OF ACCOUNT the settlement of an account **4.** ACCOUNT a bill or a statement of money owing **5.** RETRIBUTION punishment or vengeance for wrongs committed ○ *day of reckoning*

reclaim /ri kláym/ *vt* (**-claims, -claiming, -claimed**) **1.** CLAIM SOMETHING BACK to claim back something that has been taken away or temporarily given to another **2.** CONVERT WASTELAND to convert unusable land such as desert or marsh into land suitable for farming or other use **3.** EXTRACT USEFUL SUBSTANCES to extract useful substances from waste or refuse **4.** MAKE SOMEBODY REFORM to cause somebody to return to a more moral way of life **5.** TAME BIRD to tame a hawk or falcon ■ *n* RECOVERY OR CONVERSION the act of reclaiming something, or the state of being reclaimed [14C. Via French < Latin *reclamare* 'cry out against' < *clamare* 'cry out'] —**reclaimable** *adj* —**reclaimant** *n* —**reclaimer** *n* —**reclamation** /réklə máysh'n/ *n*

réclame /ray klaám/ *n* **1.** public attention or fame **2.** the capacity or gift for attracting public attention or fame [Late 19C. < French, 'advertisement' < *réclamer* < Latin *reclamare* (see RECLAIM)]

reclinate /rékli nayt/ *adj* describes a leaf or stem that is bent backward or down

recline /ri klīn/ (**-clines, -clining, -clined**) *v* **1.** *vi* to lean back into a supported sloping or horizontal position, usually in order to rest or relax ○ *She was reclining on a chaise longue.* **2.** *vti* to tilt back from an upright position, or make something tilt back ○ *These seats are more comfortable because they recline.* [15C. Directly or via French < Latin *reclinare* 'bend back or against' < *clinare* 'bend'] —**reclinable** *adj* —**reclination** /rékli náysh'n/ *n*

recliner /ri klīnər/ *n* a chair, often one with a raisable footrest, that tilts back to a sloping or almost horizontal position to allow the person sitting in it to rest more comfortably

reclosable /ree klṓzəb'l/ *adj* able to be closed and sealed again after being opened ○ *a reclosable package*

recluse /ri kloóss/ *n* **1.** a solitary person who avoids other people **2.** somebody who lives a solitary life in prayer and meditation ■ *adj* same as **reclusive** (*archaic*) [12C. < French *reclus*, past participle of Old French *reclure* 'shut up' < Latin *recludere* 'shut again' < *claudere* 'shut'] —**reclusion** /ri kloózh'n/ *n*

reclusive /ri kloóssiv/ *adj* solitary and withdrawn from the rest of the world ○ *lead a reclusive existence* [Late 16C. < obsolete *recluse* 'shut up' < Latin *reclus-*, past participle of *recludere* (see RECLUSE)] —**reclusively** *adv* —**reclusiveness** *n*

recognisance *n* LAW, FIN another spelling of **recognizance**

recognise *vt* another spelling of **recognize**

recognition /rékəg nísh'n/ *n* **1.** ACT OF RECOGNIZING the act of identifying somebody or something on the basis of a past sighting or experience, the ability to do this, or the fact of being identified through having been seen or experienced before ○ *changed beyond recognition* ○ *disguised to avoid recognition* **2.** APPRECIATION appreciation of the value of an achievement ○ *His pioneering work never got the recognition it deserved.* **3.** ACKNOWLEDGMENT acknowledgment of the existence or validity of something ○ *They'll need recognition from the committee in order to proceed.* **4.** US PERMISSION TO SPEAK permission given by somebody chairing a meeting to somebody who has asked to speak **5.** POL ACCEPTANCE OF COUNTRY'S EXISTENCE the formal acceptance by one country of the independent and legal status of another **6.** TOKEN OF ACKNOWLEDGMENT something given or awarded as a token of acknowledgment or gratitude **7.** SENSING OF DATA BY COMPUTER the sensing and conversion of data into machine-readable form by a computer **8.** BIOL COMPATIBILITY OF MOLECULES the ability of molecules with complementary shapes to attach to one another [15C. Directly or via French < Latin *recognition-* < *recognit-*, past participle of *recognoscere* (see RECOGNIZE)] —**recognitive** /ri kógnətiv/ *adj* —**recognitory** /ri kógnətəri/ *adj*

recognizance /ri kógnizənss/, **recognisance** *n* **1.** a formal agreement made by somebody before a judge or magistrate to do something, e.g. to appear in court at a set date ○ *He was released on his own recognizance.* **2.** a sum of money pledged by somebody making a recognizance, to be forfeited if the agreed act is not carried out [14C. < Old French *reconissaunce* < *coni(s)saunce* (see COGNIZANCE)] —**recognizant** *adj*

recognize /rékəg nīz/ (**-nizes, -nizing, -nized**), **recognise** (**-nises, -nising, -nised**) *vt* **1.** IDENTIFY SOMEBODY OR SOMETHING SEEN BEFORE to identify a thing or person as a result of having seen or had some other experience of him, her, or it before ○ *If you saw him again, would you recognize him?* **2.** ACKNOWLEDGE SOMEBODY'S ACHIEVEMENT to show appreciation of, or give credit to, another's achievement ○ *I hope you recognize their contribution to the success of the campaign.* **3.** ACCEPT SOMETHING to accept the validity or truth of something ○ *I recognize that I am at fault.* **4.** ACCEPT STATE'S INDEPENDENCE to accept formally the independent and legal status of a country or regime ○ *refused to recognize the military government* **5.** US ALLOW SOMEBODY TO SPEAK to allow somebody to speak to a meeting ○ *The chair recognizes the representative.* **6.** SHOW ACKNOWLEDGMENT to show in some way that somebody is personally known ○ *She recognized old friends in the crowd with a smile and a wave.* **7.** REWARD SOMEBODY to give or award something to a person as a token of acknowledgment or gratitude ○ *The government recognized his services to industry with a knighthood.* **8.** BIOL BIND ANOTHER MOLECULE to bind another molecule that has a complementary structure [15C. < Old French *recon(n)iss-*, stem of *reconnaistre* < Latin *recognoscere* 'know again' < *cognoscere* 'know'] —**recognizability** /rékəg nīzə bílləti/ *n* —**recognizable** *adj* —**recognizably** *adv* —**recognized** *adj* —**recognizer** *n*

recoil *vi* /ri kóyl/ (**-coils, -coiling, -coiled**) **1.** MOVE BACK SUDDENLY to move back suddenly and violently, e.g. after an impact **2.** FEEL HORROR to react instinctively with fear, horror, disgust, or distaste **3.** FAIL to go wrong and, as a consequence, hurt the perpetrator ○ *a scheme to defraud the company that recoiled upon the perpetrators* **4.** PHYS CHANGE MOMENTUM to experience a change in momentum as a result of a nuclear collision or the emission of an elementary particle ■ *n* /ri kóyl, rée koyl/ **1.** SUDDEN BACKWARD MOVEMENT a sudden and violent backward movement, especially that of a firearm when it is fired **2.** MOVEMENT AWAY IN HORROR a movement back or away from something, especially in horror or disgust **3.** PHYS CHANGE IN MOMENTUM a change in the momentum of an atom, nucleus, or elementary particle as a result of a nuclear collision or the emission of an elementary particle [12C. < French *reculer* < Latin *culus* 'buttocks']

SYNONYMS ***recoil, flinch, quail, shrink, wince***

CORE MEANING: to react in fear or distaste

recoil to move back suddenly and violently, or react instinctively with fear, horror, disgust, or distaste ○ *As he leaned towards her, she instinctively recoiled.* ○ *She recoiled from the sight of the dead animal.* **flinch** to make an involuntary small backward movement in response to pain or something frightening or shocking ○ *He flinched at the needle's prick.* ○ *I'm not a coward, and I don't flinch from facing trouble.* **quail** to tremble with or feel fear or apprehension ○ *Her voice was strong and firm, but she quailed inwardly.* ○ *Preston quailed at the thought of being caught.* **shrink** to move back and away, especially out of disgust, fear, or horror, or be unwilling or reluctant to do something, especially something difficult or unpleasant ○ *She shrank away from the intruder in terror.* ○ *It was not the work I shrank from, but the lack of freedom that the job entailed.* **wince** to make an involuntary movement away from something because

of pain or fear, or feel embarrassment ○ *He shook his head and winced as she touched the cut.* ○ *Charles winced at the thought of what he was going to do.*

recoilless /ri kóyl ləss/ *adj* relating to a heavy firearm such as an antitank gun, whose recoil is reduced by venting the blast to the rear

recoil-operated *adj* using the movement caused by the recoil of a firearm to operate part of its mechanism

recollect /rékə lékt/ (**-lects, -lecting, -lected**) *vti* to bring something back to mind ○ *Can you recollect what she was wearing?* [Early 16C. < Latin *recollect-*, past participle of *recolligere* 'gather again', later 'recall' < *colligere* (see COLLECT[1])] —**recollective** *adj* —**recollectively** *adv*

re-collect /reé kə lékt/ *vt* **1.** to regain control of something, especially of the self **2.** to collect again something that has been scattered or dispersed

recollection /rékə léksh'n/ *n* **1.** the act of remembering something, or the ability to remember something **2.** something that somebody remembers about something ○ *a recollection of having met him before*

recombinant /ri kómbinənt/ *adj* **1.** OF GENETIC RECOMBINATION relating to or involved in genetic recombination ○ *a recombinant chromosome* **2.** RELATING TO RECOMBINANT DNA relating to recombinant DNA or produced by recombinant DNA technology ■ *n* **1.** RESULT OF GENETIC RECOMBINATION a cell or organism exhibiting genetic recombination **2.** GENETIC MATERIAL FROM GENE-SPLICING genetic material resulting from the splicing of DNA fragments

recombinant DNA *n* DNA extracted from two or more different sources such as genes from different organisms and joined together to form a single molecule or fragment

recombination /reé kombi náysh'n/ *n* any process that gives rise to offspring that have combinations of genes different from those of either parent, such as crossing-over and independent assortment of chromosomes during gamete formation —**recombinational** *adj*

~~**recomend**~~ incorrect spelling of **recommend**

recommence /reékə méns/ (**-mences, -mencing, -menced**) *vti* **1.** to begin again, or begin something again (*formal*) **2.** to start again or start something again [15C. < French *recommencer* 'begin again' < *commencer* (see COMMENCE)]

recommencement /reékə ménsmənt/ *n* a beginning again, or the point at which something begins or is begun again

recommend /rékə ménd/ (**-mends, -mending, -mended**) *vt* **1.** SUGGEST SOMETHING AS GOOD IDEA to suggest something as worthy of being accepted, used, or done ○ *You could sue, of course, although I don't really recommend it.* **2.** ENDORSE SOMEBODY OR SOMETHING to express approval of or support for a person or thing ○ *recommended him for promotion* **3.** GIVE SOMETHING APPEAL to make something worth doing or experiencing ○ *The film has little to recommend it other than its special effects.* **4.** ENTRUST SOMEBODY TO ANOTHER to entrust a person or thing to the care of another (*formal*) ○ *She was recommended to our care until her family returned.* [14C. < medieval Latin *recommendare* 'commit thoroughly' < Latin *commendare* 'entrust completely'] —**recommendable** *adj* —**recommendatory** *adj* —**recommender** *n*

SYNONYMS ***recommend, advise, advocate, counsel, suggest***

CORE MEANING: to put forward ideas to somebody who has to decide what to do

recommend to suggest something as worthy of being accepted, used, or done ○ *The report recommended a number of wide-ranging changes.* ○ *I would recommend that you try growing the following plant varieties for a shady garden.* **advise** to give advice to somebody on a subject or course of action, or offer a personal opinion about something to somebody ○ *Your solicitor can advise you on all the matters mentioned in this leaflet.* ○ *I would strongly advise against buying this model.* **advocate** to support or speak in favour of something ○ *They have never used nor advocated the use of violence.* ○ *We strongly advocate sustainable use of coastal resources.* **counsel** (*formal*) to advise somebody on a particular course of action ○ *The doctor counselled Anne to calm down and accept the things she could not change.* ○ *The team manager counselled caution as the best ally in the forthcoming match.* **suggest** to propose somebody or something as a possible choice, plan, or course of action for somebody else to consider ○ *I suggest that we open the subject for discussion.* ○ *This issue is suggested as an area for further research.*

recommendation /rékə men dáysh'n/ *n* **1.** SUGGESTION RECOMMENDING SOMETHING a suggestion as to what is a good or sensible thing to do or use in the circumstances ○ *My recommendation would be to leave on the next train.* **2.** ENDORSEMENT an expression of praise, approval, or support for somebody or something ○ *This comes with the chef's personal recommendation.* **3.** ACT OF RECOMMENDING the act of recommending something

recompense /rékəm penss/ *vt* (**-penses, -pensing, -pensed**) **1.** GIVE COMPENSATION to give compensation to somebody for an injury or loss ○ *The state will recompense you for the accidental destruction of your property.* **2.** PAY OR REWARD SOMEBODY to pay somebody for doing work or for performing a service ○ *was recompensed for her heroism* ■ *n* **1.** COMPENSATION compensation for a loss or injury **2.** REMUNERATION payment for services or work performed [14C. Directly or via French < late Latin *recompensare* 'balance out again' < Latin *compensare* 'balance out']

reconcile /rékən sīl/ (**-ciles, -ciling, -ciled**) *v* **1.** *vti* PUT PEOPLE BACK ON FRIENDLY TERMS to bring two or more people back into a friendly relationship with each other after a dispute or estrangement, or return to a friendly relationship ○ *The two clans were finally reconciled after a century-long feud.* **2.** *vt* END CONFLICT to solve a dispute or end a quarrel ○ *reconciled their differences* **3.** *vt* MAKE SOMEBODY ACCEPT SOMETHING to persuade somebody or yourself to accept that something undesirable cannot be changed ○ *He reconciled himself to the fact that his sporting career was over.* **4.** *vti* MAKE CONSISTENT OR COMPATIBLE to make two or more apparently conflicting things consistent or compatible, or to become consistent or compatible ○ *trying to reconcile fitness with a penchant for fast food* [14C. Directly or via French < Latin *reconciliare* 'make friendly again' < *conciliare* 'make friendly' < *concilium* 'meeting'] —**reconcilability** /rékən sīlə bílləti/ *n* —**reconcilable** /rékən sīləb'l/ *adj* —**reconcilably** *adv* —**reconcilement** *n* —**reconciler** *n*

reconciliation /rékən sili áysh'n/ *n* **1.** RECONCILING OF PEOPLE the ending of conflict or renewing of a friendly relationship between disputing people or groups ○ *a series of quarrels and reconciliations* **2.** ACHIEVEMENT OF CONSISTENCY OR COMPATIBILITY the making of two or more apparently conflicting things consistent or compatible ○ *the reconciliation of such action with his pacifist principles* **3.** CHR SACRAMENT OF PENANCE the sacrament in the Roman Catholic Church whereby a person's sins are absolved through confession and penance [14C. Directly or via French < Latin *reconciliation-* < *reconciliare* (see RECONCILE)] —**reconciliatory** /rékən sílli ətəri/ *adj*

recondite /rékən dīt, ri kón-/ *adj* **1.** requiring a high degree of scholarship or specialist knowledge to be understood ○ *the recondite lore of the ancients* **2.** dealing with material that is too difficult to be understood by those without special knowledge ○ *recondite learning* [Mid-17C. < Latin *reconditus*, past participle of *recondere* 'store away' < *condere* 'store, hide'] —**reconditely** *adv* —**reconditeness** *n*

SYNONYMS See ***obscure***.

recondition /reékən dísh'n/ (**-tions, -tioning, -tioned**) *vt* to bring something back into good condition, especially by repairing it and replacing worn-out parts

SYNONYMS See ***renew***.

~~**reconize**~~ incorrect spelling of **recognize**

~~**reconnaisance**~~ incorrect spelling of **reconnaissance**

reconnaissance /ri kónniss'nss/ *n* **1.** MIL EXPLORATION TO GATHER INFORMATION the exploration or examination of an area to gather information, especially about the strength and positioning of enemy forces **2.** PRELIMINARY SURVEY a preliminary inspection of an area to obtain geographical, hydrographic, or similar data prior to a detailed survey **3.** PRELIMINARY INVESTIGATION preliminary research or investigation of something [Early 19C. < French, < *reconnaiss-*, stem of *reconnaître* 'reconnoitre' < Latin *recognoscere* (see RECOGNIZE)]

reconnoiter *n, vti* MIL US spelling of **reconnoitre**

reconnoitre /rékə nóytər/ *vti* (**-tres, -tring, -tred**) to explore an area in order to gather information, especially about the strength and positioning of enemy forces ○ *reconnoitre the drop zone* ■ *n* an exploration of an area in order to gather information [Early 18C. Via obsolete French *reconnoître* < Latin *recognoscere* (see RECOGNIZE)] —**reconnoitrer** *n*

reconstitute /reé kónsti tyoot/ (**-tutes, -tuting, -tuted**) *vt* **1.** to bring some matter or a material back to its original state, usually by adding water to a concentrated, dried, or powdered form **2.** to alter the form of something ○ *reconstitute the government* —**reconstituent** /reékən stíttyoo ənt/ *adj, n* —**reconstitution** /reé konsti tyoósh'n/ *n*

reconstruct /reékən strúkt/ (**-structs, -structing, -structed**) *vt* **1.** PUT SOMETHING BACK TOGETHER to put something back together from its component parts, pieces, or remains **2.** RE-CREATE SOMETHING FROM EVIDENCE to show plausibly what something was like or how something happened by re-creating it on the basis of the evidence available ○ *reconstruct the culture of an ancient society* **3.** REORGANIZE SOMETHING to reorganize something, reform something, or bring somebody or something up to date **4.** RESTORE NATIONAL GOVERNMENT to restore government and the rule of law to a destroyed nation —**reconstructible** *adj* —**reconstructive** *adj* —**reconstructor** *n*

reconstruction /reékən strúksh'n/ *n* **1.** RECONSTRUCTING OF SOMETHING the act or process of reconstructing something, or of being reconstructed **2.** SOMETHING RECONSTRUCTED FROM ITS PARTS something that has been put back together from its component parts, pieces, or remains **3.** SOMETHING RESTORED something that has been reorganized, reformed, or restored **4.** SOMETHING RE-CREATED something that has been re-created from the evidence available, e.g. a re-enactment of the circumstances of a crime

Reconstruction *n* the period of US history from 1865 to 1877, during which the states that had seceded during the Civil War were reorganized under federal control and later restored to the Union

Reconstructionism /reékən strúksh'nizəm/ *n* in Judaism, a movement in the United States, begun in the 1920s, emphasizing the idea that Judaism is a worldwide religious civilization and advocating continuous adaptation to contemporary conditions —**Reconstructionist** *n, adj*

reconstructive surgery *n* the use of surgery to restore the appearance or use of a damaged body part

reconvey /reékən váy/ (**-veys, -veying, -veyed**) *vt* to transfer something such as property back to a former owner or location —**reconveyance** *n*

record *n* /ré kawrd/ **1.** LASTING ACCOUNT an account of something, preserved in a lasting form, e.g. in writing or on film ○ *Some people use a diary to keep a record of their daily lives.* **2.** ACCOUNT OF PROCEEDINGS a written account of the proceedings of something ○ *the records of the Pickwick Society* **3.** WRITTEN ACCOUNT OF COURT PROCEEDINGS an official written account of the proceedings of a court, available for use as evidence ○ *His remarks were struck from the record.* **4.** DOCUMENT CONTAINING HISTORY the document or book that bears the history of something ○ *The records are stored in the basement.* **5.** BODY OF INFORMATION a body of information or statistics, gathered over a period of time (*often used in the plural*) ○ *the hottest summer since records began* **6.** EVIDENCE something that acts as evidence or a memorial ○ *The Egyptian pyramids are a record of human engineering expertise.* **7.** BEST ACCOMPLISHMENT something that represents the greatest attainment so far, especially in sports ○ *a world record* **8.** PAST PERFORMANCE a person's accomplishments or performance to date **9.** PAST CRIMES a background of criminal convictions, or a list of the crimes committed by a person **10.** MUSIC DISC something on which sound is copied, especially a

plastic disc with a groove that can be played using a gramophone **11.** COPY OF MUSIC a piece of music in a format that can be listened to repeatedly (*informal*) ○ *Their new record is only available on CD.* **12.** COLLECTION OF DATA a collection of related items of information treated as a unit by a computer, e.g. in a database ■ *v* /ri káwrd/ (**-cords, -cording, -corded**) **1.** *vt* PUT SOMETHING INTO LASTING FORM to put something into a form in which it can be kept, especially to write something down or film it ○ *Her journal records the last days of the Empire.* **2.** *vt* NOTE SOMETHING to make a note of something, often for official purposes or for subsequent consultation ○ *The clerk recorded their names in the register.* **3.** *vti* INDICATE MEASUREMENT to register or show something, usually on a scale of a measurement **4.** *vti* COPY SOUNDS OR IMAGES to make a copy of sounds or pictures, e.g. on magnetic tape ○ *I recorded my grandmother reminiscing about the war.* ■ *adj* /ré kawrd/ GREATEST YET exceeding any previous achievement or example in, e.g. size or speed ○ *A record crowd turned up for the game.* [12C. < French, < *recorder* 'bring to mind' < Latin *recordare, recordari*, literally 'bring back to the heart' < *cord-* 'heart, mind'] —**recordable** /ri káwrdəb'l/ *adj* ◇ **go on record** to make a public statement of fact ◇ **off the record** said informally or privately and not intended to be recorded or made public ◇ **on record 1.** publicly stated or known **2.** having published or having said in public ◇ **on the record** said formally or publicly with the knowledge that it may be recorded or disseminated ◇ **set the record straight** to put right a mistake or misunderstanding

recorded /ri káwrdid/ *adj* **1.** copied to a record, tape, CD, or other form of permanent copy, rather than listened to or performed live ○ *recorded music* **2.** sent through the mail by recorded delivery ○ *a recorded parcel*

recorded delivery *n* a class of postage in which an official record is kept of the sending and delivery of the item concerned. Aus, N Am term **certified mail**

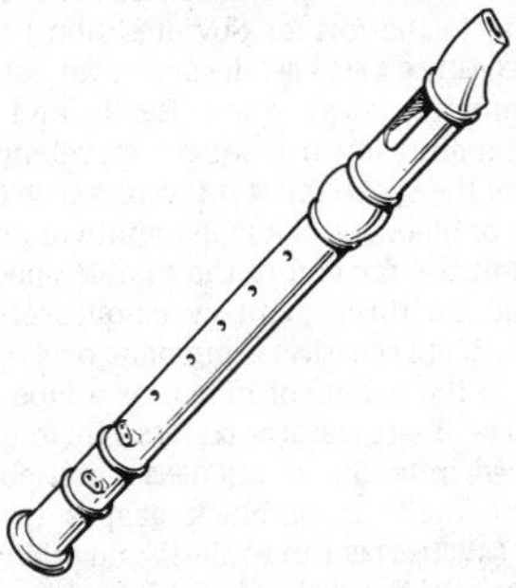

recorder (sense 3)

recorder /ri káwrdər/ *n* **1.** MACHINE FOR RECORDING a machine that makes a permanent copy of sounds or pictures, e.g. a tape recorder or a video recorder **2.** SOMEBODY NOTING SOMETHING somebody who records something, especially official proceedings **3.** MUSICAL INSTRUMENT a wind instrument of the flute family that has finger holes and is blown through a whistle-shaped mouthpiece at one end **4.** *also* **Recorder** TYPE OF JUDGE a barrister or solicitor in England and Wales who acts as a part-time judge in the crown court [15C. Partly < Anglo-Norman *recordour*, Old French *recordeur* 'person who records' < *recorder* (see RECORD); partly < RECORD] —**recordership** *n*

recording /ri káwrding/ *n* **1.** COPY OF MUSIC a permanent copy of sounds or images, e.g. a tape, CD, or video ○ *She was eager to buy the band's latest recording.* **2.** ACT OF MAKING RECORD the act of making a record, especially a permanent copy of sounds or images **3.** RECORDED BROADCAST a broadcast that is not live but has been recorded on an earlier occasion ○ *I watched a recording of the opera on TV.*

Recording Angel *n* an angel supposed to keep an account of every person's good and bad deeds

recordist /ri káwrdist/ *n* somebody who records sound during the making of a film or broadcast

record of achievement *n* a document that details the personal and educational development of a school pupil

record player *n* a machine for reproducing the sounds recorded on records, consisting of a turntable on which the disc revolves and a needle that follows the groove to pick up sound

recount /ri kównt/ (**-counts, -counting, -counted**) *vt* to tell the story or details of something ○ *a tale recounting the deeds of King Arthur* [15C. < Anglo-Norman, Old N French *reconter* 'relate again, count again' < *conter* (see COUNT[1])] —**recountal** *n* —**recounter** *n*

re-count /ree kównt/ *n* a second counting of the votes cast in an election, usually done because the first counting indicated a very close result ■ *vti* to count something, especially the votes cast in an election, a second time

recoup /ri ko͞op/ (**-coups, -couping, -couped**) *v* **1.** *vt* GET SOMETHING BACK to regain something lost or its equivalent **2.** *vt* REIMBURSE ANOTHER to give another party something to make up for that which has been lost ○ *We were adequately recouped for our losses.* **3.** *vi* MAKE UP FOR LOSS to make up for something lost ○ *It will take us years to recoup.* **4.** *vt* LAW DEDUCT SOMETHING to deduct legally part of what is due to a claim [Early 17C. < Old French *recouper* 'cut back' < *couper* 'cut' < *coup* 'blow'] —**recoupable** *adj* —**recoupment** *n*

~~**recouperate**~~ incorrect spelling of **recuperate**

recourse /ri káwrss/ *n* **1.** USE OF OTHERS FOR ASSISTANCE the act of seeking assistance from somebody or something else in a time of difficulty ○ *Can we resolve our financial problems without recourse to further borrowing?* **2.** SOURCE OF HELP OR SOLUTION somebody, something, or a course of action to which a person turns for help or to solve a problem ○ *She felt she had no recourse but to sue.* **3.** FIN, LAW RIGHT TO DEMAND PAYMENT the right to demand payment of a bill of exchange from the person who draws or endorses it, when the person who accepts it fails to pay [14C. Directly or via French < Latin *recursus* 'a running back' < *cursus* (see COURSE)]

recover /ri kúvvər/ (**-ers, -ering, -ered**) *v* **1.** *vt* REGAIN SOMETHING to get back something previously lost or its equivalent **2.** *vi* RETURN TO FORMER STATE to return to a previous state of health, prosperity, or equanimity **3. recover yourself** *vr* CONTROL OR CORRECT YOURSELF to return to a composed state, or make good an error ○ *He soon recovered himself sufficiently to feign a friendly welcome.* **4.** *vi* RETURN TO RIGHT POSITION to return to a suitable or correct state or position ○ *The goalkeeper stumbled, but recovered enough to save the goal.* **5.** *vt* EXTRACT SOMETHING to extract something from a source, e.g. to reclaim useful substances from waste or refuse **6.** *vt* LAW OBTAIN SOMETHING THROUGH COURT to obtain something by the ruling of a court **7.** *vi* LAW SUCCEED IN LITIGATION to be successful in a lawsuit [13C. Via Anglo-Norman *recoverer*, Old French *recovrer* < Latin *recuperare* 'take back' < *capere* 'take'] —**recoverability** /ri kúvvərə bílləti/ *n* —**recoverable** *adj* —**recoverer** *n*

re-cover /ree kúvvər/ *vt* **1.** to put a new cover on something **2.** to cover something again

recoverable error *n* a program error that can be corrected without causing a computer program to fail or data to be erased irretrievably. For example, if a user enters obviously wrong data, the program might request a different entry.

recovery /ri kúvvəri/ (*plural* **-ies**) *n* **1.** RETURN TO HEALTH the return to normal health of somebody who has been ill or injured **2.** RETURN TO NORMAL STATE the return of something to a normal or improved state after a setback or loss ○ *an economic recovery* **3.** GAINING BACK OF SOMETHING LOST the regaining of something lost or taken away ○ *The arrests led to the recovery of large amounts of stolen property.* **4.** EXTRACTION the extraction of a substance or energy from a source, e.g. the reclamation of useful substances from waste or refuse **5.** SHOT OUT OF OBSTACLE in golf, a shot played out of the rough or an obstacle onto the green or fairway **6.** RETURN TO GUARD in fencing, a return to the guard position after making an attack **7.** BRINGING ARM FORWARD in swimming or rowing, the bringing forward of the arm to make another stroke **8.** LAW OBTAINING SOMETHING THROUGH COURT the obtaining of something by the ruling of a court [14C. < Anglo-Norman *recoverie*, Old French *reco(u)vree* < *recov(e)rer* (see RECOVER)] ◇ **in recovery** in the process of recovering from an addiction or other destructive habit

recovery party *n Aus* a social event at which people gather to recover and relax after a night's revelling at another major social event or celebration ○ *The streets were full of people going from one recovery party to another.*

recovery room *n* a hospital room equipped for the care of patients who have just undergone surgery and are recovering from anaesthesia

recreant /rékri ənt/ *adj* (*archaic*) **1.** disloyal to a cause or duty **2.** same as **cowardly** (sense 1) [13C. < Old French, present participle of *recroire* 'surrender' < Latin *credere* 'entrust'] —**recreance** *n* —**recreancy** *n* —**recreant** *n* —**recreantly** *adv*

recreate /rékri ayt/ (**-ates, -ating, -ated**) *vt* to refresh somebody, especially yourself, mentally or physically (*archaic*) [15C. < Latin *recreat-*, past participle of *recreare* 'bring forth again' < *creare* 'bring forth'; partly back-formation < RECREATION] —**recreative** *adj* —**recreator** *n*

re-create /reé kri áyt/ *vt* to make something that appears to be the same as something that no longer exists or that exists in a different place ○ *The decor aims to re-create a 19th-century interior.* —**re-creatable** *adj* —**re-creative** *adj*

SYNONYMS See *copy.*

recreation /rékri áysh'n/ *n* **1.** the refreshment of the mind and body after work, especially by engaging in enjoyable activities **2.** an activity that a person takes part in for pleasure or relaxation rather than as work ○ *She took up sketching as a recreation.*

re-creation /reé kri áysh'n/ *n* **1.** the action or process of re-creating something **2.** something created or reproduced again

recreational /rékri áyshn'l/ *adj* **1.** done or used for pleasure or relaxation rather than work **2.** describes controlled drugs taken illegally —**recreationally** *adv*

recreational vehicle *n N Am* a large motor vehicle, usually with facilities for sleeping and eating, used for recreational activities such as camping

recreation ground *n* a public area for sports and games, often incorporating a children's playground

recreation room *n* **1.** a room set aside for games, social events, and other kinds of recreation in a public building **2.** *N Am* a room used by the occupants of a house for relaxation and recreational activities ○ *a new TV for the recreation room*

recriminate /ri krímmi nayt/ (**-nates, -nating, -nated**) *vi* to accuse somebody who has already brought an accusation [Early 17C. < medieval Latin *recriminat-*, past participle of *recriminari* 'accuse back or again' < Latin *criminari, criminare* 'accuse'] —**recriminative** /-nətiv/ *adj* —**recriminator** *n* —**recriminatory** /-nətəri/ *adj*

recrimination /ri krímmi náysh'n/ *n* **1.** an accusation made against somebody who has brought a previous accusation ○ *It started out as a calm discussion and ended in tears and recriminations.* **2.** an accusation that somebody accused of a crime makes against the accuser

rec room *n N Am* same as **recreation room** (*informal*)

recrudesce /reé kroo déss/ (**-desces, -descing, -desced**) *vi* to break out or become active again after a dormant period [Mid-17C. Back-formation < *recrudescence* < Latin *recrudescere* 'become raw again' < *crudus* 'raw, bloody'] —**recrudescence** *n* —**recrudescent** *adj*

recruit /ri kro͞ot/ *v* (**-cruits, -cruiting, -cruited**) **1.** *vti* ENROL OR TAKE ON SOMEBODY to enrol somebody as a worker or member, or to take on people as workers or members ○ *The company has stopped recruiting.* **2.** *vti* ENLIST SOMEBODY to enlist somebody in a military force, or take part in enlisting people for a military force ○ *She was recruited by the Marines.* **3.** *vt* RAISE ARMY to put together a military force ■ *n* **1.** NEW MEMBER a new member, worker, player, or supporter **2.** NEW SOLDIER a member of a military force who has joined it recently [Mid-17C. < French *recruter* < *recrue* 'new growth' < *recroître* 'increase again' < Latin *crescere* 'grow'] —**recruiter** *n* —**recruiting** *n* —**recruitment** *n*

rec. sec. *abbr* recording secretary

rect, rec't *abbr* COMM receipt

rect. *abbr* rectangle

Rect. *abbr* CHR **1.** Rector **2.** Rectory

recta ANAT plural of **rectum**

rectangle /rék tang g'l/ *n* a two-dimensional geometric figure formed of four sides in which each angle is a right angle, especially one with adjacent sides of different length [Late 16C. Directly or via French < medieval Latin *rect(i)angulum*, < form of late Latin *rectiangulus* 'straight angle' < Latin *rectus* 'straight, right' + *angulus* 'angle']

rectangular /rek táng gyōōlər/ *adj* **1.** with four sides, usually with adjacent sides of different length, and four right angles ○ *The yard is rectangular rather than square.* **2.** involving, having, or meeting at right angles [Early 17C. < ANGULAR after French *rectangulaire*] —**rectangularity** /rek táng gyōō lárrəti/ *n* —**rectangularly** *adv*

rectangular coordinate *n* a Cartesian coordinate used in a system of axes that meet at right angles

rectangular hyperbola *n* a hyperbola with asymptotes that are at right angles

recti ANAT plural of **rectus**

rectifier /rékti fī ər/ *n* **1.** ELECTRONIC DEVICE an electronic device that converts alternating current to direct current, e.g. a set of semiconductor diodes connected in a bridge circuit **2.** CONDENSING APPARATUS an apparatus that condenses vapour to liquid during distillation **3.** SOMEBODY OR SOMETHING THAT RECTIFIES SOMETHING somebody or something that puts a matter or situation right

rectify /rékti fī/ (-fies, -fying, -fied) *vt* **1.** CORRECT SOMETHING to put something right **2.** ELECTRONICS CONVERT CURRENT to convert alternating current to direct current **3.** CHEM PURIFY SOMETHING to purify a substance, especially by distillation **4.** MATHS FIND LENGTH OF CURVE to find the length of a curve [14C. Directly or via French *rectifier* < medieval Latin *rectificare* 'make right' < *rectus* 'straight, right'] —**rectifiability** /rékti fī ə bíllәti/ *n* —**rectifiable** *adj* —**rectification** /réktifi káysh'n/ *n*

rectilinear /rékti línni ər/, **rectilineal** /-ni əl/ *adj* **1.** formed or consisting of straight lines **2.** moving in a straight line [Mid-17C. < late Latin *rectilineus* < Latin *rectus* 'straight, right' + *linea* 'line'] —**rectilinearly** *adv*

rectitude /rékti tyood/ *n* **1.** RIGHTEOUSNESS strong moral integrity in character or actions **2.** CORRECTNESS correctness in judgment (*formal*) ○ *the admirable rectitude of her assessments* **3.** STRAIGHTNESS straightness in form or shape (*formal*) [15C. Directly or via French < late Latin *rectitudo* < Latin *rectus* 'straight, right'] —**rectitudinous** /rékti tyōōdinəss/ *adj*

recto /réktō/ (*plural* **-tos**) *n* **1.** the front side of a printed sheet **2.** the right-hand page of an open book [Early 19C. < modern Latin *(folio) recto* '(the page) being on the right', form of Latin *rectus* 'straight, right']

rector /réktər/ *n* **1.** CLERIC IN CHARGE OF ANGLICAN PARISH a member of the clergy of the Church of England who is in charge of a parish. Rectors, unlike vicars, were formerly entitled to the whole of the tithes from their parish. **2.** CLERIC IN CHARGE OF CATHOLIC CONGREGATION a member of the Roman Catholic clergy who is in charge of a congregation, a college, or a religious community **3.** CLERIC IN CHARGE OF EPISCOPAL PARISH a member of the Episcopal clergy who is in charge of a parish **4.** HEAD OF SCHOOL the head of some schools, colleges, or universities **5.** OFFICER ELECTED BY STUDENTS in some Scottish universities, somebody elected by students to represent them on the University Court [14C. Directly or via Old French, 'captain (of a ship), head of a university' < Latin, 'ruler, governor' < *regere* 'rule'] —**rectorate** *n* —**rectorial** /rek táwri əl/ *adj* —**rectorship** *n*

rectory /réktəri/ (*plural* **-ries**) *n* **1.** the house that a rector lives in, provided by the church **2.** the post of rector and the income that goes with it [Late 16C. < Old French *rectorie* or medieval Latin *rectoria* < Latin *rector* (see RECTOR)]

rectrix /rék triks/ (*plural* **-trices** /-tri seez, -trī seez/) *n* a tail feather of a bird [Mid-18C. < Latin, feminine of *rector* (see RECTOR)]

rectum /réktəm/ (*plural* **-tums** or **-ta** /-tə/) *n* the lower part of the large intestine, between the colon and the anal canal [15C. < Latin *(intestinum) rectum* 'straight (intestine)' < *rectus* 'straight, right'] —**rectal** *adj*

rectus /réktəss/ (*plural* **-ti** /-tī/) *n* any straight muscle, e.g. any of the muscles in the abdomen or the thigh [Early 18C. < Latin, 'straight, right']

recumbent /ri kúmbənt/ *adj* **1.** LYING lying back or lying down ○ *a colossal recumbent statue* **2.** BIOL RESTING OR LEANING describes a plant or animal part that rests or leans against something else **3.** GEOL HORIZONTAL describes a geological fold whose axis is more or less horizontal [Early 18C. < Latin *recumbent-*, present participle of *recumbere* 'lie back' < *-cumbere* 'lie down'] —**recumbence** *n* —**recumbently** *adv*

recuperate /ri kōōpə rayt/ (-ates, -ating, -ated) *v* **1.** *vi* to recover from an illness or injury **2.** *vt* to recover something lost, especially a sum of money ○ *recuperate investment losses* [Mid-16C. < Latin *recuperat-*, past participle of *recuperare* (see RECOVER)] —**recuperation** /ri kōōpə ráysh'n/ *n* —**recuperative** /-ətiv, -raytiv/ *adj* —**recuperatory** /-rətəri/ *adj*

USAGE *Recuperate* is sometimes mistakenly spelt *recouperate*, by confusion with the unrelated verb *recoup*.

USAGE *Recuperate* is normally used intransitively, that is, without an object, as in *She needed several weeks to recuperate.* When a noun such as *health* is the object, *recover* is a better choice: *She needed several weeks to recover* [not *recuperate*] *her health.*

---

recuperator /ri kōōpə raytər/ *n* **1.** a device used to recover energy that would otherwise be lost, especially one that takes heat from exhaust gases and uses it to preheat incoming combustion air **2.** a device in a gun that returns it to its firing position following recoil

recur /ri kúr/ (-curs, -curring, -curred) *vi* **1.** ⚠ OCCUR AGAIN to happen or appear once again or repeatedly **2.** BE REPEATED INDEFINITELY to occur as an infinitely repeated digit or series of digits at the end of a decimal fraction **3.** RETURN to return to a subject in speech, writing, or thought (*literary*) [Early 16C. < Latin *recurrere* 'run back' < *currere* 'run']

USAGE As the idea of *again* is an integral part of the meaning of *recur*, it is unnecessary to say things like *The disease recurred again.* Simply say *recurred.*

---

recurrent /ri kúrrənt/ *adj* **1.** happening or appearing again, especially repeatedly **2.** describes a blood vessel or nerve that turns back on itself and runs in the opposite direction —**recurrence** *n* —**recurrently** *adv*

recurrent fever *n* MED same as **relapsing fever**

recurring decimal /ri kúrring-/ *n* a decimal number in which one or more digits repeat indefinitely after the decimal point, e.g. 3.77777.... or 8.691691691.... N Am term **repeating decimal**

recursion /ri kúrsh'n/ *n* **1.** RETURN OF SOMETHING the return of something, often repeatedly **2.** LOGIC, MATHS REPETITION OF STEPS TO GIVE RESULT the use of repeated steps, each based on the result of the one before, to define a function or calculate a number **3.** COMPUT DELEGATION AS PROGRAMMING TECHNIQUE a programming technique where a routine performs its task by delegating part of it to another instance of itself [Early 17C. < late Latin *recursion-* 'a running back' < Latin *recurs-*, past participle of *recurrere* (see RECUR)]

recursive /ri kúrssiv/ *adj* **1.** repeating itself, either indefinitely or until a specific point is reached **2.** involving the repeated application of a function to its own values [Late 18C. < Latin *recurs-* (see RECURSION)] —**recursively** *adv* —**recursiveness** *n*

recurvate /ri kúrvət, -vayt/ *adj* curved backwards, inwards, or downwards

recurve /ri kúrv/ (-curves, -curving, -curved) *vti* to curve backwards, inwards, or downwards, or cause something to curve in this way [Late 16C. < Latin *recurvare* 'curve back' < *curvus* 'curved, crooked'] —**recurvation** /reé kur váysh'n/ *n* —**recurved** *adj*

recusant /rékyōōz'nt, ri kyōō-/ *n* **1.** CATHOLIC REFUSING TO ATTEND ANGLICAN SERVICES a Roman Catholic who broke the law by refusing to attend Church of England services in England between the 16th and 18th centuries **2.** SOMEBODY DISOBEYING AUTHORITY somebody who refuses to obey authority ■ *adj* DISOBEYING AUTHORITY refusing to obey authority —**recusance** *n*

recuse /ri kyōōz/ (-cuses, -cusing, -cused) *vti* to declare yourself to be, or to render somebody, disqualified to judge something or participate in something because of possible bias or personal interest [Early 19C. < Latin *recusare* 'refuse' < *causa* 'cause, case'] —**recusal** *n*

recyclable /ree sīk'ləb'l/ *adj* suitable or adapted for recycling ■ *n* a material or product that is able to be recycled —**recyclability** /ree sīk'lə bílləti/ *n*

recycle /ree sīk'l/ *v* (-cles, -cling, -cled) **1.** *vti* PROCESS FOR REUSE to process used or waste material so that it can be used again **2.** *vti* SAVE FOR REUSE to save or collect used or waste material for reprocessing into something useful **3.** *vti* USE AGAIN DIFFERENTLY to adapt or convert something to a new use **4.** *vt* REUSE SOMETHING to use something again for the same purpose **5.** *vt* USE AGAIN UNIMAGINATIVELY to use something abstract again in the same form, often at the expense of freshness or originality ○ *recycling the same old ideas* **6.** *vti* REPEAT PROCESS to repeat a process, or pass something through a process again ■ *n* RECYCLING PROCESS the process of recycling material, especially used or waste material —**recycler** *n*

recycled /ree sīk'ld/ *adj* **1.** manufactured from used or waste materials that have been reprocessed **2.** used again or repeatedly, often at the expense of freshness or originality

recycling /ree sīkling/ *n* **1.** the processing of used or waste material so that it can be used again, instead of being wasted **2.** the saving or collection of used or waste material for reprocessing

red /red/ *adj* (redder, reddest) **1.** OF COLOUR OF BLOOD of or near the colour of blood, or of a ripe tomato or strawberry **2.** REDDISH-BROWN describes hair or fur that is reddish-brown, orange, or golden-brown **3.** BLOODSHOT describes eyes that are bloodshot or with red rims, e.g. from tiredness **4.** WITH TEMPORARILY RED FACE blushing, e.g. from shame or embarrassment **5.** MADE FROM BLACK GRAPES describes wine made from black grapes. Pigments in the purple skins of these grapes give the wine a deep red colour. **6.** REPRESENTING DEBT representing debt or financial loss **7.** *also* **Red** POL LEFT-WING socialist or communist (*informal disapproving*) **8.** *also* **Red** SOVIET relating or belonging to the former Soviet Union (*informal*) **9.** ASTRON EXHIBITING A REDSHIFT describes an astronomical object moving away from Earth and therefore showing a shift towards longer wavelengths at the red end of the spectrum ■ *n* **1.** COLOUR OF BLOOD a colour like that of blood, or of a ripe tomato or strawberry. Red lies at the far end of the visible spectrum and is one of the three primary colours of light and pigment. **2.** RED COLOURING a pigment or dye that is of or near to the colour of blood, or a ripe tomato or strawberry **3.** RED FABRIC OR CLOTHES fabric or clothing that is red in colour **4.** RED THING a red object **5.** RED WINE wine made from black grapes (*informal*) **6.** SECTION OF GAMBLING TABLE in roulette and other gambling games, one of the two coloured areas on the table on which players may place bets, the other being black **7.** RING ON ARCHERY TARGET in archery, a red ring immediately outside the gold disc at the centre of a target **8.** RED BALL in billiards, snooker, and other cue games, a red ball **9.** *also* **Red** A SOCIALIST OR COMMUNIST somebody with socialist or communist views (*informal disapproving*) [Old English *rēad* < Indo-European] —**redly** *adv* —**redness** *n* ◇ **in the red** in debt, e.g. to a bank ◇ **see red** to suddenly become very angry (*informal*)

USAGE See *read.*

---

red. *abbr* **1.** FIN redeemable **2.** reduced **3.** reduction

redact /ri dákt/ (-dacts, -dacting, -dacted) *vt* (*formal*) **1.** to edit or revise something in preparation for publication ○ *formerly classified documents that were redacted before release to protect still confidential material* **2.** to compose or draft something for publication or for an announcement [Mid-19C. < Latin *redact-*, past participle of *redigere* 'reduce', literally 'bring down' < *agere* 'do'] —**redaction** *n* —**redactional** *adj* —**redactor** *n*

red admiral *n* a brightly coloured butterfly with broad orange-red bands on its forewings. Native to: Europe, North America. Latin name: *Vanessa atalanta.*

red alert *n* a warning or alarm that indicates a situation of the highest priority or greatest urgency, especially an imminent attack, or the state of readiness to deal with such a situation ◇ **on red alert**

prepared for any trouble or danger that may occur

red algae *npl* sea algae that contain a red pigment as well as chlorophyll, e.g. dulse, laver, and carrageen. Family: Rhodophyceae.

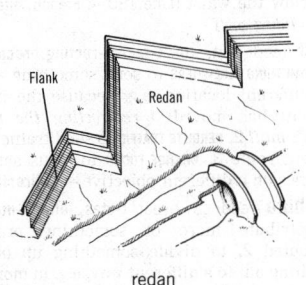

Flank   Redan

redan

redan /ri dán/ *n* a pair of parapets that form a V-shaped projection from the wall of a castle or other fortification [Late 17C. < French, variant of *redent* < *dent* 'tooth' < Latin *dent*-]

red ant *n* a reddish ant, especially a Pharaoh ant

Red Army *n* the military organization put into place by Leon Trotsky at the time of the Russian revolution. Its members were recruited from the worker and peasant classes.

redback /réd bak/, **redback spider** *n* a small venomous dark brown or black spider, the female of which has a red stripe or patch on the back of the abdomen. Native to: Australia, New Zealand. Latin name: *Latrodectus hasselti*.

red-bellied black snake *n* a large poisonous snake that is glossy black with an orange-red underside. Native to: eastern Australian woodlands. Latin name: *Pseudechis porphyriacus*.

Red Belt *n* in France, the working-class suburban area outside Paris, historically administered by communist mayors and populated chiefly by immigrants from North Africa and the Middle East

red biddy *n* a strong cheap alcoholic drink made by mixing red wine with methylated spirits (*dated informal*)

red blood cell *n* any red-coloured cell in blood that contains haemoglobin and carries oxygen to the tissues. Technical name **erythrocyte**

red-blooded *adj* behaving in ways stereotypically associated with men, e.g. by showing strength or active sexual desire

redbreast /réd brest/ (*plural* -**breasts** or *same*) *n* 1. same as **robin** (*informal*) 2. a freshwater sunfish with a reddish belly. Native to: eastern United States. Latin name: *Lepomis auritus*.

redbrick /rédbrik/ *adj* 1. relating to British universities that were founded in the late 19th and early 20th centuries, e.g. Manchester and Leeds. The term was originally intended to emphasize their modernity in contrast to the older British universities such as Oxford and St Andrews, and now also distinguishes them from newer universities. 2. constructed of red bricks

Red Brigades *npl* a left-wing urban organization that was active in Italy during the 1970s and was responsible for the kidnapping and murder of the Italian prime minister Aldo Moro in 1978 [Translation of Italian *brigate rosse*]

redbud /réd bud/ (*plural* -**buds** or *same*) *n* a tree with heart-shaped leaves and small pale pink flowers. Native to: North America. Genus: *Cercis*.

redcap /réd kap/ *n* 1. an officer in the military police (*slang*) 2. *N Am* in the United States, a porter at an airport or railway station (*informal*) [Early 20C. < the red caps traditionally worn by such personnel]

red card *n* 1. in soccer, a red card displayed by the referee when dismissing a player from the field for a serious infringement of the rules 2. any dismissal or rejection, e.g. from a job (*informal*) ○ *Even his girlfriend has threatened to give him the red card.*

red carpet *n* 1. a strip of red-coloured carpet laid on the ground for an important visitor to walk on when

arriving or departing 2. attentive or deferential treatment given to a dignitary, celebrity, or other important person (*hyphenated when used before a noun*) ○ *Everywhere we went we got the red-carpet treatment.*

red cedar /-séedər/ *n* 1. **TREE OF EASTERN N AMERICA** an evergreen tree of the juniper family with reddish wood and fleshy cones. Native to: eastern North America. Latin name: *Juniperus virginiana*. 2. **TREE OF WESTERN N AMERICA** an evergreen timber tree of the cypress family with reddish wood and small oval cones. Native to: western North America. Latin name: *Thuja plicata*. 3. **WOOD FROM RED CEDAR** the weather-resistant close-grained wood of either of the red cedar trees. Use: building material. 4. **EVERGREEN CONIFEROUS TREE** an evergreen coniferous tree with reddish timber, e.g. the Japanese red cedar

red cell *n* BIOL same as **red blood cell**

red cent *n* *N Am* the smallest amount of money (*informal*) [From the fact that the one-cent coin is made of copper]

Red Centre *n* *Aus* the desert region of central Australia, characterized by red rock and sand (*informal*)

red-chested cuckoo *n* a cuckoo with a reddish band on its chest. Native to: Africa. Latin name: *Cuculus solitarius*.

AKG London

Red Cloud

Red Cloud /red klówd/ (1822–1909) Oglala Sioux leader. He resisted the US government's occupation of Native North American territory in present-day Wyoming and Montana, but his defeat in the Sioux War (1875–76) resulted in the relocation of his people to South Dakota.

> '...the white soldier's...presence...is...an insult to the spirits of our ancestors.... Dakotas, I am for war!'
> [Red Cloud, *Speech, council at Fort Laramie*; 1866]

red clover *n* a clover often grown as a forage crop for horses or cattle. Flowers: fragrant, red. Native to: Europe, Asia, North America. Latin name: *Trifolium pratense*.

redcoat /réd kōt/ *n* 1. a British soldier serving overseas in former times, especially during the War of American Independence 2. a uniformed attendant at a Butlin's holiday camp [Early 16C. < their bright-red uniform coats]

red coral *n* a coral with hard deep pink skeletons. Use: ornaments, jewellery. Genus: *Corallium*.

red corpuscle *n* BIOL same as **red blood cell**

Red Crescent *n* in Islamic countries, the name under which the Red Cross operates

Red Cross *n* an international organization founded in 1864 and dedicated to the medical care of the sick or wounded in wars and natural disasters

redcurrant /red kúrrənt/ *n* 1. a red berry with a tart flavour that grows in clusters. Use: jam or jelly. 2. a flowering bush that produces redcurrants. Native to: northern temperate regions. Latin name: *Ribes rubrum*.

redd[1] /red/ *regional* *vti* (**redds, redding, redd** or **redded**) to tidy something, or tidy things generally ■ *n* a spell of tidying [15C. Origin ?] —**redder** *n*

redd[2] /red/ *n* a hollow that is scooped out in the sand or gravel of a river bed for spawning by fish such as trout and salmon [Early 19C. Origin ?]

red deer *n* a large deer that has spreading antlers and a reddish-brown summer coat. Native to: Europe, Asia. Latin name: *Cervus elaphus*.

redden /rédd'n/ (**-dens, -dening, -dened**) *v* 1. *vti* to become red or redder, or make something red or redder 2. *vi* to go red in the face, e.g. with embarrassment, anger, or exertion

Popperfoto

Otis Redding

Redding /rédding/, **Otis** (1941–67) US singer and songwriter. He won popular and critical acclaim for his southern soul rhythm-and-blues style, an emotional blend of gospel, country, and traditional blues.

reddish /réddish/ *adj* of a colour that is a shade of red or strongly tinged with red —**reddishness** *n*

Redditch /réddich/ town in Worcestershire, western England. It was designated a new town in 1964. Population: 78,807 (2001).

reddle *n, vt* MINERALS, AGRIC same as **ruddle**

red-dog *vt* in American football, to charge directly at the quarterback the moment the ball is put into play (*informal*)

rede /reed/ (*archaic*) *n* 1. same as **advice** 2. **EXPLANATION** a story, account, or explanation ■ *vt* (**redes, reding, reded**) 1. **ADVISE SOMEBODY** to advise or counsel somebody 2. **INTERPRET SOMETHING** to explain, understand, or interpret something in a particular way [The noun is from Old English *ræd*; the verb from Old English *rædan* (see READ)]

redear /réd eer/ (*plural* -**ears** or *same*), **redear sunfish** (*plural* **redear sunfishes** or *same*) *n* a freshwater sunfish with a scarlet margin around the gill cover. Native to: southern and eastern United States. Latin name: *Lepomis microlophus*.

red earth *n* a clayey soil found in tropical grasslands, coloured red by the presence of iron compounds

redecorate /ree déka rayt/ (**-rates, -rating, -rated**) *vti* to change or renew the interior decoration of a building or room —**redecoration** /rèe deka ráysh'n/ *n*

redeem /ri deém/ (**-deems, -deeming, -deemed**) *vt* 1. **MAKE SOMETHING ACCEPTABLE** to make something acceptable or pleasant in spite of its negative qualities or aspects 2. **RESTORE REPUTATION** to do something that changes a negative opinion to a positive one 3. **ATONE FOR HUMAN SIN** to pay for the sins of humanity with death on the Cross (*refers to Jesus Christ*) 4. **BUY SOMETHING BACK** to buy back an item given, e.g. to a pawnbroker, as security for a loan 5. **KEEP PROMISE** to fulfil a pledge or promise 6. **EXCHANGE SOMETHING FOR MONEY** to exchange or convert something such as a voucher for money or its equivalent 7. **PAY SOMETHING OFF** to pay off the outstanding portion of a debt [15C. Directly or via French < Latin *redimere* 'buy back' < *emere* 'buy'] —**redeemable** *adj*

redeemer /ri deémər/ *n* somebody who redeems somebody or something, especially somebody who rescues another

Redeemer *n* Jesus Christ regarded as the saviour of humanity through his death on the Cross

redeeming /ri deéming/ *adj* compensating for faults or flaws

redefine /reédi fín/ (**-fines, -fining, -fined**) *vt* 1. to interpret the meaning of something, especially a word, differently, or give something a new meaning 2. to change the nature or scope of something or the character or role of somebody, or cause something or somebody to be understood differently

○ *The parameters of the enquiry were redefined overnight.* —**redefinition** /-deffə nísh'n/ *n*

redemption /ri démpsh'n/ *n* **1.** IMPROVING OF SOMETHING the act of saving something or somebody from a declined, dilapidated, or corrupted state and restoring it, him, or her to a better condition ○ *The house was a wreck, and the garden seemed entirely beyond redemption.* **2.** REDEEMED STATE the improved state of somebody or something saved from apparently irreversible decline **3.** ATONEMENT FOR HUMAN SIN deliverance from the sins of humanity by the death of Jesus Christ on the Cross **4.** BUYING BACK OF SOMETHING the buying back of something given, e.g. to a pawnbroker, as security for a loan **5.** ENDING OF FINANCIAL OBLIGATION the removal of a financial obligation, e.g. the repayment of a loan or promissory note [14C. Via French < Latin *redemption-* < past participle of *redimere* (see REDEEM)]

redemptioner /ri démpsh'nər/ *n* an emigrant from Europe in the 18th and 19th centuries who worked as a servant on arriving in North America to pay for the cost of the voyage

redemptive /ri démptiv/ *adj* bringing about the redemption of somebody or something [15C. < Latin *redempt-*, past participle of *redimere* (see REDEEM)]

Redemptorist /ri démptərist/ *n* a member of the Congregation of the Most Holy Redeemer, a Roman Catholic order specializing in preaching and missionary work, founded in Italy in 1732 [Mid-19C. < French *rédemptoriste* < Latin *redemptor* 'redeemer' < *redempt-* (see REDEMPTIVE)]

red ensign *n* a red flag with the Union Jack in the upper corner of the vertical edge near the staff. It is flown by British merchant ships and pleasure craft.

redeploy /reedi plóy/ (**-ploys, -ploying, -ployed**) *vti* to move people or equipment from one area or activity to another —**redeployment** *n*

redevelop /reedi véllap/ (**-ops, -oping, -oped**) *vt* to improve an area that has become run down by renovating buildings, making better use of wasteland, and encouraging inward investment —**redevelopment** *n*

redeye /réd ī/ *n* **1.** PHOTOGRAPHIC FAULT red pupils in the eyes of a subject in flash photography (*informal*) **2.** N Am NIGHT FLIGHT a late night or overnight airline service (*informal*) **3.** US CHEAP WHISKY cheap inferior whisky (*slang*)

red-faced *adj* blushing, especially with embarrassment

redfin /réd fin/ (*plural* **-fins** or *same*), **redfin shiner** (*plural* **redfin shiners** or *same*) *n* a small freshwater fish with reddish fins, often kept in aquariums. Native to: central North America. Genus: *Notropis*.

red fire *n* a chemical mixture, especially one containing strontium salts, that burns with a vivid red flame and is used in fireworks and flares

redfish /réd fish/ (*plural* **-fishes** or *same*) *n* **1.** a reddish rockfish. Native to: northern Atlantic. **2.** a male salmon that has recently spawned

red flag *n* **1.** US same as **red rag 2.** a flag waved as a danger signal or a command to stop **3.** a plain red flag or banner used as an international symbol of communism or socialism

Redford /rédfərd/, **Robert** (*b.* 1937) US actor, producer, and director. His many films include *Butch Cassidy and the Sundance Kid* (1969). He also founded the Sundance Film Festival. Full name **Redford, Jr., Charles Robert**

red fox *n* a common fox with sharply pointed ears, a reddish-orange to reddish-brown coat, and a white-tipped tail. Native to: fields and open woods of Europe, Asia, and North America. Latin name: *Vulpes vulpes.*

red giant *n* a red-coloured star with a relatively low surface temperature and a diameter much greater than that of the Sun

Redgrave /réd grayv/, **Sir Michael** (1908–85) British actor. One of the outstanding actors of his generation, he played both classical and contemporary roles in films and on stage. Full name **Redgrave, Michael Scudamore**

Redgrave, Sir Steve (*b.* 1962) British rower. Between 1987 and 2000 he won nine world titles and was Olympic Games gold medallist on five consecutive occasions.

Redgrave, Vanessa (*b.* 1937) British actor. The daughter of Michael Redgrave, she is acclaimed for her sensitive and intelligent portrayals of strong-willed independent women.

red-green colourblindness *n* MED same as **deuteranopia**

Red Guard *n* **1.** the 1960s Chinese Communist youth movement that attempted to bring about the Cultural Revolution of Mao Zedong **2.** a member of the Red Guard

red gum *n* **1.** a eucalyptus tree with aromatic leaves and distinctive red wood. Native to: Australia. Latin name: *Eucalyptus camaldulensis.* **2.** TREES same as **sweet gum**

red-handed *adj* in the act of committing a crime or doing something wrong ○ *was caught red-handed* [From the notion of having blood on the hands]

red hat *n* **1.** the broad-brimmed crimson hat that a Roman Catholic cardinal wears on ceremonial occasions **2.** the rank or position of cardinal in the Roman Catholic Church

redhead /réd hed/ *n* **1.** somebody, especially a woman, who has reddish-coloured hair **2.** a diving duck, the male of which has a bright chestnut head. Native to: North America. Latin name: *Aythya americana.*

redheaded /réd héddid/ *adj* **1.** with reddish-coloured hair **2.** describes an animal, especially a bird, with a red head

red heat *n* the temperature at which something is red-hot, or the state of being at such a temperature

red herring *n* **1.** MISLEADING CLUE something introduced, e.g. into a crime or mystery story, in order to divert attention or mislead **2.** SMOKED HERRING a herring salted and smoked to a reddish-brown colour **3.** US BUSINESS PRELIMINARY BUSINESS PROSPECTUS a preliminary prospectus for a new stock issue, filed with the US Securities and Exchange Commission, that does not include the offering price of the shares or the size of the issue. It is often issued in order to gauge the market for shares in the proposed issue. (*slang*) [< dragging smoked fish across a scent trail to teach hounds not to be distracted]

red-hot *adj* **1.** GLOWING RED WITH HEAT heated to such a high temperature as to glow red **2.** VERY HOT extremely hot **3.** EXTREMELY POPULAR in great demand (*informal*) **4.** EXCITING very exciting (*informal*) ○ *red-hot news* **5.** PASSIONATE feeling or expressing intense enthusiasm, passion, or anger (*informal*)

red-hot poker *n* a tall perennial ornamental plant. Flowers: erect spikes, red at the top and orange below. Native to: South Africa. Genus: *Kniphofia.*

redia /reedi ə/ (*plural* **-diae** /-di ee/) *n* one of the forms of the larvae of trematode worms. Rediae are found as parasites in the gut of snails. [Late 19C. < modern Latin, after Francesco *Redi* (1626–98), Italian biologist]

redial /ree dī əl/ *vti* (**-als, -alling, -alled**) to dial a telephone number again, e.g. because the line was engaged when the number was dialled earlier ■ *n* the function or button on a telephone that permits automatic redialling of a telephone number

~~rediculous~~ incorrect spelling of **ridiculous**

redid past tense of **redo**

Red Indian *n* an offensive term for a Native North American (*dated*)

redingote

redingote /rédding gōt/ *n* **1.** WOMAN'S FULL-SKIRTED COAT a woman's coat with an open full skirt and close-fitting top **2.** WOMAN'S BELTED DRESS OR COAT a belted woman's dress or coat of 18th-century Europe that was open at the front to show a petticoat or dress **3.** MAN'S OVERCOAT a man's double-breasted coat of 18th-century Europe that had wide flat cuffs and flared out below the waist [Late 18C. < French, alteration of English *riding-coat*]

redirect /reedi rékt, -dī-/ (**-rects, -recting, -rected**) *vt* **1.** SEND SOMETHING ELSEWHERE to send something received to a different location, e.g. because the intended recipient has moved ○ *redirecting the previous tenant's mail* **2.** REROUTE TRAFFIC to send traffic along a different route **3.** CHANGE FOCUS to focus actions or activities on a different objective —**redirection** *n*

redistribute /reedi strí byoot/ (**-utes, -uting, -uted**) *vt* **1.** to distribute more of something previously distributed **2.** to divide something up or share something out in a different way, e.g. in more equal proportions or among a wider range of people —**redistribution** /reedistri byoosh'n/ *n* —**redistributionist** *n* —**redistributive** /-byootiv/ *adj*

redivivus /réddi vívəss, -vee-/ *adj* revived, reborn, or brought back to life (*literary*) [Late 16C. < Latin, 'alive again' < *vivus* 'alive']

red kangaroo *n* a kangaroo of the largest species, varying in colour from brick red to grey. Native to: desert areas of Australia. Latin name: *Megaleia rufa.*

red lead *n* a bright red poisonous oxide of lead. Use: pigment in paints. Formula: Pb_3O_4.

redleg /réd leg/ *n* (*slang*) **1.** US MIL same as **artilleryman 2.** *Carib* an offensive term for a white person from a lower income group

red-letter day *n* a very special day or occasion [< the marking of feast days in red on church calendars]

red light *n* **1.** a red warning signal, especially an instruction to drivers to stop **2.** a sign of disapproval or rejection, e.g. an instruction not to proceed with something (*informal*) ○ *Our proposal got the red light.*

red-light *adj* relating to the part of a town or city where brothels and other commercial sex-based activities are concentrated [< the red lights traditionally displayed in the doors and windows of brothels]

redline /réd līn/ (**-lines, -lining, -lined**) *v* **1.** *vti* to refuse loans, insurance, or other financial services to people or businesses in a supposedly high-risk area **2.** *vt* to select something such as an aircraft for removal from service [Mid-20C. < the traditional use of red ink to cross out deleted items in a budget]

red marrow *n* the reddish bone marrow where red blood cells and some white blood cells are formed

red mass *n* a special Roman Catholic mass celebrated in red vestments for the opening of a court or congress

red meat *n* meat that is relatively dark red in colour when raw, e.g. beef or lamb

Redmond /rédmənd/, **John** (1856–1918) Irish politician. The leader of the Irish Nationalist Party, he campaigned for Home Rule for Ireland and served in the Constitutional Convention that led to the establishment of the Irish Free State (1922). Full name **Redmond, John Edward**

red mullet *n* **1.** a smallish orange-red sea fish with slender feelers like whiskers on its jaw. Native to: Mediterranean and eastern Atlantic. Latin name: *Mullus surmuletus.* US term **goatfish 2.** the flesh of a red mullet used as food

redneck /réd nek/ *n* **1.** an offensive term for a white farmworker in the southern United States, especially one regarded as uneducated or aggressively prejudiced **2.** an offensive term for somebody who is opposed to liberal social changes, especially somebody regarded as prejudiced [Mid-19C. < the sunburnt necks of those who work outdoors in sunny climates] —**rednecked** *adj*

redo /ree doo/ (**-does** /-dúz/, **-doing, -did** /-díd/, **-done** /-dún/) *vt* **1.** to do something again, e.g. in order to correct mistakes in an earlier effort **2.** to change the appearance of something such as a hairstyle or the interior decoration of a room

red oak *n* an oak tree with bristly lobed leaves that turn red in the autumn. Native to: eastern North America. Genus: *Quercus*.

red ochre *n* **1.** a rich reddish-brown colour used in painting **2.** a reddish earth that is rich in iron oxide. Use: red pigment in paints.

redolent /rédd'lənt/ *adj* **1.** SUGGESTING suggestive or reminiscent of something ○ *redolent of corruption* **2.** HAVING PARTICULAR SMELL with a particular scent or odour ○ *redolent of beeswax* **3.** AROMATIC with a strong pleasant aroma (*literary*) [15C. < Old French < Latin *redolere* 'smell strongly' < *olere* 'to smell'] —**redolence** *n* —**redolently** *adv*

Redon /rə dón, rə dóN/, **Odilon** (1840–1916) French painter and lithographer. A central figure in the symbolist movement and a forerunner of surrealism, he used dream images in lithographs such as *La Nuit (Night)* (1886).

redone past participle of **redo**

red osier *n* **1.** a willow tree with reddish branches used in basketry **2.** *also* **red osier dogwood** a bush of the dogwood family with red twigs and clusters of white fruits. Native to: North America. Latin name: *Cornus stolonifera*.

redouble /ri dúbb'l/ *vti* (**-bles, -bling, -bled**) **1.** INCREASE to increase something considerably, especially the amount of effort expended on something, or become much greater **2.** ECHO to echo or re-echo, or cause something to echo or re-echo **3.** CARDS DOUBLE DOUBLE BID in bridge, to double an opponent's double as a bid ■ *n* CARDS DOUBLING OF DOUBLE BID in bridge, a redoubling of a bid [15C. < French *redoubler* 'double again' < *double* 'double']

redoubt /ri dówt/ *n* **1.** a temporary fortification built to defend a position such as a hilltop **2.** a castle, fortress, or other stronghold (*literary*) [Early 17C. Alteration (influenced by REDOUBTABLE) of French *redoute*, via Italian *ridotto* < medieval Latin *reductus* 'refuge' < Latin, past participle of *reducere* (see REDUCE)]

redoubtable /ri dówtəb'l/ *adj* with personal qualities worthy of respect or fear [14C. < French *redoutable* < *do(u)ter* (see DOUBT)] —**redoubtably** *adv*

redound /ri dównd/ (**-dounds, -dounding, -dounded**) *vi* **1.** to have a particular consequence, usually something good or positive ○ *a decision that redounded to her credit* **2.** to return to affect somebody as a repercussion or consequence (*formal*) ○ *His attempts at revenge redounded upon his own head.* [14C. Via French *redonder* < Latin *redundare* 'overflow' (see REDUNDANT)]

USAGE See *rebound.*

redout /réd owt/ *n* sudden headache and reddening of the field of vision experienced by pilots or astronauts during rapid deceleration and other manoeuvres

redowa /réddəvə, -wə/ *n* a Bohemian folk dance similar to a waltz or a polka [Mid-19C. Via French or German < Czech *rejdovák* < *rejdovat* 'whirl around']

redox /rée doks/ *n* CHEM same as **oxidation-reduction** [Early 20C. Contraction of REDUCTION + OXIDATION]

red packet *n Hong Kong, Malaysia, Singapore* money enclosed in a red envelope and given for luck by married people to unmarried young people during the first 15 days of the Chinese New Year

red panda *n* a reddish-brown animal that resembles a raccoon in appearance. Native to: Himalayan forests and nearby areas of East Asia. Latin name: *Ailurus fulgens*.

red-pencil *vt* to revise, correct, or censor written material

red pepper *n* **1.** a red pod that belongs to the capsicum family of vegetables, especially a ripe sweet pepper **2.** FOOD same as **cayenne pepper**

red pine *n* **1.** a pine tree with reddish bark and needles grouped in twos. Native to: northeastern North America. Latin name: *Pinus resinosa*. **2.** a coniferous tree with narrow pointed leaves. Native to: New Zealand. Latin name: *Dacrydium cupressinum*.

red planet *n* the planet Mars (*informal*)

redpoll /réd pōl/ *n* a small bird of the finch family with a red crown and a pink breast. Native to: North America, Europe, Asia. Genus: *Carduelis*.

Red Poll *n* a hornless cow with short reddish hair, belonging to a breed originating in England. Kept for: beef, milk.

redraft *vt* /ree dráaft/ (**-drafts, -drafting, -drafted**) to rewrite something, making changes in it ■ *n* /rée draaft/ a second or further draft or rewriting

red rag *n UK, ANZ, Can* something that provokes or infuriates somebody. US term **red flag** [Because bulls are said to be enraged at the sight of red objects]

red rattle *n* a plant with a seed capsule that rattles. Native to: Europe. Latin name: *Pedicularis palustris*.

redress /ri dréss/ *vt* (**-dresses, -dressing, -dressed**) **1.** MAKE UP FOR SOMETHING to provide compensation or reparation for a loss or wrong experienced **2.** IMPOSE FAIRNESS ON SOMETHING to adjust a situation in order to make things fair or equal ■ *n* **1.** COMPENSATION compensation or reparation for a loss or wrong somebody has experienced **2.** ACT OF COMPENSATING the compensating of somebody for a loss or wrong experienced [14C. < Old French *redrecier* < *drecier* < Latin *directus* 'straight' (see DIRECT)] —**redresser** *n*

redrew past tense of **redraw**

red ribbon *n N Am* a red-coloured ribbon, badge, or other decoration awarded to somebody who comes second in a competition

Red River 1. river in Southeast Asia, rising in southern China and emptying into the Gulf of Tonkin. Length: 800 km/500 mi. **2.** river in the north-central United States and south-central Canada, flowing northwards from Minnesota and emptying into Lake Winnipeg. Length: 877 km/545 mi.

red roman *n* FISH same as **roman**[3]

redroot /réd root/ *n* **1.** a perennial bog plant with red roots and woolly yellow flowers. Native to: eastern North America. Latin name: *Lachnanthes caroliana*. **2.** a plant with red roots, e.g. a bloodroot or pigweed

red route *n* a major urban road where loading and parking is restricted by a system of red lines and signs at the kerb, enforced by patrols, in order to maintain traffic flows

red salmon *n* FISH same as **sockeye**

Red Sea inland sea between the Arabian peninsula and northeastern Africa. It is linked to the Mediterranean in the north by the Suez Canal. Area: 438,000 sq. km/169,000 sq. mi.

red setter *n* BREED same as **Irish setter**

red shank *n* an annual plant with red stems. Flowers: pink, in spikes. Native to: northern temperate regions. Latin name: *Polygonum persicaria*. N Am term **lady's thumb**

redshank /réd shangk/ *n* a large slender wading bird of the sandpiper family with red legs and a red beak. Native to: Europe, Asia. Genus: *Tringa*.

redshift /réd shift/ *n* a shift in the spectrum of an astronomical object towards longer wavelengths, or towards the red end of the spectrum, caused by its motion away from Earth —**redshifted** *adj*

redshirt /réd shurt/ *n US* a college or university athlete who is kept out of competitions for one year in order to improve his or her skills and extend his or her period of eligibility [Mid-19C. < the red jerseys that customarily distinguish these players at practices] —**redshirt** *vt*

redskin /réd skin/ *n* **1.** an offensive term for a Native North American (*dated*) **2.** *Carib* a light-skinned person with African features, usually of mixed European and African origin (*sometimes offensive*) —**red-skinned** *adj*

red snapper *n* **1.** a large reddish-coloured fish. Native to: Atlantic coasts of North, South, and Central America. Genus: *Lutjanus*. **2.** the flesh of a red snapper used as food

red snow *n* fallen snow that is reddish in colour, either from the presence of airborne dust or from red algae growing in it. It is commonly seen in Arctic and Alpine regions.

Red Spot *n* a large reddish oval and variable marking in the southern hemisphere of Jupiter

red spruce *n* a spruce tree with reddish-brown bark and cones, and light soft wood. Native to: eastern North America. Latin name: *Picea rubens*.

Red Square *n* a large square in central Moscow, bordered by the Kremlin and Lenin's tomb. It was the site of military parades on public holidays in the former Soviet Union.

red squirrel *n* **1.** a reddish-brown squirrel with tufted ears. Native to: Europe, Asia. Latin name: *Sciurus vulgaris*. **2.** a squirrel with reddish fur. Native to: coniferous forests of North America. Latin name: *Tamiasciurus hudsonicus*.

redstart /réd staart/ *n* **1.** a bird of the thrush family, the male of which often has a black throat and a reddish-brown tail. Native to: Europe, Asia, Africa. Genus: *Phoenicurus*. **2.** a bird of the warbler family, the male of which has reddish-orange patches on its black and white feathers. Native to: North and South America. Latin name: *Setophaga ruticilla*. [Late 16C. < Old English *steort* 'animal's tail' < Germanic]

red steenbras /-steén brass/ *n* a red game fish, about 1.2 m/4 ft long. Native to: Cape of Good Hope, South Africa. Latin name: *Dentex rupestris*.

red tape *n* official procedure regarded as unnecessary, overcomplicated, or obstructive (*informal*) [< the red tape once widely used to seal official documents]

red tide *n* a brownish-red discoloration in seawater, caused by an increased presence of plant-based plankton that sometimes leads to the poisoning of fish and, consequently, of those who eat fish

redtop /réd top/ *n* a grass plant that has clusters of red flowers and is used in North America for lawns and forage. Genus: *Agrostis*.

red-top *n* MEDIA same as **tabloid** *n* (sense 1) (*informal*) ○ *'There is now a debate about whether the red-tops should "go up-market" to find their audiences.'* (*The Guardian*; November 1998) [< the red masthead of such a newspaper]

reduce /ri dyóoss/ (**-duces, -ducing, -duced**) *v* **1.** *vti* DECREASE to become smaller in size, number, extent, degree, or intensity, or make something smaller in this way **2.** *vt* WORSEN STATE OF SOMEBODY OR SOMETHING to bring somebody or something into a particular undesirable state ○ *Bombing had reduced the town to rubble.* ○ *reduced them to tears* **3.** *vt* MAKE SOMETHING CHEAPER to lower the price or cost of an item for sale **4.** *vt* SIMPLIFY SOMETHING to make something simpler, especially by extracting or summarizing essential components **5.** *vt* ANALYSE SOMETHING SYSTEMATICALLY to analyse something in terms of a system or rule, usually as an aid to explaining or understanding it **6.** *vt* DEMOTE SOMEBODY to place somebody officially in a lower rank or grade, e.g. as a punishment for breaking rules **7.** *vt* TAKE CONTROL OF PLACE OR PEOPLE to bring a place or people under authority using force **8.** *vti* COOK THICKEN to make a sauce or stock thicker by boiling off some of the liquid, or become thicker in this way **9.** *vt* PHOTOGRAPHY DECREASE DENSITY OF NEGATIVE to lessen the density of a photographic negative using a chemical substance **10.** *vt* METALL REFINE ORE to remove the impurities from an ore in order to obtain the pure metal **11.** *vti* BIOL UNDERGO CELL DIVISION to undergo the type of cell division (**meiosis**) that halves the number of chromosomes in the two resultant cells, or cause cells to undergo this **12.** *vti* CHEM UNDERGO CHEMICAL REACTION to undergo a chemical reaction in which there is a gain in hydrogen or a loss of oxygen, or cause a substance to undergo this **13.** *vti* CHEM GAIN ELECTRONS to undergo a chemical reaction in which there is an increase in the number of electrons, or cause a substance to undergo this **14.** *vt* MATHS SIMPLIFY EQUATION to simplify an expression or equation without changing its value **15.** *vi* LOSE WEIGHT to lose weight, especially by dieting [14C. < Latin *reducere* 'bring back' < *ducere* 'to lead'] —**reducibility** /ri dyóossə bílləti/ *n* —**reducible** *adj*

reducer /ri dyóossər/ *n* **1.** a chemical solution that lessens the density of a photographic negative by oxidizing it **2.** a pipe fitting that connects two pipes of different diameters

reducing agent /ri dyóossing-/ *n* a chemical substance

that reduces the amount of oxygen in another substance and becomes oxidized in the process

reductant /ri dúktənt/ *n* CHEM same as **reducing agent** [Early 20C. < REDUCTION, after OXIDANT]

reductase /ri dúk tayz, -tayss/ *n* an enzyme that catalyses the chemical reduction of an organic compound [Early 20C. < REDUCTION]

reductio ad absurdum /ri dúkti ō ad ab súrdəm/ *n* **1.** **TAKING SOMETHING TO ABSURD LENGTHS** the application of a rule or principle so strictly or literally that the result is ridiculous **2.** **LOGICAL DISPROOF** the disproving of a logical argument by showing that its ultimate conclusion is absurd **3.** **LOGICAL PROOF** the proving of a logical argument indirectly, by showing that the contradictory argument is absurd [Mid-18C. < Latin, 'reduction to the absurd']

reduction /ri dúksh'n/ *n* **1.** **REDUCING OF SOMETHING** the decreasing of something in size, number, extent, degree, or intensity **2.** **AMOUNT BY WHICH SOMETHING IS REDUCED** the amount by which something is made smaller or less **3.** **SIMPLIFICATION** a simplification or condensation of something **4.** **SMALLER COPY** a copy of something made on a smaller scale, e.g. a reduced photocopy **5.** COOK **THICKENED SAUCE** a sauce or stock that has been thickened by boiling off some of the liquid **6.** MATHS **MAKING FRACTION SIMPLER** the cancelling of common factors in the numerator and denominator of a fraction **7.** MATHS **DECIMALIZATION OF FRACTION** the converting of a fraction into decimal form **8.** BIOL same as **meiosis** (sense 1) **9.** CHEM **CHEMICAL REACTION** a chemical reaction that brings about a gain in hydrogen, a loss of oxygen, or an increase in electrons [15C. Via French < Latin *reduction-* < past participle of *reducere* (see REDUCE)] —**reductional** *adj*

reduction division *n* BIOL same as **meiosis** (sense 1)

reduction firing *n* the firing of pottery in an oxygen-starved atmosphere in order to change the nature of the glaze applied

reduction gear *n* a set of gears in an engine used to reduce output speed relative to that of the engine while providing greater turning power, e.g. when climbing a hill

reductionism /ri dúksh'nizəm/ *n* **1.** the analysis of something into simpler parts or organized systems, especially with a view to explaining or understanding it **2.** the oversimplifying of something complex, or the misguided belief that everything can be explained in simple terms —**reductionist** *n, adj* —**reductionistic** /ri dúkshə nístik/ *adj*

reductive /ri dúktiv/ *adj* **1.** seeking to explain complex things in terms of simple structures and systems **2.** oversimplifying complex things and ignoring their subtleties or important details [Mid-16C. < medieval Latin *reductivus* < past participle of Latin *reducere* (see REDUCE)] —**reductively** *adv* —**reductiveness** *n*

redundancy /ri dúndənssi/ (*plural* **-cies**) *n* **1.** *UK, ANZ, Can* **DISMISSAL FROM WORK** dismissal from employment because the job or the worker has been deemed no longer necessary ○ *There may be more redundancies if sales do not improve.* US term **severance** **2.** **SUPERFLUOUSNESS** the state or fact of not or no longer being needed or wanted **3.** **SOMETHING SUPERFLUOUS** something that is not or no longer needed or wanted ○ *eliminated the redundancies in the system* **4.** **USE OF SUPERFLUOUS WORDS** the use of a word or words whose meaning is already conveyed elsewhere in a passage, without a rhetorical purpose **5.** **DUPLICATION OF COMPONENTS** the fitting of duplicate electronic or mechanical components or backup systems that are designed to come into use to keep equipment working if their counterparts fail **6.** TELECOM **DUPLICATION OF MESSAGE** duplication of information in telecommunications in order to reduce the risk of error

redundancy payment *n* an amount paid to an employee who has been made redundant, often calculated in relation to length of employment

redundant /ri dúndənt/ *adj* **1.** **DISMISSED FROM WORK** dismissed from employment because the job or the worker has been deemed no longer necessary ○ *The companies merged and half the workers were made redundant.* **2.** **SUPERFLUOUS** not or no longer needed or wanted **3.** **BACKUP** fitted as a backup component or system **4.** **REPEATING MEANING** with the same meaning as a word used elsewhere in a passage and without a rhetorical purpose [Late 16C. < Latin *redundant-*, present participle of *redundare* 'overflow' < *undare* 'rise in waves' < *unda* 'wave'] —**redundantly** *adv*

reduplicate /ri dyóopli kayt/ *v* (**-cates, -cating, -cated**) **1.** *vti* **REPEAT OR DOUBLE** to repeat or double something, or be repeated or doubled **2.** *vt* LING **REPEAT SPEECH SOUND** to repeat a vowel, syllable, or word in order to create a new linguistic element or word such as 'wishy-washy' or 'goody-goody' ■ *adj* **1.** LING **REPEATED** repeated in order to create a new word or other linguistic element **2.** BOT **CURVING INWARDS** describes leaves or petals that have their edges curved inwards [Late 16C. < late Latin *reduplicat-*, past participle of *reduplicare* < Latin *duplicare* (see DUPLICATE)] —**reduplication** /ri dyóopli káysh'n/ *n* —**reduplicative** /-kətiv/ *adj* —**reduplicatively** *adv*

reduviid /ri dyóovi id/ *n* INSECTS same as **assassin bug** [Late 19C. < modern Latin *Reduviidae* < Latin *reduvia* 'hangnail']

redux /ree dúks/ *adj* brought back, especially in being restored to former importance or prominence (*literary*) [Late 19C. < Latin *reducere* (see REDUCE)]

red valerian *n* PLANTS same as **valerian** (sense 3)

redware[1] /réd wair/ *n* MARINE BIOL same as **kelp** (sense 1) [Early 18C. < northern dialect *ware* 'seaweed' < Germanic, 'bind']

redware[2] /réd wair/ *n* reddish earthenware pottery made from clay with a high iron oxide content [Late 17C. < WARE[1]]

red water *n* a cattle disease characterized by the passage of reddish urine

redwing /réd wing/ *n* a bird of the thrush family that has reddish feathers under its wings and a spotted breast. Native to: Europe, Asia. Latin name: *Turdus iliacus.*

redwood /réd wŏŏd/ *n* a coniferous evergreen tree with fibrous reddish bark. Some California redwoods are the tallest trees in the world and can grow to 110 m/360 ft. Native to: northern coastal California, southwestern China. Latin name: *Sequoia sempervirens* or *Sequoiadendron giganteum* or *Metasequoia glyptostroboides.*

REE *abbr* CHEM rare-earth element

reebok *n* ZOOL another spelling of **rhebok**

re-echo *v* **1.** *vi* to resound or echo back **2.** *vt* to repeat again something that has already been repeated

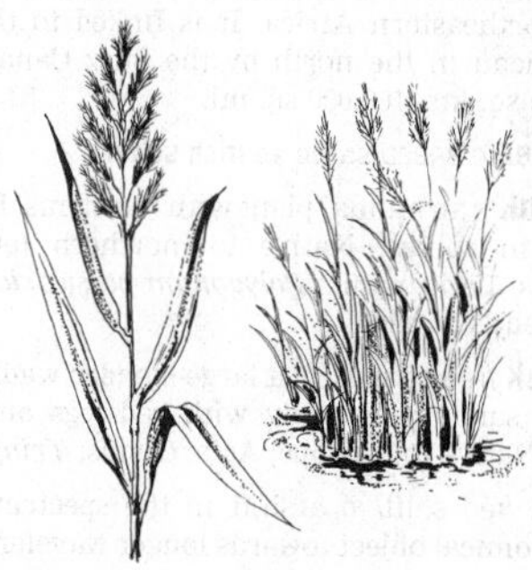

reed

reed /reed/ *n* **1.** **TALL WATER PLANT** a tall slender plant with jointed stalks that grows in marshes and other wet areas. Genera: *Phragmites* or *Arundo.* **2.** **STALK OF REED** a reed stalk, or a bundle of reed stalks. Use: thatching, basketry, crafts. **3.** MUSIC **VIBRATING PART OF MUSICAL INSTRUMENT** a thin piece of cane, metal, or plastic fitted inside a musical instrument that vibrates to produce sound, usually when the player blows into the instrument **4.** MUSIC **MUSICAL INSTRUMENT** a wind instrument fitted with a reed, e.g. an oboe or a clarinet (*informal*) **5.** TEXTILES **WIRES ON LOOM** a series of parallel wires on a loom that separate the threads of the warp evenly **6.** MEASURE **UNIT OF LENGTH** an ancient Hebrew unit of length equal to six cubits [Old English *hrēod* < Germanic]

SPELLCHECK See *read.*

Reed /reed/, **Sir Carol** (1906–76) British film director. His films include *The Third Man* (1949) and *Our Man in Havana* (1959), both written by Graham Greene, and *Oliver!* (1968), for which he won an Academy Award.

Reed, Walter (1851–1902) US army surgeon and bacteriologist. His discovery in 1900 that yellow fever is transmitted by mosquitoes led to the near-eradication of the disease.

reed bed *n* an area of marshy ground where reeds grow or are grown

reedbuck /réed buk/ *n* a tawny antelope with long horns that curve slightly forwards. Native to: sub-Saharan Africa. Genus: *Redunca.* [Mid-19C. Translation of Afrikaans *rietbok*]

reed grass *n* a tall grass plant that grows in rivers and ponds. Native to: Europe, Asia, North America. Latin name: *Glyceria maxima.*

reeding /réeding/ *n* **1.** a set of small convex decorative mouldings on a building **2.** the narrow vertical grooves on the edge of a coin

reedling /réedling/ *n* BIRDS same as **bearded tit**

reed mace *n* same as **bulrush** (sense 1)

reedman /réedmən/ (*plural* **-men** /-mən/) *n* a musician who plays a reed instrument, especially a jazz clarinettist or saxophonist (*informal*)

reed organ *n* a musical instrument in which air passing over a set of reeds produces sound, e.g. a harmonica or accordion

reed pipe *n* an organ pipe containing a reed that vibrates to make the pipe sound

reed stop *n* an organ stop that controls a set of reed pipes

reedy /réedi/ (**-ier, -iest**) *adj* **1.** **FULL OF REEDS** full of or thickly planted with reeds ○ *a reedy pond* **2.** **HIGH-PITCHED** thin and high-pitched, rather than deep or full-toned ○ *a reedy voice* **3.** **THIN** long, thin, or flexible, like a reed ○ *a reedy physique* —**reedily** *adv* —**reediness** *n*

reef[1] /reef/ *n* **1.** a ridge of coral or rock in a body of water, with the top just below or just above the surface **2.** a lode or vein of ore [Late 16C. < Dutch *rif*] —**reefy** *adj*

reef[2] /reef/ *n* **PART OF SAIL** a section of a sail that can be gathered in and tied down to reduce the sail's surface ■ *vt* (**reefs, reefing, reefed**) **1.** **MAKE SAIL SMALLER BY GATHERING** to reduce the area of a sail by gathering part of it in **2.** **SHORTEN RIGGING PIECE** to shorten or bring in one of the pieces that support the rigging on a ship [14C. Via Dutch *reef* < Old Norse *rif* 'reef (of a sail)'] —**reefable** *adj*

reefer[1] /réefər/ *n* **1.** *ANZ, N Am* same as **reefer jacket** **2.** somebody who reefs sails [Early 19C. < REEF[2]]

reefer[2] /réefər/ *n* a marijuana cigarette (*slang*) [Mid-20C. Origin ?]

reefer[3] /réefər/ *n US* a refrigerated railway wagon or truck trailer (*informal*) [Early 20C. < REFRIGERATOR]

reefer jacket *n UK* a heavy double-breasted woollen jacket or coat, usually dark blue and hip-length, originally worn by sailors. ANZ, N Am term **reefer**[1]

reef knot *n UK, ANZ, Can* a symmetrical knot that will not slip after tying, made by passing one end of rope over and around another first in one direction, then again in the opposite direction. US term **square knot**

reek /reek/ *v* (**reeks, reeking, reeked**) **1.** *vti* **SMELL STRONGLY** to have a very strong and unpleasant smell, or give off such a smell ○ *The room reeked of smoke.* **2.** *vti* **GIVE CLEAR EVIDENCE OF SOMETHING UNPLEASANT** to show very strong evidence of an unpleasant quality ○ *The document reeks of the double standard.* **3.** *vi* **GIVE OFF SMOKE** to give off smoke, steam, or fumes ○ *a reeking pile of burning tyres* **4.** *vt US* **TREAT SOMETHING WITH SMOKE** to process or treat something with smoke ■ *n* **1.** **UNPLEASANT SMELL** a very strong unpleasant smell ○ *a reek of disinfectant* **2.** *regional* **VISIBLE VAPOUR** smoke, steam, or other visible vapour [Old English *rēocan* < Indo-European] —**reeker** *n* —**reeky** *adj*

SPELLCHECK reek or **wreak**? Do not confuse the spelling of ***reek*** and ***wreak***, which sound similar. ***Reek*** is a noun or verb referring to a strong unpleasant smell (as in *the reek of rotting vegetables; the place reeked of disinfectant*) or to smoke or fumes given off (as in *reeking heaps of burning refuse*). As a verb it can also mean 'be evidence of something unpleasant', as in *the*

whole affair reeked of incompetence. ***Wreak*** is a verb only meaning 'cause havoc or destruction' or 'inflict revenge or punishment'.

SYNONYMS See ***smell***.

reel[1] /reel/ *n* **1. REVOLVING STORAGE DEVICE** a usually revolving wheel-shaped device around which something such as thread, film, or wire can be wound for storage **2. QUANTITY ON REEL** the amount of a material that a reel can hold **3.** CINEMA **SECTION OF CINEMA FILM** the amount of cinema film stored on one reel **4.** FISHING **WINDER ON FISHING ROD** a winding device attached to a fishing rod that holds the fishing line and enables it to be cast and wound back ■ *vt* (**reels, reeling, reeled**) **WIND SOMETHING ONTO REEL** to wind something such as thread or fishing line onto or off a reel [Old English *hrēol* 'spool (for winding thread)', origin ?] —**reeler** *n* —**reelful** *n*

SPELLCHECK See *real*[1].

reel in *vt* **1.** to draw something in, especially a fish, by winding a line from a fishing rod on a reel **2.** to bring in or acquire somebody or something by using the appropriate skills or offering suitable inducements

reel off *vt* to list things in rapid succession and with no apparent effort

reel[2] /reel/ *vi* (**reels, reeling, reeled**) **1. STAGGER BACKWARDS** to move in a sudden and uncontrolled fashion, especially backwards as if struck by a blow ○ *reeled back in horror* **2. MOVE UNSTEADILY** to move about unsteadily, staggering or swaying from side to side **3. FEEL GIDDY OR CONFUSED** to feel giddy or shocked and confused ○ *still reeling from the shock* **4. WHIRL ROUND AND ROUND** to move or whirl round in circles ■ *n* **STAGGERING MOTION** an unsteady or circling movement [14C. Probably < REEL[1]]

reel[3] /reel/ *n* **1.** a lively Scottish folk dance in 2/4 time for sets of two, three, or four couples **2.** the music for a reel [Late 16C. Probably < REEL[2]] —**reel** *vi*

reelman /réelmən/ (*plural* **-men** /-mən/) *n ANZ* the member of a lifesaving team who is in charge of the reel used to haul people in from the sea

reel-to-reel *adj* describes magnetic tape that must be wound off a full source reel, threaded through the heads of the machine, and rewound on an empty take-up reel ■ *n* a tape recorder or player that uses reel-to-reel tape

re-engineering /rée enji néering/ *n* **1.** a business management theory that advocates the reorganization of a business on the basis of the market value each department adds to the products produced by the business **2.** the examination and modification of an existing process or system in order to improve it —**re-engineer** *vt*

re-enter /ree éntər/ *v* **1.** *vti* **RETURN** to come back into a place again **2.** *vt* **ENTER DATA AGAIN** to key or write something in again **3.** *vti* **GO IN FOR SOMETHING AGAIN** to decide to take part in something such as a competition again —**re-entrance** *n*

re-entrant /ree éntrənt/ *n* MATHS same as **re-entrant angle** ■ *adj* relating to a re-entrant angle

re-entrant angle *n* an inward-pointing angle in a polygon that is greater than 180° when viewed or measured from inside the polygon

re-entry /ree éntri/ *n* **1. ENTERING AGAIN** the act of entering again **2.** AEROSP **RETURN TO EARTH'S ATMOSPHERE** the penetration of the Earth's atmosphere by a spacecraft or missile returning from space (*often used before a noun*) ○ *a re-entry vehicle* **3.** LAW **REPOSSESSION OF LAND** the repossession of land or other property under the terms of a previous agreement, e.g. where the terms of a lease have not been complied with **4.** CARDS **TAKING OF LEAD IN CARD GAME** in some card games such as bridge, the regaining of control by taking a trick, or the card played to take the trick

Rees /reess/, **Lloyd** (1895–1988) Australian painter. His lyrical landscape paintings often incorporate large bold forms. Full name **Rees, Lloyd Frederic**

reeve[1] /reev/ *n* **1. US DISTRICT OFFICIAL** in the United States, an administrative officer in a local district or parish who usually has the responsibility of enforcing the regulations connected with a particular area of activity **2. CANADIAN TOWN COUNCIL PRESIDENT** in Ontario and some western provinces of Canada, the elected president of a town or village council **3.** HIST **REPRESENTATIVE OF KING** in Anglo-Saxon times, the representative of the monarch in a shire **4.** HIST **STEWARD OF FEUDAL MANOR** in medieval times, a steward responsible for running the everyday affairs of a feudal manor [Old English *gerēfa* 'official over an assembly of soldiers' < Germanic]

reeve[2] /reev/ (**reeves, reeving, rove** /rōv/, **reeved**) *vt* **1.** to thread a rope or rod through a ring or other opening **2.** to fasten a line or rope by passing it around or through some solid object [Early 17C. Origin ?]

reeve[3] /reev/ *n* a female ruff, a bird of the sandpiper family [Mid-17C. Origin ?]

Reeves /reevz/, **William Pember** (1857–1932) New Zealand politician and writer. As a government minister in New Zealand, he introduced important reforms in industrial relations. He wrote a history of New Zealand, *The Long White Cloud* (1898).

re-export *vt* **EXPORT SOMETHING AFTER IMPORTING** to export goods that were previously imported from another country, especially after reprocessing them ■ *n* **1. PROCESS OF RE-EXPORTING** the business or process of re-exporting imported goods **2. SOMETHING RE-EXPORTED** something that is re-exported —**re-exportation** *n*

ref /ref/ (*informal*) *n* a sports referee ■ *vti* (**refs, reffing, reffed**) to referee a sport or game [Late 19C. Shortening of REFEREE]

ref. *abbr* **1.** reference **2.** refining **3.** reformed **4.** refunding

reface /ree fáyss/ (**-faces, -facing, -faced**) *vt* **1.** to restore or replace the exterior surface of a building or monument **2.** to replace the facing of a garment

Ref. Ch. *abbr* CHR Reformed Church

refection /ri féksh'n/ *n* (*literary*) **1.** refreshment, especially in the form of food and drink **2.** a portion of food, or a light meal [14C. < Latin *refection-* 'restoration' < *refect-* (see REFECTORY)]

refectory /ri féktəri/ (*plural* **-ries**) *n* a dining hall, especially in a monastery, convent, or college [15C. < late Latin *refectorium* 'place where somebody is restored' < Latin *refect-*, past participle of *reficere* 'remake' < *facere* 'make']

refectory table *n* a long narrow dining table with straight heavy legs

refer /ri fúr/ (**-fers, -ferring, -ferred**) *v* **1.** *vi* **MENTION** to make a comment in speech or writing that either specifically mentions somebody or something or is intended to bring somebody or something to mind ○ *referred to him by name* **2.** *vi* **GIVE DESCRIPTION** to describe somebody or something ○ *refers to her sister as 'the princess'* **3.** *vi* **BE RELATED** to relate to or be connected with something ○ *This clause refers to your responsibilities as the homeowner.* **4.** *vt* **DIRECT SOMEBODY TO SOURCE OF HELP** to direct somebody to something or somebody else for information, help, treatment, or judgment ○ *referred me to a specialist* **5.** *vi* **CONSULT FOR INFORMATION** to consult a source in order to find information or assistance ○ *refer to the manual* **6.** *vt* **ATTRIBUTE SOMETHING TO CAUSE** to attribute the cause or source of something to something else ○ *They referred the high gains to the timing of their investment.* **7.** *vt* EDUC **FAIL EXAM CANDIDATE** to fail an examination candidate, or ask a candidate to retake an exam **8.** *vt* EDUC **RETURN THESIS FOR REVISION** to return a thesis to a student for further work or revision before it can be accepted [14C. Via French < Latin *referre* 'carry back' < *ferre* 'carry'] —**referable** /ri fúrəb'l, réffərəb'l/ *adj* —**referrer** *n*

USAGE Some people think that ***refer back*** involves redundancy, because one of the implicit meanings of *re-* is 'back'. But a person may ***refer*** a problem or request, for example ***on*** to a new authority for a decision, or ***refer*** it ***back*** to the original decision-maker for reconsideration. If ***refer*** directs people to something already mentioned, for example a text quoted, it is better to say *In referring* [not *referring back*] *to page 321 of the course book, I would like to add the following information.*

USAGE See ***allude***.

referee /réffə rée/ *n* **1. OFFICIAL OVERSEEING SPORT** an official who oversees the play in a sport or game, judges whether the rules are being followed, and penalizes fouls or infringements **2. ARBITRATOR** somebody not directly involved in a matter who is called in to settle disputes, make decisions, or pass judgments concerning the matter **3.** *UK* **PERSON WHO GIVES INFORMATION ABOUT SOMEBODY** somebody who is asked to comment on the character or qualifications of another person, especially when that person is applying for a job. ANZ, N Am term **reference 4.** LAW **SOMEBODY WHO REVIEWS CASE** somebody appointed by a court to review and make a report or judgment on a case ■ *vti* (**-rees, -reeing, -reed**) **ACT AS REFEREE** to act as a referee in a sport, in a dispute, or for an applicant

reference /réffərənss/ *n* **1. MENTION** a spoken or written comment that either specifically mentions or calls attention to somebody or something or is intended to bring somebody or something to mind **2. PROCESS OF MENTIONING** the process of mentioning or alluding to somebody or something ○ *The document makes reference to three similar incidents.* **3.** HR **STATEMENT OF CHARACTER AND QUALIFICATIONS** a statement concerning somebody's character or qualifications, usually given to a potential employer **4.** *ANZ, N Am* same as **referee** *n* (sense 3) **5. APPLICABILITY** applicability or relevance to or connection with a particular subject or person ○ *Does what you're saying have any reference at all to the matter in hand?* **6. SOURCE OF INFORMATION** a source of information, e.g. a dictionary or an encyclopedia (*often used before a noun*) ○ *a reference book* **7. SOURCE REFERRED TO** a source of information referred to by a footnote or citation **8. FOOTNOTE OR BIBLIOGRAPHICAL CITATION** a note directing a reader's attention to another source of information **9.** PUBL same as **reference mark 10. IDENTIFYING CODE** something, usually a set of letters or figures, that serves to identify somebody or something such as a customer, client, business letter, or a spot on a map (*often used before a noun*) ○ *a reference number* ■ *vt* (**-ences, -encing, -enced**) **1. COMPILE REFERENCES FOR BOOK** to compile a list of references for a book, essay, or thesis **2. USE SOMETHING AS SOURCE** to use or refer to somebody or something as a source in the writing of something ○ *The author referenced some rather obscure works.* ■ *prep* **WITH REFERENCE TO** in connection with ○ *Reference our discussion of 5 June, I believe our prior decision stands.*

reference book *n* **1.** a book that is intended to be used for looking up facts, definitions, or other information **2.** POL same as **passbook** (sense 3)

reference mark *n* a typographical symbol used to draw the attention of a reader to a note or bibliographical entry, e.g. an asterisk or number

referendum /réffə réndəm/ (*plural* **-dums** or **-da** /-də/) *n* a vote by the whole of an electorate on a specific question or questions put to it by a government or similar body [Mid-19C. < Latin, '(something) to be referred (to the Senate)', form of *referre* (see REFER)]

referent /réffərənt/ *n* the thing or idea that a symbol, word, or phrase denotes or refers to

referential /réffə rénsh'l/ *adj* **1.** relating to references or in the form of a reference **2.** describes a work of art that imitates other works or contains oblique references or homages to them, often at the expense of original content or style —**referentiality** /réffə renshi állәti/ *n* —**referentially** *adv*

referral /ri fúrəl/ *n* **1.** the act or process of referring somebody or something to somebody else, especially of sending a patient to consult a medical specialist **2.** somebody or something that has been referred, especially a patient who has been sent to a medical specialist

referred pain /ri fúrd-/ *n* pain that is felt not at its source but in another part of the body

~~**referrence**~~ incorrect spelling of **reference**

refill *vti* /ree fíl/ (**-fills, -filling, -filled**) **FILL AGAIN** to fill a container again, or become filled again ■ *n* /rée fil/ **1. ANOTHER FILLING OF SOMETHING** a sufficient amount of something to fill a container again after it has been emptied **2. ANOTHER DRINK** another drink to refill an empty glass or cup **3.** COMM **REPLACEMENT FOR CONTENTS OF CONTAINER** an amount of a product packaged as a replacement for the used-up contents of a previously purchased product **4.** *N Am* MED **FURTHER AMOUNT OF PRESCRIBED MEDICINE** a further amount of a

medication prescribed on a previous occasion —**refillable** *adj*

refinance /reé fī nánss, reé fi-, ree fī nanss/ (**-nances, -nancing, -nanced**) *vti* to obtain new financing for something on different terms, often involving the paying off of an existing high-interest loan by means of a new lower-interest one —**refinancer** *n*

refine /ri fīn/ (**-fines, -fining, -fined**) *vti* **1.** MAKE SOMETHING MORE EFFECTIVE to improve something through small changes that make it more effective or more subtle ○ *refining the plan* **2.** MAKE OR BECOME MORE ELEGANT to make somebody or something more cultured or elegant by eliminating less acceptable habits and tastes, or become more cultured in this way **3.** REMOVE IMPURITIES to produce a purer form of something by removing the impurities from it, or become pure through such a process —**refinable** *adj* —**refiner** *n*

refined /ri fīnd/ *adj* **1.** CULTURED AND POLITE cultured and polite in habits, tastes, or appearance **2.** PURIFIED made purer by an industrial refining process **3.** SOPHISTICATED AND EFFECTIVE developed to or possessing a high degree of precision and effectiveness ○ *a refined technique*

refinement /ri fīnmənt/ *n* **1.** IMPROVEMENT an addition or alteration that improves something by making it more sophisticated or effective **2.** ELEGANCE elegance, politeness, and good taste **3.** SUPERIOR QUALITY superior quality and sophistication ○ *a dish of great refinement* **4.** PROCESS OF REFINING the process of making something purer by industrial refining **5.** SUBTLE PRECISE POINT a subtle or precise distinction in language or point in an argument

refinery /ri fīnəri/ (*plural* **-ies**) *n* an industrial site where substances such as oil or sugar are processed and purified

refit *vti* /reefít/ (**-fits, -fitting, -fitted**) to make something, especially a ship, ready for further use by repairing and re-equipping it, or undergo such a process ■ *n* /reé fit/ a thorough overhaul of something, especially a ship, in which it is repaired and re-equipped

refl. *abbr* **1.** MATHS reflection **2.** ANAT reflective **3.** MED reflex **4.** GRAM reflexive

reflag /ree flág/ (**-flags, -flagging, -flagged**) *vt* to register a ship or plane with a different national authority

reflation /ree fláysh'n/ *n* the process of bringing an economy out of recession by increasing the amount of money in circulation within it [Mid-20C. After DEFLATION, INFLATION] —**reflate** *vti*

reflect /ri flékt/ (**-flects, -flecting, -flected**) *v* **1.** *vti* SEND SOMETHING BACK to redirect something that strikes a surface, especially light, sound, or heat, usually back towards its point of origin ○ *The Moon reflects light from the Sun towards the Earth.* **2.** *vti* SHOW MIRROR IMAGE OF SOMEBODY OR SOMETHING to show a reverse image of somebody or something on a mirror or other reflective surface **3.** *vt* SHOW SOMETHING to express or be an indicator of something ○ *The election results reflect discontent among voters.* **4.** *vi* THINK SERIOUSLY to think seriously, carefully, and relatively calmly ○ *The retreat will give us time to reflect.* **5.** *vt* SAY SOMETHING TO SELF THOUGHTFULLY to have a relatively complex thought that may or may not be voiced ○ *reflected that withdrawal might be the safest option* **6.** *vti* BRING CREDIT OR DISCREDIT to bring credit, discredit, or another judgment on somebody or something ○ *an action that reflects badly on the school* [14C. Via French < Latin *reflectere* 'bend back' < *flectere* 'to bend']

reflectance /ri fléktənss/ *n* PHYS same as **reflectivity**

reflecting telescope /ri flékting-/ *n* a telescope in which light from the object is initially focused by a concave mirror

reflection /ri fléksh'n/, **reflexion** *n* **1.** REFLECTED IMAGE the image of somebody or something that appears in a mirror or other reflecting surface **2.** ACT OF REFLECTING SOMETHING the process or act of reflecting something, especially light, sound, or heat **3.** CAREFUL THOUGHT careful thought, especially the process of reconsidering previous actions, events, or decisions **4.** CONSIDERED IDEA an idea or thought, especially one produced by careful consideration **5.** INDICATION a clear indication or result of something ○ *a reflection of your hard work* **6.** CAUSE OF BLAME OR CREDIT a cause of blame or credit to somebody or something ○ *The failure of the experiment is no reflection on you.* **7.** ANAT BENDING BACK OF STRUCTURE the bending back upon itself of a membrane or other anatomical structure **8.** MATHS SYMMETRICAL TRANSFORMATION a symmetrical transformation in which a figure is reversed along an axis so that the new figure produced is a mirror image of the original one —**reflectional** *adj*

reflective /ri fléktiv/ *adj* **1.** THOUGHTFUL characterized by deep careful thought **2.** ABLE TO REFLECT able to reflect light, sound, or other forms of energy **3.** RESULTING FROM REFLECTION produced by reflection from a surface —**reflectively** *adv* —**reflectiveness** *n*

reflectivity /reé flek tívvəti/ (*plural* **-ties**) *n* the ratio of the energy of a wave reflected from a surface to the energy of the incident wave. Symbol ρ

reflectometer /reé flek tómmitər/ *n* an instrument used to measure the ratio of the energy of a wave after reflection to the energy of the wave before reflection

reflector /ri fléktər/ *n* **1.** an object, usually glass, plastic, or metal, that reflects light **2.** ASTRON same as **reflecting telescope**

reflet /ri fláy/ *n* a shiny or iridescent effect, especially in ceramic finishes [Mid-19C. Via French *reflet*, earlier *reflès* < Italian *riflesso* 'reflection']

reflex *adj* /reé fleks/ **1.** AUTOMATIC AND INVOLUNTARY occurring automatically and involuntarily as a result of the nervous system's reaction to a stimulus **2.** EXTREMELY FAST very fast in reacting **3.** WITHOUT THOUGHT OR PREPARATION produced automatically, unthinkingly, and totally predictably in response to events ○ *reflex opposition* **4.** MATHS OF OR OVER 180° describes an angle of between 180° and 360° **5.** BOT BENT BACK bent or folded back ○ *reflex leaves* **6.** PHYS REFLECTED involving a reflection of energy, e.g. of light or a stream of electrons ○ *reflex light* ■ *n* /reé fleks/ **1.** INVOLUNTARY BODILY REACTION an involuntary physiological reaction, e.g. a sneeze, triggered by a nerve impulse sent from a nerve centre in response to a nerve receptor's reaction to a stimulus **2.** PHYS SOMETHING REFLECTED a reflected image, or a reflection of light, sound, or heat **3.** LING WORD DEVELOPED FROM EARLIER FORM a later form of a word or other linguistic element that has developed from an earlier one ■ *vti* /reé fléks/ (**-flexes, -flexing, -flexed**) BEND BACK to bend back, or cause something to bend back on itself [Early 16C. < Latin *reflexus* 'bent back', past participle of *reflectere* (see REFLECT)] —**reflexly** /reé fleksli, ri flékslі/ *adv*

reflex arc *n* a nerve pathway that is responsible for triggering a reflex action

reflex camera *n* a camera with an internal mirror that reflects the actual image from the lens into the viewfinder so that the photographer can check the composition and focus exactly

reflexion *n* another spelling of **reflection**

reflexive /ri fléksiv/ *adj* **1.** REFERRING TO PREVIOUS NOUN describes a pronoun referring to the same person or thing as another noun or pronoun in the same sentence. The reflexive pronouns in English end in '-self' or '-selves', e.g. 'myself', 'yourself', 'ourselves'. **2.** DENOTING SELF-DIRECTED ACTION describes a verb that takes a reflexive pronoun as an object, thereby indicating an action that the subject does to or for itself **3.** OF OR BY REFLEX relating to or being the product of a reflex ○ *a reflexive action in response to the explosive sound* **4.** WITHOUT THINKING automatic and involuntary or unthinking **5.** LOGIC, MATHS BEING SAME describes a relation between pairs of logical objects or numbers that are the same or of the same size ■ *n* GRAM REFLEXIVE WORD a reflexive verb or pronoun —**reflexively** *adv* —**reflexiveness** *n*

reflexology /reé flek sólləji/ *n* **1.** ALTERN MED MASSAGE THERAPY a form of massage in which pressure is applied to parts of the feet and hands in order to promote relaxation and healing elsewhere in the body **2.** PHYSIOL STUDY OF REFLEXES AND BEHAVIOUR the scientific study of physiological reflexes and their relation to behaviour **3.** PSYCHOL BEHAVIOURAL THEORY a theory that explains human behaviour as complex chains of conditioned and unconditioned reflexes —**reflexologist** *n*

refluent /réffloo ənt/ *adj* flowing back (*literary*) [Late 17C. < Latin *refluent-*, present participle of *refluere* 'flow back' < *fluere* 'to flow']

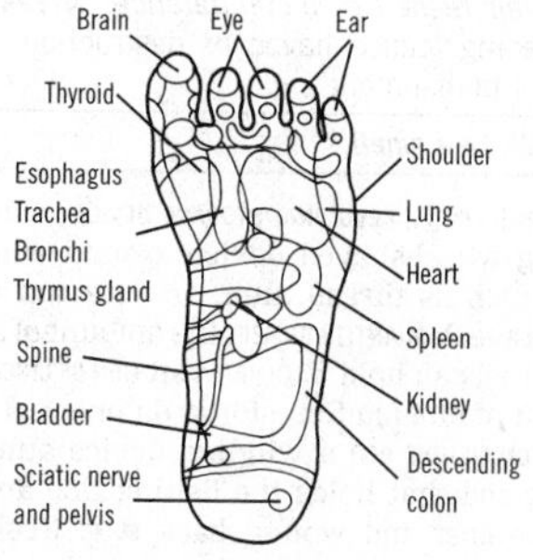

reflexology

reflux /reé fluks/ *n* **1.** BACKWARD FLOW a returning flow of something **2.** MED REGURGITATION OF STOMACH FLUID a backflow of liquid in the opposite direction to its normal movement, e.g. the regurgitation of stomach and peptic juices associated with acid indigestion and hiatal hernia **3.** PHYS HEATING WHILE CONDENSING VAPOUR a method of heating liquid so that escaping vapour is condensed and returned to the liquid ■ *vt* (**-fluxes, -fluxing, -fluxed**) PHYS HEAT SOMETHING WHILE CONDENSING VAPOUR to heat a liquid in a container with a condenser that catches and returns escaping vapour

refocus /ree fṓkəss/ (**-cuses, -cusing, -cused**) *vti* **1.** to change or adjust the focus of something such as a camera or telescope **2.** to concentrate attention or efforts on something different ○ *Let's refocus our discussion.*

reforest /ree fórrist/ (**-forests** or **-afforests, -foresting** or **-afforesting, -forested** or **-afforested**) *vti* to replant an area with trees after its original trees have been cut down —**reforestation** /reé forri stáysh'n/ *n*

reform /ri fáwrm/ *v* (**-forms, -forming, -formed**) **1.** *vt* IMPROVE SOMETHING BY REMOVING FAULTS to change and improve something by correcting faults, removing inconsistencies and abuses, and imposing modern methods or values **2.** *vti* GET RID OF UNACCEPTABLE HABITS to adopt a more acceptable way of life and mode of behaviour, or persuade or force somebody else to do so **3.** *vt* INDUST CHANGE MOLECULAR STRUCTURE OF PETROLEUM to subject petroleum to a chemical process such as catalytic cracking, in order to convert it into petrol ■ *n* **1.** REORGANIZATION AND IMPROVEMENT the reorganization and improvement of something such as a political institution or system that is considered to be faulty, ineffective, or unjust ○ *electoral reform* ○ *the reform candidate* **2.** IMPROVING CHANGE a change and improvement, especially in the social or political sphere ○ *reforms designed to prevent fraud* **3.** CHARACTER IMPROVEMENT the adoption by somebody of a more acceptable way of life and mode of behaviour [14C. Directly or via French < Latin *reformare* 'form again' < *forma* 'form'] —**reformability** /ri fáwrmə bílləti/ *n* —**reformable** *adj* —**reformative** *adj*

Reform *adj* relating or belonging to Reform Judaism ■ *n* JUDAISM same as **Reform Judaism**

re-form /ree fáwrm/ *vti* to return to a previous form, or cause something to return to a previous form

Reform Act *n* any 19th-century act of Parliament in Britain, especially those of 1832 and 1867, that gave the vote to wider sections of society and redistributed parliamentary seats

reformation /réffər máysh'n/ *n* **1.** the act or process of reforming somebody or something **2.** a reformed state, especially a general improvement in somebody's behaviour [15C. Directly or via French < Latin *reformation* < past participle of *reformare* (see REFORM)] —**reformational** *adj*

Reformation *n* the 16th-century religious movement in Europe that set out to reform some of the doctrines and practices of the Roman Catholic Church and resulted in the development of Protestantism

re-formation *n* the process or result of returning to a previous form

reformatory /ri fáwrmətəri/ *n* (*plural* **-ries**) in former times, a penal institution for young offenders ■ *adj* intended for the reform of somebody or something (*formal*) [Late 16C. < REFORMATION]

reformed /ri fáwrmd/ *adj* **1.** improved by the removal of outdated, ineffective, or unjust qualities **2.** no longer behaving in an unacceptable way

Reformed *adj* relating or belonging to a Protestant Church, especially one based on the teachings of John Calvin rather than those of Martin Luther

reformer /ri fáwrmər/ *n* a person or movement that reforms or tries to reform others

Reformer *n* an active participant in the Reformation

reformism /ri fáwrmizəm/ *n* a philosophy or movement that advocates the reform of an existing institution

reformist /ri fáwrmist/ *adj* advocating reform to an existing institution ■ *n* somebody who advocates reform

Reform Judaism *n* the branch of Judaism that seeks to adapt religious practice to modern times and rejects the belief that Moses was literally given the Torah by God

refract /ri frákt/ (**-fracts, -fracting, -fracted**) *vt* **1.** PHYS ALTER COURSE OF WAVE OF ENERGY to alter the course of a wave of energy that passes into something from another medium, as water does to light entering it from the air **2.** OPHTHALMOL MEASURE REFRACTION IN SOMETHING to measure the degree of refraction in a lens or eye **3.** SHOW SOMETHING DIFFERENTLY to alter the appearance of something by viewing or showing it through a different medium [Early 17C. < Latin *refract-*, past participle of *refringere* 'break off, break back' < *frangere* 'to break']

refracting telescope /ri frákting-/ *n* a telescope in which a lens receives and focuses light that is then viewed through a second, magnifying lens in the eyepiece

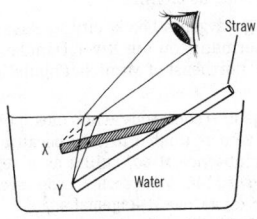

refraction

refraction /ri fráksh'n/ *n* **1.** PHYS CHANGE OF DIRECTION OF WAVE the change in direction that occurs when a wave of energy such as light passes from one medium to another of a different density, e.g. from air to water **2.** PHYS DEGREE OF WAVE REDIRECTION the degree to which a wave of energy is refracted **3.** ASTRON DISTORTION OF POSITION OF ASTRONOMICAL OBJECT the degree to which the apparent position of an astronomical object is distorted by the redirection of its light as it passes through the Earth's atmosphere **4.** OPHTHALMOL ABILITY OF EYE TO BEND LIGHT the ability of the eye to change the direction of light in order to focus it on the retina **5.** OPHTHALMOL MEASURING OF REFRACTIVE CAPACITY OF EYE the process of measuring the eye's ability to refract light —**refractional** *adj*

refractive /ri fráktiv/ *adj* relating to, involving, or capable of refraction —**refractively** *adv*

refractive index *n* UK, ANZ, Can the ratio of the speed of refracted light in a vacuum or reference medium to its speed in the medium under examination. US term **index of refraction**. Symbol *n*

refractometer /reé frak tómmitər/ *n* an instrument that measures the refractive index of a medium — **refractometric** /ri fráktə méttrik/ *adj*

refractor /ri fráktər/ *n* **1.** ASTRON same as **refracting telescope 2.** a device that alters the direction of a beam of light by passing it between two transparent materials of different density

refractory /ri fráktəri/ *adj* **1.** UNCONTROLLABLE stubborn, rebellious, and uncontrollable **2.** PHYS, INDUST HEAT-RESISTANT resistant to high temperatures and therefore not easily melted or worked **3.** MED NOT RESPONSIVE TO TREATMENT unresponsive to medical treatment ○ *a refractory infection* **4.** MED DISEASE-RESISTANT resistant

to infection or disease **5.** PHYSIOL UNRESPONSIVE TO STIMULUS not able to respond to a stimulus ○ *a refractory nerve* ■ *n* INDUST, PHYS HIGHLY HEAT-RESISTANT MATERIAL a material that is able to withstand high temperatures without melting, e.g. the fire clay used to line furnaces [Early 17C. Variant of *refractary* < Latin *refractarius* 'stubborn' < *refract-* (see REFRACT)] —**refractorily** *adv* —**refractoriness** *n*

refractory period *n* the time after receiving a stimulus during which a nerve or muscle cell cannot respond to further stimuli

refrain[1] /ri fráyn/ (**-frains, -fraining, -frained**) *vi* to avoid doing something or hold yourself back from doing something [14C. Via French < Latin *refrenare* 'hold back, curb' < *frenum* 'bridle'] —**refrainment** *n*

refrain[2] /ri fráyn/ *n* **1.** RECURRING PIECE OF VERSE a line or group of lines that recurs at regular intervals in a poem, especially at the ends of verses **2.** CHORUS the chorus in a song, or the music that accompanies it **3.** MELODY a melody or tune **4.** SOMETHING REPEATED OFTEN something that is frequently repeated, e.g. a saying or an idea [14C. < Old French, past participle of *refraindre* 'to repeat', < assumed Vulgar Latin *refrangere*, alteration of Latin *refringere* (see REFRACT)]

refrangible /ri fránjəb'l/ *adj* able to be refracted [Late 17C. < modern Latin *refrangibilis*, < *refrangere*, alteration of Latin *refringere* (see REFRACT)] —**refrangibility** /ri fránjə bílləti/ *n*

~~refrence~~ incorrect spelling of **reference**

refresh /ri frésh/ (**-freshes, -freshing, -freshed**) *v* **1.** *vt* RENEW SOMEBODY'S ENERGY to make somebody feel more energetic, especially with rest, food, or drink ○ *feel refreshed after a nap* **2.** *vt* MAKE SOMEBODY FRESH AND COOL to make somebody feel fresh and cool or clean **3.** *vt* REACTIVATE MEMORY to prompt or reactivate the memory with a piece of information ○ *Just refresh my memory.* **4.** *vt* MAKE SOMETHING FRESH OR BRIGHT AGAIN to bring the freshness or the brightness and colour back to something that is stale, wilting, or faded ○ *Plunge the carrots in ice water to refresh them.* **5.** *vt* REPLENISH SOMETHING to replenish the supplies of something ○ *Can I refresh your drink?* **6.** *vt* COMPUT UPDATE ELECTRONIC DEVICE WITH DATA to update an electronic device, especially a visual display unit or active memory chip, with data **7.** *vti* COMPUT UPDATE INFORMATION to update the information on a website, or to be updated ○ *This page refreshes every two minutes.* [14C. < Old French *refreschir* 'make fresh again' < *freis* 'fresh']

refresher /ri fréshər/ *n* **1.** something that refreshes **2.** an additional payment made to a lawyer during a lengthy case

refresher course *n* a course of instruction designed to bring somebody's knowledge and skills up to date

refreshing /ri fréshing/ *adj* **1.** serving to restore energy and vitality **2.** pleasingly different and exciting — **refreshingly** *adv*

refreshment /ri fréshmənt/ *n* **1.** SOMETHING REFRESHING something that refreshes, especially food and drink **2.** ACT OF REFRESHING the process of refreshing somebody or something, or a refreshing quality in something ■ **refreshments** *npl* SOMETHING TO EAT AND DRINK something to eat and drink, usually snacks or a light meal and drinks

refresh rate *n* the number of times per second that an image displayed on a screen needs to be regenerated to prevent flicker when viewed by the human eye. The refresh rate is dependent upon the persistence of the material used on the screen and the retina's retentivity

~~refridgerator~~ incorrect spelling of **refrigerator**

refried beans /reé frid-/ *npl* in Mexican and Tex-Mex cuisine, beans cooked with spices, mashed, then fried

refrigerant /ri fríjjərənt/ *n* **1.** COOLING SUBSTANCE a substance used to cool or freeze something, especially the liquid that circulates in a refrigerator **2.** MED FEVER-REDUCING MEDICATION a medication that alleviates fever or reduces body heat ■ *adj* **1.** COOLING having a cooling or freezing effect **2.** MED REDUCING BODY HEAT reducing fever or body heat [Late 16C. < Latin *refrigerant-*, present participle of *refrigerare* (see REFRIGERATE)]

refrigerate /ri fríjjə rayt/ (**-ates, -ating, -ated**) *vt* to cool food or other heat-sensitive products to prevent deterioration in quality [Mid-16C. < Latin *refrigerare*, 'chill again, cool', *friger-*, obsolete stem of *frigus* 'cold'] — **refrigeration** /ri fríjjə ráysh'n/ *n* —**refrigerative** /-rətiv/ *adj*

refrigerated /ri fríjjə raytid/ *adj* **1.** describes a vehicle or container designed to keep its contents or cargo at a low temperature in order to preserve them **2.** kept or preserved at a low temperature in a refrigerator

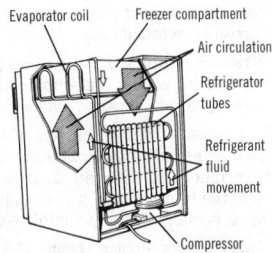

refrigerator: cross section of a refrigerator

refrigerator /ri fríjjə raytər/ *n* an electrical appliance in the form of an insulated cabinet that keeps items cool through artificial means, or an insulated walk-in chamber artificially cooled for this purpose

refringent /ri frínjənt/ *adj* PHYS same as **refractive** [Late 18C. < Latin *refringent-*, present participle of *refringere* (see REFRACT)] —**refringence** *n*

reft past participle, past tense of **reave**

refuel /ree fyoó əl, -fyoól/ (**-els, -elling, -elled**) *vti* **1.** to refill a vehicle's tank with fuel **2.** to provide additional material for or give a renewed impetus to something

refuge /réff yooj/ *n* **1.** SHELTER OR PROTECTION a sheltered or protected state safe from something threatening, harmful, or unpleasant **2.** SHELTERING PLACE a place, or sometimes a person, offering protection or safe shelter from something **3.** SAFE ACCOMMODATION FOR BATTERED WOMEN a place offering accommodation to women who are victims of violence, especially in the home **4.** TRANSP same as **traffic island** [14C. Via French < Latin *refugium* 'place to flee back to' < *fugere* 'flee']

refugee /réffyoo jeé/ *n* somebody who seeks or takes refuge in a foreign country, especially to avoid war or persecution (*often used before a noun*) [Late 17C. < French *réfugié*, past participle of *réfugier* 'take refuge' < *refuge* (see REFUGE); assimilated to -EE]

refugium /ri fyoóji əm/ (*plural* **-gia** /-ji ə/) *n* an area whose climate remains habitable, especially for rare or endangered species, when that of the surrounding areas has changed [Mid-20C. < Latin (see REFUGE)]

refulgent /ri fúljənt/ *adj* shining brilliantly or splendidly (*formal*) [Early 16C. < Latin *refulgent-*, present participle of *refulgere* 'shine back, reflect' < *fulgere* 'shine, flash'] —**refulgence** *n* —**refulgently** *adv*

refund *vt* /ri fúnd/ (**-funds, -funding, -funded**) RETURN MONEY TO SOMEBODY to return money to somebody, usually because he or she paid too much or did not receive what was paid for ■ *n* /reé fund/ **1.** RETURNED MONEY an amount of money that is returned to somebody **2.** PROCESS OF REPAYMENT the act or process of returning money [14C. Via Old French *refunder* < Latin *refundere* 'pour back' < *fundere* 'pour'] —**refundable** /ri fúndəb'l/ *adj*

re-fund /ree fúnd/ *vt* **1.** FUND SOMETHING ANEW to fund something again **2.** FIN BORROW TO REPAY DEBT to pay off a debt with new borrowing **3.** FIN REPLACE BOND ISSUE WITH NEW ISSUE to replace an existing issue of bonds with a new issue [Mid-19C. < RE- + FUND]

refurbish /ree fúrbish/ (**-bishes, -bishing, -bished**) *vt* to bring something back to a cleaner, brighter, or more functional state —**refurbishment** *n*

refusal /ri fyooz'l/ *n* **1.** UNWILLINGNESS TO DO SOMETHING a declaration or an attitude of unwillingness to do or accept something **2.** FIRST OFFER OF SOMETHING the chance

to accept or reject something before it is offered to others **3.** RIDING **HORSE'S REFUSAL TO JUMP OBSTACLE** a horse's stopping and not attempting to jump an obstacle in a race or competition

refuse[1] /ri fyo͞oz/ (**-fuses, -fusing, -fused**) *v* **1.** *vti* **INDICATE UNWILLINGNESS** to declare a decision or intention not to do something **2.** *vt* **NOT ACCEPT SOMETHING** to decline to accept something offered ○ *refused the promotion* **3.** *vt* **DENY SOMETHING** to be unwilling to give, allow, or agree to something asked for by somebody ○ *I refused them the use of my tools.* **4.** *vti* RIDING **BALK AT JUMP** to stop and not jump over an obstacle (*refers to horses*) [14C. Via Old French *refuser* < assumed Vulgar Latin *refusare*, perhaps blend of Latin *recusare* 'to refuse' + *refutare* 'to repel'] —**refusable** *adj*

refuse[2] /réffyooss/ *n* things thrown away as being of no value or use, especially household rubbish [14C. Old French *refus*, literally 'refusal' < *refuser* (see REFUSE[1])]

refusenik /ri fyo͞oznik/ *n* **1.** a citizen of the former Soviet Union, especially a Jew, who was not allowed by the government to emigrate **2.** somebody who refuses to agree to, take part in, or cooperate with something, especially out of principle (*informal*)

refute /ri fyo͞ot/ (**-futes, -futing, -futed**) *vt* **1.** to prove something to be false or somebody to be in error, either through logical argument or by providing evidence to the contrary **2.** to deny an allegation or contradict a statement without disproving it [Early 16C. < Latin *refutare* 'drive back, rebut' < *-futare* 'to beat'] —**refutability** /ri fyo͞otə bíllәti, réffyo͞otə-/ *n* —**refutable** /réffyo͞otəb'l, ri fyo͞otəb'l/ *adj* —**refutably** *adv* —**refutation** /réffyo͞o táysh'n/ *n*

USAGE refute, rebut, or **rebuff**? The core meaning of ***refute*** is 'to prove false or in error', though a more general sense 'to deny' has developed and is now widely established. In US English especially, it is acceptable to use ***refute*** and ***rebut*** interchangeably in the sense 'to deny or contradict something', as in *a spokesperson who refuted/rebutted all allegations of impropriety.* Nonetheless, if you want to emphasize the idea of proving wrongness as opposed to mere denial or contradiction, then use ***refute***, as in *used unimpeachable facts to refute opposing counsel's allegations,* and use ***rebut*** to mean 'contradict', as in *rebutted opposing counsel's opening statement in her closing statement.* Do not confuse ***rebuff*** ('to reject or snub') with ***rebut*** (*I rebuffed [not rebutted] his unwanted advances; I rebuffed [not rebutted] his protestations).*

reg[1] /rej/ *n* a vehicle's registration number, especially the first or last letter that indicates the vehicle's age (*informal*) ○ *an H-reg hatchback* [Late 20C. Shortening]

reg[2] /reg/ *n* same as **regulation** *n* (sense 1) (*informal*) ○ *rules and regs* [Early 20C. Shortening]

reg. *abbr* **1.** GEOG region **2.** registered **3.** EDUC registrar **4.** registry **5.** GRAM regular **6.** regularly **7.** GENETICS regulation **8.** ENG regulator **9.** MEASURE regulo

Reg. *abbr* **1.** Regent **2.** Regina

regain /ri gáyn/ (**-gains, -gaining, -gained**) *vt* **1.** to recover something after losing it **2.** to reach a place again ○ *She regained her seat and sat down.*

regal /reég'l/ *adj* characteristic of or suitable for a king or queen, especially in grandeur or magnificence [14C. Via French < Latin *regalis* < *reg-*, 'king'] —**regality** /ree gállәti/ *n* —**regally** *adv*

regale /ri gáyl/ (**-gales, -galing, -galed**) *vt* **1.** to entertain or amuse somebody, especially by telling stories ○ *regaled us with stories from the early days* **2.** to give somebody plenty of good things to eat and drink [Mid-17C. < French *régaler* 'entertain', literally 'give pleasure again' < Old French *gale* 'merriment, pleasure']

regalia /ri gáyli ə/ *n* (*takes a singular or plural verb*) **1. ROYAL INSIGNIA** the ceremonial and symbolic objects and clothing used and worn by royalty or other holders of high office on formal occasions **2. DISTINCTIVE CLOTHING** the distinctive clothing or trappings showing the status of a group of people, worn especially on formal occasions **3. SPLENDID ATTIRE** splendid attire for a formal occasion ○ *The general appeared in full regalia.* [Mid-16C. < medieval Latin *regalia* 'royal privileges, royal residence', form of Latin *regalis* (see REGAL)]

regard /ri gaárd/ *vt* (**-gards, -garding, -garded**) **1. CONSIDER SOMEBODY OR SOMETHING** to think of somebody or something as having a particular nature or quality or a particular role or function ○ *I regard his gift as an apology.* **2. HAVE FEELINGS IN RELATION TO SOMETHING** to have a particular feeling towards somebody or something ○ *At first they regarded the idea of early retirement with horror.* **3. JUDGE SOMEBODY OR SOMETHING** to have an opinion as to the quality or worth of somebody or something ○ *I regard her highly.* **4. LOOK AT SOMEBODY OR SOMETHING** to look at something or somebody steadily or attentively ○ *regarded the photograph with interest* **5. BE ABOUT SOMETHING** to be about or concerned with something ○ *This memo regards your performance review.* ■ *n* **1. ATTENTION** attention to or concern for somebody or something ○ *with no regard for my feelings* **2. FAVOURABLE OPINION** a mixture of liking and respect, often coupled with affection ○ *I hold her in the highest regard.* **3. GAZE** a look, or somebody's gaze (*formal*) ■ **regards** *npl* **FRIENDLY GREETINGS** friendly good wishes and greetings ○ *Give my regards to your father.* [14C. < French *regarder* 'look at fully' < *garder* (see GUARD)] ◇ **as regards** as far as somebody or something is concerned ◇ **in this** *or* **that regard** as far as this or that is concerned, or from this or that point of view (*formal*)

SYNONYMS ***regard, admiration, esteem, favour, respect, reverence, veneration***

CORE MEANING: appreciation of the worth of somebody or something

regard a mixture of liking and respect, often coupled with affection ○ *He is held in high regard by customers and colleagues alike.* ○ *She has little regard for other people's property.* **admiration** warm approval and appreciation of somebody or something ○ *The garden was so beautiful that Joanna gasped in admiration.* ○ *All the people who took part were very brave and I have nothing but admiration for them all.* **esteem** a high opinion and appreciation of somebody or something ○ *One of the reasons why teachers have fallen in public esteem is that the public have lost confidence in teaching methods.* ○ *Intelligence testing was held in high esteem fifty years ago, but has since gone out of fashion.* **favour** an approving, friendly, or supportive attitude ○ *struggles between board members competing for the chairman's favour* ○ *The proposals have not found favour with the public.* **respect** a feeling or attitude of admiration and deference towards somebody or something ○ *She obviously has the highest respect for her father.* ○ *Their customs and beliefs must be treated with respect.* **reverence** feelings of deep respect or devotion ○ *The prince was accustomed to being listened to with reverence.* ○ *A crucifix hangs on every classroom wall to help instil reverence for God.* **veneration** feelings of deep respect or awe ○ *A player of great distinction, he was regarded with veneration by his fellow guitarists.* ○ *My childhood experiences gave me a lasting veneration for long-established custom and ritual.*

regardant /ri gaárd'nt/ *adj* describes a heraldic figure that is looking backwards over its shoulder ○ *three lions regardant* [15C. < French, present participle of *regarder* (see REGARD)]

regardful /ri gaárdf'l/ *adj* **1.** paying due attention **2.** full of esteem and often deferential respect for somebody —**regardfully** *adv* —**regardfulness** *n*

regarding /ri gaárding/ *prep* about or on the subject of ○ *I'd like a word with you regarding the schedule.*

regardless /ri gaárdləss/ *adv* in spite of or ignoring setbacks, hindrances, or problems ■ *adj* paying no attention, especially failing to pay proper attention —**regardlessly** *adv*

USAGE See ***irregardless.***

regardless of *prep* **1.** in spite of ○ *Regardless of what you were told, I cannot help you.* **2.** no matter what or taking no account of ○ *We're going on holiday regardless of the weather.*

regatta /ri gáttə/ *n* a sports event consisting of a series of boat or yacht races [Mid-17C. < (Venetian) Italian, 'gondola race (on the Grand Canal)', originally 'contest for mastery' < *regattare* 'compete']

regd *abbr* registered

regelation /reéji láysh'n/ *n* **1.** the process by which water melted by pressure beneath a glacier is refrozen **2.** reduction of the freezing point of water by force of pressure

regency /reéjənssi/ (*plural* **-cies**) *n* **1.** a group of people ruling on behalf of a monarch who is unable to rule because of youth, illness, or absence **2.** the authority and responsibilities or period in office of a regent

Regency *n* **1. 1811–20 IN GREAT BRITAIN** the period from 1811–20 in Great Britain during which George, Prince of Wales, ruled as regent for his father King George III **2. 1715–23 IN FRANCE** the period from 1715–23 in France during which Philip, Duke of Orleans, ruled as regent on behalf of King Louis XV ■ *adj* **IN STYLE OF REGENCY** in the style prevalent and fashionable during either of the Regency periods

regenerate *v* /ri jénnə rayt/ (**-ates, -ating, -ated**) **1.** *vti* **FORM AGAIN** to form again, or become formed again **2.** *vti* **RECOVER FROM DECLINE** to return from a state of decline to a revitalized state, or cause something to do this **3.** *vti* BIOL **REPLACE BODY PART BY NEW GROWTH** to replace lost tissue or a lost limb or organ with a new growth, or grow again after loss **4.** *vt* RELIG **RESTORE SOMEBODY SPIRITUALLY** to restore and renew somebody morally or spiritually **5.** *vt* ELECTRONICS **RESTORE SIGNALS TO ORIGINAL WAVE SHAPE** to restore digital electrical signals to their original wave shape after transmission over long distances ■ *n* /ri jénnərət/ **1. SOMEBODY SPIRITUALLY REFORMED** somebody who is spiritually reborn or renewed **2.** BIOL **REPLACEMENT TISSUE** tissue that has grown to replace lost tissue, or a regenerated part, organ, or organism ■ *adj* /ri jénnərət/ **1. SPIRITUALLY REBORN OR RENEWED** spiritually reborn, renewed, or restored to health **2.** BIOL **NEWLY FORMED OR GROWN** newly formed or grown as a replacement for something lost —**regenerable** *adj* —**regeneracy** *n* —**regeneration** /ri jénnə ráysh'n/ *n* —**regenerative** /-rətiv/ *adj* —**regenerator** *n*

regenerative medicine *n* the branch of medicine that deals with repairing or replacing tissues and organs by using advanced materials and methodologies such as cloning

Regensburg /ráygənss bo͝ork/ city in Bavaria, southeastern Germany, on the River Danube, about 105 km/65 mi. northeast of Munich. Population: 125,608 (1997).

regent /reéjənt/ *n* somebody who rules on behalf of a monarch who is unable to rule because of youth, illness, or absence ■ *adj* ruling as a regent ○ *the prince regent* [14C. Via French < Latin *regent-*, present participle of *regere* 'rule'] —**regental** *adj*

ORIGIN The Latin word *regere* 'to rule', from which ***regent*** is derived, is also the source of the English words *correct, erect, escort, realm, rector, regime, regiment,* and *region.*

reggae /réggay/ *n* popular music, originally from Jamaica, that combines rock, calypso, and soul and is characterized by heavy accentuation of the second and fourth beats of a four-beat bar (*often used before a noun*) ○ *a reggae beat* [Mid-20C. Perhaps < Jamaican English *reggay*, alteration of *rege* 'ragged fellow' < RAG[1]]

Reggio di Calabria /réji ō dee ka laábrya/ city and administrative centre of Reggio di Calabria Province in Calabria Region, southern Italy. Population: 180,353 (2001).

Reggio nell'Emilia /-nel ay meélya/ capital city of Reggio nell'Emilia Province in Emilia Romagna Region, northern Italy. Population: 141,877 (2001).

regicide /réjji sīd/ *n* **1.** the killing of a king **2.** somebody who kills a king [Mid-16C. < Latin *reg-* 'king'] —**regicidal** /réjji sīd'l/ *adj*

regime /ray zheém, re-/, **régime** *n* **1. FORM OF GOVERNMENT** a system or style of government **2. PARTICULAR GOVERNMENT** the government of a particular country, especially one that is considered to be oppressive **3. CONTROLLING GROUP** any controlling or managing group, or the system of control and management adopted by it **4. ESTABLISHED SYSTEM** an established system or way of doing things **5. CHARACTERISTIC CONDITIONS FOR PROCESS** the characteristic conditions under which a natural, scientific, or industrial process occurs **6.** MED same as **regimen** (sense 1) [15C. Via French < Latin *regimen* (see REGIMEN)]

regime change *n* **1.** the forcible overthrow of another nation's government by outside intervention (*used euphemistically*) **2.** a change in leadership, e.g. of a country or political party

regimen /réjjimən, -men/ *n* **1.** a prescribed or recommended programme of medication, diet, exercise, or other measures intended to improve health or fitness, or stabilize a medical condition **2.** a government or form of government (*archaic*) **3.** INDUST, SCI same as **regime** (sense 5) [14C. < Latin *regimen* 'rule, government' < *regere* 'to rule']

regiment *n* /réjjimənt/ **1.** ARMY UNIT a permanent military unit usually consisting of two or three battalions of ground troops divided into smaller companies or troops under the command of a colonel **2.** LARGE NUMBER OF PEOPLE OR THINGS a large number of people or things, especially an orderly group **3.** GOVERNMENTAL RULE governmental rule or administration (*archaic*) ■ *vt* /réjji ment/ (**-ments, -menting, -mented**) **1.** CONTROL SOMEBODY OR SOMETHING STRICTLY to impose strict control or discipline on somebody or something, often to the extent of stifling flexibility, individuality, or imagination **2.** GROUP SOMETHING SYSTEMATICALLY to organize something systematically into groups **3.** GROUP SOLDIERS INTO REGIMENTS to form regiments out of a group of soldiers [14C. Via French < late Latin *regimentum* < Latin *regere* 'to rule'] —**regimental** /réjji mént'l/ *adj* —**regimentally** *adv* —**regimented** /-mentid/ *adj*

regimentals /réjji mént'lz/ *npl* **1.** the uniform and insignia worn by the members of a particular regiment **2.** military dress and insignia, especially as worn for ceremonial occasions

regimentation /réjji men táysh'n/ *n* the act of placing somebody or something under strict and inflexible organization or control, or the condition of being very strictly organized and controlled ○ *They are individuals and do not respond well to regimentation.*

Regina[1] /ri jínə/ *n* **1.** the reigning queen **2.** the Crown as the prosecuting authority in lawsuits when the ruling monarch is a queen ○ *the case of Regina versus Higgins* [Early 18C. From Latin, literally 'queen']

Regina[2] /ri jínə/ capital city of Saskatchewan Province, Canada. Population: 178,225 (2001).

region /réejən/ *n* **1.** AREA OF LAND a large land area that has geographical, political, or cultural characteristics that distinguish it from others, whether existing within one country or extending over several **2.** ADMINISTRATIVE UNIT a large separate political or administrative unit within a country **3.** ECOLOGICAL AREA an area of the world with particular animal and plant life **4.** LARGE INDEFINITE AREA any large indefinite area of a surface **5.** AREA OR ASPECT an imprecisely defined area or part of something such as a sphere of activity **6.** RANGE WITHIN WHICH FIGURE FALLS the range within which something such as a figure, sum, or price might fall ○ *in the region of £1,000* **7.** ANAT AREA OF BODY an area of the body, usually an area surrounding a particular organ or part ■ **regions** *npl* PROVINCES the rest of a country outside its capital, or the rest of an area outside its main city [14C. Via French < Latin *region-* 'boundary, district', literally 'area that is ruled' < *regere* 'to rule']

regional /réejən'l/ *adj* **1.** RELATING TO REGION belonging to or characteristic of a geographical region **2.** CONNECTED WITH ADMINISTRATIVE REGION serving or connected with one of the administrative regions of a country ○ *a regional authority* **3.** CHARACTERISTIC OF AREA characteristic of or limited to an area of a country, especially typical of the speech and usage of a particular area and different from standard speech and usage ○ *a regional accent* —**regionally** *adv*

regionalise *vt* GEOG, POL another spelling of **regionalize**

regionalism /réejənəlizəm/ *n* **1.** DIVISION INTO ADMINISTRATIVE AREAS the policy of dividing a political territory into areas with separate administrations, or support for such a policy **2.** LOYALTY TO HOME REGION loyalty to or prejudice in favour of a region **3.** LING LINGUISTIC FEATURE RESTRICTED TO ONE AREA a linguistic feature, e.g. a word, pronunciation, or expression, that is found only in a particular region —**regionalist** *n, adj*

regionalize /réejənə līz/ (**-izes, -izing, -ized**), **regionalise** (**-ises, -ising, -ised**) *vt* **1.** to divide an area into administrative regions **2.** to allocate something to regional administrations —**regionalization** /réejənə lī záysh'n/ *n*

régisseur /rézhi súr/ *n* a director who is responsible for staging a theatrical work, especially a ballet [Early 19C. < French, 'agent, manager' < *régir* 'to manage, rule' < Latin *regere*]

register /réjjistər/ *n* **1.** OFFICIAL LIST an official record, often in the form of a list **2.** BOOK FOR OFFICIAL RECORDS a book in which a register of names, attendance, or events is kept **3.** ITEM IN OFFICIAL LIST an item recorded in an official register **4.** MEASURING DEVICE THAT RECORDS a device that automatically records numbers, degrees, or quantities **5.** COMM same as **cash register** **6.** CORRECT ALIGNMENT correct alignment or positioning with respect to something else **7.** HEATING GRATE a closable grill or grate through which warm or cool air is forced in a household heating system **8.** COMPUT COMPUTER MEMORY LOCATION a memory location in a processor or microprocessor that has a particular storage capacity, is usually intended for a particular purpose, and is accessible at very high speeds **9.** MUSIC MUSICAL RANGE the range of a voice or instrument, or a part of this range **10.** MUSIC ORGAN STOP one of a group of organ stops that are similar in tonal quality **11.** LING SITUATION-SPECIFIC LANGUAGE VARIETY language of a type that is appropriate to a social situation or used for communicating with a particular set of people ○ *The word is informal in register.* ■ *v* (**-ters, -tering, -tered**) **1.** *vti* WRITE SOMETHING IN REGISTER to enter something in a register, or have something entered there by an official ○ *They registered at the hotel.* **2.** *vti* ENROL to record your name with an organization, e.g. to enrol for an academic course or fulfil a legal requirement ○ *register for the course in September* **3.** *vt* MAKE RECORD OF SOMETHING to make a record of something, or have something recorded ○ *I want to register a complaint with the manager.* **4.** *vt* SHOW SOMETHING AS MEASUREMENT to indicate or record a measurement on a device or scale **5.** *vti* DISPLAY FEELING OR THOUGHT to be visible in somebody's facial expression or body language, or to display something in this way ○ *registered her disapproval* **6.** *vt* NOTE SOMETHING MENTALLY to make a mental note of something ○ *I registered the time before moving on.* **7.** *vi* BE UNDERSTOOD to be understood or remembered by somebody ○ *The implications finally registered with me.* **8.** *vt* ACHIEVE SOMETHING to achieve or accomplish something ○ *The team registered several notable successes last season.* **9.** *vt* SEND SOMETHING BY REGISTERED POST to send a letter or package using a postage system that guarantees compensation if the item is lost **10.** *vi* BE ALIGNED to be correctly aligned [14C. Via French < medieval Latin *registrum*, alteration of late Latin *regesta* 'list', literally 'things collected or brought back' < Latin *gerere* 'bring'] —**registered** *adj* —**registrable** *adj* —**registrant** *n*

registered general nurse /réjjistərd-/ *n UK* a nurse who is qualified to practise, having undergone a three-year course of study and clinical training attached to a university

registered mail *n ANZ, N Am* same as **registered post**

registered nurse *n ANZ, N Am* a nurse who has passed a qualifying examination in order to be licensed to practise

registered post *n UK* a service provided by post offices for an additional fee to ensure safe delivery of valuable items, providing certified delivery and compensation in case of loss. ANZ, N Am term **registered mail**

registered trademark *n* LAW same as **trademark** *n* (sense 1)

register office *n* in the United Kingdom, an office where civil marriages are performed and births, marriages, and deaths are recorded (*used as the official name for 'registry office'*)

register ton *n* MEASURE same as **ton**[1] (sense 5)

registrar /réjji straár, réjji straar/ *n* **1.** RECORDER OF BIRTHS, MARRIAGES, AND DEATHS a public official who records births, marriages, and deaths **2.** SOMEBODY WHO KEEPS OFFICIAL RECORDS somebody who keeps official records **3.** OFFICIAL RESPONSIBLE FOR STUDENT RECORDS the most senior administrative officer in a university, or any university, college, or school official responsible for keeping records of such things as student enrolments and examination results **4.** MED SENIOR HOSPITAL DOCTOR a senior doctor in a hospital, of a rank lower than consultant, who specializes in a branch of medicine or surgery and may train junior doctors **5.** *US* MED HOSPITAL ADMINISTRATOR an administrative officer in a hospital responsible for admitting patients **6.** *US* BUSINESS OFFICIAL RESPONSIBLE FOR SHARE RECORDS a company official who keeps records of shares issued **7.** LAW LAW COURT OFFICIAL in the United Kingdom, an official who oversees the administration of justice in the High Court and other courts —**registrarship** *n*

Registrar General (*plural* **Registrars General**) *n* in the United Kingdom, a senior civil servant responsible for population records and censuses

registration /réjji stráysh'n/ *n* **1.** ACT OF REGISTERING OR BEING REGISTERED the act or an instance of registering somebody or something, or the process of being registered **2.** ENTRY IN REGISTER an entry in a register, or somebody or something whose name or designation is entered in a register **3.** TIME OF REGISTERING STUDENTS the act of recording school students as present or absent at the beginning of the school day, or the time or session at which this takes place **4.** ENROLMENT PROCESS the process of enrolling at a college or university, choosing courses, and paying fees at the beginning of an academic term **5.** LETTER SHOWING VEHICLE'S AGE a letter or number that identifies the year or part of a year in which a vehicle was registered and put on the road, forming part of its registration number **6.** *N Am* LEGAL PROOF FOR VEHICLE a certificate showing that a motor vehicle has been properly registered with a state's department of motor vehicles **7.** PEOPLE REGISTERING TOGETHER the number of people who register for something at a particular place at one time **8.** MUSIC COMBINATION OF ORGAN STOPS a combination of organ stops used to play a piece of music **9.** MUSIC CHOICE OF COMBINATIONS OF ORGAN STOPS the art of choosing combinations of organ stops appropriate for a piece or passage

registration document *n* an official document stating the name of the owner of a motor vehicle and giving details by which it can be identified

registration number *n* a sequence of letters and numbers by which a motor vehicle can be identified, printed on plates (**number plates**) fastened to the front and back of the vehicle

registration plate *n ANZ* a metal or plastic plate on the front and back of a motor vehicle, carrying the vehicle's registration number

registry /réjjistri/ (*plural* **-tries**) *n* **1.** RECORDS OFFICE a place where registers and other records are kept **2.** REGISTERING OF SOMETHING the act of registering somebody or something **3.** SHIP REGISTRATION IN PARTICULAR COUNTRY the nationality of a ship, as defined by where it is registered not by the nationality of its owner or its usual place of operation

registry office *n* PUBLIC ADMIN same as **register office** (*not used in official contexts*)

regius professor /réeji əss-, réejəss-/ *n* in the United Kingdom, a professor whose professorship was established by a king or queen, especially Henry VIII, and who is officially appointed by the current king or queen [*Regius* from Latin, 'royal', from *rex* 'king']

reglet /régglit/ *n* **1.** a flat narrow architectural moulding, or a narrow strip separating mouldings or panels **2.** in traditional hot-metal printing, a piece of wood used to separate lines of type [Late 16C. < Old French *régelet*, literally 'small rule']

regmaker /rékh maakər/ *n S Africa* a drink taken to relieve the symptoms of a hangover [Mid-20C. From Afrikaans, from *reg* 'right' + *maker* 'maker']

regnal /régn'l/ *adj* relating to a king or queen's reign, calculated from the date when he or she became the sovereign ○ *the third regnal year* [Early 17C. < Anglo-Latin *regnalis* < Latin *regnum* 'kingdom']

regnant /régnənt/ *adj* (*formal*) **1.** actually reigning, usually as opposed to having a royal title by marriage ○ *queen regnant* **2.** widespread, predominant, or especially fashionable ○ *according to the regnant custom* [Early 17C. < Latin *regnant-*, present participle of *regnare* 'reign']

rego /réjjō/ (*plural* **-os**) *n Aus* the annual reregistration of a motor vehicle, usually including a roadworthiness check (*informal*) [Mid-20C. < REGISTRATION]

Rego /ráygō/, **Paula** (b. 1935) Portuguese-born British painter. She was appointed first associate artist of the National Gallery, London, in 1990. An exhibition of her *Nursery Rhymes* etchings (1989) received international acclaim.

regolith /réggə lith/ *n* the layer of loose rock particles that covers the bedrock of most land on the Earth and the Moon [Late 19C. < Greek *rhēgos* 'blanket']

regorge /ree gáwrj/ (**-gorges, -gorging, -gorged**) *v* **1.** *vt* to bring up something that has been swallowed **2.** *vi* to flow or gush back along a channel or out of a pit [Early 17C. Either < Old French *regorger* < *gorge* (see GORGE), or < RE- + GORGE]

Reg. Prof. *abbr* EDUC Regius Professor

regress *v* /ri gréss/ (**-gresses, -gressing, -gressed**) **1.** *vi* RETURN TO EARLIER WORSE CONDITION to return to an earlier and less advanced, less healthy, or generally worse state from a more advanced, healthier, or generally better one **2.** *vi* GO BACK to move backwards ○ *regress in time* **3.** *vti* PSYCHOL GO BACK TO EARLIER PERIOD PSYCHOLOGICALLY to go back to an earlier emotional state and exhibit the type of behaviour associated with it, or cause somebody to do this **4.** *vt* PARAPSYCHOL SUPPOSEDLY MAKE SOMEBODY RECALL EARLIER LIVES to cause somebody to think of and describe supposed earlier lifetimes while under hypnosis **5.** *vi* STATS TEND TOWARDS MEAN to tend towards a statistical mean ■ *n* /rée gress/ **1.** MOVEMENT BACKWARDS a going backwards, especially from a more advanced or better state to a less advanced or worse one **2.** LOGIC REASONING FROM EFFECT TO CAUSE a process of reasoning backwards from effects to their causes [Early 16C. < Latin *regress-*, past participle of *regredi* 'move backwards' < *gradi* 'to walk'] —**regressor** *n*

regression /ri grésh'n/ *n* **1.** REVERSION TO EARLIER STATE a return to an earlier or less developed condition or way of behaving **2.** MOVEMENT BACKWARDS a going backwards or a backward movement or progress, especially through the earlier stages or forms of something **3.** PSYCHOL REVERSION TO LESS MATURE STATE reversion to an earlier, less mature, and less adaptive emotional or mental level, often involving the appearance of forms of behaviour associated with childhood **4.** STATS ASSOCIATION BETWEEN VARIABLES a process for determining the statistical relationship between a random variable and one or more independent variables that is used to predict the value of the random variable **5.** BIOL RETURN TO EARLIER PHYSICAL TYPE the recurrence of an earlier, less complicated physical type among later generations of a population **6.** ASTRON RETROGRADE MOTION the apparent backward motion of an astronomical object, caused by the differing orbital periods of Earth and the object being observed **7.** ASTRON MOVEMENT OF MOON'S ORBIT the slow movement around the ecliptic of the two points where the Moon's orbit crosses it. A complete revolution happens once in about every 19 years.

regressive /ri gréssiv/ *adj* **1.** reverting to an earlier, less developed condition or way of behaving **2.** describes a tax system in which those with low incomes pay proportionally higher taxes than the wealthy —**regressively** *adv* —**regressiveness** *n*

regret /ri grét/ *vt* (**-grets, -gretting, -gretted**) **1.** FEEL SORRY FOR SOMETHING to feel sorry and sad about something previously done or said that now appears wrong, mistaken, or hurtful to others **2.** USED POLITELY WHEN GIVING BAD NEWS used as a polite expression of sorrow when making an apology or delivering a piece of bad or unwelcome news ○ *We regret to inform you that this service is no longer available.* ○ *We regret any inconvenience caused.* **3.** MOURN FOR SOMEBODY OR SOMETHING to feel sadness about something, or feel a sense of loss and longing for somebody or something that is no longer there (*formal*) ■ *n* **1.** SAD OR DISAPPOINTED FEELING a feeling or expression of sorrow and guilt for a past action or event that you now wish had not happened or had happened differently **2.** FEELING OF SADNESS a feeling of sadness, disappointment, or longing for somebody or something that is no longer there ○ *I let them go with regret, knowing that the visit would not be soon repeated.* ■ **regrets** *npl* EXPRESSION OF SADNESS a polite expression of real or pretended sadness, used especially when refusing something such as an invitation ○ *Do give them my regrets. I won't be able*

to come on Saturday. [15C. < Old French *regreter*] —**regretter** *n*

regretful /ri grétf'l/ *adj* feeling or showing regret for something —**regretfully** *adv* —**regretfulness** *n*

USAGE regretful or regrettable? *Regrettable* is used of something that is a cause for regret, whereas *regretful* describes somebody who has feelings of regret for something: *These mistakes are regrettable. They felt regretful at missing the opportunity.* The adverbs *regrettably* and *regretfully* are even more vulnerable to confusion, but again *regrettably* relates to the cause of regret and *regretfully* to the feeling itself: *The exam results are regrettably poor. She regretfully turned down the invitation.*

regrettable /ri gréttəb'l/ *adj* unfortunate or blameworthy, and causing feelings of regret, embarrassment, or shame ○ *It was a regrettable lapse by a person of otherwise exemplary character.* —**regrettableness** *n* —**regrettably** *adv*

USAGE See *regretful.*

regroup /ree groóp/ (**-groups, -grouping, -grouped**) *v* **1.** *vti* MIL FORM INTO ORGANIZED BODY AGAIN to re-form into organized units or an effective fighting force, or re-form troops in this way, especially after their being dispersed or defeated **2.** *vi* REORGANIZE to recover, reorganize, and prepare for a further effort after receiving a setback **3.** *vt* ARRANGE THINGS IN NEW GROUPS to arrange people or things in new or different groups —**regroupment** *n*

Regt *abbr* **1.** POL Regent **2.** MIL Regiment

regular /réggyŏŏlər/ *adj* **1.** HAVING EQUAL TIMES OR SPACES BETWEEN occurring in a fixed, unvarying, or predictable pattern, with equal amounts of time or space between each one ○ *the regular tick-tock of the clock* **2.** HAPPENING FREQUENTLY occurring or doing something frequently enough over a period of time to establish a pattern, though not necessarily a strict one ○ *Floods are becoming a regular occurrence round here.* **3.** USUAL normally expected, or most often used or done ○ *He's not our regular postman.* **4.** FOLLOWING ROUTINE carried out according to an established routine or schedule ○ *keep very regular hours* **5.** STANDARD OR MEDIUM of a standard or medium size or strength, as opposed to something of a larger size or greater strength ○ *a regular coffee* **6.** SYMMETRICAL evenly and pleasingly shaped and symmetrical ○ *a regular facial profile* **7.** PROPER conforming to the normal or accepted rules or standards **8.** QUALIFIED officially or properly qualified to perform a specific job ○ *not a regular doctor* **9.** COMPLETE AND UTTER thoroughly deserving a particular description (*informal*) ○ *a regular tyrant in the office* **10.** *N Am* NICE pleasant, reliable, and thoughtful (*informal*) ○ *a regular guy* **11.** PHYSIOL PHYSICALLY PREDICTABLE AND CONSISTENT having predictable physical processes, especially menstruating or having bowel movements at predictable times **12.** MIL FORMING PART OF PROFESSIONAL FORCE belonging to or constituting a full-time professional military or police force ○ *an officer in the regular army* **13.** GRAM GRAMMATICALLY NORMAL following the normal or common grammatical patterns of a language ○ *a regular verb* **14.** CHR OF RELIGIOUS ORDER belonging to a religious or monastic order ○ *the regular clergy* **15.** *US* POL POLITICALLY LOYAL connected with or loyal to a particular political party **16.** MATHS HAVING EQUAL SIDES AND ANGLES having both equal sides and equal angles ○ *a regular polygon* **17.** MATHS COMPOSED OF IDENTICAL POLYGONS having faces that are congruent identical polygons and that make equal angles with each other ○ *a regular polyhedron* **18.** BOT SYMMETRICAL having flower parts that are similar in size and shape and are arranged symmetrically **19.** WITH RIGHT FOOT FORWARD in skateboarding and similar sports, used to describe a stance on the board in which the rider's left foot is nearer the front end (*slang*) ■ *n* **1.** SOMETHING STANDARD OR MEDIUM something of a medium or standard size or strength, as opposed to something larger, smaller, stronger, or weaker **2.** FREQUENT VISITOR a frequent visitor to a place (*informal*) **3.** HABITUAL ORDER something that somebody usually asks for or buys, e.g. a drink (*informal*) **4.** MIL PROFESSIONAL SOLDIER a full-time professional soldier (*often used in the plural*) **5.** CHR MEMBER OF RELIGIOUS ORDER a member of a religious or monastic order **6.** *US* POL LOYAL PARTY SUPPORTER

somebody who is loyal to a political party ■ *adv* FREQUENTLY most or all of the time (*informal*) ○ *We come here regular, don't we?* [14C. < Latin *regularis* < *regula* 'rule' < Indo-European] —**regularity** /réggyŏŏ lárrəti/ *n* —**regularly** *adv*

regularize /réggyŏŏlə rīz/ (**-izes, -izing, -ized**), **regularise** (**-ises, -ising, -ised**) *vt* to make something fit in with or conform to usual or accepted standards or practice —**regularization** /réggyŏŏlə rī záysh'n/ *n* —**regularizer** *n*

regulate /réggyŏŏ layt/ (**-lates, -lating, -lated**) *vt* **1.** CONTROL SOMETHING to control something and bring it to the desired level, e.g. by adjusting the output of a machine or by imposing restrictions on the flow of something **2.** ADJUST MACHINERY OR SELECT OUTPUT to adjust a piece of machinery or a control device on it so that the machine works correctly **3.** MAKE SOMETHING REGULAR to cause something to occur at predictable intervals or in a regular way **4.** CONTROL SOMETHING BY RULES OR LAWS to organize and control an activity or process by making it subject to rules or laws (*formal*) [15C. < late Latin *regulat-*, past participle of *regulare* < Latin *regula* (see REGULAR)] —**regulative** /-lətiv/ *adj* —**regulatory** /-lətəri/ *adj*

regulation /réggyŏŏ láysh'n/ *n* **1.** RULE OR ORDER an official rule, law, or order stating what may or may not be done or how something must be done (*often used in the plural*) **2.** GOVERNMENT ORDER WITH FORCE OF LAW an order issued by a government department or agency that has the force of law **3.** REGULATING OF SOMETHING the adjusting, organizing, or controlling of something, or the state of being adjusted, organized, or controlled **4.** BIOL ABILITY OF EMBRYO TO GROW NORMALLY the process or mechanism by which an embryo restores its ability to develop normally after being damaged or altered without creating new tissue **5.** DIRECT EU LAW a European Union law that automatically applies in all member states without the need for domestic legislation in the individual states ■ *adj* **1.** OFFICIALLY APPROVED FOR USE officially approved for use, or conforming to the official guidelines for something **2.** STANDARD AND UNADVENTUROUS like everyone has or does, and completely standard and unadventurous

regulator /réggyŏŏ laytər/ *n* **1.** CONTROL MECHANISM a mechanism that controls something such as pressure, temperature, speed, or voltage (*often used in combination*) **2.** CONTROLLING OFFICIAL an official who controls a particular activity and makes certain that regulations are complied with (*often used in combination*) ○ *the industry regulator* **3.** VERY ACCURATE TIMEPIECE a very accurate watch or clock, used as a standard by which others are set **4.** GENETICS same as *regulator gene*

regulator gene, **regulatory gene** *n* a gene that regulates the expression of one or more structural genes, thereby controlling the synthesis of their corresponding proteins. In the simplest case, the regulator gene encodes a repressor molecule that binds to a site adjacent to the structural gene, so preventing transcription of the latter.

reguli METALL plural of *regulus*

Regulo /réggyŏŏlō/ *tdmk* a trademark for a gas mark

regulus /réggyŏŏləss/ (*plural* **-luses** or **-li** /-lī/) *n* **1.** the semipurified mass of metal that forms beneath the slag in the smelting of ore **2.** an impure intermediate metal product created by the smelting process [Late 16C. < Latin, diminutive of *reg-* 'king', originally in *regulus of antimony*, a metallic antimony so called because it combined readily with gold, a kingly metal] —**reguline** /réggyŏŏlin, -līn/ *adj*

Regulus *n* a bright double star in the constellation Leo

regurgitate /ri gúrji tayt/ (**-tates, -tating, -tated**) *v* **1.** *vt* BRING FOOD UP FROM STOMACH to bring undigested or partially digested food up from the stomach to the mouth, as some birds and animals do to feed their young **2.** *vt* REPEAT INFORMATION MECHANICALLY to repeat or reproduce what has been heard, read, or taught, in a purely mechanical way, with no evidence of personal thought or understanding **3.** *vi* FLOW OUT to flow out or be ejected, especially from the mouth (*formal*) **4.** *vi* MED FLOW IN OPPOSITE DIRECTION TO NORMAL to flow in the opposite direction to the normal or usual direction, especially through a faulty heart valve [Late 16C. < medieval Latin *regurgitat-*, past participle of

regurgitare, literally 'to flood back' < Latin *gurge* 'whirlpool'] —**regurgitant** *n, adj* —**regurgitation** /ri gúrji táysh'n/ *n* —**regurgitative** /-tətiv/ *adj*

rehab /rée hab/ (*informal*) *n* **1.** *N Am* REHABILITATION the period or process of rehabilitation, e.g. for somebody addicted to a chemical substance (*often used before a noun*) ○ *a rehab clinic* **2.** SOMETHING RESTORED something that has been restored to good condition, especially a rehabilitated building ■ *vt* (**-habs, -habbing, -habbed**) *N Am* RESTORE BUILDING to restore something, especially a building [Mid-20C. Shortening] —**rehabber** *n*

rehabilitate /rée ə bílli tayt, rée hə-/ (**-tates, -tating, -tated**) *vt* **1.** HELP SOMEBODY RETURN TO NORMAL LIFE to help somebody to return to good health or a normal life by providing training or therapy **2.** RESTORE SOMEBODY TO RANK OR RIGHTS to restore somebody to a former position or rank and grant rights and privileges once more (*often passive*) **3.** RESTORE SOMEBODY'S REPUTATION to restore somebody's good reputation and standing after he or she has been disgraced or neglected **4.** RESTORE PLACE TO GOOD CONDITION to restore a building, or part of a town, to its former good condition [Late 16C. < medieval Latin *rehabilitat-*, past participle of *rehabilitare*, literally 'habilitate again' (see HABILITATE)] —**rehabilitatable** *adj* —**rehabilitation** /rée ə bílli táysh'n, rée hə-/ *n* —**rehabilitative** /-tətiv/ *adj* —**rehabilitator** *n*

rehash *vt* /ree hásh/ (**-hashes, -hashing, -hashed**) to repeat something or reuse and rework old material, making some changes but without introducing anything new ■ *n* /rée hash/ a tiresome reuse of ideas or material to which nothing new or significant has been added

rehearsal /ri húrss'l/ *n* **1.** a session or series of sessions in which something that is to be done later, especially a public performance, is practised **2.** a detailed listing or repetition of something (*formal*)

rehearse /ri húrss/ (**-hearses, -hearsing, -hearsed**) *v* **1.** *vti* PRACTISE SOMETHING BEFORE PERFORMING to practise something before doing it, especially to practise something such as a play, speech, or piece of music before performing it for the public **2.** *vt* TRAIN SOMEBODY FOR PERFORMANCE to train or instruct somebody who is practising before doing something, especially before giving a public performance **3.** *vt* GO OVER LIST to go over a list of items, often reasons, complaints, or troubles **4.** *vti* SAY SOMETHING to tell or repeat something such as a story (*literary*) [13C. < Old French *rehercer* 'rake over' < *herce, herse* (see HEARSE)] —**rehearser** *n*

Rehnquist /rén kwist/, **William H.** (*b.* 1924) chief justice of the US Supreme Court (1986–). Appointed as an associate justice in 1971 and as chief justice in 1986, he presided over a court noted for its judicial restraint. Full name **Rehnquist, William Hubbs**

rehoboam /rée ə bṓ əm/ *n* a large wine bottle, six times the size of a normal bottle [Mid-19C. Named after *Rehoboam*, who 'fortified the strongholds, and put captains in them...and stores of oil and wine' (2 Chronicles 11:11)]

Rehoboam /rée ə bṓ əm/ *n* in the Bible, the son of Solomon and king of ancient Judah (922? BC–915? BC). His reign was marked by conflict with the rival kingdom of the northern tribes of Israel (1 Kings 11–14).

rehouse /ree hówz/ (**-houses, -housing, -housed**) *vt* to provide a person or group of people with a new or different place to live in, often one that is better than the previous dwelling

rehydrate /rée hī drayt, rée hī dráyt/ (**-drates, -drating, -drated**) *v* **1.** *vt* RETURN WATER TO SOMETHING to add water to something that has been dried in order to return it to its natural state **2.** *vi* ABSORB WATER to absorb water after dehydration **3.** *vt* MED REPLENISH SOMEBODY'S BODY FLUIDS to restore somebody's body fluids to a normal or healthy level —**rehydratable** *adj* —**rehydration** /rée hī dráysh'n/ *n*

Reibey /rée bee/, **Mary** (1777–1855) British-born Australian entrepreneur. Transported to New South Wales, Australia, at the age of 15, she subsequently became one of the colony's leading business figures. Born **Haydock, Molly**

Reich /rīk, rī*kh*/ *n* the German state or empire, especially the Holy Roman Empire (926–1806) or First Reich, the German Empire (1871–1919) or Second Reich, or the Nazi state (1933–45) or Third Reich [Early 20C. < German, 'kingdom, state, empire']

Reich /rīk/, **Steve** (*b.* 1936) US composer in minimalist style whose music has a strong steady pulse and short repeating melodic figures

reichsmark /rīks maark, rī*kh*s-/ (*plural same* or **-marks**), **Reichsmark** *n* the basic unit of German currency from 1923 to 1948 [Mid-20C. < German < *Reich* 'kingdom, state, empire' + *Mark* 'mark (currency)']

Reichstag /rīks taag, rī*kh*s-/ *n* **1.** HIST GERMAN LEGISLATIVE ASSEMBLY 1867–1919 the legislative assembly of both the North German Confederation, from 1867 to 1871, and the German Empire, from 1871 to 1919 **2.** HIST LEGISLATIVE ASSEMBLY OF WEIMAR REPUBLIC the sovereign legislative assembly of the Weimar Republic, from 1919 to 1933 **3.** PARLIAMENT BUILDING IN BERLIN the building in Berlin in which the Reichstag formerly met, destroyed by fire in 1933, and now rebuilt to house the parliament of the reunified German federal state [Mid-19C. < German < *Reich* 'kingdom, state, empire' + *Tag* 'diet, legislative assembly']

Reid /reed/, **Sir George** (1845–1918) Scottish-born prime minister of Australia (1904–05). After his premiership, he was appointed the first High Commissioner of Australia (1910–16) before being elected to the House of Commons in 1916. He thus became the only Australian to have held a seat in the Colonial, Commonwealth, and Westminster parliaments. See table at **prime minister**. Full name **Reid, Sir George Houston**

reify /rée i fī/ (**-fies, -fying, -fied**) *vt* to think of or treat something abstract as if it existed as a real and tangible object [Mid-19C. Coined from Latin *re-* (stem of *res* 'thing') + -FY] —**reification** /rée ifi káysh'n/ *n* —**reificatory** /rée ifi káytəri/ *adj* —**reifier** *n*

Reigate /rīg ayt/ market town in Surrey, southeastern England. Population: 64,589 (1991).

reign /rayn/ *n* **1.** PERIOD OF RULE the period of time during which somebody, especially a king or queen, rules a nation **2.** CONTROL OR INFLUENCE the fact of being the dominant or controlling power or factor in something, or the period of time during which this dominance persists ■ *vi* (**reigns, reigning, reigned**) **1.** RULE NATION to exercise sovereign power or a controlling influence over something, especially to rule a country as its king or queen **2.** BE TITULAR SOVEREIGN to hold a royal title and be head of state while possessing only limited powers, as in a constitutional monarchy **3.** BE MOST IMPORTANT FEATURE to be the main or most noticeable feature of a situation, place, or period of time ○ *For a while, silence reigned.* [13C. Via Old French *reignier* from Latin *regnare* 'to be king', from *regnum* 'kingship']

SPELLCHECK See *rain*.

---

reign of terror *n* a time when systematic violence is used by a government, person, or group to intimidate other people and obtain or maintain dominance over them

Reign of Terror *n* the period of the French Revolution between September 1793 and July 1794, during which thousands of people were executed as enemies of the revolution

reiki /ráy ki/ *n* in alternative medicine, a treatment in which healing energy is channelled from the practitioner to the patient to enhance energy and reduce stress, pain, and fatigue [Late 20C. < Japanese, 'universal life force energy']

reimagine /rée i májjin/ (**-ines, -ining, -ined**) *vt* **1.** to recreate something, or plan to recreate something, in a fundamentally different way ○ *to reimagine the Shakespearean corpus for television* **2.** to create a new and improved image or lifestyle for yourself

reimburse /rée im búrss/ (**-burses, -bursing, -bursed**) *vt* to pay somebody back money spent for an official or approved reason or taken as a loan, or give somebody money as compensation for loss or damage [Early 17C. Formed from obsolete *imburse* 'to pay, put in a purse', ultimately from Old French *borse* 'purse', from medieval Latin *bursa* (source of English *purse*)] —**reimbursable** *adj* —**reimbursement** *n* —**reimburser** *n*

reimpression /rée im présh'n/ *n* a reprint of a book without any changes in the text

Reims /reemz/, **Rheims** city in Marne Department, Champagne-Ardenne Region, northeastern France. It is home to the 13th-century Cathedral of Notre Dame where the coronations of most of the French kings took place. Population: 187,206 (1999).

rein /rayn/ *n* (*often used in the plural*) **1.** STRAP FOR CONTROLLING HORSE a strap, or each half of a strap, by which a horse is controlled by its rider or by the driver of a coach or cart it is pulling **2.** EXERCISE OF POWER any means of guiding, controlling, or restraining somebody or something ■ **reins** *npl* STRAP FOR GUIDING CHILD a harness that fits around the body of a very young child, with straps attached by means of which the child can be controlled and guided, especially when walking out ■ *vt* (**reins, reining, reined**) CONTROL SOMEBODY OR SOMETHING to guide, control, or restrain somebody or something [13C. < Old French *rene, resne*] —**reinless** *adj* ◇ **give (free) rein to somebody** *or* **something** to allow somebody or something complete freedom, imposing no restraints or limitations ◇ **have** *or* **keep a (tight) rein on somebody** *or* **something** to maintain strict control over somebody or something ◇ **take (up) the reins** to take charge of something or somebody ○ *The new team coach will take the reins next week.*

SPELLCHECK See *rain*.

---

rein back *vt* to subject something or somebody to stricter control, often to reduce the amount of something or restrict somebody's freedom of action

rein in *v* **1.** *vti* to make a horse stop or slow down by pulling on the reins **2.** *vt* to bring somebody or something under control

reincarnate *vt* /ree ín kaar nayt, rée in káar-/ (**-nates, -nating, -nated**) **1.** GIVE SOMEBODY NEW BIRTH in some systems of belief, to return to live another life in a different body (*often passive*) **2.** PUT SOMETHING INTO NEW FORM to present something again in a new form after it has been abandoned or discontinued ■ *adj* /rée in káarnət, -nayt/ **1.** REBORN in some systems of belief, living again in a new body after death **2.** REPACKAGED embodied or presented in a new form

reincarnation /rée in kaar náysh'n/ *n* **1.** RELIG REBIRTH OF SOUL in some systems of belief, the cyclic return of a soul to live another life in a new body **2.** RELIG BODY IN WHICH SOMEBODY IS REBORN in some systems of belief, a person or animal in whose body somebody's soul is born again after he, she, or it has died **3.** APPEARANCE IN NEW GUISE a reappearance of something in a new form —**reincarnationism** *n* —**reincarnationist** *n*

reindeer /ráyn deer/ (*plural same* or **-deers**) *n* a large deer with large branched antlers in both males and females. Native to: northern and Arctic regions. Latin name: *Rangifer tarandus*. [14C. < Old Norse *hreinn* 'reindeer' + *dýr* 'animal']

Reindeer Lake /ráyn deer-/ lake in Canada, on the Saskatchewan-Manitoba border, discharging into the Reindeer River. Area: 6,390 sq. km/2,467 sq. mi.

reindeer moss, **reindeer lichen** *n* a grey lichen that grows in large erect branching tufts and provides food for reindeer and other animals. Native to: subarctic and Arctic regions. Latin name: *Cladonia rangiferia*.

reindustrialize /rée in dústri ə līz/ (**-izes, -izing, -ized**), **reindustrialise** (**-ises, -ising, -ised**) *vti* to undergo a process of renewal, usually involving government help in the modernization of factories and equipment, or subject an industry or industrial society to such a process —**reindustrialization** /rée in dustri ə lī záysh'n/ *n*

reinforce /rée in fáwrss/ (**-forces, -forcing, -forced**) *vt* **1.** STRENGTHEN SOMETHING to make something stronger by providing additional external support or internal stiffening for it **2.** GIVE SOMETHING SUPPORT to give additional strength, force, or conviction to something such as an idea, opinion, or feeling, e.g. by providing further evidence to support it **3.** STRENGTHEN MILITARY FORCE to make a military force stronger by providing it with more troops or weapons **4.** PSYCHOL INFLUENCE BEHAVIOUR BY REWARD OR PUNISHMENT to reward an action or type of behaviour to increase the probability that it will be repeated or punish an action in order to discourage it [15C. Formed from ENFORCE, probably on the model of Italian *rinforzare*] —**reinforceable** *adj*

reinforced concrete /rée in fawrst-/ *n* concrete made with metal wire or rods embedded in it to increase its strength

reinforced plastic *n* plastic with carbon or similar fibres embedded in it to make it stronger

reinforcement /rée in fáwrssmənt/ *n* **1. ADDED SUPPORT** the addition of strengthening or supporting material to make something stronger or more durable **2. SOMETHING ADDED TO INCREASE STRENGTH** something that is added to strengthen or support something else **3.** PSYCHOL **REWARD OR PUNISHMENT** the rewarding (**positive reinforcement**) or punishing (**negative reinforcement**) of actions, especially in an experimental situation, for the purpose of changing a subject's behaviour ■ **reinforcements** *npl* **ADDITIONAL TROOPS OR WEAPONS** additional troops, police, or weapons provided to make an existing force stronger

reinforcer /rée in fáwrssər/ *n* in behavioural psychology, a reward or stimulus used to encourage an action in order to increase the probability that it will be repeated

Reinga, Cape /ri ángə/ cape at the northwestern tip of the North Island, New Zealand. In Maori folklore, it is the departure point for the souls of the dead returning to the spiritual homeland of Hawaiki.

Reinhardt /rín haart/, **Django** (1910–53) Belgian musician. He is generally regarded as the finest jazz guitarist of all time. He often performed with Stephane Grappelli. Born **Reinhardt, Jean-Baptiste**

Reinhardt, Max (1873–1943) Austrian-born US theatre director. His productions were known for their elaborate settings and costumes and highly disciplined actors. He founded a music and dance festival in Salzburg, Austria. Born **Goldmann, Max**

reinsman /ráynzmən/ (*plural* **-men** /-mən/) *n ANZ* a man who is highly skilled as a jockey or as the driver of a gig in trotting races

reinstate /rée in stáyt/ (**-states, -stating, -stated**) *vt* **1.** to give somebody back a job or position of influence that he or she once had and from which he or she was dismissed or deposed **2.** to bring something back into use or force again after it has been out of use —**reinstatement** *n* —**reinstator** *n*

reinsure /rée in shóor, -sháwr/ (**-sures, -suring, -sured**) *vt* to insure something again, especially to obtain, as an insurer, additional cover from another insurer for a risk that a customer has been insured against —**reinsurance** *n* —**reinsurer** *n*

reinswoman /ráynz wŏomən/ (*plural* **-women** /-wimin/) *n ANZ* a woman who is highly skilled as a horsewoman or as the driver of a gig in trotting races

reinvent /rée in vént/ (**-vents, -venting, -vented**) *vt* **1.** to invent something again, or bring something back into existence, use, or popularity after a period of neglect or obscurity **2.** to change radically the appearance, form, or presentation of something or somebody —**reinvention** *n*

reinvest /rée in vést/ (**-vests, -vesting, -vested**) *vti* **1.** to invest money again, especially to buy more shares with the income made on a previous investment **2.** to put income back into a business instead of distributing it as profit —**reinvestment** *n*

reis MONEY plural of **real**[3]

reiterate /ree ítti rayt/ (**-ates, -ating, -ated**) *vt* ⚠ to say or do something again, once or several times, sometimes in a tiresome way —**reiterant** *adj* —**reiteration** /ree íttə ráysh'n/ *n* —**reiterative** /-rətiv, -raytiv/ *adj* —**reiteratively** *adv*

USAGE The use of *again*, *once more*, *yet again*, and other such expressions with ***reiterate***, whose meaning includes the sense of 'again', is unnecessary and to be avoided.

Reiter's syndrome /rítərz-/, **Reiter's disease** *n* a disease that begins as an infection in genetically predisposed people and is characterized by recurring bouts of arthritis, conjunctivitis, and urethritis [Early 20C. Named after Hans *Reiter* (1881–1969), German bacteriologist]

Reith /reeth/, **John, 1st Baron** (1889–1971) British broadcasting executive. He was the first general manager (1922–27) and director (1927–38) of the BBC. Full name **Reith, John Charles Walsham**

reject *vt* /ri jékt/ (**-jects, -jecting, -jected**) **1. NOT ACCEPT SOMETHING** to refuse to accept, agree to, believe in, or make use of something, e.g. because it is not good enough or not the right thing **2. TURN SOMEBODY DOWN** to decide not to give somebody something asked or applied for such as a job or membership of an organization **3. BE UNKIND TO SOMEBODY** to behave in an unkind and unfriendly way towards somebody who expects or has a right to expect love, kindness, and friendship **4. NOT KEEP SOMETHING** to put something aside or throw it away ○ *rejected the faulty disk* **5.** MED **NOT ACCEPT TRANSPLANT** to fail to accept foreign tissue or an organ transplant because of immunological incompatibility **6.** MED **BRING UP FOOD** to be unable to keep food down and vomit it up again ■ *n* /rée jekt/ **SOMETHING OR SOMEBODY NOT WANTED** somebody or something that is refused as not meeting a required standard or is otherwise unsuitable [15C. < Latin *reject-*, past participle of *rejicere* 'throw back' < *jacere* 'throw'] —**rejectable** *adj* —**rejecter** *n* —**rejective** *adj* —**rejector** *n*

rejection /ri jéksh'n/ *n* **1.** the rejecting of something or somebody, or the fact of being rejected **2.** the destruction by immune mechanisms of transplanted tissue or a transplanted organ from another individual

rejectionist /ri jéksh'nist/ *n* somebody who refuses to accept a policy, proposal, or plan that others have agreed to

rejection slip *n* an official note stating that something has been rejected such as a book submitted to a publisher or a painting submitted for exhibition

rejig /ree jíg/ (**-jigs, -jigging, -jigged**) *vt* **1.** *UK, ANZ, Can* to alter, rearrange, or readjust something, or set it up differently, sometimes with the intention of deceiving a purchaser or user (*informal*) US term **rejigger 2.** to re-equip a factory so that it can do a different kind of work

rejigger /ree jíggər/ (**-gers, -gering, -gered**) *vt US* same as **rejig** (sense 1) (*informal*)

rejoice /ri jóyss/ (**-joices, -joicing, -joiced**) *v* **1.** *vi* to feel very happy or show great happiness about something (*literary*) **2.** *vt* to fill somebody with happiness (*archaic*) [14C. Via Old French *rejoir* 'to be most joyful' from, ultimately, Latin *gaudere* 'to rejoice' (source of English *joy*)] —**rejoicer** *n* —**rejoicing** *n* —**rejoicingly** *adv*

rejoice in *vt* to be lucky enough to have or own something (*often used ironically*) ○ *They rejoice in their good health.*

rejoin[1] /ree jóyn/ (**-joins, -joining, -joined**) *vti* **1. RETURN TO SOMEBODY AFTER BEING APART** to meet up again with somebody, or go back to somebody or something, after a usually brief period of being away or apart **2. BECOME MEMBER AGAIN** to become a member again of an organization or group that you formerly belonged to **3. JOIN TOGETHER AGAIN** to join two things together again, or become joined together or merged with something again [Mid-16C. < RE- + JOIN]

rejoin[2] /ri jóyn/ (**-joins, -joining, -joined**) *v* **1.** *vti* to say something in reply, especially to reply with a sharp, critical, angry, defensive, or clever remark (*formal*) **2.** *vi* in law, to respond to a plaintiff's reply or replication [15C. < French *rejoign-*, stem of *rejoindre* 'join again' < *joindre* (see JOIN)]

rejoinder /ri jóyndər/ *n* **1.** a reply to something said, especially one that is sharp, critical, angry, defensive, or clever (*formal*) **2.** in law, the answer that a defendant makes during pleading to the plaintiff's reply or replication [15C. Via Anglo-Norman from Old French (see REJOIN[2])]

SYNONYMS See ***answer***.

rejuvenate /ri jóovi nayt/ (**-nates, -nating, -nated**) *vt* **1. MAKE SOMEBODY YOUNG AGAIN** to make somebody become, feel, or appear young again **2. RETURN SOMETHING TO ORIGINAL CONDITION** to restore something to its condition when new, or make it more vigorous, dynamic, and effective **3.** GEOL **CAUSE RIVER TO ERODE MORE** to cause a river to start eroding the land it runs over again, usually as a result of the land being uplifted **4.** GEOL **MAKE AREA DEVELOP TOPOGRAPHICALLY YOUNG FEATURES** to cause the redevelopment of younger, more rugged topographical features in a landscape through increased erosion [Early 19C. < RE- + Latin *juvenis* 'young'] —**rejuvenation** /ri jóovi náysh'n/ *n* —**rejuvenative** *adj* —**rejuvenator** *n*

rejuvenesce /ri jóovə néss/ (**-nesces, -nescing, -nesced**) *vti* to become young again, or make somebody feel or look young again (*formal*) [Late 19C. < late Latin *rejuvenescere* < Latin *juvenis* 'young'] —**rejuvenescence** *n* —**rejuvenescent** *adj*

rekey /ree kée/ (**-keys, -keying, -keyed**) *vt* to re-enter lost text or data into a computer, or input text or data in a different form, using a keyboard

rekindle /ree kínd'l/ (**-dles, -dling, -dled**) *vt* **1.** to revive or renew something such as a feeling or interest **2.** to set a fire burning again

rel. *abbr* **1.** relating **2.** GRAM relative **3.** relatively **4.** released **5.** religion **6.** religious

relapse *vi* /ri láps/ (**-lapses, -lapsing, -lapsed**) **1. GO INTO FORMER STATE** to fall back into a former mood, state, or way of life, especially a bad or undesirable one, after coming out of it for a while **2.** MED **BECOME ILL AFTER APPARENT RECOVERY** to become ill again after seeming to have made a recovery ■ *n* /ri láps, rée laps/ **1. ACT OF RETURNING TO PREVIOUS CONDITION** a return to a former mood, state, or way of life, especially a bad or undesirable one, after coming out of it for a while **2.** MED **WORSENING OF HEALTH** a sudden worsening in the condition of a patient who was ill but who seemed to have made a recovery from the illness [15C. < Latin *relaps-*, past participle of *relabi* 'slip again' < *labi* 'to slip'] —**relapser** *n*

relapsing fever /ri lápsing-/ *n* an infectious disease, characterized by chills and recurring fever, caused by a bacterium transmitted to people by ticks and lice

relate /ri láyt/ (**-lates, -lating, -lated**) *v* **1.** *vi* **HAVE CONNECTION WITH SOMETHING** to have a significant connection with or bearing on something ○ *How does this story relate to our conversation?* **2.** *vt* **CONNECT PEOPLE OR THINGS** to find or show a connection between two or more people or things **3.** *vi* **BE RELEVANT SPECIFICALLY** to concern, involve, or apply to somebody or something specifically ○ *These regulations relate only to imported goods.* **4.** ⚠ *vi* **FORM FRIENDLY ASSOCIATION** to have a friendly relationship with or friendly feelings towards somebody, based on an understanding of the person or on shared views or concerns **5.** *vi* **RESPOND TO SOMEBODY OR SOMETHING** to understand and respond favourably to something, or feel that it has a personal meaning or relevance (*informal*) ○ *I just can't seem to relate to the cynicism of that generation.* **6.** *vt* **TELL OR DESCRIBE SOMETHING** to tell a story or describe an event ○ *related a tale of sorrow* [15C. < French *relater* 'to report' < Latin *relat-*, past participle of *referre* 'carry back' < *ferre* 'carry'] —**relatable** *adj* —**relater** *n*

USAGE The use of ***relate*** without a prepositional phrase in the context of personal dealings between people is much used in the language of sociology but in general use is sometimes regarded as jargon, as in *Children who find it hard to relate tend to be inadequately socialized.* A clearer way to express this would be *Children who find it hard to relate to their peers....*

related /ri láytid/ *adj* **1. ASSOCIATED** connected by similarities or a common source **2. BELONGING TO SAME FAMILY** belonging to the same family by birth or through adoption or marriage **3.** MUSIC **HAVING CLOSE HARMONIC CONNECTION** describes a musical key or chord that, harmonically speaking, is closely connected with another, e.g. by having particular notes in common with it —**relatedly** *adv* —**relatedness** *n*

relation /ri láysh'n/ *n* **1. CONNECTION BETWEEN THINGS** a meaningful connection or association between two or more things, e.g. one based on the similarity or relevance of one thing to another **2. MEMBER OF FAMILY** a member of the same family as somebody else, by birth or through adoption or marriage **3. CONNECTION BY FAMILY** connection by birth, adoption, or marriage **4. NARRATION** the narration of a story or description of something that has happened, or what is conveyed in the narration or description (*formal*) **5.** LAW **TAKING OF SOMETHING AS DONE EARLIER** a procedure whereby an act done at a later time is, for legal purposes, deemed to have been done at an earlier

time **6.** LOGIC, MATHS **SHARED PROPERTY OF ASSOCIATION** a property of association, e.g. 'greater than' or 'less than', shared by ordered pairs of terms or objects ■ **relations** *npl* **1. CONTACTS BETWEEN GROUPS OR PEOPLE** contacts or dealings between two or more people or groups **2. SEXUAL ACTS** sexual activities between people (*euphemistic*) [14C. Directly or via French < Latin *relation-* < *relat-* (see RELATE)] ◇ **in** *or* **with relation to** with reference or regard to, or in comparison with something

relational /ri láysh'nəl/ *adj* **1. INVOLVING RELATIONSHIP** involving or expressing a relationship **2.** GRAM **CONVEYING SYNTACTIC RELATION** expressing or relating to a syntactic relation between elements in a phrase or sentence ○ *Prepositions are relational words.* **3.** COMPUT **OF ORGANIZATION OF DATABASE** describes a way of organizing and presenting information in a database so that the user perceives it as a set of tables —**relationally** *adv*

relational grammar *n* a theory of descriptive grammar in which syntactic relationships such as subject and object are used to define grammatical processes rather than syntactic structures

relationship /ri láysh'nship/ *n* **1. CONNECTION** a significant connection or similarity between two or more things, or the state of being related to something else **2. BEHAVIOUR OR FEELINGS TOWARDS SOMEBODY ELSE** the connection between two or more people or groups and their involvement with one another, especially as regards the way they behave towards and feel about one another **3. FRIENDSHIP** an emotionally close friendship, especially one involving sexual activity **4. CONNECTION BY FAMILY** the way in which two or more people are related by birth, adoption, or marriage, or the fact of being related by birth, adoption, or marriage **5.** LOGIC, MATHS same as **relation** (sense 6)

relative /réllətiv/ *adj* **1. COMPARATIVE** measured or considered in comparison with each other or with something else ○ *discussing the relative merits of various methods of transport* **2. CHANGING WITH CIRCUMSTANCES** not permanently fixed, but having a meaning or value that can only be established in relation to something else and will change according to circumstances or context ○ *'Big' and 'small' are relative terms.* **3. DEPENDENT ON SOMETHING** depending on or in proportion to something else **4. CONNECTED WITH SOMETHING** connected with or referring to something **5.** GRAM **REFERRING TO PREVIOUSLY USED WORD** used to describe words or clauses that refer to a word previously used in the same sentence **6.** MUSIC **HAVING IDENTICAL KEY SIGNATURES** describes a musical key that has the same key signature as another, usually a minor key with the same sharps and flats as a major key, or vice versa ■ *n* **1. MEMBER OF FAMILY** a member of the same family by birth, marriage, or adoption **2.** BIOL **THING RELATED TO SOMETHING ELSE** one thing that is related to something else, especially a species that has developed from the same origin as another species **3.** GRAM **RELATIVE WORD** a relative word, especially a relative pronoun, or a relative clause —**relativeness** *n*

relative atomic mass *n* the ratio of the average mass per atom of an element to one twelfth of the mass of a carbon-12 atom. Symbol A_r

relative clause *n* a clause that refers to and provides additional information about a preceding noun or pronoun, often beginning with a relative pronoun such as 'who', 'which', or 'that'

relative density *n* the ratio of the density of a substance to the density of a standard substance at the same temperature and pressure. For liquids and solids the standard substance is usually water, for gases, air. Symbol **d**

relative humidity *n* the ratio of the amount of water vapour in the air at a given temperature to the maximum amount air can hold at the same temperature, expressed as a percentage

relatively /rélləttivli/ *adv* in comparison with other things ○ *a relatively cool day, given the summer weather*

relative molecular mass *n* same as **molecular weight** (*technical*) Symbol M_r

relative permittivity *n* a measure of the resistance of a substance to an applied electric field equivalent to the ratio of the permittivity of a substance divided by that of free space. Symbol υ_r

relative pitch *n* **1.** the pitch of a tone, determined by its position in a scale with respect to other tones **2.** the ability to identify or produce a tone by mentally comparing it to another tone recently heard

relative pronoun *n* a pronoun that refers to a previously used noun and introduces a relative clause, e.g. 'that', 'which', or 'who'

relativise *vti* another spelling of **relativize**

relativism /rélləttivizəm/ *n* the belief that concepts such as right and wrong, goodness and badness, or truth and falsehood are not absolute but change from culture to culture and situation to situation —**relativist** *n*

relativistic /rélləti vístik/ *adj* **1.** PHYS **MOVING CLOSE TO SPEED OF LIGHT** moving at a velocity approaching the speed of light, the point at which properties such as mass act in accordance with the theory of relativity **2.** PHYS **RELATING TO RELATIVITY** relating to or characterized by relativity **3.** PHILOSOPHY **RELATING TO RELATIVISM** involving or characterized by relativism —**relativistically** *adv*

relativity /rélla tívvəti/ *n* **1.** PHYS **EQUIVALENCE OF MASS AND ENERGY** the first of two theories describing the relationship of matter, time, and space, showing that mass and energy are equivalent, and that mass, length, and time change with velocity. The theory is based on two assumptions: that the speed of light in a vacuum is constant, and that physical laws have the same mathematical form throughout the universe. **2.** PHYS **THEORY OF GRAVITATION AND ACCELERATION** the second of two theories describing the relationship of matter, time, and space, extending the principles of the first to gravitation and phenomena related to acceleration **3.** PHILOSOPHY **DEPENDENCE ON CONTEXTUALLY VARIABLE FACTOR** dependence on a factor that varies according to context **4. FACT OF BEING RELATIVE** the fact or state of being relative to something else

relativize /rélləti vīz/ (**-izes, -izing, -ized**), **relativise** (**-ises, -ising, -ised**) *vti* to make one thing relative to something else, or regard one thing as relative to something else

relator /ri láytər/ *n* **1.** somebody who tells a story or gives an account of something **2.** somebody who provides information used by the attorney general to bring a court action

relax /ri láks/ (**-laxes, -laxing, -laxed**) *v* **1.** *vi* **SPEND TIME DOING SOMETHING ENJOYABLE** to spend time resting or doing things for pleasure, especially in contrast to or as a relief from the effort and stress of everyday life **2.** *vti* **MAKE OR BECOME LOOSER** to slacken something that is tensed or tight such as a muscle or a grip on something, or become looser, less tense, or less tight **3.** *vti* **MAKE OR BECOME LESS STRICT** to make something such as a rule less strict or less severe, or become less strict **4.** *vti* **MAKE OR BECOME LESS TENSE** to become less anxious, hostile, defensive, or formal, or make somebody or something so **5.** *vti* **MAKE OR BECOME LESS INTENSE** to become less intense and concentrated, or make something less intense and concentrated **6.** *vt* **STRAIGHTEN HAIR** to weaken or remove the curl from hair, usually by chemical means [14C. < Latin *relaxare* 'loosen' < *laxus* 'loose'] —**relaxable** *adj* —**relaxer** *n* —**relaxing** *adj*

relaxant /ri láks'nt/ *n* a drug that reduces tension and strain, particularly in muscles ■ *adj* causing something such as a muscle to become less tense

relaxation /reé lak sáysh'n/ *n* **1. ENJOYABLE ACTIVITY** a form of activity that provides a change and relief from effort, work, or tension, and gives pleasure **2. LOOSENING PROCESS** the process of becoming or making something less firm, rigid, or tight **3. LESSENING OF SEVERITY** a lessening of the strictness or severity of regulations, restrictions, or controls **4. REDUCTION IN INTENSITY** a lessening or weakening of something that was previously concentrated or intense **5.** PHYS **RETURN OF SYSTEM TO EQUILIBRIUM** the return of a system to equilibrium after it has been displaced or changed **6.** MATHS **WAY OF SOLVING EQUATIONS** a way of solving equations using a series of approximate solutions, each of which reduces the number of errors contained in the previous one, until the errors fall within acceptable limits

relaxed /ri lákst/ *adj* **1. EXPERIENCING NO STRAIN OR TENSION** under no strain or tension, and not exerting much strain or force on anything else **2. NOT FEELING ANXIOUS OR WORRIED** feeling no anxiety, tension, pressure, or sense of threat **3. ENCOURAGING INFORMALITY** encouraging informality and casual unhurried behaviour —**relaxedly** /ri láksidli/ *adv* —**relaxedness** *n*

relaxin /ri láksin/ *n* a polypeptide hormone that relaxes the pelvic ligaments of female mammals during pregnancy and is produced by the corpus luteum

relay *n* /reé lay/ **1. PASSING OF SOMETHING TO SOMEBODY** the passing on of something, especially a message or information received, to somebody else, or the process of being passed on **2. REPLACEMENT TEAM** one of two or more teams of people or animals that relieve or replace each other in turn, e.g. as the previous team tires **3.** SPORTS same as **relay race** (*informal*) **4.** SPORTS **SECTION OF RELAY RACE** a section or lap of a relay race, run or swum by an individual athlete **5.** ELECTRONICS **DEVICE THAT REGULATES ANOTHER** an electronic or electromechanical switching device, typically operated by a low voltage, that controls a higher-voltage circuit and switches it on or off **6.** TELECOM **APPARATUS THAT RECEIVES AND TRANSMITS SIGNALS** an apparatus consisting of a receiver and a transmitter, used to receive and retransmit signals **7.** TELECOM **SIGNAL** a message or broadcast passed on by an apparatus that receives and retransmits signals ■ *vt* /ri láy/ (**-lays, -laying, -layed**) **1. PASS SOMETHING ON TO SOMEBODY** to pass information or a message on to somebody **2. REPLACE TEAM WITH FRESH PEOPLE** to replace or relieve a team, squad, or crew with a new one **3. ARRANGE PEOPLE INTO TEAMS** to organize somebody or something, especially workers, into relays **4.** TELECOM **RETRANSMIT SIGNAL** to receive and retransmit a signal [14C. < Old French *relayer* 'exchange tired horses' < Latin *relaxare* 'loosen' (see RELAX)]

re-lay /ree láy/ *vt* to lay something such as a carpet again [Late 16C. < RE- + LAY[1]]

relay race *n* a race between teams of competitors in which each member of a team runs or swims only part of the total distance to be covered. In a running race, the current runner must pass a baton to the person running the next section.

release /ri leéss/ *vt* (**-leases, -leasing, -leased**) **1. LET SOMEBODY OR SOMETHING GO** to set free a person or animal who is imprisoned, trapped, or confined in some way **2. STOP CLUTCHING SOMETHING** to stop gripping or holding something **3. LET SOMETHING OUT** to let out something that has been contained or confined within something or that is pent up or latent inside somebody ○ *released a plume of smoke* **4. FREE SOMEBODY FROM OBLIGATION** to make somebody free of a debt, obligation, promise, or task **5. MAKE SOMETHING AVAILABLE** to make something available, e.g. by putting it on sale, distributing it to the press or public, or allowing access to it **6.** *US* **FIRE EMPLOYEE** to dismiss somebody from a job or position (*formal; used euphemistically*) **7.** ENG **OPERATE CATCH TO LET MECHANISM WORK** to take the tension off a mechanism such as a spring, brake, or catch and so allow something to move, open, or operate ○ *released the clutch* **8.** LAW **RELINQUISH SOMETHING** to relinquish something such as a right or claim to another party ■ *n* **1. LIBERATION** the act of setting somebody or something free, or the fact of being freed, from imprisonment, restraint, an obligation, or anything burdensome and oppressive **2. AUTHORIZATION FOR FREEDOM** a document or message stating that somebody is to be set free **3.** HR **LEAVE OF ABSENCE** leave of absence from a place, especially the workplace, or the granting of leave of absence, to enable somebody to do something else such as attend an educational course **4. EMISSION** the emission of something such as heat or radioactivity from the place where it is generated into the atmosphere or the environment **5. ACT OF MAKING SOMETHING AVAILABLE** the act of making something generally available or in use for the first time, or the fact of being made available in this way ○ *His latest film is expected to be on general release in the autumn.* **6. SOMETHING MADE AVAILABLE TO PUBLIC** something that is made available to the public, put on show, or put on sale, e.g. a film, recording, or item of information **7.** ENG **CONTROL MECHANISM** a mechanism, catch, or handle that is moved or pressed so that something it controls can be used or allowed to operate **8. OPERATING OF DEVICE**

the moving or pressing of a mechanism so that what it controls can be used or allowed to operate **9.** LAW **RELINQUISHING OF CLAIM TO SOMETHING** the relinquishment of a right or claim to another party **10.** LAW **DOCUMENT CONFIRMING SURRENDER OF SOMETHING** a document stating that somebody has surrendered something such as a claim or right [13C. Via Old French *relaisser* 'let go' < Latin *relaxare* 'loosen' (see RELAX)] —**releasability** /ri lèessə bílləti/ *n* —**releasable** *adj*—**releasably** *adv*—**releasee** /ri lèe sée/ *n*—**releaser** *n*

re-lease /ree léess/ *vt* to lease something such as a flat again [< RE- + LEASE]

released time /ri léest-/ *n* time given to somebody by an authority or manager to allow personal matters or interests to be attended to

release print *n* the version of a film released for distribution to commercial cinemas

releasing factor /ri léessing-/ *n* a hormone produced by the hypothalamus that causes the pituitary gland to secrete other hormones

relegate /rélli gayt/ (**-gates, -gating, -gated**) *vt* **1. DEMOTE SOMEBODY OR SOMETHING** to move somebody or something to a less important position, category, or status **2. TRANSFER TEAM TO LOWER DIVISION** to transfer a sports team from a higher to a lower division in a competition, usually because it is one of the least successful teams in the higher division (*often passive*) **3. EXILE SOMEBODY** to banish somebody from a country or community **4. HAND SOMETHING ON** to pass something on to somebody for that person to deal with it or provide information about it (*formal*) [15C. < Latin *relegat-*, past participle of *relegare* 'send away, refer' < *legare* 'send as an envoy, bequeath'] —**relegation** /rélli gáysh'n/ *n*

~~**releive**~~ incorrect spelling of **relieve**

relent /ri lént/ (**-lents, -lenting, -lented**) *vi* **1.** to become more sympathetic or amenable and do something previously ruled out or allow something previously forbidden **2.** to slacken or become less intense ○ *At last my headache relented.* [14C. < RE- + Latin *lentare* 'bend, soften' < *lentus* 'flexible']

relentless /ri léntləss/ *adj* **1.** never slackening, but continuing always at the same intense, demanding, or punishing level **2.** pursuing, attacking, or opposing somebody or something persistently and without mercy —**relentlessly** *adv*—**relentlessness** *n*

relevant /rélləvənt/ *adj* **1.** having some sensible or logical connection with something else such as a matter being discussed or investigated **2.** having some bearing on or importance for real-world issues, present-day events, or the current state of society **3.** LING same as **distinctive** (sense 2) [Early 16C. < medieval Latin *relevant-*, present participle of Latin *relevare* 'relieve', later 'take possession of'] —**relevance** *n*—**relevantly** *adv*

USAGE The misspelling and mispronunciation *revelant* for ***relevant*** is increasingly common and should be avoided.

~~**relevent**~~ incorrect spelling of **relevant**

reliable /ri lī́ əb'l/ *adj* **1.** able to be trusted to do what is expected or has been promised ○ *She is extremely reliable and a hard worker.* **2.** able to be trusted to be accurate or to provide a correct result ○ *That clock is not very reliable.* —**reliability** /ri lī́ ə bílləti/ *n*—**reliableness** *n*—**reliably** *adv*

reliance /ri lī́ ənss/ *n* **1. DEPENDENCE** dependence on another person or on something such as a service or a device, and the need for something that he, she, or it provides ○ *a reliance on painkillers* **2. CONFIDENCE** trust or confidence in the eventual fulfilment of a promise or in the eventual success of a plan **3. PRIMARY SUPPORT** somebody or something needed or depended on

reliant /ri lī́ ənt/ *adj* depending on or needing somebody or something —**reliantly** *adv*

relic /réllik/ *n* **1. OLD THING SURVIVING FROM PAST** something that has survived from a long time ago, often a part of something old that has remained when the rest of it has decayed or been destroyed **2. OLD CUSTOM** a tradition, practice, or rule that dates from some time in the past, especially one that is considered out of date or inappropriate at the present time **3. KEEPSAKE** something that is kept for its interesting associations, e.g. with somebody famous or with a historic event **4.** RELIG **SOMETHING FROM DECEASED HOLY PERSON** something that is kept and venerated because it once belonged to a saint, martyr, or religious leader, especially a part of his or her body [13C. Via Old French *relique* < Latin *reliquiae* 'remains' (particularly of a dead saint), plural of *reliquus* 'remaining']

relict /rèllikt/ *n* **1.** BIOL **SURVIVING SPECIES** a species of organism surviving long after the extinction of related species, or a once widespread natural population surviving only in isolated localities because of environmental changes **2.** GEOL **MINERAL UNALTERED BY METAMORPHISM** a mineral that did not change when the host rock metamorphosed **3.** GEOL **REMNANT OF PRE-EXISTING FORMATION** a remnant of a pre-existing land or rock formation left behind after a destructive event has taken place **4.** LAW same as **widow** *n* (sense 1) (*archaic*) ■ *adj* BIOL **SURVIVING UNCHANGED** surviving in its original form when other related organisms have become extinct or its environment has changed completely [15C. < Latin *relictus* 'left behind' < *relinquere* (see RELINQUISH)]

reliction /ri líksh'n/ *n* the gradual withdrawal of water from land, leaving it permanently dry

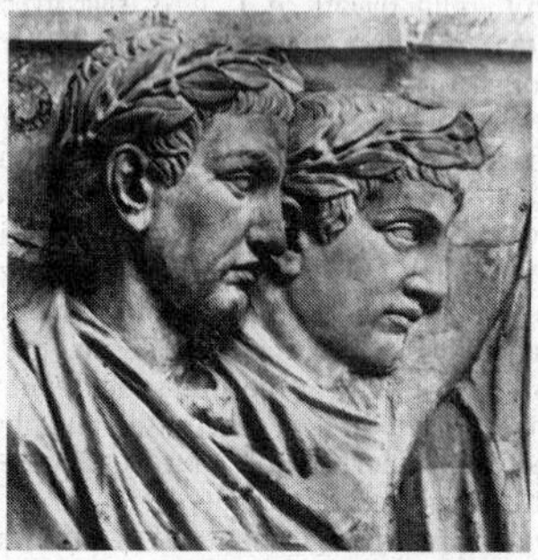

relief: 9th-century Roman relief sculpture

relief /ri léef/ *n* **1. FREEING OF SOMEBODY FROM ANXIETY** a release from anxiety or tension, or the feeling of release, lightness, and cheerfulness that accompanies this **2. FACTOR THAT ENDS ANXIETY** a factor that ends a painful or stressful experience such as pain, hunger, or boredom **3. STARK CONTRAST CREATING DIVERSION** a factor forming a contrast to the general character of something else, especially something that breaks the monotony or tension of a longer experience **4. PROMINENCE CAUSED BY CONTRAST** uniqueness or prominence caused by contrast ○ *to bring out the differences in clear relief* **5.** SOC WELFARE **AID TO THOSE IN NEED** public help in the form of money, food, clothing, shelter, or medicine, provided to people who are temporarily unable to care for themselves **6.** FIN **PAYMENT REDUCTION OR FINANCIAL HELP** a reduction somebody is entitled to in tax or other payments, or money given to him or her to help pay for something **7.** HR **REPLACEMENT** somebody who takes over a task or duty when another completes his or her spell of work, or somebody who replaces another who is unable to work **8.** TRANSP **EXTRA TRANSPORT** a train, bus, or other public transport vehicle that is brought in to provide extra places for passengers when the regular scheduled service is full **9.** ART, SCULPTURE **PROJECTION FROM SURFACE** the elevation of figures or shapes from a flat surface, as seen in sculpture, or their apparent elevation, as seen in painting **10.** SCULPTURE, ART **WORK OF ART** a work of art with figures or shapes in relief **11.** GEOG, MAPS **ELEVATIONS OF LAND** the variations in height of a land surface and its being shaped into hills and valleys **12.** PRINTING **PRINTING PROCESS** a printing process that uses raised surfaces to apply ink to the paper, e.g. engraving **13.** MIL **LIBERATION FROM SIEGE** the freeing of a besieged town, castle, fort, or strategic position by soldiers belonging to the same side as those under siege **14.** LAW **REDRESS AWARDED BY COURT** compensation or redress for a wrong or hardship, awarded to a party by a court **15.** HIST **PAYMENT TO FEUDAL LORD** a payment made to a feudal lord by the descendant of a tenant in order to inherit a fief [14C. < Old French < *relever* (see RELIEVE)]

relief map *n* a map that shows variations in land height, usually by means of contour lines or different colours

relief road *n* ROADS same as **bypass** *n* (sense 1)

relief teacher *n ANZ* same as **supply teacher**

relieve /ri léev/ (**-lieves, -lieving, -lieved**) *v* **1.** *vt* **STOP SOMETHING UNPLEASANT** to end, lessen, or provide a temporary break from something unpleasant such as pain, hunger, tension, or boredom **2.** *vt* **EASE SOMEBODY'S BURDEN** to remove something such as a burden or difficulty from the person on whom it is imposed ○ *They were relieved of responsibility for the children.* **3.** *vt* **REMOVE SOMETHING FROM SOMEBODY** to take something from somebody, usually something that the person is carrying or wearing ○ *Let me relieve you of your coat.* **4.** *vt* HR **REPLACE SOMEBODY** to replace somebody on a shift or at a job **5.** *vt* HR **FIRE EMPLOYEE** to dismiss or suspend somebody from a job or position (*formal*) ○ *After the collision, the skipper was relieved of command.* **6. relieve yourself** *vr* same as **urinate 7.** *vt* **MAKE SOMETHING PROMINENT** to make something stand out by contrast (*formal*) **8.** *vt* SOC WELFARE **HELP SOMEBODY** to provide help to people who are temporarily unable to care for themselves **9.** *vt* MIL **LIBERATE SOMETHING FROM MILITARY SIEGE** to liberate a besieged town, castle, fort, or strategic field position [14C. Via Old French *relever* < Latin *relevare* 'raise again, help', literally 'make light again' < *levis* 'light'] —**relievable** *adj*—**reliever** *n*

relievo /ri lèe vō/ (*plural* **-vos**), **rilievo** *n* ARTS same as **relief** (sense 9) [Early 17C. < Italian *rilievo* < *rilevare* 'to raise' < Latin *relevare* (see RELIEVE)]

relig. *abbr* religion

religion /ri líjjən/ *n* **1. BELIEFS AND WORSHIP** people's beliefs and opinions concerning the existence, nature, and worship of God, a god, or gods, and divine involvement in the universe and human life **2. SYSTEM** an institutionalized or personal system of beliefs and practices relating to the divine **3. PERSONAL BELIEFS OR VALUES** a set of strongly-held beliefs, values, and attitudes that somebody lives by **4. OBSESSION** an object, practice, cause, or activity that somebody is completely devoted to or obsessed by ○ *The danger is that you start to make fitness a religion.* **5.** CHR **MONK'S OR NUN'S LIFE** life as a monk or a nun, especially in the Roman Catholic Church [12C. Via French < Latin *religion-* 'obligation, reverence'] —**religionless** *adj* ◇ **get religion** (*informal*) **1.** to become a believer or join a religious organization, and, usually, start to lead a life that follows its teachings **2.** *US* to conform to the rules, regulations, customs, or expectations of somebody or something

religionism /ri líjjənizəm/ *n* religious enthusiasm when regarded as affected or excessive (*disapproving*) —**religionist** *n*

religiose /ri líjji ōss/ *adj* regarded as excessively, sentimentally, or affectedly pious (*disapproving*) [Mid-19C. < Latin *religiosus* (see RELIGIOUS)] —**religiosely** *adv*—**religiosity** /ri líjji óssəti/ *n*

religious /ri líjjəss/ *adj* **1. RELATING TO RELIGION** relating to belief in religion, the teaching of religion, or the practice of a religion ○ *religious freedom* **2. BELIEVING IN A HIGHER BEING** believing in and showing devotion or reverence for a deity or deities **3. THOROUGH** very thorough or conscientious ○ *a religious attention to detail* **4.** CHR **BELONGING TO MONASTIC ORDER** in Christianity, used to describe those who have committed themselves to a monastic order by taking vows, e.g. of poverty, chastity, or obedience ■ *n* (*plural same*) CHR **MONK OR NUN** a member of a monastic order [13C. Via French < Latin *religiosus* < *religio(n-)* 'obligation, reverence'] —**religiousness** *n*

religiously /ri líjjəssli/ *adv* **1.** carefully and conscientiously **2.** in a way that relates to religion or to a particular religion

Religious Society of Friends *n* CHR same as **Society of Friends**

~~**religous**~~ incorrect spelling of **religious**

relinquish /ri língkwish/ (**-quishes, -quishing, -quished**) *vt* **1. CEDE SOMETHING** to renounce or surrender something **2. ABANDON SOMETHING** to give something up or put something aside **3. LET SOMETHING GO** to let go of something physically [15C. < Old French *relinquiss-* < Latin *relinquere* 'leave behind' < *linquere* 'leave'] —**relinquisher** *n*—**relinquishment** *n*

reliquary: bust of reliquary of Charlemagne

reliquary /réllikwəri/ (*plural* **-ies**) *n* a container or shrine where relics such as the remains of a saint are kept [Mid-16C. < French *reliquaire* < *relique* (see RELIC)]

reliquiae /ri líkwi ee/ *npl* the remains of something, especially fossil remains of plants or animals [Mid-17C. < Latin (see RELIC)]

relish /réllish/ *vt* (**-ishes, -ishing, -ished**) **1.** ENJOY SOMETHING to enjoy or take great pleasure in an experience ○ *relished every minute of their trip* **2.** ENJOY EATING SOMETHING to enjoy the taste of a particular food or drink ■ *n* **1.** ENJOYMENT a liking or appreciation of food or of an experience ○ *a relish for adventure* **2.** SPICY SIDE DISH OR ACCOMPANIMENT a spiced side dish or accompaniment to food **3.** STRONG TASTE a pleasing sensation of strong taste or flavour **4.** INTEREST OR EXCITEMENT interest or excitement, especially when it makes something more enjoyable ○ *The incident added relish to an otherwise dull weekend.* [Early 16C. < Old French *relais* 'remainder' < *relaisser* (see RELEASE)] — **relishable** *adj*

relit past participle, past tense of **relight**

relive /ree lív/ (**-lives, -living, -lived**) *vt* to experience something again, especially as a result of thinking about it

~~rellevant~~ incorrect spelling of **relevant**

rellies /rélliz/ *npl* somebody's relatives (*informal*) ○ *We'll be seeing all the rellies again at Christmas.* [Late 20C. Shortening]

relocate /reé lō káyt/ (**-cates, -cating, -cated**) *vti* to move to a new place on a long-term basis, or move somebody or something such as personnel or a business to a new place —**relocation** /reé lō káysh'n/ *n*

reluctance /ri lúktənss/ *n* **1.** unwillingness or lack of enthusiasm **2.** a measure of the resistance of a closed magnetic circuit to a magnetic flux. It is equal to the ratio of the magnetic potential difference to the magnetic flux.

reluctant /ri lúktənt/ *adj* feeling or showing no willingness or enthusiasm to do something ○ *I am reluctant to drive in this weather.* [Mid-17C. < Latin *reluctant-*, present participle of *reluctari* 'struggle against' < *luctari* 'to struggle'] —**reluctantly** *adv*

USAGE See *reticent*.

SYNONYMS See *unwilling*.

relume /ri loóm/ (**-lumes, -luming, -lumed**), **relumine** /ri loómin/ (**-lumines, -lumining, -lumined**) *vt* to relight or rekindle something such as a light or flame [Early 17C. < RE- + *illume* 'illuminate', contraction of *illumine* < French *illuminer* < Latin *illuminare* (see ILLUMINATE)]

rely /ri lí/ (**-lies, -lying, -lied**) *vi* **1.** to be dependent on somebody or something **2.** to have faith or confidence in somebody or something [14C. Via Old French *relier* < Latin *religare* 'tie back' < *ligare* 'to bind']

rem /rem/ (*plural* same) *n* a unit for measuring amounts of radiation, equal to the effect that one roentgen of X-rays or gamma-rays would produce in a human being. It is used in radiation protection and monitoring. Full form **roentgen equivalent in man**

REM /rem, aár ee ém/ *abbr* MED rapid eye movement

remade past participle, past tense of **remake**

remain /ri máyn/ (**-mains, -maining, -mained**) *v* **1.** *vi* STAY BEHIND to stay behind or wait somewhere **2.** *vti* CONTINUE IN SPECIFIED CONDITION to continue in a particular state without changing **3.** *vi* BE LEFT to be left after everything else has gone **4.** *vi* REQUIRE MORE WORK to continue to need to be dealt with after everything else has been attended to ○ *The question still remains.* [14C. < Old French *remaindre, remanoir* < Latin *remanere* < *manere* 'to stay']

remainder /ri máyndər/ *n* **1.** PART OF SOMETHING LEFT the part of something that is left after other parts have gone or been used up **2.** MATHS AMOUNT LEFT OVER AFTER DIVISION the amount left over when a number or quantity cannot be divided exactly by another **3.** PUBL UNSOLD BOOKS the unsold copies of a book, sold by a publisher at a reduced price after demand has fallen off **4.** LAW INTEREST IN SOMEBODY ELSE'S ESTATE an interest in an estate that passes to somebody only after a prior interest terminates, e.g. when the current holder of the estate dies ■ *vt* (**-ders, -dering, -dered**) PUBL SELL BOOK AT REDUCED PRICE to sell copies of a book at a reduced price after demand has fallen off [14C. < Anglo-Norman, variant of Old French *remaindre* (see REMAIN)]

remainderman /ri máyndər man/ (*plural* **-men** /-men/) *n* the person who is entitled to an estate once everything has been resolved

remaining /ri máyning/ *adj* still left or still existing

remains /ri máynz/ *npl* **1.** ALL THAT IS LEFT all that is left of something ○ *the remains of the barn after the fire* **2.** CORPSE a dead body, or what is left of a body **3.** ANCIENT RUINS the parts of something old that are still left ○ *the remains of ancient Roman baths* **4.** DEAD AUTHOR'S UNPUBLISHED WRITINGS all of an author's work that was still unpublished at the time of the author's death

remake *n* /reé mayk/ something that has been made again or differently, especially a new version of an old film ■ *vt* /ree máyk/ (**-makes, -making, -made** /-máyd/) to produce a remake of something

remand /ri maánd/ *vt* (**-mands, -manding, -manded**) **1.** RETURN PRISONER TO CUSTODY to return a prisoner or accused person to custody, or arrange for somebody to be released on bail when a court case is adjourned ○ *The judge ordered the prisoner to be remanded in custody.* **2.** SEND SOMEBODY BACK to send or order somebody back ■ *n* RETURNING OF SOMEBODY UNTRIED TO PRISON the return of a prisoner or accused person to custody, or the arrangement of bail for somebody, while waiting for trial [15C. Via French < late Latin *remandare* 'send word back' < Latin *mandare* 'to command'] —**remandment** *n*

remand centre *n* in the United Kingdom and Canada, a place where accused people are detained while awaiting criminal trial

remand home *n* a remand centre for young offenders. US term **detention home**

remanence /rémmənənss/ *n* the magnetic inductance that remains in a substance after the magnetizing field has been removed [Mid-16C. < Latin *remanent-*, present participle of *remanere* (see REMAIN)] —**remanent** *adj*

remanent magnetism *n* magnetism shown by ferromagnetic minerals, which preserve the sense and direction of the Earth's magnetic field from the time of their formation

remark /ri maárk/ *n* **1.** CASUAL COMMENT a casual or brief observation **2.** ACT OF COMMENTING the act of making a remark about something, or an occasion on which this takes place ○ *They consumed their meal without remark.* **3.** ACT OF NOTICING an act or instance of noticing something, especially something that deserves attention (*formal*) ○ *How could such a major change take place without remark?* **4.** COMPUT same as **comment** *n* (sense 5) ■ *v* (**-marks, -marking, -marked**) **1.** *vti* MAKE COMMENT ON SOMETHING to make a casual comment or observation about something **2.** *vt* OBSERVE SOMETHING to notice or observe something (*formal*) ○ *remarked the complexity of the investigation* [Late 16C. < French *remarquer* < *marquer* 'to mark'] —**remarker** *n*

remarkable /ri maárkəb'l/ *adj* **1.** worth noticing or commenting on **2.** unusual or exceptional, and attracting attention because of this —**remarkableness** *n*

remarkably /ri maárkəbli/ *adv* **1.** to an extent or degree that is remarkable **2.** used to emphasize that something is worth noticing or commenting on ○ *Remarkably, no one was arrested.*

remarque /ri maárk/ *n* **1.** a mark in the margin of an engraved plate, made to indicate its stage of production and removed before final printing, or the plate with the mark itself **2.** a proof of an engraving made from a plate with a remarque [Late 19C. < French < *remarquer* (see REMARK)]

Remarque /ri maárk/, **Erich Maria** (1898–1970) German-born US writer. After he was wounded fighting for Germany in World War I, he wrote *All Quiet on the Western Front* (1929), which became a classic war novel. He lived in the United States after 1939. See Cultural note at **front**

'Monotonously…falls the rain. It falls on our heads and on the heads of the dead up the line, on the body of the little recruit with the wound that is much too big for his hip;…it falls in our hearts.'
[Erich Maria Remarque, *All Quiet on the Western Front*; 1929]

remaster /ree maástər/ (**-ters, -tering, -tered**) *vt* to make a new master copy of an earlier audio recording or film to improve its quality of reproduction

rematch *n* /ree mach/ a second or return contest between opponents ■ *vt* /ree mách, ree mach/ (**-matches, -matching, -matched**) to arrange for opponents to meet in a second or return contest

Rembrandt van Rijn

Rembrandt van Rijn /rém brant vaan rín/ (1606–69) Dutch artist. A major painter of the Dutch Golden Age, he imbued his portraits and religious and historical works with a moving spirituality. Full name **Rembrandt Harmenszoon van Rijn**

REME /ree mee/ *abbr* Royal Electrical and Mechanical Engineers

remedial /ri meédi əl/ *adj* **1.** ACTING AS REMEDY acting as a remedy or solution to a problem **2.** EDUC HELPING TO IMPROVE SKILLS designed to help people with learning difficulties to improve their skills or knowledge, or relating to education designed to do this **3.** MED INTENDED TO IMPROVE HEALTH intended to cure or relieve the symptoms of somebody who is ill or has a physical disability ○ *remedial exercises* —**remedially** *adv*

remediation /ri meédi áysh'n/ *n* the use of remedial methods to improve skills or reverse environmental damage ○ *soil remediation*

remedy /rémmədi/ *n* (*plural* **-dies**) **1.** WAY OF PUTTING SOMETHING RIGHT a means of putting something right or getting rid of something undesirable ○ *no easy remedy for society's ills* **2.** MED TREATMENT FOR DISEASE a medication or treatment that cures a disease or disorder or relieves its symptoms **3.** ALTERN MED HOMEOPATHIC TREATMENT a substance prescribed by a homeopath, and taken in minute quantities **4.** LAW LEGAL REDRESS a legal means of enforcing a right or of providing redress **5.** COINS PERMITTED VARIATION IN COINS the legally permitted variation from an established standard in the weight or quality of a coin ■ *vt* (**-dies, -dying, -died**) **1.** PUT SOMETHING RIGHT to put something right, or get rid of something undesirable **2.** MED CURE DISEASE to cure or relieve a disease or disorder [13C. Via Anglo-Norman *remedie* < Latin *remedium* 'medicine'] —**remediable** /ri meédi ab'l/ *adj* —**remediably** *adv*

remember /ri mémbər/ (**-bers, -bering, -bered**) *v* **1.** *vti*

RECALL SOMETHING FORGOTTEN to recall something to mind or become aware of something that had been forgotten **2.** *vti* **KEEP SOMETHING IN MEMORY** to retain an idea in the memory without forgetting it **3.** *vt* **KEEP SOMEBODY IN MIND** to keep somebody in mind for attention or consideration **4.** *vt* **GIVE SOMEBODY A GIFT** to give somebody a gift, money, or a tip ○ *She always remembered him on his birthday.* **5.** *vt* **SEND SOMEBODY'S GREETINGS** to mention somebody to somebody else as a way of passing on a greeting ○ *Remember me to your parents.* **6. remember yourself** *vr* **BECOME POLITE AGAIN** to resume behaving in a mannerly way after having briefly acted badly **7.** *vt* **COMMEMORATE SOMEBODY OR SOMETHING** to commemorate somebody or something, e.g. in a ceremony or funeral service [14C. Via Old French *remembrer* < late Latin *rememorari* < Latin *memor* 'mindful'] —**rememberer** *n*

remembrance /ri mémbrənss/ *n* **1. REMEMBERING** the act or process of remembering people, things, or events **2. BEING REMEMBERED** the state of being remembered, or of remaining in people's minds ○ *We hold her name in fond remembrance.* **3. ACT OF HONOURING** the act of honouring the memory of a person or event ○ *a service of remembrance* **4. SOMETHING REMEMBERED** something that is remembered **5. EXTENT OF MEMORY** the period of time over which memory extends **6. MEMENTO** something that reminds somebody of a thing, event, or another person **7. FRIENDLY EXPRESSION** a greeting, gift, or other expression of affection and friendship

CULTURAL NOTE ***Remembrance of Things Past***, a series of novels (1913–22) by French writer Marcel Proust. Regarded as one of the greatest works of 20th-century literature, this remarkable meditation on time and memory describes the narrator's childhood encounters with his aristocratic neighbours and his subsequent introduction to Parisian society. A series of unconscious recollections triggers the realization that the past is not lost but can be retrieved by memory and preserved as art.

Remembrance Day *n Can* in Canada, a public holiday in remembrance of those who died in World Wars I and II and subsequent conflicts. Date: 11 November.

remembrancer /ri mémbrənssər/ *n* somebody who reminds somebody else about something (*archaic*)

Remembrancer *n* **1.** a British official of the Exchequer, the Queen's or King's Remembrancer, who collects debts owed to the Crown **2.** an official appointed by the Corporation of the City of London, the City Remembrancer, to represent its interests

Remembrance Sunday *n* the Sunday nearest to 11 November (**Armistice Day**), on which those who died in World Wars I and II and subsequent conflicts are remembered, especially in church

remex /reé meks/ (*plural* **remiges** /rémmi jeez/) *n* a flight feather of a bird's wing (*technical*) [Late 17C. < Latin, 'oarsman' < *remus* 'oar'] —**remigial** /ri míjji əl/ *adj*

remind /ri mínd/ (**-minds, -minding, -minded**) *vt* to cause somebody to remember or think of something or somebody else ○ *Remind me to collect the dry cleaning.* ○ *He reminds me of his grandfather.*

reminder /ri míndər/ *n* **1.** a letter or message sent to remind somebody about something ○ *If they don't settle the bill next week, send them a reminder.* **2.** somebody or something that reminds a person or people of somebody or something else ○ *The monument is a reminder of their bravery.*

~~reminice~~ incorrect spelling of **reminisce**

reminisce /rémmi níss/ (**-nisces, -niscing, -nisced**) *vi* to talk or write about events remembered from the past [Early 19C. Back-formation < REMINISCENCE] —**reminiscer** *n*

reminiscence /rémmi níss'nss/ *n* **1. RECOLLECTION OF PAST** the recollection of past experiences or events in speech or writing, or the act of recalling the past **2. SOMETHING REMEMBERED** an experience or event remembered from the past **3. REMINDER** something that recalls or suggests something similar **4.** PHILOSOPHY **IDEA FROM PLATO** the Platonic doctrine that anything we encounter is an imperfect recollection of an idea that our souls have encountered in a previous disembodied existence **5.** PSYCHOL **ABILITY TO PERFORM TASK BETTER** the ability to perform a task or remember information better some time after it has been learnt than was possible immediately after it was learnt

reminiscent /rémmi níss'nt/ *adj* **1. RESEMBLING SOMETHING OR SOMEBODY ELSE** suggesting similarities or comparisons with something or somebody else **2. SUGGESTING MEMORIES OF PAST** characterized by or containing recollections of the past ○ *scenes reminiscent of her childhood* **3. RECALLING PAST** given to reminiscing about the past [Mid-18C. < Latin *reminiscent-*, present participle of *reminisci* 'recollect'] —**reminiscently** *adv*

remise /ri meéz/ *n* in fencing, a further thrust made on the same lunge to follow up a first thrust that has missed ■ *vi* (**-mises, -mising, -mised**) in fencing, to make a remise when a first thrust has missed [15C. < French < Latin *remittere* 'send back' (see REMIT)]

remiss /ri míss/ *adj* careless or negligent about doing something that is expected [15C. < Latin *remissus*, past participle of *remittere* 'send back' (see REMIT)]

remissible /ri míssəb'l/ *adj* worthy of forgiveness (*formal*) ○ *remissible sins* —**remissibility** /ri míssə bílləti/ *n*

remission /ri mísh'n/ *n* **1. SLOWING OF DISEASE** a lessening of the symptoms of a disease, or their temporary reduction or disappearance **2.** CRIME **REDUCTION IN PRISON TERM** the reduction of somebody's prison sentence for good conduct **3. LESSENING OF SOMETHING** a lessening or a reduction in the severity of something ○ *The afternoon sun beat down without remission.* **4. RELEASE FROM SOMETHING** a release from a debt, penalty, or obligation **5. FORGIVENESS** pardon or forgiveness **6. ACT OF REMITTING** an instance or the action of remitting something

remit *v* /ri mít/ (**-mits, -mitting, -mitted**) **1.** *vti* **SEND PAYMENT** to send money to pay for goods or services, especially by post **2.** *vt* **CANCEL SOMETHING** to cancel or hold back from enforcing something **3.** *vti* **REDUCE INTENSITY OF SOMETHING** to reduce in intensity, or reduce the intensity of something **4.** *vt* **DEFER SOMETHING** to postpone or defer something **5.** *vt* **PARDON SOMETHING** to pardon or forgive something such as a sin or other transgression **6.** *vt* LAW **SEND CASE BACK TO LOWER COURT** to send a case back to a lower court for further action to be taken ■ *n* /reémit, ri mít/ **1. AREA OF RESPONSIBILITY** the scope or area of responsibility belonging to a particular person, group, or investigation ○ *This matter is beyond the remit of the committee.* **2. SOMETHING REMITTED** something sent to another person or authority for consideration **3.** *NZ* **PROPOSAL** an item submitted by a person or organization for consideration at a conference **4.** LAW **TRANSFER OF LEGAL CASE** the transfer of a legal case from a higher to a lower court for further action to be taken [14C. < Latin *remittere* 'send back' < *mittere* 'send'] —**remittable** *adj* —**remittal** *n* —**remitter** *n*

remittance /ri mítt'nss/ *n* **1. ACT OF PAYING** the sending of money to pay for goods or services **2. MONEY** money sent as payment for goods or services **3. ACT OF REMITTING** the act of remitting something

remittance man *n* a man living abroad who is dependent on money sent from home, especially, in former times, a man who lived abroad while working for the British Empire (*dated*)

remittent /ri mítt'nt/ *adj* lessening and then intensifying again at intervals ○ *slowed down by a remittent fever* —**remittence** *n* —**remittency** *n* —**remittently** *adv*

remix *vt* /ree míks/ (**-mixes, -mixing, -mixed**) to produce a new version of a piece of music by altering the emphasis of the sound and, in pop music, often adding new tracks in place of existing ones ■ *n* /reémiks/ a recording that has been remixed

remnant /rémnənt/ *n* **1. SMALL PART STILL LEFT** a small part of something that remains after the rest has gone **2. SMALL AMOUNT OF CLOTH OR CARPET** a small amount of unsold cloth or flooring material left at the end of a roll, often sold at a reduced price **3. TRACE OF SOMETHING** a small amount or trace of something such as a feeling or emotion **4.** ANTHROP **SMALL SURVIVING GROUP OF PEOPLE** a small isolated group of people surviving from a culture or group [14C. < Old French *remanant*, present participle of *remanoir* (see REMAIN)]

remodel /ree módd'l/ (**-els, -elling, -elled**) *vt* to renovate or alter the structure or style of something such as a building, room, or design

remonstrance /ri mónstrənss/ *n* **1.** a forceful argument in favour of or against something, or the act of making such an argument **2.** a formal protest, usually in the form of a document or petition

Remonstrance *n* **1.** HIST same as **Grand Remonstrance** **2.** the statement expressing Arminian Protestant principles, drawn up in 1610 in Gouda, the Netherlands. The doctrines of Jacob Arminius rejected Calvinist predestination and supported the notion of free will, and had a profound effect on Wesleyan and Methodist theology.

remonstrant /ri mónstrənt/ (*formal*) *n* somebody who remonstrates ■ *adj* involved in or used for a protest [Early 17C. < medieval Latin *remonstrant-*, present participle of *remonstrare* (see REMONSTRATE)]

Remonstrant *n* a Dutch dissenter and supporter of the Remonstrance of 1610

remonstrate /rémmən strayt/ (**-strates, -strating, -strated**) *vi* to reason or argue forcefully with somebody about something (*formal*) [Late 16C. < medieval Latin *remonstrat-*, past participle of *remonstrare* 'demonstrate' < Latin *monstrare* 'to show'] —**remonstration** /rémmən stráysh'n/ *n* —**remonstrative** /ri mónstrətiv/ *adj* —**remonstratively** *adv* —**remonstrator** *n*

SYNONYMS See ***object***.

remontant /ri móntənt/ *adj* blooming or bearing fruit more than once in a season ■ *n* a plant that blooms or bears fruit more than once a season [Late 19C. < French, present participle of *remonter* 'rise again' < *monter* 'to rise']

remora /rémmərə/ *n* a bony saltwater fish with a suction disc on the top of its head that it uses to attach itself to a larger fish or a ship's hull. Family: Echeneidae. [Mid-16C. < Latin, 'hindrance'; from the belief that it slowed ships down]

remorse /ri máwrss/ *n* a strong feeling of guilt and regret [14C. < Old French *remors* < Latin *remordere* 'to torment' < *mordere* 'to bite'] —**remorseful** *adj* —**remorsefully** *adv* —**remorsefulness** *n*

remorseless /ri máwrssləss/ *adj* **1.** showing no pity or compassion **2.** continuing without lessening in strength or intensity —**remorselessly** *adv* —**remorselessness** *n*

remortgage /ree máwrgij/ *vt* (**-gages, -gaging, -gaged**) **1. CHANGE MORTGAGE TERMS** to revise the terms of a mortgage on a property **2. MORTGAGE SOMETHING AGAIN** to mortgage something again after the original mortgage has been paid off ■ *n* **NEW MORTGAGE** a revised or second mortgage taken out on something

remote /ri mṓt/ *adj* (**-moter, -motest**) **1. FAR AWAY** situated a long way away **2. OUT-OF-THE-WAY** far away from civilization, society, or any other populated area **3. DISTANTLY RELATED** distantly related by blood, adoption, or marriage **4. LONG AGO** distant in time **5. SLIGHT** faint or slight ○ *not the remotest possibility of her coming here* **6. DISTANTLY RELEVANT** distant in connection, relevance, or effect **7. ALOOF** distant in manner or behaviour **8. OPERATED FROM DISTANCE** operated or performed from a distance ○ *a remote camera* ○ *a remote shopping service* ■ *n* **1.** ELEC same as **remote control** (sense 1) (*informal*) **2. COMPUTER FAR FROM CENTRAL COMPUTER** a device or computer system that is situated at a distance from a central computer and that can be accessed via a network **3.** *US* BROADCAST same as **outside broadcast** [15C. < Latin *remotus*, past participle of *removere* (see REMOVE)] —**remoteness** *n*

remote access *n* access that is gained to a computer by means of a separate terminal

remote control *n* **1.** a hand-held device used to operate a television set, video cassette recorder, or other electronic device from a distance **2.** the control of a device, system, or activity from a distance, usually by radio signals (*hyphenated before a noun*) ○ *a remote-control transmitter* —**remote-controlled** *adj*

remotely /ri mṓtli/ *adv* **1. SLIGHTLY** in a slight or tenuous way ○ *The two events were only remotely connected.* **2. AT ALL** in the least possible way or to the least possible extent ○ *I am not even remotely interested in what they say.* **3. BY REMOTE CONTROL** using remote control **4. FROM DISTANCE** from a distance, especially via e-mail, fax, or telephone ○ *working remotely* **5. IN DETACHED WAY** in a distant or aloof manner **6. DISTANTLY**

IN TIME far in the future or past ○ *looking to a remotely future epoch* **7.** DISTANTLY IN RELATION distantly in terms of family or biological connection ○ *We are remotely related.* **8.** FAR AWAY at a distance or far away

remote sensor *n* an instrument that gathers information about Earth or another astronomical object from an airborne platform or from space, e.g. a radar or photographic device

rémoulade /rémmoo laád, rémmə láyd/ *n* mayonnaise with herbs, mustard, capers, and gherkins added, and sometimes chopped hard-boiled egg [Mid-19C. < French]

remould *n* /reé mōld/ TYRE WITH NEW TREAD a second-hand tyre with a new tread bonded to it. N Am term **retread** ■ *vt* /ree mṓld/ (**-moulds, -moulding, -moulded**) **1.** CHANGE SOMETHING to change or remodel something such as an idea or principle **2.** FIT TYRE WITH NEW TREAD to bond a new tread onto an old tyre. N Am term **retread**

remount *v* /ree mównt/ (**-mounts, -mounting, -mounted**) **1.** *vt* PUT SOMETHING ON AGAIN to mount something again or anew **2.** *vti* GET BACK INTO SADDLE to get back on a horse or bicycle ■ *n* /reé mownt/ SUBSTITUTE HORSE a replacement horse to ride

removal /ri moóv'l/ *n* **1.** REMOVING OF SOMETHING the taking away or getting rid of something **2.** CHANGE OF LOCATION a change in location, or in the place where somebody lives **3.** HR DISMISSAL dismissal from office or from a position

removalist /ri moóvəlist/ *n Aus* a person or company that transports people's furniture and personal effects from one house to another

removal van *n* a van that is used to transport somebody's furniture and personal effects from one house to another. N Am term **moving van**

remove /ri moóv/ *v* (**-moves, -moving, -moved**) **1.** *vt* TAKE SOMETHING AWAY to take something away from somebody or from a place **2.** *vti* RELOCATE OR BE RELOCATED to transfer somebody or something to another place, or change a place of residence **3.** *vt* TAKE OFF CLOTHING to take off an item of clothing ○ *removed his hat* **4.** *vt* GET RID OF SOMETHING to make something go away or disappear ○ *a detergent that can remove stains even more quickly* **5.** *vt* HR DISMISS SOMEBODY to dismiss somebody from office or from a position ■ *n* **1.** DISTANCE the degree of distance or closeness between people or things ○ *He has only experienced war at one remove.* **2.** CHANGE OF LOCATION a change of residence or business (*formal*) **3.** EDUC CLASS a class or form in some British secondary schools, especially public schools (*dated*) **4.** FOOD INDIVIDUAL DISH IN MEAL a dish that is taken away during a formal meal to make way for another (*dated formal*) [14C. Via French < Latin *removere* < *movere* 'to move'] —**removable** *adj* —**remover** *n*

removed /ri moóvd/ *adj* **1.** separate or distant in space, time, or character from something or somebody else **2.** separated from somebody by a particular degree of descent ○ *a cousin twice removed* —**removedness** /ri moóvidnəss, ri moóvdnəss/ *n*

REM sleep /rém-/ *n* a stage of sleep that recurs several times during the night and is marked by dreaming, rapid eye movements under closed lids, and elevated pulse rate and brain activity

remunerate /ri myoónə rayt/ (**-ates, -ating, -ated**) *vt* to pay somebody for goods or services, or compensate somebody financially for losses sustained or inconvenience caused [Early 16C. < Latin *remunerat-*, past participle of *remunerari* 'reward' < *munus* 'gift'] —**remunerability** /ri myoónərə bílləti/ *n* —**remunerable** *adj* —**remunerator** *n* —**remuneratory** *adj*

remuneration /ri myoónə ráysh'n/ *n* **1.** a payment or reward for goods or services or for losses sustained or inconvenience caused **2.** the paying or rewarding of somebody for goods or services or for losses sustained or inconvenience caused

SYNONYMS See ***wage***.

remunerative /ri myoónərativ/ *adj* paying somebody or rewarding somebody with money —**remuneratively** *adv*

Remus /reémǝss/ *n* in Roman mythology, the son of Mars and twin brother of Romulus, the founder of the city of Rome

renaissance /ri náys'nss/ *n* a rebirth or revival, e.g. of culture, skills, or learning forgotten or previously ignored [Late 19C. < French *renaître* 'be reborn' < Latin *renasci* < *nasci* 'be born']

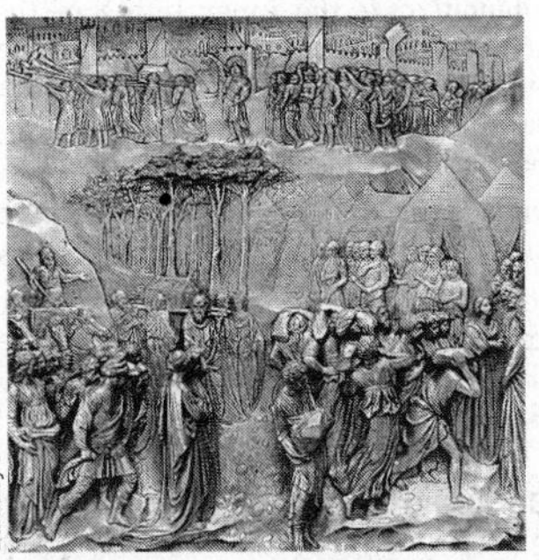
Barnaby's

Renaissance: detail of the bronze doors of the Baptistery, Florence, Italy, by Lorenzo Ghiberti

Renaissance *n* **1.** END OF MIDDLE AGES the period in European history from about the 14th to 16th centuries regarded as marking the end of the Middle Ages and featuring major cultural and artistic change **2.** CLASSICAL REVIVAL the cultural and religious spirit that characterized the Renaissance, including the decline of Gothic architecture, the revival of classical culture, the beginnings of modern science, and geographical exploration ■ *adj* **1.** OF RENAISSANCE relating to the history and culture of the Renaissance **2.** IN ARCHITECTURAL STYLE OF RENAISSANCE in the architectural style of classical revival that characterized the Renaissance

Renaissance man *n* a man who has a wide range of accomplishments and intellectual interests

Renaissance woman *n* a woman who has a wide range of accomplishments and intellectual interests

renal /reén'l/ *adj* relating to or affecting the kidneys [Mid-17C. Via French < late Latin *renalis* < Latin *renes* 'kidneys']

renal clearance *n* a measure of the removal of waste products from the blood by the kidneys, expressed as the volume of blood cleared of a specific substance in one minute

renal pelvis *n* the cavity in the kidney where urine collects before passing into the ureter

renascence /ri náss'nss, -náy-/ *n* same as **renaissance** [Early 18C. < RENASCENT]

renascent /ri náss'nt, ri náyss'nt/ *adj* showing new life or activity [Early 18C. < Latin *renascent-*, present participle of *renasci* 'be reborn' (see RENAISSANCE)]

renature /ree náychər/ (**-tures, -turing, -tured**) *vt* to restore the physical and chemical properties of a denatured protein or nucleic acid

rencounter /ren kówntər/ *n* (*archaic*) **1.** a hostile meeting between adversaries **2.** an unexpected casual meeting [Early 16C. < French *rencontrer* 'have a (hostile) meeting' < *encontrer* 'confront' (see ENCOUNTER)]

rend /rend/ (**rends, rending, rent** /rent/) *v* **1.** *vti* TEAR SOMETHING APART to pull something apart violently, or be pulled apart violently **2.** *vt* TEAR CLOTHES to tear or pull clothes or hair, out of rage, frustration, or grief **3.** *vt* TAKE SOMEBODY OR SOMETHING AWAY FORCIBLY to tear or wrest something or somebody away **4.** *vt* SHATTER SOMETHING to disturb the silence or pierce the air with a loud sound ○ *A scream rent the air.* **5.** *vt* DISTRESS SOMEBODY to cause pain or distress to the heart or emotions [Old English *rendan* < Germanic]

SYNONYMS See ***tear***[1].

Rendell /rénd'l/, **Ruth** (*b.* 1930) British novelist. Her popular crime novels include the Chief Inspector Wexford series. She also writes under the pseudonym 'Barbara Vine'. Full name **Rendell, Ruth Barbara**

render /réndər/ *v* (**-ders, -dering, -dered**) **1.** *vt* GIVE HELP to give help or provide a service (*formal*) **2.** *vt* TRANSLATE SOMETHING to translate something into another language (*formal*) ○ *fragments of poetry, hastily rendered into English* **3.** *vt* ARTS PORTRAY SOMETHING ARTISTICALLY to portray something or somebody in art, literature, music, or acting (*formal*) ○ *a scene of utter desolation, skilfully rendered without sentiment* **4.** *vt* GIVE DECISION to deliver a verdict or decision officially (*formal*) **5.** *vt* COMPUT DRAW SOMETHING to draw something in computer graphics **6.** *vt* SUBMIT SOMETHING FOR ACTION to submit something for consideration, approval, or payment (*formal*) ○ *render all passports for inspection* **7.** *vt* GIVE SOMETHING AS DUE to give what is due or appropriate to somebody who has authority or power (*formal*) ○ *'Render therefore unto Caesar the things which are Caesar's'* (Matthew 22:21, *The Bible*) **8.** *vt* PUT SOMEBODY OR SOMETHING IN PARTICULAR STATE to make somebody or something be or become something (*formal*) ○ *His actions rendered us powerless.* **9.** *vt* PURIFY FAT to purify or extract something by melting, especially to heat solid fat slowly until as much liquid fat as possible has been extracted from it, leaving small crisp remains **10.** *vti* GIVE UP SOMETHING to surrender something (*formal or literary*) **11.** *vt* TRADE SOMETHING to give something in exchange for something else (*formal or literary*) **12.** *vt* RETURN SOMETHING to give something back (*formal or literary*) **13.** *vt* CONSTR COVER WALL WITH PLASTER to cover masonry with a thin coat of plaster ■ *n* **1.** CONSTR COAT OF PLASTER the first thin coat of plaster applied to masonry **2.** HIST TENANT'S PAYMENT a payment in goods, services, or money made by a tenant to a feudal lord [14C. Via French *rendre* < alteration of Latin *reddere* 'give back' < *dare* 'give'] —**renderable** *adj* —**renderer** *n*

render farm *n* a cluster of networked computers used to create computer graphic effects such as animation

rendering /réndəring/ *n* **1.** ARTISTIC PORTRAYAL a portrayal of somebody or something in art, music, literature, or drama **2.** TRANSLATION a translation of a literary work **3.** HEATING ANIMAL REMAINS TO EXTRACT FAT the process or business of separating fat from meat or animal remains by slow heating **4.** CONSTR COAT OF PLASTER a coat of plaster applied to masonry **5.** ARCHIT ARCHITECT'S PERSPECTIVE DRAWING an architect's representation of the inside and outside of a finished building, drawn in perspective

rendezvous /róndi voo, -day-/ *n* (*plural* **-vous** /-voóz/) **1.** MEETING a meeting arranged for an agreed time and place **2.** PLACE OF MEETING the location of a prearranged meeting **3.** PLACE WHERE PEOPLE MEET a popular meeting place for people ■ *vti* (**-vouses** /-vooz/, **-vousing** /-voo ing/, **-voused** /-vood/) MEET SOMEBODY to meet, meet somebody, or bring people together at an agreed time and place [Late 16C. < French, literally 'present yourself']

rendition /ren dísh'n/ *n* **1.** VERSION OF MUSICAL OR THEATRICAL PIECE an interpretation or performance of a piece of music or drama **2.** WORK IN TRANSLATION a translation of a literary work **3.** TRANSLATING the act of translating something into another language (*formal*) [Early 17C. < French *rendre* (see RENDER)]

rendzina /ren dzeénə/ *n* a dark rich soil that develops beneath grassland above a layer of limestone or chalk [Early 20C. < Polish *rędzina*]

Rene /reen/, **Roy** (1892–1954) Australian actor. He created the music-hall act Mo the clown, and starred in the film *Strike Me Lucky* (1934). Born **Rene, Henry van der Sluys**

renegade /rénni gayd/ *n* **1.** somebody who abandons previously held beliefs or loyalties **2.** somebody who chooses to live outside laws or conventions [15C. < Spanish *renegado* < medieval Latin *renegatus* < past participle of *renegare* 'deny' (see RENEGE)]

renege /ri neég, ri náyg/ (**-neges, -neging, -neged**) *vi* **1.** to go back on a promise or commitment **2.** in cards, to fail to follow suit when able and required to do so [Mid-16C. < medieval Latin *renegare* 'deny' < Latin *negare*] —**reneger** *n*

renew /ri nyoó/ (**-news, -newing, -newed**) *v* **1.** *vti* RETURN TO DOING SOMETHING to begin something or doing something again, or be begun again ○ *renewed their friendship after several years* ○ *renewed his calls for an investigation* **2.** *vti* EXTEND SOMETHING to make something such as a contract, lease, or licence effective for a longer period, or be made effective for a longer period ○ *You'll need to renew your lease at the end of the year.* **3.** *vt* REPLACE SOMETHING WORN to replace something that is worn, broken, or no longer suitable for use **4.** *vt* BORROW LIBRARY BOOK FOR LONGER to extend the period of time a book or other

item is borrowed from a library **5.** *vt* REPEAT PROMISE to reaffirm or restate a promise or commitment ○ *renewed their marriage vows* **6.** *vt* GIVE SOMEBODY OR SOMETHING NEW ENERGY to give somebody or something new energy, strength, or enthusiasm ○ *A day of rest renewed his strength.* **7.** *vt* REPLACE SOMETHING USED UP to get a new supply of something **8.** *vt* MAKE SOMETHING NEW AGAIN to make something new or as if new again — **renewal** *n* —**renewer** *n*

SYNONYMS *renew, recondition, renovate, restore, revamp*
CORE MEANING: to improve the condition of something
renew to replace something that is worn, broken, or no longer suitable for use ○ *He added a room and renewed the roof.* ○ *Bones should constantly renew and rebuild themselves, but in osteoporosis this doesn't happen.* **recondition** to bring something back into good condition, especially by repairing it and replacing worn-out parts ○ *Their business was reconditioning used cars.* ○ *the workshop where they reconditioned the aircraft engines* **renovate** to bring something such as a building back to a former better state by means of repairs, redecoration, or remodelling ○ *newly renovated offices* ○ *the money needed to renovate crumbling school buildings* **restore** to bring something back to an earlier and better condition ○ *a fully restored flour mill dating back to 1730* ○ *The wall hanging has been recently cleaned and restored.* **revamp** to improve the appearance, condition, or structure of something by making sometimes superficial changes ○ *a major construction programme to revamp the city's shabby waterfront* ○ *As the airline revamped its business, the workforce was reduced by about 900.* **overhaul** to carry out comprehensive repairs and adjustments, especially to a piece of machinery ○ *We stayed in the town while the ship was being overhauled.* ○ *Industry watchers had expected the company to overhaul its corporate structure.* **refurbish** to bring something back to a cleaner, brighter, more functional state ○ *It would cost about 1 million less to refurbish the school than to build a new one.* ○ *a major advertising drive designed to refurbish the company's safety image.*

renewable /ri nyóō əb'l/ *adj* **1.** able to be sustained or renewed indefinitely, either because of inexhaustible supplies or because of new growth **2.** capable of being begun or done again ■ *n* ENVIRON same as **renewable resource** (*often used in the plural*) —**renewability** /ri nyóō ə bílləti/ *n* —**renewably** *adv*

renewable energy *n* INDUST same as **alternative energy**

renewable resource *n* **1.** RESOURCE THAT CAN BE SUSTAINED a resource that can be renewed as quickly as it is used up and can, in theory, last indefinitely. Timber, unlike mineral resources, is a renewable resource. **2.** RESOURCE THAT REPLACES ITSELF a natural resource that replaces itself unless overused, e.g. animal or plant life or fresh water **3.** RENEWABLE FORM OF ENERGY a source of alternative energy, e.g. sunlight, wind, or waves

renewed /ri nyóōd/ *adj* **1.** resuming after an interruption, usually with more intensity or energy ○ *renewed efforts to force a breakthrough* **2.** feeling stronger, or more relaxed, energetic, or enthusiastic

Renfrew /rén froo/ town near the River Clyde, near Glasgow, Scotland. Population: 20,764 (1991).

Renfrewshire /rén froоshər/ council area in Scotland. Paisley is the administrative centre. Population: 173,212 (2001).

reniform /rénni fawrm, reéni-/ *adj* shaped like or suggestive of a kidney [Mid-18C. < Latin *ren* 'kidney']

renin /reénin/ *n* an enzyme released by the kidneys that breaks down proteins and helps regulate blood pressure [Late 19C. < Latin *ren* 'kidney']

renitent /ri nít'nt, rénnitənt/ *adj* (*formal*) **1.** resisting physical pressure, as opposed to being flexible or pliant **2.** reluctant to have a change of mind or concede to others [Early 18C. < Latin *renitent-*, present participle of *reniti* 'struggle against'] —**renitence** *n* —**renitency** *n*

renk /rengk/ *adj* (*slang; used in Black English*) **1.** same as **rank**[2] (sense 3) **2.** same as **impudent**

renminbi /rén minbee/ (*plural same*) *n* the national currency of the People's Republic of China, equivalent in value to the yuan [Mid-20C. < Chinese *rénmín* 'people' + *bi* 'currency']

Rennes /ren/ capital city of Ile-Vilaine Department, Brittany Region, western France. It is situated about 97 km/60 mi. north of Nantes. Population: 206,229 (1999).

rennet /rénnit/ *n* **1.** the inner lining of the fourth stomach of calves and other young ruminants **2.** a substance made from rennet that contains the enzyme rennin, used in cheese making **3.** BIOCHEM same as **rennin** [15C. Probably < Germanic]

rennin /rénnin/ *n* a milk-curdling enzyme produced in the stomachs of young mammals [Late 19C. < RENNET]

Reno /reénō/ city in western Nevada, located on the Truckee River, near Lake Tahoe in the Sierra Nevada Mountains. It is a resort and commercial centre, and is home to the University of Nevada-Reno. Population: 190,248 (2002 estimate).

renogram /reénə gram/ *n* **1.** a photographic record of kidney function, showing how quickly a radioactive substance injected into the bloodstream is removed when it passes through the kidneys **2.** an X-ray image of a kidney [Early 20C. < Latin *ren* 'kidney']

AKG London
Pierre Auguste Renoir

Renoir /rén waar, rən waár/, **Auguste** (1841–1919) French painter and sculptor. One of the leading impressionists, he is noted for the harmony of his lines, the brilliance of his colours, and the intimate charm of his wide variety of subjects. Full name **Renoir, Pierre Auguste**

> 'I have a predilection for a painting that lends joyousness to a wall.'
> [Auguste Renoir, *Renoir*, Ambrose Vollard; 1919]

Renoir, Jean (1894–1979) French film director. The son of Auguste Renoir, he was a technical innovator known for the fluidity of his work. His greatest film is *The Rules of the Game* (1939). He lived in the United States after 1941.

> 'Is it possible to succeed without any act of betrayal?'
> [Jean Renoir, 'Nana', *My Life and My Films*; 1974]

renormalization /reé nawrmə lī záysh'n/ *n* a mathematical technique used in quantum physics that eliminates infinite terms by carefully defining fundamental quantities such as mass and charge — **renormalize** /ree náwrmə līz/ *vt*

renounce /ri nównss/ *v* (-**nounces**, -**nouncing**, -**nounced**) **1.** *vt* GIVE UP CLAIM to give up formally a claim, title, position, or right **2.** *vt* REJECT BELIEF to reject or disavow a belief or theory **3.** *vt* STOP DOING SOMETHING to give up a habit, pursuit, or practice **4.** *vi* CARDS NOT FOLLOW SUIT in cards, to be unable to follow suit and be forced to play a card from a different suit ■ *n* CARDS ACT OF NOT FOLLOWING SUIT in cards, a failure to follow suit [14C. Via French *renoncer* < Latin *renuntiare* 'report' < *nuntiare* 'announce'] —**renouncement** *n* —**renouncer** *n*

renovascular /reénō váskyoōlər/ *adj* relating to the blood vessels of the kidneys [Mid-20C. < Latin *ren* 'kidney']

renovate /rénnə vayt/ (-**vates**, -**vating**, -**vated**) *vt* **1.** to bring something such as a building back to a former better state by means of repairs, redecoration, or remodelling **2.** to give new vigour to somebody or something [15C. < Latin *renovat-*, past participle of *renovare* < *novus* 'new'] —**renovation** /rénnə váysh'n/ *n* —**renovative** *adj* —**renovator** *n*

SYNONYMS See *renew*.

renown /ri nówn/ *n* widespread fame or honour [14C. < Old French *renon* < *renomer* 'make famous' < *nomer* 'to name' < Latin *nominare*]

renowned /ri nównd/ *adj* well known or famous, especially for a skill or expertise

rent[1] /rent/ *n* **1.** PAYMENT BY TENANT a regular payment made by a tenant to an owner or landlord for the right to occupy or use property **2.** PAYMENT TO USE EQUIPMENT a regular payment to the owner for the right to use equipment or personal property **3.** PROFIT FROM CULTIVATED LAND the financial return from cultivated land after production costs have been deducted **4.** INCOME OF LANDOWNERS the portion of the national income that is earned by landowners **5.** ECON same as **economic rent** (sense 2) ■ *vti* (**rents**, **renting**, **rented**) **1.** PAY TO USE SOMEBODY'S PROPERTY to occupy somebody else's property or use somebody else's equipment in return for regular payments **2.** ALLOW USE OF PROPERTY FOR PAYMENT to allow somebody to occupy property or use equipment in return for regular payments [12C. < French *rente* < alteration of Latin *reddere* 'give back' (see RENDER)] —**rentable** *adj*

rent[2] /rent/ *n* **1.** an opening or hole made by tearing something **2.** a rift in a relationship, or a breach in friendly relations [Mid-16C. < obsolete variant of REND]

rent[3] /rent/ past participle, past tense of **rend**

rent-a-dread *n* same as **rental** *n* (sense 6) (*slang; used in Black English*)

rental /rént'l/ *n* **1.** RENT PAYMENT an amount paid in rent **2.** RENT INCOME an amount received in rent **3.** ACT OF RENTING SOMETHING the renting of property or equipment **4.** *N Am* SOMETHING RENTABLE something rented or available to rent **5.** *US* RENTING BUSINESS a business that rents out property or equipment **6.** ESCORT PRETENDING TO BE RASTAFARIAN a man employed as an escort who pretends to be Rastafarian (*slang; used in Black English*) ■ *adj* RELATING TO RENT relating to property for rent or with rent payments

rent boy *n* an offensive term for a young man working as a prostitute (*slang*) [< RENT[1]]

rent control *n* government regulation of the amount charged for housing rental and sometimes of eviction procedures [< RENT[1]] —**rent-controlled** *adj*

renter /réntər/ *n* **1.** SOMEBODY WHO RENTS FROM SOMEBODY somebody who rents property or equipment from somebody else **2.** SOMEBODY WHO RENTS TO SOMEBODY somebody who rents property or equipment to somebody else **3.** FILM DISTRIBUTOR a film distributor renting films to cinemas [14C. < RENT[1]]

rent-free *adj* not subject to rent payments ■ *adv* without having to pay rent [< RENT[1]]

rentier /raáaN tyay, rónti ay/ *n* somebody whose income is primarily from rent and securities [Mid-19C. < French < *rente* (see RENT[1])]

rent strike *n* an organized refusal by tenants to pay their rent [< RENT[1]]

renunciation /ri núnssi áysh'n/ *n* **1.** a denial or rejection of something or somebody, usually for moral or religious reasons **2.** an official declaration giving up a title, office, claim, or privilege [14C. Directly or via French < Latin *renuntiation-* 'announcement, (in late Latin) renunciation' < past participle of *renuntiare* (see RENOUNCE)] —**renunciatory** /ri núnssi ətəri/ *adj*

renvoi /ren vóy/ *n* the referral of a case or dispute from the country in which it arose to the laws of another [Late 19C. < French < *renvoyer* 'send back' < *envoyer* 'send']

reoffend /reé ə fénd/ (-**fends**, -**fending**, -**fended**) *vi* to commit a second or subsequent offence —**reoffender** *n*

reopen /ree ốpən/ (-**pens**, -**pening**, -**pened**) *vti* to open again, or cause something to be opened again ○ *I don't want to reopen old wounds.* ○ *The store will reopen in March.*

reorganise, etc. another spelling of **reorganize**, etc.

reorganization /ree áwrgə nī záysh'n/, **reorganisation** *n* **1.** a change in the way something is organized, arranged, or done **2.** the thorough physical or financial restructuring of a business or organization —**reorganizational** *adj*

reorganize /ree áwrgə nīz/ (**-izes, -izing, -ized**), **reorganise** (**-ises, -ising, -ised**) *vti* **1.** to impose organization on something again after its being disturbed **2.** to change the way that something is organized, or be changed —**reorganizer** *n*

reorient /ree áwri ənt/ (**-ents, -enting, -ented**), **reorientate** /ree áwri ən tayt/ (**-tates, -tating, -tated**) *v* **1. reorient yourself** *vr* to find out where you are or where you are going after being lost **2.** *vti* to change the direction or management of something, or your behaviour or ideas, to deal with a new situation —**reorientation** /ree áwri ən táysh'n/ *n*

reovirus /reé ō vīrəss/ *n* a virus that contains double-stranded RNA and is associated with various infections in plants and animals. Reoviruses are often found in people with breathing and stomach disorders. [Mid-20C. < acronym < *respiratory enteric orphan*]

rep[1] /rep/, **repp** *n* a ribbed or corded silk, wool, rayon, or cotton fabric [Mid-19C. < French *reps*]

rep[2] /rep/ *n* repertory theatre, or a repertory company (*informal*) [Early 20C. Shortening of REPERTORY]

rep[3] /rep/ (*informal*) *n* **1.** COMM same as **sales representative 2.** *NZ* FOOTBALL same as **representative** *n* (sense 6) ■ *vi* (**reps, repping, repped**) to work as a sales representative [Late 19C. Shortening of REPRESENTATIVE]

rep[4] /rep/ *n* same as **reputation** (*informal*) [Early 18C. Shortening]

rep[5] /rep/ *n* a repetition of a fitness exercise (*informal*) [Mid-19C. Shortening of REPETITION]

rep. *abbr* **1.** PUBL repair **2.** PUBL report **3.** PUBL reported **4.** LAW reporter **5.** PUBL reprint

Rep. *abbr* POL **1.** *US* Representative **2.** Republic **3.** *US* Republican

repaid past participle, past tense of **repay**

repair[1] /ri páir/ *vt* (**-pairs, -pairing, -paired**) **1.** FIX OR MEND SOMETHING to restore something broken or damaged to good condition ○ *repair a flat tyre* **2.** RESTORE RELATIONSHIP to restore a relationship or friendship by resolving a difficulty or disagreement **3.** ATONE FOR SOMETHING to make amends for something wrong ○ *How can I repair this wrong?* ■ *n* **1.** JOB OF MENDING SOMETHING the process of mending something, or the job that is done in order to achieve this ○ *carry out repairs* **2.** REPAIRED ITEM something that has been repaired **3.** CONDITION OF SOMETHING the condition of something with respect to whether it needs mending or fixing ○ *an air conditioner no longer in good repair* [14C. Via French < Latin *reparare* < *parare* 'make ready'] —**repairability** /ri páirə bílləti/ *n* —**repairable** *adj* —**repairer** *n*

repair[2] /ri páir/ *vi* (**-pairs, -pairing, -paired**) (*formal*) **1.** GO SOMEWHERE to go to a particular place ○ *repaired to the library after dinner* **2.** CONSULT SOMEBODY to go to somebody for help or advice ■ *n* (*archaic*) **1.** ACT OF GOING SOMEWHERE the act of going to a particular place, especially frequently **2.** HAUNT a place where a person or animal is frequently found [14C. Via French < late Latin *repatriare* 'go back home' (see REPATRIATE)]

repairman /ri páir man/ (*plural* **-men** /-men/) *n* a man whose job is making repairs to equipment or machinery

repairperson /ri páir purss'n/ (*plural* **-people** /-peep'l/ or **-persons**) *n* somebody whose job is making repairs to equipment or machinery

repairwoman /ri páir wŏŏmən/ (*plural* **-women** /-wimin/) *n* a woman whose job is making repairs to equipment or machinery

repand /ri pánd/ *adj* with a wavy edge ○ *a repand leaf* [Mid-18C. < Latin *repandus* 'curving back' < *pandere* 'become curved']

reparable /réppərəb'l/ *adj* able to be repaired, recovered, or put right —**reparability** /réppərə bílləti/ *n* —**reparably** *adv*

reparation /réppə ráysh'n/ *n* **1.** AMENDS compensation for a wrong, or something that is done to achieve this **2.** REPAIR restoration of something to good condition, or the process of doing this (*formal*) ■ **reparations** *npl* COMPENSATION FOR WAR compensation demanded of a defeated nation by the victor in a war, especially that demanded of Germany by the Treaty of Versailles after World War I —**reparative** /ri párrətiv/ *adj* —**reparatory** /ri párrətəri/ *adj*

repartee /réppaar teé/ *n* **1.** WITTY TALK conversation consisting of witty remarks **2.** WIT skill in making witty remarks or conversation **3.** WITTY REMARK a witty remark or reply [Mid-17C. < French *repartie* < *repartir* 'set out again' < *partir* 'leave']

repartition /reé paar tísh'n/ *n* **1.** DISTRIBUTION distribution or division of something **2.** DIVIDING OF SOMETHING AGAIN the act of dividing or distributing something again, either in the same way or differently ■ *vt* (**-tions, -tioning, -tioned**) DIVIDE SOMETHING UP AGAIN to divide something up again, either in the same way or differently

repast /ri paást/ *n* a meal, or the food eaten at a meal (*literary*) [14C. < Old French < *repaistre* 'to feed' < Latin *pascere*]

repatriate *vt* /ree páttri ayt/ (**-ates, -ating, -ated**) **1.** SEND SOMEBODY BACK to send somebody back to his or her country of birth, the country of which he or she is a citizen, or the country from which he or she arrived **2.** SEND BACK MONEY to send money that has been earned or invested abroad back to its owner's country of origin **3.** SEND BACK ARTEFACT to send a cultural artefact or works of art back to country of origin ■ *n* /ree páttri ət/ SOMEBODY REPATRIATED somebody who has been repatriated [Early 17C. < late Latin *repatriat-*, past participle of *repatriare* 'go back home' < Latin *patria* 'homeland'] —**repatriation** /ree páttri áysh'n/ *n*

repay /ri páy/ (**-pays, -paying, -paid** /-páyd/) *vt* **1.** PAY BACK MONEY TO SOMEBODY to pay back money that is owed to somebody ○ *I was repaid in full within the week.* ○ *We will repay the loan.* **2.** RETURN FAVOUR TO SOMEBODY to reward somebody for his or her effort, aid, or success ○ *We can never repay you for your kindness.* ○ *Your hard work will be repaid with success.* **3.** RETURN SOMETHING to return something in kind ○ *repaid the visit* —**repayable** *adj* —**repayment** *n*

repeal /ri peél/ *vt* (**-peals, -pealing, -pealed**) to officially end the validity of something such as a law ■ *n* the act of repealing something such as a law [14C. < Anglo-Norman *repeler*, variant of Old French *rapeler* < *re-* 'again, back' + *apeler* (see APPEAL)] —**repealable** *adj* —**repealer** *n*

SYNONYMS See *nullify*.

repeat /ri peét/ *v* (**-peats, -peating, -peated**) **1.** *vt* SAY SOMETHING AGAIN to say or write something again **2.** *vti* DO OR UNDERGO SOMETHING AGAIN to do, produce, or experience something again or several times ○ *She repeated the exercises every day.* **3.** *vti* ECHO SOMEBODY'S WORDS to say again what somebody else has said **4.** *vt* TELL WHAT HAS BEEN HEARD to tell another person something that was told to you, especially when it was done in confidence ○ *I'll tell you, but you mustn't repeat it to anyone else.* **5.** *vt* SAY SOMETHING MEMORIZED to recite something that has been learned **6. repeat yourself** *vr* SAY SAME THING AGAIN to do or say something again, especially more than once ○ *You get tired of repeating yourself after a while.* **7. repeat itself** *vr* HAPPEN AGAIN to happen again in the same way as previously ○ *History is repeating itself.* **8.** *vti* BROADCAST BROADCAST AGAIN to broadcast a television or radio programme again, or be broadcast again **9.** *vi* BE TASTED AGAIN to be tasted again after having been eaten, through wind or partial regurgitation (*informal*) ○ *Those spicy meatballs are repeating on me.* **10.** *vi* TIME SIGNAL TIME to make a sound signalling the latest hour, or sometimes quarter hour, when somebody presses a spring (*refers to clocks or watches*) ■ *n* **1.** RECURRING EVENT OR SITUATION an event or situation that is the same as a previous one **2.** SOMETHING SHOWN AGAIN something that is broadcast, shown, or performed again **3.** MUSIC RECURRING MUSICAL PASSAGE a passage of music played again within a single piece, or the notation indicating that this is to be done **4.** UNIFORMLY REPRODUCED PATTERN a pattern reproduced uniformly across a surface ○ *upholstery fabric with a large floral repeat* **5.** ACT OF REORDERING SOMETHING a reorder of the same goods or by the same customer [14C. Via French < Latin *repetere* 'demand again' < *petere* 'to demand'] —**repeatability** /ri peétə bílləti/ *n* —**repeatable** *adj* —**repeated** *adj*

repeatedly /ri peétidli/ *adv* again and again, or on several occasions

repeater /ri peétər/ *n* **1.** SOMEBODY OR SOMETHING REPEATING somebody or something that repeats something **2.** ARMS GUN FIRING SEVERAL SHOTS WITHOUT RELOADING a firearm with a magazine that can fire several shots before it has to be reloaded, e.g. a rifle **3.** TIME TIMEPIECE THAT REPEATS CHIMES a clock or watch that can be made to repeat its latest chime when somebody presses a spring **4.** ELEC ENG DEVICE FOR AMPLIFYING SIGNALS an electrical device that boosts and amplifies incoming communications signals and retransmits them

repeat fee *n* an amount of money that a performer or writer is paid each time a piece of his or her work is broadcast (*often used in the plural*)

repeating decimal /ri peéting-/ *n N Am* same as **recurring decimal**

repeating firearm *n* ARMS same as **repeater** (sense 2)

repeat performance *n* an event that is the same as one that happened before

repeat prescription *n UK, Can* a prescription for a regularly needed medicine that has been prescribed before and can be renewed without the doctor having to see the patient

repechage /réppə shaázh/ *n* a heat within a competition during which runners-up in earlier heats have a final chance to qualify for the next round. Fencing, rowing, and cycling competitions often have a repechage. [Early 20C. < French < *repêcher*, literally 'fish out']

repel /ri pél/ (**-pels, -pelling, -pelled**) *v* **1.** *vti* CAUSE GREAT DISTASTE to make somebody feel intense aversion, disgust, or revulsion **2.** *vt* KEEP SOMETHING AWAY to ward something off, or keep something away ○ *a cream that is effective in repelling mosquitoes* **3.** *vt* RESIST ATTACK to ward off or force back an attack or invasion **4.** *vti* FAIL TO MIX to fail to mix or blend with something else ○ *Oil and water repel each other.* **5.** *vti* PHYS EXERT OPPOSING FORCE to exert a force that tends to push something away ○ *Particles of like charge repel each other.* **6.** *vt* SPURN SOMEBODY OR SOMETHING to reject or refuse to accept something or somebody [15C. Via French < Latin *repellere* 'drive back' < *pellere* 'to drive'] —**repeller** *n*

repellent /ri péllənt/, **repellant** *adj* **1.** CAUSING DISGUST making somebody feel intense dislike, disgust, or revulsion **2.** RESISTANT TO SOMETHING resistant or impervious to something (*often used in combination*) ○ *water-repellent material* **3.** PUSHING AWAY pushing something away or driving something back ■ *n* **1.** SOMETHING THAT REPELS INSECTS a substance that drives away insects **2.** SUBSTANCE THAT RESISTS SOMETHING HARMFUL a substance that is applied to a surface of something to resist water, mould, or mildew —**repellence** *n* —**repellently** *adv*

USAGE Note that the adjective is usually spelt *-ent* and not *-ant*. The *-ant* variant is rather more commonly found for the noun (*an insect repellant*) than for the adjective.

USAGE repellent or **repulsive**? Both words mean 'causing disgust', but ***repulsive*** is rather stronger in effect than ***repellent***. ***Repellent*** is common in combinations such as *insect-repellent* and *water-repellent*, denoting substances that physically repel or resist a particular thing. ***Repulsive*** does not have a literal meaning corresponding to this.

repent[1] /ri pént/ (**-pents, -penting, -pented**) *vti* **1.** to recognize the wrong in something you have done and be sorry about it **2.** to feel regret about a sin or past actions and change your ways or habits [13C. < French *repentir* < *pentir* < Latin *paenitere*] —**repentance** *n* —**repentant** *adj* —**repenter** *n*

repent[2] /ri pént/ *adj* growing or lying along the ground [Mid-17C. < Latin *repent-*, present participle of *repere* 'creep']

~~repentence~~ incorrect spelling of **repentance**

repercussion /reépər kúsh'n/ *n* **1.** RESULT OF ACTION something, especially an unforeseen problem, that results from an action (*often used in the plural*) **2.** REBOUND the rebounding of a force after impact **3.** PHYS REFLECTION the reflection of light or sound **4.** MUSIC POINT OF REAPPEARANCE IN FUGUE in a fugue, the return of the theme after an episode [Mid-16C. Directly or via French < Latin *repercussion-* < past participle of *repercutere* 'strike back through' < *percutere* 'strike through'] —**repercussive** *adj*

repertoire /réppər twaar/ *n* **1.** MATERIAL AVAILABLE FOR PERFORMANCE a stock of musical or dramatic material that is known and can be performed **2.** BODY OF ARTISTIC

WORKS the entire body of works in a specific area of the arts **3. RANGE OF RESOURCES THAT SOMEBODY HAS** the range of techniques, abilities, or skills that somebody or something has ○ *the surgeon's repertoire* [Mid-19C. Via French < late Latin *repertorium* (see REPERTORY)] ◇ **in repertoire** used to refer to performances of different plays or ballets given on different days

repertory /réppərtəri/ (*plural* **-ries**) *n* **1.** *UK, ANZ, Can* **SYSTEM OF PRESENTING PLAYS** a system by which a permanent theatre company presents a set of works during a season, usually in its own theatre. US term **stock 2. USER OF REPERTORY SYSTEM** a theatre or company that uses the repertory system **3.** ARTS same as **repertoire** (senses 1–2) **4. COLLECTION OF AVAILABLE THINGS** a store or stock of available items ○ *a comedian with a large repertory of jokes* [Late 16C. < late Latin *repertorium* 'inventory' < Latin *reperire* 'get completely' < *parire* 'get'] —**repertorial** /réppər táwri əl/ *adj*

repertory company *n UK, ANZ, Can* a theatre company that performs different plays on different days in the same theatre. US term **stock company**

repetend /réppi tend, réppi ténd/ *n* **1.** the part of a repeating decimal that is repeated infinitely, e.g. '37' in '0.373737' **2.** something that is repeated [Early 18C. < Latin *repetendum* 'thing to be repeated' < *repetere* 'demand again']

répétiteur /ray pétti túr, ri-/ *n* a musician in an opera company who coaches the singers and accompanies them on the piano in rehearsal [Mid-20C. < French, 'somebody who repeats']

repetition /réppə tísh'n/ *n* **1. REPEATING OF SOMETHING** an act of doing something again **2. SOMETHING SAME AS BEFORE** an event or situation that is the same as one that happened previously **3. PROCEDURE OF STATING SOMETHING AGAIN** the act or process of saying or writing something again **4. REPEATED WORDS** something that is repeated, especially unnecessary words [Early 16C. Via French < Latin *repetition-* < *repetere* 'demand again']

repetitious /réppə tíshəss/ *adj* full of repetition, especially unnecessary or tiresome repetition —**repetitiously** *adv* —**repetitiousness** *n*

repetitive /ri péttətiv/ *adj* full of or involving repetition ○ *a boring repetitive task* —**repetitively** *adv* —**repetitiveness** *n*

repetitive strain injury, repetitive stress injury *n* MED full form of **RSI**

repine /ri pīn/ (**-pines, -pining, -pined**) *vi* to feel dissatisfied or fretful about something and complain or grumble about it (*literary*) [Early 16C. < PINE[2] 'fret', after REPENT[1]] —**repiner** *n*

~~**repitition**~~ incorrect spelling of **repetition**

replace /ri pláyss/ (**-places, -placing, -placed**) *vt* **1. SUBSTITUTE FOR SOMETHING** to take the place of or substitute for somebody or something ○ *The new ways rapidly replaced the old.* **2. SUPPLANT SOMEBODY OR SOMETHING** to fill the place of somebody or something with somebody or something else ○ *You can be replaced.* **3. PUT SOMETHING IN ANOTHER'S PLACE** to provide or find a substitute for something ○ *can't afford to replace his car* **4. PUT SOMETHING BACK IN ITS PLACE** to put an object back in its usual place ○ *She replaced the receiver slowly.* —**replaceable** *adj* —**replacer** *n*

USAGE replace or **substitute**? The constructions involving these two words are different, although the resulting meaning is usually the same. You ***replace*** item B *with* (or less often *by*) item A, but ***substitute*** item A *for* item B.

replacement /ri pláyssmənt/ *n* **1. SUBSTITUTION** the act or process of taking the place of or substituting for somebody or something **2. FILLING OF SOMEBODY'S OR SOMETHING'S PLACE** the filling of the place of somebody or something with somebody or something else **3. SUBSTITUTE** somebody or something that replaces another **4.** CHEM **CHANGE OF ONE MINERAL TO ANOTHER** the partial or complete transformation of one mineral into another in response to changing conditions such as the presence of water **5.** *US* MIL **SOMEBODY FILLING MILITARY VACANCY** somebody who fills a vacancy in a military force

replant /ree plaánt/ (**-plants, -planting, -planted**) *vt* **1. TRANSFER PLANT TO NEW PLACE** to transfer a plant or part of a plant into new soil or a new area **2. PROVIDE PLACE WITH NEW PLANTS** to put new plants in a place or container to replace previous plants ○ *replant the flower boxes every spring* **3.** MED, DENT **REATTACH OR REINSERT BODY PART** to reattach or reinsert a severed body part such as a limb or tooth —**replantation** /reé plaan táysh'n/ *n*

replay *vt* /ree pláy/ (**-plays, -playing, -played**) **1. PLAY RECORDING AGAIN** to play again something that has been recorded on tape, video, or film **2. PLAY MATCH AGAIN** to play a game, match, or contest again ■ *n* /reé play/ **1. CONTEST PLAYED AGAIN** a game, match, or contest that is played again **2. RECORDED MATERIAL REPLAYED** something recorded on tape, video, or film that is played again **3. REPEAT OF PREVIOUS EVENT** an event that repeats or appears to repeat something in the past ○ *The latest business failure was a replay of the previous one.*

replenish /ri plénnish/ (**-ishes, -ishing, -ished**) *vt* **1. NOURISH SOMEBODY OR SOMETHING** to fill somebody or something with needed energy or nourishment **2. REPLACE USED ITEMS** to restock depleted items or material ○ *time for the campers to replenish their supplies* **3. REFUEL FIRE** to resupply a fire with fuel [Early 17C. < Old French *repleniss-*, stem of *replenir* 'fill again' < *plenir* 'fill' < Latin *plenus* 'full'] —**replenisher** *n* —**replenishment** *n*

replete /ri pleét/ *adj* **1.** amply, completely, or fully supplied with something ○ *a kitchen replete with all the latest gadgets* **2.** having eaten enough to be fully satisfied [14C. Directly or via French < Latin *repletus*, past participle of *replere* 'fill up' < *plere* 'fill'] —**repleteness** *n*

repletion /ri pleésh'n/ *n* **1.** a condition of being overfull after eating too much **2.** the condition of being fully satisfied

replevin /ri plévvin/ *n* an act or writ to recover goods by somebody who claims to own them and who promises to have the claim later tested in court ■ *vt* (**-ins, -ining, -ined**) LAW same as **replevy** [14C. < Anglo-Norman < *replevir* (see REPLEVY)]

replevy /ri plévvi/ *vt* (**-ies, -ying, -ied**) to seize goods on the grounds of ownership after promising to test the claim in court ■ *n* (*plural* **-ies**) a seizure of claimed goods after a promise that the claim will be tested in court later [Late 16C. < Anglo-Norman *replevir* 'recover thoroughly' < *plevir* 'recover'] —**repleviable** *adj*

replica /répplikə/ *n* **1.** an accurate reproduction of an object **2.** a scrupulous copy of a work of art, especially one made, authorized, or supervised by the original artist [Early 19C. < Italian, 'repeat' < Latin *replicare* (see REPLICATE)]

replicant /répplikənt/ *n* especially in science fiction, an imaginary being that has been constructed from organic and computerized components to look like a human being

replicate *v* /réppli kayt/ (**-cates, -cating, -cated**) **1.** *vt* **DO SOMETHING AGAIN** to make an identical version of something repeatedly and exactly, or do something again in exactly the same way **2.** *vi* **BE DONE AGAIN** to undergo a repetition or reproduction **3.** *vt* BIOL **COPY CELLULAR OR GENETIC MATERIAL** to reproduce exactly an organism, genetic material, or a cell ■ *adj* /répplikət, -kayt/ BOT **BENT BACK** describes a leaf or other part that is folded back on itself [Mid-16C. < Latin *replicat-*, past participle of *replicare* 'fold back' < *plicare* 'to fold'] —**replicative** /-kətiv/ *adj*

SYNONYMS See ***copy***.

replication /réppli káysh'n/ *n* **1. PROCESS OF REPEATING** the process of repeating, duplicating, or reproducing something **2.** BIOL **MAKING OF CELLULAR OR GENETIC COPY** the production of exact copies of molecules, genetic material, or cells **3.** LAW **REPLY OF PLAINTIFF** a plaintiff's reply to the plea of a defendant (*dated*) **4.** BOT **FOLD** a fold or folding back of a leaf or other part

replicon /répli kon/ *n* a segment of DNA or RNA that replicates itself as a unit, distinct from adjacent segments in a chromosome or other genetic element [Mid-20C. < REPLICATION]

reply /ri plī/ *v* (**-plies, -plying, -plied**) **1.** *vti* **RESPOND TO WHAT SOMEBODY SAYS** to say or write something in response to what somebody else has said or written ○ *replied that she wouldn't be available to take the job* **2.** *vi* **RESPOND WITH ACTION OR GESTURE** to respond to somebody's action with a countering action or gesture **3.** *vi* LAW **ANSWER DEFENDANT'S PLEA** to speak in response to the plea of a defendant in a court of law **4.** *vi* **ECHO** to echo or return a sound ■ *n* (*plural* **-plies**) **1. SPOKEN OR WRITTEN RESPONSE** a reaction, usually written or spoken, to a question, letter, or situation **2. ACTION PERFORMED AS RESPONSE** something done as a response to somebody else's action ○ *Her only reply was to turn on her heel and leave.* **3.** LAW **ANSWER TO DEFENDANT'S PLEA** a statement made in response to the plea of a defendant in a court of law [14C. Via Old French *replier* < Latin *replicare* (see REPLICATE)] —**replier** *n*

SYNONYMS See ***answer***.

reply-paid *adj* MAIL same as **postpaid**

repoint /ree póynt/ (**-points, -pointing, -pointed**) *vt* to repair a brick wall by putting new mortar or cement between the bricks

repolarization /ree pōlə rī záysh'n/ *n* the restoration of the normal electrical polarity of a nerve or muscle cell membrane following reversal of its polarity (**depolarization**) during passage of a nerve impulse or muscle contraction —**repolarize** *vt*

report /ri páwrt/ *v* (**-ports, -porting, -ported**) **1.** *vti* **TELL ABOUT WHAT HAPPENED** to give information about something that has happened ○ *reported that negotiations were proceeding slowly* **2.** *vti* **TELL PEOPLE NEWS USING MEDIA** to find out facts and tell people about them in print or a broadcast **3.** *vt* **INFORM AUTHORITIES ABOUT SOMETHING OR SOMEBODY** to inform somebody in authority about something that has happened, especially a crime or an accident, or about somebody who has done something wrong ○ *reported him missing two days ago* ○ *reported the break-in to the police* **4.** *vti* **TELL ABOUT RESEARCH** to give detailed information about research or an investigation ○ *The committee will report their findings early next week.* **5.** *vti* **MAKE OFFICIAL STATEMENT** to make a formal statement regarding something **6.** *vt* **RECORD COURT PROCEEDINGS** to record the proceedings of a court of law **7.** *vi* **INFORM ABOUT ARRIVAL** to let somebody know you have arrived ○ *Guests should report to reception on arrival.* **8.** *vi* **DECLARE STATE OF HEALTH** to declare that you are in a particular condition of health ○ *another worker reporting sick* **9.** *vi* **BE UNDER SOMEBODY'S AUTHORITY** to be subordinate and responsible to somebody or something ○ *You'll be reporting to me from now on.* ■ *n* **1. ACCOUNT OF SOMETHING** an account of an event, situation, or episode **2. NEWS ITEM** an account of news presented by a journalist, in a print or broadcast medium **3. DOCUMENT GIVING INFORMATION** a document that gives information about an investigation or a piece of research, often put together by a group of people working together **4. UNCONFIRMED ACCOUNT** a widely-known account of something that may be true but has not been confirmed ○ *Report had it that the company was approaching bankruptcy.* **5.** BUSINESS **PERIODIC STATEMENT OF COMPANY'S FINANCES** a detailed periodic account of a company's activities, financial condition, and prospects that is made available to shareholders and investors ○ *a quarterly report* **6.** *UK* EDUC **WRITTEN ACCOUNT OF CHILD'S SCHOOLWORK** a record of a child's academic performance at school over a specific period, prepared by teachers and given to the child's parents or guardians. ANZ, N Am term **report card 7. SHARP LOUD NOISE** a very sharp loud noise, especially that of an explosion or gunshot **8. REPUTATION** reputation or perceived character ■ **reports** *npl* LAW **ACCOUNTS OF CASE AT LAW** written accounts of a court's adjudication, summarizing arguments and findings [14C. Via French < Latin *reportare* 'carry back' < *portare* 'carry'] —**reportable** *adj*

reportage /ri páwr tij, réppawr taázh/ *n* **1. PROCESS OF TELLING NEWS** the use of print and electronic media to inform people about news and current events **2. THINGS REPORTED** a body of reported news **3. WAY OF GIVING NEWS** a particular way of gathering and presenting news [Late 19C. < REPORT, after French *reportage*]

report card *n ANZ, N Am* same as **report** *n* (sense 6)

reportedly /ri páwrtidli/ *adv* according to an unconfirmed report ○ *Reportedly he lost all his money.*

reported speech /ri páwrtid-/ *n* GRAM same as **indirect speech**

reporter /ri páwrtər/ *n* **1. SOMEBODY WHO REPORTS NEWS** somebody whose job is to find out facts and use the print or broadcast media to tell people about them

2. SOMEBODY WHO REPORTS somebody who makes a report about something that has happened or the results of research or an investigation **3.** POL RECORDER OF LEGISLATIVE PROCEEDINGS an official who makes a written record of the proceedings of a legislature —**reportorial** /réppawr táwri əl/ *adj* —**reportorially** *adv*

report stage *n* a phase in the passage of a piece of legislation in the British and Canadian parliaments, following the report of a committee and preceding a third reading

repose[1] /ri pṓz/ *n* **1.** REST a state of rest or inactivity **2.** TRANQUILLITY a condition of peacefulness and tranquillity, e.g. in a place **3.** COMPOSURE calmness and composure of manner **4.** RELIG REST AFTER DEATH in some beliefs, eternal or heavenly rest ■ *v* (**-poses, -posing, -posed**) (*formal*) **1.** *vti* LIE RESTING to lie at rest, or lay something at rest **2.** *vi* LIE RESTING ON TOP OF SOMETHING to lie while resting on or supported by something **3.** *vi* BE DEAD to lie dead (*used euphemistically*) **4. repose yourself** *vr* SETTLE SELF AT REST to settle yourself in a relaxed or restful position **5.** *vi* TAKE SUPPORT FROM SOMETHING to be supported or based on something ○ *Your argument reposes on false analogies.* [15C. Via French *reposer* < Latin *repausare* 'rest completely' < *pausare* 'to rest'] —**reposal** *n*

repose[2] /ri pṓz/ (**-poses, -posing, -posed**) *vt* to place faith, confidence, or trust in somebody or something (*formal*) ○ *reposed a great deal of confidence in him* [Mid-16C. < Latin *repos-*, stem of *reponere* 'place again' < *ponere* 'to place']

reposeful /ri pṓzf'l/ *adj* showing or giving rise to restfulness or calm —**reposefully** *adv* —**reposefulness** *n*

repository /ri pózzitəri/ (*plural* **-ries**) *n* **1.** PLACE FOR STORAGE a place or container in which something is stored **2.** POSSESSOR OF EXTENSIVE KNOWLEDGE somebody with, or something such as a book that contains, extensive detailed knowledge of something ○ *She was a repository of information about the history of the island.* **3.** CONFIDANT somebody in whom something is confided **4.** WAREHOUSE FOR COMMODITIES a place where goods are stored prior to sale **5.** TOMB a burial vault or sepulchre [15C. Directly or via French < Latin *repositorium* < past participle of *reponere* (see REPOSE[1])]

repossess /reé pə zéss/ (**-sesses, -sessing, -sessed**) *vt* to take back goods or property from a buyer who has failed to keep up payments on them —**repossession** *n* —**repossessor** *n*

repoussé /rə póossay/ *adj* **1.** FORMING PATTERN IN RELIEF formed as a raised pattern on a thin piece of metal by having been hammered through from the reverse side **2.** DECORATED WITH HAMMERED PATTERN decorated with a raised pattern that has been hammered through from the reverse side ■ *n* **1.** HAMMERED DESIGN a repoussé design on metal **2.** TECHNIQUE OF HAMMERING DESIGN the technique of producing repoussé designs [Mid-19C. < French, past participle of *repousser* 'push back' < *pousser* 'push']

repp *n* TEXTILES another spelling of **rep**[1]

repr. *abbr* **1.** representative **2.** represented **3.** representing **4.** PUBL reprint

reprehend /réppri hénd/ (**-hends, -hending, -hended**) *vt* to criticize or reprove somebody or something [14C. < Latin *reprehendere* 'seize again' < *prehendere* 'seize'] —**reprehendable** *adj* —**reprehender** *n*

reprehensible /réppri hénssəb'l/ *adj* highly unacceptable and deserving censure [14C. < late Latin *reprehensibilis* < past participle of Latin *reprehendere* (see REPREHEND)] —**reprehensibility** /réppri hénssə bílləti/ *n* —**reprehensibly** *adv*

reprehension /réppri hénsh'n/ *n* reproof or criticism for wrongdoing [14C. < Latin *reprehension-* < past participle of *reprehendere* (see REPREHEND)] —**reprehensive** *adj* —**reprehensively** *adv*

represent /réppri zént/ (**-sents, -senting, -sented**) *v* **1.** *vt* ACT OR SPEAK FOR ANOTHER to act or speak on behalf of somebody or something **2.** *vt* GO SOMEWHERE ON BEHALF OF ANOTHER to go or be present somewhere, or participate in a competition, on behalf of a person, constituency, organization, or other group **3.** *vt* ACT FOR ANOTHER OFFICIALLY to speak and act for somebody else in an official way ○ *Who will be representing France at the conference?* **4.** *vt* BE EQUIVALENT OF SOMETHING to be a sign or equivalent of something **5.** *vt* SYMBOLIZE SOMETHING to symbolize something, especially as a sign on a map showing the position of something ○ *On the map a blue line represents a river.* **6.** *vt* DEPICT SOMETHING OR SOMEBODY to portray or present an image of somebody or something as being something in particular **7. represent yourself** *vr* UNTRUTHFULLY CLAIM TO BE SOMETHING to describe yourself as something you are not ○ *He was arrested at the airport despite trying to represent himself as a tourist.* **8.** *vt* THEATRE DEPICT SOMEBODY ON STAGE to portray or perform a character or role on stage [14C. Directly or via French < Latin *repraesentare*, literally 'show back' < *praesentare* 'to show'] —**representability** /réppri zentə bílləti/ *n* —**representable** *adj* —**representer** *n* ◇ **be represented** to be present somewhere to a particular degree ○ *Women are now well represented at all levels.*

USAGE See *denote*.

---

re-present /reé pri zént/ *vt* to send, offer, or present something again

representation /réppri zen táysh'n/ *n* **1.** PICTURE a visual depiction of somebody or something **2.** FACT OF BEING SERVED BY REPRESENTATIVE the fact or right of being represented by somebody, especially of having a member in a legislature with power to vote or speak for an electorate **3.** VOTING SYSTEM OR BODY OF ELECTORS the system by which electors vote for people to represent them as legislators, administrators, or judges, or the group of people so elected **4.** SOMETHING SPOKEN OR DONE FOR ANOTHER an action done or speech made on behalf of another, especially as an agent or deputy **5.** SOMETHING DESCRIBED OR STATED a description, account, or statement of something real or alleged, especially one meant to induce a response from authority (*often used in the plural*) **6.** LAW STATEMENT INDUCING SOMEBODY TO MAKE CONTRACT a statement, real or implied, that encourages somebody to make an agreement **7.** THEATRE PERFORMANCE a theatrical performance or production

representational /réppri zen táysh'nəl/ *adj* **1.** relating to or characterized by representation **2.** depicting something in a physically recognizable form, especially in art —**representationally** *adv*

representationalism /réppri zen táysh'nəlizəm/, **representationism** /-táysh'nizəm/ *n* **1.** the practice or principle of depicting objects in recognizable form, especially in art **2.** the theory that the mind directly apprehends external objects only through ideas or data provided by the senses —**representationalist** *n* —**representationalistic** /-taysh'nə lístik/ *adj*

representative /réppri zéntətiv/ *n* **1.** SOMEBODY WHO SPEAKS FOR OTHERS somebody who speaks, acts, or votes on behalf of others **2.** MEMBER OF LEGISLATURE a member of a legislative assembly **3.** *also* **Representative** *US* MEMBER OF HOUSE OF REPRESENTATIVES a member of the House of Representatives, the lower chamber in the US Congress, or of a state legislature **4.** COMMERCIAL AGENT OR SALESPERSON an agent or salesperson for a company **5.** EXAMPLE an example or type of something **6.** *NZ* PLAYER REPRESENTING PROVINCE a rugby or football player who represents a province during interprovincial competition ■ *adj* **1.** CHARACTERISTIC characteristic of something, especially of a class or kind **2.** MADE UP OF ELECTED PEOPLE composed of elected or authorized people ○ *a representative assembly* **3.** LETTING PEOPLE ELECT SOMEBODY allowing people to vote for somebody to represent them in a legislative body such as the House of Commons in the United Kingdom or the Congress in the United States ○ *a representative form of government* **4.** MADE UP OF ALL TYPES including a complete range of examples of something ○ *a representative sample* **5.** ACTING ON SOMEBODY'S BEHALF acting as somebody's agent, deputy, or delegate —**representatively** *adv* —**representativeness** *n*

~~**representitive**~~ incorrect spelling of **representative**

repress /ri préss/ (**-presses, -pressing, -pressed**) *vt* **1.** CURB ACTIONS THAT SHOW FEELINGS to check or restrain an action that would reveal feelings ○ *He had to repress a smile.* **2.** SUPPRESS SOMETHING BY FORCE to control a population or an expression of people's freedom by force or military means ○ *repressed any uprising* **3.** PSYCHOL BLOCK SOMETHING FROM MIND in Freudian psychology, to block unacceptable or painful impulses, desires, or memories from the conscious mind [14C. < Latin *repress-*, past participle of *reprimere* 'press back' < *premere* 'to press'] —**repressibility** /ri préssə bílləti/ *n* —**repressible** *adj*

re-press /ree préss/ *vt* to press something again, especially to manufacture another issue of a recording

repressed /ri prést/ *adj* **1.** WITH CURBED EMOTIONS not acknowledging strong personal feelings, particularly of anger or sexual desire **2.** SUBDUED FORCIBLY kept under control by force or military means ○ *the repressed peoples of the invaded islands* **3.** PSYCHOL BLOCKED FROM CONSCIOUSNESS in Freudian psychology, blocked from the conscious mind and relegated to the unconscious

represser *n* another spelling of **repressor**

repression /ri présh'n/ *n* **1.** the process of suppressing a population, or the condition of having political, social, or cultural freedom controlled by force or military means **2.** in Freudian psychology, a mechanism by which people protect themselves from threatening thoughts by blocking them out of the conscious mind

repressive /ri préssiv/ *adj* exerting strict control on the freedom of others —**repressively** *adv* —**repressiveness** *n*

repressor /ri préssər/, **represser** *n* **1.** a means of repressing something or somebody **2.** a protein that stops gene transcription

reprieve /ri preév/ *vt* (**-prieves, -prieving, -prieved**) **1.** STOP OR POSTPONE SOMEBODY'S PUNISHMENT to halt or delay the punishment of somebody, especially when the punishment is death (*often passive*) **2.** OFFER RESPITE TO SOMEBODY to provide somebody with temporary relief from something harmful, especially danger or pain ■ *n* **1.** STOPPING OR POSTPONEMENT OF PUNISHMENT the halting or delay of somebody's punishment, especially when the punishment is death **2.** WARRANT HALTING OR POSTPONING PUNISHMENT a warrant giving the authority to stop or postpone somebody's punishment, especially when the punishment is death **3.** RESPITE FROM SOMETHING HARMFUL a relief from something harmful, especially danger or pain [Mid-17C. Alteration of obsolete *repry* 'take back to prison, escape the death sentence' < Old French *repris* 'taken back' < Latin *reprehendere* (see REPREHEND)] —**reprievable** *adj* —**repriever** *n*

reprimand /réppri maand/ *vt* (**-mands, -manding, -manded**) to rebuke somebody for a wrongdoing ■ *n* a rebuke given for having done something wrong [Mid-17C. Via French *réprimande* < Latin *reprimenda* 'that is to be suppressed' < *reprimere* 'press back']

reprint *vt* /ree prínt/ (**-prints, -printing, -printed**) PRINT SOMETHING AGAIN to print something again, especially with few or no changes ■ *n* /reé print/ **1.** COPY OF SOMETHING ALREADY PUBLISHED a printed copy of something that has already been in print **2.** PUBL same as **offprint 3.** REISSUE OF PRINTED WORK a book or other printed work that is the same as or has only minor changes from one that was previously issued —**reprinter** /ree príntər/ *n*

reprisal /ri prīz'l/ *n* **1.** RETALIATION IN WAR a violent military action, e.g. the killing of prisoners or civilians, carried out in retaliation for an enemy's action **2.** STRONG OR VIOLENT RETALIATION a strong or violent retaliation for an action that somebody has taken **3.** RETALIATORY SEIZURE FROM ANOTHER COUNTRY the forcible seizure of property or people from another country as retaliation for some injury [15C. Via Anglo-Norman *reprisaille* < medieval Latin *reprisalia*, *represalia*, contraction of *reprehensalia* < Latin *reprehendere* (see REPREHEND)]

reprise /ri preéz/ *n* **1.** REPEAT OF MUSICAL PASSAGE a repeated passage of music, or a return to an earlier musical theme **2.** MUSIC same as **chorus** *n* (sense 1) **3.** REPETITION a repetition or recurrence of something ■ *vt* (**-prises, -prising, -prised**) **1.** REPEAT MUSIC to repeat a passage of music or return to an earlier theme **2.** REPEAT ACTION to repeat an action or performance ○ *reprised her role as Gertrude in the New York production* [Mid-20C. < French < past participle of *reprendre* 'take again' < *prendre* 'take' < Latin *prehendere*]

repro /reé prō/ *n* (*informal*) **1.** a reproduction, especially of a painting or piece of furniture **2.** PRINTING same as **reproduction proof** [Mid-20C. Shortening]

reproach /ri prṓch/ *v* (**-proaches, -proaching, -proached**) **1.** *vt* CRITICIZE SOMEBODY to criticize somebody for doing

something wrong **2. reproach yourself** *vr* FEEL BLAMEWORTHY to feel ashamed because you know you have done something wrong ■ *n* **1.** CRITICISM criticism or disapproval for having done something wrong, or an expression of this **2.** SOMETHING DISGRACEFUL something that reflects badly on somebody who has failed to improve or deal with it **3.** DISCREDIT shame or disgrace that somebody or something incurs ○ *actions that brought reproach upon his family* [15C. < Old French *reprochier* < Latin *prope* 'near'] —**reproachable** *adj* —**reproachableness** *n* —**reproachably** *adv* —**reproacher** *n* —**reproachingly** *adv* ◇ **above** *or* **beyond reproach** so good that no criticism can be made

reproachful /ri próchf'l/ *adj* expressing disapproval or blame —**reproachfully** *adv* —**reproachfulness** *n*

reprobate /répprō bayt/ *n* **1.** SOMEBODY IMMORAL a disreputable or immoral person **2.** RELIG SOMEBODY DAMNED somebody whose soul is believed to be damned ■ *adj* **1.** DISREPUTABLE disreputable or immoral **2.** RELIG DAMNED having a soul that is believed to be damned ■ *vt* (**-bates, -bating, -bated**) **1.** CENSURE SOMEBODY to censure or condemn somebody (*formal*) **2.** RELIG DENY SALVATION TO SOMEBODY to condemn somebody to supposed eternal damnation [Mid-16C. < late Latin *reprobatus* < Latin *reprobat-*, past participle of *reprobare* 'prove to be unworthy' < *probare* 'prove'] —**reprobacy** *n* —**reprobater** *n* —**reprobative** *adj*

reprobation /répprō báysh'n/ *n* **1.** strong condemnation or disapproval of somebody or something **2.** the supposed condemnation of somebody's soul to eternal damnation [15C. Directly or via French < Latin *reprobation-* < *reprobat-* (see REPROBATE)] —**reprobationary** *adj*

reproduce /reéprə dyoóss/ (**-duces, -ducing, -duced**) *v* **1.** *vti* MAKE DUPLICATE OF SOMETHING to copy something by photographing, scanning, printing, or another process, or be copied in this way **2.** *vi* BIOL PRODUCE OFFSPRING to produce offspring or new individuals through a sexual or asexual process **3.** *vt* REPEAT SOMETHING to do something in the same way as before **4.** *vt* REMEMBER SOMETHING to remember or imagine something again —**reproducer** *n* —**reproducibility** /reéprə dyoóssə bílləti/ *n* —**reproducible** *adj* —**reproducibly** *adv*

SYNONYMS See *copy*.

reproduction /reéprə dúksh'n/ *n* **1.** ACT OF REPRODUCING SOMETHING the act or process of reproducing something **2.** PRODUCTION OF OFFSPRING the production of offspring or new individuals through a sexual or asexual process **3.** COPY OF OBJECT a copy of something in an earlier style, especially a painting or a piece of furniture **4.** PRINT, ELECTRONIC, OR PHOTOGRAPHIC DUPLICATE a copy of something printed, scanned, photographed, or produced by other means **5.** RECORDING OF SOUND the recording of sound, or the quality of recorded sound [Mid-17C. < REPRODUCE, after *production*]

reproduction proof *n* a printed proof, usually on glossy paper, of such high quality that it can be photographed for making a printing plate

reproductive /reéprə dúktiv/ *adj* relating to, taking part in, or enabling the production of new offspring or individuals ○ *reproductive organs* [Mid-18C. < REPRODUCE, after *productive*] —**reproductively** *adv* —**reproductiveness** *n*

reproductive cloning *n* the use of cloning to produce a new genetically identical human or animal from the cells of another human or animal. ◊ **therapeutic cloning**

reproductive system *n* the combination of bodily organs and tissues used in the process of producing offspring

reprography /ri próggrəfi/ *n* the reproduction of something printed, e.g. by offset printing, microfilming, photography, or xerography [Mid-20C. < German *Reprographie*, blend of *Reproduktion* 'reproduction' + *Photographie* 'photography'] —**reprographic** /réppra gráffik/ *adj*

reproof /ri proóf/, **reproval** /ri proóv'l/ *n* the act of criticizing somebody for having done something wrong, or something said as a rebuke [14C. < Old French *reprove* < *reprover* (see REPROVE)]

reprove /ri proóv/ (**-proves, -proving, -proved**) *vt* to speak to somebody in a way that shows disapproval of something he or she has done [14C. Via Old French *reprover* < Latin *reprobare* 'prove to be unworthy' (see REPROBATE)] —**reprovable** *adj* —**reprover** *n* —**reprovingly** *adv*

Reps /reps/ *n Aus* POL same as **House of Representatives** (sense 2) (*informal*)

rept *abbr* **1.** FIN receipt **2.** report

reptant /réptənt/ *adj* creeping or lying along the ground [Mid-17C. < Latin *reptant-*, present participle of *reptare* 'keep creeping' < *repere* 'to creep']

reptile /rép tīl/ *n* **1.** COLD-BLOODED SCALY VERTEBRATE an air-breathing cold-blooded egg-laying vertebrate with an outer covering of scales or plates and a bony skeleton, e.g. the crocodile, tortoise, snake, or lizard. Class: Reptilia. **2.** OFFENSIVE TERM an offensive term that deliberately insults somebody whose behaviour or character is regarded as suspicious, untrustworthy, or sickeningly ingratiating (*insult*) ■ *adj* BEING REPTILE belonging to the class of reptiles [14C. Via French < late Latin *reptilis* 'creeping' < Latin *rept-*, past participle of *repere* 'creep'] —**reptilian** /rep tílli ən/ *adj, n*

Repton /réptən/, **Humphry** (1752–1818) British landscape architect. He designed many parks of English country houses, working in the picturesque style.

Repub. *abbr* POL **1.** Republic **2.** Republican

republic /ri púbblik/ *n* **1.** POLITICAL SYSTEM WITH ELECTED REPRESENTATIVES a political system or form of government in which people elect representatives to exercise power for them **2.** STATE WITH ELECTED REPRESENTATIVES a country or other political unit whose government or political system is that of a republic **3.** GROUP WITH COLLECTIVE INTERESTS a group of people who are considered to be equals and who have a collective interest, objective, or vocation (*formal*) ○ *the republic of letters* [Late 16C. Via French *république* < Latin *res publica* 'public matter']

CULTURAL NOTE ***The Republic***, a political treatise (early 4th century BC) by the Greek philosopher Plato. Presented in the form of a series of dialogues between Socrates and his pupils, it begins with a discussion of the nature of justice that leads in turn to an attempt to define the ideal society. For Plato, this would consist of an aristocracy run by a class of legislators groomed for leadership by a state education system.

republican /ri púbblikən/ *n* somebody who believes that the best government is one in which supreme power is vested in an electorate ■ *adj* relating to, belonging to, or characteristic of a republic

Republican *adj* **1.** supporting the idea that Northern Ireland should be united politically with the Republic of Ireland and should cease to form part of the United Kingdom **2.** belonging to or supporting the republican party in the United States —**Republican** *n*

republicanise *vt* POL another spelling of **republicanize**

republicanism /ri púbblikənizəm/ *n* **1.** the belief that the supreme power of a country should be vested in an electorate **2.** the theory and principles of republican government

Republicanism *n* **1.** support for the idea of uniting Northern Ireland politically with the Republic of Ireland **2.** support for the Republican Party in the United States

republicanize /ri púbblikə nīz/ (**-izes, -izing, -ized**), **republicanise** (**-ises, -ising, -ised**) *vt* to make a state or other political unit into a republic —**republicanization** /ri púbblikə nī záysh'n/ *n*

Republican Party *n* in the United States, a political party at state and national level, founded in 1854–56

Republic Day *n* in India, a statutory holiday to commemorate the day on which the Republic was founded and the Constitution adopted. Date: 26 January.

repudiate /ri pyoódi ayt/ (**-ates, -ating, -ated**) *vt* **1.** DISOWN SOMETHING to disapprove of something formally and strongly and renounce any connection with it ○ *She repudiated the committee's actions.* **2.** DENY SOMETHING to state that something is untrue **3.** REJECT SOMETHING to reject something that is offered **4.** DISOWN LOVED ONE to disown a family member or lover **5.** REJECT SOMETHING AS INVALID to refuse to accept the validity of something **6.** REFUSE TO PAY DEBT to refuse to acknowledge or pay a debt [Mid-16C. < Latin *repudiat-*, past participle of *repudiare* 'to divorce' < *repudium* 'divorce'] —**repudiable** *adj* —**repudiation** /ri pyoódi áysh'n/ *n* —**repudiative** *adj* —**repudiator** *n*

repugnance /ri púgnənss/, **repugnancy** *n* a very strong feeling of disgust about something

SYNONYMS See *dislike*.

repugnant /ri púgnənt/ *adj* **1.** offensive and completely unacceptable **2.** making somebody feel physically repelled ○ *a repugnant odour* [Late 18C. Via Old French, 'contrary' < Latin *repugnant-*, present participle of *repugnare* 'fight back' < *pugnare* 'to fight'] —**repugnantly** *adv*

repulse /ri púlss/ *vt* (**-pulses, -pulsing, -pulsed**) **1.** FORCE BACK MILITARY ATTACK to repel an attacking military force **2.** DISGUST SOMEBODY to cause disgust or revulsion in somebody (*informal*) **3.** SPURN SOMEBODY to reject or rebuff an approach from somebody ■ *n* **1.** REJECTION a refusal or rejection of somebody **2.** ACT OF FORCING BACK ATTACK the forcing back of an attacking military force [Mid-16C. < Latin *repuls-*, past participle of *repellere* 'drive back' (see REPEL)]

repulsion /ri púlsh'n/ *n* **1.** a feeling of disgust or very strong dislike **2.** a force between two bodies of the same electric charge or magnetic polarity that tends to repel or separate them. It is this repulsive force between atoms and molecules at very short distances that tends to keep them separated.

repulsive /ri púlssiv/ *adj* **1.** making somebody feel disgust or very strong dislike **2.** tending to repel —**repulsively** *adv* —**repulsiveness** *n*

USAGE See *repellent*.

repurchase agreement *n* **1.** an agreement between a dealer and an investor in which the investor agrees to sell purchased securities back to the dealer on a fixed date for a specific profit **2.** an agreement between a buyer and a seller in which the seller agrees to buy back the purchased item at the end of a fixed period

reputable /réppyoótəb'l/ *adj* known to be honest, reliable, or respectable [Late 17C. Directly or via French < medieval Latin *reputabilis* < Latin *reputare* (see REPUTE)] —**reputability** /réppyoótə bílləti/ *n* —**reputably** *adv*

reputation /réppyoo táysh'n/ *n* **1.** the views that are generally held about somebody or something **2.** a high opinion that people hold about somebody or something [14C. < Latin *reputation-* 'consideration' < *reputare* (see REPUTE)]

repute /ri pyoót/ *n* (*formal*) **1.** estimation or character according to what people in general think **2.** good reputation or standing [Mid-16C. Directly or via French < Latin *reputare* 'think repeatedly' < *putare* 'think']

reputed /ri pyoótid/ *adj* widely believed, although not necessarily established as fact [Late 16C. < REPUTE used as a verb]

reputedly /ri pyoótidli/ *adv* according to popular belief

req. *abbr* **1.** request **2.** require **3.** required **4.** requirement **5.** requisition

request /ri kwést/ *vt* (**-quests, -questing, -quested**) **1.** ASK POLITELY FOR SOMETHING to ask formally or courteously for something to be given or done ○ *requested that he be excused* ○ *requested her favourite song* **2.** ASK SOMEBODY FOR SOMETHING to ask somebody to do something ○ *requested Father Peter to perform their marriage ceremony* ■ *n* **1.** ACT OF EXPRESSING WISH the act of asking or petitioning for something to be done or given **2.** EXPRESSION OF POLITE WISH an act of politely or formally asking that something be done or given **3.** MUSIC THAT IS ASKED FOR a piece of music played on a radio programme, at a live performance, or at a disco because somebody asks for it ○ *We'll be playing requests later tonight.* [14C. < Old French *requeste* < Latin *requisit-*, past participle of *requirere* (see REQUIRE)] —**requester** *n*

request stop *n* a bus stop at which the bus does not halt unless somebody at the stop signals for it to do so or if somebody wants to get off there

requiem /rékwi əm, -wi em/, **Requiem** *n* **1.** ROMAN CATHOLIC SERVICE FOR DEAD a Roman Catholic mass held to offer prayers for somebody who has died **2.** MUSIC FOR REQUIEM a piece of music written to accompany a

requiem mass 3. COMMEMORATIVE MUSIC a piece of music written to commemorate somebody who has died [14C. < Latin, 'rest', in *Requiem aeternam dona eis Domine* 'Grant them eternal rest, O Lord']

requiem shark *n* a voracious grey or brownish shark with a slender body and rounded snout. Tiger sharks and blue sharks are requiem sharks. Native to: tropical waters. Family: Carcharhinidae. [By folk etymology < French *requin* 'shark']

requiescat /rékwi éss kat/ *n* a prayer asking that the soul of a dead person might be at rest [Early 19C. < Latin, 'may he or she rest']

require /ri kwír/ (**-quires, -quiring, -quired**) *vt* **1. NEED SOMETHING OR SOMEBODY** to be in need of something or somebody for a purpose ○ *The recipe requires a cup of milk.* **2. MAKE SOMETHING NECESSARY** to have something as a necessary precondition ○ *A password is required for entry to the system.* **3. DEMAND SOMETHING BY LAW** to demand something by a law or regulation (*often passive*) ○ *Notification was required by law.* **4. INSIST ON SOMETHING** to insist that somebody do something ○ *All applicants are required to pass a medical exam.* [14C. < Old French *requi(i)er-*, stem of *requere* < Latin *requirere* 'seek in return' < *quaerere* 'seek'] —**requirement** *n* —**requirer** *n*

required /ri kwírd/ *adj* **1.** necessary or appropriate for a specific purpose ○ *He lacks the required degree of expertise.* **2.** insisted upon or imposed as a condition ○ *required reading for a course*

requisite /rékwizit/ *adj* necessary or appropriate for a specific purpose (*formal*) ○ *the requisite skills for the job* ■ *n* something that is necessary or indispensable [15C. < Latin *requisitus*, past participle of *requirere* (see REQUIRE)] —**requisitely** *adv* —**requisiteness** *n*

SYNONYMS See *necessary*.

requisition /rékwi zísh'n/ *n* **1. DEMAND FOR SOMETHING** a demand for something that is required **2. OFFICIAL FORM** a written or printed request for something that is needed **3. FACT OF MAKING FORMAL DEMAND** the act or process of making a formal demand for something **4. REQUEST FOR FUGITIVE** a request by a government that another government return a fugitive from the law ■ *vt* (**-tions, -tioning, -tioned**) **1. TAKE SOMETHING OFFICIALLY** to demand and take something that is needed, especially for official or military use **2. OBTAIN SOMEBODY FOR JOB** to require and obtain the services of somebody to do something ○ *requisitioned a few friends for the weekend to help paint the house* [Mid-16C. Directly or via French < Latin *requisition-* < past participle of *requirere* (see REQUIRE)] —**requisitionary** *adj*

requite /ri kwít/ (**-quites, -quiting, -quited**) *vt* **1.** to return in kind a kindness or hurt that somebody has done **2.** to pay somebody back for a service performed [Early 16C. < RE- + earlier form of QUIT 'pay up'] —**requitable** *adj* —**requital** *n* —**requitement** *n*

reradiate /ree ráydi ayt/ (**-ates, -ating, -ated**) *vt* to emit radiation after absorbing incident radiation —**reradiation** /ree raydi áysh'n/ *n*

reredos

reredos /reér doss/ *n* **1.** an artistic decoration behind the altar in a church, e.g. a wood or stone screen or a wall-hanging **2.** the back of an open fireplace [14C. Via Anglo-Norman < Old French *areredos* < *arere* 'behind' + *dos* 'back' < Latin *dorsum*]

rerelease /ree ri leéss/ *vt* (**-leases, -leasing, -leased**) to release a music recording or a film again for

distribution to the public ■ *n* a music recording or a film that has been released again to the public

rerun *vt* /ree rún/ (**-runs, -running, -ran** /-rán/, **-run**) **1. SHOW SOMETHING AGAIN** to show or broadcast a TV series, video, or film again **2. REPEAT RACE** to run a race again, or cause a race to be run again, after the result on the first occasion has been disallowed because of an infringement ■ *n* /ree run/ (*plural* **-runs**) **1. REPEAT OF PROGRAM** a repeat showing of recorded entertainment, especially a TV series **2. REPEAT OF RACE** the repeat running of a race after an infringement

res /rayz, rayss/ (*plural same*) *n* in law, a matter or thing [< Latin, 'thing, legal matter']

RES *abbr* **1.** renewable energy source **2.** renewable energy system **3.** Royal Entomological Society

res. *abbr* **1.** research **2.** reservation **3.** reserved **4.** reservoir **5.** residence **6.** resident **7.** resigned **8.** resolution

res adjudicata *n* LAW same as **res judicata**

resale /ree sayl, ree sáyl/ *n* **1.** the selling of something again ○ *Not for resale.* **2.** the selling of something second-hand —**resalability** /ree sáylə bílləti/ *n* —**resalable** /ree sáyləb'l/ *adj*

resale price maintenance *n* COMM same as **retail price maintenance**

resat EDUC past participle, past tense of **resit**

rescale /ree skáyl/ (**-scales, -scaling, -scaled**) *vt* to modify the scale of something, especially to reduce it ○ *rescale a budget* ○ *rescale a drawing*

reschedule /ree shéddyool, -skédd-/ (**-ules, -uling, -uled**) *vt* **1.** to arrange a new time slot for something **2.** to extend the payment schedule of a loan

rescind /ri sínd/ (**-scinds, -scinding, -scinded**) *vt* **1. CANCEL SOMETHING** to remove the validity or authority of something **2. REVOKE CONTRACT** to revoke a contract and return the parties to their former positions before the contract **3. REPEAL DECISION OR ENACTMENT** to declare a decision or enactment null and void [Mid-16C. < Latin *rescindere* 'cut back' < *scindere* 'to cut'] —**rescindable** *adj* —**rescinder** *n* —**rescindment** *n*

rescission /ri sízh'n/ *n* the act of rescinding something [Early 17C. < late Latin *rescission-* < Latin *resciss-*, past participle of *rescindere* (see RESCIND)]

rescore /ree skáwr/ (**-scores, -scoring, -scored**) *vt* to write new instrumentation for a piece of music

rescript /ree skript/ *n* **1. REWRITE** an act of rewriting something **2. ECCLESIASTICAL RULING** a formal reply by the pope or some other high dignitary of the Roman Catholic Church on a matter of doctrine or discipline **3. ROMAN EMPEROR'S LEGAL RULING** a formal reply by an ancient Roman or Holy Roman emperor on a point of law [14C. < Latin *rescriptum*, form of past participle of *rescribere* 'write back' < *scribere* 'write']

rescue /réskyoo/ *v* (**-cues, -cuing, -cued**) **1.** *vt* **REMOVE SOMEBODY FROM DANGER** to save somebody or something from a dangerous or harmful situation ○ *The boys had to be rescued from the rocks by helicopter.* **2. SAVE SOMETHING** to prevent something from being discarded, rejected, or put out of operation ○ *At the last minute the factory was rescued from closure.* **3.** *vt* LAW **GET SOMEBODY OUT OF JAIL** to release somebody from legal custody by force **4.** *vt* LAW **TAKE FORCIBLE POSSESSION OF SOMETHING** to seize property or goods by force ■ *n* **1. REMOVAL FROM DANGER OR HARM** an act or instance of saving somebody or something from a dangerous or harmful situation (*often used before a noun*) ○ *a daring rescue attempt* **2. PROVISION OF HELP** an instance of helping somebody in an awkward or difficult situation ○ *I couldn't think what to say, but luckily he came to my rescue.* **3.** LAW **RELEASE FROM JAIL** the release of somebody from legal custody by force **4.** LAW **SEIZURE OF GOODS** the seizure of property or goods by force [14C. < Old French *rescourre* 'shake loose' < *escourre* 'shake' < escutere < *ex-* 'out' + *quatere* 'to strike'] —**rescuable** *adj* —**rescuer** *n*

rescue worker *n* a member of a medical or emergency service

research /ri súrch, ree súrch/ *n* methodical investigation into a subject in order to discover facts, to establish or revise a theory, or to develop a plan of action based on the facts discovered ■ *vti* (**-searches, -searching, -searched**) to carry out research into a subject [Late 16C. < obsolete French

recerche < Old French *recercher* 'search closely' < *cerchier* 'explore'] —**researchable** *adj* —**researcher** *n*

USAGE The traditional pronunciation is with the stress on the second syllable (ri súrch), both for the noun and the verb. More recently, a pronunciation with the stress on the first syllable (ree surch) has become common, especially in broadcasting.

research and development *n* in business and industry, the work of investigating improved processes, products, and services and of developing new ones

reseat /ree seét/ (**-seats, -seating, -seated**) *vt* **1. SEAT SOMEBODY ELSEWHERE** to seat somebody in another place **2. SEAT SOMEBODY AS BEFORE** to return somebody to the seat previously occupied **3. REPLACE SEATS IN BUILDING** to fit new seats in an auditorium or hall **4. PUT NEW MATERIAL ON SEAT** to replace the material on a seat **5.** ENG **REPLACE VALVE SEATING** to return the seating of a valve to good condition

reseau /rézzō/ (*plural* **-seaux** /rézzō, rézzōz/ or **-seaus**) *n* **1.** a mesh foundation on which lace is made **2.** a grid of lines photographed onto or cut into a glass plate and used as a reference for astronomical observations [Late 16C. < French *réseau* 'network', later form of Old French *reseuil* 'little net' < *raiz* 'net' < Latin *rete*]

resect /ri sékt/ (**-sects, -secting, -sected**) *vt* to cut through and surgically remove part of an organ, bone, or other body part [Mid-17C. < Latin *resect-*, past participle of *resecare* 'cut back' < *secare* 'to cut']

resection /ri séksh'n/ *n* **1.** the surgical removal of part of an organ, bone, or other body part **2.** the establishment of the location of a point when surveying by sighting from that point to two other points whose locations are known

resectoscope /ri séktə skōp/ *n* a surgical instrument that allows a resection to be made without a bigger incision than that caused by the instrument itself

reseda

reseda /réssidə, ri seédə/ (*plural* **-das** or *same*) *n* **1.** a plant that has small dense spikes of greyish-green flowers with divided petals. Native to: Mediterranean. Genus: *Reseda*. **2.** a greyish-green colour [Mid-18C. Via modern Latin genus name < Latin] —**reseda** *adj*

reseed /ree seéd/ (**-seeds, -seeding, -seeded**) *v* **1.** *vt* to plant seeds on an area of land again **2.** *vti* to grow a plant from seed dropped by the previous generation, or grow in this way

resemblance /ri zémblənss/ *n* **1. SIMILARITY** similarity in appearance or quality to somebody or something else **2. DEGREE OF SIMILARITY** the extent to which somebody or something resembles somebody or something else ○ *The resemblance between them is remarkable.* **3. POINT OF SIMILARITY** a respect in which somebody or something resembles somebody or something else **4. SOMETHING SIMILAR** something that resembles something else

resemble /ri zémb'əl/ (**-bles, -bling, -bled**) *vt* to be similar to somebody or something in appearance or behaviour [14C. < Old French *resembler* 'be very like' < *sembler* 'seem' < Latin *simulare* (see SIMULATE)] —**resembler** *n*

~~**resemblence**~~ incorrect spelling of **resemblance**

resent /ri zént/ (**-sents, -senting, -sented**) *vt* to feel aggrieved about something or towards somebody, often because of a perceived wrong or injustice [Late

16C. < obsolete French *ressentir* 'feel strongly' < *sentir* 'feel' < Latin *sentire*]

resentful /ri zéntf'l/ *adj* annoyed about having been badly treated, or characterized by such a feeling of annoyance —**resentfully** *adv* —**resentfulness** *n*

resentment /ri zéntmənt/ *n* aggrieved feelings caused by a sense of having been badly treated [Early 17C. < obsolete French *ressentiment* 'strong feeling' < *ressentir* (see RESENT)]

SYNONYMS See *anger.*

reservation /rézzər váysh'n/ *n* **1. ARRANGEMENT MADE BEFOREHAND** an advance booking, e.g. of a seat, hotel room, or ticket **2. PLACE ARRANGED BEFOREHAND** something booked in advance, e.g. a seat, hotel room, or ticket **3. ACT OF ARRANGING BEFOREHAND** the act of booking something in advance **4. LAND SET ASIDE** an area of land set aside for a special purpose, especially in North America for the use of a Native North American people **5.** ROADS same as **central reservation 6. KEEPING SOMETHING BACK** the act of withholding something, or an instance of so doing **7. LIMITING CONDITION** a limiting condition to an agreement **8.** LAW **RETAINED LEGAL INTEREST** a clause in a deed by which somebody retains an interest in something being granted or leased, or such an interest itself **9.** CHR **PRESERVATION OF CONSECRATED ELEMENTS FOR LATER** the practice of retaining part of the consecrated bread and wine after celebrating Communion for later use, e.g. when visiting the sick ■ **reservations** *npl* **MISGIVINGS** doubts that prevent wholehearted agreement to or approval of something —**reservationist** *n*

reserve /ri zúrv/ *vt* (**-serves, -serving, -served**) **1. SET SOMETHING ASIDE** to keep something back for future use or for some specific purpose **2. BOOK PLACE BEFOREHAND** to make arrangements in advance to secure a place such as a seat, ticket, table, or hotel room **3. RETAIN SOMETHING FOR YOUR OWN BENEFIT** to retain the option of future action on somebody's or your own behalf ○ *I reserve the right to change my mind.* **4. POSTPONE DECISION** to defer making a decision until all the issues have been considered ○ *reserve judgment* ■ *n* **1. EMERGENCY SUPPLY** something kept back for later use, especially in an emergency **2.** ENVIRON **WILDLIFE CONSERVATION AREA** an area of land set aside for conserving wildlife. N Am term **preserve 3. COOLNESS OF MANNER** emotional restraint, resulting in a reticent or composed manner **4. SUBSTITUTE PLAYER** a team member called to play when a member of the original team withdraws, either before or during a game **5. INACTIVE PART OF ARMED SERVICES** the part of a country's armed services that is not on active service at a given time **6. REINFORCEMENT FORCE** the part of an armed force that is not initially committed during a military engagement but supplies reinforcements as necessary **7. MEMBER OF RESERVE** a member of a military reserve **8.** FIN **MONEY RETAINED FOR FUTURE USE** an amount of capital or revenue retained by a company or financial institution to meet future contingencies (*often used in the plural*) **9.** ECON **NATIONAL FUNDS** a country's supply of gold and foreign currency that is held by the central bank against future liabilities or to support the currency when the exchange rates fluctuate **10.** GEOL **UNEXPLOITED NATURAL RESOURCE** a supply of a natural resource such as a mineral or petrochemical that is estimated to exist from geological data but is not yet utilized **11.** *ANZ* **LAND FOR PUBLIC RECREATION** an area of land set aside for public recreation **12.** *Can* **LAND USED AS RESERVATION** an area of land set aside as a reservation for use by a Native North American people **13. NEXT RUNNER-UP** a competitor or exhibit, e.g. an animal at an agricultural show, that places immediately after the prizewinners and will receive a prize if a prizewinner is disqualified **14.** COMM same as **reserve price** ■ **reserves** *npl* **EXTRA STAMINA, USABLE IN EMERGENCY** additional personal resources of energy or strength that can be called upon in an emergency [14C. Directly or via French *réserver* < Latin *reservare* 'keep back' < *servare* 'keep'] —**reservable** *adj* —**reserver** *n* ◇ **have** *or* **keep something in reserve** to use only part of something, keeping some of it back in case it is needed at a later time

reserve bank *n* **1.** any of the 12 banks in the US Federal Reserve system **2.** in Australia and New Zealand, the central bank responsible for the issuing of currency, banking for federal and state governments, and regulating financial systems

reserve clause *n* in former times, a clause in the contract of a professional sportsperson stating that the club, not the sportsperson, has the exclusive right to renew the contract

reserve currency *n* foreign currency that is acceptable for settling international transactions and that is held in reserve for that purpose by a central bank

reserved /ri zúrvd/ *adj* **1. BOOKED** booked in advance **2. EARMARKED FOR SPECIFIC USE** set aside for a specific purpose **3. HAVING COOL MANNER** having a tendency to emotional restraint and so appearing reticent or composed —**reservedly** /ri zúrvidli/ *adv* —**reservedness** *n*

reserved list *n* a list of officers retired from the armed forces who are willing and available to be recalled to active service in an emergency

reserved occupation *n* an occupation of such national importance in wartime that those working in it are exempted from military service

reserve-grade *adj Aus* relating to or made up of players at the reserve level

reserve price *n* the lowest price that a seller is willing to accept for something being sold at auction. ◊ **upset price**

reservist /ri zúrvist/ *n* a member of a military force not on active service at a given time

reservoir /rézzər vwaar/ *n* **1. LAKE OR TANK FOR STORING WATER** a large tank or natural or artificial lake used for collecting and storing water for human consumption or agricultural use **2. LARGE BACKUP SUPPLY** a substantial reserve supply of something intangible **3. LIQUID STORE IN DEVICE** a part of a machine or device where liquid is stored for use by the machine or device **4. UNDERGROUND SUPPLY OF GAS OR OIL** a natural chamber in porous rock where a supply of natural gas or crude oil collects **5.** BIOL **PARASITE CARRIER** an organism in which a parasite lives and develops without damaging it, but from which the parasite passes to another species that is damaged by it **6.** ANAT same as **cisterna** [Mid-17C. < French < *réserver* (see RESERVE)]

reset[1] /ree sét/ (**-sets, -setting, -set**) *vt* **1.** to set something again **2.** to change the reading of a dial or counter to zero or a different number [Mid-17C. < RE- + SET[1]] —**resettable** *adj* —**resetter** *n*

reset[2] *Scotland vti* /ree sét/ (**-sets, -setting, -set**) to receive stolen goods ■ *n* /reé set/ the crime of receiving stolen goods [14C. < Old French *recet(t)er* < Latin *receptare* < past participle of *recipere* (see RECEIVE)] —**resetter** *n*

resettle /ree sétt'l/ (**-tles, -tling, -tled**) *vt* to provide a group or population with a new place to live and transfer it there —**resettlement** *n*

~~**resevoir**~~ incorrect spelling of **reservoir**

res gestae /ráyz gést ī, ráyss jésti/ *npl* circumstances and facts that may be admitted as evidence in a lawsuit because they shed light on the matters in question [< Latin, 'things done']

resh /raysh/ *n* the 20th letter of the Hebrew alphabet, represented in the English alphabet as 'r'. See table at **alphabet** [Early 19C. < Aramaic *rēš* 'head']

reshape /ree sháyp/ (**-shapes, -shaping, -shaped**) *vt* **1.** to alter or restore the shape of something **2.** to change the form or organization of something

reshuffle *n* /reé shuff'l/ **1. REDISTRIBUTION OF JOBS** a reorganization of the jobs of a group of people, especially a change by a prime minister or president of the posts or personnel of a cabinet **2. SHUFFLING OF CARDS AGAIN** an act of shuffling playing cards again ■ *vt* /ree shúff'l/ (**-fles, -fling, -fled**) **1. REDISTRIBUTE JOBS** to carry out a reshuffle of jobs **2. SHUFFLE CARDS AGAIN** to shuffle playing cards again

reside /ri zīd/ (**-sides, -siding, -sided**) *vi* **1. LIVE SOMEWHERE** to have a home in a particular place **2. BE PRESENT** to be present in or belong to somebody or something **3. BE VESTED** to be vested or placed in somebody or something [15C. Probably via French *résider* < Latin *residere* 'remain behind' < *sedere* 'sit']

residence /rézzidənss/ *n* **1. HOME** the house, flat, or other dwelling in which somebody lives **2. LARGE HOUSE** a grand and imposing dwelling **3. COLONIAL GOVERNOR'S HOUSE** the governor's official house in a colony or former colony **4. LIVING SOMEWHERE** the fact of living in a place **5. TIME LIVED IN PLACE** the period of time that somebody lives in a place **6.** *US* MED same as **residency** (sense 4) ◇ **in residence 1.** living in a place at a particular time **2.** employed as a creative artist by an educational or other institution to foster interest in a subject

residency /rézzidənssi/ (*plural* **-cies**) *n* **1. PERFORMING AND TEACHING ENGAGEMENT** an engagement at a university or conservatory for a performer or group of performers, usually for at least a term, that involves performance, teaching, and master classes **2. RESIDENCE OF INDIAN GOVERNOR** in former times, the official residence of a governor in India **3. TERRITORY ADMINISTERED BY RESIDENT AGENT** formerly, a territory that was administered by the resident agent of a protecting state, e.g. the East Indies **4.** *N Am* **MEDICAL TRAINING** a period of specialized training in clinical medicine or surgery in a US hospital on completion of an internship **5.** same as **residence** (senses 4–5)

resident /rézzidənt/ *n* **1. SOMEBODY LIVING IN PLACE** a permanent or long-term dweller in a place **2. DOCTOR LIVING IN HOSPITAL** a junior doctor who lives in the hospital where he or she is working **3.** *N Am* **DOCTOR COMPLETING RESIDENCY** a doctor or surgeon engaged in a residency **4. SOMEBODY LIVING IN RESIDENTIAL SITUATION** somebody who lives in a nursing home, children's home, retirement home, or other communal housing **5. BRITISH COLONIAL OFFICIAL** a representative of the British government in a British colony or protectorate **6. DIPLOMAT** a diplomatic official based in a foreign country **7. NONMIGRATORY ANIMAL** a bird or other animal that does not migrate seasonally ■ *adj* **1. LIVING IN A PLACE** living permanently or for a considerable period in a place **2. LIVE-IN** living somewhere as part of a particular job **3. BELONGING TO GROUP** forming part of a group of people **4. INHERENT** present or inherent in something **5. NONMIGRATORY** not migrating seasonally **6.** COMPUT **PERMANENTLY INSTALLED IN A COMPUTER'S MEMORY** describes a computer program or data intentionally retained in random-access memory after being loaded so that it can be accessed quickly [14C. Directly or via French < Latin *resident-*, present participle of *residere* (see RESIDE)] —**residentship** *n*

resident commissioner *n* in the United States, a representative from a dependency who is allowed to speak but not vote in the US House of Representatives

residential /rézzi dénsh'l/ *adj* **1. RELATING TO HOUSING** relating to or consisting of private housing rather than offices or factories **2. FOR LONG-TERM LIVING** used as a place to live for the long term **3. WITH LIVING ACCOMMODATION** providing living accommodation ○ *a residential post* [Mid-17C. < RESIDENCE] —**residentially** *adv*

residential care *n* a supervised home environment provided by a welfare agency for people unable to live alone, e.g. children in care or adults with severe learning disabilities

residential school *n* **1.** a government-run school providing education and living accommodation for children with disabilities **2.** *Can* in former times, a boarding school provided by the Canadian government and run by Christian organizations for the education and assimilation of Aboriginal children from thinly populated areas

residentiary /rézzi dénshəri/ *adj* **1.** requiring the incumbent to live in an official residence **2.** residing in an official residence

residents' association *n* an association of people living in the same building or neighbourhood that deals with matters of common interest such as vandalism, traffic problems, or changes in local bylaws

residual /ri zíddyoo əl/ *adj* **1. LEFT OVER** remaining after the majority of something has been removed ○ *residual damp* **2.** GEOL **RELATING TO WEATHERED ROCK RESIDUE** relating to the material left after the weathering of a rock has removed its soluble constituents ■ *n* **1. SOMETHING LEFT OVER** something that remains after part of something has been removed **2.** STATS **DIFFERENCE**

BETWEEN ACTUAL AND THEORETICAL the difference between results obtained through theoretical calculation and those obtained through observation **3.** CINEMA, MEDIA REPEAT FEE a payment to performers, directors, or writers when their filmed work is shown again, especially on television —**residually** *adv*

residual oil *n* the low-grade hydrocarbons that remain after the process of petroleum distillation. Use: in asphalt, furnace fuel.

residual unemployment *n* unemployment remaining during times of full employment, made up of people unable to work because of poor physical or mental health

residuary /ri zíddyoo əri/ *adj* **1.** entitled to the residue of a deceased person's estate after debts have been paid and bequests distributed **2.** remaining after a process has been gone through [Early 18C. < RESIDUUM]

residue /rézzi dyoo/ *n* **1.** something that remains after a process involving the removal of part of the original has been completed **2.** the remainder of a deceased person's estate after debts have been paid and bequests distributed [14C. Via French < Latin *residuum* 'something remaining' < *residere* (see RESIDE)]

residuum /ri zíddyoo əm/ (*plural* **-ua** /-yoo ə/) *n* LAW same as **residue** (sense 2) [Late 17C. < Latin (see RESIDUE)]

resign /ri zīn/ (**-signs, -signing, -signed**) *v* **1.** *vti* LEAVE JOB to give up a paid or unpaid post voluntarily **2. resign yourself** *vr* ACCEPT SOMETHING RELUCTANTLY to come to terms with something and acquiesce in it reluctantly ○ *He resigned himself to giving up work.* **3.** *vt* RELINQUISH CLAIM to give up a right or claim to something [14C. Via French < Latin *resignare* 'unseal, cancel, give back' < *signare* 'to seal' < *signum* 'mark'] —**resigned** *adj* —**resigner** *n*

re-sign /ree sīn/ *v* **1.** *vti* to sign another contract, or cause a player to sign another contract **2.** *vt* to sign a document again

resignation /rézzig náysh'n/ *n* **1.** NOTIFICATION OF LEAVING JOB a formal notification of leaving a paid or unpaid post ○ *I've handed in my resignation.* **2.** DEPARTURE FROM JOB an instance of leaving a paid or unpaid post **3.** UNPROTESTING ACCEPTANCE OF SOMETHING agreement to something, usually given reluctantly but without protest

resile /ri zīl/ (**-siles, -siling, -siled**) *vi* (*formal*) **1.** to spring back into the same shape or position **2.** to jump or leap back [Early 16C. Directly or via French < Latin *resilire* (see RESILIENT)]

resilience /ri zílli ənss/, **resiliency** /-ənssi/ *n* **1.** SPEEDY RECOVERY FROM PROBLEMS the ability to recover quickly from setbacks **2.** ABILITY TO REACT TO POTENTIAL CRISIS the ability of government to identify, assess, and respond to a potentially disruptive situation in order to prevent it from becoming a crisis **3.** ELASTICITY the ability of matter to spring back quickly into shape after being bent, stretched, or deformed

resilient /ri zílli ənt/ *adj* **1.** able to recover quickly from setbacks **2.** able to spring back quickly into shape after being bent, stretched, or squashed [Mid-17C. < Latin *resilient-*, present participle of *resilire* 'jump back' < *salire* 'to jump'] —**resiliently** *adv*

resin /rézzin/ *n* **1.** SUBSTANCE FROM PLANTS a semisolid substance secreted in the sap of some plants and trees. It is used in varnishes, paints, adhesives, inks, and medicines. **2.** SYNTHETIC RESEMBLING RESIN a synthetic polymeric compound physically resembling natural resin, e.g. polyvinyl, polystyrene, or epoxy. Use: manufacture of petrochemicals and plastics. ■ *vt* (**-ins, -ining, -ined**) TREAT SOMETHING WITH RESIN to coat or rub something with resin [14C. Via Old French *resine* and Latin *resina* < Greek *rhētinē*] —**resinoid** *adj, n* —**resinous** *adj* —**resinously** *adv* —**resinousness** *n*

resinate /rézzi nayt/ (**-ates, -ating, -ated**) *vt* to impregnate, saturate, or flavour something with resin

res ipsa loquitur /ráyz ipsə lókwitər, ráyss-/ *n* a rule of evidence that allows that mere proof that an injury occurred establishes a presumption of negligence on the part of the defendant [< Latin, 'the thing speaks for itself']

resist /ri zíst/ *v* (**-sists, -sisting, -sisted**) **1.** *vti* FIGHT AGAINST SOMEBODY OR SOMETHING to oppose and stand firm against somebody or something **2.** *vt* REFUSE TO GIVE IN TO SOMETHING to refuse to accept or comply with something ○ *resisted all attempts to force them out of their homes* **3.** *vt* BE UNHARMED BY SOMETHING to remain unaltered by the damaging effect of something ○ *ability to resist infection* **4.** *vti* SAY NO TO SOMETHING TEMPTING to refrain from something in spite of being tempted ○ *I couldn't resist having a peek.* ■ *n* INDUST PROTECTIVE COATING a protective coating used to prevent corrosion or oxidation, provide electrical insulation in a printed circuit, or prevent part of a fabric from accepting dye [14C. Directly or via French < Latin *resistere* 'stand against' < *sistere* 'make stand' < *stare* 'to stand'] —**resister** *n* —**resistibility** /ri zístə bílləti/ *n* —**resistible** *adj* —**resistibly** *adv*

resistance /ri zístənss/ *n* **1.** OPPOSITION opposition to somebody or something **2.** REFUSAL TO GIVE IN refusal to accept or comply with something **3.** ABILITY TO WITHSTAND DAMAGING EFFECT the ability to remain unaltered by the damaging effect of something, e.g. an organism's ability not to succumb to disease or infection **4.** ABILITY TO SAY NO TO TEMPTATION the ability to refrain from something in spite of being tempted **5.** PHYS FORCE OPPOSING ANOTHER FORCE a force that opposes or slows down another force. Symbol *R* **6.** ELEC OPPOSITION TO ELECTRIC CURRENT the opposition that a circuit, component, or substance presents to the flow of electricity. Symbol *R* **7.** ELEC SOURCE OF RESISTANCE something that is a source of opposition to the flow of electricity, e.g. a resistor. Symbol *R* **8.** PSYCHOANAL REPRESSION OF THOUGHTS in psychology, the process by which the ego keeps repressed thoughts and feelings from the conscious mind

Resistance *n* an illegal secret organization that fights for national freedom against an occupying power, especially one that fought in France, the Netherlands, Denmark, or Italy during World War II

resistant /ri zístənt/ *adj* **1.** RESISTING offering resistance to something ○ *resistant to change* **2.** NOT DAMAGED BY SOMETHING unaltered by or impervious to the damaging effect of something (*often used in combination*) ○ *moisture-resistant* ■ *n* SOMEBODY OR SOMETHING THAT RESISTS somebody or something that offers resistance

~~**resistence**~~ incorrect spelling of **resistance**

resistin /ri zístin/ *n* a hormone that increases the resistance of cells to insulin, so causing levels of sugar in the bloodstream to rise

resistive /ri zístiv/ *adj* **1.** same as **resistant 2.** having the property of electrical resistance —**resistively** *adv* —**resistiveness** *n*

resistivity /reézi stívvəti/ *n* **1.** the electrical resistance of a substance of a standard length and cross section. Symbol ρ **2.** the capacity to resist something

resistless /ri zístləss/ *adj* (*archaic*) **1.** not able to be resisted **2.** not able to resist something

resistor /ri zístər/ *n* a component of an electrical circuit that has resistance and is used to control the flow of electric current

resit *vti* /ree sít/ (**-sits, -sitting, -sat** /-sát/) to take an examination again after failing the first time ■ *n* /reé sit/ a later examination in the same subject for those who failed the first time

res judicata /ráyzz joodi kaátə, ráyss-/, **res adjudicata** /-ə joodi kaátə/ *n* an issue already decided by a court [< Latin, 'judged matter']

reskill /ree skíl/ (**-skills, -skilling**) *vt* to teach somebody new skills, especially with a view to his or her finding or changing employment —**reskilling** *n*

Resnais /rénnay/, **Alain** (*b.* 1922) French film director. Among his noted films are *Hiroshima mon amour* (1959) and *Last Year at Marienbad* (1961).

resoluble /ri zóllyoob'l/ *adj* able to be resolved or analysed [Early 17C. Directly or via French < Latin *resolubilis* < *resolvere* (see RESOLVE)]

re-soluble /ree sóllyoob'l/ *adj* able to be dissolved again [15C. < RE- + SOLUBLE]

resolute /rézzə loot/ *adj* **1.** possessing determination and purposefulness **2.** motivated by or displaying determination and purposefulness [15C. < Latin *resolutus*, past participle of *resolvere* (see RESOLVE)] —**resolutely** *adv* —**resoluteness** *n*

resolution /rézzə loósh'n/ *n* **1.** PROCESS OF RESOLVING the process of resolving something such as a problem or dispute ○ *the resolution of a difficulty* **2.** DECISION a firm decision to do something **3.** DETERMINATION firmness of mind or purpose **4.** SOLUTION an answer to a problem **5.** EXPRESSION OF COLLECTIVE OPINION a formal expression of the consensus at a meeting, arrived at after discussion and usually as the result of a vote **6.** QUALITY OF DETAIL IN IMAGE the quality of detail offered by a TV or computer screen or a photographic image **7.** PHYS, CHEM SEPARATION INTO CONSTITUENT PARTS the process or act of separating something such as a chemical compound or a source of light into its constituent parts **8.** MED SUBSIDING OF SYMPTOMS the disappearance or coming to an end of a medical symptom or condition **9.** MUSIC HARMONIC PROGRESSION the musical progression from a dissonant to a consonant chord or note **10.** MUSIC FINAL NOTE the musical note or chord to which the harmony moves when progressing from dissonance to consonance **11.** THEATRE, LITERAT PART OF NARRATIVE WHEN CONFLICT IS RESOLVED the point in a literary work when the conflict is resolved **12.** PHYS same as **resolving power 13.** LITERAT SYLLABLE REPLACEMENT the substitution of a long syllable for two short ones in the rhythm of a line of poetry [14C. Directly or via French < Latin *resolution-* < past participle of *resolvere* (see RESOLVE)] —**resolutioner** *n*

resolve /ri zólv/ *v* (**-solves, -solving, -solved**) **1.** *vt* SOLVE DIFFICULTY to find a solution to a problem **2.** *vt* SETTLE ARGUMENT to bring a disagreement to an end **3.** *vt* DISPEL DOUBTS to dispel doubts or anxieties **4.** *vti* MAKE DECISION to come to a firm decision about something, or cause somebody to do this ○ *He resolved to leave.* **5. resolve itself** *vr* CHANGE to change into something else ○ *'O! that this too too solid flesh would melt,/Thaw, and resolve itself into a dew'* (William Shakespeare, *Hamlet*) **6.** *vt* EXPRESS JOINT OPINION FORMALLY to express the opinion of a meeting formally as a consensus, after discussion and usually as the result of a vote **7.** *vti* MED MAKE OR BECOME LESS SWOLLEN to subside, or cause an inflammation, swelling, or tumour to subside **8.** *vti* SPLIT INTO CONSTITUENT PARTS to cause something to separate into its constituent elements, or become separated into constituent parts **9.** *vt* CHEM SEPARATE RACEMIC MIXTURE to separate a racemic compound or mixture into its two components **10.** *vti* MUSIC MOVE FROM DISSONANT TO CONSONANT to move from dissonant to consonant, or cause a chord or note to move from dissonant to consonant **11.** *vt* PHYS MAKE PARTS OF IMAGE DISTINCT to make parts of an image distinct, e.g. in a microscope or telescope **12.** *vt* MATHS SPLIT VECTOR INTO DIRECTIONAL COMPONENTS to separate a vector into its directional components ■ *n* **1.** DETERMINATION firmness of purpose **2.** DECISION a firm decision to do something [14C. Directly or via French < Latin *resolvere* 'loosen up' < *solvere* 'loosen, dissolve'] —**resolvability** /ri zólvə bílləti/ *n* —**resolvable** *adj* —**resolver** *n*

resolved /ri zólvd/ *adj* determined in purpose —**resolvedly** /ri zólvidli/ *adv*

resolvent /ri zólvənt/ *adj* **1.** CAUSING SEPARATION INTO CONSTITUENT PARTS causing or capable of causing something to separate into its constituent parts **2.** MED ANTI-INFLAMMATORY able to cause reduction in inflammation or swelling ■ *n* **1.** SOMETHING CAUSING SEPARATION INTO CONSTITUENT PARTS a substance that causes or is capable of causing something to separate into its constituent parts **2.** MED ANTI-INFLAMMATORY MEDICINE a medicine that reduces inflammation or swelling

resolving power /ri zólving-/ *n* the ability of an optical system such as a telescope or microscope to distinguish objects separated by small angular distances

resonance /rézzənənss/ *n* **1.** UNDERLYING MEANING the effect of an event or work of art beyond its immediate or surface meaning **2.** AMPLIFIED SOUND an intense and prolonged sound produced by sympathetic vibration **3.** RINGING QUALITY OF INSTRUMENT OR VOICE an amplification of a sound, e.g. that of an instrument or the human voice, caused by sympathetic vibration in a chamber such as an auditorium or a singer's chest **4.** PHYS LARGE OSCILLATION AT NATURAL FREQUENCY increased amplitude of oscillation of a mechanical system when it is subjected to vibration from another source at or near its own natural frequency **5.** ELEC OSCILLATION IN ELECTRICAL CIRCUIT a state of oscillation that occurs at a very specific frequency in an electrical circuit consisting of inductive and capacitive components **6.** MED SOUND WHEN

BODY CAVITY IS TAPPED the sound heard during tapping (**percussion**) of a healthy chest or abdomen **7.** CHEM PROPERTY OF SOME CHEMICAL COMPOUNDS the property of some chemical compounds of having simultaneously the characteristics of two or more structures that differ in the arrangement of electrons

resonant /rézzənənt/ *adj* **1.** DEEP IN SOUND deep and rich in sound **2.** RESOUNDING continuing to sound for some time **3.** CAUSING ECHOES producing or increasing amplification of sound or echoes, usually by sympathetic vibration [Late 16C. Directly or via French < Latin *resonant-*, present participle of *resonare* (see RESONATE)] —**resonantly** *adv*

resonate /rézzə nayt/ (**-nates, -nating, -nated**) *v* **1.** *vti* RESOUND to echo, or cause something to echo **2.** *vi* HAVE EXTENDED EFFECT to have an effect or impact beyond that which is immediately apparent **3.** *vti* PRODUCE RESONANCE to produce or exhibit chemical, mechanical, or electrical resonance, or cause a chemical compound or a electrical system to produce or exhibit resonance **4.** *vi* BE FAMILIAR to produce a response in somebody, especially by reminding that person of something or prompting feelings of support or approval [Late 19C. < Latin *resonat-*, past participle of *resonare* 'resound' < *sonare* 'to sound' < *sonus* 'sound'] —**resonation** /rézzə náysh'n/ *n*

resonator /rézzə naytər/ *n* **1.** a device or part that resonates, especially one that produces sound or microwaves **2.** a part of a musical instrument designed to produce resonance, e.g. the hollow body of a violin or the tubes in a vibraphone

resorb /ri sáwrb, -záwrb/ (**-sorbs, -sorbing, -sorbed**) *vt* to absorb something again [Mid-17C. < Latin *resorbere* 'drink in again' < *sorbere* 'suck in'] —**resorbent** *adj*

resorcinol /ri záwrssi nol/ *n* a colourless crystalline phenol. Use: manufacture of dyes, resins, drugs, in tanning. Formula: $C_6H_6O_2$. [Late 19C. < RESIN + *orcin*, crystalline substance obtained from orchils]

resorption /ri sáwrpsh'n/ *n* **1.** the process or state of resorbing or being resorbed **2.** the partial fusion of a crystal in a magma in response to changing conditions of temperature and pressure [Early 19C. < RESORB, after *absorption*] —**resorptive** *adj*

resort /ri záwrt/ *n* **1.** HOLIDAY PLACE a place that is popular for recreation and holidays and provides accommodation and entertainment **2.** SOURCE OF HELP a person, place, or course of action seen as a source of help in dealing with a problem ○ *As a last resort we could sell the car.* **3.** ACT OF HAVING RECOURSE TO SOMETHING the act of turning to somebody or something for help in dealing with a problem ○ *resolve the dispute without resort to industrial action* **4.** FREQUENT VISITING the act of going somewhere frequently or in large numbers **5.** MUCH-VISITED PLACE a place frequently visited [14C. < Old French *resortir* 'come back' < *sortir* 'go out']

resort to (**resorts to, resorting to, resorted to**) *vt* **1.** to turn to something, sometimes something extreme, for help in dealing with a problem **2.** to go somewhere that is frequently visited, or go somewhere in large numbers

re-sort /ree sáwrt/ *vt* to sort things into categories or a sequence

resound /ri zównd/ (**-sounds, -sounding, -sounded**) *vi* **1.** BE FILLED WITH REVERBERATING SOUND to be filled with a long reverberating sound ○ *The hall resounded to the cheers of the audience.* **2.** MAKE REVERBERATING SOUND to produce a long reverberating sound **3.** BE EXTREMELY WELL KNOWN to be extremely well known, especially over a long period or a wide area [14C. Alteration (after SOUND¹) of Old French *resoner* < Latin *resonare* (see RESONATE)]

resounding /ri zównding/ *adj* **1.** clear and unequivocal ○ *a resounding defeat* **2.** making a loud noise that echoes —**resoundingly** *adv*

resource /ri záwrss, -sáwrss/ *n* **1.** SOURCE OF HELP somebody or something that is a source of help or information **2.** BACKUP SUPPLY a reserve supply of something such as money, personnel, or equipment **3.** ABILITY TO FIND SOLUTIONS adeptness at finding solutions to problems **4.** ECOL same as **natural resource ■ resources** *npl* **1.** TALENT DRAWN ON WHEN NECESSARY an inner ability or capacity that is drawn on in time of need, or such abilities considered collectively **2.**

NATION'S NATURAL, ECONOMIC, OR MILITARY ASSETS the natural, economic, political, or military assets enjoyed by a nation, e.g. mineral wealth, labour, capital, or military personnel **3.** COMM CORPORATE ASSETS any or all of the sources drawn on by a company for making profit, e.g. personnel, capital, machinery, or stock **■** *vt* (**-sources, -sourcing, -sourced**) PROVIDE SOMETHING WITH RESOURCES to provide something with monetary or other resources ○ *not adequately resourced to carry out their responsibilities* [Early 17C. < French *ressource* < Latin *resurgere* 'rise again, be replenished' < *surgere* 'rise up from below'] —**resourceless** *adj*

resourceful /ri záwrsf'l, -sáwrs-/ *adj* full of initiative and good at problem-solving, especially in difficult situations —**resourcefully** *adv* —**resourcefulness** *n*

resourcing *n* the work of finding and providing the material, financial, or human resources required for a task

resp. *abbr* **1.** respective **2.** respectively **3.** BIOL respiration **4.** LAW respondent

respect /ri spékt/ *n* **1.** ESTEEM a feeling or attitude of admiration and deference towards somebody or something ○ *He has no respect for authority.* **2.** STATE OF BEING ADMIRED the state of being admired deferentially **3.** THOUGHTFULNESS consideration or thoughtfulness **4.** CHARACTERISTIC an individual characteristic or point ○ *satisfactory in every respect* **■ respects** *npl* REGARDS polite greetings offered to somebody **■** *vt* (**-spects, -specting, -spected**) **1.** ESTEEM SOMEBODY OR SOMETHING to feel or show admiration and deference towards somebody or something **2.** NOT GO AGAINST OR VIOLATE SOMETHING to pay due attention to and refrain from violating something ○ *respect the law* ○ *respect another's privacy* **3.** BE CONSIDERATE TOWARDS SOMEBODY OR SOMETHING to show consideration or thoughtfulness in relation to somebody or something **■** *interj* HELLO used to greet somebody (*slang; used in Black English*) [14C. Via French < Latin *respectus*, past participle of *respicere* 'regard, look back at' < *specere* 'look at'] —**respected** *adj* —**respecter** *n* ◇ **maximum respect, nuff respect** used to greet somebody (*slang; used in Black English*)

SYNONYMS See **regard**.

respectable /ri spéktəb'l/ *adj* **1.** MORALLY ABOVE REPROACH in accordance with accepted standards of correctness or decency ○ *a respectable district* **2.** SATISFACTORY meeting an adequate standard ○ *a respectable piece of work* **3.** LARGE ENOUGH sufficiently large ○ *a respectable salary* **4.** ACCEPTABLE IN APPEARANCE tidy and fit to be seen by others, especially in public (*informal*) —**respectability** /ri spéktə bílləti/ *n* —**respectably** *adv*

respectful /ri spéktf'l/ *adj* showing appropriate deference and respect —**respectfulness** *n*

respectfully /ri spéktfəli/ *adv* with respect or in a respectful manner

USAGE **respectfully** or **respectively**? *Respectfully* means 'with respect or in a respectful manner', as in the complimentary close of a letter (*Respectfully, Jane Smith*), and in *We respectfully* [not *respectively*] *reserve the right to disagree with the ruling. Respectively* matches one list with another in the order given for both, as in *The captain and the first officer have 20 and 15 years' experience, respectively* [not *respectfully*].

respecting /ri spékting/ *prep* with reference to or concerning somebody or something

respective /ri spéktiv/ *adj* varying according to each of the people or things concerned ○ *They returned to their respective homes.* —**respectiveness** *n*

respectively *adv* matching one list with another in the order given for both ○ *Mr Jones and his wife are aged 52 and 51, respectively.*

USAGE See **respectfully**.

respell /ree spél/ (**-spells, -spelling, -spelt** or **-spelled**) *vt* to spell something again or in a different way, especially using a different alphabet in order to give guidance on pronunciation —**respelling** *n*

respirable /réspərəb'l, ri spírəb'l/ *adj* fit or able to be breathed —**respirability** /réspərə bílləti, ri spírə bílləti/ *n*

respiration /réspə ráysh'n/ *n* **1.** PHYSIOL BREATHING the act of breathing air in and out **2.** PROCESS OF SUPPLYING OXYGEN TO CELLS the chemical and physical process in which oxygen is delivered to tissues or cells in an organism and carbon dioxide and water are given off (**external respiration**) **3.** ENERGY-PRODUCING PROCESS IN CELLS a metabolic process in cells leading to the production of energy by the breakdown of organic substances (**internal respiration**) —**respirational** *adj*

respirator /réspə raytər/ *n* **1.** a machine used in hospitals to maintain breathing for patients unable to breathe unaided **2.** a device placed over the nose and mouth to filter out noxious particles and fumes from inhaled air or to warm chilled air before it is inhaled

respiratory /ri spírrətəri, réspərətəri/ *adj* relating to or used in breathing or the system in the body that takes in and distributes oxygen

respiratory distress syndrome *n* a respiratory disease of newborns, especially premature infants, caused by the inability of the lungs to take in oxygen and marked by cyanosis and difficult breathing

respiratory pigment *n* a protein that can bind with oxygen, e.g. haemoglobin

respiratory quotient *n* the ratio of the volume of carbon dioxide released to the volume of oxygen absorbed by an organism, cell, or tissue over a given time period

respiratory system *n* the system of organs in the body responsible for the intake of oxygen and the expiration of carbon dioxide. In mammals it consists of the lungs, bronchi, bronchioles, trachea, diaphragm, and nerve supply.

respire /ri spír/ (**-spires, -spiring, -spired**) *v* **1.** *vti* to breathe air in and out **2.** *vi* to breathe again in a normal way after anxiety or exertion (*literary*) [14C. Directly or via French < Latin *respirare* 'breathe again' < *spirare* 'breathe']

respirometer /réspə rómmitər/ *n* an instrument for measuring and studying the process in which oxygen is taken into the body, delivered to tissues and cells, and used by them [Late 19C. < RESPIRATION] —**respirometric** /réspərō méttrik/ *adj* —**respirometry** *n*

respite /ré spīt, réspit/ *n* **1.** BRIEF INTERVAL OF REST a brief period of rest and recovery between periods of exertion or after something disagreeable **2.** DELAY a temporary delay **3.** LAW REPRIEVE a temporary stay of execution of a criminal [13C. Via Old French, 'refuge' < Latin *respectus*, past participle of *respicere* (see RESPECT)]

respite care *n* temporary residential care for patients that provides relief for the permanent caregivers

~~**resplendant**~~ incorrect spelling of **resplendent**

resplendent /ri spléndənt/ *adj* having a dazzlingly impressive appearance ○ *resplendent in his dress uniform* [15C. < Latin *resplendent-*, present participle of *resplendere* 'shine brightly' < *splendere* 'shine'] —**resplendence** *n* —**resplendently** *adv*

respond /ri spónd/ *v* (**-sponds, -sponding, -sponded**) **1.** *vti* PROVIDE ANSWER to say or write something in reply **2.** *vi* REACT to act or do something in reaction to something else ○ *was unsure of how to respond to his moods* **3.** *vi* MED HAVE POSITIVE MEDICAL REACTION to react positively to medical treatment **■** *n* **1.** ARCHIT PILASTER OR PILLAR SUPPORTING ARCH a pilaster or pillar that supports an arch **2.** CHR, MUSIC CHORAL PART OF ANTHEM the choral part in an anthem for priest and choir in a church service [Mid-16C. Via French < Latin *respondere* 'promise in return' < *spondere* 'to pledge'] —**respondence** *n* —**responder** *n*

~~**respondant**~~ incorrect spelling of **respondent**

respondent /ri spóndənt/ *n* **1.** ANSWERER somebody who replies to something **2.** LAW DEFENDANT the person against whom a divorce petition or an appeal is brought **■** *adj* **1.** RESPONDING giving a response **2.** LAW DEFENDING IN DIVORCE acting as the defendant in a divorce petition or appeal

responsa JUDAISM plural of **responsum**

~~**responsability**~~ incorrect spelling of **responsibility**

---

a at; aa father; aw all; ay day; ai hair; ə about, item, edible, common, circus; e egg; ee eel; hw when; i it, happy; ī ice; 'l apple; 'm rhythm; 'n fashion; o odd; ō open; oo good; oo pool; ow owl; oy oil; th thin; th this; u up; ur urge;

response /ri spónss/ *n* **1.** REPLY GIVEN TO A QUESTION something said or written in reply to a statement or question from somebody else **2.** REACTION something done in reaction to something else **3.** CARDS BID IN BRIDGE in bridge, a bid that is in reply to a partner's bid or double **4.** CHR REPLY MADE BY CHURCH CHOIR a phrase sung or spoken by the choir or congregation in reply to the officiant during a church service **5.** MED BODY'S REACTION TO STIMULUS the reaction of an organism or any of its parts to a stimulus [14C. Directly or via French < Latin *responsum* < past participle of *respondere* (see RESPOND)]

SYNONYMS See *answer*.

responsibility /ri spónssə bílləti/ (*plural* **-ties**) *n* **1.** ACCOUNTABILITY the state, fact, or position of being accountable to somebody or for something **2.** SOMETHING TO BE RESPONSIBLE FOR somebody or something for which a person or organization is responsible **3.** BLAME the blame for something that has happened ○ *took full responsibility for the mix-up* **4.** AUTHORITY TO ACT authority to take decisions independently

responsible /ri spónssəb'l/ *adj* **1.** ANSWERABLE TO SOMEBODY accountable to somebody for an action or for the successful carrying out of a duty ○ *Jo was responsible for that phase of the project.* **2.** BEING TO BLAME FOR SOMETHING being the cause of something, usually something wrong or disapproved of ○ *Who's responsible for this mess?* **3.** IMPORTANT conferring the authority to take decisions independently and requiring conscientiousness and trustworthiness ○ *in a responsible position* **4.** RELIABLE able to be counted on owing to qualities of conscientiousness and trustworthiness ○ *very responsible for his age* **5.** FIN FINANCIALLY SOUND having adequate means to meet financial obligations [Late 16C. < obsolete French, 'corresponding' < Latin *respons-*, past participle of *respondere* (see RESPOND)] —**responsibleness** *n* —**responsibly** *adv*

responsions /ri spónsh'nz/ *npl* an examination required for graduation from Oxford University [Early 19C. < Latin *responsion-* < *respons-* (see RESPONSIBLE)]

responsive /ri spónssiv/ *adj* **1.** SHOWING POSITIVE RESPONSE reacting quickly, strongly, or favourably to something, especially a suggestion or proposal **2.** RESPONDING TO TREATMENT reacting positively to medical treatment **3.** DONE IN RESPONSE serving to respond to something **4.** BIOL REACTING TO STIMULUS showing reaction to a stimulus **5.** CHR CONSISTING OF CHOIR'S OR CONGREGATION'S RESPONSES consisting of responses by a choir or congregation in a church service —**responsively** *adv* —**responsiveness** *n*

responsory /ri spónssəri/ (*plural* **-ries**) *n* an anthem consisting of short verses sung or spoken by the officiant and responses sung or spoken by the choir, especially after the lesson in a church service —**responsorial** /ri spón sáwri əl/ *adj*

responsum /ri spónssəm/ (*plural* **-sa** /-sə/) *n* in Judaism, definitive written reply by a rabbinic authority to a question on religion [Late 19C. < Latin, form of past participle of *respondere* (see RESPOND)]

res publica /ráyz pòobli kaa, ráyss-/ *n* **1.** the state, a republic, or the commonwealth as a concept **2.** the public or common good [From Latin, literally 'public matter']

ressentiment /rə sóNti móN/ *n* a feeling of resentment and hostility characterized by an inability to act to change the situation [Mid-20C. Directly or via German < French, < *ressentir* 'feel strongly' < *sentir* 'feel']

rest[1] /rest/ *n* **1.** STOPPING OF WORK OR ACTIVITY a state or period of refreshing freedom from exertion **2.** SLEEP the repose of sleep that is refreshing to body and mind and is marked by a reduction in metabolic activity **3.** ABSENCE OF MOVEMENT the cessation of movement or action ○ *The boat lay at rest in the harbour.* **4.** DEATH death perceived as freedom from earthly toil ○ *He is now at rest.* **5.** FREEDOM FROM ANXIETY freedom from mental or emotional anxiety ○ *I put her mind at rest.* **6.** PLACE TO STOP AND RELAX a stopping place for shelter and relaxation **7.** SUPPORT something used for support, especially on a piece of furniture **8.** MUSIC PAUSE IN MUSIC a rhythmic pause between musical notes, or the mark indicating a musical pause **9.** LITERAT same as **caesura** (sense 1) ■ *v* (**rests, resting, rested**) **1.** *vi* SLEEP OR RELAX to restore your energy by means of relaxation or sleep ○ *Put your feet up and rest.* **2.** *vt* LET SOMEBODY SLEEP OR RELAX to allow a person or animal to regain energy by means of relaxation or sleep, or allow a limb or body part to be inactive to restore its strength ○ *rest the horses* ○ *sat down to rest my feet* **3.** *vi* BE TRANQUIL to be in a state of tranquillity **4.** *vi* BE DEAD to be dead, and so free from earthly concerns **5.** *vti* STOP MOVING to cease activity, or cause something to cease activity **6.** *vi* BE LEFT ALONE to be subject to no further discussion or attention ○ *Let the matter rest.* **7.** *vi* LIE FALLOW to lie unfarmed **8.** *vti* SUPPORT OR BE SUPPORTED to support something on or against something, or be supported on or against something ○ *The ornament was resting on a narrow ledge.* **9.** *vi* COME TO STOP to allow the eyes to come to a stop on somebody or something **10.** *vi* BE VESTED to be vested or placed in somebody or something ○ *The authority rests with him.* **11.** *vi* DEPEND ON SOMEBODY OR SOMETHING to depend on somebody or something for action or as a burden or responsibility **12.** *vi* BE BASED ON SOMETHING to rely on something for proof or explanation **13.** *vti* LAW CONCLUDE A LEGAL CASE to conclude the presentation of evidence in a case ○ *I rest my case.* [Old English *ræst* (noun), *ræstan* (verb) < Germanic] —**rested** *adj* —**rester** *n*

rest[2] /rest/ *n* something left as a remainder (*takes a singular or plural verb*) ■ *vi* (**rests, resting, rested**) to remain or continue to be (*usually used as a command*) ○ *Rest assured that we're doing everything possible.* [15C. < French *reste* 'remnant' < *rester* 'remain' < Latin *restare* 'stay behind' < *stare* 'to stand']

~~restaraunt~~ incorrect spelling of **restaurant**

rest area *n ANZ, N Am* an area at the side of a major road where motorists can rest

restate /ree stáyt/ (**-states, -stating, -stated**) *vt* to say something again, especially in order to clarify or summarize what has already been said ○ *time to restate our goals* —**restatement** *n*

restaurant /réstə ront, -roN, -rənt/ *n* a place where meals and drinks are sold and served to customers [Early 19C. < French, < present participle of *restaurer* < Latin *restaurare* 'set upright again']

restaurant car *n* a railway carriage in which meals are served to passengers. N Am term **dining car**

~~restauranteur~~ incorrect spelling of **restaurateur**

restaurateur /réstərə túr/ *n* an owner or manager of a restaurant [Late 18C. < French, 'restorer' < *restaurer* (see RESTAURANT)]

USAGE Note that there is no *-n-* in this word as there is in *restaurant*.

rest cure *n* a treatment involving complete rest, e.g. as a remedy for stress

restful /réstf'l/ *adj* **1.** giving, promoting, or involving rest ○ *a restful holiday* **2.** at rest or tranquil —**restfully** *adv* —**restfulness** *n*

restharrow /rést harō/ *n* a pod-bearing plant with three-lobed leaves and woody stems and roots. Flowers: white, purple, or pink, in clusters. Native to: Europe, Asia. Latin name: *Ononis repens* or *Ononis spinosa*. [Because its tough roots can stop, or 'arrest', the progress of a harrow]

rest home *n* a place where senior citizens and chronically ill people live and are cared for

restiform /résti fawrm/ *adj* shaped like a rope or cord [Mid-19C. < modern Latin *restiformis* < Latin *restis* 'cord']

resting /résting/ *adj* **1.** UNEMPLOYED not currently employed as an actor (*informal; often used euphemistically*) **2.** BIOL IMMOBILE describes organisms that are not moving or active **3.** BIOL NOT DIVIDING not undergoing cell division **4.** BOT DORMANT describes spores, seeds, and eggs that are dormant before germination

restitution /résti tyóosh'n/ *n* **1.** GIVING BACK the return of something to its rightful owner **2.** PAYING BACK compensation for a loss, damage, or injury **3.** RESTORATION the return of something to the condition it was in before it was changed [13C. Directly or via French < Latin *restitution-* < past participle of *restituere* 'restore' < *statuere* 'set up'] —**restitute** /résti tyoot/ *vt* —**restitutive** /résti tyootiv/ *adj* —**restitutory** *adj*

restive /réstiv/ *adj* **1.** UNEASY uneasy and on the verge of resisting control ○ *The people grew restive under the rule of the occupying force.* **2.** IMPATIENT having little patience and unwilling to tolerate annoyances **3.** OBSTINATE OR AWKWARD unwilling to be guided or controlled ○ *a restive horse* [Late 16C. Alteration of *restiff* < Old French *restif* < Latin *restare* 'to rest'] —**restively** *adv* —**restiveness** *n*

restless /réstləss/ *adj* **1.** CONSTANTLY MOVING constantly moving, or unable to be still ○ *Some waited patiently but others were restless.* **2.** DISCONTENTED seeking a change because of discontent ○ *He began to feel restless after only a few weeks in the job.* **3.** SLEEPLESS lacking rest or sleep ○ *She spent a restless night worrying.* —**restlessly** *adv* —**restlessness** *n*

restless leg syndrome *n* a condition of the legs characterized by a painful discomfort when inactive that can cause interrupted sleep and fatigue

rest mass *n* the mass a body has when it is not moving, as opposed to the additional mass it gains as a result of its movement, according to the theory of relativity

restock /ree stók/ (**-stocks, -stocking, -stocked**) *vti* to replace or refill something after it has been used or its contents emptied

restoration /réstə ráysh'n/ *n* **1.** RESTORING OF SOMETHING REMOVED the return of something that was removed or abolished ○ *calls for the restoration of curfews* **2.** RESTORING OF SOMETHING TO FORMER CONDITION the restoring of something such as buildings or furniture to an earlier and usually better condition ○ *Restoration work will begin next week.* **3.** THING RESTORED something, especially a building, that has been brought back to an earlier and usually better condition **4.** MODEL a model made to resemble or represent something in its original condition ○ *a restoration of a Neandertal dwelling*

Restoration *n* the re-establishment of monarchy in Great Britain under Charles II in 1660, or the period of his reign

restorative /ri stáwrətiv/ *adj* tending or meant to give somebody new strength or vigour ○ *a restorative tonic* ■ *n* something that gives somebody new strength or vigour, especially an activity or medication —**restoratively** *adv* —**restorativeness** *n*

restore /ri stáwr/ (**-stores, -storing, -stored**) *vt* **1.** GIVE SOMETHING BACK to return something to its proper owner or place **2.** RETURN SOMETHING TO PREVIOUS CONDITION to bring something back to an earlier and better condition ○ *techniques used to restore old oil paintings* **3.** ENERGIZE SOMEBODY to give somebody new strength or vigour ○ *I felt restored after my weekend away.* **4.** RETURN SOMEBODY TO PREVIOUS POSITION to return somebody to a previously held rank, office, or position ○ *restore her to the throne* **5.** PUT SOMETHING BACK to re-establish or put back something that was once but is no longer there ○ *restore order in the capital* [13C. Via French < Latin *restaurare* 'set upright again'] —**restorable** *adj* —**restorer** *n*

SYNONYMS See *renew*.

restrain /ri stráyn/ (**-strains, -straining, -strained**) *vt* **1.** STOP SOMEBODY FROM DOING SOMETHING to prevent somebody or yourself from doing something ○ *I couldn't restrain myself from calling out.* **2.** CONTROL SOMETHING to keep somebody or something under control or within limits ○ *finally able to restrain the violence* ○ *barriers to restrain the crowds* **3.** CONTROL SOMEBODY to physically control the movements of a person or animal ○ *Restrain him before he hurts someone.* **4.** IMPRISON SOMEBODY to put somebody in prison or otherwise take away his or her freedom [14C. Via Old French *restreindre* < Latin *restringere* 'bind fast, confine' < *stringere* 'draw tight'] —**restrainable** *adj*

SYNONYMS See *hinder*[1].

restrained /ri stráynd/ *adj* characterized by control, especially in not being excessively emotional or aggressive ○ *the artist's restrained use of colour* —**restrainedly** /-idli/ *adv*

restraining order /ri stráyning-/ *n* **1.** *ANZ, N Am* LAW a court order that commands somebody to have no contact or communication with another person. UK term **stay away order** **2.** *N Am* a preliminary court order that prohibits an action that might cause harm to the person seeking the order. A restraining order can be granted immediately without a

hearing and often stays in effect pending a hearing and decision on the granting of an injunction.

restraint /ri stráynt/ *n* **1.** HOLDING BACK an act or the quality of holding back, limiting, or controlling something ○ *Although severely provoked, she showed admirable restraint in not retaliating.* **2.** RESTRAINING THING something that controls or limits somebody or something ○ *His poverty was no restraint on his ambition.* **3.** HOLDING DEVICE something that is fastened to limit somebody's freedom of movement [14C. < Old French *restreinte*, form of past participle of *restreindre* (see RESTRAIN)]

restraint of trade *n* the limiting of commercial competition by means such as price-fixing or monopolistic practices

~~**restraunt**~~ incorrect spelling of **restaurant**

restrict /ri stríkt/ (**-stricts, -stricting, -stricted**) *vt* to keep something within fixed limits ○ *Entry is restricted to members only.* [15C. < Latin *restrict*, past participle of *restringere* (see RESTRAIN)]

restricted /ri stríktid/ *adj* **1.** LIMITED limited or made smaller or less than might be desired ○ *It's difficult to turn the vehicle in such a restricted space.* **2.** SUBJECT TO CONTROLS subject to controls or limits, e.g. of time or availability ○ *restricted use of the facilities* **3.** REQUIRING AUTHORIZATION intended only for authorized people ○ *You are entering a restricted area.* —**restrictedly** *adv* —**restrictedness** *n*

restriction /ri stríksh'n/ *n* **1.** something that limits or controls something else ○ *There are restrictions on the use of the photocopier.* **2.** a restricting of something, or the condition of being restricted ○ *the restriction of a person's freedom*

restriction enzyme, **restriction endonuclease** *n* an enzyme that splits DNA into segments at precise locations. Use: genetic engineering.

restriction fragment *n* a specific portion of DNA produced by a restriction enzyme

restriction fragment length polymorphism *n* a variation between individuals in the length of the DNA fragments produced by a specific restriction enzyme. They are caused by mutations and can be used to detect genetic anomalies.

restrictive /ri stríktiv/ *adj* **1.** acting as a limit or control on something **2.** limiting the range of reference or application of a word, phrase, or clause —**restrictively** *adv* —**restrictiveness** *n*

restrictive covenant *n* a stipulation on a party buying or leasing land to refrain from uses or activities that would lessen its value

restrictive practice *n* **1.** something done customarily by a group of workers, especially a trade union, that places limits on the work of others or the freedom of operation of employers **2.** something done by companies in trade that is against the public interest, e.g. price-fixing

restrike /reé strīk/ *n* a coin struck at a later date from a die that has already been used to produce the original issue —**restrike** /ree strīk/ *vt*

rest room *n N Am* same as **cloakroom** (sense 2)

restructure /ree strúkchər/ (**-tures, -turing, -tured**) *v* **1.** *vti* to change the way in which something is organized or arranged ○ *restructure the firm* **2.** *vt* to alter the terms of a loan, especially to relieve its burden on the debtor

restructuring /ree strúkchəring/ *n* the process or an instance of changing the way in which something is organized or arranged

Restylane /ree stīlayn/ *tdmk* a trademark for a gel based on hyaluronic acid that is injected under the skin to smooth wrinkles and create a more youthful appearance

restyle /ree stīl/ (**-styles, -styling, -styled**) *vt* **1.** to give something a new design or shape **2.** to give somebody or something a new name or designation —**restyle** /reé stīl/ *n*

result /ri zúlt/ *n* **1.** CONSEQUENCE something that follows as a consequence of another action, condition, or event **2.** SCORE an outcome, especially the final score in a sporting competition or the grade awarded to somebody who has sat an examination ○ *The results were in Saturday's paper.* **3.** NUMBER a number arrived at by a calculation **4.** SUCCESS a successful outcome to something, especially a sporting competition (*informal*) ○ *If the lads play like this next week they'll definitely get a result.* ■ **results** *npl* DESIRED OUTCOME the desired outcome from an action ○ *The new policy is already showing results.* ■ *v* (**-sults, -sulting, -sulted**) **1.** *vi* FOLLOW AS CONSEQUENCE to follow as a consequence of a particular action, condition, or event ○ *This kind of error results from inattention.* **2.** *vi* CAUSE OUTCOME to produce a particular outcome ○ *Overgrazing results in soil erosion.* **3.** *vt* LAW same as **revert** (sense 5) [15C. < Latin *resultare* 'spring back, reverberate' ('result' in medieval Latin) < *saltare* 'to jump']

resultant /ri zúltənt/ *adj* happening as a consequence of something else ■ *n* a single vector that is equivalent to two or more other vectors

resultant tone *n* a tone that is created by the sounding together of two other tones but is different from both of them

resulting /ri zúlting/ *adj* happening as a consequence ○ *the heavy snowfall and the resulting chaos on the roads*

resume /ri zyoóm/ (**-sumes, -suming, -sumed**) *v* **1.** *vti* to continue with something after a temporary halt, or be continued **2.** *vt* to take, assume, or occupy a position again ○ *She came in and resumed her place at the head of the table.* [15C. Directly or via French *résumer* < Latin *resumere* 'take up again' < *sumere* 'take'] —**resumable** *adj*

résumé /rézzyoō may, ráy-/ *n* **1.** a summary of something such as events that have happened ○ *a résumé of the afternoon's activities* **2.** *N Am* same as **CV**[2] [Early 19C. < French, past participle of *résumer* (see RESUME)]

resumption /ri zúmpsh'n/ *n* the act or an instance of continuing with something that has been stopped for a while ○ *hoping for a resumption of negotiations* [15C. Directly or via French < Latin *resumption-* < past participle of *resumere* (see RESUME)]

resupinate /ri syoópinit/ *adj* describes a plant part, especially the flower of an orchid, that grows upside down or appears to do so [Late 18C. < Latin *resupinatus*, past participle of *resupinare* 'bend back' < *supinus* 'turned upwards'] —**resupination** /ri syoōpi náysh'n/ *n*

resurface /ree súrfiss/ (**-faces, -facing, -faced**) *v* **1.** *vi* COME TO SURFACE AGAIN to come back to the surface of a body of water after having submerged **2.** *vi* APPEAR AGAIN to appear again after having disappeared or been absent ○ *He resurfaced in Bangkok after the war.* **3.** *vt* PUT NEW SURFACE ON SOMETHING to put a new surface on something, especially a road

resurfacing /ree súrfissing/ *n* the process of putting a new surface on something, especially a road

resurge /ri súrj/ (**-surges, -surging, -surged**) *vi* to rise or grow strong again (*formal*) [Late 16C. < Latin *resurgere* (see RESURGENT)]

resurgence /ri súrjənss/ *n* the act or process of rising again or becoming stronger again ○ *a resurgence of patriotism*

resurgent /ri súrjənt/ *adj* rising or becoming stronger again [Late 18C. < Latin *resurgent-*, present participle of *resurgere* 'rise again' < *surgere* 'rise up from below']

resurrect /rézzə rékt/ (**-rects, -recting, -rected**) *v* **1.** *vti* to come back to life after apparent death, or bring somebody back to life **2.** *vt* to bring back into use something that had been stopped or discarded ○ *resurrect an old argument* [Late 18C. Back-formation < RESURRECTION]

resurrection /rézzə réksh'n/ *n* **1.** in some systems of belief, a rising from or raising of somebody from the dead, or the state of having risen from the dead **2.** the revival of something old or long disused ○ *the resurrection of a youthful dream* [13C. Via French < late Latin *resurrection-* < Latin *resurrect-*, past participle of *resurgere* (see RESURGENT)] —**resurrectional** *adj*

Resurrection *n* **1.** in Christian belief, the rising of Jesus Christ from the dead after his crucifixion and entombment **2.** in Christianity, Judaism, and Islam, the rising of the dead on Judgment Day

resurrection plant *n* a plant that survives well in hot dry conditions, e.g. the rose of Jericho

resuscitate /ri sússi tayt/ (**-tates, -tating, -tated**) *vti* to revive somebody from unconsciousness or apparent death, or be revived [Early 16C. < Latin *resuscitat-*, past participle of *resuscitare* < *suscitare* 'raise' < *citare* 'summon repeatedly'] —**resuscitable** /ri sússitəb'l/ *adj* —**resuscitation** /ri sússitáysh'n/ *n* —**resuscitative** *adj* —**resuscitator** *n*

resveratrol /ress vérrə trol/ *n* an antioxidant present in many plants and plant products, especially in red grape skins [Late 20C. &lt: RESORCINOL + Latin *veratrum* 'hellebore']

ret /ret/ (**rets, retting, retted**) *vti* to soak plant fibres such as flax or hemp so that they become easier to separate, or be soaked and become easier to separate [15C. < Middle Dutch *reeten*]

ret. *abbr* **1.** LAW retain **2.** retired **3.** LAW return **4.** COMM returned

retable /ri táyb'l/ *n* a shelf or setting behind an altar for holding candles, flowers, or religious images [Early 19C. Via French *rétable* and Spanish *retablo* < medieval Latin *retrotabulum* < Latin *retro-* 'back' + *tabula* 'table']

retail /reé tayl/ *n* SALE TO CONSUMERS the selling of goods directly to customers, e.g. in shops ○ *retail outlets* ■ *adv* NOT WHOLESALE from an ordinary shop or at the normal customer price and in small amounts rather than in bulk ○ *I bought it retail.* ■ *v* (**-tails, -tailing, -tailed**) **1.** *vti* SELL GOODS to sell goods to customers in small amounts and without a discount, or be sold in this way ○ *This item usually retails at a much higher price.* **2.** *vt* REPEAT SOMETHING HEARD to repeat regularly what is heard, especially gossip [14C. < Old French *retaille* 'piece cut off' < *taillier* 'to cut']

retailer /reé taylər/ *n* a person, shop, or business that sells goods directly to the public ○ *You can buy these at any local retailer.*

retail price index *n* a list of the prices of essential consumer goods that is published each month by the government to show how much prices in general have risen or fallen

retail price maintenance *n* the setting by the manufacturer of a minimum price at which its goods are to be sold at retail

retail therapy *n* shopping for enjoyment (*humorous*)

retain /ri táyn/ (**-tains, -taining, -tained**) *vt* **1.** KEEP SOMETHING to keep possession of something ○ *Despite losing the court case he retains all rights to the magazine article.* **2.** REMEMBER THINGS to be able to keep ideas or information in the memory **3.** KEEP SOMETHING IN POSITION to keep or hold something in a place or position ○ *water retained by a dam* **4.** HOLD SOMETHING WITHIN to be able to hold or accumulate something, especially liquid **5.** PAY SOMEBODY TO DO WORK to pay somebody regularly to do work **6.** HIRE PROFESSIONAL PERSON to pay a preliminary fee to reserve the services of a barrister, accountant, or other professional person whenever needed [14C. Via Anglo-Norman *retaign-* < Latin *retinere* 'hold back' < *tenere* 'hold'] —**retainability** /ri táynə bílləti/ *n* —**retainable** *adj* —**retainment** *n*

retained object /ri táynd-/ *n* the direct or indirect object of a passive verb, e.g. 'letter' in 'She was sent a letter by her brother'

retained profits *npl* the part of the after-tax profits of a business that is not distributed to shareholders

retainer /ri táynər/ *n* **1.** FEE RESERVING PROFESSIONAL SERVICES a fee paid to reserve the services of a professional person, especially a barrister or accountant, whenever needed **2.** FEE RESERVING ACCOMMODATION a fee paid by somebody who rents accommodation to reserve it while they are temporarily away **3.** HOLDER a device for holding something in place **4.** DENT DEVICE HOLDING TEETH IN POSITION a device for holding a tooth or teeth in position after orthodontic treatment **5.** HR SERVANT a paid servant, especially one who has been employed for many years ○ *one of the old family retainers* **6.** HIST FOLLOWER in former times, a soldier or other person who supported or was dependent on somebody of high rank ◇ **on (a) retainer** paid regularly in order to be consulted whenever necessary, rather than being paid for each job

retaining wall /ri táyning-/ *n* a wall built to keep earth or water in place

retake *vt* /ree táyk/ (**-takes, -taking, -took** /-toók/, **-taken** /-táykən/) **1.** RECAPTURE SOMETHING to recapture a place that has been captured by an enemy **2.** RECORDING,

CINEMA **FILM SOMETHING AGAIN** to record, photograph, or film something again in order to get it right **3.** SPORTS **TAKE SHOT AGAIN** to take a shot in a game again because of an infringement of the rules during the first attempt **4.** EDUC **TAKE EXAM AGAIN** to take an examination again ■ *n* /reé tayk/ RECORDING, CINEMA **ACT OF RECORDING SOMETHING AGAIN** an instance of recording, photographing, or filming something again, or the product that results from this

retaliate /ri tálli ayt/ (**-ates, -ating, -ated**) *vi* to deliberately harm somebody in response or revenge for a harm he or she has done [Early 17C. < Latin *retaliat-*, past participle of *retaliare* 'pay back in kind' < *talio* 'punishment in kind'] —**retaliation** /ri tálli áysh'n/ *n* —**retaliative** /-ətiv/ *adj* —**retaliator** *n* —**retaliatory** /-ətəri/ *adj*

retard *vt* /ri taárd/ (**-tards, -tarding, -tarded**) to slow or delay the progress of something ■ *n* /reé taard/ *N Am* an offensive term that deliberately insults somebody with a learning disability or somebody regarded as unintelligent (*slang insult*) [15C. Via French < Latin *retardare* < *tardus* 'slow']

retardant /ri taárd'nt/ *n* something designed to slow down a particular process or change, especially a chemical substance that inhibits change (*often used in combination*) ■ *adj* capable of making something move or happen more slowly ○ *flame-retardant fabric*

retardation /reé taar dáysh'n/ *n* **1. SLOWING** the process or fact of slowing down **2. DELAY** something that acts as a delay or obstacle to progress **3. DECELERATION** deceleration, or the rate of deceleration **4.** *N Am* **DEVELOPMENTAL DISABILITIES** the condition of having developmental disabilities (*dated; sometimes considered offensive*)

retarded /ri taárdid/ *adj* **1.** not fully developed ○ *the retarded growth of the plant* **2.** an offensive term meaning not intellectually or emotionally developed

retch /rech/ *v* (**retches, retching, retched**) **1.** *vi* **EXPERIENCE A VOMITING SPASM** to experience a spasm of vomiting without bringing anything up **2.** *vti* **VOMIT** to vomit, or vomit something ■ *n* **VOMITING SPASM** a spasm of vomiting without bringing anything up [Mid-16C. Variant of obsolete *reach* 'spit, vomit' < Old English *hrǣcan* < Germanic, an imitation of the sound]

SPELLCHECK retch or **wretch**? Do not confuse the spelling of ***retch*** and ***wretch***, which sound similar. ***Retch*** is a noun or verb referring to a spasm of vomiting or trying to vomit, as in *a foul smell that made him retch.* ***Wretch*** is a noun denoting a person who arouses pity, irritation, or contempt: *The poor wretch had nowhere else to go.*

retd *abbr* **1.** LAW retained **2.** retired **3.** COMM returned

rete /reéti/ (*plural* **-tia** /-shi ə, -ti ə/) *n* a network of veins, arteries, or nerve fibres in the body [14C. < Latin, 'net'] —**retial** /reéshi əl/ *adj*

retell /ree tél/ (**-tells, -telling, -told** /-tṓld/) *vt* to tell something such as a story or joke again, especially in a different form or to somebody who has not heard it

retelling /ree télling/ *n* a repeating of an account or story that has been told before, often in a different form ○ *a modern retelling of an ancient fable*

retene /reé teen, ré-/ *n* a yellow crystalline hydrocarbon. Source: pine tar, some fossil resins. Formula: $C_{18}H_{18}$. [Mid-19C. < Greek *rhētinē* 'resin' + -ENE]

retention /ri ténsh'n/ *n* **1. KEEPING OR HOLDING OF SOMETHING** the act of retaining something or the condition of being retained **2. MEMORY** the ability to remember things **3.** PHYSIOL **HOLDING IN OF WASTE** the holding in the body of waste that is normally excreted **4.** FIN **AMOUNT OF MONEY HELD BACK** an amount of money that is part of a sum agreed to be paid to somebody but which is not paid until a condition has been satisfied ○ *a mortgage of £80,000 with a retention of £10,000 pending major repairs* [14C. Directly or via French < Latin *retention-* < past participle of *retinere* (see RETAIN)]

retentive /ri téntiv/ *adj* **1.** able to or tending to hold something ○ *a soil that is highly retentive of rainwater* **2.** able to remember a great deal of information [14C. Directly or via French < medieval Latin *retentivus* < Latin *retent-*, past participle of *retinere* (see RETAIN)] —**retentively** *adv* —**retentiveness** *n*

retentivity /reé ten tívvəti/ *n* **1.** the power or condition of retaining something **2.** the capacity of a material to remain magnetized after the force that magnetized it has been taken away

rethink *vti* /ree thíngk/ (**-thinks, -thinking, -thought** /-tháwt/) to think about something again, especially using new information or in order to produce a better result ■ *n* /reé thingk/ an attempt to rethink something, or an occasion on which something is rethought ○ *Let's have a rethink before we proceed.*

retia ANAT plural of **rete**

retiarius /rétti aári əss, reéti áiri əss, reéshi-/ (*plural* **-ii** /-i ī/) *n* an ancient Roman gladiator who fought using a net and a trident [Mid-17C. < Latin, < *rete* 'net']

reticent /réttis'nt/ *adj* **1.** unwilling to communicate very much, talk freely, or reveal all the facts about something ○ *rather reticent on the subject of her finances* **2.** ⚠ unwilling to do something —**reticence** *n* —**reticently** *adv*

USAGE In its traditional sense, ***reticent*** means unwilling to communicate. Thus it is more nearly a synonym for *silent* than it is for *reluctant*: *He was never reticent about wanting the job.* It is, however, increasingly seen in contexts in which it conveys other kinds of reluctance: *He was reticent to travel so much.* Many regard this as a misuse, and in fact such usages tend to convey nothing that *reluctant* would not convey better.

SYNONYMS See ***silent***.

reticle /réttik'l/ *n* a grid of fine lines in the focus of an optical instrument, used for determining the scale or position of what is being looked at [Mid-17C. < Latin *reticulum* (see RETICULUM)]

reticula BIOL plural of **reticulum**

reticular /ri tíkyŏŏlər/ *adj* relating to, involving, or structurally resembling a net or network [Late 16C. < modern Latin *reticularis* < Latin *reticulum* (see RETICULUM)]

reticular formation *n* a formation of neurons in the brain stem that regulates many body functions, including respiration, blood pressure, sleeping and waking, and transmission of stimuli

reticulate *adj* /ri tíkyŏŏ lət, -layt/ same as **reticular** ■ *vti* /ri tíkyŏŏ layt/ (**-lates, -lating, -lated**) to form a network, or be formed into a network [Mid-17C. < Latin *reticulatus* < *reticulum* (see RETICULUM)] —**reticulately** /-lətli/ *adv* —**reticulation** /ri tíkyŏŏ láysh'n/ *n*

reticule /rétti kyool/ *n* **1.** a small fabric handbag, usually closed with a drawstring, carried by women in the late 18th and early 19th centuries **2.** OPTICS same as **reticle** [Early 18C. Via French < Latin *reticulum* (see RETICULUM)]

reticulocyte /ri tíkyŏŏlə sīt/ *n* an immature red blood cell containing a network of fibres of ribosomal remains that show up with laboratory staining [Early 20C. < RETICULUM] —**reticulocytic** /ri tíkyŏŏlə síttik/ *adj*

reticulum /ri tíkyŏŏləm/ (*plural* **-la** /-lə/) *n* **1.** a network, or something resembling a network in structure **2.** the second stomach or stomach compartment in cows, sheep, and other ruminants [Mid-17C. < Latin, 'little net' < *rete* 'net']

Reticulum *n* a small constellation of the southern hemisphere lying between Dorado and Horologium near to the Large Magellanic Cloud

retin- *prefix* same as **retino-** (*used before vowels*)

retina /réttinə/ (*plural* **-nas** or **-nae** /-nee/) *n* a light-sensitive membrane in the back of the eye containing rods and cones that receive an image from the lens and send it to the brain through the optic nerve [14C. < medieval Latin < Latin *rete* 'net'; from the network of blood vessels]

retinaculum /rétti nákyŏŏləm/ (*plural* **-la** /-lə/) *n* a part of the forewings of moths and butterflies that connects to the bristle (**frenulum**) on the hind wings that keeps the wings together in flight [Mid-18C. < Latin, 'band', literally 'little thing that holds back' < *retinire* (see RETAIN)] —**retinacular** *adj*

retinae ANAT plural of **retina**

retinal[1] /réttin'l/ *adj* involving or in the retina [Mid-19C. < RETINA + -AL[1]]

retinal[2] /réttin'l/, **retinene** /rétti neen/ *n* a derivative of vitamin A that forms part of the light-sensitive pigment in the eye [Mid-20C. < RETINA + -AL[2]]

retinite /rétti nīt/ *n* a fossil resin, especially one in which the plant matter has not formed a hard coal [Early 19C. < French < Greek *rhētinē* 'resin']

retinitis /rétti nítiss/ *n* inflammation of the retina

retinitis pigmentosa /-pígmən tṓzə/ *n* an inherited disorder of the eye involving progressive disintegration of the retina and optic nerve and leading eventually to tunnel vision or inability to see [*Pigmentosa* from modern Latin, 'pigmented']

retino- *prefix* retina ○ *retinoblastoma* [From RETINA]

retinoblastoma /réttinō bla stṓmə/ (*plural* **-mata** /-mətə/ or **-mas**) *n* a malignant tumour of the eye, usually resulting from a genetic disorder and appearing in early childhood

retinoic acid /réttinō ik-/ *n* PHARM same as **tretinoin** ['Retinoic' formed from RETINOL]

retinol /rétti nol/ *n* **1.** BIOCHEM same as **vitamin A 2.** CHEM same as **rosin oil** [Mid-20C. < RETINA]

retinopathy /rétti nóppəthi/ (*plural* **-thies**) *n* a disease of the retina, especially one that is noninflammatory and associated with damage to the blood vessels of the retina ○ *diabetic retinopathy* —**retinopathic** /réttinō páthik/ *adj*

retinoscope /réttinə skōp/ *n* an instrument for identifying refractive errors in the eye by measuring the angle of a beam of light reflected from the retina and back out through the pupil

retinoscopy /rétti nóskəpi/ *n* a method of measuring refractive errors in the eye using a retinoscope —**retinoscopic** /réttinə skóppik/ *adj* —**retinoscopically** *adv* —**retinoscopist** *n*

retinue /rétti nyoo/ *n* a group of people who travel with and attend an important person [14C. < Old French, 'retained (in service)' < past participle of *retenir* < Latin *retinere* (see RETAIN)]

retiral /ri tīrəl/ *n Scotland* retirement from a job or post ○ *He's due for retiral next year.*

retire /ri tīr/ (**-tires, -tiring, -tired**) *v* **1.** *vi* **STOP WORKING WILLINGLY** to leave a job or career voluntarily, at or near the usual age for doing so **2.** *vi* **GO TO BED** to stop engaging in daily activities and go to bed **3.** *vi* **WITHDRAW** to leave a place, position, or way of life and go to a place of less activity ○ *retire from public life* **4.** *vt* **MAKE SOMEBODY STOP WORKING** to stop a person or animal performing some activity because of illness or an inability to continue ○ *injuries so extensive that the horse was retired* **5.** *vt* **WITHDRAW SOMETHING FROM SERVICE** to take a machine or piece of equipment out of service **6.** *vti* MIL **GO BACK OR MOVE TROOPS BACK** to fall back, or move troops away from a position, action, or danger **7.** *vti* SPORTS **WITHDRAW FROM SPORTS CONTEST** to withdraw from a sports contest, or withdraw somebody from a sports contest, because of an inability to continue **8.** *vt* FIN **WITHDRAW SOMETHING FROM CIRCULATION** to take a loan, stock, bond, or other financial instrument out of circulation by paying for it [Mid-16C. < French *retirer* 'retreat' < *tirer* 'draw'] —**retirer** *n*

retired /ri tīrd/ *adj* **1.** having given up working, typically after having worked many years ○ *a retired bus driver* **2.** having withdrawn from a busy way of life ○ *a retired lifestyle*

retiree /ri tī reé/ *n* somebody who has retired from a job or career

retirement /ri tīrmənt/ *n* **1. LEAVING OF JOB OR CAREER** the act of leaving a job or career at or near the usual age for doing so, or the state of having left a job or career **2. TIME AFTER HAVING STOPPED WORKING** the time that follows the end of somebody's working life **3. BEING AWAY FROM BUSY LIFE** a state of being withdrawn from the rest of the world or from a former busy life ○ *He lives in retirement in the country.*

retirement pension *n* a pension paid to a retired person, usually by the state

retiring /ri tīring/ *adj* **1.** avoiding social contact with other people **2.** at, involving, or undergoing retirement from a job or career ○ *The retiring chairman made an emotional speech.* —**retiringly** *adv*

retold *vt* past participle, past tense of **retell**

retook past tense of **retake**

retool /ree to͞ol/ (**-tools, -tooling, -tooled**) *vti* **1.** to replace the tools or machinery in a factory, or obtain new tools or machinery **2.** *N Am* to reorganize something in order to make it more efficient or powerful ○ *The company will have to retool if it's to remain competitive.*

retorsion /ri táwrsh'n/ (*plural* **-sions** or **-tions**) *n* an act of retaliation by a government against citizens of another country for a similar offence committed by the other country [Mid-17C. < French *rétorsion* < Latin *retort-* (see RETORT[1])]

retort[1] /ri táwrt/ *vt* (**-torts, -torting, -torted**) **1. RESPOND SHARPLY** to say something sharp, angry, witty, or insulting in quick response to something somebody else has said **2. ARGUE SOMETHING IN REPLY** to put forward something as an argument in reply to somebody else's argument ■ *n* **SHARP ANSWER** something sharp, angry, witty, or insulting said quickly in response to something somebody else has said [15C. < Latin *retort-*, past participle of *retorquere* 'twist again, twist back' < *torquere* 'twist'] —**retorter** *n*

SYNONYMS See *answer*.

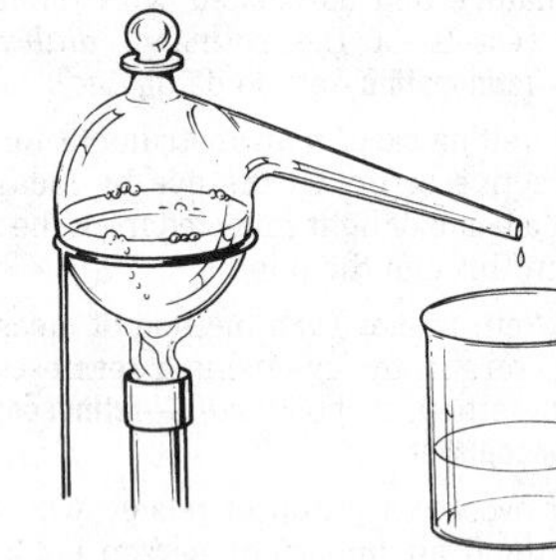

retort

retort[2] /ri táwrt/ *n* **1. GLASS VESSEL** a glass vessel with a long downward-pointing tapering spout, used for distilling by heat **2. CLOSED CONTAINER FOR HEATING SUBSTANCES** a closed container in which large quantities of a substance are heated to extract something such as metal from ore ■ *vt* (**-torts, -torting, -torted**) **HEAT SOMETHING IN RETORT** to heat or distil something in a retort [Early 17C. Via French < medieval Latin *retorta* < Latin *retorquere* 'twist back' (see RETORT[1]), from the shape of the neck]

retortion *n* **1.** an act or the process of saying something as a retort to somebody else **2.** INTERNAT REL same as **retorsion**

retouch *vt* /ree túch/ (**-touches, -touching, -touched**) **1. IMPROVE SOMETHING** to make small finishing, correcting, or improving changes to something **2.** PHOTOGRAPHY **ALTER PHOTOGRAPH** to alter a photographic negative or print by removing imperfections or adding details ■ *n* /rée tuch/ **1. ACTIVITY OF RETOUCHING** the process of retouching something, or an occasion on which something is retouched **2. SOMETHING ALTERED** something that has been retouched, especially a photograph **3. IMPROVING CHANGE** a small finishing, correcting, or improving change to something —**retoucher** *n*

retrace /ri tráyss/ (**-traces, -tracing, -traced**) *vt* **1.** to go back over a path or route again **2.** to review something in the mind such as an argument, account, or series of events ○ *retraced the events leading up to the war* —**retraceable** *adj*

retract /ri trákt/ (**-tracts, -tracting, -tracted**) *v* **1.** *vti* **MOVE, OR MOVE SOMETHING, BACK INSIDE** to draw something in from an extended position, or be drawn in ○ *Cats can retract their claws but dogs can't.* **2.** *vti* **WITHDRAW STATEMENT** to withdraw or deny something previously said, published, or promised ○ *She has since retracted her earlier statement.* **3.** *vi* **MOVE BACK** to move back from something **4.** *vt* PHON **CHANGE VOWEL SOUND** to alter a vowel sound by drawing the tongue inwards from the lips [15C. < Latin *retract-*, past participle of *retrahere* 'draw back' < *trahere* 'pull'] —**retractability** /ri tráktə bílləti/ *n* —**retractable** *adj* —**retractation** /rée trak táysh'n/ *n*

retractile /ri trák tīl/ *adj* capable of being retracted —**retractility** /rée trak tílləti/ *n*

retraction /ri tráksh'n/ *n* **1.** the act of retracting something, or the condition of being retracted **2.** a statement, sometimes formal, that withdraws or denies a previous statement

retractor /ri tráktər/ *n* **1.** a surgical instrument used to hold back skin or tissue during surgery **2.** a muscle that retracts a body part, e.g. one that closes the jaw

retrain /ree tráyn/ (**-trains, -training, -trained**) *vti* to teach somebody new skills, or learn new skills

retraining /ree tráyning/ *n* the process or activity of learning new skills or of updating existing skills

retread *n* /rée tred/ **1.** *N Am* AUTOMOT same as **remould** **2.** *N Am* a revised or remade version of something **3.** *US* somebody who returns to a job previously given up (*informal*) ■ *vt* /ree tréd/ (**-treads, -treading, -treaded**) *N Am* INDUST same as **remould** *v* (sense 2)

re-tread /ree tréd/ *vt* to walk again on a route that has already been walked over

retreat /ri tréet/ *n* **1. MOVEMENT BACK** a movement away from danger or a confrontation, back along the original route ○ *The bear had the hunters in full retreat.* **2. WITHDRAWAL FROM POSITION** a withdrawal from a position or point of view to one intended to lessen conflict ○ *their retreat from a previously inflexible position* **3. TROOP WITHDRAWAL** a withdrawal of military forces following a defeat or preceding a change of position **4. SIGNAL TO MOVE BACK** a signal, usually a bugle call or drumbeat, telling soldiers to perform a retreat **5. QUIET TIME** a period of quiet rest and contemplation in a secluded place **6. QUIET PLACE** a quiet secluded place where people go for rest and privacy **7. SAFE PLACE** a place where people or animals go to avoid danger or capture **8. SPECIAL HOSPITAL** a place for the long-term care and treatment of people who are incapable of caring for themselves (*dated*) **9.** RELIG **PERIOD OF SECLUSION** a period away from normal activities, devoted to prayer and meditation, often spent in a religious community **10.** MIL **FLAG-LOWERING CEREMONY** the ceremony of lowering the flag at a military institution, or the signal given to lower the flag ■ *v* (**-treats, -treating, -treated**) **1.** *vi* **MOVE BACK** to move back away from danger or a confrontation **2.** *vi* **WITHDRAW FROM POSITION** to withdraw from a position or point of view to one intended to lessen conflict **3.** *vi* **MAKE MILITARY WITHDRAWAL** to withdraw following a defeat or prior to a change of position **4.** *vi* **RECEDE** to recede or fall back from a previous position ○ *when the glaciers retreated* **5.** *vt* CHESS **MOVE PIECE BACK** to move a chesspiece back to an earlier position [13C. < Old French *retret* < past participle of *retraire* < Latin *retrahere* (see RETRACT)] ◇ **beat a (hasty) retreat** to leave, especially in a hurry

retreatant /ri tréet'nt/ *n* a participant in a spiritual or religious retreat

retrench /ri trénch/ (**-trenches, -trenching, -trenched**) *v* **1.** *vti* to reduce something such as costs **2.** *vt* to cut out, cut back, or omit something [Late 16C. < French *retrancher* 'cut again' < *trenchier* 'to cut'] —**retrenchment** *n*

retrial /ree trī əl, rée trī əl/ *n* a second trial in a court of law replacing a prior one that was flawed or ended in a hung jury

retribution /réttri byo͞osh'n/ *n* something done or given to somebody as punishment or vengeance for something he or she has done ○ *a just retribution for their crime* [14C. < Latin *retribution-* < past participle of *retribuere* 'hand back, repay' < *tribuere* 'allot'] —**retributive** /ri tríbbyo͞otiv/ *adj* —**retributively** *adv* —**retributory** /ri tríbbyo͞otəri/ *adj*

retrieval /ri tréev'l/ *n* **1. RECOVERY OF SOMETHING** the act of getting something back, or a particular occasion on which this is done **2. POSSIBILITY OF BEING RESTORED** the possibility of something being brought back, saved, or restored to an original condition ○ *Their business seemed beyond retrieval.* **3.** COMPUT **DATA ACCESS** the process of reading data from a storage device and returning it to the program or device that requested it

retrieve /ri tréev/ *v* (**-trieves, -trieving, -trieved**) **1.** *vt* **GET SOMETHING BACK** to get something back **2.** *vt* **SAVE SOMETHING** to save something from being lost, damaged, or destroyed **3.** *vt* **REMEDY SOMETHING** to set something right or make it better ○ *attempt to retrieve the situation before it worsens* **4.** *vt* **RESTORE SOMETHING** to revive or restore something to its original condition ○ *She quickly retrieved her sense of humour.* **5.** *vt* **REMEMBER SOMETHING** to recall something from memory **6.** *vt* COMPUT **GET DATA** to read data from a storage device and return it to the program or device that requested it **7.** *vti* RACKET GAMES **RETURN SHOT** in a game such as tennis or badminton, to return a difficult shot **8.** *vti* FIELD SPORTS **FETCH GAME** to fetch small game that has been shot by a hunter ■ *n* **RETRIEVING OF SOMETHING** the act of retrieving something ○ *a successful retrieve* [15C. < Old French *retroev-*, stem of *retrover* 'find again' < *trover* 'to find'] —**retrievability** /ri tréevə bílləti/ *n* —**retrievable** *adj* —**retrievably** *adv*

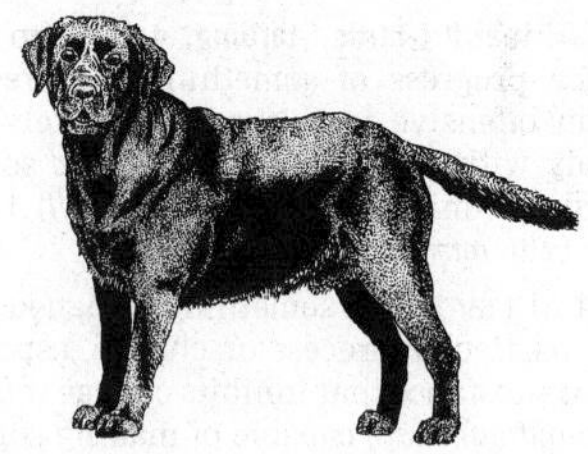

retriever

retriever /ri tréevər/ *n* **1.** a large dog belonging to a breed originally used to fetch game shot by a hunter **2.** somebody or something that retrieves something

retro /réttrō/ *adj* modelled on something from the past such as a style of fashion or music ○ *retro clothing* ■ *n* (*plural* **-ros**) **1.** the practice of modelling things such as clothes or music on styles from the past, or an example of such a practice ○ *The band is heavily into sixties retro.* **2.** AEROSP same as **retrorocket** [Late 20C. < French *rétro*, shortening of *rétrograde* 'retrograde' < Latin *retrogradus* (see RETROGRADE); influenced by RETRO-]

retro- *prefix* **1.** back, backward, after ○ *retrorocket* ○ *retrofit* **2.** behind ○ *retrochoir* [< Latin *retro*]

retroact /réttrō ákt/ (**-acts, -acting, -acted**) *vi* **1.** to act in a way that opposes something else **2.** to apply to things that have happened in the past

retroaction /réttrō áksh'n/ *n* **1. APPLICABILITY TO PAST** the applicability of something to past circumstances or events **2. ACTION REACTING TO PAST SITUATION** an action that responds or reacts to something in the past **3. COUNTERACTION** an action that goes against or balances a previous action

retroactive /réttrō áktiv/ *adj* relating or applying to things that have happened in the past as well as the present ○ *retroactive pay increases*

retroactive inhibition *n* the tendency of recently gained knowledge or skills to degenerate when new learning in a similar area is acquired

retrocede /réttrō séed/ (**-cedes, -ceding, -ceded**) *v* **1.** *vi* to go back or return **2.** *vt* to give something such as land or a territory back to somebody [Mid-17C. < French *rétrocéder* < *céder* 'give way'] —**retrocedent** *adj* —**retrocession** *n* —**retrocessive** *adj*

retrochoir /réttrō kwīr/ *n* the area behind the high altar in a large church or cathedral [Mid-19C. After medieval Latin *retrochorus* 'back choir']

retro-engine *n* AEROSP same as **retrorocket**

retrofire /réttrō fīr/ *vti* (**-fires, -firing, -fired**) to fire a retrorocket in order to decelerate, or be fired to cause deceleration ■ *n* the process of firing a retrorocket, or an occasion of doing this

retrofit /réttrō fit/ *vt* (**-fits, -fitting, -fitted**) **1. MODIFY SOMETHING WITH NEW PARTS** to modify something such as a machine or a building by adding newly developed parts or devices that were not available when the machine or building was made ○ *older cars retrofitted with catalytic converters* **2. INSTALL NEW PARTS** to install newly developed parts or devices into a machine or building, that were not available when the machine or building was made ○ *retrofit a microchip in the alarm system* ■ *n* **1. NEW PART, OR SOMETHING WITH ONE** something that has been equipped with a newly developed component, or such a component designed for something that is already in use **2. PROCESS OF ADDING NEW PART** the process or an

instance of modifying something such as a machine or a building by adding newly developed parts or devices

retroflection *n* another spelling of **retroflexion**

retroflex /réttrō fleks/, **retroflexed** /-flekst/ *adj* 1. bent or curved backwards 2. describes speech sounds that are pronounced with the tip of the tongue raised and bent backwards [Late 18C. < Latin *retroflex-*, past participle of *retroflectere* 'bend back' < *flectere* 'bend']

retroflexion /réttrō fléksh'n/, **retroflection** *n* 1. BENT CONDITION the condition of bending or being bent backwards 2. PHON PRONUNCIATION WITH TONGUE BENT BACK the pronunciation of a letter or sound with the tongue raised and bent backwards 3. PSYCHOL INABILITY TO EXTERNALIZE EMOTION in Gestalt therapy, the act of directing a difficult emotion such as anger at yourself rather than at somebody who has provoked the emotion [Early 19C. < RETRO- after REFLECTION]

retrograde /réttrō grayd/ *adj* 1. MOVING BACKWARDS moving backwards in space or time 2. GETTING WORSE worsening or returning to an earlier worse condition 3. INVERSE in writing, inverse or reversed, especially in syntactic order 4. ASTRON HAVING CONTRARY ORBIT orbiting in a direction opposite to that of Earth's orbit around the Sun, or of the Moon's orbit around the Earth 5. ASTRON MOVING EAST TO WEST moving or appearing to move from east to west in the sky, counter to the direction of most astronomical objects 6. MUSIC REVERSING NOTES reversing the sequence of notes of an earlier version of a musical composition ■ *vi* (**-grades, -grading, -graded**) 1. GO BACKWARDS to go back or appear to be moving backwards in space or time 2. same as **retrogress** (sense 1) [14C. < Latin *retrogradus* 'going backwards' < *gradus* 'step'] —**retrogradation** /réttrō gray dáysh'n/ *n* —**retrogradely** *adv*

retrogress /réttrō gréss/ (**-gresses, -gressing, -gressed**) *vi* 1. REVERT OR DEGENERATE to return to an earlier and usually worse condition 2. GO BACKWARDS to move or travel backwards 3. BIOL HAVE LESS COMPLEX FEATURES to show or develop the less complex features of simpler organisms [Early 19C. < RETRO- after PROGRESS] —**retrogressive** *adj* —**retrogressively** *adv*

retrogression /réttrō grésh'n/ *n* 1. the process of returning to an earlier and usually worse condition 2. the development of less complex features usually associated with simpler organisms

retrolental /réttrō lént'l/ *adj* located behind the lens of the eye or the lens of an optical instrument [Mid-20C. < RETRO- + modern Latin *lent-* 'lens' < Latin, 'lentil']

retronym /réttrō nim/ *n* US a term that distinguishes a subclass from members of a superclass, e.g. 'snail mail' is a retronym coined by those for whom 'mail' is likely to mean 'e-mail' [< RETRO- after SYNONYM]

retropack /réttrō pak/ *n* an array of retrorockets on a spacecraft, used for slowing down or for changing direction

retropulsion /réttrō púlsh'n/ *n* a tendency to walk backwards involuntarily, associated with Parkinson's disease [Late 18C. < RETRO- after PROPULSION]

retrorocket /réttrō rokit/ *n* a small rocket engine on a spacecraft or missile that produces thrust to act against the main engines, used for decelerating

retrorse /ri tráwrss/ *adj* describes plant parts that are turned back or down [Early 19C. < Latin *retrorsus*, contraction of *retroversus* 'turning backwards' < *versus* 'turning'] —**retrorsely** *adv*

retrospect /réttrō spekt/ *n* the remembering of past events [Early 17C. < RETRO- after PROSPECT] ◇ **in retrospect** thinking about or reviewing the past, especially from a new perspective or with new information

retrospection /réttrō spéksh'n/ *n* the act of looking back over things in the past, especially personal memories

retrospective /réttrō spéktiv/ *adj* 1. REVIEWING PAST looking back over things in the past 2. APPLYING TO PAST EVENTS applying to things that have happened in the past as well as the present ○ *a retrospective ruling* 3. ARTS CONTAINING PAST WORKS containing examples of work from many periods of an artist's life ○ *a retrospective exhibition* ■ *n* ARTS EXHIBITION OF PAST WORKS an exhibition of the work of an artist or artistic movement that shows examples from all

periods or styles ○ *a Degas retrospective* —**retrospectively** *adv*

retroussé /rə troó say/ *adj* describes a nose that is turned up at the end [Early 19C. < French, 'turned up']

retroversion /réttrō vúrsh'n/ *n* 1. the act or condition of being turned backwards 2. the turning or tilting backwards of a body part such as the uterus, but without folding [Late 16C. < Latin *retroversus* (see RETRORSE)] —**retroverse** /réttrō vúrss/ *adj* —**retroverted** /réttrō vurtid/ *adj*

retrovirus /réttrō vīrəss/ *n* a virus whose genetic information is contained in RNA rather than DNA. Some retroviruses cause Aids and cancer and they contain the enzyme reverse transcriptase for generating DNA from RNA. —**retroviral** /-vīrəl/ *adj*

retry *v* /ree trí/ (**-tries, -trying, -tried**) 1. *vt* TRY SOMEBODY AGAIN to try a person or case again in a court of law 2. *vti* ATTEMPT SOMETHING AGAIN to try to do something again ■ *n* /rée trī/ (*plural* **-tries**) SECOND ATTEMPT another attempt to do something

retsina /ret seénə/ *n* a Greek wine flavoured with pine resin [Early 20C. < modern Greek < Greek *rētinē* 'pine resin']

return /ri túrn/ *v* (**-turns, -turning, -turned**) 1. *vi* COME OR GO BACK to come or go back to a place after leaving it, or come or go back to a former condition 2. *vi* MENTION OR CONSIDER SOMETHING AGAIN to go back to something that has already been mentioned or considered, especially in order to deal with it more thoroughly or conclusively ○ *Let's return to the matter in hand.* 3. *vi* APPEAR AGAIN to appear or happen again 4. *vt* SAY SOMETHING to say something in reply ○ *'Do it yourself!' she returned.* 5. *vt* PUT SOMETHING BACK to put, bring, send, or take something back to where it came from 6. *vt* REPAY SOMETHING to give back something of equivalent value ○ *I hope that some day I'll be able to return your kindness.* 7. *vt* YIELD PROFIT to yield something as a profit on an investment ○ *returns 6% annually* 8. *vt* RE-ELECT SOMEBODY TO OFFICE to re-elect somebody to an office or position ○ *returned her to Parliament for a second term* 9. *vt* PRODUCE VERDICT to give a particular verdict in a court of law ○ *return a guilty verdict* 10. *vt* REFLECT SOMETHING to send back or reflect something such as an echo ○ *The cliff wall returned the sound of their laughter.* 11. *vt* SUBMIT OFFICIAL REPORT to give an official report, usually in response to a request or legal requirement 12. *vt* COMPUT GIVE RESPONSE of a computer, to give a particular response to a command, routine, or subroutine ○ *returns zero if the condition is false* 13. *vti* SPORTS HIT BALL BACK in sports such as tennis, to hit a ball, especially a service, back to an opponent 14. *vt* CARDS LEAD SAME SUIT to lead the same suit as a partner in a card game such as bridge or whist 15. *vt* ARCHIT BUILD SOMETHING TO FACE OPPOSITE DIRECTION to construct part of a building such as a wall or decoration so that it turns away from its original direction ■ *n* 1. INSTANCE OF GOING BACK an instance of going or coming back to a place after having left it or to a former condition 2. REPLACEMENT an instance of putting, taking, sending, or bringing back something to where it came from 3. SOMETHING GIVEN BACK something that has come or been brought back, especially unsold merchandise ○ *Returns go in that bin over there.* 4. REAPPEARANCE a reappearance or recurrence of something 5. RECIPROCATION a response to something done or given ○ *If you are kind to your puppy it will give you love in return.* 6. ANSWER something said in response to something else ○ *If you ask her an absurd question you can expect an angry return.* 7. FIN PROFIT a profit made on an investment or business venture (*often used in the plural*) 8. TRAVEL same as **return ticket** 9. FIN same as **tax return** 10. FIN FINANCIAL REPORT a periodic financial report of an organization 11. COMPUT same as **return key** 12. SPORTS BALL PLAYED BACK an instance of hitting or playing the ball back to an opponent in a sport such as tennis 13. LAW LEGAL REPORT a report on a legal document previously issued by a court, prepared by an officer of that court 14. CARDS LEAD OF SAME SUIT an instance of leading the same suit as a partner in a card game such as bridge or pinochle 15. ARCHIT ANGLED PART part of a building, e.g. a wall or decoration, built so that it turns away from its original direction 16. N Ireland BUILDINGS BUILDING EXTENSION a rearward extension to a

building ■ **returns** *npl* ELECTION RESULTS the results from an election or election district ○ *We sat up late waiting for the election returns.* ■ *adj* 1. CONNECTED WITH GOING BACK AGAIN relating to an act of going or coming back to an earlier place or position ○ *I hope the return flight isn't delayed.* 2. UK, ANZ, Can GOING THERE AND BACK involving travel to somewhere and back again ○ *How much is the return fare?* US term **round-trip** 3. HAPPENING AGAIN given or done again ○ *We enjoyed the resort so much that we decided to make a return visit the next year.* [14C. < Old French *reto(u)rner* 'turn again' < *to(u)rner* 'to turn' < Latin *tornare*] —**returnable** *adj*, *n* —**returnee** /ri túr neé/ *n* ◇ **by return (of post)** by the next post back to the sender ◇ **in return (for something)** as an exchange for something ◇ **many happy returns (of the day)** a conventional way of expressing good wishes to somebody whose birthday it is, often as an exclamation

Returned Services League *n* Aus full form of **RSL**

returner /ri túrnər/ *n* somebody who returns to work or rejoins the workforce of an organization after a prolonged break, e.g. after bringing up a family

returning officer /ri túrning-/ *n* UK, Aus, Can a constituency official who is responsible for overseeing the count in an election and for announcing the result

return key *n* the key on a computer or typewriter keyboard, usually marked with an angled arrow, that can be used to execute an instruction or create a new line

return ticket *n* UK, ANZ, Can a ticket that entitles a passenger to travel both to and back from a place. US term **round-trip ticket**

retuse /ri tyoóss/ *adj* describes leaves that have a blunt notched apex [Mid-18C. < Latin *retusus*, past participle of *retundere* 'beat back' < *tundere* 'beat']

Reuben /roóbin/ *n* in the Bible, a Hebrew patriarch and the eldest son of Jacob and his first wife Leah. He was the ancestor of one of the tribes of Israel.

reunify /ree yoóni fī/ (**-fies, -fying, -fied**) *vti* to come together, or bring people or factions together again, after they have been divided —**reunification** /ree yoónifi káysh'n/ *n*

reunion /ree yoónyən/ *n* 1. a gathering of old friends, relatives, or colleagues ○ *a class reunion* 2. the coming together again of things or people that have been divided, or the condition of having come together in this way

Réunion /ree yoónyən, rayoo nyáwN/ island in the Indian Ocean, south-east of Madagascar. It is an overseas department of France. Population: 653,000 (1995). Area: 2,512 sq. km/970 sq. mi.

reunionist /ree yoónyənist/ *n* a supporter of reunion between divided groups or parties, especially somebody who seeks reunion between the Anglican and Roman Catholic churches —**reunionism** *n* —**reunionistic** /ree yoónyə nístik/ *adj*

reunite /ree yoo nít/ (**-nites, -niting, -nited**) *vti* to bring people together after a separation, or come together after a separation

reuptake /ree úp tayk/ *n* the reabsorption of neurotransmitters by the nerve cells that produced them. Prozac™ and similar drugs work by inhibiting reuptake of the neurotransmitter serotonin so that circulating levels are high and depression is eased.

reuse *vt* /ree yoóz/ (**-uses, -using, -used**) to use something again, often for a different purpose and usually as an alternative to throwing it away ■ *n* /ree yoóss/ the use of something again, often for a different purpose and usually as an alternative to throwing it away —**reusability** /ree yoózə bílləti/ *n* —**reusable** *adj*

Reuter /róytər/, **Paul Julius, Baron von** (1816–99) German-born British journalist. In 1851, he established the pioneer Reuters Telegrams, now Reuters, the first news agency in the world. Born **Josaphat, Israel Beer**

Reuters /róytərz/ *n* a London news agency providing international news reports [Mid-19C. After Paul Julius, Baron von REUTER]

rev /rev/ *vti* (**revs, revving, revved**) to increase a vehicle's engine speed by pressing down on the accelerator or advancing the throttle, especially while the vehicle is stationary, or undergo this process ■ *n* a

single revolution of a vehicle's engine (*informal; usually plural*) [Early 20C. Shortening of REVOLUTION]

rev up *vt* (*informal*) **1.** to increase the tempo, intensity, or amount of something ○ *We'd better rev up production if we're to meet our deadline.* **2.** to stir up intense feelings in somebody, usually feelings of excitement, desire, or anger

rev. *abbr* **1.** revenue **2.** FIN reverse **3.** MIL review **4.** PUBL revised **5.** EDUC revision **6.** revolution **7.** ARMS revolver **8.** revolving

Rev. *abbr* CHR Reverend

revamp *vt* /ree vámp/ (**-vamps, -vamping, -vamped**) to improve the appearance, condition, or structure of something by making sometimes superficial changes ■ *n* /rée vamp/ a change made in something in order to improve its appearance or functioning [Mid-19C. < RE- + VAMP[2]]

SYNONYMS See ***renew***.

revanche /ri vánch/ *n* a nation's or an ethnic group's policy of regaining lost territory [Mid-19C. < French < Old French *revancher* 'avenge' < *vengier*] —**revanchism** *n* —**revanchist** *adj, n* —**revanchistic** /ri ván chístik/ *adj*

rev counter *n* AUTOMOT same as **tachometer** (*informal*)

Revd *abbr* CHR Reverend

reveal[1] /ri véel/ (**-veals, -vealing, -vealed**) *vt* **1.** MAKE SOMETHING KNOWN to disclose something that was unknown or secret **2.** EXPOSE SOMETHING to make something visible that had been hidden or covered **3.** RELIG MAKE KNOWN DIVINE TRUTH to make something known by what is believed to be divine or supernatural means [14C. Via French < Latin *revelare* 'unveil' < *velum* 'sail, curtain, veil'] —**revealer** *n*

reveal[2] /ri véel/ *n* the vertical section of wall that lies between a doorframe or window frame and the outer wall [Late 17C. Alteration of obsolete *revale* 'lower, bring down' < Old French *revaler* < *val* 'valley']

revealed religion /ri véeld-/ *n* a religion based on what its adherents believe to be the word of a supreme deity

revealing /ri véeling/ *adj* **1.** exposing part of the body that would normally be kept covered **2.** giving away new, surprising, or valuable information —**revealingly** *adv*

revegetate /ree véjji tayt/ (**-tates, -tating, -tated**) *vti* to provide eroded or otherwise barren land with new plant life —**revegetation** /-véjji táysh'n/ *n*

reveille /ri válli/ *n* **1.** WAKE-UP CALL the sounding of a bugle to awaken and summon military personnel in a camp **2.** TIME OF REVEILLE the time of day at which reveille is sounded **3.** EARLY-MORNING MILITARY FORMATION the military formation that begins the day **4.** SIGNAL TO AWAKE any signal that tells somebody it is time to get out of bed [Mid-17C. Alteration of French *réveillez* 'wake up!' < Old French *resveiller* 'awaken' < *esveiller* < Latin *vigil* 'awake, alert']

revel /révv'l/ *vi* (**-els, -elling, -elled**) **1.** TAKE PLEASURE to take great pleasure in something **2.** ENJOY PARTY to have an enjoyable time in the company of others, especially at a party ■ *n* NOISY CELEBRATION an uproarious party or celebration (*often used in the plural*) [14C. Via Old French *reveler* 'rebel, carouse' < Latin *rebellare* 'to rebel' < *bellum* 'war'] —**reveller** *n*

~~**revelant**~~ incorrect spelling of **relevant**

revelation /révvə láysh'n/ *n* **1.** INFORMATION REVEALED information that is newly disclosed, especially surprising, or valuable **2.** SURPRISING THING a surprisingly good or valuable experience **3.** DISCLOSURE the revealing of something previously hidden or secret **4.** CHR DEMONSTRATION OF DIVINE WILL a showing or revealing of what is believed to be divine will or truth [14C. < French < Latin *revelat-* past participle of *revelare* (see REVEAL[1])] —**revelational** *adj* —**revelatory** /révvə láytəri/ *adj*

Revelation, Revelations /révvə láysh'ns/ *n* a book of the Bible that includes a description of the end of the world. See table at **Bible**

revelator /révvə laytər/ *n* somebody or something believed to reveal divine will or truth [15C. < late Latin < Latin *revelat-* past participle of *revelare* (see REVEAL[1])]

revelry /révvəlri/ (*plural* **-ries**) *n* lively enjoyment or celebration, usually involving eating, drinking, dancing, and noise (*often used in the plural*)

revenant /révvənənt/ *n* a dead person believed to have come back as a ghost (*formal*) [Early 19C. < French < present participle of *revenir* 'return' (see REVENUE)]

revenge /ri vénj/ *n* **1.** PUNISHMENT the punishment of somebody in retaliation for harm done **2.** RETALIATION ACT something done to get even with somebody else who has caused harm **3.** DESIRE FOR RETALIATION the desire or urge to get even with somebody ■ *vt* (**-venges, -venging, -venged**) PUNISH SOMEBODY FOR SOMETHING to punish somebody who has harmed you or harmed a friend ○ *Those who seek to revenge themselves often regret the effort.* [14C. < Old French *revengier* < *vengier* 'avenge' < late Latin *vindicare* 'claim, set free, avenge'] —**revengeful** *adj* —**revengefully** *adv* —**revenger** *n*

revenue /révvə nyoo/ *n* **1.** INCOME FROM BUSINESS money that comes into a business from the sale of goods or services **2.** GOVERNMENT INCOME the income of a government from all sources, used to pay for a nation's expenses **3.** PERSONAL INCOME income or salary received from employment **4.** FIN YIELD ON INVESTMENT the total return produced by an investment **5.** GOV TAX-COLLECTING DEPARTMENT the department of a nation's government that is responsible for collecting taxes [15C. < French *revenu* < past participle of *revenir* 'return' < Latin *revenire* 'come back' < *venire* 'come']

revenue bond *n* a bond issued by a US government agency in order to build or improve a public property. The income from the property pays for the bond.

revenue cutter *n* a small lightly armed boat used to patrol coastlines, enforce customs regulations, and prevent smuggling

revenuer /révvə nyoo ər/ *n* a US government agent who is in charge of collecting revenue, especially those in charge of stopping the illegal manufacture of alcoholic beverages (*informal*)

revenue tariff *n* a tax or duty imposed to produce public revenue, as distinct from one imposed to protect a domestic economy

reverb *n* /rée vurb/ **1.** ECHO IN MUSIC an echoing effect produced in live or recorded music by electronic means **2.** ECHO-PRODUCING DEVICE an electronic device used to produce an echoing effect in live or recorded music ■ *vi* /ri vúrb/ (**-verbs, -verbing, -verbed**) PRODUCE ELECTRONIC ECHO to produce an echoing effect in live or recorded music [Early 17C. Shortening of REVERBERATE]

reverberate /ri vúrbə rayt/ (**-ates, -ating, -ated**) *v* **1.** *vi* ECHO to echo repeatedly **2.** *vi* HAVE CONTINUING EFFECT to have a far-reaching or lasting impact, especially as a result of being circulated widely **3.** *vi* PHYS BOUNCE BACK to be reflected repeatedly off different surfaces (*refers to heat, light, or sound waves*) **4.** *vt* CAUSE SOUND TO ECHO to cause sound to bounce back from a surface **5.** *vt* METALL HEAT OR REFINE METAL to treat metal in a furnace (**reverberatory furnace**) that reflects flame or heat [15C. < Latin *reverberat-*, past participle of *reverberare* 'beat again' < *verberare* 'beat' < *verber* 'scourge'] —**reverberant** *adj* —**reverberation** /ri vúrbə ráysh'n/ *n* —**reverberative** /-rətiv/ *adj* —**reverberator** *n*

reverberation time *n* the time it takes for a sound in a room to be reduced by 60 decibels

reverberatory /ri vúrbərətəri/ *adj* produced or functioning by the process of deflection of sound, light, or heat

reverberatory furnace *n* a furnace in which material is heated by heat reflected from above

revere /ri véer/ (**-veres, -vering, -vered**) *vt* to regard somebody with admiration and deep respect [Mid-17C. Via French < Latin *revereri* < *vereri* 'be in awe of']

Revere /ri véer/, **Paul** (1735–1818) American patriot. A leading Boston silversmith, he made an historic midnight ride, on 18 April 1775, from Boston to Concord to warn of an impending British attack.

> '[We agreed] that if the British went out by water, we would show two lanterns in the North Church steeple; and if by land, one as a signal....'
> [Paul Revere, *on signals to be used if British troops moved out of Boston, in plans made with the Charlestown Committee of Safety*; 16 April 1775]

reverence /révvərənss/ *n* **1.** RESPECT FELT feelings of deep respect or devotion **2.** RESPECT GAINED the respect or devotion that others show somebody or something **3.** *also* **Reverence** CHR USED TO ADDRESS CHRISTIAN CLERGY used as a form of address for some members of the Christian clergy ■ *vt* (**-ences, -encing, -enced**) RESPECT SOMEBODY OR SOMETHING DEEPLY to regard somebody or something with deep respect (*formal*)

SYNONYMS See ***regard***.

reverend /révvrənd/ *adj* **1.** ⚠ OF CLERGY relating or belonging to the Christian clergy **2.** RESPECTED deserving to be shown respect (*formal*) ■ *n* CHRISTIAN CLERIC a member of the Christian clergy (*informal*) [15C. Directly or via French < Latin *reverendus* 'to be revered' < *revereri* (see REVERE)]

USAGE reverend or **reverent**? Care should be taken in distinguishing between ***reverend***, a noun and adjective referring to a member of the clergy, and ***reverent***, which is a descriptive adjective meaning 'feeling or expressing reverence', not restricted to religious contexts.

Reverend *n* used as a title and form of address for some members of the clergy in many Christian churches

Reverend Mother *n* used as a title of respect to address the nun in charge of a convent

reverent /révvərənt/ *adj* ⚠ feeling or expressing profound respect or awe [14C. < Latin *reverent-*, present participle of *revereri* (see REVERE)] —**reverently** *adv*

USAGE See ***reverend***.

reverential /révvə rénsh'l/ *adj* **1.** feeling or expressing deep respect or awe **2.** worthy of deep respect or awe —**reverentially** *adv*

reverie /révvəri/ (*plural* **-ies**) *n* a state of idle and pleasant contemplation [Early 17C. < French < *rêver* 'to dream']

revers /ri véer/ (*plural* **-vers** /ri véerz/) *n* a part of a garment turned back so that the reverse side shows, e.g. a lapel [Mid-19C. < French (see REVERSE)]

reversal /ri vúrss'l/ *n* **1.** CHANGE TO OPPOSITE DIRECTION a change to an opposite direction or state **2.** REVERSING OF SOMETHING the act or process of changing something to an opposite direction or state **3.** PROBLEM an unfortunate experience or setback, particularly in business or financial affairs **4.** LAW CHANGE OF JUDICIAL DECISION a ruling made by a higher court that sets aside the decision of a lower court

reverse /ri vúrss/ *v* (**-verses, -versing, -versed**) **1.** *vt* CHANGE SOMETHING TO OPPOSITE to change something to the opposite direction, order, or position ○ *reversing the trend of population growth* **2.** *vti* GO BACKWARDS to go backwards, or move something in a backwards direction ○ *reverse the car* **3.** *vt* TURN SOMETHING INSIDE OUT to change something so that the opposite side or part shows ○ *You can reverse the cloak and wear it with the lining on the outside.* **4.** *vt* LAW REVOKE RULING to overturn a previous ruling made by a lower court **5.** *vt* PRINTING PRINT SOMETHING WHITE AGAINST DARK BACKGROUND to print text or graphics in white against a dark or colour background **6.** *vt* MIL TURN WEAPON UPSIDE DOWN to turn a weapon upside down, especially as a sign of mourning ■ *n* **1.** GEAR FOR BACKWARDS MOVEMENT the gear in a vehicle or machine that makes it run backwards ○ *It's easier to get out of here in reverse.* **2.** THE OPPOSITE the contrary of something ○ *She always does the reverse of what I tell her.* **3.** BACK SIDE the rear or back side of something ○ *The names are written on the reverse of the photo.* **4.** CHANGE TO OPPOSITE DIRECTION a change or turn to the opposite direction, position, or condition **5.** SETBACK a change for the worse ○ *a military reverse* **6.** COINS BACK SIDE OF COIN the side of a coin, medal, or seal on which the primary design does not appear ○ *The reverse of some coins carries the national motto.* **7.** AMERICAN FOOTBALL OFFENSIVE PLAY IN AMERICAN FOOTBALL in American football, a move in which a back receives the hand off from the quarterback and then hands the ball to another back running in the opposite direction ■ *adj* **1.** OPPOSITE TO USUAL OR PREVIOUS ARRANGEMENT opposite to what is usual or what was previously said or arranged ○ *announce the results in reverse order* **2.** ON BACK SIDE on the other side or the back side of something **3.** FOR BACKWARDS MOVEMENT used to make a machine or vehicle go backwards ○

reverse gear [14C. Via Old French *revers* 'reversed' < Latin *reversus*, past participle of *revertere* 'turn back' < *vertere* 'turn'] —**reversely** *adv* —**reverser** *n*

reverse bias *n* a voltage applied to a semiconductor or a junction in a semiconductor in a direction such that little or no current flows

reverse-charge *adj* describes a telephone call paid for by the person receiving it. N Am term **collect**[1]

reverse charges *adv* so as to be charged to the receiver of a call that is placed. N Am term **collect**[1]

reverse commuting *n* the practice of travelling regularly between a home in a city and a job in the suburbs —**reverse commuter** *n*

reverse discrimination *n N Am* discrimination against a member of a social group generally regarded as dominant or privileged, e.g. in employment or admission to university

reverse engineering *n* the pirating of a competitor's technology by dismantling an existing product and reproducing its parts and construction to manufacture a replica —**reverse-engineer** *vt* —**reverse-engineered** *adj*

reverse genetics *n* the process of discovering the biological function of a gene by modifying or deleting it and then looking for the effect the change has on the organism carrying the gene

reverse mortgage *n* a financial document in the United States and Canada in which a residential mortgage is transferred to a bank, which then pays an annuity to the homeowner

reverse osmosis *n* a process of purifying water or other liquids such as fruit juices by passing them through a semipermeable membrane that filters out unwanted substances

reverse takeover *n* the sale of a company to another company in order to avoid takeover by an unwanted predatory company

reverse transcriptase *n* an enzyme, found naturally in retroviruses, that assists in the formation of DNA in genetic engineering, using RNA as a template

reverse video *n* the reversal of the usual character and background colour combination on a computer display, used in highlighting

reversi /ri vúrssi/ *n* a board game for two players, played on a draughtboard, in which captured pieces are turned upside down [Early 19C. < French, alteration of *reversin* < Italian *rovescina* 'reversal' < Latin *reversus* (see REVERSE)]

reversible /ri vúrssəb'l/ *adj* **1.** ABLE TO BE REVERSED able to be changed or undone **2.** USABLE INSIDE OUT made so that either side can be used as the outer or upper side **3.** CHEM ABLE TO UNDERGO REVERSE REACTION capable of going through a stage such as a chemical reaction and then reversing the process —**reversibility** /ri vùrssə bílləti/ *n* —**reversibly** *adv*

reversing light /ri vúrssing-/ *n* either two of white lights on the rear of a vehicle that shine when the vehicle is being reversed. N Am term **backup light**

reversing prism *n* a prism that reverses the positions of parallel rays by a combination of refraction and internal reflection

reversion /ri vúrsh'n/ *n* **1.** RETURN TO FORMER CONDITION a return to an earlier condition often perceived as less desirable or inferior **2.** REVERSAL a change to the opposite direction **3.** GENETICS RETURN TO ORIGINAL CHARACTERISTICS the restoration of the normal genetic constitution in a mutant organism, e.g. by means of a second mutation that cancels out the effects of an earlier one **4.** GENETICS REVERTED ORGANISM an organism that has reverted to ancestral genetic characteristics **5.** LAW RETURN TO FORMER OWNER the return of property to its former owner or his or her heirs at the end of a specific period, usually when the present owner dies **6.** LAW PROPERTY RETURNED TO FORMER OWNER property that has been returned to its former owner or his or her heirs **7.** LAW RIGHT TO INHERIT PROPERTY the right to succeed to property, granted to somebody by the former owner ■ *vti* MAKE DIFFERENT VERSION OF SOMETHING to make a new or different version of an existing thing, especially a radio or television programme or piece of software —**reversional** *adj* —**reversionally** *adv* —**reversionary** *adj*

reversioner /ri vúrsh'nər/ *n* somebody to whom ownership of property will be returned after a specific period of time

revert /ri vúrt/ (**-verts, -verting, -verted**) *vi* **1.** GO BACK TO PREVIOUS STATE to return to a former state, often one perceived as less desirable or inferior **2.** RETURN IN DISCUSSION to return to an earlier topic in the course of a discussion **3.** RETURN TO OLD HABITS to return to a former pattern of behaviour, usually something less acceptable **4.** GENETICS REACQUIRE ORIGINAL FEATURES to acquire or develop original genetic features again **5.** LAW BE RETURNED TO OWNER to become once again the property of the former owner or his or her heirs [14C. Via French < Latin *revertere* (see REVERSE)] —**reverter** *n* —**revertible** *adj*

revertant /ri vúrt'nt/ *adj* describes an organism or part of an organism that has reacquired features that are original or simpler ■ *n* a revertant organism or part

revest /ree vést/ (**-vests, -vesting, -vested**) *vt* **1.** to reinstate somebody in a position or office **2.** to restore power or property to somebody

revet /ri vét/ (**-vets, -vetting, -vetted**) *vti* to give a structure additional support by adding a facing of bricks, stone, or concrete [Early 19C. Via French *revêtir* < late Latin *revestire* 'clothe again' < Latin *vestire* 'clothe' < *vestis* 'clothing, garment']

revetment /ri vétmənt/ *n* **1.** a facing added to a structure such as a wall or building that provides additional support **2.** a barricade constructed to protect against damage or injury from explosives

revhead /rév hed/ *n Aus* somebody whose main interest is fast cars or motor racing (*informal*)

review /ri vyoō/ *v* (**-views, -viewing, -viewed**) **1.** *vt* LOOK AT SOMETHING CRITICALLY to examine something to make sure that it is adequate, accurate, or correct ○ *They need to review their sales strategy.* **2.** *vt* GIVE OPINION ON SOMETHING to write a journalistic report on the quality of a new play, book, film, concert, or other public performance ○ *He reviews films for a newspaper.* **3.** *vt* CONSIDER SOMETHING AGAIN to consider, study, or check something again **4.** *vi N Am* EDUC same as **revise** *v* (sense 4) **5.** *vt* LOOK BACK ON SOMETHING to discuss or examine something again ○ *She's writing an article reviewing the company's history.* **6.** *vt* LAW RECONSIDER JUDICIAL DECISION to re-examine a judicial decision made in a lower court in order to consider whether it should be overturned **7.** *vt* MIL SUBJECT TROOPS TO INSPECTION to make a formal inspection of a military force ■ *n* **1.** SURVEY OF PAST a report or survey of past actions, performance, or events ○ *a review of stock market performance during the past five years* **2.** ARTICLE GIVING OPINION a journalistic article giving an assessment of a book, play, film, concert, or other public performance ○ *The book got unexpectedly bad reviews.* **3.** PUBLICATION FEATURING REVIEWS a magazine or journal that publishes reviews ○ *the Literary Review* **4.** RE-EXAMINATION OF SOMETHING another look at or consideration of something **5.** *N Am* EDUC DISCUSSION OF MATERIAL ALREADY LEARNED a brief discussion of subject matter already learned, in preparation for a test **6.** MIL INSPECTION a formal military inspection **7.** MIL FORMAL CEREMONY a formal military ceremony staged to honour a person or an occasion **8.** LAW JUDICIAL RE-EXAMINATION a critical examination by a higher court of a decision taken by a lower court **9.** THEATRE same as **revue** [15C. < obsolete French *reveue* 'inspection', < *revoir* 'inspect' < Latin *revidere* 'see again' < *videre* 'see'] —**reviewable** *adj* —**reviewer** *n*

USAGE review or **revue**? ***Review*** is the only spelling for the verb (meaning 'to examine for accuracy or completeness', 'to examine again', 'to write a critique of', etc.) and for most noun senses: *The novel had both good and bad reviews in the popular press.* ***Revue*** is only used as a noun denoting a form of theatrical entertainment, and is the usual form in this meaning.

review copy *n* a copy of a new book that a publisher sends to potential critics and reviewers to encourage published reviews

revile /ri vīl/ (**-viles, -viling, -viled**) *v* **1.** *vt* to make a fierce or abusive verbal attack on somebody or something **2.** *vi* to use insulting or abusive language [14C. < Old French *reviler* < *vil(e)* (see VILE)] —**revilement** *n* —**reviler** *n*

revise /ri vīz/ *v* (**-vises, -vising, -vised**) **1.** *vt* RETHINK SOMETHING to come to different conclusions about somebody or something after thinking again **2.** *vt* GIVE UPDATED VERSION OF SOMETHING to change a previous estimate in order to make it more accurate or realistic **3.** *vt* ALTER TEXT to amend a text in order to correct, update, or improve it **4.** *vti* STUDY FOR EXAM to study for a test by looking over notes and course materials. N Am term **review** ■ *n* **1.** SOMETHING REVISED something that has been revised **2.** PUBL STAGE OF PRINTED PROOF a late stage of a printed proof that incorporates corrections to earlier proofs (*often used in the plural*) [Mid-16C. Via French < Latin *revisere* 'look over again' < *visere* 'keep watching' < *videre* 'see'] —**revisable** *adj* —**reviser** *n* —**revisory** *adj*

Revised Standard Version /ri vīzd-/ *n* a modern US revision of the American Standard Version of the Bible, published in full in 1953

Revised Version *n* a 19th-century British revision of the Authorized Version of the Bible

revision /ri vízh'n/ *n* **1.** ACT OF CHANGING TEXT the amendment of a text in order to correct, update, improve, or adapt it **2.** ACT OF CHANGING SOMETHING the act or process of changing a decision, estimate, statistic, or set of figures in order to correct it or make it more realistic **3.** NEW EDITION a revised and republished version of a text **4.** STUDY FOR EXAM study that involves looking over notes and course materials, in preparation for a test —**revisionary** *adj*

revisionism /ri vízh'nizəm/ *n* **1.** the re-examining of long-established practices, views, or beliefs, especially when such re-examination is regarded as unnecessary or misguided **2.** a socialist movement arguing against revolutionary Marxist theory and believing in the peaceful achievement of social progress through reforms —**revisionist** *adj, n*

revisit /ree vízzit/ *vt* (**-its, -iting, -ited**) **1.** GO TO PLACE AGAIN to visit a place again **2.** RECONSIDER SOMETHING to reconsider something such as an issue of public policy or a course of action, especially when additional facts indicate that an earlier decision was inappropriate ■ *n* SUBSEQUENT VISIT another visit to a place

revitalize /ree vītə līz/ (**-izes, -izing, -ized**), **revitalise** (**-ises, -ising, -ised**) *vt* to give new life or energy to somebody or something —**revitalization** /ree vītə lī záysh'n/ *n*

revival /ri vīv'l/ *n* **1.** RENEWAL OF INTEREST a renewal of interest in something that results in its becoming popular once more **2.** NEW PRODUCTION a new production of a play or opera that has not been performed recently **3.** PROCESS OF REVIVING SOMEBODY the process of bringing somebody back to life, consciousness, or full strength **4.** RECOVERY the recovering of life, consciousness, or full strength **5.** RELIG RENEWED RELIGIOUS INTEREST a new interest in religion, or the reawakening of such interest **6.** CHR EVANGELICAL CHRISTIAN MEETING a meeting or a series of meetings of evangelical Christians intended to awaken religious fervour in those who attend **7.** LAW RE-ESTABLISHING OF LEGAL VALIDITY the renewal of the validity of a contract or the effect of a judicial decision

revivalism /ri vīvəlizəm/ *n* **1.** a desire or tendency to renew interest in something old such as old customs or beliefs **2.** the efforts of a religious movement, especially an evangelical Christian movement, to reawaken religious commitment

revivalist /ri vīvəlist/ *n* **1.** RELIG EVANGELIST a promoter, organizer, or preacher at a religious revival meeting, especially one for evangelical Christians **2.** ADVOCATE OF PAST CUSTOMS somebody who wishes to revive customs, ideas, or institutions ■ *adj* RELIG REAWAKENING RELIGIOUS FAITH dedicated to reawakening or stimulating religious fervour in evangelical Christians —**revivalistic** /ri vīvə lístik/ *adj*

revive /ri vīv/ (**-vives, -viving, -vived**) *v* **1.** *vti* RECOVER CONSCIOUSNESS to come back to life, consciousness, or full strength, or bring somebody back to life, consciousness, or full strength **2.** *vti* FLOURISH AGAIN to become active, accepted, or popular once more, or make something active, accepted, or popular once more **3.** *vt* CAUSE EXPERIENCE TO RETURN to cause something to be experienced again as a memory or feeling **4.** *vt* STAGE SOMETHING AGAIN to stage a new

production of an old play or opera [15C. Directly or via French < late Latin *revivere* 'make live again' < Latin *vivere* 'live'] —**revivable** adj —**reviver** n

revivify /ree vívvi fī/ (**-fies, -fying, -fied**) vt to impart new life, energy, or spirit to something or somebody — **revivification** /ree vívvifi káysh'n/ n

revocable /révvəkəb'l, ri vṓk-/ adj able to be revoked or cancelled —**revocability** /révvəkə bílləti, ri vṓkə bílləti/ n —**revocably** adv

revoke /ri vṓk/ v (**-vokes, -voking, -voked**) **1.** vt LAW FORMALLY CANCEL SOMETHING to make something null and void by withdrawing, recalling, or reversing it **2.** vt SUMMON SOMEBODY BACK to call somebody back, e.g. from exile or from an overseas position **3.** vi CARDS NOT FOLLOW SUIT in a card game, to fail to follow suit when able to do so ■ n CARDS FAILURE TO FOLLOW SUIT failure to follow suit in a card game when able to do so [14C. Via French < Latin *revocare* 'call back' < *vocare* 'call'] — **revocation** /révvə káysh'n/ n —**revoker** n

revolt /ri vṓlt/ v (**-volts, -volting, -volted**) **1.** vi REBEL AGAINST STATE to try to overthrow an existing government **2.** vi DEFY AUTHORITY to resist authority or rules **3.** vti FEEL DISGUST to feel disgust or repulsion, or cause somebody to feel disgust or repulsion ■ n **1.** UPRISING AGAINST GOVERNMENT an uprising that attempts to overthrow a government **2.** DEFIANCE OF AUTHORITY a protest against authority or rules [Mid-16C. Via French < Italian *revoltare* < Latin *revolvere* 'roll back' (see REVOLVE)] —**revolter** n

revolting /ri vṓlting/ adj **1.** arousing feelings of disgust, nausea, or repulsion **2.** unattractive or otherwise unpleasant (informal) —**revoltingly** adv

revolute /révvə loot/ adj describes leaves and other plant parts that are rolled backwards and downwards from the tip or edge [Mid-18C. < Latin *revolutus*, past participle of *revolvere* (see REVOLVE)]

revolution /révvə loosh'n/ n **1.** OVERTHROW OF GOVERNMENT the overthrow of a ruler or political system **2.** MAJOR CHANGE a dramatic change in ideas or practice **3.** COMPLETE CIRCULAR TURN one complete circular movement made by something round or cylindrical, e.g. a wheel, around a fixed point **4.** CIRCLE ROUND SOMETHING a complete circle made round something, e.g. the orbit made by a planet or satellite round another body **5.** GEOL PERIOD OF MAJOR GEOLOGICAL CHANGE a period during which the Earth's crust changes considerably and major features such as mountain ranges may emerge [14C. Directly or via French < late Latin *revolution-* < Latin *revolut-*, past participle of *revolvere* (see REVOLVE)]

revolutionary /révvə loosh'nəri/ adj **1.** OF POLITICAL REVOLUTION relating to or involving a political or social revolution **2.** STIRRING REBELLION causing, supporting, or advocating revolution **3.** NEW AND DIFFERENT so new and different as to cause a major change in something ■ n (plural **-ies**) REBEL somebody committed to a political or social revolution

Revolutionary adj **1.** relating to a particular revolution that has taken place such as the Russian Revolution or the French Revolution **2.** US relating to the war with Great Britain fought by the American colonists

Revolutionary Calendar n HIST same as **French Republican Calendar**

revolutionise vt another spelling of **revolutionize**

revolutionist /révvə loosh'nist/ n POL same as **revolutionary**

revolutionize (**-izes, -izing, -ized**), **revolutionise** (**-ises, -ising, -ised**) vt **1.** CHANGE SOMETHING RADICALLY to cause a radical change in something such as a method or approach **2.** INCITE PEOPLE TO REBELLION to inspire people with revolutionary ideas **3.** CAUSE REBELLION IN COUNTRY to bring about a revolution in a country

revolve /ri vólv/ v (**-volves, -volving, -volved**) **1.** vti MOVE IN CIRCULAR FASHION to move in a circular movement, or send something in a circular movement, either around an object or on a central axis **2.** vi BE FOCUSED to have something as a primary focus or theme **3.** vi RECUR to happen in cycles or regular periodic intervals ■ n THEATRE TURNING STAGE a circular part of a stage that can be turned mechanically in order to change a scene [14C. < Latin *revolvere* 'roll back' < *volvere* 'to roll'] —**revolvable** adj

revolver /ri vólvər/ n a handgun with a revolving cylinder of chambers, allowing several shots to be fired without reloading

revolving credit /ri vólving-/ n a credit scheme that imposes regular repayments and a predetermined spending limit

revolving door n **1.** a door, usually in a large building, consisting of four panels that intersect at right angles and turn on a central pivot **2.** any system in which people frequently enter and leave, e.g. a corporation that repeatedly hires and fires staff or a criminal justice system that returns offenders to society (hyphenated when used before a noun)

revolving door syndrome n **1.** the phenomenon of adult children returning to live with their parents, often for financial reasons, after a period of living away from home (humorous informal) **2.** the phenomenon of people joining or attending something such as an educational institution or a drug treatment programme, leaving, and then returning later (informal)

revolving fund n a fund that can be drawn upon and repaid repeatedly from the revenue of the projects that it finances

revue /ri vyoo/ (plural **-vues**) n a musical variety show consisting of skits, dance routines, and songs that often satirize current events and personalities [Late 19C. < French < *revoir* 'inspect' (see REVIEW)]

USAGE See *review*.

revulsion /ri vúlsh'n/ n **1.** FEELING OF DISGUST a sudden violent feeling of disgust **2.** WITHDRAWAL a pulling back or turning back (formal) **3.** MED DIVERSION OF BLOOD the diversion of blood or disease from one part of the body to another [Mid-16C. < French < Latin *revuls-* past participle of *revellere* 'pull back' < *vellere* 'tear, pull'] —**revulsive** adj

SYNONYMS See *dislike*.

Rev. Ver. abbr BIBLE Revised Version

reward /ri wáwrd/ n **1.** THING GIVEN IN RETURN something desirable given in return for what somebody has done **2.** MONEY OFFERED IN RETURN money offered for information about the whereabouts of a criminal or the return of something lost or stolen **3.** BENEFIT RECEIVED a benefit obtained as a result of an action taken or a job done **4.** PSYCHOL SOMETHING REINFORCING DESIRED BEHAVIOUR something positive that follows a desired response and acts to encourage desired behaviour ■ vt (**-wards, -warding, -warded**) **1.** GIVE SOMEBODY SOMETHING AS REWARD to give somebody something in return, especially in thanks for kindness or help **2.** REPAY EFFORT to be worth the effort or attention that is given [14C. < Anglo-Norman, variant of Old French *reguard* 'regard'] —**rewardable** adj —**rewarder** n

rewarding /ri wáwrding/ adj **1.** providing somebody with personal satisfaction or great pleasure **2.** intended as a reward for something —**rewardingly** adv

rewind vt /ree wínd/ (**-winds, -winding, -wound** /-wównd/) WIND SOMETHING BACK to wind something such as video or audio tape back onto its original spool or back to an earlier point ■ n /ree wínd/ **1.** REWINDING PROCESS the process of rewinding something **2.** REWINDING FUNCTION a function that rewinds film or tape, e.g. on a camera or video recorder

rewire /ree wîr/ (**-wires, -wiring, -wired**) vt to install new electrical wiring in a building, vehicle, or electrical device

reword /ree wúrd/ (**-words, -wording, -worded**) vt to change the wording of something written or spoken

rework vt /ree wúrk/ (**-works, -working, -worked**) **1.** to alter something in order to improve or update it **2.** to alter something in order to reuse it in a different context ■ n /ree wurk/ US same as **reworking**

reworking /ree wúrking/ n UK, ANZ, Can a new version of something, especially a spoken or written text. US term **rework**

rewritable /ree rítəb'l/ adj describes a magnetic disk that can be written on repeatedly

rewrite vt /ree rít/ (**-writes, -writing, -wrote** /-rṓt/, **-written** /-rítt'n/) **1.** AMEND WORDING to redraft a text by changing the wording or structure **2.** EDIT SOMETHING FOR PUBLICATION to edit a reporter's copy for publication in a newspaper or magazine **3.** ALTER INTERPRETATION to change the way the past is perceived or known about ■ n /ree rít, ree rīt/ AMENDED TEXT an amended version of a written document —**rewriter** n

Rex /reks/ n a word used in the formal title of a reigning king, especially on coins and official documents [Early 17C. < Latin, 'king']

Reye's syndrome /ríz-, ráyz-/ n a rare and serious childhood disease, usually following a respiratory infection, causing vomiting, fatty deposits in the liver, disorientation, and swelling of the kidneys and brain [After Ralph Douglas *Reye* (1912–78), Australian paediatrician]

Reykjavik /ráykyə vik/ capital city of Iceland, situated on Faxaflói Bay, in the southwest of the country. Population: 108,351 (1998).

Reynolds /rénn'ldz/, **Henry** (b. 1938) Australian historian and author of several works on the relationship between Aboriginal peoples and European settlers, including *The Other Side of the Frontier* (1981)

Reynolds, Sir Joshua (1723–92) British painter. He painted portraits of many notable people of his day, and was the founding president of the Royal Academy of Arts (1768).

> 'He who resolves never to ransack any mind but his own, will be soon reduced, from mere barrenness, to the poorest of all imitations; he will be obliged to imitate himself, and to repeat what he has before often repeated.'
> [Sir Joshua Reynolds, *Discourse to the students of the Royal Academy*; 10 December 1774]

Reynold's number /rénn'ldz-/ n a number used to indicate the flow of fluid through a pipe or around an obstruction. Symbol **Re** [After Osborne *Reynolds* (1842–1912), Irish physicist]

Rf[1] symbol CHEM ELEM rutherfordium

Rf[2] abbr MONEY rufiyaa

RF abbr **1.** MEDIA radio frequency **2.** AIR FORCE reconnaissance fighter **3.** MIL regular forces **4.** GENETICS releasing factor **5.** MAPS representative fraction **6.** République Française **7.** MIL Reserve Force **8.** CHEM retention factor **9.** BASEBALL right fielder **10.** MIL Royal Fusiliers

rf. abbr **1.** GEOG reef **2.** COMM refund

r.f. abbr **1.** MEDIA radio frequency **2.** MIL rapid fire **3.** TELECOM reception fair **4.** PAPER rough finish

R factor n a combination of genes that makes some bacteria resistant to antibiotics. It can be transferred to other bacteria through conjugation. [< abbreviation of RESISTANCE]

RFC abbr **1.** AIR FORCE Royal Flying Corps **2.** Rugby Football Club

RFD abbr **1.** MEDIA radio-frequency device **2.** MIL reporting for duty

RFLP abbr BIOTECH restriction fragment length polymorphism

Rfn abbr MIL Rifleman

RG abbr AMERICAN FOOTBALL right guard

RGB abbr red, green, blue (used to describe a colour monitor or colour value)

RGN abbr MED Registered General Nurse

RGS abbr Royal Geographical Society

Rgt abbr MIL regiment

rh abbr **1.** METEOROL relative humidity **2.** right hand

Rh[1] symbol CHEM ELEM rhodium

Rh[2] adj relating to or involving the Rh factor ○ presence of the Rh antigen

RH abbr **1.** METEOROL relative humidity **2.** right hand **3.** Royal Highness

RHA abbr **1.** Regional Health Authority **2.** Royal Horse Artillery

rhabdom /rábdəm/ n a transparent rod-shaped part of the compound eye of insects, spiders, and other arthropods [Late 19C. < late Greek *rhabdōma* < Greek *rhabdos* 'rod']

rhabdomancy /rábdō manssi/ *n* the use of a divining rod to locate underground water or mineral ores [Mid-17C. < Greek *rhabdomanteia* < *rhabdos* 'rod'] —**rhabdomancer** *n*

rhabdovirus /rábdō vírəss/ *n* a rod-shaped virus that contains RNA, e.g. the virus that causes rabies [Mid-20C. < Greek *rhabdos* 'rod']

rhachilla *n* BOT another spelling of **rachilla**

rhachis *n* BOT another spelling of **rachis**

Rhadamanthus /ráddə mánthəss/ *n* in Greek mythology, the son of Zeus and Europa, who became one of the three judges of the dead in the underworld

Rhaetian /reésh'n/ *n* LANG same as **Rhaeto-Romance** ■ *adj* **1.** relating to Rhaeto-Romance **2.** relating to Rhaetia, an Alpine province of ancient Rome, or the section of the Alps in this area [Late 16C. < *Rhaetia*, province of ancient Rome]

Rhaeto-Romance /reétō-/ *n* a group of Romance dialects spoken in some Alpine regions of Switzerland and Italy, including Romansch, Ladin, and Friulian —**Rhaeto-Romance** *adj*

rhamnose /rámnōss, -nōz/ *n* a white crystalline sugar found in plant cells and the protective cell wall of some bacteria. Formula: $C_6H_{12}O_5$. [Late 19C. < modern Latin *Rhamnus*, genus name of the buckthorn (in whose berries the substance is found) < Greek *rhamnos*]

rhapsode /rápsōd/ *n* ANCIENT HIST same as **rhapsodist** (sense 2) [Mid-19C. < Greek *rhapsōidēs* < *rhapsōidein* 'recite' (see RHAPSODY)]

rhapsodic /rap sóddik/, **rhapsodical** /-ik'l/ *adj* **1.** relating to a rhapsody, or with the emotional and improvisational qualities of a rhapsody **2.** joyfully enthusiastic or ecstatic about something —**rhapsodically** *adv*

rhapsodise *vti* another spelling of **rhapsodize**

rhapsodist /rápsədist/ *n* **1.** somebody who is joyfully enthusiastic or ecstatic about something (*literary*) **2.** an ancient Greek poet who recited epic poetry professionally

rhapsodize /rápsə dīz/ (**-dizes, -dizing, -dized**), **rhapsodise** (**-dises, -dising, -dised**) *v* **1.** *vi* to speak or write in an enthusiastic or ecstatic manner **2.** *vti* to write or recite a rhapsody

rhapsody /rápsədi/ (*plural* **-dies**) *n* **1.** ENTHUSIASTIC TALK an expression of intense enthusiasm (*often used in the plural*) ○ *went into rhapsodies about the garden* **2.** MUSIC FREE-FORM MUSICAL COMPOSITION a composition that is often irregular in form, emotional in effect, and improvisational in nature **3.** LITERAT ANCIENT GREEK RECITED POEM in ancient Greece, an epic poem recited by a professional reciter **4.** LITERAT EXALTED LITERARY COMPOSITION a literary work written in an intense or exalted style [Mid-16C. Via Latin < Greek *rhapsōdia* < *rhapsōidein* 'recite poems' < *rhaptein* 'stitch together' + *ōidē* 'song']

CULTURAL NOTE ***Rhapsody in Blue***, a musical composition (1924) by US composer George Gershwin. Originally written for piano and jazz band, it was later rearranged for orchestra by Ferde Grofé. One of the first classical works to incorporate jazz influences such as syncopated rhythms, it was inspired by the vibrancy of contemporary urban life, particularly that of New York City.

rhatany /ráttəni/ (*plural same* or **-nies**) *n* **1.** the dried root of a South American bush. Use: toothpaste, mouthwash. **2.** a bush with spiny globular fruits and thick roots that are dried as rhatany. Native to: South America. Genus: *Krameria*. [Early 19C. Via modern Latin *rhatania* < Quechua *ratánya*]

rhd *abbr* AUTOMOT right-hand drive

rhea /reé ə/ (*plural* **-as** or *same*) *n* a large flightless bird that looks like an ostrich but is slightly smaller. Native to: South America. Family: Rheidae. [Early 19C. < modern Latin]

Rhea /reé ə/ *n* **1.** in Greek mythology, a Titan who was the wife of Cronus and mother of the gods. Roman equivalent **Cybele 2.** a large natural satellite of Saturn

rhebok /reé bok/ (*plural* **-boks** or *same*), **reebok** *n* a straight-horned antelope with brownish-grey woolly hair. Native to: southern Africa. Latin name: *Pelea capreolus*. [Late 18C. < Dutch *reebok* 'roebuck']

Rhee /ree/, **Syngman** (1875–1965) president of South Korea (1948–60). He led the fight for Korean independence from Japan and served as South Korea's first president.

Rheims another spelling of **Reims**

rheme /reem/ *n* the part of a sentence, often the predicate, that adds the greatest amount of new information to what is already available in the discourse [Late 19C. < Greek *rhēma* 'what is said']

Rhenish /rénnish, reé-/ *adj* coming from or relating to the Rhineland area of Germany [14C. < Anglo-Norman *reneis* < Latin *Rhenus* 'the Rhine']

rhenium /reéni əm/ *n* a rare heavy silvery-white metallic element with a high melting point. Source: molybdenite. Use: catalyst, with tungsten in thermocouples. Symbol **Re**. See table at **element** [Early 20C. < German < Latin *Rhenus* 'the Rhine']

rheo- *prefix* flow, current ○ *rheometer* [< Greek *rheos* 'stream, current' < *rhein* 'to flow' < Indo-European]

rheobase /reé ō bayss/ *n* the minimum electrical nerve impulse necessary to cause a twitch in a muscle

rheology /ri óllə ji/ *n* a branch of physics dealing with the way matter flows and changes shape —**rheological** /reé ə lójjik'l/ *adj* —**rheologically** *adv* —**rheologist** *n*

rheometer /ri ómmitər/ *n* an instrument that measures the flow of thick liquids such as blood —**rheometric** /reé ə méttrik/ *adj* —**rheometry** *n*

rheomorphism /reé ə máwrfizəm/ *n* the liquefying of rock

rheostat /reé ə stat/ *n* a resistor designed to allow variation in resistance without breaking the electrical circuit of which it is a part —**rheostatic** /reé ə státtik/ *adj*

rheotaxis /reé ə táksiss/ *n* the motion of an organism towards or away from a current of water or air —**rheotactic** /-táktik/ *adj*

rheotropism /reé ə trópizəm/ *n* growth of a plant, or of an immobile animal such as a coral, in the direction of a flow of water

Rhesus /reéssəss/ *n* in Greek mythology, one of the kings of Thrace

rhesus baby /reéssəss-/ *n* a baby born with a serious condition requiring blood transfusion because the baby's Rh-positive blood has been attacked by antibodies in the blood of its Rh-negative mother [See RHESUS FACTOR]

Rhesus factor *n* MED same as **Rh factor** [Because the antigens were first discovered in the blood of rhesus monkeys]

rhesus monkey /reéssəss-/ *n* a common brownish monkey of the macaque family. Native to: South Asia. Latin name: *Macaca mulatta*. [< modern Latin, arbitrarily after RHESUS]

Rhesus negative *adj* MED same as **Rh negative**

Rhesus positive *adj* MED same as **Rh positive**

rhetoric /réttərik/ *n* **1.** PERSUASIVE SPEECH OR WRITING speech or writing that communicates its point persuasively **2.** PRETENTIOUS WORDS complex or elaborate language that only succeeds in sounding pretentious **3.** SKILL WITH LANGUAGE the ability to use language effectively, especially to persuade or influence people **4.** STUDY OF WRITING OR SPEAKING EFFECTIVELY the study of methods employed to write or speak effectively and persuasively [14C. Via Old French *rethorique* < Greek *rhetorikē (tekhnē)* '(art) of public speaking' < *rhētōr* 'speaker']

rhetorical /ri tórrik'l/ *adj* **1.** relating to the skill of using language effectively and persuasively **2.** relating to or using language that is elaborate or fine-sounding but insincere —**rhetorically** *adv*

rhetorical question *n* a question asked for effect that neither expects nor requires an answer

rhetorician /réttə rísh'n/ *n* **1.** SKILLED SPEAKER OR WRITER a skilled and effective speaker or writer **2.** PRETENTIOUS SPEAKER OR WRITER a speaker or writer of elaborate or fine-sounding but insincere language **3.** EDUC RHETORIC TEACHER a teacher of the effective and persuasive use of language

rheum /room/ *n* watery discharge coming from the

eyes, nose, or mouth [14C. Via French < Greek *rheuma* 'flow, bodily humour'] —**rheumy** *adj*

rheumatic /roo máttik/ *adj* relating to or affected with rheumatism ■ *n* somebody who is affected with rheumatism —**rheumatically** *adv*

rheumatic fever *n* an acute infectious disease that causes fever and swelling in the joints, and often damage to the heart valves

rheumatic heart disease *n* damage to the valves or muscular tissue of the heart caused by rheumatic fever

rheumatics /roo máttiks/ *n* same as **rheumatism** (*informal*; *takes a singular verb*)

rheumatism /roómətizəm/ *n* **1.** a painful condition of the joints or muscles in which neither infection nor injury is a contributing cause **2.** MED same as **rheumatoid arthritis** (*not in technical use*)

rheumatoid /roómə toyd/ *adj* relating to or affected with rheumatism or rheumatoid arthritis —**rheumatoidally** /roómə tóyd'li/ *adv*

rheumatoid arthritis *n* a chronic disease of joints that causes stiffness, swelling, weakness, loss of mobility, and leads to damage and eventual destruction of the joints

rheumatoid factor *n* an antibody found in the blood serum of many people who have rheumatoid arthritis

rheumatology /roómə tólləji/ *n* the branch of medicine dealing with the study and treatment of rheumatic diseases —**rheumatological** /roómətə lójjik'l/ *adj* —**rheumatologist** *n*

Rh factor /aar áych-/ *n* a group of antibody-producing substances (**antigens**) present in most people's red blood cells. Rh compatibility is important in matching blood for transfusions and between pregnant women and their foetuses. [Abbreviation of RHESUS FACTOR]

RHG *abbr* Royal Horse Guards

rhin- *prefix* same as **rhino-** (*used before vowels*)

rhinal /rín'l/ *adj* relating to the nose

Rhine /rīn/ river in western Europe, flowing north-westwards from southeastern Switzerland through Germany and the Netherlands, emptying into the North Sea. Length: 1,320 km/820 mi.

Rhineland /rín land/ region in western Germany, west of the Rhine

rhinencephalon /rín en séffə lon/ (*plural* **-lons** or **-la** /-lə/) *n* the area of the forebrain that controls the sense of smell —**rhinencephalic** /-ensə fállik/ *adj*

rhinestone /rín stōn/ *n* a small piece of paste or glass used as an imitation diamond [Late 19C. Translation of French *caillou du Rhin*; because the stones were first made in the city of Strasbourg, on the Rhine]

rhinitis /rī nítiss/ *n* inflammation of the mucous membranes of the nose, usually accompanied by a discharge of mucus

rhino[1] /rínō/ (*plural* **-nos** or *same*) *n* same as **rhinoceros** (*informal*) [Late 19C. Shortening]

rhino[2] /rínō/ *n* same as **money** (*archaic slang*) [Early 17C. < ?]

rhino- *prefix* nose, nasal ○ *rhinoplasty* [< Greek *rhin-*, stem of *rhis* 'nose']

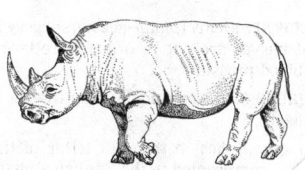

rhinoceros

rhinoceros /rī nóssərəss/ (*plur* very large herbivorous animal and one or two horns on its snout.

Asia. Family: Rhinocerotidae. [13C. Via Latin < Greek *rhinokerōs* < *rhin-* 'nose' + *keras* 'horn'] —**rhinocerotic** /rī nóssə róttik/ *adj*

rhinoceros beetle *n* a large tropical scarab beetle that has horns on its head and thorax

rhinoceros bird *n* BIRDS same as **oxpecker**

~~**rhinocerous**~~ incorrect spelling of **rhinoceros**

rhinology /rī nólləji/ *n* the branch of medicine dealing with conditions and structures of the nose —**rhinological** /rīnə lójjik'l/ *adj* —**rhinologist** *n*

rhinopharyngitis /rīnō fárrən jītiss/ *n* inflammation of the mucous membranes in the nose and pharynx

rhinoplasty /rīnō plasti/ (*plural* **-ties**) *n* plastic surgery performed on the nose, whether for medical or cosmetic reasons —**rhinoplastic** /rīnō plástik/ *adj*

rhinoscope /rīnō skōp/ *n* a device used by doctors to examine the nasal passages —**rhinoscopy** /rī nóskəpi/ *n*

rhinovirus /rīnō vīrəss/ *n* a virus containing RNA that causes infections of the upper respiratory system, including the common cold

rhiz- *prefix* same as **rhizo-** (*used before vowels*)

rhizo- *prefix* root ○ *rhizosphere* [< Greek *rhiza* 'root']

rhizobium /rī zṓbi əm/ (*plural* **-bia** /-bi ə/) *n* a soil bacterium that forms nodules on the roots of legumes and takes up nitrogen from the atmosphere. Genus: *Rhizobium*. [Early 20C. < modern Latin < Greek *rhiza* 'root' + *bios* 'life']

rhizocarpous /rīzō kaárpəss/ *adj* describes plants that produce their fruit underground

rhizocephalan /rīzō séffələn/ *n* a small crustacean that lives in water as a parasite on crabs. Order: Rhizocephala. [Late 19C. < modern Latin *Rhizocephala* < Greek *rhiza* 'root' + *kephalē* 'head'] —**rhizocephalous** *adj*

rhizofiltration /rīzō fil tráysh'n/ *n* the use of plant roots to absorb or precipitate ground-water contaminants

rhizogenic /rīzō jénnik/, **rhizogenetic** /rīzōjə néttik/, **rhizogenous** /rī zójjənəss/ *adj* describes plant cells and tissues from which roots develop

rhizoid /rī zoyd/ *n* a slender outgrowth on mosses, liverworts, and the reproductive cells of ferns that absorbs nourishment in much the same way as a root —**rhizoidal** /rī zóyd'l/ *adj*

rhizome /rīzōm/ *n* a thick underground horizontal stem that produces roots and has shoots that develop into new plants [Mid-19C. < Greek *rhizōma* 'mass of roots' < *rhiza* 'root'] —**rhizomatous** /rī zómmətəss/ *adj*

rhizomorph /rīzō mawrf/ *n* a structure in some pathogenic fungi that allows them to move from host to host —**rhizomorphous** /rīzō máwrfəss/ *adj*

rhizophagous /rī zóffəgəss/ *adj* feeding on roots

rhizoplane /rīzō playn/ *n* the part of a plant's root that lies at the surface of the soil, where many microorganisms adhere to it

rhizopod /rīzō pod/ *n* a single-celled organism (**protozoan**) that moves and eats by means of filaments that it can extend temporarily. Subphylum: Rhizopoda. —**rhizopodous** /rī zóppədəss/ *adj*

rhizopus /rīzōpəss/ *n* a mould that causes decay, e.g. the common bread mould. Genus: *Rhizopus*. [Late 19C. < modern Latin < Greek *rhiza* 'root' + *pous* 'foot'; because of its shape]

rhizosphere /rīzō sfeer/ *n* the area of soil that immediately surrounds and is affected by a plant's roots

rhizotomy /rī zóttəmi/ (*plural* **-mies**) *n* surgery in which spinal nerves are cut in order to relieve pain or high blood pressure

Rh negative /aár aych-/ *adj* lacking the Rh factor in the blood

rho /rō/ (*plural* **rhos**) *n* the 17th letter of the Greek alphabet, represented in the English alphabet as 'r'. See table at **alphabet** [14C. < Greek *rhō* < Phoenician]

rhod- *prefix* same as **rhodo-** (*used before vowels*)

rhodamine /rōdə meen/ *n* a red or pink fluorescent dye. Use: colouring wool and silk, as a biological stain. [Late 19C. < Greek *rhodon* 'rose']

Rhode Island /rōd-/ state in the northeastern United States, bordered by Massachusetts, the Atlantic Ocean, and Connecticut. Capital: Providence. Population: 1,069,725 (2002 estimate). Area: 3,188 sq. km/1,231 sq. mi. Official name **State of Rhode Island and Providence Plantations** —**Rhode Islander** *n*

Rhodes /rōdz/ **1.** largest island of the Dodecanese, Greece. Population: 87,831 (1981). Area: 1,400 sq. km/540 sq. mi. **2.** capital of Rhodes, Greece. Population: 43,619 (1991).

Rhodes, Cecil (1853–1902) British financier and colonial administrator. He made a fortune mining diamonds in South Africa before serving as prime minister of Cape Colony (1890–96). He later helped to develop the area that became modern-day Zimbabwe. Full name **Rhodes, Cecil John**

> 'Remember that you are an Englishman, and have consequently won first prize in the lottery of life.'
> [Cecil Rhodes. Quoted in *Dear Me*, Peter Ustinov; 1977]

Rhodesia /rō deeshə, -zhə/ former name for **Zimbabwe** (1964–79) —**Rhodesian** *adj*

Rhodesian man *n* an early human being sharing features with the Neandertals and with modern human beings and living in Africa in the late Pleistocene period. Latin name: *Homo sapiens rhodesiensis*. [Early 20C. Because the fossils were first found in Rhodesia (Zimbabwe)]

Rhodesian ridgeback *n* a large dog with a ridge of hair growing down its back, belonging to a breed originally developed in Africa

Rhodes scholar *n* a student from the United States, South Africa, or another Commonwealth country who holds a scholarship founded by Cecil rhodes to study at Oxford University [Early 19C. After Cecil RHODES] —**Rhodes scholarship** *n*

rhodinal /rōdin'l/ *n* CHEM same as **citronellal** [Early 20C. < German < Greek *rhodinos* 'of roses' < *rhodon* 'rose']

rhodium /rōdi əm/ *n* a hard, silvery-white, corrosion-resistant metallic element. Source: platinum and nickel ores. Use: alloys, in plating other metals. Symbol Rh. See table at **element** [Early 19C. < Greek *rhodon* 'rose', from the pink colour of its compounds]

rhodo- *prefix* red, rosy ○ *rhodolite* [< Greek *rhodon* 'rose']

rhodochrosite /rōdō krṓ sīt/ *n* a pink, red, brown, or grey manganese carbonate mineral. Use: source of manganese. [Mid-19C. < Greek *rhodokhrōs* 'rose-coloured']

rhododendron

rhododendron /rōdə déndrən/ *n* an evergreen tree widely grown in temperate regions. Flowers: brightly coloured. Native to: South Asia. Genus: *Rhododendron*. [Early 17C. Via Latin, 'oleander' < Greek < *rhodon* 'rose' + *dendron* 'tree']

rhodolite /rōddə līt/ *n* a pink to rose-red variety of garnet. Use: gems.

rhodonite /rōddə nīt/ *n* a pink to brown manganese silicate mineral. Source: metamorphic rock. Use: ornamental stone. [Early 19C. < Greek *rhodon* 'rose']

Rhodope Mountains /róddəpi-/ mountain range in southwestern Bulgaria and northern Greece. Highest peak: Musala 2,925 m/9,596 ft.

rhodopsin /rō dópsin/ *n* a reddish light-sensitive pigment found in the rod cells of the retina [Late 19C. < RHODO- + Greek *opsis* 'sight']

rhodora /rō dáwrə/ *n* a marshland bush of the rhododendron family that blooms in spring before the leaves emerge. Flowers: deep pink. Native to: northeastern North America. Latin name: *Rhododendron canadense*. [Late 18C. < modern Latin < Greek *rhodon* 'rose']

rhomb /rom, romb/ *n* MATHS same as **rhombus** [Late 16C. Directly or via French *rhombe* < Latin *rhombus* (see RHOMBUS)]

rhombencephalon /rómb en séffə lon/ (*plural* **-lons** or **-la** /-lə/) *n* ANAT same as **hindbrain** [Late 19C. < RHOMBUS]

rhombi MATHS plural of **rhombus**

rhombohedron /rómbō heédrən/ (*plural* **-drons** or **-dra** /-drə/) *n* a prism with six faces, each one a rhombus [Mid-19C. < RHOMBUS, after POLYHEDRON] —**rhombohedral** *adj*

rhomboid /róm boyd/ *n* PARALLELOGRAM WITH UNEQUAL SIDES a parallelogram with adjacent sides that are not equal ■ *adj* **1.** RHOMBOID-SHAPED shaped like a rhomboid **2.** RELATING TO RHOMBUS relating to or characteristic of a rhombus [Late 16C. < Greek *rhomboeidēs* 'lozenge-shaped' < *rhombos*]

rhombus /rómbəss/ (*plural* **-buses** or **-bi** /-bī/) *n* a parallelogram that has four equal sides and oblique angles [Mid-16C. Via Latin < Greek *rhombos*] —**rhombic** *adj*

rhonchus /róngkəss/ (*plural* **-chi** /-kī/) *n* a harsh rattling or whistling sound heard through a stethoscope on examination of the chest, caused by partial obstruction of the airways [Early 19C. Via Latin, 'snoring' < Greek *rhegkhos* < *rhegkein* 'to snore'] —**rhonchal** *adj*

Rhondda /róndə/ community in southern Wales, formerly an important coalmining centre. Population: 56,059 (2001).

Rhône /rōn/ river in Switzerland and France, flowing southwestwards from the Alps into the Mediterranean Sea. Length: 813 km/505 mi.

rhotacism /rṓtəsizəm/ *n* unusual pronunciation of the letter 'r', or too much emphasis on this sound [Late 19C. < modern Latin *rhotacismus* < Greek *rhōtakizein* 'make wrong use of the letter *r*' < *rhō*]

rhotic /rṓtik/ *adj* pronouncing the letter 'r' when it occurs after a vowel or at the end of a syllable ○ *a rhotic accent* [Mid-20C. < RHOTACISM]

r.h.p. *abbr* MEASURE rated horsepower

Rh positive /aár aych-/ *adj* containing the Rh factor in the blood, or having blood that contains the Rh factor

RHS *abbr* Royal Horticultural Society

rhubarb

rhubarb /roō baarb/ *n* **1.** STALKS COOKED AS FRUIT the pink stalks of a cultivated perennial plant, cooked as fruit **2.** PLANT WITH EDIBLE STALKS a perennial plant with poisonous leaves that produces rhubarb. Genus: *Rheum*. **3.** PHARM MEDICINAL ASIAN PLANT a medicinal rhubarb plant native to central and eastern Asia. Use: dried underground stems as laxative. **4.** THEATRE, ARTS APPARENT CONVERSATION IN PLAY the word 'rhubarb' used repeatedly by several actors simultaneously to give the impression that they are talking to one another [14C. Via Old French *reubarbe* < Latin *rha barbarum* 'barbarian rhubarb' < Greek *Rha*, the river Volga]

ORIGIN The Greeks had two words for *rhubarb*: *rhēon* (which evolved into Latin *rheum*, now the plant's scientific name) and *rha*, which is said to have come from *Rha*, an ancient name of the river Volga, in allusion to

the fact that *rhubarb* was once grown on its banks (*rhubarb* is native to China, and was once imported to Europe via Russia). In medieval Latin *rhubarb* became known as *rha barbarum* 'barbarian rhubarb, foreign rhubarb', again with reference to the plant's exotic origins; and in due course association with Latin *rheum* altered this to *rheubarbarum*.

rhumb /rum/ *n* **1.** NAVIG same as **rhumb line** (sense 2) **2.** any of the 32 points of a compass [Late 16C. < French *rumb* 'compass point', probably < Dutch *ruim* 'space, room']

rhumba *n* DANCE, MUSIC another spelling of **rumba**

rhumb line *n* **1.** an imaginary line on the surface of the Earth intersecting all meridians at the same angle **2.** a steady course along one compass setting taken by a ship or aircraft

rhyme /rīm/ *n* **1.** SIMILARITY IN SOUND a similarity in the sound of word endings, especially in poetry **2.** WORD SOUNDING SAME AS ANOTHER a word with an ending that sounds similar to the ending of another word **3.** POEM a poem, or poetry generally, of a lighthearted kind with a pattern of similar sounds at the ends of the lines ■ *v* (**rhymes, rhyming, rhymed**) **1.** *vi* SOUND SIMILAR to have an ending that sounds similar to the ending of another word or line of poetry, or have endings that sound similar ○ *'Rough' rhymes with 'cuff'.* **2.** *vt* CHOOSE RHYMING WORD to find or choose a particular word and use it with another because its ending sounds similar **3.** *vti* WRITE POETRY to write rhyming poetry, or express something in rhyme [12C. Via French *rime* < medieval Latin use of Latin *rhythmus* (see RHYTHM); because accented verse usually rhymed] —**rhymeless** *adj* ◇ **without rhyme or reason** without any rational explanation or apparent sense

rhymer /rīmər/ *n* LITERAT same as **rhymester**

rhyme royal *n* **1.** a form of poetry using verses with seven lines of iambic pentameter with a rhyme scheme ababbcc **2.** a verse written in rhyme royal [Mid-19C. Because the form was used by James I of Scotland]

rhyme scheme *n* the pattern of rhyming lines in a poem or in a verse of a poem

rhymester /rīmstər/ *n* a writer of poems with rhyming lines, especially popular or amateur verse

rhyming /rīming/ *adj* with lines that end in similar sounding words, forming a pattern

rhyming slang *n* a form of slang that replaces a word with an expression that rhymes with the word but has no meaningful connection with it, used especially in Cockney

rhynchocephalian /ríngkōssə fálli ən/ *adj* relating to an order of primitive reptiles resembling lizards with only one living representative, the tuatara of New Zealand. Order: Rhynchocephalia. ■ *n* a member of the rhynchocephalian order [Mid-19C. < modern Latin *Rhyncocephalia* < Greek *rhugkhos* 'snout' + *kephalē* 'head']

rhyolite /rī ə līt/ *n* a fine-grained acid rock that is the volcanic form of granite [Mid-19C. < Greek *rhuax* 'stream (of lava)' < *rhein* 'to flow'] —**rhyolitic** /rī ə líttik/ *adj*

Rhys /reess/, **Jean** (1894–1979) Caribbean-born British writer. Her work reflects her Caribbean background and often reveals a pessimistic view of the world. Pseudonym of **Rees Williams, Ellen Gwendolen**

> 'We can't all be happy, we can't all be rich, we can't all be lucky—and it would be so much less fun if we were.... Some must cry so that others may be able to laugh more heartily.'
> [Jean Rhys, *Good Morning, Midnight*; 1939]

rhythm /rítham/ *n* **1.** PATTERN OF BEATS IN MUSIC the regular pattern of beats and emphasis in a piece of music ○ *The audience clapped in rhythm as we sang.* **2.** PARTICULAR MUSIC PATTERN a pattern of beats in a piece or a particular kind of music ○ *boogie-woogie rhythm* **3.** PATTERN OF STRESS IN POETRY in poetry, the pattern formed by stressed and unstressed syllables **4.** PARTICULAR POETRY PATTERN a pattern of stress in a poem or a particular kind of poetry **5.** REGULAR PATTERN a regularly recurring pattern of activity, e.g. the cycle of the seasons, night and day, or repeated functions of the body **6.** CHARACTERISTIC PATTERN the characteristic pattern of an activity **7.** ARTS PATTERN IN ART a pattern suggesting movement or pace in something such as a work of art **8.** LANGUAGE SOUND PATTERN the pattern of sound that characterizes a language, dialect, or accent **9.** CINEMA, LITERAT PATTERN FROM REPETITION a mood or effect in a book, play, or film created from repetition [Mid-16C. Via Latin *rhythmus* < Greek *rhuthmos* < Indo-European, 'to flow']

rhythm and blues *n* a style of music combining blues and jazz, originally developed by African American musicians

rhythm guitar *n* a chordal accompaniment from a guitar that does not play the melody

rhythmic /ríthmik/, **rhythmical** /ríthmik'l/ *adj* **1.** with a regularly recurring pattern or beat **2.** relating to rhythm —**rhythmically** *adv* —**rhythmicity** /rith míssəti/ *n*

rhythmic gymnastics *n* a sport in which athletes combine gymnastic dance movements with the use of apparatus such as ribbons and hoops (*takes a singular or plural verb*)

rhythmics /ríth miks/ *n* the study of rhythms and rhythmic forms (*takes a singular verb*)

rhythm method *n* a method of contraception in which sexual intercourse is avoided at the times when a woman is most likely to conceive

rhythm section *n* the instruments in a band that provide the basic rhythm, e.g. the drums, bass, piano, or guitar

rhythm stick *n* either of a pair of wooden sticks, often with notches, used as a simple percussion instrument

rhytidectomy /rìtidéktəmi/ (*plural* **-mies**) *n* MED same as **facelift** (*technical*) [Mid-20C. < Greek *rhutid-* 'wrinkle']

rhyton /rī ton/ *n* a drinking vessel in ancient Greece with a hole in the bottom through which to drink [Mid-19C. < Greek *rhuton* < *rhutos* 'flowing']

RI[1] *abbr* **1.** EDUC religious instruction **2.** Rhode Island **3.** Royal Institution

RI[2] *abbr* **1.** King and Emperor **2.** Queen and Empress [Latin *rex et imperator, regina et imperatrix*]

ria /rée ə/ *n* a narrow inlet running inland from the coastline, formed when a valley is permanently flooded as a result of a rise in sea level [Late 19C. < Spanish, 'estuary' < form of *río* 'river' < Latin *rivus* 'stream']

RIA *abbr* **1.** MED radioimmunoassay **2.** Royal Irish Academy

rial /ri áal/ *n* the main unit of currency in Iran and Oman. See table at **currency** [Mid-20C. Via Persian, Arabic *riyāl* < Spanish *real* (see REAL[2])]

rialto /ri ált ō/ (*plural* **-tos**) *n* **1.** a market or marketplace **2.** a place where securities or commodities such as grain or raw materials are traded [Mid-16C. After *Rialto*, district of Venice in which the exchange was located]

riata /ri áatə/ *n* a lasso or lariat [Mid-19C. < Spanish *reata* < *reatar* 'retie' < *atar* 'tie' < Latin *aptare* 'join' < *apere* 'tie']

rib /rib/ *n* **1.** CURVED BONE OF CHEST any of the curved bones extending from the vertebrae and in some cases meeting the sternum, forming a cavity housing vital organs in many vertebrates **2.** FOOD MEAT a cut of meat that contains ribs **3.** HANDICRAFT RIDGED KNITTING a portion of knitted material with raised vertical lines of stitches, made by alternating purl stitches with plain stitches **4.** BOT LEAF VEIN a raised vein on a leaf **5.** ARCHIT MOULDING ON VAULT a ridge or moulding on the underside of a vault or arched ceiling **6.** NAUT PART OF SHIP'S HULL a beam extending from the keel to the top of the hull of a ship, giving it its shape **7.** AVIAT PART OF AIRCRAFT'S WING a part of an aircraft's wing crossing from the leading to the trailing edge of the wing **8.** PIECE RESEMBLING RIB a bar, rod, or other supporting part that has the shape or function of a rib ○ *a broken rib on the umbrella* **9.** TEASING COMMENT a comment or action meant as a joke or to tease somebody (*informal*) ■ **ribs** *npl* RIBS WITH LITTLE MEAT the ribs of an animal from which most of the meat has been removed, eaten as food ■ *v* (**ribs, ribbing, ribbed**) **1.** *vti* TEASE to make playful teasing remarks to somebody (*informal*) ○ *They ribbed me about my haircut.* **2.** *vt* PROVIDE SOMETHING WITH RIBS to provide or strengthen something with ribs **3.** *vti* HANDICRAFT KNIT PLAIN AND PURL STITCHES to knit plain stitches alternately with purl stitches to make raised lines, or form a piece of knitting in this way [Old English *ribb* < Germanic, 'covering (of the chest cavity)'] ◇ **stick to your ribs** *N Am* to be substantial, nourishing, or hearty as a meal (*informal*)

RIB *abbr* rigid inflatable boat

RIBA /áar ī bee áy, réebə/ *abbr* Royal Institute of British Architects

ribald /ríbb'ld/ *adj* humorous but rude and vulgar, often involving jokes about sex [14C. < Old French *ribau(l)t* < *riber* 'sleep around' < Germanic] —**ribaldly** *adv*

ribaldry /ríbb'ldri/ *n* language or behaviour that is humorous but rude and vulgar, often involving jokes about sex

riband /ríbbənd/, **ribband** *n* **1.** a ribbon, especially one that is presented to somebody as an award or prize (*archaic*) **2.** a rail attached to the upright posts in a defensive fence (**palisade**) [14C. < Old French *riban*]

ribavirin /rībə vīrin/ *n* a synthetic antiviral agent that inhibits the synthesis of viral DNA and RNA. Use: treatment of viral diseases. [Late 20C. < *riba-* < ?]

ribband *n* another spelling of **riband**

ribbed /ribd/ *adj* **1.** KNITTED INTO PATTERN OF VERTICAL LINES knitted to form a pattern of raised vertical lines, giving a stretchy fabric **2.** STRIPED with a surface marked by raised, roughly parallel bands **3.** HAVING RIBS with structural support or decoration in the form of ribs

Ribbentrop /ríbbən trop/, **Joachim von** (1893–1946) German Nazi official. As Germany's ambassador to Britain (1936) and foreign minister (1938–43), he helped promote the expansionist programme of the Nazis. After World War II he was tried at Nuremberg and executed.

> 'We want war!'
> [Joachim von Ribbentrop. Quoted in *Germany, 1866–1945*, Gordon A. Craig; 1978]

ribbing /ríbbing/ *n* **1.** SECTION OF RIB IN KNITTING a section of knitting in a pattern of raised vertical lines, making a stretchy fabric **2.** RIB FRAMEWORK a supporting structure or framework of ribs, e.g. in the hull of a boat **3.** TEASING playful or friendly teasing (*informal*)

Ribble /ríbb'l/ river in northwestern England that flows through Lancashire to the Irish Sea. Length: 120 km/75 mi.

ribbon /ríbbən/ *n* **1.** DECORATIVE STRIP OF FABRIC a strip of fabric used to tie something or for decoration **2.** RIBBON AS AWARD OR BADGE a decorative strip of fabric given to somebody as an award or worn as a sign of rank or membership **3.** LONG NARROW STRIP something that is long, narrow, and thin, in the shape of a ribbon **4.** COMM STRIP OF INKED MATERIAL a strip of material with ink on it, used in some printers and typewriters **5.** COMPUT FLAT CABLE a flat cable in which all the wires are parallel to one another in a single plane **6.** CONSTR same as **ledger board** (sense 2) ■ **ribbons** *npl* BADLY DAMAGED STATE a damaged state in which something is cut or torn very badly ○ *My shirt was in ribbons.* ■ *vt* (**-bons, -boning, -boned**) **1.** DECORATE SOMETHING WITH RIBBONS to decorate something by attaching ribbons to it **2.** TEAR SOMETHING INTO STRIPS to tear something into long thin strips [Early 16C. Variant of RIBAND] —**ribbony** *adj*

ribbon development *n* a planning scheme or development with houses built in a single row on each side of main roads leading out of a town or city centre

ribbonfish /ríbbən fish/ (*plural same or* **-fishes**) *n* a fish with a long tapering ribbon-shaped body and, typically, a dorsal fin extending from head to tail. Some species can exceed 10 m/32 ft in length. Native to: deeper parts of seas. Family: Trachypteridae.

ribbon grass *n* a grass that is grown as an ornamental in northern temperate regions for its drooping cream-striped leaves. Native to: Europe, North America. Latin name: *Phalaris arundinacea picta*.

ribbon snake *n* a nonvenomous snake with longitudinal reddish or yellow stripes that gives birth to live young and feeds on frogs and worms. Native to: North America. Latin name: *Thamnophis sauritus*.

ribbon worm *n* a worm with a long flat unsegmented body that burrows in the mud covered by sea tides. Phylum: Nemertea.

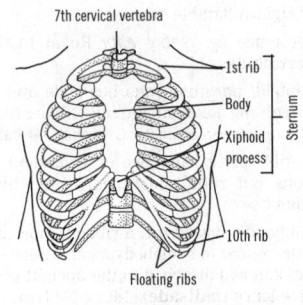

7th cervical vertebra

1st rib

Body

Xiphoid process

Sternum

10th rib

Floating ribs

rib cage

rib cage *n* the ribs as a whole, forming a protective bony enclosure surrounding the heart and lungs

ribo- *prefix* ribose ○ *riboflavin* [< RIBOSE]

riboflavin /ríbō fláyvin/, **riboflavine** /ríbō fláyveen/ *n* vitamin B₂, the yellow component of the B complex group, an important coenzyme in many biochemical processes. Formula: $C_{17}H_{20}N_4O_6$.

ribonuclease /ríbō nyóokli ayz, -ayss/ *n* BIOCHEM full form of **RNase**

ribonucleic acid /ríbō nyóo kleé ik-/ *n* BIOCHEM full form of **RNA**

ribonucleoprotein /ríbō nyóokli ō prṓ teen/ *n* a complex of RNA and a protein formed during the synthesis of RNA

ribonucleoside /ríbō nyóokli ō síd/ *n* a nucleoside in which the sugar group is ribose

ribonucleotide /ríbō nyóokli ō tíd/ *n* a nucleotide that contains the sugar ribose, making up units in important molecules such as RNA and ATP

ribose

ribose /ríbōz/ *n* a white crystalline sugar found in all living cells as a constituent of RNA and many other metabolically important compounds, including ribonucleotides, nucleic acids, and riboflavin. Formula: $C_5H_{10}O_5$. [Late 19C. < German, alteration of ARABINOSE]

ribosomal /ríbə sṓm'l/ *adj* relating to ribosomes

ribosomal RNA *n* an RNA that is a structural and functional component of ribosomes

ribosome /ríbə sōm/ *n* a submicroscopic cluster of proteins and RNA, occurring in great numbers in the cytoplasm of living cells, that takes part in the manufacture of proteins [Mid-20C. < RIBONUCLEIC ACID]

ribozyme /ríbō zīm/ *n* an RNA that can catalyse changes to its own structure [Late 20C. Blend of RIBONUCLEIC ACID + ENZYME]

rib-tickler *n* a very funny joke or story (*informal*) — **rib-tickling** *adj*

ribulose /ríbyoó lōz, -lōss/ *n* a sugar that occurs in plants and is used in photosynthesis. Formula: $C_5H_{10}O_5$. [Mid-20C. < RIBOSE + -ULE]

ribwort /ríb wurt/, **ribwort plantain** *n* a plant with long slender ribbed leaves. Flowers: small, white, in a dense rounded spike. Native to: Europe, Asia. Latin name: *Plantago lanceolata*. [14C. Because the leaves resemble ribs]

Ricardo /ri kaárdō/, **David** (1772–1823) British economist. He introduced the concept of an 'economic model' in his major work *Principles of Political Economy and Taxation* (1817).

> 'The natural price of labour is that price which is necessary to enable the labourers, one with another, to subsist and perpetuate their race, without either increase or diminution.'
> [David Ricardo, *Principles of Political Economy and Taxation*; 1817]

Riccio /ree chee ō/, **David** (1533?–66) Italian courtier. As adviser to Mary, Queen of Scots, he arranged her marriage with Lord Darnley, who later plotted his murder.

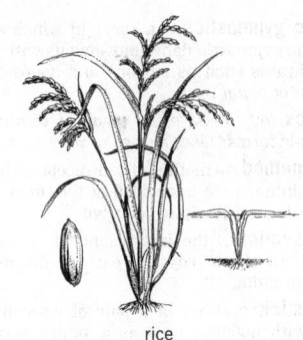

rice

rice /ríss/ *n* **1.** the edible grains of a cereal plant of South Asian origin. Rice is served hot or cold after cooking in water or other liquid. **2.** a cereal plant that produces rice, cultivated in tropical and warm regions of the world. Native to: South Asia. Latin name: *Oryza sativa*. [13C. Via Old French *ris* and Italian *riso* < Greek *oruza* < Indo-Iranian]

Rice /ríss/, **Anne** (*b.* 1941) US writer. She is best known for the Vampire Chronicles, beginning with *Interview with the Vampire* (1976). Born **O'Brien, Howard Allen**

Rice, Condoleezza (*b.* 1954) US national security adviser. A former provost of Stanford University, in 2002 she became the first woman to be appointed national security adviser.

rice paper *n* **1.** a thin brittle edible paper made from the rice-paper plant and other plant sources, used to undercoat baked food that would otherwise stick to the tin during baking **2.** a thin artist's paper made from the pith of the rice-paper plant

rice-paper plant *n* a bush grown for its fibre. Use: rice paper. Native to: China. Latin name: *Tetrapanax papyriferus*.

rice pudding *n* a hot dessert made by baking rice slowly in milk and sugar

ricer /ríssər/ *n* a kitchen utensil consisting of a perforated plate in one end of an open cylinder through which foods can be pressed to form long strings

rice rat *n* a rat that inhabits the marshes where rice fields are located. Native to: southern United States, Central and South America. Genus: *Oryzomys*.

ricercare /reechər kaá ray/ (*plural* **-ri** /-ree/) *n* a fugal composition for musical instruments, analogous to a motet for voices, involving lines of melody interwoven in an often complicated pattern [Late 18C. < Italian, 'seek out']

rich /rich/ *adj* **1.** WEALTHY owning a lot of money or expensive property **2.** WORTH MUCH worth a great deal of money ○ *a rich endowment* **3.** COSTLY AND FINE made from or consisting of things of the highest quality ○ *rich fabrics* **4.** WITH GOOD SUPPLY OF SOMETHING with a good supply of a resource or substance ○ *an area rich in minerals* ○ *a city rich in culture* ○ *cotton-rich fabric* **5.** PLENTIFUL existing in large quantities and in plentiful supply ○ *a rich supply of conscripts* **6.** PRODUCTIVE productive and so potentially very profitable **7.** FERTILE very fertile and able to produce strong healthy plants **8.** WITH FATTY INGREDIENTS containing a high proportion of foods such as cream, eggs, or butter that are full of fat ○ *a very rich chocolate cake* **9.** STRONG AND SMOOTH-FLAVOURED with a pleasantly strong, smooth flavour ○ *rich coffee* **10.** WITH STRONG

PLEASANT SMELL having a strong and pleasant smell **11.** STRONGLY COLOURED deep or fully saturated in colour ○ *a rich shade of brown* **12.** WITH DEEP FULL SOUND with a deep smooth full sound **13.** WITH TOO MUCH FUEL IN MIXTURE with a higher than normal proportion of fuel to air in the mixture supplied to an engine **14.** UNLIKELY hard to believe because ridiculous (*informal*) ○ *That's rich, coming from her!* ■ *npl* WELL-OFF wealthy people in general ○ *a playground for the rich and famous* [Old English *ríce* 'strong, powerful' and Old French *riche*, via Germanic < Indo-European, 'king'] —**richness** *n*

Richard I /ríchərd/ (1157–99) king of England. He spent most of his reign (1189–99) overseas, fighting in the Third Crusade and against Philip II of France. Known as **Richard the Lionheart**

> 'Dear Lord, I pray thee to suffer me not to see thy holy city, since I cannot deliver it from the hands of thy enemies.'
> [Richard I. Referring to Jerusalem. *Prayer*; 1192]

Richard II (1367–1400) king of England. His reign (1377–99) was marked by national disunity and civil strife that culminated in his being deposed.

Richard III (1452–85) king of England. He usurped the throne while protector of the young Edward V (1483), but was defeated at the Battle of Bosworth Field (1485) in a rebellion led by the future King Henry VII.

Richards /ríchərdz/, **I. A.** (1893–1979) British critic, poet, and teacher. He founded the New Criticism movement, which was influential in the teaching of English literature in universities. Full name **Richards, Ivor Armstrong**

Richards, Mark (*b.* 1957) Australian surfer. He won the world championship for four consecutive years (1979–82).

Richards, Maxwell (*b.* 1931) president of Trinidad and Tobago (2003–). A chemical engineer, he held posts in industry and academia before becoming the country's second elected president. Full name **Richards, George Maxwell**

Richards, Viv (*b.* 1952) Jamaican cricketer. A powerful batsman and skilled fielder, he was captain of the West Indies cricket team (1985–91). Full name **Richards, Isaac Vivian Alexander**

Richardson /ríchərdss'n/, **Henry Handel** (1870–1946) Australian novelist. She wrote the trilogy *The Fortunes of Richard Mahony* (1917–29). Pseudonym of **Robertson, Ethel Florence Lindesay**. Born **Richardson, Ethel Florence Lindesay**

Richardson, Sir Ralph (1902–83) British actor. He appeared in many Shakespearean and classical stage roles, and in numerous films. Full name **Richardson, Sir Ralph David**

Richardson, Samuel (1689–1761) British novelist. He wrote *Pamela* (1740), *Clarissa* (1747–48), and other novels in epistolary form, and had a major influence on the early development of the English novel.

Richardson's ground squirrel /ríchərdsənz-/ *n* a ground squirrel that can be a pest of grain crops. Native to: northwestern United States and Canadian prairies. Latin name: *Citellus richardsoni*. [Mid-20C. After Sir John *Richardson* (1787–1865), Scottish naturalist]

Richelieu /reésh lyṓ/, **Armand Jean du Plessis, Duc de** (1585–1642) French cardinal and royal minister. As chief minister to Louis XIII after 1624, he wielded supreme power in France. He strengthened the monarchy and made France the pre-eminent military power in Europe. Known as **Cardinal Richelieu**

> 'Authority compels people to obedience, but reason persuades them to it.'
> [Armand Jean du Plessis Richelieu, *Testament politique*; 1688]

rich e-mail *n* an e-mail that has a voice message attached to it

riches /ríchiz/ *npl* **1.** great wealth or many valuable possessions **2.** things occurring naturally in abundance ○ *enjoy the riches of the forest* [12C. Variant of obsolete *richesse* (singular) 'wealth' < Old French *richeise* < *riche* (see RICH), misunderstood as plural]

Richler /ríchlər/, **Mordecai** (1931–2001) Canadian

MEASURING EARTHQUAKES USING THE RICHTER SCALE

The Richter scale measures the magnitude of an earthquake based on how much the ground shakes at a distance of 100 km (60 miles) from the epicenter of the earthquake (the site on the Earth's surface directly above its origin). Other systems used by seismologists to measure earthquakes include the Modified Mercalli scale, a 12-point scale that measures intensity at different locations.

Richter number	Increase in the motion of the ground	Results
1	1	Generally not felt, but recorded on seismometers
2	10	Generally not felt, but recorded on seismometers
3	100	Generally not felt, but recorded on seismometers
4	1,000	Felt by many people; trees sway
5	10,000	Poorly built structures damaged
6	100,000	Specially designed structures damaged; others collapse
7	1,000,000	Many structures destroyed; cracks in ground
8+	10,000,000	Severe destruction; very wide cracks in ground

writer. He has drawn on his working-class Jewish background in *The Apprenticeship of Duddy Kravitz* (1959) and other works.

'Remember this, Griffin. The revolution eats its own. Capitalism re-creates itself.'
[Mordecai Richler, *Cocksure*; 1968]

richly /ríchli/ *adv* **1. ELABORATELY** beautifully and elaborately ◇ *richly decorated* **2. WITH DEEP COLOUR** with a deep, fully saturated colour **3. COMPLETELY** completely and suitably ◇ *a richly deserved award* **4. PLENTIFULLY** plentifully or very fully

Richmond /ríchmənd/ **1.** market town in North Yorkshire, northern England, on the banks of the River Swale. Population: 7,862 (1991). **2.** capital of Virginia, United States, in the eastern part of the state. Population: 197,456 (2002 estimate). **3.** town in eastern New South Wales, Australia, on the River Hawkesbury. Population: 3,099 (2002 estimate).

Richmond-upon-Thames borough of southwestern London, on the River Thames

Richter /ríktər, ríkhtər/, **Johann Paul Friedrich** (1763–1825) German novelist and humorist. He wrote *Hesperus* (1795), *Titan* (1800–03), and other romances and satirical works. Pseudonym **Jean Paul**

Richter scale /ríktər-, ríkhtər-/ *n* a scale from 1 to 10 used to measure the severity of earthquakes according to the amount of energy released, with a higher number indicating stronger tremors [Mid-20C. After Charles Francis *Richter* (1900–85), US seismologist]

rich text *n* computer text that includes formatting codes, e.g. for bold or italic

Richthofen /ríkt höfən, ríkht-/, **Manfred, Baron von** (1892–1918) German aviator. As the leader of a German air squadron during World War I, he is thought to have shot down 80 Allied aircraft. Known as the **Red Baron**

ricin /ríssin/ *n* a highly toxic protein. Source: seeds of the castor oil plant. Use: destruction of cancer cells in treatments such as bone marrow transplants. [Late 19C. < Latin *ricinus* 'castor oil plant']

ricinoleic acid /ríssinō lee ik-/ *n* an unsaturated fatty acid that is the main constituent of castor oil. Use: soap, plastics, textile finishing. Formula: C$_{18}$H$_{34}$O$_3$. [< Latin *ricinus* 'castor oil plant' + OLEIC]

rick[1] /rik/ *n* a large quantity of hay or straw stacked into a rectangular shape for storage and covered at the top to protect it from the weather ■ *vt* (**ricks, ricking, ricked**) to stack hay or straw to form a rick [Old English *hrēac*, origin ?]

rick[2] /rik/, **wrick** *vt* (**ricks, ricking, ricked; wricks, wricking, wricked**) to wrench or sprain a joint of the body slightly ■ *n* a slight injury to a joint caused by wrenching or spraining it [Late 18C. < ?]

rickets /ríkits/ *n* a disease, especially of children, caused by a deficiency in vitamin D that makes the bones become soft and prone to bending and

structural change. Technical name **rachitis** [Mid-17C. Origin ?]

rickettsia /ri kétsi ə/ (*plural* **-siae** /-si ee/ or **-sias**) *n* a parasitic bacterium that typically lives inside ticks and can be transmitted to humans, causing Rocky Mountain spotted fever, forms of typhus, and other diseases. Order: Rickettsiales. [Early 20C. < modern Latin, after H. T. *Ricketts* (1871–1910), US pathologist] —**rickettsial** *adj*

rickety /ríkiti/ (**-ier, -iest**) *adj* **1. UNSTABLE** in bad condition, unstable, and likely to collapse ◇ *a rickety chair* **2. INFIRM** weakened by the ageing process or illness **3. MED WITH RICKETS** affected by rickets **4. MED RELATING TO RICKETS** relating to or resembling rickets [Late 17C. < RICKETS, from the unsteadiness that the disease causes] —**ricketiness** *n*

rickey /ríki/ (*plural* **-eys**) *n* a cocktail made from soda water, lime or lemon juice, sugar, and gin or vodka [Late 19C. Probably < a surname]

rickrack /rík rak/, **ricrac** *n* a narrow decorative braid in a zigzag shape [Late 19C. Doubling of RACK[1]]

rickshaw /rík shaw/, **ricksha** *n* **1.** a small vehicle with two wheels and a seat for passengers, pulled along by somebody walking in front of it, used especially in South and East Asia **2.** a small three-wheeled vehicle, like a tricycle with a seat at the back for passengers, that is driven by somebody sitting at the front and pedalling [Late 19C. Shortening of Japanese *jinrikisha* < *jin* 'man' + *riki* 'strength' + *sha* 'vehicle']

ricochet /ríkə shay/ *vi* (**-chets, -cheting** /-shaying/ or **-chetting** /-sheting/, **-cheted** /-shayd/ or **-chetted** /-shetid/) to hit a surface and bounce, travelling away in a different direction ■ *n* the rebounding action of something that hits a surface and bounces off in a different direction [Mid-18C. < Old French, 'give-and-take, repetition']

ricotta /ri kóttə/ *n* a soft white mild-tasting Italian cheese made from whey and used mostly in cooking, or a cheese made to resemble this [Late 19C. Via Italian, 'recooked' < Latin *recocta*, form of past participle of *recoquere* 'recook' < *coquere* 'cook']

ricrac *n* **HANDICRAFT** another spelling of **rickrack**

RICS *abbr* Royal Institution of Chartered Surveyors

rictus /ríktəss/ (*plural* same or **-tuses**) *n* **1.** a fixed open-mouthed grin or grimace, especially an expression of horror **2.** the gape of a bird's beak [Mid-18C. < Latin < past participle of *ringi* 'gape'] —**rictal** *adj*

rid /rid/ (**rids, ridding, rid** or **ridded** *archaic*) *vt* **1.** to free, relieve, or empty a place or thing of something, usually something undesirable ◇ *an attempt to rid the town of crime* **2.** to free somebody or yourself from something undesirable ◇ *trying to rid myself of the habit* [12C. < Old Norse *rýðja* 'to clear land' < *hrjóða* 'to strip'] —**ridder** *n* ◇ **be well rid of somebody** or **something** to be in a better position because you no longer have to deal with somebody or something burdensome, unpleasant, or unnecessary ◇ **get rid of somebody** or **something** to make somebody or some-

thing burdensome, unpleasant, or unnecessary go away

rid up *vti N England, Scotland* to tidy up a place

riddance /rídd'nss/ *n* the removal or destruction of something unwanted ◇ **good riddance (to somebody** or **something)** used to show that you are glad to be free of somebody or something

ridden past participle of **ride**

riddle[1] /rídd'l/ *n* **1. WORD PUZZLE** a puzzle in the form of a question or rhyme that contains clues to its answer **2. PUZZLING THING** something that is puzzling or confusing ■ *v* (**-dles, -dling, -dled**) **1.** *vti* **ANSWER RIDDLE** to find or explain the answer to a riddle **2.** *vi* **TALK IN RIDDLES** to speak in an intentionally obscure way [Old English *rǣdels* < Indo-European] —**riddler** *n*

SYNONYMS See *problem*.

riddle[2] /rídd'l/ *vt* (**-dles, -dling, -dled**) **1. MAKE HOLES IN SOMETHING** to damage something by making a large number of small holes in it **2. AFFECT EVERY PART** to affect every part of something, e.g. by spreading throughout **3. SIEVE SOIL OR STONES** to put soil or stones through a sieve to separate the large pieces from the small ones **4. SHAKE ASHES FROM FIRE** to shake ashes from the bottom of a fire by poking it with a metal rod or moving a mechanism under the grate ■ *n* **SIEVE** a large flat shallow sieve for sifting soil or stones [Old English *hriddel* 'sieve', alteration of *hridder* < Indo-European, 'to sort'] —**riddler** *n*

riddling /rídd'ling/ *adj* communicating in riddles, or in a deliberately obscure and confusing way

ride /rīd/ *v* (**rides, riding, rode** /rōd/, **ridden** /rídd'n/) **1.** *vti* **SIT ON AND CONTROL HORSE** to sit on a horse or other animal and control it as it moves along **2.** *vti* **TRAVEL ON BIKE** to travel mounted on a bicycle or motorcycle **3.** *vt* **USE SPORTS EQUIPMENT** to support your weight and move on a skateboard, surfboard, or other piece of gliding or rolling sport equipment **4.** *vi* **TRAVEL AS PASSENGER** to travel as a passenger in a vehicle **5.** *vti* **US TRAVEL IN LIFT** to travel in a lift **6.** *vt* **TRAVEL OVER AREA** to travel across an area of land ◇ *ride the range* **7.** *vt* **BE IN RACE** to take part in a race or other event on a horse or bike **8.** *vt* **CARRY SOMEBODY ALONG** to carry or take somebody along sitting or mounted on something ◇ *His mother rode him around on her bicycle.* **9.** *vi* **APPEAR TO BE FLOATING** to appear to be floating in the sky or moving like a floating object ◇ *riding the air currents* **10.** *vi* **DO SOMETHING EFFORTLESSLY** to do something successfully and apparently effortlessly, as if carried along by a wave ◇ *riding on a tide of sympathy* **11.** *vi* **DEPEND ON SOMETHING** to depend on something for success ◇ *Her future rides on this interview.* **12.** *vi* **BE ALLOWED TO CONTINUE** to continue without intervention or alteration ◇ *Let it ride for now.* **13.** *vt* **DEAL WITH PROBLEM AND SURVIVE** to manage to deal with a difficult situation successfully and survive without too much harm ◇ *managed to ride the storm during the recession* **14.** *vi N Am* **HANDLE WELL OR BADLY** to function in a particular way while moving ◇ *a car that rides well over rough ground* **15.** *vt* **AUTOMOT PARTIALLY DEPRESS CLUTCH OR BRAKE** to put your foot on the clutch or brake, partially depressing it, while driving **16.** *vt* **NAUT, SWIMMING, SURFING RISE ON TOP OF WAVE** to rise up on a wave and move forward with it **17.** *vti* **NAUT ANCHOR** to be moored with the anchor down, or moor a ship by dropping its anchor ◇ *a ship riding at anchor* **18.** *vi* **ENG BE SUPPORTED BY SOMETHING** to be supported by something such as a pivot or an axle ◇ *Most of the weight rides on the central shaft.* **19.** *vt* **OVERLAP** to overlap or encroach on something such as another part **20.** *vt* **YIELD TO BLOW** to move in the direction of something forceful such as a blow, in order to lessen the impact **21.** *vt N Am* **TEASE OR TORMENT SOMEBODY** to tease or torment somebody with criticism or mockery (*informal*) ◇ *riding me about my hair* ■ *n* **1. JOURNEY BY VEHICLE OR ANIMAL** a journey or outing in a motor vehicle or on an animal ◇ *Let's go for a ride.* **2.** *N Am* **TRANSPORT IN VEHICLE** a lift in a vehicle **3.** **AUTOMOT QUALITY OF TRAVEL** the quality of travel in a motor vehicle ◇ *The new model offers a very smooth ride.* **4.** **LEISURE FAIRGROUND ENTERTAINMENT** an entertainment at an amusement park or fairground that offers a physically thrilling experience, e.g. a roller coaster **5.** **RIDING, ROADS PATH FOR HORSES** a broad grassy path where horses can be ridden **6.** **MUSIC**

JAZZ CYMBAL one of the three cymbals in a drum set, used to keep time and mark rhythmic accents in jazz [Old English *rīdan* < Indo-European] —**ridable** *adj* ◇ **be riding high** to be enjoying a period or feeling of success ◇ **ride roughshod over somebody** to treat somebody very arrogantly without justice or consideration for his or her feelings ◇ **ride roughshod over something** to disregard a rule, law, or agreement ◇ **take somebody for a ride** to cheat or deceive somebody

ride down *vt* **1.** to hit and knock down somebody while riding, especially on horseback **2.** to catch up with or overtake somebody

ride out *vt* to manage to deal with a difficult situation successfully and survive without too much harm ○ *ride out the storm*

ride up *vi* to gradually move upwards out of the correct position ○ *Her skirt was riding up.*

rider /rīdər/ *n* **1.** SOMEBODY ON HORSE OR BIKE somebody who rides on an animal or a vehicle **2.** ADDITIONAL COMMENT an extra comment or clause added to a document or statement **3.** LAW ADDITIONAL CLAUSE TO BILL an extra clause added to a parliamentary or legislative bill, often not directly related to the main issue **4.** LAW ADDITIONAL STATEMENT BY JURY a secondary statement made by a jury, giving a comment in addition to the verdict **5.** STRENGTHENING ELEMENT something that rests on or strengthens something else, e.g. the horizontal rail of a fence or additional timbers in the frame of a ship **6.** SLIDING ADJUSTMENT a small sliding weight on the arm of a chemical balance, used for adjusting the scales **7.** GEOL MINERAL SEAM a thin seam of a mineral lying above a thicker one **8.** SPORTS SNOWBOARDER somebody riding a snowboard

ridership /rīdər ship/ *n* the number of passengers using a public transport system

ridesharing /rīd shairing/ *n N Am* an arrangement in which commuters take turns using their cars for going to work, taking one another as passengers to cut down the number of cars on the roads

ridge /rij/ *n* **1.** RAISED LAND FORMATION a long narrow hilltop or range of hills **2.** RAISED AREA ON OCEAN FLOOR an elevation on the ocean floor resembling a ridge on land and resulting from volcanic eruption along the fissures between tectonic plates **3.** RAISED STRIP a long narrow raised area of something **4.** TOP OF ROOF the line along the top of a roof or a tent where the two sloping sides meet **5.** METEOROL AREA OF HIGH PRESSURE a long area of high pressure in a weather system **6.** ANAT RAISED BIT ON BONE a long narrow protuberance or crest, e.g. on a bone **7.** ZOOL BACKBONE OF ANIMAL the backbone of an animal, especially a whale ■ *v* (**ridges, ridging, ridged**) **1.** *vt* FORM SOMETHING INTO RIDGES to mark or provide something with ridges, or make something into the shape of a ridge **2.** *vi* FORM A RIDGE to form or rise up into a ridge or series of ridges [Old English *hrycg* < Germanic, 'back, spine'] —**ridgy** *adj*

ridgeback /rij bak/ *n* ZOOL same as **Rhodesian ridgeback**

ridgeline /rij līn/ *n* GEOG same as **ridge** *n* (sense 1)

ridgeling /rījling/, **ridgling** *n* a male animal in which one or both testes fail to descend into the scrotum at the usual time [Mid-16C. < dialect *ridgel* < ?]

ridgepole /rij pōl/ *n* **1.** a long beam of wood that runs along the ridge of a roof, supporting the upper ends of the rafters **2.** the horizontal pole supporting the top of a ridge tent

ridge tent *n* a tent with rectangular sides that stands chiefly by suspension from a supported horizontal pole

ridgetree /rij tree/ *n* CONSTR, CAMPING same as **ridgepole**

ridgeway /rij way/ *n* a track, usually of ancient origin, running along the top of a ridge of hills

ridgling *n* ZOOL another spelling of **ridgeling**

ridgy-didge *adj Aus* genuine or true (*informal*) [Mid-20C. Doubling of slang *ridge* 'genuine, authentic', originally 'gold' < ?]

ridicule /riddi kyool/ *vt* (**-cules, -culing, -culed**) to reduce or dismiss the importance or quality of somebody or something in a contemptuous way ■ *n* mocking laughter, mimicry, or comments intended to make fun of somebody in a contemptuous way [Late 17C. Directly or via French < Latin *ridiculum* 'joke' < *ridiculus* (see RIDICULOUS)] —**ridiculer** *n*

SYNONYMS *ridicule, deride, laugh, mock, make fun of, send up*

CORE MEANING: to belittle somebody or something by making them appear ridiculous

ridicule to reduce or dismiss the importance or quality of somebody or something in a contemptuous way ○ *His feat has been ridiculed by reporters, who question whether he really swam most of the way or actually came aboard his support boat.* **deride** to show contempt for somebody or something ○ *Critics have derided his recent works, but he still commands huge advances.* **laugh** to make scornful fun of somebody or something ○ *He laughed at our old-fashioned journalistic methods and called our newspapers 'country sheets'.* **mock** to treat somebody or something with scorn or contempt ○ *The show's host delights in mocking her narcissistic celebrity guests.* **make fun of** to make somebody or something appear ridiculous ○ *The children made fun of his shoes.* **send up** (*informal*) to make somebody or something appear ridiculous by humorous imitation ○ *We'd mercilessly send up Dad's complete incompetence with tools.*

ridiculous /ri díkyŏŏləss/ *adj* **1.** completely unreasonable and not at all sensible or acceptable **2.** silly and funny [Mid-16C. < Latin *ridiculus* 'laughable' < *ridere* 'to laugh'] —**ridiculously** *adv* —**ridiculousness** *n*

riding[1] /rīding/ *n* **1.** BEING ON HORSE the sport or hobby of sitting on a horse and controlling it as it moves along **2.** TRAVELLING ON ANIMAL OR VEHICLE the act of travelling on an animal or vehicle ■ *adj* USED ON HORSEBACK used while riding a horse ○ *riding breeches* [13C. < RIDE]

riding[2] /rīding/ *n* **1.** *also* **Riding** DISTRICT OF YORKSHIRE one of the three administrative districts into which Yorkshire was formerly split **2.** CANADIAN CONSTITUENCY in Canada, a constituency represented by either a federal member of parliament or a member of the provincial legislature **3.** *NZ* RURAL ELECTORATE a rural electorate for local government **4.** *also* **Riding** AREA OF TIPPERARY either of two counties into which the former county of Tipperary in the Republic of Ireland is now split [Pre-12C. < Old Norse *þriðungr* 'third part' < *þriði* 'third']

riding coat *n* a coat with cutaway front and tails worn in the 19th century for riding

riding crop *n* a straight short riding whip with a loop at the end

riding habit *n* a jacket with a matching skirt worn by women for riding between the late 17th and the early 20th centuries

Riding Mountain National Park /rīding-/ national park in southwestern Manitoba, Canada. Area: 2,973 sq. km/1,148 sq. mi.

ridley /ridli/ (*plural* **-leys**) *n* a small turtle, especially the grey-shelled Kemp's ridley found in the Atlantic, or the larger greenish olive ridley found in the Pacific [Early 20C. Origin ?]

ridotto /ri dóttō/ (*plural* **-tos**) *n* a musical entertainment with dancing, popular in the 18th century [Early 18C. Via Italian, 'retreat, entertainment' < medieval Latin *reductus* < past participle of Latin *reducere* (see REDUCE)]

riebeckite /reé bek īt/ *n* a blue-black silicate mineral of the amphibole group containing iron and sodium. Source: acidic igneous rocks, schists. [Late 19C. After Emil *Riebeck* (1853–85), German explorer]

Riefenstahl /reéf'n shtaal/, **Leni** (1902–2003) German film director and photographer. Her documentary films of a Nazi rally and of the 1936 Berlin Olympic Games glorified the Nazis, but are nevertheless masterpieces of cinematic technique. Born **Riefenstahl, Helena Bertha Amalie**

riel /reé əl/ *n* the main unit of Cambodian currency. See table at **currency** [Mid-20C. < Khmer]

Riemann /reémən/, **Georg Friedrich Bernhard** (1826–66) German mathematician. He studied function theory and developed a system of geometry relevant to modern theoretical physics.

Riemannian geometry /ree mánni ən-/ *n* a non-Euclidean geometry in which it is assumed that in a plane all pairs of straight lines intersect

riempie /rímpi, reémpi/ *n S Africa* a strip of leather used for weaving chair seats [Mid-19C. Via Afrikaans < Dutch *riempje* 'small thong' < *riem* 'thong']

~~rien~~ incorrect spelling of **rein**

Riesling /reézling/ *n* **1.** a fruity dry to sweet white wine made from a variety of white grape grown mainly in Germany, Austria, Alsace, and Australia **2.** a white grape that is used to make Riesling [Mid-19C. < German]

rif /rif/ (**rifs, riffing, riffed**) *vt* to lay off members of a workforce or to be laid off (*informal*) [< RIF]

RIF *n US* the laying off of members of a workforce. Full form **reduction in force**

rifampicin /ri fámpissin/, **rifampin** /ri fámpin/ *n* a semisynthetic derivative of rifamycin that works by interfering with RNA synthesis in the infecting bacteria Use: treatment of bacterial infections, especially tuberculosis [Mid-20C. Blend of RIFAMYCIN + PIPERAZINE]

rifamycin /reéfə míssin/ *n* an antibiotic belonging to a group originally isolated from the soil bacterium *Streptomyces mediterranei*. Use: treatment of leprosy, tuberculosis, other bacterial infections. [Mid-20C. Probably < Italian *riformare* 'to reform' < *formare* 'to form' < Latin (see REFORM)]

rife /rīf/ *adj* **1.** found widely or frequently ○ *areas where poverty is rife* ○ *Rumours were rife that the factory was about to be closed down.* **2.** full of something undesirable, or experiencing a widespread and very frequent occurrence of something, especially something undesirable ○ *an organization rife with corruption* [Old English *rȳfe* < Germanic] —**rifely** *adv* —**rifeness** *n*

SYNONYMS See *widespread*.

riff /rif/ *n* **1.** SERIES OF NOTES a short, often repeated series of notes in pop music or jazz that forms a distinctive part of the accompaniment **2.** *US* QUIP a quick, witty remark, especially one that is part of a rapid exchange ■ *vi* (**riffs, riffing, riffed**) USE RIFFS to play riffs as a musical accompaniment to something [Early 20C. Probably shortening of RIFFLE]

Riffian /riffi ən/ *n* a dialect of Berber spoken in Morocco, especially in the Riff Mountains of northern Morocco [Mid-19C. < the *Riff*, Mountains] —**Riffian** *adj*

riffle /riff'l/ *v* (**-fles, -fling, -fled**) **1.** *vti* FLICK THROUGH PAGES to flick through the pages of a book, magazine, or newspaper, glancing casually at the contents **2.** *vt* SHUFFLE CARDS to shuffle playing cards by halving the pack, lifting the corners, and flicking the cards so that they overlap as they fall **3.** *vi* BECOME CHOPPY to become rough and choppy when passing over submerged rocks (*refers to water*) ○ *Water riffles over the rocks.* ■ *n* **1.** QUICK LOOK AT BOOK a quick flick through the pages of a book, magazine, or newspaper **2.** SHUFFLING OF CARDS the shuffling of playing cards **3.** GROOVED PART OF SLUICE the bottom part of a sluice that has grooves for collecting gold or other mineral particles **4.** *US* SUBMERGED ROCKS OR SANDBAR an area of rocks or a sandbar lying just below the surface of the water **5.** *N Am* ROUGH WATER an area of rough water caused by submerged rocks or a sandbar [Mid-18C. < ?]

riffler /riff'lər/ *n* a curved file for smoothing concave surfaces [Late 18C. < French *rifloir* < *rifler* 'to scratch']

riffraff /rif raf/ *n* **1.** an offensive term that deliberately insults somebody's social status, importance, and manners (*insult*) **2.** rubbish or worthless objects (*informal*) [15C. < French *rif et raf* 'pieces of plunder of small value' < *rifler* 'plunder' and *raffler* 'snatch']

rifle[1] /rīf'l/ *n* **1.** LONG GUN a gun with a long barrel that is fired from the shoulder. Spiral grooves inside the barrel make the bullet spin, improving its accuracy over a long distance. **2.** CANNON a large cannon with spirals cut into the bore ■ *rifles, Rifles npl* SOLDIERS WITH RIFLES a unit, especially a regiment, of soldiers armed with rifles ■ *vt* (**-fles, -fling, -fled**) **1.** CUT GROOVE IN GUN BARREL to cut spiral grooves on the inside of a gun barrel **2.** THROW VERY FAST BALL to hit or throw a ball hard, making it travel very fast [Late 17C. < French *rifler* 'scratch']

rifle[2] /rīf'l/ (**-fles, -fling, -fled**) *v* **1.** *vti* to search through something, e.g. a drawer or room, vigorously, hurriedly, and recklessly, often leaving things in

disorder, sometimes with the intent to steal **2.** *vt* to rob or plunder somebody or something [14C. < French *rifler* 'plunder, scratch'] —**rifler** *n*

riflebird /ríf'l burd/ *n* a bird of paradise, the male of which performs an elaborate courtship dance. Native to: Australia, New Guinea. Genus: *Ptiloris*. [Mid-19C. *Rifle* < ?]

rifle green *n* a dark-green colour, similar to that of the uniform of a British army rifleman —**rifle-green** *adj*

rifle grenade *n* a grenade propelled to its target by a rifle-fired bullet, requiring special adapting hardware

rifleman /ríf'lmən/ (*plural* -**men** /-mən/) *n* **1.** SOLDIER WITH RIFLE a soldier, especially a man, who has been trained to use a rifle, or who is a member of a unit armed with rifles **2.** RIFLE USER somebody, especially a man, skilled in the use of a rifle **3.** NEW ZEALAND WREN a tiny wren found in bush areas, with a short tail, round wings, and a broad head. Native to: New Zealand. Latin name: *Acanthisitta chloris*.

rifle range *n* an area with targets where people can practise shooting rifles

riflery /ríf'lri/ *n US* **1.** the skill or practice of firing rifles **2.** fire from rifles

riflescope /ríf'l skōp/ *n* a telescopic sight designed to be used on a rifle [Mid-20C. < RIFLE[1] + TELESCOPE]

riflewoman /ríf'l woŏmən/ (*plural* -**women** /-wimin/) *n* **1.** a woman skilled in the use of a rifle **2.** a female soldier who has been trained to use a rifle, or who is a member of a unit armed with rifles

rifling /rífling/ *n* **1.** the cutting of spiral grooves in the barrel of a gun **2.** a series of spiral grooves cut in the barrel of a gun

rift /rift/ *n* **1.** GAP OR BREAK a gap or break in something where it has split apart **2.** DISAGREEMENT a serious disagreement that disrupts good relations **3.** GEOL same as **fault** *n* (sense 6) ■ *vti* (**rifts, rifting, rifted**) SPLIT APART to split apart, or make something split apart [14C. < N Germanic]

rift valley *n* a valley formed by geological faulting, where the land between two parallel faults drops down to give a broad central plain with steep sides

rift zone *n* an area of Earth's surface, often associated with the margins of continental plates, that is especially heavily faulted and may be subject to earth tremors

rig[1] /rig/ *vt* (**rigs, rigging, rigged**) **1.** EQUIP VESSEL WITH RIGGING to fit a boat or its mast with sails and rigging **2.** ERECT SOMETHING to erect, set up, or assemble something so that it is ready for use ○ *rig the aerial* **3.** MAKE SOMETHING HASTILY to construct something temporary but serviceable, usually in haste and without the proper materials ○ *rigged up a makeshift shelter* **4.** same as **rig out** (*informal*) ■ *n* **1.** ARRANGEMENT OF SAILS AND MASTS the arrangement of sails and masts on a boat **2.** DRILLING STRUCTURE FOR OIL a structure and the apparatus used for drilling for oil and gas **3.** SPECIALIST EQUIPMENT the special equipment used for an activity, especially fishing tackle or the radio equipment used by an amateur radio operator **4.** CLOTHES an outfit that somebody is wearing (*informal*) **5.** LORRY an articulated lorry or lorry with a trailer (*informal*) **6.** *US* HORSE CARRIAGE in former times, a carriage or cart pulled by one or more horses [15C. Probably < N Germanic]
rig out *vt* (*informal*) **1.** to put a special kind of clothing on somebody ○ *rigged himself out for a heavyweight bout* **2.** to fit a person, place, or object with proper or necessary equipment ○ *rigged out for a long mountain biking trip*

rig[2] /rig/ (*informal*) *vt* (**rigs, rigging, rigged**) to affect the outcome of something by intervening dishonestly or unfairly to gain an advantage ○ *tried to rig the election* ■ *n* a trick or swindle [Early 18C. < ?]

rig[3] /rig/ *n* a male animal in which one or both testes fail to descend into the scrotum at the usual time. The condition is most common in horses and pigs. (*informal*) [15C. Variant of RIDGE]

Riga /réégə/ capital city of Latvia, in the east of the country, on the Baltic Sea. Population: 764,328 (2000).

rigadoon /ríggə doōn/, **rigaudon** /ri gaw dáwN/ *n* **1.** a French dance for couples in duple or quadruple time. Originally a traditional dance from the Provence region, it became popular in the 17th and 18th centuries at the French court, where it was danced in a more dignified manner. **2.** the music for a rigadoon [Late 17C. < French *rigaudon*]

rigatoni /ríggə tóni/ *n* short rounded tubes of pasta with narrow ridges running along them [Mid-20C. < Italian < *rigato* 'ridged', past participle of *rigare* 'draw a line' < *riga* 'line']

rigaudon *n* DANCE, MUSIC same as **rigadoon**

Rigel /ríg'l/ *n* a blue-white double star in the constellation Orion [< Arabic *rijl* 'foot', because it appears at the base of the constellation]

rigger /ríggər/ *n* **1.** RIGGED SHIP a ship with a specific kind of rigging (*usually used in combination*) ○ *square-rigger* **2.** SOMEBODY WHO RIGS BOATS somebody whose job is to rig a sailing boat **3.** BRACKET ON ROWING BOAT a bracket supporting a rowlock on a rowing boat **4.** SCAFFOLDING WORKER somebody whose job is to erect and maintain scaffolding and lifting equipment **5.** OIL-RIG WORKER a worker on an oil or gas rig **6.** LARGE CRANE FOR LIFTING a mechanized crane used for hoisting very large and heavy construction materials to great heights [Early 17C. < RIG[1]]

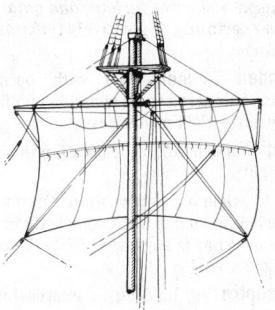

rigging

rigging /rígging/ *n* **1.** ROPES, WIRES, AND PULLEYS the ropes, wires, and pulleys that support the masts and control the sails of a boat **2.** THEATRE EQUIPMENT the system of ropes, pulleys, and other equipment used to shift scenery on a stage **3.** SUPPORTING EQUIPMENT a system of ropes, pulleys, or other equipment used as a support for something, e.g. construction scaffolding [15C. < RIG[1]]

rigging loft *n* **1.** a raised area or gallery in a boatyard where workers stand while fitting rigging **2.** an area above a stage equipped with lifting gear for raising and lowering scenery

right /rīt/ *adj* **1.** CORRECT accurate, or consistent with the facts or general belief ○ *gave the right answer* **2.** HAVING CORRECT OPINION holding a correct opinion about somebody or something ○ *hard to tell who's right in this situation* **3.** PROPER correct with regard to use, function, or operation ○ *You're not holding the thing by the right end.* ○ *It has to be stored right side up.* **4.** MORALLY GOOD morally justified and correct, or consistent with generally held ideas of morality and proper conduct ○ *I only wanted to do what is right.* **5.** USUAL in the usual or expected state, or in a desirable state for good functioning or good relations ○ *Something didn't seem right when I walked in.* ○ *You can't expect to put everything right overnight.* **6.** BEST most suitable or desirable ○ *waiting for the right offer to come along* **7.** HEALTHY in good physical and mental health ○ *hasn't felt right in weeks* **8.** PROMINENT prominent in business, society, or some other sphere ○ *knows all the right people* **9.** EAST WHEN FACING NORTH on the side of the body that is east when you face north, or on the corresponding side of an object **10.** FITTING RIGHT HAND OR FOOT designed to fit the right hand, foot, arm, or leg **11.** *also* **Right** RIGHT-WING holding generally conservative political views and tending to be cautious about social change **12.** MATHS PERPENDICULAR being perpendicular or forming an angle of 90° **13.** TOTAL complete and utter (*informal*) ○ *felt a right fool* ■ *adv* **1.** PROPERLY in the best and most effective way, or a way that will be successful ○ *You didn't do it right.* **2.** CORRECTLY

accurately with regard to fact ○ *If you'd answered right you would have won £100.* **3.** MORALLY AND APPROPRIATELY in a way that is morally good or acceptable, or conducive to somebody's benefit or happiness ○ *treat sb right* **4.** DESIRABLY desirably or advantageously ○ *afraid that it won't turn out right* **5.** COMPLETELY used to emphasize how completely something happens, or that something is situated at, or moves or extends to, an extreme point ○ *went right through the wall* ○ *right at the end of the book* ○ *reaches right across the room* **6.** IMMEDIATELY used to emphasize the immediacy with which something happens or should happen ○ *You'll do it right this minute.* **7.** EXACTLY used to emphasize the preciseness of something ○ *right in the middle* ○ *right at that moment* **8.** DIRECTLY without deviating from a course ○ *Keep right on down this road.* **9.** TOWARDS EAST WHEN FACING NORTH in or towards the east when you are facing or moving north, and correspondingly for other directions ○ *turn right at the church* **10.** USED AS PART OF TITLE used as part of a title of respect ○ *Right Reverend* **11.** *regional* same as **very** ○ *a right good deal* ■ *n* **1.** MORALLY APPROPRIATE THING that which is morally good or in accordance with accepted principles of justice, fairness, and honesty ○ *She's too young to know right from wrong.* ○ *Right will prevail!* **2.** ENTITLEMENT OR FREEDOM a justified claim or entitlement, or the freedom to do something (*often used in the plural*) ○ *You're within your rights to complain.* ○ *a declaration of the rights of civilized people* **3.** LAW CLAIM TO PROPERTY somebody's interest in a property (*often used in the plural*) **4.** EAST WHEN FACING NORTH the side of something that lies east when it is facing north, or the corresponding direction **5.** RIGHT-HAND TURN a turn to the right **6.** ONE OF PAIR the one of a pair of things that is designed for the right hand or foot **7.** BLOW MADE WITH RIGHT HAND a blow delivered with the right hand **8.** *also* **Right** CONSERVATIVES AS GROUP political conservatives considered as a group, or the opinions they hold **9.** FIN SECURITIES OPTION an option to purchase or receive securities not offered for sale openly, or the certificate indicating it (*often used in the plural*) ■ *v* (**rights, righting, righted**) **1.** *vti* MAKE OR BECOME UPRIGHT to put something upright, or return to an upright position ○ *I righted the vase and mopped up the water.* **2.** *vt* IMPROVE SOMETHING to return something to its normal, well-functioning state, or bring it to a better or more equitable one ○ *She did everything she could to right the situation.* **3.** *vt* MAKE AMENDS FOR WRONG to redress an error or misdeed ■ *interj* (*informal*) **1.** OK used to indicate assent or understanding ○ *Right, I'm with you now.* **2.** IS THAT SO? used to ask for confirmation of a statement ○ *You just got here, right?* [Old English *riht* < Indo-European, 'go straight'] —**rightable** *adj* —**righter** *n* —**rightness** *n* ◇ **by rights** if things were justly or correctly done ○ *By rights, he should be head teacher by now.* ◇ **have** *or* **catch somebody bang to rights** to catch a criminal in the act of committing a crime (*informal*) ◇ **in the right** correct in what you say or do, especially legally or morally justified in saying or doing it ◇ **in your own right** because of your birth, ability, or other entitlement, without reference to anyone else ◇ **set** *or* **put somebody right 1.** to restore somebody to good health **2.** to make the true facts or the truth of a situation clear to somebody ◇ **set** *or* **put something to rights** to put something into a correct or well-ordered state ◇ **she'll be right** *Aus* everything will be fine (*informal*)

REGIONAL NOTE Right is used as an intensifier meaning 'very' in such phrases as *right tasty, right tidy*. In-

tensifiers are often specific to a particular region. Northern Ireland speakers use 'right and' and 'brave and' to mean 'quite', as in *right and tall, brave and tricky*, and there is a growing tendency in England to use 'well', as in *well happy*.

rightabout /rítə bowt/ *n* a turn through 180° to face in the opposite direction ■ *adj, adv* facing in the opposite direction

right angle *n* an angle of 90° —**right-angled** *adj* ◇ **at right angles** placed at an angle of 90° to something or forming an angle of 90° with something

right-angled triangle *n* a triangle with one right angle. N Am term **right triangle**

right ascension *n* one of the two reference points in the equatorial coordinate system for specifying the position of an astronomical object on the celestial sphere. Corresponding to longitude on the Earth, it is measured in hours, minutes, and seconds eastwards from the vernal equinox, the point where the ecliptic intersects the celestial equator.

right atrioventricular valve *n* ANAT same as **tricuspid valve**

right away *adv* immediately, without waiting or any delay

Right Bank /rít-/ a residential and commercial area north of the River Seine in central Paris, near the Champs-Élysées

right-brain *adj* relating to or involving the emotions or creative ability, these being believed to be associated with the right half of the cerebrum

right circular cone *n* MATHS same as **cone** *n* (sense 2)

right-click *vi* to press and release the right-hand button of a computer mouse

righteous /ríchəss/ *adj* **1.** STRICTLY OBSERVANT OF MORALITY always behaving according to a religious or moral code **2.** JUSTIFIABLE considered to be correct or justifiable **3.** RESPONDING TO INJUSTICE arising from the perception of great injustice or wrongdoing ○ *righteous indignation* ■ *n* MORALLY UPRIGHT PEOPLE righteous people viewed as a group ○ *believing that the righteous will prevail* [Old English *rihtwīs* < earlier forms of RIGHT + -WISE] —**righteously** *adv* —**righteousness** *n*

right field *n* **1.** the right side of the outfield on a baseball field, when looking from home plate **2.** in baseball, the position of the player responsible for fielding balls hit to right field —**right fielder** *n*

right-footed *adj* **1.** having a natural tendency to lead with or use the right foot, especially in playing sports such as football **2.** performed using the right foot ○ *a right-footed shot onto the goal*

right-footer *n* somebody who has a natural tendency to lead with or use the right foot, especially in playing sports such as football

rightful /rítf'l/ *adj* **1.** HAVING CLAIM with a legal or moral claim to something ○ *the rightful owner* **2.** OWNED BY SOMEBODY WITH RIGHT owned by somebody who has a right to it ○ *rightful property* **3.** FAIR considered to be right and fair ○ *a rightful objection* —**rightfully** *adv* —**rightfulness** *n*

right hand *n* **1.** the side of something that lies east when it is facing north, or the corresponding direction **2.** somebody who is of invaluable help to another person

right-hand *adj* **1.** ON OR TO RIGHT on the right or leading towards the right **2.** FOR RIGHT HAND designed for or done with the right hand **3.** MOST IMPORTANT AND TRUSTED most important and trusted, and relied upon to the greatest extent

right-hand drive *adj* describes a motor vehicle driven by somebody sitting in the right-hand front seat —**right-hand drive** *n*

right-handed *adj* **1.** PREFERRING TO USE RIGHT HAND using the right hand in preference to the left for writing, throwing, and other activities that require skill and careful control **2.** DONE WITH RIGHT HAND carried out with the right hand **3.** DESIGNED FOR RIGHT HAND designed to be done with or used by the right hand **4.** MOVING TOWARDS RIGHT turning towards the right in a clockwise direction ■ *adv* **1.** WITH RIGHT HAND using the right hand **2.** TOWARDS LEFT with a swing or direction

towards the left ○ *hit a ball right-handed* —**right-handedly** *adv* —**right-handedness** *n*

right-hander *n* **1.** a right-handed person, especially a sportsperson **2.** a blow delivered with the right hand

Right Honourable *n* **1.** USED TO REFER TO GOVERNMENT MINISTERS a title used in the British House of Commons when referring to, but not talking directly to, a government minister **2.** TITLE OF PRIVY COUNCILLOR OR JUDGE a title used in Britain when referring to, but not talking directly to, a member of the Privy Council or a judge who presides over an appeal court **3.** TITLE OF RESPECT a title used in Britain when referring to, but not talking directly to, a baron, viscount, or earl, and to lord mayors and lord provosts of some cities **4.** Can CANADIAN TITLE OF RESPECT a title of respect used to refer to the governor general, prime minister, or chief justice of Canada, and other eminent Canadians

rightio *interj* same as **righto** (*dated informal*)

rightist /rítist/ *adj* favouring or relating to political conservatism ■ *n* somebody with politically conservative views —**rightism** *n*

rightly /rítli/ *adv* **1.** CORRECTLY correctly, properly, and appropriately ○ *As you quite rightly said, we agreed to this at the last meeting.* **2.** UNDERSTANDABLY with very good reason ○ *She was furious, and quite rightly so!* **3.** CERTAINLY certainly or positively (*informal*) ○ *I don't rightly know.*

right-minded /-míndid/ *adj* with opinions and attitudes considered to be sensible and fair —**right-mindedly** *adv* —**right-mindedness** *n*

rightmost /rít mōst/ *adj* in the position that is farthest to the right

righto /rí tó/, **right oh**, **rightio** /ríti ó/ *interj* used to say that you acknowledge what somebody has just said and will do what is suggested (*dated informal*) [Late 19C. < RIGHT + HO²]

right-of-centre *adj* holding or expressing political views that are slightly right-wing

right off *adv* immediately, without waiting or any delay

right of search *n* the right of a country at war to stop and search the merchant ships of neutral nations to determine if they are carrying forbidden goods that may be seized

right of way *n* **1.** PERMISSION TO GO FIRST the legal or accepted right of a vehicle or craft to proceed ahead of another **2.** RIGHT TO CROSS PROPERTY the right to cross somebody else's property by a specific route, e.g. as a means of accessing your own property **3.** LAWFUL ROUTE ACROSS SOMEBODY'S PROPERTY a lawful route that may be taken across somebody else's property **4.** N Am LAND USED FOR ROAD OR LINE a narrow length of land used for the route of a railway, electric power line, or public road

right oh *interj* another spelling of **righto**

right on *interj* N Am used to show enthusiastic agreement with something said or done (*dated informal*)

right-on *adj* **1.** socially and politically fashionable and forward-looking, particularly in a way that corresponds to the attitudes of the political left (*dated informal*) **2.** N Am perfectly true (*informal*)

Right Reverend *n* a form of address for a Roman Catholic, Anglican, or Episcopal bishop, or for a Roman Catholic abbot or cleric with the title 'M'

right shoulder arms *n* the command or act of bringing a weapon to rest on the right shoulder during a military drill

rights issue *n* an instance of an organization offering shares to existing holders on favourable terms so that they can maintain their percentage share of ownership

right-size *vi* to bring a company to what is considered to be its optimal size, usually by dismissing some of its employees —**right-sizing** *n*

right stuff *n* exactly the psychological and physical characteristics called for by a task (*informal*)

right-thinking *adj* same as **right-minded**

right-to-die *adj* having or concerned with the right

to end one's own life by obliging others not to intervene and thereby let nature take its course ○ *the right-to-die question*

right-to-life *adj* SOC SCI same as **pro-life**

right triangle *n* N Am same as **right-angled triangle**

rightward /rítwərd/ *adj* moving towards or positioned on the right ■ *adv* same as **rightwards**

rightwards /rítwərdz/ *adv* towards the right

right whale *n* a large-headed whale with a deeply curved jawline and notched tail. Native to: North Atlantic, Pacific Ocean. Family: Balaenidae. [Early 18C. Because once regarded as the 'right' whale to harpoon and kill]

right wing *n* **1.** CONSERVATIVE those members of a group or political party who hold more conservative views than the others **2.** PLAYER OR POSITION AT RIGHT in some team games, the space or position on the right-hand side of a playing area when facing an opponent, or a player who plays in this area **3.** RIGHT-HAND SECTION OF MILITARY FORCE the right-hand part or position of a military force while facing the enemy

right-wing *adj* **1.** POL CONSERVATIVE conservative in conviction or temperament **2.** SPORTS POSITIONED ON RIGHT FACING OPPONENT in some games, occupying the right-hand part of a playing area when facing an opponent **3.** MIL OCCUPYING RIGHT DURING MILITARY ENGAGEMENT occupying the right-hand part or position of a military force when it is facing the enemy —**right-winger** *n*

rigid /ríjjid/ *adj* **1.** FIRM AND STIFF not bending or easily moved into a different shape or position ○ *lengths of rigid plastic pipe* **2.** INFLEXIBLE applied or carried out strictly, with no allowances or exceptions ○ *a rigid set of rules* **3.** INFLEXIBLY ADHERED TO kept unchanged and strictly adhered to ○ *rigid opinions* **4.** REFUSING TO CHANGE unwilling to change or adapt behaviour, opinions, or attitudes ○ *Despite arguments to the contrary, she remained rigid in her stand.* [15C. < Latin *rigidus* < *rigere* 'be stiff'] —**rigidity** /ri jíddəti/ *n* —**rigidly** *adv* —**rigidness** *n*

rigid designator *n* in philosophy, a name that stands for the same thing in every possible world as opposed to a description that could stand for somebody or something else in some possible world

rigidify /ri jíddi fī/ (**-fies, -fying, -fied**) *vti* to become stiff and inflexible, or cause something to become stiff and inflexible

rigid inflatable boat *n* a medium-sized motor-powered boat with a standard boat-shaped hull, the lower section of which is made of a rigid material while the upper section consists of an inflatable flotation collar

rigmarole /rígmərōl/ *n* **1.** an irritating, tedious, or confusing sequence of tasks, especially tasks that seem unnecessary or absurd **2.** a tediously long, complicated, or unhelpful explanation [Mid-18C. Probably alteration of *ragman roll*, parchment scroll used in the gambling game of *ragman*]

ORIGIN A *ragman roll* was a parchment scroll used in a medieval gambling game. The roll had things such as names written on it, with pieces of string attached to them, and participants had to select a string at random. The word *ragman* may have been a contraction of *ragged man*, perhaps in allusion to the appearance of the scroll, with all its bits of string hanging from it. *Ragman roll* eventually came to be used for any list or catalogue, and *ragman* itself denoted a 'long rambling discourse' in 16th-century Scottish English – a meaning that seems to have transferred itself eventually to ***rigmarole***.

rigor¹ /ríggər/ *n* **1.** RIGIDITY OF BODY stiffness and lack of response to stimuli in body organs or tissues **2.** SUDDEN FEELING OF CHILLINESS an abrupt attack of shivering and coldness, typically marking a rise in body temperature, e.g. at the onset of fever **3.** INERTIA IN PLANTS lack of growth and normal functions in a plant caused by unfavourable conditions [14C. < Latin (see RIGOUR)]

rigor² *n* US spelling of **rigour**

rigorism /ríggərizəm/ *n* **1.** great strictness or severity **2.** in Roman Catholic philosophy, the theory that in matters of moral choice the stricter course should be taken —**rigoristic** /ríggə rístik/ *adj*

rigor mortis /ríggər máwrtiss/ *n* the progressive stiffening of the body that occurs several hours after death as a result of the coagulation of protein in the muscles. It usually starts to wane after about 24 hours. [< Latin, 'stiffness of death']

rigorous /ríggərəss/ *adj* **1. STRICT, HARSH, OR UNRELENTING** characterized by unrelenting demands, and allowing little or no scope for variation or relaxation ○ *a rigorous training programme* **2. EXACTING** extremely precise and exacting ○ *rigorous standards of cleanliness* **3. SEVERE** experienced as severe or extreme ○ *climbing in rigorous conditions* **4.** LOGIC **PRECISE** precise and formalized ○ *a rigorous proof* —**rigorously** *adv* —**rigorousness** *n*

rigour /ríggər/ *n* **1. USE OF DEMANDING STANDARDS** the application of precise and exacting standards in the doing of something **2. SEVERITY OR HARSHNESS** unrelenting strictness or toughness in dealing with people or things and an unwillingness to make allowances **3. HARDSHIP** an experience of great hardship or difficulty (*usually used in the plural*) ○ *the rigours of life on the battlefront* **4. SEVERE WEATHER** harshness of weather or climate **5.** MED same as **rigor mortis** (*informal*) [14C. Directly or via French < Latin *rigor* 'stiffness' < *rigere* 'be stiff']

rig-out *n* (*informal*) **1.** an outfit of clothes **2.** a set of equipment

Rig-Veda /ríg váydə/ *n* a large collection of Hindu hymns dating from 2,000 BC or earlier [Late 18C. < Sanskrit *ṛgvedaḥ* < *ṛc* 'verse' + *vedaḥ* 'knowledge' (see VEDA)]

Rijeka /ri ékə/ city and port in northwestern Croatia, situated on the Gulf of Kvarner, on the Adriatic Sea. Population: 167,964 (1991).

rijsttafel /ríss taaf'l/, **rijstafel** *n* a Dutch meal of Indonesian origin based on rice with many small side dishes such as Indonesian-style curry, seafood, satay, soups, sauces, and condiments [Late 19C. < Dutch < *rijs* 'rice' + *tafel* 'table']

rikishi /ríkishi/ (*plural same*) *n* a sumo wrestler [Early 20C. < Japanese, 'strength warrior']

Riksdag /réeks dag/ *n* the parliament of Sweden [Late 19C. < Swedish < *rike* 'realm' + *dag* 'day']

rile /rīl/ (**riles, riling, riled**) *vt* **1.** to irritate somebody enough that it provokes anger (*informal; often passive*) **2.** *N Am* to stir up water or other liquid violently [Early 19C. Variant of ROIL]

Riley /ríli/ [Early 20C. < ?] ◇ **the life of Riley** a comfortable well-off life with no worries

Riley /ríli/, **Bridget** (*b.* 1931) British painter. She was a leading figure in the 1960s art movement known as op art. Full name **Riley, Bridget Louise**

rilievo *n* ARTS another spelling of **relievo**

Rilke /rílkə/, **Rainer Maria** (1875–1926) Bohemian-born German poet. The mystic lyricism and precise imagery of his verse exerted a profound influence on 20th-century poetry. His works include *Duino Elegies* and *Sonnets to Orpheus* (both 1923).

> 'We need in love to practice only this: letting each other go. For holding on comes easily; we do not need to learn it.'
> [Rainer Maria Rilke, *Requiem für eine Freundin (Requiem for a Friend)*; 1908]

rill /ril/ *n* **1. STREAM** a little stream or brook **2. GROOVE IN SOIL** a small channel cut in soil **3.** *also* **rille TRENCH ON MOON** a long narrow valley on the Moon's surface **4. GARDEN FEATURE** an artificial channel, often a straight and narrow one, along which water is made to flow, forming a water feature in a garden ■ *vt* (**rills, rilling, rilled**) **FORM CHANNELS IN FIELD** to form small channels in a ploughed field as a result of the runoff of rainwater [Mid-16C. < Low German *rille* < Indo-European, 'run']

rillet /rillit/ *n* **1.** a little brook or stream **2.** a short narrow valley on the Moon's surface

rillettes /ri léts/ *n* seasoned pork or goose cooked in its own fat until very tender and potted as a type of soft spreadable pâté (*takes a singular or plural verb*) [Late 19C. < French, 'small pieces of pork' < *rille* 'piece of pork', variant of *reille* 'board' < Latin *regula* 'straight stick, standard']

rim /rim/ *n* **1. OUTER EDGE OF SOMETHING CIRCULAR** an outer edge, often slightly raised, that runs along the outside of something curved or circular **2. PART AROUND WHEEL'S EDGE** the curved outer edge of a wheel of a motor vehicle or bicycle **3. PART OF GLASSES FRAME** a usually curved part that holds and forms an edge to lenses in a pair of glasses **4. HOOP FOR BASKETBALL NET** the metal hoop to which a basketball net is attached **5. LIMIT** the farthest limit of something (*literary*) ○ *a novel that probes the rim of human imagination* ■ *vt* (**rims, rimming, rimmed**) **FORM OUTER EDGE** to form an edge, usually a slightly raised edge, along the edge of something curved or circular [Old English *rima* 'border, coast' < ?] —**rimless** *adj* —**rimmed** *adj*

rimaye /ri máy/ *n* GEOG same as **bergschrund** [Early 20C. < French, 'group of fissures' < Latin *rima* (see RIMOSE)]

Rimbaud /rámb ō/, **Arthur** (1854–91) French poet. Although he stopped writing at only 19 years of age, his poems were an important influence upon symbolism. Full name **Rimbaud, Jean Nicholas Arthur**

> 'I have bathed in the Poem / Of the Sea, immersed in stars, and milky, / Devouring the green azures.'
> [Arthur Rimbaud, *Le Bateau ivre (The Drunken Boat)*; 1871]

rim brake *n* a brake that acts on the rim of a wheel

rime[1] /rīm/ *n* a thin coating of frost formed on cold objects exposed to fog or cloud ■ *vt* (**rimes, riming, rimed**) to cover something with a thin frost or with something resembling it (*often passive*) [Old English *hrīm* < Germanic] —**rimy** *adj*

rime[2] /rīm/ LITERAT (*archaic*) *n* same as **rhyme** ■ *vti* (**rimes, riming, rimed**) same as **rhyme** *v* [Early variant]

rime riche /reém reésh/ *n* the use of rhyme in which stressed syllables or words are identical in pronunciation, as in 'weigh' and 'away' [< French, 'rich rhyme']

rimfire /rím fīr/ *adj* describes a firearm designed for or using a cartridge with its primer located in the rim of the base, rather than in the centre

Rimini /rímməni/ city and port in Forlì Province, Emilia-Romagna Region, northern Italy, on the Adriatic Sea. Population: 128,656 (2001).

rimose /rī mṓss/ *adj* covered with cracks, fissures, or crevices [Early 18C. < Latin *rimosus* < *rima* 'fissure' < Indo-European, 'to scratch'] —**rimosely** *adv* —**rimosity** /rī móssəti/ *n*

Rimouski /ri mo͝oski/ town in Canada, in Quebec State, on the St Lawrence River, northeast of Quebec City. Population: 35,561 (2001).

rimrock /rím rok/ *n* a layer of rock that forms a vertical boundary to a plateau, valley, or deposit of gravel

Rimsky-Korsakov /rímski káwssə kof/, **Nikolay** (1844–1908) Russian composer. He was renowned as a consummate orchestrator. His works, often inspired by Russian folk music, include *Scheherazade* (1888). Full name **Rimsky-Korsakov, Nikolay Andreyevich**

rimu /reé moo/ *n* TREES same as **red pine** (sense 2) [Mid-19C. < Maori]

rind /rīnd/ *n* **1. TOUGH OUTSIDE LAYER OF FRUIT** the thick tough outer skin of a fruit **2. HARD OUTER LAYER OF FOOD** a tough outer protective layer of a food product such as a cheese **3. BARK** the bark of a tree or bush [Old English *rind(e)* 'something torn off' < Indo-European, 'to tear']

rinderpest /ríndər pest/ *n* a sometimes fatal viral disease mainly affecting cattle, sheep, and goats that occurs chiefly in central Africa and Asia and is marked by fever, haemorrhage, and diarrhoea. Animals can be vaccinated against rinderpest, and importation of animals from affected regions is strictly controlled. [Mid-19C. < German < *Rinder* 'cattle' + *Pest* 'plague']

rinforzando /reén fawr tsándō/ *adj, adv* loud and with emphasis (*used as a musical direction*) [Early 19C. < Italian, 'getting stronger']

ring[1] /ring/ *n* **1. BAND** a durable circular band of something, especially a small band made of a particular material or for some special use **2. CIRCULAR PIECE OF JEWELLERY** a band, usually made of precious metal and often engraved or mounted with gemstones, worn as an ornament, especially round a finger **3. ENCIRCLING MARK** an outline, mark, or figure in the shape of a circle (*often used in the plural*) **4. CIRCLE** a circular arrangement of people or objects ○ *a ring of chairs* **5. CIRCULAR MOTION** a movement of steps, especially by people skipping or dancing, that goes round in a continuous circle ○ *dancing in a ring* **6. ROUND COOKING SURFACE** a circular device on a stove designed to stand a pan on so that heat may be turned on and adjusted for cooking **7. GROUP OF PEOPLE OPERATING DISHONESTLY** an organized group of people who work together in a dishonest or unethical way ○ *a gambling ring* **8. CIRCULAR AREA FOR PERFORMANCE** a round stage or piece of ground, usually surrounded by seating, on which a spectator event such as a circus or a theatrical performance takes place ○ *a small circus of only one ring* **9. PLATFORM FOR BOXING OR WRESTLING** a raised square roped platform on which a boxing or wrestling match takes place **10. BOXING** the sport of boxing ○ *choose the ring as a career* **11.** SPORTS same as **bullring** **12. COMPETITION** a competition or contest, especially a political one ○ *still debating whether to enter the ring* **13. BETTING ENCLOSURE** an enclosed area in which bets are taken at a racecourse **14.** AGRIC **ENCLOSURE FOR LIVESTOCK AT FAIR** an enclosure at a market or agricultural show in which livestock are shown, paraded, or auctioned **15.** ASTRON **BAND OF MATTER CIRCLING PLANET** a band of dust, particles, and small bodies revolving around a planet. Such bands are known to circle Saturn, Jupiter, Uranus, and Neptune. **16.** TREES same as **growth ring** **17. TURN OF SPIRAL** a single turn of a spiral **18.** CHEM **CLOSED LOOP OF ATOMS** a collection of bound atoms represented graphically in cyclic form **19.** MATHS **SET OF MATHEMATICAL ELEMENTS** a set of elements that is associative under multiplication and distributive under addition **20.** MATHS **SPACE BETWEEN CIRCLES** a space between two concentric circles ■ **rings** *npl* **GYMNASTIC APPARATUS** a pair of metal rings that are suspended from a ceiling and used to perform gymnastic routines ■ *vt* (**rings, ringing, ringed**) **1. ENCIRCLE SOMETHING** to form a circle, or move in a circle, around something (*often passive*) ○ *We were ringed by the herd of cattle.* **2. DRAW CIRCLE ROUND SOMETHING** to draw or mark a circle round something such as a word or number **3. IDENTIFY ANIMAL WITH TAG** to attach a ring-shaped tag to an animal, especially to the leg of a bird, for subsequent identification **4.** FORESTRY same as **girdle**[1] *v* (sense 2) [Old English *hring* < Indo-European, 'to curl'] ◇ **run rings around somebody** to be effortlessly superior in intelligence, skill, or performance to somebody else (*informal*)

SPELLCHECK ring or **wring**? Do not confuse the spelling of *ring* and *wring*, which sound similar. ***Ring***, the more common of the two words, is used as a noun or verb referring to something circular (as in *a diamond ring on her finger, ring the correct answer*) or to the sound of a bell: *The telephone is ringing. His story had a familiar ring.* ***Wring*** means 'twist or extract forcefully', as in *wring the wet towels, wringing his hands in despair, wring the truth out of her.*

CULTURAL NOTE *The Ring of the Nibelung*, a series of musical dramas by German composer Richard Wagner. Based on Teutonic legends, this massive tetralogy — *The Rhinegold* (1869), *The Valkyrie* (1870), *Siegfried* (1876), and *The Twilight of the Gods* (1876) — a full performance of which lasts up to 15 hours, recounts the complex chain of events triggered by the theft of a magical gold ring. It represents Wagner's most successful attempt to create a new form of theatre in which poetic drama is set to a musical score unified by recurring themes or leitmotifs.

ring[2] /ring/ *v* (**rings, ringing, rang** /rang/, **rung** /rung/) **1.** *vti* **MAKE SOUND OF BELL** to make a metallic sound when struck or played, or cause something such as a bell to make this sound **2.** *vti* **MAKE SOUND TO ALERT SOMEBODY** to produce a continuous or regular high-pitched sound to alert somebody, or make something produce such a sound **3.** *vti* **TELEPHONE SOMEBODY** to make a telephone call to somebody ○ *He rang me to cancel the appointment.* **4.** *vi* **ECHO LOUDLY** to be full of a loud, high-pitched, or reverberating sound, especially laughter or applause ○ *The hall rang with applause.* **5.** *vi* **MAKE CALL FOR SOMETHING** to call for somebody or something by sounding a bell or buzzer ○ *You rang, sir?* **6.** *vi* **IMPRESS SOMEBODY AS SOMETHING** to

make a particular impression on somebody ○ *His excuse didn't ring true.* **7.** *vi* **HAVE SENSATION OF HIGH-PITCHED SOUNDS** to have a sensation of a repeated or continuous high-pitched sound ○ *It made my ears ring.* ■ *n* **1. ACT OF SOUNDING BELL** the act of making a bell sound **2. BELL SOUND** the sound of a bell or something like a bell **3. PHONE CALL** a call on the telephone (*informal*) ○ *She gave us a ring about noon.* **4. GENERAL IMPRESSION** a general impression made by somebody or something ○ *It had a familiar ring to it.* **5. REPEATED SOUND** a loud continuous repeated or reverberating sound **6. SET OF BELLS** a set of bells in a tower or belfry [Old English *hringan*, probably < Germanic, 'make a noise']

ring back *vti* to make a return telephone call to somebody (*informal*) ○ *I left several messages but she never rang back.*

ring in *vt* **1.** to celebrate the beginning of something by or as if by ringing bells **2.** *Aus* to substitute something fraudulently, especially a horse in a race

ring off *vi* to finish speaking on the telephone and break the connection, usually by replacing the receiver

ring out *v* **1.** *vi* to be heard loudly and clearly **2.** *vt* to celebrate the end of something by or as if by ringing bells

ring up *v* **1.** *vti* to make a telephone call to somebody **2.** *vt* to press keys on a cash register to record the amount of money being paid for something (*dated*)

ring-a-ring-a-roses /-rōziz/ *n* a young children's game in which players sing while moving round in a circle and abruptly squat when the words 'all fall down' are sung [Late 19C. < ?]

ringbark /ríng baark/ *vt* FORESTRY same as **girdle**[1] *v* (sense 2)

ring binder *n* a stiff cover with metal rings inside the spine that snap open for insertion or removal of punched loose-leaf paper

ring-bolt *n* a bolt with a ring fitted through the eye at its head

ringbone /ríng bōn/ *n* **1.** a condition of a horse's pastern bone in which bony outgrowths develop, sometimes leading to pain and lameness. It is treated with rest, medication, or surgery. **2.** a bony outgrowth characteristic of ringbone [Because the outgrowths encircle the bone]

ring buoy *n* a buoy in the shape of a ring

ring circuit *n* a wiring arrangement in which electrical power is distributed to sockets and appliances through a single loop of cable that begins and ends in a fuse box

ring dance *n* DANCE same as **round dance** (sense 1)

ringdove /ríng duv/ *n* BIRDS same as **wood pigeon**

ring-dyke *n* a system of volcanic outcrops of magma (**dykes**) that form a circular structure

ringed /ringd/ *adj* **1. WEARING RING** wearing one or more rings **2. ENCIRCLED** encircled by a ring **3. HAVING MARKS THAT FORM RING** having markings that form a ring round the neck, bill, or other body part

ringed seal *n* a seal that has a dark greyish coat with lighter markings that encircle the body. Native to: Arctic and subarctic regions. Latin name: *Pusa hispida*.

ringent /rínjənt/ *adj* having an opening bordered by parts resembling the lips of a gaping mouth, as in the flower of an antirrhinum [Mid-18C. < Latin *ringent-*, present participle of *ringi* 'gape']

ringer[1] /ríngər/ *n* **1. SOMETHING THROWN AT AND ENCIRCLING PEG** a quoit thrown skilfully so that it encircles a peg or stake **2.** *Aus* **DROVER** a man who looks after the livestock on a farm, especially somebody whose job is to move herds or flocks of animals from one place to another **3.** *Aus* **FASTEST SHEARER** the fastest shearer in a shed **4.** *Aus* **FASTEST PERSON** the fastest or best person at something [Late 17C. < RING[1]]

ringer[2] /ríngər/ *n* **1.** somebody who rings a bell **2.** *N Am* somebody or something fraudulently substituted in a competition (*informal*) [15C. < RING[2]]

Ringer's solution /ríngərz-/, **Ringer solution** *n* a solution of inorganic salts used to sustain cells, tissues, or organs outside the body [Late 19C. After Sydney *Ringer* (1834–1910), British physician]

ring-fence *vt* **1. SPECIFY USE OF MONEY** to specify that money be used for a specific purpose **2. ENCLOSE SOMETHING WITH RING-FENCE** to erect a fence around an area, completely encircling it ■ *n* **1. AGREEMENT RESTRICTING USE OF MONEY** an agreement in which money is reserved for a specific purpose **2. FENCE ENCLOSING AREA** a fence that encircles a large area or a whole estate within one enclosure

ring finger *n* the third finger of the hand, especially the left hand, on which an engagement or wedding ring is traditionally worn

ringgit /ríng git/ *n* the main unit of currency of Malaysia. See table at **currency** [Mid-20C. < Malay]

ringhals /ríng halss/ (*plural same* or **-halses**) *n* a snake related to the cobra that has a small rough-skinned black or brown body and can spit jets of venom from its fangs at an aggressor. Native to: southern Africa. Latin name: *Hemachatus hemachatus*. [Late 18C. < Afrikaans, 'ring-neck', from the one or two white rings across the snake's neck]

ring-in *n Aus* an outsider brought into a team or group, usually to replace somebody or make up the numbers (*informal*)

ringing /rínging/ *n* a clear, continuing, usually high-pitched sound ■ *adj* expressed in a definite, unrestrained way —**ringingly** *adv*

ringing tone *n* a sequence of paired sounds heard in a telephone receiver when a number has been dialled successfully to a phone that is not already engaged

ringleader /ríng leedər/ *n* the member of a circle or gang who organizes and encourages others, especially in unlawful or rebellious activities [Early 16C. < *lead the ring* 'go first']

ringlet /rínglət/ *n* **1. CURLY LOCK OF HAIR** a spiral curl of hair **2. BROWN EUROPEAN BUTTERFLY** a brown butterfly with dark eyespots on the wings, found in hedges, wood margins, and other shady places. Native to: southern Europe. Genus: *Erebia*. **3. SMALL RING** a small ring or circle —**ringleted** *adj*

ring main *n* a wiring circuit in which a number of outlet sockets are connected in parallel to a ring circuit which starts and finishes at a mains supply point

ringmaster /ríng maastər/ *n* **1.** a presider over a circus show who announces and comments on performances **2.** somebody who starts, maintains, or is responsible for verifying the links on a web ring

Ring Nebula *n* a ring-shaped nebula in the constellation Lyra

ring-necked /ríng nek/, **ringneck** *adj* with markings resembling a ring round the neck in a colour that contrasts with adjacent feathers, scales, or hair

ring-necked pheasant *n* a pheasant widely introduced to the United States and Europe as a game bird, the male of which has a white neck collar, a red head, and lustrous coppery-red and green plumage. Native to: Asia. Latin name: *Phasianus colchicus*.

ringneck snake, **ring-necked snake** *n* a small non-venomous snake that has a yellowish or orange neck band. Native to: North America. Genus: *Diadophis*.

ring ouzel *n* BIRDS same as **ouzel**

ring-porous *adj* describes a tree or wood with annual rings marked by prominent bands of large pores. These rings are readily apparent when a cross section of a trunk or branch is examined.

ring-pull *n* a ring or tab of metal on the top of a drinks can that is pulled in order to open it. N Am term **pull-tab**

ring road *n* a main road designed and built to take traffic round the edge of an urban area so that the urban centre can be kept free of traffic congestion. N Am term **beltway**

ringside /ríng sīd/ *n* **1.** the row of seats or area directly in front of a boxing, wrestling, or circus ring **2.** a place or location offering a clear and close view of something (*informal*) —**ringsider** *n*

ring-spot *n* **1.** a pale or yellowish ring-shaped discoloration occurring in plants infected with a virus disease **2.** a fungus disease affecting members of the cabbage family, with brown spots appearing on the leaves

ringtail /ríng tayl/ *n* **1.** a ring-tailed mammal, especially a member of the family that includes the cacomistle and raccoon. Family: Procyonidae. **2.** ZOOL same as **ringtail possum**

ring-tailed *adj* with a tail encircled by coloured bands or markings in a colour that contrasts with adjacent feathers, scales, or hair

ring-tailed lemur *n* a lemur with a grey coat and a long tail with black and white bands. Latin name: *Lemur catta*.

ringtail possum *n* an opossum with a curly-tipped striped tail that it uses for grasping branches and carrying objects. Native to: Australasia, New Guinea. Family: Pseudocheiridae.

ringtone /ríng tōn/ *n* the sound that notifies somebody of an incoming call on a mobile phone, e.g., a series of beeps or a musical tune

ringworm /ríng wurm/ *n* a fungal disease of the skin, scalp, or nails in which intensely itchy ring-shaped patches develop. Infection is transmitted to humans from pets or livestock, or from infected bedding.

rink /ringk/ *n* **1. AREA OF ICE USED FOR SPORTS** a smooth, enclosed, and often artificially prepared ice surface used for ice-skating, ice hockey, or curling **2. SURFACE USED FOR ROLLER-SKATING** a smooth, enclosed, usually wooden surface used for roller- or in-line skating **3. BUILDING FOR ICE SPORTS** a building or arena in which ice-skating, ice hockey, or curling takes place **4. PART OF BOWLING GREEN FOR MATCH** an area of a bowling green on which a single match takes place **5. PLAYING SIDE** a team of players in curling, bowls, or quoits [14C. < ?]

rinky-dink /ríngki dingk/ *adj N Am* (*informal*) **1. OUT-OF-DATE** broken down or no longer useful **2. OLD-FASHIONED** old-fashioned or outmoded **3. INSIGNIFICANT** small and insignificant [Late 19C. < ?]

rinse /rinss/ *vt* (**rinses, rinsing, rinsed**) **1. LIGHTLY CLEAN SOMETHING IN LIQUID** to wash something lightly by dipping it in a liquid, especially clean water, or by running liquid over it **2. FLUSH MOUTH WITH WATER** to flush the mouth or teeth with clean water **3. DIP SOMETHING INTO DYE** to dip fabrics or garments into a dye solution ■ *n* **1. GENTLE WASH** the act of washing something lightly by running a liquid, usually clean water, over or around it **2. COSMETIC TREATMENT FOR HAIR** a solution that is applied to somebody's wet hair to alter or enhance its colour or condition temporarily **3. CLEANSING LIQUID** a liquid, usually water or a water-based solution, used to wash away something lightly [13C. < Old French *reincier*] —**rinsable** *adj* —**rinser** *n* —**rinsible** *adj*

rinsing /rínssing/ *n* the process or action of washing something quickly, gently, or finally in clean water or a cleaning solution

Rio de Janeiro /rée ō də zhə néer ō, -day-, -di-/ city and port in Brazil, in the southeast of the country. It is the capital of Rio de Janeiro State, and the former capital of the country. Population: 5,857,904 (2000).

Río de la Plata /rée ō də la pláatə/ ♦ **Plate, River**

Rio Grande /rée ō gránd, -grándi/ river of North America, rising in Colorado, flowing through New Mexico and along the Texas-Mexico boundary, and emptying into the Gulf of Mexico. Length: 3,100 km/1,900 mi.

Rioja /ri ōhə, ri ókhə/ *n* a dry red or white wine with a distinctive flavour, produced in northern Spain [Early 20C. After a district in N Spain]

Río Muni /rée ō mòoni/ mainland region of Equatorial Guinea, in western-central Africa. Population: 240,804 (1983). Area: 26,017 sq. km/10,045 sq. mi.

riot /rī ət/ *n* **1. VIOLENT DISTURBANCE** a public disturbance during which a group of angry people becomes noisy and out of control, often damaging property and acting violently. In law, a riot is typically defined as a group of three or more persons disturbing the public peace for private purposes. **2. GREAT DISPLAY** a spectacular visual display **3. SOMETHING EXTREMELY ENJOYABLE** a social occasion, event, or experience that people enjoy in a wild, noisy, and

energetic way (*informal*) **4. FUNNY PERSON OR EVENT** an extremely amusing person or event (*informal*) **5. UNCONTROLLED WAY OF LIFE** behaviour that shows complete lack of control, especially financially or sexually (*archaic*) ■ *vi* (**-ots, -oting, -oted**) **1. CAUSE PUBLIC DISTURBANCE** to get out of control and act in an unruly, violent, and destructive way, especially so as to cause a public disturbance **2. BE WILD AND SELF-INDULGENT** to behave with a complete lack of personal restraint, especially in financial or sexual matters (*archaic*) [12C. < Old French, 'quarrel' < *rioter* 'to quarrel'] —**rioter** *n* ◇ **read (somebody) the riot act** to reprimand somebody severely for doing something, often including a threat of punishment if the offending behaviour does not stop ◇ **run riot 1.** to behave in a wild and uncontrolled way **2.** to grow in profusion

Riot Act *n* an English law, passed in 1713, providing that persons making a public disturbance had to disperse within one hour of having had the act read to them by a magistrate

riot gun *n* a short-barrelled gun used to disperse crowds. It fires plastic or rubber bullets, or CS gas cartridges.

riotous /rī́ ətəss/ *adj* **1.** loud, conspicuous, and unrestrained **2.** involved in or taking part in serious public unrest (*formal*) —**riotously** *adv* —**riotousness** *n*

riot police *n* a police reserve specially equipped for controlling a rioting crowd

riot shield *n* a large oblong transparent shield used to protect the face and upper body of a police officer attempting to disperse a crowd

rip[1] /rip/ *v* (**rips, ripping, ripped**) **1.** *vti* **TEAR OR BE TORN** to roughly tear something apart or off, or become torn in this way **2.** *vt* **USE FORCE TO REMOVE SOMETHING** to forcibly and carelessly remove something from a place where it has been firmly fixed ◦ *Most of the original features of the house were ripped out.* **3.** *vt* **TAKE SOMETHING FROM SOMEBODY** to take something from somebody, or remove somebody from a place in a way that seems unjust ◦ *families ripped from their communities* **4.** *vi* **MOVE WITH EXTREME SPEED** to move with dangerous or destructive speed ◦ *The tornado ripped through northern Nebraska.* **5.** *vt* **WOODWORK DIVIDE TIMBER LENGTHWAYS** to split or saw a piece of timber along its grain ■ *n* **1. ROUGHLY TORN PLACE** a rough tear or split **2.** same as **ripsaw** (*informal*) [14C. < ?] ◇ **let rip** to speak rapidly and without restraint, especially with a series of curses (*informal*)

SYNONYMS See *tear*[1].

rip into *vt* to attack somebody or something, especially with a sudden and damaging criticism (*informal*)
rip off *vt* (*informal*) **1.** to charge somebody an unfair price, or cheat somebody financially **2.** to rob somebody, or steal something
rip up *vt* to tear something up into pieces or strips

rip[2] /rip/ *n* **1.** an area of rough water caused by waves meeting opposing currents **2.** OCEANOG same as **rip current** [Late 18C. Probably < RIP[1]]

rip[3] /rip/ *n* (*archaic informal*) **1.** somebody considered to be corrupt and dissolute **2.** something, especially a horse, that is old and of no value [Late 18C. < ?]

RIP *abbr* rest in peace [Latin *requiescat in pace* or *requiescant in pace*]

riparian /rī́ paíri ən, ri-/ *adj* situated or taking place along or near the bank of a river ■ *n* an owner of land along a river [Mid-19C. < Latin *riparius* (see RIVER)]

ripcord /ríp kawrd/ *n* **1.** a cord that, when pulled, opens a parachute **2.** a cord used to release gas from a hot air balloon during an emergency [Early 20C. < RIP[1]]

rip curl *n* a large and powerful wave with a curling crest that is particularly good for surfers to ride on

rip current *n* a strong narrow subsurface current flowing away from shore, visible as a band of agitated water [< RIP[2]]

ripe /rīp/ (**riper, ripest**) *adj* **1. READY TO EAT** mature and ready to be picked and eaten ◦ *a ripe plum* **2. READY TO HARVEST** having developed to the stage for harvesting ◦ *fields of ripe wheat* **3. MATURE AND MELLOW** matured or aged enough to have developed the best flavour and body ◦ *ripe cheese* **4. EXACTLY READY** at the

most suitable stage of preparation or development ◦ *The occasion was ripe for asking for a pay rise.* **5. ADVANCED IN YEARS** representing or constituting a long life ◦ *a ripe old age* **6. EXPERIENCED AND KNOWLEDGEABLE** showing maturity and judgment acquired by experience and study **7. FULL AND RED** full and ruddy, suggesting ripe fruit **8. SMELLY** giving off a strong and unpleasant smell, especially caused by sweat from part of the body (*informal*) **9. IMPOLITE OR LEWD** containing offensive language and sexual references (*informal*) [Old English *rīpe* < Germanic] —**ripely** *adv* —**ripeness** *n*

ripen /rī́pən/ (**-ens, -ening, -ened**) *vti* **1.** to become ripe for eating or harvesting, or make a fruit or crop ripe **2.** to become fully developed, mature, or ready, or make something fully developed, mature, or ready (*often passive*) —**ripener** *n*

ripieno /ríppi áyn ō/ *n* in a baroque concerto, the full ensemble, as contrasted with the soloist or group of soloists (**concertino**) [Mid-18C. < Italian, 'filled up' < *pieno* 'full']

rip-off *n* (*informal*) **1. UNFAIRLY PRICED ITEM** something that is not worth the price asked or paid **2. ACT OF BEING DISHONESTLY TREATED** an act or example of being cheated, tricked, or exploited **3. CHEAP COPY** a cheap imitation of a prestigious product [< RIP[1]]

Ripon /ríppən/ city in North Yorkshire, England, on the River Ure. Population: 13,806 (1991).

riposte /ri póst/ *n* **1.** a quick or witty reaction to something, usually spoken **2.** in fencing, a quick deft thrust made after parrying the lunge of an opponent [Early 18C. Via French < Italian *risposta*, past participle of *rispondere* 'respond' < Latin *respondere* (see RESPOND)]

SYNONYMS See *answer*.

ripper /ríppər/ *n* **1. MURDERER USING KNIFE** a murderer who uses a knife to kill and mutilate people (*informal*) **2.** *Aus* **EXCELLENT THING** something or somebody outstandingly good (*informal*) ◦ *a ripper of a shot* **3. PROGRAM FOR COPYING DIGITAL MUSIC** a program used to copy digital music from a compact disc onto a computer before converting it into a format storable as a computer file ■ *interj* *Aus* **EXPRESSES ENTHUSIASM** used to express enthusiasm or delight (*informal*) [Early 17C. < RIP[1]]

ripping /rípping/ *n* the process of copying digitized music as a stored computer file ■ *adj* wonderful or excellent (*dated informal*) [Mid-16C. < RIP[1]] —**rippingly** *adv*

ripple[1] /rípp'l/ *v* (**-ples, -pling, -pled**) **1.** *vti* **HAVE OR GIVE SOMETHING WAVY FLOW** to flow or move in tiny gentle waves, or disturb a surface with such waves ◦ *a breeze rippled the water* **2.** *vti* **APPEAR WAVY ON SURFACE** to have a wavy appearance or form, or make something have a wavy appearance or form ◦ *shiny black rippled hair* **3.** *vi* **MAKE LAPPING SOUND** to make a gentle lapping sound **4.** *vi* **RISE AND FALL IN VOLUME** to pass through a group or place, increasing and decreasing in loudness ◦ *Laughter rippled round the room.* ■ *n* **1. TINY WAVE OR SERIES OF WAVES** a small wave or series of gentle waves across a surface **2. GENTLE WAVY SHAPE OR MARK** something that resembles a ripple in its smooth undulating shape **3. SOUND RISING AND FALLING IN VOLUME** a sound that passes through a group or place, increasing and decreasing in loudness ◦ *a ripple of scorn* **4.** GEOL **SHALLOW BROKEN RIVER WATER** an area of shallow water in a river broken by rocks or sand bars **5.** ELEC **OSCILLATION OF CURRENT** a small oscillation of electrical current ■ **ripples** *npl* **CONSEQUENCES** a series of repercussions or consequences ◦ *The ripples of the sector's downturn continue to be felt.* ■ *adj* FOOD **WITH SECOND FLAVOUR MIXED IN** with a second flavour partly combined or marbled through ◦ *raspberry ripple ice cream* [Late 17C. < ?] —**rippler** *n* —**ripply** *adj*

ripple[2] /rípp'l/ *vt* (**-ples, -pling, -pled**) to remove seeds from a plant with a comb-shaped tool ■ *n* a comb-shaped tool used to remove seeds from a plant [Mid-17C. < ?]

ripple effect *n* a spreading series of effects or consequences caused by a single event [< RIPPLE[1] from the ripples that spread across the surface of a pool when something is dropped into the water]

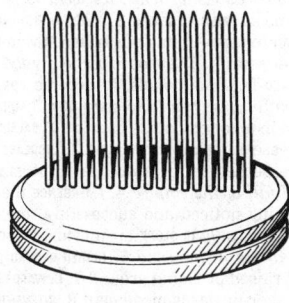
ripple

ripple mark *n* a series of small wavy ridges created in sand or silt by wind or water. Ripple marks can be preserved in sedimentary rocks. [< RIPPLE[1]] —**ripple-marked** *adj*

rippling /rípp'ling/ *adj* **1. IN SMOOTH GENTLE WAVES** moving in or resembling the flow of small gentle waves **2. SOUNDING LIKE SOFTLY FLOWING WATER** moving with a gentle lapping sound ■ *n* **SOUND OF SOFTLY FLOWING WATER** the lapping sound of gently flowing water [Mid-17C. < RIPPLE[1]]

riprap /ríp rap/ *n* **1. SOMETHING BUILT OF LOOSE STONE** a stabilizing foundation or embankment of loose and broken stone in or along the edge of water **2. STONE USED IN RIPRAP** loose and broken stone used for riprap ■ *vt* (**-raps, -rapping, -rapped**) **CONSTRUCT SOMETHING WITH BROKEN STONE** to build or stabilize something with riprap [Late 16C. Doubling of RAP[1]]

rip-roaring /-ráwring/ *adj* boisterous, lively, and exciting (*informal*) [Mid-19C. < RIP[1] + UPROARIOUS] —**rip-roaringly** *adv*

ripsaw /ríp saw/ *n* a saw with coarse teeth used to cut along the grain of wood [Mid-19C. < RIP[1]]

ripsnorter /ríp snawrtər/ *n* *N Am* something or somebody exceptionally impressive (*informal*) [Mid-19C. < RIP[1] + slang *snorter* 'something big and impressive']

ripstop /ríp stop/ *adj* woven with extra threads at regular intervals to make tearing less likely ◦ *ripstop nylon* [Late 20C. < RIP[1]]

riptide /ríp tīd/ *n* same as **rip current** [< RIP[2]]

Ripuarian /ríppyoo aíri ən/ *adj* relating to the Frankish people who lived beside the Rhine in the 4th century BC [Late 18C. < medieval Latin *Ripuarius*]

RISC /risk/ *abbr* reduced-instruction-set computer

rise /rīz/ *v* (**rises, rising, rose** /rōz/, **risen** /rízz'n/) **1.** *vi* **STAND UP** to assume a standing or nearly vertical position after sitting, kneeling, or lying **2.** *vi* **ASCEND** to go up to a higher position or location ◦ *Disturbed by our footsteps, the birds rose above the trees.* **3.** *vi* **GET HIGHER** to gain a greater height or level ◦ *After heavy rains the river rose dangerously.* **4.** *vi* **GROW LARGER** to increase in amount, degree, or quantity ◦ *Prices are rising.* **5.** *vi* **ACHIEVE GREATER SOCIAL PROMINENCE** to achieve higher wealth, status, or importance ◦ *rose through the ranks* **6.** *vi* **EXTEND UPWARDS** to become elevated, or extend upwards ◦ *The church tower rose above the village.* **7.** *vi* **GROW LOUDER OR MORE INTENSE** to increase in volume or intensity of sound ◦ *Their voices rose.* **8.** *vi* **INTENSIFY EMOTIONALLY** to become emotionally more intense or powerful ◦ *Tempers were rising.* **9.** *vi* **DEVELOP** to develop or intensify, especially until a particular state is reached ◦ *When we woke, the wind had risen.* **10.** *vi* **SWELL** to swell and puff out, e.g. in the manner of dough containing yeast ◦ *The bread is rising.* **11.** *vi* **REBEL OR REVOLT** to make an organized rebellion against something or somebody ◦ *The entire region rose up against the authorities in protest.* **12.** *vi* **END MEETING** to adjourn after a meeting or assembly **13.** *vi* **BECOME ERECT** to become stiff and erect ◦ *felt the hairs rise on the back of his neck* **14.** *vi* **ORIGINATE** to have an origin or beginning ◦ *The stream rises a few miles back.* **15.** *vi* **GROW** to spring up or grow **16.** *vi* **BECOME APPARENT** to become visible or apparent ◦ *Suddenly Africa rose before the astonished sailors' eyes.* **17.** *vi* CONSTR **BE BUILT** to become larger during the process of building **18.** *vi* **GET UP IN MORNING** to get out of bed, especially in the morning **19.** *vi* ASTRON **APPEAR IN SKY** to appear above the horizon

○ *The sun was rising when we went to bed.* **20.** *vt* NAUT same as **raise** *v* (sense 27) **21.** *vi* FISHING **MOVE UP TO TAKE BAIT** to move up to the surface of water to take an angler's bait ○ *The trout rose to my fly.* **22.** *vi* **BE RESURRECTED** in some beliefs, to become resurrected after death ○ *rise from the dead* ■ *n* **1. INCREASE** an increase in amount ○ *a rise in prices* **2. SALARY INCREASE** an increase in salary or wages **3. INCREASE IN STATUS** an increase in wealth, status, or importance ○ *the rise and fall of the empire* **4. EMERGENCE** the process of becoming noticed and successful ○ *the rise of a new talent* **5. UPWARD SLOPE** an upward slope or gradient ○ *a rise in the road* **6. HIGHER GROUND** a hill or piece of raised or rising ground **7. UPWARDS MOVEMENT** an ascent or upwards movement **8. INTENSIFICATION** an increase in degree, intensity, or force ○ *a rise in her fever* **9. INCREASE OF SOUND** an increase in loudness or pitch **10. HEIGHT** the vertical extent of something **11.** ASTRON **APPEARANCE IN SKY** the appearance of the Sun, Moon, or other astronomical object above the horizon **12. ORIGIN** a beginning or origin of something **13. REBELLION** a rebellion against authority **14.** CLOTHING **DISTANCE BETWEEN CROTCH AND WAIST** the length between the crotch and the waist of a pair of trousers **15.** FISHING **APPEARANCE ON WATER SURFACE** the appearance of something, especially a number of feeding fish, at the surface of the water ○ *There was a good rise of trout this evening.* [Old English *rīsan* < Germanic] ◇ **give rise to something** to cause something ◇ **take** *or* **get a rise out of somebody** to produce a desired response, usually anger or annoyance, by teasing or taunting somebody (*informal*)

rise above *vt* to overcome something unpleasant by not letting it become too important

rise to *vt* (*informal*) **1.** to behave well in response to a challenge or difficulty ○ *rose to the occasion* **2.** to react to something with anger or excitement

riser /rīzər/ *n* **1. SOMEBODY WHO RISES FROM BED** somebody who gets out of bed at a particular time ○ *We are late risers at the weekend.* **2. HEIGHT OF STEP** the vertical part of a step or stair **3.** CONSTR **VERTICAL PIPE** a vertical pipe, duct, or conduit **4. SOMEBODY RISING** somebody who or something that rises

risible /rízzəb'l/ *adj* **1.** causing or capable of causing laughter **2.** able or inclined to laugh (*formal*) [Mid-16C. < late Latin *risibilis* < Latin *ris-*, past participle of *ridere* 'laugh'] —**risibility** /rízzi bílləti/ *n* —**risibly** *adv*

rising /rīzing/ *adj* **1. GETTING MORE IMPORTANT** becoming increasingly respected or significant in an occupation or activity **2. BECOMING POWERFUL** becoming more influential and powerful **3. GETTING HIGHER** going up or becoming higher ■ *adv* **CLOSE TO AGE** getting close to a particular age (*dated informal*) ○ *rising sixty* ■ *n* **1. UPRISING** a rebellion or revolt **2. SOMETHING GETTING HIGHER** something that rises in height **3. UPWARDS MOVEMENT** the process of moving upwards or to a higher level **4. ACTION OF STANDING UP** the act of assuming a standing or nearly vertical position after sitting, kneeling, or lying **5. LEAVENING PROCESS** the process of leavening in bread

rising damp *n* moisture that is absorbed from the ground into walls, resulting in structural damage

rising diphthong *n* a diphthong in which the second of two sounds has more stress or sonority than the first

rising rhythm *n* a rhythmic pattern produced by a succession of metrical feet, each foot having an accented syllable preceded by one or more syllables that are unaccented

rising trot *n* a horse-riding technique used at the trot, in which the rider rises from the saddle every second beat

risk /risk/ *n* **1. CHANCE OF SOMETHING GOING WRONG** the danger that injury, damage, or loss will occur **2. HAZARD** somebody or something likely to cause injury, damage, or loss **3.** INSUR **CHANCE OF LOSS TO INSURER** the probability of loss to an insurer, or the amount that an insurer is in danger of losing **4.** FIN **POSSIBILITY OF INVESTMENT LOSS** the possibility of loss in an investment or speculation **5. STATISTICAL ODDS OF DANGER** the statistical chance of danger from something, especially from the failure of an engineered system ■ *vt* (**risks, risking, risked**) **1. ENDANGER SOMEBODY OR SOMETHING** to expose somebody or something to harm, danger, or loss **2. INVITE BAD CONSEQUENCE** to incur the chance of something harmful, dangerous, or detrimental ○ *risked imprisonment by their action* [Mid-17C. Via French *risque* < obsolete Italian *rischo* < *rischiare* 'run into danger'] —**risker** *n* —**riskless** *adj* —**risky** *adj* ◇ **at risk 1.** in danger of injury, damage, or loss ○ *needlessly putting lives at risk* **2.** SOC SCI in danger of being harmed or of harming others ◇ **run** *or* **take a risk** to do something that involves the possibility of injury, damage, or harm

risk arbitrage *n* the technique of using price discrepancies in a market in order to profit, e.g. by buying shares in a company being acquired while selling shares in the acquiring company —**risk arbitrageur** *n*

risk-averse *adj* **1.** wanting to avoid risk in an investment or speculation **2.** having an investment strategy that is designed to preserve capital

risk-benefit *adj* studying or testing whether the benefits of a procedure, process, or treatment outweigh the risks involved

risk capital *n* FIN same as **venture capital**

risk factor *n* a feature of somebody's habits, genetic makeup, or personal history that increases the probability of disease or harm to health

risk management *n* the profession or technique of determining, minimizing, and preventing accidental loss in a business, e.g. by taking safety measures and buying insurance

risk society *n* a society exposed to harm as a consequence of human activities such as environmental damage or nuclear accidents rather than naturally occurring events such as earthquakes or volcanic eruptions

Risorgimento /ri sáwrji méntō/ *n* the movement for, and period of, political unification in Italy beginning about 1750 and culminating in the occupation of Rome by Italian troops in 1870 [Late 19C. < Italian, 'resurgence']

risotto /ri zóttō/ *n* a dish of short-grained rice and other ingredients cooked in stock [Mid-19C. < Italian < *riso* (see RICE)]

risqué /rísk ay, ree skáy/ *adj* alluding to sexual conduct in a way that verges on indecency or bad taste [Mid-19C. < French, past participle of *risquer* 'risk' < *risque* (see RISK)]

Riss /riss/ *n* one of the four major glacial periods in Europe, at its peak 150,000 years ago [Early 20C. After the River *Riss* in Germany, where signs of the glaciation were observed]

rissole[1] /ríssōl/ *n* a small fried cake of minced seasoned meat or poultry, coated with breadcrumbs [Early 18C. Via French < late Latin *russeolus* 'reddish' < Latin *russus* 'red']

rissole[2] /ríssōl/ *n Aus* same as **RSL club** (*slang*) ○ *There's a show on at the rissole tonight; shall we go?* [Alteration after RISSOLE[1]]

Risso's dolphin /ríssōz-/ *n* ZOOL same as **grampus** [Late 19C. After Giovanni Antonio *Risso* (1777–1845), Italian naturalist]

risus sardonicus /réessəss saar dónnikəss/ *n* a distorted grinning expression caused by involuntary prolonged contraction of the facial muscles, especially as a result of tetanus [< modern Latin, 'sardonic grin']

rit. *abbr* MUSIC **1.** ritardando **2.** ritenuto

ritardando /ríttaar dándō/ *adj, adv* becoming gradually slower (*used as a musical direction*) [Early 19C. < Italian, present participle of *ritardare* 'slow down' < Latin *retardare* (see RETARD)]

rite /rīt/ *n* **1. CEREMONIAL ACT** a solemn ceremony or procedure customary to a community, especially a religious group (*often used in the plural*) ○ *the rite of baptism* **2. SET PROCEDURE** a formal and established observance or practice (*often used in the plural*) ○ *rites of courtship* **3. CEREMONIAL WAY OF PROCEEDING** a system of ceremonial procedures ○ *the Roman rite* **4.** *also* **Rite** CHR **LITURGICAL PROCEDURE** a liturgy or version of a liturgy, especially of a Communion service **5.** *also* **Rite** CHR **DIVISION OF CHURCHES** a historical division of Christian churches based on their liturgies [14C. Directly or via French < Latin *ritus* < Indo-European, 'fit together']

SPELLCHECK See ***right***.

ritenuto /rítta nyóotō/ *adj, adv* played slightly slower than the rest of a piece of music (*used as a musical direction*) [Early 19C. < Italian, 'held back']

rite of passage *n* **1.** an event or act that marks a significant transition in a human life **2.** a ceremony that marks somebody's passage from one stage of life to another, e.g. from childhood to puberty or from unmarried to married life [Translation of French *rite de passage*]

ritornello /rittər néllō/ (*plural* **-los** or **-li** /-lee/) *n* **1.** a short musical passage used as an orchestral refrain between verses of a song or aria **2.** in a concerto grosso, the return of full orchestral music after a solo [Late 17C. < Italian, 'little return']

ritual /rίchoo əl/ *n* **1. ESTABLISHED FORMAL BEHAVIOUR** an established and prescribed pattern of observance, e.g. in a religion **2. PERFORMANCE OF FORMAL ACTS** the observance of actions or procedures in a set, ordered, and ceremonial way (*often used before a noun*) ○ *a ritual dance* **3. SYSTEM OF RITES** the system of set procedures and actions of a group ○ *Orthodox ritual* **4. UNCHANGING PATTERN** a pattern of actions or words followed regularly and precisely (*informal*) ○ *the weekend car-washing ritual* **5.** BIOL **SET FORM OF COMMUNICATION** a set sequence of actions that an animal uses to communicate information or to reinforce social cohesion ○ *mating rituals* **6.** PSYCHOL **REPETITIVE BEHAVIOUR** an inflexible, stylized, and often repetitive sequence of actions, e.g. repeated hand-washing, that may indicate an obsession **7. BOOK OF CEREMONIES** a book containing rites or ceremonial procedures, especially religious rites ■ *adj* **1. FOLLOWING PATTERN** done regularly and in precisely the same way each time ○ *her ritual morning exercises* **2. OF RITE** relating to or done as a ceremonial rite ○ *ritual observance* [Late 16C. < Latin *ritualis* < *ritus* (see RITE)] —**ritually** *adv*

ritual abuse *n* the physical and psychological abuse of children and adults believed by some to exist as part of supposed satanic rituals

ritualisation, etc. SOCIOL another spelling of **ritualization, etc.**

ritualism /rίchoo əlizəm/ *n* devotion or adherence to rituals

ritualistic /rίchoo ə lístik/ *adj* forming part of or adhering to a ritual —**ritualistically** *adv*

ritualization /rίchoo ə lī záysh'n/, **ritualisation** *n* **1.** the act of making something into a ritual **2.** the process in which different forms of behaviour are modified and combined to form a ritual

ritualize /rίchoo ə līz/ (**-izes, -izing, -ized**), **ritualise** (**-ises, -ising, -ised**) *v* **1.** *vt* to make a ritual of something **2.** *vi* to promote the use of rituals —**ritualized** *adj*

ritual murder *n* **1.** a human sacrifice, especially to appease a deity **2.** a murder performed in a methodical, formalized, or ritualistic way

ritz /rits/ [Early 20C. Back-formation < RITZY] ◇ **put on the ritz** to make a show of wealth and extravagance (*dated informal*)

ritzy /rítsi/ (**-ier, -iest**) *adj* expensively stylish and elegant (*informal*) [Early 20C. < *Ritz*, name given to luxurious hotels established by César *Ritz* (1850–1918), Swiss-born entrepreneur] —**ritzily** *adv* —**ritziness** *n*

riv. *abbr* river

rival /rīv'l/ *n* **1. COMPETING PERSON OR GROUP** a person or group that competes with another **2. EQUAL OR BETTER COMPETITOR** somebody or something that can equal or surpass another in a specific respect ■ *v* (**-vals, -valling, -valled**) **1.** *vt* **BETTER SOMEBODY OR SOMETHING** to equal or surpass somebody or something **2.** *vti* **COMPETE WITH SOMEBODY** to engage in competition with somebody **3.** *vt* **TRY TO BETTER SOMEBODY** to try to equal or surpass somebody or something ■ *adj* **COMPETING** in competition with somebody or something [Late 16C. < Latin *rivalis* 'using the same stream' < *rivus* 'stream'] —**rivalrous** *adj*

CULTURAL NOTE ***The Rivals***, a play (1775) by Irish dramatist Richard Brinsley Sheridan. This lively comedy of manners portrays the attempts of Captain Jack Absolute

to woo Lydia Languish, the idealistic niece and ward of Mrs Malaprop. The latter's habit of misusing similar-sounding words created one of the most memorable characters in English drama and gave rise to a new term: *malapropism*.

rivalry /rívəlri/ (*plural* **-ries**) *n* **1.** the condition or fact of competing with somebody or something **2.** an act of competitiveness

rive /rīv/ (**rives, riving, rived, rived** or **riven** /rívv'n/) *v* **1.** *vt* to tear something apart (*literary*) **2.** *vti* to split a material such as wood by striking it, or become split in this way (*archaic*) [12C. < Old Norse *rífa* < Indo-European, 'to cut']

riven /rívv'n/ *adj* torn apart (*literary*) ○ *a political party riven by dissent* [Past participle of RIVE]

WORLD'S LONGEST RIVERS

	River	Length	Location
1	Nile	[4,160 mi. / 6,695 km]	Africa
2	Amazon	[4,000 mi. / 6,400 km]	South America
3	Yangtze (Chang Jiang)	[3,900 mi. / 6,300 km]	Asia
4	Mississippi-Missouri	[3,710 mi. / 5,970 km]	North America
5	Huang He (Yellow River)	[3,395 mi. / 5,464 km]	Asia
6	Ob'-Irtysh	[3,362 mi. / 5,410 km]	Asia
7	Lena	[2,730 mi. / 4,400 km]	Asia
8	Congo	[2,718 mi. / 4,374 km]	Africa
9	Amur	[2,700 mi. / 4,345 km]	Asia
10	Mekong	[2,610 mi. / 4,200 km]	Asia
11	Niger	[2,600 mi. / 4,180 km]	Africa

river /rívvər/ *n* **1.** a natural stream of water that flows through land and empties into a body of water such as a sea or lake **2.** a large flow or stream of something (*often used in the plural*) ○ *a river of mud* [13C. Via Anglo-Norman *rivere*, Old French *rivière* < Latin *riparius* < *ripa* 'riverbank' < Indo-European, 'to cut'] ◇ **sell somebody down the river** to betray or desert somebody, usually for a selfish or mercenary motive (*informal*)

Rivera /ree vérraa/, **Diego** (1886–1957) Mexican artist.

CORBIS/Bettmann
Diego Rivera

He is known for his murals portraying Mexican social issues, influenced by Native American art.

riverbank /rívvər bangk/ *n* a piece of sloping ground at the edge of a river

river basin *n* an area of land drained by a river and its tributaries

riverbed /rívvər bed/ *n* the usually water-covered ground between the banks of a river

river blindness *n* MED same as **onchocerciasis**

riverboat /rívvər bōt/ *n* a boat built with a flat bottom or shallow draft, used on rivers

river catchment *n* GEOG same as **river basin**

river dolphin *n* a dolphin that is found in rivers and coastal waters. Family: Platanistidae.

riverfront /rívvər frunt/ *n* the property or land along the edge of a river (*often used before a noun*) ○ *a riverfront park*

riverhead /rívvər hed/ *n* the source of a river and the land surrounding it

Riverina /rívvə reénə/ region of south-central New South Wales, Australia. It is heavily irrigated and predominantly agricultural. Area: 68,658 sq. km/26,509 sq. mi.

riverine /rívvə rīn/ *adj* **1.** OF RIVER relating to or resembling a river **2.** BESIDE RIVER located or living beside a river ○ *a riverine people* **3.** OPERATING ON RIVER operating or capable of operating on a river

river red gum *n* a large eucalyptus tree with pale smooth bark and durable dark-red timber. Native to: inland waterways of Australia. Latin name: *Eucalyptus camaldulensis*.

riverside /rívvər sīd/ *n* the area of land beside a river
■ *adj* located beside a river

Riverside /rívvər sīd/ city in southwestern California, on the Santa Ana River. It is a citrus-growing centre, and is home to the University of California-Riverside. Population: 274,226 (2002 estimate).

riverweed /rívvər weed/ *n* a small many-branched freshwater plant that clings to rock with roots that function as suckers. Genus: *Podostema*.

rivet /rívvit/ *n* SHORT METAL FASTENER a fastener with a head attached to a metal shaft that is passed through a hole in a material and flattened on the other side
■ *vt* (**-ets, -eting, -eted**) **1.** FIRMLY FIX ATTENTION to fix or direct the attention completely (*informal; often passive*) ○ *Jurors appeared riveted by the testimony*. **2.** FASTEN SOMETHING WITH RIVET to fasten something using a rivet or rivets **3.** HOLD SOMEBODY'S GAZE to attract and hold onto somebody's gaze or attention firmly (*informal*) ○ *'Old Grannis dared not move, but sat rigid, his eyes riveted on his empty soup plate.'* (Frank Norris, *McTeague – A Story of San Francisco*; 1899) **4.** FIX SOMETHING FIRMLY to fix or secure something firmly [14C. < Old French < *river* 'fasten']

riveter /rívvitər/ *n* a worker or machine that joins metal plates together with rivets

riveting /rívviting/ *adj* completely fixing and holding the attention (*informal*) —**rivetingly** *adv*

~~rivetting~~ incorrect spelling of **riveting**

riviera /rívvi áirə/ *n* a coastal beach area with a warm climate and fashionable resorts [Mid-18C. < ITALIAN]

Riviera /rívvi áirə/ coastal region of southeastern France and northwestern Italy, bordering the Mediterranean Sea

rivière /rívvi áir/ *n* a necklace made of a string of precious gemstones [Mid-19C. < French (see RIVER)]

rivulet /rívvyōōlət/ *n* **1.** a small quick-flowing stream of something **2.** a small stream or river (*literary*) [Late 16C. Alteration of obsolete *riveret* < earlier form of French *riviérette*, diminutive of *rivière* (see RIVER)]

rix-dollar /ríks-/ *n* a silver coin formerly used in Denmark, the Netherlands, and Germany [Late 16C. < obsolete Dutch *rijksdaler* 'dollar of the realm']

Riyadh /reé ad, ree aád/ capital city of Saudi Arabia, located in the east-central part of the country. Population: 3,180,000 (1999).

riyal /ri aál/ *n* the main unit of currency in Qatar, Saudi Arabia, and Yemen. See table at **currency** [Mid-20C. Via Arabic < Spanish *real* (see REAL[2])]

RJ *abbr* ROADS road junction

RK *abbr* EDUC religious knowledge

RL *abbr* Rugby League

Rls *symbol* MONEY rial

rly *abbr* railway

rm *abbr* **1.** MEASURE ream **2.** room

Rm *abbr* BIBLE Romans

RM *abbr* **1.** MED Registered Midwife **2.** Royal Mail **3.** MIL Royal Marines

RMA *abbr* **1.** Royal Marine Artillery **2.** Royal Military Academy

RMB *abbr Aus* roadside mail box (*used in addresses in rural areas*)

RMD *abbr Aus* roadside mail delivery (*used in addresses in rural areas*)

r.m.m. *abbr* PHYS relative molecular mass

rms *abbr* MATHS root mean square

RMS *abbr* MAIL **1.** Royal Mail Service **2.** Royal Mail Ship

RMT *abbr* National Union of Rail, Maritime, and Transport Workers

Rn *symbol* CHEM ELEM radon

RN *abbr also* **R.N.** NAVY Royal Navy

RNA *n* a nucleic acid containing ribose found in all living cells, essential for protein synthesis. RNA also acts instead of DNA as the genetic material in some viruses. Full form **ribonucleic acid**

RNA polymerase *n* a polymerase that catalyses the synthesis of RNA

RNAS *abbr* **1.** Royal Naval Air Service(s) **2.** Royal Naval Air Station

RNase /aár en ayz, -ayss/ *n* an enzyme that splits or degrades RNA. Full form **ribonuclease**

RNA virus *n* a virus in which the core of nucleic acid consists of RNA

R'n'B, R & B *abbr* MUSIC rhythm and blues

rnd *abbr* round

RNIB *abbr* Royal National Institute for the Blind

RNLI *abbr* Royal National Lifeboat Institution

RNP *abbr* BIOCHEM ribonucleoprotein

RNR *abbr* Royal Naval Reserve

rns *abbr* CRICKET runs

RNVR *abbr* Royal Naval Volunteer Force

RNZAF *abbr* Royal New Zealand Air Force

RNZN *abbr* Royal New Zealand Navy

ro *abbr* **1.** PUBL recto **2.** ONLINE Romania (*used in Internet addresses*) See table at **domain name**

ro. *abbr* MEASURE rood

roach[1] /rōch/ (*plural same* or **roaches**) *n* **1.** a freshwater fish of the carp family with an olive-green or grey-green back and reddish fins, popular as a game fish. Native to: northern Europe. Latin name: *Rutilus rutilus*. **2.** a small sunfish resembling a European roach. Native to: eastern North America. Latin name: *Hesperoleucus symmetricus*. [12C. < Old French *roche*]

roach[2] /rōch/ *n* **1.** INSECTS same as **cockroach** (*informal*) **2.** the end of a marijuana cigarette after the rest of it has been smoked (*slang*) [Mid-19C. Shortening of COCKROACH]

roach[3] /rōch/ *n* the upward curve at the foot of a square sail ■ *vt* (**roaches, roaching, roached**) to cut a horse's mane short so that the hairs stand up [Late 18C. <?]

road /rōd/ *n* **1.** HARD TRACK FOR VEHICLES a long surfaced route broad enough for vehicles to be driven on it **2.** COURSE OF ACTION a course of action or behaviour that leads to a particular outcome ○ *the road to financial success* **3.** N England, Scotland PATH the

route to somewhere (*informal*) ○ *I went the wrong road.* ○ *Get out of my road!* **4.** MIN EXTRACT **MINE TUNNEL** a tunnel used for hauling coal or ore in a mine **5.** NAUT same as **roadstead** (*often used in the plural*) [Old English *rād* 'act of riding' < Indo-European, 'ride'] ◇ **down the road** in the future ◇ **one for the road** an alcoholic drink taken just before leaving a place (*informal*) ◇ **on the road** travelling from place to place ○ *The band have been on the road all summer.*

CULTURAL NOTE *On the Road*, a novel (1957) by US writer Jack Kerouac. A thinly disguised memoir, it describes a series of cross-country journeys undertaken by a group of people united by their quest for new experiences and disregard for traditional values. It is both an engaging chronicle of the Beat generation and a lyrical evocation of the energy and passion of youth.

roadbed /rṓd bed/ *n* a foundation of soil, cinders, or crushed rock that supports a road or railway

roadblock /rṓd blok/ *n* **1.** a temporary barrier used to stop vehicles on a road, so they can be checked or their drivers questioned by authorities **2.** a hindrance or obstacle to something

road book *n* a publication for road users showing maps and an index for all the routes in an area

road company *n* US a group of actors who tour with a show

road-fund licence *n* a disc affixed to a motor vehicle to show that its road tax has been paid (*formal*)

road hog *n* an inconsiderate motorist who obstructs traffic, especially one who refuses to let other drivers overtake or go first, or forces them to move out of the way (*informal*)

roadholding /rṓd hṓlding/ *n* the ability of a motor vehicle to remain controlled and safely positioned on the road, especially in bad conditions or on sharp corners

roadhouse /rṓd howss/ (*plural* **-houses** /-howziz/) *n* a hotel or pub located beside a main road (*dated*)

road hump *n* ROADS same as **speed bump**

roadie /rṓdi/ *n* somebody who is responsible for the equipment used by a musical or theatrical group on tour, especially a rock band —**roadie** *vi*

roadkill /rṓd kil/ *n* N Am an animal that has been killed by a motor vehicle on a road

road manager *n* somebody who organizes and supervises a performing tour for a group of musicians, especially a rock band

road map *n* **1.** a map or atlas that shows routes, mileage, and often other features of interest to travellers **2.** a plan or guide for something (*informal*) ○ *a road map for the months ahead* ○ *a road map to the Internet*

road metal *n* the cinders, crushed rock, and other materials used in the construction of roads

road movie *n* a film that depicts the adventures of a person or people who leave home and travel from place to place by road, often to find or escape from something

road pricing *n* a system for controlling road use in which drivers pay a charge to use their cars in specific situations, e.g. at peak periods

road race *n* a competitive event in which participants race on foot, bicycles, or in motorized vehicles on public roads instead of on a track — **road-race** *vi*

road racing *n* the sport of racing motor vehicles or bicycles on public roads temporarily reserved for the purpose or on racing courses resembling public roads

road rage *n* uncontrollable anger experienced by a driver in difficult road conditions, often leading to violent behaviour

roadroller /rṓd rṓlər/ *n* a machine with wide heavy wheels used to roll flat a new or repaired road

roadrunner

roadrunner /rṓd runər/ *n* a swift-running bird of the cuckoo family with streaked brown-and-white feathers, a head crest, small round wings, and a long tail. Native to: deserts of western United States, and Mexico. Latin name: *Geococcyx californianus*.

roadshow /rṓd shō/ *n* **1.** TRAVELLING BROADCAST a live open-air radio show that travels to a series of locations, usually during the summer months **2.** TRAVELLING CAMPAIGN a travelling promotional or political campaign **3.** PERFORMANCE BY TRAVELLING ACTORS a show staged by a touring company of entertainers, or the company performing such a show

roadside /rṓd sīd/ *n* an area along or bordering a road

road sign *n* a sign by the side of the road giving directions or instructions

roadstead /rṓd sted/ *n* a partly sheltered area for anchored vessels

roadster /rṓdstər/ *n* **1.** BICYCLE a bicycle designed for riding on a road **2.** N Am SPORTS CAR a small open-topped car with a single seat in front and often an additional folding seat at the back (*dated*) **3.** HORSE FOR RIDING ON ROAD formerly, a sturdy horse for riding on a road

road test *n* **1.** TEST OF VEHICLE OR TYRE PERFORMANCE a test of a motor vehicle or tyre under actual operating conditions **2.** MANUF TEST OF HOW WELL SOMETHING WORKS a series of tests to determine how well a new product or design performs during actual use **3.** N Am AUTOMOT PRACTICAL DRIVING TEST a driving test to determine whether a driver of a motor vehicle is competent to be issued a licence to drive —**road-test** *vt*

road-train *n* Aus a truck that pulls several large connected trailers, often to transport livestock or bulk goods over long distances

roadway /rṓd way/ *n* the part of a road intended to be driven on

roadwork /rṓd wurk/ *n* **1.** N Am ROADS REPAIR OF ROADS the repairing and maintaining of public roads **2.** SPORTS TRAINING EXERCISE a form of exercise consisting of long runs on roads, done especially as part of a training programme **3.** MUSIC WORK OF TOURING the activity of taking a band, especially a rock band, on a lengthy tour of performances ■ **roadworks** *npl* ROADS REPAIRS TO ROAD construction or repair work being carried out on a section of public road, or on the utilities located beneath it, creating a temporary obstruction for road users. N Am term **roadwork**

roadworthy /rṓd wurthi/ *adj* in a safe condition to be driven on public roads [Early 19C. After SEAWORTHY] — **roadworthiness** *n*

roam /rōm/ *vti* (**roams, roaming, roamed**) to move about a large area, especially without a specific purpose or definite destination ■ *n* an act of roaming [14C. < ?] —**roamer** *n*

roaming /rṓming/ *n* the use of a mobile phone outside your home country

roan /rōn/ *adj* WITH LIGHT SPECKLES IN DARK COAT having a reddish-brown, brown, or black coat speckled with white or grey hairs ■ *n* **1.** ROAN HORSE an animal, especially a horse, with a roan coat **2.** COLOURS ROAN COLOUR the colour of a roan animal **3.** INDUST FINE-GRAINED LEATHER a soft pliable sheepskin leather used in bookbinding [Early 16C. Via French < Old Spanish *roano*]

Roanoke Island /rṓ ə nōk-/ island off eastern North Carolina. Expeditions sent out by the English explorer Sir Walter Raleigh twice attempted to establish colonies. The first returned to England in 1586, the second disappeared between 1587 and 1591.

roar /rawr/ *v* (**roars, roaring, roared**) **1.** *vi* GROWL LOUDLY to make a loud growling noise (*refers to large animals*) **2.** *vti* SHOUT LOUDLY to utter a loud shout or cry, or utter something with a loud shout or cry **3.** *vi* LAUGH LOUDLY to laugh loudly and without restraint **4.** *vi* BURN NOISILY to burn noisily and intensely ○ *a roaring fire* **5.** *vi* CRASH OR BLOW LOUDLY to produce a crashing or blowing noise ○ *The storm roared through the area causing extensive damage.* **6.** *vi* PRODUCE HARSH NOISE to move or operate with a loud harsh or droning noise ○ *Jets roared overhead.* **7.** **roar yourself** *vr* BECOME SOMETHING BY ROARING to cause your voice to be in a particular condition, e.g. by shouting or cheering ○ *roared themselves hoarse* **8.** *vi* VET BREATHE NOISILY to breathe with difficulty, making a rasping or wheezing noise (*refers to horses*) ■ *n* **1.** LOUD SHOUT a loud shout or cry ○ *the roar of the fans* **2.** LOUD LAUGH a loud unrestrained laugh **3.** LOUD GROWL a loud growling noise made by a large animal, especially a lion **4.** NOISE OF FIRE a loud noise made by an intense fire **5.** CRASHING NOISE a loud crashing or blowing noise ○ *the roar of the tempest* **6.** LOUD MECHANICAL NOISE a loud harsh or droning noise of a machine or vehicle [Old English *rārian*, origin ?] —**roarer** *n*

roaring /rawring/ *adj* **1.** BURNING INTENSELY describes a fire that is burning brightly and with extreme heat **2.** VERY GREAT extreme, or extremely great or good ○ *a roaring success* ■ *n* VET BREATHING DIFFICULTIES IN HORSES noisy breathing in horses, especially when caused by loss of function of the recurrent laryngeal nerve ■ *adv* EXCEEDINGLY to an extreme degree ○ *roaring drunk* —**roaringly** *adv*

Roaring Forties *npl* the area of the ocean in the southern hemisphere lying between 40° and 50° latitude that is noted for its strong winds, storms, and difficult sailing conditions

Roaring Twenties *npl* the 1920s, thought of as being a time of exuberance, hedonism, and prosperity in contrast to the hardship of World War I

roast /rōst/ *v* (**roasts, roasting, roasted**) **1.** *vti* COOK IN OVEN to cook meat or vegetables by dry heat, usually in an oven **2.** *vti* PREPARE BY DRYING OR BROWNING to heat something until it is dry or brown, or be heated in this way ○ *roast coffee beans* **3.** *vt* METALL HEAT ORE IN FURNACE to heat ore in a furnace without fusing in order to concentrate, dehydrate, or purify it or to cause a chemical change that will facilitate smelting **4.** *vti* OVERHEAT to become too warm, or make something or somebody too warm ○ *roasting in front of the log fire* **5.** *vt* CRITICIZE SOMEBODY to subject somebody to harsh criticism (*informal*) **6.** *vt* N Am MOCK SOMEBODY to make fun of somebody (*informal*) ■ *n* **1.** OVEN-COOKED MEAT a piece of meat that is suitable for roasting, or that has been roasted **2.** N Am OPEN-AIR MEAL an outside gathering or party with food cooked on an open fire **3.** N Am CELEBRATION a gathering, party, or other celebration at which the guest of honour is the subject of speeches that alternate between praise and humorous criticism ■ *adj* OVEN-COOKED cooked by dry heat, usually in an oven [13C. < Old French *rostir* < Germanic]

roaster /rṓstər/ *n* **1.** EQUIPMENT FOR ROASTING FOOD a pan, dish, or oven for roasting food in **2.** SOMEBODY WHO ROASTS somebody who roasts something **3.** FOOD FOR ROASTING an item of food, especially a chicken, that is suitable for roasting

roasting /rṓsting/ (*informal*) *adj* VERY HOT feeling or causing somebody to feel very hot ■ *n* HARSH CRITICISM a harsh criticism of somebody ■ *adv* EXTREMELY to a high degree of temperature ○ *roasting hot*

rob /rob/ (**robs, robbing, robbed**) *v* **1.** *vt* DEPRIVE SOMEBODY ILLEGALLY to take something illegally from a person or place, especially by using force, threats, or violence **2.** *vt* DEPRIVE SOMEBODY UNFAIRLY to deprive somebody of something due, expected, or wanted ○ *Many claimed the team was robbed of another title.* **3.** *vt* DEPRIVE SOMEBODY OR SOMETHING INJURIOUSLY to deprive somebody or something of something, causing harm ○ *Excessive stress robs the body of nutrients.* **4.** *vi* COMMIT ROBBERY to commit robbery, especially ha-

bitually **5.** *vt* CRIME same as **steal** *v* (sense 1) ○ *They broke in and robbed the TV and video.* [12C. < Old French *rober* < Germanic]

robalo /róbbəlō, rŏ́-/ (*plural* **-los** or *same*) *n* a fish belonging to a large diverse family that ranges from large ocean fish such as the snook to the tiny glass fish kept in aquariums. Family: Centropomidae. [Late 19C. < Spanish *robalo*, probably < *lobo* 'wolf' < Latin *lupus*]

roband /róbbənd, rŏ́-/, **robbin** /róbbin/ *n* a piece of rope used to attach a sail to a spar [15C. Probably < Dutch *raband* < *ra* 'yard for a sail' + *band* 'band']

Robbe-Grillet /rob grée ay/, **Alain** (*b.* 1922) French novelist and screenwriter. He was one of the leading experimental writers in France in the 1950s and wrote the screenplay of *Last Year in Marienbad* (1961).

> 'The true writer has nothing to say, just a way of saying it.'
> [Alain Robbe-Grillet, *Pour un nouveau roman (Towards a New Novel)*; 1963]

Robben Island /róbb'n-/ island 12 km/7 mi. off the coast of Cape Town, used for centuries as a place for isolating the sick or confining criminals and political prisoners. During the apartheid era many political activists were imprisoned there, including Nelson Mandela, Govan Mbeki, and Walter Sisulu. It was declared a World Heritage Site by UNESCO in 1999.

robber /róbbər/ *n* somebody who commits robbery

robber baron *n* **1.** in the United States, a wealthy industrialist or businessman of the late 19th century who used unscrupulous business practices **2.** a land-holding nobleman who, in feudal Europe, habitually stole from people travelling through his lands

robber fly *n* a predatory fly that catches other insects in its long bristly legs and pierces them with its sharp mouthparts. Family: Leptidae.

robbery /róbbəri/ (*plural* **-ies**) *n* the act or an instance of illegally taking something that belongs to somebody else, especially by using force, threats, or violence

Robbia ♦ Della Robbia, Luca

robbin *n* SAILING same as **roband**

robe /rōb/ *n* **1.** DRESSING GOWN OR BATHROBE a loose garment for wear at home, especially a dressing gown or bathrobe **2.** CEREMONIAL DRESS a long loose garment worn on ceremonial occasions or as a symbol of authority, especially by the peerage, judiciary, academics, and members of the clergy (*often used in the plural*) **3.** WOMAN'S OUTER DRESS in Europe in the 17th and 18th centuries, a woman's outer dress, especially a heavy brocade or ornately decorated one worn over a plainer one **4.** *N Am* MATERIAL FOR KEEPING LEGS WARM a fur or fabric covering put over the lap to keep the lower part of the body warm ■ *vti* (**robes, robing, robed**) DRESS IN ROBE to dress somebody in a robe, or be dressed in a robe [13C. < Old French, '(clothes taken as) booty, spoil' < Germanic]

robe de chambre /rŏb də shaámbrə, rŏ́b-/ (*plural* **robes de chambre** /*pronunc. same*/) *n* CLOTHING same as **dressing gown** [Mid-18C. < French, 'chamber robe, dressing gown']

Robert I /róbbərt/ (1274–1329) king of Scotland. During his reign (1306–29) he fought successfully for Scottish independence from the English, whom he defeated at the Battle of Bannockburn (1314). Known as **Robert the Bruce**

Robert II (1316–90) king of Scotland. The grandson of Robert I, he founded the Stuart dynasty.

Robert III (1337–1406) king of Scotland. The son of Robert II and father of James I of Scotland, he ruled Scotland (1390–1406) during a time of civil strife and war with England.

Roberts /róbbərts/, **Tom** (1856–1931) British-born Australian painter. He was a pioneer of Australian impressionism, and was one of the founders of the group of painters known as the Heidelberg School. Full name **Roberts, Thomas William**

Robertson /róbbərts'n/, **George** (1860–1933) British-

born Australian publisher. He was one of the founders of the Australian publishing company Angus and Robertson.

Paul Robeson

Robeson /róbsən/, **Paul** (1898–1976) US singer and actor. He acted in both stage and film productions of *Show Boat* (1928, 1936) and in other musical and Shakespearean roles including Othello. He stood against racism and racial segregation, and his socialist sympathies led to his being driven from the stage during the McCarthy era. Full name **Robeson, Paul Bustill**

> 'No barriers can stand against the mightiest river of all, the people's will for peace and freedom now surging in floodtide throughout the world!'
> [Paul Robeson, *Here I Stand*; 1958]

Robespierre /róbz pyair/, **Maximilien** (1758–94) French lawyer and revolutionary. He was elected as first deputy for Paris to the National Convention after the fall of the monarchy in 1792. As commissioner of public safety (1793) he instituted the Reign of Terror and was later guillotined. Full name **Robespierre, Maximilien François Marie Isidore de**

> 'Any law which violates the inalienable rights of man is in essence unjust and tyrannical; it is no law.'
> [Maximilien Robespierre, *Article 6, Déclaration des droits de l'homme (Declaration of the Rights of Man)*; 1793]

Robey /rŏ́bi/, **Sir George** (1869–1954) British comedian. He appeared in musicals and was celebrated for his role as the Shakespearean character Falstaff. Born **Wade, George Edward**. Known as **the Prime Minister of Mirth**

robin /róbbin/ *n* **1.** EUROPEAN SONGBIRD a small thrush, the adult male of which has a reddish-orange breast and head. Native to: Europe. Latin name: *Erithacus rubecula*. **2.** LARGE N AMERICAN THRUSH a large thrush with a rust-coloured breast and dark grey or brown upper parts. Native to: North America. Latin name: *Turdus migratorius*. **3.** BIRD WITH REDDISH BREAST LIKE ROBIN a bird with a reddish breast that is similar to the European or North American robin, especially one of numerous Australian species [14C. < the name *Robin*, diminutive of *Robert*; originally in ROBIN REDBREAST]

Robin Goodfellow /róbbin good fellō/ *n* same as **Puck**

robing room /rŏ́bing-/ *n* a room set aside for putting on ceremonial or official robes, e.g. in a court, church, parliament, or other building

Robin Hood /róbbin hood/ *n* in English legend, an outlaw of the 12th century, famous for his courage, chivalry, and practice of stealing from the rich to give to the poor

robin redbreast *n* BIRDS same as **robin** (senses 1–2)

robin's-egg blue *n* a pale greenish-blue colour — **robin's-egg blue** *adj*

Robinson /róbbinss'n/, **Arthur** (*b.* 1926) prime minister (1986–91) and president (1997–2003) of Trinidad and Tobago. He was the country's first elected president. Full name **Robinson, Arthur Napoleon Raymond**

Robinson, **Edward G.** (1893–1973) Romanian-born US actor. He is best known as the tough-talking gangster in the film *Little Caesar* (1930). Born **Goldenberg, Emanuel**

Robinson, **Heath** (1872–1944) British cartoonist. His

humorous drawings of imaginary elaborate machinery designed to perform simple tasks gave rise to the term 'Heath Robinson contraption'. Full name **Robinson, William Heath**

Robinson, **Jackie** (1919–72) US baseball player and civil rights activist. He broke baseball's colour barrier. Full name **Robinson, Jack Roosevelt**

> 'Baseball is a poker game. Nobody wants to quit when he's losing; nobody wants you to quit when you're ahead.'
> [Jackie Robinson. Quoted in *Giants of Baseball*, Bill Gutman; 1975]

Mary Robinson

Robinson, **Mary** (*b.* 1944) president of the Republic of Ireland (1990–97). She was the first woman to serve as Irish president, and later became the United Nations High Commissioner for Human Rights (1997–). Born **Bourke, Mary Terese Winifred**

Robinson, **Sugar Ray** (1921–89) US boxer. He was the world welterweight champion (1946–51) and five times world middleweight champion between 1951 and 1960. Born **Smith, Walker**

> 'I can hurt anybody. The question is, can I hurt him enough?'
> [Sugar Ray Robinson, *The Black Lights: Inside the World of Professional Boxing*, Thomas Hauser; 1987]

robocall /róbō kawl/ *US* (*informal*) *n* a telephone call made using a computer that plays a voice recording, used in election campaigning and telemarketing ■ *vti* (**-calls, -calling, -called**) to place a telephone call to somebody using a computer that plays a voice recording, in election campaigning or telemarketing [Late 20C. < ROBOT]

robot: part of an automated car assembly line

robot /rŏ́ bot/ *n* **1.** PROGRAMMABLE MACHINE FOR PERFORMING TASKS a mechanical device that can be programmed to carry out instructions and perform complicated tasks usually done by people **2.** IMAGINARY MACHINE a machine that resembles a human in appearance and can function like a human, especially in science fiction **3.** PERSON LIKE MACHINE somebody who works or behaves mechanically and emotionlessly **4.** *S Africa* TRAFFIC LIGHT a set of automatic traffic lights (*informal*) [Early 20C. Via German < Czech, < *robota* 'forced labour'; coined by Karel Čapek in his play *R.U.R.* (Rossum's Universal Robots) (1920)] —**robotic** /rŏ bóttik/ *adj* —**robotically** *adv*

robot bomb *n* a jet-propelled bomb whose flight to a target is governed by a gyroscopic guidance system, e.g. the V-1 used by Germany against London in World War II

robot dancing, **robotic dancing** *n* a dance of the 1980s that has stiff jerky body movements

robotics /rō bóttiks/ *n* **1.** the science and technology relating to computer-controlled mechanical devices such as the automated tools commonly found on automobile assembly lines (*takes a singular verb*) **2.** DANCE same as **robot dancing** (*takes a singular or plural verb*)

robotize /rō bo tīz/ (**-izes, -izing, -ized**), **robotise** (**-ises, -ising, -ised**) *vt* **1.** to introduce automation into something, especially a factory or factory process **2.** to make somebody act in an automated and unemotional or insensitive fashion —**robotization** /rō bo tī záysh'n, -bə-/ *n*

robot pilot *n* AVIAT same as **automatic pilot**

Rob Roy /rób róy/ (1671–1734) Scottish brigand. Forced into life as an outlaw by debts, he led raids against both the English and the Scots. His life was romanticized in a novel by Sir Walter Scott. Born **MacGregor, Robert**

Robson /róbss'n/, **Dame Flora** (1902–84) British actor. She performed in classical and contemporary roles in both films and plays. Full name **Robson, Dame Flora McKenzie**

robust /rō búst/ *adj* **1.** STRONG AND HEALTHY strong, healthy, and hardy in constitution **2.** STRONGLY CONSTRUCTED built, constructed, or designed to be sturdy, durable, or hard-wearing **3.** NEEDING PHYSICAL STRENGTH involving or requiring great physical strength and stamina ○ *Rugby is a robust sport.* **4.** DETERMINED characterized by firmness and determination and a refusal to make concessions ○ *a robust defence* **5.** STRAIGHTFORWARD showing clear thought and common sense **6.** BLUNT OR CRUDE rough and direct or crude **7.** FULL-FLAVOURED rich, strong-tasting, and full-bodied **8.** COMPUT CAPABLE OF RECOVERY describes a computer program or system that is able to recover from unexpected conditions during operation ○ *a robust operating system* [Mid-16C. < Latin *robustus* 'made of oak, hard, strong' < *robur* 'oak tree, hardness, strength'] —**robustly** *adv* —**robustness** *n*

robusta /rō bústə/ *n* **1.** beans from a widely cultivated coffee bush, or coffee made from them **2.** a widely cultivated species of coffee bush that produces robusta beans. Native to: west-central Africa. Latin name: *Coffea canephora*. [Early 20C. < Latin, form of *robustus* (see ROBUST)]

robustious /rō búschəss/ *adj* same as **robust** (senses 1, 6) (*archaic*) —**robustiously** *adv* —**robustiousness** *n*

roc /rok/ *n* in Arabian mythology, a large bird of prey strong enough to lift and fly with an elephant in its talons [Late 16C. Via Arabic < Persian *ruk*]

ROC *abbr* Royal Observer Corps

rocaille /ro kī, rō-/ *n* decorative rococo stonework or shellwork, especially scrollwork [Mid-19C. < French, 'pebble work, rock work' < *roc* 'rock']

rocambole /rókəm bōl/ *n* a plant related to garlic sometimes used to flavour food. Native to: Europe, Asia. Latin name: *Allium scorodoprasum*. [Late 17C. Via French < German *Rockenbolle* 'distaff bulb' (from its shape) < *Rocken* 'distaff' + *Bolle* 'bulb']

Rochdale /róch dayl/ town in Lancashire, northwestern England. Population: 207,563 (1996).

Roche /rōch/ ♦ **de la Roche, Mazo**

Roche, Tony (*b.* 1945) Australian tennis player. He was the runner-up at Wimbledon in 1968 and four-time Wimbledon doubles champion with John Newcombe. He was appointed coach of the Australian Davis Cup team in 1994. Full name **Roche, Anthony**

Roche limit /rósh-/ *n* the closest a satellite can come to the astronomical object it is orbiting before being destroyed by tidal forces generated by gravity. The distance varies with relative density but is approximately 2.45 times the radius of the primary object. [Late 19C. After Édouard *Roche* (1820–83), French astronomer]

Rochelle salt /ro shél-/ *n* PHARM same as **potassium sodium tartrate** [Mid-18C. After LA ROCHELLE]

roche moutonnée /rósh moo tónnay/ (*plural* **roches moutonnées** /*pronunc. same*/) *n* an elongated mound of bare rock, modified by glacial erosion, that is smooth and striated on one side and shattered rubble on the other [Mid-19C. < French, 'fleecy rock', because rounded like a sheep's back]

Rochester /róchistər/ **1.** city on the River Medway, in Kent, England. Population: 145,000 (1994). **2.** city and port in western New York State, south of Lake Ontario and northeast of Buffalo. Population: 217,158 (2002 estimate).

rochet /róchit/ *n* a white linen garment, similar to a surplice but with tight-fitting sleeves, worn on ceremonial occasions by bishops and other high-ranking members of the clergy [14C. < Old French, 'little mantle' < *roc* 'mantle' < Germanic]

rock[1] /rok/ *n* **1.** HARD MINERAL AGGREGATE any consolidated material consisting of more than one mineral and, sometimes, organic material, e.g. granite or limestone **2.** *also* **Rock** PROJECTING MASS OF ROCK a large mass of mineral material, especially an isolated or projecting one (*often used in placenames*) ○ *Ayers Rock* **3.** BOULDER a large stone or boulder **4.** DEPENDABLE PERSON a stable, dependable, or supportive person or thing, especially in times of trouble **5.** HARD SWEET a hard, often brightly coloured sweet made from boiled sugar, usually in the form of a long cylindrical stick and sometimes with the name of a seaside resort through it ○ *a stick of Blackpool rock* **6.** GEM a large gemstone, especially a diamond (*informal*) **7.** DRUGS CRACK COCAINE crack cocaine, or a small piece of crack cocaine (*slang*) **8.** FISH same as **rockfish** (sense 2) ■ **rocks** *npl* **1.** *US* same as **money** (*informal*) **2.** OFFENSIVE TERM an offensive term for the testicles (*slang*) [14C. < Old French *ro(c)que*] ◇ **between a rock and a hard place** faced with a choice between two equally unpleasant or undesirable alternatives ◇ **get your rocks off** (*slang*) **1.** an offensive phrase meaning to have an orgasm (*refers to men*) **2.** an offensive phrase meaning to get a great deal of pleasure or excitement from some activity ◇ **on the rocks 1.** in great difficulties and heading for ruin or disaster, especially financially or emotionally (*informal*) **2.** served with ice cubes

rock up *vi Aus* to turn up or arrive, especially unannounced (*informal*)

rock[2] /rok/ *v* (**rocks, rocking, rocked**) **1.** *vti* SWAY TO AND FRO to swing or sway backwards and forwards or from side to side, or cause something or somebody to swing or sway in this way, especially with a slow gentle rhythm **2.** *vti* SHAKE OR TREMBLE to move or shake violently, or cause somebody or something to move or shake violently ○ *A tremor rocked the city.* **3.** *vt* SHOCK SOMEBODY to disturb, upset, or shock somebody (*informal*) ○ *The ruling rocked the legal profession.* **4.** *vi* PLAY MUSIC OR DANCE to sing, play, or dance to music, especially to rock music (*informal*) **5.** *vi* BE FILLED WITH ROCK MUSIC to contain people performing or enjoying music, especially rock music (*informal*) ○ *The joint was really rocking.* **6.** *vi* MUSIC HAVE STRONG BEAT to have or play music with a strong solid beat (*informal*) **7.** *vi* TRAVEL to advance steadily or quickly (*informal*) ○ *rocking along at 60 miles an hour* **8.** *vti* MIN EXTRACT WASH ORE IN CRADLE to wash gold-bearing or gem-bearing sands or gravel in a pivoting cradle **9.** *vt* ART ROUGHEN COPPER PLATE in engraving a mezzotint, to prepare a copper plate with a tool with a short curved jagged blade (**rocker**) ■ *n* **1.** ACT OF ROCKING an act or the process of rocking somebody or something **2.** MUSIC TYPE OF POP MUSIC a style of pop music, derived from rock and roll, usually played on electric or electronic instruments and equipment [Old English *roccian*, probably < Germanic, 'move']

Rock *n* the Rock of Gibraltar (*informal*) [< ROCK[1]]

rockabilly /rókə bili/ *n* a style of pop music, originating in the late 1950s, that combines rock and roll with country music [Mid-20C. Blend of ROCK AND ROLL + HILLBILLY]

rockabye /rókə bī/, **rockaby** *interj* used to encourage a baby or child to go to sleep [Early 19C. < ROCK[2] + LULLABY]

Rockall /rók awl/ rocky islet in the Atlantic Ocean, 354 km/220 mi. west of the Outer Hebrides. The small islet is the subject of a maritime dispute between several countries. Area: 743 sq. m./8,000 sq. ft.

rock and roll /rókən rōl/, **rock'n'roll** *n* **1.** POP MUSIC WITH HEAVY BEAT pop music derived from blues music that has heavily stressed beats. It is usually played on electric instruments and has simple, often repetitive, lyrics. **2.** DANCE DONE TO ROCK AND ROLL dancing done to rock and roll music ■ *vi* (**rocks and rolls, rocking and rolling, rocked and rolled; rock'n'rolls, rock'n'rolling, rock'n'rolled**) DANCE TO ROCK AND ROLL to do a rock and roll dance —**rock and roller** *n*

rock bass /-bass/ *n* a sunfish with a dark olive back, white undersides, and red eyes. Native to: central and eastern North America. Latin name: *Ambloplites rupestris*.

rock bottom *n* the lowest level or price possible —**rock-bottom** *adj*

rockbound /rók bownd/ *adj* **1.** entirely, or almost entirely, surrounded by rocks **2.** so rocky as to be inaccessible

rock brake *n* a fern that has compound fronds and grows on rocky ground. Genus: *Crytogramma*.

rock cake, **rock bun** *n* a small individual cake containing dried fruit and sometimes spices and candied peel [< its lumpy, uneven, crusty surface]

rock candy *n N Am* a hard sweet consisting of dissolved sugar that is cooled to form large crystals. It is sometimes made on a piece of string or a stick.

rock climb *n* **1.** an act or instance of scaling a rock face, usually using ropes and other specialized equipment **2.** the route followed on a rock climb

rock climbing *n* the activity of scaling rock faces, usually using ropes and other specialized equipment and often in a team —**rock-climb** *vi* —**rock-climber** *n*

rock cod *n* FISH same as **blue cod**

rock crab *n* a fast-moving crab. Native to: rocky coastal areas of North America. Genus: *Cancer*.

rock crystal *n* a colourless transparent variety of quartz. Use: electronic and optical instruments.

rock dove *n* a bluish-grey dove from which domestic and wild pigeons are descended. Native to: Europe, southern Asia. Latin name: *Columba livia*.

Rockefeller /rókə felər/, **John D.** (1839–1937) US industrialist and philanthropist. He founded Standard Oil and established the Rockefeller Foundation (1913). Full name **Rockefeller, John Davison**

> 'I believe it is my duty to make money and still more money and to use the money I make for the good of my fellow man according to the dictates of my conscience.'
> [John D. Rockefeller, *Interview*; 1905]

Rockefeller, John D., Jr. (1874–1960) US industrialist and philanthropist. The son of John D. Rockefeller, he donated the land for the United Nations headquarters in New York. Full name **Rockefeller, John Davison, Jr.**

> 'Good management consists in showing average people how to do the work of superior people.'
> [Attributed to John D. Rockefeller, Jr.]

Rockefeller, Nelson A. (1908–79) vice president of the United States (1974–77). The son of John D. Rockefeller, Jr., he replaced Vice President Gerald Ford, who had become President when Richard Nixon resigned in 1974.

rock elm *n* a deciduous tree with corky branches. Native to: eastern North America. Latin name: *Ulmus thomasii*.

rocker /rókər/ *n* **1.** ROCKING DEVICE a device that functions by way of a rocking movement **2.** FURNITURE STAND an upwardly curved piece of wood or metal that allows something such as a rocking chair or baby's cradle to move backwards and forwards or from side to side **3.** FURNITURE same as **rocking chair** **4.** HOUSEHOLD same as **rocker switch** **5.** MIN EXTRACT same as **cradle** *n* (sense 8) **6.** ART ENGRAVER'S TOOL a tool with a short curved jagged blade used in the engraving of mezzotints for roughening the copper plates **7.** ICE SKATING TYPE OF ICE SKATE an ice skate with a curved blade, or the curved blade itself (*often used in the plural*) **8.** MUSIC ROCK MUSICIAN a rock singer or musician (*informal*) **9.** MUSIC ROCK FAN a fan of rock music or rock and roll (*informal*) **10.** HIST MEMBER OF 60S YOUTH

GROUP a follower of a youth group in 1960s Britain who rode motorcycles, liked rock and roll, wore leather jackets, and sometimes fought with smart youths on motor scooters (**mods**) ◇ **off his** *or* **her rocker** an offensive term that deliberately insults somebody's state of mental balance

rocker arm *n* a pivoted lever, e.g. in an internal-combustion engine, that transmits motion from a cam or push rod at one end to open and close a valve at the other

rocker cam *n* a cam that oscillates or rocks but does not revolve

rocker panel *n* on a passenger vehicle, the exterior panel located below the doorsill of the passenger compartment

rocker switch *n* a switch on a central pivot, especially one that operates between an 'on' and 'off' position on an electrical appliance

rockery /rókəri/ (*plural* **-ies**) ANZ a garden or area of a garden that has large stones in it with plants, especially low-growing colourful hardy ones such as edelweiss, gentian, and heathers growing in between them. N Am term **rock garden**

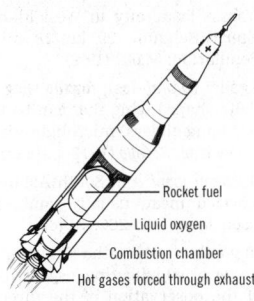

Rocket fuel
Liquid oxygen
Combustion chamber
Hot gases forced through exhaust

rocket

rocket[1] /rókit/ *n* **1.** SELF-PROPELLED FIREWORK OR FLARE a firework, flare, or similar device, usually cylindrical in shape, containing combustible propellants **2.** AEROSP SPACE VEHICLE a vehicle designed for space travel, propelled by a rocket engines **3.** AEROSP same as **rocket engine 4.** ARMS ROCKET-PROPELLED WEAPON a weapon consisting of an explosive, nuclear, or other warhead that is propelled by a rocket engine **5.** TELLING OFF a stern reprimand or rebuke (*informal*) ■ *v* (**-ets, -eting, -eted**) **1.** *vi* MOVE FAST to move or begin to move at great speed **2.** *vti* ATTAIN SOMETHING QUICKLY to get to a particular condition or position very quickly, or cause somebody or something to do this (*informal*) ○ *They rocketed to fame with their first single.* **3.** *vi* INCREASE QUICKLY to increase very quickly and dramatically (*informal*) ○ *House prices have rocketed in the last year or so.* **4.** *vt* MIL, AEROSP POWER SOMETHING USING ROCKET ENGINE to send something, especially a spacecraft, warhead, or missile, into the air or atmosphere by means of a rocket engine or rocket engines **5.** *vt* BOMBARD SOMETHING WITH ROCKET to fire a rocket at a target **6.** *vi* FLY UP QUICKLY to fly up vertically at speed (*refers to game birds*) [Early 17C. < Italian *rocchetta* 'small distaff' (from its shape) < *rocca* 'distaff' < Germanic]

rocket[2] /rókit/ *n* **1.** a plant with peppery leaves that are eaten cooked or raw in salads. Native to: Mediterranean. Latin name: *Eruca vesicaria.* N Am term **arugula 2.** a fast-growing plant with pale-yellow flowers, typically growing on waste ground. Genus: *Sisymbrium.* **3.** PLANTS same as **dame's violet 4.** PLANTS same as **sea rocket** [Early 16C. Via French *roquette* < Italian *ruchetta* 'small ruca' (a cabbage) < Latin *eruca* 'caterpillar, cole']

rocketeer /róki teér/ *n* **1.** a scientist or engineer who designs space rockets **2.** somebody who launches, operates, or travels in a space rocket

rocket engine *n* a device that carries both fuel and oxidizer, which it burns in a combustion chamber, producing thrust by expelling the expanding hot gases through a nozzle. The fuel and oxidizer may be liquefied gases such as oxygen and hydrogen, or solids such as powdered aluminium and ammonium perchloride.

rocket-launched grenade *n* ARMS same as **rocket-propelled grenade**

rocket plane *n* an aircraft that is designed to carry and launch rockets, missiles, or warheads

rocket-propelled grenade *n* a heavy grenade with a rocket attachment that is fired from a launching tube, usually against armoured vehicles or helicopters

rocketry /rókitri/ *n* the science and technology of the design, construction, operation, flying, and maintenance of rockets

rocket science *n* a complex and intellectually demanding activity (*informal*) ○ *Using the Internet isn't exactly rocket science.* [Late 20C. Because the province of a few highly qualified specialists]

rocket scientist *n* (*informal*) **1.** an extremely intelligent person ○ *It doesn't take a rocket scientist to figure that one out!* **2.** somebody highly skilled in quantitative analysis who studies the capital markets

rocket sled *n* a rocket-propelled vehicle that runs on a rail or rails and can be accelerated rapidly to high speeds, used in aeronautical applications such as crash and G-force tolerance testing

rocketsonde /rókit sond/ *n* an instrument transported by rocket to the upper atmosphere to carry out weather observations

rockfall /rók fawl/ *n* **1.** a collection or mass of fallen rocks **2.** an avalanche of falling rocks

rockfish /rók fish/ (*plural same* or **-fishes**) *n* **1.** a fish that lives among rocks. Native to: Pacific Ocean. **2.** the flesh of a dogfish or catfish as food

rock flour *n* fine powdery rock produced by grinding or abrasion, e.g. by the movement of a glacier

Rockford /rókfərd/ city in northern Illinois, south of the Wisconsin border, east of Freeport and northwest of Chicago. Population: 151,068 (2002 estimate).

rock garden *n* **1.** N Am same as **rockery 2.** a rocky area in which plants suited to the habitat are grown

Rockhampton /rok hámptən/ city in eastern Queensland, Australia, on the River Fitzroy. Population: 59,410 (2002 estimate).

rockhopper /rók hopər/ *n* a small penguin with a short bill and a yellow crest. Native to: Antarctica, New Zealand, Falkland Islands. Latin name: *Eudyptes crestatus.*

rock hound *n* N Am (*informal*) **1.** a collector of rocks and minerals **2.** an expert in or student of geology —**rockhounding** *n*

rock hyrax *n* a small plant-eating hyrax that lives in large colonies in rocky outcrops. Native to: Africa. Genus: *Procavia.*

Rockies /rókiz/ ♦ **Rocky Mountains**

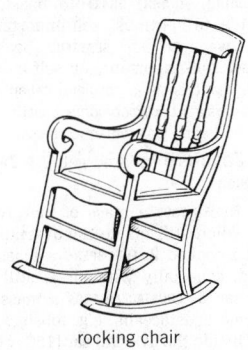

rocking chair

rocking chair /róking-/ *n* a chair that is set on a pair of curved pieces of wood so that somebody sitting in it can be rocked backwards and forwards

Rockingham /rókingəm/ coastal town in southwestern Western Australia, near Perth. Population: 76,262 (2002 estimate).

Rockingham, Charles Watson-Wentworth, 2nd Marquess (1730–82) British prime minister (1765–66, 1782). His government is best known for its repeal of the Stamp Act and sympathetic attitude towards Britain's colonies in America.

rocking horse *n* a small model horse fitted with reins and a saddle and set on a pair of rockers, on which a child can sit and rock backwards and forwards

rocking stone *n* a large stone or boulder that is so finely balanced, e.g. on another stone or stones, that it can be made to rock backwards and forwards with little effort

rockling /rókling/ (*plural* **-lings** or *same*) *n* **1.** a small fish of the cod family. Native to: northern Atlantic. Family: Gadidae. **2.** Aus FISH same as **ling**[1] (sense 2)

rock lobster *n* MARINE BIOL same as **spiny lobster**

rock mechanics *n* the study of the physical properties of rocks such as density, elasticity, and strength, especially with relation to their behaviour in tunnels and mines and when subjected to environmental forces (*takes a singular verb*)

rock melon *n* ANZ same as **cantaloupe**

rock music *n* same as **rock**[2] *n* (sense 2)

rock'n'roll *n*, *vi* MUSIC, DANCE same as **rock and roll**

rock oil *n* INDUST same as **petroleum**

rock pigeon *n* BIRDS same as **rock dove**

rock plant *n* a plant that has adapted to living on rocks or rocky ground

rock rabbit *n* ZOOL same as **rock hyrax**

rock-ribbed *adj* characterized by rocks or rocky outcrops

rockrose /rók rōz/ *n* a low-growing woody bush or perennial plant. Flowers: small, white, light-yellow or reddish, resembling wild roses. Native to: warm regions. Genera: *Cistus* or *Helianthemum.*

rock salmon *n* FISH same as **rockfish** (sense 2)

rock salt *n* MINERALS same as **halite**

rockslide /rók slīd/ *n* **1.** a collection or mass of rocks that have slipped downwards **2.** an avalanche of rocks that occurs as a result of surface movement

rock snake *n* a large snake. Native to: Australia, Asia. Genus: *Liasis.*

rock-solid *adj* **1.** firm and unshakable **2.** extremely hard and unlikely to break

rock steady *n* Jamaican reggae of the early 1960s, popular as dance music

rock-steady *adj* firm, unshaking, and calm

rockumentary /rókyoō méntəri/ (*plural* **-ries**) *n* a film documentary about rock music in general or a particular rock band or musician, containing film footage of relevant performances (*informal*) [Late 20C. Blend of ROCK AND ROLL + DOCUMENTARY]

rock wallaby *n* a medium-sized marsupial with large padded hind feet, found in open rocky country. Native to: Australia. Genus: *Petrogale.*

Rockwell /rókwəl/, **Norman** (1894–1978) US illustrator. He is best known for his magazine covers and illustrations of everyday small-town life, published in US periodicals such as *The Saturday Evening Post* and the *Ladies' Home Journal.*

rock wool *n* INDUST same as **mineral wool**

rockwork /rók wurk/ *n* **1.** artificial or decorative stonework designed to resemble the irregularity of natural rocks **2.** a collection or mass of large stones or rocks

rocky[1] /róki/ (**-ier, -iest**) *adj* **1.** WITH ROCKS consisting of or covered with rocks ○ *rocky terrain* **2.** HARD resembling rock in its hardness or firmness **3.** UNEMOTIONAL unyielding, unwavering, or lacking in human emotions —**rockiness** *n*

rocky[2] /róki/ (**-ier, -iest**) *adj* **1.** DIFFICULT characterized by difficulties, obstacles, or troubles ○ *a rocky start* ○ *a rocky reception* **2.** UNSTEADY wobbly and unsteady **3.** UNWELL unwell, especially feeling sick or dizzy (*informal*) —**rockily** *adv* —**rockiness** *n*

Rocky Mountain goat *n* ZOOL same as **mountain goat**

Rocky Mountains /róki-/ major mountain system of North America. Its highest point is Mount Elbert, at 4,399 m/14,433 ft. Length: 3,200 km/2,000 mi.

Rocky Mountain spotted fever an acute infectious disease transmitted by the bite of ticks infected with the microorganism *Rickettsia rickettsi.* Symptoms

include chills, fever, muscle and joint pain, skin rash, and prostration. [Because first reported in the area of the ROCKY MOUNTAINS]

~~rococco~~ incorrect spelling of **rococo**

rococo: detail of stucco at Wies church, Bavaria, Germany (1745–54)

rococo /rə kṓkō/ n 1. also ROCOCO ORNATE 18C ART STYLE a style of architecture and the decorative arts characterized by intricate ornamentation that was popular throughout Europe in the early 18th century 2. also ROCOCO ORNATE 18C MUSIC STYLE a style of music characterized by the use of ornamentation and embellishment that was popular in Europe in the 18th century 3. ORNATE STYLE any very ornate style ■ adj 1. also ROCOCO ARTS IN STYLE OF ROCOCO belonging to, relating to, or in the style of 18th-century rococo 2. ORNATE very ornate in style [Mid-19C. < French, fanciful alteration of *rocaille* (see ROCAILLE)]

rod /rod/ n 1. THIN STICK a narrow, usually cylindrical length of wood, metal, plastic, or other material 2. FISHING same as **fishing rod** 3. WHIPPING STICK a stick, or bundle of sticks tied together, used for whipping somebody as a punishment 4. SURVEYING POLE a graduated pole used by surveyors for sighting with a levelling instrument to determine elevation differences 5. STAFF OF OFFICE a staff, especially one that indicates somebody's standing, office, authority, or power 6. POWER WIELDED tyrannical or oppressive power 7. PLANT STEM a straight stem or shoot that has been cut from, or that is growing on, a woody plant 8. N Am RAIL METAL BAR SUPPORTING RAILWAY CARRIAGE one of the metal bars that form the framework of the underside of a railway carriage, especially one on a goods carriage (often used in the plural) 9. ANAT RECEPTOR CELL IN EYE a rod-shaped receptor in the retina of the eye that is sensitive to dim light but not colour 10. MICROBIOL BACTERIUM a rod-shaped bacterium 11. BOARD MARKED WITH FULL-SCALE JOINERY PATTERN a board on which the dimensions of a joinery assembly such as a window or door frame are marked in full scale 12. MEASURE UNIT OF LENGTH a unit of length equal to 5.03 m/5½ yd, now largely obsolete 13. MEASURE UNIT OF AREA a unit of area equal to 25.3 m²/30.25 sq. yd, now largely obsolete 14. PISTOL a gun, especially a pistol (slang) 15. OFFENSIVE TERM an offensive term for a penis (slang) ■ vt (rods, rodding, rodded) CLEAR SOMETHING OUT USING ROD to use a rod to clear an obstruction from something [Old English *rodd* 'pole, rod', origin ?]—**rodless** adj—**rodlike** adj

Rodchenko /rod chénkō/, Aleksandr (1891–1956) Russian painter, designer, and photographer. He was a central figure of the constructivist movement in Revolutionary Russia.

Roddick /róddik/, Dame Anita (b. 1942) British businessperson and campaigner. She started The Body Shop in 1976. Born **Perella, Anita Lucia**

rode[1] past tense of **ride**

rode[2] /rōd/ n a rope or chain, especially one attached to an anchor [Early17C. < ?]

rode[3] /rōd/ (rodes, roding, roded) vi 1. to fly to roost at nightfall (refers to wildfowl) 2. to fly at nightfall as a mating display (refers to male European woodcock) [Mid-18C. < ?]—**roding** n

rodent /rṓd'nt/ n a small animal of an order with large gnawing incisor teeth that continue growing throughout the animal's life, e.g. a mouse, rat, squirrel, or marmot. Rodents make up more than a third of all living mammal species and are adapted to

all terrestrial habitats. Order: Rodentia. [Mid-19C. < modern Latin *Rodentia* < Latin *rodent-*, present participle of *rodere* 'gnaw']

rodenticide /rō dénti sīd/ n a substance designed to kill rodents, especially rats and mice

rodent ulcer n a persistent, usually cancerous ulcer of the skin, especially of the face [< RODENT as adjective, 'gnawing']

rodeo /rō dáy ō, rṓdi-/ (plural -os) n 1. COMPETITION IN COWBOY SKILLS a competition or display of lassoing, riding unbroken horses, calf-roping, and cattle-wrestling 2. MOTORCYCLING COMPETITION a competition or display of motorcycle riding that often includes stunts 3. Southwest US CATTLE ROUND-UP an occasion when cattle are rounded up, especially so that they can be branded, counted, or have their health checked 4. Southwest US CATTLE PEN a pen for rounded-up cattle [Mid-19C. < Spanish, 'cattle ring' < *rodear* 'go round, surround' < Latin *rotare* (see ROTATE)]

Rodgers /rójjərz/, Richard (1902–79) US composer. His collaborations with Lorenz Hart and Oscar Hammerstein II produced popular musicals such as *Pal Joey* (1940) and *Oklahoma!* (1943).

Auguste Rodin: bronze portrait bust (1888–89) by Camille Claudel

Rodin /rō dáN/, Auguste (1840–1917) French sculptor. Among his bronze sculptures are *The Thinker* (1880), *The Kiss* (1880), and *The Burghers of Calais* (1886). Full name **Rodin, François Auguste René**

'What is ugly in Art is only that which is without character, that is, that which offers no truth at all, either exterior or interior.'
[Attributed to Auguste Rodin]

rodman /ródmən, -man/ (plural -men /-mən, -men/) n N Am same as **staffman**

rodomontade /róddə mon táyd, -taád/ (literary) n BOASTFULNESS pretentious, self-important, or self-indulgent boasting, speech, or behaviour ■ vi (-tades, -tading, -taded) BOAST to boast, speak, or behave in a pretentious, self-important, or self-indulgent way ■ adj BOASTFUL boastful in a pretentious, self-important, or self-indulgent way [Early 17C. Via French < obsolete Italian *rodomontada* < *rodomonte* 'braggart' < *Rodomonte*, boastful Saracen king in 15 and 16C Italian long romantic poems]

Rodríguez Zapatero /ro dree geth-/ ♦ Zapatero, José Luis Rodríguez

roe[1] /rō/ n 1. FISH EGGS a mass of mature fish eggs, especially when still inside the ovarian sac, sometimes eaten cooked 2. FISH SPERM a mass of mature fish sperm, especially when it is still inside the testicular sac 3. CRUSTACEAN EGGS a mass of mature eggs of some crustaceans, e.g. lobsters, especially when still inside the ovarian sac [15C. < Middle Dutch or Middle Low German *roge*]

roe[2] /rō/ (plural roes or same) n ZOOL same as **roe deer** [Old English *rā* < Germanic]

roebuck /rṓ buk/ (plural -bucks or same) n a male roe deer, especially an adult one

Roedean /rṓ deen/ n a public school for girls in southern England. It was founded in 1885.

roe deer n a medium-sized reddish-brown deer. Native to: deciduous woodlands of Europe and Asia. Latin name: *Capreolus capreolus*.

Roeg /rōg/, Nicolas (b. 1928) British film director. He

is noted especially for *Performance* (1970), which he made with Donald Cammell, and for *Don't Look Now* (1973). Full name **Roeg, Nicolas Jack**

roentgen /róntgən/, röntgen n a unit of radiation, used to measure the exposure of somebody or something to X-rays and gamma rays, defined in terms of the ionization effect on air. It is equal to the quantity of radiation that produces ionization equal to one electrostatic unit of charge at 0° and standard atmospheric pressure. Symbol **R** [Late 19C. After W. C. ROENTGEN]

Roentgen /róntgən/, Wilhelm Conrad (1845–1923) German physicist. He discovered X-rays, originally known also as 'Roentgen rays'. He was awarded the Nobel Prize (1901).

'All bodies are transparent to this agent …For brevity's sake I shall use the expression "rays"; and to distinguish them from others of this name I shall call them "X-rays".'
[Wilhelm Conrad Roentgen. Quoted in *William Conrad Roentgen and the Early History of the Roentgen Rays*, Otto Glasser; 1933]

Roeslare /róossə laarə/ city in West Flanders Province, western Belgium, 29 km/18 mi. south of Bruges. Population: 54,002 (1999).

rogallo /rō gállō/ (plural -los), rogallo wing n a fabric-covered delta-shaped wing that can be folded compactly. Use: hang-gliders, microlight aircraft. [Mid-20C. After Francis M. *Rogallo* (1912–), US engineer]

rogan josh /rṓgən jósh/ n in South Asian cooking, a dish of curried meat, usually lamb, in a thick tomato-based sauce [Mid-20C. < Urdu]

rogation /rō gáysh'n/ n 1. in the Christian Church, a solemn prayer or supplication, especially one made as part of the observation of the three days preceding Ascension Day (**Rogation Days**) (often used in the plural) 2. in ancient Rome, the submission of a law by a consul or tribune to the people for their approval, or a law so submitted [14C. < Latin *rogation-* < *rogat-*, past participle of *rogare* 'ask, beg']

Rogation Day n any of the three days preceding Ascension Day (often used in the plural)

Rogation Sunday n the Sunday before the Christian festival of Ascension Day. Date: five weeks after Easter.

rogatory /róggətəri, rṓgətəri/ adj requesting information, especially information that might be pertinent to a court case [Mid-19C. Via French < medieval Latin *rogatorius* < Latin *rogat-* (see ROGATION)]

roger /rójjər/ interj 1. MESSAGE RECEIVED indicates that the speaker has received and understood a transmitted message (in telecommunications) 2. OK used to indicate the speaker's agreement to something (informal) ■ vti (-ers, -ering, -ered) OFFENSIVE TERM an offensive term meaning to have sexual intercourse with somebody (slang) [Mid-20C. < the name *Roger*, used in radio communications for the letter *r*, for 'received']

Roger II /rójjər/ (1095–1154) king of Sicily. He was a Norman whose sovereignty also extended over southern Italy, and his domain was called the Kingdom of the Two Sicilies.

Rogers /rójjərz/, Ginger (1911–95) US dancer and actor. She was Fred Astaire's dance partner in many Hollywood musicals (1933–49), including *Top Hat* (1935). Born **McMath, Virginia Katherine**

Rogers, Sir Richard George, Baron Rogers of Riverside (b. 1933) British architect. A prominent exponent of postmodernism, he developed a high-tech style, exemplified by the Lloyd's Building, London (1986).

Roget /rṓ zhay, rō zháy/, Peter Mark (1779–1869) British scholar and doctor. He compiled the *Thesaurus of English Words and Phrases* (1852), now known as *Roget's Thesaurus*.

rogue /rōg/ n 1. SOMEBODY DISHONEST an unscrupulous or dishonest person, especially somebody who is also likable 2. SOMEBODY MISCHIEVOUS a mischievously playful person, especially a naughty child 3. DANGEROUS SOLITARY ANIMAL a vicious or uncontrolled animal that lives apart from the rest of its herd or group 4. BOT BIOLOGICALLY INFERIOR VARIANT a plant that is

a biologically inferior variant of its type ■ *adj* 1. **UNORTHODOX AND UNPREDICTABLE** acting independently and using unorthodox methods that are unpredictable and are likely to cause trouble ○ *a rogue trader* 2. **DANGEROUS AND SOLITARY** describes an animal that is vicious and uncontrolled and lives apart from the rest of the herd or group ○ *a rogue male* 3. BOT **STRAY** describes a plant that is inferior and unwanted ■ *vt* (**rogues, roguing, rogued**) AGRIC, PLANTS **CLEAR PLANTS** to remove inferior plants from a crop or a group of plants [Mid-16C. < ?] —**roguery** /rṓgəri/ *n*

rogues' gallery *n* a set of photographs of known criminals that the police show to witnesses to crimes for possible identification (*informal*)

rogue site *n* website that acquires visitors by having a domain name similar to that of a popular site

rogue state *n* a nation whose leadership intentionally refuses to adhere to the conventions of international law, does not honour established treaties, and may engage in terrorism and warfare

roguish /rṓgish/ *adj* 1. unscrupulous or dishonest in the manner of a rogue 2. mischievously playful —**roguishly** *adv* —**roguishness** *n*

Rohe ➧ **Mies van der Rohe, Ludwig**

Röhm /röm/, **Ernst** (1887–1934) German Nazi leader. As the commander of the Nazi storm troopers, he advocated that they take control of the German army. He was murdered on Adolf Hitler's orders.

Roh Moo-hyun /rṓmoo hyún/ (*b.* 1946) president of South Korea. A human rights lawyer, he entered politics in 1988 and was elected president in 2002. He was suspended in March 2004 pending impeachment proceedings.

Rohypnol /rō hípnol/ *tdmk* a trademark for flunitrazepam, a powerful sedative sometimes associated with date rape

ROI *abbr* 1. GEOG region of interest 2. FIN return on investment

'roid /royd/ *n* same as **steroid** (*slang*) [Late 20C. Shortening]

'roid rage *n* an outburst of violent or aggressive behaviour supposedly caused by taking too many anabolic steroids to improve athletic performance (*slang*)

roil /royl/ (**roils, roiling, roiled**) *v* 1. *vti* **MAKE OR BECOME OPAQUE** to stir up a liquid so that the sediment becomes dispersed through the liquid and makes it cloudy, or become cloudy with sediment by being stirred 2. *vt N Am* **MAKE SOMEBODY ANGRY** to anger or annoy somebody 3. *vi regional* **BE BOISTEROUS** to behave in a loud, rowdy way [Late 16C. < ?] —**roily** *adj*

Roisín Dubh /ro sheén dóov/ *n Ireland* Ireland personified as a woman (*literary*) [< Irish, 'black rose']

roister /róystər/ (**-ters, -tering, -tered**) *vi* 1. to take part in loud rowdy partying or celebrations (*dated*) 2. to behave in a loud bragging manner (*archaic*) [Mid-16C. Probably < Old French *ru(i)stre* 'boor, churl' < Latin *rusticus* 'rustic'] —**roisterer** *n* —**roisterous** *adj* —**roisterously** *adv*

rojak /rṓ jak/ *n Malaysia, Singapore* 1. a mixed salad of fruit and vegetables 2. an offensive term for a person of mixed ethnic background (*slang*) [Late 20C. < Malay, 'mixed']

Roland /rṓlənd/ [After the legendary nephew of Charlemagne and comrade of Oliver in medieval romance] ◇ **a Roland for an Oliver** an equally good retort, response, or retaliation (*archaic*)

role /rōl/, **rôle** *n* 1. **ACTING PART** an individual part in a play, film, opera, or other performance 2. **SPECIFIC FUNCTION** the usual or expected function of somebody or something, or the part somebody or something plays in an action or event 3. **PART PLAYED IN SOCIAL CONTEXT** the part played by somebody in a given social context, with any characteristic or expected pattern of behaviour that it entails [Early 17C. < French *rôle* '(paper) roll on which an actor's part is written' < Old French *rol(l)e* (see ROLL)]

SPELLCHECK role or **roll**? Do not confuse the spelling of ***role*** and ***roll***, which sound similar. ***Role*** is a noun denoting a part played by somebody or something: *She has a leading role in the film. What was the role of the president in this affair? Teachers are role models for their students. We engaged in role-playing exercises.* ***Roll*** is a noun or verb referring to a round shape or movement (as in *roll into a ball, roll down the hill, a roll of film*) or an official list (as in *call the roll, on the electoral roll*).

role model *n* a worthy person who is a good example for other people

role-play *n* 1. **ACTING OUT OF PART** the acting out of a part, especially that of somebody with a particular social role, in order to understand it better 2. **GAME SESSION INVOLVING TAKING ON ROLES** in a computer or other game, a session during which players take on the roles of characters ■ *v* 1. *vti* **ACT OUT PART** to engage or act out a part in role-playing 2. *vt* **PLAYING CHARACTER IN GAME** in a computer or other game, to take on the role of a character in a game

role-playing *n* the acting out of a part, especially as a learning aid in language learning, or as an aid to better understanding a well-defined social role in psychotherapy

role-playing game COMPUT GAMES full form of **RPG**

Rolfing /rólfing/ *n* a proprietary name for a therapy using vigorous massage to alleviate physical or psychological tension

roll /rōl/ *v* (**rolls, rolling, rolled**) 1. *vti* **TURN OVER AND OVER** to move with repeated turning or rotating motions, or cause something to move in this way 2. *vti* **MOVE ON WHEELS** to move on wheels or rollers, or cause something to move on wheels or rollers 3. *vi* **DRIVE IN VEHICLE** to move in a wheeled vehicle 4. *vti* **ROTATE** to turn in a complete or partial rotation, or cause something to turn in this way 5. *vi* ASTRON **ORBIT** to revolve in an orbit (*refers to astronomical objects*) 6. *vti* AVIAT **ROTATE AIRCRAFT** to cause an aircraft to perform a single complete rotation about its lengthways axis while maintaining the same altitude and direction, or perform such a rotation 7. *vi* **WRITHE** to lie on the back and move about or from side to side, but without moving very far, often with a writhing motion (*refers to animals*) 8. *vi* **BE CARRIED BY RIVER** to be transported by river 9. *vti* **OVERTURN CAR** to overturn a motor vehicle, especially a car, or be overturned 10. *vti* **THROW DICE** to throw a die or dice 11. *vt* **SCORE NUMBER BY THROWING DICE** to achieve a particular number, position, or score by throwing a die or dice 12. *vt* **FLATTEN SOMETHING WITH ROLLER** to flatten or spread something, especially by using a roller or rolling pin 13. *vti* **FORM INTO ROUND SHAPE** to form something into a ball, tube, cylinder, or other rounded shape, or be formed into such a shape 14. *vt* **TURN BETWEEN OR ON SOMETHING** to revolve something between two surfaces or on a coating material ○ *Roll the chocolates in icing sugar.* 15. *vi* **STRETCH OUT OR AWAY IN UNDULATIONS** to have or take the form of a succession of gentle slopes ○ *green hills rolling away into the distance* 16. *vti* **MOVE WITH UNDULATIONS** to move in a steady flowing motion, or cause something to move in a steady flowing motion 17. *vti* **ROCK FROM SIDE TO SIDE** to move with a sideways swaying or rocking motion on waves or a swell, or cause something, especially a ship, to move in this way 18. *vi* **WALK UNSTEADILY** to walk with an unsteady or staggering motion 19. *vi* **WALK WITH SWAY** to sway rhythmically in walking 20. *vti* **OPERATE SOMETHING** to function, or cause something to function, especially a cine camera or printing press 21. *vti* CINEMA, MEDIA **SEND OR GO UP ON SCREEN** to cause credits, titles, or other captions to move in a continuous upwards direction on a cinema or television screen, or move in this way 22. *vi* **ELAPSE** to go by or elapse, especially uneventfully or imperceptibly (*refers especially to time*) 23. *vi* **TRAVEL AROUND** to travel from place to place 24. *vi* **BE UNDER WAY** to proceed or continue successfully (*informal*) ○ *Now this project is finally rolling.* ○ *We're ready to roll.* 25. *vi* **MOVE AS CROWD** to move or arrive in large numbers or in a crowd 26. *vi* **REVERBERATE LOUDLY** to make a low prolonged rumbling noise 27. *vi* **BEAT DRUM** to make a series of quick beats on a drum 28. *vt* MUSIC **PLAY CHORD WITH SPREAD NOTES** to play a chord sounding its notes in rapid succession (**arpeggio**) rather than simultaneously 29. *vt* **ROB SOMEBODY** to take money or belongings from somebody who cannot offer any resistance (*informal*) 30. *vt* PHON **TRILL SOUND** to pronounce a sound, especially an 'r', with a trill 31. *vt* PRINTING **INK SOMETHING WITH ROLLER** to apply ink to type or a plate with a roller 32. *vti* **HAVE SEX** to have sexual intercourse or engage in sexual foreplay with somebody (*informal; sometimes offensive*) ■ *n* 1. **SOMETHING TUBE-SHAPED** a tube, cylinder, or coil of something, especially something that is wrapped around itself 2. **EQUIPMENT HOLDER WITH POCKETS** a length of fabric or leather that has pockets to hold tools, medical instruments, or other equipment and can usually be wrapped around itself and tied up 3. **WAD OF MONEY** a cylindrical wad of banknotes formed by coiling the wad around itself (*informal*) 4. **BREAD ROLL** a small individual bread, usually round or long in shape, or a sandwich made from one 5. **FILLED FOOD** a food made by wrapping pastry around a filling or by spreading a filling on something such as sponge cake and wrapping it around itself (*usually used in combination*) 6. **REPEATED TURN** a repeated turning or rotating motion 7. **TOSS OF DICE** a throw of a dice 8. AVIAT **ROTATION OF AIRCRAFT** a midair flight manoeuvre in which an aircraft maintains the same height and direction while doing a single complete rotation about its lengthways axis 9. GYMNASTICS **SOMERSAULT** a gentle somersault 10. **MOVEMENT ON WHEELS** a movement on wheels or rollers 11. **SINGLE TURN** a complete or partial rotation 12. **WRITHING MOTION** an action that involves writhing while turning backwards and forwards or from side to side, but without moving very far 13. **MOVEMENT FROM SIDE TO SIDE** a swaying or rocking motion, especially by a ship 14. **SWAYING WALK** a rhythmic sway in walking 15. **OFFICIAL LIST** an official register or list of names, especially of school pupils, members of a club, or people entitled to vote 16. **TOTAL ON OFFICIAL LIST** the total number of people registered on a school, club, or electoral roll 17. **ROUNDED LAYER** a thick rounded layer of something, especially of flesh 18. ARCHIT **SPIRAL SCROLL** in Greek architecture, a spiral scroll on an Ionic column 19. **ACT OF FLATTENING** an act of flattening or spreading something, especially by using a roller or rolling pin 20. **SOMETHING UNDULATING** a gentle rounded hump on a surface, often one of a series 21. **UNDULATING MOVEMENT** a steady, flowing, undulating movement 22. **RHYTHMIC STREAM OF WORDS** a continuous stream of words with a rhythmic quality 23. **ROLLER FOR METAL** a cylinder or roller used for pressing, shaping, or flattening something, especially one used for shaping metal in a rolling mill 24. **BOOKBINDER'S TOOL** a bookbinder's tool for embossing decorative lines on book covers 25. **TRILLING SOUND** a trilling noise, especially the sound of a trilled 'r' or the song of a canary 26. **RUMBLING NOISE** a low prolonged rumbling noise 27. **DRUM BEATS** a series of quick beats on a drum 28. MUSIC **CHORD WITH SPREAD NOTES** a chord with its notes played in rapid succession (**arpeggio**) rather than simultaneously 29. **ACT OF ROBBERY** an act or the process of taking money or belongings from somebody who cannot offer any resistance (*informal*) 30. **SEX ACT** an act of sexual intercourse or foreplay (*informal; sometimes offensive*) [12C. Via Old French *rolle* 'scroll' < Latin *rotul-* 'little wheel' < Latin *rota* 'wheel'] ◇ **a roll in the hay** an instance of having sex with somebody (*informal*) ◇ **be rolling in it** to be very rich (*informal*) ◇ **on a roll** enjoying a period of good luck or of doing something well (*informal*) ◇ **rolled into one** forming a single unit consisting of a number of different aspects or qualities

SPELLCHECK See *role*.

roll back *vt* 1. to cause something, especially prices or wages, to decrease 2. to reduce or nullify the influence or effectiveness of something

roll in *vi* 1. to come home or arrive at a destination, especially in a leisurely way, often later than expected 2. to arrive or attend in large numbers or quantities

roll off *vi* 1. to flow, especially with ease or in large numbers 2. to display a gradually decreasing response in the upper and lower portions of the amplitude-frequency range (*refers to an electronic system or transducer*)

roll on *vi* used in interjections to express a wish that a time or occasion may arrive soon (*informal*) ○ *Roll on summer!*

roll out *vt* 1. **FLATTEN PASTRY** to flatten pastry, dough, or other uncooked food by shaping it with a rolling pin 2. **UNCOIL SOMETHING** to unfold or uncoil something

3. SHOW SOMETHING TO PUBLIC to put a new product on public display for the first time **4.** MARKETING **LAUNCH PRODUCT GRADUALLY** to launch a new product or service by gradually increasing the number of outlets where it is available to the public

roll over *v* **1.** *vi* **CAPSIZE** to capsize, tip over, or overturn **2.** *vt* **DEFEAT SOMEBODY** to defeat a person or team overwhelmingly (*informal*) **3.** *vti* **ACCUMULATE PRIZE MONEY** to add the amount of prize money not won on one occasion to the prize money available on a subsequent occasion, or be added to future prize money in this way **4.** *vt* FIN **EXTEND LOAN** to allow a loan to be paid at a later date **5.** *vt* FIN **NEGOTIATE NEW FINANCIAL TERMS FOR SOMETHING** to achieve new terms for a financial contract through discussion **6.** *vt* FIN **REINVEST FUNDS** to transfer funds from one investment to a similar investment

roll up *v* **1.** *vt* **PRODUCE CYLINDER SHAPE** to turn something into a cylindrical form **2.** *vt US* **ACCUMULATE SOMETHING** to accumulate something, especially money **3.** *vi* **ARRIVE** to come to a place or destination, often in a vehicle and especially when later than expected or when not expected at all

rollaway /rṓlə way/ *adj* fitted with wheels or castors so as to be easily moved or stored

rollback /rṓl bak/ *n* **1.** a decrease in something, especially in something such as prices and wages **2.** a reduction or nullification of the influence or effectiveness of something

rollbar /rṓl baar/ *n* a reinforcing bar across the top of a vehicle, especially an open-top sports car or rally car, to protect the occupants if the vehicle overturns

roll cage *n* **1.** a protective network of metal bars enclosing the driver of a racing car **2.** a reinforcing framework, usually built into the bodywork of a car, around and over the passenger cabin to protect the occupants if the vehicle turns over

roll call *n* **1.** a check on attendance, especially in a school or military establishment, by calling out the names of those expected to be present, with each of those present responding **2.** a time when a roll call is read out, especially one that is fixed at a regular time of day

roll down *n* in financial markets, the closure of one option position and the opening of another one of the same class, but with a lower strike price

rolled gold /rṓld-/ *n UK, ANZ, Can* a thin layer of gold bonded to a backing layer of brass or other base metal. It is used in the manufacture of inexpensive and costume jewellery. US term **filled gold**

rolled oats *npl* oats that have had the husks removed and been flattened and are used in making porridge

rolled paperwork *n* a decorative covering for boxes and other small objects that consists of curls of paper laid in a pattern

rolled steel *n* steel produced to a desired thickness by being passed through a set of rollers

rolled steel joist *n* a beam made of rolled steel with a cross-section shaped like the letter H

roller[1] /rṓlər/ *n* **1. DEVICE FOR APPLYING PAINT** a painting tool in the form of a revolving tube with a soft absorbent covering and a handle, used for applying paint to large surface areas **2. DEVICE FOR FLATTENING LAWNS** a large heavy revolving cylinder or pair of cylinders with a handle, used for flattening a lawn or green **3. HAIR CURLER** a short tube around which hair is wrapped in order to make it curly or wavy **4. HEAVY WAVE** a long heavy wave that does not break until it reaches the shoreline **5. SMALL SOLID WHEEL** a small wheel without spokes, especially on a skate or a piece of heavy furniture **6. TUBE WRAPPED IN MATERIAL** a long cylinder wrapped in material, e.g. a window blind or towel **7. COILED BANDAGE** a long bandage that is rolled up tightly upon itself to form a dense cylinder. The required amount is then cut off for use. **8.** ENG **CYLINDER THAT TRANSMITS FORCE AND MOTION** a cylindrically shaped rotating device that transmits force and motion via its rotation, often used in sets or pairs and machine-operated **9.** RIDING **BELT FOR HORSE BLANKET** a strap around the belly of a horse to hold a blanket in place **10.** PRINTING **INKED TUBE** a hard tube, usually of compressed rubber, on which ink is spread and rolled over type or an engraved plate before printing **11. SOMEBODY OR SOMETHING THAT ROLLS** somebody or something that rolls **12.** *US* BASEBALL **WEAKLY HIT BASEBALL** in baseball, a batted ball that rolls along the ground slowly [14C. < ROLL]

roller[2] /rṓlər/ *n* a blue and brown bird that performs rolling dives and flies erratically during the breeding season. Native to: Europe. Family: Coraciidae. [Late 17C. < German < *rollen* 'to roll']

rollerball /rṓlər bawl/ *n* **1.** a pen with a writing tip in the form of a small movable metal or plastic ball **2.** a device containing a freely rotating ball that is moved by the fingers to control a cursor on a computer screen

roller bearing *n* a set of rotating cylindrically shaped parallel steel rollers contained within a closed track, used to prevent friction between machine parts

Rollerblade /rṓlər blayd/ *tdmk* a trademark for a type of roller skate on which the wheels are arranged in one straight line

roller blind *n* a blind consisting of a length of fabric rolled around a pole and fitted to the top of a window. It unrolls when lowered and rolls up when raised.

roller chain *n* a power transmission chain consisting of freely rotating hollow cylindrical rollers mounted on pins that connect the plates that link adjacent rollers

roller coaster *n* **1.** an amusement park ride consisting of a narrow rail track on a metal framework shaped into extreme peaks and troughs and sharp bends **2.** a situation that is characterized by sudden, extreme, and often repeated changes (*hyphenated when used before a noun*)

roller hockey *n* hockey played on a roller-skating rink or other hard surface by players wearing roller skates

roller rink *n N Am* a place where people can go to roller-skate

roller skate *n* **1.** a metal or plastic frame with wheels attached, usually one pair at the front and another at the back, fastened onto a shoe and used for skating **2.** a specially designed shoe or boot to which a roller skate is attached —**roller-skate** *vi* —**roller skater** *n* —**roller skating** *n*

roller towel *n* a continuous roll of material housed inside a metal box and used for drying the hands. Each user pulls down a fresh section of towel.

roll film *n* a length of film rolled around a spool and put inside a protective case ready to be loaded into a camera

roll forward *n* the closure of one financial option position and the opening of another one of the same class, but with a later expiry date

rollick /róllik/ *vi* (**-licks, -licking, -licked**) to have fun, especially in a loud, rowdy way ■ *n* a loud, rowdy session of having fun [Early 19C. Probably blend of ROLL or ROMP + FROLIC] —**rollicksome** *adj* —**rollicky** *adj*

rollicking /rólliking/ *adj* loud and rowdy ■ *n* a severe reprimand or scolding (*informal*) —**rollickingly** *adv*

rolling /rṓling/ *adj* **1. GRADUALLY DEVELOPING** proceeding in successive phases and usually gaining in momentum, intensity, or effectiveness ○ *a rolling program of reform* **2. CONSTANTLY UPDATED** responsive to change and constantly updated **3. FOLDABLE UP OR DOWN** able to be turned up or down **4. RICH** very well-off (*informal*) ■ *adv* **EXTREMELY** to the extent of staggering (*informal*) ○ *rolling drunk*

rolling bearing *n* a bearing in which the rolling action of components such as balls or cylinders reduces friction

rolling contract *n* **1.** a contract that is open-ended and runs until one of the contracting parties cancels it **2.** a contract for a period of more than one year that is renewed annually for the initial period, subject to a favourable review

rolling hitch *n* a knot used for joining two pieces of rope together or shortening a length of rope, or for attaching a rope to a spar

rolling launch *n* COMM same as **roll-out** (sense 2)

rolling mill *n* **1.** a factory, or part of a factory, where metal, usually in ingot form, is processed by being rolled into sheets or bars of the desired shape and size **2.** a machine with rollers that press metal into sheets or bars of the desired shape and size

rolling paper *n* a small piece of fine paper used for rolling a handmade cigarette (*often used in the plural*)

rolling pin *n* a cylinder, sometimes with small handles at either end, used for rolling out and flattening dough, pastry, or other uncooked food

rolling stock *n* **1.** railway vehicles, e.g. locomotives, passenger carriages, and goods wagons, thought of collectively, especially those belonging to a particular company **2.** *N Am* road vehicles thought of collectively, especially those belonging to a particular company

rolling stone *n* somebody who is incapable of staying in the same job or place for very long [Originally in the proverb 'a rolling stone gathers no moss']

Rolling Stones /rṓling stṓnz/ British rock group, formed in 1962, that rivalled the popularity of the group's early contemporaries, the Beatles. The group was formed by Mick Jagger, Keith Richards, Brian Jones, Charlie Watts, and Bill Wyman, who left the band in late 1992. After Jones' death (1968), Mick Taylor replaced him until 1975, when Ron Wood took his place.

rollmop /rṓl mop/ *n* a fillet of raw herring wrapped around a slice of onion or a pickle and left to marinate in spiced vinegar. It is usually served as an hors d'oeuvre. [Early 20C. < German < *rollen* 'to roll' + *Mops* 'pug dog']

roll neck *n* **1.** a garment neck that is loose-fitting and worn folded down (*hyphenated*) **2.** a garment, especially a sweater, with a roll neck —**rollnecked** *adj*

Rollo /róllō/ (860?–932?) Viking leader. An ancestor of William the Conqueror, he founded the duchy of Normandy (911?).

roll of honour *n* **1.** a list of names of people who have all excelled in some way **2.** a list of names of people who have died during a battle or war in the service of their country, especially people from one area

roll-on *adj* **WITH ROTATING-BALL APPLICATOR** applied to the skin by means of a rotating ball in the top of the container ■ *n* **1. DEODORANT WITH ROTATING-BALL APPLICATOR** a deodorant, cosmetic, or other product that comes in a container with a rotating ball in its top **2. WOMAN'S UNDERGARMENT** a woman's elasticated girdle that is pulled on rather than fastened down the front

roll-on roll-off *adj* describes a method of transport, especially a ferry, designed so that vehicles are driven on one end and, on arrival at their destination, are driven off the other end ■ *n* a roll-on roll-off vessel, especially a ferry

roll-out /rṓl owt/ *n* **1.** the first public display of a new product **2.** a launch of a new product that involves gradually increasing the number of outlets where it is available to the public

rollover /rṓl ōvər/ *n* **1. ACCUMULATION OF PRIZE MONEY** the addition of prize money not won on one occasion to the prize money available on a subsequent occasion **2. LOTTERY DRAW WITH DOUBLE PRIZE MONEY** a National Lottery draw to which the prize fund from the previous draw has been added because no one won the jackpot on that occasion **3.** FIN **TRANSFER OF FUNDS** a transfer of funds from one investment to another similar investment, often without taking possession of the funds **4. CAPSIZING INCIDENT** an act or the process of capsizing, tipping over, or overturning

roll-top desk, roll-top *n* a desk with a rounded cover consisting of connected parallel wooden slats that can be pulled down over the writing area and, usually, locked

roll-up *n UK* a hand-rolled cigarette made using a cigarette paper and loose tobacco (*informal*) ANZ, N Am term **roll-your-own**

rollway /rṓl way/ *n* **1.** a natural or artificial sloping area along which cylindrical objects are rolled, especially a slope used by lumberjacks to move

felled timber to water for transportation **2.** a series of parallel rollers used to facilitate the transportation of heavy loads

roll-your-own *n* ANZ, N Am same as **roll-up** (*informal*)

Rolodex /rólə deks/ *tdmk* a trademark for a desktop card-index system in which cards containing names, addresses, and telephone numbers are attached to but removable from a central cylinder

roly-poly /róli póli/ *adj* of greater body weight than is considered desirable (*sometimes offensive*) ■ *n* (*plural* **roly-polies**) **1.** *also* **roly-poly pudding** a hot pudding made with suet pastry spread with jam or fruit, rolled to form a coil, and baked or steamed **2.** *Aus* PLANTS same as **tumbleweed** (*informal*) [Early 17C. Probably rhyming compound of ROLL + POLL]

Rom /rom/ (*plural* **Roma** /rómmə/) *n* **1.** a member of a nomadic people who migrated from South Asia to Europe in the 15th century and now live throughout the world **2.** a man belonging to the Roma [Mid-19C. < Romany, 'married man'] —**Roma** *adj*

ROM /rom/ *abbr* COMPUT read-only memory

rom., rom *abbr* PRINTING roman

Rom. *abbr* **1.** Roman **2.** LANG Romance **3.** Romania **4.** LANG Romanian **5.** BIBLE Romans

Roma PEOPLES plural of **Rom**

Romagna /rō mányə/ historical region of north-central Italy. It was under Byzantine rule between the 6th and the 8th centuries, when it became incorporated into the Papal States.

romaine /rō máyn/, **romaine lettuce** *n* N Am same as **cos**[1] [Early 20C. < French, form of *romain* 'Roman']

romaji /ró maaji/ *n* the Roman alphabet as used for transliterating Japanese [Late 19C. < Japanese < *roma* 'Roman' + *ji* 'character']

roman[1] /rómən/ *adj* relating to a typeface with upright as opposed to slanting characters that is the standard type used in printing books, newspapers, and magazines ■ *n* roman type or characters [Early 16C. Because it imitates the style of Roman inscriptions]

roman[2] /rō maaN, rōmaaN/ *n* **1.** a novel, especially a French one or one in a French genre (*literary*) **2.** a medieval French narrative poem, especially one that has heroic exploits as its main theme [Mid-18C. < French, 'romance, romantic narrative']

roman[3] /rómən/ *n* a reddish coloured sea bream. Native to: southern Africa. Latin name: *Chrysoblephus laticeps*. [Late 18C. Afrikaans *rooiman*, 'red man']

Roman /rómən/ *adj* **1.** OF MODERN ROME relating to the modern city of Rome and its inhabitants **2.** ANCIENT HIST OF ANCIENT ROME relating to the ancient city of Rome and its territories and inhabitants **3.** ARCHIT OF ANCIENT ROMAN ARCHITECTURAL STYLE relating to, or built in, a style characteristic of the buildings of ancient Rome, especially in having rounded arches, vaults, and domes **4.** CHR OF ROMAN CATHOLIC CHURCH belonging to or characteristic of the Roman Catholic Church ■ *n* **1.** SOMEBODY FROM MODERN ROME somebody who comes from the modern city of Rome **2.** ANCIENT HIST SOMEBODY FROM ANCIENT ROME somebody who came from ancient Rome **3.** CHR OFFENSIVE TERM an offensive term for a member of the Roman Catholic Church [Pre-12C. < Latin *Romanus* 'Roman, a Roman' < *Roma* 'Rome'; later reinforced by French *Romain*]

roman à clef /rō maaN a kláy, rō maán aa-/ (*plural* **romans à clef** /*pronunc. same*/) *n* a novel in which some or all of the characters are based on real people and that usually includes clues to the characters' true identities [< French, 'novel with a key']

Roman alphabet *n* the writing system that represents sounds by 26 letters from A to Z, used for most languages in Western Europe and many elsewhere. It is based on the alphabet developed in ancient Rome.

roman à thèse /rō maaN a téz, rō maán aa-/ (*plural* **romans à thèse** /*pronunc. same*/) *n* a novel in which the author focuses on an injustice and suggests how it might be rectified, especially by putting forward a political message or social theory [< French, 'novel with a thesis']

Roman calendar *n* the lunar calendar, comprising 10 months and an intercalated month, that was used

by the ancient Romans until the introduction of the Julian calendar in 46 BC

Roman candle *n* a short cylindrical firework that when placed on the ground and lit produces showers of sparks and occasional coloured balls or stars of fire

Roman Catholic *adj* relating to the Roman Catholic Church, its members, or its beliefs ■ *n* a member of the Roman Catholic Church

Roman Catholic Church *n* a Christian church that has a pope as the head of a hierarchy of bishops and priests and is administered from the Vatican City in Rome

Roman Catholicism *n* the system of beliefs, practices, and organization of the Roman Catholic Church

romance /rō mánss, ró manss/ *n* **1.** LOVE AFFAIR a love affair, especially a brief and intense one ○ *This is more than just a holiday romance.* **2.** PHYSICAL LOVE sexual love, especially when the other person or the relationship is idealized or when it is exciting and intense **3.** SPIRIT OF ADVENTURE a spirit or feeling of adventure, excitement, the potential for heroic achievement, and the exotic ○ *the romance of cruising down the Nile* **4.** FASCINATION WITH SOMETHING a fascination or enthusiasm for something, especially of an uncritical or inexplicable kind ○ *his lifelong romance with football* **5.** STORY OF LOVE a novel, film, or play with a love story as its main theme ○ *a writer of cheap romances* **6.** LOVE STORIES COLLECTIVELY love stories considered as a genre **7.** MEDIEVAL ADVENTURE STORY a story of the adventures of chivalrous heroes written in verse or prose in a vernacular language in the Middle Ages **8.** MEDIEVAL ADVENTURE STORIES COLLECTIVELY the genre of medieval adventure stories ○ *Arthurian romance* **9.** NARRATIVE OF ADVENTURES a fictional narrative dealing with exciting and extravagant adventures ○ *a romance of piracy on the high seas* **10.** FICTITIOUS ACCOUNT an extravagant or absurd fictitious account of something **11.** MUSIC SHORT LYRICAL PIECE a short lyrical song or instrumental composition, usually expressing or evoking tender emotions ■ *v* (**-mances, -mancing, -manced**) **1.** *vi* TELL ADVENTUROUS STORIES to tell or write extravagant or idealized fictitious accounts **2.** *vi* TELL LOVE STORIES to tell or write stories about love **3.** *vi* THINK ROMANTICALLY to think or behave in a romantic way **4.** *vt* TREAT SOMEBODY ROMANTICALLY to treat somebody in a special way during a love relationship or with a view to entering on one **5.** *vt* HAVE AFFAIR WITH SOMEBODY to have a love affair with somebody [13C. < Old French *romanz* '(work composed) in French' < assumed Vulgar Latin *romanice* 'in the vernacular', form of Latin *romanicus* 'Roman' < *Roma* 'Rome'] —**romancer** *n*

Romance *n* the branch of Indo-European languages that includes French, Italian, Portuguese, Romanian, and Spanish, all of which are descended from Latin. Native speakers: 500 million. —**Romance** *adj*

Roman collar *n* CLOTHING, CHR same as **clerical collar**

Roman Empire *n* **1.** the territories ruled by ancient Rome under its emperors, from 27 BC to BC 395. In 395, these territories were split into the Byzantine or Eastern Roman Empire and the Western Roman Empire. **2.** the rule or form of government of ancient Rome under its emperors

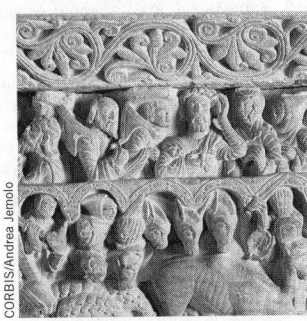

CORBIS/Andrea Jemolo

Romanesque: carved stone capital (1127–45), Pamplona cathedral, Spain

Romanesque /rōmə nésk/ *adj* **1.** TYPICAL OF EARLY EUROPEAN ARCHITECTURAL STYLE relating to or built in the style characteristic of European architecture in the 11th and the 12th centuries, especially in having rounded arches and barrel vaults **2.** RELATING TO EARLY EUROPEAN ART WORKS characteristic of or relating to the style of European painting, sculpture, or decorative arts contemporary with Romanesque architecture. Romanesque works of art show a Byzantine influence and often feature elaborate ornamentation. ■ *n* ROMANESQUE STYLE the Romanesque style in architecture or art

roman-fleuve /rō maaN flŏv, rō maán-/ (*plural* **romans-fleuves** /*pronunc. same*/) *n* a long novel or series of novels telling the stories of a linked group of people over many years [< French, 'river-novel']

Roman holiday *n* **1.** an entertainment in which people are killed, e.g. a gladiatorial contest **2.** a feeling of pleasure derived from watching other people be maimed or killed

Romani *n*, *adj* LANG, PEOPLES another spelling of **Romany**

Romania

Romania /rōō máyni ə, rō-/ country in southeastern Europe, bordered by Ukraine, Moldova, the Black Sea, Bulgaria, Yugoslavia, and Hungary. Language: Romanian. Currency: Romanian leu. Capital: Bucharest. Population: 22,271,839 (2003). Area: 237,500 sq. km/91,700 sq. mi.

Romanian /rōō máyni ən, rō-/ (*plural* **Romanians** or **Rumanians**) *n* **1.** somebody who comes from Romania **2.** the official language of Romania, belonging to the Romance group of Indo-European languages that developed from Latin —**Romanian** *adj*

Romanic /rō mánnik/ *adj* **1.** OF ANCIENT ROME belonging or relating to ancient Rome or the ancient Romans **2.** OF ROMANCE LANGUAGES relating to the Romance family of languages ■ *n* ROMANCE LANGUAGES COLLECTIVELY the Romance family of languages as a group

romanise, etc. *vti* another spelling of **romanize, etc.**

Romanism /rómənizəm/ *n* an offensive term for Roman Catholicism, especially its rituals

Romanist /rómənist/ *n* **1.** SOMEBODY INFLUENCED BY CATHOLICISM a member of a church, especially the Church of England, who is sympathetic to or influenced by Roman Catholicism **2.** OFFENSIVE TERM an offensive term for a member of the Roman Catholic Church **3.** STUDENT OF ANCIENT ROME a student of or expert in ancient Roman history or law ■ *adj* **1.** OFFENSIVE TERM an offensive term meaning belonging or relating to the Roman Catholic Church **2.** OF ANCIENT ROMAN HISTORY relating to or involving ancient Roman history or law —**Romanistic** /rōmə nístik/ *adj*

romanize /rómə nīz/ (**-izes, -izing, -ized**), **romanise** (**-ises, -ising, -ised**) *vt* to transcribe something such as a language or text in the characters of the Roman alphabet

Romanize (**-izes, -izing, -ized**), **Romanise** (**-ises, -ising, -ised**) *v* **1.** *vti* MAKE OR BECOME ROMAN to take on Roman characteristics, or make somebody or something take on Roman characteristics ○ *the Romanized Celts* **2.** *vt* MAKE SOMETHING ROMAN CATHOLIC to make something take on a Roman Catholic character or influence **3.** *vti* CONVERT TO ROMAN CATHOLICISM to become a Roman Catholic, or convert somebody to Roman Catholicism —**Romanization** /rómə nī záysh'n/ *n*

Roman law *n* **1.** the system of law established in

ancient Rome, forming the basis of many modern legal systems **2.** LAW same as **civil law** (sense 3)

Roman mile *n* a measure of distance used in ancient Rome, approximately equal to 1,481 m/1,620 yards

Roman nose *n* a nose with a high and prominent bridge

Roman numeral *n* a letter or sequence of letters used by the ancient Romans to represent cardinal numbers, including I for 1, V for 5, and X for 10

Romano /rō maánō/ *n* a hard sharp-tasting Italian cheese similar to Parmesan [Early 20C. Via Italian, 'Roman' < Latin *Romanus* < *Roma* 'Rome']

Romano /rō maánō/ ➧ **Giulio Romano**

Romans /rṓmənz/ *n* a book of the Bible, originally a letter addressed to the Church in Rome and traditionally attributed to St Paul. Written in about AD 58, it explains his theory of religious thinking. (*takes a singular verb*) See table at **Bible**

Romansch /rō mánsh/, **Romansh** *n* a Rhaeto-Romance language that is one of the official languages of Switzerland. Native speakers: 50,000. [Mid-17C. < Romansch < assumed Vulgar Latin *romanice* (see ROMANCE)] —**Romansch** *adj*

romantic /rō mántik/ *adj* **1.** INVOLVING SEXUAL LOVE involving or characteristic of a love affair or sexual love, especially when the relationship is idealized or exciting and intense ○ *I don't think there's any romantic attachment between them.* **2.** SUITABLE FOR LOVE characterized by or suitable for lovemaking or the expression of tender emotions ○ *a romantic candle-lit dinner for two* **3.** IDEALISTIC characterized by or arising from idealistic or impractical attitudes and expectations ○ *a romantic dreamer* **4.** IMAGINARY imaginary or fictitious in an extravagant or glamorizing way ○ *a romantic version of the events of her life* **5.** INVOLVING ADVENTURE relating to or characterized by adventure, excitement, the potential for heroic achievement, or the exotic ○ *a romantic tale about life in the outback* **6.** ARTS another spelling of **Romantic** ■ *n* **1.** SOMEBODY ROMANTIC somebody who has a romantic personality or outlook **2.** ARTS another spelling of **Romantic** [Mid-17C. < obsolete *romaunt* 'romance, romantic narrative' < Old French, variant of *romanz* (see ROMANCE)] —**romantically** *adv*

Romantic *adj* relating to a movement in late 18th- and early 19th-century music, literature, and art that departed from classicism and emphasized sensibility, the free expression of feelings, nature, and interest in other cultures ■ *n* a writer, composer, or artist who was involved in the Romantic movement during the late 18th and early 19th centuries

romantic comedy *n* **1.** a humorous film, play, or novel about a love story that ends happily **2.** the genre of romantic comedies

romanticise *vti* another spelling of **romanticize**

romanticism /rō mántissizəm/ *n* the quality of being romantic or having romantic inclinations

Romanticism *n* in the arts, the style and theories of the Romantic movement, or the movement itself —**Romanticist** *n*

romanticize /rō mánti sīz/ (**-cizes, -cizing, -cized**), **romanticise** (**-cises, -cising, -cised**) *v* **1.** *vt* to make something seem or believe something to be more glamorous or ideal than it really is ○ *The film tends to romanticize a rather sordid period in history.* **2.** *vi* to think or express something in an amorous, idealistic, or sentimental way —**romanticization** /rō mánti sī záysh'n/ *n*

Romany /rṓməni, rómməni/ (*plural* **-nies**), **Romani** *n* **1.** the Indic language of the Roma people. Native speakers: 250,000. **2.** a member of the Roma people (*dated*) [Early 19C. < Romany *Romani*, form of *Romano* 'Roma' (adjective) < *Rom* 'man'] —**Romany** *adj*

romcom /róm kom/ same as **romantic comedy** (*informal*) [Late 20C. Contraction]

Rome /rōm/ capital city of Italy, located in the centre of the country. The former capital of the Roman Empire, it includes within its boundaries the independent state of the Vatican City. Population: 2,546,804 (2001). ◇ **fiddle while Rome burns** to occupy yourself with unimportant things when there are extremely important things requiring to be done ◇ **when in Rome (do as the Romans do)** used to indicate the advisability of adopting the behaviour and customs of the place or circumstances in which you find yourself

Romeo /rṓmi ō/ (*plural* **-os**) *n* **1.** a man with a reputation for having or seeking romantic or sexual involvement with a large number of women **2.** a code word for the letter 'R', used in international radio communications [Mid-18C. After the lover of Juliet in William Shakespeare's play *Romeo and Juliet* (1594)]

Romish /rṓmish/ *adj* an offensive term meaning belonging to, characteristic of, or influenced by the Roman Catholic Church —**Romishly** *adv* —**Romishness** *n*

Rommel /rómməl/, **Erwin** (1891–1944) German general. He is renowned for his victories in the North African deserts during World War II. Known as **the Desert Fox**

Romney /rómni, rúmni/, **George** (1734–1802) British painter. He is noted for his portraits of British aristocrats in neoclassical settings, especially Emma, Lady Hamilton, whom he depicted in more than 50 portraits.

Romney Marsh[1] /rómni-, rúmni-/ *n* a sheep that has long wool and produces mutton, belonging to a breed originating in the Romney Marsh area

Romney Marsh[2] /rómni-, rúmni-/ region in southern Kent, England. It is protected from the sea by a sea wall. Area: 176 sq. km/68 sq. mi.

romp /romp/ *vi* (**romps, romping, romped**) **1.** PLAY BOISTEROUSLY to run around or play in a boisterous way ○ *kids romping in the playground* **2.** MAKE EASY PROGRESS to progress swiftly and effortlessly ○ *romped through her final exam* **3.** WIN WITH EASE to win a contest easily (*informal*) ○ *The horse romped home* ■ *n* **1.** BOISTEROUS ACTIVITY boisterous or playful activity ○ *The dogs had a romp in the park.* **2.** LIGHTHEARTED WORK a book, play, or film that is lighthearted and lively as opposed to serious or weighty (*informal*) ○ *The novel is an exhilarating romp through the pages of recent history.* **3.** CASUAL SEX a casual or lighthearted sexual encounter (*informal*) **4.** EASY VICTORY a victory that is remarkably or unexpectedly easy (*informal*) [Early 18C. Origin ?]

rompers /rómpərz/ *npl* a one-piece suit of trousers, often short, and a bib held up by shoulder straps, worn by babies and small children

Romulus /rómmyŏŏləss/ *n* in Roman mythology, the founder of the city of Rome. He was the son of Mars and twin brother of Remus, whom he is said to have killed.

Romulus Augustulus /-aw gústyŏŏləss/ (461?–476?) Roman emperor. He was the last Roman emperor in the West, and his deposition by Odoacer in 475–476 marked the end of the Western Roman Empire.

ROMvelope /rómvə lōp/, **romvelope** *n* a protective cardboard or similar cover for a CD [Late 20C. < ROM + ENVELOPE]

RONA *abbr* ACCT return on net assets

rondavel /ron daávəl/ *n S Africa* a circular hut or other building, usually with a conical thatched roof [Late 19C. < Afrikaans *rondawel*]

rondeau /róndō/ (*plural* **-deaux** /-dōz/) *n* **1.** a poem of 13 or 10 lines in 3 stanzas, with 2 rhymes and with the opening phrase repeated twice as an unrhymed refrain **2.** a medieval French song, especially a trouvère song with a two-part refrain [Early 16C. < French, later form of *rondel* (see RONDEL)]

rondel /rónd'l/, **rondelle** /ron dél/ *n* a poem, similar to a rondeau, that has 13 or 14 lines in 3 stanzas, with 2 rhymes and with the opening 2 lines repeated as a refrain [14C. < Old French, 'small round' (from the repetition of the opening two lines) < *ro(u)nd-* (see ROUND[1])]

rondelet /róndə let, -lay/ *n* a short form of rondeau, with 5 or 7 lines and the first line repeated as a refrain. The first line is of 4 syllables and is repeated as line 3 and, in the longer form, line 7, while the other lines have 8 syllables.

rondelle *n* LITERAT same as **rondel**

rondo /róndō/ (*plural* **-dos**) *n* a piece of instrumental music or movement in which the principal theme is repeated between at least two sections that contrast with it, often forming the last movement of a sonata [Late 18C. Via Italian < French *rondeau* (see RONDEAU)]

rone /rōn/ *n Scotland* **1.** a gutter at the edge of a roof, for channelling rain away **2.** *also* **ronepipe** /rōn pīp/ a drainpipe that channels rainwater down the side of a building away from a roof gutter [Late 16C. < ?]

röntgen *n* MEASURE another spelling of **roentgen**

roo /roo/ (*plural* **roos**) *n Aus* same as **kangaroo** (*informal*) [Early 20C. Shortening]

roo bar *n Aus* a metal bar on the front of a car or truck that prevents the vehicle from being damaged in the event of a collision with an animal

rood /rood/ *n* **1.** CRUCIFIX a crucifix, especially one mounted at the entrance to the choir or chancel of a church **2.** JESUS CHRIST'S CROSS the cross on which Jesus Christ was crucified (*archaic*) **3.** QUARTER OF ACRE a unit of area equal to 0.1 hectare/0.25 acre [Old English *rōd* 'cross, pole' < Germanic]

rood screen *n* a partition separating the choir or chancel of a church from the nave or main part

roof /roof/ *n* **1.** UPPER COVERING OF BUILDING the outside covering of the top of a building, or the framework supporting this. See illustration on next page **2.** TOP PART the top part of something, forming a covering, e.g. the top of a vehicle ○ *a blue car with a black roof* **3.** TOP OF INSIDE CAVITY the top of the inside of a hollow structure ○ *the roof of the cave* **4.** STRUCTURE COVERING BODY CAVITY the upper covering structure of a body part, especially one with a vaulted structure such as the mouth **5.** HIGHEST POINT the highest point or upper limit of something ■ *vt* (**roofs, roofing, roofed**) FIX ROOF ON SOMETHING to fix a top covering onto something, especially a building ○ *The house is roofed with slate tiles.* [Old English *hrōf* 'roof, ceiling, top' < Germanic] —**roofless** *adj* —**rooflike** *adj* ◇ **hit the roof** to be extremely angry (*informal*) ◇ **go through the roof** to rise to an extremely high level (*informal*) ◇ **have a roof over your head** to have a residence of your own as a basic necessity of life or as a shelter, e.g. during severe weather ◇ **hit the roof** to be extremely angry (*informal*)

CULTURAL NOTE ***Cat on a Hot Tin Roof***, a play (1955) by US dramatist Tennessee Williams. Set in the US South, it depicts the Pollitt family gathering to celebrate the 65th birthday of patriarch Big Daddy. The simmering conflicts between Daddy and sons Gooper and Buck and their wives reflect the lies and deceit that underpin many family relationships. It was made into a film by Richard Brooks in 1958.

roofer /rŏŏfər/ *n* somebody whose job is to build or repair the roofs of buildings

roof garden *n* a garden on the flat roof of a building

roofie /rŏŏfi/ *n* flunitrazepam, or a dose of flunitrazepam, especially when used as a date-rape drug (*slang*) [Late 20C. Probably alteration of ROHYPNOL]

roofing /rŏŏfing/ *n* **1.** MATERIAL FOR ROOF material used to make a roof **2.** TOP OF SOMETHING something forming a top or roof **3.** OCCUPATION OF ROOFER the business or occupation of making or repairing roofs

roofline /rŏŏf līn/ *n* the outline of the roof of a building or a series of buildings

roof rack *n UK, ANZ, Can* a frame attached to the top of a motor vehicle, used for carrying things, especially luggage. US term **luggage rack**

roof rat *n* ZOOL same as **black rat**

rooftop /rŏŏf top/ *n* the outer surface of the roof of a building ◇ **shout something from the rooftops** to make something publicly known or announce something to everybody, often in a jubilant manner

rooftree /rŏŏf tree/ *n* CONSTR same as **ridgepole** (sense 1)

rooibos /róy boss/ (*plural same*) *n S Africa* **1.** an evergreen bush with leaves that are often used to make tea. Native to: southern Africa. Genus: *Aspalathus*. **2.** *also* **rooibos tea** tea made from the leaves of the rooibos, drunk for its healthful properties [Early 20C. < Afrikaans, 'red bush']

rooigras /róy graass, -khraass/ *n S Africa* a grass with a reddish tinge in winter, used for pasture. Native

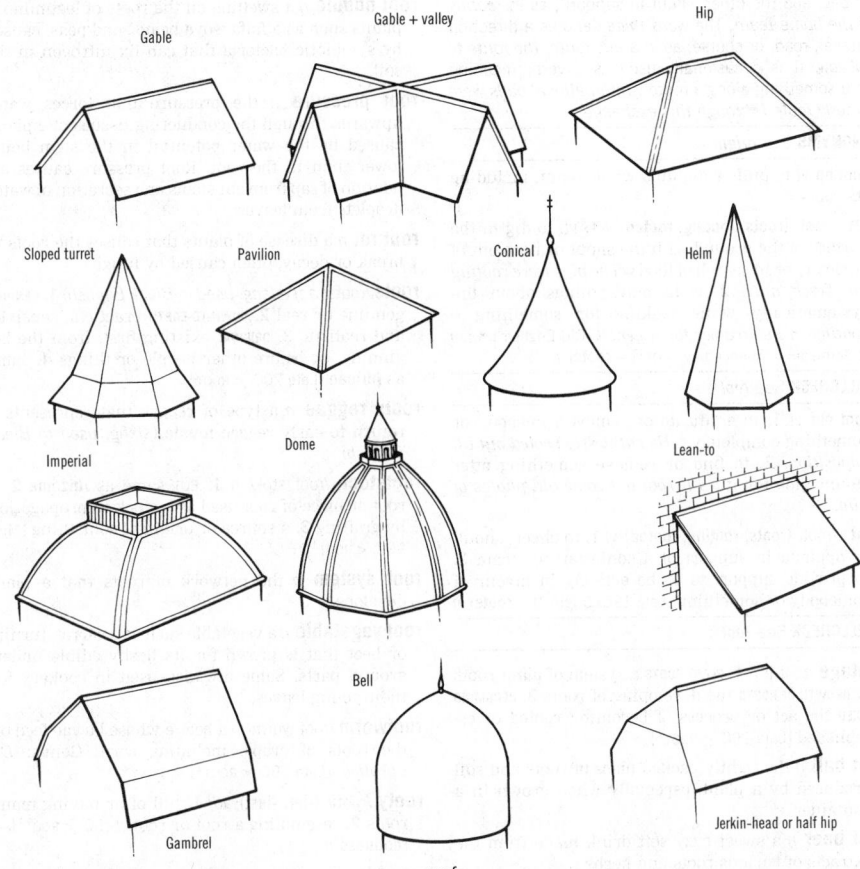

Gable

Gable + valley

Hip

Sloped turret

Pavilion

Conical

Helm

Imperial

Dome

Lean-to

Bell

Gambrel

Jerkin-head or half hip

roof

Eleanor Roosevelt

Roosevelt /rṓzə velt/, **Eleanor** (1884–1962) US first lady (1933–45), social activist, and writer. As the wife of President Franklin D. Roosevelt, she made national broadcasts and wrote a syndicated newspaper column, establishing her reputation as a campaigner for progressive social causes. She was a US delegate to the United Nations (1945–53) and chaired the commission that drafted the Universal Declaration of Human Rights. Born **Roosevelt, Anna Eleanor**

'No one can make you feel inferior without your consent.'
[Eleanor Roosevelt, *Catholic Digest*; August 1960]

Franklin D. Roosevelt

Roosevelt, Franklin D. (1882–1945) 32nd president of the United States. A Democrat, he served longer than any other president (1933–45), with an unprecedented election to four terms. He held office during the Great Depression of the 1930s and World War II. Full name **Roosevelt, Franklin Delano**. See table at **president**

'We look forward to a world founded upon four essential human freedoms. The first is freedom of speech and expression—everywhere in the world. The second is freedom of every person to worship God in his own way—everywhere in the world. The third is freedom from want—everywhere in the world. The fourth is freedom from fear—anywhere in the world.'
[Franklin D. Roosevelt, *Speech to Congress, Public Papers*; 6 January 1941]

Theodore Roosevelt

Roosevelt, Theodore (1858–1919) 26th president of the United States (1901–09). During his Republican

to: southern Africa. Latin name: *Themeda triandra*. [Late 19C. < Afrikaans, 'red grass']

rooikat /róy kat/ *n S Africa* same as **caracal** [Late 18C. < Afrikaans, 'red cat']

rooinek /roŏ i nek, róy nek/ *n S Africa* a British person, or an English-speaking South African (*slang disapproving*) [Late 19C. < Afrikaans, 'red neck']

rook

rook[1] /roŏk/ *n* **1. BIRD OF CROW FAMILY** a large bird of the crow family with black feathers and a pale area at the base of its beak, that nests in colonies in treetops. Native to: Europe, Asia. Latin name: *Corvus frugilegus*. **2. SWINDLER** a swindler or cheat, especially at cards (*slang*) ■ *vt* (**rooks, rooking, rooked**) **CHEAT SOMEBODY** to overcharge, swindle, or cheat somebody (*slang*) ○ *If you paid that amount you've been rooked.* [Old English *hrōc* < Germanic] —**rooky** *adj*

rook[2] /roŏk/ *n* any of four chess pieces that begin a game in the corner squares and that can move in a straight line in any direction over any number of unoccupied squares [13C. Via French < Arabic *rukk*]

rookery /roŏkəri/ (*plural* **-ies**) *n* **1. GROUP OF ROOKS** a colony of rooks nesting in treetops **2. GROUP OF PENGUINS** a colony of nesting penguins **3. ANIMALS' COLLECTIVE BREEDING PLACE** a breeding or living area for large numbers of animals, especially birds or mammals, that come together in colonies to nest or breed **4.**

SLUM AREA a slum or overcrowded group of run-down houses, especially tenements (*archaic*) [Early 18C. < ROOK[1]]

rookie /roŏki/ *n N Am* somebody who is new to an activity or job (*informal*) [Late 19C. Origin ?]

room /room, roŏm/ *n* **1. SPACE** space that may or may not be filled with something or where something can happen ○ *no room to move* ○ *need more room* ○ *room for another chair* **2. PART OF BUILDING** an area within a building that is enclosed by a floor, walls, and a ceiling ○ *a hotel room* **3. PEOPLE IN ROOM** the people in a room considered as a group ○ *Her entrance silenced the room.* **4. SCOPE** the scope, opportunity, or possibility for something to exist, happen, or be done ○ *There's room for improvement.* ■ **rooms** *npl* **ACCOMMODATION** part of a house or hotel that may be rented as separate accommodation ○ *I managed to find myself rooms in town.* ■ *vi* (**rooms, rooming, roomed**) *N Am* **SHARE LIVING QUARTERS** to occupy or share living quarters with one person or several people [Old English *rūm* < Germanic, 'spacious'] —**roomful** *n* ◇ **not enough room to swing a cat** very little space

room and board *n* accommodation with all meals provided, given in return for work

~~roomate~~ incorrect spelling of **roommate**

roomer /roŏmər, roŏmər/ *n N Am* same as **lodger** (*dated*)

roomette /roo mét, roŏ-/ *n N Am* a private single compartment in a railway sleeping car

roommate /roŏm mayt, roŏm-/ *n* somebody with whom a person shares a room

room service *n* a service providing food and drinks served to hotel guests in their rooms ○ *Room service is available 24 hours a day.*

room temperature *n* the average normal temperature of a living room, usually thought of as around 20°C/68°F or slightly above ○ *This cheese should be served at room temperature.*

roomy /roŏmi, roŏ-/ (**-ier, -iest**) *adj* having plenty of space in which to move around —**roomily** *adv* —**roominess** *n*

presidency he expanded US involvement in world affairs, established domestic reforms, and promoted conservation. Known as **Teddy Roosevelt**. See table at **president**

> 'We have room in this country for but one flag, the Stars and Stripes...We have room for but one loyalty, loyalty to the United States...We have room for but one language, the English language.'
> [Theodore Roosevelt, *Message to the American Defense Society*; 3 January 1919]

> 'There is a homely adage which runs "Speak softly and carry a big stick, you will go far".'
> [Theodore Roosevelt, *Speech at Minnesota State Fair*; 2 September 1901]

roost /roost/ *n* **1. PLACE WHERE BIRDS SLEEP** a place where a bird rests or sleeps, e.g. a perch or a building with perches for domestic fowl **2. BIRDS SHARING ROOST** a group of birds sharing a roost **3. TEMPORARY ACCOMMODATION** a place where somebody may rest or sleep temporarily (*slang*) ■ *vi* (**roosts, roosting, roosted**) **GO TO SLEEP** to rest or sleep on or in a roost ○ *Starlings were roosting in the trees.* [Old English *hrōst*, origin ?] ◇ **rule the roost** to be the person who is in charge and who must be obeyed (*informal*)

rooster /rōōstər/ *n N Am* same as **cock** *n* (sense 1)

root[1] /root/ *n* **1. UNDERGROUND BASE OF PLANT** the part of a plant that has no leaves or buds and usually spreads underground, anchoring the plant and absorbing water and nutrients from the soil **2. UNDERGROUND EDIBLE PART OF PLANT** an underground plant part that is used as a vegetable, e.g. a carrot or turnip ○ *diced roots* ○ *root crops* **3. ATTACHMENT OF BODY PART** the portion of a body part such as a tooth or hair that is embedded in tissue **4. BASE OF SOMETHING** the bottom or base of something, or the part by which something is attached to the body ○ *the root of the tongue* **5. CAUSE OF SOMETHING** the fundamental cause, basis, or essence of something, or the source from which something derives ○ *the roots of discontent* **6. ANCESTOR** an ancestor or progenitor, especially one from whom many people are descended **7.** MATHS **NUMBER MULTIPLIED BY ITSELF** a number that when multiplied by itself a particular number of times equals another number ○ *2 is the square root of 4.* **8.** MATHS **NUMBER SUBSTITUTABLE FOR VARIABLE** a number that can take the place of the variable in an equation and solve the equation **9.** LING **BASIC PART OF WORD** the basic meaningful part of a word that is left when any affixes are removed and that cannot be analysed further **10.** LING **ORIGINAL FORM OF WORD** the original reconstructed form from which a recorded word is derived, e.g. by phonetic change or the addition of affixes **11.** MUSIC **FOUNDATION OF CHORD** the note that forms the foundation of a chord **12.** ANAT **END OF NERVE** the end of a nerve that is nearer to the centre of the body **13.** *ANZ* **OFFENSIVE TERM** an offensive term for a sexual partner, especially of a man (*slang*) ■ **roots** *npl* **1. ORIGINS** cultural or family origins, especially as the basis for a feeling of belonging in a particular place or environment ○ *I live in the city but my roots are in the country.* **2. SOMEBODY'S GENETIC ORIGIN** somebody's genetic origins or ancestry ■ *v* (**roots, rooting, rooted**) **1.** *vti* **GROW ROOTS** to develop a root or roots, or cause a plant to grow roots **2.** *vti* **BE FIXED** to become fixed, embedded, or immobile, or cause somebody or something to become fixed, embedded, or immobile ○ *news that rooted me to the spot* **3.** *vi* **BE BASED** to have a basis or origin in something ○ *herbal remedies that are rooted in folk medicine* **4.** *vti ANZ* **OFFENSIVE TERM** an offensive term meaning to have sexual intercourse with somebody (*slang*) [Pre-12C. < Old Norse *rót* < Indo-European, 'branch, root'] —**rooter** *n* ◇ **root and branch** in every respect, or to the fullest extent ○ *reformed the system root and branch* ◇ **take root** to become established and accepted

SPELLCHECK root or **route**? Do not confuse the spelling of ***root*** and ***route***, which sound similar. The word ***root*** denotes an underground plant part, or the base of something, as in *root vegetables, the square root of 2401, the root of the problem.* It is also used as a verb, meaning 'fix', 'base', as in *rooted to the spot, rooted in tradition,* and there are also two other verbs ***root***, one meaning 'dig', as in *pigs rooting for truffles, rooted a pen out of her bag,* and the other 'shout in support', as in *rooting for the home team.* The word ***route*** denotes a direction of travel, road, or course, as in *a bus route, the route to Glasgow.* It is occasionally used as a verb, meaning 'send something along a route': *International calls were formerly routed through this exchange.*

SYNONYMS See ***origin***.

root up *vt* to pull or dig up a whole plant, including its roots

root[2] /root/ (**roots, rooting, rooted**) *v* **1.** *vti* to dig in the surface of the ground with the snout or nose out of curiosity or in search of food ○ *The pigs were rooting for beech nuts.* **2.** *vi* to move things about unsystematically while looking for something ○ *rooting in the drawer for a pencil* [Old English *wrōtan* < Germanic; influenced by ROOT[1]] —**rooter** *n*

SPELLCHECK See ***root***[1].

root out *vt* **1.** to eradicate or remove somebody or something completely ○ *He ruthlessly rooted out all opposition.* **2.** to find or remove something after rummaging for it ○ *I'll root out some old photos of him.*

root[3] /root/ (**roots, rooting, rooted**) *vi* **1.** to cheer, shout, or applaud in support of a contestant or team **2.** to provide support to or be actively in favour of somebody or something [Late 19C. Origin ?] —**rooter** *n*

SPELLCHECK See ***root***[1].

rootage /rōōtij/ *n* **1. PLANT ROOTS** a system of plant roots **2. GROWTH OF ROOTS** the developing of roots **3. BECOMING FIXED** the act or process of becoming rooted or established [Late 19C. < ROOT[1]]

root ball *n* the tightly packed mass of roots and soil produced by a plant, especially when grown in a container

root beer *n* a sweet fizzy soft drink made from the extracts of various roots and herbs

root canal *n* the cavity in the root of a tooth, containing pulp, nerves, and blood vessels

root cap *n* a thick protective mass of cells that covers the growing tip of the root of a plant

root climber *n* a vine that climbs up a structure by developing small roots on its stems that grip the structure. Ivy is a root climber.

root crop *n* a crop grown for its edible underground parts, e.g. turnips, potatoes, or sugar beet

root directory *n* the top-level directory in a computer's filing system, represented by a backslash (\), as in C:\

rooted /rōōtid/ *adj* **1. HAVING ROOTS** on which strong roots have developed ○ *a rooted plant* **2. WELL ESTABLISHED** arising from firmly held beliefs or long-standing traditions or practices ○ *a rooted conviction* **3. UNABLE TO MOVE** unable to move because of shock or fear **4. HAVING STRONG TIES** having strong emotional or cultural roots **5.** *ANZ* **TIRED OR NOT FUNCTIONING** exhausted, or unable to function (*slang*) [14C. < ROOT[1]] —**rootedness** *n* ◇ **get rooted** *ANZ* an offensive phrase used when angry or irritated to tell somebody to go away (*slang*)

root hair *n* a fine growth from the outer cells of a plant root that resembles a hair and absorbs nutrients. Root hairs are elongated epidermal cells that increase the surface area of roots to improve absorption of water and minerals.

root knot *n* a disease of plants caused by nematodes in which the roots become enlarged and plant growth is stunted

rootle /rōōt'l/ (**-tles, -tling, -tled**) *vi* to root or rummage (*informal*) [Early 19C. < ROOT[2]]

rootless /rōōtləss/ *adj* **1.** lacking close ties to people or places **2.** with roots cut off or underdeveloped [14C. < ROOT[1]] —**rootlessly** *adv* —**rootlessness** *n*

rootlet /rōōtlət/ *n* a small root or part of a root [Late 18C. < ROOT[1]]

root mean square *n* the square root of the mean of the squares of a set of numbers. Sometimes the root mean square is a more useful measure of central tendency than the mean or the median.

root nodule *n* a swelling on the roots of leguminous plants such as alfalfa, soya beans, and peas, caused by symbiotic bacteria that can fix nitrogen in the soil

root pressure *n* the pressure that forces water upwards through the conducting tissues of a plant, caused by the water potential in the stem being lower than in the root. Root pressure causes exudation of sap from cut stems and secretion of water droplets from leaves.

root rot *n* a disease of plants that causes the roots to break or decay, often caused by fungi

roots /roots/ *adj* (*slang; used in Black English*) **1. GENUINE** genuine or real **2. DOWN-TO-EARTH** practical, sensible, and realistic **3. ORIGINAL** existing first, from the beginning, or before other people or things **4.** same as **African** [Late 20C. < ROOT[1]]

roots reggae *n* a type of reggae that represents a return to early reggae music (*slang; used in Black English*)

rootstock /rōōt stok/ *n* **1.** BOT same as **rhizome** **2.** a root or piece of root used as a stock in propagation by grafting **3.** a source or origin of something [Mid-19C. < ROOT[1]]

root system *n* the network of roots that a plant develops

root vegetable *n* a vegetable such as a carrot, turnip, or beet that is grown for its fleshy edible underground parts. Some are also used in cookery for their young leaves.

rootworm /rōōt wurm/ *n* a beetle whose larvae feed on the roots of crops, including corn. Genus: *Diabrotica.* [Late 19C. < ROOT[1]]

rooty /rōōti/ (**-ier, -iest**) *adj* **1.** full of or having many roots **2.** resembling a root or roots [15C. < ROOT[1]] —**rootiness** *n*

ropable /rōpəb'l/, **ropeable** *adj* **1.** able to be caught or restrained using a rope ○ *ropable steers* **2.** *ANZ* extremely angry (*informal*)

rope /rōp/ *n* **1. STRONG CORD** a strong cord made by twisting together strands of hemp or other fibres or wire **2. STRING OF THINGS** a row of things strung or twisted together ○ *a rope of pearls* **3. STRAND OF STICKY MATERIAL** a stringy strand of a sticky substance ○ *a rope of saliva* **4. CORD FOR HANGING SOMEBODY** a cord with a noose at one end that is used for hanging people **5. DEATH BY HANGING** execution by hanging **6. FREEDOM** freedom or latitude to do something ■ **ropes** *npl* **1. CORDS OF RING USED FOR FIGHTING** the cords used to enclose a boxing or wrestling ring **2. USUAL PROCEDURES** the appropriate means and procedures for doing something or for functioning in an environment (*informal*) ○ *Her task was to show the new employee the ropes.* ■ *v* (**ropes, roping, roped**) **1.** *vt* **SECURE SOMETHING WITH ROPE** to tie, link, or bind somebody or something with rope ○ *The two climbers were roped together for the ascent.* **2.** *vt* **ENCLOSE AREA** to enclose or partition an area using ropes as barriers ○ *The museum staff had roped off the area.* **3.** *vt* **LASSO ANIMAL** to catch an animal with a lasso ○ *rope a steer* **4.** *vi* **FORM STRANDS** to form strands that resemble rope in shape or texture [Old English *rāp* < Germanic] —**roper** *n* ◇ **give somebody enough rope to hang himself** *or* **herself** to give somebody enough freedom to make mistakes or reveal his or her shortcomings ◇ **on the ropes** in a desperate or hopeless position and likely to fail (*informal*)

rope in *vt* to involve somebody in an activity, especially somebody who was initially reluctant or unwilling (*informal*) ○ *We got roped in to help with the cleaning up.*

ropeable *adj* another spelling of **ropable**

rope-a-dope *adj US* describes a strategy in which somebody feigns weakness until an opponent becomes exhausted in an effort to win, then defeats the opponent decisively (*slang*)

ropedancer /rōp daanssər/ *n* an acrobat who dances or performs feats on a rope, especially a tightrope, stretched above the ground —**ropedancing** *n*

Roper /rōpər/ river in northern Australia, in the Northern Territory. Length: 400 km/250 mi.

ropewalk /róp wawk/ *n* a long shed or covered walk where ropes are made

rope walker *n* an acrobat who performs on a rope stretched above the ground, especially a tightrope walker

ropeway /róp way/ *n* a system of cables strung from high supports and used to carry heavy objects such as logs from one place to another through the air

ropy /rópi/ (**-ier, -iest**), **ropey** *adj* **1. SIMILAR TO ROPE** resembling a rope or ropes **2. FORMING STICKY THREADS** forming into sticky, stringy strands **3. INFERIOR** not meeting an acceptable standard (*informal*) ○ *a rather ropy performance* **4. ILL** slightly unwell (*informal*) —**ropily** *adv* —**ropiness** *n*

roque /rōk/ *n* a US game developed from croquet and played on a hard court with a surrounding wall from which the ball can rebound and still be in play [Late 19C. Alteration of CROQUET]

Roquefort /rók fawr/ *n* a moist, strongly flavoured, blue-veined cheese made from ewes' milk and matured in caves [Mid-19C. After ROQUEFORT-SUR-SOULZON]

Roquefort-sur-Soulzon /rók fawr syoor sóo zoN/ town in Aveyron Region, in south-central France, famous for its blue cheese. Population: 679 (1999).

roquelaure /róka lawr/ *n* a knee-length hooded cloak worn by men in Europe in the 18th and 19th centuries [Early 18C. After Antoine-Gaston (1656–1738), Duc de *Roquelaure* and Marshal of France]

roquet /rókay, -ki/ *vti* (**-quets** /-kayz/, **-queting** /-kay ing, -ki ing/, **-queted** /-kayd, -kid/) in croquet, to strike another player's ball with your own ball ■ *n* in croquet, a stroke that makes the player's ball strike that of another player [Mid-19C. Probably alteration of CROQUET]

roquette /ro két/ *n* PLANTS, FOOD same as **rocket**[2] (sense 1) [Early 20C. < French (see ROCKET[2])]

ro-ro /rō rō/ *n* TRANSP same as **roll-on roll-off**

rorqual /ráwrkwəl/ *n* a large streamlined baleen whale that has a small pointed dorsal fin and longitudinal grooves on the throat, e.g. the blue whale or the humpback whale. Genus: *Balaenoptera*. [Early 19C. Via French < Norwegian *røyrkval* < Old Norse *reyðarhvalr* < *reyðr* 'rorqual' (< *rauðr* 'red') + *hvalr* 'whale']

Rorschach test /ráwr shaak-, -shakh-/ *n* a projective test of personality or mental state based on somebody's interpretation of a series of standard inkblots [Early 20C. After Hermann Rorschach (1884–1922), Swiss psychiatrist]

rort /rawrt/ *Aus* (*informal*) *n* a dishonest scheme or practice ■ *vt* (**rorts, rorting, rorted**) to manipulate something to personal advantage dishonestly or fraudulently ○ *accused of rorting their travel expenses* [Mid-20C. Back-formation < slang *rorty* 'boisterous, rowdy' < ?]

rorter /ráwrtər/ *n* Aus somebody who dishonestly or fraudulently manipulates a system to their own advantage —**rorting** *n*

Rosa /róza/ ♦ **Monte Rosa**

rosace /róz ayss/ *n* **1. ARCHIT** same as **rose window 2.** an ornament resembling the open flower of a rose [Mid-19C. Via French < Latin *rosaceus* 'made of roses' < *rosa* (see ROSE[1])]

rosacea /rō záyshə/ *n* a recurring inflammatory disorder of the skin of the nose, cheeks, and forehead that is characterized by swelling, dilation of capillaries, pimples, and a reddened appearance [Late 19C. < modern Latin (*acne*) *rosacea* 'rose-coloured (acne)' < form of Latin *rosaceus* < *rosa* (see ROSE[1])]

rosaceous /rō záyshəss/ *adj* **1.** belonging or relating to the rose family (**Rosaceae**) of flowering plants **2.** resembling a rose flower [Mid-18C. < Latin *rosaceus* < *rosa* (see ROSE[1])]

Rosalind /rózza lind/ *n* a small inner natural satellite of Uranus, discovered in 1986 by the Voyager 2 planetary probe. It is approximately 58 km in diameter.

rosaniline /rō zánnə leen, -līn/, **rosanilin** /rō zánnə lin/ *n* a brownish-red crystalline compound. Source: aniline. Use: dye, dye manufacture, antifungal drug,

in Schiff's reagent. Formula: $C_{20}H_{21}N_3O$. [Mid-19C. < ROSE[1]]

rosarian /rō záiri ən/ *n* a cultivator of or expert in the growing of roses [Mid-19C. < Latin *rosarium* 'rose garden' < form of *rosarius* 'of roses' < *rosa* (see ROSE[1])]

Rosario /rō saári ō/ city in east-central Argentina, situated on the River Parana. Population: 1,157,372 (1991).

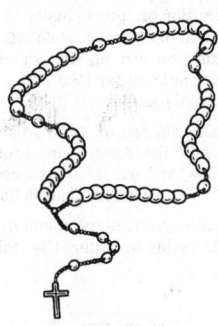

rosary (sense 2)

rosary /rózəri/ (*plural* **-ries**) *n* **1. SERIES OF PRAYERS** a series of Roman Catholic prayers, usually made up of five or 15 decades of Hail Marys, each decade beginning with an Our Father and ending with a Gloria **2. CATHOLIC PRAYER BEADS** a string of beads used in counting the prayers said in a rosary **3.** *also* **rosary bead NON-CATHOLIC PRAYER BEADS** a string of beads used in praying by members of religions or denominations other than Roman Catholicism [15C. < Latin *rosarium*, Anglo-Latin *rosarius* 'rose garden' (see ROSARIAN)]

ORIGIN It was a common stylistic device in the Middle Ages to name collections of verse or similar short pieces after bunches of flowers (*anthology* comes from the Greek word for 'flower', and a similar inspiration underlies *florilegium*). This was the background against which a collection of Roman Catholic prayers came to be known as a *rosary*. The metaphor was probably encouraged by the symbolic association of roses and rose gardens with, respectively, the Virgin Mary and paradise.

ROSCO /róskō/ *n* a company that leases trains to train-operating companies under the arrangements by which the UK national railway system was privatized. Full form **rolling stock operating company**

Roscommon /ross kómmən/ **1.** county in Connacht province, west-central Republic of Ireland. Population: 51,975 (2002). Area: 2,463 sq. km/951 sq. mi. **2.** town and administrative centre of County Roscommon, in the Republic of Ireland. Population: 3,427 (1991).

rose

rose[1] /rōz/ *n* **1. PRICKLY BUSH WITH ORNAMENTAL FLOWERS** a prickly bush with compound leaves that is cultivated in many varieties and hybrids for its flowers. Genus: *Rosa*. **2. FLOWER OF ROSE** a flower of the rose. Roses are usually red, pink, yellow, or white and are often fragrant. The wild rose has five petals, but cultivated varieties are usually double or partly double. **3. PLANT SIMILAR TO ROSE** a member of the family of flowering plants that includes the rose, or a plant that resembles it, especially in having similar flowers. Family: Rosaceae. **4. REDDISH COLOUR** a reddish-pink colour **5. ORNAMENT RESEMBLING ROSE** a representation of a rose flower as an emblem or

decoration, or an ornament or design resembling a rose flower **6. ARCHIT** same as **rose window 7. SPRINKLER NOZZLE** a perforated nozzle on a watering can or hose for producing a spray **8. CEILING FITMENT FOR WIRES** a circular fitting on a ceiling through which the lead of an electric light passes **9. HANDICRAFT, MANUF** same as **rose cut 10. MINERALS FORM OF MINERAL** a mineral form that is round and resembles a rose ■ **roses** *npl* **1. PINK COLOURING** pink colouration, especially in the cheeks ○ *a baby with roses in his cheeks* **2. EASY CIRCUMSTANCES** favourable, comfortable, or easy circumstances (*informal*) ○ *She thinks the exam will be roses, but is she ever wrong!* ■ *adj* **1. REDDISH-PINK** of a reddish-pink colour **2. HAVING OR RESEMBLING ROSES** containing or resembling rose plants or blossoms, or smelling like rose blossoms **3. RELATING TO ROSES** relating to or used for roses [Old English *rōse*, via Germanic < Latin *rosa*, probably < Greek *rhodon* < Iranian] ◇ **everything's coming up roses** everything is going very well (*informal*)

rose[2] past tense of **rise**

rosé /ró zay/ *n* a pink-coloured wine, especially one made by fermenting red grapes and removing the skins from the juice before all the colour has been extracted [Late 19C. < French < (*vin*) *rosé* 'pink (wine)']

Rose /rōz/, **Murray** (b. 1939) British-born Australian swimmer. He won gold medals at the 1956 and 1960 Olympics. Full name **Rose, Iain Murray**

rose apple *n* **1.** a rose-scented oval fruit. Use: jellies, confections. **2.** an evergreen tree with decorative flowers, that produces rose apples. Native to: Southeast Asia. Latin name: *Syzygium jambos*.

roseate /rózi ət/ *adj* **1.** having plumage of a reddish-pink colour **2.** optimistic or idealistic, especially to an absurd degree [15C. < Latin *roseus* 'rosy' < *rosa* (see ROSE[1])] —**roseately** *adv*

Roseau /rō sō/ coastal town and capital of Dominica, in the southwestern part of the island. Population: 15,853 (1991).

rosebay /róz bay/ *n* PLANTS **1.** same as **rosebay willowherb 2.** same as **oleander**

rosebay willowherb *n* a perennial plant with spikes of pink flowers. Native to: northern temperate regions. Latin name: *Epilobium augustifolium*. N Am term **fireweed**

Rosebery /róz berri/ lake in the centre of the North Island, New Zealand, originally formed by a volcanic eruption. It is a major tourist attraction. Area: 80 sq. km/31 sq. mi.

Rosebery, Archibald Philip Primrose, 5th Earl of (1847–1929) British prime minister (1894–95). He served twice as foreign secretary before succeeding W. E. Gladstone as Liberal Party leader and prime minister.

rosebud /róz bud/ *n* the unopened flower of a rose

rosebush /róz boosh/ *n* a rose growing as a bush rather than as a climber or as ground cover

rose campion *n* a plant with white woolly down on its stems and leaves. Flowers: pink. Native to: Europe, Asia. Latin name: *Lychnis coronaria*.

rose chafer *n* a greenish-gold beetle that feeds on the roots, leaves, and flowers of roses and other garden plants. Latin name: *Cetonia aurata*.

rose-coloured *adj* **1.** a reddish-pink colour **2.** optimistic or idealistic, especially to an unjustifiable degree ○ *He tends to take a rose-coloured view of things.* ◇ **through** *or* **with rose-coloured glasses** with unwarranted, unwise, or inappropriate optimism (*informal*) ○ *looked at the world through rose-coloured glasses, never facing up to dangers*

rose cut *n* a way of cutting gemstones that gives them a flat base and a hemispherical crown with facets rising to a low point —**rose-cut** *adj*

rosefish /róz fish/ *n* (*plural same* or **-fishes**) *n* **1.** a spiny-finned red fish. Native to: northern Atlantic. Latin name: *Sebastes marinus*. **2. FISH** same as **redfish** (sense 1)

rose geranium *n* a pelargonium with scented leaves. Flowers: pink. Use: leaves: flavouring, perfumes. Latin name: *Pelargonium graveolens*.

rosehip /róz hip/ *n* the fleshy fruit of a rose, re-

sembling a berry. Use: jelly, herbal tea, medicinal syrups.

rosella /rō zéllə/ *n* a parrot with bright colourful feathers and a long graduated tail, sometimes kept as a cagebird. Native to: Australia. Genus: *Platycercus*. [Early 19C. Probably alteration of *Rose Hiller*, after *Rose Hill*, Parramatta, near Sydney, Australia]

rose mallow *n* **1.** a tall plant that grows in marshy areas and has downy leaves. Flowers: pink or white. Native to: eastern North America. Genus: *Hibiscus*. **2.** *US* PLANTS same as **hollyhock**

rosemary

rosemary /rṓzməri/ *n* **1.** aromatic grey green needle-shaped leaves. Use: food flavouring, perfume. **2.** an aromatic bush with grey-green needle-shaped leaves that are rosemary. Native to: southern Europe. Latin name: *Rosmarinus officinalis*. [14C. By folk etymology < obsolete *rosmarine* < Latin *rosmarinus* < *ros* 'dew' + *marinus* 'of the sea'; from its growth near seacoasts and its blossom's resemblance to dew]

rose moss *n* a low-growing fleshy-leaved plant widely grown for its bright flowers. Native to: Brazil. Latin name: *Portulaca grandiflora*.

Rosenberg /rṓz'n burg/, **Julius** (1918–53) US Soviet spy. He and his wife Ethel Rosenberg (1915–53), both members of the Communist Party, were convicted in 1951 of passing nuclear weapons information to the Soviets during World War II. They were the first US civilians to be executed for espionage.

rose of Jericho *n* a plant that curls up into a ball in dry conditions and unfolds and grows in wet conditions. Native to: desert regions. Latin name: *Anastatica hierochuntica* or *Selaginella lepidophylla*.

rose of Sharon /-shárən/ *n* **1.** a creeping bush, widely grown as ground cover. Flowers: large, yellow. Native to: southern Europe. Latin name: *Hypericum calycinum*. **2.** a bush widely grown as an ornamental. Flowers: large, red, purple, or white. Native to: Syria. Latin name: *Hibiscus syriacus*. [Early 17C. < *Sharon*, fertile plain south of Mount Carmel, Israel]

rose oil *n* an essential oil. Source: rose flowers. Use: in perfumes, flavourings, medicines.

roseola /rō zeé ələ, rṓzi ṓlə/ *n* a red rash on the skin, seen in diseases such as measles, scarlet fever, and syphilis [Early 19C. < Latin *roseus* 'rosy' < *rosa* (see ROSE¹), after RUBEOLA] —**roseolar** *adj*

roseola infantum /-in fántəm/ *n* a mild disease of young children, typically involving a three-day fever and the eruption of pink spots

rose quartz *n* a pink translucent variety of quartz. Use: gems, ornaments.

roseroot /rṓz root/ *n* a perennial mountain plant with fleshy leaves and a pinkish underground stem. Flowers: yellow. Native to: Europe, Asia. Latin name: *Sedum rosea*. [Late 16C. Because its root smells of roses when bruised]

rose topaz *n* a pink form of topaz made by applying heat to yellowish-brown topaz

Rosetta /rō zéttə/ ♦ **Rashîd**

Rosetta stone *n* a stone tablet found in 1799 near Rashîd in Egypt that contained the same text repeated in Egyptian hieroglyphics, Egyptian demotic script, and Greek. It supplied the key to deciphering hieroglyphics.

rosette /rō zét/ *n* **1.** ROSE-SHAPED BADGE a circular badge made from gathered loops of ribbon or pleated material, worn to demonstrate support for a team or political party or to indicate having won a prize **2.** ORNAMENT RESEMBLING ROSE a carved or painted ornament resembling the open flower of a rose **3.** ZOOL MARKING RESEMBLING ROSE a patch of colour or a marking resembling the open flower of a rose, especially a cluster of spots on the fur of a leopard **4.** BOT CLUSTER OF LEAVES a circular or spiral cluster of leaves at the base of the stem of a plant **5.** MUSIC DECORATIVE BAND ON GUITAR a decoration around the edge of the sound hole of an acoustic guitar [Mid-18C. < French, 'small rose' < *rose* < Latin *rosa* (see ROSE¹)]

Rosewall /rṓz wawl/, **Ken** (*b.* 1934) Australian tennis player. He won the Australian, French, and US championships, and was also a successful doubles player. Full name **Rosewall, Kenneth Robert**

rose water *n* a fragrant liquid made by distilling or steeping rose petals in water. Use: toilet water, in cooking.

rose window

rose window *n* a round window with tracery radiating from the centre in a pattern that resembles a rose and often made of stained glass

rosewood /rṓz woŏd/ *n* **1.** the dark, heavy, rose-scented wood of various tropical trees, especially those belonging to the genus *Dalbergia*. Use: furniture. **2.** a tree that yields rosewood. Genus: *Dalbergia*.

Rosh Chodesh /rósh khóddəsh/ *n* the first day of a new month in the Jewish religious calendar [< Hebrew *rōʾšhōdeš* 'head of the month']

Rosh Hashanah /rósh hə shaánə/, **Rosh Hashana**, **Rosh Hashona**, **Rosh Hashonah** *n* the festival that marks the Jewish New Year and the beginning of the Days of Awe. Date: 1st and 2nd of Tishri in the autumn. [Mid-18C. < Hebrew *rōʾš haššānāh* 'head of the year']

Rosicrucian /rózi kroósh'n/ *n* a member of an international organization concerned with esoteric wisdom derived from ancient mystical and philosophical doctrines [Early 17C. < modern Latin *rosa crucis* 'rose of the cross', translation of German *Rosenkreuz*, after Christian *Rosenkreuz*, the organization's reputed founder] —**Rosicrucianism** *n*

rosin /rózzin/ *n* a hard translucent resin ranging in colour from amber to dark brown. Source: sap, stumps, or other parts of pine trees. Use: varnishes and other products, to increase friction, e.g. between the bow and strings of some stringed instruments. ■ *vt* (-ins, -ining, -ined) to treat something with rosin, especially to rub rosin on the bow of a stringed instrument to increase friction [13C. Alteration of Old French *raisine*, variant of *resine* < Latin *resina*; also via Anglo-Latin *rosina* < Latin *resina*] —**rosiny** *adj*

Rosinante /rózzi nánti/ *n* **1.** the bony old horse that belongs to Don Quixote, the hero of the novel by Cervantes published in 1605 **2.** a worn-out old horse (*literary*)

rosin oil *n* a thick yellowish sticky liquid distilled from rosin. Use: manufacture of varnishes and inks.

Roskilde /róss killə/ town in Denmark, in eastern Sjælland, situated about 24 km/15 mi. west of Copenhagen. Population: 42,739 (1999).

RoSPA /róspə/ *abbr* Royal Society for the Prevention of Accidents

Diana Ross

Ross /ross/, **Diana** (*b.* 1944) US pop singer. Known for her seductive vocal style and glamorous appearance, she helped her 1960s female group the Supremes become one of the most successful acts in the history of popular music before pursuing a solo career. Born **Ross, Diane Ernestine**

> 'I've always said if one person believes in me, I will try to move mountains.'
> [Diana Ross, *Secrets of a Sparrow*; 1993]

Ross, Sir James Clark (1800–62) British explorer. He determined the position of the north magnetic pole (1831) and discovered Victoria Land, Ross Island, and the Ross Sea (1839–43).

Rossellini /róssə leéni/, **Roberto** (1906–77) Italian film director. He directed several neorealist films after World War II, including *Rome, Open City* (1945) and historical films for television.

AKG London

Christina Rossetti

Rossetti /rə zétti/, **Christina** (1830–94) British poet. She wrote in a variety of styles and forms, often exploring the themes of religion and death. She was the sister of Dante Gabriel Rossetti. Full name **Rossetti, Christina Georgina**

> 'When I am dead, my dearest, / Sing no sad songs for me; / Plant thou no roses at my head, / Nor shady cypress tree; / Be the green grass above me / With showers and dewdrops wet; / And if thou wilt, remember, / And if thou wilt, forget.'
> [Christina Rossetti, 'When I am Dead'; 1862]

Rossetti, Dante Gabriel (1828–82) British painter and poet. A founder of the Pre-Raphaelite Brotherhood (1848), he brought medieval and Italianate influences to bear on idealized, emotionally charged paintings such as *The Annunciation* (1850) and *Proserpina* (1874). His last volume of verse was *Ballads and Sonnets* (1881). He was the brother of Christina Rossetti. Full name **Rossetti, Gabriel Charles Dante**

> 'I have been here before. /But when or how I cannot tell: /I know the grass beyond the door, /The sweet keen smell, /The sighing sound, the lights around the shore.'
> [Dante Gabriel Rossetti, 'Sudden Light'; 1881]

Rossetti, William Michael (1829–1919) British art critic. He was a member of the Pre-Raphaelite Brotherhood and the brother of Dante Gabriel and Christina Rossetti.

Rossini /ro seéni/, **Gioacchino** (1792–1868) Italian composer. The most successful operatic composer of his

time, he was a master of the bel canto style and excelled in comedy. His 37 operas, all written before 1831, include *The Barber of Seville* (1816) and *William Tell* (1829). Full name **Rossini, Gioacchino Antonio**

> 'Give me a laundry list and I'll set it to music.'
> [Attributed to Gioacchino Rossini]

Rosslare /róss láir/ town in County Wexford, on the southeastern coast of the Republic of Ireland. Population: 1,578 (2002).

Ross River virus /ross rívvər-/ n an Australian virus transmitted by mosquitoes that causes recurring fever, headaches, lethargy, rashes, and muscle and joint pains [Mid-20C. After a river near Townsville, NE Australia, near which the virus was first isolated]

Ross Sea /róss-/ southern extension of the Pacific Ocean, bordering Antarctica. A large part of its surface is frozen, forming the Ross Ice Shelf. Ross Island, in the Ross Sea, is the location of the volcano Mount Erebus.

Rostand /rás taaN/, **Edmond** (1868–1918) French playwright. He is best known for the romantic verse play *Cyrano de Bergerac* (1898).

> 'My nose is huge!...let me inform you that I am proud of such an appendage, since a big nose is the proper sign of a friendly, good, courteous, witty, liberal, and brave man, such as I am.'
> [Edmond Rostand, *Cyrano de Bergerac*; 1898]

> 'The dream, alone, is of interest. What is life, without a dream?'
> [Edmond Rostand, *La Princesse Lointaine*; 1895]

rostellum /ro stélləm/ (*plural* **-la** /-lə/) n a part of an animal or plant that resembles a beak, e.g. the hooked projection from the head of a tapeworm [Mid-18C. < Latin, 'small beak' < *rostrum* (see ROSTRUM)] —**rostellar** adj —**rostellate** adj

roster /róstər/ n 1. LIST OF NAMES a list of personnel, especially employees, athletes, or members of the armed forces, often detailing their duties and the times when they are to be carried out 2. PEOPLE ON LIST the people listed on a roster ■ vt (**-ters, -tering, -tered**) PUT SOMEBODY ON ROSTER to name somebody on a roster [Early 18C. < Dutch *rooster* 'gridiron', (from the resemblance of its pattern to lines on paper) 'list' < *roosten* 'roast']

rösti /rósti/ n a Swiss fried potato cake made from thinly sliced or grated potatoes, sometimes with added onions and bacon [Mid-20C. < Swiss German]

Rostock /rós tok/ city and port in northeastern Germany, in the state of Mecklenburg-Western Pomerania, on the Baltic Sea. Population: 232,634 (1997).

Rostov /rós tov/ city in southwestern European Russia, on the River Don. Population: 1,127,339 (1995).

rostrum /róstrəm/ (*plural* **-trums** or **-tra** /-trə/) n 1. PLATFORM FOR PUBLIC SPEAKING a platform or raised area where somebody stands to address an audience 2. MUSIC CONDUCTOR'S PLATFORM a platform on a stage or in front of an orchestra where the conductor stands 3. MEDIA, CINEMA PLATFORM FOR CAMERA a platform, stand, or raised area supporting a film or television camera 4. ANCIENT HIST PROW OF ROMAN SHIP the beak-shaped prow of an ancient Roman ship, especially a war galley 5. BIOL BEAK-SHAPED PART a beak or beak-shaped part of an organism [Mid-16C. < Latin, 'beak, ship's prow', in plural 'platform' (because ships' prows decorated the orator's platform in the Roman forum) < *rodere* 'gnaw'] —**rostral** adj —**rostrally** adv —**rostrate** adj

rosy /rózi/ (**-ier, -iest**) adj 1. ROSE-COLOURED of the reddish-pink colour of roses ○ *the sunset turning the sky a rosy hue* 2. HAVING PINKISH COMPLEXION having a pinkish complexion that is regarded as indicating good health in white people 3. PROMISING likely to be characterized by success or happiness ○ *predicts a rosy future for the business* 4. OPTIMISTIC optimistic, especially to an unreasonable degree ○ *takes a rosy view of things* 5. LOOKING OR SMELLING LIKE ROSES resembling roses, characteristic of roses, or full of roses —**rosily** adv —**rosiness** n

rosy pastor n BIRDS same as **pastor** (sense 3)

rot /rot/ v (**rots, rotting, rotted**) 1. vti DECOMPOSE to be broken down by the action of bacteria or fungi, or break something organic down in this way ○ *The fruit rotted quickly in the heat.* 2. vti CHANGE BY DECOMPOSITION to be reduced, damaged, or broken by the action of bacteria or fungi, or affect something organic in this way ○ *allow the compost to rot* 3. vi LANGUISH to endure the effects of complete neglect ○ *thrown into prison and left to rot* ■ n 1. PROCESS OF DECAYING the process or condition of decaying, or decayed matter ○ *acted immediately to try to stop the rot* 2. NONSENSE irrelevant or ridiculous talk (*informal*) 3. VET, FUNGI FUNGAL DISEASE a disease caused by fungi, e.g. foot rot of sheep, dry rot of timber and plants, and wet rot of timber 4. ANIMAL DISEASE infestation with liver flukes 5. BACTERIAL PLANT DISEASE a plant disease in which the tissue is broken down by the action of bacteria ■ interj EXPRESSION OF DISAGREEMENT used to disagree with what somebody has said or to express annoyance or exasperation (*informal*) [Old English *rotian* (verb) < Germanic]

rot. abbr MATHS rotation

rota /rótə/ n a list of people's names and the order in which they are to carry out duties [Mid-17C. < Latin, 'wheel']

ORIGIN The Latin word *rota* 'wheel', from which *rota* is derived, is also the source of English *control*, *rodeo*, *roll*, *rondo*, *rotate*, *rotund*, *roué*, and *round*[1].

Rota n the supreme ecclesiastical tribunal of the Roman Catholic Church

Rotarian /rō táiri ən/ n a member of a Rotary Club [Early 20C. < ROTARY CLUB] —**Rotarianism** n

rotary /rótəri/ (*plural* **-ries**) n a machine or part of a machine that rotates around an axis or a fixed point [Mid-18C. < medieval Latin *rotarius* < Latin *rota* 'wheel']

Rotary Club n a local club that is a member of an international organization of business and professional people that encourages service to the community [From the organization's early practice of holding meetings in rotation at members' business premises]

rotary cultivator n AGRIC same as **rotary plough**

rotary engine n 1. an internal-combustion engine with cylinders that rotate about a fixed crankshaft 2. an engine that produces torque or power entirely by a rotating mechanism rather than by a crankshaft and reciprocating piston arrangement

Rotary International n an international organization of business and professional people formed in the United States in 1905 to encourage service to the community [See ROTARY CLUB]

rotary mower n a lawn mower with a single blade attached in the middle and sharpened at both ends that rotates as the mower is moved

rotary plough n a machine for breaking up and tilling soil, consisting of a series of blades mounted on a revolving power-driven shaft. N Am term **rototiller**

rotary press n a printing press that prints from curved plates mounted on a revolving cylinder, often onto a continuous roll of paper

rotary pump n a pump that imparts motion by internal sets of rotating vanes or screws, used to move water or other fluids

rotary tiller n AGRIC same as **rotary plough**

rotary-wing aircraft n an aircraft, especially a helicopter, that is lifted or propelled by rotating aerofoils

rotate /rō táyt/ vti (**-tates, -tating, -tated**) 1. TURN AROUND AXIS to turn like a wheel around an axis or a fixed point, or make something turn around an axis or a fixed point ○ *Earth rotates around the axis through its poles.* ○ *The windmill's sails are rotated by the wind.* 2. FOLLOW IN ORDER to follow in a sequence, taking turns, or make things follow in such a sequence ○ *Rotate the plates in the pile so that they all get used.* 3. HR REPLACE PERSONNEL to be replaced by somebody else, or replace one person or group by another, e.g. in a sports team or military unit ○ *The manager rotates first-team players with promising newcomers*

in less important games. 4. AGRIC VARY CROPS to vary the crops grown on the same piece of ground so as not to exhaust the soil or make it susceptible to disease, or be varied in this way ■ adj WHEEL-SHAPED having parts that radiate from a central point [Late 17C. Either < Latin *rotat-*, past participle of *rotare* < *rota* 'wheel'; or back-formation < ROTATION] —**rotatable** adj —**rotative** adj —**rotatory** adj

rotation /rō táysh'n/ n 1. TURNING MOTION a turning motion like that of a wheel around an axis or a fixed point, or the act or process of turning in such a way ○ *the rotation of the Earth* 2. SINGLE REVOLUTION a single turn of something around an axis or a fixed point ○ *one full rotation of the wheel* 3. REGULAR VARIATION a regular or planned recurrent sequence of events or changes of position ○ *The families use the holiday cottage by strict rotation.* 4. AGRIC same as crop rotation 5. MATHS MATHEMATICAL TRANSFORMATION a mathematical transformation in which axes are rotated by a fixed angle while the origin remains unchanged [15C. Directly or via French < Latin *rotation-* < *rotat-* (see ROTATE)] —**rotational** adj

rotator /rō táytər/ n 1. somebody or something that rotates or causes rotation 2. (*plural* **rotatores** /rótə táwr eez/) a muscle that rotates part of the body on an axis

rotator cuff n the deep muscles of the shoulder and their tendons that connect the arm to the shoulder joint, encircle it, and provide strength and stability while permitting rotation of the arm

rotatores n ANAT plural of **rotator** (sense 2)

rotavate /rótə vayt/ (**-vates, -vating, -vated**), **rotovate** vt to break up or till soil using a rotary plough

Rotavator /rótə vaytər/, **Rotovator** tdmk a trademark for a type of rotary plough

rotavirus /rótə vírəss/ n a wheel-shaped RNA virus that causes gastroenteritis, especially in infants [Late 20C. < modern Latin < Latin *rota* 'wheel' + *virus* 'poison, virus']

rotaxane /rō ták sayn/ n a chemical compound consisting of two unbonded portions, a long thin molecule that is encircled by a molecule held in its position by large end groups

rote[1] /rōt/ n mechanical repetition of something so that it is remembered, often without real understanding of its meaning or significance ○ *learned it by rote* [13C. < ?]

rote[2] /rōt/ n a medieval stringed instrument played by plucking [14C. < Old French, probably < late Latin *chrotta* 'British musical instrument' < Welsh *crwth* 'crowd (Celtic stringed instrument)' or Old Irish *crot* 'harp, cithara']

rotenone /rótə nōn/ n a white crystalline insecticide. Source: roots of derris. Formula: $C_{23}H_{22}O_6$. [Early 20C. < Japanese *roten* 'derris']

rotgut /rót gut/ n cheap and rough alcoholic drink (*informal*)

Roth /roth/, **Philip** (b. 1933) US writer. His novels, which often concern American Jewish life, include *Goodbye, Columbus* (1959) and *Portnoy's Complaint* (1969). Full name **Roth, Philip Milton**

> 'Just like those who are incurably ill, the aged know everything about their dying except exactly when.'
> [Philip Roth, 'Opening letter to Zuckerman', *The Facts*; 1988]

Rother /róthər/ river in East Sussex and Kent, southeastern England. Length: 50 km/31 mi.

Rotherham /róthərəm/ town in South Yorkshire, northern England. Population: 248,175 (2001).

Rothermere /róthər meer/, **Harold Sydney, 1st Viscount Harmsworth** (1868–1940) British newspaper magnate. The brother of Alfred Harmsworth, he controlled a newspaper empire that included the *Daily Mail* and *Sunday Dispatch*.

Rothesay /róthsi, -say/ town in Argyll and Bute council area, Scotland. Population: 5,264 (1991).

Rothko /róth kō/, **Mark** (1903–70) Russian-born US artist. He is known for large colour-field abstract expressionist paintings, often in sombre tones.

> 'It is a widely accepted notion among painters that it does not matter what one paints

as long as it is well painted. This is the essence of academism. There is no such thing as good painting about nothing.'
[Mark Rothko, *Letter to Edwin A. Jewell, New York Times; 13 June 1943*]

Rothschild /róth chīld, róths-/, **Lionel Nathan** (1808–79) British financier. The eldest son of Nathan Mayer Rothschild, he was the manager of the London branch of the family business and the first Jewish MP.

Rothschild, Mayer Amschel (1743–1812) German financier. The father of Nathan Mayer Rothschild, he was a financial agent of the British government.

Rothschild, Nathan Mayer (1777–1836) German financier. The son of Mayer Amschel Rothschild and father of Lionel Nathan Rothschild, he founded the British branch of the family firm in 1805.

Rothschild, Salomon (1774–1855) German financier. The son of Mayer Amschel Rothschild, he established a branch of the House of Rothschild in Vienna.

roti /róti/ (*plural* **-tis**) *n* an unleavened bread made from wheat flour and cooked on a griddle, originally from northern South Asia but also eaten in the Caribbean [Early 20C. < Hindi *rotī*]

rotifer /rótifər/ *n* a microscopic invertebrate that has a wheel-shaped crown of projecting threads (**cilia**) at the anterior end and lives mostly in freshwater habitats. Phylum: Rotifera. [Late 18C. < modern Latin, 'wheel-bearing, wheel-bearer' < Latin *rota* 'wheel'] —**rotiferal** /rō tíffərəl/ *adj* —**rotiferous** /rō tíffərəss/ *adj*

rotisserie /rō tíssəri/ *n* **1.** a cooking appliance for roasting meat using a rotating spit **2.** a shop or restaurant where meat is roasted and sold [Mid-19C. < French *rôtisserie* < *rôtir* 'to roast' < Germanic]

rotl /róttʼl/ (*plural* **artal** /aar taal/) *n* in many Islamic countries, a unit of weight varying from approximately 0.45 to 2.25 kg/1 to 5 lb [Early 17C. < Arabic *raṭl*]

rotogravure /rō tōgrə vyoór/ *n* **1.** a printing process in which images are etched photomechanically onto copper cylinders mounted in a rotary press, from which they are printed onto a moving web of paper **2.** something printed using rotogravure, e.g. a magazine or a photographic section of a newspaper [Early 20C. < German *Rotogravur*, company name]

rotor /rótər/ *n* **1.** ROTATING AEROFOILS ON HELICOPTER an assembly consisting of several flat blades attached to a hub, which rotates either horizontally to give lift and thrust to a helicopter, or vertically to help control it **2.** ROTOR BLADE a blade or aerofoil of a rotor (*informal*) **3.** ROTATING PART OF MACHINE a rotating part of an electrical apparatus, e.g. the armature of a generator, or of a mechanical device [Late 19C. Contraction of ROTATOR]

rotorcraft /rótər kraaft/ (*plural* **same**) *n* **1.** AVIAT same as **rotary-wing aircraft 2.** a helicopter or any similar aircraft that uses a rotor to gain lift

Rotorua /rótə roŏ ə/ city in the centre of the North Island, New Zealand, noted for its volcanic activity and thermal springs. Population: 52,608 (2001).

Rotorua, Lake lake in the centre of the North Island, New Zealand, originally formed by a volcanic eruption. It is a major tourist centre. Area: 80 sq. km/31 sq. mi.

rototiller /rótə tillər/ *n N Am* same as **rotary plough** [Early 20C. < Latin *rota* 'wheel' + TILLER[2]]

rotovate *vt* AGRIC another spelling of **rotavate**

Rotovator *tdmk* AGRIC another spelling of **Rotavator**

rotten /róttʼn/ *adj* **1.** DECAYED affected by rot or decay ○ *a rotten apple* **2.** CORRUPT characterized by a lack of honesty or moral principles ○ *The administration was rotten to the core.* **3.** NASTY mean and nasty in attitude and behaviour towards others (*informal*) ○ *He's been rotten to his sister.* **4.** FOUL extremely unpleasant or unfortunate (*informal*) ○ *They've had rotten luck.* **5.** INFERIOR bad, incompetent, or substandard (*informal*) ○ *He's a rotten driver.* **6.** UNWELL generally unwell, usually without a specific complaint (*informal*) ○ *I woke up feeling rotten the morning after the party.* **7.** UNHAPPY unhappy or uncomfortable, especially through guilt

or embarrassment (*informal*) ○ *I feel rotten about letting you down.* **8.** *UK regional, ANZ* DRUNK very drunk ■ *adv* TO GREAT DEGREE to a great degree, especially so much as to be disapproved of (*informal*) ○ *She fancies you rotten.* ○ *spoils those kids rotten* [13C. < Old Norse *rotinn*] —**rottenly** *adv* —**rottenness** *n*

rotten borough *n* formerly, a political constituency with few electors but the same right to elect a representative as a more populous constituency, especially any of various parliamentary constituencies in England before 1832

rottenstone /róttʼn stōn/ *n* a form of silica-rich limestone that has been decomposed by weathering and is used in powdered form for polishing metal

rotter /róttər/ *n* somebody considered to be nasty or unpleasant (*dated informal*) [Early 17C. < ROT]

Rotterdam /róttər dam/ city and port in Zuid-Holland Province, southwestern Netherlands. Population: 593,321 (2000).

Rottnest Island /rót nest-/ island off the coast of Western Australia, 18 km/11 mi. west of Fremantle. It is noted for its picturesque scenery and marine life, and is a popular day trip and holiday destination.

Rottweiler /rót vīlər, -wīlər/ *n* a large powerful dog belonging to a breed that has a black smooth coat with tan markings [Early 20C. After *Rottweil*, town in SW Germany]

rotund /rō túnd/ *adj* **1.** having a rounded body shape and, usually, a greater body weight than is advisable **2.** having a full, rich sound [15C. Directly or via Italian *rotondo* < Latin *rotundus* 'round' < *rotare* 'rotate' < *rota* 'wheel'] —**rotundity** *n* —**rotundly** *adv* —**rotundness** *n*

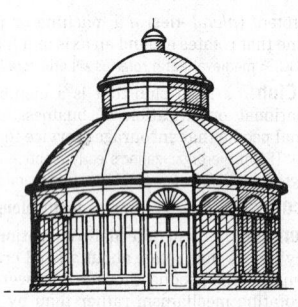

rotunda

rotunda /rō túndə/ *n* **1.** ROUND BUILDING a round building, usually covered with a dome **2.** ROUND ROOM a large round hall or room **3.** *N Am* OPEN AREA IN PUBLIC BUILDING a large open area at an airport, railway station, or other public building [Early 17C. < Italian *rotonda* < Latin *rotunda*, form of *rotundus* 'round' (see ROTUND); altered after the Latin]

ROU *abbr* Republic of Uruguay

Rouault /roo ō/, **Georges** (1871–1958) French painter and engraver. A member of the Fauves, his work is characterized by glowing colours, impasto, and heavy outlines. Full name **Roualt, Georges Henri**

Roubaix /roo bé/ city in Nord Department, Nord-Pas-de-Calais Region, northern France, situated northeast of Lille. Population: 96,984 (1999).

rouble /roŏbʼl/, **ruble** *n* the main unit of currency in Russia, Belarus, and Tajikistan. See table at **currency** [Mid-16C. Via French < Russian *rubl'*]

roué /roŏ ay/ *n* a man who regularly engages in drinking, gambling, and womanizing (*literary*) [Early 19C. < French < past participle of *rouer* 'break on the wheel' (a medieval instrument of torture) < Latin *rotare* (see ROTATE)]

ORIGIN The term *roué* is thought to stem from Philip, duke of Orléans and regent of France (1715–23), who humorously designated his debauched companions as *roués*, either to suggest that they deserved to be broken upon the wheel or because their behaviour was so exhausting that they felt they had undergone this torture. See also *rota*.

Rouen /roŏ aaN/ capital of Seine-Maritime Department, Haute-Normandie Region, northwestern France. Population: 106,592 (1999).

rouge /roozh/ *n* **1.** REDDISH MAKEUP FOR CHEEKS red or pink makeup in powder or cream form used to add colour to the cheeks or lips or to accentuate the shape of the cheekbones (*dated*) **2.** POLISH IN POWDER FORM a polish in powder form containing metallic oxides, especially a polish for metal (**jeweller's rouge**) that contains ferric oxide ■ *vt* (**rouges, rouging, rouged**) COLOUR SOMETHING WITH ROUGE to put rouge on the cheeks or lips (*dated*) [Mid-18C. Via French < Latin *rubeus* 'red']

rouge et noir /-ay nwaár/ *n* a card game in which gamblers place their stakes on a table marked with two red and two black diamonds and all betting is against the house at even money [< French, 'red and black']

rough /ruf/ *adj* **1.** NOT SMOOTH OR FLAT having a bumpy, knobbly, or uneven surface rather than being smooth, flat, and regular **2.** NOT SOFT not soft and smooth, but rather coarse in texture ○ *a dog with a rough bristly coat* **3.** WINDY OR TURBULENT stormy, or unpleasantly turbulent as a result of stormy conditions ○ *The weather had been rough for days.* **4.** NOT GENTLE characterized by or done with a lot of force or violence ○ *toys that will stand up to rough handling* **5.** BOORISH not refined or polite in manner and behaviour, but tending to be noisy and rowdy ○ *rough talk* **6.** FREQUENTED BY UNSAVOURY PEOPLE frequented or inhabited by people who tend to be noisy, rowdy, or violent ○ *a rough part of town* **7.** HARSH harsh in sound or to the taste **8.** GENERAL not exact, precise, or detailed, but broadly correct ○ *a rough estimate* **9.** THROWN TOGETHER made quickly and without using proper or good-quality materials, or reaching only the most basic standard ○ *a rough shelter made from branches* **10.** CRUDE hastily or incompletely made ○ *a rough wooden carving* **11.** WILD AND UNCULTIVATED not cleared, flattened, and cultivated, but in a natural state with wild vegetation, and often difficult to travel over ○ *marching over rough terrain* **12.** SEVERE OR UNPLEASANT severe, unfair, or generally unpleasant (*informal*) ○ *They felt they had received rough treatment at the hands of the judge.* ○ *It's rough on the children when the parents split up.* **13.** SLIGHTLY ILL rather ill, especially as a result of tiredness or overindulgence rather than because of illness (*informal*) ○ *She felt a bit rough the next morning.* ■ *n* **1.** UNMOWN PART OF GOLF COURSE the area of a golf course on which grass and other vegetation is allowed to grow higher than on the fairway **2.** PRELIMINARY OUTLINE a preliminary version of something, e.g. a sketch giving the broad layout of an artwork **3.** VIOLENT PERSON a violent or brutal person, especially a hired thug **4.** SIDE OF RACQUET the side of a tennis or other racquet where the binding of the strings is not smooth **5.** same as **rough trade** (*slang offensive*) ■ *vt* (**roughs, roughing, roughed**) ROUGHEN SOMETHING to make something rough [Old English *rūh* < Germanic] —**roughish** *adj* —**roughness** *n* ◇ **in the rough** in a crude, unfinished, or uncultivated state ◇ **rough it** to live in a less comfortable or less sophisticated way than usual (*informal*) ◇ **rough or smooth** used as a call when spinning a racket in a game of tennis or squash to decide which player should serve first or choose the end to serve from ◇ **take the rough with the smooth** to accept the disadvantages of a situation as well as the advantages

SPELLCHECK rough or **ruff?** Do not confuse the spelling of **rough** and **ruff**, which sound similar. **Rough** is chiefly used as an adjective, meaning 'coarse', 'bumpy', 'harsh', or 'approximate', as in *a rough surface, a rough sea, rough treatment, a rough draft.* It is occasionally used as a noun or verb, as in *take the rough with the smooth, roughing it in makeshift accommodation.* **Ruff** is a noun denoting a stiff pleated collar worn in the 16th and 17th centuries, or a bird with neck feathers resembling such a collar.

rough out *vt* to prepare a rough model, plan, or sketch of something ○ *roughed out a scene-by-scene narrative*

rough up *vt* **1.** to subject somebody to a violent beating (*informal*) **2.** to make something, e.g. somebody's hair, look untidy by rubbing it to make it stick up or stick out

roughage /rúffij/ *n* MED same as **fibre** (sense 7)

rough-and-ready *adj* **1.** not elegant or stylish and often hastily made or improvised, but practical or usable ○ *rough-and-ready accommodation in a hostel* **2.** crude and vigorous in behaviour rather then gentle, polite, or well-mannered, but not malicious

rough-and-tumble *n* **1.** a situation characterized by aggressive tactics and a disregard for rules and conventions **2.** a bout of rough physical horseplay or free-for-all fighting —**rough-and-tumble** *adj*

rough breathing *n* in ancient Greek, a sound like that of the English 'h', occurring with an initial vowel or the letter ρ and indicated by the symbol '

roughcast /rúf kaast/ *n* **1.** PEBBLED SURFACE ON WALLS a surface of coarse plaster covered with pebbles on the outside walls of a building (*often used before a noun*) ○ *roughcast walls* **2.** ROUGH MODEL a preliminary form or model of something ○ *made a roughcast in clay before starting to work the marble* ■ *vt* (**-casts, -casting, -cast**) **1.** COVER WALL WITH ROUGHCAST to cover the surface of a wall or the walls of a building with roughcast **2.** FORM SOMETHING ROUGHLY to shape or form something in a crude fashion or as a preliminary to more polished work —**roughcaster** *n*

rough collie *n* a long-haired collie dog that is black and white or black, white, and tan and has a band of thick hair round its neck and shoulders

rough copy *n* a preliminary draft of a piece of writing, usually raw and unedited

rough cut *n* the preliminary version of a cinema film, with only basic editing done to put the scenes together in sequence

rough-cut *adj* **1.** NOT SMOOTHED cut or shaped only roughly, with the surface and the edges not smoothed ○ *rough-cut planks* **2.** UNREFINED lacking polish or finesse in manner ■ *vt* CUT ROUGHLY to cut or carve something roughly without smoothing the surface or edges ○ *rough-cut timbers for the barn*

rough diamond *n* **1.** a diamond in its natural state, before it has been cut into shape and polished **2.** somebody who does not care about good manners or formality but is likeable or trustworthy. N Am term **diamond in the rough**

rough-dry *vt* to dry washed laundry but not iron it —**rough-dry** *adj*

roughen /rúff'n/ (**-ens, -ening, -ened**) *vti* to make something rough, or become rough

rough endoplasmic reticulum *n* endoplasmic reticulum containing ribosomes that give its surface an uneven appearance, involved in the synthesis of proteins in plant and animal cells

rough fish *n* a species of fish that is neither caught for food nor fished for by anglers

rough-hew *vt* **1.** to cut or carve something roughly without smoothing the surface or edges ○ *He rough-hewed the wood to make a crude table.* **2.** to shape or form something crudely

rough-hewn *adj* **1.** NOT SMOOTHED cut or shaped only roughly, with the surface and the edges not smoothed ○ *blocks of rough-hewn sandstone* **2.** CRUDELY MADE crudely shaped or formed **3.** UNREFINED uncouth and unrefined in character

roughhouse /rúf howss/ (*informal*) *n* a situation characterized by rough behaviour or excessively boisterous play ○ *The party turned into a roughhouse.* ■ *vti* (**-houses** /-howziz/, **-housing** /-howzing/, **-housed, -housed** /-howzd/) to behave or treat somebody in a rough boisterous way

roughly /rúf li/ *adv* **1.** APPROXIMATELY as a fairly close estimate, or in a manner that is broadly correct but without any claim to exactness ○ *Roughly one-third of the funding comes from government.* **2.** VIOLENTLY OR RUDELY in a violent way or a manner lacking in gentleness and politeness ○ *shoved him roughly to one side* **3.** CRUDELY in a crude, preliminary, or incomplete way ○ *sketched the design out roughly on a scrap of paper*

roughneck /rúf nek/ *n* **1.** COARSE PERSON a rough, bad-mannered person (*informal*) **2.** HIRED THUG a violent person, especially a hired thug (*informal*) **3.** CRIME same as **don**[1] (sense 4) (*slang; used in Black English*) **4.** OIL-FIELD WORKER an unskilled worker on an oil rig or at an oil well (*slang*)

roughrider /rúf rīdər/ *n* a breaker or trainer of wild or untrained horses

roughshod /rúf shod/ *adj* **1.** fitted with horseshoes that have short spikes to prevent slipping in wet weather **2.** displaying great forcefulness and a lack of consideration ◇ **ride roughshod over somebody** *or* **something** to treat somebody with no justice or consideration, or disregard something completely

rough shooting *n* shooting prey on moorland without using beaters

rough sledding *n US* a hard or difficult time or experience (*informal*)

rough stuff *n* violent behaviour or acts (*informal*)

rough trade *n* an offensive term for a man whose physicality and lack of refinement are found sexually attractive by a gay man from a higher social class (*slang*)

rouille /roo ée/ *n* a sauce made from chillies, garlic, and olive oil served as an accompaniment to Provençal foods such as bouillabaisse [Mid-20C. Via French, 'rust' (from its colour) < Latin *robigo*]

roulade /roo laád/ *n* **1.** a dish in which a piece of food is coated with a sauce or filling and rolled up before being cooked, so that each slice has a spiral appearance **2.** a run of several musical notes sung rapidly to one syllable [Early 18C. < French < *rouler* 'to roll']

rouleau /róolō/ (*plural* **-leaux** /-lō/ or **-leaus** /-lōz/) *n* **1.** a stack of coins wrapped in a paper cylinder **2.** a rolled or folded ribbon used as decorative piping or trimming [Late 17C. Via French, 'small roll' < Latin *rotula* 'small wheel' < *rota* 'wheel']

roulette /roo lét/ *n* **1.** GAMBLING GAME WITH WHEEL a game in which a ball is rolled onto a spinning horizontal wheel divided into compartments, with players betting on which compartment the ball will come to rest in (*often used before a noun*) **2.** TOOL WITH TOOTHED WHEEL a tool with a toothed wheel used for making dots, e.g. in engraving, or for making perforations in paper, e.g. on a sheet of postage stamps **3.** SLITS CUT IN PAPER a line of slits or perforations made by a cutting tool on a sheet of paper ■ *vt* (**-lettes, -letting, -letted**) MARK SOMETHING WITH DOTS OR PERFORATIONS to use a roulette to mark a surface with a line of dots or make perforations in a sheet of paper [Mid-18C. < French, 'small wheel' < late Latin *rotella* < Latin *rota* 'wheel']

Roumanian /roo máyni ən/ *n* LANG, PEOPLES another spelling of **Romanian** (*dated*) [Variant] —**Roumanian** *adj*

round[1] /rownd/ *adj* **1.** CIRCULAR OR SPHERICAL shaped like a circle or a ball ○ *a big, perfectly round bowl* **2.** CURVED curved rather than square or angular **3.** IN CIRCULAR MOTION done with or involving a circular motion **4.** COMPLETE not less or more than ○ *a round dozen* **5.** EXPRESSED BY INTEGER expressed as an approximate value, especially to the nearest integer or power of ten ○ *use 1,500 as a round number* **6.** CONSIDERABLE large in amount or size ○ *a round sum* **7.** ROUNDED fully developed, or fully depicted, as a character with a broad spread of interests, accomplishments, or personality traits **8.** PLUMP full and plump, especially in facial features ○ *kindly eyes in a round face* **9.** SONOROUS mellow and rich in tone **10.** BRISK lively and rather fast ○ *We set off at a round pace.* **11.** STRAIGHTFORWARD plain and outspoken ○ *'I said in good round English 'I'm going to knock the stuffing out of you'.'* (John Buchan, *Greenmantle*; 1916) **12.** PHON PRONOUNCED WITH ROUNDED LIPS describes speech sounds articulated with the lips forming an oval opening ○ *a round vowel sound* ■ *n* **1.** ROUND SHAPE a round shape or object ○ *little rounds of cheese* **2.** SESSION a session or instance of an event, usually in a series of similar or related events ○ *the first round of talks* **3.** STAGE OF COMPETITION a game, or series of games, forming a stage in a competition ○ *lost to the reigning champion in the third round* **4.** DIVISION OF BOXING OR WRESTLING MATCH one the periods of actual fighting, usually three minutes in length, into which a boxing or wrestling match is divided **5.** GAME OF GOLF a session of golf in which all the holes on a golf course are played once **6.** PERIOD OF PLAY IN CARDS a period of play, especially in a game of cards, during which each player takes his or her turn **7.** CHARGE OF AMMUNITION FOR ONE SHOT an item of ammunition, e.g. a cartridge, or the quantity of ammunition required to fire one shot ○ *hundreds of mortar rounds* **8.** GUN DISCHARGE a single discharge by a gun or guns ○ *fired a few rounds* **9.** ARROWS SHOT a specific number of arrows shot from a set distance **10.** SERIES OF VISITS a series of visits made on a regular basis to different places or people (*often used in the plural*) **11.** APPLAUSE an outburst of applause or cheering **12.** SET OF DRINKS a number of drinks bought, one for each person in a group **13.** PART SONG a song sung by several voices in which each voice sings the same tune at the same pitch, but the voices enter one after the other so that they end up singing different parts of the song at the same time **14.** MOVEMENT IN CIRCLE movement in a circle or around an axis **15.** BELLS RUNG a sequence of bells rung in order from treble to tenor **16.** CIRCULAR DANCE a dance with a sequence of movements in a circle **17.** SLICE OF BREAD a slice of bread or toast, or a sandwich made from two slices of bread **18.** CUT OF BEEF a cut of beef from between the rump and the shank ■ *v* (**rounds, rounding, rounded**) **1.** *vt* MOVE PAST OBSTACLE to move in a curve past the edge or corner of something **2.** *vti* EXPRESS AS ROUND NUMBER to express a number containing several units as the nearest significant number above or below it, e.g. treating 5,753 as 6,000, or 6.375 as 6 ○ *The estimate was rounded to the nearest pound.* **3.** *vt* PRONOUNCE SOUNDS to pronounce a sound with rounded lips ○ *Try to round your vowels.* **4.** *vt* PURSE LIPS to purse the lips [13C. < Old French *ro(u)nd-* < Latin *rotundus* (see ROTUND)] —**roundish** *adj* —**roundness** *n* ◇ **in the round 1.** THEATRE having a stage in the centre and the audience seated around it (*refers to a theatre or performance*) **2.** SCULPTURE free-standing and viewable from all sides, rather than being carved from a background **3.** considered from a variety of different perspectives and as a whole ◇ **make** *or* **do** *or* **go the rounds 1.** to circulate and become widespread ○ *a new rumour making the rounds* **2.** to go from place to place in a regular pattern

round down *vt* to express a number as a smaller, less exact, but more manageable number for ease of calculation

round off *vt* **1.** FINISH SOMETHING IN PLEASING WAY to bring something to a pleasant or satisfactory end by doing or adding one last thing **2.** MAKE SOMETHING MORE ROUNDED to make the edges, sides, or corners of something less straight or angular and more rounded **3.** EXPRESS SOMETHING AS ROUND NUMBER to express a number as the nearest significant number above or below it for ease of calculation

round on *vt* to attack somebody suddenly, either physically or verbally, in a fit of anger

round out *vti* to achieve a more complete or satisfactory form, or cause something to achieve this

round up *vt* **1.** to gather people or animals together in one place **2.** to express a number as a larger, less exact, but more manageable number for ease of calculation

round[2] /rownd/ CORE MEANING: a grammatical word used to indicate that a circle of people, a place, or an object surrounds or encloses something ○ (prep) *She sat clasping her hands round her knees.* ○ (prep) *an area of green belt round the town* ○ (adv) *A crowd soon gathered round.*

1. *prep, adv* SURROUNDING so as to surround or be on all sides of ○ (adv) *gathered round to watch* ○ (prep) *put his arm round her* **2.** *prep, adv* IN DIFFERENT PARTS OF situated at various points in, or moving to various places in ○ (prep) *newspapers and books scattered round the room* ○ (adv) *We managed to find someone to show us round.* ○ (adv) *She keeps moving things round and I can't find anything!* **3.** *prep, adv* IN ALL DIRECTIONS situated or moving in all directions from a central point of reference ○ (prep) *gazing round him at the strange sights of this new country* ○ (adv) *They could see nothing but green fields for 10 miles round.* ○ *driving round for hours looking for them* **4.** *prep* TO OTHER SIDE OF moving or looking to the other side of ○ *The lorry came round the bend at breakneck speed.* **5.** *prep, adv* TURNING ON AXIS revolving round a centre or axis ○ (prep) *the movement of the planets round the Sun* ○ (adv) *propellers going round at*

1,000 revolutions per minute. **6.** *adv* **TO REVERSED POSITION** in or to a different or the opposite direction ○ *She turned round when he called her name.* ○ *The road then bends round to the left.* **7.** *prep, adv* **IN CIRCUMFERENCE** on or outside the circumference or perimeter ○ (prep) *It measures 25 centimetres round the base.* ○ (adv) *The tower was 100 metres tall and 30 metres round.* **8.** *prep, adv* **TO EVERYONE** to all members in a group, from person to person ○ (adv) *She handed round the drinks.* ○ (prep) *News of the closure was passed round the factory.* **9.** *adv* **FOR VISIT** so as to visit somebody or something ○ *She went round to give them the news.* **10.** *prep* **HAVING BASIS IN** used to indicate the thing that is the basis for something such as a concept or a story line ○ *The plot is centred round the relationship between two brothers.* [14C. Partly < ROUND[1]; partly shortening of AROUND] ◇ **round about 1.** approximately ○ *round about midnight* **2.** surrounding somebody or something on all sides

USAGE round or **around**? In British English, ***round*** and ***around*** are interchangeable in many contexts: *She wore a silver chain round* [or *around*] *her neck. There was nothing but sand for miles around* [or *round*]. ***Round*** is often preferred, however, where circular movement is involved, as in *He spun round to face me*, and in fixed phrases such as *the wrong way round* and *round and round*. In US English *around* is the usual form, and it may be regarded as an Americanism by some British people. ***Round*** and ***around*** can sometimes be replaced by ***about*** in British English: *children running about in the garden.* ***About*** and ***around*** can also be used to mean 'approximately': *We left at about* [or *around*] *midnight.*

roundabout /równdə bowt/ *n* **1. CIRCULAR ROAD JUNCTION** a road junction with a central island around which traffic moves in one direction. N Am term **traffic circle 2. REVOLVING RIDE IN PLAYGROUND** a piece of playground equipment in the form of a revolving structure for children to sit on and push or be pushed round and round. N Am term **merry-go-round** ■ *adj* **INDIRECT** proceeding in a way that is not direct or straightforward ○ *went by a roundabout route* ○ *answered in a roundabout way*

round-arm *adj* **1.** made with a near-horizontal swing of the arm **2.** in cricket, with the bowler's arm coming over the shoulder at an angle nearer horizontal than vertical ○ *a round-arm action*

round bracket *n* PRINTING same as **bracket** *n* (sense 1)

round clam *n* ZOOL same as **quahog**

round dance *n* **1. FOLK DANCE** a folk dance in which several dancers or couples form a circle **2. BALLROOM DANCE** a ballroom dance in which couples revolve as they move round the room, as in a waltz **3. BEE'S MOVEMENT** a more or less circular sequence of movements that a honeybee performs in or near the hive to show other bees that food is nearby

rounded /równdid/ *adj* **1. CURVED** having curved, not straight or angular, surfaces or edges ○ *a rounded lawn* **2. COMPLEX OR DIVERSE** having many different features or aspects that together form a whole that is complete and interestingly complex or diverse ○ *received a very rounded education* **3.** PHON **PRONOUNCED WITH PURSED LIPS** pronounced with the lips pursed to form a round shape —**roundedness** *n*

roundel /równd'l/ *n* **1. ROUND PART** a round part or piece, e.g. a round section in a stained-glass window or a round panel in a section of wood panelling **2. IDENTIFYING DISC ON AIRCRAFT WING** a coloured disc on a military aircraft wing identifying the aircraft's country of origin **3. ROUND PIECE OF ARMOUR** a circular section of armour that protects the wearer's armpit **4.** LITERAT **MODIFIED FORM OF RONDEAU** an English form of the rondeau that has eleven lines arranged in three stanzas of three lines and a one-line refrain after the first and third stanzas **5.** LITERAT **TYPE OF RONDEL** a modified form of the rondel that has ten lines arranged in two stanzas of three lines and one of four lines, with the opening line repeated as a refrain **6.** DANCE same as **roundelay** (sense 2) [13C. < Old French *rondel* 'small circle' < *ro(u)nd-* (see ROUND[1])]

roundelay /równdə lay/ *n* **1.** a simple song in which one of the verses is repeated at intervals, or the music for such a song **2.** a slow medieval dance performed by a group who form a circle [15C. Anglicization of French *rondelet* 'small roundel' < *rondel* 'small circle' < *ro(u)nd-* (see ROUND[1])]

rounder /równdər/ *n* **1. COMPLETE CIRCUIT IN ROUNDERS** a score in the game of rounders made when the batter runs round all four bases after a single hit of the ball **2. TOOL MAKING THINGS ROUND** a tool that makes edges or surfaces round **3. BOXING MATCH** a boxing match that lasts for a particular number of rounds (*usually used in combination*) ○ *fighting a ten-rounder*

rounders /równdərz/ *n* a ball game in which batters score a point, or rounder, if they run round all four marked fielding positions or bases after a single hit of the ball (*takes a singular verb*)

round hand *n* handwriting with broad rounded letters

Roundhead /równd hed/ *n* a supporter of Oliver Cromwell and the Parliamentarians against King Charles I during the English Civil War [Mid-17C. < their close-cropped hair (contrasted with that of the Cavaliers)]

roundhouse /równd howss/ (*plural* **-houses** /-howziz/) *n* **1. BUILDING FOR RAILWAY ENGINES** a circular building in which railway engines are stored or serviced, consisting of a central turntable with several sections of track radiating from it **2. CABIN ON SAILING SHIP** a large cabin or set of cabins at the rear of an old-fashioned sailing ship **3. PINOCHLE MELD** in the card game pinochle, a meld of four kings and four queens in all suits **4. PUNCH DELIVERED WITH CIRCULAR SWING** a punch made with a wide circular swing of the arm (*slang*)

roundlet /równdlət/ *n* a small circular or disc-shaped object (*formal*)

round lot *n* a regular number of stocks or bonds as a trading unit, usually 100 shares of stock or 5 bonds

roundly /równdli/ *adv* **1.** forcefully and thoroughly ○ *was roundly criticized* **2.** so as to form a circle or sphere (*dated*)

round robin *n* **1. TOURNAMENT WITH EVERYONE PLAYING ONE ANOTHER** a tournament in which each player or team plays against every other player or team in turn (*hyphenated before a noun*) ○ *a round-robin contest* **2. DOCUMENT EACH PERSON PASSES ON** a letter or other document circulated in turn to all members of a group, with each of them adding comments if they wish **3. PETITION WITH SIGNATURES IN CIRCLE** a letter, especially a petition or letter of protest, on which the signatures are arranged in a circle in order to hide the identity of the first person to sign [< the man's first name *Robin*]

round-shouldered *adj* with the shoulders hunched or drooping and the upper back bent forward slightly

roundsman /równdzmən/ (*plural* **-men** /-mən/) *n* **1.** somebody, especially a man, who is a regular visitor to places on a route, e.g. to make deliveries or inspections **2.** *ANZ* a journalist, especially a man, employed to cover stories on a specific topic or field of interest

roundsperson /równdz purss'n/ (*plural* **-people** /-peep'l/ or **-persons**) *n* **1.** a regular visitor to places on a route, e.g. to make deliveries or inspections **2.** *ANZ* a journalist employed to cover stories on a specific topic or field of interest

round steak *n* a lean cut of beef from between the rump and shank

round table *n* a discussion or negotiation between several parties or groups who all take part on equal terms (*hyphenated before a noun*) [< ROUND TABLE]

Round Table *n* **1. KING ARTHUR'S TABLE** in Arthurian legend, the table at which King Arthur and his knights sat, made round so that no one would appear to have precedence **2. KING ARTHUR'S KNIGHTS** the knights of King Arthur as a group **3. INTERNATIONAL CHARITABLE ASSOCIATION** an international association of businessmen set up in 1927 to carry out charitable work in local communities worldwide, or a local branch of the association

round-the-clock *adj* lasting or operating throughout the day and night ○ *round-the-clock nursing care*

round-the-world ticket *n* an airline ticket that entitles a passenger to travel to various destinations around the world, returning to the point of departure

round trip *n* **1.** a journey to a place and back again, usually returning by the same route (*hyphenated before a noun*) ○ *the round-trip fare* **2.** CARDS same as **roundhouse** (sense 3)

round-trip *adj N Am* same as **return** (sense 2)

round-trip ticket *n N Am* same as **return ticket**

round-up *n* **1.** a gathering together of people or animals, e.g. suspects in a criminal investigation or livestock on a farm or ranch **2.** a gathering together of things of any kind, especially information or news ○ *a news round-up on the hour*

roundworm /równd wurm/ *n* a parasitic round-bodied worm (**nematode**) that infests the intestine of people and some animals. Latin name: *Ascaris lumbricoides.*

roup /roop/ *n* an infectious respiratory disease that affects poultry [14C. Probably < N Germanic]

rouse /rowz/ (**rouses, rousing, roused**) *v* **1.** *vti* **WAKE** to wake somebody, or to awaken, from sleep or unconsciousness **2.** *vt* **SHAKE SOMEBODY OUT OF APATHY** to stir somebody into action or a more active state, or become more active ○ *He roused even the most apathetic students to something like enthusiasm for the subject.* **3.** *vt* **CAUSE EMOTION** to cause a particular emotion to be felt ○ *the feelings of guilt that the whole affair roused in us* **4.** *vt* **SCARE HUNTED ANIMAL INTO OPEN** to scare a hunted animal or bird out of its hiding place [15C. < ?] —**rouser** *n*

rouseabout /rówzə bowt/ *n ANZ* an unskilled worker who carries out menial tasks, especially on a sheep or cattle station (*dated*)

rousing /rówzing/ *adj* **1.** filling people with passion, emotion, and enthusiasm ○ *a rousing speech* **2.** full of energy and vigour ○ *a rousing chorus* —**rousingly** *adv*

Rous sarcoma /rówss-/ *n* a cancerous tumour found in chickens, caused by a tumour-producing RNA virus [Early 20C. After Francis Peyton *Rous* (1879–1970), US physician]

Rousseau /roo sṓ/, **Henri** (1844–1910) French painter. He painted in a bold primitive style, and is especially known for dreamscapes and jungle landscapes, painted after his retirement from a post as a customs official. Full name **Rousseau, Henri Julien Félix**. Known as **Le Douanier Rousseau**

Rousseau, Jean Jacques (1712–78) French philosopher and writer. He was one of the great authors of the Age of Enlightenment. His works include *The Social Contract* (1762), *The New Heloise* (1761), and *Émile* (1762).

> 'The passing from the state of nature to the civil society produces a remarkable change in man; it puts justice as a rule of conduct in place of instinct, and gives his actions the moral quality they previously lacked.'
>
> [Jean Jacques Rousseau, *The Social Contract*; 1762]

Rousseau, Théodore (1812–67) French painter. Best known for his naturalistic landscapes, he was the leader of the Barbizon School and a forerunner of impressionism. Full name **Rousseau, Pierre Étienne Théodore**

roust /rowst/ *vt* (**rousts, rousting, rousted**) **1. FORCE SOMEBODY TO GET UP** to make somebody get up, make a move, or take action, especially abruptly or roughly **2.** *N Am* **HARASS SOMEBODY** to bother, annoy, or jostle somebody (*slang*) ■ *n US* **HARASSING** a harassing of somebody (*slang*) [Mid-17C. Probably alteration of ROUSE]

roustabout /rówstə bowt/ *n* **1.** *N Am* an unskilled labourer, especially on an oil rig, on a ship or wharf, or in a circus **2.** *ANZ* same as **rouseabout** (*dated*)

rout[1] /rowt/ *n* **1. DEFEATED ARMY'S RETREAT** a swift and disorderly retreat by a defeated army **2. CRUSHING DEFEAT** a severe and humiliating defeat ○ *the rout suffered at the general election* **3. RABBLE** a noisy and disorganized group of people ■ *vt* (**routs, routing,**

routed) **1. FORCE ARMY TO RETREAT** to defeat an army completely and force it to make a swift and disorderly retreat **2. DEFEAT SOMEBODY THOROUGHLY** to subject an opponent to a thorough and humiliating defeat [13C. < Anglo-Norman *rute*, Old French *route* 'dispersed group' < Latin *rupta* (see ROUTE)]

rout out *vt* **1.** to drive a person or animal from a place, especially by the use of force **2.** to reveal or uncover something, especially after a search ○ *routed out his true motives*

rout² /rowt/ (**routs, routing, routed**) *v* **1.** *vt* to cut a groove in wood or metal, especially with a router **2.** *vti* to search for something by poking about, as pigs do with their snouts [Mid-16C. Variant of ROOT²]

route /root/; *in military usage also* /rowt/ *n* **1. COURSE** a sequence of roads or paths taken, or places passed through, in travelling from one place to another, or a plan of these **2. PROGRESSION** the course that something follows, or the way it progresses or develops ○ *My career might have taken an entirely different route.* **3. REGULAR JOURNEY** a journey somebody regularly makes, especially a set sequence of calls or stops made, e.g. by somebody delivering something ○ *Their store wasn't on my usual route.* ■ *vt* (**routes, routeing, routed**) **SEND SOMEBODY OR SOMETHING ALONG ROUTE** to direct or arrange for somebody or something to follow a particular course ○ *All phone calls were routed through my office.* [12C. < Old French *route* < Latin *rupta*, form of past participle of *rumpere* 'break']

SPELLCHECK See *root*¹.

routeman /rootmən/ (*plural* **-men** /-mən/) *n US* somebody who regularly calls or stops in the course of a job, especially somebody selling or delivering something

route march *n* a long march over rough ground, often used as training in physical endurance for soldiers, in which discipline is often relaxed and route step is allowed —**route-march** *vti*

router¹ /rootər/ *n* a computer switching program that transfers incoming messages to outgoing links via the most efficient route possible, e.g. over the Internet [Late 20C. < ROUTE]

router² /rowtər/ *n* a tool that cuts shaped grooves and hollows in wood or metal, originally a hand tool but now usually driven by electricity [Early 19C. < ROUT²]

route step *n* a mode of marching in military formation where there is no requirement to keep in step and talking and singing are allowed

routine /roo teen/ *n* **1. USUAL PATTERN OF ACTIVITY** the usual sequence for a set of activities **2. SOMETHING REPETITIVE** something that is unvarying or boringly repetitive ○ *a life of mindless routine* **3. REHEARSED PERFORMANCE** a rehearsed set of movements, actions, or speeches that make up a performance ○ *her gymnastic routine on the parallel bars* **4. REGULAR PATTERN OF BEHAVIOUR** a pattern of behaviour adopted to suit particular circumstances (*informal*) ○ *The salesman went into his routine about the car's unique reliability and performance.* **5. PART OF COMPUTER PROGRAM** a part of a computer program that performs a task ○ *a dump routine* ■ *adj* **1. USUAL OR STANDARD** regular or standard and not out of the ordinary ○ *carrying out routine maintenance* **2. REPETITIVE** boringly predictable, monotonous, and unchanging ○ *found the work pretty routine* [Late 17C. < French < *route* (see ROUTE)] —**routinely** *adv*

SYNONYMS See *habit*.

routinize /roo teen īz, rootin īz/ (**-izes, -izing, -ized**), **routinise** (**-ises, -ising, -ised**) *vt* to arrange or plan something so that it follows a regular or unchanging pattern —**routinization** /roo teen ī zaysh'n, rooti nī-/ *n*

roux /roo/ *n* a mixture of flour and fat that is cooked briefly and used as the thickening base of a sauce or soup [Early 19C. Via French, 'browned' < Old French *rous* 'reddish brown' < Latin *russus* 'red']

rove¹ /rōv/ (**roves, roving, roved**) *v* **1.** *vti* to wander or travel about without any definite purpose, often over a wide area, or travel over an area in this way **2.** *vi* to move, especially to look, in changing directions ○ *as his gaze roved around the room* [Early 16C. < ?]

rove² /rōv/ *vt* (**roves, roving, roved**) to twist fibres slightly before they are spun into yarn or thread ■ *n* wool, cotton, or other fibres twisted slightly in preparation for spinning [Late 18C. < ?]

rove³ NAUT past participle, past tense of REEVE²

rove beetle *n* a carnivorous or scavenging beetle with a long body and short wing covers. Family: Staphylinidae. [< ?]

rover¹ /rōvər/ *n* **1. WANDERER** somebody who wanders from place to place, never settling anywhere for long **2. VEHICLE FOR EXPLORING PLANET** a small vehicle launched from a lander and used to explore the surface of the moon or a planet **3. ARCHERY TARGET** a mark or object selected randomly as a target in archery **4. CROQUET BALL** a ball in croquet that has been through all the hoops but has not yet hit the final peg **5.** FOOTBALL *Aus* **AUSTRALIAN RULES PLAYER** in Australian Rules, a player, usually smaller than the others, who plays alongside the two ruckmen, and who gathers and clears the ball when it emerges from a ruck [15C. < ROVE¹]

rover² /rōvər/ *n* a machine or attachment for twisting fibres slightly in preparation for spinning [Mid-18C. < ROVE²]

rover³ /rōvər/ *n* a pirate or pirate ship (*archaic*) [14C. < Middle Low German or Middle Dutch *rōver* < *rōven* 'rob']

Rover Scout *n* YOUTH ORG same as **Venture Scout**

roving /rōving/ *adj* **1.** moving or travelling from one place or thing to another ○ *a bulletin from our roving reporter* **2.** tending to wander or waver rather than settle or concentrate on one thing ○ *a roving mind*

roving eye *n* a wide and often promiscuous sexual interest

row¹ /rō/ *n* **1. THINGS OR PEOPLE PLACED IN LINE** a group of things or people arranged in a line that is usually straight ○ *a row of cabbages* **2. LINE OF THINGS OR PEOPLE** a line along which things or people are placed next to one another ○ *arranged us in rows* **3. LINE OF SEATS** a line of seats in a theatre, cinema, lecture hall, or similar public place ○ *the second row in the balcony* **4. NARROW STREET BETWEEN LINES OF HOUSES** a narrow street that is lined with houses or other buildings on both sides **5. STREET WITH PARTICULAR CHARACTER** a street where a particular occupation or type of person predominates ○ *lawyer's row* **6.** MUSIC same as **tone row** [Old English *rāw* < Germanic] ◇ **in a row** one after the other in succession ◇ **a hard row to hoe** something difficult to do

row² /rō/ (**rows, rowing, rowed**) *v* **1.** *vti* to propel a boat across water by using oars **2.** *vi* to take part in the sport of rowing [Old English *rōwan* < Germanic, 'to steer'] —**rower** *n*

row back *vi* to moderate or modify a previous assertion, claim, or opinion, or retreat from a previous position on an issue (*informal*)

row³ /row/ *n* **1. LOUD FIGHT** a noisy quarrel or dispute **2. RACKET** an unpleasant or excessively loud noise ■ *vi* (**rows, rowing, rowed**) **ARGUE NOISILY** to have a noisy argument [Mid-18C. < ?]

rowan /rō ən, row ən/ *n* **1.** a deciduous tree with greyish compound leaves, clusters of white flowers, and bright red berries. Native to: Europe, Southwest Asia, North Africa. Latin name: *Sorbus aucuparia*. **2.** *also* **rowanberry** /-berri/ (*plural* **-ries**) a red to orange berry from a rowan tree [Early 19C. < N Germanic < Indo-European, 'red']

rowboat /rō bōt/ *n N Am* same as **rowing boat**

rowdy /rowdi/ *adj* (**-dier, -diest**) noisy and disorderly ○ *The debate was a pretty rowdy affair.* ■ *n* (*plural* **-dies**) a rough and noisy person who often causes disturbances ○ *local rowdies hanging out on the streets* [Early 19C. Probably < ROW³] —**rowdily** *adv* —**rowdiness** *n* —**rowdyism** *n*

rowel /row əl/ *n* a small spiked revolving wheel on the end of a horse-rider's spur ■ *vt* (**-els, -elling, -elled**) to urge a horse on by digging rowels into its sides [14C. Via Old French *roel(e)* 'small wheel' < late Latin *rotella* (see ROULETTE)]

row house /rō-/ *n N Am* same as **terraced house**

rowing /rō ing/ *n* the propelling of a small boat through the water using oars, especially the sport of racing in specially designed lightweight boats

(often used before a noun) ○ *a member of the rowing team*

rowing boat *n* a small lightweight boat designed to be propelled through the water by one or more people rowing with oars. N Am term **rowboat**

rowing machine *n* a fitness machine that imitates the action of rowing a boat

Rowlandson /rōlənds'n/, **Thomas** (1756–1827) British painter and caricaturist. He created satirical illustrations of life in Georgian and Regency England.

Rowling /rōling/, **Bill** (1927–95) prime minister of New Zealand (1974–75). He took over as leader of the Labour Party and Prime Minister after the death of Norman Kirk, but lost the general election the following year. Full name **Rowling, Sir Wallace Edward**. See table at **prime minister**

Rowling, J. K. (*b.* 1965) British author of the *Harry Potter* series of children's books. Full name **Joanne Kathleen Rowling**

rowlock /rollək, rullək/ *n* a more or less U-shaped pivoting metal rest fitted to the side of a rowing boat, in which an oar rests. N Am term **oarlock** [Mid-18C. < ROW² + OARLOCK]

Rowntree /rown tree/, **Benjamin Seebohm** (1871–1954) British manufacturer and philanthropist. He was the head of the chocolate firm founded by his father Joseph Rowntree, and was noted for his concern for social welfare.

Popperfoto

Arundhati Roy

Roy /roy/, **Arundhati** (*b.* 1961) Indian writer. She achieved success with her first novel, *The God of Small Things* (1997), which won the Booker Prize.

'In an unconscious gesture of television-enforced democracy, mistress and servant both scrabbled unseeingly in the same bowl of nuts.'
[Arundhati Roy, *The God of Small Things*; 1997]

royal /roy əl/ *adj* **1. OF KINGS AND QUEENS** relating to, belonging to, or consisting of a king, queen, or other member of a monarch's family ○ *members of the royal household* **2. ENJOYING MONARCH'S PATRONAGE** used in the titles of organizations and societies established by a monarch or a member of a monarch's family, or given his or her formal approval and support **3. LARGEST OR BEST** of the largest size or of the highest standard **4. EXCELLENT** of the most excellent kind ○ *given a royal welcome* **5. EXTREMELY BAD** used to emphasize how extremely bad something is (*informal*) ○ *a right royal pain in the neck* **6.** SAILING **ABOVE TOPGALLANT** located in the area of a sailing ship's rigging that is above the topgallant ■ *n* **1. MONARCH OR MEMBER OF MONARCH'S FAMILY** a monarch, or a member of a monarch's family, especially his or her immediate family (*informal*) **2. STAG WITH LARGE ANTLERS** a stag with large antlers that have 12 or more points on them **3.** SAILING **SAIL ABOVE TOPGALLANT SAIL** the sail above the topgallant sail on a full-rigged ship **4.** PRINTING **SIZE OF PAPER** a size of paper, especially a British size of writing paper 483 x 610 mm/19 x 24 in or a size of printing paper 508 x 635 mm/20 x 25 in [13C. Via Old French *roial* < Latin *regalis* (see REGAL)]

Royal Academy, Royal Academy of Arts *n* an independent British institution, based in London, that promotes the fine arts, especially through exhibitions and education programmes —**Royal Academician** *n*

Royal Academy of Dramatic Art *n* a British institution, based in London, that trains students for the acting profession

Royal Academy of Music *n* a British conservatoire, founded in 1822 and based in London, that trains students for a career in music

Royal Air Force *n* the air force of the United Kingdom, formed on 1 April 1918 from the amalgamation of the Royal Flying Corps and the Royal Naval Air Service

Royal Assent *n* the British monarch's formal signing of an act of Parliament, making it law

royal blue *adj* of a bright deep blue colour (*hyphenated before a noun*) —**royal blue** *n*

Royal British Legion *n* same as **British Legion**

Royal Canadian Mounted Police *n* a police force that operates throughout Canada except in cities and provinces with their own police forces

Royal Commission *n* in the United Kingdom, a committee set up by the monarch on the prime minister's advice to enquire into an issue ○ *set up a Royal Commission to investigate environmental pollution*

royal fern *n* a deep-rooted fern with branched stems. Native to: worldwide. Latin name: *Osmunda regalis.*

royal flush *n* in poker, a hand that consists of a ten, jack, queen, king, and ace of the same suit

Royal Flying Doctor Service *n* a medical service operated in remote parts of Australia that involves doctors and emergency medical services travelling to patients by light aircraft

Royal Highness *n* a title used when speaking or referring to a member of a royal family other than a king or queen

royal icing *n* a crisp icing made by mixing icing sugar with egg whites instead of water

royalist /róy əlist/ *n* a supporter of a monarch or the monarchic system of government (*often used before a noun*) —**royalism** *n*

Royalist *n* **1.** a Cavalier or supporter of Charles I during the English Civil War **2.** HIST same as **Tory** *n* (sense 5) **3.** in France, a supporter of the Bourbon dynasty after the Revolution

royal jelly *n* a protein-rich substance that worker bees secrete and feed to larvae in the early stages of their development and to the larvae of queen bees in all stages of their development

Royal Leamington Spa ♦ **Leamington Spa**

royally /róy əli/ *adv* **1.** GENEROUSLY with impressive generosity and hospitality ○ *royally entertained* **2.** EXPENSIVELY with great magnificence or at great expense ○ *paid royally for their front-row seats* **3.** WITH DIGNITY in a stately or dignified manner as befits a king or queen ○ *swept royally through the crowd*

Royal Marines *n* a body belonging to the British armed forces, part of the Royal Navy, whose members serve primarily at sea and in amphibious operations

royal mast *n* the highest section of a sailing ship's mast that is immediately above the topgallant

Royal Mencap Society /-mén kap-/ *n* a UK charity for people with learning disabilities [*Mencap* contraction of *mental handicap* or *mentally handicapped*]

royal palm *n* a palm tree with a tall naked trunk. Native to: tropical America. Genus: *Roystonea.*

royal poinciana *n* a tropical tree widely grown for ornament. Flowers: bright red, in clusters. Native to: Madagascar. Latin name: *Delonix regia.*

royal prerogative *n* the power or right of a monarch to do something or be exempt from something, especially as formerly exercised by British monarchs

royal purple *adj* of a deep vivid reddish-purple colour (*hyphenated before a noun*) —**royal purple** *n*

royal road *n* the route or method by which progress or a particular result is guaranteed, often by virtue of special privileges ○ *a young singer on the royal road to stardom*

royal standard *n* the flag of the British monarch,

flown from the place he or she is staying in at the time

royalty /róy əlti/ (*plural* **-ties**) *n* **1.** ROYAL PERSON OR PEOPLE a king, queen, or other member of a monarch's family, or members of a royal family generally ○ *mixing with royalty at garden parties* **2.** ROYAL PERSON'S STATUS the status or authority of a king, queen, or other member of a monarch's family **3.** KINGLY OR QUEENLY QUALITIES the personal qualities conventionally ascribed to a king or queen, especially great dignity **4.** MONARCH'S PERMISSION TO HAVE SOMETHING the right to have or take something, especially minerals, granted by a king or queen to a person or company **5.** PERCENTAGE OF INCOME PAID TO CREATOR a percentage of the income from a book, piece of music, or invention that is paid to the author, composer, or inventor (*often used in the plural*) ○ *still living on the royalties from her first novel* **6.** MINING COMPANY'S PAYMENT TO LANDOWNER money paid to a landowner by a company taking minerals, oil, or gas from his or her land (*often used in the plural*)

royal warrant *n* a king's or queen's official authorization to a company to supply goods to a royal household

rozzer /rózzər/ *n* a member of a police force (*dated slang*) [Late 19C. < ?]

RP *abbr* **1.** LING Received Pronunciation **2.** EDUC Regius Professor **3.** Republic of the Philippines **4.** role-play

RPB *abbr* recognized professional body

RPG[1] *n* a high-level computer language used primarily for business reports. Full form **report program generator**

RPG[2] *n* a computer or other game in which the participants assume roles, often as fantasy characters such as heroes or elves, in a scenario that develops as the game progresses. Full form **role-playing game**

RPG[3] *abbr* ARMS rocket-propelled grenade

RPI *abbr* COMM retail price index

rpm *abbr* RECORDING, MECH ENG revolutions per minute

RPM *abbr* COMM resale price maintenance

RPO *abbr* Royal Philharmonic Orchestra

rps *abbr* MECH ENG revolutions per second

RPS *abbr* Royal Photographic Society

rpt *abbr* **1.** repeat **2.** report

RPV *abbr* MIL remotely piloted vehicle

RQ *abbr* MED respiratory quotient

RR *abbr* **1.** TRANSP railroad **2.** CHR Right Reverend

-rrhagia *suffix* unusual or excessive flow or discharge ○ *metrorrhagia* [< Greek < *rhag-* stem of *rhēgnunai* 'burst out']

-rrhoea, -rrhea *suffix* flow, discharge ○ *pyorrhoea* [< modern Latin < Greek *rhein* 'to flow']

rRNA *abbr* BIOCHEM ribosomal RNA

RRP *abbr* COMM recommended retail price

Rs *symbol* MONEY rupees

RS *abbr* **1.** recording secretary **2.** right side **3.** Royal Society

RSA[1] *abbr* **1.** Republic of South Africa **2.** Returned Services Association (New Zealand) **3.** Royal Scottish Academician **4.** Royal Scottish Academy **5.** Royal Society of Arts

RSA[2] *n* in computing, a system of encryption based on the difficulty of factoring very large numbers [< *RSA Security Inc.*]

RSC *abbr* **1.** Royal Shakespeare Company **2.** Royal Society of Chemistry

RSFSR *abbr* Russian Soviet Federated Socialist Republic

RSI *n* UK, ANZ, Can a painful condition affecting some people who overuse muscles as a result of activities such as regularly operating a computer keyboard and mouse or playing the piano. Full form **repetitive strain injury**. US term **cumulative trauma disorder**

RSJ *abbr* CONSTR rolled steel joist

RSL[1] *n* an organization established in Australia in 1916 to provide help for former members of the armed forces and their families. Full form **Returned Services League**

RSL[2] *abbr* Royal Society of Literature

RSL club *n* Aus a social club run by the RSL

RSM *abbr* **1.** MIL regimental sergeant major **2.** Republic of San Marino **3.** MED Royal Society of Medicine

RSPB *abbr* Royal Society for the Protection of Birds

RSPCA *abbr* Royal Society for the Prevention of Cruelty to Animals

RSV *abbr* BIBLE Revised Standard Version

RSVP *v* used on an invitation to request a response to it [Abbreviation of French *répondez s'il vous plaît*]

rt *abbr* right

RT *abbr* **1.** TELECOM radio telegraph **2.** TELECOM radio telegraphy **3.** TELECOM radiotelephone **4.** real time **5.** AMERICAN FOOTBALL right tackle **6.** room temperature **7.** TRAVEL round trip

RTDS *abbr* COMPUT real-time data system

Rte *abbr* MAIL route

RTE *abbr* Ireland Radio Telefís Éireann [Irish, 'Irish Radio and Television']

rtf[1] *n* **1.** a format for a computer file that contains rich text **2.** a computer file in rich text format [Abbreviation of *rich text format*]

rtf[2] *abbr* a file extension for an rtf file

RTFM *v* a highly offensive term used as a response in e-mail communications to an obvious technical question (*taboo*) Full form **read the fucking manual**

Rt Hon. *abbr* POL Right Honourable

RTM *abbr* read the manual (*used in e-mails or text messages*)

Rt Rev. *abbr* CHR Right Reverend

RTS *n* in computer gaming, a strategy game in which the action is continuous rather than turn-based [Abbreviation of real-time strategy]

RTW *abbr* CLOTHING ready-to-wear

ru *abbr* Russian Federation (*used in Internet addresses*) See table at **domain name**

Ru *symbol* CHEM ELEM ruthenium

RU *abbr* **1.** are you (*used in e-mails or text messages*) **2.** SPORTS Rugby Union

Ruahine Range /roō ə heē nay-/ mountain range in the south of the North Island, New Zealand. Its highest point is Mount Mangaweka, 1,733 m/5,686 ft.

Ruanda-Urundi /roō ándə oö roōndi/ former name for **Burundi** (until 1962)

Ruapehu /roō ə páy hoo/ active volcano in the central part of the North Island, New Zealand. It last erupted in 1996. Height: 2,797 m/9,177 ft.

rub /rub/ *v* (**rubs, rubbing, rubbed**) **1.** *vt* PRESS AND MOVE HAND ON SOMETHING to move the hand or an object over the surface of something, pressing down with a repeated circular or backwards and forwards motion ○ *rubbed his aching shoulders with ointment* **2.** *vi* TOUCH WITH DRAGGING PRESSURE to make dragging contact with a surface ○ *metal parts rubbing against one another* **3.** *vti* CLEAN WITH REPEATED STROKES to clean, dry, or polish something, or be able to be cleaned, dried, or polished, by moving a cloth, sponge, or other implement over the surface repeatedly ○ *rubbed the stain from the tablecloth* **4.** *vti* CAUSE ABRASION ON SKIN to cause discomfort or pain by repeatedly scraping the skin ○ *These shoes are rubbing my heels.* **5.** *vi* BOWLS BE SLOWED DOWN IN BOWLS in bowls, to be slowed by an uneven patch on the green ■ *n* **1.** RUBBING ACTION a rubbing motion, or a rubbing of something with or against something else **2.** MASSAGE a massaging of part of the body ○ *a soothing back rub* **3.** DIFFICULTY a problem or difficulty ○ *That's the rub: too little time.* **4.** IRRITATING THING something that somebody does or says that irritates or offends somebody else **5.** BOWLS UNEVEN PATCH IN BOWLS in bowls, an uneven patch of grass in the green [14C. < ?]

rub along *vi* to have a friendly enough relationship or existence together (*informal*)

rub down *vt* **1.** MAKE SURFACE SMOOTH FOR PAINTING to prepare a surface for painting or varnishing by smoothing it or removing the old paint or varnish with sandpaper or some other abrasive **2.** MASSAGE SOMEBODY to massage somebody or part of the body vigorously **3.** DRY BODY WITH VIGOROUS RUBBING to dry a person's or animal's body by vigorous rubbing with a towel

rub in *vt* **1.** to keep referring to something that the hearer does not want to be reminded of, usually because it is embarrassing (*informal*) **2.** to mix fat, usually butter, into flour in small pieces between the fingertips

rub off *vi* to be passed to somebody, or be an influence on somebody who is exposed to it

rub out *v* **1.** *vti* to remove something written, or be removed, with a rubber **2.** *vt N Am* to murder somebody (*slang*)

rub up *vt* to polish something by vigorous rubbing ○ *Let the polish soak into the leather before you rub them up.* ◇ **rub somebody up the wrong way** to irritate or annoy somebody

rubab /roo bab/ *n* a short-necked lute played in Afghanistan [Via Afghan Persian or Pashto < Arabic *rabāb*]

Rub al-Khali /roob al kaáli/ desert in the Arabian Peninsula. Also called the 'Empty Quarter', it extends from central Saudi Arabia into Yemen, the United Arab Emirates, and Oman. Area: 650,000 sq. km/250,000 sq. mi.

rubasse /roo bass, roo báss/ *n* a ruby-red variety of quartz containing iron oxide [Late 19C. < French *rubace* < *rubis* 'ruby' < Latin *rubeus* 'red']

rubato /roo baátō/ *n* rhythmic freedom in musical performance, often against a steady accompaniment ■ *adj, adv* performed with rubato [Late 18C. < Italian (*tempo*) *rubato* 'robbed (time)', past participle of *rubare* 'rob']

rubber[1] /rúbbər/ *n* **1.** NATURALLY OCCURRING ELASTIC SUBSTANCE a strong elastic material made by drying the sap from various tropical trees, especially the American rubber tree **2.** ELASTIC SYNTHETIC SUBSTANCE a strong elastic synthetic substance made either by improving the qualities of natural rubber or by an industrial process using petroleum and coal products **3.** DEVICE FOR ERASING a piece of rubber used for erasing writing. N Am term **eraser 4.** N Am CONDOM a contraceptive sheath that fits over a man's penis (*slang; sometimes offensive*) **5.** N Am CLOTHING WATERPROOF OVERSHOE a waterproof overshoe worn over normal shoes to protect them in wet weather (*usually used in the plural*) **6.** RUBBING OR POLISHING CLOTH a cloth or pad used for rubbing or polishing something, especially the pad that a cabinetmaker uses to apply varnish or French polish **7.** DEVICE THAT RUBS SOMETHING any machine or device that rubs a surface **8.** BASEBALL SPOT PITCHER STANDS ON in baseball, the rectangle of hard rubber on the mound that the pitcher stands on to throw the ball [Mid-16C. < RUB] ◇ **burn rubber** to drive very fast (*informal*)

rubber[2] /rúbbər/ *n* **1.** BRIDGE MATCH OF THREE GAMES a match of three or five games in cards, especially bridge and whist **2.** DECIDING GAME IN CARDS MATCH in some card games, an extra game played to decide a tied match **3.** SESSION OF PLAY IN CARD GAME a match or session of playing in a card game (*informal*) **4.** SET OF GAMES a series of games in some sports (*informal*) [Late 16C. Origin ?]

rubber band *n* a loop of thin rubber that is wrapped round objects to hold them together

rubber bridge *n* a form of contract bridge in which a new hand is dealt for each round

rubber bullet *n* a cylindrical block of hard rubber fired by police officers or troops during crowd-control operations, designed as a deterrent but capable of inflicting serious injury

rubber cement *n* an adhesive made by dissolving rubber in an organic solvent

rubber cheque *n* a cheque that is returned by a bank because the person who wrote it has insufficient funds in his or her account to cover it (*informal humorous*) [Because it bounces]

rubber-chicken circuit *n N Am* a series of events that people feel obliged to attend, especially lunches or dinners for politicians or other public figures

(*informal*) [Because the food served is usually unappetizing]

rubber duck *n S Africa* an inflatable dinghy with an outboard motor

rubber goods *npl* condoms (*euphemistic*)

rubberize /rúbbə rīz/ (*-izes, -izing, -ized*), **rubberise** (*-ises, -ising, -ised*) *vt* to coat or impregnate something, especially fabric, with rubber

rubberneck /rúbbər nek/ (*informal*) *vi* (*-necks, -necking, -necked*) to stare at somebody or something in an excessively inquisitive or insensitive way ■ *n* somebody who stares in an over-inquisitive or insensitive way. N Am term **rubbernecker** [Late 19C. < craning or turning the neck as if it were made of rubber] — **rubbernecking** *n*

SYNONYMS See *gaze*.

rubbernecked /rúbbər nekt/ *adj* staring insensitively or in an excessively inquisitive way (*informal*) ○ *a crowd of rubbernecked onlookers*

rubbernecker /rúbbər nekər/ *n N Am* same as **rubberneck** (*informal*)

rubber plant *n* **1.** a tropical plant with thick glossy leaves and a rubbery sap, widely grown as a houseplant but growing as a full-size tree in Southeast Asia. Latin name: *Ficus elastica*. **2.** any plant that produces a rubbery sap

rubber stamp *n* **1.** STAMPING DEVICE a device for stamping words or numbers on paper, consisting of an embossed flat rubber pad that is inked **2.** AUTOMATIC AUTHORIZATION authorization or approval that is given automatically **3.** SOMEBODY GIVING APPROVAL AUTOMATICALLY a person or group who gives authorization or approval automatically, without thinking, questioning, or dissenting

rubber-stamp *vt* **1.** to authorize or approve something automatically, without thinking, questioning, or dissenting **2.** to mark a document with an imprint from a rubber stamp

rubber tree

rubber tree *n* **1.** a tree whose sap is the main source of natural rubber. Native to: tropical America. Latin name: *Hevea brasiliensis*. **2.** any tree whose sap is made into rubber

rubbery /rúbbəri/ *adj* with the elastic or tough texture of rubber

rubbing /rúbbing/ *n* an impression of a textured surface, e.g. a raised design on a tombstone, made by placing paper over the surface and rubbing with a drawing implement

rubbing alcohol *n N Am* same as **surgical spirit**

rubbish /rúbbish/ *n* **1.** WASTE MATERIAL things that are thrown away as unwanted, usually the remains of things that have been used or used up (*often used before a noun*) **2.** WORTHLESS THINGS things that are worthless or of very poor quality ○ *Most of what he's written is utter rubbish.* **3.** NONSENSE foolish things said or written, or things dismissed as wrong or not to be believed ○ *Don't talk rubbish!* ■ *vt* (*-bishes, -bishing, -bished*) DISMISS SOMETHING OR CRITICIZE SOMEBODY to dismiss something as worthless, or criticize somebody severely (*informal*) ○ *The scheme has been rubbished in the national press.* [14C. < Anglo-Norman *rubbous*] —**rubbish** *adj* —**rubbishy** *adj*

rubbish bin *n* a large usually cylindrical container with a lid for household rubbish, kept outdoors

rubble /rúbb'l/ *n* **1.** FRAGMENTS OF BROKEN BUILDINGS broken stones, bricks, and other materials from buildings that have fallen down or been demolished **2.** ROUGH STONES AS FILLER OR BULK rough unfinished stones used to fill space between walls or to build the bulk of a wall that will have a finishing surface of dressed stone **3.** *also* **rubblework** /rúbb'l wurk/ MASONRY OF ROUGH STONES masonry that is constructed using rough unfinished stones [14C. Origin ?] —**rubbly** *adj*

Rubbra /rúbbrə/, **Edmund** (1901–86) British composer. In his symphonies, chamber music, and choral compositions, he made much use of counterpoint and polyphony.

rubdown /rúb down/ *n* a brisk rubbing down, usually of a person's or animal's body after exercising

rube /roob/ *n N Am* an offensive term for somebody who is regarded as naive or unsophisticated, especially somebody from the country who is not used to city ways (*slang*) [Late 19C. Shortening of the forename *Reuben*]

rubefacient /roobi fáysh'nt/ *adj* causing the skin to become red (*formal*) ■ *n* a substance that causes the skin to become red, especially a cream or ointment used as a counterirritant [Early 19C. < Latin *rubefacient-*, present participle of *rubefacere* 'make red' < *rubeus* 'red' + *facere* 'make'] —**rubefaction** /-fáksh'n/ *n*

rubefy /roobi fī/ (*-fies, -fying, -fied*) *vt* to use a rubefacient on skin [14C. < Old French *rubifier* 'make red' < Latin *rubeus* 'red']

Rube Goldberg /roob góld burg/ *adj N Am* same as **Heath Robinson** [Mid-20C. After Reuben 'Rube' Goldberg (1883–1970), US cartoonist known for depictions of complex devices performing elementary tasks]

rubella /roo béllə/ *n ANZ, N Am* a highly contagious viral disease, especially affecting children, that causes swelling of the lymph glands and a reddish-pink rash on the skin. It can be harmful to the unborn baby of a pregnant woman who contracts it. (*technical*) UK term **German measles** [Late 19C. < modern Latin, 'rash' < form of Latin *rubellus* 'reddish' < *rubeus* 'red']

rubellite /roobi līt, roo bélīt/ *n* a red variety of tourmaline. Use: jewellery. [Late 18C. < Latin *rubellus* (see RUBELLA)]

Rubens /roobənz/, **Peter Paul** (1577–1640) Flemish painter. He is considered one of the most important artists of the 17th century, and his style has come to define the sensuous aspects of baroque painting.

rubeola /roo beé ələ, roobi ólə/ *n* same as **measles** (*technical*) [Late 17C. < modern Latin < Latin *rubeus* 'red'] —**rubeolar** *adj*

rubescent /roo béss'nt/ *adj* turning red or reddish, e.g. by blushing (*literary*) [Mid-18C. < Latin *rubescent-*, present participle of *rubescere* 'redden' < *rubeus* 'red'] —**rubescence** *n*

Rubicon /roobikən, -kon/, **rubicon** *n* a point at which any action taken commits the person taking it to a further course of action that cannot be avoided [Early 17C. After the stream in N Italy that Julius Caesar crossed illegally with his army in 49 BC, making civil war inevitable] ◇ **cross the Rubicon** to do something that commits you to a particular course of action

rubicund /roobikənd/ *adj* with the reddish skin colour that is widely regarded as a sign of good health in people with white skin (*literary*) [15C. < Latin *rubicundus* < *rubeus* 'red'] —**rubicundity** /roobi kúndəti/ *n*

rubidium /roo bíddi əm/ *n* a soft silvery-white radioactive element of the alkali metal group that reacts strongly with water and bursts into flame when exposed to air. Source: lepidolite, carnallite. Use: photocells. Symbol **Rb**. See table at **element** [Mid-19C. < modern Latin < Latin *rubidus* 'red' < *rubere* 'be red' < *ruber* 'red'; from the two red lines in its spectrum]

Rubik's cube /roobiks-/, **Rubik cube** *tdmk* a trademark for a puzzle that is a cube composed of smaller rotating coloured cubes, the aim being to rotate them to make each of the large cube's faces a uniform colour

Rubinstein /roobin stīn/, **Anton** (1829–94) Russian composer and pianist. He is best known for his small

piano pieces, e.g. *Melody in F* (1859). Full name **Rubinstein, Anton Grigoryevich**

Rubinstein, Arthur (1887–1982) Polish-born US pianist. He is known for his interpretations of works by the romantic composers, notably Frédéric Chopin.

'Sometimes, I think, not so much am I a pianist, but a vampire. All my life I have lived off the blood of Chopin.'
[Attributed to Arthur Rubinstein]

ruble *n* MONEY another spelling of **rouble**

rubric /ro͝obrik/ *n* **1. TITLE OR HEADING** a printed title or heading, usually distinguished from the body of the text in some way, especially the heading of a section of a legal statute, originally underlined in red **2. SET OF PRINTED INSTRUCTIONS** a set of printed rules or instructions, e.g. the rules governing how Christian services are to be conducted, often printed in red in a prayer book **3. ESTABLISHED CUSTOM** a well-established custom or tradition that provides rules for conduct **4. CATEGORY** a class or category of things ■ *adj* **IN RED** printed or marked in red [13C. Directly or via French < Latin *rubrica* 'red ochre' < *ruber* 'red'] —**rubrical** *adj* —**rubrically** *adv*

rubricate /ro͝obri kayt/ (**-cates, -cating, -cated**) *vt* (*formal*) **1. ADD HEADINGS TO TEXT** to add titles or heading to a text, or print them in red **2. MARK SOMETHING IN RED** to print or mark something in red **3. REGULATE SOMETHING** to apply a set of rules to something —**rubrication** /ro͝obri káysh'n/ *n* —**rubricator** *n*

rubrician /roo brísh'n/ *n* an expert in the way religious services should be conducted

ruby /ro͝obi/ (*plural* **-bies**) *n* **1.** a red precious stone that is a form of corundum. Use: jewellery, manufacture of watches, precision instruments. **2.** a deep glowing purplish-red colour like that of a ruby [14C. Via Old French *rubi* < medieval Latin *rubinus* < Latin *rubeus* 'red'] —**ruby** *adj*

ruby port *n* a port that is matured for a minimal period in the barrel and then bottled for immediate drinking

ruby spinel *n* a red transparent form of the mineral spinel. Use: jewellery.

ruby wedding *n* the 40th anniversary of a couple's wedding

RUC *abbr* Royal Ulster Constabulary

ruche /roosh/ *n* a decorative strip of gathered, pleated, or frilled fabric on a garment ■ *vt* (**ruches, ruching, ruched**) to decorate the edges of a garment with ruches [Early 19C. Via French < medieval Latin *rusca* 'tree bark' < Celtic]

ruching /ro͝oshing/ *n* decorative edges of gathered, pleated, or frilled fabric

ruck[1] /ruk/ *n* **1. LARGE NUMBER** a large number of people or things **2. ORDINARY PEOPLE OR THINGS** the great mass of unexceptional people or things **3. FOLLOWERS** the group of competitors behind the leader in a race **4.** RUGBY **LOOSE SCRUM** in rugby, a loose scrum formed around the ball when it is on the ground **5.** FOOTBALL **GROUP OF ROVING PLAYERS** in Australian Rules football, three players who have no fixed positions but follow play, trying to win possession of the ball for their team ■ *vi* (**rucks, rucking, rucked**) RUGBY **FORM RUCK** in rugby, to form a loose scrum around the ball on the ground [13C. Probably < N Germanic, 'pile of combustible material']

ruck[2] /ruk/ *vti* (**rucks, rucking, rucked**) to become creased, or cause something, especially fabric, to become creased ○ *The carpet is rucked up under your chair.* ■ *n* a crease, especially in a fabric [Late 18C. < Old Norse *hrukka* 'wrinkle']

ruckman /rúk man/ (*plural* **-men** /-men/) *n* in Australian Rules football, either of two players who do not have fixed positions but follow play, trying to win possession of the ball for their team. They are assisted by a third player, a rover.

rucksack /rúk sak, ro͝ok-/ *n* a large bag, usually with two straps and often with a supporting frame, carried on the back and used especially by walkers and climbers [Mid-19C. < German, 'back sack']

ruckus /rúkəss/ *n* a noisy and unpleasant disturbance [Late 19C. < ?]

ruction /rúksh'n/ *n* a noisy, often violent, quarrel or fight ■ **ructions** *npl* angry reactions, protests, or arguments ○ *There'll be ructions if the boss finds out!* [Early 18C. < ?]

rudbeckia /rud béki ə/ (*plural* **-as** or *same*) *n* a plant with alternate leaves and showy yellow flowers that have green or black centres. Native to: North America. Genus: *Rudbeckia*. [Mid-19C. < modern Latin, after Olof *Rudbeck* the elder (1630–1702) and the younger (1660–1740), Swedish botanists]

rudd /rud/ (*plural* **rudds** or *same*) *n* a freshwater fish of the carp family with a thin greenish-brown body and red fins. Native to: Europe. Latin name: *Scardinius erythrophthalmus*. [Early 16C. Variant of obsolete *rud* 'redness' < Germanic, 'red']

Rudd /rud/, **Steele** (1868–1935) Australian writer. He wrote comic sketches, collected in works such as *On Our Selection* (1899). Pseudonym of **Davis, Arthur Hoey**

rudder /rúddər/ *n* **1. MEANS OF STEERING BOAT OR SHIP** a means of steering a boat or ship, usually in the form of a pivoting blade under the water, mounted at the stern and controlled by a wheel or handle (**tiller**) **2. AEROFOIL FOR STEERING AEROPLANE** an aerofoil, usually on the tail of an aeroplane, that pivots vertically and controls left-to-right movement **3. CONTROLLING FORCE** a guiding or controlling force or influence [Old English *rōþer* < Germanic] —**rudderless** *adj*

ruddle /rúdd'l/, **reddle** /rédd'l/, **raddle** /rádd'l/ *n* a red ochre. Use: dye, formerly to mark sheep. ■ *vt* (**-dles, -dling, -dled**) to dye or mark something such as a sheep with ruddle [Mid-16C. < obsolete *rud* 'redness' < Germanic, 'red']

ruddy /rúddi/ *adj* (**-dier, -diest**) **1. ROSY WITH HEALTH** with a healthy reddish glow ○ *ruddy cheeks* **2. REDDISH** red or reddish in colour ○ *ruddy sky* ■ *adj, adv* **SWEARWORD** used as a swearword to emphasize how good, bad, or severe something is (*slang; sometimes offensive*) [Old English *rudig* < Germanic, 'red'] —**ruddily** *adv* —**ruddiness** *n*

ruddy duck *n* a duck with a broad beak, upright tail, and white cheeks, the male of which is brownish-red with a black crown and blue beak during the mating season. Native to: North America. Latin name: *Oxyura jamaicensis*.

rude /rood/ (**ruder, rudest**) *adj* **1. ILL-MANNERED** disagreeable or discourteous in manner or action ○ *Don't be rude!* **2. INDECENT** offensive to accepted standards of decency ○ *rude words* **3. UNREFINED** lacking refinement or social skills **4. SUDDEN AND UNPLEASANT** happening with unexpected suddenness and unpleasantness ○ *a rude awakening* **5. ROUGHLY MADE** in a rough or incomplete state ○ *a rude wooden bench* **6. UNSKILLED** showing a lack of skill or training ○ *rude paintings* **7. INEXPERIENCED** without schooling or experience ○ *a rude youth raised in the wilderness* **8. RAW** in a raw or unprocessed state ○ *rude fibres* **9. VAGUE** lacking precision ○ *a rude guess* **10. UNDEVELOPED** technologically or economically undeveloped **11. ROBUST** strong and energetic ○ *in rude health* [13C. Via French < Latin *rudis* 'raw, rough'] —**rudely** *adv* —**rudeness** *n*

rudeboy /ro͞od boy/ *n* a criminal, especially a gang leader, gunman, or drug dealer (*slang; used in Black English*)

ruderal /ro͞odərəl/ *adj* describes a plant growing in wasteland, rubbish, or disturbed ground [Mid-19C. < Latin *ruder-* 'rubble'] —**ruderal** *n*

rudiment /ro͞odimənt/ *n* **1. SOMETHING BASIC TO SUBJECT** a basic principle or skill, especially in a particular field or subject (*often used in the plural*) ○ *the rudiments of computer programming* **2. BEGINNING** an early stage in the development of something such as a plan (*often used in the plural*) **3.** BIOL **UNDEVELOPED BODY PART** a body part that does not develop fully and performs no useful function. The mammary gland in males is a rudiment. **4.** BIOL **EMBRYO OF ORGAN** an embryonic stage of an organ or body part [Mid-16C. Directly or via French < Latin *rudimentum* < *rudis* 'raw, rough']

rudimentary /ro͞odi méntəri/, **rudimental** /-mént'l/ *adj* **1. BASIC** existing at an elementary or basic level ○ *a rudimentary knowledge of French* **2. DEVELOPING** in an early or partially developed stage **3.** BIOL **UNDEVELOPED** not fully developed ○ *a rudimentary tail* **4.** BIOL **IN FORM OF EMBRYO** in an embryonic state —**rudimentarily** *adv* —**rudimentariness** *n*

Rudolf /ro͞o dolf/, **archduke and crown prince of Austria** (1858–89) The son of Franz Josef of Austria, he was a well-travelled patron of the arts

Rudolf I (1218–91) king of Germany and Holy Roman Emperor. His acquisition of Bohemian territories in 1278 greatly strengthened the house of Habsburg. He is considered the founder of the Habsburg dynasty.

Rudolf, Lake /ro͞o dolf/ former name for **Turkana, Lake**

rue[1] /roo/ *vti* (**rues, ruing, rued**) to feel regret or sorrow for something in the past ○ *I rue the day I offered to help.* ■ *n* a feeling of regret or sorrow (*archaic*) [Old English *hrēowan* < Germanic]

rue[2] /roo/ (*plural* **rues** or *same*) *n* a woody plant with bitter, strongly scented leaves that yield an oil formerly used in medicines. Flowers: small, yellow. Native to: Europe, Asia. Latin name: *Ruta graveolens*. [14C. Via French and Latin *ruta* < Greek *rhutē*]

rueful /ro͞of'l/ *adj* **1.** feeling, showing, or causing regret **2.** causing people to feel pity —**ruefully** *adv* —**ruefulness** *n*

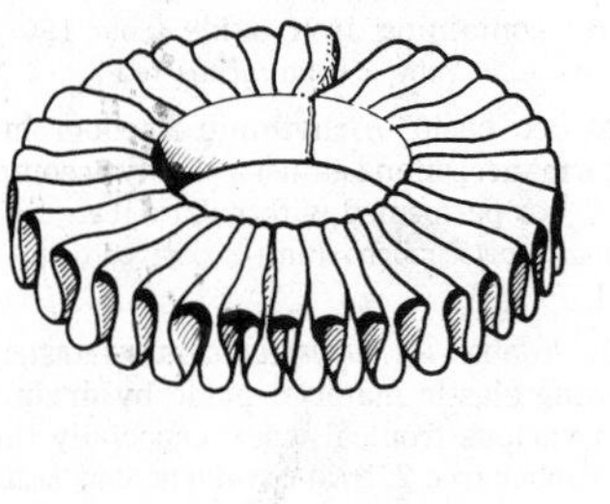

ruff

ruff[1] /ruf/ *n* **1. FANCY PLEATED COLLAR** a separate collar of starched pleated linen or lace worn by men and women in the 16th and 17th centuries **2. NECK HAIR OR FEATHERS** a growth of long, colourful, or bushy hair or feathers on the neck of a bird or other animal **3.** (*plural* **ruffs** or *same*) **BIRD WITH ELABORATE RUFF** a bird of the sandpiper family, the male of which, in spring, grows a ruff of feathers that are raised during courtship displays. Native to: Europe, Asia. Latin name: *Philomachus pugnax*. [Early 16C. Probably < variant of ROUGH] —**ruffed** *adj*

SPELLCHECK See *rough*.

ruff[2] /ruf/ *n* **1. PLAYING OF TRUMP CARD** in bridge or whist, the act of playing a trump card **2. CARD GAME** an old card game similar to whist ■ *vti* (**ruffs, ruffing, ruffed**) **PLAY TRUMP ON DIFFERENT SUIT** in bridge or whist, to play a trump card on a card from a different suit [Late 16C. < Old French *roffle*, a card game]

ruffe /ruf/ (*plural* **ruffes** or *same*), **ruff** (*plural* **ruffs** or *same*) *n* a small freshwater fish of the perch family with a single spiny dorsal fin. Native to: Europe. Latin name: *Acerina cernua*. [15C. Probably < variant of ROUGH, from its rough scales]

ruffian /rúffi ən/ *n* a rough, bullying, or violent person, often a member of a gang of thugs (*dated*) ■ *adj* behaving in a rough, bullying, or violent way (*literary*) [15C. Via French < Italian *ruffiano* < Germanic] —**ruffianism** *n* —**ruffianly** *adj*

ruffle[1] /rúff'l/ *v* (**-fles, -fling, -fled**) **1.** *vt* **MAKE FEATHERS ERECT** to erect feathers, e.g. in defence, as a display, or for warmth or grooming (*refers to birds*) **2.** *vti* **MAKE WAVES IN SURFACE** to disturb or ripple something, especially a surface, or become disturbed or rippled **3.** *vti* **ANNOY SOMEBODY** to bother or fluster somebody, or become bothered or flustered ○ *gets ruffled so easily* **4.** *vt* **GATHER OR PLEAT FABRIC** to draw a strip of material into pleats or gathers to use as trim **5.** *vt* **GLANCE QUICKLY THROUGH SOMETHING** to flick rapidly through the pages of a book or magazine (*dated*) **6.** *vt* **SHUFFLE CARDS** to shuffle playing cards (*dated*) ■ *n* **1. WAVE IN SURFACE** a disturbance or ripple in something, especially a

surface **2.** IRRITATING THING a source of irritation or annoyance **3.** TRIM OF PLEATED FABRIC a strip of closely pleated or gathered material used as trim **4.** ZOOL same as **ruff**[1] (sense 2) [14C. < ?] —**ruffled** adj —**ruffly** adj

ruffle[2] /rúff'l/ n a low continuous drumbeat ■ vt (**-fles, -fling, -fled**) to play a ruffle on a drum [Early 18C. Probably an imitation of the sound]

rufiyaa /roo feé yaa/ (plural same) n the main unit of currency in the Maldives. See table at **currency** [Late 20C. Via Divehi < Hindi rūpiyā (see RUPEE)]

rug /rug/ n **1.** FABRIC FLOOR COVERING a thick heavy fabric covering for a floor, especially one that is smaller than a carpet **2.** ANIMAL SKIN MAT an animal skin used as a mat or small carpet **3.** BLANKET a thick blanket, especially one formerly used by car or carriage passengers to cover their legs and feet **4.** HAIRPIECE a toupee or wig (informal) [Mid-16C. Probably < N Germanic]

ruga /roógə/ (plural **-gae** /-jee, -gī/) n a natural crease or ridge in a body part, especially in the internal organs (often used in the plural) [Late 18C. < Latin, 'wrinkle'] —**rugate** /-gayt/ adj

rugby: a player attempts a kick

rugby /rúgbi/, **rugby football** n a team sport in which players run with an oval ball, pass it laterally from hand to hand, and kick it (often used before a noun) [Mid-19C. After RUGBY School, where it was reputedly invented]

Rugby /rúgbi/ town in Warwickshire, central England. Rugby School, a leading public school, is located there. Population: 87,453 (2001).

rugby league n a form of rugby that has teams of 13 players. Throughout the history of the game, rugby league players have always been allowed to turn professional.

rugby union n a form of rugby that has teams of 15 players. Rugby union players have only been allowed to turn professional since 1995.

rugged /rúggid/ adj **1.** WITH IRREGULAR SURFACE with a sharply rising and falling, rough, or jagged surface ○ over rugged terrain **2.** STRONG-FEATURED with furrowed facial features thought to suggest physical strength or strength of character, especially in men ○ their rugged faces **3.** PHYSICALLY RESILIENT physically strong enough to endure harsh conditions, or used to enduring them **4.** SEVERE IN MANNER harsh and forbidding in manner **5.** LACKING REFINEMENT coarse or unrefined in behaviour **6.** TESTING requiring strength, skill, or endurance **7.** STRONGLY BUILT designed and manufactured to withstand hard use or harsh environments **8.** STORMY affected by violent and dangerous storms ■ n COMPUT DURABLE DEVICE a device such as a laptop that is made of durable materials resistant to extreme conditions such as heat, cold, liquids, and impact [13C. Probably < N Germanic] —**ruggedly** adv —**ruggedness** n

ruggedize /rúggi dīz/ (**-izes, -izing, -ized**), **ruggedise** (**-ises, -ising, -ised**) vt to make something such as a piece of computer equipment capable of withstanding rough treatment —**ruggedization** /rúggi dī záysh'n/ n —**ruggedized** adj

rugger /rúggər/ n same as **rugby** (informal) [Late 19C. Alteration]

rugosa rose /roo góssə-/ n a common wild hedge rose. Flowers: fragrant, pink or white. Native to: eastern North America. Latin name: Rosa rugosa. [< Latin, form of rugosus (see RUGOSE)]

rugose /roó gōss, roó-, roo góss/, **rugous** /roógəss/ adj **1.** with creases, wrinkles, or ridges **2.** describes a leaf or other plant part that has a surface of alternating depressions and ridges [15C. < Latin rugosus < ruga 'wrinkle'] —**rugosely** adv —**rugosity** /roo góssəti/ n

rug rat n a young child, especially an infant or toddler (informal humorous)

rug up (**rugs up, rugging up, rugged up**) vi Aus to put on warm clothes in cold weather ○ There's quite a wind, so we'd better rug up.

Ruhr /roor/ **1.** river in western Germany. It rises near Winterberg and flows northwest and west to join the River Rhine at Duisburg. Length: 235 km/146 mi. **2.** region of western Germany, comprising the valley of the River Ruhr and adjacent areas, and including the cities of Düsseldorf and Dortmund. It contains the largest coalfield and industrial region in western Europe. Area: 4,500 sq. km/1,737 sq. mi.

ruin /roó in/ n **1.** BROKEN REMAINS the physical remains of something such as a building or city that has decayed or been destroyed (often used in the plural) **2.** COMPLETE DEVASTATION a state of complete destruction, decay, collapse, or loss (often plural) ○ The buildings had gone to ruin. **3.** COMPLETE FAILURE complete moral, social, or economic failure ○ facing financial ruin **4.** SOMEBODY OR SOMETHING DESTROYED somebody or something completely lost or destroyed **5.** CAUSE OF DESTRUCTION a cause of complete loss or destruction ○ Alcohol was their ruin. ■ **ruins** npl COMPLETE DEVASTATION a state of complete destruction, decay, collapse, or loss ○ Her dreams lay in ruins. ■ v (**-ins, -ining, -ined**) **1.** vt DESTROY SOMETHING to cause something to be destroyed or lost **2.** vt DESTROY SOMEBODY FINANCIALLY to bring about somebody's financial demise **3.** vt DAMAGE SOMETHING BEYOND REPAIR to spoil something so severely that it cannot be restored **4.** vi DECLINE to fall into a state of complete destruction or loss (literary) [14C. Via French < Latin ruina < ruere 'fall'] —**ruined** adj —**ruiner** n

ruination /roó i náysh'n/ n **1.** the destruction or loss of something **2.** something that brings about destruction or loss

ruinous /roó inəss/ adj **1.** causing severe damage or complete destruction or loss **2.** decayed or deteriorated beyond repair —**ruinously** adv —**ruinousness** n

rule /rool/ n **1.** PRINCIPLE GOVERNING CONDUCT an authoritative principle set forth to guide behaviour or action ○ the rules of the game **2.** NORM something regarded as customary or normal **3.** USUAL CONDITION a prevailing condition or quality **4.** GOVERNING POWER a governing or reigning power ○ under Communist rule **5.** PERIOD OF GOVERNING a period during which a person or group reigns or governs **6.** RELIGIOUS PRINCIPLES a body of principles governing a religious order or group ○ the Benedictine rule **7.** METHOD OF CALCULATING a mathematical procedure for performing an operation or solving a problem **8.** PRINTING LINE BETWEEN PRINTED COLUMNS a thin strip or design used for borders or for separating columns of type **9.** LAW LAW GOVERNING COURT PROCEDURE a law made to govern procedure in court **10.** LAW COURT ORDER an order issued by a court of law or judge **11.** MEASURE same as **ruler** (sense 2) ■ v (**rules, ruling, ruled**) **1.** vti GOVERN to exercise controlling authority over somebody or something ○ She ruled for almost 50 years. **2.** vt CONTROL SOMETHING to subject something to control, or restrain something **3.** vti LAW MAKE LEGAL DECISION to issue a legal decision or order ○ The judge ruled against the plaintiff. **4.** vti DOMINATE to prevail, or be the prevailing influence over something ○ He let his heart rule his head. **5.** vt MARK SOMETHING WITH LINES to make a straight line or mark something with straight lines [13C. Via French riule < Latin regula 'straight stick, standard'] —**rulable** adj —**ruleless** adj

rule out vt **1.** to exclude something, or take a decision not to consider something **2.** to consider something impossible

rulebook /rool book/ n **1.** a book or pamphlet containing the official rules of a game, sport, organization, or job **2.** the strictly correct or orthodox

way of doing something ○ doing everything by the rulebook

rule of thumb n **1.** a way of proceeding based on experience or sound judgment **2.** any practical, though not entirely accurate, method that can be relied on for an acceptable result [Probably < the practice of using the thumb as a rough measure] —**rule-of-thumb** adj

ruler /roólər/ n **1.** somebody who governs a state or nation, e.g. a sovereign **2.** a strip of plastic, wood, or metal with at least one straight edge and units of length marked on it. It is used for measuring and for drawing straight lines.

Rules /roolz/ n Aus SPORTS same as **Australian Rules** (informal)

ruling /roóling/ adj **1.** IN POWER exercising controlling or governing authority ○ the ruling party ○ joined the ruling body **2.** MOST POWERFUL exerting the strongest influence ○ a ruling passion ■ n DECISION BY AUTHORITY an official or binding decision such as one made by a court or judge

rum[1] /rum/ n **1.** an alcoholic spirit made from sugar cane or molasses. It can be clear but is usually coloured brownish-red by storage in oak casks or by the addition of caramel. **2.** US any intoxicating liquor [Mid-17C. Shortening of obsolete rumbullion, origin ?]

rum[2] /rum/ (**rummer, rummest**) adj out of the ordinary (informal dated) [Late 18C. Origin ?] —**rumly** adv —**rumness** n

Rum /rum/ island in the Inner Hebrides, western Scotland. Area: 109 sq. km/42 sq. mi.

Rumanian /roo máyni ən, roo-/ n, adj LANG, PEOPLES another spelling of **Romanian** (dated) [Variant] —**Rumanian** adj

rumba /rúmbə, room-/, **rhumba** n **1.** CUBAN DANCE a rhythmically complex Cuban dance **2.** RHYTHMIC BALLROOM DANCE a ballroom dance based on the Cuban rumba, with exaggerated swinging of the hips **3.** MUSIC the music for a rumba ■ vi (**-bas, -baing, -baed**) DANCE RUMBA to dance a Cuban rumba or the ballroom dance based on it [Early 20C. Via American Spanish < Spanish rumbo 'course, direction' < Latin rhombus 'rhombus']

rumble /rúmb'l/ v (**-bles, -bling, -bled**) **1.** vi MAKE DEEP SOUND to make a deep rolling sound ○ thunder rumbling in the distance **2.** vi MOVE NOISILY to travel, e.g. along a road, with a deep rolling sound ○ Trucks rumbled past. **3.** vt UTTER SOMETHING WITH RUMBLE to say something in a deep continuous voice **4.** vt FIND OUT ABOUT SOMEBODY OR SOMETHING to discover the truth about somebody or something (informal) ○ We've been rumbled! **5.** vi NZ, N Am FIGHT to be involved in a street fight, especially one between members of rival gangs (slang) **6.** vt MINERALS, MECH ENG CLEAN STONES OR METAL to polish stones or metal in a rotating drum (**tumbler**) ■ n **1.** DEEP SOUND a deep rolling sound **2.** MURMUR OF DISSATISFACTION a feeling of dissatisfaction quietly expressed by several people (informal) **3.** NZ, N Am STREET FIGHT a street fight, especially one fought by members of rival gangs (slang) **4.** MINERALS, MECH ENG same as **tumbler** (sense 10) [14C. Probably < obsolete Dutch rommelen, an imitation of the sound] —**rumbler** n —**rumbly** adj

rumble strip n a strip of textured road surface that alerts drivers by vibration or tyre noise to an approaching junction, speed restriction, or hazard

rumbling /rúmbling/ n **1.** DEEP SOUND a deep rolling sound **2.** FIRST INDICATION an early sign of growing discontent, or an indication of an unpleasant event that is about to happen (often used in the plural) ■ adj MAKING DEEP SOUND making a deep rolling sound ○ rumbling stomach

rumbustious /rum búschəss/ adj full of noisy uncontrollable exuberance [Late 18C. Probably alteration of archaic robustious < ROBUST] —**rumbustiously** adv —**rumbustiousness** n

rumen /roó men, roómən/ (plural **-mens** or **-mina** /roómina/) n the large first chamber of a ruminant animal's stomach in which microorganisms break down plant cellulose before the food is returned to the mouth as cud for additional chewing [Early 18C. < Latin] —**ruminal** /roómin əl/ adj

Rumi /ro͝omee/, **Jalal ad-Din Muhammad Din ar-** (1207–73) Persian mystic and poet. His works, which include the six-volume *Masnavi-ye Manavi* (*Spiritual Couplets*), had an important influence on Islamic literature and thought.

rumina ZOOL plural of **rumen**

ruminant /ro͝ominənt/ *n* **HOOFED ANIMAL THAT CHEWS CUD** any cud-chewing hoofed mammal with an even number of toes and a stomach with multiple chambers, e.g. cattle, camels, and giraffes. Suborder: Ruminantia. ■ *adj* **1. OF RUMINANTS** relating or belonging to the suborder of animals that chew the cud **2. THOUGHTFUL** inclined to be thoughtful and reflective [Mid-17C. < Latin *ruminant-*, present participle of *ruminare* (see RUMINATE)] —**ruminantly** *adv*

ruminate /ro͝omi nayt/ (**-nates, -nating, -nated**) *v* **1.** *vti* to think carefully and at length about something **2.** *vi* to regurgitate partially digested food and chew it again (*refers to ruminants*) [Mid-16C. < Latin *ruminat-*, past participle of *ruminare* < *rumen* 'rumen'] —**rumination** /ro͝omi náysh'n/ *n* —**ruminative** /-nətiv/ *adj* —**ruminatively** *adv*

rummage /rúmmij/ *v* (**-mages, -maging, -maged**) **1.** *vti* **SEARCH THROUGH THINGS** to make a rapid search for or through something by carelessly moving and disarranging things **2.** *vt* **FIND SOMETHING** to find something by searching ■ *n* **1. THOROUGH SEARCH** a thorough search for or through something **2. GROUP OF THINGS** a miscellaneous collection of items **3.** *US* same as **jumble**[1] *n* (sense 2) [15C. < Old French *arrumage* 'arrangement of cargo in a ship' < *run* 'ship's hold' < Dutch *ruim* 'space'] —**rummager** *n*

rummage sale *n N Am* same as **jumble sale**

rummer /rúmmər/ *n* a large drinking glass, especially one with a short stem [Mid-17C. Directly or via German *Römer* < Dutch *roemer* < *roemen* 'praise']

rummy[1] /rúmmi/ *n* a card game in which the players try to get three or more cards of the same rank or a sequence of three or more cards of the same suit [Early 20C. Origin ?]

rummy[2] /rúmmi/ *adj* tasting or smelling of rum, or similar to rum in smell or taste ■ *n* (*plural* **-mies**) *N Am* same as **drunkard** (*slang*) [Mid-19C. < RUM[1]]

rumor *n, vt* US spelling of **rumour**

rumour /ro͝omər/ *n* **1. UNVERIFIED REPORT** a generally circulated story, report, or statement without facts to confirm its truth **2. IDLE SPECULATION** general talk or opinions of uncertain reliability ■ *vt* (**-mours, -mouring, -moured**) **TO PASS ON RUMOURS** to pass along information by rumour (*usually passive*) ○ *It is rumoured that they are leaving the company.* [14C. Via French < Latin *rumor* 'noise, rumour']

rumour mill *n* the process by which rumours are started and spread

rumourmonger /ro͝omər mung gər/ *n* somebody who habitually spreads rumours ■ *vi* (**-gers, -gering, -gered**) to participate actively in spreading rumours

rump /rump/ *n* **1. ANIMAL'S HINDQUARTERS** the fleshy hindquarters of a four-legged mammal, not including its legs **2. BEEF FROM HINDQUARTERS** a cut of beef that is tender and contains some fat, taken from the animal's rump ○ *rump steak* **3. BOTTOM** the buttocks (*informal*) **4.** LAW **REMAINS OF LEGISLATURE** the remnant of a legislative body after the majority of its members have resigned or been expelled **5. BIRD'S TAIL END** the lower part of a bird's back nearest the tail that is sometimes coloured distinctively [15C. Probably < N Germanic]

rumple /rúmp'l/ *vti* (**-ples, -pling, -pled**) to take on a dishevelled appearance, or make clothes or hair untidy, e.g. by creasing clothes or pulling hair out of style ■ *n* a wrinkle or crease [Early 16C. Origin ?]

rumpus /rúmpəss/ *n* an outcry or noisy disturbance [Mid-18C. < ?]

rumpus room *n ANZ, N Am* a room in a house for recreational activities such as parties and children's play

run /run/ *v* (**runs, running, ran** /ran/, **run**) **1.** *vi* **GO AT FAST PACE** to move rapidly on foot so that both feet are momentarily off the ground in each step **2.** *vi* **GALLOP** to go at a fast pace in which all four feet are momentarily off the ground in each stride (*refers to four-footed animals*) **3.** *vt* **TRAVEL DISTANCE BY RUNNING** to cover a particular distance while running **4.** *vti* **PARTICIPATE IN RACE** to compete in a race on foot or on a horse or other animal **5.** *vt* **ENTER ANIMAL IN RACE** to enter a horse or other animal in a race **6.** *vti N Am* **CAMPAIGN IN ELECTION** to be a candidate in an election, or enter somebody as a candidate in an election ○ *will be running for president* **7.** *vi* **BE IN RELATIVE POSITION** to be or end in a particular position, e.g. in a race, election, or contest ○ *running behind until the last lap* **8.** *vt* **PERFORM SOMETHING** to carry out or accomplish something ○ *run a test* **9.** *vi* **LEAVE QUICKLY** to leave a place quickly or in a hurry, usually in order to escape notice or capture ○ *take the money and run* **10.** *vi* **MOVE FREELY** to move around without restraint ○ *allow the cats to run* **11.** *vt* **SPEED ACROSS SOMETHING** to travel quickly across, over, or through something ○ *ran the rapids* **12.** *vt* **TRANSPORT SOMEBODY OR SOMETHING** to take or transport somebody or something, usually by motor vehicle ○ *ran me into town* **13.** *vi* **GO FOR HELP** to turn to somebody for assistance, especially in desperation or as a dependant to a protector ○ *ran to his brother for money* **14.** *vi* **VISIT** to make a brief trip or visit somewhere ○ *ran out to the mountains for the weekend* **15.** *vti* **MOVE SMOOTHLY** to pass quickly or smoothly through or over something, or cause something to pass quickly or smoothly through or over something ○ *ropes running easily through the pulleys* **16.** *vi* **ENTER CONDITION** to enter into a particular state or condition ○ *Supplies were running low.* **17.** *vti* **OPERATE** to be functioning, or put or leave something in a functioning mode ○ *Let the engine run.* **18.** *vt* **CONTROL SOMETHING** to direct the activities, affairs, or operation of something ○ *responsible for running the whole department* **19.** *vti* **POUR OR FLOW** to flow, or cause water or another liquid to flow from or to something ○ *run a tap* **20.** *vi* **RELEASE MUCUS** to discharge a fluid such as pus or mucus ○ *a nose that was constantly running* **21.** *vti* **GO BACK AND FORTH** to travel regularly over a set route, or cause somebody or something to travel regularly over a set route ○ *runs a shuttle between stations* **22.** *vi* **ROLL FREELY** to roll unhindered or unchecked ○ *could only stand and watch it run down the hill* **23.** *vti* **GO OR TAKE OFF COURSE** to deviate from the usual or proper course, or allow something such as a ship or car to deviate from the usual or proper course ○ *run a car off the road* **24.** *vi* **SPREAD OR LEAK UNDESIRABLY** to spread as a result of unwanted dissolving or mixing ○ *The red stripes ran into the white.* **25.** *vi* **RANGE** to range between particular limits ○ *The work ran from difficult to impossible.* **26.** *vi* **KEEP COMPANY** to associate with a particular person or group **27.** *vti* **EXTEND SOMETHING** to route something in a particular direction or for a particular distance, or be routed in this way ○ *They plan to run the cable under the road.* **28.** *vi* **CONTINUE** to continue for a particular length or period ○ *a report running to ten pages* **29.** *vt* **EXPERIENCE SOMETHING** to experience, undergo, or be subject to something ○ *a child running a high temperature* **30.** *vti* **BE COVERED WITH SOMETHING** to be covered or flowing with something ○ *The valley was running with lava.* **31.** *vti* **TOTAL** to total a particular amount ○ *The bill runs to four figures.* **32.** *vt* **BREACH SOMETHING** to break through a barrier of some kind ○ *ran a checkpoint* **33.** *vi* **BE WORDED** to be worded in a particular way ○ *in a statement that runs as follows* **34.** *vi* **EXHIBIT TENDENCY** to tend or be inclined in a particular direction ○ *His tastes in art run towards abstractions.* **35.** *vi* **RECUR** to appear recurrently as a feature or quality ○ *Stubbornness runs in the family.* **36.** *vi* **BE COMMUNICATED** to be communicated from person to person ○ *a story running round the office* **37.** *vi* **UNRAVEL** to come undone, causing damage to a garment (*refers to stitches*) **38.** *vi* **REMAIN LEGALLY VALID** to continue to have force in law ○ *The contract has a year to run.* **39.** *vt* **TRADE GOODS ILLEGALLY** to import or export goods illegally ○ *running guns to the rebels* **40.** *vi* **GO UPSTREAM TO SPAWN** to migrate in large numbers, usually upstream, to spawn (*refers to fish*) **41.** *vti* PUBL, BROADCAST **SHOW PUBLICLY** to print, broadcast, or exhibit something, or be printed, broadcast, or exhibited ○ *run a news story* **42.** *vti* AMERICAN FOOTBALL **CARRY FOOTBALL DOWNFIELD** in American football, to advance the ball while running as opposed to passing **43.** *vt* METALL **PRODUCE METAL BY CASTING** to cast or mould molten metal ■ *n* **1. FAST PACE** a rapid pace faster than a walk or jog **2. GALLOPING PACE** an animal's fastest pace **3. SPELL OF RUNNING** a spell of running, especially for pleasure or exercise **4. RACE** a race in which the competitors run **5. REGULAR TRIP** a regular or scheduled trip or route ○ *the run to work each day* **6. DISTANCE OR TIME COVERED** a distance or period covered while travelling or running **7. ERRAND** a brief trip made in order to get something **8. FREE USE OF PLACE** unrestricted access to, use of, and movement around a place ○ *given the run of the whole house* **9. UNINTERRUPTED PERIOD** an extended period during which a particular condition or circumstance prevails ○ *a run of bad luck* **10. QUANTITY MANUFACTURED** an amount of something produced in a period of continuous operation of a machine or factory ○ *an initial print run of five thousand copies* **11. OPERATING PERIOD** a period of continuous operation of a machine or factory **12.** CARDS **SEQUENCE OF CARDS** in card games, a sequence of playing cards in one suit **13.** CUE GAMES **SUCCESSIVE SHOTS** in billiards and some other cue games, a series of successful shots **14.** ARTS **SERIES OF PERFORMANCES** a series of continuous showings or performances **15. URGENT REQUIREMENT** a sudden large demand for something such as goods or payment ○ *Rumours of a shortage led to a run on coffee.* **16. FLOW** a flow of liquid **17. PIPE FOR LIQUID** a channel or pipe in which a liquid flows **18. PERIOD OF FLOW** a period during which a liquid flows **19. AMOUNT OF LIQUID** an amount of liquid in a flow **20. STEEP ROUTE** a sloping course or track for a particular activity ○ *a ski run* **21. PASSAGE DOWN TRACK** a single trip along a course or down a slope **22. DIRECTION OF PATTERN** the natural direction of a pattern in something such as wood grain **23. TENDENCY** the general direction in which things or events are moving ○ *the usual run of things* **24. SOMETHING ORDINARY** an average or typical kind of person or thing ○ *the general run of merchandise* **25. TRIP FOR PLEASURE** a trip in a vehicle, especially for pleasure ○ *went for a run along the coast road* **26. UNRAVELLING OF STITCHES** a damaged section of a stocking or other knitted garment caused by unravelling stitches **27. ANIMAL ENCLOSURE** an outdoor enclosure for domestic animals, often one attached to or used as a temporary break from a standard enclosure that allows less freedom of movement **28. ANIMAL TRAIL** a trail followed regularly by a group or herd of animals **29. REPORTER'S TERRITORY** a media reporter's regular territory **30.** MUSIC **RAPID MUSICAL PASSAGE** a rapid musical scale or melodic passage, especially one for the piano **31.** CRICKET **POINT SCORED IN CRICKET** a point scored in cricket, usually when one or both batsmen run between the wickets **32.** BASEBALL **SCORE IN BASEBALL** a score in baseball made by travelling round all the bases to home plate ■ *adj* **1. MELTED** in a melted state **2. WORN OUT** exhausted or out of breath, especially from running [Old English *rinnan* < Germanic] ◇ **be on the run** to be fleeing from something, especially the law ◇ **give somebody a run for his** *or* **her money** to provide somebody with some serious, sometimes unexpected, competition ◇ **in the long run** eventually or finally ◇ **in the short run** in the near future ◇ **run yourself** *or* **somebody ragged** to work yourself or somebody else to the point of exhaustion

run about *vi* to move hurriedly from place to place

run across *vt* to meet somebody or find something unexpectedly

run after *vt* **1.** to chase after somebody or something **2.** to pursue somebody romantically or sexually (*informal*)

run along *vi* to go away (*usually used as a command*)

run around *vi* (*informal*) **1.** to behave promiscuously **2.** to spend a lot of time with somebody ○ *running around with a bad crowd*

run away *vi* to escape or flee from somebody or something

run away with *vt* **1. TAKE SOMETHING AND LEAVE** to steal something and escape with it **2. ELOPE WITH SOMEBODY** to leave secretly with a lover, especially in order to marry **3. TAKE CONTROL OF SOMEBODY** to cause somebody to lose self-control ○ *His excitement ran away with him.* **4. WIN SOMETHING EASILY** to win a competition, contest, or election easily

run by *vt* to tell somebody about something in order to find out his or her opinions or ideas about it ○ *Could I run these figures by you before I send them out?*

run down *v* **1.** *vti* STOP FUNCTIONING to lose power and cease to function, or allow a device to lose its power **2.** *vt* HIT SOMEBODY WITH VEHICLE to knock somebody or something to the ground with a vehicle **3.** *vti* REDUCE to shrink in size or amount, or reduce the size or amount of something **4.** *vt* BELITTLE SOMEBODY to speak of somebody in a disparaging or critical manner **5.** *vt* CATCH SOMEBODY EVENTUALLY to find or capture somebody after a long search or chase **6.** *vt* US TRACE SOMETHING to find the source of something ○ *run down a lead* **7.** *vt* READ SOMETHING QUICKLY to read or review something quickly **8.** *vt* NAUT CAUSE SHIP TO SINK to collide with a ship and cause it to sink **9.** *vt* BASEBALL REMOVE BASEBALL PLAYER in baseball, to chase and tag out a base runner trapped between two bases

run in *v* **1.** *vt* TREAT VEHICLE CAREFULLY WHILE STILL NEW to operate a new vehicle or engine carefully until it is functioning efficiently **2.** *vt* ARREST SOMEBODY to take somebody into police custody (*informal*) **3.** *vi* US VISIT to pay somebody a quick visit (*informal*) **4.** *vt* PRINTING ADD SOMETHING AS TEXT to insert additional text in printed matter

run into *v* **1.** *vt* MEET SOMEBODY BY CHANCE to meet somebody unexpectedly **2.** *vti* COLLIDE WITH SOMETHING to collide with somebody or something, or cause something to collide with somebody or something **3.** *vt* ENCOUNTER SOMETHING to encounter something unanticipated, usually problems or trouble **4.** *vt* AMOUNT TO SOMETHING to add up to something, or be approximately equal to something ○ *left debts running into millions*

run off *v* **1.** *vi* LEAVE IN HASTE to leave quickly without notifying anyone **2.** *vt* MAKE COPIES to produce or print copies, e.g. on a photocopier **3.** *vt* FORCE SOMEBODY TO LEAVE to force trespassers off property **4.** *vt* SETTLE TIED CONTEST to settle a tied competition or election by running a final deciding contest

run off with *vt* **1.** to steal and escape with something **2.** to leave secretly with a lover, especially in order to marry

run on *v* **1.** *vi* TALK AT LENGTH to talk at length, especially about trivial things **2.** *vi* CONTINUE to continue without interruption, often boringly or frustratingly **3.** *vt* PRINTING PRINT TEXT WITHOUT PARAGRAPH BREAK to print or typeset following text without a paragraph break

run out *v* **1.** *vi* COME TO END to be consumed completely ○ *Time is running out.* **2.** *vi* EXHAUST SUPPLIES to consume all of a supply of something ○ *We've run out of milk.* **3.** *vi* BECOME INVALID to become invalid because of time restrictions **4.** *vt* US CHASE SOMEBODY AWAY to expel somebody using force **5.** *vt* CRICKET DISMISS RUNNING BATSMAN in cricket, to dismiss a player who is trying to complete a run by breaking the wicket with the ball at the end he or she is running to

run out on *vt* to leave somebody or something in a helpless state or at a time when support is needed (*informal*)

run over *v* **1.** *vt* KNOCK SOMEBODY DOWN WITH VEHICLE to hit somebody or something with a vehicle while driving it **2.** *vi* OVERFLOW to overflow the limits or capacity of a container **3.** *vti* TAKE LONGER THAN PLANNED to go beyond a limit or time previously set **4.** *vt* REVIEW SOMETHING to examine or consider something again, especially reviewing its main points

run past *vt* same as **run by**

run through *vt* **1.** USE SOMETHING UP to exhaust a supply of something, especially money, quickly and without much consideration **2.** REVIEW SOMETHING to examine or consider something again, especially reviewing its main points **3.** REHEARSE SOMETHING QUICKLY to read or perform at speed the whole or part of a play, script, piece of music, lecture, or other prepared text in order to rehearse it **4.** STAB SOMEBODY WITH SWORD to push a sword all the way through somebody's body (*literary*)

run to *vt* **1.** to be or have sufficient resources for something ○ *finances might run to two holidays this year* **2.** to have a particular length ○ *The report runs to 500 pages.*

run up *vt* **1.** INCUR EXPENSE to amass or accumulate a large expense **2.** SEW SOMETHING to make something, usually a garment, by means of fast sewing **3.** RAISE FLAG to hoist a flag on a flagpole

run up against *vt* to suddenly encounter an unexpected problem

runabout /rúnnə bowt/ *n* **1.** a small car, motorboat, or aircraft, especially one used for short trips **2.** somebody who wanders from place to place

runaround /rún ə rownd/ *n* **1.** inconvenience deliberately engineered in order to mislead or delay somebody (*informal*) ○ *They've been giving me the runaround.* **2.** an arrangement of printed type in which lines are shortened to leave room for an illustration or symbol

runaway /rúnnə way/ *n* SOMEBODY WHO ESCAPES somebody who escapes from something such as confinement or harm (*often used before a noun*) ■ *adj* **1.** OUT OF CONTROL moving too fast to be stopped or controlled **2.** EASILY WON OR ACHIEVED won by an overwhelming margin, or achieved to an impressive degree (*informal*) ○ *a runaway success*

Runaway, Cape /rúnnə way/ cape on the northeastern coast of the North Island, New Zealand, situated at the eastern end of the Bay of Plenty

runcible spoon /rúnssib'l-/ *n* a fork with three curved prongs, one of which is sharp [< nonsense word coined by Edward Lear in *The Owl and the Pussy Cat* (1871)]

Runcorn /rún kawrn/ town and port in Cheshire, northwestern England, on the River Mersey. It was designated a new town in 1964. Population: 64,154 (1991).

rundown /rún down/ *n* **1.** a summary of the main points of a subject **2.** a deliberate and controlled decrease in size, amount, or production (*often used before a noun*)

run-down *adj* **1.** EXHAUSTED tired out, e.g. from overwork or poor health **2.** SHABBY in poor repair from neglect or hard use **3.** OUT OF POWER depleted of energy or power and unable to operate

Rundstedt /rúnt shtet, roónt-/, **Karl von** (1875–1953) German military commander. He led the German offensives on the western front (1942–44) during World War II. Full name **Rundstedt, Karl Rudolf Gerd von**

Fehu (f)	Uruz (u)	Thurisaz (th)	Ansuz (a)
Raido (r)	Kaunaz (k)	Gebo (g)	Wunjo (w)
Hagalaz (h)	Nauthiz (n)	Isa (i)	Jera (j)
Eihwaz (æ)	Thorp (p)	Alhiz (z)	Sowulo (s)
Teiwaz (t)	Berkana (b)	Ehwaz (e)	Mannaz (m)
Laguz (l)	Inguz (ng)	Odal (o)	Dagaz (d)

rune

rune /roon/ *n* **1.** OLD GERMANIC ALPHABET CHARACTER a character in an ancient Germanic alphabet used between the 3rd and the 13th centuries **2.** MAGICAL SYMBOL OR SPELL a mysterious symbol, inscription, or incantation, especially one with supposed magical power **3.** POEM IN FINNISH a Finnish poem or stanza [Old English *rūn* < Germanic] —**runic** *adj*

rung[1] /rung/ *n* **1.** LADDER STEP a step of a ladder **2.** CROSSPIECE OF CHAIR a horizontal bar used to strengthen the legs of a chair or stool **3.** LEVEL IN HIERARCHY a position in a hierarchy, e.g. of a profession **4.** NAUT PART OF SHIP'S WHEEL a spoke or handle on the wheel of a ship by which the wheel is turned [Old English *hrung* < Germanic]

rung[2] past participle of **ring**[2]

run-in *n* **1.** a heated argument or quarrel (*informal*) **2.** a section of text added to a page that has already been typeset or printed

~~runing~~ incorrect spelling of **running**

runnel /rúnn'l/ *n* **1.** a small brook or stream **2.** any narrow channel for water, e.g. a gutter [Late 16C. Alteration of obsolete *rindle* < Germanic, 'run']

runner /rúnnər/ *n* **1.** RACER somebody or something that runs, especially an athlete or a horse in a flat race **2.** DOOR OR DRAWER SLIDE a guide on which a drawer or door slides **3.** SLED BLADE either of the long blades that a sledge or sleigh slides on **4.** SKATE BLADE the blade of an ice skate **5.** SMUGGLER somebody involved in smuggling (*often used in combination*) ○ *gun runner* **6.** SMUGGLER'S VESSEL a boat or ship used for smuggling (*often used in combination*) **7.** MESSENGER a messenger or undertaker of errands for a bank, brokerage firm, or other business **8.** CARPET STRIP a long narrow piece of carpet **9.** FABRIC STRIP a strip of fabric, often linen or lace, used to protect or decorate the top of a piece of furniture such as a dressing table **10.** CREEPING STEM THAT GROWS ROOTS a thin horizontal plant stem that grows roots from nodes at regular intervals **11.** PLANT GROWING FROM STEM NODES a plant that has runners or grows by runners, e.g. a strawberry **12.** CLIMBING PLANT any plant that climbs and twists, e.g. a bean plant **13.** CANDIDATE somebody entered as a candidate in an election **14.** OPERATOR a manager or operator of something such as a business or a machine **15.** FLEEING PERSON somebody who flees, e.g. an escaped prisoner (*informal*) **16.** ANCHORING LOOP in mountaineering, a continuous loop of webbing used to provide an anchor to a rock, tree, or other point **17.** DEEP-WATER SEA FISH a swift streamlined deep-water sea fish of the jack family, especially either of two edible bluish species. Latin name: *Caranx crysos* or *Elagatis bipinnulata*.

runner bean *n* **1.** a long flat green seed pod, cooked and eaten as a vegetable **2.** a climbing bean plant that produces runner beans. Latin name: *Phaseolus coccineus*. N Am term **scarlet runner**

runner-up (*plural* **runners-up**) *n* **1.** a contestant or competitor who comes second, e.g. in a sports event or an election **2.** a contestant or competitor who comes near the winner in an event or race and often receives a small prize

running /rúnning/ *n* **1.** FAST MOVEMENT rapid movement on foot, with long strides and both feet momentarily off the ground **2.** RUNNING AS EXERCISE the sport or exercise of running **3.** MANAGEMENT the managing of a business or organization ■ **runnings** *npl* (*slang; used in Black English*) **1.** GOINGS-ON events or activities **2.** BUSINESS same as **running** (sense 3) ■ *adj* **1.** FLOWING flowing continuously in a stream **2.** FUNCTIONING in operation or in working order **3.** FOR USE OR WEAR BY RUNNERS relating to or intended for the sport or exercise of running ○ *running shoes* **4.** WHILE RUNNING begun with a run, or performed during a run ○ *a running jump* **5.** LONG-STANDING begun long ago and still continuing ○ *a running joke* **6.** MADE DURING EVENT made while something is operating or happening ○ *a running commentary* **7.** MED OPEN open and discharging fluid or pus ○ *a running sore* **8.** BOT CREEPING growing by means of horizontal stems that creep along the ground **9.** AMERICAN FOOTBALL GAINING YARDS WHILE RUNNING in American football, advancing the ball while running rather than passing ■ *adv* CONSECUTIVELY in succession ○ *for five days running* ◇ **be in** *or* **out of the running** to have *or* not have a chance of success

running back *n* in American football, an offensive back who advances the ball in running plays

running board *n* a narrow step beneath the doors of some motor vehicles, typically vintage cars

running hand *n* handwriting done without lifting the pen or pencil from the writing surface

running head *n* a heading printed on every page or every other page of a book

running light *n* a light displayed on a ship or aircraft at night to show its location and size

running mate *n* **1.** in horseracing, a horse that is entered in a race for the purpose of setting the pace for a stronger horse from the same stable **2.** *N Am* a candidate for the lesser of two associated political offices, e.g. a vice-presidential candidate

running stitch *n* a simple sewing stitch that goes down and up evenly through cloth without being looped

running title *n* PUBL same as **running head**

runnin's /rúnninz/ *npl* same as **runnings** (sense 1; *see* **running**), **running** (sense 3) (*slang; used in Black English*) [Representing a pronunciation]

runny /rúnni/ (**-nier, -niest**) *adj* **1.** OF LIQUID CONSISTENCY of a liquid or semiliquid consistency that pours or flows **2.** WATERY of a consistency that is too thin **3.** RELEASING MUCUS producing excessive flowing mucus ○ *a runny nose* —**runniness** *n*

Runnymede /rúnni meed/ meadow on the southern bank of the River Thames, near Windsor, south-eastern England. King John granted the Magna Carta there in 1215.

runoff /rún of/ *n* **1.** GEOG WATER NOT ABSORBED BY SOIL rainfall that does not soak into the soil but flows into surface waters **2.** ENVIRON WATER POLLUTION agricultural or industrial waste products that are carried by rainfall and melting snow into surface waters **3.** SPORTS, POL SECOND CONTEST TO DETERMINE WINNER an election, race, or other contest held after an earlier one that produced no clear winner

run-of-the-mill *adj* with no exceptional or distinguishing qualities

run-on *adj* PRINTING ON SAME LINE added to a line of text without a line break ■ *n* **1.** PRINTING TEXT ADDED WITHOUT LINE BREAK an added section of text that continues a line, without a line break **2.** LING WORD UNDERSTOOD BUT UNDEFINED an undefined word appearing at the end of a dictionary entry, whose meaning can be understood from the previous defined senses

runrig /rúnrig/ *n* formerly in Scotland, a system of land-sharing in which tenants each worked several separate strips (**rigs**) of land allocated by lot each year ■ *adv* using a runrig system [15C. < RUN + *rig,* dialect variant of RIDGE]

runs /runz/ *n* an attack of diarrhoea (*informal; takes a singular or plural verb*) ○ *have the runs*

runt /runt/ *n* **1.** SMALLEST ANIMAL an animal that is considerably smaller than others of the same kind, especially the smallest or weakest animal in a litter **2.** OFFENSIVE TERM an offensive term that deliberately insults somebody's stature as short or physical strength as lacking (*insult*) **3.** PIGEON a large domestic show pigeon [Mid-16C. < ?] —**runtiness** *n* —**runtish** *adj* —**runty** *adj*

REGIONAL NOTE See *underling.*

run-through *n* **1.** a practice or rehearsal of something, especially a dramatic performance **2.** a brief review of something such as an agenda or report

run time *n* **1.** the time during which a computer program runs **2.** a version of a computer program that allows a user to perform some, but not all, of the program's functions (*hyphenated before a noun*) ○ *a run-time module* **3.** COMPUT same as **execution time**

run-up *n* **1.** a run taken to gather momentum, e.g. for a jump or kick in an athletics or sports event **2.** the period of time that leads up to an important event

runway /rún way/ *n* **1.** STRIP FOR AIRCRAFT LANDINGS AND TAKEOFFS a long wide level roadway or other strip of land on which aircraft land and take off **2.** EXTENSION OF STAGE INTO AUDIENCE a narrow ramp or platform that is part of a stage and extends into the auditorium, especially as used in fashion shows **3.** TRACK a track,

passageway, or channel along which something runs **4.** *N Am* CHUTE FOR LOGS a chute down which logs are slid

Popperfoto
Damon Runyon

Runyon /rúny'n/, **Damon** (1884–1946) US journalist and short-story writer. His writings, mainly about gangsters, are distinguished by their use of slang and colourful characterizations. His collected stories include *Guys and Dolls* (1932), which formed the basis of the Broadway musical of the same name (1950). Full name **Runyon, Alfred Damon**

> 'A freeloader is a confirmed guest.'
> [Damon Runyon, 'Freeloading Ethics', *Short Takes*; 1946]

rupee /roo pée/ *n* the main unit of currency in India, Mauritius, Nepal, Pakistan, the Seychelles, and Sri Lanka. See table at **currency** [Early 17C. Via Hindi *rūpiyā* < Sanskrit *rūpya* 'wrought silver' < *rūpa* 'shape']

Rupert (of the Rhine) /roopart-/ (1619–82) German prince. A nephew of Charles I of England, he commanded Royalist troops in the English Civil War and was a founder of the Hudson's Bay Company.

Rupes Recta /roopez réktə/ fault on the surface of the Moon running north-south for 120 km/75 mi. along the eastern edge of Mare Nubium

rupiah /roo pée ə/ (*plural* **-ahs** or *same*) *n* the main unit of Indonesian currency. See table at **currency** [Mid-20C. Via Malay < Hindi *rūpiyā* (see RUPEE)]

rupicolous /roo píkələss/ *adj* describes organisms that live or grow on or among rocks [Mid-19C. < Latin *rupes* 'rock' + *-cola* 'inhabitant']

rupture /rúpchər/ *n* **1.** BROKEN STATE a break in something, or a breaking apart of something ○ *a rupture in the fabric of the balloon* **2.** BREACH IN RELATIONS a breakdown in a friendly or peaceful relationship **3.** MED TORN TISSUE a tear in bodily tissue, or a tearing of bodily tissue ○ *the rupture of a blood vessel* **4.** MED same as **hernia** ■ *vti* (**-tures, -turing, -tured**) **1.** BREAK, BURST, OR TEAR SOMETHING to break, burst, or tear something, or become broken, burst, or torn **2.** CAUSE RIFT IN RELATIONSHIP to cause a breakdown in a friendly or peaceful relationship, or undergo such a breakdown **3.** MED TEAR TISSUE to cause a tearing of body tissue, or experience it **4.** MED PRODUCE OR HAVE HERNIA to cause a hernia, or be affected by a hernia [15C. Via French < Latin *ruptura* < *rupt-,* past participle of *rumpere* 'break'] —**rupturable** *adj*

ORIGIN Latin *rumpere* 'to break', from which **rupture** is derived, is also the source of English *corrupt, disrupt, erupt, rout*[1], *route,* and *routine.*

rural /rooral/ *adj* **1.** OUTSIDE CITY found in or living in the country **2.** TYPICAL OF COUNTRY relating to or characteristic of country or country living **3.** AGRICULTURAL relating to, characteristic of, or involving farming [15C. Via French < Latin *rural-* < *rur-* 'country, countryside'] —**rurality** /roor rálləti/ *n* —**rurally** *adv*

rural dean *n* a member of the Christian clergy with authority over the clergy of a number of parishes

rural district *n* formerly, an administrative division of a county in England, Wales, and Northern Ireland, abolished in the 1970s

ruralise *vti* another spelling of **ruralize**

ruralist /rooralist/ *n* **1.** somebody who lives in the

countryside **2.** a supporter or promoter of a rural lifestyle and rural interests

ruralize /roora líz/ (**-izes, -izing, -ized**), **ruralise** (**-ises, -ising, -ised**) *v* **1.** *vt* to make something rural in character or habit **2.** *vi* to live or pass time in the country after having lived in a city or town —**ruralization** /roora līzáysh'n/ *n*

rurban /rúrbən, roorbən/ *adj* relating to an area, usually on the edge of a city, that incorporates both residential and agricultural development [Early 20C. < RURAL + URBAN]

Rurik /roorik/ (d. AD 879) Scandinavian military leader. He established the first kingdom and royal dynasty of Russia, which continued until 1598.

Ruritania /roori táyni ə/ *n* a place of romance, adventure, and intrigue [Late 19C. After a fictional central European kingdom in novels by Anthony Hope (1863–1933)] —**Ruritanian** *adj, n*

rurp /rurp/ *n* a small piton used by mountain climbers [Mid-20C. Acronym < *realized ultimate reality piton*]

ruse /rooz/ *n* a clever trick or plot used to deceive others [15C. Old French *ruser* 'repulse, retreat, dodge']

Ruse /rooss ay/ city in Ruse Province, northern Bulgaria. Population: 168,051 (1996).

Ruse /rooss/, **James** (1760–1837) British-born Australian farmer. He was transported to New South Wales, Australia, for burglary in 1788, and went on to become the first self-sufficient farmer in the colony.

Rusedski /roo zédski/, **Greg** (*b.* 1973) Canadian-born British tennis player. Known for his fast serve, he has won 11 singles titles and was runner-up in the US Open (1997). Full name **Rusedski, Gregory**

rush[1] /rush/ *v* (**rushes, rushing, rushed**) **1.** *vi* MOVE FAST to move, act, or proceed quickly **2.** *vt* HURRY SOMEBODY OR SOMETHING ALONG to make somebody or something move, act, or proceed quickly ○ *Don't rush me.* **3.** *vt* TAKE SOMEBODY OR SOMETHING URGENTLY to take or send somebody or something to a place quickly and urgently ○ *We rushed him to the airport to catch his flight.* **4.** *vt* DO SOMETHING HASTILY to do something in a hurry and without careful thought ○ *rushed the job* **5.** *vi* GO RECKLESSLY to proceed in a quick and reckless way ○ *We mustn't rush into things.* ○*'For fools rush in where angels fear to tread.'* (Alexander Pope, *An Essay on Criticism;* 1711) **6.** *vi* FLOW FAST to flow quickly and in quantity **7.** *vt* CAPTURE ENEMY QUICKLY to seize a position or overcome an enemy by a sudden quick attack **8.** *vt* CHEAT SOMEBODY to cheat somebody, especially by overcharging for something (*slang*) ○ *How much did they rush you for that jacket?* **9.** *vt* PASS RUGBY BALL UP PITCH in rugby, to move the ball up the field by giving it short kicks and running after it in a loose group ■ *n* **1.** GREAT HURRY a hurry, or a need for hurry ○ *Slow down; you're always in a rush!* ○ *There's no great rush for it.* **2.** SUDDEN FAST MOVEMENT BY CROWD a sudden and quick movement of a person or group of people towards a place or objective ○ *There was a rush to the door.* **3.** BUSY TIME a very busy period, e.g. a time when large numbers of people try to do something at the same time ○ *a rush during the store's sale* **4.** GREAT DEMAND a sudden and high demand for something **5.** SUDDEN ATTACK a sudden quick forward movement in an attack **6.** SUDDEN FLOW a sudden quick flow or movement of something **7.** SUDDEN FEELING a sudden powerful onset of an emotion **8.** SUDDEN PLEASURABLE SENSATION a sudden feeling of elation and pleasure (*informal*) **9.** RUGBY ACT OF RUSHING RUGBY BALL in rugby, the act or an instance of rushing the ball ■ **rushes** *npl* CINEMA UNEDITED PRINTS OF FILM SCENES the first unedited prints of a scene or scenes shot for a film ■ *adj* **1.** DONE QUICKLY done or needing to be done quickly ○ *a rush job* **2.** VERY BUSY very busy, especially with many people travelling at the same time [14C. < Old French *re(h)usser* 'repel'] —**rushed** *adj* —**rusher** *n*

rush into *vt* to do or agree to something with little consideration of the consequences, or cause somebody to do this

rush through *vt* **1.** to get something approved or put in place hurriedly, often without allowing time for full consideration ○ *The government hoped to rush the bill through Parliament before the election.* ○ *The plans for the new building were rushed through.* **2.**

to do something quickly and with little thought or preparation

rush² /rush/ *n* **1.** STEM OF PLANT the cylindrical and sometimes hollow stem of a marsh plant. Use: weaving baskets and mats, bottoming chairs. (*often used before a noun*) ○ *a rush mat* **2.** PLANT GROWING IN WET AREAS a marsh plant with stems that are rushes and leaves that resemble blades of grass. Genus: *Juncus.* **3.** SOMETHING UNIMPORTANT something of very little importance or value (*archaic*) **4.** HOUSEHOLD same as **rush light** [Old English *rysc* < Germanic] —**rushy** *adj*

Rush /rush/, **Geoffrey** (*b.* 1951) Australian actor. He won an Academy Award for his role in *Shine* (1996).

rush candle *n* HOUSEHOLD same as **rush light**

Rushdie /rúshdi/, **Salman** (*b.* 1947) Indian-born British novelist. A master of the magic realist style, his novels include *Midnight's Children* (1981), which won the Booker Prize, *The Satanic Verses* (1988), and *The Ground Beneath Her Feet* (1999). Full name **Rushdie, Ahmed Salman**

> 'I call upon the intellectual community in this country and abroad to stand up for freedom of the imagination, an issue much larger than my book or indeed my life.'
> [Salman Rushdie, *Public statement*; 14 February 1989]

rush hour *n* a period of heavy traffic in the morning and evening during which people are travelling to and from work (*hyphenated before a noun*)

rush light *n* a candle made from pith of the stem of a rush that has been dipped in tallow

Mount Rushmore

Rushmore, Mount /rúsh mawr/ mountain in the Black Hills, western South Dakota, carved with the faces of the US presidents George Washington, Thomas Jefferson, Abraham Lincoln, and Theodore Roosevelt. Height: 1,745 m/5,725 ft.

rusk /rusk/ *n* a sweet crisp golden-brown biscuit, often given to children and babies [Late 16C. Alteration of Portuguese or Spanish *rosca* 'screw, coil, bread twist']

Ruskin /rússkin/, **John** (1819–1900) British art and social critic. He argued for the moral and religious significance of art in works such as *Modern Painters* (1843–60) and *The Stones of Venice* (1851–53).

> 'Life without industry is guilt, and industry without art is brutality.'
> [John Ruskin, 'The Relation of Art to Morals', *Lectures on Art*; 1870]

Russell /rúss'l/, **Bertrand, 3rd Earl Russell** (1872–1970) British philosopher and mathematician. A pacifist, he wrote many highly influential philosophical works. He was awarded a Nobel Prize in literature (1950). Full name **Russell, Bertrand Arthur William**

> 'Mathematics may be defined as the subject in which we never know what we are talking about, nor whether what we are saying is true.'
> [Bertrand Russell, *Mysticism and Logic*; 1918]

> 'Fear is the main source of superstition, and one of the main sources of cruelty.'
> [Bertrand Russell, 'An Outline of Intellectual Rubbish', *Unpopular Essays*; 1950]

Russell, Ken (*b.* 1927) British film director. His vivid

Russia

adaptation of D. H. Lawrence's *Women in Love* (1969) and biographies of composers have often attracted controversy. Full name **Russell, Henry Kenneth Alfred**

Russell's paradox /rúss'lz-/ *n* the contradiction in set theory resulting from assuming that it is possible to form any set whatsoever, contradicted by the set of all and only things that are not members of themselves [Early 20C. After Bertrand RUSSELL]

Russell's viper *n* a venomous snake that has a yellowish-brown body with black markings. Native to: South Asia. Latin name: *Vipera russelli.* [Early 20C. After Patrick *Russell* (1727–1805), Scottish naturalist and physician]

russet /rússit/ *n* **1.** REDDISH BROWN a reddish-brown colour **2.** *also* **russet apple** APPLE WITH ROUGH SKIN an apple with a rough brownish skin, a deep sweetsharp flavour, and a firm texture **3.** HOMESPUN FABRIC a coarse homespun fabric with a reddish-brown colour [13C. < Old French *rousset*, literally 'small red' < *rous* 'red' < Latin *russus*] —**russet** *adj*

Russia /rúshə/ country in eastern Europe and northern and western Asia. In the past the term referred to the Russian Empire, a state that included several republics that are now independent. Russia was also the largest part of the former Soviet Union. Language: Russian. Currency: rouble. Capital: Moscow. Population: 144,526,280 (2003). Area: 17,075,200 sq. km/6,592,770 sq. mi. Official name **Russian Federation**

Russia leather *n* a smooth brownish-red leather impregnated with oil from birch bark. Use: binding books.

Russian /rúsh'n/ *n* **1.** SOMEBODY FROM RUSSIA somebody who comes from Russia **2.** OFFICIAL LANGUAGE OF RUSSIA the official Balto-Slavic language of Russia, also spoken elsewhere in the world. Native speakers: 160 million. Other speakers: 110 million. See panel on next page ■ *adj* **1.** OF RUSSIA relating to Russia, or its people, language, or culture **2.** OF SOVIET UNION relating to the former Soviet Union, or its peoples or cultures (*dated*)

Russian blue *n* a short-haired domestic cat belonging to a breed with a slender body and bluish-grey fur

Russian doll *n* a hollow painted wooden doll in which the top and bottom come apart to reveal a smaller, similar doll inside that similarly comes apart, and so on [Because made in Russia]

Russian dressing *n* a salad dressing with a mayonnaise or vinaigrette base and sometimes added chilli sauce or pickles

Russian Federation ♦ **Russia**

Russianize /rúshə nīz/ (**-izes, -izing, -ized**), **Russianise** (**-ises, -ising, -ised**) *vti* to become Russian in style, character, or appearance, or make somebody or something do this —**Russianization** /rúshə nī záysh'n/ *n*

Russian olive *n* BOT same as **oleaster** (sense 2)

Russian Orthodox Church *n* the national church of Russia, an independent branch of the Orthodox Church with the Patriarch of Moscow at its head

Russian roulette *n* **1.** a deadly game in which people take turns to fire a revolver loaded with only one bullet at their own heads, after spinning the cylinder **2.** a dangerous or reckless action or activity

[Because reportedly played by Russian officers in Romania in 1917]

Russian salad *n* a mixed salad of cooked diced vegetables in a mayonnaise or Russian dressing

Russian tea *n* tea boiled with lemon and orange juice and spices such as cinnamon and cloves, and often served in a glass rather than a cup

Russian thistle, **Russian tumbleweed** *n* a saltwort with narrow spiny leaves that has become a troublesome weed in western North America. Native to: Europe. Latin name: *Salsola kali.*

Russki /rúski/ (*plural* **-skis**), **Russky** (*plural* **-skies**) *n* N Am an offensive term for a Russian person (*slang*) [Mid-19C. < Russian *russkiĭ*]

Russo- *prefix* Russia, Russian ○ *Russo-Japanese* [< RUSSIA]

Russo-Japanese War /rússō-/ *n* a war fought in 1904–05 between Russia and Japan, mainly over control of Korea, in which Russia was unexpectedly defeated

Russolo /ru ssólō/, **Luigi** (1885–1947) Italian painter and composer. He was one of the leading figures in the futurist movement.

russula /rússyŏolə/ (*plural* **-lae** /-lee/ or **-las**) *n* a common mushroom that usually has a bright flattish cap and a white stem and gills. Native to: Europe, North America. Genus: *Russula.* [Mid-20C. < modern Latin *Russula*]

rust /rust/ *n* **1.** REDDISH-BROWN COATING ON METAL a reddish-brown coating of iron oxide on the surface of iron or steel that forms when the metal is exposed to air and moisture **2.** SOMETHING RESEMBLING RUST something that resembles rust, especially in colour, e.g. another type of corrosion or a stain **3.** COLOURS REDDISH-BROWN a reddish-brown colour **4.** BOT PLANT DISEASE a plant disease caused by fungus in which reddish-brown spots form on the leaves and stems **5.** FUNGI same as **rust fungus** ■ *v* (**rusts, rusting, rusted**) **1.** *vti* CORRODE WITH RUST to cause something to corrode with rust, or become corroded with rust **2.** *vi* DETERIORATE to deteriorate from neglect or lack of use ○ *His knowledge of German had rusted over the years.* [Old English *rūst* < Germanic, 'red'] —**rust** *adj*

rust bucket *n* a car that is badly affected by rust (*slang humorous*)

rust fungus *n* a fungus that lives as a parasite on many plants, causing reddish-brown spots on the plant parts. Order: Uredinales.

rustic /rústik/ *adj* **1.** OF COUNTRY LIFESTYLE relating to, characteristic of, or appropriate to the country or country living **2.** PLAIN AND SIMPLE lacking excessive refinement or elegance **3.** MADE OF ROUGH BRANCHES made of rough wood, especially branches with the bark left on them ○ *rustic chairs on the patio* **4.** CONSTR HAVING ROUGH SURFACE with a rough finish ○ *rustic bricks* ■ *n* **1.** SOMEBODY LIVING IN COUNTRY somebody who lives in the country, especially somebody who is unsophisticated (*dated*; *sometimes offensive*) **2.** CONSTR BRICK WITH ROUGH FINISH brick or stone with a rough finish [15C. < Latin *rusticus* < *rus* 'country, countryside'] —**rustically** *adv* —**rusticity** /ru stísseti/ *n*

rusticate /rústi kayt/ (**-cates, -cating, -cated**) *v* **1.** *vi* MOVE TO COUNTRY to go to the country to live **2.** *vt* SEND SOMEBODY TO COUNTRY to send somebody to the country to live **3.** *vti* MAKE SOMEBODY OR SOMETHING APPEAR RUSTIC to become rustic in appearance or quality, or cause

LANGUAGE HERITAGE *Russian* Much of English is made up of words from other languages, and Russian is a small but significant contributor in this respect. English absorbed many words relating to prerevolutionary Russian life, from *muzhik* (peasant), through *kulak* (land-owning peasant) and *boyar* (member of the higher nobility), to *tsar*, the *dacha*, *samovar*, and *troika*, and, alas, the *pogrom*. The word *ukase*, an order from the tsar with the force of law, developed in English to refer to any decree by a self-styled expert. Soviet politics also provided a vocabulary able to travel beyond its original boundaries: the unquestioningly loyal *apparatchik* is found outside its ruling Communist Party; *agitprop* can be disseminated under other regimes; the *gulag* is available for dissenters anywhere, whether in totalitarian nations or unsavoury work environments; *Bolshevik* has been reduced to *bolshie*. The end of the Soviet Union gave the world *glasnost* (greater accountability, openness, discussion, and freer disclosure of information) and *perestroika*, which became able to refer to any political, economic, or bureaucratic restructuring.

Keen interest in Soviet politics and society led to many other Russian words becoming familiar to English-speakers: *commissar*, *kremlin*, *Menshevik*, *nomenklatura*, *samizdat*, and *soviet* itself, to name a few. Early Soviet successes in space gave us the *sputnik* (literally 'fellow traveller') and *cosmonaut*, not in itself a Russian form, but modelled on Russian *kosmonavt*. Russia's vast landscapes have provided *steppe* (via German) and *tundra* (ultimately from Sami). Soil science is indebted to Russian for *chernozem*, *podzol*, *solonchak*, and other terms.

Translations of Russian literature, as well as travels and Russian émigrés, have brought awareness and enjoyment of Russian food and cuisine: *blini*, *borscht*, *kvass*, *pirozhki*, *shashlik* (ultimately from Crimean Turkish), and *zakuski*, for instance; *knish* and *latke* came via Yiddish. Russian also gave us *vodka* and *beluga* caviar. The dish *bitok* (fried mince patties served with a sour cream sauce) has come a complete linguistic circle: English *beefsteak* passed into French as *bifteck* then into Russian as *bitok*, only to be returned to English in a new guise.

Names of the many peoples and languages of European and Asian Russia have naturally come to English via Russian: *Cossack* (ultimately from Turkic), *Evenki* (via Russian from Evenki, a language of parts of eastern Asia), *Kalmyck*, *Ostyak* (via Russian from Tatar), *Osset* (via Russian from Georgian), *Udmurt*, and *Yakut* (via Russian from Yakut, a Turkic language), for example. Some names are formed from Russian words combined with English suffixes, as *Ugrian* and *Ugric* (from *Ugry* 'Hungarians') and *Zyrian* (from *Zyryanin*).

Russian words appear in many places in English, expected and unexpected: the *balalaika* is a Russian string instrument and the *borzoi* a Russian dog; *babushka*, a word for 'grandmother', applies also to a headscarf; *parka* came from Russian via Aleut; *mammoth* derives from an obsolete Russian word (the first remains were found in Siberia); *shaman* goes back through Tungus to Sanskrit, but was adopted into English from Russian. The suffix *-nik*, now thoroughly anglicized, came from Russian, either directly or through Yiddish. Self-conscious awareness of Russian – and a Soviet stereotype – is manifested in the hybrid form *nyetwork*, 'computer network that is not functional', from *nyet* 'no'.

---

somebody or something to do this **4.** *vt* EDUC SUSPEND STUDENT FROM UNIVERSITY to suspend a student from university for a set time as a punishment **5.** *vt* CONSTR FINISH WALL WITH ROUGH MASONRY to finish the outside of a wall with large blocks of masonry that are left with a rough surface, bevelled, and have deep joints between them —**rustication** /rústi káysh'n/ *n* —**rusticator** *n*

rusticle /rústik'l/ *n* a long structure formed as iron rusts underwater, consisting of iron compounds produced as waste by a complex community of microorganisms that use the rusting metal as a source of food

rusticwork /rústik wurk/ *n* CONSTR same as **rustic** *n* (sense 2)

rustle /rúss'l/ *v* (-tles, -tling, -tled) **1.** *vti* MAKE SWISHING SOUND to make a swishing or soft crackling sound such as that made by dry leaves rubbing together, or cause something to make such a sound **2.** *vi* MOVE WITH SWISHING SOUND to move with a swishing or soft crackling sound **3.** *vti* N Am STEAL LIVESTOCK to steal livestock, especially cattle or horses **4.** *vi* N Am MOVE QUICKLY AND ENERGETICALLY to move or work quickly and energetically ■ *n* RUSTLING SOUND a swishing or soft crackling sound ○ *the rustle of paper money* [14C. An imitation of the sound] —**rustler** *n* —**rustlingly** *adv*

rustle up *vt* (*informal*) **1.** to prepare a meal or snack quickly using any food that is immediately available **2.** to quickly find and bring together things or people

rust mite *n* a gall mite that produces brown spots on leaves and fruit by burrowing into them

rustproof /rúst proof/ *adj* not susceptible to rust, or treated so as not to be susceptible to rust ■ *vt* (-proofs, -proofing, -proofed) to treat metal to prevent it from rusting —**rustproofing** *n*

rusty /rústi/ (-ier, -iest) *adj* **1.** CORRODED covered with or corroded by rust **2.** OUT OF PRACTICE out of practice or impaired because of advanced age, neglect, or lack of use ○ *My German is very rusty.* **3.** COLOURS same as **rust** *n* (sense 3) **4.** DISCOLOURED faded and threadbare from wear and age **5.** OLD old or old-fashioned ○ *rusty ideas* **6.** ROUGH-SOUNDING croaking or rough-sounding ○ *a rusty voice* **7.** BOT INFECTED WITH RUST FUNGUS affected by rust fungus —**rustily** *adv* —**rustiness** *n*

rut[1] /rut/ *n* **1.** NARROW GROOVE a narrow channel or groove in something, especially one made by the wheels of vehicles **2.** BORING SITUATION a routine procedure,

situation, or way of life that has become uninteresting and tiresome ○ *I felt I was in a rut.* ■ *vt* (**ruts, rutting, rutted**) MAKE RUTS IN SOMETHING to make ruts in a road, track, or other surface [Late 16C. Probably < Old French *route* (see ROUTE)]

rut[2] /rut/ *n* a period of sexual excitement that recurs annually in male ruminants, especially deer ■ *vi* (**ruts, rutting, rutted**) ZOOL to be in a state of sexual excitement (*refers to male ruminants*) [12C. < Old French, 'bellowing, roaring (of a stag in rut)' < late Latin *rugitus* 'roaring' < Latin *rugire* 'to roar'] —**ruttish** *adj*

rutabaga /róotə baygə, róotə báygə/ *n* N Am FOOD same as **swede** (sense 2) [Late 18C. < Swedish dialect *rotabagge* < *rot* 'root' + *bagge* 'bag']

ruth /rooth/ *n* (*archaic*) **1.** pity for another person's troubles **2.** sorrow or remorse for having done something wrong [12C. < RUE[1] after words like TRUTH]

Ruth /rooth/ *n* **1.** in the Bible, a Moabite widow who left her own people to live with her mother-in-law Naomi, married Boaz, and was an ancestor of King David **2.** a book of the Bible that tells the story of Ruth. See table at **Bible**

Babe Ruth

Ruth /rooth/, **Babe** (1895–1948) US baseball player. When he played for the New York Yankees in the 1920s and 1930s, his legendary home run hitting dominated the sport and made him one of the most popular players in the history of baseball. Born **Ruth, George Herman**

'All I can tell them is pick a good one and sock it. I get back to the dugout and they ask me what it was I hit and I tell them I don't know except it looked good.'

[Babe Ruth. Quoted in *The American Treasury, 1455–1955*, Clifton Fadiman; 1955]

Ruthenia /roo theeni ə/ former region of central Europe, corresponding to present-day Zakarpats'ka Oblast, Ukraine —**Ruthenian** *n, adj*

ruthenic /roo thénnik, -theenik/ *adj* relating to or containing ruthenium, especially with a high valency [Mid-19C. < RUTHENIUM]

ruthenious /roo theeni əss/ *adj* relating to or containing ruthenium, especially with a low valency [Mid-19C. < RUTHENIUM]

ruthenium /roo theeni əm/ *n* a brittle white metallic element. Source: platinum ores. Use: hardening of platinum and palladium alloys. Symbol **Ru**. See table at **element** [Mid-19C. After RUTHENIA]

Rutherford /rúthərfərd/, **Ernest, 1st Baron Rutherford of Nelson and Cambridge** (1871–1937) New Zealand-born British physicist. He discovered the nuclear structure of the atom (1909), and was awarded the Nobel Prize in chemistry (1908).

'All science is either physics or stamp collecting.'
[Ernest Rutherford. Quoted in *Rutherford at Manchester*, J. B. Birks; 1962]

Dame Margaret Rutherford

Rutherford, Dame Margaret (1892–1972) British actor. A character and comic actor in films and on stage, she is best known for her role as Miss Marple in film adaptations of novels by Agatha Christie.

rutherfordium /rúthər fáwrdi əm/ *n* a radioactive element. Source: produced artificially in high-energy atomic collisions. Symbol **Rf**. See table at **element** [Mid-20C. After Ernest RUTHERFORD]

ruthless /róothləss/ *adj* having or showing no pity or mercy —**ruthlessly** *adv* —**ruthlessness** *n*

rutilant /róotilənt/ *adj* shining or glowing with a red light (*archaic*) [15C. < Latin *rutilant-*, present participle of *rutilare* 'redden' < *rutilus* 'reddish']

rutile /róo tïl/ *n* a dark reddish-brown or lustrous black titanium dioxide mineral forming needle-shaped crystals. Source: igneous and metamorphic rocks. Use: source of titanium. [Early 19C. Via French and German < Latin *rutilus* 'reddish']

Rutland /rúttlənd/ county in the eastern Midlands, central England. Between 1974 and 1997 it was part of Leicestershire. Population: 34,563 (2001). Area: 394 sq. km/152 sq. mi.

rutting /rútting/ *adj* describes male ruminants, especially deer, that are in a state of sexual excitement

Ruwenzori Range /róo ən záwri-/ mountain range in central Africa, on the northeastern border of the Democratic Republic of the Congo and the southwestern border of Uganda, between lakes Edward and Albert

rv *abbr* STATS random variable

RV *abbr* **1.** N Am CAMPING recreational vehicle **2.** AEROSP re-entry vehicle **3.** *also* **Rv.** BIBLE Revised Version

R-value *n* a measure of the ability of a material such as insulation to retard heat flow. A higher number indicates better insulating properties. [Mid-20C. < R[2] 'resistance']

rw *abbr* Rwanda (*used in Internet addresses*) See table at **domain name**

RW *abbr* **1.** Right Worshipful **2.** Right Worthy

Rwanda[1] /rŏŏ ándə/ *n* a Bantu official language of Rwanda, also spoken in other parts of east-central Africa. Native speakers: 15 million. [Early 20C. < Bantu] —**Rwanda** *adj*

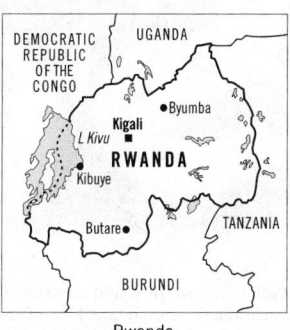

Rwanda

Rwanda[2] /rŏŏ ándə/ country in east-central Africa bordered by Uganda, Tanzania, Burundi, Lake Kivu, and the Democratic Republic of the Congo. During the civil war that broke out between the Hutu and Tutsi peoples in 1994, an estimated quarter of the population was either killed or displaced to neighbouring countries. Language: Rwanda, French. Currency: Rwanda franc. Capital: Kigali. Population: 7,810,056 (2003). Area: 26,338 sq. km/10,169 sq. mi. Official name **Rwandese Republic** — **Rwandan** *n, adj* —**Rwandese** /rŏŏ an deèz/ *n, adj*

RWD *abbr* TRANSP rear-wheel drive

rwy, Rwy, ry, Ry *abbr* TRANSP railway

-ry *suffix* same as **-ery**

rya /reè ə/ *n* **1.** a handwoven Scandinavian rug with a deep pile and a colourful pattern **2.** the weaving pattern or style used in making a rya [Mid-20C. After *Rya*, Sweden]

rye[1] /rī/ *n* **1.** the light brown grain of an annual cereal grass. Use: to make flour and whisky, as fodder. **2.** a tall hardy annual cereal plant that has bluish-green leaves and is widely cultivated for rye. Latin name: *Secale cereale.* **3.** BEVERAGES same as **rye whisky** [Old English *ryge* < Germanic]

CULTURAL NOTE *Catcher in the Rye*, a novel (1951) by US writer J. D. Salinger. A moving and realistic account of a young boy's attempt to come to terms with encroaching adulthood, it describes two days in the life of disaffected teenager Holden Caulfield. Holden absconds to New York, then resolves to leave home for good; his failure to accomplish this results in his mental collapse.

rye[2] /rī/ *n* same as **gentleman** (*used by Roma people*) [Mid-19C. Via Romany *rai* < Sanskrit *rājan* 'king']

Rye /rī/ historic market town in East Sussex, southeastern England, and a Cinque Port since 1350. Population: 3,708 (1991).

rye bread *n* a dark or light bread made using rye flour, often flavoured with caraway seed

rye-grass *n* a grass that is widely cultivated as forage, as a cover crop, and for lawns. Native to: Europe. Latin name: *Lolium perenne.*

rye whisky *n* whisky distilled from fermented rye

Ryle /rīl/, **Sir Martin** (1918–84) British astronomer. As Astronomer Royal (1972–82) he developed aperture synthesis in radio astronomy. He received the Nobel Prize in physics (1974).

rye

~~ryme~~ incorrect spelling of **rhyme**

ryokan /ri ŏkən/ *n* a traditional Japanese establishment providing food and lodging for travellers [Mid-20C. < Japanese < *ryo*- 'travel' + *kan*- 'building']

ryot /rī ət/ *n* in South Asia, a subsistence farmer who owns or rents a small piece of land [Early 17C. Via Persian and Urdu < Arabic *ra'īyya(t)* 'subjects', literally 'herd, flock' < *ra'ā* 'pasture']

RYS *abbr* ONLINE read your screen (*used in e-mails or text messages*)

~~rythm~~ incorrect spelling of **rhythm**

ryu /ri ŏŏ/ (*plural same* or **-us**) *n* a style or method of practising a Japanese art, especially a martial art [Early 19C. < Japanese]

Ryukyu Islands /ri ŏŏkoo-/ chain of islands in southwestern Japan, between Kyushu and Taiwan. Population: 1,222,458 (1990). Area: 2,260 sq. km/873 sq. mi.

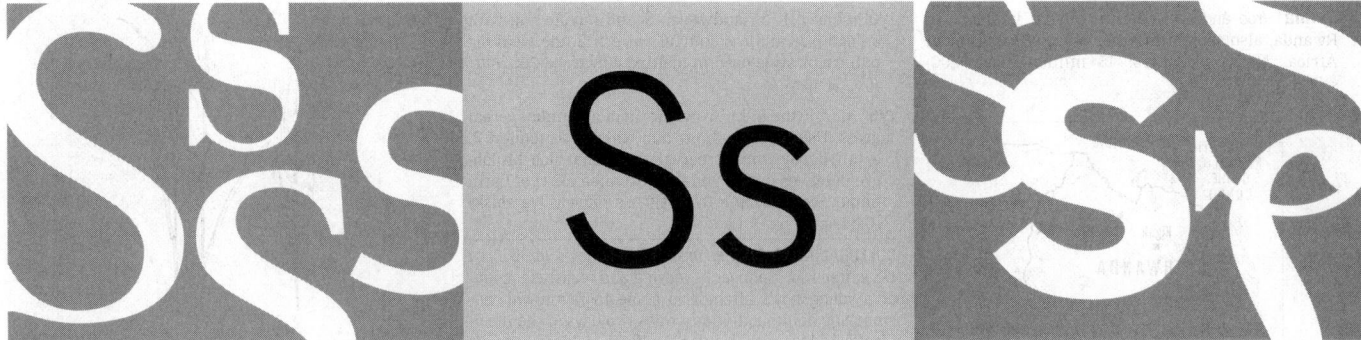

s¹ (*plural* **s's**), **S** (*plural* **S's** or **Ss**) *n* **1.** the 19th letter of the English alphabet, representing a consonant sound **2.** a written representation of the letter 's'

s² *symbol* TIME, MATHS second

s³ *abbr* **1.** semi- **2.** MONEY shilling **3.** GRAM singular **4.** sire **5.** sister **6.** MUSIC solo **7.** son **8.** MUSIC soprano **9.** MEASURE stere **10.** FIN stock **11.** QUANTUM PHYS strange quark **12.** GRAM substantive

S¹ /ess/ (*plural* **S's** or **Ss**) *n* something shaped like a letter 'S'

S² *symbol* **1.** QUANTUM PHYS entropy **2.** PHYS siemens **3.** CHEM ELEM sulphur

S³ *abbr* **1.** JUD-CHR Sabbath **2.** RELIG Saint **3.** BIBLE Samuel **4.** EDUC satisfactory **5.** Saturday **6.** HIST Saxon **7.** MONEY schilling **8.** GEOG Sea **9.** September **10.** CLOTHING small (*used in clothes sizes*) **11.** ONLINE smile (*used in e-mails or text messages*) **12.** ONLINE smiling (*used in e-mails or text messages*) **13.** POL Socialist **14.** south **15.** QUANTUM PHYS strangeness **16.** Sunday

-'s *suffix* used to form the possessive of nouns ○ *school's* ○ *person's* ○ *men's* [Old English *-es*]

-s, -es *suffix* **1.** used to form the plural of many regular nouns ○ *dogs* ○ *bananas* **2.** used to form the 3rd person present singular of regular verbs and most irregular verbs ○ *speaks* [Old English *-as*]

S2P *abbr* GOV state second pension

sa *abbr* ONLINE Saudi Arabia (*used in Internet addresses*) See table at **domain name**

SA *abbr* **1.** CHR Salvation Army **2.** South Africa **3.** South America **4.** South Australia

s.a.¹ *abbr* **1.** semiannual **2.** COMM subject to approval

s.a.² *abbr* without date [Latin *sine anno*]

SAA *abbr* COMPUT systems application architecture

Saadi another spelling of **Sadi**

Saadia ben Joseph /saʹadi ə ben jõzif/ (882–942) Arabian philosopher and scholar. His *Book of Opinions and Beliefs* (933) is a classic exegesis of Jewish traditions and laws.

saag /saag/ *n S Asia* green leaf vegetables, especially spinach [Mid-20C. < Hindi]

Saakashvili /saʹakash villi/, **Mikhail** *or* **Mikheil** (*b.* 1967) president of Georgia (2004–). A US-trained lawyer, he formed the National Movement that forced the resignation of President Eduard Shevardnadze in 2003.

Saar /saar/ river in eastern France and western Germany. It rises in the Vosges Mountains and flows north to join the River Moselle. Length: 241 km/150 mi. French name **Sarre**

Saarbrücken /sá broŏkən, za brykən/ capital city of Saarland State, in southwestern Germany. Population: 189,012 (1997).

Saarinen /saʹarinən/, **Eero** (1910–61) Finnish-born US architect. He is known for his innovative and elegant buildings such as the TWA terminal at New York's Kennedy International Airport (1962). He was the son of Eliel Saarinen.

Saarinen, Eliel (1873–1950) Finnish-born US architect. His most admired work was the Helsinki Railway Station (1904–14). He emigrated to the United States (1923), where he headed the Cranbrook Academy of Art (1932–48). He often worked in collaboration with his son, Eero Saarinen. Full name **Saarinen, Gottlieb Eliel**

sab /sab/ (*slang*) *vti* (**sabs, sabbing, sabbed**) to obstruct a fox hunt because of opposition to blood sports ■ *n* somebody who obstructs a fox hunt because of opposition to blood sports [Late 20C. Shortening of SABOTAGE, SABOTEUR]

Sab. *abbr* JUD-CHR Sabbath

sabadilla /sábbə dílla/ (*plural* **-las** or *same*) *n* **1.** the seeds of a plant of the lily family that contain veratrine. Use: insecticides, source of veratrine. **2.** a plant of the lily family whose seeds are sabadilla. Flowers: long spikelets. Native to: Mexico. Latin name: *Schoenocaulon officinale*. [Early 19C. < Spanish *cebadilla*, diminutive of *cebada* 'barley' < Latin *cibus* 'food']

Sabah /saʹa baa/ second largest state in Malaysia, on the northeast of the island of Borneo. Capital: Kota Kinabalu. Population: 2,593,400 (1997). Area: 73,620 sq. km/28,425 sq. mi. Former name **North Borneo** (until 1963)

Sabatier /saa baa tyáy/, **Paul** (1854–1941) French chemist. His research on the catalytic hydrogenation of oils made possible the manufacture of margarine. He shared the Nobel Prize in chemistry (1912).

sabayon /sábay yón/ *n* a light frothy dessert sauce made by whisking together egg yolks, sugar, and wine over a gentle heat [Early 20C. Via French < Italian dialect *zabaione*]

sabbat /sábbət/ *n* PARANORMAL same as **witches' Sabbath** [Via French < Latin *sabbatum* (see SABBATH)]

Sabbatarian /sábbə táiri ən/ *n* **1.** STRICT OBSERVER OF SABBATH a believer in the strict observance of a designated day of worship and rest **2.** OBSERVER OF SATURDAY AS SABBATH somebody who observes the Sabbath on Saturday, e.g. in Judaism ■ *adj* OF SABBATH OR SABBATARIANS relating to the Sabbath or its observance, or to Sabbatarians [Early 17C. < late Latin *Sabbatarius* < Latin *sabbatum* (see SABBATH)] —**Sabbatarianism** *n*

Sabbath /sábbəth/ *n* **1.** Sunday, observed by most Christians as the day of worship and rest from work **2.** Saturday, observed as a day of religious worship and rest from work in Judaism and some Christian denominations **3.** PARANORMAL same as **witches' Sabbath** [Pre-12C. Via Latin *sabbatum* < Greek *sabbaton* < Hebrew *šabbāt* 'rest' < *šābat* 'to rest']

Sabbath school *n* in the tradition of the Seventh-Day Adventists, a school for religious teaching held on Saturday

sabbatical /sə báttik'l/, **sabbatic** /-báttik/ *n* a period of leave from work for research, study, or travel, often with pay and usually granted to university lecturers every seven years ■ *adj* relating to a sabbatical [Late 16C. < late Latin *sabbaticus* < Greek *sabbatikos* 'of the Sabbath' < *sabbaton*, (see SABBATH)]

Sabbatical, Sabbatic *adj* relating to or suitable for the Sabbath ■ *n* BIBLE same as **Sabbatical Year**

sabbatical year, sabbatical leave *n* EDUC same as **sabbatical**

Sabbatical Year *n* in biblical times, every seventh year, during which the ancient Israelites allowed their land to lie fallow

SABC *abbr* South African Broadcasting Corporation

saber *n*, *vt* ARMS US spelling of **sabre**

sabin /sáybin/ *n* a unit of sound absorption equal to the absorption of one square foot of a perfectly absorbing surface [Mid-20C. After Wallace Clement Ware *Sabine* (1868–1919), US physicist]

Sabin /sáybin/, **Albert** (1906–93) Polish-born US microbiologist and immunologist. Best known for developing an oral live-virus polio vaccine (1960), he also developed vaccines against dengue and sandfly fever. Full name **Sabin, Albert Bruce**

Sabine /sábbīn/ *n* **1.** a member of an ancient people who lived in central Italy. By the 3rd century BC, after centuries of rivalry and fighting, the Romans had defeated them. **2.** the Italic language of the Sabine people [14C. < Latin *Sabinus*] —**Sabine** *adj*

Sabin vaccine *n* an oral vaccine used to immunize against poliomyelitis and containing live poliovirus [Mid-20C. After Albert SABIN]

sabji /súbji/ *n S Asia* a raw or cooked vegetable dish [Early 19C. < Urdu *sabzī* 'greenness' < *sabz* 'green' < Persian *sebz*]

sable /sáyb'l/ *n* (*plural* **-bles** or *same*) **1.** INDUST BROWN FUR the soft dark fur of a marten (*often used before a noun*) **2.** CLOTHING SABLE GARMENT a garment made of sable fur **3.** ZOOL N ASIAN MARTEN a short-tailed marten whose fur is sable. Native to: northern Asia. Latin name: *Martes zibellina*. **4.** ART ARTIST'S BRUSH an artist's brush made with the hairs of a sable **5.** HERALDRY COLOUR BLACK IN HERALDRY in heraldry, the colour black ■ **sables** *npl* MOURNING CLOTHES black clothes worn in mourning (*archaic*) ■ *adj* (*literary*) **1.** COLOURS, HERALDRY OF BLACK COLOUR of the colour black, e.g. in heraldry **2.** DARK very dark or gloomy [15C. Via French < medieval Latin *sabelum*, probably < Lithuanian *sàbalas* or Russian *sobol'*]

sable antelope *n* a large antelope with long backward-curving horns. The male has a black coat. Native to: Africa. Latin name: *Hippotragus niger*.

sablefish /sáyb'l fish/ (*plural same* or **-fishes**) *n* a large dark-coloured fish that is important for commercial fisheries. Native to: North American Pacific coast. Latin name: *Anoplopoma fimbria*.

sabot /sábbō/ *n* **1.** a wooden shoe, or a shoe with a wooden sole, formerly worn in Belgium, France, the Netherlands, and Germany **2.** a sleeve placed around a projectile so that it can be fired from a weapon with a larger bore. The sabot drops away shortly after the projectile is fired. [Early 17C. < French]

sabotage /sábbə taazh/ *n* **1.** DELIBERATE DESTRUCTION the deliberate damaging or destroying of property or equipment, e.g. by resistance fighters, enemy agents, or disgruntled workers **2.** ACTION TO HINDER an action taken to undermine or destroy somebody's efforts or achievements ■ *vt* (**-tages, -taging, -taged**) **1.** DAMAGE SOMETHING to damage, destroy, or disrupt something deliberately, especially in a war **2.** HINDER SOMETHING to undermine or destroy somebody's efforts or achievements [Mid-19C. < French *saboter* 'clatter in sabots', hence 'act clumsily, work badly, ruin' < *sabot* 'sabot']

saboteur /sábbə túr/ *n* somebody who commits sabotage [Early 20C. < French, < *saboter* (see SABOTAGE)]

sabra /saʹabrə/ *n* a Jew who was born in Israel [Mid-20C. Directly or via colloquial modern Hebrew *ṣābrāh* < Arabic *ṣabr* 'prickly pear']

sabre /sáybər/ *n* **1.** HEAVY SWORD WITH CURVED BLADE a heavy

cavalry sword with a slightly curved blade that is sharp on one edge **2. FENCING SWORD WITH TAPERING BLADE** a light sword with a guard to cover the hand and a tapering flexible blade, used in fencing **3. FENCING WITH SABRE** the sport or technique of fencing with a sabre **4. CAVALRY SOLDIER** a soldier in a cavalry regiment (*dated*) ■ *vt* (**sabres, sabring, sabred**) **INJURE SOMEBODY WITH SABRE** to jab, injure, or kill somebody with a sabre [Late 17C. Via French *sabre* < obsolete German *Sabel*]

sabre-rattling *n* an aggressive display or threat of force, especially military force

sabretache /sábbər tash/ *n* a small leather case worn on a cavalryman's belt [Early 19C. < French, translation of German *Säbeltasche* 'sabre pocket']

sabre-toothed tiger, **sabre-toothed cat** *n* an extinct animal of the cat family that lived in the Oligocene and Pleistocene epochs and had long curving upper canine teeth. Genus: *Smilodon*.

sabulose /sábbyŏŏ lōss/, **sabulous** /-ləss/ *adj* **1.** having a gritty texture like sand **2.** growing in sand or sandy soil [Mid-19C. < Latin *sabulum* 'sand'] —**sabulosity** /sábbyŏŏ lóssəti/ *n*

sac /sak/ *n* a small bag or pouch, especially one that contains a fluid, formed by a membrane in an animal or plant [Mid-18C. Via French < Latin *saccus* (see SACK[1])] —**saccate** *adj*

SPELLCHECK sac or **sack?** Do not confuse the spelling of *sac* and *sack*, which sound similar. The word *sac* is largely restricted to scientific contexts, denoting a small bag or pouch inside an animal or plant, as in *air sac, yolk sac*. It is also found in *cul-de-sac*, meaning 'a road with no exit at one end'. *Sack* is a more common word, denoting a large cloth or paper bag, as in *a sack of potatoes*. It is also used as a noun or verb referring to dismissal from a job: *She threatened to give him the sack. They will sack anybody who is persistently late for work.*

Sac *n, adj* **PEOPLES, LANG** same as **Sauk**

saccade /sa kaad, -káyd/ *n* **1.** a rapid irregular movement of the eye as it changes focus moving from one point to another, e.g. while reading **2.** a sudden brief pull by a rider on a horse's reins in order to check the horse [Early 18C. < French, 'twitch' < *sac* 'sack' < Latin *saccus* (see SACK[1])] —**saccadic** *adj* —**saccadically** *adv*

sacchar- *prefix* same as **saccharo-** (*used before vowels*)

saccharase /sákə rayss, -rayz/ *n* **BIOCHEM** same as **invertase**

saccharate /sákə rayt/ *n* a compound that is a salt or ester of saccharic acid [Early 19C. < SACCHARIC ACID]

saccharic acid /sə kárrik-/ *n* a white soluble solid formed by the oxidation of sugar or starch. Formula: COOH(CHOH)$_4$COOH.

saccharide /sákə rīd/ *n* a sweet-tasting, water-soluble carbohydrate based on a ring of four or five carbon atoms and one oxygen atom

saccharify /sə kárri fī/ (**-fies, -fying, -fied**) *vt* to convert a starch into simple sugars [Mid-19C. < SACCHARINE] —**saccharification** /sə kárrifi káysh'n/ *n*

saccharimeter /sákə rímmitər/ *n* an instrument used to measure the concentration of sugar in a solution, e.g. a polarimeter —**saccharimetry** *n*

saccharin /sákərin/ *n* a white crystalline compound

saccharin

that is several hundred times sweeter than sugar. Use: sugar substitute. Formula: C$_7$H$_5$NO$_3$S.

saccharine /sákə reen, -rīn, -rin/ *adj* **1. OF OR LIKE SUGAR** relating to, resembling, or containing sugar **2. TOO SWEET** excessively sweet and ingratiating ○ *a saccharine smile* **3. TOO SENTIMENTAL** excessively sentimental and cloying —**saccharinely** *adv* —**saccharinity** /sákə rínnəti/ *n*

saccharo- *prefix* sugar ○ *saccharometer* [Via Latin and Greek < Sanskrit *śarkarā* 'sugar']

saccharoid /sákə royd/, **saccharoidal** /sákə róydl/ *adj* describes rocks and minerals that have a texture resembling loaf sugar

saccharometer /sákə rómmitər/ *n* a hydrometer used to determine the strength of a sugar solution by measuring its density —**saccharometry** *n*

saccharomycete /sákərō mī́ seet/ (*plural* **-mycetes** /-mī́ seets, -mī́ seéteez/) *n* a single-celled yeast that has no mycelium, reproduces asexually, and ferments sugar. Genus: *Saccharomyces*. [Late 19C. < SACCHARO- + Greek *mukētes* 'mushrooms, fungi']

saccharose /sákə rōss, -rōz/ *n* **CHEM** same as **sucrose**

saccular /sákyŏŏlər/ *adj* resembling a sac or saccule [Mid-19C. < Latin *sacculus* (see SACCULE)]

saccule /sákyool/, **sacculus** /sákyŏŏləss/ (*plural* **-li** /-lī/) *n* **1.** a small membranous bag or pouch in an animal or plant **2.** the smaller of two sacs in the vestibule of the inner ear [Mid-19C. < Latin *sacculus* 'little sack' < *saccus* (see SACK[1])] —**sacculate** *adj*

sacerdotal /sássər dṓt'l, sákər-/ *adj* relating to or characteristic of a priest or the priesthood [14C. Via French < Latin *sacerdotalis* 'priestly' < *sacerdot-* 'priest'] —**sacerdotally** *adv*

sacerdotalism /sássər dṓt'lizəm, sákər-/ *n* **1. PRINCIPLES OF PRIESTHOOD** the beliefs or methods of priests **2. BELIEF IN PRIEST'S POWER AS MEDIATOR** the belief that a priest is able to mediate between God and human beings **3. PRIEST'S POWER OVER ORDINARY PEOPLE** power that a priest has over ordinary people, especially when this is seen as excessive or dishonestly achieved —**sacerdotalist** *n*

SACEUR *abbr* **MIL** Supreme Allied Commander, Europe

sac fungus *n* **FUNGI** same as **ascomycete**

sachem /sáychəm/ *n* a chief of a Native North American people or confederation, especially of the Algonquian people [Early 17C. < Algonquian] —**sachemic** /say chémmik/ *adj*

sachertorte /sákər tawrt, zaákhər tawrtə/ *n* a dark rich chocolate cake covered with glossy chocolate icing [Early 20C. < German, after Franz *Sacher*, German pastry chef]

sachet /sásh ay/ *n* **1.** a small flat sealed packet that contains a powder, cream, or liquid **2.** a small bag containing perfumed powder or potpourri, used to perfume clothes in wardrobes or drawers [15C. < Old French, 'little sack' < *sac* 'sack' < Latin *saccus* (see SACK[1])]

sack[1] /sak/ *n* **1. LARGE BAG** a large bag, especially one that is made from hessian, other coarse cloth, or thick heavy-duty paper **2. AMOUNT IN BAG** the amount that a sack will hold **3. JOB DISMISSAL** dismissal from a job (*informal*) ○ *got the sack* **4. BED** a bed as a place to sleep (*slang*) ○ *in the sack trying to get some shut-eye* **5. CLOTHING WOMAN'S DRESS** a woman's loose-fitting dress that narrows below the knee **6. CLOTHING, HIST 18C WOMAN'S GOWN** a gown worn by women in the 18th century that had a bodice with loose pleats at the back ■ *vt* (**sacks, sacking, sacked**) **1. FIRE SOMEBODY** to dismiss somebody from a job (*informal*) **2. PUT SOMETHING IN SACK** to put something in a sack, e.g. for storage or transport [Pre-12C. < Latin *saccus* 'bag, wallet' < Greek *sakkos* 'packing material' < Semitic] —**sacker** *n* ◊ **hit the sack** to go to bed (*slang*)

SPELLCHECK See *sac.*

sack out *vi* **N Am** to go to sleep or to bed (*informal*)

sack[2] /sak/ *vt* (**sacks, sacking, sacked**) to destroy a captured town or city and plunder its goods and valuables ■ *n* the destruction of a captured town or city and the plundering of its goods and valuables [Mid-16C. < Old French (*a*) *sac*, call to plunder, literally '(to the) sack' < Latin *saccus* (see SACK[1])]

sack[3] /sak/ *n* dry white wine from Spain, Portugal, or the Canary Islands (*archaic*) [Early 16C. < French (*vin*) *sec* 'dry (wine)' < Latin *siccus* 'dry']

sackbut /sák but/ *n* a medieval wind instrument with a long slide like a trombone [Early 16C. < Old French *saqueb(o)ute* 'hooked lance for pulling riders from their horses']

sackcloth /sák kloth/ *n* **1.** a coarse cloth made from goat or camel's hair or cotton, hemp, or flax. Use: sacks. **2.** clothes made from sackcloth, formerly worn as a sign of mourning or penitence [14C. < SACK[1]] ◊ **sackcloth and ashes** a show of mourning or repentance (*dated*)

sacking /sáking/ *n* a coarse cloth woven from hemp or jute. Use: sacks. [Late 16C. < SACK[1]]

sack race *n* a race in which each competitor stands in a sack and jumps towards the finish line while holding up the sack [< SACK[1]]

Sackville /sákvil/, **Thomas, 1st Earl of Dorset** (1536–1608) English poet, playwright, and diplomat. He was the co-author (with Thomas Norton) of *Gorboduc* (1565), the first blank-verse tragedy in English. He served at the court of Elizabeth I.

Vita Sackville-West

Sackville-West /sák vil wést/, **Vita** (1892–1962) British writer. She is remembered for poems such as 'The Land' (1926) and novels including *The Edwardians* (1930). Virginia Woolf celebrated their friendship in her novel *Orlando* (1928). Full name **Sackville-West, Victoria Mary**

'For observe, that to hope for Paradise is to live in Paradise, a very different thing from actually getting there.'
[Vita Sackville-West, *Passenger to Tehran*; 1926]

sacra **ANAT** plural of **sacrum**

~~sacrafice~~ incorrect spelling of **sacrifice**

sacral[1] /sáykrəl, sák-/ *adj* relating to or near the sacrum at the base of the spine [Mid-18C. < SACRUM]

sacral[2] /sáykrəl, sák-/ *adj* relating to or used in sacred rites [Late 19C. < Latin *sacr-* 'sacred']

sacrament /sákrəmənt/ *n* **1. RELIGIOUS RITE OR CEREMONY** in Christianity, a rite that is considered to have been established by Jesus Christ to bring grace to those participating in or receiving it. In the Protestant Church, the sacraments are baptism and Communion. The Roman Catholic and Eastern Orthodox Churches also include penance, confirmation, holy orders, matrimony, and the anointing of the sick. **2.** *also* **Sacrament CONSECRATED ITEMS** the bread and wine consecrated at Communion **3. SOMETHING SACRED** something considered to be sacred or to have a special significance [12C. Via French < Latin *sacramentum* 'soldier's oath, solemn obligation', later 'rite, mystery, revelation' < *sacr-* 'sacred']

sacramental /sákrə mént'l/ *adj* **1. USED IN SACRAMENT** relating to or used in a Christian sacrament **2. SACRED** bound by a sacrament or in a way considered inviolable ■ *n* **RITUAL ACTION OR SIGN** in the Roman Catholic Church, an object, act, or ritual that is used to show religious devotion, e.g. the sign of the cross —**sacramentality** /sákrə men tálləti/ *n* —**sacramentally** *adv*

sacramentalism /sákrə mént'lizəm/ *n* in Christianity, the belief in the necessity of the sacraments to attain salvation and God's grace —**sacramentalist** *n*

Sacramentarian /sákrə men táiri ən/ *n* **1.** **BELIEVER IN SYMBOLIC NATURE OF COMMUNION** in Christianity, a believer that the consecrated bread and wine of the Communion merely symbolize the body and blood of Jesus Christ **2.** *also* **sacramentarian** **SACRAMENTALIST** a believer in sacramentalism ■ *adj* **OF SACRAMENTARIANS** relating to or characteristic of Sacramentarians —**Sacramentarianism** *n*

Sacramento /sákrə méntō/ capital city of California, at the confluence of the Sacramento and American rivers. Population: 435,425 (2002 estimate).

sacrarium /sa kráiri əm/ (*plural* **-ia** /-i ə/) *n* **1.** a Christian church's sanctuary or sacristy **2.** CHR same as **piscina** (sense 1) [Early 18C. < Latin, 'shrine' < *sacr-* 'sacred']

sacred /sáykrid/ *adj* **1.** **DEVOTED TO DEITY** dedicated to a deity or religious purpose **2.** **OF RELIGION** relating to or used in religious worship **3.** **WORTHY OF WORSHIP** worthy of or regarded with religious veneration, worship, and respect **4.** **DEDICATED TO SOMEBODY** dedicated to or in honour of somebody **5.** **INVIOLABLE** not to be challenged or disrespected [14C. < past participle of obsolete *sacre* 'consecrate', via French < Latin *sacrare* < *sacr-* 'sacred'] —**sacredly** *adv* —**sacredness** *n*

ORIGIN The Latin word *sacer, sacr-* 'holy, sacred', from which ***sacred*** is derived, is also the source of English *consecrate, execrate, sacrament, sacrifice, sacrilege, sacristan,* and *sexton.*

sacred cow *n* somebody or something exempt from any criticism or interference [Because cattle are sacred to Hindus]

Sacred Heart *n* **1.** in the Roman Catholic Church, the heart of Jesus Christ, seen as a symbol of his love **2.** an image representing the Sacred Heart, often shown as bleeding

sacred mushroom *n* a hallucinogenic mushroom. Native to: Americas. Genus: *Psilocybe.* [Because formerly eaten in Native American rituals]

sacred site *n* in Australia, a place that has religious or historical significance for Aboriginal people

sacred thread *n* a cotton thread worn by Brahmin men to symbolize initiation into adulthood

~~**sacreligious**~~ incorrect spelling of **sacrilegious**

sacrifice /sákri fīss/ *n* **1.** **GIVING UP OF SOMETHING VALUED** a giving up of something valuable or important for somebody or something else considered to be of more value or importance **2.** **SOMETHING VALUED AND GIVEN UP** something valuable or important given up as a sacrifice **3.** **LOSS IN GIVING UP SOMETHING VALUED** a loss incurred by giving away or selling something below its value **4.** RELIG **OFFERING TO GOD** an offering to honour or appease a god, especially of a ritually slaughtered animal or person **5.** CHESS **STRATEGIC GIVING UP OF CHESS PIECE** in chess, an act or instance of allowing or forcing an opponent to take one of your pieces or pawns so that you can gain an advantage position ■ *v* (**-fices, -ficing, -ficed**) **1.** *vt* **GIVE UP SOMEBODY OR SOMETHING VALUED** to give up somebody or something important or valued in exchange for somebody or something else that is considered more important or valuable **2.** *vt* **ABANDON SOMEBODY OR SOMETHING FOR ADVANTAGE** to allow somebody or something to be hurt, killed, or destroyed for your own advantage **3.** *vti* RELIG **MAKE OFFERING TO GOD** to make an offering of a ritually slaughtered animal or person to a god **4.** *vt* CHESS **STRATEGICALLY GIVE UP CHESS PIECE** in chess, to allow or force one of your pieces or pawns to be taken by an opponent so that you can gain an advantage in position [13C. Via French < Latin *sacrificium* 'making sacred' < *sacr-* 'sacred'] —**sacrificeable** *adj* —**sacrificer** *n*

sacrifice bunt *n* in baseball, an act of bunting the ball, expecting to be put out, in order to advance a base runner

sacrifice fly *n* in baseball, a fly ball that is caught in the outfield and on which a runner scores

sacrifice hit *n* BASEBALL same as **sacrifice bunt**

sacrificial /sákri fish'l/ *adj* relating to, used in, or offered as a sacrifice —**sacrificially** *adv*

sacrilege /sákrilij/ *n* **1.** the violation, desecration, or theft of something considered holy or sacred **2.** the disrespectful or irreverent treatment of something other people consider worthy of respect or reverence [14C. Via French < Latin *sacrilegium* 'temple robbery' < *sacrilegus* 'collector of sacred things' < *sacr-* 'sacred' + *legere* 'collect'] —**sacrilegious** /sákri líjjəss/ *adj* —**sacrilegist** /sákri leéjist/ *n*

sacristan /sákristən/, **sacrist** /sákrist, sáy-/ *n* **1.** somebody in charge of the contents of a Christian church, especially objects kept in the sacristy **2.** CHR same as **sexton** (*dated*) [14C. < medieval Latin *sacristanus* < *sacrista* 'keeper of sacred things' < Latin *sacr-* 'sacred']

sacristy /sákristi/ (*plural* **-ties**) *n* a room in a Christian church in which sacred objects such as vessels and vestments are kept [15C. Via French < medieval Latin *sacristia* < *sacrista* (see SACRISTAN)]

sacroiliac /sáykrō ílli ak, sák-/ *adj* relating to the sacrum and the upper portion of the hip bone (**ilium**), or to the joint between the sacrum and ilium ■ *n* the joint in the back where the sacrum and the ilium meet [Mid-19C. < SACRUM]

sacrosanct /sákrō sangkt/ *adj* **1.** very holy and sacred **2.** not to be criticized or tampered with [Early 17C. < Latin *sacrosanctus*, 'made holy through religious rites' < *sacr-* 'sacred' + *sanctus*, past participle of *sacrare* 'make holy'] —**sacrosanctity** /sákrō sángktəti/ *n*

sacrum /sáykrəm, sák-/ (*plural* **-crums** or **-cra** /-krə/) *n* a triangular bone at the base of the spine that joins to a hip bone on each side and forms part of the pelvis. In human beings it consists of five fused vertebrae. [Mid-18C. < Latin *(os) sacrum*, translation of Greek *hieron (osteon)* 'sacred (bone)'; from the belief that the soul resided there]

sad /sad/ (**sadder, saddest**) *adj* **1.** **UNHAPPY** feeling or showing unhappiness, grief, or sorrow ○ *a sad expression* **2.** **CAUSING UNHAPPINESS** causing or containing unhappiness ○ *sad news* **3.** **REGRETTABLE** unfortunate or to be deplored ○ *The sad fact is that there are not enough funds available to support this project.* **4.** **PITIABLE OR CONTEMPTIBLE** uninteresting and pitiable or contemptible (*slang*) ○ *wearing a really sad shirt* **5.** **DULL IN COLOUR** dull or dark in colour **6.** COOK **NOT HAVING RISEN PROPERLY** doughy, or not having risen properly [Old English *sæd* 'weary, heavy, sated' < Indo-European] —**sadly** *adv* —**sadness** *n*

SAD *abbr* MED seasonal affective disorder

AKG London

Anwar al-Sadat

Sadat /sə dát/, **Anwar al-** (1918–81) president of Egypt (1970–81). He was the first Arab leader to recognize Israel and, together with Israeli prime minister Menachem Begin, negotiated a historic peace treaty in 1978, for which they shared the Nobel Peace Prize. He was assassinated by members of his own army.

> 'Most people seek after what they do not possess and they are enslaved by the very things they want to acquire.'
> [Anwar al- Sadat, *In Search of Identity*; 1978]

Saddam /sa dám/ ➧ **Hussein, Saddam**

sadden /sádd'n/ (**-dens, -dening, -dened**) *vti* to become sad, or cause somebody to become sad (*often passive*)

saddhu *n* HINDUISM another spelling of **sadhu**

saddle /sádd'l/ *n* **1.** **SEAT FOR RIDING ANIMAL** a seat, usually made of leather, used by a rider on the back of an animal such as a horse or donkey **2.** **SEAT ON BICYCLE OR MOTORCYCLE** a padded seat for a rider on a vehicle such as a bicycle, motorcycle, or tractor **3.** **PART OF ANIMAL'S BACK** the part of an animal where a saddle is placed **4.** **PART OF HARNESS** a pad that forms part of a harness and fits across the back of an animal carrying or pulling something **5.** **SOMETHING RESEMBLING SADDLE** something that looks like or is used like a saddle **6.** GEOG **LOW POINT OF RIDGE** a low point of a ridge connecting two peaks **7.** FOOD **CUT OF MEAT** a cut of meat that includes part of the backbone and both loins **8.** FOOD **BACK PART OF CHICKEN** the back part of a chicken or other fowl nearest its tail ■ *v* (**-dles, -dling, -dled**) **1.** *vt* **STRAP SADDLE ONTO ANIMAL** to put a saddle onto a horse or other animal **2.** *vi* **MOUNT ANIMAL** to mount a horse, or other animal, that has a saddle on it [Old English *sadol* < Indo-European, 'sit'] ◇ **in the saddle** in control of something

saddle up *vti* to put a saddle on a horse in readiness for riding it

saddle with *vt* to give somebody an unwelcome or unpleasant task or responsibility

saddleback /sádd'l bak/ *n* **1.** an animal, e.g. a bird, fish, or other vertebrate, that has a saddle-shaped marking on its back **2.** ARCHIT same as **saddle roof** **3.** GEOG same as **saddle** *n* (sense 6)

saddle-backed *adj* **1.** with its back curved into a shape like a saddle **2.** with a saddle-shaped marking on its back

saddlebag /sádd'l bag/ *n* a bag, sometimes one of a pair, carried near or attached to an animal's saddle or attached to a frame over a wheel of a bicycle or motorcycle

saddlebill /sádd'l bil/ (*plural* **-bills** or *same*) *n* a stork with black and white feathers, black legs with red joints, and a red beak with a black band. Native to: sub-Saharan Africa. Latin name: *Ephippiorhynchus senegalensis.*

saddle blanket *n* a blanket or other pad placed under a saddle to prevent it from chafing the animal's back

saddlebow /sádd'l bō/ *n* the high arch or raised part (**pommel**) at the front of a horse's saddle

saddlecloth /sádd'l kloth/ *n* **1.** a cloth placed under a saddle to prevent it from chafing the horse's back **2.** a cloth placed under or over a racehorse's saddle that shows the horse's number

saddle horn *n* a projection like a horn on the arch at the front of a horse's saddle

saddle horse *n* a horse that is used or trained for riding

saddler /sáddlər/ *n* a maker, repairer, or seller of saddlery

saddle roof *n* a roof that has two gables and a ridge

saddlery /sáddləri/ (*plural* **-ies**) *n* **1.** **EQUIPMENT FOR HORSES** saddles, harnesses, and other equipment for horses **2.** **JOB OF SADDLER** the work done by a saddler **3.** **SADDLER'S SHOP** a shop that sells equipment for horses **4.** **PLACE FOR STORING SADDLES** a room in or near a stable used for making, repairing, or storing equipment for horses

saddle soap *n* a mild soap containing neat's-foot oil. Use: cleaning, softening, and preserving leather.

saddle sore *n* **1.** a sore on the buttocks, groin, or inner thighs of a rider, caused by the rubbing of the saddle **2.** a sore on a horse's body, caused by the rubbing of an ill-fitting saddle

saddle-sore *adj* **1.** sore from having ridden a horse, bicycle, or other mode of transport with a saddle **2.** sore, or affected by sores, from the wearing of a saddle

saddle stitch *n* **1.** a long running stitch, usually made with a contrasting colour for ornamentation **2.** in bookbinding, a method of binding the pages of a small book or magazine together by folding it in half and stitching along the line of the fold —**saddle-stitch** *vti*

saddletree /sádd'l tree/ *n* the frame of a saddle

saddo /sáddō/ (*plural* **-dos**) *n* somebody considered uninteresting and pitiable or contemptible, especially because of a perceived lack of taste and style (*slang insult*)

Sadducee /sáddyoŏ see/ *n* a member of an ancient Jewish group of priests and aristocrats who accepted the literal interpretation of the Torah but rejected Oral Law and belief in the afterlife. Sadducees favoured accommodation with the Roman occupiers of Palestine. [Pre-12C. Via late Latin < late Greek *Saddoukaios* < post-biblical Hebrew *Ṣĕḏūqī* 'follower

of Zadok' < *Ṣāḏōq* 'Zadok', high priest who supposedly founded the group] —**Sadducean** /sáddyoō sée ən/ *adj* —**Sadduceeism** *n*

sade *n* another spelling of **sadhe**

Sade /saad/, **Marquis de** (1740–1814) French philosopher and novelist. His own cruel sexual practices, for which he was imprisoned, were reflected in novels such as *Juliette* (1797). Full name **Donatien Alphonse François, Comte de Sade**

> 'All universal moral principles are idle fancies.'
> [Marquis de Sade, *The 120 Days of Sodom*; 1785]

sadhe /saádi/, **sade, tsade** *n* the 18th letter of the Hebrew alphabet, represented in the English alphabet as 's' or 'ts'. See table at **alphabet** [Late 19C. < Hebrew *ṣāḏhē*]

sadhu /saádoo/, **saddhu** *n* a Hindu holy man who lives by begging [Mid-19C. < Sanskrit *sādhu-* 'good, holy']

Sadi /saa dée/, **Saadi** (1200?–92) Persian poet. His contributions to classical Persian literature include the *The Rose Garden* (1258). Full name **Musilh-ud-Din**

sadiron /sád ī ərn/ *n* a heavy iron that curves to a point at both ends, has a removable handle, is heated on an external source, and is used for pressing clothes and linens [Mid-18C. < SAD in the obsolete sense 'solid, heavy']

sadism /sáydizəm/ *n* **1. HURTING OTHERS FOR SEXUAL PLEASURE** the gaining of sexual gratification by causing physical or mental pain to other people, or the acts that produce such gratification **2. BEING CRUEL FOR FUN** the gaining of pleasure from causing physical or mental pain to people or animals **3. CRUELTY** great physical or mental cruelty [Late 19C. < French *sadisme*, after the Marquis de SADE] —**sadist** *n* —**sadistic** /sə dístik/ *adj* —**sadistically** *adv*

sadomasochism /sáydō mássəkizəm/ *n* **1.** the gaining of sexual gratification by alternately or simultaneously enduring pain and causing pain to somebody else, or the acts that produce such gratification **2.** a combination of sadistic and masochistic sexual tendencies within an individual person, who may derive sexual pleasure both from inflicting and from enduring pain and cruelty [Mid-20C. < SADISM] —**sadomasochist** *n* —**sadomasochistic** /sáydō mássə kístik/ *adj*

sad sack *n N Am* somebody, especially a soldier, who means well but is hopelessly inept (*informal*) [Mid-20C. < a melancholy cartoon soldier created by US cartoonist George Baker]

s.a.e., SAE *abbr* MAIL **1.** self-addressed envelope **2.** stamped addressed envelope

SAEF /sayf/ *abbr* Stock Exchange Automatic Execution Facility

Safar /sə faár/, **Saphar** *n* in the Islamic calendar, the second month of the year. See table at **calendar** [Late 18C. < Arabic *safar*]

safari /sə faári/ *n* **1.** a journey across a stretch of land, especially in Africa, for the purpose of hunting or observing wild animals ○ *go on safari* **2.** a group of people on a safari, together with the animals or vehicles that transport them [Late 19C. Via Kiswahili < Arabic *safar* 'journey']

safari jacket *n* a casual jacket with four large pockets and a belt

safari park *n* a large enclosed area of land where wild animals wander relatively freely and people pay to drive around and observe them

safari suit *n* a short-sleeved safari jacket with matching trousers, shorts, or skirt

Safavid dynasty /sa faávid-/ *n* a Persian dynasty that ruled from 1500 to 1722 and established the Shiite branch of Islam as the state religion [Early 20C. < Arabic *ṣafawī*, < *Ṣfī* al-Din Isḥaq, the dynasty's founder]

safe /sayf/ *adj* (**safer, safest**) **1. NOT DANGEROUS** unlikely to cause or result in harm, injury, or damage ○ *Have a safe journey!* **2. NOT IN DANGER** in a position or situation that offers protection, so that harm, damage, loss, or unwanted tampering is unlikely ○ *You'll be safe with me.* ○ *It's hidden in a safe place.* **3. UNHARMED OR UNDAMAGED** in an unharmed, uninjured, or undamaged condition ○ *They're safe, but the car's a write-off.* **4. SURE TO BE SUCCESSFUL** certain to be successful or profitable, and not at risk of failure or loss ○ *a safe bet* ○ *This investment is as safe as houses.* **5. UNLIKELY TO CAUSE TROUBLE** unlikely to cause trouble or controversy ○ *Is it safe to talk about politics with them?* **6. PROBABLY CORRECT** unlikely to be wrong ○ *It's safe to assume that the weather will be good.* **7. CAUTIOUS AND CONSERVATIVE** cautious with regard to risks or unforeseen problems, conservative with regard to estimates, or unadventurous with regard to choices and decisions ○ *The safe option is just to put the money in the bank.* **8. DEPENDABLE** able to be trusted or depended on ○ *Don't worry, your child's in safe hands.* **9. HAVING REACHED BASE SUCCESSFULLY** in baseball, having reached a base or home plate without being put out ■ *n* **1. CONTAINER FOR VALUABLES** a strong metal container, often with a complex locking system, for the storage of money and other valuables **2. STORAGE CONTAINER** a container for storage or protection, especially a ventilated box or small cupboard for keeping food cool or fresh **3.** *N Am* same as **condom** (*slang*) [13C. Via Old French *sauf* < Latin *salvus*] —**safely** *adv* —**safeness** *n*

safeblower /sáyf blō ər/ *n* somebody who uses explosives to open a safe in order to steal the contents

safebreaker /sáyf braykər/ *n* somebody who breaks into a safe, with or without the use of force, in order to steal the contents. N Am term **safecracker** —**safebreaking** *n*

safe-conduct *n* **1.** official protection from harm or immunity from arrest for somebody passing through a dangerous area such as enemy territory in wartime **2.** a document or escort providing safe-conduct

safecracker /sáyf krakər/ *n N Am* same as **safebreaker** —**safecracking** *n*

safe-deposit *n* a place where money and other valuables can be stored without risk of loss or damage by fire or theft, e.g. a bank vault or strongroom

safe-deposit box *n* a strong metal container for valuables such as jewellery or documents, usually kept in a bank vault or strongroom

safeguard /sáyf gaard/ *n* **1. PROTECTIVE MEASURE** something intended to prevent undesirable consequences from happening, e.g. a safety device or measure, or a proviso in a legal document **2. SAFE-CONDUCT DOCUMENT** a document providing safe-conduct ■ *vt* (**-guards, -guarding, -guarded**) **KEEP SOMETHING SAFE** to prevent something or somebody from being harmed, damaged, badly treated, or lost [14C. < Anglo-Norman *salve garde*, French *sauve garde* < *sauf* (see SAFE) + *garde* (see GUARD)] —**safeguarder** *n*

SYNONYMS ***safeguard, protect, defend, guard, shield***

CORE MEANING: to keep something or somebody safe from actual or potential damage or attack

safeguard to prevent something or somebody from being harmed, damaged, badly treated, or lost ○ *Assistance worth £326 million has been committed to the north-west, safeguarding 60,000 jobs.* ○ *measures to safeguard our citizens against terrorism* **protect** to prevent somebody or something from being harmed or damaged ○ *protect your skin from direct sunlight* ○ *efforts to protect our national parks from overuse* **defend** to protect somebody or something from attack, harm, or danger ○ *The stallion will defend his mares against the attentions of other males.* ○ *Charlie defended himself well, using the ropes and corner as he ducked and dived.* **guard** to protect somebody or something against danger or loss by being vigilant and taking defensive measures ○ *The main prison was guarded by armed officers.* ○ *Guard against identity theft.* **shield** to prevent harm or damage to somebody or something by using a physical barrier or by intervening in a protective way ○ *His broad-brimmed hat shielded his eyes from the sun.* ○ *The president's children are protectively shielded from the public spotlight at home.*

---

safe haven *n* a place guaranteed safe from danger or attack

safe house *n* a house or other place of refuge where people in danger can hide or meet in secret

safekeeping /sayf kéeping/ *n* protection from harm, damage, loss, or theft ○ *I put the documents in my desk for safekeeping.*

safelight /sáyf līt/ *n* a light used in darkrooms to filter out the rays that are harmful to sensitive film and photographic paper

safe room *n* a room in a building reinforced against intruders, attack, or severe weather

safe seat *n* a parliamentary seat that is likely to continue to be held by the same party after an election

safe sex *n* sexual activity in which precautions are taken to avoid spreading sexually transmitted diseases, e.g. intercourse using a condom

safety /sáyfti/ (*plural* **-ties**) *n* **1. FREEDOM FROM DANGER** protection from, or not being exposed to, the risk of harm or injury ○ *a safety device* ○ *The captain is responsible for the safety of the crew.* **2. LACK OF DANGER** inability to cause or result in harm, injury, or damage ○ *People are beginning to question the safety of the medication.* **3. SAFE PLACE** a place or situation where harm, damage, or loss is unlikely ○ *She led the passengers to safety.* **4. BEING UNHARMED OR UNDAMAGED** the fact of being or remaining unharmed, uninjured, or undamaged ○ *There are fears for their safety.* **5. SAFETY CATCH** a safety catch or other device intended to prevent harm, injury, or damage **6. DEFENSIVE BACK** in American football, a player defending the back of the field **7. PLAY GIVING POINTS TO DEFENSIVE TEAM** in American football, a play in which a member of the offensive team downs the ball intentionally or unintentionally in his own end zone, resulting in the defensive team being awarded two points **8.** *US* HEALTH same as **condom** (*slang*) [14C. Via French *sauveté* < medieval Latin *salvitas* < Latin *salvus* 'safe']

safety belt *n* **1.** TRANSP same as **seat belt 2.** a strong strap attached to a fixed point, worn by somebody in danger of falling such as somebody working in a high place

safety catch *n* a device designed to prevent a mechanism from being operated unintentionally, e.g. one that stops a gun from being fired or a hoisting device from falling

safety-critical *adj* describes an electronic, electromechanical, or computer feature or system whose failure may cause injury or death to human beings ○ *a workshop on safety-critical software and systems*

safety curtain *n* a fireproof curtain that can be lowered at the front of the stage in a theatre to isolate the auditorium from the stage in the event of fire

safety film *n* nonflammable cinema film made with a cellulose acetate or polyester base. Formerly, film was made with cellulose nitrate and was prone to catch fire as it aged.

safety glass *n* **1.** strong laminated glass designed not to shatter, made with a layer of clear plastic sandwiched between two glass sheets **2.** glass that, if it breaks, forms rounded fragments rather than sharp splinters

safety harness *n* an arrangement of straps or belts designed to restrain or support somebody at risk of falling or injury

safety lamp *n* a miner's lamp in which the flame is enclosed in fine wire gauze to prevent the combustion of flammable gases

safety match *n* a match that will only produce a flame if it is struck against a specially prepared surface

safety net *n* **1.** a net installed below a high place such as a circus tightrope or trapeze from which somebody might fall or jump **2.** something intended to help people in the event of hardship or misfortune, especially something providing financial security, e.g. insurance or benefit payments

safety pin *n* **1.** a loop-shaped pin that fastens into itself with its point under a protective cover to prevent accidental opening or injury **2.** a pin that when properly seated prevents accidental or premature detonation, e.g. in a grenade

safety razor *n* a razor in which the blade is partially covered to minimize the risk of accidental injury

safety valve *n* **1.** a valve that will automatically open and release a fluid when the pressure in a chamber,

e.g. the boiler of a steam engine, approaches a dangerous level **2.** something that enables people to get rid of strong feelings such as anger, grief, anxiety, or excitement without harming themselves or others

safflower /sá flow ər/ *n* **1.** PLANT YIELDING OIL AND DYE an annual composite plant. Flowers: orange or red. Use: dye, cooking oil, paints, medicines. Native to: South Asia. Latin name: *Carthamus tinctorius*. **2.** DRIED FLOWERS the dried flowers of the safflower plant. Use: red dye. **3.** RED DYE a red dye made from the dried flowers of the safflower plant. Use: colourant for fabric, food, and cosmetics. [15C. Via Dutch or German < Old French *saffleur*, via Italian < Arabic *asfar* 'yellow plant']

saffron /sáffrən/ (*plural* **-frons** or *same*) *n* **1.** COOKING SPICE the deep orange-coloured stigmas of a type of crocus, sometimes ground to a powder. Use: food colourant, flavouring. **2.** SPICE-PRODUCING CROCUS a crocus thought to have originated from the Greek island of Crete whose flowers produce saffron. Native to: Europe, South and Southwest Asia. Flowers: showy, purple or white. Latin name: *Crocus sativus*. **3.** BRIGHT ORANGE-YELLOW COLOUR a bright orange-yellow colour [Pre-12C. Via French *safran* and medieval Latin *safranum* < Arabic *za'farān*] —**saffron** *adj*

Saffron Walden /sáffrən wáwld'n/ market town in Essex, eastern England. The first part of the name comes from the saffron crocuses that were once grown there. Population: 13,201 (1991).

Safi /saa fee/ capital city of Safi Province and a port on the Atlantic Ocean, in western Morocco. Population: 376,038 (1994).

S. Afr. *abbr* South Africa

safranine /sáffrə neen/, **safranin** /sáffrə nin/ *n* a red organic azine. Use: textile colour, biological stain. [Mid-19C. < French < *safran* (see SAFFRON)]

safrole

safrole /sáffrōl/ *n* a colourless or yellow poisonous oily liquid. Source: sassafras, camphor oils. Use: manufacture of perfumes and soaps. Formula: $C_{10}H_{10}O_2$. [Mid-19C. < SASSAFRAS]

~~saftey~~ incorrect spelling of **safety**

sag /sag/ *v* (**sags, sagging, sagged**) **1.** *vti* BEND UNDER WEIGHT to bend downwards in the middle, hang, or droop instead of remaining firm or level, usually through having to support excessive weight, or make something bend in this way ○ *My cakes always sag in the middle.* **2.** *vi* BECOME WEAKER OR LOSE INTENSITY to become weaker or lose intensity or enthusiasm **3.** *vi* FALL IN VALUE to decrease in value **4.** *vi* NAUT DRIFT LEEWARD to drift to leeward ■ *n* **1.** PLACE WHERE SOMETHING SAGS a bend, depression, or slackness in something where it has sagged **2.** DECLINE IN STRENGTH a decline in strength, intensity, or value ○ *a sag in the stock market* **3.** NAUT LEEWARD DRIFT a tendency of a boat or ship to drift to leeward [14C. < Middle Low German *sacken* 'to sink'] —**saggy** *adj*

saga /saáagə/ *n* **1.** SERIES OF EVENTS a complicated series of events or personal experiences stretching over a considerable period of time, or a detailed account of such a series of events or experiences (*informal*) ○ *Have you heard the saga of our house move?* **2.** LONG NOVEL OR SERIES OF NOVELS a long story or novel, or a series of stories or novels, often following the lives of a family or community over several generations **3.** NORSE LITERARY GENRE an epic tale in Old Norse literature, usually in prose, recounting events in the lives of historical and mythological figures from

medieval Iceland and Norway [Early 18C. < Old Icelandic]

CULTURAL NOTE *The Forsyte Saga*, a series of novels (1906–22) by John Galsworthy. Set in early 20th-century England, it charts the decline of traditional Victorian values in upper-middle-class society through the story of three generations of the Forsyte family. It was made into a popular television series in 1967 and again in 2002.

sagacious /sə gáyshəss/ *adj* having or based on a profound knowledge and understanding of the world combined with intelligence and good judgment [Early 17C. < Latin *sagac-* 'of quick perception'] —**sagaciously** *adv* —**sagaciousness** *n*

sagacity /sə gássəti/ *n* profound knowledge and understanding, coupled with foresight and good judgment [15C. Via French < Latin *sagacitas* < *sagac-* 'of quick perception']

sagamore /sággə mawr/ *n* among the Native North American Algonquian people, a subordinate chief [Early 17C. < Algonquian *sangman* 'he overcomes', 'chief']

Françoise Sagan

Sagan /saa gaán/, **Françoise** (*b.* 1935) French writer. Among her best known novels are *Bonjour Tristesse* (1954) and *A Certain Smile* (1956). Pseudonym of **Quoirez, Françoise**

'To jealousy, nothing is more frightful than laughter.'
[Françoise Sagan, *La Chamade (Heartbeat)*; 1965]

saga novel *n* LITERAT same as **roman-fleuve**

sag bag *n* FURNITURE same as **beanbag** (sense 2)

sage[1] /sayj/ (*literary*) *n* somebody who is regarded as knowledgeable, wise, and experienced, especially a man of advanced years revered for his wisdom and good judgment ■ *adj* having or showing great wisdom, especially that gained from long experience of life [14C. < French. < Latin *sapere* 'be wise, have taste'] —**sagely** *adv* —**sageness** *n*

sage[2] /sayj/ (*plural* **sages** or *same*) *n* **1.** a plant or bush with aromatic greyish-green leaves. Use: flavouring food. Latin name: *Salvia officinalis*. **2.** PLANTS same as **sagebrush 3.** COLOURS same as **sage green** [14C. Via French *sauge* < Latin *salvia* 'healing plant' < *salvus* 'healthy, uninjured'] —**sage** *adj*

sagebrush /sáyj brush/ (*plural* **-brushes** or *same*) *n* a bush of dry regions with silvery wedge-shaped leaves and large flower clusters. Native to: western North America. Genus: *Artemisia*.

Sage Derby *n* a hard British cheese that is flavoured with sage and marbled with a green colour

sage green *adj* of a greyish-green colour, like sage leaves —**sage green** *n*

saggar /sággər/, **sagger** *n* a clay box into which delicate ceramic objects are placed to protect them in the kiln during firing. It is now seldom used. [Mid-18C. Probably contraction of SAFEGUARD]

Sagitta /sə gíttə/ *n* a small prominent constellation of the northern hemisphere. See illustration at **constellation**

sagittal /sájjit'l/ *adj* **1.** relating to or situated on the imaginary plane that divides a human or animal body into right and left halves **2.** resembling an arrow or an arrowhead in shape [Mid-16C. < medieval Latin *sagittalis* < Latin *sagitta* 'arrow'] —**sagittally** *adv*

Sagittarius /sájji táiri əss/ *n* **1.** CONSTELLATION IN SOUTHERN HEMISPHERE a zodiacal constellation of the southern hemisphere. See illustration at **constellation 2.** 9TH SIGN OF ZODIAC the ninth sign of the zodiac, represented by an archer and lasting from approximately 22 November to 21 December. Sagittarius is classified as a fire sign and its ruling planet is Jupiter. **3.** SOMEBODY BORN UNDER SAGITTARIUS somebody whose birthday falls between 22 November and 21 December [Pre-12C. < Latin, 'archer' < *sagitta* 'arrow'] —**Sagittarian** *adj, n* —**Sagittarius** *adj*

sagittate /sájji tayt/, **sagittiform** /sá jítti fawrm/ *adj* describes a leaf that is shaped like an arrowhead [Mid-18C. < Latin *sagitta* 'arrow']

sago /sáygō/ *n* a powdery substance obtained from the pith of the sago palm. Use: cookery, fabric stiffener. [Mid-16C. < Malay *sagu*]

sago palm *n* a tall palm tree that yields sago. Native to: Asia. Genus: *Metroxylan*.

saguaro /sə gwaárō, sə waárō/ (*plural* **-ros** or *same*), **sahuaro** /sə waárō/ *n* a large cactus growing up to 18 m/60 ft tall, with upwards-curving branches and edible red fruit. Flowers: white, nocturnal. Native to: southwestern United States, Mexico. Latin name: *Carnegiea gigantea*. [Mid-19C. < Mexican Spanish]

Sahaptin /sə háptin/ (*plural same* or **-tins**) *n* **1.** a member of a group of Native North American peoples who once lived in a wide area around the Columbia River and who now mainly live in its basin **2.** the language of the Sahaptin peoples, in some classifications belonging to the Penutian group of Native American languages. Native speakers: 4,000. [Mid-19C. < Salish *Sʔaptnx*] —**Sahaptin** *adj*

Sahaptin-Chinook *n* in some language classifications, a northern branch of the Penutian family of Native American languages consisting of Sahaptin and Chinook —**Sahaptin-Chinook** *adj*

Sahara /sə haárə/ the largest desert in the world, covering much of northern Africa between the Atlantic Ocean and the Red Sea. Area: 9,100,000 sq. km/3,500,000 sq. mi. —**Saharan** *adj, n*

saheb *n* S Asia same as **sahib**

Sahel /sə hél/ a dry zone, extending from Sudan in the east to Senegal in the west, and separating the Sahara from the tropical regions of western and central Africa

sahib /saab, saá hib, -ib/, **saheb** /saab, saá heb/ *n* S Asia a respectful form of address for men, formerly widely used to address white men during the colonial period. The term is also used as a title, placed after the man's name. [Late 17C. Via Urdu and Persian < Arabic *ṣāḥib* 'friend, lord']

sahitya /saa híttyə/ *n* S Asia **1.** literature **2.** song lyrics, especially for songs in Hindi films [Mid-20C. < Sanskrit *sāhitya* 'composition']

Sahitya Akademi /-híttyaa ə kaddəmi/ *n* an institute set up by the Indian government to promote literature in the Indian languages and in English

sahuaro *n* PLANTS same as **saguaro**

saice *n* HIST another spelling of **syce**

said[1] /sed/ *v* past participle, past tense of **say** ■ *adj* previously named or mentioned ○ *The said car was later found abandoned.* ○ *discovered the said car*

said[2] /sí yid/ *n* ISLAM another spelling of **sayyid**

saiga /sáygə/ (*plural* **-gas** or *same*) *n* an antelope with a thick tawny coat and enlarged snout. Native to: steppes of Central Asia. Genus: *Saiga*. [Early 19C. < Russian]

Saigon /sí gón/ former name for **Ho Chi Minh City** (until 1975)

sail /sayl/ *n* **1.** FABRIC CATCHING WIND ON BOAT a large piece of strong fabric, usually triangular or rectangular in shape, fixed by rigging, masts, and booms to catch the wind and propel a vessel forward **2.** JOURNEY IN VESSEL a trip in a boat or ship, especially a sailing vessel ○ *a pleasant sail across the bay* **3.** SAILS OF VESSEL the sails of a boat or ship considered collectively ○ *a ship under full sail* **4.** SAILING SHIPS COLLECTIVELY ships and boats with sails considered collectively or as a means of transport ○ *Steam gives way to sail.* **5.** THING OR PART RESEMBLING SAIL something that resembles

AKG London

a sail of a boat or ship in form, function, or position **6.** **BLADE OF WINDMILL** a long flat structure on the outside of a windmill that is designed to be turned by the wind in order to drive machinery **7.** **PART OF SUBMARINE** the conning tower of a submarine **8.** (*plural same*) **VESSEL WITH SAILS** a boat or ship with sails (*archaic*) ○ *a fleet of 200 sail* ■ *v* (**sails, sailing, sailed**) **1.** *vti* **GO BY VESSEL ON WATER** to be transported in a boat or ship across a stretch of water ○ *We sailed to Shanghai on a large cruise ship.* **2.** *vti* **MOVE ON WATER** to move across the surface of water, or across a particular stretch of water, driven by wind or engine power ○ *pirate ships that sailed the high seas* **3.** *vt* **DRIVE BOAT OR SHIP** to control the movement of a boat or ship, especially one with sails ○ *She sailed the boat into the harbour.* **4.** *vi* **BEGIN SEA JOURNEY** to depart in a boat or ship, or to leave a harbour, mooring, or anchorage ○ *The ferry sails at noon.* **5.** *vi* **MOVE SMOOTHLY** to move smoothly or swiftly and usually in a graceful way ○ *The ball sailed over the fence.* [Old English *segl* < Germanic] —**sailable** *adj* —**sailless** *adj* ◇ **set sail** to depart in a boat or ship, or to leave a harbour, mooring, or anchorage ◇ **under sail** with sails hoisted, and not propelled by an engine

SPELLCHECK sail or **sale**? Do not confuse the spelling of *sail* and *sale*, which sound similar. A *sail* is something that catches the wind, as in *the sails of a boat, the sails of a windmill*. *Sail* is also used as a verb, meaning 'be transported by a boat or ship' or 'move smoothly and swiftly', as in *sailing down the river, sailing through the air*. The word *sale* is only used as a noun, referring to the selling of goods or services, as in *houses for sale, a sale of second-hand books, the sales manager of the company.*

sail into *vt* (*informal*) **1.** to make a violent physical or verbal attack on somebody ○ *She sailed into me for forgetting to post the letter.* **2.** to tackle something with vigour and enthusiasm ○ *He sailed into the task of redesigning the building.*

sail through *vti* to do something, especially to pass a test, with ease ○ *He sailed through the exam.*

sailboard /sáyl bawrd/ *n* a large surfboard with a keel and a mast and a sail mounted on it that is operated by one person standing up ■ *vi* to ride on a sailboard —**sailboarder** *n* —**sailboarding** *n*

sailboat /sáyl bōt/ *n N Am* same as **sailing boat**

sailcloth /sáyl kloth/ *n* **1.** any strong fabric used to make sails, originally a heavy cotton canvas **2.** a lightweight cotton fabric with a texture like that of canvas. Use: clothes.

sailer /sáylər/ *n* a boat or ship, especially a sailing vessel, that has particular sailing characteristics

sailfish /sáyl fish/ (*plural same* or **-fishes**) *n* a warm-water sea fish with a large high dorsal fin resembling a sail and an elongated upper jaw that projects forward like a spear. Genus: *Istiophorus*.

sailing /sáyling/ *n* **1.** **TRAVELLING IN VESSEL WITH SAILS** the sport, leisure activity, or occupation of travelling in or operating a boat or ship propelled by sails **2.** **SKILL OF OPERATING VESSEL** the art or a method of controlling a boat or ship, especially one with sails ○ *Expert sailing is required in such conditions.* **3.** **SHIP'S DEPARTURE OR DEPARTURE TIME** the departure of a ship, or the time at which a ship is scheduled to leave port ○ *The next sailing is at noon.*

sailing boat *n* a boat with one or more masts and sails that is propelled by the wind, chiefly used for sport and leisure. N Am term **sailboat**

sailing ship *n* a ship with masts and sails that is propelled by the wind, formerly used for transporting passengers and goods

sailor /sáylər/ *n* **1.** somebody who works aboard a boat or ship, especially a low-ranking member of the crew of a merchant or naval ship **2.** somebody who frequently sails or travels on a boat or ship, especially with reference to his or her susceptibility to seasickness ○ *I'm not a good sailor.*

sailor blouse *n* a pull-on top with a collar that is large and square at the back and comes to a V in the front, of the type often worn by sailors

sailor collar *n* a collar that is V-shaped in front and has a broad square shape at the back, traditionally worn by sailors

sailor hat *n* a hat with a flat top, a low crown, and wide brim that is either straight or rolled upwards all around

sailor's-choice *n* a small fish such as the pinfish or pigfish. Native to: North American Atlantic coast.

sailor suit *n* an outfit for children resembling the traditional sailor uniform, consisting of a top with a sailor collar and trousers or a skirt, usually in dark blue and white

sailplane /sáyl playn/ *n* a light glider particularly well adapted to making use of rising air currents, used for soaring ■ *vi* (**-planes, -planing, -planed**) to travel in a sailplane —**sailplaner** *n*

Saimaa, Lake /sī́maa/ lake in southeastern Finland. Area: 1,300 sq. km/500 sq. mi.

sainfoin /sán foyn/ (*plural* **-foins** or *same*) *n* a forage plant with feathery leaves. Flowers: pink, in clusters. Native to: Europe, Asia. Latin name: *Onobrychis viciifolia*. [Early 17C. Via obsolete French < modern Latin *sanctum foenum* 'holy hay', alteration of *sanum foenum* 'wholesome hay']

saint *stressed* /saynt/; *unstressed* /sənt, sən/; *in French names often* /saN/ *n* **1.** **SOMEBODY HONOURED BY CHURCH AFTER DEATH** a member of a religion who after death is formally designated as having led a life of exceptional holiness **2.** **MEMBER OF CHOSEN PEOPLE** somebody chosen by God because of personal righteousness or the nature of his or her faith, sometimes used by religious groups to refer to their own members (*often used in the plural*) **3.** **VIRTUOUS PERSON** a particularly good or holy person, or one who is exceptionally kind and patient in dealing with difficult people or situations ■ *vt* (**saints, sainting, sainted**) **RECOGNIZE SOMEBODY AS SAINT** to declare somebody officially to be a saint of a Christian church [Pre-12C. < Latin *sanctus* 'holy', past participle of *sancire* 'confirm, consecrate'] —**saintdom** *n*

St Agnes's Eve /-ágnəssəz-/ *n* the eve of St Agnes's Day, on which, according to British folklore, people dream of their future partners if they have performed special rituals before going to sleep. Date: 20 January.

St Albans /-áwlbənz/ city in Hertfordshire, southeastern England. Nearby are the ruins of the Roman town of Verulamium. Population: 129,005 (2001).

St Andrews /-ándrooz/ university town in Fife, Scotland. It is famous for its historic connections with the game of golf. Population: 69,181 (1991).

St Andrew's cross *n* a diagonal cross with arms of equal length, especially a white one on a blue background, as on the flags of St Andrew and Scotland

St Andrew's Day *n* the day commemorating St Andrew, the patron saint of Scotland. Date: 30 November.

St Anthony's cross *n* same as **tau cross**

St Anthony's fire *n* any acutely painful inflammatory skin disorder, e.g. cellulitis, shingles, or erysipelas (*archaic*)

St Austell /-óst'l/ market town in Cornwall, southwestern England. It is a centre of the china clay industry. Population: 21,622 (1991).

St Bartholomew's Day Massacre /-baar thóllə myooz-/ *n* a massacre of Huguenots that began in Paris on St Bartholomew's Day, 24 August 1572

St Bernard /-búrnərd/ *n* a very large working dog belonging to a breed developed in Switzerland to rescue lost mountain travellers [Mid-19C. After the Hospice of the Great ST BERNARD PASS]

St Bernard Pass either of two mountain passes running between Italy and Switzerland

St-Brieuc /saN bri ő́/ city and administrative centre of Côtes-du-Nord Department, Brittany, northwestern France. Population: 46,087 (1999).

St Catharines /-káth'rinz/ city in Ontario, Canada, on the Welland Canal, across Lake Ontario from Toronto. Population: 299,935 (2001).

St Croix /-króy/ largest island of the US Virgin Islands. Population: 50,139 (1990). Area: 207 sq. km/80 sq. mi.

St David's /-dáyvidz/ small city in Pembrokeshire, Wales. Its cathedral was a pilgrimage centre in the Middle Ages. Population: 1,589 (1999).

St David's Day *n* the day commemorating St David, the patron saint of Wales. Date: 1 March.

St-Denis /saN də neé/ city in north-central France, in Seine-St-Denis Department, on the River Seine. It is a northern suburb of Paris. Population: 85,832 (1999).

sainted /sáyntid/ *adj* **1.** **RECOGNIZED AS SAINT** officially declared to be a saint of a Christian church **2.** **IN HEAVEN** dead and thought to be in heaven **3.** **VIRTUOUS** exceptionally good, virtuous, or holy (*literary*)

St Elias, Mount /-ə lī́ əss/ second highest mountain in Canada, on the Alaska-Yukon Territory border, in the St Elias Range. Height: 5,489 m/18,008 ft.

St Elmo's fire /-élmōz-/ *n* a luminous region of electrical discharge that appears during stormy weather around a narrow pointed object such as a church spire or the mast of a ship [Early 19C. After *St Elmo* (d. AD 303), patron saint of sailors]

St-Émilion /sánt e meéli on/ *n* a prestigious red wine from the Bordeaux region of southwestern France

St-Étienne /sánt eti én/ city and administrative centre of Loire Department, Rhône-Alpes Region, east-central France. Population: 180,210 (1999).

St. Ex. *abbr* Stock Exchange

Saint-Exupéry /sánt eg zoópe ree/, **Antoine** (1900–44) French aviator and writer. He wrote novels, essays and autobiographical works, but is chiefly remembered for his much-loved children's story, *The Little Prince* (1943). Full name **Saint-Exupéry, Antoine Marie Roger de**

'Although human life is precious, we always act as if something had an even greater price than life... But what is that something?'
[Antoine Saint-Exupéry, *Vol de Nuit (Night Flight)*; 1931]

St Gallen /sənt gaálən/, **St Gall** /-gáll/ capital of St Gallen Canton, northeastern Switzerland, situated about 64 km/40 mi. east of Zurich. Population: 69,747 (1998).

St George's capital, main port, and tourist centre of Grenada, in the southwest of the island. Population: 30,000 (1994).

St George's Channel sea passage between southeastern Ireland and southwestern Wales

St George's cross *n* a red cross on a white background, as on the flags of St George and England

St George's Day *n* the day commemorating St George, the patron saint of England. Date: 23 April.

St Gotthard Pass /-góttərd-/ pass through the central Alps between southern Switzerland and Italy. Length: 26 km/16 mi.

St Helena /-hə leénə/ volcanic island in the South Atlantic Ocean off the western coast of Angola. It was the site of Napoleon's death in exile in 1821 and became a British dependency in 1834. Language: English. Capital: Jamestown. Population: 7,367 (2003). Area: 122 sq. km/47 sq. mi.

St Helens /-héllənz/ town in Lancashire, northwestern England. Population: 179,483 (1996).

St Helens, Mount active volcano in southwestern Washington State, in the Cascade Range. Its last major eruption was in 1980. Height: 2,550 m/8,365 ft.

St Helier /-hélli ər/ port and chief town of Jersey, in the Channel Islands. Population: 27,083 (1991).

sainthood /sáynt hŏod/ *n* **1.** the condition or status of being a saint or saintly **2.** saints regarded as a group

St Ives /-ī́vz/ town and fishing port in Cornwall, southwestern England. Population: 9,700 (1994).

St John /-jón/ **1.** river in east-central North America. It rises in northwestern Maine, flows northeastwards into New Brunswick, and empties into the Atlantic Ocean. It forms part of the border between the United States and Canada. Length: 673 km/418 mi. **2.** largest city and principal port of New

Brunswick, Canada, situated on the Bay of Fundy. Population: 72,494 (1996).

St John's /-jónz/ **1.** capital city and principal port of Newfoundland, Canada, situated on the Atlantic Ocean. Population: 122,709 (2001). **2.** capital of Antigua and Barbuda. It is situated in the northwestern part of Antigua, on an inlet of the Caribbean Sea. Population: 25,000 (1999).

St John's bread *n* FOOD same as **carob** (sense 2)

St John's day *n* CALENDAR same as **Midsummer Day**

St John's wort *n* a herb or bush with five-petalled yellow flowers. Genus: *Hypericum*. [Because it is said to flower on the feast of St JOHN the Baptist]

St Kilda /-kíldə/ group of small, now uninhabited islands in the Outer Hebrides, Scotland. They became home to a seabird sanctuary and a National Nature Reserve.

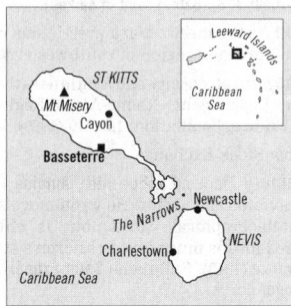
St Kitts and Nevis

St Kitts and Nevis /-kíts ənd neéviss/ independent state in the Caribbean, comprising two islands that are part of the Leeward Islands group. It became an independent member of the Commonwealth in 1983. Capital: Basseterre. Population: 38,763 (2003). Area: 269 sq. km/104 sq. mi. Official name **Federation of St Kitts and Nevis**

St Laurent /sán lo róN/, **Louis** (1882–1973) prime minister of Canada (1948–57). A prominent member of the Liberal Party of Canada, he was instrumental in establishing the United Nations before becoming prime minister. See table at **prime minister**. Full name **St Laurent, Louis Stephen**

St Lawrence /sənt lórrənss/ river in southeastern Canada, flowing northeastwards from Lake Ontario into the Gulf of St Lawrence. Length: 1,300 km/800 mi.

St Lawrence, Gulf of deep inlet of the Atlantic Ocean between Newfoundland and the Canadian mainland. Area: 259,000 sq. km/100,000 sq. mi.

St Lawrence Seaway system of canals bypassing unnavigable sections of the St Lawrence River and allowing oceangoing vessels to reach the Great Lakes, sometimes also including the canals between the Great Lakes

St Leger /-léjjər/ *n* a horse race run annually since 1776 at Doncaster, England

St-Lô /saN lố/ town and administrative centre of Manche Department, Basse-Normandie Region, northwestern France. Population: 20,090 (1999).

St Louis /sənt loó iss, -loó i/ city in eastern Missouri, extending along the western bank of the Mississippi River. It is one of the principal industrial and cultural centres of the Midwest. Population: 338,353 (2002 estimate).

St-Louis /sáN loo eé/ town and port in northwestern Senegal, situated 177 km/110 mi. northeast of Dakar. Population: 132,499 (1994).

St Louis encephalitis *n* a viral inflammation of the brain, found in parts of North America and transmitted by mosquitoes [Mid-20C. After ST LOUIS, Missouri]

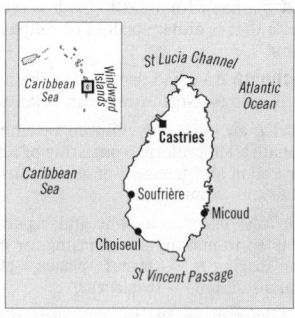
St Lucia

St Lucia /sənt loóshə/ independent island state in the Caribbean, one of the Windward Islands. It became an independent member of the Commonwealth in 1979. Capital: Castries. Population: 162,157 (2003). Area: 616 sq. km/238 sq. mi.

St Luke's summer /-loóks-/ *n* a period of warm weather occurring in the autumn, around 18 October, the festival of St Luke (*archaic*)

saintly /sáyntli/ (**-lier, -liest**) *adj* **1.** characteristic of or associated with a saint of a Christian church **2.** very good, virtuous, or holy —**saintliness** *n*

St Martin /-maártin/ one of the Leeward Islands, divided between a dependency of Guadeloupe in the north and part of the Netherlands Antilles in the south. Area: 52 sq. km/20 sq. mi. Population: 65,774 (1994).

St Martin's summer *n* a period of warm weather occurring in the autumn, around 11 November, the festival of St Martin (*archaic*)

St Michael's Mount /-mík'lz-/ small granite island off the coast of Cornwall, in southwestern England. A causeway links it to the mainland at low tide. Area: 0.03 sq. mi. / 0.08 sq. km. Population: 25 (1991).

St Moritz /sáN mə ríts/ spa town in southeastern Switzerland, situated 14 km/9 mi. from the Italian border. Population: 5,600 (1994).

St-Nazaire /sáN na záir/ city and port in Loire-Atlantique Department, Pays de la Loire Region, western France. Population: 65,874 (1999).

St Neots /sənt neé əts/ market town in east-central England. Population: 13,471 (1991).

St Patrick's Day /-páttriks-/ *n* the day commemorating St Patrick, the patron saint of Ireland. Date: 17 March.

St Paul /-páwl/ capital city of Minnesota, in the southeastern part of the state on the banks of the Mississippi River, and near Minneapolis. Population: 284,037 (2002 estimate).

saintpaulia /sənt páwli ə/ (*plural* **-lias** or *same*) *n* PLANTS same as **African violet** [Late 19C. After Baron Walter von Saint-Paul (1860–1910), German explorer]

St Paul's Cathedral *n* a large domed baroque cathedral in the City of London, designed by Christopher Wren and completed in 1710

St Peter Port /-peétər-/ port and chief town of Guernsey, in the Channel Islands. Population: 15,587 (1981).

St Peter's *n* a large baroque basilica in the Vatican City, Rome, that was completed in 1612. It is one of the largest churches in the world.

St Petersburg /-peétərz burg/ **1.** second largest city in Russia, located in the northwestern part of the country. Situated at the head of the Gulf of Finland, an arm of the Baltic Sea, it is also the country's largest port. It was the capital of Russia from 1712 until 1918. Population: 4,695,400 (1999). Former name **Petrograd** (1914–24) **Leningrad** (1924–90) **2.** city in western Florida, located on Pinellas Peninsula between Tampa Bay and the Gulf of Mexico. Population: 248,546 (2002 estimate).

St-Pierre /san pyáir/ town and tourist centre on Martinique Island in the eastern Caribbean, near the base of the volcano Montagne Pelée. Population: 4,453 (1999).

St-Pierre and Miquelon /-meé kloN/ overseas

territory of France, in the North Atlantic Ocean, off the coast of Newfoundland, Canada. It consists of two small groups of islands. The capital is St Pierre on the island with that name. The islands' proximity to the Grand Banks makes them a base for fishing vessels. Population: 6,976 (2003). Area: 242 sq. km/93 sq. mi.

Saint-Saëns /sáN sóNss, -sóN/, **Camille** (1835–1921) French composer. His works, including symphonies, church music, concertos, songs, and operas, are in the classical French tradition. Full name **Saint-Saëns, Charles Camille**

saint's day *n* a day of the year on which a specific saint is remembered or honoured. Some saint's days are marked by traditional festivities or associated with popular superstitions.

St Swithin's Day /-swíthinz-/ *n* the day commemorating St Swithin. According to superstition, rain on this day presages rain on the next 40 days, and lack of rain presages 40 days of dry weather. Date: 15 July.

St Thomas /-tómməss/ island of the US Virgin Islands. Population: 48,166 (1990). Area: 73 sq. km/28 sq. mi.

St-Tropez /sáN trō páy/ resort town on the Mediterranean coast, southern France. It is situated 155 km/60 mi. east of Marseille. Population: 5,444 (1999).

St Valentine's Day /sənt válləntīnz-/ *n* CALENDAR same as **Valentine's Day**

St Vincent, Cape /sənt vínsənt/ cape at the most southwesterly point of Portugal

St Vincent, Gulf of gulf in southern Australia, located between the Yorke and Fleurieu peninsulas

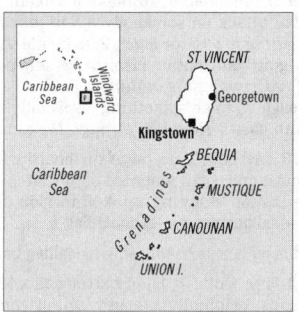
St Vincent and the Grenadines

St Vincent and the Grenadines /-grénnə deenz/ independent state in the Caribbean comprising the island of St Vincent and 32 of the islands of the Grenadine group. It became an independent member of the Commonwealth in 1979. Capital: Kingstown. Population: 116,812 (2003). Area: 389 sq. km/150 sq. mi.

St Vitus's dance /sənt vítəssiz-/ *n* former name for **Sydenham's chorea** (*not in technical use*) [Early 17C. After *St Vitus* (3C), patron saint of those affected by this condition]

Saipan /sī pán, -paán/ largest island, seat of government, and main port of the Northern Mariana Islands, in the western Pacific Ocean. Capital: Tanapeg. Population: 38,896 (1990). Area: 122 sq. km/47 sq. mi.

saith /seth/ 3rd person singular present of **say** (*archaic*)

Saiva /sívə/ *n* a member of a Hindu religious group that worships Shiva [Late 18C. < Sanskrit *śaiva-* 'sacred to Shiva'] —**Saiva** *adj* —**Saivism** *n* —**Saivite** *n*

sakai /sákī/ *n* a member of an aboriginal people who live in the forests of Malaysia [Mid-19C. < Malay, 'dependent, subject']

Sakai /saa kí/ town south of Osaka, situated on Osaka bay in Osaka Prefecture, on western Honshu, Japan. Population: 787,833 (2002).

sake[1] /sayk/ *n* **1.** the good, benefit, or welfare of somebody or something ○ *I hope you're right, for all our sakes!* **2.** the purpose of doing, obtaining, achieving, or maintaining something ○ *It's not worth risking your life for the sake of getting there a few minutes earlier.* [Old English *sacu* < Germanic, 'seeking', hence 'accusation, cause']

sake[2] /saaki/, **saki**, **saké** *n* a Japanese alcoholic beverage made from fermented rice and usually served warm [Late 17C. < Japanese]

saker /sáykər/ *n* a large falcon with brown feathers on its body and a pale-coloured head, used in falconry. Native to: central Asia, eastern Europe. Latin name: *Falco cherrug*. [15C. Via French < Arabic *ṣaḳr* 'hawk, falcon']

Sakhalin /sáke leén/ island off eastern Russia, lying in the Sea of Okhotsk north of the Japanese island of Hokkaido. Area: 76,400 sq. km/29,500 sq. mi. Population: 660,000 (1983).

Sakharov /sákərov/, **Andrei** (1921–89) Soviet physicist and political dissident. His research led to the development of the Soviet hydrogen bomb, but he became a spokesman for civil liberties and international disarmament, and was exiled to Gorky (1980). He was awarded the Nobel Peace Prize (1975). Full name **Sakharov, Andrei Dmitriyevich**

saki *n* BEVERAGES another spelling of **sake**[2]

Sakkara /sə kaárə/ village near Cairo, Egypt. It is the site of a stepped pyramid built by King Zoser between 2737 and 2717 BC, the first monumental royal tomb, and one of the oldest stone structures in Egypt.

Sakta /shaáktə/, **Shakta** *n* a member of a Hindu religious group who particularly worship the female principle or the female gods [Early 19C. < Sanskrit *śākta* (see SAKTI)]

Sakti /sákti/, **Shakti** /shúkti/ *n* in Hinduism, the vital generative and creative principle at work in the universe, typically associated with the feminine component of the divine, often embodied as a goddess [Early 19C. < Sanskrit *śaktiḥ* 'power' < *śak-* 'be strong']

Sakyamuni /saákyə moőni/ *n* one of the names of the Buddha, deriving from Sakya, the name of his clan

sal /sal/ *n* in pharmacy, salt (*usually used in combination*) ○ *sal ammoniac* [14C. < Latin]

salaam /sə laám/ *n* **1.** DEEP BOW WITH HAND ON FOREHEAD a deeply respectful or deferential gesture of greeting or acknowledgment, used especially in Islamic countries, made by bowing low with the palm of the right hand against the forehead **2.** RESPECTFUL GREETING the word 'salaam', meaning 'peace', used as a respectful greeting ■ *vti* (**-laams, -laaming, -laamed**) MAKE SALUTATION OF GREETING OR RESPECT to perform a salaam, or greet somebody with a salaam [Early 17C. < Arabic *salām* 'peace']

salable *adj* COMM another spelling of **saleable**

salacious /sə láyshəss/ *adj* **1.** intended to titillate or arouse people sexually, usually by having an explicit erotic content **2.** having or showing explicit or crude sexual desire or interest [Mid-17C. < Latin *salac-* < *salire* 'to leap'] —**salaciously** *adv* —**salaciousness** *n* —**salacity** /sə lássəti/ *n*

salad /sálləd/ *n* **1.** MIXTURE OF RAW VEGETABLES a cold savoury dish consisting mainly of a mixture of raw vegetables, whole, sliced, chopped, or in pieces, usually served with a dressing for flavour. Many other ingredients may be incorporated into a salad, which can be served as a separate course or as an accompaniment to other food. **2.** COLD MEAL a dish consisting of cold meat, fish, cheese, or egg served with a salad of lettuce, tomato, cucumber, and other vegetables ○ *chicken salad* **3.** DISH OF COLD INGREDIENTS a cold dish consisting of a particular type of food such as a single vegetable or a selection of fruit, cut into pieces or slices, and served usually with a dressing ○ *potato salad* **4.** LEAFY VEGETABLES any leafy vegetable commonly used to make a green salad, typically the many types of lettuce, watercress, chicory, endive, mustard, and cress **5.** CONFUSED MIXTURE a confused or varied mixture ○ *a salad of ideas* [14C. < French *salade* < Latin *sal* 'salt']

salad bar *n* a counter in a restaurant or shop where salads of various types are available, often set up as a buffet where customers can choose their own ingredients

salad cream *n* a ready-made creamy white dressing with a flowing consistency, for eating with salad

salad days *npl* the period of a person's life when he or she is young, innocent, naive, and inexperienced (*literary*) [< the words of Cleopatra in Shakespeare's *Antony and Cleopatra*: 'My salad days, When I was green in judgment, cold in blood']

salad dressing *n* a well-seasoned sauce poured over or mixed with the ingredients of a salad, e.g. a vinaigrette made from oil and vinegar

salade niçoise /sálləd nee swaáz/ *n* a cold dish originally from the region around Nice in France, containing anchovies, tuna fillets, olives, green beans, and sometimes other ingredients, served with a dressing of olive oil and garlic [Early 20C. < French, 'salad in the style of Nice']

Saladin /sálládin/ (1138–93) sultan of Egypt and Syria. During his sultanate (1174–93), he led the Muslims successfully against the Christian crusaders in Palestine until he was defeated and captured at Acre (1191). Full name **Salah ad-din Yussuf ibn Ayub**

salad spinner *n* a kitchen utensil for draining washed salad vegetables consisting of a perforated basket able to revolve inside a circular container. The basket is turned by a handle, and the water forced out through the perforations.

Salafism /sə laáfizəm/ *n* an Islamic movement associated with Wahhabism that in its radical form emphasizes strict interpretation of religious texts and opposition to non-Islamic influences [Early 20C. < Arabic *as-salaf as-salah* 'pious forebears'] —**Salafist** *n*, *adj*

salal /sə lál/ (*plural* **salals** or **salal**) *n* an evergreen bush with leathery leaves and edible purple berries. Flowers: pink or white, in clusters. Native to: coast of western North America. Latin name: *Gaultheria shallon*. [Early 19C. < Chinook Jargon *sallal*]

Salam /saa laám/, **Abdus** (1926–96) Pakistani physicist. He was noted for his study of the interactions of elementary particles, in particular his formulation of the electroweak theory. He shared the Nobel Prize in physics (1979).

Salamanca /sállə mángkə/ city in the autonomous region of Castile-León, west-central Spain. It is the site of the University of Salamanca, founded in 1218. Population: 156,006 (2002).

salamander

salamander /sállə mandər/ *n* **1.** SMALL ANIMAL RESEMBLING LIZARD an amphibian that resembles a lizard but has porous moist skin instead of scales, and that lives in water as a larva and on land as an adult. Order: Caudata. **2.** MYTHICAL REPTILE LIVING IN FIRE a mythical lizard that can live in fire **3.** HOT METAL PLATE FOR BROWNING FOOD a cooking utensil, most often in the form of a metal plate with a handle, designed to be heated until very hot then held over food to produce a browned or caramelized surface **4.** PORTABLE STOVE a stove that is used on construction projects to heat or dry out buildings or to thaw frozen water pipes [14C. Directly or via French < Latin *salamandra* < Greek] —**salamandrine** /sállə mándrin/ *adj*

salami /sə laámi/ *n* a large, thick, highly seasoned, and often cured type of sausage, Italian in origin and usually served cold in thin slices [Mid-19C. < Italian, plural of *salame* < Latin *sal* 'salt']

Salamis /sálləmiss/ island in eastern Greece 13 km/8 mi. west of the port of Piraeus. It was the location of a major sea battle in 480 BC in which the Greeks defeated the Persians. Population: 28,574 (1981). Area: 104 sq. km/40 sq. mi.

sal ammoniac /sál ə móni ak/ *n* CHEM same as **ammonium chloride** [< Latin *sal ammoniacus* (see AMMONIA)]

salary /sálləri/ (*plural* **-ries**) *n* a fixed annual sum, paid at regular intervals, usually monthly, to an employee, especially for professional or clerical work [13C. Directly or via French < Latin *salarium* 'money given to a Roman soldier to buy salt' < *sal* 'salt'] —**salaried** *adj*

SYNONYMS See **wage**.

salaryman /sálləri man/ (*plural* **-men** /-men/) *n* in Japan, a loyal and unambitious employee of a large company

salbutamol /sal byoótə mol/ *n* a drug that relaxes and dilates the bronchi. Use: relief of asthma, emphysema, and chronic bronchitis. Formula: $C_{13}H_{21}NO_3$. [Mid-20C. < SALICYLIC ACID + BUTYL + AMINE]

salchow /sálkō/ *n* a jump in figure skating in which the skater takes off from one skate, does a complete rotation in the air, and lands on the opposite skate [Early 20C. After Ulrich *Salchow* (1877–1949), Swedish figure skater]

sale /sayl/ *n* **1.** SELLING OF SOMETHING the transfer of something to the ownership or use of somebody else, or the provision of something, e.g. a service, in exchange for an agreed amount of money ○ *The sale of alcohol to children is illegal.* **2.** OPPORTUNITY TO BUY GOODS AT DISCOUNT a period of time when a shop sells goods at reduced prices, often in order to clear stocks ○ *I never go shopping during the sales.* **3.** OPPORTUNITY TO BUY SECOND-HAND GOODS an event at which personal possessions or other second-hand items are sold, usually at low prices, sometimes to raise money for a charitable or other cause **4.** AUCTION an event at which goods are sold to the highest bidder **5.** AMOUNT SOLD OR RATE OF SELLING a quantity of things sold, or the rate at which they are sold ○ *disappointed by the slow sale of the new model* **6.** MARKET OR DEMAND demand that creates an opportunity to sell something ○ *found no sale for the goods at that price* ■ **sales** *npl* (*often used before a noun*) **1.** DEPARTMENT SELLING THINGS the department of a company involved with selling its products or services ○ *sales manager* **2.** THINGS SOLD the total number or value of items sold ○ *Sales fell by 10 per cent last month.* [Pre-12C. < Old Norse *sala* < Germanic] ◇ **for sale** available for purchase ◇ **on sale** available for purchase, usually from a shop or other commercial organization

SPELLCHECK See **sail**.

Sale /sayl/ town on the River Mersey in Cheshire, northwestern England, near Manchester. Population: 56,052 (1991).

Salé /saa láy/ city on the Atlantic coast of Morocco. Population: 289,391 (1982).

saleable /sáyləb'l/, **salable** *adj* suitable for selling or capable of being sold —**saleability** /sáylə bílləti/ *n* —**saleableness** *n* —**saleably** *adv*

sale and leaseback *n* the sale of an asset that the vendor rents back from the buyer immediately after the sale, thereby raising cash and allowing a tax deduction

sale and return *n* COMM same as **sale or return**

Saleh /saa lékh/, **Ali Abdullah** (b. 1942) Yemeni soldier and politician. He became president of the Yemen Arab Republic, or North Yemen, in 1978 and in 1990 unified the country with the People's Democratic Republic of Yemen, or South Yemen, as the Republic of Yemen.

Salem /sáyləm/ **1.** city in northeastern Massachusetts, on Massachusetts Bay, northeast of Boston. It was the site of witchcraft trials and executions in 1692. Population: 42,149 (2002 estimate). **2.** capital city of Oregon, on the Willamette River, in the northwest of the state. Population: 140,977 (2002 estimate).

sale of work *n* an event at which home-made goods are sold, usually to raise money for a church or other charitable cause

sale or return *n* an agreement between a supplier and a purchaser or retailer whereby the latter returns any unused or unsold goods, paying only for those that have been used or sold

salep /sálləp/ *n* a starchy powder produced from ground dried tubers of various orchids. Use: food thickener. [Mid-18C. Via French < Turkish *sālep*, < Arabic

ta'lab, shortening of *kusat-ta'lab* 'orchid', literally 'fox's testicles']

Salerno /sə lúrnō/ capital city and port in Salerno Province, Campania Region, southern Italy. Population: 138,188 (2001).

saleroom /sáyl room, -rŏŏm/ *n UK* a large room where goods are sold by auction. ANZ, N Am term **salesroom**

~~salery~~ incorrect spelling of **salary**

sales assistant *n* COMM same as **shop assistant**

salesclerk /sáylz klaark/ *n N Am* same as **shop assistant**

sales force *n* the body of salespeople employed by a company to sell its goods and services

Salesian /sə leézi ən, -leézh'n/ *n* a member of the Roman Catholic order of St Francis de Sales founded in Turin, Italy, in 1845 and dedicated to educational and missionary work [Mid-19C. < French *salésien* < St Francis de *Sales*] —**Salesian** *adj*

salesman /sáylzmən/ (*plural* **-men** /-mən/) *n* a man who sells goods or services, either in a shop or by contacting potential customers

CULTURAL NOTE *Death of a Salesman*, a play (1949) by US dramatist Arthur Miller. The tragic story of Willy Loman, an ageing salesman tormented by an overwhelming sense of failure, highlights the false values of contemporary consumer society and questions traditional ideas of success and failure. It was made into a film by Volker Schlöndorff in 1985.

salesmanship /sáylzmən ship/ *n* the skills, techniques, and tactics involved in persuading people to buy goods or services

salesperson /sáylz purss'n/ (*plural* **-people** /-peep'l/ or **-persons**) *n* somebody who sells goods or services, either in a shop or by contacting potential customers

sales pitch *n* the statements made, arguments used, and assurances given by somebody trying to sell something

sales rep *n* COMM same as **sales representative** (*informal*)

sales representative *n* somebody employed by a company to visit prospective customers with a view to selling them the company's products

sales resistance *n* reluctance or refusal to buy, especially when aggressive selling techniques are used

salesroom /sáylz room, -rŏŏm/ *n* **1.** a large room where goods for sale are put on display **2.** ANZ, N Am same as **saleroom**

sales slip *n N Am* a record of a purchase or sale made in a store, usually given to the customer as a receipt

sales tax *n* a tax on retail merchandise that is levied by the government and collected at the point of sale by the retailer

sales team *n* BUSINESS same as **sales force**

saleswoman /sáylz wŏŏmən/ (*plural* **-women** /-wimin/) *n* a woman who sells goods or services, either in a shop or by contacting potential customers

Salford /sáwlfərd, sólfərd/ city in Lancashire, northwestern England. It is adjacent to Manchester, from which it is separated by the River Irwell. Population: 216,103 (2001).

Salian /sáyli ən/ *n* a member of an ancient Frankish people who settled in the Rhine valley in the Netherlands during the 4th century AD. They subsequently spread into and conquered large parts of Northern Gaul. [Early 17C. < late Latin *Salii* 'Salian Franks']

Salic /sáylik, sállik, **Salique** *adj* **1.** relating to Salic law **2.** relating to the Salian people or their culture [Mid-16C. < French *salique* or medieval Latin *Salicus* < late Latin *Salii* 'Salian Franks']

salicaceous /sálli káyshəss/ *adj* describes trees or woody shrubs that have catkins, e.g. the willow and poplar. Family: Salicaceae. [Mid-19C. < modern Latin *salicaceus* < Latin *salic-* 'willow']

salicin /sállissin/, **salicine** *n* a colourless crystalline substance obtained from the bark of willow trees. Use: formerly, as an analgesic. [Mid-19C. < French *salicine* < Latin *salic-* 'willow']

salicional /sə lísh'nəl/ *n* a stop and pipes on an organ that produce a soft, gentle tone [Mid-19C. < German < Latin *salic-* 'willow']

Salic law *n* a law excluding women from the right to succeed to the throne that formerly applied in France and some other European monarchies. The prohibition was supposedly founded on a law of the Salians that prevented women from inheriting land in some areas.

salicylate /sə líssi layt/ *n* a salt or ester of salicylic acid [Mid-19C. < French *salicyle* < Latin *salictum* < *salic-* 'willow']

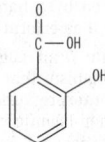

salicylic acid

salicylic acid /sálli síllik-/ *n* a white crystalline acid. Use: as a preservative, in the manufacture of aspirin and dyes. Formula: $C_7H_6O_3$. [< French *salicyle* (see SALICYLATE)]

salient /sáyli ənt/ *adj* **1.** NOTICEABLE OR STRIKING particularly noticeable, striking, or relevant **2.** PROJECTING sticking out from a surface **3.** MATHS PROJECTING OUTWARDS describes an angle that projects outwards from a polygon **4.** HERALDRY JUMPING in heraldry, represented as a jumping or leaping animal ■ *n* **1.** MIL PROJECTING PART OF DEFENSIVE ALIGNMENT a part of a military front, line, or fortification that projects outwards into enemy-held territory or towards the enemy **2.** MATHS SALIENT ANGLE an angle that projects outward from a polygon [Mid-17C. < Latin *salient-*, present participle of *salire* 'leap'] —**salience** *n* —**saliently** *adv*

ORIGIN The Latin word *salire* 'to jump, leap', from which *salient* is derived, is also the source of English *assail*, *assault*, *desultory*, *insult*, *salacious*, *sally*, and *sauté*.

salientian /sáyli énshi ən/ *adj* AMPHIB same as **anuran** [Mid-20C. < modern Latin *Salientia* < Latin *salient-* (see SALIENT)]

Salieri /sálli áiri/, **Antonio** (1750–1825) Italian composer. As a successful writer of operas and church music in Vienna, he was a rival of Mozart.

salimeter /sə límmitər/ *n* CHEM same as **salinometer** [Mid-19C. < Latin *sal* 'salt'] —**salimetric** /sálli méttrik/ *adj* —**salimetry** *n*

salina /sə línə, sə leénə/ *n* a salt marsh, lake, pond, or spring [Late 16C. Via Spanish < medieval Latin, 'salt pit' < *sal* 'salt']

saline /sáy līn/ *adj* **1.** CONTAINING SALT containing or impregnated with salt **2.** CHEM CONTAINING SALTS relating to or containing alkali metal salts or magnesium salt ■ *n* MED SOLUTION OF SALT AND DISTILLED WATER a solution of common salt (**sodium chloride**) and distilled water, especially one having the same concentration as body fluids. It is used as a diluent for drugs and as a plasma substitute. [15C. < Latin *salinum* 'saltcellar' < *sal* 'salt'] —**salinity** /sə línnəti/ *n*

saline solution *n* MED same as **saline**

Salinger /sállinjər/, **J. D.** (*b.* 1919) US writer. After great success with *The Catcher in the Rye* (1951) and his short stories, in the mid-1960s he became a recluse. Full name **Salinger, Jerome David**. See Cultural note at **rye**[1]

'What really knocks me out is a book that, when you're all done reading it, you wish the author that wrote it was a terrific

friend of yours and you could call him up on the phone whenever you felt like it.' [J. D. Salinger, *The Catcher in the Rye*; 1951]

Salingeresque /sállinjə résk/ *adj* relating or characteristic of the writings of J. D. Salinger. [Mid-20C. Surname of US writer J. D. Salinger (*b.* 1919) + -ESQUE]

salinize /sálli nīz/ (**-nizes, -nizing, -nized**), **salinise** (**-nises, -nising, -nised**) *vt* to treat or contaminate something with salt —**salinization** /sálli nī záysh'n/ *n*

salinometer /sálli nómmitər/, **salometer** *n* an instrument used to measure the concentration of salt in solutions —**salinometric** /sállinə méttrik/ *adj* —**salinometry** *n*

Salique *adj* PEOPLES, HIST another spelling of **Salic**

Salisbury /sáwlzbəri, -bri/ city in Wiltshire, southwestern England. Salisbury Cathedral dates from the 12th century and has the highest spire in the country at 125 m/404 ft. Population: 114,613 (2001). Former name **Sarum**

Salisbury, Robert Arthur Talbot Gascoyne-Cecil, 3rd Marquess of (1830–1903) British prime minister. As foreign secretary (1878–80) and prime minister (1885–86, 1886–92, 1895–1902) he extended British influence abroad, especially in Africa.

Salisbury Plain area of rolling chalky downs in Wiltshire, southwestern England. Stonehenge is located there. Area: 775 sq. km/300 sq. mi.

Salish /sáylish/ *n* **1.** a small family of Native North American languages spoken in the northwestern United States and British Columbia. Native speakers: 2,000. **2.** a member of a Salish-speaking Native North American people who live in British Columbia [Mid-19C. < Salish *sé'liš* 'Flatheads'] —**Salishan** *adj, n*

saliva /sə lívə/ *n* the clear liquid secreted into the mouth by the salivary glands, consisting of water, mucin, protein, and enzymes. It moistens food and starts the breakdown of starches. [15C. < Latin]

salivary /sə lívəri, sállivəri/ *adj* relating to saliva or the salivary glands

salivary gland *n* any gland in mammals that produces and secretes saliva into the mouth

salivate /sálli vayt/ (**-vates, -vating, -vated**) *v* **1.** *vi* PRODUCE SALIVA to produce saliva in the mouth, especially at an increased rate, e.g. when food is seen, smelled, or expected **2.** *vt* CAUSE ANIMAL TO DROOL to cause an animal in an experiment to produce large amounts of saliva **3.** *vi* LONG FOR SOMETHING to feel or show an immense desire for or appreciation of something (*informal*) ○ *salivating over the magnificent range of fitted kitchens* [Mid-17C. Back-formation < *salivation* < Latin *salivation-* < past participle of *salivare* 'salivate' < *saliva* 'saliva'] —**salivation** /sálli váysh'n/ *n*

Jonas Salk

Salk /sawk/, **Jonas** (1914–95) US physician and epidemiologist. He developed the first vaccine against poliomyelitis. Full name **Salk, Jonas Edward**

Salk vaccine *n* a vaccine against poliomyelitis, containing a form of the virus causing the disease made inactive by treatment with a solution of formaldehyde [Mid-20C. After Jonas SALK]

sallet /sállit/, **salet** *n* a light helmet protecting the head and the back of the neck, worn in the late Middle Ages [15C. Via French *salade* < Latin *caelata* 'engraved (helmet)' < *caelum* 'chisel']

sallow[1] /sállō/ *adj* unnaturally pale and yellowish ○ *a sallow complexion* ■ *vt* (**-lows, -lowing, -lowed**) to

make something unnaturally pale and yellowish ○ *The illness had sallowed her skin.* [Old English *salo* 'dark, dusky' < Germanic] —**sallowish** *adj* —**sallowly** *adv*—**sallowness** *n*

sallow[2] /sállō/ (*plural* **-lows** or *same*) *n* a willow tree with large catkins that yields a hard wood used to produce charcoal. Native to: Europe. Latin name: *Salix caprea.* [Old English *salh* < Indo-European] —**sallowy** *adj*

Sallust /sálləst/ (86–35? BC) Roman historian. His histories of Catiline's conspiracy and the Romans' war with the African king Jugurtha, written after he retired from holding colonial governorships, influenced the work of later historians. Full name **Gaius Sallustius Crispus**

'To like and dislike the same things, that is indeed true friendship.'
[Sallust, *Bellum Catilinae*; 43 BC]

sally /sálli/ *vi* (**-lies, -lying, -lied**) **1. SET OUT** to set out on a journey or excursion ○ *Ena sallied forth to face the day, her gait determinedly nonchalant.* **2. RUSH OUT SUDDENLY** to rush or spring out suddenly **3.** MIL **MAKE SALLY** to make an offensive thrust from a defensive position ■ *n* (*plural* **-lies**) **1. WITTY REMARK** a witty remark, reply, or retort **2. SUDDEN RUSH FORWARD** a sudden rush or spring forward **3. SUDDEN ACTION** a sudden burst of activity or springing into action **4. SUDDEN EXPRESSION** a sudden outburst of speech or expression of emotion **5. EXPEDITION** an expedition or excursion **6.** MIL **ATTACK FROM DEFENSIVE POSITION** an offensive thrust from a defensive position, especially, formerly, a sudden attack by the defenders of a besieged position on the people besieging them [Mid-16C. < French *saillie* < past participle of *saillir* 'leap' < Latin *salire*]

Sally Army /sálli-/ *n* same as **Salvation Army** (*informal*) [< shortening and alteration]

Sally Lunn /sálli lún/ *n* **1.** a light teacake, usually served hot **2.** a sweet bread leavened with yeast that is typically baked in a tin and served warm in slices with butter. It is particularly popular in the southern United States. [Late 18C. Probably < the name of a woman who sold teacakes in Bath]

sallyport /sálli pawrt/ *n* an opening in a fortification from which the defenders can make sallies

salmagundi /sálmə gúndi/ *n* **1.** a mixed salad of various ingredients such as meat, poultry, fish, and vegetables, arranged in rows on a platter **2.** a mixture of different types of thing (*literary*) [Late 17C. < French *salmagondis*, originally 'seasoned salt meats']

Salmanazar /sálmə názzər/, **salmanazar** *n* a large wine bottle that holds the equivalent of 12 standard bottles, used especially for champagne [Mid-20C. After *Salmanasar* or *Shalmaneser*, a king of Assyria in the Bible]

salmi /sálmi/, **salmis** (*plural same*) *n* a dish made from pieces of partly roasted game stewed with mushrooms and served with a rich wine sauce [Mid-18C. Shortening of French *salmagondis* (see SALMAGUNDI)]

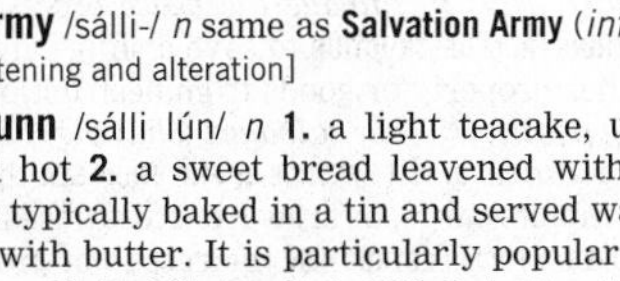

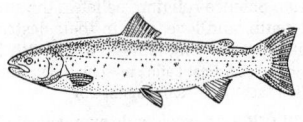

salmon

salmon /sámmən/ (*plural same* or **-ons**) *n* **1.** a large food fish with soft fins that spends most of its life in the sea but migrates up freshwater rivers to spawn. Native to: northern Atlantic, northern Pacific. Family: Salmonidae; Genera: *Salmo* or *Oncorhynchus.* **2.** FOOD the red or pink flesh of salmon as food **3.** COLOURS same as **salmon pink** [13C. Via French < Latin *salmon-*] —**salmon** *adj*

salmonberry /sámmənbəri/ (*plural* **-ries** /sámmən beri/) *n* **1.** a salmon-pink raspberry **2.** a plant that produces salmonberries. Flowers: red. Native to: Pacific coast of North America. Latin name: *Rubus spectabilis.*

salmon day *n US* a day on which continuous and strenuous efforts produce no progress and no worthwhile result (*humorous*)

salmonella /sálmə néllə/ (*plural* **-lae** /-lee/) *n* **1.** a rod-shaped bacterium found in the intestine that can cause food poisoning, gastroenteritis, and typhoid fever. Genus: *Salmonella.* **2.** MED same as **salmonellosis** [Early 20C. < modern Latin, after Daniel Elmer *Salmon* (1850–1914), US veterinary surgeon]

salmonellosis /sálmə ne lṓssiss/ *n* food poisoning caused by infection with salmonella organisms, usually characterized by gastrointestinal upset, diarrhoea, fever, and occasionally death. It is usually contracted by eating undercooked contaminated food.

salmonid /sálmənid/ *n* a bony soft-finned fish of the family that includes salmon, trout, whitefish, and char. Family: Salmonidae.

salmon pink *n* a pale orange-pink colour, like salmon flesh —**salmon-pink** *adj*

Salome /sə lṓmi/ *n* in the Bible, the daughter of Herodias who demanded and received John the Baptist's head as reward for dancing before her stepfather, Herod Antipas (Matthew 14:6–11 and Mark 6:21–28)

salometer /sa lómmitər/ *n* CHEM same as **salinometer** [Mid-19C. < Latin *sal* 'salt']

salon /sállon/ *n* **1. GRAND SITTING ROOM** an elegantly furnished room in a large house where guests are received and entertained **2. SOCIAL GATHERING OF INTELLECTUALS** a regular gathering of prominent people from the worlds of literature, art, music, or politics, especially one held at the home of a wealthy woman. Salons were especially popular in the 17th, 18th, and 19th centuries. **3. PLACE FOR HAIRDRESSING OR BEAUTY TREATMENTS** a commercial establishment where hairdressers or beauticians work, sometimes part of a larger shop or department store or a hotel **4. EXPENSIVE CLOTHES SHOP** a shop selling elegant or fashionable women's clothes, especially expensive designer clothes **5. ART EXHIBITION OR GALLERY** an art exhibition, especially one devoted to the work of living artists, or the hall in which the exhibits are displayed [Late 17C. Via French < Italian *salone* 'large hall' < *sala* 'hall' < Germanic]

Salonika /sə lónnikə/ ♦ **Thessaloníki**

salon music *n* light classical music for easy listening

saloon /sə lóon/ *n* **1.** *UK* **CLOSED CAR WITH BOOT** a car with two or four doors, four to six seats, a fixed roof, and a separate boot. ANZ, N Am term **sedan 2.** LEISURE same as **lounge bar 3. PART OF SHIP OR TRAIN** a large room on a ship or, formerly, a carriage on a train where passengers can sit and relax **4. DRINKING PLACE** in North America, a commercial establishment serving alcoholic drinks to the general public **5. LARGE PUBLIC ROOM** a large public room used for any of various purposes such as receptions, dances, entertainment, or sport **6.** *S Asia* **BARBER'S SHOP** a men's barber's shop [Early 18C. Alteration of SALON]

saloon bar *n* LEISURE same as **lounge bar**

salopettes /sállə péts/ *npl* a garment worn by skiers, comprising a pair of usually padded, water-resistant trousers that reach up to the chest with straps passing over the shoulders [Late 20C. < French]

salp /salp/, **salpa** /sálpə/ (*plural* **-pae** /-pee/ or **-pas**) *n* a tiny free-swimming organism (**tunicate**) that has a transparent barrel-shaped body. Native to: warm seas. Genus: *Salpa.* [Mid-19C. Via French < modern Latin *salpa*, < Greek *salpē* 'fish'] —**salpiform** *adj*

salpicon /sálpikən/ *n* a mixture of chopped ingredients such as meat, fish, or vegetables, bound together by a thick sauce and used to make croquettes or as a filling for pastries [Early 20C. Via French < Spanish < *salpicar* 'sprinkle with salt']

salpiglossis /sálpi glóssiss/ (*plural* **-glosses** /-glós seez/ or *same*) *n* a tall annual plant. Flowers: large, funnel-shaped. Native to: Chile. Genus: *Salpiglossis.* [Early 19C. < modern Latin < Greek *salpigx* 'trumpet' + *glossa* 'tongue'; from the plant's shape]

salpingectomy /sálpin jéktəmi/ (*plural* **-mies**) *n* the severing or surgical removal of a fallopian tube [Late 19C. < Greek *salpigg-* 'trumpet']

salpingitis /sálpin jítiss/ *n* inflammation of a fallopian tube [Mid-19C. < Greek *salpigg-* 'trumpet'] —**salpingitic** /-jíttik/ *adj*

salsa /sálssə/ *n* **1. SPICY MEXICAN SAUCE** a spicy sauce of finely chopped vegetables including tomatoes, onions, and chillies, eaten with tortilla chips and other Mexican foods **2. LATIN AMERICAN DANCE MUSIC** Latin American dance music combining aspects of jazz and rock with African-Cuban melodies **3. DANCE TO SALSA MUSIC** a dance performed to salsa music [Late 20C. < Spanish, 'sauce' < Latin, 'salted', form of past participle of *sallere* 'to salt' < *sal* 'salt']

salsify /sálssəfi/ (*plural* **-fies** or *same*) *n* **1.** a long earth-coloured edible root of a plant of the daisy family, which is said to have a taste resembling oysters, cooked as a vegetable **2.** a plant of the daisy family with long thin leaves and roots that are salsify. Native to: Europe. Latin name: *Tragopogon porrifolius.* [Early 18C. Via French *salsifis* < Italian *salsefica*]

sal soda *n* CHEM same as **washing soda**

salt /sawlt, solt/ *n* **1. WHITE CRYSTALS USED IN FOOD PREPARATION** small white tangy-tasting crystals consisting largely of sodium chloride. Source: seawater, mineral deposits. Use: food seasoning and preservative. **2. SALT CONTAINER** a container of salt, especially one for use at the table ○ *Please pass the salt.* **3. CRYSTALLINE CHEMICAL COMPOUND** a crystalline compound formed from the neutralization of an acid by a base containing a metal or group acting like a metal **4. SOMETHING THAT ADDS ZEST** something that adds zest, piquancy, liveliness, or vigour **5. DRY WIT** sharp or dry wit **6.** NAUT same as **old salt** ■ **salts** *npl* **SUBSTANCE RESEMBLING SALT** a chemical or crystalline solution used for a particular purpose ○ *smelling salts* ■ *adj* **1. PRESERVED WITH SALT** preserved with salt or a salt solution ○ *salt cod* **2. CONTAINING SALT** containing or consisting of salt ○ *salt tears* **3. CONTAINING OR ASSOCIATED WITH SALT WATER** containing, covered with, or growing near salt water ○ *a salt marsh* **4. TASTING OF SALT** tasting or smelling of salt ■ *vt* (**salts, salting, salted**) **1. SEASON FOOD WITH SALT** to add salt to food, during or after preparation, to emphasize its flavour **2. PRESERVE FOOD WITH SALT** to preserve food by treating it with salt or a salt solution **3. PUT SALT ON COLD GROUND** to scatter salt over a road or pavement to melt ice or prevent it from forming **4. ADD ZEST TO SOMETHING** to add a more lively or entertaining quality to something ○ *She salted her speech with jokes.* **5. ENRICH ORE SAMPLE** to enrich a mining area or sample with a valuable ore artificially introduced in order to increase its apparent value [Old English *sealt* < Indo-European] —**saltness** *n* ◇ **rub salt in the wound** to add to somebody's distress, embarrassment, or sense of shame, often deliberately ◇ **take something with a grain** *or* **pinch of salt** to listen to something without fully believing it ◇ **the salt of the earth** a very good, worthy person or group of people ◇ **worth your salt** efficient and doing the job well

ORIGIN The Indo-European word from which ***salt*** is ultimately derived is also the ancestor of English *halogen, salad, salami, salary, saline, sauce, sausage,* and *souse.*

salt away *vt* to save money for future use, often carefully over time [Probably < the practice of preserving food in salt]

salt out *vt* to separate a dissolved substance from a solution by adding a salt

SALT /sawlt, solt/ *abbr* Strategic Arms Limitation Talks (or Treaty)

salt-and-pepper *adj N Am* same as **pepper-and-salt**

saltarello /sáltə réllō/ (*plural* **-los** or **-li** /-li/) *n* **1.** a dance in triple time originating in medieval times and especially popular in Spain and Italy **2.** the music for a saltarello [Late 16C. < Italian < Latin *saltare* 'to dance' (see SALTATION)]

Saltash /sáwlt ash, sólt-/ town in Cornwall, southwestern England, on the estuary of the River Tamar. Population: 14,139 (1991).

saltation /sal táysh'n, sawl-/ *n* **1. JUMPING OR JUMP** leaping or jumping, or a sudden jump or leap (*formal*) **2.**

SUDDEN CHANGE development or transition that takes place in jumps or leaps (formal) **3. BIOL ABRUPT EVOLUTIONARY DEVELOPMENT** the abrupt evolutionary development of a new species or property, especially as a result of genetic mutation **4. GEOL JUMPING MOTION OF PARTICLES** the transportation of particles of soil or sand in the wind or in running water, characterized by bouncing movements [Early 17C. < Latin *saltation-* < *saltare* 'keep leaping, dance' < *salire* 'to leap']

saltatorial /sáltə táwri əl, sáwltə-, sóltə-/, **saltatory** /sáltətəri, sáwltətəri/ *adj* **1. RELATING TO JUMPING** relating to or adapted for jumping ○ *an insect with saltatorial legs* **2. ASSOCIATED WITH JUMPING OR DANCING** associated with or involving jumping, leaping, or dancing **3. DEVELOPING IN JUMPS OR LEAPS** involving or characterized by sudden change rather than gradual transition

saltbox /sáwlt boks, sólt-/ *n* **1.** a box in which salt is stored, especially one with a sloping lid **2.** *N Am* a wood-frame house that has two floors at the front but only one at the back, and with a long sloping roof on the rear side

saltbush /sáwlt boosh, sólt-/ (*plural* **-bushes** or *same*) *n* **PLANTS** same as **orache**

salt cake *n* an impure form of sodium sulphate. Use: manufacture of glass, paper pulp, soap, and ceramic glazes.

saltcellar /sáwlt selər, sólt-/ *n* **1.** a small container for salt, especially one used at the table to season food after it is served **2.** one of two depressions above the collarbone, at either side of the neck, especially prominent in very slim people (*informal*)

saltchuck /sáwlt chuk, sólt-/ *n Can* a stretch of salt water flowing into a freshwater lake or river

salt dome *n* a dome-shaped structure formed in sedimentary rock when buried salt deposits move up through overlying rocks, owing to their low density and high buoyancy

salted /sáwltid, sól-/ *adj* **1.** with salt added for seasoning, preservation, or some other purpose **2.** hardened or experienced, e.g. in a trade or profession

salter /sáwltər, sól-/ *n* **1.** a producer or seller of salt **2.** a preserver of food by using salt

saltern /sáwltərn, sól-/ *n* **1.** a place where salt is produced commercially **2.** a place where salt is produced naturally when pools of sea water evaporate [Pre-12C. < SALT + Old English *ærn* 'building']

saltfish /sáwlt fish, sólt-/ *n Carib* cod or other fish preserved with salt

salt flat *n* a broad flat area in hot deserts encrusted with salt left after the evaporation of water from shallow saline lakes (*often used in the plural*)

salt gland *n* a gland in some sea birds or reptiles, used to excrete excess ingested salt

salt glaze *n* a glaze formed by throwing salt into a kiln during the firing process

salt grass *n* any grass native to salt marshes or alkaline regions

salt hay *n* hay produced from salt grass, used as fodder

saltie /sáwlti, sólt-/ *n Aus* REPT same as **saltwater crocodile** (*informal*)

Saltillo /sal teél yō/ capital of Coahuila State in northern Mexico, founded in 1575. Population: 577,372 (2000).

saltimbocca /sáltim bókə/ *n* a dish consisting of thin slices of veal rolled up with prosciutto ham and fresh sage leaves, lightly fried and braised in white wine [Mid-20C. < Italian < *saltare* 'to leap' + *in* 'into, in' + *bocca* 'mouth']

saltine /sawl teén, sol-/ *n N Am* a thin crisp cracker sprinkled with salt

salting /sáwlting, sól-/ *n* a low-lying area of land regularly flooded with salt water (*often used in the plural*)

saltire /sáwl tīr, sál-/ *n* in heraldry, one of the basic designs used on coats of arms, consisting of a diagonal cross [15C. Via Old French *sau(l)toir* 'stirrup, stile' < medieval Latin *saltatorium* < Latin *saltare* (see SALTATION)]

salt-kind *n Carib* salted meat or meat soaked in brine, including pig's feet and oxtails, used in making soup or cooking beans

salt lake *n* a lake with no outlet and having a high salt content as a result of evaporation, e.g. the Dead Sea

Salt Lake City /sáwlt layk-, sólt-/ capital city of Utah, located in the north-central part of the state, 24 km/15 mi. east of the Great Salt Lake. Population: 181,266 (2002 estimate).

salt lick *n* **1.** a place where animals go to lick salt deposits that occur naturally **2.** a block of salt or other preparation that livestock lick in order to supplement their salt intake. It may also contain other essential minerals such as magnesium or iodine.

salt marsh *n* a marshy grassland area regularly flooded with salt water

saltpan /sáwlt pan, sólt-/ *n* a basin in a semiarid region where salts are precipitated after saline floodwaters evaporate

saltpeter *n* CHEM US spelling of **saltpetre**

saltpetre /sawlt peétər, solt-/ *n* CHEM **1.** same as **Chile saltpetre 2.** same as **potassium nitrate** [14C. Directly or via French < medieval Latin *salpetra* < Latin *sal* 'salt' + *petra* 'rock'; from its appearance as a crust on rock]

salt pork *n* a fat cut of pork from the belly, back, or sides, cured by salting

salt water *n* **1.** water containing a lot of salt **2.** the water of the sea and coastal inlets

saltwater /sáwlt wawtər, sólt-/ *adj* **1.** containing or involving salt water **2.** living or growing in salt water

saltwater crocodile *n* a large crocodile that inhabits coastal waterways and feeds on fish, birds, reptiles, and small mammals. Native to: northern Australia, Southeast Asia. Latin name: *Crocodylus porosus*.

saltworks /sáwlt wurks, sólt-/ *n* a place or factory where salt is produced commercially (*takes a singular or plural verb*)

saltwort /sáwlt wurt, sólt-/ (*plural* **-worts** or *same*) *n* a prickly leaved seashore plant. Native to: Europe, Asia. Genus: *Salsoa*.

salty /sáwlti, sól-/ (**-ier, -iest**) *adj* **1. TASTING OF SALT** containing or tasting of salt **2. OF SEA OR SAILORS** associated with the sea or with nautical life **3. LIVELY AND AMUSING** lively, amusing, and sometimes mildly indecent ○ *salty jokes* —**saltily** *adv* —**saltiness** *n*

salubrious /sə loóbri əss/ *adj* **1.** beneficial to or promoting health and wellbeing **2.** decent, respectable, or generally pleasant (*informal humorous*) ○ *advised to avoid the less salubrious parts of the old quarter* [Mid-16C. < Latin *salubris* < *salus* 'health'] —**salubriously** *adv* —**salubriousness** *n* —**salubrity** *n*

saluki /sə loóki/ *n* a tall slender dog with a smooth coat and long fringes on the ears and tail, belonging to a breed originally developed in Arabia and Egypt [Early 19C. < Arabic *salūkī* < *Salūk*, town in Yemen]

salutary /sállyoŏtəri/ *adj* **1.** of value or benefit to somebody or something ○ *We asked if military service had been a salutary experience for him.* **2.** promoting good health (*formal*) [15C. Via French < Latin *salutaris* < *salut-*, stem of *salus* 'health'] —**salutarily** *adv* —**salutariness** *n*

salutation /sállyoŏ táysh'n/ *n* **1. SIGN OF GREETING** a gesture or phrase that is used to greet, welcome, or recognize somebody **2. ACT OF GREETING SOMEBODY** the expression of greetings, welcome, or recognition **3. OPENING GREETING** the opening phrase of a letter or speech, used to address the recipient or audience, e.g. 'Dear Sir or Madam' or 'Ladies and Gentlemen' ■ *npl*, *interj* **salutations GREETINGS** greetings or regards (*formal*) ○ *Salutations from us all!* —**salutational** *adj*

salutatorian /sə loótə táwri ən/ *n* in the United States, a student in a graduating class who is second highest in academic ranking and is usually required to give a welcoming speech (**salutatory**) at the graduation ceremony

salutatory /sə loótə təri/ *adj* expressing or conveying greetings ■ *n* (*plural* **-ries**) a welcoming speech, especially one given at a US graduation ceremony [Mid-17C. < Latin *salutatorius* < *salutare* (see SALUTE)]

salute /sə loót/ *v* (**-lutes, -luting, -luted**) **1.** *vti* **GIVE FORMAL SIGN OF RESPECT** to formally signal respect to another member of the armed forces or to a flag, usually by raising the right hand to the forehead or by presenting arms **2.** *vt* **GREET SOMEBODY** to greet, welcome, or acknowledge somebody, either with a gesture or in words **3.** *vt* **FORMALLY PRAISE OR HONOUR SOMEBODY** to praise or honour somebody for something, especially in a formal ceremony ○ *We salute you for your contribution.* ■ *n* **1. GESTURE OF RESPECT** a gesture used by members of the armed forces and some other organized groups as a formal sign of respect **2. FIRING GUNS AS MILITARY HONOUR** a military display of honour for a dignitary or on a special occasion, e.g. the firing of guns into the air at the funeral of an officer ○ *a 21-gun salute* **3. ACT OF SALUTING** an act or an occasion of saluting [14C. < Latin *salutare* < *salut-*, stem of *salus* 'health'] —**saluter** *n* ◇ **salute the judge** *Aus* to win a race (*refers to a racehorse*)

Salvador /sálvə dawr/ port and capital city of Bahia State in eastern Brazil, on the Atlantic Ocean. Population: 2,211,539 (1996). Former name **Bahia**

Salvador, El ♦ **El Salvador**

Salvadoran /sálvə dáwrən/, **Salvadorian** /-dáwri ən/, **Salvadorean** *n* somebody who comes from El Salvador ■ *adj* relating to El Salvador or its people or culture

salvage /sálvij/ *vt* (**-vages, -vaging, -vaged**) **1. SAVE SOMETHING FOR FURTHER USE** to save used, damaged, or rejected goods for recycling or further use ○ *Maybe we can salvage some spare parts from your old car.* **2. RESCUE SOMETHING FROM BAD SITUATION** to save something of worth or merit from a situation or event that is otherwise a failure ○ *Diplomats are meeting to consider ways to salvage the peace process.* **3. SAVE SOMETHING FROM DESTRUCTION** to save a ship, cargo, crew, or other property or goods from destruction or loss (*often passive*) ○ *They salvaged what they could from the wreckage.* ■ *n* **1. RESCUE OF SHIP FROM SEA** the rescue of a ship, its cargo, or crew from loss at sea **2. RESCUE OF PROPERTY FROM DESTRUCTION** the rescue of property or goods from destruction or loss, e.g. because of a flood or fire **3. RESCUED GOODS** something that has been saved from destruction or loss **4. SOMETHING REUSED** something that would otherwise be destroyed or discarded but is recycled or put to further use **5. COMPENSATION FOR RESCUERS** compensation to volunteers who help in the rescue of ships, property, or goods from destruction or loss **6. MONEY FROM SALE OF RESCUED GOODS** money from the sale of property or goods that have been salvaged [Mid-17C. Via French (noun) < medieval Latin *salvgium* < late Latin *salvare* 'save' < Latin *salvus* 'safe'] —**salvageability** /sálvijə bílləti/ *n* —**salvageable** *adj* —**salvager** *n*

salvation /sal váysh'n/ *n* **1. ACT OF SAVING FROM HARM** the saving of somebody or something from harm, destruction, difficulty, or failure ○ *The business was clearly beyond salvation.* **2. MEANS OF SAVING SOMEBODY OR SOMETHING** somebody or something that protects or delivers another from harm, destruction, difficulty, or failure ○ *Those long walks were my salvation.* **3.** CHR **DELIVERANCE FROM SIN THROUGH JESUS CHRIST** in the Christian religion, deliverance from sin or the consequences of sin through Jesus Christ's death on the cross **4. CHRISTIAN SCIENCE PHILOSOPHY OF LIFE** in the Christian Science religion, belief in the supremacy of life, truth, and love, and in their destruction of such illusions as sin, illness, and death [13C. Via French < ecclesiastical Latin *salvation-* < late Latin *salvare* 'save' (see SALVAGE)] —**salvational** *adj*

Salvation Army *n* a worldwide evangelical Christian organization that provides aid to those in need. It was founded by William Booth in London in 1865.

salvationist /sal váysh'nist/ *n* a Christian who preaches the doctrine that Jesus Christ died on the cross to save people from sin or the consequences of sin —**salvationism** *n*

Salvationist *n* a member of the Salvation Army

salve[1] /salv/ *n* **1. SOOTHING OINTMENT** an ointment that soothes and heals **2. SOMETHING CALMING** something that eases pain or anxiety ○ *Her forgiveness was a salve to my conscience.* ■ *vt* (**salves, salving, salved**) **EASE PAIN OR WORRY** to soothe or ease pain or anxiety ○ *salve your wounded pride* [Old English *salf* < Germanic]

salve[2] /salv/ (**salves, salving, salved**) *vt* to save something from destruction or loss [Early 18C. Back-formation < SALVAGE] —**salvor** *n*

salver /sálvər/ *n* a tray, especially a silver one, used to serve food or drinks, or to present things such as letters or visiting cards [Mid-17C. Via French *salve* 'tray for presenting things to the king' < Spanish *salva* < late Latin *salvare* 'save' (see SALVAGE)]

salverform /sálvər fawrm/ *adj* describes the corolla of a flower with joined petals that is long and tube-shaped with a spreading upper part

salvia /sálvi ə/ (*plural* **-as** or **same**) *n* an ornamental plant with opposite leaves. Flowers: red, whorled, with two-lipped corolla. Latin name: *Salvia splendens*. [Mid-19C. Via modern Latin, genus name < Latin, 'sage (plant)' < *salvus* 'safe']

salvo[1] /sálvō/ (*plural* **-vos** or **-voes**) *n* **1.** SIMULTANEOUS DISCHARGE OF WEAPONS the firing of several weapons simultaneously, especially at a formal military ceremony **2.** HEAVY BURST OF FIRING OR BOMBING a concentrated burst of firing or bombing from several different sources during a battle **3.** NUMBER OF BOMBS RELEASED AT ONCE a number of bombs or projectiles released simultaneously **4.** OUTBURST a sudden burst of applause or cheering **5.** VERBAL ATTACK a vigorous written or spoken attack ○ *a blistering salvo* [Mid-17C. Alteration of obsolete *salva* < Italian, 'greeting' < Latin *salvus* 'safe']

salvo[2] /sálvō/ *n* something that is used to save a reputation or soothe somebody's conscience or wounded pride [Early 17C. < Latin, form of *salvus* 'safe']

Salvo /sálvō/ (*plural* **-vos**) *n* Aus a member of the Salvation Army (*informal*) [Late 19C. Shortening and alteration]

sal volatile /sál və láttəli/ *n* **1.** a solution of ammonium carbonate in alcohol and ammonia in water, often mixed with aromatic oils. Use: smelling salts. **2.** CHEM same as **ammonium carbonate** [Mid-17C. < modern Latin, 'volatile salt']

salwar /shál vaar/, **shalwar** *n* a pair of loose-fitting pleated trousers tapering to the ankle, worn by women from northern India and Pakistan, especially in the Punjab region, usually under a long tunic (**kameez**) [Early 19C. < Persian, Urdu *šalwār*]

Salween /sál ween/ river in Southeast Asia, flowing through China, including Tibet, and Myanmar (Burma). Length: 2,800 km/1,740 mi.

Salzburg /sálts burg/ capital city of Salzburg Province in western Austria. The Salzburg Festival, which concentrates on the music of Mozart, who was born in the city, is held there annually. Population: 143,941 (1999).

Salzgitter /záalts gittər/ city in Lower Saxony State, north-central Germany, situated 169 km/105 mi. south of Hamburg. Population: 117,842 (1997).

SAM /sam, éss ay ém/ *abbr* ARMS surface-to-air missile

Sam. *abbr* BIBLE Samuel

samadhi /su maádi/ *n* in Buddhism and Hinduism, a state of intense meditation believed to lead to spiritual enlightenment [Late 18C. < Sanskrit *samādhiḥ*]

samara /sə maárə, sámmərə/ *n* BOT same as **key**[1] *n* (sense 25) [Late 16C. < Latin, 'elm seed']

Samaria /sə máiri ə/ ancient city and state in Palestine, located north of present-day Jerusalem, east of the Mediterranean Sea —**Samarian** *n, adj*

Samaritan /sə márritən/ *n* **1.** SOMEBODY FROM SAMARIA somebody who came from ancient Samaria **2.** same as **Good Samaritan 3.** WORKER FOR SAMARITANS ORGANIZATION a volunteer who works for the Samaritans organization ■ **Samaritans** *npl* ORGANIZATION HELPING PEOPLE IN CRISIS a charitable organization that runs a telephone helpline for people in crisis [Pre-12C. < late Latin *Samaritanus* < Greek *Samareitēs* < *Samareia* 'Samaria'] —**Samaritanism** *n*

samarium /sə máiri əm/ *n* a silvery-grey metallic element. Source: monazite, bastnaesite. Use: strong magnets, carbon-arc lighting, laser materials, neutron absorber. Symbol **Sm**. See table at **element** [Late 19C. < SAMARSKITE]

Samarqand /sámmaar kánd, sámmər kand/, **Samarkand** capital city of Samarqand Oblast, central Uzbekistan. Located in the valley of the River Zerav-

shan, it is the oldest city in Central Asia. Population: 368,000 (1994).

samarskite /sə maár skīt/ *n* a black mineral containing uranium and rare-earth elements. Source: pegmatite. [Mid-19C. After V. E. *Samarskii*-Vykhovets (1803–70), Russian mining engineer]

Sama-Veda /saámə váydə/ *n* one of the four collections of chants (**Vedas**) used during Hindu sacrifices, containing songs based on the Rig-Veda with instructions on their recitation [Late 18C. < Sanskrit < *sāman* 'chant' + *vedaḥ* 'knowledge']

samba /sámbə/ *n* **1.** BRAZILIAN DANCE a lively Brazilian ballroom dance with strong African influences in 4/4 time **2.** BRAZILIAN MUSIC the music for a samba ■ *vi* (**-bas, -baing, -baed**) DANCE SAMBA to dance the samba [Late 19C. < Portuguese]

sambal /sám bal/, **sambol** /-bol/ *n* a spicy condiment or relish of Southeast Asia made of chilli, spices, tomato, and vegetables [Early 19C. < Malay]

sambar /sámbər/ (*plural* **-bars** or **same**), **sambur** (*plural* **-burs** or **same**) *n* a large deer that has a reddish-brown coat and three-pronged antlers. Native to: Southeast Asia. Latin name: *Cervus unicolor*. [Late 17C. Via Hindi < Sanskrit *śambaraḥ*]

sambhar /súm baar/ *n* in southern Indian cooking, a stew of highly spiced lentils and vegetables eaten mixed with rice [Mid-20C. Via Tamil < Sanskrit *sambhāra* 'collection']

sambo[1] /sámbō/ (*plural* **-bos** or **-boes**) *n* a highly offensive term for a Black person (*dated taboo insult*) [Early 18C. Probably < Fulah, 'uncle']

sambo[2] /sámbō/, **sambo wrestling** *n* a form of wrestling based on judo that originated in the former Soviet Union and is now practised internationally [Mid-20C. Acronym < Russian *samozashchita bez oruzhiya* 'unarmed self-defence'] —**sambo wrestler** *n*

sambo[3] /sámbō/ (*plural* **-bos** or **-boes**) *n* Aus FOOD same as **sandwich** (*informal*) [Late 20C. Alteration]

Sam Browne belt /sám brówn-/, **Sam Browne** *n* a wide belt supported by a diagonal strap that passes from the left-hand side over the right shoulder, worn as part of military or police uniforms [After Sir *Samuel Browne* (1824–1901), British military commander]

sambuca /sam boókə/ *n* an Italian liqueur made from elderberries and flavoured with liquorice or aniseed [Late 20C. Via Italian < Latin *sambucus* 'elder tree']

same /saym/ CORE MEANING: a word indicating that one thing or person is involved rather than two or more different things or people ○ (adj) *I can't drive and talk at the same time.* ○ (adj) *He lives in the same street as I do.*
1. *adj, pron, adv* IDENTICAL identical, or alike in every significant respect ○ (adj) *They turned up at the party wearing the same dress.* ○ (adj) *All the houses looked exactly the same.* ○ (adj) *Look – their curtains are the same as ours!* ○ (pron) *All the experts say the same.* **2.** *adj, pron* PREVIOUSLY MENTIONED previously mentioned, or as previously described or identified (*used as a pronoun without 'the' in business and legal contexts; see Usage note below*) ○ (adj) *She left because she was bored, and I left two months later for the same reason.* ○ (pron) *Wool should always be washed carefully. The same applies to silk.* ○ (pron) *'Are you Lee Smith?' 'The same'.* **3.** *adj* UNCHANGED not changed or changing ○ *After the accident, he just wasn't the same person.* ○ *The house looked the same as always.* ○ *I want things to stay the same.* [12C. < Old Norse *samr* < Indo-European, 'one'] —**sameness** *n*
◇ **all** *or* **just the same 1.** despite a particular situation or comment ○ *All the same, I wish she hadn't said it.* ○ *They tried to stop us but we took it just the same.*
2. nevertheless ◇ **same old, same old** used to say that a situation is unchanged or unexciting (*informal*) ◇ **the same as** in the identical way that (*informal*) ○ *He wants to win, the same as I do.*

USAGE The use of *same* as a pronoun as in *We have received your order and have pleasure in completing same* is characteristic of commercial language and is not normally found in general use, except with special or humorous effect: *She poured out a large glass of water and drank same.*

samekh /saá mek, -mekh/ *n* the 15th letter of the

Hebrew alphabet, represented in the English alphabet as 's'. See table at **alphabet** [Early 19C. < Hebrew *sāmekh* 'a support']

same-sex *adj* relating to gays or lesbians ○ *involved in a same-sex relationship*

samey /sáymi/ *adj* boringly repetitive or unchanging (*informal*)

Sami /saámi/ (*plural* **same** or **-mis**) *n* **1.** a member of an indigenous people of Lapland **2.** the Finno-Ugric language of the Sami people. Native speakers: 80,000. [Late 18C. < Sami *Sabme*] —**Sami** *adj*

Samian /sáymi ən/ *n* somebody who comes from the Greek island of Samos [Late 16C. < Latin *Saniius* 'Samos'] —**Samian** *adj*

Samian ware *n* reddish-brown or black earthenware pottery found in large quantities at Roman archaeological sites

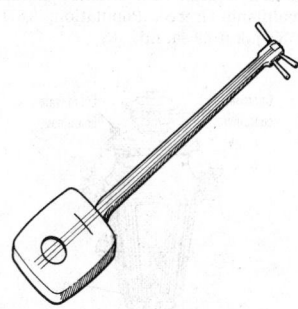

samisen

samisen /sámmi sen/ *n* a Japanese three-stringed musical instrument that has a long fretless neck and is plucked with a plectrum [Early 17C. Via Japanese < Chinese *sānxián* 'three strings']

samite /sámm īt, sáy-/ *n* a heavy silk fabric, often interwoven with gold or silver threads. Use: formerly, clothing. [12C. Via Old French *samit* < medieval Latin *examitum* < Greek *hexamiton* 'six threads']

samiti /súmmiti/, **samithi** *n* S Asia same as **committee** [Mid-20C. < Sanskrit *samitiḥ* 'assembly']

samizdat /sámmiz dát/ *n* **1.** SOVIET UNDERGROUND PUBLISHING in the former Soviet Union, the printing and distribution of secret or banned literature **2.** BANNED LITERATURE literature produced by the samizdat system **3.** SECRET PRINTING PRESS a secret printing press, especially in the former Soviet Union [Mid-20C. < Russian < *sam-* 'self' + shortening of *izdatel'stvo* 'publishing house']

Sammarinese /sa márri neéz/ (*plural* **-nesi** /-náyzi/) *n* somebody who comes from San Marino [Mid-20C. < Italian < SAN MARINO] —**Sammarinese** *adj*

Samnite /sám nīt/ *n* a member of an ancient people who lived in central and southern Italy in the 4th and 3rd centuries BC. They repeatedly tried to spread into territory held by Rome and were eventually defeated by the Romans around 290 BC. ■ *adj* relating to the Samnites, or their culture or empire ○ *the Samnite wars* [14C. < Latin *Samnites* 'the Samnites']

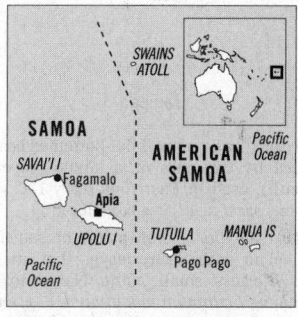

Samoa

Samoa /sə mó ə/ independent island state in the southern Pacific Ocean, situated west of American Samoa. It became an independent member of the Commonwealth in 1970. Language: Samoan,

English. Currency: tala. Capital: Apia. Population: 178,173 (2003). Area: 2,831 sq. km/1,093 sq. mi. Official name **Independent State of Samoa**. Former name **Western Samoa** (until 1997)

Samoan /sə mṓ ən/ n **1.** somebody who comes from American Samoa or the Independent State of Samoa **2.** the Polynesian language of the Independent State of Samoa. Native speakers: 300,000. —**Samoan** adj

Samos /sámmoss/ Greek island in the Aegean Sea, separated from the southwestern coast of Turkey by the narrow Samos Strait. Population: 41,965 (1991). Area: 477 sq. km/184 sq. mi.

samosa /sə mṓssə, -mṓzə/ (plural **-sas** or same) n a savoury South Asian snack consisting of a thin pastry case filled with spiced vegetables or meat and then deep-fried [Mid-20C. < Urdu]

Samothrace /sámmə thrayss/ Greek island in the northeastern Aegean Sea, situated 40 km/25 mi. from mainland Greece. Population: 2,871 (1981). Area: 178 sq. km/69 sq. mi.

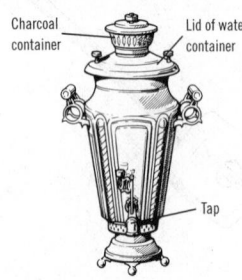

samovar

samovar /sámmə vaar/ n a large and often ornate Russian tea urn, originally heated by a built-in charcoal burner [Mid-19C. < Russian < samo- 'self' + varit' 'boil']

Samoyed /sámmə yed, sə mṓy ed/ n **1.** (plural **Samoyeds** or same) MEMBER OF SIBERIAN PEOPLE a member of a people living in northeastern European Russia and western Siberia **2.** LANGUAGE OF SAMOYEDS the group of Uralic languages spoken by the Samoyed people, related to Finno-Ugric. Native speakers: 35,000. **3.** SIBERIAN DOG a dog with a thick creamy-white coat, distinctive ruff, and tightly-curled tail, belonging to a Siberian breed [Late 16C. < Russian] —**Samoyed** adj

samp /samp/ n **1.** S Africa coarsely crushed maize, frequently cooked with dried beans as a staple food by Black South Africans **2.** New England cornmeal porridge [Mid-17C. < Algonquian nasàump]

sampan

sampan /sám pan/ n a small flat-bottomed boat (**skiff**) propelled by two oars or a single rear-mounted oar (**scull**), used in East Asia [Early 17C. < Chinese (Cantonese) saam-paán 'three-board (boat)']

samphire /sám fīr/ (plural **-phires** or same) n **1.** a coastal plant with fleshy leaves that are used in pickles. Flowers: small, white. Native to: Europe. Latin name: Crithmum maritimum. **2.** PLANTS same as **glasswort** [Mid-16C. Contraction of French herbe de Saint Pierre 'St Peter's herb']

sample /saámp'l/ n **1.** EXAMPLE a small amount or part of something, used as an example of the character, features, or quality of the whole ○ a free sample of the new shampoo **2.** SPECIMEN FOR ANALYSIS a small part

or quantity of something such as blood or soil, for scientific or medical examination or analysis ○ took a blood sample **3.** RECORDING PIECE OF RECORDED SOUND a piece of recorded sound or a musical phrase taken from an existing recording, especially in digital form, and used as part of a new recording ○ a CD of drum samples **4.** STATS GROUP SELECTED FOR TESTING a representative selection of a population that is examined to gain statistical information about the whole ■ vti (**-ples, -pling, -pled**) **1.** GET SAMPLE OF SOMETHING to take a sample of something, especially in order to determine its character, features, or quality ○ sample the river water **2.** RECORDING CONVERT SOUND INTO DIGITAL INFORMATION to convert sound into digital information in order to store or manipulate it electronically **3.** RECORDING TAKE SAMPLE OF SOMETHING FOR RECORDING to take a sample of recorded music, especially in order to use it in another recording ○ sampled whatever albums happened to be lying around [13C. Shortening of Anglo-Norman assample 'example' < Latin exemplum (see EXAMPLE)]

sampler /saámplər/ n **1.** EMBROIDERED CLOTH a piece of embroidered cloth containing rows of different stitches, either as a practice piece or, originally, as a demonstration of the embroiderer's skill **2.** REPRESENTATIVE SELECTION a selection that is intended to represent what is available in a range **3.** SOMEBODY WHO ANALYSES SAMPLES somebody who samples small quantities of something, especially to determine quality **4.** DEVICE FOR TAKING SAMPLES a machine or device used to take and analyse samples **5.** RECORDING ELECTRONIC EQUIPMENT FOR SAMPLING MUSICAL PHRASES an electronic device that can record sounds or take short musical phrases from an existing recording and allow them to be manipulated digitally before being used to make a new recording **6.** RECORDING MACHINE CONVERTING SOUND TO DIGITAL INFORMATION an electronic device that converts sound to digital information for electronic storage or manipulation

sample space n the set of all possible outcomes of a statistical experiment, represented by points

sampling /saámpling/ n **1.** PROCESS OF SELECTING SAMPLE GROUP the process of selecting a group of people or products to be used as a representative or random sample **2.** SOMETHING USED AS SAMPLE a small part, number, or quantity of something that has been taken or selected as a sample **3.** RECORDING REUSE OF RECORDED MUSICAL PHRASES the process of taking a short musical phrase from one recording and using it in another recording, often in repeated sequences and sometimes in an adapted or edited form ○ recent advances in sampling technology

sampling frame n a list of the people or items from which a statistical sample is taken

Pete Sampras

Sampras /sámprəss/, **Pete** (b. 1971) US tennis player. At 19, he became the youngest man to win the US Open. His many Grand Slam titles include seven Wimbledon trophies. Full name **Peter Sampras**. Known as **Pistol Pete**

samsara /səm saárə/ n **1.** in Hinduism, the endless cycle of birth, life, death, and rebirth **2.** in Buddhism, somebody's rebirth [Late 19C. < Sanskrit saṃsā-raḥ < sam 'together' + sarati 'it flows']

samshu /sám shoo/ n a Chinese alcoholic drink made from fermented rice [Late 17C. < Pidgin English]

samskara /sum skaárə/ n a Hindu purification ceremony that marks a transition in a person's life [Early 19C. < Sanskrit saṃskārah 'preparation, making perfect']

Samson /sámss'n/ n **1.** in the Bible, an Israelite judge and warrior. He used his enormous strength to fight the Philistines, to whom he was ultimately betrayed by his mistress, Delilah (Judges 13–16). **2.** any very strong man —**Samsonian** /sam sṓni ən/ adj

Samuel /sámmyoo əl/ n **1.** in the Bible, the leader of the Israelites in the 11th century BC. He was the first prophet after Moses. **2.** either of two books of the Bible that describe the history of the Israelites from the birth of Samuel to the end of the reign of King David, traditionally attributed to Samuel. See table at **Bible**

samurai /sámmŏŏ rī, -myŏŏ-/ (plural same or **-rais**) n an aristocratic Japanese warrior of a class that dominated the military aristocracy between the 11th and the 19th centuries [Early 18C. < Japanese]

san[1] /san/ n MED same as **sanatorium** (dated informal) [Early 20C. Shortening]

san[2] /san/, **-san** used in Japanese after somebody's first name, last name, or title, as a polite form of address [Late 19C. < Japanese]

San[1] /san/ n used as a title, usually in placenames, before the name of a man who has been made a saint [< Spanish and Italian, form of Santo (see SANTO) used before vowels]

San[2] /saan/ (plural same or **Sans**) n **1.** a member of a people living in southern Africa. The San traditionally live in small nomadic groups as hunters and gatherers. **2.** the group of Khoisan languages spoken by the San people [Late 19C. < Nama] —**San** adj

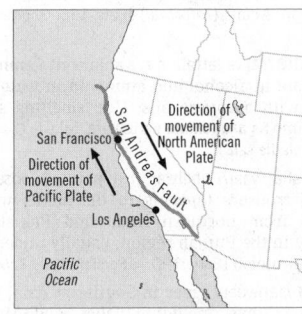

San Andreas Fault

San Andreas Fault /sán an dráy əss-/ n a geological fault zone between two tectonic plates that runs from San Francisco south to San Diego in California. It is an area of frequent earthquakes caused by the plates sliding past each other. Length: 1,000 km/600 mi. [Because it runs along the San Andreas valley]

San Antonio /sán an tṓni ō/ city in south-central Texas. It is the cultural and commercial centre of the Rio Grande Valley, and was the site of the battle of the Alamo in 1836. Population: 1,194,222 (2002 estimate).

sanative /sánnətiv/ adj able to restore health (archaic formal) [15C. Via French < late Latin sanativus < Latin sanare 'heal' (see SANATORIUM)]

sanatorium /sánnə táwri əm/ (plural **-riums** or **-ria** /-ri ə/) n **1.** MEDICAL FACILITY FOR LONG-TERM ILLNESS a medical facility where people affected by long-term illnesses can receive treatment and those recovering from severe illnesses can recuperate **2.** MEDICAL ROOM IN BOARDING SCHOOL a room or unit in a boarding school where pupils who are ill can receive treatment and recuperate **3.** HEALTH RESORT a resort for maintaining or improving health (dated) [Mid-19C. < modern Latin < Latin sanat-, past participle of sanare 'heal' < sanus 'healthy']

sanbenito /sánbə neetṓ/ (plural **-tos**) n a sackcloth garment worn by those declared heretics by the Spanish Inquisition. Penitent heretics wore a yellow one with a red cross on it and impenitent heretics wore a black one decorated with flames and devils. [Mid-16C. < Spanish sambenito, alteration of San Benito 'St Benedict', because it resembles the scapular of a Benedictine monk]

sancoche /sang kóch, -kósh, -kóchee/ n Carib a Caribbean soup made with a variety of vegetables,

split peas, and meat [Mid-20C. Alteration of American Spanish *sancocho* < Spanish *sancochar* 'parboil']

San Cristobal /sang krístə baal/ one of the Galapagos Islands, off the coast of Ecuador. Area: 505 sq. km/195 sq. mi.

San Cristóbal /sang kri stó bal/ capital city of Táchira State, western Venezuela. Population: 238,670 (1992).

sancta RELIG plural of **sanctum**

sanctify /sángkti fī/ (**-fies, -fying, -fied**) vt **1.** MAKE SOMETHING HOLY to give something holy status **2.** FREE SOMEBODY FROM SIN to perform a ritual or other act intended to free somebody from sin **3.** BLESS SOMETHING THROUGH RELIGIOUS VOW to give a religious blessing to something such as a marriage, usually through an oath or vow ○ *sanctified the marriage* **4.** OFFICIALLY APPROVE SOMETHING to give social, moral, or official approval to something ○ *rules sanctified by tradition* **5.** MAKE SOMETHING ROUTE TO HOLINESS to make something a means of achieving holiness or a source of grace [14C. < Old French *saintifier*, later *sanctifier* < Latin *sanctus* 'holy' (see SAINT)] —**sanctifiable** adj —**sanctification** /sángktifi káysh'n/ n —**sanctifier** n

sanctimonious /sángkti mṓni əss/ adj making an exaggerated show of holiness or moral superiority [Early 17C. < Latin *sanctimonia* 'sanctity' < *sanctus* 'holy' (see SAINT)] —**sanctimoniously** adv —**sanctimoniousness** n —**sanctimony** /sángktiməni/ n

sanction /sángksh'n/ n **1.** AUTHORIZATION official permission or approval for a course of action ○ *unable to proceed without the sanction of the board* **2.** SUPPORT something that serves as approval or encouragement, e.g. social acceptance or custom **3.** LAW a law or rule that leads to a penalty being imposed when it is disobeyed **4.** PENALTY IMPOSED FOR BREAKING RULE a punishment imposed as a result of breaking a law or rule **5.** INTERNAT REL PUNITIVE MEASURE TO PRESSURE COUNTRY a measure taken by one or more nations to apply pressure on another nation to conform to international law or opinion (*often used in the plural*) ○ *imposed trade sanctions* **6.** ETHICS PRINCIPLE DETERMINING BEHAVIOUR an ethical principle or consideration that determines or influences somebody's conduct ■ vt (**-tions, -tioning, -tioned**) **1.** AUTHORIZE SOMETHING to grant official approval or permission for something ○ *The town council refused to sanction the proposed design.* **2.** TACITLY APPROVE OF SOMETHING to allow something to be tolerated or accepted ○ *The school's inaction further sanctions this behaviour.* [15C. Via French < Latin *sanction-* < *sanctus* 'holy' (see SAINT)] —**sanctionable** adj —**sanctioner** n —**sanctionless** adj

sanctity /sángktəti/ (*plural* **-ties**) n **1.** the condition of being considered sacred or holy, and therefore entitled to respect and reverence **2.** something considered holy or sacred (*formal*) [14C. Via French < Latin *sanctitas* < *sanctus* 'holy' (see SAINT)]

sanctuary /sángkchoo əri/ (*plural* **-ies**) n **1.** REFUGE a safe place, especially for people being persecuted **2.** PLACE WHERE WILDLIFE IS PROTECTED a place or area of land where wildlife is protected from predators and from being destroyed or hunted by human beings ○ *a bird sanctuary* **3.** SAFETY PROVIDED BY REFUGE the safety and protection afforded by a place of refuge ○ *immigrants seeking sanctuary in the United States* **4.** CHR CHURCH PROTECTING FUGITIVES in medieval times, a holy place, usually a church, that provided immunity from the law **5.** CHR CHURCH PROTECTION FOR FUGITIVES the immunity from arrest, violence, or execution provided to fugitives under medieval church law **6.** RELIG HOLY PLACE a holy place, e.g. a church, mosque, or temple **7.** RELIG MOST SACRED PART OF HOLY BUILDING the most sacred part of a consecrated building, e.g. the area around the altar in a Christian church **8.** JUDAISM same as **holy of holies** [14C. Via French < Latin *sanctuarium* < *sanctus* 'holy' (see SAINT)]

sanctum /sángktəm/ (*plural* **-tums** or **-ta** /-tə/) n **1.** a sacred place inside a church, temple, or mosque **2.** a quiet private place where somebody is free from interference or interruption [Late 16C. < late Latin < form of Latin *sanctus* 'holy' (see SAINT)]

sanctum sanctorum /sángktəm saángk táwrəm/ (*plural* **sancta sanctorum** /sángktə-/ or **sanctum sanctorums**) n **1.** JUDAISM same as **holy of holies** (sense

1) **2.** same as **sanctum** (sense 2) [14C. < late Latin, 'holy of holies']

Sanctus /sángktəss, -tǒoss/ n **1.** in some Christian churches, a hymn praising the power and holiness of God that is part of the Mass **2.** a musical setting for the Sanctus [14C. < Latin, 'holy' (see SAINT), the first word of the hymn]

Sanctus bell n in the Roman Catholic Church, a bell rung at the beginning of the Sanctus and at other times during Mass

sand /sand/ n **1.** MATERIAL MADE OF TINY GRAINS a substance consisting of fine loose grains of rock or minerals, usually quartz fragments, found on beaches, in deserts, and in soil, sometimes used as a building material **2.** AREA OF SAND an area covered with or made up of sand, e.g. a beach or a desert ○ *playing on the sand and swimming in the sea* **3.** COLOURS BROWNISH YELLOW a brownish-yellow colour like sand **4.** PARTICLES IN HOURGLASS the tiny grains in an hourglass **5.** GEOL FINE SEDIMENTARY MATERIAL a sedimentary material that is finer than gravel but coarser than silt, with particle sizes between 0.06 mm and 2 mm (*technical*) ■ **sands** npl MOMENTS moments remaining or allotted (*literary*) ○ *The sands of time are running out for the old king.* ■ v (**sands, sanding, sanded**) **1.** vt SMOOTH SOMETHING USING SANDPAPER to rub a surface with sandpaper or sand to make it smoother **2.** vt SPRINKLE SOMETHING WITH SAND to cover or sprinkle something such as an icy road with sand **3.** vt MIX SAND WITH SOMETHING to add sand to something, e.g. to a mixture of materials when making mortar **4.** vti FILL WITH SAND to become filled with sand, or fill something with sand [Old English < Germanic] —**sand** adj —**sandlike** adj ◇ **kick sand in somebody's face** to show contempt for or dominance over somebody less strong or powerful

George Sand: portrait (1839) by Auguste Charpentier

Sand /saan, saaN/, **George** (1804–76) French writer. She wrote many volumes of essays, novels, and plays, which reflect her feminist and libertarian ideals. Pseudonym of **Dudevant, Amandine Aurore Lucille, Baronne**

> 'Where love is absent there can be no woman.'
> [George Sand, *Lelia*; 1833]

sandal /sánd'l/ n **1.** a light open shoe that is held on by straps across the instep or around the heel or ankle, usually worn during warm weather **2.** a strap for going around the ankle or across the instep to keep a shoe on a foot [14C. Via Latin < Greek *sandalion*, diminutive of *sandalon*] —**sandalled** adj

sandalwood /sánd'l wǒod/ n **1.** PALE YELLOW FRAGRANT WOOD a fragrant close-grained pale yellow wood. Use: furniture-making, carving, incense. **2.** AROMATIC OIL OF SANDALWOOD an aromatic oil extracted from sandalwood. Use: perfumes, incense, aromatherapy oil. **3.** TROPICAL EVERGREEN TREE a parasitic tropical evergreen tree that produces sandalwood. Native to: South Asia, Australia. Latin name: *Santalum album*. **4.** TREE RESEMBLING SANDALWOOD TREE a tree that resembles true sandalwood and is harvested for wood. Native to: South Asia, Australia. Genera: *Adenanthera* or *Myroporum* or *Pterocarpus*.

sandarac /sándə rak/, **sandarach** n **1.** BRITTLE RESIN a brittle yellowish translucent resin exuded by a coniferous tree. Use: varnishes, incense. **2.** WOOD FOR BUILDING a hard dark aromatic wood. Use: building material. **3.** EVERGREEN TREE a coniferous tree with flat branches and leaves with overlapping scales, which

produces sandarac. Native to: northwestern Africa, Spain. Latin name: *Tetraclinis articulata*. [Mid-17C. Via Latin < Greek *sandarakē*]

sandbag /sánd bag/ n **1.** SACK OF SAND a sealed bag full of sand, used in building defences against gunfire or flooding, or as ballast in hot air balloons **2.** BAG OF SAND USED AS WEAPON a small bag filled with sand and used as a weapon in the same way as a cosh ■ v (**-bags, -bagging, -bagged**) **1.** vt PROTECT SOMETHING WITH SANDBAGS to put sandbags in or around something as protection **2.** vt KNOCK SOMEBODY OR SOMETHING DOWN to attack or hit somebody or something with a sandbag (*informal*) **3.** vti DELAY NEGOTIATIONS to delay negotiations or a business deal in the hope of receiving a more favourable offer from somebody else (*slang*) —**sandbagger** n

sandbank /sánd bangk/ n a mound, hillside, or shoal of sand formed by the action of wind or water

sandbar /sánd baar/ n a long ridge of sand formed in a body of water by currents or tides

sandblast /sánd blaast/ vti (**-blasts, -blasting, -blasted**) POLISH WITH SAND to clean, polish, or mark the surface of glass, metal, or stone by applying a jet of pressurized air or steam mixed with sand ■ n **1.** JET OF SAND FIRED UNDER PRESSURE a jet of pressurized air or steam mixed with sand or grit that is used for sandblasting **2.** MACHINE FOR SANDBLASTING a machine that produces a jet of pressurized air or steam mixed with sand or grit for sandblasting —**sandblaster** n

sand-blind adj having reduced ability to see (*archaic or literary*) [15C. Alteration of Old English *samblind*, literally 'half blind'] —**sand-blindness** n

sandboard /sánd bawrd/ n a board similar to a surfboard or snowboard used for riding down sand dunes or performing stunts on a course covered in sand —**sandboarder** n —**sandboarding** n

sandbox /sánd boks/ n **1.** a container on a railway locomotive that releases sand onto the track to increase traction **2.** N Am same as **sandpit** (sense 1)

sandbox tree n a spiny tree with woody seed capsules that explode when ripe. Native to: tropical America. Latin name: *Hura crepitans*. [Because the seed capsules formerly served as boxes for sand]

sandboy /sánd boy/ ◇ **(as) happy** or **jolly as a sandboy** extremely happy or cheerful

sand-cast vt to make a casting by pouring molten metal into a sand mould

sand casting n a casting made by pouring molten metal into a sand mould

sandcastle /sánd kaass'l/ n a small model of a castle that is made out of damp sand, usually by children on a beach

sand crack n a crack in a horse's hoof that starts at the top (**coronet**) and extends vertically towards the sole

sand dab n a small flatfish caught for food. Native to: North American Pacific coast. Genus: *Citharichthys*.

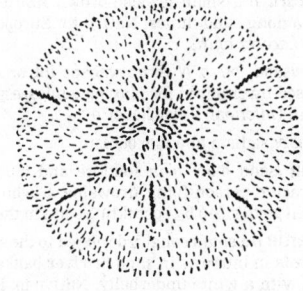
sand dollar

sand dollar n a flat circular sea animal related to the starfish and sea urchin, that is enclosed in white shell with an imprint that resembles a flower. Native to: shallow sandy coastal waters of North America. Genus: *Citharichthys*.

sand eel n a small slender sea fish resembling an eel. Genus: *Ammodytes*.

sander /sándər/ n **1.** an electric power tool that is used to smooth wooden or metal surfaces **2.** somebody who sands something or operates a sander

sanderling /sándərling/ (plural **-lings** or same) n a small bird of the sandpiper family with grey and white plumage in winter. Native to: coastal regions worldwide. Latin name: Calidris alba. [Early 17C. Origin ?]

Sanderson /sáandərss'n/, **Tessa** (b. 1956) British athlete. A gold medallist in the javelin at the 1984 Olympic Games and winner of the 1992 World Cup, she has also pursued a career in the media. Full name **Sanderson, Teresa Ione**

sand flea n **1.** INSECTS same as **chigoe 2.** MARINE BIOL same as **sand hopper**

sandfly /sánd flī/ n a hairy fly that resembles a moth. Bloodsucking females transmit several tropical diseases. Native to: tropics. Genus: Phlebotomus.

sandfly fever n a mild viral illness transmitted by the bite of a female sandfly. It causes fever, headaches, eye pain, and general discomfort.

sandglass /sánd glaass/ n TIME same as **hourglass**

sandgroper /sánd grōpər/, **Sandgroper** n Aus somebody who comes from Western Australia (informal humorous) [Late 19C. Because of the sandy soil of Western Australia]

sandgrouse /sánd growss/ (plural **-grouses** or same) n a bird related to the pigeon that has long pointed wings and a short beak and feet. Native to: dry and semiarid regions of Europe and Asia. Genus: Pterocles.

S & H abbr COMM shipping and handling

sandhi /sándi/ n the modification of the sound or form of a word under the influence of a preceding or following sound. The variation between 'a' and 'an' for the indefinite article in English is a form of sandhi. [Early 19C. < Sanskrit samdhih 'combination']

sandhog /sánd hog/ n N Am a worker inside a caisson in underwater building projects such as tunnels (slang)

sand hopper n a tiny jumping crustacean that lives on sandy tidal beaches. Genus: Orchestia.

San Diego /-di áygō/ city and major port of entry in southwestern California, on San Diego Bay. It is the second largest city in California, and the sixth largest in the United States. Population: 1,259,532 (2002 estimate).

Sandinista /sándi néestə/ n a member of a socialist movement in Nicaragua that successfully overthrew the government of President Anastasio Somoza in 1979 and fought a US-backed insurgent force in the 1980s [Early 20C. < Spanish, after Augusto César Sandino (1893–1934), Nicaraguan revolutionary leader]

S & L abbr BANKING savings and loan association

sand lance n FISH same as **sand eel**

sand leek n a plant that has a bulb shaped like that of garlic, e.g. rocambole. Flowers: reddish-pink. Native to: Europe, Asia. Latin name: Allium scorodoprasum.

sand lizard n a small greyish-brown lizard that is found among sand dunes. Native to: Europe. Latin name: Lacerta agilis.

sandlot /sánd lot/ n N Am a vacant lot or area of land used by children for playing games, especially baseball (informal) —**sandlotter** n

S & M abbr sadism and masochism

sandman /sánd man/ n in folklore and fairy tales, a character personifying drowsiness, who makes children go to sleep by sprinkling sand in their eyes

sand martin n a small songbird related to the swallow that nests in burrows in sand or river banks and is brown with a white underbelly. Native to: Europe. Latin name: Riparia riparia.

sand painting n **1.** a ceremonial practice of the Navajo and Pueblo peoples, in which different colours of sand are distributed over a flat surface to create symbolic pictures and designs **2.** a picture or design made by sand painting

sandpaper /sánd paypər/ n strong paper coated on one side with sand or another abrasive. Use: smoothing surfaces. ■ vt (**-pers, -pering, -pered**) to rub a surface such as a piece of wood or a wall with sandpaper — **sandpapery** adj

sandpiper /sánd pīpər/ (plural **-pers** or same) n a shorebird with a long slender beak that it uses to catch insects, worms, and soft molluscs in sand and mud. Family: Scolopacidae. [Late 17C. < its piping voice]

sandpit /sánd pit/ n **1.** an area of sand for children to play in, often contained in a box or frame. N Am term **sandbox 2.** a large deep pit from which sand is excavated

sand shark n a shark of mainly shallow waters. Native to: central and southern Atlantic, western Pacific coasts. Genus: Carcharias.

sandshoe /sánd shoo/ n a light low-cut canvas shoe with a rubber sole

sandsoap /sánd sōp/ n a gritty abrasive soap used for heavy cleaning

sandstone /sánd stōn/ n a sedimentary rock made up of particles of sand bound together with a mineral cement. Use: building material.

sandstorm /sánd stawrm/ n a strong windstorm, especially in the desert, that carries clouds of sand or dust, reducing visibility

sand table n a table covered with a layer of sand moulded to imitate the relief of a battleground terrain, used to plan military tactics

sand trap n N Am same as **bunker** n (sense 2)

sand viper n **1.** REPT same as **horned viper 2.** a viper with a yellowish-brown zigzag pattern along its back. Native to: southern Europe. Latin name: Vipera ammodytes.

sand wedge n a golf club with a face angle of more than 50° that is used for chipping the ball out of a bunker

sandwich /sánwij, -wich/ n **1.** BREAD SLICES WITH FILLING IN BETWEEN a snack or light meal made of two slices of bread or a split roll with a filling, or a single slice of bread with a topping **2.** FOOD same as **sandwich cake 3.** SOMETHING LIKE SANDWICH something resembling a sandwich, especially something in which various things are squashed together or arranged in layers ■ vt (**-wiches, -wiching, -wiched**) SQUEEZE SOMEBODY OR SOMETHING BETWEEN OTHERS to fit something or somebody tightly between two other things in space or time ○ I'll see if I can sandwich you in on Tuesday. [Mid-18C. After John Montague (1718–92), 4th Earl of Sandwich]

ORIGIN The Earl of Sandwich is said to have been so addicted to the gambling table that in order to sustain him through an entire 24-hour session uninterrupted, he had a portable meal of cold beef between slices of toast brought to him. The idea was not new, but the earl's patronage ensured that it became a vogue, and by the early 1760s we have the first evidence of his name being attached to it: the historian Edward Gibbon recorded in his diary in 1762 how he dined at the Cocoa Tree and saw 'twenty or thirty of the best men in the kingdom … supping at little tables … upon a bit of cold meat, or a *Sandwich*'.

Sandwich /sán wich/ market town in southern Kent, England. It was one of the original Cinque Ports. Population: 4,164 (1991).

sandwich board n **1.** a pair of boards, usually displaying advertisements or notices, joined by straps and hung from the shoulders with one displayed in front and one behind **2.** either of the two boards that make up a sandwich board [Because the boards sandwich the person wearing them]

sandwich cake n a cake with two or more layers separated by a filling such as jam or cream

sandwich coin n a three-layered coin that has a middle layer made of a different metal from the outside layers

sandwich course n an educational course in which work experience or practical training alternates with periods of study

sandwich man n a man who carries a sandwich board

~~sandwitch~~ incorrect spelling of **sandwich**

sandworm /sánd wurm/ n a segmented worm living in coastal sand or mud, often used as fishing bait. Genera: Nereis or Anicola.

sandwort /sánd wurt/ (plural **-worts** or same) n a plant that grows in thick tufts close to the ground on sandy soil. Flowers: single, white or pink. Genus: Arenaria.

sandy /sándi/ (**-ier, -iest**) adj **1.** FULL OF SAND made up of, covered in, or full of sand **2.** LIKE SAND having a grainy texture or consistency similar to that of sand **3.** OF COLOUR OF SAND of a reddish- or brownish-yellow colour ○ sandy hair —**sandiness** n

sand yacht n a small light boat equipped with a sail and wheels that allow it to be propelled by the wind over flat land, especially beaches

sane /sayn/ (**saner, sanest**) adj **1.** mentally healthy and able to make rational decisions **2.** based on sensible, reasonable, or rational thinking ○ a sane and practical solution to the problem [Early 17C. < Latin sanus 'healthy'] —**sanely** adv —**saneness** n

San Fernando Valley /-fər nándō-/ residential and industrial region in southern California, north of Los Angeles. It is bounded by the Transverse Range on the north, the Santa Susana Mountains on the west, and the Santa Monica Mountains on the south. Population: 1,300,000 (1998).

San Francisco /-frən sískō/ city in western California, the largest West Coast US port, located on San Francisco Bay. The famous Golden Gate Bridge, a suspension bridge that connects Marin County with San Francisco, was opened there in 1937. Population: 764,049 (2002 estimate). —**San Franciscan** n, adj

San Francisco Bay inlet in California, linked to the Pacific Ocean by the Golden Gate Strait. Length: 100 km/60 mi.

sang past tense of **sing**

sangar /sángər/ n a small low temporary defensive work (**breastwork**), usually built of stone around an existing hollow in the ground [Mid-19C. < Persian and Pashto]

sangaree /sáng gə reé/ n a chilled drink of wine mixed with fruit juice, nutmeg, and sometimes other spirits [Mid-18C. Alteration of Spanish sangría (see SANGRIA)]

sanger /sángər/ n Aus FOOD same as **sandwich** n (sense 1) (informal) [Probably alteration]

Sanger /sángər/, **Frederick** (b. 1918) British biochemist. He was noted for his work on insulin, the structure of proteins, and the nucleotide sequence of nucleic acids. He twice won the Nobel Prize in chemistry (1958, 1980).

Margaret Sanger

Sanger, Margaret (1883–1966) US social reformer. She founded and led the US birth control movement in the 1910s and 1920s. Born **Higgins, Margaret Louise**

sang-froid /song frwaá, sang-/ n self-possession or calmness, especially in a dangerous or stressful situation [Mid-18C. < French, 'cold blood']

Sangiovese /sánjō váyzi/ n **1.** a red wine made from a black grape grown mainly in Italy **2.** a black grape variety. Use: to make Sangiovese. [Early 20C. < Italian]

sangoma /sang gṓmə/ n S Africa in South Africa, a traditional healer (**shaman**) or herbalist [Late 19C. < Nguni]

Sangrail /sang gráyl/, **Sangraal, Sangreal** /san grī əl/ n CHR same as **Grail** [15C. < Old French saint graal 'Holy Grail']

Sangre de Cristo Mountains /sáng gri də krístō-/ range of the Rocky Mountains in southeastern

Colorado and northern New Mexico. Its highest peak is Blanca Peak, 4,372 m/14,345 ft. Length: 354 km/220 mi.

sangria /sang greě ə, sáng gri ə/ *n* a chilled Spanish drink of red wine, fruit juice, lemonade or soda water, and brandy or another spirit, usually served in a jug with pieces of fruit [Mid-20C. < Spanish *sangría* 'act of bleeding' < Latin *sanguis* 'blood']

sanguinaria /sáng gwi náiri ə/ *n* the dried rhizome and roots of the bloodroot plant. Use: antiplaque agent in toothpaste, formerly, internally as medicine. [Early 19C. < modern Latin < Latin *sanguis* 'blood']

sanguinary /sáng gwinəri/ *adj* (*formal*) **1.** INVOLVING BLOODSHED involving death or bloodshed **2.** BLOODTHIRSTY bloodthirsty or eager to kill **3.** BLOODIED consisting of or stained with blood [15C. < Latin *sanguinarius* < *sanguis* 'blood']

sanguine /sáng gwin/ *adj* **1.** CONFIDENT cheerfully optimistic **2.** RUDDY flushed with a healthy rosy colour ○ *a sanguine complexion* **3.** BLOOD-RED of a blood-red colour **4.** BLOODTHIRSTY eager to shed blood (*archaic*) **5.** PHYSIOL, HIST HAVING BLOOD AS DOMINANT HUMOUR in medieval physiology, having blood as the dominant humour and therefore characterized by a ruddy complexion and a courageous, optimistic, and romantic temperament ■ *n* RED CRAYON a red crayon that contains ferric oxide, used for drawing [14C. Via French < Latin *sanguin-*, stem of *sanguis* 'blood'] —**sanguinely** *adv* —**sanguineness** *n* —**sanguinity** /sang gwínnəti/ *n*

sanguineous /sang gwínni əss/ *adj* **1.** relating to or containing blood, especially mixed with other fluids (*often used in combination*) ○ *a sero-sanguineous discharge* **2.** COLOURS same as **sanguine** *adj* (sense 3) **3.** involving or enjoying bloodshed (*literary*) [Early 16C. < Latin *sanguineus* < *sanguin-* (see SANGUINE)]

Sanhedrin /sánnədrin/ *n* the supreme Jewish judicial, ecclesiastical, and administrative council in ancient Jerusalem before AD 70, having 71 members from the nobility and presided over by the high priest [Late 16C. Via Hebrew < Greek *sunedrion* 'council' < *sun* 'together' + *hedra* 'seat']

sanicle /sánnik'l/ *n* a widely distributed plant with oval fruits and hooked bristles. Flowers: small, variously coloured, in clusters. Use: formerly, astringent. Genus: *Sanicula*. [15C. Via French < medieval Latin *sanicula*]

sanidine /sánnidin/ *n* a glassy high-temperature form of the mineral orthoclase. Source: lavas. [Early 19C. < Greek *sanid-* 'board'; from the shape of the mineral's crystals]

sanitary /sánnitəri/ *adj* **1.** relating to public health, especially general hygiene and the removal of human waste through the sewage system **2.** clean and free from agents that cause disease or infection [Mid-19C. < French *sanitaire* < Latin *sanitas* 'health' < *sanus* 'healthy'] —**sanitarian** /sánni táiri ən/ *adj, n* —**sanitarily** *adv* —**sanitariness** *n*

sanitary engineering *n* the branch of civil engineering concerned with the building, maintenance, and development of water and sewage systems and other public health services —**sanitary engineer** *n*

sanitary pad, **sanitary napkin** *n* ANZ, N Am same as **sanitary towel**

sanitary protection *n* sanitary towels and tampons as means of absorbing the blood flow during menstruation

sanitary towel *n* UK a disposable cotton pad worn by women to absorb the blood flow during menstruation. ANZ, N Am term **sanitary pad**

sanitation /sánni táysh'n/ *n* **1.** the study and maintenance of public health and hygiene, especially the water supply and sewage systems ○ *sanitation laws* **2.** conditions or procedures related to the collection and disposal of sewage and refuse [Mid-19C. < SANITARY]

sanitize /sánni tīz/ (**-tizes, -tizing, -tized**), **sanitise** (**-tises, -tising, -tised**) *vt* **1.** to clean something thoroughly by disinfecting or sterilizing it **2.** to make something more likely to be acceptable by removing anything that might be considered offensive or controversial (*usually passive*) ○ *a sanitized version*

of the article [Mid-19C. < SANITARY] —**sanitization** /sánni tī záysh'n/ *n* —**sanitizer** *n*

~~sanitorium~~ incorrect spelling of **sanatorium**

sanity /sánnəti/ *n* **1.** the condition of being mentally healthy and able to make rational decisions **2.** common sense, reasonableness, and predictability ○ *to restore a little sanity to the situation* [Early 17C. < Latin *sanitas* < *sanus* 'healthy']

San Jose /-hō záy/ city and county seat of Santa Clara county in western California, situated in Santa Clara Valley, south of San Francisco Bay. Historically an agricultural centre, it is now regarded as the capital of Silicon Valley. Population: 900,403 (2002 estimate).

San José /-hō záy/ capital city of Costa Rica, and of San José Province, situated in the centre of the country. It is the country's largest city and its economic and political centre. Population: 309,672 (2000).

San Juan /-waán/ capital city and port of Puerto Rico, situated in the northeast of the island. Population: 421,958 (2000).

sank past tense of **sink**

> USAGE See *sink*.

Sankhya /sángkyə/ *n* one of six systems of orthodox Hindu philosophy, based on the perpetual interaction of spirit and matter [Late 18C. < Sanskrit *sāṁkhya-* 'relating to number']

San Luis Potosí /-loo éess potō seé/ **1.** state in east-central Mexico. Capital: San Luis Potosí. Population: 2,299,360 (2000). Area: 63,038 sq. km/24,339 sq. mi. **2.** industrial centre and capital city of San Luis Potosí State, east-central Mexico. Population: 670,532 (2000).

San Marino

San Marino /-mə reénō/ small independent enclave in northeastern Italy. It has been independent since AD 885 and a republic since the 14th century. Language: Italian. Currency: euro. Capital: San Marino. Population: 28,119 (2003). Area: 61 sq. km/23 sq. mi. Official name **Republic of San Marino** —**San Marinese** /sán mari neéz/ *n, adj*

San Martín /-maar teén/, **José Francisco de** (1778–1850) Argentine revolutionary leader. He helped to liberate Argentina (1812), Chile (1818), and Peru (1821) from Spanish rule. Frustrated by political quarrels, he retired to France in 1824.

San Miguel de Tucumán /-mi gél də too koo maán/ capital city of Tucumán Province, northwestern Argentina, on the Río Salí. Population: 470,809 (1991).

sannyasi /sun yaássi/ (*plural* **-sis**), **sannyasin** /sun yaássin/ *n* in Hinduism, a Brahmin who has reached the fourth and final stage of life as a mendicant [Early 17C. < Sanskrit *saṁnyāsī* 'somebody who renounces']

S-A node *abbr* ANAT sinoatrial node

San Pedro Sula /-péddrō soó laa/ capital city of Cortés Department, northwestern Honduras, in the Sula Valley. Population: 383,900 (1995).

sanpro /sánprō/ *n* same as **sanitary protection** (*informal*) [Late 20C. Contraction]

San Remo /-reémō/ city and port in Imperia Province, Liguria Region, northwestern Italy. Population: 50,608 (2001).

sans /sanz/ *prep* same as **without** (*archaic or literary or humorous*) ○ *looking forward to a well-earned break*

sans children [13C. < Old French *sanz* < alteration of Latin *sine* 'without']

San Salvador /-sálvə dawr/ **1.** capital city of El Salvador and of San Salvador Department, located in central El Salvador. Population: 415,346 (1992). **2.** island of the Bahamas, in the Atlantic Ocean, near Cat Island. Population: 465 (1990). Area: 155 sq. km/60 sq. mi.

sans-culotte /sánz kyoŏ lót/ *n* **1.** during the French Revolution, a revolutionary either from the poorer classes or with extreme republican sympathies **2.** a revolutionary in any country who has extremist views (*formal*) [Late 18C. < French, 'without breeches'] —**sans-culottism** *n*

San Sebastián /-sə básti ən/ city and administrative centre of Guipúzcoa Province in the Basque Country, northern Spain. It is the site of an annual international film festival. Population: 178,229 (1998).

sanserif *n* PRINTING another spelling of **sans serif**

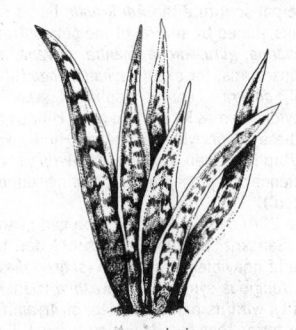

sansevieria

sansevieria /sánssi veéri ə/ (*plural* **-as** or *same*) *n* a tropical plant with thick variegated blade-shaped leaves, commonly grown as a houseplant. Use: bowstring hemp. Native to: Africa, Asia. Genus: *Sansevieria*. [Early 19C. After Raimondo de Sangro, prince of Sansevero (1710–70), Italian patron of horticulture]

Sanskrit /sánskrit/ *n* an Indo-European language that is the ancestor of most of the languages of northern South Asia and of Sri Lanka. The language of the Vedas and other Hindu scriptures, classical literature, and a vast body of scientific, philosophical, and religious scholarship, it is now used by a tiny minority, but its cultural influence far outstrips its tiny base of speakers. See panel on next page [Early 17C. < Sanskrit *saṁskṛta-* 'perfected'] —**Sanskrit** *adj* —**Sanskritic** /san skríttik/ *n, adj* —**Sanskritist** *n*

sans serif, **sanserif** /sán sérrif/ *n* a typeface in which there are no fine lines (**serifs**) at the ends of the main strokes of the characters

Santa[1] /sántə/ *n* used as a title, usually in placenames, before the name of a woman who has been made a saint [< Spanish and Italian, form of *Santo* (see SANTO)]

Santa[2] /sántə/ *n* same as **Father Christmas** (*informal*) [Early 20C. Shortening of SANTA CLAUS]

Santa Ana /sántə ánnə/ city in Orange County, southwestern California, in the south of the large metropolitan region surrounding Los Angeles. Population: 343,413 (2002 estimate).

Santa Barbara /-baárbərə/ city and county seat of Santa Barbara County in southwestern California, situated on the Pacific coast northwest of Los Angeles. A resort and industrial centre, it is home to the University of California-Santa Barbara. Population: 89,380 (2002 estimate).

Santa Claus /sántə klawz, sántə kláwz/ *n* Christmas personified as a jolly old man with a white beard and a red suit who brings presents to children [Late 18C. < Dutch dialect *Sante Klaas* 'St Nicholas']

Santa Cruz /-kroŏz/ **1.** river in southern Argentina that flows eastwards out of Lake Argentino in western Santa Cruz Province, and empties into the Atlantic Ocean at the port of Santa Cruz. Length: 400 km/250 mi. **2.** city in Santa Cruz Department, central Bolivia, on the River Piray, in the tropical plains region east of the Andes Mountains. Population: 914,795 (1997).

LANGUAGE HERITAGE *Sanskrit* Much of English is made up of words from other languages, and Sanskrit, an ancient language of South Asia, is an important contributor in this respect. Sanskrit is the ancestor of modern languages including Hindi, Urdu, Gujarati, Sinhalese, Punjabi, Bangla (formerly called Bengali), and Romany, but it also survives as the language of classical literary and religious texts. Trade brought Europeans into contact with South Asia early, but scholarly interest in Sanskrit blossomed from the late 18th century, especially with the development of comparative and historical linguistics during the 19th, and most words of direct Sanskrit origin are recognizably émigrés and arrived in or after this period. However migrants that took a circuitous route are often fully naturalized.

The familiar foodstuffs *pepper*, *sugar*, and the *orange*, for example, are ultimately from Sanskrit. *Pepper* existed in Old English as *piper*, and comes from a prehistoric West Germanic word itself ultimately, through Latin and Greek, from Sanskrit *pippalī* 'berry, peppercorn'. *Sugar* arrived in the 13th century, via French, medieval Latin, and Arabic from Sanskrit *śarkarā* 'grit, ground sugar'. *Orange* is from the same century, having reached English from Sanskrit through Old French, Italian, Arabic, and Persian.

Some well-established words also arrived through Sanskrit's descendants – via Hindi, for example, *cheetah*, *chit* ('official note'), *jungle*, *pundit*, and *thug*; via Bangla *jute*; and via English Romany *pal* (ultimately from Sanskrit *bhrātṛ* 'brother').

Nevertheless words of Eastern religion, philosophy, scholarship, and society dominate the Sanskritic émigré community. Religious migrants include: Hindu deities such as *Kali*, *Krishna*, *Shiva*, and *Vishnu*; texts, for example *Bhagavadgita*, *Veda*, and *Upanishad*; terms of the practice of Hinduism, including *ashram*, *avatar* (now also transformed into a computer game persona), and *saddhu*; terms of Buddhism, including its forms *Hinayana* and *Mahayana*, the name *Buddha* itself, and the sacred syllable *Om*; terms of Sikhism, including *Sikh* itself and its principal scripture the *Adi Granth*; terms of Jainism, including *Jain* and *Tirthankara* ('traditional holy man'); and terms shared by several of the subcontinent's religions, for example *ahimsa* ('the philosophy of revering all life', *dharma*, *guru*, *karma*, *mantra*, *nirvana*, and *sutra*. Closely associated with Hindu philosophy is *yoga*, with its various forms, for example *hatha yoga* (literally 'force yoga'); yoga terms used in English include *asana* ('a posture'), *chakra* ('a centre of spiritual power'), and *prana* ('inhaling, holding the breath, and exhaling'). Sanskrit also provided names for the four great Hindu castes: *Brahman*, *Kshatriya*, *Vaisya*, and *Sudra*, with the untouchables below these (*Dalit*, which came via Hindi, with the alternative name *Harijan* directly from Sanskrit). Sanskrit scholarship has given linguists *bahuvrihi* (a type of compound word) and *sandhi* ('modification of a word under the influence of a preceding or following sound'), the *Devanagari* alphabet, and *Sanskrit* itself (Sanskrit *saṃskṛta*-'perfected').

In the 20th century Sanskrit emerged in social movements in South Asia, where Mahatma Gandhi (*mahatma* is from Sanskrit, literally 'great soul') and his followers sought a new social order (*Sarvodaya*) through the doctrine of nonviolent resistance (*satyagraha*). It also emerged, in a totally different way, in Europe, where the ancient religious symbol the *swastika* (Sanskrit *svastikaḥ* 'good-luck sign') was appropriated by the German Nazi party, with its perverted ideal of *Aryan* (from Sanskrit *ārya* 'of good family') superiority.

Other terms that have travelled through Sanskrit's descendants include, for example, in social and cultural life *rajah*, *rupee*, *sari*, and *wallah* from Hindi; trees, *deodar* and *pipal* from Hindi, the *bo tree* from Sinhalese, the *banyan* from Gujarati (via Portuguese); animals, *cheetah*, *langur*, *nilgai*, and *sambar* from Hindi. However a few words of Sanskrit origin – again mostly with a spiritual or religious theme – have migrated to English by less expected routes, for example *shaman* (via Russian and Tungus), *wat* ('Buddhist monastery or temple', via Thai), and *Zen* (via Japanese and Chinese).

Santa Cruz de Tenerife /-də tenə reéf/ capital city and port of Tenerife Island and of Santa Cruz de Tenerife Province, in the Canary Islands, Spain. Population: 217,415 (2002).

Santa Fe /-fáy/ **1.** capital city of Santa Fe Province in northeastern Argentina. It is a port on the Salado River. Population: 353,063 (1991). **2.** capital city of New Mexico, on the Santa Fe River, in the north of the state. Population: 65,127 (2002 estimate).

Santa Gertrudis /-gər troódiss/ (*plural* **Santa Gertrudises** or *same*) *n* a large red beef cow that is highly resistant to heat and insects, belonging to a breed developed in Texas from Brahman and shorthorn cattle [After a section of the King Ranch in Kingsville, Texas, where the breed was developed]

Santamaria /sántə mə reé ə/, **B. A.** (1915–98) Australian writer and political activist. He was active in various Roman Catholic organizations, and as a staunch anticommunist helped establish the Australian Democratic Labor Party. Full name **Santamaria, Bartholomew Augustine**

Santa Marta /-maártə/ port and capital city of Magdalena Department in northern Colombia, on the Caribbean Sea. Population: 343,038 (1997).

Santa Monica /-mónnikə/ city near Los Angeles in southwestern California, on Santa Monica Bay. It is chiefly a resort and residential city. Population: 86,799 (2002 estimate).

Santander /sántən dáir/ port and capital city of Cantabria Province in the autonomous region of Cantabria, northern Spain. Population: 184,661 (2002).

Santayana /sán tī yaánə/, **George** (1863–1952) Spanish-born US philosopher. He maintained that reality is external to consciousness, and that all beliefs about the external world rest on 'animal faith'. His major work is *Realms of Being* (1927–40).

'For an idea ever to be fashionable is ominous, since it must afterwards be always old-fashioned.'
[George Santayana, 'Modernism and Christianity', *Winds of Doctrine*; 1913]

Santee /san teé/ (*plural same* or **-tees**) *n* a member of the eastern branch of the Sioux people, who now mainly live in Nebraska, Minnesota, North and South Dakota, and Canada —**Santee** *adj*

Sant'Elia /san télyə/, **Antonio** (1888–1916) Italian architect. His futurist drawings of buildings with sheer vertical lines and external lifts were a major influence on modern architecture.

Santería /sántə reé ə/, **santería** *n* a religion that combines the West African Yoruba religion with Roman Catholicism. The religion recognizes a supreme God as well as other spirits. Originally developed in Cuba by West African slaves, it is now practised in the Caribbean and the United States. [Mid-20C. < Spanish *santería* 'holiness' < Latin *sanctus* 'holy' (see SAINT)]

Santiago /sánti aágō/ capital and largest city of Chile, on the River Mapocho, in the central part of the country. Population: 5,493,062 (2000).

Santiago de Compostela /-day kompo stáylə/ capital city of the autonomous region of Galicia, northwestern Spain. Its cathedral has been a major place of pilgrimage since medieval times. Population: 93,273 (2002).

Santiago de Cuba /-koóbə/ second largest city in Cuba, situated in the southeast of the country. It is a major port. Population: 432,396 (1996).

santim /sán teem/ *n* a subunit of Latvian currency. See table at **currency** [Late 20C. < Latvian *santims* < French *centime* (see CENTIME)]

Santo /sántō/ (*plural* **-tos**) *n* used as a title, usually in placenames, before the name of a man who has been made a saint [< Spanish and Italian < Latin *sanctus* 'holy' (see SAINT)]

Santo Domingo /sántō də míng gō/ capital and largest city of the Dominican Republic, situated in the south of the country. Population: 2,677,056 (2001).

santolina /sántə leénə/ (*plural* **-nas** or *same*) *n* an evergreen plant with distinctive silvery-grey velvety foliage. Native to: Mediterranean. Latin name: *Santolina chamaecyparissus*. [Late 16C. < modern Latin]

santonica /san tónnikə/ (*plural* **-cas** or *same*) *n* **1.** the dried unopened flower heads of a wormwood plant. Use: source of santonin. **2.** a wormwood plant with twin needle-shaped leaves grown for its abundant flower heads, which when dried are santonica. Native to: Europe, Asia. Genus: *Artemisia*. [Mid-17C. < modern Latin < form of Latin *santonicus* < *Santoni*, tribe of the Gauls]

santonin /sántənin/ *n* a white crystalline compound. Source: extracted from santonica flower heads. Use: formerly, to eradicate parasitic worms. Formula: $C_{15}H_{18}O_3$. [Mid-19C. < SANTONICA]

Santorini /sánto reé ni/ ♦ **Thera**

Santos /sántooss/ city and port in São Paulo State, in southeastern Brazil, situated on the Atlantic island of São Vicente. Population: 412,243 (1996).

Sanusi /se noóssi/ *n* a member of an Islamic Sufi religious group in Arabia and North Africa [Late 19C. After Sīdī Muḥammad ibn 'Alī as-*Sanūsī* (d. 1859), the group's founder]

San Yu /sán yoó/ (1919–96) soldier and president of Burma (1981–88). A retired general, he took over the presidency from Ne Win.

São Miguel /sow mi gél/ largest island of the Azores, located in the North Atlantic Ocean 1,200 km/740 mi. from the western coast of Portugal. Population: 126,388 (1991). Area: 746 sq. km/288 sq. mi.

Saône /sōn/ river in east-central France. It is a tributary of the Rhône. Length: 480 km/298 mi.

São Paulo /-pówlō/ capital of São Paulo State in southeastern Brazil. It is the largest city in South America, and an industrial and commercial metropolis. Population: 9,839,436 (1996).

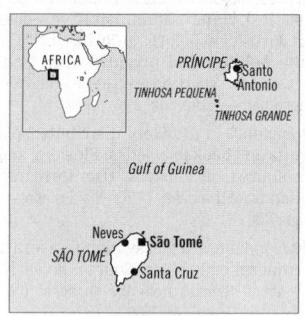

São Tomé and Príncipe

São Tomé and Príncipe /-tō máy ənd prínssi pay/ island country in the Gulf of Guinea, approximately 290 km/180 mi. west of Gabon, West Africa. Formerly Portuguese, the territory became an independent republic in 1975. Language: Portuguese. Currency: dobra. Capital: São Tomé. Population: 175,883 (2003). Area: 1,001 sq. km/386 sq. mi. Official name **Democratic Republic of São Tomé and Príncipe**

sap[1] /sap/ *n* **1.** PLANT FLUID a watery liquid containing mineral salts, sugars, and other nutrients that circulates through the conducting tissues of a plant **2.** BOT same as **sapwood 3.** BODY FLUID any essential body fluid **4.** ENERGY bodily strength or vitality ○ *feel the sap rising* **5.** OFFENSIVE TERM an offensive term that deliberately insults somebody's intelligence and judgment (*slang insult*) **6.** *US* SMALL CLUB a weapon such as a cosh ■ *vt* (**saps, sapping, sapped**) **1.** DRAW SAP FROM PLANT to drain a plant of sap **2.** *US* HIT SOMEBODY WITH SAP to hit or knock somebody out with a sap [Old English *sæp* < Germanic] —**sapless** *adj*

sap[2] /sap/ *v* (**saps, sapping, sapped**) **1.** *vt* TAKE AWAY SOMEBODY'S ENERGY to gradually weaken or reduce something, especially somebody's strength or energy ○ *The long hours were sapping his strength.* **2.** *vt* TUNNEL UNDER FORTIFICATIONS to weaken the foundations of an enemy fortification with a tunnel **3.** *vi* DIG TUNNEL LEADING TO ENEMY to dig a covered trench to approach or get inside enemy territory ■ *n* TUNNEL LEADING TO ENEMY a covered trench, dug to approach or get inside enemy territory [Late 16C. Via French and Italian < late Latin *sappa*]

sapanwood *n* TREES, INDUST another spelling of **sappanwood**

sapele /sə peéli/ (*plural* **-les** or *same*) *n* **1.** a wood that resembles mahogany. Use: furniture-making. **2.** a tall rainforest tree that produces sapele. Native to: West Africa. Genus: *Entandrophragma*. [Early 20C. After *Sapele*, port in Nigeria]

Saphar *n* CALENDAR, ISLAM another spelling of **Safar**

saphead /sáp hed/ *n* an offensive term that deliberately insults somebody's intelligence and judgment (*slang insult*) [Late 18C. < SAP¹] —**sapheaded** *adj*

saphenous vein /sə feénəss/ *n* either of two major veins in the leg that run from the foot to the thigh near the surface of the skin [< medieval Latin *saphena* 'vein']

~~saphire~~ incorrect spelling of **sapphire**

sapid /sáppid/ *adj* (*formal*) **1.** having a strong and pleasant taste **2.** engaging or pleasant to think about [Early 17C. < Latin *sapidus* < *sapere* 'to taste'] —**sapidity** /sə píddəti/ *n* —**sapidness** *n*

sapient /sáypi ənt/ *adj* wise or learned [15C. Via French < Latin *sapient-*, present participle of *sapere* 'be wise'] —**sapience** *n* —**sapiently** *adv*

Sapir-Whorf hypothesis /sə peér wáwrf-/ *n* the theory that the structure of a language helps determine how its native speakers perceive and categorize experience [Mid 20C. After Edward *Sapir* (1884–1939) and Benjamin Lee *Whorf* (1897–1941), US linguists]

sapling /sáppling/ *n* **1.** a young tree with a slender trunk **2.** a young person (*literary*) [14C. < SAP¹]

sapodilla /sáppə díllə/ *n* **1.** *also* **sapodilla plum** a brown rough-skinned fruit with sweet yellowish pulp **2.** an evergreen tree that produces chicle and sapodillas. Native to: Mexico, Central America, Caribbean. Latin name: *Manilkara zapota*. [Late 17C. Alteration of Spanish *zapotillo* < *zapote* (see SAPOTE)]

saponify /sə pónni fī/ (**-fies, -fying, -fied**) *vti* to be converted into soap, or convert a fat into soap, especially by reaction with an alkali [Early 19C. < French *saponifier* < Latin *sapon-*, stem of *sapo* 'soap' < Germanic] —**saponifiable** /sə pónni fíəbl/ *adj* —**saponification** /sə pónnifi káysh'n/ *n* —**saponifier** *n*

saponin /sáppənin/ *n* a glucoside extracted from plants that forms a soapy lather when mixed with water. Use: detergents. [Mid-19C. < French *saponine* < Latin *sapon-* (see SAPONIFY)]

saponite /sáppə nīt/ *n* a soft soapy clay mineral. Source: veins and cavities of rocks altered by hot water. [Mid-19C. < Latin *sapon-* (see SAPONIFY)]

sapote /sə pótə/ *n* **1.** an oval brown sweet fruit **2.** a tree that produces sapotes. Native to: Mexico, Central America. Latin name: *Poulteria sapota*. [Mid-16C. Via modern Latin < Spanish *zapote* < Nahuatl *tzapotl*]

sappanwood /sáppən woòd/, **sapanwood** *n* **1.** a wood from which a red dye is obtained **2.** the leguminous tree whose wood is sappanwood. Native to: tropical Asia. Latin name: *Caesalpina sappan*. [Early 17C. < obsolete *sappan*, via Dutch < Malay *sapang*]

sapper /sáppər/ *n* **1.** SPECIALIST IN TRENCHES AND TUNNELS a military engineer who specializes in fortifications, especially tunnels dug under enemy territory **2.** SPECIALIST IN MINES a military engineer who lays, detects, and disarms mines **3.** PRIVATE IN ROYAL ENGINEERS in the British Army, a private in the Royal Engineers [Early 17C. < SAP²]

Sapphic /sáffik/ *adj* **1.** relating to the Greek poet Sappho or her poetry, largely written in 11-syllable lines, with stanzas of three such lines and a shorter fourth line **2.** same as **lesbian** (*literary*) ■ *n* a Sapphic line, stanza, or poem

sapphire /sáff īr/ *n* **1.** a clear hard precious stone that is a variety of the mineral corundum and is usually deep blue in colour **2.** a brilliant blue colour like that of a sapphire [13C. Via French and Latin < Greek *sappheiros*] —**sapphire** *adj*

sapphirine /sáffə reen/ *adj* resembling a sapphire, especially in being a brilliant blue colour ■ *n* a rare blue or green aluminium magnesium silicate mineral

sapphism /sáffizəm/ *n* same as **lesbianism** (*literary*) [Late 19C. After SAPPHO]

Sappho /sáffō/ (*fl* 7th century BC) Greek poet. She wrote odes, wedding songs, and hymns notable for their depth of feeling. Few fragments of her work remain.

Sapporo /sáppōrō, sa pórō/ commercial centre and capital of Hokkaido Prefecture, on western Hokkaido Island, Japan. Population: 1,822,992 (2002).

sappy /sáppi/ (**-pier, -piest**) *adj* **1.** FULL OF SAP containing a large quantity of sap **2.** OVERLY SENTIMENTAL expressing or portraying emotion in an excessively sentimental way (*slang*) ○ *a sappy film* **3.** OFFENSIVE TERM an offensive term meaning silly or unintelligent (*slang insult*) [Pre-12C. < SAP¹] —**sappily** *adv*

sapr- *prefix* same as **sapro-** (*used before vowels*)

sapro- *prefix* **1.** death, decay, putrefaction ○ *saprozoic* **2.** dead or decaying organic matter ○ *saprophagous* [< Greek *sapros* 'rotten']

saprobe /sá prōb/ *n* an organism that gets its nourishment from inorganic or decaying organic matter [Mid-20C. < SAPRO-, after MICROBE] —**saprobic** /sə próbik/ *adj*

saprobiology /sápprō bī ólləji/ *n* the study of environments that support organisms (**saprobes**) that feed on decaying organic matter —**saprobiological** /-ə lójjik'l/ *adj* —**saprobiologist** *n*

saprogenic /sápprō jénnik/ *adj* causing or resulting from decay —**saprogenicity** /-jə níssəti/ *n*

saprolite /sápprō līt/ *n* soft disintegrating igneous rock that remains where it was located when solid, formed by heavy weathering in a humid environment —**saprolitic** /sápprō líttik/ *adj*

sapropel /sápprə pel/ *n* a soft black layer of decaying organic matter at the bottom of a body of water [Early 20C. < German < Greek *sapros* 'rotten' + *pēlos* 'mud'] —**sapropelic** /sápprə péllik/ *adj*

saprophagous /sa próffəgəss/ *adj* feeding on or obtaining food from decaying organic matter

saprophyte /sápprō fīt/ *n* an organism, especially a fungus or bacterium, that obtains food from dead or decaying organic matter —**saprophytic** /sápprō fíttik/ *adj* —**saprophytically** *adv*

saprophytism /sápprō fítizəm/ *n* the process of obtaining nourishment from dissolved decaying organic matter

saprozoic /sáp prō zó ik/ *adj* getting nourishment by absorbing dissolved organic matter and salts

sapsago /sápsəgō/ *n* a hard green Swiss cheese made with sour skimmed milk and flavoured with sweet clover [Mid-19C. Alteration of German *Schabzieger* < *schaben* 'scrape' + *zieger* 'curd cheese']

sapsucker /sáp sukər/ *n* a small woodpecker that drills holes in trees in order to drink the sap and eat insects attracted by the sap. Native to: North America. Genus: *Sphyrapicus*. [Early 19C. < SAP¹]

sapwood /sáp woòd/ *n* the soft wood of a tree between the inner bark and the heartwood [Late 18C. < SAP¹]

SAR¹ *n* the rate, measured in watts or milliwatts per kilogram, at which a mass, especially human tissue, absorbs radiated electrical energy, e.g. that produced by a mobile phone. Full form **specific absorption rate**

SAR² *abbr* search and rescue

saraband /sárrə band/, **sarabande** *n* **1.** a dignified Spanish dance of the 17th and 18th centuries in triple time **2.** the music for a saraband [Early 17C. Via French < Spanish *zarabanda*]

Saracen /sárrəss'n/ *n* **1.** MUSLIM OPPOSING CHRISTIAN CRUSADES a Muslim who fought against the Christian Crusaders in the Middle Ages **2.** MEMBER OF ANCIENT DESERT PEOPLE a member of an ancient desert people of Syria and Arabia living on the fringes of the Roman Empire **3.** same as **Arab** (*archaic*) ■ *adj* RELATING TO SARACENS relating to the ancient or medieval Saracens or their culture [Pre-12C. Via French < late Latin *Saracenus* < late Greek *sarakēnos*] —**Saracenic** /sárrə sénnik/ *adj* —**Saracenical** *adj*

Saragossa /sárrə góssə/ ♦ **Zaragoza**

Sarah /sáirə/ *n* in the Bible, the wife and half-sister of Abraham, and mother of Isaac (Genesis 17:15–22)

Sarajevo /sárrə yáyvō/ capital city of Bosnia-Herzegovina, in the east-central part of the country. Population: 360,000 (1997).

saran /sə rán/ *n* a thermoplastic resin produced from a vinyl compound. Use: fabrics, plastic wrap. [Mid-20C. Originally a trademark]

sarangi /saa rúng gi/ (*plural* **-gis**) *n* a musical instrument of South Asia that resembles a violin, with a rectangular soundbox and three playing strings that have sympathetic strings [Mid-19C. < Sanskrit *sārangī*]

sarape *n* CLOTHING another spelling of **serape**

Sarawak /sə raáwək/ state in Malaysia, in the northwestern portion of the island of Borneo. Capital: Kuching. Population: 1,954,300 (1997). Area: 124,449 sq. km/48,050 sq. mi.

Sarazen /sárrəzən/, **Gene** (1902–99) US golfer. He was the first golfer to win the four championships that comprise the grand slam of golf. Born **Saraceni, Eugene**

sarc- *prefix* same as **sarco-** (*used before vowels*)

sarcasm /saár kazəm/ *n* remarks that mean the opposite of what they seem to say and are intended to mock or deride [Mid-16C. Directly or via French < late Latin *sarcasmus* < Greek *sarkazein* 'tear flesh' < *sarx* 'flesh']

sarcastic /saar kástik/ *adj* **1.** characterized by words that mean the opposite of what they seem to say and are intended to mock or deride **2.** fond of or habitually using sarcasm —**sarcastically** *adv*

SYNONYMS *sarcastic, ironic, sardonic, satirical, caustic*

CORE MEANING: used to describe remarks that are designed to hurt or mock

sarcastic characterized by words that mean the opposite of what they seem to say and are intended to mock or deride ○ *She cared little for his sarcastic jokes.* ○ *As a politician, he is eloquent and sometimes bitingly sarcastic.* **ironic** deliberately stating the opposite of the truth, usually with the intention of being amusing ○ *The nickname Charles the Bald may not have been descriptive but ironic, implying Charles was exceptionally hairy.* ○ *songs bristling with ironic observation and vivid imagery* **sardonic** disdainfully or cynically mocking ○ *a sardonic smile* ○ *He gradually evolved into a more polished politician – his sardonic humour emerged, his views became more refined.* **satirical** using wit, especially irony, sarcasm, and ridicule, to criticize faults, particularly in the arts or politics ○ *a satirical TV show* ○ *He was a sharp, satirical observer of the social scene.* **caustic** very sarcastic and intended to mock, offend, or belittle somebody ○ *a barrage of caustic editorials* ○ *His caustic style made him the most controversial broadcaster of his time.*

sarcenet /saárssnət/, **sarsenet** *n* a soft delicate silk cloth. Use: formerly, veils, linings, ribbons. [15C. < Old French *sarzinet*]

sarco- *prefix* **1.** striated muscle ○ *sarcolemma* **2.** flesh ○ *sarcoid* [< Greek *sark-*, stem of *sarx* 'flesh' < Indo-European, 'cut, tear']

sarcodinian /saárkə dínni ən/ *adj* belonging to the class of protozoans that includes amoebas ■ *n* a protozoan that belongs to the same class as amoebas [< modern Latin *Sarcodina* < Greek *sarkōdēs* 'fleshy' < *sarx* 'flesh']

sarcoid /saár koyd/ *n* a small area of chronic infection in the body of a person affected by sarcoidosis ■ *adj* relating to or resembling flesh

sarcoidosis /saár koy dōssiss/ *n* a disease in which lumps of fibrous tissue and collections of cells (**granulomas**) appear on the skin and internal organs

sarcolactic acid /saárkō láktik-/ *n* a form of lactic acid produced by muscle tissue during anaerobic activity

sarcolemma /saárkō lémmə/ (*plural* **-mas** or **-mata** /-lémmətə/) *n* a thin clear membrane that covers a striated muscle fibre

sarcoma /saar kṓmə/ (*plural* **-mas** or **-mata** /-mətə/) *n* a malignant tumour that begins growing in connective tissue such as muscle, bone, fat, or cartilage. Sarcomas may occur in any part of the body, and are typically fast-growing and quick to

spread. —**sarcomatoid** *adj* —**sarcomatosis** /saar kṓmə tṓssiss/ *n* —**sarcomatous** *adj*

sarcomere /sáarkō meer/ *n* a segment of a fibril of striated muscle

sarcophagus /saar kóffəgəss/ (*plural* -**gi** /-gī/ or -**guses**) *n* an ancient stone or marble coffin, often decorated with sculpture and inscriptions [Early 17C. Via Latin < Greek *sarkophagos* 'flesh-eater']

sarcoplasm /sáarkō plazəm/ *n* the cytoplasm of a striated muscle fibre —**sarcoplasmic** /saárkō plázmik/ *adj* —**sarcoplasmous** /saárkō plázməss/ *adj*

sarcoplasmic reticulum *n* the endoplasmic reticulum of a striated muscle fibre that regulates the concentration of calcium ions in the cell cytoplasm

sarcoptic mange /saar kóptik-/ *n* a form of mange caused by a parasitic mite that burrows into the skin [< modern Latin *Sarcoptes*, genus of mites < Greek *sarx* 'flesh' + *koptein* 'cut']

sarcous /sáarkəss/ *adj* consisting of or relating to flesh or muscle tissue

sard /saard/ *n* a deep orange-red variety of chalcedony. Use: jewellery. [15C. < Latin *sarda* < Greek *sardios*]

Sardanapalus /saárdə náppələss/ (*fl* 7th century BC) legendary Assyrian monarch. He was reputedly the last Assyrian king and died in a fire in his palace during an enemy siege. He is probably an amalgam of several Assyrian rulers.

sardar /sər daár/ *n* POL, MIL same as **sirdar** [Late 16C. < Persian, Urdu *sardār*, 'holding the position of chief']

sardine /saar deén/ *n* **1.** a small sea fish related to the herring, especially the European pilchard. Sardines are netted in large numbers for food and preserved in cans, packed tightly in oil. Latin name: *Sardinia pilchardus*. **2.** the flesh of a sardine as food, usually preserved in cans, packed tightly in oil [15C. Via French < Latin *sardina* < Latin *Sardō* 'Sardinia'] ◇ **be packed like sardines** to be crowded closely together

Sardinia /saar dínni ə/ Italian island in the Mediterranean Sea. It is the second largest island in the Mediterranean after Sicily. Capital: Cagliari. Population: 1,659,466 (1995). Area: 23,813 sq. km/9,194 sq. mi. —**Sardinian** *adj*, *n*

Sardis /sáardiss/ ancient city of Asia Minor, in present-day Turkey. It was the capital city of Lydia and an early seat of Christianity.

sardius /sáardi əss/ *n* CRYSTALS same as **sard** [15C. < Latin < *sarda* (see SARD)]

sardonic /saar dónnik/ *adj* disdainfully or cynically mocking [Mid-17C. < French *sardonique*, alteration of obsolete *sardonien* < Latin *sardonios* < Greek *sardanios* 'scornful'] —**sardonically** *adv* —**sardonicism** *n*

SYNONYMS See *sarcastic*.

sardonyx /sáardəniks/ *n* a variety of onyx with alternating bands of light orange-brown and white chalcedony. Use: formerly, cameos. [14C. Via Latin < Greek *sardonux*, literally 'sard onyx']

saree *n* CLOTHING another spelling of **sari**

sargasso /saar gássō/ *n* MARINE BIOL same as **gulfweed** [Late 16C. < Portuguese *sargaço*]

Sargasso Sea /saar gássō-/ section of the North Atlantic Ocean, between the Greater Antilles and the Azores. It is noted for its predominantly still waters. Area: 5,200,000 sq. km/2,000,000 sq. mi.

sargasso weed *n* PLANTS same as **gulfweed**

sargassum /saar gássəm/ *n* PLANTS same as **gulfweed** [Early 20C. < modern Latin < SARGASSO]

sargassum fish *n* a brown and black fish that lives in floating gulfweed. Native to: Atlantic and western Pacific oceans. Latin name: *Histrio histrio*.

sarge /saarj/ *n* a sergeant in the armed forces or police (*informal*) [Mid-19C. Shortening]

John Singer Sargent

Sargent /sáarjənt/, **John Singer** (1856–1925) Italian-born US artist. Possessing a brilliant technique, he was known for oil portraits of well-known people, e.g. *Madame Gautreau* (1883–84). He later turned to watercolours.

'Every time I paint a portrait I lose a friend.'
[John Singer Sargent, *Treasury of Humorous Quotations*, N. Bentley and E. Esar; 1951]

Sargeson /sáarjəss'n/, **Frank** (1903–82) New Zealand writer. His short-story collections include *A Man and His Wife* (1940). Pseudonym of **Davey, Norris Frank**

Sargodha /saar gṓdə/ city in Punjab Province, Pakistan, about 177 km/110 mi. northwest of Lahore. Population: 291,361 (1981).

Sargon II /sáargon/ (763?–705 BC) king of Assyria. During his reign (721–705 BC) he extended the Assyrian empire through a series of military campaigns and deported thousands of Israelites.

sari

sari /sáari/, **saree** *n* a garment, traditionally worn by South Asian women, consisting of a long rectangle of fabric reaching the feet, wrapped and pleated around the waist over an underskirt and short-sleeved fitted top (**choli**), and draped over the shoulder [Late 18C. Via Hindi *saṛī* < Sanskrit *śāṭī* 'garment']

sarin /sáarin, sárrin/ *n* an extremely toxic gas that attacks the central nervous system, causing convulsions and death. It has been used for chemical warfare. Formula: $C_4H_{10}FO_2P$. [Mid-20C. < German]

Sark /saark/ one of the Channel Islands, in the English Channel, forming a dependency of Guernsey. It comprises Great Sark and Little Sark, linked to each other by a narrow isthmus. Population: 550 (1996). Area: 5 sq. km/2 sq. mi.

sarking /sáarking/ *n* N England, Scotland, NZ planks of wood nailed to the rafters of a building to support a slate or tile roof [15C. < dialect *sark* 'shirt' < Germanic]

sarky /sáarki/ (**sarkier, sarkiest**) *adj* sarcastic in tone or manner (*informal*) [Early 20C. Shortening of SARCASTIC]

sarmentose /saar mént ōss/, **sarmentous** /-təss/ *adj* producing long slender stems that reach out and take root along the ground [Mid-18C. < Latin *sarmentosus* 'full of twigs' < *sarmentum* 'twig']

sarmie /sáarmi/ *n* S Africa same as **sandwich** *n* (sense 1) (*informal*) [Late 20C. Probably alteration]

Sarnia /sáarni ə/ city at the southern tip of Lake Huron, on the St Clair River, Ontario, Canada. Population: 78,577 (2001).

sarnie /sáarni/ *n* same as **sandwich** *n* (sense 1) (*informal*) [Mid-20C. Probably alteration]

sarod /sa rṓd/ *n* a stringed instrument of northern South Asia that resembles a lute with two resonating gourds [Mid-19C. Via Urdu < Persian *sarūd*]

sarong

sarong /sə róng/ *n* **1.** TRADITIONAL MALAYSIAN GARMENT a traditional Malayan and Javanese garment for men or women, consisting of a length of fabric wrapped and tied around the body at the waist or under the arms **2.** FASHION VERSION OF SARONG a fashion version of the sarong worn by a woman as a wrapped skirt, often for the beach **3.** CLOTH FOR MALAYSIAN GARMENTS cloth for a sarong, often brightly coloured [Mid-19C. < Malay, 'covering']

Saronic Gulf /sə rónnik-/ gulf of the Aegean Sea, on the coast of southeastern Greece

saros /sáir oss/ *n* the cycle of 6,585.32 days, or approximately 18 years 11 days, after which a sequence of eclipses of the Sun and Moon repeats itself. It was known to the Babylonians and some other ancient civilizations. [Early 19C. Via Greek < Babylonian *sāru* 'the number 3,600'] —**saronic** /sə rónnik/ *adj*

sarpanch /sər púnch/ *n* S Asia the head of a village council (**panchayat**) [Mid-20C. < Hindi, Urdu < *sar* 'head' + *panch* 'five']

sarracenia /sárrə seéni ə/ (*plural* -**as** or same) *n* a pitcher plant with hollow tubular leaves that trap insects. Native to: eastern North America. Genus: *Sarracenia*. [Mid-18C. < modern Latin, after D. *Sarrazin*, 17C North American botanist]

sarrusophone /sə roózə fōn/ *n* a woodwind musical instrument resembling a bassoon but made of brass [Late 19C. After Pierre-Auguste *Sarrus* (1813–76), French bandmaster]

SARS /saarz/ *n* a serious respiratory illness that is caused by a coronavirus and often develops into pneumonia. It was first reported in Asia in 2003 and includes symptoms such as high fever and aching limbs. Full form **severe acute respiratory syndrome**

sarsaparilla /saárspə ríllə/ (*plural* -**las** or same) *n* **1.** MEDICINAL ROOT the dried root of a tropical creeper or temperate plant. Use: traditional or herbal medicine, soft drink. **2.** SOFT DRINK a carbonated drink flavoured with sarsaparilla root **3.** TROPICAL VINE a tropical vine with aromatic roots and heart-shaped leaves. Native to: America. Genus: *Smilax*. **4.** PLANT LIKE SARSAPARILLA VINE a plant similar to the sarsaparilla vine. Genera: *Aralia* or *Smilax*. [Late 16C. < Spanish *zarzaparrilla* < *zarza* 'bramble' + *parra* 'vine']

sarsen /sáarssn/ *n* any large sedimentary rock that has been broken into blocks by frost action and is found on the chalk downs of southern England [Late 17C. Alteration of SARACEN]

sarsenet *n* TEXTILES another spelling of **sarcenet**

sartor /sáartər/ *n* same as **tailor** *n* (sense 1) (*archaic*) [Mid-17C. < Latin < *sart-* past participle of *sarcire* 'patch']

sartorial /saar táwri əl/ *adj* **1.** relating to tailoring or clothing in general **2.** relating to the sartorius muscle in the thigh

sartorius /saar táwri əss/ (*plural* -**rii** /-ri ī/) *n* a flat narrow muscle that extends from the hip to the inner thigh and helps rotate the leg to a cross-legged position. It is the longest muscle in the human body. [Early 18C. < modern Latin *musculus sartorius* 'tailor's muscle' < *sartor* (see SARTOR)]

Jean-Paul Sartre

Sartre /saártrə/, **Jean-Paul** (1905–80) French philosopher, playwright, and novelist. The principal exponent of existentialism, he wrote *Being and Nothingness* (1943) and the novel *Nausea* (1938).

'Hell is other people.'
[Jean-Paul Sartre, *Huis Clos (In Camera)*; 1944]

'The one and only basis of the moral life must be spontaneity, that is, the immediate, the unreflective.'
[Jean-Paul Sartre, *Notebooks for an Ethics*; 1983]

Sarum /sáirəm/ former name for **Salisbury**

Sarvodaya /saar vṓdəyə/ *n* the name that Mahatma Gandhi and his followers gave to the new social order that they sought to establish in India [Early 20C. < Sanskrit, 'prosperity for all']

SAS *n* a British army regiment that is specially trained to undertake dangerous clandestine operations. Full form **Special Air Service**

SASE *abbr* MAIL self-addressed stamped envelope

sash /sash/ *n* **1.** FABRIC BELT a strip of cloth tied around the waist, e.g. as part of ceremonial dress **2.** WIDE RIBBON WORN ACROSS CHEST a band of cloth draped over one shoulder and across the chest as a symbol of rank or office **3.** FRAME FOR GLASS a frame holding the glass panes of a window or door [Late 17C. < Arabic *šāš* 'muslin']

sashay /sásh ay/ *vi* (-shays, -shaying, -shayed) **1.** FLOUNCE GRACEFULLY to walk in a way that is intended to attract attention, especially by swaying the hips or swinging the elbows (*humorous*) **2.** PERFORM STEPS IN SQUARE DANCING to dance a sequence of gliding or sideways steps in square dancing ■ *n* **1.** DANCE same as **chassé 2.** PATTERN IN SQUARE DANCING a figure in square dancing in which partners circle each other using sideways steps [Mid-19C. Alteration of French *chassé* 'chasing, chase']

sashimi /sáshimi/ *n* a Japanese dish consisting of slices of raw fish, usually served with a dipping sauce, e.g. a seasoned soy sauce. Small quantities of other ingredients such as finely shredded white radish or pickles may also be added as garnishes and palate-refreshing accompaniments. [Late 19C. < Japanese]

sashing /sáshing/ *n* strips of fabric used to separate blocks in a patchwork

sash saw *n* a small saw with a thin blade, used in making window sashes

sash window *n* a window that consists of two frames, one above the other in vertical grooves, allowing either to be opened or shut by sliding it up or down

sasin /sássin/ *n* ZOOL same as **blackbuck**

Sask. *abbr* Saskatchewan

Saskatchewan /sa skáchəwən/ **1.** river in Canada, rising in central Saskatchewan and flowing into Lake Winnipeg, in Manitoba. Length: 550 km/340 mi. **2.** the central Prairie Province of Canada, between Alberta and Manitoba. Capital: Regina. Population: 1,011,800 (2002). Area: 651,036 sq. km/251,366 sq. mi. —**Saskatchewanian** /sə skáchə wáyni ən/ *n, adj*

saskatoon /sáskə toõn/ *n* **1.** a sweet purplish-black fruit **2.** a bush that produces saskatoons. Flowers: white. Native to: northwestern North America.

Latin name: *Amelanchier alnifolia*. [Early 19C. < Cree *misaaskwatoomin* 'amelanchier berry']

Saskatoon /sáskə toõn/ second largest city in Saskatchewan, Canada, 242 km/150 mi. northwest of Regina. Population: 196,211 (2001).

sasquatch /sásk wach, -woch/ *n* same as **Bigfoot** [Early 20C. < Salish]

sass /sass/ *N Am* (*informal*) *vt* (**sasses, sassing, sassed**) to talk disrespectfully or impudently to somebody, especially somebody who is older or in authority ■ *n* disrespectful or impudent remarks, especially in reply to an older person or somebody in authority [Mid-19C. Back-formation < SASSY¹]

sassaby /sássəbi/ (*plural* -**bies**) *n* an antelope that is a type of topi. Native to: southern Africa. Latin name: *Damaliscus lunatus lunatus*. [Early 19C. Alteration of Setswana *tsessébí*]

sassafras /sássə frass/ (*plural same*) *n* **1.** a deciduous tree with aromatic bark, lobed leaves, and small bluish fruits. Native to: eastern North America. Latin name: *Sassafras albidum*. **2.** the dried root bark of the sassafras tree. Use: flavouring, perfumes, medicines. [Late 16C. < Spanish *sasafrás*]

~~sassafrass~~ incorrect spelling of **sassafras**

Sassanid /sássənid/ *n* a member of a Persian dynasty that ruled from AD 224–651. The dynasty superseded the Parthian Empire, and challenged Roman power in the East. It was the last line of Persian kings before the Arab conquests. [Late 18C. After *Sasan*, Persian monarch and grandfather of the first Sassanid] —**Sassanian** /sə sáyni ən/ *adj*

Sassari /sássəri/ capital of Sassari Province, Sardinia, Italy, situated near the northwestern coast of the island. Population: 120,729 (2001).

Sassenach /sássə nak, -nakh/ (*plural* -**nachs**) *n Ireland, Scotland* an offensive term for an English person [Early 18C. Via Gaelic *Sassunach* < Latin *Saxones* 'Saxons' < Germanic]

Sassoon /sə soõn/, **Siegfried** (1886–1967) British poet and novelist. He is known for his searing poems about the horrors of World War I and for his semi-autobiographical fictional trilogy, collected as *The Complete Memoirs of George Sherston* (1937). Full name **Sassoon, Siegfried Lorraine**

'And when the war is done and youth stone dead / I'd toddle safely home and die—in bed.'
[Siegfried Sassoon, 'Base Details'; 1918]

sassy¹ /sássi/ (-**sier**, -**siest**) *adj* **1.** *N Am* IMPUDENT impudent or disrespectful **2.** *N Am* HIGH-SPIRITED lively and high-spirited ○ *The show has refreshingly sassy hoedown-style choreography*. **3.** *US* STYLISH stylish or fashionable ○ *a sassy look for spring* [Mid-19C. Alteration of SAUCY]

sassy² /sássi/ (*plural* -**sies**) *n* a tree with poisonous bark and insect-resistant wood used for building. Native to: West Africa. Latin name: *Erythrophleum suaveolens*. [Mid-19C. Probably < an African language]

sastra *n* HINDUISM another spelling of **shastra**

sastruga /sə stroõgə/ *n* a long wave-shaped ridge of hard snow formed by the wind, common in polar regions [Mid-19C. Via German < Russian *zastruga*]

sat past participle, past tense of **sit**

USAGE See **sit**.

SAT¹ /éss ay teé/ *abbr* EDUC standard assessment task

SAT² /éss ay teé/ *tdmk* a trademark for a standardized test taken by applicants to colleges in the United States. Full form **Scholastic Assessment Test**

Sat. *abbr* CALENDAR Saturday

~~satalite~~ incorrect spelling of **satellite**

Satan /sáyt'n/ *n* in Christianity, the enemy of God, the lord of evil, and the tempter of human beings. He is sometimes identified with Lucifer, the leader of the fallen angels. [Pre-12C. Via Latin and Greek < Hebrew *śāṭān* 'adversary' < *śāṭan* 'accuse']

satang /sa táng/ (*plural same*) *n* a subunit of Thai currency. See table at **currency** [Late 19C. Via Thai < Pali *sata* 'hundred']

satanic /sə tánnik/ *adj* **1.** relating to Satan or the

worship of Satan **2.** extremely evil or cruel —**satanically** *adv*

Satanism /sáyt'nizəm/ *n* the worship of Satan, especially as a parody of Christian rites

satay /sáttay/ *n* a popular Indonesian and Malaysian dish consisting of marinated pieces of meat, chicken, or fish grilled on wooden skewers and served with peanut sauce [Mid-20C. < Malay]

SATB *abbr* MUSIC soprano, alto, tenor, bass

satchel /sáchəl/ *n* a small bag, especially one with shoulder straps used for carrying schoolbooks [14C. Via Old French *sachel* < Latin *sacellus* < *saccus* 'bag']

sate /sayt/ (**sates, sating, sated**) *vt* **1.** to satisfy completely somebody's hunger or some other desire **2.** to provide somebody with more than enough, to the point of exhaustion or disgust [Old English *sadian* < Indo-European]

sateen /sə teén/ *n* a cotton or polyester fabric with a shiny side intended to look like satin [Late 19C. Alteration of SATIN, after VELVETEEN]

~~satelite~~ incorrect spelling of **satellite**

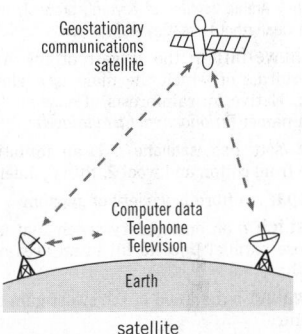
Geostatationary communications satellite
Computer data
Telephone
Television
Earth
satellite

satellite /sáttə līt/ *n* **1.** DEVICE THAT ORBITS PLANET an object put into orbit around Earth or another planet in order to relay communications signals or transmit scientific data **2.** MOON ORBITING OTHER BODY an astronomical object that orbits a larger one **3.** COUNTRY DEPENDENT ON ANOTHER COUNTRY a nation or political unit that is dependent economically and politically on another more powerful nation **4.** SUBURB a town or small city located near and dependent on a larger city **5.** ATTENDANT an attendant of an important person [Mid-16C. Via French < Latin *satellit-* 'attendant']

satellite broadcasting *n* the global transmission of television programmes via satellite

satellite cell *n* one of the cells forming the capsule that encloses the nerve cells in many spinal ganglia

satellite dish *n* a dish-shaped device for receiving television signals broadcast via satellite

satellite DNA *n* a component of an animal's DNA that differs in density from surrounding DNA, consists of short repeating sequences of nucleotide pairs, and does not undergo transcription

satellite link *n* a communications signal or link from a transmitting Earth station to a satellite and back to a receiving Earth station

satellite phone *n* a wireless phone that connects callers via a communications satellite that receives transmissions, then relays them back to Earth

satellite station *n* a radio or television station that receives programmes from another station and re-broadcasts them immediately on a different wavelength

satellite telephone *n* a mobile phone that can send voice messages over extremely long distances via links to communications satellites

satellite television *n* a television service for which the signal is relayed via satellite to be broadcast to customers who have appropriate receiving equipment

satellitium /sáttə lítti əm/ *n* in astrology, a group of planets in one sign of the zodiac

satem /sáatəm/ *adj* relating to Indo-European languages in which the consonant sounding like 'k' developed into the sound 's' or 'sh' [Early 20C. < Avestan, 'hundred']

~~Saterday~~ incorrect spelling of **Saturday**

sati *n* RELIG same as **suttee**

satiate /sáyshi ayt/ *vt* (**-ates, -ating, -ated**) **1. GLUT SOMEBODY** to provide somebody with too much of something desirable, to the point of overindulgence (*often passive*) **2. GRATIFY DESIRE** to satisfy hunger or another appetite completely ■ *adj* **HAVING TOO MUCH** having had enough or too much [15C. < Latin *satiat-*, past participle of *satiare* < *satis* 'enough'] —**satiable** *adj* —**satiation** /sáyshi áysh'n/ *n*

Satie /saáti/, **Erik** (1866–1925) French composer. His light, innovative ballets, dramas, and piano pieces influenced Maurice Ravel, Claude Debussy, and the composers known as Les Six. Full name **Satie, Erik Alfred Leslie**

satiety /sə tī əti/ *n* a state in which somebody has had enough or too much [Mid-16C. Via French < Latin *satietas* < *satis* 'enough']

satin /sáttin/ *n* **GLOSSY SILK OR RAYON FABRIC** a fabric woven of silk or rayon, with a smooth glossy finish and a dull back ■ *adj* **1. OF SATIN** made of satin fabric **2. GLOSSY LIKE SATIN** smooth and glossy like satin [14C. Via French < Arabic *zaytūnī* 'of Zaytun', probably the Chinese city of Quangzhou] —**satiny** *adj*

satin bowerbird *n* the largest of the Australian bowerbirds, of which the male is a glossy blue-black. Native to: rainforests of eastern Australia. Latin name: *Ptilonorhynchus violaceus*.

satinet /sátti nét/, **satinette** *n* **1.** an imitation satin made from cotton and wool **2.** thin or inferior satin

satin spar *n* a fibrous variety of gypsum

satin stitch *n* an embroidery stitch that is worked in close parallel lines to fill in an area or form a solid line

satin walnut *n* the wood of the sweet gum tree. Use: furniture.

satin weave *n* a weave in which the face of the fabric is covered entirely with warp threads, producing a smooth finish

satinwood /sáttin wŏŏd/ *n* **1. WOOD FROM S ASIAN TREE** a smooth hard yellow-brown wood. Use: furniture making. **2. S ASIAN TREE** a deciduous tree with hard yellow-brown wood. Native to: South Asia. Latin name: *Chloroxylon swietenia*. **3. CARIBBEAN TREE** an evergreen tree with smooth lustrous wood. Native to: Caribbean. Latin name: *Zanthoxylum flavum*.

satire /sáttīr/ *n* **1.** the use of wit, especially irony, sarcasm, and ridicule, to criticize faults **2.** a literary work that uses satire, or the branch of literature made up of such works [Early 16C. Directly or via French < Latin *satira* 'poetic medley, satire']

satirical /sə tírrik'l/, **satiric** /sə tírrik/ *adj* using wit, especially irony, sarcasm, and ridicule, to criticize faults —**satirically** *adv*

SYNONYMS See *sarcastic*.

satirise *vt* another spelling of **satirize**

satirist /sáttərist/ *n* a writer or performer of satires

satirize /sáttə rīz/ (**-rizes, -rizing, -rized**), **satirise** (**-rises, -rising, -rised**) *vt* to attack or criticize somebody or something by means of satire —**satirization** /sáttə rī záysh'n/ *n* —**satirizer** *n*

satisfaction /sáttiss fáksh'n/ *n* **1. GRATIFICATION** the feeling of pleasure that comes when a need or desire is fulfilled ○ *job satisfaction* **2. HAPPINESS WITH ARRANGEMENT** happiness with the way that something has been arranged or done ○ *was organized to her satisfaction* **3. COMPENSATION** compensation for an injury or loss ○ *demanded satisfaction for their mistreatment* **4. FULFILMENT** the fulfilment of a need, claim, or desire ○ *the satisfaction of their hunger* [14C. Via French < Latin *satisfaction-* < past participle of *satisfacere* (see SATISFY)]

satisfactory /sáttiss fáktəri/ *adj* good enough to meet a requirement or to be considered acceptable [15C. Directly or via French < medieval Latin *satisfactorius* < past participle of Latin *satisfacere* (see SATISFY)] —**satisfactorily** *adv*

satisfy /sáttiss fī/ (**-fies, -fying, -fied**) *v* **1.** *vt* **CONTENT SOMEBODY** to do or offer enough to make somebody feel pleased or content **2.** *vti* **FULFIL NEED** to fulfil a need or gratify a desire **3.** *vt* **MEET CONDITION** to achieve or be of sufficient standard to meet a requirement or condition **4.** *vt* MATHS **SOLVE MATHEMATICAL PROBLEM** to make both sides of an equation equal by finding the values of the unknown variables **5.** *vt* LAW **PAY DEBT** to pay a debt in full **6.** *vt* **COMPENSATE SOMEBODY** to compensate somebody for an injury or loss [15C. Via Old French *satisfier* < Latin *satisfacere* < *satis* 'enough' + *facere* 'make'] —**satisfied** *adj* —**satisfier** *n* —**satisfyingly** *adv*

Sato Eisaku /saátō áyss akoo, -ay saákoo/ (1901–75) prime minister of Japan (1964–72). He was awarded the Nobel Peace Prize (1974) for his role in negotiating a nuclear nonproliferation pact.

satori /sə táwri/ *n* in Zen Buddhism, a state of spiritual enlightenment that is a spiritual objective [Early 18C. < Japanese, 'awakening']

SAT phone /sát-/ *n* TELECOM same as **satellite telephone** (*informal*)

satrap /sáttrap/ *n* **1.** in ancient Persia, the governor of a province **2.** a subordinate official, especially a self-important one [15C. Via French and Latin < Old Persian *kšathrapāvā* 'protector of the country']

satrapy /sáttrəpi/ (*plural* **-pies**) *n* in ancient Persia, a province or territory governed by a satrap

satsuma /sat sṓmə/ *n* **1.** a cultivated variety of mandarin orange, with a thin orange skin **2.** a citrus tree that bears satsumas. Native to: Japan. Latin name: *Citrus reticulata*. [Late 19C. After *Satsuma*, province in Kyushu, Japan]

Satsuma ware, **Satsuma** *n* cream-coloured Japanese pottery [After a province in Kyushu, Japan]

~~sattelite~~ incorrect spelling of **satellite**

saturant /sáchərənt/ *n* a substance that is used to saturate another substance ■ *adj* causing saturation [Mid-18C. < Latin *saturant-*, present participle of *saturare* (see SATURATE)]

saturate *vt* /sáchə rayt/ (**-rates, -rating, -rated**) **1. MAKE SOMETHING WET** to soak something with liquid **2. FILL SOMETHING COMPLETELY** to fill something with so many people or things that no more can be added **3.** COMM **SUPPLY MARKET FULLY** to supply a market fully, so that all existing demand for a product is met **4.** CHEM **FILL SOLUTION WITH ANOTHER SUBSTANCE** to add as much of a liquid, solid, or gas to a solution as it can absorb at a given temperature **5.** MIL **BOMB ENEMY HEAVILY** to overwhelm an enemy with intensive bombing ■ *adj* /sáchərət/ **SATURATED** saturated with liquid (*archaic*) [Mid-16C. < Latin *saturat-*, past participle of *saturare* < *satur* 'satiated'] —**saturable** *adj*

saturated /sáchə raytid/ *adj* **1. WET** soaked with liquid **2. PACKED FULL** completely packed or full so that no more can be added **3.** CHEM **CONTAINING MAXIMUM SOLUTE** containing the maximum amount of solute that can be absorbed at a given temperature **4.** CHEM **CONTAINING SINGLE BONDS BETWEEN CARBON ATOMS** containing only single bonds between carbon atoms

SYNONYMS See *wet*.

saturated fat *n* a fat in which the carbon atoms are fully hydrogenated, found in animal products. A diet heavy in saturated fat is thought to raise cholesterol in the bloodstream.

saturation /sáchə ráysh'n/ *n* **1. STATE OF TOTAL WETNESS** a state in which something is completely soaked with liquid **2. STATE OF BEING PACKED FULL** a state in which something is so full or packed that no more can be added **3.** MIL **HEAVY BOMBING** intensive bombing of a military target in order to overwhelm an enemy **4.** COMM **FULL SUPPLYING OF MARKET** the full supplying of a commercial market, to the point where all existing demand for a product is met **5.** CHEM **MAXIMUM ABSORPTION** the absorption of the greatest possible amount of a liquid, solid, or gas by a solution at a given temperature **6.** PHYS **STATE OF MAGNETIZATION** a state of complete magnetization **7.** METEOROL **100 PER CENT HUMIDITY** the condition of the atmosphere when it contains as much water vapour as it can hold at a specific temperature **8.** PHYS **COLOUR INTENSITY** the intensity of a colour **9.** ELECTRONICS **CONDITION OF STABLE OUTPUT CURRENT** a condition where the output current of an electronic device is substantially constant and no longer increases as a function of increasing input ■ *adj* **COMPREHENSIVE** comprehensive in the use of outlets or other resources ○ *The event had saturation coverage in the press.*

saturation diving *n* a method of diving in which the diver's bloodstream is saturated with an inert gas so that the time required for decompression is unaffected by the duration of the dive

saturation point *n* **1.** the point at which no more can be added **2.** the point at which the greatest possible amount of a substance has been absorbed by a solution at a given temperature

saturation zone *n* the zone below the water table that is saturated with ground water

Saturday /sáttər day, -di/ *n* the day of the week after Friday and before Sunday [Pre-12C. Contraction of *Saturn's day*, translation of Latin *Saturni dies*]

Saturday night special *n US* a small cheap handgun that is easy to obtain and conceal (*informal*) [Because the guns are most often used in the types of crime that typically occur on a Saturday night]

Saturdays /sáttər dayz, -diz/ *adv* every Saturday

Saturn /sáttərn/ *n* **1.** the second-largest planet in the solar system and the sixth planet from the Sun. It has bright rings made up of orbiting fragments of rock. **2.** in Roman mythology, the god of agriculture and ruler of the universe during the Golden Age. Greek equivalent **Cronus** [Pre-12C. < Latin *Saturnus*] —**Saturnian** /sa túrni ən/ *adj*

saturnalia /sáttər náyli ə/ (*plural* **-as** or *same*) *n* a wild celebration or orgy [Late 18C. < SATURNALIA]

Saturnalia /sáttər náyli ə/ *npl* an ancient Roman festival of feasting and revelry in celebration of the god Saturn and the winter solstice. Date: mid-December. [Late 16C. < Latin < *Saturnus* 'Saturn']

saturniid /sa túrni id/ *n* a large brightly coloured moth with a hairy body. Family: Saturniidae. [Late 19C. < modern Latin *Saturniidae* < Latin *Saturnus* 'Saturn']

saturnine /sáttər nīn/ *adj* gloomy and morose [15C. Directly or via French < medieval Latin *saturninus* < Latin *Saturnus* 'Saturn'] —**saturninely** *adv*

satyagraha /sut yaágrəhə/ *n* the doctrine of nonviolent resistance originated by Mohandas Gandhi and used in the opposition to British rule in India [Early 20C. < Sanskrit *satyāgrahaḥ* 'force born out of truth']

satyagrahi /sut yaágrəhi/ *n* a practitioner of nonviolent resistance or satyagraha [Early 20C. < Sanskrit *satyāgrahī*]

satyr /sáttər/ *n* **1. HALF-MAN, HALF-GOAT** in Greek mythology, a wood-dwelling creature with the head and body of a man and the ears, horns, and legs of a goat. Satyrs were characterized as being fond of lechery and drunken merriment. Roman equivalent **faun 2. MAN DISPLAYING INAPPROPRIATE SEXUAL BEHAVIOUR** a man who displays inappropriate or excessively sexual behaviour **3.** INSECTS **BUTTERFLY** a brown or grey butterfly with spotted wings. Family: Satyridae. [14C. Via French < Latin *satyrus* < Greek *saturos*] —**satyric** /sə tírrik/ *adj* —**satyrical** *adj*

satyriasis /sáttə rī́ əssiss/ *n* excessive and uncontrollable sexual desire in a man

satyrid /sə teérid/ *n* a small brown butterfly. Family: Satyridae.

satyr play *n* in ancient Greece, a comic play that mocked a mythological subject and included a chorus of satyrs

sauce /sawss/ *n* **1. FLAVOURING LIQUID FOR FOOD** a thick liquid that is served with food to add extra flavour **2.** *N Am* **STEWED FRUIT** stewed fruit served with a meal ○ *cranberry sauce* **3. ZEST** something that adds zest or excitement **4. IMPUDENT REMARKS** impudent or disrespectful remarks (*informal*) **5. ALCOHOL** alcoholic drinks (*slang*) ■ *vt* (**sauces, saucing, sauced**) **1. ADD SAUCE TO FOOD** to add flavour to food using a sauce **2. ENLIVEN SOMETHING** to add zest or interest to something **3. SPEAK TO SOMEBODY DISRESPECTFULLY** to make impudent or disrespectful remarks to somebody (*informal*) [14C. Via French < Latin *salsus*, past participle of *sallere* 'to salt' < *sal* 'salt']

sauce boat

sauce boat *n* a low boat-shaped jug used for serving sauce or gravy

saucepan /sáwspən/ *n* a cooking pot with a handle, used on top of a cooker

saucer /sáwssər/ *n* 1. a small shallow dish designed to hold a matching cup 2. anything circular and shallow like a saucer

saucy /sáwssi/ (-ier, -iest) *adj* 1. CHEEKY showing a lack of respect 2. PERT cheerfully pert ○ *a hat at a saucy angle* 3. SEXUALLY EXPLICIT intended to be amusingly vulgar, especially in sexual innuendo ○ *a range of saucy postcards* —**saucily** *adv* —**sauciness** *n*

Saud[1] /sowd, saa oód/ ♦ **Ibn Saud, Abdul Aziz**

Saud[2] /sowd, saa oód/ (1902–69) king of Saudi Arabia. The son of King Ibn Saud, he ruled (1953–64) until he was peacefully deposed and replaced by his brother Faisal.

Saudi /sówdi, sáwdi/ *n* somebody who comes from Saudi Arabia ■ *adj* relating to Saudi Arabia or its people or culture [Mid-20C. After the *Saud* family, the ruling dynasty]

Saudi Arabia

Saudi Arabia /sówdi ə ráybi ə/ country in Southwest Asia, on the Arabian Peninsula. Language: Arabic. Currency: riyal. Capital: Riyadh. Population: 24,293,844 (2003). Area: 2,240,000 sq. km/864,900 sq. mi. Official name **Kingdom of Saudi Arabia** —**Saudi Arabian** *n*, *adj*

sauerbraten /sówər braat'n/ *n* a German dish of beef marinated and cooked in vinegar [Late 19C. < German, 'sour roast meat']

sauerkraut /sów ər krowt/ *n* a German dish of shredded cabbage fermented in its own juice with salt [Mid-17C. < German, 'sour cabbage']

sauger /sáwgər/ *n* a freshwater fish similar to but smaller than a walleyed pike and valued in sport fishing. Native to: North America. Latin name: *Stizostedion canadense*. [Late 19C. Origin ?]

Sauk /sawk/ (*plural same* or **Sauks**), **Sac** /sak/ (*plural same* or **Sacs**) *n* 1. a member of a Native North American people who lived in Wisconsin, Illinois, and Iowa and who now live mainly in Oklahoma. The Sauk joined with the Fox to fight in the Black Hawk War of 1832, following US attempts to move the Fox from their lands in Illinois. 2. the Algonquian language of the Sauk people, related to Fox [Early 18C. Via Canadian French *Saki* < Ojibwa *osāki*] —**Sauk** *adj*

Saul /sawl/ (*fl* 11th century BC) Israelite monarch, mentioned in the Bible (1 Samuel 8–15). He defeated the Philistines but later died in battle against them. He was succeeded by his son-in-law, David.

sault /soo, sō/ *n N Am* a waterfall or rapids [14C. Via French < Latin *saltus* 'leap' < *salire* 'to leap']

Sault Sainte Marie /soo sənt mə reé/ 1. city in northern Michigan, opposite Sault Sainte Marie, Ontario. Population: 14,264 (2002 estimate). 2. city in Ontario, Canada, between Lakes Superior and Huron, on the St Marys River. Population: 67,384 (2001).

sauna /sáwnə/ *n* 1. a bath involving a spell in a hot steamy room followed by a plunge into cold water or a light brushing with birch or cedar boughs 2. a room designed or prepared for having a sauna [Late 19C. < Finnish]

saunf /sawnf/ *n S Asia* aniseed used as a flavouring, snack, or mouth freshener after food [< Hindi *saūph*]

saunter /sáwntər/ *vi* (-ters, -tering, -tered) STROLL to walk at an easy unhurried pace ■ *n* 1. EASY PACE an easy unhurried pace ○ *walk at a saunter* 2. SLOW WALK a slow leisurely walk ○ *go for a saunter round the grounds* [Mid-17C. Origin ?] —**saunterer** *n*

saurel /sáwrəl/ *n US* FISH same as **horse mackerel** [Late 19C. < French < late Latin *saurus* < Greek *sauros* 'lizard, horse mackerel']

saurian /sáwri ən/ *n* any of a former suborder of reptiles that included all lizards. Suborder: Sauria. ■ *adj* relating to or resembling a lizard [Early 19C. < modern Latin *Sauria* < Latin *saurus* 'lizard' < Greek *sauros*]

saurischian /saw ríski ən/ *n* a dinosaur that had a pelvis like that of a modern lizard. Order: Saurischia. ■ *adj* relating to the saurischians [Late 19C. < modern Latin *Saurischia* 'lizard hip-joint']

~~saurkraut~~ incorrect spelling of **sauerkraut**

sauropod /sáwrō pod/ *n* a gigantic plant-eating dinosaur that had a long neck and tail and a small head. Suborder: Sauropoda. ■ *adj* relating to the sauropods [Late 19C. < modern Latin *Sauropoda* 'lizard foot'] —**sauropodous** /saw róppədəss/ *adj*

saury /sáwri/ (*plural* -ries) *n* a small offshore fish resembling a needlefish but with shorter jaws and a series of small fins behind the dorsal and anal fins. Native to: tropical and temperate seas. Family: Scomberosocidae. [Late 18C. < modern Latin *saurus* 'lizard' < Greek *sauros*]

sausage /sóssij/ *n* 1. a tube of animal intestine or another tube-shaped casing stuffed with finely chopped pork or other meat 2. FOOD same as **sausagemeat** [15C. Via Old French *saussiche* < medieval Latin *salsicius* 'made by salting' < Latin *salsus* (see SAUCE)] ◇ **not a sausage** nothing at all (*informal*)

sausage dog *n* BREED same as **dachshund** (*informal*)

sausagemeat /sóssij meet/ *n* seasoned minced pork, usually mixed with fat and bread or cereal. It can be encased in pastry in a sausage roll or encase an egg in a Scotch egg.

sausage roll *n* a short length of sausagemeat wrapped in pastry and baked

sausage tree *n* a tree with long hard-shelled fruits that hang down on very long stalks. Flowers: large, red, bell-shaped. Native to: tropical Africa. Latin name: *Kigelia pinnata*.

Saussure /sō syoor, -soor/, **Ferdinand de** (1857–1913) Swiss linguist. His masterwork, *Course in General Linguistics* (1916), was assembled from his students' lecture notes. He is considered the founder of structural linguistics, structuralism, and semiotics.

sauté /sō tay/ *vt* (-tés, -téing, -téed) FRY SOMETHING LIGHTLY to cook food quickly and lightly in a little butter, oil, or fat ■ *n* SAUTÉED DISH a dish consisting of food, usually meat, that has been sautéed and prepared with a sauce ■ *adj* COOKED LIGHTLY cooked by being sautéed [Early 19C. < French, past participle of *sauter* 'leap' < Latin *salire*]

Sauternes /sō túrn/ (*plural same*), **sauternes** *n* a sweet white wine from southwestern France [Early 18C. After a French region]

sauve qui peut /sóv kee pó/ *n* a disordered or panicked escape [< French, 'save who can']

Sauvignon Blanc /sō veen yon blaáN/ *n* 1. a typically light white wine made from a white grape originally grown in west-central France 2. a white grape variety. Use: to make Sauvignon Blanc. [< French, 'white Sauvignon']

sav /sav/ *n Aus* FOOD same as **saveloy** (*informal*) [Mid-20C. Shortening]

savage /sávvij/ *adj* 1. VIOLENT unrestrained, violent, or vicious 2. BRUTAL brutal and severe ○ *savage cuts in funding* 3. UNDOMESTICATED living wild, beyond the control of people ○ *savage beasts* 4. OFFENSIVE TERM an offensive term meaning relating to a culture that is unfamiliar and perceived as inferior, especially one not using complex modern technologies ■ *n* 1. VICIOUS OR VIOLENT PERSON somebody who enjoys treating people and animals cruelly and violently 2. OFFENSIVE TERM an offensive term for a member of a people considered inferior to or not as advanced as your own group ■ *vt* (-ages, -aging, -aged) 1. ATTACK SOMEBODY OR SOMETHING VIOLENTLY to attack somebody or something violently, viciously, and without restraint 2. CRITICIZE SOMEBODY OR SOMETHING CRUELLY to criticize somebody or something cruelly and unrestrainedly ○ *The same critics who praised her first book savaged her second.* [13C. Via French *sauvage* < Latin *silvaticus* 'wild' < *silva* 'forest'] —**savagely** *adv* —**savageness** *n*

USAGE The use of *savage* to refer to peoples not using complex modern technologies and with an unfamiliar culture was a feature of 19th-century and earlier English (*Vouchsafe to show the sunshine of your face, that we, like savages, may worship it*, Shakespeare, *Love's Labour's Lost* Act 5, scene 2) but is regarded as inappropriate and offensive in current use.

Savage, **Michael Joseph** (1872–1940) Australian-born prime minister of New Zealand (1935–40). He won a landslide victory to become the country's first Labour Party prime minister. See table at **prime minister**

savagery /sávvijəri/ *n* 1. barbarity or violent cruelty 2. an offensive term for a culture perceived to be inferior to or less advanced than your own

savanna /sə vánnə/, **savannah** *n* a flat grassland, sometimes with scattered trees, in a tropical or subtropical region [Mid-16C. Via Spanish *zavana* < Taino]

Savannah /sə vánnə/ 1. river rising in northeastern South Carolina and emptying into the Atlantic Ocean below Savannah, Georgia, United States. Length: 505 km/314 mi. 2. city and seaport in southeastern Georgia, United States, on the Savannah River near its mouth on the Atlantic Ocean. Population: 127,691 (2002 estimate).

savant /sávvənt/ *n* a wise or scholarly person [Early 18C. < French, present participle of *savoir* 'know' < Latin *sapere* 'be wise']

savate /sə vát/ *n* a form of boxing in which kicking as well as hitting is allowed [Mid-19C. < French, originally a kind of shoe]

save[1] /sayv/ *v* (**saves**, **saving**, **saved**) 1. *vt* RESCUE SOMEBODY OR SOMETHING to rescue somebody or something from harm or danger ○ *The entire crew were saved.* 2. *vti* ACCUMULATE MONEY to set aside money for later use, often adding to the sum periodically ○ *She's saving for a new computer.* 3. *vt* CONSERVE SOMETHING to avoid wasting something or using something unnecessarily ○ *take a short-cut to save time* ○ *switched it off to save the batteries* 4. *vt* KEEP SOMETHING BACK FOR LATER to set something aside, keep something back, or protect something so that it can be used later ○ *Save some of the pie for tomorrow.* 5. *vti* REDUCE EXPENSE to reduce or limit the expense of something ○ *Extra insulation helps us to save on fuel.* 6. *vt* COLLECT ITEMS FOR LATER to collect as many items of a particular kind as possible, usually in order to do something with them later ○ *She saves old jam jars for when she makes marmalade.* 7. *vt* SPARE SOMEBODY FROM SOMETHING to make it possible for somebody to be spared from a situation or activity ○ *It will save me from having to decide.* 8. *vt* PRESERVE SOMETHING to treat something carefully or stop using it in order to keep it from being used up or worn out ○ *Switch the radio off to save the batteries.* 9. *vt* COMPUT COPY DATA FOR STORAGE to store a copy of a data file on a storage medium such as a hard drive or disk 10. *vt* SPORTS PREVENT GOAL to prevent a goal from being scored by an opponent 11. *vt* RELIG REDEEM SOMEBODY in some beliefs, to free somebody from the con-

sequences of sin ■ *n* SPORTS **BLOCK** an action that keeps an opponent from scoring [13C. Via French < late Latin *salvare* < Latin *salvus* 'safe']

save[2] /sayv/ *prep, conj* same as **except** (sense 1) ○ *Everyone agreed save one.* [13C. Via Old French *sauf, sauve* < form of Latin *salvus* 'safe']

save-all *n* **1.** a receptacle for catching waste products so that they can be reused **2.** something that prevents waste or loss

save as you earn *n* in the United Kingdom, a savings plan in which monthly deposits are made over a five-year period. The savings are tax-free and they accumulate interest as well as earning a bonus at the end of five years.

saveloy /sávvə loy/ *n* a spicy smoked pork sausage [Mid-19C. Via French *cervelas* < Italian *cervellata* 'sausage']

saver /sáyvər/ *n* **1.** SOMEBODY WHO SAVES MONEY somebody who saves money, especially in a bank or building society account ○ *The fall in interest rates is not such good news for savers.* **2.** SOMETHING THAT CONSERVES RESOURCES something that avoids wasting resources or using them unnecessarily (*used in combination*) ○ *E-mail is a great time-saver.* **3.** CHEAP TRAVEL TICKET an airline, coach, or train ticket that is cheaper than the normal price and usually places a number of restrictions on the date and time of travel ○ *A weekend saver to Leeds, please.*

Savernake Forest /sávvər nayk-/ ancient beech forest near Marlborough in Wiltshire, southwestern England. It was formerly a royal hunting ground. Area: 18 sq. km/7 sq. mi.

Savery /sáyvəri/, **Thomas** (1650?–1715) English engineer and inventor. He patented a method of paddle-wheel propulsion for vessels and a steam pump, and, with Thomas Newcomen, developed a steam piston engine.

Save the Children Fund *n* an organization that provides international aid directed towards children's well-being

Savimbi /sa vímbi/, **Jonas** (1934–2002) Angolan soldier and revolutionary. He was a founder and leader of the independence movement UNITA. After independence, he led UNITA in a long civil war against the ruling MPLA until his death. Full name **Savimbi, Jonas Malheiro**

savin /sávvin/, **savine** *n* an evergreen bush that yields an oil formerly used medicinally and in perfumes. Native to: Europe, northern Asia, North America. Latin name: *Juniperus sabina.* [Pre-12C. Via Old French *savine* < Latin *herba Sabina* 'Sabine plant']

saving /sáyving/ *n* **1.** SOMETHING KEPT FROM BEING USED an amount of time or money that is not spent or used ○ *a saving of ten per cent* **2.** AMOUNT SAVED a particular amount of money saved by buying the equivalent at a lower rate **3.** RESCUE FROM DANGER rescue of somebody or something from harm or danger **4.** LAW LEGAL EXCEPTION an exception or reservation in law ■ **savings** *npl* MONEY SAVED money set aside for future use ■ *prep, conj* same as **except** (sense 1) (*literary*)

USAGE **saving** or **savings**? *Savings* means 'money saved', as in *Substantial savings are essential to a secure retirement.* In this sense it takes a plural verb. In US English, *savings* is commonly used with a singular verb to mean 'a specific amount of money not spent', as in *A savings of $3,000 was gained during the transaction.* This usage undoubtedly has its origins in the well-established expressions *a savings and loan association, a savings bank,* and *a savings account.*

----

saving grace *n* a quality or feature that redeems a person or situation

savings /sáyvingz/ *n US* same as **saving** (sense 2) (*takes a singular verb*)

savings account *n* a bank or building society account that earns interest on money deposited

savings and loan association *n US* a financial institution that issues shares to members who deposit savings and invests the money mainly in home mortgage loans. Members receive interest on their savings in the form of dividends.

savings bank *n* a bank that invests the savings of depositors and pays interest on the deposits

savings bond *n* **1.** a registered bond issued by the US government in denominations of $50 to $10,000. It allows people to earn interest on the savings they entrust to the government in exchange for the bond. **2.** *Can* a bond issued by the Canadian government in denominations of $100 to $100,000. The bond is offered to most working Canadians through a payroll deduction scheme.

savings method *n US* a method of testing memory by assessing how much faster somebody can learn information already previously learned, seen, or read

savings ratio *n* the ratio of national disposable income to consumer spending, used as a measure of national saving

savior *n US* spelling of **saviour**

saviour /sáyvyər/ *n* somebody who rescues somebody or something from harm or danger [13C. Via Old French *sauveour* < ecclesiastical Latin *salvator* < late Latin *salvare* (see SAVE[1])]

Saviour *n* used by Christians as a name for Jesus Christ

savoir-faire /sáv waar fáir/ *n* the ability to act appropriately and adroitly in any situation [Early 19C. < French, 'know how to do']

savoir-vivre /-véevrə/ *n* a combination of worldly wisdom, self-confidence, and refinement in a person [Mid-18C. < French, 'know how to live']

Savonarola /sávvənə rólə/, **Girolamo** (1452–98) Italian religious leader and martyr. He criticized the corruption of the Medici family and Pope Alexander VI and was excommunicated (1497), declared guilty of heresy, and hanged (1498).

> 'Art cannot imitate nature entirely, even if the artist is perfect, because, even if a painter makes something similar to man in everything, yet it will not have life.'
> [Girolamo Savonarola, *Sermon on the Psalm Quam Bonus*; 1493]

savor *n, vti US* spelling of **savour**

savory[1] /sáyvəri/ *n* a herb with aromatic leaves. Use: flavouring food. Latin name: *Satureja hortensis.* [14C. Via Old French *sarree* < Latin *satureia*]

savory[2] /sáyvəri/ *adj, n* (*plural* **-ies**) FOOD US spelling of **savoury**

savour /sáyvər/ *v* (**savours, savouring, savoured**) **1.** *vt* ENJOY SOMETHING UNHURRIEDLY to enjoy something with unhurried appreciation ○ *savour the moment* **2.** *vt* RELISH SOMETHING to enjoy the taste or smell of something **3.** *vi* SHOW TRACES to show traces of something ○ *something in his manner that savoured of deceit* ■ *n* **1.** ENJOYMENT enjoyment and relish **2.** TASTE OR SMELL SOMETHING HAS the way that something tastes or smells **3.** DISTINCTIVE QUALITY a quality that identifies or distinguishes something [12C. Via Old French < Latin *sapor* 'taste' < *sapere* 'have a taste'] —**savourless** *adj* —**savorous** *adj*

savoury /sáyvəri/ *adj* **1.** NOT SWEET salty or sharp-tasting rather than sweet **2.** APPETIZING having an appetizing taste or smell **3.** RESPECTABLE respectable or morally acceptable ○ *not a very savoury character* ■ *n* (*plural* **savouries**) DISH THAT ADDS RELISH a light salty or spicy dish served before or at the end of a meal [13C. < Old French *savoure*, past participle of *savourer* 'taste' < Latin *sapor* (see SAVOUR)] —**savourily** *adv* —**savouriness** *n*

savoy /sə vóy/ *n* a winter cabbage with crinkled leaves [16C. After *Savoy*, region of SE France]

Savoyard /sə vóy aard, sávvoy aárd/ *n* **1.** somebody who comes from the Savoy region of southeastern France **2.** a performer, producer, or admirer of the operettas of W. S. Gilbert and Arthur Sullivan. [Early 17C. < French < *Savoie* 'Savoy'; in sense 2, after the *Savoy* Theatre in London]

savoy cabbage *n* PLANTS, FOOD same as **savoy**

Savoy opera *n* an operetta by Gilbert and Sullivan or a work composed in the same style

savvy /sávvi/ (*informal*) *n* SHREWDNESS shrewdness and practical knowledge ■ *adj* SHREWD shrewd and well informed ■ *vti* (**-vies, -vying, -vied**) COMPREHEND SOMETHING to understand something, especially what somebody has said [Late 18C. < Spanish *sabe (usted)?* 'you know?']

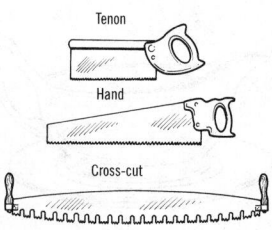

Tenon   Hand   Cross-cut

saw

saw[1] /saw/ *n* TOOL FOR CUTTING WOOD a hand-operated or power-driven tool with a toothed metal blade, used to cut wood or other hard materials ■ *v* (**saws, sawing, sawed, sawed** or **sawn** /sawn/) **1.** *vti* CUT SOMETHING WITH SAW to cut something using a saw **2.** *vt* MOVE FORWARD AND BACK to make back-and-forth motions through something such as the air, as if using a handsaw [Old English *saga* < Indo-European]

SPELLCHECK **saw, soar,** or **sore**? Do not confuse the spelling of *saw, soar,* and *sore,* which may sound similar. *Saw* is a noun denoting a cutting tool with a toothed blade, a verb referring to the use or movement of a saw (as in *saw the plank in half, sawing the air with his arms*), or the past tense of see: *I saw her last week. Soar* is chiefly used as a verb, meaning 'fly high' or 'rise rapidly': *The plane soared into the clouds. Prices are soaring. Sore* is an adjective meaning 'painful' (as in a *sore finger*) or a noun meaning 'a painful area of infection on the skin' (as in *open sores on his arms and legs*).

----

saw[2] /saw/ *n* an old saying, especially a cliché [Old English *sagu* < Germanic]

saw[3] /saw/ past tense of **see**[1]

SAW *abbr* ELECTRONICS surface acoustic wave

sawbill /sáw bil/ *n* ZOOL same as **merganser**

sawbones /sáw bōnz/ (*plural same* or **-boneses**) *n* a surgeon or physician (*slang*) [Mid-19C. < early surgeons' role as amputators]

sawbuck /sáw buk/ *n N Am* **1.** CONSTR same as **sawhorse** **2.** a ten-dollar bill (*slang*) [Mid-19C. < Dutch *zaagbok*; in sense 2, from the resemblance between the X-shaped end of a sawhorse and the Roman numeral for 'ten']

saw doctor *n* **1.** a machine that gives a saw a serrated edge **2.** *NZ* somebody employed to sharpen the blades in a sawmill

sawdust /sáw dust/ *n* tiny particles of wood produced when wood is sawn

sawed-off *adj US* ARMS same as **sawn-off**

sawfish

sawfish /sáw fish/ (*plural same* or **-fishes**) *n* a ray having a long snout with projections resembling teeth that it uses as a weapon. Native to: tropical seas. Family: Pristidae.

sawfly /sáw flī/ (*plural* **-flies**) *n* an insect in which the female has a prominent, often serrated appendage at the tip of its abdomen, for boring holes and laying eggs in wood and plants. Family: Tenthredinidae.

saw grass *n* any of various sedges that have serrated leaves. Genus: *Cladium.*

sawhorse /sáw hawrss/ *n* a support for wood during sawing

sawine /saá wīn/ *n Carib* a Trinidadian dessert consisting of milk with fried vermicelli, spiced with cinnamon, raisins, and other additions, usually made and shared with others during the Muslim festival of Eid al-Fitr [< Urdu, Hindi, contraction of *sivaiyārh* 'noodles']

saw log *n* **1.** LOG BIG ENOUGH TO SAW a log of sufficient size to be suitable for sawing **2.** TREE TRUNK USED FOR TIMBER a trunk of a tree that has been felled and can be cut up into timber **3.** *US* HARVESTABLE LOG a log that meets the minimum commercial requirements of diameter, length, and quality for harvesting

Saw Maung /sow maa oóng/ (1928–97) Myanmar general, who was dictatorial premier of Burma (1988–92). In 1989 he oversaw its renaming as Myanmar.

sawmill /sáw mil/ *n* **1.** a factory in which wood is sawn into planks or boards by machine **2.** a powerful sawing machine

sawn past participle of **saw**¹

sawn-off *adj* **1.** describes a firearm that has the barrel cut short so that it is less cumbersome or obtrusive and its field of fire is increased ○ *a sawn-off shotgun* **2.** an offensive term meaning of small stature (*slang*)

saw palmetto *n* a palm tree with spiny-toothed leafstalks. Native to: southeastern United States. Latin name: *Serenoa repens*.

saw-scaled viper *n* a small venomous snake that lives in dry areas and is believed to have the most powerful venom of all the vipers. Native to: North Africa, central Asia. Latin name: *Echis carinaus*.

saw set *n* an instrument that bends alternating teeth of a saw in opposite directions

Sawtell /saw tél/ coastal town in northeastern New South Wales, Australia. Population: 10,810 (1991).

sawtooth /sáw tooth/ *n* (*plural* **-teeth** /-teeth/) any of the teeth of a saw ■ *adj* in a zigzag shape, like the teeth of a saw

saw-toothed *adj* **1.** having notched teeth like a saw **2.** DESIGN same as **sawtooth**

sawyer /sáw yər/ *n* **1.** SOMEBODY WHO SAWS WOOD somebody who saws wood for a living **2.** HORNED BEETLE a horned beetle whose larvae bore into coniferous trees. Genus: *Monochamus*. **3.** *NZ* NOCTURNAL TREE INSECT a nocturnal insect related to grasshoppers and locusts that lives in holes in trees. Native to: New Zealand. Latin name: *Hemideina*. [13C. < SAW¹ + -*yer*, variant of -IER]

sax /saks/ *n* MUSIC same as **saxophone** (*informal*) [Early 20C. Shortening]

saxatile /sáksə tīl/ *adj* growing on or living in rocks [Mid-17C. < Latin *saxatilis* < *saxum* 'rock']

saxe blue /sáks-/ *adj* of a light greyish-blue colour [Via French < German *Sachsen* 'Saxony'] —**saxe blue** *n*

saxhorn /sáks hawrn/ *n* a valved brass wind instrument, often used in military brass bands [Mid-19C. After Charles Joseph *Sax* (1791–1865) and his son Antoine Joseph *Sax* (1814–94) (known as 'Adolphe'), Belgian instrument makers]

saxicolous /sak síkələss/, **saxicoline** /-līn/ *adj* BIOL same as **saxatile** [Mid-19C. < modern Latin *saxicola* < Latin *saxum* 'rock' + *colere* 'inhabit']

saxifrage /sáksi frayj/ (*plural* **-frages** or *same*) *n* a plant that grows on rocky ground. Flowers: small, white, yellow, purple, or red. Genus: *Saxifraga*. [14C. Via French < Latin *saxifraga* 'rock-breaking' < *saxum* 'rock, stone']

saxitoxin /sáksi tóksin/ *n* a strong neurotoxin found in plankton (**dinoflagellates**) and concentrating in shellfish, causing food poisoning in humans. It is found in red tides. [Mid-20C. < modern Latin *Saxodomus*, genus of clams]

Saxon /sáks'n/ *n* **1.** MEMBER OF ANCIENT GERMANIC PEOPLE a member of a West Germanic people who started to spread west during Roman times, establishing powerful kingdoms with the Angles in southern Britain in the 7th century AD **2.** LANGUAGE OF ANCIENT SAXONS the group of West Germanic dialects spoken by the ancient Saxons **3.** SOMEBODY FROM SAXONY somebody who comes from Saxony [12C. Via French < Latin *Saxones* 'Saxons' < Germanic] —**Saxon** *adj*

Saxon blue *n* a dye made from a solution of indigo in sulphuric acid

Saxonism /sáks'nizəm/ *n* a word, phrase, or idiom in English supposedly from an Anglo-Saxon rather than Latin source

saxony /sáksəni/ *n* **1.** a fine three-ply knitting yarn **2.** a fine woollen fabric. Use: coats. [Mid-19C. After SAXONY]

Saxony /sáksəni/ state in eastern Germany. It was a kingdom until 1918, although part of the North German Confederation from 1866. Between 1945 and 1989 the area was part of East Germany. Capital: Dresden. Population: 4,489,415 (1998). Area: 18,337 sq. km/7,078 sq. mi.

saxophone /sáksə fōn/ *n* a metal wind instrument with keys and a reed that comes in several sizes and registers and is particularly associated with jazz music. The alto and tenor saxophones are the most popular. [Mid-19C. After Antoine Joseph *Sax* (see SAXHORN)] —**saxophonic** /sáksə fónnik/ *adj* —**saxophonist** /sak sóffənist/ *n*

saxtuba /sáks tyoobə/ *n* a large bass saxhorn [Mid-19C. < SAXHORN + TUBA]

say /say/ *v* (**says**, **saying**, **said** /sed/) **1.** *vt* UTTER SOMETHING to utter something in a normal voice, not singing, shouting, or whispering **2.** *vti* EXPRESS VERBALLY to convey information or express feelings in spoken words **3.** *vt* STATE SOMETHING to utter something as a matter of fact, belief, or prediction ○ *was said to be the largest in captivity* **4.** *vt* INDICATE SOMETHING to convey information in written or printed words, numbers, or symbols ○ *The clock said midnight.* ○ *The rules say that you should not kick your opponent.* **5.** *vt* MAKE CASE FOR OR AGAINST SOMETHING to utter something by way of argument, explanation, or excuse ○ *There's much to be said for being rich.* **6.** *vt* COMMAND SOMETHING to utter something as an instruction ○ *said to go* **7.** *vt* SUPPOSE SOMETHING to assume something for the sake of argument, or take something as a suitable example ○ *Let's say we can't afford it.* **8.** *vt* RECITE SOMETHING to utter something that has a formula or set form of words ○ *says his prayers* **9.** *vt* CONVEY SOMETHING INDIRECTLY to convey something over and above the immediate words or superficial sound or appearance ○ *The finale says we can all triumph.* **10.** *vt* CONVEY SOMETHING IMPORTANT to convey something substantial or significant in what is spoken or written ○ *We talked for hours but didn't really say anything.* ■ *n* **1.** CHANCE TO SPEAK a chance or turn to say something, especially to give an opinion ○ *You've already had your say.* **2.** RIGHT TO GIVE OPINION the right to express an opinion and have it considered by others ○ *had no say in the decision* ■ *adv* APPROXIMATELY approximately, or as a possibility or example ○ *if we get, say, three gallons* ■ *interj N Am* (*informal*) **1.** EXPRESSING SURPRISE used to express surprise, admiration, or protest **2.** ATTRACTING ATTENTION used to attract somebody's attention [Old English *secgan* < Germanic] —**sayer** *n* ◇ **easier said than done** used to describe something that is more difficult than it sounds ◇ **enough said** used to indicate that nothing more need be said for a situation to be understood ◇ **I say** (*dated*) **1.** used to express surprise, admiration, or protest **2.** used to attract somebody's attention ◇ **it goes without saying** used to emphasize that there should be no doubt concerning something ◇ **say when** used to ask somebody to indicate when enough drink has been poured or food served (*informal*) ◇ **that is to say** used to indicate that you are repeating something more clearly or in other words ◇ **there's no saying** used to emphasize the uncertainty of a situation ◇ **you can say that again** used to indicate complete agreement with what has just been said (*informal*)

Sayda ▸ **Sidon**

SAYE *abbr* FIN save as you earn

Sayers /sáy ərz/, **Dorothy L.** (1893–1957) British writer. She wrote detective stories, including *Whose Body?* (1923) and *Gaudy Night* (1936). Full name **Sayers, Dorothy Leigh**

> 'The worst sin—perhaps the only sin—passion can commit, is to be joyless.'
> [Dorothy L. Sayers, *Gaudy Night*; 1936]

Dorothy L. Sayers

sayest /sáy əst/, **sayst** /sáyst/ 2nd person singular present of **say** (*archaic*)

saying /sáy ing/ *n* a frequently offered piece of advice or information, or a frequently heard reflection on the way things are

sayonara /sī ə naárə/ *interj US* same as **goodbye** (*informal*) [Late 19C. < Japanese, 'if it be so']

say-so *n* (*informal*) **1.** AUTHORIZATION permission or authorization from somebody **2.** ASSERTION a mere assertion by somebody that something is so **3.** AUTHORITY the right to decide something

sayyid /sī yid/, **sayid**, **said** *n* **1.** a Muslim who claims to be descended from Muhammad's grandson Husain **2.** an Islamic title of respect for a man [Mid-17C. < Arabic, 'prince']

sb *abbr* ONLINE Solomon Islands (*used in Internet addresses*) See table at **domain name**

Sb *symbol* CHEM ELEM antimony [Abbreviation of Latin *stibium*]

SB *abbr* BROADCAST simultaneous broadcast

SBA *n* a system of radio navigation that provides an aircraft with lateral guidance and marker beam indicators at set points during its landing approach. Full form **standard beam approach**

S band *n* a microwave band in the 2655–3353 MHz range, used in radio astronomy and satellite communications

SbE *abbr* south by east

S-bend *n* an S-shaped bend in a road or a pipe

SBS *abbr* **1.** HEALTH sick building syndrome **2.** MIL Special Boat Service **3.** *Aus* Special Broadcasting Service

SBU *abbr* strategic business unit

SbW *abbr* south by west

sc¹ *abbr* Seychelles (*used in Internet addresses*) See table at **domain name**

sc², **s.c.** *abbr* PRINTING small capital

Sc *symbol* CHEM ELEM scandium

SC *abbr* **1.** POL Security Council **2.** MIL Signal Corps

sc. *abbr* **1.** LITERAT, THEATRE scene **2.** scilicet. **3.** MEASURE scruple

s/c *abbr* self-contained (*used in advertisements*)

scab /skab/ *n* **1.** CRUST OVER HEALING WOUND a hard crust of dried blood, serum, or pus that forms over a wound during healing **2.** STRIKEBREAKER somebody who continues to work or replaces a worker during a strike (*disapproving*) **3.** VET SKIN DISEASE OF SHEEP a skin disease of sheep and other animals that resembles mange **4.** BOT PLANT DISEASE CAUSING CRUSTY SPOTS a fungal plant disease causing crusty spots on the affected parts **5.** BOT CRUSTY SPOT ON PLANT a crusty spot on a plant caused by a fungal disease **6.** DISLIKABLE PERSON somebody regarded as despicable or dislikable (*slang insult*) ■ *vi* (**scabs**, **scabbing**, **scabbed**) **1.** BECOME COVERED WITH SCAB to become covered with a scab during healing **2.** WORK DURING STRIKE to continue to work during a strike, or do a striker's job during a strike (*disapproving*) [13C. < Old Norse *skabb* < Indo-European, 'to scrape']

scabbard

scabbard /skábbərd/ *n* a sheath, hanging from a belt, for a sword, dagger, or bayonet ■ *vt* (**-bards, -barding, -barded**) to put a sword, dagger, or bayonet into a sheath [13C. < Anglo-Norman *escauberge*]

scabbard fish *n* a sea fish with an elongated body and long sharp teeth. Family: Trichiuridae.

scabble /skább'l/ (**-bles, -bling, -bled**) *vt* to give a rough shape to stone [Early 17C. Alteration of obsolete *scapple* < Old French *escapeler* 'shape timber' < *capler* 'to cut']

scabby /skábbi/ (**-bier, -biest**) *adj* **1.** having or covered in scabs **2.** despicable or dislikable (*slang*) —**scabbily** *adv* —**scabbiness** *n*

scabies /skáy beez/ *n* a contagious skin disease marked by intense itching, inflammation, and red papules [14C. < Latin *scabere* 'to scratch'] —**scabietic** /skáybi éttik/ *adj*

scabious /skáybi əss/ *n* (*plural* **-ouses** or *same*) a plant with blue, pink, or white dome-shaped flowers. Genera: *Scabiosa* or *Knautia*. ■ *adj* having scabs or scabies [14C. Directly or via French < Latin *scabiosus* < *scabies* (see SCABIES)]

scablands /skábbləndz/ *npl* tracts of elevated land with bare rock, thin soil, and sparse vegetation, crossed by dry channels formed by glacial floodwaters

scabrous /skáybrəss, skább-/ *adj* **1.** WITH ROUGH SURFACE having a rough surface because of scales or short stiff hairs **2.** REQUIRING TACT having to be handled with tact and care **3.** OBSCENE dealing with or referring to sex in an obscene way (*literary*) [Late 16C. < late Latin *scabrosus* < Latin *scaber* 'scurfy, scaly'] —**scabrously** *adv* —**scabrousness** *n*

scad /skad/ (*plural* *same* or **scads**) *n* **1.** a fish with a long body and sharp bony plates on either side of the narrow point of the tail. Native to: tropical and subtropical seas. Family: Caringidae. **2.** FISH same as **horse mackerel** [Early 17C. Origin ?]

scads /skadz/ *npl* large numbers or quantities (*informal*) ○ *scads of money* [Mid-19C. Origin ?]

Scafell Pike /skáw fel-/ highest mountain in the Lake District in Cumbria, northwestern England. Height: 978 m/3,209 ft.

scaffold /skáffōld, -f'ld/ *n* **1.** FRAMEWORK TO SUPPORT WORKERS a temporary framework of poles and planks that is used to support workers and materials during the erection, repair, or decoration of a building **2.** PLATFORM FOR EXECUTIONS a raised platform on which somebody is executed by hanging or beheading **3.** DEATH BY HANGING death by hanging or beheading as a form of punishment **4.** SUPPORT a supporting framework ■ *vt* (**-folds, -folding, -folded**) ERECT SCAFFOLD AROUND BUILDING to put up a scaffold around or against a building [13C. Via Old French *(e)schaffaut* < Vulgar Latin *catafalcum*] —**scaffolder** *n*

scaffolding /skáffōlding, -f'lding/ *n* **1.** a scaffold or system of scaffolds around or against a building **2.** the poles and planks used to build a scaffold

scag /skag/, **skag** *n* DRUGS same as **heroin** (*slang*) [Early 20C. Origin ?]

scagliola /skal yŏlə/ *n* imitation marble made of gypsum mixed with glue, with a polished surface of marble or granite dust [Late 16C. < Italian, 'tiny scale, chip of marble' < Germanic]

scalable /skáyləb'l/ *adj* **1.** CLIMBABLE able to be climbed up or over **2.** VARIABLE describes computer graphics fonts generated by an algorithm that permits the size to vary proportionately over a wide range **3.** EXPANDABLE describes a computer, component, or network that can be expanded to meet future needs —**scalability** /skáylə bílləti/ *n* —**scalableness** *n* —**scalably** *adv*

scalage /skáylij/ *n US* **1.** an allowance in the form of a percentage deducted from the cost of goods to reflect loss in amount or size during storage or shipping **2.** the estimated yield of lumber from a log

scalar /skáylər/ *n* PHYS, MATHS a quantity that has magnitude but no direction, e.g. mass or time ■ *adj* describes a quantity that has magnitude but no direction [Mid-17C. < Latin *scalaris* < *scala* 'staircase, ladder']

scalare /skə laári/ (*plural* *same* or **-res**) *n* FISH same as **angelfish** (sense 1) [Early 20C. < Latin *scalaris* 'of a ladder' (from its markings) < *scala* 'staircase, ladder']

scalariform /skə laári fawrm/ *adj* describes the walls of a cell that have parallel structural formations resembling the rungs of a ladder [Mid-19C. < Latin *scalaris* (see SCALAR)]

scalar product *n* a number (**scalar**) equal to the product of the magnitudes of any two vectors and the cosine of the angle formed between them

scalawag *n* same as **scallywag**

scald /skawld/ *vt* (**scalds, scalding, scalded**) **1.** BURN SOMEBODY WITH HOT LIQUID to burn somebody or a part of the body with hot liquid or steam **2.** HEAT LIQUID TO NEAR BOILING POINT to heat a liquid to just below the boiling point **3.** STERILIZE SOMETHING WITH BOILING LIQUID to subject something to the action of boiling liquid or steam in order to clean or sterilize it **4.** TREAT FRUIT WITH BOILING WATER to plunge a fruit or vegetable into boiling water, or pour boiling water over it and leave it briefly before draining, to prevent cooking **5.** BREW TEA to pour boiling water on tea and leave it to brew (*informal*) ■ *n* **1.** BURN CAUSED BY HOT LIQUID a burn caused by hot liquid or steam **2.** BOT PLANT DISEASE a plant disease or condition that produces brownish discoloration of leaves and fruit [12C. Via Anglo-Norman *escalder* < late Latin *excaldere* 'bathe in hot water' < Latin *calidus* 'hot']

scalding /skáwlding/ *adj* **1.** extremely hot, especially hot enough to scald somebody **2.** severely critical ○ *a scalding remark*

scale[1] /skayl/ *n* **1.** BONY PLATE ON FISH any of the small flat bony or horny overlapping plates that cover the bodies of fish and some reptiles and mammals **2.** FLAKE a thin flat piece or flake of something such as dead skin **3.** INSECTS COVERING OF BUTTERFLY WING a small structure that overlaps others to form the covering of the wings of butterflies and moths **4.** HOUSEHOLD DEPOSIT INSIDE KETTLE OR BOILER a white deposit sometimes formed on the inside of a kettle or boiler by the action of heat on the water **5.** DENT same as **tartar** (sense 1) **6.** METALL FLAKY OXIDE ON HEATED METAL a flaky oxide that forms on the surface of some metals undergoing heat treatment, especially the black oxide that forms on iron or steel at high temperatures **7.** BOT same as **scale leaf 8.** BOT PLANT DISEASE the diseased condition of plants caused by scale insects **9.** INSECTS same as **scale insect** ■ *v* (**scales, scaling, scaled**) **1.** *vt* CLEAN SCALES OR SCALE FROM SOMETHING to remove the scales or scale from something ○ *scaling the fish* **2.** *vi* FLAKE OFF to come off in scales **3.** *vt* THROW FLAT OBJECT to throw a thin flat object through the air, especially a flat stone in order to make it skip across a surface of water **4.** *vt* DENT SCRAPE TOOTH to remove the tartar from a tooth by scraping the surface with a sharp instrument **5.** *vi* REPT SHED SCALES to shed scales from the body **6.** *vi Aus* DODGE FARE to travel by public transport without paying (*informal*) [13C. < Old French *escale* < Germanic, 'husk'] —**scaleless** *adj*

scale[2] /skayl/ *n* **1.** MEASURING SYSTEM a system of measurement based on a series of marks laid down at regular intervals and representing numerical values **2.** SIZE RATIO a ratio representing the size of an illustration or reproduction, especially a map or a model, in relation to the object it represents ○ *The scale of the map is 1:50,000.* **3.** MEASURING INSTRUMENT an instrument or apparatus with graduated markings for measuring something **4.** SYSTEM OF CLASSIFICATION a system of classification in which people or things are ranked progressively according to a specific criterion ○ *rated their satisfaction on a scale of 1 to 5* **5.** LEVEL the extent or relative size of something ○ *the scale of the devastation* **6.** CLASSIFICATION SYSTEM a system of classification based on differing quantity or value, e.g. one used in paying employees ○ *a pay scale* **7.** MUSIC SERIES OF MUSICAL NOTES a series of musical notes, usually sequential, arranged in ascending or descending order of pitch ■ *v* (**scales, scaling, scaled**) **1.** *vt* CLIMB SOMETHING to climb up something, especially a steep incline, often using a ladder **2.** *vt* MAKE SOMETHING IN DIFFERENT SIZE to make a model or draw a map of something in a regular proportion to the size of the original **3.** *vi* RISE IN STAGES to go upward in stages or steps [14C. < Latin *scala* 'staircase, ladder'] —**scalable** *adj* ◇ **to scale** with the same proportion of reduction or enlargement throughout, e.g. in a map or model

scale down *vt* to reduce something in size, amount, or extent

scale up *vt* to increase something in size, amount, or extent

scale[3] /skayl/ *n* **1.** WEIGHING MACHINE a device on which something or somebody can be weighed (*often used in the plural*) **2.** PAN OF BALANCE either of the dishes or pans of a balance ■ *vt* (**scales, scaling, scaled**) **1.** WEIGH SOMETHING OR SOMEBODY to weigh something or somebody with a scale **2.** WEIGH SO MUCH to have a particular weight when put on a scale [12C. < Old Norse *skál* 'bowl, scales' < Germanic, 'shell'] ◇ **tip the scales at** to weigh a particular amount

scaleboard /skáyl bawrd/ *n* **1.** very thin board used, especially formerly, to back a picture or mirror **2.** a thin strip of wood used to justify hand-set type [< SCALE[1]]

scale insect *n* a plant-sucking insect that covers itself with a waxy secretion resembling scales. Superfamily: Coccoidea. [< SCALE[1]]

scale leaf *n* a leaf that protects a plant bud before the bud expands [< SCALE[1]]

scale moss *n* a liverwort with leaves resembling scales. Order: Jungermanniales. [< SCALE[1]]

scalene /skáyl een/ *adj* describes a triangle in which each side is a different length [Mid-17C. Via Latin < Greek *skalenos* 'unequal']

scaler /skáylər/ *n* an electronic circuit that produces an output pulse for every specific number of input pulses received [Mid-20C. < SCALE[2]]

Scales /skaylz/ *npl* ZODIAC same as **Libra** (sense 2) [Plural of SCALE[3]]

scaling /skáyling/ *n* in social research, the creation of a measurement system for such qualities as attitudes and strength of feeling, where there is no existing scale [< SCALE[2]]

scaling ladder *n* a ladder used to climb high walls, especially those of a besieged fortress

scallion /skálli ən/ *n* an onion with a small bulb and long green leaves, e.g.spring onion or shallot [13C. Via Anglo-Norman *scal(o)un* < Old French *esc(h)aloigne* < Latin *Ascalonia (caepa)* '(onion) of Ascalon', port in ancient Palestine]

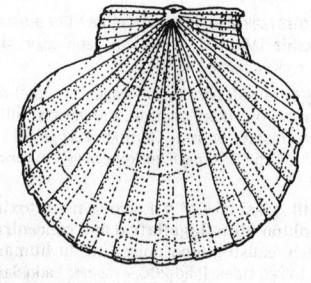

scallop

scallop /skólləp, skáll-/, **scollop** *n* **1.** SEA MOLLUSC a sea bivalve mollusc that has a fan-shaped shell with radial ribs and wavy edges. Family: Pectinidae. **2.** SCALLOP AS FOOD the round white edible muscle of a scallop, often with bright red roe around one side, as food **3.** MARINE BIOL same as **scallop shell 4.** DISH

SHAPED LIKE SCALLOP SHELL a dish shaped like a scallop shell, used for cooking and serving food in **5.** DECORATIVE EDGING an ornamental undulating edging, especially in fabric **6.** PILGRIM'S BADGE a representation of a scallop shell worn as a badge by pilgrims in the Middle Ages **7.** *US* FOOD same as **escalope 8.** *Aus* FRIED POTATO CAKE a slice of potato deep-fried in batter ■ *v* (**-lops, -loping, -loped**) **1.** *vt* MAKE EDGE WAVY to decorate the edge of a fabric or object with an undulating pattern **2.** *vt* COOK FOOD IN SCALLOP SHELL to cook food in a scallop shell or in a dish shaped like a scallop shell **3.** *vt* COOK FOOD IN CREAM SAUCE to bake food in a cream sauce, usually with breadcrumbs on top **4.** *vi* COLLECT SCALLOPS to gather or dredge for scallops [14C. < Old French *escalope*] —**scalloped** *adj* —**scalloper** *n* —**scalloping** *n*

scallop shell *n* either of the fan-shaped shell valves of the scallop, with radial ribs and a wavy edge

scally /skálli/ (*plural* **-lies**) *n N England* a mischievous or naughty person (*informal*) [Late 20C. Shortening of SCALLYWAG]

scallywag /skálli wag/, **scalawag** /skállə-/ *n* **1.** a rascal or scamp (*dated informal*) **2.** in the United States, a white person in the South who worked with the federal government during the Reconstruction period after the Civil War [Mid-19C. Origin ?]

scalogram /skáylə gram/ *n* a test of attitudes or opinions in which the questions are ranked so that the answer to one implies the same answer to all questions lower on the scale [Mid-20C. < SCALE², probably after CARDIOGRAM]

scalp /skalp/ *n* **1.** SKIN ON TOP OF HEAD the skin and underlying tissues covering the dome of the skull **2.** SCALP CUT OFF AS TROPHY the scalp of an enemy cut off as a trophy **3.** TROPHY a trophy or achievement belonging to somebody that somebody else wants to win or take away ■ *vt* (**scalps, scalping, scalped**) **1.** CUT OFF SOMEBODY'S SCALP to cut off the scalp of an enemy as a trophy **2.** *N Am* RESELL SOMETHING FOR QUICK PROFIT to resell something quickly or at an inflated price in order to make a quick profit ○ *scalping tickets* [14C. Probably < N Germanic] —**scalper** *n*

scalpel /skálp'l/ *n* a surgical knife with a short, very sharp blade [Mid-18C. Directly or via French < Latin *scalpellum* 'small cutting tool']

scalp lock *n* a tuft or plait of hair left on the otherwise shaven scalp by the men among some Native North American peoples

scaly /skáyli/ (**-ier, -iest**) *adj* covered in scales or flakes [15C. < SCALE¹] —**scaliness** *n*

scaly anteater *n* ZOOL same as **pangolin**

scam /skam/ (*slang*) *n* a scheme for making money by dishonest means ■ *vt* (**scams, scamming, scammed**) to obtain money or other goods from somebody by dishonest means [Mid-20C. Origin ?] —**scammer** *n*

scammony /skámməni/ (*plural* **-nies** or *same*) *n* **1.** a twining plant with arrow-shaped leaves. Flowers: white, pink, or purple, funnel-shaped. Native to: Asia. Latin name: *Convulvulus scammonia*. **2.** a resin obtained from the roots of the scammony or similar plants. Use: purgative. [Pre-12C. Via French and Latin < Greek *skammōnia*]

scamp¹ /skamp/ *n* **1.** MISCHIEVOUS CHILD a mischievous person, especially a child who misbehaves in harmless or humorous ways (*informal*) **2.** ROGUE a rascally or dishonest person (*dated informal*) **3.** *Carib* WICKED PERSON a wicked or immoral person, or a criminal [Mid-18C. Probably < Middle Dutch *schampen* (see SCAMPER)] —**scampish** *adj*

scamp² /skamp/ (**scamps, scamping, scamped**) *vt* to do something hastily, carelessly, or in a perfunctory manner [Mid-19C. Origin ?]

scamper /skámpər/ *vi* (**-pers, -pering, -pered**) to run quickly or playfully ■ *n* a quick or playful run [Late 17C. Probably via Middle Dutch *schampen* 'slip away, decamp' < Old French *esc(h)amper* < Latin *campus* 'field'] —**scamperer** *n*

scampi /skámpi/ *n* pieces of tail meat from Dublin Bay prawns, usually fried in batter or breadcrumbs (*takes a singular or plural verb*) [Mid-20C. < Italian, plural of *scampo*, kind of lobster < Greek *kampē* 'bending'; from its shape]

scan /skan/ *v* (**scans, scanning, scanned**) **1.** *vt* EXAMINE SOMETHING IN DETAIL to subject something to a thorough examination ○ *scanning the horizon* **2.** *vt* LOOK THROUGH SOMETHING QUICKLY to look through or read something quickly **3.** *vt* LOOK AT SOMETHING INTENTLY to look over and around something intently **4.** *vt* MED OBTAIN IMAGE OF BODY to obtain an image of internal organs with any of various devices, especially in order to make a diagnosis without the need for exploratory surgery **5.** *vt* COMPUT EXAMINE SOMETHING WITH BEAM OF LIGHT to direct a light-sensitive device over a surface in order to convert an image into digital or electronic form for further storage, retrieval, and transmission ○ *scanned the document* **6.** *vt* COMPUT EXAMINE STORED DATA to make an automatic search of a computer storage medium such as a magnetic disk or tape for data in anticipation of retrieving that data **7.** *vti* ELECTRONICS SEARCH AREA USING RADAR to search a region for something, e.g. aircraft, by systematically sweeping a radar or sonar beam across it **8.** *vi* LITERAT CONFORM TO VERSE RULES to conform to the rules of metre ○ *That line doesn't scan.* **9.** *vt* LITERAT ANALYSE VERSE to analyse verse according to the rules of metre ■ *n* **1.** IMAGE OF BODY an image of an internal body part taken using a scanner **2.** BRIEF PERUSAL a quick look at or through something **3.** ACT OF SCANNING the act or process of scanning something **4.** SWEEP OF RADAR BEAM a single sweep of a radar or sonar beam across a region [14C. < Latin *scandere* 'climb, (in late Latin) scan a verse'] —**scannable** *adj*

scandal /skánd'l/ *n* **1.** SOMETHING CAUSING PUBLIC OUTRAGE a situation or event that causes public outrage or censure **2.** PUBLIC OUTRAGE an outburst of public outrage or censure as a consequence of an event **3.** MALICIOUS TALK malicious talk, especially about other people's private lives [12C. Via French < Latin *scandalum* 'trap, temptation' < Greek *skandalon*]

CULTURAL NOTE ***School for Scandal***, a play (1777) by Irish dramatist Richard Brinsley Sheridan. In this satire on contemporary middle-class mores, Sir Oliver Surface attempts to spy on his nephews Charles and Joseph in order to discover their true characters. Among the play's many targets are the hypocrisy and vindictiveness of gossipmongers, personified by the characters of Lady Sneerwell, Sir Benjamin Backbite, and Mrs Candour.

scandalize /skándə līz/ (**-izes, -izing, -ized**), **scandalise** (**-ises, -ising, -ised**) *vt* to shock somebody by outrageous or improper behaviour —**scandalization** /skándə lī záysh'n/ *n* —**scandalizer** *n*

scandalmonger /skánd'l mung gər/ *n* a spreader of malicious talk about other people's private lives —**scandalmongering** *n*

scandalous /skándələss/ *adj* **1.** causing or deserving to cause public outrage or censure **2.** causing or having the potential to cause damage to somebody's reputation —**scandalously** *adv* —**scandalousness** *n*

scandal sheet *n* a periodical publication that features scandalous stories about people's private lives (*disapproving*)

scandent /skándənt/ *adj* describes a plant that climbs as it grows [Late 17C. < Latin *scandent-*, present participle of *scandere* 'climb']

scandic /skándik/ *adj* relating to or containing the element scandium

Scandinavia /skándi náyvi ə/ region in northern Europe comprising Norway, Sweden, Denmark, Finland, Iceland, and the Faroe Islands

Scandinavian /skándi náyvi ən/ *n* **1.** somebody who comes from one of the countries of Scandinavia **2.** LANG same as **North Germanic** ▶ See panel on next page —**Scandinavian** *adj*

scandium /skándi əm/ *n* a rare silvery-white metallic element. Source: wolframite. Use: tracer. Symbol **Sc**. See table at **element** [Late 19C. < Latin *Scandia*, shortening of *Scandinavia*; because found in various minerals there]

~~**scandle**~~ incorrect spelling of **scandal**

scanner /skánnər/ *n* **1.** DEVICE PUTTING SOMETHING INTO DIGITAL FORM an input device used to convert an image or text into digital form for storage or display **2.** DATA-SCANNING DEVICE a device for examining written or recorded data, e.g. for reading a product bar code for inventory and pricing purposes **3.** BODY-SCANNING DEVICE a device used to obtain information about the internal parts of the body without the need for surgery, or the contents of something without the need for opening it **4.** RADIO RECEIVER a receiver that continuously broadcasts radio signals it picks up from specific frequencies ○ *a police scanner* **5.** RADAR SEARCHING DEVICE a rotating directional radar antenna that emits a beam to search for or locate objects **6.** SOMEBODY WHO SCANS TEXTS somebody who scans texts, e.g. for errors or in poetic analysis

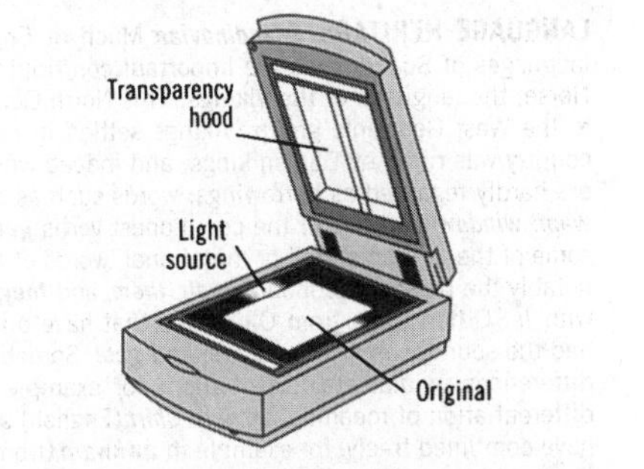

scanner

scanning electron microscope /skánning-/ *n* a microscope that uses a beam of electrons to scan an object and produce an enlarged image of it on a cathode-ray tube —**scanning electron microscopy** *n*

scanning tunnelling microscope *n* a microscope used to study surfaces in which a very small probe is moved across a sample and quantum mechanical effects give information about the surface structure —**scanning tunnelling microscopy** *n*

scansion /skánsh'n/ *n* **1.** the analysis of verse according to the rules of metre **2.** the way that a line, verse, or poem scans [Mid-17C. < Latin *scansion-* 'climbing, (in late Latin) scansion' < *scandere* 'to climb']

scant /skant/ *adj* **1.** not sufficient **2.** only just at or just below a particular amount ○ *a scant twenty votes* [14C. < Old Norse *skamt*, form of *skammr* 'short'] —**scantly** *adv* —**scantness** *n*

scantling /skántling/ *n* **1.** THIN PIECE OF TIMBER a piece of timber with a small cross section, e.g. a rafter **2.** SIZE the dimension of a building material or a structural part of a ship **3.** SMALL AMOUNT a small amount or quantity [Early 16C. Alteration of obsolete *scantillon* 'gauge' < late Latin *scandaculum* 'ladder' < Latin *scandere* 'to climb']

scanty /skánti/ (**-ier, -iest**) *adj* **1.** INADEQUATE not much, and less than is needed ○ *can't tell much from the scanty evidence* **2.** MEAGRE only just enough ○ *found the remains of a scanty meal* **3.** REVEALING not covering much of the part of the body that it is worn on —**scantily** *adv* —**scantiness** *n*

Scapa Flow /skaápə-/ anchorage in the Orkney Islands, Scotland. It was used as a base for Britain's home fleet during both world wars. Area: 310 sq. km/120 sq. mi.

scape¹ /skayp/ *n* **1.** BOT LEAFLESS FLOWER STALK a leafless flower stalk rising directly from the root **2.** ZOOL PART OF FEATHER OR ANTENNA a shaft of a feather or other animal part, or a segment of an antenna **3.** ARCHIT ARCHITECTURAL COLUMN the shaft of an architectural column [Early 17C. Via Latin < Greek *skapos* 'rod'] —**scapose** /skáppōss/ *adj*

scape² /skayp/ (**scapes, scaping, scaped**) *vti* same as **escape** (*archaic*) [13C. Shortening]

-scape *suffix* a scene or view ○ *seascape* [< LANDSCAPE]

scapegoat /skáyp gōt/ *n* **1.** SOMEBODY MADE TO TAKE BLAME somebody who is made to take the blame for others **2.** PSYCHOL SOMEBODY WRONGLY BLAMED somebody who is unjustly blamed for another's misdeeds **3.** BIBLE GOAT GIVEN SINS IN JEWISH RITUAL on the Jewish Day of Atonement, a goat on which the high priest symbolically loaded all the sins of the community before sending the animal out into the wilderness ■ *v* (**-goats, -goating, -goated**) **1.** *vt* MAKE SOMEBODY TAKE BLAME to force somebody to take the blame for others **2.** PSYCHOL BLAME SOMEBODY TO AVOID TAKING RESPONSIBILITY to blame another person unjustly for causing upset or distress as a way of avoiding taking personal responsibility [Mid-16C. < SCAPE²; because in Jewish ritual the goat, having had the sins of the people symbolically laid on it, was allowed to 'escape' into the desert]

LANGUAGE HERITAGE ***Scandinavian*** Much of English is made up of words from other languages, and the languages of Scandinavia are important contributors in this respect, especially in their shared early form Old Norse, the language of the Vikings. This North Germanic language is closely related to English, which belongs to the West Germanic group. Vikings settled in much of England, and between 1016 and 1042 part of the country was ruled by Danish kings, and indeed words from the early period are so integral to English that they are hardly regarded as borrowings: words such as ***anger, bag, call, dirt, husband, ill, law, near, odd, sale, seem, want, window,*** and two of the commonest verbs ***get*** and ***take.*** The penetration of Norse is such that it provides some of the 'grammatical' or 'functional' words of English, for example ***both*** and the preposition ***like,*** and most notably the personal pronouns ***their, them,*** and ***they,*** which replaced their Old English equivalents, which began with *h-*. Other forms from Old Norse that have ousted related native English words include ***egg*** (Old English had the sound *y* as in *yes*), ***ankle,*** and ***gate.*** Sometimes both Anglo-Saxon and Viking forms survive, either with differences in dialectal distribution, for example Scottish ***kirk*** alongside standard English ***church,*** or with differentiation of meaning, as with ***shirt*** (English) alongside ***skirt*** (from Old Norse). Native and Norse elements have combined freely, for example in ***awkward*** (from obsolete *awk* 'turned the wrong way', from Old Norse *afugr* 'turned backwards' + the English suffix *-ward*) and ***blackmail*** (from *black* + obsolete *mail* 'tribute, tax' from Old Norse *mál* 'speech, agreement'), and English idiom has modelled itself on Norse, as in ***afoot,*** partly based on Old Norse *á fótum* 'on foot', and ***upon,*** based on Old Norse *upp á.*

Some relatively modern words also trace their ancestry to Old Norse. ***Berserk,*** for instance, is recorded only from the early 19th century, but derives from a Norse word meaning 'wild warrior', which is probably formed from the stem of *bjorn* 'bear' with *serkr* 'shirt'.

The modern Scandinavian languages such as Norwegian, Danish, and Swedish have provided in particular terms reflecting occupations and activities of northern peoples: seafaring, fisheries, and winter sports. The ***minke whale, narwhal, rorqual*** (via French from Norwegian *røyrkval,* from an Old Norse word meaning literally 'red whale'), and ***sei whale*** may feed on ***krill,*** and whalers might ***flense*** (strip the skin or blubber from) them (from Danish). Other sea creatures with North Germanic names include the ***auk, brisling, eider*** (from Icelandic), ***fulmar,*** and ***kraken,*** a huge sea monster shaped like a giant squid, periodically reported by Norwegian fishermen since the 16th century; from the land come the ***lemming, mink,*** and, perhaps surprisingly, the ***vole.*** In winter sports Norwegian has provided ***ski, slalom,*** and ***skijoring,*** a sport in which a skier is towed across a frozen surface by a horse or vehicle. Swedish has made its sporting contribution with ***orienteering*** (an anglicization of Swedish *orientering*) and ***fartlek*** (literally 'speed play'), another name for interval training.

Scandinavian foods have inevitably been welcomed into English: ***gravlax, rutabaga*** (the usual North American term for the swede), and the Swedish ***smorgasbord*** (literally 'bread-and-butter table'), which has become familiar enough to develop a figurative meaning, 'a wide variety'. Adopted geographical features include the ***fjord*** and the ***geyser*** (named after *Geysir,* a hot spring in Iceland). In science Scandinavia has provided the name for the element ***tungsten,*** and the prefixes for units ***atto-*** and ***femto-,*** from words meaning 'eighteen' and 'fifteen' respectively. In cultural life Sweden has made the significant contribution of the ***ombudsman.***

One word of individual interest is ***gauntlet*** (the kind that you 'run'). Its Scandinavian origin has been concealed by identification with the completely different word (from French) for a long glove with a wide cuff. The ***gauntlet*** was a punishment formerly used in the military in which a soldier was forced to run between two lines of men armed with weapons who beat him as he passed; its earlier form in English was *gantlope,* which came from Swedish *gatlopp* 'passageway'.

scapegrace /skáyp grayss/ *n* a lazy, mischievous, or irresponsible person, especially a child (*archaic*) [Early 19C. < SCAPE[2]]

scaphoid /skáffoyd/ *adj* same as **navicular** ■ *n* the navicular bone in the wrist [Mid-18C. Via modern Latin < Greek *skaphoeidēs* < *skaphē* 'boat']

scapolite /skáppō līt/ *n* a variously coloured aluminosilicate mineral. Source: metamorphic rocks, weathered basic igneous rocks. Use: semiprecious gems. [Early 19C. < Greek *skapos* 'rod']

scapula /skáppyŏŏlə/ (*plural* **-lae** /-lee/ or **-las**) *n* **1.** either of two large flat triangular bones that form the back of the shoulder in humans **2.** a bone in vertebrates that corresponds to the human shoulder blade [Late 16C. < late Latin, singular < Latin *scapulae* 'shoulder blades']

scapular[1] /skáppyŏŏlər/ *n* any of the feathers on a bird's shoulder ■ *adj* relating to or associated with the shoulder blade [Late 17C. < SCAPULA]

scapular[2] /skáppyŏŏlər/, **scapulary** /-ləri/ (*plural* **-ies**) *n* **1.** a loose sleeveless garment worn by Christian monks **2.** two small pieces of cloth joined together and worn over the shoulder and back underneath other garments to signify membership in a Christian religious order or some other devotional purpose [15C. < late Latin *scapulare* < *scapula* (see SCAPULA)]

scar[1] /skaar/ *n* **1.** MARK ON SKIN AFTER DAMAGE a mark left on the skin after a wound, burn, or sore has healed over **2.** MENTAL EFFECT OF DISTRESSING EXPERIENCE a lasting effect left on somebody's mind by a personal misfortune or unpleasant experience **3.** MARK ON SURFACE a mark on a surface caused by damage **4.** BOT MARK OF FORMER ATTACHMENT ON PLANT the mark on a plant indicating the place where a part such as a leaf was formerly attached ■ *v* (**scars, scarring, scarred**) **1.** *vt* MARK SOMEBODY OR SOMETHING WITH SCARS to leave somebody or something with a physical or emotional scar **2.** *vi* FORM SCAR to form or become marked by a scar [14C. Directly or via French < late Latin *eschara* 'scab' < Greek *eskhara* 'brazier, scab formed after a burn']

scar[2] /skaar/ *n* **1.** a steep bare rocky cliff, typically in the limestones of the Yorkshire Dales **2.** a rock submerged or partly submerged in the ocean [14C. < Old Norse *sker* 'low reef' < Germanic, 'something cut off']

scarab /skárrəb/ *n* **1.** a beetle regarded as sacred by the ancient Egyptians. Family: Scarabaeidae. **2.** a representation of a beetle used on amulets and signets by the ancient Egyptians [Late 16C. < Latin *scarabaeus* < Greek *karabos* 'crab, beetle']

scarabaeid /skárrə beé id/, **scarabaean** /-ən/ *n* INSECTS same as **scarab** (sense 1) [Mid-19C. < modern Latin *Scarabaeidae* < Latin *scarabaeus* (see SCARAB)]

Scaramouch /skárrə mooch, -moosh, -mowch/, **Scaramouche** *n* a boastful and cowardly man (*literary*) [Mid-17C. Via French < Italian *Scaramuccia,* character in the commedia dell'arte]

Scarborough /skaárbərə/ town in northeastern England, on the North Sea. A market centre in the Middle Ages, it is now primarily a resort. Population: 116,243 (2001).

scarce /skairss/ *adj* (**scarcer, scarcest**) **1.** being in insufficient supply ○ *scarce resources* **2.** rarely found or rarely occurring ○ *Elephants are becoming scarce.* ■ *adv* same as **scarcely** (*archaic or literary*) [13C. < Anglo-Norman *(e)scars* < Latin *excerpere* 'pick out' < *carpere* 'pluck'] —**scarceness** *n* ◇ **make yourself scarce** to go or stay away, often in order to avoid some kind of trouble or difficulty (*informal*)

scarcely /skáirssli/ *adv* **1.** HARDLY only just ○ *scarcely arrived when she was put to work* **2.** HARDLY AT ALL only to the slightest degree ○ *scarcely slept all night* **3.** SURELY NOT surely or almost certainly not ○ *scarcely a good reason*

USAGE See ***hardly.***

---

scarcement /skáirssmənt/ *n* a ledge in a wall [Early 16C. < SCARCE in obsolete sense 'make scarce']

scarcity /skáirssəti/ (*plural* **-ties**) *n* **1.** an insufficient supply of something **2.** an infrequency of occurrence of something

scare /skair/ *v* (**scares, scaring, scared**) **1.** *vt* FRIGHTEN SOMEBODY to make somebody afraid or alarmed **2.** *vi* BE FRIGHTENED to be or become frightened ■ *n* **1.** FRIGHT a sudden fright or feeling of fear **2.** SOMETHING THAT FRIGHTENS a situation causing general fear or alarm ○ *another food scare* [12C. < Old Norse *skirra* 'frighten' < *skjarr* 'timid'] —**scarer** *n*

scare off, scare away *vt* to frighten a person or an animal into going away

scare up *vt N Am* to manage to find something or put something together with difficulty or skill (*informal*)

scarecrow /skáir krō/ *n* **1.** OBJECT FOR SCARING BIRDS AWAY an object in the shape of a person dressed in old clothes, set up in a field to scare birds away from the crops **2.** SOMETHING FRIGHTENING BUT NOT DANGEROUS somebody or something that may have a frightening effect but is not dangerous **3.** POORLY DRESSED PERSON a wearer of ragged clothes (*informal*)

scared /skaird/ *adj* feeling full of worry or fear —**scaredly** *adv* —**scaredness** *n*

scaredy-cat /skáirdi-/ *n UK, ANZ, Can* somebody who is unusually timid and frightened (*informal; usually used by or to children*) US term **fraidy-cat**

scaremonger /skáir mung gər/ *n* a spreader of alarming rumours —**scaremongering** *n*

scarf[1] /skaarf/ *n* (*plural* **scarfs** or **scarves** /skaarvz/) **1.** CLOTH WORN ROUND NECK a piece of cloth worn round the neck or on the head for warmth, decoration, or concealment **2.** MILITARY SASH an official sash, usually indicating military rank ■ *vt* (**scarfs, scarfing, scarfed**) WRAP SOMETHING IN SCARF to wrap a scarf round something (*literary*) [Mid-16C. Shortened < Old N French *escarpe,* probably variant of Old French *escherpe* 'bag hung around the neck' < Frankish *skirpja* 'bag woven from rushes' < Latin *scirpus* 'rush']

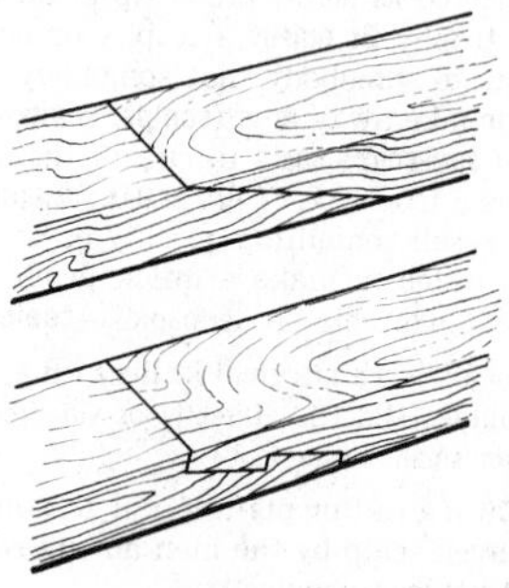

scarf

scarf[2] /skaarf/ *n* **1.** JOINT MADE BETWEEN NOTCHED ENDS a joint made by joining two notched boards together **2.** NOTCHED END either of the notched ends of a scarf joint ■ *vt* (**scarfs, scarfing, scarfed**) JOIN BOARDS USING NOTCHES to join boards together by means of a scarf joint [13C. Probably via French < N Germanic]

scarf[3] /skaarf/ *vt N Am* to eat or drink something greedily or noisily (*slang*) ○ *scarfed down the food* [Mid-20C. Variant of SCOFF[2]]

scarf joint *n* CONSTR same as **scarf**[2] *n* (sense 2)

scarfskin /skaárf skin/ *n* the outermost layer of skin, especially the cuticle of a nail [Early 16C. Probably < SCARF[1]]

scarify[1] /skárri fī, skáiri-/ (**-fies, -fying, -fied**) *vt* **1.** MAKE SCRATCHES ON SKIN to make scratches on or superficial incisions in the skin, as a traditional cosmetic practice in some cultures or as a medical procedure **2.** LOOSEN SOIL to break up and loosen the surface of soil **3.** SCRATCH SEEDS to break the outer cover of hard seeds to aid germination [14C. Via French *scarifier* < late Latin *skarificare* < Greek *skariphasthai* 'scratch an outline' < *skariphos* 'stylus'] —**scarification** /skárrifi káysh'n, skáiri-/ *n* —**scarificator** /-fi kaytər/ *n* —**scarifier** *n*

scarify[2] /skáiri fī/ (**-fies, -fying, -fied**) *vt* to make somebody afraid or alarmed (*informal*) [Late 18C. < SCARE, probably after TERRIFY] —**scarifyingly** *adv*

scarious /skáiri əss/, **scariose** /-ōss/ *adj* describes parts of plants that have a thin dry membranous appearance [Late 18C. Directly or via French < modern Latin *scariosus*]

scarlatina /skaárlə teénə/ *n* MED same as **scarlet fever** (*technical*) [Early 19C. Via modern Latin < Italian *scarlattina* 'little scarlet things' < *scarlatto* 'scarlet' < Arabic *siqillāt* (see SCARLET)] —**scarlatinal** *adj*

Scarlatti /skaar látti/, **Alessandro** (1659–1725) Italian composer. The father of Domenico Scarlatti, he was a major contributor to the establishment of the Neapolitan style of opera. Full name **Scarlatti, Pietro Alessandro Gaspare**

Scarlatti, Domenico (1685–1757) Italian composer. The son of Alessandro Scarlatti, he composed operas and church music, but is best known for over 550 sonatas for harpsichord. Full name **Scarlatti, Giuseppe Domenico**

scarlet /skaárlət/ *n* **1.** a bright orange-tinged red colour **2.** scarlet clothing or cloth, especially the traditional red uniforms of the British army [13C. Via Old French *escarlate* < Arabic *siqillāt*, a rich red cloth < Latin *sigillatus* 'decorated with raised figures' < *signum* 'sign'] —**scarlet** *adj*

scarlet fever *n* a contagious bacterial infection marked by fever, a sore throat, and a red rash, mainly affecting children

scarlet letter *n* a scarlet letter 'A' that a woman convicted of adultery was formerly made to wear, especially among the Puritans of 17th-century New England

CULTURAL NOTE ***The Scarlet Letter***, a novel (1850) by US writer Nathaniel Hawthorne. The title of this eloquent plea for tolerance refers to the red letter 'A' that Hester Prynne, a woman living in mid-17th-century New England, is forced to wear as punishment for an adulterous affair. While her husband and lover are consumed by anger and guilt respectively, Hester's honesty and strength of character help her to survive the scandal.

scarlet pimpernel *n* a common pimpernel whose flowers close in cloudy weather. Flowers: small, scarlet, purple, or white. Latin name: *Anagallis arvensis*.

scarlet runner *n N Am* same as **runner bean**

scarlet woman *n* an offensive term for a woman believed to be an adulterer or prostitute or to engage excessively in sexual activity (*literary*) [< Revelations 17:1–6 in the Bible, in which a sinful woman appears 'in purple and scarlet colour']

scarp /skaarp/ *n* **1.** a steep slope or cliff, formed by erosion or faulting **2.** a steep slope in front of a fortification, e.g. the inner wall of a ditch [Late 16C. < Italian *scarpa*]

scarper /skaárpər/ (**-ers, -ering, -ered**) *vi* to leave a place quickly (*slang*) [Mid-19C. Probably < Italian *scappare* 'to escape']

scart /skaart/ (**scarts, scarting, scarted**) *vti Scotland* to scratch the skin or another surface (*nonstandard*) [Late 16C. Alteration of dialect *scrat*, origin ?]

Scart /skaart/, **SCART** *n* an electrical device for connecting video equipment that has a socket and plug with 21 pins ○ *a Scart lead* [Late 20C. < French, acronym < *Syndicat des Constructeurs des Appareils Radiorécepteurs et Téléviseurs*, the committee that designed the connector]

scar tissue *n* dense fibrous tissue that forms the scar over a healed wound

scarves CLOTHING plural of **scarf**[1]

scary /skáiri/ (**-ier, -iest**) *adj* (*informal*) **1.** causing fear or alarm **2.** easily frightened —**scarily** *adv* —**scariness** *n*

scat[1] /skat/ (**scats, scatting, scatted**) *vi* to leave immediately and quickly (*informal; usually used as a command*) [Mid-19C. Origin ?]

scat[2] /skat/ *n* a style of jazz singing that uses nonsense syllables to approximate the sound of a solo instrument ■ *vi* (**scats, scatting, scatted**) to sing in scat style [Early 20C. Probably an imitation of the sound]

scat[3] /skat/ (*plural* **scats** or *same*) *n* a small tropical sea fish, often kept in aquariums because of its bright colour. Native to: Indian and Pacific oceans. Family: Scatophagidae. [Mid-20C. Shortening of modern Latin *Scatophagidae* < Greek *scatophagos* 'dung-eating'; because it frequents sewage outlets]

scat[4] /skat/ *n* a faecal dropping of an animal [Mid-20C. < Greek *skat-* (see SCATO-)]

scathe /skayth/ *vt* (**scathes, scathing, scathed**) **1.** CRITICIZE SOMEBODY to subject somebody to severe criticism (*literary*) **2.** DAMAGE SOMETHING BY BLASTING to damage something by blasting or scorching it (*archaic*) ■ *n* HARM injury or harm (*archaic*) [12C. < Old Norse *skaða* 'harm, damage'] —**scatheless** *adj*

scathing /skáything/ *adj* severely critical and scornful —**scathingly** *adv*

scato- *prefix* excrement ○ *scatology* [< Greek *skat-*, stem of *skōr* 'excrement' < Indo-European, 'cut off']

scatology /ska tólləji/ *n* **1.** a preoccupation with excrement or obscenity **2.** the scientific study of excrement, especially for diagnostic purposes —**scatological** /skáttə lójjik'l/ *adj* —**scatologist** *n*

scatter /skáttər/ *v* (**-ters, -tering, -tered**) **1.** *vt* THROW THINGS ABOUT to throw things about so that they land with an irregular distribution over a relatively wide area ○ *scatter seed* **2.** *vt* SCATTER SOMETHING OVER AREA to cover an area by throwing things about over it **3.** *vti* DISPERSE to separate and move suddenly in different directions, or cause people or animals to move in this way **4.** *vti* PHYS DEVIATE to cause waves or a beam of particles to be irregularly deflected, dispersed, or reflected, or be turned aside in this way ■ *n* THINGS SCATTERED ABOUT a number of things spread untidily about an area (*literary*) [12C. Probably variant of SHATTER] —**scatterable** *adj* —**scatterer** *n*

scatterbrain /skáttər brayn/ *n* a person regarded as unable to think seriously or systematically or to remember important things —**scatterbrained** *adj*

scatter cushion *n* a small moveable cushion placed on a sofa or armchair (*often used in the pl*) *N Am* term **throw pillow**

scatter diagram *n* a graph that represents the joint relationship of two variables by depicting the data as points along two axes at right angles to each other

scattered /skáttərd/ *adj* **1.** in a number of different places far away from each other ○ *scattered communities* **2.** few in number and far apart in distance or time ○ *scattered showers*

scattergun /skáttər gun/ *n N Am* same as **shotgun**

scattering /skáttəring/ *n* **1.** a small amount or number of things irregularly spread over a large area **2.** the deflection of a wave or beam of particles caused by collisions with other particles

scattering layer *n* an undersea zone where there is a high concentration of plankton that causes sound waves to become scattered

scatter pin *n* a small decorative pin typically worn as part of a cluster on clothing

scatter rug *n* a small decorative rug

scattershot /skáttər shot/ *adj* indiscriminate and lacking in focus ○ *a scattershot approach to the operation*

scatty /skátti/ (**-tier, -tiest**) *adj* (*informal*) **1.** *UK, Can* lacking in serious or organized thought, forgetful, and often eccentric in behaviour **2.** extremely muddled, irritated, or angry ○ *These children are driving me scatty.* [Early 20C. Probably < shortening of *scatterbrained*] —**scattily** *adv* —**scattiness** *n*

scaup /skawp/ (*plural* **scaups** or *same*), **scaup duck** *n* a diving duck, the male of which has a black and white body. Native to: Europe, North America. Genus: *Aythya*. [Late 17C. Variant of *scalp* 'shellfish bed', origin ?]

scauper /skáwpər/ *n* an engraving tool used to clear away lines or other unwanted areas on wood [Mid-19C. Variant of *scalper*]

scaur /skawr/ *n Scotland* a steep eroded hill or precipice (*often used in placenames*) [Early 18C. Variant of SCAR[2]]

scavenge /skávvinj/ (**-enges, -enging, -enged**) *vti* **1.** LOOK FOR SOMETHING USABLE to search for or through discarded material in order to find something usable **2.** FEED ON CARRION OR SCRAPS to feed on dead and rotting flesh or discarded food scraps **3.** CLEAN PLACE UP to remove waste material and dirt from an area **4.** CHEM GET RID OF IMPURITIES to neutralize or remove impurities in a chemical reaction or mixture [Mid-17C. Back-formation < SCAVENGER]

scavenger /skávvinjər/ *n* **1.** ANIMAL FEEDING ON CARRION OR SCRAPS an animal, bird, or other organism that feeds on dead and rotting flesh or discarded food scraps **2.** SOMEBODY LOOKING FOR SOMETHING USABLE somebody who seeks or looks through discarded items in the hope of finding something usable **3.** CHEM SUBSTANCE REMOVING IMPURITIES something that is added to a chemical reaction or mixture to neutralize or remove impurities **4.** STREET CLEANER a paid street cleaner or refuse collector (*archaic*) [Mid-16C. Alteration of *scavager*, former official whose responsibilities included street-cleaning < Anglo-Norman *scawager* < Flemish *scauwen* 'look at']

ORIGIN The term *scavager* was originally, in the Middle Ages, an official who collected taxes levied on overseas merchants. Later the term came to denote a street-cleaner, and by the time it had metamorphosed into ***scavenger*** (by the same process as produced *messenger* from *messager* and *passenger* from *passager*) it had completed its descent to its modern meaning.

scavenger beetle *n* a dark oval-shaped beetle that lives in water and feeds on decaying vegetation. Family: Hydrophilidae.

scavenger hunt *n* a game in which people must obtain items on a list within a time limit and without buying them

scavenger moth *n* a small moth that is commonly found scavenging stored food such as grains and oils. Family: Tineidae.

ScB *abbr* EDUC Bachelor of Science [Latin *Scientiae Baccalaureus*]

SCC *abbr* storage connecting circuit

ScD *abbr* EDUC Doctor of Science [Latin *Scientiae Doctor*]

SCE *n* in Scotland, any of three levels of examinations in a wide range of subjects taken in the last three years of secondary school. Standard Grades are usually taken at the age of 16, Highers at 17, and Advanced Highers at 18. Full form **Scottish Certificate of Education**

~~scedule~~ incorrect spelling of **schedule**

~~sceince~~ incorrect spelling of **science**

~~sceme~~ incorrect spelling of **scheme**

scena /sháynə/ (*plural* **-ne** /-nay/) *n* **1.** a division of an opera that is equivalent in length or structure to a scene in a play **2.** a dramatic concert piece written and performed in the style of an operatic scena [Early 19C. Via Italian < Latin *scaena* (see SCENE[1])]

scenario /si naári ō/ (*plural* **-os**) *n* **1.** POSSIBLE SITUATION an imagined sequence of possible events, or an imagined set of circumstances ○ *the worst-case scenario* **2.** LITERAT, MUSIC PLOT OUTLINE an outline of the plot of a play or opera **3.** CINEMA SCREENPLAY a screenplay for a film [Late 19C. < Italian, < *scena* 'scene' < Latin *scaena* (see SCENE[1])]

USAGE The use of ***scenario*** in a generalized way to denote an imagined sequence of possible events or set of circumstances (*an alternative scenario if the vote goes the other way*) is widely deprecated in dictionaries and books on usage, although it is hard to see why this figurative use of a word is to be rejected when so many others (for example *scene*) are accepted without comment. It is a useful word when the imagined events or circumstances can be regarded as a whole and are therefore directly comparable to the elements of a film or theatre plot.

scenarist /seénərist, sə naárist, si-/ *n* a writer of film scripts [Early 20C. < SCENARIO]

scend /send/, **send** *n* the upward movement of a ship that is moving up and down in heavy seas ■ *vi* (**scends, scending, scended; sends, sending, sended**) to rise up high under the force of a strong wave (*refers to boats*) [15C. Probably shortening of DESCEND or ASCEND]

scene[1] /seen/ *n* **1.** PLACE WHERE SOMETHING HAPPENS a location at which an event or action happens ○ *the scene of many battles* **2.** VIEW OR PICTURE a view of a place or an activity, especially one presented in a painting or photograph **3.** EMBARRASSING PUBLIC DISPLAY an embarrassing or disconcerting public display of emotion ○ *Don't make a scene, but I think they've lost your coat.* **4.** MILIEU the characteristic environment in which an activity or pursuit is carried out ○ *new to the fashion scene* **5.** THEATRE, MUSIC DIVISION OF ACT OF PLAY a division of an act of a play or opera, presenting continuous action in one place **6.** ARTS SHORT SECTION OF PLAY OR FILM a short section of a play, film, opera, or work of literature that presents a single event ○ *the love scene* **7.** ARTS SETTING IN DRAMATIC WORK a setting

for the whole or a part of a play, film, opera, or work of literature **8.** ARTS SCENERY FOR DRAMATIC WORK the backgrounds, sets, or props for a play, film, or opera (*often used before a noun*) ○ *a couple of quick scene changes* **9.** *US* SITUATION a set of circumstances of any kind (*informal*) ○ *a bad scene* [Mid-16C. Via Latin *scaena* < Greek *skēnē* 'tent, stage'] ◇ **behind the scenes 1.** in private and away from public view **2.** out of sight of somebody at a performance or spectacle ◇ **it's not somebody's scene** it is not the kind of thing that somebody likes to do or takes an interest in ◇ **set the scene 1.** to describe a situation or the background to an event **2.** to create the circumstances in which something can or does happen

scene² /sháynay/ MUSIC plural of **scena**

scene-of-crime *adj* relating or belonging to a civilian branch of the police force responsible for collecting forensic evidence at crime scenes

scenery /seénəri/ *n* **1.** landscape or natural surroundings, especially when regarded as picturesque ○ *admired the scenery from the hotel balcony* **2.** the set or decorated background for a play, film, or opera [Mid-18C. Alteration of obsolete *scenary* 'scenario of a play or opera' < Italian *scenario* (see SCENARIO)]

sceneshifter /seén shiftər/ *n* somebody employed to move sets or props in a theatre or opera house

scene-stealer *n* a performer who, by his or her performance or personal qualities, takes the audience's attention away from another performer who is supposedly the focus of the scene

scenic /seénik/ *adj* **1.** PICTURESQUE with attractive or impressive natural scenery **2.** OF NATURAL SCENERY relating to the natural scenery of an area ○ *famous for its scenic beauty* **3.** ARTS OF DRAMATIC SCENES relating to scenes in a play, film, or opera **4.** THEATRE OF STAGE SCENERY relating to the scenery for a play or opera —**scenically** *adv*

scenic railway *n* **1.** a miniature railway that carries customers past artificial scenery in a theme park or other place of entertainment **2.** LEISURE same as **roller coaster** (sense 1) (*dated*)

scenography /see nógrəfi/ *n* **1.** the artistic representation of objects according to the rules of perspective **2.** the painting of theatrical scenery —**scenographer** *n* —**scenographic** /seénə gráffik/ *adj* —**scenographical** *adj* —**scenographically** *adv*

scent /sent/ *n* **1.** PLEASANT SMELL a pleasant sweet smell such as that of a flower ○ *the scent of jasmine* **2.** SMELL USED IN TRACKING the characteristic smell given off by a person or animal and used especially for tracking ○ *They followed the scent deep into the forest.* **3.** PERFUME cosmetic liquid worn on the skin, especially women's perfume **4.** SMELLING SENSE the sense of smell **5.** ABILITY TO SENSE SOMETHING an ability to sense or detect something as likely to happen **6.** HINT a faint indication that something is likely to happen ○ *There was the scent of danger in the air.* ■ *v* (**scents, scenting, scented**) **1.** *vti* SMELL SOMEBODY OR SOMETHING to perceive somebody or something by smelling **2.** *vt* DETECT SOMETHING AS IMMINENT to sense that something is likely to happen ○ *They could scent victory.* **3.** *vt* IMBUE SOMETHING WITH PLEASANT SMELL to fill something with a distinctive odour, especially a pleasant one ○ *Roses scented the room.* [14C. Via French *sentir* 'to sense' < Latin *sentire* 'feel'] —**scentless** *adj* ◇ **put** or **throw somebody off the scent** to divert somebody from finding or discovering something

SYNONYMS See *smell*.

scented orchid /séntid-/ *n* a wild orchid that has fragrant pink flowers. Latin name: *Gymnadenia conopsea*.

scent gland *n* a specialized skin gland that enables an animal to secrete a scent designed to send social or sexual signals or serve as a deterrent

scent strip *n* a strip of perfumed paper used to advertise a commercially available perfume to potential customers

scepter *n*, *vt* POL US spelling of **sceptre**

sceptic /sképtik/ *n* **1.** a doubter of accepted beliefs **2.** a doubter of religious doctrines and principles **3.** PHILOSOPHY another spelling of **Sceptic** [Early 17C. < SCEPTIC]

SYNONYMS See *doubtful*.

Sceptic /sképtik/ *n* a member of an ancient Greek school of philosophy holding the doctrine that real knowledge is impossible, or a later follower of this doctrine [Late 16C. Via Latin < Greek *skeptikos* 'follower of the Greek philosopher Pyrrho' < *skeptesthai* 'look about'] —**Sceptic** *adj*

sceptical /sképtik'l/ *adj* **1.** tending not to believe or accept things but to question them **2.** marked by a doubting attitude —**sceptically** *adv* —**scepticalness** *n*

SYNONYMS See *doubtful*.

scepticism /sképtisizəm/ *n* **1.** an attitude marked by a tendency to doubt what others accept to be true **2.** a doubting attitude towards religious beliefs **3.** PHILOSOPHY another spelling of **Scepticism**

Scepticism *n* the doctrine that holds that true knowledge is not possible

sceptre

sceptre /séptər/ *n* **1.** STAFF USED AS ROYAL EMBLEM a ceremonial staff, rod, or wand used as an emblem of a monarch's authority **2.** ROYAL AUTHORITY royal or imperial power or authority ■ *vt* (**-tres, -tring, -tred**) GIVE SOMEBODY ROYAL AUTHORITY to endow somebody with royal power or authority [13C. Via French and Latin < Greek *skēptron* 'staff' < *skēptein* 'lean on'] —**sceptred** *adj*

SCF *abbr* Save the Children Fund

SCG *abbr* Aus Sydney Cricket Ground

sch. *abbr* school

schadenfreude /shaád'n froydə/, **Schadenfreude** *n* malicious or smug pleasure taken in somebody else's misfortune [Late 19C. < German < *Schaden* 'harm' + *Freude* 'joy']

Schaffhausen /shaaf hówzən/ town in north-central Switzerland, on the River Rhine. Population: 33,789 (1998).

schappe /sháppə/ *n* yarn or fabric made from the waste products of silk [Late 19C. < German]

schedule /shéddyool, skéd-/ *n* **1.** WORK PLAN a plan of work to be done, showing the order in which tasks are to be carried out and the amounts of time allocated to them ○ *The project was completed ahead of schedule.* ○ *draw up a production schedule* **2.** LIST OF MEETINGS, COMMITMENTS, OR APPOINTMENTS an outline description of the things somebody is to do and the times at which they are to be done ○ *Her busy work schedule didn't permit us to meet for lunch.* **3.** *N Am* same as **timetable 4.** LIST OF ITEMS a table of items of information ○ *a schedule of tariffs* **5.** SUPPLEMENTARY LIST a list of details, often in the form of an appendix to a legal or legislative document **6.** *US* EDUC STUDENT'S TIMETABLE a list of the classes and the times at which they occur for a student or teacher in a given period ■ *vt* (**-ules, -uling, -uled**) **1.** PLAN SOMETHING FOR A PARTICULAR TIME to plan something to happen at a particular time ○ *They are scheduled to arrive at midday.* **2.** MAKE A LIST OF THINGS to put together a table of items of information, or place an item in the table **3.** PROTECT BUILDING BY LAW to put a building on a list of officially protected buildings [14C. Via French < late Latin *schedula* 'small piece of paper' < Greek *skhedē* 'page'] —**schedular** *adj* —**scheduler** *n*

Scheduled Castes /shéddyool-, skéd-/ *npl* in India, castes that are officially considered disadvantaged and granted special treatment, including Dalits

[Because listed in a 'schedule' of the Indian constitution, 1950]

scheduled territories *npl* FIN same as **sterling area**

Scheduled Tribes *npl* in India, the indigenous rural communities who are officially considered disadvantaged and granted special treatment

Scheele /sheélə, sháy-/, **Carl Wilhelm** (1742–86) Swedish chemist. He discovered many elements, compounds, and chemical reactions, and isolated oxygen before the British chemist Joseph Priestley.

scheelite /sheé līt/ *n* a variously coloured calcium tungstate mineral. Use: source of tungsten. [Mid-19C. After Carl Wilhelm SCHEELE]

schefflera /shéfflərə/ (*plural* **-ras** or *same*) *n* a tropical tree or bush with glossy leaves, often cultivated as a house plant. Genus: *Schefflera*. [Mid-20C. After J. C. Scheffler (1742–86), German botanist]

Schelling /shélling/, **Friedrich** (1775–1854) German philosopher. He was one of the leading exponents of idealism and the Romantic tendency in German philosophy. Full name **Schelling, Friedrich Wilhelm Joseph von**

Schelte /skéltə/ river in Europe that flows through France, Belgium, and the Netherlands. Length: 435 km/270 mi.

schema /skeémə/ (*plural* **-mata** /skeémətə, skee maátə/) *n* **1.** DIAGRAM a diagram or plan showing the basic outline of something **2.** MENTAL PATTERN an organizational or conceptual pattern in the mind **3.** KANTIAN PHILOSOPHICAL PRINCIPLE in the philosophy of Kant, a method that allows the understanding to apply concepts to the evidence of the senses **4.** DUMMY EXPRESSION IN LOGIC in logic, a dummy expression indicating where particular words should appear, e.g. in 'S and R', 'S' and 'R' are schemata for sentences [Late 18C. Directly or via German < Greek *skhēma*]

schematic /skee máttik, ski-/ *adj* showing the basic form or layout of something ○ *a schematic drawing* ■ *n* a diagram, especially of electrical circuits

schematise *vt* another spelling of **schematize**

schematism /skeémətizəm/ *n* the basic arrangement or layout of parts in a complex object or system

schematize /skeémə tīz/ (**-tizes, -tizing, -tized**), **schematise** (**-tises, -tising, -tised**) *vt* to arrange or organize something according to a system —**schematization** /skeémə tī záysh'n/ *n*

scheme /skeem/ *n* **1.** SECRET PLOT a secret and cunning plan, especially one designed to cause damage or harm ○ *Luckily, we got wise to their little scheme.* **2.** PLAN OF ACTION a systematic plan of action ○ *money-making schemes* **3.** GOVERNMENT OR BUSINESS PROGRAMME a plan, policy, or programme carried out by a government or business ○ *a training scheme* ○ *pension scheme* **4.** SYSTEM a systematic and coherent arrangement of parts **5.** DIAGRAM OF SOMETHING a diagram, chart, or map **6.** ASTROLOGER'S CHART an astrological chart of the sky **7.** *Scotland* TOWN PLAN same as **housing scheme** ■ *v* (**schemes, scheming, schemed**) **1.** *vi* MAKE A SECRET PLAN to devise plots and plans, especially secret or cunning ones intended to cause damage or harm **2.** *vt* FOLLOW COLOUR SCHEME WHEN DECORATING SOMETHING to decorate or arrange something in accordance with a colour scheme [Mid-16C. Via Latin *schema* 'form' < Greek *skhēma*] —**schemer** *n*

scheming /skeéming/ *adj* continually devising plots and plans, especially cunning or underhand ones, or using them to achieve objectives —**schemingly** *adv*

Schengen Agreement /shéngən-/ *n* an agreement between some countries in the European Union and associated states, abolishing internal border controls over the movement of people and goods between member countries [After a village on the borders of Luxembourg, France, and Germany where the agreement was signed]

Schepisi /sképsi/, **Fred** (*b.* 1939) Australian filmmaker. He directed *The Chant of Jimmie Blacksmith* (1978). After the 1980s he made films in Hollywood, including *Six Degrees of Separation* (1994). Full name **Schepisi, Frederick Alan**

scherzando /skairt sándō/ *adj*, *adv* performed in a playful musical style and tempo (*used as a musical*

direction) ■ n (plural **-dos** or **-di** /-di/) a scherzando piece or passage of music [Early 19C. < Italian, < scherzare 'to joke']

scherzo /skáirtsō/ (plural **-zos** or **-zi** /-tsi/) n **1.** a lively and often playful or humorous movement in a musical composition, usually the third of four **2.** an independent musical work in a lively and often playful or humorous style [Mid-19C. < Italian, < scherzare 'to joke']

Scheveningen /skáyvən ingən/ resort town in the western Netherlands, on the North Sea. It is now a district of The Hague.

Elsa Schiaparelli

Schiaparelli /skee aápə rélli, skáppə-/, **Elsa** (1896–1973) Italian fashion designer. Her designs were often extravagant with deliberately overstated effects.

> 'A dress has no life of its own unless it is worn, and as soon as this happens another personality takes over from you and animates it, or tries to, glorifies or destroys it, or makes it into a song of beauty.'
> [Elsa Schiaparelli, *A Shocking Life*; 1954]

Schick test /shík-/ n an injection of nontoxic diphtheria under the skin, used to determine whether a patient is immune to diphtheria. A patch of reddened skin at the point of injection indicates no immunity. [Early 20C. After Bela Schick (1877–1967), Hungarian-born US paediatrician]

Schiele /sheélə/, **Egon** (1890–1918) Austrian painter. His depictions of the human figure, in the expressionist style, have a strongly erotic quality.

Schiff's reagent /shífs-/, **Schiff reagent** n an acid solution of fuchsin. Use: test for aldehydes. [Late 19C. After Hugo Schiff (1834–1915), German chemist]

schiller /shíllər/ n an iridescent lustre in some minerals [Early 19C. < German, 'iridescence']

Schiller /shíllər/, **Friedrich von** (1759–1805) German poet, dramatist, historian, and philosopher. Regarded as Germany's greatest playwright, he wrote works in praise of the freedom of the human spirit, including the dramas *Wallenstein* (1799), *Maria Stuart* (1800), and *Wilhelm Tell* (1804). Full name **Schiller, Johann Christoph Friedrich von**

> 'Kings are only slaves of their own position who may not follow their own heart.'
> [Friedrich von Schiller, *Maria Stuart*; 1800]

schilling /shílling/ n the main unit of the former Austrian currency [Mid-18C. < German]

schipperke /shíppərki, skíp-/ (plural **-kes** or same) n a small black tailless dog belonging to a breed with pointed ears and a thick coat [Late 19C. < Dutch dialect, diminutive of Dutch schipper (see SKIPPER¹)]

schipperke

schism /skízzəm, sízzəm/ n **1.** DIVISION IN RELIGIOUS DENOMINATION a major split within an established religious denomination, usually on the grounds of differences in belief or practice, leading to the setting up of a separate breakaway organization, or the offence of causing such a split **2.** DIVISIVE UNPLEASANT SPLIT the division of a group into mutually antagonistic factions **3.** FACTION a faction formed as a result of a schism [14C. Via French < late Latin schisma < Greek schizein 'to split']

schismatic /skiz máttik, siz-/, **schismatical** /-máttik'l/ adj relating to, involved in, or causing schism ■ n a participant in or cause of a schism —**schismatically** adv

schist /shist/ n a rock whose minerals have aligned themselves in one direction in response to deformation stresses, with the result that the rock can be split in parallel layers [Late 18C. Via French schiste < Latin (lapis) schistos 'fissile (stone)' < Greek skhistos < skhizein 'to split'] —**schistose** /-tōss, -tōz/ adj —**schistosity** /shiss tóssəti/ n

schistocyte /shísto sīt/ n a red blood cell undergoing fragmentation, or any one of the fragments that are formed as a result

schistosome /shísto sōm/ n a tiny flatworm that often lives as a parasite in the blood of birds and mammals. In humans, it causes the disease schistosomiasis.

schistosomiasis /shísto sō mí əssiss/ n an often chronic illness that results from infection of the blood with a parasitic flatworm (**schistosome**). It causes debilitation and can cause liver and intestinal damage. It is most common in Asia, Africa, and South America, especially in areas where the water is contaminated by freshwater snails that carry the parasite.

schiz- prefix same as **schizo-** (used before vowels)

schizanthus /skit sánthəss, ski zánth-/ (plural same) n an annual plant that grows in cool, moist conditions. Flowers: colourful with distinctive markings, resembling orchids. Native to: South America. Genus: *Schizanthus*. [Early 19C. < modern Latin, < Greek skhizein 'to split' + anthos 'flower']

schizo /skítsō/ (slang insult) n (plural **-os**) an offensive term for somebody who has schizophrenia ■ adj an offensive term meaning having characteristics thought of, though often erroneously, as symptomatic of schizophrenia [Mid-20C. Shortening of SCHIZOPHRENIC]

schizo- prefix **1.** split, cleft ○ schizocarp **2.** cleavage, fission ○ schizogony **3.** schizophrenia ○ schizothymia [< modern Latin, < Greek skhizein 'to split' < Indo-European]

schizocarp /skítsō kaarp, shízō-/ n a dry fruit that splits into individually seeded parts (**carpels**) when ripe —**schizocarpic** /skítsō kaárpik, shízo-/ adj —**schizocarpous** /skítsō kaárpəss, shízo-/ adj

schizogony /skit zóggəni, shī zóg-/ n a form of asexual reproduction that occurs in some single-celled organisms (**protozoans**), in which the nucleus of an individual divides many times before the cytoplasm divides to form the daughter cells. This process enables some parasites, including the malaria parasite, to undergo rapid proliferation in the body tissues of an infected host.

schizoid /skít soyd/ adj **1.** showing some of the symptoms of schizophrenia such as withdrawal into the self and a tendency to fantasize (technical) ○ exhibits a schizoid personality **2.** an offensive term describing a personality that suggests inner conflicts and exhibits outer contradictions (insult)

schizont /skítsont, shí zont/ n a cell formed during the asexual phase of the life cycle of some single-celled organisms (**protozoans**)

schizophrenia /skítsō freéni ə/ n **1.** a severe psychiatric disorder with symptoms of emotional instability, detachment from reality, and withdrawal into the self **2.** an offensive term for a state characterized by contradictory or conflicting attitudes, behaviour, or qualities (insult) [Early 20C. < SCHIZO- + Greek phrēn 'mind']

schizophrenic /skítsō frénnik/ adj **1.** relating to or resulting from schizophrenia **2.** an offensive term meaning characterized by conflicts and contradictions (insult) —**schizophrenic** n

schizophyte /skítsə fīt, shízə-/ n a microorganism that reproduces by fission. Bacteria and bluish-green algae are schizophytes. —**schizophytic** /skítsə fíttik, shízə-/ adj

schizopod /skítsə pod, shízə-/ (plural **-pods** or same) n a crustacean resembling a shrimp, e.g. a krill. Order: Mysidacea or Euphausiacea.

schizothymia /skítsō thími ə/ n an introverted psychiatric condition that resembles a mild form of schizophrenia (technical) [Mid-20C. < SCHIZO- + Greek thumos 'soul, mind'] —**schizothymic** adj

schizy /skítsi/ (**-ier**, **-iest**) adj an offensive term for somebody regarded as emotionally sensitive or moody to a degree that makes others feel uneasy (slang insult) [Mid-20C. Shortening of SCHIZOPHRENIC or SCHIZOID with alteration]

schlemiel /shlə meél/, **schlemihl** n N Am an offensive term that deliberately insults somebody's ability to cope or do things or somebody's failure to experience good fortune (slang insult) [Late 19C. < Yiddish shlemiel]

schlep /shlep/, **shlep** v (**schleps**, **schlepping**, **schlepped**; **shleps**, **shlepping**, **shlepped**) (informal) **1.** vt MOVE SOMETHING WITH DIFFICULTY to lug or haul something from one place to another **2.** vi GO WITH DIFFICULTY to move slowly, clumsily, or tediously ■ n **1.** TEDIOUS JOURNEY a long, tedious, or difficult journey (informal) ○ It's such a schlep all the way across town. **2.** OFFENSIVE TERM an offensive term that deliberately insults somebody's intelligence or physical coordination (informal insult) [Early 20C. Via Yiddish < German schleppen 'to drag'] —**schlepper** n

Schleswig-Holstein /shléz vig hólstīn/ state in northern Germany occupying the southern part of the Jutland peninsula. Capital: Kiel. Population: 2,766,057 (1998). Area: 15,769 sq. km/6,088 sq. mi.

Schliemann /shleémən/, **Heinrich** (1822–90) German archaeologist who discovered and excavated the remains of ancient Troy (1870–80)

schlieren /shleérən/ npl **1.** zones of different density and refraction in a transparent fluid, visible as streaks and caused by pressure or temperature variations **2.** a texture observed in some igneous rocks where the darker, more basic minerals form linear aggregates in the paler host rock [Late 19C. < German, 'streaks']

schlieren photography n a form of flash photography that records schlieren present in a fluid

schlock /shlok/ N Am (slang) n something that has no value and is shoddily made ■ adj cheap and lacking any redeeming quality ○ a schlock horror film [Early 20C. Probably via Yiddish shlak 'evil blow' < Middle High German slag] —**schlocky** adj

schm-, **shm-** prefix somebody or something purported or purporting to be genuine, real, or of the expected high quality but really not (used dismissively in rhyming compounds) ○ doctor-schmoctor [< Yiddish]

schmaltz /shmawlts, shmolts/, **schmalz**, **shmaltz** n cloying or exaggerated sentimentality (informal) [Mid-20C. Via Yiddish shmalts 'melted fat' < German Schmalz] —**schmaltzily** adv —**schmaltziness** n —**schmaltzy** adj

schmatte /shmáttə/, **shmatte** n N Am a rag or worthless thing (informal) [Late 20C. Via Yiddish < Polish szmata 'rag']

Schmeling /shmáyling/, **Max** (b. 1905) German boxer. He was holder of the world heavyweight title (1930–32 and 1936–38). After serving in the German army, he retired in 1945 to pursue a business career. Full name **Schmeling, Maximilian**

Schmidt /shmit/, **Helmut** (b. 1918) chancellor of West Germany (1974–82). He was a prominent leader of the European Union, and, from 1983, publisher of the weekly newspaper *Die Zeit*. Full name **Schmidt, Helmut Heinrich Waldemar**

Schmidt camera n ASTRON same as **Schmidt telescope**

Schmidt system n an optical system that uses a special concave spherical mirror to correct optical

aberrations [Mid-20C. After Bernhard Voldemar *Schmidt* (1879–1935), Estonian-born German specialist in optics]

Schmidt telescope *n* a wide-angle photographic telescope used in astronomy. It has a special internal mirror to correct optical aberrations. [Mid-20C. Because it uses a Schmidt system]

Schmitt trigger /shmít-/ *n* an electronic circuit that produces an output when the input exceeds a predetermined turn-on or threshold level. The output is maintained until the input falls below the threshold level. [Mid-20C. After Otto H. *Schmitt* (b. 1913), US electronics engineer]

schmo /shmō/ (*plural* **schmoes**), **shmo** (*plural* **shmoes**) *n N Am* an offensive term that deliberately insults somebody's character or perceptiveness (*slang insult*) [Mid-20C. Alteration of SCHMUCK]

schmooze /shmooz/ (*slang*) *v* (**schmoozes, schmoozing, schmoozed**) **1.** *vi* CHAT INFORMALLY to chat socially and agreeably **2.** *vt* BE INGRATIATING TOWARDS SOMEBODY to talk persuasively to somebody, often to gain personal advantage ■ *n* INFORMAL CHAT an informal chat about trivial matters [Late 19C. Via Yiddish *schmuesn* 'talk' < Hebrew *šĕmū'āh* 'rumour'] —**schmoozer** *n*

schmuck /shmuk/, **shmuck** *n N Am* a highly offensive term that deliberately insults somebody's personal worth (*slang insult*) [Late 19C. < Yiddish *shmok* 'penis']

Schnabel /shnaab'l/, **Artur** (1882–1951) Austrian pianist and composer. He was known for his interpretations of Beethoven, Schubert, and Mozart. His own compositions include chamber music and piano works. After 1938 he settled in the United States.

> 'When a piece gets difficult make faces.'
> [Artur Schnabel. Quoted in *The Unimportance of Being Oscar*, Oscar Levant; 1968]

schnapps /shnaps/ (*plural same*), **schnaps** *n* **1.** a strong alcoholic spirit, resembling gin, made in Germany and the Netherlands **2.** a glass or measure of schnapps [Early 19C. Via German < Low German or Dutch *snaps* 'mouthful']

~~schnaps~~ incorrect spelling of **schnapps**

schnauzer /shnówtsər/ *n* a wiry-coated dog with bushy eyebrows and whiskers that grow like a beard, belonging to any one of three breeds (giant, standard, and miniature) that originated in Germany [Early 20C. < German, < *Schnauze* 'snout']

schnitzel /shníts'l/ *n* a piece of meat, typically veal, beaten flat and served fried, usually coated in egg and breadcrumbs [Mid-19C. < German, < Old High German *snidan* 'to cut']

Schnitzler /shnítslər/, **Arthur** (1862–1931) Austrian doctor, playwright, and novelist. His works, inspired by psychoanalysis and focusing on human relationships, include *Reigen* (1897), later staged and filmed as *La Ronde*.

schnozzle /shnózz'l/, **schnoz** /shnoz/ (*plural* **schnozes**) *n US* a nose, especially a large one (*slang*) [Mid-20C. < Yiddish *shnoytsl*, diminutive of *shnoyts* 'snout' < German *Schnauze*]

Schoenberg /shúrn burg, shön bŏŏrk/, **Arnold** (1874–1951) Austrian composer. He is best known for his revolutionary 12-tone, or serial, system, which broke with traditional harmony. Full name **Schoenberg, Arnold Franz Walter**

> 'If it is art, it is not for the masses.'
> [Arnold Schoenberg, *Letter to W. S. Schlamm*; 1 July 1945]

schola cantorum /skōlə kan táwrəm/ (*plural* **scholae cantorum** /skōlee-/) *n* a choir or choir school housed in a church or cathedral [< medieval Latin, 'school of singers']

scholar /skóllər/ *n* **1.** LEARNED PERSON a learned person, especially an academic specialist in one area of knowledge **2.** SCHOLARSHIP STUDENT a student who receives a scholarship **3.** PUPIL a school pupil (*formal*) [Pre-12C. < late Latin *scholaris* < Latin *schola* (see SCHOOL 1)]

scholarly /skóllərli/ *adj* **1.** LEARNED possessing or showing a great deal of knowledge, especially knowledge of an academic subject **2.** OF SCHOLARS relating to scholars or to formal study ○ *scholarly journals* **3.** ACCORDING TO PRINCIPLES OF FORMAL STUDY in keeping with a rigorous and systematic approach to acquiring knowledge or to setting out the results of study —**scholarliness** *n*

scholarship /skóllər ship/ *n* **1.** FINANCIAL HELP FOR STUDENT a sum of money awarded to a student on the basis of academic merit, to help with living expenses, study, or travel **2.** FORMAL STUDY academic learning or achievement **3.** ACADEMIC WORKS a body of learning on an academic subject ○ *a review of German scholarship on the topic*

SYNONYMS See ***knowledge***.

scholastic /skə lástik/ *adj* **1.** OF SCHOOLS OR STUDYING relating to students, schools, or studying **2.** PEDANTIC too concerned with details or fine distinctions and too ready to criticize minor errors (*disapproving*) **3.** OF SCHOLASTICISM relating to the medieval movement of religious and philosophical learning known as scholasticism ■ *n* **1.** STUDENT OR TEACHER UNDER SCHOLASTICISM a student or teacher in the medieval intellectual movement known as scholasticism **2.** PEDANT a person regarded as pedantic or quibbling (*disapproving*) **3.** CHR SOMEBODY UNDERGOING ROMAN CATHOLIC SCHOLASTICATE a probationer in a scholasticate at a Roman Catholic seminary [Late 16C. Via Latin < Greek *skholastikos* 'learned' < *skholē* 'learned discussion, school'] —**scholastically** *adv*

scholasticate /skə lástikət/ *n* **1.** a probationary period of study for a Jesuit student at a Roman Catholic seminary **2.** a seminary where a scholasticate is undertaken

scholasticism /skə lástissizəm/ *n* **1.** a medieval theological and philosophical system of learning based on the authority of St Augustine and other leaders of the early Christian Church, and on the works of Aristotle. It sought to bridge the gap between religion and reason. **2.** narrowly traditional learning, or adherence to traditional educational methods

scholia LITERAT plural of **scholium**

scholiast /skōli ast/ *n* a medieval scholar who wrote commentaries on ancient Greek and Latin texts [Late 16C. < medieval Greek *skholiastēs* < *skholion* (see SCHOLIUM)] —**scholiastic** /skōli ástik/ *adj*

scholium /skōli əm/ (*plural* **-lia** /-li ə/) *n* a medieval annotation or commentary written on an ancient Greek or Latin text [Mid-16C. < Greek *skholion* 'interpretation' < *skholē* 'learned discussion, school']

school[1] /skool/ *n* **1.** INSTITUTION FOR TEACHING CHILDREN an institution in which children and teenagers are taught, usually up to the age of 16 or 18, or a building housing such an institution (*often used before a noun*) **2.** DEPARTMENT SPECIALIZING IN AN ACADEMIC SUBJECT a faculty, department, or institution that offers specialized instruction in an academic subject ○ *medical school* **3.** INSTITUTION TEACHING A NONACADEMIC SKILL an institution that specializes in teaching a particular skill, especially a practical or sports skill ○ *tennis school* **4.** STAFF AND STUDENTS all the staff and students of an educational institution (*often used before a noun*) **5.** DAY AT SCHOOL the part of a day spent teaching or being taught in a school ○ *School was over for another day.* **6.** YEARS SPENT AT SCHOOL the part of somebody's life spent being taught in a school ○ *After school, he went abroad for two years.* **7.** INSTRUCTIVE PLACE OR PERIOD a place or period of activity regarded as providing knowledge or experience ○ *the school of life* **8.** ARTISTS OR WRITERS SHARING SAME APPROACH a group of people, especially artists, writers, or philosophers, who share the same principles, methods, ideals, or style ○ *the Impressionist school* ○ *the Aristotelian school* **9.** *N Am* EDUC UNIVERSITY-LEVEL INSTITUTION a college or university ■ *vt* (**schools, schooling, schooled**) **1.** DEVELOP SOMEBODY'S SKILL to train somebody in a particular skill or area of expertise in a thorough and detailed way ○ *were schooled in the art of debate* **2.** EDUCATE SOMEBODY IN SCHOOL to educate a child or teenager formally in a school **3.** DISCIPLINE SOMEBODY to exert control or discipline over somebody or yourself **4.** RIDING TRAIN A HORSE to train a horse, especially for riding and dressage [Pre-12C. Via Latin *schola* < Greek *skholē* 'learned discussion, school']

SYNONYMS See ***teach***.

school[2] /skool/ *n* a group of fish, whales, porpoises, or other sea animals of a single type ■ *vi* (**schools, schooling, schooled**) to congregate in a school or swim in a school [14C. < Middle Dutch *schole* < W Germanic]

school age *n* the age at which a child is required legally to attend school —**school-age** *adj*

school board *n* in Britain, between 1870 and 1902, an elected committee that supervised local elementary schools

schoolbook /skóol bŏŏk/ *n* a textbook or other book used at school

schoolboy /skóol boy/ *n* a boy who attends school ■ *adj* at a level of maturity regarded as characteristic of, or designed to appeal to, boys of school age ○ *schoolboy clothes*

school bus *n* a large motor vehicle that takes children to and from school or on school-related trips

school captain *n Scotland, Aus* a boy or girl appointed or elected to be the senior representative of a school's pupils

School Certificate *n* in New Zealand, and from 1917 to 1951 in England and Wales, a public examination taken by 16-year-olds

schoolchild /skóol chīld/ (*plural* **-children** /-childrən/) *n* a child who attends school

school crossing patrol *n* somebody employed to stop traffic to allow schoolchildren to cross a road

school day *n* **1.** DAY OF SCHOOL OR SCHOOLING a day on which school is conducted, or the hours of instruction in that day **2.** PORTION OF DAY IN SCHOOL the part of a day spent at school ■ **school days** *npl* YEARS SPENT AT SCHOOL the period of time in somebody's life spent attending school

schoolfellow /skóol felō/ *n* same as **schoolmate** (*formal*)

school figure *n* in figure skating, one of a number of basic movements that used to be required as a part of competition (*often used in the plural*)

schoolgirl /skóol gurl/ *n* a girl who attends school ■ *adj* at a level of maturity regarded as characteristic of, or designed to appeal to, girls of school age ○ *schoolgirl clothes*

schoolhouse /skóol howss/ (*plural* **-houses** /-howziz/) *n* **1.** a building that houses a school, especially a rural primary school **2.** a house attached to a school, where a teacher, often the head teacher, lives

schoolie /skóoli/ *n Aus* **1.** a school pupil, especially one who has finished his or her final-year exams and is on holiday (*informal*) **2.** same as **schoolteacher** (*dated informal*)

schoolies week /skóoliz-/ *n Aus* the week after the final-year school examinations, when school pupils traditionally congregate in holiday resorts to celebrate leaving school (*informal*)

schooling /skóoling/ *n* **1.** EDUCATION AT SCHOOL the education or skills acquired at school **2.** INSTRUCTION instruction or training in something, carried out systematically and in a disciplined way **3.** TRAINING OF HORSE the training of a horse, especially for riding and dressage

school inspector *n* in the United Kingdom, an official appointed by the government to check on the standards of education in state-funded schools

schoolkid /skóol kid/ *n* a child or teenager who attends school (*informal*)

school-leaver *n* a pupil who has left school or is about to do so, especially one who leaves at the minimum age and does not go on to further or higher education

schoolman /skóol man/ (*plural* **-men** /-men/) *n* a university teacher, philosopher, or theologian in the late medieval period who espoused scholasticism

schoolmarm /skóol maarm/ *n* **1.** an offensive term for a woman thought to live in a way regarded as old-fashioned (*insult*) **2.** an offensive term for a woman schoolteacher, especially one considered too proper and old-fashioned (*dated insult*) —**schoolmarmish** *adj*

schoolmaster[1] /skóol maastər/ (*dated*) *n* a man who teaches in a school, especially in a private school or as a headmaster ■ *vi* (**-ters, -tering, -tered**) to be

a schoolmaster by profession [13C. < SCHOOL[1]] — **schoolmasterish** *adj* —**schoolmasterly** *adj* —**schoolmastership** *n*

schoolmaster[2] /skool maastər/ (*plural same*) *n* a fish of the snapper family that has yellow fins. Native to: Caribbean, tropical Atlantic. Latin name: *Lutjanus apodus*. [Mid-19C. < SCHOOL[2]]

schoolmate /skool mayt/ *n* a friend or companion at school

school milk *n* a third of a pint of milk formerly provided free to British schoolchildren each school day

schoolmistress /skool mistrəss/ *n* a female schoolteacher, especially in a private school (*dated*) — **schoolmistressy** *adj*

school of arts *n Aus* a building used for adult education classes in a rural town

school of hard knocks *n* difficult or challenging experiences that are considered to be instructive

School of the Air *n* in Australia, an education service provided for children living in remote regions. Lessons are carried out by radio as well as through video, tape, fax, and computer networks.

school of thought *n* a way of thinking about something, or a group of people who share the same attitude or opinion

school psychologist *n* a psychologist who visits a group of schools to give teachers and parents advice on the psychological and developmental problems of individual schoolchildren

schoolroom /skool room, -room/ *n* a classroom in a school

Schools /skoolz/ *npl* MEDIEVAL UNIVERSITIES OR SCHOLASTICS the universities of medieval Europe, or the scholastics who taught in them (*takes a plural verb*) ■ *n* (*takes a singular or plural verb*) **1.** OXFORD UNIVERSITY EXAMINATIONS BUILDING at Oxford University, the university building in which examinations are held **2.** OXFORD UNIVERSITY FINAL EXAMINATIONS at Oxford University, the final examinations for the degree of BA that are held in the Examination Schools

schoolteacher /skool teechər/ *n* a teacher in a school —**schoolteaching** *n*

schoolwork /skool wurk/ *n* the work that a pupil does in or after school

schoolyard /skool yaard/ *n N Am* same as **playground** (sense 2)

school year *n* **1.** a period of 12 months, beginning usually in late August or early September, throughout which pupils are assigned to the same class **2.** the months during which instruction is given at a school

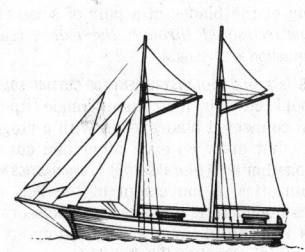
schooner

schooner /skoonər/ *n* **1.** SAILING VESSEL a fast sailing ship with at least two masts and with sails set lengthways (**fore-and-aft**) **2.** HIST same as **prairie schooner 3.** SHERRY GLASS a large glass for sherry **4.** *N Am* BEER GLASS a tall slim glass for beer **5.** *Aus* NEW SOUTH WALES BEER GLASS in New South Wales, a large beer glass containing 425 ml/15 fl oz **6.** *Aus* SOUTH AUSTRALIAN BEER GLASS in South Australia, a medium-sized beer glass containing 257 ml/9 fl oz [Early 18C. Origin ?]

schooner rig *n* an arrangement of masts and sails (**rig**) in which the mainmast is taller than the foremast —**schooner-rigged** *adj*

Schopenhauer /shópən howər/, **Arthur** (1788–1860) German philosopher. His atheistic, deeply pessimistic philosophy was most fully expounded in *The World as Will and Idea* (1819).

> 'I cannot here withhold the statement that *optimism*...seems to me to be not merely an absurd, but also a really *wicked*, way of thinking, a bitter mockery of the unspeakable sufferings of mankind.'
> [Arthur Schopenhauer, *The World as Will and Idea*; 1819]

schorl /shawrl/ *n* a black opaque form of the mineral tourmaline, often occurring in needle-shaped radiating crystals [Late 18C. < German *Schörl*] —**schorlaceous** /shawr láyshəss/ *adj*

schottische /sho teesh/ *n* **1.** a round dance of German origin, resembling a slow polka **2.** the music for a schottische [Mid-19C. < German *schottische (Tanz)* 'Scottish dance']

Schottky effect /shótki-/ *n* a reduction in the energy needed to remove an electron from a solid surface caused by the application of an electric field [Mid-20C. After Walter *Schottky* (1886–1976), German physicist]

Schröder /shrürdər, shródər/, **Gerhard** (*b.* 1944) chancellor of Germany (1998–). A former lawyer, and member of the centre-left Social Democratic Party since 1963, he ended 16 years of government by the Christian Democratic Union when he won the general election in 1998.

Schrödinger /shrürdingər, shród-, shród-/, **Erwin** (1887–1961) Austrian physicist. His mathematical analysis of the wave mechanics of orbiting electrons made a major contribution to quantum theory. He shared the Nobel Prize in physics (1933).

schtetl *n* another spelling of **shtetl**

schtick *n* another spelling of **shtick** (*informal*)

schtoom *adj* another spelling of **shtoom**

Franz Schubert

Schubert /shoobərt/, **Franz** (1797–1828) Austrian composer. He is particularly noted for his songs and chamber works, although he also wrote choral and orchestral music. Full name **Schubert, Franz Peter**

schul *n* JUDAISM another spelling of **shul**

Schulz /shoolts/, **Charles** (1922–2000) US cartoonist. He created the successful *Peanuts* comic strip (1950), featuring Snoopy and Charlie Brown. Full name **Schulz, Charles Monroe**

Schumacher /shoo makər/, **E. F.** (1911–77) German-born British economist and conservationist. He was the author of *Small is Beautiful* (1973) and an advocate of intermediate technology and the preservation of natural resources. Full name **Schumacher, Ernst Friederich**

> 'Modern economic thinking...is peculiarly unable to consider the long term and to appreciate man's dependence on the natural world.'
> [E. F. Schumacher, *Lecture, Blackpool*, 'Clean Air and Future Energy'; 19 October 1967]

Schumacher /shoo maakər, -maakher/, **Michael** (*b.* 1969) German racing driver. He was Formula One world champion six times between 1994 and 2003.

Schumann /shooman/, **Robert** (1810–56) German composer. He was a major exponent of the romantic style, noted for his songs, piano music, and or-

chestral and chamber works. Full name **Schumann, Robert Alexander**

> 'Music owes as much to Bach as religion to its founder.'
> [Attributed to Robert Schumann]

Schumpeter /shoom paytər/, **Joseph** (1883–1950) Austrian-born US economist. A professor at Harvard University (1932–50), he promoted entrepreneurship for the 'creative destruction' by which it drives economies forwards. Full name **Schumpeter, Joseph Alois**

schuss /shooss/ *vi* (**schusses, schussing, schussed**) to ski straight downhill at high speed ■ *n* a straight fast downhill run on skis [Mid-20C. < German, 'shot']

schussboomer /shooss boomər/ *n* a skier adept at making fast straight downhill runs (*informal*)

Schüssel /shooss'l/, **Wolfgang** (*b.* 1945) chancellor of Austria. A former lawyer, he became leader of the Austrian People's Party in 1995, chancellor in 2000.

schwa /shwaa/, **shwa** *n* an unstressed vowel, e.g. 'a' in 'above' or 'e' in 'sicken'. It is represented in the International Phonetic Alphabet by the symbol ə. [Late 19C. Via German < Hebrew *šĕwā*]

Schwann cell /shwon-, shván-/ *n* a cell of the peripheral nervous system that wraps around a nerve fibre and forms the myelin sheath [Early 20C. After Theodor *Schwann* (1810–82), German physiologist]

Schwarzenegger /shvaártsə neggər, swáwrtsə-/, **Arnold** (*b.* 1947) Austrian-born US body builder, film actor and politician. He has appeared in numerous films, usually in action roles such as in *The Terminator* (1984). In 2003 he was elected governor of California in a gubernatorial recall.

> 'I'll be back.'
> [Arnold Schwarzenegger, line in *The Terminator*; 1984]

Schwarzkopf /shvaárts kopf, shwáwrts kopf/, **Dame Elisabeth** (*b.* 1915) German soprano. She was noted for her operatic roles, especially in operas by Wolfgang Amadeus Mozart and Richard Strauss, and for her interpretation of lieder. Full name **Schwarzkopf, Olga Maria Elisabeth Friederike**

Schwarzkopf /shwáwrts kopf/, **H. Norman** (*b.* 1934) US general and commander of the Allied Forces during the Gulf War. Full name **Schwarzkopf, Herbert Norman**

Schwarzschild radius /shwáwrts shild-/ *n* the critical radius within which the gravitational force of a gravitationally collapsing astronomical object becomes so great that neither matter nor energy can escape, creating a black hole [Mid-20C. After Karl *Schwarzschild* (1873–1916), German astronomer]

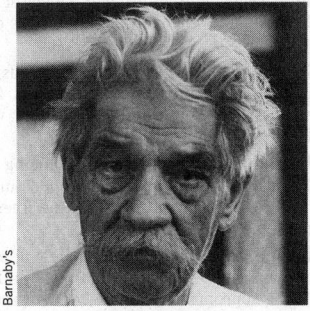
Albert Schweitzer

Schweitzer /shwítsər/, **Albert** (1875–1965) German-born theologian, musicologist, and missionary. He wrote important works on J.S. Bach and theology before setting up a hospital in 1913 at Lambaréné, in present-day Gabon, where he spent most of the rest of his life. He was awarded the Nobel Peace Prize (1952).

> 'Pain is a more terrible lord of mankind than even death himself.'
> [Albert Schweitzer, *On the Edge of the Primeval Forest*; 1922]

Schwitters /shvíttərz/, **Kurt** (1887–1948) German artist. He was noted for his collages, in which ephemera

are a prominent element, and his sculpture composed from junk.

sci *abbr* PRINTING single column inch

sci. *abbr* 1. science 2. scientific

sciamachy /sī ámməki/ (*plural* **-chies**), **skiamachy** /skī ámməki/ *n* the activity of fighting or arguing against imaginary opponents, usually for practice, or a fight or argument against an imagined opponent (*literary*) [Early 17C. < Greek *skiamakhia* < *skia* 'shadow' + *makhē* 'fight']

sciatic /sī áttik/ *adj* 1. relating to or affecting the back of the human hip or the sciatic nerve 2. causing sciatica or caused by sciatica [Early 16C. Via French < medieval Latin *sciaticus* < Greek *iskhion* 'hip joint']

sciatica /sī áttikə/ *n* pain and tenderness extending from the back of the hip down to the calf, usually caused by a protrusion of vertebral disc substance pressing on the roots of the sciatic nerve [15C. < medieval Latin, form of *sciaticus* (see SCIATIC)]

sciatic nerve *n* either of two nerves, one in each leg, that run from the back of the hip down the thigh to the calf and have the largest diameter of any nerves in the human body

SCID *abbr* MED severe combined immunodeficiency

science /sī ənss/ *n* 1. STUDY OF PHYSICAL WORLD the study of the physical and natural world and phenomena, especially by using systematic observation and experiment (*often used before a noun*) 2. BRANCH OF SCIENCE a particular area of study or knowledge of the physical world ○ *the life sciences* 3. SYSTEMATIC BODY OF KNOWLEDGE a systematically organized body of knowledge about a particular subject ○ *the behavioural sciences* 4. SOMETHING STUDIED OR PERFORMED METHODICALLY an activity that is the object of careful study or that is carried out according to a developed method ○ *the science of dressing for success* 5. KNOWLEDGE GAINED FROM SCIENCE the knowledge gained by the study of the physical world [14C. Via French < Latin *scientia* < *scient-*, present participle of *scire* 'know, discern' < Indo-European, 'cut'] ◇ **blind somebody with science** to confuse or overwhelm somebody by giving an impenetrable explanation using technical terms and concepts

science fiction *n* a form of fiction, usually set in the future, that deals with imaginary scientific and technological developments and contact with other worlds —**science-fiction** *adj*

science park *n* an area, usually associated with a university, where scientific research is carried out by commercial companies

scienter /sī éntər/ *adv* in law, with full knowledge or awareness [Early 19C. < Latin, 'knowingly' < *scient-* (see SCIENCE)]

sciential /sī énsh'l/ *adj* 1. relating to science or knowledge 2. possessing considerable knowledge or skill (*formal*)

scientific /sī ən tíffik/ *adj* 1. relating to, using, or conforming to science or its principles 2. proceeding in a systematic and methodical way —**scientifically** *adv*

scientific method *n* the system of advancing knowledge by formulating a question, collecting data about it through observation and experiment, and testing a hypothetical answer

scientific notation *n* a way of expressing a given number as a number between 1 and 10 multiplied by 10 to the appropriate power. 5,743.6 expressed in scientific notation is 5.7436 ± 10^3.

scientific revolution *n* the period of advances in science that was at its height in the 17th century and produced widespread change in traditional beliefs held since the Middle Ages

scientism /sī əntizəm/ *n* 1. the use of the scientific method of acquiring knowledge, whether in the traditional sciences or in other fields of enquiry 2. the belief that science alone can explain phenomena, or the application of scientific methods to fields unsuitable for it ○ *We feel that the attitude that predominates in science at present is arrogance, which has fostered dogmatism and scientism.'* (Brian D. Josephson, Beverly A. Rubik, *The Challenge of Consciousness Research*; 1992) —**scientist** /sī ən tístik/ *adj*

scientist /sī əntist/ *n* somebody who has scientific training or works in one of the sciences ○ *a forensic scientist*

Scientist *n* 1. in Christian Science belief, Jesus Christ as the paramount spiritual healer 2. a member of the Church of Christ, Scientist

sci-fi /sī fí/ *n* same as **science fiction** (*informal*) [Mid-20C. Shortening]

scilicet /sílli set, síli-, sílla-, skeéli ket/ *adv* used to introduce a word or phrase of clarification, or a missing word or phrase (*formal*) [14C. < Latin, contraction of *scire licet* 'it is permitted to know']

scilla /síllə/ (*plural* **-las** or *same*) *n* a plant with glossy narrow leaves that grows from a bulb. Flowers: small, blue, star- or bell-shaped. Native to: Europe, Asia. Genus: *Scilla*. [Early 19C. Via Latin < Greek *skilla* 'squill']

Scilly Isles /sílli-/ group of about 150 islands, only four of which are inhabited, in the Atlantic Ocean off Cornwall, southwestern England. Population: 2,153 (2001). Area: 16 sq. km/6 sq. mi.

scimitar

scimitar /símmitər, -taar/, **simitar** *n* an Arab or Turkish sword with a curved blade that broadens out as it nears the point [Mid-16C. < French *cimeterre* or Italian *scimitarra*]

scindapsus /skin dápsəss/ (*plural* **-suses** or *same*) *n* a climbing plant with heart-shaped, often variegated leaves that is popular as a house plant. Native to: Asia. Genus: *Scindapsus*. [Mid-20C. Via modern Latin < Greek *skindapsos*, plant like ivy]

scintigram /sínti gram/ *n* a two-dimensional image of the distribution of a radioactive tracer in a body organ such as the brain or a kidney, obtained using a special scanner (**scintiscanner**) [Mid-20C. < SCINTILLATION]

scintilla /sin tíllə/ *n* a tiny amount of something ○ *There's not a scintilla of truth in what he said.* [Late 17C. < Latin, 'spark']

scintillate /sínti layt/ (**-lates**, **-lating**, **-lated**) *vi* 1. SPARKLE AND FLASH BRIGHTLY to give off or reflect light in sparks or flashes 2. BE CLEVER OR WITTY to be very lively, exciting, and entertaining, especially by saying brilliantly clever or witty things 3. PHYS EMIT LIGHT FLASHES to produce sparks of light when hit by particles or photons [Early 17C. < Latin *scintillat-*, past participle of *scintillare* < *scintilla* 'spark'] —**scintillant** *adj* —**scintillantly** *adv* —**scintillator** *n*

scintillating /sínti layting/ *adj* possessing or displaying a dazzlingly impressive liveliness, cleverness, or wit —**scintillatingly** *adv*

scintillation /sínti láysh'n/ *n* 1. FLASH a bright flash of light or spark 2. EMISSION the emission of flashes and sparks of light 3. ASTRON TWINKLING OF STARS the twinkling of stars, caused by refraction of light rays from the stars because of different densities in the Earth's atmosphere 4. PHYS FLASH OF LIGHT a flash of light caused by the impact of particles or photons 5. LIVELINESS dazzling liveliness, cleverness, or wit (*formal*)

scintillation counter *n* a device that detects and measures high-energy radiation through flashes of light produced when ionizing radiation impacts on a phosphorescent substance

scintiscan /sínti skan/ *n* MED same as **scintigram** [Mid-20C. < SCINTILLATION]

scintiscanner /sínti skanər/ *n* an apparatus used in

diagnosing some diseases that produces an image (**scintigram**) of the distribution in the body of a radioactive tracer that has been administered to the patient

sciolism /sī əlizəm/ *n* displays of sham learning designed to deceive or impress [Early 19C. < late Latin *sciolus*, diminutive of *scius* 'having knowledge' < *scire* 'know'] —**sciolist** *n* —**sciolistic** /sī ə lístik/ *adj*

scion /sī ən/ *n* 1. a living shoot or twig of a plant used for grafting to a stock 2. a child or descendant of a family, especially a rich, famous, or important family [13C. < Old French *ciun*]

Scipio /skíppi ō, síppi ō/, **Publius Cornelius** (*d.* 211 BC) Roman general. He was the father of Scipio Africanus the Elder. Although he failed to defeat the Carthaginians in northern Italy and Spain, he helped to check their advances on Rome.

Scipio Africanus (the Elder) /-áffri káanəss/ (234?–183 BC) Roman general. He was the grandfather by adoption of Scipio Africanus the Younger. His defeat of Hannibal in 202 BC ended the Second Punic War. Full name **Publius Cornelius Scipio**

Scipio Africanus (the Younger) /-áffri káanəss/ (185?–129 BC) Roman general. He was the grandson by adoption of Scipio Africanus the Elder. A successful military commander, he destroyed Carthage to end the Third Punic War (146 BC). As a government official in Rome, he opposed the populist Gracchi brothers. Full name **Publius Cornelius Scipio Aemilianus**

scire facias /síri fáyshi ass/ *n* 1. a writ that requires a defendant to appear in court and show why the plaintiff should not be permitted to take a specific legal step 2. the judicial proceeding that produces a writ of scire facias [< Latin, 'you should cause (him or her) to know']

scirocco *n* METEOROL another spelling of **sirocco**

scirrhous /sírrəss, skírrəss/ *adj* describes a cancerous tumour (**carcinoma**) that is hard and fibrous [Mid-16C. < modern Latin *scirrhosus* < *scirrhus* 'hard growth', alteration of Latin *scirrus* < Greek *skirros* 'hard'] —**scirrhosity** /si róssəti, ski-/ *n*

scissel /skíss'l/ *n* metal clippings left over after discs, especially coins, have been punched out of sheets of metal [Early 17C. < French *cisaille* < *cisailler* 'clip with shears']

scissile /síssīl/ *adj* capable of being easily and smoothly cut, separated, or divided (*technical*) [Early 17C. < Latin *scissilis* < *sciss-* (see SCISSION)]

scission /sízh'n, sísh'n/ *n* the act or process of cutting, separating, or dividing (*technical*) [15C. Via French < Latin *scission-* < *sciss-*, past participle of *scindere* 'cut']

scissor /sízzər/ (**-sors**, **-soring**, **-sored**) *vti* 1. to use scissors to cut something 2. to move the legs, arms, or body in a way that resembles the opening and shutting of the blades of a pair of scissors ○ *The swimmer scissored through the water.* [Early 17C. Back-formation < SCISSORS]

scissors /sízzərz/ *npl* INSTRUMENT FOR CUTTING SOMETHING a hand-held cutting instrument made up of two crossed connected blades, each with a ring-shaped handle, that pivot on each other and cut as they come together ■ *n* (*plural same*) 1. GYMNASTICS MOVEMENT in gymnastics, a movement of the legs that resembles the opening and closing of scissors 2. TECHNIQUE IN HIGH-JUMPING in the high jump, a simple technique of clearing the bar sideways on with a leading leg and then the other in a fast separating and closing movement. This technique is now rarely used. 3. WRESTLING same as **scissors hold** 4. RUGBY MANOEUVRE in rugby, a tactic in which a player passes the ball to another player running diagonally to his or her line of advance, thus changing the direction of an attack [14C. Via French *cisoires* < late Latin *cisoria* 'cutting tool' < Latin *cis-*, past participle of *caedere* 'cut']

scissors-and-paste *adj* crudely or hastily put together

scissors hold *n* a wrestling hold in which the legs are wrapped and the feet locked around an opponent's head or body

scissors kick *n* 1. in swimming, a kicking motion that resembles the opening and closing of scissors,

used especially when doing the sidestroke **2.** in soccer, a mid-air kick of the ball with the legs moving in a way that resembles the movement of scissor blades

scissortail /sízzər tayl/ (*plural* **-tails** or *same*) *n* a bird with a long forked tail

sciurine /sī yŏŏrīn/, **sciurid** /sī yŏŏrid/ *n* a rodent belonging to the family that includes squirrels, marmots, and chipmunks. Family: Sciuridae. ■ *adj* relating to or belonging to the squirrel family of rodents [Mid-19C. < Latin *sciurus* (see SQUIRREL)]

sclaff /sklaf/ *vti* (**sclaffs, sclaffing, sclaffed**) in golf, to scrape the ground with the club head in making a stroke, or hit the ball after scraping the ground with the club head ■ *n* a golf stroke in which the ground and ball are sclaffed [Early 19C. Probably an imitation of the sound] —**sclaffer** *n*

scler- *prefix* same as **sclero-** (*used before vowels*)

sclera /skléérə/ *n* the dense outer coating of the eyeball that forms the white of the eye [Late 19C. < modern Latin, < Greek *sklēros* 'hard']

sclereid /skléérid/ *n* a short thick-walled plant cell that makes up a plant's supporting tissue (**sclerenchyma**) [Late 19C. < SCLERENCHYMA]

sclerenchyma /skleer éngkimə/ *n* strengthening or supporting walls of plant tissue made up of long cells or fibres and short cells (**sclereids**) [Mid-19C. < SCLERO- after PARENCHYMA] —**sclerenchymatous** /skleer eng kímmətəss/ *adj*

scleriasis /skleer ī́ əssiss/ *n* MED same as **scleroderma**

sclerite /skléér īt/ *n* a hard plate or layer of chitin or calcium on the outer skeleton of an arthropod —**scleritic** /skleer íttik/ *adj*

scleritis /skleer ī́tiss/ *n* inflammation of the tough outer coat of the eyeball that forms the white of the eye (**sclera**)

sclero- *prefix* **1.** hard ○ *scleroderma* **2.** hardness ○ *sclerometer* **3.** sclera ○ *scleritis* [< Greek *sklēros* 'hard' < Indo-European, 'dried up']

scleroderma /skléérō dúrmə/ *n* a disease in which the skin becomes progressively hard and thickened

sclerodermatous /skléérō dúrmətəss/ *adj* **1.** describes an organism having a hard external covering of scales or plates **2.** relating to or characteristic of the skin disease scleroderma

sclerometer /sklə rómmətər, skli-, skleer rómmitər/ *n* an instrument that determines the hardness of a metal or mineral by measuring the force required to scratch or pierce it —**sclerometric** /sklérrə méttrik, skléérō-/ *adj*

sclerophyll /skléérəfil, sklérrəfil/ *n* a woody plant of dry areas with thick leathery evergreen foliage that retains water —**sclerophyllous** /sklə róffiləss, skleer-/ *adj*

scleroprotein /skléérō prṓ teen, sklerrō-/ *n* any of a group of fibrous insoluble proteins that are found in body tissue, e.g. keratin, elastin, and collagen

sclerosis /sklə róssiss, skleer-/ (*plural* **-roses** /-rṓ seez/) *n* **1.** the hardening and thickening of body tissue as a result of unwarranted growth, degeneration of nerve fibres, or deposition of minerals, especially calcium **2.** the hardening and thickening of a plant cell wall that occurs as lignin is deposited, turning young green growth woody —**sclerosal** *adj* —**sclerosed** *adj*

sclerotia FUNGI plural of **sclerotium**

sclerotic /sklə róttik, skleer-/ *adj* **1.** OF PLANT CELL WALL HARDENING relating to the hardening and thickening of plant cell walls that turns young green growth woody **2.** OF WHITE OF THE EYE relating to the dense outer coating of the eyeball that forms the white of the eye (**sclera**) **3.** OF SCLEROSIS OF BODY TISSUE relating to or suffering from sclerosis of body tissue **4.** INFLEXIBLE having become unresponsively rigid, especially from longevity ○ *a political party grown sclerotic from too many years in power* ■ *n* ANAT same as **sclera** [Mid-16C. < Greek *sklēros* 'hard' + -OTIC]

sclerotin /skléérōtin, sklérrō-/ *n* an insoluble protein that hardens and darkens the chitin on the outer skeleton of arthropods [Mid-20C. < SCLERO- after words such as KERATIN]

sclerotise *vt* INSECTS another spelling of **sclerotize**

sclerotium /sklə rṓti əm/ (*plural* **-tia** /-ti ə/) *n* a compact hard mass in a fungus that contains stored food [Mid-19C. < modern Latin, genus of fungi < Greek *sklērotēs* 'hardness' < *sklēros* 'hard'] —**sclerotial** *adj* —**sclerotioid** *adj*

sclerotize /skléérō tīz, sklérrō-/ (**-tizes, -tizing, -tized**), **sclerotise** (**-tises, -tising, -tised**) *vt* to harden and darken an arthropod's outer skeleton [Mid-20C. < SCLEROTIC] —**sclerotization** /skléérō tī záysh'n, sklérrō tī-/ *n*

sclerotomy /sklə róttəmi, skleer-/ (*plural* **-mies**) *n* a surgical operation in which the outer coat (**sclera**) of the eyeball is cut, e.g. in order to remove an underlying tumour

sclerous /skléérəss, sklérrəss/ *adj* **1.** describes animal parts that are bony or scaly **2.** describes body tissue or body parts that have become especially hardened, as a result of the deposition of minerals

SCM *abbr* **1.** MED State Certified Midwife **2.** CHR Student Christian Movement

Sc.M. *abbr* EDUC Master of Science

SCN *abbr* ANAT suprachiasmatic nucleus

scoff[1] /skof/ *vi* (**scoffs, scoffing, scoffed**) BE DERISIVE OR SCORNFUL to express derision or scorn about somebody or something ○ *She scoffed at all our suggestions.* ■ *n* **1.** EXPRESSION OF SCORN an expression of derision or scorn **2.** OBJECT OF SCORN somebody or something that is derided or scorned [14C. Probably < N Germanic] —**scoffer** *n* —**scoffing** *adj* —**scoffingly** *adv*

scoff[2] /skof/ *vti* (**scoffs, scoffing, scoffed**) to eat food quickly and hungrily or greedily (*informal*) ■ *n* food (*slang*) [Late 18C. Origin ?]

Scofield /skṓ feeld/, **Sir Paul** (*b.* 1922) British actor. He won an Academy Award for *A Man for All Seasons* (1966) and is known for his versatility in numerous stage and screen roles, from Shakespeare to contemporary drama. Full name **Scofield, Sir David Paul**

scold /skōld/ *v* (**scolds, scolding, scolded**) **1.** *vt* TELL SOMEBODY OFF to rebuke somebody angrily **2.** *vi* SPEAK HARSHLY to use harsh language, especially when complaining or finding fault ■ *n* **1.** PERSON WHO REBUKES OTHERS an insistent rebuker of others **2.** OFFENSIVE TERM an offensive term for a woman regarded as making a habit of using abusive language, especially when constantly reminding a man to do something (*archaic*) [13C. Probably < Old Norse *skáld* 'poet, bard'; from the poet's role of satirizing people] —**scolder** *n* —**scoldingly** *adv*

scolecite /skólli sīt, skṓli sīt/ *n* a white zeolite mineral consisting of hydrated calcium aluminium silicate and found in both crystalline and massive forms [Early 19C. < Greek *skōlēk-*, stem of *skōlēx* 'worm']

scolex /skṓ leks/ (*plural* **-lices** /-li seez/) *n* the head of a tapeworm, with suckers or hooks that enable the parasitic worm to attach itself to its host [Mid-19C. Via modern Latin < Greek *skōlēx* 'worm']

scoliosis /skṓli ṓssiss/ *n* an excessive sideways curvature of the human spine [Early 18C. Via modern Latin < Greek *skoliōsis* < *skolios* 'bent, curved'] —**scoliotic** /-óttik/ *adj*

scollop *n* MARINE BIOL another spelling of **scallop**

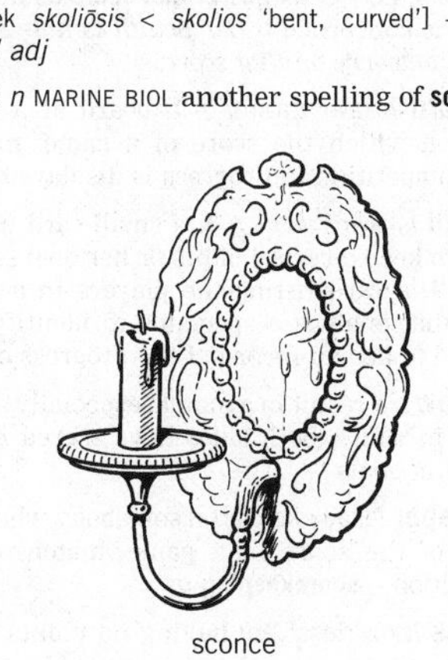

sconce

sconce[1] /skonss/ *n* a wall bracket for holding candles or, sometimes, electric light bulbs [14C. < Old French *esconse* < medieval Latin *absconsa (laterna)* 'hidden (lantern)' < *abscondere* (see ABSCOND)]

sconce[2] /skonss/ *n* a small defensive fort or earthwork [Late 16C. < Dutch *schans* 'brushwood, earthwork']

scone /skon, skōn/ *n* **1.** a generally small, sweet or savoury, unyeasted cake, made of flour, a little fat, and milk and usually served split and buttered. Plain scones are served with jam and clotted cream as part of the traditional British cream tea. **2.** *ANZ* the human head (*informal humorous*) [Early 16C. Origin ?]

Scone /skoon/ village in central Scotland, near the River Tay. It is famous for the Stone of Destiny on which Scottish kings were crowned, which was originally located there. The stone was moved to Westminster Abbey, London, by Edward I in 1296 then returned to Edinburgh Castle in 1996. Population: 4,533 (1991).

scoob /skoob/, **scooby** /skoobi/ (*plural* **-ies**) *n Aus* a cigarette containing cannabis (*slang*) [Late 20C. Perhaps < *Scooby Doo*, children's cartoon series interpreted as having a drugs theme]

scoop /skoop/ *n* **1.** SHOVEL a utensil with a short handle and deep rounded sides, used for shovelling or ladling grain, flour, or other dry or semisolid substances **2.** LADLE FOR SERVING LIQUIDS a utensil with a long handle and round bowl, used for transferring liquids **3.** UTENSIL WITH A BOWL-SHAPED HEAD a utensil with a long handle and a small hemispherical bowl, used for serving such things as ice cream and mashed potato or making melon balls **4.** DIGGING PART the part of a dredge or digging machine that is used for excavating **5.** QUANTITY LIFTED BY SCOOP the quantity that is taken by a scoop ○ *three scoops of ice cream* **6.** DIGGING MOTION a curving digging movement made with a scoop or the hand **7.** CAVITY a shallow cavity, hole, or other hollow area in something **8.** ACT OF SLIDING TO PITCH in vocal and instrumental music, a sliding up to a pitch **9.** EXCLUSIVE a news story that is published by a newspaper, magazine, or news programme before its rivals (*informal*) ○ *the scoop of the year* **10.** QUICK PROFIT a large amount of money made quickly (*informal*) **11.** *N Am* NEWS the latest news or gossip (*informal*) ○ *What's the scoop?* ■ *v* (**scoops, scooping, scooped**) **1.** *vt* HOLLOW SOMETHING OUT to create a shallow hole in something with a scoop or similar object, or a curved hand ○ *He scooped out a hole in the ground.* **2.** *vt* REMOVE SOMETHING to remove an amount of a liquid or solid substance with a scoop or similar object, or a curved hand ○ *scooping up water with a ladle* **3.** *vt* LIFT SOMEBODY OR SOMETHING SWIFTLY to pick somebody or something up swiftly and without ceremony ○ *She scooped the tiny puppy up in her arms.* **4.** *vti* HIT BALL UPWARDS to hit a ball upwards from underneath so that it rises into the air **5.** *vt* PUBLISH OR BROADCAST SOMETHING FIRST to publish or broadcast an item of news before any other newspaper, magazine, or news programme (*informal*) ○ *The newspaper scooped its rivals for the second time in a week.* ○ *scooping the hottest story of the year* **6.** *vt* GET A GREAT DEAL OF MONEY to win or otherwise obtain a large amount of money (*informal*) ○ *scoop the jackpot* [14C. < Middle Low German, Middle Dutch *schōpe* 'bucket for bailing, bucket of a water wheel'] —**scooper** *n*

scoop neck *n* a low curved neckline on an article of women's clothing

scoosh /skŏŏsh/ *Scotland* (*informal*) *vti* (**scooshes, scooshing, scooshed**) same as **squirt** *v* (sense 1) ■ *n* **1.** an act of squirting something **2.** a sweet fizzy drink, especially lemonade [19C. An imitation of the sound]

scoot /skoot/ (*informal*) *v* (**scoots, scooting, scooted**) **1.** *vi* LEAVE FAST to go away quickly (*usually used as a command*) **2.** *vi* MOVE QUICKLY to move, run, or go somewhere quickly **3.** *vt N Am* SEND QUICKLY to move or send something quickly ○ *Scoot that file to me as soon as you can.* **4.** *vti Scotland* same as **squirt** *v* (sense 1) ■ *n* **1.** SWIFT MOVEMENT a swift movement or trip ○ *a quick scoot to the supermarket* **2.** *Scotland* same as **squirt** *n* (sense 1) [Mid-18C. Origin ?]

scooter /skŏŏtər/ *n* **1.** a child's toy consisting of handlebars attached by a long rod to a footboard on two wheels. One foot is placed on the board and

the other pushes against the ground to propel the scooter along. **2.** AUTOMOT same as **motor scooter**

scop /skop/ *n* a bard or poet in Anglo-Saxon England [Old English *sc(e)op* < Germanic]

scope[1] /skōp/ *n* **1. ROOM TO ACT** freedom, space, or capacity to act ○ *not much scope for originality* **2. RANGE COVERED** the range covered by an activity, subject, or topic ○ *a question that is beyond the scope of this lecture* **3. MENTAL CAPACITY** the extent of somebody's mental capacity **4.** NAUT **MOORING CABLE** the length of a ship's mooring cable **5.** LOGIC **RANGE OF LOGICAL OPERATOR** the range of application or boundaries of a logical operator, usually indicated by parentheses. The scope of 'and' in '(p and q) or r' is limited to 'p' and 'q'. ■ *vt* **(scopes, scoping, scoped) LOOK AT SOMETHING** to look at or examine something (*slang*) ○ *Let's send the biopsy to the lab to be scoped.* [Mid-16C. Via Italian *scopo* 'aim, purpose' < Greek *skopos* 'target'] ◇ **scope out** *N Am* to investigate or study something (*informal*)

scope[2] /skōp/ *n* an optical device or tool for viewing something (*informal*) ○ *a hunting rifle with a high-powered scope* [Early 17C. < -SCOPE]

-scope *suffix* an instrument for viewing or observing ○ *nephroscope* ○ *periscope* [< modern Latin *-scopium* < Greek *skopein* 'look, see' < Indo-European] —**-scopic** *suffix* —**-scopy** *suffix*

scopolamine /skə póllə meen, -min/ *n* a colourless thick liquid poisonous alkaloid found in some plants of the nightshade family and used as a truth serum, to prevent motion sickness, and as a sedative. Formula: $C_{17}H_{21}NO_4$. [Late 19C. < modern Latin *Scopolia japonica*, the Japanese belladonna, after G. A. *Scopoli* (1723–88), Italian naturalist]

scopula /skóppyŏŏlə/ (*plural* **-las** or **-lae** /-lee/) *n* a tuft of dense hairs on the back of the legs of some insects or spiders [Early 19C. < late Latin, 'little broom']

scorbutic /skawr byóotik/ *adj* relating to, affected with, or causing scurvy [Mid-17C. < modern Latin *scorbuticus* < medieval Latin *scorbutus* 'scurvy'] —**scorbutically** *adv*

scorch /skawrch/ *v* **(scorches, scorching, scorched) 1.** *vti* **BURN SURFACE** to burn the surface of something, or be burnt so as to cause pain, injury, or discolouring ○ *scorched the handkerchief with the iron* **2.** *vti* **DRY OUT** to dry or parch something with intense heat, or become dried out or parched because of intense heat ○ *The plains had been scorched by the Sun.* **3.** *vt* **CRITICIZE SOMEBODY** to subject somebody to severe criticism (*informal*) **4.** *vi* **DRIVE FAST** to drive or travel extremely fast (*informal*) ○ *scorching down the motorway in a Porsche* ■ *n* **1. SURFACE BURN** a burn, or burn mark on the surface of something ○ *The iron left a slight scorch on the blouse.* **2. DISCOLORATION ON PLANTS** a brown marking on plants or vegetables caused by disease, insecticide, or heat [12C. Probably < N Germanic]

scorched /skawrcht/ *adj* dried out or parched from the intense heat of the Sun

scorched earth policy *n* **1.** a policy of destroying crops or buildings, especially by burning, or of removing anything that might be useful to an advancing enemy in wartime **2.** a strategy adopted by a company facing a hostile takeover whereby it makes itself appear a financially less attractive acquisition until the threat has gone

scorcher /skáwrchər/ *n* **1. SOMETHING THAT BURNS** somebody or something that scorches **2. HOT DAY** an extremely hot day (*informal*) ○ *Yesterday was fairly warm but today is a scorcher!* **3. CRITICAL REMARK** a severely critical remark (*informal*) **4. SOMETHING VERY GOOD** something extraordinary or excellent (*informal*)

scorching /skáwrching/ *adj* extremely hot (*informal*)

score /skawr/ *n* **1. POINTS GAINED** the total number of points gained by a player or team at the end of or during a match or game **2. TALLY OF POINTS GAINED** a record of the number of points gained by a player or team in a match or game ○ *Who's keeping the score?* **3. GAINING OF POINT** an action that leads to the gaining of a point or points in a match or game **4. EXAM RESULT** the result of a test or examination, usually presented in numerical form **5.** (*plural same* or **scores**) **GROUP OF 20** a group of twenty things or people ○ *A score or more people showed up.* **6. PRINTED MUSIC** a written or printed copy of a musical composition ○ *distributed copies of the score to the chorus* **7. MUSIC COMPOSED** the music that has been composed for a film, play, or musical ○ *a film with a breathtaking score* **8. COPY OF CHOREOGRAPHIC NOTATION** a written record of the choreography for a dance or ballet **9. NOTCH CUT ONTO SURFACE** a notch or incision cut into the surface of something **10. PARTIAL CUT** a crease or superficial cut made in something such as a piece of paper to enable it to be folded or separated easily **11. RECORD OF MONEY OWED** a record of an amount of money due for payment **12. MONEY OWED** an amount of money due for payment **13. FESTERING GRUDGE** a grievance that is not resolved and incurs resentment ○ *settling old scores* **14. PRESENT SITUATION** the present state or actual facts of a situation (*informal*) ○ *What's the score? Are you coming or not?* **15. SUCCESS** a successful result or achievement, especially one that is significant (*slang*) ○ *made a big score on the stock market* **16. DRUG DEAL** a purchase of illegal drugs (*slang*) **17. ROBBERY** the successful theft of something (*slang*) **18. SEXUAL CONQUEST** a successful seduction of somebody or the sexual encounter itself (*slang*) **19.** NAUT **GROOVE FOR ROPE** a groove cut in wood to hold a rope ■ **scores** *npl* **MANY** a great many ○ *Scores of members protested at the decision.* ■ *v* **(scores, scoring, scored) 1.** *vti* **GAIN POINTS** to gain a point or points in a match or game ○ *scored twice in the second half* **2.** *vt* **AMASS POINTS TOTAL** to gain a particular number of points in total during a match, game, or other competition ○ *Cambridge scored ten in the final round.* **3.** *vti* **RECORD POINTS** to keep a record of the number of points gained in a match, game, or other competition ○ *Who's scoring?* **4.** *vt* **ASSIGN SOMEBODY POINTS** to award a particular number of points to somebody in a match, game, or other competition ○ *Three of the judges scored the skater perfect 6.0s.* **5.** *vt* **BE WORTH POINTS IN A GAME** to count for a particular number of points in a match, game, or other competition ○ *Hitting the red area scores ten.* **6.** *vti* **GET POINTS IN EXAM** to achieve a particular number of points in a test or examination **7.** *vt* **CUT LINES IN SOMETHING** to make notches, cuts, or lines in a surface **8.** *vt* **CUT SOMETHING SUPERFICIALLY TO SEPARATE IT** to make a superficial cut or crease in something such as a piece of paper in order to fold, tear, or break it easily **9.** *vt* **WRITE SOMETHING BY MAKING INCISIONS** to write something by means of notches, incisions, or lines cut into a surface ○ *names scored on the back of the bench with a penknife* **10.** *vti* **CROSS SOMETHING OUT** to draw a line through something in order to mark it as cancelled or deleted **11.** *vt* **RECORD MONEY OWED** to keep a record of an amount of money owed by somebody by making a series of marks next to his or her name **12.** *vt* **ORCHESTRATE SOMETHING** to orchestrate or arrange a piece of music **13.** *vt* **COMPOSE THE MUSIC FOR SOMETHING** to write the music for a film, play, or musical **14.** *vt* **WRITE THE CHOREOGRAPHY FOR SOMETHING** to write out the choreography for a dance or ballet **15.** *vi* **DO WELL** to secure an advantage (*informal*) ○ *She scores because she can communicate.* **16.** *vt* **GET SOMETHING** to succeed in getting something (*slang*) ○ *scored front-row tickets for the concert* **17.** *vti* DRUGS **BUY DRUGS** to buy illegal drugs (*slang*) **18.** *vi* **HAVE SEX** to succeed in having sex with somebody, especially a new sexual partner (*slang*) [Pre-12C. < Old Norse *skor* 'notch, tally, 20'] ◇ **on this** *or* **that score** as far as this or that is concerned ○ *Her health is fine, so there's no need to worry on that score.*

scoreboard /skáwr bawrd/ *n* a board at a sporting venue on which the score of a game, match, or other competition in progress is displayed

scorecard /skáwr kaard/ *n* **1.** a small card used by a player to keep a record of his or her own score, e.g. in golf **2.** a card listing the players in a game or match that enables a spectator to identify who is who and to keep a record of the progress of play

score draw *n* a result in a match, especially a football match, in which both sides have scored the same number of goals

scorekeeper /skáwr keepər/ *n* somebody who keeps a record of the score in a game, match, or other competition —**scorekeeping** *n*

scoreless /skáwrləss/ *adj* having no points or goals scored

scoreline /skáwr līn/ *n* the total number of points gained by players or teams in a match or game

scorer /skáwrər/ *n* **1.** somebody who scores a point or goal in a game or match **2.** SPORTS, LEISURE same as **scorekeeper 3.** a device for cutting a notch or incision into something

Scoresby Sound /skáwrzbi-/ arm of the Norwegian Sea touching eastern Greenland. It is the largest fjord in the world. Length: 451 km/280 mi.

scoresheet /skáwr sheet/ *n* a record of who has scored a point or goal in a game or match, especially in football or rugby

scoria /skáwri ə/ *n* **1.** loose rubbly porous solidified lava that is ejected from a volcano and builds up round the crater **2.** METALL same as **slag** *n* (sense 1) [14C. Via Latin < Greek *skōria* 'refuse, dross' < *skōr* 'dung'] —**scoriaceous** /skáwri áyshəss/ *adj*

scorify /skáwri fī/ (**-fies, -fying, -fied**) *vt* to purify ore by separating it out into metal and slag —**scorification** /skáwrifi káysh'n/ *n* —**scorifier** *n*

scorn /skawrn/ *n* **1. DISDAIN** a strong feeling of contempt ○ *poured scorn on my attempts at writing* **2. OBJECT OF CONTEMPT** somebody or something that is held in contempt ○ *Their behaviour made them the scorn of the entire community.* ■ *v* **(scorns, scorning, scorned) 1.** *vt* **DISDAIN SOMEBODY OR SOMETHING** to hold somebody or something in contempt **2.** *vti* **REJECT SOMETHING CONTEMPTUOUSLY** to reject something with contempt ○ *They had scorned our attempts at peace.* [12C. < Old French *escarn* < *escharnir* 'mock, despise' < Germanic] —**scorner** *n*

scornful /skáwrnf'l/ *adj* feeling or expressing great contempt for somebody or something —**scornfully** *adv* —**scornfulness** *n*

Scorpio /skáwrpi ō/ *n* **1.** ASTRON same as **Scorpius 2.** the eighth sign of the zodiac, represented by a scorpion and lasting from approximately 23 October to 21 November. Scorpio is classified as a water sign and its ruling planets are Mars and Pluto. **3.** somebody whose birthday falls between 23 October and 21 November [14C. < Latin (see SCORPION)] —**Scorpian** *n* —**Scorpio** *adj*

scorpioid /skáwrpi oyd/ *adj* **1.** having the main stem curled at the end ○ *a scorpioid inflorescence* **2.** relating to or resembling a scorpion [Mid-19C. < Greek *skorpioeidēs* < *skorpios* 'scorpion']

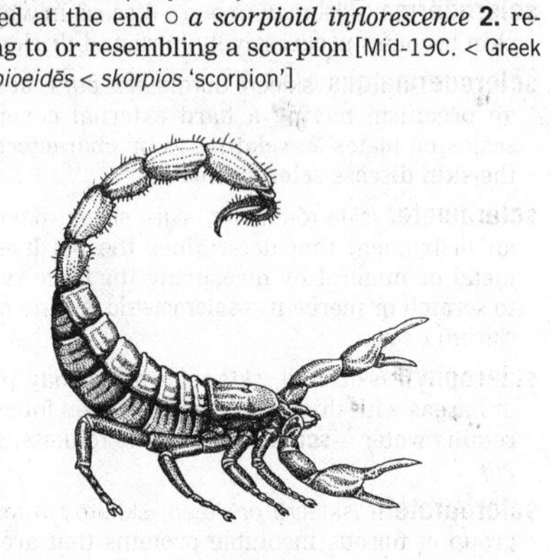

scorpion

scorpion /skáwrpi ən/ *n* **1.** a nocturnal arachnid of warm dry regions that has a long body with pincers in front and a thin segmented upturned tail tipped with a venomous sting. Order: Scorpionida. **2.** in the Bible, a whip with metal barbs [12C. Via French < Latin *scorpion-*, stem of *scorpio*, alteration of *scorpius* < Greek *skorpios* 'scorpion, scorpion fish']

Scorpion *n* **1.** ASTRON same as **Scorpius 2.** ZODIAC same as **Scorpio** (sense 2)

scorpion fish *n* a small brightly coloured fish with venomous spines in its fins. Family: Scorpaenidae.

scorpion fly *n* a nonvenomous insect that has downward-pointing mouthparts and a reproductive organ in the male resembling the sting of a scorpion. Order: Mecoptera.

Scorpius /skáwrpi əss/ *n* a zodiacal constellation of the southern hemisphere. See illustration at **constellation** [15C. < Latin *scorpius* (see SCORPION)]

Scorsese /skawr sáyzi/, **Martin** (*b.* 1942) US film director. His films, including *Taxi Driver* (1976) and *Goodfellas* (1990), often depict urban violence.

'I don't think there is any difference

between fantasy and reality in the way these should be approached in a film. Of course if you live that way you are clinically insane.'
[Martin Scorsese, 'Mean Streets—Alice Doesn't Live Here Anymore—Taxi Driver', *Scorsese on Scorsese*; 1989]

scot /skot/ *n* formerly, a type of tax (*archaic*) [Pre-12C. Partly < Old Norse *skot* 'shot', partly < Old French *escot* < Germanic]

Scot /skot/ *n* 1. ⚠ somebody who comes from Scotland or who has Scottish ancestry 2. a member of a people who lived in Ireland and who, after making invasions of western Britain from the 3rd century AD, settled in northern Britain during the 6th century [Pre-12C. < late Latin *Scottus*]

USAGE Scot, Scotch, Scots, or **Scottish**? All these words make a direct connection to Scotland, but they are used in different ways. *Scottish* is the most generally used adjective to describe the country and people of Scotland (*Scottish history*; *a Scottish accent*), whereas *Scots* is normally applied to people from the Lowlands or to a language related to English that is spoken there (*the Scots Guards*, *a Scots speaker*). A *Scot* is a person who comes from Scotland or who has Scottish ancestry; more specific words are *Scotsman* and *Scotswoman*. *Scotch* as an adjective is a literary word more closely associated with the writings of Robert Burns and Sir Walter Scott and has fallen out of general use, usually being considered offensive except in fixed expressions such as *Scotch whisky* and *Scotch mist*.

Scot. *abbr* 1. Scotch 2. Scotland 3. Scottish

scot and lot *n* formerly, a municipal tax that entitled those who paid it to receive the vote [< LOT in obsolete sense 'tax, due']

scotch[1] /skoch/ *vt* (**scotches, scotching, scotched**) 1. STOP SOMETHING to put a stop to something such as an idea, plan, or rumour 2. DISABLE SOMEBODY to disable somebody by wounding (*archaic*) 3. GASH SOMETHING to make a gash or score in something (*archaic*) ∎ *n* (*archaic*) 1. CUT OR SCORE a cut or score in something 2. LINE a line drawn on the ground, especially one used to mark out a grid for hopscotch [15C. Origin ?]

scotch[2] /skoch/ *n* a wedge used to prevent something from moving ∎ *vt* (**scotches, scotching, scotched**) to wedge something in order to prevent it from moving [Early 17C. Origin ?]

Scotch /skoch/ *n* 1. WHISKY whisky produced in Scotland 2. LANG same as **Scots** ∎ *npl* ⚠ OFFENSIVE TERM an offensive term for people who come from Scotland or who are of Scottish descent ∎ *adj* 1. ⚠ OFFENSIVE TERM an offensive term meaning relating to Scotland, its people, or its culture 2. CHARACTERISTIC OF SCOTLAND made in Scotland, or characteristic of a style prevalent in Scotland ○ *Scotch broth* [Late 16C. Contraction of SCOTTISH]

USAGE See *Scot*.

Scotch broom *n* a deciduous bush of the broom family. Flowers: bright yellow. Native to: western Europe. Latin name: *Cytisus scoparius*.

Scotch broth *n* a traditional Scottish soup made with lamb or beef, mixed root vegetables, and pearl barley

Scotch catch *n* MUSIC same as **Scotch snap**

Scotch egg *n* a hard-boiled egg wrapped in sausagemeat, coated with breadcrumbs, and deep fried. It is usually served cut in half, either hot or cold.

Scotch-Irish *npl* N Am same as **Scottish-Irish** —**Scotch-Irish** *adj*

Scotchman /skóchmən/ (*plural* -**men** /-mən/) *n* an offensive term for a Scotsman (*archaic*)

Scotch mist *n* 1. a fine, damp mist 2. a figment of somebody's imagination (*humorous*)

Scotch pancake *n* FOOD same as **drop scone**

Scotch pine *n* N Am 1. TREES same as **Scots pine** (sense 1) 2. INDUST same as **Scots pine** (sense 2)

Scotch snap *n* in music, a rhythmic figure consisting of a dotted note preceded by a note the value of the dot

Scotch terrier *n* DOGS same as **Scottish terrier**

Scotch whisky *n* BEVERAGES same as **Scotch** *n* (sense 1)

Scotchwoman /skóch wŏomən/ (*plural* -**women** /-wimmin/) *n* an offensive term for a Scotswoman (*archaic*)

Scotch woodcock *n* a snack or light meal of toast spread with an anchovy paste and topped with scrambled eggs [Fanciful]

scoter /skóter/ (*plural* -**ters** or same) *n* a large sea duck, the male of which has black feathers with white spots on its head. Native to: northern coasts of North America, southern Asia, and Europe. Genus: *Melanitta*. [Late 17C. Origin ?]

scot-free *adv* without punishment being exacted or payment being made

scotia /skóshə/ *n* a deep concave moulding, especially on the base of a column [Mid-16C. Via Latin < Greek *skotia* < *skotos* 'darkness' (from the shadow inside the moulding)]

Scotia /skóshə/ *n* a former name for Scotland, still sometimes used in literary contexts (*archaic* or *literary*) [Early 17C. < medieval Latin] —**Scotian** *adj*

Scotism /skótizəm/ *n* the philosophical tenets of, or school of scholastic philosophy founded by, the 13th-century Scottish philosopher and theologian Duns Scotus —**Scotist** *adj* —**Scotistic** /skō tístik/ *adj*

Scotland /skótlənd/ *n* country forming the northernmost part of Great Britain and of the United Kingdom. It became united with England by the Act of Union in 1707, though the crowns had been united since 1603. Following a referendum in 1997, a separate Scottish Parliament was established in 1999 giving the country a limited degree of self-government. Capital: Edinburgh. Population: 5,062,011 (2001). Area: 78,790 sq. km/30,420 sq. mi.

Scotland Yard *n* the headquarters of the Metropolitan Police in London, from which national criminal investigations are coordinated. The headquarters moved to new premises in 1890 and 1967 and is officially known as New Scotland Yard. [Because originally located in *Great Scotland Yard*, where the palace used by visiting kings of Scotland once stood]

Scot Nat /skót nát/ *n* same as **Scottish Nationalist** (*informal*) [Shortening]

scotoma /skə tőmə/ (*plural* -**mas** or -**mata** /-mətə/) *n* a permanent or temporary area of diminished sight in the field of vision [Mid-16C. Via late Latin < Greek *skotōma* 'dizziness' < *skotos* 'darkness'] —**scotomatous** *adj*

scotopia /skə tőpi ə, skō-/ *n* the ability to see in poor light or in the dark [Early 20C. < Greek *skotos* 'darkness'] —**scotopic** /skə tóppik, skō tőpik/ *adj*

Scots /skots/ *adj* 1. OF SCOTLAND relating to Scotland, especially the Lowlands 2. OF LANGUAGE OF SCOTS relating to the Germanic language, closely related to English, spoken in parts of Scotland, especially the Lowlands ∎ *n* LANGUAGE OF SCOTS a Germanic language closely related to English, spoken in parts of Scotland, especially the Lowlands [14C. Contraction of SCOTTISH]

USAGE See *Scot*.

Scots Gaelic *n* LANG same as **Scottish Gaelic**

Scots Guards *n* one of the regiments of the Household Division in the British Army (*takes a singular or plural verb*)

Scots-Irish *npl* PEOPLES same as **Scottish-Irish** —**Scots-Irish** *adj*

Scots law *n* the Scottish legal system, different from that of England and Wales and based on Roman law

Scotsman /skótsmən/ (*plural* -**men** /-mən/) *n* a man who comes from Scotland or who has Scottish ancestry

USAGE See *Scot*.

Scots pine *n* 1. a pine with a reddish trunk, twisted needles, and hard yellow wood. Native to: Europe, southern Asia. Latin name: *Pinus sylvestris*. 2. the wood of the Scots pine, valuable as timber ▶ N Am term **Scotch pine**

Scotswoman /skóts wŏomən/ (*plural* -**women** /-wimmin/) *n* a woman who comes from Scotland or who has Scottish ancestry

USAGE See *Scot*.

Scott, Dred (1795–1858) US slave. He sued for his freedom in 1846. The case came before the United States Supreme Court (1856–57) and was among the causes of the American Civil War.

Scott, Sir Peter (1909–89) British ornithologist and painter. The son of Robert Falcon Scott, he was the founder of the Severn Wild Fowl Trust (1948) and leader of ornithological expeditions. He was noted for his bird paintings. Full name **Scott, Sir Peter Markham**

Scott, Robert Falcon (1868–1912) British naval officer and explorer. On his second expedition to Antarctica (1910–12) he was beaten to the South Pole by Roald Amundsen. He died on the return journey. Known as **Scott of the Antarctic**

Sir Walter Scott

Barnaby's

Scott, Sir Walter (1771–1832) Scottish novelist and poet. His ballads and historical novels, which mainly dealt with Scottish subjects, made him one of the most popular writers of his day and did much to establish widespread European interest in Scottish history and culture. See Cultural note at **heart**

'O Caledonia! stern and wild, / Meet nurse for a poetic child! / Land of brown heath and shaggy wood, / Land of the mountain and the flood, / Land of my sires! what mortal hand / Can e'er untie the filial band /

WORLD ENGLISH *Scottish English* is the variety of English used in Scotland, considered by some to include traditional (Lowland) Scots, and by others to be distinct from it, despite overlap. A compromise with the English of England began to emerge after the Act of Union in 1707, when many among the upper and middle classes began to adopt the pronunciation, grammar, and vocabulary of 'refined' London. The Scottish aristocracy became socially and linguistically indistinguishable from their peers in England, while the middle class developed a shaky compromise.

That knits me to thy rugged strand!'
[Sir Walter Scott, *The Lay of the Last Minstrel*; 1805]

'O what a tangled web we weave, / When first we practise to deceive!'
[Sir Walter Scott, *Marmion*; 1808]

Scotticism /skóttissizəm/ *n* a word, phrase, or idiom that is characteristic of the Scots language or the English spoken in Scotland

Scottie /skótti/, **Scotty** (*plural* **-ties**) *n* (*informal*) **1.** BREED same as **Scottish terrier 2.** an offensive term for somebody, especially a man, who is Scottish

Scottish /skóttish/ *adj* relating to Scotland or its people or culture ■ *npl* people who come from Scotland ■ *n* LANG same as **Scots** [12C. < SCOT] — **Scottishness** *n*

USAGE See *Scot.*

Scottish Blackface /-blák fayss/ *n* a mountain sheep with horns and a black face, belonging to a breed originating in Scotland and northern Britain

Scottish Borders council area in southeastern Scotland, on the English border. Population: 103,881 (2001). Area: 4,734 sq. km/1,828 sq. mi.

Scottish Certificate of Education *n* EDUC full form of **SCE**

Scottish Cup *n* **1.** a yearly competition in which teams are gradually eliminated, open to football teams that belong to the Scottish Football Association **2.** the trophy awarded to the winning team in the Scottish Cup

Scottish English *n* a variety of English spoken in Scotland

Scottish Executive *n* the devolved government of Scotland

Scottish Executive Development Department *n* a department of the Scottish Executive, responsible for planning, building control and housing, social justice, and economic advice

Scottish Executive Education Department *n* a department of the Scottish Executive, responsible for education at school level, social services, culture, sport, and tourism

Scottish Executive Environment and Rural Affairs Department *n* a department of the Scottish Executive, responsible for agriculture, rural development, food, and fisheries

Scottish Executive Health Department *n* a department of the Scottish Executive, responsible for health and ambulance services

Scottish FA Cup *n* SOCCER same as **Scottish Cup**

Scottish Gaelic *n* the Celtic language spoken in parts of the Highlands and Western Isles of Scotland

Scottish-Irish *npl* Irish people of Scottish descent or Americans descended from these people. N Am term **Scotch-Irish** —**Scottish-Irish** *adj*

Scottish Land Court *n* a Scottish court whose jurisdiction covers the various forms of agricultural tenancy

Scottish Nationalist *n* a member or supporter of the Scottish National Party ■ *adj* relating to or belonging to the Scottish National Party

Scottish National Party *n* a Scottish political party founded in 1934 that advocates full political independence for Scotland

Scottish Parliament *n* the centre of devolved government for Scotland, made up of elected members. It has the power to make laws affecting local matters and to raise or lower Scottish taxes.

Scottish terrier

Scottish terrier *n* a terrier belonging to a breed with short sturdy legs, pointed ears, and thick, wiry, usually black hair

scoundrel /skówndrəl/ *n* a dishonourable or unprincipled person [Late 16C. Origin ?] —**scoundrelly** *adj*

scour[1] /skowr/ *v* (**scours, scouring, scoured**) **1.** *vti* CLEAN SOMETHING BY RUBBING to clean or brighten something by rubbing it with an abrasive substance or material **2.** *vti* REMOVE SOMETHING BY RUBBING to remove something by rubbing with an abrasive substance or material **3.** *vt* FREE SOMETHING FROM DIRT to remove dirt or impurities from something by washing **4.** *vt* FLUSH SOMETHING OUT to clear something out by passing water through it **5.** *vi* VET HAVE DIARRHOEA to be affected by diarrhoea (*refers to cattle*) ■ *n* **1.** SCOURING a scouring of something **2.** CLEANING SUBSTANCE a substance or tool that can be used for scouring **3.** PLACE SCOURED a place that has been scoured, especially by water **4.** VET DIARRHOEA diarrhoea affecting cattle and pigs [12C. Via Middle Low German, Middle Dutch *schüren* < late Latin *excurare* 'clean out, take care of' < Latin *cura* 'care'] — **scourer** *n*

scour[2] /skowr/ (**scours, scouring, scoured**) *vti* **1.** to search something thoroughly and quickly for somebody or something ○ *They scoured the countryside for him, but to no avail.* **2.** to move quickly over or through an area [15C. Probably < N Germanic] —**scourer** *n*

scourge /skurj/ *n* **1.** TORMENTOR somebody or something that is perceived as an agent of punishment, destruction, or severe criticism ○ *the scourge of my childhood* **2.** WHIP a whip that is used for inflicting punishment ■ *vt* (**scourges, scourging, scourged**) **1.** PUNISH SOMEBODY to punish or criticize somebody severely **2.** WHIP SOMEBODY to whip somebody severely [12C. < Old French *escorgier* 'to whip' < Latin *corrigia* 'thong, whip'] —**scourger** *n*

scouring rush /skówring-/ *n* a horsetail with a rough stem, especially the Dutch rush. Use: formerly, scouring. Genus: *Equisetum.*

scourings /skówringz/ *npl* the material removed or left after scouring something, especially that left after scouring grain

scours /skowrz/ *n* VET same as **scour**[1] *v* (sense 5) (*takes a singular or plural verb*)

scouse /skowss/ *n regional* a stew made from leftover cooked meat with potatoes and vegetables [Mid-19C. Shortening of LOBSCOUSE]

Scouse /skowss/ (*informal*) *n* **1.** the dialect spoken in Liverpool **2.** PEOPLES same as **Scouser** ■ *adj* relating to Liverpool, its people, or its dialect [Mid-20C. < SCOUSE]

Scouser /skowssər/ *n* somebody who comes from Liverpool, especially somebody whose speech is marked by the local accent and dialect (*informal*)

scout /skowt/ *n* **1.** SOLDIER SENT TO GATHER INFORMATION somebody, especially a soldier, who is sent to gather information about an enemy's position or movements **2.** SPORTS, ARTS same as **talent scout 3.** RE-

CONNAISSANCE CRAFT OR VEHICLE a ship, aircraft, or vehicle designed and used by the armed forces for reconnaissance purposes **4.** SEARCH a search for somebody or something ○ *have a scout around for the missing keys* **5.** RECONNOITRING a gathering of information concerning an enemy's position or movements **6.** OXFORD COLLEGE SERVANT somebody employed to clean students' rooms at Oxford University **7.** PERSON a person, usually a boy or man (*dated informal*) ○ *Be a good scout and give me a hand here.* ■ *v* (**scouts, scouting, scouted**) **1.** *vti* SEARCH AREA to make a search of an area for somebody or something ○ *scouting around for a place to camp* **2.** *vi* GATHER INFORMATION to seek out information about somebody or something, especially about an enemy's position or movements **3.** *vti* SPORTS, ARTS SEEK OUT NEW TALENT to look for talented players for a sports team, or talented performers for a show or group [14C. < Old French *escouter* 'to listen' < Latin *auscultare*] —**scouter** *n*

Scout *n* a member of the Scout Association

Scout Association *n* an international youth organization founded for boys in 1908 by Lord Baden-Powell

Scouter /skówtər/ *n* an adult who is a troop leader in the Scout Association

Scouting /skówting/ *n* the activities of the Scout Association

scoutmaster /skówt maastər/ *n* a man who is in charge of a troop of Scouts

scow /skow/ *n* **1.** a barge for transporting freight **2.** a flat-bottomed sailing boat [Mid-17C. < Dutch *schouw*]

scowl /skowl/ *n* an expression of anger, displeasure, or menace made by drawing the eyebrows together towards the middle of the forehead ■ *vi* (**scowls, scowling, scowled**) to draw the eyebrows together towards the middle of the forehead in an expression of anger, displeasure, or menace [14C. Probably < N Germanic] —**scowler** *n*

SCPO *abbr* NAVY Senior Chief Petty Officer

SCPS *abbr* Society of Civil and Public Servants

SCR *abbr* EDUC senior common room

scrabble /skrább'l/ *v* (**-bles, -bling, -bled**) **1.** *vi* SCRATCH AT SOMETHING to scrape or scratch at something with small, hurried movements of the fingers, toes, or claws ○ *The cat was scrabbling at the door.* **2.** *vi* FEEL WITH FINGERS to grope about frantically in an effort to find something ○ *She scrabbled around trying to find the torch.* **3.** *vi* CLIMB OVER SOMETHING to climb hastily or clumsily up or over something **4.** *vi* STRUGGLE TO GET SOMETHING to struggle desperately to get something ○ *scrabbling for enough money to make ends meet* **5.** *vt* PRODUCE SOMETHING WITH DIFFICULTY to produce something hastily and with difficulty from scarce resources ○ *scrabble together a meal* **6.** *vti* SCRIBBLE to scribble something ■ *n* **1.** ACT OF SCRATCHING a scraping or scratching at something with short hurried movements of the fingers, toes, or claws **2.** A SEARCH WITH FINGERS a frantic groping about in an effort to find something **3.** HASTY CLIMB a climb up or over something, performed hastily or clumsily **4.** DESPERATE STRUGGLE a desperate struggle to acquire or gain something ○ *scrabble together a meal* **5.** SCRIBBLING a scribbling of something **6.** SOMETHING SCRIBBLED something that somebody has scribbled [Mid-16C. < Middle Dutch *schrabbelen* 'scratch repeatedly' < *schrabben* 'scratch, scrape'] —**scrabbler** *n*

Scrabble /skrább'l/ *tdmk* a trademark for a board game in which players score points by placing lettered tiles on the squares of a board to form words

scrabbly /skrábbli/ (**-blier, -bliest**) *adj* characterized by a scratching sound

scrag /skrag/ *n* **1.** THIN PERSON OR ANIMAL an unattractively thin person or animal **2.** NECK somebody's neck (*informal*) **3.** N Am FOOD same as **scrag end** ■ *vt* (**scrags, scragging, scragged**) STRANGLE SOMEBODY to throttle or strangle somebody (*informal*) [Mid-16C. Probably < dialect *crag* 'neck' < Middle Dutch *crāghe* 'throat']

scrag end *n* the bony neck joint of a sheep or lamb, usually cut up and used in soup or stew. N Am term **scrag**

scraggly /skrággli/ (**-glier, -gliest**) *adj* untidy in

appearance or shape [Mid-19C. < SCRAG] —**scraggliness** *n*

scraggy /skrággi/ (**-gier, -giest**) *adj* bony and thin ○ *a scraggy little cat* —**scraggily** *adv* —**scragginess** *n*

SYNONYMS See *thin.*

scram /skram/ *v* (**scrams, scramming, scrammed**) **1.** *vi* **LEAVE QUICKLY** to get out or leave quickly (*informal; usually used as a command*) **2.** *vti* INDUST **SHUT DOWN NUCLEAR REACTOR** to shut down a nuclear reactor rapidly in an emergency, or be shut down rapidly ■ *n* INDUST **REACTOR SHUTDOWN** a rapid shutting-down of a nuclear reactor in an emergency [Early 20C. Origin ?]

scramble /skrámb'l/ *v* (**-bles, -bling, -bled**) **1.** *vi* **CLAMBER** to climb or advance over something using hands and feet ○ *We managed to scramble over the fence.* **2.** *vi* **HURRY** to move in haste and with a sense of urgency **3.** *vi* **COMPETE FRANTICALLY** to struggle or compete frantically in order to get something ○ *Everyone was scrambling for the best seats.* **4.** *vt* **JUMBLE THINGS TOGETHER** to mix or gather a number of things together haphazardly **5.** *vt* COOK **BEAT AND COOK EGGS** to beat eggs, usually with some milk, and cook while stirring in a pan **6.** *vt* TELECOM **ENCODE TRANSMITTED SIGNALS** to render a telecommunications or broadcast signal unintelligible by means of an electronic device **7.** *vti* AIR FORCE **LAUNCH AIRCRAFT AGAINST ATTACK** to launch a large number of aircraft in a short space of time in response to an impending attack, or be launched in these circumstances ■ *n* **1. HARD CLIMB** a difficult climb or walk that involves using the hands as well as the feet but no ropes **2. DASH OR STRUGGLE** a hasty, undignified, or disorganized struggle for something or in order to do something **3. CONFUSED MASS** a jumbled mass of people or things **4.** MOTORCYCLES **MOTORCYCLE RACE** a motorcycle race over rough terrain **5.** AIR FORCE **LAUNCH OF AIRCRAFT** the scrambling of military aircraft [Late 16C. Probably to suggest the action]

scrambled eggs /skrámb'ld égz/ *n* (*takes a singular or plural verb*) **1.** a dish made by beating eggs and a little milk together and cooking them in a pan **2.** gold braid attached to the peak of the cap of a senior military officer (*slang*)

scrambler /skrámblər/ *n* **1. STRAGGLING PLANT** a plant with long straggling shoots that are held up by adjacent plants **2. DEVICE TO ENCODE TRANSMITTED SIGNALS** an electronic device that renders telecommunications or broadcast signals unintelligible without a special receiver **3. ROUGH-TERRAIN MOTORCYCLE** a motorcycle designed for racing across rough terrain

scramjet /skrám jet/ *n* a ramjet aircraft in which fuel is burned in air that is moving at supersonic speeds [Mid-20C. < initial letters of SUPERSONIC and COMBUSTION + RAMJET]

scran /skran/ *n regional* food [Early 19C. Origin ?] ◇ **bad scran to somebody** *Ireland* used to wish somebody bad luck (*informal*)

scrap[1] /skrap/ *n* **1. FRAGMENT** a small piece or remnant that has been detached from or torn off a larger piece **2. WASTE MATERIAL** waste material, especially metal awaiting reprocessing **3. SMALL PIECE** a very small piece of something ○ *There's not a scrap of evidence to prove it.* **4. BIT OF WRITTEN OR PRINTED MATERIAL** a short piece of writing, or a cutting from something printed ■ **scraps** *npl* **LEFTOVERS** pieces of leftover food ○ *table scraps* ■ *vt* (**scraps, scrapping, scrapped**) **1. GET RID OF SOMETHING** to discard or discontinue something because it is considered useless or ineffective **2. CONVERT SOMETHING TO SCRAP** to convert something into scrap material ○ *scrapping old warships* [14C. < Old Norse *skrap* 'scraps, trifles']

scrap[2] /skrap/ (*informal*) *n* a minor fight or disagreement ■ *vi* (**scraps, scrapping, scrapped**) to have a minor fight or disagreement with somebody [Late 17C. Origin ?]

scrapbook /skráp bŏŏk/ *n* a blank book or album for pasting in photos, pictures, cuttings, or other material

scrape /skrayp/ *v* (**scrapes, scraping, scraped**) **1.** *vti* **RUB SURFACE** to move something hard, sharp, or rough across a surface, especially in order to clean it ○ *scraping the wall to remove the paint* **2.** *vt* **TAKE SOMETHING OFF** to remove something by drawing or rubbing a hard or sharp edge over it ○ *My efforts to scrape the paint off failed.* ○ *scraped out the burnt contents of the pot* **3.** *vt* **SCRATCH SOMETHING** to scratch, cut, or damage something by bringing it into contact with a rough or abrasive surface ○ *fell and scraped my knees* **4.** *vti* **MAKE GRATING NOISE** to make a harsh grating sound, or cause something to make such a sound ○ *scraping his chair along the floor* **5.** *vi* **SCRIMP** to live economically in an effort to save money ○ *scraping by on a single income* **6.** *vti* **ONLY JUST DO SOMETHING** to barely manage to do or achieve something ○ *He just scraped through law school.* **7.** *vt* **DRAW HAIR BACK** to draw something, especially the hair, back tightly ■ *n* **1. SCRAPING** a scraping of something ○ *I'll give the paint a quick scrape.* **2. LIGHT SCRATCH** a light cut, graze, or area of damage caused by contact with a rough or abrasive surface **3. GRATING SOUND** a sharp grating sound ○ *the scrape of chairs on the bare floor* **4. DANGEROUS SITUATION** a dangerous, difficult, or awkward situation (*informal*) **5. MINOR FIGHT** a minor fight or disagreement (*informal*) [Old English *scrapian* 'to scratch' < Germanic] —**scraper** *n*

scrape together, scrape up *vt* to manage with difficulty to collect together an amount of something, especially money, or a number of people or things

scraperboard /skráypər bawrd/ *n* **1.** a drawing board that is covered with a layer of white clay on top of which is a layer of black that can be scraped away to make white-line drawings. N Am term **scratchboard 2.** a drawing produced on a scraperboard

scrapheap /skráp heep/ *n* **1.** a large pile of unwanted or discarded items, especially those being used as scrap material **2.** an imagined place to which people and things regarded as worn out and useless are consigned (*informal*) ○ *workers who find themselves on the scrapheap at 50*

scrapie /skráypi/ *n* a usually fatal disease affecting the nervous system of sheep and goats that is marked by intense itching and loss of muscular control. It is now thought to be one of the diseases caused by a prion, and is similar to BSE in cattle and CJD in humans. [Early 20C. < SCRAPE, because the animals rub against objects to alleviate itching]

scrapper /skráppər/ *n* an enthusiastic, determined fighter, especially a boxer (*slang*) [Late 19C. < SCRAP[2]]

scrapple /skrápp'l/ *n US* scraps of pork cooked with cornmeal and seasonings, formed into a loaf, and cooled. It is sliced and fried before serving. [Mid-19C. < SCRAP[1]]

scrappy[1] /skráppi/ (**-pier, -piest**) *adj* **1.** consisting of scraps or fragments **2.** poorly held together or structured —**scrappily** *adv* —**scrappiness** *n*

scrappy[2] /skráppi/ (**-pier, -piest**) *adj N Am* plucky, determined, and willing to fight or argue (*informal*) —**scrappily** *adv* —**scrappiness** *n*

scrapyard /skráp yaard/ *n* a place where scrap is brought and kept before being reprocessed or discarded

scratch /skrach/ *v* (**scratches, scratching, scratched**) **1.** *vt* **SCRAPE SURFACE** to make a slight mark on the surface of something with something sharp or rough ○ *He scratched the table top with the knife.* **2.** *vti* **TEAR SKIN** to make a thin tear in the surface of the skin of a person or animal ○ *The cat scratched me.* **3.** *vti* **RELIEVE ITCHING** to rub the skin with nails or claws, especially to relieve itching or discomfort **4.** *vti* **MAKE SCRAPING MOVEMENT** to rub or scrape a surface, e.g. with claws or a scraping instrument ○ *The cat was scratching at the door.* **5.** *vi* **MAKE HARSH NOISE** to make a scraping sound **6.** *vt* **DRAG SOMETHING ALONG SURFACE** to drag something along a rough surface so that the object is scraped **7.** *vti* **CAUSE ITCHING** to irritate the surface of the skin by being rough or prickly ○ *a wool sweater that scratches* **8.** *vt* **WRITE SOMETHING WITH SHARP INSTRUMENT** to write or draw something by marking a surface with a pointed or sharp instrument ○ *names scratched on the tree* **9.** *vti* **PEN QUICKLY** to write or draw something hastily **10.** *vt* **DELETE SOMETHING** to delete or erase something by scraping it off, crossing it out, or rendering it illegible **11.** *vt* **CANCEL SOMETHING** to cancel or abandon a project, plan, or proposal completely **12.** *vi* **SEARCH AIMLESSLY** to search for something in an unsystematic way by picking through things or looking on the ground ○ *scratching around for evidence* **13.** *vti* **JUST GET BY** to make a barely adequate living ○ *scratching out a living* **14.** *vti* MUSIC **PRODUCE SCRAPING SOUND FROM RECORD** to run a record backwards and forwards on a turntable in order to repeat and distort the original sound of the record **15.** *vti* **WITHDRAW FROM COMPETITION** to withdraw a person or team from a race or competition **16.** *vi* CUE GAMES **INCUR PENALTY** to make a billiard shot that incurs a penalty, e.g. by hitting the cue ball into a pocket **17.** *vi* CUE GAMES **MAKE FLUKE SHOT** in billiards, to make a mishit that produces a score ■ *n* **1. MARK ON SURFACE** a slight mark on a surface made with something sharp or rough **2. TEAR IN SKIN** a thin cut or tear in the surface of the skin of a person or animal **3. SCRAPING SOUND** a scraping sound, especially one made with the claws or nails **4. ACTION TO RELIEVE ITCHING** a rubbing of the skin with the nails or claws, especially to relieve itching or discomfort **5. SCRIBBLY WRITING** something written hastily or illegibly **6. MONEY** money or cash (*slang*) **7.** SPORTS **WITHDRAWN COMPETITOR** a person or team withdrawn from a race or competition **8.** GOLF **HANDICAP OF ZERO** in golf, a zero handicap **9.** CUE GAMES **SHOT INCURRING PENALTY** a billiard shot that incurs a penalty **10.** CUE GAMES **FLUKE SHOT** in billiards, a mishit that produces a score **11.** MUSIC **TYPE OF POP MUSIC** music produced by running a record backwards and forwards on a turntable, repeating and distorting the original sound. Scratch is performed especially by disc jockeys in clubs. ■ *adj* **1. FOR JOTTED NOTES** used for making quick or preliminary notes ○ *scratch paper* **2.** SPORTS **DONE RANDOMLY** done randomly or by chance ○ *a scratch shot* **3. ASSEMBLED HASTILY** assembled hastily from available resources ○ *a scratch team* **4.** GOLF **WITH NO HANDICAP** playing golf with a handicap of zero [14C. Probably blend of dialect *scrat* 'scratch' (< ?) + dialect *cratch* 'scratch' (< ?)] ◇ **from scratch** right from the beginning, or with nothing having been done previously (*informal*) ◇ **up to scratch** of or up to a satisfactory standard (*informal*) ○ *exam results that aren't really up to scratch*

scratch together, scratch up *vt* same as **scrape together**

scratch-and-sniff *adj* designed to release a smell when scratched, especially as a complement to a visual experience

scratchboard /skrách bawrd/ *n N Am* ART same as **scraperboard** (sense 1)

scratchbook /skrách bŏŏk/ *n US* a tiny notepad encased in a cardboard cover resembling that of a matchbook [Early 21C. Modelled on MATCHBOOK]

scratch card *n* a card containing one or more sections covered in an overlay that can be scratched off to reveal a possible prize printed beneath

scratch file *n* a temporary computer file created in a memory device as a work area or for use when executing a program

scratchie /skráchi/ *n* GAMBLING same as **scratch card** (*informal*)

scratchings /skráchingz/ *npl* FOOD same as **pork scratchings** [14C. Origin ?]

scratch line *n* **1.** a starting line in a race **2.** a line that a competitor may not step over without committing a foul

scratchpad /skrách pad/ *n* **1.** a high-speed temporary storage area in a computer memory **2.** *N Am* a pad of paper for making rough notes

scratchproof /skrách proof/ *adj* resistant to being scratched

scratch test *n* a test to discover if somebody is allergic to a substance (**allergen**), in which a small amount of the substance is rubbed into a lightly scratched area of skin. A reaction, e.g. the formation of a weal, indicates an allergy to the substance.

scratch ticket *n* GAMBLING same as **scratch card** (*informal*)

scratchy /skráchi/ (**-ier, -iest**) *adj* **1. ITCHY** causing or feeling itchiness on the skin ○ *a scratchy sweater* **2. WITH SCRAPING SOUND** making a scratching or scraping sound ○ *a scratchy recording* **3. PENNED QUICKLY** written or drawn hastily or illegibly —**scratchily** *adv* —**scratchiness** *n*

scrawl /skrawl/ *vti* (**scrawls, scrawling, scrawled**) to write or draw something untidily or hastily, especially in large letters that are difficult to read ■ *n*

untidy or hurried-looking handwriting or drawing [Early 17C. Origin ?] —**scrawler** n —**scrawly** adj

scrawny /skráwni/ (-**nier**, -**niest**) adj unpleasantly or unhealthily thin and bony [Mid-19C. Variant of dialect *scranny*, origin ?] —**scrawnily** adv —**scrawniness** n

SYNONYMS See **thin**.

screak /skreek/ US vi (**screaks**, **screaking**, **screaked**) 1. MAKE SCREECHING SOUND to produce a screech 2. MAKE CREAKING SOUND to produce a creak ■ n 1. SCREECH a screeching sound 2. CREAK a creaking sound [15C. < Old Norse *skrækja*, an imitation of the sound] —**screaky** adj

scream /skreem/ n 1. PIERCING CRY a loud, piercing, high-pitched cry, uttered in fear, pain, excitement, or amusement 2. HIGH-PITCHED NOISE a very loud, high-pitched sound, e.g. that of a siren or jet engine 3. SOMEBODY OR SOMETHING HIGHLY AMUSING an extremely funny or entertaining person, event, or activity (*informal*) ■ v (**screams**, **screaming**, **screamed**) 1. vi CRY to utter a loud, piercing, high-pitched cry, especially in fear, pain, or excitement ○ *He screamed for help.* 2. vt SHOUT SOMETHING IN PIERCING VOICE to utter something in a loud, piercing, high-pitched voice, especially in fear, panic, desperation, or excitement ○ *'Get out'! he screamed.* 3. vi LAUGH LOUDLY to laugh shrilly and loudly 4. vi MAKE HIGH-PITCHED SOUND to make a loud high-pitched sound ○ *The ambulance went by, sirens screaming.* 5. vi MOVE AT SPEED to move extremely quickly while producing a loud high-pitched sound ○ *The police car screamed by.* 6. vi BE OBVIOUS to be extremely obvious or noticeable ○ *The mistakes just scream out at you.* [13C. Origin ?] —**screamingly** adv

CULTURAL NOTE *The Scream*, a painting (1893) by the Norwegian painter Edvard Munch. Painted in a bold, expressionist style, it depicts a panic-stricken human figure standing on a bridge or pier. The skull-like face appears to emit a cry that reverberates through the surrounding landscape. A powerful symbol of despair, it is one of the best-known icons of modern art.

screamer /skreémər/ n 1. SOMETHING THAT SCREAMS somebody or something that screams 2. HILARIOUS PERSON OR THING somebody or something that is extremely funny or entertaining (*informal*) 3. BIRDS BIRD RESEMBLING GOOSE a water bird that resembles a goose, but has a smaller beak and a harsher call. Native to: South America. Family: Anhimidae. 4. US MEDIA SENSATIONAL HEADLINE a sensational headline set in large letters (*slang*) 5. PRINTING same as **exclamation mark** (*slang*) 6. SOCCER FAST SHOT OR BALL a shot or ball that travels extremely fast (*informal*) ○ *fired a screamer that went whistling past the post* 7. Aus LEAPING FREE KICK in Australian Rules football, a free kick taken by leaping high off the ground (*informal*) ○ *With five minutes to go, Ablett took a real screamer, after which his team never lost possession.*

screaming abdabs /skreéming áb dabz/, **screaming habdabs** /-háb dabz/ npl an attack of nervous anxiety (*informal*) N Am term **screaming meemies** [Abdabs, origin ?]

screaming meemies /-meémiz/ n n N Am same as **screaming abdabs** (*informal; takes a singular or plural verb*) [Meemies, origin ?]

scree /skree/ n 1. an accumulation of rock debris at the base of a cliff, hill, or mountain slope, often forming a heap 2. a slope covered with a layer of scree [Early 18C. < Old Norse *skriða* 'landslide']

screech /skreech/ n 1. SHRILL SCREAM OR CRY a high-pitched grating cry or scream ○ *the screech of an owl* 2. HIGH-PITCHED SOUND a loud high-pitched grating sound ○ *a screech of brakes* ■ v (**screeches**, **screeching**, **screeched**) 1. vi UTTER SHRILL SCREAM to utter a high-pitched grating cry or scream ○ *They screeched with delight.* 2. vt SHRIEK SOMETHING to utter something in a high-pitched and grating tone of voice 3. vi MAKE SCREECHING SOUND to make a loud high-pitched grating sound 4. vi PRODUCE SCREECHING SOUND BY MOVING FAST to move, usually extremely fast, while producing a screeching sound ○ *The car screeched to a stop.* [Mid-16C. Alteration of archaic *scritch*, ultimately an imitation of the sound] —**screecher** n —**screechiness** n —**screechy** adj

screechie /skreéchi/ n Aus a manoeuvre performed in a car in which the driver accelerates quickly in

order to cause the wheels to spin and make a loud screeching sound (*slang*)

screech owl n any owl that has a characteristic screeching cry. Native to: Europe.

screed /skreed/ n 1. LENGTHY PIECE OF WRITING a long and often tedious piece of writing or speech (*often used in the pl*) 2. CONSTR GUIDE FOR PLASTERING a strip of plaster, wood, or other material placed on a surface as a guide to the correct thickness of plaster or concrete to be applied there 3. CONSTR BOARD FOR LEVELLING a board or tool used to level a layer of concrete, sand, or other loose material 4. CONSTR TOP LAYER a smooth top layer on a concrete floor or other surface 5. Scotland TEAR a tear or tearing sound [14C. Variant of SHRED 'torn strip']

screel /skreel/ (**screels**, **screeling**, **screeled**) vi Carib 1. to complain 2. to squeal or scream [Late 19C. An imitation of the sound, or related to SKIRL]

screen /skreen/ n 1. PARTITION OR SHELTER a fixed or movable partition or frame that is used to conceal, divide, separate, or provide shelter ○ *You may get changed behind the screen.* 2. DECORATIVE FRAME a decorative frame or partition, e.g. in a church choir ○ *a rood screen* 3. MESH FRAME OR MESH a frame with a fine wire or plastic mesh designed to prevent the entry of mosquitoes or other insects, or the mesh itself 4. SIEVE a sieve used to filter out fine particles, e.g. of sand or gravel 5. SOMETHING THAT CONCEALS anything that serves to conceal, divide, separate, or provide shelter ○ *A screen of leaves protected her from the sun.* 6. CONCEALMENT a measure taken to conceal something ○ *This report is just a screen for the government's inaction.* 7. SELECTION SYSTEM a system for selecting suitable people, e.g. for a post, membership of an organization, or tenancy of property 8. COMPUT, MEDIA ELECTRONIC DISPLAY SURFACE the broad flat end of a cathode-ray tube or liquid crystal display on which images are displayed, e.g. in a television set or computer monitor 9. COMPUT DATA DISPLAYED ON MONITOR the data displayed on the screen of a computer monitor ○ *to print the screen* 10. CINEMA, PHOTOGRAPHY SURFACE FOR PROJECTING FILM ONTO a large flat white or silver surface onto which a film or slide is projected 11. CINEMA CINEMA INDUSTRY the film industry 12. PHOTOGRAPHY CAMERA PLATE FOR FOCUSING a ground-glass plate in a camera that is used in focusing an image before photographing it 13. AUTOMOT same as **windscreen** 14. MIL ADVANCE DETACHMENT a military detachment sent in advance of a main force to protect it from the enemy or give warning of enemy approach 15. PRINTING GLASS PLATE FOR HALF-TONE REPRODUCTIONS a glass plate marked with very fine lines and used in producing half-tone reproductions 16. PSYCHOANAL EMOTIONAL BLOCK something that prevents somebody from understanding his or her real feelings ■ v (**screens**, **screening**, **screened**) 1. vt CONCEAL OR SHELTER SOMEBODY OR SOMETHING to provide somebody or something with shelter, protection, or concealment from somebody or something 2. vt PARTITION SOMETHING OFF to partition, separate, or divide something off from something else ○ *They had screened the area into cubicles.* 3. vt FIT SOMETHING WITH SCREEN to provide something with a screen 4. vt PROTECT SOMEBODY to protect somebody from something unpleasant or dangerous 5. vt SIEVE SOMETHING to filter something through a sieve 6. vti TEST FOR DISEASE to test somebody or something for an illness or disease 7. vti SELECT BY WEEDING OUT to examine a candidate or candidates for something such as a post, membership of an organization, or tenancy of property as part of a selection process 8. vti CINEMA SHOW IN CINEMA to project a film onto a screen in a cinema, or be projected in a cinema 9. vti MEDIA SHOW ON TELEVISION to broadcast a film, programme, or other item on television, or be broadcast on television 10. vt PRINTING PHOTOGRAPH FOR HALF-TONE REPRODUCTION to photograph something through a glass plate to make a half-tone reproduction [14C < Old N French escren] —**screener** n —**screenful** n

screenager /skreén ayjər/ n a young person who has grown up watching TV and playing with computers and is knowledgeable about and skilled in operating electronic devices (*informal*)

screen dump n the process of printing or saving the contents of a computer display screen

screened shot /skreénd-/ n COMPUT same as **screen shot**

screen font n a font used to display text on a computer screen

screening /skreéning/ n 1. A SHOWING IN CINEMA a projection of a film on a screen in a cinema 2. A SHOWING ON TELEVISION a showing of a film, programme, or other item on television 3. TEST FOR DISEASE a test or testing carried out routinely on supposedly healthy people in order to establish, as early as possible, whether or not they have an illness or disease 4. PROTECTING SCREENS screens for providing shelter, protection, or concealment, or for separating or dividing 5. WIRE MESH fine wire or plastic mesh used on a door or window to prevent the entry of mosquitoes or other insects ■ **screenings** npl SIEVED MATERIAL waste material that has been screened from something

screen memory n an early childhood memory that is used subconsciously to mask another related, often distressing, memory

screenplay /skreén play/ n a script or scenario for a film

screen-print n a print produced by silk-screen printing —**screen-print** vti —**screen-printing** n

screen rage n extreme anger and frustration experienced by a computer user who encounters difficulties (*slang*)

screen saver n a computer utility that automatically makes the screen go blank or display a preselected image after a given period of time

screen shot n a photograph or printout showing what appears on a computer screen, especially for the purposes of demonstrating a program

screen test n an audition for a film role in which an actor is filmed, or the film made of the audition — **screen-test** vti

screenwriter /skreén rítər/ n the writer of a script that is intended to be filmed —**screenwriting** n

screich /skreékh/, **screigh** vti (**screichs**, **screiching**, **screiched**; **screighs**, **screighing**, **screighed**), n Scotland same as **screech** [Late 16C. Alteration of SCREAK]

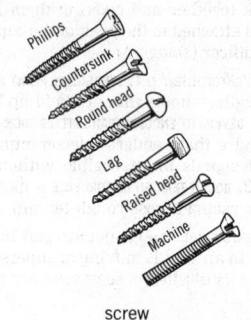

Phillips
Countersunk
Round head
Lag
Raised head
Machine

screw

screw /skroo/ n 1. THREADED FASTENER INSERTED INTO MATERIAL a piece of metal with a tapering threaded body and grooved head by which it is turned into something in order to fasten things together 2. SCREW FOR NUT a screw with a blunt end onto which a nut is fitted to hold two objects together 3. DEVICE SIMILAR TO SCREW anything that has a form similar to a tapering metal screw, e.g. a corkscrew 4. TWISTING ACTION a turn of a screw or of a device like a screw 5. same as **miser** (*informal*) 6. OLD HORSE a decrepit old horse (*informal*) 7. OFFENSIVE TERM an offensive term for an act or instance of sexual intercourse (*slang*) 8. OFFENSIVE TERM an offensive term for a sexual partner considered with regard to his or her sexual performance (*slang*) 9. OFFICER a prison officer (*slang*) 10. PAPER TWIST a small twist of paper, especially one containing tobacco (*dated informal*) 11. SALARY a salary or wages earned by somebody (*dated informal*) 12. ENG same as **propeller** 13. CUE GAMES SHOT IN WHICH CUE BALL REBOUNDS a shot in billiards or snooker in which the cue ball returns towards the player after hitting the ball it was aimed at ■ v (**screws**, **screwing**, **screwed**) 1. vti FASTEN WITH SCREWS to fasten or tighten something with a screw or screws, or be fastened or tightened in this way ○ *He screwed the shelf to the wall.* 2. vti FASTEN BY ROTATING to rotate something along a thread in order to fasten or tighten it, or be rotated in this way ○ *screwed the bulb in carefully* 3. vt CRUSH SOMETHING to crumple or

crush something into a tight ball ○ *screwed up the letter and threw it away* **4.** *vti* **CONTORT THE FACE** to contort or crumple a part or all of the face, or be contorted or crumpled ○ *She screwed her eyes up against the glare.* **5.** *vt* **CHEAT SOMEBODY** to cheat or swindle somebody (*informal*) **6.** *vt* **EXTORT SOMETHING** to get something out of somebody with great difficulty (*informal*) ○ *We managed to screw some money out of him in the end.* **7.** *vti* **OFFENSIVE TERM** an offensive term meaning to have sexual intercourse with somebody (*slang*) **8.** *vt* **OFFENSIVE TERM** an offensive term expressive of anger or frustration with somebody or something (*slang*) **9.** *vt* CUE GAMES **CAUSE CUE BALL TO REBOUND** in billiards or snooker, to hit the cue ball below its centre of gravity so that, when it strikes a ball it is aimed at, it rolls back on itself [15C. < Old French *escroue*, directly or via Germanic < Latin *scrofa* 'sow' (from its curly tail)] —**screwer** *n* ◇ **have a screw loose** to be irrational or lack common sense or good judgment (*informal*) ◇ **put the screws on somebody** to use force or pressure on somebody (*slang*)

screw around *vi* (*slang*) **1.** an offensive term meaning to have sex with a number of different people, especially when married or in an established relationship **2.** an offensive term meaning to waste time in trivial or pointless activities

screw up *v* **1.** **MUSTER SOMETHING** to gather courage or nerve before doing something **2.** *vti* **OFFENSIVE TERM** an offensive term meaning to mismanage, disrupt, or make a mess of something (*slang*) **3.** *vt* **OFFENSIVE TERM** an offensive term meaning to disturb somebody psychologically or emotionally (*slang*)

screwball /skróo bawl/ (*slang insult*) *n* an offensive term for somebody who is regarded as behaving in an unconventional, irrational, or strange way ■ *adj* an offensive term meaning regarded as unconventional, irrational, or strange

screwball comedy *n* a film, especially a Hollywood comedy of the 1930s, featuring the amusing antics of appealing characters in a glamorous world. These films often feature an emancipated and strong-willed heroine.

screw bean *n* **1.** a bush of the legume family that produces twisted pods. Native to: southwestern United States, Mexico. Latin name: *Prosopis pubescens.* **2.** a pod of the screw bean plant. Use: fodder.

screwdriver /skróo drīvər/ *n* **1.** a tool for driving screws that consists of a handle with a metal rod shaped at the tip to fit into the head of a screw **2.** a cocktail made from vodka and orange juice

screwed up /skrood-/ *adj* (*slang*) **1.** an offensive term meaning affected by or displaying symptoms of psychological or emotional disorder (*hyphenated before a noun*) **2.** an offensive term meaning mismanaged, disrupted, or bungled (*hyphenated when used before a noun*)

screw eye *n* a screw with a looped instead of a flat head

screw jack *n* a jack used for lifting heavy items such as vehicles, operated by a screw mechanism

screw pine *n* TREES same as **pandanus**

screw propeller *n* ENG, NAUT same as **propeller**

screw tap *n* same as **tap**² *n* (sense 7)

screw thread *n* **1.** the continuous helical outer surface of a screw or the inner surface of a nut **2.** a full turn of a screw thread

screw top *n* a lid or cap that screws onto a container (*hyphenated before a noun*) ○ *a screw-top jar*

screwup /skróo up/ *n* an offensive term for a mess, muddle, or bungled event (*slang*)

screwworm /skróo wurm/ *n* the larva of the screwworm fly that grows under the skin of livestock and other mammals, causing injury and death [Late 19C. < the spiny hairs of the larva, which encircle each segment]

screwworm fly *n* a bluish blowfly whose eggs, laid on the skin of livestock and other large mammals, hatch as larvae (**screwworms**) that grow under the skin. Latin name: *Cochliomyia hominivorax.*

screwy /skróo i/ (**-ier, -iest**) *adj* an offensive term meaning regarded as irrational, unconventional, or strange (*slang insult*) —**screwily** *adv* —**screwiness** *n*

scribble¹ /skríbb'l/ *v* (**-bles, -bling, -bled**) **1.** *vti* **WRITE MESSILY** to write something hastily or untidily, often in smallish letters **2.** *vti* **MAKE MEANINGLESS MARKINGS** to write or draw meaningless or undecipherable marks on something ○ *Don't scribble on the wall!* **3.** *vi* **BE WRITER** to be a writer, especially one of little merit (*humorous*) ■ *n* **1.** **MESSY HANDWRITING** untidy or careless handwriting **2.** **HASTY NOTE** something written untidily or hastily **3.** **DOODLES** meaningless marks written or drawn on something [15C. < medieval Latin *scribillare* < Latin *scribere* 'write'] —**scribbler** *n* —**scribbly** /skríbbli/ *adj*

scribble² /skríbb'l/ (**-bles, -bling, -bled**) *vt* to card wool roughly [Late 17C. Origin ?]

scribbly gum *n* a eucalyptus tree whose bark has patterns resembling scribbles that are created by burrowing insect larvae. Genus: *Eucalyptus.*

scribe /skrīb/ *n* **1.** **BOOK COPIER** a copier or transcriber of documents, especially somebody who copied manuscripts in medieval times **2.** **COPIER OF JEWISH RELIGIOUS DOCUMENTS** a copier of the Sefer Torah and other Jewish religious documents using a quill pen on parchment **3.** **CLERK** an official public clerk **4.** **JOURNALIST** a writer, especially a journalist (*humorous*) **5.** same as **scriber** ■ *vti* (**scribes, scribing, scribed**) CONSTR **MARK LINES ON SOMETHING** to mark something such as wood or metal with a line using a pointed instrument, especially as a guide for cutting [12C. < Latin *scriba* 'official or public writer' < *scribere* 'write'] —**scribal** *adj*

scriber /skrībər/ *n* a sharp instrument for marking lines on wood or other material

scrim /skrim/ *n* **1.** a drop curtain in the theatre that appears opaque to the audience when lit from the front but transparent when lit from behind **2.** a durable open-weave cotton or linen fabric. Use: curtains, clothing, upholstery lining. [Late 18C. Origin ?]

scrimmage /skrímmij/ *n* **1.** **FIGHT** a skirmish or minor battle **2.** **STRUGGLE** a rough or confused struggle **3.** AMERICAN FOOTBALL **PLAY IN US FOOTBALL** in American football, the action from the moment the ball is put into play to the moment the ball is declared out of play **4.** RUGBY same as **scrum** (*archaic*) **5.** FOOTBALL **GROUP OF PLAYERS PURSUING LOOSE BALL** in Australian Rules football, a cluster of players attempting to take possession of a loose ball ■ *vti* (**-mages, -maging, -maged**) **TAKE PART IN SCRIMMAGE** to engage in a scrimmage against somebody [15C. Alteration of SKIRMISH]

scrimp /skrimp/ (**scrimps, scrimping, scrimped**) *v* **1.** *vi* **ECONOMIZE** to economize drastically or be extremely frugal ○ *scrimp on food* **2.** *vt* **LIMIT SOMEBODY'S PROVISIONS** to severely limit provision to somebody **3.** *vt* **MAKE SOMETHING TOO SMALL** to make something too small or scanty [Mid-18C. < obsolete *scrimp* 'scant, meagre', origin ?] —**scrimpily** *adv* —**scrimpiness** *n* —**scrimpy** *adj*

scrimshank /skrím shangk/ (**-shanks, -shanking, -shanked**) *vi* to shirk work or obligations (*dated slang*) [Late 19C. Origin ?] —**scrimshanker** *n*

scrimshaw /skrím shaw/ *n* **1.** **CARVED WHALE IVORY** a carved or engraved object made originally by North American whalers from the teeth and bones of whales, or such objects collectively **2.** **MAKING OF SCRIMSHAW** the skill or pastime of making scrimshaw ■ *v* (**-shaws, -shawing, -shawed**) **1.** *vi* **MAKE SCRIMSHAW** to make scrimshaw **2.** *vt* **CARVE OR ENGRAVE SOMETHING** to carve or engrave something into scrimshaw [Mid-19C. Origin ?]

scrip¹ /skrip/ *n* **1.** **BRIEF PIECE OF WRITING** a list, receipt, or other short piece of writing **2.** *US* **TEMPORARY PAPER CURRENCY** paper currency issued for temporary emergency use, e.g. by an occupying force **3.** *US* **PRESCRIPTION** a doctor's prescription (*slang*) [Late 16C. Alteration of SCRIPT, influenced by SCRAP¹]

scrip² /skrip/ *n* a document or certificate representing a fraction of a share or stock [Mid-18C. Contraction of obsolete *subscription receipt* 'receipt for shares']

scrip issue *n* FIN same as **bonus issue**

scripophily /skri póffili/ *n* the hobby of collecting share and bond certificates, especially those of historical interest [Late 20C. < SCRIP²] —**scripophile** /skríppə fīl/ *n*

script /skript/ *n* **1.** **TEXT OF PLAY OR BROADCAST** the printed version of a stage play, film screenplay, or radio or television broadcast, including the words to be spoken and often also technical directions **2.** **TEXT INSTRUCTING SOMEBODY WHAT TO SAY** a real or imagined piece of text setting out what somebody is to say or do on a specific occasion ○ *The prime minister stuck to his script and refused to be drawn on side issues.* **3.** **MANUSCRIPT** an original document or manuscript **4.** **SYSTEM OF WRITING** any system of characters used in writing **5.** **HANDWRITING** characters written by hand, especially in cursive form **6.** **PRINTED TYPE RESEMBLING WRITING** printed type designed to imitate handwriting **7.** **ANSWER PAPER** an answer paper in an examination **8.** **SERIES OF COMMANDS IN COMPUTER PROGRAM** a sequence of automated computer commands embedded in a program that tells the program to execute a specific procedure when a Web page is opened or a hypertext link is clicked ■ *vt* (**scripts, scripting, scripted**) **1.** **WRITE SCRIPT FOR SOMETHING** to write or prepare a script for something, especially a play, film, or broadcast **2.** **DIRECT SOMEBODY TO SAY OR DO SOMETHING** to make or arrange something as if according to a script ○ *carefully scripted comments* [14C. Via French < Latin *scriptus* < *scribere* 'write'] —**scripted** *adj*

Script. *abbr* RELIG, BIBLE Scripture

scriptorium /skrip táwri əm/ (*plural* **-riums** or **-ria** /-ri ə/) *n* a room in a monastery for storing, copying, illustrating, or reading manuscripts [Late 18C. < medieval Latin, < Latin *script-* (see SCRIPTURE)]

scripture /skrípchər/, **Scripture** *n* **1.** **BIBLICAL WRITINGS** the sacred writings of the Bible **2.** **BIBLICAL TEXT** a passage from the Bible **3.** **SACRED WRITING** any sacred writing or book ○ *Buddhist scripture* **4.** **AUTHORITATIVE STATEMENT** a statement regarded as authoritative [14C. < Latin *scriptura* 'what is written' < *script-*, past participle of *scribere* 'write'] —**scriptural** *adj*

scriptwriter /skrípt rītər/ *n* a writer of scripts for broadcasts or films

scrivener /skrívvənər/ *n* **1.** in former times, somebody whose job involved writing or making handwritten copies of documents, books, or other texts **2.** LAW same as **notary public** (*archaic*) [14C < Old French *escrivein* < Latin *scriba* (see SCRIBE)]

scrobiculate /skrō bíkyoolət, -layt/ *adj* with a grooved or pitted surface [Early 19C. < late Latin *scrobiculus* 'groove' < Latin *scrobis* 'trench']

scrod /skrod/, **schrod** *n N Am* a young cod or haddock [Mid-19C. Origin ?]

scrofula /skróffyoolə/ *n* tuberculosis of the lymph glands, especially of the neck. If untreated, the glands burst through the skin to form running sores. [14C. < medieval Latin, 'swelling of glands' < *scrofa* 'breeding sow'; because sows were thought to be subject to the disease]

scrofulous /skróffyooləss/ *adj* **1.** **HAVING OR RESEMBLING SCROFULA** affected with or characteristic of scrofula **2.** **SHABBY IN APPEARANCE** run-down, diseased, or shabby in appearance **3.** **MORALLY CORRUPT** morally corrupt and degenerate —**scrofulously** *adv* —**scrofulousness** *n*

scroggin /skróggin/ *n NZ* a mixture of dried fruit, nuts, chocolate, and other high-energy foods eaten as a snack by hikers [Mid-20C. Origin ?]

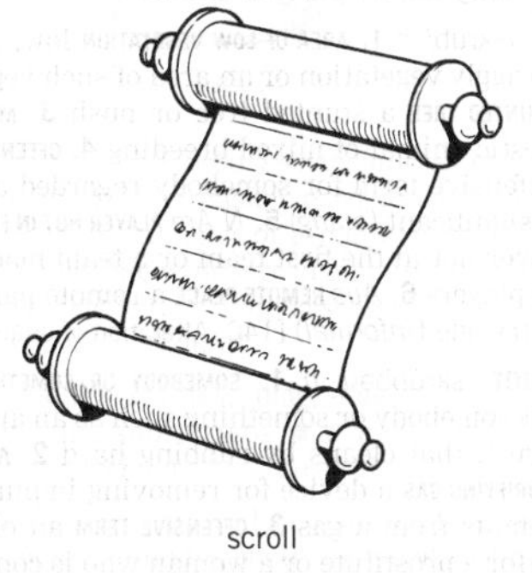

scroll

scroll /skrōl/ *n* **1.** **ROLL OF PARCHMENT** a roll of paper, parchment, leather, or other material, used for a written document, or a document written on such a roll **2.** **LIST** a list, roll, or roster **3.** **ORNAMENTAL DESIGN RESEMBLING ROLL OF PAPER** an ornamental design shaped

Scutum *n* a small faint constellation of the southern hemisphere

scuzz /skuz/ *n* **1.** something dirty, disgusting, or disreputable (*slang*) **2.** *N Am* an offensive term for somebody regarded as unpleasant and contemptible (*slang insult*) [Mid-20C. Origin ?] —**scuzzily** *adv* —**scuzziness** *n* —**scuzzy** *adj*

scuzzbag /skúz bag/, **scuzzball** /skúz bawl/, **scuzzbucket** /skúz búkət/ *n N Am* same as **scuzz** (sense 2) (*slang insult*)

Scylla /síllə/ *n* in Greek mythology, a sea monster who attacked sailors. In later times, Scylla was thought to be a rock on the Italian side of the Straits of Messina. ◇ **be between Scylla and Charybdis** to be faced with the necessity of choosing between two equally undesirable or unpleasant things

scyphistoma /sī fístəmə/ (*plural* **-mae** /-mee/ or **-mas**) *n* the form taken by a jellyfish or other scyphozoan during the stage in its life cycle when it remains fixed in one place and reproduces asexually to produce free-swimming offspring [Late 19C. < Latin *scyphus* 'large cup' < Greek *skuphos*]

scyphozoan /sīfə zṓ ən/ *n* a member of a class of marine invertebrate animal that are generally free-swimming and only sedentary when reproducing, especially a jellyfish [Early 20C. < modern Latin *Scyphozoa* < Greek *skuphos* 'cup' + *zōa* 'animals']

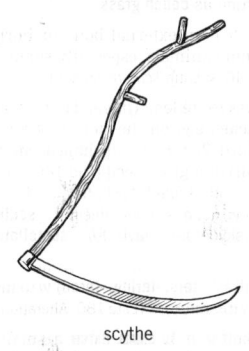
scythe

scythe /sīth/ *n* **TOOL FOR MOWING OR REAPING** an implement with a long handle and a long curved single-edged blade, used to cut grass, crops, or similar plants by swinging the blade horizontally close to the ground ■ *v* (**scythes, scything, scythed**) **1.** *vti* **CUT SOMETHING WITH SCYTHE** to cut or reap something with or as if with a scythe ○ *scythed grass* ○ *a scything tackle* **2.** *vi* **MOVE SWIFTLY AND IRRESISTIBLY** to move, proceed, or cut through something swiftly and with irresistible force ○ *took the ball on the halfway line and scythed through the defence* [Old English *sipe* < Indo-European, 'to cut']

Scythia /síthi ə, síthi ə/ ancient region in what is now Moldova, Ukraine, and eastern Russia

Scythian /síthi ən, síthi ən/ *n* a member of an ancient people who lived in Scythia ■ *adj* relating to ancient Scythia or its people or culture

sd[1] *abbr* **1.** sine die **2.** STATS standard deviation

sd[2] *abbr* Sudan (*used in Internet addresses*) See table at **domain name**

SD *abbr* STATS standard deviation

SDA *abbr Scotland* Scottish Development Agency

SDI *abbr US* MIL, POL Strategic Defense Initiative

SDLP *abbr* Social Democratic and Labour Party

SDP *abbr* Social Democratic Party

SDR, **SDRs** *abbr* ECON special drawing rights

SDRAM *abbr* COMPUT synchronous dynamic random-access memory

se *abbr* Sweden (*used in Internet addresses*) See table at **domain name**

Se *symbol* CHEM ELEM selenium

SE *abbr* **1.** COMPASS southeast **2.** COMPASS southeastern **3.** FIN stock exchange

sea /see/ *n* **1.** **SALT WATERS OF EARTH** the great body of salt water that covers a large portion of Earth ○ *swimming in the sea* ○ *sea air* ○ *a sea fish* **2.** **BODY OF SALT WATER** a body of salt water that is surrounded by land on all or most sides, or that is part of one of the oceans ○ *the Caribbean Sea* **3.** **LARGE LAKE** a large inland body of fresh water **4.** ASTRON same as **mare**[2] **5.** **TURBULENCE OF OCEAN** the motion and disturbance of a large body of water such as the ocean, or the waves themselves ○ *big seas* **6.** **SEAFARER'S JOB OR LIFE** the occupation or way of life of a sailor ○ *ran away to sea* **7.** **VAST BODY** a large area or great number of something ○ *a sea of faces* [Old English *sæ* < Germanic] ◇ **at sea 1.** travelling on the ocean **2.** bewildered and confused

SPELLCHECK sea or **see**? Do not confuse the spelling of *sea* and *see*, which sound similar. *Sea* denotes a large body of water, as in *the Mediterranean Sea*, and is used figuratively in such phrases as *a sea of faces*. *See* is chiefly used as a verb, meaning 'perceive with the eyes', 'have a clear understanding', etc.: *She couldn't see him anywhere. I see what you mean.* There is also a different word *see*, a noun, referring to the area of jurisdiction of a bishop or archbishop.

sea anchor *n* a device, e.g. a conical canvas bag, that is thrown overboard and dragged behind a ship to control its speed or heading

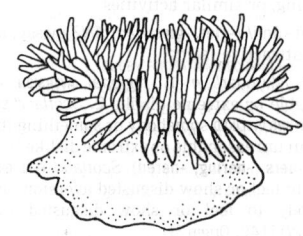
sea anemone

sea anemone *n* a solitary and often colourful sea animal with a squat cylindrical body topped by a ring of tentacles that attaches itself to rock or other nonliving material. Order: Actiniaria.

sea aster *n* a biennial or perennial plant with narrow fleshy leaves. Flowers: purple-and-yellow. Native to: salt marshes throughout Europe. Latin name: *Aster tripolium*.

sea bass /-bass/ *n* a bony sea fish that has a long body, large mouth, and spiny dorsal fin and is a popular game fish. Native to: Atlantic coast of North America. Latin name: *Centropristis striata*.

seabed /see bed/ *n* the ground at the bottom of the sea

Seabee /see bee/ *n* a member of one of the construction battalions of the US Navy that build naval shore facilities in combat zones [Mid-20C. < pronunciation of *CB*, abbreviation of *construction battalion*]

sea beet *n* a wild beet with leathery leaves. Flowers: inconspicuous, green, in long spikes. Native to: European seashores. Latin name: *Beta vulgaris*.

seabird /see burd/ *n* a bird that frequents the open sea, e.g. a gull, albatross, or petrel

sea biscuit *n* FOOD same as **hardtack**

seablite /see blīt/ *n* an annual plant that grows in salt marshes. Latin name: *Suaeda maritima*. [Mid-18C. < *blite* 'plant of the goosefoot family', via Latin < Greek *bliton*]

seaboard /see bawrd/ *n* **1.** same as **seacoast 2.** land near a seacoast

seaborgium /see báwrgi əm/ *n* a very unstable chemical element produced by high-energy collisions of atoms. Symbol **Sg**. See table at **element** [Late 20C. After Glenn T. *Seaborg* (1912–99), US nuclear chemist]

seaborne /see bawrn/ *adj* **1.** transported by ship across the sea **2.** carried on or in the sea

sea bream *n* a sea fish that resembles a freshwater bream. Native to: European waters. Family: Sparidae.

sea breeze *n* a cooling breeze that blows inland from the sea during the daytime when the land is warmer than the surface of the water

sea buckthorn *n* a bush with silvery leaves and orange-red berries. Native to: sandy coasts of Europe and Asia. Latin name: *Hippophaë rhamnoides*.

sea captain *n* somebody in charge of a ship, especially a merchant ship

sea change *n* a substantial transformation ○ *a sea change in attitudes about legalized gambling*

seachanger /see chaynjər/ *n Aus* somebody who has moved out of a city to seek a more tranquil life in a rural, especially coastal, area

sea chest *n* a large box or trunk in which a sailor's personal belongings are stored

seacoast /see kṓst/ *n* the land that borders the sea

seacock /see kok/ *n* a valve in the hull of a ship used to let water in or out

Seacole /see kṓl/, **Mary Jane** (1805–81) Jamaican nurse. She worked in the Crimean War and received honours from the British, French, and Turkish governments for her courage on the battlefields.

sea cow *n* MARINE BIOL same as **sirenian**

sea crayfish *n* ZOOL same as **spiny lobster**

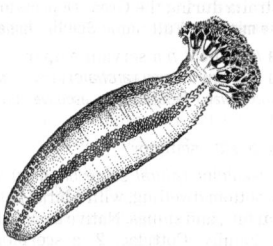
sea cucumber

sea cucumber *n* an invertebrate (**echinoderm**) that has a long tough muscular body and a mouth encircled by tentacles, and lives on the seabed. Class: Holothuroidea.

sea dog *n* a sailor of long experience

seadog /see dog/ *n* METEOROL same as **fogbow**

sea eagle *n* a fish-eating eagle that lives near the sea. Genus: *Haliaeetus*.

sea-ear (*plural* **sea-ears** or *same*) *n* MARINE BIOL same as **abalone**

sea elephant *n* MARINE BIOL same as **elephant seal**

sea fan *n* a coral with a fan-shaped skeleton. Native to: Florida, Caribbean. Genus: *Gorgonia*.

seafarer /see fairər/ *n* somebody who travels by sea

seafaring /see fairing/ *adj* **1.** **REGULARLY GOING TO SEA** regularly travelling by sea or working at sea **2.** **OF SEA TRAVEL OR TRANSPORT** relating to travel or transport by sea ■ *n* **SAILOR'S WAY OF LIFE** the work and way of life of a sailor

sea fire *n* light that is produced by sea organisms

seafloor /see flawr/ *n* OCEANOG same as **seabed**

seafloor spreading *n* a process in which molten material from the Earth's mantle rises up at ocean ridges, causing volcanic and seismic activity, spreads out, and creates a new seafloor

seafood /see food/ *n* fish and shellfish from the sea eaten as food

seafowl /see fowl/ (*plural same* or **-fowls**) *n* BIRDS same as **seabird**

seafront /see frunt/ *n* land or property along the edge of the sea

sea-girt *adj* encircled by the sea (*literary*)

seagoing /see gṓ ing/ *adj* **1.** made or fit for sailing on the open sea **2.** NAUT same as **seafaring** *adj* (sense 1)

sea gooseberry *n* a sea invertebrate (**ctenophore**) that resembles a gooseberry in having a round body and fine tentacles like hairs. Genus: *Pleurobrachia*.

sea grape *n* a tree with large rounded leaves and clusters of purple-to-whitish berries. Native to:

sandy shores from Florida to South America. Latin name: *Coccoloba uvifera*.

seagrass /sée graass/ *n* an underwater sea grass with long thick blades that is harvested and processed into a material, similar to twine or jute, used for making baskets and matting

sea green *n* a blue-green colour in which the green is predominant —**sea-green** *adj*

seagull /sée gul/ *n* BIRDS same as **gull**[1]

CULTURAL NOTE *The Seagull*, a play (1896) by the Russian writer Anton Chekhov. The plot centres on the young writer Triplev's love for the aspiring actress Nina, who, to Triplev's dismay, allows herself to be seduced by an older, more famous writer, Trigorin. One of Chekhov's most successful plays, it typically eschews melodrama for social and psychological analysis.

seagull manager *n* a manager whose interaction with the workforce consists in arriving, criticizing everything and everybody harshly, and leaving again (*slang*)

sea hare *n* a large sea mollusc that has an arched back, a reduced or absent external shell, and two tentacles resembling rabbit ears. Genus: *Aplysia*.

sea heath *n* a small perennial plant with pink flowers. Native to: salt marshes of Europe and Asia. Latin name: *Frankenia laevis*.

sea holly *n* a spiny-leaved perennial plant. Flowers: blue, resembling thistles. Native to: European seashores. Latin name: *Eryngium maritimum*.

sea horse

sea horse *n* 1. a small bony fish with a head shaped like that of a horse, a vertical swimming position, and a tail that it uses to cling to seaweed. Genus: *Hippocampus*. 2. a mythological creature with the head and forelegs of a horse and the body of a fish 3. MARINE BIOL same as **walrus** (*archaic*)

sea-island cotton *n* a cotton with long silky fibres, grown chiefly in the Caribbean. Latin name: *Gossypium barbadense*. [After the SEA ISLANDS]

Sea Islands chain of several hundred low islands in the southern United States, lying in the Atlantic Ocean off the coast of South Carolina, Georgia, and Florida. The main islands include Parris and Hilton Head in South Carolina and Amelia in Florida. The Sea Islands are a popular tourist destination and home to the Gullah people.

sea kale *n* a plant related to the cabbage, with edible leaves and shoots. Native to: seashores of Europe and Asia. Latin name: *Crambe maritima*.

seakale beet /sée kayl-/ *n* PLANTS same as **Swiss chard**

sea king *n* a Norse pirate chief of the early Middle Ages

seal[1] /seel/ *n* 1. TIGHT OR PERFECT CLOSURE a tight closure that prevents the entrance or escape of, e.g. air or water, or a substance or device that forms such a closure 2. SPECIAL CLOSURE THAT REVEALS TAMPERING a closure for a package or container that must be broken when the package or container is opened and can therefore reveal tampering 3. AUTHENTICATING STAMP a ring or stamp with a raised or engraved symbol or emblem that is pressed into wax in order to certify a signature or authenticate a document 4. WAX MARKED WITH SEAL a piece of wax bearing the mark of a seal 5. SYMBOL OF OFFICE a device, emblem, or symbol that is a mark of office 6. ORNAMENTAL ADHESIVE STAMP an ornamental adhesive stamp used to

close a letter or package 7. SOMETHING GIVING CONFIRMATION something that gives confirmation or assurance ○ *Mother gave our plans for the party her seal of approval.* ■ *vt* (**seals, sealing, sealed**) 1. CLOSE SOMETHING FIRMLY to close something tightly or securely with a seal 2. MAKE SOMETHING WATERTIGHT OR AIRTIGHT to make something watertight, airtight, or nonporous, e.g. by filling gaps or applying a coating 3. ATTACH AUTHENTICATING SEAL TO SOMETHING to affix a marked piece of wax to something in order to authenticate or certify it 4. CONFIRM SOMETHING to confirm a decision or come to an agreement on something ○ *seal a contract* 5. SETTLE SOMETHING to determine something irrevocably ○ *His fate was sealed when his lies were discovered.* 6. SOLEMNIZE MARRIAGE OR ADOPTION in the Church of Jesus Christ of Latter-Day Saints, to solemnize a marriage or adoption [12C. Via Anglo-Norman < Latin *sigillum* 'little mark' < *signum* 'sign, token']—**sealable** *adj* ◇ **set the seal on something** 1. to be the thing that ensures that something happens or that completes and perfects something 2. to give final approval or authorization for something ◇ **set your seal on something** to have a decisive influence on the character of something

seal off *vt* to prevent people or things from entering or leaving a place, e.g. by surrounding it or closing it securely ○ *Police sealed off the area.*

seal

seal[2] /seel/ *n* 1. FISH-EATING SEA MAMMAL a carnivorous sea mammal with a sleek body adapted for swimming and living in cold regions and webbed feet modified as flippers. Families: Otariidae or Phocidae. 2. SEAL'S PELT the pelt or fur of a seal 3. LEATHER FROM SEAL'S SKIN leather made from the skin of a seal ■ *vi* (**seals, sealing, sealed**) HUNT SEALS to hunt seals, usually for their skins or blubber [Old English *seol*-, stem of *seolh* < Germanic]

sea lace *n* a seaweed with long thin blackish fronds. Latin name: *Chorda filum*.

sea lamprey *n* a large eel-shaped jawless sea fish that swims up rivers to spawn and lives as a parasite on other fish. Native to: Atlantic coast of North America. Latin name: *Petromyzon marinus*.

sea lane *n* an established and commonly used sea route for large ships

sealant /séelənt/ *n* a substance used to seal something, e.g. by filling gaps or making a surface nonporous

sea lavender *n* a perennial plant of the thrift family with a rosette of slender leaves at the base. Flowers: bluish-purple, in branching spikes. Native to: temperate salt marshes. Genus: *Limonium*.

sea lawyer *n* an argumentative sailor, or any contentious person (*informal*)

sealed-beam headlight /séeld-/ *n* a vehicle headlight with a prefocused reflector and lens sealed in one unit

sealed orders *npl* written instructions not to be opened or read before a specific time

sealed road *n* ANZ a road with a surface of bitumen or tar

sea legs *npl* the ability to maintain balance and not experience motion sickness from the rolling and pitching of a boat (*informal*)

sealer[1] /séelər/ *n* 1. a person, substance, or device that seals something 2. an official who inspects and certifies weights and measures [14C. < SEAL[1]]

sealer[2] /séelər/ *n* a hunter of seals, or a boat used by such hunters [Mid-18C. < SEAL[2]]

sealery /séeləri/ (*plural* **-ies**) *n* 1. BREEDING PLACE FOR SEALS a place where seals are reared or where seals congregate and breed 2. HUNTING GROUND FOR SEALS a place where seals are hunted 3. HUNTING OF SEALS the occupation or practice of hunting seals [Late 19C. < SEAL[2]]

sea letter *n* a passport issued to a neutral ship in wartime that entitles the ship to sail under the flag of the nation to which it belongs

sea lettuce *n* a seaweed sometimes used as food in salads. Genus: *Ulva*.

sea level *n* the level of the surface of the sea relative to the land, halfway between high and low tide, used as a standard in calculating elevation

sealift /sée lift/ *n* a large-scale operation to transport people or cargo, often troops and their equipment, by sea, especially in a time of emergency ■ *vt* (**-lifts, -lifting, -lifted**) to transport people or cargo by ship, especially at short notice

sea lily *n* an invertebrate that has a stalk anchored to the seabed and a flower-shaped body. Class: Crinoidea.

sealing wax /séeling-/ *n* a resinous substance that is soft when heated and used for sealing letters, documents, batteries, or jars

sea lion

sea lion *n* a large gregarious seal that has external ears and coarse hair with no underfur. Family: Otariidae.

sea loch *n* Scotland GEOG same as **loch** (sense 2)

Sea Lord *n* either of the two most senior serving naval officers on the Admiralty Board of the British Ministry of Defence

seal point *n* a Siamese cat with a cream or fawn body and a dark brown face, paws, and tail

seal ring *n* JEWELLERY same as **signet ring**

sealskin /séel skin/ *n* 1. the pelt or fur of a seal, or a garment made from this 2. leather made from a seal's skin

Sealyham terrier /séeli əm-/ *n* a dog with short legs, a long head, powerful jaws, and a wiry, mostly white coat, belonging to a breed developed in Wales for catching rabbits and similar animals [Late 19C. After a village in South Wales]

seam /seem/ *n* 1. PLACE WHERE PIECES JOIN the line along which pieces of cloth or leather are joined by sewing 2. STITCHES FORMING SEAM the stitches used to form a seam 3. LINE FORMED BY ADJACENT SECTIONS any line, groove, or ridge formed by joining or fitting together two sections along their edges 4. LINEAR INDENTATION a scar, wrinkle, or other linear indentation 5. GEOL THIN LAYER OF ROCK a thin layer of a rock or mineral such as a coal deposit occurring between different strata of bedrock ■ *v* (**seams, seaming, seamed**) 1. *vt* JOIN THINGS ALONG EDGES to join two parts or pieces along their edges, e.g. by sewing them together 2. *vti* MARK WITH LINES to mark something with wrinkles, scars, furrows, or other lines, or become marked in this way [Old English *seam* < Germanic, 'sew'] ◇ **bulging** or **bursting at the seams** extremely full ◇ **come** or **fall apart at the seams** to show signs of imminent failure or collapse

SPELLCHECK seam or **seem**? Do not confuse the spelling of *seam* and *seem*, which sound similar. *Seam* is usually a noun, denoting a line, layer, or ridge where things join,

as in *sewed a seam, a rock seam.* **Seem** is a verb, meaning 'give a particular impression or sensation': *He seemed to be looking for someone. They seem very pleasant.*

seaman /seémən/ (*plural* **-men** /-mən/) *n* **1.** somebody, especially a man, who works aboard a boat or ship, especially a low-ranking member of the crew of a merchant or naval ship **2.** an enlisted person in the US Navy or Coast Guard of a rank above seaman apprentice —**seamanship** *n*

seamark /seé maark/ *n* an object on land easily visible from the sea that serves as an aid to navigation

sea mat *n* MARINE BIOL same as **bryozoan**

seam bowler *n* in cricket, a fast bowler who makes the ball bounce on its seam and so deviate from a straight line —**seam bowling** *n*

seamer /seémər/ *n* **1.** a person or machine that makes seams, or the operator of such a machine **2.** CRICKET same as **seam bowler 3.** a ball that bounces on its seam and so deviates from a straight line

sea mile *n* MEASURE same as **nautical mile**

sea milkwort *n* a plant of the primula family. Flowers: small, pink. Native to: northern temperate coasts. Latin name: *Glaux maritima.*

seamless /seémləss/ *adj* **1.** WITHOUT SEAMS having no seams **2.** PERFECTLY SMOOTH free from awkward transitions and creating perfectly smooth continuity **3.** COMPUT FULLY INTEGRATED characterized by integration into an existing software or hardware system without causing any disruption, as if the new item were part of the original design —**seamlessly** *adv* —**seamlessness** *n*

seamoss /seé moss/ *n Carib* a drink popular in the Caribbean, made of seaweed that is boiled until it dissolves and then mixed with milk and spices

seamount /seé mownt/ *n* an isolated undersea mountain of volcanic origin that rises from the seabed to a height of up to 1,000 m/3,300 ft, usually 1,000 m/3,300 ft to 2,000 m/6,500 ft below the surface of the sea

sea mouse *n* a large sea worm with a broad flat body covered in bristles resembling hair. Genus: *Aphrodite.*

seamstress /sémstrəss, seém-/ *n* a woman who sews or whose occupation is sewing [Late 16C. < archaic *seamster* 'tailor, somebody who sews' < SEAM]

seamy /seémi/ (**-ier, -iest**) *adj* having unpleasant qualities associated with a degraded or degenerate way of living —**seaminess** *n*

Seanad Éireann /shánnəth áirən, -nəd-/ *n* the upper chamber of parliament in the Republic of Ireland [Early 20C. < Irish, 'Senate of Ireland']

seance /sáy oNss, -onss, -aanss/ *n* **1.** a meeting at which a spiritualist attempts to receive communications from the spirits of the dead **2.** a sitting, session, or meeting, e.g. of a society or a legislative body [Late 18C. < French, 'sitting' < Old French *seoir* 'sit' < Latin *sedere*]

sea nettle *n* a stinging jellyfish. Native to: Atlantic estuaries from Cape Cod to the Caribbean.

sea onion *n ANZ, N Am* same as **sea squill**

sea otter *n* a sea animal of the weasel family that has a thick brown coat and feeds mainly on shellfish. Native to: northern Pacific coasts. Latin name: *Enhydra lutris.*

sea pen *n* a sea organism related to coral that forms feathery colonies. Native to: warm seas. Genus: *Pennatula.*

sea pink *n* PLANTS same as **thrift** (sense 3)

seaplane /seé playn/ *n* a plane designed in such a way that it can take off from and land on water

sea poacher *n* a small slender sea fish that has an armour of bony plates and is found near the bottom of the North Pacific and other cold waters. Family: Agonidae.

seaport /seé pawrt/ *n* a port, town, or harbour that can accommodate seagoing ships

sea power *n* **1.** a nation that has formidable naval strength **2.** the military power that a nation can deploy to fight on water

SEAQ /seé ak/ *n* a computerized system for displaying prices and transactions in securities on the UK Stock Exchange. Full form **Stock Exchange Automated Quotation**

seaquake /seé kwayk/ *n* an earthquake occurring under the sea

sear[1] /seer/ *v* (**sears, searing, seared**) **1.** *vt* BURN SOMETHING to burn or scorch something with intense heat **2.** *vt* HAVE UNPLEASANT EFFECT to have a sudden painful or unpleasant effect on somebody or something **3.** *vti* WITHER to wither, shrivel, or dry up, or cause something to wither, shrivel, or dry up ■ *n* BURN OR SCORCH MARK a mark or scar made by searing [Old English *sēarian* 'wither away' < Germanic]

sear[2] /seer/ *n* the catch that holds a gunlock cocked or at half-cock [Mid-16C. < French *serre* 'grasp, lock' < *serrer* 'to grasp' < Latin *sera* 'bar for a door']

sear[3] /seer/ *adj* another spelling of **sere**[1] (*archaic or literary*)

Sea Ranger *n* a senior Guide aged between 14 and 20 who specializes in activities at sea

search /surch/ *v* (**searches, searching, searched**) **1.** *vti* EXAMINE SOMETHING THOROUGHLY to look into, over, or through something carefully in order to find somebody or something ○ *searched his pockets for some change* ○ *searching through the pile of papers on the desk* **2.** *vt* EXAMINE SOMEBODY FOR CONCEALED ITEMS to examine the clothing, personal effects, or body of somebody in order to discover something such as weapons or illegal drugs that have been deliberately concealed **3.** *vt* DISCOVER SOMETHING BY EXAMINATION to discover, come to know, or find something by examination ○ *searched out the relevant file* **4.** *vt* COMPUT EXAMINE COMPUTER FILE to examine a computer file, disk, database, or network for information ■ *n* **1.** THOROUGH EXAMINATION a careful and thorough examination in order to find somebody or something **2.** COMPUT EXAMINATION OF COMPUTER FILE the examination of a computer file, disk, database, or network in order to find information **3.** LAW ACT OF BOARDING SHIP TO SEARCH the act of boarding a ship in accordance with international law in order to search it, especially during wartime [14C. Via Anglo-Norman *sercher*, Old French *cerchier* 'explore' < Latin *circare* 'go around in circles' < *circus* 'circle'] —**searchable** *adj* —**searcher** *n* ◇ **search me** used for emphasizing your lack of knowledge about something (*informal*)

search and rescue *n* **1.** a rapid coordinated response to an emergency situation involving human casualties by volunteer or professional personnel ○ *trained in search and rescue* **2.** a voluntary or professional organization that provides search and rescue facilities

search directory *n* a website in which links to information are organized into a categorical, alphabetical hierarchy to provide the broadest response to a query

search dog *n* a dog that is trained to find people who are lost or have become trapped after an accident or disaster, or to uncover specific substances such as drugs

search engine *n* a computer program that searches for specific words and returns a list of documents in which they were found, especially a commercial Internet service

searching /súrching/ *adj* observing acutely or examining thoroughly —**searchingly** *adv*

searchlight /súrch līt/ *n* **1.** an apparatus for projecting a high-intensity beam of light in any direction **2.** the light from a searchlight

search party *n* a group of volunteers or professionals organized to search for a missing person

search warrant *n* a court order authorizing entry to somebody's property to look for unlawful possessions

searing /seéring/ *adj* **1.** extremely intense or strong ○ *felt a searing pain* **2.** extremely critical of something ○ *wrote a searing criticism of the performance* —**searingly** *adv*

sea robin *n N Am* FISH same as **gurnard** (sense 1)

sea rocket *n* a plant of the mustard family that grows along seashores and has sharp-tasting leaves. Flowers: white or lavender. Native to: Europe, North America, Asia, Australia. Genus: *Cakile.*

searoom /seé room, -ro͝om/ *n* open space at sea in which to turn or manoeuvre a ship

sea rover *n* a pirate or a pirate ship (*literary*)

sea salt *n* coarse salt obtained from the evaporation of seawater

seascape /seé skayp/ *n* a painting or picture of the sea, or a view of the sea

Sea Scout *n* a member of a scouting organization who learns sailing, boating, canoeing, and other water activities

sea serpent *n* **1.** a giant snake often reported to have been seen at sea, but never proved to exist **2.** REPT same as **sea snake** (sense 1)

seashell /seé shel/ *n* the empty shell of a sea organism, especially a mollusc

seashore /seé shawr/ *n* **1.** the land lying next to the sea, especially a beach **2.** in law, the land lying between the usual high and low water marks

seasick /seé sik/ *adj* feeling sick or dizzy as a result of the rocking movement of a vessel on water —**seasickness** *n*

seaside /seé sīd/ *n* the area of land bordering the sea, especially as a place for holidays and leisure activities ■ *adj* situated or taking place at the seaside ○ *a seaside cottage*

sea slater *n* a marine organism that resembles a large woodlouse, lives in cracks in the rocks around the high-water mark, and is active mainly at night. Latin name: *Ligea oceanica.*

sea slug *n* a marine invertebrate animal that resembles a sea snail with no shell and is often brightly coloured. Order: Nudibranchia.

sea snail *n* **1.** a small marine organism with a spiral shell resembling that of a snail, e.g. a whelk or periwinkle. Class: Gastropoda. **2.** FISH same as **snailfish**

sea snake *n* **1.** a venomous snake that swims by means of an oar-shaped tail and bears live young. Native to: tropical waters. Family: Hydrophidae. **2.** MYTHOL same as **sea serpent** (sense 1)

season /seéz'n/ *n* **1.** TRADITIONAL DIVISION OF YEAR a traditional division of the year based on distinctive weather conditions. In temperate regions, there are four seasons, spring, summer, autumn, and winter, while in tropical countries there are often only two, a dry season and a rainy season. **2.** PERIOD FOR PARTICULAR ACTIVITY a period of the year during which a particular activity usually takes place in the human world or among plants and animals ○ *planting season* ○ *mating season* **3.** PERIOD SET ASIDE FOR ACTIVITY a fixed period of every year during which particular activities, especially sports, take place or are permitted ○ *cricket season* **4.** PLAYER'S OR TEAM'S PERFORMANCE the performance of a player or team during a sporting season in relation to others ○ *had his best season ever* **5.** TIME FOR FOOD the time of year when something, especially a kind of food, is abundant and at its best ○ *asparagus season* **6.** ARTS CONNECTED SERIES OF PERFORMANCES a period of time during which artistic works of a particular kind are shown or performed **7.** HIGH SEASON AT RESORTS the time of year at which resorts receive most visitors and charge their highest rates ○ *the height of the season* **8.** SOCIAL SEASON the time during which the important social events of the year involving members of high society take place **9.** TIME AROUND HOLIDAY the period of time just before, after, and including a holiday ○ *the Christmas season* **10.** VET SEXUAL RECEPTIVENESS the period during which a female animal is sexually receptive and ready to be mated **11.** PERIOD OF TIME a period of time of unspecified length ○ *a brief season* **12.** SUITABLE TIME an appropriate time for something (*literary*) **13.** TRANSP same as **season ticket** (*informal*) ■ *v* (**-sons, -soning, -soned**) **1.** *vti* ADD FLAVOURINGS to add flavourings such as salt, spices, or herbs to food **2.** *vt* ENLIVEN SOMETHING to liven up something such as a speech or piece of writing by inserting exciting or amusing material ○ *a speech seasoned with wit* **3.** *vti* DRY OUT BEFORE USE to allow wood to dry out fully before use, or become fully dried out before being used **4.** *vt* CAUSE SOMEBODY TO GAIN EXPERIENCE to cause or enable somebody to gain experience and become more

skilled, or to gain toughness and strength ○ *seasoned troops* **5.** *vt* PREPARE NEW PAN FOR USE to prepare a new frying pan or wok for use by rubbing vegetable oil into the heated cooking surface **6.** *vt* MODERATE SOMETHING to temper something such as a strong emotion (*literary*) [14C. Via Old French < Latin *sation*-'sowing' < *sat*-, past participle of *serere* 'sow'] —**seasoner** *n* ◇ **in season 1.** plentifully available and at a peak of quality ○ *Strawberries are in season now.* **2.** allowed to be hunted, caught, or killed **3.** VET sexually receptive to males **4.** at an appropriate time (*literary*) ◇ **out of season 1.** not widely available or not of good quality because of the time of year ○ *Tulips are out of season at this time of year.* **2.** not allowed to be hunted, caught, or killed because of the time of year **3.** at an inappropriate time (*literary*)

CULTURAL NOTE *The Four Seasons*, a violin concerto (1725) by the Italian composer Antonio Vivaldi. Vivaldi's best-known work (Opus 8) consists of four movements, each of which describes a season with appropriate music. The section called 'Spring', for example, features birdsong, while 'Autumn' incorporates sounds that suggest rustling leaves. Vivaldi provided a commentary on each movement in a series of sonnets he wrote to accompany the concerto.

seasonable /seéz'nəb'l/ *adj* **1.** typical of or appropriate for the time of year **2.** done, given, or occurring at a time when needed or appropriate — **seasonableness** *n* —**seasonably** *adv*

seasonal /seéz'nəl/ *adj* **1.** dependent on or determined by the time of year **2.** available or employed only during one season or at specific times of the year — **seasonally** *adv*

seasonal affective disorder, seasonal affective disorder syndrome *n* medical depression associated with the onset of winter and thought to be caused by decreasing amounts of daylight

seasoning /seéz'ning/ *n* **1.** salt, pepper, or any herb or spice used to give additional flavour to food **2.** the process of treating timber to reduce its moisture sufficiently so that it is suitable for the function for which it will be used

season ticket *n* a ticket valid for a specific period of time for travel on public transport, use of leisure facilities, or attendance at sporting or cultural events

sea spider *n* a marine organism resembling a spider, with a fairly small body and four to six pairs of long jointed legs. Class: Pycnogonida.

sea squill *n UK* a plant that has an onion-shaped bulb with medicinal properties. Flowers: small, white, in dense spikes. Native to: Mediterranean. Latin name: *Urginea maritima*. ANZ, N Am term **sea onion**

sea squirt *n* a marine invertebrate animal that has a transparent sac-shaped body with openings through which water passes in and out. It squirts out a stream of water when disturbed. Class: Ascidiacea.

sea star *n* ZOOL same as **starfish**

sea steps *npl* a set of metal bars fixed to the side of a ship to allow people to climb on or off

sea swallow *n* a bird of the tern family, especially a common tern. Latin name: *Sterna hirundo*.

seat /seet/ *n* **1.** PLACE TO SIT something for sitting on, especially something designed for this, e.g. a chair or bench **2.** PART OF CHAIR SAT ON the usually horizontal part of a chair or other seat that takes most of the weight of the person sitting on it **3.** VIEWER'S OR TRAVELLER'S SITTING PLACE a place to sit and watch an event or travel in a vehicle, for which a ticket is usually required ○ *We reserved seats in the front row.* **4.** PART OF GARMENT COVERING BUTTOCKS the part of a garment that covers the buttocks **5.** MEMBERSHIP IN OFFICIAL GROUP a position as a member of an official body or group, especially in an elected legislature ○ *won a seat in the legislature* **6.** CONSTITUENCY the constituency represented by a member of parliament **7.** BASE a place where something is located or based (*formal*) ○ *the seat of consciousness* **8.** RESIDENCE a residence, especially a large house associated with a specific family **9.** OBJECT ON WHICH SOMETHING RESTS an object, part, or space on which something rests or into which it fits **10.** RIDER'S POSITION the position in which a rider sits on a horse ■ *v* (**seats, seating, seated**) **1.** *vt* PLACE SOMEBODY IN SEAT to place somebody

or yourself in a chair or other seat **2.** *vt* PROVIDE SEATS FOR PEOPLE to have or provide seats for a particular number of people ○ *The hall seats five hundred.* **3.** *vti* REST OR FIT SECURELY to rest something securely on or fit something firmly into another thing, or be firmly resting on or fitted into something ○ *The valve isn't seating properly.* **4.** *vt* INSTALL SOMEBODY IN POWERFUL POSITION to establish somebody in a position of power or authority (*literary*) **5.** *vt* FIT SEAT ON SOMETHING to put or refurbish a seat in or on something [12C. < Old Icelandic *sæti* < Germanic, 'sit'] ◇ **by the seat of your pants 1.** using intuition and guesswork rather than theory or specialized knowledge **2.** without the help of any instruments or technical aids

seatback /seét bak/ *n* the part of a seat against which the back rests

seat belt *n* a strong strap or harness designed to keep the wearer securely in a seat in a vehicle or aircraft

-seater *suffix* a venue, vehicle, or piece of furniture that can seat a particular number of people ○ *a three-seater sofa* ○ *drove up in a two-seater*

seating /seéting/ *n* **1.** SEATS the places provided for people to sit, especially in a public building or a vehicle **2.** ARRANGEMENT OF SEATS OR SITTERS the way in which seats or people sitting are arranged ○ *a seating plan* **3.** SOMETHING THAT OBJECT RESTS ON something on which an object rests or into which it fits **4.** UPHOLSTERING MATERIAL material for upholstering the seat of a chair

SEATO /seétō/ *abbr* Southeast Asia Treaty Organization

seat-of-the-pants *adj* relying on intuition or guesswork rather than mechanical aids, rules and procedures, or planning (*slang*) [Because pilots claim to feel an aircraft's motion through the seat]

sea trout *n* **1.** a large silvery-coloured trout living mainly in the sea but returning to fresh water to spawn. Native to: Europe, North Africa. Latin name: *Salmo trutta*. **2.** a sea fish of the croaker family resembling a trout. Native to: Atlantic coast of North America. Latin name: *Cynoscion regalis*.

SEATS /seets/ *abbr* Stock Exchange Alternative Trading Service

Seattle /si átt'l/ city in west-central Washington State, between Puget Sound and Lake Washington. The most important city in the Pacific Northwest, it is a major port and commercial centre. Population: 570,426 (2002 estimate).

sea turtle *n N Am* REPT same as **turtle**[1] (sense 1)

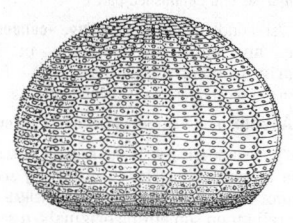
sea urchin

sea urchin *n* a small marine invertebrate animal with a soft body enclosed in a spherical shell that is covered in spines when the animal is alive. Class: Echinoidea.

sea wall *n* a wall built to prevent flooding or coastal erosion by the sea

seaward /seéwərd/ *adj* **1.** moving towards or facing the sea **2.** describes wind that blows in towards the shore from the sea ■ *adv* same as **seawards**

seawards /seéwərdz/ *adv* in a direction towards the sea

seaware /seé wair/ *n* seaweed collected from the shore and used as fertilizer

sea wasp *n* a jellyfish that has a cube-shaped body with tentacles hanging from the lower corners. Its

sting is very venomous and sometimes fatal. Order: Cubomedusae.

seawater /seé wawtər/ *n* salt water in or from the sea

seaway /seé way/ *n* **1.** INLAND CHANNEL FOR SHIPS an inland canal, passage, or channel large enough for sea-going ships to navigate ○ *the St Lawrence Seaway* **2.** ROUTE ACROSS SEA a shipping route across a sea **3.** SHIP'S PROGRESS the progress of a ship through the sea **4.** ROUGH SEAS seas that are moderate to rough

seaweed

seaweed /seé weed/ *n* plants that grow in the sea, e.g. kelp

sea whip *n* a coral that forms long flexible structures with few or no branches and is common on Atlantic reefs. Class: Anthozoa.

seawoman /seé woomən/ (*plural* **-women** /-wimin/) *n* a woman who works aboard a boat or ship, especially a low-ranking member of the crew of a merchant or naval ship

seaworthy /seé wurthi/ *adj* suitable or in a fit state to sail safely on the sea —**seaworthiness** *n*

sea wrack *n* seaweed, especially clumps of the larger varieties, found cast up on the shore

sebaceous /sə báyshəss/ *adj* relating to or producing a waxy yellowish body secretion (**sebum**) [Early 18C. < Latin *sebaceus* < *sebum* 'grease, tallow']

sebaceous gland *n* a gland that secretes sebum into hair follicles to lubricate the hair and skin. Sebaceous glands are found all over the human body except for the palms of the hands and the soles of the feet.

sebacic acid /sə bássik-, -báyssik-/ *n* a white crystalline acid. Use: manufacture of synthetic resins, rubbers, plasticizers. Formula: $COOH(CH_2)_8COOH$. [< SEBACEOUS]

Sebastian /sə básti ən/, **St** (*fl* 3rd century) Roman Christian martyr. He is said to have survived execution by archers ordered by the emperor Diocletian, who then had him beaten to death.

Sebastopol /sə bástə pol/, **Sevastopol** city and port on the Black Sea, in southern Ukraine, on the southern coast of the Crimean Peninsula. Population: 356,000 (1998).

SEbE *abbr* southeast by east

seborrhea *n* MED US spelling of **seborrhoea**

seborrhoea /sébbə reé ə/ *n* excessively oily skin caused by heavy discharge from the sebaceous glands [Late 19C. < SEBUM] —**seborrhoeal** *adj* —**seborrhoeic** *adj*

SEbS *abbr* southeast by south

sebum /seébəm/ *n* an oily substance secreted by the sebaceous glands that lubricates the hair and skin and gives some protection against bacteria [Late 19C. < Latin, 'grease, tallow']

sec[1] /sek/ *n* a very short period of time (*informal*) [Late 19C. Shortening of SECOND[2]]

sec[2] /sek/ *adj* describes a wine, especially champagne, that is dry in taste [Mid-19C. Via French < Latin *siccus* 'dry']

sec[3] /sek/ *abbr* MATHS secant

SEC *abbr* Securities and Exchange Commission

sec. *abbr* **1.** second **2.** secondary **3.** BUSINESS, GOV, FURNITURE secretary **4.** section **5.** sector **6.** security

SECAM /seé kam/ *n* a broadcasting system for colour television used in France, Russia, and a number

of other countries. Full form **séquentiel couleur à mémoire**

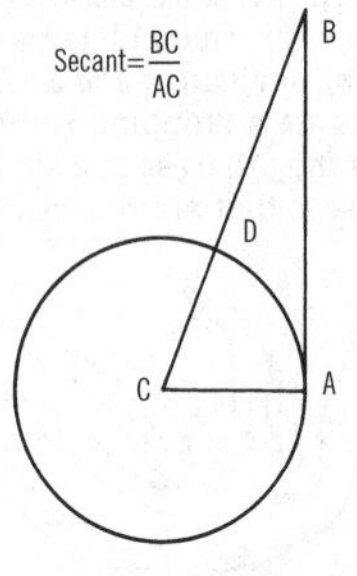

secant

secant /seékənt/ *n* **1.** a straight line that intersects with a curve in two or more places **2.** the ratio of the hypotenuse to the side adjacent to a given angle in a right-angled triangle [Late 16C. < Latin *secant-*, present participle of *secare* 'cut']

secateurs /sékə turz, -túrz/ *npl* a gardening tool used for pruning that has two short heavy blades with a spring mechanism [Mid-19C. < French < Latin *secare* 'to cut']

secco /sékō/ *n* (*plural* **-cos**) **1.** ART **WALL PAINTING TECHNIQUE** the technique of wall painting on dry plaster using tempera or pigments ground in limewater **2.** ART **PICTURE PAINTED ON WALL** a painting on a wall made by the secco method **3.** MUSIC **RECITATIVE STYLE** a style of vocal recitative in which the natural stress of the words is paramount and, if accompanied at all, is supported only by occasional chords of continuo instruments ■ *adj* MUSIC **1. ACCOMPANIED ONLY BY CONTINUO INSTRUMENTS** used to refer to vocal recitatives that are unaccompanied or accompanied only by occasional chords of continuo instruments **2. STACCATO** played and released quickly and lacking resonance (*used as a musical direction*) ■ *adv* MUSIC **IN STACCATO MANNER** with the notes played and released quickly and without resonance (*used as a musical direction*) [Mid-19C. Via Italian < Latin *siccus* 'dry']

secede /si seéd/ (**-cedes, -ceding, -ceded**) *vi* to make a formal withdrawal of membership from an organization, state, or alliance [Early 18C. < Latin *secedere* 'go apart' < *cedere* 'give way'] —**seceder** *n*

~~**seceed**~~ incorrect spelling of **secede**

secession /si sésh'n/ *n* a formal withdrawal from an organization, state, or alliance [Mid-16C. Directly or via French < Latin *secession-* < *secedere* (see SECEDE)] —**secessional** *adj*

Secession *n* the withdrawal from the Union of 11 Southern States in 1860–61 that led to the formation of the Confederacy and the beginning of the American Civil War

secessionism /si sésh'n izəm/ *n* a belief or policy in favour of withdrawal from a nation, state, or organization, or alliance —**secessionist** *n, adj*

seclude /si kloód/ (**-cludes, -cluding, -cluded**) *vt* **1.** to remove somebody from contact with others **2.** to make a place private and quiet by screening or isolating it [15C. < Latin *secludere* 'shut out' < *claudere* 'shut']

secluded /si kloódid/ *adj* **1.** cut off from other places and therefore private and quiet **2.** having or involving little or no contact with others —**secludedly** *adv* —**secludedness** *n*

seclusion /si kloózh'n/ *n* **1. CONDITION OF BEING SECLUDED** the condition of being cut off from others, or from other places **2. ACT OF SECLUDING** an act of setting somebody or something apart from others **3. SECLUDED PLACE** a quiet place removed from activity and people [Early 17C. < Latin *seclusion-* < past participle of *secludere* (see SECLUDE)]

seclusive /si kloóssiv/ *adj* preferring to be solitary [Mid-19C. < SECLUDE, after INCLUSIVE] —**seclusively** *adv* —**seclusiveness** *n*

second[1] /sékənd/ *adj* **1. COMING AFTER FIRST** coming after the first in a series **2. ANOTHER** additional to, repeating, or following one that came before or was previously mentioned ○ *I need a second look at those figures.* **3. ADDITIONAL AND LESS IMPORTANT** additional to and less important than the first or main one ○ *a second home* **4. SIMILAR TO PREDECESSOR** similar or comparable in many respects to a particular renowned personality or event ○ *a second Watergate* **5. INFERIOR** inferior to or less important than somebody or something else ○ *second only to the President* **6.** MUSIC **PERFORMING LOWER OR LESS IMPORTANT PART** singing or playing a lower or less important part ■ *n* **1. 2 IN SERIES** the ordinal number assigned to item number two in a series **2. ANOTHER PERSON OR THING** another person or thing of the same kind as one previously mentioned **3. COMPETITOR'S OR DUELLIST'S ASSISTANT** an official assistant to a contestant in a boxing match or a participant in a duel **4. SECONDER** a seconder for a proposal, a motion, or nomination in a debate **5. ITEM WITH FAULT** an imperfectly manufactured item that is sold at a discount **6.** AUTOMOT **FORWARD GEAR** a forward gear of a transmission that is higher than first gear and lower than third gear **7.** BASEBALL same as **second base** (sense 1) **8.** EDUC **SECOND CLASS DEGREE** a second class degree from a university or college **9.** MUSIC **INTERVAL OF TWO NOTES** in a standard musical scale, the interval between one note and another that lies one note above or below it. In the scale of C major, C and D form a second. **10.** MUSIC **NOTE SECOND AWAY FROM ANOTHER** in a standard musical scale, a note that is a second away from another note **11.** BALLET same as **second position** ■ **seconds** *npl* (*informal*) **1. ANOTHER HELPING OR SERVING** another helping or serving of a dish or type of food **2. SECOND COURSE OF MEAL** the second course of a meal, usually the dessert ■ *vt* (**-onds, -onding, -onded**) **1. ACT AS SECONDER** to state support officially for a proposal, motion, or nomination introduced by somebody else, so that discussion or voting can take place **2. EXPRESS AGREEMENT AND SUPPORT** to express agreement and support for something that somebody has just said (*informal*) ○ *I second that.* **3. ACT AS COMPETITOR'S OR DUELLIST'S SECOND** to act as second to a contestant in a boxing match or duel **4. ASSIST OR SUPPORT** to assist or support somebody or something (*formal*) ○ *seconded her efforts* ■ *adv* **1. EXCEPT FOR ONE** the one that exceeds all the rest, except for one, in a particular way (*used to qualify a superlative*) ○ *the second-highest mountain in the world* **2.** same as **secondly** [14C. Via French < Latin *secundus* 'following' < *sequi* 'follow'] ◇ **second to none** better than anyone or anything else

second[2] /sékənd/ *n* **1. 60TH OF MINUTE** a unit of time that is equal to 1/60th of a minute. Symbol **s** **2. UNIT OF MEASUREMENT OF ANGLES** a unit of measurement of angles equal to 1/60th of a minute or 1/360th of a degree. Symbol **"** **3. VERY SHORT TIME** a very short period of time [14C. Via French < medieval Latin *secunda* < *secunda pars minuta* 'second diminished part']

second[3] /si kónd/ (**-conds, -conding, -conded**) *vt* to transfer an employee, official, or soldier temporarily to other duties [Early 19C. < French *en second* 'in the second rank'] —**secondment** *n*

Second Advent *n* CHR same as **Second Coming**

secondary /sékəndəri/ *adj* **1. NOT PRIMARY OR MAJOR** subordinate to something else ○ *matters of secondary importance* **2. DERIVED FROM SOMETHING ORIGINAL** derived from or reliant on something original ○ *a secondary source* **3.** MED **HAPPENING AS RESULT OF OTHER ILLNESS** happening as a result of another disorder or condition ○ *secondary tumours* **4.** EDUC **OCCURRING AFTER PRIMARY SCHOOL** intended for students who have completed their primary education, usually for children aged between eleven and eighteen ○ *a secondary school* **5.** BIRDS **GROWING ALONG INNER EDGE OF WING** describes feathers that grow along the trailing edge of the inner segment of a bird's wing **6.** ELEC **ELECTRICALLY INDUCED** describes a circuit or coil that has an electric current produced by induction **7.** INDUST **INVOLVED IN MANUFACTURING** involved in the manufacture of goods from raw materials ○ *a secondary industry* **8.** CHEM **ORGANIC CARBON COMPOUND** describes an organic compound that has a carbon atom attached to three organic groups, at least one of which is chemically active **9.** CHEM **RELATING TO ORGANIC NITROGEN COMPOUND** describes an amine that has two alkyl groups and one hydrogen atom attached to a nitrogen atom **10.** BOT **OF RAPIDLY DIVIDING TISSUE** relating to or derived from rapidly dividing tissue (**cambium**) that gives rise to increased girth, not increased length ■ *n* (*plural* **-ies**) **1. SOMEBODY OR SOMETHING SECONDARY** somebody or something that is secondary or subordinate **2.** MED **SECONDARY TUMOUR** a cancerous growth at a site remote from that of the original malignant tumour **3.** BIRDS **SECONDARY FEATHER** a feather that grows along the trailing edge of the inner segment of a bird's wing **4.** ELEC **INDUCED COIL OR CIRCUIT** a coil or circuit in which an induced current flows [14C. < Latin *secondarius* < *secundus* (see SECOND[1])] —**secondarily** *adv* —**secondariness** *n*

secondary accent *n* **1.** *US* PHON same as **secondary stress** **2.** a mark used to indicate where a secondary accent is placed in a word

secondary cell *n* an electric cell in which electricity is produced by a reversible chemical reaction. It is therefore rechargeable and able to store electrical energy.

secondary colour *n* a colour produced by mixing two primary colours in roughly equal quantities, e.g. orange, green, or purple

secondary electron *n* an electron released by secondary emission

secondary emission *n* the emission of electrons from the surface of a substance bombarded with electrons or ions

secondary infection *n* an infection that is acquired during the course of a separate initial infection

secondary modern school, **secondary modern** *n* formerly, a secondary school offering a more practical and less academic education than a grammar school and attended by students who did not pass the eleven-plus exam

secondary picketing *n* the picketing by strikers of premises other than those of the company with which they are in dispute, often those of the suppliers or distributors of their company's products

secondary school *n* a school for students who have completed their primary education, usually attended by children aged between eleven and eighteen

secondary sexual characteristic *n* a characteristic that develops at puberty but is not directly concerned with reproduction, e.g. a woman's breasts or a man's facial hair

secondary stress *n UK, ANZ, Can* an accentuation on a syllable that is weaker than that on the syllable receiving the main accent (**primary stress**). For example, in the word 'secondary', the primary stress falls on the first syllable and the secondary stress on the third. US term **secondary accent**

secondary syphilis *n* the second, highly infectious stage of syphilis that appears several weeks or months after primary infection and is marked by a faint skin rash, fever, and muscular pain

second ballot *n* a second round of voting in an election in which no candidate obtained a winning majority in the first round. In a second ballot, the candidates who received the fewest votes in the first round are usually left out.

second base *n* **1.** the base opposite home plate in the baseball diamond, or the position of the infielder playing nearest to second base on the first-base side **2.** BASEBALL same as **second baseman**

second baseman *n* in baseball, the player positioned closest to second base, on the first-base side of it

second best *n* **1. SOMEBODY OR SOMETHING NEXT TO BEST** somebody or something that is next in quality to, or surpassed only by, the best **2. SOMEBODY OR SOMETHING INFERIOR TO BEST** somebody or something inferior to the best or the favourite ■ *adj* (*hyphenated when used before a noun*) **1. NEXT IN QUALITY TO BEST** next in quality to, or surpassed only by, the best ○ *my second-best suit* **2. INFERIOR TO BEST** inferior to the best or the favourite ○ *had to make do with a second-best alternative*

second chamber *n* the upper house in a two-chamber legislative assembly, e.g. the British House of Lords

second childhood *n* an offensive term for a condition associated with ageing that manifests itself in behaviour regarded as resembling that of a child

second class *n* **1. CATEGORY AFTER BEST** the category or

standard of something, especially of accommodation or travel, that comes immediately below the best **2.** MAIL DELIVERY SERVICE a mail delivery service for letters and packets that is slower but less expensive than first class **3.** SECOND HIGHEST DEGREE the second highest division on the classification of university results, or a degree awarded for a result in this division ■ *adj* (*hyphenated when used before a noun*) **1.** BELONGING TO SECOND CLASS belonging to or meeting the standards of second class, especially regarding mail service or travel accommodation ○ *second-class cabins* **2.** INFERIOR inferior to, or less important than, somebody or something else ○ *treated as second-class citizens*

second-class *adv* by second-class mail delivery service or travel accommodation ○ *travelled second-class*

second-class citizen *n* somebody who does not have the same rights, privileges, or opportunities as a full citizen

Second Coming *n* in Christian belief, the anticipated and prophesied return of Jesus Christ to judge humanity at the end of the world

second cousin *n* a child of a first cousin of either of your parents

second-degree burn *n* a burn that causes blistering on the skin but does not damage the deeper layers of the skin or require grafting

seconde /sə kóNd/ *n* the second of the eight classic parrying positions in fencing [Early 18C. < French, 'second (in order)']

Second Empire *n* **1.** the reign or the government of the Emperor Napoleon III of France, lasting from 1852 until 1870 **2.** the weighty, grandiose, and highly ornamented style of architecture, furnishing, and decoration typical of the Second Empire

seconder /sékəndər/ *n* somebody who states support for a proposal, motion, or nomination introduced by somebody else, so that discussion or voting can take place

second estate *n* the nobility, as one of the three broad traditional classes of people within a monarchic state

second fiddle *n* a less important or less prominent role, or somebody or something in such a role

second generation *n* **1.** the children of immigrants **2.** a later stage in the development of something that benefits from what was learned from the first stage of development —**second-generation** *adj*

second growth *n* the trees and plants that grow back naturally in an area of forest after the original trees have been removed by cutting or fire

second-guess *vti* **1.** to predict a course of events, an outcome, or somebody's intentions from a position of relative ignorance ○ *no point in trying to second-guess what they'll do* **2.** *N Am* to criticize, assess, or correct somebody or something after an event is over and the outcome is known —**second-guesser** *n*

second hand *n* the hand of a clock or watch that shows time passing second by second and rotates once around the dial in the space of a minute

second-hand *adj* **1.** PREVIOUSLY OWNED previously owned or used **2.** SELLING USED GOODS selling or dealing in used goods **3.** NOT ORIGINAL received from or reliant on somebody or something other than the original source ○ *second-hand accounts of the incident* ■ *adv* **1.** IN USED CONDITION after being owned or used by somebody else ○ *bought it second-hand* **2.** THROUGH INTERMEDIARY from or through somebody or something else and not by direct experience or personal effort ○ *acquires the information second-hand* ◇ **at second-hand** from or through somebody or something else

secondi MUSIC plural of **secondo**

second-in-command *n* a person ranking next below somebody in command

Second International *n* an international socialist association established in 1889 in Paris and lasting until World War I

second language *n* **1.** a language learned by somebody after the first language he or she learns at home (*hyphenated before a noun*) **2.** a language in widespread use in a country, sometimes having official status (*hyphenated when used before a noun*)

second lieutenant *n* **1.** an officer in the US and Canadian armies or air forces, the US Marine Corps, or the Royal Marines **2.** in many military forces, the lowest commissioned rank

secondly /sékəndli/ *adv* used to introduce the second point in an argument or discussion

second man *n* especially in the past, a crew member who assists the driver of a railway train

second mate *n* the officer on a merchant ship next in the line of command after the first mate, usually the third-highest-ranking officer on board

second mortgage *n* an additional mortgage on a property that has been mortgaged once already, secondary to the main loan that is secured on the property

second name *n* **1.** somebody's surname **2.** somebody's second forename

second nature *n* a habit or tendency so well-developed and long-practised that it seems to be done unconsciously

secondo /se kóndō/ (*plural* **-di** /-di/) *n* the second or lower part in a piece of music for two players, especially a piano duet [Late 18C. < Italian, 'second (in order)']

second opinion *n* an opinion, especially one of a professional nature, from somebody other than the usual or first person consulted

second person *n* **1.** the form of a verb or pronoun used when addressing somebody. In English, the second-person singular and plural pronoun is 'you'. **2.** the grammatical set containing the forms indicating the second person

second position *n* in ballet, a position in which the feet are turned outwards with the feet slightly apart

second-rate *adj* inadequate in quality or performance ○ *a second-rate pianist* —**second-rater** *n*

second reading *n* the second presentation of a bill to a legislature as part of the process of turning the bill into law. In the British Parliament, it precedes a debate on its merits and its submission to committee.

Second Republic *n* the period of the Republican government in France from 1848 to 1852

second sight *n* the supposed ability to see things that the physical eye cannot see, especially events taking place in the future or elsewhere —**second-sighted** *adj* —**second-sightedness** *n*

second-strike *adj* relating to, involving, or intended for use in a retaliatory nuclear attack with weapons designed to survive a first nuclear strike by an enemy ○ *second-strike capabilities*

second string, **second team** *n* **1.** a fallback plan of action **2.** *N Am* a lineup of players, any of whom may substitute for a starting player during the course of the game, but who do not play at the beginning of a game —**second-string** *adj*

second thought *n* a reconsideration of something tentatively decided, e.g. in light of new developments or something not previously taken into account (*often used in the plural*) ○ *having second thoughts about getting married* ◇ **on second thoughts** after reconsideration

second wind /-wínd/ *n* a renewal of energy following a period of effort and exertion

Second World War *n* HIST same as **World War II**

~~secratary~~ incorrect spelling of **secretary**

secrecy /séekrəssi/ *n* **1.** STATE OF CONCEALMENT the state of being concealed or secret ○ *talks held in secrecy* **2.** KEEPING OF SECRET the keeping of a secret ○ *sworn to secrecy* **3.** SECRETIVENESS a tendency to keep things secret [Late 16C. < SECRET]

secret /séekrət/ *adj* **1.** NOT WIDELY KNOWN known by only a few people and intentionally withheld from general knowledge **2.** UNDERCOVER working or operating without the knowledge of the general public **3.** UNADMITTED acting or feeling in a particular way without admitting to it ○ *a secret admirer* **4.** PRIVATE AND SECLUDED known to very few people and consequently quiet and secluded **5.** SECRETIVE tending by nature to keep things secret (*informal*) **6.** MYSTERIOUS mysterious and often beyond common understanding ■ *n* **1.** INFORMATION NOT WIDELY KNOWN a piece of information that is known only to a few people and is intentionally withheld from general knowledge **2.** MYSTERY something that is unknown, hidden, or not understood ○ *still trying to unravel the secrets of the atom* **3.** SOMETHING ENSURING SUCCESS a little-known technique, approach, or piece of information that is the key to success in an endeavour ○ *the secret of making a good soufflé* [14C. Via French < Latin *secretus* 'separate, hidden' < *secernere* 'separate apart' < *cernere* 'to separate'] —**secretly** *adv* ◇ **in secret** without anyone else's knowledge ○ *meet in secret*

SYNONYMS ***secret, clandestine, covert, furtive, stealthy, surreptitious, secretive***

CORE MEANING: conveying a desire or need for concealment

secret known by only a few people and intentionally withheld from general knowledge ○ *was supported by a majority in a secret ballot* ○ *The find was kept secret until it had been properly excavated by the archaeological department.* **clandestine** needing to be concealed, usually because it is illegal or unauthorized ○ *clandestine arms deals* ○ *It appeared he was having a clandestine relationship with the owner, from whom he had received the information.* **covert** not intended to be known, seen, or found out ○ *a covert police operation* ○ *a covert intelligence and sabotage campaign* **furtive** done in a way that is intended to escape notice ○ *Sandra was whispering to her neighbour, with occasional furtive glances in Edward's direction.* ○ *The stranger looked about him, then walked in an unexpectedly furtive manner towards the gate.* **stealthy** done quietly, slowly, and cautiously in order to escape notice ○ *Casting a stealthy glance around, he leaned forward and lowered his voice.* **surreptitious** done in a concealed or underhand way to escape notice, especially disapproval ○ *surreptitious methods for getting your own way* ○ *If she did a little surreptitious investigating she might find something, she thought.* **secretive** unwilling to reveal or share information ○ *Even as a child he had a very secretive nature.*

Secret /séekrət/, **secret** *n* formerly, the Prayer over the Gifts in the Roman Catholic Mass (*dated*) [14C. < ecclesiastical Latin *secreta oratio* 'concealed speech'; from the low voice used]

secret agent *n* somebody engaged in espionage for a government or organization

secretagogue /si kréetə gog/ *n* a substance that causes or stimulates secretion, e.g. a hormone [Early 20C. < SECRETE[1]] —**secretagogic** /si kréetə gójjik/ *adj*

secretaire /sékrə táir/ *n UK, ANZ, Can* a large cabinet with a fold-down desktop, usually with drawers below and an enclosed bookcase above. US term **secretary** [Late 18C. Via French < late Latin *secretarius* (see SECRETARY)]

secretariat /sékrə táiri ət/ *n* **1.** ADMINISTRATIVE DEPARTMENT a department that carries out the administrative and clerical work of an organization or legislature **2.** SECRETARIAL STAFF the secretarial staff under the direction of a secretary-general **3.** BUILDING HOUSING SECRETARIAT the headquarters or offices of a secretariat [Early 19C. Via French < medieval Latin *secretariatus* < late Latin *secretarius* (see SECRETARY)]

secretary /sékritəri/ (*plural* **-ies**) *n* **1.** CLERICAL WORKER an employee who does clerical and administrative work in an office for a person or organization **2.** OFFICER OF ORGANIZATION somebody elected or appointed to keep the records of the meetings of an organization such as a club, society, or committee, and to write or answer letters on its behalf **3.** GOV same as **Secretary of State** (sense 1) **4.** SENIOR CIVIL SERVANT a senior civil servant who advises a government minister **5.** *also* **Secretary** *US* CABINET MEMBER a cabinet-level official of a national government **6.** *US* FURNITURE same as **secretaire** [14C. < late Latin *secretarius* 'confidential officer' < *secretus* (see SECRET)] —**secretarial** /sékri táiri əl/ *adj* —**secretaryship** *n*

secretary bird *n* a large long-legged bird of prey that has grey-and-black feathers and a crest projecting from the back of its head and which feeds mainly on snakes. Native to: Africa. Latin name: *Sagittarius serpentarius*. See illustration on next page [< the

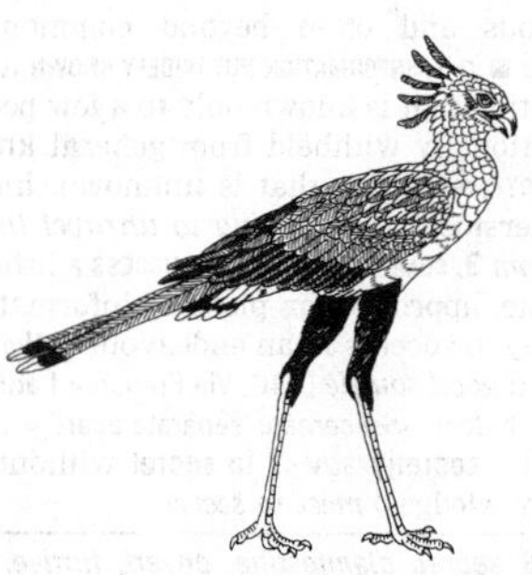

secretary bird

resemblance of the bird's crest to quill pens stuck behind a secretary's ear]

secretary-general (*plural* **secretaries-general**) *n* the chief executive officer of a large organization such as the United Nations, who oversees a secretariat

Secretary of State *n* **1.** a member of the British government and cabinet who is in charge of a major department such as Education or Defence **2.** the US government official and cabinet member who is in charge of foreign affairs

secret ballot *n* a situation in which people cast votes secretly in order to determine the outcome of an election or some other decision

secrete[1] /si kréet/ (**-cretes, -creting, -creted**) *vti* to produce and discharge a substance [Early 18C. < Latin *secret-*, past participle of *secernere* (see SECRET)] —**secretor** *n* —**secretory** *adj*

secrete[2] /si kréet/ (**-cretes, -creting, -creted**) *vt* to conceal somebody or something [Mid-18C. Alteration of SECRET in the obsolete sense 'to hide']

secretin /si kréetin/ *n* a hormone secreted in the duodenum that stimulates the pancreas and the bowel to produce digestive enzymes and the liver to produce bile [Early 20C. < SECRETION[1]]

secretion[1] /si kréesh'n/ *n* **1.** the process of producing a substance from the cells and fluids within a gland or organ and discharging it **2.** a substance formed and discharged by a cell, tissue, gland, or organ [Mid-17C. Directly or via French < Latin *secretion-* < past participle of *secernere* (see SECRET)] —**secretionary** *adj*

secretion[2] /si kréesh'n/ *n* the act of concealing somebody or something [Mid-20C. < SECRETE[2]]

secretive /séekrətiv/ *adj* unwilling to reveal information —**secretively** *adv* —**secretiveness** *n*

SYNONYMS See *secret*.

secret partner *n* a partner whose involvement in a business is kept secret

secret police *npl* a police force that operates in secret and whose function is to prevent subversion or suppress political opposition to a regime

secret service *n* a government department that carries out secret investigations and covert operations

Secret Service *n* a branch of the US Treasury Department whose main function is the protection of the president and vice president and their families

secret society *n* an organization that requires its members to keep all or some of its activities secret from nonmembers

sect /sekt/ *n* **1.** NONMAINSTREAM RELIGIOUS GROUP a religious group with beliefs and practices at variance with those of the more established main groups **2.** RELIGIOUS DENOMINATION a denomination of a larger religious group **3.** CLOSE-KNIT GROUP a small close-knit group with strongly held views that are sometimes regarded as extreme by the majority [14C. Via French < Latin *secta* 'school of thought' < *sequi* 'follow']

-sect *suffix* **1.** to cut or divide ○ *quadrisect* **2.** cut, divided ○ *pinnatisect* [< Latin *sectus*, past participle of *secare* 'cut']

sectarian /sek táiri ən/ *adj* **1.** OF RELIGIOUS GROUP relating to or involving relations between religious groups or denominations **2.** OF SINGLE RELIGIOUS GROUP relating to, involved with, or devoted to a single religious group or denomination **3.** DOGMATIC AND INTOLERANT rigidly adhering to a set of doctrines and intolerant of other views ■ *n* **1.** MEMBER OF RELIGIOUS GROUP a member of a religious group or denomination **2.** SOMEBODY DOGMATIC AND INTOLERANT somebody who rigidly adheres to a set of doctrines and is intolerant of other views —**sectarianism** *n*

sectarianize /sek táiri ə nīz/ (**-izes, -izing, -ized**), **sectarianise** (**-ises, -ising, -ised**) *vt* to cause somebody or something to become sectarian

sectary /séktəri/ (*plural* **-ries**) *n* a member of a religious group or denomination (*archaic*)

sectile /sék tīl/ *adj* describes minerals that can be cut so as to leave a smooth surface [Early 18C. < Latin *sectilis* < *sect-* (see SECTION)] —**sectility** /sek tílləti/ *n*

section /séksh'n/ *n* **1.** DISTINCT PART a distinct part that can be separated or considered separately from the whole of something **2.** UNIT OF PEOPLE a group of people forming a unit within a larger group, e.g. a subdivision of a military unit, or the musicians playing a particular kind of instrument in an orchestra **3.** SUBDIVISION OF DOCUMENT a major subdivision of a written work such as a book or newspaper, or of an official or legal document, often numbered **4.** VIEW OF SOMETHING CUT THROUGH a view or representation of something cut through to show its internal structure or workings **5.** SCI VERY THIN SLICE a very thin slice of something removed for examination under a microscope ○ *a tissue section* **6.** SURG SURGICAL CUT a surgical incision **7.** MED same as **Caesarean** *adj* (sense 2) (*informal*) **8.** RAIL LENGTH OF TRACK a length of railway track maintained by a single crew or controlled from a single signal box **9.** BOT SEGMENT OF CITRUS FRUIT a segment of an orange, grapefruit, or other citrus fruit **10.** PRINTING same as **section mark** **11.** *N Am* TOWN PLAN AREA OF ONE SQUARE MILE an area of land, for purposes of land surveying, equal to one square mile, 2.59 square kilometres, or one thirty-sixth of a township **12.** *NZ* RESIDENTIAL PLOT a piece of residential land in a town or city **13.** *Aus* PIECE OF LAND FROM GOVERNMENT a piece of Australian government land released for agricultural or residential use ■ *vt* (**-tions, -tioning, -tioned**) **1.** DIVIDE SOMETHING to divide something up into separate parts **2.** CUT SOMETHING SURGICALLY to make a surgical incision in something **3.** CONFINE SOMEBODY TO PSYCHIATRIC HOSPITAL to order somebody who is mentally ill to be confined in a psychiatric hospital under the appropriate section of the Mental Health Act [14C. Via French < Latin *section-* < *sect-*, past participle of *secare* 'cut']

ORIGIN The Latin word *secare* 'to cut', from which ***section*** is derived, is also the source of the English words *bisect, dissect, insect, intersect, secateurs, sector,* and *segment.*

sectional /séksh'nəl/ *adj* **1.** OF SECTION relating to a group or section **2.** INVOLVING DIFFERENT SECTIONS involving different groups or sections **3.** CONSISTING OF SECTIONS divided into or made up of sections —**sectionally** *adv*

sectionalism /séksh'nəlizəm/ *n* excessive concern for the interests of one group or area to the detriment of the whole —**sectionalist** *n, adj*

sectionalize /séksh'nə līz/ (**-izes, -izing, -ized**), **sectionalise** (**-ises, -ising, -ised**) *vt* to divide something, especially a geographical area, into sections —**sectionalization** /séksh'nə lī záysh'n/ *n*

section mark *n* a symbol (§) sometimes used in printing to mark the beginning of a section of a book or one of a series of footnotes, and for various other purposes

sector /séktər/ *n* **1.** COMPONENT PART a component of an integrated system such as an economy or a society **2.** MIL PART OF AREA OF MILITARY OPERATIONS a part of an area where military forces are operating or in control **3.** MATHS PART OF CIRCLE a part of a circle bounded by two radii and the part of the circumference that lies between them **4.** MATHS MEASURING INSTRUMENT a measuring instrument consisting of two arms marked with graduations, hinged together at one end **5.** COMPUT UNIT OF MAGNETIC STORAGE DEVICE the smallest addressable unit of a magnetic storage device ■ *vt* (**-tors, -toring, -tored**) DIVIDE SOMETHING to divide something into sectors [Late 16C. < late Latin, 'something that cuts' < Latin *sect-* (see SECTION)] —**sectoral** *adj*

sectorial /sek táwri əl/ *adj* **1.** relating to a sector or consisting of sectors **2.** adapted or specialized for cutting ○ *sectorial teeth*

secular /sékyoolər/ *adj* **1.** NOT CONCERNED WITH RELIGION not controlled by a religious body or concerned with religious or spiritual matters ○ *secular education* **2.** NOT RELIGIOUS not religious or spiritual in nature ○ *secular music* **3.** NOT MONASTIC not belonging to a monastic order ○ *secular clergy* **4.** OCCURRING ONCE IN CENTURY occurring only once in the course of an age or century ○ *a secular change* **5.** ASTRON, GEOL OCCURRING OVER LONG PERIOD taking place over an extremely or indefinitely long period of time ■ *n* **1.** MEMBER OF SECULAR CLERGY a member of the secular clergy **2.** LAY PERSON a member of the laity [14C. Via French < Latin *saecularis* < *saeculum* 'world, generation'] —**secularity** /sékyoo lárrəti/ *n* —**secularly** *adv*

secular humanism *n* a philosophy or world view that stresses human values without reference to religion or spirituality

secularise /sékyələ rīz/ *vt* RELIG another spelling of **secularize**

secularism /sékyoolərizəm/ *n* **1.** the belief that religion and religious bodies should have no part in political or civic affairs or in running public institutions, especially schools **2.** the rejection of religion or its exclusion from a philosophical or moral system —**secularist** *n* —**secularistic** /sékyoolə rístik/ *adj*

secularize /sékyoolə rīz/ (**-izes, -izing, -ized**), **secularise** (**-ises, -ising, -ised**) *vt* **1.** to transfer something from a religious to a nonreligious use, or from control by a religious body to control by the state or a lay body **2.** to remove the religious dimension or element from something, or otherwise make it secular —**secularization** /sékyoolə rī záysh'n/ *n* —**secularizer** *n*

secund /si kúnd/ *adj* BOT arranged on or curving towards only one side of an axis [Late 18C. < Latin *secundus* (see SECOND[1])] —**secundly** *adv*

secure /si kyóor, -kyáwr/ *adj* **1.** FIRMLY FIXED firmly fixed or placed in position and unlikely to come loose or give way ○ *made the rope secure* **2.** NOT WORRIED untroubled by feelings of fear, doubt, or vulnerability **3.** RELIABLE reliable and unlikely to fail or be lost ○ *a secure investment* **4.** WELL GUARDED AND FORTIFIED well guarded and strongly fortified or protected **5.** SAFE safe, especially against attack or theft **6.** SAFE FOR SECRET COMMUNICATIONS safe to use for secret or confidential communication ○ *a secure line* **7.** ASSURED certain to be achieved or gained ○ *Just when victory seemed secure, we let it slip from our grasp.* ■ *v* (**-cures, -curing, -cured**) **1.** *vt* FIX SOMETHING FIRMLY to fix something firmly in position **2.** *vti* MAKE SAFE to make a building or area safe to occupy, usually by ensuring that all internal sources of danger are removed or that it is defended against attack **3.** *vt* ACQUIRE SOMETHING to obtain something, especially after using considerable effort to persuade somebody to grant or allow it ○ *secure an agreement* **4.** *vt* FIN ENSURE PAYMENT FOR SOMETHING to provide security for something or otherwise guarantee payment ○ *a loan secured against your house* **5.** *vti* GUARANTEE to guarantee or ensure something **6.** *vt* PREVENT SOMEBODY FROM ESCAPING to ensure that somebody cannot escape ○ *secure a prisoner* **7.** *vt* MAKE SOMETHING SAFE FOR SECRET COMMUNICATIONS to ensure that a means of communication can be safely used for secret or confidential messages ○ *secure a telephone line* **8.** *vt* MAKE SOMETHING SAFE ON SHIP to make sure that everything on board a ship or aircraft is safely stowed and that openings are covered or doors closed ○ *secure a ship* ○ *secure the cargo* [Mid-16C. < Latin *securus* 'without care' < *cura* 'care'] —**securable** *adj* —**securely** *adv* —**securement** *n* —**secureness** *n* —**securer** *n*

SYNONYMS See *get*[1].

Secure Electronic Transaction *tdmk* a trademark for a standard protocol for secure Internet credit card transactions (*used in e-commerce*)

secure server *n* an Internet server that allows for the encryption of data and thus is suitable for use in e-commerce

secure tenancy *n* a form of tenancy with a landlord such as a local authority or housing association in which the tenant has security of tenure

Securities and Exchange Commission *n* an agency of the US government set up to regulate transactions in securities and protect investors against malpractice

Securities and Investment Board *n* a regulatory body set up in 1986 to oversee financial markets in the City of London. In 1997, it was replaced by the Financial Services Authority.

securitization /si kyoŏrəti tī záysh'n, -kyáwri-/, **securitisation** *n* the preparation of readily marketable securities representing an ownership interest in an asset such as credit card loans or forestry land that is not otherwise conveniently traded

security /si kyoŏrəti, -kyáwr-/ (*plural* **-ties**) *n* **1.** STATE OR FEELING OF SAFETY the state or feeling of being safe and protected **2.** FREEDOM FROM WORRIES OF LOSS the assurance that something of value will not be taken away ○ *job security* **3.** SOMETHING GIVING ASSURANCE something that provides a sense of protection against loss, attack, or harm ○ *the security of knowing that the vehicle has been thoroughly checked* **4.** SAFETY protection against attack from without or subversion from within ○ *a matter of national security* **5.** PRECAUTIONS TO MAINTAIN SAFETY precautions taken to keep somebody or something safe from crime, attack, or danger ○ *security measures* **6.** GUARDS people or an organization entrusted with the job of protecting somebody or something, especially a building or institution, against crime ○ *If you don't leave, I'll call security.* **7.** ASSET DEPOSITED TO GUARANTEE REPAYMENT something pledged to guarantee fulfilment of an obligation, especially an asset guaranteeing repayment of a loan that becomes the property of the creditor if the loan is not repaid **8.** GUARANTOR somebody who pledges to fulfil somebody else's obligation should that person fail to do so **9.** FINANCIAL INSTRUMENT a tradable document that shows evidence of debt or ownership, e.g. a share certificate or bond

security blanket *n* **1.** a familiar blanket, toy, or other object that a child carries around for the feeling of security it gives, or any object that fulfils the same function for an adult **2.** a policy of withholding information in the interests of security adopted as a temporary measure by the police or any other official body

security clearance *n* official permission for somebody to have access to a secure facility or to information that has been classified for reasons of national security

Security Council *n* the permanent committee of the United Nations that oversees its peacekeeping operations throughout the world. The Security Council has five permanent members, Great Britain, China, France, Russia, and the United States, and ten other members chosen in rotation from among the other member states.

security guard *n* somebody employed by a private organization to guard and protect a building or other property

security of tenure *n* the right of a tenant to continue occupying a property unless or until the landlord obtains a court order to regain possession of the property or terminate the tenancy

security risk *n* somebody or something considered a threat to security, especially somebody whose behaviour is thought likely to compromise the security of a country

securocrat /sə kyoŏrə krat, -kyáwrə-/ *n* a senior military, police or intelligence officer with power to influence government policy, often from behind the scenes [Blend of SECURITY + BUREAUCRAT]

secy, sec'y *abbr* secretary

SED *abbr* Scottish Education Department

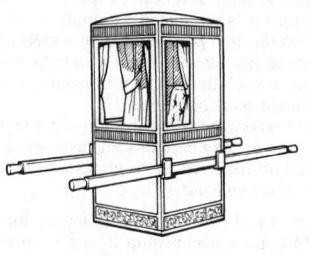

sedan

sedan /si dán/ *n* **1.** in the 17th and 18th centuries, an enclosed chair carried by porters at the front and rear on two long poles passed through handles on the sides of the box **2.** ANZ, N Am a car with a fully enclosed passenger compartment, a permanent roof, two or four doors, front and rear seats, and a separate boot. UK term **saloon** [Mid-17C. Origin ?]

Sedan /sə dán, sə dóN/ *n* town in northeastern France. It was the location of a decisive French defeat in 1870 during the Franco-Prussian war. Population: 20,548 (1999).

sedan chair *n* VEHICLES same as **sedan** (sense 1)

sedate[1] /si dáyt/ *adj* dignified, subdued, and lacking any sense of hurry or urgency [Mid-17C. < Latin *sedatus*, past participle of *sedare* 'to calm' < *sedere* 'sit'] —**sedately** *adv* —**sedateness** *n*

sedate[2] /si dáyt/ (**-dates, -dating, -dated**) *vt* to administer a sedative to somebody [Mid-20C. Back-formation < SEDATIVE or SEDATION]

sedation /si dáysh'n/ *n* **1.** the use of a sedative or tranquillizing drug to induce a state of calm, restfulness, or drowsiness **2.** a state of calm, restfulness, or drowsiness, especially as induced by a sedative or tranquillizing drug [Mid-16C. Directly or via French < Latin *sedation-* < *sedatus* (see SEDATE[1])]

sedative /séddətiv/ *n* a drug or other agent that induces sedation ■ *adj* inducing sedation, especially by means of a tranquillizing drug ○ *a sedative effect* [15C. Directly or via French < medieval Latin *sedativus* < Latin *sedatus* (see SEDATE[1])]

SEDD *abbr* GOV Scottish Executive Development Department

Seddon /sédd'n/, **Richard** (1845–1906) British-born prime minister of New Zealand (1893–1906). A Liberal politician, he was New Zealand's longest serving premier. Full name **Seddon, Richard John**. Known as **King Dick**. See table at **prime minister**

sedentary /sédd'ntəri/ *adj* **1.** INVOLVING SITTING involving a lot of sitting and correspondingly little exercise ○ *sedentary work* **2.** USUALLY SITTING tending to sit most of the time and taking little exercise ○ *a sedentary person* **3.** MARINE BIOL NOT MOVING describes shellfish that remain in one place, usually attached to a rock, for most of their lives **4.** BIRDS NONMIGRATORY describes birds that remain in the same area throughout the year and do not migrate [Late 16C. Via French < Latin *sedentarius* < *sedere* 'sit'] —**sedentarily** *adv* —**sedentariness** *n*

Seder /sáydər/ *n* in Judaism, a ceremonial meal eaten on either of the first two nights of Passover, commemorating the exodus of the Jews from Egypt [Mid-19C. < Hebrew *seder* 'order, procedure']

sederunt /si déerənt/ *n* Scotland **1.** a formula used to introduce the list of those present at a sitting of a body such as an ecclesiastical assembly or a court, or the list itself **2.** a sitting of a body such as an ecclesiastical assembly or a court [Early 17C. < Latin, 'they sat', form of *sedere* 'sit']

sedge /sej/ *n* a wetland plant that resembles grass and has a triangular stem, leaves growing in three vertical rows, and inconspicuous spikes of flowers. Genus: *Carex*. [Old English *secg* < Indo-European, 'to cut'] —**sedgy** *adj*

Sedgemoor /séj moor, -mawr/ former marshland in Somerset, southwestern England, where the Duke of Monmouth's rebellion was defeated in 1685

sedge warbler *n* a songbird with streaked brownish feathers and a white strip around its eye. Native to: marshes of Europe and central Asia. Latin name: *Acrocephalus schoenobaenus*.

sedge wren *n* a bird of the wren family that lives in grassy meadows and sedge marshes. Native to: eastern North America. Latin name: *Cistothorus platensis*.

Sedgwick /séjjwik/, **Adam** (1785–1873) British geologist. His studies of rock strata contributed to the identification of the Cambrian period, and to a scientific approach to geology, but he opposed Charles Darwin's theory of evolution.

sedilia /si dílli ə/ *npl* a set of three seats placed near the altar of a Christian church and often recessed into the wall, used by priests celebrating Mass or Communion [Late 18C. < Latin, plural of *sedile* 'seat' < *sedere* 'sit']

sediment /séddimənt/ *n* **1.** material, originally suspended in a liquid, that settles at the bottom of the liquid when it is left standing for a long time **2.** material eroded from preexisting rocks that is transported by water, wind, or ice and deposited elsewhere [Mid-16C. < Latin *sedimentum* 'settling' < *sedere* 'sit'] —**sedimentous** /séddi méntəss/ *adj*

sedimentary /séddi méntəri/ *adj* **1.** forming at the bottom of a liquid **2.** describes rocks formed from material deposited as sediment by water, wind, or ice and then consolidated by pressure —**sedimentarily** *adv*

sedimentation /séddi men táysh'n/ *n* **1.** the process by which particles in suspension in a liquid form sediment **2.** the process by which rocks are formed by the accumulation of sediment

sedimentation tank *n* a tank in which sewage is left in order to allow its solid constituents to separate out

sedimentology /séddi men tólləji/ *n* the branch of geology concerned with the nature and formation of sedimentary rocks —**sedimentologic** /séddi mentə lójjik/ *adj* —**sedimentologist** *n*

sedition /si dísh'n/ *n* actions or words intended to provoke or incite rebellion against government authority, or actual rebellion against government authority [14C. Via French < Latin *sedition-* 'coming apart' < *se(d)-* 'apart' + *ition-* 'going' < *ire* 'go']

seditious /si díshəss/ *adj* **1.** involving or encouraging rebellion against a government or other authority **2.** taking part in activities that are directed against a government or other authority [15C. Via French < Latin *seditiosus* < *sedition-* (see SEDITION)] —**seditiously** *adv* —**seditiousness** *n*

seduce /si dyoóss/ (**-duces, -ducing, -duced**) *vt* **1.** ENCOURAGE SOMEBODY TO HAVE SEX to persuade somebody to have sex, especially by using a romantic or deceptive approach **2.** LEAD SOMEBODY ASTRAY to persuade somebody to do something by making it seem desirable or exciting **3.** WIN SOMEBODY OVER to persuade somebody into giving support or agreement [15C. < Latin *seducere* 'lead astray' < *se(d)-* 'apart' + *ducere* 'to lead'] —**seducer** *n* —**seducible** *adj*

seducement /si dyoóssmənt/ *n* something that tempts or persuades ○ *'ere any flattering seducement, or vain principle seize them'* (John Milton, *Civil War Polemic, part I*)

seduction /si dúksh'n/ *n* **1.** LURING OF SOMEBODY INTO SEX the act of persuading somebody to have sex, especially by using a romantic or deceptive approach **2.** LEADING ASTRAY OF SOMEBODY the act of persuading somebody to do something wrong ○ *their easy seduction into a life of crime* **3.** TEMPTING THING something that tempts, persuades, or attracts [15C. Directly or via French < Latin *seduction-* < *seduct-*, past participle of *seducere* 'lead astray' (see SEDUCE)]

seductive /si dúktiv/ *adj* **1.** aiming to be or regarded as being sexually inviting ○ *his seductive smile* **2.** serving to tempt, persuade, or attract ○ *made me a very seductive offer* [Mid-18C. < SEDUCTION] —**seductively** *adv* —**seductiveness** *n*

seductress /si dúktrəss/ *n* a woman who seduces people [Early 19C. < obsolete *seductor* 'seducer' < Latin *seduct-* (see SEDUCTION)]

sedulous /séddyoōləss/ *adj* (*literary*) **1.** working with

great zeal and persistence **2.** carried out with great care, concentration, and commitment ○ *sedulous attention to detail* [Mid-16C. < Latin *sedulus* < *se* 'without' + *dolus* 'deception'] —**sedulity** /si dyóoləti/ *n* —**sedulously** *adv* —**sedulousness** *n*

sedum /seédəm/ *n* a low-growing herbaceous plant that grows naturally in rocky places and has fleshy leaves. Flowers: white, yellow, or pink, in clusters. Genus: *Sedum.* [Mid-16C. < Latin, 'houseleek']

see[1] /see/ (**sees, seeing, saw** /saw/, **seen** /seen/) *v* **1.** *vti* **PERCEIVE WITH EYES** to perceive, or perceive something, with the eyes **2.** *vi* **HAVE VISION** to have the faculty of sight ○ *sees fine without his glasses* **3.** *vti* **VIEW OR WATCH SOMETHING** to examine, look at, or watch somebody or something using the eyes ○ *He asked to see my passport.* **4.** *vti* **COMPREHEND SOMETHING** to have a clear understanding of something ○ *I'm not sure I see what you mean.* **5.** *vti* **REALIZE SOMETHING BY SEEING** to realize that something is true or exists by using the eyes, e.g. by reading about it ○ *I see from his letter that he's worked here before.* **6.** *vt* **PERCEIVE SOMETHING AS PLEASING OR GOOD** to perceive or find a trait in somebody, especially one that is interesting or pleasing ○ *I don't understand what she sees in him.* **7.** *vt* **MEET OR CONSULT WITH SOMEBODY** to meet somebody or spend time with somebody, either socially or professionally ○ *I'm seeing an old friend for lunch.* **8.** *vt* **HAVE RELATIONSHIP WITH SOMEBODY** to meet somebody in a romantic context, or have a romantic or sexual relationship with somebody ○ *Is he seeing anyone at the moment?* **9.** *vt* **HAVE INTERVIEW WITH SOMEBODY** to meet somebody in order to raise or discuss an issue such as a complaint ○ *She asked to see the customer care manager.* **10.** *vt* **RECEIVE SOMEBODY FOR INTERVIEW** to admit or receive somebody who has come for a visit or an interview ○ *The doctor can't see you until next week.* **11.** *vt* **IMAGINE SOMETHING** to picture something in the mind ○ *I couldn't see someone like him in a jacket and tie.* **12.** *vt* **BELIEVE SOMETHING** to regard it as likely that somebody will do something ○ *We couldn't see them agreeing to that.* **13.** *vt* **CONSIDER SOMEBODY OR SOMETHING** to regard somebody or something in a particular way ○ *see her as a potential rival* **14.** *vt* **UNDERGO SOMETHING** to experience something firsthand ○ *saw active service* **15.** *vt* **ESCORT SOMEBODY** to go somewhere with somebody, usually as a guide, for company, or for protection ○ *Would you see me to my car?* **16.** *vt* **MAKE SURE THAT SOMETHING HAPPENS** to be sure to do something, or make sure that somebody does something ○ *See that they wash their hands.* **17.** *vt* **REFER TO SOMETHING** to consult or refer to something for information ○ *See our main advertisement on page 25.* **18.** *vti* **ASCERTAIN SOMETHING** to act to find something out ○ *see what he wants* **19.** *vi* **WAIT UNTIL LATER TO DECIDE** to allow time to elapse, either in order to be better able to judge what the outcome will be or in order to delay making a decision ○ *I don't know; we'll have to see.* **20.** *vt* GAMBLING **MATCH BET** to match an opponent's bet by staking the same amount [Old English *sēon* < Germanic] —**seeable** *adj* ◇ **what you see is what you get** used to emphasize that nothing is disguised, hidden, or insincere

SPELLCHECK See *sea.*

see about *vt* to take care of a matter

see into *vt* **1.** to discern the true nature or content of something hidden such as somebody's thoughts **2.** to be able to predict future events

see off *vt* **1. ATTEND SOMEBODY'S DEPARTURE** to accompany somebody to a place of departure and say goodbye **2. FORCE SOMEBODY TO GO** to make somebody leave a place, especially by force (*informal*) ○ *The dogs soon saw them off.* **3. DEFEAT SOMEBODY** to withstand a challenge, e.g. by beating an opponent in a sporting contest ○ *There's no question that the Brazilians will see off the others in their group.*

see out *vt* **1. ESCORT SOMEBODY OUT** to accompany somebody who is leaving a room, building, or other place **2. STAY UNTIL END OF SOMETHING** to stay in a place or stay committed to something until the end **3. OUTLIVE SOMEBODY** to last until the end of somebody's life and beyond (*informal*) ○ *I reckon this old car will see me out.*

see over, see round *vt* to make a tour of a place, especially a building, in order to inspect it ○ *We can arrange for you to see over the property.*

see through *vt* **1. PERCEIVE TRUTH BENEATH EXTERIOR** to discern the true nature of somebody or something beneath a facade or disguise ○ *I saw through his bravado.* **2. FINISH SOMETHING** to continue with something until it is completed ○ *a professional who sees every job through personally* **3. HELP SOMEBODY THROUGH DIFFICULTY** to provide somebody with help, advice, and support, especially in times of trouble ○ *He's seen me through some bad times.*

see to *vt* to do what is required in order to deal with something or take care of somebody successfully ○ *We need an usher to see to guests as they arrive.* ○ *I'll see to it immediately.*

see[2] /see/ *n* **1.** the area that is under the jurisdiction of a bishop or archbishop **2.** the position or authority of a bishop or archbishop [13C Via Old French *se* < Latin *sedes* 'seat' < *sedere* 'sit']

SPELLCHECK See *sea.*

Seebeck effect /seé bek-/ *n* the production of an electric current in a circuit containing junctions between different metals or semiconductors kept at different temperatures [Early 20C. After Thomas *Seebeck* (1770–1831), Russian-born German physicist]

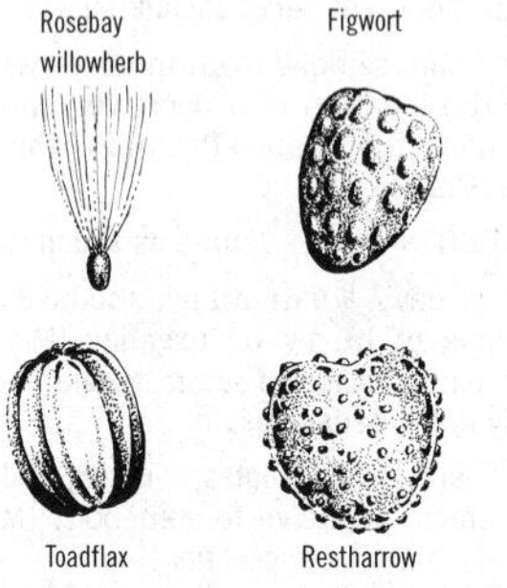
Rosebay willowherb
Figwort
Toadflax
Restharrow
seed

seed /seed/ *n* **1. PLANT PART CONTAINING EMBRYO** a plant part produced by sexual reproduction that contains the embryo and gives rise to a new individual. In flowering plants it is enclosed within the fruit. **2. FRUIT OF GRASS PLANT** the small dry hard fruit produced by cereal plants or grasses **3. PROPAGATIVE PART OF PLANT** a compact part of a plant that is used for propagation, e.g. a bulb, tuber, or spore **4. PROPAGATIVE PLANT PARTS COLLECTIVELY** propagative plant parts as a whole, including seeds, tubers, rhizomes, spores, and bulbs ○ *a dry place to store seed* **5. SOURCE** something that is the source of a significant change in outlook or action ○ *the seeds of doubt* **6. SOMETHING RESEMBLING SEED** something that resembles a seed in shape, size, or function **7.** SPORTS **GRADED COMPETITOR** a competitor who is graded according to the perceived likelihood of his or her winning a specific tournament **8.** CHEM **CRYSTAL** a small crystal added to a supersaturated or supercooled solution to induce crystallization **9. SPERM** sperm or semen as a vehicle of reproduction (*literary*) **10. DESCENDANTS** a person's children or descendants (*literary*) ○ *the seed of Abraham* **11.** MARINE BIOL same as **seed oyster** ■ *v* (**seeds, seeding, seeded**) **1.** *vt* **PLANT SEEDS IN PLACE** to plant seeds in the soil of a place, or plant an area by sowing seeds ○ *The lower field was seeded with barley.* **2.** *vr* **DROP SEEDS** to shed seeds that develop into new plants (*refers to plants*) ○ *Those poppies have seeded themselves everywhere.* **3.** *vt* **REMOVE SEEDS FROM SOMETHING** to take the seeds out of a fruit or vegetable before eating or cooking **4.** *vt* SPORTS **RANK PLAYER** to rank a player according to the perceived likelihood of his or her winning a specific tournament **5.** *vt* SPORTS **STRUCTURE TOURNAMENT** to arrange the draw of a tournament so that the best players meet in the later rounds **6.** *vt* METEOROL **SPRINKLE CLOUD WITH CRYSTALS** to release silver iodide into clouds to encourage precipitation **7.** *vt* CHEM **ADD CRYSTAL TO SOLUTION** to add a small crystal to a supersaturated or supercooled solution to induce crystallization **8.** *vt N Am* BUSINESS **ENCOURAGE ENTERPRISE** to give financial or other assistance to something such as a business during the early stages of its development ○*'Big venture capital funds have helped seed a start-up culture...'* (*Newsweek*; November 1998) ■ *adj* AGRIC **RESERVED FOR USE AS SEED** reserved for planting to grow the next crop ○ *seed potatoes* [Old English *sǣd* < Germanic, 'to sow'] —**seedless** *adj* ◇ **go** *or* **run to seed 1.** to become shabby or unhealthy from lack of proper care or attention **2.** to reach the stage of producing seeds and stop flowering or become unusable

SPELLCHECK See *cede.*

SEED *abbr* GOV Scottish Executive Education Department

seedbed /seéd bed/ *n* **1.** a plot of ground in which seeds and seedlings are cultivated before being transplanted **2.** a place where conditions encourage the development of a significant change in outlook or action ○ *Small business is the seedbed of job creation.*

seedcake /seéd kayk/ *n* a cake flavoured with seeds, usually caraway seeds

seed capital *n* money provided to enable a business venture to be developed. N Am term **seed money**

seed coat *n* BOT same as **testa**

seed corn *n* **1.** cereal grain that is reserved for use as seed **2.** investments that are expected to yield good profits in the future

seedeater /seéd eetər/ *n* a bird that relies on seeds for its food and usually has a strong conical bill adapted to cracking the seeds open. Finches are seedeaters.

seeder /seédər/ *n* **1.** a mechanical device designed to scatter seed on the surface of the ground. Seeders are usually either pulled by a tractor or have wheels and a handle that is pushed. **2.** a kitchen device used to remove the seeds from fruit and vegetables

seed fern *n* PLANTS same as **pteridosperm**

seedhead /seéd hed/ *n* a fertilized flower or flower cluster that contains numerous seeds

seed leaf *n* BOT same as **cotyledon** (sense 1)

seedling /seédling/ *n* a young developing plant that has been grown from a seed

seed money *n N Am* same as **seed capital**

seed oyster *n* a small young oyster, especially one that is transplanted to a commercial oyster bed

seed pearl *n* a very small round pearl, natural or cultured, weighing less than one quarter of a grain

seed plant *n* BOT same as **spermatophyte**

seed pod *n* BOT same as **pod**[1] *n* (sense 1)

seedsman /seédzmən/ (*plural* **-men** /-mən/) *n* a commercial producer or seller of seeds

seed stock *n* **1.** a supply of seed for planting **2.** a supply of animals kept or provided for breeding purposes, capable of founding a new population or sustaining an existing population (*hyphenated before a noun*) ○ *They introduced seed-stock trout to the lake.*

seed tick *n* the tiny larva of a tick

seedtime /seéd tīm/ *n* **1.** the time of the year when seeds are sown **2.** a period of new development or growth

seed weevil *n* an insect of the weevil family that lays its eggs in seeds, where the larvae then develop. There are several species.

seedy /seédi/ (**-ier, -iest**) *adj* **1. DINGY** shabby, dirty-looking, and often disreputable ○ *a seedy hotel* **2. HAVING SEEDS** containing many seeds ○ *seedy raspberry jam* **3. UNWELL** somewhat ill, especially with a stomach complaint (*informal*) —**seedily** *adv* —**seediness** *n*

Seeger /seégər/, **Pete** (*b.* 1919) US singer and songwriter. He led the 1960s folk music revival with songs including 'Where Have All the Flowers Gone?' (1956).

> 'Where have all the flowers gone? / Young girls picked them every one.'
> [Pete Seeger, 'Where Have All the Flowers Gone?'; 1956]

seeing /seé ing/ *n* **1. VISION** vision or perception with the eyes ○ *My seeing isn't too good.* **2.** ASTRON **ATMOSPHERIC CONDITIONS** the clarity of the Earth's atmosphere for astronomical observations using an optical telescope **3.** ASTRON **QUALITY OF ASTRONOMICAL IMAGES** the quality of the images obtained using an optical telescope ■ *conj* **seeing that, seeing as (how)** *informal* ⚠ **IN VIEW OF** used to introduce a statement

that takes into account something mentioned before or after ○ *Seeing that you're an old friend, I'll give you a special price.*

USAGE The use of ***seeing that*** as a conjunction not grammatically attached to a particular subject is established in current English and conforms to a pattern used also in *given that, granted that,* and others, as in the sentence: *Perhaps a bonus on my wages might be an idea, seeing that I shall be doing this out of hours* (Paula Marshall, *An American Princess*). On the other hand, ***seeing as***, used in the same way, is informal only: *I'll leave now seeing as you look tired.* To avoid using *seeing that*, substitute *since*.

seek /seek/ (**seeks, seeking, sought** /sawt/) *v* **1.** *vti* **SEARCH FOR SOMETHING** to try to find a person, thing, or place ○ *journeyed to America to seek their fortune* **2.** *vt* **STRIVE FOR SOMETHING** to try to achieve or obtain something ○ *candidates seeking election* **3.** *vt* **HEAD FOR SOMETHING** to go to or towards a place or thing ○ *As the water rose, they sought higher ground.* **4.** *vt* **ASK FOR SOMETHING** to consult somebody in order to obtain something such as help or advice **5.** *vt* **ATTEMPT SOMETHING** to try to do something ○ *seeking to exploit the rift between them* [Old English *sēcan* < Indo-European, 'seek out'] —**seeker** *n*

seek out *vt* to find somebody or something as a result of active searching

seel /seel/ (**seels, seeling, seeled**) *vt* to sew up the eyelids of a hawk or falcon in order to make it tame [15C. Via Old French *siller* < medieval Latin *ciliare* < Latin *cilium* 'eyelid']

seem /seem/ (**seems, seeming, seemed**) *v* **1.** *vti* to give a particular impression or sensation, either of a quality or of something happening ○ *It's not as easy as it seems.* ○ *It seems that I was wrong.* **2.** *vt* used to lessen the force of a following statement, usually by suggesting uncertainty or mitigating criticism, often for the sake of politeness ○ *We seem to have a misunderstanding.* [12C. < Old Norse *sœma* 'conform to' < *sœmr* 'fitting']

SPELLCHECK See *seam*.

seeming /seéming/ *adj* apparent to the senses or to the mind, but not necessarily true or real ○ *her seeming joy at his return* —**seemingly** *adv*

seemly /seémli/ (**-lier, -liest**) *adj* in keeping with accepted standards and appropriate to the circumstances [12C. < Old Norse *sœmiligr* < *sœmr* 'fitting'.] —**seemliness** *n*

seen past participle of **see**[1] ■ *interj* used to check that somebody has understood what has just been said (*used in Black English*)

seep /seep/ *vi* (**seeps, seeping, seeped**) **1. PASS THROUGH** to pass or escape through an opening very slowly and in small quantities (*refers to liquids or gases*) ○ *water seeping out of the cracks* **2. DISAPPEAR** to diminish slowly but steadily ○ *with her resistance gradually seeping away* **3. GO SLOWLY** to enter or escape slowly but inexorably ○ *new sensations seeping into his consciousness* ■ *n* **1.** GEOL **PLACE WHERE LIQUID ESCAPES** a small pool or spring where liquid escapes from the ground **2.** same as **seepage** [Late 18C. Variant of dialect *sipe*, origin ?]

seepage /seépij/ *n* **1.** a slow discharge or escape of liquid **2.** the amount of a liquid that has seeped

seer[1] /seer, seé ər/ *n* **1.** somebody believed to be able to predict the future **2.** somebody with supposed supernatural powers [14C. < SEE[1]]

seer[2] /seer/ (*plural* **seers** or *same*) *n* in South Asia, a former unit of measurement approximately equal to 0.9 kg/2 lbs or 1 litre/1.75 pt [Early 17C. Via Hindi *ser* < Greek *statēr*, unit of weight]

SEERAD /seérad/ *abbr* GOV Scottish Executive Environment and Rural Affairs Department

seersucker /seér sukər/ *n* a lightweight cotton, linen, or synthetic fabric with a pattern of alternate puckered and smooth stripes [Early 18C. Via Hindi < Persian *šīr o šakar* 'milk and sugar']

seesaw /seé saw/ *n* **1. PLAYGROUND TOY** a playground toy in which two people sit at either end of a bar balanced in the middle and take turns at riding up into the air **2. SEESAW RIDING** the game of riding a seesaw **3. UP-AND-DOWN MOVEMENT** an up-and-down, back-and-forth, or otherwise alternating movement, e.g. in the popularity of one political party over another ■ *vi* (**-saws, -sawing, -sawed**) **1. RIDE SEESAW** to ride up and down on a seesaw **2. MOVE LIKE SEESAW** to move in an alternating fashion, especially back and forth or up and down **3. ALTERNATE** to change regularly and repeatedly from one thing to another, e.g. one state of mind to another [Mid-17C. Probably to suggest the repetitive action of a two-handled saw]

seethe /seeth/ *v* (**seethes, seething, seethed**) **1.** *vi* **BE ANGRY** to be in a state of extreme emotion, especially unexpressed anger ○ *I sat in my office quietly seething.* **2.** *vi* **BE BUSY** to be full of bustling activity, especially with crowds of people moving in many different directions **3.** *vi* **MAKE BOILING MOVEMENTS** to boil, or churn or foam as if boiling **4.** *vt* COOK **BOIL SOMETHING** to cook food by boiling it, or boil something to extract its essence (*archaic*) ■ *n* **ACT OF SEETHING** a seething movement or action [Old English *sēothan* < Germanic]

seething /seéthing/ *adj* **1. ANGRY** full of anger, especially pent-up anger **2. BUSTLING** moving in all directions, busily or frantically ○ *'the seething crowd of Paris'* (Baroness Orczy, *The Scarlet Pimpernel*; 1905) **3. BOILING** boiling and bubbling or foaming —**seethingly** *adv*

see-through *adj* made of transparent material, especially so as to reveal clothes or skin underneath

Sefer Torah /séyffər táwrə/ (*plural* **Sefer Torahs** or **Sifrei Torah** /sí fray-/) *n* a parchment scroll on which the Pentateuch is handwritten [Mid-17C. < Hebrew *sēper tōrāh* 'book of (the) Law']

segment *n* /ségmənt/ **1. COMPONENT PART** any of the parts or sections into which an object or group is divided **2.** ZOOL **ORGANISM'S BODY PART** any of the individual units that make up the body or part of the body of some animals **3.** MATHS **PART OF GEOMETRIC FIGURE** the portion of a line or curve between any two of its points, or the portion of a solid cut by a plane **4.** LING **SPEECH SOUND** any of the individual speech sounds that make up a longer string of sounds ■ *vt* /seg mént/ (**-ments, -menting, -mented**) **SPLIT SOMETHING INTO SEGMENTS** to divide an object or group into segments [Late 16C. < Latin *segmentum* < *secare* 'to cut'] —**segmental** /seg mént'l/ *adj* —**segmentary** /ségməntəri/ *adj*

segmentation /ség men táysh'n/ *n* **1. SPLITTING INTO SEGMENTS** the dividing of something into segments **2. SEGMENTED STRUCTURE** the structure of something that is made up of a series of similar segments **3.** ZOOL **BODY STRUCTURE** the structure of the body of an organism such as a worm or centipede that consists of a linear series of similar subunits

segmentation cavity *n* BIOL same as **blastocoel**

segno /sénnyō/ (*plural* **segni** /-yi/ or **segnos**) *n* a symbol used on sheet music to mark the beginning or end of a repeated section [Early 20C. Via Italian < Latin *signum* 'sign']

Ségou /sáy goo/ capital of Ségou Region, southwestern Mali. Population: 107,000 (1998).

Segovia /sə gṓvi ə/ capital of Segovia Province, central Spain. Population: 54,945 (2002).

Segovia, Andrés (1893–1987) Spanish guitarist. His successful international career revived interest in the classical guitar.

Segre /sé gray/, **Emilio** (1905–89) Italian-born US physicist. He discovered the antiproton with physicist Owen Chamberlain (1955) and they shared the Nobel Prize in physics (1959) for their research into atomic nuclei. Full name **Segre, Emilio Gino**

segregant /séggrigənt/ *adj* describes an organism having a genetic makeup that differs from that of either parent because of genetic segregation —**segregant** *n*

segregate /séggri gayt/ (**-gates, -gating, -gated**) *v* **1.** *vt* **SEPARATE PEOPLE OR THINGS** to separate one person or group from the rest, or divide a group into smaller units that are kept apart **2.** *vti* SOCIOL **KEEP GROUPS SEPARATE** to keep different groups within a population separate, especially different ethnic, racial, religious, or gender groups **3.** *vti* GENETICS **UNDERGO GENETIC SEGREGATION** to undergo genetic segregation, or cause cells to undergo genetic segregation [Mid-16C. < Latin *segregat-*, past participle of *segregare* 'separate from the flock' < *grex* 'flock'] —**segregable** *adj* —**segregate** /séggrigət/ *n* —**segregative** *adj* —**segregator** *n*

segregation /séggri gáysh'n/ *n* **1. ENFORCED SEPARATION OF GROUPS** the practice of keeping ethnic, racial, religious, or gender groups separate, especially by enforcing the use of separate schools, transport, housing, and other facilities, and usually discriminating against a minority group **2. ACT OF SEGREGATING** the separating of one person, group, or thing from others, or the dividing of people or things into separate groups kept apart from each other **3. SEGREGATED STATE** the state or position of somebody or something kept separate from others **4.** GENETICS **GENE SEPARATION** the separation of the two versions (**alleles**) of each gene and their distribution to separate sex cells during the formation (**meiosis**) of these cells in organisms with paired chromosomes —**segregational** *adj*

segregationist /séggri gáysh'nist/ *n* an advocate or enforcer of segregation, especially racial or religious segregation —**segregationist** *adj*

segue /sé gway/ *vi* (**-gues, -gueing, -gued**) **1. MOVE SMOOTHLY** to make a smooth, almost imperceptible transition from one state, situation, or subject to another ○ *segued into a discussion of the play-offs without skipping a beat* **2.** MUSIC **CONTINUE PLAYING** in music, to continue by playing the following piece or passage without a pause ■ *n* **1. SMOOTH TRANSITION** the act of making a smooth transition from one state, situation, or subject to another **2.** MUSIC **CONTINUATION OF MUSIC** the act of moving without a pause from one musical piece or passage into another **3.** MUSIC **INSTRUCTION TO CONTINUE** an instruction to a musician to begin playing a following piece or passage without a pause [Mid-18C. < Italian < *seguire* 'follow' < Latin *sequi*]

seguidilla /séggi deélyə/ *n* **1.** DANCE **SPANISH DANCE** a Spanish dance in triple time, usually accompanied by castanets and guitars **2.** MUSIC **SPANISH MUSIC** the music for a seguidilla **3.** LITERAT **SPANISH VERSE FORM** a Spanish verse form with either four or seven very short lines that makes use of assonance rather than rhyme [Mid-18C. < Spanish < *seguida* 'sequence' < *seguir* 'follow' < Latin *sequi*]

SEHD *abbr* GOV Scottish Executive Health Department

seicento /say chéntō/ *n* the 17th century, with reference to Italian art and literature [Early 20C. < Italian, shortening of *milseicento* 'one thousand six hundred']

seiche /saysh/ *n* a movement on the surface of an enclosed body of water such as a lake, usually caused by intense storm activity [Mid-19C. < Swiss French]

seidel /sīd'l, zīd'l/ *n* a large beer glass [Early 20C. Via German < Latin *situla* 'bucket']

Seidler /zīdlər/, **Harry** (*b.* 1923) Austrian-born Australian architect. He was a modernist who studied under Walter Gropius at Harvard. He designed Australia Square in Sydney.

Seidlitz powder /séddlits-/ *n* a powdered preparation containing sodium bicarbonate, tartaric acid, and potassium sodium tartrate formerly taken dissolved in water. Use: laxative. [Late 18C. After a village in Bohemia that had a mineral spring]

seif dune /sáyf-, seéf-/ *n* a sand dune with curved edges, found in hot deserts in a series of parallel ridges and often reaching several miles in length and up to 100 m/300 ft in height [Early 20C. < Arabic *sayf* 'sword']

~~**seige**~~ incorrect spelling of **siege**

seigneur /say nyúr/ *n* **1.** HIST same as **seignior** **2.** in French Canada until 1854, the owner of an estate originally granted by the king of France and farmed by tenants holding a form of feudal tenure over the land [Late 16C. < French, later form of *seignor* (see SEIGNIOR)]

seigneury /sáynyəri/ (*plural* **-ies**) *n* **1.** the estate of a seigneur **2.** the rank or authority of a seigneur

seignior /sáynyər/ *n* a feudal lord, especially in medieval England [13C. Via Anglo-Norman *segnour*, Old French *seignor* < Latin *senior* 'older'] —**seigniorial** /say nyáwri əl/ *adj*

seigniorage /sáynyərij/ *n* **1. PROFIT FROM MINTING COINS** the

profit represented by the difference between the value of bullion and the face value of the coins minted from it **2.** HIST **MONARCH'S PERCENTAGE OF BULLION** in former times, a monarch's right to a percentage of the bullion brought to a mint for the minting of coins **3.** HIST **ARISTOCRAT'S PRIVILEGE** in former times, a right or privilege claimed by a sovereign or other person of high rank

seigniory /sáynyəri/ (*plural* **-ies**), **signiory** /sín-/, **signory** *n* **1. SEIGNIOR'S LAND** the estate of a seignior **2. SEIGNIOR'S RANK** the rank or authority of a seignior **3. LORDS COLLECTIVELY** lords considered as a group, especially English lords under the feudal system

seine /sayn/ *n* a large commercial fishing net that is weighted so that it hangs vertically in the water ■ *vti* (**seines, seining, seined**) to catch fish with a seine [Old English *segne*, via W Germanic < Latin *sagena* 'net' < Greek *sagēnē*] —**seiner** *n*

Seine /sayn, sen/ river rising in eastern France and flowing northwestwards through Paris into the English Channel. Length: 776 km/482 mi.

seise /seez/ (**seises, seising, seised**) *vt* LAW same as **seize** (sense 11) [Early 17C. Variant of SEIZE]

seisin /séezin/, **seizin** *n* **1. LAND OWNERSHIP** the legal freehold possession of land **2. ACT OF TAKING POSSESSION OF LAND** the act of taking legal freehold possession of land **3. OWNED LAND** land that is wholly and legally owned, especially land taken possession of legally [13C. < Anglo-Norman *sesine* < Old French *saisir* (see SEIZE)]

seism /sízəm/ *n* same as **earthquake** (sense 1) (*technical*) [Late 19C. < Greek *seismos* (see SEISMO-)]

seism- *prefix* same as **seismo-** (*used before vowels*)

seismic /sízmik/ *adj* **1.** relating to or caused by an earthquake or earth tremor **2.** extremely large or great (*informal*) ○ *had a seismic impact* —**seismically** *adv*

seismic array *n* a network of seismometers positioned so as to maximize the sensitivity of each of them and best monitor seismic activity in a specific region of the world

seismicity /sīz míssəti/ *n* the distribution and frequency of seismic events

seismic wave *n* a shock wave travelling through the Earth from the epicentre of an earthquake

seismo- *prefix* earthquake ○ *seismograph* [Late 19C. < Greek *seismos* 'earthquake' < *seiein* 'to shake']

seismogram /sízmə gram/ *n* a record of an earthquake made by a seismograph

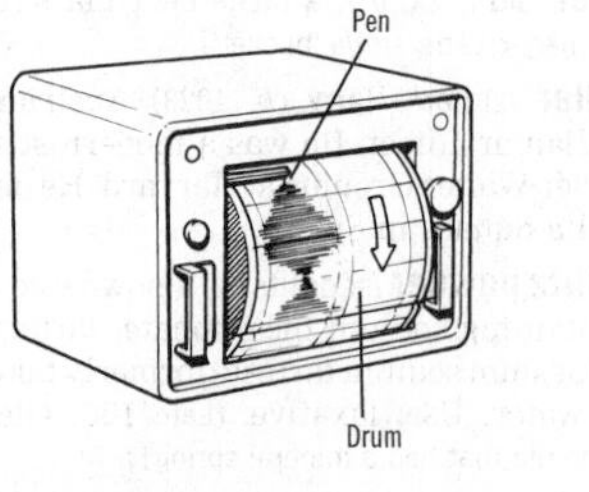

seismograph

seismograph /sízmə graaf, -graf/ *n* an instrument that detects the presence of an earthquake and measures and records its magnitude —**seismographer** /sīz móggrəfər/ *n* —**seismographic** /sízmə gráffik/ *adj* —**seismography** /sīz móggrəfi/ *n*

seismology /sīz mólləji/ *n* the scientific study of earthquakes —**seismological** /sízmə lójjik'l/ *adj* —**seismologically** *adv* —**seismologist** *n*

seismometer /sīz mómmitər/ *n* an instrument used to measure vibrations caused by an earthquake —**seismometric** /sízmə méttrik/ *adj* —**seismometry** *n*

~~**seive**~~ incorrect spelling of **sieve**

sei whale /sáy-/ *n* a dark bluish-grey whale similar to the blue whale but smaller and more streamlined. It lives in all but the polar oceans and belongs to the rorqual family of whales. Latin name: *Balaenoptera borealis*. [Early 20C. < Norwegian *sejhval* < *sei* 'coalfish' + *hval* 'whale']

seize /seez/ (**seizes, seizing, seized**) *v* **1.** *vt* **TAKE HOLD OF SOMETHING** to take hold of an object quickly and firmly ○ *seized the letter from his hand* **2.** *vt* **EXPLOIT SOMETHING IMMEDIATELY** to take advantage of something such as a chance eagerly and immediately ○ *seize an opportunity* **3.** *vt* **AFFECT SOMEBODY SUDDENLY** to overwhelm the mind or emotions suddenly ○ *seized by panic* **4.** *vt* **AFFECT SOMEBODY PHYSICALLY** to overwhelm somebody physically ○ *Yet another spasm seized him.* **5.** *vt* **APPROPRIATE SOMETHING** to take official or legal possession of something, often something held illegally such as arms, drugs, or stolen goods ○ *The shipment was seized by customs officials.* **6.** *vt* **ARREST SOMEBODY** to take somebody into custody ○ *seized the suspects after a chase* **7.** *vti* **COMPREHEND SOMETHING** to understand an idea or concept, especially quickly **8.** *vi* **STOP WORKING** to become jammed, especially as a result of great heat, pressure, or friction, often arising from lack of lubrication ○ *The clutch has seized up.* **9.** *vi* **STIFFEN UP** to become painfully stiff and immobile ○ *My leg's just seized up.* **10.** *vi* **STOP** to come to a sudden and sometimes permanent halt ○ *The negotiations seized up after the most recent incident.* **11.** *vt* LAW **GIVE LEGAL POSSESSION TO SOMEBODY** to make somebody the legal owner of property or goods ○ *The families were seized of all the relevant documentation.* **12.** *vt* NAUT **LASH SOMETHING** to tie or secure something by lashing it using several turns of thin rope or wire [13C. Via Old French *saisir* < medieval Latin *sacire* 'to claim' < Germanic] —**seizable** *adj* —**seizer** *n* ◇ **seized of 1.** LAW in control of **2.** engaged with and interested in (*formal*)

seizin *n* LAW another spelling of **seisin**

seizing /séezing/ *n* a knot or lashing made using thin rope or wire, e.g. to join two ropes or to secure an item of ship's gear

seizure /séezhər/ *n* **1. ACT OF SEIZING SOMETHING** the seizing of something, especially the taking of something by force or the official or legal appropriation of something **2. FACT OF BEING SEIZED** capture or appropriation **3. DISEASE ATTACK** a sudden attack of an illness or condition, especially of the kind experienced by people with epilepsy **4. EMOTIONAL FIT** a sudden and intense rush of emotion ○ *a seizure of panic*

sejant /séejənt/, **sejeant** *adj* in heraldry, used to describe a figure on a coat of arms that is in a sitting position [15C. < French *séant* < Latin *sedere* 'sit']

Sejm /saym/ *n* the national parliament of Poland. It has a single legislative chamber. [Late 19C. < Polish, 'assembly']

Sekondi-Takoradi /sekən dée takə raádi/ capital of Western Region, southwestern Ghana, situated 193 km/120 mi. southwest of Accra. Population: 116,500 (1990).

selachian /si láyki ən/ *n* a fish of the order that includes all sharks, rays, and skates. Order: Selachii. [Mid-19C. < modern Latin *selachii* < Greek *selakhē* 'shark'] —**selachian** *adj*

selaginella /si lájji néllə, sélləji-/ *n* a mossy plant with branching stems and small leaves bearing spores. Genus: *Selaginella*. [Mid-19C. < modern Latin < Latin *selago*, herb similar to savin]

selah /séelə, -laa/ *interj* used to perform a punctuating function between verses of the Bible. It is an ancient Hebrew word of unknown meaning and uncertain grammatical status that appears in some books of the Bible and is therefore, when included in English translations, left untranslated. [Mid-16C. < Hebrew *selāh*]

Selby /sélbi/ market town and port on the River Ouse in North Yorkshire, northern England. Population: 76,468 (2001).

seldom /séldəm/ *adv* not often [Old English *seldum*, *seldan* < Germanic] —**seldomness** *n*

select /si lékt/ *vti* (**-lects, -lecting, -lected**) **CHOOSE FROM OTHERS** to choose somebody or something from among several ○ *selected a chocolate from the box* ■ *adj* **1. OF GOOD QUALITY** chosen on grounds of particularly high quality **2. HAVING LIMITED MEMBERSHIP** admitting only a few carefully chosen members ○ *one of the more select gentlemen's clubs* **3. SPECIALLY CHOSEN** chosen from several others and given special treatment or a special privilege ○ *advance copies sent to a select few* **4. DISCRIMINATING** showing care and discernment when choosing ○ *'foreign films which generally attract a select audience'* (James Berardinelli, *Review: Deception*; 1993) ■ *n* **SOMEBODY OR SOMETHING CHOSEN** somebody or something chosen from among others, often on the basis of high quality (*often used in the plural*) [Mid-16C. < Latin *select-*, past participle of *seligere* < *legere* 'pick out'] —**selectable** *adj* —**selectee** /si lék tée/ *n* —**selectness** *n*

select committee *n* a small group of members of parliament instructed by either the House of Commons or the House of Lords to investigate and report on a specific matter

selection /si léksh'n/ *n* **1. SOMEBODY OR SOMETHING CHOSEN** somebody or something chosen from among others ○ *among the judges' final selection* **2. AVAILABLE CHOICE** the range from which somebody or something can be selected ○ *a fantastic selection of carpets* **3. ACT OF CHOOSING** an act of choosing somebody or something from a wide variety of others **4. CHOSEN STATE** the status of somebody or something chosen from among others **5.** GENETICS **SURVIVAL OF FITTEST** the process by which organisms that adapt well to their environment produce offspring, while those that do not adapt die out, resulting in gradual changes in a species. Selection may take place naturally (**natural selection**) or as the result of breeding for specific characteristics (**artificial selection**). **6.** GAMBLING **GAMBLER'S CHOICE** a competitor on whom a bet is placed, especially in horse-racing ○ *always a popular selection here at Goodwood* **7.** *Aus* **PIECE OF LAND FROM GOVERNMENT** in colonial Australia, a plot of land acquired through the system of free selection [Early 17C. < Latin *selection-* < *select-* (see SELECT)]

selection box *n* a selection of chocolate bars and other sweets made by the same manufacturer, packaged in a seasonally decorated box to be used as a gift to a child at Christmas

selectionist /si léksh'nist/ *n* a believer or promoter of the theory that natural selection is the chief or only force governing biological development

selection rule *n* a rule derived from quantum mechanics that governs whether changes may or may not occur in quantized systems such as molecules, atoms, or nuclei

selective /si léktiv/ *adj* **1. NOT UNIVERSAL** applying to some but not others **2. DISCERNING** tending to make careful choices **3.** ELECTRONICS **RECEIVING ON SOME FREQUENCIES ONLY** describes an electronic receiver capable of selecting some frequencies or frequency bands and blocking out all others, and therefore eliminating interference in reception —**selectively** *adv* —**selectiveness** *n*

selective attention *n* the ability to pay attention to those things that are considered important and to ignore those that are not

selective high school *n* in Australia, a secondary school open to students who have achieved a specific academic standard in specially set exams

selective serotonin reuptake inhibitor *n* a drug that increases serotonin levels in synapses, resulting in elevation of mood. Use: antidepressant.

selective service *n* a system for calling up men for US military service, which requires almost all men between the ages of 18 and 25 to register with the relevant agency. In the event of a draft, men will be called in a sequence determined by a random lottery number and year of birth.

selectivity /si lék tívvəti/ *n* **1. CHOOSING ONLY SOME** the choosing of only some, not all, and the exercising of judgment in making the choice **2. ABILITY TO DISTINGUISH FREQUENCIES** the degree to which an electronic device or circuit can distinguish a desired frequency from other adjacent frequencies, as in the tuning circuits in radio or television receivers **3.** PUBLIC ADMIN **WELFARE PRINCIPLE** the principle that government aid should be given only to those shown to be in greatest need

selector /si léktər/ *n* **1.** a person that selects something, especially somebody responsible for selecting the members of a team ○ *in meetings between the team captain and selectors* **2.** a device for selecting a particular function or setting of a machine

selen- *prefix* same as **seleno-** (*used before vowels*)

selenate /séllə nayt/ *n* a salt or ester of selenic acid [Early 19C. < SELENIUM]

Selene /sə leé ni/ *n* in Greek mythology, the goddess of the Moon. Roman equivalent **Luna**

selenic /si leénik/ *adj* relating to or containing selenium, especially with a valency of six [Early 19C. < SELENIUM]

selenic acid *n* a highly corrosive acid usually found in the form of a whitish solid. Formula: H_2SeO_4.

seleniferous /séllə nífərəss/ *adj* containing or producing selenium [Early 19C. < SELENIUM]

selenious /si leéni əss/ *adj* relating to or containing selenium, especially with a valency of two or four [Early 19C. < SELENIUM]

selenite /sélli nīt/ *n* a transparent colourless variety of gypsum that cleaves to reveal lustrous crystal faces [Mid-16C. Via Latin < Greek *selēnitēs lithos* 'moon stone' < *selēnē* (see SELENIUM)]

selenium /si leéni əm/ *n* a nonmetallic element that occurs in several forms ranging from a red powder to grey-black crystals and is an essential trace element, although toxic in excess. Source: copper refining. Use: photocells, photocopiers. Symbol **Se**. See table at **element** [Early 19C. < modern Latin < Greek *selēnē* 'moon' < *selas* 'light']

selenium cell *n* a photoelectric cell based on the light-sensitive properties of selenium and containing a strip of selenium mounted between two metal electrodes

seleno- *prefix* the moon ○ *selenography* [< Greek *selēnē* 'moon' (see SELENIUM)]

selenography /seélə nóggrəfi/ *n* the branch of astronomy that is concerned with mapping the surface features of the Moon —**selenographic** /si leénə gráffik/ *adj* —**selenographically** *adv* —**selenographist** *n*

selenology /seélə nólləji/ *n* the branch of astronomy concerned with the origin and physical characteristics of the Moon —**selenological** /si leénə lójjik'l/ *adj* —**selenologist** *n*

Seles /sél ez, -esh/, **Monica** (*b.* 1973) Yugoslavian-born US tennis player. She has won numerous Grand Slam tennis championships since turning professional at the age of 15. Her career was interrupted for two years after she was stabbed by a spectator in 1993.

Seleucid /si lóossid/ (*plural* **-cids** or **-cidae** /-sidee/) *n* a member of a dynasty of rulers who ruled Asia Minor from 312 to 64 BC, after the death of Alexander the Great [Mid-19C. < Latin *Seleucides* < Greek *Seleukidēs* < *Seleukos*, the dynasty's founder] —**Seleucid** *adj*

Seleucus I /si lóokəss/ (358?–280 BC) Macedonian general. One of Alexander the Great's successors, he founded the Seleucid dynasty. He became king of Babylonia in 312 BC and gained control of territory from India to Asia Minor, but died trying to seize the throne of Macedonia. Known as **Seleucus Nicator**

Seleucus II (265?–226? BC) Syrian monarch. During his reign over the Seleucid kingdom (247–226 BC), the Bactrians and Parthians won independence.

self /self/ *n* (*plural* **selves** /selvz/) **1.** PERCEIVED PERSONALITY somebody's personality, or an aspect of somebody's personality, especially as perceived by others ○ *not his usual self* **2.** COMPLETE PERSONALITY a complete and individual personality, especially one that somebody recognizes as his or her own and with which there is a sense of ease ○ *develop a sense of self* **3.** SELF-INTEREST somebody's own individual interests and welfare, especially when placed before those of other people **4.** IMMUNOL OWN BODY PARTS the set of organs and tissues that the body recognizes as its own and does not attack with antibodies **5.** ZOOL SELF-COLOURED ANIMAL an animal that is one colour all over, especially a pigeon ■ *pron* ONESELF myself, yourself, himself, or herself (*informal*) ○ *not enough to sustain self and family* ■ *adj* **1.** SELF-COLOURED having the same colour all over **2.** OF SAME FABRIC made of the same material as the garment it is worn with ○ *a self belt* [Old English < Indo-European]

USAGE The two main uses of ***-self*** compounds such as *himself*, *herself*, and *myself* are, first, to serve as a reflexive pronoun when the object of the verb is the same as the subject (*He saw himself in the mirror*) and, second, to reinforce or emphasize a noun (*Jane herself had wanted to go with them*). In formal contexts, compounds with ***-self*** should not be used simply as alternatives for other pronouns such as *him*, *her*, *me*, and *I*: *It was up to her* [not *herself*] *whether she came or not. This is between him and me* [not *myself*]. The plural of *-self* is *-selves*; thus you should use *themselves* not *themself*.

self- *prefix* **1.** of, by, for, to, or in somebody's own self or a thing itself ○ *self-adhesive* ○ *self-control* **2.** automatic ○ *self-winding* [< SELF]

self-abandoned *adj*
self-abandonment *n*
self-abasement *n*
self-abnegating *adj*
self-abnegation *n*
self-acceptance *n*
self-accusation *n*
self-accusing *adj*
self-acting *adj*
self-action *n*
self-actualization *n*
self-actualize *vi*
self-adjusting *adj*
self-administer *vt*
self-administered *adj*
self-administrating *adj*
self-administration *n*
self-admiration *n*
self-advancement *n*
self-advertisement *n*
self-aggrandizement *n*
self-aggrandizer *n*
self-aggrandizing *adj*
self-anointed *adj*
self-approval *n*
self-approved *adj*
self-avowed *adj*
self-betrayal *n*
self-betterment *n*
self-censorship *n*
self-closing *adj*
self-command *n*
self-complacency *n*
self-complacent *adj*
self-conceit *n*
self-concept *n*
self-conception *n*
self-concern *n*
self-concerned *adj*
self-condemnation *n*
self-condemned *adj*
self-conducted *adj*
self-consistent *adj*
self-consuming *adj*
self-contempt *n*
self-content *adj, n*
self-contradicting *adj*
self-contradiction *n*
self-contradictory *adj*
self-created *adj*
self-critical *adj*
self-critically *adv*
self-criticism *n*
self-cultivation *n*
self-debasement *n*
self-deceit *n*
self-deceived *adj*
self-deceiving *adj*
self-deception *n*
self-deceptive *adj*
self-deceptively *adv*
self-defining *adj*
self-definition *n*
self-deluded *adj*
self-deluding *adj*
self-delusion *n*
self-deprecating *adj*
self-deprecation *n*
self-depreciation *n*
self-described *adj*
self-development *n*
self-devouring *adj*
self-diagnosis *n*
self-directed *adj*
self-directing *adj*
self-direction *n*
self-disgust *n*
self-distrust *n*
self-distrustful *adj*
self-educated *adj*
self-education *n*
self-elected *adj*
self-enclosed *adj*
self-engrossed *adj*
self-enrichment *n*
self-evaluation *n*
self-explaining *adj*
self-flattery *n*
self-forgetful *adj*
self-forgetfully *adv*
self-forgetfulness *n*
self-generating *adj*
self-giving *adj*
self-gratification *n*
self-guidance *n*
self-guided *adj*
self-hate *n*
self-hating *adj*
self-hatred *n*
self-healing *adj*
self-humiliation *n*
self-hypnosis *n*
self-identification *n*
self-identify *vi*
self-identity *n*
self-ignite *vi*
self-improvement *n*
self-initiated *adj*
self-instructed *adj*
self-involved *adj*
self-involvement *n*
self-labelled *adj*
self-liquidation *n*
self-loathing *n*
self-love *n*
self-loving *adj*
self-management *n*
self-mastery *n*
self-medication *n*
self-medicator *n*
self-mockery *n*
self-moving *adj*
self-observation *n*
self-obsessed *adj*
self-occupied *adj*
self-ordained *adj*
self-parody *n*
self-penned *adj*
self-perception *n*
self-praise *n*
self-produced *adj*
self-professed *adj*
self-promoter *n*
self-promotion *n*
self-propagating *adj*
self-propelled *adj*
self-propelling *adj*
self-propulsion *n*
self-published *adj*
self-punishment *n*
self-purification *n*
self-questioning *adj*
self-recording *adj*
self-recrimination *n*
self-reflection *n*
self-reliance *n*
self-reliant *adj*
self-renewal *n*
self-renunciation *n*
self-replicating *adj*
self-replication *n*
self-respectful *adj*
self-revealing *adj*
self-revelation *n*
self-ridicule *n*
self-satirizing *adj*
self-satisfaction *n*
self-satisfied *adj*
self-scrutiny *n*
self-study *n*
self-support *n*
self-supported *adj*
self-supporting *adj*
self-sustaining *adj*
self-torture *n*
self-transformation *n*
self-treatment *n*
self-trust *n*
self-understanding *n*
self-validating *adj*

self-absorbed *adj* excessively concerned with your own life and interests

self-absorption *n* **1.** excessive concern with your own life and interests **2.** a radioactive material's absorption of part of the radiation that it emits

self-abuse *n* **1.** masturbation when viewed as being detrimental to character (*sometimes humorous*) **2.** somebody's deprecation or deliberate misuse of his or her talents and abilities —**self-abuser** *n*

self-addressed *adj* **1.** addressed to the sender for return by post ○ *enclose a self-addressed envelope* **2.** directed by somebody towards himself or herself

self-adhesive *adj* having adhesive on one side and able to be stuck in position without needing to be moistened or to have adhesive applied

self-advocacy *n* **1.** the principle and practice of allowing people with psychiatric disorders to assume legal and practical responsibility for their own lives, rather than making them dependent on others **2.** somebody's legal representation of himself or herself, especially in court

self-analysis *n* a systematic attempt to try and gain insight into your own personality and emotions

self-annihilation *n* **1.** loss of awareness of being an individual person, achieved through meditation or other mystical means **2.** an act or instance of suicide

self-appointed *adj* assuming a role personally, rather than being given it or being regarded as worthy of it by others ○ *a self-appointed arbiter of good taste*

self-assembly *n* the construction by the purchaser of something such as a piece of furniture sold in kit form

self-assertive *adj* tending to be aggressively confident in making your views heard and your presence felt —**self-asserting** *adj* —**self-assertion** *n* —**self-assertively** *adv* —**self-assertiveness** *n*

self-assured *adj* behaving in a relaxed manner that displays confidence that your views and abilities are of value —**self-assurance** *n* —**self-assuredly** *adv* —**self-assuredness** *n*

self-aware *adj* having a balanced and honest view of your own personality, and often an ability to interact with others frankly and confidently —**self-awareness** *n*

self-basting *adj* commercially prepared with added fat to prevent drying out when cooked in an oven ○ *a self-basting turkey*

self-catering *adj* describes accommodation, especially for holidaymakers or students, in which meals are not provided but cooking facilities are ■ *n* holidaying in self-catering accommodation ○ *decided on two weeks self-catering in Corfu*

self-centred *adj* tending to concentrate selfishly on your own needs and affairs and to show little or no interest in those of others —**self-centredly** *adv* —**self-centredness** *n*

self-certification *n* the UK system under which employees claim sick pay by making a formal statement to their employer declaring they have been unfit for work, rather than by submitting a doctor's statement

self-cleaning *adj* designed to stay clean when being used, usually by virtue of being coated with materials that shed dirt ○ *a self-cleaning oven*

self-coloured *adj* **1.** UNIFORM IN COLOUR of the same colour all over or throughout **2.** BOT RETAINING NATURAL COLOUR describes a flower whose colour has not been artificially changed by hybridization **3.** TEXTILES

UNDYED describes cloth that has not been dyed and so retains its natural colour

self-compatible adj describes a plant that is capable of pollinating itself

self-confessed adj admitting freely to having a particular characteristic, quality, or behaviour —**self-confessedly** adv

self-confidence n confidence in yourself and your own abilities —**self-confident** adj

self-congratulation n the frequent mentioning of personal achievements and the displaying of the smug satisfaction taken in them —**self-congratulatory** adj

self-conscious adj 1. feeling acutely and uncomfortably aware of your failings and shortcomings when in the company of others and believing that others are noticing them too ○ *too self-conscious to speak in public* 2. highly conscious of the impression made on others and tending to act in a way that reinforces this impression ○ *swinging his car keys in a self-conscious manner* —**self-consciously** adv —**self-consciousness** n

self-contained adj 1. HAVING OWN FACILITIES AND ENTRANCE describes accommodation that has its own kitchen, bathroom, and entrance ○ *self-contained two-bed flat near tube* 2. HAVING EVERYTHING REQUIRED possessing all the features and facilities required to function independently ○ *a number of self-contained holiday villages* 3. KEEPING FEELINGS PRIVATE able or tending to keep feelings and opinions private or to control feelings and reactions in front of others 4. INDEPENDENT not needing the company or support of other people to be a complete and fulfilled person —**self-containedly** adv —**self-containment** n

self-contented adj feeling contented with personal achievements and good fortune —**self-contentedly** adv —**self-contentedness** n

self-control n the ability to control your own behaviour, especially in terms of reactions and impulses —**self-controlled** adj

self-correcting adj 1. describes a word processor that automatically corrects typing errors as they occur 2. able or tending to notice personal mistakes and correct them

self-dealing n the benefiting or attempting to benefit from a financial transaction carried out on behalf of somebody else

self-defeating adj defeating the very aim or purpose it is designed to fulfil

self-defence n 1. LEGAL RIGHT TO DEFEND SELF the use of reasonable force to defend yourself, your family, and your property against physical attack, or the right to do this 2. FIGHTING TECHNIQUES fighting techniques used to defend yourself against physical attack, especially unarmed combat techniques such as any of the martial arts 3. JUSTIFYING OF SELF the defending of your own ideas, principles, or actions —**self-defensive** adj

self-denial n the setting aside of your own wishes, needs, or interests, whether voluntary, altruistic, or enforced by circumstances —**self-denying** adj —**self-denyingly** adv

self-destruct /-di strúkt/ vi 1. DESTROY ITSELF AUTOMATICALLY to destroy itself by means of a built-in mechanism 2. RUIN OWN LIFE to behave in a way that destroys any chance of your success, credibility, or effectiveness ■ adj CAUSING DESTRUCTION OF ITSELF causing a device or machine to destroy itself if given conditions are met

self-destruction n 1. AUTOMATIC DESTRUCTION OF DEVICE the automatic destruction of a device fitted with a self-destruct mechanism 2. RUINING OF OWN LIFE the ruining of your own life or an aspect of it such as your health, happiness, or career 3. SUICIDE an act or instance of suicide

self-destructive adj causing or tending to cause harm to yourself

self-determination n 1. the right of a people to determine their own form of government without interference from outside 2. the ability or right to make your own decisions without interference from others —**self-determining** adj

self-discipline n the ability to do what is necessary or sensible without needing to be urged by somebody else —**self-disciplined** adj

self-discovery n the process of learning about your true personality and motives

self-divinization n in philosophical terms, the elevation by human beings of humankind to godlike status

self-doubt n feelings of doubt about your own worth and abilities

self-drive adj describes a hired car or van that is driven by the hirer

self-effacing adj tending to be modest about your achievements and to avoid drawing attention to yourself in company —**self-effacement** n —**self-effacingly** adv

self-employed adj earning a living by working independently of an employer, either freelance or by running a business —**self-employment** n

self-esteem n confidence in your own merit as an individual person

self-evident adj obvious without explanation or proof —**self-evidently** adv

self-examination n 1. careful reflection on your own thoughts, beliefs, behaviour, and circumstances 2. the regular examination of parts of your own body for signs of disease —**self-examining** adj

self-excited adj describes an electrical device with a field system that is excited by a current the device generates for itself

self-executing adj legally effective without intervention ○ *self-executing clauses in the contract*

self-exile /sélf ék síl/ n 1. a person who leaves his or her own country voluntarily to live elsewhere, especially for political reasons 2. a voluntary state of exile —**self-exiled** adj

self-explanatory adj clear and easy to understand with no need for explanation

self-expression n the expressing of your own ideas, emotions, or individuality through behaviour or an activity such as painting, music, or writing

self-feeder n a machine or device that automatically supplies or replaces materials as they are needed, e.g. a device for feeding animals

self-fertile adj describes a plant or organism that uses its own pollen or sperm to fertilize itself

self-fertilization n fertilization of a plant or animal ovum using pollen or sperm from the same individual —**self-fertilized** adj —**self-fertilizing** adj

self-financed adj describes a business or venture that is paid for or run using its own money, rather than being supported by somebody else

self-financing adj paid for or run without outside financial support

self-flagellation n 1. very strong or harsh self-criticism 2. severe self-administered physical punishment, formerly used as an act of penance, often in the form of beatings or floggings

self-focusing adj focusing automatically rather than manually ○ *a camera with a self-focusing lens*

self-fulfilling adj 1. brought about or proved true because of having been expected or predicted 2. providing satisfaction or pleasure through personal labour, initiative, or talent

self-fulfilment n contentment or happiness as a result of personal work, initiative, or talent

self-gifting n the practice of making purchases for yourself rather than as gifts for other people —**self-gift** n, vi

self-glorification n promotion of your own qualities and abilities, especially beyond what is true or appropriate

self-governed adj run by the people who live or work in an area or place rather than by external government

self-governing adj run by its own members, employees, or citizens, rather than being run from outside

self-government n 1. the ability or right of the citizens of a region to choose their own government

rather than having it imposed from outside 2. the ability to exercise self-control (*archaic*)

self-hardening adj becoming harder without special treatment after being heated above a specific temperature

self-harm n the practice of injuring yourself, especially by cutting, in order to relieve emotional distress —**self-harm** vi —**self-harming** n

selfheal /sélf heel/ n a low-growing creeping mint that grows as a weed in North America. Flowers: purple-blue, in small spikes. Native to: Europe, Asia. Latin name: *Prunella vulgaris*. [14C. Because it is believed to have medicinal properties]

self-help n 1. the practice of meeting or working with others who share a common problem rather than relying on professional or government help 2. the practice of dealing with your own problems and challenges without seeking outside help

selfhood /sélf hood/ n 1. INDIVIDUALITY the possession of a unique identity, distinct from others 2. COMPLETE SENSE OF SELF the possession of a fully developed personality and sense of identity 3. SOMEBODY'S CHARACTER OR PERSONALITY all the qualities and characteristics that make up somebody's character or personality

self-image n the opinion that you have of your own worth, attractiveness, or intelligence

self-immolation n suicide, usually by burning, as an act of sacrifice or protest

self-importance n an unrealistically high evaluation of your own importance or worth —**self-important** adj —**self-importantly** adv

self-imposed adj chosen willingly as a burden or limit ○ *a self-imposed deadline*

self-incrimination n speech or action that suggests your own guilt, especially during court testimony —**self-incriminating** adj —**self-incriminatory** adj

self-induced adj 1. brought on by your own actions 2. produced by the process of self-induction

self-induction n induction of an electromotive force in a circuit by means of a changing current in that circuit —**self-inductive** adj

self-indulgence n 1. lack of self-control in pursuing your own pleasure or satisfaction 2. something that reveals lack of self-restraint —**self-indulgent** adj —**self-indulgently** adv

self-inflicted adj caused or done by your own actions ○ *a self-inflicted wound*

self-insurance n the saving of money to protect against a loss instead of buying an insurance policy

self-interest n 1. the placing of your own needs or desires before those of others 2. your own needs and desires —**self-interested** adj —**self-interestedness** n

selfish /sélfish/ adj 1. concerned with your own interests, needs, and wishes while ignoring those of others 2. showing that personal needs and wishes are thought to be more important than those of other people —**selfishly** adv —**selfishness** n

selfish DNA n a segment of DNA that increases itself, e.g. as repeated sequences, within the total genetic material of a population over successive generations without apparent benefit to the organisms concerned

selfish gene n a gene that exploits the organism in which it occurs as a vehicle for its self-perpetuation. Posited by the biologist Richard Dawkins in 1976, it overturns the traditional concept of the gene serving as a vehicle of inheritance for the organism.

self-justification n 1. an attempt to explain your own behaviour or actions by making excuses 2. something that somebody does or says in an attempt to explain personal behaviour or actions

self-justifying adj 1. ATTEMPTING TO EXPLAIN making excuses in an attempt to explain your own behaviour or actions 2. AUTOMATICALLY MAKING TEXT UNIFORM ON MARGIN automatically providing an even right or left margin for text printed on a page 3. LOGICALLY COMPLETE describes an argument or rule that justifies or explains itself without referring to something else because of being regarded as completely logical or obvious

self-knowledge *n* awareness or understanding of your own motives and behaviour

selfless /sélfləss/ *adj* putting other people's needs, interests, or wishes before your own —**selflessly** *adv* —**selflessness** *n*

self-limited, **self-limiting** *adj* 1. limited by internal or personal characteristics rather than by outside influences 2. describes a disease that lasts for a specific length of time time whether or not it is treated

self-liquidating *adj* 1. describes a loan to fund a transaction that is expected to make money before the loan is due to be repaid 2. describes a business transaction that makes enough money to cover its costs

self-loading *adj* describes a firearm that automatically ejects a spent cartridge and puts a new round into the chamber each time it is fired —**self-loader** *n*

self-locking *adj* describes a window or door that locks automatically when closed

self-lubricating *adj* not requiring external application of lubrication to parts that experience friction because the lubricant is self-contained

self-made *adj* 1. successful or wealthy through your own efforts, rather than through birth or from the work of others 2. made without the help of others

self-mortification *n* self-administered punishment, often as prescribed by religious precepts, because of some perceived fault or flaw

self-motivated *adj* energetic and ambitious, and so able to make plans and get things done without being directed by others —**self-motivation** *n*

self-mutilation *n* self-inflicted injury, especially with a sharp object

self-opinion *n* a very high opinion of your own abilities or worth

self-opinionated *adj* 1. confident of holding the correct opinions 2. very conceited

self-perpetuating *adj* continuing because of having the power to preserve or renew itself indefinitely —**self-perpetuation** *n*

self-pity *n* the self-indulgent belief that your life is harder and sadder than everyone else's —**self-pitying** *adj* —**self-pityingly** *adv*

self-pollination *n* pollination that takes place within a flower through the transfer of pollen from its anthers to its stigmas —**self-pollinate** *vi* —**self-pollinating** *adj*

self-portrait *n* a visual image, sculpture, or written description of somebody, produced by that person —**self-portraiture** *n*

self-possessed *adj* confident and in control of your own emotions

self-possession *n* the ability to remain calm and confident, especially in difficult or emotional circumstances

self-preservation *n* the instinctive need to do what is necessary to survive danger

self-proclaimed *adj* claiming to be something, often without justification

self-protection *n* action taken to protect against attack on or injury to yourself —**self-protecting** *adj*—**self-protective** *adj*

self-raising *adj* having a leavening agent added, so that baking powder need not be added when baking ○ *self-raising flour* N Am term **self-rising**

self-realization *n* fulfilment of personal potential

self-referential *adj* describes an art form that employs references to the art itself or to personal experience or character —**self-reference** *n* —**self-referentially** *adv*

self-regard *n* 1. self-interest rather than concern for the well-being of others 2. belief in your own worth and dignity —**self-regarding** *adj*

self-regulating, **self-regulatory** *adj* 1. regulating its own affairs rather than being regulated by an outside organization or by law 2. capable of regulating its functions automatically —**self-regulation** *n*

self-regulation *n* the system by which an organization or institution deals with its own disciplinary and legal problems, often in private, rather than being publicly regulated by somebody else

self-reproach *n* self-criticism or blame —**self-reproachful** *adj* —**self-reproachfully** *adv*

self-respect *n* belief in your own worth and dignity —**self-respecting** *adj*

self-restraint *n* the ability to restrain the urge to do or say something

self-righteous *adj* sure of the moral superiority of personal beliefs and actions, usually to an irritating degree —**self-righteously** *adv* —**self-righteousness** *n*

self-righting *adj* able to right itself after being capsized

self-rising *adj* N Am FOOD same as **self-raising**

self-rule *n* POL same as **self-government** (sense 1)

self-sacrifice *n* the giving up of personal wants and needs, either from a sense of duty or in order to benefit others —**self-sacrificing** *adj*—**self-sacrificingly** *adv*

selfsame /sélf saym/ *adj* being the very same

self-scanner *n* a hand-held electronic device that supermarket customers can use to scan the prices of goods they intend to buy and add up their total bill in order to save time at the checkout

self-sealing *adj* 1. describes an envelope that has a flap coated with adhesive that can be closed without being moistened 2. describes a tyre that can seal itself after being punctured. The tyre contains a compound that hardens in contact with air.

self-seeded *adj* BOT same as **self-sown**

self-seeking *adj* interested only in gaining an advantage over others, not in sharing or cooperating ■ *n* behaviour intended to secure an advantage over others —**self-seeker** *n*

self-selection *n* 1. COMM same as **self-service** 2. the choosing of yourself for something, or the choosing of something for yourself —**self-selected** *adj* —**self-selective** *adj*

self-service *adj* describes a retail outlet or device used by customers or users helping themselves ○ *a self-service petrol station* ○ *a self-service drinks machine* —**self-service** *n*

self-serving *adj* putting personal concerns and interests before those of others

self-sown *adj* describes plants that grow from seeds that have fallen to the soil naturally, without being deliberately planted

self-starter *n* 1. somebody with the initiative and motivation to work without needing help or supervision 2. an electrically operated device for starting an internal-combustion engine —**self-starting** *adj*

self-sterile *adj* describes organisms that are unable to fertilize their female sex cells using their own male sex cells, as flowering plants are

self-stick, **self-sticking** *adj* US same as **self-adhesive**

self-storage *n* a property divided into storage units of varying sizes that are rented to people who store their personal property there

self-styled *adj* using a particular name or title or professing knowledge of a subject without having training or independent proof

USAGE See *so-called*.

self-sufficient, **self-sufficing** *adj* 1. able to provide what is needed, e.g. by making enough money or growing enough food, without having to borrow or buy from others 2. able to live independently of others —**self-sufficiency** *n* —**self-sufficiently** *adv*

self-suggestion *n* PSYCHOL same as **autosuggestion**

self-talk *n* the things that an individual says to himself or herself mentally

self-tanner *n* an ointment or lotion that can be applied to the skin in order to produce the effect of a suntan

self-tapping *adj* describes a screw that cuts a thread for itself when it is screwed into a hole in metal

self-taught *adj* having learned a skill, job, or subject without formal instruction

self-tender *n* an offer made by a company to buy back shares from its shareholders, e.g. to avoid a hostile takeover bid

self-test *n* 1. SELF-ADMINISTERED TEST a diagnostic test that you give yourself to determine your health, e.g. for blood pressure 2. TEST OF KNOWLEDGE a test you give yourself to find out how well you know a subject ■ *v* (**self-tests**, **self-testing**, **self-tested**) 1. *vti* TEST YOUR HEALTH to perform a diagnostic test of something on yourself in order to determine your health 2. *vi* TEST YOURSELF ON KNOWLEDGE to test yourself on a subject to find out how well you know it

self-will *n* stubborn determination to hold to personal views and behaviour —**self-willed** *adj*

self-winding *adj* not needing to be wound ○ *a self-winding watch*

self-worth *n* confidence in personal value and worth as an individual person

Seljuk /sél jook/ *n* a member of one of the Turkish dynasties that ruled large areas of central and western Asia between the 11th and 13th centuries before the Ottoman Empire [Mid-19C. < Turkish *Selčŭk*, the dynasty's reputed founder] —**Seljuk** *adj*

selkie /sélki/ *n* Scotland 1. MARINE BIOL same as **seal²** 2. a mythical creature which assumes human form on land and that of a seal in water [Mid-16C. < later form of Old English *seolh* (see SEAL²)]

Selkirk /sél kurk/, **Alexander** (1676–1721) Scottish sailor. His solitary life for 52 months on the Juan Fernández Islands 400 miles off Chile is said to have inspired Daniel Defoe's *Robinson Crusoe* (1719).

Selkirk Mountains mountain range in southeastern British Columbia, Canada, west of the Rocky Mountains. The highest point is Mount Sandford, 3,522 m/11,555 ft.

sell /sel/ *v* (**sells**, **selling**, **sold** /sōld/) 1. *vti* EXCHANGE FOR MONEY to exchange a product or service for money, or be exchanged for money 2. *vt* OFFER SOMETHING FOR SALE to offer a particular product or range of products for sale 3. *vi* BE BOUGHT IN QUANTITY to be bought in large numbers ○ *The book is selling well.* 4. *vt* MAKE PEOPLE WANT TO BUY SOMETHING to increase the sale of or the demand for a product ○ *Advertising sells products.* 5. *vt* PERSUADE SOMEBODY OF SOMETHING to make an idea or proposal acceptable to somebody ○ *You've convinced me but now you have to sell it to the shareholders.* 6. *vt* GIVE SOMETHING UP FOR MONEY to sacrifice an important personal quality in order to obtain wealth or success ○ *He's sold his integrity for a long-term contract.* 7. **sell yourself** *vr* to work hard to persuade others that you are talented, pleasant, well-qualified, or suitable for a particular job 8. *vr* to abandon your principles in order to get something you want or need, e.g. money or success 9. *vt* CHEAT SOMEBODY to cheat or trick somebody (*informal*) ■ *n* 1. PROCESS OF SELLING the activity or process of persuading people to buy a product or service (*informal*) ○ *use an aggressive sell* 2. TRICK a trick or deception (*informal*) 3. Ireland DISAPPOINTMENT a big disappointment [Old English *sellan* 'hand over' < Germanic] —**sellable** *adj* ◇ **sell somebody** or **something short** 1. to make an estimate of the quality and worth of somebody or something that is too low ○ *You've a lot in your favour – don't sell yourself short.* 2. to sell goods or securities without owning them, expecting to buy them at a price lower than the selling price ◇ **sold on something** enthusiastic about something (*informal*)

sell off *vt* to sell something, especially at a low price, in order to get rid of it

sell out *v* 1. *vi* SELL ALL OF SOMETHING to sell the entire stock of a product or range 2. *vti* SELL ALL TICKETS to sell all the tickets for a show, concert, or sports event 3. *vti* BETRAY PRINCIPLES to be disloyal to personal principles or to another person for reasons of short-term advantage (*informal*)

sellback /sél bak/ *n* US the act of selling something back to the person it was bought from

sell-by date *n* a date displayed on food and pharmaceutical products, after which they should not be sold ◇ **past its** or **your sell-by date** thought to be too advanced in years or old-fashioned to be useful or taken seriously (*informal; sometimes offensive*)

seller /séllər/ *n* **1.** a person, shop, or company that offers something for sale **2.** a product that sells in a particular way, especially well or badly **3.** HORSERACING same as **selling race**

Sellers /séllərz/, **Peter** (1925–80) British actor. A member of the Goons radio comedy team (1952–60), he was later a screen actor. He played the eccentric detective Inspector Clouseau in the hugely successful Pink Panther films (1964–82).

> 'There used to be a me behind the mask, but I had it surgically removed.'
> [Attributed to Peter Sellers]

seller's market *n* a situation or market in which the demand for something is greater than the supply, so that its price can be forced up

selling climax /sélling-/ *n* a large volume of trading at the end of a downturn in the stock markets (*informal*)

selling plate *n* HORSERACING same as **selling race**

selling-plater *n* **1.** a horse that races in or is only good enough to race in a selling race **2.** somebody or something that is not very good, important, or valuable

selling point *n* a feature of something such as a product or an idea that makes people more likely to want to buy or support it

selling race *n* a horse race in which the winner is auctioned and sold

sell-off *n* the quick sale of a large amount of goods, especially at low prices

Sellotape /séllō tayp/ *tdmk* a trademark for a type of transparent adhesive tape

sellout /séll owt/ *n* **1.** a show, concert, or sports event for which all the tickets are sold **2.** betrayal of personal principles or of another person (*informal*)

selsyn /sél sin/ *n* a system used to transmit angular rotation or position in a generator to a motor [Early 20C. Blend of SELF + SYNCHRONOUS]

Seltzer /séltsər/, **Seltzer water** *n* **1.** mineral water that contains naturally occurring dissolved gases that make it slightly fizzy, often used for medicinal purposes **2.** BEVERAGES same as **soda water** (sense 1) (*dated*) [Mid-18C. Alteration of German *Selterser* 'from Selters' < *Nieder- Selters*, village near Wiesbaden with mineral springs]

selva /sélvə/ *n* a dense tropical rainforest, especially in the Amazon basin [Mid-19C. Via Spanish or Portuguese < Latin *silva* 'wood']

selvage /sél vij/, **selvedge** *n* **1.** NONFRAYING EDGE OF FABRIC an edge of a piece of fabric that is woven so that it will not fray **2.** STRIP OF MATERIAL an edge or strip of material included when manufacturing something such as a metal or plastic object or a sheet of postage stamps that allows it to be handled **3.** LOCK PLATE a slotted plate or surface through which the bolt of a lock passes **4.** RUG FRINGE a decorative fringe on the ends of an Oriental rug [15C. Contraction of SELF + EDGE; because it 'edges' itself and does not need hemming] — **selvaged** *adj*

selves plural of **self**

David O. Selznick

Selznick /sélznik/, **David O.** (1902–65) US film producer. His many classic productions included *Gone With the Wind* (1939). Full name **Selznick, David Oliver**

SEM *abbr* PHYS scanning electron microscope

semanteme /sə mán teem/ *n* the smallest possible unit of meaning in language, expressing a single image or idea, e.g. cat, sit, or non- [Early 20C. < French *sémantème* < Greek *semantikos* (see SEMANTIC), after *morphème* 'morpheme']

semantic /sə mántik/ *adj* **1.** LING RELATING TO WORD MEANINGS relating to meaning or the differences between meanings of words or symbols **2.** LING OF SEMANTICS relating to semantics **3.** LOGIC RELATING TO TRUTH relating to the conditions in which a system or theory can be said to be true [Mid-17C. Via French < Greek *sēmantikos* 'significant' < *sēmainein* 'signify' < *sēma* 'sign, mark'] — **semantically** *adv*

semantics /sə mántiks/ *n* (*takes a singular verb*) **1.** STUDY OF MEANING IN LANGUAGE the study of how meaning in language is created by the use and interrelationships of words, phrases, and sentences **2.** STUDY OF SYMBOLS the study of the relationship between symbols and what they represent **3.** STUDY OF LOGIC the study of ways of interpreting and analysing theories of logic —**semanticist** /sə mántissist/ *n*

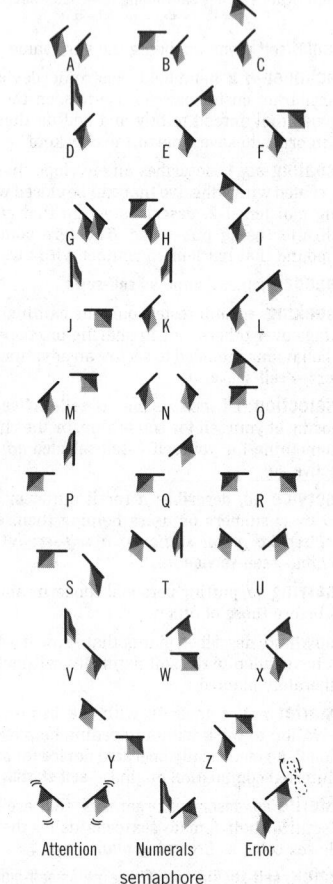

Attention   Numerals   Error
semaphore

semaphore /sémmə fawr/ *n* **1.** SYSTEM OF SIGNALLING a system for sending messages using hand-held flags that are moved to represent alphabetical letters **2.** MECHANICAL SIGNALLING DEVICE a signalling device for sending information over distances using mechanically operated arms or flags mounted on a post, especially on a railway ■ *vti* (**-phores, -phoring, -phored**) USE SEMAPHORE TO SIGNAL to send messages using semaphore [Early 19C. Via French *sémaphore* 'sign-bearer' < Greek *sēma* 'sign, mark'] —**semaphoric** /sémmə fórrik/ *adj* —**semaphorically** *adv*

Semarang /sémmə ráng/ *city and port on the island of Java, Indonesia, located east of Jakarta. Population: 812,979 (1997).*

semasiology /sə máyzi ólləji/ *n* LING, LOGIC same as **semantics** (senses 1–2) [Mid-19C. < German *Semasiologie* 'science of meaning' < Greek *sēmasia* 'meaning' < *sēmainein* (see SEMANTIC)] —**semasiological** /sə máyzi ə lójjik'l/ *adj* —**semasiologically** *adv* —**semasiologist** *n*

sematic /sə máttik/ *adj* describes bright colourings on animals that act as a warning to predators, e.g.

because the animals are poisonous [Late 19C. < Greek *sēmat-*, stem of *sēma* 'sign, mark']

semblable /sémbləb'l/ *adj* resembling or similar to something or somebody else (*formal*) ■ *n* somebody or something that closely resembles another (*archaic*) [13C. < Old French < *sembler* (see SEMBLANCE)] — **semblably** *adv*

semblance /sémblənss/ *n* **1.** TRACE OF SOMETHING a small amount of something ○ *a semblance of dignity* **2.** LOOK OF BEING SOMETHING an outward appearance or imitation of something ○ *a semblance of competence* **3.** COPY a representation, likeness, or copy (*literary*) [14C. < Old French < *sembler* 'seem' < Latin *simulare* (see SIMULATE)]

semé /sémmay/ *adj* in heraldry, covered with many small dots or delicate designs [15C. < French, past participle of *semer* 'sow' < Latin *semere*]

sememe /seé meem/ *n* the meaning that a morpheme has in a linguistic system [Early 20C. < Greek *sēma* 'sign, mark', after MORPHEME]

semen /seémən/ *n* the thick white fluid containing sperm that a male ejaculates [14C. < Latin, 'seed']

semester /sə méstər/ *n* **1.** especially in the United States, either of two periods of 15 to 18 weeks into which the academic year is divided in some universities and colleges **2.** in German universities, an academic session lasting six months [Early 19C. Via German < Latin *semestris* 'of six months' < *sex* 'six' + *mensis* 'month'] —**semestral** *adj*

semi /sémmi/ *n* **1.** a house with a wall in common with the next house (*informal*) **2.** N Am VEHICLES same as **tractor-trailer** **3.** SPORTS same as **semifinal** (*informal*) [Early 20C. Shortening]

semi- *prefix* **1.** partial, partially, somewhat ○ *semisweet* ○ *semiterrestrial* **2.** half ○ *semicircle* **3.** resembling, having some characteristics of something ○ *semitropical* ○ *semivowel* **4.** occurring twice during a particular period ○ *semiweekly* [< Latin, 'half' < Indo-European]

semiacoustic *adj*	**semiliquid** *adj, n*
semiallegorical *adj*	**semiliquidity** *n*
semialphabetical *adj*	**semilustrous** *adj*
semianimate *adj*	**semimajor** *adj*
semiantique *adj*	**semimatt** *adj*
semiarboreal *adj*	**semiminor** *adj*
semiaware *adj*	**semimodal** *n*
semiawareness *adj*	**semimoist** *adj*
semibasement *n*	**semimolten** *adj*
semicivilized *adj*	**semimonastic** *adj*
semicolonial *adj*	**semimonocoque** *adj*
semicolony *n*	**semimystical** *adj*
semicommercial *adj*	**semimythical** *adj*
semicontinuous *adj*	**seminatural** *adj*
semicrystalline *adj*	**semiopacity** *n*
semicubist *adj*	**semiopaque** *adj*
semicylinder *n*	**semiopen** *adj*
semicylindrical *adj*	**semiopera** *n*
semideity *n*	**semiphilosophical** *adj*
semideponent *adj, n*	**semipolitical** *adj*
semiderelict *adj*	**semipopular** *adj*
semidictatorial *adj*	**semipornographic** *adj*
semidominant *adj*	**semiprone** *adj*
semidouble *adj*	**semipublic** *adj*
semidrying *adj*	**semipurified** *adj*
semidurable *adj*	**semiquantitative** *adj*
semielectronic *adj*	**semirefined** *adj*
semiempirical *adj*	**semireligious** *adj*
semierect *adj*	**semisacred** *adj*
semievergreen *adj*	**semisedentary** *adj*
semifabricated *adj*	**semishrubby** *adj*
semifeudal *adj*	**semispherical** *adj*
semifictional *adj*	**semistaged** *adj*
semifitted *adj*	**semistagger** *vti*
semiflexible *adj*	**semisterile** *adj*
semiformed *adj*	**semisubterranean** *adj*
semifree *adj*	**semisynthetic** *adj*
semigovernmental *adj*	**semitrained** *adj*
semihardy *adj*	**semitranslucent** *adj*
semihistorical *adj*	**semitransparent** *adj*
semihumid *adj*	**semiunconscious** *adj*
semi-invalid *n*	**semiunconsciousness** *n*
semilegendary *adj*	**semiwild** *adj*

semiabstract /sémmi áb strakt/ *adj* describes art that has heavily stylized but still recognizable subject matter —**semiabstraction** /sémmi ab straksh'n/ *n*

semiannual /sémmi ánnyŏŏ əl/ adj **1. HAPPENING TWICE YEAR** happening or issued every six months or twice a year **2. LASTING SIX MONTHS** lasting for half a year ■ n **SEMIANNUAL PLANT** a semiannual plant or flower — **semiannually** adv

semiaquatic /sémmi ə kwáttik/ adj growing or living near water as well as in it

semiarid /sémmi árrid/ adj with little rainfall and scrubby vegetation —**semiaridity** /sémmi ə ríddəti/ n

semiautobiographical /sémmi áwtə bī ə gráffik'l/ adj describes something such as a novel or film that is based in part on the life or experiences of its author

semiautomatic /sémmi awtə máttik/ adj **1. RELOADING AUTOMATICALLY** automatically ejecting a spent shell from a weapon's chamber and replacing it with another round each time the weapon is fired **2. PARTIALLY AUTOMATED** operated partly automatically and partly manually ■ n **SEMIAUTOMATIC WEAPON** a weapon that is semiautomatic —**semiautomatically** adv

semiautonomous /sémmi aw tónnəməss/ adj **1.** ruled partly by its own citizens or rulers and partly by another country or region **2.** self-governing but remaining within a larger organization of which it is part —**semiautonomously** adv —**semiautonomy** n

semibold /sémmi bṓld/ adj darker than ordinary type but not as dark as bold type

semibreve /sémmi breev/ n the longest musical note in common use, written as an open note-head without a stem or tail, with a duration equivalent to four crotchets or two minims. N Am term **whole note**

semibreve rest n the longest musical rest in common use, with a duration equivalent to a semibreve. N Am term **whole rest**

semicentennial /sémmi sen ténni əl/ adj **1. MARKING 50TH ANNIVERSARY** marking the date or year that is 50 years after an event **2. HAPPENING EVERY 50 YEARS** happening every 50 years ■ n **50TH ANNIVERSARY OF EVENT** the 50th anniversary of an important event

semicircle /sémmi surk'l/ n **1.** half of the area or circumference of a circle **2.** a curved or crescent-shaped line of things or people in the shape of a semicircle [Early 16C. < Latin *semicirculus* < *circulus* 'small circle'] —**semicircular** /sémmi súrkyŏŏlər/ adj —**semicircularly** adv

semicircular canal n each of three tubes in the inner ear, semicircular in shape and set at right angles to one another, that help to maintain balance

semiclassical /sémmi klássik'l/ adj classical in musical style, pleasant, easy to listen to, and usually written relatively recently —**semiclassically** adv

semicolon /sémmi kṓlən, -lon/ n a punctuation mark (;) used to separate parts of a sentence or list and indicate a pause longer than a comma but shorter than a full stop

---

USAGE A **semicolon** is used to separate two parts of a sentence that have a relationship to each other in terms of meaning when each part could stand alone as a sentence in its own right: *The building is chiefly a tourist attraction; it is rarely used as a church these days.* There is no proof that the disease is caused by agricultural use of this chemical; however, experts admit that there could be a link. Semicolons may also separate parts of a complex list when it would be confusing to use commas for this purpose: *We invited Jack and Kate, who live next door; Maria, my sister-in-law; Tom, an old school friend of my husband's; and some of our colleagues from work.* Like commas, semicolons are sometimes used to break up a lengthy complicated sentence, but it is often better and clearer to split the sentence up into smaller units.

---

semicoma /sémmi kṓmə/ n a partial or light comatose state from which it is sometimes possible to rouse people by stimulating them

semicomatose /sémmi kṓmətoss/ adj **1.** bordering on being unconscious but capable of being awakened **2.** almost unconscious or half asleep

semiconductor /sémmi kən dúktər/ n a solid material that has electrical conductivity between that of a conductor and an insulator —**semiconducting** adj —**semiconduction** n —**semiconductive** adj —**semiconductivity** /sémmi kon duk tívvəti/ n

semiconscious /sémmi kónshəss/ adj only partly conscious —**semiconsciously** adv —**semiconsciousness** n

semiconservative /sémmi kən súrvətiv/ adj relating to the replication of a nucleic acid molecule such as DNA in which a double stranded molecule separates into two templates for the formation of complementary strands —**semiconservatively** adv

semidarkness /sémmi dáarknəss/ n a state in which it is neither fully dark nor fully light

semidesert /sémmi dézzərt/ n a region that is not completely dry, usually one lying between desert and a more heavily vegetated area

semidetached /sémmi di tácht/ adj joined to a neighbouring building by a shared wall ■ n a house with a wall in common with the next house

semidiameter /sémmi dī ámmitər/ n half of the angular diameter of the visible disc of an astronomical object as measured by an observer

semidiurnal /sémmi dī úrn'l/ adj **1.** continuing or happening over half a day **2.** happening approximately once every twelve hours

semidivine /sémmi di vín/ adj having some of the characteristics or powers of a deity, or existing on a higher spiritual plane than ordinary mortals but not wholly divine

semidocumentary /sémmi dokyŏŏ méntəri/ (*plural* **-ries**) n a film or TV programme that is fictional but makes use of or is based on factual details or events

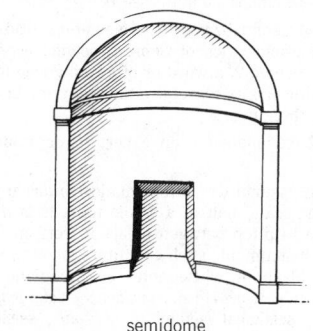

semidome

semidome /sémmi dṓm/ n a half dome, especially one used as the roof for a semicircular space or recess

semidomesticated /sémmi də mésti kaytid/ adj describes animals that are wild but live near or with humans to mutual benefit —**semidomestication** /sémmi də mésti káysh'n/ n

semidry /sémmi drī/ adj US describes wine that is partially or moderately dry

semidwarf /sémmi dwáwrf/ adj describes plants that grow to heights greater than true dwarf plants but less than standard specimens

semielliptical /sémmi i lípptik'l/ adj resembling half an ellipse in shape, especially one that is divided along its major axis

semifinal /sémmi fín'l/ n either of two matches or games, the winners of which will play each other in the final round of a competition —**semifinal** adj —**semifinalist** n

semifinished /sémmi fínnisht/ adj partially finished, treated, or processed

semifluid /sémmi flŏŏ id/ adj having properties between those of a fluid and a solid —**semifluid** n —**semifluidity** /sémmi flŏŏ íddəti/ n

semiformal /sémmi fáwrm'l/ adj designed to be worn on moderately formal occasions

semigloss /sémmi glóss/ n a paint or varnish with a finish that is midway between gloss and matt when it dries

semigroup /sémmi group/ n a mathematical set for which there is a closed and associative binary operation

semihard /sémmi háard/ adj describes cheese that has a consistency firm enough to slice but that is moist and pliable

semi-infinite adj unbounded in one dimension or direction

semilethal /sémmi leéth'l/ adj lethal in more than 50 per cent but fewer than 100 per cent of cases

semiliterate /sémmi líttərət/ adj **1.** unable to read or write properly **2.** N Am having only limited understanding of a particular subject, especially a technical one —**semiliteracy** n

Sémillon /sémmi yoN/ n **1.** a white wine made from a variety of white grape originally grown in southwestern France **2.** a white grape variety. Use: to make Sémillon. [Mid-19C. < French < Latin *semen* 'seed']

semilogarithmic /sémmi loggə rith mik/ adj having one logarithmic scale and one arithmetic scale

semilunar /sémmi lŏŏnər/ adj shaped like a crescent or a half moon

semilunar cartilage n either of two crescent-shaped pieces of cartilage in the knee joint

semilunar valve n either of two crescent-shaped valves in the heart that prevent blood from flowing back into the ventricles. The two valves are called the aortic valve and the pulmonary valve.

semimetal /sémmi métt'l/ n CHEM same as **metalloid** —**semimetallic** /sémmi mə tállik/ adj

semimonthly /sémmi múnthli/ adj **HAPPENING TWICE IN MONTH** happening or published twice each month, usually at equal intervals ■ adv **TWICE DURING MONTH** twice each month, usually at equal intervals ■ n (*plural* **-lies**) **SEMIMONTHLY PUBLICATION** a publication that appears twice each month, usually at equal intervals

seminal /sémmin'l/ adj **1. INFLUENTIAL** highly original and influential **2. CAPABLE OF DEVELOPMENT** containing an idea or set of ideas that forms a basis for later developments **3. OF SEMEN OR SEEDS** relating to, containing, or carrying semen or seeds [14C. Via French < Latin *seminalis* < *semin-*, stem of *semen* 'seed'] —**seminality** /sémmi nálləti/ n —**seminally** adv

seminal fluid n ANAT same as **semen**

seminal vesicle n either of a pair of glands that secrete the fluid component of semen into the ejaculatory duct in males

seminar /sémmi naar/ n **1. MEETING OF STUDENTS AND TUTOR** a meeting of university or college students for study or discussion with a tutor, or the group that participates in it **2. MEETING ON SPECIALIZED SUBJECT** a single session or short, often one-day meeting devoted to presentations on and discussion of a specialized topic, usually at an advanced or professional level ○ *a seminar on the industrial applications of biotechnology* **3. SPECIALIZED EDUCATIONAL CLASS** a course of specialized, especially postgraduate study under academic supervision, in which ideas, approaches, and advances are regularly shared among participants [Late 19C. Via German, 'advanced class' < Latin *seminarium* 'seed plot, breeding ground' < *semin-* (see SEMINAL)]

seminary /sémminəri/ (*plural* **-ies**) n a college for the training of priests, ministers, or rabbis [15C. < Latin *seminarium* 'seed plot, breeding ground' < *semin-* (see SEMINAL)] —**seminarian** /sémmi naíri ən/ n

seminiferous /sémmi nífferəss/ adj **1.** carrying, containing, or producing semen **2.** bearing or producing seeds [Late 17C. < Latin *semin-* (see SEMINAL)]

Seminole /sémmi nṓl/ (*plural* same or **-noles**) n **1.** a member of a Native North American people who lived in Georgia and Florida, and now live mainly in Oklahoma and Florida. The Seminole were one of the Five Civilized Nations who, under the Removal Act of 1830, were forced to settle in Indian Territory. **2.** the Muskogean language of the Seminole people [Mid-18C. < Creek *simanó:li*, alteration of *simaló:ni*, alteration of American Spanish *cimarrón* 'wild, untamed'] —**Seminole** adj

seminoma /sémmi nṓmə/ (*plural* **-mas** or **-mata** /-mətə/) n a malignant tumour of the sperm-producing tissue in the testicle [Early 20C. < modern Latin *seminoma* < Latin *semin-* (see SEMINAL)]

seminomadic /sémmi nō máddik/ adj belonging or relating to an ethnic group or people who migrate seasonally and cultivate crops during periods of settlement

seminude /sémmi nyŏŏd/ adj only partly clothed, usually in underclothes or skimpy outer clothing —**seminude** —**seminudity** n

semiochemical /sémmi ō kémmik'l/ *n* an organic chemical that plays a role in animal communication, e.g. pheromone [Late 20C. < Greek *sēmeion* 'sign' (see SEMIOLOGY)]

semiofficial /sémmi ə físh'l/ *adj* with only some degree of authority or official status and therefore not completely reliable —**semiofficially** *adv*

semiology /sémmi ólləji, seém-/ *n* LING, MED same as **semiotics** [Late 17C. < Greek *sēmeion* 'sign'] —**semiologic** /sémmi ə lójik, seém-/ *adj* —**semiological** *adj* —**semiologically** *adv* —**semiologist** *n*

semiotics /sémmi óttiks, seémi-/ *n* (*takes a singular verb*) **1.** the study of signs and symbols of all kinds, what they mean, and how they relate to the things or ideas they refer to **2.** the study of identifying the ways that various symptoms indicate the diseases that underlie them —**semiotic** *adj* —**semiotician** /-ə tísh'n/ *n*

semipalmate /sémmi pál mayt/, **semipalmated** /sémmi pál máytid/ *adj* with feet or toes that are partially webbed. Some shore birds have semipalmate feet.

semipermanent /sémmi púrmənent/ *adj* set up or arranged to last quite a long time but not indefinitely —**semipermanently** *adv*

semipermeable /sémmi púrmi əb'l/ *adj* describes a membrane or tissue that allows some types of particle to pass through, but not others —**semipermeability** /sémmi púrmi ə bílləti/ *n*

semipolar bond /sémmi pōlər-/ *n* CHEM same as **coordinate bond**

semiporcelain /sémmi páwrssəlin, -layn/ *n* a durable glazed ceramic material widely used for tableware. It resembles porcelain but is opaque.

semiprecious /sémmi préshəss/ *adj* describes stones, gems, and minerals that have commercial value but are not valued as highly as those called precious

semipro /sémmi prō/ (*informal*) *n* (*plural* -**pros**) same as **semiprofessional** ■ *adj* relating to or being semiprofessional

semiprofessional /sémmi prə fésh'nəl/ *adj* **1.** PAID BUT NOT FULL-TIME participating in a sport or artistic activity for pay but not as a full-time professional **2.** FOR SEMIPROFESSIONAL ATHLETES played in or contested by semiprofessional athletes **3.** LIKE PROFESSIONAL displaying some aspects of a professional ■ *n* PART PROFESSIONAL somebody, especially an athlete or performing artist, who is intermediate between an amateur and a professional —**semiprofessionally** *adv*

semiquaver /sémmi kwayvər/ *n* a musical note with the time value of one-sixteenth of a semibreve. It is written as a filled note-head with a stem and two tails. N Am term **sixteenth note**

semiquaver rest *n* a musical rest with the time value of a semiquaver. N Am term **sixteenth rest**

semiretired /sémmi ri tírd/ *adj* working only part-time following the end of a full-time career —**semiretirement** *n*

semirigid /sémmi ríjjid/ *adj* **1.** partly rigid, or rigid only in some parts **2.** describes an airship with a rigid keel that maintains its shape

semirugged /sémi rúggid/ *adj* **1.** designed and made to be resilient enough to withstand a moderate amount of rough treatment or fairly harsh environmental conditions **2.** moderately rough or moderately difficult to walk or drive over ○ *semirugged terrain* —**semirugged** *n*

semirural /sémmi roóərəl/ *adj* intermediate between rural and urban

semisecret /sémmi seékrət/ *adj* intended or supposedly intended to be secret but actually known about

semiskilled /sémmi skíld/ *adj* with or requiring relatively few skills or little training ○ *semiskilled workers* ○ *a semiskilled job*

semi-skimmed *adj* describes milk that has part of the cream removed, so it contains less animal fat and fewer calories than full cream milk

semisoft /sémmi sóft/ *adj* softer than most things, especially foods, of its type

semisolid /sémmi sóllid/ *adj* not quite solid or liquid, but somewhere in between, like a gel ■ *n* a sub-

stance that has most of the qualities of a solid but can also flow, e.g. a gel

semisubmersible /sémmi səb múrssəb'l/, **semi-submersible rig** *n* a self-propelled oil-drilling platform resting on vertical pontoons that can be flooded for stability in deep water

semisweet /sémmi sweét/ *adj* slightly sweet, or having only a small amount of sugar or other sweetening ingredient added ○ *semisweet biscuits*

Semite /seé mīt, sémm-/ *n* **1.** a member of a Semitic-speaking people of Southwest Asia, including the Arab and Jewish peoples, and the ancient Assyrians, Babylonians, Carthaginians, Ethiopians, and Phoenicians **2.** an offensive term for a Jew [Mid-19C. < modern Latin *Semita* < Greek *Sēm* 'Shem', son of Noah < Hebrew *Šēm*]

semitendinosus /sémmi tendi nóssəss/ *n* a muscle extending from the hip to just below mid-thigh

semiterrestrial /sémmi tə réstri əl/ *adj* living partly on land but requiring a watery environment

Semitic /sə míttik/ *n* LANGUAGES SPOKEN BY SEMITES a group of languages belonging to the Afro-Asiatic family and spoken in North Africa and Southwest Asia, including Hebrew, Arabic, Aramaic, Maltese, and Amharic ■ *adj* **1.** OF SEMITIC in or relating to Semitic **2.** OF SEMITIC-SPEAKING PEOPLES relating to the peoples who speak Semitic languages

Semitics /sə míttiks/ *n* the study of the Semitic peoples, languages, and culture (*takes a singular verb*) —**Semiticist** /sə míttissist/ *n*

Semitism /sémmətizəm/ *n* **1.** the customs, traditions, and characteristics of Semitic people, especially Jewish people **2.** a word or other language feature of Semitic origin, especially one occurring in a non-Semitic language

Semitist /sémmətist/ *n* an expert in or student of Semitics

semitone /sémmi tōn/ *n* the smallest interval of the diatonic scale, half of a whole tone. It is the difference in pitch between adjacent frets on fretted string instruments such as guitars, or between adjacent black or white notes on the piano. [15C. Via French < medieval Latin *semitonus* < Latin *tonus* (see TONE)] —**semitonal** /sémmi tō n'l/ *adj* —**semitonally** *adv* —**semitonic** /sémmi tónnik/ *adj*

semitrailer /sémmi tráylər/ *n* **1.** a large rectangular vehicle with wheels only at the rear and a hitch at the front that attaches to a tractor or other towing vehicle **2.** a tractor with an attached semitrailer

semitropical /sémmi tróppik'l/ *adj* GEOG same as **subtropical** —**semitropics** *npl*

semivowel /sémmi vowəl/ *n* a sound that is like a vowel in involving no major obstruction of the airflow but that functions as a consonant in preceding vowels that form the nucleus of syllables. Examples in English are initial 'w' and 'y'.

semiweekly /sémmi weékli/ *adj* happening or published twice each week ■ *adv* twice each week

semiyearly *adj* happening or published twice each year ■ *adv* twice each year

semolina /sémmə leénə/ *n* gritty ground-up grains of wheat that are a by-product of flour milling. Use: pasta, couscous, other foods. [Late 18C. Alteration of Italian *semolino* 'small bran' < *semola* 'bran' < Latin *simila* 'fine wheat flour']

semper fidelis /sémpər fi dáyliss/ *adj* 'always faithful', the motto of the US Marine Corps [< Latin]

sempervivum

sempervivum /sémpər veévəm/ *n* a widely grown ornamental garden plant that has rosettes of fleshy leaves. Flowers: pink, in clusters on stems. Genus: *Sempervivum*. [Late 16C. < modern Latin < form of Latin *sempervivus* 'ever-living' < *semper* 'ever' + *vivus* (see VIVID)]

sempiternal /sémpi túrn'l/ *adj* lasting forever (*literary*) [15C. Via French < late Latin *sempiternalis* < Latin *sempiternus* < *semper* 'always' + *-ternus*, suffix of time] —**sempiternally** *adv* —**sempiternity** *n*

semplice /sémmplichi, -chay/ *adv* in a simple manner, without rubato (*used in musical directions*) [Mid-18C. < Italian, 'simple']

sempre /sémpri, -pray/ *adv* to be played or sung throughout in the manner indicated (*used in musical directions*) ○ *sempre largo* [Early 19C. < Italian, 'always']

sempstress /sémpstrəss/ *n* OCCUPATIONS same as **seamstress** (*archaic*) [Mid-17C. < *sempster*, variant of *seamster* (see SEAMSTRESS)]

Semtex /sém teks/ *tdmk* a trademark for a plastic explosive of Czech origin

sen /sen/ (*plural same*) *n* a subunit of currency in several countries in East and Southeast Asia. See table at **currency** [Early 18C. Via Japanese < Chinese *qián* 'money, coin']

SEN *abbr* **1.** EDUC special educational needs **2.** MED State Enrolled Nurse (*dated*)

Sen. *abbr* **1.** POL senate **2.** POL senator **3.** senior

Senanayake /sénnə ní yəkə/, **D. S.** (1884–1952) prime minister of Ceylon (1947–52). As the country's first prime minister, he presided over its transition to independence (1948). Full name **Senanayake, Don Stephen**

Senanayake, Dudley (1911–73) prime minister of Ceylon (1952–53, 1960, 1965–70). The son of D. S. Senanayake, he began the first of his three terms as prime minister after his father's death. Full name **Senanayake, Dudley Shelton**

senate /sénnət, sénnit/ *n* **1.** LEGISLATIVE BODY the sole or upper law-making chamber of government in many countries or states, past or present **2.** US STATE LEGISLATURE the higher of two elected legislative bodies in many states of the United States **3.** ANCIENT ROMAN ASSEMBLY the highest council of the ancient Roman Republic and of the Roman Empire **4.** SENATE BUILDING the building where a senate meets **5.** UNIVERSITY BODY the main faculty governing body in some universities and colleges [12C. Via French < Latin *senatus* 'assembly of elders' < *senex* 'male elder']

Senate *n* **1.** US LEGISLATURE the upper of the two elected legislative bodies of the United States government. It is made up of two senators from each state. **2.** UPPER HOUSE OF CANADIAN PARLIAMENT the upper chamber of the federal parliament of Canada. It is made up of 104 senators appointed by the ruling government. **3.** UPPER HOUSE OF AUSTRALIAN PARLIAMENT the upper house of the federal parliament of Australia. It is made up of 76 members, 12 from each state plus two each from the Northern Territory and Australian Capital Territory. **4.** POL another spelling of **senate** (sense 1)

senator /sénnətər/ *n* an elected or appointed member of a senate, e.g. in the United States, Australia, or ancient Rome [13C. Via French < Latin, related to *senatus* (see SENATE)]

senatorial /sénnə táwri əl/ *adj* **1.** relating to or characteristic of a senate or the post of senator ○ *senatorial privileges* **2.** made up of senators —**senatorially** *adv*

Senatus Academicus /sə náatəss akə démmikəss/ *n* in the older Scottish universities, the body that superintends and regulates the teaching and discipline of the university [< Latin, 'academic senate']

send[1] /send/ *v* (**sends, sending, sent** /sent/) **1.** *vt* CAUSE SOMEBODY OR SOMETHING TO GO to cause somebody or something to be moved or taken to another place **2.** *vt* COMMUNICATE SOMETHING to transmit information or a message to somebody who is somewhere else **3.** *vt* COMMAND SOMEBODY TO GO to ask or command somebody to come or go **4.** *vt* ENABLE SOMEBODY TO GO to enable somebody to go somewhere special ○ *Let's send the children to camp this summer.* **5.** *vt* REFER SOMEBODY SOMEWHERE to suggest that somebody go somewhere

or see somebody, usually for a specific kind of information ○ *He sent the student to his colleague for advice.* **6.** vt BRING SOMETHING ABOUT to make something happen ○ *Our blessings were sent by a higher power.* **7.** vt PROPEL SOMETHING to make something move or travel by pushing it or hitting it ○ *A gust of wind sent the papers swirling round the office.* **8.** vt DRIVE SOMEBODY INTO PARTICULAR STATE to make somebody enter a particular condition ○ *The delay is sending her crazy.* **9.** vt EXCITE SOMEBODY GREATLY to excite or thrill somebody intensely (*dated slang*) **10.** vi COMPUT BE TRANSMITTED to be transmitted or transmittable ○ *This e-mail won't send.* **11.** vi TELECOM BROADCAST INFORMATION to transmit information by telecommunication ○ *The operator was still sending when the power was cut off.* ■ *n* COMPUT COMMAND TO TRANSMIT COMPUTER DATA a command, key, or icon on a computer monitor or keyboard that is used to start the transmission of data [Old English *sendan* < Germanic, 'cause to go'] —**sender** *n* ◇ **send flying** to make somebody or something fly through the air by force of impact ◇ **send somebody packing** to dismiss or send somebody away in a firm, not very polite way (*informal*)

send away for *vt* to order something by post or through a mail order catalogue

send down *vt* **1.** to expel a student from a university, especially Oxford or Cambridge (*often passive*) **2.** to imprison somebody following conviction (*informal*) ○ *He got sent down for armed robbery.*

send for *vt* to request the delivery, dispatch, or appearance of somebody or something ○ *send for reinforcements*

send in *vt* to post something such as an application form for processing along with those sent by other people

send off *vt* **1.** DISPATCH SOMETHING to dispatch something in the post **2.** SEND SOMEBODY AWAY to send somebody away, either on an errand or by way of dismissal ○ *We sent him off to buy some things.* **3.** DISMISS SOMEBODY FROM GAME to dismiss a player from a game or competition for breaking the rules, e.g. in football, rugby, or hockey (*often passive*) **4.** BID SOMEBODY FAREWELL to say goodbye or good luck to somebody who is leaving ○ *Who was there to send her off?*

send on *vt* **1.** to send something such as mail or belongings to a second place for somebody or ahead of somebody or yourself **2.** to send something received to a subsequent place or person

send out for *vt* to order food by telephone, to be delivered to you and paid for when it arrives (*informal*) ○ *Let's send out for a pizza.*

send up *vt* **1.** MOCK SOMEBODY OR SOMETHING BY IMITATION to make somebody or something appear ridiculous by humorous imitation (*informal*) **2.** RAISE SOMETHING to make something rise or climb, especially a scale or index such as on a thermometer or a listing of stock market values **3.** *N Am* SEND SOMEBODY TO PRISON to imprison somebody following conviction (*informal*) ○ *He was sent up for armed robbery.*

SYNONYMS See *ridicule.*

send² /send/ *n, vi* NAUT another spelling of **scend**

Sendai /sen dí/ capital city of Miyagi Prefecture, on northeastern Honshu Island, Japan. Population: 986,713 (2002).

Sendak /sén dak/, **Maurice** (*b.* 1928) US writer and illustrator best known for the popular children's book *Where the Wild Things Are* (1963)

sendoff /sénd of/ *n* an occasion when people gather to give good wishes to somebody who is leaving, e.g. at an airport ◇ **give somebody a good sendoff** to have a good party after somebody's funeral (*informal*)

sendup /sénd up/ *n* a parody done as a joke (*informal*)

sene /seen/ (*plural same*) *n* a subunit of Samoan currency. See table at **currency** [Mid-20C. < Samoan, 'cent']

Seneca /séннikə/ (*plural same* or *-cas*) *n* **1.** a member of an Iroquois people who lived in western New York State and who now mainly live there and in southern Ontario, Canada. The Seneca were one of the five peoples who formed the Iroquois Confederacy, which later became known as the Six Nations. **2.** the Iroquoian language of the Seneca people. It now has few speakers. [Mid-17C. < Dutch

Sennecaas 'the Upper Iroquois peoples'] —**Seneca** *adj* —**Senecan** *adj*

Seneca /séннikə/ (4? BC–AD 65) Spanish-born Roman philosopher and writer. He was Nero's tutor, and influenced the early years of his reign. He committed suicide after being condemned for conspiracy against the state. His writings as a dramatist, rhetorician, and Stoic moralist were influential in shaping the thought and literature of the European Renaissance. Full name **Seneca, Lucius Annaeus**

senecio /sə neéshi ō, -neéssi ō/ (*plural -os*) *n* PLANTS same as **ragwort** [Mid-16C. < Latin, 'groundsel' < *senex* 'male elder'; from the plant's white hairs]

Senegal

Senegal /sénni gáwl, -gaál/ **1.** country in West Africa. Formerly a French territory, it became an independent republic in 1960. Language: French. Currency: C.F.A. franc. Capital: Dakar. Population: 10,580,307 (2003). Area: 196,722 sq. km/75,955 sq. mi. Official name **Republic of Senegal 2.** river in western Africa that forms the border between Senegal and Mauritania and empties into the Atlantic Ocean near St-Louis, Senegal. Length: 1,610 km/1,000 mi. —**Senegalese** /sénni gə leéz/ *n, adj*

senery incorrect spelling of **scenery**

senescent /si néss'nt/ *adj* approaching an advanced age (*literary*) [Mid-17C. < Latin *senescent-*, present participle of *senescere* < *senex* 'advanced in age'] —**senescence** *n*

seneschal /sénnish'l/ *n* in medieval times, a steward who managed the domestic staff of a noble house [14C. Via French < medieval Latin *seniscalcus* < Germanic]

Senghor /sáN gawr/, **Léopold Sédar** (1906–2001) Senegalese president and writer. He was the first president of Senegal (1960–80) and a leading African intellectual. He promoted the cultural heritage of Africans, developing the idea of negritude.

senhor /se nyáwr/ (*plural -hors* or *-hores* /-yáw ress/) *n* a Portuguese title equivalent to English 'Mr' [Late 18C. Via Portuguese < medieval Latin *senior* 'lord, superior' < Latin (see SENIOR)]

senhora /sen yáwrə/ *n* a Portuguese title equivalent to English 'Mrs' [Early 19C. < Portuguese < *senhor* (see SENHOR)]

senhorita /sénnyə reétə/ *n* a Portuguese title equivalent to English 'Miss' [Late 19C. < Portuguese < *senhor* (see SENHOR)]

senile /seé nīl/ *adj* **1.** forgetful, confused, or otherwise mentally less acute in later life **2.** occurring in or believed to be characteristic of later life, especially the period after the age of 65 years ○ *senile dementia* [Mid-17C. < Latin *senilis* 'advanced in age' < *senex* 'old'] —**senilely** *adv* —**senility** /sə nilləti/ *n*

senile dementia *n* a form of brain disorder marked by progressive and irreversible mental deterioration, memory loss, and disorientation, known to affect some people in later life

senior /seé ni ər/ *adj* **1.** MORE ADVANCED IN AGE of a more advanced age **2.** HIGHER IN RANK of higher rank or having longer service or employment than another ○ *Everyone on the committee is senior to me.* **3.** *also* **Senior** BELONGING TO EARLIER GENERATION used to distinguish the elder of two members of the same family with the same name from the younger person of that name ■ *n* **1.** PERSON OF GREATER AGE somebody who is older than somebody else **2.** HIGHER-RANKING PERSON somebody who ranks higher than somebody else or

has worked in the same place longer ○ *She is my only senior in the department.* **3.** *N Am* FINAL-YEAR STUDENT a student in the last year of high school or college **4.** *Aus* LAW AUSTRALIAN BARRISTER in Australia, a barrister who has qualified as a Queen's Counsel [14C. < Latin, 'elder, older' < *senex* 'old']

senior aircraftman *n* a man in the Royal Air Force of a rank above leading aircraftman

senior aircraftwoman *n* a woman in the Royal Air Force of a rank above leading aircraftwoman

senior chief petty officer *n* a noncommissioned officer in the US Navy or Coast Guard of a rank above chief petty officer

senior citizen *n* somebody of retirement age or beyond

senior common room *n* a common room for the use of academic staff in some colleges and universities

senior debt *n* an indebtedness with no claims ahead of it and the first in line to be paid off

senior executive officer *n* *US* **1.** any of the most important managers in an organization **2.** the most important manager in an organization

senior high school *n* in the United States, a school for the last three or four years of secondary education grades 9 or 10 to 12

seniority /seéni órrəti/ (*plural -ties*) *n* **1.** status accorded to greater age, higher rank, or longer service or employment ○ *Days off will be awarded on the basis of seniority.* **2.** the state of being of greater age or higher rank than somebody else

senior lecturer *n* a university teacher of a rank above lecturer

senior master sergeant *n* a noncommissioned officer in the US Air Force of a rank above master sergeant

senior moment *n* a temporary lapse in memory or performance, which may be characteristic of an older person (*informal*)

senior service *n* the Royal Navy, especially as viewed in relation to the army

seniti /sénni ti/ (*plural same*) *n* a subunit of Tongan currency. See table at **currency** [Mid-20C. Via Tongan < CENT]

senna /sénnə/ *n* **1.** a leguminous plant. Flowers: yellow, in clusters. Native to: temperate regions. Genus: *Cassia.* **2.** dried plant leaves or pods of the senna plant. Use: purgative, laxative. [Mid-16C. Via modern Latin *senna* < Arabic *sanā'*]

Ayrton Senna

Senna /sénnə/, **Ayrton** (1960–94) Brazilian racing driver. One of the most celebrated Brazilian sportsmen of the 20th century, he won the World Grand Prix Formula One championship three times (1988, 1990, 1991). Full name **Senna da Silva, Ayrton**

'To survive in grand prix racing, you need to be afraid. Fear is an important feeling. It helps you to race longer and live longer.'
[Ayrton Senna, *Times*; 3 May 1994]

Sennacherib /sen ákərib/ (*d.* 681 BC) king of Assyria. During his reign (705–681 BC) he conquered Babylon (689 BC) and rebuilt Nineveh.

sennet /sénnit/ *n* a trumpet call that announced the exits and entrances of actors in Elizabethan drama [Late 16C. Probably alteration of SIGNET in obsolete sense 'signal']

Sennett /sénnit/, **Mack** (1880–1960) Canadian-born US film director. A leading director of silent films, he was known for slapstick films featuring Charlie Chaplin and the Keystone Cops. Born **Sinnott, Mikall (or Michael)**

sennit

sennit /sénnit/ n 1. braided cord in flat strands, used on ships 2. braided straw, reeds, or leaves, used to make hats [Mid-18C. Origin ?]

señor /se nyáwr/ (plural -**ñors** or -**ñores** /-nyáw ress/) n a Spanish title equivalent to English 'Mr' [Early 17C. Via Spanish < medieval Latin senior 'lord, superior' < Latin (see SENIOR)]

señora /se nyáwrə/ n a Spanish title equivalent to English 'Mrs' [Late 16C. < Spanish < señor (see SEÑOR)]

señorita /sénnyaw réetə/ n a Spanish title equivalent to English 'Miss' [Early 19C. < Spanish < señora (see SEÑOR)]

senryu /sénnri oo/ (plural same) n a three-line ironic or satirical Japanese poem, similar in structure to a haiku [Mid-20C. After Karai Senryu (1718–90), Japanese poet]

sensate /sén sayt/ adj 1. perceived through any of the senses 2. able to feel sensation [15C. < late Latin sensatus 'equipped with senses' < Latin sensus (see SENSE)] —**sensately** adv

sensation /sen sáysh'n/ n 1. PHYSICAL FEELING a physical feeling caused by having one or more of the sense organs stimulated ○ a burning sensation in my mouth and throat 2. POWER TO PERCEIVE the capacity to receive impressions through the sense organs ○ He has lost all sensation in his legs. 3. MENTAL IMPRESSION a vague or general feeling, especially one not attributable to an obvious cause ○ a sensation of falling 4. PUBLIC INTEREST a state of avid public interest in a phenomenon ○ Her speech caused a sensation. 5. INTERESTING PHENOMENON a phenomenon that creates avid public interest [Early 17C. Via French < medieval Latin sensation- 'perception' < Latin sensus (see SENSE)]

sensational /sen sáysh'nəl/ adj 1. EXTRAORDINARY attracting a great deal of attention and interest ○ a sensational defeat 2. EMPHASIZING LURID DETAILS giving too much emphasis to the most shocking and lurid aspects of something ○ sensational coverage of the murder trial 3. OUTSTANDING exceptionally good (informal) ○ sensational results 4. PHYSIOL, PHILOSOPHY SENSORY connected with the senses or sense impressions —**sensationally** adv

sensationalise vt another spelling of **sensationalize**

sensationalism /sen sáysh'nəlizəm/ n 1. the practice of emphasizing the most lurid, shocking, and emotive aspects of something under discussion or investigation, especially by the media 2. the belief that all knowledge is obtained only through the senses —**sensationalist** n, adj —**sensationalistic** /sen sáysh'nə lístik/ adj

sensationalize /sen sáysh'nə līz/ (-izes, -izing, -ized), **sensationalise** (-ises, -ising, -ised) vt to place excessive emphasis on the most shocking and emotive aspects of a subject —**sensationalization** /sen sáysh'nə līz zaysh'n/ n

sense /senss/ n 1. PHYSICAL FACULTY any of the faculties by which a person or animal obtains information about the physical world, e.g. sight or taste 2. FEELING DERIVED FROM SENSES a feeling derived from multiple or subtle sense impressions ○ a sense of security 3. ABILITY TO APPRECIATE SOMETHING the faculty whereby somebody appreciates a particular quality ○ a sense

of humour 4. MORAL DISCERNMENT the ability to perceive and be motivated by moral or ethical principles ○ instil a sense of right and wrong in the children 5. INTELLIGENCE the ability to make intelligent decisions or sound judgments ○ He's got no sense at all. 6. POINT useful purpose or good reason ○ There's no sense in waiting any longer. 7. REASONED OPINION an opinion arrived at through reflection or perception, often as a consensus ○ The sense of the meeting was clearly against the proposal. 8. MAIN IDEA the essence or gist of something ○ What was the sense of her argument? 9. MEANING a single meaning of a word or phrase that may have many 10. LOGIC MEANING OF TERM the meaning as opposed to the reference of a word or sentence ■ **senses** npl RATIONAL MIND a sensible, rational state of mind ○ I must be out of my senses. ■ vt (**senses, sensing, sensed**) 1. PERCEIVE SOMEBODY OR SOMETHING to perceive somebody or something with a sense or the senses ○ I sensed a movement behind me. 2. INFER SOMETHING to understand something intuitively ○ He must have sensed that I was disappointed. 3. DETECT AND IDENTIFY CHANGE to detect and identify a change in something ○ The device senses when the door is opened and sounds the alarm. [14C. Via French < Latin sensus 'perception' < sens-, past participle of sentire 'feel'] ◇ **in a sense** 1. considered from a point of view that may not be the most obvious or the most popular 2. used when saying that something could be described in a particular way, but that the description is not complete or accurate ◇ **make sense** to be understandable and consistent with reason ◇ **make sense of something** to understand something well enough to be able to act on it or evaluate it

---

CULTURAL NOTE **Sense and Sensibility**, a novel (1811) by Jane Austen. Set in Devon, Austen's first novel describes the emotional development of two sisters, Elinor and Marianne Dashwood, who live with their widowed mother in a modest cottage. Outwardly, Elinor appears dull and practical, Marianne sensitive and passionate, but the story of their involvement with two seemingly appropriate suitors warns against simplistic character judgments.

ORIGIN The Latin word sentire 'to feel', from which **sense** is derived, is also the source of English assent, consensus, consent, dissent, resent, sensible, sensual, sentence, and sentiment.

---

sense datum n in the philosophical doctrine of phenomenalism, a sensation

senseh fowl /sénse-/ n Carib same as **frizzle fowl** [< Twi asense 'hen without a tail']

sensei /sen sáy/ (plural same) n 1. a teacher of a martial art such as karate or T'ai Chi 2. used as a title to address somebody who is a teacher, especially in the martial arts [Late 19C. Via Japanese < Middle Chinese senshiaj 'first person']

senseless /sénssləss/ adj 1. WITHOUT INTELLIGENCE demonstrating a lack of reason and intelligence ○ a senseless decision 2. UNCONSCIOUS unconscious, or unable to perceive anything ○ was knocked senseless by the blow 3. WITH NO APPARENT PURPOSE apparently or really without purpose or meaning ○ a senseless activity ○ a senseless crime —**senselessly** adv —**senselessness** n

sensemilla n DRUGS, PLANTS same as **sinsemilla**

sense organ n an organ such as an eye or ear that is specialized to receive stimuli from the physical world and transmit them via nerve impulses to the brain

sensi /sénssi/ n DRUGS same as **sinsemilla** (slang; used in Black English) [Late 20C. Shortening of sensemilla]

sensibilia /sén sə bílli ə/ npl things that can be sensed, considered collectively [Mid-19C. < late Latin < Latin sensibilis (see SENSIBLE)]

sensibility /sénn sə bílləti/ n 1. △ CAPACITY TO RESPOND the capacity to respond emotionally or aesthetically ○ the sensibility of a child 2. CAPACITY TO FEEL the capacity to perceive or feel 3. BOT CAPACITY OF PLANTS FOR RESPONSE the sensitivity of plants to external stimuli ■ **sensibilities** npl MORAL SCRUPLES sensitivity about moral or ethical issues ○ careful not to offend their sensibilities

USAGE **sensibility** or **sensitivity**? Sensitivity is used in ways corresponding to the meanings of the adjective sensitive, and is mainly concerned with physical or emotional reactions of various kinds: a sensitivity to bright light. Sensibility is less closely related in meaning to sensible than sensitivity is to sensitive, and chiefly denotes somebody's capacity to respond emotionally or aesthetically, as in poetry that appealed to his sensibility.

---

sensible /sénssəb'l/ adj 1. SHOWING GOOD SENSE having or demonstrating sound reason and judgment ○ a sensible decision ○ She's not very sensible. 2. PRACTICAL practical, usually comfortable and hard-wearing, and not worn as an adornment ○ a pair of sensible shoes 3. SUBJECT TO PERCEPTION able to be perceived through the senses ○ sensible objects in the world around us 4. CONSCIOUS awake or conscious, and having the capacity to understand 5. △ AWARE OF SOMETHING very aware of something, emotionally or intellectually (formal) ○ not sensible of the tragic mistake he'd made [14C. Via French < Latin sensibilis 'perceptible by the senses, able to perceive' < sens- (see SENSE)] —**sensibleness** n —**sensibly** adv

USAGE **sensible** or **sensitive**? The two words overlap in meaning to some extent in the sense illustrated by the sentence I am sensible of your difficult situation ('I can appreciate your difficult situation'). In this meaning, **sensible** is normally used to express emotional or intellectual awareness. In a comparable use, **sensitive** is followed by to and denotes a a tactful and sympathetic feeling about or for something: He was always sensitive to their needs.

SYNONYMS See **aware**.

sensible horizon n ASTRON same as **horizon** (sense 2)

sensillum /sen sílləm/ (plural -**la** /-lə/) n a simple sense organ made up of one or a few cells connected by a nerve cell, often found in insects [Early 20C. < modern Latin < Latin sensus (see SENSE)]

sensitise vt another spelling of **sensitize**

sensitive /sénssətiv/ adj 1. ACUTELY PERCEPTIVE unusually responsive to stimuli from the physical world ○ a sensitive nose 2. ABLE TO MEASURE SMALL DIFFERENCES capable of detecting minute changes in levels, conditions, or amounts ○ a sensitive scientific instrument 3. AFFECTED BY EXTERNAL STIMULUS affected in some way by a particular external stimulus such as an allergen (often used in combination) ○ sensitive to light ○ a touch-sensitive screen 4. DELICATE easily damaged or irritated physically ○ a toothpaste for people with sensitive teeth 5. TOUCHY easily offended or annoyed if something is spoken about ○ He's very sensitive about his driving. 6. THOUGHTFUL AND SYMPATHETIC tactful and sympathetic in relation to the feelings of others 7. REQUIRING TACTFULNESS needing to be dealt with tactfully to avoid embarrassment ○ a sensitive issue 8. SECRET OR CONFIDENTIAL not to be mentioned or divulged ○ sensitive matters of national security 9. ABLE TO SENSE with the capacity to perceive via the sense organs 10. SUBTLE IN ARTISTIC EXPRESSION subtly expressive in one of the arts 11. ARTISTICALLY IMPRESSIONABLE susceptible to artistic effects, e.g. in music, writing, or painting 12. FIN FLUCTUATING volatile and subject to fluctuation ○ a sensitive market 13. PHOTOGRAPHY RESPONSIVE TO LIGHT extremely responsive to radiation, especially to light of a specific wavelength ○ light-sensitive film 14. ELECTRONICS RESPONSIVE TO SIGNALS able to respond to transmitted signals ■ n PSYCHIC PERSON a person with supposedly clairvoyant or psychic powers [14C. Via French < medieval Latin sensitivus < Latin sens- (see SENSE)] —**sensitively** adv —**sensitiveness** n

USAGE See **sensible**.

sensitive plant n 1. a plant that recoils when touched. Flowers: purplish. Native to: tropical Americas. Latin name: Mimosa pudica. 2. somebody who is easily upset (informal)

sensitive site exploitation n MIL full form of SSE[1]

sensitivity /sénssə tívvəti/ n 1. CONSIDERATION care and understanding of needs and requirements ○ sensitivity to different cultural traditions 2. RESPONSIVENESS capacity for physical sensation or response ○ sensitivity to heat 3. ELECTRONICS RE-

SPONSIVENESS TO RADIO SIGNALS the ability of a radio or other receiver to respond to transmitted signals ■ **sensitivities** *npl* FEELINGS somebody's feelings, especially feelings that might be offended

USAGE See *sensibility*.

sensitize /sénssə tīz/ (**-tizes, -tizing, -tized**), **sensitise** (**-tises, -tising, -tised**) *vt* **1.** MAKE SOMEBODY SENSITIVE to make somebody sensitive, especially to a situation **2.** MAKE SOMEBODY ALLERGIC to induce undue sensitivity in somebody to a substance such as a food ingredient or drug so that subsequent exposure to the substance triggers an allergic reaction **3.** PHOTOGRAPHY MAKE FILM SENSITIVE TO LIGHT to make a photographic film, plate, or other medium sensitive to light by coating it with an emulsion [Mid-19C. < SENSITIVE] —**sensitization** /sénssə tī záysh'n/ *n* —**sensitizer** *n*

sensitometer /sénssə tómmitər/ *n* an instrument for measuring degrees of sensitivity, especially one used on photographic materials [Late 19C. < SENSITIVE] —**sensitometry** *n*

sensor /sénssər/ *n* a device capable of detecting and responding to physical stimuli such as movement, light, or heat [Mid-20C. < SENSE or Latin *sens-* (see SENSE)]

sensoria PHYSIOL plural of **sensorium**

sensorial /sen sáwri əl/ *adj* relating to sensation and the sense organs [Mid-18C. < SENSORIUM] —**sensorially** *adv*

sensorimotor /sénssəri mṓtər/ *adj* **1.** relating to both the motor and sensory functions in the brain or the neurological structures underlying these functions **2.** relating to motor functions arising from sensory stimuli

sensorimotor stage *n* the first major stage in Jean Piaget's theory of cognitive development, from birth to approximately two years, in which children begin to understand their world through sensory and motor experience

sensorineural /sénssəri nyóorəl/ *adj* involving or relating to sensory nerves

sensorium /sen sáwri əm/ (*plural* **-ria** /-ri ə/) *n* **1.** the sensory components of the brain and nervous system that deal with the receiving and interpreting of external stimuli **2.** all the sensory functions in the body, considered as a single unit [Mid-17C. < late Latin, 'organ of sensation' < Latin *sens-* (see SENSE)]

sensory /sénssəri/ *adj* relating to sensation and the sense organs ○ *heightened sensory awareness* [Mid-18C. < SENSE or Latin *sens-* (see SENSE)]

sensory deprivation *n* the elimination of or a sharp reduction in sensory stimulation, usually as part of an experiment in psychology or as part of repressive interrogation procedures or brainwashing

sensory integration dysfunction *n* a neurological disorder of children caused by the inability of the brain to process sensory information correctly, making them either oversensitive or not sensitive enough to touch, taste, and sound, and resulting in inappropriate behaviour

sensual /sénssyoo əl, -shoo əl/ *adj* **1.** CARNAL relating to physical or, especially, sexual pleasure **2.** VOLUPTUOUS suggesting a great deal of physical or, especially, sexual pleasure ○ *sensual lips* **3.** SENSORY relating to the body or the senses as opposed to the mind or the intellect [15C. < late Latin *sensualis* 'equipped with feeling or sensation' < Latin *sensus* (see SENSE)] —**sensually** *adv*

USAGE sensual or **sensuous**? Both words are connected with gratification of the human senses. ***Sensual*** is the older word, and in the 17th century it developed special meanings associated with the bodily appetites, especially eating and above all sexual satisfaction: *Her mouth looked sensual and inviting. They enjoyed the sensual pleasures of the table.* About this time the poet John Milton seems to have invented the word ***sensuous*** to refer more specifically to the aesthetic and spiritual senses (seeing, hearing, thinking), and it was taken up by Samuel Taylor Coleridge in the 19th century. In current use, it is almost impossible to keep the two sets of meanings apart, since the senses cannot readily be compartmentalized in this way, but it is prudent to have regard for the main distinction when using these words. ***Sensuous***, for example, is the word to use in connection with music or poetry: *The conductor relished the sensuous parts of Ravel's score.*

sensualism /sénssyoo əlizəm, -shoo-/ *n* **1.** devotion to sensual gratification **2.** PHILOSOPHY, ETHICS same as **sensationalism** (sense 2) —**sensualist** *n* —**sensualistic** /sénssyoo ə lístik, -shoo-/ *adj*

sensuality /sénssyoo álləti, -shoo-/ *n* **1.** the capacity for enjoying the pleasures of the senses **2.** the quality of being pleasing to the senses

sensuous /sénssyoo əss, -shoo əss/ *adj* **1.** OF SENSE STIMULATION relating to stimulation of the senses **2.** APPRECIATING STIMULATION enjoying or appreciating pleasurable stimulation of the senses ○ *a sensuous lover* **3.** CAUSING STIMULATION causing pleasurable stimulation of the senses ○ *a sensuous experience* [Mid-17C. < Latin *sensus* (see SENSE)] —**sensuously** *adv* —**sensuousness** *n*

USAGE See *sensual*.

sent[1] /sent/ past participle, past tense of **send**[1]

sent[2] /sent/ (*plural* **senti** /sénti/) *n* a subunit of Estonian currency. See table at **currency** [Late 20C. Via Estonian < CENT]

~~**sentance**~~ incorrect spelling of **sentence**

sente /sénti/ (*plural* **lisente** /li sénti/) *n* a subunit of currency in Lesotho. See table at **currency** [Late 20C. Via Sesotho < CENT]

sentence /séntənss/ *n* **1.** GRAM MEANINGFUL LINGUISTIC UNIT a group of words or a single word that expresses a complete thought, feeling, or idea. It usually contains an explicit or implied subject and a predicate containing a finite verb. **2.** LAW JUDGMENT a judgment by a court specifying the punishment of somebody convicted of a crime **3.** LAW JUDICIAL PUNISHMENT the punishment imposed by a court on somebody convicted of a crime ○ *a sentence of 15 years in prison* **4.** LOGIC WELL-FORMED EXPRESSION a well-formed expression in a symbolic language ■ *vt* (**-tences, -tencing, -tenced**) LAW ALLOCATE SOMEBODY PUNISHMENT to allocate a punishment to somebody convicted of a crime, usually stating its nature and its duration ○ *was sentenced to 90 hours of community service* [13C. Via French < Latin *sententia* 'feeling, opinion' < *sentient-*, present participle of *sentire* 'feel'] —**sentencer** *n*

sentence adverb *n* an adverb that modifies an entire sentence

USAGE Many English adverbs can be used to modify whole sentences, for example: *Obviously there must be some mistake. Regrettably I shall be away that week. Financially it was a disaster. I've never liked him, frankly.* They are known as sentence adverbs. Sentence adverbs are concise; they allow you to express in a single word what you might otherwise have to say in several words. Sentence adverbs form a completely standard aspect of English grammar, but there are a few, for example *ironically* and *hopefully*, that give rise to widespread criticism as they express the user's attitude to the sentence content rather than modify the sentence as a whole. Others that may incur criticism in the same way are *mercifully*, *thankfully*, and *truthfully*. In formal contexts, writers are advised to avoid all these and simply recast their sentences accordingly.

sentence substitute *n* a single word that, when used in the proper context, meets all the semantic requirements of a sentence. Words such as 'yes' and 'no' are sentence substitutes.

sentencing /séntənssing/ *n* **1.** the phase of a court trial in which a sentence is arrived at and pronounced **2.** the act of pronouncing a judicial sentence on a defendant

sentential /sen ténsh'l/ *adj* relating to sentences in natural language or logic —**sententially** *adv*

sentential calculus *n* LOGIC same as **propositional calculus**

sententious /sen ténshəss/ *adj* **1.** FULL OF APHORISMS tending to use, or full of, maxims and aphorisms **2.** OVERLY MORALIZING inclined to moralize more than is merited or appreciated **3.** PITHY expressing much in few words [15C. Via French < Latin *sententiosus* 'meaningful' < *sententia* (see SENTENCE)] —**sententiously** *adv* —**sententiousness** *n*

senti MONEY plural of **sent**[2]

sentient /sénsh'nt, -shi ənt/ *adj* **1.** capable of feeling and perception ○ *a sentient being* **2.** capable of responding emotionally rather than intellectually [Mid-17C. < Latin *sentient-*, present participle of *sentire* 'feel'] —**sentience** *n* —**sentiently** *adv*

sentiment /séntimənt/ *n* **1.** MENTAL FEELING a thought or idea based on a feeling or emotion **2.** GENERAL FEELING a feeling or opinion prevailing among a group of people ○ *The sentiment emerged that we were acting too soon.* **3.** UNDERLYING FEELING an underlying feeling, as distinct from the action that it brings about ○ *His speech was awkward but the sentiment was right.* **4.** APPEAL TO FEELING a calculated appeal to feeling or emotion, especially one that is excessive and unreasoning ○ *The book ends on a note of cheap sentiment.* **5.** DEEP FEELING refined or tender feeling, especially when expressed in a work of art (*formal*) ■ **sentiments** *npl* OPINION a point of view or judgment on something ○ *What are her sentiments on the matter?* [14C. Via French < medieval Latin *sentimentum* 'opinion, feeling' < Latin *sentire* 'feel']

sentimental /sénti mént'l/ *adj* **1.** MAWKISH IN FEELING affected acutely by emotional matters, often to the point of mawkishness **2.** MAWKISH IN EXPRESSION displaying too much uncontrolled or self-indulgent emotion **3.** APPEALING TO TENDER FEELINGS experiencing, appealing to, or expressing tender, often romantic or nostalgic, feelings ○ *a sentimental portrait of our town* **4.** EXPRESSING DEEP FEELING expressing deep, refined feeling (*formal*) —**sentimentally** *adv*

CULTURAL NOTE ***A Sentimental Journey***, a novel (1768) by Laurence Sterne. Sterne's second and last novel was intended as a riposte to Tobias Smollett's ill-tempered *Travels Through France and Italy* (1766) and even features a Smollett-like curmudgeon called Smellfungus. A rambling account of a journey through France from Calais to Lyons, it is transformed into an engaging work of art by the author's wit, sensitivity, and sharp social observation. Not surprisingly, the word *smellfungus* came to mean a carping faultfinder in general parlance.

sentimentalise *vti* another spelling of **sentimentalize**

sentimentalism /sénti méntəlizəm/ *n* **1.** a tendency to express or use obvious or powerful feelings or emotions without appealing to reason **2.** something that expresses excessive emotion, especially something that is self-indulgent or nostalgic —**sentimentalist** *n*

sentimentality /sénti men tálləti/ *n* the tendency or practice of indulging in emotion or nostalgia

sentimentalize /sénti mént'l īz/ (**-izes, -izing, -ized**), **sentimentalise** (**-ises, -ising, -ised**) *v* **1.** *vi* to indulge excessively in emotion or nostalgia **2.** *vt* to treat somebody or something, or express something, with undue emphasis on feeling —**sentimentalization** /sénti mént'l ī záysh'n/ *n*

sentimental value *n* a value placed on something because of its emotional associations rather than its monetary worth

sentinel /séntinəl/ *n* SENTRY a guard or lookout ■ *vt* (**-nels, -nelling, -nelled**) **1.** GUARD SOMETHING to stand guard over something or a group of people **2.** PROVIDE GUARD FOR SOMETHING to provide a guard for something or for a group of people [16C. Via French < Italian *sentinella*]

sentry /séntri/ (*plural* **-tries**) *n* a member of the armed services who is assigned to keep watch to warn of danger and to guard entrances and exits [Early 17C. Origin ?]

sentry box *n* a covered shelter for a sentry, typically at an entrance or crossing

senza /séntsə, -zə/ *prep* without something indicated by a following Italian noun (*used in musical directions*) ○ *senza ritenuto* [Early 18C. < Italian]

Seoul /sōl/ capital and largest city of South Korea, in the northwest of the country, on the Han River. Population: 9,895,217 (2000).

Sep. *abbr* **1.** CALENDAR September **2.** BIBLE Septuagint

sepal /sépp'l/ *n* a modified leaf in the outermost whorl (**calyx**) of a flower that encloses the petals and other parts [Early 19C. Via French < modern Latin *sepalum*, blend of Greek *skepē* 'covering' + Latin *petalum* 'petal'] —**sepalled** *adj* —**sepalous** /séppələss/ *adj*

sepaloid /séppə loyd/ *adj* resembling or functioning as a sepal

separable /séppərəb'l/ *adj* capable of being divided, taken apart, or removed, either from each other or from something else —**separability** /séppərə bílləti/ *n* —**separableness** *n* —**separably** *adv*

separate *adj* /séppərət/ **1.** APART not touching or connected, not together, or not in the same place ○ *They slept in separate rooms.* **2.** UNRELATED distinct from or unrelated to something else ○ *treated it as a separate issue* **3.** DIFFERENT not shared with somebody or something else ○ *The book will be sent to you under separate cover.* ■ *v* /séppə rayt/ (**-rates, -rating, -rated**) **1.** *vt* MOVE OR KEEP SOMETHING APART to move two or more people or things away from each other, or prevent people or things from coming into contact with each other ○ *Somehow we got separated in the crowd.* **2.** *vt* BE BETWEEN THINGS to stand or lie between one person or thing and another **3.** *vt* DISTINGUISH PEOPLE OR THINGS to be the factor that makes two people or things different from one another ○ *His ready wit separated him from his classmates.* **4.** *vi* COME APART to come apart or stop being attached or connected **5.** *vi* PART COMPANY to leave one another and go off in different directions ○ *The group separated soon after lunch.* **6.** *vi* CEASE LIVING AS COUPLE to stop living together as a couple **7.** *vt* CATEGORIZE SOMEBODY OR SOMETHING to put somebody or something into different categories or groups **8.** *vt* SHOW HOW THINGS DIFFER to see or show that two or more things are different or not ○ *Try to separate the issues and establish priorities.* **9.** *vti* DIVIDE to split something into component parts, or be split into component parts **10.** *vti* MAKE OR BECOME INDEPENDENT to leave a larger group and become independent, or cause part of a larger group to leave and form an independent unit **11.** *vt* N Am RELEASE OR FIRE SOMEBODY to dismiss somebody from a job, or release somebody from military service ■ **separates** /séppərəts/ *npl* CLOTHING INDIVIDUAL ITEMS OF CLOTHING articles of women's clothing that can be bought as individual items and worn in various combinations, e.g. blouses, skirts, jackets, and trousers [15C. < Latin *separat-*, past participle of *separare*, literally 'arrange apart' < *parare* 'make ready'] —**separately** *adv* —**separateness** *n* —**separator** /-raytər/ *n*

separate off *vt* to divide somebody or something from a larger group or unity

separate out *v* **1.** *vti* to come out of a mixture and form a distinct mass, or make something do so **2.** *vt* to be the factor that makes two people or things different from one another

separated /séppə raytid/ *adj* **1.** LIVING APART WHILE MARRIED no longer living together as a couple but still legally married **2.** POSITIONED APART moved apart so as not to be touching or connected, not together, or not in the same place ○ *geographically separated families* **3.** DIVIDED split into component parts ○ *separated eggs*

separating funnel /séppə rayting-/ *n* a large funnel that has a valve in its output tube. Use: separation of liquids that do not mix.

separation /séppə ráysh'n/ *n* **1.** KEEPING OF THINGS APART the act or process of separating things or people **2.** STATE OF BEING APART the state or duration of being apart from other things or people **3.** PLACE OF MEETING OR SPACE BETWEEN a place, line, or mark that shows where two things meet, or the gap between them **4.** AGREEMENT NOT TO LIVE TOGETHER the act of stopping living together as husband and wife while remaining married, or a formal agreement to do so, especially one made in a court of law **5.** DIVISION the splitting of something into its component parts **6.** DUMPING PART OF ROCKET the act of detaching the rear section of a multistage rocket when it is burnt out, or the time when this happens **7.** N Am DEPARTURE FROM GROUP dismissal from a job, or release from military service [15C. Via French < Latin *separation-* < *separat-* (see SEPARATE)]

separation anxiety *n* a state of anxiety caused in somebody, especially a young child, by the thought or fact of being separated from his or her mother or primary caregiver

separationist /séppə ráysh'nist/ *n, adj* POL same as separatist

separation of powers *n* in the United States, the constitutional requirement that each of the three branches of government, executive, judicial, and

legislative, be autonomous and distinct from the others

separatist /séppərətist/ *n* **1.** somebody who breaks away from or who is in favour of breaking away from a group, organization, or country **2.** somebody who favours keeping members of racial, religious, gender, or cultural groups separate —**separatism** *n* —**separatist** *adj* —**separatistic** /séppərə tístik/ *adj*

separative /séppərətiv/ *adj* tending to become separate or make something become separate —**separatively** *adv*

sepd. *abbr US* separated

~~seperate~~ incorrect spelling of **separate**

Sephardi /se faárdi/ (*plural* **-dim** /-dim/) *n* a Jew of Spanish or Portuguese origin, or one who is not of German or eastern European descent (**Ashkenazi**) [Mid-19C. < modern Hebrew < *sĕp̄araḏ*, land of exile mentioned in the Bible] —**Sephardic** *adj*

sepia /sée pi ə/ *n* **1.** REDDISH-BROWN PIGMENT a deep reddish-brown pigment made from the dark liquid in the ink sacs of various species of cuttlefish, or an artificial form of it, used in painting **2.** ARTS SEPIA DRAWING OR PHOTOGRAPH a drawing done in sepia, or a photograph with a brownish tone **3.** COLOURS DARK BROWN a dark brown colour tinged with yellow or red **4.** PHOTOGRAPHY BROWNISH COLOUR IN PHOTOGRAPHS a brownish tone produced by some photographic processes, especially seen in early photographs [14C. Via Latin < Greek *sēpia* 'cuttlefish'] —**sepia** *adj*

Sepik /séppik/ river on eastern New Guinea. Length: 1,100 km/700 mi.

sepiolite /sée̊epi ə līt/ *n* a clayey hydrated magnesium silicate mineral, formed by hydrothermal alteration of basic igneous rocks. N Am term **meerschaum** [Mid-19C. < German *Sepiolith* < Greek *sēpion* 'cuttlefish bone' < *sēpia* 'cuttlefish']

sepoy /sée̊ poy/ *n* in former British India, an Indian soldier under British command, especially one who served in the British East India Company [Early 18C. < Persian, Urdu *sipāhī* 'horseman, soldier']

Sepoy Mutiny, Sepoy Rebellion *n* HIST same as **Indian Mutiny**

seppo /séppō/ (*plural* **-pos**) *n* ANZ an offensive term for a citizen of the United States [Late 20C. < shortening of SEPTIC TANK, rhyming slang for YANK]

seppuku /se pookoo/ *n* CULTL ANTHROP same as **harakiri** [Late 19C. < Japanese < *setsu* 'to cut' (< Middle Chinese *tshet*) + *fuku* 'abdomen' (< Middle Chinese *fuwk*)]

sepsis /sépsiss/ *n* the condition or syndrome caused by the presence of microorganisms or their toxins in the tissue or the bloodstream [Late 19C. < Greek *sēpsis* < *sēpein* 'make rotten']

sept /sept/ *n* **1.** a branch of a Scottish or Irish clan **2.** a section of a people that believes itself to be descended from one particular ancestor [Early 16C. Probably alteration of SECT]

Sept. *abbr* **1.** CALENDAR September **2.** BIBLE Septuagint

septa ANAT, ENG plural of **septum**

septarium /sep táiri əm/ (*plural* **-ia** /-i ə/) *n* a nodule of mineral containing cracks filled with crystalline material [Late 18C. < modern Latin < Latin *septum* (see SEPTUM)] —**septarian** *adj*

September /sep témbər, səp-/ *n* in the Gregorian calendar, the ninth month of the year, lasting 30 days. See table at **calendar** [Pre-12C. Via French < Latin < *septem* 'seven'; because September was the 7th month of the Roman year]

September Massacre *n* the massacre of hundreds of prisoners by mobs in Paris in September 1792, during the French Revolution. The killings were caused by fears of a counter-revolution by royalist prisoners, but most of those who were killed were ordinary criminals.

Septembrist /sep témbrist, səp-/ *n* a member of the Paris mob that carried out the September Massacre in 1792

septenary /séptinəri, sep tée̊nəri/ *adj* **1.** OF 7 relating to the number seven **2.** CONTAINING 7 made up of seven people or things **3.** TIME same as **septennial** ■ *n* (*plural* **-ries**) **1.** NUMBER 7 the number seven **2.** GROUP OF 7 a group of seven people or things **3.** 7 YEARS a period of seven years **4.** LITERAT LINE OF VERSE CONTAINING 7 FEET

a line of verse consisting of seven metrical feet [15C. < Latin *septenarius* < *septeni* 'seven each' < *septem* 'seven']

septennia plural of **septennium**

septennial /sep ténni əl/ *adj* **1.** FOR 7 YEARS lasting seven years **2.** HAPPENING EVERY 7 YEARS occurring once every seven years ■ *n* SEPTENNIAL EVENT something that happens every seven years [Mid-17C. < Latin *septennium* (see SEPTENNIUM)] —**septennially** *adv*

septennium /sep ténni əm/ (*plural* **-niums** or **-nia** /-ni ə/) *n* a period of seven years [Mid-19C. < Latin < *septem* 'seven' + *annus* 'year']

septet /sep tét/, **septette** *n* **1.** 7 MUSICAL PERFORMERS a group of seven instrumentalists or singers **2.** MUSIC FOR 7 PERFORMERS a musical piece composed for seven instrumentalists or singers **3.** GROUP OF 7 a group of seven people or things [Early 19C. < German *Septett* < Latin *septem* 'seven']

septi- *prefix* seven ○ *septivalent* [< Latin *septem*]

septic /séptik/ *adj* **1.** full of or generating pus **2.** relating to, involving, or causing sepsis ■ *n* Aus same as **seppo** (*slang offensive*) [Early 17C. Via Latin < Greek *sēptikos* < *sēpein* 'make rotten'] —**septically** *adv* —**septicity** /sep tíssəti/ *n*

septicaemia /sépti sée̊mi ə/ *n* a disease caused by toxic microorganisms in the bloodstream —**septicaemic** *adj*

septicemia *n* MED US spelling of **septicaemia**

septicidal /sépti síd'l/ *adj* describes a fruit that splits open along a septa, dividing the component carpels [Early 19C. < SEPTUM + Latin *-cidere* 'to cut' < *caedere*] —**septicidally** *adv*

septic tank *n* a tank, usually underground, in which human waste matter is decomposed by bacteria

Sept-Îles /se té̊el/ city in southeastern Quebec, Canada, on the St Lawrence River. Population: 23,636 (2001).

septillion /sep tíllyən/ (*plural* **-lions** or *same*) *n* **1.** US the number equal to 10^{24}, written as 1 followed by 24 zeros **2.** the number equal to 10^{42}, written as 1 followed by 42 zeros (*dated*) [Late 17C. < French < *sept* 'seven' + *-illion* as in *million*] —**septillion** *adj* —**septillionth** *adj, n*

septime /sep té̊em/ *n* in fencing, the seventh of eight positions from which a parry or attack can be made [Late 19C. Via French < Latin *septimus* 'seventh' < *septem* 'seven']

septuagenarian /séptyoo əjə náiri ən/ *n* a person between 70 and 79 years of age ■ *adj* between 70 and 79 years old [Early 18C. < Latin *septuaginarius* < *septuaginta* 'seventy']

Septuagesima /séptyoo ə jéssimə/ *n* in the Christian calendar, the third Sunday before Lent [14C. < Latin *septuagesima (dies)* 'seventieth (day)' < *septuaginta* 'seventy']

Septuagint /séptyoo əjint/ *n* a Greek translation of the Hebrew Bible made in the 3rd and 2nd centuries BC to meet the needs of Greek-speaking Jews outside Palestine. The Septuagint contains some books not in the Hebrew canon. [Mid-16C. < Latin *septuaginta* 'seventy'; because about seventy translators were said to have worked on it]

septum /séptəm/ (*plural* **-ta** /-tə/) *n* **1.** a thin partition or membrane dividing something into two or more cavities. Examples include the tissue separating the nostrils, each of the muscular membranes separating the chambers of the heart, and the internal dividing walls in the seed heads of poppies. **2.** a thin partition that separates components in a machine [Mid-17C. < Latin, 'partition' < *sepire* 'enclose' < *sepes* 'hedge'] —**septal** *adj* —**septate** *adj*

septuple /séptyoo̊p'l, sép tyoo̊p'l/ *adj* **1.** 7 TIMES AS MUCH seven times as many or as much as something else **2.** HAVING 7 PARTS consisting of seven parts ■ *vti* (**-ples, -pling, -pled**) INCREASE BY 7 TIMES to multiply something by seven, or become seven times as much or as many (*formal*) [Early 17C. < late Latin *septuplus* < Latin *septem* 'seven']

septuplet /séptyoo̊plət, séptyoo̊plét/ *n* **1.** ONE OF 7 BORN TOGETHER one of seven babies or animals born to the same mother at one time **2.** GROUP OF 7 a group of seven people or things **3.** MUSIC GROUP OF 7 NOTES a

group of seven notes to be played or sung in the time of four, six, or eight of the same notated value [Late 19C. < SEPTUPLE, after TRIPLET]

sepulcher *n, vt* BUILDINGS, RELIG US spelling of **sepulchre**

sepulchral /si púlkrəl/ *adj* **1.** suggesting or possessing characteristics associated with the grave, e.g. gloominess **2.** relating to burial vaults or funerals and burials (*formal*) —**sepulchrally** *adv*

sepulchre /sépp'lkər/ *n* a vault in which a corpse is buried ■ *vt* (**-chres, -chring, -chred**) to put a corpse into a sepulchre (*literary*) [12C. Via French < Latin *sepulc(h)rum* < *sepult-*, past participle of *sepelire* 'bury']

seq. *abbr* sequel

sequacious /si kwáyshəss/ *adj* **1.** argued, or developing an argument, in a logically consistent and coherent way (*formal*) **2.** too willing to follow a leader uncritically (*archaic*) [Mid-17C. < Latin *sequax* 'inclined to follow' < *sequi* 'follow'] —**sequaciously** *adv* —**sequaciousness** *n* —**sequacity** /si kwássəti/ *n*

sequel /seékwəl/ *n* **1.** a film, novel, or play that continues a story begun in a previous film, novel, or play **2.** something that happens after something else, especially as a consequence of it [15C. Via French < Latin *sequel(l)a* < *sequi* 'follow']

sequela /si kweélə/ (*plural* **-quelae** /-kweé lee/) *n* a disease or disorder that is caused by a preceding disease or injury in the same individual [Late 18C. < Latin (see SEQUEL)]

sequelitis /seékwəl ítiss/ *n* the tendency of authors and filmmakers to continue to produce sequels to their works as long as they are financially successful

sequence /seékwənss/ *n* **1.** SERIES OF THINGS a number of things, actions, or events arranged or happening in a specific order or having a specific connection **2.** ORDER OF THINGS the order in which things are arranged, actions are carried out, or events happen ○ *a chronological sequence* **3.** CINEMA SECTION OF FILM a section of a film showing a single incident or set of related actions or events ○ *a chase sequence* **4.** CARDS CARDS OF CONSECUTIVE VALUES three or more consecutive playing cards, usually of the same suit **5.** MUSIC REPEATED MUSICAL PHRASE a musical passage or chant consisting of three or more related short phrases repeated several times at successively higher or lower pitch levels **6.** CHR HYMN in the Roman Catholic Church, a hymn sung or said between the gradual and the gospel **7.** MATHS ORDERED SET OF ELEMENTS in mathematics, an ordered set of elements that can be put into a one-to-one correspondence with the set of positive integers **8.** BIOCHEM ORDER DETERMINING BIOLOGICAL PROPERTIES the order of the amino acids in a protein or of the nucleotides in a nucleic acid ■ *vt* (**-quences, -quencing, -quenced**) **1.** PUT OR DO THINGS IN ORDER to arrange things or perform actions in a definite order **2.** BIOCHEM DETERMINE MOLECULE'S SEQUENCE to determine the sequence of a protein or nucleic acid [14C. < late Latin *sequentia* 'what follows' < Latin *sequent-*, present participle of *sequi* 'follow']

ORIGIN The Latin word *sequi* 'to follow', from which ***sequence*** is derived, is also the source of English *consecutive, consequence, ensue, obsequious, persecute, prosecute, pursue, second*[1] in a series, *sect, sequel, set*[2], *subsequent, sue,* and *suit.*

sequence of tenses *n* the grammatical relationship that causes the tense of a verb in a subordinate clause to be influenced or dictated by the tense of the verb in the related main clause

sequencer /seékwənssər/ *n* **1.** ELECTRONICS DEVICE FOR SORTING DATA an instrument for sorting information into the correct order for data processing **2.** MUSIC ELECTRONIC DEVICE FOR STORING MUSIC an electronic device or piece of software that digitally stores sequences of musical notes, chords, or rhythms that can be transmitted to an electronic musical instrument **3.** BIOCHEM DEVICE FOR DETERMINING SEQUENCES an apparatus for automatically determining the sequence of a protein or nucleic acid

sequence tagged site *n* a short DNA sequence, usually 200 to 500 base pairs, that has a single occurrence in the human genome and whose location and base sequence are known

sequent /seékwənt/ *adj* **1.** CONSEQUENT following as a consequence or result (*formal*) **2.** FOLLOWING following one after another (*formal or archaic*) ■ *n* **1.** CONSEQUENCE a consequence or result (*formal*) **2.** LOGIC FORMAL LOGICAL REPRESENTATION in logic, a formal representation of an argument showing that an element is a theorem [Mid-16C. < Latin *sequent-* (see SEQUENCE)] —**sequently** *adv*

sequential /si kwénsh'l/ *adj* **1.** happening in chronological order, or forming a sequence **2.** being a consequence or result of something else [Early 19C. < SEQUENCE, after CONSEQUENCE, CONSEQUENTIAL] —**sequentiality** /si kwénshi állәti/ *n* —**sequentially** *adv*

sequential access *n* a way of accessing and reading a computer file by starting at the beginning

sequential scanning *n* a system that scans a television picture using lines in a numerical sequence

sequester /si kwéstər/ (**-ters, -tering, -tered**) *vt* **1.** PUT SOMEBODY INTO ISOLATION to put somebody in an isolated or lonely place away from other people, the pressures of everyday life, or possible disturbances (*formal*) **2.** LAW TAKE PROPERTY TO COVER OBLIGATION to take legal possession of somebody's property temporarily until a debt that person owes is paid, a dispute is settled, or a court order is obeyed **3.** LAW TAKE ENEMY'S PROPERTY to demand or seize the property of an enemy [14C. Via French < late Latin *sequestrare* 'place in safe keeping' < *sequester* 'follower, trustee'] —**sequestrable** *adj*

sequestrant /si kwéstrənt/ *n* a chemical that in effect removes ions from a solution. Use: soil treatment to correct mineral deficiencies.

sequestrate /seékwə strayt, si kwé-/ (**-trates, -trating, -trated**) *vt* **1.** TAKE SOMEBODY'S PROPERTY TEMPORARILY to take legal possession of somebody's property temporarily until a debt that person owes is paid, a dispute is settled, or a court order obeyed **2.** *Scotland* DECLARE SOMEBODY BANKRUPT in Scottish law, to declare somebody bankrupt **3.** *Scotland* TAKE BANKRUPT'S PROPERTY in Scottish law, to hand over the property of a bankrupt to a trustee so that it can be used to pay off the bankrupt's debts [15C. < late Latin *sequestrat-*, past participle of *sequestrare* (see SEQUESTER)] —**sequestrator** /seékwi straytər/ *n*

sequestration /seékwe stráysh'n, sék-/ *n* **1.** CONFISCATING OR BEING CONFISCATED the act or process of legally confiscating somebody's property temporarily until a debt that person owes is paid, a dispute is settled, or a court order obeyed **2.** LAW SEIZING OR BEING SEIZED the seizing of an enemy's property, or the fact or process of being seized **3.** GOING INTO OR BEING IN ISOLATION the act of going into or putting somebody in an isolated place, away from people or everyday pressures, or the fact of being in such a place (*formal*) **4.** CHEM ION-BINDING PROCESS the chemical process of binding an ion, especially a metallic ion, in a coordination complex

sequestrum /si kwéstrəm/ (*plural* **-tra** /-trə/) *n* a fragment of dead tissue, usually bone, that separates from surrounding living tissue [Mid-19C. < medieval Latin *sequestrum* 'sequestration' < late Latin *sequester* 'follower, trustee'] —**sequestral** *adj*

sequin /seékwin/ *n* **1.** a small round flat piece of shiny metal or plastic that is sewn onto clothing as a decoration, usually in large numbers **2.** a gold coin that was used in Venice and Turkey between the 16th and 18th centuries [Late 16C. Via French < Italian *zecchino* < *zecca* 'mint' < Arabic *sikka* 'coin, die for making coins'] —**sequinned** *adj*

sequoia /si kwóy ə/ (*plural same or* **-as**) *n* **1.** a large redwood tree that grows in California. Latin name: *Sequoia sempervirens* or *Sequoiadendron giganteum.* **2.** same as **giant sequoia** [Mid-19C. < modern Latin, after *Sequoya* (1766?–1843), US Cherokee leader]

Sequoia National Park /si kwóy ə-/ park in south-central California, established in 1890. It includes Mount Whitney, and is noted for its giant sequoia trees. Area: 1,629 sq. km/629 sq. mi.

sera BIOL plural of **serum**

serac /sə rák/, **sérac** *n* a ridge, pinnacle, or block of ice in the crevasses or slope of a glacier [Mid-19C. < Swiss French *sérac*, originally 'kind of firm white cheese']

seraglio /sə raáli ō/ (*plural* **-glios**) *n* **1.** ISLAM same as **harem** (senses 1–2) **2.** a Turkish palace, especially the Ottoman sultan's palace at Istanbul [Late 16C. < Italian *serraglio*, alteration of Turkish *saray* 'palace' < Persian *sarāī* 'inn']

serai /sə rí/ *n* **1.** BUILDINGS same as **caravanserai** (sense 1) **2.** HIST same as **seraglio** (sense 2) [Early 17C. < Turkish *saray* (see SERAGLIO)]

serail /sə rí/ *n* BUILDINGS same as **seraglio** [Late 16C. Via French < Italian *serraglio* (see SERAGLIO)]

serape /sə raápi, -pay/, **sarape** *n* a usually brightly coloured woollen blanket worn as a cloak by some men in Mexico and Central and South America [Early 19C. < Mexican Spanish *sarape*]

seraph /sérrəf/ (*plural* **-aphs** or **-aphim** /-əfim/) *n* an angel of the highest rank of nine orders of angels in the traditional Christian hierarchy [Pre-12C. Via late Latin *seraphim* (plural) < Hebrew *šərāpīm*] —**seraphic** /sə ráffik/ *adj* —**seraphically** *adv*

Serb /surb/ *n* a member of a Slavic people living mainly in Serbia, as well as other parts of the Balkan region [Early 19C. < Serbo-Croatian *Srb*]

Serbia /súrbi ə/ larger constituent republic of Serbia and Montenegro, in southeastern Europe. Capital: Belgrade. Population: 9,979,752 (2002). Area: 88,361 sq. km/34,116 sq. mi.

Serbia and Montenegro

Serbia and Montenegro country in the Balkans, southeastern Europe, consisting of Serbia and Montenegro, two of the six republics that made up the former Federal People's Republic of Yugoslavia. Language: Serbian. Currency: Yugoslav dinar, euro. Capital: Belgrade. Population: 10,655,774 (2003). Area: 102,173 sq. km/39,449 sq. mi. Former name **Yugoslavia, Federal Republic of**

Serbian /súrbi ən/ *n* **1.** PEOPLES SOMEBODY FROM SERBIA somebody who comes from Serbia **2.** LANG DIALECT OF SERBO-CROATIAN the Slavic language of Serbia, written in the Roman or Cyrillic alphabet and closely related to Bosnian and Croatian ■ *adj* OF SERBIA relating to Serbia or its language, people, or culture

Serbo-Croatian /súrbō-/, **Serbo-Croat** *n* **1.** the Slavic language spoken by the Serbians and Croatians, now considered as Bosnian, Croatian, and Serbian **2.** somebody whose native language is Serbo-Croatian —**Serbo-Croatian** *adj*

sere[1] /seer/, **sear** *adj* dry and withered (*literary*) [Old English *sēar* 'withered' < Indo-European]

SYNONYMS See ***dry.***

sere[2] /seer/ *n* the series of different communities of plants and animals that occupy a specific site and create a stable system during the process of ecological succession [Early 20C. < Latin *serere* 'join, connect'] —**seral** *adj*

serein /se ráyn, sə ráN/ *n* in the tropics, a very fine rain that falls from a clear sky at dusk [Late 19C. Via French < Latin *serum* 'evening' < *serus* 'late']

serenade /sérrə náyd/ *n* **1.** LOVE SONG a song used to court somebody, traditionally sung by a man in the evening outside a woman's window, or the performance of such a song **2.** INSTRUMENTAL COMPOSITION FOR SMALL ENSEMBLE an instrumental work similar to a sonata, designed for evening outdoor performance by a small ensemble of musicians ■ *vti* (**-nades, -nading, -naded**) PERFORM LOVE SONG to sing or play a serenade for somebody ○ *A mockingbird serenades us every evening.* [Mid-17C. Via French *sérénade* < Italian

a particular player serves ○ *He's lost his serve three times in a row.* [12C. Via French *servir* < Latin *servire* < *servus* 'slave'] —**servable** *adj* ◇ **give somebody a serve** *Aus* to give somebody a strong reprimand ◇ **serve somebody right** to be a deserved punishment for doing something wrong ◇ **serve two masters** to attempt to focus on two projects, activities, goals, or responsibilities at the same time, or to try to be loyal to two competing or parallel groups or organizations ○ *A reporter cannot serve two masters—the media and the politicians.*

ORIGIN The Latin word *servire* 'to serve', from which ***serve*** is derived, is also the source of English *deserve, dessert, sergeant,* and *serviette* (but not of *conserve, observe, preserve,* and *reserve,* which come from the unrelated Latin *servare* 'to watch, pay attention, keep').

serve up *v* **1.** *vti* to make food ready for serving or present it to people ○ *How do they get away with serving up this muck every day?* ○ *We're just about to serve up.* **2.** *vt* to offer or present something ○ *They're still serving up the same old platitudes.*

server /súrvər/ *n* **1.** SOMEBODY WHO STARTS GAME in racket games, the player who starts a point or game by hitting the ball or shuttlecock across the net to an opponent **2.** FOOD UTENSIL a utensil for serving food **3.** TRAY FOR SERVING SOMETHING a tray for serving food or drinks on **4.** SOMEBODY WHO SERVES somebody, especially a waiter, who serves food to patrons at a meal **5.** CHR ASSISTANT AT MASS OR LITURGY an assistant to a Roman Catholic, Anglican, or Eastern Orthodox priest during Mass or a liturgy **6.** COMPUT same as **file server**

server farm *n* **1.** a group of networked servers that distributes tasks in a way that maximizes the efficiency of the computers and minimizes the risk of losing data **2.** E-COMMERCE same as **web server farm**

~~**servicable**~~ incorrect spelling of **serviceable**

service[1] /súrviss/ *n* **1.** WORK DONE FOR SOMEBODY ELSE work done by somebody for somebody else as a job, duty, punishment, or favour ○ *After 25 years of service to the company, all I got was a watch.* **2.** HELPFUL ACTION an action done to help somebody or as a favour to somebody ○ *Would you do me one small service?* **3.** WORK FOR CUSTOMERS work done for the customers of a shop, restaurant, hotel, or similar establishment, often with regard to whether it pleases them or not ○ *The service in this restaurant is lousy.* ○ *You can never get any service in this place!* **4.** HOUSE SERVANT'S WORK work done as a servant in a private house **5.** USE the use that can be had from a machine or piece of equipment ○ *Treat it carefully, and it'll give you years of good service.* **6.** USE OR OPERATION current use or operation **7.** MECH ENG MAINTENANCE OF MACHINERY the act of cleaning, checking, adjusting, or making minor repairs to a piece of machinery, especially a motor vehicle, to make sure that it works properly ○ *take the car in for a service* **8.** MEETING OF PUBLIC NEED a system or organization that provides people with something that they need, e.g. public transport or a utility ○ *the tourist information service* ○ *a bus service* **9.** GOVERNMENT AGENCY a body of people who carry out work for the public benefit within an organization run by local or national government ○ *the diplomatic service* ○ *the police service* **10.** ONE OF ARMED FORCES one of the branches of the armed forces of a country (*often used in the plural*) **11.** FORM OF PUBLIC WORSHIP a religious ceremony usually involving specific forms for worship and prayer ○ *a memorial service* **12.** RELIG RELIGIOUS RITUAL the prescribed form for a particular act of public worship or religious ceremony ○ *the marriage service* **13.** COLLECTION OF RELIGIOUS MUSICAL SETTINGS a collection of musical settings of parts of the liturgy prescribed for use in the Church of England **14.** SET OF DISHES a set of dishes and cups for use in serving a particular meal ○ *dinner service* **15.** RACKET GAMES same as **serve 16.** SERVING OF LEGAL DOCUMENT TO SOMEBODY the delivery of a legal document such as a writ or summons **17.** NAUT MATERIAL USED TO BIND ROPE something used to bind a rope to prevent it from fraying, e.g. fine wire or cord ■ *npl* **1.** SKILLS AND WORK the work that somebody can do or does by virtue of their job, profession, or training ○ *You seem to need the services of a plumber.* ○ *I'm afraid we've decided to dispense with your services.* **2.** WORK THAT DOES NOT MAKE ANYTHING jobs and businesses that provide something for other people but do not produce tangible goods, e.g. banking and insurance **3.** THINGS PROVIDED BY GOVERNMENT things that are provided by national or local government and paid for by taxation, e.g. education, health care, and roads **4.** FACILITIES FOR TRAVELLERS facilities for travellers available at intervals along a motorway, e.g. shops, cafés, toilets, and a service station ○ *There are no services at the next exit.* ■ *vt* (**-vices, -vicing, -viced**) **1.** PROVIDE SOMETHING FOR COMMUNITY to provide a community or organization with something that it needs ○ *The electric company services all nine counties.* **2.** MECH ENG CLEAN AND ADJUST MACHINERY to clean, check, adjust, and make minor repairs to a piece of machinery in order to make sure that it works properly ○ *It's time to have my car serviced.* **3.** PAY INTEREST ON DEBT to pay interest on a debt **4.** ZOOL MATE WITH FEMALE to copulate with a female (*refers to male animals*) ■ *adj* **1.** PROVIDING SERVICE NOT GOODS relating to jobs or businesses that provide services but do not manufacture goods **2.** FOR MAINTENANCE AND REPAIR providing maintenance and repair for manufactured products ○ *automotive service technicians* **3.** USED BY EMPLOYEES OR FOR DELIVERIES intended for employees or deliveries rather than for members of the public (*often used before a noun*) ○ *a service elevator* [Pre-12C. Via French < Latin *servitium* 'servitude' < *servus* 'slave'] —**servicer** *n* ◇ **press somebody** *or* **something into service** to use something or somebody for an unusual purpose, especially in an emergency situation ○ *At the last minute, she was pressed into service as the organist at her brother's wedding.*

service[2] /súrviss/ *n* TREES same as **service tree** [Mid-16C. Plural of obsolete *serve* < Latin *sorbus* 'service tree']

serviceable /súrvissəb'l/ *adj* **1.** MADE TO WEAR WELL suitable for everyday use and hard wear **2.** WORKING in working condition **3.** EFFECTIVE useful or effective —**serviceableness** *n* —**serviceably** *adv*

service area *n* **1.** a place beside a motorway where there are facilities for travellers such as a shops, cafés, toilets, and a service station **2.** the area over which a radio or television broadcasting station can transmit a satisfactory signal for reception

serviceberry /súrviss berri/ (*plural* **-ries**) *n* **1.** SMALL EDIBLE FRUIT a small round dark blue edible fruit from a small North American tree **2.** N AMERICAN PLANT PRODUCING SERVICEBERRIES a commonly cultivated small tree or bush that produces serviceberries. Flowers: white, in clusters. Native to: North America. Genus: *Amelanchier*. **3.** FRUIT OF SERVICE TREE the dark brown fruit of the service tree, similar to an apple and sometimes used to make cider [< SERVICE[2]]

service book *n* a book containing the correct forms of worship authorized for use in a church

service break *n* in racket games, a game won by a player when an opponent was serving

service centre *n* **1.** a garage that sells parts and carries out repairs on motor vehicles **2.** a retail store that provides repairs and parts for the items it sells

service charge *n* **1.** MONEY ADDED TO BILL FOR SERVICE a sum of money, usually calculated as a percentage of a customer's bill, added to the bill in a restaurant or hotel to pay the staff for their service **2.** CHARGE FOR CARRYING BALANCE a fee added to the balance of a bill when it is paid in instalments rather than being paid in one lump sum **3.** MONEY CHARGED FOR PERFORMING SERVICE a sum of money charged by a business or bank for handling a transaction

service contract *n* **1.** a contract between a company and a senior employee such as a director or senior executive **2.** a contract with a company or manufacturer to maintain equipment in working order at an agreed price over a fixed period

service court *n* in tennis, badminton, and similar games, the marked-out area on the opposite side of the net into which a ball or shuttlecock must be served for play to continue

service dog *n US* a dog that has been specially trained to assist people with disabilities, e.g. by opening doors and retrieving needed objects

service flat *n* a flat in which some domestic services such as cleaning and laundry and sometimes also meals are provided by the management

service industry *n* an industry that provides a service rather than goods, or such industries as a whole

service line *n* in racket games and volleyball, a line on a court that the server must not cross before serving

serviceman /súrvissmən/ (*plural* **-men** /-mən/) *n* **1.** a man serving in the armed forces **2.** *also* **service man** a man whose job is repairing and servicing equipment

service mark *n* a sign or symbol used by people or companies who provide a service to identify themselves and set them apart from other companies

servicemember /súrviss membər/ *n US* a member of the US armed forces [20C.]

service module *n* the section of an Apollo spacecraft in which parts of the propulsion and navigation systems are kept and which is jettisoned when the craft re-enters the Earth's atmosphere

serviceperson /súrviss purss'n/ (*plural* **-people** /-peep'l/ or **-persons**) *n* **1.** somebody serving in the armed forces **2.** *also* **service person** somebody whose job is maintaining and servicing equipment

service provider *n* **1.** a company that provides people and businesses with access to the Internet, usually charging a monthly fee **2.** a company that provides a specific service or services, e.g. health or life insurance

service road *n* a minor road that runs alongside a main road, giving access to houses, shops, offices, and other businesses

service station *n* a place where petrol, oil, and other requirements for motor vehicles can be bought, and that usually also provides other facilities for motorists such as toilets and a shop

service tree *n* tree that has leaves consisting of numerous toothed leaflets and produces fruits (**serviceberries**) sometimes used for cider-making. Native to: central and southern Europe. Latin name: *Sorbus domestica*.

servicewoman /súrviss wŏŏmən/ (*plural* **-women** /-wimin/) *n* **1.** a woman serving in the armed forces **2.** *also* **service woman** a woman whose job is repairing and servicing equipment

serviette /súrvi étt/ *n* HOUSEHOLD same as **napkin** (sense 1) [15C. < French < *servir* (see SERVE)]

servile /súr vīl/ *adj* **1.** TOO OBEDIENT too willing to agree with somebody or to do anything, however demeaning, that somebody wants **2.** MENIAL relating to work that is considered menial or degrading ○ *servile tasks* **3.** RELATING TO SLAVERY relating to slaves or the condition of slavery [14C. < Latin *servilis* < *servus* 'slave'] —**servilely** *adv* —**servileness** *n* —**servility** /sur víllәti/ *n*

serving /súrving/ *n* a portion of food, or of a particular type of food, served to one person

serving dish *n* a large dish used to serve food at table, especially vegetables or rice

serving hatch *n* an opening in the wall between a kitchen and a dining area, through which food and dishes may be passed. N Am term **pass-through**

serving spoon *n* a large spoon used to serve food, especially liquids such as gravy, and vegetables

servitor /súrvitər/ *n* a servant or attendant (*archaic*) [14C. Via French < late Latin < Latin *servire* (see SERVE)]

servitude /súrvi tyood/ *n* **1.** STATE OF SLAVERY the state of being a slave **2.** SUBJECTION the state of being ruled or dominated by somebody or something **3.** WORK IMPOSED AS PUNISHMENT work imposed as a punishment for a crime **4.** LAW RESTRICTION OR OBLIGATION ON PROPERTY a restriction or obligation attached to a property that entitles somebody other than the owner to a specific use of it such as the right to cross it [15C. Via French < Latin *servitudo* < *servus* 'slave']

servo[1] /súrvō/ *adj* relating to, forming part of, or activated by a servomechanism ■ *n* (*plural* **-vos**) MECH ENG **1.** same as **servomechanism 2.** same as **servomotor** [Late 19C. Shortening of French *servo-moteur* 'auxiliary motor' < Latin *servus* 'slave']

servo[2] /súrvō/ (*plural* **-vos**) *n Aus* TRANSP same as **service station** (*informal*) [Late 20C. Shortening]

servomechanism /súrvō mekənizəm/ *n* a closed-circuit device in which a small input power controls a much larger power, as in a radio telescope —**servomechanical** /súrvō mi kánnik'l/ *adj*

servomotor /súrvō mōtər/ *n* a motor that supplies the initial power in a servomechanism

sesame

sesame /séssəmi/ (*plural* **-mes** or *same*) *n* **1.** the small oval white seeds of the sesame plant. Use: cooking, oil extraction. **2.** an annual plant cultivated for its oil-rich seeds. Native to: tropical and subtropical Asia. Latin name: *Sesamum indicum.* [15C. Via Latin < Greek *sēsamon*]

sesame oil *n* a strongly flavoured oil from sesame seeds, widely used in East and Southeast Asian cooking

sesamoid /séssə moyd/ *n* a small, roughly spherical bone lying within a tendon to assist in its mechanical action or to bear pressure ■ *adj* relating to or being various small bones or cartilages in a tendon or joint such as the knee [Late 17C. < SESAME]

Sesotho /si sóotoo/ *n* the dialect of Sotho spoken by the Basotho people in Lesotho [Mid-19C. < Sesotho] —**Sesotho** *adj*

sesqui- *prefix* one and a half ○ *sesquicentennial* [< Latin < *semis* 'half' + *-que* 'and']

sesquicentennial /séskwi sen ténni əl/, **sesquicentenary** /séskwi sen teénəri, -ténnəri/ *n* (*plural* **-als**; *plural* **-ies**) **1. 150TH ANNIVERSARY** a 150th anniversary or the celebration of one **2. 150 YEARS** a period of 150 years ■ *adj* **OCCURRING EVERY 150 YEARS** relating to or happening after a period of 150 years —**sesquicentennially** *adv*

sesquipedalian /séskwi pi dáyli ən/, **sesquipedal** /se skwíppid'l/ (*literary*) *adj* **1. USING LONG WORDS** characterized by the use of long words **2. LONG** containing a great many letters or syllables ■ *n* **LONG WORD** a word with many letters or syllables [Early 17C. < Latin *sesquipedalis* 'measuring one and one-half feet' < *sesqui-* (see SESQUI-) + *ped-* 'foot'] —**sesquipedalianism** *n*

sess. *abbr* session

sessile /séssīl/ *adj* **1.** describes a leaf or flower that has no stalk but is attached directly to the stem **2.** describes an animal that is permanently attached to something rather than free-moving, e.g. a barnacle [Early 18C. < Latin *sessilis* 'lying close to the ground' < *sess-*, past participle of *sedere* 'sit'] —**sessility** /sə sílləti/ *n*

sessile oak *n* TREES same as **durmast oak**

session /sésh'n/ *n* **1. MEETING** a meeting of an official body, especially a court or legislature **2. PERIOD OF MEETING** a period during which an official body meets or does business **3. SERIES OF MEETINGS** a series of meetings of an official body **4. TEACHING PERIOD** the time of year or the time of day during which a school or university holds classes **5. PERIOD OF DOING SOMETHING** a period of time during which people are involved in an activity together **6. PERIOD OF PLAYING MUSIC** a period during which musicians play together, especially in a recording studio **7. GOVERNING BODY OF PRESBYTERIAN CONGREGATION** the governing body of a Presbyterian congregation, consisting of the minister and elders ■ **sessions** *npl* LAW **SITTINGS OF JUSTICE OF PEACE** the sittings of a justice of the peace in court ■ *adj* **1. RELATING TO FREELANCE MUSICIAN** relating to or being a musician paid to play or sing on recordings in a studio but not a permanent member of a band **2. RELATING TO FREELANCE MUSIC** relating to playing or singing done by a session musician [14C. Via French < Latin *session-* 'a sitting' < *sess-* (see SESSILE)] —**sessional** *adj*

ORIGIN The Latin word *sedere* 'to sit', from which ***session*** is derived, is also the source of English *assess, assiduous, assize, hostage, insidious, obsess, reside, seance, sedentary, sediment, sessile, size*[1], *subsidy,* and *supersede.*

sesterce /séstursś/, **sestertius** /se stúrti əss, -stúrshəss/ (*plural* **-tii** /-ti ī, -hi ī/) *n* an ancient Roman coin, originally silver but later bronze, worth a quarter of a denarius [Late 16C. < Latin *sestertius* 'two and one-half times as great' < *semis* 'half' + *tertius* 'third']

sestertium /se stúrti əm, -stúrshəm/ (*plural* **-tia** /-ti ə, -shə/) *n* an ancient Roman unit of currency equal to 1,000 sesterces [Mid-16C. < Latin *(mille) sestertium* '(a thousand) sesterces' (see SESTERCE)]

sestet /se stét/ *n* a stanza or poem of six lines, especially the last six lines of a Petrarchan sonnet [Early 19C. < Italian *sestetto* < *sesto* 'sixth' < Latin *sextus*]

sestina /se steénə/ *n* a poem of six six-line stanzas and a three-line envoy, with the last words of the first six lines repeated, in different order, at the ends of the other lines [Mid-19C. < Italian < *sesto* (see SESTET)]

set[1] /set/ *v* (**sets, setting, set**) **1.** *vt* **PLACE SOMETHING** to put somebody or something somewhere ○ *Set the books on the table.* **2.** *vt* **CAUSE SOMEBODY TO BE SOMETHING** to put somebody or something into a particular condition ○ *finally set the hostages free* **3.** *vt* **INITIATE ACTION OR PROCESS** to cause something or somebody to begin doing something, or begin to do something ○ *set my heart thumping* ○ *set to work* **4.** *vt* **APPLY FIRE** to apply something to an object or material that will cause it to burn ○ *set fire to the house* **5.** *vt* **CONCENTRATE MIND** to focus your mind on a goal or task ○ *Once he sets his mind to it, he can usually come up with a solution.* **6.** *vti* **SOLIDIFY** to become, or cause something to become, solid or hard ○ *Let the concrete set.* **7.** *vi* **BECOME PERMANENT** to become permanent or fast (*refers to dyes or colours*) **8.** *vt* **ARRANGE SOMETHING FOR USE** to arrange, place, or prepare something to be used ○ *set a trap* ○ *set the table* **9.** *vt* **ADJUST MEASURING DEVICE** to adjust a mechanical or electronic device such as a clock to a desired time, level, or position ○ *set the counter at zero* **10.** *vt* **DECIDE ON SOMETHING** to reach a decision about something such as a price or time ○ *We've set a date for the wedding.* **11.** *vt* **IMPOSE SOMETHING** to establish or impose something that determines the scope or direction of future action ○ *set a limit to government spending* ○ *set a course for home* **12.** *vt* **ESTABLISH EXAMPLE OR STANDARD** to establish something that others have to emulate, follow, or try to beat ○ *tried to set an example for her younger siblings* ○ *set a precedent* **13.** *vt* **CONSIDER AS HAVING VALUE** to consider something as having a particular value ○ *set a high value on his own work* **14.** *vt* **ASSIGN SOMETHING FOR STUDY** to make something, usually a particular book or subject, an obligatory object of study for a course or examination ○ *Which Shakespeare play has been set for A level this year?* **15.** *vt* **INSTRUCT SOMEBODY TO DO SOMETHING** to assign a task to somebody or give somebody instructions to do something ○ *set homework for the children* ○ *set two men to guard the gate* **16.** *vt* **ARRANGE HAIR** to arrange hair by using styling products or clips **17.** *vt* **PUT BROKEN BONE IN POSITION** to put a broken bone back in its normal position so it can heal properly **18.** *vi* **HEAL** to heal up and become solid after being broken (*refers to bones*) **19.** *vt* **PROVIDE MUSIC FOR SOMETHING** to provide the music that a particular text is to be sung to ○ *set his words to music* **20.** *vt* **PORTRAY IN PARTICULAR SETTING** to portray something as happening in a particular place or time period (*usually passive*) ○ *The play is set in the 19th century.* **21.** *vt* **PUT SCENERY ON STAGE** to place scenery on a stage **22.** *vt* **ARRANGE TYPE** to arrange type for printing **23.** *vt* **PUT GEM IN SETTING** to put a gem or stone in a metal setting **24.** *vt* **ADORN** to adorn something with decorations ○ *set a gown with sequins* **25.** *vti* **POSITION SAIL** to rig a sail to catch the wind, or be rigged in this way **26.** *vi* **GO BELOW HORIZON** to move below the horizon ○ *watched the sun set* **27.** *vi* **COME TO GRADUAL END** to come to a gradual end and pass into eclipse or obscurity (*literary*) ○ *a glorious writing career that has at last begun to set* **28.** *vi* **FIT WELL OR POORLY** to fit in a particular way (*refers to clothes*) ○ *The skirt sets well.* **29.** *vi* SPORTS **GET READY TO START RACE** to get into a position ready to start a race ○ *Ready, get set, go!* **30.** *vt* **LET DOUGH RISE** to place dough aside to allow it to rise **31.** *vt* **SHARPEN SOMETHING** to sharpen a blade **32.** *vt* **DISPLACE TEETH ON SAW** to bend the teeth of a saw alternately to either side of the blade **33.** *vt* **DRIVE NAIL HEAD BELOW SURFACE** to drive the head of a nail below the surface **34.** *vti* PLANTS **PRODUCE FRUIT OR SEEDS** to produce fruit or seeds after being pollinated, or be produced in this way **35.** *vt* AGRIC, GARDENING **PLANT** to plant something **36.** *vti* AGRIC **SIT OR MAKE SIT ON EGGS** to sit on eggs, or put a hen to sit on eggs, to keep them warm **37.** *vti* FIELD SPORTS **INDICATE GAME** to indicate the presence of game by turning towards it and holding that position (*refers to hunting dogs*) **38.** *vt* **BEAT IN BRIDGE** in bridge, to prevent an opponent meeting the contract **39.** *vi* METALL **BECOME BENT** to become bent from strain **40.** *vt regional* **SIT SOMEBODY** to cause somebody to sit somewhere ○ *Set yourself here.* ■ *n* **1. CONDITION OF SOLIDITY** the condition of being solid **2. POSTURE** the particular position, angle, or posture of a part of the body, often considered suggestive of a character trait or emotion ○ *the set of his shoulders* **3. FIT OF CLOTHES** the way something hangs when worn **4. DIRECTION OF WIND OR MOVING WATER** the direction of a wind, tide, or current **5. ARRANGEMENT OF SAILS** the way the sails and other rigging are arranged on a sailing boat **6. THEATRICAL SCENERY** an arrangement of scenery for a scene in a play or film **7. PLACE WHERE SCENE IS FILMED** the place or area where the actors perform when a scene in a film is shot **8. HAIR-STYLING TECHNIQUE** a method of styling hair that involves giving it a particular shape when wet and then drying it so that it retains that shape **9. PREFERENCE** a preference for or increased ability in a particular activity **10. BIAS INFLUENCING REACTION TO STIMULUS** the psychological state that causes a living being to react to a stimulus in a particular way **11.** PRINTING **WIDTH OF PIECE OF TYPE** the width of a piece of type **12.** PRINTING **WIDTH OF LINE OF TYPE** the width of a column or a page of type **13.** AGRIC, GARDENING **SEEDLING READY FOR PLANTING** a plant that is ready to be planted, e.g. a seedling **14.** AGRIC **CLUTCH OF EGGS** the number of eggs that a hen lays at one time **15.** METALL **DISTORTION UNDER STRESS** a distortion or bending that occurs in metal as a result of stress **16.** INDUST, ZOOL, TEXTILES same as **sett** ■ *adj* **1. ESTABLISHED** previously established, arranged, or decided upon ○ *There's no set way of doing this.* ○ *a set menu* **2. ACCORDING TO STEREOTYPE** conforming to an established, often conventional formula ○ *rattled off a set speech* **3. ASSIGNED TO STUDY** assigned for students to study ○ *a set text* **4. READY** prepared for somebody or something, or to do something ○ *We're all set to go.* **5. DETERMINED** determined to do something ○ *We're set on the idea and won't consider changing.* [Old English *settan* 'cause to sit' < Germanic, 'sit'] ◇ **set in your ways** unwilling to change your habitual ways of doing things ○ *Living alone he's become more set in his ways.*

set about *vt* **1.** to begin doing something **2.** to attack somebody

set against *vt* **1.** to consider something in relation to something else, or consider something as being offset by something else ○ *Set against her previous good work, this is only a minor lapse.* **2.** to make people or groups start to fight with or be hostile to people who used to be their friends ○ *The civil war set brother against brother and father against son.*

set apart *vt* **1.** to keep something for a specific use or purpose **2.** to make somebody conspicuous or different ○ *Her knowledge sets her apart.*

set aside *vt* **1. RESERVE SOMETHING** to keep something, especially time or money, for a specific purpose **2. PUT SOMETHING TO ONE SIDE** to put something to one side **3. REJECT PREVIOUS DECISION** to discard, reject, or annul a previous decision or judgment

set back *vt* **1.** to block or delay the progress of something or somebody **2.** to cost somebody a lot of money (*informal*)

set down *vt* **1. LAY SOMETHING ON HORIZONTAL SURFACE** to put something down on a surface **2. WRITE SOMETHING DOWN** to write something down, especially on paper **3. ASSESS SOMEBODY OR SOMETHING** to judge somebody or something as being a particular thing ○ *set the whole thing down as a failure* ○ *set her down as very ambitious* **4. ATTRIBUTE SOMETHING TO CAUSE** to attribute an event or quality to a cause ○ *set his mistake down to inexperience* **5. LET SOMEBODY GET OFF** to allow a passenger in a vehicle to get off at a specific place

6. **SCOLD SOMEBODY** to snub or rebuke somebody 7. **LAND AIRCRAFT** to land an aircraft or a space shuttle

set forth *v* 1. *vt* to state or present an argument or a set of figures in speech or writing 2. *vi* to leave on a journey (*literary*)

set in *v* 1. *vi* **BEGIN** to begin and become established ○ *once the winter snows set in* 2. *vt* **ADD ON SOMETHING TO GARMENT** to add a separately made part to a garment 3. *vi* **MOVE SHOREWARDS** to move in a shorewards direction (*refers to winds, tides, or currents*)

set off *v* 1. *vi* **START OUT ON TRIP** to start out on a journey 2. *vt* **MAKE SOMETHING WORK** to make something such as an alarm or a firework operate or explode 3. *vt* **MAKE SOMEBODY START DOING SOMETHING** to make somebody start doing something such as laughing, crying, or complaining ○ *When she started giggling, it set us all off too.* 4. *vt* **START SOMETHING** to make something start happening ○ *set off a chain of events that eventually led to war* 5. *vt* **MAKE SOMETHING LOOK ATTRACTIVE** to provide a contrast to something in a way that makes it look more attractive ○ *The new frame really sets off the painting.* 6. *vt* ACCT **COUNTERBALANCE CREDIT** to counterbalance a credit in the accounts of one person or organization against a debit in those of another

set on *vt* 1. to attack somebody, or encourage a person or animal to attack somebody or something 2. to encourage somebody to do something

set out *v* 1. *vi* **BEGIN JOURNEY** to begin something, especially a journey ○ *The caravan set out across the desert.* 2. *vi* **PLAN TO DO SOMETHING** to plan or intend to do something, or take action to realize a deliberate plan or intention to do something ○ *set out to ruin the performance* 3. *vt* **DISPLAY SOMETHING** to arrange or display something ○ *merchants setting out their wares* 4. *vt* **LAY SOMETHING OUT IN PLAN** to lay out something in a planned way ○ *The gardens are beautifully set out.* 5. *vt* **PRESENT SOMETHING FULLY** to present or explain something, especially in a well-planned way ○ *a book that clearly sets out the author's philosophy*

set to *vi* 1. to start doing something, especially work 2. to start fighting

set up *v* 1. *vt* **ERECT SOMETHING** to erect something or put something in an upright or usable position ○ *set up road blocks* 2. *vti* **PREPARE EQUIPMENT FOR EVENT** to prepare the equipment needed for an event ○ *The band is setting up on stage.* 3. *vt* **ESTABLISH SOMETHING** to establish something, or bring something into being ○ *The charity set up a fund for the refugees.* 4. *vt* **PLAN SOMETHING** to make necessary arrangements for something such as a meeting or conference ○ *Please set up a meeting for the five of us early next week.* 5. *vti* **START BUSINESS** to start a business, or give somebody everything needed to start a business ○ *His family set him up in business.* 6. *vt* **PRODUCE LOUD SOUND** to start making a loud noise or giving voice to something ○ *The spectators set up a howl of protest.* 7. *vt* **PRESENT AS MODEL** to give prominence to something or somebody and present it, him, or her as an example to a group ○ *They've set him up as a model for the younger generation.* 8. *vti* **CLAIM TO BE EXPERT** to claim to be something, or claim somebody to be something, especially an expert or authority in a particular area ○ *She set herself up as an expert on childcare.* 9. *vt* **MAKE HEALTHY** to make somebody feel healthy or invigorated, especially after having been ill 10. *vt* **CAUSE SOMEBODY TO BE BLAMED** to cause somebody to be caught and blamed for something (*informal*) ○ *claims he was set up* 11. *vt* **GIVE DRINKS** to buy or provide an alcoholic drink for somebody (*informal*) ○ *asked the barman to set up another two beers*

set upon *vt* to attack somebody violently

set[2] /set/ *n* 1. **COLLECTION CONSIDERED AS UNIT** a collection of people or things considered together and usually having something in common 2. **SOCIAL GROUP** a group of people who form a social group ○ *They were the first in our set to have kids.* 3. **DEVICE RECEIVING SIGNALS** a device that receives radio or television signals 4. **PART OF TENNIS MATCH** a part of a tennis match that is won when one player or couple wins a minimum of six games 5. **SONGS PLAYED IN ONE SESSION** a number of songs or acts that an entertainer or band performs on a single occasion 6. **NUMBER OF REPETITIONS OF EXERCISE** a number of repetitions of an exercise done at one time 7. **COLLECTION OF ELEMENTS** a collection of elements in mathematics or logic, e.g. numbers or terms 8. **COUPLES REQUIRED FOR DANCE** a number of couples required for a dance ○ *We need another couple to complete our set.* ■ *vi* (**sets, setting, set**) **DANCE FACING PARTNER** to perform a series of moves while facing another dancer [14C. Via Old French *sette* < Latin *secta* (see SECT)]

SET *abbr* E-COMMERCE Secure Electronic Transaction

seta /séetə/ (*plural* **-tae** /-tee/) *n* a slender, usually rigid bristle or hair [Late 18C. < Latin, 'bristle'] —**setal** *adj*

setaceous /si táyshəss/ *adj* 1. having bristles or made up of bristles 2. having the appearance or feel of bristles (*formal*) [Mid-17C. < modern Latin *setaceus* < Latin *seta* 'bristle']

set-aside *n* a European Union scheme whereby farmers are paid not to produce crops on some areas of land as a way of reducing surpluses or controlling prices

set back *n* in American football, an offensive back who takes up position behind the quarterback

setback /sét bak/ *n* 1. something that reverses or delays the progress of somebody or something 2. a place in the wall of a building where there is a shelf or recess

se tenant /sə tə naaN/ *adj* describes two stamps that are joined together but have different values or designs ■ *n* a pair of stamps that are joined together but have different values or designs [Early 20C. < French, 'holding together']

seth /seth/ *n S Asia* a rich man or a man who finances a legal or illegal enterprise

SETI /sétti/ *n* a scientific attempt to detect or communicate with intelligent beings from beyond Earth, especially using radio signals. Full form **search for extraterrestrial intelligence**

setiferous /sə tíffərəss/, **setigerous** /sə tíjjərəss/ *adj* describes an organism that has bristles or projections that resemble bristles [Early 19C. < SETA]

set-in *adj* describes a part of a garment that is made separately and stitched in

setline /sét līn/ *n* a fishing line suspended over a stream or between buoys with shorter hooked and baited lines hanging down from it into the water

set-off *n* 1. **COUNTERBALANCE TO SOMETHING ELSE** something that compensates for something else 2. **FEATURE IMPROVING APPEARANCE** a quality or feature that contrasts with something else and in that way improves its appearance 3. ARCHIT same as **setback** (sense 2) 4. PRINTING same as **offset** *n* (sense 4) 5. ACCT **COUNTERBALANCING CLAIM** a claim brought by a debtor against a creditor that counterbalances the debt owed

Seton /séet'n/, **Ernest Thompson** (1860–1946) British-born US writer and illustrator. He was one of the founders of the Boy Scouts of America (1910). He is known for his stories about animals for young people such as *Wild Animals I Have Known* (1898). Born **Seton-Thompson, Ernest**

setose /séetōss/ *adj* covered with bristles [Mid-17C. < Latin *setosus* < *seta* 'bristle']

set phrase *n* a phrase which does not vary and whose meaning is different from the literal combination of its parts, e.g. 'the apple of somebody's eye' or 'make waves'

set piece *n* 1. **PLANNED ACTION** a carefully planned and rehearsed performance or action, especially a military or diplomatic operation 2. **FORMAL WORK OF ART** a work of art with a formal theme, undertaken to show the artist's skill 3. **PLANNED MANOEUVRE** a planned manoeuvre used by a team in a game, e.g. the way a soccer team takes a corner or free kick (*hyphenated when used before a noun*) 4. **PIECE OF SCENERY** a piece of stage scenery that can stand unsupported 5. **FIXED FIREWORKS IN DISPLAY** a fixed arrangement of fireworks in a display

set point *n* 1. a situation in a tennis match when a player can win a set by winning the next point, or the point he or she has to win 2. the natural weight that somebody's body will assume if provided with a balanced diet

setscrew /sét skroo/ *n* a screw that fixes one part of a mechanism to another and prevents it moving relative to the part to which it is fixed

set square *n* a flat metal or plastic instrument in the shape of a right-angled triangle, used in technical drawing. N Am term **triangle**

Setswana /set swaanə/ *n* the Bantu language of the Tswana people of southern Africa, belonging to the Sotho group. Native speakers: 4 million. [Early 19C. < Setswana] —**Setswana** *adj*

sett /set/ *n* 1. **PAVING STONE** a rectangular stone paving block 2. **BADGER'S BURROW** the burrow of a badger 3. **TARTAN PATTERN** the precise pattern of squares and stripes in a tartan, including the colours and numbers of threads 4. **SQUARE OF TARTAN** an individual square in a tartan pattern [Variant of SET[1]]

settee /se tée, sə-/ *n* 1. a comfortable seat for two or more people, with a cushioned back and arms 2. *US* a long wooden bench with a back [Early 18C. Origin ?]

setter /séttər/ *n* 1. a long-haired gun dog of any of several breeds that is trained to crouch in a set position when it finds game 2. somebody or something that sets something

set theory *n* 1. the branch of mathematics that deals with the properties and relationships of sets 2. the system of axioms for sets

setting /sétting/ *n* 1. **SURROUNDINGS** the surroundings or environment in which something exists or takes place ○ *a lovely setting for the wedding* 2. **PERIOD OR PLACE OF STORY** the period in time or the place in which the events of a story are said to occur 3. **SET FOR PERFORMANCE** the set, including props and scenery, where actors perform for a film or play 4. **MUSIC FOR POEM** the music composed for a text such as a poem or hymn 5. **SURROUNDINGS OF JEWEL** the metal fixture into which a jewel is fixed 6. **OPERATIONAL LEVEL OF DEVICE** something, often represented by a mark on a dial or scale, that determines how a machine will operate, e.g. at what temperature or speed ○ *Put the stove on its highest setting.* 7. **CUTLERY** the cutlery, napkin, table mat, and any other items placed on a table to be used by one person during a meal 8. **CLUTCH OF EGGS** a batch of eggs in a bird's nest, especially a hen's

setting circle *n* a scale on the mounting of an equatorial telescope, used to show right ascension or declination

settle /sétt'l/ *v* (**-tles, -tling, -tled**) 1. *vti* **DECIDE ON SOMETHING** to come to a decision or agreement about something, usually so that further arrangements can be made ○ *That's settled then.* ○ *Can we settle on a date for the meeting first?* 2. *vti* **SOLVE** to solve a problem or end a dispute 3. *vti* **END LEGAL DISPUTE** to end a legal dispute by mutual agreement out of court 4. *vti* **PAY WHAT IS OWED** to pay a bill, debt, or claim ○ *She settled the lunch bill and left the restaurant.* ○ *Our client settled up with us yesterday.* 5. *vt* **PUT DETAILS IN ORDER** to put all the details of a piece of business in order or into a desired arrangement ○ *settle your affairs* 6. *vt* LAW **ASSIGN PROPERTY** to give something, especially property or money, to somebody legally and formally ○ *settled her with a substantial inheritance* 7. *vti* **MAKE OR BECOME RESIDENT** to become a resident of a place, or cause somebody to become a resident of a place ○ *Her family settled in Minnesota in the 1890s.* 8. *vt* **COLONIZE PLACE** to populate an area with permanent residents 9. *vti* **ESTABLISH OR BECOME ESTABLISHED** to establish somebody in a place, occupation, or way of life, or become established in this way 10. *vti* **MAKE SOMEBODY COMFORTABLE** to make somebody feel comfortable in a particular position, or get yourself into a position where you feel comfortable ○ *Father settled back in his chair and sighed.* 11. *vti* **MAKE OR BECOME CALM** to become calm, quiet, or stable, or cause somebody or something to become calm, quiet, or stable 12. *vt* **PUT SOMETHING IN PLACE** to put something in a place firmly or permanently 13. *vi* **STOP MOVING** to stop moving and come to rest somewhere 14. *vi* **MOVE DOWNWARDS** to move downwards and spread over something ○ *A blanket of mist settled over the field.* 15. *vi* **SUBSIDE** to sink slowly to a lower level ○ *Cracks sometimes appear in a new building as the foundations settle.* 16. *vti* **STOP FLOATING** to stop floating and sink to the bottom or the ground, or cause something to do so ○ *waited for the dust to settle before opening their eyes* 17. *vti* **MAKE OR BECOME CLEAR** to cause a cloudy liquid to become clear after a sediment has sunk to the bottom, or become clear in this way 18. *vti* **STOP**

SOMEBODY CAUSING TROUBLE to deal with somebody who is causing trouble, or end an outstanding issue or grievance (*dated informal*) ○ *Tell me who did it, I'll settle him soon enough.* **19.** *vti* VET IMPREGNATE OR BE IMPREGNATED to make an animal pregnant ■ *n* LONG WOODEN SEAT WITH HIGH BACK a long wooden seat with a high back, and often with storage space inside the box-shaped seat [Old English *setlan* < *setl* 'chair, bench' < Indo-European, 'sit'] —**settleable** *adj*

settle down *v* **1.** *vti* MAKE OR BECOME CALM to become calm, quiet, or orderly, or cause somebody or something to become calm, quiet, or orderly **2.** *vi* LIVE ORDERLY LIFE to begin a stable, orderly, and often conventional way of life **3.** *vi* DO SOMETHING DILIGENTLY to begin doing something in a diligent and orderly way ○ *settled down to her morning's work*

settle for *vt* to accept or agree to something that is not ideal or exactly what was wanted

settle in *v* **1.** *vti* to adapt to a new environment, or cause somebody to adapt to a new environment ○ *settling in at a new school* **2.** *vi* to get comfortable in a place because the intention is to stay there for a long time ○ *decided to settle in for the night*

settlement /sétt'lmənt/ *n* **1.** ACT OR STATE OF SETTLING an act of settling, or the state of being settled **2.** AGREEMENT an agreement reached after discussion or negotiation **3.** AGREEMENT REACHED OUT OF COURT an agreement reached without completing legal proceedings **4.** PAYMENT the payment of a bill, debt, or claim **5.** ACT OF POPULATING the act of populating a place with permanent residents or becoming a permanent resident in a place **6.** COLONY a place that has recently been populated with permanent residents **7.** SMALL COMMUNITY a small group of dwellings or a small community **8.** CONSTR SUBSIDENCE subsidence in a building **9.** LAW SETTLING OF PROPERTY ON SOMEBODY a conveyance of property to somebody or to the trustees for somebody **10.** LAW CONVEYANCE DOCUMENT a document recording a conveyance of property

settler /séttlər/ *n* a new resident of a place, especially a place that is unpopulated or populated by people of a different race or civilization

settlings /séttlings/ *npl* solid material that has sunk to the bottom of a liquid

settlor /séttlər/ *n* somebody who creates a trust or settlement

set-to (*plural* **set-tos**) *n* a brief and hot-tempered argument or fight (*informal*)

set-top box *n* a device used with a traditional television set to enable the reception and decoding of satellite, cable, or digital signals

Setubal /se tōob'l/, **Setúbal** city and port in western Portugal, situated 32 km/20 mi. southeast of Lisbon. Population: 104,270 (1995).

setup /sét up/ *n* **1.** ORGANIZATION OF SOMETHING the way that something is organized or arranged **2.** SET OF PREPARED OBJECTS FOR TASK a set of the tools or apparatus required to perform a task, properly assembled and prepared for its performance **3.** POSITION OF CAMERA FOR SCENE the position of a camera at the beginning of a film scene **4.** DISHONEST PLAN OR TRICK something that is planned to bring about a desired result dishonestly (*informal*) **5.** *US* TABLE SETTING a table setting for a single person

set width *n* PRINTING same as **set**[1] *n* (senses 11–12)

Georges Seurat: portrait drawing (1890?) by Maximilien Luce

Seurat /súr aa, sör a/, **Georges** (1859–91) French painter. He developed the theory and practice of pointillism, seen in works such as *A Sunday Afternoon on the Island of La Grande Jatte* 1884–86.

Seuss /syooss/, **Dr** (1904–91) US writer and illustrator. His children's books, replete with fanciful word play and illustrated with his own drawings, include *Horton Hatches the Egg* (1940) and *The Cat in the Hat* (1957). Pseudonym of **Geisel, Theodor Seuss**

Sevan, Lake /se vaán/ largest lake in Armenia, in the north of the country, in the Caucasus Mountains. It is drained by the River Razdau. Area: 1,397 sq. km/540 sq. mi.

Sevastopol another spelling of **Sebastopol**

seven /sévv'n/ *n* **1.** 7 the number 7 **2.** SOMETHING WITH VALUE OF 7 something in a numbered series, e.g. a playing card, with a value of 7 ○ *the seven of clubs* ○ *to play the seven* **3.** GROUP OF 7 a group of seven objects or people [Old English *seofon* < Indo-European] —**seven** *adj, pron*

seven deadly sins *npl* CHR same as **deadly sins**

sevenfold /sévv'n fōld/ *adj* **1.** BEING SEVEN TIMES AS MUCH relating to something that is seven times as much as something else **2.** CONSISTING OF SEVEN PARTS relating to something that is made up of seven parts ■ *adv* BY SEVEN TIMES by seven times as much or as many

Seven Hills of Rome the Capitoline, Quirinal, Viminal, Esquiline, Caelian, Aventine, and Palatine hills surrounding the centre of ancient Rome

sevens /sévv'nz/ *n* a fast and open form of rugby played by teams of seven players (*takes a singular verb*)

seven seas *npl* all the oceans of the world. They are the North and South Atlantic, North and South Pacific, Arctic, Antarctic, and Indian oceans.

Seven Sisters *n* ASTRON, MYTHOL same as **Pleiades**

seventeen /sévv'n teén/ *n* **1.** the number 17 **2.** a group of 17 objects or people [Old English *seofontīene* < *seofon* 'seven' + *-tīene* 'ten more than'] —**seventeen** *adj, pron*

seventeenth /sévv'n teénth/ *n* one of 17 equal parts of something —**seventeenth** *adj, adv*

seventeen-year locust *n* a cicada that spends most of its 17 years of life as an underground nymph, living as a winged adult for only a few weeks. Native to: eastern North America. Latin name: *Magicicada septendec.*

seventh /sévv'nth/ *n* **1.** ONE OF 7 PARTS OF SOMETHING one of seven equal parts of something **2.** INTERVAL OF SEVEN NOTES in a standard musical scale, the interval between one note and another that lies six notes above or below it. In the scale of C major, C and B form a seventh. **3.** NOTE SEVENTH AWAY FROM ANOTHER in a standard musical scale, a note that is a seventh away from another note **4.** MUSIC same as **seventh chord** —**seventh** *adj, adv* —**seventhly** *adv*

Seventh Avenue *n* the US garment industry ○ *Seventh Avenue is showing leopard prints this year.* [After a street in Manhattan where garments are designed, manufactured, shown, and sold wholesale]

seventh chord *n* a chord with a seventh note above the base note

Seventh-Day Adventist *n* a member of a Protestant denomination that believes in the imminent Second Coming of Jesus Christ and observes Saturday as the Sabbath

seventh heaven *n* **1.** a state of extreme happiness (*informal*) **2.** in Islamic and Talmudic belief, the highest of the seven heavens

seventieth /sévv'nti əth/ *n* one of 70 equal parts of something —**seventieth** *adj, adv*

seventy /sévv'nti/ *n* (*plural* **-ties**) **1.** 70 the number 70 **2.** GROUP OF 70 a group of 70 objects or people ■ **seventies** *npl* **1.** NUMBERS 70 TO 79 the numbers 70 to 79, particularly as a range of Fahrenheit temperatures ○ *in the low seventies* **2.** YEARS FROM 70 TO 79 the years from 70 to 79 in a century **3.** PERIOD FROM AGE 70 TO 79 the period of somebody's life from the age of 70 to 79 [Old English *hundseofontig* < *hund* (origin ?) + *seofon* 'seven' + *-tig* 'ten'] —**seventy** *adj, pron*

seventy-eight, **78** *n* a gramophone record designed to be played at 78 revolutions per minute, a former standard speed

seventy four *n* either of two large, colourfully striped sea fish related to the sea bream. Native to: southern Africa. Latin name: *Polysteganus undulosus*. [Origin ?]

seven-up *n* a card game in which the first person to reach seven points wins the game

seven-year itch *n* an inclination towards sexual infidelity, popularly believed to begin after seven years of marriage (*informal*)

Seven Years' War *n* a war fought from 1756 to 1763 by Prussia, assisted by British subsidies and Hanoverian troops, against France and Austria

sever /sévvər/ (**-ers, -ering, -ered**) *vti* **1.** CUT THROUGH OR OFF to cut through something or cut something off, or be cut through or off **2.** BREAK OFF RELATIONSHIP to break off a relationship or tie with somebody, or become broken off ○ *severed her relationship with him* **3.** SEPARATE to separate or put things or people apart, or become separated or put apart [14C. Via Anglo-Norman *severer* < Latin *separare* (see SEPARATE)] —**severable** *adj*

several /sévvərəl/ CORE MEANING: a grammatical word indicating a small number ○ (det) *I sent the cheque several days ago.* ○ (pron) *Several of the apples were bruised.*

1. *det, pron* FEW a small number, though more than two or three ○ *several years later* ○ *several of the children* **2.** *adj* VARIOUS various or separate ○ *They all went their several ways.* **3.** *adj* LAW SEPARATE relating to separate persons ○ *joint and several liability* [15C. Via Anglo-Norman < medieval Latin *separalis*, < Latin *separare* (see SEPARATE)]

severalfold /sévvərəl fōld/ *adj* **1.** BEING SEVERAL TIMES AS MUCH amounting to several times as much as something else **2.** CONSISTING OF SEVERAL PARTS relating to something that is made up of several parts ■ *adv* BY SEVERAL TIMES by several times as much or as many

severally /sévvrəli/ *adv* (*formal or literary*) **1.** in a separate or individual way **2.** in turn or respectively

severance /sévvərənss/ *n* **1.** an act of severing, or the state of being severed **2.** *US* BUSINESS same as **redundancy** (sense 1) **3.** BUSINESS same as **redundancy payment 4.** LAW the act or process of splitting into separate parts something that was held jointly, e.g. an estate

severance pay *n* money given as redundancy payment

severe /si veér/ *adj* **1.** HARSH very harsh or strict ○ *a severe punishment* **2.** DANGEROUS extremely bad or dangerous ○ *severe injuries* **3.** STERN looking stern or serious **4.** EXTREMELY UNPLEASANT causing great discomfort by being extreme ○ *a severe frost* **5.** DIFFICULT difficult to do or endure ○ *severe hardship* **6.** EXACTING having standards or other criteria that are difficult to meet ○ *a severe test* **7.** PLAIN plain or austere in style, with little or no decoration ○ *severe clothing* [Mid-16C. < Latin *severus* 'serious'] —**severely** *adv*

Severini /sevə reéni/, **Gino** (1883–1966) Italian artist. One of the founders of futurism, his painting shows strong cubist influences, as in *Dynamic Hieroglyphic of the Bal Tabarin* (1912).

severity /si vérrəti/ *n* **1.** STATE OR EXTENT OF BADNESS the state of being very bad, or the extent to which something is bad **2.** STRICTNESS OR STERNNESS the state of being very strict or stern **3.** PLAINNESS the plainness or austerity of something such as a building or style of dress **4.** (*plural* **severities**) HARSH ACT OR CRITICISM an instance of harsh treatment or censure

Severn /sévvərn/ **1.** longest river in Britain, rising in Wales and flowing into the Bristol Channel. Its estuary is crossed by two suspension bridges. Length: 354 km/220 mi. **2.** river that originates in lakes in western Ontario, Canada, and flows northeast into Hudson Bay. Length: 982 km/610 mi.

Severus /si veérəss/, **Lucius Septimus** (146–211) North African-born Roman emperor. As emperor (193–211), he was noted for his civil, judicial, and military reforms and his military expeditions to maintain his control of the Roman Empire.

Seveso /se vássō/ town situated near Milan, in northern Italy. It was the scene of an industrial accident in 1976, when the poisonous gas dioxin escaped into the atmosphere.

seviche *n* FOOD another spelling of **ceviche**

Seville /sə víl/ city and river port in the autonomous region of Andalusia, southwestern Spain. Population: 704,114 (2002).

Seville orange *n* **1.** a bitter orange often used to make marmalade **2.** an orange tree cultivated to produce Seville oranges. Native to: tropical and subtropical regions. Latin name: *Citrus aurantium.*
▶ N Am term **bitter orange**

~~sevral~~ incorrect spelling of **several**

Sèvres /sévvrə/ *n* a highly decorated French porcelain [Mid-18C. After a suburb of Paris (formerly a separate town)]

sew /sō/ (**sews, sewing, sewed, sewn** /sōn/ or **sewed**) *vti* to join things or repair or make something by using a needle to pass thread repeatedly through material [Old English *siowan* < Indo-European] —**sewable** *adj*

SPELLCHECK sew, so, or sow? Do not confuse the spelling of *sew*, *so*, and *sow*, which sound similar. Both *sew* and *sow* are verbs: *sew* means 'to join things or repair or make something using a needle and thread' and *sow* means 'plant seed'. *So* is an adverb or conjunction introducing a reason, consequence, etc.: *Put your coat on so that you won't get cold. He asked me outright, so I had to tell him. So* is also used in numerous fixed phrases, as in *office equipment, stationery, and so on; so many things to do; so be it; so what?*

sew up *vt* to finish a business deal or other endeavour successfully

sewage /soó ij, syoó-/ *n* human and domestic waste matter from buildings, especially houses, that is carried away through sewers [Mid-19C. < SEWER[1]]

sewage farm *n* a place where sewage is treated to make it nontoxic, and especially to make it into manure. N Am term **sewage plant**

Sewell /syoó əl, soó-/, **Anna** (1820–78) British writer. Her only book, *Black Beauty* (1877), was written to advocate humane treatment of animals and became a children's classic.

Sewell /soó əl/, **Henry** (1807–79) British-born premier of New Zealand (1856). He was New Zealand's first premier.

sewellel /sə wéllǝl/ *n* ZOOL same as **mountain beaver** [Early 19C. < Chinook *šwalál* 'robe made of mountain beaver skin']

sewen *n* Ireland, Wales ZOOL another spelling of **sewin**

sewer[1] /soó ər, syoó-/ *n* a pipe or drain, usually underground, that carries away waste or rainwater ■ *vt* (**-ers, -ering, -ered**) to provide a place with sewers [15C. Via Anglo-Norman *sever* < Vulgar Latin *exaquare* 'remove water' < Latin *ex-* 'out' + *aqua* 'water']

sewer[2] /soó ər, syoó-/ *n* a medieval servant who served meals [14C. < Anglo-Norman *asseour* < French *asseoir* 'place a seat for' < Latin *sedere* 'sit']

sewer[3] /sō ər/ *n* somebody or something that sews [14C. < SEW]

sewerage /soó ərij, syoó-/ *n* **1.** a system of sewers **2.** the removal of waste by means of sewers **3.** INDUST same as **sewage**

sewin /syoó in/ (*plural* **-ins** or *same*), **sewen** (*plural* **-ens** or *same*) *n* Ireland, Wales same as **sea trout** (sense 1) [Mid-16C. Origin ?]

sewing /sō ing/ *n* **1.** the act or work of using a needle and thread to join or repair material **2.** a piece of material that somebody is sewing

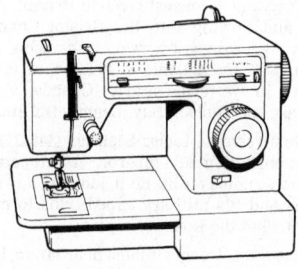

sewing machine

sewing machine *n* a machine for sewing material

sewn HANDICRAFT past participle of **sew**

sex /seks/ *n* **1.** same as **sexual intercourse 2.** SEXUAL BEHAVIOUR sexual activity, or behaviour leading to it **3.** MALE OR FEMALE GENDER either of the two reproductive categories, male or female, of animals and plants **4.** ANAT same as **genitals** (*literary*) **5.** BIOL REPRODUCTIVE CHARACTERISTICS the set of characteristics that determine whether the reproductive role of an animal or plant is male or female ■ *adj* OF SEX relating to sexual matters or to the sexes ■ *vt* (**sexes, sexing, sexed**) DETERMINE SEX OF SOMETHING to determine the sex of an animal or plant [14C. Directly or via French < Latin *sexus*]

USAGE See *gender*.

sex up *v* **1.** *vti US* to arouse somebody sexually, or become aroused **2.** *vt* to make changes to something such as a piece of writing or an artistic production so that it appears more interesting, exciting, or significant than before (*slang*) ○ *the report had been sexed-up for the media*

sex- *prefix* six ○ *sexennial* [< Latin *sex* < Indo-European]

sexagenarian /séksəjə náiri ən/, **sexagenary** /sek sájjinəri/ *n* somebody aged between 60 and 69 — **sexagenarian** *adj*

Sexagesima /séksə jéssimə/ *n* in the Christian calendar, the second Sunday before Lent, eight weeks before Easter [14C. < ecclesiastical Latin < Latin *sexagesimus* (see SEXAGESIMAL)]

sexagesimal /séksə jéssim'l/ *adj* relating to or based on the number 60 ■ *n* a fraction in which the denominator is a power of 60 [Late 17C. < Latin *sexagesimus* 'sixtieth' < *sexaginta* 'sixty']

sex appeal *n* the quality of being sexually attractive

sexavalent /séksə váylənt/ *adj* CHEM same as **hexavalent**

sex cell *n* GENETICS same as **gamete**

sexcentenary /sék sen teénəri/ *adj* **1.** OF 600 relating to the number 600 or a period of 600 years **2.** OF 600TH ANNIVERSARY relating to a 600th anniversary ■ *n* (*plural* **-ies**) 600TH ANNIVERSARY a 600th anniversary, or the celebration of one

sex change *n* an operation with accompanying hormonal treatment that changes somebody's physical characteristics from those of one sex to those of the other

sex chromatin *n* GENETICS same as **Barr body**

sex chromosome *n* a chromosome that determines the sex of an organism, e.g. the X and Y chromosomes in human beings and other mammals. In each cell nucleus, a male mammal has one X and one Y chromosome, and a female has two X chromosomes.

sexduction /seks dúksh'n/ *n* the transfer of a fragment of chromosome from one bacterial cell to another by its incorporation into a special DNA particle (**plasmid**) that initiates sexual conjugation between the cells [Mid-20C. < SEX + TRANSDUCTION]

sexed /sekst/ *adj* **1.** having a particular degree of interest in sex ○ *highly sexed* **2.** possessing sexual characteristics

sexennial /sek sénni əl/ *adj* happening every six years or over a period of six years ■ *n* something that happens every six years or over a period of six years [Mid-17C. < Latin *sexennium* 'period of six years' < *sex* 'six' + *annus* 'year'] —**sexennially** *adv*

sex factor *n* a genetic element found in some bacteria that enables the cell to put out a fine tube to another bacterial cell and transfer some of its genetic material

sex gland *n* ANAT same as **gonad**

sex hormone *n* a hormone that affects the development of the reproductive organs and sexual characteristics

sex industry *n* prostitution or the provision of sexual services considered as a business or an area of employment (*often used euphemistically*)

sexism /séksizəm/ *n* **1.** discrimination against women or men because of their sex **2.** the tendency to treat people as cultural stereotypes of their sex

sexist /séksist/ *adj* **1.** BELIEVING ONE SEX IS INFERIOR believing that one sex is inferior to the other in a variety of attributes ○ *sexist colleagues* **2.** OF BELIEF IN ONE SEX'S INFERIORITY resulting from or relating to the belief that one sex is inferior to the other in a variety of attributes ○ *a sexist employment policy* ■ *n* SOMEBODY SEXIST somebody who believes that one sex is inferior to the other

sexivalent /séksi váylənt/ *adj* CHEM same as **hexavalent**

sex kitten *n* an offensive term for a young woman perceived as sexually appealing

sexless /séksləss/ *adj* **1.** NOT SEXY sexually unattractive **2.** WITHOUT SEXUAL ACTIVITY living without sexual intercourse or interest in sex **3.** WITHOUT SEXUAL CHARACTERISTICS describes an animal or plant that has no, or no obvious, sexual characteristics —**sexlessly** *adv* —**sexlessness** *n*

sex-limited *adj* describes genetically inherited traits or conditions that appear in one sex only, although the genes themselves may be found in either sex

sex-linked *adj* relating to a gene located on a sex chromosome, typically the X chromosome, or to inheritance determined by such a gene —**sex-linkage** *n*

sex object *n* somebody treated or seen as worthy of notice solely because of characteristics perceived as sexually appealing

sex offender *n* somebody who has committed a crime involving a sexual act

sexology /sek sólləji/ *n* the study of human sexual behaviour —**sexological** /séksə lójjik'l/ *adj* —**sexologist** *n*

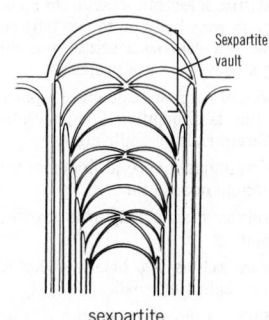

Sexpartite vault

sexpartite

sexpartite /seks paár tīt/ *adj* **1.** divided into or made up of six parts ○ *a sexpartite vault* **2.** involving six participants [Mid-18C. < SEX-]

sexploitation /séks ploy táysh'n/ *n* the deliberate use of sexual material to make a product, especially a film, commercially successful [Mid-20C. Blend of SEX + EXPLOITATION]

sexpot /séks pot/ *n* an offensive term for a woman who appears to radiate sexuality

sex role *n* a set of behaviours characteristic of or expected of members of one sex or the other

sex selection *n* sex determination before conception by separating spermatozoa carrying Y chromosomes from those carrying X chromosomes

sex shop *n* a shop that sells items intended to aid sexual arousal or add to the pleasure of sexual intercourse

sex-starved *adj* frustrated by an absence of sexual activity

sex symbol *n* somebody whose fame is linked to a widely perceived sex appeal

sext /sekst/ *n* in the Roman Catholic Church, the fourth of the seven separate hours (**canonical hours**) that are set aside for prayer each day. This was originally the sixth hour of the day, midday. [14C. < Latin *sexta (hora)* 'sixth (hour)']

Sextans /sékstənz/ *n* a faint constellation near the celestial equator. See illustration at **constellation**

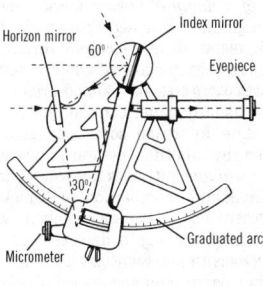

sextant

sextant /sékstənt/ *n* a navigational instrument incorporating a telescope and an angular scale that is used to work out latitude and longitude. An astronomical object is viewed through the telescope and its angular distance above the horizon is read off the scale. The data is then used to calculate the viewer's position. [Late 16C. < Latin *sextant-* 'sixth part (of a circle)' (from the arc on which the scale is marked) < *sextus* 'sixth']

sextet /sek stét/, **sextette** *n* 1. a group of six musicians or singers, or a piece of music composed for them 2. any group of six people or things [Mid-19C. Alteration of SESTET after Latin *sex* 'six']

sex therapy *n* the treatment of sexual problems through counselling and psychotherapy —**sex therapist** *n*

sextile /séks tīl/ *n* 1. STATISTICAL DIVISION any of the six equal groups into which a statistical sample can be divided 2. STATISTICAL VALUE any of the five statistical values that divide a frequency distribution into six parts, with each containing a sixth of the sample population 3. ANGLE BETWEEN PLANETS a position of two astronomical objects in which they are 60° apart as viewed from Earth [Mid-16C. < Latin *sextilis* < *sextus* 'sixth'] —**sextile** *adj*

sextillion /seks tíli ən/ (*plural* **-lions** or *same*) *n* 1. the number equal to 10²¹, written as 1 followed by 21 zeros 2. the number equal to 10³⁶, written as 1 followed by 36 zeros (*dated*) [Late 17C. < French < Latin *sex* 'six', after MILLION] —**sextillion** *adj*, *pron* —**sextillionth** *n, adj*

sextodecimo /sékstō déssimō/ (*plural* **-mos**) *n* a size of book page traditionally created by folding a single sheet of standard-sized printing paper four times, giving 16 leaves or 32 pages [Mid-17C. < Latin *sexto decimo*, form of *sextus decimus* 'sixteenth']

sexton /sékstən/ *n* 1. the caretaker of a church and its graveyard whose duties often include ringing the bell and digging graves 2. *also* **sexton beetle** a beetle that buries the bodies of dead small animals such as mice by digging beneath them, using the bodies as food for itself and its larvae. Genus: *Necrophorus*. [14C. Via Anglo-Norman *segerstein* < medieval Latin *sacristanus* (see SACRISTAN)]

sex tourism *n* travel undertaken or organized to take advantage of the relatively lax laws on prostitution and sexual activities in some countries —**sex tourist** *n*

sextuple /sékstyōōp'l, seks tyōōp'l/ *n* NUMBER SIX TIMES ANOTHER a number or quantity that is six times another number or quantity ■ *adj* 1. BEING SIX TIMES ANOTHER relating to or being a number or quantity that is six times greater than another number or quantity 2. CONSISTING OF SIX PARTS made up of six parts or members 3. MUSIC HAVING SIX BEATS TO BAR describes a time or rhythm in which there are six beats to the bar ■ *vti* (**-ples, -pling, -pled**) MULTIPLY BY SIX to multiply something by six, or be multiplied by six [Early 17C. < medieval Latin *sextuplus* < Latin *sex* 'six']

sextuplet /sékstyōōplət, seks tyōōplət/ *n* 1. ONE OF SIX OFFSPRING BORN TOGETHER one of six babies or young animals born in a single birth 2. GROUP OF SIX a group of six things 3. MUSIC GROUP OF SIX NOTES in music, a group of six notes played in a time normally given to four [Mid-19C. < SEXTUPLE, after TRIPLET]

sextuplicate *n* /seks tyōōplikət/ SET OF SIX THINGS a set of six things, especially identical copies ■ *adj* /seks tyōōplikət/ BEING SIX TIMES ANOTHER relating to or being

a number or quantity that is six times greater than another number or quantity ■ *v* /seks tyōōpli kayt/ (**-cates, -cating, -cated**) 1. *vti* MULTIPLY BY SIX to multiply something by six, or be multiplied by six 2. *vt* COPY SOMETHING SIX TIMES to make six copies of something [Mid-17C. < medieval Latin *sextuplicat-*, past participle of *sextuplicare* 'increase sixfold' < *sextuplus* (see SEXTUPLE)]

sex-typed *adj* intended for or conventionally perceived as appropriate for one sex and not the other —**sex-typing** *n*

sexual /sékshoo əl/ *adj* 1. OF SEX relating to sex, sexuality, or the sexual organs ○ *a sexual disease* 2. RELATING TO EITHER SEX relating to the two sexes or to either of them ○ *sexual differences* 3. BIOL INVOLVING REPRODUCTIVE UNION relating to the union of male and female gametes in reproduction [Mid-17C. < late Latin *sexualis* < Latin *sexus* 'sex'] —**sexually** *adv*

sexual assault *n* an incident that involves sexual contact that is forced on somebody

sexual dimorphism *n* the existence of differences in the appearance of the male and female of a species

sexual harassment *n* unwanted sex-related behaviour towards somebody, e.g. touching somebody or making suggestive remarks, especially by somebody with authority towards a subordinate

sexual intercourse *n* an act carried out for reproduction or pleasure involving penetration, especially one in which a man inserts his erect penis into a woman's vagina

sexualise *vt* another spelling of **sexualize**

sexuality /sékshoo álləti/ *n* 1. SEXUAL APPEAL sexual appeal or potency 2. STATE OF BEING SEXUAL the state of being sexual 3. INVOLVEMENT IN SEXUAL ACTIVITY involvement or interest in sexual activity 4. same as **sexual orientation**

sexualize /sékshoo ə līz/ (**-izes, -izing, -ized**), **sexualise** (**-ises, -ising, -ised**) *vt* to impose a sexual interpretation or perception on something or somebody

sexually transmitted infection, **sexually transmitted disease** *n* a disease that is normally passed from one person to another through sexual activity, e.g. syphilis or genital herpes

sexual orientation *n* the direction of somebody's sexual desire, towards people of the opposite sex, people of the same sex, or people of both sexes

sexual relations *npl* same as **sexual intercourse**

sexual reproduction *n* reproduction that involves the union of male and female gametes, each contributing half of the genetic makeup of the resulting zygote

sexual selection *n* the choice by a female animal of a mate on the basis of a characteristic such as a bird song or bright plumage

sexvalent /seks váylənt/ *adj* CHEM same as **hexavalent**

sex work *n* the work of somebody in one of the sex industries such as pornography or prostitution —**sex worker** *n*

sexy /séksi/ (**-ier, -iest**) *adj* 1. AROUSING DESIRE arousing or intended to arouse sexual desire 2. AROUSED sexually aroused 3. APPEALING appealing because of being new, interesting, or trendy (*informal*) ○ *a sexy new slogan* —**sexily** *adv* —**sexiness** *n*

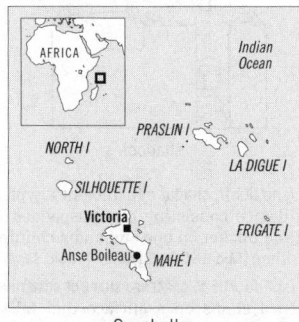

Seychelles

Seychelles /say shélz/ island country in the western Indian Ocean. It contains four main islands and

many islets. It became an independent member of the Commonwealth in 1976. Language: Creole, English, French. Currency: Seychelles rupee. Capital: Victoria. Population: 79,715 (2001). Area: 454 sq. km/175 sq. mi. Official name **Republic of Seychelles** —**Seychellois** /sáy shel wǎa/ *adj, n*

Seyfert galaxy /sífərt-/ *n* a small spiral galaxy that varies in brightness and emits radio waves and X-rays [Mid-20C. After Carl K. *Seyfert* (1911–60), US astronomer]

Seymour /seém awr/, **Jane** (1509?–37) queen of England and Ireland. She was the third wife of Henry VIII of England, and died shortly after giving birth to Edward VI, Henry's only male heir.

Sezer /sé zair/, **Ahmet Necdet** (*b.* 1941) president of Turkey. A former chief justice of the Constitutional Court (1998–2000), he became president in 2000.

sf *abbr* 1. LITERAT science fiction 2. MUSIC sforzando

SF *abbr* 1. LITERAT science fiction 2. FIN sinking fund

SFA *abbr* 1. Scottish Football Association 2. Securities and Futures Authority Ltd

Sfax /sfaks/ port and capital city of Safaqis Governorate, east-central Tunisia. Population: 230,900 (1994).

sferics *npl* METEOROL US spelling of **spherics**

SFO *abbr* 1. Serious Fraud Office 2. Superannuation Funds Office

sforzando /sfawrt sándō/, **sforzato** /sfawrt saátō/ *adv* with a sudden strong accent (*used as a musical direction*) ■ *n* (*plural* **-dos** or **-di** /-di/; *plural* **-tos** or **-ti** /-ti/) a note or chord that is to be played with a sudden strong accent, or a symbol indicating this [Early 19C. < Italian < *sforzare* 'use force' < Latin *fortis* 'strong'] —**sforzando** *adj*

sfumato /sfoo maátō/ *n* the gradual blending of one area of colour into another without a sharp outline [Mid-19C. < Italian, past participle of *sfumare* 'tone down', < Latin *fumus* 'smoke']

sfz. *abbr* MUSIC sforzando

sg *abbr* ONLINE Singapore (*used in Internet addresses*) See table at **domain name**

Sg[1] *symbol* CHEM ELEM seaborgium

Sg[2] *abbr* BIBLE Song of Songs

SG *abbr* 1. GRAM singular 2. LAW solicitor general 3. PHYS specific gravity

sgd *abbr* signed

SGHWR *abbr* ENG steam-generating heavy-water reactor

sgian-dhu, **sgian-dubh** *n* Scotland ARMS, CLOTHING another spelling of **skean-dhu**

SGM *abbr* US MIL Sergeant Major

SGML *n* an international standard markup system for the definition of system-independent methods of representing texts in electronic form by describing the relationship between a document's form and its structure. SGML is used widely to manage large documents that are subject to frequent revisions and need to be printed in different formats. Full form **Standard Generalized Markup Language**

SGR *abbr* ASTRON soft gamma repeater

sgraffito /sgraa feétō/ (*plural* **-ti** /-ti/) *n* 1. DECORATION TECHNIQUE a technique used to decorate ceramics or plaster walls, in which the top layer has patterns scratched into it, revealing the different-coloured layer beneath 2. DECORATION a decoration made using the sgraffito technique 3. DECORATED OBJECT an object decorated using the sgraffito technique [Mid-18C. < Italian, past participle of *sgraffire* 'to scratch' < *sgraffio* 'scratch']

Sgt *abbr* MIL Sergeant

Sgt Maj. *abbr* MIL Sergeant Major

sh[1] /sh/, **shh** *interj* used to tell somebody to be silent or quieter [Mid-19C. Natural exclamation]

sh[2] *abbr* ONLINE St Helena (*in Internet addresses*) See table at **domain name**

sh. *abbr* 1. FIN share 2. AGRIC sheep 3. AGRIC sheet

SHA *abbr* NAVIG sidereal hour angle

Shaaban *n* CALENDAR, ISLAM another spelling of **Sha'ban**

Shaanxi /shaa aánshi/ province in China bordered by Ningxia Hui, Nei Monggol, Shanxi, Henan, Hubei, Sichuan, and Gansu. Capital: Xi'an. Population: 35,430,000 (1997). Area: 195,799 sq. km/75,598 sq. mi.

Sha'ban /shaa baán, shaa-/, **Shaban**, **Shaaban** *n* in the Islamic calendar, the eighth month of the year. See table at **calendar** [Mid-18C. < Arabic *ša'bān*]

Shabbat /shaa baát/ *n* the Jewish Sabbath, celebrated on Saturday [Mid-19C. < Hebrew *šabbāṭ* 'day of rest']

shabby /shábbi/ (**-bier**, **-biest**) *adj* **1. WORN AND THREADBARE** worn out, frayed, or threadbare after long use **2. WEARING WORN CLOTHES** wearing worn-out clothing and perceived as being unappealing to the eye **3. INCONSIDERATE** inconsiderate and unfair ○ *won't put up with shabby treatment* **4. INFERIOR IN QUALITY** inferior in quality ○ *shabby goods* **5. RUN DOWN** poorly maintained and thus falling apart or dirty ○ *a shabby section of town* [Mid-17C. < obsolete *shab* 'disreputable person' < Old English *sceabb* 'scab' < Indo-European, 'to scrape'] —**shabbily** *adv* —**shabbiness** *n*

shabby-genteel *adj* trying to keep up the appearances that a middle- or upper-middle-class lifestyle demands, despite not having enough money

shabushabu /shaáboo shaáboo/ *n* a Japanese dish in which thinly sliced beef and vegetables are cooked at table in a pot of simmering stock, then dipped into a sauce and eaten [Late 20C. < Japanese, literally 'swish swish', an imitation of the sound of bubbling water]

Shacharis /shaákhariss/ *n* the Jewish morning liturgy [< Hebrew *šaḥăriṭ* 'morning time']

shack /shak/ *n* a small crude building typically made of boards or sheets of material, usually without a foundation [Late 19C. Origin ?]

shack up (**shacks up**, **shacking up**, **shacked up**) *vi* to live with a lover without being married (*informal disapproving*)

shackle (sense 3)

shackle /shák'l/ *n* **1. METAL BAND ON PRISONER** a round metal band that can be opened or locked in order to hold the wrist or ankle of a captive, usually attached by chains in pairs or fours (*often used in the plural*) **2. BINDER FOR ANIMAL LEGS** a device used to hold together the legs of horses and other animals **3. U-SHAPED FASTENER** a U-shaped bar that is fastened with a straight pin or bolt to hold something securely **4. RESTRAINT ON FREEDOM** an oppressive restraint on something or somebody (*often used in the plural*) ○ *mental shackles* ■ *vt* (**-les**, **-ling**, **-led**) **1. RESTRICT SOMEBODY** to restrict the freedom of somebody or something ○ *felt shackled by the inflexible rules* **2. RESTRAIN SOMEBODY WITH SHACKLES** to restrain somebody or an animal using shackles **3. SECURE SOMETHING WITH SHACKLE** to connect or secure something with a shackle [Old English *sceacul* < Germanic, 'fastening'] —**shackler** *n*

Shackleton /shák'ltən/, **Sir Ernest** (1874–1922) Irish explorer. He was the leader of an expedition that almost reached the South Pole (1907–09). He was the first to cross South Georgia (1916), but died there on his fourth expedition. Full name **Shackleton, Sir Ernest Henry**

shad /shad/ (*plural* **shads** *or* same) *n* a fish similar to herring that spawns upstream in rivers. Native to: northern Atlantic. Genus: *Alosa*. [Old English *sceadd*. Origin ?]

shadberry /shádbəri/ (*plural* **-ries**) *n* TREES same as **serviceberry** (sense 1) [Mid-19C. Because it flowers when shad appear in N American rivers to spawn]

Shadbolt /shád bōlt/, **Maurice** (*b.* 1932) New Zealand writer. He wrote the short-story collection *The New Zealanders* (1959) and novels including *Season of the Jew* (1986). Full name **Shadbolt, Maurice Francis Richard**

shadbush /shád boõsh/ *n* N Am TREES same as **serviceberry** (sense 2)

shadchan /shaad kha̱an, shaádkhən/ (*plural* **-chanim** /-kha̱anīm/ *or* **-chans**), **shadkhan** (*plural* **-khanim** *or* **-khans**) *n* a marriage broker for Jewish couples [Mid-19C. Via Yiddish *shadkhn* < medieval Hebrew *šaddĕkān* < *šiddēk* 'make marriage proposals']

shaddock /sháddək/ *n* TREES, FOOD same as **pomelo** [Late 17C. After a 17C English ship's captain named *Shaddock*]

shade /shayd/ *n* **1. AREA OUT OF DIRECT SUNLIGHT** an area of relative darkness where direct sunlight is blocked or obscured **2. SLIGHTLY DIFFERENT COLOUR** a colour that is a variation on a basic colour, e.g. by being more or less bright or dark ○ *a pretty shade of blue* **3. SOMETHING THAT BLOCKS LIGHT** something used to block a direct light source, e.g. a lampshade **4.** *N Am* **BLIND** a window blind **5. DARK PARTS OF PAINTING** the darker areas of a painting, drawing, or photograph **6. SMALL AMOUNT** a slight degree or amount ○ *a shade too close* **7. VARIATION** a slight variation on something similar ○ *different shades of opinion* **8. OBSCURITY** a position of relative obscurity **9. GHOST** a ghost or phantom (*literary*) ■ **shades** *npl* same as **sunglasses** (*see* **sunglass**) (*informal*) ■ *v* (**shades**, **shading**, **shaded**) **1.** *vt* **PROTECT SOMETHING FROM SUNLIGHT** to protect or block it off from direct light, particularly from direct sunlight ○ *The awning shades the porch well.* **2.** *vt* **DARKEN PART OF PICTURE** to darken part of a drawing or picture using pencil, ink, or some other dark medium ○ *He shaded in the trees in the background.* **3.** *vi* **CHANGE SLIGHTLY OR GRADUALLY** to change imperceptibly into something slightly different ○ *The cream gradually shades into gold.* **4.** *vt* **DARKEN SOMETHING** to make a place or area darker **5.** *vt* BUSINESS **REDUCE PRICE** to reduce a price slightly [Old English *sceadu* < Indo-European, 'darkness'] ◇ **put somebody or something in the shade** to make somebody or something seem unimportant by appearing much more special or attractive ◇ **shades of somebody or something** used to say that somebody or something is reminiscent of somebody or something else, especially a time in the past or the work of a writer or other artist ○ *You can take tea on the terrace – shades of E. M. Forster – or ride on an elephant.*

Shades /shaydz/ *npl* MYTHOL same as **underworld** (*literary*)

shade tree *n* a tree planted to provide shade

shading /sháyding/ *n* **1.** an area of relatively dark tone or close lines, dots, or hatching that produces darkness or shadow in a drawing or picture **2.** a subtle difference or variation

shadkhan *n* JUDAISM another spelling of **shadchan**

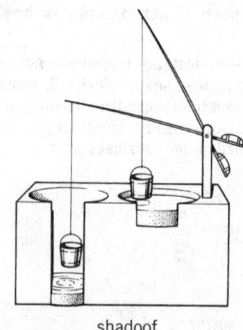

shadoof

shadoof /shə doóf/, **shaduf** *n* in ancient Egypt, a water-raising device consisting of a suspended pivoting pole with a bucket on one end and a counterweight on the other [Mid-19C. < Egyptian Arabic *šādūf*]

shadow /sháddō/ *n* **1. DARKENED SHAPE OF SOMETHING IN LIGHT** a darkened shape on a surface that falls behind somebody or something blocking the light **2. DARKNESS** relative darkness in a place that is being screened or blocked off from direct sunlight ○ *Part of the room was in shadow.* **3. HINT OF SOMETHING** a slight suggestion or hint of something ○ *beyond the shadow of a doubt* **4. OMINOUS GLOOM** a depressing or ominous gloom ○ *The news cast a shadow over the party.* **5. THREAT** an ever-present threat or blight ○ *living under the shadow of environmental disaster* **6. DARK AREA UNDER EYES** a darkened area of skin under the eyes, usually caused by fatigue **7. OVERSHADOWED STATE** a state in which somebody is always overshadowed by another person ○ *grew up in his brother's shadow* **8. REGULAR COMPANION** somebody who is the invariable companion of somebody else **9. PERSON SECRETLY TRAILING ANOTHER** somebody who secretly follows somebody, e.g. a detective or spy **10.** POL **OPPOSITION MINISTER WITH PARTICULAR JOB** a politician in an opposition party who speaks on a particular area of policy and would hold a ministerial job if the party were in government **11.** ARTS, PARANORMAL same as **shade** (senses 5, 9) **12. REFLECTION** a reflection of something in water ○ *the shadow of the stars in the dark lake* **13. COPY** an imitation or copy of something **14. INFERIOR REMNANT** a remnant of somebody or something formerly greater or more important ○ *now a shadow of her former self* **15.** BUSINESS **SOMEBODY LEARNING BY OBSERVATION** somebody who learns a job by observing the person who regularly does the job **16.** MED **ATYPICAL AREA IN X-RAY** an atypical area showing up on an X-ray **17.** PSYCHOANAL **JUNGIAN ARCHETYPE** in Jungian psychology, the archetype that represents sexual and aggressive instincts inherited from a more primitive stage of humanity **18. SHELTER** something that provides protection ■ *vt* (**-ows**, **-owing**, **-owed**) **1. PROTECT SOMETHING FROM LIGHT** to shade something from the light ○ *Her face was shadowed by a wide-brimmed straw hat.* **2. FOLLOW SOMEBODY** to go everywhere that somebody else goes in order to watch what they are doing, especially secretly ○ *The police had been shadowing him for days.* **3.** BUSINESS **LEARN JOB BY FOLLOWING WORKER** to accompany and observe somebody who is doing a job in order to learn how it is done **4. REPRESENT SOMETHING VAGUELY** to represent something vaguely or in outline ■ *adj* POL **IN CAPACITY OF OPPOSITION COUNTERPART** describes a member of the largest opposition party who speaks on a particular area of policy and would hold a ministerial job if that party were in government ○ *the shadow cabinet* [Old English *sceaduwe*, form of *sceadu* (see SHADE)] —**shadower** *n*

SYNONYMS See *follow*.

shadow-box *vi* to practise boxing moves by sparring with an imaginary partner —**shadow-boxer** *n* —**shadow-boxing** *n*

shadow dance *n* a dance performance in which the dancers' shadows are seen on a screen

shadow economy (*plural* **shadow economies**) *n* ECON same as **black economy**

shadowgraph /sháddō graaf, -graf/ *n* **1.** an image of a shape made by casting a shadow onto a surface, e.g. by shaping the hands so that their shadow resembles the silhouette of an animal **2.** MED same as **radiograph**

shadow mask *n* a perforated metal sheet mounted close to the rear of the phosphor dot faceplate of a three gun colour picture tube. The shadow mask is used to direct the electron beam to the desired phosphor colour element.

shadow play *n* a theatrical performance in which the audience views a screen on which the shadows of puppets or performers are cast by a light source behind them

shadow price *n* the estimated price of goods or a service for which no market price exists

shadow senator *n* a nonvoting representative of the District of Columbia in the US Senate

shadowy /sháddō i/ (**-ier**, **-iest**) *adj* **1. FULL OF SHADOWS** full of shadows or shade **2. NOT CLEARLY SEEN** seen only vaguely **3. MYSTERIOUS** mysteriously little-known or obscure —**shadowiness** *n*

shaduf *n* AGRIC another spelling of **shadoof**

shady /sháydi/ (**-ier**, **-iest**) *adj* **1. HAVING SHADE** having little natural light, often giving shelter from harsh sunlight ○ *a shady corner of the park* **2. DISHONEST** probably dishonest or illegal ○ *shady dealings with foreign investors* **3. PROVIDING SHADE** providing shade ○ *a shady tree* —**shadily** *adv* —**shadiness** *n*

SHAEF /shayf/ *abbr* MIL Supreme Headquarters Allied Expeditionary Forces

shaft /shaaft/ *n* **1.** LONG HANDLE the long slender handle on various instruments and tools such as golf clubs and hammers **2.** BODY OF PROJECTILE a long narrow rod that forms the body of a spear, arrow, harpoon, or other projectile **3.** POLE FOR HARNESSING HORSE either of the two parallel bars by which an animal is harnessed to a cart or wagon **4.** ROTATING ROD IN MACHINE a rotating rod that provides motion or power for a machine **5.** VERTICAL PASSAGE a vertical passage, especially one in which a lift travels or one that gives access to a mine **6.** PASSAGE FOR VENTILATION IN BUILDING a small passageway in a building, particularly in a wall, ceiling, or floor, to allow for air circulation **7.** LIGHT BEAM a beam of light ○ *a shaft of sunlight* **8.** SHARP COMMENT a sharp or barbed comment directed at somebody ○ *a shaft of wit* **9.** *N Am* HARSH TREATMENT unkind or harsh treatment or dismissal (*informal*) ○ *His girlfriend gave him the shaft.* **10.** ARMS same as **arrow** *n* (sense 1) (*literary*) **11.** ANAT MIDDLE OF LONG BONE the middle part of a long bone **12.** ANAT BODY OF PENIS the cylindrical body of the penis **13.** ANAT MAIN PART OF HAIR the part of a hair that is visible above the skin **14.** ARCHIT BODY OF COLUMN the main body of a column, between the capital and base **15.** ARCHIT COLUMN a column, especially one of a pair supporting an arch **16.** BIRDS FEATHER RIB the central rib of a feather **17.** TREES TRUNK the trunk of a tree **18.** UPRIGHT PART OF CROSS the upright bar in a cross ■ *vt* (**shafts, shafting, shafted**) (*slang*) **1.** TREAT SOMEBODY UNFAIRLY to cheat somebody or treat somebody unfairly ○ *She got shafted on her book contract.* **2.** OFFENSIVE TERM an offensive term meaning to have sexual intercourse with somebody [Old English *sceaft* < Germanic]

Shaftesbury /sháaftsbəri/ market town in Dorset, southwestern England. Population: 6,203 (1991).

Shaftesbury, Anthony Ashley Cooper, 7th Earl of (1801–85) British philanthropist. An influential figure of the social reform movement, he established schools for the poor and a ten-hour day for factory workers (1847).

shag¹ /shag/ *n* **1.** LONG PILE ON TEXTILE a long rough nap or pile on a textile **2.** SHREDDED TOBACCO a strong coarse tobacco that is finely shredded **3.** LAYERED HAIRCUT a hairstyle with layers that are cut progressively shorter from base to crown **4.** MATTED TANGLE OF HAIR a rough matted tangle of hair or wool ■ *v* (**shags, shagging, shagged**) **1.** *vt* MAKE SOMETHING ROUGH to cause something to be rough-looking and shaggy **2.** *vi* HANG UNTIDILY to hang in an untidy manner **3.** *vt* PROVIDE SOMETHING WITH SHAFT to provide something such as a tool with a shaft [Old English *sceacga* < Germanic]

shag² /shag/ *n* a small crested cormorant. Native to: Europe, North Africa. Latin name: *Phalacrocorax aristotelis.* [Mid-16C. Origin ?]

shag³ /shag/ (*slang*) *vti* (**shags, shagging, shagged**) an offensive term meaning to have sexual intercourse with somebody ■ *n* an offensive term for an act of sexual intercourse [Late 18C. Origin ?] —**shagger** *n*

shag⁴ /shag/ *n* a 1930s dance step involving hopping alternately on each foot ■ *vi* (**shags, shagging, shagged**) to dance the shag [Early 20C. Origin ?]

shag⁵ /shag/ (**shags, shagging, shagged**) *vt US* **1.** to run and retrieve something **2.** to chase somebody or something away [Early 20C. Origin ?]

shagbark /shág baark/, **shagbark hickory** *n* a hickory that has grey shaggy bark, hard wood, and bears edible nuts. Native to: eastern North America. Latin name: *Carya ovata.*

shagged /shagd/, **shagged out** *adj* extremely tired (*slang*)

shaggy /shággi/ (**-gier, -giest**) *adj* **1.** LONG AND UNTIDY growing long and untidily **2.** HAVING COARSE LONG FIBRES covered with or resembling coarse, long, and usually uneven hair, wool, or similar fibres **3.** ROUGH NAPPED having a rough, relatively long nap or pile

shaggy cap *n* FUNGI same as **shaggymane**

shaggy dog story *n* a long drawn-out absurd story or joke, often with an ending or punchline that is anticlimactic [< one such anecdote involving a shaggy dog]

shaggymane /shággi mayn/ *n* a common edible mushroom with shaggy scales on its cap that contain black spores. Latin name: *Coprinus comatus.*

shagreen /shə gréen/ *n* **1.** the rough skin of some sharks and rays, used as an abrasive or as leather **2.** rough untanned leather with a grainy surface, made from the hide of various animals and often dyed green [Late 17C. Via French *chagrin* 'untanned leather', < Turkish *saġri* 'back of a horse']

shah /shaa/ *n* in former times, the hereditary monarch of some Southwest Asian nations, especially Iran [Mid-16C. < Persian *šāh*] —**shahdom** *n*

Shah Jahan /sháa jə háan/ (1592–1666) emperor of India. The fifth Mughal emperor (1628–58), he made Delhi the capital of India and built the Taj Mahal and Pearl Mosque in Agra.

shaikh *n* POL another spelling of **sheik**

shaikha *n* POL another spelling of **sheika**

shaitan /shī táan/ *n* in Islamic countries, an evil spirit or person [Late 17C. < SHAITAN]

Shaitan /shī táan/ *n* in Islamic belief, the devil [Mid-17C. Via Arabic < Hebrew *śāṭān* (see SATAN)]

Shaka /sháakə/ (1787?–1828) southern African ruler. Through conquest he centralized and expanded the Zulu nation, taking control of Natal (now KwaZulu-Natal, South Africa) and initiating the period of warfare and migrations known as the mfecane.

shake /shayk/ *v* (**shakes, shaking, shook** /shŏŏk/, **shaken** /sháykən/) **1.** *vti* MOVE BACK AND FORTH to move back and forth or up and down in short quick movements, or make something or somebody move in this way ○ *I shook my coat to see if my keys were in the pockets.* **2.** *vi* TREMBLE to tremble uncontrollably ○ *shaking with fright* **3.** *vti* BECOME SOMETHING BY SHAKING to achieve a particular state by shaking, or shake something in order to achieve a particular state ○ *The door finally shook free of its hinges.* ○ *We shook the apples from the tree.* **4.** *vi* QUAVER WITH EMOTION to sound uncertain, nervous, angry, or distressed ○ *Her voice was shaking.* **5.** *vt* SHOCK AND UPSET SOMEBODY to shock and upset or disturb somebody ○ *He was badly shaken by the accident.* **6.** *vt* MAKE SOMEBODY LESS CONFIDENT to cause somebody to lose confidence or certainty ○ *Nothing could shake his faith.* **7.** *vti* CLASP HANDS AS GREETING to grasp another person's hand and move it up and down as a greeting or sign of trust **8.** *vt N Am* same as **shake off** (sense 1) **9.** *vt* MIX INGREDIENTS BY SHAKING to mix ingredients together in a container by shaking the container **10.** *vt* MOVE HEAD TO EXPRESS 'NO' to move the head from side to side in order to express disagreement, disbelief, commiseration, or sorrow **11.** *vt* WAVE SOMETHING THREATENINGLY to wave something in the air in a threatening way ○ *She shook her fist at them.* **12.** *vti* RATTLE DICE BEFORE THROWING to rattle a dice in the hand or in a dice cup before throwing **13.** *vti* MUSIC TRILL to trill a note ■ *n* **1.** ACT OF SHAKING a shaking of something ○ *She gave the bag a good shake.* **2.** VIBRATION a trembling motion or vibration ○ *The device moves smoothly along the track without shake.* **3.** MOMENT a brief moment (*informal*) ○ *I'll do it in two shakes.* **4.** BEVERAGES same as **milk shake 5.** SHAKEN BEVERAGE a beverage made without milk or ice cream but blended or shaken like a milk shake ○ *a fruit and yogurt shake* **6.** HANDSHAKE an act of grasping somebody's hand as a greeting **7.** *US* REASONABLE CHANCE reasonable treatment or a reasonable opportunity to succeed ○ *give everybody a fair shake* **8.** GEOL, FORESTRY FISSURE OR CRACK a fissure or crack in a rock or timber **9.** MUSIC TRILL a trilled note **10.** SEISMOL same as **earthquake** (sense 1) (*informal*) **11.** CONSTR WOODEN SHINGLE a rough wooden shingle cut with a hatchet ■ **shakes** *npl* UNCONTROLLABLE TREMBLING uncontrollable trembling, especially caused by fear or illness [Old English *sceacan* < Germanic] —**shakable** *adj*
◇ **no great shakes** not very good or not very important (*informal*)

shake down *v* **1.** *vt N Am* EXTORT MONEY FROM SOMEBODY to extort money from somebody (*slang*) **2.** *vt US* TAKE SOMETHING FOR TRIAL RUN to subject a ship or aircraft to a trial run in order to look for faults or train the crew **3.** *vi* BECOME ACCUSTOMED to become comfortable in a new setting (*informal*) **4.** *vi* SLEEP IN MAKESHIFT BED to go to bed in a makeshift bed

shake off *vt* **1.** to get rid of something unwanted. N Am term **shake 2.** to get away from a pursuer

shake out *vt* to open something, spread something, or dislodge things from something by holding it and shaking it

shake up *vt* **1.** MAKE MAJOR CHANGES to make major changes in an organization or institution, especially with the intention of improving or modernizing it **2.** UPSET SOMEBODY to make somebody feel upset and disturbed **3.** MIX SOMETHING BY SHAKING to mix something by shaking it in a container

shakedown /sháyk down/ *n* **1.** TRIAL RUN OF VESSEL a trial run of a ship or aircraft carried out in order to locate and fix problems or to familiarize the crew with their duties (*informal*) **2.** MAKESHIFT BED a makeshift bed, e.g. a pile of blankets on a floor (*dated informal*) **3.** *N Am* THOROUGH SEARCH a thorough search of somebody or a place (*informal*) **4.** *N Am* ACT OF EXTORTION an act of extorting money from somebody using threats (*slang*)

shaken past participle of **shake**

shaken baby syndrome, shaken infant syndrome *n* in young babies, a series of often life-threatening internal head injuries sustained through being shaken violently

shake-out *n* a major change in an organization or system resulting in some streamlining ○ *a shake-out in the voluntary sector*

shaker /sháykər/ *n* **1.** CONTAINER FOR DISPERSING PARTICLES a container with small holes in its lid that can be shaken to disperse the contents **2.** CONTAINER FOR MIXING DRINKS a container with a lid in which drinks are mixed by shaking the container **3.** SOMEBODY CAUSING CHANGE somebody who is active in something, especially somebody who brings about change (*informal*) ○ *a real shaker in the industry* **4.** SOMETHING THAT SHAKES somebody or something that shakes, or shakes something ■ *adj* HANDICRAFT another spelling of **Shaker** *adj* (sense 2)

Shaker: wooden Shaker box

Shaker *n* MEMBER OF ASCETIC DENOMINATION a member of a Christian denomination related to the Quakers who live communally, simply, and celibately. The denomination originated in England in the 18th century but settled in the United States. ■ *adj* **1.** SIMPLE AND FUNCTIONAL designed or made in the simple, functional style that originated with the Shakers **2.** PARALLEL RIBBED knitted in a large gauge in thin parallel ribs [Late 18C. < shaking movements in their ritual dances]

~~**Shakespear**~~ incorrect spelling of **Shakespeare**

William Shakespeare

Shakespeare /sháyks peer/, **William** (1564–1616) English poet and playwright. He is widely recognized as the greatest dramatist in the English-speaking world. Although much about his life is

obscure, it is known that he was born in Stratford-upon-Avon, and was established as an actor-playwright in London by about 1590. Over the next 23 years he wrote 36 tragedies, histories, and comedies, including *Hamlet* (1601?), *Richard III* (1593?), and *Twelfth Night* (1600?). His poetry includes over 150 sonnets. See Cultural note at **ado, labour, like**[2], **measure, merchant, merry, shrew, tempest, Twelfth Night** —**Shakespearean** /shayk spéeri ən/ *adj, n*

> 'JAQUES All the world's a stage, / And all the men and women merely players; / They have their exits and their entrances; / And one man in his time plays many parts, / His acts being seven ages.'
> [William Shakespeare, *As You Like It*; 1599]

> 'HAMLET To be, or not to be—that is the question; /Whether 'tis nobler in the mind to suffer / The slings and arrows of outrageous fortune, / Or to take arms against a sea of troubles, / And by opposing end them? To die, to sleep—/ No more; and by a sleep to say we end / The heart-ache and the thousand natural shocks / That flesh is heir to, 'tis a consummation / Devoutly to be wish'd. To die, to sleep; / To sleep, perchance to dream. Ay, there's the rub; / For in that sleep of death what dreams may come, / When we have shuffled off this mortal coil, / Must give us pause.'
> [William Shakespeare, *Hamlet*; 1601?]

> 'Shall I compare thee to a summer's day? / Thou art more lovely and more temperate. / Rough winds do shake the darling buds of May, / And summer's lease hath all too short a date.'
> [William Shakespeare, *Sonnet 18*; 1609]

Shakespeareana /shayk spéeri áanə/, **Shakespeariana** *n* collectively, things relating to William Shakespeare

Shakespearean sonnet *n* a sonnet in iambic pentameter composed of three quatrains followed by a couplet. The rhyme pattern is abab cdcd efef gg. This is the form perfected by William Shakespeare.

Shakespeariana *n* LITERAT another spelling of **Shakespeareana**

shake-up *n* a major reorganization or change

shaking palsy *n* MED same as **Parkinson's disease** (*dated informal*)

shako /shákō, sháykō/ (*plural* **-os** or **-oes**) *n* a tall cylindrical military hat made of stiff material with a short visor and a plume at the front [Early 19C. Via French *schako* < Hungarian *csákós (süveg)* 'peaked (cap)']

Shakta /shúktə/, **Sakta** *n* a Hindu who worships Sakti, the female consort of Shiva [Early 19C. < Sanskrit *śāktaḥ* < *śaktiḥ* (see SAKTI)] —**Shaktism** *n* —**Shaktist** *n*

Shakti *n* HINDUISM another spelling of **Sakti**

shakuhachi /shákoo haáchi/ (*plural* **-chis**) *n* a Japanese bamboo flute [Late 19C. < Japanese]

shaky /sháyki/ (**-ier, -iest**) *adj* **1.** TREMBLING trembling or unsteady **2.** NOT STURDY not sturdy or firm and likely to collapse **3.** WEAK AND NOT LIKELY TO LAST weak or wavering and unlikely to last long or to be successful ○ *a shaky financial venture* **4.** UNRELIABLE unreliable or uncertain ○ *made us a rather shaky promise* —**shakily** *adv* —**shakiness** *n*

shale /shayl/ *n* a dark fine-grained sedimentary rock composed of layers of compressed clay, silt, or mud [Mid-18C. Ultimately < Germanic, 'split'] —**shaly** *adj*

shale oil *n* crude oil distilled from heated shale

shall *stressed* /shal/; *unstressed* /sh'l/ CORE MEANING: will happen in the future, or intended to happen ○ *I shall as president promote measures that keep families whole.*

modal v **1.** FUTURE EVENTS indicates that something will or ought to happen in the future **2.** DETERMINATION used especially in formal speech and writing to indicate determination on the part of the speaker that something will happen or somebody will do something ○ *If you want to behave like that you shall certainly not do it here.* **3.** RULES AND LAWS indicating that something must happen or somebody is obliged to do something because of a rule or law ○ *The department shall issue an account number to the vehicle owner.* **4.** OFFERS AND SUGGESTIONS used to make offers and suggestions or to ask for advice (*used in questions*) ○ *Shall I arrange it for you?* ○ *What shall I do next?* **5.** CERTAINTY indicating the certainty or inevitability of something happening in the future (*usually used with 'you'*) ○ *If you want a new outfit that badly then you shall have one.* [Old English *sceal* < Germanic, 'owe']

USAGE shall or **will**? The traditional rule, often stated in grammars and usage books, is that to express a simple future tense ***shall*** is used after *I* and *we* and ***will*** in other cases, and to express intention or wish their roles are reversed; but it is unlikely that this rule has ever been regularly observed, and many examples of written English can be found that contradict it. (The distinction is often difficult to establish, especially in the first person when the speaker is also the performer of the future action, and intention must always be involved to some extent.) Although ***will*** and, occasionally, ***shall*** are used as auxiliary verbs with reference to future action or state, there are other ways of expressing this that are often preferred as more natural, for example *am going to*. When ***shall*** and ***will*** are used in conversation, they are normally contracted to *'ll*, so that the difference between the two words becomes irrelevant. In all parts of the English-speaking world other than England, ***shall*** has been more or less replaced by ***will***. It survives mostly in the contracted negative form *shan't*. In the English of England (not Britain as a whole), ***shall*** is still sometimes used in such cases as *Shall we go now?*, *They shall apologize immediately* (a command), and *Shall you bring the children?* (an enquiry rather than a request), but the last two examples sound old-fashioned.

shalloon /shə lóon/ *n* a light wool twill. Use: garment lining. [Mid-17C. < French *chalon*]

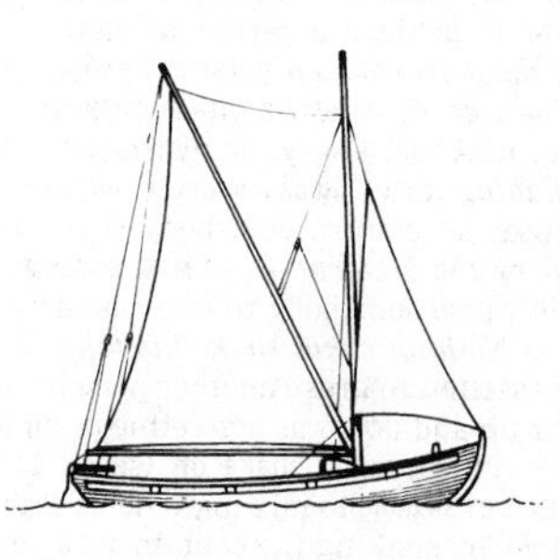

shallop

shallop /shálləp/ *n* a light boat with oars, sails, or both, used in shallow waters [Late 16C. < French *chaloupe*]

shallot /shə lót/ *n* **1.** an edible bulb with a delicate onion flavour **2.** a cultivated plant of the onion family that produces shallots. Latin name: *Allium ascalonicum*. [Mid-17C. < French *échalotte*, alteration of Old French *esc(h)aloigne* (see SCALLION)]

shallow /shállō/ *adj* **1.** NOT DEEP with little space between the bottom and the surface or top **2.** NOT THINKING OR FEELING DEEPLY having or displaying little intellectual or emotional complexity or value **3.** TAKING IN LITTLE AIR characterized by the inhaling and exhaling of only a small amount of air ■ **shallows** *npl* SHALLOW WATER an area of shallow water ■ *vti* (**-lows, -lowing, -lowed**) MAKE OR BECOME SHALLOW to become less deep, or make water less deep [15C. Origin ?] —**shallowly** *adv* —**shallowness** *n*

shallow water blackout *n* the sudden loss of consciousness by a diver upon resurfacing caused by oxygen starvation

shalom /she lóm/ *interj* used as a greeting or leave-taking among Jews [Late 19C. < Hebrew *šālōm* 'peace']

shalt /shalt/ 2nd person singular present of **shall**. 2nd person plural present of **shall** (*archaic*)

shalwar *n* CLOTHING another spelling of **salwar**

sham /sham/ *n* **1.** SOMETHING FAKE something that is presented as genuine but that is not **2.** IMPOSTER somebody who pretends to be something that he or she is not ■ *adj* NOT GENUINE not genuine and used for deception ○ *sham credentials* ■ *vti* (**shams, shamming, shammed**) FEIGN SOMETHING to pretend to be experiencing a condition such as illness or an emotion in order to deceive ○ *He shammed a migraine to avoid the exam.* ○ *Is the patient really ill or just shamming?* [Late 17C. Probably variant of SHAME] —**shammer** *n*

shaman /shámmən, sháymən, shaá-/ *n* a spiritual leader who is believed to have special powers such as prophecy and the ability to heal [Late 17C. Via Russian < Tungus *šaman* < Sanskrit *śramanáḥ* 'Buddhist ascetic' < *śrámas* 'religious exercise'] —**shamanic** /shə mánnik/ *adj*

shamanism /shámmən izəm, sháymən-, shaá-/ *n* **1.** a religion of northern Asia, in which shamans are believed to be able to intercede between humanity and powerful good and evil spirits **2.** an animistic belief system involving shamans

shamash *n* JUDAISM another spelling of **shammash**

shamateur /shámmətər, shámmə choor/ *n* an athlete who is officially an amateur but who is secretly paid [Late 19C. Blend of SHAM + AMATEUR]

shamble /shámb'l/ *vi* (**-bles, -bling, -bled**) to walk clumsily keeping the feet close to the ground ■ *n* a shuffling awkward walking style [Late 16C. Probably < obsolete *shamble legs* 'ungainly legs']

shambles /shámb'lz/ (*plural same*) *n* **1.** DISORGANIZED FAILURE a failure caused by inadequate planning or organization (*takes a singular verb*) **2.** MESSY DISORDER a state of messy disorder or chaos (*takes a singular verb*) **3.** PLACE OF CARNAGE a place of great destruction and carnage (*literary; takes a singular verb*) **4.** same as **abattoir** (*archaic*) **5.** MEAT MARKET a meat or fish market (*archaic*) [15C. < obsolete *shamble* 'stool, table, meat vendor's stall', via W Germanic < Latin *scamellum* 'small bench']

ORIGIN The Old English ancestor of *shamble*, the source of ***shambles***, meant simply 'stool, table'. It gradually acquired the specialized meaning 'meat table', being applied to meat sellers' stalls at markets (a street in the old butchers' quarter of York is still known as the Shambles). By a natural extension the plural form ***shambles*** came to denote a 'slaughterhouse', and hence metaphorically any 'place of carnage', but the milder modern sense 'state of disorder or chaos' did not emerge until as recently as the early 20th century.

shambolic /sham bóllik/ *adj* poorly organized and in a messy or chaotic state (*informal*) [Late 20C. < SHAMBLES]

shame /shaym/ *n* **1.** NEGATIVE EMOTION a negative emotion that combines feelings of dishonour, unworthiness, and embarrassment **2.** CAPACITY TO FEEL UNWORTHY the capacity or tendency to feel shame ○ *He has no shame.* **3.** STATE OF DISGRACE a state of disgrace or dishonour ○ *bring shame on the family* **4.** CAUSE FOR REGRET a cause for regret or disappointment ○ *It's a shame you couldn't stay for lunch.* **5.** CAUSE OF SHAME somebody or something that causes somebody else to feel shame ■ *vt* (**shames, shaming, shamed**) **1.** MAKE SOMEBODY FEEL ASHAMED to make somebody feel the negative emotion of shame ○ *It shamed her that she had cheated.* **2.** FORCE SOMEBODY THROUGH SHAME to make somebody do something by exploiting the fact that he or she would be ashamed not to do it ○ *He shamed us into making higher donations to the ministry.* **3.** MAKE SOMEBODY FEEL INFERIOR to be so much better or more successful than others as to expose their comparative inadequacy ○ *Their exam results shame other local schools.* ■ *interj* **1.** EXPRESSING SYMPATHETIC REACTION used to react sympathetically to something disappointing ○ *Shame, old friend, we would have invited you if we'd known you were free.* **2.** *S Africa* EXPRESSING SENTIMENTAL APPROVAL used to show that you think that something or somebody is attractive in an endearing way ○ *'Have you seen our new puppy?' 'Oh, shame! Isn't it cute!'* [Old English *sceamu* < Germanic] ◇ **put somebody** *or* **something to shame** to make somebody or something seem inferior or of inferior quality by comparison

shamefaced /sháym fáyst/ *adj* **1.** showing a feeling of shame or embarrassment **2.** timid or easily embarrassed [Mid-16C. Alteration of obsolete *shamefast* 'bashful'] —**shamefacedly** /-fáyssidli, -fáystli/ *adv* —**shamefacedness** /-fáyssidnəss, -fáystnəss/ *n*

shameful /sháymf'l/ *adj* bad enough to inspire shame

in those responsible —**shamefully** adv —**shamefulness** n

shameless /sháymləss/ adj **1.** untroubled or unaffected by shame, especially in situations where others would be ashamed **2.** done without shame, especially where others would feel shame —**shamelessly** adv —**shamelessness** n

shamiana /shámmi áanə, sháymi-/ n S Asia a decorative circus-style tent used for outdoor entertaining or weddings [Early 17C. < Persian, Urdu shāmiyāna]

Shamir /sha méer/, **Yitzhak** (b. 1914) Polish-born prime minister of Israel (1983–84, 1986–92). He has held many other government positions, including foreign minister (1980–92) and leader of the Likud Party (1983–93). Born **Jazernicki, Yitzhak**

shammash /shámməss/ (plural -**mashim** /sha móssim/), **shamosh**, **shammes** (plural -**mosim**) n **1.** the beadle of a synagogue **2.** a candle used to light the candles in a Hanukkah candlestick [Mid-17C. Via Yiddish shames < Hebrew šāmmaš 'attendant' < šimmēš 'serve']

shammy /shámmi/ (plural -**mies**) n INDUST, HOUSEHOLD same as **chamois** (senses 2–3) [Early 18C. Representing the pronunciation]

shampoo /sham póo/ n **1.** HAIR-CLEANING SOAP soap for cleaning the hair and scalp, usually in liquid or gel form **2.** SUDSY DETERGENT sudsy detergent for cleaning upholstery and carpets **3.** USE OF SHAMPOO a cleaning of the hair with shampoo ■ vt (-**poos**, -**pooing**, -**pooed**) CLEAN SOMETHING WITH SHAMPOO to clean the hair and scalp, upholstery, or a carpet with shampoo [Mid-18C. < Hindi cā̃pō < cā̃pnā 'knead, massage']

shamrock

shamrock /shám rok/ n a three-leafed clover or a plant similar to clover that serves as the national emblem of Ireland [Late 16C. < Irish seamróg 'small clover' < seamar 'clover']

shamus /sháyməss, shaá-/ n (slang) **1.** US a police officer **2.** N Am same as **private detective** [Early 20C. Origin ?]

Shan /shaan, shan/ (plural same or **Shans**) n **1.** a member of a people living mainly in northeastern Myanmar and also in neighbouring parts of China, Laos, and Thailand **2.** the Tai language of the Shan people. Native speakers: 2.5 million. [Early 19C. < Burmese] —**Shan** adj

Shandong /shan dóong/ province on the eastern coast of China, bordered by Hebei, the Yellow Sea, Henan, and Jiangsu. Capital: Jinan. Population: 87,380,000 (1997). Area: 153,300 sq. km/59,190 sq. mi.

shandy /shándi/ n a drink made of beer and lemonade [Late 19C. Shortening of SHANDYGAFF]

shandygaff /shándi gaf/ n US a drink made of beer and ginger beer [Mid-19C. Origin ?]

Shang /shang/ n a Chinese dynasty that ruled from about 1766 to about 1027 BC, a period that coincided with the development of China's system of handwriting and work in bronze (often used before a noun) [Mid-17C. < Chinese Shāng]

Shangaan /shán gaan/ (plural same or -**gaans**) n PEOPLES, LANG same as **Tsonga** [Late 19C. < Bantu] —**Shangaan** adj

shanghai[1] /shán hī/ (-**hais**, -**haiing**, -**haied**) vt **1.** to trick or force somebody to do something or go somewhere **2.** to recruit somebody forcibly into a navy [Late 19C. After SHANGHAI, typical destination of ships with enforced crews]

shanghai[2] /shán hī, shang hī/ ANZ n (plural -**hais**) ARMS same as **catapult** n (sense 1) ■ vt (-**hais**, -**haiing**, -**haied**) to shoot something with a catapult [Mid-19C. Origin ?]

Shanghai /shang hī/ city and port on the River Huangpu in eastern China. Population: 13,580,000 (1995). —**Shanghainese** /sháng hī néez/ npl, adj

Shango /sháng gō/ n Carib an African-based religion based on the worship of numerous deities, who also have Catholic counterparts. Worship includes animal sacrifice, spirit possession, drumming, dancing, and chanting. [Mid-20C. < Yoruba, the god of thunder]

Shangri-la /sháng gri laá/ n an imaginary and remote paradise [Mid-20C. After an imaginary land in The Lost Horizon (1933) by English novelist James Hilton]

shank /shangk/ n **1.** LONG NARROW PART the long narrowest part of something such as a key or pipe, especially when it connects two functional parts **2.** CUT OF MEAT a cut of meat from the leg of cattle, pigs, or sheep **3.** BOTTOM OF ANIMAL LEG the lower part of an animal's leg, between the bottom and middle joints **4.** LOWER LEG the lower part of the human leg, from ankle to knee **5.** LEG a human leg (informal) **6.** MECH ENG BODY OF PIN OR NAIL the long narrow part of a pin, nail, screw, or bolt, between the head and the pointed or threaded part **7.** MECH ENG PART CONNECTING TOOL HEAD TO HANDLE a part sticking out from the head of a tool, by which it can be fitted into a handle **8.** JEWELLERY RING BAND the plain band part of a ring, not including any jewels and their settings **9.** CLOTHING NARROW PART OF SHOE SOLE the narrow part of the sole of a shoe, beneath the arch of the foot, or any fitting at this part of a shoe **10.** NAUT ANCHOR'S STEM the stem of an anchor **11.** PRINTING PART OF PRINTING TYPE the body of a piece of type, between the foot and shoulder **12.** CLOTHING BUTTON STEM a loop or stem at the back of a button, by which it is sewn to the cloth **13.** CRIME HOMEMADE DAGGER a makeshift dagger, e.g. one made from a shard of glass, especially one made by a prisoner (slang) ■ v (shanks, shanking, shanked) **1.** vt GOLF MISHIT GOLF BALL to hit a golf ball with the heel of the club, sending it in the wrong direction **2.** vi BOT SHOW DISEASE FROM BASE UP to shrivel, or show other signs of disease spreading upwards from the base of the stem (refers to plants) [Old English sceanca 'shinbone' < W Germanic]

Popperfoto
Ravi Shankar

Shankar /shángk aar/, **Ravi** (b. 1920) Indian sitarist, composer, and teacher. His international tours popularized Indian music in the West. His compositions include film scores and sitar concertos.

shanking /shángking/ n a disease of plants marked by shrivelling and decay from the base of the stems

shanks's pony n the legs or feet, as a means of transportation (dated informal humorous)

shannachie /shánna khee/ n Ireland a traditional Irish storyteller [Mid-16C. < Irish seanchaidhe]

Shannon /shánnən/ longest river in the British Isles. It rises in northwestern County Cavan, north-central Republic of Ireland, and empties into the Atlantic Ocean. Length: 370 km/230 mi.

shanny /shánni/ (plural -**nies** or same) n a fish with a small tapering body and a long dorsal fin. Native to: rocky European coasts. Latin name: Blennius pholis. [Mid-19C. Origin ?]

shan't /shaant/ contr shall not

shantey n MUSIC, NAUT another spelling of **shanty**[2]

shantung /shan túng/ n **1.** heavy silk cloth with a nubby uneven weave **2.** cotton or synthetic fabric made to resemble silk shantung [Late 19C. After SHANDONG]

shanty[1] /shánti/ (plural -**ties**) n a crudely built shack or hut [Early 19C. Probably < Canadian French chantier 'lumberjack's hut', via French, 'timberyard' < Latin cant(h)erius 'rafter']

shanty[2] /shánti/ (plural -**ties**), **shantey** (plural -**teys**) n a rhythmic song of a kind originally sung by sailors while they were working in groups [Mid-19C. Probably < French chantez 'sing!']

shantytown /shánti town/ n a settlement consisting of shacks [Late 19C. < SHANTY[1]]

Shanxi /shánshi/ agricultural province in northeastern China, bordered by Nei Monggol, Hebei, Henan, and Shaanxi. Capital: Taiyuan. Population: 31,090,000 (1997). Area: 157,099 sq. km/60,656 sq. mi.

shape /shayp/ n **1.** OUTLINE the outline of something's form ○ His face has a square shape. **2.** SOMETHING NOT CLEARLY SEEN something that has bulk but is not clearly seen in outline ○ She could see a shape through the fog. **3.** MATHS GEOMETRIC FORM a geometric form, e.g. a square, triangle, cone, or cube **4.** GENERAL CHARACTER OF SOMETHING the broad character that something has ○ the overall shape of the proposals **5.** ORIGINAL FORM the original or optimal form of something ○ The pleats lost their shape in the wash. **6.** HEALTH the condition of somebody's health or fitness ○ She exercises regularly and is in pretty good shape. **7.** SOMETHING'S CONDITION the condition that something is in ○ The lawn is in great shape. **8.** MOULD FOR SOMETHING a mould or pattern for making something or giving something its form **9.** GHOST a ghostly form or phantom ■ v (shapes, shaping, shaped) **1.** vt INFLUENCE SOMETHING GREATLY to have a profound or crucial influence over something ○ His beliefs were shaped by his upbringing. **2.** vt PLAN FOR NATURE OF SOMETHING to plan or decide on what the character of something should be ○ They are meeting to shape the nation's future. **3.** vt GIVE SHAPE TO SOMETHING to mould something into a different shape ○ She shapes the clay into little animals. **4.** vi HAPPEN to happen or occur **5.** vt PSYCHOL TRAIN WITH REWARD AND PUNISHMENT to change somebody's behaviour gradually using reward as the person comes closer to the desired behaviour, and punishment for moving away from it [Old English gesceap 'creation' < Germanic, 'cut out'] —**shaped** adj —**shaper** n ◇ **knock** or **lick** or **whip somebody** or **something into shape** to bring somebody or something to a desired state quickly, roughly, or haphazardly (informal) ◇ **take shape** to take a definite form

shape up vi **1.** REACH ACCEPTABLE STANDARD to reach an acceptably high standard of behaviour, skill, or attitude **2.** DEVELOP IN PARTICULAR WAY to seem to be developing in a particular way ○ It's shaping up to be an environmental disaster. **3.** IMPROVE to improve or develop in the way that is wanted (informal)

SHAPE /shayp/ abbr MIL Supreme Headquarters Allied Powers Europe

shapeless /sháypləss/ adj **1.** with an indefinite or imprecise shape **2.** put together in a very haphazard way —**shapelessly** adv —**shapelessness** n

shapely /sháypli/ (-**lier**, -**liest**) adj having a shape that is visually appealing —**shapeliness** n

shape memory alloy n a metallic alloy that has the ability when it is heated to return to a previously defined shape or size after deformation

shape-shifter n in fiction, somebody or something that is able to change form

shape-up n US a method of hiring dock workers in which those seeking work arrive at the docks in the morning and employers select from among them

shard /shaard/, **sherd** /shurd/ n **1.** BROKEN PIECE OF GLASS a sharp broken piece of glass or metal **2.** ARCHAEOL same as **potsherd 3.** ZOOL ANIMAL'S SCALE OR SHELL an animal's scales, shell, or other tough outer covering **4.** INSECTS BEETLE'S OUTER WING the outer wing covering of a beetle [Old English sceard 'cut, notch' < Indo-European, 'to cut']

share[1] /shair/ v (shares, sharing, shared) **1.** vti USE SOMETHING ALONG WITH OTHERS to have or use something in common with other people ○ We shared a flat. **2.** vti

TAKE RESPONSIBILITY TOGETHER to take equal responsibility for something along with other people ○ *We shared the blame.* **3.** *vti* **LET SOMEBODY USE SOMETHING** to allow somebody to use something or have part of something ○ *I shared my ice cream with him.* **4.** *vt* **DIVIDE SOMETHING EQUALLY BETWEEN PEOPLE** to allocate equal parts of something to different people or groups ○ *She shared out the money among her six grandchildren.* **5.** *vt* **HAVE SIMILAR FEELING OR EXPERIENCE** to have something the same as or in common with somebody else ○ *He shared my view that the plan would not work.* **6.** *vt* **TELL SOMEBODY SOMETHING** to express something to another person rather than keeping silent ○ *Do you want to share your feelings?* ■ *n* **1.** **PART OF SOMETHING ALLOTTED** a part of something that is owned by, paid for by, done by, or set aside for each of several people ○ *He hasn't had his share of the cake.* **2.** **FIN PART OF COMPANY'S STOCK** any of the equal, usually small, parts into which a company's capital stock is divided ○ *She owns shares in several companies.* **3.** **REASONABLE OR APPROPRIATE PORTION** the portion that somebody deserves or should be responsible for ○ *She does more than her share of the work.* [Old English *scearu* 'division, portion' < Indo-European, 'to cut'] —**sharer** *n*

SYNONYMS *share, divide up, allocate, allot, distribute, dispense, dole out*

CORE MEANING: to give something to or divide it between different people or groups

share to divide something, especially equally, between different people or groups ○ *Occasionally the role of chairperson may be shared between several people.* ○ *The new agreement calls for added revenue to be shared equally among the players.* **divide up** to divide something into several parts ○ *There is no way of dividing up the work that will satisfy everybody.* **allocate** to divide something and give it for a specific purpose, or to divide something between different people or groups ○ *allocate funds for recurrent expenditures* ○ *Warranties serve as a means of allocating business risk between the vendor and the purchaser.* **allot** to give something to somebody as a share of what is available or what has to be done ○ *We rejected the plan, which would allot us control of 49 per cent of the undertaking.* ○ *Some tasks now allotted to local government might more efficiently be handled by the state* **distribute** to give things to a number of people ○ *The remaining funds will be distributed among good causes around the world.* ○ *The premier's speech was distributed to reporters beforehand.* **dispense** to give a service or advice to several recipients ○ *the agency responsible for dispensing nonmilitary foreign aid* ○ *The prime role of the law courts is to dispense justice.* **dole out** (*informal*) to give something to each of a group of people ○ *Dad began to dole out the porridge from the saucepan.* ○ *a need to dole out sympathy to the losers of today's match*

share[2] /shair/ *n* AGRIC same as **ploughshare** [Old English *scear* < Indo-European, 'to cut']

share accommodation *n Aus* rented property shared by two or more individual tenants

share certificate *n* a document certifying ownership of shares, issued by a company to somebody who holds shares in that company. N Am term **stock certificate**

sharecropper /sháir kropər/ *n US* a tenant farmer who farms land for the owner and is paid a share of the value of the yielded crop —**sharecrop** *vti*

shared ownership /shaird-/ *n* a form of home ownership in which the resident buys part of the property and rents part of it from a housing association

shareholder /sháir hōldər/ *n* somebody who owns one or more shares of a company's stock. N Am term **stockholder**

share house *n Aus* a rented house shared by two or more individual tenants

share index *n* an index showing movement of share prices

share-milker *n NZ* somebody who tends and milks a herd of cows as a tenant on somebody else's farm and shares in the profits of the business [After SHARE-CROPPER]

share option *n* a benefit by which an employee of a company can buy its shares at a special price. US term **stock option**

shareware /sháir wair/ *n* software made available for free trial with the understanding that users will voluntarily pay a fee to the author or publisher for continued use

sharia /shə ree ə/, **shari'a**, **shari'ah** *n* Islamic religious law, based on the Koran (*often used before a noun*) [Mid-19C. < Arabic *šar'īya* 'lawfulness' < *aš-šar* 'Islamic law']

sharif /sha reef/, **sherif** /she reef/, **shereef** *n* **1.** **DESCENDANT OF MUHAMMAD** a descendant of the prophet Muhammad through his daughter Fatima **2.** **GOVERNOR OF MECCA** the governor or chief magistrate of Mecca during the years of Ottoman Turkish rule **3.** **ARAB RULER** an Arab prince or ruler [Late 16C. < Arabic *sharīf* 'illustrious'] —**sharifian** *adj*

Sharjah /shá'arjə/ one of the seven member states of the United Arab Emirates. Capital: Sharjah. Population: 200,000 (1989). Area: 2,590 sq. km/1,000 sq. mi.

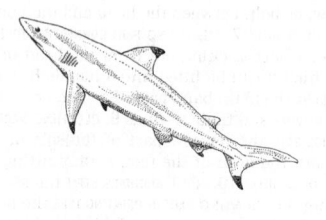

shark

shark /shaark/ *n* **1.** **CARNIVOROUS FISH** a carnivorous fish with a long body, two dorsal fins, sharp teeth, a cartilaginous skeleton, and thick, rough skin. Class: Chondrichthyes. **2.** **RUTHLESS PERSON** a ruthless greedy person (*informal*) **3.** same as **loan shark** (*informal*) ■ *vi* (**sharks, sharking, sharked**) **CHEAT OTHERS PROFESSIONALLY** to make a living as a cheater or fraud [Mid-16C. Origin ?] ◊ **jump the shark** to do something atypical or out of place that seems to mark the beginning of an inevitable decline in quality or popularity (*informal*)

shark bait *n Aus, US* somebody who foolishly swims beyond most other swimmers into waters that might be dangerous because of sharks (*informal humorous*)

Shark Bay /shá'ark-/ bay on the coast of Western Australia

shark bell *n Aus* LEISURE same as **shark siren**

shark patrol *n Aus* a patrol carried out by boat or plane to watch for sharks that may approach public swimming areas

shark siren *n Aus* a siren or similar mechanism sounded to warn swimmers and surfers that sharks have been spotted offshore

sharkskin /shá'ark skin/ *n* **1.** a smooth glossy fabric made from a mixture of acetate and rayon **2.** leather made from a shark's skin

sharksucker /shá'ark sukər/ *n* FISH same as **remora** [Mid-19C. < its habit of attaching itself to sharks]

Helen Sharman

Sharman /shá'armən/, **Helen** (*b.* 1963) British astronaut. With her participation in the Anglo-Soviet scientific space mission Project Juno, she became Britain's first astronaut (1991). Full name **Sharman, Helen Patricia**

Sharon, Plain of /shárrən/ plain between the Mediterranean coast and the Samarian foothills in western Israel. It extends southwards from Haifa to Tel Aviv and is the most densely populated region of the country.

Sharon /shə rón/, **Ariel** (*b.* 1928) Israeli soldier and prime minister (2001–). A prominent member of the Likud Party, he became party leader in 1999 and prime minister in 2001.

sharon fruit /shárrən-/ *n* FOOD same as **persimmon** (sense 1) [After the Plain of SHARON]

sharp /shaarp/ *adj* **1.** **ABLE TO CUT** having an edge or point that is very acute and able to cut or puncture things ○ *a sharp blade* **2.** **POINTED** ending in a point or sharp angle ○ *a sharp nose* **3.** **ABRUPT IN CHANGING DIRECTION** making a change in direction that forms an acute angle ○ *a sharp turn* **4.** **QUICK-WITTED** quick-witted and intelligent or quick to notice and understand **5.** **CRITICAL** critical and unsympathetic ○ *a sharp rebuke* **6.** **IRRITABLE** irritable or angry ○ *a sharp temper* **7.** **SUDDEN** sudden and significant or noticeable ○ *a sharp rise in prices* ○ *a sharp intake of breath* **8.** **DISTINCT** clearly and definitely distinct ○ *Her soft voice was in sharp contrast to her forbidding expression.* **9.** **CLEARLY DETAILED** with the detail clear and distinct ○ *a sharp image* **10.** **PIERCING** loud, piercing, and abrupt or unexpected ○ *a sharp cry* **11.** **STRONG IN TASTE** strong and slightly bitter in taste ○ *a sharp cheese* **12.** **INTENSE** penetrating and intense ○ *a sharp frost* **13.** MUSIC **HIGHER BY SEMITONE** higher in pitch by a semitone ○ *F sharp* **14.** MUSIC **TOO HIGH PITCHED** a little too high in pitch and therefore slightly out of tune **15.** **STYLISH** neat, stylish, and fashionable (*informal*) ○ *a sharp dresser* **16.** **FRAUDULENT** deceitful or fraudulent ○ *sharp practice* ■ *adv* **1.** **PRECISELY** exactly and not before or after ○ *at 9 o'clock sharp* **2.** MUSIC **AT SLIGHTLY TOO HIGH PITCH** at higher than the usual pitch and therefore slightly out of tune ○ *She's singing sharp.* ■ *n* **1.** MUSIC **NOTE HIGHER BY SEMITONE** a note or tone that is a semitone higher in pitch than the natural or unmodified pitch. Symbol ♯ **2.** MUSIC **SHARP SYMBOL** the symbol for a sharp note **3.** HANDICRAFT **LONG SEWING NEEDLE** a long thin needle for hand-sewing **4.** MED **SHARP MEDICAL INSTRUMENT** a pointed or cutting medical instrument that requires careful disposal, e.g. a hypodermic needle or surgical blade (*usually used in the plural*) ○ *a container labelled 'sharps only'* **5.** **SKILLED CHEATER** somebody who is skilled at cheating others, especially in gambling and at cards (*informal*) **6.** **EXPERT** somebody expert at something (*informal*) [Old English *scearp* < Indo-European, 'to cut'] —**sharply** *adv* —**sharpness** *n*

Sharp /shaarp/, **Cecil** (1859–1924) British musicologist. His collections of folk songs and dances from Britain and the United States reawakened interest in folk song and folk dance. Full name **Sharp, Cecil James**

sharpbill /shá'arp bil/ *n* a small fruit-eating bird with a straight sharp beak, green and yellow feathers, and a red crest. Native to: rainforests of Central and South America. Latin name: *Oxyruncus cristatus.*

shar-pei /shaar páy/, **Shar-Pei** *n* a medium-sized dog with a squarish snout, blue tongue, short hair, and loose skin that falls in folds over its body, especially when young. It belongs to a breed originating in China. [Late 20C. < Chinese *shā pí* 'sand skin']

sharpen /shá'arpən/ (**-ens, -ening, -ened**) *v* **1.** *vti* **BECOME OR MAKE SHARPER** to become sharp or sharper, or make something sharp or sharper **2.** *vt* **RAISE PITCH OF NOTE** to raise a note in pitch, especially by a semitone **3.** *vt* **IMPROVE SOMETHING** to improve something so that it is more efficient or stylish than before —**sharpener** *n*

sharper /shá'arpər/ *n* GAMBLING same as **sharp** *n* (sense 5) (*informal*)

Sharpeville /shá'arp vil/ township near Vereeniging, South Africa. It was the scene of a massacre of antiapartheid demonstrators in 1960. Population: 42,000 (1972).

sharp-eyed *adj* **1.** alert and able to notice detail **2.** with very keen eyesight

sharpie /sha´arpi/, **sharpy** (*plural* **-ies**) *n* **1.** *US* GAMBLING same as **sharp** *n* (sense 5) (*informal*) **2.** *Aus* in Australia, a member of a youth subculture of the late 1960s and early 1970s whose members tended to wear short hair with long strands at the nape of the neck and baggy trousers and cardigans (*slang*)

sharpish /sha´arpish/ *adv* quickly or without delay (*informal*)

sharp-nosed puffer *n* a sea fish that is a puffer and can inflate its body like other puffers but also has a long snout with prominent nostrils. Native to: tropics. Family: Canthigasteridae.

sharp-set *adj* eagerly wanting something, especially food (*dated*)

sharpshooter /sha´arp shootər/ *n* somebody who can shoot a firearm extremely accurately

sharp-sighted *adj* same as **sharp-eyed** —**sharp-sightedly** *adv* —**sharp-sightedness** *n*

sharp-tongued *adj* critical or sarcastic and unsympathetic in speech

sharp-witted *adj* quick to think, understand, or react —**sharp-wittedly** *adv* —**sharp-wittedness** *n*

sharpy *n* another spelling of **sharpie** (*informal*)

shashlik /shásh lik, shaásh-/, **shashlick** *n* FOOD same as **shish kebab** [Early 20C. Via Russian *shashlyk* < Crimean Turkish *şişlik* 'small skewer' < *şiş* 'skewer']

Shasta /shástə/ (*plural same* or **-tas**) *n* **1.** a member of a group of Native North American peoples of the highlands of northern California **2.** the Hokan language of the Shasta people, which is nearly extinct [Mid-19C. Origin ?] —**Shasta** *adj*

Shasta, Mount /shástə/ mountain and extinct volcano in the Cascade Range, northern California. It has five glaciers. Height: 4,317 m/14,162 ft.

Shasta daisy *n* a chrysanthemum with large white flower heads. Latin name: *Chrysanthemum maximum*.

shastra /shaástrə/, **sastra** *n* in Hinduism, a sacred text [Mid-17C. < Sanskrit *śāstra* 'lesson' < *śās-* 'instruct']

shat past participle, past tense of **shit** (*taboo offensive*)

Shatt al-Arab /shát al árrəb/ river in Southwest Asia. It rises at the confluence of the Tigris and Euphrates rivers, flows along the border between Iran and Iraq, and empties into the Persian Gulf, near Kuwait. Length: 170 km/110 mi.

Shatten /shátt´n/, **Gerald P.** (*b.* 1949) US developmental biologist. He led the research team that produced the first genetically modified monkey.

shatter /sháttər/ *v* (**-ters, -tering, -tered**) **1.** *vti* SMASH INTO PIECES to break suddenly into many small brittle pieces, or cause something to break in this way **2.** *vt* DESTROY HOPE OR BELIEF to destroy something that somebody believed in or hoped for **3.** *vt* SHOCK SOMEBODY to shock and distress somebody badly ■ **shatters** *npl* FRAGMENTS fragments made by shattering something [14C. Ultimately < Indo-European, 'split apart'] —**shatterer** *n*

shatter cone *n* a cone-shaped rock piece that has stripes running from its point, created by volcanic pressure or meteoric impact

shattered /sháttərd/ *adj* thoroughly tired out (*informal*)

shatterproof /sháttər proof/ *adj* made to resist shattering

shave /shayv/ *v* (**shaves, shaving, shaved, shaved** or **shaven** /sháyvən/) **1.** *vti* REMOVE HAIR WITH RAZOR to remove hair from the body using a razor **2.** *vt* REDUCE AMOUNT SLIGHTLY to reduce an amount, price, or time taken by a very slight amount ○ *shaved two seconds off her best time* **3.** *vt* BARELY TOUCH SOMETHING to barely touch something when passing **4.** *vt* REMOVE THIN LAYER to remove a thin layer from something using a razor, rasp, or similar tool **5.** *vt* TRIM SOMETHING to trim something closely ■ *n* **1.** ACT OF SHAVING the act, process, or result of shaving **2.** same as **shaving** (sense 1) **3.** SHAVING TOOL a tool for shaving or scraping [Old English *scafan* < Indo-European, 'to scrape, scratch']

shaven /sháyvən/ past participle of **shave** ■ *adj* (*often used in combination*) **1.** with the beard or the hair shaved off **2.** trimmed or cropped

shaver /sháyvər/ *n* **1.** a device that is used to shave

the beard or hair, especially an electric razor (*often used before a noun*) **2.** a boy who is not old enough to shave (*dated informal*)

Shavian /sháyvi ən/ *adj* **1.** BY OR LIKE G. B. SHAW written by or in the style of the work of the playwright George Bernard Shaw **2.** OF G. B. SHAW relating to or studying George Bernard Shaw or his works ■ *n* STUDENT OF G. B. SHAW an admirer or student of George Bernard Shaw or his works [Early 20C. < modern Latin *Shavius* 'Shaw']

shaving /sháyving/ *n* **1.** a thin slice shaved off **2.** the removing of hair or a beard with a razor (*often used before a noun*)

Shavuoth /shə voó ŏth/, **Shavuot** /-ŏt/ *n* a Jewish festival marking the Law being given by God to Moses on Mount Sinai. Date: 6th of Sivan, in May or June. [Late 19C. < Hebrew *šāḇūʿōṯ* 'weeks' (between Passover and Pentecost)]

shaw /shaw/ *n* UK, Midwest a thicket of shrubs or small trees [Old English *sceaga* < Germanic, 'something sticking out']

George Bernard Shaw

Shaw /shaw/, **George Bernard** (1856–1950) Irish playwright. His plays, including *Pygmalion* (1913) and *Heartbreak House* (1919), established him as the leading English-language playwright of his time. He promoted socialism in works such as *The Intelligent Woman's Guide to Socialism and Capitalism* (1928).

> 'All professions are conspiracies against the laity.'
> [George Bernard Shaw, *The Doctor's Dilemma*, Act I; 1911]

> 'I don't want to talk grammar, I want to talk like a lady.'
> [George Bernard Shaw, *Pygmalion*, Act II; 1913]

Shaw, Norman (1831–1912) British architect. He was noted for his designs for town and country houses and for New Scotland Yard, London (1888–90). He formulated the Queen Anne style. Full name **Shaw, Richard Norman**

Shawano *n, adj* PEOPLES, LANG same as **Shawnee**

Shawinigan /shə wínnigən/ town in southern Quebec, Canada, northwest of Trois Rivières on the St Maurice River. Population: 48,366 (2001).

shawl /shawl/ *n* a fabric square worn by women over the shoulders or head and shoulders or used to wrap a baby in ■ *vt* (**shawls, shawling, shawled**) to cover somebody or something with a shawl or with something performing a similar function [Early 17C. < Persian, Urdu *šāl*]

shawm /shawm/ *n* a woodwind instrument of the Middle Ages and Renaissance that has a double reed and was the predecessor of the modern oboe [14C. Via Old French *chalemie* < Latin *calamus* 'reed']

Shawnee /shaw neé/ (*plural same* or **-nees**), **Shawano** /shə waánŏ/ (*plural same* or **-nos**) *n* **1.** a member of an Algonquian people who lived along the Ohio, Cumberland, and Tennessee rivers, and now live mainly in Oklahoma **2.** the Algonquian language of the Shawnee people. Few people now speak Shawnee. [Late 17C. < Delaware *ša:wano:w*] —**Shawnee** *adj*

Shawwal /shə wól/ *n* in the Islamic calendar, the tenth month of the year. See table at **calendar** [Late 18C. < Arabic *shawwāl*]

she stressed /shee/; unstressed /shi/ *pron* (*used as the subject of a verb*) **1.** PREVIOUSLY MENTIONED FEMALE PERSON OR ANIMAL used to refer to a female person or animal who has been previously mentioned or whose identity is known ○ *Ms Jones continues to enjoy high approval ratings as she starts her third year in office.* **2.** OBJECT PERCEIVED AS FEMALE used to refer to something previously mentioned or known that has been traditionally thought of as female, e.g. a nation, car, machine, boat, or ship ○ *Brazil stated that she is ready to start talks on the issue.* ○ *The tanker is 25 years old but she is still very seaworthy.* ■ *n* FEMALE ANIMAL OR GIRL a female animal or person, sometimes used of a new baby ○ *Is it a he or a she?* [12C. Probably alteration of Old English *hēo*, feminine form of HE[1]]

s/he /shee awr heé/ *pron* used in writing as a pronoun to mean 'she or he' (*intended to avoid sexism in writing*) ○ *If a student wishes to change courses s/he should consult me before the end of next week.*

shea /shay/ *n* TREES same as **shea tree** [Late 18C. < Mande *sí*]

shea butter *n* a white fat obtained from the seeds of the shea tree. Use: food, soap and candle manufacture.

sheading /sheéding/ *n* any of the six administrative districts of the Isle of Man [Late 16C. Variant of *shedding* 'division', originally verbal noun of SHED[1] 'to divide']

sheaf /sheef/ *n* (*plural* **sheaves** /sheevz/) **1.** a bundle of the harvested stalks of a plant, especially wheat or another cereal, with the heads still containing their seeds **2.** a bundle of objects gathered or tied together ■ *vt* (**sheafs, sheafing, sheafed**) AGRIC same as **sheave**[1] [Old English *sceaf* < Germanic]

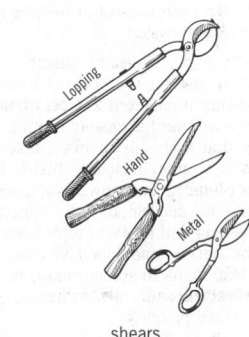

shears

shear /sheer/ *v* (**shears, shearing, sheared, sheared** or **shorn** /shawrn/) **1.** *vti* CUT SOMETHING OFF to remove something with a sharp tool **2.** *vti* CUT HAIR OR FOLIAGE FROM SOMETHING to cut hair, fleece, or foliage from the surface of something using a sharp tool **3.** *vt* DEPRIVE SOMEBODY OF SOMETHING VALUABLE to take something valuable or prized away from somebody ○ *sheared of all self-respect* **4.** *vti* MOVE SMOOTHLY THROUGH SOMETHING to move quickly and cleanly through something **5.** *vti* DEFORM BY TWISTING FORCE to cause something to deform or break by applying a twisting force, or deform or break in this way ■ *n* **1.** REMOVAL OF FLEECE a cutting off of a sheep's wool, often used as a measure of the age of a sheep **2.** WOOL CUT OFF a quantity of wool cut off a sheep **3.** PHYS, ENG same as **shear strain 4.** PHYS, ENG same as **shear stress** ■ **shears** *npl* **1.** CUTTING TOOL a tool with a large pair of scissors, used for cutting or trimming **2.** ENG same as **sheerlegs** [Old English *sceran* < Indo-European, 'to cut']

SPELLCHECK **shear** or **sheer**? Do not confuse the spelling of **shear** and **sheer**, which sound similar. **Shear** is chiefly used as a verb, meaning 'remove something with a sharp tool', 'deprive somebody of something valuable' (as in *shear them of their self-respect*), or 'deform or break by a twisting force': *The head of the bolt has sheared off*. **Shears** is a plural noun denoting a cutting tool. The most commonly used word spelt **sheer** is chiefly used as an adjective, meaning 'complete and utter', 'vertical', or 'thin and almost transparent' (as in *sheer folly, a sheer drop, sheer fabric*). Another **sheer** is primarily a verb, meaning 'swerve from a course': *The boat sheered away, narrowly avoiding a collision*. A third **sheer** is a nautical term referring to the upward curve of a boat's hull.

shearer /sheérər/ *n* a farm worker who shears sheep

for a living, especially in Australia and New Zealand

Shearer /sheérər/, **Alan** (*b.* 1970) English footballer. A skilled centre-forward, he played for Blackburn Rovers (1992–96) before joining Newcastle United (1996). He has captained England.

shear force *n* a force, or a component of a force, that acts parallel to a plane

shearing shed *n* a large building on a sheep farm, especially in Australia and New Zealand, where shearers work

shearlegs *n* ENG another spelling of **sheerlegs**

shearling /sheérling/ *n* **1.** a young sheep, usually between six and twelve months old, after its first shearing **2.** the tanned skin of a recently sheared lamb or sheep, with the short wool that remains after shearing still attached

shear modulus *n* the ratio of the shear stress to the shear strain, taken as an indication of the strength of a material under shear forces

shear pin *n* a pin inserted in a machine as a safety device. If safe loads are exceeded, the pin breaks and the machine shuts down.

shear strain *n* the angular deformation of a body, quantitatively taken to be the sideways displacement of two adjacent planes divided by the distance between them

shear stress *n* the forces acting on a body that produce shear strain

shearwater /sheér waatər/ (*plural* **-ters** or *same*) *n* a long-winged seabird with a short hooked beak, that flies low over the water in search of food. Genus: *Puffinus*. [< the impression when the bird flies that its wings are shearing the water]

sheath /sheeth/ *n* (*plural* **sheaths** /sheethz, sheeths/) **1.** CASE FOR BLADE a case for the blade of a knife, sword, or other cutting implement **2.** CLOSE-FITTING COVERING a covering or case that fits closely around something in the way that a sheath covers a blade **3.** CLOSELY FITTING DRESS a woman's closely fitting dress, originally floor-length, but now also knee-length **4.** HEALTH same as **condom 5.** BIOL PROTECTIVE TUBE a tubular covering that protects some body parts, e.g. some of the nerves and blood vessels, and plant parts, e.g. leaf stems in some grasses ■ *vt* (**sheaths**, **sheathing**, **sheathed**) same as **sheathe** [Old English *scæð* < Germanic, 'to divide, split']

sheathbill /sheéth bil/ *n* an all-white shorebird resembling a pigeon, which has a horny sheath on its face, around the beak, and is a scavenger. Native to: rocky Antarctic and subantarctic coasts. Latin name: *Chionis alba* or *Chionis minor*.

sheathe /sheeth/ (**sheathes**, **sheathing**, **sheathed**) *vt* **1.** PUT INTO SHEATH to put a knife, sword, or other cutting implement into a sheath **2.** ENCLOSE SOMETHING to enclose something in a covering or case ○ *PVC-sheathed cable* ○ *sheathed in a tight silk dress* **3.** RETRACT CLAWS to retract the claws, in the way a cat does **4.** THRUST CUTTING IMPLEMENT to thrust a knife or sword into somebody's flesh (*literary*) [14C. < SHEATH]

sheathing /sheéthing/ *n* something that encloses and protects, e.g. a covering of boards on a building's framework or a protective material applied to the underwater surfaces of a boat's hull

sheath knife *n* a knife with a fixed blade that is carried in a sheath

shea tree *n* a tropical tree with seeds from which shea butter is obtained. Native to: West Africa. Latin name: *Vitellaria paradoxa* or *Butyrospermum parkii*.

sheave[1] /sheev/ (**sheaves**, **sheaving**, **sheaved**) *vt* to gather something, especially the cut stalks of a cereal crop, into a sheaf [Late 16C. Back-formation < SHEAVES]

sheave[2] /sheev/ *n* a wheel with a grooved rim for a rope, cable, or belt, especially one used as a pulley [13C. Ultimately < Germanic, 'disc, slice of bread']

sheaves AGRIC plural of **sheaf**

Sheba /sheébə/ ancient kingdom of southwestern Arabia, in present-day Yemen. It reached the height of its wealth and power in the 8th century BC. In

the Bible, it is the meeting place of Solomon and the Queen of Sheba (1 Kings 10:1–13).

shebang /shi báng/ [Mid-19C. Origin ?] ◇ **the whole shebang** the entirety of something (*slang*) ○ *They sold their house, car, furniture, and boat – the whole shebang.*

Shebat *n* CALENDAR, JUDAISM another spelling of **Shevat**

shebeen /shi beén/ *n* a small establishment that sells alcoholic beverages illegally or without a licence, traditionally operating in the poorer regions of Ireland, Scotland, and South Africa [Late 18C. < Irish *síbín* 'little mug' < *séibe* 'mug']

Shechina /shə kínə, -keénə/, **Shechinah**, **Shekhinah** *n* in the theology of Judaism, God's presence in and throughout the world [Mid-17C. < late Hebrew *šĕkīnāh* < *šākan* 'rest, dwell']

shechita /shə kheétə/, **schechita** *n* under Jewish dietary laws, the prescribed method of slaughter of animals and birds. The act is performed by a trained and licensed slaughterer (**shochet**) who draws a very sharp knife across the animal's throat and allows the blood to drain out. [Late 19C. < Hebrew *šĕhītāh* 'slaughter' < *šāhat* 'to slaughter']

shed[1] /shed/ *v* (**sheds**, **shedding**, **shed**) **1.** *vt* CAUSE SOMETHING TO FLOW to cause tears or blood to pour out **2.** *vt* RADIATE SOMETHING to radiate or disperse something, especially light **3.** *vti* BIOL LOSE GROWING PART NATURALLY to cast off a growing part such as hair or leaves as a result of a natural process such as moulting **4.** *vt* GET RID OF UNDESIRABLE to get rid of somebody or something that is unwanted or unnecessary **5.** *vti* REPEL OR BE REPELLED to flow off or drop off, or cause something, especially water, to flow off or drop off **6.** *vt* LOSE LOAD ACCIDENTALLY to have a transported load accidentally fall off onto the road **7.** *vt Scotland* PART HAIR to put a parting in the hair ■ *n Scotland* DIVISION IN HAIR a parting in the hair [Old English *scēadan* 'divide, separate' < Germanic]

shed[2] /shed/ *n* **1.** SMALL BUILDING a small structure, either free-standing or attached to a larger building, used especially for storage or shelter **2.** LARGE OPEN BUILDING a large building with an open interior and sometimes no walls, used for storage or shelter or as a work area **3.** LARGE ENCLOSED BUILDING a large rectangular enclosed building containing an open space, used especially for commercial and retail purposes [15C. Probably variant of SHADE]

she'd /sheed/ *contr* **1.** she had **2.** she would

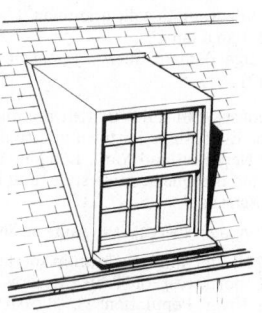

shed dormer

shed dormer *n* a dormer window with a flat roof that slopes in the same direction as the main roof that surrounds it [< SHED[2]]

she-devil *n* an offensive term for a woman who is regarded as treating people with cruelty or gross contempt (*insult*)

shedload /shéd lōd/ *n* a very large amount or number of something (*informal*; *often used in the plural*) ○ *He always turns up with shedloads of gear, even if we're only camping for the weekend.*

sheen /sheen/ *n* **1.** GLOSSY APPEARANCE a bright, softly shining surface or appearance **2.** FINE CLOTHING fine or brightly coloured clothing (*literary*) ■ *vi* (**sheens**, **sheening**, **sheened**) *regional* SHINE to have a sheen [14C. < archaic *sheen* 'beautiful' < Germanic, 'to see'] — **sheeny** *adj*

Sheene /sheen/, **Barry** (1950–2003) British motorcyclist. He was a world champion at 500cc (1976 and 1977) and winner of 23 Grand Prix (1971–81). He

went on to work as a television commentator in Australia.

sheeny /sheéni/ (*plural* **-nies**) *n* a highly offensive term for a Jew (*slang insult*) [Early 19C. Origin ?]

sheep

sheep /sheep/ (*plural same*) *n* **1.** DOMESTICATED MAMMAL a stocky hooved animal, with ribbed horns in the male. Kept for: wool, meat. Genus: *Ovis*. **2.** LEATHER FROM SHEEP leather made from the skin of a sheep **3.** OFFENSIVE TERM an offensive term that deliberately insults somebody's courage, self-assertion or leadership qualities (*insult*) [Old English *scēap* < Germanic] ◇ **on the sheep's back** ANZ deriving a high percentage of income from the sale of wool ◇ **separate the sheep from the goats** to distinguish good or competent members of a group from the bad or incompetent

sheep-dip *n* **1.** a disinfectant in which sheep are immersed to rid them of external parasites such as mites, ticks, and flies **2.** a bath containing a disinfectant in which sheep are immersed to rid them of external parasites

sheepdog

sheepdog /sheép dog/ *n* a dog that is used to herd sheep, or belongs to a breed traditionally used to herd sheep

sheepfold /sheép fōld/ *n* an enclosure or shelter for sheep

sheepish /sheépish/ *adj* **1.** showing embarrassment as a result of having done something awkward or wrong **2.** showing the meekness popularly associated with sheep —**sheepishly** *adv* —**sheepishness** *n*

sheep ked /-ked/ *n* INSECTS same as **sheep tick** [< *ked* 'sheep tick', origin ?]

sheep laurel *n* a low-growing evergreen bush with leaves that are poisonous to young grazing animals. Flowers: crimson or pink. Native to: eastern United States, Canada. Latin name: *Kalmia angustifolia*.

sheep's eyes *npl* shy glances full of love and longing (*dated*) [< the large size and the docile appearance of the eyes of sheep]

sheepshank /sheép shangk/ *n* a knot used to shorten a rope in which the rope is doubled up upon itself

sheepshead /sheéps hed/ (*plural same* or **-heads**) *n* **1.** a sea fish with a deep body marked with dark vertical bands. Native to: Atlantic coastal waters of North America. Latin name: *Archosargus rhomboidalis*. **2.** a freshwater fish of the drum family. Native to: eastern North America. Latin name: *Aplodinotus grunniens*. [Mid-16C. < a supposed resemblance of its head to that of a sheep]

sheepskin /shéep skin/ *n* **1.** SHEEP LEATHER WITH OR WITHOUT WOOL the skin of a sheep used as leather, with or without the wool still attached (*often used before a noun*) **2.** SHEEPSKIN GARMENT OR RUG a rug or a garment, especially a coat or jacket, made from sheepskin with the wool attached **3.** PARCHMENT a parchment made from the skin of a sheep (*often used before a noun*) **4.** *N Am* DIPLOMA a diploma, traditionally made of sheepskin parchment (*informal*)

sheep tick *n* a wingless fly that lives as a blood-sucking parasite on sheep and can cause serious skin irritations. Latin name: *Melophagus ovinus*.

sheer[1] /sheer/ *adj* **1.** COMPLETE AND UTTER used to emphasize the unlimited extent or unmitigated quality of something ○ *That explanation is sheer nonsense.* **2.** EXCLUSIVE OF ANYTHING ELSE considered by itself without reference to anything else, or acting by itself without help from anything else ○ *She won the race by sheer endurance.* **3.** PURE OR UNADULTERATED free of any impurities, or not mixed with anything else **4.** VERTICAL rising nearly straight up or falling nearly straight down over a long distance ○ *They looked over the edge and there was a sheer drop.* **5.** THIN AND ALMOST TRANSPARENT so thin and fine as to be almost transparent ○ *a sheer summer blouse* ■ *adv* **1.** VERTICALLY with an almost vertical rise or fall **2.** COMPLETELY completely and utterly ■ *n* NEARLY TRANSPARENT FABRIC a fabric or piece of clothing that is very thin and fine and almost transparent [Mid-16C. Origin ?] —**sheerly** *adv* —**sheerness** *n*

SPELLCHECK See *shear*.

sheer[2] /sheer/ *vti* (**sheers, sheering, sheered**) SWERVE FROM COURSE to swerve from a course, or cause a vehicle or vessel to swerve from its course ■ *n* **1.** CHANGE OF COURSE an abrupt or sudden change of course **2.** POSITION OF SHIP AT ANCHOR the position of a ship in relation to its anchor [Early 17C. Origin ?]

SPELLCHECK See *shear*.

sheer[3] /sheer/ *n* the upward curve of a boat's hull as seen from the side, or the degree to which the hull curves upwards [Late 17C. Origin ?]

SPELLCHECK See *shear*.

sheerlegs /sheér legz/, **shearlegs** *n* a lifting device consisting of two poles tied together at the top and spread apart at the bottom with a pulley suspended from the apex (*takes a singular or plural verb*) [Mid-19C. < variant of SHEAR]

Sheerness /sheér néss/ town and river port on the Isle of Sheppey, Kent, southeastern England. Population: 11,653 (1991).

sheet[1] /sheet/ *n* **1.** CLOTH USED ON BED a large rectangular piece of cloth that is used to cover the mattress of a bed or somebody sleeping on the mattress **2.** FLAT THIN RECTANGULAR PIECE a broad flat thin piece of a material, especially a rectangular piece of paper, metal, or glass **3.** BROAD THIN EXPANSE a broad flat thin expanse of a substance, especially ice or water **4.** EXPANSE OF SOMETHING MOVING a broad expanse of something that is in motion, e.g. falling water **5.** STAMPS PAGE OF STAMPS an entire rectangular page of postage stamps that were printed as a unit **6.** PUBL NEWSPAPER a newspaper or periodical, especially one dismissed as trivial ■ *v* (**sheets, sheeting, sheeted**) **1.** *vt* PUT SHEET OVER SOMETHING to cover or wrap something in a sheet **2.** *vt* COVER SOMETHING WITH THIN LAYER to cover something with a thin layer of a material **3.** *vt* FORM SOMETHING INTO THIN PIECES to form something, especially metal, into broad flat thin pieces **4.** *vi* FALL OVER BROAD EXPANSE to fall, flow, or spread out over a broad area ○ *Rain sheeted over the parking lot.* ■ *adj* **1.** BROAD, FLAT, AND THIN made in broad flat thin, usually rectangular pieces **2.** COVERING THINLY covering a broad area thinly [Old English *scēte* 'cloth' < Germanic, 'to project']

sheet down *vi* to fall in torrents (*refers to rain*)

sheet[2] /sheet/ *n* a rope or line attached to a bottom corner of a sail and used to change the sail's position ■ **sheets** *npl* the spaces in the bow and stern of an open boat that are not occupied by the seats [Old English *scēata* 'corner, lower part of a sail' < Germanic]

sheet anchor *n* **1.** a large anchor that is dropped only in emergencies **2.** a personal source of help in a time of crisis or danger [Origin ?]

sheet bend *n* a knot used for tying one rope to a loop formed in another [< SHEET[2]]

sheetcake /sheét kayk/ *n US* a rectangular or square, one-layer, iced cake [< SHEET[1]]

sheeting /sheéting/ *n* **1.** wide cotton or linen cloth. Use: sheets. **2.** thin material for lining and covering surfaces [Early 18C. < SHEET[1]]

sheet lightning *n* lightning that appears in a broad sheet as a result of being diffused by cloud cover [< SHEET[1]]

sheet metal *n* metal that has been formed into a sheet by being pressed between rollers until it is thinner than plate but thicker than foil [< SHEET[1]]

sheet music *n* music printed on folded or unfolded sheets of paper that have not been bound into a book

sheet pile *n* a vertical column of steel, wood, or concrete driven into the ground alongside others to form an underground barrier impeding the movement of earth or water [< SHEET[1]]

Sheffield /shéffeeld/ city in South Yorkshire, northern England. It was for many years the centre of the British steel industry. Population: 513,234 (2001).

Sheffield Shield *n* in Australia, a trophy competed for annually by the state cricket teams [Early 20C. After Henry North Holroyd (1832–1909), 3rd Earl of SHEFFIELD]

shegetz /sháygits/ (*plural* **shkotzim** /shkótsim/) *n* an offensive term for a boy or man who is not Jewish (*insult*) [Early 20C. Via Yiddish *sheygets* < Hebrew *sheqeṣ* 'abomination, detested thing']

sheik /shayk, sheek/, **sheikh, shaikh** *n* **1.** ARAB CHIEF the leader of an Arab family or village **2.** ISLAMIC RELIGIOUS LEADER a senior official in an Islamic religious organization **3.** PHYSICALLY APPEALING MAN a handsome and physically appealing man (*dated informal*) [Late 16C. < Arabic *šayk* 'man of advanced years' < *šāka* 'be aged'] —**sheikdom** *n*

sheika /sháy kaa/, **sheikha, shaikha** *n* the wife of a sheik [Mid-19C. < Arabic *šayka*]

sheikh, etc. ISLAM another spelling of **sheik, etc.**

sheila /sheélə/ *n ANZ* a woman, especially a girl or young woman (*informal*) [Mid-19C. Origin ?]

~~**sheild**~~ incorrect spelling of **shield**

sheitel /sháyt'l/ *n* a wig worn by a married Orthodox Jewish woman to avoid showing her natural hair in accordance with Orthodox belief [Late 19C. Via Yiddish *sheytl* < Middle High German *scheitel* 'crown of the head']

shekel /shék'l/ *n* **1.** ISRAELI CURRENCY UNIT the main unit of Israeli currency. See table at **currency 2.** ANCIENT JEWISH UNIT OF WEIGHT an ancient Jewish unit of weight equivalent to approximately 16 g/0.5 oz **3.** ANCIENT JEWISH COIN an ancient Jewish coin that was a unit of currency between 66 AD and 130 AD ■ **shekels** *npl* MONEY money or cash (*slang*) [Mid-16C. < Hebrew *šeqel* < *šaqal* 'weigh']

Shekhinah *n* JUDAISM another spelling of **Shechina**

Shelburne /shélbərn, -burn/, **William Petty Fitzmaurice, 2nd Earl of** (1737–1805) British prime minister (1782–83). He helped draw up the Treaty of Paris (1783), which granted independence to Britain's North American colonies.

sheldrake /shél drayk/ (*plural* **-drakes** or *same*) *n* a male shelduck [14C. Origin ?]

shelduck /shél duk/ (*plural* **-ducks** or *same*) *n* a large thick-set, often brightly coloured or variegated duck with a thick beak. Native to: Europe, Asia. Genus: *Tadorna*. [Early 18C. Alteration of SHELDRAKE after DUCK[1]]

shelf /shelf/ (*plural* **shelves** /shelvz/) *n* **1.** FLAT SURFACE FOR HOLDING OBJECTS a flat, usually rectangular board on which things are stored or displayed. It can be attached to a wall or can form part of a cabinet. **2.** CONTENTS OF SHELF the contents of a shelf, or the quantity of something that a shelf holds **3.** GEOG LEDGE ON LANDSCAPE a ledge of rock, ice, or sand **4.** MIN EXTRACT LAYER OF UNDERGROUND ROCK a layer of underground rock encountered when sinking a shaft **5.** ARCHERY HEEL OF HAND the part of the heel of the hand on which the back end of an arrow is supported before being fired from a bow [14C. < Low German *schelf*] —**shelfful** *n* ◇ **be (left) on the shelf 1.** to be thought too old to have any chance of marrying (*sometimes offensive*) **2.** to be no longer wanted, used, or taken account of

shelf fungus *n* FUNGI same as **bracket fungus**

shelf ice *n* a large plate of floating ice that has broken off from an ice shelf

shelf life *n* **1.** the length of time a product may be stored before it begins to lose its freshness or effectiveness **2.** the length of time that somebody or something is popular or lasts (*informal*)

shelf mark *n* a series of numbers or letters on a book indicating its location in a library

shell /shel/ *n* **1.** COVERING OF TURTLE OR CRAB the hard protective outer covering of turtles, crabs, and other molluscs and crustaceans, or the calcium-based material this covering is made of **2.** COVERING OF INSECT'S BODY the hard outer covering (**exoskeleton**) of an insect's body **3.** COVERING OF EGG the hard or tough protective outer covering of the eggs of birds, reptiles, and a few mammals **4.** OUTER COVERING OF NUT the hard or fibrous protective outer covering of some seeds and fruits such as nuts **5.** PROTECTIVE CASING a hard casing or covering that protects or holds its contents **6.** CONSTR FRAMEWORK OF BUILDING the basic framework of a building, especially while under construction or after damage by fire **7.** NAUT HULL OF SHIP the outer hull of a ship **8.** COOK PASTRY CASE a casing of pastry that has a filling put into it **9.** SOMETHING HOLLOW OR EMPTY an external form that contains nothing ○ *a mere shell of her former self* **10.** RESERVED MANNER a reserved manner behind which a shy person hides feelings or thoughts ○ *eventually came out of her shell and joined in* **11.** ARMS LARGE EXPLOSIVE PROJECTILE an explosive projectile fired from a large-bore gun such as a field gun or tank gun **12.** ARMS GUN CARTRIDGE a piece of ammunition fired by a gun, especially a shotgun cartridge, which holds the shot and explosive powder **13.** INDUST FIREWORK CARTRIDGE the cartridge that forms the outside of a firework and contains the explosive powder **14.** *US* HOUSEHOLD SMALL GLASS a small beer glass **15.** CLOTHING UNLINED JACKET an unlined, usually lightweight jacket **16.** *US* CLOTHING SLEEVELESS BLOUSE a sleeveless blouse or sweater for a woman **17.** BUSINESS same as **shell company 18.** ROWING NARROW RACING BOAT a narrow light boat used for racing, rowed by one or more people **19.** PHYS GROUP OF ELECTRONS IN SIMILAR ORBITS a group of electrons with the same principal quantum number that orbit the nucleus of an atom **20.** COMPUT COMMAND PROGRAM a computer program that simplifies the interface between a user and the operating system by allowing the user to pick from a set of menus instead of entering commands ■ *v* (**shells, shelling, shelled**) **1.** *vti* TAKE SOMETHING OUT OF SHELL to take something out of a shell, or be taken out of a shell ○ *shell peas* **2.** *vti* SEPARATE KERNELS FROM COB to separate kernels from a cob, or be separated from a cob ○ *shell sweet corn* **3.** *vti* MIL BOMBARD TARGET to fire artillery shells at something **4.** *vi* FLAKE OFF to fall off in thin scales **5.** *vi N Am* COLLECT SEASHELLS to look for and gather shells at the seashore [Old English *scell* < Germanic]

shell out *vti* to pay out money, especially a great deal of money (*informal*)

she'll /sheel/ *contr* **1.** she shall **2.** she will

shellac /shə lák, shéllak/ *n* **1.** PURIFIED RESIN yellowish-orange flakes of a resin (**lac**) secreted by a tropical insect **2.** VARNISH a thin varnish made of purified lac dissolved in alcohol. Use: formerly, as a coating on wooden items. **3.** 78 RPM GRAMOPHONE RECORD an old type of gramophone record originally made from a material containing purified lac, played at 78 rpm ■ *vt* (**-lacs, -lacking, -lacked**) **1.** APPLY SHELLAC TO SOMETHING to coat something with shellac varnish **2.** *N Am* HIT SOMEBODY REPEATEDLY to beat somebody repeatedly with hard blows (*slang*) **3.** *N Am* DEFEAT SOMEBODY EASILY to defeat somebody easily or decisively (*slang*) [Mid-17C. < SHELL + LAC[1], after French *laque en écailles* 'lac (melted) in thin plates']

shellacking /shə láking, shéllaking/ *n N Am* (*slang*) **1.** a severe physical beating **2.** an easy or decisive defeat

shellback /shél bak/ *n* **1.** a sailor who has crossed the equator, especially one whose crossing was marked by a traditional initiation ceremony **2.** an experienced sailor or somebody who has been a

sailor for many years [< the idea that limpets and barnacles have grown on the sailor's back during the long time at sea]

shell company *n* a company that has no independent assets or operations of its own, but is used by its owners to conduct specific business dealings or maintain control of other companies

Mary Shelley

Shelley /shélli/, **Mary** (1797–1851) British writer. Her most famous work is *Frankenstein* (1818). She was the daughter of Mary Wollstonecraft and the wife of Percy Bysshe Shelley. Born **Godwin, Mary Wollstonecraft**

Shelley, Percy Bysshe (1792–1822) British poet. His lyric poetry was at the forefront of the English romantic movement and included odes such as 'To a Skylark' (1819) and an elegy on Keats, 'Adonais' (1821). He was the husband of Mary Shelley.

> 'Hail to thee, blithe Spirit! / Bird thou never wert, / That from Heaven, or near it, / Pourest thy full heart / In profuse strains of unpremeditated art.'
> [Percy Bysshe Shelley, 'To a Skylark'; 1819]

> 'Poets are...the trumpets which sing to battle and feel not what they inspire...Poets are the unacknowledged legislators of the world.'
> [Percy Bysshe Shelley, *A Defence of Poetry*; 1821]

shellfire /shél fīr/ *n* **1.** artillery shells or projectiles fired at a target **2.** the firing or exploding of artillery shells or projectiles

shellfish /shél fish/ (*plural same* or **-fishes**) *n* an invertebrate water animal with a shell, especially an edible mollusc or crustacean such as an oyster, shrimp, or lobster

shell game *n N Am* **1.** a form of the game thimblerig in which spectators bet on the final location of an object hidden under one of three walnut shells or cups that have been shuffled **2.** a scheme for defrauding or deceiving people

shell jacket *n* a tight-fitting military jacket that extends only to the waist and is worn on semiformal occasions

shell-like *n* somebody's ear (*slang humorous*)

shell pink *adj* of a pale pink colour (*hyphenated when used before a noun*) —**shell pink** *n*

shell shock *n* a psychiatric disorder caused by exposure to warfare, especially shellfire (*dated*)

shell-shocked *adj* **1.** stunned, upset, or exhausted as a result of a stressful experience (*informal*) **2.** experiencing severe psychological effects from exposure to warfare, especially shellfire (*dated*)

shell star *n* a star that is thought to have a surrounding shell of gas

shell suit *n* a lightweight shiny brightly coloured tracksuit worn casually or for sport. It is usually made of nylon with a soft lining.

shellwork /shél wurk/ *n* seashells stuck on furniture and other items to give a decorative finish

Shelta /shéltə/ *n* an ancient secret language used by the Roma and other travelling people in the Republic of Ireland and the United Kingdom, based on Gaelic [Late 19C. Origin ?] —**Shelta** *adj*

shelter /shéltər/ *n* **1.** STRUCTURE THAT PROTECTS OR COVERS a structure or building that provides cover from weather or protection against danger **2.** REFUGE an establishment providing temporary accommodation and food for people in need or without a home **3.** PROTECTION OR COVER the protection, cover, refuge, or safety that a shelter provides **4.** DWELLING OR HOUSING a place to live, considered as one of life's necessities **5.** *N Am* REFUGE FOR ANIMALS an establishment that takes in and looks after lost or unwanted animals ■ *v* (**-ters, -tering, -tered**) **1.** *vt* PROVIDE SOMEBODY OR SOMETHING WITH PROTECTION to provide somebody or something with protection, cover, refuge, or safety **2.** *vi* FIND PROTECTION to find protection, cover, refuge, or safety **3.** *vt* INVEST MONEY TO AVOID TAXES to put money into an investment that is subject to a lower tax rate or is free from taxes [Late 16C. Origin ?]

sheltered /shéltərd/ *adj* **1.** protected from the adverse effects of the weather, especially wind **2.** protected from the unpleasant, upsetting, or testing experiences of life

sheltered housing, **sheltered accommodation** *n* accommodation specially designed for people unable to live independently. It usually consists of self-contained self-catering units with some communal facilities and live-in staff to help when required.

sheltered workshop *n N Am* a workplace specially designed to provide a noncompetitive environment where people with disabilities can acquire job skills and experience

shelter tent *n US* a small tent for two people usually made from two similar pieces of waterproof fabric

sheltie /shélti/, **shelty** (*plural* **-ties**) *n* (*informal*) **1.** ZOOL same as **Shetland pony 2.** BREED same as **Shetland sheepdog** [Early 16C. Probably < Old Norse *Hjalti* 'Shetlander']

shelve[1] /shelv/ (**shelves, shelving, shelved**) *vt* **1.** PUT SOMETHING ON SHELF to put or store something on a shelf **2.** SET SOMETHING ASIDE to put something off until later, or set something aside **3.** DISMISS SOMEBODY OR SOMETHING to dismiss or withdraw somebody or something from active service [Late 16C. Back-formation < SHELVES]

shelve[2] /shelv/ (**shelves, shelving, shelved**) *vi* to descend with a flat, usually gradual slope [Late 16C. Origin ?]

shelves plural of **shelf**

shelving /shélving/ *n* **1.** the shelves in a place, or shelves in general **2.** material used for making shelves

Shema /shə maá/ *n* the confession of faith made in Jewish religious practice [Early 18C. < Hebrew *šĕma* 'hear!']

shemozzle /shə mózz'l/ *n* (*dated informal*) **1.** a confused or muddled situation **2.** a noisy quarrel or argument [Late 19C. Via Yiddish, 'crooked luck' < Middle High German *slim* 'crooked' + *mazzāl* 'luck']

Shenandoah National Park /shénnən dō ə-/ national park in the Blue Ridge Mountains, northern Virginia, established in 1935. Area: 802 sq. km/310 sq. mi.

shenanigan /shi nánnigən/ *n* (*informal*) **1.** something that is deceitful, underhand, or otherwise questionable (*usually used in the plural*) **2.** a playful trick, mischievous prank, or other display of high spirits [Mid-19C. Origin ?]

Shenyang /shən yúng/ city in Liaoning Province, northeastern China. Population: 5,120,000 (1995).

she-oak *n Aus* same as **casuarina** [< SHE used for 'timber that is inferior in texture and colour']

Sheol /shee ol, shee ōl/ *n* in ancient Hebrew theology, the dwelling place of the dead [Late 16C. < Hebrew *šĕ'ōl*]

~~shepard~~ incorrect spelling of **shepherd**

Shepard /shéppərd/, **Alan, Jr** (1923–98) US astronaut. He was the first US astronaut in space (5 May 1961) and the fifth person to walk on the moon (1971). Full name **Shepard, Alan Bartlett Jr**

Shepard, Sam (*b.* 1943) US playwright and actor. His offbeat plays include the Pulitzer Prize-winning *Buried Child* (1978). Full name **Rogers, Samuel Shepard, Jr**

'In this business we make movies, American movies. Leave the films to the French.' [Sam Shepard, *True West*; 1980]

shepherd /shéppərd/ *n* **1.** SOMEBODY TENDING SHEEP somebody who looks after sheep **2.** SOMEBODY PROVIDING GUIDANCE somebody who is responsible for looking after and guiding a group of people, especially a Christian minister ■ *v* (**-herds, -herding, -herded**) **1.** *vti* TEND SHEEP to look after sheep **2.** *vt* GUIDE to guide a group of people somewhere **3.** *vt* TAKE CARE OF OTHERS to look after the well-being of a group of people **4.** *vti Aus* SHIELD TEAM-MATE in Australian Rules football, to shield a team-mate by blocking the approach of an opposing player [Old English *scēaphirde* < *scēap* 'sheep' + *hierde* 'herder']

shepherdess /shéppər déss, shéppərdiss/ *n* a girl or woman who looks after sheep (*dated*)

shepherd's check *n* (*often used before a noun*) **1.** a pattern of small black-and-white squares **2.** a fabric in a shepherd's check pattern

shepherd's pie *n* a baked dish made of cooked minced meat, traditionally lamb or mutton, in gravy with a topping of mashed potato

shepherd's purse *n* an annual plant that has heart-shaped seed pods and is a common garden weed. Latin name: *Capsella bursa-pastoris*. [< the pod's resemblance to a bag used by shepherds to carry food]

Sheppard /shéppərd/, **Jack** (1702–24) English robber. Notorious for his repeated escapes, he was hanged in London. His exploits were later romanticized in ballads, plays, and novels. Born **Sheppard, John**

Sheppard, Kate (1848–1934) British-born New Zealand suffragist. She was the leader of a successful campaign for the extension of political suffrage to women, which resulted in New Zealand's being the first country to grant women the vote (1893). Born **Malcolm, Catherine Wilson**

Shepparton /shéppərtən/ city in northern Victoria, Australia. It is an industrial, agricultural, and food-processing centre. Population: 17,001 (1991).

Sheppey, Isle of /shéppi/ island off the coast of northern Kent, southeastern England, at the mouth of the River Medway. Area: 91 sq. km/35 sq. mi.

Sheraton: a Sheraton chair

Sheraton /shérrətən/ *adj* describes furniture designed by or in the simple graceful style of Thomas Sheraton, who favoured straight lines, considered classical ornamentation, and light thin legs

Sheraton /shérrətən/, **Thomas** (1751–1806) British cabinetmaker. He wrote *The Cabinet-Maker and Upholsterer's Drawing Book* (1793–94), which was influential in formulating the neoclassical style in English furniture.

sherbert *n N Am* FOOD another spelling of **sherbet** (sense 3)

sherbet /shúrbət/ *n* **1.** FIZZY POWDER a fruit-flavoured sweet powder that fizzes when moistened on the tongue and is eaten as a confection or is stirred into water to make a fizzy drink (*often used before a noun*) **2.** FRUIT DRINK a drink made from fruit juice, water, and sugar and served chilled **3.** *N Am* FROZEN DESSERT a frozen dessert made with fruit syrup, milk and the white of an egg, whisked until smooth and opaque **4.** BEVERAGES same as **beer** (*dated slang humorous*) [Early 17C. Via Turkish *şerbet* and Persian *šerbet* < Arabic *šarbat* 'drink' < *šariba* 'to drink']

Sherborne /shúr bawrn/ market town in Dorset, south-

ern England, known for its 8th-century abbey. Population: 7,606 (1991).

Sherbrooke /shúr brŏŏk/ city situated south of the St Lawrence River in Quebec, Canada, 160 km/100 mi. east of Montreal. Population: 127,354 (2001).

sherd n ARCHAEOL same as **shard**

shereef n ISLAM, POL, HIST same as **sharif**

Sheridan /shérridən/, **Richard Brinsley** (1751–1816) Irish-born British playwright. His comedies of manners include *The Rivals* (1775) and *The School for Scandal* (1777). He was a Whig MP (1780–1812). See Cultural note at **rival, scandal**

'MRS. MALAPROP If I reprehend any thing in this world, it is the use of my oracular tongue, and a nice derangement of epitaphs!'
[Richard Brinsley Sheridan, *The Rivals*; 1775]

sherif n ISLAM, POL, HIST same as **sharif**

sheriff /shérrif/ n 1. SENIOR OFFICIAL OF ENGLISH COUNTY in England and Wales, the senior representative of the monarch in a county, who performs ceremonial and some judicial duties 2. SCOTTISH JUDGE in Scotland, a judge who presides over one of the lower courts for civil and criminal cases (**sheriff courts**) 3. US COUNTY LAW ENFORCEMENT OFFICER in the United States, the chief law enforcement officer for a county, whose duties are sometimes restricted to the enforcement of the orders of the courts 4. CANADIAN COURT OFFICER in Canada, an officer of the courts who assists with the administration of the justice system, e.g. by serving writs 5. AUSTRALIAN COURT OFFICIAL in Australia, a court official charged with managing juries and implementing orders from the Supreme Court [Old English scīrgerēfa 'reeve of the shire' < scīr 'shire' + gerēfa 'reeve'] —**sheriffdom** n

sheriff court n in Scotland, the lower court for civil and criminal cases

sheriff officer n in Scotland, a court official who carries out warrants and serves writs

Sherlock Holmes /shúr lok hómz/ n 1. somebody with exceptional powers of deduction or perception (*humorous*) 2. CRIME same as **private detective** (*informal*) [Early 20C. After the detective in the stories of Sir Arthur Conan Doyle]

AKG London
Cindy Sherman

Sherman /shúrmən/, **Cindy** (b. 1954) US photographer. Her carefully staged and composed photographs, featuring herself in various roles, gained widespread notice in the 1980s.

Sherman, **William T.** (1820–91) US Union army general. A Mexican War veteran, he rejoined the army in 1861 as the American Civil War broke out and became one of the Union army's most aggressive and successful generals, marching on Atlanta and then to the sea (1864). Full name **Sherman, William Tecumseh**

'There is many a boy here today who looks on war as all glory, but, boys, it is all hell.'
[William T. Sherman, *Speech, Columbus, OH*; 11 August 1880]

sherpa /shúrpə/ n 1. a fabric with a fleecy pile. Use: lining for winter outdoor wear. 2. CLIMBING another spelling of **Sherpa** (senses 2–3) [Mid-20C. < SHERPA]

Sherpa /shúrpə/ (*plural* -**pas** or same) n 1. MEMBER OF HIMALAYAN PEOPLE a member of a people originally from Tibet who live on the southern slopes of the

Himalayan range in Nepal and Sikkim. Sherpas are noted for their mountaineering skills. 2. HIMALAYAN GUIDE a Sherpa who works as a guide for mountaineers in the Himalayan range 3. EXPERT POLITICAL AIDE an expert who helps a government leader prepare for a summit meeting [Mid-19C. < Tibetan *sharpa* 'inhabitant of an eastern country']

~~sherrif~~ incorrect spelling of **sheriff**

sherry /shérri/ n a wine, especially one made near Jerez de la Frontera, Spain, that has a higher alcohol content as a result of adding brandy, and ranges from very sweet to very dry [Late 16C. Alteration of archaic *sherris*, interpreted as plural, after *Xeres* (now JEREZ DE LA FRONTERA)]

sherwani /shər waáni/ (*plural* -**nis**) n a knee-length formal coat without lapels that buttons up to the neck, worn by men in and from South Asia [Early 20C. < Urdu, Persian *širwānī* 'from Shirvan', town in NE Persia]

Sherwood Forest /shúr wŏŏd-/ ancient forest in Nottinghamshire, central England, now reduced to a small fraction of its former extent. According to legend it was the haunt of Robin Hood.

she's /sheez/ contr 1. she has 2. she is

Shetland /shétlənd/ n 1. ZOOL same as **Shetland pony** 2. BREED same as **Shetland sheepdog** 3. TEXTILES same as **Shetland wool** 4. CLOTHING an item of clothing made of Shetland wool, especially a sweater ■ adj made of Shetland wool

Shetland Islands /shétlənd-/ group of about 150 islands lying 209 km/130 mi. north of mainland Scotland. The islands serve as a base for the North Sea oil industry. Mainland is the chief island. Capital: Lerwick. Population: 22,522 (2001). Area: 1,438 sq. km/555 sq. mi. —**Shetlander** n

Shetland pony

Shetland pony n a small sturdy pony with a long shaggy mane and tail, belonging to a breed that originated in the Shetland Islands

Shetland sheepdog n a small herding dog with a heavy coat that resembles a collie, belonging to a breed that originated in the Shetland Islands

Shetland wool n a fine wool from sheep raised in the Shetland Islands, or a yarn spun from this wool

Shevardnadze /shévvərd naádzi/, **Eduard** (b. 1928) Georgian chairman (1992–96) and president (1995–2003). As foreign minister of the former Soviet Union, he helped to implement democratic reforms. After his native Georgia became an independent republic, he became its head of state, but was forced to resign following election disputes. Full name **Shevardnadze, Eduard Amvrosiyevich**

Shevat /shə vót/, **Shebat** /-bót, -vót/ n in the Jewish calendar, the 11th month of the religious year, lasting 30 days and falling about the same time as January to February. See table at **calendar** [Mid-16C. < Hebrew *šĕḇaṭ*]

shew /shṓ/ (**shews, shewing, shewed, shewed** or **shewn** /shṓn/) vti same as **show** (*archaic*) [Variant]

shewbread /shṓ bred/ n in the Bible, the twelve loaves of bread placed in the tabernacle every Sabbath by the Hebrew priests of ancient Israel (*archaic*)

SHF, **shf** abbr PHYS superhigh frequency

shh interj another spelling of **sh**

Shia /shee ə/, **Shi'a, Shi'ah** n (*plural* same or -**as**; *plural* same or -**'as**; *plural* same or -**'ahs**) 1. the branch of Islam that considers Ali, the cousin of Muhammad,

and his descendants as Muhammad's true successors 2. ISLAM same as **Shiite** ■ adj ISLAM same as **Shiite** [Early 17C. < Arabic *šī'a* 'faction, party']

shiatsu /shi aát soo/, **shiatzu** n a form of healing massage in which the hands are used to apply pressure at acupuncture points on the body in order to stimulate and redistribute energy. Originating in Japan, it is used to treat various conditions such as back pain, migraine, insomnia, depression, and digestive pain. [Mid-20C. < Japanese, 'finger pressure']

shibboleth /shíbbə leth/ n 1. CATCHWORD OR SLOGAN a word or phrase frequently used, or a belief strongly held, by members of a group that is usually regarded by outsiders as meaningless, unimportant, or misguided 2. COMMON SAYING OR BELIEF a saying that is widely used or a belief that is widely held, especially one that interferes with somebody's ability to speak or think about things without preconception 3. IDENTIFYING WORD OR CUSTOM a unique pronunciation, word, behaviour, or practice used to distinguish one group of people from another and to identify somebody as either a member of the group or an outsider [Mid-17C. < Hebrew *šibbōleṭ* 'stream']

ORIGIN According to the Bible, the people of Gilead used the word *šibbōleṭ* as a password, because they knew their enemies the Ephraimites could not pronounce the 'sh' properly ('And it was so, that when those Ephraimites which were escaped said, Let me go over; that the men of Gilead said unto him, Art thou an Ephraimite? If he said, Nay, then they said unto him, Say now Shibboleth; and he said Sibboleth: for he could not frame to pronounce it right') (Judges 12:5–6).

shidduch /shí dakh/ (*plural* -**duchim** /shi dóokhim/) n a Jewish marriage, in former times usually arranged by a professional matchmaker (**shadchan**) [Late 19C. Via Yiddish < Hebrew *šiddūk* 'negotiation']

~~shiek~~ incorrect spelling of **sheik**

Shiel, Loch /sheel/ long narrow lake in western Scotland, linked to the sea by the River Shiel. It is a National Scenic Area. Length: 27 km/17 mi.

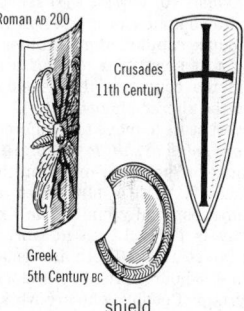
Roman AD 200
Crusades 11th Century
Greek 5th Century BC
shield

shield /sheeld/ n 1. PIECE OF ARMOUR CARRIED ON ARM a flat or convex piece of armour carried on the arm and used as a protection against weapon blows, arrows, bullets, or projectiles 2. PROTECTION OR DEFENCE somebody or something that serves as protection or acts as a defence 3. COAT OF ARMS a shield or a shield-shaped insignia that contains somebody's coat of arms 4. PRIZE OR TROPHY a prize or trophy, especially in a sports competition, that is made in the shape of a shield 5. DECORATIVE OFFICIAL EMBLEM a decorative device used as an official emblem by a government or organization, usually containing symbolic images associated with the government's territory or the organization's purpose 6. US POLICE OFFICER'S BADGE the official badge that a US police officer wears or carries 7. CLOTHING same as **dress shield** 8. ARMS PROTECTIVE PLATE ATTACHED TO ARTILLERY a steel plate attached to a piece of artillery to protect those operating the artillery from bullets and shrapnel 9. MECH ENG MACHINE'S SAFETY BARRIER a protective barrier around the moving parts of a piece of machinery, e.g. a screen or housing 10. ELEC ENG ANTISTATIC OR ANTIMAGNETIC SCREEN a screen used to protect equipment or people from unwanted electric or magnetic fields 11. PHYS WALL PROTECTING FROM RADIATION an encasing structure or wall, usually made of lead or concrete that is put around a nuclear reactor or

other source of radiation to prevent the release of radiation **12.** GEOL **FLAT AREA OF ROCK** a broad flat area of exposed Precambrian basement rock that lies at the centre of each continent **13.** ZOOL **PROTECTIVE PART COVERING ANIMAL** a protective part covering an animal, e.g. a shell, scale, or plate **14.** BOT same as **apothecium** ■ *v* (**shields, shielding, shielded**) **1.** *vt* **PROTECT SOMEBODY OR SOMETHING WITH SHIELD** to prevent harm or damage to somebody or something by using a physical barrier or by intervening in a protective way **2.** *vi* **ACT AS SHIELD** to serve or act as a protection or defence **3.** *vt* **HIDE SOMEBODY OR SOMETHING** to conceal or shelter somebody or something from view [Old English *scield* < Germanic] —**shielder** *n*

SYNONYMS See *safeguard.*

shielding /sheélding/ *n* the use of material such as lead or concrete around a source of radiation to prevent the harmful release of radiation

Shield of David *n* JUDAISM same as **Star of David**

shieling /sheéling/ *n Scotland* **1.** a mountain hut used by a cowherd **2.** a mountain pasture that is used by cattle in the summer [Mid-16C. < *shiel* 'shieling', origin ?]

shift /shift/ *v* (**shifts, shifting, shifted**) **1.** *vti* **MOVE** to move somebody or something to a different position, or be moved to a different position **2.** *vti* **CHANGE OR EXCHANGE** to change or exchange something for something else of the same group, set, or class, or be changed or exchanged in this way ○ *I've shifted jobs three times in the last year.* **3.** *vti* **REMOVE STAIN** to remove a mark or stain from a material or surface, especially with difficulty, or be removed from a material or surface **4.** *vti ANZ, N Am* AUTOMOT same as **change** *v* (sense 9) **5.** *vi* **PROVIDE FOR OWN NEEDS** to provide for your own personal needs or manage your personal affairs ○ *You need to learn to shift for yourself.* **6.** *vi* **GET BY WITH DECEIT** to get by through the use of deceit, tricks, or underhand methods **7.** *vi* **MOVE FAST** to move at great speed (*informal*) **8.** *vt* **EAT OR DRINK SOMETHING QUICKLY** to eat or drink something quickly or in large amounts (*informal*) **9.** *vt* **SELL SOMETHING QUICKLY** to sell something quickly or in large amounts, often when it is stolen or illegal or difficult to sell (*informal*) **10.** *vi* **PRESS SHIFT KEY** to press the shift key on a computer or typewriter keyboard in order to produce capital letters or other characters **11.** *vti* LING **ALTER PHONETICALLY** to alter a sound phonetically in the course of the development of a language, or be altered phonetically **12.** *vi Malaysia, Singapore* **MOVE HOUSE** to move to a different house or area ○ *We are going to shift to Penang.* ■ *n* **1. CHANGE MADE** a change in position, direction, makeup, or circumstances **2. PERIOD OF TIME WORKED** a period of working time, especially one of the fixed periods that the day is divided into in workplaces that operate 24 hours a day. There are usually two 12-hour or three 8-hour shifts. **3. PEOPLE WORKING DURING PERIOD** the group of people who are working during a particular period of time **4.** COMPUT same as **shift key 5.** CLOTHING **DRESS** a loose-fitting dress that hangs down from the shoulders **6.** CLOTHING **WOMAN'S UNDERGARMENT** a woman's shirt-shaped undergarment of the 17th and 18th centuries **7. PLAN** a tactic or plan required to accomplish something difficult **8. TRICK** a deceitful or underhand scheme or plan **9.** GEOL **ROCK DISPLACEMENT AT FAULT** a displacement of rocks on a fault line **10.** MUSIC **CHANGE IN HAND POSITION** a change in hand position in order to play a different set of notes in a different register on a keyboard or stringed instrument **11.** LING **CHANGE IN PRONUNCIATION** a change in the pronunciation of a sound in the course of the development of a language **12.** PHYS **CHANGE IN FREQUENCY** a change in the position of a spectral line representing a change of frequency, e.g. that caused by the Doppler effect [Old English *sciftan* 'divide, arrange' < Germanic]

SYNONYMS See *change.*

shifta /shíftə/ (*plural same* or **-tas**) *n* in parts of Africa, somebody who commits a robbery, usually of a traveller, on or near a public road [Mid-20C. Via Somali *shúfto* 'bandit' < Amharic]

shifting spanner *n Aus* a spanner with a head that can be adjusted by means of a screw to fit different sizes of nuts and bolts. UK term **adjustable spanner**. NZ term **adjustable wrench**

shift key *n* a key on a computer or typewriter keyboard that is pressed to produce capital letters or other characters

shiftless /shíftləss/ *adj* **1.** unwilling to make the effort to be successful or do something properly **2.** lacking the abilities or knowledge required to do something successfully or properly —**shiftlessly** *adv* —**shiftlessness** *n*

shiftwork /shíft wurk/ *n* a system of working in which people work one of a set of usually two 12-hour or three 8-hour shifts in a 24-hour period —**shiftworker** *n*

shifty /shífti/ (**-ier, -iest**) *adj* **1. UNTRUSTWORTHY** likely to try to deceive or avoid responsibility **2.** *N Am* **CHANGING DIRECTION OR POSITION** changing direction or position often or quickly, or able to do so **3. RESOURCEFUL** having the abilities and knowledge needed to do something successfully —**shiftily** *adv* —**shiftiness** *n*

shigella /shi géllə/ (*plural* **-lae** /-lee/ or **-las**) *n* a rod-shaped bacterium that lives in the intestinal tracts of human beings and animals and causes dysentery. There are four species, all causing dysentery, but with varying degrees of severity. Genus: *Shigella.* [Mid-20C. < modern Latin, after Kiyoshi *Shiga* (1870–1957), Japanese bacteriologist]

shigellosis /shíggə lṓssiss/ (*plural* **-loses** /-lṓseez/) *n* a highly infectious form of dysentery caused by the shigella bacterium. It occurs mainly in tropical countries, especially under insanitary conditions and among children and people with weakened immune systems.

shih tzu /sheé tsóo/ (*plural same* or **shih tzus**) *n* a small short-legged dog with a short muzzle, long dense coat, and a tail that curls over its back, belonging to a breed developed in Tibet [Early 20C. < Chinese *shīzigǒu* 'lion dog']

Shiism /sheé izəm/, **Shi'ism** *n* the Shiite branch of the Islamic religion [Late 19C. < SHIA or SHIITE]

shiitake /shi táaki/, **shiitake mushroom, shitake, shitake mushroom** *n* a dark-coloured mushroom with an edible fleshy cap. Native to: East Asia. Latin name: *Lentinus edodes.* [Late 19C. < Japanese, 'oak-tree mushroom']

Shiite /sheé īt/, **Shi'ite** *n* a follower of the Shia branch of Islam, which considers Ali, the cousin of Muhammad, and his descendants as Muhammad's true successors ■ *adj* relating to Shiites or the Shia branch of Islam —**Shiitic** /shee íttik/ *adj*

Shijiazhuang /sheéji ə zhwáng/ industrial centre and capital of Hebei Province, southwest of Beijing, in northeastern China. Population: 1,600,000 (1995).

shikari /shi káari/ (*plural* **-ris** or **-rees**) *n S Asia* a big-game hunter, especially a professional hunter who works as a guide [Early 19C. Via Urdu < Persian *šikārī* 'of hunting' < *šikār* 'hunting']

Shikoku /shi kṓkoo/ smallest of the four main islands of Japan. Area: 18,800 sq. km/7,259 sq. mi. Population: 4,195,000 (1990).

shiksa /shíksə/, **shikse** *n* an offensive Jewish term for a girl or woman who is not Jewish (*insult*) [Late 19C. < Yiddish *shikse*, feminine of *sheygets* (see SHEGETZ)]

shill /shil/ *N Am n* **1. PRETENDED CUSTOMER OR GAMBLER** an accomplice who pretends to be an interested customer or gambler in order to lure others into buying or gambling **2. SELF-INTERESTED PROMOTER** somebody who promotes somebody else or makes a sales pitch for something for reasons of self-interest ■ *v* (**shills, shilling, shilled**) **1.** *vi* **BE SHILL** to be or work as a shill **2.** *vt* **PROMOTE SOMEBODY OR SOMETHING AS SHILL** to promote somebody or make a sales pitch for something using the tactics of a shill [Early 20C. Origin ?]

shillelagh /shi láylə, -li/, **shillalah** *n Ireland* a stick or club, traditionally made of oak or blackthorn wood [Late 18C. After *Shillelagh*, town in Co. Wicklow, Ireland, famous for oaks]

shilling /shílling/ *n* **1.** a former subunit of British currency **2.** the main unit of currency in several East African countries. See table at **currency 3.** *Malaysia, Singapore* COINS same as **coin** (*informal*) [Old English *scilling* < Germanic] ◇ **not the full shilling** an offensive phrase meaning extremely unintelligent or affected to some extent by mental illness (*informal*)

Shillong /shi lóng/ capital of Meghalaya State, northeastern India. Population: 267,881 (2001).

Shilluk /shi lóok/ (*plural same* or **-luks**) *n* **1.** a member of a people who live in northeastern Africa, mainly along the western bank of the Nile in southern Sudan **2.** the Nilo-Saharan language of the Shilluk people. Native speakers: 110,000. [Late 18C. < Shilluk] —**Shilluk** *adj*

shilly-shally /shílli shali/ *vi* (**shilly-shallies, shilly-shallying, shilly-shallied**) **1. HESITATE OR VACILLATE** to be unable to make a choice or decision when one is needed **2. WASTE TIME** to waste time on unimportant things ■ *adv* **IRRESOLUTELY** with hesitation or a lack of decision ■ *adj* **LACKING DECISIVENESS** feeling or showing a lack of decisiveness ■ *n* (*plural* **shilly-shallies**) **HESITATION** a failure or inability to make a choice or decision [Early 18C. Alteration of *shall I? shall I?*] —**shilly-shallier** *n*

shim /shim/ *n* a thin, usually wedge-shaped piece of wood, metal, plastic, or other material that is used to help position something properly, usually by adjusting a level or filling a gap ■ *vt* (**shims, shimming, shimmed**) to position or adjust something using a shim [Early 18C. Origin ?]

shimmer /shímmər/ *vti* (**-mers, -mering, -mered**) **1. SHINE WITH WAVERING LIGHT** to shine softly with a wavering or flickering light, or make something do this **2. BE VISIBLE AS WAVERING IMAGE** to be visible as a wavering or flickering and sometimes distorted image, or make something do this ■ *n* **1. WAVERING LIGHT OR GLOW** a wavering or flickering soft light or glow **2. WAVERING IMAGE OR APPEARANCE** a wavering or flickering and sometimes distorted image such as that caused by hot air rising from the ground [Old English *scymrian* < Germanic, 'shine'] —**shimmery** *adj*

shimmy /shímmi/ *n* **1. WOBBLING OF VEHICLE** a wobbling motion or vibration, especially in the front wheels of a motor vehicle **2. POPULAR 1920S DANCE** a 1920s jazz dance in which the body was held straight and shaken rhythmically and rapidly from the shoulders down **3. QUICK SIDEWAYS MOVEMENT** a quick movement of the body to the side **4.** CLOTHING same as **chemise** (*informal*) ■ *vi* (**-mies, -mying, -mied**) **1. MOVE WITH WOBBLE** to wobble or be shaken with a wobbling motion, especially in the front wheels (*refers to vehicles*) **2. DANCE SHIMMY** to dance the shimmy **3. MOVE WITH SHAKE** to move the body in a shaking or swaying way **4. MOVE QUICKLY SIDEWAYS** to make a quick movement of the body to the side [Early 20C. Origin ?]

Shimonoseki /shímmənō seéki/ city and port in Yamaguchi Prefecture on southwestern Honshu Island, Japan, across the Shimonoseki Strait from Kitakyushu. Population: 246,924 (2002).

shin[1] /shin/ *n* **1. FRONT OF LOWER LEG** the front part of the leg from below the knee to above the ankle **2.** ANAT same as **shinbone 3. CUT OF BEEF** the lower portion of the foreleg in cattle, used as a cut of beef in stews ■ *v* (**shins, shinning, shinned**) **1.** *vti* **CLIMB USING ARMS AND LEGS** to climb a rope, tree, or pole with speed and agility by gripping with the arms and legs and then pulling up with the arms and sliding upwards. N Am term **shinny**[1] **2.** *vt* **KICK SOMEBODY IN SHIN** to kick or hit somebody in the shin [Old English *scinu* < Germanic]

shin[2] /shin/ *n* the 22nd letter of the Hebrew alphabet, represented in the English alphabet as 'sh'. See table at **alphabet** [Early 19C. < Hebrew *šīn*]

shinbone /shín bōn/ *n* the flat bone immediately under the skin on the front of the lower leg. Technical name **tibia** (sense 1)

shindig /shíndig/ *n* (*informal*) **1.** a noisy and festive party or celebration **2.** same as **shindy** (sense 1) [Late 19C. Probably alteration of SHINDY]

shindy /shíndi/ (*plural* **-dies**) *n* (*informal*) **1.** a disturbance or commotion **2.** same as **shindig** (sense 1) [Early 19C. Probably variant of SHINTY]

shine /shīn/ *v* (**shines, shining, shone** /shon/) **1.** *vi* **EMIT LIGHT** to give out light **2.** *vi* **BE BRIGHT** to be bright or reflect light **3.** *vt* **DIRECT LIGHT OF SOMETHING** to direct the light emitted by something ○ *Shine the torch over here.* **4.** *vi* **EXCEL** to be very good at or do very well in an activity **5.** *vi* **BE OBVIOUS** to appear clearly **6.** *vi*

HAVE RADIANT QUALITY to appear to have a specially bright or radiant quality as a result of good health or a strong positive emotion ○ *Her face shone with happiness.* **7.** (*past and past participle* **shined**) *vt* **POLISH SOMETHING** to make something bright and gleaming by polishing it ■ *n* **1. BRIGHTNESS FROM LIGHT SOURCE** brightness or radiance emitted by a source of light **2. BRIGHT SURFACE** the bright or gleaming surface of something **3. ACT OF POLISHING SOMETHING** an act of polishing something to make it shiny **4.** *US* BEVERAGES same as **moonshine** (sense 1) (*informal*) [Old English *scīnan* < Indo-European, 'to glimmer'] ◇ **take a shine to somebody** to develop a liking for somebody (*informal*)

CULTURAL NOTE ***Shine***, a film (1996) by Australian director Scott Hicks. It tells the true story of pianist David Helfgott's return to performance after a major mental illness and years in psychiatric hospitals. Geoffrey Rush won an Oscar for his portrayal of Helfgott.

shiner /shīnər/ *n* **1.** MED same as **black eye** (*informal*) **2.** a small silvery freshwater fish. Native to: North America. Genus: *Notropis*. **3.** something that shines or makes something shine

shingle[1] /shíng g'l/ *n* **1. ROOF OR WALL TILE** a small flat tile, especially one made of wood, used in overlapping rows to cover a roof or wall **2. HAIRSTYLE** a short hairstyle for women, popular in the 1920s, in which the back hair was cut to taper at the nape of the neck **3.** *N Am* **SIGN OR NAMEPLATE** a nameplate or a small sign giving the name of a doctor, lawyer, or other professional person, fixed outside that person's office ■ *vt* (**-gles, -gling, -gled**) **1. COVER SOMETHING WITH TILES** to cover something with small overlapping tiles **2. TAPER HAIR AT BACK** to cut hair so that it is tapered at the nape of the neck [12C. Alteration of late Latin *scindula*, variant of Latin *scandula*] —**shingler** *n* ◇ **hang out your shingle** *N Am* to begin working as a professional from your own office (*informal*)

shingle[2] /shíng g'l/ *n* **1.** small round pebbles on a beach **2.** an area of beach covered in shingle [Mid-16C. Origin ?] —**shingly** *adj*

shingle[3] /shíng g'l/ (**-gles, -gling, -gled**) *vt* to remove the slag from iron by hammering or squeezing it in the process of making wrought iron [Late 17C. Via French *cingler* < German *zängeln* < *Zange* 'tongs']

shingles /shíng g'lz/ *n* a disease of adults caused by the reactivation of chickenpox viruses in a nerve ganglion and resulting in inflammation, pain, and a rash of small skin blisters. Technical name **herpes zoster, zoster** (sense 1) [14C. Alteration of Latin *cingulum* 'girdle' < *cingere* 'gird']

shining /shīning/ *adj* **1. EMITTING LIGHT** giving out or reflecting light **2. BRIGHT** having a bright or radiant quality **3. EXCELLENT** conspicuously excellent and admirable ○ *a shining example to all* —**shiningly** *adv*

shinney /shínni/ *n, vi* HOCKEY another spelling of **shinny**[2]

shinny[1] /shínni/ (**-nies, -nying, -nied**) *vi N Am* same as **shin**[1] *v* (sense 1) [Late 19C. < SHIN[1]]

shinny[2] /shínni/, **shinney** *n* (*plural* **-nies**; *plural* **-neys**) **1. N AMERICAN GAME RESEMBLING HOCKEY** in the United States and Canada, an informal game similar to hockey, played with a small hard ball and curved wooden sticks **2. STICK USED IN SHINNY** the stick that is used to play shinny ■ *vi* (**-nies, -nying, -nied; -neys, -neying, -neyed**) **PLAY SHINNY** to play the game of shinny [Late 17C. Variant of SHINTY]

shinplaster /shín plaastər/ *n N Am* a piece of low-value paper money, especially one issued in the United States during the American Civil War [Early 19C. Because it resembled plaster used for leg plasters]

shin splints *n* a painful inflammation of the muscles surrounding the shinbone, often caused by running or jogging on hard roads (*takes a singular or plural verb*)

shintaido /shin tīdō/ *n* a form of exercise based on the movements used in Japanese martial arts, performed by a group [Late 20C. < Japanese *shintaidō* < *shintai* 'Shinto object'+ *dō* 'art']

Shinto /shíntō/ *n* a Japanese religion in which devotees worship and make offerings to numerous gods and spirits associated with the natural world [Early 18C. < Japanese *shintō* < *shin* 'gods' (< Middle Chinese) + *tō* 'way' (< Middle Chinese *daw*')] —**Shintoism** *n* —**Shintoist** *n, adj*

shinty /shínti/ *n* (*plural* **-ties**) **1. SCOTTISH GAME RESEMBLING HOCKEY** a game resembling hockey traditionally played in the Highlands of Scotland **2. STICK USED IN SHINTY** the stick that is used to play shinty ■ *vi* (**-ties, -tying, -tied**) **PLAY SHINTY** to play the game of shinty [Late 17C. Probably < *shin (t')ye!*, uttered by players of the game]

shiny /shīni/ (**-ier, -iest**) *adj* **1.** bright or highly polished, with a glossy or glistening surface **2.** smooth and glossy on the surface through too much wear ○ *a shiny patch on the seat of his trousers* —**shininess** *n*

ship /ship/ *n* **1. LARGE BOAT** a large wind-driven or engine-powered vessel designed to carry passengers or cargo over water, especially across the sea **2. LARGE SQUARE-RIGGED SAILING VESSEL** a large sailing vessel with three, four, or five square-rigged masts **3. SHIP'S CREW** the crew of a ship **4. AIRCRAFT OR SPACECRAFT** a large aircraft or spacecraft ■ *v* (**ships, shipping, shipped**) **1.** *vti* **TRANSPORT SOMETHING OVER WATER** to transport something by ship **2.** *vt* **TRANSPORT SOMETHING OVERLAND OR BY AIR** to send or transport something overland or by air, using a common carrier **3.** *vt* **SEND SOMEBODY** to send somebody to a place ○ *shipped the children off to their grandparents for the holidays* **4.** *vti* COMM **SEND OR BE SENT TO SHOPS** to send a product to shops and make it available for purchase, or be sent in this way ○ *If all goes well, the new software will be shipping early next year.* **5.** *vt* **TAKE IN WATER** to take in water over the sides of a ship or boat ○ *We're shipping water.* **6.** *vt* **BRING OARS INSIDE BOAT** to bring oars inside a boat and lay them down **7.** *vi* **GO ON VOYAGE** to travel on a ship **8.** *vi* **WORK ON SHIP** to take a job aboard a ship [Old English *scip* < Germanic] —**shippable** *adj* ◇ **desert** *or* **leave a sinking ship** to leave an organization that is having difficulties ◇ **when your ship comes in** when you become rich

-ship *suffix* **1.** condition, state, quality ○ *companionship* **2.** skill, art, craft ○ *musicianship* **3.** office, title, position, profession ○ *governorship* **4.** group of people collectively ○ *membership* **5.** somebody holding a particular title ○ *ladyship* **6.** something showing a particular quality or condition ○ *township* [Old English *-scipe* < Germanic]

ship biscuit *n* FOOD same as **hardtack**

shipboard /shíp bawrd/ *adj* used, intended for, or occurring on board a ship ◇ **on shipboard** on board a ship

shipborne /shíp bawrn/ *adj* transported by ship

shipbroker /shíp brōkər/ *n* an agent who acts on behalf of ship owners, organizing cargoes, passengers, and insurance for their ships

shipbuilder /shíp bildər/ *n* a person or business that constructs ships —**shipbuilding** *n*

ship canal *n* a canal that is wide and deep enough for ships to pass through

ship chandler *n* a person, shop, or company that sells supplies for ships or boats —**ship chandlery** *n*

Corbis Sygma

Jenny Shipley

Shipley /shíppli/, **Jenny** (*b.* 1952) prime minister of New Zealand (1997–99). A National Party politician, she introduced wide-ranging conservative welfare and health reforms. Full name **Shipley, Jennifer Mary**. See table at **prime minister**

shipload /shíp lōd/ *n* the quantity of cargo carried by a ship

shipmaster /shíp maastər/ *n* the captain or master of a ship

shipmate /shíp mayt/ *n* a sailor or passenger on the same ship as another

shipment /shípmənt/ *n* **1.** a quantity of goods that are shipped together as part of the same cargo **2.** the act of shipping something

ship money *n* a tax formerly levied by English monarchs, especially by King Charles I, to raise money to provide ships for the navy

ship of the line *n* in former times, a sailing warship large enough to be in the line of battle

shipowner /shíp ōnər/ *n* a person or company owning one or more ships

shipper /shíppər/ *n* a person or company that sends or receives goods by sea, land, or air

shipping /shípping/ *n* **1.** the act or business of transporting goods **2.** ships considered collectively, especially those belonging to a single port, country, or industry, and often referred to in terms of their tonnage

shipping agent *n* a person or company that prepares the documents required for cargoes to be transported and deals with insurance and customs matters on behalf of ships

shipping clerk *n* an employee who prepares, sends, receives, and records shipments of goods

shipping forecast *n* a weather forecast for ships and sailors around the UK coast broadcast at regular times by the BBC

shipping lane *n* a route regularly used by ships when crossing a body of water

ship rat *n* ZOOL same as **black rat**

ship-rigged *adj* describes a sailing ship with three, four, or five masts and square sails set at right angles to the hull

ship's biscuit *n* FOOD same as **hardtack**

shipshape /shíp shayp/ *adj* neat, tidy, and in good order ■ *adv* in a neat, tidy, and orderly way [Mid-17C. Shortening of obsolete *shipshapen* 'made appropriate for use aboard ship']

shipside /shíp sīd/ *n* the area, especially at a dock, beside a ship

ship's papers *npl* documents stating the ownership, nationality, cargo, and destination of a ship or boat, required by international law to be carried by all vessels

shipt *abbr* MAIL shipment

shipway /shíp way/ *n* **1.** a structure on which a ship is built and down which it slides when it is launched **2.** NAUT same as **ship canal**

shipworm /shíp wurm/ *n* a burrowing sea mollusc that drills into wood, damaging wharves and ships. Family: Teredinidae.

shipwreck /shíp rek/ *n* **1. SINKING OR DESTRUCTION OF SHIP** the sinking, destruction, or damaging of a ship while at sea **2. SUNKEN SHIP** a ship that has been sunk or destroyed **3. DESTRUCTION** the destruction or failure of something ■ *v* (**-wrecks, -wrecking, -wrecked**) **1.** *vti* **INVOLVE SOMEBODY IN SHIPWRECK** to experience the sinking or destruction of a ship, or cause somebody to experience this (*usually passive*) ○ *was shipwrecked on a desert island* **2.** *vti* **SINK SHIP** to sink or destroy a ship, or be sunk or destroyed at sea (*usually passive*) **3.** *vt* **RUIN SOMETHING** to ruin or destroy something utterly (*literary*)

shipwright /shíp rīt/ *n* somebody who builds or repairs ships [Pre-12C. < SHIP + Old English *wyrhta*, *wryhta* 'maker, builder' < W Germanic]

shipyard /shíp yaard/ *n* a place where ships are built or repaired

Shiraz /shi ráz/ *n* **1.** a red wine made from a variety of black grape grown mainly in Australia and South Africa **2.** a black grape variety. Use: to make Shiraz. [Mid-17C. After *Shiraz*, port in Iran]

shire[1] /shīr/ *n* **1.** a county in England or Wales **2.** *also* **Shire** ZOOL same as **shire horse** [Old English *scīr* 'administrative office, district'. Origin ?]

shire[2] /shīr/ (**shires, shiring, shired**) *vt Ireland* to clear the head by taking fresh air (*informal*) [Old English *scīr* 'bright, clear' < Germanic]

Shire /shéeray/ river flowing from Malawi to Mo-

zambique in south-central Africa. Length: 402 km/250 mi.

Shire Highlands plateau in southern Malawi, east of the River Shire. Height: 900 m/2,953 ft.

shire horse, **Shire horse** *n* a large heavy carthorse with long hair growing from its fetlocks, belonging to a breed originating in the Midlands of England

Shires /shīrz/ *npl* a group of counties in the Midlands of England, especially Northamptonshire and Leicestershire, famous as fox-hunting country

shire town *n* the administrative capital of a British county, especially one whose name ends in '-shire'

shirk /shurk/ (**shirks, shirking, shirked**) *v* **1.** *vt* to avoid having to carry out something such as an obligation, task, or responsibility through lack of initiative, cowardice, or distaste for it **2.** *vi* to lack initiative, or deliberately avoid work or duty [Mid-17C. Origin ?] —**shirker** *n*

Shirley poppy /shúrli-/ *n* an annual poppy. Flowers: red, pink, or white, single or double. [Late 19C. After a district in Croydon, Surrey]

shirr /shur/ (**shirrs, shirring, shirred**) *v* **1.** *vti* to gather fabric into two or more parallel rows for decoration on a garment such as a skirt, usually using elasticated thread **2.** *vt N Am* to bake an egg without its shell, e.g. in a ramekin dish [Mid-19C. Origin ?]

shirt /shurt/ *n* **1.** an item of clothing for the upper part of the body, usually made of a fairly light material and fitted with a collar, sleeves, and buttons down the front **2.** a usually loose linen garment for the upper body with sleeves that was worn by men as underwear until the early 20th century **3.** CLOTHING same as **nightshirt** [Old English *scyrte* < Indo-European, 'to cut'] ◇ **keep your shirt on** to keep your temper (*informal; usually used as a command*) ◇ **lose your shirt** to lose everything you have, especially as a result of losing a bet (*informal*) ◇ **put your shirt on something** to bet or risk everything you have on something (*informal*)

shirtdress /shúrt dress/ *n N Am* CLOTHING same as **shirtwaister**

shirtfront /shúrt frunt/ *n* the front part of a shirt, especially the stiffened fabric on the front of a dress shirt ■ *vt* (**shirtfronts, shirtfronts, shirtfronted**) in Australian Rules football, to bring an opponent down by charging him head-on

shirt-fronter *n* in Australian Rules football, a tackle made by charging an opponent head-on

shirting /shúrting/ *n* plain or striped cotton fabric. Use: men's shirts.

shirtlifter /shúrt liftər/ *n* an offensive term for a gay man (*slang*)

shirtsleeve /shúrt sleev/ *n* the part of a shirt that covers all or part of the arm ◇ **in (your) shirtsleeves** not wearing a jacket

shirt-tail *n* the lower part of a shirt, usually cut in a curved shape, that extends below the waist at the back and is usually tucked into trousers

shirtwaist /shúrt wayst/ *n N Am* a woman's blouse styled like a man's shirt

shirtwaister /shúrt waystər/ *n* a woman's dress that is tailored to resemble a shirt, with buttons fastening down the front. N Am term **shirtdress**

shirty /shúrti/ (**-ier, -iest**) *adj* aggressive or bad-tempered because of being annoyed about something (*informal*) [Mid-19C. < taking shirts off to fight] —**shirtily** *adv* —**shirtiness** *n*

shisha mirror /shíshə-/ *n* a small mirrored disc. Use: surface decoration on textiles. [Mid-20C. < Persian *šīša*, Urdu *šīšah* 'mirror']

shishito /shə shéetō/ *n* in Japanese cuisine, a mild sweet pepper used, e.g., in tempura

shish kebab /shísh-/ *n* a dish of cubes of marinated meat and vegetables grilled and served on a skewer [Early 20C. Via Armenian < Turkish *şiş kebabiu* < *şiş* 'skewer' + *kebab* 'roast meat']

shiso /shéessō/ *n* in Japanese cuisine, an aromatic herb in the mint-basil family, used as seasoning in salads and sushi. Latin name: *Perilla frutescens.*

shit /shit/ *n* **1.** a highly offensive term for human or animal excrement (*taboo*) **2.** a highly offensive term for an act of defecating (*taboo*) **3.** a highly offensive term for somebody regarded as unpleasant or malicious (*taboo insult*) **4.** a highly offensive term for something that is unpleasant, of no value, or of inferior quality (*taboo*) **5.** a highly offensive term for useless or unnecessary things (*taboo*) **6.** a highly offensive term for nonsense or lies (*taboo*) **7.** a highly offensive term for difficulty or trouble (*taboo*) **8.** a highly offensive term for criticism perceived as unhelpful or mean-spirited (*taboo*) **9.** a highly offensive term for illegal drugs, especially cannabis (*taboo*) ■ **shits** *npl* a highly offensive term for an attack of diarrhoea (*taboo*) ■ *interj* a highly offensive term used as a swearword (*taboo*) ■ *v* (**shits, shitting, shitted** or **shit** or **shat** /shat/) (*taboo*) **1.** *vti* a highly offensive term meaning to eliminate waste from the body via the rectum **2.** *vi* a highly offensive term meaning to behave towards or criticize somebody with arrogant contempt and a total disregard for his or her feelings, especially from a position of power **3.** *vt US* a highly offensive term meaning to tease somebody or deceive somebody for amusement ■ *adj* a highly offensive term meaning very bad or inferior (*taboo*) [Old English *scitte* < Indo-European, 'to cut, split'] ◇ **get your shit together** a highly offensive phrase meaning to get organized (*taboo*) ◇ **in deep shit** a highly offensive phrase meaning in trouble or in a difficult situation (*taboo*) ◇ **knock** *or* **beat the shit out of somebody** a highly offensive phrase meaning to strike or kick somebody violently and repeatedly (*taboo*) ◇ **no shit** a highly offensive term indicating surprise, disbelief, or sarcasm (*taboo*) ◇ **tough shit** a highly offensive phrase indicating in an unfriendly way that there is no alternative to a difficult or undesirable situation (*taboo*) ◇ **when the shit hits the fan** a highly offensive phrase meaning when trouble starts (*taboo*)

shitake *n* FUNGI, FOOD another spelling of **shiitake**

shite /shīt/ *regional n* **1.** a highly offensive term for human or animal excrement (*taboo*) **2.** a highly offensive term somebody regarded as unpleasant or malicious (*taboo insult*) **3.** a highly offensive term for something that is unpleasant, of no value, or of inferior quality (*taboo*) **4.** a highly offensive term for nonsense or lies (*taboo*) ■ *interj* a highly offensive term used as a swearword (*taboo*) [Variant of SHIT]

shitfaced /shít fayst/ *adj* a highly offensive term meaning extremely intoxicated by alcohol (*taboo*)

shithead /shít hed/ *n* a highly offensive term that deliberately insults somebody's intelligence or character (*taboo*)

shit hot *adj* a highly offensive term indicating emphatic approval (*taboo*)

shithouse /shít howss/ *n* a highly offensive term for a toilet (*taboo*)

shitless /shíttləss/ *adv* a highly offensive term meaning to a very great extent (*taboo*) [Mid-20C. < the tendency to lose control of the bowels when terror-stricken]

shitlist /shít list/ *n* a highly offensive term meaning a list of people who are out of favour, especially in the view of somebody in authority (*taboo*)

shitload /shít lōd/ *n N Am* a highly offensive term meaning an undesirably large amount or quantity of something (*taboo*)

shittah /shíttə/ (*plural* **-tim** /-tim/ or **-tahs**) *n* the tree that yielded the shittim wood of the Bible, probably a species of acacia [Early 17C. < Hebrew *šiṭṭāh*]

shittim wood /shíttim-/ *n* the wood of the shittah tree that according to the Bible was used to make the Ark of the Covenant

shitty /shítti/ *adj* (*taboo*) **1.** a highly offensive term meaning regarded as inferior, unpleasant, or unenjoyable **2.** a highly offensive term meaning wretched or miserable **3.** a highly offensive term meaning of very poor quality **4.** a highly offensive term meaning covered with excrement —**shittily** *adv* —**shittiness** *n*

shiv /shiv/ (*slang*) *n* a pocketknife, often a flick knife or razor, used as a weapon ■ *vt* (**shivs, shivving, shivved**) to slash or stab somebody with a shiv [Late 17C. Origin ?]

shiva /sheévə/, **shivah** *n* seven days of formal mourning observed by close relatives of a deceased Jew during which they sit on low stools and do not go out, work, bathe, or shave [Late 19C. Via Yiddish < Hebrew *šiḇ'āh* 'seven']

Shiva /sheévə/, **Siva** /seévə/ *n* in Hinduism, an important deity, worshipped as the god of destruction [Late 18C. < Sanskrit, 'the auspicious one']

shivah *n* JUDAISM another spelling of **shiva**

Shiva Ratri /-raátri/ *n* a Hindu festival honouring the god Shiva. Date: middle of Magha. [*Ratri* < Hindi, 'night']

shivaree /shívvə reé, shívvəri/ *n N Am* same as **charivari** [Mid-19C. Alteration of French *charivari*]

shiver[1] /shívvər/ *v* (**-ers, -ering, -ered**) **1.** *vi* TREMBLE to tremble or shake slightly because of cold, fear, or illness **2.** *vti* FLAP OR MAKE SAIL FLAP to flap, or make a sail flap, when a sailing vessel is too close to the wind ■ *n* BODY TREMOR a tremor or shudder in the body caused by fear, cold, or illness ■ **shivers** *npl* ATTACK OF SHIVERING an attack of shivering caused by fear, cold, or illness (*informal*) [13C. Origin ?] —**shiverer** *n* —**shiveringly** *adv*

shiver[2] /shívvər/ *vti* (**-ers, -ering, -ered**) to splinter into fragments, or cause something to splinter into fragments ■ *n* a very small piece of something such as glass that has splintered off a larger piece [12C. < assumed Old English *scifer* < Indo-European, 'to split']

shivery /shívvəri/ *adj* trembling from cold, fear, or illness [Mid-18C. < SHIVER[1]]

Shizuoka /sheé zoo ṓkə/ city on southeastern Honshu Island, Japan, west of Suruga Bay. Population: 468,775 (2002).

Shkodër /shkṓdair/ capital city of Shkodër District, northwestern Albania, situated near the southern end of Lake Shkodër. Population: 81,900 (1990).

shkotzim JUDAISM plural of **shegetz** (*offensive insult*)

shlemiel *n* JUDAISM another spelling of **schlemiel** (*informal*)

shlep *vti, n* another spelling of **schlep** (*informal*)

Shluh /shloo/ (*plural same* or **Shluhs**) *n* **1.** a member of a Berber people who live mainly in the Atlas Mountains of Morocco and Algeria **2.** the Berber dialect of the Shluh people [Early 18C. < Berber] —**Shluh** *adj*

SHM *abbr* PHYS simple harmonic motion

shm- *prefix* another spelling of **schm-** (*used dismissively in rhyming compounds*)

shmaltz *n* another spelling of **schmaltz** (*informal*)

shmatte *n* another spelling of **schmatte** (*informal*)

shmegegge /shmə géggə/ *n* an offensive term for a person who is regarded variously as petty, humourless, dull, clumsy, or sycophantic (*slang insult*) [Yiddish SH- + *megege* 'dawdler, idler']

shmo *n N Am* another spelling of **schmo** (*slang insult*)

shmuck *n N Am* another spelling of **schmuck** (*slang offensive*)

SHO *abbr* Senior House Officer

Shoah /shṓ ə/ *n* HIST same as **Holocaust** (*used by Jews*) [Mid-20C. < Hebrew *šōāh* 'catastrophe']

shoal[1] /shōl/ *n* **1.** GROUP OF FISH a large group of fish or other sea animals swimming together **2.** GROUP OF PEOPLE a large group of similar people or things ○ *a shoal of reporters* ■ *vi* (**shoals, shoaling, shoaled**) FORM SHOAL to group together to form a shoal [Late 16C. < Middle Dutch *scōle* or Middle Low German *schōle* (see SCHOOL[2])]

shoal[2] /shōl/ *n* **1.** SHALLOW WATER an area of shallow water in a larger body of water **2.** UNDERWATER SANDBANK an underwater sandbank or sandbar that is visible at low water ■ *v* (**shoals, shoaling, shoaled**) **1.** *vti* MAKE OR BECOME SHALLOW to become shallow or shallower, or make something shallow **2.** *vi* ENTER SHALLOWER WATER to enter a shallower area of water ■ *adj also* **shoaly** /shṓli/ SHALLOW describes water that is shallow [Old English *sceald* 'shallow' < Germanic]

shoat /shōt/, **shote** *n* a young pig that has just been weaned [15C. Origin ?]

shochet /shṓkhət/ (*plural* **-etim** /-ətim/) *n* somebody licensed to perform the ritual kosher slaughter of

animals for food (**shechita**) [Late 19C. < Hebrew *šōḥēṯ*, present participle of *šāḥaṯ* 'slaughter']

shock[1] /shok/ *n* **1.** SOMETHING SURPRISING AND UPSETTING an unexpected, intense, and distressing experience that has a sudden and powerful effect on somebody's emotions or physical reactions ○ *The news of her death came as a great shock to us all.* **2.** DISTRESSING FEELINGS AFTER SHOCK the feeling of distress or numbness experienced by somebody who has had a shock **3.** MED PHYSIOLOGICAL COLLAPSE a state of physiological collapse, marked by a weak pulse, coldness, sweating, and irregular breathing, and resulting from a situation such as blood loss, heart failure, allergic reaction, or emotional trauma ○ *in shock* **4.** PHYSICAL IMPACT a sudden and violent impact, collision, or blow **5.** MOVEMENT AFTER IMPACT the movement or violent shaking felt after a collision, explosion, or earthquake **6.** SOMETHING THREATENING OR DAMAGING an unexpected event that threatens or damages a system, organization, or conventional situation ○ *the announcement was a shock to international markets* **7.** ELEC same as **electric shock 8.** N Am MECH ENG same as **shock absorber** ■ *v* (**shocks, shocking, shocked**) **1.** *vt* UPSET SOMEBODY to make somebody feel suddenly and acutely distressed or upset **2.** *vti* OFFEND OR BE OFFENDED to make somebody feel deeply offended or disgusted, or be likely to feel offended or disgusted ○ *He shocks easily.* **3.** *vt* GIVE SOMEBODY ELECTRIC SHOCK to give an electric shock to a person or animal **4.** *vt* MED PUT SOMEBODY INTO SHOCK to cause a state of shock in somebody **5.** *vti* COLLIDE to collide, or cause people or things to collide (*archaic*) [Mid-16C. < French *choc* < French *choquer* 'to strike'] —**shockability** /shókə bílləti/ *n* —**shockable** *adj*

shock[2] /shok/ *n* a group of sheaves of corn set upright in a field for drying ■ *vt* (**shocks, shocking, shocked**) to arrange sheaves of corn in a shock [14C. Origin ?]

shock[3] /shok/ *n* a large amount of thick shaggy hair [Early 19C. Origin ?]

shock absorber

shock absorber *n* a device on a vehicle designed to absorb jarring or jolting such as that caused by wheels moving over a rough surface [< SHOCK[1]]

shocker /shókər/ *n* (*informal*) **1.** SOMETHING UNPLEASANT a difficult, troublesome, or unpleasant experience, thing, or person **2.** SHOCKING STORY, PLAY, OR FILM a story, play, or film that is particularly lurid and intended to shock people **3.** *Aus* BAD SPORTS PERFORMANCE a very poor performance, especially at sport [Early 19C. < SHOCK[1]]

shockheaded /shók héddid/ *adj* having a large amount of thick shaggy hair that sticks up or is tousled [Early 19C. < SHOCK[3]]

shock-horror *adj* lurid, sensational, and apparently intended to cause a shocked or horrified reaction (*informal; used ironically*) [< SHOCK[1]]

shocking /shóking/ *adj* **1.** OUTRAGEOUS provoking a deeply offended or outraged response **2.** DISTRESSING emotionally distressing or horrifying **3.** VERY BAD very bad or unpleasant (*informal*) ■ *adj, adv* VERY BRIGHT very bright or glaring in shade of colour [Early 18C. < SHOCK[1]] —**shockingly** *adv* —**shockingness** *n*

shocking pink *adj* of a garish pink colour —**shocking pink** *n*

shock jock *n* a DJ or radio host who uses provocative language and broadcasts his or her extreme views (*slang*) [< SHOCK[1]]

Shockley /shókli/, **William B.** (1910–89) US physicist. He codeveloped the transistor (1948) and shared the Nobel Prize in physics (1956). He went on to promote controversial theories about intelligence and race. Full name **Shockley, William Bradford**

shockproof /shók proof/ *adj* designed or able to withstand the effects of jarring or impact [Early 20C. < SHOCK[1]]

shock tactics *npl* methods that are likely to shock people, deliberately used in order to achieve a goal [< SHOCK[1]]

shock therapy, **shock treatment** *n* a method of treating patients affected with psychiatric disorders that involves passing an electric current through the brain [< SHOCK[1]]

shock troops *npl* soldiers who are specially trained and equipped to be in the forefront of an attack [< SHOCK[1]; translation of German *Stosstruppen*]

shock wave *n* **1.** a wave of increased temperature or pressure as a result of an explosion or earthquake or the movement of a supersonic body **2.** a widespread reaction of shock or distress caused by an event or piece of news (*often used in the plural*) [< SHOCK[1]]

shod CLOTHING past participle, past tense of **shoe**

shoddy /shóddi/ *adj* (**-dier, -diest**) **1.** POORLY MADE poorly or carelessly made or done **2.** OF INFERIOR MATERIAL made from inferior material **3.** DISHONEST dishonest or disgraceful ○ *shoddy treatment* ■ *n* (*plural* **-dies**) **1.** CLOTH MADE WITH OLD WOOL cloth made using a mixture of old unravelled woollen cloth and new wool **2.** SOMETHING INFERIOR something that is of inferior quality, especially if it is imitating something better [Mid-19C. Origin ?] —**shoddily** *adv* —**shoddiness** *n*

shoe /shoo/ *n* **1.** STIFF OUTER COVERING FOR FOOT an outer covering for the foot, usually made of leather, fabric, or plastic, with a stiff sole and usually not reaching above the ankle **2.** same as **horseshoe** *n* (sense 1) **3.** MECH ENG DEVICE TO SLOW SOMETHING DOWN a device that slows or stops the movement of an object, e.g. the part of a brake that presses against the drum **4.** MECH ENG PROTECTIVE PART IN ENGINE a lining or part in an engine or machine that protects another part from being worn down **5.** CARDS PLAYING CARD DISPENSER a special box that dispenses playing cards one at a time **6.** RAIL POWER COLLECTOR ON ELECTRIC TRAIN the part of an electric train that connects with the electrified rail from which it draws power **7.** SPORTS METAL STRIP ON SLEDGE a strip of metal along the runner of a sledge **8.** CIV ENG PART OF BRIDGE a base that supports the upper part of a bridge ■ *vt* (**shoes, shoeing, shod** /shod/) **1.** PROVIDE HORSE WITH HORSESHOES to fix a horseshoe on a horse **2.** SUPPLY SOMEBODY WITH SHOES to provide somebody with shoes (*usually passive*) **3.** MECH ENG PUT PROTECTIVE COVERING ON SOMETHING to cover something with a hard, especially metal plate to protect against wear [Old English *scōh* < Germanic] —**shoeless** *adj* ◇ **be in somebody's shoes** to be in somebody else's position (*informal*)

shoebill /shóobil/ *n* a large tropical wading bird with shaggy grey feathers, a large head, black legs, and a broad hooked beak. Native to: East Africa. Latin name: *Balaeniceps rex.*

shoeblack /shóo blak/ *n* same as **bootblack**

shoebox /shóo boks/ *n* **1.** a box, usually made of cardboard, in which shoes are packed for sale **2.** a small and cramped living or working space (*informal*)

shoegazing /shóo gayzing/ *n* a style of early 1990s guitar music characterized by ambient sounds and static performances [Late 20C. < the typical stance of the performers and audience]

shoehorn /shóo hawrn/ *n* a curved piece of plastic, metal, or horn used to help ease the heel into a tight-fitting shoe or boot ■ *vt* (**-horns, -horning, -horned**) to squeeze somebody or something into a space that is barely large enough

shoelace /shóo layss/ *n* a thin cord of leather or fabric, used as a shoe fastener

shoemaker /shóo maykər/ *n* a maker or repairer of footwear —**shoemaking** *n*

shoepac /shóo pak/, **shoepack** *n* N Am a heavy laced waterproof boot [Mid-18C. Alteration of pidgin Delaware *seppock* 'shoes' < Unami Delaware *čipahko* 'moccasins']

Trainer

Ballet shoe

Mule

Court shoe

Galosh

Moccasin

Espadrille

Lace-up

Stiletto

Slip-on

Flip-flop/Thong

Clog

Boot

shoe

shoeshine /shóo shīn/ *n* **1.** the act of giving a clean or shiny finish to shoes by polishing them **2.** a polished finish on shoes

shoestring /shóo string/ *adj* **1.** consisting of or running on a very limited amount of money ○ *a shoestring allocation for new classrooms* **2.** US FOOD cut or made long and narrow in shape ○ *shoestring licorice* ■ *n* US CLOTHING same as **shoelace** ◇ **on a shoestring** using very little money

shoetree /shóo tree/ *n* a wooden or metal block that is inserted into a boot or shoe to stretch it or help it to keep its shape when not being worn

shofar /shó faar/ (*plural* **-fars** or **-froth** /-frōt/) *n* a horn, usually a ram's horn, blown by the ancient Hebrews in battle and during religious ceremonies, now sounded in a synagogue on Rosh Hashanah [Mid-19C. < Hebrew *šōpār* 'ram's horn']

shogi /shógi/ *n* a Japanese board game for two players that resembles chess [Mid-19C. Via Japanese < Chinese *jiàng qí* < *jiàng* 'commander in chief' + *qí* 'board game, chess']

shogun /shṓ gun/ n a hereditary military commander in feudal Japan who ruled the country under the nominal rule of an emperor between the years 1192 and 1867 [Mid-17C. Via Japanese < Chinese *jiāng jūn* 'general'] —**shogunal** *adj*

shogunate /shṓgǝ nayt/ n the office, period in office, or rule of a shogun

shoji /shṓji/ (*plural same* or **-jis**) n a rice-paper screen in a wooden frame used as a sliding partition or door in traditional Japanese houses [Late 19C. < Japanese *shōji* < *shō* 'screen, barrier' (< Middle Chinese *tsiang*) + *-ji* 'seed' (< Middle Chinese *tsz*)]

Sholapur /shṓlǝ poŏr/ city in west-central India. Population: 604,215 (1991).

~~**sholder**~~ incorrect spelling of **shoulder**

Shona /shṓnǝ/ (*plural same* or **-nas**) n 1. a member of a people living in parts of southern central Africa, mainly in Zimbabwe and Mozambique 2. the Bantu language of the Shona people. Native speakers: 8 million. [Mid-20C. < Bantu] —**Shona** *adj*

shone past participle, past tense of **shine**

shoneen /shṓ neen/ n Ireland an Irish person who, in order to seem of a higher social class, imitates an English person, especially in accent [Mid-19C. < Irish *seóinín* 'little John' < *Seón* 'John, John Bull']

shongololo n same as **songololo** (*informal*) [Early 20C. Zulu]

shonky /shóngki/ (**-kier**, **-kiest**) *adj* ANZ unreliable, untrustworthy, or inferior (*informal*) [Late 20C. < shortening of offensive slang *shonicker* 'Jew', origin ?]

shoo /shoo/ *interj* used to tell a child or animal to go away ■ *vti* (**shoos**, **shooing**, **shooed**) to say shoo and gesture to a child or animal to go away ○ *shooed the pigeons away* [15C. Natural exclamation]

shoofly pie /shoo flī-/ n N Am a pie made with a filling of crumbs, butter, and brown sugar or molasses [< its sweet filling, which is apt to attract flies]

shoofty /shoofti/ (*plural* **-ties**), **shooftee** /shooftee/ n Aus same as **shufti** (*informal*) [Mid-20C. Variant]

shoogle /shoogg'l/ Scotland (*informal*) *vti* (**-gles**, **-gling**, **-gled**) to rock back and forth with small rapid movements, or cause something to do this ■ *n* a small rapid rocking movement [Late 16C. < dialect *shog* 'shake']

shoogly /shooggli/ *adj* Scotland wobbling or liable to wobble (*informal*)

shoo-in n N Am a certain winner

shook[1] /shook/ past tense of **shake**

shook[2] /shook/ n 1. AGRIC same as **shock**[2] 2. N Am a set of timber parts for assembling a barrel or box [Late 18C. Origin ?]

shook-up *adj* N Am disturbed and upset (*informal*)

shoon /shoon/ Scotland CLOTHING plural of **shoe** n (sense 1)

shoot /shoot/ v (**shoots**, **shooting**, **shot** /shot/) 1. *vti* FIRE WEAPON OR PROJECTILE to fire a projectile such as a bullet, missile, or arrow from a weapon, or make a weapon fire a projectile ○ *Don't shoot!* 2. *vt* HIT SOMEBODY OR SOMETHING WITH BULLET to fire a weapon at and hit, injure, or kill a person or animal ○ *She shot herself.* 3. *vti* HUNT ANIMALS WITH GUN to hunt animals with a gun for sport 4. *vti* MOVE FAST to move quickly and suddenly, or cause something to move quickly and suddenly ○ *She shot out her hand to catch the ball.* 5. *vi* DASH to go somewhere quickly and suddenly (*informal*) ○ *He shot off to his interview.* 6. *vt* TRAVEL OVER SOMETHING FAST to travel quickly over a stretch of water where the current is fast ○ *shoot the rapids* 7. *vi* PROGRESS VERY RAPIDLY to make extremely rapid progress, or undergo a startlingly rapid change of state ○ *She shot to fame.* 8. *vi* MOVE SWIFTLY THROUGH BODY to seem to move very swiftly, and usually painfully, through the body ○ *Pain shot up her leg.* 9. *vti* SEND SOMETHING OUT RAPIDLY to send out something rapidly or forcefully or in a beam or ray, or be sent out in this way 10. *vt* DIRECT SOMETHING QUICKLY to direct a look or glance at something briefly and rapidly ○ *He shot a glance at her.* 11. *vt* ASK OR SAY SOMETHING RAPIDLY to say something or ask a question rapidly 12. *vti* KICK BALL TO GET POINT in a sport such as football or basketball, to kick, hit, or throw a ball in an attempt to score a goal or point 13. *vt* N Am SPORTS SCORE

POINT in a sport, to score a goal or point 14. *vt* N Am CUE GAMES PLAY CUE GAME to play a game of pool or billiards 15. *vti* LEISURE THROW DICE to throw a die or dice 16. *vt* SPORTS, LEISURE MAKE PARTICULAR SCORE in a game such as golf or dice, to score a particular amount ○ *shot a 72* 17. *vti* CINEMA, PHOTOGRAPHY, MEDIA RECORD SOMETHING ON FILM to record a shot, scene, film, or programme on film with a camera 18. *vt* MOVE BOLT INTO PLACE to move something such as a bolt into or out of a fastening ■ *n* 1. NEW PLANT GROWTH a newly grown aerial part of a plant, e.g. a leaf bud or branch 2. OCCASION FOR PHOTOGRAPHING OR FILMING an occasion when a professional photographer or filmmaker is photographing or filming something 3. ACT OF FIRING an act of firing a weapon ■ *v* (**shoots, shooting, shot** /shot/) *vi* BOT GERMINATE to germinate or begin to grow ■ *n* HUNTING EVENT an occasion for hunting animals with guns for sport ■ *v* (**shoots, shooting, shot** /shot/) *vt* ASTRON MEASURE DISTANCE TO ASTRONOMICAL OBJECT to measure the altitude of a star or other astronomical object ■ *n* HUNTING PARTY a party of people gathered together to hunt animals with guns for sport ■ *v* (**shoots, shooting, shot** /shot/) *vt* DRUGS same as **shoot up** (sense 4) (*slang*) ■ *n* HUNTING AREA an area where people shoot animals with guns for sport ■ *v* (**shoots, shooting, shot** /shot/) *vi* US STRIVE TO ACHIEVE SOMETHING to try to achieve something difficult (*informal*) ○ *shooting for a five per cent increase in productivity* ■ *n* GEOL VEIN OF ORE a narrow vein of ore ■ *interj* (*informal*) 1. USED TO TELL SOMEBODY TO START used to tell somebody to go ahead and start talking 2. N Am USED TO EXPRESS ANNOYANCE used as an exclamation of annoyance or disappointment [Old English *scēotan* < Germanic]

SPELLCHECK See *chute*[1].

shoot down *vt* 1. BRING DOWN AIRCRAFT to bring down an aircraft while it is in the air by firing a weapon or missile 2. KILL SOMEBODY OR SOMETHING BY SHOOTING to fire a weapon at and hit, injure, or kill a person or animal 3. DESTROY ARGUMENT to destroy somebody's argument, theory, or idea by disproving, criticizing, or discrediting it

shoot through *vi Aus* to leave a place, usually abruptly (*informal*)

shoot up *v* 1. *vi* INCREASE SUDDENLY to increase suddenly by a large amount 2. *vi* GET TALLER to grow considerably taller in a short space of time 3. *vt* HARM SOMEBODY OR SOMETHING BY GUNFIRE to cause serious injuries to somebody or damage to something with gunfire 4. *vti* DRUGS INJECT DRUG to inject an illegal drug (*slang*)

shootdown /shoot down/ n the process or an instance of destroying an aircraft in flight by means of a gun or missile attack

shoot-'em-up n 1. COMPUTER GAME WITH SHOOTING a video or computer game in which a player scores points by shooting at figures on the screen 2. FAIRGROUND SHOOTING STALL a stall in a fairground where a player shoots a rifle at a sequence of targets in order to win a prize 3. N Am FILM WITH SHOOTING a film or television programme featuring a large amount of shooting and bloodshed (*dated*)

shooter /shootǝr/ n 1. SOMEBODY SHOOTING somebody or something that shoots 2. PLAYER WHO SHOOTS BALL in a sport such as soccer or basketball, a player who shoots a ball to score a goal or point 3. GUN a pistol or other gun (*informal*)

shooting box /shooting-/ n a cabin or small house in the country in which guests stay while on a shoot for game

shooting brake n CARS same as **estate car** (*dated*)

shooting gallery n 1. a place used for target practice using guns or rifles 2. a place where addicts inject drugs, e.g. an abandoned building (*slang*)

shooting iron n US ARMS same as **handgun** (*informal*)

shooting lodge n FIELD SPORTS same as **shooting box**

shooting match ◇ **the whole shooting match** everything, or everything connected with the thing or issue in question (*informal*) ○ *They're planning to demolish the factory, the warehouse, the offices – the whole shooting match.*

shooting party n a group of people who gather together in the country to hunt game with guns for sport

shooting script n the final screenplay for a cinema or television film that includes directions for shooting and is broken down into scenes with the shots numbered consecutively

shooting star n 1. ASTRON same as **meteor** (sense 2) 2. a plant with slender flower stems rising above the leaves. Flowers: drooping, with backward-curving petals. Native to: North America. Genus: *Dodecatheon*.

shooting stick

shooting stick n a walking stick with handles at one end that fold out to form a small seat, often used by a spectator at an outdoor sporting event

shoot-out n 1. a fight to the finish with guns 2. in a football match, a means of resolving a tie in which five players from each side take alternate penalty shots at the goal

shoot-to-kill *adj* relating to or involving the aiming of a gun to kill, not wound, somebody

shop /shop/ n 1. RETAIL BUSINESS a retail business that sells consumer merchandise and sometimes services 2. WORKSHOP a place where goods are manufactured or repaired 3. ACT OF BUYING GOODS the act of going out to buy goods, especially food and household supplies (*informal*) 4. N Am INDUSTRIAL ARTS SCHOOL SUBJECT a school subject in which students are taught to work with tools and machinery, especially on wood 5. N Am SCHOOLROOM FOR LEARNING INDUSTRIAL ARTS a schoolroom or building with tools and equipment for students to learn industrial arts ■ *v* (**shops, shopping, shopped**) 1. *vi* BUY GOODS to go to a shop or shops in order to buy things 2. *vt* INFORM ON SOMEBODY to inform on somebody to the police or authorities (*slang*) 3. *vt* N Am VISIT PARTICULAR SHOP to buy goods from a particular shop 4. *vt* US TRY TO SELL SOMETHING to try to sell something such as a company or creative work by bringing it to the attention of potential buyers ○ *His agent shopped his manuscript around to various publishers.* [Old English *sceoppa* 'booth, pedlar's stall' < W Germanic] ◇ **all over the shop** (*informal*) 1. scattered or spread out over a wide area, usually untidily 2. in a confused or disorganized state ◇ **shut up shop** 1. to stop working or doing something 2. to close down a business ◇ **talk shop** to talk about your work or some other specialized activity

shop around *vi* 1. to look around for the best deal or bargain 2. to review a number of possibilities before making a choice

shopaholic /shóppǝ hóllik/ n a compulsive shopper (*informal*)

shop assistant n somebody who serves customers in a shop. N Am term **salesclerk**

shopbot /shóp bot/ n an automated device that allows potential customers to search the Internet for specific products and compare prices and specifications

shop-bought *adj* bought ready-made from a shop as opposed to being homemade. N Am term **storebought**

shop floor n 1. the area in a factory where goods are manufactured 2. the manual workers in a factory

shopfront /shóp frunt/ n the front facade of a shop building, facing onto the street. N Am term **storefront**

shopkeeper /shóp keepǝr/ n somebody who owns or manages a shop. N Am term **storekeeper**

shoplift /shóp lift/ (**-lifts, -lifting, -lifted**) *vti* to steal something from a shop or store while pretending to shop for goods —**shoplifter** n —**shoplifting** n

shoppe /shop/ *n* used in shop names in order to create a quaint old-fashioned impression [Early 20C. Alteration of SHOP]

shopper /shóppər/ *n* **1.** SOMEBODY DOING SHOPPING somebody who searches for things to buy, especially in a shop **2.** SHOPPING TROLLEY OR BAG a trolley or large bag for putting shopping in **3.** *N Am* LOCAL NEWSPAPER a usually free newspaper that carries advertising and some local news

shopping /shópping/ *n* **1.** the activity of visiting shops and stores to look at and buy things **2.** goods bought in a shop or shops, especially food and household items

shopping agent *n* a computer program used to browse websites searching for a product or service

shopping bag *n* a large strong bag with handles used for carrying purchases when shopping

shopping basket *n* **1.** a basket used to carry shopping **2.** *UK* E-COMMERCE same as **shopping cart**

shopping cart *n* **1.** *N Am* same as **shopping trolley 2.** a storage area on a seller's website in which a customer lists the items that he or she intends to buy

shopping centre *n* **1.** a large enclosed purpose-built area consisting of shops and other facilities, together with a large area for parking. N Am term **mall 2.** *US* a group of shops, usually with restaurants and other businesses, built around a shared parking area

shopping experience *n* the virtual environment in which a buyer browses a retailer's website, places items in a virtual shopping trolley, and sends the order to the merchant

shopping list *n* **1.** a list of all the things somebody wants to buy when shopping **2.** a list of demands, requirements, or things wanted

shopping mall *n* a pedestrianized shopping area with enclosed walkways in a town

shopping precinct *n UK* a pedestrianized area in a town where shops and other facilities are grouped together

shopping trolley *n* a small trolley consisting either of a square bag on a frame or a basket on wheels that is pushed or pulled along to carry shopping. N Am term **shopping cart**

shopsoiled /shóp soyld/ *adj* **1.** faded, tarnished, or otherwise slightly spoiled from being on display in a shop. N Am term **shopworn 2.** old, overused, and hackneyed

shop steward *n* a worker elected by fellow union members as their representative in dealings with the management

shoptalk /shóp tawk/ *n* **1.** conversation about work or another specialized activity at a time when more lighthearted chat is the norm, especially outside working hours **2.** *US* jargon used in a specific field, job, or profession

shopwalker /shóp wawkər/ *n* an employee in a department store who supervises sales staff and assists customers. N Am term **floorwalker**

shopworn /shóp wawrn/ *adj N Am* same as **shopsoiled** (sense 1)

shoran /sháw ran/ *n* a short-range navigational system in which a ship's or aircraft's precise location is determined by the time taken for a signal to travel to two fixed stations and back [Mid-20C. Contraction of *short-range (navigation)*]

shore[1] /shawr/ *n* **1.** LAND AT EDGE OF WATER the land that runs along the edge of a sea or lake **2.** DRY LAND dry land as opposed to water ○ *on shore* **3.** COUNTRY a land or country (*literary; often used in the plural*) ○ *on the shores of Tripoli* **4.** LAW COAST BETWEEN LOW AND HIGH TIDES the area of land that lies between normal low and high tide marks [Old English *scora* < Indo-European, 'to cut']

shore[2] /shawr/ *vt* (**shores, shoring, shored**) **1.** PROP UP STRUCTURE to stop something such as a wall from falling down or over by propping a support against it **2.** HELP TO STOP SOMETHING FAILING to give support or help in order to stop something failing ○ *took measures to shore up the exchange rate* ■ *n* PROP TO SUPPORT SOMETHING a beam or other prop set at an angle to support something such as a wall or tree [14C. < Middle Low German, Middle Dutch *schōre* 'prop']

shorebird /sháwr burd/ *n* a bird that lives and feeds near the shores of coastal or inland waters, e.g. a plover, sandpiper, or avocet. Suborder: Charadrii. [Late 17C. < SHORE[1]]

shore dinner *n N Am* a meal consisting mainly of fish and seafood [< SHORE[1]]

shorefront /sháwr frunt/ *n N Am* land situated immediately next to a body of water [< SHORE[1]]

shore leave *n* **1.** permission for a member of a ship's crew to go ashore **2.** a period of time spent ashore by a member of a ship's crew [< SHORE[1]]

shoreless /sháwrləss/ *adj* having no flat shore on which a boat can land [Early 17C. < SHORE[1]]

shoreline /sháwr līn/ *n* the land where a body of water, especially a sea, meets the shore [Mid-19C. < SHORE[1]]

shore patrol *n* the military police of the Royal Navy or the US Navy, Coast Guard, or Marine Corps while on duty on shore [< SHORE[1]]

shoreward /sháwrwərd/ *adj* facing or near the shore ■ *adv* same as **shorewards** [Late 16C. < SHORE[1]]

shorewards /sháwrwərdz/ *adv* towards the shore

shoring /sháwring/ *n* **1.** a structure or arrangement designed to shore something up **2.** the act or process of shoring something up with a support [15C. < SHORE[2]]

shorn /shawrn/ past participle of **shear** ■ *adj* **1.** with hair cut short **2.** having had something removed or taken away ○ *shorn of all the trappings of power*

short /shawrt/ *adj* **1.** NOT LONG having little or relatively little length or distance ○ *short hair* **2.** NOT TALL having little or relatively little height ○ *shorter than her sister* **3.** NOT LASTING LONG lasting for only a small amount of time ○ *a short stay* **4.** NOT SEEMING LONG IN DURATION seeming or imagined not to last very long ○ *in a few short weeks* **5.** CONCISE expressed economically and briefly ○ *a short summary* **6.** ABBREVIATED expressed in fewer words or using fewer letters or characters than the full form ○ *Typo is short for typographical error.* ○ *the short form of the word* **7.** HAVING LESS THAN NEEDED having less than the amount needed, expected, or thought to be sufficient ○ *I'm rather short of cash at the moment.* **8.** INSUFFICIENTLY LONG OR TALL not long or tall enough by a particular amount ○ *All the beams are six inches short.* **9.** NOT REMEMBERING MORE DISTANT EVENTS unable or unwilling to recall events that happened before the comparatively recent past ○ *a short memory* **10.** DISCOURTEOUS rude and abrupt when speaking to somebody ○ *She was very short with the cashier.* **11.** FULL OF FAT made with lots of fat so as to be flaky or crumbly when baked ○ *short pastry* **12.** FIN SOLD WITHOUT POSSESSING SHARES SOLD involving a seller who, at the time of sale, does not possess the shares he or she is selling and has to borrow them before being able to deliver. Once the share price has fallen, the short seller buys the shares and returns them to the person from whom they were borrowed, resulting in a gain on the deal. **13.** FIN MATURING SOON being due for payment or repayment within a comparatively short space of time ○ *a short bill* **14.** PHON PRONOUNCED WITH RELATIVELY BRIEF SOUND describes phonemes or syllables that, when spoken, are comparatively brief in duration or are categorized as being of this type. The vowel 'a' in the word 'pat' is short compared with the similar vowel in the word 'part'. **15.** CRICKET PITCHING CLOSE TO BOWLER describes a cricket ball pitching comparatively close to the bowler and likely to bounce higher than usual before reaching the batsman ○ *bowled a short ball* **16.** BEVERAGES NEAT not diluted with water or a mixer drink ■ *adv* **1.** ABRUPTLY abruptly and unexpectedly ○ *stop short* **2.** NOT REACHING TARGET before reaching a goal, target, or destination ○ *The pass fell three yards short.* **3.** FIN WITHOUT ACTUAL POSSESSION without actually possessing the things being sold when the sale is agreed on ○ *sell short* ■ *n* **1.** FILM OF SHORT DURATION a film whose running time is approximately 30 minutes or less **2.** ELEC ENG same as **short-circuit 3.** BASEBALL same as **shortstop 4.** GARMENT SIZE a size of garment for a short person **5.** SMALL DRINK a drink consisting of a small measure of spirits in a small glass (*informal*) ■ **shorts** *npl* **1.** SHORT TROUSERS trousers that end somewhere between the upper thigh and the knee **2.** *N Am* UNDERPANTS men's underpants **3.** AGRIC MIXTURE OF BRAN AND COARSE FLOUR a mixture of bran and coarse flour left over from the milling of wheat **4.** FIN SHORT-DATED ITEMS bills or securities that are due to mature within a comparatively short space of time ■ *vti* (**shorts, shorting, shorted**) ELEC same as **short-circuit** (sense 1) [Old English *sceort* < Indo-European, 'to cut'] —**shortness** *n* ◇ **for short** as an abbreviation or shortened form ◇ **go short** to have insufficient money or food ◇ **in short** used to introduce a rephrasing of something in a more concise form ◇ **short and sweet** pleasant or bearable because brief ◇ **short of 1.** not having something, or not having enough of something **2.** less than ○ *Nothing short of an apology will do.* **3.** without actually doing something ○ *praised the candidate, but stopped short of endorsing him*

short-acting *adj* effective for a short period

shortage /sháwrtij/ *n* an absence of something that is needed or required

---

SYNONYMS See *lack*.

---

short back and sides *n* a hairstyle in which the hair at the back and sides of the head is cut short

short black *n ANZ* a strong black coffee served in a small cup

shortboard /sháwrt bawrd/ *n* a surfboard that is below a specific length, shorter than a longboard —**shortboarding** *n*

shortbread /sháwrt bred/ *n* a rich crumbly biscuit made with a high proportion of butter to flour and a comparatively small proportion of sugar

short break *n* a holiday away from home lasting a few days, but usually less than a week

shortcake /sháwrt kayk/ *n* **1.** FOOD same as **shortbread 2.** a dessert consisting of a shortbread base topped with fruit and cream

shortchange /sháwrt cháynj/ (**-changes, -changing, -changed**) *vt* **1.** to give somebody less change than is due to him or her **2.** to behave unfairly towards somebody by giving him or her less of something than he or she deserves or expects —**shortchanger** *n*

short circuit *n* a failure in an electrical circuit caused by an accidental flow of excessive current

short-circuit *v* **1.** *vti* HAVE OR CAUSE FAILURE IN CIRCUIT to have a failure in an electrical circuit by creating a connection of low resistance across which an excessive current flows, or cause such a failure in a circuit **2.** *vt* AVOID STANDARD PROCEDURE to ignore or bypass a standard procedure by using a much quicker or more direct method to achieve something **3.** *vt N Am* FRUSTRATE OR HINDER PLANS to hinder a plan or project by erecting obstacles

shortcoming /sháwrt kuming/ *n* a failure or flaw in somebody's character or in a system or organization (*often used in the plural*)

shortcrust pastry /sháwrt krust-/ *n* pastry with a crisp crumbly texture made with one measure of fat to every two measures of flour

short cut *n* **1.** SHORTER ROUTE a route that is shorter or more direct than the usual one **2.** TIMESAVER a way of saving time and effort in doing something **3.** COMPUT QUICK WAY OF PERFORMING COMPUTER FUNCTION a means of quickly ordering a computer to perform a complicated function, e.g. an icon on a computer screen or a short series of keystrokes —**short-cut** *vti*

short-day *adj* able to flower only upon exposure to relatively short periods of sunlight, e.g. during spring or autumn

short division *n* a method of dividing relatively simple numbers without writing down all the steps in the process

shorten /sháwrt'n/ (**-ens, -ening, -ened**) *v* **1.** *vti* BECOME OR MAKE SHORTER to make something shorter, or become shorter **2.** *vti* GAMBLING MAKE ODDS SHORTER to reduce the odds on a bet, or be reduced **3.** *vt* SAILING REDUCE SAIL to reduce the area of a sail **4.** *vt* COOK MAKE PASTRY SHORTER to make pastry more crumbly by adding more fat —**shortener** *n*

shortening /sháwrtning/ *n* **1.** ACT OF MAKING SOMETHING SHORTER the act or process of making something shorter, or of becoming shorter **2.** GRAM ABBREVIATION

shaped head. Native to: shallow Atlantic and Pacific waters. Latin name: *Sphyrna tiburo.*

shoveller /shúvvələr/ *n* somebody or something that uses a shovel to move or throw something

shovel-nosed *adj* having a broad shovel-shaped head, snout, or bill

shovelware /shúvv'l wair/ *n* software or material that is put on the Web or on a CD-ROM indiscriminately without regard for its appearance or usefulness (*informal*)

show /shō/ *v* (**shows, showing, showed, shown** /shōn/) **1.** *vt* MAKE SOMETHING VISIBLE to cause or allow something to come into view, or present something to be looked at ○ *Show me your hand.* **2.** *vti* BE VISIBLE to be visible, or allow something to be seen easily, often inadvertently or against inclination ○ *Does the spot on my shirt show?* **3.** *vti* EXHIBIT to put on an exhibition or performance, or be presented for the public to see ○ *She's showing her paintings all over the world now.* ○ *Several new films are showing this week.* **4.** *vti* PRESENT SOMETHING TO PUBLIC to display something publicly, e.g. in a sale, exhibition, or competition, or be displayed publicly ○ *His work was showing at the Museum of Modern Art.* **5.** *vt* DEMONSTRATE SOMETHING FOR INSTRUCTION to give a demonstration of something in order to teach others ○ *She showed us how to apply the glaze to the pot.* **6.** *vt* ESTABLISH SOMETHING USING REASON to explain, demonstrate, or prove something in a logical way ○ *The teacher showed them the solution.* **7.** *vt* GIVE INFORMATION to register information ○ *This chart shows the sudden increase in temperature.* **8.** *vt* GUIDE SOMEBODY to guide or accompany somebody ○ *Show them to the office.* **9.** *vt* POINT SOMETHING OUT TO SOMEBODY to call somebody's attention to something ○ *She showed him the mistake.* **10.** *vt* DEMONSTRATE QUALITIES to make fundamental qualities or characteristics evident ○ *He has shown that he is honest.* **11.** *vt* DISPLAY ATTITUDE to display a personal feeling or attitude ○ *She's never shown much interest in art.* **12.** *vi* HAVE A PARTICULAR APPEARANCE to have a particular appearance when being viewed ○ *The horse shows well.* **13.** *vi* ARRIVE to put in an appearance at a place (*informal*) ○ *They never showed.* **14.** *vi N Am* COME IN THIRD to finish at least third in a race, especially a horse race or a dog race **15.** *vt* LAW PLEAD SOMETHING IN LAWSUIT to allege or plead something in a legal document ■ *n* **1.** PUBLIC PRESENTATION a public entertainment, e.g. a theatre performance, film, or radio or television programme ○ *Shall we go to a show tonight?* **2.** EXHIBITION an exhibition, e.g. of art, flowers, animals, or an industry's products ○ *a flower show* **3.** EVENT WITH FARM COMPETITIONS AND AMUSEMENTS an annual outdoor event with competitions for the best livestock, produce, and prepared foods and with entertainments, rides, and other amusements. N Am term **fair**[2] **4.** DEMONSTRATION an expression or demonstration of something ○ *a show of force* **5.** APPEARANCE an appearance given, either as an outward display of an emotion or trait, or as a demonstration of falseness and pretence ○ *a show of diligence* **6.** SIZABLE VENTURE an undertaking or task, especially one of some size and complexity (*informal*) ○ *You decide – it's your show!* **7.** IMPRESSIVE DISPLAY an extravagant or impressive display ○ *Their lawyers put on quite a show!* **8.** *ANZ, US* OPPORTUNITY a chance or opportunity (*informal*) ○ *no show of winning* **9.** INDICATION a trace of something indicating its presence, e.g. oil in the ground **10.** MED BLOOD INDICATING START OF LABOUR a bloody mucous discharge indicating the onset of labour in childbirth ■ **shows** *npl N England, Scotland* LEISURE same as **fair**[2] (sense 1) (*informal*) [Old English *scēawian* 'look at' < W Germanic, 'to look'] —**showable** *adj* ◇ **get the** *or* **this show on the road** to begin an activity or start an event (*informal*) ◇ **good show** used to express approval or to congratulate somebody on doing well (*dated*) ◇ **steal the show** to attract the most attention or admiration

show off *v* **1.** *vi* ATTRACT ATTENTION OF OTHERS to try to impress others by behaving in a way that attracts attention **2.** *vt* PRESENT SOMETHING FOR APPROVAL to display somebody or something proudly for others to admire **3.** *vt* PRESENT SOMETHING IN APPEALING WAY to display something in a way that enhances it

show up *v* **1.** *vi* ARRIVE to arrive or put in an appearance (*informal*) **2.** *vt* BRING SOMETHING TO LIGHT to expose or reveal something, especially an error or personal shortcoming **3.** *vi* BE SEEN to be easily seen **4.** *vt* EMBARRASS SOMEBODY BEFORE OTHERS to embarrass or humiliate somebody publicly **5.** *vt* MAKE SOMEBODY LOOK BAD to perform in a superior way and make somebody look inferior by comparison

show-and-tell *n* a classroom activity for children in which each child brings an object to school and tells the other children about it

show bill *n* a poster advertising or publicizing something

show biz *n* ARTS same as **show business** (*informal*)

showboat /shō bōt/ *n* a river steamboat equipped with a theatre and carrying an acting company that performs for communities along the river

show business *n* the entertainment industry, including films, radio, television, theatre, and music recording

showcase /shō kayss/ *n* **1.** GLASS CASE FOR DISPLAYING OBJECTS a box or case, usually one made of glass, used to display objects, especially in a museum or shop **2.** MOST FAVOURABLE SETTING an event, setting, or medium in which something or somebody is presented to advantage ■ *vt* (**-cases, -casing, -cased**) PRESENT SOMETHING TO ADVANTAGE to present something or somebody in a way that is designed to attract attention and admiration

showdown /shō down/ *n* **1.** a confrontation to settle a conflict or dispute **2.** in poker, the moment at the end of a round when the players show their cards to see who has the best hand

shower[1] /shów ər/ *n* **1.** BATH UNDER SPRAY a method of washing in which somebody stands upright under a spray of water from a nozzle **2.** PLACE AND EQUIPMENT FOR SHOWER an enclosure or the plumbing apparatus for a shower **3.** PERIOD OF PRECIPITATION a short period of rain, snow, hail, or sleet **4.** SOMETHING LIKE RAIN a sudden spray or fall of something such as meteors, sparks, or bullets ○ *a meteor shower* **5.** LARGE AMOUNT OF SOMETHING something that somebody receives all at once in quantity **6.** *ANZ, N Am* PARTY WITH GIFTS a party given by friends, especially in honour of a woman who is about to be married or is expecting a baby, at which gifts are given **7.** *UK* DISAGREEABLE GROUP a group of people considered unpleasant, worthless, or inferior (*informal*) **8.** PHYS IONIZING PARTICLES CAUSED BY COSMIC RAY a large number of ionizing particles and photons caused by the collision of a cosmic-ray particle with the upper atmosphere ■ *v* (**-ers, -ering, -ered**) **1.** *vi* WASH UNDER SHOWER to wash using a shower **2.** *vti* RAIN DOWN ON SOMEBODY to fall in a spray, or make things fall in a spray **3.** *vt* GIVE SOMEBODY SOMETHING PLENTIFULLY to give somebody something in abundance ○ *They were showered with gifts.* [Old English *scūr* < W Germanic] —**showery** *adj*

shower[2] /shō ər/ *n* somebody or something that shows, especially an exhibitor at a public exhibition [Old English *scēawere* 'scout, watchman' < *scēawian* (see SHOW)]

shower bath *n* HOUSEHOLD same as **shower**[1] *n* (sense 1) (*dated*)

shower gel *n* a liquid soap with the consistency of a gel, used especially when in the shower and often scented

showerhead /shów ər hed/ *n* a spray nozzle that is part of an overhead plumbing fixture used in a shower

showerproof /shów ər proof/ *adj* resistant to light but not heavy rain —**showerproofing** *n*

shower tea /shów ər-/ *n ANZ* same as **kitchen tea**

showgirl /shō gurl/ *n* a young woman who performs in the chorus of a stage show, usually a musical, as a dancer or singer

showground /shō grownd/ *n* an area of land where an open-air event such as an agricultural show is held

show house, show home *n* a house decorated and furnished for prospective buyers to view as an example of the type of house for sale on a newly built estate. US term **model home**

showing /shō ing/ *n* **1.** DISPLAY a presentation or exhibition, e.g. of a film or artwork **2.** TYPE OF PERFORMANCE the way a person, group, or team performs **3.** PRESENTATION OF FACTS a presentation of facts

showjumping /shō jumping/ *n* a competitive sport in which riders on horseback take turns jumping over a series of obstacles on a set course and are judged on speed and ability —**showjump** *vi* —**showjumper** *n*

showman /shōmən/ (*plural* **-men** /-mən/) *n* **1.** GIFTED ENTERTAINER somebody, especially a man, who is naturally talented in dramatic presentation or entertainment **2.** PRODUCER OF SHOW a producer or promoter of commercial entertainment ventures, especially in musical theatre **3.** CIRCUS MANAGER a manager or owner of a circus or fairground, especially a man —**showmanship** *n*

shown past participle of **show**

show-off *n* a flamboyant person who seeks attention (*informal*)

show of hands *n* a form of voting that involves counting the hands raised by people to vote for or against a proposal

showperson /shō purss'n/ (*plural* **-people** /-peep'l/ or **-persons**) *n* somebody who is in show business

showpiece /shō peess/ *n* something considered or offered as a fine example of something

showplace /shō playss/ *n* **1.** a place visited for its beauty or historical significance **2.** a place that is considered or offered as an example of beauty

show pony *n Aus* somebody who appears impressive but lacks substance or depth

showroom /shō room, -ro͝om/ *n* a room in which goods for sale, especially cars or electrical appliances, are displayed

showstopper /shō stopər/ *n* **1.** a performance receiving so much applause from an audience that the show is interrupted **2.** somebody or something so spectacular as to attract and hold everyone's attention

showtime /shō tīm/ *n N Am* **1.** the scheduled time for an entertainment such as a film or play to begin **2.** the scheduled time for any event or activity to begin (*informal*)

show trial *n* a trial with a predetermined verdict held for propaganda purposes

showwoman /shō wo͝omən/ (*plural* **-women** /-wimin/) *n* **1.** a woman who is naturally talented in dramatic presentation or entertainment **2.** a woman who manages or owns a circus or fairground

showy /shō i/ (**-ier, -iest**) *adj* **1.** making an attractive or impressive display **2.** appearing tasteless and ostentatious —**showily** *adv* —**showiness** *n*

shoyu /shō yoo/ *n* a Japanese variety of soy sauce [Early 18C. < Japanese]

shp *abbr* MECH ENG shaft horsepower

shpilkes /shpílkəss/ *npl* a state of great nervousness or anxiety [< Yiddish]

shpt *abbr* shipment

shr. *abbr* FIN share

shraddh *n* CULTL ANTHROP another spelling of **sraddhaa**

shrank past tense of **shrink**

shrapnel /shrápnəl/ *n* **1.** metal balls or fragments that are scattered when a shell, bomb, or bullet explodes **2.** an artillery shell designed to explode before impact producing a shower of metal balls and fragments [Early 19C. After General Henry *Shrapnel* (1761–1842), British artillery officer]

shred /shred/ *n* **1.** LONG TORN STRIP a ragged scrap or strip cut or torn from something **2.** SMALL PART a very small amount or fragment of something ■ *v* (**shreds, shredding, shredded**) **1.** *vt* TEAR SOMETHING INTO SHREDS to cut or tear something into shreds **2.** *vt* PUT DOCUMENT THROUGH SHREDDER to reduce a document to unreadable strips in a shredder **3.** *vti Aus, N Am* SURF OR SNOWBOARD EXPERTLY to ride a wave on a surfboard or descend a slope on a snowboard with expert skill (*informal*) [Old English *scrēade* < W Germanic, 'to cut']

shredder /shréddər/ *n* **1.** an office machine used to destroy documents by cutting them into very small pieces so that they cannot be read **2.** *Aus, N Am* an expert surfer or snowboarder (*informal*)

Shreveport /shreév pawrt/ city in northwestern Louisiana, on the western bank of the Red River, east of the Texas border. The city is an important pro-

ducer of oil, natural gas, and cotton. Population: 199,033 (2002 estimate).

shrew

shrew /shroo/ *n* **1.** a small nocturnal animal that resembles a mouse but is an insectivore, with velvety fur, a long pointed snout, and small eyes and ears. Native to: found worldwide, except New Guinea, Australia, and New Zealand. Family: Soricidae. **2.** an offensive term for a woman who is regarded as quarrelsome, nagging, or ill-tempered [Old English *scrēawa*. Origin ?]

CULTURAL NOTE *The Taming of the Shrew*, a play (1593–94?) by William Shakespeare. The central story of this play within a play is set in Verona and describes Petruchio's attempts to woo the wealthy but haughty and temperamental Katharina (the 'shrew' of the title). The rounded and convincing protagonists make this an intriguing character study as well as a boisterous farce. The expression 'Kiss me, Kate' comes from Act II, scene i: 'Kiss me, Kate, we will be married o' Sunday'.

shrewd /shrood/ *adj* **1.** GOOD AT JUDGING PEOPLE OR SITUATIONS showing or possessing intelligence, insight, and sound judgment, especially in business or politics **2.** CLEVER AND PROBABLY ACCURATE based on good judgment and probably correct ○ *a shrewd assessment of the situation* ○ *a shrewd guess* **3.** CRAFTY inclined to deal with others in a clever underhand way **4.** SHARP piercing or sharp (*archaic*) [13C. < SHREW in the obsolete sense 'wicked person'] —**shrewdly** *adv* —**shrewdness** *n*

shrewish /shroo ish/ *adj* with a quarrelsome ill-tempered disposition —**shrewishly** *adv* —**shrewishness** *n*

Shrewsbury /shrṓzbəri, shroozbəri/ county town of Shropshire, England. Population: 32,751 (2002).

Shri *n* same as **Sri**

shriek /shreek/ *v* (**shrieks, shrieking, shrieked**) **1.** *vi* MAKE SHRILL SOUND to make a loud high-pitched piercing sound **2.** *vt* SAY SOMETHING IN SHRILL VOICE to utter something in a loud high-pitched piercing voice ■ *n* SHRILL CRY a loud high-pitched piercing cry or sound [15C. < N Germanic] —**shrieker** *n*

shrieval /shree'v'l/ *adj* belonging or relating to a sheriff [Late 17C. < obsolete *shrieve* 'sheriff']

shrievalty /shree'v'lti/ (*plural* **-ties**) *n* **1.** SHERIFF'S OFFICE the office or position of sheriff **2.** SHERIFF'S TERM the term of office of a sheriff **3.** SHERIFF'S JURISDICTION the jurisdiction of a sheriff [Early 16C. < obsolete *shrieve* 'sheriff']

shrift /shrift/ *n* (*archaic*) **1.** SHRIVING SOMEBODY the act of shriving or of being shriven **2.** CONFESSION confession to a priest **3.** ABSOLUTION absolution granted by a priest. ◊ **short shrift** [Old English *scrift* < *scrīfan* (see SHRIVE)]

shrike

shrike /shrīk/ (*plural* **shrikes** or *same*) *n* a brown or grey songbird with a screeching call and a hooked beak that eats insects and small animals that it impales on sharp objects such as thorns. Family: Laniidae. [Mid-16C. Origin ?]

shrill /shril/ *adj* **1.** PENETRATINGLY HIGH-PITCHED with a high-pitched penetrating quality **2.** MAKING SHRILL SOUND making a high-pitched penetrating sound **3.** INSISTENT with an obtrusive insistent quality ■ *v* (**shrills, shrilling, shrilled**) **1.** *vi* MAKE SHRILL SOUND to make a high-pitched penetrating sound (*literary*) **2.** *vt* SAY SOMETHING IN PIERCING VOICE to utter something in a high-pitched penetrating voice [13C. Origin ?] —**shrillness** *n* —**shrilly** /shríl li/ *adv*

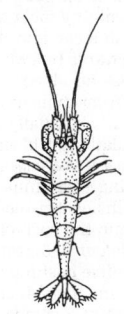

shrimp

shrimp /shrimp/ *n* **1.** SMALL SEA CRUSTACEAN a small, mainly sea-dwelling crustacean with ten legs, belonging to a suborder that includes several edible species. A shrimp has a long thin semi-transparent body, five pairs of jointed legs, a tail resembling a fan, and a pair of pincers. Suborder: Natantia. **2.** SOMETHING UNDERSIZED somebody or something very small or considered insignificant (*informal*) ■ *vi* (**shrimps, shrimping, shrimped**) FISH FOR SHRIMPS to fish for shrimps [14C. Origin ?] —**shrimper** *n*

shrimp plant *n* an ornamental plant with long curving flower spikes within overlapping pink bracts. Native to: tropical America. Latin name: *Beloperone guttata*.

shrine /shrīn/ *n* **1.** HOLY PLACE OF WORSHIP a sacred place of worship associated with a holy person or event **2.** CONTAINER FOR HOLY RELICS a case or other container for sacred relics such as the bones of a saint **3.** TOMB OF HOLY PERSON the tomb of a saint or other revered figure **4.** NICHE FOR RELIGIOUS ICON a ledge or alcove for a religious icon, e.g. in a church **5.** SOMETHING REVERED an object or place revered for its associations or history ■ *vt* (**shrines, shrining, shrined**) same as **enshrine** (sense 2) (*literary*) [Pre-12C. < Latin *scrinium* 'case for books or papers']

shrink /shringk/ *v* (**shrinks, shrinking, shrank** /shrangk/ or **shrunk** /shrungk/, **shrunk** or **shrunken** /shrúngkən/) **1.** *vti* MAKE OR BECOME SMALLER to become smaller, or cause something to become smaller, e.g. when exposed to cold, heat, or damp **2.** *vti* REDUCE SIZE to decrease in amount, extent, value, or weight, or cause something to decrease in this way **3.** *vi* DRAW AWAY FROM SOMETHING to move back and away, especially out of disgust, fear, or horror ○ *shrinking back in revulsion* **4.** *vi* BE DISINCLINED TO DO SOMETHING to be unwilling or reluctant to do something, especially something difficult or unpleasant ○ *She does not shrink from tackling tough problems.* ■ *n* **1.** same as **psychiatrist** (*slang; considered offensive by some people*) **2.** ACT OF SHRINKING AWAY an act of shrinking away from something [Old English *scrincan* 'to wither' < Indo-European, 'to turn, bend'] —**shrinkable** *adj* —**shrinker** *n*

SYNONYMS See *recoil*.

shrinkage /shríngkij/ *n* **1.** DECREASE AFTER SHRINKING the amount lost when something is decreased or reduced, or when it shrinks **2.** ACT OF SHRINKING the shrinking of something **3.** MERCHANDISE STOLEN OR BROKEN the loss of goods through theft or breakage **4.** LOSS OF VALUE the decrease in value of something **5.** WEIGHT REDUCTION IN CARCASSES the loss in body weight of livestock carcasses during shipping, storage, and preparation for sale **6.** REDUCED SIZE OF CLAY ITEM the reduction in size of a clay object when it is fired in a kiln, caused by the moisture burning off

shrink fit *n* the fit of two interlocking parts in which the outer is heated and therefore expands before being put in position, the contraction during cooling ensuring that it is tight

shrinking violet /shrinking-/ *n* a shy or retiring person (*informal*)

shrink-wrap *n* a clear thermoplastic film that is wrapped around a product and shrunk to its original smaller size using heat, thereby forming a tightly sealed package ■ *vt* to wrap goods in shrink-wrap

shrive /shrīv/ (**shrives, shriving, shrove** /shrōv/ or **shrived, shriven** /shrívv'n/ or **shrived**) *v* **1.** *vt* ABSOLVE SOMEBODY OF SINS in Christianity, to hear somebody's confession of sins and give the person absolution **2.** *vt* IMPOSE PENANCE in Christianity, to impose a penance on a sinner **3.** *vi* CONFESS to confess to a priest (*archaic*) [Old English *scrīfan*, via Germanic < Latin *scribere* 'write'] —**shriver** *n*

shrivel /shrívv'l/ (**-els, -elling, -elled**) *vti* **1.** SHRINK to become shrunken or wrinkled, or cause somebody or something to become shrunken or wrinkled, especially from drying out or ageing **2.** WEAKEN to become useless or ineffectual, or cause somebody to become useless or ineffectual **3.** BECOME OR MAKE SMALLER to become gradually smaller or less, or cause something to become gradually smaller or less [Mid-16C. Origin ?]

shriven CHR past participle of **shrive**

Shrivijaya HIST another spelling of **Sri Vijaya**

shroff /shrof/ *n* **1.** SOUTH ASIAN BANKER in South Asia, a banker or moneychanger **2.** EXPERT IN COUNTERFEIT COINS somebody employed in eastern Asia to separate counterfeit from real coins ■ *vt* (**shroffs, shroffing, shroffed**) SEPARATE COUNTERFEIT COINS to separate counterfeit from real coins [Early 17C. Alteration of Hindi *śarāf* < Arabic *ṣarrāf*]

Shropshire /shrópshər/ county on the Welsh border in the Midlands, England. It is mainly agricultural, and was an early centre of the iron industry. Shrewsbury is the county town. Population: 283,173 (2001). Area: 3,490 sq. km/1,348 sq. mi.

shroud /shrowd/ *n* **1.** BURIAL CLOTH a cloth in which a dead body is wrapped before burial **2.** COVERING something that covers or conceals something or somebody **3.** PROTECTIVE COVERING a protective covering, e.g. a guard for a piece of machinery **4.** NAUT MAST STAY any one of the supporting ropes or wires that extend down from the top of a mast to the deck **5.** AEROSP PROTECTIVE COVERING FOR SPACECRAFT a shield that protects a spacecraft from heat during launch **6.** AEROSP REARWARD AEROFOIL SURFACE a rearward extension of a fixed aerofoil surface covering the leading edge of a movable surface hinged to it **7.** CONSTR CABLE TO STOP SWAY a supporting cable that extends from the top of a tall structure such as a smokestack to the ground **8.** AVIAT PARACHUTE LINE any one of the lines by which the harness of a parachute is attached to the canopy ■ *vt* (**shrouds, shrouding, shrouded**) **1.** COVER OR CONCEAL to cover or conceal somebody or something **2.** WRAP CORPSE to wrap a dead body in a cloth [Old English *scrūd* 'garment' < W Germanic, 'to cut']

shroud-laid *adj* describes a rope that is made up of four twisted strands

shroud-waving *n* the calculated use of distressing events or statistics to publicize issues or gain political advantage (*slang*) —**shroud-waving** *adj*

shrove CHR past tense of **shrive**

Shrovetide /shrṓv tīd/ *n* in the Christian calendar, the three-day period preceding Ash Wednesday and the season of Lent

Shrove Tuesday *n* in the Christian calendar, the last day before the beginning of Lent [< past tense of SHRIVE; from the practice of going to confession at the beginning of Lent]

shrub[1] /shrub/ *n* a woody plant without a trunk but with several stems growing from the base [Old English *scrybb* 'shrubbery' < Indo-European, 'to cut']

shrub[2] /shrub/ *n* a drink made with fruit juice, sugar, spices, and rum or other alcohol [Early 18C. < Arabic *surb* 'a drink']

shrubbery /shrúbbəri/ (*plural* **-ies**) *n* **1.** a part of a

garden where shrubs grow **2.** shrubs considered collectively

shrubby /shrúbbi/ (**-bier, -biest**) *adj* **1.** planted or covered with shrubs **2.** resembling a shrub in size or in having little or no trunk —**shrubbiness** *n*

shrug /shrug/ *vti* (**shrugs, shrugging, shrugged**) to raise and drop the shoulders briefly, especially to indicate indifference or lack of knowledge ■ *n* a gesture of raising and dropping the shoulders briefly [14C. Origin ?]

shrug off *vt* **1. DISMISS SOMETHING** to reject or disregard something as unimportant **2. GET FREE OF SOMETHING** to become free of something such as a disease **3. REMOVE CLOTHING** to get out of clothing by wriggling

shrunk past participle, past tense of **shrink**

shrunken past participle of **shrink**

sht *abbr* sheet

shtetl /shtétt'l/ (*plural* **shtetls** or **shtetlach** /shtét laak/), **schtetl** (*plural* **schtetls** or **schtetlach**) *n* in former times, a small Jewish town or village in Eastern Europe [Mid-20C. < Yiddish, 'little town' < German *Stadt* 'town']

shtg. *abbr* shortage

shtick /shtik/, **schtick, shtik** *n* **1.** something that especially characterizes somebody, e.g. an interest, talent, trait, job, or hobby (*slang*) **2.** a comedian's or entertainer's act or gimmick (*informal*) [Mid-20C. Via Yiddish, 'piece, routine' < Old High German *stucki*]

shtoom /shtŏŏm/, **schtoom, shtum, stumm** *adj* quiet or silent (*informal*) [Mid-20C. Via Yiddish < German *stumm*]

shtuck /shtŏŏk/ *n* trouble resulting from a failing such as an error or misjudgment (*informal*) [Mid-20C. Origin ?]

shtum *adj* another spelling of **shtoom** (*informal*)

shuck /shuk/ *n* **1.** *N Am* **OUTER COVERING OF GRAIN OR FRUIT** the husk, pod, or shell of something such as a nut, pea, or ear of corn **2. OYSTER OR CLAM SHELL** the shell of a clam or oyster ■ *vt* (**shucks, shucking, shucked**) **GET RID OF SOMETHING** to get rid of or remove something or throw something off (*informal*) [Late 17C. Origin ?] —**shucker** *n*

shucks /shuks/ *interj N Am* used to express disappointment, bashfulness, or irritation (*dated informal*) [Mid-19C. < *shucks* 'worthless things']

shudder /shúddər/ *vi* (**-ders, -dering, -dered**) **1. SHIVER VIOLENTLY** to shake or tremble uncontrollably from a reaction such as cold, fear, or disgust **2. VIBRATE** to vibrate rapidly and heavily ■ *n* **1. VIOLENT SHAKING MOVEMENT** an uncontrolled shaking or trembling movement **2. VIBRATION** a rapid heavy vibrating movement [12C. Probably < Middle Low German *schōderen* or Middle Dutch *shūderen* 'keep on shuddering'] —**shuddery** *adj*

Shudra *n* HINDUISM same as **Sudra**

shuffle /shúff'l/ *v* (**-fles, -fling, -fled**) **1.** *vi* **WALK WITHOUT LIFTING FEET** to walk slowly without picking up the feet **2.** *vt* **DRAG FEET** to move the feet without picking them up **3.** *vi* **MOVE AWKWARDLY** to move in an awkward clumsy way **4.** *vi* **DANCE BY SHUFFLING FEET** to slide the feet in a dance step **5.** *vt* **CHANGE WHERE SOMETHING IS LOCATED** to move things around from one place to another **6.** *vt* **MIX THINGS UP** to mix things together carelessly **7.** *vti* **REARRANGE ORDER OF PLAYING CARDS** to rearrange playing cards randomly so that the order is not known **8.** *vi* **BEHAVE EVASIVELY** to be deliberately evasive or shifty in addressing an issue ■ *n* **1. FOOT-DRAGGING WALK** a slow walk while dragging the feet **2. SLIDING DANCE STEP** a dance or dance step in which the feet drag or slide on the floor **3. REORDERING OF CARDS** a random reordering of playing cards **4. SOMEBODY'S CHANCE TO SHUFFLE SOMETHING** a player's turn to shuffle playing cards **5. EVASION** a deliberate evasion of an issue [Mid-16C. Origin ?] —**shuffler** *n*

shuffleboard /shúff'l bawrd/ *n* **1.** a game in which players use a long pronged cue to push discs along a smooth hard surface into numbered scoring areas **2.** the surface on which shuffleboard is played [Mid-19C. Alteration of *shovelboard*, alteration of obsolete *shove-board*, earlier name for the game]

shufti /shŏŏfti/ (*plural* **-tis**), **shufty** (*plural* **-ties**) *n* a quick look or glance (*informal*) [Mid-20C. < colloquial Arabic *šufti* 'have you seen?' < *šāfa* 'see']

shul /shool/, **schul** *n* JUDAISM same as **synagogue** (sense 1) [Late 19C. Via Yiddish < German *Schule* 'school']

shun /shun/ (**shuns, shunning, shunned**) *vt* to avoid somebody or something intentionally [Old English *scunian*. Origin ?] —**shunner** *n*

shunt /shunt/ *v* (**shunts, shunting, shunted**) **1.** *vt* **MOVE SOMEBODY OR SOMETHING ELSEWHERE** to move somebody or something to a different place, especially for convenience rather than fairness or kindness **2.** *vti* **CHANGE TRACKS** to move rolling railway stock from one track to another, either by using an engine or by means of an automatic switch, especially when assembling trains, or be moved in this way **3.** *vt* **GET RID OF RESPONSIBILITY** to avoid something by ignoring it or shifting responsibility for it to somebody else **4.** *vt* **CRASH CAR** to crash a car into the back of another car, pushing it forwards (*informal*) **5.** *vt* ELECTRONICS **DIVERT CURRENT** to use an electrical device to divert electrical current from an instrument **6.** *vt* **SURGICALLY DIVERT FLOW** to use an artificially created passage to redirect the circulation of blood or cerebrospinal fluid ■ *n* **1. DIVERSION OF SOMETHING** a turning aside, or a means of turning something aside **2. MINOR CAR CRASH** a minor collision between road vehicles in which one runs into the back of another at a relatively low speed (*informal*) **3. SORTING OF RAILWAY VEHICLES** the act of a locomotive pushing railway vehicles in the process of sorting them **4.** ELECTRONICS **DEVICE FOR DIVERTING ELECTRIC CURRENT** a component in an electric circuit that is connected in parallel with an instrument and diverts the majority of current from the instrument **5. BYPASS FOR BODILY FLUID** a passage in the body that diverts the flow of blood or other bodily fluid from one channel to another, created either as a result of disease or injury or artificially by surgery. Artificial shunts are used to facilitate regular connection to a kidney dialysis machine or to relieve the pressure of cerebrospinal fluid on the brain in the condition of hydrocephalus. [13C. Origin ?]

shush /shŏŏsh, shush/ *interj* used to tell somebody to be quiet ■ *vti* (**shushes, shushing, shushed**) to silence somebody, or become silent (*informal*) [Early 20C. Natural exclamation]

shu-shu /shŏŏ shoo/ *n Carib* whispering or gossip [Origin ?]

Shuswap /shŏŏss wop/ (*plural same* or **-waps**) *n* **1.** a member of a Native North American people of southern British Columbia **2.** the Salishan language of the Shuswap people. Native speakers: 500. [Mid-19C. < Shuswap] —**Shuswap** *adj*

shut /shut/ *v* (**shuts, shutting, shut**) **1.** *vti* **CLOSE OPENING** to move something into a position that blocks or covers an opening, or move into such a position ○ *leaned over to shut the window* **2.** *vt* **STOP ACCESS OR EXIT** to prevent entrance to or exit from something, e.g. by locking doors ○ *Rising water levels meant that they had to shut the tunnel.* **3.** *vt* **FOLD PARTS CLOSED** to close something by bringing its covering or parts together ○ *had to shut her eyes against the light* **4.** *vt* **LOCK SOMETHING** to secure something with a lock or latch ○ *The gate had not been shut properly.* **5.** *vti* **STOP OPERATION** to discontinue operation temporarily or permanently, or cause something to discontinue operation ○ *Another factory shut because it was losing money.* ■ *adj* **SECURED** closed or fastened against entrance or exit ■ *n* METALL **CONNECTION BETWEEN WELDED PIECES** the region of connection between pieces of metal that are welded together [Old English *scyttan* < Germanic]

shut down *v* **1.** *vti* to cease operation or activity, or cause something to cease operation or activity **2.** *vt* to reduce the power output of a nuclear reactor by maintaining it at its lowest possible level

shut in *vt* to confine or enclose somebody or something

shut off *v* **1.** *vti* **STOP SOMETHING WORKING** to stop operating, or cause something to stop operating **2.** *vt* **CUT OFF FLOW** to stop the passage, flow, or supply of something **3.** *vt* **BLOCK SOMETHING OFF** to impede the flow or progress of something **4.** *vt* **ISOLATE SOMEBODY** to put somebody or something into a state of isolation

shut out *vt* **1. EXCLUDE SOMEBODY** to exclude somebody or something **2. STOP SOMEBODY ENTERING** to prevent somebody or something from entering a place **3. HIDE SOMETHING** to hide something from sight **4.** *N Am* **KEEP SOMEBODY FROM SCORING** to prevent an opponent from scoring in a game

shut up *v* **1.** *vi* **STOP TALKING** to be quiet or stop talking (*informal*) ○ *I shut up before saying something I would regret.* **2.** *vt* **SILENCE SOMEBODY** to cause somebody to be quiet or stop talking (*informal*) ○ *She shot me a look that shut me up instantly.* **3.** *vt* **CONFINE SOMEBODY** to confine or imprison somebody or something ○ *She shut the dog up in the pen.* **4.** *vt* **CLOSE SOMETHING** to close or prevent entrance to something ○ *The building is all shut up.*

shutdown /shút down/ *n* **1.** the cessation or suspension of activities at a business, factory, or plant **2.** the reduction of power in a nuclear reactor by maintaining the core at the lowest level possible

Shute /shoot/, **Nevil** (1899–1960) British novelist and aeronautical engineer. His experiences during World War II inspired many of his novels. Others, including *A Town Like Alice* (1950), are set in Australia. Born **Norway, Nevil Shute**

shuteye /shút ī/ *n* a short sleep (*informal*)

shut-in *n* somebody who is rarely or never able to leave home, especially because of illness or lack of physical mobility (*informal*)

shut-off *n* **1.** a device, usually a valve, that shuts something off **2.** an interruption or stoppage, e.g. in flow or supply

shutout /shút owt/ *n* **1.** MANAGEMT same as **lockout 2.** *N Am* a game in which one team does not score

shutter /shúttər/ *n* **1. DOOR OR WINDOW COVER** a hinged cover for a door or window, often with louvres and usually fitted in pairs **2. CAMERA DEVICE** a mechanical part of a camera that opens and closes the lens aperture to expose the film or plate to light ■ *vt* (**-ters, -tering, -tered**) **1. CLOSE SOMETHING USING SHUTTERS** to close or protect something by means of shutters **2. FIT SOMETHING WITH SHUTTERS** to equip something with shutters

shuttering /shúttəring/ *n* BUILDINGS same as **formwork**

shuttle /shútt'l/ *n* **1. ROUTE TAKEN OR VEHICLE USED** the route taken or the aircraft, bus, or train used to travel frequently between two places, often relatively near each other **2.** AEROSP same as **space shuttle 3. GOING BACK AND FORTH** frequent travel by vehicle between two places **4.** RACKET GAMES same as **shuttlecock** *n* (sense 1) **5. WEAVING DEVICE** a device in weaving that holds the weft thread and is used to pass it between the warp threads **6. SPINDLE OR BOBBIN** a thread holder, e.g. in tatting or netting or for the lower thread in a sewing machine ■ *vti* (**-tles, -tling, -tled**) **1. GO BACK AND FORTH** to move between two places frequently, or cause somebody or something to move in this way **2. GO BY SHUTTLE** to transport somebody or something by a shuttle, or be transported by a shuttle [Old English *scytel* 'arrow, dart' < Germanic, 'shoot']

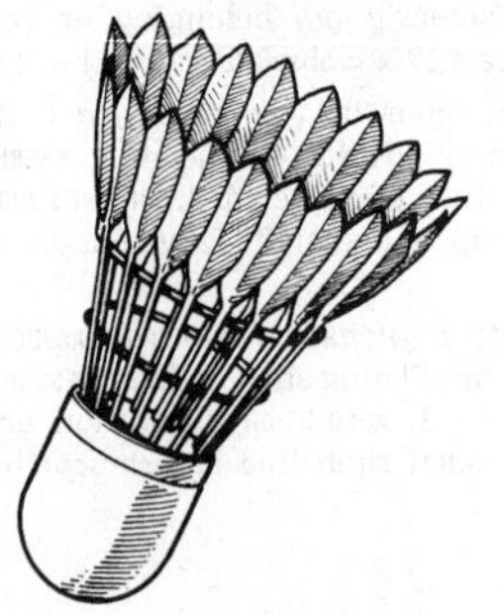

shuttlecock

shuttlecock /shútt'l kok/ *n* **1. OBJECT HIT IN BADMINTON** a small rounded piece of cork or rubber attached to a cone of feathers that is hit back and forth in badminton and in the old game of battledore **2. SUBJECT OF ARGUMENT** something that is continually argued about by two opposing sides ○ *The sovereignty of the island became a shuttlecock between the two countries.* ■ *vt* (**-cocks, -cocking, -cocked**) **SEND SOMETHING BACK AND FORTH** to toss or send something back and forth [Early 16C. *Shuttle* probably < its going back and forth, like the shuttle in a loom; *cock* < the feathers, like a bird's crest]

shuttlecraft /shútt'l kraaft/ (*plural same*) *n* a reusable spacecraft for carrying astronauts or material between Earth and space or between objects in space

shuttle diplomacy *n* diplomatic negotiations carried on between countries by a mediator who travels back and forth between the countries

shwa *n* PHON another spelling of **schwa**

Shwe /shə wáy/, **Than** (*b.* 1933) national leader of Myanmar (1992–). A senior general and specialist in psychological warfare, he became head of the State Law and Order Restoration Council (1992) and refuses to transfer power to the National League for Democracy, despite its election victory in 1990.

shy[1] /shī/ *adj* (**shyer, shyest**) **1.** UNCOMFORTABLE WITH OTHERS reserved, diffident, and uncomfortable in the company of others ○ *She was always shy at parties.* **2.** TIMID easily frightened ○ *The deer were shy and ran when we tried to approach them.* **3.** CAUTIOUS unwilling to trust or put confidence in somebody or something ○ *The children were shy of their new classmates.* **4.** RELUCTANT fearful of making a commitment ○ *Don't be shy of speaking your mind.* **5.** DISLIKING SOMETHING showing a disinclination for something (*usually used in combination*) ○ *workshy* **6.** SHORT OF SOMETHING short of the full or a particular amount ○ *We are £100 shy of the down payment.* **7.** BIOL NOT REPRODUCING EASILY describes plants and animals that do not breed readily or freely ■ *vi* (**shies, shying, shied**) **1.** MOVE SUDDENLY to move suddenly in fright or alarm ○ *That horse shies at anything on the road.* **2.** STAY AWAY to avoid or evade something ○ *He always shies away from public speaking.* ■ *n* (*plural* **shies**) SUDDEN MOVE a sudden movement in fright or alarm [Old English *scēoh* < Germanic] —**shyer** *n* —**shyly** *adv* —**shyness** *n*

shy[2] /shī/ *vt* (**shies, shying, shied**) THROW SOMETHING to toss something quickly and suddenly ■ *n* (*plural* **shies**) **1.** QUICK THROW a quick sudden throw of something **2.** VERBAL ATTACK a rude or insulting remark **3.** ATTEMPT an attempt made to do or get something (*informal*) ○ *We'll have a shy at it.* [Late 18C. Origin ?] —**shyer** *n*

shylock /shī lok/ *n* a ruthless and demanding money-lender or creditor [Late 18C. After *Shylock*, a money-lender in Shakespeare's play *The Merchant of Venice*]

shyster /shīstər/ *n* an unscrupulous person, especially a lawyer or political representative (*slang insult*) [Mid-19C. Origin ?]

si[1] /see/ *n* MUSIC same as **te** [Early 18C. < the initial letters of Latin *Sancte Iohannes* 'St John', the words sung to this note in the hymn for St John's day]

si[2] *abbr* ONLINE Slovenia (*used in Internet addresses*) See table at **domain name**

Si *symbol* CHEM ELEM silicon

SI[1] *abbr* MEASURE International System of Units [< French *Système International (d'Unités)*]

SI[2] *abbr* NZ South Island

sial /sī əl/ *n* rocks rich in silicon and aluminium that form the crust of the continental masses (*dated*) [Early 20C. Blend of *silicon + aluminium*] —**sialic** /sī állik/ *adj*

sialagogue /sī ́állə gog/, **sialogogue** *n* a drug or agent that stimulates the flow of saliva [Late 18C. < Greek *sialon* 'saliva'] —**sialagogic** /sī ́allə góggik/ *adj*

sialic acid /sī állik-/ *n* an amino sugar found in animal tissues [< Greek *sialon* 'saliva']

Sialkot /si álkot/ town in Punjab Province, north-eastern Pakistan, situated about 97 km/60 mi. north of Lahore. Population: 302,009 (1981).

sialoid /sī ́ə loyd/ *adj* resembling saliva [< Greek *sialon* 'saliva']

Siam /sī ́ám/ former name for **Thailand** (until 1939)

Siam, Gulf of former name for **Thailand, Gulf of**

siamang /seé ə mang/ *n* the largest species of gibbon, with a large throat sac that inflates during calls. Native to: Sumatra, Malaysia. Latin name: *Hylobates syndactylus*. [Early 19C. < Malay]

Siamese /sī ́ə meéz/ *adj* relating to Siam, now Thailand, or to its people or culture (*dated*) ■ *n* (*plural same*) **1.** BREED same as **Siamese cat 2.** SOMEBODY FROM THAILAND somebody who comes from Thailand (*dated*) **3.** THAI the Thai language (*dated*)

Siamese cat

Siamese cat *n* a short-haired domestic cat belonging to a breed that originated in Thailand (formerly Siam) with blue eyes and a long cream-coloured body with dark ears, paws, face, and tail

Siamese fighting fish *n* a brightly coloured long-finned freshwater fish often kept in aquariums, the male of which is very aggressive. Native to: Thailand, Malaysia. Latin name: *Betta splendens*.

Siamese twin *n* same as **conjoined twin** (*informal*) [After twins, Chang and Eng (1811–74), born in Siam (Thailand)]

sib /sib/ *n* **1.** BROTHER OR SISTER a brother or sister **2.** GENETICS INDIVIDUAL WITH SAME PARENTS AS ANOTHER an individual that has the same parents as another individual **3.** ANTHROP GROUP WITH SINGLE COMMON ANCESTOR a group of people who trace their descent lineally from a single real or presumed ancestor ■ **sibs** *npl* WIDER FAMILY members of an extended family considered as a group ■ *adj* CLOSELY RELATED with the same parents or closely related [Old English *sib(b)*, origin ?]

SIB *abbr* FIN Securities and Investments Board

AKG London

Jean Sibelius

Sibelius /si báyli əss/, **Jean** (1865–1957) Finnish composer. One of the leading symphonic composers of the 20th century, his works are much influenced by the culture and landscape of his native Finland. Born **Sibelius, Johan Julius Christian**

'My heart sings, full of sadness—the shadows lengthen.'
[Jean Sibelius, *Diary entry*; October 1914]

Siberia /sī beéri ə/ *n* vast region of eastern Russia, extending from the Ural Mountains in the west to the Pacific Ocean in the east, and from the Arctic Ocean in the North to China, Mongolia, and Kazakhstan in the south. Much of it is frozen for over half the year. Sparsely populated, it was used during Soviet rule (1917–91) as a place of exile. —**Siberian** *n, adj*

sibilant /síbbilənt/ *adj* **1.** PRONOUNCED WITH HISSING SOUND describes consonants that are pronounced with a hissing sound **2.** PRODUCING HISSING SOUND producing a hissing sound ○ *the sibilant sound of air escaping from a tyre* ■ *n* SIBILANT CONSONANT a consonant that is pronounced with a hissing sound [Mid-17C. < Latin *sibilant-*, present participle of *sibilare* 'hiss', probably an imitation of the sound] —**sibilance** *n* —**sibilantly** *adv*

sibilate /síbbi layt/ (**-lates, -lating, -lated**) *vti* to pronounce sounds with a hiss [Mid-17C. < Latin *sibilat-*, past participle of *sibilare* (see SIBILANT)]

sibling /síbbling/ *n* **1.** a brother or sister (*often used before a noun*) **2.** a member of a group of people who

trace their descent from a single real or presumed ancestor [Old English < *sib(b)* (see SIB)]

sibling species *n* a species that closely resembles another in appearance and other characteristics but cannot interbreed with it

sibyl /síbbil, síbb'l/ *n* **1.** a woman of ancient Greece and Rome believed to be an oracle or a prophet **2.** a female prophet or fortune teller [13C. Via French and Latin < Greek *Sibulla*] —**sibyllic** /si bíllik/ *adj* —**sybilline** /síbbi līn, -leen/ *adj*

sic[1] /sik/ *adv* thus or so, used within brackets to indicate that what precedes it is written intentionally or is copied verbatim from the original, even if it appears to be a mistake [Late 19C. < Latin] ◇ **sic passim** /sik pássim/ used to indicate that a word or term is used in the same form throughout a printed work ◇ **sic transit gloria mundi** 'thus passes the glory of the world', used, e.g., when a distinguished person dies or an important era comes to an end

sic[2] /sik/ (**sics, siccing, sicced**), **sick** (**sicks, sicking, sicked**) *vt* **1.** to attack somebody physically, usually used as a command to a dog **2.** to urge a person or animal, especially a dog, to attack somebody physically [Mid-19C. Dialect variant of SEEK]

Sica ♦ De Sica, Vittorio

siccar /síkər/, **sicker** *adj* Scotland free from doubt or uncertainty [Old English *sicor*, via Germanic < Latin *securus* (see SECURE)]

siccative /síkətiv/ *n* a substance added to liquids to speed drying ■ *adj* absorbing moisture to promote drying [15C. < late Latin *siccativus* < past participle of Latin *siccare* 'to dry' < *siccus* 'dry']

sice *n* HIST another spelling of **syce**

Sichuan /si chwaán/, **Szechwan** /se-/ province in southern China bordered by Qinghai, Gansu, Shaanxi, Hubei, Hunan, Guizhou, Yunnan, and Tibet. Capital: Chengdu. Population: 114,300,000 (1997). Area: 569,000 sq. km/220,000 sq. mi.

Sichuan pepper *n* a spice with a hot aniseed flavour, one of the ingredients of Chinese five-spice powder

siciliano /si sílli aánō/ (*plural* **-nos**), **siciliana** /-nə/ *n* **1.** an old Sicilian folk dance **2.** the music for a siciliano, in a minor key with six or twelve beats to the bar [Early 18C. < Italian, 'Sicilian']

Sicily /síssəli/ largest island in the Mediterranean Sea, in southern Italy. Population: 5,082,697 (1995). Area: 25,710 sq. km/9,927 sq. mi. —**Sicilian** /si sílli ən/ *n, adj*

sick[1] /sik/ *adj* **1.** ILL affected by an illness **2.** RELATING TO ILLNESS relating to illness or to people who are ill ○ *sick leave* **3.** LIKELY TO VOMIT feeling on the point of vomiting **4.** OFFENSIVE TERM an offensive term for somebody thought to have a mental illness that makes him or her dangerous to others **5.** DISTRESSED spiritually or emotionally distraught ○ *sick with anxiety* **6.** VERY BORED WITH SOMETHING utterly tired of something because of having had too much of it ○ *I am sick of watching television.* **7.** YEARNING feeling a deep or passionate longing for something or somebody **8.** DISGUSTED filled with disgust or repulsion ○ *Such rudeness makes me sick.* **9.** IMPAIRED in need of repair or improvement ○ *a sick economy* **10.** SUGGESTING ILLNESS pale and unhealthy-looking **11.** IN BAD TASTE dealing with subjects regarded by most people as bizarre, gruesome, or otherwise unsuitable for lighthearted treatment (*informal*) **12.** AGRIC UN-PRODUCTIVE unable to produce a profitable crop ○ *a sick field* **13.** MED FORMING UNHEALTHY ENVIRONMENT describes a building or other location that is seen as an unhealthy environment for people **14.** EXTREME SPORTS EXCELLENT in snowboarding, so brilliantly performed as to cause envy (*slang*) ○ *sick tricks* ■ *npl* ILL PEOPLE people who are ill ■ *n* VOMIT vomited stomach contents (*informal*) [Old English *sēoc*, origin ?]

USAGE See **ill**.

sick up *vti* to vomit something (*informal*)

sick[2] /sik/ *vt* another spelling of **sic**[2]

sickbag /sík bag/ *n* a bag made of stiff paper, used for vomiting into by somebody who is travel-sick, e.g. on an aircraft (*informal*)

sickbay /sík bay/ *n* **1.** a place for treating the sick or

Sidney /sídni/, **Sir Philip** (1554–86) English soldier, courtier, and poet. He was a favourite of Elizabeth I and an accomplished diplomat and soldier. His *Arcadia*, posthumously published in 1590, became the model for later English pastoral poetry.

Sidon /síd'n/, **Sayda** /sáydə/ town and seaport in south-western Lebanon, on the Mediterranean Sea south of Beirut. It was a Phoenician city-state in the 3rd millennium BC. Population: 38,000 (1998).

Sidra, Gulf of /sídrə/ arm of the Mediterranean Sea that forms a bay on the coast of Libya, northern Africa

SIDS /sidz/ *abbr* MED sudden infant death syndrome

siege /seej/ *n* **1.** MILITARY OPERATION a military or police operation in which troops or the police surround a place and cut off all outside access to force surrender (*often used before a noun*) ○ *siege warfare* **2.** PROLONGED EFFORT a prolonged effort to gain or overcome something **3.** TIRESOME PERIOD a prolonged and tedious period ■ *vt* (**sieges, sieging, sieged**) MIL SUBJECT PLACE TO SIEGE to assail or besiege an enemy's fortifications [12C. < Old French *sege* 'seat' < Latin *sedere* 'sit'] ◇ **lay siege to something 1.** to besiege a place **2.** to make a persistent attempt to gain something

Siegfried /seég freed/ *n* in medieval Germanic mythology, a prince who kills the dragon guarding the treasure of the Nibelungs, and wins Brunhild for Gunther

Siegfried line *n* the line of fortifications constructed by Germany before and during World War II on its western frontier, facing the Maginot line in France

Sieg Heil /seég híl/ *interj* a Nazi salute usually accompanied by the right arm raised with the palm facing downward [Mid-20C. < German, 'hail victory!']

siemens /seémənz/ (*plural same*) *n* the SI unit of electrical conductance equal to one ampere per volt. Symbol **S** [Mid-20C. After Werner von *Siemens* (1816–92), German inventor]

Siena /si énnə/ capital of Siena Province, Tuscany Region, in north-central Italy. Population: 52,625 (2001). —**Sienese** /seé ə neéz/ *n, adj*

~~sience~~ incorrect spelling of **science**

~~siene~~ incorrect spelling of **scene**

sienna /si énnə/ *n* **1.** artists' paint made with iron-rich soil **2.** an iron-rich soil. Use: paint pigment. [Late 18C. After SIENA] —**sienna** *adj*

sierra /si érrə/ *n* a range of mountains with jagged peaks, or the country surrounding such a range [Mid-16C. Via Spanish < Latin *serra* 'saw'] —**sierran** *adj*

Sierra *n* a code word for the letter 'S', used in international radio communications

Sierra Leone

Sierra Leone /si érrə li ón/ country in West Africa, bordered by Guinea, Liberia, and the Atlantic Ocean. It became an independent member of the Commonwealth in 1961. Language: English. Currency: leone. Capital: Freetown. Population: 5,732,681 (2003). Area: 71,740 sq. km/27,699 sq. mi. Official name **Republic of Sierra Leone** —**Sierra Leonean** *n, adj*

Sierra Madre /-maá dray/ mountain system in Mexico that stretches southeastwards from the US border in the north to the border with Guatemala in the south. Its highest peak is Orizaba, 5,610 m/18,406 ft. Length: 1,100 km/680 mi.

Sierra Nevada /-nə vaádə/ **1.** mountain range in southeastern Spain. Its highest peak is Cerro de Mulhacén, 3,480 m/11,411 ft. **2.** mountain range in eastern California, extending from the Mojave Desert to the Coast Range. Its highest peak is Mount Whitney, 4,417 m/14,491 ft. Length: 600 km/400 mi.

siesta /si éstə/ *n* an early afternoon rest or nap [Mid-17C. Via Spanish < Latin *sexta (hora)* 'sixth (hour of the day), noon']

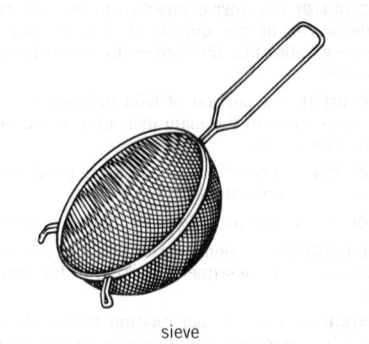
sieve

sieve /siv/ *n* a utensil consisting of a round frame surrounding a mesh and used to separate solids from liquids or large particles from small particles, or to purée foods ■ *vt* (**sieves, sieving, sieved**) to pass something through a sieve [Old English *sife* < Germanic]

sieve element *n* BOT same as **sieve tube element**

sieve plate *n* an area of perforations in the end walls of the cells that make up a sieve tube in plants

sievert /seévərt/ *n* the SI unit measuring the probability that a specific dose of a particular radiation type will cause a biological effect. 1 sievert is equal to 1 joule per kilogram. Symbol **Sv** [Mid-20C. After R. M. *Sievert* (1896–1966), Swedish radiologist]

sieve tube *n* a sap-conducting tube within the phloem tissue of a plant. It is composed of numerous cells (**sieve tube elements**) connected end to end and separated by porous sieve plates.

sieve tube element *n* any one of the numerous cells connected end to end and separated by porous sieve plates in a sieve tube

~~sieze~~ incorrect spelling of **seize**

sifaka /si faákə/ *n* a large rare tree-dwelling lemur that has a black face and long soft fur variously patterned in white, black, or brown. Native to: Madagascar. Latin name: *Propithecus verreauxi* or *Propithecus diadema*. [Mid-19C. < Malagasy]

sift /sift/ (**sifts, sifting, sifted**) *v* **1.** *vti* SEPARATE PARTICLES to pass a substance through a sieve to separate out or break up coarse particles **2.** *vt* TAKE SOMETHING OUT to separate something with a sieve, or by a process of selection or elimination ○ *sift the good from the bad* **3.** *vt* SCATTER SOMETHING to scatter something with or as if with a sieve ○ *We sifted sugar onto the strawberries.* **4.** *vti* EXAMINE to sort or examine something carefully ○ *sift evidence* **5.** *vi* PASS THROUGH to pass or fall through or as if through a sieve [Old English *siftan* < Germanic] —**sifter** *n*

siftings /síftingz/ *npl* parts separated out using a sieve or by a process of elimination

SIG /sig/ *abbr* special-interest group

sig. *abbr* **1.** signature **2.** signor **3.** signore

Sig. *abbr* Signor

sig file *n* ONLINE same as **signature file** (*informal*)

sigh /sī/ *v* (**sighs, sighing, sighed**) **1.** *vi* BREATHE LONG AND LOUD to take in and let out a deep audible breath in relief or weariness **2.** *vi* MAKE EXHALING SOUND to make a sound like the exhalation of a deep breath ○ *The wind sighed in the trees.* **3.** *vi* YEARN to long for somebody or something ○ *sigh for simpler times* **4.** *vt* EXPRESS FEELING IN SIGHS to express an emotion by sighs ○ *She sighed her relief when she found us.* ■ *n* **1.** EXHALATION an audible exhalation of a deep breath **2.** SOUND OF EXHALING a sound like that of somebody exhaling a deep breath [13C. Probably back-formation < past tense of Old English *sīcan*, origin ?]

sight /sīt/ *n* **1.** FACULTY OF SEEING the ability to see using the eyes **2.** ACT OF SEEING the perception of something using the visual sense **3.** RANGE OF SEEING the range or field of vision ○ *By now the coastline was out of* sight. **4.** SOMETHING SEEN something that somebody sees **5.** SOMETHING WORTH SEEING something that is worth seeing, especially the landmarks of a place (*often used in the plural*) ○ *the sights of the city* **6.** ALIGNMENT DEVICE an alignment device on a gun or surveying instrument used to guide the eye in aiming or determining direction **7.** AIM a determination of direction made with a gun or surveying instrument **8.** OPPORTUNITY FOR OBSERVATION an opportunity to observe or inspect something **9.** OPINION a point of view ○ *In the sight of his followers he was infallible.* **10.** SOMETHING UNPLEASANT TO LOOK AT something or somebody that has an unpleasant, distressing, or disarranged appearance (*informal*) ○ *He was a sight after falling in the mud.* ■ *v* (**sights, sighting, sighted**) **1.** *vt* SEE SOMETHING to see or notice somebody or something ○ *They sighted the plane in the distance.* **2.** *vti* OBSERVE USING OPTICAL DEVICE to observe something, or take measurements of something, using an optical device **3.** *vti* AIM AT SOMETHING WITH GUN to take aim at something with a firearm **4.** *vt* ADJUST GUN'S SIGHTS to adjust the sights of a gun **5.** *vi* DIRECT EYES to look carefully in a particular direction ○ *sight down a line* [Old English *(ge)siht* < W Germanic] —**sighted** *adj* ◇ **a sight** a great deal or quantity (*informal*) ○ *He's feeling a sight better today.* ◇ **a sight for sore eyes** a very welcome sight ◇ **at** *or* **on sight** as soon as something or somebody is able to be seen ◇ **in sight 1.** able to be seen **2.** likely to happen in the near future ◇ **know somebody by sight** to be able to recognize somebody whom you have never actually met or spoken to ◇ **out of sight 1.** no longer able to be seen **2.** used as an exclamation to express approval and surprise (*slang*) ◇ **out of sight, out of mind** it is easy to forget or ignore somebody or something not present or visible ◇ **set** *or* **have your sights on something** to decide to try to get something ◇ **sight unseen** without seeing or inspecting first ○ *buy something sight unseen*

SPELLCHECK See *cite*.

sighter /sítər/ *n* a practice shot allowed in a shooting or archery tournament, or a shot used to assess the setting of the sights of a gun

sight gag *n* a joke or comic episode whose humour depends on its being seen (*informal*)

sighting /síting/ *n* an occasion on which something is seen, usually something unusual or searched for ○ *alleged sightings of the long-dead superstar*

sightless /sítləss/ *adj* **1.** without the faculty of sight **2.** invisible (*literary*) ○'*heaven's cherubim, hors'd upon the sightless couriers of the air*' (William Shakespeare, *Macbeth*; 1623) —**sightlessly** *adv* —**sightlessness** *n*

sightline /sít līn/ *n* a line of vision between a person and an object, especially between a member of an audience and the stage in a theatre

sightly /sítli/ (**-lier, -liest**) *adj* pleasing to look at

sight-read *vti* to read or perform something such as music without having seen or practised it beforehand —**sight-reader** *n*

sight rhyme *n* LITERAT same as **eye rhyme**

sightscreen /sít skreen/ *n* a large white screen placed near the boundary of a cricket field behind the bowler to help the batsman see the ball

sightsee /sít see/ (**-sees, -seeing, -saw** /-saw/, **-seen** /-seen/) *vi* to visit a place's interesting sights — **sightseer** *n*

sightseeing /sít see ing/ *n* visiting places of interest (*often used before a noun*) ○ *a sightseeing tour*

sightseen past participle of **sightsee**

sigil /síjjəl/ *n* **1.** a seal or signet **2.** a sign or image that is supposed to have magical power [15C. < late Latin *sigillum* 'sign, trace, (in medieval Latin) seal', singular < Latin *sigilla* 'small images' < *signum* 'mark, sign'] —**sigillary** /si jílləri/ *adj*

sigint /síggint/, **SIGINT** *n* intelligence data acquired electronically. Full form **signals intelligence**

Sigismund /síggissmənd/ (1368–1437) king of Hungary and Holy Roman Emperor. As king of Hungary (1387–1437), he conquered much Balkan territory. He was Holy Roman Emperor from 1411 to 1437. His rule over Bohemia (1419–37) was constantly

challenged by Bohemians opposed to his role in the execution of John Huss (1415).

'Only do always in health what you have often promised to do when you are sick.'
[Sigismund, *Biographiana*; 14th-15th century]

sigma /sígmə/ *n* **1.** the 18th letter of the Greek alphabet, represented in the English alphabet as 's'. See table at **alphabet** **2.** MATHS the symbol (σ) indicating the addition of the numbers or quantities indicated **3.** PHYS same as **sigma hyperon** [Early 17C. Via Latin < Greek] —**sigmate** *adj*

sigma hyperon, sigma particle *n* an unstable elementary particle of the baryon group with a positive, negative, or neutral electric charge and mass of 2,328 to 2,343 times that of an electron

sigmoid /síg moyd/ *adj* **1.** shaped like the letter 'S' **2.** relating to the sigmoid colon of the large intestine

sigmoid colon *n* the final S-shaped portion of the large intestine leading to the rectum

sigmoid flexure *n* **1.** ANAT same as **sigmoid colon** **2.** an S-shaped curve or bend, e.g. in the neck of a bird or turtle

sigmoidoscope /sig móydə skōp/ *n* a fibre-optic tubular instrument inserted through the anus for examining the interior of the rectum and sigmoid colon —**sigmoidoscopic** /sig móydə skóppik/ *adj* —**sigmoidoscopy** /síg moy dóskəpi/ *n*

sign /sīn/ *n* **1.** THING REPRESENTING SOMETHING ELSE something that indicates or expresses the existence of something else not immediately apparent ○ *a sign of wealth* **2.** SOMETHING CONVEYING IDEA an action or gesture used to convey an idea, information, a wish, or a command ○ *His kick under the table was a sign that we should leave.* **3.** ADVERTISING NOTICE a publicly displayed structure carrying lettering or designs intended to advertise a business or product, e.g. a painted board or neon lights **4.** INFORMATION NOTICE a publicly displayed notice or board bearing directions, instructions, or warnings ○ *a road sign* **5.** INDICATION something that indicates the presence of something or somebody ○ *no sign of life* **6.** TRACE LEFT BY ANIMAL a trace of a wild animal, e.g. spoor, scent, or footprints **7.** OMEN something interpreted as being an omen **8.** ASTROL DIVISION OF ZODIAC any one of the 12 equal parts into which the zodiac is divided, each represented by a symbol **9.** MED EVIDENCE OF DISEASE an indication of the presence of a disease or disorder, especially one observed by a doctor but not apparent to the patient ○ *Fever is a sign of an infection.* **10.** MATHS, LOGIC SYMBOL USED IN MATHS OR LOGIC a symbol indicating an operation or relation in mathematics or logic ○ *the plus sign* **11.** MUSIC MUSICAL NOTATION SYMBOL a symbol used in musical notation **12.** COMMUNICATION same as **sign language** ■ *v* (**signs, signing, signed**) **1.** *vti* WRITE NAME to write a signature on something **2.** *vti* APPROVE DOCUMENT to affirm or approve a document formally by affixing a signature or seal **3.** *vti* EMPLOY SOMEBODY to engage the services of somebody by written agreement ○ *The manager signed two promising young players.* **4.** *vi* AGREE TO TAKE JOB to agree to be employed by writing a signature on a contract **5.** *vti* SIGNAL INFORMATION to convey information using a signal or signals **6.** *vt* PORTEND SOMETHING to be an omen of something to come ○ *That signs danger.* **7.** *vti* COMMUNICATION COMMUNICATE IN SIGN LANGUAGE to use sign language to communicate a message ○ *She signed 'yes'.* **8.** *vt* CHR GIVE BLESSING TO SOMEBODY to bless somebody or something by making the sign of the cross [13C. Via French < Latin *signum* 'mark, sign'] —**signer** *n*

SPELLCHECK sign or **sine**? Do not confuse the spelling of ***sign*** and ***sine***, which sound similar. The general and commoner word is ***sign***, which usually refers to something that indicates or expresses something or that provides information (*a sign of the times, a road sign*), and is also used as a verb (*sign a document*). ***Sine*** is a specialized noun referring to a trigonometric function.

ORIGIN The Latin word *signum* 'mark', from which ***sign*** is derived, is also the source of English *assign, consign, design, designate, ensign, insignia, resign, seal*[1], *signal, signature, signet,* and *significant.*

sign away *vt* to convey rights or property to somebody by signing a document ○ *He signed away his property to pay his debts.*

sign in *v* **1.** *vi* to write a signature in a register, usually as a way of recording presence or attendance **2.** *vt* to secure admission of a guest, especially in a members-only club, by putting your signature on a register

sign off *v* **1.** *vi* END SOME FORM OF COMMUNICATION to bring to an end a communication or transmission such as a radio or TV programme, a letter, or an e-mail message, by announcing its conclusion **2.** *vt* CERTIFY SOMEBODY AS UNFIT FOR WORK to state that somebody is not fit to work because of illness or injury (*often used in the passive*) **3.** *vi* STOP DOING SOMETHING to stop doing something, especially work, or to record or announce the end of some activity

sign on *v* **1.** *vi* REGISTER AS UNEMPLOYED to register as unemployed in order to receive state benefits **2.** *vi* CONSENT BY SIGNING to agree to do some activity, especially by signing a contract **3.** *vt* EMPLOY SOMEBODY to take somebody on as an employee or to do a particular job

sign out *v* **1.** *vi* to write a signature as a record of having left somewhere, especially a workplace **2.** *vt* to sign your name as an acknowledgment of having received something, especially as being temporarily in possession of it

sign over *vt* to transfer possession of something to somebody else by writing a signature on a document

sign up *vti* **1.** to agree to participate in something, or get somebody to agree to participate in something, especially by way of a signature **2.** to enlist for military service, or enlist somebody for military service

signa., Signa. *abbr* signorina

Signac /sín yak/, **Paul** (1863–1935) French painter. In his earlier years he was a major exponent of divisionism, which he developed to produce an effect resembling mosaic.

signage /sínij/ *n* **1.** signs collectively **2.** the design and display of signs

signal /sígn'l/ *n* **1.** MEANS OF COMMUNICATION an action, gesture, or sign used as a means of communication **2.** COMMUNICATED INFORMATION a piece of information communicated by an action, gesture, or sign **3.** INCITEMENT something that incites somebody to action ○ *The threat of a shortage was a signal to hoard.* **4.** ELECTRONICS TRANSMITTED INFORMATION information transmitted by means of a modulated current or an electromagnetic wave and received by telephone, telegraph, radio, television, or radar ■ *adj* NOTABLE of considerable importance ○ *a signal accomplishment* ■ *v* (**-nals, -nalling, -nalled**) **1.** *vti* SEND MESSAGE USING SIGNAL to communicate a message to somebody using a signal or signals **2.** *vt* COMMUNICATE SOMETHING to communicate something with an action or gesture ○ *She signalled her impatience.* **3.** *vt* INDICATE SOMETHING to be a sign that something has happened or is about to happen ○ *This event signalled the end of the conflict.* [14C. Via French < medieval Latin *signale* < Latin *signum* 'mark, sign'] —**signaller** *n*

signal box *n* a building from which a stretch or system of railway track is controlled, either manually by means of levers, or electrically and semi-automatically. US term **signal tower**

signal generator *n* a device used to test electronic equipment by generating a signal whose frequency, wave shape, and amplitude are independently adjustable over a wide range of settings

signalize /sígnə līz/ (**-izes, -izing, -ized**), **signalise** (**-ises, -ising, -ised**) *vt* **1.** to make something conspicuous or remarkable **2.** to indicate something distinctly —**signalization** /sígnə lī záysh'n/ *n*

signally /sígnəli/ *adv* completely and unmistakably

signalman /sígnəlmən/ (*plural* **-men** /-mən/) *n* **1.** a railway employee who is in charge of operating signals **2.** a member of the armed forces who sends and receives signals

signal-to-noise ratio *n* the ratio of the strength of a signal carrying information to unwanted interference in an electronic circuit

signal tower *n US* RAIL same as **signal box**

signatory /sígnətəri/ *n* (*plural* **-ries**) a person, government, or organization that has signed a treaty or contract and is bound by it ■ *adj* bound by the terms of a treaty or contract ○ *a signatory nation*

signature /sígnəchər/ *n* **1.** SIGNED NAME somebody's name written by him or her in a characteristic way **2.** SIGNING OF NAME the act of signing your name ○ *payable on signature of contract* **3.** DISTINCTIVE CHARACTERISTIC a distinctive mark, characteristic, or thing that identifies somebody (*often used before a noun*) ○ *The interior design had her signature all over it.* **4.** MED DIRECTIONS ON PRESCRIPTION the part of a doctor's prescription that contains the directions for use **5.** MUSIC same as **key signature** **6.** MUSIC same as **time signature** **7.** PRINTING MARK INDICATING PAGE ORDER a letter or mark printed on what will become the first page of a section of a book, indicating its order in binding **8.** PRINTING SHEET FORMING SECTION OF BOOK a sheet of paper printed with several pages that, when folded and cut, makes up a section of a book ■ *adj* MOST CLOSELY ASSOCIATED distinctive and closely associated with or identifying somebody or something ○ *the marathon, signature race of the Olympics* [Mid-16C. Via French < medieval Latin *signatura* < Latin *signare* 'to sign' < *signum* 'mark, sign']

signature file *n* a short text file with information such as the user's name and address, serving as a signature at the end of e-mails and Usenet messages

signature tune *n* a piece of music used to introduce or identify a performer, group, or television or radio programme. N Am term **theme song**

signboard /sín bawrd/ *n* a board carrying a notice or advertisement

signed /sīnd/ *adj* **1.** bearing a signature, e.g. for authentication or as an autograph **2.** with a positive or negative value, as indicated by a plus or minus sign

signed-ranks test *n* STATS same as **Wilcoxon test**

signet /sígnət/ *n* **1.** SMALL SEAL a small seal, e.g. one that is engraved on a ring **2.** STAMP FOR DOCUMENTS a seal used to stamp official documents **3.** IMPRESSION MADE BY SEAL an impression made on a document by a seal ■ *vt* (**-nets, -neting, -neted**) STAMP DOCUMENT WITH SEAL to stamp a document with a seal [14C. Via French < medieval Latin *signetum* 'small seal' < Latin *signum* 'mark, sign']

signet ring *n* a finger ring containing a small seal

significance /sig níffikənss/, **significancy** /-kənssi/ *n* **1.** IMPORTANCE the quality of having importance or being regarded as having great meaning **2.** MEANING implied or intended meaning **3.** STATS VALUE AS STATISTICAL POINTER status as a statistical value that is not accidental or random (*often used before a noun*)

significant /sig níffikənt/ *adj* **1.** MEANINGFUL having or expressing a meaning **2.** COMMUNICATING SECRET MEANING having a hidden or implied meaning ○ *a significant nod of the head* **3.** MOMENTOUS AND INFLUENTIAL having a major or important effect ○ *a significant idea* **4.** SUBSTANTIAL relatively large in amount ○ *Her work was a significant contribution to the project.* **5.** STATS OCCURRING NOT MERELY BY CHANCE relating to the occurrence of events or outcomes that are too closely linked statistically to be mere chance [Late 16C. < Latin *significant-*, present participle of *significare* (see SIGNIFY)]

significant figures *npl* the figures necessary in a decimal number to express accuracy, beginning with the first nonzero figure to the left and ending with the figure farthest to the right. N Am term **significant digits**

significantly /sig níffikəntli/ *adv* **1.** to a large extent or degree ○ *significantly higher* **2.** in an important or fundamental way ○ *Your ideas will contribute significantly.*

significant other *n* **1.** a spouse or somebody with whom a person has a long-term sexual relationship **2.** an influential or supportive person in somebody's life

signification /sígnifi káysh'n/ *n* **1.** the meaning of something such as a word, event, or other phenomenon **2.** the signifying or indicating of something [13C. Via French < Latin *signification-* 'indication, sign' < past participle of *significare* (see SIGNIFY)]

~~**significent**~~ incorrect spelling of **significant**

signify /sígni fī/ (**-fies, -fying, -fied**) *v* **1.** *vt* MEAN SOMETHING to have something as a particular meaning **2.** *vt* BE SIGN OF SOMETHING to be a sign or symbol of something **3.** *vi* BE IMPORTANT to be important or significant [13C. Via French *signifier* < Latin *significare* < *signum* 'mark, sign'] —**signifiable** *adj* —**significative** /sig níffi kətiv/ *adj* —**signifier** *n*

signing /sīning/ *n* COMMUNICATION same as **sign language**

signing bonus *n N Am* an extra amount paid to somebody when he or she signs a contract, especially in entertainment and sports

signior *n* another spelling of **signor**

signiory *n* HIST same as **seigniory**

sign language *n* communication, or a system of communication, by gestures as opposed to written or spoken language, especially the highly developed system of hand signs used by or to people who are hearing-impaired

sign manual (*plural* **signs manual**) *n* in law, somebody's signature, especially that of a king or queen on an official document [Translation of Anglo-Latin *signum manuale* 'sign made with the hand']

sign of the cross *n* in Christianity, a movement of the hand as if tracing a cross in the air or on the body, usually by touching the forehead, chest, and shoulders in turn. The gesture is made, e.g. by Roman Catholics, in order to invoke the blessing of God or as a declaration of Christian faith.

signor /sée nyawr/ (*plural* **-gnors** or **-gnori** /-nyáwri/), **signior** (*plural* **-gniors** or **-gniori**), **Signor, Signior** *n* the usual Italian form of title or address for a man. It is the equivalent of English 'Mr'. [Late 16C. < Italian, shortened form of *signore* (see SIGNORE[1])]

signora /see nyáwrə/ (*plural* **-ras** or **-re** /-ray/), **Signora** *n* the usual Italian form of title or address for a married or older woman. It is equivalent to English 'Mrs' or 'madam'. [Mid-17C. < Italian, feminine form of *signore* (see SIGNORE[1])]

signore[1] /see nyáw ray/ (*plural* **-ri** /-ri/) *n* the Italian form of title or address for a highly respected man or a man of advanced age. It is equivalent to English 'sir'. [Late 16C. Via Italian < medieval Latin *senior* 'lord, superior' < Latin (see SENIOR)]

signore[2] /see nyáw ray/ plural of **signora**

signori plural of **signor, signore**

signorina /see nyaw réenə/ (*plural* **-nas** or **-ne** /-rée nay/) *n* the usual Italian form of title or address for a young or unmarried woman. It is equivalent to English 'Miss'. [Early 19C. < Italian < *signora* (see SIGNORA)]

signory *n* HIST same as **seigniory**

sign painting *n N Am* same as **signwriting** —**sign painter** *n*

signpost /sīn pōst/ *n* **1.** INFORMATION SIGN a pole with a sign on it, especially one that gives directions or similar information **2.** SOMETHING THAT INDICATES SOMETHING something that gives a clue, indication, hint, or guide ■ *vt* (**-posts, -posting, -posted**) **1.** DIRECT SOMEBODY TO PLACE to direct somebody or mark the way to a place with signposts or similar indications ○ *a series of notices signposting patients to the X-ray department* **2.** GIVE INDICATION to give a clear indication of something, especially some future action or decision

signwriting /sīn rīting/ *n* the activity or profession of designing and painting signs, especially for shops, hotels, and other businesses. N Am term **sign painting** —**signwriter** *n*

sigra., Sigra. *abbr* signora

sigri /séegri/ (*plural* **-ris**) *n S Asia* a brazier usually burning charcoal and used for cooking [Mid-20C. < Punjabi *sagṛī*]

Sigurd /síggōord/ *n* in Norse mythology, a warrior with a cursed hoard of gold whom Brynhild contrives to have killed after he has woken her from an enchanted sleep

Sihanouk /sée ə nook/, **Norodom** (*b.* 1922) king of Cambodia. As king of Cambodia (1941–55) and intermittently prime minister and head of state, he helped win independence from French rule (1954) and protested against the Vietnamese occupation (1975–82). He was restored to the throne after negotiating a political settlement in 1993.

sika /séekə/ *n* a small deer that has a brown, often spotted coat with a white patch on the rump. Native to: Japan, China. Latin name: *Cervus nippon.* [Late 19C. < Japanese, 'deer']

sike /sīk/ *n N England, Scotland* **1.** a small, usually slow-moving stream, especially one that tends to dry up in summer **2.** AGRIC same as **ditch** *n* (sense 1) [Old English *sīc* < Germanic]

Sikh /seek/ *n* a member of a religious group that broke away from Hinduism during the 16th century and advocated a monotheistic doctrine, incorporating some aspects of Islam ■ *adj* belonging or relating to the Sikhs or their religion, beliefs, customs, or history [Late 18C. Via Punjabi or Hindi < Sanskrit *śiṣya* 'disciple'] —**Sikhism** *n*

Sikkim /síkim/ mountainous state in northeastern India, in the eastern Himalaya range, bordered by Tibet, Bhutan, and Nepal. Capital: Gangtok. Population: 540,493 (2001). Area: 7,096 sq. km/2,740 sq. mi. —**Sikkimese** /síki méez/ *n, adj*

Sikorski /si káwrski/, **Władysław** (1881–1943) Polish general and prime minister (1922–26). He fought in the Russian-Polish War (1920–21) and was also prime minister of the Polish government in exile (1940–43) during World War II. Full name **Sikorski, Władysław Eugeniusz**

Sikorsky /si káwrski/, **Igor** (1889–1972) Russian-born US aeronautical engineer and corporate executive. He built the first multiengine airplane (1913) and produced the first helicopter that could be controlled during sustained flight (1939). He founded an aircraft company bearing his name. Full name **Sikorsky, Igor Ivanovich**

sila /séelə/ *n* in Buddhism, morality, representing three aspects of the eightfold path, right speech, right action, and right livelihood [Mid-20C. < Pali]

silage /sīlij/ *n* animal fodder that is made by storing green plant material in a silo where it is preserved by partial fermentation [Late 19C. < French *ensilage* < Spanish *ensilar* 'store in a silo' < *silo* (see SILO)]

silane /sīlayn, síllayn/ *n* a compound of silicon and hydrogen belonging to a group analogous to the paraffin hydrocarbons. Formula: Si_nH_{2n+2}. [Early 20C. < SILICON]

Silbury Hill /sílbəri-/ artificial mound near Avebury, Wiltshire, England. It was made about 2100 BC. Height: 40 m/130 ft.

sild /sild/ (*plural* **silds** or *same*) *n* an immature herring, especially one that has been processed and canned [Early 20C. Via Danish and Norwegian < Old Norse *sīld* 'herring']

sildenafil citrate /sil dénnəfil-/ *n* a drug used to treat impotence [Late 20C. < *sil-* + *-denafil*, informal INN stem]

silence /sīlənss/ *n* **1.** QUIETNESS the absence or lack of noise **2.** NOT SPEAKING a refusal, failure, or inability to speak **3.** IGNORING OF SOMETHING a failure to notice or acknowledge something ○ *Most remarkable was the statement's silence about the recent policy change.* ■ *vt* (**-lences, -lencing, -lenced**) **1.** STOP SOMEBODY OR SOMETHING MAKING NOISE to stop somebody or something from making a noise **2.** SUPPRESS SOMETHING to suppress the expression of something, or stop a person or group from speaking out ○ *silence criticism* **3.** END HOSTILE BEHAVIOUR OF SOMEBODY to cause somebody to stop hostile or aggressive behaviour [13C. Via French < Latin *silentium* < *silent-* (see SILENT)]

silencer /sīlənssər/ *n* **1.** *UK* CAR PART a drum-shaped part of a car's exhaust pipe designed to reduce the amount of noise made by the engine. ANZ, N Am term **muffler** **2.** ARMS FIREARM MUFFLER a device that muffles the noise of a gun **3.** SOMEBODY OR SOMETHING IMPOSING SILENCE somebody or something that causes silence or lessens noise

silene /sī léeni/ *n* a widespread perennial plant. Flowers: pink or red. Genus: *Silene.* [Late 18C. < modern Latin < Latin *silenus* (see SILENUS)]

silent /sīlənt/ *adj* **1.** UTTERLY QUIET lacking any noise or sound ○ *a silent country lane* **2.** NOT SPEAKING not speaking or communicating at a particular time, especially through choice ○ *The children all remained silent.* **3.** SAYING LITTLE not inclined to say much ○ *the strong silent type* **4.** UNSPOKEN communicated without words or sound ○ *a silent warning* ○ *rolled her eyes in silent disbelief* **5.** INACTIVE currently inactive or not operating ○ *a silent volcano* **6.** NOT PRONOUNCED describes a letter that appears in a word but is not pronounced, e.g. the 'k' in 'knight' or the 'b' in 'debt' **7.** CINEMA WITHOUT SOUNDTRACK describes films made without sound, especially those made before 1927 **8.** RELIG NOT ALLOWED TO SPEAK not allowed to speak because of a religious vow of silence ○ *a silent order of monks* ■ *n* CINEMA SILENT FILM a film made without sound [15C. < Latin *silent-*, present participle of *silere* 'be silent'] —**silently** *adv* —**silentness** *n*

CULTURAL NOTE ***Silent Spring***, (1962) by US scientist and writer Rachel Carson. In passionate prose it presented to a popular audience evidence that the indiscriminate use of pesticides like DDT was killing wildlife. It foresaw an eerie future: 'A spring without voices. On the mornings that had once throbbed with the dawn chorus of scores of bird voices there was now no sound; only silence lay over the fields and woods and marsh'. *Silent Spring* was fiercely attacked by the chemical industry, but its findings were endorsed by a Presidential Commission, and its publication is credited with launching the environmental movement in the United States.

SYNONYMS ***silent, quiet, reticent, taciturn, uncommunicative***

CORE MEANING: not speaking or not saying much

silent not speaking or communicating at a specific time, especially through choice, or not inclined to speak much ○ *Both girls fell silent for a moment.* ○ *He's a rather silent type where women are concerned.* **quiet** displaying calmness and self-control and not inclined to speak much, or not speaking or communicating at a specific time ○ *Jed, who was coming up to five years old, was very bright, but very quiet.* ○ *Keep quiet and sit still for a minute, please!* **reticent** unwilling to communicate very much, talk freely, or reveal all the facts about something ○ *On Tuesday, the usually reticent athlete even ventured some fighting talk.* ○ *The boss of the lucrative cosmetics empire had been reticent in the past when it came to revealing details of his bank account.* **taciturn** habitually uncommunicative or reserved in speech and manner ○ *Both men were taciturn and found it difficult to put ideas into words.* ○ *The team's coach, never particularly talkative, has been even more taciturn than usual.* **uncommunicative** not willing to say much, especially not to reveal information, or tending not to say much ○ *Fred was somewhat reserved and uncommunicative concerning his recent experiences.* ○ *Luke stopped trying to salvage the relationship, becoming increasingly uncommunicative.*

silent auction *n* an auction that is conducted by submitting bids in sealed envelopes before the sale

silent cop *n Aus* a large metal disc located at an intersection that is designed to prevent drivers from cutting corners (*informal*)

silent majority *n* a significant proportion of a population who choose not to express their views, often because of apathy or because they do not believe their views matter

silent partner *n ANZ, N Am* BUSINESS somebody who invests capital in a business but who takes no part in managing it. UK term **sleeping partner**

silent policeman *n NZ* a dome or mound located at an intersection to prevent drivers from cutting corners

silenus /sī léenəss/ (*plural* **-ni** /-nī/) *n* in Greek mythology, a spirit of woodlands and forests, usually depicted as an elderly satyr [Early 18C. Via Latin < Greek *Silēnos* 'Silenus']

Silenus /sī léenəss/ *n* in Greek mythology, an aged woodland god who was in charge of Dionysus' education. In art, Silenus is often depicted as a drunken old man.

silesia /sī léezi ə, sī léessi ə, sī léeshə/ *n* a hard-wearing cotton twill fabric. Use: pockets, linings. [Late 17C. After SILESIA]

Silesia /sī léezi ə, sī léessi ə/ historic region in east-central Europe, lying mostly within present-day southwestern Poland —**Silesian** *n, adj*

silex /sī leks/ *n* **1.** powdered silica or tripoli, used as

silhouette

a filter material **2.** a heat-resistant glass with high quartz content [Late 16C. < Latin, 'flint']

silhouette /sílloo ét/ *n* **1.** SHADOWED CONTOUR an outline of somebody or something filled in with black or a dark colour on a light background, especially when done as a likeness or work of art **2.** SOMETHING DARK ON LIGHT BACKGROUND something lit in such a way as to appear dark, but surrounded by light, or the effect produced by such lighting ○ *silhouettes dancing in front of the bonfire* ■ *vt* (**-ettes, -etting, -etted**) MAKE SOMETHING APPEAR AS SILHOUETTE to cause somebody or something to appear surrounded by light (*often passive*) ○ *The buildings were silhouetted against the rising sun.* [Late 18C. < French, after Étienne de *Silhouette* (1709–67), French finance minister]

ORIGIN As French finance minister in the late 1750s, Étienne de Silhouette gained a reputation for stinginess, and *silhouette* came to be used for anything skimped on. One account of the application of the word to a simple picture showing a dark shape against a light background is that it carries on this notion of 'simplicity' or 'lack of finish', but an alternative theory is that Silhouette himself was in the habit of making such pictures.

silic- *prefix* same as **silici-** (*used before vowels*)

silica /síllikə/ *n* silicon dioxide found naturally in various crystalline and amorphous forms, e.g. quartz, opal, sand, flint, and agate. Use: manufacture of glass, abrasives, concrete. [Early 19C. Via modern Latin < Latin *silic-*, stem of *silex* 'flint'] —**siliceous** /si líshəss/ *adj*

silica gel *n* gelatinous silica in a form that readily absorbs water from the air. Use: drying agent, carrier for catalysts, anticaking agent.

silica glass *n* glass made from fused silica, which expands minimally when heated

silicate /síllikət, -kayt/ *n* a common rock-forming mineral belonging to a group formed from silicon and oxygen combined with various elements and classified by their crystalline structures

silici- *prefix* **1.** silica ○ *silicosis* **2.** silicon ○ *silicate* [< SILICON, SILICA]

silicic /si líssik/ *adj* relating to or containing silica or silicon

silicic acid *n* a weak gelatinous acid obtained by adding an acid to sodium silicate

silicide /sílli sīd/ *n* a binary compound of silicon with another element

siliciferous /sílli síffərəss/ *adj* containing or yielding silica

silicify /si líssi fī/ (**-fies, -fying, -fied**) *vti* to convert something into silica, or become converted into silica —**silicification** /si líssifi káysh'n/ *n*

silicle *n* BOT same as **silicula**

silicon /síllikən/ *n* an abundant brittle nonmetallic element. Source: sand, granite, clay, many minerals. Use: alloys, semiconductors, building materials. Symbol **Si**. See table at **element** [Early 19C. < SILICA]

silicon carbide *n* an extremely hard bluish-black crystalline compound. Use: abrasive, refractory, semiconductor. Formula: SiC.

silicon chip *n* a small wafer of silicon forming the base on which an integrated circuit is laid out, or such a wafer together with its integrated circuit

silicon dioxide *n* a colourless transparent solid that melts at a very high temperature. Use: manufacture of microchips. Formula: SiO_2.

silicone /sílli kōn/ *n* a heat-resistant silicon-based synthetic substance in the form of a grease, oil, or plastic. Use: lubricants, insulators, water-repellents, resins, adhesives, coatings, paints, prosthetics.

Silicon Valley /síllikən-/ region in Santa Clara County, western California, that is an important centre for electronics and computer manufacturing industries

silicosis /sílli kóssiss/ *n* a lung disease caused by prolonged inhalation of dust containing silica and marked by the development of fibrous tissue in the lungs and a resultant chronic shortness of breath — **silicotic** /-kóttik/ *adj*

silicula /si líkyŏŏlə/ (*plural* **-lae** /-lee/ or **-las**), **silicule** /sílli kyool/, **silicle** /síllik'l/ *n* a dry fruit consisting of a broad flat pod divided by a membrane into two seed chambers, e.g. that of honesty [Mid-18C. < modern Latin, 'little pod' < Latin *siliqua* 'seed pod']

silique /si leek/, **siliqua** /síllikwə/ (*plural* **-quae** /-kwee/ or **-quas**) *n* a long dry seed capsule of plants of the mustard family that has two valves that open, leaving a central partition to which seeds are attached [Late 18C. Via French < Latin *siliqua* 'seed pod'] —**siliquaceous** /sílli kwáyshəss/ *adj* —**siliquose** /síllikwōss/ *adj* —**siliquous** /síllikwəss/ *adj*

silk /silk/ *n* **1.** THREAD FROM SILKWORMS the fine fibre that silkworms secrete to make their cocoons. Use: threads, fabrics. **2.** TEXTILES SILK FABRIC fabric woven from spun silk **3.** ZOOL THREAD FROM SPIDERS a fine fibre that spiders secrete and use to make their webs, nests, and cocoons **4.** LAW KING'S OR QUEEN'S COUNSEL a lawyer who has the right to practise as a King's or Queen's Counsel (*informal*) **5.** LAW HIGH BARRISTER'S GARMENT the gown worn by a King's or Queen's Counsel ■ **silks** *npl* HORSERACING JOCKEY'S SILK GARMENTS the distinctively coloured silk clothes worn by a jockey as a mark of identification [Old English *seoloc*, via Slavic or Latin < Greek *sērikos* 'silken' < *Sēres* 'people from E Asian countries producing silk'] ◇ **take silk** to become a King's or Queen's Counsel

silkaline /sílkə leen/, **silkalene** *n* a fine cotton fabric with a glossy finish [Late 19C. < SILK]

silk cotton *n* TEXTILES same as **kapok**

silk-cotton tree *n* ANZ, N Am a large tropical tree whose seed pods yield the silky fibre kapok. Latin name: *Ceiba pentandra*. UK term **ceiba**

silken /sílkən/ *adj* **1.** MADE OF SILK made or consisting of silk **2.** LIKE SILK IN TEXTURE OR APPEARANCE resembling silk, especially in smoothness, softness, or shininess ○ *Spaniels have lovely silken ears.* **3.** IN SILK CLOTHES dressed in garments made of silk **4.** SOFT OR GENTLE pleasingly soft, gentle, or delicate ○ *silken phrases* **5.** LUXURIOUS luxurious or opulent (*dated*)

silk gland *n* a salivary gland of a cocoon-spinning insect or an abdominal gland of a web-spinning spider that produces a viscous liquid that is expelled in a thread and polymerizes into a filament

silk hat *n* a man's top hat with an outer covering made of silk or a similar fabric

silkie *n* Scotland ZOOL, MYTHOL same as **selkie**

silk-screen *vti* to print a design on paper or fabric using the silk-screen printing technique ■ *n* **1.** a print made using the silk-screen printing technique **2.** PRINTING same as **silk-screen printing**

silk-screen printing *n* a method of printing on paper or fabric in which ink is forced through areas of a silk screen that are not blocked out with an impermeable substance

silk tree *n* a widely cultivated tree of the mimosa family. Flowers: showy, pink, with silky filaments. Native to: Asia. Latin name: *Albizia julibrissin*.

silkweed /sílk weed/ *n* PLANTS same as **milkweed**

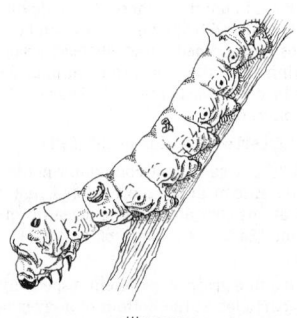

silkworm

silkworm /sílk wurm/ *n* **1.** a yellowish caterpillar, the larva of an Asian moth, that feeds on mulberry leaves and is a commercial source of silk. Latin name: *Bombyx mori*. **2.** a moth larva that excretes a substance resembling silk. Family: Bombycidae.

silkworm moth *n* a moth with larvae that spin silk for cocoons. Family: Bombycidae.

silky /sílki/ (**-ier, -iest**) *adj* **1.** LOOKING OR FEELING LIKE SILK resembling silk, especially in smoothness, softness, or shininess ○ *silky hair* **2.** MADE OF SILK made of silk or a similar fibre or fabric ○ *a silky blouse* **3.** SMOOTH IN MANNER smooth, refined, elegant, or sophisticated, often to the extent of being unctuous ○ *a silky manner* **4.** COVERED WITH FINE HAIRS covered with delicate downy hairs or feathers —**silkily** *adv* —**silkiness** *n*

silky oak *n* an ornamental evergreen tree with feathery leaves and smooth silky wood. Flowers: orange. Native to: Australia. Latin name: *Grevillea robusta*.

silky terrier *n* a small slender terrier with a long silky grey or grey-and-tan coat, belonging to a breed developed from a cross between the Australian terrier and the Yorkshire terrier

sill /sil/ *n* **1.** WINDOW LEDGE a ledge below a window, especially one on the inside of a building **2.** BOTTOM OF FRAME the horizontal part at the bottom of a window or door frame **3.** GEOL LAYER OF IGNEOUS ROCK a more or less horizontal layer of igneous rock forced between layers of sedimentary rock or older volcanic beds [Old English *syll* 'foundation of a wall' < Germanic]

sillimanite /síllimə nīt/ *n* a white or greenish-brown fibrous mineral consisting of aluminium silicate. Source: metamorphic rocks. [Mid-19C. After Benjamin *Silliman* (1779–1864), US geologist]

Sillitoe /síllitō/, **Alan** (*b.* 1928) British novelist, short story writer, and poet. The theme of social exclusion and of the individual's rebellion against society runs through much of his work, including *Saturday Night and Sunday Morning* (1958).

silly /sílli/ *adj* (**-lier, -liest**) **1.** FOOLISH lacking common sense **2.** TRIVIAL unworthy of serious concern **3.** DAZED OR HELPLESS in or into a stunned, dazed, or helpless condition ○ *be scared silly* **4.** CRICKET NEAR BATSMAN in cricket, used to describe a fielder or fielding position near the batsman ○ *silly mid-on* ■ *n* (*plural* **-lies**) FOOLISH PERSON somebody regarded as lacking in common sense (*informal*) [Old English *sǣlig* 'happy' < W Germanic, 'luck, happiness'] —**sillily** *adv* —**silliness** *n*

ORIGIN *Silly* has undergone one of the most astonishing semantic about-turns in the history of the English lexicon. In a thousand years it has gone from 'blessed, happy' to 'foolish'. The transformation began with 'blessed' becoming 'pious'. This led on via 'innocent, harmless', 'pitiable', and 'feeble' to 'feeble in mind, foolish'. The related German *selig* retains its original meaning 'happy, blessed'.

silly billy *n* somebody regarded as silly or foolish (*informal*)

silly season *n* a period in summer when newspapers print frivolous articles because there is a lack of political news

silo /sílō/ *n* (*plural* **-los**) **1.** CONTAINER FOR GRAIN OR ANIMAL FEED a tall cylindrical tower used for storing grain, animal feed, or other material, or for making silage **2.** MISSILE SAFETY CHAMBER a reinforced protective

underground chamber where a missile or missiles can be stored and from which they can be launched ■ *vt* (**-los, -loing, -loed**) STORE SOMETHING IN SILO to store something in a silo, e.g. grain, animal feed, or a missile [Mid-19C. Via Spanish < Latin *sirus* < Greek *siros* 'storage pit for corn']

~~silouette~~ incorrect spelling of **silhouette**

siloxane /si lók sayn/ *n* a compound containing alternating silicon and oxygen atoms in which the silicon atoms are attached to organic groups or hydrogen [Early 20C. Blend of SILICON + OXYGEN + METHANE]

silt /silt/ *n* a fine-grained sediment, especially of mud or clay particles at the bottom of a river or lake ■ *vti* (**silts, silting, silted**) to become full or obstructed with silt, or fill or obstruct something with silt [15C. Probably < N Germanic] —**siltation** /sil táysh'n/ *n* —**silty** *adj*

siltstone /sílt stōn/ *n* a form of fine-grained sandstone consisting of compressed silt

Silures /sī lyoó reez/ *npl* an ancient people who lived in western Britain, especially South Wales, and who strongly resisted the invading Romans during the 1st century AD [Late 19C. < Latin]

Silurian /sī lyoóri ən/ *n* 1. the period of geological time, 435 million to 410 million years ago, during which the first air-breathing animal and land plants appeared. See table at **geological time** 2. a member of the Silures [Early 18C. < Latin *Silures*; from the discovery of rocks of this period in SE Wales, home of the ancient people the Silures] —**Silurian** *adj*

silurid /sī loórid/ *n* a freshwater catfish with an elongated scaleless body, a short dorsal fin, and a long anal fin. Native to: Europe, Asia. Family: Siluridae. ■ *adj* relating to or belonging to the silurids [< modern Latin *Siluridae* (plural) < Latin *silurus*, type of catfish < Greek *silouros*]

silva /sílvə/ (*plural* **-vas** or **-vae** /-vee/), **sylva** *n* 1. the forests or trees of a region 2. a book or treatise on the forests or trees of a region

Silva /sílvə/, **Luis Inacio Lula da** (*b.* 1945) president of Brazil. A former union activist, he helped to organize the Workers' Party (1980) and in 2002 became the first left-wing leader to be elected president of Brazil. Known as **Lula**

silvan *adj* another spelling of **sylvan**

Silvanus /sil váynəss/, **Sylvanus** *n* in Roman mythology, the god of fields and forests, protector of flocks and cattle. He later came to be identified with the gods Pan and Faunus.

Silvassa /sil vússə/ capital of the Union Territory of Dadra and Nagar Haveli, western India. Population: 11,720 (1991).

silver /sílvər/ *n* 1. SHINY GREYISH ELEMENT a shiny greyish-white metallic element that has the highest thermal and electrical conductivity of any substance. Use: coins, ornaments, jewellery, dental materials, solders, photographic chemicals, conductors. Symbol **Ag**. See table at **element** 2. HOUSEHOLD SILVER ARTICLES items of tableware or other household goods that are made of silver, coated with silver plate, or made of a silver-coloured metal 3. COINS COINS money, especially coins made of silver or a silver-coloured metal 4. COLOURS LUSTROUS GREYISH-WHITE a lustrous greyish-white colour 5. PHOTOGRAPHY SILVER COMPOUND a compound of silver used in photography, e.g. to make paper sensitive to light 6. same as **silver medal** (*informal*) ■ *adj* 1. MADE OF SILVER made of, plated with, or containing silver ○ *a silver bracelet* 2. WITH COLOUR OF SILVER of the colour silver 3. SHINY shining like silver ○ *silver moonlight* 4. OF 25TH ANNIVERSARY relating to the 25th anniversary of something ○ *silver wedding anniversary* 5. RESONANT pleasingly resonant and clear in tone 6. FLUENT fluent or persuasively eloquent ○ *a silver tongue* ■ *v* (**-vers, -vering, -vered**) 1. *vt* COAT SOMETHING WITH SILVER to coat something with a layer of silver or a similar shiny material 2. *vti* MAKE OR BECOME LIKE SILVER to become like silver in colour or sheen, or cause something to do this ○ *Frost silvered the trees.* [Old English *siolfor* < Germanic] —**silverer** *n* —**silvering** *n*

Silver Age *n* in classical mythology, the epoch following the Golden Age that was characterized by a refusal to serve the gods and a love of luxury

silverback /sílvər bak/ *n* an older adult male gorilla with greyish-white hair on its back

silver beet *n* ANZ a beet with large heavily veined green leaves and white stems, eaten as a vegetable. Native to: Australia, New Zealand. Latin name: *Beta vulgaris* var. cicla. [Because of its white stalks and midribs]

silverbell /sílvər bel/, **silverbell tree** *n* a deciduous tree or bush with toothed leaves. Flowers: drooping, white, bell-shaped. Native to: southeastern United States, Asia. Genus: *Halesia*.

silverberry /sílvər beri/ (*plural* **-ries**) *n* 1. a bush with silvery leaves and berries. Native to: North America. Latin name: *Elaeagnus commutata*. 2. PLANTS same as **oleaster** (sense 2)

silver birch *n* a deciduous tree with peeling silvery-white bark. Native to: Europe, Asia. Latin name: *Betula pendula*.

silver bromide *n* a yellowish powder that darkens when exposed to light. Use: photographic emulsions. Formula: AgBr.

silver ceiling *n* discrimination in the workplace against employees and job applicants who are no longer considered young

silver chloride *n* a white powder that darkens when exposed to light. Use: photographic emulsions. Formula: AgCl.

silver dollar *n* 1. US a one-dollar coin with a high silver content, minted from time to time in the United States 2. *Can* a commemorative Canadian dollar coin issued annually

silver dollar fish *n* a freshwater fish with a flattened round silver body. Native to: tropical Central and South America. Genera: *Metynnis* or *Myleus*.

silvereye /sílvər ī/ *n* a bird of the white-eye family that has yellow and grey feathers and a white ring around each eye. Native to: Australia. Latin name: *Zosterops lateralis*.

silver fern *n* 1. PLANTS same as **ponga** 2. *NZ* a stylized depiction of a silver fern leaf on a dark background. It is an emblem of some of New Zealand's sporting teams, especially the All Blacks rugby team. [< the colour of its foliage]

silver fir *n* a fir tree with leaves that have a white or silvery underside. Genus: *Abies*.

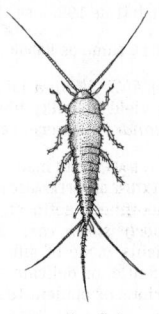

silverfish

silverfish /sílvər fish/ (*plural same* or **-fishes**) *n* 1. a small silvery wingless insect with three long tail bristles and two long antennae that feeds on the starch of books, wallpaper, food, and other materials. Latin name: *Lepisma saccharina*. 2. a silvery fish, e.g. a tarpon

silver fox *n* 1. a North American red fox in the colour phase in which the black fur is silver-tipped 2. the pelt of the silver fox, once valued for making fur coats and other articles

silver frost *n* METEOROL same as **glaze ice**

silver-gilt *n* 1. silver that has been coated with a very thin layer of gold 2. a decorative coating of silver leaf

silver-grey *n* a pale lustrous grey colour —**silver-grey** *adj*

silver gull *n* a common seagull with a white head and breast, a grey back, black-tipped wing feathers, and red beak, legs, and ring around each eye. Native to: Australia. Latin name: *Larus novaehollandiae*.

silver hake *n* a fish resembling a cod with silvery scales. Native to: North American Atlantic coastal waters. Latin name: *Merluccius bilinearis*.

silver iodide *n* a yellow powder that darkens when exposed to light. Use: photographic emulsions, antiseptics, seeding of clouds to make rain. Formula: AgI.

silver lining *n* something that offers hope or benefit in a situation that is generally adverse [< the proverb 'Every (dark) cloud has a silver lining']

silver maple *n* 1. the hard wood of a maple tree 2. a common maple tree with deeply cut five-lobed leaves that are silvery-white underneath. Native to: North America. Latin name: *Acer saccharinum*.

silver medal *n* an award for taking second place in a race or other competition, usually in the form of a silver disc on a ribbon —**silver medallist** *n*

silvern /sílvərn/ *adj* made of or resembling silver (*archaic or literary*) [Old English *silfren* < *siolfor* (see SILVER)]

silver nitrate *n* a white poisonous compound that turns black when it is exposed to light while in contact with organic matter. Use: photographic emulsion, reagent, antiseptic, astringent. Formula: AgNO₃.

silver plate *n* 1. a thin layer of silver, especially one that is used to coat a base metal 2. items, especially of tableware, that are made from a base metal coated with a thin layer of silver

silver-plate *vt* to coat something, especially a base metal, with a thin layer of silver, usually by electroplating

silverpoint /sílvər poynt/ *n* 1. a drawing technique that involves using a silver-tipped pencil on specially prepared paper or parchment 2. a drawing made using the silverpoint technique

silver screen *n* 1. films or the cinema industry in general 2. the screen that a film is projected onto

silver service *n* 1. a method of serving food in restaurants that includes correct table settings, changing cutlery to suit dishes ordered, and serving vegetables and other side dishes to diners at table (*hyphenated before a noun*) 2. *N Am* a silver tray, coffee pot, teapot, sugar bowl, and cream jug used in formal entertaining

silverside /sílvər sīd/ *n* 1. a cut of beef taken from behind and below the rump and topside, usually used for roasting or pot-roasting 2. a small bony fish with a broad silvery stripe along each side of its body. Family: Atherinidae.

silversmith /sílvər smith/ *n* somebody who makes or repairs silver or silver-plated objects —**silversmithing** *n*

silver spoon *n* inherited wealth and high social status [< the expression 'be born with a silver spoon in your mouth']

silverspot /sílvər spot/ *n* a butterfly that has silver-coloured spots on its wings. Native to: northern temperate areas. Family: Nymphalidae.

silver standard *n* a basis for currency consisting of a reserve of silver for which issued bills are redeemable at a fixed rate

silvertail /sílvər tayl/ *n* Aus an affluent and influential member of society (*slang*)

silver-tongued *adj* having the gift of persuading or complimenting people eloquently and with charm

silverware /sílvər wair/ *n* 1. items made of silver or silver plate, especially tableware 2. *N Am* metal knives, forks, and other items of tableware

silverweed /sílvər weed/ *n* a creeping plant that has leaves with silvery undersides, used in herbal medicine for its mildly astringent properties. Flowers: yellow. Native to: northern temperate regions. Latin name: *Potentila anserina*.

silvery /sílvəri/ *adj* 1. LIKE SILVER resembling silver, especially in colour or sheen 2. WITH SILVER containing silver or coated with a thin layer of silver 3. CLEAR AND RESONANT clear and ringing in tone ○ *silvery peals of laughter* —**silveriness** *n*

silvicolous /sil víkələss/ *adj* describes plants and

animals that grow or live in woods or forests [< Latin *silvicola* 'living in woods' < *silva* 'a wood']

silviculture /sílvi kulchər/, **sylviculture** *n* the study, cultivation, and management of forest trees [Late 19C. < French < Latin *silva* 'a wood' + French *culture* 'cultivation'] —**silvicultural** /sílvi kúlchərəl/ *adj* —**silviculturist** *n*

sim /sim/ *n* COMPUT GAMES same as **simulation** (sense 5) (*informal*) [Shortening]

sim. *abbr* similar

sima[1] /síma/ *n* an area consecrated for the ordination of Buddhist monks, and for other formal monastic activities [< Sanskrit *sīmā*, 'border, boundary']

sima[2] /síma/ *n* the rocks that form the lower part of the Earth's crust, lying beneath the oceans and the continents and consisting mainly of silica and magnesia [Early 20C. < SILICA + MAGNESIUM]

simarouba /símmə roóbə/, **simaruba** *n* a tree of the quassia family whose bark has medicinal properties. Native to: tropical America. Genus: *Simaruba*. [Mid-18C. Via French and Portugese < Galibi *simaruppa*]

~~simbol~~ incorrect spelling of **symbol**

SIM card *n* a smart card inserted into a mobile phone that holds personal information relating to the subscriber such as the subscriber's PIN number or stored phone numbers. Full form **Subscriber Identity Module card**

Simchat Torah /símchat-, -khat-/, **Simchas Torah** /símchas-, -khas-/, **Simchath Torah** /-at-/ *n* a Jewish festival marking the end of the annual cycle of reading from the Torah. Date: end of Sukkoth. [Late 19C. < Hebrew *śimḥath tōrā* 'rejoicing of the Torah']

Georges Simenon

Simenon /seemə nóN/, **Georges** (1903–89) Belgian-born French writer. He published more than 400 novels under a variety of pseudonyms, but is best known for the 80 crime novels featuring his tough and intuitive sleuth, Inspector Maigret. Full name **Simenon, Georges Joseph Christian**

'Writing is not a profession but a vocation of unhappiness.'
[Georges Simenon, *Interview, Paris Review*; Summer 1955]

Simeon Stylites /símmi ən stī lít eez/, **St** (390?–459) Syrian ascetic. He was the first 'pillar saint', so called after the stone pillar near Antakya on which he resided for long periods of time and from which he preached.

Simferopol /simfə rópp'l/, **Simferopol'** city on the Crimean peninsula, southern Ukraine, situated about 48 km/30 mi. northeast of Sebastopol. Population: 341,000 (1998).

simian /símmi ən/ *adj* **1.** OF MONKEYS OR APES relating to or characteristic of monkeys or apes **2.** LIKE MONKEY OR APE resembling a monkey or ape in appearance or behaviour ■ *n* MONKEY a monkey or an ape [Early 17C. < Latin *simia* 'ape' < Greek *simos* 'snub-nosed']

similar /símmilər/ *adj* **1.** ⚠ ALIKE sharing some qualities, but not identical **2.** MATHS WITH SAME SHAPE OR ANGLES describes geometric figures that differ in size or proportion but not in shape or angular measurements **3.** *Malaysia, Singapore* IDENTICAL exactly the same [Late 16C. Via French < medieval Latin *similaris* < Latin *similis* 'like, similar']

USAGE In its meaning 'sharing some qualities', *similar* is followed by *to: My own experience has been similar to yours.* Use with *as*, though occasionally found, is incorrect: *I had a similar experience as yours.*

similarity /símmi lárrəti/ (*plural* **-ties**) *n* **1.** the possession of one or more qualities or features in common **2.** a quality or feature that two or more people or things have in common

similarly /símmilərli/ *adv* **1.** so as to share some qualities but not exactly identical **2.** used to indicate that something corresponds to or is similar to something else

simile /símmili/ *n* a figure of speech that draws a comparison between two different things, especially a phrase containing the word 'like' or 'as', e.g. 'as white as a sheet' [14C. < Latin, 'like thing' < *similis* 'like, similar']

~~similer~~ incorrect spelling of **similar**

~~similie~~ incorrect spelling of **simile**

similitude /si mílli tyood/ *n* **1.** CONDITION OF BEING SIMILAR likeness or resemblance (*formal*) **2.** SOMEBODY OR SOMETHING RESEMBLING ANOTHER somebody or something that is like somebody or something else **3.** SHARED CHARACTERISTIC a quality or feature shared by two or more people or things (*formal*) **4.** FORM OR SEMBLANCE a form or semblance of somebody or something (*formal or literary*) [14C. Via French < Latin *similitudo* 'likeness' < *similis* 'like, similar']

Simla /símlə, shímlə/ capital city of Himachal Pradesh State, northwestern India. Population: 110,360 (1991).

SIMM /sim/ *n* a module plugged into the motherboard of a computer to add memory. Full form **single inline memory module**

Simmental /símmen taal/ (*plural* **-tals** or *same*), **Simmenthal** (*plural* **-thals** or *same*) *n* a large cow with a yellowish-brown or reddish coat, a white head, and white legs. It belongs to a breed originating in Switzerland and is bred for beef and milk. [Early 20C. After a valley in Switzerland]

simmer[1] /símmər/ *v* (**-mers, -mering, -mered**) **1.** *vti* COOK COOK JUST BELOW BOIL to cook something gently just below boiling point, usually with the occasional bubble breaking on the surface, or be cooked in this way **2.** *vti* COOK STAY OR KEEP SOMETHING BELOW BOIL to keep a liquid just below boiling point, or be kept at this point **3.** *vi* GROW ANGRY to have anger or another strong emotion building up inside ○ *simmering with rage* **4.** *vi* BUILD UP to build up inside somebody, often without being expressed (*refers to strong emotions*) ○ *'with grief and rage and laughter all simmering within me like a boiling pot'* (Arthur Conan Doyle, *The Lost World*; 1912) ■ *n* COOK GENTLE COOKING TEMPERATURE a cooking temperature that cooks food or keeps liquid at just below boiling point [Mid-17C. Alteration of obsolete *simper*, probably an imitation of the sound]

simmer down *v* **1.** *vi* to become calm, e.g. after an outburst of anger or a state of excitement **2.** *vti* to condense something by simmering it gently, or be condensed in this way

simmer[2] /símmər/ *n* somebody who plays computer or video simulation games [< SIM.]

simmet /símmət/, **simmit** *n regional* same as **vest** [15C. Origin ?]

REGIONAL NOTE See *vest*.

simnel cake /símnəl-/ *n* a fruitcake covered with marzipan or with a layer of marzipan baked in the middle, traditionally served during the Christian celebrations of Lent or Easter. It is traditionally decorated with 11 balls of marzipan representing the loyal apostles of Jesus Christ, excluding Judas Iscariot. [13C. Via Old French *simenel* < Latin *simila* 'fine flour']

Simon /símən/ (*fl* AD 1st century) one of the 12 apostles of Jesus Christ in the Bible, he is traditionally believed to have been martyred in Persia with St Jude. Known as **Simon the Zealot**

Simon, Neil (*b.* 1927) US playwright. Plays such as *The Odd Couple* (1965) and *Sweet Charity* (1966) made him the country's most successful writer of comedies. He later wrote more serious works in-

cluding *Lost in Yonkers* (1991), which won a Pulitzer Prize. Full name **Simon, Marvin Neil**

Nina Simone

Simone /si móN/, **Nina** (1933–2003) US jazz singer and composer. She wrote and sang protest songs against racism in the 1960s, using her smoky contralto voice to great dramatic effect. Born **Waymon, Eunice Kathleen**

'Getting stardom and, once you've got it, keeping it, is like fighting a war. You plan your campaign, recruit your troops, equip them properly, and then fight until you've stormed the cities you want. Then you dig in and defend your position.'
[Nina Simone, *I Put a Spell On You: The Autobiography*; 1991]

simoniac /si móni ak/ *n* somebody who buys and sells sacred Christian objects ■ *adj also* **simoniacal** /síma nī ək'l/ relating to the buying or selling of sacred Christian objects [14C. < French *simoniaque* < late Latin *simonia* (see SIMONY)]

simon-pure /símən-/ *adj* completely genuine or authentic [Late 18C. After *Simon Pure*, character in Susannah Centlivre's play *A Bold Stroke for a Wife* (1717)]

Simons /símənss/, **Menno** (1496–1591) Dutch religious reformer who believed in adult baptism and pacifism. The Protestant sect of Mennonites takes its name from him.

Simon's Town /síməns-/ town and naval base in Western Cape Province, South Africa, situated about 32 km/20 mi. south of Cape Town. Population: 6,500 (1997).

simony /síməni, símməni/ *n* the buying or selling of sacred Christian objects [13C. Via French < late Latin *simonia* < *Simon* Magus, Samaritan who tried to buy the power of conferring the Holy Spirit] —**simonist** *n*

simoom /si moóm/, **simoon** /si moón/ *n* a hot dry wind that blows across northern Africa and the Arabian Peninsula, carrying dust and sand particles [Late 18C. < Arabic *samūm* < *samma* 'poison']

simp /simp/ *n N Am* an offensive term that deliberately insults somebody's intelligence or common sense (*slang*) [Early 20C. Shortening of SIMPLETON]

simpatico /sim páttikō/ *adj* **1.** sharing similar temperaments or interests and, therefore, able to get on well together **2.** easy to like because pleasant and friendly [Mid-19C. < Spanish or Italian, 'sympathetic' < Latin *sympathia* (see SYMPATHY)]

simper /símpər/ *v* (**-pers, -pering, -pered**) **1.** *vi* SMILE COYLY to smile in an affected, coy, and usually irritating way **2.** *vt* SAY SOMETHING COYLY to say something while smiling in an affected, coy, and usually irritating way ■ *n* COY SMILE an affected, coy, and usually irritating smile [Mid-16C. Origin ?] —**simperer** *n* —**simpering** *adj, n* —**simperingly** *adv*

simple /símp'l/ *adj* (**-pler, -plest**) **1.** EASY able to be done or understood quickly, or with very little effort ○ *a simple task* **2.** NOT ELABORATE lacking decoration or embellishment and therefore plain in appearance ○ *a simple black dress* **3.** NOT COMPLEX made up of or having only one part or element ○ *a simple organism* **4.** WITHOUT COMPLICATIONS having no complications, luxuries, or embellishments ○ *the simple life* **5.** STRAIGHTFORWARD ordinary or straightforward ○ *It's a simple case of the flu and I should be back to work in a couple of days.* **6.** OFFENSIVE TERM an offensive term meaning having an intellectual capacity that does

not permit the performance of higher-level cognitive processes **7. NAIVE** naive and lacking in depth and detail **8. HUMBLE** humble and unsophisticated ○ *simple folk* **9. GUILELESS** direct, sincere, or lacking any form of deceitfulness **10.** CHEM **CONTAINING ONE COMPOUND ONLY** consisting of a single chemical compound **11.** BIOL **NOT DIVIDED** not divided, either totally or partially, into separate segments ○ *a simple leaf* ■ *n* **HERBAL MEDICINE** a herbal medicine, or a herb that yields medicine (*archaic*) [Pre-12C. Via French < Latin *simplus*] —**simpleness** *n*

USAGE See ***simplistic***.

SYNONYMS See ***easy***.

simple closed curve *n* a plane curve that is closed and does not intersect itself, e.g. a circle or ellipse

simple equation *n* MATHS same as **linear equation**

simple fraction *n* a fraction that consists of two whole numbers separated by a horizontal or slanting line, as opposed to a decimal fraction

simple fracture *n* e. Same as **closed fracture**

simple fruit *n* a fruit that forms from a single pistil, e.g. a pea pod or a tomato

simple harmonic motion *n* a type of periodic motion in which a body experiences a force proportional to its distance from a fixed point and directed towards the fixed point. N Am term **harmonic motion**

simple-hearted *adj* honest, open, and lacking deceit or deviousness

simple interest *n* interest on an investment that is calculated once per period, usually annually, on the amount of the capital alone and not on any interest already earned

simple machine *n* each of the six devices formerly considered to be the basic components from which all machines were composed. They were the inclined plane, lever, pulley, screw, wedge, and wheel and axle.

simple-minded *adj* **1. LACKING DUE THOUGHT** showing a lack of intelligent thinking or proper consideration **2. OFFENSIVE TERM** an offensive term meaning regarded as having limited intellectual ability **3. UNSOPHISTICATED** lacking guile or complexity —**simple-mindedly** *adv* —**simple-mindedness** *n*

simple protein *n* a protein such as globulin that yields only amino acids on complete hydrolysis

simple sentence *n* a sentence that takes the form of a single main clause with no relative or subordinate clauses, e.g. 'I read the book'

Simple Simon *n* an offensive term for somebody, especially a man or boy, who is perceived as lacking intelligence or sophistication (*insult*) [After a character in a nursery rhyme]

simple sugar *n* CHEM same as **monosaccharide**

simple tense *n* a grammatical form of a verb that expresses a relationship of time without using any auxiliary or modal verbs. In English, there are only two simple tenses, the simple present, as in 'I walk', and the simple past, as in 'I walked'.

simple time *n* a musical tempo in which the main beats are divisible by two, e.g. 2/2 or 4/4 time

simpleton /símp'ltən/ *n* an offensive term for somebody regarded as lacking intelligence or common sense (*insult*)

simplex /sím pleks/ *adj* **1. SIMPLE** containing, using, or designed for a single element or component **2.** TELECOM **ALLOWING TRANSMISSION IN ONE DIRECTION** allowing transmission of signals or communication in only one direction at a time ■ *n* **1.** *US* **FLAT ON ONE FLOOR** a flat with all rooms on one floor **2.** LING **ROOT FORM OF WORD** a word in its base form, without any inflections, prefixes, or suffixes, and not formed by putting two distinct words together. The words 'book' and 'mark' are simplexes, whereas 'bookmark', 'books', 'marked', and 'remark' are not. **3.** MATHS **GEOMETRICAL FIGURE OR ELEMENT** a geometrical element in a Euclidean space that exhibits the minimum number of dimensions of the space, e.g. a line in one-dimensional space or a triangle in two-dimensional space [Late 16C. < Latin (see SIMPLICITY)]

~~simpley~~ incorrect spelling of **simply**

simplicity /sim plíssəti/ (*plural* **-ties**) *n* **1.** a lack of complexity, complication, embellishment, or difficulty **2.** a simple quality or thing [14C. Via French < Latin *simplicitas* < *simplic-*, stem of *simplex* < *simplus* 'simple']

simplify /símpli fī/ (**-fies, -fying, -fied**) *vt* **1.** to make something less complicated or easier to understand **2.** to convert a mathematical expression such as a fraction or equation to a simpler form by removing common factors or regrouping elements [Mid-17C. Via French *simplifier* < medieval Latin *simplificare* < Latin *simplus* 'simple'] —**simplification** /símplifi káysh'n/ *n* —**simplificative** /-kətiv/ *adj* —**simplifier** *n*

simplism /símplizəm/ *n* a tendency to avoid or ignore the complexities of something —**simplist** *n*

simplistic /sim plístik/ *adj* **1.** tending to oversimplify, especially by avoiding or ignoring complexities **2.** ⚠ characterized by simplicity —**simplistically** *adv*

USAGE simple or **simplistic**? ***Simplistic*** is normally a derogatory word, implying that something is oversimplified rather than naturally simple: *He argued that it was simplistic to reject these methods as unscientific.* It should not be used as an alternative or supposedly stronger word for ***simple***: *A simple* [not *simplistic*] *approach would be helpful here.*

Simplon Pass /sím plon-/ mountain pass in the Swiss Alps, between Brig in Switzerland, and Iselle in northern Italy. Height: 2,009 m/6,590 ft.

simply /símpli/ *adv* **1. NOTHING OTHER THAN** with nothing else involved ○ *It was simply a misunderstanding.* **2. PLAINLY** in an uncomplicated, straightforward, or plain way ○ *To put it simply, I can't afford it.* **3. ABSOLUTELY** absolutely or utterly ○ *simply astonishing* ○ *This kind of behaviour simply won't be tolerated.* **4. FRANKLY** frankly and without embellishment ○ *It was, quite simply, the best they had in stock.* **5. NAIVELY** without full understanding

Simpson /símps'n/, **Sir James Young** (1811–70) British obstetrician. The founder of gynaecology, he pioneered the use of ether in childbirth, later replacing it with chloroform (1847).

Simpson, O. J. (*b.* 1947) US American football player, sportscaster, and actor. He was one of the National Football League's greatest running backs in a ten-year career, mostly with the Buffalo Bills. He was acquitted of murdering his wife after a controversial criminal trial (1995), but deemed guilty in a civil trial (1997). Full name **Simpson, Orenthal James**

Simpson Desert desert in central Australia, at the junction of the South Australia, Northern Territory, and Queensland borders. Area: 100,000 sq. km/40,000 sq. mi.

simulacrum /símmyōō láykrəm/ (*plural* **-cra** /-krə/) *n* **1.** a representation or image of something **2.** something that has a vague, tentative, or shadowy resemblance to something else [Late 16C. < Latin < *simulare* (see SIMULATE)]

simulant /símmyōōlənt/ *adj* serving to imitate or reproduce the essential features of something (*formal*) ■ *n* ENG same as **simulator** (sense 1) [Mid-18C. < Latin *simulant-*, present participle of *simulare* (see SIMULATE)]

simulate /símmyōō layt/ (**-lates, -lating, -lated**) *vt* **1. REPRODUCE FEATURES OF SOMETHING** to reproduce the essential features of something, e.g. as an aid to study or training ○ *a computer model simulating the process of continental drift* **2. FAKE SOMETHING** to feign or pretend to experience something ○ *simulating enjoyment* **3. MIMIC SOMEBODY OR SOMETHING** to mimic or imitate somebody or something [15C. < Latin *simulat-*, past participle of *simulare* < *similis* 'like, similar'] —**simulative** *adj* —**simulatively** *adv*

simulated /símmyoo laytid, símmyə-/ *adj* **1. REPRODUCED BY SIMULATION** reproduced or realized by simulation, especially computer simulation **2. NOT GENUINE** artificial, especially made in imitation of a genuine article, fabric, or other substance **3. FALSE** feigned or faked

simulation /símmyōō láysh'n/ *n* **1. REPRODUCTION OF FEATURES OF SOMETHING** the reproduction of the essential features of something, e.g. as an aid to study or training **2. FALSE APPEARANCE** the imitation or feigning of something **3. FAKE** an artificial or imitation object **4.** COMPUT **CONSTRUCTION OF MATHEMATICAL MODEL** the construction of a mathematical model to reproduce the characteristics of a phenomenon, system, or process, often using a computer, in order to infer information or solve problems **5.** COMPUT GAMES **COMPUTER GAME** a computer game that simulates a real activity such as flying

simulator /símmyōō laytər/ *n* **1. DEVICE THAT SIMULATES SOMETHING** a device, instrument, or piece of equipment designed to reproduce the essential features of something, e.g. as an aid to study or training **2.** COMPUT **COMPUTER PROGRAM SIMULATING REAL WORLD** a computer program that simulates something else such as a board game, a vehicle, or a complex system like a city or railway system **3. SOMEBODY WHO SIMULATES SOMETHING** somebody who feigns or imitates something —**simulatory** *adj*

simulcast /símm'l kaast/ *n* **1. SIMULTANEOUS TV AND RADIO BROADCAST** a programme that is broadcast simultaneously on both television and radio, on multiple channels, or in multiple languages **2. LIVE BROADCAST** a live broadcast of an event on closed-circuit television ■ *vt* (**-casts, -casting, -cast**) **MAKE SIMULTANEOUS BROADCAST** to broadcast a programme as a simulcast [Mid-20C. Blend of SIMULTANEOUS + BROADCAST]

simultaneous /símm'l táyni əss/ *adj* **1. AT SAME TIME** done, happening, or existing at the same time **2. TAKING SAME VARIABLES** describes equations that are satisfied by the same values of the variables ■ *n* **DISPLAY OF CHESS-PLAYING** an exhibition of chess-playing skills in which one player is involved in several games at the same time, systematically moving from one board to the next [Mid-17C. < medieval Latin *simultaneus* < Latin *simul* 'at the same time', probably after late Latin *momentaneus* 'momentary'] —**simultaneity** /símm'ltə neé əti/ *n* —**simultaneously** *adv* —**simultaneousness** *n*

~~simultanious~~ incorrect spelling of **simultaneous**

simvastatin /símvə státtin/ *n* a drug that lowers lipid levels in the blood. Use: treatment of high cholesterol. [Late 20C. < *sim-*, perhaps alteration of SYN- + *vastatin*, INN stem]

sin[1] /sin/ *n* **1. TRANSGRESSION OF THEOLOGICAL PRINCIPLES** an act, thought, or way of behaving that goes against the law or teachings of a religion, especially when the person who commits it is aware of this **2. ESTRANGEMENT FROM GOD** in Christian theology, the condition of being denied God's grace because of a sin or sins committed **3. SHAMEFUL OFFENCE** something that offends a moral or ethical principle ■ *vi* (**sins, sinning, sinned**) **1. KNOWINGLY DO WRONG** to commit a sin, especially by knowingly violating the law or teachings of a religion **2. COMMIT SHAMEFUL OFFENCE** to commit a serious moral or ethical offence [Old English *synn* < Indo-European] —**sinless** *adj* —**sinlessly** *adv* —**sinlessness** *n* ◇ **live in sin** to live together as husband and wife without being married (*dated or humorous*)

sin[2] /seen, sin/ *n* the 21st letter of the Hebrew alphabet, represented in the English alphabet as 's'. See table at **alphabet** [< Hebrew *śīn*, after *šīn* 'shin (the 22nd letter)']

sin[3] /sīn/ *abbr* MATHS sine

Sinai /sī nī/ peninsula of northeastern Egypt bounded on the east by the Gulf of Aqaba, on the north by the Mediterranean Sea, and on the west by the Gulf of Suez. A sparsely populated wilderness, it has long been the land bridge between Africa and Asia. Area: 60,900 sq. km/23,500 sq. mi.

Sinai, Mount mountain in northeastern Egypt on the south-central Sinai Peninsula, about 2,888 m/7,500 ft high. According to the Bible, it is the place where Moses received the Ten Commandments (Exodus 19).

sinamay /sínnə mī/ *n* a stiff open-weave fabric spun from the fibres of the banana plant. Use: hats. [Mid-20C. < Tagalog]

Sinanthropus /sin ánthrəpəss/ *n* the original scientific name for Peking man [Early 20C. < modern Latin < late Latin *Sinae* 'the Chinese' + Greek *anthrōpos* 'person']

a at; aa father; aw all; ay day; air hair; ə about, item, edible, common, circus; e egg; ee eel; hw when; i it, happy; ī ice; 'l apple; 'm rhythm; 'n fashion; o odd; ō open; ōō good; oo pool; ow owl; oy oil; th thin; th this; u up; ur urge;

Frank Sinatra

Sinatra /si naátrə/, **Frank** (1915–98) US singer and actor. He won an Academy Award for *From Here to Eternity* (1953), and is generally recognized as the supreme master of the popular song. Full name **Sinatra, Francis Albert**

'Luck is only important in so far as getting the chance to sell yourself at the right moment. After that, you've got to have talent and know how to use it.' [Frank Sinatra]

sin bin *n* an area with a bench beside an ice hockey rink or a rugby pitch where penalized players must stay during the period that they have to serve as a time penalty for an offence (*informal*)

since /sinss/ CORE MEANING: a grammatical word used to indicate that a situation has continued from a particular time or event in the past ○ (*prep*) *Karen has lived in London since 1988.* ○ (*adv*) *She left the firm in 1980 and has since been self-employed.* ○ (*conj*) *He has been on a high since he got married in January.* **1.** *prep, conj* HAPPENING AFTER happening at some point or points after the period of time or event mentioned ○ *The rate of job growth is higher than under any administration since 1920.* ○ *Since Ryland became commissioner in 1994, all complaints are investigated fully.* **2.** *adv* SUBSEQUENTLY at some point between then and now ○ *The department had an engineer, who has since retired.* **3.** *conj* BECAUSE because, seeing that ○ *Since it was still light, they were allowed to play in the park.* [15C. Contraction of obsolete *sithence* 'then, afterwards' < Old English *siððan* (< Germanic) + *-s* forming adverbs]

USAGE See *ago* and *because*.

sincere /sin seér/ (**-cerer, -cerest**) *adj* **1.** honest and unaffected in a way that shows what is said is really meant **2.** based on what is truly and deeply felt [Mid-16C. < Latin *sincerus* 'pure, whole'] —**sincereness** *n*

sincerely /sin seérli/ *adv* in an honest and unaffected way ○ *He sincerely told her everything that was in his heart.* ◇ **yours sincerely** used immediately before the signature to end a letter that is addressed to somebody by name ○ *Yours sincerely, John Smith*

sincerity /sin sérrəti/ *n* honesty in the expression of true or deep feelings ○ *We had no reason to doubt her sincerity.*

~~sincerly~~ incorrect spelling of **sincerely**

sinciput /sínssi put, -pət/ (*plural* **-ciputs** or **-cipita** /-síppətə/) *n* the part of the skull that includes the forehead and the area above it [Late 16C. < Latin, 'half head'] —**sincipital** /sin síppít'l/ *adj*

Sinclair /síng klair, sing kláir/, **Sir Clive** (*b.* 1940) British engineer and inventor. He made pocket calculators and digital watches available to the mass market, and developed the C5, an electrically powered vehicle. Full name **Sinclair, Sir Clive Marles**

'It has suddenly become cheaper to have a machine to do a mental task than for a man to do it…Just as men's muscles were replaced in the first industrial revolution, men's minds will be replaced in this second one.' [Sir Clive Sinclair. Quoted in 'Creativity and Inventiveness', *The Roots of Excellence*, Ronnie Lessem; 1985]

Sinclair /sin kláir, sing-/, **Upton** (1878–1968) US writer

and reformer. His social and political novels include *The Jungle* (1906). He ran unsuccessfully for several public offices including governor of California (1934). Full name **Sinclair, Upton Beall**

Sind /sind/ region of southeastern Pakistan in the lower Indus valley. A province of British India from 1843, it became part of Pakistan after partition in 1947. Capital: Karachi. Population: 29,991,000 (1998). Area: 140,914 sq. km/54,407 sq. mi.

Sindbis virus /síndbiss-/ *n* a virus found in Africa, Asia, Australia, and Europe that can be transmitted by mosquitoes from mammals and birds to human beings, causing rash, joint pain, and headache [Mid-20C. After a village in Egypt]

Sindhi /síndi/ (*plural same* or **-dhis**) *n* **1.** somebody who comes from Sind **2.** the Indic language of the people of Sind. Native speakers: 14 million. [Early 19C. < Persian, Urdu *sindī* < Sind 'the river Indus' < Sanskrit *sindhu*] —**Sindhi** *adj*

sine /sīn/ *n* **1.** for a given angle in a right-angled triangle, a trigonometric function equal to the length of the side opposite the angle divided by the hypotenuse **2.** a mathematical function equal to the vertical coordinate of a circumference point divided by the radius of a circle with its centre at the origin of a Cartesian coordinate system [Late 16C. < Latin *sinus* 'curve, fold']

SPELLCHECK See *sign*.

sinecure /sínni kyoŏr, sīni-, -kyawr/ *n* **1.** a job or position that provides a regular income, but requires little or no work **2.** a church office whose holder is paid, but is not required to do pastoral work [Mid-17C. < medieval Latin *beneficium sine cura* 'benefice without care (of souls)']

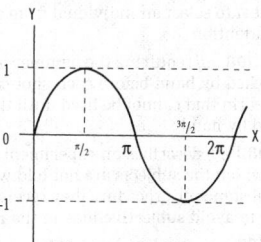

sine curve

sine curve *n* a graph of the sine equation 'y = a sin bx', with 'a' and 'b' being constants

sine die /sīni dī ee, sínni deé ay/ *adv* without a day being fixed for a further meeting ○ *The committee was adjourned sine die.* [< Latin, 'without a day']

sine prole /sínee prṓ lee, sínnay prṓlay/ *adv* without offspring ○ *She died in 1985, aged 59, sine prole.* [< Latin, 'without offspring']

sine qua non /sínnay kwaa nṓn, sīni kway nón, sīni kway nṓn, sínni kwaa nṓn/ *n* an essential condition or prerequisite ○ *The suspension of industrial activity is considered a sine qua non for talks to proceed.* [< Latin, 'without which (cause) not']

sinew /sínnyoo/ *n* **1.** ANAT same as **tendon 2.** STRENGTH strength, power, or resilience (*literary*) **3.** SOURCE OF POWER a source of strength or power (*literary; often used in the plural*) ■ *vt* (**-ews, -ewing, -ewed**) STRENGTHEN SOMEBODY OR SOMETHING to give added strength to somebody or something [Old English *sin(e)we* < Germanic] —**sinewless** *adj*

sine wave *n* a waveform with the shape of a sine curve, representing a single frequency indefinitely repeated in time

sinewy /sínnyoo i/ *adj* **1.** THIN AND STRONG lean, tough, and muscular ○ *a sinewy 20-year-old* **2.** CONTAINING OR RESEMBLING TENDONS consisting of or containing tendons or stringy parts resembling tendons ○ *a rather sinewy steak* **3.** FORCEFUL vigorous and forceful (*literary*) ○ *rich, sinewy prose* —**sinewiness** *n*

sinfonia /sínfə neé ə, sin fṓni ə/ (*plural* **-nias** or **-nie** /-neé ay, -ni ə/) *n* **1.** a piece of orchestral music used as an overture or interlude in an opera **2.** a complex

instrumental composition, usually for a group of stringed instruments or an orchestra [Late 18C. Via Italian < Latin *symphonia* 'sound of instruments, harmony' (see SYMPHONY)]

sinfonietta /sínfōni éttə, sínfəni-/ *n* **1.** an orchestral piece that resembles a symphony but is shorter or written for fewer instruments, often for strings only **2.** a small symphony orchestra, often composed of stringed instruments only [Early 20C. < Italian, 'little sinfonia' < *sinfonia* (see SINFONIA)]

sinful /sínf'l/ *adj* **1.** engaging in or characterized by behaviour that goes against the law or teachings of a religion **2.** morally or ethically wrong ○ *a sinful waste of an expensive education* —**sinfully** *adv* —**sinfulness** *n*

sing /sing/ *v* (**sings, singing, sang** /sang/, **sung** /sung/) **1.** *vti* MAKE MUSIC WITH VOICE to use the voice to produce words or sounds in a musical way ○ *Sing me that song again.* ○ *Paul was sitting in a chair singing to himself.* **2.** *vti* PERFORM SONGS PROFESSIONALLY to perform songs as a trained or professional singer ○ *The last I heard she was singing with a group in Edinburgh.* **3.** *vti* MAKE TUNEFUL ANIMAL SOUND to make the melodious sound that is characteristic of an animal species ○ *I could hear a nightingale singing in the distance.* **4.** *vi* MAKE CONTINUOUS MUSICAL SOUND to make a continuous whistling, humming, or ringing sound ○ *A strong wind was making the wires sing.* **5.** *vi* MAKE BRIEF SPEEDING SOUND to make a brief whistling or whizzing sound **6.** *vi* EXPERIENCE RINGING OR HUMMING IN HEAD to experience a continuous ringing or humming sound in the head **7.** *vt* INTONE SOMETHING to chant something, especially a religious text, on a single note or a small range of notes **8.** *vt* AFFECT SOMEBODY BY SINGING to bring somebody to a particular condition by singing ○ *sing the baby to sleep* **9.** *vti* TELL ABOUT SOMETHING to praise somebody or proclaim something, especially in verse **10.** *vi* BE HAPPY to rejoice or be extremely happy ○ *Her heart was singing.* **11.** *vi* CONFESS to confess to or implicate others in a crime (*slang*) ○ *McGrath had a reputation for making even the toughest criminals sing.* ■ *n* SINGING SESSION a session of singing (*informal*) [Old English *singan* < Indo-European] —**singability** /síngə bílləti/ *n* —**singable** *adj* —**singingly** *adv* ◇ **sing from the same hymn-sheet** or **song-sheet** to express the same opinion or act in the same way (*informal*)

sing along *vi* to join in a song that somebody else is singing

sing out *vi* to call out in a loud voice, especially to warn somebody (*informal*) ○ *Sing out if you see any rocks ahead.*

sing. *abbr* GRAM singular

singalong /síng əlong/ *n N Am* same as **singsong** *n* (sense 1)

Singapore

Singapore /síngə páwr/ city-state in Southeast Asia, comprising one major island and several islets, situated south of Malaysia. It became an independent member of the Commonwealth in 1965. Language: Chinese, Malay, Singapore English, Tamil. Currency: Singapore dollar. Population: 4,608,595 (2003). Area: 648 sq. km/250 sq. mi. Official name **Republic of Singapore** —**Singaporean** *n, adj*

Singapore English *n* a variety of English spoken in Singapore. See panel on next page

singe /sinj/ *v* (**singes, singeing, singed**) **1.** *vti* SCORCH SOMETHING SLIGHTLY to burn something slightly so that only the surface, edge, or tip is affected, or be burnt

WORLD ENGLISH *Singapore English* is the variety of English used in the city-state of Singapore, where it has been co-official since 1965 with Mandarin Chinese, Malay, and Tamil, having already been a regional lingua franca since the early 19th century. As the key language of government, business, and education, it has uniquely acquired a large fully native-speaking community of non-Western origin. There are two varieties: educated, more formal usage, and a patois influenced by Chinese and Malay (and often referred to pejoratively, humorously, or affectionately as Singlish). Singapore English does not pronounce *r* in words such as *art*, *door*, and *worker*. It tends to have full vowels in all syllables (e.g., *seven* is pronounced 'seh-ven' not 'sev'n'). Words ending in *k*, *p*, and *t*, e.g. *kick*, *stop*, and *put*, are generally pronounced with 'glottal stops'. Those words ending in clusters such as *-st* and *-ld* are reduced to the vowel and the first of the last two consonants e.g., 'fas' for *fast*, 'sol' for *sold*. Colloquial usage diverges considerably from the standard, as in: *You come or not?* for *Are you coming?*; *My dad, he come from Penang* for *My dad comes from Penang*; *This hotel cheap* for *This hotel is cheap*.

in this way ○ *The heat from the fire had singed his jacket.* **2.** *vt* REMOVE FEATHERS OR HAIR WITH FLAME to expose the carcass of a bird or animal to a flame in order to remove unwanted feathers, bristles, or hair **3.** *vt* BURN ENDS OF CLOTH FIBRES to burn the short fuzzy ends of fibres from cloth in the manufacturing process ■ *n* SCORCH a superficial burn [Old English *sencgan* < W Germanic]

singer /síngər/ *n* **1.** somebody who sings, especially professionally **2.** a bird that sings **3.** LITERAT same as **poet** (*literary*)

Singer /síngər/, **Isaac Bashevis** (1904–91) Polish-born US writer. His novels often concern Polish-Jewish subjects, and, like most of his works, were written first in Yiddish. He won the Nobel Prize in literature (1978).

> 'It seems that the analysis of character is the highest human entertainment. And literature does it, unlike gossip, without mentioning real names.'
> [Isaac Bashevis Singer, *Interview, New York Times Magazine*; 26 November 1978]

> 'Originality is not seen in single words or even sentences. Originality is the sum total of a man's thinking on his writing.'
> [Isaac Bashevis Singer, *Interview, New York Times Magazine*; 3 December 1978]

Singer, **Isaac M.** (1811–75) US inventor and entrepreneur. He patented a home sewing machine (1851) and founded the Singer Manufacturing Company. Full name **Singer, Isaac Merritt**

Singer, **Peter** (b. 1946) Australian philosopher and ethicist. His works include *Animal Liberation* (1976) and *Practical Ethics* (1979). Full name **Singer, Peter Albert David**

Singh /sing/ *n* a title adopted as a surname by a Sikh boy when he is initiated at puberty into the fraternity of warriors [Early 17C. Via Punjabi *singh* 'lion' < Sanskrit *simha*]

Singh /sing/, **Manmohan** (b. 1932) economist and prime minister of India (2004–). As finance minister for the Congress Party (1991–96), he instituted wide-ranging economic reforms. He is the first non-Hindu prime minister of India.

Singh. *abbr* Singhalese

Singhalese *n, adj* PEOPLES, LANG same as **Sinhalese**

singing /sínging/ *n* **1.** USE OF VOICE TO PRODUCE SONGS the technique of producing musical sounds with the voice, or the performance of songs **2.** MELODIC SOUNDS the melodic or other sounds made by somebody or something that sings ■ *adj* MAKING MUSICAL SOUND performing songs or making a melodic, whistling, humming, or ringing sound ◇ **all-singing, all-dancing** elaborate and containing many interesting or useful features (*informal*)

singing telegram *n* a message sung by a messenger paid to do so, or the service of providing sung messages

single /síng g'l/ *adj* **1.** ONE only or even one ○ *in the space of a single day* ○ *didn't get a single reply* **2.** CONSIDERED INDIVIDUALLY considered separately as something distinct or unique ○ *Every single piece must be accurately measured.* **3.** WITHOUT SPOUSE OR PARTNER unmarried or unattached, or characteristic of being unmarried or unattached ○ *decided to give up the single life and get married* **4.** FOR ONE PERSON suitable or designed for one person ○ *He has a single room on the third floor.* ○ *a single bed* **5.** CONSISTING OF ONE THING consisting of one part, element, or quality ○

single malt whisky **6.** BETWEEN ONLY TWO PEOPLE taking place as a contest or competition between two persons only, one on each side ○ *single combat* **7.** FORMING ONE UNDIVIDED UNIT forming a whole and left undivided or unbroken ○ *carved the sculpture from a single block of ice* **8.** UNIFORM sole and the same for all ○ *a single rate for the job* **9.** BOT WITH ONE PETAL ROW describes a flower that has only one whorl or row of petals ■ *n* **1.** ACCOMMODATION FOR ONE a room, cabin, or bed for one person **2.** RECORDING OF ONE SONG a recording of one individual song released for sale on its own, or of one featured song together with another less publicized one **3.** OUTWARD-BOUND TICKET a ticket that covers the outward-bound part of a journey to a destination but not the return **4.** CRICKET CRICKET STROKE a stroke in cricket that scores one run **5.** TWO-PLAYER GOLF MATCH a match between two golfers **6.** ONE-POUND NOTE a banknote of the value of one pound or one dollar (*dated*) **7.** BASEBALL HIT a hit in baseball that allows the batter to reach first base ■ *vti* (**-gles, -gling, -gled**) HIT BASEBALL SINGLE in baseball, to hit a single, or advance a runner by hitting a single [13C. Via French < Latin *singulus* < *simplus* 'simple'] —**singleness** *n*

single out *vt* to select an individual from a group for special attention

single-action *adj* requiring the hammer of a firearm to be cocked by hand before each shot can be fired ■ *n* a firearm that cannot be fired until the hammer is cocked by hand

single-blind *adj* describes an experiment or clinical trial in which the subjects are not told whether the tested substance or procedure they receive is active, in order to avoid subjective bias in the results

single bond *n* a covalent bond between two atoms formed through the sharing of a pair of electrons

single-breasted *adj* with a small overlap at the front and fastened with a single row of buttons

single-cell protein *n* a protein derived from one-celled organisms grown in various cultures

single cream *n UK* cream with a butterfat content of 18 per cent that cannot be whipped and is used for pouring over desserts or enriching sweet or savoury dishes

single cross *n* the first generation of offspring resulting from hybridization between two inbred lines

single currency *n* a monetary unit that is shared by several countries

single-cut file *n* a metal file that has all its teeth pointing in one direction

single-decker *n* a bus that has only one passenger deck

single-end *n Scotland* a flat with one room only

single-ended *adj* designed for use with an unbalanced electrical signal and having one input and one output permanently earthed

single entry *n* a system of bookkeeping in which the amounts owed and due are kept in a single account (*hyphenated before a noun*)

single file *n* a line of people, animals, or vehicles standing or moving one behind another ○ *We moved along the track in single file.* ■ *adv* moving in a line, one behind another

single-foot RIDING *n* same as **rack**[4] ■ *vti* same as **rack**[4] *v*

single-handed *adj* **1.** UNAIDED accomplished alone and unaided ○ *the first single-handed circumnavigation of the world* **2.** WITH ONE HAND ONLY made with only one

hand or the use of one hand ○ *a single-handed shot* **3.** FOR ONE HAND ONLY using or requiring only one hand ■ *adv* WITHOUT HELP without any help from anyone ○ *sailed round the world single-handed* —**single-handedly** *adv*

single-hearted /-háartid/ *adj* sincere, faithful, and straightforward [< SINGLE in the obsolete sense 'honest'] —**single-heartedly** *adv*

single-issue *adj* concerned with only a single public issue ○ *the multiplication of single-issue groups*

single-lens reflex *n* a camera in which the light passes through one lens to the film and, by means of a mirror and prism system, to the focusing screen

single-minded *adj* concentrated on attaining only one goal or accomplishing only one task ○ *their single-minded attention to quality* —**single-mindedly** *adv* —**single-mindedness** *n*

single nucleotide polymorphism *n* a commonly found change in a single nucleotide base in a DNA sequence, occurring about every 1,000 bases. It is of significance in biomedical research.

single parent *n* a parent who brings up a child or children alone, usually because he or she is unmarried, widowed, or divorced (*hyphenated before a noun*) —**single-parenting** *n*

single-phase *adj* with, generating, or powered by a single alternating voltage

single photon emission computed tomography *n* a technique used in diagnosing some diseases that generates a three-dimensional computer image of the distribution of a radioactive tracer in an organ

single-player *adj* describes computer games that are played alone —**single-player** *n*

singles /síng g'lz/ *n* (*plural same*) a game of tennis or badminton between two people ○ *played singles* ■ *npl* unmarried people or unattached people considered as a group

singles bar *n* a bar frequented by men and women, usually unmarried, who are seeking romance, companionship, or sex

single-serve *adj* packaged in small amounts intended for one person ○ *available in single-serve sizes*

single-sex *adj* restricted to either men or to women

single-space *vt* to type or print text without a blank space between the lines

singlestick /síng g'l stik/ *n* **1.** a stick fitted with a hand guard, formerly used in fencing **2.** the former sport or skill of fencing with a singlestick

single supplement *n* an additional charge made to somebody on a package holiday who is not sharing a hotel room

singlet /síng glət/ *n* **1.** a sleeveless undershirt **2.** a sleeveless shirt worn with shorts in sports such as basketball or amateur boxing [Mid-18C. < SINGLE after DOUBLET, because originally an unlined one-layered garment]

REGIONAL NOTE See *vest*.

singleton /síng g'ltən/ *n* **1.** somebody or something that occurs singly and not as part of a group, e.g. the only child in a family **2.** a playing card that is the only one of its suit in a hand

Singleton /síng g'ltən/ town in eastern New South Wales, in Australia. It is a centre for coal mining, agriculture, and light industry. Population: 21,480 (2002 estimate).

single-tongue *vti* to articulate notes on a wind instrument by raising the tip of the tongue against the palate, temporarily obstructing the flow of air

single-track *adj* **1.** FIXED ON SINGLE IDEA fixed on one thought or idea only **2.** WITH ONE TRACK ONLY with only one track and passing places for trains coming from opposite directions **3.** WIDE ENOUGH FOR ONE VEHICLE ONLY not wide enough to allow motor vehicles to pass each other

single transferable vote *n* a system of voting in a multimember constituency in which voters list the candidates in order of preference and any candidate receiving the required number of votes is elected. The excess votes and the votes of the bottom candidate are then redistributed among the other candidates

didates until the required number of members has been chosen.

singletree /síng g'l tree/ *n US* AGRIC same as **swingletree** [Mid-19C. Alteration of SWINGLETREE, after DOUBLETREE]

Singlish /síng glish/ *n* the variety of English spoken by many people in Singapore, showing the influence of Malay and Chinese (*informal*) [Mid-20C. Blend of SINGAPORE + ENGLISH] —**Singlish** *adj*

singly /síng gli/ *adv* **1.** INDIVIDUALLY IN SEQUENCE one at a time or one by one ○ *They drifted back into camp singly or in small groups.* **2.** WITHOUT HELP alone and by unaided efforts **3.** SEPARATELY solely and separately

singsong /síng song/ *adj* WITH REPEATEDLY RISING AND FALLING INTONATION having an intonation that regularly rises and falls in pitch ■ *n* **1.** OCCASION WHEN PEOPLE SING TOGETHER a meeting of a group of people to sing songs together for fun, or an impromptu session of singing ○ *After we've eaten we'll have a singsong.* N Am term **singalong 2.** RISING AND FALLING INTONATION a way of speaking in which the voice rises and falls regularly in pitch **3.** SINGSONG VERSE RHYTHMS OR RHYMES a singsong rhythm or rhyme in verse, or a verse marked by such monotony

singspiel /síng speel, zíng shpeel/, **Singspiel** *n* an 18th-century German comic opera in which folk songs, or arias written mainly in a simple popular style, are interspersed with spoken dialogue [Late 19C. < German, 'singing play']

singular /síng gyŏŏlər/ *adj* **1.** EXCEPTIONAL especially great or remarkable ○ *He had the singular misfortune of encountering a man-eating tiger on a day when he had left his gun at home.* **2.** UNUSUAL unusual, odd, or striking ○ *The room had a singular colour scheme.* **3.** SOLE being only one, or the only one of a kind ○ *He had hitherto thought of himself as singular, as Rachael's only son.* **4.** GRAM NOT PLURAL referring to one person or thing **5.** LOGIC STANDING FOR INDIVIDUAL THING used to describe a term intended to stand for an individual thing, or a proposition containing such a term ■ *n* **1.** GRAM SINGULAR FORM OF WORD the form of a word that is used when referring to one person or thing **2.** LOGIC THING IN ISOLATION something considered solely by itself [14C. Via French < Latin *singularis* 'alone of its kind' < *singulus* (see SINGLE)] —**singularly** *adv* —**singularness** *n*

singularise *vti* GRAM another spelling of **singularize**

singularity /síng gyŏŏ lárrəti/ (*plural* **-ties**) *n* **1.** SINGULAR QUALITY a singular, exceptional, or unusual quality **2.** SOMETHING UNIQUE OR UNUSUAL something that is unique, distinctive, or remarkable **3.** CHARACTERISTIC a distinguishing trait **4.** ASTRON HYPOTHETICAL POINT IN SPACE a hypothetical region in space in which gravitational forces cause matter to be infinitely compressed and space and time to become infinitely distorted **5.** MATHS FUNCTION THAT IS NOT DIFFERENTIABLE in mathematics, a point at which a complex function is undefined because it is neither differentiable nor single-valued while the function is defined in every neighbourhood of the point [13C. Via French < late Latin *singularitas* < Latin *singularis* (see SINGULAR)]

singularize /síng gyŏŏlə rīz/ (**-izes, -izing, -ized**), **singularise** (**-ises, -ising, -ised**) *v* **1.** *vti* to make a word singular, or become singular **2.** *vt* to distinguish somebody or something or make somebody or something stand out from the rest (*formal*) —**singularization** /síng gyŏŏlə rī záysh'n/ *n*

singular point *n* MATHS same as **singularity** (sense 5)

Sinhala /sin haalə/ *n* LANG same as **Sinhalese** (sense 2) [Early 20C. < Sanskrit *Siṁhala* (see SINHALESE)] —**Sinhala** *adj*

Sinhalese /sínhə leez/ (*plural same*), **Singhalese** /síngə-, síng gə-/ *n* **1.** a member of a people who live mainly in Sri Lanka **2.** the Indic language of the Sinhalese people. Native speakers: 13 million. [Late 18C. < Portuguese *Singhalez* < Sanskrit *Siṁhala*, variant of *Siṁhala* 'Sri Lanka'] —**Sinhalese** *adj*

Sinicize /síni sīz, sínni-/ (**-cizes, -cizing, -cized**), **Sinicise** (**-cises, -cising, -cised**) *vti* to acquire a Chinese idiom, form, or cultural trait, or give somebody or something a Chinese idiom, form, or cultural trait (*often passive*) [Late 16C. < obsolete *Sinic* 'Chinese' < late Latin *Sinae* (see SINO-)]

sinister /sínnistər/ *adj* **1.** threatening or suggesting malevolence, menace, or harm **2.** on the left side of a heraldic shield as seen by the holder ○ *a bend sinister* [15C. Via French < Latin, 'left'; from the superstition that the left side is unlucky] —**sinisterly** *adv* —**sinisterness** *n*

sinistral /sínnistrəl/ *adj* **1.** relating to or located on the left side, especially the left side of the body (*archaic*) **2.** same as **left-handed** (*archaic*) **3.** MARINE BIOL describes gastropod shells coiling in a clockwise direction from the apex to the aperture —**sinistrally** *adv*

sinistrorse /sínni strawrss/ *adj* describes plants growing upwards in a clockwise spiral [Mid-19C. < Latin *sinistrorsus* < *sinister* 'left'] —**sinistrorsely** *adv*

Sinitic /sī níttik, si-/ *n* the branch of the Sino-Tibetan language group that includes the Chinese languages [Late 19C. < late Latin *Sinae* 'the Chinese' (see SINO-)]

sink /singk/ *v* (**sinks, sinking, sank** /sangk/, **sunk** /sungk/) **1.** *vti* GO BENEATH SURFACE OF LIQUID to descend, or cause something to descend, beneath the surface of a liquid or a soft substance and become partly or wholly submerged ○ *The paper boat began to sink.* ○ *We think the ship was sunk by a freak wave.* **2.** *vi* FALL TO LOWER LEVEL to descend, or appear to descend, from a higher position or level to a lower one ○ *The water level has sunk because of drought.* ○ *The sun was sinking in the west.* **3.** *vi* SUBSIDE to become gradually more deeply embedded in something, e.g. the ground or mud ○ *This corner of the foundation is sinking.* **4.** *vi* BE ABSORBED to become absorbed in something ○ *Smear a little oil on the surface and leave it to sink in.* **5.** *vi* FALL GENTLY to fall or collapse slowly ○ *sank to his knees* **6.** *vi* LIE BACK ON SOMETHING to lower yourself gently or luxuriously ○ *She sank back into the cushions.* **7.** *vi* SUBSIDE to diminish in degree, volume, or strength ○ *The wind sank towards evening.* **8.** *vi* BECOME LESS AUDIBLE to become quieter or weaker in sound ○ *voice sank to a whisper* **9.** *vi* LOSE STANDING to pass to a less desirable condition, e.g. a lower social status ○ *sink into obscurity* **10.** *vi* PASS INTO SPECIFIC STATE to pass to a less active, quieter, or less healthy state ○ *sink into a coma* **11.** *vi* FEEL DISCOURAGEMENT to pass into a condition of hopelessness, dejection, or despair ○ *His heart sank.* **12.** *vi* DECLINE IN VALUE to decline in value or amount ○ *The pound sank again yesterday.* **13.** *vi* BE DYING to be approaching death ○ *The old lady was sinking fast.* **14.** *vi* DISAPPEAR to be no longer in existence, come to an end, or disappear, often as a result of failure ○ *I don't know what happened to the project, it seems to have sunk without trace.* **15.** *vti* PENETRATE OR MAKE PENETRATE to penetrate something, or cause something to penetrate something ○ *sank its fangs into her leg* **16.** *vt* DRILL SOMETHING INTO GROUND to drill a well, tunnel, or shaft in the ground **17.** *vt* DRIVE SOMETHING INTO GROUND to force something into the ground ○ *sinking piles for a dock* **18.** *vt* INVEST IN SOMETHING to invest or lose money in a business or project ○ *He must have sunk millions into these theatres.* **19.** *vt* BRING SOMEBODY OR SOMETHING TO RUIN to defeat, undo, or ruin somebody or something ○ *If they won't accept our offer, we're sunk.* **20.** *vt* DEFEAT SOMEBODY IN CONTEST to defeat an opponent easily in a game or contest (*informal*) **21.** *vt* SHOOT OR HIT SOMETHING SUCCESSFULLY to take aim at something and make a successful shot or stroke (*informal*) ○ *sink a critical putt* **22.** *vt* DRINK SOMETHING to drink something, usually quickly (*informal*) ○ *sink a pint* ■ *n* **1.** BASIN FOR WASHING SOMETHING a basin that is fixed or mounted against a wall, and has a piped water supply and drainage ○ *Just put the pans in the sink.* **2.** CESSPOOL a cesspool, drain, or sewer **3.** BAD OR CORRUPT PLACE a place considered to be wicked and corrupt **4.** POORLY DRAINED LAND an area of low-lying, poorly drained land in which water collects, sometimes in the form of a salt lake, and evaporates or sinks into the ground **5.** GEOG same as **sinkhole** (sense 1) **6.** PHYS DEVICE ABSORBING ENERGY a device or component of a system in which a physical entity such as energy or neutrons is absorbed **7.** MIN EXTRACT MINE SHAFT a shaft in a mine [Old English *sincan* < Germanic] —**sinkable** *adj* ◇ **sink or swim** to have no alternative but to succeed or fail without help from anyone else

SPELLCHECK sink or **sync**? Do not confuse the spelling of ***sink*** and ***sync***, which sound similar. ***Sink*** is a common verb referring to movement to a lower or deeper level (*The ship sank beneath the waves. Her success hasn't sunk in yet.*). It is also a noun denoting a basin with piped water. ***Sync*** is an informal word relating to synchronization: *out of sync.*

USAGE sank, sunk, or **sunken**? The inflections of the verb ***sink*** have been variable over many centuries of use. In current British usage, the past tense is ***sank***, although ***sunk*** is also used in US English. For the past participle, ***sunk*** is used (*Six enemy ships were sunk on a single day*); the old form ***sunken*** is now used only as an adjective: *a sunken garden.*

sink in *vi* **1.** to become absorbed **2.** to become fully understood ○ *I don't think the news of her death has sunk in yet.*

sinkage /síngkij/ *n* the process of sinking or the extent to which something sinks

sinker /síngkər/ *n* **1.** a weight used to take a fishing line or net to the bottom **2.** in baseball, a pitched ball that curves sharply downward as it reaches the plate **3.** *US* FOOD same as **doughnut** *n* (sense 1) (*informal*)

sinkhole /síngk hōl/ *n* **1.** a natural depression in the land surface, especially in limestone, where a stream flows underground into a passage or cave **2.** a sunken area where waste collects

sinking fund /síngking-/ *n* a fund created by setting aside regular sums for investment, usually in bonds, in order to repay a debt that will fall due at a future date

sinner /sínnər/ *n* somebody who commits a sin or who habitually does wrong

Sinn Féin /shín fáyn/ *n* a nationalist Irish republican party founded in 1905 [Early 20C. < Irish *sinn féin* 'we ourselves'] —**Sinn Féiner** *n* —**Sinn Féinism** *n*

Sino- *prefix* China or Chinese ○ *Sino-American* [< late Latin *Sinae* 'the Chinese' < Arabic *Sīn* 'China']

sinoatrial /sīnō áytri əl/ *adj* relating to the sinus venosus and the right atrium of the heart

sinoatrial node *n* a small mass of specialized cardiac muscle fibres in the wall of the right atrium of the heart which originates the regular electrical impulses that stimulate the heartbeat

Sinology /sī nóləji, si-/ *n* the study of Chinese civilization, literature, and language —**Sinological** /sīnə lójjik'l, sínnə-/ *adj* —**Sinologist** *n*

Sinope /si nōpi/ *n* a small natural satellite of Jupiter

Sino-Tibetan /sīnoti bétt'n/ *n* a family of languages of East and Southeast Asia, including two main branches, Chinese (**Sinitic**) and Tibeto-Burman. Native speakers: 1,200 million. —**Sino-Tibetan** *adj*

sinsemilla /sínssə meelyə, -míllə/, **sensemilla** /sénssə-/ *n* a very strong form of marijuana obtained from unpollinated female hemp plants [Late 20C. < American Spanish, 'seedless']

sin tax *n* a tax on something such as tobacco, alcoholic beverages, or gambling that is considered to have harmful personal and social effects

sinter /síntər/ *vti* (**-ters, -tering, -tered**) BOND METAL PARTICLES to use pressure and heat below the melting point to bond and partly fuse masses of metal particles, or be bonded in this way ■ *n* **1.** BONDED METAL PARTICLES a mass of metal particles bonded and partly fused by the use of pressure and heat below the melting point **2.** POROUS MINERAL SEDIMENT a whitish chemical sediment consisting of porous silica or calcium carbonate deposited by a mineral spring [Late 18C. < German, 'cinder']

Sintra /síntrə/ resort town in western Portugal, situated 24 km/15 mi. west of Lisbon. Population: 20,000 (1981).

Sintu /sín too/ *n* LANG same as **Bantu** (sense 1) [Mid-20C. < Bantu *(i)si-* 'language, culture' + *-ntu* 'person'] —**Sintu** *adj*

sinuate *adj* /sínnyoo ət, -ayt/ *also* **sinuated** /sínnyoo áytid/ describes a leaf with a wavy indented edge ■ *vi* /sínnyoo ayt/ (**-ates, -ating, -ated**) to wind in and out [Late 16C. < Latin *sinuat-*, past participle of *sinuare* 'to bend, curve' < *sinus* 'curve'] —**sinuately** *adv* —**sinuation** /sínnyoo áysh'n/ *n*

sinuosity /sínnyoo óssəti/ (*plural* **-ties**) *n* **1.** the condition of being winding or curving in shape or movement **2.** a winding bend or curving movement

sinuous /sínnyoo əss/ *adj* **1.** SUPPLE AND GRACEFUL lithe and graceful, especially making graceful winding or curving movements ○ *the dancer's sinuous gestures* **2.** WINDING OR SERPENTINE full of bends and curves ○ *the sinuous course of a hill stream* **3.** DEVIOUS indirect and devious **4.** BOT same as **sinuate** [Late 16C. < Latin *sinuosus* < *sinus* 'curve'] —**sinuously** *adv* —**sinuousness** *n*

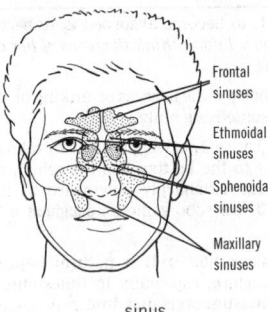

Frontal sinuses
Ethmoidal sinuses
Sphenoidal sinuses
Maxillary sinuses

sinus

sinus /sínəss/ *n* **1.** CAVITY IN BONE OF SKULL a cavity filled with air in the bones of the face and skull, especially one opening into the nasal passages **2.** CHANNEL FOR BLOOD a widened channel containing blood, especially venous blood **3.** CHANNEL LEADING FROM BODY CAVITY an elongated tract leading from a pus-filled region of the body to the exterior or to the cavity of a hollow organ **4.** NOTCH BETWEEN LEAVES a cleft or indentation between the lobes of a leaf or the fused petals of a corolla [15C < Latin, 'curve, fold, hollow']

Sinus Iridum /sínəss írridəm/ *n* a large half-crater on the Moon adjoining the northwestern side of Mare Imbrium. Its walled perimeter forms the Montes Jura and it is approximately 260 km/160 mi. in diameter.

sinusitis /sínə sítiss/ *n* inflammation of the membrane lining a sinus of the skull

sinus node *n* ANAT same as **sinoatrial node**

sinusoid /sínə soyd/ *n* **1.** a small blood vessel or cavity in the tissue of an organ such as the liver, heart, or pancreas **2.** MATHS same as **sine curve** ■ *adj* resembling a sinus in shape or function —**sinusoidal** /sínə sóyd'l/ *adj* —**sinusoidally** *adv*

sinusoidal projection *n* a map projection on which equal areas appear equal, the parallels of latitude are regularly spaced straight lines, and all the lines of longitude except the prime meridian are curved

sinus venosus /-vee nóssəss/ (*plural* **sinus venosi** /-sī/) *n* an enlarged pouch attached to the heart of fish, amphibians, and reptiles through which blood from the veins is forced into the atrium [< modern Latin, 'veined sinus']

Siouan /sóo ən/ *n* **1.** a family of Native North American languages that includes Dakota, Omaha, and Choctaw. Native speakers: 30,000. **2.** a speaker of a Siouan language —**Siouan** *adj*

Sioux /soo/ (*plural* same) *n* a member of a group of Native North American peoples who lived throughout the Great Plains, and now live mainly in North and South Dakota [Early 18C. < North American French, shortening of *Nadouessioux* < Ojibwa (Ottawa dialect) *nātowēssiwak*] —**Sioux** *adj*

sip /sip/ *vti* (**sips, sipping, sipped**) to drink something slowly, taking only a small amount at a time ■ *n* a very small amount of liquid taken into the mouth ○ *a few sips of champagne* [14C. Probably variant of SUP¹] —**sipper** *n*

siphon /sîf'n/, **syphon** *v* (**-phons, -phoning, -phoned**) **1.** *vt* DRAW LIQUID THROUGH TUBE to transfer liquid from one container to another through a tube using atmospheric pressure to make it flow ○ *Why not siphon some petrol from the tank?* **2.** *vti* ILLEGALLY TAP FUNDS OR RESOURCES to convey or draw money or resources from something, especially illegally ○ *It looks as though they were siphoning money from the pension fund.* ■ *n* **1.** BENT TUBE FOR DRAWING OFF LIQUID a bent tube or pipe used to transfer liquid from one container to another using atmospheric pressure to make it flow **2.** BEVERAGES, HOUSEHOLD same as **soda siphon 3.** TUBULAR ORGAN a tubular organ, especially of

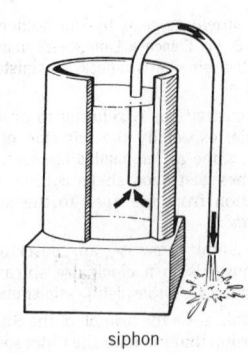

siphon

arthropods and molluscs, by which water is taken in or expelled [14C. Via Latin *siphon-* < Greek *siphōn* 'pipe, tube'] —**siphonage** *n* —**siphonal** *adj* —**siphonic** /sī fónnik/ *adj*

siphon bottle *n* N Am same as **soda siphon**

siphonophore /sífənə fawr, sī fónnə-/ *n* a sea hydrozoan that forms floating or swimming transparent or lightly-coloured colonies, e.g. the Portuguese man-of-war. Order: Siphonophora. —**siphonophorous** /sífə nóffərəss/ *adj*

SIPP /sip/ *n* a pension scheme that allows somebody to manage his or her own investments. Full form **Self-Invest Personal Pension**

sippet /síppit/ *n* a small piece of toast or fried bread cut in a triangle or small neat shape and usually eaten with stews or dishes served with sauce (*archaic*) [Mid-16C. < alteration of SOP]

sir *stressed* /sur/; *unstressed* /sər/ *n* **1.** a form of address to a man often used in speech as a sign of respect ○ *Excuse me, sir, do you know what time it is?* **2.** a form of address or way of referring to a male teacher, mainly used by his students ○ *Let's ask sir if we can leave early.* [13C. Variant of SIRE]

Sir *n* **1.** a title of honour used before the name of a knight or baronet ○ *Have you met Sir Robin?* **2.** used at the beginning of a formal letter to a man, especially one whose name is not known to you (*formal*) ○ *Dear Sir*

Siraj-ud-Dawlah /sí raaj ood dówlə/, **Siraj-ud-Daula** (1729?–57) Bengali ruler. In his attack on the British settlement of Fort William in India, he lethally imprisoned people in a tiny room, known as the Black Hole of Calcutta (1756). He was defeated by the British at the Battle of Plassey and executed (1757). Born **Muhammad, Mirza**

sirdar /súr daar/ *n* **1.** HIGH-RANKING LEADER in India or Pakistan, a political or military leader of high rank **2.** TITLE FOR SIKH MAN a title of respect for a Sikh man **3.** FORMER BRITISH COMMANDER OF EGYPTIAN ARMY formerly, the title given to the British commander of the Egyptian army [Early 17C. Via Hindi *sardār* < Persian, 'head holder']

sire /sīr/ *n* **1.** MALE PARENT OF FOUR-LEGGED ANIMAL the male parent of a four-legged animal, especially a domesticated animal such as a stallion or bull **2.** *also* **Sire** ADDRESS TO KING OR LORD a respectful form of address for a king or lord (*archaic*) ○ *We are honoured by your presence, Sire.* ■ *vt* (**sires, siring, sired**) FATHER OFFSPRING to father young, especially animals ○ *A filly sired by the great Man o' War.* [12C. Via French < Latin *senior* (see SENIOR)]

siren /sírən/ *n* **1.** STATIONARY WARNING DEVICE a warning device that produces a loud wailing sound when a current of compressed air or steam is forced through a rotating perforated disk ○ *The siren sounded the all clear.* **2.** PORTABLE WARNING DEVICE an electronic warning device, often mounted or placed on a moving vehicle, that produces a loud wailing sound **3.** SEA NYMPH LURING SAILORS ONTO ROCKS in Greek mythology, a sea nymph, half-woman and half-bird, who was believed to sing beguilingly to passing sailors in order to lure them to their doom on the rocks she sat on **4.** OFFENSIVE TERM an offensive term for a woman whose sexual attractiveness is considered dangerous **5.** SALAMANDER RESEMBLING EEL a salamander with a long thin body and tail, permanent external gills, lungs, small forelegs, and no hind limbs.

Family: Sirenidae. [14C. Via French < Latin *Siren* 'sea nymph' < Greek *Seirēn*]

siren call *n* same as **siren song**

sirenian /sī rēeni ən/ *n* a herbivorous placental sea mammal that has forelimbs like paddles, no hind limbs, and a broad flat tail. The dugong and manatee are sirenians. Order: Sirenia. [Late 19C. < modern Latin *Sirenia* < Latin *Siren* (see SIREN)] —**sirenian** *adj*

siren song *n* an alluring appeal, possessed by something or made by somebody, that has the power to tempt people, though yielding to the temptation may have unfortunate effects ○ *He resisted the siren songs of cheque-book journalists.*

siren suit *n* a long-sleeved one-piece garment that covers the whole body [< its original use as an air-raid shelter garment]

Sirius /sírri əss/ *n* a binary star in the constellation Canis Major, the brightest star in the sky

sirloin /súr loyn/ *n* an expensive prime cut of beef used for roasting or steaks, taken from the lower part of the ribs or the upper loin [15C. < Old French, 'above the loin']

ORIGIN One of the most persistent of etymological fictions is that the *sirloin* got its name because a particular English king found the joint of beef so excellent that he knighted it. The monarch in question has been variously identified as Henry VIII, James I, and Charles II, but none of these is chronologically possible, and in fact the story has no truth in it at all. The spelling *sir-*, which began to replace the original *sur-* (from Old French *sur* 'above') in the 18th century, no doubt owes something to the 'knighting' story.

sirocco /si rókō/ (*plural* **-cos**), **scirocco** *n* a hot dusty humid southeast wind in southern Europe that begins in the Sahara and picks up moisture as it crosses the Mediterranean [Early 17C. Via French < Italian *scirocco* < Arabic *sharūq* 'east']

sirrah /sírrə/ *n* a form of address for a man or boy that was used to express contempt (*archaic*) [Early 16C. Alteration of SIRE]

sirree /sur rée, sə rée/ [Early 19C. Alteration of SIR] ◇ **yes** *or* **no sirree** US used to emphasize agreement *or* disagreement (*informal*)

Sir Roger de Coverley /-rójjər də kúvvərli/ *n* an English country dance performed to a traditional tune by two rows of dancers facing each other [Fictitious personal name]

sis /siss/ *n* a form of address for a sister (*informal*) [Mid-17C. Shortening]

sisal /síss'l, síz'l/, **sisal hemp** *n* **1.** a strong white fibre obtained from the leaves of an agave plant. Use: rope, rugs. **2.** an agave plant that produces sisal. Native to: Mexico. Latin name: *Agave sisalana*. [Mid-19C. After *Sisal*, port in Yucatán, Mexico]

siskin /sískin/ *n* a yellow-and-black finch related to the goldfinch. Native to: Europe, Asia, North Africa. Latin name: *Carduelis spinus*. [Mid-16C. < Middle Dutch *siseken*, early Flemish *sijsken* 'little siskin']

Sisley /sízzli, síssli/, **Alfred** (1839–99) French painter. He was one of the early impressionist painters, noted for his landscapes and village scenes of northern France.

~~sissors~~ incorrect spelling of **scissors**

sissy /síssi/, **cissy** *n* (*plural* **-sies**) an offensive term for a boy or man who is considered not to exhibit stereotypical masculine behaviour, especially by other boys or men (*informal offensive insult*) ■ *adj* an offensive term referring to a boy, man, behaviour, or object that is considered not to exhibit or be characteristic of stereotypical masculinity (*informal*) [Mid-19C. < SIS] —**sissiness** *n* —**sissyish** *adj*

sister /sístər/ *n* **1.** FEMALE SIBLING a girl or woman who has the same parents as another person **2.** STEPSISTER OR HALF-SISTER a girl or woman who has one parent in common with another person **3.** *also* **Sister** NUN a female member of a Christian religious community **4.** *also* **Sister** WAY TO ADDRESS NUN a form of address to a female member of a Christian religious community **5.** WOMAN SENIOR NURSE a female hospital nurse of the most senior grade, above staff nurse and often in charge of a ward (*dated*) **6.** SURGERY NURSE a female nurse working in a doctor's surgery or a

clinic (*dated*) **7. WOMAN MEMBER OF SAME ORGANIZATION** a woman who belongs to the same organization as another **8. WOMAN SUPPORTER OF FEMINISM** a woman who advocates or supports feminist principles **9. AFRICAN AMERICAN WOMAN** a form of address or way of referring to an African American woman, used especially by other African Americans **10. CLOSE WOMAN FRIEND** a close woman friend, especially of another woman ■ *adj* **1. CLOSELY LINKED** belonging to or closely associated with something ○ *links with sister organizations in Europe* **2. GENETICS WITH PAIRED CELL** describes either of an identical pair of cells or cell components formed by division of a parent cell or component [Old English *sweostor* < Indo-European]

CULTURAL NOTE *The Three Sisters*, a play (1900) by the Russian dramatist Anton Chekhov. Set in rural Russia, this powerful and compassionate study of the quiet desperation of bourgeois life centres on the three Pozarov sisters. Stifled by the dreariness of local society, they look to the officers of the local garrison for romance and entertainment. But when the army departs, the sisters are left with only their dreams and each other.

sisterhood /síster hŏŏd/ *n* **1. SOLIDARITY AMONG WOMEN** the empathy and loyalty that women feel for other women who have shared goals, experiences, or viewpoints **2. WOMEN'S GROUP** a group of women who have shared goals, experiences, or viewpoints (*takes a singular or plural verb*) **3. STATUS AS SISTER** the status of a sister or the relationship of sisters **4. COMMUNITY OF NUNS** a religious community of Christian nuns

sister-in-law (*plural* **sisters-in-law**) *n* **1.** the sister of somebody's husband or wife **2.** the wife of somebody's brother

sisterly /sísterli/ *adj, adv* relating to, coming from, or characteristic of a sister, especially in an affectionate, kind, or caring way —**sisterliness** *n*

Sistine /sís teen, -tīn/ *adj* **1.** relating to any of the popes named Sixtus, especially Sixtus IV, who was pope 1471–84 **2.** relating to the Sistine Chapel in the Vatican [Late 18C. < Italian *Sistino* 'of Sixtus']

sistra MUSIC plural of **sistrum**

sistren /sístren/ (*plural same*) *n* (*slang; used in Black English*) **1.** a form of address for, or way of referring to, another Rastafarian woman **2.** a form of address for, or way of referring to, a woman who is a close friend

sistrum

sistrum /sístrem/ (*plural* **-tra** /-trə/) *n* an ancient Egyptian percussion instrument consisting of a thin metal frame with rods or loops attached that jingle when shaken [14C. Via Latin < Greek *seistron* < *seiein* 'shake']

Sisulu /si sŏŏ loo/, **Walter** (1912–2003) South African political activist. He served a prison sentence (1963–89) for his membership of the African National Congress, and was later the party's deputy president (1991–94).

Sisyphean /síssi fée ən/ *adj* **1.** involving endless but futile labour **2.** relating to Sisyphus [Late 16C. < Latin *Sisypheius* < Greek *Sisuphos* 'Sisyphus']

Sisyphus /síssifess/ *n* in Greek mythology, a cruel king of Corinth who was condemned for eternity to roll a boulder up a hill only to have it roll down again just before it reached the top

sit /sit/ *v* (**sits, sitting, sat** /sat/) **1.** *vi* **REST WITH WEIGHT ON BUTTOCKS** to assume a position of rest in which the weight is largely supported by the buttocks, usually with the body vertical and the thighs horizontal ○

Where would you like to sit? **2.** *vt* **PLACE SOMEBODY IN SEAT** to place somebody or yourself in a seat or a sitting position ○ *They sat us down to hear the whole story.* **3.** *vi* **REST BODY ON HINDQUARTERS** to rest the body with the weight supported by the lowered hindquarters (*refers to four-legged animals*) ○ *The hound sat in the corner, looking strangely thoughtful* **4.** *vi* **PERCH, ROOST, OR COVER EGGS** to perch, roost, or cover and warm eggs for hatching (*refers to birds*) ○ *A falcon sat on the telephone wire, staring down at us.* **5.** *vi* **OCCUPY POSITION OF AUTHORITY** to be a member of an official decision-making or governing body, e.g. a jury, council, or committee, or preside in a court ○ *sits on the board of directors* **6.** *vi* **MEET IN OFFICIAL SESSION** to hold an official session or be in session (*refers to a legislative or judicial body*) ○ *The legislature sat through the night.* **7.** *vi* **POSE FOR SOMETHING** to pose for a portrait or picture ○ *She sat for an official portrait.* **8.** *vti* **EDUC TAKE EXAM** to take an examination for something ○ *She sat her finals last week.* **9.** *vt* **HAVE SEATS FOR NUMBER OF PEOPLE** to have seats or seating space for a particular number of people ○ *We can sit ten around the dining table.* **10.** *vt* **BE ASTRIDE SOMETHING** to keep astride of a horse or similar animal ○ *She sat her gelding with great poise.* **11.** *vi* **BE IDLE** to be or remain idle or unused ○ *sat around all day* **12.** *vi* **BE PLACED OR SITUATED** to be located or positioned somewhere ○ *The dishes were still sitting on the table.* **13.** *vi* **FIT OR HANG** to fit or hang on somebody in a particular way ○ *a gown that sat beautifully on her* **14.** *vi* **REST OR WEIGH IN PARTICULAR WAY** to rest, weigh, or lie in a particular way ○ *The responsibility sat heavily on his shoulders.* **15.** *vi* **BE COMPATIBLE** to accord with or seem appropriate in conjunction with something ○ *It was not, they thought in those days, a role that sat well with motherhood.* **16.** *vti* same as **babysit** (sense 1) (*informal*) **17.** *vi* **US BE REGARDED IN PARTICULAR WAY** to be accepted or considered by somebody in a particular way ○ *The news didn't sit well with her.* **18.** *vi* **US BE DIGESTIBLE** to be digestible (*informal*) ■ *n* **1. TIME SPENT BEING SEATED** a period of being seated, especially while waiting ○ *We had a long sit waiting for the dentist.* **2. CLOTHING WAY GARMENT FITS** the way a garment hangs on somebody **3. MOUNTED POSITION** a position astride a horse or similar animal [Old English *sittan* < Indo-European] ◇ **sit tight** to refrain from moving or acting until the right time (*informal*) ◇ **sitting pretty** in a good or favourable position (*informal*)

USAGE sat or **sitting**? *Sat*, the past participle of the verb *sit*, is sometimes wrongly used in place of the present participle *sitting* in sentences like this: *I was sitting* [not *sat*] *by the telephone, waiting for it to ring.* The only correct use of *I was sat* is as the passive form of *sit* in the sense 'place somebody in a seat', as in *I asked for a seat near the president, but I was sat at the opposite end of the table.* The same mistake sometimes occurs with *stood* and *standing*, the past and present participles of the verb *stand: I've been standing* [not *stood*] *here for almost an hour.*

sit back *vi* to take no action ○ *sat back and watched the crisis develop*

sit down *vti* to become seated, or make somebody become seated ○ *time to sit him down and tell him the truth*

sit in *vi* **1. ATTEND WITHOUT TAKING PART** to attend something but not take an active part in it ○ *Do you mind if I sit in on your meeting?* **2. TEMPORARILY REPLACE SOMEBODY** to do a job for the person who normally does it ○ *sitting in for the regular announcer* **3. OCCUPY BUILDING AS PROTEST** to take part in a sit-in

sit on *vt* (*informal*) **1. DELAY DEALING WITH SOMETHING** to fail to take action on or reveal something over a period of time, although in a position to do so ○ *The government sat on the information for weeks.* **2. SUPPRESS SOMETHING** to put a stop to something or prevent it from going ahead **3.** *US* **NAG SOMEBODY** to nag somebody continually **4. QUELL SOMEBODY** to prevent somebody from saying or doing anything more, especially by means of a crushing remark or rebuke

sit out *v* **1.** *vt* **STAY UNTIL END OF** to remain until the end of something, especially something unpleasant **2.** *vt* **NOT PARTICIPATE IN** to remain seated during something and not join in ○ *I think I'll sit this one out.* **3.** *vi* **KEEP SAILING BOAT UPRIGHT** to lean backwards over the side of a sailing boat to counterbalance the wind in the sails and keep the boat flat in the water. N Am term **hike out**

sit up *vi* **1. SIT STRAIGHT** to sit upright or rise from lying down **2. BECOME ALERT** to become alert or interested **3. STAY UP LATE** to stay up past the usual time of going to bed

Sita /sée taa/ *n* in Hinduism, an incarnation of the goddess Lakshmi

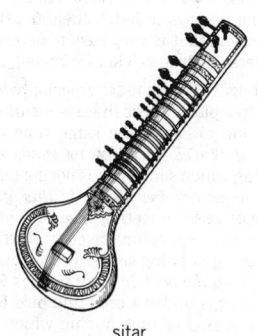

sitar

sitar /si taár, síttaar/ *n* a South Asian stringed instrument with a rounded resonating body and a long fretted neck. There are several playing strings and a larger number that vibrate sympathetically. [Mid-19C. Via Hindi < Persian, 'three-stringed'] —**sitarist** *n*

sitcom /sít kom/ *n* MEDIA same as **situation comedy** (*informal*) [Mid-20C. Shortening]

sit-down *n* **1.** a short spell of sitting in order to relax (*informal*) ○ *After all that shopping I could do with a sit-down.* **2.** HR same as **sit-down strike 3.** HR same as **sit-in** ■ *adj* served to people sitting at a table ○ *There's a sit-down dinner before the dancing.*

sit-down strike *n* a form of industrial action in which workers occupy their workplace and refuse to leave it until their demands are granted or negotiated

site /sīt/ *n* **1. PLACE WHERE SOMETHING STANDS** an area or piece of land where something was, is, or will be located ○ *The whole area has become one vast building site.* ○ *the site of an ancient temple* **2. PLACE OF SIGNIFICANT EVENT** a place where something important happened ○ *The field was the site of a terrible massacre.* **3.** ONLINE same as **website** ■ *vt* (**sites, siting, sited**) **POSITION SOMETHING** to locate something in a particular place or position ○ *The heavy artillery had been sited in the hills.* [14C. Via Anglo-Norman < Latin *situs* 'place, position' < *sinere* 'put']

SPELLCHECK See **cite**.

sitella *n* BIRDS another spelling of **sittella**

site-specific *adj* designed, built, or intended for one individual site

Sithole /si tóli/, **Ndabaningi** (1920–2000) Zimbabwean cleric and politician. He founded the Zimbabwe African National Union (1963), which he led in a guerrilla war against Rhodesia that was instrumental in gaining majority rule in present-day Zimbabwe (1980).

sit-in *n* **1.** a form of protest in which people occupy a building or public place and refuse to leave until their demands have been met or negotiated **2.** a protest against racial discrimination in which people occupy the seats or an area of a segregated business or place and refuse to leave

sitka spruce /sítkə-/ *n* a spruce tree with reddish-brown bark and silvery-white needles, widely planted for timber. Native to: northwestern coast of North America. Latin name: *Picea sitchensis*. [Late 19C. After *Sitka*, town in Alaska]

sit spin *n* a spin on one ice skate made in a squatting position with one leg stretched out in front of the body

sittella /si téllə/, **sitella** *n* a small gregarious songbird, similar to a nuthatch in its build, short tail, and habit of hopping up and down trees. Native to: New Guinea, Australasia. Family: Neosittidae. [Mid-19C. < modern Latin *Sittella*, literally 'little nuthatch' < Greek *sittē* 'nuthatch']

sitter /síttər/ *n* **1. BABYSITTER** somebody who babysits a child **2. HIRED MINDER** somebody who agrees or is

employed to look after something or somebody (*often used in combination*) ○ *a house-sitter* **3. SOMEBODY HIRED TO WATCH PATIENTS** somebody who watches over a sick person in order to respond to urgent needs, ensure safety, or provide companionship **4. POSER FOR PICTURE** an artist's or photographer's model, especially for a portrait **5. BROODY HEN** a hen or other bird sitting on eggs to hatch them **6. EXTREMELY EASY TASK** something that is very easy to accomplish, e.g. an effortless catch in cricket (*informal*)

sitting /sítting/ *n* **1. TURN TO EAT** a period when a meal is served in a place where there is insufficient room for everyone to eat at the same time ○ *The first sitting is at 12 o'clock.* **2. TIME FOR POSING** a period of time during which somebody is posing for a portrait ○ *I'd like to get another sitting in this afternoon.* **3. SESSION OF PUBLIC BODY** a meeting or session of an official body such as a legislature or court **4. PERIOD OF BEING SEATED** a period of being seated while engaged in an activity ○ *read the book in three sittings* **5. SET OF EGGS** a clutch of eggs under a brooding bird **6. INCUBATION OF EGGS** the period of time during which a hen sits on eggs to hatch them ■ *adj* **1. SEATED** seated or for being seated ○ *a sitting area* **2. DONE SEATED** done or performed while seated ○ *prescribed some simple sitting exercises* **3. IN OFFICE** holding office at the present time ○ *the sitting MP for Southgate*

USAGE See *sit*.

Sitting Bull

Sitting Bull /sítting bool/ (1831?–90) Sioux leader. He defeated General George Custer at the Battle of Little Big Horn (1876). He was killed during a later outbreak of hostilities.

> 'What treaty that the white man ever made with us have they kept? Not one.'
> [Attributed to Sitting Bull]

sitting duck *n* somebody or something that is defenceless, exposed to danger, and easy to attack or exploit (*informal*) ○ *The company's competitors regarded it as a sitting duck for a takeover.*

sitting room *n* a room in a house or flat used for relaxing or entertaining guests in comfortable seats

sitting target *n* same as **sitting duck**

sitting tenant *n* a tenant who has a legal right to continue living in a property when it changes ownership

sitting trot *n* a horse-riding technique used while trotting in which the rider does not rise from the horse's saddle

situate /síttyoo ayt/ (-ates, -ating, -ated) *vt* **1.** to put something in a particular place or position **2.** to place something in a context or set of circumstances and show its connections ○ *I shall endeavour to situate these ideas in the early Gnostic tradition.* [15C. < late Latin *situat-*, past participle of *situare* 'place' < Latin *situs* (see SITE)]

situated /síttyoo aytid/ *adj* (*often used in combination*) **1.** located in a place or position ○ *The hotel is situated within the medieval walls of the old town.* ○ *a conveniently situated building* **2.** in a particular financial condition ○ *comfortably situated, living off their investments*

situation /síttyoo áysh'n/ *n* **1. STATE OF AFFAIRS** a particular set of circumstances existing in a particular place or at a particular time ○ *Kaye assessed the situation and decided to call you.* **2. CURRENT CIRCUMSTANCES** the current conditions that characterize somebody's

life or events in a particular place, country, or society ○ *In your situation, I'd sell my car.* ○ *destabilized the political situation* **3. LOCATION** the location of a property ○ *The property is in an idyllic situation on the southern slope of a hill.* **4.** ARTS **SET OF CIRCUMSTANCES IN PLOT** a significant combination of circumstances in a drama, film, or work of literature **5. JOB** a job or position of employment (*formal*) **6. COMBINATION OF DIFFICULT CIRCUMSTANCES** a difficult or problematic set of circumstances ○ *I'm afraid we have a situation on our hands.* —**situational** *adj*

USAGE In its generalized meaning, *situation* serves a useful purpose when a word that is not too specific is wanted: *We shall have to discuss our financial situation with the bank next week.* In some cases it is superfluous, and such uses are best avoided: *The government is concerned about the unemployment situation* could be expressed equally well as *The government is concerned about unemployment* and *We are facing a crisis situation* as *We are facing a crisis.*

situation comedy *n* a television or radio comedy series in which a regular cast of characters, usually working or living together, respond to everyday situations in a humorous way

situation ethics *n* a system of ethics in which moral judgments are thought to depend on the context in which they are to be made, rather than on general moral principles (*takes a singular verb*)

sit-up *n* an exercise in which you lie flat on your back with your legs bent and then raise the upper part of your body to a sitting position without using your hands

situs /sítɘss/ (*plural same*) *n* the position of an organ or part of the body, especially the normal position [Early 18C. < Latin (see SITE)]

situs inversus /-in vúrssɘss/ *n* an uncommon reversal of organs in the body in which the apex of the heart points to the right and the liver and appendix are on the left side [< Latin, shortening of *situs inversus viscerum* 'inverted position of the internal organs']

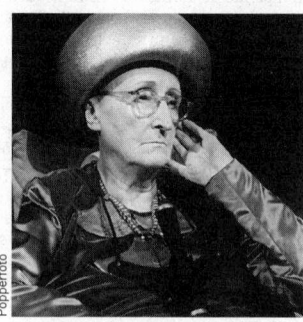
Dame Edith Sitwell

Sitwell /sít wel, síttwɘl/, **Dame Edith** (1887–1964) British writer. Unconventional in her writing, behaviour, and dress, she is best known for her poetic work *Façade* (1922), which was set to music by Sir William Walton. She was the sister of Osbert and Sacheverell Sitwell. Full name **Sitwell, Dame Edith Louisa**

Sitwell, **Sir Osbert, 5th Baronet Sitwell** (1892–1969) British writer. He wrote satirical and serious poetry and five volumes of memoirs (1944–50). He was the brother of Edith and Sacheverell Sitwell. Full name **Sitwell, Sir Francis Osbert Sacheverell**

Sitwell, **Sir Sacheverell, 6th Baronet Sitwell** (1897–1988) British writer. He was known for his biographies and studies in baroque art, which included *Sacred and Profane Love* (1940). He was the brother of Osbert and Edith Sitwell.

sitz bath /síts-/ *n* **1.** a bath shaped like a chair in which the bather sits immersed up to the waist in water, to which salts may be added for therapeutic purposes **2.** an act of immersion in a sitz bath, especially for therapeutic purposes [Partial translation of German *Sitzbad* 'sitting bath']

sitzkrieg /síts kreeg/ *n* a period in a war during which there is little offensive activity or change in the

positions of the combatants [Mid-20C. < German *sitzen* 'sit', after BLITZKRIEG]

sitzmark /síts maark/ *n* a depression in the snow made by a skier who has fallen backwards [Mid-20C. < German *Sitzmarke* 'sitting mark']

SI unit *n* a unit adopted for international use under the Système International d'Unités in science and technology. The seven fundamental units are the metre, kilogram, second, ampere, kelvin, candela, and mole.

Siva *n* HINDUISM another spelling of **Shiva**

Sivan /sívv'n, see vaan/ *n* in the Jewish calendar, the third month of the religious year, lasting 30 days and falling about the same time as May to June. See table at **calendar** [14C. < Hebrew *sīwān*]

six /siks/ *n* **1.** **6** the number 6 **2. SOMETHING WITH VALUE OF 6** something in a numbered series, e.g. a playing card, with a value of 6 **3. GROUP OF SIX** a group of six objects or people **4. GROUP OF CUBS OR BROWNIES** a division of a Cub Scout pack or Brownie Guide troop **5. BALL CROSSING BOUNDARY** a stroke in cricket that clears the boundary without bouncing, or the six runs scored by this stroke [Old English *si(e)x* < Indo-European] —**six** *adj, pron* ◇ **at sixes and sevens** (*informal*) **1.** disorganized or in disarray **2.** in disagreement ◇ **knock** *or* **hit somebody for six** to surprise somebody completely (*informal*) ◇ **six of one and half-a-dozen of the other** used when there is not much difference between two alternatives, or either of two people may be equally to blame

Six MUSIC ◗ **Les Six**

sixain /síks ayn/ *n* a six-line stanza in poetry [Late 16C. < French < *six* 'six']

Six-Day War *n* a war between Israel and the states of Egypt, Jordan, and Syria that lasted six days in June 1967

six-eight time *n* a time signature in which there are six beats to the bar and each beat is a quaver

sixer /síksɘr/ *n* a Cub Scout or Brownie who leads one of the divisions of the pack [Early 20C. < the six members of the division]

sixfold /síks fold/ *adj* **1. SIX TIMES GREATER** with six times as much or as many ○ *a sixfold increase in absenteeism* **2. WITH SIX PARTS** with six parts ■ *adv* MULTIPLIED BY SIX by six times as much or as many ○ *The number of teenagers who enrolled increased sixfold.*

six-footer *n* somebody who is six feet tall or taller (*informal*)

six-gun *n* US ARMS same as **six-shooter**

Six Nations *n* **1.** a confederacy of six Iroquois peoples, the Cayuga, Mohawk, Oneida, Onondaga, Seneca, and Tuscarora, that was formed in 1722 **2.** an international rugby championship held annually since 2000 between teams representing England, France, Ireland, Italy, Scotland, and Wales

six-pack *n* **1.** six cans or bottles, usually of beer, sold together in a pack **2.** a well-developed block of abdominal muscles (*informal*)

sixpence /síkspɘnss/ *n* a small silver-coloured coin used in Britain between 1550 and 1980, worth 6 old pennies or 2.5 new pence

sixpenny nail /síkspɘni-/ *n* a nail that is 5 cm/2 in long [< the original price of a hundred such nails]

six-shooter *n* a handgun whose bullets are loaded into a revolving cylinder containing six chambers (*informal*)

sixte /sikst/ *n* in fencing, the sixth of the eight basic defensive positions [Late 19C. < French, 'sixth']

sixteen /síks teen/ *n* **1.** **16** the number 16 **2. SOMETHING WITH VALUE OF 16** something in a numbered series with a value of 16 **3. GROUP OF 16** a group of sixteen objects or people [Old English *si(e)xtiene* < Germanic, 'ten more than six'] —**sixteen** *adj, pron*

sixteenmo /síks teen mō/ (*plural* **-mos**) *n* PRINTING same as **sextodecimo**

sixteenth /síks teenth/ *n* **1.** one of 16 equal parts of something **2.** one sixteenth of a drug such as cannabis (*slang*) —**sixteenth** *adj, adv*

sixteenth note *n* N Am same as **semiquaver**

sixteenth rest *n* N Am same as **semiquaver rest**

sixth /siksth/ n **1.** ONE OF 6 PARTS OF SOMETHING one of six equal parts of something **2.** INTERVAL OF SIX NOTES in a standard musical scale, the interval between one note and another that lies five notes above or below it. In the scale of C major, C and A form a sixth. **3.** NOTE SIXTH AWAY FROM ANOTHER in a standard musical scale, a note that is a sixth away from another note **4.** ONE NOTE IN SIXTH one of the two notes in a sixth **5.** HARMONY OF SIXTH the harmony created by playing two notes a sixth apart —**sixth** adj, adv

sixth chord n a musical chord that is made up of a note plus a note a third above and a note a sixth above

sixth form n the final optional stage of school education for students in England and Wales aged 16 to 18 in which they study for and sit A-level and A/S-level examinations (hyphenated before a noun) —**sixth-former** n

sixth-form college n a college for students in England and Wales between the ages of 16 and 18 that offers mainly A-level and A/S-level courses

sixth sense n a supposed special ability to perceive something not using any of the five senses of sight, hearing, touch, smell, and taste

sixth year n Scotland **1.** the final optional year in Scottish secondary schools during which students can study for additional Highers (hyphenated before a noun) **2.** a student in the sixth year of school

sixth-year studies npl Scotland a one-year course of study formerly taken in the final year at Scottish secondary schools after the completion of Highers

sixtieth /siksti əth/ n one of 60 equal parts of something —**sixtieth** adj, adv

Sixtus V /sikstəss/ (1521–90) pope. As pope (1585–90) he reformed the administration of the Roman Catholic Church, ordered the construction of public buildings in Rome, and supported missions abroad.

sixty /siksti/ n (plural **-ties**) **1.** 60 the number 60 **2.** GROUP OF 60 a group of sixty objects or people ■ **sixties** npl **1.** NUMBERS 60 TO 69 the numbers 60 to 69, particularly as a range of Fahrenheit temperatures ○ in the low sixties **2.** YEARS FROM 60 TO 69 the years from 60 to 69 in a century **3.** PERIOD FROM AGE 60 TO 69 the period of somebody's life from the age of 60 to 69 [Old English sixtig < SIX + -tig 'ten'] —**sixty** adj, pron

64 bit key /sikstee fawr bit-/ n an industry standard encryption key length for e-commerce transactions

sixty-fourmo /-fáwrmō/ (plural **sixty-fourmos**) n a size of book page traditionally created by folding a single sheet of standard-sized printing paper 6 times, giving 64 leaves or 128 pages

sixty-fourth note n N Am MUSIC same as **hemidemisemiquaver**

sixty-four thousand dollar question, **$64,000 question**, **64,000 dollar question** n a question whose answer is not yet known but is significant and important (informal) ○ Yes, but will it actually work? That's the sixty-four thousand dollar question! [< the top prize in a popular TV quiz show of the 1950s]

sixty-nine n an offensive term for a sexual activity in which two people simultaneously stimulate each other's genitals orally (slang) [< the position of the couple]

six-yard box n a rectangle of lines on the pitch in front of the goal in association football. It extends six yards from the goal line and goal kicks are taken within it.

sizable /síz əb'l/, **sizeable** adj fairly large —**sizableness** n —**sizably** adv

sizar /sízər/ n at some universities, an undergraduate student who receives a grant for expenses from a college [Late 16C. < SIZE[1] in the obsolete sense 'quantity of bread or ale'] —**sizarship** n

size[1] /síz/ n **1.** HOW BIG SOMETHING IS the dimensions, extent, amount, or degree of something, in terms of how large or small it is ○ I think this table is about the right size for our dining room. **2.** BIGNESS the fact of being large, often very large, in dimensions or degree ○ Did you see the size of that fish? **3.** STANDARD MEASUREMENT OF MANUFACTURED ITEM a set of measurements used when making or classifying articles such as clothing or shoes that are produced and

sold ○ He takes a size 11 shoe, I think. ■ vt (**sizes, sizing, sized**) **1.** SORT THINGS ACCORDING TO SIZE to put things into different groups according to their size **2.** MAKE SOMETHING TO PARTICULAR SIZE to cut, shape, or manufacture goods so that they have the necessary or chosen measurements **3.** MEASURE to work out or find out the measurements of something [13C. < Old French sise, shortening of assise (see ASSIZE)] —**sized** adj ◇ **cut somebody down to size** to make somebody be less self-important and arrogant ◇ **that's about the size of it** used to indicate that something describes a situation very well (informal) ◇ **try something (on) for size 1.** to put something on to see whether it fits you or not **2.** to find out how much you like something

size up vt to assess a person or situation and form a judgment

size[2] /síz/ n a gelatinous mixture made from glue, starch, or varnish. Use: filling pores in the surface of paper, textiles, or plaster. ■ vt (**sizes, sizing, sized**) to coat a porous surface such as paper, textile, or plaster with size [15C. Origin ?]

sizeable adj another spelling of **sizable**

sizeism /sízizəm/ n discrimination against somebody on the basis of the person's size, especially in the person's unusual tallness, shortness, fatness, or thinness —**sizeist** adj

sizing /sízing/ n **1.** INDUST, ARTS same as **size[2] 2.** the process of coating something with size

sizzle /sízz'l/ v (**-zles, -zling, -zled**) **1.** vti MAKE NOISE OF FOOD FRYING to make the hissing and spattering sound typical of frying fat, or cook food so that it makes a hissing sound **2.** vi BE HOT to be extremely hot (informal) **3.** vi BE PHYSICALLY APPEALING to be physically appealing or very popular (informal) **4.** vi BE FURIOUS to show or feel great anger (informal) ■ n FRYING NOISE the hissing and splattering sound of something frying, or a sound resembling this [Early 17C. An imitation of the sound]

sizzler /sízzlər/ n **1.** SOMETHING THAT SIZZLES something that makes a sizzling noise **2.** HOT DAY an extremely hot day (informal) **3.** US SOMETHING EXCITING an exciting event (informal)

sizzling /sízzling/ adj (informal) **1.** extremely hot **2.** physically appealing or very popular —**sizzlingly** adv

sj abbr Svalbard and Jan Mayen Islands (used in Internet addresses) See table at **domain name**

SJ abbr Society of Jesus

SJA abbr Saint John Ambulance (Brigade or Association)

Sjælland /syéllənd/ the main island of Denmark, on which Copenhagen is situated. Population: 2,159,260 (1994). Area: 7,031 sq. km/2,715 sq. mi. English name **Zealand**

sjambok /shám bok/ S Africa n a sturdy whip or riding crop made from the hide of a rhinoceros or hippopotamus ■ vt (**-boks, -bokking, -bokked**) to whip somebody or something with a sjambok [Late 18C. Via Afrikaans < Malay chambuk < Persian chābuk 'whip']

SJD abbr Doctor of Juridical Science [Latin Scientiae Juridicae Doctor]

sk abbr Slovakia (used in Internet addresses) See table at **domain name**

SK abbr Saskatchewan

ska /skaa/ n dance music in 4/4 time, marked by emphasis on the second and fourth beats, originating in Jamaica in the late 1950s. It combines traditional Caribbean music and jazz, and was a predecessor of reggae. [Mid-20C. Origin ?]

skag n DRUGS another spelling of **scag** (slang)

Skagerrak /skággə rak/ arm of the North Sea between Norway and the Jutland Peninsula, Denmark. Length: 210 km/130 mi.

skald /skawld/, **scald** n a medieval Scandinavian poet or travelling minstrel (archaic or literary) [Mid-18C. < Old Norse skáld] —**skaldic** adj

Skåne /skőnə/ province forming the southern tip of Sweden. It consists of the counties of Kristianstad and Malmöhus. Population: 1,120,038 (1998). Area: 10,984 sq. km/4,241 sq. mi.

skank /skangk/ vi (**skanks, skanking, skanked**) **1.** DANCE TO REGGAE to dance to reggae music, especially in a jerky way **2.** CHEAT to be deceitful (used in Black English) ■ n OFFENSIVE TERM an offensive term for a girl or woman who is regarded as unpleasant-looking and sexually promiscuous (slang insult) [Late 20C. Origin ?]

skanky /skángki/ adj disgusting or unpleasant (slang) [Late 20C. Origin ?]

skat /skat/ n a card game for three players played with 32 cards and involving bids, contracts, and the taking of tricks [Mid-19C. Via German < Italian scarto 'discarded card' < Latin c(h)arta (see CARD[1])]

skate[1] /skayt/ n **1.** ICE SKATING same as **ice skate 2.** ROLLER-SKATING same as **roller skate 3.** METAL BLADE FOR ICE SKATE a steel runner that is fastened to the sole of a boot or shoe to make an ice skate **4.** TIME SPENT SKATING a period of time spent skating ■ vi (**skates, skating, skated**) **1.** MOVE AROUND ON SKATES to glide along a surface wearing ice skates or roller skates **2.** SLIDE SMOOTHLY to slide along a slippery surface [Mid-17C. < Dutch schaats 'skate, stilt' < Old French eschasse 'stilt'] ◇ **get your skates on** to hurry (informal)

skate over vt to mention or deal with something in a cursory way, often in order to avoid an unpleasant truth (informal)

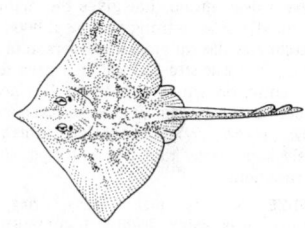

skate

skate[2] /skayt/ (plural same or **skates**) n **1.** a bottom-dwelling cartilaginous sea fish with a flat body, very large flat pectoral fins, two small dorsal fins, a long snout, and short slender tail. Family: Rajidae. **2.** the flesh of a skate as food [14C. < Old Norse skata]

skateboard /skáyt bawrd/ n a short narrow board to which a set of small wheels is fitted on the underside, used to move rapidly or to perform jumps and stunts ■ vi (**-boards, -boarding, -boarded**) to ride on a skateboard —**skateboarder** n

skateboarding /skáyt bawrding/ n the sport or pastime of riding a skateboard

skatepark /skáyt paark/ n an area specially designed and constructed for people practising and performing on skateboards and in-line skates

skater /skáytər/ n **1.** somebody who skates on ice skates or roller skates **2.** INSECTS same as **pond-skater**

skating /skáyt ing/ n the pastime or sport of sliding on ice skates or rolling on roller skates

skatole /skáttōl/ n an organic crystalline solid that has a strong faecal odour. Source: faeces, beetroot, coal tar. Use: perfume fixative. Formula: C_9H_9N. [Late 19C. < Greek skat- (see SCATO-)]

skean /skeen/ n a dagger with a double-edged blade formerly used in Scotland and Ireland [Early 16C. Via Gaelic < Old Irish scían]

skean-dhu /skeén doó/, **sgian-dhu** n a small dagger with a black hilt that is tucked into the top of a man's stocking in Highland dress [< Gaelic, 'black skean']

skedaddle /ski dádd'l/ (slang) vi (**-dles, -dling, -dled**) to run away quickly ■ n a very quick or agitated departure [Mid-19C. Origin ?] —**skedaddler** n

skeet /skeet/, **skeet shooting** n a form of clay-pigeon shooting in which clay targets are tossed into the air [Early 20C. Invented word, supposedly archaic form of SHOOT]

skeg /skeg/ n **1.** a part of the keel of a ship, near the stern, that connects the keel with the rudder post **2.** the short stabilizing fin on the rear underside of

a surfboard or sailboard [Early 17C. Via Dutch < Old Norse *skegg* 'beard, point of a ship's stern']

Skegness /skeg néss/ *n* town and seaside resort in Lincolnshire, eastern England. Population: 15,149 (1991).

skein /skayn/ *n* **1. BUNDLE OF YARN** a length of yarn or thread wound loosely and coiled together **2. TANGLE** a tangled or complex mass of material **3. GROUP OF GEESE IN FLIGHT** a flock of geese flying across the sky in a line [15C. < Old French *escaigne*]

skeletal /skéllitəl/ *adj* **1.** relating to a skeleton **2.** extremely thin or emaciated —**skeletally** *adv*

skeleton /skéllitən/ *n* **1. BONES OF PERSON OR ANIMAL** the rigid framework of interconnected bones and cartilage that protects and supports the internal organs and provides attachment for muscles in humans and other vertebrate animals **2. SUPPORTIVE PROTECTIVE STRUCTURE OF INVERTEBRATES** something that provides support, gives protection, or maintains shape in an invertebrate animal, e.g. the shell of a snail or the cuticle of a crab **3. BASIC FRAME SOMETHING IS BUILT AROUND** a structure that is needed to support and hold something together as an internal framework, onto which the connecting or covering parts are attached **4. SOMETHING WITH ONLY ESSENTIAL PARTS LEFT** a plan, organization, or structure that has been reduced so that only its most basic and necessary parts are still functioning or in place **5. OUTLINE OR LAYOUT OF SOMETHING** a description that gives the main points but no details of something such as a book or plan **6. SOMEBODY VERY THIN** an emaciated person or animal (*informal*) **7. RACING SLED** a small sled used for high-speed racing, on which the driver lies head first [Late 16C. Via modern Latin < Greek *skeleton (sōma)* 'dried up (body)' < *skellein* 'dry up'] ◇ **a skeleton in the cupboard** a closely kept secret that is a source of shame or embarrassment

skeletonize /skéllitə nīz/ (**-izes, -izing, -ized**), **skeletonise** (**-ises, -ising, -ised**) *vt* **1. CUT SOMETHING BACK TO BASICS** to reduce something until only its most basic structure or outline remains **2. CREATE OUTLINE OF SOMETHING** to create something in basic outline **3. REDUCE SOMETHING TO SKELETAL FORM** to reduce something to a skeleton

skeleton key *n* a key with the usually serrated part that connects with the lever of a lock (**bit**) filed down so that it can open many different unsophisticated locks [< its basic cut-back shape]

skelf /skelf/ *n N England, Scotland* a thin splinter of wood, especially one that has gone into the skin [14C. Probably < Low German *schelf* 'shelf']

skell /skel/ *n US* a homeless or jobless person who lives on the street (*slang*) [Late 20C. Origin ?]

skelly /skélli/ *adj Scotland* with a squint or with crossed eyes [Late 18C. < Old Norse *skjelga* < *skjálgr* 'wry, oblique']

Skelmersdale /skélmərz dayl/ town in Lancashire, northwestern England. It was designated a new town in 1961. Population: 42,104 (1991).

skelp /skelp/ *v* (**skelps, skelping, skelped**) *N England, Scotland* **1.** *vt* **SMACK SOMEBODY** to slap somebody sharply with the hand or with something flat **2.** *vi* **MOVE AT GREAT SPEED** to hustle along quickly and energetically ■ *n* **1.** *N England, Scotland* **A SMACK** a slap, usually with the hand **2. CRIME** same as **criminal** (*slang*) [14C. Probably an imitation of the sound of a slap]

skep /skep/ *n* **1.** a beehive made of straw or similar material **2.** *regional* a large basket woven from straw, reeds, or twigs [Pre-12C. < Old Norse *skeppa* 'basket, bushel']

skeptic, etc. *n US* spelling of **sceptic, etc.**

skerrick /skérrik/ *n Aus, NZ* a tiny scrap or trace of something (*informal*) [Early 19C. Origin ?]

Skerrit /skérrit/, **Pierre** (b. 1972?) prime minister of Dominica (2004–). A member of the Dominican Labour Party, he served as minister for education before becoming the country's youngest ever prime minister.

skerry /skérri/ (*plural* **-ries**) *n Scotland* a rocky islet or reef [Early 17C. < Old Norse *sker* 'reef']

sketch /skech/ *n* **1. PICTURE DONE QUICKLY AND ROUGHLY** a drawing or painting that is done quickly without concern for detail. A sketch might be made to

capture the general mood of a scene, or to help the artist work out an idea for a finished composition. **2. SHORT PERFORMANCE** a quick comic routine or piece of acting that is part of a variety show or comedy revue **3. ROUGH DESCRIPTION OR EXPLANATION** a short written or spoken account that conveys just a general outline or idea, with little detail **4. SHORT PIECE OF WRITING** a short, often descriptive piece of writing **5. SHORT MUSICAL COMPOSITION** a short piece of instrumental music, often for piano ■ *vti* (**sketches, sketching, sketched**) **MAKE SKETCH** to create a sketch of something [Mid-17C. Via Dutch *schets* or German *Skizze* < Italian *schizzo* < Vulgar Latin *schediare* 'do hastily' < Latin *schedius* < Greek *skhedios* 'on the spur of the moment'] —**sketchable** *adj* —**sketcher** *n*

sketchbook /skéch book/, **sketchpad** /-pad/ *n* **1.** a book of plain paper for making sketches on **2.** a book containing a collection of literary sketches

sketchy /skéchi/ (**-ier, -iest**) *adj* **1. GIVING ONLY ROUGH IDEA** giving only the main points, with little detail **2. SUPERFICIAL** lacking in substance, depth, or finality **3. DRAWN LIKE A SKETCH** drawn or painted quickly without concern for detail —**sketchily** *adv* —**sketchiness** *n*

skew /skyoo/ *v* (**skews, skewing, skewed**) **1.** *vti* **SLANT, OR CAUSE SOMETHING TO SLANT** to make something uneven, sloping, or unsymmetrical, or be in this state **2.** *vt* **DISTORT SOMETHING** to misrepresent the true meaning or nature of something **3.** *vi* **SQUINT** to look sideways at something ■ *adj* **1. IN SLANTED POSITION OR LINE** being in a slanted or unsymmetrical position **2. DISTORTING TRUTH** giving an unfair or untrue account of something, especially statistics **3. MATHS NOT PARALLEL OR INTERSECTING** describes a line that is neither parallel nor intersecting ■ *n* **1. TILTED OR INACCURATE POSITION** a position that is not straight but that slants or twists out of correct alignment **2. SLANTING DIRECTION** a slanting movement, line, or direction [14C. Shortening of Old N French *eskiuer*, variant of Old French *eschiver* 'eschew']

skew arch *n* an arch with sides that are not at right angles to the span, e.g. on a bridge or tunnel

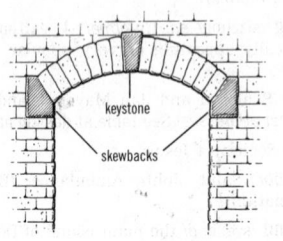

keystone

skewbacks

skewback

skewback /skyoo bak/ *n* either of the sloping surfaces on which the sides of a segmental arch abut

skewbald /skyoo bawld/ *adj* describes a horse that has a spotted coat consisting of white and another colour other than black, generally brown ■ *n* a skewbald horse [Mid-17C. Blend of obsolete *skewed* 'having mixed colours' (origin ?) + PIEBALD]

skewer /skyoo ər/ *n* **1. THIN ROD TO COOK FOOD ON** a thin metal or wooden rod with a sharp end used to hold meat or meat and vegetables during cooking **2. SOMETHING SIMILAR TO SKEWER** a thin pointed object used to pierce something or hold it in place ■ *vt* (**-ers, -ering, -ered**) **PIERCE SOMETHING WITH SKEWER** to pierce somebody or something with a skewer or with something else that is thin and sharp [15C. Origin ?]

skewness /skyoo nəss/ *n* **1.** the way or amount that something is tilted or distorted from the true or straight position **2.** in statistics, a lack of symmetry about the mean in a frequency distribution

skewwhiff /skyoo wif/ *adj* not level or straight, but crooked, tilted, or lopsided (*informal*) [Mid-18C. Fanciful < SKEW]

ski /skee/ *n* (*plural* **skis**) **1. BOARD USED TO SLIDE ACROSS SNOW** either of a pair of long thin boards made of wood, metal, or other material that curve up at the front and are used to slide across snow **2. WATER SKIING** same as **waterski 3. RUNNER FOR VEHICLES TRAVELLING ON**

SNOW a runner fitted to vehicles such as snowmobiles and aeroplanes for landing or travelling on snow and ice ■ *vti* (**skis, skiing, skied** or **ski'd**) **MOVE ALONG ON SKIS** to glide over the surface of snow or water wearing skis, as a means of travel or as a leisure pursuit or sport [Mid-18C. Via Norwegian < Old Norse *skið* 'piece of split wood, snowshoe'] —**skiable** *adj* —**skier** *n*

skiboard /skee bawrd/ *n* either of a pair of boards, shorter and wider than standard skis and often with sharp edges, worn and used like skis —**skiboarder** *n*

skiboarding /skee bawrding/ *n* the sport of travelling over snow or performing stunts on skiboards

skibob /skee bob/ *n* a vehicle similar to a bicycle that has skis instead of wheels and is used to travel over snow [Mid-20C. < SKI + *bob*, shortening of BOBSLEIGH] —**skibobber** *n* —**skibobbing** *n*

skid /skid/ *n* **1. UNCONTROLLED SLIDE** an uncontrolled slide across a surface in a wheeled vehicle **2. AIRCRAFT RUNNER** a runner on the underside of an aircraft, used as part of its landing gear **3. PALLET** a low pallet on which goods are loaded for handling or transport **4. MECH ENG BLOCK USED TO PREVENT WHEEL TURNING** a shoe or block used to prevent a wheel from turning, e.g. when a vehicle is descending a hill **5. NAUT SHIP'S FENDER** a wooden structure hung over the side of a ship to protect the ship in loading and unloading cargo ■ *v* (**skids, skidding, skidded**) **1.** *vti* **SLIDE DANGEROUSLY ACROSS SURFACE** to slide across a surface, or make a vehicle slide across a surface, usually unintentionally, so that the wheels lose their grip and control is lost **2.** *vi* **SLIDE OVER SURFACE WITHOUT ROLLING** to slide across a surface without turning round and gripping it in the proper way **3.** *vti* **SLIDE SIDEWAYS** to slide sideways, or make an aircraft slide sideways away from the centre of curvature when it is insufficiently banked in making a turn [Early 17C. Origin ?] —**skiddy** *adj* ◇ **on the skids** in difficulties and heading for failure (*informal*)

ski'd SPORTS past participle, past tense of **ski**

skidlid /skídlid/ *n* MOTORCYCLES same as **crash helmet** (*dated informal*)

skidpan /skíd pan/ *n* an area with a surface that is deliberately made slippery so that drivers can practise dealing with a skidding vehicle

skidproof /skíd proof/ *adj* designed to prevent skidding

skid road *n N Am* **1.** same as **skid row** (*informal*) **2.** a road with logs embedded in it, along which timber is hauled to a mill or loading area

skid row *n* an area of a city that has cheap bars and rundown hotels and is frequented by members of the city's underclass (*informal*) [Alteration of *skid road*, originally an area of a town frequented by loggers]

skied[1] /skeed/ SPORTS past participle, past tense of **ski**

skied[2] /skīd/ SPORTS past participle, past tense of **sky**

skiff /skif/ *n* a small flat-bottomed boat of shallow draft that can be propelled with oars, a sail, or a motor [15C. Via French *esquif* < Italian *schifo*, probably < Old High German *schif*]

skiffle /skíff'l/ *n* music popular in the 1950s, usually played by a small group on guitars with improvised instruments such as a washboard used as percussion [Early 20C. Origin ?]

Barnaby's

skiing

skiing /skee ing/ *n* the activity, sport, or pastime of travelling on skis [< SKI]

SKI-ing /skeé ing/ *n* the spending by retired people of their savings for their own enjoyment, rather than leaving the money to their children when they die (*humorous*) [< acronym < 'spending the kids' inheritance'] —**SKI-er** *n*

skijoring /skeé jawring/ *n* a sport in which a skier is towed across a frozen surface by a horse or vehicle [Early 20C. < Norwegian *skijøring* 'ski driving'] —**skijorer** *n*

ski jump *n* **1.** a steep artificial slope with a sharp upturn at the bottom. People ski down this and then leap into the air, competing to travel the longest distance before landing. **2.** a jump made by a skier from a ski jump —**ski-jump** *vi* —**ski jumper** *n*

Skikda /skík daa/ city and port in northeastern Algeria, situated about 354 km/220 mi. east of Algiers. Population: 128,747 (1987).

skilful /skílf'l/ *adj* **1.** with special ability and dexterity in doing something **2.** requiring or done with specialized techniques and abilities developed over a period of time —**skilfully** *adv* —**skilfulness** *n*

~~skilfull~~ incorrect spelling of **skilful**

ski lift *n* a motor-driven apparatus consisting of a continuously moving cable with seats, gondolas, or tow bars suspended from it, built to transport skiers to the top of a ski run

skill /skil/ *n* **1.** the ability to do something well, usually gained through training or experience **2.** something that requires training and experience to do well, e.g. an art or trade [12C. < Old Norse *skil* 'discernment'] —**skilled** *adj* —**skill-less** *adj* —**skill-less-ness** *n*

SYNONYMS See *ability*.

skillet /skíllit/ *n* **1.** in former times, a small shallow pan with a long handle and usually legs, used for frying or braising food **2.** HOUSEHOLD same as **frying pan** [15C. Probably < Old French *escuelete* 'small platter' < *escuele* 'platter' < Latin *scutella* 'flat dish']

skillful *adj* US spelling of **skilful**

skillion /skíllyən/ *n* Aus **1.** an outhouse **2.** a type of roof that includes a wide, flat, gently sloping section of the type formerly found on outhouses

skilly /skílli/ *n* a watery type of soup, made from oatmeal or something similar [Mid-19C. Nonsense word]

skim /skim/ *v* (**skims, skimming, skimmed**) **1.** *vt* SCOOP SOMETHING FROM TOP OF LIQUID to remove a substance such as fat forming a layer on the surface of a liquid, usually with a large shallow spoon **2.** *vt* RID LIQUID OF FLOATING MATERIAL to rid a liquid of material accumulating on its surface **3.** *vti* PASS CLOSELY OVER SURFACE OF SOMETHING to pass quickly across and just above the surface of something, or make something pass in this way, sometimes touching it lightly and briefly **4.** *vt* GLANCE THROUGH BOOK OR PAPER to read something very quickly, looking only at occasional lines or words, in order to get a general idea of its contents **5.** *vt* SEND SOMETHING BOUNCING ALONG to throw something so that it bounces lightly along the surface of water **6.** *vt* TREAT SOMETHING IN CURSORY WAY to deal with something in a superficial way **7.** *vti* COAT OR BECOME COATED WITH LAYER to develop a thin surface layer of something, or coat an object so that its surface is covered in a thin layer of something **8.** *vti* EMBEZZLE to embezzle some of the proceeds from a business (*informal*) **9.** *vt* N Am HIDE PROFITS TO AVOID TAXES to hide earnings or profits in order to avoid paying taxes on them (*informal*) ■ *n* **1.** THIN FILM a thin layer of something on a surface **2.** CURSORY LOOK a cursory look at or treatment of something ○ *a quick skim over the main topics on the agenda* **3.** SUBSTANCE REMOVED FROM SURFACE OF SOMETHING the matter that forms a layer on a surface and is skimmed off **4.** SKIMMING PROCESS the process of removing a substance from a surface [15C. < Old French *escumer* < *escume* 'scum'] —**skim off** *vt* to cull the best people or items from a group

ski mask *n* a covering for the face and head, usually made of knitted material and having openings for the eyes, the mouth, and sometimes the nose, worn by skiers as protection against the cold

skimmed milk *n* milk with most or all of its fat content removed. Aus, US term **skim milk**

skimmer /skímmər/ *n* **1.** SOMEBODY OR SOMETHING THAT SKIMS a person, object, or device that skims **2.** LONG-WINGED FRESHWATER BIRD a long-winged freshwater bird that has a beak with the lower half longer than the upper, used for skimming food from the surface of water while in flight. Native to: South America, Africa, Asia. Genus: *Rynchops*. **3.** UTENSIL USED FOR SKIMMING a broad flat spoon with small perforations in it, used to skim something such as fat from the surface of a liquid

skim milk *n* ANZ, N Am FOOD same as **skimmed milk**

skimming /skímming/ *n* the crime of fraudulently reusing the electronic information from a swiped credit card or payment card ■ **skimmings** *npl* the floating fat or debris skimmed off the surface of a liquid

skimp /skimp/ (**skimps, skimping, skimped**) *v* **1.** *vti* USE TOO LITTLE OF SOMETHING to use or provide hardly enough of something **2.** *vt* DO SOMETHING IMPROPERLY to carry out a piece of work poorly, without spending enough time, trouble, or materials on it **3.** *vt* NOT PROVIDE SOMEBODY WITH ENOUGH to give or allow yourself or another person only an inadequate amount of money, food, or other necessary items [Late 18C. Origin ?]

skimpy /skímpi/ (**-ier, -iest**) *adj* **1.** made or done using barely enough of the necessary materials **2.** not giving somebody enough of something through meanness —**skimpily** *adv* —**skimpiness** *n*

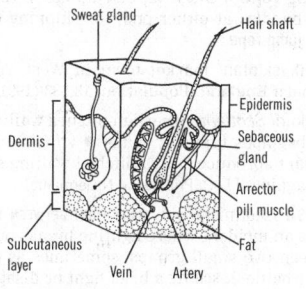

skin: cross-section of human skin

skin /skin/ *n* **1.** NATURAL LAYER COVERING BODY the external protective membrane or covering of an animal's body, consisting of the dermis and epidermis and often covered in hair, fur, scales, or feathers **2.** SKIN ON FACE somebody's skin, especially on the face, in terms of its colour and appearance ○ *Do you have oily, dry, or combination skin?* ○ *skin tone* **3.** NATURAL COVERING OF FRUIT OR VEGETABLE a relatively thin but protective layer closely surrounding the flesh of a fruit or vegetable **4.** FUR OR LEATHER FROM DEAD ANIMAL skin or a piece of skin removed from an animal's body, especially once it has been cleaned and treated to use as fur or leather **5.** SOLID SURFACE LAYER ON LIQUID a thin pliant surface that forms on the top of some liquids, e.g. on hot milk left to cool **6.** TIGHT-FITTING COVERING a thin tough casing or cover that fits closely round something such as a sausage to hold in, protect, or preserve the enclosed material **7.** OUTER COVERING OF STRUCTURE the outer protective covering of a structure such as an aircraft **8.** SMALL LEATHER SACK a bag made from animal hide used to hold liquid such as wine or water **9.** COMPUT SOFTWARE FOR EDITING IMAGES a piece of software that enables the user to change the appearance of images produced by existing software without changing their function, or the changed image that results **10.** CIGARETTE PAPER a piece of paper used for making marijuana joints or other roll-up cigarettes (*slang*) **11.** same as **skinhead** (sense 1) (*informal*) ■ **skins** *npl* MUSIC JAZZ DRUMS drums, especially in a jazz band (*informal*) ■ *v* (**skins, skinning, skinned**) **1.** *vt* TAKE SKIN OFF FRUIT OR VEGETABLE to remove the skin from a fruit or vegetable, or from an animal or person, especially by cutting or ripping it **2.** *vt* SCRAPE SKIN to make the skin on a part of the body red, sore, and broken, especially by falling on it or scraping it **3.** *vt* REMOVE OUTSIDE LAYER OF SOMETHING to strip off an outer, covering layer of something that resembles a skin **4.** *vi* ACQUIRE LAYER LIKE SKIN to become covered with a layer that resembles a skin **5.** *vti* COMPUT ALTER SOFTWARE IMAGES to change the appearance of images produced by existing soft-

ware, without changing their function **6.** *vt* CRIME SWINDLE SOMEBODY to trick somebody out of money or property (*slang*) ■ *adj* US PORNOGRAPHIC relating to or containing pornographic material (*informal*) [12C. < Old Norse *skinn*] —**skinless** *adj* ◇ **get under somebody's nose** to be a matter that does not harm somebody at all and therefore may be of little interest (*informal*) ◇ **by the skin of your teeth** by a very narrow margin, or only just (*informal*) ◇ **get under somebody's skin** (*informal*) **1.** to annoy or irritate somebody **2.** to make somebody feel great interest or attraction ◇ **jump out of your skin** to get a bad fright or a shock (*informal*) ◇ **save somebody's skin** to prevent somebody from suffering hurt, loss, or punishment by giving vital help (*informal*)

skin up *vi* to roll a marijuana joint or cigarette (*slang*)

skincare /skín kair/ *adj* intended to keep the skin healthy, supple, or young-looking

skin-deep *adj* appearing to be important, meaningful, or valuable but having little deep or lasting importance ■ *adv* in a superficial way

skinder /skínnər/, **skinner** S Africa (*informal*) *n* same as **gossip** *n* (sense 1) ■ *vi* (**-ders, -dering, -dered; -ners, -nering, -nered**) same as **gossip** [Mid-20C. < Afrikaans]

skin diving *n* the sport of underwater diving using flippers, a mask, and a snorkel —**skin-dive** *vi* —**skin diver** *n*

skin effect *n* the tendency of a high-frequency alternating current to flow near the surface of the conductor rather than in its interior

skin flick *n* a pornographic film (*slang*)

skinflint /skín flint/ *n* same as **miser** (sense 1) [Late 17C. < the idea of somebody so miserly as to try to remove the skin from a piece of flint]

skin friction *n* a frictional force that acts on the surface of an aerofoil or other object immersed in and moving through a fluid

skinful /skín fòol/ *n* **1.** a large amount of alcoholic drink, especially as much as somebody can drink (*informal*) **2.** the amount of liquid that a skin bag holds

~~skiing~~ incorrect spelling of **skiing**

skin game *n* a confidence trick or scheme used to cheat people of their money (*slang*) [< SKIN 'swindle']

skin graft *n* a piece of skin taken from part of the body and used to replace lost or damaged skin

skinhead /skín hed/ *n* (*slang*) **1.** somebody whose hair is very short or whose head is shaved **2.** one of a group of young white men with closely-cropped or shaven hair, characterized by extreme right-wing views and aggressive behaviour

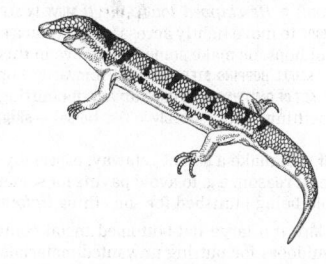

skink

skink /skingk/ *n* a small smooth insect-eating lizard with a long thin body and small limbs. It lives in temperate and tropical regions, especially in Asia and Africa. Family: Scincidae. [Late 16C. Via Latin *scincus* < Greek *skigkos*]

skinner[1] /skínnər/ *n* **1.** somebody who skins animals, or deals in animal skins **2.** somebody who creates software to change the appearance of images on a computer screen [14C. < SKIN]

skinner[2] /skínnər/ *n*, *vi* S Africa same as **gossip**

Skinner /skínnər/, **B. F.** (1904–90) US behavioural psychologist. His stimulus-response experiments and behaviourist theories profoundly influenced

methods of education and behaviour therapy. His works include *Beyond Freedom and Dignity* (1971). Full name **Skinner, Burrhus Frederic** —**Skinnerian** /ski néeri ən/ *adj, n*

'The real problem is not whether machines think but whether men do.'
[B. F. Skinner, *Contingencies of Reinforcement*; 1969]

Skinner box *n* an enclosure for isolating an animal during studies of learning behaviour or operant conditioning that contains a device the animal may operate to receive a reward or avoid punishment [Mid-20C. After B. F. SKINNER]

skinny /skínni/ (**-nier, -niest**) *adj* **1.** thin, especially in an unappealing or unhealthy way **2.** made with skimmed milk (*slang*) ○ *One skinny latte to go.* [Mid-16C. < SKIN] —**skinniness** *n*

SYNONYMS See ***thin***.

skinny-dip (*informal*) *vi* to go swimming in the nude ■ *n* a swim in the nude [< SKINNY 'of the skin'] —**skinny-dipper** *n* —**skinny-dipping** *n*

skinny rib *adj* describes a jumper or similar garment that is knitted with a narrow rib pattern and fits closely to the body

skin-pop *vti* to take narcotic drugs by inserting the needle under the skin, not straight into a vein (*slang*)

skint /skint/ *adj* without any money (*informal*) [Early 20C. Variant of *skinned*]

skin-teeth /skín teet/ *vi* same as **smile** (*slang; used in Black English*)

skin test *n* a test in which a substance is applied to the skin to determine somebody's allergic sensitivity or immunity to it

skintight /skín tīt/ *adj* fitting tightly to the body

skip[1] /skip/ *v* (**skips, skipping, skipped**) **1.** *vi* MOVE WITH SMALL HOPPING STEPS to move along by hopping from one foot to the other **2.** *vti* JUMP REPEATEDLY OVER CIRCLING ROPE to jump repeatedly over a rope as it is swung round over the head and under the feet **3.** *vt* JUMP OVER SOMETHING to jump nimbly over something **4.** *vti* OMIT SOMETHING to pass over or leave out something that should properly follow as part of a sequence or a complete work **5.** *vi* DEAL WITH SOMETHING CURSORILY to deal with or look at something in a cursory way ○ *Can we just skip through the draft document before we break for lunch?* **6.** *vt* NOT ATTEND SOMETHING to decide to miss an event or activity (*informal*) **7.** *vi* NOT PLAY CORRECTLY to fail to play properly by jumping from one place to another (*refers to CDs or records*) **8.** *vti N Am* LEAVE SOMEWHERE SECRETLY to make a secret getaway from a place, especially for some dishonest reason, e.g. to avoid being punished for something (*informal*) ○ *He skipped town.* **9.** *vti* MOVE IN SERIES OF SMALL HOPS to move lightly across a surface in a series of small hops, or make something move in this way ■ *n* **1.** SMALL HOPPING STEP a small forwards hopping step **2.** ACT OF OMITTING SOMETHING an act of omitting part of something [13C. Probably < Old Norse] —**skippable** *adj*

skip off *vi* to make a secret getaway, especially for a dishonest reason, e.g. to avoid paying for something or avoid being punished for something (*informal*)

skip[2] /skip/ *n* a large flat-bottomed metal container kept outdoors for putting unwanted materials, furniture, or any bulky refuse in, especially when a building is being renovated or constructed [Early 19C. Variant of SKEP]

skip[3] /skip/ (*slang*) *n* NAUT same as **skipper**[1] *n* (sense 1) ■ *vi* (**skips, skipping, skipped**) to be the skipper of a vessel [Early 19C. Shortening]

ski pants *npl* **1.** *UK* women's trousers made of stretchy fabric with elasticated straps that go under the feet. ANZ, N Am term **stirrup pants** **2.** lined, windproof, water-resistant trousers that are worn for skiing and other cold weather activities

skip distance *n* the shortest distance between a radio transmitter and receiver that permits waves of a specific frequency to be sent and received by reflection from the ionosphere

skipjack /skíp jak/ (*plural same* or **-jacks**) *n* **1.** LEAPING SEA FISH a sea fish that leaps out of the water, e.g. the bonito or bluefish **2.** *also* **skipjack tuna** SEA FISH a tropical sea fish of the tuna family that is blue and silver with dark stripes on its abdomen. Latin name: *Euthynnus pelamus.* **3.** INSECTS same as **click beetle** **4.** *US* SAILING BOAT a sailing boat with straight sides and a V-shaped bottom

skiplane /skée playn/ *n* an aircraft equipped with skis for taking off from and landing on snow

ski pole *n* either of a pair of lightweight poles held by skiers for balance and control. The bottom end has a point surrounded by a disc for gaining a hold on the snow.

skipper[1] /skíppər/ *n* **1.** SOMEBODY IN CHARGE OF SHIP somebody in charge of a ship or boat **2.** LEADER OF TEAM somebody in charge of a squad or group of others, especially the captain or coach of a sports team (*informal*) ■ *vt* (**-pers, -pering, -pered**) BE SKIPPER OF SOMETHING to be in charge of a ship, team, or aircraft (*informal*) [14C. < Middle Dutch *schipper* < *schip* 'ship']

skipper[2] /skíppər/ *n* **1.** somebody or something that skips **2.** a quick-flying insect that has a hairy body and clubbed antennae with hooked tips, and is closely related to true butterflies. Families: Hesperiidae or Megathymidae. **3.** FISH same as **saury** [Mid-18C. < SKIP[1]]

skipping /skípping/ *n* a children's pastime or adult exercise in which you skip over a rope as it swings round over your head and under your feet

skipping rope *n UK, ANZ, Can* a piece of rope, often with handles at either end, for skipping over. US term **jump rope**

Skipton /skíptən/ market town in West Yorkshire, northern England. Population: 13,583 (1991).

skirl /skurl/ *Scotland n* the high-pitched wailing sound that bagpipes typically make ■ *vti* (**skirls, skirling, skirled**) to produce a high-pitched wailing sound on the bagpipes [14C. Probably < N Germanic]

skirmish /skúrmish/ *n* **1.** BRIEF FIGHT BETWEEN TWO ARMED GROUPS an incident where fighting breaks out briefly between two small groups, sometimes as part of a larger battle **2.** SCUFFLE a brief fight or disagreement between people ■ *vi* (**-mishes, -mishing, -mished**) ENGAGE IN MINOR BATTLE to become involved in a skirmish [14C. < Old French *eskermiss-* 'to fence' < Germanic, 'defend'] —**skirmisher** *n*

SYNONYMS See ***fight***.

skirr /skur/ *vti* (**skirrs, skirring, skirred**) to rush along, or rush through an area ■ *n* a whirring sound [Mid-16C. Origin ?]

skirret /skírrət/ *n* a plant with sweetish edible roots resembling carrots. Native to: East Asia. Latin name: *Sium sisarum.* [14C. Origin ?]

skirt /skurt/ *n* **1.** GARMENT THAT HANGS FROM WAIST a piece of clothing that hangs from the waist and does not divide into two separate legs, usually worn by women and girls **2.** AREA OF GARMENT FALLING FROM WAISTLINE the section from the waist to the hem on a dress, coat, or robe **3.** SOMETHING SIMILAR TO SKIRT an attachment shaped like a skirt, or covering the lower part of something like a skirt **4.** OFFENSIVE TERM an offensive term for a girl or woman, or women in general (*slang*) **5.** FOOD CUT OF BEEF a stewing cut of beef taken from the flank, below the sirloin and rump, and cut from the inside of flank steak **6.** ENG FLAP AROUND BOTTOM OF HOVERCRAFT the lower outer section of a rocket or the flap around the bottom of a hovercraft **7.** RIDING FLAP ON SADDLE one of a pair of leather flaps that hang from a saddle ■ *v* (**skirts, skirting, skirted**) **1.** *vti* BE AROUND OUTSIDE OF SOMETHING to form a border along the edge of an area or object **2.** *vti* MOVE AROUND OUTSIDE OF SOMETHING to travel along the edge of something such as an area, structure, or geographical feature **3.** *vt* NOT DEAL WITH SOMETHING to avoid dealing with a subject in any depth, usually because it is tricky or unpleasant **4.** *vt* GIVE EDGE TO SOMETHING to provide something with an attachment shaped like a skirt or border [13C. < Old Norse *skyrta* 'shirt' < Germanic, 'cut'] —**skirter** *n*

skirt-chaser *n* an offensive term for a man who is regarded as being excessively interested in pursuing women sexually (*slang*) —**skirt-chasing** *n*

skirting /skúrting/ *n* **1.** CONSTR same as **skirting board** **2.** material used to make skirts ■ **skirtings** *npl ANZ* inferior pieces trimmed off a shorn fleece

skirting board *n* a narrow board, attached to the base of an interior wall, that covers the joint between the wall and the floor. N Am term **baseboard**

ski run *n* a snow-covered slope or course used for skiing

ski stick *n* SKIING same as **ski pole**

skit /skit/ *n* **1.** a short comic sketch **2.** a short piece of comic writing that satirizes somebody or something [Early 18C. Origin ?]

skite[1] /skīt/ *Scotland v* (**skites, skiting, skited**) **1.** *vi* SLIP to slip on a slippery surface **2.** *vti* HIT SOMETHING SHARPLY to hit something or somebody else with a sharp blow, or hit something and bounce sharply from it ■ *n* **1.** ACT OF SKIDDING OR SLIPPING an instance of sliding suddenly across a slippery surface **2.** SHARP KNOCK OR SLAP a sudden forceful glancing blow [Early 18C. Origin ?]

skite[2] /skīt/ *Aus vi* (**skites, skiting, skited**) BOAST to talk with excessive pride about personal abilities or achievements (*informal*) ■ *n* **1.** BOASTING TALK talk that exaggerates somebody's personal abilities or achievements **2.** BOASTER an arrogant or boastful person [Mid-19C. Origin ?]

ski touring *n* travelling over long distances on skis, especially in wilderness areas

ski tow *n* an apparatus consisting of a motor-driven rope that skiers hang onto to be towed up a mountain

skitter /skíttər/ *v* (**-ters, -tering, -tered**) **1.** *vi* RUN WITH TINY STEPS to move about or run off quickly with small scampering steps **2.** *vti* SKID LIGHTLY ACROSS SOMETHING to pass quickly across something, touching its surface very lightly and briefly, or send something skidding rapidly over the surface of something ■ *n Ireland* UNRELIABLE PERSON somebody regarded as unreliable (*slang insult*) ■ **skitters** *npl Ireland, Scotland* DIARRHOEA an attack of diarrhoea (*slang*) [Mid-19C. Origin ?]

skittish /skíttish/ *adj* **1.** SILLY AND IRRESPONSIBLE with moods or ideas that constantly change, in a frivolous and unreliable way **2.** NERVOUS easily agitated or alarmed **3.** LIVELY tending to dash about in an energetic or restless way [14C. Origin ?] —**skittishly** *adv* —**skittishness** *n*

skittle /skítt'l/ *n* one of the set of wooden or plastic bottle-shaped pins that are stood upright in a group for players to aim at in the game of skittles. N Am term **ninepin** [Mid-17C. Origin ?]

skittle out *vt* to put a batting side out quickly in cricket

skittles /skítt'lz/ *n* a game played on an alley in which players bowl a wooden ball at a set of nine bottle-shaped pins (*takes a singular verb*) N Am term **ninepins**

skive[1] /skīv/ (*informal*) *vti* (**skives, skiving, skived**) to avoid doing work, studies, or duties ■ *n* time spent avoiding work, studies, or duties, or something that somebody uses to disguise doing this [Early 20C. Origin ?]

skive[2] /skīv/ (**skives, skiving, skived**) *vt* to scrape thin slices off leather in preparing it [Early 19C. < N Germanic]

skiver[1] /skívər/ *n* somebody who avoids work (*informal*) [Mid-20C. < SKIVE[1]]

skiver[2] /skívər/ *n* **1.** a thin soft tanned leather taken from the outer side of a skin **2.** somebody or something that skives leather [Early 19C. < SKIVE[2]]

skivvy /skívvi/ *n* (*plural* **-vies**) **1.** SERVANT a domestic servant, usually a woman, who performs menial tasks (*informal insult*) **2.** *US* MAN'S UNDERSHIRT a man's short-sleeved undershirt (*slang*) **3.** *ANZ, US* LONG-SLEEVED COTTON TOP a long-sleeved, usually cotton piece of clothing with a rolled neck worn on the upper part of the body ■ **skivvies** *npl US* MEN'S UNDERWEAR men's underwear consisting of an undershirt and shorts (*slang*) ■ *vi* (**-vies, -vying, -vied**) PERFORM MENIAL WORK to perform menial tasks for somebody else (*informal*) [Mid-20C. Origin ?]

skiwear /skée wayr/ *n* clothing designed for skiers to wear

skoal *interj* another spelling of **skol**

Skobelev /skóbbə lef/ former name for **Fergana** (1907–24)

skol /skōl/, **skoal** *interj* used as a drinking toast [Early 17C. Via Danish, Swedish, and Norwegian < Old Norse *skál* 'bowl']

skollie /skólli/, **skolly** (*plural* **-lies**) *n S Africa* an offensive term for a young man, usually Black or of mixed race, who is involved in petty crime and violence and often belongs to a gang (*slang*) [Mid-20C. < Afrikaans, probably < Dutch *schoelje* 'scoundrel']

Skomer /skómər/ islet in St Bride's Bay, off the Pembrokeshire coast, Wales

Skopje /skóp yi/ capital of the Former Yugoslav Republic of Macedonia, situated in the north-central part of the country. Population: 440,577 (1994).

Skr., **Skt** *abbr* LANG Sanskrit

SKU /éss kay yoó, skyoó/, **Sku** *n* a unique code, consisting of numbers or letters and numbers, assigned to a product by a retailer for identification and stock control. Full form **stockkeeping unit**

skua /skyoó ə/ *n* a large brown predatory seabird with slender wings that chases other birds to make them drop their prey. Genera: *Catharacta* or *Stercorarius*. N Am term **jaeger** [Late 17C. Via modern Latin < variant of Faeroese *skugvur* < Old Norse *skufr*]

skulduggery /skul dúggəri/, **skullduggery** *n* unfair and dishonest practices carried out in a secretive way in order to trick other people (*humorous*) [Mid-19C. Alteration of *sculduddery* 'sexual impropriety, indecency', origin ?]

skulk /skulk/ *vi* (**skulks**, **skulking**, **skulked**) 1. MOVE FURTIVELY to move about in a furtive way 2. HIDE SOMEWHERE to hide, especially in order to do something sinister 3. SHIRK to avoid work or responsibilities ■ *n* 1. SOMEBODY WHO SKULKS a furtive person, or somebody who conceals a sinister purpose 2. GROUP OF FOXES a pack of foxes [12C. < N Germanic]

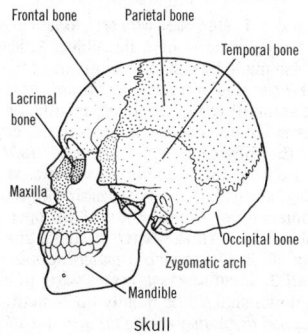

Frontal bone · Parietal bone · Temporal bone · Lacrimal bone · Maxilla · Occipital bone · Zygomatic arch · Mandible

skull

skull /skul/ *n* 1. the skeletal part of the head in humans and other vertebrates, consisting of the cranium, which encases the brain, and the bones of the face and jaws 2. a person's head or mind (*informal*) ○ *tried to din the principles of thermodynamics into his skull* [13C. Probably < N Germanic] —**-skulled** *suffix*

skull and crossbones *n* 1. a representation of a human skull above two human thighbones crossed over each other, used as a symbol of danger or death 2. same as **Jolly Roger**

skullcap /skúl kap/ *n* 1. SMALL ROUND BRIMLESS HAT a simple hat consisting of a small circle of fabric shaped to fit over the crown of the head 2. TOP OF SKULL the top part of the skull 3. PERENNIAL MINT PLANT a perennial plant of the mint family. Flowers: blue or pinkish, with helmet-shaped calyx. Genus: *Scutellaria*.

skullduggery *n* another spelling of **skulduggery** (*humorous*)

skunk /skungk/ *n* (*plural* same or **skunks**) 1. BLACK-AND-WHITE MAMMAL a black-and-white animal of the weasel family that ejects a foul-smelling liquid from an anal gland as a defensive action. Native to: North, South America. 2. OFFENSIVE TERM an offensive term for a person considered to be despicable (*slang insult*) 3. DRUGS same as **skunkweed** (sense 1) (*slang*) ■ *vt* (**skunks**, **skunking**, **skunked**) *N Am* DEFEAT SOMEBODY SOUNDLY to defeat an opponent soundly, especially by not allowing him or her to score any points in a sporting competition (*slang*) [Mid-17C. < Massachuset]

skunk

skunk cabbage *n* 1. a foul-smelling broad-leaved perennial herb with small flowers enclosed in greenish spathes. Native to: swampy areas of eastern North America. Latin name: *Symplocarpus foetidus*. 2. a plant similar to skunk cabbage that has a large yellow spathe. Native to: western North America. Latin name: *Lysichitum americanum*.

skunkweed /skúng weed/ (*plural* **-weeds** or same) *n* 1. marijuana with a pungent smell (*slang*) 2. PLANTS same as **skunk cabbage**

skunkworks /skúngk wurks/ *n US* a department or laboratory, especially one involved in secret cutting-edge research and development (*informal*; *usually takes a singular verb*) [Mid-20C. < *Skonk Works*, place in the comic strip *L'il Abner* by Al Capp]

skutchy-bell /skúchi bel/ *n regional* same as **earwig** [Probably < *scutch* 'two-pronged pick' < variant of SCOTCH¹, because the pincers of the insect resemble the prongs]

REGIONAL NOTE See **earwig**.

sky /skī/ *n* (*plural* **skies**) 1. REGION ABOVE EARTH the area high above the trees, buildings, landscape, or horizon. The sky is made up of the various layers of the Earth's atmosphere and the part of space beyond it, as seen from one place on the Earth's surface. 2. WAY SKY APPEARS the way the sky looks (*often used in the plural*) ○ *clear blue skies* 3. *also* **Sky** HEAVEN the plane, thought of as being high above the Earth, in which immortal powers or beings such as God exist (*literary*; *often used in the plural*) 4. HIGHEST LIMIT the topmost limit or the best and most it is possible to achieve ○ *reach for the sky* ■ *vti* (**skies**, **skying**, **skied**) MAKE BALL GO VERY HIGH to kick, hit, or throw a ball high up into the air [13C. < Old Norse *ský* 'cloud'] ◇ **praise somebody** or **something to the skies** to praise somebody or something very highly ◇ **the sky's the limit** there is no upper limit on something (*informal*)

sky blue *n* a pale blue colour like that of the sky on a clear day —**sky blue** *adj*

skycap /skī kap/ *n US* a porter who works at an airport [Mid-20C. After REDCAP]

skydive /skī dīv/ (**-dives**, **-diving**, **-dived**) *vi* to jump from an aeroplane and descend in free fall, sometimes performing acrobatic manoeuvres, before pulling the ripcord of a parachute —**skydiver** *n* —**skydiving** *n*

Skye /skī/ largest island in the Inner Hebrides, in Scotland. Portree is the chief town and port. Population: 8,843 (1991). Area: 1,676 sq. km/647 sq. mi.

Skye terrier *n* a small terrier with short legs, a long body, and a long straight coat, belonging to a breed originating in Scotland

sky-high *adv*, *adj* up to or at the highest level ■ *adv* high into the air or in all directions, forcefully and often in pieces

sky-hook *n* 1. an imaginary hook conceived as hanging from the sky 2. a helicopter that is specially configured with a hook-and-cable apparatus in its fuselage, used to lift, drop, and transport heavy objects

skyjack /skī jak/ (**-jacks**, **-jacking**, **-jacked**) *vt* to use force to take over control of an aircraft, especially a commercial aircraft, when it is in the air [Mid-20C. After HIJACK] —**skyjacker** *n* —**skyjacking** *n*

skylark /skī laark/ *n* a lark with streaked brown-and-white feathers that is noted for singing melodiously while hovering high in the air. Native to: Europe, Asia. Latin name: *Alauda arvensis*. ■ *vi* (**-larks**, **-larking**, **-larked**) to take part in lively physical playful behaviour (*dated informal*) —**skylarker** *n*

skylight /skī līt/ *n* an opening in a roof or ceiling that is fitted with glass to let in daylight

skylight filter *n* a photographic filter that is slightly pink and is used to filter out ultraviolet light and reduce blueness

skyline /skī līn/ *n* 1. the pattern of shapes made by the various features of a landscape, e.g. hills or buildings, against the sky 2. the place where the ground appears to join the sky

sky marshal *n US* an armed guard providing in-flight security on commercial passenger aircraft

sky pilot *n* an offensive term for a priest or chaplain, associated especially with the armed forces (*slang*)

skyrocket /skī rokit/ *n* INDUST same as **rocket**¹ *n* (sense 1) ■ *vti* (**-ets**, **-eting**, **-eted**) to rise suddenly to a very high level or value, or make something do this (*informal*)

Skyros /skeé ross/ largest and most easterly of the Greek Sporades Islands, in the Aegean Sea. Population: 2,757 (1981). Area: 205 sq. km/79 sq. mi.

skysail /skī sayl/ *n* a small light square sail that goes above the royal on a square-rigged sailing vessel

skyscape /skī skayp/ *n* a scene or picture showing chiefly sky, especially an artistic study of a section of sky

skyscraper /skī skraypər/ *n* a modern building that is extremely tall

skysurfing /skī surfing/ *n* the sport of jumping from an aeroplane and performing a series of moves before descending by parachute —**skysurf** *vi* —**skysurfer** *n*

skywalk /skī wawk/ *n N Am* a raised walkway, usually joining two buildings

skyward /skī wərd/ *adj* heading towards the sky ■ *adv* same as **skywards**

skywards /skī wərdz/ *adv* in the direction of the sky

sky wave *n* a radio wave that is transmitted around the curved surface of the Earth by being reflected back to Earth by the ionosphere

skyway /skī way/ *n* 1. a route used by aircraft 2. *N Am* an elevated highway, supported by tall spans ○ *the Chicago Skyway*

skywriting /skī rīting/ *n* 1. the use of an aircraft releasing coloured smoke to form letters in the sky 2. letters or a message formed in the sky by coloured smoke released from an aircraft —**skywrite** *vti* —**skywriter** *n*

sl *abbr* Sierra Leone (*used in Internet addresses*) See table at **domain name**

SL *abbr* 1. INSUR salvage loss 2. GEOG sea level 3. Solicitor-at-Law 4. LING source language 5. GEOG south latitude

slab /slab/ *n* 1. THICK PIECE a thick flat broad piece of something, especially when cut or trimmed 2. STONE BASE FOR SOMETHING a flat rectangular base or foundation of concrete or stone 3. MORTUARY TABLE a table on which a body is laid in a mortuary (*informal*) 4. GEOL SHEET OF ROCK a smooth flat sheet of rock sharply angled to the horizontal 5. OFFCUT FROM LOG any large outer section of a log that is sawn off before it is made into planks 6. *Aus* PACK OF BEER a pack or box of 24 cans or bottles of beer (*informal*) ■ *adj* ANZ MADE OF ROUGH BOARDS made of coarse wooden planks ■ *vt* (**slabs**, **slabbing**, **slabbed**) 1. COVER AREA WITH SLABS to cover something by laying stone or concrete slabs on it 2. MAKE SOMETHING INTO SLABS to cut or saw something into slabs 3. TRIM SOMETHING BY SAWING to saw off the rough outer parts of a log [13C. Origin ?]

slabber /slábbər/ *regional vi* (**-bers**, **-bering**, **-bered**) to dribble saliva from the mouth ■ *n* saliva dribbled from the mouth [Mid-16C. Probably related to dialect *slab* 'muddy place, puddle' < N Germanic]

slabbing /slábbing/ *n* 1. the laying of stone or concrete slabs to form a surface such as a pathway 2. stone or concrete slabs, collectively

slab pottery *n* pottery made by hand using rolled-out sheets of clay

slack /slak/ *adj* **1. NOT TIGHT** not tight or stretched taut, but hanging loosely or having a good deal of give ○ *The reins are too slack.* **2. NOT SHOWING ENOUGH CARE** not showing enough care, attention, or rigour ○ *They've been rather slack about keeping to performance targets.* **3. NOT BUSY** not busy or active, or less busy than usual ○ *the slack period following the main tourist season* **4. MOVING SLOWLY** moving slowly or sluggishly **5.** PHON same as **lax** (sense 4) ■ *adv* **LOOSELY** in a loose or limp way ○ *His clothes hung slack on him.* ■ *n* **1. LOOSENESS** looseness or give in something such as a rope, or the extra length or fullness in it that needs to be taken in to make it taut **2. UNUSED POTENTIAL** productive potential in an organization or system that is not being fully made use of ○ *take in some of the slack in the administrative division* **3. QUIET TIME** a period of time that is not busy **4. STILL WATER** a stretch of water that is still or moving only slowly ■ **slacks** *npl* **TROUSERS** casual trousers, especially loose-fitting ones ■ *v* (**slacks, slacking, slacked**) **1.** *vi* **AVOID WORK** to be lazy, avoid work, or work with insufficient vigour or concentration **2.** *vt* **NEGLECT SOMETHING** to neglect something such as duty, or leave something undone **3.** *vti* same as **slacken** (sense 1) **4.** *vti* CHEM same as **slake** (sense 2) [Old English *slæc* < Indo-European, 'be loose'] —**slackly** *adv* —**slackness** *n*

slackarse *n* /slák aarss/ *Aus* a highly offensive term that deliberately insults somebody's willingness to work or make an effort (*slang taboo*)

slacken /slákən/ (**-ens, -ening, -ened**) *vti* **1.** to become less intense, vigorous, or fast, or make something become less intense, vigorous, or fast **2.** to become looser or more relaxed, or make something become looser or more relaxed

slacker /slákər/ *n* **1.** somebody who avoids doing something, especially work or military service **2.** an offensive term for a young educated person who is regarded as being disaffected or apathetic and underachieving (*slang*)

slack water *n* the period of time during which the tide is turning and the water is still or slow-moving because of this

SLADE /slayd/ *abbr* Society of Lithographic Artists, Designers, Engravers, and Process Workers

slag /slag/ *n* **1. WASTE MATERIAL FROM SMELTING** fused glassy material that is produced when a metal is separated from its ore during smelting **2. COAL WASTE** the mixture of coal dust and mineral waste produced after coal has been mined **3.** GEOL same as **scoria** (sense 1) **4. OFFENSIVE TERM** an offensive term for a woman who is considered to be sexually promiscuous or generally coarse and sluttish (*slang*) **5. SOMEBODY DESPISED** any individual, especially a man, regarded as despicable (*slang insult*) ■ *v* (**slags, slagging, slagged**) **1.** *vti* **TURN SOMETHING INTO SLAG** to convert something into slag, or become slag **2.** *vt* **INSULT OR CRITICIZE** to make insulting, mocking, or critical comments about somebody or something (*slang*) ○ *Don't you dare slag off my team!* **3.** *vi Aus* **SPIT** to spit (*slang*) [Mid-16C. < Middle Low German *slagge* < Germanic, 'strike']

slagging /slágging/ *n* a series of insulting, mocking, or critical comments (*slang*) ○ *I took a right slagging over that haircut.*

slag heap *n* a large mound of waste material from a coal mine or factory

slain past participle of **slay**

slàinte /slaáanchə/, **slàinte mhath** /slaáanchə vaá/ *interj Scotland* used as a drinking toast to wish somebody good health [Early 19C. < Gaelic *slàinte (mhath)* '(good) health']

slake /slayk/ (**slakes, slaking, slaked**) *v* **1.** *vt* to satisfy a desire for something, especially a drink **2.** *vti* to treat lime with water to produce calcium hydroxide, or undergo this process [Old English *slacian* 'relax' < Germanic] —**slakable** *adj*

slaked lime /slaykt-/ *n* CHEM same as **calcium hydroxide**

slalom /slaáləm/ *n* **1. ZIGZAG SKI RACE** a downhill ski race in which competitors follow a winding course and zigzag through flags on poles or other obstacles **2. ZIGZAG RACE** any race that involves following a zigzag course through obstacles ■ *vi* (**-loms, -loming, -lomed**) **FOLLOW ZIGZAG COURSE** to follow a zigzag or winding course, especially in a race [Early 20C. < Norwegian *slalåm* 'sloping track']

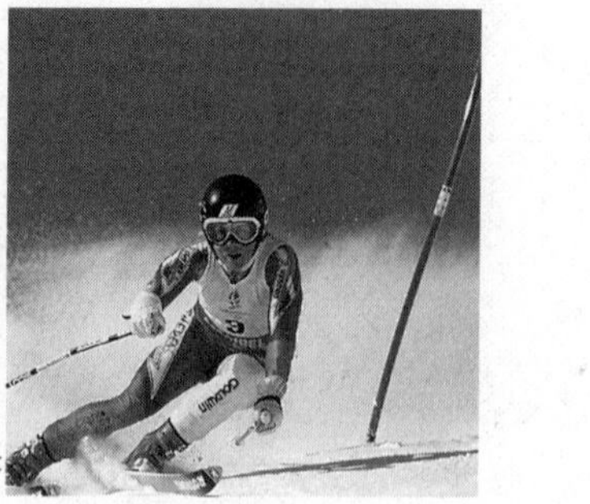

Popperfoto

slalom

slam[1] /slam/ *v* (**slams, slamming, slammed**) **1.** *vti* **CLOSE FORCEFULLY** to close something forcefully and noisily, or be closed in this way **2.** *vti* **PUT SOMETHING DOWN VIOLENTLY** to put something down violently and noisily, or be put down in this way **3.** *vti* **HIT SOMETHING VIOLENTLY** to hit something with sudden or violent force ○ *The waves slammed into the dock.* **4.** *vt* **CRITICIZE SOMEBODY OR SOMETHING** to criticize somebody or something forcefully (*informal*) ○ *The press slammed the government's performance.* **5.** *vt US* TELECOM **CHANGE SOMEBODY'S PHONE SERVICE** to change the telephone service provider of a customer without his or her consent or authorization (*informal*) ■ *n* **1. IMPACT** a heavy, noisy, or violent blow or impact **2. CRITICISM** a forceful piece of criticism or critical remark [Late 17C. Origin ?]

slam[2] /slam/ *n* **1.** the winning of all, or all but one, of the tricks in a hand of bridge or whist **2.** LITERAT same as **poetry slam** [Mid-17C. Origin ?]

slam-bang *N Am* (*informal*) *adv* **1.** same as **slap-bang** (sense 2) **2. CARELESSLY** in a careless and reckless way **3. EXCITINGLY** in an exciting and vigorous way ○ *The novel ended slam-bang with a fight to the finish.* ■ *adj* **1. SUDDEN AND NOISY** sudden, noisy, or violent ○ *a slam-bang fight* **2. CARELESS AND RECKLESS** careless and reckless ○ *a slam-bang approach to his work* **3. EXCITING** exciting and vigorous ○ *slam-bang action scenes*

slam dancing *n* boisterous dancing to rock music in which young people hurl their bodies against one another, more out of enthusiasm than aggression —**slam dance** *vi*

slam dunk *n* **1.** in basketball, a shot in which a player jumps up and jams or slams the ball forcefully down into the basket **2.** *N Am* something dramatically successful and effective (*informal*)

slam-dunk *vt* **1. SLAM BALL INTO BASKET** in basketball, to jam or slam the ball through the hoop from above with great force **2.** *US* **TREAT SOMEBODY HARSHLY** to speak of or treat somebody in a dramatic, hostile, or disrespectful way (*slang*) **3.** *US* **DEFEAT SOMEBODY COMPLETELY** to defeat a person or a group of people completely (*slang*) ■ *adj US* **CERTAIN OF SUCCESS** without risk and sure to be successful ○ *a slam-dunk scenario*

slammer /slámmər/ *n* CRIME same as **prison** *n* (sense 1) (*slang*) [Mid-20C. < the idea of the doors slamming shut]

s.l.a.n. *abbr* PUBL without place, year, or name [Latin *sine loco, anno, vel nomine*]

slander /slaándər/ *n* **1. SAYING OF SOMETHING FALSE AND DAMAGING** the act or offence of saying something false or malicious that damages somebody's reputation **2. FALSE AND DAMAGING STATEMENT** a false and malicious statement that damages somebody's reputation ■ *vt* (**-ders, -dering, -dered**) **UTTER SLANDER AGAINST SOMEBODY** to make a false and malicious oral statement about somebody [13C. Via Old French *esclandre* < ecclesiastical Latin *scandalum* 'cause of offence' (see SCANDAL)] —**slanderer** *n* —**slanderous** *adj* —**slanderously** *adv* —**slanderousness** *n*

SYNONYMS See *malign.*

slang /slang/ *n* **1. VERY CASUAL SPEECH OR WRITING** words, expressions, and usages that are casual, vivid, racy, or playful replacements for standard ones, are often short-lived, and are usually considered unsuitable for formal contexts **2. LANGUAGE OF EXCLUSIVE GROUP** a form of language used by a particular group of people, often deliberately created and used to exclude people outside the group ○ *a word that came from surfers' slang* ■ *adj* **IN SLANG** belonging to, expressed in, or containing slang ○ *a slang dictionary* ■ *vt* (**slangs, slanging, slanged**) **ATTACK VERBALLY** to use abusive language, usually slang, to attack somebody verbally ○ *We'll get nowhere just slanging each other.* [Mid-18C. Origin ?] —**slangily** *adv* —**slanginess** *n* —**slangy** *adj*

SYNONYMS See *jargon*[1].

slanging match /slánging-/ *n UK, Can* a dispute in which people insult and accuse each other ○ *Political debate had deteriorated into a series of slanging matches.*

slant /slaant/ *v* (**slants, slanting, slanted**) **1.** *vti* **BE OR SET SOMETHING AT ANGLE** to be at an angle, or set something at an angle **2.** *vt* **CAUSE SOMETHING TO HAVE PARTICULAR APPEAL** to make something appeal to a particular group of people ○ *a magazine slanted towards the youth market* **3.** *vt* **PRESENT INFORMATION WITH BIAS** to present something in a way that is biased towards a particular person, group, or viewpoint ○ *The news report was slanted in favour of the nationalists.* ■ *n* **1. ANGLED POSITION** an angled position or a direction that is at an angle to something else ○ *the roof was built on a slant* **2. BIASED PERSPECTIVE** a particular bias, or a perspective on something that is likely to appeal to a particular group ○ *The news was given a pro-government slant.* **3. POINT OF VIEW** a point of view or way of looking at something ○ *Her diaries give us a new slant on the events of the time.* ■ *adj* **SLOPING** sloping, or at an angle (*informal*) [15C. Variant of dialect *slent* < N Germanic] —**slanted** *adj* —**slanting** *adj* —**slantingly** *adv*

slantways /slaánt wayz/, **slantwise** /-wīz/ *adv* at an angle to something else

slanty /slánti/ *adj* sloping, or at an angle (*informal*)

slap /slap/ *n* **1. BLOW MADE WITH OPEN HAND** a blow made with the open hand or a flat object **2. NOISE OF SLAP** the noise made by a slap, or something that sounds like it ○ *the slap of a wave on the side of the boat* **3. REBUKE** something that rebukes, insults, or hurts **4. MAKE-UP** make-up, whether for personal everyday use or for the theatre (*slang*) ○ *She said she'd just put some slap on and meet us downstairs.* ■ *v* (**slaps, slapping, slapped**) **1.** *vt* **HIT SOMEBODY WITH OPEN HAND** to hit somebody or something with an open hand or flat object **2.** *vi* **STRIKE SHARPLY** to strike sharply and noisily, as if with a slap ○ *water slapping against the hull* **3.** *vt* **PUT SOMETHING DOWN SHARPLY** to put something down sharply or noisily on something else ○ *He slapped the money on the table and walked away.* **4.** *vt* **APPLY SOMETHING CARELESSLY** to put something on, make something, or do something, quickly and carelessly ○ *I slapped on some makeup and ran for the car.* ○ *Just slap it in the oven for an hour.* **5.** *vt* **APPLY SOMETHING AS PENALTY** to apply something as a punishment, penalty, or restriction to somebody or something (*informal*) ○ *The government slapped an embargo on the story.* ○ *They slapped me with a fine.* ■ *adv* (*informal*) **1. FORCEFULLY** forcefully, and often with the sound or effect of a slap ○ *landed slap on the floor* **2. EXACTLY** exactly, and usually with suddenness and force ○ *slap in the middle of the target* [Mid-17C. An imitation of the sound] ◇ **a slap in the face** a rebuke or rebuff (*informal*) ◇ **a slap on the back** congratulations (*informal*) ◇ **a slap on the wrist** a mild rebuke or punishment (*informal*) ◇ **slap and tickle** playful sexual behaviour (*informal*)

slap down *vt* (*informal*) **1.** to rebuke somebody sharply or cruelly **2.** to suppress or check something thought to be unacceptable ○ *Any disrespect is slapped down immediately.*

slap-bang *adv* (*informal*) **1.** exactly or directly, and usually with suddenness and force ○ *The ball landed slap-bang in the middle of the pond.* N Am term **smack-dab** **2.** in a sudden, noisy, or violent way. N Am term **slam-bang**

slapdash /sláp dash/ *adj* careless, hasty, and unskilful ■ *adv* in a careless, hasty, and unskilful way ■ *n* CONSTR same as **roughcast** *n* (sense 1)

slaphappy /sláp hapi/ *adj* (*informal*) **1.** irresponsible or careless in a cheerful way **2.** dazed or disorientated,

like a boxer who has been hit on the head too many times

slaphead /sláp hed/ *n* an offensive term for a bald person, especially a man who has gone bald naturally rather than a man who has shaved his head by fashion choice (*slang insult*)

slapper /sláppər/ *n* an offensive term for a woman who is considered sexually promiscuous or vulgar (*slang*) [Late 18C. < SLAP in an obsolete dialectal sense]

slap shot *n* in ice hockey, a shot in which the player swings the stick with a fast powerful stroke [< the loud sound made when the stick hits the ice]

slapstick /sláp stik/ *n* comedy with the emphasis on fast physical action, farcical situations, and obvious jokes that do not depend on language (*often used before a noun*) ○ *slapstick comedy* [Early 20C. < *slapstick*, a device made of two flat linked pieces of wood, formerly used in comic performances to simulate the sound of a blow]

slap-up *adj* with lots of good food to eat and served in style (*informal*) ○ *First prize is a slap-up dinner at the restaurant of your choice.*

slash /slash/ *vt* (**slashes, slashing, slashed**) **1.** MAKE CUTS IN SOMETHING to make long deep cuts in something **2.** ATTACK SOMEBODY WITH SHARP OBJECT to cut or attack somebody with the sharp sweeping strokes of a sword, knife, stick, or whip **3.** REDUCE OR CUT SOMETHING SHORT to reduce or shorten something greatly ○ *All prices slashed!* **4.** CLOTHING SLIT FABRIC to make a slit in fabric or a garment to reveal the lining **5.** FORESTRY CLEAR GROWTH BY CUTTING to cut bushes and undergrowth from a wooded area ■ *n* **1.** SHARP SWEEPING STROKE a sharp sweeping stroke of a sword, knife, stick, or whip **2.** LONG AND DEEP CUT a long deep cut or wound **3.** CLOTHING SLIT IN FABRIC a slit in fabric or a garment, made to reveal the lining **4.** PRINTING PRINT CHARACTER a punctuation mark (/) that is used to separate optional items in a list or to express fractions or division, and that has various uses in computer programming. Technical name **solidus** (sense 1) **5.** URINATION an act of urination, usually by a male (*slang*) ○ *Hang on a minute while I go for a quick slash.* **6.** *N Am* FORESTRY DEBRIS FROM CUT TREES the debris left after trees have been cut down **7.** *US* SWAMPY GROUND swampy ground covered with bushes and small trees (*often used in the plural*) [Late 16C. Probably < French *esclachier* 'break'] —**slasher** *n*

USAGE A *slash* is used between optional or alternative elements: *He refused to work with children and/or animals. Please place unwanted clothes/toys/books in the box.* It may also mean 'to' or 'between': *the academic year 2001/2002; the parent/child relationship.* Slashes are used to separate numbers in fractions: *33/140 of the total weight*; dates: *your invoice of 9/12/04*; to stand for 'per': *at the rate of 2 mm/sec*; and in some abbreviations, e.g. *c/o* meaning 'care of'. They are also used to indicate line breaks when quoting poetry, when they are usually followed (and sometimes preceded) by a space: *The weight of the world/ is love* (Allen Ginsberg). In computing the slash (/) is called a *forward slash* to distinguish it from the *backslash* (\\), which is used for specific purposes, e.g. to show the location of a computer file or document: *c:\letters\surfclub.doc.* Internet locations usually have forward slashes.

slash-and-burn *adj* **1.** describes a form of agriculture characterized by the cutting down and burning of trees and vegetation in order to plant crops **2.** having or showing the intention to deal with somebody or something drastically and ruthlessly or to destroy somebody or something completely (*informal*) ○ *her slash-and-burn approach to budget cuts*

slasher movie *n* a horror film featuring gory effects such as people being slashed with blades (*slang*)

slashing /sláshing/ *adj* **1.** CRITICAL aggressively critical **2.** REDUCING severely reducing or shortening something ○ *make slashing cuts to the budget* ■ *n* **1.** SPORTS ILLEGAL ACT IN HOCKEY AND LACROSSE the illegal striking or swinging of a stick at an opposing player in hockey or lacrosse **2.** CUTTING ATTACK an act of attacking and cutting somebody with a blade —**slashingly** *adv*

slash neck *n* a wide shallow neckline in a jumper, blouse, or dress

slash pine *n* **1.** a pine of swampy regions that yields turpentine, pulp, and timber. Native to: southeastern United States. Latin name: *Pinus caribaea*. **2.** the hard durable wood of the slash pine [< *slash* 'swamp'. Origin ?]

slash pocket *n* a pocket in a garment fitted with a diagonal slit for easy access

slat /slat/ *n* **1.** THIN STRIP a light thin narrow strip of wood or metal **2.** AEROFOIL ON AIRCRAFT WING an auxiliary aerofoil fixed to the leading edge of a wing to give extra lift ■ *vt* (**slats, slatting, slatted**) ADD SLATS TO SOMETHING to put slats in something [Mid-18C. < Old French *esclat* 'splinter, piece broken off']

slate /slayt/ *n* **1.** LAYERED ROCK a fine-grained metamorphic rock that splits easily into layers and is widely used as a roofing material **2.** ROOFING TILE a roofing tile made of slate **3.** WRITING TABLET a small square piece of slate formerly used for writing on, especially by school students. It could be wiped clean and reused indefinitely. **4.** IDENTIFYING BOARD ON FILM SET a board used on a film set to give information identifying something such as the number of the scene being shot **5.** DARK GREY a dark grey colour **6.** *N Am* POL LIST OF CANDIDATES a list of the candidates in an election ■ *vt* (**slates, slating, slated**) **1.** TILE ROOF WITH SLATE to cover a roof with tiles made of slate **2.** SUBJECT SOMEBODY TO HARSH CRITICISM to criticize somebody or something severely (*informal*) ○ *His last play was slated by the critics.* **3.** *N Am* POL INCLUDE SOMEBODY IN LIST OF CANDIDATES to put somebody's name on a list of candidates for election **4.** *N Am* DESIGNATE SOMEBODY to choose or schedule somebody or something for a particular job or time ○ *You've been slated to be our next director.* ○ *The satellite is slated for launch in December.* [14C. < Old French *esclate*, feminine of *esclat* 'splinter, piece broken off'] —**slate** *adj* —**slaty** *adj* ◇ **a clean slate** an imaginary record of somebody's past, with no transgressions recorded on it or with all previous transgressions forgotten (*informal*) ◇ **have a slate loose** *Scotland* an offensive phrase meaning to be irrational or very odd ◇ **on the slate** on credit (*informal*) ◇ **wipe the slate clean** to forget about what has happened and make a fresh start (*informal*)

slate grey *adj* of a light grey colour —**slate grey** *n*

slater /sláytər/ *n* **1.** somebody whose job is to lay roofing tiles made of slate **2.** *Scotland, ANZ, US* ZOOL same as **woodlouse**

slather /sláthər/ *vt* (**-ers, -ering, -ered**) *N Am* **1.** SPREAD SOMETHING THICKLY to spread something thickly or excessively on something else ○ *slather jelly on toast* **2.** SQUANDER SOMETHING to use something wastefully (*informal*) ■ *slathers* *npl US* LARGE AMOUNT a large or generous quantity (*informal*) [Mid-19C. Origin ?]

slating /sláyting/ *n* **1.** the process of covering something with slates, or slates collectively as a covering material **2.** harsh criticism, or a severe reprimand (*informal*)

slattern /sláttərn/ *n* (*dated*) **1.** an offensive term that deliberately insults a woman's standards of hygiene and grooming **2.** an offensive term that deliberately insults a woman for the number of her supposed sexual partners [Mid-17C. Origin ?] —**slatternliness** *n* —**slatternly** *adj*

slaughter /sláwtər/ *n* **1.** KILLING OF PEOPLE the brutal killing of a person or large numbers of people **2.** KILLING OF ANIMALS the killing of animals for their meat **3.** MAJOR DEFEAT an overwhelming defeat (*slang*) ■ *vt* (**-ters, -tering, -tered**) **1.** KILL PEOPLE BRUTALLY to kill a person or large numbers of people brutally **2.** KILL ANIMAL FOR MEAT to kill an animal or animals, usually for their meat **3.** DEFEAT SOMEBODY CONVINCINGLY to defeat a person or a group of people overwhelmingly (*slang*) [13C. < Old Norse *slátr* 'meat, butchery'] —**slaughterer** *n* —**slaughterous** *adj*

SYNONYMS See *kill*.

slaughterhouse /sláwtər howss/ (*plural* **-houses** /-howziz/) *n* FOOD INDUST same as **abattoir**

CULTURAL NOTE *Slaughterhouse-Five*, a novel (1970) by US writer Kurt Vonnegut. In this highly original blend of realism and science fiction, World War II veteran Billy Pilgrim is kidnapped by aliens who enable him to revisit his past. He subsequently relives the Allied firebombing of Dresden in 1945, an event witnessed by Vonnegut

himself and here presented as a symbol of the unending cruelty and suffering of humanity.

slaughterman /sláwtərmən/ (*plural* **-men** /-mən/) *n* a worker in a slaughterhouse

Slav /slaav/ *n* a member of any of the peoples of eastern Europe and northwestern Asia who speak a Slavonic language [14C. < medieval Latin *S(c)lavus*, same as *s(c)lavus* (see SLAVE); because the Slavs were reduced to an enslaved state in the 9C]

slave /slayv/ *n* **1.** SOMEBODY FORCED TO WORK FOR ANOTHER somebody who is forced to work for somebody else for no payment and is regarded as the property of that person **2.** DOMINATED PERSON somebody who is dominated by somebody or by something **3.** SOMEBODY ACCEPTING ANOTHER'S RULE somebody who meekly accepts being ruled by somebody else **4.** VERY HARD WORKER somebody who works hard, in bad conditions, and for low pay **5.** DEVICE CONTROLLED BY ANOTHER an electronic or mechanical device that is controlled by another (*often used before a noun*) ■ *vi* (**slaves, slaving, slaved**) WORK VERY HARD to work very hard ○ *I've been slaving away over this manuscript all day.* ■ *adj* **1.** USING SLAVES using or relating to enslaved workers **2.** HARSH very harsh and unfair ○ *slave conditions* [13C. Shortening of Old French *esclave* < medieval Latin *s(c)lavus* 'captive', *S(c)lavus* 'Slav' < Slavic]

slave ant *n* an ant captured and forced to work for an ant colony of another species

slave cylinder *n* a small, piston-bearing cylinder in a hydraulic system [Because its action is linked to a master cylinder]

slave-driver *n* **1.** somebody who makes employees work unduly hard **2.** formerly, somebody who was employed to make sure that enslaved people worked hard

slaveholder /sláyv hōldər/ *n* somebody who owns enslaved workers

slave labour *n* **1.** a workforce consisting of people who are forced to work against their will **2.** hard or demanding work, in poor conditions, that is not well paid (*informal*)

slave-making ant, **slave-maker ant** *n* an ant of a species that raids the colonies of other ant species, capturing larvae and pupae to be used in its own colony

slaver[1] /sláyvər/ *n* **1.** an owner of or dealer in enslaved workers **2.** HIST same as **slave ship** [Early 19C. < SLAVE]

slaver[2] /slávvər, sláyvər/ *vi* (**-ers, -ering, -ered**) **1.** DRIBBLE SALIVA to dribble saliva from the mouth **2.** BEHAVE OBSEQUIOUSLY to fawn or behave obsequiously to somebody **3.** LUST AFTER to desire or lust after something or somebody greatly ■ *n* DRIPPING SALIVA saliva that drips from somebody's mouth [14C. Probably < N Germanic]

slavery /sláyvəri/ *n* **1.** CONDITION OF BEING ENSLAVED LABOURER the state or condition of being held in involuntary servitude as the property of somebody else **2.** SYSTEM BASED ON ENSLAVED LABOUR the practice of, or a system based on, using the enforced labour of other people **3.** STATE OF BEING DOMINATED a state of being completely dominated by another **4.** HARD WORK very hard work, especially for low pay and under bad conditions

slave ship *n* a ship used to carry captured people, especially from Africa, to countries where they were bought as enslaved workers

Slave State *n* any of the 15 US states in which slavery was legal until the Civil War

slave trade *n* the business of capturing people and buying and selling them as enslaved workers

Slavic /sláavik/ *n* a branch of the Indo-European family of languages that includes Bulgarian, Russian, and Polish ■ *adj* relating to Slavic or the people who speak a language belonging to Slavic

slavish /sláyvish/ *adj* (*sometimes offensive*) **1.** showing total unquestioning obedience or devotion ○ *slavish loyalty to the cause* **2.** showing a complete lack of originality or independence of thought ○ *a slavish copy* —**slavishly** *adv* —**slavishness** *n*

Slavism /sláavizəm/ *n* a feature or characteristic of the Slavs or Slavic languages

slavocracy /slay vókrəssi/ *n* owners of slaves con-

sidered collectively as a ruling group, or rule by owners of slaves

Slavonic /slə vónnik/ *n, adj* LANG same as **Slavic** [Early 17C. < medieval Latin *S(c)lavonicus* < *S(c)lavonia* 'country of the Slavs' < *S(c)lavus* (see SLAVE)]

Slavophile /slaávō fīl/, **Slavophil** *n* (*often used before a noun*) **1.** an admirer of Slavic culture or people **2.** somebody who, in 19th-century Russia, advocated the supremacy of Slavic culture over European culture —**Slavophilism** /slaávōfilizəm/ *n*

slaw /slaw/ *n N Am* FOOD same as **coleslaw** [Late 18C. < Dutch *sla*, contraction of French *salade* (see SALAD)]

slay /slay/ (**slays, slaying, slew** /sloo/, **slain** /slayn/) *vt* **1.** to kill a person or animal (*formal or literary*) ○ *slew the beast with one stroke of his sword* **2.** (*past* **slayed,** *past participle* **slayed** or **slain**) to amuse somebody very much (*informal*) [Old English *slēan* < Germanic, 'strike'] —**slayer** *n*

SPELLCHECK Do not confuse the spelling of ***slay*** and ***sleigh***, which sound similar. ***Slay*** is a verb meaning 'kill'; ***sleigh*** is a noun denoting 'a horse-drawn vehicle used on snow and ice' ('a one-horse open sleigh'), or a verb meaning 'move in a sleigh'.

SYNONYMS See ***kill***.

slaying /sláy ing/ *n* a killing or murder

SLBM *abbr* ARMS submarine-launched ballistic missile

SLCM *abbr* ARMS sea-launched cruise missile

SLE *abbr* MED systemic lupus erythematosus

sleaze /sleez/ *n* **1.** corruption, dishonesty, or scandal, especially among public figures **2.** same as **sleazebag** (*slang insult*) [Mid-20C. Back-formation < SLEAZY]

sleazebag /sleéz bag/, **sleazeball** /sleéz bawl/ *n* an offensive term for somebody whose behaviour is perceived as immoral, unethical, or despicable (*slang insult*)

sleazy /sleézi/ (**-zier, -ziest**) *adj* **1.** dirty, disreputable, or sordid in character or appearance **2.** dishonest or immoral ○ *You get some pretty sleazy types in here.* [Mid-17C. Origin ?] —**sleazily** *adv* —**sleaziness** *n*

sled /sled/ *n, vti* VEHICLES same as **sledge**[1] [14C. < Middle Low German *sledde* < Germanic, 'slip, slide']

sledge[1] /slej/ *n* **1.** SMALL VEHICLE SLIDING OVER SNOW a small, low vehicle on ski-style or other runners, designed to be pulled over snow or ice by people or dogs **2.** CHILD'S TOY VEHICLE FOR SNOW a child's toy vehicle on runners, used for sliding down snowy hills ■ *vti* (**sledges, sledging, sledged**) MOVE USING SLEDGE to ride, travel, or transport something by sledge [Late 16C. < Dutch dialect *sleedse*] —**sledger** *n*

sledge[2] /slej/ *n* same as **sledgehammer** ■ *vt* (**sledges, sledging, sledged**) (*informal*) **1.** in cricket, to attempt to undermine an opposing batsman's confidence by verbal abuse **2.** *Aus* to subject somebody to verbal abuse or taunting [Old English *slecg* < Germanic, 'strike']

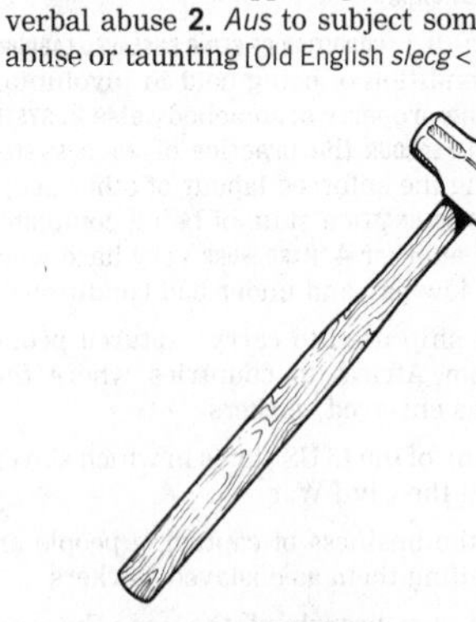

sledgehammer

sledgehammer /sléj hamər/ *n* LARGE HAMMER a large heavy hammer swung with both hands ■ *vt* (**-mers, -mering, -mered**) STRIKE SOMETHING WITH SLEDGEHAMMER to hit something with a sledgehammer or with the force of one ■ *adj* VERY FORCEFUL delivered with tremendous force and power ○ *sledgehammer blows*

sledging[1] /sléjjing/ *n* the activity, sport, or pastime of sliding over snow or ice on a sledge [Mid-19C. < SLEDGE[1]]

sledging[2] /sléjjing/ *n* (*informal*) **1.** in cricket, the attempt by a fielder or bowler to undermine a batsman's confidence by verbal abuse **2.** *Aus* the act of verbally abusing or taunting somebody [Late 20C. < SLEDGE[2]]

sleek /sleek/ *adj* **1.** SMOOTH AND SHINY attractively smooth and shiny **2.** WELL-GROOMED well-groomed and healthy looking **3.** SUAVE smooth and polished in behaviour or speech, often insincerely or suspiciously so ○ *a sleek sales pitch* ■ *vt* (**sleeks, sleeking, sleeked**) MAKE SOMETHING SLEEK to make something appear smooth or shiny [Late 16C. Variant of SLICK] —**sleekly** *adv* —**sleekness** *n*

sleekit /sleékit/ *adj Scotland* superficially charming but cunning and untrustworthy ○ *He's the kind of sleekit character that gets round people.* [14C. Variant of *sleeked*, past participle of SLEEK]

sleep /sleep/ *n* **1.** STATE OF NOT BEING AWAKE a state of partial or full unconsciousness in people and animals, during which voluntary functions are suspended and the body rests and restores itself, or a period spent in this state **2.** STATE RESEMBLING SLEEP any state that is inactive or dormant, like sleep **3.** same as **death** (sense 1) (*literary; also euphemistic*) **4.** MUCUS IN EYES small amounts of dried mucus that collect in the eyes during sleep (*informal*) **5.** BOT same as **nyctitropism** ■ *v* (**sleeps, sleeping, slept** /slept/) **1.** *vi* BE IN STATE OF SLEEP to be in or go into a state of sleep **2.** *vt* SPEND TIME IN SLEEP to spend a period of time sleeping ○ *We slept the night in a hotel.* **3.** *vt* PROVIDE BEDS FOR PEOPLE to provide sleeping accommodation for a particular number of people ○ *The yacht sleeps eight.* **4.** *vi* BE INACTIVE to be in an inactive or dormant state ○ *a city that never sleeps* **5.** *vi* BE DEAD to be dead (*literary; also euphemistic*) ○ *He sleeps in the bosom of Abraham.* **6.** *vi* BOT CHANGE POSITION AT NIGHT in plants, to assume a position at night that is different from the daytime position [Old English *slǣp* (noun), *slǣpan* (verb) < Germanic] ◇ **get** *or* **go to sleep** to begin sleeping ◇ **in your sleep 1.** while you are sleeping **2.** with ease, as if not having to be fully awake (*informal*) ○ *I could find my way there in my sleep, I've been so often.* ◇ **not lose (any) sleep over something** to not worry about something because it is thought to be trivial or irrelevant ◇ **put somebody to sleep** to anaesthetize somebody ◇ **put something to sleep** to kill an animal in a humane way, especially because it is ill, injured, or in pain ◇ **sleep on it** to postpone a decision until at least the next day in order to give it more thought ◇ **sleep rough** to sleep outdoors, especially in the street, usually as a result of being homeless

SYNONYMS See ***kill***.

sleep around *vi* to have a lot of casual sexual relationships with different people (*informal*)
sleep in *vi* to sleep longer than you usually do
sleep off *vt* to recover from something such as an illness or hangover by sleeping
sleep out *vi* to sleep out of doors
sleep over *vi* to sleep at somebody else's house as part of a visit
sleep together *vi* to have sex (*used euphemistically*)
sleep with *vt* to have sex with somebody (*used euphemistically*)

sleep apnoea *n* a temporary cessation of breathing during sleep, experienced by some people

sleeper /sleépər/ *n* **1.** SOMEBODY WHO SLEEPS somebody who is asleep, or somebody who sleeps in a particular way ○ *a light sleeper* **2.** RAILWAY CARRIAGE WITH BEDS a railway carriage or compartment with beds for passengers **3.** TRAIN WITH BEDS an overnight train with beds for passengers to sleep in ○ *Should I go down on the sleeper or get an early-morning flight?* **4.** BEAM SUPPORTING RAILS any of the beams of wood or concrete on which the rails of a railway track are laid. N Am term **tie 5.** HEAVY BEAM a heavy beam used as a sill, footing, or support **6.** SMALL GOLD EARRING a small gold stud or ring worn to keep the hole of a pierced ear from closing **7.** BELATED SUCCESS somebody who or something that is not an immediate success but, often surprisingly, later becomes one **8.** SPY INACTIVE UNTIL CALLED INTO ACTION a spy or secret agent who lives an ordinary life until called into action **9.** TROPICAL FISH a sea or freshwater tropical fish related to the goby that often lies immobile. Family: Eleotridae. ■ **sleepers** *npl N Am* CHILDREN'S PYJAMAS children's one-piece pyjamas with feet

sleeper cell *n* a cell of trained terrorists who are awaiting instructions to commit a terrorist act against the country in which they are living seemingly ordinary lives

sleeping bag /sleéping-/ *n* a long padded or lined fabric bag for sleeping in, especially when camping

sleeping car *n* a railway carriage that has bunks or compartments in which passengers can sleep

sleeping draught *n* a drink containing a drug that is meant to help somebody sleep

sleeping partner *n UK* somebody who puts money into a business but does not play an active part in running it. ANZ, N Am term **silent partner**

sleeping pill (*plural* **sleeping pills** or **sleeping tablets**) *n* a pill containing a drug that is meant to induce sleep

sleeping policeman *n* ROADS same as **speed bump**

sleeping sickness *n* **1.** a disease in tropical Africa caused by parasitic protozoans that are carried by tsetse flies. Affected people and animals experience fever, weight loss, and lethargy. **2.** an epidemic form of encephalitis causing lethargy, muscular weakness, and impaired vision

sleeping tablet *n* PHARM same as **sleeping pill**

sleep-learning *n* a method of learning something that involves the continuous playing of recordings of it to a sleeping learner

sleepless /sleépləss/ *adj* **1.** without sleep, or unable to sleep ○ *a sleepless night* **2.** always awake, active, or busy —**sleeplessly** *adv* —**sleeplessness** *n*

sleep mode *n* an energy-saving state that a device may go into automatically if it is not used over a period of time, in which some of its functions shut down

sleep-out *n* **1.** a night or period spent sleeping outdoors **2.** *ANZ* an extra room attached to or separated from a house, or a part of a veranda or yard that has been turned into an outdoor sleeping area, usually partially or fully enclosed with glass or insect screens

sleepover /sleép ōvər/ *n* a children's party that includes an overnight stay at somebody's house (*informal*)

sleepsuit /sleép syoot/ *n* a one-piece sleeping garment for a baby or child, usually with feet

sleep terror disorder *n N Am* a condition of persistent nightmares from which the sleeper awakens in a state of terror and disorientation but remembers nothing of the episode in the morning

sleepwalk /sleép wawk/ (**-walks, -walking, -walked**) *vi* **1.** to walk while asleep **2.** to do something in an inattentive or lethargic way (*informal*) —**sleepwalker** *n* —**sleepwalking** *n*

sleepwear /sleép wair/ *n N Am* same as **nightwear**

sleepy /sleépi/ (**-ier, -iest**) *adj* **1.** DROWSY feeling drowsy and wanting to sleep **2.** QUIET AND WITHOUT MUCH ACTIVITY quiet and not very lively or exciting ○ *a sleepy mining town* **3.** CAUSING SLEEP tending to make somebody fall asleep —**sleepily** *adv* —**sleepiness** *n*

sleepyhead /sleépi hed/ *n* somebody who is drowsy and is nearly falling asleep or has just woken up (*informal*) —**sleepyheaded** *adj*

sleepy sickness *n* MED same as **sleeping sickness** (sense 2)

sleet /sleet/ *n* **1.** MIXTURE OF RAIN AND SNOW rainfall that is partly frozen or mixed with snow **2.** *N Am* THIN COATING OF ICE the thin coating of ice formed when rain freezes on something ■ *vi* (**sleets, sleeting, sleeted**) FALL AS SLEET to have sleet falling from the sky [13C. Probably ultimately < Germanic]

sleeve /sleev/ *n* **1.** COVERING FOR ARM either of the two parts of a garment that wholly or partially cover the arms **2.** RECORD COVER a decorated protective cover for a record or CD that usually lists the performers and contents. N Am term **jacket 3.** ENG TUBULAR PIECE a tubular piece designed to fit inside or over a cylinder ■ *vt* (**sleeves, sleeving, sleeved**) FIT WITH SLEEVE to provide something with a sleeve [Old English *slēfe* < Indo-European, 'slide, slip'] —**sleeveless** *adj* ◇ **roll up your sleeves** to get ready to do something vigorously

(*informal*) ◇ **up your sleeve** kept hidden or secret but available for use

sleeve board *n* a small, narrow ironing board used for pressing sleeves

sleeveen /slee veen/ *n Ireland* somebody who is sly, plausible, and ingratiating [Mid-19C. < Irish *slíbhín* 'sly person, trickster']

sleeve notes *npl* information about a record, printed on its cover. N Am term **liner notes**

sleeve valve *n* a valve for an internal-combustion engine, fitted and reciprocating inside a cylinder

sleeving /sleeving/ *n UK, NZ, Can* flexible, tubular insulation inside which wires that carry electric current can be fitted. Aus, US term **spaghetti**

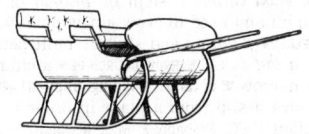
sleigh

sleigh /slay/ *n* an open, usually horse-drawn vehicle on runners, used for travel on snow and ice ■ *vi* (**sleighs, sleighing, sleighed**) to move over snow or ice in a sleigh [Early 18C. < Dutch *slee*, later form of Middle Dutch *slēde* < Germanic, 'slip, slide']

SPELLCHECK See *slay*.

sleighbell /slay bel/ *n* a small bell attached to a sleigh or to the harness of horses pulling it. Sometimes a number of them are used together as a musical instrument.

sleight /slīt/ *n* (*archaic*) **1.** dexterity or skill in doing something **2.** cunning or trickery [13C. < Old Norse *slœgð* 'cunning' < *slœgr* 'crafty']

sleight of hand *n* **1.** skill or dexterity with the hands in conjuring, card tricks, or juggling **2.** any kind of skill by which something happens without it being obvious how it is done

slender /sléndər/ *adj* **1.** SLIM gracefully and attractively thin **2.** SMALL IN WIDTH small or slight in width in proportion to height or length ○ *a flower with a slender stem* **3.** LIMITED small or limited in degree, extent, or size ○ *The home team won by a slender margin.* [13C. Origin ?] —**slenderly** *adv* —**slenderness** *n*

SYNONYMS See *thin*.

slenderize /sléndə rīz/ (**-izes, -izing, -ized**), **slenderise** (**-ises, -ising, -ised**) *vti US* to become slender, or make somebody or something slender

slender loris *n* a small tailless slow-moving primate. Native to: rainforests of India and Sri Lanka. Latin name: *Loris tardigradus*.

slept past participle, past tense of **sleep**

Slessor /sléssər/, **Kenneth** (1901–71) Australian poet. His work, mostly written between 1919 and 1939, includes 'Five Bells' (1939). Full name **Slessor, Kenneth Adolf**. See Cultural note at **bell**[1]

sleuth /slooth/ *n* **1.** same as **detective** (*informal*) **2.** BREED same as **sleuthhound** (sense 1) (*dated*) ■ *v* (**sleuths, sleuthing, sleuthed**) **1.** *vi* to make investigations as, or in a similar way to, a detective (*informal*) **2.** *vt* to track or find somebody or something [Early 19C. Shortening of SLEUTHHOUND]

sleuthhound /slooth hownd/ *n* **1.** a dog used for tracking people, especially a bloodhound (*dated*) **2.** same as **detective** (*dated informal*) [14C. < Old Norse *slóð* 'track, trail']

S level *n* an advanced qualification, above and in addition to A level, taken in a subject in England and Wales for the General Certificate of Education. Full form **special level**

slew[1] /sloo/ past tense of **slay**

slew[2] /sloo/ *vti* (**slews, slewing, slewed**) to turn or twist something around, or be turned or twisted around, especially suddenly, violently, or uncontrollably ○ *She jammed on the brakes and the car slewed to a halt.* ■ *n* a forceful or uncontrolled turn or twist around

slew[3] /sloo/ *n N Am* a large quantity or number of something (*informal*) ○ *They hit us with a whole slew of complaints.* [Mid-19C. < Irish *sluagh* 'multitude', later form of Old Irish *slúag* 'host, army']

slewed /slood/ *adj* drunk (*slang*) [Mid-19C. < SLEW[2]]

slice /slīss/ *n* **1.** PIECE CUT FROM SOMETHING a thin broad piece cut from something larger ○ *a slice of ham* **2.** SHARE a part, portion, or share of something ○ *a slice of the profits* **3.** SERVING UTENSIL a utensil with a thin flat triangular blade, used for cutting and serving food, especially fish or cake **4.** OBLIQUE STRIKE OF BALL a stroke in which the ball is hit off-centre so that it follows a curving path **5.** FLIGHT OF BALL the flight of a ball that has been hit with a slice **6.** TENNIS SHOT a tennis shot that makes the ball spin and stay low when it bounces in the opponent's court ■ *v* (**slices, slicing, sliced**) **1.** *vti* CUT SOMETHING INTO PORTIONS to cut something into slices or portions, or be cut into slices or portions ○ *slice the ham* **2.** *vti* CUT CLEANLY to cut something cleanly and effortlessly, or be cut in this way ○ *The sword sliced the rope in half.* **3.** *vi* MOVE SWIFTLY AND CLEANLY to move swiftly and cleanly, especially through a medium such as air or water **4.** *vti* CUT SOMETHING OFF to cut a slice or piece off something else, or be cut off with a slice or piece ○ *The spinning blade sliced off log after log.* **5.** *vt* SET BALL ON CURVING PATH to hit a ball off-centre so that it follows a curving path, whether intentionally or as a result of a bad swing or stroke **6.** *vti* HIT BALL WITH CHOPPING ACTION to hit a tennis shot with a chopping stroke so that the ball spins and stays low when it bounces in the opponent's court **7.** *vt* PUT OAR IN WATER AT ANGLE to put the blade of an oar into the water at an angle [15C. < Old French *esclice* 'splinter' < *esclicier* 'to splinter' < Germanic] —**sliceable** *adj* —**slicer** *n*

slice of life *n* a realistic portrayal of life, especially a harsh or unpleasant life, e.g. in literature or a film (*hyphenated before a noun*) ○ *a slice-of-life drama* [< the idea of cutting into something to see inside]

slick /slik/ *adj* **1.** EFFORTLESS done with great skill and apparently effortless ease and smooth continuity, or able to do things in this way ○ *a slick presentation* **2.** CRAFTY clever and resourceful or suave and sophisticated but not entirely trustworthy **3.** GLIB superficially impressive or persuasive but lacking substance or sincerity ○ *a slick sales pitch* **4.** SLIPPERY having a smooth, glossy, or slippery surface ○ *a slick runway* ■ *n* **1.** SLIPPERY PATCH a thinly spread or slippery patch of something, especially of oil floating on water **2.** TREADLESS TYRE a wide treadless tyre used in motor racing **3.** *N Am* PUBL same as **glossy magazine** ■ *vt* (**slicks, slicking, slicked**) SMOOTH SOMETHING to make something smooth, glossy, or presentable [14C. Ultimately < Indo-European, 'slippery'] —**slickly** *adv* —**slickness** *n*

slickenside /slíkən sīd/ *n* a rock surface that is smooth and marked with fine scratches caused by friction with another rock surface [Early 19C. < dialect variant of SLICK + SIDE]

slicker /slíkər/ *n* **1.** SOPHISTICATED BUT UNTRUSTWORTHY PERSON an apparently sophisticated, stylish, or clever person who is not honest or trustworthy (*informal*) **2.** *N Am* RAINCOAT a shiny raincoat, often made of a plastic or rubber material **3.** SMOOTHING TOOL a tool used for smoothing something

slide /slīd/ *v* (**slides, sliding, slid** /slid/) **1.** *vti* MOVE SMOOTHLY to move, or make something move, in an uninterrupted glide across a smooth surface, remaining in continuous contact with it but experiencing little friction or unable to get a grip on it ○ *The car slid for 50 yards when the brakes locked.* **2.** *vti* MOVE UNOBTRUSIVELY to move unobtrusively, or move something unobtrusively ○ *He slid the letter into his pocket.* **3.** *vi* SLIP to lose your grip or secure footing on a surface ○ *I slid on an icy patch and nearly ended up flat on my back.* **4.** *vi* TO CHANGE TO DIFFERENT CONDITION to change to a different, usually worse, state or condition ○ *unable to stop the*

economy from sliding into recession **5.** *vi* MUSIC PLAY GLIDE BETWEEN NOTES to make a gliding change from one note to another **6.** *vti* BASEBALL APPROACH BASE HORIZONTALLY in baseball or softball, to approach a base while skidding feet first, low to the ground ■ *n* **1.** STRUCTURE THAT CHILDREN PLAY ON a structure with a sloping surface that children slide down for fun **2.** SLIDING MOVEMENT a swift, gliding, and often uncontrollable movement across a smooth surface **3.** FALL OF ROCK, MUD, OR EARTH a downhill displacement of rock, mud, or earth, often caused by rainfall or erosion **4.** SMALL POSITIVE PHOTOGRAPH a positive photograph reproduced on a small piece of film that can be viewed by projection on a screen or through a magnifying device **5.** SPECIMEN HOLDER a small glass plate on which a specimen is mounted for viewing under a microscope **6.** HAIR same as **hair slide 7.** CLOTHING SHOE WITH NO HEEL OR TOE a slip-on shoe with an open heel and often an open toe **8.** SLIDING MACHINE PART a machine part that slides, or the track on which it slides **9.** ROWING same as **sliding seat 10.** TROMBONE MECHANISM the U-shaped tube of a trombone that is pushed in and out to allow for changes in pitch **11.** MUSIC MUSICAL FEATURE a sliding change from one note to another [Old English *slīdan* < Germanic] ◇ **let things** or **something slide** to let a situation gradually deteriorate ◇ **on the slide** in the process of becoming worse (*informal*)

slide-action *adj* describes a shotgun or rifle with a lever that ejects the case of a spent round and loads a new one

slide guitar *n* a method of playing a guitar in which the player moves a metal or glass object along the strings to produce a gliding effect between notes

slider /slídər/ *n* **1.** a control knob or lever that moves horizontally or vertically, e.g. to change the volume of a radio or CD player **2.** *regional* in Scotland and Northern Ireland, a serving of ice cream between two wafers

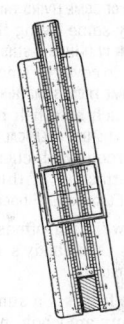
slide rule

slide rule *n* a manual calculating device, now largely obsolete, consisting of two rulers marked with graduated logarithmic scales, one sliding inside the other

slide show *n* a sequence of photographic slides projected on a screen or wall as education or entertainment

slide tackle *n* in football, an aggressive tackle in which the tackler slides in, feet first, on the ground

slide trombone *n* a trombone with a slide that is moved to select different pitches as distinct from a trombone fitted with valves

sliding /slíding/ *adj* **1.** varying according to changing conditions **2.** moved by sliding ○ *a sliding door*

sliding scale *n* a scale that varies according to changes in some other factor, e.g. a scale of wages, costs, or fees

sliding seat *n* a seat in a rowing boat that slides backwards and forwards, allowing a rower to lengthen the stroke of the oars

slieght incorrect spelling of **sleight**

Slieve Donard /sleev dónnərd/ mountain in Northern Ireland. It is the highest peak in the Mourne Mountains. Height: 852 m/2,795 ft.

slight /slīt/ *adj* **1.** VERY SMALL very small in size, degree, amount, or importance ○ *a slight resemblance* **2.** THIN having a slim body that does not look very strong **3.** INSUBSTANTIAL not very substantial or convincing ○

an assertion made without the slightest evidence ■ *vt* (**slights, slighting, slighted**) **1. SNUB SOMEBODY** to treat somebody rudely, e.g. by deliberately ignoring him or her **2. TREAT SOMETHING AS UNIMPORTANT** to think of or treat something as unimportant **3.** *US* **DO SOMETHING CARELESSLY** to handle duties or responsibilities carelessly ■ *n* **IMPOLITE ACT** an action that shows contempt for somebody or something [14C. Probably partly < Old Norse *sléttr* 'level, smooth', partly < Middle Dutch *slicht* 'simple, defective', both < Germanic] —**slightness** *n* ◇ **not in the slightest** not at all (*informal*)

slighting /slīting/ *adj* showing contempt or disrespect ○ *made slighting remarks about it* —**slightingly** *adv*

slightly /slītli/ *adv* **1.** to a small extent or degree ○ *slightly injured* **2.** slimly and rather delicately ○ *slightly built*

Sligo /slīgō/ county in Connacht Province, north-western Ireland. Capital: Sligo. Population: 55,821 (2002). Area: 1,796 sq. km/693 sq. mi.

slim /slim/ *adj* (**slimmer, slimmest**) **1. PLEASINGLY THIN** slender and well-proportioned **2. SMALLER IN WIDTH THAN HEIGHT** small in width, thickness, or girth and generally long and narrow in shape **3. SMALL** small in degree, quality, or extent ○ *Hopes of their survival were slim.* ■ *v* (**slims, slimming, slimmed**) **1.** *vi* **LOSE WEIGHT** to lose weight, especially by dieting **2.** *vt* **REDUCE SOMETHING IN EXTENT** to reduce the size or scope of something ○ *slim down the bloated bureaucracy* [Mid-17C. < Dutch, 'inferior, small' < Germanic] —**slimly** *adv* —**slimmer** *n* —**slimness** *n*

SYNONYMS See *thin*.

Slim /slim/, **William Joseph, 1st Viscount** (1891–1970) British general. He led the British forces to victory in Burma (Myanmar) during World War II and was governor general of Australia (1952–60).

slime /slīm/ *n* **1. SLIPPERY LIQUID** a fluid that is thick and slippery, especially one that is unpleasant to touch **2. MUCOUS SECRETION OF SOME LIVING THINGS** a mucous substance secreted by some living things such as fish, snails, and fungi ■ *vt* (**slimes, sliming, slimed**) **1. COVER SOMETHING WITH SLIME** to cover or smear something with slime **2. REMOVE SLIME FROM SOMETHING** to remove slime from something such as a fish before preparing it for cooking **3.** *US MIL* **USE CHEMICAL OR BIOLOGICAL WEAPONS** to attack enemy troops with chemical or biological weapons, or be attacked in this way (*slang*) [Old English *slīm* < Indo-European, 'slippery']

slimeball /slīm bawl/ *n* an offensive term that deliberately insults somebody's character or appearance (*slang insult*)

slime mould, slime fungus *n* a simple organism that forms a small slimy amoeboid mass, e.g. on fallen logs, and produces spore-bearing reproductive organs similar to those of a fungus

slimline /slim līn/ *adj* **1.** thinner than the standard type or model ○ *a slimline pocket tape recorder* **2.** designed to help with a weight-reducing diet ○ *slimline tonic*

slimming /slimming/ *n* **EFFORT TO LOSE WEIGHT** the process of trying to lose weight, especially by dieting ■ *adj* **1. USED IN LOSING WEIGHT** used for losing weight or intended to help with losing weight **2. GIVING SLIM APPEARANCE** tending to make somebody look slimmer (*informal*) ○ *That dress is very slimming on you.*

slimsy /slimzi/ (**-sier, -siest**), **slimpsy** *adj US* both slight and flimsy (*informal*) [Mid-19C. Blend of SLIM + FLIMSY]

slimy /slīmi/ (**-ier, -iest**) *adj* **1. LIKE SLIME** covered with or having the consistency of slime ○ *a slimy secretion* **2. DISGUSTING** extremely unpleasant, especially to the touch ○ *a slimy mess* **3. OFFENSIVE TERM** an offensive term meaning thought to behave in an excessively ingratiating way (*insult*) —**slimily** *adv* —**sliminess** *n*

sling¹ /sling/ *n* **1. SUPPORTING BANDAGE** a wide bandage suspended from somebody's neck to support an injured arm or hand **2. CARRYING STRAP** a carrying strap attached to something such as a rifle **3. LOOP FOR CARRYING SOMETHING HEAVY** a loop of rope, leather, chain, or net used to lift, lower, or carry something heavy **4. LOOP USED AS WEAPON** a weapon used for throwing a stone or other object, consisting of a loop of leather or other material in which the missile is twirled before being released **5. NAUT SUPPORT FOR YARD** a rope or chain that supports a ship's beam **6.** *Aus*

BRIBE MONEY a payment made as a bribe or protection money ■ *slings npl* **CLIMBING ANCHORING LOOP** a fixed loop of webbing used to provide an anchor to a rock, tree, or other point ■ *v* (**slings, slinging, slung** /slung/) **1.** *vt* **THROW WITH FORCE** to throw something with a lot of force **2. CARRY OR MOVE SOMETHING IN SLING** to attach something to, carry something with, or hang something from a sling ○ *sling a hammock* **3.** *vt* **PASS OR PUT SOMETHING CASUALLY** to throw, pass, or put something somewhere in a casual or careless way (*informal*) ○ *Sling me that newspaper, will you?* **4.** *vt* **HANG SOMETHING LOOSELY** to hang or suspend something loosely, e.g. a piece of clothing from a part of the body (*often passive*) ○ *with his coat slung over one arm* **5.** *vt* **GET RID OF SOMETHING** to throw something away (*informal*) ○ *Do you want to keep this letter, or shall I sling it?* ■ *n Aus* **PAY BRIBE** to pay a bribe or protection money [13C. Origin ?] —**slinger** *n*

sling off *vi ANZ* to speak abusively, often while blaming or criticizing ○ *I'm sick of my boss slinging off at me.*

sling² /sling/ *n* a mixed alcoholic drink made with spirits, sugar, lemon or lime juice, and water [Mid-18C. Origin ?]

slingback /sling bak/ *n* a woman's shoe that is open at the heel and is held on the foot by a strap (*often used before a noun*)

slingshot /sling shot/ *n N Am* same as **catapult** *n* (sense 1)

slink /slingk/ *v* (**slinks, slinking, slunk** /slungk/) **1.** *vi* **MOVE FURTIVELY** to move or behave quietly and secretively ○ *I could see her trying to slink away through the back door.* **2.** *vi* **MOVE SEXILY** to walk in a sexually alluring way **3.** *vt* **VET BEAR PREMATURE YOUNG** to give birth to young prematurely, especially to a calf ■ *n VET* **PREMATURE ANIMAL** a prematurely born animal, especially a calf ■ *adj VET* **BORN EARLY** describes an animal, especially a calf, that is born prematurely [Old English *slincan* < Germanic, 'slide, throw']

slinky /slingki/ (**-ier, -iest**) *adj* **1.** having a seductive appearance or way of moving **2.** close-fitting and emphasizing the curves of the body ○ *a slinky outfit* —**slinkily** *adv* —**slinkiness** *n*

sliotar /slōtər/ *n* the ball used in the sport of hurling [Early 19C. < Irish]

slip¹ /slip/ *v* (**slips, slipping, slipped**) **1.** *vi* **LOSE YOUR FOOTING** to lose your footing or grip on a slippery surface ○ *I slipped and fell.* **2.** *vi* **MOVE FROM PROPER POSITION** to slide or move accidentally out of the proper or desired position ○ *This strap keeps slipping off my shoulder.* **3.** *vti* **MOVE SMOOTHLY** to move smoothly and easily and usually with a sliding motion, or make something move in this way ○ *It slips easily in and out of its case.* **4.** *vi* **GO QUIETLY** to go somewhere in a quiet, furtive, or unnoticed way ○ *He slipped out while nobody was looking.* **5.** *vt* **PASS SOMETHING SECRETLY** to give somebody something furtively or secretly ○ *I saw the man slip her an envelope.* **6.** *vti* **PUT ON OR TAKE OFF** to put something on or take something off quickly and easily, or be put on or taken off in this way **7.** *vti* **BE FORGOTTEN** to escape from somebody's memory or mind and be forgotten or overlooked ○ *It slipped my mind.* **8.** *vi* **GET WORSE** to decline from a previous standard, e.g. a standard of performance or awareness ○ *He's slipping – two years ago he would have spotted that mistake at once.* ○ *She's in danger of slipping back into her bad old ways.* **9.** *vt* **DISLOCATE BONE** to dislocate or displace a bone, especially in the spine **10.** *vti* **RELEASE** to release an animal from a restraint, or be released in this way **11.** *vti* **AUTOMOT DISENGAGE CLUTCH** to disengage the clutch of a motor vehicle, or be disengaged **12.** *vi* **MECH ENG FAIL TO ENGAGE** to fail to engage properly, usually because of wear (*refers to mechanical parts*) **13.** *vt* **NAUT LET RESTRAINING CABLE GO** to release a line or cable that is securing a vessel to a mooring or anchor ■ *n* **1. ACT OF SLIPPING** an act of slipping, especially a sudden slide on a slippery surface **2. ERROR** a minor mistake, especially one caused by carelessness **3. LAPSE** a moral lapse or an instance of misconduct **4. DECLINE** a fall from some previous standard or level **5. CLOTHING UNDERGARMENT** a light sleeveless woman's undergarment worn under a dress **6. CLOTH COVERING** a cloth covering for something **7.** *NAUT* same as **slipway 8. CRICKET FIELDING POSITION** in cricket, the position of a fielder behind and near

the wicketkeeper, especially on the off side, or the fielder who takes up this position **9. CRYSTALS DEFORMATION OF CRYSTAL** the deformation of a metallic crystal by shearing along a plane **10. GEOL** same as **landslide** (sense 1) **11. AVIAT** same as **sideslip** *n* (sense 2) [13C. Probably < Middle Dutch, Middle Low German *slippen* < Germanic] ◇ **give somebody the slip** to get away from somebody who is pursuing you ◇ **let slip 1.** to say something without meaning to, or reveal something that should be kept secret **2.** to allow somebody or something to escape ◇ **slip one over on somebody** to trick or deceive somebody (*informal*)

SYNONYMS See *mistake*.

slip up *vi* **1.** to make a mistake (*informal*) ○ *Somebody slipped up and forgot to put your name on the guest list.* **2.** to slip and fall while walking or running

slip² /slip/ *n* **1. NARROW PIECE** a narrow strip of something ○ *a slip of paper* **2. SMALL DOCUMENT** a small form, document, or record of a transaction ○ *a paying-in slip* **3. PLANT CUTTING** a stem or branch of a plant broken off and used to grow a new plant **4. DELICATE YOUNG PERSON** a young and slightly built person ○ *a slip of a lad* **5.** *US* **NARROW CHURCH PEW** a church pew that is narrow ■ *vt* (**slips, slipping, slipped**) **REMOVE SLIP** to remove a slip from a plant in order to grow a new plant [15C. Probably < Middle Dutch, Middle Low German *slippe* 'flap, split']

slip³ /slip/ *n* a mixture of clay and water used as a decorative layer on pottery or for casting in moulds to form an actual piece [Old English *slipa, slyppe* 'slime']

SLIP /slip/ *n* the older of two protocols for dial-up access to the Internet using a modem. It has now been largely replaced by a higher-level protocol (**PPP**). Full form **serial line Internet protocol**

slipcase /slip kayss/ *n* a box for protecting a book or set of books, usually made of sturdy cardboard, with one or more open ends

slipcover /slip kuvər/ *n N Am* same as **loose cover**

slipe /slīp/ *n* **1.** *N England, Scotland* a sledge or sledge runner used in a mine **2.** *NZ* wool that is taken from a slaughtered sheep by immersing the pelt in a chemical bath [15C. < Low German *slīpe*, variant of *slēpe* 'sledge, train']

slipknot /slip not/ *n* **1.** a knot that slips easily along the rope or cord around which it is tied **2.** a knot that can be unfastened by pulling

slip-on *n* a shoe that does not have a fastening ■ *adj* used to describe a shoe that does not have a fastening

slipover /slipōvər/ *n* **CLOTHING** same as **pullover**

slippage /slippij/ *n* **1. SLIDE** the process or an instance of slipping, especially from a stable or desired position ○ *Recent thunderstorms have caused slippage in the banks along rivers.* **2. AMOUNT OF SLIPPING** an amount or extent that something slips **3. DECLINE** a decrease in the quality, performance, or production of something **4. MECH ENG LOSS OF POWER** a loss of power or forward motion caused by the slipping of a mechanical part

slipped disc *n* one of the discs of cartilage separating the bones of the spine that has become displaced or protrusive and causes pain by pressing on a nerve

slipper /slippər/ *n* a flat shoe of soft or lightweight material, usually worn indoors —**slippered** *adj*

slipper bath *n* a bath that is covered at one end ■ **slipper baths** *npl* a place where people can pay to have a bath (*dated*)

slipper flower *n US* **PLANTS** same as **calceolaria**

slipperwort /slippər wurt/ *n* **PLANTS** same as **calceolaria**

slippery /slippəri/ (**-ier, -iest**) *adj* **1. CAUSING SLIDING** likely to cause somebody or something to slip **2. HARD TO HOLD FIRMLY** sliding easily from the grasp or from a position **3. PRECARIOUS** unstable and liable to change ○ *We're in a slippery situation; things could go either way.* **4. UNTRUSTWORTHY** behaving in a devious or deceitful way ○ *a slippery character* —**slipperily** *adv* —**slipperiness** *n*

slippery dip *n Aus* a children's slide in a playground or funfair

slippery elm *n* **1.** the moist sticky inner bark of an elm. Use: natural remedy in alternative medicine to relieve inflammation in the digestive tract. **2.** a

deciduous hardwood tree that yields slippery elm. Native to: North America. Latin name: *Ulmus rubra*.

slippery slope *n* a dangerous situation that can lead to ultimate downfall

slippy /slíppi/ (**-pier, -piest**) *adj* likely to cause somebody or something to slip, or sliding easily from the grasp or from a position (*informal*) —**slippiness** *n*

slip ring *n* a metal ring in a generator or motor to which current is delivered or from which it is removed by brushes

slip road *n* a short road for driving onto or off a motorway or fast road

slipsheet /slíp sheet/ *n* a sheet of blank paper placed between newly printed sheets to prevent wet ink on the printed sheets from rubbing off or smearing ■ *vt* (**-sheets, -sheeting, -sheeted**) to place a blank sheet of paper between newly printed papers on which the ink is still wet

slipshod /slíp shod/ *adj* **1.** done in a sloppy way without attention to details **2.** not neat in appearance [Late 16C. < SLIP[1] 'slide' + SHOD 'wearing shoes']

slip step *n* a step in Scottish reels and jigs in which the left foot moves one step to the side and the right foot moves to the left

slip stitch *n* a hidden stitch used to connect two layers of fabric —**slip stitch** *vt*

slipstream /slíp streem/ *n* **1.** AREA BEHIND FAST-MOVING VEHICLE an area of reduced air pressure and forward suction that is directly behind and caused by a rapidly moving vehicle **2.** AIR FROM PROPELLER a stream of air driven backwards by an aircraft's propeller ■ *vi* (**-streams, -streaming, -streamed**) FOLLOW IN SLIPSTREAM to follow in another vehicle's slipstream, taking advantage of the decreased air resistance

slip-up *n* an accidental mistake or blunder (*informal*)

slipware /slíp wair/ *n* pottery that has been coated or decorated with slip

slipway /slíp way/ *n* a sloping surface used to build or repair boats before returning them to the water

slit /slit/ *vt* (**slits, slitting, slit**) **1.** SLICE SOMETHING to make a long straight cut in something ○ *She slit the bag open with a knife.* **2.** CUT SOMETHING INTO STRIPS to cut something into thin strips ■ *n* NARROW OPENING a long narrow cut or opening [12C. < Old English *slitan* 'cut up' < Germanic] —**slitter** *n*

SYNONYMS See *tear*[1].

slither /slíthər/ *v* (**-ers, -ering, -ered**) **1.** *vti* SLIDE OR CAUSE SOMETHING TO SLIDE to move along a slippery or uneven surface, or make something slide along ○ *We slithered down the muddy river bank.* **2.** *vi* GLIDE to slide along easily, using friction to move forward, as a snake does ■ *n* GLIDING MOVEMENT a gliding, effortless movement [12C. Alteration of Old English *slidrian* 'slide repeatedly' < SLIDE]

slithery /slíthəri/ *adj* **1.** moving with a slithering motion ○ *slithery snake* **2.** having a smooth and slippery surface ○ *slithery surface*

slit trench *n* a narrow trench dug as protection against shelling during a battle

sliver /slívvər/ *n* **1.** SPLINTER a thin piece of something that has been split, cut, or broken off **2.** SMALL PIECE a small narrow portion or piece of something **3.** LOOSE FIBRE a loose strand of wool, cotton, or some other material prepared for drawing and twisting by carding ■ *vti* (**-ers, -ering, -ered**) BREAK INTO SPLINTERS to break something into splinters, or become splintered [14C. < obsolete *slive* 'cleave, split' < Germanic]

slivovitz /slívvəvits/ *n* a dry colourless plum brandy made in eastern Europe [Late 19C. < Serbo-Croatian *sljivovica* 'plum brandy' < *sljiva* 'plum']

Sloane Ranger /slón-/, **Sloane** *n* a fashionable and conventional upper-class young person, usually a woman, who lives in London and has a lively social life among people of the same kind (*informal*) [Late 20C. Pun on *Sloane* Square, London, and the Lone *Ranger*, fictional cowboy]

slob /slob/ *n* an offensive term that deliberately insults somebody regarded as having an unhealthy lifestyle or poor standards of hygiene or manners

(*insult*) [Late 18C. Via Irish *slab* 'mud' < English *slab* 'bog' < N Germanic] —**slobbish** *adj*

slob around *vi* to spend time relaxing and doing nothing much (*informal*) ○ *I spent the day slobbing around in my pyjamas.*

slobber /slóbbər/ *v* (**-bers, -bering, -bered**) **1.** *vti* DRIBBLE SALIVA to allow saliva or a liquid to run from the mouth **2.** *vi* EXPRESS EXTREME EMOTION to be overly sentimental or emotional **3.** *vt* SMEAR SOMETHING WITH SALIVA to soak or cover something with saliva or liquid from the mouth ■ *n* **1.** SALIVA saliva or liquid that has been drooled from the mouth **2.** SENTIMENTAL WRITING OR TALK overemotional or sentimental talk or writing ○ *I can't stand to read such slobber.* [14C. Probably < Middle Dutch *slobberen* 'feed noisily, walk through mud'] —**slobberer** *n* —**slobbery** *adj*

slob ice *n* Can floating ice in slushy masses

sloe /slō/ (*plural* **sloes** or same) *n* **1.** SOUR BLUE-BLACK FRUIT a small sour blue-black fruit of the blackthorn **2.** DARK RED OR YELLOW FRUIT a dark purple fruit, or a red or yellow fruit, produced by different species of North American plum trees **3.** TREES same as **blackthorn** (sense 1) **4.** N AMERICAN PLUM TREE a plum tree that bears sloes. Native to: eastern North America. Latin name: *Prunus alleghaniensis* or *Prunus americana*. [Old English *slah* < Indo-European, 'bluish']

sloe-eyed *adj* with dark almond-shaped eyes [Because of the blue-black colour of the fruit]

sloe gin *n* a liqueur made of gin flavoured with sloes

slog /slog/ *v* (**slogs, slogging, slogged**) **1.** *vi* PLOD to walk slowly with great effort ○ *How long did it take us to slog up that mountain?* **2.** *vi* WORK LONG AND HARD to work at something for a long time with little progress ○ *They've all been down at the office, slogging through endless reams of paperwork.* **3.** *vt* MAKE YOUR WAY to make your way through something with great difficulty ○ *We had to slog our way through several muddy fields.* **4.** *vt* HIT SOMEBODY OR SOMETHING HARD to hit somebody or something with great force ○ *It was like being slogged by a heavyweight boxer.* ■ *n* **1.** LONG HARD WALK a long difficult trip or walk ○ *It was quite a slog from the station to the hotel.* **2.** HARD WORK a long period of hard work ○ *Hard slog is the only way you'll pass those exams.* **3.** HARD HIT a hard blow or swipe [Early 19C. Origin ?] —**slogger** *n*

slogan /slṓgən/ *n* **1.** MOTTO a short distinctive phrase used to identify a company or organization or its goals **2.** ADVERTISING PHRASE a short catchy phrase used in advertising to promote something **3.** *Scotland* SCOTTISH BATTLE CRY the battle cry of a Highland clan (*archaic*) [Early 16C. < Gaelic *sluagh-ghairm* < *sluagh* 'army' + *gairm* 'cry']

sloganeer /slṓgə néer/ *n* a creator or frequent user of slogans ○ *the kind of politician who is little more than a clever sloganeer* ■ *vi* (**-eers, -eering, -eered**) to create or use slogans

sloganize /slṓgə nīz/ (**-izes, -izing, -ized**), **sloganise** (**-ises, -ising, -ised**) *vt* to express something in a slogan, or make a slogan of something ○ *the sloganizing of political ideals* —**sloganizer** *n*

sloop /sloop/ *n* a single-masted sailing boat, rigged fore-and-aft, with one headsail extending from the foremast to the bowsprit [Early 17C. < Dutch *sloep*]

sloop of war *n* a small armed sailing ship that is larger than a gunboat and carries guns on only one deck

slop[1] /slop/ *n* **1.** SOMETHING SPILLED a liquid that has spilled or overflowed ○ *Look at all the slop on the floor!* **2.** MUD OR SLUSH soft mud or slushy snow ○ *How far do we have to wade through this slop?* **3.** UNAPPEALING FOOD poor-quality unappetizing or watery food (*often used in the plural*) **4.** HUMAN WASTE human waste, e.g. urine **5.** OVERLY SENTIMENTAL WRITING OR SPEECH overly emotional or sentimental speech or writing without any literary value (*informal*) ○ *Not all romantic novels are slop.* **6.** FOOD INDUST MASH what remains of the mash after an alcoholic beverage has been distilled (*often used in the plural*) ■ **slops** *npl* PIG FOOD leftover food, especially kitchen waste, that is fed to pigs ■ *v* (**slops, slopping, slopped**) **1.** *vti* SPILL LIQUID to spill a liquid, or be spilled on or over somebody or something **2.** *vi* WALK THROUGH MUD OR WATER to trudge or splash through water, mud, or slush **3.** *vt* SERVE FOOD MESSILY to serve food in a careless and unappetizing way **4.** *vt* FEED ANIMALS SLOPS to feed

kitchen waste to pigs and other livestock **5.** *vi* WRITE GUSHILY to write or speak about something in an overly emotional or sentimental way (*informal*) [14C. < Old English *sloppe* 'dung' < Germanic]

slop out *vi* to empty a chamber pot as part of prison routine ○ *All prisoners must slop out every morning.*

slop[2] /slop/ (*archaic*) *n* a loose smock or pair of overalls ■ **slops** *npl* clothes and personal articles that are sold from a slop chest to sailors on a merchant ship [14C. Probably < Middle Dutch]

slop basin *n* a bowl or other container into which tea or coffee dregs are emptied. N Am term **slop bowl**

slop chest *n* a store of merchandise such as tobacco or clothes, kept aboard merchant ships to be sold to the crew

slope /slōp/ *n* **1.** SLANTED GROUND ground that inclines slightly **2.** SIDE OF HILL OR MOUNTAIN the part of a hill or mountain that is at an angle ○ *thousands of skiers hitting the slopes this weekend* **3.** SLANT a slant upwards or downwards, or the degree of such a slant **4.** SOMETHING SLANTED a line, surface, direction, or plane that is inclined **5.** MATHS TANGENT the tangent of the angle between a straight line and the x-axis **6.** MATHS FIRST DERIVATIVE OF CURVE the first derivative of a curve at a point ■ *v* (**slopes, sloping, sloped**) **1.** *vti* GO UP OR DOWN to ascend or descend, or make something ascend or descend ○ *From here, the road slopes gently down to the valley.* **2.** *vi* BE AT SLANT to be at or have an angle that deviates from horizontal ○ *Does the floor in this room slope?* **3.** *vt* TAKE SOMETHING UP OR DOWN to make something rise or descend gradually ○ *We had a landscaper slope the path through our garden.* [Late 16C. < *slope* 'so as to slope, on a slope', shortening of *aslope*, origin ?] —**sloper** *n* —**sloping** *adj*

slope off *vi* to leave unobtrusively or furtively (*informal*) ○ *I managed to slope off before the end of the talk.*

sloppy /slóppi/ (**-pier, -piest**) *adj* **1.** MESSY lacking order or tidiness **2.** WET slushy, muddy, or very wet **3.** WATERY cooked or prepared in a way that results in excessive wateriness **4.** NOT DONE WELL carelessly or badly done (*informal*) **5.** GUSHY excessively sentimental or emotional (*informal*) **6.** CLOTHING BAGGY loose-fitting so as to be casual and comfortable ○ *a big sloppy sweater*

sloppy joe *n* a long, baggy, loose-fitting sweater (*informal*)

slopwork /slóp wurk/ *n* **1.** any kind of work that has been done quickly and carelessly **2.** clothing that is cheap and of inferior quality, or the manufacture of such clothing (*dated*) —**slopworker** *n*

slosh /slosh/ *v* (**sloshes, sloshing, sloshed**) **1.** *vt* SPILL LIQUID CLUMSILY to spill or splash a liquid on or over something **2.** *vi* WADE IN LIQUID to wade or splash around in water, mud, or slush (*informal*) **3.** *vti* STIR SOMETHING IN LIQUID to move or splash something, or move or splash in a liquid (*informal*) ○ *Slosh the shirt in some warm water before the stain sets.* **4.** *vt* HIT SOMEBODY to hit somebody very hard (*informal*) ■ *n* **1.** SLUSH wet snow or mud **2.** LIQUID SPLASHING liquid splashing, or its sound ○ *We could hear the slosh of water against the docks all night because of the storm.* **3.** HIT a heavy blow (*informal*) [Early 19C. Probably blend of SLOP[1] 'bog' + SLUSH] —**sloshy** *adj*

sloshed /slosht/ *adj* thoroughly intoxicated (*informal*)

slot[1] /slot/ *n* **1.** OPENING a narrow vertical or horizontal opening into which something can be inserted ○ *Put the coin in the slot.* **2.** SCHEDULED TIME an assigned place and time in a sequence or schedule ○ *The station is moving the new comedy to a prime-time slot next month.* **3.** JOB a position in a company or organization **4.** AVIAT AIR PASSAGE an air passage in an aerofoil that directs air from the lower to the upper surface **5.** ELEC ENG same as **expansion slot** ■ *v* (**slots, slotting, slotted**) **1.** *vti* ASSIGN PLACE TO SOMETHING to put something in a place, position, or time, or be put in a place ○ *Slot the shelves into the grooves.* **2.** *vt* MAKE SLOT IN SOMETHING to cut a slot or slots in something [14C. < Old French *esclot* 'hollow of the breastbone']

slot in *vti* to find a suitable time or place for somebody or something in a plan, organization, or series of events, or be found a time or place ○ *The doctor is busy this morning but she could slot you in at 2 o'clock.*

slot[2] /slot/ n the track of an animal, especially a deer [Late 16C. < Old French esclot 'horse's hoofprint']

slot car n US an electric toy racing car that is operated by a rheostat and has a pin underneath that fits into a groove on a slotted track

sloth

sloth /slōth/ n 1. a slow-moving mammal that uses its long claws to hang upside down from tree branches. Native to: Central, South America. Genera: *Bradypus* or *Choloepus*. 2. a dislike of work or any kind of physical exertion [12C. < SLOW + -th, suffix forming nouns < Indo-European]

sloth bear n a bear with long shaggy fur and a long snout that enables it to feed on plants and insects. Native to: India, Sri Lanka. Latin name: *Melursus ursinus*.

slothful /slōthf'l/ adj disliking work or any form of physical exertion —**slothfully** adv —**slothfulness** n

slot machine n 1. N Am same as **fruit machine** 2. a coin-operated vending machine

slouch /slowch/ vti (**slouches, slouching, slouched**) WALK OR SIT IN LAZY WAY to stand, sit, or walk in a careless drooping way, or make a part of the body droop carelessly ○ *He slouched his back and shoulders and leaned against the wall.* ■ n 1. EXTREMELY CASUAL POSTURE an extremely relaxed or ungainly way of sitting, standing, or walking 2. LAZY OR INEPT PERSON somebody who will not or cannot do something well (*informal; usually used in negative statements*) ○ *very good with children and no slouch around the house either* [Early 16C. Probably < N Germanic] —**sloucher** n —**slouchily** adv —**slouchiness** n —**slouchy** adj

slouch hat n a hat made of a soft material such as felt that has a broad drooping brim, especially an Australian army hat

slouch pants npl comfortable loose-fitting trousers, usually made of jersey or similar fabric

slough[1] /slow/ n 1. DEEP MUDDY HOLE a hole or low area in the ground filled with mud or water 2. N Am SWAMPY AREA a stagnant area of water connected to a larger body of water such as a marsh, inlet, bayou, or backwater 3. N Am ESTUARY a saltwater estuary 4. N Am HOLE FILLED WITH WATER on the prairies, a low area filled with water, especially from melting snow 5. SPIRITUAL LOW POINT deep despair or disgrace [Old English slōh, origin ?] —**sloughy** adj

slough[2] /sluf/ n 1. SOMETHING CAST OFF something discarded or shed 2. ZOOL DEAD OUTER COVERING the dead outer skin shed by a reptile or an amphibian 3. MED DEAD TISSUE LAYER a layer of dead skin that separates from healthy skin after an infection or inflammation 4. *also* **sluff** CARDS DISCARDED CARD in card games, a card that has been discarded ■ v (**sloughs, sloughing, sloughed**) 1. vti CAST SOMETHING OFF to shed something, or be shed ○ *Snakes slough off their dead skins.* 2. vt DISCARD SOMETHING OR SOMEBODY to get rid of somebody or something that is no longer wanted or needed ○ *She sloughs off friends when she no longer has a use for them.* 3. vt IGNORE SOMETHING to pay no attention to something 4. vi MED SEPARATE FROM HEALED TISSUE to separate from surrounding healthy skin (*refers to dead skin*) 5. *also* **sluff** vti CARDS DISCARD CARD to get rid of an unwanted card [14C. Origin ?]

Slough /slow/ town in south-central England. Population: 119,067 (2001).

slough of despond /slow-/ n a state of extreme despair and depression [After the deep bog in *Pilgrim's Progress, Part 1* (1678) by John Bunyan (1628–88)]

Slovak /slō vak/ (*plural* **-vaks** or **-vakians**) n 1. somebody who comes from Slovakia 2. the Slavic national language of Slovakia. Native speakers: 5 million. [Early 19C. < Slovak, Czech, Russian] —**Slovak** adj

Slovakia

Slovakia /slō vaaki ə/ country in east-central Europe. It was part of Czechoslovakia until 1993 and became a member of the European Union in 2004. Language: Slovak. Currency: Slovak koruna. Capital: Bratislava. Population: 5,430,033 (2003). Area: 49,035 sq. km/18,933 sq. mi. Official name **Slovak Republic**

Slovakian /slō vaki ən/ n PEOPLES, LANG same as **Slovak** —**Slovakian** adj

sloven /slúvv'n/ n an offensive term that deliberately insults somebody whose standards of personal hygiene and tidiness are considered too low [15C. Probably < Middle Flemish *sloovin* 'a scold']

Slovene /slō veen/ n 1. somebody who comes from Slovenia 2. the Slavic national language of Slovenia. Native speakers: 2 million. [Late 19C. Via German < Slovene *Sloven(ec)* < Slavic] —**Slovene** adj

Slovenia

Slovenia /slō veeni ə/ country in eastern Europe, on the Balkan Peninsula. It was part of Yugoslavia until 1991. It became a member of the European Union in 2004. Language: Slovene. Currency: tolar. Capital: Ljubljana. Population: 1,935,677 (2003). Area: 20,253 sq. km/7,820 sq. mi. Official name **Republic of Slovenia**

Slovenian /slō veeni ən/ n PEOPLES, LANG same as **Slovene** —**Slovenian** adj

slovenly /slúvv'nli/ (**-lier, -liest**) adj an offensive term meaning not concerned about conventional standards of personal hygiene and tidiness —**slovenliness** n

Slovo /slóvō/, Joe (1926–95) Lithuanian-born South African political leader. He was one of the leading architects of the Freedom Charter, and served in Nelson Mandela's government (1994–95). Full name **Yossel Mashel Slovo**

slow /slō/ adj 1. NOT FAST not moving at a fast pace 2. LENGTHY taking a long time to do or create something ○ *Writing software is a slow process.* 3. TAKING TOO MUCH TIME requiring more time than is usual or expected 4. NOT KEEPING ACCURATE TIME showing a time that is earlier than the correct time ○ *I was late for my appointment because my watch was slow.* 5. HESITANT doing something hesitantly or unwillingly ○ *Why were you so slow to answer my question?* 6. SLUGGISH lacking the usual volume of sales or customers ○ *Business is usually slow during the summer months.* 7. DULL lacking in interest or activity ○ *The acting* was good but the plot was terribly slow. 8. REDUCING SPEED OF BALL OR RUNNER tending to reduce the speed or ability to travel of a ball, runner, or other competitor ○ *a slow track* 9. UNINTELLIGENT lacking in intelligence or mental sharpness (*informal insult*) 10. COOK WARM operating at a low temperature that ensures thorough cooking throughout ○ *A turkey should be cooked in a slow oven.* 11. CRICKET DELIVERING BALL SLOWLY in cricket, delivering a ball at a slow pace with spin ○ *a slow bowler* ■ adv 1. BEHIND behind the correct time or pace ○ *My watch seems to be running slow.* 2. ⚠ AT LOW SPEED at a reduced speed or pace (*nonstandard*) ○ *The law requires motorists to drive slow through residential areas.* ■ vti (**slows, slowing, slowed**) 1. MAKE OR BECOME SLOW to make somebody or something slow or slower, or become slow or slower ○ *Could you slow your speed a little on those sharp turns?* 2. DELAY OR BE DELAYED to reduce the speed or progress of something, or become reduced in speed or progress ○ *slowed down the company's rate of expansion* [Old English *slaw* 'sluggish' < Indo-European] —**slowly** adv —**slowness** n ◇ **go slow** to officially work more slowly than usual as a form of protest

USAGE **slowly** or **slow**? The normal adverb is **slowly**: *The car moved slowly up the hill.* **Slow**, although usually an adjective, is used as an adverb of keeping time (*My watch is running slow*), and informally more generally (*Don't walk so slow*), though this is not regarded as standard. However, in some expressions, for example *go slow*, and *slow-moving*, **slow** is idiomatic and acceptable.

slow burn, **slow boil** n a state of steadily becoming angrier (*informal*) ○ *doing a slow burn*

slowcoach /slō kōch/ n somebody who moves or does something too slowly (*informal*) N Am term **slowpoke**

slowdown /slō down/ n N Am same as **go-slow**

slow-footed adj happening or proceeding at an extremely slow pace ○ *Congress has been slow-footed in passing the bill.* —**slow-footedness** n

slow handclap n a very slow, steady clapping used by an audience to show its dislike of a performance ○ *The audience broke into a slow handclap.*

slow loris n a small slow-moving primate that has a rounded, almost tailless body. Native to: Indonesia. Latin name: *Nycticebus coucang*.

slow match n a match or fuse that burns without a flame very slowly or at a known rate and is used to set off explosives

slow motion n a method of filming action at a rate faster than the normal projection rate, so that it appears on the screen at a slower than normal rate

slow-motion adj 1. photographed or shown in slow motion 2. taking place at a slower pace than normal ○ *her slow-motion reaction*

slow neutron n a relatively slow-moving neutron that possesses less than 100 electron volts of kinetic energy and is capable of bringing about nuclear fission

slowpoke /slōw pōk/ n N Am same as **slowcoach** (*informal*) [Mid-19C. < POKE[1] 'dawdling person']

slow time n a very slow marching step, used especially in funeral ceremonies

slow virus n any virus, or any agent resembling a virus, that causes diseases with very long incubation periods. Technical name **lentivirus**

slow-wave sleep n a state of dreamless sleep characterized by slow brain waves and lowered heart rate, respiration, and blood pressure

slow-witted adj an offensive term meaning slow to understand ideas, events, or situations

slowworm /slō wurm/ n a legless lizard with a smooth body resembling that of a snake. Native to: Europe, North Africa, western Asia. Latin name: *Anguis fragilis*. [< WORM 'snake']

SLP abbr POL Scottish Labour Party

SLR abbr PHOTOGRAPHY single-lens reflex

slub /slub/ n 1. KNOT IN YARN a lump in yarn or fabric that is sometimes an imperfection, but is often made to provide a knobbly effect 2. TWISTED THREAD a loosely twisted roll of fibre, e.g. of silk or cotton, prepared for spinning ■ vt (**slubs, slubbing, slubbed**) PREPARE FIBRE FOR SPINNING to draw out and twist a strand

of fibre to prepare it for spinning [Early 19C. Origin ?]

sludge /sluj/ *n* **1. SOLID WASTE** the solids in sewage that separate out during treatment **2. SLUSH** wet material, especially watery mud or snow **3. SEDIMENT** a solid deposit found at the bottom of a liquid **4. BROKEN ICE** a layer of broken or half-formed ice on a body of water, especially the sea **5. MED MASS OF BLOOD CELLS** a sticky grouping of blood cells that form a mass and hinder the circulation of blood [Mid-17C. Origin ?] —**sludgy** *adj*

slue /sloo/ *vti* (**slues, sluing, slued**) same as **slew**¹ *v* ■ *n* same as **slew**² [Variant of SLOUGH¹ and SLEW² 'turn']

sluff *n, vti* CARDS another spelling of **slough**² *n* (sense 4)

slug¹ /slug/ *n* **1. BULLET** a metal projectile that is fired from a gun or rifle **2. DRINK OF SOMETHING** a single shot of a strong alcoholic drink (*informal*) **3. PRINTING TYPE-METAL** a strip of type-metal, less than type-high, used for spacing in traditional hot-metal printing **4. PRINTING LINE OF TYPE** a strip of cast type in a single strip of metal in traditional hot-metal printing **5. PRINTING TEMPORARY TYPE LINE** a temporary type line inserted in copy that carries identifying marks or a compositor's instructions **6. MANUF METAL OR GLASS BLANK FOR PROCESSING** a metal or glass blank that will receive further processing to make it into a finished object **7. MEASURE UNIT OF MASS** a foot-pound-second unit of mass equal to 32.17 pounds that will acquire an acceleration of one foot per second per second when acted on by a one pound force ■ *vt* **1. DRINK SOMETHING QUICKLY** to gulp down a drink (*informal*) **2. PRINTING ADD SLUGS TO COPY** to add printers' slugs to copy in traditional hot-metal printing [Early 17C. Origin ?]

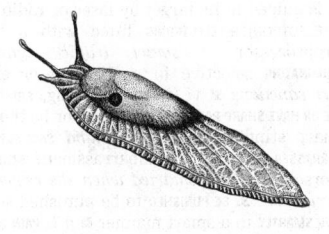

slug

slug² /slug/ *n* **1. MOLLUSC WITHOUT SHELL** a small slow-moving terrestrial mollusc that resembles a snail but has no shell, or only a rudimentary one. Order: Stylommatophora. **2. SOFT INSECT LARVA** a soft smooth larva of some insects such as the sawfly **3. OFFENSIVE TERM** an offensive term that deliberately insults somebody's level of energy or activity **4. BIOL CELLS THAT DEVELOP INTO SPORE-BEARING STRUCTURE** a sticky mass of cells from which the sporophore of a slime mould develops [15C. Probably < N Germanic]

slug³ /slug/ *vt* (**slugs, slugging, slugged**) **1. HIT SOMEBODY OR SOMETHING HARD** to strike somebody or something very hard with the fist or a bat **2. Aus CHARGE SOMEBODY TOO MUCH** to charge somebody a price that is unfairly high (*informal*) ■ *n* **HARD HIT** a hard strike or blow [Mid-19C. Variant of SLOG] ◇ **slug it out** *N Am* to fight to a conclusion (*informal*)

slugabed /slúggə bed/ *n* somebody who likes to stay in bed late (*archaic*) [Late 16C. < SLUG² + ABED]

slugfest /slúg fest/ *n N Am* **1. BASEBALL GAME WITH MANY HITS** a baseball game in which both teams make a large number of hits and score a large number of runs **2. HEATED ARGUMENT** an intense debate or dispute **3. BRAWL** a long fight in which many heavy blows are exchanged (*slang*) [Early 20C. < SLUG³]

sluggard /slúggərd/ *n* somebody who avoids work or physical exertion (*archaic*) ■ *adj* sluggishly lazy [14C. < SLUG²] —**sluggardliness** *n* —**sluggardly** *adj* —**sluggardness** *n*

slugger /slúggər/ *n* a fighter who delivers hard blows [< SLUG³]

sluggish /slúggish/ *adj* **1. NOT MOVING MUCH** inactive and moving slowly or very little **2. NOT VERY RESPONSIVE** slow to react or respond to stimulation **3. LACKING ALERTNESS AND ENERGY** not alert and showing little energy or vitality —**sluggishly** *adv* —**sluggishness** *n*

sluice

sluice /slooss/ *n* **1. WATER CHANNEL** an artificial channel for a flow of water that is controlled by a valve or gate **2. FLOODGATE** a valve or floodgate that controls the water in a sluice **3. WATER BEHIND FLOODGATE** a body of water contained by a floodgate **4. DRAINAGE CHANNEL** a channel for carrying away excess water **5. TROUGH** a long inclined trough used to separate gold ore from sand or gravel **6. CHANNEL TO MOVE LOGS** an artificial stream or channel for floating logs ■ *v* (**sluices, sluicing, sluiced**) **1. *vt* FLUSH SOMETHING WITH WATER** to flood or clean something with a sudden heavy flow of water **2. *vt* WASH SOMETHING** to wash something in running water ○ *He sluiced his hands under the tap.* **3. *vt* WASH GOLD** to wash gold or other minerals in water flowing in a sluice **4. *vti* RELEASE SOMETHING FROM SLUICE** to flow from a sluice, or let something out of a sluice **5. *vt* MOVE SOMETHING IN SLUICE** to float something, especially logs, down a sluice [14C. < Old French *escluse* < Latin *exclus-*, past participle of *excludere* (see EXCLUDE)]

sluicegate /slóoss gayt/ *n* ENG same as **sluice** *n* (sense 2)

sluiceway /slóoss way/ *n* an artificial channel into which water flows from a sluice

slum /slum/ *n* **POOR AREA** an overcrowded area of a city in which the housing is typically in very bad condition (*often used in the plural*) ■ *v* (**slums, slumming, slummed**) **1. *vti* ACCEPT LOWER STANDARDS THAN USUAL** to stay in or go to a place that you would usually consider unacceptable (*often used humorously*) ○ *We'll have to slum it and stay here until we can find a better place.* **2. *vi* VISIT SLUMS** to go into a slum out of curiosity [Mid-19C. < *back slum* 'street housing poor people' < obsolete *slum* 'room' origin ?] —**slummer** *n*

slumber /slúmbər/ *vi* (**-bers, -bering, -bered**) **1. SLEEP** to be asleep **2. BE IN QUIET STATE** to be in a state of inactivity or rest ■ *n* **1. SLEEPING** the state of being asleep, or a period of sleep ○ *A loud noise disturbed my slumber.* **2. INACTIVITY** a state of being dormant or quiet [14C. Alteration of obsolete *sloom* 'light sleep' < Germanic] —**slumberless** *adj*

slumberous /slúmbərəss/ *adj* **1. DROWSY** feeling sleepy **2. INACTIVE** characterized by inactivity or sluggishness ○ *A slumberous atmosphere seemed to stifle sound and motion in the town.* **3. CAUSING SLEEP** inducing lethargy or sleep ○ *She dozed in the slumberous heat of the afternoon.* —**slumberously** *adv* —**slumberousness** *n*

slumber party *n N Am* a party at which a group of girls, wearing nightgowns or pyjamas, talk, eat, and stay overnight at one of the girls' homes

slumlord /slúm lawrd/ *n N Am* somebody who owns housing in slum areas, especially a neglectful landlord who overcharges tenants [Mid-20C. < SLUM + LANDLORD]

slump /slump/ *vi* (**slumps, slumping, slumped**) **1. COLLAPSE** to sink or fall suddenly and heavily **2. SLOUCH** to have a hunched drooping posture ○ *She was slumped over her desk.* **3. DECREASE** to decline suddenly and sharply in value ○ *share prices slumped* ■ *n* **1. SLOUCHED POSTURE** a drooping or hunched posture **2. ECONOMIC RECESSION** a sudden decline in business, stock prices, or productivity ○ *an economy fluctuating between boom and slump* [Mid-17C. Origin ?]

slumpflation /slump fláysh'n/ *n* an economic situation in which an economic depression is accompanied by increasing inflation [Late 20C. < SLUMP + INFLATION]

slung past participle, past tense of **sling**¹

slungshot /slúng shot/ *n* a weight or weights attached to the end of a cord and used as a weapon

slunk past participle, past tense of **slink**

slur /slur/ *v* (**slurs, slurring, slurred**) **1. *vti* SPEAK INDISTINCTLY** to pronounce sounds or words so that they cannot be distinguished, or be pronounced in this way **2. *vt* DEMEAN SOMEBODY** to speak of somebody in an insulting or demeaning way **3. *vt* GLOSS OVER SOMETHING** to ignore something or treat it superficially ○ *The committee slurred over my protests.* **4. *vti* SMEAR OR BE SMEARED** to blur or smear wet ink on a page, or be blurred or smeared **5. *vt* MUSIC PERFORM MUSIC SMOOTHLY** to play musical notes in a smooth, uninterrupted way ■ *n* **1. INSULT** an insulting or demeaning statement about somebody **2. SLURRED PRONUNCIATION** an indistinct pronunciation or sound **3. BLURRED IMAGE** an image that has been smeared or blurred **4. MUSIC MUSIC SYMBOL** a curved line that connects two or more notes on a score, indicating that they are to be performed smoothly [Early 17C. Origin ?]

slurp /slurp/ *vti* (**slurps, slurping, slurped**) **DRINK SOMETHING NOISILY** to make a loud sucking sound while drinking or eating something ○ *Would you stop slurping your milk shake?* ■ *n* **1. SUCKING SOUND** a loud sucking sound made while drinking or eating **2. LIQUID MOUTHFUL** a mouthful of a liquid (*informal*) ○ *Can I have a slurp of your lemonade?* [Mid-17C. < Dutch *slurpen*] —**slurpingly** *adv*

slurry /slúrri/ *n* a liquid mixture of water and an insoluble solid material such as cement or clay [15C. < dialect *slur* 'thin mud', origin?]

slush /slush/ *n* **1. MELTING SNOW OR ICE** snow or ice that has begun to melt **2. SEMILIQUID SUBSTANCE** a solid substance that has become wet and sloppy, e.g. mud **3. OVERLY SENTIMENTAL EXPRESSION** extremely sentimental speech or writing **4. ICE DRINK** a drink made of finely crushed ice with a flavoured syrup poured over it **5. GREASE** a greasy substance used to lubricate machine parts **6. NAUT GREASE FROM SHIP'S GALLEY** the waste grease or fat produced by a ship's galley ■ *v* (**slushes, slushing, slushed**) **1. *vt* SOAK SOMETHING WITH SLUSH** to splash or cover something with mud or slush **2. *vi* WALK THROUGH SLUSH** to walk through wet snow or mud ○ *It had been raining so hard we had to slush through mud to get there.* **3. *vi* MAKE SPLASHING SOUND** to make a splashing or squelching sound **4. *vt* ENG GREASE MACHINERY** to lubricate the parts of a machine **5. *vt* CONSTR PUT MORTAR IN JOINTS** to fill masonry joints with mortar, or cover a surface with cement [Mid-17C. Origin ?]

slush fund *n* **1. MONEY FOR ILLEGAL ACTIVITIES** money set aside by a business or other organization for corrupt activities such as the bribery of public officials **2. MONEY FOR ENTERTAINMENT** money set aside to use for fun or entertainment expenses **3. LUXURY FUND FOR SHIP'S CREW** money raised by selling refuse from a ship to pay for small luxuries for the crew [< SLUSH 'grease collected in a ship's galley (and sold)'; from the idea of 'greasing' somebody's palm with money]

slush pile *n* a pile of unsolicited manuscripts accumulated in a publisher's office (*informal*)

slushy /slúshi/ (**-ier, -iest**) *adj* **1. FULL OF SLUSH** covered with or full of melting snow and ice **2. RESEMBLING SLUSH** with the consistency of slush **3. OVERLY SENTIMENTAL** filled with or expressing excessive sentiment ○ *a slushy love story* —**slushiness** *n*

slut /slut/ *n* **1.** an offensive term for a woman thought to be sexually promiscuous **2.** an offensive term for a woman who charges for engaging in sexual activities **3.** an offensive term for a woman who is regarded as not concerned about conventional standards of domestic cleanliness (*dated*) [15C. Origin ?] —**sluttish** *adj* —**sluttishly** *adv* —**sluttishness** *n* —**slutty** *adj*

Sluter /slóotər/, **Claus** (1350?–1406) Dutch sculptor noted for the intense facial expressions of his figures. His best-known work is *Well of Moses* (1395–1403).

SLV *abbr* AEROSP space launch vehicle *or* standard launch vehicle

sly /slī/ (**slier, sliest**) *adj* **1.** CRAFTY cleverly skilful and cunning **2.** EVASIVE lacking honesty or straightforwardness **3.** MISCHIEVOUS full of playful mischief [13C. < Old Norse *slœgr* 'clever, crafty'] —**slyly** *adv* —**slyness** *n* ◇ **on the sly** without the knowledge or permission of others

slyboots /slī boots/ *n* somebody considered to be cunning or devious (*insult; takes a singular verb*)

sly grog *n* ANZ alcoholic beverages sold illegally (*informal*)

slype /slīp/ *n* a covered passage in a cathedral or church that joins the transept to a chapter house [Mid-19C. Origin ?]

sm *abbr* San Marino (*used in Internet addresses*) See table at **domain name**

Sm *symbol* CHEM ELEM samarium

SM *abbr* MIL sergeant major

sm. *abbr* small

S/M, S-M *abbr* sadomasochism

SMA *abbr* METALL shape memory alloy

smack[1] /smak/ *v* (**smacks, smacking, smacked**) **1.** *vti* SLAP SOMEBODY to hit somebody with a quick stinging and usually noisy blow with the palm of the hand **2.** *vi* HIT AGAINST SOMETHING NOISILY to strike against, collide with, or land in something with a sharp loud noise **3.** *vt* PRESS LIPS TOGETHER to press the lips together and then open them with a short loud noise ■ *n* **1.** SLAP a sharp quick blow with the palm of the hand **2.** NOISY SOUND a sharp loud noise made when one thing strikes another **3.** LOUD KISS a brief noisy kiss ■ *adv* **1.** WITH LOUD NOISE with a sharp loud noise or collision **2.** DIRECTLY directly or precisely ○ *I was smack in the middle of getting ready to leave when you called.* [Mid-16C. < Middle Low German *smacken* 'open the lips noisily', an imitation of the sound]

smack[2] /smak/ *n* **1.** DISTINCTIVE TASTE a unique flavour or taste of something **2.** HINT a small amount or trace ■ *vi* (**smacks, smacking, smacked**) **1.** BE DISTINCTIVELY FLAVOURED to have a unique flavour or taste **2.** EXPRESS SOMETHING INDIRECTLY to suggest or hint at something ○ *an editorial that smacked of snobbery* [Old English *smæc* 'taste' < Germanic]

smack[3] /smak/ *n* a sailing vessel used for fishing, usually for carrying the catch to market [Early 17C. < Dutch *smak*]

smack[4] /smak/ *n* DRUGS same as **heroin** (*slang*) [Mid-20C. Probably alteration of slang *schmeck* < Yiddish, 'a sniff' < Middle High German *smecken* 'to smell']

smack-dab *adv* N Am same as **slap-bang** (sense 1) (*informal*)

smacker /smákər/ *n* (*informal*) **1.** a noisy smacking kiss **2.** MONEY same as **pound**

smacking /smáking/ *adj* very brisk or lively ○ *a smacking breeze*

small /smawl/ *adj* **1.** LITTLE of a relatively little size ○ *a small animal* **2.** NOT MUCH little in quantity or value ○ *a small sum of money* **3.** INSIGNIFICANT unimportant or trivial ○ *a small matter* **4.** LIMITED operating on a limited scale ○ *small businesses* **5.** MINOR lacking in power, influence, or status ○ *a small fish in a big pond* **6.** NOT YET MATURE young or not fully grown ○ *small children* **7.** ORDINARY humble or modest ○ *He came from small beginnings.* **8.** MEAN petty and mean-spirited ○ *He's too small to apologize.* **9.** LOWER CASE in lower case rather than capitals ○ *small letters* **10.** WITHOUT SELF-RESPECT humiliated or feeling little self-worth ○ *Her criticisms and ridicule made me feel very small.* ■ *adv* **1.** IN SMALL PIECES in or into little pieces ○ *Cut it up small.* **2.** IN SMALL WAY in a moderate or limited way ○ *start out small* **3.** QUIETLY quietly or softly (*archaic*) ■ *n* **1.** NARROW PART a part of something that is narrower or smaller than the rest of it ○ *the small of the back* **2.** SIZE FOR SOMEBODY SMALL a size that fits somebody who is of less than average proportions, or a garment in that size ■ **smalls** *npl* UK UNDERGARMENTS items of underwear (*informal or humorous*) [Old English *smæl* 'slender, small' < Germanic, 'small animal'] —**smallish** *adj* —**smallness** *n*

small ad *n* same as **classified advertisement** (*informal; usually used in the plural*)

small arms *npl* firearms that can be held in one or both hands while firing, e.g. pistols and rifles

small beer *n* **1.** something of little or no importance (*informal*) ○ *A thousand pounds is small beer to people like him.* **2.** weak or inferior beer (*dated*)

small-bore *adj* describes .22-calibre firearms or ammunition

small calorie *n* MEASURE same as **calorie** (sense 1)

small capital *n* a capital letter that is the same height as a lower-case letter

small change *n* **1.** coins that have a low denomination **2.** something considered to be comparatively insignificant

small circle *n* the circumference of a plane that cuts a sphere but does not pass through its centre

small claims court *n* a local court that has jurisdiction to try civil actions involving claims worth only a small sum of money

Smalley /smáwli/, **Richard E.** (*b.* 1943) US chemical physicist. Together with Robert Curl and Harold Kroto, he discovered the family of carbon molecules called fullerenes, and shared the Nobel Prize in chemistry (1996).

small fry *npl* **1.** TRIVIAL THINGS people, events, or issues that are thought to be of little importance **2.** CHILDREN a young child or young children (*informal*) **3.** YOUNG FISH young, immature, or small fish

small game *n* small animals and birds that are hunted for sport

small goods *npl* ANZ processed meats, e.g. sausages and salamis

smallholding /smáwl hōlding/ *n* a piece of farmland that is smaller than the average farm —**smallholder** *n*

small hours *npl* the early morning hours after midnight

small intestine *n* the part of the intestine between the stomach and the large intestine, consisting of the duodenum, jejunum, and ileum, where digestion of food and most absorption of nutrients takes place

small island *n* Carib any of the small Caribbean islands northwest of Trinidad such as St Vincent and Grenada (*disapproving*)

small-minded *adj* petty and intolerant of the ideas and beliefs of others —**small-mindedly** *adv* —**small-mindedness** *n*

smallmouth bass /smáwl mowth báss/ *n* a greenish-brown freshwater bass found in clear streams and lakes that is a popular game fish. Native to: North America. Latin name: *Micropterus dolomieu*.

smallpox /smáwl poks/ *n* a highly contagious disease caused by a poxvirus and marked by high fever and the formation of scar-producing pustules. A worldwide inoculation programme has almost eradicated the smallpox virus from the human population. Technical name **variola**

small print *n* UK the very fine, hard-to-read print in a contract or other legal document that often contains important information that could be overlooked. ANZ, N Am term **fine print**

small-scale *adj* **1.** limited in scope or size ○ *small-scale businesses* **2.** made or constructed on a small scale ○ *She built a small-scale replica of the ship.*

small screen *n* the medium of television, especially as distinct from the cinema (*informal*)

small slam *n* CARDS same as **little slam**

small stores *npl* small items sold on a ship or at a naval base, e.g. clothing

small stuff *n* light twine or yarn used on a ship

smallsword /smáwl sawrd/ *n* a light sword used in the 17th and 18th centuries for duelling and fencing (*archaic*)

small talk *n* polite conversation about matters of little importance, especially between people who do not know each other well

small-time *adj* of minor importance or influence (*informal*) ○ *He's just a small-time crook.*

smalmy /smáami/ (**smalmier, smalmiest**) *adj* regional dirty

REGIONAL NOTE See *manky*.

smalt /smawlt/ *n* **1.** silica glass that has been coloured a deep blue by cobalt oxide **2.** a deep blue pigment made by crushing smalt [Mid-16C. Via French < Italian *smalto* (see SMALTO)]

smaltite /smáwl tīt/ *n* a blue-grey cobalt nickel arsenide mineral. Use: source of cobalt.

smalto /smáaltō/ *n* small bits of pottery, glass, and tiles used in mosaics [Early 18C. < Italian < Germanic]

smaragdite /smə rág dīt/ *n* a fibrous green amphibole mineral [Early 19C. < Latin *smaragdus*, via Greek < Hebrew *bāreqet* 'emerald' < *bāraq* 'flash, sparkle']

smarm /smaarm/ (*informal*) *n* **1.** SELF-SERVING FLATTERY ingratiating or servile flattery **2.** INSINCERE CHARM charm that is distastefully self-conscious or insincere ■ *v* (**smarms, smarming, smarmed**) **1.** *vi* FLATTER SOMEBODY to make a lot of fuss over somebody in order to ingratiate yourself **2.** *vt* GREASE HAIR to flatten hair by smoothing it down with grease [Early 20C. Origin ?]

smarmy /smáarmi/ (**-ier, -iest**) *adj* excessively and unpleasantly polite and ingratiating (*informal*) —**smarmily** *adv* —**smarminess** *n*

smart /smaart/ *adj* **1.** WELL-GROOMED having a neat and well-cared-for appearance **2.** FASHIONABLE fashionable and stylish ○ *smart restaurants* **3.** CLEVER showing intelligence and mental alertness ○ *smart students* **4.** KEEN shrewd and calculating in business and other dealings ○ *a smart dealer* **5.** WITTY AND AMUSING amusingly clever and possessing a quick wit **6.** INSOLENT disrespectful or impertinent ○ *Whatever you say to him, he has some smart answer.* **7.** LIVELY vigorous and brisk ○ *a smart pace* **8.** STINGING causing a sharp stinging sensation ○ *a smart slap* **9.** MIL LASER- OR RADIO-GUIDED describes a missile or weapon that is guided to its target by laser or radio beams **10.** ELECTRONICS ELECTRONIC fitted with a built-in microprocessor ○ *smart traffic lights* **11.** DISCRIMINATING selective in application or effect ○ *smart sanctions* ■ *vi* (**smarts, smarting, smarted**) **1.** CAUSE OR HAVE SHARP PAIN to feel, cause, or be the site of a sharp stinging pain ○ *My hand smarts.* **2.** BE EMBARRASSED to feel acute embarrassment, shame, or remorse ○ *She still smarted when she remembered his criticism.* **3.** BE PUNISHED to be punished severely ■ *adv* SMARTLY in a smart manner ■ *n* **1.** PAIN a sharp stinging localized pain **2.** EMBARRASSMENT OR MENTAL DISCOMFORT a feeling such as acute embarrassment, shame, or remorse [Old English *smeortan* 'be painful' origin ?] —**smartly** *adv* —**smartness** *n*

SYNONYMS See *intelligent*.

Smart /smaart/, **Jeffrey** (*b.* 1921) Australian painter. He is renowned for his stylized, often surreal paintings of urban environments. Full name **Smart, Frank Jeffrey Edson**

smart aleck /-alik/, **smart alec** *n* somebody who makes an annoying show of knowing something or of being cleverer than others (*informal*) [Mid-19C. Origin ?] —**smart-aleck** *adj*

smartarse /smáart aarss/ *n* same as **smart aleck** (*slang offensive*)

smartass /smáart ass/, **smart-ass** *n* N Am same as **smart aleck** (*slang offensive*)

smart bomb *n* a missile that is guided to its target by laser or radio beams

smart card *n* a small plastic card containing a microchip that can store personal data such as bank-account details, used for identification and for payment of purchases

smarten /smáart'n/ (**-ens, -ening, -ened**) *vt* **1.** to improve the appearance of somebody or something **2.** to increase the speed of something
smarten up *vti* **1.** IMPROVE APPEARANCE to improve your appearance, or the appearance of somebody or something else **2.** MAKE OR BECOME LIVELIER to make somebody or something brighter or livelier, or become brighter or livelier **3.** N Am MAKE OR BECOME WISER to make somebody wiser or more knowing, or become wiser or more knowing

smart growth *n* economic growth that consciously seeks to avoid wastefulness and damage to the environment and communities

smartish /smáartish/ *adv* without delay or quickly (*informal*) ○ *You'd better make up your mind smartish!*

smart money *n* **1.** WISE INVESTMENT OR BET money invested in or bet on something likely to yield a good profit **2.** WISE INVESTORS people who know what to invest in or bet on to make a good profit **3.** *US* LAW DAMAGES AWARDED TO PUNISH DEFENDANT damages awarded to a plaintiff in excess of the usual level of compensation to punish a defendant in cases of serious negligence or wilful misconduct

smartsizing /smáart sīzing/ *n* the process of reducing the size of a workforce by eliminating staff positions (*slang*)

smart terminal *n* a network terminal that carries out processing but uses another computer for data and program storage

smarty-pants /smáarti-/ (*plural same*), **smarty** (*plural* **-ies**) *n* same as **smart aleck** (*informal*)

smash /smash/ *v* (**smashes, smashing, smashed**) **1.** *vti* BREAK SOMETHING WITH FORCE to break something with great force or violence, or move violently so as to break something **2.** *vti* BREAK SOMETHING INTO PIECES to break something into many small pieces, or be broken in this way **3.** *vti* HIT SOMETHING FORCEFULLY to hit something with great force, or make something do this **4.** *vt* DEFEAT OR DESTROY SOMETHING to ruin, defeat, or put an end to somebody or something completely **5.** *vt* RACKET GAMES HIT BALL WITH OVERHEAD STROKE in racket games, to hit a ball or shuttlecock downwards with great force with an overhead stroke ■ *n* **1.** LOUD NOISE the loud sound of something hitting or being hit by something else and breaking into pieces ○ *The mirror hit the floor with a smash.* **2.** HEAVY BLOW a blow delivered with great force **3.** COLLISION a crash or collision ○ *There's been a bad smash on the motorway.* **4.** RACKET GAMES OVERHEAD STROKE in racket games, an overhead stroke hit downwards with great force **5.** VOLLEYBALL same as **spike** (sense 12) **6.** BUSINESS, THEATRE GREAT SUCCESS an unqualified success (*often used before a noun*) ○ *The new show was a smash hit.* **7.** BUSINESS BIG FAILURE a major failure, especially one involving finances ■ *adv* WITH SMASH with the sound of a smash [Late 17C. Origin ?] —**smashable** *adj*

smash up *v* **1.** *vti* to damage something severely in a collision with something solid, or be damaged in this way **2.** *vt* to damage or destroy something by breaking

smash-and-grab *adj* describes a robbery committed by breaking a shop window in order to steal the goods on display —**smash-and-grab** *n*

smashed /smasht/ *adj* very drunk or under the influence of drugs (*informal*)

smasher /smáshər/ *n* somebody or something that is extremely impressive or attractive (*dated informal*)

smashing /smáshing/ *adj* extremely good or pleasing (*dated informal*)

smash repairs *npl Aus* a business that specializes in repairing car bodies

smash-up *n* a road accident between vehicles in which all the machines involved are badly damaged

smattering /smáttəring/, **smatter** /smáttər/ *n* **1.** a slight knowledge of something such as a subject or language **2.** a small amount or number ○ *a smattering of rain* [Mid-16C. < *smatter* 'dabble, speak without proper knowledge', origin?]

SMATV *abbr* satellite master antenna television

smear /smeer/ *v* (**smears, smearing, smeared**) **1.** *vti* SPREAD SOMETHING OVER SURFACE to spread something liquid or greasy over a surface, or be spread over a surface ○ *This lipstick is made not to smear.* **2.** *vt* SAY BAD THINGS ABOUT SOMEBODY to deliberately spread damaging rumours about somebody **3.** *vt US* DEFEAT SOMEBODY to severely defeat a competitor or enemy (*informal; usually passive*) ○ *We got smeared.* ■ *n* **1.** PATCH OF SMEARED SUBSTANCE an act of smearing, or a smeared patch of something **2.** HARMFUL RUMOUR a damaging rumour about somebody **3.** MED SAMPLE OF CELLS a sample of cells taken from body tissue or a bodily secretion or discharge and smeared on a microscope slide for examination **4.** MED same as **cervical smear** (*informal*) [Old English *smeirwan* (verb), *smeoru* (noun) < Germanic] —**smearer** *n*

smear campaign *n* a concerted effort to damage somebody's reputation by spreading harmful rumours about him or her

smear test *n* MED same as **cervical smear**

smeary /smeéri/ (**-ier, -iest**) *adj* **1.** smeared on, easily smeared, or likely to smear **2.** having or covered with smears

smectic /sméktik/ *adj* describes materials such as liquid crystals whose liquid phase consists of elongated molecules arranged in layers and with their axes parallel to each other [Late 17C. Via Latin < Greek *smēktikos* < *smēkhein* 'rub, cleanse']

smectite /smék tīt/ *n* a clay mineral belonging to the group that swell in water. Use: ion exchange materials. [Early 19C. < Greek *smēktis* 'fuller's earth']

smeddum /sméddəm/ *n Scotland* **1.** spirit, energy, and determination **2.** fine dust, powder, or flour [Old English *smedena* 'fine flour', origin ?]

smegma /smégmə/ *n* a secretion of the sebaceous glands that collects under the foreskin or around the clitoris [Early 19C. Via Latin < Greek *smēgma* 'soap' < *smēkhein* 'rub, cleanse']

smell /smel/ *v* (**smells, smelling, smelt** /smelt/ or **smelled**) **1.** *vti* DETECT SOMETHING USING NOSE to detect or recognize something by means of sensitive nerves in the nose **2.** *vt* USE NOSE TO ASSESS SOMETHING to use the sensitive nerves in the nose to assess something ○ *Smell that and see if it's still good.* **3.** *vi* BE DETECTED WHEN BREATHED IN to seem to be in a particular condition or give a particular impression, when judged by somebody breathing in through the nose ○ *Something smells good.* **4.** *vi* GIVE UNPLEASANT IMPRESSION WHEN BREATHED IN to be considered unpleasant when breathed in through the nose ○ *That really smells!* **5.** *vi* GIVE IMPRESSION to give off a suggestion or impression of something ○ *It smells dangerous.* **6.** *vt* FEEL OR DETECT SOMETHING to detect the presence or existence of something, usually something bad ○ *I smell trouble here.* ■ *n* **1.** SENSE BASED ON NERVES IN NOSE the sense based on the sensitive nerves in the nose that distinguish odours **2.** QUALITY DETECTED BY NOSE the quality of something that can be detected by the sensitive nerves in the nose **3.** UNPLEASANT ODOUR the unpleasant impression that something gives when breathed in through the nose ○ *What's that smell?* **4.** ACT OF SMELLING an act or instance of breathing something in through the nose in order to make a judgment about it **5.** SUGGESTION OF SOMETHING a suggestion or impression of something [12C. Origin ?] —**smeller** *n*

SYNONYMS *smell, odour, aroma, bouquet, scent, perfume, fragrance, stink, stench, reek*

CORE MEANING: the way something smells

smell a neutral, pleasant, or unpleasant quality detected by the nerves of the nose ○ *the smell of newly mown grass* ○ *a black substance that had the most awful smell* **odour** a smell, whether pleasant or unpleasant ○ *the rank odour of sweat* ○ *Horses can smell dry oats, which for us have no strong odour.* **aroma** a distinctive pleasant smell, especially one related to cooking or food ○ *the appealing aroma of fresh coffee* **bouquet** the characteristic pleasant smell of a wine ○ *There is seldom much of a bouquet from Pinot Blanc wines.* **scent** a pleasant sweet smell such as that of a flower, or the characteristic smell given off by a particular animal or person and used in tracking ○ *The air was heavy with the scent of flowers.* ○ *Badgers can sometimes become nervous if they catch the scent of a stranger.* **perfume** a sweet, pleasant, and heady smell, especially the smell of flowers or plants ○ *the heady perfume of the old roses* **fragrance** a pleasant sweet smell, especially a delicate or subtle one ○ *the faint, elusive fragrance of his aftershave* ○ *The jasmine filled the evening air with its fragrance.* **stink** a strong and unpleasant smell ○ *the stink of sewage* **stench** a very strong unpleasant smell, especially a lingering smell associated with death or decay ○ *The stench of rotting fish hung in the air.* ○ *Rescue workers wore face masks to guard against the foul stench.* **reek** a strong unpleasant smell ○ *the pungent reek of stable manure*

smellfungus /sméll fung gəss/ (*plural* **-gi** /-gī/ or **-guses**) *n* a carping faultfinder (*archaic*) [Early 19C. After *Smellfungus*, name given to Tobias Smollett by Laurence Sterne in *A Sentimental Journey* (1768), because of the ill-tempered tone of Smollett's *Travels through France and Italy* (1766)]

smellies /smélliz/ *npl* toiletries with an appealing scent (*informal*)

smelling salts /smélling-/ *npl* a mixture of ammonium carbonate and perfume. Use: especially formerly, to revive somebody who felt faint or had fainted.

smelly /smélli/ (**-ier, -iest**) *adj* giving off a strong or unpleasant smell —**smelliness** *n*

smelt[1] /smelt/ (**smelts, smelting, smelted**) *v* **1.** *vt* to melt ore in order to get metal from it, or produce metal in this way. The separation of the metal usually requires a chemical change. **2.** *vi* to undergo fusing or melting in the process of smelting [Mid-16C. < Middle Low German *smelten*]

smelt[2] /smelt/ (*plural* **smelts** or *same*) *n* **1.** a small silvery sea or freshwater fish. Native to: northern waters. Family: Osmeridae. **2.** the oily flesh of a smelt as food [Pre-12C. Origin ?]

smelt[3] /smelt/ past participle, past tense of **smell**

smelter /sméltər/ *n* **1.** SOMEBODY WHO SMELTS ORE somebody who smelts ore or who owns a place where ore is smelted **2.** SMELTING FACTORY a place where smelting is carried out **3.** SMELTING APPARATUS an apparatus used for smelting

Smetana /sméttənə/, **Bedřich** (1824–84) Czech composer. The founder of Czech nationalist music, he is best known for his opera *The Bartered Bride* (1866) and the six symphonic poems *Ma Vlast* (My Homeland) (1874–79).

smew /smyoo/ (*plural* **smews** or *same*) *n* a sub-Arctic duck with a hooked serrated beak, the male of which has predominantly white feathers with black markings. Native to: Europe, Asia. Latin name: *Mergus albellus.* [Late 17C. Probably ultimately < W Germanic]

smidgen /smíjjən/, **smidgin, smidgeon, smidge** /smij/ *n* a small amount (*informal*) [Mid-19C. Origin ?]

smilax /smī laks/ *n* **1.** a climbing plant with red or bluish-black berries and often prickly stems. Flowers: small, white or yellowish. Native to: temperate and tropical regions. Genus: *Smilax.* **2.** a vine prized by florists for its glossy bright green leaves. Native to: southern Africa. Latin name: *Asparagus asparagoides.* [Late 16C. Via Latin < Greek, 'bindweed']

smile /smīl/ *v* (**smiles, smiling, smiled**) **1.** *vti* MAKE PLEASANT EXPRESSION WITH MOUTH to raise the corners of the mouth in an expression of amusement, pleasure, or approval **2.** *vt* EXPRESS SOMETHING BY SMILING to express something by or while smiling ○ *smiled his agreement* **3.** *vi* HAVE PLEASANT APPEARANCE to appear to be in a state of happiness or enjoying good fortune or pleasure **4.** *vi* BE FAVOURABLE to be favourably disposed to somebody or something ○ *Fortune smiled on their journey.* ■ *n* **1.** PLEASANT EXPRESSION a facial expression in which the corners of the mouth are raised, usually expressing amusement, pleasure, or approval **2.** PLEASANT APPEARANCE an appearance of pleasure or approval (*often used in the plural*) ○ *They were all smiles when we left.* **3.** SIGN OF FAVOUR an expression or sign of favour [13C. Probably < N Germanic] —**smiler** *n* —**smilingly** *adv*

smiley /smīli/ *adj* (**-ier, -iest**) smiling or often smiling ■ *n* (*plural* **-eys**) a symbol (**emoticon**), often in the form :-), keyed in e-mails and text messages to communicate feelings such as pleasure, approval, or humour

smiley face *n* **1.** a round yellow image representing a smiling face, generally consisting of two dots and an upward-curving arc, representing eyes and a mouth **2.** ONLINE same as **smiley**

smilodon /smīlə don/ *n* a large sabre-toothed tiger existing during the Pleistocene epoch, between about 2 million and 10,000 years ago. Genus: *Smilodon.* [Mid-19C. < modern Latin, 'knife-toothed' < Greek *smilē* 'knife']

smir /smur/, **smirr** *Scotland n* drizzle or very fine rain ■ *vi* (**smirs, smirring, smirred; smirrs, smirring, smirred**) to drizzle or rain with very fine droplets [Early 19C. Origin ?]

smirch /smurch/ vt (**smirches, smirching, smirched**) **1.** DAMAGE REPUTATION to damage somebody's or something's reputation or good name **2.** DIRTY SOMETHING to make something dirty by smearing or staining it (*archaic or literary*) ■ n **1.** DIRTY STAIN a dirty stain or smear (*archaic or literary*) **2.** SOMETHING DAMAGING something that damages a reputation [15C. Origin ?]

smirk /smurk/ n INSOLENT SMILE an insolent smile expressing feelings such as superiority, self-satisfaction, or conceit ■ v (**smirks, smirking, smirked**) **1.** vi SMILE INSOLENTLY to smile in an insolent, smug, or contemptuous way **2.** vt EXPRESS SOMETHING WITH SMIRK to express something with a smirk [Old English *smearcian* 'smile' < Germanic]

smirr n, vi *Scotland* METEOROL another spelling of **smir**

smite /smīt/ (**smites, smiting, smote** /smōt/, **smitten** /smítt'n/ or **smit** /smit/) v **1.** vti HIT SOMEBODY OR SOMETHING HARD to hit somebody or something with a hard blow (*archaic or literary*) **2.** vt AFFECT OR AFFLICT SOMEBODY to affect somebody strongly or disastrously, or afflict somebody with something (*literary; often passive*) **3.** vt FILL SOMEBODY WITH LOVE to fill somebody with love or longing (*literary; usually passive*) [Old English *smītan* 'smear, pollute' < Germanic] —**smiter** n

smith /smith/ n **1.** somebody who makes or repairs metal objects **2.** OCCUPATIONS same as **blacksmith** [Old English *smiþ* < Germanic, 'coppersmith']

Smith /smith/, **Adam** (1723–90) British philosopher and economist. He articulated his theory of free trade in *The Wealth of Nations* (1776).

> 'The chief enjoyment of riches consists in the parade of riches.'
> [Adam Smith, *The Wealth of Nations*; 1776]

Smith, Bernard (b. 1916) Australian art historian. He wrote *European Vision and the South Pacific* (1960). Full name **Smith, Bernard William**

Smith, Bessie (1894–1937) US singer. The leading blues singer of her day, she recorded widely with major jazz bands.

> 'It's mighty strange, without a doubt, Nobody knows you when you're down and out.'
> [Bessie Smith, 'Nobody Knows You When You're Down and Out', *Harlem: The Great Black Way*, Jervis Anderson; 1982]

Smith, Dick (b. 1944) Australian entrepreneur and aviator. In 1983 he became the first person to fly round the world solo by helicopter. Born **Smith, Richard Harold**

Smith, Grace Cossington (1892–1985) Australian painter. She was a modernist artist noted for post-impressionist works such as *The Lacquer Room* (1935).

Smith, Harvey (b. 1938) British showjumper. He was many times winner of the British Grand Prix and other championships, and a member of the British Olympic team (1968 and 1972). Full name **Smith, Robert Harvey**

Smith, Ian (b. 1919) prime minister of Rhodesia (now Zimbabwe; 1964–79). He led the ruling white minority of Rhodesia to declare unilateral independence from the United Kingdom in 1965. Full name **Smith, Ian Douglas**

> 'I don't believe in black majority rule in Rhodesia...not in a thousand years.'
> [Ian Smith, *Speech*; March 1976]

Smith, John (1579–1631) English-born North American colonist. He was president of the Virginia colony at Jamestown (1608–09) and claimed to have been rescued from Native North Americans by Pocahontas. His explorations and accounts influenced many English people to settle in North America.

> 'Two great stones were brought before *Powhatan*: then as many as could layd hands on him...to beate out his braines, *Pocahontas* the Kings dearest daughter...got his head in her armes, and laid her owne upon his to save him.'
> [John Smith, *The Generall History of Virginia, New-England, and the Summer Isles*; 1624]

Smith, Joseph (1805–44) US religious leader. He was the visionary founder of the Church of Jesus Christ of Latter-Day Saints (1830). Amid local controversy, he established communities in Missouri and Illinois. He was killed by a mob opposed to his philosophy.

> 'He called me by name, and said unto me that he was a messenger sent from the presence of God to me, and that...God had a work for me to do.'
> [Joseph Smith, *In His Own Words*; 1844]

Dame Maggie Smith

Smith, Dame Maggie (b. 1934) British actor. Her work in classical theatre was complemented by her comedy performances and extensive film appearances. Full name **Smith, Dame Margaret Nathalie**

Smith, Stevie (1902–71) British poet and novelist. Her works include the autobiographical *Novel on Yellow Paper* (1936) and collections of sharp, wry verse such as *Not Waving but Drowning* (1957). Her *Collected Poems* (1975) were published posthumously. Born **Smith, Florence Margaret**

> 'Nobody heard him, the dead man, / But still he lay moaning: / I was much further out than you thought / And not waving but drowning.'
> [Stevie Smith, 'Not Waving But Drowning'; 1957]

smithereens /smíthə réenz/ npl very small broken pieces (*informal*) [Early 19C. Probably < Irish *smidirín* 'small fragment' < *smiodar* 'fragment']

smithery /smíthəri/ (*plural* -**ies**) n **1.** the work or craft of a smith **2.** MANUF same as **smithy**

Smithson /smíths'n/, **James** (1765–1829) British mineralogist and chemist. His legacy helped to establish the Smithsonian Institution (1846).

Smithsonian Institution /smith sōni ən-/, **Smithsonian** n a government trust founded in Washington, D.C., by an act of Congress in 1846 to promote research and education. It sponsors scientific research and publications and maintains the national collections. The fourteen museums it administers include the National Museum of American History and the National Air and Space Museum in Washington, DC, and the National Museum of the Native American in New York City. [Early 19C. After James SMITHSON]

smithsonite /smíthsə nīt/ n a white or yellow-to-brown zinc carbonate mineral. Use: source of zinc. [Mid-19C. After James SMITHSON]

smithy /smíthi/ (*plural* -**ies**) n the place where a blacksmith works

smitten past participle of **smite** (*archaic or literary*)

smock /smok/ n **1.** LOOSE DRESS a loose dress with the cloth gathered at the chest worn by a child or woman **2.** OVERSHIRT a loose garment worn to protect the clothes **3.** UNDERGARMENT a woman's loose-fitting undergarment or chemise of a type used until the 18th century ■ vt (**smocks, smocking, smocked**) SEW SOMETHING WITH GATHERING STITCHES to sew or decorate something with decorative gathering stitches [Old English *smoc* < Germanic, 'creep']

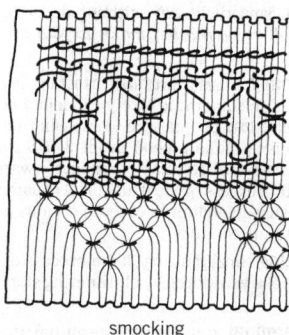

smocking

smocking /smóking/ n decorative stitching in a honeycomb or zigzag pattern, used to gather fabric evenly

smog /smog/ n a mixture of fog and smoke or other airborne pollutants such as exhaust fumes [Early 20C. Blend of SMOKE + FOG] —**smoggy** adj

smoke /smōk/ n **1.** CLOUD OF TINY PARTICLES a mass of tiny particles in the air that rises up from something burning **2.** VAPOUR RESEMBLING SMOKE something that resembles smoke, usually consisting of minute particles suspended in a gas ○ *a white, stinging smoke of chemical fumes* **3.** INHALING OF BURNING TOBACCO FUMES an act of smoking a cigarette, cigar, or pipe **4.** CIGARETTE a cigarette or other tobacco product (*informal*) **5.** SMOKABLE SUBSTANCE something that can be smoked, e.g. tobacco (*informal*) ○ *picked up some great smoke last week* **6.** SOMETHING THAT OBSCURES something that obscures or obstructs information, understanding, or awareness **7.** SOMETHING TRANSIENT something transient or illusory **8.** COLOURS GREY COLOUR a grey colour tinged with blue or brown ■ v (**smokes, smoking, smoked**) **1.** vti USE TOBACCO to inhale and exhale the smoke of burning tobacco or a drug, or smoke from a cigarette, cigar, or pipe **2.** vti INHALE VAPOURS to inhale the smoke of any substance that can burn and be inhaled **3.** vi GIVE OFF SMOKE to give off smoke, often in a way that indicates a malfunction **4.** vt FUMIGATE SOMETHING WITH SMOKE to fumigate, clean, or clear something with smoke **5.** vt STUPEFY SOMETHING to stupefy something with smoke ○ *smoke a hive* **6.** vt HANDICRAFT DARKEN SOMETHING to darken something so as to give it the colour of smoke ○ *smoked glass* **7.** vt FOOD CURE FOOD WITH WOOD SMOKE to cure or treat food such as meat, fish, or cheese with wood smoke **8.** vt US BEAT SOMEBODY EASILY to defeat somebody heavily, or outclass a competitor (*informal*) [Old English *smoca* < Germanic] —**smokable** adj —**smoke** adj ◇ **go up in smoke 1.** to be destroyed by burning **2.** to fail completely to happen as planned or hoped

smoke out vt **1.** to drive a person or animal from a hiding place by using smoke **2.** to bring something to light by clever or assertive enquiry

smoke alarm n a device intended to give a warning of fire by triggering an alarm when it detects the presence of smoke. N Am term **smoke detector**

smoke and mirrors n something that is intended to draw attention away from something else that somebody would prefer remained unnoticed [< the use of smoke and mirrors in magic acts]

smoke bomb n a device that gives off dense clouds of irritating chemical smoke, used to drive people or animals out of a place

smoke detector n N Am same as **smoke alarm**

smoke-dried adj cured with or dried in smoke

smoked rubber /smṓkt-/ n crude rubber prepared by drying coagulated latex sheets in smokehouses before they are packed into bales. The smoking process hinders the formation of bacteria and moulds, and aids in the preservation of the rubber against oxidation.

smoke-filled room n a room where deals are negotiated in private, traditionally considered to be filled with the smoke of the negotiators' cigarettes, cigars, or pipes

smoke hood *n* a plastic head covering designed to be used with a breathing apparatus

smokehouse /smók howss/ (*plural* **-houses** /-howziz/) *n* a small building where meat, fish, or other materials are cured in smoke

smokejack /smók jak/ *n* a device that turns a roasting spit and is powered by rising gases in a chimney

smokeless /smókləss/ *adj* **1.** producing little or no smoke **2.** describes an area where smoke, e.g. from coal fires, is not permitted

smokeless powder *n* a nitrocellulose-based explosive or propellant that produces little smoke

smokeless zone *n* an area in which only smokeless fuels can be burned

smoker /smókər/ *n* **1.** SOMEBODY WHO SMOKES somebody who smokes something, especially tobacco products **2.** GATHERING OF MEN a social gathering of men **3.** RAIL RAILWAY CARRIAGE DESIGNATED FOR SMOKING a railway compartment where smoking is permitted **4.** HOUSEHOLD APPARATUS FOR SMOKING FOOD an apparatus for smoking food in

smoker's cough *n* a hacking cough, often accompanied by phlegm, caused by excessive smoking

smoke screen *n* **1.** a mass of smoke produced to conceal the movements of ships, troops, or equipment **2.** an action taken to mislead somebody or obscure something

smokestack /smók stak/ *n* **1.** a tall, often cylindrical industrial chimney, often attached to a factory **2.** *N Am* ENG same as **chimney** (sense 4)

smokestack industry *n* an industry characterized by large factories, heavy equipment, high energy consumption, and usually pollution of the environment

smoke tree *n* a bush or small tree whose clusters of small flowers resemble puffs of smoke. Genus: *Cotinus*.

smoking gun /smóking-/ *n* conclusive evidence or proof, especially of wrongdoing [< the idea of finding a recently fired gun in a suspect's hand]

smoking jacket

smoking jacket *n* a loose-fitting jacket made of a rich fabric such as velvet or silk, worn in the past by men while smoking or relaxing

smoking room *n* a room designated for people to smoke in

smoky /smóki/ (**-ier, -iest**) *adj* **1.** FILLED WITH SMOKE filled with or smelling of smoke **2.** GIVING OFF EXCESSIVE SMOKE giving off smoke, especially excessively **3.** AFFECTED BY SMOKE discoloured or marked with smoke **4.** FOOD TASTING OF SMOKE having or suggesting a taste imparted by smoke or an open flame **5.** COLOURS COLOURED LIKE SMOKE of a grey colour, like smoke —**smokily** *adv* —**smokiness** *n*

smoky quartz *n* MINERALS same as **cairngorm**

smolder *vi, n* US spelling of **smoulder**

Smolensk /smo lénsk/ city in western Russia, on the River Dnieper. It is the capital of Smolensk Oblast. Population: 398,405 (1995).

Smollett /smóllət/, **Tobias** (1721–71) British novelist whose picaresque novels, including *The Adventures of Roderick Random* (1748) and *The Expedition of Humphry Clinker* (1771), successfully combined adventure, comedy, and satire. Full name **Smollett, Tobias George**

'Some folk are wise, and some are otherwise.'
[Tobias Smollett, *The Adventures of Roderick Random*; 1748]

smolt /smōlt/ *n* a young salmon before it has swum to the sea. It is characterized by physiological changes undergone in preparation for living in salt water, e.g. silver coloration. [15C. Origin ?]

smooch /smooch/ (*informal*) *v* (**smooches, smooching, smooched**) **1.** *vti* KISS SOMEBODY to kiss and caress somebody **2.** *vi* DANCE INTIMATELY to dance slowly and closely ■ *n* **1.** KISS an act of kissing and caressing somebody **2.** SLOW DANCE a period of slow intimate dancing in which a couple hold each other closely [Mid-20C. An imitation of the sound of kissing] —**smoochy** *adj*

smoodge /smooj/, **smooge** ANZ (*informal*) *vi* (**smoodges, smoodging, smoodged; smooges, smooging, smooged**) **1.** KISS to kiss **2.** INGRATIATE YOURSELF to try to please or win the favour of somebody by being extremely flattering or attentive ■ *n* INGRATIATING BEHAVIOUR extremely flattering or attentive behaviour intended to please or win the favour of somebody [Early 20C. Probably variant of SCHMOOZE]

smooth /smooth/ *adj* **1.** NOT ROUGH OR BUMPY not having a rough or uneven surface ○ *The sea was calm and as smooth as glass.* **2.** WITHOUT LUMPS having no lumps or pieces of solid matter ○ *Beat the mixture to a smooth paste.* **3.** WITHOUT UPHEAVAL OR DIFFICULTIES proceeding without interruption, upheaval, or problems **4.** WITHOUT JERKS OR JOLTS in a steady flowing motion, without jolts or interruptions **5.** NOT HARSH having no harshness ○ *spoke in smooth tones* **6.** NOT SHARP OR SOUR not tasting sharp, sour, or unpleasant **7.** NOT EASILY UPSET not easily ruffled or upset ○ *a smooth and serene personality* **8.** INSINCERELY CONVINCING using insincere flattery and pleasantness, especially in order to persuade somebody to do something ○ *his smooth talk* **9.** HAIRLESS having no beard or moustache ○ *a smooth-faced young man* **10.** WITHOUT FRICTION offering no apparent resistance to sliding **11.** PHON UNASPIRATED spoken without audible breath ■ *vt* (**smoothes, smoothing, smoothed**) **1.** EVEN OUT ROUGHNESS OF SOMETHING to remove bumps, unevenness, or roughness from something **2.** PRESS OUT CREASES IN SOMETHING to remove lines and creases from something **3.** MAKE SOMETHING CREAMY to remove lumps from a liquid mixture so that it becomes creamy ○ *smooth the gravy by whisking* **4.** REMOVE DIFFICULTIES FROM SOMETHING to remove obstacles and difficulties from something ○ *Influential allies smoothed his path to power.* **5.** LESSEN BAD FEELINGS to remove or lessen bad feeling or disagreement between people ○ *I tried to smooth things over with her.* **6.** STATS REMOVE IRREGULARITIES FROM DATA to modify a sequential set of numerical data by reducing the differences in magnitude between adjacent numbers **7.** PHYS, ELEC ENG REMOVE IRREGULARITIES IN CURRENT to remove the slight irregularities (**ripples**) in a rectified current ■ *adv* WITHOUT PROBLEMS without problems or difficulties ○ *The path of true love never did run smooth.* ■ *n* **1.** ACT OF SMOOTHING the action of smoothing something **2.** SOMETHING SMOOTH a smooth part of something [Old English *smōþ* origin ?] —**smoothable** *adj* —**smoother** *n* —**smoothly** *adv* —**smoothness** *n*

smooth down *vti* to make something flat by a smoothing action, or become flat in this way

smooth out *vti* **1.** to make something smooth by the removal of lines and creases, or become smooth in this way **2.** to make something easier or calmer after a period of difficulty, or become easier or calmer in this way

smooth over *vt* to remove or lessen difficulties or tensions

smoothbore /smóoth bawr/ *adj* having a barrel without ridges or grooves in the bore. Early firearms and modern shotguns and mortars are characterized by smooth bores. ■ *n* a firearm that has a barrel without ridges or grooves in the bore

smooth breathing *n* a mark (') written over some initial Greek vowels to show that they are not aspirated

smooth collie *n* a dog belonging to a breed of collie with a thick short-haired coat

smoothen /smóoth'n/ (**-ens, -ening, -ened**) *vti* to make something smooth, or become smooth

smooth endoplasmic reticulum *n* endoplasmic reticulum that stores key enzymes in plant and animal cells and is involved in various processes including the synthesis of fatty acids and the detoxification of chemicals such as drugs and alcohol

smooth hound *n* a small bottom-dwelling shark. Native to: Atlantic from southern Brazil to northern Gulf of Mexico. Latin name: *Mustelus norrisi*.

smoothie /smóothi/ *n* **1.** a drink made from puréed fruit, sometimes with milk, yoghurt, or ice cream **2.** *also* **smoothy** (*plural* **-ies**) an attractive and charming man perceived as being insincere (*informal*)

smoothing circuit /smóothing-/ *n* a circuit used to remove the alternating current component from a direct current power source

smooth muscle *n* a muscle found in the viscera that functions by slow contraction and is made up of layers of spindle-shaped cells lacking cross striations. Smooth muscle is not under voluntary control and is activated by the autonomic nervous system, hormones, or drugs.

smooth snake *n* a brownish snake with dark markings and small, smooth scales. Native to: Europe. Latin name: *Coronella austriaca*.

smooth-spoken *adj* speaking in a gentle, quiet, and agreeable way

smooth-tongued *adj* speaking or spoken skilfully and persuasively

smoothy *n* another spelling of **smoothie** (sense 2) (*informal*)

smorgasbord /smáwrgəss bawrd/ *n* **1.** a meal served buffet-style, consisting of a large variety of hot and cold dishes **2.** a wide variety (*informal*) [Late 19C. < Swedish *smörgåsbord*, literally 'bread-and-butter table']

smote past tense of **smite** (*archaic or literary*)

smother /smúthər/ *v* (**-ers, -ering, -ered**) **1.** *vti* ALLOW OR GET TOO LITTLE AIR to deprive somebody or something of air, or be deprived of air **2.** *vti* SUFFOCATE to kill somebody or something by suffocation, or die by suffocation **3.** *vt* OVERWHELM SOMEBODY WITH AFFECTION to give somebody too much love or affection with the effect that he or she feels restricted **4.** *vti* PUT OUT FIRE to extinguish something such as a fire, or go out from lack of oxygen **5.** *vt* SUPPRESS OR HIDE SOMETHING to suppress or hide the expression of something **6.** *vt* COVER SOMETHING THICKLY to cover something with a thick layer of something else ■ *n* **1.** DENSE SMOKE dense smoke or gas **2.** THICK COATING a thick coating of something [12C. < Old English *smorian* 'suffocate, choke (with smoke)'] —**smotherer** *n* —**smotheringly** *adv* —**smothery** *adj*

smothered mate /smúthərd-/ *n* a checkmate resulting when a surrounded king is unable to move and thus escape a threatening knight

smoulder /smóldər/ *vi* (**-ders, -dering, -dered**) **1.** BURN SLOWLY to burn slowly and gently, usually with some smoke, but without a flame **2.** HAVE SUPPRESSED EMOTION to have or show a strong emotion that is suppressed, but liable to flare up at any time **3.** EXIST IN BACKGROUND to exist in the background, liable to appear or reappear at any moment ■ *n* **1.** THICK SMOKE thick smoke from a slow-burning fire **2.** SMOKY FIRE a slow-burning fire [14C. Origin ?]

smout /smowt/, **smowt** *n Scotland* a small person, especially a young child [Variant of SMOLT]

SMP *abbr* statutory maternity pay

smriti /smrítti/ *n* a group of Hindu scriptures giving instruction on social and domestic matters [< Sanskrit, 'what is remembered']

SMS *n* a service that allows short text messages to be sent, e.g. between mobile phones and pagers. Full form **short message service, short messaging service**

SMTP *n* the main protocol used to send electronic mail on the Internet, consisting of rules for how programs sending mail should interact with programs receiving mail. Full form **Simple Mail Transfer Protocol**

smudge /smuj/ *n* **1.** SMEARED INK OR PAINT a patch of smeared ink or paint blurring what has been written or painted **2.** DIRTY MARK a dirty or greasy mark **3.** INDISTINCT AREA something visible, but blurred or indistinct, and not easily identifiable **4.** *N Am*

AGRIC **SMOKE OR FIRE** smoke produced to protect trees from frost or insect damage, or a fire that produces such smoke ■ *v* (**smudges, smudging, smudged**) **1.** *vti* **SMEAR OR BE SMEARED** to smear or blur something by rubbing it, or become smeared or blurred by being rubbed **2.** *vti* **MAKE OR BECOME DIRTY** to smear something with dirt or grease, or become smeared with dirt or grease **3.** *vt N Am* AGRIC **PROTECT TREES WITH SMOKE** to fill an orchard with smoke to protect the trees from frost or insects [15C. Origin ?] —**smudgily** *adv* —**smudginess** *n* —**smudgy** *adj*

smudge pot *n N Am* a container in which material is burned to produce smoke for protecting trees from frost or insects

smug /smug/ (**smugger, smuggest**) *adj* conceited and self-satisfied [Mid-16C. Origin ?] —**smugly** *adv* —**smugness** *n*

smuggle /smúgg'l/ (**-gles, -gling, -gled**) *v* **1.** *vti* to carry goods into a country secretly because they are illegal or in order to avoid paying duty on them **2.** *vt* to take, bring, or carry somebody or something secretly into or out of a place [Late 17C. < Low German *smukkelen* or Dutch *smokkelen*] —**smuggler** *n*

smut /smut/ *n* **1. OBSCENE MATERIAL** obscene jokes, stories, or pictures **2. SMALL PIECE OF SOOT** a speck of dirt or soot **3.** PLANTS **PLANT DISEASE** a plant disease, especially of cereals and other grasses, caused by fungi and characterized by sooty black masses of spores forming on leaves and other parts **4.** FUNGI **FUNGUS CAUSING DISEASE** a parasitic fungus that causes smut. Order: Ustilaginales. ■ *v* (**smuts, smutting, smutted**) **1.** *vt* **MAKE SOMETHING DIRTY** to mark or dirty something with smuts **2.** *vi* BOT **BECOME AFFECTED WITH SMUT** to become affected with smut [15C. Ultimately < Germanic]

smutch /smuch/ *n* a smudge of something dirty or greasy ■ *vt* (**smutches, smutching, smutched**) to mark something with a smudge of something dirty or greasy [Mid-16C. Origin ?] —**smutchy** *adj*

Smuts /smutss, smöts s/, **Jan** (1870–1950) South African general and prime minister (1919–24, 1939–48). He was instrumental in forming the Union of South Africa (1910) and, as prime minister, was sometimes unpopular for his pro-British policies. Full name **Smuts, Jan Christiaan**

smutty /smútti/ (**-tier, -tiest**) *adj* **1. OBSCENE** obscene or pornographic **2. MARKED WITH SMUTS** covered with sooty marks of dirt **3.** BOT **AFFECTED BY SMUT** affected by the disease smut —**smuttily** *adv* —**smuttiness** *n*

Smyrna /smúrnə/ former name for **Izmir**

Smyth /smīth/, **Dame Ethel** (1858–1944) British composer and social reformer. She composed numerous works, and her six operas, written to her own libretti, contributed to the establishment of British opera. She campaigned for women's right to vote. Full name **Smyth, Dame Ethel Mary**

SN *abbr* Senegal (*used in Internet addresses*) See table at **domain name**

Sn *symbol* CHEM ELEM tin

SN *abbr US* NAVY seaman

SNA *abbr* COMPUT systems network architecture

snack /snak/ *n* **1. SMALL MEAL** a small meal of prepared or easy-to-prepare food eaten in place of a main meal or between main meals **2. FOOD FOR SNACK** a food suitable for eating between meals or instead of a main meal ■ *vi* (**snacks, snacking, snacked**) **EAT BETWEEN MEALS** to eat between the times that meals are usually served, or eat a snack instead of a main meal ○ *I've been snacking all afternoon.* [15C. < Middle Dutch *snac* 'bite']

snack bar *n* a small restaurant or food outlet that sells snacks

snaffle /snáff'l/ *n also* **snaffle bit BIT FOR HORSES** a bit for a horse that is jointed in the middle and has rings on either end where the reins are attached ■ *vt* (**-fles, -fling, -fled**) **1. STEAL SOMETHING** to steal or take something, usually something worth relatively little (*informal*) **2. FIT HORSE WITH BIT** to fit a horse or pony with a snaffle bit [Mid-16C. < Low Dutch]

snafu /sna fóo/ (*informal*) *n* a mishap or mistake generally caused by incompetence and resulting in delay or confusion ■ *vti* (**-fus, -fuing, -fued**) *N Am* to cause a situation or process to become confused or delayed, generally by incompetence, or become confused or delayed in this way [Mid-20C < SNAFU]

SNAFU *abbr* situation normal all fouled up

snag /snag/ *n* **1. SMALL PROBLEM** a minor problem or obstacle to progress **2. INCONVENIENT SHARP PROJECTION** a sharp projection on which something may catch and tear **3. HOLE IN FABRIC** a hole or loose thread in a fabric resulting from catching it on something sharp **4.** NAUT **NAVIGATIONAL OBSTRUCTION** an object underwater that may obstruct boats, e.g. a tree stump **5.** *ANZ* FOOD same as **sausage** (*slang*) ■ *v* (**snags, snagging, snagged**) **1.** *vti* **CATCH ON SNAG** to catch on or collide with a sharp projection, or be caught or struck in this way ○ *snagged my sleeve on a nail* **2.** *vt N Am* **OBTAIN SOMETHING** to obtain something by luck or skilful manoeuvring **3.** *vt US* **OBSTRUCT SOMETHING** to obstruct the progress of something **4.** *vt US* **CLEAR SOMETHING OF OBSTRUCTIONS** to clear a river or lake of underwater obstructions **5.** *vi US* **MEET PROBLEM** to come up against a problem or obstacle that deters progress [Late 16C. Probably < N Germanic] —**snaggy** *adj*

snagging item /snágging-/ *n* an outstanding minor unsatisfactory detail of workmanship detected during final inspection of a building project and listed for repair or completion (*usually pl*)

snaggletooth /snágg'l tooth/ (*plural* **-teeth** /-teeth/) *n* a broken, projecting, or crooked tooth [Early 19C. < SNAG + *-le*, suffix indicating repetition] —**snaggletoothed** *adj*

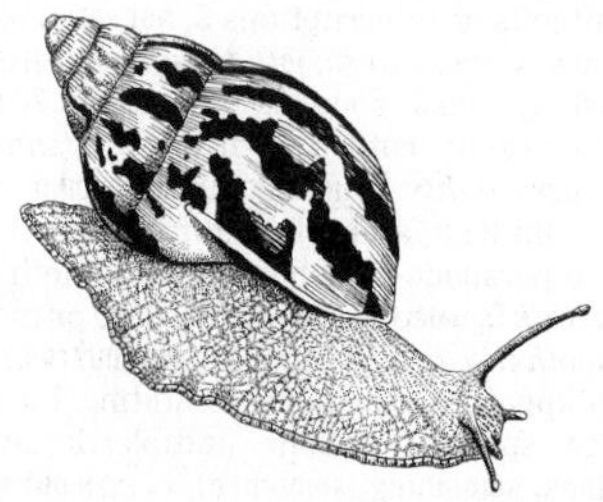

snail

snail /snayl/ *n* **1.** a small organism with a coiled shell and a retractable muscular foot on which it crawls. Class: Gastropoda. **2.** somebody or something that moves very slowly (*informal*) [Old English *snægel* < Germanic, 'to crawl']

snailfish /snáyl fish/ (*plural same* or **-fishes**) *n* a small elongated flabby bottom-dwelling sea fish, often with ventral fins modified to form a sucking disc. Native to: cold oceans, especially northern Pacific. Family: Liparidae. [Origin ?]

snail mail *n* mail sent through the postal service, as distinct from the faster electronic mail (*informal*)

snail's pace *n* a speed that is thought unbearably or unaccountably slow —**snail-paced** *adj*

snake /snayk/ *n* **1. LEGLESS REPTILE** a legless reptile with a scaly tubular body tapering towards the tail, lidless eyes, and often venomous fangs. Suborder: Serpentes. **2. OFFENSIVE TERM** an offensive term that deliberately insults somebody's reliability and honesty, especially in personal dealings (*insult*) **3. PLUMBER'S TOOL** a plumber's tool consisting of a long flexible wire that can be inserted into and rotated inside drains to unblock them **4.** FIN **EC CURRENCY RESTRICTION** a former system restricting the amount by which the values of the currencies of EC countries were allowed to vary against each other ■ *v* (**snakes, snaking, snaked**) **1.** *vi* **MOVE LIKE SNAKE** to move or lie like a snake, with many bends or twists **2.** *vt US* **DRAG SOMETHING** to drag something by a rope or chain **3.** *vt US* **TUG SOMETHING** to pull or jerk something suddenly [Old English *snaca* < Germanic, 'to crawl'] ◇ **a snake in the grass** an offensive term for somebody perceived as betraying or deceiving others

snakebird /snáyk burd/ *n* BIRDS same as **darter** (sense 2)

snakebite /snáyk bīt/ *n* **1.** the bite of a poisonous snake, or illness resulting from this **2.** an alcoholic drink that is a mixture of cider and lager

snake charmer *n* an entertainer who elicits a swaying movement from snakes, especially cobras, by means of music and rhythmic body movements

snake dance *n* a ritual dance of some Native North American peoples in which live snakes are handled

snakefish /snáyk fish/ (*plural same* or **-fishes**) *n* a fish with a long slender body, e.g. a lizard fish

snakehead /snáyk hed/ *n* **1.** a freshwater fish that has a protruding lower jaw and possesses an accessory organ for breathing atmospheric air in oxygen-depleted water. Many snakeheads are valued as food and others are kept as aquarium fish. Native to: Africa, Asia. Family: Channidae. **2.** *Hong Kong* somebody who smuggles illegal immigrants from mainland China into Hong Kong

snake lizard *n* a legless lizard, resembling a snake except that its tongue is flat and fleshy like a lizard's. Native to: Australia, New Guinea. Family: Pygopodidae.

snake oil *n* **1.** any worthless liquid preparation sold as a medicine, especially in the past by travelling pedlars **2.** something said or written with the intention of deceiving, pacifying, or persuading others

snake pit *n* **1.** a place or situation of aggression and destruction (*informal*) **2.** *US* an offensive term for a place used to house and care for people judged to have a psychiatric disorder

snakeroot /snáyk root/ *n* a plant with roots used in folk medicine to treat snakebite, or the root of any of these plants used as medicine

snakes and ladders *n* a game played on a board marked out with squares and with a number of snakes and ladders printed on it, in which players move counters towards the finishing point. Players may climb a ladder to a point closer to the finish, but must go down a snake to a square closer to the starting point. (*takes a singular verb*)

snake's head *n* a plant that grows in damp areas such as water meadows. Flowers: drooping, purplish, chequered. Native to: Europe. Latin name: *Fritillaria meleagris.*

snakeskin /snáyk skin/ *n* **1.** the skin of a snake **2.** the skin of a snake or snakes made into leather, e.g. for shoes

snakeweed /snáyk weed/ *n* a plant, especially bistort, traditionally used in folk medicine to cure snakebite

snaky /snáyki/ (**-ier, -iest**) *adj* **1.** resembling a snake in being long and narrow with bends or coils, or like a snake's twisting and turning movements **2.** treacherous and deceitful —**snakily** *adv* —**snakiness** *n*

snap /snap/ *v* (**snaps, snapping, snapped**) **1.** *vti* **BREAK WITH SHARP NOISE** to break suddenly with a sharp cracking sound, or make something do this **2.** *vti* **DO SOMETHING WITH SHARP NOISE** to move, strike, or operate something in a way that makes a sharp noise, or be moved, struck, or operated in this way **3.** *vti* **BREAK UNDER PRESSURE** to break something by excessive force or pressure, or be broken in this way ○ *The rope snapped under the weight of the log.* **4.** *vi* **LOSE CONTROL OF EMOTIONS** to lose control or erupt in anger suddenly **5.** *vti* **SPEAK ANGRILY** to say something or reply in anger or irritation **6.** *vt* **PHOTOGRAPH SOMEBODY OR SOMETHING** to take a photograph of somebody or something, especially in a casual way (*informal*) **7.** *vti* **BITE SOMEBODY OR SOMETHING** to bite or try to bite somebody or something with a quick movement or movements ○ *He ran off, with the little dog snapping and yapping behind him.* **8.** *vti US* **TAKE SOMETHING** to take or grasp something eagerly, or take something away from somebody suddenly ○ *She suddenly snapped the paper away from me.* **9.** *vti* **MOVE SHARPLY** to move something quickly and sharply, or be moved quickly and sharply ○ *The sentries snapped to attention.* **10.** *vi* **APPEAR ANGRY** to flash, especially in anger (*refers to eyes*) **11.** *vt US* **FLICK SOMETHING AWAY** to flick something away with a finger coming forward sharply from the thumb **12.** *vt* **PLAY BALL** in American football, to put the ball into play by passing it back to the quarterback behind the line of scrimmage ■ *n* **1. SHARP SOUND** a short sharp sound, e.g. of something brittle suddenly breaking or of something clicking

shut **2.** SHORT TIME a short period of time, especially one with cold weather ○ *a sudden cold snap* **3.** SWEET BISCUIT a crisp thin sweet biscuit **4.** CARDS CARD GAME a game where players lay cards face up in a pile and try to be the first to shout 'snap' when two identical cards are played one after the other. The object of the game is to win the whole pack of cards. **5.** PHOTOGRAPHY same as **snapshot** (sense 1) **6.** LIVELINESS liveliness and vigour ○ *His campaign needs more snap.* **7.** *N Am* CLOTHING same as **press stud** **8.** *N Am* SOMETHING EASY something easily done ○ *The test was a snap.* **9.** *N England* SNACK a meal or snack, especially a packed lunch (*informal*) **10.** AMERICAN FOOTBALL FOOTBALL PLAY in American football, the action required to start play, when the ball is passed to the quarterback behind the line of scrimmage ■ *adj* **1.** DECIDED WITHOUT REFLECTION arrived at quickly and without reflection ○ *a snap decision* **2.** COMING WITHOUT WARNING coming suddenly and without warning ○ *a snap election* **3.** OPERATING WITH SHARP SOUND operating with interlocking parts that snap when being shut ○ *a snap lid* **4.** *US* EASILY DONE easily done with success ○ *a snap job* ■ *adv* WITH SNAP in such a way as to make a sharp sound ■ *interj* NOTING TWO IDENTICAL THINGS used to acknowledge or draw attention to the simultaneous presence of two identical people or things, and also in the game of snap when attempting to win cards [15C. Partly an imitation of the sound, partly < Middle Dutch *snappen* 'seize']

snap up *vt* to quickly buy or take up something offered or available

snap bean *n N Am* an edible bean with long tubular pods that are harvested and eaten when immature [< its crispness, or because the pods are broken into pieces before being cooked]

snap-brim, **snap-brim hat** *n US* a man's hat with a flexible brim all around that is usually turned up at the back and down at the front

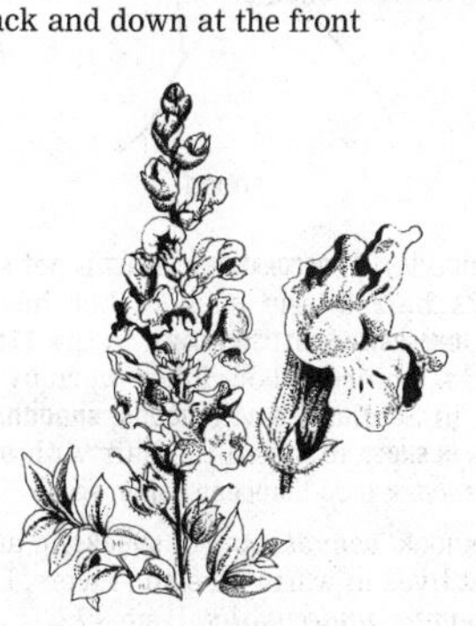

snapdragon

snapdragon /snáp dragən/ *n* a common perennial plant with spikes of flowers of various colours. Genus: *Antirrhinum.* [Late 16C. Because the flowers are said to be similar to a dragon's mouth]

snap link *n* CLIMBING same as **karabiner**

snap-on *adj* designed to attach to something quickly and easily, especially with a click when pressed into position, or designed to take attachments of this kind ○ *snap-on cover*

snapper /snáppər/ *n* **1.** (*plural* **snappers** or *same*) CARNIVOROUS FISH a carnivorous reddish sea fish. Native to: tropical waters. Family: Lutjanidae. **2.** (*plural* **snappers** or *same*) AUSTRALIAN FISH a fish with a reddish body and bright blue spots, popular as a game fish. Native to: Australian and New Zealand waters. Latin name: *Chrysophrys auratus.* **3.** SNAPPER AS FOOD the flesh of a snapper as food **4.** SNAPPING PERSON OR THING somebody or something that snaps **5.** ZOOL same as **snapping turtle**

snapping beetle /snápping-/ *n US* INSECTS same as **click beetle**

snapping turtle *n* a freshwater turtle with a large head and powerful hooked jaws. Native to: North America. Family: Chelydridae.

snappish /snáppish/ *adj* **1.** showing a sharpness or curtness caused by irritation or impatience **2.** describes an animal that tends to snap at people — **snappishly** *adv* —**snappishness** *n*

snappy /snáppi/ (**-pier, -piest**) *adj* **1.** SHOWING IMPATIENCE expressing or showing impatience or irritation **2.** INTERESTING interesting and to the point, or able to write something interesting and to the point (*informal*) **3.** HASTY done or produced without delay **4.** STYLISH fashionable and stylish (*informal*) ○ *a snappy dresser* —**snappily** *adv* —**snappiness** *n* ◇ **make it snappy** to do something quickly (*informal*)

snap ring *n* CLIMBING same as **karabiner**

snap roll *n* an aerial manoeuvre in which an aeroplane turns a complete circle longitudinally while maintaining altitude and direction of flight

snapshot /snáp shot/ *n* **1.** a photograph, especially one taken by an amateur with simple equipment **2.** a record or view of a particular point in a sequence of events or a continuing process [Early 19C. < SNAP 'quick, sudden']

snare[1] /snair/ *n* **1.** ANIMAL TRAP a trap for small animals that operates like a noose **2.** TRAP FOR UNWARY a situation that is both alluring and dangerous **3.** SURG SURGICAL DEVICE a surgical instrument consisting of a wire loop that can be tightened like a noose around the base of polyps or tumours to sever and remove them ■ *vt* (**snares, snaring, snared**) **1.** CATCH IN TRAP to catch somebody or something in a snare **2.** ENTRAP SOMEBODY to entrap somebody by alluring deception [Pre-12C. < Old Norse *snara*] —**snarer** *n*

snare[2] /snair/ *n* a gut or wire cord stretched across the bottom skin of a drum to create a rattling sound when the drum is hit (*often used in the plural*) [Late 17C. Probably < Dutch *snaar* 'string']

snare drum *n* a drum fitted with snares to produce a rattling effect

Snares Islands /snáirz-/ group of uninhabited islands situated 100 km/62 mi south of Stewart Island, New Zealand. They are home to several large bird colonies. Area: 39 sq. km/15 sq. mi.

snarf /snaarf/ (**snarfs, snarfing, snarfed**) *vt US* to eat or drink something noisily or greedily (*informal*) [Mid-20C. Probably an imitation of the sound]

snarky /snáarki/ (**-ier, -iest**) *adj US* sarcastically critical or mocking and malicious (*informal*) ○ *a snarky remark*

snarl[1] /snaarl/ *v* (**snarls, snarling, snarled**) **1.** *vi* GROWL to growl threateningly **2.** *vti* SAY SOMETHING ANGRILY to speak or say something angrily or threateningly ■ *n* GROWLING NOISE the sound of somebody or something snarling [Late 16C. < obsolete *snar* 'to snarl' (ultimately an imitation of the sound) + *-le*, suffix indicating repetition] —**snarlingly** *adv*

snarl[2] /snaarl/ *n* **1.** TANGLE a tangled mass of something such as hair or wool **2.** KNOT IN WOOD a knot in wood **3.** *US* same as **snarl-up** ■ *vti* (**snarls, snarling, snarled**) **1.** TANGLE SOMETHING to tangle something, or become tangled **2.** *US* same as **snarl up** [14C. Probably < SNARE[1] + *-le*, diminutive suffix]

snarl up *vti UK, ANZ, Can* to become complicated, confused, or too congested to move, or cause something to be in such a state (*often passive*) US term **snarl**[2]

snarler /snáarlər/ *n* **1.** a person or animal that snarls **2.** *NZ* same as **sausage** (*informal*)

snarl-up *n UK, ANZ, Can* a complicated, disordered, or congested situation, especially a traffic jam. US term **snarl**[2]

snash /snash/ *n Scotland* abusive language or insolent behaviour [Late 18C. Probably an imitation of the sound]

snatch /snach/ *vt* (**snatches, snatching, snatched**) **1.** TAKE SOMETHING QUICKLY to grab or grasp somebody or something hastily **2.** MOVE SOMETHING QUICKLY to move or remove something quickly **3.** TAKE SOMETHING WHEN OPPORTUNITY ARISES to take or get something while there is an opportunity ○ *snatched a few hours of sleep* **4.** *N Am* same as **kidnap** (*informal*) ■ *n* **1.** GRABBING an instance of grabbing or grasping somebody or something **2.** SMALL AMOUNT a small incomplete bit or short period of something **3.** THEFT an act of stealing (*informal*) **4.** *N Am* same as **kidnapping** (*informal*) **5.** *US* TABOO TERM a highly offensive term for the outer sexual organs of a woman (*taboo*) **6.** GYM LIFTING FEAT a weightlifting feat in which the barbell is raised from the floor over the lifter's head in one motion [12C. Origin ?] —**snatcher** *n*

snatch block *n* a block that can be opened on one side to insert a rope, thereby avoiding the necessity of threading the rope through from one end

snatch squad *n* **1.** a group of soldiers or police officers trained to single out and seize the apparent ringleaders in situations of public disorder **2.** *US* a special operations unit trained to capture targeted individuals and disable enemy sentries or patrols

snatch theft *n* the theft in a public place of an item of personal property such as a bag or mobile phone, or an instance of this

snatchy /snáchi/ (**-ier, -iest**) *adj* occurring or done in short spells

snath /snath/, **snathe** /snay*th*/ *n* the handle of a scythe [Late 16C. Variant of dialect *snead*, origin ?]

snazzy /snázzi/ (**-zier, -ziest**) *adj* attractively new, bright, or fashionable (*informal*) [Mid-20C. Origin ?] —**snazzily** *adv* —**snazziness** *n*

SNCF *n* the national railway system in France. Full form **Société Nationale des Chemins de Fer**

sneak /sneek/ *v* (**sneaks, sneaking, sneaked**) **1.** *vi* MOVE ABOUT STEALTHILY to go or move in a stealthy, secretive way **2.** *vt* DO SOMETHING FURTIVELY to do something stealthily, furtively, and without being noticed ○ *He sneaked a look over the wall.* **3.** *vt* BRING STEALTHILY to bring, take, or carry somebody or something secretly and furtively ○ *sneak friends into the house for a surprise party* **4.** *vi* TELL TALES to tell somebody in authority about something wrong that somebody else has done ■ *n* **1.** SOMEBODY WHO TELLS TALES somebody who informs those in authority about another's wrongdoing **2.** STEALTHY DEPARTURE a departure intended to be unobserved **3.** UNTRUSTWORTHY PERSON a person regarded as cunning and deceitful (*insult*) ■ *adj* STEALTHILY DONE done stealthily or furtively ○ *a sneak peek at the gifts* [Late 16C. Origin ?]

sneak up on *vt* **1.** to approach stealthily, with the intention of surprising or frightening somebody or something **2.** to arrive more quickly than expected ○ *The weekend sneaked up on me.*

sneakbox /sneék boks/ *n US* a flat-bottomed boat with low sides and usually camouflaged, used by hunters of duck and other waterfowl

sneaker /sneékər/ *n ANZ, N Am* a shoe with a rubber sole and, usually, a cloth upper (*often used in the plural*)

sneaking /sneéking/ *adj* **1.** HIDDEN FROM OTHERS unknown to or hidden from others **2.** SLIGHT slight but persistent ○ *a sneaking suspicion* **3.** DECEPTIVE deceptive or given to cunning and deception —**sneakingly** *adv*

sneak preview *n* a brief, private, or unofficial viewing of something before its general release or launch

sneak thief *n* a thief who surreptitiously steals unguarded or unsecured articles when the opportunity arises

sneaky /sneéki/ (**-ier, -iest**) *adj* done, doing something, or in the habit of behaving in an underhanded and unfair way —**sneakily** *adv* —**sneakiness** *n*

sneck /snek/ *N England, Scotland n* a latch on a door or a catch on a door lock that allows it to be left open or shut ■ *vt* (**snecks, snecking, snecked**) to operate or set the sneck on a door or lock [14C. Origin ?]

sneer /sneer/ *n* EXPRESSION OF SCORN a facial expression of scorn or hostility in which the upper lip may be raised ■ *v* (**sneers, sneering, sneered**) **1.** *vi* FEEL OR SHOW SCORN to feel or show scorn, contempt, or hostility, either in speech or facial expression **2.** *vt* UTTER SOMETHING WITH SCORN to say something with scorn or contempt [14C. Origin ?] —**sneerer** *n* —**sneering** *adj* —**sneeringly** *adv*

sneeze /sneez/ *vi* (**sneezes, sneezing, sneezed**) to suddenly, forcefully, and involuntarily expel air through the nose and mouth because of irritation of the nasal passages ■ *n* an act or sound of sneezing [15C. Alteration of obsolete *fnese* < Old English *fneosan*, an imitation of the sound of breathing] —**sneezer** *n* —**sneezy** *adj*

sneezeweed /sneéz weed/ *n* a perennial wild plant. Flowers: yellow to dark red, resembling daisies. Native to: North America. Genus: *Helenium.*

sneezewood /sneéz wo͝od/ *n* a tree whose pepperysmelling wood is used for posts and beams. Native

to: southern Africa. Latin name: *Ptaeroxylon utile*. [Mid-19C. Probably alteration of Cape Dutch *nieshout*]

sneezewort /sneéz wurt/ *n* a plant with silvery leaves that when powdered induce sneezing. Flowers: small, white, resembling daisies. Native to: Europe, Asia. Latin name: *Achillea ptarmica*.

snell /snel/ *adj Scotland* bitingly cold [Old English, < Germanic]

Snell /snel/, **Peter** (*b.* 1938) New Zealand runner. He won gold medals at the 1960 and 1964 Olympics. Full name **Snell, Peter George**

Snellen chart /snéllən-/ *n* a chart for vision testing on which are printed rows of letters and numbers in decreasing size from top to bottom [Mid-19C. After Herman *Snellen* (1834–1908), Dutch ophthalmologist]

Snell's law /snélz-/ *n* the law stating that for a light ray passing between two media the ratio of the sines of the angle of incidence and the angle of refraction is a constant [Late 19C. After Willebrord Van Roijen *Snell* (1591–1626), Dutch astronomer and mathematician]

SNG *abbr* INDUST synthetic (or substitute) natural gas

snib /snib/ *Ireland, Scotland n* a bolt or catch on a door or a catch on a lock ■ *vt* (**snibs, snibbing, snibbed**) to operate or fasten the snib on a door or lock [Early 19C. Origin ?]

snick /snik/ *n* **1.** SNIP a small cut or notch **2.** CRICKET GLANCING BLOW a glancing blow to the ball from a cricket bat ■ *vt* (**snicks, snicking, snicked**) **1.** SNIP SOMETHING to cut something slightly **2.** CRICKET HIT OBLIQUELY in cricket, to hit the ball with a glancing blow [Late 17C. Probably < *snick* in obsolete *snick or snee* 'to cut or thrust with a knife in a fight' < alteration of Dutch *steken* 'thrust' + dialect variant of *snij(d)en* 'cut']

snicker /s nikər/ *v* (**-ers, -ering, -ered**) **1.** *vi* to neigh or whinny **2.** *vi N Am* same as **snigger** *v* (sense 1) **3.** *vt N Am* same as **snigger** *v* (sense 2) ■ *n* **1.** a horse's neigh or whinny **2.** *N Am* same as **snigger** [Late 17C. Origin ?]

snide /snīd/ (**snider, snidest**) *adj* derisively sarcastic [Mid-19C. Origin ?] —**snidely** *adv*

sniff /snif/ *v* (**sniffs, sniffing, sniffed**) **1.** *vti* BREATHE IN THROUGH NOSE to breathe in through the nose quickly, briefly, and audibly, e.g. in smelling something or to prevent mucus from dripping, or smell something by breathing in quickly **2.** *vt* SUSPECT SOMETHING to have a suspicion of something, especially something bad ○ *sniff trouble* ■ *n* **1.** BRIEF INHALATION an instance or sound of sniffing **2.** SUSPICION a hint or suspicion, especially of something bad [14C. An imitation of the sound]

sniff at *vt* to show contempt or disdain for somebody or something

sniff out *vt* to discover something, especially something bad, by investigation (*informal*)

sniffer /sníffər/ *n* **1.** SOMEBODY WHO SNIFFS somebody who sniffs, especially who takes drugs by inhaling them **2.** DEVICE MONITORING DATA TRANSMISSION a device or program that monitors and analyses computer network traffic, detecting bottlenecks and problems **3.** PROGRAM TO CAPTURE NETWORK DATA a program on a computer system designed legitimately or illegitimately to capture data being transmitted on a network, often used by hackers to appropriate passwords and user names

sniffer dog *n* a dog trained to detect explosives or drugs by scent

sniffle /sniff'l/ *vi* (**-fles, -fling, -fled**) **1.** INHALE MUCUS to inhale through the nose to prevent mucus from dripping out of it **2.** WEEP QUIETLY to sniff repeatedly while gently weeping ■ *n* ACT OF SNIFFLING an instance or sound of sniffling ■ **sniffles** *npl* SLIGHT COLD a slight cold that causes sniffling (*informal*) [Mid-17C. An imitation of the sound] —**sniffler** *n*

sniffy /sníffi/ (**-ier, -iest**) *adj* (*informal*) **1.** behaving in a haughty, disdainful way **2.** tending to sniff a lot, e.g. because of a cold —**sniffily** *adv* —**sniffiness** *n*

snifter /sníftər/ *n* **1.** a stemmed glass with a bowl that tapers upwards, typically used for brandy **2.** a small amount of drink, especially of alcohol (*informal*) [Mid-18C. An imitation of the sound of sniffing or snuffling]

snig /snig/ (**snigs, snigging, snigged**) *vt ANZ, Can* to drag something heavy, especially a log, by means of ropes or chains [Late 18C. Origin ?]

snigger /sníggər/ *v* (**-gers, -gering, -gered**) **1.** *vi* LAUGH DISRESPECTFULLY to laugh disrespectfully in a covert way **2.** *vt* SAY DISRESPECTFULLY to speak or say something while laughing disrespectfully ■ *n* DISRESPECTFUL LAUGH an instance or sound of sniggering ▶ N Am term (all senses) **snicker** [Early 18C. Variant of SNICKER]

snigging track, **snigging trail** *n ANZ, Can* an access track through a forest to a logging area, along which logs are transported

sniggle /snígg'l/ *vti* (**-gles, -gling, -gled**) to fish for or catch eels by putting a baited hook into crevices where they hide ■ *n* a baited hook used for catching eels [Mid-17C. < *snig* 'young eel', origin ?] —**sniggler** *n*

snip /snip/ *vti* (**snips, snipping, snipped**) CUT SOMETHING WITH SMALL STROKES to cut something with scissors or shears, especially using small strokes ■ *n* **1.** A CUT a short quick cut, made with scissors **2.** SMALL PIECE a small piece of something that has been snipped off **3.** ACT OR SOUND OF SNIPPING the act or sound of using scissors to snip something **4.** BARGAIN something costing less than its real value (*informal*) **5.** EASY THING something that is a certainty or is easily done (*informal*) ■ **snips** *npl* ENG SHEARS shears used for cutting sheet metal ■ *interj* SOUND OF SNIPPING used to represent the sound that scissors make [Mid-16C. < Dutch or Low German *snippen*, an imitation of the sound]

snipe /snīp/ *n* (*plural* **snipes** or *same*) **1.** WADING BIRD a wading bird with a long straight beak. Native to: marshes and riverbanks of the northern hemisphere. Genus: *Gallinago*. **2.** SHOT FIRED FROM CONCEALMENT a shot fired from a concealed place ■ *vi* (**snipes, sniping, sniped**) SHOOT FROM CONCEALED PLACE to shoot at people from a concealed position [14C. Probably < Old Norse *snípa*]

snipefish /snīp fish/ (*plural same* or **-fishes**) *n* a fish with a long snout and a spine extending from its dorsal fin to its tail. Native to: tropical and temperate waters. Family: Macrorhamphosidae.

snipe fly *n* a fly with a long body and long legs that eats other insects. Family: Leptidae.

sniper /snīpər/ *n* **1.** somebody who shoots people from a concealed position **2.** a member of the armed forces who is trained to shoot enemy soldiers from a concealed position

snippet /sníppət/ *n* a small piece of something such as information or music [Mid-17C. < SNIP]

snipping /snípping/ *n* same as **snip** *n* (sense 2)

snippy /snípi/ (**-pier, -piest**) *adj* **1.** FRAGMENTARY made up of scraps or fragments **2.** SHARP-TONGUED behaving in a curt and irritable way (*informal*) **3.** *regional* MEAN stingy or mean with money —**snippily** *adv* —**snippiness** *n*

snit /snit/ *n N Am* a state of mild irritation or bad temper [Mid-20C. Origin ?]

snitch /snich/ *v* (**snitches, snitching, snitched**) (*slang*) **1.** *vi* INFORM ON SOMEBODY to tell somebody in authority about another person's wrongdoing ○ *Friends don't snitch on each other.* **2.** *vt* PILFER SOMETHING to steal something in a sneaky way, especially something of little value ■ *n* **1.** INFORMER somebody who informs on others (*slang*) **2.** NOSE a person's nose (*dated slang*) [Late 17C. Origin ?] —**snitcher** *n*

snivel /snívv'l/ *vi* (**-els, -elling, -elled**) **1.** SNIFF to sniff repeatedly **2.** WHINE to behave in a whining, tearful, or self-pitying way **3.** SNIFFLE to have a runny nose ■ *n* SNIVELLING an act of snivelling [Assumed Old English *snyflan* < Germanic] —**sniveller** *n* —**snivelling** *n, adj* —**snivelly** *adj*

snob /snob/ *n* **1.** an admirer and cultivator of people with high social status who disdains those considered inferior **2.** somebody who disdains people considered to have inferior knowledge or tastes [Late 18C. Origin ?] —**snobbery** *n* —**snobbism** *n* —**snobby** *adj*

ORIGIN ***Snob*** originally meant 'shoemaker' (a sense that survives in places). Cambridge University students of the late 18th century adopted it as a slang term for a 'townsman, somebody not a member of the university', and it seems to have been this usage that formed the basis in the 1830s for the emergence of a new general sense 'member of the lower classes'. The modern sense 'somebody who admires and cultivates social superiors' received a considerable boost when Thackeray used it in his *Book of Snobs* (1848). As for the origins of the word itself, the suggestion that it comes from *s.nob.*, short for Latin *sine nobilitate* 'without nobility', is ingenious but ignores the word's early history.

snobbish /snóbbish/ *adj* displaying an offensively superior condescending manner —**snobbishly** *adv* —**snobbishness** *n*

SNOBOL /snṓ bawl/ *n* a high-level computer programming language designed for dealing with strings of symbols [Mid-20C. < letters in *string-oriented symbolic language*, after COBOL]

snob value *n* worth or desirability arising from being seen as superior (*informal*)

snoek /snook/ (*plural* **snoeks** or *same*) *n* a long predatory fish of the mackerel family. Native to: Australia, New Zealand, southern Africa. Latin name: *Thyrsites atun*. [Late 18C. Via Afrikaans < Middle Dutch *snoec* 'pike']

snog /snog/ *UK* (*slang*) *vti* (**snogs, snogging, snogged**) to kiss and cuddle somebody, especially for a long time ■ *n* a long kiss or a prolonged kissing and cuddling session [Mid-20C. Origin ?]

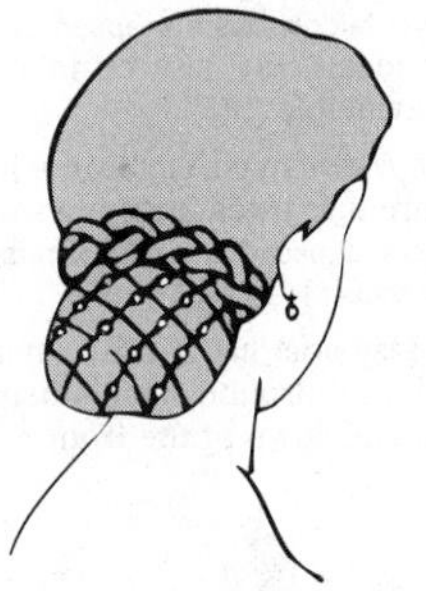

snood

snood /snood/ *n* **1.** DECORATIVE HAIR NET a net that holds a woman's hair at the back of her head **2.** RIBBON WORN BY UNMARRIED SCOTTISH WOMEN in the 17th and 18th centuries, a hairband or ribbon worn by unmarried women in Scotland ■ *vt* (**snoods, snooding, snooded**) HOLD HAIR IN SNOOD to fasten the hair with a snood [Old English *snōd*, < Indo-European, 'spin, sew']

snook[1] /snook/ (*plural same* or **snooks**) *n* a large bony fish that lives in warm seas and rivers. Latin name: *Centropomus undecimalis*. [Late 17C. < Dutch *snoek* 'pike', later form of Middle Dutch *snoec*]

snook[2] /snook, snŏŏk/ *n* a gesture made as a sign of contempt, by putting the thumb to the nose with the fingers outstretched [Late 18C. Origin ?]

snooker /snŏŏkər/ *n* **1.** BALL AND CUE GAME a game played on a table in which a white ball struck with a cue is used to hit fifteen red balls and six balls of different colours into pockets **2.** POSITION IN SNOOKER a position in snooker in which a player is forced to play an indirect shot because another ball is between the cue ball and the target ball ■ *vt* (**-ers, -ering, -ered**) **1.** PUT SOMEBODY AT DISADVANTAGE IN SNOOKER to put a snooker player in the position of being forced to play an indirect shot because another ball is between the cue ball and the target ball **2.** THWART SOMEBODY OR SOMETHING to thwart somebody or put somebody in a position of being unable to proceed (*informal*) [Late 19C. Origin ?]

ORIGIN The most widely canvassed theory of the origins of the word ***snooker*** is that it is an adaptation of late 19th-century British army slang *snooker* 'new recruit'. The game was invented, as a diversion perhaps from the monotony of billiards, by British army officers serving in India in the 1870s, and the story goes that the term ***snooker*** was applied to it by Colonel Sir Neville Chamberlain (1856–1944), at that time a subaltern stationed in Jubbulpore, in allusion to the inept play of one of his brother officers.

snoop /snoop/ (*informal*) *vi* (**snoops, snooping, snooped**) PRY to pry into other people's business or affairs, especially surreptitiously ■ *n* **1.** SOMEBODY WHO SNOOPS somebody who pries into other people's lives **2.**

SECRET INVESTIGATION a surreptitious investigation of somebody's private life or property [Mid-19C. < Dutch *snoepen* 'eat on the sly'] **—snooper** *n*

snooperscope /snooˈpər skōp/ *n* a device that converts infrared radiation into a visual image and is used for seeing in the dark

snoopy /snooˈpi/ (**-ier, -iest**) *adj* tending to pry into the affairs of others

snoot /snoot/ *n* a nose or snout (*informal*) [Mid-19C. Variant of SNOUT]

snooty /snooˈti/ (**-ier, -iest**) *adj* (*informal*) **1.** having or showing a haughty condescending manner, especially to those considered socially inferior **2.** catering to people regarded as having high social status ○ *a snooty country club* [Early 20C. < snooty 'treat somebody in a haughty manner'] **—snootily** *adv* **—snootiness** *n*

snooze /snooz/ (*informal*) *vi* (**snoozes, snoozing, snoozed**) to have a short sleep ▪ *n* a short sleep [Late 18C. Origin ?] **—snoozer** *n* **—snoozy** *adj*

snore /snawr/ *vi* (**snores, snoring, snored**) to breathe noisily while asleep because of vibrations of the soft palate ▪ *n* a snorting or whistling sound made while sleeping [14C. Origin ?] **—snorer** *n*

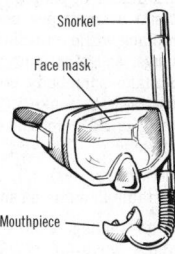

snorkel

snorkel /snawrkˈl/ *n* **1.** BREATHING APPARATUS a curved tube that projects above the water and enables somebody to breathe while swimming face-down near the surface **2.** VENTILATOR ON SUBMARINE a shaft on a diesel-powered submarine for ventilation and for engine intake and exhaust, which enables the submarine to stay submerged near the surface for long periods **3.** DEVICE ON TANK a device on a tank or other vehicle that functions like the snorkel on a submarine and enables the vehicle to go through shallow water ▪ *vi* (**-kels, -kelling, -kelled**) SWIM WITH SNORKEL to swim underwater breathing air through a snorkel [Mid-20C. < German dialect *Schnorchel* 'nose'] **—snorkeller** *n*

snorkelling /snawrkˈling/ *n* the activity or pastime of swimming with a snorkel

snort /snawrt/ *v* (**snorts, snorting, snorted**) **1.** *vi* FORCE AIR THROUGH NOSE to make a harsh sound by forcing air through the nostrils **2.** *vi* SHOW CONTEMPT to express a feeling, especially of contempt or impatience, by snorting **3.** *vti* DRUGS INHALE DRUG to inhale a powdered drug through the nostrils (*informal*) ▪ *n* **1.** HARSH SOUND an instance or sound of snorting **2.** GULP OF ALCOHOL a short drink, especially of alcohol, taken all at once (*informal*) **3.** DRUGS INHALATION OF DRUG an act of snorting a drug (*informal*) **4.** NAVY same as **snorkel** *n* (sense 2) (*slang*) [14C. Probably variant of SNORE] **—snorter** *n* **—snorting** *n, adj*

snot /snot/ *n* **1.** an offensive term for mucus produced in the nose (*slang*) **2.** an offensive term for somebody whose behaviour is regarded as arrogant or condescending (*slang insult*) [Old English *gesnot* < Germanic]

snot-nosed *adj* an offensive term meaning regarded as being young and precocious but not to be taken seriously (*slang*)

snotter /snotˈər/ *Scotland n* NASAL MUCUS a lump of mucus in or from somebody's nose ▪ *vi* (**-ters, -tering, -tered**) **1.** SNUFFLE to breathe through the nose while it is partially blocked up with mucus **2.** SNIVEL to cry in a way that produces nasal mucus [Early 18C. < SNOT]

snotty /snotˈi/ (**-tier, -tiest**) *adj* (*slang*) **1.** an offensive term meaning wet or dirty with nasal mucus **2.** an offensive term meaning behaving in an arrogant and condescending manner **3.** an offensive term describing actions that are regarded as malicious or rude **—snottily** *adv* **—snottiness** *n*

snotty-nosed *adj* same as **snot-nosed** (*slang offensive*)

snout /snowt/ *n* **1.** ANIMAL'S NOSE the projecting part of a vertebrate's head, consisting of the nose and mouth, especially that of a mammal such as a pig **2.** PROJECTING PART OF INSECT'S HEAD the projecting part of the head of an insect or other invertebrate such as a weevil **3.** PROJECTION something that sticks out, e.g. the muzzle of a gun **4.** same as **nose** (*slang*) **5.** SOMETHING TO SMOKE tobacco, or a cigarette (*slang*) **6.** INFORMER somebody who informs on another person to the police (*slang*) **7.** GEOG STEEP END OF GLACIER the leading face of a glacier, usually heavily loaded with rock debris [13C. < Middle High German, Middle Dutch *snūt(e)* < Germanic] **—snouted** *adj*

snout beetle *n* INSECTS same as **weevil** (sense 1) [< the shape of its head]

snow /snō/ *n* **1.** ICE CRYSTAL FLAKES water vapour in the atmosphere that has frozen into ice crystals and falls to the ground in the form of flakes **2.** SNOW ON GROUND a layer of fallen snow **3.** SUBSTANCE RESEMBLING SNOW a substance that resembles snow in colour or texture **4.** ELEC WHITE SPECKS ON TELEVISION SCREEN random patterns of small white specks on a television or radar screen caused by electrical interference **5.** METEOROL FALL OF SNOW an amount of snow that falls at one time ○ *had a heavy snow last night* **6.** DRUGS NARCOTIC DRUG cocaine or heroin in the form of a white powder (*slang*) ▪ *v* (**snows, snowing, snowed**) **1.** *vi* TO FALL AS SNOW to fall from the sky as snow ○ *It's snowing!* **2.** *vt* COVER SOMETHING WITH SNOW to cover, close in, or block something with a fall of snow **3.** *vti* FALL LIKE SNOW to fall or scatter like snow, or make something fall in this way **4.** *vt N Am* PERSUADE SOMEBODY WITH GLIB TALK to overwhelm or deceive somebody especially with flattery or charm (*slang*) ○ *She snowed us into buying worthless stock.* [Old English *snāw* < Indo-European]

snow under *vt US* to defeat an opposing team soundly ◇ **be snowed under (with something)** to be overwhelmed with something, especially work

Snow /snō/, **C. P., Baron Snow of Leicester** (1905–80) British novelist and critic. His 11-novel series *Strangers and Brothers* examines English life in the mid-20th century. Full name **Snow, Charles Percy**

'The official world, the corridors of power.' [C.P. Snow, *Homecomings*; 1956]

snowball /snō bawl/ *n* **1.** BALL OF SNOW a ball of compacted snow that is thrown, especially by children **2.** ALCOHOLIC DRINK a drink made from advocaat mixed with lemonade ▪ *v* (**-balls, -balling, -balled**) **1.** *vi* INCREASE RAPIDLY to increase rapidly or at an accelerating rate ○ *The event snowballed and this year more than a hundred people took part.* **2.** *vti* THROW SNOWBALLS to throw snowballs at each other or at somebody else ◇ **not have a snowball's chance (in hell)** to have no chance at all (*informal*)

snowberry /snō bəri/ (*plural* **-ries**) *n* an ornamental bush with white berries. Flowers: pink. Native to: North America, naturalized in Great Britain. Genus: *Symphoricarpos*.

snowbiking /snō bīking/ *n* the sport of riding mountain bikes with studded tyres over snow-covered slopes or trails

snowbird /snō burd/ *n* any bird that is seen chiefly in winter, e.g. a snow bunting or a fieldfare

snowblading /snō blayding/ *n* SKIING same as **ski-boarding**

snow-blind *adj* affected by snow blindness

snow blindness *n* a condition of temporary blindness caused by the bright sunlight and intense radiation reflected from snow or ice, which causes swelling of parts of the eyeball and severe pain

snowblink /snō blingk/ *n* a white glow in the sky, especially in polar regions, caused by the reflection of light from distant snowfields

snowblower /snō blō ər/ *n* a machine that clears snow from roads by scooping it into a fast-rotating spiral blade and ejecting it to one side

snowboard /snō bawrd/ *n* a board with bindings for the feet that somebody stands on to slide down snow slopes ▪ *vi* (**-boards, -boarding, -boarded**) to slide down snow slopes using a snowboard **—snowboarder** *n* **—snowboarding** *n*

snowbound /snō bownd/ *adj* prevented from moving or leaving a place by a heavy fall of snow

snow bunting *n* a white finch with dark markings that nests on tundra and winters in coastal regions. Latin name: *Plectrophenax nivalis*.

snowcap /snō kap/ *n* a covering of snow on a mountain peak **—snowcapped** *adj*

snow cone *n Carib, N Am* a snack consisting of crushed flavoured ice served in a paper cone or cup

Snowdon, Mount /snōd'n/ mountain in Gwynedd, northwestern Wales. It is the highest peak in Wales. Height: 1,085 m/3,560 ft.

Snowdonia National Park /snō dōni ə-/ national park incorporating Mount Snowdon, in northwestern Wales, established in 1951. Area: 2,171 sq. km/840 sq. mi.

snowdrift /snō drift/ *n* a bank of snow piled up by the wind

snowdrop /snō drop/ *n* an early spring-flowering plant that grows from a bulb. Flowers: small, white, drooping. Native to: Europe, Asia. Latin name: *Galanthus nivalis*.

snowfall /snō fawl/ *n* **1.** a period during which snow falls or an instance of snow falling **2.** the amount of snow that falls in a location over a period of time ○ *What is the average snowfall for the area?*

snow fence *n* a portable flexible fence made of upright slats or heavy plastic mesh, designed to stop snow from drifting onto roads or ski runs

snowfield /snō feeld/ *n* a large area permanently covered in snow

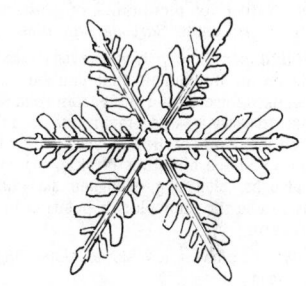

snowflake

snowflake /snō flayk/ *n* **1.** an individual mass of ice crystals that falls with others as snow **2.** a garden plant grown from a bulb. Flowers: white, drooping. Genus: *Leucojum*.

snow goose *n* a goose with white feathers and black wing tips. Native to: Arctic regions, migrating to coastal areas of North America. Latin name: *Anser caerulescens*.

snow grass *n* **1.** a grey-green grass that grows in upland areas of Australia. Genus: *Poa*. **2.** a grass that grows in the hills of New Zealand. Genus: *Danthonia*.

snow gum *n* a gum tree that grows at high altitudes. Native to: Australia. Genus: *Eucalyptus*.

snow-in-summer *n* a perennial plant with woolly stems and notched silvery green leaves. Flowers: white. Native to: Europe. Latin name: *Cerastium tomentosum*.

snow job *n N Am* an attempt to mislead or persuade somebody by insincere talk or flattery (*slang*)

snow leopard *n* a large cat with a thick pale-grey or brown coat marked with dark patches. Native to: mountainous regions of Central Asia. Latin name: *Panthera uncia*.

snow line *n* **1.** the line of altitude above which there is permanent snow **2.** the line of latitude marking the edge of a perennial snow field or polar region

snowman /snō man/ (*plural* **-men** /-men/) *n* a roughly human figure made by piling up and shaping snow

snowmelt /snṓ melt/ *n* N Am **1.** water produced when snow melts that does not soak into the soil **2.** the season when snow melts

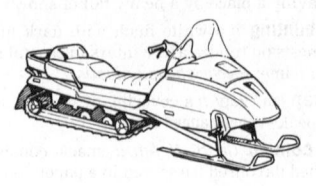

snowmobile

snowmobile /snṓmə beel, -mō beel/ *n* a small motorized vehicle with runners and a continuous track, used for travelling over snow

snow-on-the-mountain *n* a bush with white-edged leaves and white modified leaves (**bracts**) at the base of the flower petals. Native to: North America. Latin name: *Euphorbia marginata*.

snowpack /snṓ pak/ *n* accumulated snow, usually in a mountainous area

snow pea *n* ANZ, N Am a variety of garden pea with an edible thin flat pod. Latin name: *Pisum sativum*. UK term **mangetout**

snow pellet *n* a soft white round mass of ice that falls as precipitation (*often used in the plural*)

snowperson /snṓ purss'n/ (*plural* **-people** /-peep'l/ or **-persons**) *n* a snowman or snowwoman

snow plant *n* a plant with a fleshy reddish stalk that often flowers before the snow has melted. Flowers: scarlet. Native to: mountains of western North America. Latin name: *Sarcodes sanguinea*.

snowplough /snṓ plow/ *n* **1.** VEHICLE FOR CLEARING SNOW a vehicle or an implement that can be fixed to a vehicle, used for clearing snow from roads or paths **2.** CONTROL TECHNIQUE IN SKIING a technique used in skiing in which the points of the skis are brought together to make a V-shape, enabling the skier to turn or stop ■ *vi* (**-ploughs, -ploughing, -ploughed**) SKI IN SNOWPLOUGH POSITION to use the snowplough position to turn or stop in skiing

snowplow /snṓ plow/ *n, vi* VEHICLES, SKIING US spelling of **snowplough**

snow scooter *n* **1.** a vehicle used on snow for fun, consisting usually of a single flat runner like a ski with a seat and a steering mechanism mounted on it **2.** a small motorized vehicle on runners for travelling over snow —**snow scooting** *n*

snowshed /snṓ shed/ *n* a shelter over an open section of a railway track, especially on a mountainside, to prevent it getting covered in snow

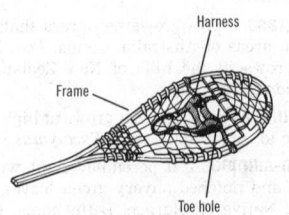

snowshoe

snowshoe /snṓ shoo/ *n* a metal or wood framework with interwoven straps that is attached to a boot allowing the wearer to walk on snow without sinking ■ *vi* (**-shoes, -shoeing, -shoed**) to walk on snow wearing snowshoes

snowshoe hare, snowshoe rabbit *n* a hare with a white winter coat that turns brown in summer and large, heavily furred hind feet that allow it to move

quickly in snow. Native to: North America. Latin name: *Lepus americanus*.

snowstorm /snṓ stawrm/ *n* a storm with heavy snow

snow tyre *n* a tyre with a deep tread pattern or studs to provide extra traction for a vehicle driving in snowy conditions

snow-white *adj* as white as fresh snow

snowwoman /snṓ woomən/ (*plural* **-women** /-wimin/) *n* a roughly human figure made by piling up and shaping snow and with features suggesting a woman

snowy /snṓ i/ (**-ier, -iest**) *adj* **1.** characterized by the presence of snow ○ *a snowy day* **2.** resembling snow, especially in colour or purity ○ *a snowy beard* —**snowily** *adv* —**snowiness** *n*

Snowy /snṓ i/ river in southeastern Australia. It rises in the Snowy Mountains in New South Wales and flows into the Tasman Sea, near the town of Orbost in Victoria. Length: 430 km/270 mi.

CULTURAL NOTE *The Man From Snowy River*, a long poem (1895) by Australian writer A. B. Paterson. Set in the high country of southeastern Australia, this verse sequence tells of the heroic exploits of a horseman as he rounds up a mob of wild and escaped horses. It is one of Australia's best-known poems.

snowy egret *n* a small egret with white feathers, black legs, and yellow feet. Native to: North and South America. Latin name: *Egretta thula*.

Snowy Mountains range of peaks within the Australian Alps, in southeastern New South Wales, Australia. The highest point, and the highest peak in Australia, is Mount Kosciuszko, 2,228 m/7,310 ft.

snowy owl *n* a large white owl that builds its nest on the ground and feeds mainly on lemmings. Native to: Arctic. Latin name: *Nyctea scandiaca*.

SNP[1] *abbr* POL Scottish National Party

SNP[2] /snip/ *abbr* BIOTECH single nucleotide polymorphism

Snr, snr *abbr* Senior

snub /snub/ *vt* (**snubs, snubbing, snubbed**) **1.** TREAT SOMEBODY RUDELY to treat somebody with deliberate coldness or contempt **2.** BRING SOMETHING TO STOP to stop a line from paying out or something attached to a line from getting away by wrapping the line around something ■ *n* HUMILIATING ACTION a remark or act intended to humiliate or insult somebody ■ *adj* SMALL short and flat or turned up at the end ○ *a snub nose* [14C. < Old Norse *snubba*] —**snubber** *n*

snub-nosed *adj* **1.** having a nose that is short and flat or turned up **2.** having a very short barrel or a blunt end ○ *snub-nosed pliers*

snuff[1] /snuf/ *v* (**snuffs, snuffing, snuffed**) **1.** *vt* INHALE SOMETHING to inhale something through the nose **2.** *vti* SNIFF to sniff noisily, or to examine something by sniffing it ○ *The hounds snuffed the ground searching for the trail.* ■ *n* SNIFFING SOUND an instance or sound of snuffing [Early 16C. < Dutch *snuffen* 'snuffle' < Germanic, 'of the nose']

snuff[2] /snuf/ *vt* (**snuffs, snuffing, snuffed**) **1.** EXTINGUISH FLAME to extinguish a flame, e.g. that of a burning candle **2.** TRIM WICK OF CANDLE to remove the burnt end from the wick of a candle **3.** DESTROY SOMETHING to put an end to somebody or something (*informal*) ○ *snuff out enthusiasm* ■ *n* SOOTY WICK the sooty, charred end of a candle wick [14C. Origin ?] ◇ **snuff it** to die (*informal*)

snuff[3] /snuf/ *n* **1.** POWDERED TOBACCO tobacco in the form of powder, taken by sniffing it up the nostrils **2.** AMOUNT OF SNUFF a portion of snuff ■ *vi* (**snuffs, snuffing, snuffed**) TAKE SNUFF to inhale snuff [Late 17C. < Dutch *snuf*, shortening of *snuftabak* 'sniffing tobacco']

snuffbox /snúf boks/ *n* a small ornamental box for powdered tobacco

snuff-coloured *adj* of a dark yellowish-brown colour

snuffer /snúffər/ *n* a device used to extinguish a candle, consisting of a long handle with a cone shape at one end

snuffers /snúffərz/ *n* an instrument resembling a pair of scissors, used for trimming wicks or extinguishing candles or oil lamps (*takes a singular or plural verb*)

snuff film *n* a pornographic film or video that allegedly ends with the murder of one of the participants in a sex act (*slang*)

snuffle /snúff'l/ *v* (**-fles, -fling, -fled**) **1.** *vi* BREATHE NOISILY to breathe noisily through a partially blocked nose **2.** *vti* SPEAK NASALLY to speak or say something in a nasal or whining way **3.** *vi* SNIFF to make repeated sniffing sounds ■ *n* SOUND OF SNUFFLING an instance or sound of snuffling ■ **snuffles** *npl* RUNNY NOSE a cold or other condition in which somebody sniffs a lot [Late 16C. Probably < Low German, Dutch *snuffelen*, ultimately an imitation of the sound] —**snuffler** *n* —**snuffly** *adj*

snuff movie *n* CINEMA same as **snuff film**

snuffy /snúffi/ (**-ier, -iest**) *adj* **1.** LIKE SNUFF like snuff in colour or smell **2.** COVERED WITH SNUFF soiled or marked with snuff **3.** IRRITABLE in a bad temper and easily annoyed —**snuffiness** *n*

snug /snug/ *adj* (**snugger, snuggest**) **1.** COSY warm and comfortable **2.** SMALL BUT COMFORTABLE small in size but offering a comfortable well-arranged space ○ *a snug cottage* **3.** SHELTERED protected from the weather ○ *The fishing boats were snug in the harbour.* **4.** CLOSE-FITTING fitting comfortably close or too close ○ *The sweater was perhaps a little too snug.* **5.** CONCEALED offering a safe and private hiding place ■ *n* **1.** SMALL ROOM IN PUB a small room or enclosed area in a pub allowing a small number of people to sit in private **2.** PEG FOR HOLDING BOLT a small peg used to hold the head of a bolt in place while a nut is tightened onto the end ■ *v* (**snugs, snugging, snugged**) **1.** *vt* MAKE SOMEBODY SNUG to make somebody comfortable and warm **2.** *vti* SECURE BOAT to make a boat secure to weather a storm [Late 16C. Probably < N Germanic or Low Dutch] —**snugly** *adv*

snuggery /snúggəri/ (*plural* **-ies**) *n* **1.** a place that is warm and comfortable **2.** same as **snug** (sense 1)

snuggle /snúgg'l/ (**-gles, -gling, -gled**) *v* **1.** *vi* to get into a comfortable, cosy position, especially close to another person **2.** *vt* to draw close to somebody or something to offer or receive comfort and affection [Late 17C. < SNUG]

so[1] /sō/ CORE MEANING: a conjunction indicating the reason for an action or situation, or its result ○ *Let's go upstairs and talk, so as to get a bit of privacy.* ○ *Keep your password secret so that others cannot access your account.* ○ *I had the flu, so I couldn't attend the meeting.*

1. *conj* IN ORDER THAT introduces the reason for doing what has just been mentioned ○ *The poles are joined together so as to strengthen the structure.* ○ *He held her tight so that she wouldn't fall.* **2.** *conj* INTRODUCES RESULT introduces the result of the situation that has just been mentioned ○ *Everything is done on a shoestring, so their prices are very low.* **3.** *conj* INDICATES SIMILARITY indicates that two events or situations are alike in some way ○ *Just as my circumstances have changed, so too have my aims in life.* **4.** *adv* INDICATES IDENTITY indicates that what is true of one person or thing is also true of another person or thing (*followed by auxiliary or modal, or by the main verb 'do', 'have', or 'be'*) ○ *If you can keep a secret, so can I.* **5.** *adv* AS IT IS indicates that something is the way it has been described ○ *The city has the potential to be very important, and will soon be so, both politically and commercially.* **6.** *adv* REFERS BACK refers back to something that has just been mentioned ○ *Lunch may be purchased on the island, for those who desire to do so.* **7.** *adv* TO SUCH EXTENT emphasizes the degree of something by mentioning its result ○ *He is so busy working at Nathan's, he doesn't have time to study.* **8.** *adv* EMPHASIZES QUALITY adds emphasis to the meaning of an adverb or adjective ○ *I was so scared.* ○ *He acts so stubbornly sometimes.* **9.** *conj* THEREFORE OR IN CONSEQUENCE introduces an event in a sequence ○ *It's not working out so we'll have to go back to the beginning and start again.* ○ *She said she would like to see me again so I gave her my phone number.* **10.** *conj* INVITES COMMENT introduces a new topic, or a question or comment about something ○ *So what are we going to do about it?* ○ *So I see you've changed your mind.* **11.** *adv* INDICATES POSITION OR DIMENSIONS indicates the position or dimensions of something, using actions or gestures ○ *Hold onto the boat like so, and hold yourself up.* **12.** *adv* INDEED used to contradict a negative statement (*nonstandard*) ○ *'You never explained what to do'. 'I*

did so!' **13.** *adv* N Am INTRODUCES COMMAND used to introduce commands (*informal*) ○ *So stop it already!* [Old English *swā* < Indo-European] ◇ **and so on** or **forth** used at the end of a list to indicate that there are other things that could be mentioned ○ *These systems are traditionally used in industries such as insurance, banking, universities, and so on.* ○ *Remove any additional hardware from the system (mouse, network card, fax board, modem, and so forth.)* ◇ **so be it** expresses agreement or resignation ○ *I wish you'd think again, but never mind – so be it!* ◇ **so much, so many** a limited or unspecified degree or amount ○ *The government can only do so much.* ○ *I can only take so many insults.* ◇ **so much for** (*informal*) **1.** used to indicate that there is nothing more that can be said or done about something ○ *So much for the morning. I still had the afternoon to get through.* **2.** used to indicate that something or somebody has not been successful or helpful ○ *So much for that brilliant plan!* ◇ **so that** in order that ◇ **so there** used to express defiance, triumph, or finality ◇ **so what?** used to ask rather rudely why something is important, implying that it is not

SPELLCHECK See *sew*.

USAGE See *order*.

so² /sō/ *n* MUSIC another spelling of **soh**

so³ *abbr* Somalia (*used in Internet addresses*) See table at **domain name**

SO *abbr* **1.** significant other **2.** COMM standing order

s.o. *abbr* FIN seller's option

soak /sōk/ *v* (**soaks, soaking, soaked**) **1.** *vti* STEEP IN LIQUID to immerse something in liquid for a period of time, or be immersed in liquid **2.** *vt* MAKE SOMEBODY OR SOMETHING WET to make something or somebody completely wet (*often passive*) ○ *We got soaked in the rain on the way home.* **3.** *vti* ABSORB to draw something such as moisture in through the pores or other small holes ○ *Use a paper towel to soak up the spillage.* **4.** *vti* PERMEATE SOMETHING to penetrate something by saturating it and passing into pores or small holes ○ *The water quickly soaked through her shoes.* **5.** *vti* REMOVE STAIN BY SOAKING to remove something, e.g. a mark or a stain from an item of clothing, by leaving it in liquid for a time **6.** *vti* GET DRUNK to drink too much alcohol, or make somebody drunk (*informal*) **7.** *vt* OVERCHARGE SOMEBODY to charge or tax somebody an excessive amount (*slang*) ■ *n* **1.** ACT OF SOAKING an act or instance of immersing something in liquid ○ *had a long, leisurely soak in the bath* **2.** SOAKING LIQUID a solution or liquid in which to soak something **3.** same as **drunkard** (*slang*) [Old English *socian*, form of *sūcan* (see SUCK)] —**soaker** *n*

soakaway /sōkə way/ *n* a hole where waste water can drain away by filtering down through the soil

soaking /sōking/ *n* **1.** STEEPING an act or the process of steeping something in liquid **2.** DRENCHING an instance of being made very wet (*informal*) ■ *adj* VERY WET very wet, especially because of being rained on (*informal*)

SYNONYMS See *wet*.

so-and-so (*plural* **so-and-sos**) *n* **1.** somebody or something not named or specified (*informal*) **2.** somebody regarded as annoying or disagreeable (*informal insult*)

Soane /sōn/, **Sir John** (1753–1837) British architect. He was an exponent of the neoclassical style, seen in his churches, private houses, and public buildings, most notably the Bank of England, London (1792–1833).

soap /sōp/ *n* **1.** CLEANSING AGENT a solid, liquid, or powdered preparation made by reacting potassium or sodium hydroxide with animal or vegetable oils. Use: cleaning. **2.** METALLIC SALT COMBINED WITH FATTY ACID a metallic salt of a fatty acid, often made with calcium, copper, aluminium, or lithium. Use: bases for waterproofing agents, ointments, greases. **3.** same as **soap opera** (*informal*) ■ *vt* (**soaps, soaping, soaped**) PUT SOAP ON SOMETHING OR SOMEBODY to put soap on something or somebody, especially in the process of washing [Old English *sāpe* < Germanic]

soapbark /sōp baark/ *n* **1.** a bark containing saponin. Use: formerly, soap substitute. **2.** an evergreen tree

that yields soapbark. Native to: South America. Latin name: *Quillaja saponaria.*

soapberry /sōp beri/ (*plural* **-ries**) *n* **1.** a pulpy fruit that is rich in saponins. Use: soap substitute. **2.** a tree or bush that bears soapberries. Native to: tropical America. Genus: *Sapindus.*

soapbox /sōp boks/ *n* **1.** a box in which soap is packed, especially when travelling **2.** something used as a platform for making an impromptu speech

soap bubble *n* **1.** a bubble formed with soapy water **2.** something that is beautiful but that does not last

soap opera *n* a serial on television or radio that deals with the everyday lives of a group of characters, especially in a melodramatic or sentimental way [Because originally often sponsored by soap manufacturers]

soap powder *n* a detergent in powdered form used in washing machines

soapstone: Nigerian carving (12th to 15th centuries)

soapstone /sōp stōn/ *n* a dark grey or green soft soapy compact variety of talc. Use: decorative carving.

soapsuds /sōp sudz/ *npl* same as **suds** *npl* (sense 1)

soapwort /sōp wurt/ *n* UK, ANZ, Can a plant with roots and leaves that yield saponin. Flowers: pink and white. Native to: Europe. Latin name: *Saponaria officinalis.* US term **bouncing Bet**

soapy /sōpi/ (**-ier, -iest**) *adj* **1.** WITH SOAP full of or covered with soap **2.** LIKE SOAP having the look or feel of soap ○ *a soapy texture* **3.** INSINCERE given to excessive insincere flattery (*slang*) —**soapiness** *adv*

soar /sawr/ *vi* (**soars, soaring, soared**) **1.** INCREASE RAPIDLY to increase rapidly in number, volume, size, or amount ○ *soaring prices* **2.** FLY to fly or rise high in the air **3.** GLIDE HIGH to glide on rising currents of air **4.** BECOME MORE INTENSE to rise to a higher, more intense, or exalted level ○ *Hopes for peace soared at the end of the day's talks.* ■ *n* ACT OF SOARING the act of soaring, or the height or range reached by soaring [14C. < Old French *essorer* < Latin *ex-* 'out' + *aura* 'air'] —**soarer** *n*

SPELLCHECK See *saw¹*.

Soares /swaaresh/, **Mário** (b. 1924) prime minister (1976–78, 1983–85) and president (1986–96) of Portugal. He was instrumental in the restoration of democratic government there. Full name **Soares, Mário Alberto Nobre Lopes**

Soave /sō aa vay, swaa vay/ *n* a dry white blended wine from northeastern Italy [Mid-20C. After a village in N Italy]

Soay /sō ay, sóy/ *n* a small dark brown horned sheep, belonging to an ancient breed originating in Soay, Outer Hebrides

sob /sob/ *v* (**sobs, sobbing, sobbed**) **1.** *vi* GASP WHILE CRYING to make gasping sounds while crying **2.** *vt* SPEAK WHILE SOBBING to say something while sobbing **3.** **sob yourself** *vr* BECOME BY SOBBING to get into a particular state by sobbing ○ *sobbed herself to sleep* ■ *n* SOUND OF SOBBING an act or sound of sobbing ○ *stifled a sob* [12C. Probably < Low Dutch] —**sobbingly** *adv*

soba /sōbə/ *n* a Japanese dish of buckwheat noodles [Late 19C. < Japanese]

sober /sóbər/ *adj* **1.** NOT INTOXICATED not under the influence of alcohol **2.** TENDING NOT TO DRINK not in the habit of drinking much alcohol **3.** SERIOUS serious and thoughtful in demeanour or quality ○ *a sober face* **4.** DULL lacking vitality or brightness in appearance ○ *He always dresses in sober colours.* **5.** NOT

FANCIFUL OR SPECULATIVE based on facts and rational thinking rather than on speculation ○ *a sober assessment of the situation* ■ *vti* (**-bers, -bering, -bered**) **1.** same as **sober up 2.** BECOME OR MAKE SOMEBODY SERIOUS to become more serious or thoughtful, or make somebody become so ○ *His expression sobered.* [14C. Via French < Latin *sobrius*] —**soberly** *adv* —**soberness** *n*
sober up *vti* make somebody sober after being drunk, or become sober

sobering /sóbəring/ *adj* making somebody give serious thought to important things ○ *a sobering experience* ○ *had a sobering effect* —**soberingly** *adv*

sobersides /sóbər sīdz/ *n* somebody who is solemn and serious —**sobersided** *adj*

sobriety /sə brí əti/ *n* **1.** ABSTINENCE abstinence from or moderation in the use of alcohol **2.** SERIOUSNESS the quality of being serious and thoughtful **3.** DULLNESS a lack of vitality or brightness [15C. Directly or via French < Latin *sobrietas* < *sobrius* 'sober']

sobriquet /sóbri kay/, **soubriquet** *n* an unofficial name or nickname, especially a humorous one [Mid-17C. < French, 'a tap under the chin']

sob sister *n* a journalist who writes or edits sentimental stories or answers problems sent in by readers (*informal*)

sob story *n* a story told to gain somebody's sympathy or pity, especially when offered as an excuse (*informal*)

sob stuff *n* something such as a film, intended to provoke feelings of sadness or sentimentality (*informal*)

soca /sókə/ *n* a style of Caribbean music that combines calypso and soul and has a fast beat [Late 20C. < SOUL + CALYPSO]

socage /sókkij/, **soccage** *n* a feudal system of holding land in which the tenant either paid rent or performed a fixed service, usually agricultural and nonmilitary in nature [14C. < Anglo-Norman < *soc* variant of *soke* 'right of jurisdiction'] —**socager** *n*

SoCal /sō kal/ *adj* US relating to the southern part of California, or to the people living there and their culture (*informal*) —**SoCal** *n*

so-called *adj* **1.** popularly known as, but not necessarily by the speaker or writer ○ *the so-called information superhighway* **2.** incorrectly known as ○ *a so-called art expert*

USAGE Quotation marks should not be used around expressions immediately following words like *so-called* and *self-styled: He is a so-called generalissimo of capitalism* [not *a so-called 'generalissimo of capitalism'*].

soccage *n* HIST another spelling of **socage**

soccer /sókər/ *n* ANZ, N Am a game in which two teams of 11 players try to score by kicking or butting a round ball into the net goals on either end of a rectangular field. UK term **football** ■ *vt* (**-cers, -cering, -cered**) *Aus* in Australian Rules football, to move the ball along the ground by repeatedly kicking and running after it ○ *He soccered it towards the centre circle.* [Late 19C. < Assoc., abbreviation of ASSOCIATION (in ASSOCIATION FOOTBALL) + *-er*, suffix added to shortened forms of words]

Socceroos /sókə roöz/ *n* Aus an informal name for the Australian national soccer team (*informal*; takes a singular or plural verb)

~~soceity~~ incorrect spelling of **society**

sociable /sóshəb'l/ *adj* **1.** GREGARIOUS inclined to seek out the company of other people **2.** FRIENDLY friendly and pleasant to other people **3.** OFFERING OPPORTUNITY FOR SOCIAL INTERACTION allowing people to mix in an informal way ○ *a sociable occasion* [Mid-16C. Directly or via French < Latin *sociabilis* < *socius* 'companion'] —**sociability** /sóshə bílləti/ *n* —**sociableness** *n* —**sociably** *adv*

USAGE **sociable** or **social**? *Social* is a neutral word that classifies a person or thing as being concerned in some way with society or its organization. A *social club* is a place provided for people to enjoy themselves, and a *social worker* is involved in work done for people's welfare. *Sociable*, by contrast, refers to a person's capacity to deal with other people in social contexts, so a *sociable worker* is a worker who enjoys the company of colleagues.

social /sṓsh'l/ *adj* **1. RELATING TO SOCIETY** relating to human society and how it is organized **2. RELATING TO INTERACTION OF PEOPLE** relating to the way in which people in groups behave and interact ○ *the social sciences* **3. LIVING IN A COMMUNITY** living or preferring to live as part of a community or colony rather than alone ○ *social insects such as ants* **4. OFFERING OPPORTUNITY FOR INTERACTION** allowing people to meet and interact with others in a friendly way ○ *a social club* **5. RELATING TO HUMAN WELFARE** relating to human welfare and the organized welfare services that a community provides ○ *social services* **6. OF RANK IN SOCIETY** relating to or considered appropriate to a rank in society, especially the upper classes **7. SOCIABLE** tending to seek out the company of others (*informal*) ○ *a very social person* **8. GROWING IN CLUMPS** describes plants that grow in clumps or masses ■ *n* **INFORMAL GET-TOGETHER** an informal gathering or party, usually of a particular group of people who meet regularly [Mid-17C. Via French < Latin *socialis* < *socius* 'companion'] —**socially** *adv*

USAGE See ***sociable***.

social anthropology *n* same as **cultural anthropology** —**social anthropologist** *n*

social assistance *n Can* same as **social security**

social capital *n* the educational, social, and cultural advantages that somebody from the upper middle classes is believed to possess

Social Charter *n* a declaration that outlines the rights of employees in countries that are part of the European Union

social climber *n* somebody who tries to rise in status by associating with people of a higher social class (*disapproving*) —**social climbing** *n*

social contract, **social compact** *n* an agreement among individual people in a society or between the people and their government that outlines the rights and duties of each party. It derives from the ideas of Hobbes, Locke, and Rousseau and involves people giving up freedoms in return for benefits such as state protection.

Social Credit *n* a Canadian conservative political party founded in 1935 —**Social Crediter** *n*

social Darwinism *n* a discredited social theory stating that the political and economic advantages in a developed society are derived from the biological advantages of its collective membership —**social Darwinist** *n*

social democracy, **Social Democracy** *n* the political belief that a change from capitalism to socialism can be achieved gradually and democratically —**social democrat** *n* —**social democratic** *adj*

Social Democratic and Labour Party *n* a political party in Northern Ireland, many of whose supporters want to unite Northern Ireland and the Republic of Ireland peacefully

Social Democratic Party *n* a British political party existing from 1981 to 1990, founded by a group who left the Labour Party. Many of its members joined the Social and Liberal Democratic Party in 1988.

social disease *n* a sexually transmitted disease (*informal; used euphemistically*)

social drinker *n* somebody who only consumes alcoholic beverages in the company of other people and in moderation

social engineering *n* the use of policies that are based on the findings of social science to deal with social problems

social exclusion *n* a form of deprivation experienced by people who are denied the benefits enjoyed by most members of an affluent society through poverty or through belonging to a marginalized group

social housing *n* housing provided by organizations such as local authorities or housing associations for renting at lower than market rates to people who cannot afford to buy their own homes or rent privately

social insurance *n* state insurance that uses compulsory contributions to pay for benefits for unemployed and retired people

socialise *vti* LEISURE, SOC SCI another spelling of **socialize**

socialism /sṓshəlizəm/, **Socialism** *n* **1. POLITICAL SYSTEM OF COMMUNAL OWNERSHIP** a political theory or system in which the means of production and distribution are controlled by the people and operated according to equity and fairness rather than market principles **2. MOVEMENT BASED ON SOCIALISM** a political movement based on principles of socialism, typically advocating an end to private property and to the exploitation of workers **3. STAGE BETWEEN CAPITALISM AND COMMUNISM** in Marxist theory, the stage after the proletarian revolution when a society is changing from capitalism to communism, marked by pay distributed according to work done rather than need

socialist /sṓshəlist/, **Socialist** *n* **BELIEVER IN SOCIALISM** somebody who believes in or supports socialism or a socialist party ■ *adj* **1. ADVOCATING SOCIALISM** relating to, based on, or advocating socialism **2. RELATING TO SOCIALISTS** relating to socialists or a socialist party —**socialistic** /sṓshə lístik/ *adj* —**socialistically** *adv*

socialist realism *n* an artistic doctrine officially sanctioned in many Communist countries, especially during the 1930s–50s, that proposed the idea that art and literature should serve to promote and glorify the ideals of a socialist state

Socialist Workers Party *n* a British political party that opposes capitalism

socialite /sṓshə līt/ *n* somebody who is well known in fashionable society

sociality /sṓshi álləti/ (*plural* **-ties**) *n* **1.** the quality of being social, or an instance of it **2.** the tendency to form social groups or live in a community

socialize /sṓshə līz/ (**-izes, -izing, -ized**), **socialise** (**-ises, -ising, -ised**) *v* **1.** *vi* **TAKE PART IN SOCIAL ACTIVITIES** to take part in social activities, or behave in a friendly way to others ○ *a group of friends who like to socialize after work* **2.** *vt* **TRAIN SOMEBODY TO BE SOCIAL** to give somebody the skills required for functioning successfully in society or in a particular society ○ *socialize a child* **3.** *vt* **MAKE SOMETHING PUBLICLY OWNED** to place something under public ownership or control —**socialization** /sṓshə lī záysh'n/ *n* —**socializer** *n*

socialized medicine /sṓshə līzd-/ *n US* a system of national health care that provides medical care to all and is regulated and subsidized by the US government

socially responsible investor *n* a person, company, or other organization with a policy of ethical investment

social mobility *n* the possibility for people in a society to change their class or social status within their lifetimes

social psychology *n* the branch of psychology that deals with how groups behave and how individual members are affected by the group to which they belong —**social psychologist** *n*

social realism *n* the use of realistic portrayals of life in art or literature to make a social or political point

social science *n* **1.** the study of people in society and how they relate to one another and to the group to which they belong **2.** a discipline that studies a specific area of human society, e.g. sociology, psychology, economics, political science, history, or anthropology —**social scientist** *n*

social secretary *n* somebody whose job is to arrange social activities and handle correspondence for a person or organization

social security *n* **1.** *also* **Social Security** a government scheme that provides economic security for people who are retired, unemployed, or unable to work **2.** money paid to somebody by a government through a social security scheme

Social Security number *n* in the United States, a unique reference number assigned to each person within the Social Security system. It remains the same throughout the person's life.

social service *n* a service provided by a government agency for the welfare of a person or community. Such services include housing, child protection, free school lunches, and health care. (*often used in the plural*) ■ **social services** *npl* a government agency that provides social services to a person or a community

social studies *n* an academic subject devoted to the study of society and including geography, economics, and history (*takes a singular or plural verb*)

social welfare *n* the social services provided by a state or by a private organization

social work *n* the profession or work of providing people in need with social services —**social worker** *n*

society /sə sī́ əti/ (*plural* **-ties**) *n* **1. RELATIONSHIPS AMONG GROUPS** the sum of social relationships among groups of humans or animals **2. STRUCTURED COMMUNITY OF PEOPLE** a structured community of people bound together by similar traditions, institutions, or nationality **3. CUSTOMS OF A COMMUNITY** the customs of a community and the way it is organized, e.g. its class structure ○ *the role of women in society* **4. SUBSET OF COMMUNITY** a particular section of a community that is distinguished by particular qualities ○ *In those days, the subject was never mentioned in polite society.* **5. PROMINENT PEOPLE** the prominent or fashionable people in a community, or their social life **6. COMPANIONSHIP** the state of being with other people **7. GROUP SHARING INTERESTS** an organized group of people who share an interest, aim, or profession [Mid-16C. Via French < Latin *societas* 'companionship' < *socius* 'companion'] —**societal** *adj*

Society of Friends *n* the Christian denomination consisting of the Quakers

Society of Jesus *n* the Roman Catholic religious order of the Jesuits

Socinian /sō sínni ən/ *n* a follower of Laelius and Faustus Socinus, Italian theologians who preached belief in God, but rejected other traditional Christian doctrines such as the Trinity and the divinity of Christ ■ *adj* relating to the Socinians and their beliefs [Mid-17C. < modern Latin *Socinianus* < *Socinus*] —**Socinianism** *n*

socio- *prefix* society, social ○ *sociopath* ○ *sociopolitical* [Via French < Latin, < *socius* 'companion']

sociobiology /sṓssi ō bī ólləji/ *n* the study of the social behaviour of animals and humans and how this is related to genetics and the survival of species —**sociobiological** /-bī ə lójjik'l/ *adj*

sociocultural /sṓssi ō kúlchərəl, sṓshi ō-/ *adj* relating to or involving cultural and social factors —**socioculturally** *adv*

socioeconomic /sṓssi ō ékkə nómmik, sṓshi ō-, -éekə-/ *adj* relating to or involving economic and social factors —**socioeconomically** *adv*

sociol. *abbr* sociology

sociolinguistics /sṓssi ō ling gwístiks, sṓshi ō-/ *n* the study of the relationships between language and social and cultural factors (*takes a singular verb*) —**sociolinguist** /-líng gwist/ *n* —**sociolinguistic** *adj*

sociology /sṓssi ólləji, sṓshi-/ *n* **1.** the study of the origin, development, and structure of human societies and the behaviour of individual people and groups in society **2.** the study of a particular social institution and the part it plays in society [Mid-19C. < French *sociologie* < Latin *socius* 'companion'] —**sociologic** /sṓssi ə lójjik, sṓshi ə-/ *adj* —**sociological** *adj* —**sociologically** *adv* —**sociologist** *n*

sociometry /sṓssi ómmətri, sṓshi-/ *n* the statistical study of behaviour and relationships within social groups, especially expressed in terms of preferences —**sociometric** /sṓssi ō méttrik, sṓshi ō-/ *adj* —**sociometrist** *n*

sociopath /sṓssi ō path, sṓshi ō-/ *n* PSYCHIAT same as **psychopath** (sense 1) (*technical*) [Mid-20C. After PSYCHOPATH] —**sociopathic** /sṓssi ō páthik, sṓshi ō-/ *adj* —**sociopathy** /sṓssi óppəthi, sṓshi-/ *n*

sociopolitical /sṓssi ō pə líttik'l, sṓshi ō-/ *adj* relating to or involving both social and political factors

sock[1] /sok/ *n* **1.** a soft, usually knitted covering for the foot and ankle that may reach as high as the knee. It is usually worn inside a shoe. **2.** METEOROL same as **windsock** **3.** a removable inner sole used for warmth or to make a shoe fit better [Old English *socc* 'light shoe, slipper', via Germanic < Latin *soccus*

< Greek *sukkhos* '(kind of) shoe'] ◇ **pull your socks up** to make an effort to improve (*informal*) ◇ **put a sock in it** used to tell somebody to stop talking (*informal*) **sock away** *vt NZ, N Am* to save money for the future (*informal*) [< the practice of storing savings in a sock]

sock² /sok/ (*informal*) *vti* (**socks, socking, socked**) to hit somebody or something hard, usually with the fist ■ *n* a hard hit or blow, usually with the fist [Late 17C. Origin ?] ◇ **sock it to somebody** to speak or behave in a way that makes a strong impression upon somebody (*dated informal*)

socket /sókit/ *n* **1. SHAPED HOLE FOR CONNECTION** a hole or recess in something specially shaped to receive a specific object or part, e.g. the hole that receives a light bulb or one that receives a plug on an electrical device **2. ELEC CONNECTION WITH ELECTRICITY SUPPLY** a receptacle, usually mounted on a wall, into which an electric plug is inserted to make a connection to a source of electric power. N Am term **outlet 3. ANAT HOLLOW IN BODY** a bony hollow in the body into which another part fits ■ *vt* (**-ets, -eting, -eted**) **1. PUT IN SOCKET** to insert something into a socket **2. FIT SOMETHING WITH SOCKET** to provide something with a socket [13C. < Anglo-Norman *soket* 'small ploughshare' < Old French *sok* 'ploughshare']

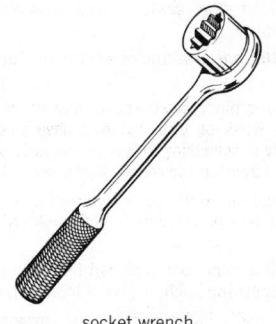

socket wrench

socket wrench, **socket spanner** *n* a long-handled wrench with interchangeable heads that fit over nuts and bolts of various sizes and a ratchet that makes tightening nuts and bolts easier

sockeye /sók ī/ (*plural* **-eyes** or *same*), **sockeye salmon** *n* a food fish of the salmon family that has red flesh. Native to: Pacific waters. Latin name: *Oncorhynchus nerka*. [Late 19C. Alteration of Salish *sukai* 'fish of fishes']

socle /sók'l/ *n* a base that sticks out from under the bottom of a wall, or the lowest part of the base of a column or pedestal [Early 18C. Via French < Latin *socculus* 'small light shoe' < *soccus* (see SOCK¹)]

SOCO /sókō/ (*plural* **SOCOs**) *n* a police officer responsible for collecting forensic evidence [Acronym < *scene-of-crime officer*]

Socrates /sókrə teez/ (469–399 BC) Greek philosopher. His philosophy has survived through the writings of his pupils, especially Plato. He employed what became known as the 'Socratic method' to question conventional assumptions about morality, justice, and other social concepts. Charged with atheism and corrupting youth, he was condemned to death.

> 'The unexamined life is not worth living.'
> [Socrates. Quoted in *Apology*, Plato; 4th century BC]

Socratic /sə kráttik/ *adj* relating to Socrates, his philosophy, or his method of arriving at the truth ■ *n* a student or follower of Socrates —**Socratically** *adv*— **Socraticism** /sə kráttisizəm/ *n* —**Socratist** /sókrətist/ *n*

Socratic irony *n* ignorance feigned in order to elicit explanations from somebody whose own ignorance can then be exposed through subsequent clever questioning

Socratic method *n* a means developed by Socrates of arriving at the truth by continually questioning, obtaining answers, and criticizing the answers

sod¹ /sod/ *n* **1. TURF** a surface section or strip of earth with growing grass and roots **2. GROUND** ground or soil (*literary*) ■ *vt* (**sods, sodding, sodded**) **COVER WITH TURF** to cover something with sods [15C. < Middle Dutch *sode* or Low German *sode* 'turf']

sod² /sod/ *n* **1. ANY PERSON** used, often humorously or affectionately, to refer to a person (*slang; sometimes offensive*) ○ *lucky sod* **2. OFFENSIVE TERM** an offensive term for somebody regarded as thoughtless, annoying, or objectionable (*slang insult*) ■ *vt* **OFFENSIVE TERM** an offensive term used to express anger with somebody or about something or defiance of somebody or something (*slang*) [Early 19C. Shortening of SODOMITE]

sod off *vi* an offensive term meaning to go away (*slang*)

soda /sódə/ *n* **1. BEVERAGES** same as **soda water** (sense 1) **2. US SOFT DRINK** a flavoured and carbonated drink, served cold **3. N Am ICE CREAM IN FLAVOURED CARBONATED WATER** a refreshment made with flavoured carbonated water and ice cream, usually served in a tall glass **4. SODIUM** sodium that is chemically combined with other elements **5. CHEM** same as **sodium bicarbonate 6. CHEM** same as **sodium carbonate** (sense 1) **7. CHEM** same as **sodium hydroxide 8. CARDS CARD THAT STARTS FARO** the card from the top of the pack that is turned face up in the dealing box at the start of the card game faro [15C. Via Italian, 'saltwort' (from which sodium carbonate is obtained) < Arabic *suwwād*]

soda ash *n* sodium carbonate when sold commercially. Use: manufacture of soap and paper.

soda biscuit *n* a biscuit leavened with bicarbonate of soda

soda bread *n* bread leavened with bicarbonate of soda instead of yeast, associated especially with Irish cooking

soda cracker *n* *N Am* a cracker leavened slightly with bicarbonate of soda and cream of tartar

soda fountain *n* *N Am* a counter or stand where beverages, ice cream, and snacks are sold (*dated*)

soda lime *n* a mixture of sodium hydroxide and calcium hydroxide. Use: moisture and carbon dioxide absorbent.

sodalite /sódə līt/ *n* a blue, greyish, or yellow translucent aluminosilicate mineral containing sodium and chlorine. Source: alkaline igneous rocks.

sodality /sō dálləti/ (*plural* **-ties**) *n* **1.** a Roman Catholic lay society that is run as a charity or a religious fellowship **2.** an association or fellowship [Early 17C. Directly or via French < Latin *sodalitas* 'fellowship' < *sodalis* 'fellow, companion']

soda nitre *n* MINERALS same as **Chile saltpetre**

soda pop *n* *US* a flavoured and carbonated drink, served cold (*informal*)

soda siphon *n* a sealed bottle containing water and carbon dioxide gas under pressure, used to produce soda water. N Am term **siphon bottle**

soda water *n* **1.** a carbonated water drunk alone or used as a mixer in alcoholic drinks **2.** a weak solution of water, bicarbonate of soda, and acid, taken to aid digestion

sodbuster /sódbustər/ *n* **1.** a plough used to break the sod **2.** *N Am* AGRIC same as **farmer 3.** *Can* a prairie homesteader, especially one growing crops (*informal*)

sodden /sódd'n/ *adj* **1. THOROUGHLY WET** extremely wet and heavy with retained moisture **2. DRUNK** having dulled senses as a result of excessive drinking ■ *vti* (**-dens, -dening, -dened**) **MAKE OR BECOME SODDEN** to make somebody or something sodden, or become sodden [13C. Obsolete past participle of SEETHE] —**soddenly** *adv*— **soddenness** *n*

SYNONYMS See *wet*.

sodium /sódi əm/ *n* a soft silver-white metallic element that reacts readily with other substances and is essential to the body's fluid balance. Source: common salt, calcium chloride. Use: catalyst, tracer, in chemical processes. Symbol **Na**. See table at **element** [Early 19C. < SODA; from its being isolated from caustic soda]

sodium benzoate *n* a white crystalline powder. Use: food preservative, antiseptic, manufacture of pharmaceuticals. Formula: $C_7H_5O_2Na$.

sodium bicarbonate *n* a white, crystalline, slightly alkaline salt. Use: leavening agent, antacid, in effervescent drinks, fire extinguishers. Formula: $NaHCO_3$.

sodium carbonate *n* **1.** a white crystalline salt of carbonic acid. Use: water softener, manufacture of glass, ceramics, cleansing agents, paper. Formula: Na_2CO_3. **2.** CHEM same as **washing soda**

sodium chlorate *n* a colourless crystalline salt. Use: weedkiller, bleaching agent, manufacture of explosives. Formula: $NaClO_3$.

sodium chloride *n* a colourless crystalline compound. Source: sea water, halite deposits. Use: preservative, food seasoning. Formula: $NaCl$.

sodium citrate *n* a white crystalline salt. Use: photography, buffering agent in foods, anticoagulant in stored blood. Formula: $Na_3C_6H_5O_7$.

sodium cyanide *n* a poisonous white crystalline salt. Use: fumigant, gold and silver mining, manufacture of steel and dyes. Formula: $NaCN$.

sodium cyclamate *n* CHEM same as **cyclamate**

sodium dichromate *n* a red or orange crystalline salt. Use: leather tanning, manufacture of dyes and inks, oxidizing agent, corrosion inhibitor. Formula: $Na_2Cr_2O_7$.

sodium fluoride *n* a poisonous colourless crystalline salt. Use: pesticide, in metallurgical processes, trace amounts for water fluoridation and tooth decay prevention. Formula: NaF.

sodium fluoroacetate *n* a white poisonous powder. Use: killing rats and mice. Formula: $C_2H_2FNaO_2$.

sodium glutamate *n* CHEM same as **monosodium glutamate**

sodium hydroxide *n* a brittle white alkaline solid. Use: manufacture of paper, rayon, soap, chemicals, pharmaceuticals. Formula: $NaOH$.

sodium hypochlorite *n* a green crystalline unstable salt, usually kept in solution. Use: bleach, disinfectant, water purifier. Formula: $NaOCl$.

sodium hyposulphite *n* CHEM same as **sodium thiosulphate**

sodium nitrate *n* a white crystalline salt. Use: curing of meats, rocket propellant, fertilizer, manufacture of explosives, pottery, glass enamels. Formula: $NaNO_3$.

sodium peroxide *n* a yellowish odourless powder. Use: bleaching agent, antiseptic, disinfectant. Formula: Na_2O_2.

sodium phosphate *n* a sodium salt of phosphoric acid. Use: medical preparations, cleaning agents.

sodium propionate *n* a colourless crystalline powder. Use: spoilage retardant in packaged foods. Formula: $C_3H_5NaO_2$.

sodium pump *n* the exchange of sodium ions for potassium ions across a cell membrane

sodium silicate *n* a compound of sodium and silica, often in solution. Use: preservatives, textile processing, cement.

sodium sulphate *n* a bitter white salt. Use: manufacture of glass, wood pulp, rayon, dyes, detergents, ceramic glazes, cathartics. Formula: Na_2SO_4.

sodium thiosulphate *n* a white crystalline salt. Use: photographic fixer, bleach. Formula: $Na_2S_2O_3$.

sodium-vapour lamp *n* an electric lamp containing neon gas and sodium vapour through which a current runs to produce an orange-yellow light used for street lighting

Sodom /sóddəm/ *n* **1.** in the Bible, a city full of moral corruption and evil that was destroyed along with Gomorrah by God **2.** a place that is regarded as corrupt

sodomise *vt* another spelling of **sodomize** (*offensive*)

sodomite /sóddə mīt/ *n* an offensive term for somebody who practises anal intercourse [14C. Via French and late Latin *Sodomitēs* 'inhabitant of Sodom' < *Sodoma* 'Sodom'] —**sodomitic** /sóddə míttik/ *adj*

sodomize /sóddə mīz/ (**-izes, -izing, -ized**), **sodomise** (**-ises, -ising, -ised**) *vt* an offensive term meaning to have anal intercourse with somebody

sodomy /sóddəmi/ *n* an offensive term for anal intercourse [13C. Directly or via medieval Latin *sodomia* < ecclesiastical Latin *peccatum Sodomiticum* 'sin of Sodom']

Sod's Law *n* UK the law or principle that if anything can go wrong, it will (*informal*) ANZ, N Am term **Murphy's Law** [Late 20C. < SOD²]

soever /sō évvər/ *adv* in any way or to any degree possible

sofa /sófə/ *n* a long upholstered seat that has a back and arms and is made to seat more than one person [Early 17C. Via French < Arabic ṣuffa 'long bench']

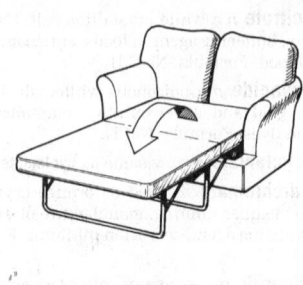

sofa bed

sofa bed *n* a sofa that can be temporarily converted into a bed as required, e.g. by unfolding its seat

sofar /sō faar/ *n* a way of locating survivors at sea by measuring the time it takes sound waves to reach three shore locations from an explosion set off underwater by the survivors [Mid-20C. Acronym < *sound fixing and ranging*]

soffit /sóffit/ *n* the underside of a structural component of a building, e.g. the underside of a roof overhang or the inner curve of an arch [Early 17C. Via French *soffite* or Italian *soffitto* < Latin *suffixus* 'fastened underneath' (see SUFFIX)]

Sofia /sófi ə/ capital city of Bulgaria, situated in the Sofia basin, about 64 km/40 mi. from the Yugoslavian border. Population: 1,096,389 (2001).

S. of Sol. *abbr* BIBLE Song of Solomon

soft /soft, sawft/ *adj* **1.** MALLEABLE easily shaped, bent, or cut **2.** YIELDING giving way to externally applied pressure or weight ○ *a soft cushion* **3.** SMOOTH-TEXTURED having a texture that is smooth to the touch ○ *soft fur* **4.** WITH SMOOTH OUTLINE having no sharp or jagged edges ○ *furniture designed with soft lines* **5.** QUIET-SOUNDING quiet and soothing in sound **6.** EASY ON EYES lacking glare or intensity of light or colour **7.** MILD not blowing strongly or falling heavily ○ *a soft rain* **8.** AFFECTIONATE conveying love and tenderness **9.** EMOTIONAL easily moved to tender emotions **10.** COWARDLY lacking determination or strength of character **11.** LENIENT lenient in treatment or punishment, often too lenient **12.** UNDEMANDING requiring little effort or attention (*informal*) ○ *a soft job* **13.** NOT WELL TONED out of good physical condition **14.** INCAPABLE OF ENDURING HARDSHIP unable or unwilling to put up with hardship or privation, especially from having lived a life of ease **15.** LACKING GOOD SENSE lacking intelligence or sound judgment (*informal*) **16.** NOT EASILY VERIFIABLE relating to, dealing with, or based on data that is not easily proved or disproved using scientific method **17.** NOT COERCIVE based on negotiation, flexibility, and good will rather than on coercion ○ *a soft sell* **18.** same as **soft-core 19.** VULNERABLE unprotected against violent attack **20.** MIL UNARMOURED describes military vehicles and sites with little or no protection against military attack **21.** POL NOT POLITICALLY EXTREME holding moderate political views **22.** FIN RELATING TO PAPER MONEY relating to currency or a monetary system that is not backed by gold and is therefore not easily convertible to a foreign currency **23.** COMM DECLINING ECONOMICALLY exhibiting a downward trend, e.g. in price, demand, or economic activity **24.** PHON SIBILANT OR FRICATIVE describes the consonant sounds 'c' and 'g' when pronounced as a fricative, as in 'dance' and 'age', instead of as a stop, as in 'cat' and 'get' **25.** PHON PALATALIZED describes a consonant that is palatalized in a Slavic language **26.** PHYS LOW-ENERGY describes radiation that has low energy and lacks penetrating ability ■ *adv* SOFTLY in a quiet, tender, or lenient way ■ *n* SOMETHING SOFT a soft thing or part of something ■ **softs** *npl* ECON same as **soft commodities** [Old English *sōfte* (earlier *sēfte*)]

< Germanic] —**softly** *adv* —**softness** *n* ◇ **be soft on** somebody to be romantically attracted to somebody

softback /sóft bak, sáwft-/ *n, adj* PUBL same as **paperback** *n, adj*

softball /sóft bawl, sáwft-/ *n* **1.** baseball played with a larger softer ball on a smaller field, between two teams of ten people **2.** the ball used to play softball

soft-boiled *adj* **1.** describes an egg that is boiled so that the yolk is soft, but the white is firm **2.** having or showing a sympathetic or sentimental nature

soft chancre *n* MED same as **chancroid** (sense 2)

soft coal *n* INDUST same as **bituminous coal**

soft commodities *npl* traded commodities that are not metals, e.g. cocoa, sugar, cotton, and cereals

soft copy *n* data stored on a computer disk, as distinct from data that is printed on paper

soft-core *adj* sexually suggestive or provocative without being explicit

softcover /sóft kuvvər/ *n, adj* PUBL same as **paperback** *n, adj*

soft drink *n* a still or carbonated nonalcoholic beverage, served cold

soft drug *n* an illegal drug that is thought by some to be less addictive and harmful than the narcotic drugs heroin and cocaine

soften /sóff'n, sáwf'n/ (**-ens, -ening, -ened**) *vti* **1.** MAKE OR BECOME LESS HARD to become soft or softer, or make something soft or softer **2.** BE KINDER to become gentler or less harsh, or make something gentler or less harsh **3.** WEAR SOMEBODY DOWN to make somebody's resolve less firm, or become less firmly resolved **4.** HARASS ENEMY to weaken an enemy's resistance or morale by continuous bombardment, or be weakened in this way **5.** REDUCE SOMETHING to decline, e.g. in price, demand, or economic activity, or make something do this

softener /sóff'nər, sáwf-/ *n* a substance added to something such as water or laundry to make it softer

soft focus *n* a deliberate slight blurring of a photograph or a filmed image, giving it a hazy appearance, so as to achieve a special effect such as romance or nostalgia (*hyphenated before a noun*)

soft fruit *n* a small stoneless fruit, e.g. the raspberry, strawberry, or blackberry

soft furnishings *npl* furnishings made from fabric that decorate a house and make it more comfortable, e.g. curtains and rugs

soft gamma repeater *n* ASTRON same as **magnetar**

soft goods *npl* textiles and the items such as clothing and bedding that are made from them

soft hail *n* METEOROL same as **graupel**

soft-hearted *adj* showing sympathy, kindness, or generosity —**soft-heartedly** *adv* —**soft-heartedness** *n*

softie *n* another spelling of **softy**

soft-kill *adj* US intended to disable, not kill, an enemy

soft landing *n* **1.** a landing of a spacecraft, especially on the moon, without enough impact to cause damage **2.** a resolution of a problem, especially an economic problem, found without undue effort

softly-softly *adj* characterized by caution or discretion

soft option *n* the easier or easiest course of action

soft palate *n* the fleshy rear portion of the roof of the mouth, extending from the hard palate at the front and tapering to the hanging uvula at the rear. It elevates to close off the nasal passages when swallowing, sucking, and pronouncing some sounds.

soft pedal *n* a pedal on a piano that reduces the usual volume. It shifts the hammers so that they do not strike all the strings of each note or so that they strike the strings with less force.

soft-pedal *vti* **1.** to reduce the volume of music played on a piano by operating the soft pedal **2.** to try to make something seem less important, noticeable, or objectionable (*informal*)

soft rock *n* rock music that tends to be slower and

more melodic than hard rock, often influenced by folk or country and western music

soft rot *n* a bacterial or fungal plant disease that causes plant parts, especially fruits and vegetables, to decay into a pulpy mass

soft sell *n* a method of selling or advertising goods and services that uses subtlety and persuasion, rather than aggressive insistence (*informal*; hyphenated before a noun)

soft-shell *adj* used to describe an animal that lives in water and has a soft or thin and brittle shell, sometimes as a result of having recently moulted

soft-shelled turtle *n* a freshwater turtle with sharp claws, a pointed snout, and a soft flat shell covered with leathery skin. Family: Trionychidae.

soft-shoe *n* tap dancing for which soft-soled shoes without metal taps are worn (*often used before a noun*)

soft soap *n* **1.** flattery used for the purpose of persuading or distracting somebody (*informal*) **2.** a liquid or semiliquid soap, usually made with potassium hydroxide

soft-soap *vt* to use flattery to persuade or distract somebody (*informal*)

softsore /sóft sawr, sáwft-/ *n* MED same as **chancroid** (sense 1)

soft-spoken *adj* speaking or said with a quiet gentle voice

soft spot *n* a place, position, or area in which something is weak or vulnerable ◇ **have a soft spot for** somebody or something to have especially tender feelings or affection for somebody or something

soft top *n* a car that has a soft roof made of fabric that can be opened and folded back. N Am term **ragtop**

soft touch *n* somebody who can be easily persuaded to do something such as give a loan or handout

software /sóft wair, sáwft-/ *n* programs and applications that can be run on a computer system, e.g. word processing or database packages (*often used before a noun*)

software engineering *n* the application of mathematics and technology to the design, implementation, and testing of computer programs to optimize their production and support

software piracy *n* the illegal duplication of copyrighted software or the installation of copyrighted software on more computers than authorized under terms of the software licence agreement

soft water *n* naturally occurring or treated water in which soap lathers easily because of low levels of calcium and magnesium salts

soft wheat *n* wheat with soft kernels and weak gluten that is relatively low in protein. Use: cakes, biscuits, pastries, livestock feed.

softwood /sóft wŏŏd, sáwft-/ *n* **1.** the open-grained wood of a pine, cedar, or other coniferous tree. Many softwoods are, in fact, hard and durable. **2.** a tree that yields softwood, e.g. a pine or cedar

softy /sófti, sáwfti/ (*plural* **-ies**), **softie** *n* somebody regarded as weak, timid, or sentimental (*informal*)

Sogdian /sógdi ən/ *n* **1.** a member of a people who lived in Central Asia **2.** the extinct Iranian language of the Sogdian people [Mid-16C. Via Latin < Greek *Sogdianos* < Old Persian *Suguda*] —**Sogdian** *adj*

soggy /sóggi/ (**-gier, -giest**) *adj* **1.** THOROUGHLY WET soaked through with moisture **2.** WITH TOO MUCH LIQUID unpleasantly wet and heavy in texture **3.** UNINTERESTING lacking animation or vitality [Early 18C. < obsolete *sog* 'area of marshy ground'] —**soggily** *adv* —**sogginess** *n*

Sogne Fjord /sóngnə-/ inlet of the North Sea in southwestern Norway. Length: 200 km/125 mi.

soh /sō, soļ/ *n* a syllable that represents the fifth note in a scale when singing solfeggio. In fixed solfeggio it represents the note G. N Am term **sol**¹

Soho /sóhō/ *n* **1.** an area of central London well known for its theatres, restaurants, and clubs **2.** *also* **SoHo** an area of the lower west side of Manhattan well known for its art studios and galleries [In sense 2 < SOUTH + *Houston Street*]

soi-disant /swaa deézaaN, swaádee zaáN/ *adj* self-styled or so-called [< French, 'saying yourself']

soigné /swaán yay/, **soignée** *adj* **1.** neat and smart in dress and appearance **2.** designed or furnished in an elegant style [Early 19C. < French, past participle of *soigner* 'care for' < Germanic]

soil[1] /soyl/ *n* **1.** TOP LAYER OF LAND the top layer of most of the Earth's land surface, consisting of the unconsolidated products of rock erosion and organic decay, along with bacteria and fungi (*often used before a noun*) **2.** TYPE OF EARTH earth or ground of a particular kind ○ *sandy soil* **3.** COUNTRY a country or state (*literary*) ○ *their native soil* **4.** FARMING agricultural life and work (*literary*) **5.** NURTURING MEDIUM a medium in which growth and development takes place (*literary*) [13C. Via Anglo-Norman, 'piece of land' < Latin *solium* 'seat', by association with *solum* 'ground, soil']

soil[2] /soyl/ *vt* (**soils, soiling, soiled**) **1.** MAKE DIRTY to make somebody or something dirty or stained **2.** BRING DISHONOUR ON SOMEBODY to damage somebody's reputation, character, or good name ■ *n* **1.** DIRT dirt or dirtiness ○ *remove soil from linens* **2.** MORAL CORRUPTION immoral behaviour or lack of moral standards (*literary*) [13C. < Old French *soill(i)er* 'to soil, wallow']

SYNONYMS See *dirty*.

soil[3] /soyl/ *n* excrement or sewage ○ *a soil pipe* [15C. < Old French *souille* 'muddy place' < *soill(i)er* 'to soil, wallow']

soiled /soyld/ *adj* stained or marked, especially during normal use

SYNONYMS See *dirty*.

soilure /sóylyər/ *n* the soiling or staining of something (*literary*) [14C. < Old French *soilleure* < *soillier* 'to soil, wallow']

soiree /swaá ray/, **soirée** *n* a party or gathering held in the evening, especially in somebody's home [Late 18C. < French, < *soir* 'evening' < Latin *sero* 'at a late hour' < *serus* 'late']

soixante-neuf /swássont núrf/ *n* same as **sixty-nine** (*slang offensive*) [< French, 'sixty-nine'; from the position of the couple]

sojourn /sójjurn, sójjərn/ (*literary*) *n* a short stay at a place ■ *vi* (**-journs, -journing, -journed**) to stay at a place for a time [13C. < Anglo-Norman *sujurn*, Old French *sojorn* < Old French *sojourner* 'spend the day' < Latin *sub-* 'under' + late Latin *diurnum* 'day'] —**sojourner** *n*

Sokoto /sókətō/ capital city of Sokoto State, northwestern Nigeria, situated about 483 km/300 mi. northwest of Abuja. Population: 199,900 (1995).

sol[1] /sol/ *n* *N Am* same as **soh** [14C. < medieval Latin, shortening of Latin *solve* 'purge!, release!', word sung to this note in a medieval hymn]

sol[2] /sol/ *n* a liquid colloidal solution [Late 19C. Shortening of SOLUTION]

sol[3] /sol/ *n* a copper or silver coin formerly used in France, worth 12 deniers [Late 16C. < obsolete French, shortening of Latin *solidus* (see SOLDIER)]

sol[4] /sol/ (*plural* **soles** /sólays/) *n* the main unit of currency in Peru. See table at **currency** [< Spanish, literally 'sun' < Latin]

Sol /sol/ *n* **1.** the personification of the Sun (*literary*) **2.** in Roman mythology, the god of the Sun. Greek equivalent **Helios** [14C. < Latin, 'sun']

sola[1] /sólə/ *adj* used as a stage direction to indicate that a girl or woman character appears alone on stage [stage Mid-18C. <. Latin, form of *solus* 'alone']

sola[2] /sólə/ GEOG *plural of* **solum**

solace /sólləss/ *n* **1.** RELIEF FROM EMOTIONAL DISTRESS comfort at a time of sadness, grief, or disappointment **2.** SOURCE OF COMFORT somebody or something that provides comfort at a time of sadness, grief, or disappointment ■ *vt* (**-aces, -acing, -aced**) PROVIDE SOMEBODY WITH COMFORT to comfort somebody at a time of sadness, grief, or disappointment [13C. Via French < Latin *solatium* < *solari* 'to comfort'] —**solacer** *n*

solan /sólən/, **solan goose** *n* a bird of the gannet family having a white body, yellowish head, and black wingtips. Native to: North Atlantic. Latin name: *Morus bassanus*. [15C. Probably < Old Norse *súla* 'gannet' + *and-* 'duck']

solanaceous /sóllə náyshəss/ *adj* relating to or belonging to the nightshade family of plants, a family that includes the potato, tomato, and tobacco [Early 19C. < modern Latin *Solanaceae* < Latin *solanum* (see SOLANUM)]

solanine /sólə neen/ *n* a bitter poisonous alkaloid found in several plants of the nightshade family. Use: formerly to treat epilepsy, bronchitis, asthma. Formula: $C_{45}H_{73}NO_{15}$.

solanum /sō láynəm, sō láynəm/ (*plural* **-nums** or *same*) *n* a plant of the nightshade family, e.g. the potato or aubergine. Genus: *Solanum*. [Late 16C. Via modern Latin < Latin < *sol* 'sun']

solar /sólər/ *adj* **1.** FROM SUN relating to or originating from the Sun **2.** OPERATING USING ENERGY FROM SUN using the Sun's radiation as a source of energy **3.** MEASURED BY SUN'S POSITION measured with reference to the Earth's movement in relation to the Sun [15C. < Latin *solaris* < *sol* 'sun']

solar apex *n* the point in space towards which the Sun appears to be moving, located in the constellation Hercules

solar battery *n* an arrangement of several solar cells for converting solar radiation into electricity

solar cell *n* an electric cell that converts solar radiation directly into electricity. Solar cells are mounted on solar panels used on satellites and spacecraft

solar constant *n* the average amount of solar radiation received at the outer atmosphere at the Earth's mean distance from the Sun, equal to 0.140 watt per square centimetre

solar cycle *n* a cycle in the Sun's activity lasting on average 11 years, during which changes in the Sun's internal magnetic field occur. Sunspot activity is greatest in the middle of the cycle.

solar day *n* the time taken for the Earth to make a complete revolution on its axis, measured with respect to the Sun

solar eclipse *n* an eclipse in which the Moon blocks all or part of the Sun's light from reaching the Earth's surface, because it passes directly between the Earth and the Sun

solar energy *n* **1.** energy radiated from the Sun in the form of heat and light, used by green plants for photosynthesis and harnessed as solar power **2.** energy obtained from radiation emitted by the Sun

solar flare *n* a brief sudden eruption of high-energy hydrogen gas from the surface of the Sun, associated with sunspots. It causes interruptions of communication systems on Earth.

solar furnace *n* a furnace equipped with a series of concave mirrors that are motorized to follow the Sun and focus its radiation to obtain and maintain extremely high temperatures

solar gain *n* the amount of heat produced in a building by solar radiation, e.g. through windows or transparent walls

solar heating *n* the use of radiation emitted by the Sun to heat water or air that is passed through heat-absorbing panels

solaria LEISURE *plural of* **solarium**

solarimeter /sólə rímmitər/ *n* an instrument used to measure solar radiation

solarise *vt* PHYS, PHOTOGRAPHY another spelling of **solarize**

solarium /sə láiri əm/ (*plural* **-ia** /-ri ə/ or **-iums**) *n* **1.** a room built for the purpose of enjoying sunlight, usually with large windows or glass walls, especially a room in a hospital or other health care establishment **2.** a room or establishment equipped with sunlamps or sunbeds for acquiring a tan [Mid-19C. < Latin, 'sundial, terrace' < *sol* 'sun']

solarize /sólə rīz/ (**-izes, -izing, -ized**), **solarise** (**-ises, -ising, -ised**) *vt* **1.** to affect or damage something with solar radiation **2.** to overexpose photographic materials to light for deliberate effect, usually in order to exaggerate highlights —**solarization** /sólə rī záysh'n/ *n*

solar month *n* one-twelfth of a solar year, equal to 30 days, 10 hours, 29 minutes, 3.8 seconds

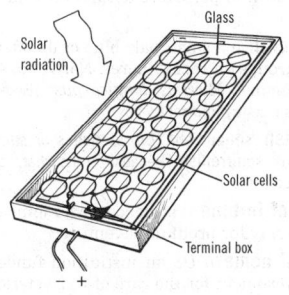

Solar radiation / Glass / Solar cells / Terminal box / − +

solar panel

solar panel *n* a large panel containing solar cells or heat-absorbing plates that convert the Sun's radiation into energy for use, e.g. in heating buildings and powering satellites and spacecraft

solar plexus *n* **1.** a mass of nerve cells in the upper abdomen behind the stomach, kidneys, and other internal organs **2.** a point on the upper abdomen just below where the ribs separate. A sharp blow to this region can cause loss of consciousness. [< its radial network of nerves]

solar system *n* the Sun and all the planets, satellites, asteroids, meteors, and comets that are subject to its gravitational pull

solar wind *n* the flow of high-speed ionized particles from the Sun's surface into interplanetary space

solar year *n* the time taken for the Earth to move around the Sun, equal to 365 days, 5 hours, 48 minutes, 45.51 seconds

solation /sō láysh'n/ *n* the process of changing from a gel to a liquid [Early 20C. < SOL[2]]

solatium /sō láyshi əm/ (*plural* **-tia** /-shi ə/) *n* damages awarded for emotional suffering, as opposed to financial loss or physical injury or suffering [Early 19C. < Latin (see SOLACE)]

sold past participle, past tense of **sell**

solder /sóldər/ *n* **1.** ALLOY FOR JOINING METAL an alloy with a low melting point, usually a mixture of tin and lead, used to join electrical components to a circuit board or to join metal objects together **2.** SOMETHING THAT UNITES something that forms a bond or union ■ *vti* (**-ders, -dering, -dered**) **1.** JOIN THINGS WITH SOLDER to work with solder, or join things using solder **2.** UNITE TO FORM WHOLE to come together in unity, or establish a bond of unity between people or things [14C. < French *soudure* < *souder* 'fasten together' < Latin *solidare* < *solidus* 'solid'] —**solderer** *n*

soldering iron /sóldəring-/ *n* a tool with a point that is heated for melting and applying solder

soldi COINS plural of **soldo**

~~soldiar~~ incorrect spelling of **soldier**

soldier /sóljər/ *n* **1.** SOMEBODY SERVING IN ARMY somebody who serves in a military organization **2.** ARMY MEMBER BELOW OFFICER RANK a member of an army, of a rank below commissioned officer **3.** DEDICATED WORKER somebody who works with dedication for a cause **4.** SKILLED WARRIOR a skilled and experienced fighter or military strategist **5.** ANT THAT PROTECTS COLONY a sterile member of an ant or termite colony with a large head and powerful jaws. Its role is to defend the colony. **6.** PIECE OF BREAD AND BUTTER a thin strip of bread or toast, usually buttered, especially one for dipping into a soft-boiled egg or the yolk of a fried egg (*informal*) ■ *vi* (**-diers, -diering, -diered**) **1.** SERVE IN ARMY to serve as a soldier in an army **2.** PRETEND TO WORK to give the appearance of working while really idling (*archaic*) [13C. < Old French, 'somebody having pay' < *soulde* 'soldier's pay' < Latin *solidus (nummus)* 'Roman gold coin', literally 'solid (coin)'] —**soldierly** *adj*

CULTURAL NOTE *The Good Soldier*, a novel (1915) by Ford Madox Ford. Considered Ford's masterpiece, it describes an American couple's tragic involvement with an English army captain (the good soldier of the title) and his domineering wife. A powerful study of the conflict between sexuality and contemporary moral values, it is

admired in particular for its innovative and intricate narrative structure.

---

soldier on *vi* to persevere despite difficulties or setbacks

soldier crab *n* a small pale blue crab, often seen in large groups on rocky shores. Native to: Australia. Latin name: *Mictyris longicarpus.* [Because it resembles a sentry in a sentry box]

soldierfish /sṓljər fish/ (*plural* **-fishes** or *same*) *n* FISH same as **squirrelfish** [Because of its sharp spines and rough scales]

soldier of fortune *n* somebody who joins or serves in an army for profit or adventure

soldiers' home *n US* an institution funded by the US government for the care of war veterans

soldiery /sṓljəri/ *n* **1.** soldiers as a group **2.** the profession or skill of a soldier

soldo /sóldō/ (*plural* **-di** /-di/) *n* a copper coin used in the former Italian states until the 19th century, worth one-twentieth of a lira [Late 16C. Via Italian < Latin *solidus (nummus)* 'Roman gold coin', literally 'solid (coin)']

sold-out *adj* describes an entertainment venue or performance for which all available tickets have been sold

sole[1] /sōl/ *n* **1. BOTTOM OF FOOT** the underside of the foot from the toes to the heel **2. BOTTOM OF SHOE** the underside of a shoe, boot, or other piece of footwear, sometimes excluding the heel **3. BOTTOM SURFACE OF GOLF CLUB** the underside of the head of a golf club ■ *vt* (**soles, soling, soled**) **1. PUT SOLE ON SHOE** to put a sole on a shoe, boot, or other piece of footwear **2. PLACE GOLF CLUB ON GROUND** to put the sole of a golf club on the ground in preparation for a stroke [14C. Via French < Latin *solea* 'sandal' < *solum* 'foot']

SPELLCHECK sole or **soul**? Do not confuse the spelling of ***sole*** and ***soul***, which sound similar. There are several words spelt***sole***: one means 'the underside of the foot or of a shoe', and can also be used as a verb meaning 'put a sole on a shoe'; another is a noun denoting a fish; a third is an adjective meaning 'only' or 'exclusive' (as in *the sole reason, sole responsibility*). ***Soul*** is a noun meaning 'a person's nonphysical aspect or spirit', 'spiritual depth', or simply 'a person', as in *heart and soul, a novel that lacks soul, not a soul to be seen.* ***Soul*** is also used in such compounds as *soul-destroying, soul mate, soul music,* and *soul-searching.*

---

sole[2] /sōl/ *adj* **1. ONLY** only one ○ *the sole reason* **2. EXCLUSIVE** belonging to one person or group ○ *has sole responsibility for the department* **3. UNFETTERED** free from the interference of others **4.** LAW **UNMARRIED** having no husband or wife [13C. Via French < Latin *sola*, form of *solus*] —**soleness** *n*

SPELLCHECK See *sole*[1].

---

sole[3] /sōl/ (*plural* **soles** or *same*) *n* **1.** a brownish sea fish with a small mouth and both eyes on the upper side of its flat body. It is valued as a food fish. Family: Soleidae. **2.** the flesh of a sole or a similar fish, as food [14C. Via French < Provençal *sola* < Latin *solea* 'sandal' (see SOLE[1])]

SPELLCHECK See *sole*[1].

---

solecism /sólləssizəm/ *n* **1. GRAMMATICAL MISTAKE** a mistake in grammar or syntax **2. ERROR** something incorrect, inappropriate, or inconsistent **3. BREACH OF GOOD MANNERS** an action that breaks the rules of etiquette or good manners [Mid-16C. Directly or via French < Latin *soloecismus* < Greek *soloikismos* < *soloikos* 'speaking incorrectly', literally 'of Soloi' (in ancient Cilicia, E Turkey), whose colonial Attic dialect was considered barbarous] —**solecist** *n* —**solecistical** /sóllə sístik'l/ *adj* —**solecistically** *adv*

solely /sṓl li/ *adv* **1.** for nothing other than ○ *sold the company solely for commercial reasons* **2.** to the exclusion of all else or others ○ *He is solely to blame.*

~~**solemly**~~ incorrect spelling of **solemnly**

solemn /sólləm/ *adj* **1. EARNEST** having or showing sincerity and gravity **2. HUMOURLESS** having or showing no joy or humour **3. FORMAL** characterized by ceremony or formality **4. RELIGIOUS** observed with sacred or religious ceremony **5. AWE-INSPIRING** inspiring wonder or reverence [14C. Via French < Latin *sol(l)emnis* 'customary, religious', < *sollus* 'whole, entire' + an unknown element] —**solemnly** *adv* —**solemnness** *n*

solemnify /sə lémni fī/ (**-fies, -fying, -fied**) *vt* to make something solemn or serious

solemnise *vt* another spelling of **solemnize**

solemnity /sə lémnəti/ (*plural* **-ties**) *n* **1. SOLEMN QUALITY** the solemn nature or quality of something **2. SOLEMN CEREMONY** a formal or solemn ceremony held to observe an occasion or event (*often used in the plural*) **3.** LAW **LEGAL FORMALITY** a formality that must be complied with before a contract or agreement can become effective

solemnize /sólləm nīz/ (**-nizes, -nizing, -nized**), **solemnise** (**-nises, -nising, -nised**) *v* **1.** *vt* **CELEBRATE WITH CEREMONY** to observe an event or occasion with ceremony or formality **2.** *vt* **PERFORM A MARRIAGE CEREMONY** to celebrate a marriage with a religious ceremony **3.** *vt* **MAKE DIGNIFIED** to bring dignity or formality to something **4.** *vi* **SPEAK SOLEMNLY** to speak or reflect with great seriousness —**solemnization** /sólləm nī záysh'n/ *n*

solenodon /sə lénnə don/ *n* a rare nocturnal insect-eating mammal with a long snout and a long scaly tail. Native to: Caribbean. Family: Solenodontidae. [Mid-19C. < modern Latin, literally 'pipe tooth' < Greek *sōlēn* 'pipe, channel']

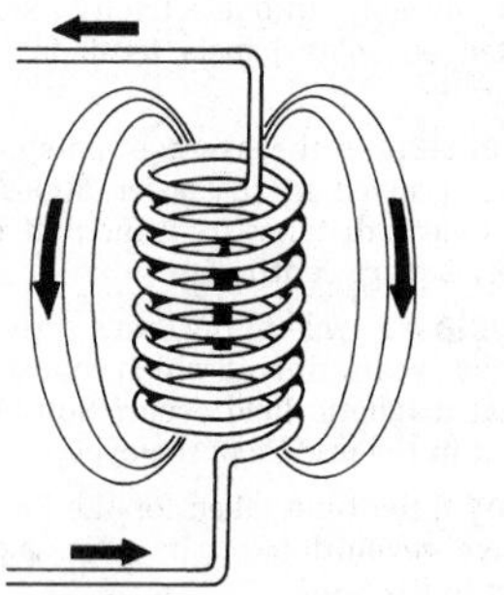

solenoid

solenoid /sóllə noyd/ *n* a device consisting of a cylindrical coil of wire surrounding a moveable iron core that moves along the length of the coil when an electric current is passed through it. Solenoids are used as switches and relays, e.g. in a motor vehicle to complete the circuit between the battery and starter motor. [Early 19C. < French *solénoïde* 'pipe-shaped' < Greek *sōlēn* 'pipe, channel'] —**solenoidal** /sóllə nóyd'l/ *adj* —**solenoidally** *adv*

Solent /sṓlənt/ arm of the English Channel separating the Isle of Wight from mainland England. Length: 24 km/15 mi.

soleplate /sṓl playt/ *n* **1.** the underside of an iron for pressing clothes **2.** the plate that supports the bases of the studs used in framing a wall

sole proprietor *n N Am* same as **sole trader**

sole trader *n* an individual who is the sole owner of a business that is neither a partnership nor a company. N Am term **sole proprietor**

soleus /sṓli əss/ (*plural* **-lei** /-li ī/) *n* a broad flat muscle in the calf of the leg that helps to flex the ankle and depress the sole of the foot [Late 17C. < modern Latin < Latin *solea* 'sandal' (see SOLE[1])]

sol-fa *n* MUSIC same as **tonic sol-fa** ■ *vti* (**sol-fas, sol-faing, sol-faed**) to sing a tune using the sol-fa syllables

solfatara /sólfə taárə/ *n* a vent in a volcano through which sulphur-rich gases and steam escape, leaving bright yellow sulphur deposits [Late 18C. < Italian, 'sulphurous volcano' < *solfo* 'sulphur' < Latin *sulfur*] —**solfataric** *adj*

solfège /sol fé<u>zh</u>/ *n* MUSIC same as **solfeggio** [Early 20C. Via French < Italian *solfeggio* (see SOLFEGGIO)]

solfeggio /sol féjji ō/ (*plural* **-gi** /-féjji/ or **-gios**) *n* an exercise in singing using the sol-fa syllables [Late 18C. < Italian < *sol-fa* 'sol-fa']

solferino /sólfə reé nō/ *adj* of a purplish-red colour [Mid-19C. After *Solferino*, Italian town near which a battle was fought just before the dye was discovered] —**solferino** *n*

soli ARTS plural of **solo**

solicit /sə líssit/ (**-its, -iting, -ited**) *v* **1.** *vti* **PLEAD FOR SOMETHING** to try to get something by making insistent requests or pleas **2.** *vt* **ASK SOMEBODY FOR SOMETHING** to plead with or petition a person or group for something **3.** *vti* **OFFER SEX FOR MONEY** to offer to participate in sexual activities with somebody in return for money **4.** *vt* **GET SOMEBODY TO DO SOMETHING WRONG** to attempt to draw somebody into participating in illegal or immoral acts [15C. Via French < Latin *sollicitare* 'disturb' < *sollicitus* 'completely moved' < *sollus* 'whole' + *citus*, past participle of *ciere* 'move'] —**solicitation** /sə líssi táysh'n/ *n*

solicitor /sə líssitər/ *n* a lawyer who gives legal advice, draws up legal documents, and does preparatory work for barristers. A solicitor who holds an advocacy qualification may also represent clients in court. —**solicitorship** *n*

Solicitor General (*plural* **Solicitors General**) *n* **1. LAW OFFICER OF CROWN** in England and Wales, the second most senior law officer of the Crown, of a rank below Attorney General **2. LAW OFFICER OF CROWN IN SCOTLAND** in Scotland, the second most senior law officer of the Crown, of a rank below Lord Advocate **3. NEW ZEALAND'S TOP LEGAL OFFICER** in New Zealand, the chief law officer and prosecutor for the Crown **4.** *Can* **FEDERAL OR PROVINCIAL LAW OFFICER** a member of a federal or provincial cabinet responsible for law enforcement, prisons, and some forms of licensing

solicitous /sə líssitəss/ *adj* **1. CONCERNED** expressing an attitude of concern and consideration **2. READY AND WILLING** full of eagerness to do something **3. METICULOUS** paying very careful attention to details [Mid-16C. < Latin *sollicitus* (see SOLICIT)] —**solicitously** *adv* —**solicitousness** *n*

solicitude /sə líssi tyood/ *n* **1.** concern and consideration shown for somebody or something **2.** a cause of concern or uneasiness (*often used in the plural*)

solid /sóllid/ *adj* **1. NOT SOFT OR YIELDING** consisting of compact unyielding material **2. NOT HOLLOW** having no open interior spaces **3. UNADULTERATED OR UNMIXED** made of the same material throughout **4. OF STRONG AND SECURE CONSTRUCTION** built out of strong substantial material and not likely to break or collapse **5. UNINTERRUPTED** continuing without breaks or openings ○ *It took a solid two hours to crack the code.* **6. NOURISHING** providing ample nourishment **7. UNANIMOUS** in complete agreement ○ *Support for the amendment was solid.* **8. RELIABLE** able to be relied or depended upon **9. FINANCIALLY SECURE** in sound financial condition **10.** MATHS **THREE-DIMENSIONAL** having the three dimensions of length, breadth, and depth, or relating to geometric figures that have three dimensions **11.** CHEM **RETAINING ITS SHAPE** of a shape that resists change, unlike a liquid or gas **12.** LANGUAGE **AS SINGLE WORD** written as one word without a space or hyphen **13.** PRINTING **WITHOUT SPACES** without spaces between lines of type in printing ■ *n* **1. SOLID THING** something that is solid **2.** MATHS **SOLID FIGURE** a three-dimensional geometric figure or object **3.** CHEM **SUBSTANCE THAT RETAINS SHAPE** a substance that resists change in shape, unlike a liquid or gas [14C. Directly or via French < Latin *solidus* 'firm, whole'] —**solidity** /sə líddəti/ *n* —**solidly** *adv* —**solidness** *n*

solid angle *n* a three-dimensional angle formed at the vertex of a cone or the intersection of three planes

solidarity /sólli dárrəti/ *n* harmony of interests and responsibilities among individuals in a group, especially as manifested in unanimous support and collective action for something [Mid-19C. < French *solidarité* < *solidaire* < *solide* 'solid']

Solidarity /sólli dárrəti/ *n* a federation of trade unions in Poland, founded in 1980. Under the leadership of Lech Walesa, it challenged the Soviet-backed government of the day. [Late 20C. Translation of Polish *Solidarność*]

solid geometry *n* the branch of geometry that deals with three-dimensional figures

solidi PRINTING, COINS plural of **solidus**

solidify /sə líddi fī/ (**-fies, -fying, -fied**) *vti* **1.** to become

compact or firm, or make something compact or firm **2.** to become strong and united, or make something strong and united —**solidifiable** *adj* —**solidification** /sə líddifi káysh'n/ *n* —**solidifier** *n*

solid of revolution *n* a three-dimensional mathematical figure formed by rotating a plane figure about an axis in its plane

solid smoke *n* a silica-based porous solid (**aerogel**) that is extremely light because it is 99.8% air

solid solution *n* a crystalline substance in which different kinds of atoms or molecules share the same structure, e.g. an alloy

solid-state *adj* **1.** working by means of the flow of electric current through solid material, as in semiconductors and transistors. The term is usually used to distinguish modern electronic equipment from earlier devices that made use of valves or heated filaments. **2.** relating to the electronic characteristics of solids, especially at the atomic or molecular level

solidus /sóllidəss/ (*plural* **-di** /-dī/) *n* **1.** UK, ANZ, Can a line sloping from right to left, used to separate items of information in dates, in fractions, and in presenting alternatives, as in 'and/or' (*technical*) US term **virgule 2.** a gold coin used in the Roman Empire from the 4th century BC. It remained in use in Europe until the 12th century AD. [14C. < Latin *solidus (nummus)* (see SOLDIER)]

solifluction /sólli flúksh'n/ *n* the slow movement of soil downhill as a result of water saturation after rainfall or the melting of ice [Early 20C. < Latin *solum* 'ground' + *fluct-*, past participle of *fluere* 'flow']

Solihull /sóli húl, sólli hul/ town in the Midlands, near Birmingham, central England. Population: 203,922 (1996).

soliloquize /sə líllə kwīz/ (**-quizes, -quizing, -quized**), **soliloquise** (**-quises, -quising, -quised**) *vi* to speak a soliloquy in the course of a play —**soliloquist** *n* —**soliloquizer** *n*

soliloquy /sə lílləkwi/ (*plural* **-quies**) *n* **1.** the act of speaking while alone, especially when used as a theatrical device that allows a character's thoughts and ideas to be conveyed to the audience **2.** a section of a play or other drama in which a soliloquy is spoken [14C. < late Latin *soliloquium* 'a speaking alone' < Latin *solus* 'alone' + *loqui* 'speak']

Solingen /zólingən/ city in North Rhine-Westphalia State, west-central Germany. Population: 165,973 (1997).

solipsism /sóllipsizəm/ *n* the belief that the only thing somebody can be sure of is that he or she exists, and that true knowledge of anything else is impossible [Late 19C. < Latin *solus* 'alone' + *ipse* 'self'] —**solipsist** *n* —**solipsistic** /sóllip sístik/ *adj* —**solipsistically** *adv*

solitaire /sólli tair, sólli táir/ *n* **1.** BOARD GAME FOR ONE a board game for one person in which pegs are eliminated from the board by being moved into empty spaces, the object being to end with one remaining centre peg **2.** N Am CARDS same as **patience** (sense 2) **3.** JEWELLERY SINGLE GEMSTONE a gem, especially a diamond, that is set alone in a ring **4.** BIRDS SONGBIRD a songbird of the thrush family. Native to: North and Central America, Caribbean. Genus: *Myadestes*. [14C. Via French, 'recluse' < Latin *solitarius* (see SOLITARY)]

solitary /sóllitəri/ *adj* **1.** DONE ALONE done without the company of other people **2.** SHUNNING COMPANY preferring to be or live alone **3.** SECLUDED in a remote location, apart from others **4.** SINGLE existing as the only one of its kind ○ *a solitary boat on the sea* **5.** ZOOL NOT LIVING IN SOCIAL GROUPS describes animals that live alone or in pairs rather than in colonies or social groups **6.** BOT GROWING SINGLY describes flowers that grow singly rather than as a cluster ■ *n* (*plural* **-ies**) **1.** RECLUSE somebody who lives alone or prefers to be alone **2.** CRIME same as **solitary confinement** [14C. < Latin *solitarius* < *solus* 'alone'] —**solitarily** *adv* —**solitariness** *n*

solitary confinement *n* confinement of a prisoner in an area or cell isolated from other prisoners, used as a punishment or for protection

solitude /sólli tyood/ *n* **1.** STATE OF BEING ALONE the state of being alone, separated from other people, whether considered as a welcome freedom from disturbance or as an unhappy loneliness **2.** REMOTENESS a quality of quiet remoteness or seclusion in places from which human activity is generally absent **3.** LONELY PLACE a remote or uninhabited place (*literary*) [14C. Directly or via French < Latin *solitudo* < *solus* 'alone'] —**solitudinous** /sólli tyood'nəss/ *adj*

CULTURAL NOTE *One Hundred Years of Solitude*, a novel (1967) by Colombian writer Gabriel García Márquez. It recounts a hundred years in the lives of the Buendía family, founders of the town of Macondo in Colombia, a story that mirrors the history of the nation. Marquez's skilful use of fantasy and myth to convey the depth of his characters' experiences makes this a key work in the magic realism school of literature.

solitudinarian /sólli tyoodi náiri ən/ *n* somebody who lives or prefers to be alone (*literary*)

solleret /sóllə ret/ *n* a shoe made of steel plates riveted together, forming part of a suit of armour [14C. Via the diminutive of Old French *soller* 'shoe' < late Latin *subtel* 'hollow of the foot' < *sub* 'under' + *talus* 'ankle']

sollicker /sóllikər/ *n* Aus a very large thing (*slang*) [Late 19C. Origin ?]

solmization /sóllmi záysh'n/ *n* the assigning of separate syllables to different musical pitches for singing or training the ear, as in solfeggio [Mid-18C. French *solmisation* < *solmiser* 'sing sol-fa']

soln *abbr* CHEM, MATHS solution

solo /sólō/ *n* (*plural* **-los** or **-li** /-li/) **1.** MUSICAL PIECE PERFORMED BY ONE PERSON a piece of music performed by one musician or singer, or a passage for a single player or singer within a longer piece for two or more, a choir, or an orchestra **2.** PERFORMANCE BY ONE ARTIST a performance by a single artist such as a musician, singer, or dancer with or without accompaniment **3.** ACT DONE BY SINGLE PERSON an action or feat carried out by one person alone, e.g. a flight in an aircraft or a climb up a mountain **4.** MOTORCYCLES MOTORCYCLE WITHOUT SIDECAR a motorcycle without a sidecar **5.** CARDS CARD GAME FOR INDIVIDUAL PLAYERS a card game in which players play on their own, not in pairs or teams, especially solo whist ■ *adj* **1.** FOR SINGLE PERFORMER intended for or executed by somebody performing singly, not as one of a group **2.** DONE BY ONE PERSON carried out by one person unaccompanied by anyone else ■ *adv* ALONE unaccompanied by anyone, or not performing or doing something as one of a group ■ *vi* (**-los, -loing, -loed**) DO SOMETHING WITHOUT ASSISTANCE to do something alone, without help or accompaniment, especially to fly an aircraft without an instructor or to perform an artistic solo [Late 17C. Via Italian < Latin *solus* 'alone']

soloist /sólō ist/ *n* somebody who performs a solo, especially a musical solo —**soloistic** /sólō ístik/ *adj*

Solo man /sólō-/ *n* an extinct variety of the human species Homo sapiens that lived 50,000 years ago during the late Pleistocene epoch [Because fossils were discovered near the River Solo, Java]

Solomon[1] /sólləmən/ *n* somebody wise (*informal*) [After SOLOMON]

Solomon[2] /sólləmən/ (*fl* 10th century BC) king of Israel. The second son of David and Bathsheba, he ruled Israel from 961 to 922 BC. Famed for his wisdom, he is generally acknowledged as the builder of the Temple in Jerusalem. He is credited with writing the biblical *Song of Solomon* and *Proverbs*.

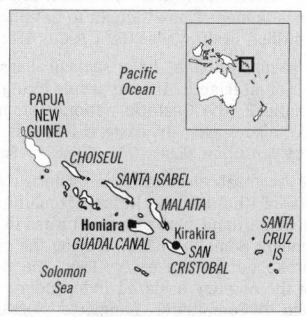

Solomon Islands

Solomon Islands country comprising over 35 islands and atolls in the southern Pacific Ocean. It became an independent member of the Commonwealth in 1978. Language: English. Currency: Solomon Islands dollar. Capital: Honiara. Population: 509,190 (2003). Area: 27,556 sq. km/10,639 sq. mi. —**Solomon Islander** *n*

Solomon Sea arm of the western South Pacific Ocean, east of New Guinea and west of the Solomon Islands

Solomon's seal *n* **1.** a perennial woodland plant. Native to: northern countries. Flowers: drooping, whitish, in pairs. Latin name: *Polygonatum multiflorum*. **2.** a six-pointed symbol resembling a star, made up of one triangle laid on top of another facing the other way. Examples are the Star of David that is the symbol of Judaism, and the hexagram that healers of former times believed had the power to cure diseases.

solon /sō lon/ *n* somebody wise, especially an experienced and wise legislator or politician (*literary*) [Early 17C. After SOLON]

Solon /sō lon/ (638?–559? BC) Athenian political leader, legislator, and poet. He introduced wide-ranging legal and political reforms and is considered the founder of Athenian democracy.

solonchak /sóllən chák/ *n* an intrazonal soil with a greyish crust that develops in semiarid and desert areas and contains large amounts of soluble salts [Early 20C. < Russian, 'salt marsh, salt lake' < *sol* 'salt']

solonetz /sóllə néts/, **solonets** *n* an intrazonal soil with a blackish crust developed from solonchak soil by leaching of the salts [Early 20C. < Russian, 'salt marsh, salt lake' < *sol* 'salt']

so long (*informal*) *interj* used to say goodbye ■ *adv* S Africa in the meantime, for the time being

solo stop *n* a stop on an organ with a penetrating tone, used in isolated passages of organ pieces to give the effect of a single instrument playing the melody

solo whist *n* a version of the card game whist in which each of the four players plays on his or her own, instead of in the usual pairs

solstice /sólstiss/ *n* **1.** either of the times when the Sun is farthest from the equator, on or about 21 June or 21 December. The summer solstice falls in June in the northern hemisphere but in December in the southern hemisphere, and vice versa for the winter solstice. **2.** either of the two points on the ecliptic when the Sun reaches its northernmost or southernmost point relative to the celestial equator [13C. Via French < Latin *solstitium* < *sol* 'Sun' + *stit-*, past participle of *sistere* 'stand still'] —**solstitial** /sol stísh'l/ *adj*

Georg Solti

Solti /shólti/, **Sir Georg** (1912–97) Hungarian conductor. Associated particularly with the music of late romantic composers, he held important posts in Germany, the United Kingdom, and the United States, where he conducted the Chicago Symphony Orchestra (1969–91).

solubilise *vti* CHEM another spelling of **solubilize**

solubility /sóllyoŏ bílləti/ (*plural* **-ties**) *n* **1.** the extent to which one substance is able to dissolve in another **2.** a measure of one substance's ability to dissolve

in a specific amount of another substance at standard temperature and pressure

solubilize /sóllyŏoba līz/ (**-lizes, -lizing, -lized**), **solubilise** /sóllyŏobi līz, sóllyəbi-/ (**-lises, -lising, -lised**) *vti* to make a substance soluble or more soluble, or become soluble or more soluble

soluble /sóllyŏob'l/ *adj* **1.** DISSOLVING able to be dissolved in another substance. The level of solubility often varies with temperature. (*often used in combination*) ○ *water-soluble* **2.** DESIGNED TO DISSOLVE designed to be dissolved in water **3.** CAPABLE OF BEING SOLVED able to be solved or answered [14C. Via French < late Latin *solubilis* < *solvere* 'loosen, dissolve'] —**solubly** *adv*

soluble glass *n* CHEM same as **sodium silicate**

soluble RNA *n* BIOCHEM same as **transfer RNA**

solum /sóləm/ *n* the upper layer of a soil profile where the formation of new soil takes place and where most plant roots and soil animals are found [Mid-19C. < Latin, 'ground, foundation']

solus /sóləss/ *adj* **1.** ALONE ON STAGE used as a stage direction to indicate that a character appears alone on stage ○ *Enter Hector solus* **2.** FEATURED ON OWN describes an advertisement that appears on its own, rather than alongside advertisements for different products or from competing companies **3.** SELLING ONE COMPANY'S PRODUCTS selling the products of one company only [Late 16C. < Latin, 'alone'] —**solus** *adv*

solute /so lyóot/ *n* a substance dissolved in another substance ■ *adj* dissolved in a solution [15C. < Latin *solut-* (see SOLUTION)]

solution /sə lóosh'n/ *n* **1.** WAY OF RESOLVING DIFFICULTY a method of successfully dealing with a problem or difficulty **2.** ANSWER TO PUZZLE the answer to a puzzle or question **3.** FINDING OF ANSWER the process of resolving a difficulty or finding the answer to a puzzle or question **4.** CHEM FLUID WITH SUBSTANCE DISSOLVED IN IT a substance consisting of two or more substances mixed together and uniformly dispersed, most commonly the result of dissolving a solid, fluid, or gas in a liquid. It is also possible, however, to form a solution by dissolving a gas or solid in a solid or one gas in another gas. **5.** CHEM PROCESS OF FORMING MIXED FLUID the process of forming a solution or dissolving one substance in another, or the state of being dissolved in another substance **6.** MATHS VALUE SATISFYING EQUATION a value for a variable that satisfies an equation **7.** LAW ENDING OF SOMETHING the termination of a dispute or payment of a debt **8.** ENDING OF SOMETHING the act of ending, breaking, or separating something (*literary*) [14C. Via French < Latin *solution-* < *solut-*, past participle of *solvere* 'loosen, dissolve']

solution set *n* the set of values for a variable that satisfy an equation

Solutrean /sə lóotri ən/ *adj* belonging to a prehistoric culture that existed in Europe between 40,000 BC and 12,000 BC, at the end of the Palaeolithic period, in which people worked with leaf-shaped flint blades [Late 19C. < French *solutréen* < *Solutré*, village in E France]

solvable /sólvəb'l/ *adj* capable of being solved —**solvability** *n*

solvate /sól vayt/ *vti* (**-vates, -vating, -vated**) to enter into solution with a solvent, or cause a solute to dissolve in solution with a solvent ■ *n* a compound consisting of an ion or molecule of solute combined with one or more of solvent [Early 20C. < SOLVENT] —**solvation** /sol váysh'n/ *n*

Solvay process /sól vay-/ *n* an industrial process for producing sodium carbonate or washing soda from common salt. A solution of salt is saturated with ammonia and carbon dioxide is passed through it, which causes sodium hydrogen carbonate to precipitate. It is then heated to obtain sodium carbonate. [Late 19C. After Ernest Solvay (1838–1922), Belgian chemist]

solve /solv/ (**solves, solving, solved**) *vt* **1.** DEAL WITH PROBLEM SUCCESSFULLY to find a way of dealing successfully with a problem or difficulty **2.** FIND ANSWER TO PUZZLE to find the answer to a question or puzzle **3.** MATHS FIND ANSWER TO MATHS PROBLEM to work out the solution to an equation or other mathematical problem [15C. < Latin *solvere* 'loosen, dissolve'] —**solver** *n*

ORIGIN The Latin word *solvere* 'to loosen, dissolve', from which *solve* is derived, is also the source of the English words *absolute*, *absolve*, *dissolve*, *resolve*, *soluble*, and *solution*.

solvent /sólvənt/ *adj* **1.** HAVING ENOUGH MONEY having enough money to cover expenses and debts **2.** DISSOLVING SOMETHING able to dissolve substances ■ *n* SUBSTANCE THAT DISSOLVES THINGS a substance in which other substances are dissolved, often a liquid [Early 17C. Directly or via French < Latin *solvent-*, present participle of *solvere* 'loosen, dissolve'] —**solvency** *n* —**solvently** *adv*

solvent misuse, **solvent abuse** *n* the inhaling of fumes from solvents such as glues and petrol in order to produce a feeling of euphoria

solvolysis /sol vólləsiss/ *n* a chemical reaction in which a dissolved solute and its solvent combine to form a new compound

Solway Firth /sól way-/ arm of the Irish Sea separating Dumfries and Galloway in Scotland from Cumbria in England. Length: 64 km/40 mi.

Farrar, Straus and Giroux, Inc.
Aleksandr Isayevich Solzhenitsyn

Solzhenitsyn /sólzhə neetsin, səlzhə nyeetsin/, **Aleksandr** (*b.* 1918) Russian writer. His imprisonment in the former Soviet Union for political dissent (1945–53) inspired early novels such as *One Day in the Life of Ivan Denisovich* (1962). He was expelled after the publication of *The Gulag Archipelago* (1974–78), and lived in exile in the United States for 20 years, returning to Russia after the collapse of the Soviet Union. He won a Nobel Prize in literature (1970). Full name **Solzhenitsyn, Aleksandr Isayevich**

'How can you expect a man who's warm to understand one who's cold?'
[Aleksandr Solzhenitsyn, *One Day in the Life of Ivan Denisovich*; 1962]

'The salvation of mankind lies only in making everything the concern of all.'
[Aleksandr Solzhenitsyn, *Nobel lecture*; 1972]

som /sōm/ (*plural same*) *n* the main unit of currency of Kyrgyzstan. See table at **currency** [Via Kyrgyz < Chuvash, 'sum, payment']

Som. *abbr* **1.** Somalia **2.** Somerset

soma[1] /sómə/ (*plural* **-mata** /-mətə/ or **-mas**) *n* **1.** all the cells and tissues in the body considered collectively, with the exception of germ cells **2.** the body considered separately from the mind or soul [Mid-19C. Via modern Latin < Greek *sōma* 'body']

soma[2] /sómə/ *n* **1.** an intoxicating drink made from plant juice, mentioned in the Vedas, the most ancient sacred writings of Hinduism **2.** the plant that soma is made from, thought to be ephedra but not identified in the Vedas [Early 19C. < Sanskrit]

Somali /sə máali/ (*plural* **-lis** or *same* or **-lians**) *n* **1.** a member of an Islamic African people living mainly in Somalia **2.** the Cushitic national language of Somalia, also spoken in eastern Ethiopia. Native speakers: 5 million. [Early 19C. < Somali] —**Somali** *adj*

Somalia /sə máali ə/ country in eastern Africa. It consists of the former Italian Somaliland and British Somaliland, both of which united to become independent Somalia in 1960. During the civil war that broke out in the early 1990s, the northern part of the country declared independence as the Republic of Somaliland. Language: Somali. Currency: Somali shilling. Capital: Mogadishu. Popu-

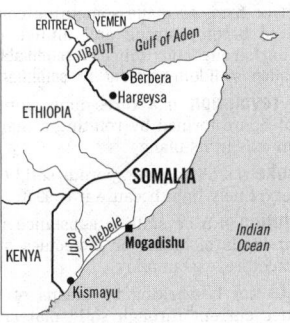
Somalia

lation: 8,025,190 (2003). Area: 637,700 sq. km/246,200 sq. mi. Official name **Somali Democratic Republic**

Somalian /sə máali ən/ *n* PEOPLES, LANG same as **Somali** —**Somalian** *adj*

Somaliland /sə máali land/ **1.** region in northeastern Africa, comprising Somalia, Djibouti, and part of Ethiopia **2.** autonomous region of northern Somalia, consisting of the former British Somaliland, which is seeking independent nation status. Language: Somali. Currency: Somaliland shilling. Capital: Hargeisa. Population: 3,500,000 (2001). Area: 137,600 sq. km/68,000 sq. mi.

Somare /sə máari/, **Sir Michael** (*b.* 1936) prime minister of Papua New Guinea. The country's first prime minister (1975–80), he was removed from office by a vote of no confidence, served again from 1982–5, with the same result, and as a member of the National Alliance Party was reappointed in 2002.

somat- *prefix* same as **somato-** (*used before vowels*)

somata BIOL *plural of* **soma**[1]

somatic /sə máttik/ *adj* **1.** AFFECTING BODY AS DISTINCT FROM MIND relating to or affecting the body, especially the body as considered to be separate from the mind **2.** ANAT RELATING TO OUTER WALLS OF BODY relating to the outer walls of the body, not the inner organs **3.** BIOL OF SOMATIC CELL relating to a somatic cell [Late 18C. < Greek *sōmatikós* 'bodily' < *sōma* 'body'] —**somatically** *adv*

somatic cell *n* any body cell except a reproductive cell

somaticize /sə mátti sīz/ (**-cizes, -cizing, -cized**), **somaticise** (**-cises, -cising, -cised**) *vti* to believe mistakenly that an emotional pain is a physical symptom

somatic nervous system *n* the part of the nervous system that serves the sense organs and muscles of the body wall and limbs, and brings about voluntary muscle activity

somato- *prefix* body ○ *somatoplasm* [< Greek *sōmat-*, stem of *sōma*]

somatology /sómə tólləji/ *n* **1.** the study of both the physiology and anatomy of the body **2.** the branch of anthropology that studies human evolution through variation and development in physical characteristics —**somatologic** /sómətə lójjik/ *adj* —**somatological** *adj* —**somatologically** *adv*

somatomedin /sómətə meedin/ *n* a hormone produced in the liver that stimulates the growth of bone and muscle [Late 20C. < SOMATO- + INTERMEDIARY]

somatoplasm /sómətə plazəm/ *n* the protoplasm of body cells as distinct from the protoplasm of germ cells —**somatoplastic** /sómətə plástik/ *adj*

somatopleure /sómətə ploor, -plur/ *n* a fold of embryonic tissue in vertebrates formed by the fusion of ectoderm and mesoderm that gives rise to an embryo's inner and outer membranes —**somatopleural** /sómətə plóorəl, -plúrəl/ *adj* —**somatopleuric** *adj*

somatosensory /sómətə sénssəri/ *adj* describes sensory stimuli coming from the skin and internal organs and the perception of these stimuli

somatostatin /sómətə státtin/ *n* a hormone produced in the hypothalamus that inhibits the release of growth hormone [Late 20C. < SOMATO- + Latin *stat-*, past participle of *stare* 'stand']

somatotrophin /sómətə trófin/, **somatotropin** /sómətə

trṓpin/ *n* BIOL same as **growth hormone** [Mid-20C. < SOMATO- + -TROPHIC[1]] —**somatotrophic** /sṓmətə tróffik/ *adj*

somatotype /sṓmətə tīp/ *n* the type of physical build that somebody has

somber *adj* US spelling of **sombre**

sombre /sómbər/ *adj* **1.** DARK AND GLOOMY lacking light or brightness and producing a dull, dark, or melancholy atmosphere **2.** DARK IN COLOUR having a colour or tone that is dark, dull, or suitable for a serious mood or occasion **3.** SERIOUS AND MELANCHOLY marked by or conveying strict seriousness combined with sadness or a troubled state of mind [Mid-18C. < French, 'gloomy' < assumed Vulgar Latin *subumbrare* 'to shadow' < Latin *sub* 'under' + *umbra* 'shade'] —**sombrely** *adv* —**sombreness** *n*

sombrero /som bráirō/ (*plural* **-ros**) *n* a straw or felt hat with a very wide upturned brim, originally worn by men in Mexico and some other Spanish-speaking countries [Late 16C. < Spanish, 'hat' < *sombra* 'shade' < assumed Vulgar Latin *subumbrare* (see SOMBRE)]

Sombrero /som bráirō/ northernmost islet in the Lesser Antilles. A dependency of Anguilla, it is the site of an important lighthouse protecting the passage between the Atlantic Ocean to the Caribbean Sea. Area: 0.4 sq. km/0.15 sq. mi.

some /stressed sum, unstressed səm/ CORE MEANING: a grammatical word used to indicate an unspecified or unknown quantity of people or things ○ (det) *There is always some risk in any project.* ○ (pron) *There was plenty of food left over, so I took some.*
1. *det, pron* A LITTLE used to indicate an unspecified number, quantity, or proportion of a total, generally a fairly small to average or reasonable one ○ *I agree with you to some extent.* ○ *Some of you, I know, will disagree with me.* **2.** *det* QUITE A FEW used with a slight emphasis to indicate an unspecified but fairly large number or quantity ○ *We have been debating this problem for some months now.* **3.** *det* PARTICULAR BUT UNSPECIFIED used to indicate an unspecified single person or thing, often in a dismissive way (*informal*) ○ *He was reading some medical book.* **4.** *det* USED FOR EMPHASIS used to emphasize that somebody or something is impressive or remarkable in some way (*informal*) ○ *That was some performance you put on for us!* **5.** *adv* APPROXIMATELY used to indicate that a number is approximate ○ *for some 30 years* **6.** *adv N Am* TO SMALL EXTENT to a small extent or degree (*informal*) ○ *I do write some, but not as much as I'd like.* **7.** *adv N Am* A GREAT DEAL a great deal, at a considerable rate, or vigorously (*informal*) ○ *I'm going to have to study some to get through this exam.* [Old English *sum* 'one, somebody' < Indo-European, 'together with'] ◇ **and then some** *N Am* used to emphasize that more, often considerably more, has been done than was suggested in a previous statement (*informal*)

SPELLCHECK some or **sum**? Do not confuse the spelling of ***some*** and ***sum***, which sound similar. ***Some*** refers to an unspecified amount, number, thing, or person, as in *buy some milk, some ten days ago, undergoing some kind of therapy, some of them refused to leave.* ***Sum*** refers to a total amount, as in *a sum of money, the sum total of his knowledge*, and is also used as a verb, especially in *sum up* meaning 'summarize' (*summed up the story in a couple of sentences*).

-some[1] *suffix* **1.** characterized by a particular quality, condition, or thing ○ *troublesome* ○ *quarrelsome* **2.** a group containing a particular number of members ○ *foursome* [Old English *-sum*]

-some[2] *suffix* **1.** body ○ *cytosome* **2.** chromosome ○ *autosome* [< Greek *sōma* 'body']

somebody /súmbədi/ *pron* an unspecified or unidentified person ○ *Somebody just rang the doorbell.* ■ *pron, n* (*plural* **-ies**) an important or well-known person ○ *She didn't want mediocre success; she wanted to be somebody.*

someday /súm day/, **some day** *adv* at some unknown, unspecified, and usually fairly distant time in the future

USAGE someday, someplace, sometime: ***Someday*** (or ***some day***) is idiomatic in British English (*Someday* [or *some day*] *I'll take you away from all this*), but ***someplace*** is not used at all except as a conscious Americanism (*I must have left it someplace*). ***Sometime*** is written as one word as an adjective meaning 'former' (*a sometime president of the Rotary Club*), and as an adverb meaning 'at some time' (*I'll see you again sometime*).

somehow /súm how/ *adv* **1.** in some unspecified or unknown way, often with great effort or difficulty ○ *He somehow managed to scramble back on board.* **2.** for some unknown or inexplicable reason ○ *She somehow forgot to tell anyone where she was going.*

someone /súm wun/ *pron* same as **somebody**

someplace /súm playss/ *adv N Am* same as **somewhere** (*informal*)

USAGE See ***someday.***

somersault /súmmər solt, -sawlt/, **summersault** /súmmər sawlt/ *n* **1.** ACROBATIC ROLLING OVER OF BODY an acrobatic movement in which the body is rolled over, feet over head, either forwards or backwards, on the ground or in midair, finally returning to an upright position **2.** REVERSAL OF OPINION OR DECISION a complete change of mind or reversal of policy (*informal*) ■ *vi* (**-saults, -saulting, -saulted**) PERFORM SOMERSAULT to perform an acrobatic somersault [Early 16C. < Middle French *sombresault*, alteration of *sobresault* < Latin *super* 'over, above' + *saltus* 'leap']

Somerset /súmmər set/ county in southwestern England that includes Glastonbury, Exmoor, and Cheddar. Taunton is the county town. Population: 498,093 (2001). Area: 3,458 sq. km/1,335 sq. mi.

Somerset /súmmər sət/, **Edward Seymour, 1st Duke of** (1506?–52) Protector of England (1547–50). The brother of Jane Seymour, he became Protector of England during the minority of the future Edward VI. Rivalry with the Duke of Northumberland led to his execution. Known as **Protector Somerset**

Somerset House *n* a building in London that formerly housed the General Register Office

Somerset Island island in Nunavut, Canada, in the Arctic Archipelago, north of the Boothia Peninsula. Area: 24,786 sq. km/9,570 sq. mi.

Somerville /súmmər vil/, **Mary** (1780–1872) British scientist. She wrote several major works explaining scientific matters, including *On the Connexion of the Physical Sciences* (1834).

something /súm thing/ *pron* **1.** UNSPECIFIED THING an unspecified or unidentified object, phenomenon, action, utterance, or feeling ○ *Don't just stand there; do something!* ○ *I had a feeling that there was something wrong.* ○ *Would you like something to eat?* **2.** UNSPECIFIED AMOUNT an unspecified and approximate amount expressed in relation to a specific number or quantity ○ *something over 50* ○ *something between 20 and 30%* **3.** SUGGESTING RESEMBLANCE used to suggest that one thing or person resembles another to an extent or has some of the qualities of the other ○ *There's definitely something of the knight errant about him.* **4.** RATHER used to qualify a description of a thing or event and tone it down or make it sound more guarded ○ *It was something of a disappointment.* **5.** IMPRESSIVE PERSON OR THING an impressive or important person or thing ○ *He's really something!* ■ *adv* **1.** SOMEWHAT slightly or to some degree ○ *It sounds something like what she might have said.* **2.** TO EXTREME DEGREE used to intensify the effect of an adjective, especially a strong adjective used as an adverb (*informal*) ○ *It hurts something awful.* **3.** AND A BIT MORE used to indicate that a number is slightly higher than the one mentioned (*informal*) ○ *She's fifty something.* ◇ **have something to do with somebody** *or* **something** to be connected with or involve somebody *or* something ◇ **something else** somebody or something really special, remarkable, or extreme (*informal*) ○ *That performance was something else!*

sometime /súm tīm/ *adv* **1.** AT SOME TIME at some unspecified or unknown time ○ *They intend to marry sometime soon.* **2.** FORMERLY at one time in the past (*formal*) ○ *our speaker today, sometime a professor at Princeton University* **3.** OCCASIONALLY occasionally or sporadically (*archaic*) ■ *adj* **1.** FORMER referring to somebody who at one time in the past had the job, position, or status in question ○ *a sometime student of this university* **2.** *N Am* OCCASIONAL occasional or sporadic ○ *an author and sometime lecturer*

USAGE See ***someday.***

sometimes /súm tīmz/ *adv* **1.** from time to time, not continually or every time ○ *We go to the theatre sometimes.* **2.** at one time in the past (*archaic*) [Early 16C. < SOMETIME + *-s*, possessive (genitive) singular suffix]

someway /súm way/ *adv* using some means or method that is not yet known or not indicated ○ *We'll figure it out someway.*

somewhat /súm wot/ *adv* to some extent or degree ○ *The hot night had cooled somewhat.*

somewhere /súm wair/ *adv* **1.** in, to, or at some unspecified place ○ *He lives somewhere in Scotland.* **2.** used in giving approximate amounts, numbers, or times ○ *somewhere around 300* ○ *somewhere between three and four o'clock* ◇ **get somewhere** to make progress towards achieving something

somite /sṓ mīt/ *n* **1.** one of a series of paired blocks of cells that develop along the back of a vertebrate embryo, giving rise to the vertebral column and most of the skeletal muscles **2.** a body segment, usually one of several, into which the bodies of some animals such as earthworms and crayfish are divided along their length [Mid-19C. < SOMA[1]] —**somital** /sṓmit'l/ *adj* —**somitic** /sō míttik/ *adj*

Somme /som/ river in northern France, flowing from near St Quentin into the English Channel. The Somme valley was the scene of a major World War I battle in 1916, which resulted in more than one million casualties. Length: 241 km/150 mi.

sommelier /sómm'l yay, sə mélli ər/ *n* a wine waiter in a restaurant, hotel, or other licensed establishment, who supervises the ordering, storing, and serving of wine [Early 20C. < French, variant of *somm(er)ier* 'officer in charge of provisions' < *somme* 'burden' < Greek *sāgma* 'covering, packsaddle']

sommer /sómmər/ *adv S Africa* just, only, or somewhat (*informal*) [Mid-19C. < Afrikaans]

somn- *prefix* same as **somni-** (*used before vowels*)

somnambulate /som námbyoǒ layt/ (**-lates, -lating, -lated**) *vi* same as **sleepwalk** (sense 1) (*technical*) —**somnambulance** /-námbyoǒlənss/ *n* —**somnambulation** /som námbyoǒ láysh'n/ *n* —**somnambulator** *n*

somnambulism /som námbyoǒlizəm/ *n* walking while asleep (*technical*) —**somnambulist** *n* —**somnambulistic** /som námbyoǒ lístik/ *adj*

somni- *prefix* sleep ○ *somnifacient* [< Latin *somnus*]

somnifacient /sómni fáysh'nt/ *adj* describes a drug designed to induce sleep

somniferous /som níffərəss/ *adj* making somebody, or designed to make somebody, feel sleepy —**somniferously** *adv*

somnolent /sómnələnt/ *adj* **1.** SLEEPY feeling sleepy or tending to fall asleep **2.** LACKING ACTIVITY quiet and with little or no activity **3.** SLEEP-INDUCING making somebody feel sleepy [15C. Via French < Latin *somnōlentus* 'sleepy' < *somnus* 'sleep'] —**somnolence** *n* —**somnolently** *adv*

~~**somthing**~~ incorrect spelling of **something**

son /sun/ *n* **1.** MALE CHILD a male child in relation to his parents **2.** MALE IN FAMILY a male descendant **3.** MALE CONNECTED WITH SOMETHING a man or boy referred to in terms of his connection with a place, a time in history, or a sphere of interest ○ *the achievements of the sons of the Industrial Revolution* **4.** ANIMAL'S YOUNG a male offspring of an animal **5.** TERM OF ADDRESS an affectionate, or sometimes condescending, way of addressing a boy or man (*informal*) [Old English *sunu* < Indo-European, 'give birth'] —**sonless** *adj* —**sonlike** *adj*

SPELLCHECK son or **sun**? Do not confuse the spelling of ***son*** and ***sun***, which sound similar. A ***son*** is 'a male child in relation to his parents': *They have two daughters and three sons.* The ***sun*** (in astronomical contexts, ***Sun***) is the star that gives us heat and light: *The sun shone all day; observations of the Sun and the stars.* The word ***sun*** is also used as a verb, as in *sunning herself on the patio*, and in phrases such as *everything under the sun*, meaning 'things of all kinds'.

CULTURAL NOTE ***Sons and Lovers***, a novel (1913) by D. H. Lawrence. Lawrence's first major novel, and his most autobiographical work, it centres on a family living in a

Nottinghamshire coalmining community. Gertrude Morel is frustrated by life with her less refined and increasingly drunken husband and devotes herself to her children, focusing on her son Paul after the death of his brother William. When Paul falls in love, first with a local girl and subsequently with a married woman, he finds it hard to break the bonds of attachment to his mother.

Son *n* a title that Christians give to Jesus Christ, especially when referred to as the second person in the Holy Trinity

sonant /sónənt/ *adj* **1.** HAVING SOUND producing or possessing a sound (*formal*) **2.** PHON VOICED describes a speech sound made with vibration of the vocal cords **3.** PHON SYLLABIC describes a consonant that is capable of forming a syllable on its own, without a vowel ■ *n* PHON **1.** VOICED SOUND a sound made with vibration of the vocal cords **2.** SYLLABIC CONSONANT a consonant capable of forming a syllable on its own, without a vowel [Mid-19C. < Latin *sonant-*, present participle of *sonare* 'sound'] —**sonance** *n* —**sonantal** /sō nántl'/ *adj* —**sonantic** /sō nántik/ *adj*

sonar /sṓ naar/ *n* **1.** a system that determines the position of unseen underwater objects by transmitting sound waves and measuring the time it takes for their echo to return after hitting the object **2.** a device that uses sonar [Mid-20C. Acronym < *sound navigation ranging*, after RADAR]

sonata /sə naátə/ *n* **1.** a piece of classical music for a solo instrument or a small ensemble. It consists of several movements, at least one of which is in sonata form. **2.** a piece of baroque keyboard music in a single movement [Late 17C. < Italian < feminine past participle of *sonare* 'sound' < Latin *sonare*]

sonata form *n* an important musical form developed in the 18th century consisting of three sections, an exposition, development, and recapitulation, and used especially for the first movement of sonatas, concertos, and symphonies

sonatina /sónnə teénə/ *n* a short, usually technically undemanding sonata [Early 18C. < Italian, 'little sonata' < *sonata* (see SONATA)]

sondage /son daázh/ *n* a deep trench dug in order to study the relative positions of human artefacts in horizontal layers [Mid-20C. < French, 'sounding, bore hole' < *sonder* (see SOUND²)]

sonde /sónd/ *n* a collection of instruments that can be lowered down a borehole or carried into the upper atmosphere by balloon or rocket to transmit information relating to the conditions encountered [Early 20C. < French, 'plumb line, sound' < *sonder* (see SOUND²)]

Express Newspapers

Stephen Sondheim

Sondheim /sónd hīm/, **Stephen** (*b.* 1930) US composer and lyricist. His innovative musicals include the Pulitzer Prize-winning *Sunday in the Park with George* (1984). Full name **Sondheim, Stephen Joshua**

'I like to be in America! / O.K. by me in America! / Ev'rything free in America / For a small fee in America!'
[Stephen Sondheim, 'America', *West Side Story*; 1957]

sone /sōn/ *n* a unit measuring the loudness of sound as subjectively perceived, equal to a tone of 1 kilohertz at 40 decibels above the threshold where sounds become audible to the listener [Mid-20C. < Latin *sonus* 'sound']

son et lumière /són ay loómi air/ *n* an outdoor nighttime spectacle that combines dramatic lighting effects with recorded sounds and music, usually staged at the site of a famous and historical building, often telling its history [< French, 'sound and light']

song /song/ *n* **1.** SET OF WORDS SUNG a usually relatively short musical composition consisting of words set to music **2.** ART OF SINGING the art or practice of singing **3.** INSTRUMENTAL WORK IN VOCAL STYLE an instrumental work written in the style of a composition for the voice, or, in popular music, any musical work **4.** ZOOL ANIMAL CALL the sounds made by a bird, insect, whale, frog, or other animal to attract a mate or defend territory **5.** LITERAT same as **poetry** (*literary*) **6.** POEM a long poem, especially one that tells a story (*literary*) ○ *the Song of Roland* [Old English *sang* < Indo-European, 'sing'] —**songlike** *adj* ◇ **for a song** very cheaply (*informal*) ◇ **on song** performing well or in good form (*informal*)

Song /song/ *n* HIST same as **Sung**

song and dance *n* (*informal*) **1.** an unnecessary fuss about something **2.** N Am a long-winded attempt to explain or justify something

songbird /sóng burd/ *n* a bird with a musical call, especially a passerine belonging to the group that includes larks, finches, and thrushes. Suborder: Oscines.

songbook /sóng bŏŏk/ *n* a book containing the words and music for a collection of songs

song cycle *n* a set of songs linked by a common subject or underlying musical theme or forming a narrative, often with words by a single poet and music by a classical composer

songfest /sóng fest/ *n* US an informal gathering of people for the purpose of singing folk or popular songs together

song form *n* the three-part structure of a song consisting of a first section that leads to a contrasting section before the original section returns, either identically or with some variation

songful /sóng fŏŏl, sóngf'l/ *adj* resembling song, especially in having a pleasing melody —**songfully** *adv* —**songfulness** *n*

Songhai¹ /song gī/ (*plural same* or **-hais**), **Songhay** (*plural same* or **-hays**) *n* **1.** a member of a people living in West Africa, mainly in Mali and Niger. The Songhai established a powerful empire in this area during the 7th century AD, and they remained the dominant ethnic group until the 16th century. **2.** the Nilo-Saharan language of the Songhai. Native speakers: 2 million. —**Songhai** *adj*

Songhai² /song gī/, **Songhay** state in western Africa during the 15th and 16th centuries. Its capital was Gao, which stood on the River Niger in what is now Mali.

songline /sóng līn/ *n* in Aboriginal culture, a traditional route across a landscape that is recorded in songs that are passed down to guide future generations

Song of Solomon *n* a book of the Bible that consists of a set of love poems, forming part of the Protestant scripture. Traditionally attributed to King Solomon, it is now thought to have been written by several later authors. See table at **Bible**

Song of Songs *n* a book of the Bible that corresponds to the Song of Solomon, forming part of the Jewish and Roman Catholic scriptures. See table at **Bible**

songololo /sóng gə lóllo/, **shongololo** /shóng go lóllo/ *n* S Africa a giant millipede (*informal*) [Early 20C. Xhosa]

songsmith /sóng smith/ *n* MUSIC same as **songwriter**

songster /sóngstər/ *n* **1.** a singer, especially a talented one **2.** a bird with a musical call **3.** same as **poet** (sense 1) (*literary*)

songstress /sóngstrəss/ *n* a female singer, songwriter, or poet (*dated*; *sometimes offensive*)

song thrush *n* a small songbird with brown upper parts and a white breast speckled with brown. Native to: Europe, Asia. Latin name: *Turdus philomelos.*

songwriter /sóng rītər/ *n* a writer of songs —**songwriting** *n*

sonic /sónnik/ *adj* **1.** RELATING TO SOUND OR SOUND WAVES relating to, using, or producing sound or sound waves **2.** AUDIBLE TO HUMAN EAR able to be heard by the human ear **3.** RELATING TO SPEED OF SOUND relating to or travelling at the speed of sound in air, approximately 1,220 km per hour/760 mi. per hour at sea level [Early 20C. < Latin *sonus* 'sound']

sonic barrier *n* PHYS same as **sound barrier**

sonic boom *n* a noise heard as a loud boom at ground level resulting from the shock waves created by an aircraft flying above the speed of sound

sonics /sónniks/ *n* the study of sound or, more generally, elastic wave motion (*takes a singular verb*)

son-in-law (*plural* **sons-in-law**) *n* the husband of somebody's daughter

sonnet /sónnət/ *n* a short poem with 14 lines, usually ten-syllable rhyming lines, divided into two, three, or four sections. There are many rhyming patterns for sonnets, and they are usually written in iambic pentameter. ■ *vi* (**-nets, -neting, -neted**) to write sonnets [Mid-16C. Directly or via French < Italian *sonnetto* < Old Provençal *son* 'poem' < Latin *sonus* 'sound']

sonneteer /sónnə teér/ *n* **1.** a poet who writes sonnets **2.** a writer whose poems are regarded as mediocre (*disapproving*)

sonnet sequence *n* a set of sonnets written by one poet and unified by a single theme or idea

sonny /súnni/, **sonny boy** *n* used as an affectionate, or sometimes condescending, way of addressing a man or boy (*informal*)

sonobuoy /sṓnə boy, sónnə-/ *n* a buoy fitted with equipment for detecting underwater noises and transmitting them by radio [Mid-20C. < Latin *sonus* 'sound']

son of a bitch N Am *n* (*plural* **sons of bitches**) **1.** TABOO TERM a highly offensive term for somebody, usually a man, regarded as hateful, despicable, or intensely annoying (*taboo insult*) **2.** ANY PERSON used as a familiar, humorous, and slightly vulgar term for a person, usually a man, who has the named characteristic (*slang*; *sometimes considered offensive*) ○ *He's a lucky son of a bitch.* ■ *interj* EXCLAMATION OF ANGER used as a swearword to express anger or defiance (*slang*; *sometimes considered offensive*)

son of a gun N Am (*informal*) *n* (*plural* **sons of guns**) a person, especially a man, and usually somebody affectionately or kindly regarded ■ *interj* used to express mild annoyance or surprise

son of God *n* **1.** a being regarded as superhuman or angelic **2.** a believer in the Christian faith

Son of God, **Son of Man** *n* Jesus Christ, considered by Christians as the Messiah

sonogram /sṓnə gram/ *n* a graphical representation of sound, especially in the three dimensions of frequency, time, and intensity

Sonoma /sə nṓmə/ town northeast of San Francisco in Sonoma County, northern California. It lies at the heart of an important wine-producing region. Population: 9,354 (2002 estimate).

Sonoma Valley region of western California, northeast of San Francisco. Extending northwards from the city of Sonoma, it is famous for its wineries and is a major tourist destination.

Sonora /sə náwrə/ state in northwestern Mexico, on the border with the United States. Capital: Hermosillo. Population: 2,216,969 (2000). Area: 180,833 sq. km/69,820 sq. mi.

Sonoran Desert /sə náwrən-/ one of the largest deserts in North America, situated in southwestern Arizona, southern California, and northwestern Mexico. Area: 310,799 sq. km/120,000 sq. mi.

sonority /sə nórəti/ (*plural* **-ties**) *n* **1.** a sonorous quality **2.** a sound, especially a rich deep sound [Early 16C. Via French < medieval Latin *sonoritas* < Latin *sonorus* (see SONOROUS)]

sonorous /sónnərəss/ *adj* **1.** PRODUCING SOUND producing or possessing sound **2.** RESONANT sounding with loud, deep, and clear tones **3.** HAVING IMPRESSIVE MANNER OF SPEAKING speaking, spoken, or expressed in a rich, full, and impressive manner [Early 17C. < Latin *sonorus* 'noisy, loud' < *sonor* 'sound' < *sonare* 'make a sound'] —**sonorously** *adv* —**sonorousness** *n*

sonsie *adj regional* another spelling of **sonsy**

Sons of Freedom *npl* a religious group in western Canada involved in antigovernment terrorism during the 1950s and 1960s

sonsy /sónssi/ (**-sier, -siest**), **sonsie** *adj* **1.** *Scotland* BUXOM buxom or chubby **2.** *regional* EASYGOING having a cheerful easygoing nature **3.** *regional* LUCKY bringing or having good luck [Mid-16C. < *sonse* 'abundance, plentifulness' < Gaelic *sonas* 'good fortune']

Popperfoto

Susan Sontag

Sontag /són tag/, **Susan** (*b.* 1933) US writer. She is best known for her social commentary such as the article *Notes on* 'Camp' (1964) and *Illness as Metaphor* (1978). She has also written novels and short stories.

> 'The camera makes everyone a tourist in other people's reality, and eventually in one's own.'
> [Susan Sontag, *New York Review of Books*; 18 April 1974]

sook /soōk/ *n* **1.** *Scotland* TOADY somebody who is regarded as sickeningly flattering or obsequious (*insult*) **2.** *ANZ* SOMEBODY WEAK OR TIMID somebody regarded as weak, timid, or cowardly (*insult*) **3.** *also* **sookie** /soōki/ *NZ* CALF a pet calf (*informal*) [Late 19C. Dialect form of SUCK]

sool on /sool-/ (**sools on, sooling on, sooled on**) *vt Aus* to order or urge a dog or person to attack somebody (*informal*) ○ *He sooled the dogs on them.* [Late 19C. Variant of English dialect *sowl* 'seize something by the ears', origin?]

soon /soon/ *adv* **1.** AFTER SHORT TIME within or after a short time ○ *She soon realized that she had made a mistake.* **2.** QUICKLY quickly or without much delay ○ *How soon will you be ready?* ○ *I'll soon see about that!* **3.** EARLY before a reasonable or the desired length of time has elapsed ○ *Do you really have to go so soon?* ○ *It's a bit soon to be thinking of leaving, isn't it?* **4.** WILLINGLY used when expressing a preference for one alternative over another or an equal willingness to accept either, and often in the comparative form 'sooner' ○ *I'd sooner stay in than go out.* ○ *I'd as soon stay in as go out.* [Old English *sōna* < W Germanic] ◇ **as soon as** immediately after ◇ **no sooner...than** immediately after one thing had happened, another took place ◇ **sooner or later** inevitably or certainly at some as yet unspecifiable time

soot /soŏt/ *n* a black powdery form of carbon produced when coal, wood, or oil is burned, which rises up in fine particles with the flames and smoke ■ *vt* (**soots, sooting, sooted**) to sprinkle or cover something with soot [Old English *sōt* 'something that sits' < Germanic, 'sit']

sooth /sooth/ *n* same as **truth** (sense 1) (*archaic or literary*) [Old English *sōþ* 'true' < Indo-European, 'be'] —**soothly** *adv*

soothe /sooth/ (**soothes, soothing, soothed**) *v* **1.** *vt* to make pain or discomfort less severe **2.** *vti* to make somebody less angry, anxious, or upset [Old English *sōpian* 'prove to be true, verify' < *sōp* (see SOOTH)] —**soother** *n* —**soothing** *adj* —**soothingly** *adv* —**soothingness** *n*

soothsayer /sooth say ər/ *n* a predictor of future events —**soothsay** *vi*

sooty /soŏti/ (**-ier, -iest**) *adj* **1.** covered in soot, or lined or blocked with soot **2.** resembling soot in its blackness, dirtiness, or powdery texture

sooty mould *n* **1.** a plant disease characterized by a black velvety fungus **2.** a fungus that causes sooty mould. Genus: *Meliola* or *Capnodium*.

sop /sop/ *n* **1.** SOMETHING GIVEN TO SATISFY DISCONTENTED PERSON something offered as a concession or gesture to pacify somebody who is angry or discontented **2.** FOOD DIPPED IN LIQUID a piece of food dipped or soaked in liquid before it is eaten **3.** OFFENSIVE TERM an offensive term that deliberately insults somebody, especially a man, regarded as lacking courage (*dated insult*) ■ *vti* (**sops, sopping, sopped**) MAKE OR BECOME SOAKING WET to make something thoroughly wet, or become thoroughly wet [Old English *sopp* 'bread dipped in liquid' < *sūpan* 'swallow, taste' < Germanic, 'take liquid']

sop up *vt* to soak up a liquid with something absorbent

SOP *abbr* standard operating procedure

sop. *abbr* MUSIC soprano

sophism /sóffizəm/ *n* an argument or explanation that seems very clever or subtle on the surface but is actually flawed, misleading, or intended to deceive [14C. Via French and Latin < Greek *sophisma* 'acquired skill, clever device' < *sophos* 'skilled in a craft, clever, wise']

sophist /sóffist/ *n* **1.** *also* **Sophist** a member of a school of ancient Greek professional philosophers who were expert in and taught the skills of rhetoric, argument, and debate, but were criticized for specious reasoning. The sophists were active before and during the time of Socrates and Plato, who were their main critics. **2.** a deceptive person who offers clever-sounding but flawed arguments or explanations [Mid-16C. Via Latin *sophista* < Greek *sophistēs* 'master of a craft, man clever in practical affairs', also 'cheat' < *sophos* 'skilled in a craft, clever, wise']

sophister /sóffistər/ *n* formerly, a second-year undergraduate student at a British university [14C. Via Old French *sophistre* < Latin *sophista* (see SOPHIST)]

sophistic /sə fístik/, **sophistical** /sə fístik'l/ *adj* **1.** clever-sounding and plausible but based on shallow or dishonest thinking or flawed logic **2.** relating to sophists [Mid-16C. Via Latin *sophisticus* < Greek *sophistikos* < *sophos* 'skilled in a craft, clever, wise'] —**sophistically** *adv*

sophisticate /sə físti kayt/ *v* (**-cates, -cating, -cated**) **1.** *vt* MAKE SOMEBODY MORE CULTURED OR WORLDLY to make somebody more cultured or worldly, especially by educating out or destroying his or her naturalness, naivety, or innocence **2.** *vt* MAKE SOMETHING MORE COMPLEX to make something more advanced or complex than before **3.** *vti* PHILOSOPHY USE SOPHISTRY to use sophistic arguments, or make reasoning or an argument sophistic **4.** *vt* CORRUPT SOMETHING to make something impure, false, or adulterated ■ *n* CULTURED OR WORLDLY PERSON a person with cultivated tastes and refined manners who knows how the world works [14C. < medieval Latin *sophisticat-*, past participle of *sophisticare* 'deceive with words, disguise' < Latin *sophisticus* (see SOPHISTIC)]

sophisticated /sə físti kaytid/ *adj* **1.** KNOWLEDGEABLE AND CULTURED knowledgeable about the ways of the world, self-confident, and not easily deceived **2.** SUITABLE FOR SOPHISTICATED PEOPLE appealing to or frequented by sophisticated people **3.** ADVANCED complex, advanced, and very up-to-date ○ *a sophisticated computer network* —**sophisticatedly** *adv*

sophistication /sə físti káysh'n/ *n* **1.** KNOWLEDGEABLENESS AND REFINEMENT a combination of worldly wisdom, self-confidence, and refinement in a person **2.** ADVANCED TECHNICAL DEVELOPMENT advanced technical development and complexity **3.** ACT OF SOPHISTICATING the process of sophisticating something or somebody

sophistry /sóffistri/ (*plural* **-tries**) *n* **1.** a method of argumentation that seems clever but is actually flawed or dishonest **2.** PHILOSOPHY same as **sophism** [14C. Via French < Latin *sophistria* < *sophista* (see SOPHIST)]

~~sophmore~~ incorrect spelling of **sophomore**

Sophocles /sóffə kleez/ (496?–406? BC) Greek dramatist. The seven tragedies of his 123 plays that survive in complete texts, including *Electra*, *Oedipus Rex*, and *Antigone*, demonstrate the powerful treatment of moral and religious themes that made him one of the greatest dramatists of all time.

> 'Wonders are many, and none is more wonderful than man.'
> [Sophocles, *Antigone*; after 441 BC]

sophomore /sóffə mawr/ *N Am* *n* **1.** SECOND-YEAR STUDENT a second-year student at high school or university **2.** SOMEBODY IN SECOND YEAR OF SOMETHING somebody in the second year of a project or activity ■ *adj* EDUC OF SOPHOMORES relating to sophomores, the sophomore or second year in school or college ○ *a sophomore dance* ○ *sophomore textbooks* [Late 17C. < obsolete *sophum*, early form of SOPHISM + ER[1], probably altered as if < Greek *sophos* 'skilled in a craft, clever, wise' + *mōros* 'dull']

sophomoric /sóffə máwrik/ *adj* **1.** showing the naive lack of judgement that accompanies immaturity (*disapproving*) **2.** *N Am* relating to sophomores at high school or university

-sophy *suffix* wisdom, knowledge, science ○ *theosophy* [< Greek *sophia* < *sophos* 'skilled in a craft, clever, wise']

sopor /sópər/ *n* a very deep sleep or state of unconsciousness [Mid-17C. < Latin, 'sleep']

soporific /sóppə ríffik/ *adj* **1.** MAKING SOMEBODY SLEEPY causing sleep or drowsiness **2.** FEELING SLEEPY experiencing sleepiness or drowsiness **3.** TEDIOUS dull and boring ■ *n* SLEEP-INDUCING DRUG a drug or other substance that induces sleep —**soporifically** *adv*

sopping /sópping/, **sopping wet** *adj* thoroughly and unpleasantly wet (*informal*)

SYNONYMS See **wet**.

soppy /sóppi/ (**-pier, -piest**) *adj* **1.** excessively affectionate or sentimental (*informal*) **2.** thoroughly wet —**soppily** *adv* —**soppiness** *n*

sopranino /sóppra neénō/ (*plural* **-nos**) *n* a musical instrument, usually a wind instrument, that has a pitch higher than any others in its family [Early 20C. < Italian, 'little soprano' < *soprano* (see SOPRANO)]

soprano /sə praánō/ (*plural* **-pranos** or **-prani** /-praáni/) *n* **1.** WOMAN OR BOY WITH HIGHEST VOICE a woman, girl, or boy with the highest register of singing voice **2.** HIGHEST SINGING VOICE the highest register of singing voice a woman, girl, or boy can have **3.** SINGING PART FOR SOPRANO VOICE a singing part written for somebody with the highest register of voice **4.** MUSICAL INSTRUMENT WITH HIGH PITCH a musical instrument, especially a wind instrument, with the highest or second-highest pitch of instruments in its family [Early 18C. < Italian < *sopra* 'above' < Latin *supra*]

soprano clef *n* a C clef in which middle C is designated by the first line of the staff, formerly used for the soprano vocal line

Sopwith /sópwith/, **Sir Thomas** (1888–1989) British aircraft designer and yachtsman. His company produced many of the British aircraft used during World War I, including the Sopwith Camel. Full name **Sopwith, Sir Thomas Octave Murdoch**

SOR, **SoR** *abbr* COMM sale or return

sorb /sawrb/ *n* **1.** TREES same as **service tree 2.** *also* **sorb apple** the berry of the service tree [Early 16C. Via French < Latin *sorbum* 'serviceberry'] —**sorbic** *adj*

Sorb /sawrb/ *n* a member of a Slavic people living mainly in the upper Spree Valley between eastern Germany and southwestern Poland. There are about 150,000 Sorbs, who are descendants of an earlier people known as Wends. [Mid-19C. Via German *Sorbe* < Wendish *serbje* 'Serb']

sorb apple *n* BOT same as **sorb** (sense 2)

sorbet /sáwr bay, sáwrbit/ *n* a frozen dessert, usually made with fruit syrup and sometimes egg whites, whisked until smooth [Late 16C. Via French *sorbet* and Italian *sorbetto* < Turkish *şerbet* 'cool drink' (see SHERBET)]

sorbic acid /sáwrbik-/ *n* a white crystalline solid acid. Source: berries of mountain ash or synthetically manufactured. Use: food preservative, fungicide. Formula: $C_6H_8O_2$.

sorbitol

sorbitol /sáwrbi tol/ *n* a white crystalline sweet alcohol. Source: berries of mountain ash or synthetically manufactured. Use: sweetener, moisturizer, manufacture of Vitamin C. Formula: $C_6H_{14}O_6$.

Sorbonne /sawr bón/ *n* a part of the University of Paris, founded in 1253, that contains the faculties of science and literature

sorbose /sáwr bōss/ *n* a six-carbon sugar that is an isomer of fructose [Late 19C. < SORBITOL]

sorcerer /sáwrssərər/ *n* somebody who is believed or claims to have magical powers [Early 16C. < French *sorcier* < Latin *sort-* 'lot, fortune']

sorceress /sáwrsəres/ *n* a woman who is believed or claims to have magical powers

sorcery /sáwrssəri/ *n* the supposed use of magic — **sorcerous** *adj*

sordid /sáwrdid/ *adj* **1.** demonstrating the worst aspects of human nature such as immorality, selfishness, and greed **2.** dirty and depressing [Late 16C. Via French and Latin *sordidus* < *sordes* 'dirt'] — **sordidly** *adv* —**sordidness** *n*

sordino /sawr deenō/ (*plural* **-ni** /-ni/) *n* a device used to muffle or soften the tone of a musical instrument, e.g. a mute for a stringed or brass instrument or a damper on a piano [Late 16C. < Italian < *sordo* 'unable to speak or hear' < Latin *surdus*]

sore /sawr/ *adj* (**sorer, sorest**) **1.** PAINFUL painful or tender because of an injury, infection, or unaccustomed exercise **2.** ANNOYING causing annoyance or embarrassment ○ *Her dismissal has always been a sore point.* **3.** DISTRESSING causing great worry or distress (*literary*) ○ *The child's illness was a sore trial to her entire family.* **4.** URGENT requiring urgent action to provide relief ○ *The survivors of the flood are in sore need of help.* **5.** *N Am* UPSET angry or irritated, especially because of something said or done by another person in the recent past (*informal*) ○ *He was still sore because I kidded him about his tie.* ■ *n* INFECTED SPOT a painful open skin infection or wound ■ *adv* same as **sorely** (*archaic*) [Old English *sār* < Germanic] —**soreness** *n*

SPELLCHECK See *saw*[1].

sorehead /sáwr hed/ *n N Am* somebody who is regarded as easily offended or angered (*informal*)

sorely /sáwrli/ *adv* to a great extent or degree ○ *I was sorely tempted to say 'I told you so'.*

sorgho *n* AGRIC another spelling of **sorgo**

sorghum /sáwrgəm/ (*plural* **-ghums** or *same*) *n* **1.** a drought-resistant cereal plant, widely cultivated in tropical and warm areas. Use: food grain, animal feed, hay and fodder. Genus: *Sorghum*. **2.** a syrup made from the juice of some varieties of sorghum [Late 16C. Via modern Latin < Italian *sorgo* (see SORGO)]

sorgo /sáwrgō/, **sorgho** *n* a variety of sorghum cultivated as a source of syrup [Mid-18C. Via Italian < Vulgar Latin *syricum (granum)* 'Syrian (grain)']

sori BOT plural of **sorus**

sorites /so rí teez/ (*plural same*) *n* an argument consisting of a series of premises arranged so that the predicate of each premise forms the subject of the next. The conclusion unites the subject of the first premise with the predicate of the last. [Mid-16C. Via Latin < Greek *sōreitēs* < *sōros* 'heap']

Soroptimist /sə róptəmist/ *n* a member of an international organization (**Soroptimist International**) of professional women and businesswomen that promotes public service. It was founded in California in 1921. [Early 20C. Blend of Latin *soror* 'sister' + OPTIMIST]

sororate /sórrə rayt/ *n* a custom in some societies in which a widower marries a younger sister of his deceased wife [Early 20C. < Latin *soror* 'sister']

sororicide /sə rórri sīd/ *n* **1.** the murder of a sister **2.** a killer of his or her sister [Mid-17C. < Latin *soror* 'sister'] —**sororicidal** /sə rórri síd'l/ *adj*

sorority /sə rórrəti/ (*plural* **-ties**) *n* a social society for women who are students at a North American college or university, with a name consisting of individually pronounced Greek letters [Mid-16C. < medieval Latin *sororitas* < Latin *soror* 'sister']

sorption /sáwrpsh'n/ *n* the taking in or holding of something, either by absorption or adsorption [Early 20C. Back-formation < ABSORPTION and ADSORPTION]

sorrel[1] /sórrəl/ (*plural* **-rels** or *same*) *n* a sharp-tasting plant of the dock family. Use: salad greens, medicines. Genus: *Rumex*. [14C. < Old French *surele* < *sur* 'sour']

sorrel[2] /sórrəl/ *adj* REDDISH-BROWN of a reddish-brown colour ■ *n* **1.** BROWN WITH RED ADDED a brown colour with a red tone **2.** REDDISH-BROWN ANIMAL a horse or other animal with a reddish-brown coat [15C. < Old French *sorel* < *sor* 'yellowish']

sorrel[3] /sórrəl/ *n Carib* a red spiced drink traditionally made from the sepals of hibiscus flowers at Christmas time [French *roselle* '*Hibiscus sabdariffa*']

Sorrento /sə réntō/ town and resort on the southern shore of the Bay of Naples, in Naples Province, Campania Region, in southern Italy. Population: 16,536 (2001).

sorrow /sórrō/ *n* **1.** GRIEF a feeling of deep sadness caused by a loss or misfortune **2.** SADDENING BURDEN an unfortunate event, experience, or other cause of sorrow ■ *vi* (**-rows, -rowing, -rowed**) GRIEVE to feel or express deep sadness over something (*literary*) [Old English *sorg* < Germanic, 'care'] —**sorrower** *n* ◇ **drown your sorrows** to take alcoholic drink in order to try to forget a source of sadness or disappointment (*informal*)

sorrowful /sórrəf'l/ *adj* **1.** feeling or expressing sorrow **2.** characterized by or causing sorrow —**sorrowfully** *adv* —**sorrowfulness** *n*

sorry /sórri/ *adj* (**-rier, -riest**) **1.** APOLOGETIC feeling or expressing regret for an action that has upset or inconvenienced somebody, or is likely to do so **2.** SYMPATHETIC feeling or expressing sympathy or empathy, especially because of something that has happened ○ *I felt sorry it had to end that way.* ○ *Don't start feeling sorry for yourself.* **3.** PITIFUL pitifully bad or neglected ○ *a sorry little cottage with an overgrown garden* **4.** VERY BAD pathetically or contemptibly unsatisfactory ○ *a sorry excuse for a car* ■ *interj* **1.** USED AS APOLOGY used as an apology for hurting, interrupting, or inconveniencing somebody ○ *Sorry – I didn't realize that I stepped on your foot.* **2.** ASKING SOMEBODY TO REPEAT SOMETHING used with an interrogative inflexion to ask somebody to repeat something (*informal*) ○ *Sorry? What did you just say?* **3.** USED AS CORRECTING REMARK used to introduce a correction in speech ○ *The company employs 10,000 – sorry, 12,000 workers nationwide.* [Old English

sārig < *sār* (see SORE)] —**sorrily** *adv* —**sorriness** *n* ◇ **say sorry** to apologize to somebody

sort /sawrt/ *n* **1.** CATEGORY a category of persons or things with shared attributes, to which somebody or something can be assigned ○ *What sort of instrument is that?* **2.** PARTICULAR TYPE a particular type of person (*informal*) ○ *She'll help – she's a good sort.* **3.** SIMILAR THING something similar to a particular thing ○ *It's a sort of play with dancing.* **4.** COMPUT SORTING OF DATA a process of arranging data in a set order **5.** PRINTING LETTER OR SYMBOL a character in a font of type (*often used in the plural*) **6.** MANNER a manner of doing something (*archaic*) ■ *vt* (**sorts, sorting, sorted**) **1.** CATEGORIZE PEOPLE OR THINGS to place people or things in categories according to shared attributes ○ *clothes sorted into piles* **2.** PUT THINGS IN SEQUENCE to arrange things in a set order, especially automatically, as some computer programs do with data **3.** same as **sort out** (senses 1, 3) [14C. Via French < Latin *sort-* 'lot, fortune'] —**sortable** *adj* —**sorter** *n* ◇ **of a sort, of sorts** used to indicate that something is not very good ○ *We had a meal of sorts at the airport.* ◇ **out of sorts 1.** slightly unwell **2.** not in a very good mood ◇ **sort of** △ rather (*informal*) ○ *This place is sort of strange.*

USAGE The expression **sort of** tends to be overused, even though it is not only vague but also very informal. In formal writing it is best to avoid usages like *He looked sort of unhappy*; the more formal words *somewhat* and *rather* are preferable.

USAGE See **kind**[2].

SYNONYMS See **type**.

sort out *vt* **1.** RESOLVE SOMETHING EFFECTIVELY to deal effectively with a problem ○ *I think we've sorted out our difficulties with the printer.* **2.** SEPARATE SOMETHING to separate something from the mixture it exists in, or from another group of things **3.** PUT SOMETHING IN ORDER organize or disentangle something ○ *It took weeks to sort out the library.* **4.** REACH CONCLUSION to think and come to a conclusion about a problem or difficulty **5.** PUNISH SOMEBODY to deal with or punish somebody who has behaved badly (*informal*) ○ *Don't worry about him – I'll soon sort him out.*

sortation /sawr táysh'n/ *n* the process of sorting items into categories or into a set order, especially when done by machine or computer

sort code *n* a number that uniquely identifies a financial institution so that banking transactions can be sent to it

sorted /sáwrtid/ *adj* **1.** PUT RIGHT put to rights, repaired, or dealt with satisfactorily (*informal*) **2.** WELL-ADJUSTED socially or emotionally well-adjusted (*slang*) **3.** WELL PREPARED well prepared for something or well provided with something, especially illegal drugs (*slang*)

sortie /sáwrti/ *n* **1.** ATTACK ON ENEMY an attack made by a small military force into enemy territory **2.** AIRCRAFT MISSION a mission flown by a combat aircraft **3.** SHORT TRIP a brief trip away from home, especially to an unfamiliar place (*humorous*) **4.** PEOPLE ON SORTIE the personnel engaged in a military sortie ■ *vi* (**-ties, -tieing, -tied**) MIL MAKE SORTIE to make a sortie against an enemy position [Late 17C. < French, past participle of *sortir* 'go out']

sortilege /sáwrtilij/ *n* **1.** the supposed foretelling of the future by drawing lots **2.** the supposed practice of magic or sorcery [14C. Via French < Latin *sortilegus* 'prophetic, soothsayer' < *sort-* 'lot, fortune' + *legere* 'read']

sorting office /sáwrting-/ *n* a place where letters and packages for delivery are sorted according to their destinations

sorus /sáwrəss/ (*plural* **-ri** /-rī/) *n* **1.** a cluster of spore cases on the underside of some fern fronds **2.** a spore-producing organ in some algae, fungi, and lichens [Mid-19C. Via modern Latin < Greek *sōros* 'heap']

SOS /éss ō éss/ *n* **1.** DISTRESS SIGNAL an international radio signal that ships or aircraft in serious distress can use to call for help. It consists of the letters 'SOS' in Morse code (... – – – ...). **2.** CALL FOR HELP a call or signal requesting help **3.** BROADCAST TO CONTACT SOMEBODY URGENTLY a radio broadcast attempting to contact somebody whose whereabouts are unknown, in an emergency [Early 20C. < letters that

sorghum

are clear and easy to transmit; popularly regarded as abbreviation of *save our souls*]

sosatie /sə saáti/ *n S Africa* curried or spicy meat grilled on a skewer [Mid-19C. Via Afrikaans < Malay *sesate*]

Sosigenes of Alexandria /so síjjə neez-/ (*fl* 50 BC) Greek astronomer. He advised Julius Caesar on the adoption of the solar, or Julian, calendar (45 BC).

so-so (*informal*) *adj* neither very good nor very bad ○ *The food was so-so, but the atmosphere was wonderful.* ■ *adv* neither very well nor very badly ○ *feeling so-so*

sostenuto /sóstə noótō/ *adv* with notes sustained to or beyond the notated value (*used as a musical direction*) ■ *n* (*plural* **sostenutos**) a piece of music, or a section of a piece, played sostenuto [Mid-18C. < Italian, past participle of *sostinere* 'sustain' < Latin *sustinere* (see SUSTAIN)] —**sostenuto** *adj*

sot /sot/ *n* an offensive term for somebody who habitually drinks alcohol to excess (*literary*) [Pre-12C. Via Old French, 'fool' < medieval Latin *sottus*]

soteriology /sō teéri ólləji/ *n* the doctrine of salvation, especially the Christian doctrine of salvation through Jesus Christ [Mid-18C. < Greek *sōtēria* 'salvation'] —**soteriologic** /sō teéri ə lójjik/ *adj*

Sothic cycle /sṓthik-/ *n* a cycle of 1460 Sothic years in the ancient Egyptian calendar [Early 19C. < Greek *Sōthis*, the star Sirius, used in calendar calculations]

Sothic year *n* a year of $365\frac{1}{4}$ days in the ancient Egyptian calendar, based on the first appearance of the dog star (**Sirius**) above the horizon [See SOTHIC CYCLE]

Sotho /soó too/ (*plural same* or **-thos**) *n* **1.** a member of a large group of peoples who live in southern Africa, mainly in Botswana, Lesotho, and South Africa **2.** the group of Bantu languages of the Sotho people. There are three main languages in the group, Sesotho or Southern Sotho, Pedi or Northern Sotho, and Tswana. [Early 20C. < Bantu] —**Sotho** *adj*

Soto ♦ **de Soto, Hernando**

sotol /sṓtōl/ *n* **1.** a prickly-leaved desert plant. Flowers: whitish, in dense clusters. Native to: southwestern United States, Mexico. Genus: *Dasylirion*. **2.** an alcoholic drink made from the sap of the sotol plant [Late 19C. Via American Spanish *sotole* < Nahuatl *tzotolli*]

sottish /sóttish/ *adj* **1.** in the habit of drinking far too much alcohol **2.** showing the effects of having drunk too much alcohol

sotto voce /sóttō vṓchi/ *adv* in a soft voice, so as not to be overheard [Mid-18C. < Italian, 'under (the) voice'] —**sotto voce** *adj*

sou /soo/ *n* **1.** a French coin no longer in use, worth only a small amount **2.** the least amount of money (*informal; used in negative statements*) ○ *I haven't a sou.* [15C. < French, back-formation < Old French *sous*, plural of *sout* 'sou' < Latin *solidus (nummus)* (see SOLDIER)]

soubrette /soo brét/ *n* **1.** MAIDSERVANT IN COMEDY a pretty, flirtatious woman's role in a comedy, especially one in which she plays a lady's maid involved in romantic intrigues **2.** ACTOR PLAYING SOUBRETTE an actor who often plays soubrettes **3.** DISMISSIVE TERM a dismissive term for a young woman whose behaviour is interpreted as flirtatious (*dated*) [Mid-18C. < French, 'lady's maid' < Provençal *soubreto* 'coy' < Latin *superare* 'surpass' < *super* 'above']

soubriquet *n* another spelling of **sobriquet**

~~**souce**~~ incorrect spelling of **source**

souchong /soó chóng/ *n* black China tea [Mid-18C. < Cantonese *síu-chúng* 'small kind']

soucouyant /soókoo yaán/ *n Carib* somebody, usually a woman, who according to legend sucks people's blood and can shed her skin, change into a ball of fire, and fly around by night. It is said that she must return to her skin before daylight, and that salt and thorn-trees offer protection against her. [Mid-20C. < Caribbean creole]

souffle /soóf'l/ *n* a soft blowing sound inside somebody's chest, heard through a stethoscope and caused by blood flowing through blood vessels [Late 19C. < French, 'breath' < *souffler* (see SOUFFLÉ)]

soufflé /soóf lay/ *n* a sweet or savoury open-textured dish that has been made light by adding whisked egg whites. Hot soufflés are usually based on a thick milk sauce and are baked, while cold soufflés are made with gelatin and set by chilling. [Early 19C. < French, past participle of *souffler* 'blow, puff up' < Latin *sufflare*] —**soufflé** *adj*

Soufriere Hills Volcano /soófri áir-/ volcano on the island of Montserrat in the Caribbean Sea. It erupted in 1997, leaving large parts of the island uninhabitable. Height: 915 m/3,002 ft.

sough /sow/ (*archaic or literary*) *vi* (**soughs, soughing, soughed**) to make a soft rustling, sighing, or murmuring sound, like the wind in trees ■ *n* a sound like that made by a gentle wind through trees [Old English *swōgan* < Germanic]

sought past participle, past tense of **seek**

sought-after *adj* in high demand because scarce ○ *Blue diamonds are among the most sought-after gems.*

souk /sook/, **suq** *n* an open-air market in North Africa or Southwest Asia [Early 19C. < Arabic *sūḳ*]

soukous /soó kooss/ *n* a style of dance music originally from the Democratic Republic of the Congo, combining guitar, drums, and vocals [Late 20C. Probably < Lingala < French *secouer* 'to shake']

soul /sōl/ *n* **1.** NONPHYSICAL ASPECT OF PERSON the complex of human attributes that manifests as consciousness, thought, feeling, and will, regarded as distinct from the physical body **2.** FEELINGS a person's emotional and moral nature, where the most private thoughts and feelings are hidden ○ *Her soul was in turmoil.* **3.** SPIRIT SURVIVING DEATH in some systems of religious belief, the spiritual part of a human being that is believed to continue to exist after the body dies. The soul is sometimes regarded as subject to future reward and punishment, and sometimes as able to take a form that allows it to remain on or return to earth. **4.** SPIRITUAL DEPTH evidence of spiritual or emotional depth and sensitivity, either in a person or in something created by a person ○ *Though technically perfect, the drawing lacked soul.* **5.** ESSENCE the deepest and truest nature of people or a nation, or what gives somebody or something a distinctive character ○ *In my travels I hoped to discover the soul of the Russian people.* **6.** TYPE OF PERSON somebody of a particular type, especially one regarded sympathetically or with familiarity ○ *Poor soul! What will he do now?* **7.** ANYONE anyone at all (*used in negative statements*) ○ *You have to promise not to tell a soul.* **8.** INDIVIDUAL PERSON an individual person, especially when thought of as making up the number of a group (*usually used in the plural*) ○ *a country of some 10 million souls* **9.** PERFECT EXAMPLE a good example, or personification, of a positive quality ○ *The hotel manager was the soul of discretion.* **10.** SOMEBODY ESSENTIAL TO SOMETHING the leader of or the most influential person in a group or movement **11.** AFRICAN AMERICAN SPIRIT a quality regarded as characterizing African American culture, especially as manifested in understanding and in social customs, speech, and music **12.** MUSIC same as **soul music** [Old English *sāwol* < Germanic] ◇ **sell your soul** to abandon your principles in order to obtain wealth or success

SPELLCHECK See ***sole***[1].

Soul *n* in the Christian Science religion, the name for God

soul-destroying *adj* extremely boring, repetitive, or unfulfilling

soul food *n* the traditional foods of African Americans of the American South. Typical dishes are yams, chitterlings, black-eyed peas, and collard greens.

soulful /sṓlf'l/ *adj* deeply or sincerely emotional —**soulfully** *adv* —**soulfulness** *n*

soulless /sṓl ləss/ *adj* **1.** lacking warmth, sensitivity, or feeling ○ *soulless bureaucrats* **2.** lacking anything that might stimulate or engage the feelings —**soullessly** *adv* —**soullessness** *n*

soul mate *n* somebody with whom somebody else naturally shares deep feelings and attitudes

soul music *n* a style of African American popular music with a strong emotional quality, related to gospel music and rhythm and blues

soul-searching *n* a thorough examination of personal thoughts and feelings, especially when faced with a difficult problem

Soult /soolt/, **Nicolas** (1769–1851) French marshal and government official. Under Napoleon I, he led many campaigns in Europe, notably in Spain and Portugal. After the restoration of the monarchy in 1814, he shifted his loyalties and held various high posts, including premier (1833–34, 1839–47). Full name **Soult, Nicholas Jean de Dieu**

sound[1] /sownd/ *n* **1.** SOMETHING AUDIBLE something that can be heard ○ *not a sound in the whole house* ○ *the sound of gunfire* **2.** VIBRATIONS SENSED BY EAR vibrations travelling through air, water, or some other medium, especially those within the range of frequencies that can be perceived by the human ear. At sea level and freezing point, the speed of sound through the air is 1,220 km/760 mi. per hour. **3.** IMPLICATION an impression of somebody or something formed from limited but significant information, especially information lately received ○ *From the sound of it she's finally found a job she really likes.* **4.** EARSHOT the distance or area within which something can be heard ○ *Our house was within the sound of the church bells.* **5.** ELECTRONICS REPRODUCED MUSIC OR SPEECH the music, speech, or other sounds heard through an electronic device such as a television, radio, or loudspeaker, especially with regard to volume or quality ○ *Please turn down the sound.* **6.** BROADCAST RECORDING OF MUSIC OR SPEECH the recording, editing, and replaying of music, speech, or sound effects in the broadcast or entertainment industry **7.** LING BASIC ELEMENT OF SPOKEN LANGUAGE a basic element of speech formed by the vocal tract and interpreted through the ear, or a combination of such sounds **8.** MUSIC TYPE OF MUSIC the distinctive quality that identifies bands or music from a particular place, area, or studio, or belonging to a particular movement or style ■ **sounds** *npl* MUSIC music, especially music that is not classical, e.g. pop, jazz, or rock (*informal*) ■ *v* (**sounds, sounding, sounded**) **1.** *vi* SEEM to give a particular impression when mentioned or described ○ *The meal sounded awful.* **2.** *vi* INDICATE CONDITION to give a particular impression about a physical or mental condition via speech or writing ○ *He sounded exhausted when I talked to him on the phone.* **3.** *vi* HAVE PARTICULAR QUALITY WHEN HEARD to give a particular impression to a hearer about the quality of the noise or the identity of the source of the noise ○ *That sounds like the postman.* **4.** *vti* MAKE A NOISE to make a particular noise so as to be heard, or make something produce such a noise ○ *Somewhere down the corridor, an alarm sounded.* **5.** *vt* ANNOUNCE SOMETHING to spread the news of or signal something by making a noise, or produce a similar effect by saying something ○ *She sounded a note of caution about the likely result of the election.* **6.** *vt* PHON ARTICULATE A SOUND to pronounce a letter or sound, especially in a context in which it might be silent ○ *You don't sound the 'p' in 'psychic'.* **7.** *vt* MED TEST BODILY CONDITION BY CAUSING SOUND to observe the sound made by an organ of the body for testing or diagnostic purposes [13C. Via French < Latin *sonus*]

sound off *vi* **1.** to express strong feelings through speech, or complain loudly about something (*informal*) ○ *always sounding off about high property taxes* **2.** to chant or count in turn while marching

sound out *vt* to find out somebody's opinions about something before committing to a course of action

sound[2] /sownd/ *adj* **1.** SENSIBLE based on good sense and valid reasoning ○ *a sound argument* **2.** NOT DAMAGED without any serious damage or decay **3.** HEALTHY free from injury, disease, or illness **4.** COMPLETELY ACCEPTABLE worthy of approval, especially as agreeing with traditional views or conforming to conventional behaviour ○ *morally sound opinions* **5.** DEEP AND PEACEFUL unbroken by waking and untroubled by dreams or discomfort ○ *She had a sound night's sleep.* **6.** COMPLETE including all necessary aspects and details ○ *sound knowledge of the subject* **7.** THOROUGH painful and thorough ○ *a sound spanking* **8.** FIN WITH LITTLE FINANCIAL RISK financially secure and likely to make money **9.** LOGIC VALID WITH TRUE PREMISES having a true conclusion that follows from true

premises **10.** LAW **LEGALLY VALID** valid in law ■ *adv* **DEEPLY** in a deep and peaceful way ○ *sound asleep* [12C. Shortening of Old English *gesund* < W Germanic] —**soundly** *adv* —**soundness** *n*

SYNONYMS See ***valid***.

sound[3] /sownd/ *v* (**sounds, sounding, sounded**) **1.** *vti* NAUT **MEASURE DEPTH** to measure the depth of water using a weighted line or sonar **2.** *vi* ZOOL **DIVE DOWN** to dive suddenly and swiftly downwards (*refers to whales*) **3.** *vt* MED **EXAMINE SOMETHING WITH PROBE** to use a surgical probe to examine a bodily cavity or passage such as the bladder or to dilate a constriction ■ *n* MED **SURGICAL PROBE** a surgical probe used to sound bodily cavities [14C. Via French *sonder* < Vulgar Latin *subundare* < Latin *sub* 'under' + *unda* 'wave'] —**sounder** *n*

sound[4] /sownd/ *n* **1.** GEOG **WIDE CHANNEL** a broad channel between two large bodies of water, or between an island and the mainland **2.** GEOG **OCEAN INLET** a long wide arm of the sea **3.** FISH **AIR BLADDER** the air bladder of a fish [Old English *sund* < Germanic]

soundalike /sównd ə līk/ *n* **1.** a performer whose voice or musical style closely resembles that of a particular well-known performer **2.** a word that sounds similar to another word but has a different spelling

sound barrier *n* a sudden increase in the force of air opposing an aircraft or other moving body as it approaches the speed of sound, producing a sonic boom

sound bite *n* a short comment intended or suitable for broadcasting in a news programme, especially one made by a politician. Their use is often regarded as manipulative. ○ *There's no substance to their policy – it's all sound bites.*

soundboard /sównd bawrd/ *n* a thin sheet of wood placed under or above the strings of a musical instrument to increase resonance. On a violin it is the top of the instrument.

sound bow *n* the thick part of a bell, where the clapper strikes

soundbox /sównd boks/ *n* the hollow chamber in a stringed instrument that increases its resonance

sound card *n* a computer circuit board that allows a personal computer to receive sound in digital form and reproduce it through speakers

sound effect *n* a recording or imitation of a sound used in a film, radio or television programme, play, or other theatrical performance ■ **sound effects** *npl* all the sounds in a film, broadcast, or theatre production other than dialogue and music (*hyphenated before a noun*)

sound hole *n* an opening near the centre of a hollow stringed instrument that increases resonance

sounding[1] /sównding/ *n* **1.** NAUT **DEPTH MEASUREMENT** a measurement of the depth of water, taken using sonar or a weighted line **2.** METEOROL **ATMOSPHERIC MEASUREMENT** a measurement of the conditions in the atmosphere at a specific altitude ■ **soundings** *npl* **1.** **PRELIMINARY ENQUIRY INTO OPINION** a sampling of the views of a group of people taken before committing to a course of action ○ *taking soundings about the popularity of the council's plans* **2.** NAUT **WATER WHERE DEPTH MEASUREMENTS ARE TAKEN** a place where the water is shallow enough for a sounding line to be used to determine its depth [14C. < SOUND[2]]

sounding[2] /sównding/ *adj* having an impressive or resonant sound (*literary*) [14C. < SOUND[1]] —**soundingly** *adv*

sounding board *n* **1.** a person or group that gives feedback on preliminary ideas before they are considered for further development **2.** MUSIC same as **soundboard 3.** ACOUSTICS a roof-like structure built above a pulpit or platform to direct the speaker's voice to the audience [< SOUND[1]]

sounding line *n* a weighted line with measurements marked on it, used for determining the depth of water [< SOUNDING[1]]

soundless /sówndləss/ *adj* not making any noise — **soundlessly** *adv* —**soundlessness** *n*

sound mixer *n* a person or machine that combines or balances sounds for a recording, broadcast, or film soundtrack

soundpost /sównd pōst/ *n* a small piece of wood inside the body of a stringed instrument that supports the bridge and transmits the vibrations to the back

soundproof /sównd proof/ *adj* constructed so that no sound can enter or escape ■ *vt* (**-proofs, -proofing, -proofed**) to line or seal a room so that no sound can enter or escape

sound ranging *n* a method of locating the source of a sound by measuring the travel time of sound waves to a microphone at a fixed position

sound shift *n* a systematic change over time in the pronunciation of a set of sounds in a language

sound spectrograph *n* an electronic instrument that makes a graphic representation of sound qualities

sound stage *n* a large room or studio, usually soundproof, where film scenes are shot

sound system *n* electronic equipment for amplifying sound, used in recording, broadcasting, or live at public gatherings

soundtrack /sównd trak/ *n* **1.** **SOUND RECORDING FOR FILM** the recorded music, dialogue, and sound effects in a film or video production **2.** **STRIP CARRYING FILM SOUND** a thin strip at the edge of a film reel or video tape on which sound is recorded **3.** **MUSIC FROM FILM** a commercially released recording of the music that has been used in a film

sound truck *n US* same as **loudspeaker van**

sound wave *n* an audible pressure wave caused by a disturbance in water or air and carried forward in a ripple effect

soup /soop/ *n* **1.** **LIQUID FOOD** a liquid food made by cooking meat, fish, vegetables, or other ingredients in water, milk, or stock **2.** **SOMETHING THICK AND SWIRLING** something with the consistency or appearance of soup, especially a swirling liquid or dense fog ○ *the primordial soup of hydrogen, oxygen, and other gases* **3.** **PHOTOGRAPHIC CHEMICALS** chemicals for developing photographs (*slang*) [Mid-17C. Via French *soupe* < late Latin *suppa* < assumed *suppare* 'soak'] ◇ **from soup to nuts** *N Am* used to emphasize the variety or the wide range of something ◇ **in the soup** in difficulties or trouble (*informal*)

soup up *vt* to make changes to a car, motorcycle, engine, or similar machine in order to make it more powerful (*informal*) [< SOUP 'drug injected into a horse to increase its speed']

soupçon /sóop son, -soN/ *n* a very small amount of something [Mid-18C. Via French, 'suspicion' < Latin *suspicion-* (see SUSPICION)]

soup du jour /sóop dyoo͞ zhoo͞r/ (*plural* **soups du jour** /*pronunc. same*/) *n* the featured soup of the day on the menu of a restaurant [Mid-20C. < French 'soup of the day']

soup kitchen *n* a place that serves free meals to people of a lower income group

soupspoon /sóop spoon/ *n* a spoon with a round bowl for eating soup

soupy /sóopi/ (**-ier, -iest**) *adj* **1.** **LIKE SOUP** like soup in appearance or consistency **2.** **DAMP OR FOGGY** unpleasantly damp or foggy (*informal*) **3.** **SENTIMENTAL** highly sentimental (*informal*)

sour /sowr/ *adj* **1.** **SHARP-TASTING** having a tart or sharp taste that is acidic though not necessarily unpleasant, like the taste of vinegar, lemons, or unripe apples **2.** **BAD THROUGH FERMENTATION** unpleasantly rancid in taste or smell because of fermentation ○ *It was so hot that the milk went sour in hours.* **3.** **DISSATISFIED** characterized by ill temper or feelings of bitterness or dissatisfaction ○ *a sour look* **4.** **UNFRIENDLY** unpleasant, unfriendly, or ill-disposed, having previously been harmonious, friendly, or approving ○ *After two years the partnership began to turn sour.* **5.** **UNPLEASANT** causing distaste or discomfort **6.** AGRIC **LACKING LIME** describes soil that is too acidic because of a lack of lime, and is therefore unfavourable to crops **7.** INDUST **SULPHUROUS AND ACIDIC** describes crude oil or gas that is foul-smelling, toxic, and acidic because of excessive levels of sulphur compounds ■ *vti* (**sours, souring, soured**) **1.** **BECOME OR MAKE SOMEBODY DISSATISFIED** to become bad-tempered, embittered, or unfriendly, or make somebody become so ○ *A breach of diplomacy soured relations between the two countries.* **2.** **BECOME OR MAKE SOMETHING SOUR** to become sour in taste, smell, or composition, or make something sour in this way ■ *n* **1.** *N Am* **COCKTAIL WITH LEMON OR LIME** a cocktail made with whisky, lemon or lime juice, and often sugar **2.** **SOMETHING SOUR OR ACID** something sour or acid, especially an acid solution used in bleaching clothes or in curing skins [Old English *sūr* < Germanic] —**sourly** *adv* —**sourness** *n*

source /sawrss/ *n* **1.** **ORIGIN** the place, person, or thing through which something has come into being or from which it has been obtained **2.** **PROVIDER OF INFORMATION** a person, organization, book, or other text that supplies information or evidence ○ *a reliable source* **3.** ARTS **WORK ON WHICH ANOTHER IS BASED** a creation that forms the basis of or inspiration for a later work, e.g. a story or work of art **4.** GEOG **BEGINNING OF RIVER** the spring or fountain from which a river or stream first issues from the ground, or the area around this **5.** ELECTRONICS **ELECTRODE SUPPLYING CURRENT** in a field effect transistor, the electrode from which the electrical current originates ■ *vt* (**sources, sourcing, sourced**) **1.** **LOCATE SOMETHING FOR USE** to get parts, materials, or information from elsewhere **2.** **SPECIFY SOURCES OF SOMETHING WRITTEN** to list the people or materials used in researching a written work ○ *The book has been thoroughly sourced.* [14C. < Old French *sourse* < past participle of *sourdre* 'rise, spring' < Latin *surgere*]

SYNONYMS See ***origin***.

source book *n* a document or collection of documents that is the main source of information about a subject of study

source code *n* computer code written in a recognized programming language that can be converted into machine code

source language *n* the language from which a translation is made

sour cherry *n* **1.** a sharp-tasting red or blackish fruit used mainly in cooking and preserves **2.** a bush or small tree that produces sour cherries. Native to: Europe, Asia. Latin name: *Prunus cerasus*.

sour cream *n* smooth thick cream that has been soured artificially, used in cooking and baking and as a topping

sourdine /soor deén/ *n* **1.** a reed instrument with a soft tone similar to a bassoon. It is no longer in use. **2.** MUSIC same as **sordino 3.** a stop on an organ that produces a low muted tone [Early 17C. Via French < Italian *sordina*, form of *sordino* (see SORDINO)]

sourdough /sówr dō/ *n* **1.** fermenting dough used as a leavening agent in making bread **2.** bread made with sourdough

sour grapes *n* the scornful denial that something is attractive or desirable because it is unobtainable [In allusion to Aesop's fable *The Fox and the Grapes* where the fox disparages some grapes as sour when he cannot reach them]

sour gum *n* a tree with glossy leaves and light wood. Native to: eastern United States. Latin name: *Nyssa sylvatica*.

sour mash *n* **1.** a grain mash that is a mixture of new and old batches, used in distilling some kinds of whisky **2.** whisky distilled using sour mash

sourpuss /sówr po͝oss/ *n* somebody regarded as gloomy or bad-tempered (*informal*)

soursop /sówr sop/ (*plural* **-sops** or *same*) *n* **1.** a spiny fruit with a tart fibrous pulp **2.** a tree with spicy fragrant leaves that produces soursops. Native to: tropical America. Latin name: *Annona muricata*.

sourwood /sówər wo͝od/ (*plural* **-woods** or *same*) *n* a tree with thick bark, small white flowers, and sour-tasting leaves. Native to: eastern United States. Latin name: *Oxydendrum arboreum*.

Sousa /sóozə/, **John Philip** (1854–1932) US military bandmaster and composer. His rousing patriotic compositions include 'The Stars and Stripes Forever' (1897). Known as **the March King**

> 'Jazz will endure just as long as people hear it through their feet instead of their brains.'
> [Attributed to John Philip Sousa]

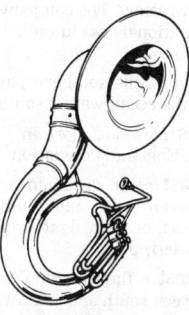

sousaphone

sousaphone /sóozə fōn/ *n* a large brass instrument with a flaring bell that resembles a tuba. It is used in military marching bands. [Early 20C. After John Philip SOUSA] —**sousaphonist** *n*

sous-chef /soo-/ *n* a head chef's assistant and deputy [Late 17C.< French, 'under chef']

souse /sowss/ *v* (**souses, sousing, soused**) **1.** *vti* DRENCH OR SOAK to make something soaking wet, or become soaking wet **2.** *vti* PLUNGE INTO LIQUID to plunge into a liquid, or plunge something into a liquid **3.** *vt* PICKLE SOMETHING to steep something in vinegar or brine in order to preserve it (*often passive*) **4.** *vt* MAKE SOMEBODY INTOXICATED to make somebody extremely intoxicated (*slang; usually passive*) ■ *n* **1.** LIQUID USED IN PICKLING the brine or vinegar used in pickling **2.** PICKLED FOOD pickled food, especially pork trimmings **3.** *Carib* BROTH MADE WITH PORK a broth made with a pig's snout, trotters, and sometimes tail, boiled with vegetables and seasonings **4.** DRUNKARD somebody who is habitually drunk (*slang*) **5.** BINGE a bout of heavy drinking (*dated*) [14C. < Old French *sous*]

souslik *n* ZOOL another spelling of **suslik**

sou-sou /sóo soo/, **susu** *n* *Carib* an arrangement for saving money whereby participants pay a sum each month for a fixed period of time and take turns borrowing the total amount accumulated [Early 20th C. < Yoruba *eesu* or *esusu* 'fund where several people pool their money, each paying a fixed sum and each drawing out the total in rotation', probably influenced by French *sou* 'coin']

Sousse /sooss/ *n* city and port in east-central Tunisia. Population: 125,000 (1994).

soutache /soo tásh/ *n* a narrow ornamental braid in a herringbone pattern, used for trimming garments [Mid-19C. Via French < Hungarian *sujtás*]

soutane /soo taán, -tán/ *n* a priest's robe or cassock, especially one with buttons down the front [Mid-19C. Via French < Italian *sottana* < *sotto* 'below' < Latin *subtus*]

souterrain /sóotə rayn/ *n* an ancient underground room or passage [Mid-18C. < French, 'underground']

south /sowth/ *n* **1.** DIRECTION TO RIGHT FACING RISING SUN the direction that lies directly to the right of somebody facing the rising sun or that is located towards the bottom of a conventional map of the world **2.** COMPASS POINT OPPOSITE NORTH the compass point that lies directly opposite north **3.** *also* **South** AREA IN SOUTH the part of an area, country, or region that is situated in or towards the south **4.** RIGHT-HAND SIDE OF CHURCH the right side of a church as you face the altar from the nave **5.** POSITION EQUIVALENT TO SOUTH the position equivalent to south in any diagram consisting of four points at 90-degree intervals ■ *adj* **1.** *also* **South** IN SOUTH situated in, facing, or coming from the south of a place, region, or country **2.** BLOWING FROM SOUTH describes a wind that blows from the south ■ *adv* TOWARDS SOUTH in or towards the south [Old English *sūp* < Germanic]

South *n* **1.** the southern region of England, roughly south of the River Severn and the Wash **2.** the nations of the world with less industrialized economies

---

WORLD ENGLISH *South African English* is the variety of English used in the Republic of South Africa. Since the early 19th century it has been the mother tongue of settlers of British origin and a second language, in varying degrees, of indigenous Afrikaners, Africans, and Asians. Since 1994, the nation has had 11 official languages: English, Afrikaans, Ndebele, Sotho (Northern and Southern), Swati, Tsonga, Tswana, Venda, Xhosa, and Zulu. South African English tends not to pronounce *r* in words such as *art*, *door*, and *worker*, and, among Africans, generally has full vowels in all syllables (e.g. *seven* is pronounced 'seh-ven' not 'sev'n'). Although middle-class British South Africans have traditionally had Received Pronunciation as their ideal, certain distinctive usages are common: e.g. the vowels in *park* and *trap*, heard by outsiders as 'pork' and 'trep', and in *fair hair* as 'fay hay'. Notably, British South Africans use the velar fricative in Scottish *ach* and *loch*, acquired primarily from Afrikaans and used for words from that language. A curiosity of the grammar is the affirmative 'no', as in *How are you? – No, I'm fine*, probably adopted from Afrikaans. With its parent Dutch, this language has provided the bulk of local borrowings: e.g. *Afrikaner* 'a white South African of Dutch or Huguenot origin', *apartheid* 'former policy of separate racial development', *bakkie* 'pick-up truck', *braai* 'barbecue', *drift* 'ford', *kloof* 'ravine', the now internationalized *trek* 'journey', and *veld*, pronounced /felt/, 'open country', with its hybrid extensions *highveld* and *backveld*. Words from African languages include *impala*, *muti* (medicine), *sangoma* (diviner), and *tshwala* (sorghum beer). Distinctive English words are the now-archaic *bioscope* (cinema), *location* (district set aside for a particular group), and *robot* (traffic light).

WORLD ENGLISH *South Asian English* is the variety of English that has been used since the 17th century in South Asia. Usage varies greatly from area to area, primarily because of the influence of local languages on pronunciation, grammar, and vocabulary, e.g. Bangla (formerly called Bengali) in Bangladesh and the Indian state of Bengal, Hindi in northern India, Tamil in southern India and Sri Lanka, Urdu in Pakistan and India, and Sinhalese in Sri Lanka. At the same time, however, there is considerable uniformity throughout the region as a consequence of British administrative, legal, and commercial usage, the presence of English-language-media schools based on British models, and, more recently, local television.

South Asian English pronounces *r* in words such as *art*, *door*, and *worker*. It tends to have full vowels in all syllables (e.g. *seven* is pronounced 'seh-ven' not 'sev'n'), and it is widely considered to have a singsong quality often compared to that of English speakers in Wales. Two widespread grammatical features are, first, questions without word-order inversion, as in *What you would like to buy, please? Where you are coming from? Why you are doing this?* Second is the sentence-final use of *only* for emphasis: *He is coming once a week only* for *He only comes once a week*. Widely used in the region are adopted local expressions such as: *gherao* (in industrial actions, surrounding people so that they cannot leave a place; also used as a verb, e.g. *He was gheraoed yesterday*); *wallah* 'man', used in compounds like *dhobiwallah* meaning 'laundry man'; and the numbers *lakh* 'one hundred thousand', e.g. *a lakh of rupees*, and *crore* 'ten million' in *They have crores of rupees*. Hybridization of English with indigenous usages is common, as in *policewallah* 'policeman', and *goondaism* 'behaving like a goonda or thug', itself a South Asian word.

South Africa

South Africa country in southern Africa. It became a fully democratic republic in 1994 when it rejoined the Commonwealth (after withdrawing in 1961). Language: Afrikaans, English, Ndebele, Northern Sotho, Southern Sotho, Swati, Tsonga, Tswana, Venda, Xhosa, Zulu. Currency: rand. Capital: Pretoria. Population: 42,768,678 (2003). Area: 1,219,090 sq. km/470,693 sq. mi. Official name **Republic of South Africa** —**South African** *n, adj*

South African Dutch *n* LANG same as **Cape Dutch** (sense 3) (*not used in South Africa*)

South African English *n* a variety of English spoken in South Africa

South America fourth largest continent in the world, lying between the Atlantic and Pacific oceans southeast of North America and stretching from the isthmus of Panama southwards to Cape Horn. Population: 317,846,000 (1996). Area: 17,819,100 sq. km/6,880,000 sq. mi. —**South American** *adj, n*

South American trypanosomiasis *n* same as **Chagas' disease**

Southampton /sow thámptən, sowth hámptən/ city in Hampshire, southern England. It is one of England's principal ports. Population: 217,445 (2001).

South Asia region comprising the countries of Bangladesh, Bhutan, India, the Maldives, Nepal, Pakistan, and Sri Lanka

South Asian English *n* a variety of English spoken in South Asia

---

South Australia state occupying the central part of southern Australia. Founded in 1834, it was the only Australian colony set up as a free settlement rather than a penal colony. Capital: Adelaide. Population: 1,527,400 (2003). Area: 984,000 sq. km/379,900 sq. mi. —**South Australian** *n, adj*

South Ayrshire council area in west central Scotland. The administrative centre is Ayr. Population: 112,658 (2001). Area: 1,202 sq. km/464 sq. mi.

South Bend city in northern Indiana, on the Kankakee and St Joseph rivers, southwest of Elkhart. It is home to the University of Notre Dame. Population: 106,558 (2002 estimate).

southbound /sówth bownd/ *adj* leading, going, or travelling towards the south

south by east *n* the direction or compass point midway between south and south-southeast —**south by east** *adj, adv*

south by west *n* the direction or compass point midway between south and south-southwest —**south by west** *adj, adv*

South Carolina state in the southeastern United States, bordered by North Carolina, the Atlantic Ocean, and Georgia. Capital: Columbia. Population: 4,107,183 (2002 estimate). Area: 80,779 sq. km/31,189 sq. mi. —**South Carolinian** *n, adj*

South Caucasian *n* LANG same as **Kartvelian** —**South Caucasian** *adj*

South China Sea part of the China Sea, bounded by southeastern China, Vietnam, Malaysia, and the Philippines. Area: 2,319,000 sq. km/895,400 sq. mi.

South Dakota state in the north-central United States, bordered by North Dakota, Minnesota, Iowa, Nebraska, Wyoming, and Montana. Capital: Pierre. Population: 761,063 (2002 estimate). Area: 199,742 sq. km/77,121 sq. mi. —**South Dakotan** *n, adj*

Southdown /sówth down/ *n* a breed of small-to-medium hornless English sheep with short dense wool. Kept for: mutton. [Late 18C. After the SOUTH DOWNS]

South Downs chalk ridge extending along the southern coast of England, through Hampshire and East Sussex

southeast /sówth éest/ *n* **1.** COMPASS POINT BETWEEN SOUTH

AND EAST the direction or compass point midway between south and east **2.** also **Southeast** AREA IN SOUTHEAST the part of an area, region, or country that is situated in or towards the southeast ■ adj **1.** also **Southeast** IN SOUTHEAST situated in, facing, or lying towards the southeast of a region, place, or country **2.** BLOWING FROM SOUTHEAST describes a wind that blows from the southeast ■ adv TOWARDS SOUTHEAST in or towards the southeast

Southeast Asia region comprising the countries of Brunei, Cambodia, East Timor, Indonesia, Laos, Malaysia, Myanmar, the Philippines, Singapore, Thailand, and Vietnam —**Southeast Asian** n, adj

Southeast Asia Treaty Organization n a former alliance of countries for economic cooperation and defence against communism in Southeast Asia and the South Pacific, formed in 1954 and disbanded in 1977. Its members were the United States, the United Kingdom, France, Australia, New Zealand, the Philippines, and Thailand.

southeast by east n the direction or compass point midway between southeast and east-southeast — **southeast by east** adj, adv

southeast by south n the direction or compass point midway between southeast and south-southeast — **southeast by south** adj, adv

southeaster /sowth eéstər/ n a storm or wind that blows from the southeast

southeasterly /sowth eéstərli/ adj **1.** IN SOUTHEAST situated in or towards the southeast **2.** BLOWING FROM SOUTHEAST describes a wind that blows from the southeast ■ n (plural **-lies**) WIND FROM SOUTHEAST a wind that blows from the southeast —**southeasterly** adv

southeastern /sówth eéstərn/ adj **1.** IN SOUTHEAST situated in the southeast of a region or country **2.** FACING SOUTHEAST facing the southeast **3.** also **Southeastern** OF SOUTHEAST native to the southeast of a region or country —**southeasternmost** adj

southeastward /sowth eéstwərd/ adj towards or in the southeast ■ n a direction towards or a point in the southeast ■ adv same as **southeastwards** —**southeastwardly** adv, adj

southeastwards /sówth eéstwərdz/ adv in a south-easterly direction

Southend-on-Sea /sówth end-/ town in Essex, eastern England, on the Thames Estuary. Population: 160,257 (2001).

souther /sówthər/ n a strong wind that blows from the south

southerly /súthərli/ adj **1.** IN SOUTH situated in or towards the south **2.** BLOWING FROM SOUTH describes a wind that blows from the south ■ n (plural **-lies**) WIND FROM SOUTH a wind that blows from the south — **southerly** adv

southerly buster n Aus a strong cold southerly wind in southeastern Australia, especially in Sydney

southern /súthərn/ adj **1.** IN SOUTH situated in the south of a region or country **2.** SOUTH OF EQUATOR lying south of the equator or south of the celestial equator **3.** FACING SOUTH facing the south **4.** also **Southern** OF SOUTH native to the south of a region or country **5.** BLOWING FROM SOUTH describes a wind that blows from the south [Old English superne < Germanic]

Southern /súthərn/, E. M. (b. 1938) British biochemist. He devised various techniques for studying genetic patterns in DNA, including Southern blot. Full name **Southern, Edwin Mallor**

Southern Alps /súthərn-/ mountain range on the South Island, New Zealand. It extends from the far north to the extreme southwest of the island. Its highest peak is Mount Cook, 3,754 m/12,316 ft.

Southern blot n a technique for transferring DNA restriction fragments onto a membrane filter enabling them to be identified with a gene probe [Late 20C. After E. M. SOUTHERN]

Southern Cross n a constellation of the southern hemisphere containing four bright stars forming a cross. The smallest of the 88 constellations, it contains the Coalsack, a dark cloud of dust obscuring the stars beyond it in the Milky Way. See illustration at **constellation**

southerner /súthərnər/ n somebody who comes from the southern part of a country or region

southern hemisphere n **1.** the half of Earth that is south of the equator **2.** the southern half of an imaginary sphere that contains the universe and is divided horizontally by the celestial equator

Southernism /súthərnizəm/ n **1.** an expression or pronunciation that is characteristic of the southern United States or southern England **2.** an attitude or custom that is characteristic of the South, especially in the United States

southernmost /súthərnmōst/ adj situated farthest south

Southern Paiute, **Southern Piute** n **1.** a member of a Native North American people who lived in Utah, Nevada, Arizona, and California, and now live in Utah **2.** the Uto-Aztecan language of the Southern Paiute people —**Southern Paiute** adj

Southern Rhodesia former name for **Zimbabwe**

Southern Sotho n LANG same as **Sesotho**

southernwood /súthərn wŏod/ (plural **-woods** or same) n an ornamental bush with fragrant grey bitter-tasting leaves. Native to: Europe. Latin name: Artemisia abrotanum.

Southey /súthi, sówthi/, **Robert.** (1774–1843) British poet. He was one of the Lake Poets, along with Wordsworth and Coleridge. He became poet laureate in 1813.

> 'Now tell us all about the war / And what they fought each other for.'
> [Robert Southey, 'The Battle of Blenheim'; 1800]

South Georgia uninhabited mountainous island in the South Atlantic Ocean, southeast of the Falkland Islands. A dependency of the United Kingdom, it was first visited by Captain James Cook in 1775. Area: 3,592 sq. km/1,387 sq. mi.

South Holland province in the west-central Netherlands. Capital: The Hague. Population: 3,397,343 (2000). Area: 2,860 sq. km/1,104 sq. mi.

southing /sówthing/ n **1.** the distance a point is south of a reference latitude **2.** the distance covered as a ship sails towards the south

South Island the larger and more southerly of the two main islands of New Zealand, in the southwestern Pacific Ocean. Population: 931,566 (1996). Area: 150,460 sq. km/58,093 sq. mi.

South Korea /-kə reé ə/ country in East Asia that occupies the southern portion of the Korean Peninsula. Language: Korean. Currency: won. Capital: Seoul. Population: 48,289,037 (2003). Area: 99,268 sq. km/38,328 sq. mi. Official name **Republic of Korea** —**South Korean** n, adj

Southland /sówthlənd/ administrative region of New Zealand, occupying the southernmost tip of the South Island. Capital: Invercargill. Population: 91,002 (2001). Area: 53,132 sq. km/20,514 sq. mi.

southpaw /sówth paw/ n a left-handed person, especially a boxer who leads with the left hand (informal) [Late 19C. Originally used of left-handed baseball players, from the pitcher's orientation on the mound (since baseball diamonds are traditionally oriented to the same points of the compass)]

south pole n **1.** GEOG another spelling of **South Pole 2.** the south end of the axis of rotation of a planet or other astronomical object **3.** the point where the southern end of the Earth's axis intersects the celestial sphere

South Pole n the southern end of the Earth's axis at the latitude of 90° S

Southport /sówth pawrt/ town in Merseyside, in northwestern England. Population: 90,959 (1991).

South Riding ♦ Tipperary

Southron /súthrən/ adj Scotland relating to England (dated) [15C. Variant of SOUTHERN]

South Saskatchewan river rising in the Rocky Mountains and flowing north into Lake Winnipeg, Canada. Length: 1,390 km/865 mi.

South Sea Bubble n frenzied speculation in the South Sea Company in early 18th-century Britain. In 1720 the company collapsed, ruining many banks

and private investors. The company had taken over much of the national debt in return for sole trading rights in the area.

South Seas npl **1.** the southern part of the Pacific Ocean **2.** all the ocean waters south of the equator

South Shields /-sheēldz/ port in Tyne and Wear, northeastern England. Population: 83,704 (1991).

south-southeast n the direction or compass point midway between south and southeast ■ adj, adv in, from, facing, or towards the south-southeast — **south-southeasterly** adv

south-southwest n the direction or compass point midway between south and southwest ■ adj, adv in, from, facing, or towards the south-southwest — **south-southwesterly** adv

South Taranaki Bight gulf on the southwestern coast of the North Island, New Zealand. It extends from Otakeho in the west to Kakaramea in the east.

South Vietnam former country in Southeast Asia between 1954 and 1976. It occupied the southern part of modern-day Vietnam. —**South Vietnamese** n, adj

southward /sówthwərd/ adj towards or in the south ■ n a direction towards or a point in the south ■ adv same as **southwards** —**southwardly** adv, adj

USAGE **southward** or **southwards**? **Southward** is the only form available for the adjective (in a southward direction); it is also used for the adverb, although **southwards** is more common: The ship was moving slowly southwards/southward.

southwards /sówthwərdz/ adv in a southerly direction

USAGE See **southward**.

southwest /sówth wést/ n **1.** COMPASS POINT BETWEEN SOUTH AND WEST the direction or compass point midway between south and west **2.** also **Southwest** AREA IN SOUTHWEST the part of an area, region, or country that is situated in or towards the southwest **3.** **Southwest** SW US STATES the region of the United States that includes Texas, New Mexico, Arizona, Nevada, and California, and sometimes regarded as extending northwards to Utah and Colorado ■ adj **1.** also **Southwest** IN SOUTHWEST situated in, facing, or lying towards the southwest of a region, place, or country **2.** BLOWING FROM SOUTHWEST describes a wind that is blowing from the southwest ■ adv TOWARDS SOUTHWEST in or towards the southwest

Southwest Asia region comprising Afghanistan, the Arabian Peninsula, and countries bordering the eastern Mediterranean

southwest by south n the direction or compass point midway between southwest and south-southwest — **southwest by south** adj, adv

southwest by west n the direction or compass point midway between southwest and west-southwest — **southwest by west** adj, adv

Southwest Cape the southernmost point in New Zealand, situated at the southern tip of Stewart Island

southwester /sowth wéstər/ n a storm or wind that blows from the southwest

southwesterly /sówth wéstərli/ adj **1.** IN SOUTHWEST situated in or towards the southwest **2.** BLOWING FROM SOUTHWEST describes a wind that blows from the southwest ■ n (plural **-lies**) WIND FROM SOUTHWEST a wind that blows from the southwest —**southwesterly** adv

southwestern /sówth wéstərn/ adj **1.** IN SOUTHWEST situated in the southwest of a region or country **2.** FACING SOUTHWEST situated in or facing the southwest **3.** also **Southwestern** OF SOUTHWEST native to the southwest of a region or country —**southwesternmost** adj

southwestward /sówth wéstwərd/ adj towards or in the southwest ■ n a direction towards or a point in the southwest ■ adv same as **southwestwards** — **southwestwardly** adv, adj

southwestwards /sówth wéstwərdz/ adv in a south-westerly direction

South Yorkshire metropolitan county in northern England. In 1986 its administrative powers were divided between Barnsley, Doncaster, Rotherham,

and Sheffield councils. Area: 1,562 sq. km/603 sq. mi.

~~souvenier~~ incorrect spelling of **souvenir**

souvenir /soóvə neér/ n something bought or kept as a reminder of a place or occasion ■ vt (**-nirs, -niring, -nired**) Aus to steal something (informal) [Late 18C. < French, 'memory', use of verb < Latin subvenire 'come into mind']

souvlakia /soov laáki ə/ npl Greek kebabs consisting of pieces of marinated meat, usually lamb, skewered and grilled [Mid-20C. < modern Greek, 'small skewers' < souvla 'skewer']

sou'wester /sow wéstər/ n 1. a long waterproof coat, originally made of oilskin, now usually of rubber or plastic, worn during stormy weather at sea 2. a waterproof hat with a broad brim covering the back of the neck, originally made of oilskin, now usually of rubber or plastic. Sou'westers were originally worn by sailors and fishermen. ■ METEOROL same as **southwester** [Mid-19C. Contraction of SOUTHWESTER]

Sov. abbr Soviet

sovereign /sóvvrin/ n 1. MONARCH the ruler or permanent head of a state, especially a king or queen 2. OLD BRITISH GOLD COIN a gold coin worth one pound, used in Britain between the early 17th and the early 20th centuries ■ adj 1. INDEPENDENT self-governing and not ruled by any other state ○ a sovereign state 2. WITH COMPLETE POWER having supreme authority or power ○ The king is the sovereign ruler of the land. 3. OUTSTANDING outstanding, e.g. in its excellence or effectiveness ○ Her voice was her sovereign talent. [13C. Via Old French souverein < Vulgar Latin superanus < Latin super 'above'] —**sovereignly** adv

sovereigntist /sóvvrintist/ n Can a supporter of sovereignty for Quebec

sovereignty /sóvvrinti/ (plural **sovereignties**) n 1. TOP AUTHORITY supreme authority, especially over a state 2. INDEPENDENCE the right to self-government without interference from outside 3. INDEPENDENT STATE a politically independent state

sovereignty association n Can a proposed type of economic and political association between a sovereign Quebec and the rest of Canada

~~sovereign~~ incorrect spelling of **sovereign**

~~soverign~~ incorrect spelling of **sovereign**

soviet /sóv i ət, sóv-/ n 1. an elected government council that existed at local, regional, and national levels in the former Soviet Union. The highest was the Supreme Soviet. 2. a council in the early political organization of the Russian Revolution in 1917 [Early 20C. < Russian sovet 'council'] —**sovietism** n

Soviet adj 1. TYPICAL OF USSR relating to the former Soviet Union, or to its people, culture, or political system 2. COMMUNIST having Communist views similar to those found in the former Soviet Union ■ n SOMEBODY FROM USSR somebody who came from the former Soviet Union

Sovietologist /sóvi ə tólləjist, sóv-/ n a scholar who studies the former Soviet Union, especially its government and political history

Soviet Union /sóvi ət yoónyən/ former federation of Communist states in Eastern Europe and northern and central Asia from 1922 until 1991. Moscow was its capital. Then the largest country in the world, the Soviet Union was the Communist superpower during the Cold War. Official name **Union of Soviet Socialist Republics**

sow[1] /sō/ (**sows, sowing, sowed, sown** /sōn/ or **sowed**) v 1. vti PLANT SEED to scatter or plant seed on an area of land in order to grow crops 2. vt INTRODUCE IDEA to instill and spread an idea, especially one which is negative or divisive ○ Increased competition will only sow discord among the members of the company. 3. vt SPREAD SOMETHING THICKLY to spread something thickly with something (often passive) ○ a sky sown with stars [Old English sāwan < Indo-European] —**sowable** adj —**sower** n

SPELLCHECK See **sew**.

sow[2] /sow/ n 1. FEMALE PIG an adult female pig 2. ADULT FEMALE ANIMAL the adult female of several animals such as the bear, mink, badger, guinea pig, and hedgehog 3. METALL CHANNEL FOR MOLTEN IRON a channel

through which molten iron runs into a mould in the process of casting pig iron 4. METALL HARDENED IRON a mass of iron that has hardened in a channel or mould in the process of casting pig iron [Old English sugu < Indo-European]

Sow. abbr S Asia Sowbhagyawati

sowback /sówbak/ n a long ridge of earth left by a glacier [Late 19C. Because supposed to resemble a pig's back]

sowbelly /sów beli/ n US fatty salt pork

Sowbhagyawati /sə bági ə wótti/ n S Asia a title used before the name of a married woman whose husband is still alive, roughly equivalent to the English term 'Mrs' [< Sanskrit]

sowbread /sów bred/ (plural **-breads** or same) n a cyclamen, especially one with a single nodding flower. Native to: southern Europe. Genus: Cyclamen. [Mid-16C. Because supposedly eaten by pigs]

sow bug /sów-/ n N Am same as **woodlouse** [Because it resembles a pig in shape]

Soweto /sə wáytō, sə wéttō/ township in southern Johannesburg, Gauteng Province, South Africa. Population: 596,632 (1991). [mid-20C Acronym for 'South Western Townships']

sown past participle of **sow**[1]

sow thistle /sów-/ n a prickly-leaved plant. Flowers: yellow. Native to: Europe, Asia. Genus: Sonchus. [Origin ?]

soya /sóy ə/, **soy** /soy/ n 1. PLANTS the soya bean plant 2. FOOD same as **soy sauce** ■ adj made or derived from soya beans [Late 17C. Via Dutch, Malay, and Japanese < Chinese jiàngyóu 'soya bean oil']

soya bean n 1. the oil- and protein-rich seed of the soya bean plant. Use: soy sauce, soya milk, tofu, textured vegetable protein. 2. a plant cultivated around the world for its nutritious seeds, for soil improvement, and to provide grazing for animals. Native to: southeastern Asia. Latin name: Glycine max.

soya milk n a milk substitute made from soya beans, often with vitamins and sugar added

soybean /sóy been/ n US PLANTS, FOOD same as **soya bean**

Soyinka /so yíngkə/, **Wole** (b. 1934) Nigerian writer and political activist. His plays, poems, and novels examine the relationship between traditional and modern African cultures, and include Poems from Prison (1969). He won a Nobel Prize in literature (1986). Full name **Soyinka, Akinwande Oluwole**

> 'There is only one home to the life of a tortoise; there is only one shell to the soul of man: there is only one world to the spirit of our race. If that world leaves its course and smashes on the boulder of the great void, whose world will give us shelter?'
> [Wole Soyinka, Death and the King's Horseman; 1975]

soy sauce n a dark salty liquid made by fermenting soya beans in brine, used to flavour foods

sozzled /sózz'ld/ adj extremely intoxicated (informal) [Late 19C. < dialect sozzle 'splash, mess', probably an imitation of the sound]

sp abbr without children [Latin sine prole]

SP abbr 1. HORSERACING starting price 2. NAVY submarine patrol

sp. abbr 1. special 2. BIOL species 3. specific 4. MED, BIOL specimen 5. spelling

Sp. abbr 1. Spain 2. Spaniard 3. Spanish

spa /spaa/ n 1. a resort with mineral springs (often used in placenames) 2. a bath with a device for aerating or swirling water [Early 17C. After Spa, resort town in Belgium, famous for mineral springs]

SpA abbr COMM limited company (used after the name of an Italian company) [Italian Società per Azioni]

space /spayss/ n 1. PERIOD OF TIME a period or interval of time ○ In the space of two hours the situation was resolved. 2. ENOUGH ROOM room to fit or accommodate something or somebody ○ There isn't space for the table. 3. AREA SET APART an area set apart or available

for use ○ floor space 4. REGION BEYOND EARTH'S ATMOSPHERE the region that lies beyond the Earth's atmosphere, and all that it contains ○ space travel 5. REGION BETWEEN ALL ASTRONOMICAL OBJECTS the region, usually of negligible density, between all astronomical objects in the universe 6. THREE-DIMENSIONAL EXPANSE WHERE MATTER EXISTS the unbounded three-dimensional expanse in which all matter exists 7. PRINTING BLANK AREA BETWEEN TYPE a blank area between characters, words, or lines of type, or an interval the width of a single character 8. MUSIC INTERVAL BETWEEN LINES OF MUSICAL STAFF an interval between the lines of the musical staff 9. COMMUNICATION TIME OR AREA AVAILABLE FOR ADVERTISING broadcast time or an area in a publication available for specific use, e.g. by advertisers 10. MATHS SET OF POINTS GOVERNED BY AXIOMS in mathematics, a collection of points that have geometric properties in that they obey set rules (**axioms**), e.g. a Euclidean space that is governed by Euclidean geometry. Each non-Euclidean geometry, having its own axioms, has its own non-Euclidean space containing a collection of points governed by those axioms. 11. PRINTING PIECE OF TYPE TO CREATE BLANK a piece of type used to create a blank interval in printing 12. FREEDOM TO ASSERT IDENTITY the freedom or opportunity to assert a personal identity or fulfil personal needs (informal) ○ I need my own personal space. 13. COMMUNICATION INTERVAL IN TELEGRAPHIC TRANSMISSION an interval during the transmission of a telegraphic message when the key is not in contact ■ vt (**spaces, spacing, spaced**) SET THINGS APART to set things some distance apart or arrange them with gaps between [13C Via French espace < Latin spatium 'space, distance']

space out v 1. vt same as **space** 2. vti to become distracted, forgetful, or inattentive, or cause somebody to become distracted, forgetful or inattentive (slang)

space age, **Space Age** n the era marked by the exploration of space, often considered as beginning in 1957 when the Soviet Union launched Sputnik — **space-age** adj

spaceband /spáyss band/ n a device used in printing to provide variable but even spacing between words in a justified line

space bar n a horizontal bar at the bottom of a keyboard or typewriter that is pressed to introduce a space

space biology n BIOL same as **exobiology**

space blanket n a plastic wrapping with aluminium foil coating that is used to restore body heat in people affected by exposure or exhaustion

spacebridge /spáyss brij/ n a way of communicating internationally by television, using transmissions from orbiting satellites

space cadet n somebody whose behaviour is regarded as mildly strange, especially somebody who seems disorientated or out of touch with a situation (slang)

space capsule n a vehicle or cabin designed to support life and used for transporting human beings or animals in outer space or at very high altitudes within the Earth's atmosphere

space charge n the net electric charge distributed in a given volume of space

spacecraft /spáyss kraaft/ (plural same or **-crafts**) n a vehicle or device designed for travel or use in space

spaced-out /spáyst-/, **spaced** /spayst/ adj inattentive, dazed, confused, or lightheaded from or as if from drug use (slang)

spacefaring /spáyss fairing/ n the use of spacecraft for the exploration of outer space —**spacefaring** adj

spaceflight /spáyss flīt/ n flight beyond the Earth's atmosphere, or an instance of this

space heater n a small portable appliance used to heat a small area

spacelab /spáyss lab/ n a laboratory in space used to carry out scientific experiments

space lattice n CRYSTALS same as **lattice** n (sense 4)

spaceless /spáyssləss/ adj (literary) 1. with no limits 2. not occupying any space

spaceman /spáyss man/ (plural **-men** /-men/) n 1. a man who is an astronaut 2. in science fiction, a traveller to Earth from outer space

space medicine *n* the branch of medicine dealing with the effects of space flight on the human body

Space Needle

Space Needle *n* a tall tower in central Seattle, Washington State, with a revolving restaurant and observation deck near the top. It was built for the 1962 World's Fair.

space opera *n US* a science fiction drama involving space travel and, often, extraterrestrial beings (*informal*)

spaceport /spáyss pawrt/ *n* an installation for launching, testing, landing, and maintaining spacecraft

space probe *n* a satellite or other spacecraft that is designed to explore the solar system and transmit data back to Earth

spacer /spáyssər/ *n* something inserted between two other things to keep them apart, e.g. a pierced bar threaded on a multistring necklace to prevent the strands from tangling

spaceship /spáyss ship/ *n* a vehicle designed to transport people or materials through outer space

space shuttle *n* a reusable spacecraft designed to transport people and cargo between Earth and space, with two solid rocket boosters and an external fuel tank that are jettisoned after takeoff

space sickness *n* motion sickness experienced as a result of space flight

space station *n* a spacecraft or satellite designed to be occupied by a crew for extended periods of time and used as a base for the exploration, observation, and research of space

spacesuit: astronaut Buzz Aldrin on the Moon

spacesuit /spáyss soot, -syoot/ *n* a sealed pressurized suit designed to support the wearer's life in space

space-time, **space-time continuum** *n* a four-dimensional system consisting of three spatial coordinates and one for time, in which it is possible to locate events

space-time foam *n PHYS* same as **quantum foam**

spacewalk /spáyss wawk/ *n* an excursion by an astronaut or cosmonaut outside the spacecraft ◾ *vi* (**-walks, -walking, -walked**) to go out of a spacecraft in order to perform a task or experiment

spacewoman /spáyss wŏomən/ (*plural* **-women** /-wimin/) *n* **1.** a female astronaut **2.** in science fiction, a female traveller to Earth from outer space

space writer *n* a writer paid according to the area of print taken up by what is written

spacey /spáyssi/ *adj* another spelling of **spacy** (*slang*)

Spacey /spáyssi/, **Kevin** (*b.* 1964) US actor. He won an

Academy Award for best actor for *American Beauty* (1999) and for best supporting actor for *The Usual Suspects* (1995).

spacial *adj* another spelling of **spatial**

spacing /spáyssing/ *n* **1.** the space between several things, e.g. between words or lines in type, or the way this space is arranged **2.** the act of arranging things in spaces

spacious /spáyshəss/ *adj* containing ample space — **spaciously** *adv* —**spaciousness** *n*

spacy /spáyssi/ (**-ier, -iest**), **spacey** *adj* same as **spaced-out** (*slang*)

spade[1] /spayd/ *n* a digging tool with a wide shallow blade flattened where it meets the shaft so it can be pushed into the ground with the foot ◾ *vti* (**spades, spading, spaded**) to dig, cut, or remove something using a spade [Old English *spadu* < Indo-European] ◊ **call a spade a spade** to say plainly and bluntly what you mean

spade[2] /spayd/ *n* **1.** PLAYING CARD a playing card of the suit of spades. ◊ **spades 2.** BLACK SYMBOL ON PLAYING CARD a black symbol shaped like a stylized spade on a playing card. ◊ **spades 3.** TABOO TERM a highly offensive term for somebody, especially a man, who is of African descent (*taboo*) [Late 16C. < Italian, plural of *spada* 'sword' (the sign used on Italian cards) < Latin *spatha* 'broadsword' (see SPATULA)] ◊ **in spades** to a very great degree (*informal*)

spadefish /spáyd fish/ (*plural same* or **-fishes**) *n* a deep-bodied bony fish. Native to: Atlantic coastal waters. Family: Ephippidae. [Early 18C. < its shape]

spade guinea *n* a British gold coin worth 21 shillings that was issued between 1787 and 1799 [< the spade-shaped shield on its reverse]

spades /spaydz/ *n* one of the four suits used in cards, with a black figure shaped like a stylized spade as its symbol (*takes a singular or plural verb*)

spadework /spáyd wurk/ *n* **1.** preliminary work that is often hard drudgery **2.** work done using a spade

spadiceous /spay díshəss/ *adj* bearing or resembling a spadix [Mid-17C. < Latin *spadic-*, stem of *spadix* (see SPADIX)]

spadices BOT plural of **spadix**

spadille /spə díl/ *n* in some card games, e.g. ombre, the highest trump card [Late 17C. Via French < Spanish *espadilla* 'small sword' < Latin *spatha* (see SPADE[2])]

spadix /spáydiks/ (*plural* **-dices** /-di seez/) *n* a fleshy or succulent plant spike that bears tiny flowers and is usually enclosed in a leafy sheath (**spathe**) [Mid-18C. Via Latin 'palm branch torn off with its fruit' < Greek < *span* 'to pull']

spaetzle /shpéts'l, shpétslə/ (*plural same* or **-les**), **spätzle** *n* a hot dish from southern Germany and Alsace consisting of very small noodles or dumplings formed by pressing batter through a colander into boiling water. It is often served with gravy or sauce. [< German dialect, literally 'little sparrows']

spaewife /spáy wīf/ (*plural* **-wives** /-wīvz/) *n Scotland* a female fortune-teller [Late 18C. < *spae* 'prophesy, prophecy' < Old Norse *spá* + WIFE 'woman']

~~spagetti~~ incorrect spelling of **spaghetti**

spaghetti /spə gétti/ *n* **1.** pasta in the shape of long thin strings **2.** a dish of long thin strings of boiled pasta, usually served with a sauce **3.** *Aus, US* ELEC same as **sleeving** [Mid-19C. < Italian (plural), diminutive of *spago* 'string']

spaghetti junction *n* a motorway interchange with complex systems of intersections, flyovers, and underpasses

spaghettini /spággə teeni/ *n* pasta that is thinner than spaghetti but thicker than vermicelli [Mid-20C. < Italian, diminutive of *spaghetti* (see SPAGHETTI)]

spaghetti squash *n* an oval winter squash with a yellow rind whose cooked flesh can be scraped out in long strands that resemble spaghetti

spaghetti Western *n* a low-budget Western made in Europe, usually Spain, by an Italian film company, characterized by extreme and melodramatic violence

spahi /spaá hee, -ee/, **spahee** *n* **1.** in former times, a cavalryman in the Turkish army **2.** in former times,

a member of a corps of Algerian cavalrymen in French service [Mid-16C. Via French and Turkish < Persian *sipāhī* 'cavalryman' < *sipāh* 'army']

Spain

Spain /spayn/ country in southwestern Europe on the Iberian Peninsula, east of Portugal. Language: Spanish. Currency: euro. Capital: Madrid. Population: 40,217,413 (2003). Area: 505,990 sq. km/195,364 sq. mi. Official name **Kingdom of Spain**

spake past tense of **speak** (*archaic*)

Spalding /spáwl ding/ market town in Lincolnshire, eastern England. Population: 18,731 (1991).

spall /spawl/ *n* a small fragment, splinter, or chip of stone or ore ◾ *vti* (**spalls, spalling, spalled**) to break up into small chips, flakes, or splinters, or to cause stone, ore, or masonry to break off in flakes [15C. Origin ?]

spallation /spaw láysh'n/ *n* **1.** a nuclear reaction in which several particles are emitted from the nucleus of an atom after bombardment with high-energy particles or radiation **2.** the removal of the surface layers of a rock by meteorite impact

spalpeen /spál peen/ *n Ireland* **1.** a mischievous and cunning person **2.** an impoverished farm labourer [Late 18C. < Irish *spailpín*]

spam /spam/ *n* ELECTRONIC JUNK MAIL an unsolicited, often commercial, message transmitted through the Internet as a mass mailing to a large number of recipients ◾ *vti* (**spams, spamming, spammed**) **1.** SEND UNWANTED E-MAIL to send an unsolicited e-mail message, often an advertisement, to many people **2.** POST UNWANTED ELECTRONIC MESSAGES to post a message many times to a newsgroup, or an inappropriate message to multiple newsgroups [Late 20C. Probably from a sketch in the television comedy series *Monty Python's Flying Circus* in which all items on a menu contained Spam™] —**spammer** *n*

Spam /spam/ *tdmk* a trademark for tinned chopped meat, mainly pork, that is pressed into a loaf

spam killer *n* a piece of software that automatically identifies and deals with spam in incoming e-mail

spamming /spámming/ *n* the sending of unsolicited electronic messages through the Internet to a large number of recipients

span[1] /span/ *n* **1.** DISTANCE BETWEEN LIMITS the distance or expanse between two extremes or limits **2.** DISTANCE BETWEEN BRIDGE SUPPORTS the extent or space between abutments or supports, e.g. on a bridge or arch, or a portion of the structure that is supported in this way **3.** same as **wingspan 4.** PERIOD FOR MAINTENANCE OF COGNITIVE FUNCTION the period of time during which a mental function or act can be maintained ○ *a short attention span* **5.** PERIOD OF TIME a period of time, especially the lifetime of a person **6.** OLD MEASUREMENT an old measurement based on the distance from the end of the thumb to the end of the little finger of a spread hand, approximately 23 cm/9 in ◾ *vt* (**spans, spanning, spanned**) **1.** EXTEND OVER OR ACROSS SOMETHING to reach or extend over or across something **2.** MEASURE SOMETHING WITH THE HAND to measure something by or as if by the hand with fingers and thumb fully extended **3.** ENCIRCLE SOMETHING WITH THE HANDS to encircle or cover something with the hands, especially in order to estimate its size [Old English *spann* < Germanic]

span[2] /span/ *n* a pair of horses or other animals harnessed and driven together [Mid-18C. < Dutch < *spannen*, 'harness']

span[3] /span/ past tense of **spin** (*archaic*)

Span. *abbr* Spanish

spanakopita /spánnə kóppitə, -kə peétə/ *n* a traditional Greek dish of spinach and feta cheese baked in filo pastry [Mid-20C. < modern Greek *spanakopēta* 'spinach pie']

Spandau /spán dow/ district of Berlin, Germany, the site of a prison where Nazi war criminals were confined after World War II. Population: 192,895 (1986).

spandex /spán deks/ *n* a synthetic stretch fabric or fibre made from polyurethane [Mid-20C. < EXPAND]

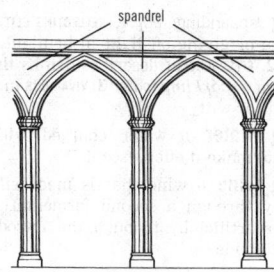

spandrel

spandrel /spándrəl/, **spandril** *n* 1. the triangular space between the right or left exterior curve of an arch and the framework of another arch 2. the area between two arches and a horizontal cornice above them [15C. Origin ?]

spang /spang/ *adv US* completely, squarely, or exactly on target or in the middle of something (*informal*) [Mid-19C. Origin ?]

spangle /spáng g'l/ *n* 1. SMALL SHINY DECORATION a small shiny piece of metal or plastic used for decoration on clothing 2. SMALL SPARKLING OBJECT a small sparkling spot or object ■ *v* (-gles, -gling, -gled) 1. *vt* SPRINKLE SOMETHING WITH SPANGLES to sprinkle or adorn something with spangles 2. *vi* GLITTER WITH SPANGLES to sparkle or glitter as if adorned with spangles [15C. < obsolete *spang* 'glittering ornament' < Dutch *spange* 'clasp'] —**spangly** *adj*

spangled drongo /spáng g'ld-/ *n* a bird that has glossy black feathers with pale blue-green patches. Native to: tropical Southeast Asia and Australia. Latin name: *Dicrurus bracteatus.*

Spanglish /spáng glish/ *n* a variety of Spanish characterized by many borrowings from English [Mid-20C. Blend of SPANISH + ENGLISH] —**Spanglish** *adj*

Spaniard /spánnyərd/ *n* 1. somebody who comes from Spain 2. a perennial rock plant with sharp leaves. Native to: New Zealand. [14C. < Old French *Espaignart* < Latin *Hispania* 'Spain']

spaniel

spaniel /spánnyəl/ *n* a small or medium-sized dog characterized by a long wavy silky coat, usually short legs, and large drooping ears [14C. < Old French *espaigneul* 'Spanish' < Latin *Hispania* 'Spain']

Spanish /spánnish/ *n* ROMANCE LANGUAGE a Romance language that is the official language of Spain and of many Central and South American countries, including Argentina, Bolivia, Chile, Colombia, Costa Rica, Cuba, Mexico, and Peru. It is also spoken widely elsewhere, including in the southwestern United States. Native speakers: 358 million. Other speakers: 59 million. ■ *npl* PEOPLE OF SPAIN the people of Spain ■ *adj* 1. RELATING TO SPAIN relating to

Spain, or its people or culture 2. OF SPANISH relating to Spanish [13C. < SPAIN]

Spanish America /spánnish-/ part of America that was colonized by the Spanish from the 16th century and where Spanish is still widely spoken. It includes much of Central and South America and some Caribbean islands. —**Spanish-American** *n, adj*

Spanish bayonet *n* a plant with stiff pointed leaves and a long woody stem. Flowers: white. Native to: America. Genus: *Yucca.* [< its sword-shaped leaves]

Spanish cedar *n* 1. a tree with reddish fragrant wood. Native to: tropical America. Genus: *Cedrela.* 2. the wood of a Spanish cedar. Use: making cigar boxes.

Spanish chestnut *n* same as **chestnut** (sense 2)

Spanish customs *npl* same as **Spanish practices** (*dated informal*)

Spanish fly *n* 1. a green European blister beetle, source of the stimulant and irritant cantharides. Latin name: *Lytta vesicatoria* or *Cantharis vesicatoria.* 2. a toxic preparation made from the crushed dried bodies of the Spanish fly. Use: formerly, as an aphrodisiac and to treat skin blisters.

Spanish guitar *n* the classical six-stringed form of guitar

Spanish Inquisition *n* an ecclesiastical tribunal of the Roman Catholic Church established in Spain in 1542, and finally suppressed in 1834, under which large numbers of people deemed to be heretics were tortured and executed

Spanish mackerel *n* 1. a large game fish of the tuna family. Native to: Atlantic coast of North and South America. Latin name: *Scomberomorus maculatus.* 2. a mackerel. Native to: Atlantic coastal waters of Europe and North America. Latin name: *Scomberomorus colias.*

Spanish Main /-máyn/ in the 16th and 17th centuries, a region of Spanish America from the isthmus of Panama to the mouth of the Orinoco river ■ the part of the Caribbean Sea crossed by Spanish ships in colonial times

Spanish moss *n* a plant of the pineapple family that grows on trees in long drooping matted clusters of greyish-green filaments. Native to: southeastern

United States, South America. Latin name: *Tillandsia usneoides.*

Spanish omelette *n* an omelette filled with a selection of vegetables, usually including tomatoes and cooked potato [Because it contains ingredients typical of Spanish cuisine]

Spanish onion *n* an onion with yellow skin and a mild flavour. Latin name: *Allium fistulosum.*

Spanish practices *npl* irregular practices that are in the interests of workers and are usually imposed on employers by trade unions, e.g. overstaffing and excessive overtime (*dated informal*)

Spanish rice *n* rice cooked with onion, green pepper, tomato, and seasonings

Spanish Sahara former name for **Western Sahara**

Spanish Town second largest city in Jamaica, in the southeast of the island on the Cobre River, near Kingston. It was the capital of the island from 1535 until the 1870s. Population: 92,383 (1991).

spank[1] /spangk/ *vt* (**spanks, spanking, spanked**) to strike somebody, usually on the buttocks with the open hand in punishment ■ *n* an open-handed slap on the buttocks [Early 18C. Probably an imitation of the sound]

spank[2] /spangk/ *vi* to move briskly, spiritedly, or smartly [Early 19C. Probably back-formation < SPANKING[2]]

spanker /spángkər/ *n* 1. the fore-and-aft sail on the mast nearest the stern of a square-rigged ship 2. somebody who spanks somebody else in punishment [Mid-17C. Origin ?]

spanking[1] /spángking/ *n* a beating with the flat of the hand on somebody's buttocks, given as punishment [Mid-19C. < SPANK[1]]

spanking[2] /spángking/ *adj* 1. EXCEPTIONAL with an unusual quality that makes something exceptional or remarkable of its kind 2. BRISK lively, or moving briskly, especially a breeze ■ *adv* VERY extremely and impressively ○ *a spanking new car* [Mid-17C. Origin ?]

spanner /spánnər/ *n* a tool with fixed or movable jaws, used to seize, turn, or twist objects such as nuts and bolts. N Am term **wrench** [Mid-17C. < German < *spannen* 'harness horses or oxen to a vehicle' < Germanic]
◇ **put** *or* **throw a spanner in the works** to ruin or impede a plan or system

spanspek /spán spek/ *n S Africa* a cantaloupe or musk melon with a ridged scaly rind and aromatic orange flesh. Latin name: *Cucumis melo cantalupensis*. Same as **cantaloupe** [Late 19C. < Afrikaans, 'Spanish bacon']

spanworm /spán wurm/ *n US* INSECTS same as **measuring worm**

spar[1] /spaar/ *n* **1.** a thick strong pole used to support rigging on a ship **2.** any of the principal lateral members supporting the wing of an aeroplane [14C. Probably < Old French *esparre* or Old Norse *sperra*]

spar[2] /spaar/ *vi* (**spars, sparring, sparred**) **1.** ENGAGE IN BOXING to box, especially to fake a blow in order to draw an opponent or create an opening **2.** USE LIGHT BLOWS to engage in a practice or exhibition bout of boxing or martial arts using light blows **3.** FIGHT USING FEET AND SPURS to fight using the feet and spurs to strike an opponent (*refers to gamecocks*) **4.** ARGUE to engage in argument ■ *n* **1.** PRACTICE BOUT a practice or exhibition bout of boxing **2.** PARTICULAR MOTION IN BOXING a motion in boxing for attack or defence **3.** CLOSE FRIEND a close friend of either sex (*used in Black English*) [Late 16C. Origin ?]

spar[3] /spaar/ *n* any light-coloured lustrous mineral that cleaves easily [Late 16C. < Low German] —**sparry** *adj*

sparable /spárrəb'l/ *n* a small headless nail used to attach the soles of shoes [Early 17C. Alteration of *sparrow-bill*]

spare /spair/ *v* (**spares, sparing, spared**) **1.** *vt* REFRAIN FROM HARMING SOMEBODY to refrain from killing, punishing, or harming somebody or something **2.** *vt* TREAT SOMEBODY LENIENTLY to treat somebody leniently or refrain from treating somebody harshly **3.** *vt* SAVE SOMEBODY FROM DOING SOMETHING to save or relieve somebody from the effort or trouble of doing something ○ *I went myself to spare her the trouble.* **4.** *vt* AFFORD SOMETHING to give up or be able to contribute something from one's resources, especially without inconvenience ○ *I can't spare any time to exercise.* **5.** *vt* WITHHOLD SOMETHING to withhold or avoid something ○ *They spared no expense on the wedding.* **6.** *vt* USE SOMETHING FRUGALLY to use or dispense something frugally **7.** *vt* REFRAIN FROM USING SOMETHING to refrain from using something **8.** *vi* BE FRUGAL to be frugal and thrifty (*archaic*) ■ *adj* **1.** KEPT IN RESERVE kept in reserve for emergency use **2.** SUPERFLUOUS more than what is needed **3.** LEAN with a muscular physique and no excess fat **4.** SCANTY lacking in quantity or extent ○ *a spare diet* **5.** PLAIN lacking embellishment or fullness ○ *spare prose* ■ *n* **1.** SOMETHING EXTRA something extra that is kept in reserve **2.** AUTOMOT same as **spare wheel, spare tyre** **3.** KNOCKING DOWN PINS IN TWO TRIES in tenpin bowling, an instance of knocking down all the pins in two successive rolls **4.** BOWLING SCORE a score made in tenpin bowling by using two successive rolls to knock down all ten pins **5.** UNATTACHED MEMBERS OF OPPOSITE SEX unattached members of the opposite sex who are potential sexual partners (*slang*) [Old English *sparian* < Germanic] —**sparely** *adv* —**spareness** *n* —**sparer** *n* ◇ **go spare** become upset, especially to lose your temper (*informal*) ◇ **to spare** more than what is needed

spare part *n* a replacement for a faulty component in a vehicle or machine (*hyphenated*)

spare-part surgery *n* surgery in which nonfunctioning organs in the body are replaced by transplanted or artificial organs

sparerib /spáir ríb/ *n* a rib of pork from which most of the meat has been removed, usually cooked in a barbecue or Chinese sauce [Late 16C. By folk etymology < Low German *ribbesper* 'pickled pork ribs roasted on a spit', by association with SPARE]

spare time *n* time not spent working or attending to other day-to-day responsibilities

spare tyre *n* **1.** an extra tyre mounted somewhere on a motor vehicle and carried in case of a flat tyre **2.** a roll of extra flesh around somebody's waist (*humorous*)

spare wheel *n* **1.** AUTOMOT same as **spare tyre** (sense 1) **2.** somebody or something whose presence is superfluous or unwanted

sparge /spaarj/ *v* (**sparges, sparging, sparged**) *vt* **1.** to scatter, spray, or sprinkle something **2.** to introduce

air or gas into a liquid to agitate it [Late 16C. Directly or via French < Latin *spargere* 'scatter'] —**sparger** *n*

sparid /spárrid/ (*plural same* or **-ids**), **sparoid** /spárroyd/ (*plural same* or **-oids**) *n* a sea fish with a compressed body, large head, and sharp teeth. Porgies and breams are sparids. Native to: warm regions. Family: Sparidae. [Late 20C. < modern Latin *Sparidae* < Greek *sparos* 'sea bream']

sparing /spáiring/ *adj* **1.** FRUGAL showing careful restraint in the use of resources **2.** SCANTY limited or restricted in quantity **3.** MERCIFUL inclined to be lenient or merciful —**sparingly** *adv*

spark[1] /spaark/ *n* **1.** FIERY PARTICLE a small piece of a burning substance thrown off in combustion or produced in friction **2.** ELECTRIC DISCHARGE a quick bright discharge of electricity between two conductors **3.** SOMETHING THAT ACTIVATES a factor or device that sets off or acts as a stimulant, inspiration, or catalyst ○ *a spark of interest* **4.** SOMETHING CAPABLE OF DEVELOPMENT a latent trace of something capable of development ○ *had a real spark of genius* ■ *v* (**sparks, sparking, sparked**) **1.** *vt* STIMULATE OR INCITE SOMETHING to stimulate or initiate a burst of activity ○ *The issue sparked an emotional debate.* **2.** *vi* RESPOND ENTHUSIASTICALLY to respond with lively enthusiasm **3.** *vi* EMIT SPARKS to throw off sparks **4.** *vi* PRODUCE SPARKS to have an electric ignition working properly so that it generates sparks (*refers to internal combustion engines*) [Old English *spærca*. Origin ?]

spark off *vt* to activate or act as a catalyst for something

spark[2] /spaark/ (*archaic*) *n* a vain young man, especially one concerned with fashion and appearance ■ *vti* (**sparks, sparking, sparked**) to try to persuade somebody to become romantically or sexually involved [Early 16C. Probably < SPARK[1]]

Dame Muriel Spark

Spark /spaark/, **Dame Muriel** (*b.* 1918) British writer. She is best known for her novels, including *Memento Mori* (1959) and *The Prime of Miss Jean Brodie* (1961). Full name **Spark, Dame Muriel Sarah**. See Cultural note at **prime**[1]

'To me education is a leading out of what is already there in the pupil's soul.'
[Dame Muriel Spark, *The Prime of Miss Jean Brodie*; 1961]

spark chamber *n* a device for tracking the path of a subatomic particle, consisting of charged plates that cause the particle to ionize the gas present and create sparks

spark coil *n* the induction coil that produces the spark discharge to start combustion in an internal combustion engine

spark erosion *n* a process for shaping metal, similar to conventional machining but using an electric arc from a moving electrode to remove metal

spark gap *n* a space between two electrodes across which a discharge of electricity occurs, e.g. the gap between electrodes of a spark plug in an internal combustion engine

sparking plug /spáarking-/ *n* AUTOMOT same as **spark plug**

sparkle /spáark'l/ *v* (**-kles, -kling, -kled**) **1.** *vti* GLITTER to give off or reflect light in brilliant glittering flashes, or make something do this **2.** *vi* BE LIVELY OR BRILLIANT to perform brilliantly or be vivacious, witty, or enthusiastic **3.** *vi* EMIT BUBBLES to effervesce (*refers to wine and other drinks*) **4.** *vi* THROW OFF SPARKS to throw

off sparks ■ *n* **1.** SHINING PARTICLE a little spark or shining particle **2.** ANIMATION lively or brilliant animation and vivacity **3.** EFFERVESCENCE effervescence in wine and other drinks [12C. < SPARK[1]] —**sparkly** *adj*

sparkler /spáarklər/ *n* **1.** HAND-HELD FIREWORK a handheld firework that throws off sparks as it burns **2.** SPARKLING GEM a diamond or other sparkling gem (*informal*) **3.** same as **sparkling wine** (*informal*) **4.** SOMETHING THAT SPARKLES something that reflects or gives off brilliant flashes of light or throws off sparks

sparkling /spáarkling/ *adj* **1.** REFLECTING GLITTERING LIGHT reflecting or giving off light in brilliant glittering flashes **2.** EFFERVESCENT describes drinks that are effervescent ○ *sparkling water* **3.** VIVACIOUS intelligently vivacious or witty

sparkling water *n* water charged with carbon dioxide to make it effervescent

sparkling wine *n* wine that is made effervescent naturally through a second fermentation in the bottle or artificially through the introduction of carbon dioxide

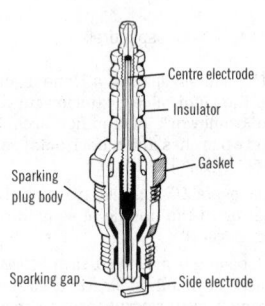

spark plug

spark plug *n* a device that ignites the fuel mixture in the cylinder in an internal-combustion engine by emitting a spark

sparks /spaarks/ *n* (*informal; takes a singular verb*) **1.** OCCUPATIONS same as **electrician** **2.** the radio operator on a ship or aircraft

spark transmitter *n* an obsolete form of radio transmitter that used power generated from the discharge of a condenser across a spark gap

sparky /spáarki/ (**-ier, -iest**) *adj* very lively and enthusiastic

sparling /spáarling/ (*plural* **-lings** or *same*) *n* **1.** a common European smelt. Native to: North Atlantic. Latin name: *Osmerus eperlanus.* **2.** an immature herring [14C. < Old French *esperlinge* < Germanic]

sparoid /spárr oyd/ *n* FISH same as **sparid**

sparring partner /spáaring-/ *n* **1.** somebody who spars with a boxer to help in training **2.** somebody who regularly debates or disputes with somebody else

sparrow /spárrō/ *n* **1.** a small dull-coloured songbird with a short sturdy beak for cracking seeds. Family: Passeridae. **2.** *N Am* a bird of the bunting family that resembles a sparrow. Family: Emberizidae. [Old English *spearwa* < Germanic]

sparrowgrass /spárrō graass/ *n US regional* FOOD same as **asparagus** (sense 1) [Mid-17C. Alteration]

sparrowhawk /spárr ō hawk/ *n* **1.** a small hawk that preys on smaller birds and has short broad wings, a long tail, and a dark grey to blackish back. Native to: Europe, Asia. Latin name: *Accipiter nisus.* **2.** *N Am* a kestrel. Native to: North America. Latin name: *Falco sparverius.*

sparse /spaarss/ (**sparser, sparsest**) *adj* thinly spread, or occurring with many spaces in between [Early 18C. < Latin *sparsus*, past participle of *spargere* 'scatter'] —**sparsely** *adv* —**sparseness** *n* —**sparsity** *n*

Sparta /spáarta/ town in the southern Peloponnese, Greece, the site of an ancient city-state that was an important military power between the 6th and 4th centuries BC. Population: 14,084 (1991).

Spartacist /spáartəssist/ *n* a member of a German revolutionary group that was organized in 1918 and promoted an extreme socialistic agenda [Early 20C.

< German *Spartakist* < *Spartakus* 'Spartacus', pen name of Karl Liebknecht, German socialist leader]

Spartacus /spaártəkəss/ (*d.* 71 BC) Roman slave and rebel leader. He led an uprising that defeated several Roman armies before he was killed in battle against the Roman commander Crassus.

spartan /spaárt'n/ *n* a strong and self-disciplined person ■ *adj* marked by stern discipline, frugality, simplicity, or courage [Mid-17C. < SPARTAN] —**spartanly** *adv*

Spartan /spaárt'n/ *n* somebody who came from ancient Sparta ■ *adj* relating to the ancient Greek city-state of Sparta, or its people or culture [15C. < SPARTA] —**Spartanism** *n*

sparteine /spaárti īn, -in/ *n* a bitter poisonous alkaloid. Source: common broom plant. Use: medicines. [Mid-19C. < modern Latin *Spartium*, genus name of broom < Greek *sparton* 'esparto']

spasm /spázzəm/ *n* **1.** an involuntary sudden muscle contraction **2.** a sudden brief emotion, sensation, or action ○ *a spasm of pain* [14C. Via French and Latin < Greek *spasmos* < *span* 'to pull']

spasmodic /spaz móddik/ *adj* **1.** AFFECTED BY SPASMS affected or characterized by spasms **2.** RESEMBLING SPASM resembling a spasm in sudden brief intensity **3.** INTERMITTENT occurring at uneven intervals **4.** EXCITABLE prone to sudden outbursts of emotion [Late 17C. < modern Latin *spasmodicus* < Greek *spasmōdēs* < *spasmos* (see SPASM)] —**spasmodically** *adv*

spasmolytic /spázmə líttik/ *n, adj* MED, PHARM same as **antispasmodic**

spastic /spástik/ *adj* **1.** AFFECTED BY SPASMS relating to or affected by spasms **2.** OFFENSIVE TERM an offensive term meaning lacking physical coordination or the ability to perform competently (*dated*) ■ *n* **1.** OFFENSIVE TERM an offensive term for somebody with a disability that affects physical coordination (*dated*) **2.** OFFENSIVE TERM an offensive term that deliberately insults somebody's coordination or competence (*slang insult*) [Mid-18C. Via Latin < Greek *spastikos* < *span* 'to pull'] —**spastically** *adv* —**spasticity** /spas tíssəti/ *n*

spastic colon *n* MED same as **irritable bowel syndrome**

spat[1] /spat/ *n* a brief quarrel usually concerning petty matters ■ *vi* (**spats, spatting, spatted**) to quarrel briefly over a petty matter [Early 19C. Origin ?]

spat[2] /spat/ past participle, past tense of **spit**[1]

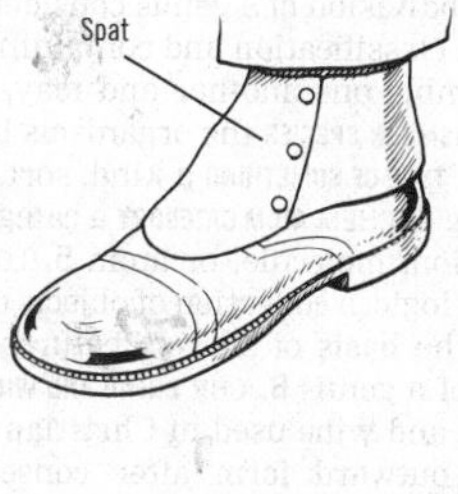

spat

spat[3] /spat/ *n* a short cloth or leather gaiter, popular in the late 19th and early 20th centuries, worn over a shoe to cover the instep and the ankle [Early 19C. Shortening of SPATTERDASH]

spat[4] /spat/ *n* an immature bivalve mollusc, e.g. an oyster [Mid-17C. < Anglo-Norman]

spatchcock /spách kok/ *n* SPLIT BIRD FOR COOKING a chicken or other fowl that is split, dressed, and grilled ■ *vt* (**-cocks, -cocking, -cocked**) **1.** PREPARE FOWL FOR ROASTING to prepare a chicken or other fowl for roasting by splitting it open **2.** INSERT SOMETHING AWKWARDLY to introduce or interpose something into a piece of writing, especially in a forced or inappropriate way [Late 18C. Origin ?]

spate /spayt/ *n* **1.** LARGE QUANTITY a large quantity of something ○ *a spate of rumours* **2.** OUTBURST a sudden strong outburst ○ *a spate of jealousy* **3.** FLOOD a flood, or the state of overflowing ○ *After the heavy rain the river was in spate.* [15C. Origin ?]

spathe /spayth/ *n* a leafy sheath (**bract**) that encloses the cluster of flowers (**spadix**) in some plants such as the arum and sometimes resembles a petal [Late 18C. < Latin *spatha* (see SPATULA)] —**spathaceous** /spə tháyshəss/ *adj* —**spathed** *adj*

spathic /spáthik/, **spathose** /spáthōss/ *adj* resembling spar minerals, especially in being easy to split [Late 18C. < German *Spat(h)* 'spar']

spathulate *n* BIOL same as **spatulate**

spatial /spáysh'l/, **spacial** *adj* relating to, occupying, or happening in space [Mid-19C < Latin *spatium* 'space, distance'] —**spatiality** /spáyshi álləti/ *n* —**spatially** *adv*

spatiotemporal /spáyshi ō témpərəl/ *adj* **1.** relating to, existing in, or having the qualities of both space and time **2.** relating to a four-dimensional space-time system [Early 20C. < Latin *spatium* 'space, distance' + TEMPORAL[1]] —**spatiotemporally** *adv*

Spätlese /shpáyt layzə/ *n* the grade of high-quality German table wine above Kabinett, made from late-picked grapes and typically medium sweet [Early 20C. < German, 'late vintage']

spatter /spáttər/ *v* (**-ters, -tering, -tered**) **1.** *vti* THROW OR COME OUT IN DROPS to expel something in small scattered drops or splashes, or come out in this way **2.** *vt* SPLASH SOMETHING WITH LIQUID to splash something with or as if with a liquid, especially if the liquid leaves a mark or residue **3.** *vt* DEFAME SOMEBODY to defame or sully somebody's character ■ *n* **1.** DROPLET OF SOMETHING SPATTERED a droplet or splash of something spattered ○ *got a few spatters of paint on the floor* **2.** SMALL AMOUNT a small amount of something ○ *a spatter of applause* **3.** ACT OF SPATTERING an act of spattering or being spattered **4.** SPATTERING SOUND the sound of spattering [Mid-16C. Ultimately < W Germanic]

spatterdash /spáttər dash/ *n* a knee-length cloth or leather legging formerly worn to protect clothing from water or mud spatters

spatula /spáttyōōlə/ *n* **1.** a flat flexible metal, plastic, or rubber utensil with a handle, used to scoop, lift, spread, or mix **2.** *UK* a flat wooden stick used to depress the tongue when the mouth or throat is being examined. ANZ, N Am term **tongue depressor** [Early 16C. < Latin, 'small broadsword', var of *spathula* < *spatha* 'broadsword' < Greek *spathē* 'broad blade'] —**spatular** *adj*

spatulate /spáttyōōlət/, **spathulate** /spáth-/ *adj* describes a leaf that is shaped like a spatula, with a narrow tapering base and a broad rounded tip

spätzle *n* FOOD another spelling of **spaetzle**

spavin /spávvin/ *n* an ailment of horses involving a swelling or enlargement of the hock joint [15C. < Old French *espavin*]

spavined /spávvind/ *adj* **1.** having a spavin or lame with a spavin ○ *a spavined horse* **2.** in extremely poor condition or badly deteriorated ○ *a spavined old car*

spawn /spawn/ *n* **1.** EGG MASS a mass of eggs of a fish, amphibian, or other water animal **2.** OFFSPRING progeny or offspring, especially if numerous **3.** FUNGAL THREADS a mass of microscopic fungal threads (**mycelium**), especially when prepared on a growth medium for starting a new culture of the fungus **4.** SEED a seed, germ, or the source of something ■ *v* (**spawns, spawning, spawned**) **1.** *vi* DEPOSIT EGGS to produce and deposit eggs **2.** *vi* PRODUCE YOUNG to produce offspring in large numbers **3.** *vt* GIVE RISE TO SOMETHING to generate or give rise to something ○ *The storm has spawned at least one tornado.* **4.** *vt* START NEW FUNGUS CULTURE to start a new culture of a fungus using spawn [15C. < Anglo-Norman *espaundre* 'shed roe', variant of Old French *espandre* 'shed, spill, pour out' < Latin *expandere* (see EXPAND)] —**spawner** *n*

spay /spay/ (**spays, spaying, spayed**) *vt* to surgically remove a female animal's ovaries and adjacent parts of the uterus [15C. < Old French *espeer* 'cut with a sword' < *espee* 'sword' < Latin *spatha* (see SPATULA)]

spaz /spaz/, **spazz** *US n* (*plural* **spazzes**) an offensive term that deliberately insults somebody's coordination or competence (*slang insult*) ■ *vi* (**spazzes, spazzing, spazzed**) same as **spaz out** (*slang offensive*) [Mid-20C. Shortening and alteration of SPASTIC]

spaz out *vi US* an offensive term meaning to do something clumsily or incompetently (*slang*)

spaza /spaázə/ *n S Africa* a small informal shop, often run from a home in a township [Late 20C. Origin?]

spazz *n, vi US* another spelling of **spaz** (*slang offensive*)

SPCK *abbr* Society for Promoting Christian Knowledge

~~**speach**~~ incorrect spelling of **speech**

speak /speek/ (**speaks, speaking, spoke** /spōk/ or **spake** *archaic* /spayk/, **spoken** /spókən/) *v* **1.** *vti* TALK to utter words or articulate sounds with the voice, or communicate something orally ○ *so shocked I could hardly speak* **2.** *vi* EXPRESS THOUGHTS AND OPINIONS to communicate thoughts, opinions, or feelings by uttering with the voice ○ *speak your mind* **3.** *vt* BE ABLE TO USE LANGUAGE to know and be able to converse in a particular language ○ *learning to speak French* **4.** *vi* BE ON GOOD TERMS to be on good and friendly terms with somebody ○ *They're not speaking any more.* **5.** *vi* DELIVER SPEECH TO AUDIENCE to make a speech or deliver an address **6.** *vti* EXPRESS IN WRITING to express something or make a statement in writing ○ *Her poetry speaks of the joy of solitude.* **7.** *vti* COMMUNICATE NONVERBALLY to communicate something by other than verbal means ○ *Actions speak louder than words.* **8.** *vi* MAKE CHARACTERISTIC SOUND to produce or make a sound characteristic of its kind **9.** *vt* COMMUNICATE WITH ANOTHER SEA-GOING VESSEL to communicate with another vessel at sea [Old English *specan, sprecan* < Indo-European] —**speakable** *adj* ◇ **so to speak** used to indicate that you are expressing something in an unusual way, e.g. that you are being euphemistic ◇ **something speaks for itself** something has an obvious meaning and needs no further explanation ◇ **to speak of** significant or worth mentioning

speak for *vt* to act as an advocate for or speak on behalf of another person or a group

speak out *vi* **1.** to express opinions boldly, freely, and frankly **2.** to talk loudly, or loudly enough to be heard

speak to *vt* to address a particular issue in a speech or discussion ○ *a speech that spoke to the needs of international students*

speak up *vi* **1.** to talk loudly enough to be heard **2.** to express opinions freely and frankly

speak up for *vt* to speak in support or on behalf of somebody or something

-speak /speek/ *suffix* vocabulary or a way of speaking that is characteristic of a particular group or sphere of activity (*disapproving*) ○ *adspeak*

SYNONYMS See *jargon*[1].

speakeasy /speék eezi/ (*plural* **-ies**) *n N Am* a place where alcoholic beverages are sold and consumed illegally, especially formerly during Prohibition in the United States [Late 19C. < speaking softly so as not to attract attention]

speaker /speékər/ *n* **1.** somebody who speaks, especially somebody able to speak a particular language ○ *Spanish speakers* **2.** somebody who makes a speech or gives a lecture **3.** BROADCAST same as **loudspeaker**

Speaker *n* the presiding officer of a legislative body such as the House of Commons or the US or Australian House of Representatives

speakerphone /speékər fōn/ *n* a telephone equipped with a loudspeaker and microphone

speaking /speéking/ *adj* **1.** INVOLVING SPEECH involving speech or speaking **2.** ABLE TO USE PARTICULAR LANGUAGE able to speak a particular language (*usually used in combination*) ○ *French-speaking students* **3.** APPARENTLY REAL resembling a real person or object ○ *the speaking image of her aunt*

speaking clock *n* a telephone service that provides an accurate verbal announcement of the time

speaking in tongues *n* the making of utterances that are not recognizable as any known language and have no formal linguistic content

speaking tube *n* a pipe through which conversation can be conducted between people in different parts of something such as a ship or building

speako /speékō/ (*plural* **-os**) *n* a mistake caused by the failure of a computer speech-recognition program to recognize a particular word correctly (*slang*)

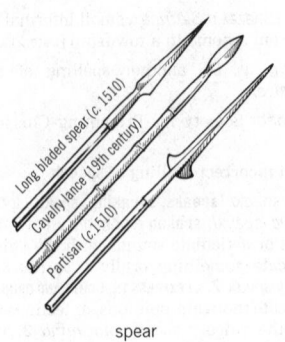

Long bladed spear (c. 1510)
Cavalry lance (19th century)
Partisan (c. 1510)

spear

spear[1] /speer/ n **1.** LONG-HANDLED WEAPON WITH BLADE a weapon for throwing or thrusting that has a long handle and a blade or head with a sharpened point **2.** WEAPON FOR SPEARING FISH a weapon with a sharp point and barbs used for catching fish by piercing them ■ vti (spears, spearing, speared) PIERCE SOMETHING WITH SPEAR to stab, pierce, or take somebody or something with or as though using a spear [Old English *spere* < Germanic] —**spearer** n —**spearman** n

spear[2] /speer/ n a young blade, shoot, or stalk of a plant such as asparagus or grass [15C. Alteration of SPIRE[1]]

spear carrier n **1.** a minor member of the cast in a play or opera **2.** an unimportant or irrelevant contributor to something (*informal*)

spearfish /speer fish/ (*plural same* or -**fishes**) n a large sea swordfish that is related to the marlin and sailfish and has a very long, pointed upper jaw. Genus: *Tetrapturus*.

spear grass n PLANTS same as **feather grass**

spear gun n a gun designed to shoot a barbed spear underwater, used to catch fish

spearhead /speer hed/ vt (-heads, -heading, -headed) ACT AS LEADER OF EVENT to act as the leader or driving force of an event or undertaking ■ n **1.** DRIVING FORCE IN EVENT the leading or driving element or force in an undertaking **2.** MIL LEADING FORCES IN MILITARY ATTACK the leading forces in a military attack **3.** ARMS POINTED HEAD OF SPEAR the pointed head of a spear **4.** Aus FOOTBALL same as **full forward**

spearmint /speer mint/ (*plural same* or -**mints**) n a common mint, the leaves and essential oil of which are used for flavouring. Latin name: *Mentha spicata*. [Mid-16C. < the stem's resemblance to a spear]

spear side n a husband's or father's side of a family (*literary*) [< SPEAR[1] as a former symbol of man's domain]

spear tackle n Aus in rugby league, an illegal tackle in which the player in possession is turned upside down and thrown headfirst at the ground

spearwort /speer wurt/ (*plural same* or -**worts**) n a buttercup with spear-shaped leaves. Flowers: small, yellow. Native to: Europe, Asia, eastern United States.

spec /spek/ n a detailed description of something, especially one that provides somebody with enough information to make that thing (*informal; usually used in the plural*) [Late 18C. Shortening of SPECIFICATION] ◇ **on spec** with a chance of achieving something but no certainty of it

spec. abbr **1.** special **2.** specification

special /spésh'l/ adj **1.** UNUSUAL OR BETTER distinct, different, unusual, or superior in comparison to others of the same kind ○ *a very special occasion* ○ *received special consideration* **2.** HELD IN ESTEEM regarded with particular esteem or affection ○ *a special friend* **3.** RESERVED unique to or reserved for a specific person or thing ○ *It's my special chair*. **4.** MADE FOR SPECIFIC PURPOSE made or used for a specific purpose or occasion ○ *Firefighters used special breathing equipment*. **5.** ARRANGED FOR SPECIFIC PURPOSE planned for a specific occasion or purpose ○ *made a special visit to the factory* **6.** ADDITIONAL in addition to or more than is usual ○ *a special issue of the newspaper* **7.** INVOLVING SPECIAL-NEEDS CHILDREN designed or intended for educating children who have physical disabilities or learning difficulties ■ n **1.** SOMETHING RESERVED FOR SPECIFIC PURPOSE something designed or reserved for

a specific purpose or occasion **2.** TELEVISION PROGRAMME NOT PART OF SCHEDULE a television programme that is not part of a network's normal schedule **3.** N Am TEMPORARY REDUCTION IN PRICE a temporary reduction in the price of an item **4.** DISH NOT ON USUAL MENU a dish that a restaurant or other food outlet offers in addition to the standard menu, or one that is available for a low price **5.** POLICE same as **special constable** [12C. Directly or via French < Latin *specialis* < *species* (see SPECIES)] —**specialness** n ◇ **on special** ANZ, N Am being sold at a reduced price

Special Air Service n ARMY full form of **SAS**

Special Boat Service n an elite British Royal Marines force that is used to spearhead amphibious operations and to reconnoitre beach landings

Special Branch n the branch of the UK police force that is the executive arm of the government intelligence agencies and specializes in matters of political security

special constable n in the United Kingdom, somebody who acts as a volunteer to supplement the police force, especially on occasions when a large police force is necessary, e.g. emergencies or demonstrations

special delivery n the delivery of mail more quickly than or outside normal delivery times for an extra fee

special drawing rights n a method of settling international debts through the International Monetary Fund in order to stabilize exchange rates

special education n teaching modified to suit students with special educational needs

special effects npl extraordinary visual effects in a film or television programme achieved by technical means, either optically, digitally, or mechanically

special interest group n a group seeking to influence government policy in favour of an interest or issue

specialise, etc. vi another spelling of **specialize, etc.**

specialism /spésh'lizam/ n **1.** concentration in a field of study ○ *There is a great deal of specialism in their education system*. **2.** same as **speciality** (sense 1)

specialist /spésh'list/ n **1.** SOMEBODY IN PARTICULAR INTEREST somebody who specializes in an occupation, interest, or field of study **2.** TYPE OF PHYSICIAN a medical doctor who practises in a specific field **3.** US ENLISTED RANK IN US ARMY an enlisted person in the US Army with special technical skills, of a rank in a series numbered from 4 to 7 between corporal and sergeant first class —**specialist** adj —**specialistic** /spésha lístik/ adj

speciality /spéshi álləti/ (*plural* -**ties**) n **1.** SOMETHING SOMEBODY SPECIALIZES IN a skill, field of study, interest, or activity in which somebody specializes **2.** PRODUCT OF SOMEBODY'S SPECIALIZATION a product or result of somebody's specialization **3.** DISTINCTIVE MARK an unusual, distinctive, or superior mark or quality ▶ N Am term **specialty**

specialization /spésha l záysh'n/, **specialisation** n **1.** ACT OF BECOMING SPECIALIZED the act or process of becoming specialized **2.** EDUC same as **speciality** (sense 1) **3.** BIOL ADAPTATION OF ORGANISM the adaptation of an organism or a part of an organism to a specific function or condition in response to environmental conditions **4.** BIOL ADAPTED BODY PART an organism or a part of an organism that has been adapted to a specific function or condition

specialize /spésha līz/ (-izes, -izing, -ized), **specialise** (-ises, -ising, -ised) v **1.** vi DEVOTE TIME TO ACTIVITY to devote time exclusively to an interest, skill, or field of study ○ *She's specializing in pediatrics*. **2.** vi CONCENTRATE ON PRODUCT to concentrate on a particular activity, area, or group of products ○ *The shop specializes in water sports*. **3.** vt ADAPT SOMETHING TO SPECIFIC PURPOSE to adapt something to suit a specific purpose **4.** vi BECOME ADAPTED to become adapted to a specific function or condition **5.** vt SPECIFY SOMETHING to specify or make specific mention of something

speciall incorrect spelling of **special**

special licence n a marriage licence that allows a marriage to take place without the usual legal conditions being enforced

specially /spésh'li/ adv for a special or particular purpose, person, or occasion ○ *It was intended specially for preschool children*. ○ *I had it specially made*.

USAGE See **especially**.

special needs npl the requirements, especially in education, that some people have because of physical disabilities or learning difficulties

Special Olympics n an international athletic competition for athletes who have a physical or mental disability (*takes a singular or plural verb*)

special operations, **special ops** n a branch of a military force engaged in covert operations, especially in enemy territory ■ npl covert operations undertaken by military personnel, especially in enemy territory

special pleading n **1.** pleading in a court trial that introduces new or special matter and that avoids allegations of matter pleaded by the opposite side, instead of direct denial of those allegations **2.** an argument that presents only one aspect of an issue and avoids any unfavourable aspects

special relativity n PHYS same as **relativity** (sense 1)

special school n a school catering to students who have special educational needs, e.g. because of learning difficulties or physical disabilities

special session n a session of a legislature, court, or council held in addition to and outside of regularly scheduled sessions

special sort n a character that is not on the usual printing font, e.g. an accented or Greek letter

special theory of relativity n PHYS same as **relativity** (sense 1)

specialty /spésh'lti/ (*plural* -**ties**) n **1.** an area of medicine in which somebody specializes **2.** N Am same as **speciality** ○ *Prime rib is the house specialty*. ○ *Evasiveness is a specialty of his*. **3.** LAW a legal agreement made under seal

speciation /speéssi áysh'n/ n the evolutionary formation of new biological species, usually by one species that divides into two or more species that are genetically unique [Early 20C. < SPECIES] —**speciate** /speéssi ayt/ vi

specie /speéshi/ n money in the form of coins [Mid-16C. Shortening of Latin *in specie* 'in kind' < *species* (see SPECIES)] ◇ **in specie 1.** in the form of coins **2.** in a similar way or kind **3.** in the form specified

speciel incorrect spelling of **special**

species /speé sheez/ (*plural same*) n **1.** BIOL TAXONOMIC GROUP a subdivision of a genus considered as a basic biological classification and containing individuals that resemble one another and may interbreed **2.** BIOL ORGANISMS IN SPECIES the organisms belonging to a species **3.** TYPE OF SOMETHING a kind, sort, or variety of something **4.** CHEM ATOM CATEGORY a category of atomic nucleus, ion, molecule, or atom **5.** LOGIC SUBDIVISION OF GENUS in logic, a collection of objects or individuals that, on the basis of shared features, form a subdivision of a genus **6.** CHR BREAD AND WINE IN COMMUNION the bread and wine used in Christian Communion, or their outward form after consecration [14C. < Latin, 'appearance, kind' < *specere* 'look at']

SYNONYMS See **type**.

species barrier n the ability of cells belonging to members of a species to identify genes alien to the species and prevent them combining with its genome. The species barrier usually prevents members of different species from producing healthy offspring if they mate, and is also thought to prevent the transmission of some diseases between species.

speciesism /speé sheezizam/ n the belief that the human race is superior to other species, and that exploitation of animals for the advantage of humans is justified

specif. abbr **1.** specific **2.** specifically

specific /spə síffik/ adj **1.** PRECISE precise and detailed, avoiding vagueness ○ *specific instructions* **2.** RELATING TO IDENTIFIED THING acting on or relating to something identified or particularized ○ *The instructions are specific to this task*. **3.** DISTINCTIVE with individual

qualities that allow a distinction to be made or make a distinction necessary ○ *discussing these specific problems* **4.** BIOL OF BIOLOGICAL SPECIES relating to a biological species **5.** MED CAUSED BY PARTICULAR INFECTIOUS AGENT describes a disease caused by a particular infectious agent **6.** PHYS DENOTING PHYSICAL PROPERTY used to indicate that a physical property is being expressed with reference to a particular quantity such as mass, volume, or length **7.** COMM LEVIED PER UNIT describes taxes or duties levied on a per-unit basis using number, weight, or volume ■ *n* DETAIL a precise quality or detail (*usually used in the plural*) ○ *The report didn't go into specifics.* [Mid-17C. < late Latin *specificus* 'constituting a kind' < Latin *species* (see SPECIES)] —**specifically** *adv* —**specificity** /spéssi físsəti/ *n*

specific absorption rate *n* MED full form of **SAR**

specification /spéssifi káysh'n/ *n* **1.** DETAILED DESCRIPTION a detailed description, especially one providing information needed to make, build, or produce something ○ *a look at the engine specification* **2.** DETAIL an item within a specification ○ *The machine's technical specifications are in Appendix A.* **3.** SPECIFYING the specifying of something **4.** LAW INTELLECTUAL PROPERTY DESCRIPTION a detailed description of intellectual property, as required by law **5.** PUBL TYPOGRAPHICAL INSTRUCTIONS detailed instructions regarding information such as font, point size, and layout that are sent with material to be typeset and printed

specific charge *n* the ratio of the electric charge of an elementary particle divided by its mass

specific gravity *n* same as **relative density**

specific heat capacity *n* UK the amount of heat needed to raise the temperature of one gram of a substance by one degree, usually measured in joules per kelvin per kilogram. Symbol *c*. ANZ, N Am term **specific heat**

specific impulse *n* a measure of the fuel efficiency of a rocket, expressed as the number of pounds of thrust produced per pound of propellant used per second

specific language impairment *n* an inability to develop the expected language skills in a child without difficulties in hearing or learning, possibly because of an inability to process sound

~~specificly~~ incorrect spelling of **specifically**

specific performance *n* a court order compelling somebody to carry out an obligation, often something stipulated in a contract

specific resistance *n* ELEC same as **resistivity** (sense 1)

specific volume *n* the volume of a unit mass of a substance, equal to the reciprocal of the density. Symbol *v*

specify /spéssi fī/ (-**fies**, -**fying**, -**fied**) *vt* **1.** STATE SOMETHING EXPLICITLY to state or identify something in detail or explicitly ○ *Can you specify a date when the order will be delivered?* **2.** STIPULATE SOMETHING to state something or make it a condition ○ *The rules specify that pets cannot be kept here.* **3.** INCLUDE SOMETHING IN SPECIFICATION to include or state something in a specification ○ *We had specified a 48-speed CD drive.* [13C. Directly or via French *spécifier* < late Latin *specificare* < *specificus* (see SPECIFIC)] —**specifiable** *adj* —**specificative** /spéssifi kaytiv, spə síffi kaytiv/ *adj*—**specifier** *n*

~~speciman~~ incorrect spelling of **specimen**

specimen /spéssimin/ *n* **1.** REPRESENTATIVE THING something that is representative because it is characteristic of its kind or of a whole, especially something that serves as an example ○ *a specimen of his handwriting* **2.** SAMPLE OF BODY MATERIAL a sample used for testing and diagnosis, e.g. of urine or blood **3.** TYPE OF PERSON somebody who displays particular characteristics (*informal*) ○'*turning away with disgust from the loathsome specimen of humanity before him*' (Baroness Orczy, *The Scarlet Pimpernel*; 1905) **4.** TYPICAL EXAMPLE an organism or one of its parts preserved as a typical example of its classification [Early 17C. < Latin < *specere* 'look at']

specious /spéeshəss/ *adj* **1.** appearing to be true but really false ○ *a specious claim* **2.** superficially attractive but actually of no real interest or value

[14C. < Latin *speciosus* 'good-looking' < *species* (see SPECIES)] —**speciously** *adv* —**speciousness** *n*

speck /spek/ *n* **1.** SMALL SPOT a very small mark or stain **2.** PARTICLE a tiny amount or particle of something ○ *a speck of dust* ■ *vt* (**specks, specking, specked**) MARK SOMETHING WITH SPECKS to mark something with specks (*usually passive*) [Old English *specca*. Origin ?]

speckle /spék'l/ *n* a small spot or mark, often a small irregular patch of contrasting colour, e.g. on plumage or an egg shell ■ *vt* (-**les**, -**ling**, -**led**) to mark something with speckles (*usually passive*) [15C. < Middle Dutch *spekkel*]

speckled /spék'ld/ *adj* **1.** with a pattern of many small spots or small irregular patches, often of a contrasting colour **2.** with parts that contrast distinctly with each other ○ *a speckled career* ○ *speckled shadows*

speckled trout *n* FISH same as **brook trout**

speckle interferometry *n* a technique for reducing distortions in photographic images of astronomical objects by combining a number of images of very short exposure

specs /speks/ *npl* same as **spectacles** (see **spectacle**) (*informal*) [Early 19C. Shortening]

SPECT *abbr* PHYS single photon emission computed tomography

spectacle /spéktək'l/ *n* **1.** SOMETHING REMARKABLE THAT CAN BE SEEN an object, phenomenon, or event that is witnessed, especially one that is impressive, unusual, or disturbing **2.** LAVISH DISPLAY an impressive performance or display, especially something staged as a form of entertainment **3.** UNPLEASANT CENTRE OF ATTENTION somebody or something that attracts attention by being unpleasant or ridiculous ○ *You are making a spectacle of yourself.* ■ **spectacles** *npl* GLASSES a pair of glass or plastic lenses worn in a frame in front of the eyes to help correct imperfect vision [14C. Via French < Latin *spectaculum* < *spectare* 'to watch' < *specere* 'look at']

ORIGIN The Latin word *specere* 'to look at' and its stem *spect-*, from which **spectacle** is derived, are also the source of English *aspect, circumspect, conspectus, conspicuous, despise, expect, inspect, perspective, prospect, respect, specimen, spectre, spectrum,* and *suspect.*

spectacled /spéktək'ld/ *adj* **1.** wearing spectacles **2.** having markings on the face that encircle the eyes in a way that resembles spectacles

spectacled bear *n* a rare bear that is black with white markings around the eyes. It is vulnerable to extinction because of habitat loss. Native to: grasslands and forests of the Andes. Latin name: *Tremarcto ornatus.*

spectacular /spek tákyŏolər/ *adj* **1.** VISUALLY IMPRESSIVE impressive or dramatic to look at or watch **2.** REMARKABLE remarkably large, great, or speedy ■ *n* EXTRAVAGANZA a lavish celebration or artistic production [Late 17C. < SPECTACLE after ORACULAR related to ORACLE and similar pairs] —**spectacularly** *adv*

spectate /spek táyt/ (-**tates, -tating, -tated**) *vi* to watch an activity or event without participating [Early 18C. Back-formation < SPECTATOR]

spectator /spek táytər/ *n* somebody who watches or observes, especially somebody who watches an activity or event [Late 16C. Directly or via French < Latin < *spectare* 'to watch' (see SPECTACLE)] —**spectatorial** /spéktə táwri əl/ *adj* —**spectatorship** *n*

spectator sport *n* a sport that attracts spectators in large numbers

specter *n* US spelling of **spectre**

spectinomycin /spéktinō mísin/ *n* an antibiotic with a wide range of effectiveness against penicillin-resistant pathogens. Use: treatment of gonorrhoea. [Mid-20C. < modern Latin *Streptomyces spectabilis*, bacterium that is its source < Latin *spectabilis*, 'visible']

spectra PHYS, PHARM plural of **spectrum**

spectral /spéktrəl/ *adj* **1.** relating to spectres or in the form of a spectre **2.** produced by a spectrum or relating to a spectrum —**spectrality** /spek trálləti/ *n* —**spectrally** *adv* —**spectralness** *n*

spectral class *n* ASTRON same as **spectral type**

spectral line *n* a discrete band of light in a spectrum associated with a specific wavelength and used to identify substances. Characteristic spectral lines are emitted by atoms and molecules and may be used to identify substances.

spectral type *n* a classification system for stars based on an analysis of the light they emit. This analysis also gives information on a star's temperature and chemical composition.

spectre /spéktər/ *n* **1.** a ghostly presence or apparition **2.** a threat or prospect of something unpleasant ○ *the spectre of my performance review* [Early 17C. Directly or via French < Latin *spectrum* 'image, apparition' (see SPECTRUM)]

spectrin /spéktrin/ *n* a fibrous protein in the membranes of red blood cells [Mid-20C. < SPECTRE, because first isolated from red blood cells lacking haemoglobin, called 'ghosts']

spectro- *prefix* spectrum ○ *spectroscope* [< SPECTRUM]

spectrochemistry /spéktrō kémmistri/ *n* the branch of chemistry that deals with the spectra formed during chemical activity, e.g. the emission spectra of substances burned in an arc or spark —**spectrochemical** *adj*

spectrogram /spéktrə gram/ *n* a photograph or representation of a spectrum

spectrograph /spéktrə graaf, -graf/ *n* an instrument consisting of a spectrometer and related equipment used to obtain a visual record of a spectrum —**spectrographic** /spéktrə gráffik/ *adj* —**spectrographically** *adv* —**spectrography** /spek tróggrəfi/ *n*

spectroheliogram /spéktrə heéli ə gram/ *n* an image of the Sun produced using a narrow wavelength band of the radiation it emits

spectroheliograph /spéktrō heéli ə graaf, -graf/ *n* an instrument used to obtain images of the Sun over a narrow band of wavelengths —**spectroheliographic** /-heeli ə gráffik/ *adj* —**spectroheliography** /-heeli óggrəfi/ *n*

spectrohelioscope /spéktrō heéli ə skōp/ *n* an instrument used for viewing the Sun's spectrum —**spectrohelioscopic** /-heeli ə skóppik/ *adj*

spectrometer /spek trómmitər/ *n* an instrument used to disperse radiant energy or particles into a spectrum and measure properties such as wavelength, mass, energy, or index of refraction —**spectrometric** /spéktrə méttrik/ *adj* —**spectrometry** *n*

spectrophotometer /spéktrōfə tómmitər/ *n* an instrument used to measure the relative intensities of wavelengths in a spectrum —**spectrophotometric** /-fōtə méttrik/ *adj* —**spectrophotometrically** *adv* —**spectrophotometry** *n*

spectropolarimeter /spéktrō pōlə rímmitər/ *n* an instrument used to determine the amount of polarized light reflected from a source such as a distant star or galaxy —**spectropolarimetric** /-pōləri méttrik/ *adj* —**spectropolarimetrical** *adj* —**spectropolarimetry** *n*

spectroscope /spéktrə skōp/ *n* an instrument for dispersing light, usually light in the visible range, into a spectrum in order to measure it —**spectroscopic** /spéktrə skóppik/ *adj* —**spectroscopically** *adv*

spectroscopic analysis *n* the use of spectroscopy to determine the chemical composition, energy levels, and molecular structure of substances

spectroscopy /spek tróskəpi/ *n* the study of spectra, especially to determine the chemical composition of substances and the physical properties of molecules, ions, and atoms —**spectroscopist** *n*

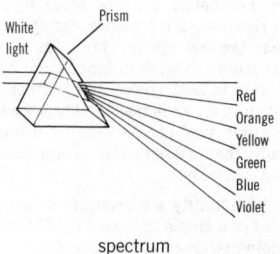

spectrum

spectrum /spéktrəm/ (*plural* **-tra** /-trə/ or **-trums**) *n* **1.** DISTRIBUTION OF COLOURED LIGHT a continuous distribution of coloured light produced when a beam of white light is dispersed into its components, e.g. by a prism **2.** PARTICULAR RADIATION FREQUENCY RANGE a range of radiation frequencies that have a particular property **3.** RECORD OF RADIATION WAVELENGTHS OF SUBSTANCE a visual record of the wavelengths of the radiation or particles emitted by a substance, used as a means of analysing its physical properties such as energy and mass **4.** RANGE OF VALUES a range of values, especially one with opposite values at its limits ○ *a spectrum of opinions between the two extremes* **5.** PHARM RANGE OF DRUG TARGETS the range of organisms that an antibiotic can kill [Late 19C. < Latin, 'image, apparition' < *specere* 'look at']

specula OPTICS, MED, BIRDS plural of **speculum**

specular /spékyŏŏlər/ *adj* **1.** relating to mirrors or having the characteristics of a mirror **2.** carried out using a speculum [Late 16C. < Latin *specularis* < *speculum* (see SPECULUM)]

speculate /spékyŏŏ layt/ (**-lates, -lating, -lated**) *v* **1.** *vti* CONJECTURE to form a conjecture on the basis of incomplete facts or information **2.** *vi* CONSIDER POSSIBILITIES to think over possibilities **3.** *vi* MAKE RISKY DEALS FOR PROFIT to engage in financial transactions such as commodity trading that have an element of risk, especially in the short term, with the hope of making a profit **4.** *vi* TAKE RISKS to take risks in an attempt to achieve something or get some benefit **5.** *vi NZ* RUGBY KICK AIMLESSLY in rugby, to kick the ball out of defence hurriedly in order to thwart an attack [Late 16C. < Latin *speculat-*, past participle of *speculari* 'observe, spy out' < *specere* 'look at']

speculation /spékyŏŏ láysh'n/ *n* **1.** OPINION BASED ON INCOMPLETE INFORMATION a conclusion, theory, or opinion based on incomplete facts or information **2.** REASONING BASED ON INCOMPLETE INFORMATION reasoning based on incomplete facts or information ○ *mere speculation* **3.** RISKY TRANSACTION a financial transaction that involves risk, but is potentially profitable ○ *a failed speculation on a dot-com* **4.** MAKING OF RISKY TRANSACTIONS the practice of engaging in financial transactions that are risky, but potentially profitable

speculative /spékyŏŏlətiv/ *adj* **1.** USING INCOMPLETE INFORMATION based on conjecture or incomplete facts or information **2.** FORMING CONCLUSIONS NOT BASED ON FACT given to forming conclusions or opinions that are not based on fact **3.** RISKY BUT POTENTIALLY PROFITABLE risky in nature, but potentially profitable ○ *speculative investments* —**speculatively** *adv* —**speculativeness** *n*

speculator /spékyŏŏ laytər/ *n* **1.** somebody who speculates, especially financially **2.** *NZ* in rugby, a hurried forward kick of the ball from a defensive position, made in order to thwart a promising attack

speculum /spékyŏŏləm/ (*plural* **-la** /-lə/ or **-lums**) *n* **1.** OPTICS MIRROR a mirror or other reflective surface in an optical instrument such as a telescope **2.** MED MEDICAL INSTRUMENT a medical instrument used to hold open a body passage such as the anus or vagina so that it can be examined **3.** BIRDS COLOURED PATCH ON BIRD'S WINGS a patch of colour on the wings of ducks and some other birds [Late 16C. < Latin, 'mirror' < *specere* 'look at']

speculum metal *n* an alloy of copper and tin, sometimes with other metals. It is hard, brittle, white, resistant to corrosion and, because it can be highly polished, is used for metal mirrors.

sped past participle, past tense of **speed**

speech /speech/ *n* **1.** SPEAKING ABILITY the ability to speak (*often used before a noun*) **2.** COMMUNICATION BY SPEAKING the act of communicating by speaking **3.** UTTERANCES things that are said ○ *recordings of human speech* **4.** SPOKEN LANGUAGE spoken language, especially as distinct from the written language ○ *effective communication in both speech and writing* **5.** ADDRESS a talk given to an audience **6.** PARTICULAR WAY OF SPEAKING a particular way of speaking or using language, especially that of a person or group [Old English *spǣc* < *specan* (see SPEAK)]

speech community *n* a group that includes all the speakers of a single language or dialect. They may be widely dispersed geographically.

speech day *n* an annual event in a school during which speeches are given by staff and guests, and pupils are presented with prizes for good work and outstanding achievements

speechify /spéechi fī/ (**-fies, -fying, -fied**) *vi* **1.** to talk in a tedious and self-important manner, especially in giving an opinion **2.** to give a speech or speeches —**speechification** /spéechifi káysh'n/ *n* —**speechifier** *n*

speechless /spéechləss/ *adj* **1.** TEMPORARILY UNABLE TO SPEAK temporarily unable to speak or unable to think of something to say, e.g. because of surprise or fear **2.** UNABLE TO SPEAK lacking the power of speech **3.** REMAINING SILENT choosing not to say anything **4.** UNSPOKEN not expressed in words **5.** HARD TO EXPRESS difficult or impossible to put into words —**speechlessly** *adv* —**speechlessness** *n*

speechmaker /spéech maykər/ *n* somebody who makes a speech, especially somebody who frequently makes speeches —**speechmaking** *n*

speech pathology *n* the study, diagnosis, and treatment of speech disorders, including failure of speech development in children and language disorders resulting from acquired brain dysfunction —**speech pathologist** *n*

speech-reading *n* COMMUNICATION same as **lip-reading**

speech recognition *n* a system of computer input and control in which the computer can recognize spoken words and transform them into digitized commands or text. With such a system, a computer can be activated and controlled by voice commands or take dictation as input to a word processor or a desktop publishing system.

speech synthesis *n* computer-generated audio output that resembles human speech

speech therapy *n* the treatment of disorders that prevent people from speaking clearly —**speech therapist** *n*

speechwriter /spéech rītər/ *n* somebody who writes speeches for other people, especially professionally

speed /speed/ *n* **1.** RATE OF MOVEMENT OR HAPPENING the rate at which something moves, happens, or functions **2.** RAPIDITY fast movement, progress, or operation **3.** RATE OF MOVEMENT IRRESPECTIVE OF DIRECTION rate of movement irrespective of direction. It is equal either to distance travelled divided by travel time, or to rate of change of distance with respect to time. **4.** DRUGS same as **amphetamine** (*slang*) **5.** MECH ENG GEAR RATIO a gear ratio in a motor, engine, or driving mechanism ○ *a ten-speed bicycle* ○ *operates at three different speeds* **6.** PHOTOGRAPHY PHOTOGRAPHIC FILM'S SENSITIVITY TO LIGHT a measure of the sensitivity of photographic film to light, expressed numerically according to any of various rating systems **7.** SUCCESS success or prosperity (*archaic*) ■ *v* (**speeds, speeding, sped** /sped/ or **speeded**) **1.** *vti* GO OR MOVE QUICKLY to go or move quickly, or make somebody or something do this **2.** *vi* DRIVE FAST to drive fast, especially in excess of the speed limit **3.** *vi* HAPPEN QUICKLY to pass or happen quickly or more quickly ○ *days speeding by* **4.** *vi* DRUGS USE AMPHETAMINES to be under the influence of amphetamines (*slang*) **5.** *vti* MAKE OR BE PROSPEROUS to prosper, or cause somebody or something to prosper (*archaic*) [Old English *spēd* 'success, prosperity' < Indo-European, 'prosper'] ◇ **be** or **get up to speed 1.** to reach the maximum or desirable rate of movement or progress **2.** to be or become fully informed about the latest developments

speed up *vti* to increase in rate or speed, or make somebody or something do this

speedball /spéed bawl/ *n* **1.** a team game similar to football, in which the ball can be passed forwards with the hands and caught when in mid-air **2.** a combination of illegal drugs such as cocaine and heroin taken by injection (*slang*)

speedboat /spéed bōt/ *n* a motorboat capable of travelling at high speeds

speed brake *n* a flap on an aircraft wing used to decrease speed in flight before landing

speed bump *n* a raised area or ridge on a road surface designed to limit traffic speeds

speed camera *n* a roadside-mounted camera that automatically photographs a vehicle passing by it at excessive speed. It provides traffic police with concrete evidence of speeding offences.

speed dating *n* an organized gathering of singles at which the participants meet privately for a few minutes of conversation with a number of potential partners and decide who among those they have met they would like to meet again

speed demon *n N Am* somebody who habitually drives too fast in a motor vehicle (*informal*)

speed dial *n* a function on a telephone that enables numbers to be stored in a memory so that they can be dialled by pressing a single button ○ *I have her number on speed dial.*

speeder /spéedər/ *n* a motorist who breaks the speed limit

speed freak *n* somebody who is addicted to amphetamines (*slang*)

speed hump *n* ROADS same as **speed bump**

speeding /spéeding/ *n* the offence of driving a vehicle at a speed above the designated speed limit ■ *adj* moving or working quickly

speed limit *n* the maximum permitted speed, usually set by law, at which a vehicle may travel on a specific stretch of road

speed merchant *n* somebody who habitually drives too fast in a motor vehicle (*informal*)

speedo /spéedō/ (*plural* **-os**) *n* TRANSP same as **speedometer** (*informal*) [Mid-20C. Shortening]

Speedo /spéedō/ *tdmk* a trademark for swimwear, especially close-fitting briefs

speed of light *n* the constant and universal speed at which all electromagnetic radiation travels through a vacuum, 2.998×10^8 metres per second. Symbol **c**

speed of sound *n* the speed at which sound waves travel through a medium

speedometer /spi dómmitər/ *n* an instrument that continuously measures a vehicle's speed and displays it either numerically or by means of a needle on a dial

speed-read *vti* to read something very fast using a learned technique of skimming the text

speed skate *n* an ice skate designed for racing. It has a blade that is much longer than on a standard skate. —**speed skater** *n*

speed skating *n* the sport of racing competitively on speed skates. Two skaters race against each other on a wide oval track divided into two lanes.

speed trap *n* a stretch of road kept under hidden surveillance by police officers monitoring vehicle speeds, usually using radar equipment

speedup /spéed up/ *n* **1.** an increase in rate or speed **2.** *US* a demand for an increase in productivity from a workforce without a corresponding pay increase

speed walking *n* ATHLETICS same as **race walking**

speedway /spéed way/ *n* **1.** a motor sport in which lightweight motorcycles race against each other on an oval cinder track (*often used before a noun*) **2.** a track or stadium used for speedway

speedwell /spéed wel/ *n* a perennial plant of the snapdragon family with opposite leaves. Flowers: blue or pinkish, in clusters. Native to: Europe. Genus: *Veronica.* [Late 16C. < SPEED (verb) + WELL[2]]

speedwriting /spéed rīting/ *n* a system of shorthand writing that uses combinations of standard letters, as distinct from other systems that use symbols

speedy /spéedi/ (**-ier, -iest**) *adj* **1.** accomplished or achieved quickly **2.** capable of moving very fast —**speedily** *adv* —**speediness** *n*

~~**speek**~~ incorrect spelling of **speak**

speiss /spīss/ *n* a compound of arsenic or antimony formed during the smelting of ores such as iron, nickel, and copper [Late 18C. < German *Speise* 'food, speiss']

spekboom /spék boom/ (*plural same* or **-booms**) *n S Africa* a succulent bush with fleshy leaves, often cultivated as an ornamental plant. Flowers: small, pinkish. Native to: South Africa. Latin name: *Portulacaria afra.* [Mid-19C. < Afrikaans, 'bacon tree']

Speke /speek/, **John Hanning** (1827–64) British explorer. Among his African explorations were expeditions to Lake Tanganyika and Lake Victoria (both 1858).

spelaean /spi leé ən/, **spelean** adj relating to caves, or found in caves [Mid-19C. Via Latin < Greek *spēlaion* 'cave']

speleology /speéli ólləji/, **spelaeology** n 1. the scientific study of caves 2. the sport or pastime of exploring caves. N Am term **spelunking** — **speleological** /-ə lójjik'l/ adj —**speleologist** n

spell [1] /spel/ (**spells, spelling, spelt** /spelt/ or **spelled**) v 1. vti NAME OR WRITE LETTERS OF WORD to name or write in correct order the constituent letters of a word, part of a word, or group of words 2. vt FORM WORD to form a word when arranged in the correct order 3. vt SIGNIFY SOMETHING to be a sign or indication of something ○ *Increased interest rates could spell trouble for some corporate borrowers.* [13C. < Old French *espeller* < Germanic]
spell out vt 1. MAKE SOMETHING COMPLETELY CLEAR to state something clearly, allowing no room for misunderstanding 2. READ SOMETHING WITH DIFFICULTY to read something with difficulty or very slowly, especially by reading out words one letter at a time 3. FIGURE SOMETHING OUT to figure something out by careful study or analysis

spell [2] /spel/ n 1. WORDS WITH SUPPOSED MAGICAL POWER a word or series of words believed to have magical power, spoken to invoke the magic 2. INFLUENCE OF MAGIC WORDS the influence that a spell has over somebody or something 3. FASCINATION a compelling fascination or attraction ■ vt (**spells, spelling, spelt** /spelt/ or **spelled**) INFLUENCE SOMEBODY OR SOMETHING USING SPELL to put somebody or something under the influence of a spell [Old English, 'talk, speech' < Germanic]

spell [3] /spel/ n 1. SHORT PERIOD a period of indeterminate, but usually short duration (*informal*) ○ *achieved great things with the club in his short spell as manager* 2. PERIOD OF PARTICULAR WEATHER a period of weather of a particular type ○ *a warm spell* 3. BOUT OF PARTICULAR ILLNESS a period in which somebody has a particular illness or medical condition ○ *a fainting spell* 4. PERIOD OF WORK a period of work or purposeful activity 5. TURN ON DUTY somebody's turn to work or perform a duty 6. *Scotland, ANZ* REST PERIOD a period of rest 7. *N Am* SHORT DISTANCE a short unspecified distance (*informal*) ○ *down the road a spell* ■ v (**spells, spelling, spelled, spelt** /spelt/ or **spelled**) 1. vt *Scotland, ANZ, N Am* RELIEVE SOMEBODY to relieve somebody of a task temporarily, especially in order to allow him or her to rest 2. vi *ANZ* TAKE TURNS to take turns working at a job [Late 16C. < variant of obsolete *spele* 'take the place of somebody' origin ?]

spellbinding /spél bīnding/ adj holding somebody's attention and interest completely [Late 20C. < SPELL[2]] —**spellbind** vt —**spellbinder** n —**spellbindingly** adv

spellbound /spél bownd/ adj having your attention and interest held completely by somebody or something [Late 18C. < SPELL[2]]

spellchecker /spél chekər/ n a computer program that compares words in a text with a file of correctly spelt words in order to detect misspellings [Late 20C. < SPELL[1]] —**spellcheck** n, vt

speller /spéllər/ n 1. somebody who spells words, especially in a particular way ○ *an excellent speller* 2. a book for teaching or improving spelling [15C. < SPELL[1]]

spellican /spéllikən/ n LEISURE another spelling of **spillikin** [Mid-18C. Variant]

spelling /spélling/ n 1. ABILITY TO SPELL the ability to spell words correctly 2. FORMING OF WORDS BY ORDERING LETTERS the forming of words with letters in a conventionally accepted order (*often used before a noun*) 3. EXAMPLE OF LETTER ORDER an example of how a word is spelt [15C. < SPELL[1]]

spelling bee n a competition in which the object is to see who can spell the most words correctly

spelling pronunciation n a variant pronunciation of a word that differs from the standard pronunciation and is influenced by the way a word is spelt

spelt [1] /spelt/ past participle, past tense of **spell** [3]. past participle of **spell** [2]. past tense of **spell** [1]

spelt [2] /spelt/ n a hardy variety of wheat of inferior quality, sometimes grown in mountainous regions. Latin name: *Triticum spelta*. [Pre-12C. < late Latin *spelta*]

spelter /spéltər/ n impure zinc, often used as a cheap alternative for bronze in cast decorative items [Mid-17C. Ultimately < W Germanic]

spelunking /spi lúngking/ n N Am LEISURE same as **speleology** (sense 2) [Mid-20C. < Latin *spelunca* 'cave' < Greek *spelunx*] —**spelunker** n

Spemann /shpáy man/, **Hans** (1869–1941) German embryologist. He discovered the organizer function in embryonic development and won the Nobel Prize in physiology or medicine (1935).

spencer /spénssər/ n 1. a short jacket worn by boys in the late 18th and early 19th centuries 2. a very short jacket worn by women over a high-waisted gown in the late 18th and early 19th centuries [Late 18C. After George John *Spencer* (1758–1834), second Earl Spencer]

Spencer /spénssər/, **Sir Baldwin** (1860–1929) British-born Australian anthropologist. He was the author of pioneering studies of Australian Aboriginals, including *Native Tribes of Central Australia* (1899). Full name **Spencer, Sir Walter Baldwin**

Spencer, Herbert (1820–1903) British philosopher and social theorist. He applied evolutionary theory to ethics and sociology, and coined the phrase 'survival of the fittest'. His major work is *A System of Synthetic Philosophy* (1862–93).

'The liberty the citizen enjoys is to be measured not by the governmental machinery he lives under, whether representative or other, but by the paucity of restraints it imposes on him.'
[Herbert Spencer, *The Man Versus the State*; 1884]

Sir Stanley Spencer

Spencer, Sir Stanley (1891–1959) British painter. Many of his works, e.g. *The Resurrection, Cookham* (1923–27), place traditional biblical scenes in contemporary settings.

Spencer Gulf large coastal inlet in South Australia, flanked by the Eyre and Yorke peninsulas. Length: 320 km/200 mi.

Spencerian /spen seéri ən/ adj describes a style of handwriting with perfectly formed letters and ornamentation of capitals [Mid-19C. After Platt Rogers *Spencer* (1800–64), US calligrapher]

spend /spend/ v (**spends, spending, spent** /spent/) 1. vti PAY MONEY to pay out money in exchange for goods or services 2. vt DEVOTE TIME OR EFFORT to devote time, energy, or thought to something ○ *spent a lot of time thinking about it* 3. vt PASS TIME to pass a particular amount of time in a particular place or way ○ *spend a week in Hawaii* 4. vt USE SOMETHING UP to deplete something totally 5. vt SACRIFICE SOMETHING to sacrifice something, especially for a cause ○ *spent her life working for reform* ■ n 1. SPREE a time or trip during which things are bought and money is spent, especially a lot of money 2. AMOUNT OF MONEY SPENT an amount of money spent or set aside for spending ○ *'...is increasing its advertising spend by 40 per cent...'* (*Marketing Week*; December 1998) [Pre-12C. Partly < Latin *expendere* 'pay' (see EXPEND); partly < Old French *despendre* 'expend' < Latin *dispendere* (see DISPENSE)] —**spender** n

Spender /spéndər/, **Dale** (b. 1943) Australian writer and feminist. Her books include *Women of Ideas and What Men Have Done to Them* (1982).

Spender, Sir Stephen (1909–95) British poet and editor. He was a prominent member of the left-wing British literary movement in the 1930s, and edited *Encounter* from 1953 to 1967. His works include *Collected Poems, 1928–85* (1986) and *Journals 1939–83* (1986). Full name **Spender, Sir Stephen Harold**

spending money /spénding-/ n cash used or available for personal expenses, especially expenditure on nonessential items

spendthrift /spénd thrift/ n somebody who spends money recklessly or extravagantly ■ adj tending to spend money recklessly or extravagantly [Late 16C. < SPEND + THRIFT in the archaic sense 'savings, earnings']

spendy /spéndi/ (**-ier, -iest**) adj US same as **expensive** (*slang*)

Spenser /spénssər/, **Edmund** (1552?–99) English poet. He wrote the epic romance *The Faerie Queene* (published in three parts, 1590–96), a panoramic historical allegory and one of the classics of English Renaissance literature. —**Spenserian** /spen seéri ən/ adj

'Upon a great adventure he was bond, / The greatest Gloriana to him gave, / (That greatest Glorious Queene of Faery lond) / To winne him worshippe, and her grace to have, / Which of all earthly thinges he most did crave.'
[Edmund Spenser, *The Faerie Queene*; 1590]

Spenserian stanza n a stanza devised by Edmund Spenser that contains eight lines of iambic pentameter and a ninth of iambic hexameter, using the rhyme scheme ababbcbcc. The scheme is used in *The Faerie Queene*.

spent /spent/ past participle, past tense of **spend** ■ adj 1. CONSUMED used or used up ○ *tossed the spent match into the fire* 2. EXHAUSTED totally depleted of energy or strength ○ *felt totally spent by the end of the day* 3. FINISHED at an end 4. FISH EXHAUSTED OF SPAWN OR SPERM describes a female fish that has deposited all its spawn or a male fish that has used up all its sperm

sperm [1] /spurm/ n PHYSIOL 1. same as **spermatozoon** 2. same as **semen** (*informal; not in technical use*) [14C. Via late Latin < Greek *sperma* 'seed, semen' < *speirein* 'to sow']

sperm [2] /spurm/ n 1. INDUST same as **spermaceti** 2. INDUST same as **sperm oil** 3. MARINE BIOL same as **sperm whale** [Mid-19C. Shortening]

spermaceti /spúrmə sétti, -seéti/ n a white waxy solid. Source: oil in the head of sperm whales and other cetaceans. Use: formerly, in cosmetics, candles, and ointments. [Late 15C. < medieval Latin, < late Latin *sperma* (see SPERM[1]) + Latin *ceti* 'of a whale']

spermary /spúrməri/ (*plural* **-ries**) n an organ in which male reproductive cells are developed. The testes are spermaries.

spermat- prefix same as **spermato-** (*used before vowels*)

spermatheca /spúrmə theékə/ n a receptacle for storing sperm in the reproductive tracts of some invertebrates such as insects [Early 19C. < late Latin *sperma* (see SPERM[1])] —**spermathecal** adj

spermatic /spur máttik/ adj 1. relating to, carrying, or containing semen 2. relating to a spermary or to the spermatic cord —**spermatically** adv

spermatic cord n a cord by which a testis is suspended in the scrotum. It contains the vas deferens as well as nerves, vessels, and veins.

spermatid /spúrmə tid/ n a cell that, with three others, forms from a spermatocyte and develops into a spermatozoon

spermatium /spur máyshəm/ (*plural* **-tia** /-shə/) n a cell that functions as a male reproductive cell in some algae, fungi, and lichens [Mid-19C. Via modern Latin < Greek *spermation*, diminutive of *sperma* (see SPERM[1])]

spermato- prefix 1. sperm, spermatozoon ○ *spermatogenesis* 2. seed ○ *spermatophyte* [< Greek *spermat-*, stem of *sperma* (see SPERM[1])]

spermatocide /spur máttō sīd/ n PHARM same as **spermicide** —**spermatocidal** /spur máttō sīd'l, spúrmətō-/ adj

spermatocyte /spur máttō sīt/ *n* a cell that develops from a spermatogonium. It divides into four spermatids by means of the kind of cell division known as meiosis.

spermatogenesis /spur máttō jénnəssiss, spúrmətō-/ *n* the formation and development of spermatozoa in the testes —**spermatogenetic** /spur máttō jə néttik, spúrmətō-/ *adj*

spermatogonium /spur máttō gṓni əm, spúrmətō-/ (*plural* **-nia** /-ni ə/) *n* a cell in the male testes that develops and divides to form spermatocytes. These subsequently divide to form spermatids, from which spermatozoa finally develop. —**spermatogonial** *adj*

spermatophore /spur máttō fawr, spúrmətə fawr/ *n* a capsule or mass that encloses spermatozoa in insects and other lower animals and is transferred to the female during insemination —**spermatophoral** /spur mátte fáwrəl, spúrmətō-/ *adj*

spermatophyte /spur máttō fīt/ *n* a plant such as an angiosperm or a gymnosperm that produces seeds —**spermatophytic** /spur máttə fíttik, spúrmətō-/ *adj*

spermatorrhoea /spur mátə reé ə/ *n* the involuntary emission of semen without orgasm

spermatozoa BIOL *plural of* **spermatozoon**

spermatozoid /spur máttō zṓ id, spúrmətō-/ *n* a male reproductive cell, resembling a ribbon, produced in algae, ferns, fungi, mosses, and some gymnosperms. It can move by means of flagella. [Mid-19C. < SPERMATOZOON]

spermatozoon /spur máttō zṓ on, spúrmətō-/ (*plural* **-zoa** /-zṓ ə/) *n* a male reproductive cell (**gamete**) that has an oval head with a nucleus, a short neck, and a tail by which it moves to find and fertilize an ovum —**spermatozoan** *adj*

sperm bank *n* a place that stores semen until it is required for use in artificial insemination

sperm count *n* **1.** the concentration of sperm in a given volume of seminal fluid, taken as an index of male fertility **2.** a test to determine a man's sperm count

spermi- *prefix same as* **spermo-**

spermic /spúrmik/ *adj* BIOL *same as* **spermatic**

spermicide /spúrmi sīd/ *n* a contraceptive cream or gel used in conjunction with a birth-control device. Use: kills spermatozoa. —**spermicidal** /spúrmi sīd'l/ *adj*

spermiogenesis /spúrmi ō jénnəssiss/ *n* the stage of spermatogenesis during which a spermatid is transformed into a spermatozoon —**spermiogenetic** /spúrmi ō jə néttik/ *adj*

spermo-, spermi- *prefix* seed, sperm [< Greek *sperma* (see SPERM[1])]

sperm oil *n* a pale yellow oil obtained from the head of the sperm whale. Use: formerly, industrial lubricant.

sperm whale *n* the largest of the toothed whales, whose massive square head has a cavity filled with a mixture of sperm oil and spermaceti [Shortening of *spermaceti whale*]

-spermy *suffix* fertilization ○ *polyspermy* [< Greek *sperma* (see SPERM[1]) + -Y[2]]

Sperrin Mountains /spérrin-/ mountain range forming the border between the counties of Londonderry and Tyrone, Northern Ireland. Its highest peak is Sawel Peak, 683 m./2,240 ft. Length: 24 km/15 mi.

sperrylite /spérri līt/ *n* a silvery white platinum arsenide mineral. Use: source of platinum. [Early 20C. After Francis L. *Sperry* (d. 1906), Canadian chemist]

spessartine /spéssər teen/, **spessartite** /spéssər tīt/ *n* a yellow or reddish-brown garnet that contains manganese. Use: gems. [Mid-19C. < French, after *Spessart*, S Germany]

spew /spyoo/ *vti* (**spews, spewing, spewed**) **1.** VOMIT SOMETHING to vomit something that has been eaten **2.** POUR OUT FORCEFULLY to flow out forcefully, or force something out in a stream ○ *a volcano spewing ash* **3.** SAY SOMETHING FORCEFULLY to utter something in an angry, forceful, or relentless way ■ *n* VOMIT some-thing ejected from the mouth, especially vomit [Old English *spīwan* < Indo-European 'to spit', an imitation of the sound] —**spewer** *n*

Spey /spay/ river in northern Scotland, flowing from Loch Lochy to the Moray Firth. Length: 171 km/107 mi.

Speyer /spī ər, shpī ər/ city in southwestern Germany. At the Diet of Speyer in 1529 the followers of Martin Luther registered a formal protest, which gave rise to the term 'Protestant'. Population: 45,100 (1989). English name **Spires**

SPF *n* the degree to which a sun cream, lotion, screen, or block provides protection for the skin against the sun. Full form **sun protection factor**

Spgs *abbr* Springs (*in placenames*)

sphagnum /sfágnəm/ *n* moss growing in wet acid temperate regions that decays and becomes compacted to form peat. Genus: *Sphagnum*. [Mid-18C. Via modern Latin < Greek *sphagnos*, type of shrub] —**sphagnous** *adj*

sphalerite /sfállə rīt, sfáylə rīt/ *n* a yellow or brownish zinc sulphide mineral. Use: source of zinc. [Mid-19C. < Greek *sphaleros* 'slippery, uncertain', because the mineral is easily confused with galena]

sphen- *prefix same as* **spheno-** (*used before vowels*)

sphene /sfeen/ *n* a brown-black mineral composed of calcium titanium silicate. Source: igneous rocks. [Early 19C. Via French < Greek *sphēn* 'wedge']

spheno- *prefix* wedge-shaped ○ *sphenodon* [< Greek *sphēn* 'wedge']

sphenodon /sfeénə don/ *n* REPT *same as* **tuatara** [Late 19C. < modern Latin < Greek *sphēn* 'wedge' + *odōn*, variant of *odous* 'tooth']

sphenoid /sfeé noyd/ *adj* **1.** shaped like a wedge **2.** relating to the sphenoid bone ■ *n* ANAT *same as* **sphenoid bone**

sphenoid bone *n* a bone with prominent wings at the base of the cranium. It forms part of the walls and roof of the nasal cavity.

spher- *prefix same as* **sphero-** (*used before vowels*)

sphere /sfeer/ *n* **1.** GLOBE an object similar in shape to a ball **2.** MATHS THREE-DIMENSIONAL SURFACE a three-dimensional closed surface consisting of all points that are a given distance from a centre **3.** MATHS ROUND SOLID FIGURE the solid figure bounded by a sphere, or the volume it encloses **4.** FIELD OF KNOWLEDGE OR ACTIVITY a field of knowledge, interest, or activity **5.** AREA OF INFLUENCE an area of control or influence ○ *took no interest in matters beyond her sphere* **6.** GROUP IN SOCIETY a level or group within a society **7.** ASTRONOMICAL OBJECT an astronomical object such as a planet, moon, or star (*literary*) **8.** ASTRON *same as* **sky** (*literary*) **9.** REVOLVING CELESTIAL SHELL in early astronomical theory, a revolving concentric transparent shell on which the Sun, Moon, planets, and stars were thought to be fixed as they moved around the Earth ■ *vt* (**spheres, sphering, sphered**) **1.** ENCIRCLE SOMETHING to surround, encircle, or enclose something (*literary*) **2.** RAISE SOMETHING ALOFT to place something in the sky or in heaven, among the celestial spheres (*literary*) **3.** FORM SOMETHING INTO BALL to form something into the shape of a ball [13C. Via French < Latin *sphaera* < Greek *sphaira* 'ball'] —**spheral** *adj* —**sphericity** /sfe ríssəti/ *n*

sphere of influence *n* a geographical region or area of activity in which a state, organization, or person is dominant

spherical /sférrik'l/, **spheric** /sférrik/ *adj* **1.** ROUND shaped like a sphere **2.** OF SPHERES relating to a sphere or to spheres in general **3.** OF ASTRONOMICAL OBJECTS relating to astronomical objects **4.** OF SPHERES OF ANCIENT ASTRONOMY relating to the spheres of ancient astronomy —**spherically** *adv* —**sphericalness** *n*

spherical aberration *n* a fault in a lens or curved mirror in which light passing through the edge has a different focal point from light passing through the centre, resulting in blurred images

spherical angle *n* an angle formed on a sphere at the point at which any two circles of maximum radius intersect

spherical coordinates *npl* a set of coordinates used for locating a point in space, representing its distance from an origin and two angles describing its orientation relative to perpendicular axes extending from that origin

spherical geometry *n* the geometry of figures formed on the surface of a sphere

spherical polygon *n* a geometric figure formed on the surface of a sphere, bounded by three or more arcs of great circles

spherical triangle *n* a spherical polygon that has three sides

spherical trigonometry *n* trigonometry dealing with spherical triangles

spherics /sférriks/ *n* the study of electromagnetic radiation emanating from natural sources in the atmosphere (*takes a singular verb*) [Mid-20C. Shortening of ATMOSPHERICS]

sphero- *prefix* sphere, spherical ○ *spheroplast* [Via Latin < Greek *sphaira* 'sphere, ball']

spheroid /sférroyd, sfeér oyd/ *n* a three-dimensional object that is shaped like a sphere, but is not perfectly round, e.g. an ellipsoid —**spheroidal** /sfi róyd'l/ *adj* —**spheroidally** *adv* —**spheroidicity** /sférroy díssəti, sfeér oy-/ *n*

spherometer /sfi rómmitər/ *n* an instrument used to measure the curvature of a surface

spheroplast /sférrō plast, -plaast/ *n* a bacterium or yeast cell that has lost part of its cell wall and is as a result spherical in shape and more sensitive to osmosis

spherule /sférrool/ *n* a minute sphere or globule [Mid-17C. < late Latin *spherula* 'small sphere' < Latin *sphaera* (see SPHERE)] —**spherular** *adj*

spherulite /sférroō līt/ *n* a spherical mass of radiating crystal fibres. Source: volcanic rocks. —**spherulitic** /sférrō líttik/ *adj*

sphery /sfeéri/ *adj* **1.** having the shape of a sphere **2.** relating to or resembling a planet, star, or other astronomical object (*literary*)

sphincter /sfíngktər/ *n* a circular band of muscle that surrounds an opening or passage in the body, especially the anus, and narrows or closes the opening by contracting [Late 16C. Via Latin < Greek *sphigktēr* < *sphiggein* 'bind tight'] —**sphincteral** *adj*

sphinges MYTHOL *plural of* **sphinx**

sphingosine /sfíng gə seen, -sin/ *n* a long-chain amino glycol that is part of the lipids found in nerve tissue [Late 19C. < Greek *sphiggos* 'of a sphinx' < *sphigg-*, stem of *sphigx* 'sphinx']

sphinx

sphinx /sfingks/ (*plural* **sphinxes** or **sphinges** /sfín jeez/) *n* **1.** COMPOSITE CREATURE IN GREEK MYTHOLOGY in Greek mythology, a winged creature with a lion's body and a woman's head. It strangled all who could not answer its riddle, but killed itself when Oedipus answered correctly. **2.** COMPOSITE CREATURE IN EGYPTIAN MYTHOLOGY in Egyptian mythology, a creature with a lion's body and the head of a man, ram, or bird **3.** STATUE a statue of a sphinx **4.** SOMEBODY MYSTERIOUS somebody regarded as mysterious or inscrutable [Late 16C. Via Latin < Greek *sphigx*]

sphinxlike /sfíngks līk/ *adj* difficult to understand or find out about

sphinx moth *n* INSECTS *same as* **hawk moth** [Because its appearance suggests a sphinx]

sphragistics /sfrə jístiks/ *n* the study of seals and signet rings (*takes a singular verb*) [Mid-19C. Directly or

via French < late Greek *sphragistikos* 'of seals (for impressing designs)' < Greek *sphragis* 'seal'] —**sphragistic** *adj*

sphygm- *prefix* same as **sphygmo-** (*used before vowels*)

sphygmic /sfígmik/ *adj* relating to the pulse of an artery [Early 18C. < Greek *sphugmikos* < *sphugmos* (see SPHYGMO-)]

sphygmo- *prefix* pulse of an artery ○ *sphygmograph* [< Greek *sphugmos* 'pulsation' < *sphug-*, stem of *spuzein* 'throb']

sphygmograph /sfígmō graaf, -graf/ *n* an apparatus used to make a graphical record of variations in blood pressure and pulse —**sphygmographic** /sfígmō gráffik/ *adj* —**sphygmography** /sfig móggrəfi/ *n*

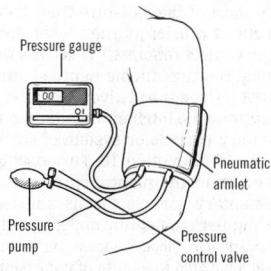

Pressure gauge

Pneumatic armlet

Pressure pump

Pressure control valve

sphygmomanometer

sphygmomanometer /sfíg mōmə nómmitər/ *n* an instrument used to measure blood pressure in an artery that consists of a pressure gauge, an inflatable cuff placed around the upper arm, and an inflator bulb or pressure pump

spic /spik/ *n* a highly offensive term for a Spanish or Italian person (*taboo*) [Early 20C. Shortening and alteration of *spiggoty*, probably < broken English *(no)speaka de (English)* 'I don't speak English']

spica /spíkə/ (*plural* **-cae** /-see/ *or* **-cas**) *n* a bandage applied to a limb in an overlapping figure-of-eight pattern to immobilize it [14C. < Latin, 'ear of grain'; from its spiralling shape]

spic-and-span *adj* another spelling of **spick-and-span**

spicate /spí kayt/ *adj* growing in the form of a spike, or having flowers that grow in spikes [Mid-17C. < Latin *spicatus*, past participle of *spicare* 'provide with sharp points' < *spica* 'spike, ear of grain']

spiccato /spi ka̓atō/ *n* a technique of playing staccato on stringed instruments, in which the bow is allowed to bounce on the string ■ *adj, adv* played using the technique of allowing the bow to bounce on the string [Early 18C. < Italian, past participle of *spiccare* 'pick off, detach']

spice /spīss/ *n* **1.** AROMATIC PLANT SUBSTANCE USED AS FLAVOURING an aromatic plant substance used as a flavouring, e.g. nutmeg or ginger **2.** FLAVOURINGS FROM PLANTS food flavourings derived from the nonleafy parts of plants (*often used before a noun*) **3.** EXCITEMENT OR INTEREST a source of excitement or interest **4.** US STRONG SMELL a pungent odour or fragrance (*often used before a noun*) **5.** TRACE OF SOMETHING a tiny amount of something ■ *vt* (**spices, spicing, spiced**) **1.** SEASON SOMETHING WITH SPICE to season food or drink with spice **2.** MAKE SOMETHING MORE EXCITING to introduce excitement or interest into something ○ *spiced the speech with joking asides* [13C. Via Old French *espice* < late Latin *species* (plural) 'goods, wares' < Latin (singular) 'appearance, kind']

spiceberry /spíssbəri/ (*plural* **-ries**) *n* **1.** a spicy orange, red, or black berry **2.** a tree or bush that produces spiceberries, e.g. the wintergreen

spicebush /spíssboosh/ *n* a bush of the laurel family with aromatic leaves. Flowers: yellow, in dense clusters. Native to: North America. Latin name: *Lindera benzoin.*

~~spicey~~ incorrect spelling of **spicy**

spick-and-span /spík-/, **spic-and-span** *adj* **1.** very clean and tidy (*not hyphenated after a verb*) **2.** showing no sign of damage or wear and tear [Late 16C. Shortening of *spick-and-span-new* < variant of SPIKE] + dialect *span-new* 'completely new' < Old Norse *spánnyr* 'new chip' < *spán* 'chip']

spicula BIOL plural of **spiculum**

spicule /spíkyool/ *n* **1.** a small hard needle-shaped part, especially one of the calcium- or silicon-containing supporting parts of some invertebrates such as sponges and corals **2.** a slender column of relatively cool high-density gas that rapidly erupts from the solar chromosphere and then falls back. There can be as many as 250,000 spicules rising above the solar surface at any moment. [Late 18C. Anglicized < SPICULUM] —**spicular** *adj* —**spiculate** *adj*

spiculum /spíkyələm/ (*plural* **-la** /-lə/) *n* BIOL same as **spicule** (sense 1) [Mid-18C. < modern Latin, 'small spike' < Latin *spica* 'spike, ear of grain']

spicy /spíssi/ (**-ier, -iest**) *adj* **1.** SEASONED WITH SPICE smelling or tasting strongly of spices **2.** INVOLVING IMPROPRIETY arousing interest as a result of involving scandal or sexual impropriety (*informal*) **3.** VIVACIOUS having a very lively personality **4.** BOT PRODUCING SPICES describes plants or plant parts from which spices are obtained —**spicily** *adv* —**spiciness** *n*

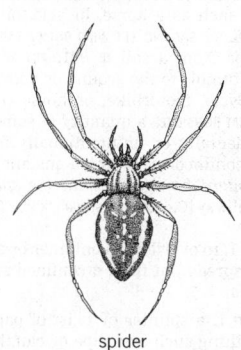

spider

spider /spídər/ *n* **1.** EIGHT-LEGGED ANIMAL THAT SPINS WEBS a predatory invertebrate animal with four pairs of legs and two or more abdominal organs (**spinnerets**) used for spinning webs that serve as nests and traps for prey. It is popularly thought to be an insect, although it is an arachnid. Order: Araneae. **2.** US TRIVET a trivet for supporting a pan on a hearth **3.** SET OF STRAPS FOR ATTACHING LOADS a bunch of elastic straps joined at a central point, usually with a hook at each free end, used especially for attaching a load to a rack on a vehicle **4.** MECH ENG MECHANICAL DEVICE a mechanical device that has radiating arms, spokes, or other parts **5.** NAUT FRAME SECURING REDUNDANT ROPES a circular frame at the base of a ship's mast, used to secure ropes when sails are not in use **6.** ONLINE PROGRAM SEARCHING INTERNET FOR INFORMATION a computer program that searches the Internet for newly accessible information to be added to the index examined by a standard search tool (**search engine**) **7.** CUE GAMES CUE REST a multiposition cue rest with wide legs designed to lift the cue tip over an intervening ball **8.** TRANSP same as **spider phaeton 9.** Aus FOOD same as **ice-cream soda** (*informal*) [Old English *spiþra* < *spinnan* (see SPIN)]

spider beetle *n* a wingless beetle, many varieties of which are pests to stored food in households and warehouses. Family: Ptinidae.

spider crab *n* a sea crab with a small triangular body and long slender legs. Family: Majidae.

spider flower *n* **1.** PLANTS same as **cleome 2.** a flowering plant whose flower heads resemble spiders. Native to: Australian. Genus: *Grevillea.*

spider food *n* words or coding embedded in a webpage in order to make it more likely to be found and indexed by search engines (*slang*) [Late 20C. < *spider* meaning 'search engine']

spidergram /spídər gram/ *n* a diagram resembling a spider's body and legs, in which information relating to a topic is noted down in boxes joined by radiating lines to a central box containing the topic

spider hole *n* (*informal*) **1.** a concealed sniper position, e.g. in a cave or a camouflaged hole dug in the ground **2.** a camouflaged and reinforced hole dug in the ground and used as a hiding place [< the habit of some spiders such as the trapdoor spider of digging concealed holes with hinged lids]

spider-hunting wasp *n* a large black or metallic-

blue solitary wasp that preys on spiders. Family: Pepsidae.

spiderman /spídər man/ (*plural* **-men** /-men/) *n* (*informal*) **1.** a construction worker who erects the steel frame of a building **2.** a worker who climbs and repairs tall buildings

spider mite *n* a tiny web-spinning mite. Some spider mites are garden and crop pests. Family: Tetranychidae.

spider monkey *n* a tree-dwelling monkey with long slender limbs, a long prehensile tail, and a small head. Native to: Central and South America. Genus: *Ateles.*

spider phaeton *n* a high-bodied lightweight fast horse carriage with large wheels

spider plant *n* a common houseplant grown for its long narrow variegated leaves and clusters of plantlets. Flowers: white. Latin name: *Chlorophytum variegatum.*

spiderweb /spídər web/ *n* a web that is constructed by a spider to entrap prey, using silk produced from fluid from its abdominal glands

spiderwort /spídər wurt/ *n* a plant widely grown as a houseplant. Flowers: pink, blue, or violet. Genus: *Tradescantia.* [< the resemblance of the stamens to a spider's legs]

spidery /spídəri/ *adj* **1.** THIN AND IRREGULAR having thin lines or constituent parts that form irregular angles **2.** SPIDER-INFESTED infested with spiders **3.** LIKE SPIDER resembling a spider in shape or movement

Spidla /spíddlə/, **Vladimir** (*b.* 1951) prime minister of the Czech Republic (2002–). A founder member of the centre-left Czech Social Democratic Party and former deputy prime minister, he was elected prime minister in 2002.

spiegeleisen /speég'l īz'n/, **spiegel** /speég'l/ *n* pig iron containing high concentrations of manganese and carbon. It is added to steel in the late stages of production to adjust the final composition. [Mid-19C. < German < *Spiegel* 'mirror' + *Eisen* 'iron']

spiel /shpeel, speel/ (*informal*) *n* an irritatingly long or predictably glib speech, e.g. a rambling apology or prepared sales patter ■ *vi* (**spiels, spieling, spieled**) to deliver a spiel [Late 19C. < German, 'play, game'] **spiel off** *vt* to say something very quickly or by rote ○ *spiel off a list of names*

Express Newspapers

Steven Spielberg

Spielberg /speél burg/, **Steven** (*b.* 1947) US film director and producer. His films include *E.T.* (1982), *Jurassic Park* (1993), and the Academy Award-winning *Schindler's List* (1993).

> 'When I grow up I still want to be a director.'
> [Steven Spielberg, *Time*; 15 July 1985]

spiff /spif/ (**spiffs, spiffing, spiffed**) [Late 19C. Origin ?] **spiff up** *vt* to make somebody or something more attractive especially by adding enhancing features (*informal*)

spiffing /spíffing/ *adj* UK exceptionally good (*dated informal*) [Late 19C. Origin ?]

spifflicate *vt* another spelling of **spiflicate**

spiffy /spíffi/ (**-ier, -iest**) *adj* stylish or modern and attractive (*informal*) ○ *a spiffy collection of supercomputers blinking away in a room of their own* (Kathleen O'Gorman *Detroit Free Press*; 1997) [Mid-19C. Origin ?] —**spiffily** *adv* —**spiffiness** *n*

spiflicate /spífflі kayt/ (**-cates, -cating, -cated**), **spif-flicate** *vt* (*dated or humorous slang*) **1.** to destroy something completely **2.** to defeat somebody resoundingly [Mid-18C. Nonsense word] —**spiflication** /spíffli káysh'n/ *n*

spignel /spígn'l/ *n* a plant with fine aromatic leaves, found mainly in mountain pastures. Flowers: small, white. Native to: Europe. Latin name: *Meum athamanticum*. [Early 16C. Origin ?]

spigot /spíggət/ *n* **1.** TAP FITTED TO CASK a tap, usually wooden, that is fitted to a cask **2.** PLUG FOR CASK HOLE a plug for the vent hole of a cask **3.** *US* OUTDOOR TAP a tap situated outdoors **4.** PIPE END JOINING OTHER the end of a pipe that is joined by insertion into the enlarged end of another pipe [14C. Origin ?]

spike[1] /spīk/ *n* **1.** POINTED METAL OR WOODEN PIECE a sharply pointed piece of metal or wood, especially one of a number along the top of a railing, fence, or wall **2.** SHARP POINT a narrow sharp point **3.** LARGE NAIL a long heavy metal nail **4.** METAL PART FOR GRIPPING AND CLIMBING a sharp pointed metal projection strapped to a boot as an aid in gripping and climbing something **5.** METAL POINT ON RUNNING SHOE SOLE a pointed metal stud, part of a set attached to the sole of an athlete's shoe to give better grip (*often used in the plural*) **6.** METAL ROD FOR LOOSE PAPERS a pointed metal rod mounted on a base onto which loose papers are thrust, especially rejected news stories (*dated*) **7.** UNBRANCHED ANTLER OF DEER the straight unbranched antler of a young deer **8.** DRUGS same as **hypodermic needle** (*slang*) **9.** VARIATION IN VOLTAGE an abrupt temporary surge in the voltage or current in an electrical circuit. The change may be caused by turning off appliances, a lightning strike, or power being restored after a power cut. **10.** IMAGE OF PEAK AND FALL a graphic representation of a sharp rise followed by a sharp fall, especially on a graph or as a reading on an instrument **11.** SUDDEN BRIEF INCREASE a sharp and brief rise in something **12.** DOWNWARD SMASH OF VOLLEYBALL a hard smash of a volleyball, hit close to the net and straight down into the opponent's court **13.** HOSTEL FOR PEOPLE WITHOUT HOMES a hostel that houses people who have no place to live (*dated slang*) ■ **spikes** *npl* PAIR OF SHOES WITH METAL STUDS a pair of athletic shoes whose soles are equipped with pointed metal studs to give better traction ■ *v* (**spikes, spiking, spiked**) **1.** *vt* SECRETLY ADD SOMETHING TO DRINK to put alcohol, a drug, or a poison into somebody's drink surreptitiously (*informal*) **2.** *vt* RENDER SOMETHING USELESS to make something useless or ineffective (*informal*) **3.** *vt* CAUSE INJURY WITH SPIKES ON SHOE to injure another player or competitor with the spikes of an athletic shoe **4.** *vi* RISE ABRUPTLY to rise sharply and briefly **5.** *vt* MEDIA DISCARD POTENTIAL NEWS STORY to reject or decide not to use a news story (*informal*) **6.** *vt* SMASH VOLLEYBALL DOWNWARD to leap high close to the net and hit a volleyball straight down into an opponent's court **7.** *vt* DISABLE CANNON WITH SPIKE to render a cannon useless by driving a spike into its vent [13C. Ultimately < Indo-European, 'sharp point'] —**spiked** *adj*

spike[2] /spīk/ *n* **1.** a long cluster of flowers attached directly to a stem, with the newest flowers at the tip **2.** an ear of corn such as wheat or barley [14C. < Latin *spica* 'ear of grain']

spike heel *n* a high pointed heel on a woman's shoe, or a shoe with such a heel

spikelet /spíklət/ *n* a small flower spike, especially one of the basic units of the flower cluster of a grass or sedge

spikenard /spík naard, spíkə naard/ (*plural* **-nards** or *same*) *n* **1.** HIMALAYAN PLANT a perennial aromatic plant of the valerian family. Flowers: pinkish-purple. Native to: Himalayan range. Latin name: *Nardostachys jatamansi*. **2.** ANCIENT FRAGRANT OINTMENT a fragrant ointment derived from spikenard, used in ancient times **3.** PLANT WITH AROMATIC ROOT a plant of the ginseng family with purplish berries and aromatic roots. Flowers: small, whitish. Native to: North America. Latin name: *Aralia racemosa*. [14C. < medieval Latin *spica nardi* 'spike of nard', translation of Greek *nardou stakhus*]

spiky /spíki/ (**-ier, -iest**) *adj* **1.** having one or more narrow sharp points **2.** easily made angry (*informal*) —**spikily** *adv* —**spikiness** *n*

spile /spīl/ *n* **1.** HEAVY SUPPORTING POST a heavy timber post driven into the ground as a foundation or support **2.** WOODEN PEG a wooden peg, especially one used as a plug or stopper **3.** *N Am* TREE-TAPPING SPOUT a tap for drawing sap from the sugar maple tree ■ *vt* (**spiles, spiling, spiled**) **1.** SUPPORT SOMETHING WITH POST to provide or support something with a heavy timber post driven into the ground **2.** *N Am* TAP TREE FOR SAP to draw sap from a tree with a spout or spigot [Early 16C. Via Dutch *spijl* < Middle Dutch or Middle Low German *spile* 'splinter, wooden pin']

spill[1] /spil/ *v* (**spills, spilling, spilt** /spilt/ or **spilled, spilt** or **spilled** /spilt/) **1.** *vti* FLOW FROM CONTAINER to flow from a container, or allow something to flow from a container, especially accidentally and usually with resulting loss or waste **2.** *vi* COME OUT OF CONFINED SPACE to come out from a building or other confined space in large numbers ○ *The fans spilled out onto the pitch.* **3.** *vt* DIVULGE SOMETHING to reveal or divulge something, often unintentionally (*informal*) ○ *spilled the news* **4.** *vti* FALL OFF SOMETHING to fall off something onto the ground or floor, or make somebody fall off something such as a horse, bicycle, or motorbike (*informal*) **5.** *vt* SAILING LET WIND OUT OF SAIL to let the wind escape from a sail ■ *n* **1.** ACT OF FALLING FROM SOMETHING a tumble to the ground or floor, especially from a bicycle, motorbike, or horse (*informal*) **2.** SOMETHING THAT RUNS OVER a quantity of something that flows accidentally or unintentionally from a container or confined area, or an instance of this ○ *Workers fought hard to contain the spill.* **3.** GEOG same as **spillway** [Old English *spillan* 'kill' < Germanic] —**spiller** *n*

spill over *vi* **1.** to overflow a container or an enclosed area **2.** to spread out from a confined space into a nearby area

spill[2] /spil/ *n* **1.** a splinter or twist of paper used to light something such as a pipe or candle **2.** CONSTR same as **spile** *n* (sense 2) [14C. < Middle Low German *spile*]

spillage /spíllij/ *n* **1.** the act of spilling something **2.** a quantity of something that has been spilled

Spillane /spi láyn/, **Mickey** (*b.* 1918) US writer. His crime fiction is known for its raw energy and violence. Many of his stories feature the detective Mike Hammer. Born **Spillane, Frank Morrison**

spillikin /spílli kin/, **spilikin, spellican** /spéllikən/ *n* a small thin stick used in the game of jackstraws (*dated*) [Mid-18C. Diminutive of SPILL[2]]

spillikins /spílli kinz/, **spilikins** *n* LEISURE same as **jackstraws** (*dated; takes a singular verb*)

spillover /spíl ōvər/ *n N Am* **1.** a spread or expansion of something from a confined space into a nearby area **2.** an indirect effect of something

spillway /spíl way/ *n* a channel for carrying away excess water, e.g. at a reservoir or dam

spilt past participle, past tense of **spill**[1]

spim /spim/ *n* unsolicited e-mail that arrives on a personal computer screen in the form of an instant message [Late 20C. Blend of SPAM + *instant message*] —**spimmer** *n*

spin /spin/ *v* (**spins, spinning, spun** /spun/ or **span** /span/, **spun**) **1.** *vti* ROTATE SOMETHING QUICKLY to turn round and round rapidly, or make something turn round and round rapidly, as if on an axis ○ *He spun a coin.* ○ *dancers spinning round the room* **2.** *vi* ROTATE FREELY to revolve or rotate rapidly around an axis ○ *Our wheels spun on the ice.* **3.** *vi* FACE ABOUT QUICKLY to turn round rapidly to face in the opposite direction **4.** *vti* CREATE YARN FROM RAW MATERIALS to twist raw fibres, e.g. of wool, silk, or cotton, so that they form a continuous yarn or thread **5.** *vti* MAKE WEB OR COCOON to make a web or cocoon from filaments extruded from the body **6.** *vt* INVENT STORY to make up an extended story or a series of lies **7.** *vti* GIVE PUBLIC BIASED INFORMATION to present information in a way meant to influence public opinion ○ *Nobody will give you an unvarnished fact; it has to be spun and interpreted.* **8.** *vti* ROTATE SOMETHING RAPIDLY IN CHANGED DIRECTION to strike, throw, or kick something in a way that makes it revolve and change direction when it hits something, or rotate and change direction in this way **9.** *vi* BECOME DIZZY to feel dazed, as if whirling round ○ *My head was spinning.* **10.** *vti* DRY SOMETHING BY ROTATION to remove water, especially from washed clothes, by rotating them rapidly in a machine **11.** *vi* DRIVE FAST AND WELL to drive smoothly and speedily **12.** *vti* AVIAT MAKE AIRCRAFT DIVE STEEPLY to go into a steep spiral dive, or make an aircraft do this **13.** *vi* FISHING FISH WITH RAPIDLY MOVING BAIT to fish with a rod, line, and reel, constantly drawing a revolving bait or lure through the water **14.** *vt* MUSIC PLAY RECORDING to play a piece of recorded music (*informal*) ■ *n* **1.** ROTATION a quick rotating movement **2.** ROTATION CAUSING CHANGED DIRECTION rotation given to a ball to make it change direction **3.** DIZZY STATE a state of mental disorientation or dizziness **4.** INTERPRETIVE POINT OF VIEW a viewpoint, bias, or interpretation meant to influence public opinion ○ *There's no way the government can put a favourable spin on this disaster.* **5.** DRYING OPERATION IN WASHING MACHINE the rapid rotation of washed clothes in a washing machine to remove most of the moisture from them **6.** SHORT JOURNEY IN VEHICLE a brief journey taken for pleasure in a motor vehicle (*informal*) **7.** ROTATION WHILE SKATING a stationary rotation during figure skating **8.** AVIAT SPIRALLING DIVE a steep spiral dive in an aircraft **9.** PHYS ANGULAR MOMENTUM the intrinsic angular momentum of an elementary particle or system of such particles independent of its motion **10.** PHYS QUANTUM PROPERTY OF ANGULAR MOMENTUM the quantum property or number of an elementary particle that is a measure of its intrinsic angular momentum and magnetic moment [Old English *spinnan* < Indo-European, 'to stretch, spin'] ◇ **in a spin, in a flat spin** in a state of confusion or panic

spin off *v* **1.** *vti* to derive a new product, material, or service from something that already exists, or be derived in this way **2.** *vt* to divest a company of a subsidiary by distributing the subsidiary's shares to shareholders in the parent corporation

spin out *v* **1.** *vt* PROLONG SOMETHING to make an activity last for an unnecessarily long time **2.** *vt* MAKE SUPPLIES LAST to make something last longer than it ordinarily would, usually by careful management **3.** *vi N Am* LOSE CONTROL OF VEHICLE to skid out of control

spina bifida /spínə bíffidə, -bífidə/ *n* a congenital condition in which part of the spinal cord or meninges protrudes through a cleft in the spinal column, resulting in loss of voluntary movement in the lower body [< modern Latin, 'spine split in two']

spinach /spínich/ *n* an annual plant widely cultivated for its edible dark green leaves. Use: eaten cooked as a vegetable or raw in salads. Latin name: *Spinacia oleracea*. [14C. Via Old French *espinache* and Spanish *espinaca* < Arabic *isbānāk* < Persian *aspānāk*]

spinal /spín'l/ *adj* **1.** OF SPINE on, in, near, or relating to the spine of a vertebrate animal **2.** LIKE SPINE resembling the spine of a vertebrate animal ■ *n* MED SPINAL ANAESTHETIC an anaesthetic used to induce spinal anaesthesia (*informal*) —**spinally** *adv*

spinal anaesthesia *n* **1.** anaesthesia of the lower half of the body induced by injecting an anaesthetic into the fluid surrounding the spinal cord **2.** the loss of sensation in part of the body caused by injury to the spinal column

spinal canal *n* a passage that runs through the opening in the middle of each vertebra of the spinal column and contains the spinal cord, the meninges, nerve roots, and blood vessels

spinal column *n* the axis of the skeleton of a vertebrate animal, extending from the head and consisting of a series of interconnected vertebrae that enclose and protect the spinal cord

spinal cord *n* a thick whitish cord of nerve tissue extending from the bottom of the brain through the spinal column and giving rise to pairs of spinal nerves that supply the body. The spinal cord and brain together form the central nervous system.

spinal meningitis *n* inflammation of the membranes surrounding the spinal cord that particularly affects young children

spinal tap *n N Am* MED same as **lumbar puncture**

spin angular momentum *n* PHYS same as **spin** *n* (sense 9)

spin bowler *n* in cricket, a bowler who specializes in bowling balls that spin

spindle /spínd'l/ *n* **1.** SPECIALLY SHAPED ROD FOR SPINNING THREAD a hand-held rod with a notched end through which strands of natural fibres are drawn, then twisted into thread and wound round the rod **2.** THREAD-SPINNING ROD ON SPINNING WHEEL a device similar to

the hand-held spindle, attached to a spinning wheel **3.** MECHANICAL THREAD-SPINNING DEVICE a device on a spinning machine for spinning thread and winding it onto bobbins **4.** SPINDLE-SHAPED PIECE OF WOOD a long thin piece of wood that is shaped like a spindle, e.g. a table leg or baluster **5.** SPINDLE-SHAPED CELL STRUCTURE a spindle-shaped structure consisting of a network of microtubule fibres along which chromosomes are distributed and drawn apart during meiosis and mitosis **6.** MECH ENG ROTATING ROD FOR DEVICE a rotating rod on a device such as a lathe, turntable, or door handle **7.** NAUT WARNING SIGNAL FOR BOATS a metal rod surmounted by a ball or lantern and fixed to a rock or shoal. Use: warning for approaching vessels. ■ *v* (-dles, -dling, -dled) **1.** *vt* EQUIP SOMETHING WITH SPINDLE to provide something with a spindle or spindles **2.** *vi* BOT GROW TALL AND THIN to grow a tall slender weak stem [Old English *spinel* < Germanic]

spindle cell *n* a narrow, elongated cell characteristic of some cancers

spindle-legged, **spindle-shanked** *adj* with legs that are long and thin (*dated*)

spindle tree *n* an evergreen or deciduous tree or bush with small flowers, red fruits, and hard wood. Use: formerly, to make spindles. Genus: *Euonymus*.

spindly /spíndli/ (-dlier, -dliest), **spindling** /spíndling/ *adj* long or tall, thin, and weak-looking

spin doctor *n* somebody whose job is to present to the public the policies, actions, or words of a person or organization in their best possible light (*informal*)

spin-drier *n* HOUSEHOLD another spelling of **spin-dryer**

spindrift /spín drift/ *n* **1.** spray that blows from the surface of the sea **2.** blowing snow or sand [Early 17C. < alteration (probably after SPIN) of obsolete *spoon* 'run before a sea', origin ?]

spin-dry *vt* to remove most of the water from washed laundry by spinning it in a washing machine or spin-dryer

spin-dryer, **spin-drier** *n* a machine that forces most of the water out of wet laundry by spinning it rapidly in a perforated drum

spine /spīn/ *n* **1.** ANAT same as **spinal column 2.** PRINTING VERTICAL BACK OF BOOK the back of a book cover to which the pages are fixed **3.** ZOOL HARD SHARP PROJECTION ON ANIMAL'S BODY a sharp stiff projection on the body of an animal, e.g. the quill of a porcupine or the ray of a fish's fin **4.** BOT SHARP POINT ON PLANT a stiff sharp pointed outgrowth on a plant, e.g. on a rose or cactus **5.** GEOG RIDGE IN MOUNTAINS a continuous ridge in a range of mountains or hills **6.** HR FLEXIBLE PAY SCALE a pay scale used by some professions and large organizations that takes into account individual circumstances such as age and location [14C. Via French < Latin *spina* 'thorn']

spine-chiller *n* something such as a novel or film that is meant to frighten people —**spine-chilling** *adj*— **spine-chillingly** *adv*

spinel /spi nél/ *n* a hard crystalline, usually red, oxide mineral containing magnesium, aluminium, iron, and sometimes manganese. Use: gems. [Early 16C. Via French < Italian *spinella* < Latin *spina* 'thorn'; from its pointed crystals]

spin electronics *n* PHYS same as **spintronics** —**spin-electronic** *adj*

spineless /spínləss/ *adj* **1.** seriously lacking willpower or strength of character **2.** lacking a spinal column —**spinelessly** *adv* —**spinelessness** *n*

SYNONYMS See *cowardly*.

spinet /spi nét/ *n* a small harpsichord, popular in the 18th century, that has the strings set at a slant to the keyboard [Mid-17C. Via French < Italian *spinetta*]

spine-tingling *adj* causing nervous fear or excitement —**spine-tinglingly** *adv*

spiniferous /spī nífferəss/ *adj* having, producing, or bearing spines or needles [Mid-17C. < Latin *spina* 'thorn']

spinifex /spínni feks/ (*plural* **-fexes** or **same**) *n* **1.** a perennial grass that has sharp pointed leaves and grows in circular mounds in dry inland areas. Native to: Australia. Genera: *Plectrachne* or *Triodia*. **2.** a plant that has silvery foliage, globular seed heads, and grows on coastal sand dunes. Native

to: Australasia. Genus: *Spinifex*. [Early 19C. < modern Latin, 'thorn-maker' < Latin *spina* 'thorn']

spinmeister /spín mīstər/ *n* POL same as **spin doctor** (*informal*)

spinnaker /spínnəkər/ *n* a large triangular sail set at the front of a yacht for running before the wind [Mid-19C. Origin ?]

spinner /spínnər/ *n* **1.** SOMEBODY OR SOMETHING THAT SPINS a person, object, or device that spins **2.** FISHING FISHING LURE an angling lure that spins in the water when the line is reeled in **3.** CRICKET same as **spin bowler 4.** CRICKET SPINNING CRICKET BALL a cricket ball bowled with spin **5.** AVIAT COVER FOR AIRCRAFT PROPELLER a streamlined dome-shaped cap (**fairing**) that fits over the hub of the propeller of an aircraft

spinneret /spínnə ret/ *n* **1.** a tiny tubular structure, usually one of two pairs, that exudes the fluid produced by the abdominal glands of a silk-producing spider **2.** a perforated device for extruding filaments of synthetic fibre

spinney /spínni/ (*plural* **-neys**) *n* a small thicket or wood [Late 16C. Via Old French *espinei* 'thorny hedge' < Latin *spinetum* < *spina* 'thorn']

spinning frame /spínning-/ *n* a machine that draws out fibres, twists them into yarn or thread, and winds them onto spindles

spinning jenny /-jénni/ *n* a spinning machine invented in the 18th century that had more than one spindle, allowing one person to spin several yarns at once

spinning mule *n* TEXTILES same as **mule**[1] (sense 5)

spinning top *n* LEISURE same as **top**[2]

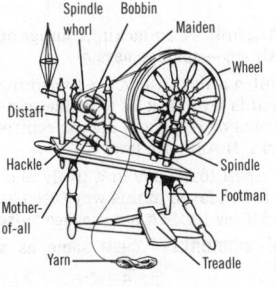

spinning wheel

spinning wheel *n* a domestic device for spinning yarn by means of a large wheel driven by hand or a treadle

spinode /spínōd/ *n* MATHS same as **cusp** (sense 7) [Mid-19C. Blend of SPINE + NODE]

spin-off /spínnof/ *n* **1.** DERIVATIVE OF SOMETHING a product, material, or service deriving from something that already exists **2.** CORPORATE DIVESTITURE a divestiture by a company of a division or subsidiary by the sale or distribution of shares of stock in a newly created independent company **3.** NEWLY CREATED COMPANY a company created by a spin-off

spin-orbit coupling *n* the interaction between two specific quantum physical properties of a particle

spinous /spínəss/ *adj* **1.** with, covered with, or resembling spines **2.** sharply pointed, like a spine of a leaf ○ *spinous process of a bone* [Mid-17C. < Latin *spinosus* < *spina* 'thorn']

spinous process *n* a long projection at the back of a vertebra

spinout /spín owt/ *n* N Am an uncontrolled skid in a motor vehicle

Spinoza /spi nózə/, **Baruch** (1632–77) Dutch philosopher. Rejecting the Judaism of his cultural background, he developed a philosophy that combined rationalist and pantheistic elements. His major work was *Ethics* (1677).

> 'The human mind is part of the infinite intellect of God. Therefore, when we say the human mind perceives this or that, we are saying nothing but that God…has this or that idea.'
> [Baruch Spinoza, *Ethics*; 1677]

Spinozism /spi nózizəm/ *n* the philosophical system developed by Baruch Spinoza, defining God as a unique impersonal deity with an infinite number of attributes and modes —**Spinozist** *n*

spin stabilization *n* a method of steadying the flight of a projectile such as a bullet, shell, or rocket by spinning it about its long axis

spinster /spínstər/ *n* **1.** OFFENSIVE TERM an offensive term for a woman who has remained unmarried beyond the usual age (*dated*) **2.** SPINNER OF YARN a woman whose livelihood is spinning yarn (*archaic*) **3.** LAW UNMARRIED WOMAN IN LEGAL DOCUMENTS in some legal documents, a woman who has never married [14C. < SPIN]

spinthariscope /spin thárri skōp/ *n* an instrument used to detect ionizing radiation such as alpha particles that produces flashes of light on a phosphorescent screen [Early 20C. < Greek *spintharis* 'spark']

spinto /spíntō/ *adj* describes an operatic voice that is both lyric and dramatic [Mid-20C. < Italian, 'pushed']

spintronics /spin trónniks/ *n* the study of magnetic and electric fields produced by electron spin (*takes a singular verb*) —**spintronic** *adj*

spinule /spī nyool/ *n* a tiny spine or thorn —**spinulose** /spínyoo lōss/ *adj*

spiny /spíni/ (-ier, -iest) *adj* **1.** WITH SPINES with or covered with spines **2.** THORNY with thorns or prickles **3.** LIKE SPINE shaped like a spine —**spininess** *n*

spiny anteater *n* ZOOL same as **echidna**

spiny eel *n* a freshwater fish resembling an eel that has a sensitive elongated snout with tubular nostrils and several sharp spines in front of the dorsal fin. Native to: Africa, Asia. Family: Mastacembelidae.

spiny-headed worm *n* a parasitic unsegmented worm that has a proboscis composed of rows of hooked spines, used for attachment to a vertebrate's intestinal wall. Phylum: Acanthocephala.

spiny lobster *n* a large edible crustacean that is like a lobster but has a spiny shell and lacks enlarged pincers. Family: Palinuridae.

spiracle /spírək'l/ *n* **1.** GEOL VENT IN LAVA FLOW a small vent in a lava flow that allows the escape of built-up gases **2.** INSECTS SMALL APERTURE IN INSECT a small paired aperture along the side of the thorax or abdomen of an insect or spider through which air enters and leaves **3.** FISH SMALL GILL SLIT a small gill slit or opening behind the eye area of some fishes such as skates and rays **4.** MARINE BIOL BLOWHOLE a blowhole of a whale, dolphin, or similar sea mammal (*technical*) [Early 17C. Via French < Latin *spiraculum* < *spirare* 'breathe'] —**spiracular** /spī rákyōōlər/ *adj*

spiraea /spī rée ə/, **spirea** *n* an ornamental flowering bush. Flowers: small white or pink, in dense clusters. Native to: northern hemisphere. Genus: *Spiraea*. [Mid-17C. Via modern Latin < Greek *speiraia* 'privet' < *speira* 'coil']

spiral /spírəl/ *n* **1.** CONTINUOUS CIRCLING FLAT CURVE in mathematics, a flat curve or series of curves that constantly increase or decrease in size in circling around a central point **2.** MATHS same as **helix** (sense 2) **3.** SOMETHING WITH CURVING CIRCULAR PATTERN something that has a helical or spiral form **4.** AVIAT FLIGHT MANOEUVRE a manoeuvre in which an aircraft makes a continuous banking turn as it descends **5.** ECON ACCELERATING ECONOMIC CHANGE a continuously accelerating increase or decrease in prices, wages, or interest rates ■ *adj* **1.** CONTINUOUSLY CIRCLING WITH FLAT CURVES with a flat curve or series of curves that constantly increase or decrease in size in circling around a central point **2.** HELICAL like a helix in shape ■ *v* (-rals, -ralling, -ralled) **1.** *vti* MOVE SOMETHING IN SPIRAL to move in a spiral, or make something move in a spiral **2.** *vi* CHANGE AT INCREASING PACE to increase or decrease at a continuously accelerating rate ○ *spiralling inflation* **3.** *vti* SHAPE SOMETHING LIKE SPIRAL to take on a spiral shape, or make something take on a spiral shape [Mid-16C. < medieval Latin *spiralis* 'coiled' < Latin *spira* (see SPIRE[2])] —**spirally** *adv* —**spiroid** *adj*

spiral binding *n* a binding in which pages are fastened together with a spiral of wire or plastic that coils through a series of punched holes —**spiral-bound** *adj*

spiral galaxy *n* a galaxy consisting of an older central nucleus of stars from which extend two spiral arms of gas, dust, and newer stars

spiral of Archimedes *n* a spiral curve formed by a point moving at constant speed to or from a fixed point and along a line rotating, also at a constant speed, about the point

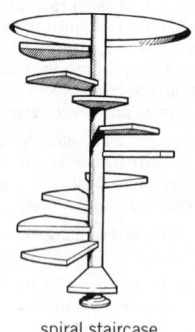

spiral staircase

spiral staircase *n* a staircase that winds round a central axis

spirant /spírənt/ *n, adj* PHON same as **fricative** [Mid-19C. < Latin *spirant-*, present participle of *spirare* 'breathe']

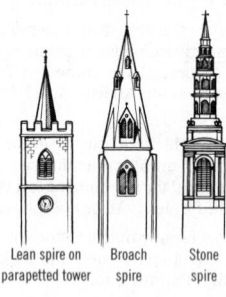

Lean spire on parapetted tower   Broach spire   Stone spire

spire

spire[1] /spīr/ *n* **1.** NARROW TAPERING STRUCTURE TOPPING SOMETHING a tall narrow pointed structure on the top of a roof, tower, or steeple **2.** POINTED PLANT SHOOT a slender pointed part of a plant, e.g. a blade of grass or the top of a tree **3.** UPWARD-FACING SPIKE the top part of something narrow and pointed such as a mountain peak ■ *vi* (**spires, spiring, spired**) RISE TO POINT to rise to a narrow point [Old English *spīr* < Indo-European, 'sharp point']

spire[2] /spīr/ *n* **1.** a spiral or coil **2.** a convolution of a spiral or coil [Late 16C. Via Latin *spira* 'coil' < Greek *speira*]

spirea *n* TREES, PLANTS another spelling of **spiraea**

spirelet /spírlət/ *n* ARCHIT same as **flèche** (sense 1) [Mid-19C. < SPIRE[1]]

spirillum /spī rílləm/ (*plural* **-la** /-lə/) *n* a spiral-shaped or curved bacterium with a rigid body, that lives only in the presence of oxygen. Genus: *Spirillum*. [Late 19C. < modern Latin, 'little spiral' < Latin *spira* (see SPIRE[2])] —**spirillar** *adj*

spirit /spírrit/ *n* **1.** LIFE FORCE OF PERSON the vital force that characterizes a human being as being alive **2.** WILL will or sense of self ○ *He retained an indomitable spirit.* **3.** ENTHUSIASM enthusiasm and energy ○ *Alice responded with spirit.* **4.** DISPOSITION somebody's personality or temperament **5.** ATTITUDE a person's attitude or state of mind **6.** GROUP LOYALTY the enthusiasm and loyalty that somebody feels through belonging to a group **7.** IMPORTANT INFLUENCE somebody or something that is a divine, inspiring, or animating influence **8.** REAL MEANING the intention behind something such as a rule or decree, rather than its literal interpretation **9.** SHARED OUTLOOK the prevailing mood or outlook characteristic of a place or time **10.** PERSON somebody who displays a particular quality **11.** SOUL in some beliefs, somebody's soul, especially that of a dead person **12.** PARANORMAL SUPERNATURAL ENTITY a supernatural being that does not have a physical body, e.g. a ghost, angel, or demon **13.** BEVERAGES ALCOHOLIC DRINK a strong alcoholic liquor made by distillation (*often used in the plural*) ○ *We drank a toast with a glass of the local spirit.* ○ *She never drank spirits.* **14.** CHEM DISTILLED LIQUID any liquid produced by distillation, especially a distilled solution of ethanol and water (*often used in the plural*) **15.** CHEM ALCOHOLIC SOLUTION a solution of an essence or volatile substance in alcohol (*often used in the plural*) ■ **spirits** *npl* MOOD a particular frame of mind or mood ○ *The group was in high spirits, talking and laughing.* ■ *adj* BURNING ALCOHOL using alcohol as fuel ○ *a spirit stove* ■ *vt* (**-its, -iting, -ited**) REMOVE SOMEBODY OR SOMETHING SECRETLY to take somebody or something away quickly in a secret or mysterious way ○ *spirited him out of the room* [13C. Via Anglo-Norman < Latin *spiritus* 'breath' < *spirare* 'breathe'] ◇ **in high spirits** elated and happy ◇ **out of spirits** sad or dejected

ORIGIN The Latin word *spirare* 'to breathe', from which **spirit** is derived, is also the source of English *aspire, conspire, expire, inspire, perspire, respire,* and *transpire.*

Spirit *n* CHR same as **Holy Spirit**

spirited /spírritid/ *adj* **1.** LIVELY lively and vigorous **2.** ANIMATED with great animation **3.** BEHAVING IN SPECIFIC WAY behaving in a way that has a particular feeling, mood, or character (*usually used in combination*) ○ *low-spirited* —**spiritedly** *adv* —**spiritedness** *n*

spirit gum *n* a glue made from a solution of gum in ether. Use: especially to stick false hair to an actor's skin.

spiritism /spírritizəm/ *n* PARANORMAL same as **spiritualism** (sense 1) —**spiritist** *n* —**spiritistic** /spírri tístik/ *adj*

spirit lamp *n* a lamp that uses methylated spirit as fuel

spiritless /spírritləss/ *adj* lacking courage or energy —**spiritlessly** *adv* —**spiritlessness** *n*

spirit level *n* a device laid on something to check whether it is level. If it is, a bubble in a tube filled with alcohol or ether will appear centred between two marks. N Am term **level**

spiritoso /spírri tóssō/ *adv* in a lively and vivacious way, or to be played in this way (*used as a musical direction*) [Early 18C. < Italian, 'spirited'] —**spiritoso** *adj*

spirits of ammonia *n* CHEM same as **sal volatile** (sense 1)

spiritual /spírrichoo əl/ *adj* **1.** OF SOUL relating to the soul or spirit, usually in contrast to material things **2.** OF RELIGION relating to religious or sacred things rather than worldly things **3.** TEMPERAMENTALLY OR INTELLECTUALLY AKIN connected by an affinity of the mind, spirit, or temperament **4.** REFINED showing great refinement and concern with the higher things in life ■ *n* **1.** FOLK HYMN a religious song, especially one arising from African American culture **2.** THINGS OF SPIRIT matters concerning the spirit ○ *He was deeply concerned with anything to do with the spiritual.* [14C. Via French *spirituel* < Latin *spiritualis* < *spiritus* (see SPIRIT)] —**spiritually** *adv*

spiritual bouquet *n* in the Roman Catholic Church, a promise of, or performance of, devotional acts, performed on behalf of another, e.g. in memory of somebody who has died

spiritualise *vt* RELIG another spelling of **spiritualize**

spiritualism /spírrichoo ə lizəm/ *n* **1.** BELIEF IN COMMUNICATION WITH DEAD PEOPLE the belief that the spirits of dead people can communicate with the living, especially through mediums **2.** PRACTICES OF COMMUNICATING WITH DEAD PEOPLE the practices used among people who believe that communication occurs between the dead and the living **3.** RELIGIOUS BELIEFS EMPHASIZING SPIRITUAL MATTERS a system of belief that emphasizes the spiritual nature of existence **4.** PHILOSOPHY EMPHASIZING SPIRITUAL NATURE OF REALITY the philosophical doctrine that all reality is spiritual, not material **5.** SPIRITUAL STATE the quality or state of being spiritual

spiritualist /spírrichoo əlist/ *n* **1.** a believer in communication between the living and the dead **2.** somebody who is interested in spiritual matters —**spiritualistic** /spírrichoo ə lístik/ *adj*

spirituality /spírrityoo álləti/ (*plural* **-ties**) *n* **1.** the quality or condition of being spiritual **2.** the property or revenue belonging to a church or church official (*often used in the plural*)

spiritualize /spírrichoo ə līz/ (**-izes, -izing, -ized**), **spiritualise** (**-ises, -ising, -ised**) *vt* **1.** to give something a spiritual content **2.** to attribute a spiritual meaning to something —**spiritualization** *n* —**spiritualizer** *n*

spiritualty /spírrichoo əlti/ (*plural* **-ties**) *n* CHR same as **spirituality** (sense 2)

spirituel /spírrityoo él/, **spirituelle** *adj* showing a refined and graceful intellect [Late 17C. < French (see SPIRITUAL)]

spirituous /spírrityoo əss/ *adj* containing alcohol or made by distillation (*formal*)

spirit varnish *n* a varnish consisting of a resin dissolved in alcohol

spirketting /spúrkiting/ *n* a thick planking used to line and reinforce the decks and ports of a wooden ship [Mid-18C. < obsolete *spurket* 'space between the deck and side of a ship', origin ?]

spiro-[1] *prefix* breathing, respiration ○ *spirograph* [< Latin *spirare* 'breathe']

spiro-[2] *prefix* **1.** spiral, coil ○ *spirochaete* **2.** molecule with two rings having one shared atom ○ *spironolactone* [< Latin *spira* (see SPIRE[2])]

spirochaete /spírō keet/, **spirochete** *n* a coiled rod-shaped bacterium, many of which cause diseases such as syphilis and relapsing fever. Order: Spirochaetales. [Late 19C. < modern Latin *Spirochaeta* < Latin *spira* (see SPIRE[2]) + *chaeta* 'hair']

spirochaetosis /spírōki tốssiss/ (*plural* **-toses** /-tōseez/), **spirochaetosis** (*plural* **-ses** /-tōseez/) *n* a disease caused by a spirochaete

spirochete, etc. *n* MICROBIOL another spelling of **spirochaete, etc.**

spirograph /spírə graaf, -graf/ *n* an instrument that makes a record of the depth and rapidity of somebody's breathing [Late 19C. < SPIRO-[1]] —**spirographic** /spírə gráffik/ *adj* —**spirography** /spī róggrəfi/ *n*

spirogyra /spírə jírə/ *n* a multicellular freshwater green alga. Genus: *Spirogyra*. [Late 19C. < modern Latin < Latin *spira* (see SPIRE[2]) + Greek *guros* 'round']

spirometer /spī rómmitər/ *n* an instrument for measuring the capacity of the lungs [Mid-19C. < SPIRO-[1]] —**spirometric** /spírə méttrik/ *adj* —**spirometry** *n*

spironolactone /spírənō láktōn/ *n* a steroid that acts as a diuretic. Use: treatment of oedema, hypertension. Formula: $C_{24}H_{32}O_4S$. [Mid-20C. < *spirolactone* earlier name < SPIRO-[1]]

spirt /spurt/ (*dated*) *vti* (**spirts, spirting, spirted**) same as **spurt** *v* ■ *n* same as **spurt** [Mid-16C. Variant]

spirulina /spírroo línə, spī-/ *npl* cyanobacteria valued as a rich source of protein, containing vitamins, minerals, essential fatty acids, and antioxidants. Spirulina are grown in tanks and harvested to be made into nutritional supplements. Genus: *Spirulina*. [< modern Latin < Latin *spirula* 'small spiral shell' < *spira* (see SPIRE[2])]

spiry[1] /spíri/ *adj* shaped like a spiral (*literary*) [Late 17C. < SPIRE[2]]

spiry[2] /spíri/ *adj* shaped like a spire (*literary*) [Early 17C. < SPIRE[1]]

spit[1] /spit/ *v* (**spits, spitting, spat** /spat/ or **spit**) **1.** *vi* EJECT SALIVA to expel saliva forcefully from the mouth **2.** *vi* EXPEL SALIVA TO SHOW CONTEMPT to show anger, contempt, or hatred by or as if by expelling saliva **3.** *vt* EXPEL SOMETHING FROM YOUR MOUTH to eject something such as food forcefully from the mouth **4.** *vti* EMIT SOMETHING to sputter and emit something such as sparks or fat **5.** *vi* HISS to make hissing explosive sounds **6.** *vi* RAIN LIGHTLY to rain lightly or in scattered drops **7.** *vt* UTTER SOMETHING ANGRILY to utter something sharply and angrily ■ *n* **1.** SPITTLE FROM MOUTH saliva, especially when ejected from the mouth **2.** EXPULSION OF SOMETHING FROM MOUTH a forceful ejection of saliva or something else from the mouth **3.** LIKENESS an exact likeness (*informal*) [Old English *spittan* < Indo-European] —**spitter** *n* ◇ **spit it out** to say something at once, especially something that has been withheld (*informal; usually used as a command*)

spit up *vt* to regurgitate or cough up something

spit[2] /spit/ *n* **1.** THIN ROD FOR ROASTING SOMETHING a thin rod on which something is impaled for roasting over a fire **2.** LAND PROJECTING FROM SHORE an elongated point of land or shoal projecting into a body of water ■ *vt* **(spits, spitting, spitted) 1.** IMPALE SOMETHING ON SPIT to impale something on a roasting spit **2.** IMPALE SOMEBODY to impale somebody on a long pointed object [Old English *spitu* < Indo-European, 'sharp point']

spit and polish *n* meticulous care in presenting a neat appearance, especially in the armed forces (*informal*)

spitball /spít bawl/ *n N Am* **1.** a tiny wad of paper chewed and moistened with saliva that is thrown as a prank **2.** in baseball, an illegal pitch that is made to curve deceptively because it has been moistened with saliva

spitchcock /spích kok/ *n* an eel split and then grilled or fried [Early 17C. Origin ?]

spit curl *n N Am* same as **kiss curl** [< its being fixed in place with saliva]

spite /spīt/ *n* a malicious, usually small-minded desire to harm or humiliate somebody ■ *vt* **(spites, spiting, spited)** to harm, hinder, or humiliate somebody out of small-mindedness [13C. Shortening of DESPITE] ◇ **in spite of** notwithstanding, or without taking account of something

spiteful /spítf'l/ *adj* full of or showing petty maliciousness —**spitefully** *adv* —**spitefulness** *n*

spitfire /spít fīr/ *n* a quick-tempered person

Spitfire *n* a British fighter plane used by the Royal Air Force during World War II

spitting cobra /spítting-/ *n US* ZOOL same as **ringhals**

spitting distance *n* a short enough distance to seem within reach (*informal*)

spitting image *n* an exact likeness (*informal*) ○ *the spitting image of his father* [Alteration of *spit and image* < SPIT[1] 'exact likeness']

spitting snake *n* REPT same as **ringhals**

spittle /spítt'l/ *n* **1.** saliva, especially that has been or is about to be expelled from the mouth **2.** something that looks like frothy saliva, especially the secretions from spittlebugs deposited on plants **(cuckoo spit)** [15C. Alteration (after SPIT[1]) of dialect *spattle* < Germanic]

spittlebug /spítt'l bug/ *n* INSECTS same as **froghopper**

spittoon /spi tóon/ *n* a container, formerly common in public places such as bars, into which tobacco chewers spit [Mid-19C. < SPIT[1]]

spitz /spits/ *n* a dog belonging to a breed that has a pointed muzzle, erect pointed ears, and a tightly curled tail [Mid-19C. Shortening of German *Spitzhund* 'pointed dog']

spiv /spiv/ *n UK* an offensive term for a man whose way of dressing is considered ostentatiously smart and whose integrity is doubted (*slang insult*) [Mid-20C. Origin ?] —**spivvy** *adj*

splanchnic /splángk nik/ *adj* relating to the intestines (*technical*) [Late 17C. Via modern Latin *splanchnicus* < Greek *splagkhnikos* < *splagkhna* 'entrails']

splash /splash/ *v* **(splashes, splashing, splashed) 1.** *vt* SPATTER LIQUID to scatter a liquid in large drops or amounts ○ *She splashed water over the side of the bath.* **2.** *vi* BE SPATTERED ABOUT to scatter or fly up in large drops or amounts ○ *The waves splashed against the rocks.* **3.** *vt* SPATTER DROPS OF LIQUID ON SOMETHING to wet or dirty something by spattering it with liquid ○ *She splashed her blouse with the hot tea.* **4.** *vti* MAKE YOUR WAY THROUGH WATER to make your way through water or another liquid, scattering it about ○ *They splashed through the puddles.* **5.** *vt* ADD CONTRASTS TO SOMETHING to apply contrasting colour or light to something **6.** *vt* DISPLAY SOMETHING PROMINENTLY to display something such as a news headline, story, or photograph conspicuously (*usually passive*) ○ *The story was splashed across the front page.* ■ *n* **1.** NOISE OR INSTANCE OF WATER SCATTERING a sound or act of splashing **2.** SOMETHING SPLASHED something or an amount that has been splashed ○ *The bathroom floor was covered with splashes.* **3.** MARK CAUSED BY SCATTERED LIQUID a mark or stain made by something splashing or being splashed ○ *The backs of her legs were covered with splashes.* **4.** PATCH OF COLOUR an area of contrasting colour or light, often irregular ○ *The dark forest was dappled with splashes of moonlight.* **5.** PROMINENT DISPLAY a conspicuous display, e.g. a prominent news headline, story, or photograph **6.** TINY AMOUNT OF LIQUID a very small quantity of one liquid added to another (*informal*) ○ *She added a splash of milk to her tea.* [Early 18C. Probably alteration of PLASH[1]] ◇ **make a splash** to attract a great deal of attention or publicity (*informal*)

splash down *vi* to land in the sea after a space flight

splashback /splásh bak/ *n* a sheet of something such as glass or plastic attached to a wall behind a basin or cooker to protect the wall from splashes. N Am term **backsplash**

splashboard /splásh bawrd/ *n* **1.** a screen for preventing water from splashing into a boat **2.** a protective guard that prevents mud or water from splashing the upper part of a motor vehicle and the people travelling in it

splashdown /splásh down/ *n* the landing of a spacecraft or missile in the sea after a flight

splashguard /splásh gaard/ *n US* same as **mud flap**

splashy /spláshi/ **(-ier, -iest)** *adj* **1.** COLOURFUL with lots of bright colours **2.** MAKING SPLASHES with great splashing of liquid **3.** ATTRACTING NOTICE attracting a lot of attention (*informal*) —**splashily** *adv* —**splashiness** *n*

splat /splat/ *n* WET SMACKING SOUND a sound made when something soft and wet hits something hard ■ *adv* WITH SMACK with a wet smacking sound ■ *interj* IMITATING IMPACT used to imitate the sound made when something soft and wet hits something hard [Late 19C. An imitation of the sound]

splatter /spláttər/ *vti* **(-ters, -tering, -tered)** to spatter or splash something, or be spattered or splashed ■ *n* a spatter or splash [Late 18C. Origin ?]

splatterpunk /spláttər pungk/ *n* a form of narrative, e.g. a story, film, or comic strip, that contains a large amount of gory violence (*slang*)

splay /splay/ *vti* **(splays, splaying, splayed) 1.** SPREAD SOMETHING WIDE AND OUTWARDS to spread out something such as the fingers or toes, or be spread out **2.** TURN SOMETHING OUT AWKWARDLY to turn something outwards in an awkward manner **3.** INCLINE SIDES OF OPENING to give the sides of an opening in a wall an oblique angle, so that the opening is wider on one side than on the other ■ *adj* **1.** *also* **splayed** /splayd/ SPREAD FLAT AND OUTWARDS sloping, turning, or spread flatly and outwards **2.** *also* **splayed** TURNED AWKWARDLY OUTWARDS turned awkwardly outwards ■ *n* INCLINE GIVEN TO SIDES OF OPENING an oblique angle given to the sides of an opening in a wall [14C. Shortening of DISPLAY]

Splayd /splayd/ *tdmk Aus* a trademark for a utensil shaped like a spoon with tines at the end like a fork and a sharp edge on one side like a knife

splayed /splayed/ *adj* same as **splay**

splayfoot /spláy fòot/ (*plural* **-feet** /-feet/) *n* **1.** a foot with fallen arches, often with widely spread toes, or the condition that causes this **2.** a foot that is excessively turned outwards, or the condition causing it —**splayfooted** /spláy fòotid/ *adj* —**splayfootedly** *adv*

spleen /spleen/ *n* **1.** a ductless vascular organ in the left upper abdomen of humans and other vertebrates that helps to destroy old red blood cells, form lymphocytes, and store blood **2.** anger or bad temper [13C. Via Latin *splen* < Greek *splēn*] —**spleenful** *adj* —**spleenish** *adj* —**spleeny** *adj*

spleenwort /spléen wurt/ (*plural* **-worts** or *same*) *n* an evergreen fern of temperate and tropical regions that has feathery fronds. Genus: *Asplenium.* [Late 16C. < the former belief that it cured illnesses of the spleen]

splendent /spléndənt/ *adj* (*literary*) **1.** reflecting light so that it shines **2.** distinguished or illustrious [15C. < Latin *splendent-*, present participle of *splendere* 'shine']

splendid /spléndid/ *adj* **1.** MAGNIFICENT impressive because of quality or size **2.** RADIANT reflecting light brilliantly **3.** EXCELLENT excellent or highly enjoyable **4.** ACCLAIMED very well known and acclaimed [Early 17C. < Latin *splendidus* < *splendere* 'shine'] —**splendidness** *n*

splendidly /spléndidli/ *adv* in a fine or admirable way ○ *The restoration work is coming along splendidly.*

splendiferous /splen díffərəss/ *adj* magnificent and wonderful (*humorous*) [Mid-19C. < SPLENDOUR] —**splendiferously** *adv* —**splendiferousness** *n*

splendor *n* US spelling of **splendour**

splendour /spléndər/ *n* **1.** the condition of being magnificent, impressive, or brilliant **2.** something that is magnificent, impressive, or brilliant ○ *the splendours of ancient Greece* [15C. Directly or via French < Latin *splendor* < *splendere* 'shine'] —**splendorous** *adj*

splenectomy /spli néktəmi/ (*plural* **-mies**) *n* surgical removal of the spleen [Mid-19C. < Greek *splēn* 'spleen']

splenetic /spli néttik/ *adj* **1.** RELATING TO SPLEEN relating to the spleen (*dated*) **2.** BAD-TEMPERED extremely bad-tempered or spiteful (*literary*) ■ *n* SOMEBODY BAD-TEMPERED somebody regarded as bad-tempered or spiteful (*literary or dated*) [Mid-16C. < Latin *spleneticus* < *splen* (see SPLEEN)] —**splenetically** *adv*

splenic /splénnik, spléé-/ *adj* relating to, in, or near the spleen [Early 17C. < Greek *splēn* 'spleen']

splenius /spléeni əss/ (*plural* **-nii** /-ni ī/) *n* either of two muscles on each side of the neck that reach from the base of the skull to the upper back and rotate and extend the head and neck [Mid-18C. Via modern Latin < Greek *splēnion* 'bandage, compress'] —**splenial** *adj*

splenomegaly /spléenō méggəli/ *n* unusual enlargement of the spleen [Early 20C. < Greek *splēn* 'spleen' + *megal-* 'great']

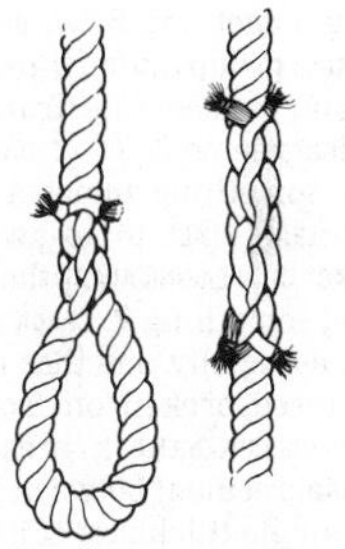

splice

splice /splīss/ *vt* **(splices, splicing, spliced) 1.** JOIN ROPES to join two pieces of rope or wire by weaving the strands of each into the other **2.** JOIN ENDS OF FILM OR TAPE to join the ends of two pieces of film or magnetic tape, e.g. in editing **3.** JOIN PIECES OF WOOD to join two pieces of wood by overlapping them and bolting or otherwise attaching them **4.** MARRY TWO PEOPLE to join a couple in marriage (*slang; often passive*) **5.** GENETICS INSERT GENETIC MATERIAL to join together or insert pieces of DNA in order to alter the genetic structure of an organism ■ *n* **1.** CONNECTION a join made by connecting two pieces of something **2.** JUNCTION OF SPLICING the junction where something has been spliced **3.** CRICKET END OF BAT HANDLE the wedge-shaped end of the handle of a cricket bat where it fits into the striking part [Early 16C. < Middle Dutch *splissen*] —**splicer** *n*

spliff /splif/ *n* a marijuana cigarette (*slang*) [Mid-20C. Origin ?]

spline /splīn/ *n* **1.** a flat, relatively narrow key that is integral to a shaft, produced by milling a longitudinal groove **2.** same as **slat** *n* (sense 1) **3.** a thin narrow piece of wood, metal, or plastic that fits onto or into the edges of tiles or boards and connects them together [Mid-18C. Origin ?]

splint /splint/ *n* **1.** DEVICE TO IMMOBILIZE BROKEN BONE a strip of rigid material used to keep a broken bone or other injured body part from moving **2.** STRIP OF WOOD USED IN BASKETRY a thin strip of wood used to weave something such as a basket or chair seat **3.** WOOD SLIVER FOR LIGHTING FIRES a sliver of wood used to carry a flame, e.g. to light a fire or a candle **4.** WOODWORK same as **splinter** *n* (sense 1) **5.** MIL, HIST METAL PLATE IN ARMOUR any overlapping metal plate or strip used in making a suit of armour **6.** VET ENLARGEMENT OF HORSE'S LEG BONE a condition that occurs in young horses, consisting of painful bony outgrowths in or near the splint bones on the inner sides of the legs ■ *vt* **(splints, splinting, splinted) 1.** IMMOBILIZE INJURED PART to immobilize a broken bone or injured body part with a rigid support **2.** STRENGTHEN SOMETHING to give support

or added strength to something [13C. < Middle Low German or Middle Dutch *splinte*]

splint bone *n* either of a pair of thin bones on either side of the cannon bone in the lower legs of horses and other hoofed animals

splinter /splíntər/ *n* **1.** THIN SHARP FRAGMENT a small thin sharp piece of wood, metal, stone, glass, or other material broken from a larger piece **2.** BOMB FRAGMENT a metal fragment thrown from an exploding bomb or shell **3.** POL same as **splinter group** ■ *vti* (**-ters, -tering, -tered**) **1.** BREAK SOMETHING INTO SHARP FRAGMENTS to break something into thin sharp fragments, or be broken into thin sharp fragments **2.** DIVIDE GROUP to split a larger group into factions or independent groups, or be split in this way [14C. < Middle Dutch] —**splintery** *adj*

splinter group *n* a group formed by individuals who have dissociated themselves from a larger organization, usually because of disagreement

split /split/ *v* (**splits, splitting, split**) **1.** *vti* DIVIDE SOMETHING LENGTHWAYS to divide something lengthways into two or more parts, or be divided lengthways into two or more parts, usually by force **2.** *vti* BURST SOMETHING to burst something apart, or rip apart **3.** *vt* AFFECT SOMETHING VIOLENTLY to disturb or disrupt something with a violently jarring presence ○ *shouts splitting the air* **4.** *vti* SEPARATE SOMETHING INTO PARTS to divide a whole into parts, or be separated from the rest or from a whole **5.** *vt* SEPARATE SOMETHING BY ADDING SOMETHING BETWEEN to separate a whole into its components by interposing something **6.** *vti* DIVIDE SOMETHING INTO FACTIONS to make a group divide into factions because of disagreement, or separate from a main group because of disagreement **7.** *vt* DIVIDE SOMETHING INTO SHARES to share something among a group ○ *split the proceeds* **8.** *vti* LEAVE PLACE to go away from a place (*slang*) ■ *n* **1.** ACT OF BREAKING APART the action of breaking or splitting something **2.** CRACK a crack or break in something, especially one that runs lengthways **3.** FRAGMENT a piece broken off from the whole **4.** DIVISION THROUGH DISAGREEMENT a breach in a group, caused by a disagreement between members **5.** LAYER OF ANIMAL HIDE a single thickness of animal hide other than the outermost layer **6.** INDUST LEATHER leather made from a single inner layer of animal hide **7.** BOWLING ARRANGEMENT OF STANDING BOWLING PINS in ten-pin bowling, a batch of remaining pins in which the pins are clustered into two groups with a large gap in between **8.** PORTION a share, especially a share of money (*informal*) **9.** FOOD ICE CREAM DESSERT a dessert of fruit with ice cream and a topping of flavoured syrup, nuts, and whipped cream **10.** HANDICRAFT STRIP OF WOOD FOR BASKETRY a strip of flexible wood, usually willow, used for basketry ■ *adj* **1.** BROKEN broken, divided, or separated into parts **2.** DISUNITED divided because of disagreement [Late 16C. < Dutch *splitten*]

split on *vt* to inform on somebody (*informal*)

split up *v* **1.** *vi* END RELATIONSHIP to end a relationship or a marriage **2.** *vti* SEND PEOPLE DIFFERENT WAYS to go off in a different direction, or send individuals off in different directions **3.** *vt* DIVIDE SOMETHING INTO PARTS to divide something into separate parts

Split /split/ chief city and port of Dalmatia, southern Croatia, on the Adriatic Sea. Population: 189,388 (1991).

split board *n* a type of snowboard that comes apart lengthways to form two separate pieces that can be used as skis

split brain *n* a brain that has the corpus callosum surgically severed or missing from birth, so that the two hemispheres of the brain are not connected

split decision *n* in boxing, a win awarded by a majority of judges, rather than by a unanimous decision

split end *n* **1.** the damaged end of a hair that has separated into strands **2.** in American football, a player at the end of an offensive line that lines up some distance outside the rest of the line

split infinitive *n* an infinitive in which the 'to' and the verb are separated by another word, as in the phrase 'to seriously think'

USAGE What is wrong with a **split infinitive**? The ***split infinitive*** is a stylistic issue that has been rationalized into a grammatical one. There is no grammatical basis for rejecting split infinitives, since to regard an infinitive with *to* as an inseparable unit has no support in the typical structures of English grammar, which freely separates particles, auxiliary verbs, and other qualifiers from the words to which they belong (e.g. *I have never been to Paris* separates *have* from *been*). The issue is one of style and not of grammar. If splitting an infinitive produces awkwardness, it is better to avoid it, but if the split is natural and supports or clarifies the meaning, there can be no objection to it. The adverb belongs closely with the verb in the infinitive in cases such as *They agreed to flatly forbid such actions* and *They were plotting to secretly copy the files,* but can be moved to a more comfortable position in other cases such as *We expect to further modernize our services* (revise as: ... *to modernize our services further*) and *I would like to briefly mention a few points* (revise as: *I would like briefly to ...*). It is usually advisable to avoid splitting the infinitive with an adverbial phrase (e.g. *They were trying to in some way improve the situation*). In some cases, however, even an adverbial phrase cannot be separated from its verb: *Prices are likely to more than double* (in which *more than double* is effectively regarded as a set verb phrase). The guiding principle is that the split infinitive has a long history of use; it is acceptable when the rhythm and meaning of the sentence call for it or when its use is that of a set verb phrase. It should be avoided (either by repositioning or by rephrasing) when it seems stilted or awkward, or creates ambiguity, especially in formal writing where its inclusion may draw criticism.

split-level *adj* **1.** describes a house or room built on two levels with steps between them **2.** describes a cooker that has the oven and hob in separate units —**split-level** *n*

split-new *adj Scotland* same as **brand-new** [Referring to a strip of wood]

split pea *n* a pea that has been shelled, dried, and split in half, used especially in soup

split personality *n* **1.** a tendency towards erratic mood or temperament changes **2.** PSYCHIAT ➧ **multiple personality disorder**

split pin *n* a two-pronged metal pin that holds things together when its prongs are passed through holes on both parts and then bent back

split ring *n* a small steel ring with two spiral turns, often used as a key ring or as a means of fastening two parts together

splits /splits/ *n* a gymnastic action in which the legs are fully extended in opposite directions until the body is sitting on or very close to the floor (*takes a singular or plural verb*) ○ *do the splits*

split screen *n* a cinema or television screen frame divided into more than one image

split second *n* an extremely brief amount of time

split-second *adj* carried out instantly, or depending on instant skill or judgment

split shift *n* a single work period that is divided into two or more sessions of work, separated by an interval that is longer than a normal rest or meal break

split stitch *n* in embroidery, a back stitch in which each new stitch is made through the centre of the previous one

splitter /splíttər/ *n* an electronic or other device that divides something into parts, e.g. a software device that enables a long file to be divided into sections or a device that splits a telephone signal so that it can carry voice and data transmissions simultaneously

split tin *n* a long narrow loaf of bread with a shallow lengthways split along the top

splitting /splítting/ *adj* causing intense pain ○ *a splitting headache* ■ *n* a Freudian defence mechanism in which somebody separates something unpleasant such as an idea into parts that are each less threatening than the whole

split-up *n* an instance or the act of separating, e.g. the ending of a relationship between two people

splodge /sploj/ *UK n* a large irregular spot, stain, or discoloration ■ *vt* (**splodges, splodging, splodged**) to mark or dirty something with splodges ▶ ANZ, N Am term (all senses) **splotch** [Early 17C. Origin ?]

splosh /splosh/ (**sploshes, sploshing, sploshed**) *vi* to move with or make a gentle splashing sound [Mid-19C. An imitation of the sound] —**splosh** *n*

splotch /sploch/ *ANZ, N Am n* same as **splodge** ■ *vt* (**splotches, splotching, splotched**) same as **splodge** [Early 17C. Origin ?]

splurge /splurj/ (*informal*) *v* (**splurges, splurging, splurged**) **1.** *vi* INDULGE to indulge in something extravagant or expensive **2.** *vt* SPEND MONEY EXTRAVAGANTLY to spend money in an extravagant or wasteful way ■ *n* **1.** BOUT OF EXTRAVAGANCE a period of indulgence or extravagant spending **2.** GRAND DISPLAY a showy display of something such as wealth [Early 19C. Origin ?]

splutter /splúttər/ *v* (**-ters, -tering, -tered**) **1.** *vi* MAKE SPITTING SOUND to make a spitting or choking sound **2.** *vti* SAY SOMETHING INCOHERENTLY to say something in a choking incoherent manner **3.** *vti* SPIT SOMETHING OUT to scatter saliva, liquid, or particles of food from the mouth ■ *n* **1.** INCOHERENT SPEECH a burst of choking incoherent speech **2.** CHOKING NOISE a spitting choking noise [Late 17C. Origin ?] —**splutterer** *n* —**spluttering** *n, adj*

Popperfoto
Dr Spock

Spock /spok/, **Dr** (1903–98) US paediatrician and political activist. His book *The Common Sense Book of Baby and Child Care*, first published in 1946, which went through numerous editions and sold tens of millions of copies worldwide, popularized a new, permissive philosophy of parenting. He was a vociferous public opponent of the Vietnam War and of nuclear weapons. Full name **Spock, Benjamin McLane**

spodumene /spóddyoo meen/ *n* a crystalline mineral that contains lithium and occurs in greyish white, greenish, or lilac forms. Use: source of lithium, gems. [Early 19C. Via French < Greek *spodoumenos* 'burnt to ashes' < *spodos* 'ashes'; from its greyish colour]

spoil /spoyl/ *v* (**spoils, spoiling, spoiled** or **spoilt** /spoylt/) **1.** *vt* IMPAIR SOMETHING to damage or ruin something in such a way that a quality such as worth, beauty, or usefulness is diminished **2.** *vt* HARM SOMEBODY BY OVERINDULGENCE to harm the character of somebody, especially a child, by repeated overindulgence **3.** *vt* TREAT SOMEBODY INDULGENTLY to treat somebody with indulgence out of a desire to please ○ *The hotel staff really spoiled us.* **4.** *vt* MAKE SOMEBODY CONSIDER SOMETHING UNSATISFACTORY to make somebody dissatisfied with what is usually offered by greatly exceeding it in quality ○ *All that sun spoils you for holidays at home.* **5.** *vi* BECOME ROTTEN to become unfit to eat because of decay **6.** *vt* TAKE PROPERTY FROM SOMEBODY to take property from somebody by force or violence (*archaic*) ■ *n* **1.** WASTE FROM EXCAVATION waste material removed from an excavation **2.** STEALING the act of plundering (*archaic*) ■ **spoils** *npl* **1.** PROPERTY SEIZED BY VICTOR valuables or property seized by the victor in a conflict **2.** SOMETHING GAINED THROUGH EFFORT something valuable or desirable gained through effort, opportunism, or other means [13C. Via Old French *espoillier* 'plunder, despoil' < Latin *spoliare* < *spolium* 'booty'] ◇ **be spoiling for** be eager for something, usually a conflict or confrontation

spoilage /spóylij/ *n* **1.** DECAYING the process of decaying or becoming damaged, or the condition of being decayed or damaged **2.** WASTE waste arising from decay or damage **3.** AMOUNT WASTED the amount of something wasted because of decay or damage

spoiled /spoyld/, **spoilt** /spoylt/ *adj* **1.** severely or irrevocably impaired, e.g. by damage or decay **2.**

wilful or selfish because of having been over-indulged

spoiled priest *n Ireland* somebody who studied for the priesthood, but withdrew or was dismissed

spoiler /spóylər/ *n* **1. AEROFOIL FOR CONTROLLING LIFT AND DRAG** a narrow hinged aerofoil attached lengthways to the upper surface of an aircraft wing. It is raised to increase drag and reduce lift during banking and descent. **2. CAR AIR DEFLECTOR** a fixed air deflector on the rear of a car, designed to keep it on the ground during high speeds **3. SOMEBODY WHO CAN RUIN ANOTHER'S WIN** a candidate for office, or a competitor in sport, who cannot win but can or does prevent an opponent from doing so **4. RIVAL PUBLICATION** a newspaper or magazine whose release is calculated to coincide with that of a rival publication in order to divert interest in it and reduce its sales **5. SOMEBODY WHO WRECKS SOMETHING** somebody or something that ruins or wrecks something **6. ROBBER** somebody or something that robs or pillages

spoilsport /spóyl spawrt/ *n* somebody whose conduct spoils the pleasure of others

spoils system *n* a practice in which a winning political party gives government jobs and public appointments to its supporters

spoilt *v* past participle, past tense of **spoil** ■ *adj* same as **spoiled**

Spokane /spō kán/ city in eastern Washington State, situated on the waterfalls on the Spokane River. It is a commercial and manufacturing centre. Population: 196,305 (2002 estimate).

spoke

spoke[1] /spōk/ *n* **1. SUPPORTING ROD FOR WHEEL RIM** a bar or rod that extends from the hub of a wheel to support or brace the rim **2. KNOB ON SHIP'S WHEEL** a knob that sticks out from the rim of a ship's wheel **3. RUNG** a rung of a ladder [Old English *spāca* < Indo-European, 'pointed object'] —**spoked** *adj* ◇ **put a spoke in somebody's wheel** to hinder or thwart somebody's plans

spoke[2] /spōk/ past tense of **speak**

spoken /spókən/ past participle of **speak** ■ *adj* **1.** expressed with the voice ○ *the spoken word* **2.** speaking in a particular way, e.g. with a particular voice quality, accent, command of the language, or attitude (*used in combination*) ○ *well-spoken* ◇ **spoken for 1.** already owned or reserved by somebody **2.** already married, engaged, or romantically committed to somebody (*dated*)

SYNONYMS See **verbal**.

spokeshave /spók shayv/ *n* a small carpenter's plane consisting of a blade with a handle at each end, formerly used to shape spokes, now used to shape and smooth convex and concave wooden surfaces

spokesman /spóksmən/ (*plural* -**men** /-mən/) *n* somebody, especially a man, authorized to speak on behalf of another person or other people [Early 16C. < SPOKE[2] after CRAFTSMAN etc.]

spokesperson /spóks purss'n/ (*plural* -**people** /-peep'l/ or -**persons**) *n* somebody authorized to speak on behalf of another person or other people [Late 20C. After SPOKESMAN]

spokeswoman /spóks woomən/ (*plural* -**women** /-wimin/) *n* a woman authorized to speak on behalf of another person or other people [Mid-17C. After SPOKESMAN]

spoliation /spóli áysh'n/ *n* **1. PLUNDERING** the seizing of things by force **2. SEIZURE OF SHIPS** the seizure or plundering of neutral ships at sea by a belligerent power in time of war **3. ALTERATION OF DOCUMENT** the alteration or destruction of a document so as to make it invalid or unusable as evidence **4. TAKING OF PRIVILEGES OF RELIGIOUS POSITION** the taking of the income or privileges that go with a religious position by somebody who is not entitled to them [15C. < Latin *spoliation-* < *spoliare* (see SPOIL)] —**spoliatory** /spóli ətəri/ *adj*

spondaic /spon dáy ik/ *adj* relating to spondees or written in spondees [Late 16C. < French *spondaïque* < Greek *spondeios* (see SPONDEE)]

spondee /spón dee/ *n* a metrical foot of two long or stressed syllables [14C. Via French < Greek *spondeios* 'libational' < *spondē* 'libation'; because the spondee was often used in songs accompanying libations]

spondylitis /spóndi lítiss/ *n* inflammation of the vertebrae and the attached discs and ligaments [Mid-19C. < Latin *spondylus* 'vertebra' < Greek *spondulos*]

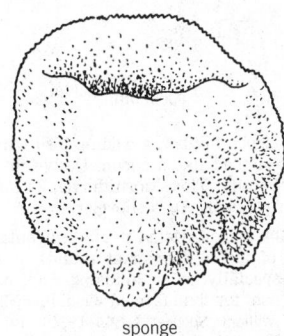
sponge

sponge /spunj/ *n* **1. SEA ANIMAL** a chiefly sea-dwelling invertebrate animal with a porous fibrous skeleton composed of calcium carbonate, silica, and spongin. Sponges often live in colonies and attach themselves to underwater objects. Phylum: Porifera. **2. NATURAL MATERIAL USED FOR WASHING** a lightweight porous absorbent piece of the skeleton of some sponges. Use: washing, cleaning. **3. SYNTHETIC MATERIAL USED FOR WASHING** a piece of cellulose or synthetic material resembling a true sponge. Use: washing, cleaning. **4. GAUZE PAD** a folded gauze pad. Use: in surgery or medicine to absorb discharges, dress wounds, or apply medications. **5.** same as **sponger** (sense 1) (*informal*) **6. HEAVY DRINKER** somebody who drinks heavily (*informal*) **7. FOOD** same as **sponge cake 8. FOOD** same as **sponge pudding 9. MASS OF RISING YEAST DOUGH** a small amount of yeast dough that is allowed to rise before being kneaded with the rest of the batch **10. ACT OF CLEANING** the act of rubbing or bathing somebody or something with a wet sponge or cloth **11. POROUS METAL** a porous metal capable of absorbing large quantities of gas, obtained by reduction without melting of a metal compound or by electrolysis ■ *v* (**sponges**, **sponging**, **sponged**) **1.** *vt* **CLEAN SOMEBODY OR SOMETHING** to wipe or clean somebody or something with a wet sponge or cloth **2.** *vt* **REMOVE SOMETHING** to remove or destroy something by rubbing **3.** *vt* **ABSORB LIQUID** to absorb liquids with a sponge or with the efficiency of a sponge **4.** *vt* **GET SOMETHING BY IMPOSING ON GENEROSITY** to get something by imposing on the generosity of others **5.** *vi* **LIVE OFF OTHERS** to live at the expense of others, repeatedly imposing on them and making no effort to live independently (*informal*) **6.** *vi* **COLLECT SPONGES** to dive for sponges under the sea [Pre-12C. Via Latin *spongia* < Greek *spoggos*] —**sponger** *n*

sponge bag *n* a small waterproof bag used to carry toiletries when travelling. N Am term **ditty bag**

sponge bath *n ANZ, N Am* a body cleansing just using a sponge and some water, without immersion, usually performed on somebody confined to bed. UK term **bed bath**

sponge cake *n* a light open-textured cake made of flour, eggs, sugar, flavouring, and traditionally no fat

sponge pudding *n* a light steamed or baked pudding made from a basic cake mixture

sponger /spúnjər/ *n* **1.** somebody who lives off others, habitually imposing on their generosity and making no effort to live independently (*informal*) **2.**

somebody who dives for sponges, or a ship used for gathering sponges

spongiform /spúnji fawrm/ *adj* having an open texture containing many holes, resembling the texture of a sponge [Early 19C. < SPONGE]

spongiform encephalopathy *n* a brain disease in humans and animals in which areas of the brain slowly degenerate and take on a spongy appearance

spongin /spúnjin/ *n* a protein that forms the skeletal framework of sponges [Mid-19C. < SPONGE]

spongioblast /spúnji ō blast/ *n* an embryonic cell in the brain and spinal cord that develops into supporting connective tissue (**neuroglia**) [Early 20C. < Latin *spongia* (see SPONGE)] —**spongioblastic** /spúnji ō blástik/ *adj*

spongy /spúnji/ (-**ier**, -**iest**) *adj* **1. OPEN-TEXTURED** having a light open texture full of holes or cavities **2. ABSORBENT** absorbent and elastic **3. SOFT AND WET** soft and full of water —**sponginess** *n*

spongy mesophyll, **spongy parenchyma** *n* a spongy tissue layer of irregularly shaped chlorophyll-bearing cells interspersed with air spaces, sandwiched between the upper and lower epidermal layers of a leaf

~~**sponser**~~ incorrect spelling of **sponsor**

sponson /spónss'n/ *n* **1. NAVY GUN PLATFORM ON SHIP** a gun platform sticking out from the side of a ship. A gun can be mounted in such a way that it can fire both fore and aft. **2. ARMS, HIST GUN TURRET** a gun turret mounted on the side of an early tank **3. CANOEING AIR CHAMBER IN CANOE** an air chamber that runs along each side of a canoe to help keep it afloat **4. AVIAT STABILIZER FOR SEAPLANE** an air-filled structure or small wing projecting from the lower hull of a seaplane to stabilize it in water **5. NAUT SUPPORT FOR PADDLE WHEEL** a structural support for a paddle wheel on a ship [Mid-19C. Origin ?]

sponsor /spónssər/ *n* **1. CONTRIBUTOR TO FUNDING OF EVENT** a person or organization that provides or pledges money to help fund an event, especially an event run by another person or group **2. CONTRIBUTOR TO CHARITY** a person or organization that donates money to a charity on the basis of the performance of a participant in an organized fundraising event **3. SUPPORTER** a country, organization, or group that supports or organizes an activity, or vouches for the acceptability of another **4. POL LEGISLATOR** a legislator who proposes and supports the passage of a bill **5.** BROADCAST **RADIO OR TELEVISION ADVERTISER** a person or a business that pays for radio or television programming by buying advertising time **6.** CHR **SOMEBODY ANSWERING AT CHILD'S BAPTISM** somebody who answers on behalf of a child at baptism and becomes responsible for the child's religious upbringing (*formal*) **7.** *N Am* **SOMEBODY RESPONSIBLE FOR ANOTHER** somebody who becomes responsible for somebody else, especially during education, apprenticeship, or probation ■ *vt* (-**sors**, -**soring**, -**sored**) **ACT AS SPONSOR TO SOMEBODY** to act as a sponsor to somebody or something [Mid-17C. < late Latin, 'baptismal sponsor' < Latin *spons-*, past participle of *spondere* 'pledge'] —**sponsorial** /spon sáwri əl/ *adj* —**sponsorship** *n*

ORIGIN The Latin word *spondere* 'to pledge', from which *sponsor* is derived, is also the source of English *despond*, *respond*, *riposte*, and *spouse*.

SYNONYMS See **backer**.

spontaneity /spóntə née əti, -náy-/ *n* **1.** behaviour that is natural and unconstrained and is the result of impulse, not planning **2.** the generating or provoking of activity from within, rather than as a result of external influences

spontaneous /spon táyni əss/ *adj* **1. ARISING FROM INTERNAL CAUSE** resulting from internal or natural processes, with no apparent external influence **2. ARISING FROM IMPULSE** arising from natural impulse or inclination, rather than from planning or in response to suggestions from others **3. UNRESTRAINED** naturally unrestrained or uninhibited **4. BOT GROWING UNCULTIVATED** growing without cultivation [Mid-17C. < late Latin *spontaneus* 'of your own accord' < Latin *sponte* in same sense] —**spontaneously** *adv* —**spontaneousness** *n*

spontaneous abortion *n* MED same as **miscarriage** (sense 1)

spontaneous combustion *n* the ignition of a combustible material such as hay as a result of internal heat generation usually caused by rapid oxidation

spontaneous generation *n* BIOL same as **abiogenesis**

spontaneous ignition *n* PHYS same as **spontaneous combustion**

spontaneous recovery *n* in psychology, the return of an extinguished conditioned response without reinforcement

~~spontanious~~ incorrect spelling of **spontaneous**

spontoon /spon to͞on/ *n* a type of halberd used by some infantry officers in the 18th century [Mid-18C. Via French < Italian *spontone* < *punto* 'point' < Latin *punctum* (see POINT)]

spoof /spoof/ *n* **1.** AMUSING SATIRE a light amusing satire **2.** HOAX a good-humoured hoax **3.** ONLINE FRAUDULENT SPAM E-MAIL a method of sending e-mail using a false name or e-mail address to make it appear that the e-mail comes from somebody other than the true sender **4.** *Aus* OFFENSIVE TERM an offensive term for semen (*slang*) ■ *v* (**spoofs, spoofing, spoofed**) **1.** *vt* SATIRIZE SOMEBODY OR SOMETHING to satirize somebody or something good-naturedly **2.** *vt* DECEIVE SOMEBODY to deceive or fool somebody **3.** *vti* ONLINE SEND FRAUDULENT E-MAIL TO SOMEBODY to send e-mail using a false name or e-mail address **4.** *vi Aus* OFFENSIVE TERM an offensive term meaning to ejaculate semen (*slang*) [Late 19C. Invented name for a game involving hoaxing] —**spoofer** *n* —**spoofing** *n*

spook /spook/ *n* (*informal*) **1.** GHOST a ghost or a ghostly figure **2.** same as **spy** *n* (sense 1) ■ *v* (**spooks, spooking, spooked**) **1.** *vt* HAUNT SOMEBODY to haunt somebody as a ghost **2.** *vt* STARTLE SOMEBODY to startle or make an animal or person feel uneasy **3.** *vi* BE FRIGHTENED to feel frightened or uneasy [Early 19C. < Dutch]

spooky /spoōki/ (**-ier, -iest**) *adj* **1.** SCARILY SUGGESTIVE OF SUPERNATURAL frightening or unnerving because suggesting the presence of supernatural forces (*informal*) **2.** AMAZING strange or amazing, often in a way that seems supernatural (*informal*) **3.** *N Am* EASILY FRIGHTENED easily frightened or startled —**spookily** *adv* —**spookiness** *n*

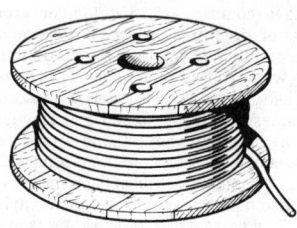

spool

spool[1] /spool/ *n* **1.** CYLINDER ON WHICH SOMETHING IS WOUND a cylinder around which thread, tape, or film is wound. It has a central hole and a rim at each end. **2.** AMOUNT ON SPOOL the amount of something wound on a spool ■ *vti* (**spools, spooling, spooled**) WIND SOMETHING ON SPOOL to wind something on a spool or on something similar to a spool such as a reel or bobbin, or be wound in this way [14C. Directly or via French < Middle Dutch *spoele*]

spool[2] /spool/ (**spools, spooling, spooled**) *vi* to transfer computer data for printing into a computer's memory store so that it can be printed later without slowing down the computer's operations [Late 20C. < SPOOL[1]; sometimes thought to be an acronym < *simultaneous peripheral operation on line*] —**spooling** *n*

spoon /spoon/ *n* **1.** EATING UTENSIL a utensil used for eating or preparing food, consisting of a shallow oval bowl attached to a handle **2.** FISHING SHINY FISHING LURE a bright oval metal fishing lure with a hook attached **3.** GOLF GOLF CLUB a number three wood, used for hitting long high drives from the fairway (*dated*) **4.** DRUGS QUANTITY OF DRUG a quantity of hard drugs, especially a two-gram measure of heroin (*slang*) ■ *v* (**spoons, spooning, spooned**) **1.** *vt* EAT FOOD USING SPOON to eat, scoop, or carry something with a spoon or with the action of somebody using a spoon **2.** *vt*

HOLLOW SOMETHING OUT to dig or scrape a hollow in something, or dig something out to leave a hollow **3.** *vt* GOLF HIT BALL UP in golf, to hit a ball upwards with a scooping action, often as a result of an imperfect stroke **4.** *vi* FISHING USE SPOON FISHING LURE to fish with a spoon lure **5.** *vi* BE AMOROUS to indulge in amorous behaviour such as kissing and cuddling (*dated informal*) [Old English *spōn* 'wood chip' < Indo-European, 'flat piece of wood'] —**spoonful** *n*

spoonbill

spoonbill /spoon bil/ *n* **1.** a wading bird with a long flat beak shaped like a spoon. Native to: tropical regions. Family: Threskiornithidae. **2.** *US* a duck with a broad beak, e.g. a shoveler

spoonerism /spoonərizəm/ *n* an accidental transposition of initial consonant sounds or parts of words, especially in an amusing way, e.g. 'half-warmed fish' for 'half-formed wish' [Early 20C. After Reverend William *Spooner* (1844–1930), British educationalist]

spooney *adj* another spelling of **spoony** (*dated*)

spoon-feed *vt* **1.** to feed somebody, especially a child or hospital patient, using a spoon **2.** to cater to somebody completely, requiring him or her to make no effort at all

spoony /spoōni/, **spooney** (**-ier, -iest**) *adj* foolishly sentimental or amorous (*dated*)

spoor /spoor, spawr/ *n* the visible trail of an animal, especially one being hunted for sport ■ *vti* (**spoors, spooring, spoored**) to track an animal by following its trail [Early 19C. Via Afrikaans < Middle Dutch] —**spoorer** *n*

spor- same as **sporo-** (*used before vowels*)

Sporades /spórrə deez/ group of Greek islands in the Aegean Sea, north of the island of Euboea

sporadic /spə ráddik/ *adj* **1.** occurring at intervals that have no apparent pattern **2.** describes a disease that appears in scattered or isolated instances or locations [Late 17C. Via medieval Latin < Greek *sporadikos* < *sporad-* 'scattered'] —**sporadically** *adv*

SYNONYMS See *periodic*.

sporangiophore /spə ránji ə fawr/ *n* a thread (**hypha**) from a fungus or a projection from the cone of a horsetail from which spore-forming sacs develop

sporangium /spə ránji əm/ (*plural* **-gia** /-ji ə/) *n* a hollow spore-producing organ in fungi, ferns, and some other plants [Early 19C. < modern Latin, 'spore vessel' < Greek *spora* 'sowing, seed' + *aggeion* 'small vessel' (see ANGIO-)]

spore /spawr/ *n* **1.** ASEXUAL REPRODUCTIVE STRUCTURE a small, usually one-celled reproductive structure produced by seedless plants, algae, fungi, and some protozoans that is capable of developing into a new individual **2.** DORMANT BACTERIUM a dormant resistant form taken by some bacteria in response to adverse conditions ■ *vi* (**spores, sporing, spored**) PRODUCE SPORES to produce or release spores [Mid-19C. Via modern Latin < Greek *spora* 'sowing, seed']

spore case *n* BOT same as **sporangium**

sporiferous /spə ríffərəss/ *adj* producing or releasing spores

sporo- *prefix* spore ○ *sporoplasm* ○ *sporocyte* [< Greek *spora* 'sowing, seed']

sporocarp /spórrō kaarp, spáwrō-/ *n* **1.** the spore-producing organ in red algae and some fungi and

slime moulds **2.** the hard round spore-producing organ of some ferns that grow in water

sporocyst /spórrō sist, spáwr-/ *n* **1.** CASE PROTECTING SPOROZOITES a protective case produced by sporozoans in which sporozoites develop **2.** ENCASED SPOROZOITE a sporozoite protected within a case **3.** STRUCTURE PRODUCING SPORES a structure that produces spores, formed by a parasite within its host

sporocyte /spórrō sīt, spáwrō-/ *n* a cell from which spores are produced

sporogenesis /spórrō jénnəssiss, spáwrō-/ *n* **1.** the production or formation of spores **2.** reproduction by means of spores —**sporogenous** /spə rójjənəss/ *adj*

sporogony /spo róggəni, spə-/ *n* the process in sporozoans by which sporozoites are formed from multiple fission of an encysted zygote

sporophore /spórrə fawr, spáwrə-/ *n* an organ in fungi that produces spores

sporophyll /spórrə fil, spáwrə-/, **sporophyl** *n* a leaf or modified leaf that bears spore-producing organs, e.g. the fertile leaf of a fern or club moss

sporophyte /spórrə fīt, spáwrə-/ *n* in plants that alternate between sexual and asexual phases, a plant in its asexual spore-producing phase —**sporophytic** /spórrə fíttik, spáwrə-/ *adj*

sporoplasm /spórrə plazəm, spáwrə-/ *n* an infective mass of protoplasm contained inside a spore that is injected into a host cell by various parasitic organisms

sporopollenin /spórrə póllənin, spáwrə-/ *n* a polymer found in the outer layer of pollen and some spores

sporotrichosis /spórrə trī kóssiss, spáwrə-/ *n* a serious infectious disease caused by a fungus *Sporothrix schenckii* that enters the body from soil or wood via a skin wound. It typically produces skin ulcers and nodules on the lymph nodes. [Early 20C. < modern Latin *Sporotrichum* < *spora* (see SPORE) + Greek *thrix* 'hair']

sporozoan /spórrə zṓ ən, spáwrə-/ *n* a parasitic single-celled organism (**protozoan**) that has alternating sexual and asexual generations and reproduces by means of spores. The malaria parasites are sporozoans. Class: Sporozoa. [Late 19C. < modern Latin *Sporozoa* < Greek *spora* 'sowing, seed' + *zōion* 'animal'] —**sporozoan** *adj*

sporozoite /spáwrə zṓ īt/ *n* a small infectious motile stage in the life of sporozoans produced by sporogony, usually within a host [Late 19C. < modern Latin *Sporozoa* (see SPOROZOAN)]

sporran /spórrən/ *n* a leather pouch, sometimes decorated with fur, worn hanging from a belt in front of the kilt in men's traditional Scottish Highland dress [Mid-18C. Via Scottish Gaelic < Middle Irish *sporán*]

sport /spawrt/ *n* **1.** COMPETITIVE PHYSICAL ACTIVITY an individual or group competitive activity involving physical exertion or skill, governed by rules, and sometimes engaged in professionally **2.** COMPETITIVE PHYSICAL ACTIVITIES AS GROUP competitive physical activities considered collectively as a group **3.** PASTIME an active pastime participated in for pleasure or exercise **4.** SOMEBODY CHEERFUL somebody who remains cheerful when losing or in an unpleasant situation (*informal*) **5.** SOMEBODY WHO PLAYS FAIRLY somebody noted for abiding by the rules in a game or for generally honourable behaviour (*informal*) **6.** GOOD COMPANION a good-natured, easy-going, or sociable person (*informal*) **7.** JOKING good-natured joking (*formal*) ○ *a harmless prank done in sport* **8.** DERISION contemptuous mockery (*formal*) **9.** OBJECT OF RIDICULE an object of ridicule or mockery (*formal*) **10.** SOMEBODY OR SOMETHING MANIPULATED BY OTHERS somebody or something manipulated by external forces (*literary*) **11.** GAMBLER a gambler, especially somebody who gambles on sporting events (*informal*) **12.** ANZ, US FORM OF ADDRESS a casual form of address, especially used between men or boys (*informal*) **13.** BIOL MUTATED ORGANISM a plant or animal that deviates markedly from its parent stock or type, usually as a result of mutation, especially mutation of somatic tissue **14.** BIOL UNUSUAL CHARACTER the mutant character of a mutated organism **15.** AMOROUS BEHAVIOUR amorous behaviour, e.g. kissing or cuddling (*archaic*) ■ *v* (**sports, sporting, sported**) **1.** *vt* WEAR SOMETHING to wear or display something, usually proudly or with the intention of impressing others (*informal*) **2.** *vi* PLAY

HAPPILY to romp and play happily (*formal*) **3.** *vi* ENJOY YOURSELF to enjoy yourself, especially by taking part in outdoor physical activity (*formal*) **4.** *vi* MAKE JOKES to joke or trifle with somebody (*formal*) **5.** *vi* BIOL MUTATE to produce or undergo a mutation [14C. Shortening of DISPORT] —**sporter** *n*

sport climbing *n* a sport in which competitors ascend walls, often artificial ones, on difficult routes that have bolts in place

sporting /spáwrting/ *adj* **1.** USED IN SPORTS relating to or used in sports activities ○ *sporting dogs* **2.** FAIR in keeping with the principles of fair competition, respect for other competitors, and personal integrity **3.** OF GAMBLING relating to gambling, or taking an interest in gambling **4.** RISKING willing to take a risk —**sportingly** *adv*

sporting chance *n* an even or good chance of succeeding

sportive /spáwrtiv/ *adj* **1.** PLAYFUL playful and frolicsome **2.** JOKING done as a joke **3.** FOND OF SPORT regularly taking part in sport **4.** SEXUALLY ACTIVE frequently indulging in sexual activity, or tending to enjoy it (*archaic*) —**sportively** *adv* —**sportiveness** *n*

sports /spawrts/ *adj* **1.** FOR SPORTING ACTIVITIES relating to or used in physical or recreational activities ○ *sports equipment* ○ *sports ground* **2.** FOR INFORMAL WEAR designed for informal or outdoor wear ○ *sports shirt* ■ *npl* SPORTS MEETING a meeting for athletics or other sports activities, especially for school pupils ○ *It's the school sports next week.*

sports car *n* a small car with a low centre of gravity designed for fast acceleration and for handling at high speeds

sportscast /spáwrts kaast/ *n* a radio or television broadcast of a sports event or of sports news [Mid-20C. After BROADCAST] —**sportscaster** *n*

sports day *n UK, Can* a day on which a school stages races and other sports competitions for its pupils

sports drink *n* a soft drink that is intended to quench thirst faster than water and replenish the sugar and minerals lost from the body during physical exercise

sports ground *n* an area of land on which competitive sports events are held

sports jacket *n* **1.** a man's jacket similar in style to a suit jacket but worn on more informal occasions with trousers of a different material or colour **2.** *US* a collarless jacket fitting closely at the wrists, hem, and collar, usually made of synthetic fabric and worn over sports clothes or for casual dress

sportsman /spáwrtsmən/ (*plural* **-men** /-mən/) *n* **1.** a man who participates in sport **2.** somebody, especially a man, who behaves fairly, observing rules, respecting others, and accepting defeat graciously —**sportsmanlike** *adj*

sportsmanship /spáwrtsmən ship/ *n* **1.** conduct considered fitting for a sportsperson, including observance of the rules of fair play, respect for others, and graciousness in losing **2.** participation in sport

sports medicine *n* the branch of medicine concerned with preventing and treating injuries resulting from sport

sportsperson /spáwrts purss'n/ (*plural* **-persons** or **-people** /-peep'l/) *n* **1.** somebody who participates in sport **2.** somebody who behaves fairly, observing rules, respecting others, and accepting defeat graciously

sports supplement *n* a dietary supplement used by athletes to enhance performance

sportswear /spáwrts wair/ *n* clothes worn for sport or outdoor leisure activities

sportswoman /spáwrts wŏŏmən/ (*plural* **-women** /-wimin/) *n* **1.** a woman who participates in sport **2.** a woman who behaves fairly, observing rules, respecting others, and accepting defeat graciously

sportswriter /spáwrts rītər/ *n* somebody who writes about sport, especially for a newspaper or magazine

sport tourer *n* a four-door motor vehicle resembling both a estate car and a four-wheel drive, capable of towing a boat and hauling gear

sport-utility vehicle, sport-utility *n* (*informal*) *N Am* a four-wheel-drive vehicle used for everyday driving, but suitable for rough terrain

sporty /spáwrti/ (**-ier, -iest**) *adj* **1.** FOR SPORT designed or appropriate for sport or leisure activities **2.** ENTHUSIASTIC ABOUT SPORT enthusiastic about sport or outdoor activities and regularly taking part in them **3.** SIMILAR TO SPORTS CAR having features resembling the style or performance of a sports car

sporulate /spórryŏŏ layt/ (**-lates, -lating, -lated**) *vi* to produce spores [Late 19C. < modern Latin *sporula* 'small spore' < *spora* (see SPORE)] —**sporulation** /spórryŏŏ láysh'n/ *n*

spot /spot/ *n* **1.** SMALL ROUND AREA a small defined area, especially one that is more or less circular, that is different in colour, material, or texture from the surrounding area **2.** STAIN a dirty mark or stain **3.** MARK ON SKIN a mark or blemish on the skin, especially a pimple **4.** PLACE a place, point, position, or location ○ *Do you remember the exact spot?* **5.** GEOGRAPHICAL LOCATION a geographical location or area ○ *a local beauty spot* **6.** ASPECT OF SOMETHING a particular aspect or part of something larger ○ *a weak spot in her argument* **7.** SMALL AMOUNT a small amount, e.g. of liquid to drink or of work to do ○ *What about a spot of lunch?* **8.** ANNOUNCEMENT OR ADVERTISEMENT a brief announcement or advertisement inserted between regular radio or television programmes **9.** TIME SLOT OF PERFORMER the appearance of a performer in a variety show, or the scheduled or regular time for that appearance **10.** AWKWARD SITUATION an awkward or difficult situation (*informal*) **11.** ENTERTAINMENT VENUE a place of entertainment **12.** POSITION IN SERIES a position in a series or sequence **13.** ARTS same as **spotlight** *n* (sense 1) **14.** *US* MONEY a piece of paper money worth a particular amount (*dated slang; usually used in combination*) ○ *She handed me a ten spot.* **15.** CUE GAMES MARKED WHITE BILLIARD BALL in billiards, the white ball that is marked with a black dot **16.** CUE GAMES BILLIARD PLAYER the player in billiards who is using the white ball with the black mark **17.** CUE GAMES DOT ON BILLIARD TABLE a small black dot on the table in billiards, snooker, or pool that marks where a ball should be placed **18.** *N Am* CARDS SYMBOL ON PLAYING CARD one of the traditional symbols, heart, diamond, spade, or club, on a playing card **19.** *US* CARDS PLAYING CARD a playing card from two to ten of any of the four suits ○ *a six spot* **20.** *N Am* LEISURE DOT ON GAME PIECE one of the dots on a domino or dice **21.** ELECTRONICS ILLUMINATED POINT ON CATHODE-RAY TUBE the point on the face of a cathode-ray tube at which the phosphor is illuminated by the impact of an electron beam **22.** CHARACTER BLEMISH a blemish on somebody's character or reputation (*archaic*) ■ *adj* **1.** COMM AVAILABLE IMMEDIATELY describes goods or currencies that are paid for and delivered immediately after a sale **2.** BROADCAST ORIGINATING LOCALLY describes a news report that is broadcast from the place where it happens ■ *v* (**spots, spotting, spotted**) **1.** *vt* SEE SOMEBODY OR SOMETHING to see or detect somebody or something suddenly **2.** *vt* IDENTIFY SOMEBODY AS PROMISING to identify somebody, especially a performer, as having a promising talent worthy of being developed to a high, often professional standard **3.** *vti* MAKE OR BECOME STAINED to mark or dirty something with stains, or become marked or dirtied with stains **4.** *vt* MARK SOMETHING WITH DOTS to mark something with dots of a different colour **5.** *vt* BLEMISH SOMEBODY'S CHARACTER to blemish somebody's character or reputation **6.** *vti* ADJUST FIRE to adjust gunfire for accuracy by observation **7.** *vi* FALL LIGHTLY to fall in light drops (*refers to rain*) **8.** *vt N Am* LEND MONEY TO SOMEBODY to give or lend money to somebody, or pay for something for somebody (*slang*) ○ *Will somebody spot me twenty bucks?* [12C. Origin ?] ◇ **hit the spot** to be absolutely what is required for total satisfaction, especially in terms of food or drink (*informal*) ◇ **in a spot** in a difficult or embarrassing position (*informal*) ◇ **on the spot 1.** in the exact place where something is happening **2.** immediately **3.** in a difficult situation or under pressure ◇ **put somebody on the spot** to put somebody in a difficult or embarrassing position, especially a position of having to make an instant judgment or decision

spot check *n* a quick random inspection usually made without prior notice —**spot-check** *vt*

spot kick *n* SOCCER same as **penalty kick** (sense 1)

spotless /spótləss/ *adj* **1.** impeccably clean ○ *a spotless kitchen* **2.** beyond reproach ○ *a spotless reputation* —**spotlessly** *adv* —**spotlessness** *n*

spotlight /spót līt/ *n* **1.** FOCUSED BEAM OF LIGHT a strong beam of light that can be directed to illuminate a small area, especially one focusing attention on a stage performer **2.** LAMP a lamp that produces a strong narrow beam of light that can be directed at will, e.g. one mounted on a police car **3.** FOCUS OF ATTENTION the focus of public attention ■ *vt* (**-lights, -lighting, -lit** /-lit/ or **-lighted**) **1.** ILLUMINATE SOMETHING WITH LIGHT BEAM to direct a beam of light on somebody or something **2.** FOCUS ATTENTION ON SOMEBODY OR SOMETHING to focus public attention on somebody or something

spot market *n* a market in which commodities, securities, or currencies are traded for immediate payment and delivery

spot-on *adj* (*informal*) **1.** absolutely correct or perfectly accurate **2.** exactly what is needed

spot price *n* the market price for goods, currencies, or securities at a specific time

spotted /spóttid/ *adj* **1.** patterned with spots **2.** stained or soiled with spots of something

spotted dick *n* a steamed suet pudding containing dried fruit [< its spotted appearance]

spotted fever *n* a fever accompanied by skin eruptions, e.g. Rocky Mountain spotted fever, typhus, or epidemic cerebrospinal meningitis

spotted-tailed quoll /-kwól/ *n* a carnivorous marsupial that has a brown coat with white spots. Native to: southeastern Australia and Tasmania. Latin name: *Dasyurus maculatus.* [Late 18C. *Quoll* < an Aboriginal language]

spotter /spóttər/ *n* **1.** SOMEBODY WATCHING OUT FOR SOMETHING somebody or something that watches for and locates something (*often used before a noun*) ○ *a spotter plane* **2.** SOMEBODY OR SOMETHING LOCATING ENEMY POSITIONS a person or aircraft that locates and reports enemy positions **3.** TALENT SCOUT somebody who looks out for new talent or material **4.** SOMEBODY WHO MARKS SOMETHING somebody who puts marks or dots on something **5.** SOMEBODY WHOSE HOBBY IS WATCHING somebody whose hobby is watching for and noting down sightings of things, especially trains and aircraft (*usually used in combination*) ○ *a train-spotter*

spotting *n* MED same as **breakthrough bleeding**

spotty /spótti/ (**-tier, -tiest**) *adj* **1.** PIMPLY covered in pimples **2.** SPOTTED patterned with spots **3.** INCONSISTENT inconsistent in quality or character —**spottily** *adv* —**spottiness** *n*

spot-weld *vt* to join overlapping pieces of metal by making a series of small welds dotted about, instead of making a large continuous weld. Spot-welding is used when the bond is subject to light temporary stresses, but not to structural loads. ■ *n* a joint between overlapping metal parts, formed by making a series of small welds —**spot-welder** *n*

spouge /spooj/ *n Carib* Barbadian dance music with a lively beat [Late 20C. Invented word]

spousal /spówz'l/ *adj* relating to a husband or wife

spousal equivalent *n N Am* somebody who becomes equivalent to a husband or wife, especially for the purposes of tax, pension, or state benefits

spouse /spowss, spowz/ *n* somebody's husband or wife [12C. Via Old French *spous* < Latin *sponsus*, past participle of *spondere* 'pledge, betroth']

spout /spowt/ *vti* (**spouts, spouting, spouted**) **1.** DISCHARGE JET OF SOMETHING to discharge a substance forcibly in a jet or stream, or be discharged in this way **2.** ZOOL DISCHARGE AIR FROM BLOWHOLE to discharge air and water through a blowhole **3.** TALK AT GREAT LENGTH ABOUT SOMETHING to talk about something tediously and at great length, usually with no regard for the listener's interest ■ *n* **1.** TUBE FOR POURING LIQUID a tube or pipe out of which a liquid is poured **2.** CHUTE FOR DISCHARGE OF SOLID SUBSTANCE a chute through which something solid such as grain is discharged **3.** STREAM OF LIQUID a continuous and forceful stream of liquid **4.** BUILDINGS, METEOROL same as **waterspout** **5.** ZOOL AIR AND WATER FROM BLOWHOLE a burst of air and water from a whale or other sea animal's blowhole [14C. < Middle Dutch *spouten*] ◇ **up the spout** (*informal*) **1.** ruined or useless **2.** an offensive phrase meaning pregnant

spouting /spówting/ *n NZ, Northeast US* the system of gutters and downpipes that carry rainwater from the roof of a building

spp. *abbr* BIOL species (*plural*)

SPQR *abbr* the senate and people of Rome [Latin *Senatus Populusque Romanus*]

Spr *abbr* MIL Sapper

sprain /sprayn/ *n* a painful injury to the ligaments of a joint caused by wrenching or overstretching ■ *vt* (**sprains, spraining, sprained**) to injure a joint by a sudden wrenching or overstretching of its ligaments [Early 17C. Origin ?]

sprang past tense of **spring**

sprat /sprat/ *n* **1.** (*plural* **sprats** or *same*) **SMALL EDIBLE FISH** a small fish of the herring family. Native to: northeastern Atlantic Ocean, North Sea. Latin name: *Sprattus sprattus*. **2. SMALL HERRING** a small or young herring or similar fish such as an anchovy **3. SPRAT AS FOOD** the flesh of a sprat as food [Old English *sprot* < W Germanic]

sprawl /sprawl/ *vi* (**sprawls, sprawling, sprawled**) **1. SIT OR LIE AWKWARDLY** to sit or lie with the arms and legs spread awkwardly in different directions **2. EXTEND IN DISORDERED WAY** to extend over or across something in a disordered, awkward, or ugly way ○ *handwritten notes sprawled across the page* ■ *n* **1. AWKWARD SITTING OR LYING POSITION** a sitting or lying position in which the arms and legs are spread out awkwardly **2. UNCHECKED GROWTH OF URBAN AREA** the scattered, unplanned, and unchecked expansion of a town or city into the surrounding countryside **3. URBANIZED AREAS ON CITY'S EDGE** the urbanized areas on the edge of a town or city that have developed as a result of unplanned and unchecked expansion [Old English *sprēawlian* 'move convulsively' < Indo-European, 'strew'] —**sprawler** *n* —**sprawling** *adj* —**sprawly** *adj*

spray[1] /spray/ *n* **1. LIQUID PARTICLES** a moving cloud or mist of water or other liquid particles **2. JET OF LIQUID** a jet of fine particles of liquid from an atomizer or pressurized container **3. CONTAINER FOR RELEASING LIQUID** an atomizer or pressurized container that releases fine particles of a liquid (*often used before a noun*) **4. LIQUID IN PRESSURIZED CONTAINER** a liquid product that is packaged in an atomizer or pressurized container, e.g. a deodorant, paint, or insecticide (*often used before a noun*) ■ *v* (**sprays, spraying, sprayed**) **1.** *vt* **DISCHARGE LIQUID FROM PRESSURIZED CONTAINER** to disperse a liquid in the form of fine particles, or apply a liquid in this form to the surface of something **2.** *vt* **PAINT SOMETHING WITH PAINT SPRAY** to paint or mark something using a paint spray ○ *spray the car red* ○ *He sprayed his name on the wall.* **3.** *vi* **URINATE** to put out a stream of urine, e.g. as a cat does when marking its territory [Early 17C. < Middle Dutch *sprayen* 'sprinkle'] —**sprayer** *n*

spray[2] /spray/ *n* **1. PLANT SPRIG** a shoot or branch of a plant, with flowers, leaves, or berries on it **2. FLOWER ARRANGEMENT** a decorative arrangement of flowers and foliage **3. DECORATION IMITATING FLOWERS AND FOLIAGE** something decorative made in imitation of a sprig of flowers and foliage, e.g. a brooch [13C. Origin ?]

spray can *n* a small pressurized container used to disperse liquids in a fine mist

spray gun *n* a device that uses pressure to apply atomized paint or other liquids, operated by means of a trigger

spread /spred/ *v* (**spreads, spreading, spread**) **1.** *vt* **OPEN SOMETHING TO FULLEST EXTENT** to open or extend something to its fullest area **2.** *vti* **EXTEND WIDELY** to extend over a large area, or cause something to extend over a large area ○ *A vast plain spread out before them.* **3.** *vti* **EXTEND IN TIME** to extend something over a period of time, or be extended over a period **4.** *vti* **EXTEND IN RANGE** to extend over a wider range, or cause something to cover a wider range than before **5.** *vt* **SEPARATE THINGS BY STRETCHING** to separate things by stretching or pulling, so that they become far apart **6.** *vti* **BECOME OR MAKE KNOWN** to become widely known, or make something widely known **7.** *vt* **APPLY COATING TO SOMETHING** to coat something with a layer of a substance, especially one smoothly applied **8.** *vti* **DISPERSE** to disperse something over a wide area, or be dispersed in this way ○ *Let's spread out so we can search over a wider area.* **9.** *vti* **SEND OUT IN ALL DIRECTIONS** to send out something in all directions, or to be sent out in all directions ○ *The lamp spread its light.* **10.** *vt* **DISPLAY SOMETHING IN FULL** to exhibit or display something in its fullest extent **11.** *vt* **DIVIDE SOMETHING UP** to divide, share, or split something up among several people or groups ○ *They decided to spread out the money more evenly among the various departments.* **12.** *vt* **GET TABLE READY FOR MEAL** to prepare a table for a meal **13.** *vt* **PUT FOOD ON TABLE** to lay out food or a meal on a table ■ *n* **1. EXTENSION OF SOMETHING** the extension, diffusion, or distribution of something over an area, range, or time **2. VARIETY** a wide variety of things **3. LIMIT OF EXTENSION** the limit to which something can be extended **4. DISTANCE BETWEEN THINGS** the distance or range between two points or things **5. BED OR TABLE COVER** a covering for a bed or table **6.** FOOD **SPREADABLE FOOD** a food with a soft texture, designed to be spread on bread or crackers **7. FOOD MEAL** a large meal laid out on a table (*informal*) **8.** MEDIA **PAIR OF FACING PAGES** two facing pages in a newspaper, magazine, or book, often with material printed across the fold **9.** MEDIA **EXTENSIVE STORY OR AD** an advertisement or story that occupies two or more columns in a newspaper or magazine **10. WIDENING OF BODY** a widening of the hips and waist owing to weight gain (*informal*) **11.** *N Am* **RANCH OR FARM** a piece of land and its buildings used for ranching or farming **12.** AVIAT **PLANE'S WINGSPAN** the wingspan of an aeroplane (*informal*) **13.** FIN **DIFFERENCE BETWEEN BID AND OFFER** the difference between the asking price and the bid price of a security **14.** JEWELLERY **GEMSTONE SIZE** the size of a gemstone when viewed from above, expressed in carats ■ *adj* **1. EXTENDED** extended or stretched out **2.** JEWELLERY **SHALLOW** describes a gemstone that is shallow and flat **3.** PHON **SAID WITH LIPS STRAIGHT** describes a speech sound that is pronounced with the lips forming a horizontal line [Old English *sprǣdan* < Indo-European, 'strew'] —**spreadable** *adj*

spread betting *n* a form of gambling that involves betting on the movement of a stock price in relation to a given range of high and low values. If the stock price moves outside the values on a given day, the better wins a multiple of the original stake times the number of points above or below the set range.

spread eagle *n* **1. SYMBOLIC IMAGE OF EAGLE** the image of an eagle with its wings and legs outstretched, especially when used as an emblem of the United States. The spread eagle appears on the Great Seal of the United States. **2. SKATING FIGURE** in ice skating, a figure performed with the blades touching heel to heel **3. POSTURE WITH SPREAD LIMBS** a way of standing or lying with arms and legs spread apart

spread-eagle *v* **1.** *vt* **FORCE SOMEBODY INTO SPREAD-OUT POSITION** to force somebody to stand or lie with arms and legs spread apart, especially when being arrested or searched **2.** *vi* **ADOPT POSITION WITH SPREAD LIMBS** to stand or lie with arms and legs spread apart **3.** *vt* **STRETCH BODY ACROSS** to stand or lie with limbs spread wide across a gap or an object **4.** *vi* **PERFORM SKATING FIGURE** in ice skating, to perform a spread eagle ■ *adj US* same as **spread-eagled**

spread-eagled *adj UK, ANZ, Can* standing or lying with arms and legs spread apart. US term **spread-eagle**

spreader /spréddər/ *n* **1. DEVICE FOR DISTRIBUTING SEED OR FERTILIZER** a machine used by farmers and gardeners to spread manure, fertilizer, seed, or similar material over the ground (*usually used in combination*) **2. IMPLEMENT FOR SPREADING** an implement used for spreading soft substances, e.g. a spatula, trowel, or broad-bladed knife (*usually used in combination*) **3. DEVICE FOR SEPARATING THINGS** a device used to hold things such as cables or wires apart, e.g. a bar

spreading factor /sprédding-/ *n* BIOL same as **hyaluronidase**

spreadsheet /spréd sheet/ *n* **1.** a computer program that displays numerical data in cells in a simulated accountant's worksheet of rows and columns in which hidden formulas can perform calculations on the visible data. Changing the contents of one cell can cause automatic recalculation of other cells. **2.** the display or printout of a spreadsheet, showing the many lines and columns of a ledger

sprechgesang /shprékgə zang, shprékh-/, **Sprechgesang** *n* a style of singing that incorporates aspects of ordinary nonmusical speech [Early 20C. < German, 'speech song']

sprechstimme /shprék shtimə, shprékh-/, **Sprechstimme** *n* **1.** the voice used to sing sprechgesang **2.** MUSIC same as **sprechgesang** [Early 20C. < German, 'speech voice']

spree /spree/ *n* **1.** a session of extravagant self-indulgent activity, especially of spending or drinking, but also of criminal activity **2.** a fun-filled sociable outing (*dated*) [Late 18C. Origin ?]

sprezzatura /sprétsə tóorə/ *n* **1.** unstudied grace in art, music, or literature **2.** elegant unstudied carelessness in attitude and personal behavior [Mid-20C. < Italian]

sprig /sprig/ *n* **1. SMALL BRANCH** a shoot, stem, or twig cut or broken from a plant ○ *garnished with a sprig of parsley* **2. DECORATION** an artistic representation of a sprig that is usually repeated in rows on fabric or wallpaper to produce a decorative pattern **3. YOUTH** a young man (*dated*) **4.** CONSTR **SMALL NAIL** a small headless tack that tapers to a point **5. STUD** a stud or spike in the sole of a boot used for various sports ■ *vt* (**sprigs, sprigging, sprigged**) **1. DECORATE SOMETHING WITH SPRIG PATTERN** to decorate fabric, wallpaper, or pottery with a pattern of sprigs ○ *a dress of sprigged cotton* **2.** BOT **CUT TWIGS FROM PLANT** to cut small twigs or branches from a plant **3.** CONSTR **NAIL SOMETHING WITH TACKS** to nail something using small headless tacks that taper to a point [14C. Origin ?] —**sprigger** *n* —**spriggy** *adj*

sprightly /sprītli/ *adj* (**-lier, -liest**) full of life and vigour, especially with a light and springy step ■ *adv* in a lively and vigorous way [Early 16C. < variant of SPRITE] —**sprightliness** *n*

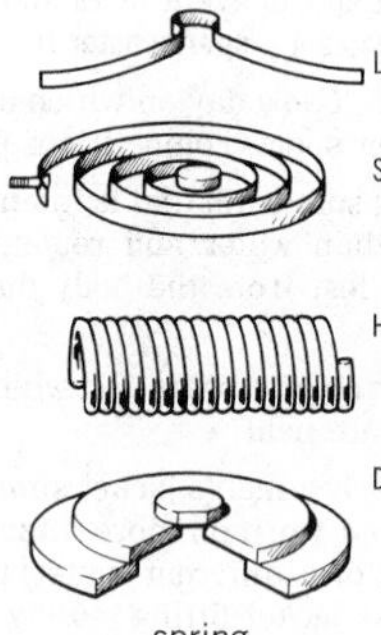
Leaf
Spiral
Helical
Disc

spring

spring /spring/ *v* (**springs, springing, sprang** /sprang/, **sprung** /sprung/) **1.** *vi* **MOVE SUDDENLY IN SINGLE MOVEMENT** to move rapidly upwards or forwards in a single movement or in a series of rapid movements ○ *He sprang to his feet.* ○ *The lid sprang open.* ○ *She sprang to my defence.* **2.** *vt* **LEAP OVER SOMETHING** to leap over a barrier **3.** *vi* **RAPIDLY RESUME ORIGINAL POSITION** to move back rapidly to an original position after being forced in another direction ○ *A branch sprang back and hit me in the face.* **4.** *vi* **EMERGE RAPIDLY** to appear or come into existence quickly ○ *There are new houses springing up all around the village.* **5.** *vi* **COME FROM SOMEBODY'S LIPS** to be uttered, especially as a sudden and almost involuntary reaction to something ○ *A cry of rage sprang from his lips.* **6.** *vi* **ORIGINATE FROM SOMETHING** to originate from a particular source ○ *His behaviour seems to spring from an innate sense of insecurity.* **7.** *vi* **BE DESCENDED** to be descended from a person or family **8.** *vt* **MAKE SOMETHING OPERATE** to operate a device or trap by releasing a mechanism that was held in check **9.** *vti* **DETONATE MINE** to explode or detonate a mine, or be detonated **10.** *vt* **FIT SOMETHING WITH SPRINGS** to provide something, e.g. a vehicle or piece of furniture with springs (*usually passive*) ○ *a sprung floor* **11.** *vi* **JUMP OUT OF PLACE** to move suddenly out of place, or come suddenly loose, within a mechanism **12.** *vti* **WARP OR SPLIT** to crack, split, or warp, or cause wood to do this **13.** *vt* **SUDDENLY REVEAL SOMETHING TO SOMEBODY** to make something known to somebody, or present somebody with something, unexpectedly or suddenly (*informal*) ○ *You can't just spring a decision like that on me!* **14.** *vt* **GET SOMEBODY OUT OF PRISON** to release somebody from prison or help somebody escape from prison (*slang*) **15.** *vi Aus, N Am* **PAY FOR SOMETHING**

to pay for something, usually on behalf of another person (*slang*) ○ *I'll spring for lunch.* **16.** *vti* FIELD SPORTS **MOVE ANIMAL FROM COVER** to move an animal or bird out into the open during a hunting expedition, or be moved in this way **17.** *vi* ARCHIT **RISE** to extend upwards from a base, e.g. from the top part of a column ■ *n* **1. COIL OF METAL** a resilient metal coil that will store energy when compressed and release energy when returning to its original shape. Use: for cushioning, in clockwork. **2. ABILITY TO REGAIN SHAPE** the ability of an object to revert rapidly to its original position after being extended, compressed, or placed under tension ○ *a mattress with a lot of spring left in it* **3. ONWARD OR UPWARD LEAP** a rapid forward or upward movement **4. SEASON OF YEAR** the season of the year between winter and summer during which many plants bring forth leaves and flowers. It runs from March to May in the northern hemisphere, and from September to November in the southern hemisphere. **5. TIME OF RENEWAL** a time of new growth and regeneration **6. WATER EMERGING FROM UNDERGROUND** a source of water that flows out of the ground as a small stream or pool **7. ORIGIN OF SOMETHING** a source from which something, e.g. a character trait, a feeling, or a situation, proceeds or develops (*literary; often used in the plural*) ○ *the springs of her ambition* **8. WARPING OR BENDING** warping, cracking, or bending, especially when caused by great force **9.** METEOROL same as **spring tide** (sense 1) ■ *adj* **1. HAPPENING IN SPRINGTIME** relating to, occurring in, or appropriate to the season of spring ○ *spring fashions* **2. GROWN IN SPRINGTIME** normally grown or growing in the season of spring ○ *spring flowers* **3. FULL OF SPRINGS** having or containing springs, especially for cushioning or as part of a clockwork mechanism ○ *a spring mattress* **4. RECOILING** acting like a spring in being held back then quickly releasing energy [Old English *springan* < Indo-European, 'rapid movement']

CULTURAL NOTE ***The Rite of Spring***, a ballet (1913) with music by the Russian composer Igor Stravinsky. This one-act work is based on traditional dances performed at pagan festivals in Russia. Its use of dissonance and irregular pulsating rhythms combined with Nijinsky's unorthodox choreography outraged contemporary audiences, resulting in a famous riot at the first performance in Paris on 29 May.

spring balance *n* a device to determine the weight of something by measuring the tension it creates on a spring

spring beauty *n* a spring-flowering succulent herbaceous plant of the purslane family. Flowers: white or pinkish. Native to: eastern North America. Genus: *Claytonia*.

springboard /spríng bawrd/ *n* **1. FLEXIBLE DIVING BOARD** a flexible board secured to a base at one end and projecting over the water at the other, used for diving **2. GYMNASTIC EQUIPMENT** a flexible board on which gymnasts bounce in order to gain height for vaulting **3. EVENT OR FACTOR HELPING ADVANCEMENT** an event, activity, or plan that provides an opportunity for something or helps to promote future success

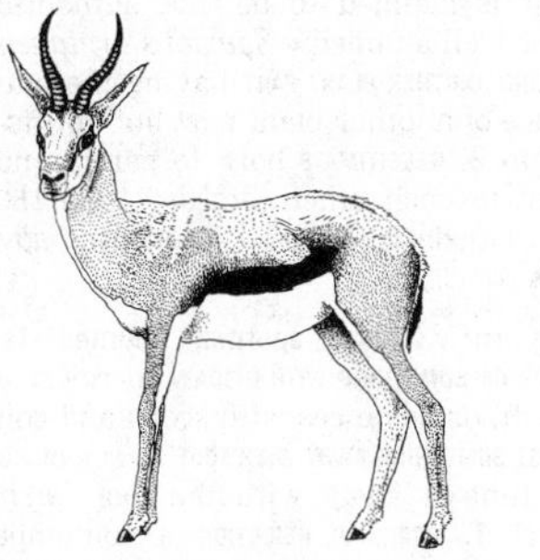

springbok

springbok /spríng bok/ (*plural same* or **-boks**) *n* a small swift gazelle noted for its ability to leap high in the air repeatedly when startled. Native to: semiarid regions of southern Africa. Latin name: *Antidorcas marsupialis*. [Late 18C. < Afrikaans, 'leaping he-goat']

Springbok *n* **1.** a member of the South African national rugby team **2.** an athlete who has represented South Africa in any of various international sporting competitions (*dated*)

spring break *n* a holiday, usually lasting a week, during the spring term at school

springbuck /spríng buk/ (*plural same* or **-bucks**) *n* ZOOL same as **springbok**

spring chicken *n* a chicken less than ten months old [Because formerly available for eating only in spring] ◇ **no spring chicken** no longer young, inexperienced, or agile

spring-clean *vti* to clean a house or room thoroughly, usually including all the contents and furnishings, at the end of the winter or during spring ■ *n* a thorough cleaning of a house or room at the end of the winter or during spring —**spring-cleaning** *n*

springe /sprinj/ *n* a snare or trap for small animals, consisting of a noose attached to a branch under tension [13C. Ultimately < Germanic]

springer /springər/ *n* **1. SOMEBODY OR SOMETHING THAT LEAPS** a person or animal that springs or leaps **2.** BREED same as **springer spaniel 3.** ARCHIT **WEDGE-SHAPED STONE** the first wedge-shaped stone (**voussoir**) of an arch resting on the top section of the arch's supporting pillar (**impost**) **4.** AGRIC **COW READY TO GIVE BIRTH** a cow that is on the point of giving birth to a calf

springer spaniel *n* a hunting dog with a long wavy coat, short legs, and floppy ears, belonging to either an English or a Welsh breed

spring fever *n* a feeling of restlessness, yearning, lust, or sometimes laziness, believed to be brought on by the coming of spring

Springfield /spring feeld/ **1.** capital of Illinois, on the southern bank of the Sangamon River, west of Decatur. US President Abraham Lincoln is buried there. Population: 111,834 (2002 estimate). **2.** city in south-central Massachusetts, on the Connecticut River, north of the Connecticut border. It is home to the Basketball Hall of Fame. Population: 151,915 (2002 estimate). **3.** town in northeastern Virginia. It is a suburb of Washington, DC. Population: 23,706 (2002 estimate).

Springfield rifle *n* a bolt-action .30-calibre rifle developed at the federal arsenal in Springfield, Massachusetts, used by the US Army in World War I

springhaas /spríng haas/ (*plural same*) *n* a jumping mammal with hind legs like a kangaroo's and a long black-tufted tail. Native to: dry regions of southern Africa. Latin name: *Pedestes capensis*. [Late 18C. < Afrikaans, 'leaping hare']

springhead /spríng hed/ *n* **1.** the source of a particular way of thinking **2.** the source of a stream

springing /springing/ *n* the point at which an arch, vault, or dome rises from its support

spring line *n* a rope by means of which a sailing vessel is made fast to an anchorage, usually one of two

spring-loaded *adj* describes a mechanism that is fixed in place or controlled by a spring

spring lock *n* a lock that is bolted automatically by means of a spring

spring onion *n* a young onion with a small white bulb and a long green shoot. N Am term **green onion**

spring peeper *n* a small brownish tree frog that has an X-shaped marking on its back and makes a shrill peeping call early in the spring. Native to: eastern North America. Latin name: *Hyla crucifer*.

spring roll *n* an appetizer of savoury ingredients formed into a slightly flattened cylindrical shape in a wrapping and fried until crisp and golden. The wrapping is usually thin dough, a pancake mixture, or edible paper. [Translation of Chinese *chūn juǎn*]

spring scale *n* same as **spring balance**

Springsteen /spríng steen/, **Bruce** (*b.* 1949) US singer and songwriter. His songs include 'Born in the USA' (1984). Full name **Springsteen, Bruce Frederick Joseph**

> 'The life of a rock-'n-roll band will last as long as you look down into the audience and can see yourself, and your audience looks up at you and can see themselves.'
> [Bruce Springsteen. Quoted in *Springsteen*, Robert Hilburn; 1985]

springtail /spríng tayl/ *n* a primitive wingless insect with a forked abdominal structure that helps it spring through the air. Order: Collembola.

spring tide *n* **1.** a tide that occurs near the times of the new moon and full moon and has a greater than average range **2.** a great rush of emotion (*literary*)

springtide /spríng tīd/ *n* same as **springtime** (*literary*)

springtime /spríng tīm/ *n* **1.** the season of spring, between winter and summer **2.** the earliest, freshest, and most pleasant stage of somebody's life, a relationship, or a period of time (*literary*)

springwood /spríng wŏŏd/ *n* young relatively soft wood that develops just beneath the bark of trees in spring

springy /springi/ *adj* (**-ier, -iest**) **1. BOUNCING BACK INTO SHAPE** springing back strongly to its original shape after being compressed or extended **2. MAKING SPRINGING MOTIONS** tending to make a lot of springing movements (*informal*) ■ *n* (*plural* **-ies**) *Aus* **WET SUIT** a wet suit with short sleeves and legs, used in warm conditions (*slang*) —**springily** *adv* —**springiness** *n*

sprinkle /springk'l/ *v* (**-kles, -kling, -kled**) **1.** *vt* **DISTRIBUTE SMALL AMOUNTS OF SOMETHING** to scatter small drops of a liquid, or particles of a fine or powdery substance, e.g. sugar, ashes, or flour, over the surface of something **2.** *vt* **SCATTER OR BE SCATTERED THROUGHOUT THINGS** to scatter things in among other things, at random or as though at random, or be scattered among other things in this way ○ *hedgerows sprinkled with poppies* **3.** *vt* **GIVE SOMETHING OUT IN SMALL AMOUNTS** to distribute a substance, emotion, or commodity in small amounts **4.** *vi N Am* **RAIN VERY SLIGHTLY** to rain very gently in fine drops, usually for a short period ■ *n* **1. ACT OF SPRINKLING** the action of scattering small drops of liquid or particles of a fine or powdery substance **2.** same as **sprinkling** (sense 1) **3.** *N Am* **FINE RAIN** a light rain falling in fine or sporadic drops [14C. Origin ?]

sprinkler /springklər/ *n* **1.** a device that sends out a moving spray of water, used for watering gardens or for suppressing fires ○ *a ban on the use of hosepipes and sprinklers* **2.** a plastic or metal nozzle perforated with many small holes that fits onto a watering can or hose

sprinkler system *n* **1.** a system for extinguishing fires, designed to release water from overhead nozzles that open automatically when a specific temperature is reached **2.** a system of sprinklers for watering a garden or lawn, operated by a single control

sprinkling /springkling/ *n* **1.** a small quantity of drops of liquid or of a fine or powdery substance, e.g. sugar, snow, or sand, scattered on or throughout something **2.** a meagre amount or a small number of something, especially spread over a wide area ○ *There was only a sprinkling of people in the hall.*

sprint /sprint/ *n* **1. SHORT SWIFT RACE** a short race run or cycled at a very high speed **2. FAST FINISHING RUN** a burst of fast running or cycling during the last part of a longer race **3. BURST OF ACTIVITY** a sudden burst of activity or speed ■ *vi* (**sprints, sprinting, sprinted**) **GO AT TOP SPEED** to run, swim, or cycle as rapidly as possible [Mid-16C. < Old Norse *spretta* 'jump'] —**sprinter** *n, vi*

sprit /sprit/ *n* a pole that crosses a fore-and-aft sail diagonally [Old English *sprēot* < Germanic]

sprite /sprīt/ *n* **1. SUPERNATURAL ELFIN CREATURE** in folklore, a small supernatural being like an elf or a fairy, especially one associated with water **2. SOMEBODY LIKE ELF** a small or delicately built person who is likened to an elf or a fairy **3. GHOST** in folklore, a ghost or spirit **4.** COMPUT **INDEPENDENT GRAPHIC OBJECT** an independent graphic object that moves freely across a computer screen [14C. Via French < Latin *spiritus* (see SPIRIT)]

spritsail /sprít sayl/; *nautical* /sprítś'l/ *n* a sail that is extended by being mounted on a sprit

spritz /sprits/ *vt* (**spritzes, spritzing, spritzed**) to spray a fine jet of liquid through a nozzle ■ *n* a fine spray of liquid squirted through a nozzle [Early 20C. < German *spritzen* 'squirt, splash']

spritzer /sprítsər/ *n* a drink consisting of wine, generally white, diluted with sparkling water or

lemonade [Mid-20C. < German, 'splash' < *spritzen* 'to squirt, splash']

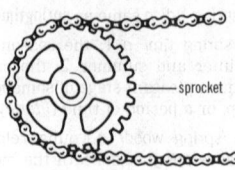

sprocket

sprocket /spróckit/ *n* **1.** a projecting tooth on a wheel or cylinder that engages with the links of a chain or with perforations in film to make the chain or film move forward **2.** *also* **sprocket wheel** a wheel with sprockets [Mid-16C. Origin ?]

sprog /sprog/ *n* (*slang*) **1.** a child or baby **2.** in the RAF, a new recruit [Mid-20C. Origin ?]

sprout /sprowt/ *v* (**sprouts, sprouting, sprouted**) **1.** *vti* DEVELOP SHOOTS to develop buds or shoots **2.** *vi* GERMINATE to begin to grow from a seed **3.** *vti* GROW to grow from something, or have something growing from or on it ○ *His chin was suddenly sprouting hair.* **4.** *vti* EMERGE to emerge and grow rapidly, or cause something to emerge and grow rapidly ○ *New tourist hotels were sprouting up all along the coast.* ■ *n* **1.** NEW GROWTH ON PLANT a new growth on a plant, e.g. a bud or shoot **2.** PLANTS, FOOD same as **Brussels sprout** **3.** SOMETHING LIKE SPROUT somebody or something that grows rapidly ■ **sprouts** *npl N Am* EDIBLE SHOOTS OF PLANTS newly sprouted seeds or beans, eaten especially in sandwiches, salads, and stir-fries [Old English *-sprūtan* < Germanic]

spruce

spruce[1] /sprooss/ (*plural* **spruces** *or same*) *n* **1.** an evergreen tree of the pine family with a pyramid shape, short needles, drooping cones, and soft light wood. Genus: *Picea.* **2.** the soft light wood of a spruce tree [Early 17C. Shortening of *Spruce fir* 'Prussian fir' < alteration of obsolete *Pruce* 'Prussia' < medieval Latin *Prussia*]

spruce[2] /sprooss/ *adj* having a clean, smart, and well-cared-for appearance ○ *a spruce young man* ■ *vti* (**spruces, sprucing, spruced**) to make a person, usually yourself, or a place cleaner and smarter in appearance ○ *sprucing up the city for the celebrations* [Late 16C. Origin ?] —**sprucely** *adv* —**spruceness** *n*

spruce beer *n* a fermented drink whose ingredients include spruce leaves and twigs

spruce pine *n* a tall pine with soft wood and needles in pairs. Native to: southeastern United States. Latin name: *Pinus glabra.*

sprue[1] /sproo/ *n* **1.** a vertical channel in a mould, used to pour in molten material **2.** a piece of waste material from moulding plastic or metal, especially one of the supporting pieces that connect small parts moulded at the same time [Early 19C. Origin ?]

sprue[2] /sproo/ *n* a tropical disease of unknown origin involving deficient absorption of nutrients from the intestine and marked by persistent diarrhoea,

weight loss, and anaemia [Late 19C. < Dutch *spruw* 'the disease thrush']

spruik /sprook/ (**spruiks, spruiking, spruiked**) *vi Aus* to promote goods, services, or a cause by addressing people in a public place (*humorous*) [Early 20C. Origin ?]

spruiker /sprookər/ *n Aus* **1.** a salesperson who addresses passing members of the public from the door of a shop, bar, or other establishment (*informal*) **2.** somebody who promotes goods, services, or a cause by addressing people in a public place (*humorous*)

sprung past participle of **spring**

sprung rhythm *n* a system of prosody that uses metrical feet with a varying number of syllables in an effort to evoke the irregular stresses and rhythms of ordinary speech

spry /sprī/ (**spryer** *or* **sprier, spryest** *or* **spriest**) *adj* markedly brisk and active, especially at an advanced age [Mid-18C. Origin ?] —**spryly** *adv* —**spryness** *n*

spt *abbr* seaport

SPUC *abbr* Society for the Protection of the Unborn Child

spud /spud/ *n* **1.** FOOD same as **potato** (senses 1–2) (*informal*) **2.** GARDENING GARDEN IMPLEMENT a spade with a sharp narrow blade, used for cutting through roots and digging up weeds **3.** FORESTRY TOOL FOR REMOVING BARK FROM TREES a tool resembling a chisel that is used to peel bark from trees ■ *v* (**spuds, spudding, spudded**) **1.** *vi* START DRILLING OIL WELL to use a large bit to drill the upper part of the bore of a new oil well **2.** *vt* GARDENING DIG SOMETHING UP WITH SPUD to use a spud to dig up weeds or cut through roots **3.** *vt* FORESTRY REMOVE BARK to remove bark from trees by the use of a spud [15C. Origin ?]

spud-bashing *n* in the British armed forces, the task of peeling potatoes as a punishment (*slang*)

spume /spyoom/ (*literary*) *n* a mass of fine bubbles on the surface of a liquid, especially on the sea ■ *vi* (**spumes, spuming, spumed**) to produce or have a mass of fine bubbles on the surface [14C. Directly or via French < Latin *spuma* 'foam'] —**spumous** *adj* —**spumy** *adj*

spumone /spoo mṓni/, **spumoni** *n* **1.** an Italian ice cream composed of differently coloured and flavoured layers, often containing nuts and candied fruit **2.** an Italian light mousse dessert [Early 20C. < Italian < *spuma* 'foam' < Latin]

spun past participle, past tense of **spin**

spun glass *n* **1.** INDUST same as **fibreglass** (sense 1) **2.** blown glass that has slender, often spiral glass threading or filigree incorporated into it

spunk /spungk/ *n* **1.** PLUCKINESS spiritedness or eager willingness (*informal*) **2.** TABOO TERM a highly offensive term for semen (*taboo*) **3.** TINDER a combustible material, especially soft wood or twigs, that can be used to kindle fires **4.** *Aus* SEXUALLY DESIRABLE PERSON a sexually desirable person (*informal*) [Mid-16C. Origin ?]

spunky /spúngki/ (**-ier, -iest**) *adj* very lively, determined, and courageous (*informal*) —**spunkily** *adv* —**spunkiness** *n*

spun silk *n* inexpensive fabric or yarn made from short-fibred silk combined with silk waste

spun sugar *n US* FOOD same as **candyfloss**

spun yarn *n* rope or cord made from several light yarns twisted or spun together

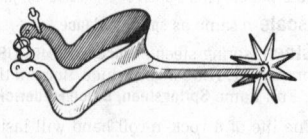

spur

spur /spur/ *n* **1.** DEVICE ATTACHED TO RIDER'S HEEL a small spike or spiked wheel attached to the heel of a rider's boot that is nudged into the horse's sides to encourage it to go faster **2.** INDUCEMENT something that encourages a person or organization to take action or to make a greater effort, e.g. the hope of a reward or the fear of punishment **3.** PROJECTION something that projects outward at an angle from a larger object **4.** PROJECTING PLANT PART a tubular extension from a flower part, as, e.g. in larkspur and columbine **5.** SHORT BRANCH OR SHOOT a short branch or lateral shoot from a stem or branch of a plant **6.** HORNY PROJECTION a sharp horny projection on the legs of some male birds such as domestic cocks above the claws **7.** PROJECTING ANIMAL PART a pointed extension or projecting part (**process**) on some animals, e.g. the stiff outgrowth on the legs of some insects and birds **8.** SHORT BONY OUTGROWTH a bony outgrowth, usually a normal part of the body but sometimes one that develops such as that on the bottom of the heel after an injury **9.** SPIKE ON LEG OF FIGHTING COCK a sharp metal spike attached to the leg of a fighting cock **10.** MOUNTAIN RIDGE a ridge that projects outwards from a mountain range and descends towards a valley floor **11.** SHORT JETTY a small jetty extending from a shore to protect a beach against erosion or to trap shifting sands **12.** PART OF RAILWAY a short section of railway track leading off a main line **13.** ROAD OFF MAJOR ROAD a short side road leading off a main road **14.** PROP a timber or masonry prop or support **15.** CERAMIC SUPPORT IN KILN a small ceramic support placed beneath a pot in a kiln ■ *v* (**spurs, spurring, spurred**) **1.** *vt* ENCOURAGE SOMEBODY TO TRY HARDER to stimulate a person or organization to take action or make greater efforts in the hope of a reward or in the fear of punishment ○ *'Public schools are spurred to perform better thanks to new reforms.'* (*US News & World Report*; December 1998) **2.** *vt* MAKE HORSE GO FASTER to encourage a horse to go faster by nudging spurs into its sides **3.** *vt* CAUSE INJURY TO HORSE WITH SPURS to injure a horse by using spurs too strongly and too frequently **4.** *vt* PUT SPURS ON SOMEBODY OR SOMETHING to equip somebody or something with spurs **5.** *vi* RIDE FAST to ride fast, using spurs (*literary*) **6.** *vi* GO QUICKLY to go or proceed hastily (*literary*) [Old English *spura* < Indo-European, 'to kick'] —**spurred** *adj* ◇ **on the spur of the moment** on impulse and without forethought ◇ **win** *or* **gain your spurs** **1.** to gain recognition and respect for the first time **2.** in the past, to be given the rank of knight

SYNONYMS See *motive.*

spurge /spurj/ *n* a herbaceous plant or bush that has flowers without petals and a bitter milky juice. Genus: *Euphorbia.* [14C. < Old French *espurge* < *espurgier* 'purge' < Latin *expurgare* (see EXPURGATE)]

spur gear *n* a gear whose teeth are arranged along the rim parallel to its axis of rotation

spurge laurel *n* a low-growing evergreen bush with elongated glossy leaves. Flowers: yellow. Native to: Europe, Asia. Latin name: *Daphne laureola.*

spurious /spyoori əs/ *adj* **1.** NOT GENUINE different from what it is claimed to be, not authentic, or not valid or well-founded ○ *spurious arguments* **2.** BOT RESEMBLING ANOTHER PLANT PART having the outward appearance of another plant part but not its function or origin **3.** ILLEGITIMATE born to parents not legally married to each other (*archaic*) [Late 16C. < Latin *spurius* 'illegitimate child'] —**spuriously** *adv* —**spuriousness** *n*

spurn /spurn/ *v* (**spurns, spurning, spurned**) **1.** *vti* REJECT SOMEBODY OR SOMETHING WITH DISDAIN to reject a person, offer, gift, or advances with scorn and contempt **2.** *vt* THRUST SOMETHING AWAY WITH FOOT to reject something by pushing it away with the foot (*archaic*) ■ *n* (*archaic*) **1.** SCORNFUL REJECTION a contemptuous or scornful rejection **2.** KICK a kick with the foot [Old English *spurnan* < Indo-European] —**spurner** *n*

spur-of-the-moment *adj* happening, made, or done in haste, without reflection or preparation ○ *a spur-of-the-moment purchase*

spurrey /spúrr i/ (*plural* **-reys**), **spurry** (*plural* **-ries**) *n* a low-growing plant of the pink family with linear whorled leaves. Flowers: small, white. Native to: Europe. Genus: *Spurgula.* [Late 16C. < Dutch *spurrie*]

spurt /spurt/ *n* **1. JET OF LIQUID OR GAS** a sudden stream of liquid or gas, forced out under pressure **2. SUDDEN BURST OF ENERGY** a short intense burst of energy, interest, action, or speed ○ *I had a spurt of energy as I was digging.* **3. SUDDEN INCREASE** a sudden increase in the amount, development, or speed of something ○ *a fourth-quarter spurt in inflation* ■ *vti* **(spurts, spurting, spurted) GUSH OUT** to gush out in a pressurized stream or jet, or cause a liquid or gas to do this ○ *Blood spurted from the wound.* [Mid-16C. Origin ?]

spurtle /spúrt'l/ *n Scotland* a short stick, frequently with a decorative end, used for stirring porridge [Early 16C. Origin ?]

spur wheel *n* MECH ENG same as **spur gear**

sputa MED plural of **sputum**

sputnik /spóotnik, spút-/ *n* one of a series of ten artificial Earth-orbiting satellites launched by the former Soviet Union starting in 1957 [Mid-20C. < Russian, 'fellow traveller']

sputter /spúttər/ *v* **(-ters, -tering, -tered) 1.** *vi* **MAKE POPPING SOUND** to make a popping, spitting sound **2.** *vi* **SPIT OUT FOOD AND SALIVA** to spray out drops of saliva or food particles, especially when talking or laughing while eating **3.** *vi* **SPEAK EXPLOSIVELY** to make sounds or pronounce words in an explosive way, especially when angry or excited **4.** *vti* PHYS **REMOVE SURFACE ATOMS BY ION BOMBARDMENT** to cause, or experience, an effect in which the atoms of a surface are removed through bombardment by ions, e.g. in cathode evaporation in a discharge tube **5.** *vt* PHYS **USE METAL TO COAT SOMETHING** to use metal removed by the process of sputtering to coat something ■ *n* **1. NOISE OF SPUTTERING** the noise of a person, fire, candle, or other object sputtering **2. INCOHERENT SPEECH** the confused or incoherent speech of somebody who is angry or excited **3. SOMETHING EMITTED WHILE SPUTTERING** drops of saliva or food particles sprayed out of the mouth while sputtering [Late 16C. < Dutch *sputteren* 'spray'] —**sputterer** *n*

sputum /spyóotəm/ (*plural* **-ta** /-tə/) *n* a substance coughed up from the respiratory tract and usually ejected by mouth, e.g. saliva, phlegm, or mucus [Late 17C. < Latin, 'saliva' < *spuere* 'to spit']

spy /spī/ *n* (*plural* **spies**) **1. SOMEBODY EMPLOYED TO OBTAIN SECRET INFORMATION** an employee of a government who seeks secret information in or from another country, especially about military matters ○ *a spy ring* **2. EMPLOYEE WHO OBTAINS INFORMATION ABOUT RIVALS** an employee of a company who seeks secret information about rival organizations **3. SECRET OBSERVER OF OTHERS** a watcher of other people in secret **4. ACT OF SPY** an instance of acting as a spy ■ *v* **(spies, spying, spied) 1.** *vi* **ACT AS SPY** to work, operate, or function as a spy **2.** *vi* **ENGAGE IN ESPIONAGE** to maintain a network of spies and gather intelligence in other clandestine ways **3.** *vi* **OBSERVE IN SECRET** to keep watch secretly or furtively on somebody or something in order to gain information ○ *Have you been spying on us again?* **4.** *vi* **INVESTIGATE** to try to discover information about something or somebody by means of intensive covert investigations ○ *trying to spy into their customers' purchasing habits* **5.** *vt* **SEE SOMEBODY OR SOMETHING SUDDENLY** to catch sight of somebody or something, often by chance ○ *I happened to look out of the window and spied him scuttling across the yard.* **6.** *vt* **DISCOVER SOMETHING BY OBSERVATION** to discover something by close observation [13C. < Old French *espie* < *espier* 'to spy' < Germanic]

spy out *vt* **1.** to discover something by close and discreet examination ○ *Once he had spied out her weaknesses, he would know how to apply pressure.* **2.** to try to gain information about something by close and discreet examination or by secret reconnaissance ○ *sent scouts ahead to spy out the land between the river and the mountains*

spyglass /spī glaass/ *n* a telescope that is small enough to be held in the hand

spyhole /spī hōl/ *n* same as **peephole** (sense 2)

spy-in-the-cab (*plural* **spies-in-the-cab**) *n* AUTOMOT same as **tachograph** (*informal*)

spymaster /spī maastər/ *n* the leader of espionage and intelligence-gathering activities for a country or organization, especially in fictional spy stories

spyware /spī wair/ *n* software surreptitiously installed on a hard disk without the user's knowledge that relays encoded information on his or her identity and Internet use via an Internet connection

sq. *abbr* **1.** sequence **2.** MIL squadron **3.** MEASURE square *adj* (sense 5) [Latin, 'the one that follows']

Sq. *abbr* **1.** MIL Squadron **2.** square *n* (sense 4) (*used in addresses*)

SQL /éss kyoo él, séekwəl/ *n* a standardized language that approximates the structure of natural English for obtaining information from databases. Full form **structured query language**

Sqn *abbr* MIL Squadron

squab /skwob/ *n* (*plural* **squabs** or *same*) **1. YOUNG BIRD** a young bird just starting to fly, especially a pigeon, sometimes cooked as a delicacy **2. CUSHION** a thick cushion used especially as the seat or sometimes as the back of a chair or sofa ■ *adj* **(squabber, squabbest) SHORT AND FAT** short and rather fat (*archaic*) [Late 17C. Origin ?]

squabble /skwóbb'l/ *n* a noisy argument over a petty matter ■ *vi* **(-bles, -bling, -bled)** to have a petty argument over a trivial matter [Early 17C. An imitation of the sound] —**squabbler** *n*

squad /skwod/ *n* **1. TEAM OF PEOPLE** a small group of people engaged in the same activity ○ *a squad of volunteers* **2. MILITARY FORMATION** a small military formation, especially one that is doing a drill **3. GROUP OF POLICE OFFICERS** a group of police officers, generally assigned to a particular task ○ *the bomb squad* **4. GROUP OF PLAYERS** a number of players from which a team is selected ○ *dropped from the England squad* **5.** *US* **SPORTS TEAM** an athletics or sports team ○ *the volleyball squad* [Mid-17C. Via French *escouade* and Italian *squadra* or Spanish *escuadra* < assumed Vulgar Latin *exquadra* (see SQUARE)]

squad car *n* a police car linked by radio with police headquarters

squaddie /skwóddi/ *n* a private soldier (*slang*)

squadron /skwóddrən/ *n* **1. AIR FORCE UNIT** a unit of a tactical air force belonging to a group and containing two or more flights **2. NAVAL UNIT** a naval unit containing two or more divisions of a fleet **3. CAVALRY UNIT** an armoured cavalry unit belonging to a regiment and containing two or more troops **4. GROUP** an organized group of people, animals, or objects [Mid-16C. < Italian *squadrone* 'large squad' < *squadra* (see SQUAD)]

squadron leader *n* in the RAF, the commander of a squadron of military aircraft

squalene /skwáy leen/ *n* a hydrocarbon that is an intermediate in the formation of cholesterol. Source: human sebum, shark-liver oil. [Early 20C. < modern Latin *Squalus* < Latin, 'a sea fish']

squalid /skwóllid/ *adj* **1.** neglected, insanitary and unpleasant **2.** lacking in honesty, dignity, and moral value ○ *a squalid little scandal* [Late 16C. < Latin *squalidus* 'filthy, rough' < *squalere* 'be filthy' < *squalus* 'filthy'] —**squalidly** *adv* —**squalidness** *n*

SYNONYMS See *dirty*.

squall[1] /skwawl/ *n* **1. WINDSTORM** a sudden strong wind, often with heavy rain or snow **2. BRIEF DISTURBANCE** a short but noisy disturbance **3. SHOW OF TEMPER** a brief but intense outburst of temper ■ *vi* **(squalls, squalling, squalled) BLOW STRONGLY** to blow strongly and suddenly (*refers to winds*) [Late 17C. Origin ?]

squall[2] /skwawl/ *vi* **(squalls, squalling, squalled)** to cry or yell hoarsely ■ *n* a noisy cry or yell [Mid-17C. Origin ?]

squall line *n* a series of small storms that occur along a cold front

squally /skwáwli/ **(-ier, -iest)** *adj* **1.** occurring in or characterized by strong gusts, often accompanied by rain or snow **2.** marked by sudden short noisy arguments

squalor /skwóllər/ *n* **1.** shabbiness and dirtiness resulting from poverty or neglect **2.** a state of moral degradation [Early 17C. < Latin, 'dirtiness, roughness' < *squalere* (see SQUALID)]

squama /skwáymə/ (*plural* **-mae** /-mi/) *n* a scale, or a structure resembling a scale, of the type that make up the covering of fish, reptiles, and some mammals [Early 18C. < Latin, 'scale']

squamate /skwáy mayt/ *n* a reptile of the order that comprises all lizards and snakes and includes about 6,000 species. Order: Squamata. ■ *adj* having scales, or structures resembling scales, of the type that make up the covering of fish, reptiles, and some mammals —**squamation** /skway máysh'n/ *n*

squamiform /skwáymi fawrm/ *adj* resembling a scale or scales of the type that make up the covering of fish, reptiles, and some mammals

squamosal /skwə móss'l/ *n* a thin plate-shaped bone of the vertebrate skull that forms the forward and upper part of the temporal bone in humans [Mid-19C. < Latin *squamosus* (see SQUAMOUS)]

squamous /skwáyməss/, **squamose** /-móss/ *adj* **1. OF SCALES ON BODY** covered with, consisting of, or resembling scales or thin plates of the type that make up the covering of fish, reptiles, and some mammals **2. CONSISTING OF SCALE-SHAPED CELLS** describes a layer of skin (**epithelium**) made up of small scale-shaped cells **3. OF SKULL BONE** relating to the squamosal in the vertebrate skull [15C. < Latin *squamosus* < *squama* 'scale'] —**squamously** *adv* —**squamousness** *n*

squamous cell carcinoma *n* a common type of cancer that usually develops in the epithelial layer of the skin but sometimes in various mucous membranes of the body

squamulose /skwáymyoo lōs, -lōz/ *adj* having or consisting of tiny scales of the type that make up the covering of fish, reptiles, and some mammals [Mid-19C. < *squamule* 'small scale' < Latin *squamula* < *squama* 'scale']

squander /skwóndər/ *vt* **(-ders, -dering, -dered)** to spend or use something precious in a wasteful and extravagant way ■ *n* extravagant spending [Late 16C. Origin ?] —**squanderer** *n*

square /skwair/ *n* **1. EQUILATERAL RECTANGLE** a geometric figure with four right angles and four equal sides **2. RECTANGULAR OBJECT** an object in the shape of a square, or a rectangle that is nearly a square **3. ON GAMES BOARD** one of the four-sided areas marked out on the board used to play chess, draughts, or other games **4. OPEN SPACE IN CITY** an open area in a city or town where two or more streets meet, often containing trees, grass, and benches for recreational use **5.** *N Am* **CITY BLOCK** a block of buildings surrounded by four streets **6. MILITARY DRILL AREA** an open space within an army barracks where soldiers practise marching and handling weapons **7. PART OF CRICKET PITCH** an area in the middle of a cricket pitch where the grass is kept shorter, from which the wicket area is chosen **8. RESULT OF MULTIPLICATION** the product resulting from multiplying a number or term by itself ○ *The square of 7 is 49.* **9. DRAWING INSTRUMENT** an 'L'- or 'T'-shaped instrument made of plastic, wood, or metal, used for drawing or measuring right angles **10. BODY OF SOLDIERS** formerly, a tactical formation of soldiers in a solid or hollow rectangle, with the soldiers on the sides facing outwards **11. UNFASHIONABLE PERSON** an unfashionable person who is out of touch with current popular culture (*dated slang*) **12.** *N Am* same as **square meal** (*informal*) ■ *adj* **1. SHAPED LIKE SQUARE** having the shape of a square, with four more or less equal sides and angles ○ *a square table* **2. FORMING RIGHT ANGLE** intersecting at, having, or making a right angle ○ *square corners* **3. CUBIC** in the shape of a cube ○ *a square block of stone* **4. VAGUELY SQUARE IN SHAPE** roughly square or angular in shape, and looking firm and solid **5. OF MEASUREMENT OF SURFACE AREA** used to describe a measurement of area in which the specified unit refers to the length of each side of a square whose surface area constitutes the measurement ○ *100 square feet* **6. WITH SIDES OF SPECIFIED LENGTH** used to describe a square area with sides of a particular length ○ *a room approximately ten feet square* **7. STRAIGHT OR LEVEL** adjusted or made to be perfectly straight, even, level, or lined up with something else ○ *Make sure the picture is square on the wall.* **8. COMPLETELY FAIR** completely fair, honest, and direct ○ *a square deal* **9. NOT OWING MONEY** with all outstanding debts paid up ○ *She paid me back this morning – we're square now.* **10. AT RIGHT ANGLES TO THE WICKET** in cricket, positioned at right angles to the wicket **11.** MUSIC **LACKING COMPLEXITY** in jazz and popular music, lacking swing or complexity **12. CLEAN** clean and tidy (*informal*) ○ *The kitchen still needs getting square.*

13. BORING AND OLD-FASHIONED dressing and behaving in an unfashionable way and out of touch with current popular culture (*dated slang*) ■ v (**squares, squaring, squared**) **1.** *vt* MAKE SOMETHING SQUARE to make something into a square or rectangular shape **2.** *vt* MULTIPLY NUMBER BY ITSELF to multiply a number or term by itself ○ *Seven squared equals 49.* **3.** *vt* DIVIDE SOMETHING INTO SQUARES to divide a surface, sheet of paper, or other object into squares **4.** *vt* SET SOMETHING STRAIGHT to move an object, item of clothing, or part of the body so that it is straight or level **5.** *vt* PUT SOMETHING AT RIGHT ANGLES to adjust something so that it is at right angles to something else, or test something for this alignment **6.** *vi* BE AT RIGHT ANGLES to be at right angles to something else **7.** *vt* BRING SCORES LEVEL to level the scores, especially in a ball game **8.** *vt* SETTLE THINGS FAIRLY to arrive at a fair and equal agreement with somebody about something, especially about paying off money owed ○ *He squared all his bills and left town.* **9.** *vti* CONCUR OR MAKE SOMETHING AGREE to agree with another person, fact, event, or idea, or make two facts, events, or ideas concur ○ *does not square with what we know* **10. square yourself** *vr US* IMPROVE IMPRESSION to try to improve a relationship or the impression that somebody has of you ○ *Have you squared yourself with the boss?* **11.** *vt* GET SOMEBODY TO APPROVE SOMETHING to obtain somebody's agreement or consent to something, sometimes by offering an inducement (*informal*) ○ *I've squared it with the landlord, it'll be OK to repaint the room.* **12.** *vt* BRIBE SOMEBODY to obtain the consent, acquiescence, or assistance of somebody by means of a bribe or a similar inducement (*informal*) ○ *You'll get a good table, I've squared the maitre d'.* ■ *adv* **1.** AT RIGHT ANGLES so as to be even, straight, level, or at right angles to something **2.** NOT FORWARDS OR BACKWARDS in ball games, to or at another point at the same distance up or down the pitch **3.** DIRECTLY in a direct or forceful way (*informal*) ○ *She drove square into the wall.* **4.** HONESTLY in an honest and straight-forward way (*informal*) [13C. < Old French *esquare* < Latin *quadrum* < Latin *quat-* 'four'] —**squareness** *n* —**squarer** *n* —**squarish** *adj* ◇ **all square 1.** in a situation in which the scores are even **2.** in a situation where all debts and obligations have been cleared and nobody owes anybody anything ◇ **on the square 1.** at right angles to something, or constructed with right angles **2.** in an honest and direct manner, or direct and honest **3.** done on equal terms, or being on equal terms with somebody **4.** being a member of the order of Freemasons ◇ **out of square 1.** not at right angles to something **2.** not in agreement with each other

square away *vt* **1.** to square the yards of a square-rigged sailing vessel **2.** *US* to put things in order or complete some necessary activities, especially in order to get ready for something ○ *I've got my equipment squared away for the trip.*

square off *vi* to take the proper stance for beginning to fight

square up *v* **1.** *vi* SETTLE DEBTS to pay bills, accounts, or other sums of money owed to somebody **2.** *vi* ADOPT AGGRESSIVE POSTURE to put up fists or adopt a similar posture that shows a readiness to fight **3.** *vi* FACE SOMETHING UNPLEASANT to confront something unpleasant or frightening **4.** *vt* ENLARGE SOMETHING USING GRID OF SQUARES to enlarge or transfer a drawing using a grid of squares **5.** *vti* *N Am* ARRANGE OR BE ARRANGED SATISFACTORILY to arrange something in an acceptable or pleasing way, or be arranged in an acceptable or pleasing way

square-bashing *n* the training of soldiers in marching and handling arms on a barracks square (*slang*)

square bracket *n* either of a pair of symbols, [ ], used in keying, printing, or writing to indicate the insertion of special commentary, e.g. that made by an editor

USAGE *Square brackets* are used around text that is added by somebody other than the original writer or speaker, especially to explain or comment on a word or phrase used in a quotation: *He wrote 'As we travelled across Rhodesia now Zimbabwe the weather changed for the worse'.* They are also used to provide information needed when a quotation is taken out of its original context: *She said 'I have never seen him the accused before'.* The word *sic* (Latin for 'thus'), enclosed in square brackets, indicates that the preceding word,

although wrong, is the one actually used: *The notice read 'In case of fire please excite sic the building by the nearest door'.*

square dance *n* **1.** a country dance featuring dancers in pairs or sets, lively music played on fiddles and other instruments, and a caller who announces the steps. It originated in the United States. **2.** a country dance in which four couples form a square —**square dancer** *n* —**square dancing** *n*

square knot *n US* same as **reef knot**

square leg *n* in cricket, a fielding position on the leg side more or less at right angles to the batsman, or somebody fielding in this position

squarely /skwáirli/ *adv* **1.** DIRECTLY in a direct or forceful way ○ *She met my gaze squarely.* **2.** HONESTLY in an honest and straightforward way **3.** AT RIGHT ANGLES in or into a position that is at right angles to something else

square matrix *n* a mathematical matrix that has equal numbers of rows and columns

square meal *n* a filling and nourishing meal

square measure *n* a unit or system of units for measuring an area, e.g. a hectare or an acre

square one *n* the beginning or starting point of an activity or process (*informal*) ○ *The experiment failed, so we're back to square one.*

square pyramid *n* a solid figure with a base that is a square and four faces that are triangles meeting at a common point

square-rigged *adj* having principal sails that are at right angles to the length of the ship

square-rigger *n* a sailing vessel equipped with square-shaped sails

$$\sqrt{81} = 9$$

$$9^2 = 81$$

square root

square root *n* a number or quantity that when multiplied by itself gives a particular number or quantity. For example, 4 or –4 is the square root of 16.

square sail *n* a sail with four sides that is usually suspended horizontally on the mast

squash[1] /skwosh/ *v* (**squashes, squashing, squashed**) **1.** *vt* CRUSH SOMETHING WITH PRESSURE to apply pressure to something so that its volume or size is reduced and it is flattened, crushed, or put out of shape ○ *managed to squash it flat before packing it* **2.** *vti* ENTER OR PUT SOMETHING INTO SMALL SPACE to force your way into a confined space, or force something into a confined space ○ *people trying to squash into the lift* **3.** *vt* PUT DOWN REBELLION to suppress a revolt or uprising completely by using force **4.** *vt* MAKE SOMEBODY FEEL SMALL to silence somebody with a crushing remark or answer **5.** *vi* BECOME FLAT to become flat, often making a squelching sound ■ *n* **1.** JUICE-BASED DRINK a mixture of concentrated fruit juice and sugar or sweeteners used as the basis for soft drinks, or a soft drink made by diluting this mixture with water **2.** MANY PEOPLE IN SMALL SPACE a situation in which a lot of people are crushed into a small space ○ *It was a terrible squash in the back seat.* **3.** ACTION OR NOISE OF SQUASHING the action or noise that results when something is being squashed **4.** SOMETHING SQUASHED a squashed object or number of objects **5.** RACKET GAMES BALL GAME IN WALLED COURT a game for two or four participants played in an enclosed court with long-handled rackets and a small ball that may be hit off any of the walls **6.** RACKET GAMES GAME LIKE SQUASH WITH TENNIS BALLS a ball game for two players resembling squash but played with a tennis ball and rackets

shaped more like conventional tennis rackets [Mid-16C. < Old French *esquasser* < medieval Latin *quassare* (see QUASH[1])] —**squasher** *n*

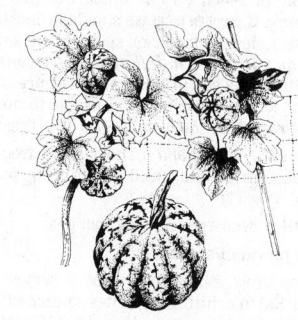

squash

squash[2] /skwosh/ (*plural same* or **squashes**) *n* **1.** the fruit of any plant of the gourd family, cooked and eaten as a vegetable **2.** a plant yielding or cultivated for its edible gourds. Genus: *Cucurbita*. [Mid-17C. Shortening of Narraganset *asquutasquash* 'green things that may be eaten raw']

squash rackets *n* RACKET GAMES same as **squash**[1] *n* (sense 5) (*takes a singular verb*)

squash tennis *n* RACKET GAMES same as **squash**[1] *n* (sense 6)

squashy /skwóshi/ (**-ier, -iest**) *adj* **1.** EASILY SQUASHED soft and easily squashed **2.** OVERRIPE overripe and full of juice **3.** SOFT AND WET soft and waterlogged **4.** LOOKING SQUASHED having a squashed appearance

squat[1] /skwot/ *vi* (**squats, squatting, squatted**) **1.** CROUCH DOWN to crouch down with the knees bent and the thighs resting on the calves **2.** CROUCH DOWN LOW to crouch close to the ground like an animal, especially in order to avoid being seen **3.** OCCUPY PROPERTY WITHOUT LEGAL CLAIM to occupy land or buildings without permission of the owner or other rights holder ■ *adj* (**squatter, squattest**) **1.** SHORT AND SOLID short and solidly built **2.** IN CROUCHED POSTURE in a crouched position ■ *n* **1.** ACTION OF SQUATTING the action of crouching down with the knees bent and the thighs resting on the calves **2.** SQUATTING POSITION a crouched posture with knees bent and thighs resting on calves **3.** WEIGHTLIFTING EXERCISE an exercise in weightlifting in which the lifter raises a barbell while rising from a crouching position **4.** PROPERTY OCCUPIED BY SQUATTERS a piece of property that is occupied by squatters **5.** HARE'S LAIR the den of a hare [14C. < Old French *esquatir* 'crush' < Latin *coactus*, past participle of *cogere* 'force together'] —**squatness** *n*

squat[2] /skwot/ *n N Am* same as **diddlysquat** (*slang*) [Mid-20C. Origin?]

squatly /skwótli/ *adv* in a solid unyielding manner ○ *The piano stood squatly by the window.*

squatter /skwóttər/ *n* **1.** ILLEGAL OCCUPANT OF LAND OR PROPERTY an illegal occupant of land or property, especially somebody who takes over and lives in somebody else's empty house **2.** HOMESTEADER an early North American homesteader **3.** *Aus* TENANT ON AUSTRALIAN GRAZING LAND an early Australian settler who farmed supposedly vacant land and subsequently obtained a lease for it from the government **4.** *Aus* LANDOWNER a wealthy landowner **5.** *NZ* SETTLER IN NEW ZEALAND an early settler in New Zealand who leased a large area of government-owned land **6.** SOMEBODY OR SOMETHING THAT CROUCHES a person or animal that crouches down

squattocracy /skwo tókrəssi/ *n Aus* wealthy landowners regarded as a powerful and influential social class (*disapproving*)

squatty /skwótti/ (**-tier, -tiest**) *adj N Am* **1.** short and thickset **2.** positioned close to the ground

squaw /skwaw/ *n* **1.** an offensive term for a Native North American woman or wife (*dated*) **2.** an offensive term for a woman or wife (*slang*) [Mid-17C. < Narraganset *squaws* 'woman' or Massachuset *squa*]

squawk /skwawk/ *v* (**squawks, squawking, squawked**) **1.** *vi* UTTER HARSH CRY to utter a loud harsh cry **2.** *vti* COMPLAIN LOUDLY to complain or protest about something noisily and annoyingly (*informal*) **3.** *vi* CRY

LOUDLY to cry or wail loudly and annoyingly (*informal*) **4.** *vti* SAY SOMETHING LOUDLY AND SHRILLY to say something in a loud harsh voice (*informal*) ■ *n* **1.** RAUCOUS CRY a loud raucous cry **2.** NOISY COMPLAINT a noisy and annoying complaint or protest (*informal*) [Early 19C. An imitation of the sound] —**squawker** *n*

squawk box *n* a public-address system or one of its speakers, originally box-shaped (*dated slang*)

squeak /skweek/ *v* (**squeaks, squeaking, squeaked**) **1.** *vi* MAKE HIGH-PITCHED SOUND to make a short high-pitched sound or cry **2.** *vt* SAY SOMETHING SHRILLY to say something in a high-pitched voice **3.** *vi* BARELY MANAGE SOMETHING to manage to pass, win, or survive something by the narrowest of margins (*informal*) ○ *squeaked through her final exams* **4.** *vi* BE INFORMER to give information or evidence about somebody to the police (*slang disapproving*) ■ *n* HIGH-PITCHED CRY a short high-pitched sound or cry [14C. An imitation of the sound] ◇ **a narrow squeak** an escape or success achieved by an extremely narrow margin

squeaker /skwéekər/ *n* **1.** SOMEBODY OR SOMETHING THAT SQUEAKS a person, animal, or device that makes a short high-pitched sound or cry **2.** SNITCH somebody who informs on somebody to the police (*slang disapproving*) **3.** *N Am* NARROWLY WON VICTORY a competition, election, race, or other event that is won by a very slight margin (*informal*)

squeaky /skwéeki/ (**-ier, -iest**) *adj* **1.** having a tendency to squeak **2.** designed to make a squeaking noise when pressed —**squeakily** *adv* —**squeakiness** *n*

squeaky-clean *adj* **1.** so clean that it squeaks when rubbed ○ *His hair was squeaky-clean.* **2.** appearing to be almost unnaturally free from general human shortcomings (*informal*)

squeal /skweel/ *n* **1.** SHRILL CRY a short high cry expressing pain, excitement, delight, or other strong emotion **2.** LOUD HIGH SOUND the screaming sound made by tyres when a vehicle brakes suddenly ■ *v* (**squeals, squealing, squealed**) **1.** *vti* GIVE SHORT HIGH CRY to say something, speak, or make a sound in a loud high-pitched tone **2.** *vi* PROTEST LOUDLY to protest or complain loudly and annoyingly (*informal*) **3.** *vi* BECOME INFORMER to give information or evidence against somebody to the police (*slang disapproving*) [13C. An imitation of the sound] —**squealer** *n*

squeamish /skwéemish/ *adj* **1.** EASILY MADE TO FEEL SICK easily sickened by such sights as blood or physical injuries **2.** EASILY OFFENDED easily shocked by such things as violence, the mention of bodily functions, or strong language **3.** FASTIDIOUS excessively scrupulous about manners or behaviour [14C. < Anglo-Norman *escoymous*] —**squeamishly** *adv*—**squeamishness** *n*

squeegee /skwée jee/ *n* **1.** a T-shaped implement edged with plastic or rubber that is drawn across the surface of windows to remove water after washing **2.** an implement, usually a rubber roller, that is used in printing and photography to remove excess water or ink [Mid-19C. < obsolete *squeege* 'press', alteration of SQUEEZE]

squeegee man *n* a man or youth who enters stopped traffic without invitation, attempting to wash motorists' windscreens for money (*slang*)

squeeze /skweez/ *v* (**squeezes, squeezing, squeezed**) **1.** *vt* PRESS SOMETHING FROM TWO SIDES to press something hard in the hand or between two other objects, especially in order to reduce its size or alter its shape **2.** *vt* PRESS SOMEBODY AFFECTIONATELY to exert slight pressure on part of somebody's body such as the hand, knee, or shoulder, usually as a sign of affection and reassurance **3.** *vti* APPLY PRESSURE to exert pressure on something ○ *Come on, squeeze harder!* **4.** *vt* HUG SOMEBODY to hold somebody tightly in your arms **5.** *vt* PUSH PERSON OR OBJECT INTO GAP to force a person, object, or part of the body into or through a small or narrow space **6.** *vi* PUSH INTO OR THROUGH SMALL SPACE to push into or through a small, narrow, or crowded space ○ *I squeezed through a gap in the hedge.* **7.** *vt* PRESS FRUIT TO OBTAIN JUICE to compress a piece of fruit, especially a citrus fruit, in order to extract its juice **8.** *vt* FIND TIME FOR SOMEBODY OR SOMETHING to find time or space for somebody or something in a busy schedule ○ *I could squeeze you in at 9.30.* **9.** *vt* OBTAIN SOMETHING USING PHYSICAL PRESSURE to extract something by exerting physical pressure on somebody or something **10.** *vt* EXTORT MONEY OR FAVOURS to obtain something such as money or favours from somebody by means of psychological pressure or threats **11.** *vt* REQUIRE MONEY FROM SOMEBODY to make financial demands on somebody, especially for rent and taxes, that place the person in a difficult situation **12.** *vt* EXCLUDE SOMEBODY to put an end to somebody's participation in a field of activity ○ *squeezed them out by means of aggressive marketing* **13.** *vt* PRODUCE SOMETHING WITH DIFFICULTY to make an effort to produce something ○ *He managed to squeeze out a timid 'thank you'.* **14.** *vi* JUST MANAGE just narrowly to succeed in winning, passing, or surviving something ○ *managed to squeeze through the exam with a D* **15.** *vt* CARDS PLAY CARD in bridge or whist, to lead a card that may force an opponent to discard a valuable card **16.** *vi* COLLAPSE to condense or collapse under pressure **17.** *vt* HANDICRAFT MAKE IMPRESSION to make an impression or mould of an object using a soft material such as wax or plaster of Paris ■ *n* **1.** PHYSICAL PRESSING a pressing action ○ *gave the sponge a quick squeeze* **2.** SOMETHING PRESSED OUT an amount pressed out of something ○ *Add a squeeze of lemon.* **3.** HUG a hug or close embrace **4.** TOUCH THAT SHOWS AFFECTION the action of briefly clasping somebody's hand, arm, knee, or other part of the body, usually as a sign of affection or reassurance **5.** CROWD OF PEOPLE OR THINGS a group of people or objects crowded together **6.** ECON RESTRICTION IN FINANCIAL CRISIS a government-imposed restriction on credit and investment to counteract inflation or some other financial crisis **7.** COMM FINANCIAL PRESSURE TO ACT an action by business competitors that influences or forces others to make some type of transaction **8.** CRIME SOMETHING EXTORTED something such as money or goods obtained from somebody as a result of threats or the use of force **9.** CARDS same as **squeeze play** (*informal*) **10.** HANDICRAFT IMPRESSION OF OBJECT an impression or mould of an object made by using a soft material such as wax or plaster of Paris **11.** COMM FINANCIAL PRESSURE a financial pressure in the form of reduced profit margins or product shortages **12.** OFFENSIVE TERM an offensive term for a sexual or romantic partner (*slang; sometimes considered offensive*) [Mid-16C. Alteration of obsolete *queise*, origin ?] —**squeezable** *adj* ◇ **put the squeeze on somebody** (*informal*) **1.** to exert pressure on somebody by means of force and threats in order to extort money or goods or to obtain some other end such as a confession **2.** to place somebody in a difficult situation, especially financially, or pressure somebody to do something

squeeze off *vt* to fire a bullet from a gun

squeezebox /skwéez boks/ *n* a concertina or small accordion (*informal*)

squeeze play *n* in bridge or whist, a play in which an opponent is forced to discard a valuable and potentially winning card

squeezer /skwéezər/ *n* a tool or device for squeezing something, especially a kitchen tool for pressing the juice out of citrus fruits ○ *a lemon squeezer*

squelch /skwelch/ *v* (**squelches, squelching, squelched**) **1.** *vt* PUT END TO SOMETHING to suppress or put a stop to something ○ *squelched the uprising* **2.** *vt* SILENCE SOMETHING to silence something such as a rumour or an unwanted remark (*slang*) **3.** *vi* MAKE SUCKING SOUND to move with or make a sucking or gurgling sound like that of somebody treading on muddy ground **4.** *vt* CRUSH SOMETHING to crush something by trampling ■ *n* **1.** SUCKING SOUND a sucking or gurgling sound like that of somebody treading on muddy ground **2.** CRUSHING RETORT a clever or cutting answer to something somebody has said (*slang*) **3.** ELECTRONICS ELECTRONIC CIRCUIT an electronic circuit that automatically reduces the gain of a receiver in response to an input signal that exceeds a predetermined level [Early 17C. An imitation of the sound] —**squelcher** *n* —**squelchy** *adj*

squeteague /skwi téeg/ (*plural same* or **-teagues**) *n* a large fish of the croaker family, especially an Atlantic weakfish. Native to: Atlantic Ocean. Genus: *Cynoscion.* [Early 19C. < Algonquian]

squib /skwib/ *n* **1.** SMALL FIREWORK a small firework, especially a banger **2.** DUD FIREWORK a faulty firework that burns without exploding **3.** PIECE OF SATIRE a short satirical piece of writing or speech **4.** SHORT JOURNALISTIC PIECE a short humorous piece that acts as a filler in a newspaper **5.** AEROSP DEVICE FOR FIRING ROCKET ENGINE a small device for firing a rocket engine **6.** SOMEBODY UNIMPORTANT somebody regarded as insignificant or mean-spirited (*archaic*) ■ *v* (**squibs, squibbing, squibbed**) **1.** *vi* SET OFF FIREWORK to set off a small firework, especially a banger **2.** *vt* SATIRIZE SOMEBODY to write a satirical piece about somebody **3.** *vt* AMERICAN FOOTBALL KICK BALL LOW in American football, to kick the ball in such a way that it wobbles as it bounces along the ground [Early 16C. Origin ?]

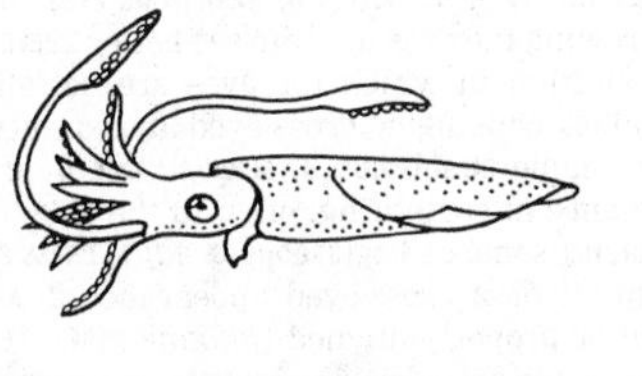

squid

squid /skwid/ (*plural same* or **squids**) *n* **1.** a sea cephalopod mollusc that has two long tentacles and eight shorter arms, a long tapered body, two triangular fins, and an internal shell. It is often cooked and eaten. Order: Teuthoidea. **2.** a dish of squid that has been prepared and cooked for eating [Late 16C. Origin ?]

squidgy /skwíjji/ (**-gier, -giest**) *adj* soft and damp or yielding, often unpleasantly so [Late 19C. Origin ?]

squiffy /skwíffi/ (**squiffier, squiffiest**) *adj* slightly drunk (*informal*) [Mid-19C. Origin ?]

squiggle /skwígg'l/ *n* **1.** WAVY LINE a wavy or curly line or movement **2.** ILLEGIBLE WORD an illegible handwritten word or words ■ *vi* (**-gles, -gling, -gled**) (*informal*) **1.** SQUIRM to twist, squirm, or wriggle **2.** DRAW SQUIGGLES to draw wavy or curly lines [Early 19C. Origin ?] —**squiggler** *n* —**squiggly** *adj*

squill /skwil/ *n* **1.** a plant grown from a bulb. Flowers: small, blue, white, pink, or purple, drooping. Native to: Europe, Asia, Africa. Genus: *Scilla* or *Pushkinia.* **2.** PLANTS same as **sea squill** **3.** PHARM dried slices of a sea squill's bulb. Use: formerly, expectorant, diuretic. [14C. Via Latin *squilla* 'shrimp, squill' < Greek *skilla*]

squilla /skwíllə/ *n* a burrowing sea crustacean that has eyes on stalks and large grasping appendages. Genus: *Squilla.* [Early 16C. < Latin, 'shrimp' (see SQUILL)]

squillion /skwíllyən/ *pron* a number of people or things so huge it cannot be counted or determined (*slang*) [Mid-20C. Fancifully after MILLION, BILLION] —**squillion** *det*

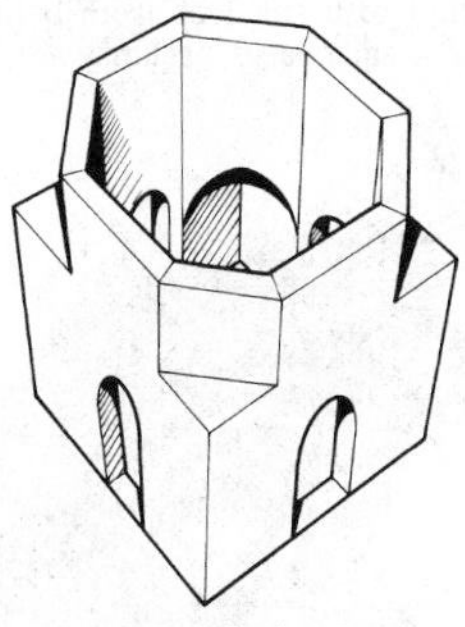

squinch

squinch[1] /skwinch/ *n* an arch, corbelling, or lintel built across the upper inside corner of a square tower to support the weight of a spire or other structure above [Mid-19C. Alteration of dialectal *scunch*, abbreviation of *scuncheon* < Old French *escoinson*, literally 'corner out' < *coin* 'corner' (see COIN)]

squinch[2] /skwinch/ (**squinches, squinching, squinched**) *v N Am* **1.** *vt* to screw up the eyes or face **2.** *vi* to

zh vision. In foreign words: kh German Bach; aN French vin; aaN French blanc; ö German schön, French feu; oN French bon; öN French un; ü as in French rue. Stress marks: ´ as in secret /séekrət/, academic /ákə démmik/

crouch so as to take up less space [Early 19C. Probably blend of SQUINT + PINCH]

squingy /skwínji/ (**-gier, -giest**) adj Carib **1.** small and dried-up in appearance **2.** worthless [Late 20C. < Caribbean alteration of SQUINCH²]

squint /skwint/ v (**squints, squinting, squinted**) **1.** vi PARTLY CLOSE EYES to half-close the eyes so as to see better ○ *a photo of them squinting into the camera in bright sunlight* **2.** vti HAVE EYES NOT LOOKING IN PARALLEL to have eyes that are not aligned in parallel, or move the eyes so that they are not aligned in parallel **3.** vi GLANCE ASIDE to glance or look at something sideways **4.** vi US LOOK ASKANCE to regard something with disapproval (*disapproving*) ○ *Congress clearly is squinting at the prospect of increased funding for the program.* ■ n **1.** ACTION OF NARROWING EYES the act of narrowing the eyes to try to see better **2.** EYE CONDITION a condition in which the eyes are not aligned in parallel, causing a cross-eyed appearance. Technical name **strabismus 3.** QUICK GLIMPSE a quick look or glance at something, often to the side (*informal*) **4.** ARCHIT same as **hagioscope** ■ adj **1.** CROSS-EYED with a squint or a cross-eyed appearance **2.** ASKEW not level or properly aligned (*informal*) [Mid-16C. Shortening of *asquint*, origin ?] —**squinter** n —**squinty** adj ◇ **have** or **take a squint at something** to have a look at something (*informal*)

squint-eyed adj **1.** WITH SQUINT with one or both eyes looking slightly inwards or outwards rather than in parallel **2.** LOOKING WITH EYES PARTLY CLOSED looking with the eyes partly closed in order to see better **3.** ASKANCE looking askance or sidelong

squirarchy n HIST another spelling of **squirearchy**

squire /skwīr/ n **1.** RURAL LANDOWNER a country landowner in England, often the main local landowner **2.** HIST ATTENDANT TO KNIGHT a young apprentice knight who acted as an attendant to a knight in the Middle Ages **3.** FORM OF ADDRESS used by a man as a term of address to another man (*informal*) **4.** MAN WHO ESCORTS WOMAN a man who is escorting a woman or going out with her regularly (*dated*) ■ vt (**squires, squiring, squired**) ESCORT SOMEBODY to escort or go out with a man or a woman (*dated; often passive*) [13C. Shortened < Old French *esquier, escuier* (see ESQUIRE)]

squirearchy /skwír aarki/, **squirarchy** n the main rural landowners collectively, especially the social, economic, or political class formed by such landed proprietors [Late 18C. < SQUIRE + HIERARCHY] —**squirearchal** /skwīr aⁱark'l/ adj —**squirearchic** adj

squireen /skwī reēn/ n Ireland a rural landowner owning a relatively small amount of land (*archaic*) [Early 19C. < SQUIRE + Irish *-ín* (suffix) 'little']

squirm /skwurm/ vi (**squirms, squirming, squirmed**) **1.** WRIGGLE FROM DISCOMFORT to wriggle the body, especially because of discomfort or in an attempt to break free from being held **2.** FEEL EMOTIONAL DISTRESS to feel very uncomfortable, especially because of shame, embarrassment, or revulsion ○ *a tough question that made the press office squirm* ■ n WRIGGLING MOVEMENT a wriggling movement, especially from discomfort or as an attempt to break free from being held [Late 17C. Origin ?] —**squirmer** n —**squirmy** adj

squirrel

squirrel /skwírrəl/ n **1.** SMALL BUSHY-TAILED RODENT a small rodent that has a long bushy tail, lives in trees, and eats nuts and seeds. Family: Sciuridae. **2.** RODENT LIKE SQUIRREL a rodent related to or resembling the true squirrel, e.g. the ground squirrel, flying squirrel, or chipmunk **3.** HOARDER somebody who hoards some-

thing (*informal*) ■ vt (**-rels, -relling, -relled**) HOARD SOMETHING to hoard or save things ○ *squirrelled away some money* [14C. < Anglo-Norman *esquirel*, literally 'little squirrel' < Latin *sciurus* < Greek *skiouros* < *skia* 'shadow' + *oura* 'tail']

squirrel cage n **1.** ROTATING FRAMEWORK FOR ANIMAL a cage containing a cylindrical wheel that goes round when a small pet rodent runs inside it **2.** DULL TASK a dull repetitive, seemingly purposeless task **3.** MECH ENG WINDING IN INDUCTION MOTORS a rotor of an induction motor consisting of copper bars mounted in slots around the periphery

squirrelfish /skwírrəl fish/ (*plural same* or **-fishes**) n a brightly coloured nocturnal fish. Native to: tropical reefs. Family: Holocentridae. [Origin ?]

squirrelly /skwírrəli/ adj **1.** resembling or characteristic of a squirrel **2.** US an offensive term meaning very irrational or odd

squirrel monkey n a small long-tailed monkey that has soft yellowish-grey, brown, or reddish fur, a white face, and a black muzzle. Native to: Central and South America. Genus: *Saimiri*.

squirt /skwurt/ v (**squirts, squirting, squirted**) **1.** vti FORCE OR BE FORCED OUT to force something out of a narrow opening in a strong quick stream, or be pushed out in this way ○ *The ketchup squirted all over the table.* ○ *managed to squirt the last of the toothpaste out of the tube* **2.** vt SQUIRT LIQUID OVER SOMETHING to hit or cover somebody or something with liquid that is forced out of a narrow opening in a strong quick stream ○ *She squirted me with her water bottle.* ■ n **1.** STREAM OF EJECTED LIQUID a small stream of liquid forced out of a narrow opening ○ *a squirt of body lotion* **2.** INSTRUMENT FOR SQUIRTING LIQUID an instrument that is used to dispense liquid in a thin quick stream, e.g. a syringe **3.** OFFENSIVE TERM an offensive term that deliberately insults somebody's young age or small size, especially in response to perceived impudence (*informal insult*) [15C. An imitation of the sound of something being squirted]

squirt gun n N Am same as **water pistol**

squirting cucumber /skwúrting-/ n a vine of the gourd family with oblong fruits that burst when ripe, ejecting seeds and juice. Native to: Mediterranean. Latin name: *Ecballium elaterium*.

squish /skwish/ v (**squishes, squishing, squished**) **1.** vt SQUEEZE SOMETHING to squeeze or crush something soft **2.** vi MAKE SOFT SPLASHING NOISE to make a sucking or soft splashing sound when subjected to pressure, as when being walked on or squeezed ■ n **1.** SOFT SPLASHING NOISE a sucking or soft splashing sound **2.** US OFFENSIVE TERM an offensive term for somebody perceived as weak or cowardly (*slang insult*) [Mid-17C. Probably alteration of SQUASH¹]

squishy /skwíshi/ adj (**-ier, -iest**) adj soft and giving under pressure

squit /skwit/ n **1.** an offensive term that deliberately insults somebody regarded as having low status or being of little importance (*informal insult*) **2.** nonsense (*dated informal*) ■ **squits** npl same as **diarrhoea** (*slang*) [Early 19C. Origin ?]

squiz /skwiz/ (*plural* **squizzes**) n ANZ a quick inquisitive look at something (*informal*) ○ *Can I have a squiz at your paper?* [Early 20C. Origin ?]

sr¹ symbol MEASURE steradian

sr² abbr Suriname (*used in Internet addresses*) See table at **domain name**

Sr¹ symbol CHEM ELEM strontium

Sr² abbr **1.** Senhor **2.** senior **3.** señor **4.** Signor **5.** Sir **6.** CHR Sister

Sra abbr **1.** Senhora **2.** Señora

SRA abbr RAIL Strategic Rail Authority

sraddhaa /shraád aa/, **shraddh** /shraad/ n an annual Hindu ritual, including the offering of food and water to dead ancestors [Late 18C. < Sanskrit *śraddha* < *śraddhā* 'faith, trust']

SRAM abbr COMPUT static random access memory

Sranantongo /sraánən tónggo/, **Sranan** /sraánən/ n a creole language based on English that is the lingua franca of Suriname [Mid-20C. < Sranantongo, 'Suriname tongue'] —**Sranantongo** adj

Sravana /sraávənə/ n in the Hindu calendar, the fifth month of the year, lasting 31 days and falling about the same time as July to August. See table at **calendar**

SRCN abbr State Registered Children's Nurse

S-R connection n in psychology, the relationship between a stimulus and a response

Srebrenica /srébbrə neētsə/ n town in Bosnia-Herzegovina, southeastern Europe, situated between Sarajevo and Tuzla. Declared a Muslim enclave during the Bosnian-Serbian-Croatian War from 1991 to 1995, it was invaded by Serb troops and subsequently placed under international protection. Population: 37,211 (1991).

Sri /sri, shri/, **Shri** /shri/ n **1.** S Asia a title of respect for a man, equivalent to 'Mr' **2.** a title of respect for a Hindu deity or holy man **3.** HINDUISM same as **Lakshmi** [Late 18C. Via Hindi < Sanskrit *śrī* 'lord', literally 'beauty, wealth, majesty']

SRI abbr FIN socially responsible investor

Sri Lanka

Sri Lanka /sri lángkə/ island country in South Asia, off the tip of southeastern India in the Indian Ocean. It became an independent member of the Commonwealth in 1948. Language: Sinhalese. Currency: Sri Lankan rupee. Capital: Colombo. Administrative capital: Sri Jayawardenepura. Population: 19,408,635 (2001). Area: 65,610 sq. km/25,332 sq. mi. Official name **Democratic Socialist Republic of Sri Lanka.** Former name **Ceylon** (until 1972) —**Sri Lankan** n, adj

Sriman /sreēmən/ n same as **Sri** (sense 1)

Srinagar /sri núggər, shrínnə gaar/, **Srīnager** capital city of the state of Jammu and Kashmir, northwestern India. Population: 971,357 (2001).

Sri Vijaya /shreēvi jay əl/, **Shrivijaya** n an Indonesian kingdom centred in Palembang, Sumatra, that dominated the maritime trade of Southeast Asia between the 7th and 14th centuries [Late 19C. < Hindi]

SRN abbr State Registered Nurse

sRNA abbr BIOCHEM soluble RNA

SRO abbr **1.** self-regulatory organization **2.** TRAVEL single room occupancy **3.** standing room only **4.** Statutory Rules and Orders

Srta abbr **1.** Senhorita **2.** Señorita

SS¹ abbr **1.** Saints **2.** SOC SCI Social Security **3.** SHIPPING, TRANSP steamship **4.** CHR Sunday school **5.** LAW sworn statement

SS² n a paramilitary organization founded by Hitler in 1925 as a personal bodyguard. During World War II, the SS was responsible for administering concentration camps. [Early 20C. < German *Schutzstaffel* 'defence squadron']

ss. abbr PUBL sections

SS. abbr CHR Saints

SSB abbr MEDIA, COMMUNICATION single sideband (transmission)

SSC abbr **1.** S Asia EDUC Secondary School Certificate **2.** Scotland LAW Solicitor to the Supreme Court

SSE¹ n the detection and removal of actual or suspected weapons of mass destruction, and precursor materials used in building them. Full form **sensitive site exploitation**

SSE² abbr COMPASS south-southeast

SSG *abbr US* MIL Staff Sergeant

SSgt *abbr* MIL Staff Sergeant

SSHA *abbr Scotland* Scottish Special Housing Association

SSM *abbr* ARMS surface-to-surface missile

SSN *abbr US* GOV Social Security Number

SSP *abbr* **1.** HR statutory sick pay **2.** GOV state second pension

ssp. *abbr* BIOL subspecies

SSR *abbr* HIST Soviet Socialist Republic

SSRI *abbr* MED selective serotonin reuptake inhibitor

SSSI /tripp'l ess ī/ *abbr* site of special scientific interest

SST *abbr* TRANSP supersonic transport

SSW *abbr* COMPASS south-southwest

st *abbr* **1.** ONLINE São Tomé and Príncipe (*used in Internet addresses*) See table at **domain name 2.** MEASURE short ton

St[1] *abbr* **1.** Saint **2.** Strait **3.** Street (*used in addresses*)

St[2] for saints, see under first name

ST *abbr* TIME standard time

st. *abbr* **1.** LITERAT stanza **2.** start **3.** state **4.** LAW statute **5.** PRINTING stet **6.** HANDICRAFT stitch

-st *suffix* same as **-est**[1]

Sta *abbr* GEOG Santa[1]

stab /stab/ *v* (**stabs, stabbing, stabbed**) **1.** *vt* **THRUST KNIFE INTO SOMEBODY OR SOMETHING** to thrust a knife or other sharp pointed instrument into somebody or something **2.** *vti* **JAB FINGER OR OBJECT** to thrust a finger or an object sharply at something ○ *He stabbed his potato angrily with his fork.* **3.** *vi* **HURT LIKE KNIFE WOUND** to cause a sudden sharp hurting sensation, like that of a knife wound ○ *Pain stabbed at her temples.* ■ *n* **1. ACT OF STABBING SOMEBODY** the action of thrusting a knife or other sharp pointed instrument into somebody (*often used before a noun*) ○ *a stab wound* **2. INJURY FROM STABBING** an injury or wound sustained from a thrust of a knife or other sharp pointed instrument ○ *The stab was deep enough to require stitches.* **3. SUDDEN PAINFUL FEELING** a sudden brief sensation, especially of pain ○ *felt a sudden stab of loss* **4. ATTEMPT** an attempt at something (*informal*) ○ *Each of us made a stab at solving the problem.* **5. SEVERE CRITICISM** a severe criticism of somebody [15C. Origin ?] —**stabber** *n* ◇ **a stab in the back** a betrayal, or an act of treachery (*informal*) ◇ **stab somebody in the back** to betray or harm somebody who trusts you

~~**stabalize**~~ incorrect spelling of **stabilize**

Stabat Mater /staá bat maátər/ *n* a Latin hymn that was composed in the 13th century and concerns the grief of the Virgin Mary at the crucifixion of Jesus Christ [Mid-19C. < Latin *stabat mater dolorosa* 'the mother stood, full of grief', first words of the hymn]

stabbing /stábbing/ *n* an incident in which somebody is deliberately stabbed with a knife or sharp object ■ *adj* brief, sharp, and sudden, as if from the thrust of a knife ○ *a stabbing pain in the side*

stabile /stáy bīl/ *n* **SCULPTURE ATTACHED TO SOMETHING** an abstract sculpture made of wire, metal, or other materials and attached to fixed supports ■ *adj* **1. STABLE** in a fixed position **2.** CHEM **NOT CHANGING CHEMICALLY** not readily undergoing chemical change [Late 18C. < Latin *stabilis* 'stable']

stabilise, etc. another spelling of **stabilize, etc.**

stability /stə bílləti/ *n* **1. STABLE QUALITY** the condition of being stable ○ *policies aimed at creating economic stability* **2. MENTAL FIRMNESS** mental or psychological firmness **3.** MECH ENG **ABILITY TO ADJUST TO LOAD CHANGES** a property of a transmission system that allows changes in load to be met without any reduction in performance **4.** METEOROL **AIR MASS WITHOUT UPWARD MOVEMENT** a condition of no upward movement in an air mass **5.** METEOROL **RESISTANCE TO AIR CURRENTS** a measure of the tendency of an air mass to be influenced by convection currents **6.** ECOL **ABILITY TO MAINTAIN BALANCE** the ability of an ecological community to resist disturbance caused by environmental changes, or the ability to return to its original state after disturbance **7.** AEROSP, NAUT **RESISTANCE TO CHANGED POSITION** the capability of an aircraft, rocket, or ship to maintain a position and to return to it if displaced **8.** CHEM **RESISTANCE TO CHEMICAL CHANGE** a resistance to chemical change **9.** PHYS **MEASURE OF MAINTAINING EQUILIBRIUM** a measure of the difficulty of displacing an object or system from equilibrium

stabilization /stáybi lī záysh'n/, **stabilisation** *n* the action of becoming stable or of making something stable

stabilization fund *n* a reserve of money that a country uses to maintain its official exchange rate by buying and selling foreign exchange

stabilize /stáybi līz/ (**-lizes, -lizing, -lized**), **stabilise** (**-lises, -lising, -lised**) *v* **1.** *vti* to become stable, or make something stable ○ *The patient's condition has stabilized.* **2.** *vt* to keep something at the same level

stabilizer /stáybi līzər/, **stabiliser** *n* **1. STABILIZING PERSON OR THING** something that or somebody who acts to bring stability **2.** AVIAT **AEROFOIL THAT STABILIZES AIRCRAFT** an aerofoil or combination of aerofoils, e.g. in the tail assembly of an aeroplane, that keeps an aircraft or missile aligned with the direction of flight. A vertical stabilizer controls yawing, or side-to-side motion, while a horizontal stabilizer controls pitching, or up-and-down motion. **3.** NAUT **FINS TO CONTROL SHIP'S ROLLING** one or more pairs of submerged fins, often gyroscopically controlled, used to minimize the rolling of a ship in rough waters **4.** CHEM **ADDITIVE THAT MAINTAINS CHEMICAL PROPERTIES** a chemical compound added to another substance to make it resistant to change **5.** ELEC **DEVICE TO PRODUCE CONSTANT VOLTAGE** a device used to maintain a constant voltage from a source of direct current **6.** INDUST **SOMETHING ADDED TO DISPERSE PAINT** a substance added to a fast-drying paint to improve the dispersion of pigment ■ **stabilizers** *npl UK* **EXTRA WHEELS TO BALANCE BICYCLE** a pair of small wheels fitted to the back wheel of a bicycle to help balance it while somebody is learning to ride. ANZ, N Am term **training wheels**

stable[1] /stáyb'l/ *adj* **1. NOT CHANGING** steady and not liable to change ○ *Prices have remained stable.* **2. NOT LIKELY TO MOVE** steady or firm and not liable to move **3. NOT EXCITABLE** having a calm and steady temperament, rather than being excitable or given to apparently irrational behaviour **4.** CHEM, PHYS **NOT READILY UNDERGOING CHANGE** not subject to changes in chemical or physical properties **5.** PHYS **NOT NATURALLY RADIOACTIVE** incapable of becoming a different isotope or element by radioactive decay [13C. Via Anglo-Norman and Old French < Latin *stabilis*] —**stably** *adv*

stable[2] /stáyb'l/ *n* **1. BUILDING FOR HORSES** a building in which horses, and sometimes other large types of livestock, are kept **2. HORSES OWNED BY SOMEBODY** the group of horses, especially racehorses, owned by one person or kept and trained at one establishment **3. PEOPLE WORKING IN STABLE** the people who work in a stable, especially a training establishment for racehorses **4. GROUP UNDER MANAGEMENT** a group of people managed by the same person or organization ○ *a stable of bestselling authors* ■ *vti* (**-bles, -bling, -bled**) **PUT OR LIVE IN STABLE** to keep or put a horse or other large animal in a particular building, or be kept in a particular building ○ *We stabled our horses in the barn.* [13C. Via Old French *estable* < Latin *stabulum*]

stable boy *n* a youth or man who looks after horses in a racing stable

stable door *n* a door split into upper and lower sections that can be closed separately. In stables the opened top section allows a confined horse to see out.

stable fly *n* a biting bloodsucking fly resembling a housefly that attacks humans and domestic animals. Latin name: *Stomoxys calcitrans.*

stable girl *n* a girl or woman who looks after horses in a racing stable

stablemate /stáyb'l mayt/ *n* **1.** a horse that belongs to the same owner or is kept and trained at the same racing stable as another **2.** an associate of somebody or something, e.g. an author who shares the same publisher as another

stabling /stáybling/ *n* **1.** a stable or stables **2.** accommodation for horses, usually but not always in a stable

~~**stablize**~~ incorrect spelling of **stabilize**

stab pass *n Aus* in rugby and Australian Rules football, a pass made by kicking the ball with the toe of the boot so that it travels low and rapidly

stab stitch *n* a very small straight stitch designed to hold pieces of fabric together without showing as more than a dot on the surface

stabvest /stáb vest/ *n* a padded waistcoat of tough material, designed to protect a police officer against attacks with knives or other sharp implements

stacc. *abbr* MUSIC staccato

staccato /stə kaátō/ *adv* **IN QUICK SEPARATE NOTES** as rapid short detached notes (*used as a musical direction*) ■ *adj* **1. PLAYED SEPARATELY** played as rapid short detached notes **2. QUICK AND CLIPPED** rapid, brief, and clipped in sound ○ *a staccato voice* ■ *n* (*plural* **-tos**) **STACCATO PASSAGE** a staccato passage in music [Early 18C. < Italian, 'detached']

stachys /stáykiss/ *n* a plant with spiked whorls of purple, reddish, or white flowers, e.g. lamb's ears or betony. Genus: *Stachys.* [Mid-16C. Via modern Latin < Greek *stakhus* 'ear of corn']

stack /stak/ *n* **1. HEAPED PILE OF THINGS** a pile of things more or less neatly arranged one on top of another ○ *a stack of chairs* **2. LARGE NUMBER** a large number or amount (*informal*) ○ *She has stacks of money.* **3. LARGE PILE OF SOMETHING STORED OUTDOORS** a large pile of hay, straw, or grain, often conical in shape, stored outdoors **4.** ARCHIT **CHIMNEY OR CHIMNEYS** a tall chimney or group of chimneys arranged together **5.** AVIAT **AIRCRAFT WAITING TO LAND** a queue of aircraft waiting a turn to land at an airport, circling at different heights **6.** GEOG **ROCKY PILLAR RISING FROM COASTAL WATERS** a steep-sided pillar of rock that has been isolated from nearby cliffs at the shoreline by the erosion of the waves **7.** COMPUT **LIST IN COMPUTER MEMORY** an area in a computer memory where data can be stored temporarily in a list in which the last item entered is the first one removed. A control program uses a stack to save register information and return addresses temporarily so that it can restore the environment on returning from another procedure to which it has jumped. **8.** ARMS **ARRANGEMENT OF FIREARMS** a group of firearms formed in a pyramid, especially three rifles with their muzzles leaning against each other **9.** CONSTR **VERTICAL PIPE** a vertical duct or waste pipe **10.** MEASURE **MEASURE FOR COAL OR WOOD** a nonmetric measure of coal or firewood equal to 108 cu. ft. ■ **stacks** *npl* **BOOK STORAGE IN LIBRARY** an area of a library, usually not open to the public, where books are stored on shelves ■ *v* (**stacks, stacking, stacked**) **1.** *vti* **PUT OR BE IN ORGANIZED PILE** to put things one on top of another to form a pile, or be arranged in this way **2.** *vt* **PUT THINGS ON SHELF** to arrange objects on a shelf **3.** *vt* **HEAP SOMETHING WITH PILES OF OBJECTS** to load or heap something with large piles of articles or objects ○ *The bins were stacked with bargains.* **4.** *vt* **MANIPULATE SITUATION UNETHICALLY** to arrange something underhandedly to ensure a desired outcome **5.** *vti* AVIAT **FLY, OR KEEP AIRCRAFT, IN STACK** to keep aircraft waiting to land at an airport circling at different heights, or be kept in this position [13C. < Old Norse *stakkr* < Germanic, 'stick, pole'] —**stackable** *adj* —**stacker** *n* ◇ **be stacked against somebody** to amount to an unfair disadvantage for somebody ◇ **blow your stack** to have a sudden angry outburst (*slang*) ◇ **stack the deck** *or* **cards** (*slang*) **1.** to arrange playing cards in a deck for the purposes of cheating **2.** to arrange something dishonestly or unethically so as to gain an unfair advantage

stack up *vi* **1. SEEM REASONABLE** to make sense (*usually with negatives*) **2. ADD UP** to add up to a total **3.** *N Am* **MEASURE UP** to be measurable against or comparable to something

stacked /stakt/ *adj* **1. DISHONESTLY ARRANGED** unfairly or dishonestly manipulated or arranged **2.** *N Am* **OFFENSIVE TERM** an offensive term meaning having large breasts (*slang*) **3.** AVIAT **DISPOSED AT DIFFERENT HEIGHTS** circling at different heights prior to landing

stacked heel *n* a wide high heel made of different coloured layers of wood or material simulating wood

stacks on the mill *n Aus* **1.** a children's game in which one child lies on the ground and then others, one by one, pile up on top (*takes a singular verb*) **2.** (*plural same*) same as **ruck**[1] *n* (sense 4)

stacte /stákti/ *n* in the Bible, a sweet spice mentioned as being used by the ancient Jews in making incense [14C. Via Latin < Greek *staktē* < *staktos*, past participle of *stazein* 'drip, ooze']

staddle /stádd'l/ *n* a supporting base to keep stored hay off the ground (*regional or archaic*) [Old English *stapol* < Indo-European, 'to stand']

stadholder /stád hōldər/, **stadtholder** *n* **1.** the chief magistrate of the Dutch republic between the 16th and 18th centuries **2.** formerly, a governor or viceroy of a province in the Netherlands [Mid-16C. Partial translation of Dutch *stadhouder* 'place-holder'] —**stadholderate** *n* —**stadholdership** *n*

stadia[1] /stáydi ə/ plural of **stadium**

stadia[2] /stáydi ə/ *n* a method of measuring distances or differences in elevation using a telescopic instrument calibrated to correspond to distances from the surveyor [Mid-19C. Directly or via Italian < Latin, plural of *stadium* (see STADIUM)]

stadium /stáydi əm/ (*plural* -**diums** or -**dia** /-di ə/) *n* **1.** ARENA WITH TIERED SEATS a place where people watch sports or other activities, usually a large enclosed flat area surrounded by tiers of seats for spectators **2.** ANCIENT HIST ANCIENT GREEK RACECOURSE in ancient Greece, a racecourse for foot races that had tiers of seats at each side and one end **3.** MEASURE, ANCIENT HIST ANCIENT GREEK MEASUREMENT UNIT in ancient Greece, a unit of linear measure equal to about 185 m/607 ft [14C. Via Latin < Greek *stadion* 'racetrack, unit of measure']

stadtholder *n* HIST, LAW another spelling of **stadholder**

Madame de Staël: portrait (1808–9)
by Elisabeth Vigee-Lebrun

AKG London

Staël /staal/, **Madame de** (1766–1817) French writer. She is credited with disseminating the theories of romanticism in works such as *Germany* (1810). Full name **Staël-Holstein, Baronne Anne Louise Germaine de**. Born **Necker, Anne Louise Germaine**

'Love is above the laws, above the opinion of men; it is the truth, the flame, the pure element, the primary idea of the moral world.'
[Madame de Staël, *Zulma and Other Tales*; 1813]

staff[1] /staaf/ *n* **1.** WORKERS people who are employed by a company or an individual employer **2.** BODY WITHIN LARGER GROUP a particular group of employees within a company, institution, or organization ○ *the teaching staff* **3.** EDUC TEACHERS the teachers in a school or other educational institution, as opposed to the students. N Am term **faculty 4.** PEOPLE WHO WORK FOR LEADER a group of people who serve a leader or an executive of a company, organization, or institution **5.** (*plural* **staffs** or **staves** /stayvz/) LARGE HEAVY STICK a stick, rod, or pole, e.g. a stick used as a support while walking, or a rod used as a symbol of authority in ceremonies **6.** (*plural* **staffs** or **staves**) same as **flagpole 7.** *Malaysia, Singapore* HR, EDUC EMPLOYEE a member of staff working for a company, organization, or school **8.** MIL GROUP OF AIDES TO COMMANDER a group of officers in the armed services who assist a commanding officer or work at headquarters as advisers or planners **9.** (*plural* **staffs** or **staves**) MUSIC SET OF LINES FOR WRITING MUSIC a set of five horizontal lines, together with the four spaces between them, on which the notes of music are written **10.** (*plural* **staffs** or **staves**) MEASURE GRADUATED ROD USED FOR MEASURING a graduated rod used for testing or measuring something, e.g. in surveying ■ *adj* **1.** EMPLOYED WITH SALARY employed full-time, not on a freelance basis **2.** HR

CONCERNED WITH STAFF for or relating to the staff of a company, institution, or organization ■ *vt* (**staffs, staffing, staffed**) PROVIDE ORGANIZATION WITH WORKERS to provide a place or organization with employees (*often passive*) [Old English *stæf* 'stick, rod' < Indo-European, 'to support']

staff[2] /staaf/ *n* a building material of plaster and fibrous material used as a temporary, especially decorative, finish on the outside of a structure [Late 19C. Origin ?]

Staffa /stáffə/ uninhabited island in the Inner Hebrides, western Scotland. Its many caverns include Fingal's Cave. Area: 0.5 sq. km/0.2 sq. mi.

staff college *n* a school in which military officers receive leadership training in preparation for higher positions, e.g. as staff officers or commanders

staffer /stáafər/ *n* a member of the staff of an organization (*informal*) ○ *White House staffers*

staffing /stáafing/ *n* **1.** the number of people working in a place or organization **2.** the act of providing people to do jobs

staffman /stáaf man/ (*plural* -**men** /-men/) *n* somebody who holds a levelling staff during surveying. N Am term **rodman**

staff nurse *n* a fully qualified hospital nurse of a rank below team leader

staff of Aesculapius /-eéskyōō láypi əss/ *n* a symbol for the medical profession consisting of a staff with a single snake entwined round it

staff officer *n* a military officer who assists a commanding officer or works as a planner or adviser at a headquarters

staff of life *n* bread, or sometimes another food, considered as an essential part of the human diet (*literary*)

Stafford /stáffərd/ county town of Staffordshire, central England. Population: 120,670 (2001).

Stafford, Sir Edward (1819–1901) Scottish-born premier of New Zealand. A moderate liberal, he was premier three times (1856–61, 1865–69, 1872) before the advent of organized political parties in New Zealand. Full name **Stafford, Sir Edward William**

Staffordshire /stáffərdshər/ county in the Midlands, central England. It includes the Potteries. Stafford is the county town. Population: 806,744 (2001). Area: 2,716 sq. km/1,049 sq. mi.

Staffordshire bull terrier, **Staffordshire terrier** *n* a bull terrier belonging to a breed with a short broad head and ears that hang down

staffroom /stáaf room, -rōōm/ *n* a room used only by the teachers in a school, e.g. for relaxation between classes

Staffs. /stafs/ *abbr* Staffordshire

staff sergeant *n* a noncommissioned officer in the US Army or Marine Corps and in the British Army of a rank above sergeant, and in the US Air Force of a rank above senior airman

stag /stag/ *n* **1.** MATURE MALE DEER an adult male deer, especially a male red deer **2.** CASTRATED ADULT ANIMAL a male animal, e.g. a pig, castrated after it reaches maturity **3.** *US* SOMEBODY UNACCOMPANIED AT SOCIAL EVENT somebody who goes to a social function without a partner (*informal*) **4.** FIN SPECULATOR IN NEW ISSUES OF SHARES a speculator who applies for a new issue of a security in the hope of making a quick profit when it begins to be traded ■ *adj* RESTRICTED TO MEN for men only, and often involving activities that would not be felt appropriate when women are present (*informal*) ■ *adv* N Am ALONE without a companion on a social occasion (*informal*) ■ *v* (**stags, stagging, stagged**) **1.** *vt* FIN BUY SHARES FOR QUICK PROFIT to buy a new issue of a security in the hope of making a quick profit when it begins to be traded **2.** *vi US* ATTEND EVENT WITHOUT DATE to attend a social event without a companion (*informal*) [Assumed Old English *stagga* < Indo-European, 'pointed']

stag beetle *n* a large beetle the male of which has long extended jaws (**mandibles**) shaped like a stag's antlers. Family: Lucanidae.

stage /stayj/ *n* **1.** PERIOD OR STEP DURING PROCESS a step, level, or period in the development or progress of

something ○ *The project is still in its early stages.* **2.** PLATFORM a raised platform where speeches are made and ceremonies are carried out, e.g. in a hall or auditorium **3.** AREA IN THEATRE the area in a theatre where a performance takes place, especially a platform on which actors perform a play **4.** DRAMATIC PROFESSION the profession of acting, drama, or the theatre **5.** SETTING IN WHICH SOMETHING HAPPENS the scene of an event or series of events ○ *The summit marks her first appearance on the world stage.* **6.** PART OF BUS ROUTE any division of a bus route that is used to calculate fares **7.** SIGNIFICANT PHASE an important phase of cultural, economic, or social development **8.** PART OF JOURNEY a distinct section of a journey, especially one after which a stop is made **9.** AEROSP DETACHABLE ROCKET UNIT a separable unit of a rocket or spacecraft that contains fuel and can be jettisoned after the fuel is exhausted **10.** *N Am* CONSTR PLATFORM FOR WORKERS a raised platform, especially a scaffolding for workers during the construction of a building **11.** EDUC SUBJECT STUDIED FOR YEAR a subject studied for one year at a university or college **12.** FOOD INDUST PLATFORM FOR DRYING FOOD a platform used to dry fish or meat **13.** RECORDING same as **sound stage 14.** BIOL PERIOD OF DEVELOPMENT OF ORGANISM a distinct period of development in the life of an organism when its form is different from earlier or later periods **15.** MEASURE ELEVATION OF RIVER SURFACE a measure of how much the surface of a river or stream rises above a given point **16.** SCI PLATFORM FOR MOUNTING MICROSCOPIC SPECIMEN the small platform of an optical microscope on which a specimen is placed for examination **17.** GEOL PERIOD OF ROCK STRATA a relatively short geological distinct period, a subdivision of a series, during which rock strata are deposited **18.** ELEC UNIT OF ELECTRICAL COMPONENTS a group of components that form part of an electronic or electrical system **19.** TRANSP same as **stagecoach** ■ *vt* (**stages, staging, staged**) **1.** ORGANIZE PERFORMANCE FOR PUBLIC to put on a play, concert, exhibition, or similar event for an audience **2.** ORGANIZE EVENT to organize or carry out something such as an event that will attract attention or publicity **3.** SET PLAY IN PLACE OR TIME to set a play in a particular place or time ○ *staged the drama in the Regency period* **4.** MED CLASSIFY PHASES OF DISEASE to classify the progress of a disease [13C. < Old French *estage* < Latin *stat-*, past participle of *stare* 'stand'] —**stageability** /stáyjə bílləti/ *n* —**stageable** *adj* —**stageably** *adv* ◇ **by** or **in easy stages** in an unhurried undemanding way ◇ **hold the stage** to continue to be the centre of attention ◇ **on stage** performing in something, especially as an actor ◇ **set the stage (for something)** to make the preparations or produce the conditions necessary for something to happen or begin ◇ **take centre stage** to draw people's or public attention

stage brace *n* a brace used to support upright pieces of scenery in a play

stage business *n* THEATRE same as **business** *n* (sense 8)

stagecoach

stagecoach /stáyj kōch/ *n* a large four-wheeled horse-drawn coach formerly used to carry passengers and mail over a regular route

CULTURAL NOTE *Stagecoach*, a film (1939) by US director John Ford. Considered the first modern Western, it portrays an encounter between a diverse group of stagecoach passengers and an intimidating outlaw, the Ringo Kid (played by John Wayne). Its convincing and intriguing characters, magnificent desert setting, gripping narrative, and exciting climax made it a landmark in US cinema.

stagecraft /stáyj kraaft/ *n* the technique or art of writing, adapting, or putting plays on stage

stage direction *n* an instruction for an actor in the script of a play

stage door *n* a door in the back or side of a theatre that leads directly backstage and is usually used by performers

stage effect *n* a special visual or auditory effect created on a theatrical stage by lighting, scenery, or sound

stage fright *n* fear or nervousness felt by somebody before going in front of an audience to speak or perform

stagehand /stáyj hand/ *n* a manual worker in a theatre, e.g. somebody who sets up and removes stage sets

stage left *n* the part of a stage that is to a performer's left when facing the audience

stage-manage *v* **1.** *vt* to control an organized event, especially in a way that is not public, so that it happens exactly as planned **2.** *vti* to carry out the work of a stage manager, especially on a particular production —**stage-management** *n*

stage manager *n* an assistant of the director of a play who supervises backstage activities

stage name *n* the name a performer or entertainer uses for professional purposes, as opposed to his or her real name

stager /stáyjər/ *n* THEATRE same as **actor** (sense 1) (*archaic*) [Late 16C. Origin ?]

stage right *n* the part of a stage that is to a performer's right when facing the audience

stage-struck *adj* loving the theatre and intensely wanting to be part of it, especially as a performer

stage wait *n* an unintentional pause in the action of a play, especially one caused by an actor's missing a cue

stage whisper *n* **1.** something said on stage that for the purposes of the play is supposed to be a whisper but is intended to be heard by the audience **2.** a loud whisper intended to be overheard

stagey *adj* another spelling of **stagy**

stagflation /stag fláysh'n/ *n* a period of rising prices and unemployment but little growth in consumer demand and business activity [Mid-20C. Blend of STAGNATION + INFLATION] —**stagflationary** *adj*

stagger /stággər/ *v* (**-gers, -gering, -gered**) **1.** *vi* **MOVE UNSTEADILY, NEARLY FALLING** to move or walk unsteadily, almost but not quite falling over **2.** *vt* **MAKE PERSON OR ANIMAL STUMBLE** to make a person or animal stumble or nearly fall, especially by a blow **3.** *vt* **ASTONISH SOMEBODY** to completely astonish or amaze somebody (*often passive*) **4.** *vi* **CONTINUE IMPERFECTLY** to keep going or operating in an incompetent or less than satisfactory way **5.** *vt* **ARRANGE ACTIVITIES FOR SEPARATE TIMES** to arrange activities so that they do not overlap **6.** *vt* **PUT THINGS INTO ALTERNATING OR ZIGZAG PATTERN** to arrange things so that they do not form a straight line, especially in an alternating or zigzag pattern (*often passive*) **7.** *vi* **HESITATE** to hesitate or falter **8.** *vt* AVIAT **ADJUST EDGE OF BIPLANE'S WING** to make the leading edge of one wing of a biplane project beyond the leading edge of the other wing ■ *n* **1. STUMBLE NEARLY RESULTING IN FALL** an unsteady movement in which a person or animal almost falls **2.** AVIAT **ARRANGEMENT OF BIPLANE WINGS** a design in which the leading edge of one wing of a biplane is ahead of that of the other wing [Mid-16C. Alteration of obsolete *stacker* < Old Norse *stakkra* < *staka* 'push' < Germanic, 'pole'] —**staggerer** *n*

staggerbush /stággər bŏŏsh/ (*plural* **-bushes** or *same*) *n* a deciduous bush of the heath family with poisonous leaves. Flowers: white or pink, in clusters. Native to: eastern United States. Latin name: *Lyonia mariana*.

staggered /stággərd/ *adj* **1.** shocked or astounded at something **2.** not arranged consecutively or in a straight line

staggered hours *npl* an arrangement in a business in which employees arrive and leave at different times but work hours that overlap for part of the time

staggering /stággəring/ *adj* with the effect of shocking or astounding people —**staggeringly** *adv*

staggers /stággərz/ *n* a form of vertigo associated with decompression sickness, with symptoms including dizziness, weakness, and confusion (*takes a singular or plural verb*)

staghorn /stág hawrn/ *n* **stag's horn 1.** a stag's antler, or a piece of this used as material for carved objects **2.** PLANTS same as **staghorn fern 3.** PLANTS same as **staghorn moss** ■ *adj* made from a piece of a stag's antlers

staghorn coral *n* a form of stony coral branched like a deer's antlers. Genus: *Acropora*.

staghorn fern *n* a fern with broad leaves like antlers and smaller clinging leaves, often cultivated as a houseplant. Genus: *Platycerium*.

staghorn moss *n* a plant with creeping stems like antlers and tiny overlapping leaves. Latin name: *Lycopodium clavatum*.

staghound /stág hownd/ *n* a hound like a large foxhound, used, especially formerly, in hunting stags

staging /stáyjing/ *n* **1. TECHNIQUE OF PRESENTING STAGE PLAY** the activity, process, or style of presenting a play on a stage **2.** CONSTR **SCAFFOLDING FOR BUILDING** a temporary structure of supports and platforms used while people are building or working on something **3.** AEROSP **TECHNIQUE FOR INCREASING SPACECRAFT'S VELOCITY** a technique to increase the velocity achieved by a spacecraft's launch vehicle by using multiple propulsive stages, each being jettisoned after use

staging area *n* **1.** a place where soldiers and military equipment are gathered for final organization, outfitting, and training before deployment on an operation **2.** a place where people stop or assemble before undertaking an activity or task

staging post *n* a place where people on a long journey stop off to take a break from travel, especially on an air route

stagnant /stágnənt/ *adj* **1. STILL AND UNMOVING** not flowing or moving **2. FOUL OR STALE** stale or impure from lack of motion **3. NOT DEVELOPING** not developing or making progress **4. INACTIVE** not active or lively ○ *a stagnant week on the share market* [Mid-17C. < Latin *stagnant-*, present participle of *stagnare* (see STAGNATE)] —**stagnancy** *n* —**stagnantly** *adv*

stagnate /stag náyt/ (**-nates, -nating, -nated**) *vi* **1. NOT DEVELOP OR MAKE PROGRESS** to fail to develop, progress, or make necessary changes **2. STOP FLOWING** to stop flowing or moving **3. BECOME FOUL** to become stale or impure through not flowing or moving **4. BECOME INACTIVE** to become listless and inactive [Mid-17C. < Latin *stagnat-*, past participle of *stagnare* < *stagnum* 'pool, swamp'] —**stagnation** *n* —**stagnatory** *adj*

stag night, stag party *n* a social occasion that only men attend, especially an evening of drinking with male friends spent by a man who is about to be married (*informal*) Aus term **buck's party.** N Am term **bachelor party**

stag's horn *n* PLANTS, ZOOL same as **staghorn**

stagy /stáyji/ (**-ier, -iest**), **stagey** *adj* exaggerated or artificial in manner, as if in a play —**stagily** *adv* —**staginess** *n*

staid /stayd/ *adj* sedate and settled in habits or temperament, sometimes to the point of dullness [Mid-16C. Obsolete past participle of STAY[1], literally 'fixed, settled'] —**staidly** *adv* —**staidness** *n*

stain /stayn/ *n* **1. DISCOLOURED PATCH** a discoloured mark made by something such as blood, wine, or ink **2. COLOUR FINISH** a liquid that is applied to something, especially wood, to darken it or change its colour without hiding its texture or grain **3.** BIOL **DYE USED TO COLOUR MICROSCOPIC SPECIMENS** a dye used to colour tissues and cells to make features more visible under a microscope **4.** INDUST **DYE FOR TEXTILES OR LEATHER** a dye used in liquid form to colour textiles or leather **5. CHARACTER BLEMISH** something that detracts from a somebody's good reputation ■ *v* (**stains, staining, stained**) **1.** *vti* **LEAVE MARK ON SOMETHING** to make a discoloured mark on something, or be liable to cause or suffer discoloured marks (*often passive*) **2.** *vt* **DYE SOMETHING** to dye something a different or deeper colour using liquid or pigment that penetrates the surface **3.** *vt* **TARNISH SOMETHING** to disgrace or detract from something ○ *reprehensible acts that stained his reputation* **4.** *vt* MICROBIOL **COLOUR ORGANIC SPECIMENS** to colour organic materials with dyes to make features more visible under a microscope [15C. Partly < Old Norse *steina* 'paint'; partly < Old French *desteindre* 'discolour' < Latin *tingere* 'to dye'] —**stainable** *adj* —**stainer** *n*

stained glass /stáynd-/ *n* glass that has been coloured so that it can be used to make a mosaic picture, especially in a window. Stained glass may be made by enamelling, burning pigments into the surface, or by fusing metallic oxides with it. (*hyphenated before a noun*)

Staines /staynz/ town in Surrey, southern England. Population: 51,167 (1991).

stainless /stáynləss/ *adj* **1. RESISTANT TO RUST** resisting rust or corrosion **2. WITHOUT STAINS** not discoloured or marked by stains **3. ENTIRELY REPUTABLE** not tarnished by any blemishes of character or reputation ■ *n* METALL same as **stainless steel** —**stainlessly** *adv*

stainless steel *n* a corrosion-resistant steel containing at least 12 per cent chromium that has many domestic and industrial uses, e.g. making cutlery, ball bearings, and turbine blades (*hyphenated before a noun*)

stair /stair/ *n* **1. SINGLE STEP** a step in a series of steps leading from one floor or level to another **2. SERIES OF STEPS** a flight of steps leading from one floor or level to another ■ **stairs** *npl* **SET OF STEPS** a set or several sets of steps leading from one floor or level to another [Old English *stæger* < Indo-European, 'to step'] ◇ **above stairs** in the upper part of a large house, formerly occupied by the employers but not the servants (*archaic*) ◇ **below stairs** in the lower part of a house, formerly occupied by the servants (*archaic*)

SPELLCHECK stair or **stare**? Do not confuse the spelling of ***stair*** and ***stare***, which sound similar. ***Stair*** is a noun denoting a step or series of steps, as in *climb up the stairs to the top floor,* and is also found in related compound words such as *staircase* and *downstairs.* ***Stare*** is a verb or noun referring to a fixed look or facial expression with the eyes wide open (as in *staring at her in astonishment, a vacant stare*) and is also used figuratively: *The solution to the problem was staring us in the face.*

staircase /stáir kayss/ *n* a set of stairs in a building, usually with banisters or handrails

stairhead /stáir hed/ *n* the landing at the top of a flight of stairs

stair rod *n* a rod laid to hold a carpet in place against the bottom of a riser in a staircase

stairway /stáir way/ *n* a passageway from one floor or level of a building to another, consisting of stairs or a staircase

stairwell /stáir wel/ *n* the vertical space in a building where stairs are located

stake[1] /stayk/ *n* **1. THIN POINTED POST IN GROUND** a thin wooden or metal post that is driven into the ground to mark or support something **2. POST TO TIE SOMEBODY TO** a wooden post to which somebody was tied and burnt in an old form of execution **3. FORM OF EXECUTION** the method of execution in which somebody was tied to a post and burnt **4. POST THAT RETAINS LOAD** an independent upright post inserted into sockets of a flat wagon or lorry to keep long loads such as logs in place **5. MORMON CHURCH DISTRICT** an administrative district in the Church of Jesus Christ of Latter-Day Saints that consists of wards, each governed by a president and two counsellors ■ *v* (**stakes, staking, staked**) **1.** *vt* **SUPPORT OR STRENGTHEN SOMETHING WITH STAKE** to support or strengthen something using a stake **2.** *vt* **TETHER SOMETHING TO STAKE** to tie or tether something to a stake **3.** *vi* **MARK OR FENCE AREA WITH STAKES** to mark out, confine, or fence off an area using stakes driven into the ground round the boundary **4.** *vt* **ASSERT SOMETHING** to assert something, usually rights, over something such as an area of land [Old English *staca* < Germanic, 'stick, pole'] ◇ **(pull) up stakes** *N Am* to leave and move to another place

stake out *vt* **1. WATCH PLACE CONTINUOUSLY** to watch a place continuously from a hidden vantage point (*informal*) **2. ESTABLISH BOUNDARIES** to establish the boundaries of an area intended to be used or controlled **3. ESTABLISH**

AND CLARIFY POSITION to establish and clarify a personal position in a situation

stake[2] /stayk/ n **1.** MONEY RISKED IN GAMBLING an amount of money risked in a bet or game **2.** SHARE OR INTEREST IN SOMETHING a share or interest in something, particularly through money risked in it **3.** PERSONAL INVOLVEMENT personal or emotional interest, concern, or involvement ○ *We had a huge stake in his success.* **4.** *N Am* MIN EXTRACT same as **grubstake** n (sense 2) ■ **stakes** npl **1.** DEGREE OF RISK the degree of hazard or danger involved in a situation **2.** PRIZE AVAILABLE the prize, reward, or success available in a gamble or competition **3.** PRIZE MADE UP OF CONTRIBUTIONS the total of bets made by players in a gambling game that is taken by the winner **4.** CARDS AMOUNT OF BETS IN POKER in poker, the cash values assigned to chips, bets, or raises ■ vt (**stakes, staking, staked**) **1.** WAGER SOMETHING to bet something, especially money, on something **2.** RISK LOSS OF SOMETHING to risk the loss of something valuable ○ *I'm prepared to stake my reputation on it.* **3.** SUPPLY SOMEBODY WITH NECESSITIES to give or lend somebody something needed or wanted ○ *staked him money to pay the rent for a month* **4.** FIN INVEST IN SOMETHING to put money into something, especially initial capital [Mid-16C. Origin ?] ◇ **at stake** at risk of being lost

stakeholder /stáyk hṓldər/ n **1.** a person or group with a direct interest, involvement, or investment in something, e.g. the employees, shareholders, and customers of a business concern ○'...*demonstrating how to build powerful stakeholder relationships based on trust...*' (*Marketing Week*; December 1998) **2.** a holder and payer of bets in a gambling game — **stakeholding** n

stakeholder pension n in the United Kingdom, a pension intended to help especially low-paid people to supplement their state pension, administered by the private financial sector but regulated by the government

stakeout /stáyk owt/ n (*informal*) **1.** hidden surveillance of somebody or something, especially by the police **2.** *N Am* the place from which surveillance is carried out, especially by the police

stakes /stayks/ (*plural same*) n a horse race in which a prize is offered, especially a sum of money made up of contributions from owners of horses that take part

Stakhanovite /stə kánnə vīt/ n in the former Soviet Union, a worker who received a reward for increasing production ■ adj rewarding people who work very hard, especially in the former Soviet Union [Mid-20C. After Aleksei Grigorevich *Stakhanov* (1906–77), Soviet mine worker]

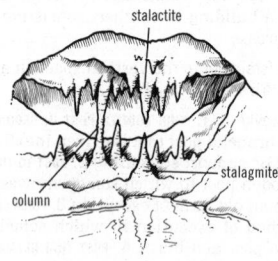

stalactite and stalagmite

stalactite /stálläk tīt/ n a conical hanging pillar in a limestone cave that has gradually built up as a deposit from ground water seeping through the cave's roof [Late 17C. < modern Latin *stalactites* < Greek *stalaktos* 'dripping' < *stalak-*, stem of *stalassein* 'to drip'] — **stalactitic** /stálläk títtik/ adj

stalag /stállag/ n a German prisoner of war camp in World War II for officers and lower ranks [Mid-20C. < German, contraction of *Stammlager* 'main camp']

stalagmite /stálläg mīt/ n a conical pillar in a limestone cave that is gradually built upwards from the floor as a deposit from ground water seeping through and dripping from the cave's roof [Late 17C. < modern Latin *stalagmites* < Greek *stalagmos* 'something dropped' < *stalak-*, stem of *stalassein* 'to drip'] — **stalagmitic** /stálläg míttik/ adj

stale[1] /stayl/ adj (**staler, stalest**) **1.** KEPT TOO LONG no longer fresh ○ *This bread has gone stale.* **2.** LOW IN OXYGEN stagnant and low in oxygen owing to lack of circulation or ventilation ○ *stale air* **3.** FREQUENTLY HEARD AND BORING heard too often before and no longer interesting or amusing ○ *his stale old jokes* **4.** OUT OF CONDITION ineffective, enervated, or bored because of doing too much of the same thing **5.** LAW LEGALLY EXPIRED having lost legal force through lack of use or elapse of time **6.** BANKING NOT NEGOTIABLE BECAUSE OF DELAY describes financial statements or cheques that are not negotiable by a bank because a time limit has expired ■ vti (**stales, staling, staled**) LOSE FRESHNESS to become stale, or make something become stale [13C. < Old French *estale* 'settled' < *estal* 'standing place' < Germanic] — **stalely** adv — **staleness** n

stale[2] /stayl/ vi (**stales, staling, staled**) VET same as **urinate** (*refers to livestock*) the urine of livestock, especially horses and cattle [14C. Origin ?]

stalemate /stáyl mayt/ n **1.** SITUATION WITH NO POTENTIAL WINNERS in a contest, a situation in which neither side can take any further worthwhile action **2.** CHESS CHESS SITUATION WITH NO WINNER in chess, a situation in which no winner is possible because neither player can move a piece without placing the king in check ■ vt (**-mates, -mating, -mated**) PUT SOMEBODY OR SOMETHING INTO STALEMATE to put somebody or something into a situation in which no further worthwhile action is possible (*often passive*) [Mid-18C. < obsolete *stale* (< Anglo-Norman *estale* 'fixed position' < Germanic) + MATE[2]]

Joseph Stalin

Stalin /staálin/, **Joseph** (1879–1953) Georgian-born Soviet leader. He was the general secretary of the Soviet Communist Party (1922–53). He ruled the former Soviet Union as a dictator after 1930, eliminating political opponents in a series of purges and causing nationwide famine with his collectivist agricultural policy. After World War II, he extended Soviet control over most of Eastern Europe. Born **Dzhugashvili, Iosif Vissarionovich**

'One death is a tragedy; a million deaths a statistic.'
[Attributed to Joseph Stalin]

Stalingrad /staálin grad/ former name for **Volgograd** (1925–61)

Stalinism /staálinizəm/ n the political principles and economic policies developed by Joseph Stalin from Marxist-Leninist thought, which included centralized autocratic rule and total suppression of dissent — **Stalinist** n, adj

Stalin Peak former name for **Ismail Samani Peak**

stalk[1] /stawk/ n **1.** PLANT STEM the main stem or axis of a plant that is fleshy rather than woody **2.** SUPPORTIVE PART OF PLANT a supporting part of a plant, e.g. a leaf stem (**petiole**) or flower stalk (**pedicel**) **3.** SLENDER SUPPORTING PART a thin cylindrical part of something that acts as a support, e.g. of a glass **4.** SLENDER STRUCTURAL PART OF ANIMAL a slender supporting structure for an organ or body of an animal [14C. Probably alteration of obsolete *stale* 'stile of a ladder, handle' < Old English *stalu* 'upright piece'] — **stalked** adj — **stalkless** adj

SPELLCHECK **stalk** or **stork?** Do not confuse the spelling of **stalk** and **stork** ('a large wading bird'), which sound similar.

stalk[2] /stawk/ v (**stalks, stalking, stalked**) **1.** vt FOLLOW SOMEBODY STEALTHILY to follow or try to get close to a person or animal unobtrusively **2.** vi WALK STIFFLY AND ANGRILY to walk in a stiff, angry, or proud way **3.** vt TROUBLE SOMEBODY STEADILY AND MALEVOLENTLY to assail somebody in a steady and sinister way ○ *villages stalked by the threat of famine* **4.** vt LAW HARASS SOMEBODY PERSISTENTLY to harass somebody criminally by persistent, inappropriate, and unwanted attention, e.g. by constantly following, telephoning, e-mailing, or writing to him or her ■ n **1.** STEALTHY PURSUIT a stealthy pursuit or hunt of something **2.** STIFF WALK a stiff, angry, or proud walk [Assumed Old English *stealcian* < Germanic, 'to steal'] — **stalkable** adj — **stalker** n

SYNONYMS See **follow**.

stalk-eyed adj used to describe crustaceans and flies that have eyes located on stalks (**pedicels**)

stalking /stáwking/ n **1.** the act or process of stealthily following or trying to approach somebody or something **2.** the crime of harassing somebody with persistent, inappropriate, and unwanted attention — **stalkingly** adv

stalking horse n **1.** MEANS TO DISGUISE OBJECTIVE something used as a means of disguising a real objective **2.** POL DECEPTIVE CANDIDATE FOR ELECTION a candidate who is in an election only to conceal the potential candidacy of somebody else, to divide the opposition, or to determine how strong the opposition is **3.** FIELD SPORTS FAKE HORSE a horse or figure of a horse that is used as cover in the hunting of game

stalky /stáwki/ (**-ier, -iest**) adj **1.** long or tall and thin like a stalk **2.** with stalks, especially many stalks ○ *stalky background plants in the garden* — **stalkily** adv — **stalkiness** n

stall[1] /stawl/ n **1.** SMALL AREA SELLING OR DISPENSING GOODS a booth, table, counter, or compartment set up to display goods for sale or information to give out **2.** COMPARTMENT FOR LARGE ANIMAL a compartment in a building where a single large animal lives or is fed or milked **3.** AUTOMOT SITUATION IN WHICH ENGINE HALTS a situation in which an engine stops abruptly because of insufficient fuel, being braked too suddenly, or mechanical failure **4.** SMALL ROOM a very small room, or partitioned area in a room, for a shower or toilet **5.** AVIAT SUDDEN DIVE BY AIRCRAFT a situation in which an aircraft suddenly dives because the airflow is obstructed and lift is lost. The loss of airflow can be caused by insufficient air speed or by an excessive angle of an aerofoil when the aircraft is climbing. **6.** CHR SEAT IN CHURCH a pew or enclosed seat in a church **7.** MED SHEATH FOR FINGER a protective covering for a finger or thumb **8.** HORSERACING COMPARTMENT OF STARTING GATE a partitioned compartment at the starting gate of a racecourse that holds a horse before the start of a race ■ **stalls** npl SEATS CLOSEST TO STAGE the seats in a theatre or cinema on the ground floor nearest the stage or screen ■ v (**stalls, stalling, stalled**) **1.** vti AUTOMOT STOP OR MAKE ENGINE STOP to stop working suddenly, or make an engine do this **2.** vti AVIAT PLUNGE OR CAUSE TO PLUNGE to go into a sudden dive, or cause a sudden dive in an aircraft **3.** vt AGRIC PUT LARGE ANIMAL INTO STALL to put a large animal into a compartment where it will live or be fed or milked **4.** vti STOP PROGRESSING, OR MAKE SOMETHING STOP to stop making progress, or cause something to stop making progress ○ *stalled the project* ○ *a project that stalled* [Old English *steall* 'standing place' < Germanic]

stall[2] /stawl/ vti (**stalls, stalling, stalled**) to delay or obstruct somebody, or use delaying tactics ■ n a pretext or ruse used to delay or deceive somebody [Early 19C. Alteration of obsolete *stale* 'decoy, pickpocket's accomplice' < Anglo-Norman *estale* 'something set up']

stall-feed vt to keep an animal in a stall while fattening it for slaughter

stallholder /stáwl hōldər/ n somebody who has a stall at a market or fair

stalling angle n the angle relative to the horizontal at which the flow of air around an aerofoil changes abruptly, resulting in significant changes in the lift and drag of an aircraft

stallion /stállyən/ n **1.** an uncastrated adult male horse, especially one kept for breeding **2.** a man who is regarded as having great sexual prowess (*informal*) [14C. < Anglo-Norman *estaloun*]

Stallone /stə lŏn, -lōni/, **Sylvester** (*b.* 1946) US actor. He is best known for playing heroes in Hollywood action films, most notably a boxer in the *Rocky* series (1976–90). Full name **Stallone, Michael Sylvester Enzio**

stalwart /stáwlwərt/ *adj* **1. DEPENDABLE** dependable and loyal **2. STRONG** sturdy and strong ■ *n* **HARD-WORKING LOYAL SUPPORTER** a faithful, dependable, and hard-working supporter of somebody or something ○ *phones manned by party stalwarts* [15C. Scottish variant of obsolete *stalworth* < Old English *stælwierþe* 'good, serviceable', literally 'having a worthy foundation' < *staþol* 'foundation' (see STADDLE) + *weorþ* (see WORTH)] —**stalwartly** *adv* —**stalwartness** *n*

stamen /stáy men, -mən/ (*plural* **-mens** or **-mina** /stámminə/) *n* the male reproductive organ of a flower, typically consisting of a stalk (**filament**) bearing a pollen-producing anther at its tip [Mid-17C. < Latin, 'thread'] —**staminal** /stámmin'l/ *adj* —**staminiferous** /stámmi níffərəss/ *adj*

Stamford /stámfərd/ **1.** market town in Lincolnshire, eastern England. Population: 17,492 (1991). **2.** city in southwestern Connecticut, founded in 1641. Population: 119,850 (2002 estimate).

Stamford Bridge village near York, in northern England. It was near here that King Harold II defeated an invasion by his brother Tostig and King Harald Hardraada of Norway in 1066. Population: 3,099 (1991).

stamina[1] /stámminə/ *n* enduring physical or mental energy and strength that allows somebody to do something for a long time [Early 18C. < Latin, plural of *stamen* 'thread'] —**staminal** *adj*

stamina[2] /stámminə/BOT plural of **stamen**

staminate /stámminət/ *adj* describes plants that have stamens, especially flowers with stamens but without female parts (**carpels**)

staminode /stámmi nōd/, **staminodium** /stámmi nōdi əm/ (*plural* **-dia** /-di ə/) *n* a sterile or vestigial stamen. It forms a conspicuous part of some flowers, e.g. in the iris. [Early 19C. < modern Latin *staminodium* < *stamen* 'thread']

stammel /stámm'l/ *n* **1.** a coarse woollen cloth, usually red. Use: in medieval times, undergarments. **2.** a bright red colour, like that of stammel cloth [Mid-16C. Alteration of obsolete *stamin*, via French < Latin *stamineus* 'consisting of threads' < *stamen* 'thread'] —**stammel** *adj*

stammer /stámmər/ *vti* (**-mers, -mering, -mered**) to speak, or say something, with many quick hesitations and repeated consonants or syllables because of a speech condition or a strong emotion ■ *n* a speech condition that makes somebody speak with involuntary hesitations and repetition of consonants or syllables. Stammering will usually respond to treatment from a speech therapist. [Old English *stamerian* < Germanic, 'halt, stutter'] —**stammerer** *n*

stamp /stamp/ *n* **1. GUMMED PAPER PAYING FOR POSTAGE** a small piece of gummed paper that is stuck on an envelope or parcel to show that postage has been paid **2. CANCELLATION ACROSS POSTAGE STAMP** a mark put across a postage stamp on an envelope or parcel to show that the stamp has been used **3. SMALL BLOCK FOR PRINTING DESIGN** a small block with a raised design or lettering that can be printed onto paper by inking the block and pressing it to the paper **4. DESIGN PRINTED ONTO PAPER WITH STAMP** a design printed onto paper using a stamp in order to show that a document has been read, cancelled, or officially approved **5. GUMMED PAPER AS OFFICIAL MARK** a piece of printed gummed paper fixed to a document as an official sign of something such as approval or validity **6. CHARACTERISTIC OF SOMETHING** a characteristic or distinguishing sign or impression **7. TYPE OR KIND** a class or type of something **8. WAY OF PAYING FOR SOMETHING** a piece of paper that can be purchased as a way of redeeming part or all of the amount charged for goods or a service **9.** PUBLIC ADMIN **NATIONAL INSURANCE CONTRIBUTION** a contribution to national insurance, recorded formerly by means of a stamp on an official card (*informal*) **10. ACT OF BANGING DOWN FOOT** the action of bringing a foot down forcefully on a surface **11.** INDUST **MACHINE FOR CRUSHING ROCKS AND ORE** a machine that crushes rocks and ore by a weight being lifted and dropped ■ *v* (**stamps, stamping, stamped**) **1.** *vt* **PUT STAMP ON DOCUMENT** to press a stamp onto a document leaving a design or lettering on it in order to show that it has been seen, dated, cancelled, or officially approved **2.** *vt* MAIL **STICK POSTAGE STAMP ON SOMETHING** to stick a stamp on an envelope or parcel **3.** *vti* **BANG FOOT DOWN** to bring a foot down forcefully on a surface **4.** *vi* **WALK FORCEFULLY** to walk by taking short forceful steps **5.** *vt* **HAVE LASTING EFFECT ON SOMEBODY** to have a lasting effect or influence on somebody **6.** *vi* **SUPPRESS SOMETHING OR SOMEBODY** to suppress or eradicate something or somebody ○ *He stamped on any suggestion he should resign.* **7.** *vt* INDUST **CRUSH ROCKS** to crush or pound rocks and ore [12C. Probably < assumed Old English *stampian* 'pound' < Germanic] —**stampable** *adj* —**stamped** *adj*

stamp out *vt* **1. ERADICATE SOMETHING** to put an end to something **2. EXTINGUISH SOMETHING** to extinguish something by stamping on it with the feet **3. CUT SOMETHING OUT USING SHARP TOOL** to cut out a shape or object by pressing a sharp-edged machine or tool onto a material

Stamp Act *n* a law passed in the British Parliament in 1765 introducing a tax on legal documents, commercial contracts, licences, publications, and playing cards in the North American colonies. Because of colonial opposition, the first Stamp Act was repealed in March 1766 but it was later replaced by others.

stamp collecting *n* the collecting of postage stamps as a hobby or investment —**stamp collector** *n*

stamp duty *n* a duty applied to some legal documents. A stamp is fixed to a document to show that the duty has been paid.

stampede /stam pēēd/ *n* **1. HEADLONG RUSH OF ANIMALS** an uncontrolled headlong rush of frightened animals **2. HEADLONG SURGE OF CROWD** an uncontrolled surging rush of a crowd of people **3. SUDDEN RUSH OF PEOPLE DOING SOMETHING** a sudden rush of many people all doing or wanting to do something at the same time ○ *There was a stampede to take advantage of the low prices.* **4.** *N Am* **FESTIVAL INCLUDING RODEO** in the western United States and especially in Canada, a celebration, usually held annually, that includes a rodeo along with contests, exhibitions, dancing, and entertainment (*regional*) ■ *v* (**-pedes, -peding, -peded**) **1.** *vti* **RUSH FORWARDS IN FRIGHTENED SURGE** to rush forwards in a frightened headlong surge, or make animals or people surge forwards **2.** *vt* **FORCE SOMEBODY INTO DOING SOMETHING** to force somebody to do something before he or she is ready or has properly thought about it [Early 19C. < Mexican Spanish *estampida* < Spanish, 'uproar'] —**stampeder** *n*

stamper /stámpər/ *n* **1. SOMEBODY OR SOMETHING THAT STAMPS** a person or device used for stamping **2. MACHINE FOR STAMPING SOMETHING** a tool or machine that stamps something, especially ore being pulverized **3.** RECORDING **MOULD FOR DISC RECORDINGS** a mould from which disc recordings are pressed

stamping ground /stámping-/ *n* a place where somebody is habitually found (*informal*)

stamp mill *n* a machine in which rocks and ore are finely crushed, usually operated by hydraulic power, or a building housing one or more such machines

stan /staan/ *n* a central Asian country, especially one bordering Afghanistan, whose name ends with the suffix '-stan' (*slang*)

stance /stanss, staanss/ *n* **1. ATTITUDE TOWARDS SOMETHING** an attitude or view that somebody takes about something **2. WAY OF STANDING** the way that a person or an animal stands **3. POSITION OF WHEELS** the position of a vehicle's wheels in relation to its bodywork ○ *The newer model has a wider stance and a taller cab.* **4. POSITION OF PLAYER** the position in which a player holds the body in attempting to hit a ball, e.g. in cricket or golf **5.** CLIMBING **PLACE FOR PITCHING AND BELAYING** a place where a mountain climber can pitch and belay **6.** *Scotland* TRANSP **TRANSPORT WAITING PLACE** a place where buses or taxis wait for passengers [Mid-16C. Via French, 'position' < Italian *stanza* (see STANZA)]

stanch *vt* same as **staunch**[2]

stanchion /staánchən/ *n* **1. UPRIGHT SUPPORTING POLE** a vertical pole, bar, or beam used to support something **2.** AGRIC **FRAME FOR CONFINING COW** an upright frame in which the neck of a cow is loosely fitted, usually to confine the cow for milking ■ *vt* (**-chions, -chioning, -chioned**) **SUPPORT SOMETHING WITH POLE** to support something using a vertical pole, bar, or beam [15C. < Old French *estanchon* < *estance* 'prop, support']

stand /stand/ *v* (**stands, standing, stood** /stŏŏd/) **1.** *vti* **BE OR SET UPRIGHT** to be in an upright position, or put something in an upright position ○ *I was standing to the left of him.* ○ *Stand the box in the corner.* **2.** *vi* **GET UP ON FEET** to get up into an upright position from a sitting or lying position ○ *The newborn foal tried to stand but only collapsed again.* **3.** *vi* **BE IN PARTICULAR PLACE** to be situated or positioned in a particular place ○ *The castle stands on a headland.* **4.** *vi* **BE IN PARTICULAR STATE** to be in a particular condition or state ○ *The old place stands in need of a few repairs.* ○ *The document can't be published as it stands.* **5.** *vi* **MEASURE IN HEIGHT** to be of a particular height when upright ○ *He stood six feet tall.* **6.** *vi* **BE AT PARTICULAR POINT** to be at a particular point while subject to change or fluctuation ○ *The balance of the account stands at four hundred pounds.* **7.** *vi* **REMAIN MOTIONLESS** to remain in a particular place without moving or being used ○ *The car stood outside the office all morning.* **8.** *vi* **REMAIN VALID** to continue to be in effect or existence ○ *Her world record still stands.* **9.** *vi* **STOP** to come to a halt ○ *I had to stand and catch my breath.* **10.** *vi* **GATHER AND LIE** to gather somewhere and not flow away ○ *rainwater standing in pools* **11.** *vt* **TOLERATE SOMETHING OR SOMEBODY UNPLEASANT** to accept or put up with something or somebody regarded as unpleasant ○ *He can't stand being kept waiting.* **12.** *vt* **UNDERGO SOMETHING WITHOUT HARM** to resist or bear something without being harmed or damaged ○ *The mechanism is too delicate to stand rough handling.* **13.** *vt* **SUBMIT TO SOMETHING** to submit or be subjected to something ○ *I am prepared to stand trial.* **14.** *vt* **BUY SOMETHING FOR SOMEBODY** to pay for something such as a drink for somebody else to have ○ *My uncle offered to stand dinner for all of us.* **15.** *vt* **BENEFIT FROM SOMETHING** to benefit from something, or be no worse for something ○ *I could stand to lose a few more pounds.* **16.** *vi* POL **SEEK ELECTION** to enter an election as a candidate ○ *She decided not to stand at the next election.* **17.** *vi* MIL **FIGHT RESOLUTELY** to fight resolutely or give battle, often after having been in retreat ○ *The general was convinced the enemy would not stand if attacked.* ■ *n* **1. ACT OF STANDING** the act or an example of standing ○ *a long stand in the airport* **2. ATTITUDE** an opinion that somebody has or an attitude that somebody adopts ○ *Management took a tough stand on absenteeism.* **3. SUPPORTING STRUCTURE** a framework or structure on which something is supported ○ *a music stand* **4. PIECE OF FURNITURE** a piece of furniture on which clothes or accessories are hung or supported (*often used in combination*) ○ *an umbrella stand* ○ *a hat stand* **5. PLACE FOR SPECTATORS** a large seating area for spectators in a sports stadium ○ *a ticket for the North Stand.* N Am term **stands** **6. STATIONARY CONDITION** a state of having stopped or being stationary ○ *The runaway vehicle came to a stand in a field.* **7. PLACE WHERE SOMETHING IS SOLD** a booth or stall where something is sold or given out (*often used in combination*) ○ *a refreshment stand* **8. EXHIBITION AREA** one of several places in an exhibition where something is displayed **9.** BOT **AREA OF GROWING THINGS** a group of several plants, especially trees, growing together in one place ○ *a stand of trees* **10. HALT TO FIGHT** a halt made, especially by a force that has been retreating, to give battle ○ *Custer's last stand* **11.** THEATRE **STOP FOR PERFORMANCE** a halt made to give a performance during a tour by a performer or theatrical company ○ *a three-week stand out of town* **12.** CRICKET **TIME AT WICKET** a period at a wicket involving two batsmen during which both bat and are not out, or the score they make **13.** *N Am* TRANSP **PLACE FOR WAITING VEHICLES** a place where vehicles, especially taxis, wait to pick up passengers (*usually used in combination*) ○ *a taxi stand* [Old English *standan* < Indo-European] —**standee** /stan dēē/ *n* ◇ **stand or fall by something** to succeed or fail depending on particular circumstances

USAGE See *sit*.

stand behind *vt* to support or back something or

somebody stalwartly ○ *I'll stand behind you on this contentious issue.*

stand by *v* **1.** *vi* REMAIN READY to wait in a state of readiness to act if required ○ *Stand by for further orders.* **2.** *vi* BE PRESENT WITHOUT ACTION to be present while something is happening but play no part in it ○ *I'm not prepared to stand by and let this go on.* **3.** *vt* SUPPORT SOMEBODY to support or remain faithful to somebody ○ *Her friends all stood by her.* **4.** *vt* ADHERE TO SOMETHING to continue to assert or believe in something ○ *I stand by what I said yesterday.*

stand down *v* **1.** *vi* RESIGN to resign from office or withdraw from a contest **2.** *vi* END TESTIMONY to leave a witness box after having been questioned ■ *Aus* HR LAY SOMEBODY OFF to stop employing somebody, often temporarily, when there is insufficient work to be done ■ *v* **1.** *vti* END DUTY to end somebody's period of duty, or go off duty, especially military duty **2.** *vti* MIL GO OFF ALERT to go off alert, or be taken off alert or out of a combat zone

stand for *vt* **1.** MEAN SOMETHING to mean or represent something else **2.** BELIEVE IN SOMETHING to believe in something strongly and fight for it ○ *To agree with this would go against everything I stand for.* **3.** POL BECOME CANDIDATE FOR SOMETHING to enter an election as a candidate for a particular office **4.** TOLERATE SOMETHING to put up with something ○ *She won't stand for any nonsense.* **5.** NAUT HEAD FOR PLACE to set a course for a particular destination ○ *The fleet stood for home.*

stand in *vi* to take the place of somebody or something else as a substitute ○ *I'm looking for someone to stand in for me next week.*

stand off *v* **1.** *vti* KEEP AWAY to keep at a distance from something, or make somebody or something stay at a distance **2.** *vti* SAIL AWAY to sail a vessel away from something such as a shore **3.** *vt* SUSPEND EMPLOYEE FROM WORK to suspend somebody from work, usually temporarily

stand on *v* **1.** *vt* to insist on something or see it as being important ○ *We don't stand on ceremony in this house.* **2.** *vi* to continue sailing on the same course

stand out *vi* **1.** BE CONSPICUOUS to be conspicuous or prominent **2.** STICK OUT to project or protrude from something **3.** REFUSE TO ACCEPT SOMETHING to refuse to accept or comply with something, especially after others have done so ○ *stood out against the court's decision and appealed it*

stand to *vti* to take up position in readiness for military action, or make somebody do this

stand up *v* **1.** *vti* to rise to an upright position, or make something do this **2.** *vi* to be seen as still valid or right despite being closely examined or criticized ○ *I don't think her testimony will stand up in court.*

stand up for *vt* **1.** to defend the interests of somebody **2.** *N Am* same as **stand up with**

stand up to *v* **1.** *vt* to resist or refuse to be cowed by somebody ○ *He'll back down if you stand up to him.* **2.** *vi* to undergo something that is potentially damaging without being badly affected ○ *These cars are able to stand up to being driven on rough terrain.*

stand up with *vt* *N Am* to act as best man or maid of honour for somebody who is getting married

stand-alone *adj* able to operate as a self-contained unit independently of a computer network or system

standard /stándərd/ *n* **1.** LEVEL OF QUALITY OR EXCELLENCE the level of quality or excellence attained by somebody or something ○ *I hadn't expected work of such a high standard from trainees.* **2.** LEVEL OF QUALITY ACCEPTED AS NORM a level of quality or excellence that is accepted as the norm or by which actual attainments are judged (*often used in the plural*) ○ *By present-day standards the sound quality of this recording is very poor.* **3.** DISTINCTIVE FLAG a flag with a distinctive design that is the emblem of, and often a focus of loyalty to, a particular nation, person, or group **4.** MIL DEVICE USED AS BATTLE RALLYING POINT a flag or other symbolic device attached to a pole and used as a rallying point for troops in battle **5.** HERALDRY LONG TAPERING FLAG a long tapering flag ending in two points and with heraldic devices on it, used in heraldry as an emblem of a person or group. It was formerly carried on ceremonial occasions by or before the nobleman to whom it belonged. **6.** MEASURE AUTHORIZED MODEL OF UNIT OF MEASUREMENT an authorized model used to define a unit of measurement **7.** COINS PROPORTION OF METAL IN COIN the proportion of gold or silver and of

nonprecious metal that a coin is legally required to contain **8.** FIN COMMODITY AS BASIS OF CURRENCY VALUE the commodity or commodities on which the value of a currency or monetary system is based **9.** HOUSEHOLD UPRIGHT POLE OR POST an upright pole or post, usually serving as a support for something **10.** BOT PLANT WITH STRAIGHT BARE STEM a plant, especially a fruit tree or rose, trained in such a way that the leaves and flowers grow at the top of a straight bare stem **11.** MUSIC ITEM IN USUAL REPERTOIRE something, especially a song or other piece of music, that is very popular or is performed as part of the usual repertoire of a performer or performers ○ *played all the old standards* **12.** BOT LARGE UPPER PETAL OF PEA the large upper petal in the flowers of plants of the pea family ■ **standards** *npl* PRINCIPLES principles or values that govern a person's behaviour ■ *adj* **1.** NORMAL constituting or not differing from the norm ○ *This clause is absolutely standard in a contract of this type.* **2.** WIDELY USED AND RESPECTED very widely used and generally regarded as authoritative ○ *the standard text in thermodynamics* **3.** GRAM GRAMMATICALLY CORRECT regarded as correct or acceptable by the majority of educated speakers of or authorities on a language **4.** BOT TRAINED TO GROW WITH STRAIGHT STEM describes plants that are trained in such a way that the leaves and flowers grow at the top of a straight bare stem [12C. Via Anglo-Norman *estaundart* 'flag to which troops rally' < Old French *estandart*] —**standardly** *adv*

standard assessment task *n* a test used to assess the progress of children in a core subject of the UK national curriculum

standard atmosphere *n* MEASURE same as **atmosphere** (sense 6)

standard-bearer *n* **1.** the bearer of a standard or flag, especially for a military unit **2.** a leader or prominent and inspiring representative of a movement, cause, or party

Standardbred /stándərd bred/ *n* a horse belonging to a North American breed specially bred for speed and stamina in harness races

standard candle *n* MEASURE same as **candela**

standard cell *n* an electric cell that produces a constant known voltage and can be used to calibrate voltage-measuring equipment

standard cost *n* the budgeted expenditure of a regular manufacturing process against which the actual cost is measured

standard deviation *n* a statistical measure of the amount by which a set of values differs from the arithmetical mean, equal to the square root of the mean of the differences' squares

standard electrode potential *n* the voltage developed by an electrode of a particular element placed in a solution of the element's ions, measured against that of hydrogen under standardized conditions

Standard English *n* the form of the English language used by educated speakers and regarded as representing correct usage in grammar, spelling, vocabulary, and punctuation

standard error *n* in statistics, the standard deviation of the sample in a frequency distribution divided by the square root of the number of values in the sample. It is a measure of the variability that a constant would be expected to show during sampling.

standard gauge *n* the gauge used for most public railway systems worldwide, the distance between the rails being 143.5 cm/4 ft 8½ in

Standard Generalized Markup Language *n* COMPUT full form of **SGML**

Standard Grade *n* **1.** in Scotland, the lower-level public examination for the Scottish Certificate of Education, usually taken by school students at the age of 15 or 16 **2.** a subject studied, an examination taken, or a pass achieved at Standard Grade

standardize /stándər dīz/ (**-izes**, **-izing**, **-ized**), **standardise** (**-ises**, **-ising**, **-ised**) *vt* **1.** to remove variations and irregularities in something and make all types or examples of it the same or bring them into conformity with one another **2.** to assess something or determine its properties by

comparing it with a standard —**standardization** /stándər dī záysh'n/ *n* —**standardizer** *n*

standardize on *vt* to choose something as a standard and remove variations and irregularities

standard lamp *n* a tall lamp with a base that stands on the floor. N Am term **floor lamp**

standard of living *n* the level of material comfort enjoyed by a person, group, or society

standard operating procedure *n* a procedure that is usually followed when carrying out an operation or dealing with a situation

Standards Australia *n* in Australia, a government-funded independent organization that sets, monitors, and certifies standards in a wide range of fields such as building and manufacturing

standard state *n* the pure form of a chemical substance that is stable at a given pressure and temperature

standard time *n* a system of measuring time in relation to the natural day, usually based on the mean solar time at the central meridian of a particular time zone

stand-by *n* **1.** PERSON OR THING READILY AVAILABLE somebody or something that can always be relied on to be available and useful, especially if needed as a substitute or in an emergency **2.** TRAVEL UNRESERVED TICKET OR PASSENGER WITHOUT RESERVATION an unreserved ticket or a passenger having no prior reservation on a mode of public transport such as an aircraft ■ *adj* **1.** HELD IN RESERVE able to be used as a replacement **2.** TRAVEL UNRESERVED AND SUBJECT TO AVAILABILITY made available, usually at a lower price, shortly before the departure of a flight when there are seats remaining unsold, or using a ticket made available in this way ■ *adv* TRAVEL ON STAND-BY BASIS on the basis of having no prior reservation to travel ○ *flew stand-by from Washington to Amsterdam* ◇ **on stand-by** available for use or service if necessary

stand-down *n* a return to normal status after being on alert, or the withdrawal of a military presence

stand-in *n* **1.** somebody or something that acts as a temporary replacement **2.** a replacement for an actor in a film, e.g. during preparatory or dangerous action —**stand-in** *adj*

standing /stánding/ *n* **1.** STATUS AND REPUTATION somebody's reputation or position, e.g. in society or business ○ *a person of some standing in computer electronics* **2.** DURATION the period over which something has been in existence ■ *adj* UPRIGHT performed while standing rather than sitting or moving ■ **standings** *npl* LISTING OF SCORES the official record of the relative positions of competitors taking part in an event ■ *adj* **1.** PERMANENT remaining permanently in existence or in force **2.** NOT FLOWING not flowing, or containing water that cannot flow or run away ○ *a pool of standing water* **3.** AGRIC NOT CUT DOWN growing where planted, having not been cut down ○ *a standing forest*

USAGE See *sit*.

standing army *n* a permanent professional military force maintained by a country in times of peace as well as war

standing committee *n* a committee that remains in existence permanently in order to deal with a particular issue

standing crop *n* the total mass of living things of all kinds or of one specific kind found in an area or ecosystem at a specific time

standing order *n* **1.** an instruction given by an account holder to a bank to pay a specific sum of money at fixed intervals to a person or account **2.** an order or rule, especially one governing military or parliamentary procedures, that remains in force on all relevant occasions until it is specifically revoked

standing rigging *n* the wires and ropes holding the masts and spars of a sailing ship or boat that are more or less permanently fixed in place

standing room *n* space where people can only stand, not sit

standing stone *n* a large stone set upright in the

ground in prehistoric times, singly or as part of a larger structure

standing wave *n* a stationary wave characterized by points of zero vibration and points of maximum vibration, occurring when two waves of equal frequency and intensity travelling in opposite directions combine [Because the points of minimum and maximum vibration remain stationary]

standish /stándish/ *n* a holder for an ink bottle, pens, and other writing equipment [14C. Probably < STAND as a verb]

standoff /stánd of/ *n* **1.** a situation in which no result or conclusion can be reached because the two sides in a contest or dispute are equally matched or are equally intransigent **2.** *N Am* a state of equality, e.g. in a sports contest or an election **3.** RUGBY same as **stand-off half**

stand-off half *n* in rugby, a player who plays behind the forwards and the scrum half, provides a link between them and the three-quarter backs, and often has control of the team's tactics

standoff insulator *n* an insulator that supports an electrical conductor and keeps it at a distance from other conducting elements. The insulators supporting power lines are examples of this.

standoffish /stand óffish/ *adj* reluctant to show friendship or enter into conversation with other people —**standoffishly** *adv* —**standoffishness** *n*

standoff missile *n* a guided missile that can be fired from an aircraft at a sufficient distance from its target to be out of range of enemy defences

stand oil *n* a thick drying oil used in oil enamel paints, made by heating linseed or another oil to a high temperature [Translation of German *Standöl*; it was formerly prepared by allowing linseed oil to stand]

standout /stánd owt/ *n N Am* somebody or something that is especially prominent or outstanding (*informal*)

standover man /stánd ōvər-/ *n Aus* somebody, especially a man, who intimidates or threatens people or extorts money or services from them

standover person *n Aus* somebody who intimidates or threatens people or extorts money or services from them

standpipe /stánd pīp/ *n* **1.** a vertical pipe with a tap on the top, used to enable householders to draw water from a water main in the street when the normal supply is disrupted **2.** a vertical open-ended pipe attached to a pipeline to act as a pressure regulator, ensuring that the pressure head at that point cannot exceed the length of the pipe

standpoint /stánd poynt/ *n* a way of considering an event or issue, or one of the contexts in which an event or issue can be considered ○ *From an ecological standpoint, this is an utter disaster.*

standstill /stánd stil/ *n* a situation in which all movement or activity ceases and further movement or activity is prevented ○ *Traffic is at a standstill.*

standstill agreement *n* an agreement that things should remain as they are, especially one between a creditor country and a debtor country that needs extra time to repay its debt

stand-to *n* the act of taking up positions ready for action

standup /stánd up/ *adj* **1.** STANDING ERECT standing erect and not folded down **2.** AT WHICH PEOPLE STAND where or at which people stand, especially to eat or drink ○ *A large standup buffet was laid out for the reception.* **3.** INTENSE AND NOISY intense and involving a lot of noise and sometimes violence ○ *a standup fight* **4.** INVOLVING SOLO PERFORMANCE BY COMEDIAN involving a performance by a comedian standing alone on stage telling jokes or stories to an audience **5.** *US* TRUSTWORTHY showing the qualities of honesty, loyalty, and dependability (*informal*) ■ *n* STANDUP COMEDY comedy in which the performer stands alone on stage telling jokes or stories to an audience

Stanford /stánfərd/, **Sir Charles** (1852–1924) British composer and teacher. He wrote operas and symphonies, but is best known for his church music. Full name **Stanford, Sir Charles Villiers**

Stanford-Binet test /stánfərd bi náy-/ *n* an intelligence test commonly used with children in the United States [Early 20C. After *Stanford* University, California + Alfred *Binet*, (1857–1911), French psychologist]

stanhope /stánnəp, stán hōp/ *n* a light open horse-drawn carriage with a single seat and two or four wheels [Early 19C. After Fitzroy H. R. *Stanhope* (1787–1864), British cleric for whom one was first made]

Stanislavsky /stánni slávski/, **Stanislavski, Konstantin** (1863–1938) Russian actor and theatre director. He helped to found the Moscow Arts Theatre (1889) and there adopted methods of training actors that greatly influenced theatre in the 20th century. Full name **Stanislavsky, Konstantin Sergeyevich Alexeyev** —**Stanislavskian** *adj*

Stanislavsky method *n* THEATRE, ARTS same as **Method**

stank past tense of **stink**

Stanley[1] /stánli/ industrial town in a coal-mining area of Durham, in England. Population: 18,905 (1991).

Stanley[2] capital of the Falkland Islands. Population: 1,232 (1986).

Stanley, Sir H. M. (1841–1904) British journalist and explorer. On his African expeditions he located David Livingstone at Ujiji on Lake Tanganyika (1871), traced the Lualaba and Congo rivers to the sea (1874–77), and laid the foundations for the establishment of the Congo Free State (1879–84). Full name **Stanley, Sir Henry Morton**. Born **Rowlands, John**

Stanley knife *tdmk* a trademark for a type of knife that is very sharp and has a retractable blade

Stanley Pool former name for **Malebo Pool**

stann- *prefix* tin ○ *stanniferous*

Stannaries /stánnəriz/ *npl* a former tin-mining district in the English counties of Devon and Cornwall

stannary /stánnəri/ (*plural* **-naries**) *n* a district with tin mines [15C. Via medieval Latin *stannaria* 'stannaries' < late Latin *stannum* 'tin']

stannic /stánnik/ *adj* relating to or containing tin, especially with a valency of four [Late 18C. < late Latin *stannum* 'tin']

stannic sulphide *n* a yellow or gold-coloured solid compound of sulphur and tin. Use: pigment.

stanniferous /sta níffərəss/ *adj* containing or yielding tin [Early 19C. < late Latin *stannum* 'tin']

stannite /stánnīt/ *n* a grey metallic oxide mineral containing copper, iron, and tin. Use: source of tin. [Mid-19C. < late Latin *stannum* 'tin']

stannous /stánnəss/ *adj* relating to or containing tin, especially with a valency of two [Mid-19C. < late Latin *stannum* 'tin']

stannous fluoride *n* a white crystalline powder with a bitter salty taste. Use: fluoride toothpaste. Formula: SnF_2.

Stansted /stán sted/ third largest airport serving London, to the northeast of the city

Stanthorpe /stán thawrp/ town in southeastern Queensland, Australia. It is one of the highest towns in the state at 811 m/2,660 ft. Population: 10,515 (2002 estimate).

stanza /stánzə/ *n* a number of lines of verse forming a separate unit within a poem. In many poems, each stanza has the same number of lines and the same rhythm and rhyme scheme. [Late 16C. Via Italian < assumed Vulgar Latin *stantia* 'a standing, stopping place' < Latin *stare* 'to stand'] —**stanzaic** /stan záy ik/ *adj*

stapedectomy /stáypi déktəmi/ (*plural* **-mies**) *n* surgical removal of the stapes of the ear. It is performed in treating some forms of hearing loss. [Late 19C. < modern Latin *staped-*, stem of *stapes* (see STAPES)]

stapedes ANAT plural of **stapes**

stapelia /stə péeli ə/ (*plural* **-as** or *same*) *n* a plant similar to the cactus, with thick fleshy four-angled stems and no leaves. Flowers: large, mottled, foul-smelling. Native to: Africa. Genus: *Stapelia*. [Late 18C. < modern Latin, after Jan Bode van *Stapel* (d. 1636), Dutch botanist]

stapes /stáy peez/ (*plural same* or **-pedes** /-péedeez/) *n* a small stirrup-shaped bone in the middle ear of mammals, the innermost of the three small bones that transmit vibration to the inner ear [Mid-17C. < medieval Latin, 'stirrup'] —**stapedial** /stə péedi əl/ *adj*

staph /staf/ *n* MED same as **staphylococcus** (*informal*) [Early 20C. Shortening]

staphylococcus /stáffilə kókəss/ (*plural* **-cocci** /-kók sī/) *n* a bacterium that typically occurs in clusters resembling grapes, normally inhabits the skin and mucous membranes, and may cause disease. These bacteria commonly infect the skin, eyes, and urinary tract, and some produce toxins responsible for septicaemia and food poisoning. Genus: *Staphylococcus*. [Late 19C. < modern Latin < Greek *staphulē* 'bunch of grapes' + *kokkos* 'berry'] —**staphylococcal** *adj*

staple[1] /stáyp'l/ *n* **1.** BENT WIRE USED TO FASTEN PAPERS a small thin piece of metal wire bent into the shape of a flattened U with square corners, used to fasten things together, especially sheets of paper. The staple is driven through the material by a device that also bends its two ends inwards and flattens them so that they grip the material firmly. **2.** U-SHAPED FASTENER FOR WOOD OR MASONRY a small U-shaped piece of strong metal wire with two sharp points, usually driven into a surface to hold something such as a bolt or cable in place ■ *vt* (**-ples, -pling, -pled**) FASTEN SOMETHING WITH STAPLES to fasten something to something else or in position with staples [Old English *stapol* 'post, pillar' < Germanic]

staple[2] /stáyp'l/ *n* **1.** MOST IMPORTANT PRODUCT OF TRADE the commodity or product that is most important to the trade of a country, region, or organization **2.** BASIC INGREDIENT OF DIET a food that forms the basis of the diet of the people of a region or of an animal **3.** PRINCIPAL OR RECURRING INGREDIENT a principal or continually recurring ingredient or feature of something ○ *I'd hardly describe opera as a staple of the entertainment offered in this theatre.* **4.** MANUF WOOL, COTTON, OR FLAX FIBRE wool, cotton, or flax fibre graded according to its length and fineness ■ *adj* BASIC AND MOST IMPORTANT used or depended on as the basic and most important element of something, especially diet or trade ■ *vt* (**-ples, -pling, -pled**) MANUF GRADE FIBRES to grade wool, cotton, or flax fibre according to its length and fineness [14C. Via French < Middle Low German, Middle Dutch *stapel* 'shop; pillar' < Germanic]

staple gun *n* a powerful device used to drive heavy metal staples into wood or masonry

stapler /stáyplər/ *n* a device that fastens paper and other materials together using staples, usually consisting of a flat metal base, a spring-loaded magazine of staples, and a top section

star /staar/ *n* **1.** POINT OF LIGHT IN NIGHT SKY an astronomical object usually visible as a small bright point of light in the night sky **2.** MASS OF GAS IN SPACE a gaseous mass in space that generates energy by thermonuclear reactions, e.g. the Sun. Stars range in size from that of a planet to one larger than the Earth's orbit. **3.** STAR SHAPE a shape representing or based on that of a star as seen in the night sky, usually having four or five triangular points radiating from a centre **4.** STAR-SHAPED SYMBOL OF MERIT OR RANK a star-shaped object or symbol used as a sign of merit, quality, or rank **5.** PRINTING, LING same as **asterisk** **6.** POPULAR PERFORMER a very famous, successful, and popular performer, especially in a field of entertainment or in sport **7.** MOST IMPORTANT OR PROFICIENT PERSON an especially proficient or important member of a group ○ *the star of the French class* **8.** HELPFUL PERSON a very nice or helpful person (*informal*) ○ *Thanks, Ben. You're a star!* **9.** ASTROL ASTRONOMICAL OBJECT IN RELATION TO FATE a planet or constellation believed to influence somebody's character or fate on Earth ■ **stars** *npl* ASTROL DESTINY somebody's future, especially as supposedly revealed in a horoscope (*informal*) ■ *v* (**stars, starring, starred**) **1.** *vt* HAVE SOMEBODY AS LEADING PERFORMER to have somebody as the leading performer or as one of the leading performers **2.** *vi* BE LEADING PERFORMER to be the leading performer or one of the leading performers in something such as a film or play ○ *starring in his first major film* **3.** *vt* PRINTING same as **asterisk** **4.** *vt* COVER OR DECORATE SOMETHING WITH STARS to cover or decorate something with stars, or with many brilliant or colourful objects so as to give an effect comparable to that of the stars in the night sky ■ *adj* OUTSTANDING very or most important, skilful, or

successful ○ *our star player* [Old English *steorra* < Indo-European] ◇ **see stars** to see flashes of light, e.g. after receiving a hard blow to the head

star anise *n* **1.** a star-shaped fruit consisting of 6 to 12 woody single-seeded carpels, with an aniseed flavour. Use: in Chinese cookery and medicine, source of oil. **2.** an evergreen tree that yields star anise. Native to: China. Latin name: *Illicium verum*.

star-apple *n* **1.** an apple-shaped fruit with a smooth greenish-purple skin and a star-shaped arrangement of seeds inside **2.** an evergreen tree that produces star-apples. Native to: tropical America. Latin name: *Chrysophyllum cainito*.

Stara Zagora /stárrə zə górrə/ city in central Bulgaria, situated about 153 km/95 mi. west of the Black Sea port of Burgas. Population: 151,218 (1996).

star billing *n* the fact of being advertised as the leading performer in something

starboard /staárbərd/ *n* RIGHT-HAND SIDE the direction to the right of somebody facing the front of a ship or aircraft ■ *adj* ON RIGHT-HAND SIDE on, towards, or from the right-hand side of somebody facing the front of a ship or aircraft ■ *adv* TOWARDS RIGHT-HAND SIDE towards starboard or the starboard side of a ship or aircraft ■ *vt* (-boards, -boarding, -boarded) TURN TOWARDS RIGHT to turn or move something, especially the helm, towards starboard [Old English *stēorbord* < *stēor* 'steering paddle' + *bord* (see BOARD)]

ORIGIN *Starboard* has no connection with the stars. *Star-* represents a form related to *steer* and meaning 'paddle'. The name derives from the ancient custom of steering boats by means of a paddle on the right-hand side.

starburst /staár burst/ *n* **1.** a pattern of lines or light rays radiating outwards from a centre **2.** a strong sudden burst of star formation

starburst galaxy *n* a galaxy in a stage of intense star production

starburst molecule *n* CHEM same as **dendrimer**

starch /staarch/ *n* **1.** CARBOHYDRATE SUBSTANCE a natural substance composed of chains of glucose units, made by plants and providing a major energy source for animals. The two main components of starch are amylose and amylopectin. Formula: $(C_6H_{10}O_5)_n$. **2.** STIFFENING SUBSTANCE FOR FABRICS a white powder extracted from potatoes and grain. Use: fabric stiffener. **3.** STARCHY FOODSTUFF a foodstuff that contains a large amount of starch **4.** STIFF AND FORMAL MANNER behaviour marked by a stiff manner and formality **5.** *N Am* COURAGE great courage or energy ■ *vt* (starches, starching, starched) STIFFEN FABRIC to stiffen fabric with starch [Assumed Old English *stercan* 'stiffen' < Germanic, 'be rigid']

star chamber *n* a court or tribunal noted for being harsh, arbitrary, and unaccountable in its proceedings

Star Chamber *n* a court established by King Henry VII of England to try civil and criminal cases, especially those involving the security of the state, in secret. It was noted for its arbitrary proceedings and was abolished in 1641. [Because the ceiling of the original courtroom was decorated with stars]

starch syrup *n* a syrup containing dextrose, maltose, and dextrin that is created through the incomplete hydrolysis of glucose

starchy /staárchi/ (-ier, -iest) *adj* **1.** containing a large amount of starch, or like starch, especially in consistency **2.** very formal and unbending, and apparently lacking in warmth or a sense of humour —**starchily** *adv* —**starchiness** *n*

star connection *n* an electrical connection in a polyphase system in which the windings have one end connected to a common junction and the other ends connected to separate load points

star-crossed *adj* believed to be destined by fate to be unhappy ○ *a star-crossed political campaign from the outset* [< the belief in the influence of the stars over human lives]

stardom /staárdəm/ *n* **1.** the status of a star performer in sport or entertainment, and the fame and prestige that go with it **2.** star performers considered as a group

stardust /staár dust/ *n* **1.** a dreamy romantic sentimental feeling, or an imaginary substance, usually represented as starry and twinkling, that is supposed to induce this feeling **2.** far distant stars in a cluster or strewn like a cloud of bright dust in the night sky

stare /stair/ *vi* (stares, staring, stared) **1.** LOOK FIXEDLY to look directly at somebody or something for a long time without moving the eyes away, usually as a result of curiosity or surprise, or to express rudeness or defiance ○ *'What is this life if, full of care,/ We have no time to stand and stare?'* (W. H. Davies *Leisure*; 1911) **2.** BE WIDE OPEN WITH SHOCK to look wide open with shock, fear, or amazement (*refers to eyes*) **3.** BE OBVIOUS to be obvious or blatant ○ *The answer was staring at you all the time you just couldn't see it.* ■ *n* **1.** LONG CONCENTRATED LOOK a long concentrated look at somebody or something, often full of curiosity or hostility **2.** FACIAL EXPRESSION a facial expression in which the eyes are wide open with shock or amazement and are looking fixedly at somebody or something [Old English *starian* < Germanic, 'be rigid'] —**starer** *n*

SPELLCHECK See *stair*.

SYNONYMS See *gaze*.

stare out *vt* to look somebody directly in the eyes until he or she is forced to look away. N Am term **stare down**

starets /staárits/ (*plural* **startsy** /staártsi/) *n* a religious teacher or spiritual adviser in the Russian Orthodox Church, especially one who is a monk or holy man [Early 20C. < Russian, 'elderly man, elder']

star facet *n* one of the eight small triangular facets that surround the table of a gem cut in the brilliant style

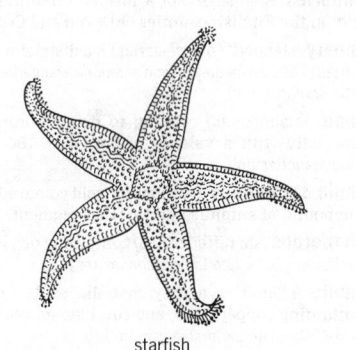

starfish

starfish /staár fish/ (*plural* **same** or **-fishes**) *n* an invertebrate sea animal (**echinoderm**) whose body consists of five or more arms radiating from a central disc. Starfish have a central mouth on the underside and feed on oysters and other molluscs on shores and the seabed. Class: Asteroidea.

starflower /staár flowər/ *n* a plant with star-shaped flowers, e.g. star-of-Bethlehem and some plants of northeastern North America

star fruit *n* FOOD same as **carambola** (sense 2)

stargaze /staár gayz/ (-gazes, -gazing, -gazed) *vi* **1.** observe the stars at night **2.** to engage in daydreaming

stargazer /staár gayzər/ *n* **1.** DAYDREAMER somebody given to daydreaming **2.** ASTRONOMER somebody who studies the stars (*informal*) **3.** TROPICAL SEA FISH a bottom-dwelling tropical sea fish that has eyes and mouth on the top of its head. Families: Uranoscopidae or Dactyloscopidae.

star grass *n* a plant of the daffodil family with long leaves that look like grass. Flowers: star-shaped, white or yellow. Native to: tropical and temperate regions. Genus: *Hypoxis*.

star jump *n* an exercise in which a person jumps in the air with legs apart and arms extended out from the shoulder in a comparable direction

stark /staark/ *adj* **1.** FORBIDDINGLY BARE AND PLAIN forbidding in its bareness and lack of any ornament, relieving feature, or pleasant prospect ○ *the stark interior of a dungeon cell* **2.** UNAMBIGUOUS AND HARSH presented in plain, unambiguous, and usually rather harsh

terms ○ *Faced with the stark choice, we had either to change or go under.* **3.** COMPLETE having reached the fullest extent or degree of something **4.** WITHOUT CLOTHES completely unclothed and uncovered **5.** RIGID showing or affected by rigor mortis (*archaic*) ■ *adv* UTTERLY to the utmost degree [Old English *stearc* < Germanic, 'be rigid'] —**starkly** *adv* —**starkness** *n*

Dame Freya Stark

Stark /staark/, **Dame Freya** (1893–1993) British writer. She wrote over 30 travel books describing aspects of Southwest Asian culture, especially life in the deserts. Full name **Stark, Dame Freya Madeline**

starkers /staárkərz/ *adj* completely unclothed and uncovered (*informal*) [Early 20C. Shortening and alteration of STARK-NAKED]

star key *n* a key or button on, e.g. a telephone or keypad, that is marked with an asterisk symbol

stark-naked *adj* completely unclothed and uncovered

starlet /staárlət/ *n* a young woman actor seen as a possible major film star of the future

starlight /staár līt/ *n* the light that comes from the stars

starling[1] /staárling/ *n* **1.** a common songbird with a stocky body, a strong beak, strong legs, and glossy greenish-black feathers covered in white spots, which gathers in large noisy flocks. Native to: Europe. Latin name: *Sturnus vulgaris*. **2.** a songbird with a stocky body, a strong beak and strong legs, which often has glossy greenish or bluish feathers. Native to: Europe, Africa, Asia, Australasia, western Pacific. Family: Sturnidae. [Old English *stærlinc* 'little starling' < *stær* 'starling' < Germanic]

starling[2] /staárling/ *n* a structure made of piles surrounding a pier of a bridge to protect the pier from floating debris [Late 17C. Origin ?]

starlit /staár lit/ *adj* lit by light from the stars

star-nosed mole *n* a mole that has a ring of small pink fleshy tentacles surrounding its nose. Native to: North America. Latin name: *Condylura cristata*.

star-of-Bethlehem (*plural* **stars-of-Bethlehem** or **same**) *n* a perennial plant of the lily family that has long slender leaves. Flowers: white, star-shaped, in clusters on a central stalk. Native to: Europe. Genus: *Ornithogalum*. [Late 16C. < its abundance in Palestine]

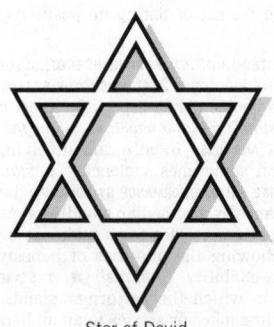

Star of David

Star of David *n* a symbol of the Jewish faith and of the state of Israel consisting of two equilateral triangles superimposed on each other to form a six-pointed star

starquake /stáar kwayk/ *n* a violent seismic event on a star, caused by flares

Starr /staar/, **Ringo** (*b.* 1940) British musician. He attained fame as the drummer of the Beatles (1962–70). Born **Starkey, Richard**

'I like Beethoven, especially the poems.' [Ringo Starr. Quoted in *The Wit and Wisdom of Rock and Roll*, Maxim Jabukowski (ed.); 1983]

star ruby *n* a ruby that reflects light in a star shape when cut with a convex surface

starry /stáari/ (**-rier, -riest**) *adj* **1.** WITH MANY STARS SHINING bright with many shining stars **2.** COVERED WITH STARS covered or decorated with stars **3.** SIMILAR TO STAR relating to stars, or similar in shape or brightness to a star

starry-eyed *adj* having a happy and enthusiastic or romantic attitude that is naive and unrealistic

Stars and Bars *n* the first flag of the Confederacy during the American Civil War, which had two red stripes and one white, and a circle of white stars representing the seceded states (*takes a singular or plural verb*)

Stars and Stripes *n* the national flag of the United States, which has 13 alternating red and white stripes and one star for each state on a blue field (*takes a singular or plural verb*)

star sapphire *n* a sapphire that reflects light in a star shape when cut with a convex surface

star shell *n* an artillery shell designed to burst in midair and release a flare or a shower of lights

starship /stáar ship/ *n* a spaceship designed to travel between stars or star systems, as yet existing only in science fiction

star sign *n* a sign of the zodiac, especially the sign under which somebody was born

star-spangled *adj* **1.** covered or decorated with stars **2.** attended by many important people, usually politicians or film stars

Star-Spangled Banner *n* **1.** the national anthem of the United States **2.** the national flag of the United States

starstruck /stáar struk/, **star-struck** *adj* **1.** feeling or showing an awed fascination with stars from the world of entertainment or with becoming such a star **2.** overawed in the presence of somebody famous

star-studded *adj* containing many well-known actors or performers

star system *n* the system of deliberately exploiting an individual star performer, both on screen and off, to sell films

start /staart/ *v* (**starts, starting, started**) **1.** *vti* BEGIN to begin doing something or begin something ○ *She started to laugh.* ○ *I'd better start getting ready.* **2.** *vti* BEGIN HAPPENING to begin happening, or make something begin happening ○ *The film starts at 7 o'clock.* **3.** *vt* CREATE SOMETHING to bring something into being as an entity or operation **4.** *vt* BEGIN WORKING to commence work on something **5.** *vt* HELP SOMEBODY BEGIN SOMETHING to help somebody out in beginning an activity such as a journey or career ○ *It was a university professor who started her on her law career.* **6.** *vi* GO FROM PARTICULAR LEVEL to begin at a particular level ○ *Prices start at fifteen pounds.* **7.** *vti* PLAY FIRST IN SPORTS MATCH to be in a race or play at the beginning of a sports match, or select somebody to do this **8.** *vi* BEGIN ARGUING to begin arguing or making a fuss (*informal*) ○ *Please don't start.* **9.** *vi* MAKE SUDDEN MOVEMENT to make a sudden movement out of surprise, pain, fear, or anger **10.** *vti* MOVE SUDDENLY to go very quickly from being still to moving, or cause a person or animal to do this ○ *start to your feet* **11.** *vt* CAUSE ANIMAL TO APPEAR to cause a hunted animal to appear suddenly from its hiding place or den **12.** *vt* RAISE SOMETHING to raise or care for something in the early stages of its growth ○ *start some plants in early spring* **13.** *vi* FLOW VIOLENTLY OUT to flow violently or suddenly out of something ○ *water starting from the barrel's seams* **14.** *vti* AUTOMOT BEGIN WORKING, OR MAKE ENGINE BEGIN to begin working, or make an engine begin to operate ○ *The car won't start.* ○ *I can't start the car.* **15.** *vti* COME LOOSE to come loose from the proper place, or cause something to come loose from its proper place ○ *timbers starting at the joints* ■ *n* **1.** BEGINNING the first part of something that proceeds through time ○ *We missed the start of the play.* **2.** PLACE OR TIME OF START the place or time at which something starts ○ *The start of the race is scheduled for noon.* **3.** QUICK SUDDEN MOVEMENT a quick sudden movement from being still to moving **4.** SUDDEN INVOLUNTARY MOVEMENT a sudden involuntary movement caused by surprise, pain, fear, or anger **5.** INSTANCE OF PARTICIPATING the fact or an instance of participating in a race or game ○ *winning three out of five starts* **6.** POSITION AHEAD OF OTHERS a position of being ahead of other competitors ○ *get a start on the rest* **7.** POSITION AT BEGINNING a set of circumstances at the beginning of something ○ *He needed a better start in life.* **8.** SIGNAL TO BEGIN the signal to begin something such as a race **9.** SURPRISING THING something that is surprising (*informal*) [12C. Probably < Old English *styrtan* 'to jump' < Germanic] ◇ **for a start** used in an argument to indicate that you are making the first point of many ◇ **to start with** at the beginning

start in *vi US* to begin to scold or criticize somebody ○ *As soon as she'd finished tearing a strip off Doreen, she started in on me.*

start off *v* **1.** *vi* SET OFF to begin moving in a particular direction, or begin a journey ○ *She turned and started off up the hill.* **2.** *vti* BEGIN to begin to do something, or cause or help somebody to begin to do something ○ *Let's start off by introducing ourselves.* **3.** *vt* MAKE SOMEBODY START TALKING OR LAUGHING to do something that causes somebody else to start doing something such as talking, laughing, crying, or misbehaving (*informal*) ○ *Stop it, or you'll start her off again.*

start on *vt* **1.** to begin to work on or deal with something or somebody, usually something that will take a long time to finish ○ *As soon as I've finished cleaning the kitchen, I'm going to start on the bathroom.* **2.** to begin to scold, criticize, or attack somebody (*informal*) ○ *Look, don't start on me. It's not my fault!*

start out *vi* **1.** BEGIN JOURNEY to set off on a journey ○ *If we start out at about nine, we should be there in time for lunch.* **2.** BEGIN to do something at the beginning of a process ○ *He starts out trying to prove she's guilty and ends up convincing everyone she's innocent.* **3.** INTEND to intend to do something, or have something as an initial intention ○ *I didn't start out to cause a lot of trouble.* **4.** BEGIN STAGE OF LIFE to make a start in something such as adult life or a career ○ *young people who are starting out in journalism*

start up *v* **1.** *vti* BEGIN TO OPERATE to begin to operate, or make something begin to operate ○ *start the engine up* **2.** *vti* OPEN BUSINESS to begin something such as a business venture ○ *started up her own accountancy firm* **3.** *vi* BEGIN TO MAKE SOUND to begin to make a sound, especially a characteristic sound, or begin to speak ○ *First a solitary blackbird started up, and soon the whole wood was alive with birdsong.* **4.** *vi* RISE SUDDENLY to rise suddenly to a standing or upright position ○ *He started up from his chair at the loud sound and rushed to the window.*

START /staart/ *abbr* INTERNAT REL Strategic Arms Reduction Talks

starter /stáartər/ *n* **1.** FIRST COURSE OF MEAL a first course of a meal, or something suitable to be eaten as a first course of a meal **2.** AUTOMOT STARTING DEVICE FOR ENGINE a device for starting a machine or engine, especially an electrically operated device that causes the internal-combustion engine in a motor vehicle to fire **3.** SPORTS SOMEBODY SIGNALLING START OF RACE somebody who gives the signal for a race to start **4.** SPORTS COMPETITOR WHO STARTS a horse or competitor who starts in a race **5.** SPORTS PLAYER AT BEGINNING OF GAME a player who takes the field for a team at the beginning of a game **6.** *N Am* BASEBALL FIRST PITCHER in baseball, the pitcher who pitches first for a team, either regularly or in a specific game ■ *adj* USED TO START used to start something or as an introduction to something for people with little experience of it ○ *a starter set of paints* ◇ **for starters** as the first thing to be done, considered, or dealt with (*informal*)

starter home *n* a small property suitable for somebody who is buying a home for the first time

starter kit *n* same as **starter pack**

starter pack *n* a set containing the materials, equipment, or information required by somebody who wishes to begin a particular activity

star thistle *n* a plant belonging to the daisy family. Flowers: purple, encircled by radiating spines. Native to: Europe, Asia. Genus: *Centaurea*.

starting /stáarting/ *adj* protruding or bulging, or appearing to do so ○ *ran with starting eyes from the horrific scene*

starting block *n* either of a pair of objects that runners brace their feet against at the start of a sprint race. The blocks are made up of a base that can be firmly fixed to the track and angled supports for the runners' feet.

starting gate *n* **1.** *ANZ, N Am* STARTING STALLS a line of starting stalls **2.** TAPES RAISED AT START OF HORSE RACE a set of tapes spanning the width of a racetrack that are raised by the starter to begin a race **3.** BARRIER CONNECTED TO TIMER a physical barrier or electronic beam that automatically starts a timing device when a competitor passes through it, e.g. at the start of a skiing race

starting grid *n* a pattern of lines marked on a motor racing track, with numbered starting positions. The cars that record the fastest times in practice or qualifying occupy the front positions.

starting gun *n* a gun fired as the signal for a race to start

starting line *n* a line marked across a racetrack to show runners where to start

starting lineup *n* an official list of the players who will begin a game or the competitors who will begin a race

starting pistol *n* SPORTS same as **starting gun**

starting point *n* **1.** a basis from which something can start or develop **2.** the place from which you start a journey

starting price *n* the odds being offered by a bookmaker on a horse just before the start of a race

starting rotation *n* the order in which the manager of a baseball or softball team plays the pitchers at the start of games

starting stalls *npl UK* a line of stalls into which racehorses are put at the start of a race that have gates at the front that spring open simultaneously when operated by the starter

startle /stáart'l/ (**-tles, -tling, -tled**) *vti* to disconcert or frighten a person or animal into making an involuntary movement, or become disconcerted or frightened by a sudden shock [Old English *steartlian* < Germanic] —**startler** *n*

startling /stáartling/ *adj* provoking surprise, fright, wonder, or alarm —**startlingly** *adv*

start page *n* the webpage to which a visitor to a website is automatically taken first, or the page to which a user is automatically taken first whenever he or she goes online

startsy CHR plural of **starets**

startup /stáart up/, **start-up** *n* **1.** SOMETHING NEWLY FORMED something that is just beginning operations, e.g. a company **2.** COMMENCEMENT OF SOMETHING the beginning of an activity such as the construction of a building ■ *adj* INVOLVED IN STARTING SOMETHING UP involved in or used for the establishment of a business venture

star turn *n* the most striking or popular item or performer in a show

starvation /staar váysh'n/ *n* **1.** the state of not having enough food, or of losing strength or dying through lack of food **2.** *Ireland, N England, Scotland* the state of feeling extremely cold

starve /staarv/ (**starves, starving, starved**) *v* **1.** *vti* WEAKEN OR DIE BECAUSE OF HUNGER to weaken or die through lack of food, or cause somebody to do this ○ *The besieged city was starved into submission.* **2.** *vi* BE HUNGRY to be very hungry (*informal*) ○ *I'm starving! What's for dinner?* **3.** *vt* DEPRIVE SOMEBODY to deprive somebody or something of something vitally needed ○ *starved of affection* **4.** *vi* NEED to feel deprived of something, or feel a great need or desire for something ○ *starving for a kind word* **5.** *vi Ireland, N England, Scotland* BE

VERY COLD to be feeling extremely cold [Old English *steorfan* 'die' < Germanic, 'be stiff'] —**starver** *n*

starve out *vt* to force an enemy to surrender by making necessary food and supplies inaccessible

starved /staarvd/ *adj* **1.** thin, gaunt, or unhealthy-looking through lack of food **2.** extremely hungry (*informal*)

starveling /staárvling/ *n* a very thin and hungry-looking person or animal (*archaic*)

starving /staárving/ *adj* **1. DYING OF HUNGER** very weak or dying because of hunger **2. HUNGRY** very hungry (*informal*) **3.** *regional* **VERY COLD** extremely cold

REGIONAL NOTE The use of **starving** to mean 'extremely cold' survives in the north of England, Scotland, Ireland, and the Isle of Man. In these areas *starved* is used in the same way.

stash /stash/ *n* **1. HIDDEN STORE** a secret store of something such as money or valuables (*informal*) **2. HIDING PLACE** a secret hiding place (*informal*) **3. DRUGS SECRET STORE OF DRUGS** a store of illegal drugs kept for personal consumption (*slang*) ■ *vt* (**stashes, stashing, stashed**) **1. HIDE SOMETHING** to put something into a secret hidden storage place (*informal*) **2.** *N Am* **PUT SOMETHING AWAY** to put something somewhere, e.g. in a convenient place or where it belongs ○ *We'll eat after we've stashed our gear.* [Late 18C. Origin ?]

stasis /stáyssiss/ *n* **1. MOTIONLESS STATE** a state in which there is neither motion nor development, often resulting from opposing forces balancing each other **2.** MED **STOPPAGE OF FLOW OF BODY FLUIDS** a condition in which body fluids such as blood or the contents of the bowel are prevented from flowing normally through their channels **3.** BIOL **STATE OF NO CHANGE** a state in which there is little or no apparent change in a species of organism over a long period of time. It is most evident in so-called living fossils such as the coelacanth, which have remained unchanged for many millions of years. [Mid-18C. Via modern Latin < Greek, 'standing, stoppage']

stat[1] /stat/ *n* same as **statistic** (senses 1–2) (*informal*) [Mid-20C. Shortening]

stat[2] /stat/, **stat.** *adv* used in prescriptions to indicate that a drug is to be given immediately ■ *adj* urgent ○ *The doctor received a stat page while on call.* [Late 19C. Shortening of Latin *statim* 'immediately']

-stat *suffix* **1.** a device for stabilizing or regulating ○ *humidistat* ○ *rheostat* **2.** a device for focusing something in a single direction ○ *siderostat* **3.** a substance or device that inhibits the growth or flow of something ○ *fungistat* ○ *haemostat* [Via modern Latin *-stata* < Greek *statos* 'standing', *statēs* 'maker of something to stand']

statampere /stat ámpair/ *n* the unit of electrical current in the cgs system formerly in use (*dated*) [Mid-20C. < STATIC]

state /stayt/ *n* **1. MOSTLY AUTONOMOUS REGION OF FEDERAL COUNTRY** an area forming part of a federal country such as the United States or Australia with its own government and legislature and control over most of its own internal affairs **2. COUNTRY** a country or nation with its own sovereign independent government **3. GOVERNMENT** a country's government and those government-controlled institutions that are responsible for its internal administration and its relationships with other countries ○ *state-owned companies* **4. CONDITION** the condition that something or somebody is in ○ *What sort of state was he in after hearing the news?* ○ *a house in a poor state of repair* **5. PHYSICAL STAGE** a growth or developmental stage of an animal or plant **6. FORM** any form or quantifiable condition in which a physical substance can be, depending on its temperature and other circumstances **7. CEREMONIOUS STYLE** a very formal, dignified, or grand way of doing something in which all the appropriate ceremonies are observed **8. NERVOUS, UPSET, OR EXCITED CONDITION** a very nervous, upset, or excited frame of mind or manner of behaving ○ *He was in a state by the time she finally arrived.* ○ *Don't get into a state worrying about money.* **9. BAD PHYSICAL CONDITION** a very untidy or disreputable condition (*informal*) ○ *The house is in such a state that we'll never get it tidy.* ■ *adj* **1. RELATING TO GOVERNMENT** involving or relating to the government of a nation or an autonomous federal

region within a nation ○ *state security* **2. HELD OR RUN BY STATE** owned, operated, or financed by a nation or an autonomous region within a federalized nation ○ *state schools* **3. DONE WITH FULL CEREMONY** involving many grand rituals and ceremonies, especially those appropriate to a head of state ○ *a state banquet* ■ *vt* (**states, stating, stated**) **1. EXPRESS SOMETHING IN WORDS** to express something in spoken or written words, especially to announce something publicly in a deliberate formal way ○ *We have already stated our position on this issue.* **2.** LAW **DECLARE SOMETHING WITH FORCE OF LAW** to declare something officially so that it has the force of a law or regulation ○ *It is expressly stated in your contract that you must not undertake work for another employer.* **3.** MUSIC **PLAY MUSICAL THEME FOR FIRST TIME** to play a musical theme or motif for the first time before it is repeated and developed within a piece of music [12C. Directly or via French < Latin *status* 'way of standing, condition' (as in *status rei publicae* 'condition of the republic')] ◇ **the state of play** a stage reached in a situation or activity

state attorney *n* LAW same as **state's attorney**

state benefit *n* money given by the government to people who do not have enough money to live on

state capitalism *n* an economic system in which the state controls the use of capital and the means of production

statecraft /stáyt kraaft/ *n* the art of governing or managing the affairs of a country well

stated /stáytid/ *adj* **1.** laid down by an official agreement or in a legal document **2.** announced previously, especially in a public medium

stated case *n* LAW same as **case stated**

State Department *n* the department of the United States government that deals with foreign affairs and is headed by a cabinet secretary and staffed by career foreign service officers

state earnings-related pension scheme *n* FIN full form of SERPS

State Enrolled Nurse *n* in the United Kingdom, a nurse certified as competent to carry out many of the functions of a nurse, but who is less qualified than and junior to a State Registered Nurse

statehood /stáyt hŏod/ *n* the status of a state in a federal union, especially in the United States, as opposed to that of a territory or dependency

statehouse /stáyt howss/ (*plural* **-houses** /-howziz/), **Statehouse** *n* a building in which a state legislature convenes in any of the US state capitals

stateless /stáytləss/ *adj* not being a citizen of any country and having no nationality

state line *n* the official boundary between two US states

stately /stáytli/ (**-lier, -liest**) *adj* **1.** characterized by an impressively weighty and dignified but graceful manner **2.** grand and imposing in appearance — **stateliness** *n*

stately home *n* a large and impressive country house, especially one that is owned by a famous or aristocratic family and is open to the public

statement /stáytmənt/ *n* **1. EXPRESSION IN WORDS** the expression in spoken or written words of something such as a fact, intention, or policy, or an instance of this ○ *a statement of intent* **2. SOMETHING SAID** something that somebody says that is not a question or an exclamation and that expresses an idea or facts in definite terms ○ *We were unable to verify the truth of that statement.* **3. SPECIALLY PREPARED PUBLIC ANNOUNCEMENT** a specially prepared announcement or reply that is made public ○ *Has she made a statement to the press?* **4. ACCOUNT OF FACTS** an account of the facts relating to a crime or case given to the police or in a court of law, usually for use as evidence ○ *The police asked me if I wished to make a statement.* **5. WORDLESS EXPRESSION OF IDEA** an expression of an idea, opinion, or concept made in a nonverbal way ○ *Her art is a powerful statement of her political beliefs.* **6.** BANKING **PRINTED RECORD OF BANK ACCOUNT** a printed record of all transactions that have taken place over a period of time in a bank account and of the amount of the holder's current credit or debt **7.** FIN **CUSTOMER'S ACCOUNT** an account issued to a customer showing charges made, payments received, and any balance

owing **8.** EDUC **ASSESSMENT OF CHILD'S SPECIAL EDUCATIONAL NEEDS** an official and legally binding assessment made by a local authority of the help required by a child with special educational needs **9.** MUSIC **FIRST PRESENTATION OF MUSICAL THEME** the first presentation of a theme or idea that is to be developed later in a piece of music **10.** COMPUT **COMPUTER INSTRUCTION** a computer instruction written in a source language ■ *vt* (**-ments, -menting, -mented**) EDUC **DRAW UP STATEMENT FOR CHILD** to draw up an official statement of the special educational needs of a particular child, so that the local education authority will have to make provision for those needs

statement of attainment *n* a programme of the objectives that school students should be able to attain within their own ability range in a subject

statement of case *n* a formal statement of the facts relating to either of the parties involved in a legal case

statement of claim *n* LAW same as **declaration** (sense 5)

Staten Island /státt'n-/ one of the five boroughs of New York City. It has a regular ferry service to Manhattan, and the Verrazano-Narrows Bridge connects it to Brooklyn. It is mainly residential. Population: 378,977 (2002 estimate).

state of affairs *n* a set of circumstances ○ *This regrettable state of affairs cannot be allowed to continue.*

state of concern *n* INTERNAT REL same as **rogue state** (*formal*)

State of Origin *n* in Australia, a match in which state teams play each other and in which the members of each team have been born in the state they represent. The term is often used to refer specifically to the annual rugby league match between New South Wales and Queensland.

state of the art *n* the most advanced level of knowledge and technology currently achieved in any field at any given time —**state-of-the-art** *adj*

state of war *n* **1.** armed conflict between states or other groups, with or without a formal declaration of war **2.** the situation brought about by a declaration of war, with or without the commencement of actual armed conflict, in which special internationally agreed laws apply

state prayers *npl* the prayers for the sovereign, royal family, clergy, and Parliament, said at services in the Anglican Church

stater[1] /stáytər/ *n* an ancient Greek coin in gold or silver [14C. Via late Latin < Greek *statēr* < base of *histanai* 'weigh']

stater[2] /stáytər/, **Stater** *n* somebody who comes from a particular state or type of state, especially in the United States (*usually used in combination*) ○ *Bay Staters are from Massachusetts.* [< STATE]

State Registered Nurse *n* in the United Kingdom, a nurse who has obtained a higher qualification in nursing than a State Enrolled Nurse and is certified as competent to carry out all the functions of a nurse

stateroom /stáyt room, -rōom/ *n* **1.** a large and luxuriously furnished private cabin on a ship or a private sleeping compartment on a train **2.** a large imposing room in a palace or government building, used for large-scale functions and for entertaining important guests

States /stayts/ *npl* **1.** GEOG same as **United States** (*informal*) **2.** the name of the legislative bodies in Jersey, Guernsey, and Alderney in the Channel Islands

state's attorney *n* a US attorney who acts as prosecutor in court cases on behalf of a state

state school *n* a school controlled and financed by a public authority in which education is free

state second pension *n* an additional pension paid by the government to supplement the basic state pension, based on an employee's earnings and National Insurance contributions

state secret *n* a piece of information, usually considered important to national security, that is

supposed to be known only to people whom the state authorizes to know

state services *npl* special forms of service for use in Anglican churches on days of national celebration

state's evidence *n* evidence given for the prosecution in a criminal trial in the United States and other nations, sometimes by one of the accused or by an accomplice to the crime

States General *npl* 1. the legislative assembly of the Netherlands 2. the legislative body in France before 1789, consisting of representatives of the three estates of the realm

stateside /stáyt sīd/ *N Am adv* in or towards the continental United States ■ *adj* relating to, in, or towards the continental United States

statesman /stáytsmən/ (*plural* **-men** /-mən/) *n* 1. a senior politician, especially a man, who plays an important role in government or international affairs 2. a senior politician, especially a man, who is widely respected for integrity and impartial concern for the public good —**statesmanlike** *adj* —**statesmanship** *n*

state socialism *n* a political and economic system in which the state controls major industries and banks and plans its economic and social welfare programmes in order to bring about an egalitarian society —**state socialist** *n*

statesperson /stáyts purss'n/ (*plural* **-persons** or **-people** /-peep'l/) *n* 1. a senior politician who plays an important role in government or international affairs 2. a senior politician who is widely respected for integrity and impartial concern for the public good

states' rights *npl* 1. the powers and rights not granted by the US Constitution to the federal government and not forbidden to the states by the Constitution 2. a political doctrine that advocates the reduction of federal rights and powers and a maximization of those of the US states —**states' righter** *n*

stateswoman /stáyts woŏmən/ (*plural* **-women** /-wimin/) *n* 1. a senior woman politician who plays an important role in government or international affairs 2. a senior woman politician who is widely respected for integrity and impartial concern for the public good

state trooper *n* a member of the highway patrol police of a US state

statewide /stáyt wīd/ *US adj* affecting or happening throughout an entire state ○ *a statewide search for the escaped prisoner* ■ *adv* throughout an entire state

static /státtik/ *adj* 1. MOTIONLESS not moving or changing, or fixed in position 2. PHYS OF FORCES NOT CAUSING MOVEMENT relating to forces, weight, or pressure that act without causing movement 3. PHYS INVOLVING STATICS relating to, involving, or characteristic of statics 4. ELEC INVOLVING STATIONARY ELECTRIC CHARGES relating to, involving, or characteristic of stationary electric charges 5. BROADCAST CAUSED BY ELECTRICAL INTERFERENCE relating to or caused by electrical interference in a radio or television broadcast 6. COMPUT NOT NEEDING TO BE REFRESHED describes a random-access-memory computer chip that retains its contents without having to be refreshed by a central processor ■ *n* 1. BROADCAST ELECTRICAL INTERFERENCE electrical interference in a radio or television broadcast, causing a random crackling noise or disruption of a picture 2. ELEC same as **static electricity** 3. *N Am* OPPOSITION OR INTERFERENCE criticism, opposition, or unwanted interference by somebody else (*informal*) ○ *getting a lot of static from the boss* [Mid-19C. Via modern Latin < Greek *statikos* 'causing to stand' < *statos* 'standing'] —**statically** *adv*

statice /státtissi/ *n* PLANTS same as **sea lavender** [Mid-18C. < modern Latin < Greek *statikos* 'causing to stand' (see STATIC); because it stops the flow of blood]

static electricity *n* a stationary electric charge that builds up on an insulated object such as a capacitor or a thundercloud

static line *n* a rope attached to an aircraft and a parachutist's parachute that automatically opens the parachute

static pressure *n* pressure not caused by motion at a point on the surface of an object moving freely in a flowing fluid

statics /státtiks/ *n* a branch of mechanics that deals with forces and systems in equilibrium (*takes a singular verb*)

static tube *n* a tube used to measure the static pressure present in a moving fluid

statin /státtin/ *n* a drug belonging to a group that reduces cholesterol in the blood

station /stáysh'n/ *n* 1. STOP ON ROUTE a place along a train or bus route where passengers are picked up or set down, often with amenities such as ticket offices, waiting rooms, refreshments, toilets, and facilities for goods and parcels 2. LOCAL BRANCH OF ORGANIZATION a local branch or headquarters of an official organization such as the police force, fire brigade, or ambulance service 3. SPECIALLY EQUIPPED BUILDING a building or group of buildings that provides a particular function or service ○ *a pumping station* 4. BROADCASTING BUILDING a place equipped to make and broadcast radio or television programmes 5. BROADCASTING CHANNEL a television or radio channel 6. USUAL PLACE the place or position where somebody or something is usually to be found or is supposed to be found 7. POSITION FOR PERFORMING TASK a position where somebody performs a task, e.g. in a factory, or the equipment used in performing a task 8. RANK the position somebody holds in society or in an organization in terms of rank 9. *ANZ* SHEEP OR CATTLE FARM a large farm in Australia or New Zealand where sheep or cattle are raised 10. MIL MILITARY POSTING a place where military personnel are sent to carry out duties 11. NAUT PLACE ON SHIP FOR CREW MEMBER a place on board a ship where a crew member carries out duties 12. NAVY PLACE WHERE SHIP IS SENT a place where a naval ship or fleet is sent for a period of duty 13. CIV ENG SURVEYOR'S REFERENCE POINT a fixed point used by surveyors as a reference 14. CHR STATION OF CROSS in Christianity, one of the Stations of the Cross 15. HIST MILITARY OR GOVERNMENT SETTLEMENT IN INDIA a place where military officers or government officials lived in India while it was under British rule 16. *S Asia* SETTLEMENT a town ○ *He's out of station today.* ■ *vt* (**-tions, -tioning, -tioned**) PUT SOMEBODY OR SOMETHING IN PLACE to assign somebody to a particular place, or put something in a particular place (*often passive*) [Mid-16C. Via French < Latin *station-* 'standing still' < *stat-*, past participle of *stare* 'stand']

stationary /stáysh'nəri/ *adj* 1. NOT MOVING not moving, especially at a standstill after being in motion 2. IMMOBILE fixed in position and not able to be moved 3. UNCHANGING not changing 4. STAYING IN ONE PLACE showing a tendency to remain in the same place [15C. Directly or via French < medieval Latin *stationarius* 'motionless, (in classical Latin) of a military station' < Latin *station-* (see STATION)]

stationary bicycle *n* FITNESS same as **exercise bike**

stationary front *n* a weather condition in which the boundary between a cold air mass and a warm air mass is stationary

stationary orbit *n* an orbit around an astronomical object that has the same period as one revolution of the astronomical object. An object in such an orbit appears stationary above the surface.

stationary point *n* a point on a graph at which the tangent to a curve is parallel to either the horizontal or vertical axis. *N Am* term **critical point**

stationary wave *n* PHYS same as **standing wave**

stationer /stáysh'nər/ *n* a person or shop that sells stationery

ORIGIN In medieval Latin, a *stationarius* was originally a 'trader who kept a permanent stall' (as opposed to an itinerant seller) – the word's source, the Latin stem *station-*, meant literally 'standing, keeping still'. Such

permanent shops were comparatively rare in the Middle Ages. Of those that did exist, the commonest were bookshops, licensed by the universities, and so English adopted the Latin term. It has since come down in the world somewhat to 'seller of paper, pens, etc.', a sense first recorded in the mid-17th century, but the earlier application is preserved in the name of the 'Stationers' Company', a London livery company to which booksellers and publishers belong.

stationery /stáysh'nəri/ *n* paper, envelopes, and other things used in writing

station hand *n* *Aus* a worker on a large sheep or cattle farm

station house *n* *N Am* a building housing a police department or precinct office, or a fire department

station manager *n* *ANZ* somebody who runs a large sheep or cattle farm

stationmaster /stáysh'n maastər/ (*plural* **-tionmasters** or **station managers**) *n* somebody whose job is to oversee the running of a railway station

Stations of the Cross *npl* 1. a series of 14 images around the inside of a Roman Catholic church, each representing a stage in Jesus Christ's road to Calvary 2. a Roman Catholic devotion in which a prayer is said before each of the Stations of the Cross

station stop *n* a railway station at which a particular train stops to set down or pick up passengers ○ *Reading is your next station stop.*

station-to-station *N Am* (*dated*) *adj* charged from the time somebody answers the telephone ■ *adv* by a station-to-station telephone call

station wagon *n* *ANZ, N Am* a car with an extended area behind the rear seats that provides extra seating or carrying capacity, usually with a tailgate. *UK* term **estate car** [Because originally a covered carriage for transporting passengers to and from train stations]

statism /stáytizəm/ *n* the theory, or its practice, that economic and political power should be controlled by a central government leaving regional government and the individual with relatively little say in political matters

statist /stáytist/ *n* an advocate, believer in, or practitioner of statism ■ *adj* belonging or relating to, or characteristic of, statism

statistic /stə tístik/ *n* 1. ELEMENT OF DATA a single element of data from a collection 2. NUMERICAL VALUE OR FUNCTION a numerical value or function, e.g. a mean or standard deviation, used to describe a sample or population 3. PIECE OF INFORMATION somebody or something treated as a piece of data or information [Late 19C. Back-formation < STATISTICS] —**statistical** *adj* —**statistically** *adv*

statistical mechanics *n* the branch of physics that analyses macroscopic systems by applying statistical principles to their microscopic constituents (*takes a singular verb*)

statistics /stə tístiks/ *n* a branch of mathematics that deals with the analysis and interpretation of numerical data in terms of samples and populations (*takes a singular verb*) ■ *npl* a collection of numerical data (*takes a plural verb*) ○ *this month's sales statistics* [Late 18C. < German *Statistik* < Latin *status* (see STATE)] —**statistician** /státti stísh'n/ *n*

stative /stáytiv/ *adj* describes a verb that deals with states, e.g. 'know' or 'own', as opposed to one that deals with actions, e.g. 'listen', 'talk', or 'go' ■ *n* a verb dealing with states not actions [Mid-17C. < Latin *stativus* < *stat-* (see STATION)]

~~statment~~ incorrect spelling of **statement**

stato- *prefix* 1. balance, equilibrium ○ *statoscope* 2. resting ○ *statoblast* [< Greek *statos* 'standing' < Indo-European, 'to stand']

statoblast /státtō blast/ *n* a chitin-encased body that serves as a means of asexual reproduction for freshwater bryozoans. It can withstand climatic extremes and prolonged dormancy.

statocyst /státtō sist/ *n* a fluid-filled organ of balance in some invertebrates such as the lobster. It

contains suspended bony granules that, along with sensory cells, help it to determine its position.

statolith /státtō lith/ *n* **1.** any tiny bony granule that is suspended in fluid within a statocyst and whose movement is detected by sensory hairs that determine an invertebrate's position **2.** a starch grain or other particle inside plant cells that moves in response to gravity and is thought to influence the way shoots or other organs grow —**statolithic** /státtō líthik/ *adj*

stator /stáytər/ *n* a stationary part in a machine, e.g. a motor or generator, about which or in which a rotor rotates [Late 19C. < modern Latin, 'somebody or something that stands' < Latin *stat-* (see STATION)]

statoscope /státtō skōp/ *n* a sensitive aneroid barometer used to detect small changes in atmospheric pressure, often used in aircraft to determine changes in altitude

statuary /státtyoo əri/ *n* **1.** statues considered collectively **2.** the art and techniques of making statues [Mid-16C. < Latin *statuarius* 'of a statue' < *statua* (see STATUE)]

statue /státtyoo/ *n* a three-dimensional image of a human being or animal that is sculpted, modelled, cast, or carved [14C. Via French < Latin *statua* < *statuere* 'set up' < *status* (see STATE)]

Statue of Liberty

Statue of Liberty *n* a huge statue of a woman holding a torch and a book inscribed '4 July 1776'. It stands in New York Harbor. At 46 m/152 ft high, it is one of the tallest statues in the world. A gift from France to the United States, it was unveiled in 1886.

statuesque /státtyoo ésk/ *adj* like a statue, especially in having classical beauty, elegance, or proportions —**statuesquely** *adv*

statuette /státtyoo ét/ *n* a small, usually portable statue

stature /státchər/ *n* **1.** the standing height of somebody or something **2.** somebody's standing or level of achievement [13C. Via French < Latin *statura* < *stat-* (see STATION)]

status /stáytəss/ *n* **1.** RANK the relative position or standing of somebody or something in a society or other group **2.** PRESTIGE high rank or standing, especially in a community, workforce, or organization **3.** CONDITION a condition that is subject to change ○ *What's the current status of the investigation?* **4.** LAW LEGAL STANDING somebody's standing in terms of the law [Late 18C. < Latin (see STATE)]

status bar *n* a bar on a computer screen that displays information about an application being used

Status Indian *n* Can a member of an indigenous people whom the federal government recognizes as having special rights and privileges, especially residence on a reserve

status quo /-kwṓ/ *n* the condition or state of affairs that currently exists [< Latin, 'the state in which']

status symbol *n* a possession that is a sign of wealth or prestige

statute /státtyoot/ *n* **1.** a law established by a legislative body, e.g. an Act of Parliament **2.** a permanent established rule or law, especially one involved in the running of a company or other organization [13C. Via French < late Latin *statutum* 'something set up' < *statuere* (see STATUE)] —**statutable** *adj*

statute book *n* a record of the acts that have been passed by a legislature and remain in force

statute law *n* the body of law that has been enacted by a legislature, or a specific law so enacted

statute mile *n* MEASURE same as **mile** (sense 1) [Because it is fixed by law]

statute of limitations *n* a statute that lays down the time within which legal proceedings must be started

statutory /státtyootəri/ *adj* **1.** CONTROLLED BY STATUTE regulated or imposed by statute **2.** OF STATUTE relating to a statute **3.** SUBJECT TO PENALTY covered by a statute, and subject to the penalty laid down by that statute —**statutorily** *adv*

statutory declaration *n* a declaration that somebody makes on oath according to statute

statutory order *n* a statute that augments an existing statute

statutory rape *n* under US law, the offence of having sexual relations with somebody who has not reached the legal age of consent

statvolt /stat vólt/ *n* the unit of electrical potential difference in the cgs system formerly in use (*dated*) [Mid-20C. < STATIC]

Stauffenberg /stówfən burg, shtówfən berk/, **Claus Schenk, Count** (1907–44) German army officer. He was the leader of the unsuccessful July Plot (1944) to assassinate Adolf Hitler.

staunch[1] /stawnch/ *adj* **1.** showing loyalty, dependability, and enthusiasm **2.** solidly built or substantial [15C. < Anglo-Norman *estaunche* < Old French *estanchier* 'to stop' (see STAUNCH[2])] —**staunchly** *adv* —**staunchness** *n*

staunch[2] /stawnch/ (**staunches, staunching, staunched**), **stanch** /staanch/ (**stanches, stanching, stanched**) *v* **1.** *vti* STOP LIQUID FLOW to stop the flow of a liquid, particularly blood, or be stopped from flowing **2.** *vt* STOP WOUND BLEEDING to stop a wound from bleeding or exuding pus **3.** *vt* ASSUAGE SOMETHING to assuage or allay something bad [14C. < Old French *estanchier* < Latin *stant-*, present participle of *stare* (see STATION)] —**staunchable** *adj* —**stauncher** *n*

staup /stawp/ *n* regional an offensive term that deliberately insults somebody's intelligence

REGIONAL NOTE See **addle-headed**.

staurolite /stáwrə līt/ *n* a reddish-brown or black aluminosilicate mineral containing iron and magnesium that often occurs in cross-shaped crystals. Source: metamorphic rocks. Use: gems. [Late 18C. < Greek *stauros* 'cross'; because it often forms twin crystals in the shape of a cross] —**staurolitic** /stáwrə líttik/ *adj*

Stavanger /stə vánggər/ city and port in southwestern Norway. Population: 108,437 (2001).

stave /stayv/ *n* **1.** BAND OF WOOD a long thin piece of wood, one of several fixed together to make the hull of a boat or the body of a container such as a barrel **2.** RUNG OR BAR OF WOOD a bar or strip of wood or other material, especially one that forms a rung in a ladder or a crosspiece between the legs of a chair **3.** MUSIC same as **staff**[1] *n* (sense 9) **4.** LITERAT POETRY STANZA a stanza of poetry **5.** *Scotland* SPRAIN an injury to a part of the body such as a toe, finger, or elbow caused by spraining or twisting it ■ *v* (**staves, staving, staved** or **stove** /stōv/, **staved**) **1.** *vti* BREAK STAVES to break a barrel, a tub, or a boat's hull by smashing its staves in, or break by having the staves smashed in **2.** *vti* BREAK HOLE IN OBJECT to smash a hole in the side of a boat or a barrel, or be smashed in this way **3.** *vt* BREAK SOMETHING INWARDS to strike something such as a door or a rib and make it break inwards **4.** *vt* FIT STAVE TO SOMETHING to fit a stave to something such as a chair or a ladder **5.** *vt* *Scotland* SPRAIN PART OF BODY to injure a part of the body such as a toe, finger, or elbow by spraining it or twisting it [14C. Back-formation < *staves*, plural of STAFF[1]]

stave off *vt* to avoid or prevent something unpleasant, often only temporarily ○ *staved off hunger*

staves plural of **staff**[1] *n* (senses 5–6, 9–10), **stave**

stavesacre /stáyvz aykər/ *n* **1.** the poisonous seeds of a species of delphinium. Use: in herbal medicine as external parasiticide; formerly, to cause vomiting. **2.** a delphinium with poisonous seeds used in herbal medicine. Flowers: purple. Native to: Europe, Asia. Latin name: *Delphinium staphisagria*. [14C. Alteration of Latin *staphisagria* < Greek *staphis agria* 'wild raisin']

Stavropol /stávrəpol/ city in southwestern Russia. It is a centre for transport and heavy industry. Population: 418,112 (1995).

Stawell Gift /stawl-/ *n* an annual 120 m/131 yd footrace held in Stawell, Victoria, Australia. It first took place in 1878 and is claimed to be the oldest event of its kind in the world. [Held at Easter, and begun as an 'Easter gift']

stay[1] /stay/ *v* (**stays, staying, stayed**) **1.** *vi* REMAIN to continue to be in the same place, condition, or state ○ *Stay there and wait for me.* ○ *Try to stay alert.* **2.** *vi* RESIDE FOR SHORT TIME to spend some time or live temporarily in a place ○ *We've stayed at some beautiful hotels.* **3.** *vi* *Scotland* RESIDE to live permanently in a place ○ *Where do you stay?* **4.** *vti* PASS SOME TIME to spend a particular length of time at a place or in doing something ○ *Alicia stayed too long in the sun and got burnt.* **5.** *vi* REMAIN IN CONTENTION to keep up with somebody or something, especially by going along with the leader or leaders of a race **6.** *vt* PERSEVERE WITH SOMETHING to continue to do something, especially to support something such as an idea, plan, or project ○ *You should stay the course until the task is completed.* **7.** *vt* UNDERGO SOMETHING to endure, put up with, or survive something, especially something trying, difficult, or unpleasant ○ *The runner had trouble staying the final mile.* **8.** *vi* BE AROUND FOR SOMETHING to be present long enough to take part in something, especially a meal ○ *It's so good to see you – I hope you can stay for tea?* **9.** *vi* LINGER to linger or wait somewhere ○ *Stay a moment.* **10.** *vt* STOP SOMETHING to put a stop to something ○ *They put sandbags across the doorway to try to stay the floodwater.* **11.** *vt* POSTPONE OR HINDER to postpone, hinder, or delay something ○ *stay a trip until the weather improves* **12.** *vt* ALLEVIATE SOMETHING IN SHORT TERM to relieve or ease temporarily something such as hunger, thirst, or other physical need **13.** *vt* RESTRAIN SOMETHING to hold something back or in check **14.** *vt* LAW SUSPEND LEGAL PROCESS TEMPORARILY to suspend a judgment or proceedings temporarily **15.** *vi* GAMBLING STAKE SAME AMOUNT to stake the same amount of money on a poker hand as the person who last raised the stake ■ *n* **1.** A VISIT a short period of temporarily residing away from home, especially as a visitor or guest ○ *planning a weekend stay with friends in the country* ○ *booked an overnight stay at a small hotel* **2.** CURB OR CHECK something that acts to stop or delay something negative happening **3.** LAW TEMPORARY HALT a temporary halt in legal proceedings, or a period during which a judgment may not be carried out ○ *a stay of execution* [15C. Via Old French *ester* < Latin *stare* 'to stand'] ◇ **stay put** to remain in a place or position

stay on *vi* to remain somewhere after others have left or after the expected time of leaving

stay out *vi* to be away from home, usually for or until a specific time

stay up *vi* to remain awake and not go to bed at the normal time

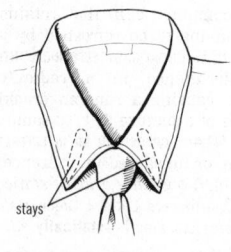
stays

stay

stay[2] /stay/ *n* **1.** A SUPPORT something that gives extra support to something else, e.g. a brace, prop, or buttress **2.** CLOTHING STIFFENER a small bone or piece of metal or plastic used as a stiffener in corsets and girdles and in shirt collars ■ **stays** *npl* STIFFENED CORSET a corset that is stiffened with strips of whalebone,

metal, or other material ■ *vt* (**stays, staying, stayed**) **1. COMFORT SOMEBODY** to give somebody comfort or strength (*formal*) **2. SUPPORT SOMETHING** to provide support for something (*archaic*) [Early 16C. < Old French *estaye* < Germanic]

stay[3] /stay/ *n* **1.** NAUT **ROPE SUPPORTING MAST** a rope or cable used to support a mast **2.** CONSTR **STEADYING ROPE** a rope used for steadying or guiding something, especially on a chimney or flagpole ■ *vti* (**stays, staying, stayed**) NAUT, SAILING **TURN ONTO OTHER TACK** to turn onto the other tack, or make a vessel turn onto the other tack [Old English *stæg* < Indo-European, 'make stand']

stay-at-home *adj* preferring a quiet domestic routine to travelling or to leading a busy social life —**stay-at-home** *n*

stay away order *n UK* a court order that commands somebody to have no contact or communication with another person. ANZ, N Am term **restraining order**

stayer /stáy ər/ *n* **1. SOMEBODY WHO STAYS** somebody or something that stays **2. SOMEBODY PERSISTENT** somebody with much stamina and persistence **3. HORSE OR DOG THAT RACES PERSISTENTLY** a racehorse or greyhound that has stamina and competes to the end of a race, even under difficult conditions

staying power /stáy ing-/ *n* the ability to keep doing something or keep trying, especially over long periods of time

staysail /stáy sayl/; *nautical* /stáyss'l/ *n* an extra sail hoisted on one of the stays of a sailing vessel

stay stitching *n* an extra line of stitches reinforcing a seam, used to prevent stretching and fraying

stbd *abbr* NAUT starboard

std *abbr* standard

STD *abbr* **1.** MED sexually transmitted disease **2.** TELECOM subscriber trunk dialling

Ste *abbr* CHR woman saint [French *Sainte*]

stead /sted/ *n* the position or role of somebody or something else [Old English *stede* 'place' < Indo-European, 'to stand'] ◇ **stand somebody in good stead** to be useful to somebody, especially at a later time

Stead /sted/, **Christina** (1902–83) Australian writer. Her short stories and novels include *The Man Who Loved Children* (1940). Full name **Stead, Christina Ellen**

> 'A mother! What are we worth really? They all grow up whether you look after them or not.'
> [Christina Stead, *The Man Who Loved Children*; 1940]

Stead, C. K. (*b.* 1932) New Zealand writer of several collections of poetry and criticism and the novel *Smith's Dream* (1971). Full name **Stead, Christian Karlson**

steadfast /stéd faast/, **stedfast** *adj* **1.** firm and unwavering in purpose, loyalty, or resolve **2.** firmly fixed or constant [Pre-12C. < STEAD + FAST[1] 'fixed'] —**steadfastly** *adv* —**steadfastness** *n*

steading /stédding/ *n* **1.** a farm, especially a small one **2.** a farm outbuilding or all of the outbuildings of a farm [15C. < STEAD]

steady /stéddi/ *adj* (**-ier, -iest**) **1. STABLE** fixed, stable, or not easily moved ○ *Can you hold the ladder so that it's steady?* **2. STAYING SAME** showing no tendency to change or fluctuate ○ *Oil prices are steady at the moment.* **3. CONSTANT OR CONTINUOUS** coming in a regular nonstop flow ○ *a steady stream of traffic* **4. REGULAR OR ORDINARY** reliable, but often rather dull or routine ○ *a steady job* **5. UNRUFFLED** not easily upset or excited ○ *It's a job that requires steady nerves.* **6. STAID OR SERIOUS** having a serious and calm attitude or character ○ *Joe was always a steady kind of guy.* **7. REGULAR OR INDUSTRIOUS** regular, habitual, or industrious ○ *a steady worker* ■ *adv* (**-ier, -iest**) **CONTINUOUSLY** in a constant or continuous way (*informal*) ■ *vti* (**-ies, -ying, -ied**) **BECOME OR MAKE SOMETHING STEADY** to become steady, or make something steady ■ *n* (*plural* **-ies**) **SOMEBODY DATED REGULARLY** somebody with whom a specific person regularly goes on dates (*informal*) ■ *interj* **1. BE CAREFUL** used to tell somebody to be careful or be calm **2.** NAUT **KEEP TO PRESENT COURSE** used to tell somebody steering a ship or boat to keep to the present course [Mid-13C. < STEAD] —**steadier** *n* —**steadily** *adv* —**steadiness** *n* ◇ **go steady** to go out together regularly as a couple (*informal*)

steady state *n* a condition of stability or equilibrium in a system, e.g. in the energy levels of an atom, in which there is little or no change over time

steady-state theory *n* a theory in astronomy that the universe has always existed at a uniform density that is maintained because new matter is created continuously as the universe expands

steak /stayk/ *n* **1. CUT OF BEEF** a thick slice of beef from a lean part of a cow **2. PIECE OF MEAT OR FISH** a piece of a meat other than beef, e.g. pork, gammon, venison, or veal, or of a large fish such as cod, salmon, or tuna **3. SERVING OF MINCED MEAT** minced meat formed into a solid shape, usually a flat roundish shape, and served grilled, fried, or barbecued [15C. < Old Norse *steik* 'meat roasted on a spit']

steakhouse /stáyk howss/ (*plural* **-houses** /-howziz/) *n* a restaurant that specializes in serving beef steaks

steak knife *n* a table knife with a sharp, usually serrated blade, suitable for cutting steak

steak tartare /-taar taár/ *n* freshly minced beef that is mixed with raw egg and chopped onions and served uncooked [*Tartare* < French, 'Tatar']

steal /steel/ *v* (**steals, stealing, stole** /stōl/, **stolen** /stōlən/) **1.** *vti* **TAKE SOMETHING UNLAWFULLY** to take something that belongs to somebody else, illegally or without the owner's permission **2.** *vt* **TAKE SOMETHING FURTIVELY** to take or get something secretly, surreptitiously, or through trickery ○ *steal a glance* **3.** *vt* **DISHONESTLY PRESENT SOMEBODY'S WORK AS YOURS** to take something that somebody else has created, especially ideas, theories, or a piece of writing, and present it as your own **4.** *vi* **SNEAK** to move quietly, especially in the hope of not been seen or caught **5.** *vi* **PASS UNNOTICED** to pass or move without being noticed (*literary*) ○ *Dawn was stealing over the mountaintops.* **6.** *vt* **SUCCEED AT SOMETHING UNEXPECTEDLY** to win or succeed at something unexpectedly, luckily, or dishonestly at the expense of another or others (*informal*) **7.** *vti* BASEBALL **GAIN BASE WITHOUT HIT** in baseball, to gain a base by running without the ball being hit by the batter and in the absence of an error by the fielding team ■ *n* **1. ACT OF STEALING** an act of stealing something **2. BARGAIN** something that does not cost very much or that costs a lot less than would be expected (*informal*) **3.** BASEBALL **STOLEN BASE** in baseball, a stolen base [Old English *stelan* < Germanic] —**stealer** *n*

SPELLCHECK steal or **steel**? Do not confuse the spelling of ***steal*** and ***steel***, which sound similar. ***Steal*** is chiefly used as a verb, meaning 'take illegally or without permission' or 'move quietly', as in *steal a car, steal past the door.* ***Steel*** can be used as a noun, denoting a hard strong metal, an alloy of iron (as in *stainless steel*), or as a verb, meaning particularly 'make unfeeling or tough enough': *He steeled himself for the blow.*

SYNONYMS ***steal, pinch, nick, filch, purloin, pilfer, embezzle, misappropriate***

CORE MEANING: to take property unlawfully

steal to take something that belongs to somebody else, illegally or without the owner's permission ○ *Last year, 22,000 cars were stolen in that region.* ○ *a robbery in which more than $20 million was stolen from a Geneva bank* **pinch** (*informal*) to steal something or take something without permission ○ *Who's pinched my pen?* ○ *I had my purse pinched on the bus.* **nick** (*slang*) to steal something ○ *He had some stuff nicked last Saturday – an expensive ski jacket and a pair of trainers.* ○ *You're crazy, giving her your purse – she's probably nicking your cash card this very minute.* **filch** (*informal*) to steal something opportunistically, usually a small item or something of little value ○ *He filched the wood he needed from railway sidings.* ○ *A navy diver has admitted filching money from a victim of the sunken ferry.* **purloin** (*formal or humorous*) to steal something ○ *Stealing from employers was widespread – workers purloined wire among other things* ○ *The former inspector told how he had once caught a member of his team purloining a top-secret document.* **pilfer** to steal small items of little value, especially habitually ○ *accused the children of pilfering fruit from her orchard* ○ *It is estimated that 25% of food sent as aid to the camps is being pilfered and sold on the black market.* **embezzle** to take for personal use money or property that has been given on trust by others, without their knowledge. ○ *She denies embezzling thousands of dollars while she was company treasurer.* ○ *The former attorney general had embezzled public funds and should be extradited to face the charge, US prosecutors argued yesterday.* **misappropriate** to take something, especially money, dishonestly or in order to use it for an improper or illegal purpose ○ *The chief executive denied any wrongdoing and said no money had been misappropriated.* ○ *The defendant was found guilty of misappropriating public funds.*

stealth /stelth/ *n* **1. ACTION TO AVOID DETECTION** the action of doing something slowly, quietly, and covertly, in order to avoid detection **2. FURTIVENESS** secretive, dishonest, or cunning behaviour or actions ■ *adj* **1.** MIL **ALMOST UNDETECTABLE BY RADAR** used to describe aircraft whose design incorporates technology and materials that minimize the likelihood of detection by enemy radar ○ *a stealth fighter* **2. SECRET** done in a highly secret way so as to be unnoticed (*slang*) ○ *conducted a stealth fundraising campaign* [13C. < assumed Old English *stǣlþ* < Germanic] —**stealthful** *adj*

stealth tax *n* a new tax or a tax increase that is introduced largely unnoticed, or an additional charge that is effectively a tax though not officially classed as one

stealth tower *n* a wireless telecommunications tower camouflaged so as to be ecologically friendly and aesthetic, e.g. one configured as a pine tree, and intended to soften the environmental and visual impact of proliferating antennae sites (*informal*)

stealthy /stélthi/ (**-ier, -iest**) *adj* **1.** done quietly, slowly, and cautiously in order to escape notice **2.** secretive, furtive, or cunning —**stealthily** *adv* —**stealthiness** *n*

SYNONYMS See ***secret***.

steam /steem/ *n* **1. VAPORIZED WATER** the vapour that is formed when water is boiled **2. MIST OF WATER VAPOUR** the visible mist that forms when water vapour condenses in the air **3. VAPOUR** a visible form of vapour of any kind **4. POWER** stamina, strength, or speed (*informal*) ○ *running out of steam* ■ *adj* **1. DRIVEN BY STEAM** driven or powered by steam ○ *a steam turbine* **2. USING STEAM** using steam to do something ○ *a steam iron* **3. OUTMODED** old-fashioned or obsolete, like the steam engine (*humorous*) ■ *v* (**steams, steaming, steamed**) **1.** *vi* **PRODUCE STEAM** to produce steam, or be produced as steam **2.** *vti* **COOK IN STEAM** to cook something in the steam of boiling water, or be cooked in this way **3.** *vi* **MOVE BY STEAM** to move or be powered by steam **4.** *vi* **MOVE FAST** to move very quickly and energetically (*informal*) **5.** *vi* **GENERATE STEAM** to generate steam (*refers especially to boilers*) **6.** *vi* **GET ANGRY** to be or become very angry (*informal*) ○ *Neighbours are steaming about the noisy late-night flights.* [Old English *stēam* < Germanic] ◇ **get up steam** to gather together enough energy and speed to do something (*informal*)

steam up *vti* to become clouded with condensation, or make something become clouded with condensation

steam bath *n* a steam-filled room or compartment that people go into to relax and refresh themselves through sweating

steamboat /steém bōt/ *n* a boat with an engine powered by steam

steam chest *n* a compartment in a steam engine from which steam is supplied to the valve of the engine

steam distillation *n* the process of separating or purifying a liquid by passing steam through it

steamed /steemd/ *adj* **1.** cooked by steaming ○ *steamed rice* **2.** very angry or upset (*informal*)

steam engine *n* an engine powered by steam, typically incorporating a flywheel attached to a reciprocating piston that in turn is driven by the expansive action of steam generated in a boiler

steamer /steémər/ *n* **1. BOAT POWERED BY STEAM** a boat or ship that is powered by a steam engine or engines **2. PAN FOR STEAMING FOOD** a covered pan with a perforated base that fits on top of a saucepan of boiling water so that the food inside is cooked by steam **3.**

CONTAINER FOR STEAMING WOOD a container in which wood is treated with steam to make it pliable **4.** MUGGER a member of a large group of youths who go to crowded areas and carry out mass mugging (*slang*) **5.** *N Am* FOOD SOFT-SHELL CLAM a soft-shell clam, especially when steamed and eaten **6.** DIVING WET SUIT FOR COLD CONDITIONS a wet suit with long sleeves and legs, for use in cold conditions (*slang*)

steamer chair *n* a collapsible adjustable outdoor chair made of wooden slats, usually with a removable cushion and used around a swimming pool, on a patio, or in a garden

steamer rug *n US* a warm blanket that can be put over the knees and legs for warmth, used especially by passengers sitting on the deck of a ship

steamer trunk *n* a traveller's trunk, especially one that is shallow enough to fit underneath a bunk on a ship

steam-generating heavy-water reactor *n* a nuclear reactor that uses ordinary water as the coolant and heavy water as the moderator

steaming /steéming/ *adj* **1.** EMITTING STEAM emitting steam or filled with steam **2.** VERY ANGRY very angry or upset (*informal*) **3.** VERY HOT extremely hot (*informal*) ○ *We were steaming by the end of the match.* **4.** DRUNK extremely drunk (*slang*) ■ *n* MASS MUGGING mass mugging carried out by a large group of youths in crowded areas such as busy streets or shopping malls, or on trains, buses, or the underground. The group quickly and systematically grab handbags, wallets, watches, and briefcases, and other valuables. (*slang*)

steam iron *n* an electric iron with a chamber for water. As the iron heats up, steam is produced and channelled through holes in the face of the iron to dampen the laundry.

steam jacket *n* a covering or casing surrounding the cylinders and heads of a steam engine to keep the surfaces hot and dry

steam organ *n UK* a musical organ with whistles sounded by steam. It is played manually by keyboard or automatically using a punched card and it used to be a popular fairground attraction. ANZ, N Am term **calliope**

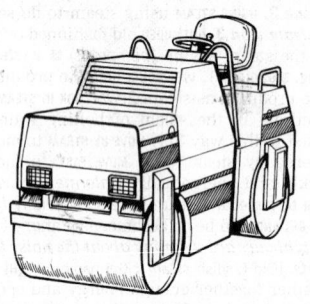

steamroller

steamroller /steém rôlər/ *n* **1.** VEHICLE FOR FLATTENING ROADS a specialized vehicle, originally steam-powered, with large heavy rollers for wheels, designed to flatten and compress newly laid road surfaces **2.** CRUSHING FORCE somebody or something that is a powerful driving force, often crushing or dismissing anybody or anything that might stand in the way ■ *v* (-lers, -lering, -lered) **1.** *also* **steamroll** /steém rôl/ (*3rd person present singular* -rolls, *present participle* -rolling, *past and past participle* -rolled) *vt* FLATTEN ROAD to flatten and compress a newly laid road surface using a steamroller **2.** *also* **steamroll** (*3rd person present singular* -rolls, *present participle* -rolling, *past and past participle* -rolled) *vt* RUTHLESSLY CRUSH SOMEBODY OR SOMETHING to crush or dismiss anybody or anything that might stand in the way ○ *steamroller everyone else's ideas* **3.** *also* **steamroll** (*3rd person present singular* -rolls, *present participle* -rolling, *past and past participle* -rolled) *vt* COMPEL SOMEBODY to force somebody to do something ○ *She felt the company had steamrollered her into taking early retirement.* **4.** *also* **steamroll** (*3rd person present singular* -rolls, *present participle* -rolling, *past and past participle* -rolled) *vt* ADVANCE SOMETHING to move

something forward in an aggressive way that does not tolerate opposition ○ *The legislation was steamrollered through Congress.* **5.** *also* **steamroll** (*3rd person present singular* -rolls, *present participle* -rolling, *past and past participle* -rolled) *vi* PROCEED FORCEFULLY to move or proceed with overwhelming force ○ *Product placement in films has steamrollered ahead.*

steam room *n* a room with a steam bath in it, or a room that can be filled with steam and used as a steam bath

steamship /steém ship/ *n* a ship with an engine powered by steam

steam shovel *n* a large steam-powered excavating machine, especially an earthmover that has a bucket on a boom fixed to a jib that can be rotated

steamtight /steém tīt/ *adj* designed or sealed so that steam cannot escape

steam turbine *n* a turbine that uses the heat energy of steam to generate the power for mechanical rotation

steamy /steémi/ (-ier, -iest) *adj* **1.** full of, affected by, or like steam **2.** involving or featuring sexual behaviour or sexual passion (*informal*) —**steamily** *adv* —**steaminess** *n*

steapsin /sti ápsin/ *n* a pancreatic lipase that aids the digestion of fats [Late 19C. Blend of Greek *stear* 'solid fat, tallow' + PEPSIN]

stearate /steér ayt/ *n* a salt or ester of stearic acid [Mid-19C. < Greek *stear* 'solid fat, tallow']

stearic /sti árrik/ *adj* **1.** relating to, containing, or typical of stearin or fat **2.** about, derived from, or containing stearic acid [Mid-19C. < Greek *stear* 'solid fat, tallow']

stearic acid *n* a colourless odourless waxy crystalline fatty acid. Source: animal tallow, vegetable oils. Use: manufacture of candles, cosmetics, soaps, lubricants, medicines. Formula: $C_{18}H_{36}O_2$.

stearin /steérin/, **stearine** /steéreen/ *n* **1.** a colourless ester of glycerol and stearic acid. Use: manufacture of soap, candles, adhesives. **2.** BIOCHEM same as **stearic acid 3.** a waxy solid mixture of stearic and palmitic acids [Early 19C. < Greek *stear* 'solid fat, tallow']

steatite /steé ə tīt/ *n* MINERALS same as **soapstone** [Mid-18C. Via Latin < Greek *steatitis (lithos)* 'tallow-like (stone)' < *stear* 'solid fat, tallow'] —**steatitic** /steé ə títtik/ *adj*

steato- *prefix* fat ○ *steatopygia* [< Greek *steat-*, stem of *stear* 'solid fat, tallow']

steatopygia /steé ətō píjji ə, -píji ə/ *n* an accumulation of fat on the buttocks [Early 19C. < STEATO- + Greek *pugē* 'buttocks'] —**steatopygous** /steé ətō pīgəss, steé ə tóppigəss/ *adj*

steatorrhea *n* MED US spelling of **steatorrhoea**

steatorrhoea /steé ətə reé ə/ *n* an unusual condition in which an excess of fat is present in stools

steed /steed/ *n* a horse, especially a lively spirited one (*literary*) [Old English *stēda* 'stallion' < Germanic]

steel! /steel/ *n* **1.** STRONG ALLOY OF IRON AND CARBON a strong alloy of iron containing up to 1.5 per cent carbon along with small amounts of other elements such as manganese, chromium, and nickel **2.** SOMETHING MADE OF STEEL something made of steel, e.g. a weapon **3.** KNIFE SHARPENER a steel rod, often with a handle, that knives are drawn back and forward along in order to sharpen them **4.** TOUGHNESS determination, toughness, or great strength of character ■ *adj* STRONG OR HARD like steel, especially in strength or hardness ■ *vt* (steels, steeling, steeled) **1.** STRENGTHEN SOMEBODY FOR ORDEAL to make somebody unfeeling or tough enough to withstand a setback or trial ○ *steeled myself for the news* **2.** TREAT SOMETHING WITH STEEL to coat, plate, edge, or point something with steel [Old English *stēli* < Indo-European, 'stand, be solid']

SPELLCHECK See *steal*.

steel band *n* a group of musicians who play steel drums and often specialize in calypsos

steel-blue *adj* of a cold greyish-blue colour —**steel blue** *n*

steel drum *n* a Caribbean percussion instrument made by hammering an oil drum into a concave shape with flattened areas that make musical notes when struck

Steele, Mount /steel/ peak in the St Elias Range, in southwestern Yukon Territory, Canada. Height: 5,073 m/16,644 ft.

Steele /steel/, **Sir Richard** (1672–1729) English playwright and essayist who founded and contributed to the influential journals the *Tatler* (1709–11) and the *Spectator* (1711–12)

steel engraving *n* **1.** a print made from an engraved steel plate **2.** the art, technique, or process of engraving on a steel plate

steel-grey *adj* of a dark bluish-grey colour —**steel grey** *n*

steel guitar *n* a fretless guitar played on a horizontal stand with a pick and a movable metal slide

steelhead /steel hed/ (*plural* -heads or *same*) *n* an anadromous rainbow trout with a silver coloration, popular for sport fishing. Native to: North Pacific Ocean.

steel pan *n* MUSIC same as **steel drum**

steel wool *n* thin strands of steel tangled together to form an abrasive mass, used for cleaning and polishing

steelwork /steel wurk/ *n* something made from steel, especially a structural framework

steelworker /steel wurkər/ *n* somebody whose job is making steel in a steelworks

steelworks /steel wurks/ (*plural same*) *n* a factory where steel is made

steely /steéli/ *adj* **1.** like steel, especially in colour or hardness, or in being tough or determined **2.** made of steel (*dated or literary*) —**steeliness** *n*

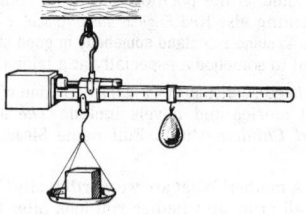

steelyard

steelyard /steel yaard/ *n* a portable balance for weighing objects. The object is hung on a hook and a counterweight is moved along a scaled arm to find the weight. [Mid-17C. < STEEL + YARD[1] 'rod, spar']

Steen /stayn/, **Jan** (1626–79) Dutch painter. His genre scenes, particularly on the theme of eating and drinking, often illustrate proverbs or have an allegorical element. Full name **Steen, Jan Havickszoon**

steenbok /steen bok/ (*plural* -boks or *same*), **steinbok** /stīn-/ *n* a small slender antelope with short straight horns, long legs, and a reddish-brown coat. Native to: grasslands of southern Africa. Latin name: *Raphicerus campestris*. [Late 18C. Via Afrikaans < Middle Dutch *steenboc* 'stone buck']

steenbras /steen brass, -braass/ (*plural same*) *n S Africa* an edible fish belonging to a family of fishes that resemble breams. Native to: shallow seas around southern Africa. Family: Sparidae. [Early 17C. < Afrikaans < Dutch *steen* 'stone' + *brasen* 'bream']

steep[1] /steep/ *adj* **1.** SLOPING SHARPLY sloping very sharply, often to the extent of being almost vertical **2.** RAPID OR HUGE faster or greater than is usual or expected ○ *a steep decline in demand* **3.** EXCESSIVE unreasonably or excessively high, especially in cost (*informal*) **4.** UNREASONABLE unreasonable, unfair, or expecting too much (*informal*) **5.** TAXING very ambitious or difficult [Old English *stēap* 'high' < Germanic, 'lofty, deep'] —**steeply** *adv* —**steepness** *n*

steep[2] /steep/ *v* (steeps, steeping, steeped) **1.** *vti* IMMERSE IN LIQUID to soak something in a liquid, or be soaked

in a liquid, especially for cleaning or softening or in order to extract something **2.** *vt* PERMEATE SOMEBODY OR SOMETHING to permeate somebody or something with a substance or quality, usually over a long period (*usually passive*) ○ *steeped in tradition* ■ *n* **1.** SOAKING an act or the process of steeping something in a liquid **2.** LIQUID FOR SOAKING a liquid that something is or can be steeped in [14C. < assumed Old English *stiepan* < Germanic] —**steeper** *n*

steepen /steepən/ (**-ens, -ening, -ened**) *vti* to become steep or steeper, or make something become steep or steeper

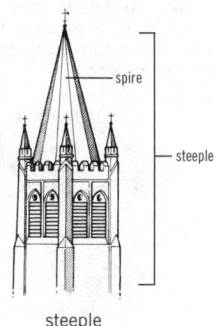

spire

steeple

steeple

steeple /steep'l/ *n* **1.** a tower forming part of a Christian church or another building, usually with a spire on top **2.** BUILDINGS same as **spire**[1] *n* (sense 1) [Old English *stēpel* < Germanic, 'lofty, deep'] —**steepled** *adj*

steeplechase /steep'l chayss/ *n* **1.** HORSE RACE WITH JUMPS ON TRACK a horse race run over a course that has constructed obstacles, e.g. hedges, ditches, and water jumps, that the horses must jump over **2.** HORSERACING HORSE RACE WITH JUMPS IN OPEN COUNTRY a cross-country horse race that has natural obstacles such as hedges and ditches for the horses to jump over **3.** ATHLETICS EVENT an athletics event in which runners must jump over a water jump as well as hurdles ■ *vi* (**-chases, -chasing, -chased**) RUN STEEPLECHASE to compete in a steeplechase [Late 18C. Because a church steeple was originally the competitors' goal] —**steeplechaser** *n*

steeplejack /steep'l jak/ *n* somebody who builds or repairs tall structures, especially steeples and chimneys

steer[1] /steer/ *v* (**steers, steering, steered**) **1.** *vti* DIRECT VEHICLE to guide the direction of movement of something such as a motor vehicle or ship using a steering wheel, rudder, or other device **2.** *vi* MANOEUVRE IN PARTICULAR WAY to go or move in a particular way or direction when being driven or propelled ○ *This car steers to the left.* **3.** *vt* INFLUENCE SOMEBODY IN PARTICULAR DIRECTION to encourage somebody to take a particular course or route by unobtrusively guiding them **4.** *vi* FOLLOW COURSE to follow a particular course ○ *steering clear of controversy* ■ *n* PIECE OF ADVICE a piece of guidance or advice (*informal*) [Old English *stīeran* < Germanic] —**steerable** *adj* —**steerer** *n*

SYNONYMS See *guide*.

steer[2] /steer/ *n* a male of the cattle family, especially a young bull, that has been castrated before reaching sexual maturity and is kept for beef [Old English *stēor* < Germanic]

steerage /steerij/ *n* **1.** the cheapest passenger accommodation on board a ship, usually in the area near the rudder and steering gear **2.** the act or process of steering a boat

steerageway /steerij way/ *n* a rate of forward movement that is fast enough to allow a boat to be steered from the helm

steering column /steering-/ *n* the part in a motor vehicle that connects the steering wheel, or the handlebars on a motorcycle, with the steering gear

steering committee *n* a group of selected people who decide agendas and topics for discussion, and prioritize urgent business, especially one acting for a legislative body or other assembly

steering gear *n* the mechanism in a vehicle or ship that allows it to be steered

steering wheel *n* **1.** a wheel in a vehicle or ship that is connected by way of the steering column to the steering gear and is turned to change direction **2.** in computer games, a wheel used to control movement

steersman /steerzmən/ (*plural* **-men** /-mən/) *n* somebody, especially a man, who steers a boat or ship [Old English *stēoresman* 'man for steering' < form of *stēor* 'steering' < Germanic]

steersperson /steerz purss'n/ *n* somebody who steers a boat or ship

steerswoman /steerz woomən/ (*plural* **-women** /-wimin/) *n* a woman who steers a boat or ship

steeve[1] /steev/ *n* a spar with a pulley block at one end that is used for stowing cargo on a boat or ship ■ *vt* (**steeves, steeving, steeved**) to stow cargo in the hold of a boat or ship and make it secure [Mid-19C. Origin ?]

steeve[2] /steev/ *vti* (**steeves, steeving, steeved**) to incline upwards, or make a bowsprit incline upwards ■ *n* the angle at which a bowsprit inclines upwards from the horizontal [Mid-17C. Origin ?]

steg analysis *n* the process of searching through computer files to find slight deviations in expected patterns that may reveal the presence of hidden messages [Late 20C. *Steg* < STEGANOGRAPHY]

steganography /stéggə nógrəffi/ *n* **1.** the production and placing in computer files of secret messages so small as to be detectable only by special software **2.** the art of secret writing [16C. < modern Latin *steganographia* < Greek *steganos* 'covered']

stegosaur /stéggə sawr/, **stegosaurus** /stéggə sáwrəss/ *n* a plant-eating dinosaur that lived in the Jurassic and Early Cretaceous periods and had tough bony dorsal plates and spikes. Genus: *Stegosauria*. [Early 20C. < modern Latin *Stegosaurus* < Greek *stegos* 'plate' + *sauros* 'lizard']

stein /stīn/ *n* **1.** a large beer mug, especially a German earthenware or pewter one, often with a hinged lid **2.** the amount of beer or other liquid that a stein holds [Mid-19C. < German, shortening of *Steinkrug* 'stoneware mug']

Gertrude Stein: photographed by Man Ray (1930)

Stein /stīn/, **Gertrude** (1874–1946) US writer. Her works, experimental in language and style, include *Three Lives* (1909), *The Autobiography of Alice B. Toklas* (1933), and *Four Saints in Three Acts* (1934), an opera with music by Virgil Thomson.

> 'Remarks are not literature.'
> [Gertrude Stein, *The Autobiography of Alice B. Toklas*; 1933]

> 'You are all a lost generation.'
> [Gertrude Stein, *on the young men who served in World War I*]

Stein /steen/, **Jock** (1922–85) Scottish football manager. He managed Glasgow Celtic during the most successful period in their history (1965–78), and as manager of Scotland (1978–85) took the team to the World Cup finals. Born **Stein, John**

John Steinbeck

Steinbeck /stín bek/, **John** (1902–68) US writer. His novels, notable for their social realism, include *Of Mice and Men* (1937) and *The Grapes of Wrath* (1939). He won a Nobel Prize in literature (1962). Full name **Steinbeck, John Ernst**. See Cultural note at **grape, mice**

> 'And where a number of men gathered together, the fear went from the faces, and anger took its place. And the women sighed with relief, for they knew it was all right—the break had not come; and the break would never come as long as fear could turn to wrath.'
> [John Steinbeck, *The Grapes of Wrath*; 1939]

steinbok *n* ZOOL same as **steenbok**

Gloria Steinem

Steinem /stínəm/, **Gloria** (b. 1934) US feminist. A leading member of the women's movement, she was one of the founders of *Ms.* magazine (1972).

> 'We are becoming the men we wanted to marry.'
> [Gloria Steinem, *Ms.*; July/August 1982]

Steiner /shtínər, stínər/, **Rudolf** (1861–1925) Austrian philosopher. He founded the Anthroposophical Society (1912) to promote his intellectually based spirituality. The Waldorf School movement is based on his work.

> 'The man of the present day would far rather believe that disease is connected only with immediate causes for the fundamental tendency in the modern view of life is always to seek what is more convenient.'
> [Rudolf Steiner, *The Manifestations of Karma*; 1925]

stela /steelə/ (*plural* **-lae** /-lee/) *n* ARCHAEOL same as **stele** (sense 1) [Late 18C. Via Latin < Greek *stēlē* 'standing stone']

stele /steel, steeli/ (*plural* **-lae** /-lee/ or **-les**) *n* **1.** an ancient stone slab or pillar, usually engraved, inscribed, or painted, and set upright **2.** the cylindrical core of the stem and roots of a plant that contains the sap-conducting vascular tissues and varying amounts of packing tissue (**pith**) [Early 19C. < Greek *stēlē* 'standing stone'] —**stelar** *adj*

stellar /stélər/ *adj* **1.** INVOLVING STARS relating to, consisting of, or like a star or stars **2.** INVOLVING FAMOUS PEOPLE full of famous people, especially those in the film or entertainment industries **3.** N Am EXCEPTIONAL exceptionally good [Mid-17C. < late Latin *stellaris* < Latin *stella* 'star']

stellar nursery *n* a region within a nebula where intense new star formation takes place

stellar wind *n* a stream of ionized particles ejected from the surface of a star

stellate /stéllət, -ayt/, **stellated** /ste láytid/ *adj* **1.** having a central part with smaller parts radiating out from it, like a starfish, some flower heads, and some crystal formations **2.** shaped like a star [Mid-17C. < Latin *stella* 'star'] —**stellately** *adv*

Stellenbosch /stéllən bosh/ city in Western Province, in southwestern South Africa. Founded by the Dutch in 1679, it was the second European settlement in the Cape. It is a major centre of wine production and in 1971 the first South African wine route was established there. Population: 58,097 (1996).

stem[1] /stem/ *n* **1.** MAIN AXIS OF PLANT the main stalk of a plant that bears buds and shoots **2.** SECONDARY PLANT BRANCH a secondary stalk of a plant, bearing a leaf, bud, or flower **3.** NARROW CONNECTING PART a long slim part of an object, e.g. the part that connects the base of a wine glass to its bowl, or the hollow tube on a smoker's pipe **4.** CYLINDRICAL WATCH PART a short rod, usually with an expanded crown at the end of it, that is used in winding a watch **5.** GENEALOGICAL LINE the major line of descent in a family tree **6.** GRAM BASE OF WORD the base of a word, to which affixes are added **7.** PHARM same as INN stem **8.** PRINTING VERTICAL LETTER PART an upright stroke, especially the main one, in a letter or character **9.** MUSIC VERTICAL PART OF MUSIC NOTE the vertical part that extends from the head of a written musical note **10.** NAUT UPRIGHT BOW TIMBER the main upright timber at the bow of a ship ■ *v* (**stems, stemming, stemmed**) **1.** *vi* ORIGINATE to derive, originate, or be caused by something ○ *This behaviour stems from some trauma in his childhood.* **2.** *vt* REMOVE STEM OF SOMETHING to take off the stem or part of the stem from something, especially a flower, fruit, or vegetable **3.** *vt* NAUT ADVANCE AGAINST TIDE OR WIND to make headway sailing against a tide or wind [Old English *stefn* < Indo-European, 'to stand'] —**stemless** *adj* —**stemmed** *adj* —**stemmer** *n* ◇ **from stem to stern** through the whole of a place, especially a ship

stem[2] /stem/ *v* (**stems, stemming, stemmed**) **1.** *vt* PREVENT SOMETHING FROM FLOWING to hinder, obstruct, or stop something from flowing, especially by creating a dam or plug **2.** *vt* STOP SOMETHING UP to plug something such as a blast or drill hole by packing it **3.** *vti* SKIING TURN SKI IN to turn the tip of a ski or skis inwards in order to turn or slow down ■ *n* SKIING TURNING IN OF SKI an act or the technique of turning the tip of a ski or skis inwards in order to turn or slow down [13C. < Old Norse *stemma* < Germanic, 'halt, stammer']

STEM *abbr* EDUC science, technology, engineering, mathematics

stem cell *n* an undifferentiated cell that can give rise to other cells of the same type indefinitely or from which specialized cells such as blood cells develop

stem christie *n* a skiing turn performed by stemming one ski and then bringing the other parallel to it during the turn [< STEM[2]]

stem ginger *n* round portions of the underground stem of a ginger plant, cooked until tender and preserved in syrup

stemma /stémmə/ (*plural* **-mata** /-mətə/) *n* **1.** FAMILY TREE a diagram of the genealogy of a person or a family **2.** LITERAT DIAGRAM OF TEXTS OF LITERARY WORK a diagram like a family tree that shows the relationships between different texts of a literary work **3.** ZOOL EYE OF ARTHROPOD a simple eye or facet of a compound eye of some arthropods [Mid-17C. Via Latin < Greek *stemma* 'garland'; from the ancient Roman practice of placing garlands on images of their ancestors]

stemson /stémss'n/ *n* a timber attached to the stem and keelson in the bow of a wooden ship [Mid-18C. < STEM[1] after KEELSON]

stem turn *n* SKIING same as **stem**[2] [< STEM[2]]

stemware /stém wair/ *n* glasses, goblets, and other glass vessels that have stems

stench /stench/ *n* a very strong unpleasant smell, especially a lingering smell associated with death or decay [Old English *stenc* 'odour' < Germanic]

SYNONYMS See *smell*.

stench trap *n* a device used in a sewer to prevent foul-smelling gases from rising, especially one that has a water seal

stencil

stencil /sténss'l/ *n* **1.** PLATE WITH CUT-OUT DESIGN a thin sheet of material with a shape cut out of it through which paint or ink is applied to mark the shape on another surface **2.** PATTERN the design, lettering, or other characters marked using a stencil ■ *vt* (**-cils, -cilling, -cilled**) **1.** MAKE PATTERN USING STENCIL to apply a design, lettering, or other characters to a surface using a stencil **2.** DECORATE SOMETHING USING STENCIL to decorate or mark a surface such as a wall or paper using a stencil [Early 18C. < Old French *estenceler* 'decorate with bright colours' < Latin *scintilla* 'spark'] —**stenciller** *n*

Stendhal /stén daal, staan dáʼal/ (1783–1842) French novelist and one of the first realists in 19th-century literature. His best-known works are *Le Rouge et le noir* (*The Red and the Black*) (1830) and *La Chartreuse de Parma* (*The Charterhouse of Parma*) (1839). Pseudonym of **Beyle, Marie-Henri**

> 'A novel is a mirror which passes over a highway. Sometimes it reflects to your eyes the blue of the skies, at others the churned-up mud of the road.'
> [Stendhal, *The Red and the Black*; 1830]

stengah /sténg gə/ *n* BEVERAGES same as **stinger**[2] (sense 2) [Late 19C. < Malay *satĕngah* 'half']

Sten gun /stén-/ *n* a light, cheaply manufactured submachine gun formerly used by the British Army, especially in World War II [Acronym < R. V. V. Shepherd + H. J. Turpin, its designers + *Enfield* in Greater London, after BREN GUN]

steno /sténnō/ (*plural* **-os**) *n* (*informal*) **1.** N Am OCCUPATIONS same as **stenographer 2.** *US* same as **stenography** (sense 1) [Early 20C. Shortening]

steno- *prefix* narrow, small ○ *stenothermal* [< Greek *stenos*]

stenobathic /sténnō báthik/ *adj* able to live only within a narrow range of depth of water [Early 20C. < STENO- + Greek *bathos* 'depth'] —**stenobath** /sténnō bath/ *n*

stenograph /sténnə graaf, -graf/ *n* **1.** SHORTHAND TYPEWRITER a machine like a small typewriter with keys for shorthand characters **2.** SHORTHAND CHARACTER a character in a system of shorthand writing ■ *vt* (**-graphs, -graphing, -graphed**) WRITE OR TYPE SOMETHING IN SHORTHAND to record something in shorthand by writing or using a stenograph

stenographer /stə nóggrəfər/ *n* **1.** somebody who uses a stenograph **2.** N Am same as **shorthand typist**

stenography /stə nóggrəfi/ (*plural* **-phies**) *n* **1.** the act, process, or skill of recording something in shorthand by writing or by using a stenograph **2.** something that has been recorded in written shorthand or by using a stenograph —**stenographic** /sténnə gráffik/ *adj* —**stenographical** *adj* —**stenographically** *adv*

stenohaline /sténnō háy leen, -lī'n/ *adj* unable to tolerate wide variations in salinity of water [Mid-20C. < STENO- + Greek *hal-* 'salt']

stenosis /stə nóssiss/ *n* a constriction or narrowing of a duct, passage, or opening in the body [Late 19C.

< modern Latin < Greek *stenos* 'narrow'] —**stenosed** /stə nõzd, -nõst/ *adj* —**stenotic** /stə nóttik/ *adj*

stenothermal /sténnə thúrm'l/ *adj* able to live only within a narrow temperature range

stenotype /sténnə tīp/ *n* a machine whose keyboard is used to record speech by means of phonetic shorthand

stenotypy /sténnə tīpi/ *n* a form of phonetic shorthand that uses combinations of letters to represent sounds and short words —**stenotypic** /sténnə típpik/ *adj* —**stenotypist** *n*

stent /stent/ *n* an open tubular structure of stainless steel or plastic that is inserted into an artery or another bodily tube to keep it from becoming blocked by disease [Mid-20C. After Charles T. *Stent* (1807–85), British dentist]

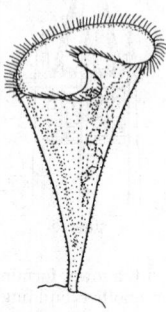

stentor (sense 2)

stentor /stén tawr/ *n* **1.** somebody with a loud powerful voice **2.** a trumpet-shaped protozoan with a mouth at the broad end. Genus: *Stentor*. [Early 17C. After *Stentor*, strong-voiced Greek herald in the Trojan war]

stentorian /sten táwri ən/ *adj* loud, powerful, or declamatory in tone

step /step/ *n* **1.** SHORT MOVEMENT WITH FOOT a short movement made by raising one foot and lowering it ahead of the other foot **2.** DISTANCE OF STEP the distance travelled in taking a step **3.** SOUND OF FOOTFALL the sound made by putting the foot down **4.** FOOTPRINT the footprint made by putting the foot down on a surface ○ *saw her steps in the snow* **5.** WAY OF WALKING a particular manner of walking **6.** SHORT WAY a very short distance ○ *a few steps away* **7.** RAISED SURFACE a raised surface for the foot, especially in a series going up or down **8.** STAGE IN PROGRESS a stage in a progression towards some goal or target ○ *a step towards lifting the embargo* **9.** DEGREE OR GRADE a degree, rank, or grade, especially on a scale ○ *took the issue one step further* **10.** MUSIC DEGREE OF MUSICAL SCALE a degree of a musical staff or scale **11.** MUSIC MUSICAL INTERVAL the interval between two degrees of a musical scale **12.** DANCE DANCE MOVE a movement of the feet and body that forms part of a dance **13.** same as **step aerobics** (*informal*) ○ *a step class* ■ **steps** *npl* **1.** OUTDOOR STAIRS a flight of stairs, usually outdoors, and made of stone or a similar material **2.** PATH MADE BY SOMEBODY ELSE a route, path, or course set by somebody else ○ *She followed in her mother's steps and became an architect.* ■ *v* (**steps, stepping, stepped**) **1.** *vti* MOVE FOOT to move a foot on top of something or in a particular direction ○ *Please step aside.* **2.** *vi* WALK FEW STEPS to walk a short distance or to a specific place ○ *Would you step into my office?* **3.** *vi* DANCE MOVE IN REGULAR RHYTHM to move at a measured pace, e.g. in a dance **4.** *vi* EASILY WALK INTO SITUATION to come into a new situation with ease or with little preparation ○ *Within a week of graduating she stepped into a fantastic job.* **5.** *vt* ARRANGE SOMETHING IN STEPS to arrange or organize something in steps **6.** *vt* MAKE STEPS IN SOMETHING to provide or furnish something with steps **7.** *vt* MEASURE SOMETHING BY STEPS to measure something by walking or pacing its length **8.** *vt* NAUT FIX MAST to place a ship's mast in its step ■ *n* NAUT MAST SUPPORT the block in which the heel of the mast of a sailing vessel is fixed (*informal*) [Old English *stæpe* < Germanic, 'to tread'] —**stepped** *adj* —**stepper** *n* ◇ **be in** *or* **out of step 1.** to agree *or* disagree with somebody or something in your attitudes or opinions **2.** to move in unison with or at a different pace and rhythm from other people ◇ **step by step** gradually ◇ **step on it** to hurry (*informal*) ◇ **take**

steps to take action ◇ **watch your step 1.** to be careful and cautious **2.** to tread carefully

SPELLCHECK step or **steppe**? Do not confuse the spelling of **step** and **steppe**, which sound similar. **Step** relates to a short movement of the foot, either as a noun or a verb (*took her first steps at nine months*, *Don't trip over the step*, *stepped inside*). **Steppe** is a noun denoting 'an extensive, usually treeless plain' (*the steppes of Central Asia*).

step aside *vi* to resign, retire, or withdraw from a position, especially so that somebody else can fill it
step down *v* **1.** *vi* WITHDRAW FROM POSITION to resign, retire, or withdraw from a position **2.** *vt* DECREASE IN STAGES to lower or decrease something in stages, or become lower in stages **3.** *vt* REDUCE VOLTAGE to reduce voltage using a transformer
step in *vi* to intervene or become involved in something
step on *vt* to treat somebody with arrogant disregard or active unkindness ○ *She's constantly stepping on other people's feelings.*
step out *vi* **1.** LEAVE BRIEFLY to leave a place for a brief period **2.** WALK WITH LONG STRIDES to walk fast, with longer strides than usual **3.** DATE SOMEBODY to go on a date or to a social gathering with somebody (*informal*) **4.** US TO BE UNFAITHFUL to be unfaithful to a spouse or partner (*informal*)
step up *v* **1.** *vt* RAISE SOMETHING IN STAGES to raise or increase something in stages **2.** *vt* RAISE VOLTAGE to raise voltage using a transformer **3.** *vi* COME FORWARD to come forward, e.g. to stand for an office or position or to take responsibility for something

step- *prefix* related because of remarriage, not by blood ○ *stepson* ○ *stepmother* [Old English *stēop-* < Germanic]

step aerobics *n* an exercise programme done to music that involves performing different movements with the arms and legs while stepping onto and off a small portable platform (*takes a singular or plural verb*)

stepbrother /stép brùthər/ *n* a boy or man who has brothers or sisters through the remarriage of a parent to somebody who has children

step change *n* a change that makes a significant difference in the size or value of something or the way in which something is done ■ *vt* to change something in a significant way

stepchild /stép chīld/ (*plural* **-children** /-chíldrən/) *n* the son or daughter of a stepparent

step dance *n* a dance in which feet and leg movements are important, often performed with the dancer remaining in one spot

stepdaughter /stép dàwtər/ *n* the daughter of somebody's spouse by a previous marriage

step-down *adj* **1.** decreasing in quantity, size, or status, especially in stages **2.** serving to lower voltage —**step-down** *n*

stepfamily /stép fàmli/ (*plural* **-lies**) *n* a family in which there is a stepparent

stepfather /stép faàthər/ *n* a man who has married somebody's mother after the death of or divorce from the person's father

step function *n* a mathematical function, e.g. a waveform, that remains constant in value over a given interval but changes abruptly in value from one interval to the next

stephanotis /stéffə nòtiss/ (*plural* **-tises** or *same*) *n* an ornamental vine or bush with leathery leaves. Flowers: fragrant, white, waxy. Genus: *Stephanotis*. [Mid-19C. < Greek *stephanōtis* 'fit for a crown' < *stephanos* 'crown, wreath' < *stephein* 'to crown']

Stephen /stéev'n/ (1090?–1154) king of England. He seized the throne on the death of Henry I (1135), but was engaged in civil war throughout his reign with supporters of Matilda, Henry's daughter.

Stephen I, St (975?–1038) king of Hungary. He founded the Hungarian state and established Christianity in Hungary. He is the country's patron saint.

Stephen, Sir Ninian (*b.* 1923) British-born Australian lawyer and politician. He was a justice of the Australian High Court (1972–82), and governor general of Australia (1982–89). Full name **Stephen, Sir Ninian Martin**

Stephen, St (*d.* AD 36) Christian martyr. Condemned to death on a charge of blasphemy, he was the first Christian martyr. Known as **the Protomartyr**

Stephens /stéev'nz/, **Frederick George** (1828–1907) British artist and art critic. A member of the Pre-Raphaelite Brotherhood, he abandoned painting for writing in the 1850s.

Stephenson /stéevənss'n/, **George** (1781–1848) British railway engineer. He built the Liverpool & Manchester Railway (opened 1830) and the *Rocket*, the steam locomotive that established the viability of the railway as a means of passenger transport.

Stephenson, Robert (1803–59) British civil engineer and politician. The son of George Stephenson, he was noted as a builder of bridges in the United Kingdom, Egypt, and Canada. He was an MP (1847–59).

step-in *adj* describes a garment without fastenings that is put on by stepping into it ■ **step-ins** *npl* a step-in article of clothing, especially panties with wide legs worn by women in the 1920s and 1930s (*dated*)

stepladder /stép ladər/ *n* a folding ladder that has flat broad steps and a hinged supporting frame

step machine *n* a type of exercise machine with two large pedals that are depressed alternately to imitate the action of stepping

stepmother /stép mùthər/ *n* a woman who has married somebody's father after the death of or divorce from the person's mother

stepparent /stép pairənt/ *n* a stepfather or stepmother —**stepparenting** *n*

steppe /stép/ *n* an extensive, usually treeless plain, often dry and grass-covered [Late 17C. Via German < Russian *step*]

SPELLCHECK See **step.**

Steppes /steps/ *npl* the vast grassy plains of Russia and Ukraine

stepping stone /stépping-/ *n* **1.** one of a series of stones on which somebody is able to step, e.g. to cross shallow water **2.** a stage or step that helps achieve a goal

stepsister /stép sìstər/ *n* a girl or woman who has brothers or sisters through the remarriage of a parent to somebody who has children

stepson /stép sùn/ *n* the son of somebody's spouse by a previous marriage

step stool *n* a stool with hinged steps that can be folded

step turn *n* a turn in which a skier lifts one ski in a desired direction, brings it down, and then aligns the other ski with it

step-up *adj* **1.** increasing in quantity, size, or status, usually in stages **2.** serving to raise voltage — **stepped-up** *adj* —**step-up** *n*

stepwife /stép wíf/ (*plural* **-wives** /-wívz/) *n* a man's ex-wife and the mother of his children, or his current wife and the stepmother of his children [Late 20C. < STEP- + *ex-wife*]

stepwise /stép wīz/ *adj* arranged in or resembling steps —**stepwise** *adv*

stepwives plural of **stepwife**

ster. *abbr* MONEY sterling

-ster *suffix* **1.** associated with, doing, or making a particular thing ○ *gangster* ○ *punster* **2.** having a particular characteristic ○ *youngster* [Old English *-estre*, feminine suffix < Germanic]

steradian /stə ráydi ən/ *n* the basic SI unit of measurement of solid angle. One steradian is the solid angle made at the centre of a sphere by an area on the surface of the sphere equal to the square of the sphere's radius. Symbol **sr** [Late 19C. < STEREO- + RADIAN]

stercoraceous /stúrkə ráyshəss/ *adj* consisting of or resembling dung or faeces [Mid-18C. < Latin *stercor-* 'dung']

stere /steer/ *n* a cubic metre, equal to 35.32 cubic ft [Late 18C. Via French *stère* < Greek *stereos* (see STEREO-)]

stere- *prefix* same as **stereo-** (*used before vowels*)

stereo /stérri ō, steéri-/ (*plural* **-os**) *n* **1.** DEVICE PRODUCING STEREOPHONIC SOUND an audio system or device that reproduces stereophonic sound **2.** STEREOPHONIC REPRODUCTION stereophonic sound reproduction **3.** STEREOSCOPIC PHOTOGRAPHY photography using stereoscopy **4.** PRINTING same as **stereotype** *n* (sense 2) [Late 19C. Shortening]

stereo- *prefix* **1.** three-dimensional ○ *stereology* **2.** solid ○ *stereotaxis* [< Greek *stereos* 'solid' < Indo-European, 'stiff']

stereobate /stérri ō bàyt, steéri-/ *n* **1.** a masonry platform that supports a building **2.** ARCHIT same as **stylobate** [Mid-19C. < Latin *stereobates* < Greek *stereos* 'solid' + *-batēs* 'walker']

stereochemistry /stérri ō kémmistri, steéri-/ *n* the study of the spatial distribution of atoms in a compound and its effects on the compound's properties —**stereochemical** *adj*

stereochrome /stérri ə krōm, steéri-/ *n* a wall painting that uses water glass as a medium or preservative [Mid-19C. < German *Stereochrom* < Greek *stereos* 'solid' + *khroma* 'colour'] —**stereochromy** *n*

stereogram /stérri ə gram, steéri-/ *n* **1.** PHOTOGRAPHY same as **stereograph 2.** a diagram or picture that shows objects as though in relief **3.** a radiogram that gives stereo sound reproduction (*dated*)

stereograph /stérri ə graaf, steéri ə-, -graf/ *n* a picture with two superimposed images or two almost identical pictures placed side by side which, when viewed through special glasses or a stereoscope, produce a three-dimensional image

stereography /stérri óggrəfi, steéri-/ *n* **1.** the technique or art of depicting a three-dimensional object on a flat surface **2.** the study and construction of defined geometric objects —**stereographic** /stérri ə gráffik, steéri-/ *adj* —**stereographically** *adv*

stereoisomer /stérri ō íssəmər, steéri-/ *n* one of a group of molecules that have identical atoms connected in the same order but in different spatial arrangements

stereoisomerism /stérri ō ī sómmərizəm, steéri-/ *n* isomerism in which the atoms in molecules are connected in the same order but in different spatial arrangements —**stereoisomeric** /-íssə mérrik/ *adj*

stereology /stérri ólləji, steéri-/ *n* the study of the properties of three-dimensional structures and objects based on two-dimensional views of them — **stereological** /stérri ə lójjik'l, steéri-/ *adj*

stereometry /stérri ómmətri, steéri-/ *n* the measurement of volume —**stereometric** /stérri ō méttrik, steéri-/ *adj*

stereomicroscope /stérri ō míkrəskōp, steéri-/ *n* a microscope with two optically separate eyepieces to make viewed objects look three-dimensional — **stereomicroscopy** /-mī króskəpee/ *n*

stereophonic /stérri ə fónnik, steéri-/ *adj* using an audio system based on two or more soundtracks to make recorded sound seem more natural when reproduced —**stereophonically** *adv* —**stereophony** /stérri óffəni, steéri-/ *n*

stereopsis /stérri ópsiss, steéri-/ *n* three-dimensional vision

stereopticon /stérri óptikən, steéri-/ *n* a slide projector able to allow one image to gradually replace another [Mid-19C. < modern Latin < Greek *stereos* 'solid' + *optikos* 'optic']

stereoscope /stérri əskōp, steéri-/ *n* a device resembling a pair of binoculars in which two-dimensional pictures of a scene taken at slightly different angles are viewed concurrently, one with each eye, creating the illusion of three dimensions

stereoscopic /stérri ə skóppik, steéri-/ *adj* **1.** involving, producing, or resembling the effects of seeing something as three-dimensional **2.** produced by or relating to a stereoscope —**stereoscopically** *adv*

stereoscopy /stérri óskəpi, steéri-/ *n* the visual perception of objects as being three-dimensional

stereoselective /stérri ō si léktiv, steéri-/ *adj* describes a chemical reaction in which one stereoisomer is affected more rapidly than another —**stereoselectively** *adv*

stereospecific /stérri ō spə síffik, steéri-/ *adj* relating to a process in which atoms are in a fixed spatial position —**stereospecifically** *adv* —**stereospecificity** /stérri ō spessə físsətee, steéri-/ *n*

stereotaxis /stérri ō táksiss, steéri-/ *n* 1. neurological surgery involving the insertion of delicate instruments that are guided to the relevant area by the use of three-dimensional scanning techniques 2. *ANZ*, *N Am* same as **thigmotaxis** —**stereotactic** *adj* —**stereotactically** *adv* —**stereotaxic** *adj* —**stereotaxically** *adv*

stereotropism /stérri óttrəpizəm, steéri-/ *n* BOT same as **thigmotropism** —**stereotropic** /stérri ə tróppik, steéri-/ *adj*

stereotype /stérri ə tīp, steéri-/ *n* 1. OVERSIMPLIFIED CONCEPTION an oversimplified standardized image of a person or group 2. PRINTING METAL PRINTING PLATE a metal printing plate cast from a mould in another material such as papier-mâché 3. PSYCHOL same as **stereotypy** (sense 1) ■ *vt* (-types, -typing, -typed) 1. REDUCE SOMEBODY TO OVERSIMPLIFIED CATEGORY to categorize individuals or groups according to an oversimplified standardized image or idea 2. PRINTING PRINT SOMETHING USING STEREOTYPE to cast or print something using a stereotype [Late 18C. < French *stéréotype* 'solid-block printing'] —**stereotyper** *n* —**stereotypical** /stérri ə típpik'l, steéri-/ *adj* —**stereotypically** *adv* —**stereotypist** *n*

stereotypy /stérri ə tīpi, steéri-/ *n* 1. a pattern of persistent, fixed, and repeated speech or movement that is apparently meaningless and is characteristic of some mental conditions 2. the process of casting or printing stereotypes

steric /stérrik, steér-/ *adj* related to the way atoms are spatially arranged [Late 19C. < STEREO-] —**sterically** *adv*

sterigma /stə rígmə/ (*plural* -mata /-mətə/ or -mas) *n* a tiny stalk that bears a spore or spores in a fungus [Mid-19C. Via modern Latin < Greek, 'support' < *sterizein* 'to support']

sterile /stérrīl/ *adj* 1. MED FREE FROM INFECTIVE ORGANISMS free from living bacteria and other microorganisms 2. BIOL INFERTILE incapable of becoming pregnant or of inducing pregnancy 3. ECOL BARREN incapable of supporting vegetation 4. BIOL NOT PRODUCING SEEDS not producing seeds, fruit, or spores 5. DULL AND UNCREATIVE unstimulating, uncreative, and lacking in ideas that will lead to any useful outcome [15C. Via French < Latin *sterilis*] —**sterilant** /stérrilənt/ *n* —**sterilely** *adv* —**sterility** /stə rílləti, ste-/ *n*

sterilize /stérri līz/ (-izes, -izing, -ized), **sterilise** (-ises, -ising, -ised) *vt* 1. to kill all living microorganisms in something in order to make it incapable of causing infection 2. to stop a person or animal from reproducing, e.g. by surgical removal or alteration of reproductive organs —**sterilizable** *adj* —**sterilization** /stérri īt záysh'n/ *n* —**sterilizer** *n*

~~sterio~~ incorrect spelling of **stereo**

sterlet /stúrlit/ (*plural* -lets or same) *n* a small sturgeon that is commercially used for caviar production. Native to: Black and Caspian seas. Latin name: *Acipenser ruthenus*. [Late 16C. < Russian *sterlyad* < Germanic]

sterling /stúrling/ *n* 1. BRITISH CURRENCY the currency in pounds and pence used in the United Kingdom 2. BRITISH STANDARD FOR COIN METAL PURITY the official standard of purity in terms of precious metal content for gold and silver coins in the United Kingdom, being 91.666% (22 carat) or 74.999% (18 carat) for gold and 92.5% for silver 3. METALL same as **sterling silver** ■ *adj* 1. OF STERLING SILVER made of sterling silver 2. ADMIRABLE admirable or valuable ○ *sterling efforts* [13C. Probably diminutive of STAR]

sterling area *n* the group of countries that use UK currency or that link the value of their own currency to that of sterling

sterling silver *n* 1. an alloy containing at least 92.5% silver with the remainder usually copper 2. objects made of sterling silver

stern[1] /sturn/ *adj* 1. rigid, strict, and uncompromising 2. grim, austere, or forbidding in appearance [Old English *styrne* < Indo-European, 'stiff'] —**sternly** *adv* —**sternness** *n*

stern[2] /sturn/ *n* 1. REAR OF SHIP the rear part of a ship or boat 2. BACK PART the rear part of something ■ *adj* IN REAR located at or resembling the stern [13C. Probably < Old Norse *stjórn* 'rudder' < Germanic]

Stern /sturn/, **Isaac** (1920–2001) Russian-born US violinist. He achieved international acclaim and recorded many of the works in the classical repertoire.

sterna ANAT plural of **sternum**

Sternberg ♦ von Sternberg, Josef

Sterne /sturn/, **Laurence** (1713–68) Irish novelist. His comic masterpiece, *The Life and Opinions of Tristram Shandy* (1759–67), anticipated many of the techniques of the modern novel. See Cultural note at **sentimental**

> 'Digressions, incontestably, are the sunshine; they are the life, the soul of reading; take them out of this book for instance, you might as well take the book along with them.'
> [Laurence Sterne, *Tristram Shandy*; 1759–67]

sternite /stúr nīt/ *n* a shield or cover on the underside of a segment of an insect [Mid-19C. < STERNUM]

sterno- *prefix* the sternum ○ *sternocostal* [< Greek *sternon* 'breastbone']

sternoclavicular /stúrnōklə víkyōōlər/ *adj* relating to or connecting the sternum and clavicle

sternocostal /stúrnō kóst'l/ *adj* situated between or relating to the sternum and ribs [Late 18C. < STERNO- + Latin *costa* 'rib']

sternpost /stúrnpōst/ *n* the main upright timber in the stern of a vessel

sternsheets /stúrn sheets/ *npl* the space at the rear of an open boat that is behind the rowers' bench [Mid-17C. < STERN[2] + SHEET[2] 'forward or after section of a boat']

sternson /stúrnss'n/ *n* a reinforcing timber at the joint of a sternpost and keelson at the stern of a wooden vessel [Mid-19C. < STERN[2] after KEELSON]

sternum /stúrnəm/ (*plural* -na /-nə/ or -nums) *n* 1. same as **breastbone** (*technical*) 2. the chitinous ventral plate covering the abdomen of an arthropod [Mid-17C. Via modern Latin < Greek *sternon* 'breastbone'] —**sternal** *adj*

sternutation /stúrnyōō táysh'n/ *n* the act or an instance of sneezing (*formal*) [Mid-16C. < Latin *sternutation-* < *sternutat-*, past participle of *sternutare* 'keep sneezing' < *sternuere* 'to sneeze']

sternutatory /stur nyōōtətəri/ *adj* causing or resulting in sneezing ■ *n* (*plural* -ries) a substance that causes sneezing [Early 17C. < late Latin *sternutatorius* < Latin *sternutat-* (see STERNUTATION)]

sternward /stúrnwərd/ *adj* located in or moving towards the stern of a boat or ship ■ *adv* same as **sternwards**

sternwards /stúrnwərdz/ *adv* in the direction of a ship's or boat's stern

sternway /stúrn way/ *n* the backward movement of a ship or boat

stern-wheeler *n* a boat propelled by a large paddle wheel at the rear, especially a riverboat

steroid /steér oyd, stérroyd/ *n* any of a large group of natural or synthetic fatty substances containing four carbon rings, including the sex hormones [Mid-20C. < STEROL + -OID] —**steroidal** /ste róyd'l/ *adj*

sterol /steér ol, stérrol/ *n* a steroid alcohol such as cholesterol that is present in animal and plant lipids [Early 20C. Shortening of CHOLESTEROL]

-sterone *suffix* steroid hormone ○ *androsterone* [< STEROL + -ONE]

stertor /stúrtər, stúr tawr/ *n* noisy or laborious snoring, heard when somebody is deeply unconscious or when there are obstructed air passages [Early 19C. < modern Latin < Latin *stertere* 'to snore'] —**stertorous** *adj* —**stertorously** *adv* —**stertorousness** *n*

stet /stet/ *vti* (stets, stetting, stetted) to restore, or direct somebody to restore, something that has previously been deleted from a printed or written text ■ *n* a word or mark indicating that previously deleted

printed or written matter should be restored [Mid-18C. < Latin, 'let it stand']

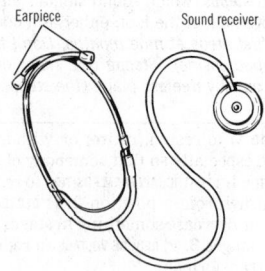

Earpiece   Sound receiver

stethoscope

stethoscope /stéthə skōp/ *n* a medical instrument used for listening to breathing, heartbeats, and other sounds made by the body [Early 19C. < Greek *stēthos* 'chest'] —**stethoscopic** /stéthə skóppik/ *adj* —**stethoscopy** /ste thóskəpi/ *n*

Stetson /stéts'n/ *tdmk* a trademark for hats with wide brims and high crowns

Stettin /shte teén/ German name for **Szczecin**

stevedore /steévə dawr/ *n* somebody whose job is to load and unload ships ■ *vti* (-dores, -doring, -dored) to work as a dockworker, loading and unloading ships, or unload a particular ship [Late 18C. < Spanish *estibador*, Portuguese *estivador* < *estibar* 'stow a cargo' < Latin *stipare* 'press together']

stevedore's knot *n* a knot that forms a lump to prevent a line from passing through a hole

Stevens /steév'nz/, **Nettie Maria** (1861–1912) US biologist and geneticist. She was one of the first scientists to prove that chromosomes determine the sex of an organism

Stevens, Siaka (1905–88) prime minister (1967, 1968) and president (1971–85) of Sierra Leone. Founder of the All-People's Congress (1960), he was the country's first president. Full name **Stevens, Siaka Probin**

AKG London

Wallace Stevens

Stevens, Wallace (1879–1955) US poet. His poems have a strongly philosophical bent. He won a Pulitzer Prize for his *Collected Poems* (1954).

> 'I do not know which to prefer, / The beauty of inflections / Or the beauty of innuendoes, / The blackbird whistling / Or just after.'
> [Wallace Stevens, 'Thirteen Ways of Looking at a Blackbird', *Harmonium*; 1923]

Stevens-Johnson syndrome *n* a severe inflammation of the skin and mucous membranes, often after a respiratory infection or as an allergic reaction to drugs [Mid-20C. After Albert Mason *Stevens* (1884–1945) and Frank Chambliss *Johnson* (1894–1934), US paediatricians]

Stevenson /steévənss'n/, **Robert Louis** (1850–94) Scottish writer. He lived in Europe, the United States, and, after 1889, in Samoa. Among his many books of travel, autobiography, and verse, he is best remembered for classic adventure tales such as *Treasure Island* (1883) and *Kidnapped* (1886). Full name **Stevenson, Robert Louis Balfour**. See Cultural note at **treasure**

'Old and young, we are all on our last cruise.'
[Robert Louis Stevenson, 'Crabbed Age and Youth', *Virginibus Puerisque*; 1881]

stew[1] /styoo/ *n* **1.** SIMMERED DISH a dish of meat, fish, or vegetables, or a combination of them, that is cooked by slow simmering **2.** MIXTURE a widely assorted mixture **3.** BROTHEL a house of prostitution (*archaic*) ■ *v* (**stews, stewing, stewed**) **1.** *vti* COOK BY SIMMERING to cook something by long slow simmering, or be cooked in this way **2.** *vi* BE UPSET to be deeply troubled or agitated **3.** *vi* BE VERY HOT to swelter or become uncomfortably hot **4.** *vti* MAKE TEA BITTER to cause tea to become bitter by infusing it for too long, or be infused for too long [14C. < Old French *estuve* 'steam bath'] ◇ **in a stew** agitated, anxious, or in a difficult situation (*informal*)

stew[2] /styoo/ *n* **1.** an artificial oyster bed **2.** same as **fishpond** (*archaic*) [14C. Via Old French *estui* 'confinement' < Latin *studium* (see STUDY)]

steward /styoo ərd/ *n* **1.** PLANE OR SHIP ATTENDANT somebody who attends to passengers on an aircraft or ship, or manages provisions and dining aboard a ship **2.** PROPERTY MANAGER somebody who manages somebody else's property, finances, or household **3.** HOTEL OR CLUB MANAGER somebody who manages arrangements concerning meals or lodging at a hotel, club, college, or other establishment **4.** OFFICIAL AT PUBLIC EVENT a marshal or official at a large public event **5.** POL same as **shop steward** ■ *v* (**-ards, -arding, -arded**) **1.** *vti* ACT AS STEWARD to act as a steward for a person or event **2.** *vt* GUIDE OR DIRECT SOMETHING to guide or direct something such as a project to completion ◇ *successfully stewarded the fundraising campaign to completion on time* ◇ *stewarded the bill through Congress to the President* [Old English *stigweard* < *stig* 'house, hall' + *weard* 'keeper' (see WARD)] —**stewardship** *n*

stewardess /styoo ərdiss/ *n* a female flight attendant on a passenger aeroplane (*dated*)

Stewart /styoo ərt/, **Jackie** (*b.* 1939) British racing driver. He scored 27 Grand Prix wins (1965–73) and was three times world champion (1969, 1971, and 1973). Born **Stewart, John Young**

'In my sport the quick are too often listed among the dead.'
[Attributed to Jackie Stewart]

Jimmy Stewart

Stewart, Jimmy (1908–97) US film actor. He was an appealing drawling presence in dozens of films, and was most closely identified with his roles in *Mr Smith Goes to Washington* (1939) and *It's a Wonderful Life* (1946). Full name **Stewart, James Maitland**

Stewart Island island in New Zealand, south of the South Island. Population: 387 (2001). Area: 1,735 sq. km/670 sq. mi.

stewed /styood/ *adj* **1.** SIMMERED cooked by slow simmering **2.** INTOXICATED very intoxicated (*slang*) **3.** MADE BITTER made bitter by being infused for too long ◇ *stewed tea*

stey /stay/ *adj Scotland* very steep ◇ *a stey brae* [14C. Origin ?]

stg *abbr* MONEY sterling

stge *abbr* storage

Sth *abbr* COMPASS South

STI *abbr* MED sexually transmitted infection

stibine /stíbeen, -īn/ *n* a highly toxic foul-smelling gas, or a derivative of one, produced by the action of hydrochloric acid on an antimony and zinc alloy. Use: fumigant. Formula: SbH_3. [Mid-19C. < Greek *stibi* 'antimony' + -INE]

stibnite /stíb nīt/ *n* a soft greyish antimony sulphide mineral. Use: source of antimony. [Mid-19C. < STIBINE]

stich /stik/ *n* a line of poetry [Early 18C. < Greek *stikhos* 'row, rank, line of verse']

Stich /stik, shtikh/, **Michael** (*b.* 1968) German tennis player. He won both the Wimbledon Men's Singles (1991) and Men's Doubles (1992), and the ATP World Championship (1993).

stichomythia /stíkō míthi ə/ *n* in ancient Greek drama, a form of dramatic dialogue in which characters speak single lines alternately [Mid-19C. < Greek *stikhomuthia* 'speaking in lines'] —**stichomythic** *adj*

stick[1] /stik/ *n* **1.** THIN BRANCH a thin branch or shoot cut or broken from a tree **2.** PIECE OF WOOD USED FOR FUEL a piece of wood used as fuel or as construction material **3.** SPECIALLY SHAPED PIECE OF WOOD a long often cylindrical piece of wood or other material used for a particular purpose ◇ *a hockey stick* **4.** ROD a rod, wand, or baton **5.** WALKING CANE OR CUDGEL a cane, club, or cudgel **6.** SHORT THIN THING a short slender part or piece ◇ *a stick of celery* **7.** SOMETHING USED TO SECURE COMPLIANCE something used to intimidate or coerce somebody into compliant behaviour ◇ *tempted them with the carrot but subtly threatened them with the stick* **8.** SHIP'S MAST a mast or spar on a ship **9.** CRITICISM strong adverse criticism (*informal*) **10.** FURNITURE a piece of furniture (*informal*) ◇ *We need a few sticks to furnish the flat.* **11.** PERSON somebody of a particular kind (*dated informal*) ◇ *He's a decent old stick.* **12.** ARMS BOMBS FALLING ON TARGET AT INTERVALS a group of bombs that are arranged to fall on a target at regular intervals **13.** AVIAT PARACHUTISTS JUMPING TOGETHER a group of parachutists all jumping at the same time **14.** *N Am* AUTOMOT CAR WITH GEAR STICK a car with a manual transmission (*informal*) **15.** *US* OFFENSIVE TERM an offensive term for somebody who is regarded as dull, unduly formal, or stuffy (*informal*) **16.** *Aus* SURFING same as **surfboard** (*slang*) **17.** *US* DRUGS CANNABIS CIGARETTE a marijuana cigarette (*dated slang*) ■ **sticks** *npl* REMOTE PLACE a rural or remote place or district, especially one that is regarded as unsophisticated or unfashionable (*informal*) ◇ *living out in the sticks* ■ *vt* (**sticks, sticking, sticked**) GARDENING SUPPORT PLANT WITH STICK to support a plant with a stake or stick [Old English *sticca* 'peg' < Indo-European, 'to stick, stab'] ◇ **in a cleft stick** in a situation where no possible course of action will bring a good result

stick[2] /stik/ *v* (**sticks, sticking, stuck** /stuk/) **1.** *vti* FASTEN SOMETHING WITH ADHESIVE to fasten or fix something by means of an adhesive, or remain fastened or fixed in this way **2.** *vt* FASTEN SOMETHING WITH POINTED OBJECT to fasten something in position by thrusting a pointed object such as a pin or nail through it **3.** *vti* PENETRATE SOMETHING to pierce, stab, or puncture something, or be pierced, stabbed, or punctured **4.** *vti* PROTRUDE to protrude, or make something protrude ◇ *She stuck her head out of the car window.* **5.** *vt* PUT SOMETHING SOMEWHERE to place or put something in a location or position (*informal*) ◇ *Stick it on the shelf.* **6.** *vti* BE UNABLE TO MOVE to be at a standstill or unable to move or proceed, or make something do this ◇ *be stuck in traffic* **7.** *vt* PUZZLE SOMEBODY to bewilder or perplex somebody (*usually passive*) ◇ *stuck for an answer* **8.** *vi* STAY IN MIND to remain in somebody's mind ◇ *He told me all the facts but they didn't stick.* **9.** *vt* STAND SOMEBODY OR SOMETHING to be able to tolerate or put up with somebody or something (*informal*) ◇ *I can't stick him.* **10.** *vt* IMPOSE SOMETHING ON SOMEBODY to impose something unpleasant on or take advantage of somebody (*usually passive*) ◇ *was always stuck with the boring jobs* **11.** *vt* KILL ANIMAL to kill an animal by stabbing ◇ *stick a pig* ■ *n* **1.** ABILITY TO ADHERE the adhesive quality of something such as glue or tape **2.** EXTREME SPORTS, SURFING BOARD a skateboard, snowboard, or surfboard (*slang*) [Old English *stician* < Indo-European] ◇ **get stuck into something** to start doing something with vigour or enthusiasm (*informal*) ◇ **stick in your craw** *or* **throat** to go against your sense of what is right and make you feel angry or resentful (*informal*) ◇ **stick it out** to persist with something to the end, even when doing so is difficult ◇ **stick it**

to somebody *N Am* to exploit somebody or treat somebody unfairly (*informal*) ◇ **stuck on somebody** infatuated with somebody (*informal*)

stick around, stick about *vi* to linger or wait for somebody or something (*informal*)

stick at *vt* to persist at something ◇ *stick at a job until it's done*

stick by *vt* to remain loyal to somebody or something ◇ *I'll stick by you no matter what.*

stick out *v* **1.** *vti* to protrude, or make something protrude **2.** *vt* to endure something disagreeable ◇ *stick out a long wait*

stick to *v* **1.** *vti* ADHERE TO SOMETHING to adhere to something, or make something adhere to something else **2.** *vt* BE LOYAL TO ANOTHER to be loyal or close to somebody or something **3.** *vt* PERSIST WITH SOMETHING to persist faithfully or stubbornly with something **4.** *vt* REMAIN FOCUSED ON SOMETHING to keep to and remain focused on something such as a topic without digression ◇ *stick to the point*

stick together *vi* to stay close physically or to remain unified ◇ *stuck together through thick and thin*

stick up *v* **1.** *vti* to protrude or point upwards, or make something do this **2.** *vt US* to carry out an armed robbery on somebody (*informal*)

stick up for *vt* to defend a belief or a person

stick with *vt* **1.** to persist with something in spite of difficulties or opposition **2.** to remain loyal or faithful to somebody or something

sticker /stíkər/ *n* **1.** SOMETHING WITH ADHESIVE an adhesive label, poster, or paper **2.** SOMETHING THAT STICKS something that sticks or attaches itself to something else **3.** SOMEBODY PERSISTENT somebody who perseveres at tasks

stick-fighting *n Carib* a highly stylized form of fighting in which two chanting combatants attempt to score points by striking each other with sticks

stick figure *n* a simple or crude drawing of a person or animal with single lines for the torso, arms, and legs, and a circle for the head

stickhandle /stík hand'l/ (**-dles, -dling, -dled**) *vt* in ice hockey and lacrosse, to control and manoeuvre a ball or puck using a stick —**stickhandler** *n* —**stickhandling** *n*

stickiness /stíkinəss/ *n* **1.** the condition or fact of being sticky **2.** the extent to which a website attracts, and especially retains, visitors

sticking plaster /stíking-/ *n* same as **plaster** *n* (sense 2)

sticking point *n* an issue, detail, or item likely to cause difficulty or prevent progress from being made, e.g. in a negotiation

stick insect

stick insect *n* a long brown or green insect that resembles a twig. Family: Phasmidae.

stick-in-the-mud *n* an offensive term for somebody who is regarded as resisting new ideas or practices (*informal*)

stickleback /stík'l bak/ (*plural* **-backs** *or same*) *n* **1.** a small spiny-backed fish found in both salt and fresh water that has distinctive nest-building and courtship behaviour. Family: Gasterosteidae. **2.** *regional* FISH same as **minnow** [15C. < Old English *sticel* 'thorn, sting' < Germanic]

stickler /stíklər/ *n* **1.** somebody who insists that every detail must be correct **2.** a puzzling or perplexing problem [Mid-16C. < *stickle*, alteration of obsolete *stightle* 'keep trying to control things' < Old English *stihtian* 'arrange, settle']

stick-on *adj* designed to be attached to something by means of an adhesive that has already been applied to one surface of the object to be stuck on ○ *stick-on labels*

stick pin *n N Am* an ornamental pin with a long shaft and a decoration or design at one end

stickseed /stík seed/ *n* a plant with prickly seeds that can stick to clothing. Native to: Europe, Asia, North America. Genus: *Lappula*.

stick shift *n N Am* 1. MANUAL TRANSMISSION a manually operated transmission in a motor vehicle 2. GEAR STICK a gear stick that operates a manual transmission 3. MANUAL VEHICLE a motor vehicle with a manual transmission

stick tackle *n* in hockey, an illegal challenge when a player hits another player's stick instead of the ball

sticktight /stík tīt/ *n* a plant with barbed fruits that can stick to clothing or fur

stickup /stík up/, **stick-up** *n N Am* an armed robbery (*informal*)

stickweed /stík weed/ (*plural* **-weeds** or *same*) *n* a plant with clinging seeds, especially ragweed. Native to: North America.

sticky /stíki/ *adj* (**-ier, -iest**) 1. COVERED IN SOMETHING GLUEY covered in something gluey or viscous 2. ADHESIVE having adhesive qualities 3. HUMID AND HOT uncomfortably warm and humid ○ *sticky weather* 4. DIFFICULT difficult, unpleasant, or involving problems (*informal*) ○ *a sticky situation* 5. ONLINE ATTRACTING VISITORS describes an Internet site that attracts, and especially retains, visitors (*informal*) ■ *n* (*plural* **-ies**) *ANZ* same as **stickybeak** (senses 1–2) (*informal*) — **stickily** *adv*

stickybeak /stíki beek/ *n ANZ* (*informal*) 1. somebody who pries into somebody else's private business 2. an inquisitive look —**stickybeak** *vi*

sticky-fingered *adj* having a tendency to steal things (*informal*)

sticky tape *n* plastic tape coated with adhesive on one side, usually sold in the form of a reel, used mainly for attaching pieces of paper together, e.g. when wrapping a parcel

sticky wicket *n* 1. in cricket, a pitch that has been made wet by rain and is in the process of being dried by sun, so that the ball bounces awkwardly 2. an awkward or difficult situation (*informal*)

Stieglitz /steéglits/, **Alfred** (1864–1946) US photographer. A promoter of photography as an art form, he was known for portraiture and wrote extensively on photographic technique. He was the husband of Georgia O'Keeffe.

stiff /stif/ *adj* 1. RIGID rigid, inflexible, or hard to move 2. NOT SUPPLE painful and not supple ○ *stiff muscles* 3. SEVERE very harsh or severe ○ *a stiff punishment* 4. TAXING difficult or demanding ○ *stiff competition* 5. FORCEFUL having force or power ○ *a stiff breeze* 6. STRONG strong or potent to the taste or in effect on the body ○ *a stiff drink of black coffee* 7. RESOLUTE showing determination and resolve ○ *stiff resistance* 8. TOO HIGH higher than is justified or usual ○ *stiff prices* 9. FORMAL rigidly formal or distant in manner ○ *a stiff manner* 10. NAUT NOT LIKELY TO CAPSIZE describes a ship or boat that is relatively stable in the water 11. INTOXICATED having had too much alcohol to drink (*slang*) ■ *adv* 1. TOTALLY totally or utterly ○ *bored stiff* ○ *scared stiff* 2. IN STIFF WAY in a stiff way or manner ■ *n* 1. CORPSE a dead body (*slang*) 2. *US* PERSON a person, especially somebody of a particular type (*slang*) ○ *a lucky stiff* 3. *US* OFFENSIVE TERM an offensive term for somebody regarded as unpleasant or excessively formal (*slang insult*) 4. *US* OFFENSIVE TERM an offensive term for a customer who leaves insufficient tips (*slang insult*) 5. FLOP something that is an utter failure (*slang*) ■ *vt* (**stiffs, stiffing, stiffed**) *N Am* NOT PAY SOMEBODY to fail to pay somebody an amount due or expected (*slang*) ○ *He stiffed me on the tip.* [Old English *stīf* < Indo-European, 'to compress, pack'] —**stiffish** *adj* —**stiffly** *adv* —**stiffness** *n*

stiff-arm *adj US* SPORTS same as **straight-arm**

stiff-arm tackle *n Aus* in rugby, an illegal straight-arm tackle

stiffen /stíff'n/ (**-ens, -ening, -ened**) *vti* 1. to become rigid or inflexible, or make something do this 2. to make something stronger or more effective, or become stronger or more effective —**stiffener** *n*

stiffie *n* another spelling of **stiffy** (sense 2) (*offensive slang*)

stiff-necked *adj* extremely obstinate and arrogant

stiffy /stíffi/ (*plural* **-fies**), **stiffie** *n* 1. FORMAL INVITATION a formal invitation card printed on high-quality stiff paper (*informal*) 2. OFFENSIVE TERM an offensive term for an erect penis (*slang*) 3. *S Africa* COMPUTER DISK a floppy disk

stifle[1] /stīf'l/ (**-fles, -fling, -fled**) *v* 1. *vti* SUFFOCATE to impair somebody's breathing, or find it hard to breathe 2. *vt* CHECK OR REPRESS SOMETHING to curb, repress, or prevent the development of something ○ *stifled the spreading discontent* 3. *vt* REPRESS PHYSICAL ACT to cut off a physical act such as a yawn or laugh before it develops [14C. Probably alteration (after Old Norse *stífla* 'stop up') of Old French *estouffer* 'smother'] —**stifler** *n*

stifle[2] /stīf'l/ *n* the joint in the hind leg of a four-legged animal that corresponds to the human knee [14C. Origin ?]

stifling /stífling/ *adj* 1. uncomfortably hot and stuffy 2. repressive in not allowing full expression —**stiflingly** *adv*

stigma /stígmə/ *n* 1. SIGN OF SOCIAL UNACCEPTABILITY the shame or disgrace attached to something regarded as socially unacceptable 2. BOT PLANT PART the part of a flower's female reproductive organ (**carpel**) that receives the male pollen grains. It is generally located at the tip of a slender stalk-shaped projection (**style**). 3. (*plural* **stigmata** /stígmətə, stig maátə/) MED MARK ON SKIN a mark on the skin indicating a medical condition 4. INSECTS SPOT ON BUTTERFLIES a coloured mark or spot, often resembling an eye, found on some protozoans and invertebrates, especially butterflies and other lepidopterans [Late 16C. Via Latin < Greek, 'mark on the skin' < *stig-*, stem of *stizein* 'to prick']

stigmasterol /stig mástərol/ *n* a sterol found in plants. Use: manufacture of progesterone. [Early 20C. < shortening of *Physostigma* + STEROL]

stigmata /stígmətə, stig maátə/ *npl* marks on the hands and feet resembling the wounds from Jesus Christ's crucifixion ■ MED plural of **stigma** (sense 3) [Mid-17C. < Greek, plural of *stigma* (see STIGMA)]

stigmatic /stig máttik/ *adj* 1. socially unacceptable (*formal*) 2. OPTICS same as **anastigmatic** ■ *n* somebody affected with stigmata [Late 16C. < Latin *stigmat-* < Greek *stigmat-*, stem of *stigma* (see STIGMA)]

stigmatise *vt* SOC SCI another spelling of **stigmatize**

stigmatism[1] /stígmətizəm/ *n* 1. the properties of an anastigmatic lens 2. the condition in which the eye focuses properly [Mid-19C. Back-formation < ASTIGMATISM]

stigmatism[2] /stígmətizəm/ *n* the condition of having stigmata [< STIGMATA]

stigmatist /stígmətist/ *n* CHR same as **stigmatic**

stigmatize /stígmə tīz/ (**-tizes, -tizing, -tized**), **stigmatise** (**-tises, -tising, -tised**) *v* 1. *vt* to label somebody or something as socially unacceptable 2. *vti* to mark somebody with stigmata, or be marked with stigmata —**stigmatization** /stígmə tī záysh'n/ *n* —**stigmatizer** *n*

stilb /stilb/ *n* a unit of luminescence equal to 1 candela per square centimetre [Mid-20C. < French < Greek *stilbein* 'to glitter']

stilbene /stíl been/ *n* a crystalline solid. Use: manufacture of dyes. Formula: $C_{14}H_{12}$. [Mid-19C. < Greek *stilbein* 'to glitter']

stilbestrol /stil beésstrol/, **stilboestrol** *n* CHEM same as **diethylstilbestrol** [Mid-20C. < STILBENE + OESTRUS]

stilbite /stíl bīt/ *n* a white or yellow zeolite mineral containing calcium and sodium [Early 19C. < Greek *stilbein* 'to glitter'; from its lustrous crystals]

stilboestrol *n* CHEM another spelling of **stilbestrol**

stile[1] /stīl/ *n* a step or rung designed to make it easier to climb over a fence or wall [Old English *stigel* < Indo-European, 'to step, climb']

SPELLCHECK **stile** or **style**? Do not confuse the spelling of ***stile*** and ***style***, which sound similar. ***Stile*** is a noun denoting a means of climbing over a fence or wall, or a noun denoting a vertical piece in a door or frame; it is also found in the compound word *turnstile*. ***Style*** is a noun or verb referring to the way something is done, designed, written, etc., as in *different styles of architecture, have your hair styled.*

stile[2] /stīl/ *n* a vertical piece in a door, frame, or panel [Late 17C. Probably via Dutch *stijl* 'prop, doorpost' < Latin *stilus* 'column, post' (see STYLUS)]

SPELLCHECK See ***stile***[1].

stilet /stílət/ *n* 1. a wire inserted in a catheter to give it rigidity 2. a fine wire used as a probe in surgery [Late 17C. Via French < Italian *stiletto* (see STILETTO)]

stiletto /sti léttō/ *n* (*plural* **-tos** or **-toes**) 1. ARMS SMALL DAGGER a small dagger with a narrow tapering blade 2. HANDICRAFT POINTED TOOL a pointed tool for making holes in fabric or leather 3. CLOTHING same as **stiletto heel** ■ *vt* (**-tos, -toing, -toed**) STAB SOMEBODY WITH STILETTO to stab somebody using a stiletto [Early 17C. < Italian, 'small dagger' < *stilo* 'dagger' < Latin *stilus* (see STYLUS)]

stiletto heel *n* a high pointed heel on a woman's shoe, or a shoe with such a heel

Stilicho /stíllikō/, **Flavius** (359?–408) Roman general and politician. As guardian of the emperor Honorius during his minority, he was in effect the ruler of the West Roman Empire.

still[1] /stil/ *adj* 1. NOT MOVING motionless and undisturbed 2. BEVERAGES NOT CARBONATED describes a drink that is not sparkling or bubbly 3. QUIET subdued, gentle, or quiet 4. PHOTOGRAPHY TAKING STATIC PHOTOGRAPHS designed for, or relating to the process of, taking photographs as opposed to making films ■ *adv* SILENTLY OR WITHOUT MOTION without sound or movement ■ *n* 1. PEACE silence or peace (*literary*) ○ *the still of the night* 2. CINEMA SCENE FROM FILM a photographic print, either made from a single frame of a film or shot independently with a still camera during production ■ *v* (**stills, stilling, stilled**) 1. *vti* MAKE SOMEBODY CALM to cause somebody to become quiet, calm, soundless, or immobile, or become quiet, calm, soundless, or immobile 2. *vt* RELIEVE EMOTION to allay or relieve an emotion such as fear or doubt ○ *stilled our fears* [Old English *stille* < Indo-European, 'stay put'] —**stillness** *n*

still[2] /stil/ *adv* 1. EXISTING NOW used to indicate that a situation that used to exist has continued and exists now ○ *The original is still my favourite.* ○ *I still believe it's a mistake.* ○ *It was still light.* 2. EVEN AT THIS TIME used to emphasize that something is the case even up to the point mentioned ○ *Her birthday is still a month away.* ○ *He may still be around.* ○ *Still to come...* 3. EVEN MORE used to emphasize that there is even more of a quality or quantity (*often used with a comparative*) ○ *Profits next year will be larger still.* ○ *The market for flour is equal to almost any in the West, and it will be still better.* 4. NEVERTHELESS used to emphasize that something remains the case in spite of the situation mentioned ○ *It's not very good. Still, it's better than nothing.* [13C. < STILL[1]] ◇ **still and all** nonetheless or notwithstanding (*informal*)

USAGE See ***yet***.

still[3] /stil/ *n* 1. an apparatus for distilling liquids, especially alcohol 2. BEVERAGES same as **distillery** [Mid-16C. Shortening of DISTIL]

stillage /stíllij/ *n* a frame, stand, or platform for keeping goods off the floor in a warehouse [Late 16C. Probably < obsolete Dutch *stellagie* 'scaffolding' < *stellen* 'set up']

stillbirth /stíl búrth/ *n* the birth of a dead foetus or baby after the 28th week of pregnancy

stillborn /stíl bawrn/ *adj* 1. dead at birth 2. useless or ineffectual from the start [Mid-16C. < STILL[1] in the obsolete sense 'dead']

~~**stilleto**~~ incorrect spelling of **stiletto**

still frame *n* a single frame from a film or television programme displayed as a photograph

still life: *Still life with Dessert and Bouquet* (1632)
by Georg Flegel

AKG London

still life (*plural* **still lifes**) *n* **1.** a representation of inanimate objects such as fruit, flowers, or food, often in a domestic setting, in paintings, pictures, or photographs (*hyphenated before a noun*) ○ *a still-life class* **2.** the style or genre of still life in paintings, pictures, or photographs

still room *n* **1.** a room in which distilling is done **2.** a pantry or storeroom off the kitchen of a large house

Still's disease /stílz-/ *n* chronic arthritis that develops in children under the age of 16 [Early 20C. After Sir George Still (1868–1941), British physician]

stilt /stilt/ *n* **1.** POLE FOR WALKING either of two poles with footrests high off the ground on which somebody balances and walks **2.** CONSTR SUPPORTING POST a tall post or column that supports a structure above land or water **3.** BIRDS LONG-LEGGED WADING BIRD a black and white shorebird with a straight beak and extremely long red legs that lives near ponds and marshes. Genera: *Himantopus* or *Cladorhynchus*. ■ *vt* (**stilts, stilting, stilted**) RAISE SOMETHING ON STILTS to place or raise something up on stilts [14C. Probably < Low German < Indo-European, 'to set up']

stilted /stíltid/ *adj* **1.** NOT FLUENT lacking fluency so as to be halting or unnatural in flow **2.** FORMAL pompous or unduly formal **3.** CONSTR RESTING ON VERTICAL PIECES OF STONE describes an arch that is joined to the top part of the pillar, column, or wall (**impost**) supporting it by vertical pieces of stone —**stiltedly** *adv* —**stiltedness** *n*

Stilton[1] /stíltən/ *n* either of two strong-flavoured British white cheeses made from whole milk, one veined with blue mould, the other plain [Mid-18C. After STILTON[2]]

Stilton[2] /stíltən/ village near Peterborough, in eastern England. It gave its name to Stilton cheese, made in the surrounding areas. Population: 2,219 (1991).

stimulant /stímmyŏŏlənt/ *n* **1.** SOURCE OF STIMULUS something that provides a stimulus, incentive, or quickening **2.** PHARM AGENT PRODUCING INCREASE IN FUNCTIONAL ACTIVITY a drug or other agent that produces a temporary increase in the functional activity of a body organ or part ■ *adj* INCREASING ACTIVITY increasing physical activity or acting as a stimulus or incentive

stimulate /stímmyŏŏ layt/ (**-lates, -lating, -lated**) *vt* **1.** ENCOURAGE SOMETHING to encourage something such as an activity or a process so that it will begin, increase, or develop ○ *stimulate discussion* **2.** MAKE SOMEBODY INTERESTED to cause somebody to become interested in or excited about something **3.** PHYSIOL CAUSE BODY PART TO RESPOND to cause physical activity in something such as a nerve or an organ [Early 16C. < Latin *stimulat-*, past participle of *stimulare* 'to goad' < *stimulus* 'goad, stake'] —**stimulable** *adj* —**stimulating** *adj* —**stimulatingly** *adv* —**stimulation** /stímmyŏŏ láysh'n/ *n* —**stimulative** *adj* —**stimulator** *n* —**stimulatory** *adj*

stimulus /stímmyŏŏləss/ (*plural* **-li** /-lī/) *n* **1.** INCENTIVE something that encourages an activity or a process to begin, increase, or develop **2.** SOMETHING AROUSING INTEREST an agent or factor that provokes interest, enthusiasm, or excitement **3.** PHYSIOL CAUSE OF PHYSICAL RESPONSE something that causes a physical response in an organism, e.g. a drug or an electrical impulse [Late 17C. < Latin, 'goad, stake']

sting /sting/ *v* (**stings, stinging, stung** /stung/) **1.** *vti* INJECT SOMEBODY WITH TOXIN to prick somebody's skin and inject a small quantity of a poisonous or irritant substance, causing a sharp pain that is often followed by itchiness and swelling **2.** *vti* FEEL OR CAUSE SHARP PAIN to feel a sharp pain, usually only for a short period of time, or make somebody do this ○ *His eyes were stinging with the onions.* **3.** *vt* UPSET SOMEBODY to make somebody feel upset, hurt, or annoyed ○ *I was stung by her harsh criticisms.* **4.** *vt* GOAD SOMEBODY to urge somebody on, usually with criticism ○ *words that stung them into action* **5.** *vt* OVERCHARGE SOMEBODY to overcharge somebody for goods or services (*informal*) ○ *They stung me £800 for repainting the wall.* **6.** *vt* BORROW FROM SOMEBODY to borrow money from somebody (*informal*) ○ *I might be able to sting my old man for a tenner.* ■ *n* **1.** WOUND CAUSED BY STING a skin wound that may hurt, swell up, and itch, caused by an insect, plant, or animal piercing the skin and injecting a small quantity of a poisonous or irritant substance **2.** POISON-INJECTING ORGAN the sharp organ through which an insect or other animal injects poison to immobilize its prey or for defence. N Am term **stinger**[1] **3.** SHARP PAIN a short sharp pain, e.g. that caused by the application of an antiseptic to a fresh wound **4.** HURTFUL QUALITY the hurtful nature of something such as criticism **5.** POWER TO UPSET the power to inflict mental or emotional discomfort ○ *threats that have lost their sting* **6.** N Am ORCHESTRATED SWINDLE an underhand scheme, especially a carefully planned and orchestrated swindle (*slang*) [Old English *stingan* < Germanic] —**stinging** *adj* —**stingingly** *adv*

stinger[1] /stíngər/ *n* **1.** SOMETHING STINGING something that stings, especially a hurtful or critical comment **2.** ANZ ZOOL STINGING ANIMAL OR PLANT an animal or plant that stings, especially the box jellyfish **3.** N Am ZOOL same as **sting** *n* (sense 2) **4.** SHARP BLOW a sharp blow or slap that causes a smarting pain (*informal*) **5.** US CRIME, POLICE UNDERCOVER OFFICER a law enforcement officer who is taking part in an undercover operation (*informal*) [Mid-16C. < STING]

stinger[2] /stíngər/ *n* **1.** N Am BEVERAGES COCKTAIL a cocktail consisting of crème de menthe and brandy **2.** BEVERAGES WHISKY DRINK a whisky and soda with crushed ice **3.** DEVICE TO STOP CARS a device used by police that is covered in spikes and can be thrown across a road to puncture a car's tyres [Early 20C. Alteration of STENGAH]

stinging nettle /stínging-/ *n* PLANTS same as **nettle** *n* (sense 1)

stingo /stíng gō/ *n* a strong beer, especially an English beer originally made in Yorkshire (*archaic slang*) [Mid-17C. < the beer's sharp taste]

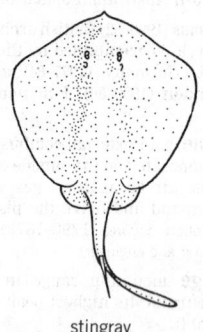

stingray

stingray /stíng ray/ (*plural* **-rays** or *same*) *n* a ray with a flexible tail shaped like a whip that has poisonous spines on it. Native to: shallow warm waters. Family: Dasyatidae.

stingy[1] /stínji/ (**-gier, -giest**) *adj* (*informal*) **1.** not generous in giving or spending money **2.** ungenerously small or inadequate ○ *a stingy tip* [Mid-17C. Origin ?] —**stingily** *adv* —**stinginess** *n*

stingy[2] /stíngi/ (*informal*) *adj* (**-ier, -iest**) stinging or capable of stinging ■ *n* (*plural* **-ies**) Wales PLANTS same as **nettle** *n* (sense 1) [Early 17C. < STING]

stink /stingk/ *vi* (**stinks, stinking, stank** /stangk/ or **stunk** /stungk/, **stunk**) **1.** SMELL HORRIBLE to have a very strong and unpleasant smell **2.** BE WORTHLESS to be very bad or worthless (*informal*) ○ *This poetry stinks.* **3.** BE CORRUPT to be despicably corrupt or dishonest (*informal*) ○ *The whole voting process stinks.* **4.** HAVE UNDESIRABLE QUALITY to have a large amount of an undesirable quality (*informal*) ○ *a career that stinks of nepotism* ■ *n* **1.** FOUL SMELL a strong and unpleasant smell **2.** SCANDAL a scandal, fuss, or trouble (*informal*) ○ *'even if there was a stink, he had plenty good friends in San Francisco'* (Robert Louis Stevenson, *The Wrecker*; 1896) [Old English *stincan* 'to smell' < W Germanic] ◇ **kick up** *or* **make** *or* **raise a stink** to cause trouble, especially by protesting (*slang*) ◇ **like stink** very hard or fast (*informal*)

SYNONYMS See *smell*.

stink out *vt* **1.** to give something a very strong and unpleasant smell ○ *The smell of rotting cabbage stank the whole place out.* N Am term **stink up 2.** to drive a person or animal out of a place by introducing a strong and unpleasant smell

stink bomb *n* a practical joker's toy in the form of a small glass or plastic capsule that, when smashed, emits a horrible smell

stinkbug /stíngk bug/ *n* an insect that emits foul-smelling secretions. It typically has a flattish body, and is often camouflaged to blend with its surroundings. Family: Pentatomidae.

stinker /stíngkər/ *n* **1.** SOMETHING UNPLEASANT something that is very difficult or unpleasant (*informal*) ○ *That last exam was a real stinker.* **2.** OFFENSIVE TERM an offensive term for somebody regarded as obnoxious or hateful (*slang insult*) **3.** SPITTING SEABIRD a seabird that feeds on offal and carrion and spits a foul-smelling oil at aggressors, e.g. a fulmar or petrel (*informal*)

stinkhorn /stíngk hawrn/ *n* a fungus with a thick white stalk and a thimble-shaped foul-smelling cap containing spores. The smell attracts flies, which disperse the spores. Order: Phallales.

stinking /stíngking/ *adj* **1.** SMELLY having or giving off a very strong and unpleasant smell **2.** EXTREMELY BAD unpleasant or contemptible as an action or behaviour (*informal*) ○ *'This was, of course, a stinking lie.'* (Richard Kadrey, *Metrophage*; 1995) **3.** INTOXICATED very intoxicated with alcohol (*slang*) ■ *adv* USED FOR EMPHASIS used to emphasize the contemptible extent of something (*informal*) ○ *stinking rich* —**stinkingly** *adv*

stinking ash *n* a deciduous tree with fragrant greenish-white flowers and fruits that are used in brewing. Native to: eastern North America. Latin name: *Ptelea trifoliata*.

stinking badger *n* ZOOL same as **teledu** [< the foul-smelling secretion that the animal ejects]

stinko /stíngkō/ *adj* **1.** very intoxicated with alcohol (*slang*) **2.** US of the poorest quality (*informal*) ○ *a stinko bowl of stew*

stinkpot /stíngk pot/ *n* **1.** SOMETHING WITH HORRIBLE SMELL something that has a very strong and unpleasant smell (*informal insult*) **2.** OFFENSIVE TERM an offensive term for somebody considered very unpleasant or unpopular (*slang insult*) **3.** REPT SMALL TURTLE a small species of musk turtle that emits a foul-smelling secretion from its cloacal glands. Native to: ponds and sluggish streams of the United States. Latin name: *Sternotherus odoratus*. **4.** ARMS STINKING WEAPON in former times, a military weapon consisting of an earthenware pot that released a suffocating vapour when thrown into an enemy position or onto an enemy ship

stinkstone /stíngk stōn/ *n* rock, especially limestone, that gives off a highly unpleasant odour when rubbed or struck [Early 20C. Translation of German *Stinkstein*]

stinkweed /stíngk weed/ (*plural* **-weeds** or *same*) *n* **1.** PLANTS same as **wall rocket 2.** a plant with unpleasant-smelling flowers or foliage, e.g. mayweed or pennycress

stinkwood /stíngk wŏŏd/ (*plural* **-woods** or *same*) *n* **1.** a hard durable unpleasant-smelling wood. Use: furniture-making. **2.** a tree with unpleasant-smelling wood, especially a South African deciduous tree with hard wood [Mid-18C. Translation of Dutch *stinkhout*]

stinky /stíngki/ *adj* (*informal*) **1.** having a very strong and unpleasant smell ○ *one of those stinky cheeses* **2.** unfair, dishonest, or devious —**stinkily** *adv*

stint[1] /stint/ v (**stints**, **stinting**, **stinted**) **1.** vi BE MISERLY to be ungenerous in offering, providing, or giving something ○ *For a really good mousse, don't stint on the chocolate.* **2.** vt DENY SOMEBODY SOMETHING to deny somebody something out of miserliness, or deny yourself something, usually in an act of sacrifice ○*'your mother and me economizing and stinting ourselves to give you a University education'* (Thomas Hardy, *Tess of the d'Urbervilles*; 1891) ■ n **1.** ALLOTTED TIME a fixed period of time spent on a task or job ○ *do a two-year stint as an apprentice* **2.** LIMITATION limitation or restriction, especially in time or amount ○*'I gave him time and thought without stint'* (Willa Cather, *The Professor's House*; 1925) [Old English *styntan* 'to blunt' < Germanic; later reinforced by related Old Norse *stytta* 'shorten'] —**stinter** n

stint[2] /stint/ n (plural **stints** or same) n BIRDS same as **sandpiper** [15C. Origin ?]

stipe /stīp/ n **1.** the stalk of a mushroom or fern **2.** ZOOL same as **stipes** (senses 1–2) [Late 18C. Via French < Latin *stipes* 'post, log']

stipel /stíp'l/ n a structure shaped like a tiny leaf or scale located at the base of a leaflet of a compound leaf [Early 19C. Via French < modern Latin *stipella* 'small stipule' < Latin *stipula* 'straw, stalk'] —**stipellate** /sti péllət/ adj

stipend /stí pend/ n a fixed amount of money paid at regular intervals as a salary or to cover living expenses, especially one paid to a member of the clergy [15C. Directly or via French < Latin *stipendium* 'soldier's pay' < *stips* 'payment' + *pendere* 'weigh out']

SYNONYMS See *wage*.

stipendiary /stī péndi əri/ adj **1.** PROVIDED WITH ALLOWANCE receiving a fixed amount of money on a regular basis as a salary or to cover living expenses **2.** WITH STIPEND paying a stipend or paid for by a stipend ■ n (plural **-ies**) SOMEBODY RECEIVING STIPEND somebody who regularly receives a fixed amount of money as a salary or to cover living expenses, e.g. a priest or magistrate

stipes /stí peez/ (plural **stipites** /stíppi teez/) n **1.** the second or bottom mouthpart of some insects and crustaceans **2.** the eyestalk of a crayfish or crab **3.** BOT same as **stipe** (sense 1) [Mid-18C. Via modern Latin < Latin, 'post, log'] —**stipitiform** /stíppiti fawrm/ adj

stipitate /stíppitət/ adj having or supported by a stipe [Late 18C. < modern Latin *stipitatus* < Latin *stipit-*, stem of *stipes* 'post, log']

stipites ZOOL, BOT plural of **stipes**

stipple /stípp'l/ vt (**-ples**, **-pling**, **-pled**) **1.** ART PAINT SOMETHING BY DABBING to paint, draw, or engrave something using dots or short dabbing strokes **2.** ART APPLY PAINT WITH DABBING STROKES to apply paint or another substance in dots or short dabbing strokes **3.** MAKE SURFACE MATERIAL APPEAR GRAINY to give something such as wet paint or plaster a rough grainy texture with dabbing strokes **4.** DAPPLE SURFACE WITH DOTS to mark something with dots or speckles (*literary*; *usually passive*) ○ *its lime-green weatherboard stippled with sunlight* ■ n **1.** ART ARTISTIC TECHNIQUE the technique of painting, drawing, or engraving using dots or short dabbing strokes **2.** CONSTR DABBED FINISH a rough grainy finish in wet paint or plaster, produced by means of dabbing strokes [Mid-18C. < Dutch *stippelen* 'keep pricking' < *stip* 'point, dot'] —**stippler** n —**stippling** n

stipulate[1] /stíppyoo̅lət/ (**-lates**, **-lating**, **-lated**) v **1.** vt SPECIFY SOMETHING to specify something such as a condition when making an agreement or an offer ○ *The contract stipulates which expenses will be covered.* **2.** vti DEMAND SOMETHING to make a specific demand for something, usually as a condition in an agreement ○ *stipulate a price* **3.** vt MAKE FORMAL PROMISE to promise something formally or legally **4.** vi LAW AGREE to agree, in terms of the conduct of a legal proceeding ○ *We will stipulate to our receipt of all pertinent discovery documents, my lord.* **5.** vti MAKE ORAL CONTRACT in Roman Law, to make an oral contract in the form of question and answer [Early 17C. < Latin *stipulat-*, past participle of *stipulari* 'demand, bargain'] —**stipulable** adj —**stipulation** /stíppyoo̅ láysh'n/ n —**stipulator** n —**stipulatory** adj

stipulate[2] /stíppyoo̅lət/ adj describes a stem or stalk

that has a pair of growths resembling leaves (**stipules**) at the base [Late 18C. < STIPULE]

stipule /stíppyool/ n either of a pair of small growths at the base of a leaf stalk or stem that resemble leaves [Late 18C. Directly or via French < Latin *stipula* 'straw, stalk'] —**stipular** /-yoo̅lər/ adj

stir[1] /stur/ v (**stirs**, **stirring**, **stirred**) **1.** vt MIX INGREDIENTS to move a liquid around with a spoon, stick, or other implement in order to mix or cool the contents ○ *Slowly stir the cream into the soup.* **2.** vi BE ABLE TO BE STIRRED to be of a consistency that allows a spoon or other implement to be moved around **3.** vti MOVE GENTLY to move gently, or make something do this **4.** vi LEAVE PLACE to move or leave, especially from a favourite or usual place ○ *The guards were told not to stir from their posts.* **5.** vi MOVE AFTER RESTING to get up and move about, especially after a rest ○ *anyone stirring at this early hour* **6.** vt MAKE SOMEBODY OUT to rouse somebody into action **7.** vt STIMULATE IMAGINATION to stimulate something such as somebody's imagination or memory (*formal*) **8.** vi BE FELT to begin to be experienced as an emotion (*formal*) ○ *Deep-seated bitterness stirred within him.* **9.** vti MAKE SOMEBODY EMOTIONAL to arouse a strong emotional reaction in somebody ○ *music that never fails to stir me* **10.** vi HAPPEN to happen or be current (*informal*) ○ *What's stirring this week at Westminster?* ■ n **1.** ACT OF STIRRING an act or instance of stirring a liquid **2.** COMMOTION a lively reaction, usually either excitement or controversy **3.** SLIGHT MOVEMENT a gentle movement **4.** *Aus* TROUBLE trouble or mischief (*informal*) ○ *He used to ring doorbells for a stir.* **5.** *NZ* LEISURE CELEBRATION a lively party (*informal*) [Old English *styrian* 'agitate' < Indo-European, 'to whirl'] —**stirrable** adj

stir up vt **1.** to cause trouble or a confrontation deliberately **2.** to cause something such as dust to rise and swirl around

stir[2] /stur/ n CRIME same as **prison** (*dated slang*) [Mid-19C. Origin ?]

stir-crazy adj mentally unsettled as a result of spending a long time in a confined space such as a prison cell (*informal or humorous*) [< STIR[2]]

stir-fry vt to fry small pieces of food rapidly in a small amount of oil over high heat, stirring continuously. This method is used extensively in Chinese cookery. ■ n a dish of food prepared by stir-frying

stirk /sturk/ n *regional* a young cow or bullock [Old English *stīrc*. Origin ?]

Stirling /stúrling/ **1.** city in central Scotland, on the River Forth. Population: 78,833 (2001). **2.** town in southern South Australia. Population: 4,698 (1991).

Stirling, Sir James (1926–92) British architect. His post-modernist style is exemplified by the Staatsgalerie in Stuttgart, Germany (1977–84) and the Clore Gallery, London (1980–86). Full name **Stirling, Sir James Frazer**

Stirling engine n an external-combustion engine in which heat generated on the outside of the cylinders causes either air or an inert gas within the cylinders to expand and drive the pistons [Mid-19C. After Revd Robert *Stirling* (1790–1878), Scottish Presbyterian minister and engineer]

Stirling Range mountain range in southwestern Western Australia. Its highest peak is Bluff Knoll, 1,073 m/3,520 ft.

Stirling's formula n a mathematical formula used to calculate the approximate value of the factorial of a very large number [Mid-20C. After James *Stirling* (1692–1770), Scottish mathematician]

stirps /sturps/ (plural **stirpes** /stúr peez/) n **1.** a line of descendants from a common ancestor **2.** a plant variety in which the characteristics are fixed through cultivation [Late 17C. < Latin, 'stem, lineage']

stirrer /stúrər/ n somebody who deliberately causes trouble or provokes confrontation, often by spreading rumours or divulging confidences (*informal*)

stirring /stúring/ adj **1.** CAUSING EMOTIONAL REACTION causing an emotional or excited reaction **2.** LIVELY full of energy and vitality ○ *a stirring rendition of a Chopin mazurka* ■ n **1.** MOVEMENT a slight movement **2.** AROUSING OF FEELING the awakening of something, especially an emotion or memory (*formal*) —**stirringly** adv

stirrup /stírrəp/ n **1.** RIDER'S FOOT SUPPORT a flat-bottomed metal ring hanging from a strap on each side of a horse's saddle to provide support for a rider's foot **2.** SUPPORTING STRAP a loop or strap that supports a foot or passes under a foot, e.g. the straps supporting a woman's feet in childbirth **3.** NAUT SHIP'S ROPE one of a set of ropes hanging from a sail-supporting spar (**yard**) on a ship. Loops at the bottom allow another rope for standing on to be threaded through. [Old English *stīgrāp* 'rope for getting up' < *stīgan* 'go up' + *rāp* (see ROPE)]

stirrup bone n ANAT same as **stapes** [< its shape]

stirrup cup n a farewell drink of alcohol, originally one shared with a departing horse rider

stirrup iron n the metal ring of a riding stirrup

stirrup leather n a leather strap that attaches a stirrup to the saddle

stirrup pants npl ANZ, N Am CLOTHING women's stretch pants with straps attached that pass under the feet. UK term **ski pants**

stirrup pump n a portable hand-operated pump, held on the ground with the feet, that draws water from a bucket and sprays it out. It is used to fight small fires. [< the shape of the foot-piece used to hold the pump in place]

stishovite /stíshə vīt/ n a rare crystalline form of quartz. Source: meteor craters. [Mid-20C. After Sergey Mikhailovich *Stishov* (b.1937), Russian mineralogist]

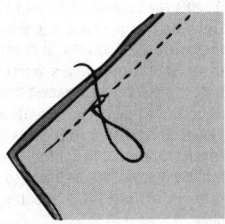

Running stitch

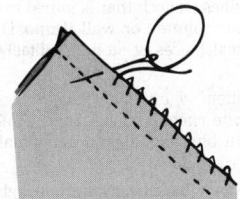

Overcast stitch

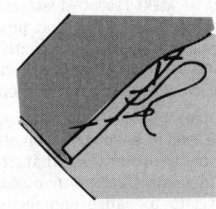

Blind stitch

stitch

stitch /stich/ n **1.** LENGTH OF THREAD IN MATERIAL a short length of thread that has been passed through one or more pieces of material, either for decoration or to join pieces together **2.** SURGICAL THREAD a single loop of surgical thread used to close up a wound **3.** LOOP OF WOOL a single loop of wool or similar material, passed around a knitting needle or a crochet hook **4.** STYLE OF NEEDLEWORK a style of sewing or knitting ○ *lock stitch* **5.** ACHING PAIN cramp in the side of the abdomen caused e.g. by exercising or laughing **6.** GARMENT a piece of clothing (*informal*) ○ *didn't have a stitch on* **7.** AGRIC RIDGE BETWEEN FURROWS the ridge between two adjacent furrows in a field ■ vt (**stitches**, **stitching**, **stitched**) **1.** SEW SOMETHING to join, finish, or

decorate something with stitches **2. CLOSE WOUND** to close a wound with one or more stitches **3. BIND PAGES** to bind the pages of a book, pamphlet, or other publication with thread or staples [Old English *stice* 'prick' < Indo-European, 'jab'] —**stitcher** *n* ◇ **a stitch in time saves nine** dealing promptly with a minor problem will prevent it from developing into a more complicated or larger-scale problem ◇ **in stitches** laughing a great deal

stitch up *vt* **1. SEW SOMETHING TOGETHER** to sew fabric or an article, or repair something by sewing it **2. CLOSE WOUND** to close a wound with stitches (*informal*) **3. ARRANGE DEAL** to complete negotiations or arrange a deal satisfactorily (*informal*) **4. MAKE SOMEBODY APPEAR GUILTY** to deliberately make somebody innocent appear to be guilty of something (*informal*) ○ *He claimed the police had stitched him up.*

stitchery /stíchəri/ *n* needlework, especially when it is functional rather than decorative

stitch-up *n* a deliberate attempt to achieve an unfair outcome (*informal*) ○ *Everyone felt her appointment to the board had been a stitch-up.*

stitchwort /stích wurt/ (*plural* **-worts** or *same*) *n* a perennial creeping wild plant of the chickweed family. Flowers: small, white, star-shaped. Genus: *Stellaria*. [< its former use to cure sharp pains in the side]

stk *abbr* COMM stock

STM *abbr* Master of Sacred Theology [Latin *Sacrae Theologiae Magister*]

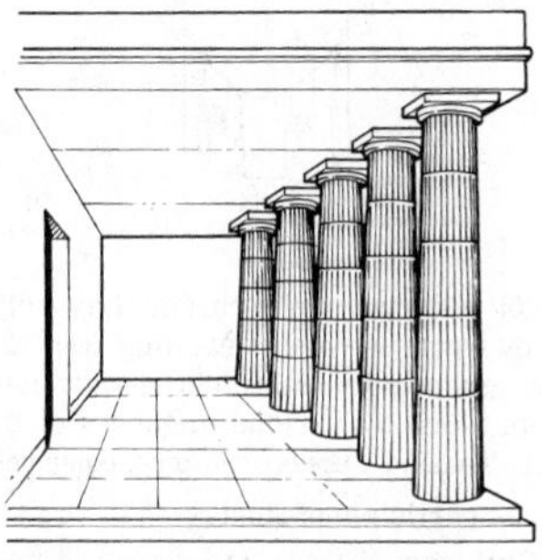

stoa

stoa /stṓ ə/ (*plural* **stoas** or **stoae** /stṓ ee/) *n* in ancient Greece, a covered walkway, usually with a row of columns on one side and a wall on the other [Early 17C. < Greek]

stoat /stōt/ (*plural* **stoats** or *same*) *n* a small animal similar to a weasel, with a sleek brown coat. Native to: Europe, Asia, North America. Latin name: *Mustela erminea*. [15C. Origin ?]

stob /stob/ *n UK regional, Southern US* a stake or stump [14C. Probably variant of STUB]

stochastic /stə kástik/ *adj* **1.** STATS **RANDOM** involving or showing random behaviour **2.** STATS **INVOLVING PROBABILITY** involving or subject to probabilistic behaviour **3. INVOLVING GUESSWORK** involving guesswork or conjecture (*formal*) [Mid-20C. < Greek *stokhastikos* < *stokhos* 'target, aim', literally 'pointed stake'] —**stochastically** *adv*

stock /stok/ *n* **1. SUPPLY OF GOODS AVAILABLE FOR SALE** a supply of goods for sale, kept on the premises by a shop or business **2. RESERVE OF SOMETHING** a supply held in reserve for future use **3. AVAILABLE AMOUNT OF SOMETHING** the amount of something such as a natural resource or a service available ○ *an alarming fall in North Atlantic fish stocks* **4.** FIN **TOTAL SHARE ISSUE** the total number of shares issued by a company or sector **5.** FIN **INVESTOR'S CAPITAL SHARE** the share of capital held by an individual investor (*often used in the plural*) **6.** *UK* FIN **MONEY RAISED** the amount of money raised by a company through the sale of shares, entitling holders to dividends, some rights of ownership, and other benefits. Aus, N Am term **capital stock 7. SOMEBODY'S REPUTATION** somebody's standing or reputation ○ *Her stock is high in terms of public opinion because of her aid work.* **8.** AGRIC same as **livestock 9. ANCESTRAL DESCENT** ancestry, usually with reference to race, ethnic group, class, region, or profession **10. ORIGINAL VARIETY** the original variety from which other similar plants, animals, or languages are descended **11.** BIOL **GROUP OF RELATED ORGANISMS** a race, family, breed, or other related group of animals or plants **12.** FOOD **BROTH** a liquid made by simmering meat, fish, bones, or vegetables with herbs in water, used in soups, stews, and sauces **13.** BOT **TRUNK** the trunk of a tree, or the main stem of a plant **14.** BOT **PLANT RECEIVING GRAFT** a plant or plant stem onto which a shoot or bud is grafted **15.** BOT **PLANT USED FOR CUTTINGS** a plant or part of a plant from which cuttings are taken **16.** AGRIC **ANIMAL PEN** a small pen or frame where a single animal can be confined, e.g. for veterinary examination or treatment (*often used in the plural*) **17.** ARMS **PART OF FIREARM** the part of a firearm to which the barrel and firing mechanism are attached. It is held in the hand or rested against the shoulder. **18.** ARMS **PART OF GUN CARRIAGE** the long beam on a field artillery carriage that extends behind it. When placed on the ground, it becomes the piece's third point of contact, along with the two wheels. **19.** AGRIC, HIST **PART OF PLOUGH** the frame of a horse-drawn plough **20. HANDLE OF SOMETHING** the handle of something such as a fishing rod, whip, or carpentry tool **21. WOODEN BLOCK** a block of wood **22. SUPPORTING PART** an upright supporting part **23.** NAUT **ANCHOR PART** the crosspiece on some types of anchor **24. RAW MATERIAL** the basic material from which something is manufactured **25.** CINEMA **UNEXPOSED FILM** cinema film that has not yet been exposed **26.** METALL **PIECE OF METAL** a piece of cut metal ready to be processed, especially by forging **27.** (*plural* **stocks** or *same*) PLANTS **FLOWERING PLANT** a widely grown ornamental plant. Flowers: fragrant, brightly coloured, in clusters. Native to: Europe, southern Asia. Genus: *Matthiola*. **28.** (*plural* **stocks** or *same*) PLANTS same as **Virginia stock 29.** CHR **CLERICAL SHIRT FRONT** a broad piece of cloth worn on the chest below a clerical collar by members of the clergy in some denominations of the Christian Church **30.** LEISURE **UNDISTRIBUTED CARDS OR COUNTERS** a pile of cards or counters not dealt out at the start of a game, but picked up during it **31.** *US* THEATRE same as **repertory** (sense 1) **32. HUB** the hub of a wheel **33.** GEOL **ROCK MASS** a roughly circular mass of exposed igneous rock **34.** RAIL same as **rolling stock** (sense 1) ■ *adj* **UNORIGINAL** typical or familiar and lacking originality ○ *When pushed for an answer, he gave the stock response.* ■ *v* (**stocks, stocking, stocked**) **1.** *vt* **HAVE PRODUCT IN STOCK** to have an item available for sale **2.** *vt* **FILL SOMETHING WITH GOODS FOR SALE** to fill something with a supply of goods for sale ○ *stocked the supermarket shelves with their new product* **3.** *vt* **FILL SOMETHING WITH SUPPLY FOR FUTURE** to fill something with a plentiful supply of something for future use ○ *We've stocked the freezer with ice cream for the children.* **4.** *vt* **SUPPLY FARM WITH ANIMALS** to supply a farm with livestock **5.** *vi* BOT **SPROUT ANEW** to sprout new shoots [Old English *stocc* 'tree trunk' < Germanic] —**stocker** *n* ◇ **take stock 1.** to think carefully about something so that you can form an opinion about it **2.** COMM to make an inventory of the stock, especially at the end of a season in a shop or business

stock up *vi* to collect a large supply of something for future use ○ *stock up on canned goods*

stockade /sto káyd/ *n* **1. DEFENSIVE BARRIER** a tall fence or enclosure made of wooden posts driven into the ground side by side to keep out enemies or intruders **2. AREA INSIDE BARRIER** an area surrounded by a stockade **3.** *N Am* MIL **MILITARY PRISON** a prison on a military base, especially an army or air force base ■ *vt* (**-ades, -ading, -aded**) **SURROUND AREA WITH STOCKADE** to enclose an area with a stockade [Early 17C. Via obsolete French *estocade* < Spanish *estacada* < *estaca* 'stake' < Germanic]

stockbreeder /stók breedər/ *n* somebody who breeds and rears livestock —**stockbreeding** *n*

stockbroker /stók brōkər/ *n* somebody who buys and sells stocks, shares, and other securities for clients —**stockbrokerage** *n* —**stockbroking** *n*

stockbroker belt *n* an affluent residential area outside a city inhabited by middle-class professional people who commute to the city to work

stock car *n* **1.** a standard passenger car that has been modified for professional racing **2.** *N Am* same as **cattle truck**

stock certificate *n N Am* FIN same as **share certificate**

stock company *n N Am* **1.** a company that has its capital divided into shares that are freely tradable **2.** same as **repertory company**

stock control *n* regulation of its stock by a retailer or other trader

stock cube *n* a small cube of dried and concentrated food extracts that, when added to hot water, makes a stock for use in soups, stews, and sauces. US term **bouillon cube**

stock dove *n* a greyish dove that nests in holes in trees and cliffs. Native to: Europe. Latin name: *Columba oenas*. [Probably < STOCK 'tree trunk'; from its nesting in trees]

stock exchange *n* **1.** FIN same as **stock market** (sense 1) **2.** a building in which a stock exchange is situated

stock farm *n* a farm on which animals such as cattle, sheep, and pigs are bred and raised

stockfish /stók fish/ (*plural same* or **-fishes**) *n* a fish, usually cod or haddock, that has been cured by being split and air-dried without the addition of salt [13C. Translation of Low German and Middle Dutch *stokvisch* < *stok* 'stick, tree trunk' + *visch* 'fish']

Stockhausen /shtók howz'n/, **Karlheinz** (*b.* 1928) German composer. A major figure in the musical avant-garde from the late 1950s, he incorporates serialism, aleatory elements, and electronic sound in his work.

> 'Music is mathematics, the mathematics of listening, mathematics for the ears.'
> [Karlheinz Stockhausen. Quoted in 'In the Service of Music: The Quest for Perfection', *Conversations with Stockhausen*, Mya Tannenbaum; 1987]

stockholder /stók hōldər/ *n* **1.** *N Am* FIN same as **shareholder 2.** *Aus* a farmer who keeps livestock —**stockholding** *n*

Stockholm /stók hōm/ capital city of Sweden, on the eastern coast of the country. Population: 754,948 (2002).

Stockholm syndrome *n* a condition experienced by some people who have been held as hostages for an extended time in which they begin to identify with and feel sympathetic towards their captors [Late 20C. Because a hostage taken during a bank robbery in Stockholm exhibited this]

stockhorse /stók hawrss/ *n Aus* a horse trained to herd livestock

stockinette /stóki nét/, **stockinet** *n* a stretchy knitted fabric. Use: bandages, dishcloths. [Late 18C. Probably alteration of *stocking net*]

stockinette stitch *n US* HANDICRAFT same as **stocking stitch**

stocking /stóking/ *n* **1.** either of a pair of tightly fitting leg coverings for women, made of silk, nylon, or wool (*often used in the plural*) **2.** CLOTHING same as **sock**[1] (sense 1) (*dated or formal*) **3.** same as **Christmas stocking** (*informal*) **4.** ZOOL a differently coloured part of the lower leg of an animal, especially a horse [Late 16C. < STOCK in the obsolete sense 'stocking'] —**stockinged** *adj*

ORIGIN The use of ***stocking*** to mean a leg covering may have arisen from the blackly humorous comparison of the stocks in which people's legs were restrained as punishment with 'leggings, hose'. Until comparatively recently ***stocking*** was a unisex term (as it still is in the expression 'in your stockinged feet'); the restriction to women's hosiery is a 20th-century development.

stocking cap *n* a tightly fitting cone-shaped knitted cap with a tapering tail that often has a tassel on the end

stocking filler *n* a small and usually inexpensive Christmas gift, especially one put into a child's Christmas stocking. N Am term **stocking stuffer**

stocking frame *n* an early type of knitting machine

stocking mask *n* a nylon stocking pulled over the head to disguise the features, usually worn by somebody committing a crime

stocking stitch *n UK, ANZ, Can* a pattern in knitting that alternates rows of plain and purl stitches. US term **stockinette stitch**

stocking stuffer *n N Am* same as **stocking filler**

stock-in-trade *n* **1.** a resource that somebody needs

and regularly makes use of, especially at work ○ *Courtesy and composure are the receptionist's stock-in-trade.* **2.** the goods and equipment that need to be kept on the premises for a business or shop to operate normally

stockist /stókist/ *n* a person or shop that stocks a particular product

stockjobber /stók jobbər/ *n* **1.** formerly, a dealer on the stock exchange who dealt only with brokers, not with members of the public **2.** *US* a stockbroker, especially an unscrupulous dealer trading in worthless securities (*dated*) —**stockjobbery** *n* —**stockjobbing** *n*

stockkeeping /stók keeping/ *n* BUSINESS same as **stock control**

stockkeeping unit *n* BUSINESS, COMPUT full form of **SKU**

stockman /stókmən/ (*plural* -**men** /-mən/) *n* **1.** a man who owns or breeds farm animals, especially cattle **2.** a man who looks after the livestock on a farm

stock market *n* **1.** FINANCIAL MARKET an organized market where brokers meet to buy and sell stocks and shares **2.** FINANCIAL TRADING the activity of buying and selling stocks and shares, or the global market for stocks and shares (*hyphenated before a noun*) **3.** PRICE LEVEL the level of prices for stocks and shares in a stock market ○ *The stock market fell to its lowest yet.* **4.** *US* AGRIC PLACE WHERE ANIMALS ARE AUCTIONED a building with an arena in which farm animals are auctioned

stock option *n* N Am same as **share option**

stockperson /stók purss'n/ (*plural* -**persons** or -**people** /-peep'l/) *n* **1.** somebody who owns or breeds farm animals, especially cattle **2.** somebody who looks after the livestock on a farm

stockpile /stók pīl/ *vti* (-**piles**, -**piling**, -**piled**) to collect and store large amounts of things such as equipment or weapons for future use ■ *n* a large supply of something such as food or weapons, often accumulated in anticipation of future difficulties —**stockpiler** *n*

SYNONYMS See *collect*[1].

Stockport /stók pawrt/ town in Cheshire, northwestern England. Population: 291,100 (2000).

stockpot /stók pot/ *n* a large pot for cooking soups and stock

stockroom /stók room, -room/ *n* a room where goods are stored in a shop, office, or factory

stockroute /stók root/ *n* ANZ a road or track that cattle are herded along

stocks /stoks/ *n* (*takes a singular or plural verb*) **1.** PUNISHMENT DEVICE in former times, a wooden frame in which an offender was secured by the hands and feet or by the head and hands and left in public to be ridiculed or abused **2.** CONSTRUCTION STAND a frame that supports a boat or ship while it is being built **3.** RUDDER SHAFT the vertical shaft at the forward edge of a rudder, attached to the steering controls [14C. Plural of STOCK, in the sense 'post, tree trunk'] ◇ **on the stocks** in the process of being made, prepared, or arranged

stock saddle *n* N Am RIDING same as **Western saddle**

stock-still *adv* absolutely motionless

stocktaking /stók tayking/ *n* **1.** the process of evaluating a situation, especially a personal situation **2.** the making of an itemized list of all merchandise in a shop or business. N Am term **inventory**

Stockton /stóktən/ city and inland port in central California, on the San Joaquin River, south of Sacramento. Population: 262,835 (2002 estimate).

Stockton-on-Tees /-on teez/ port in County Durham, northeastern England. Population: 83,576 (1991).

stockwoman /stók wooman/ (*plural* -**women** /-wimin/) *n* **1.** a woman who owns or breeds farm animals, especially cattle **2.** a woman who looks after the livestock on a farm

stocky /stóki/ (-**ier**, -**iest**) *adj* **1.** short and broad with a strong-looking physique **2.** N Am somewhat overweight —**stockily** *adv* —**stockiness** *n*

stockyard /stók yaard/ *n* a large enclosed yard with

pens or covered stables where livestock are kept before being sold, slaughtered, or shipped on

stodge /stoj/ *n* (*informal*) **1.** food that is heavy, filling, and usually fairly tasteless **2.** dull or unimaginative matter of any kind, especially writing [Late 17C. Origin ?]

stodgy /stójji/ (-**ier**, -**iest**) *adj* (*informal*) **1.** FILLING heavy and filling to eat and usually fairly tasteless **2.** FORMAL OR POMPOUS boringly or laughably conventional, formal, or pompous ○ *one of his stodgy dinner parties* **3.** UNIMAGINATIVE lacking originality, flair, or imagination ○ *another sheaf of stodgy poems* —**stodgily** *adv* —**stodginess** *n*

stoep /stoop/ *n* S Africa a porch or veranda [Late 18C. Via Afrikaans < Dutch]

stogy /stógi/ (*plural* -**gies**), **stogie**, **stogey** (*plural* -**geys**) *n* **1.** N Am a long slim inexpensive cigar **2.** US a heavy boot or shoe that is crudely made [Mid-19C. Shortening of *Conestoga*, probably because used by drivers of Conestoga wagons]

stoic /stó ik/ *n* somebody who is unemotional, especially somebody who shows patience and endurance during adversity ■ *adj also* **stoical** /stó ik'l/ showing admirable patience and endurance in the face of adversity without complaining or getting upset [Late 16C. < STOIC] —**stoically** *adv*

SYNONYMS See *impassive*.

Stoic /stó ik/ *n* a member of an ancient Greek school of philosophy that asserted that happiness can only be achieved by accepting life's ups and downs as the products of unalterable destiny. The school was founded around 308 BC by Zeno. [14C. < Latin *Stoicus* < Greek *stoa* 'porch', referring to the Painted Porch in Athens, where Zeno taught] —**Stoic** *adj*

stoical *adj* same as **stoic**

stoichiology /stóyki ólləji/ *n* the study of the elements or principles of any discipline, especially the chemical principles underlying cell and tissue physiology [Mid-19C. < Greek *stoikheion* 'element', after German *Stöchiologie*] —**stoichiological** /stóyki ə lójjik'l/ *adj*

stoichiometry /stóyki ómmətri/ *n* **1.** the branch of chemistry concerned with measuring the proportions of elements that combine during chemical reactions **2.** a measure of the relative proportions of the elements that take part in a chemical reaction [Mid-19C. < Greek *stoikheion* 'element', after German *Stochiometrie*] —**stoichiometric** /stóyki ə méttrik/ *adj*

stoicism /stó issizəm/ *n* emotional indifference, especially admirable patience and endurance shown in the face of adversity

Stoicism /stó issizəm/ *n* the beliefs of the ancient Greek school of Stoic philosophy

stoke /stōk/ (**stokes**, **stoking**, **stoked**) *vti* **1.** to add fuel to a fire and stir it up to make it burn more intensely **2.** to be responsible for adding fuel to and tending a boiler or furnace [Mid-17C. Back-formation < STOKER] **stoke up** *v* **1.** *vt* ADD FUEL TO FIRE to add fuel to a fire or a furnace and stir it up so that it burns more intensely **2.** *vt* INTENSIFY EMOTION to cause an emotion such as anger or fear to be felt more strongly **3.** *vi* EAT IN BULK to eat food in large quantities, because or as if more food may not be had (*informal*)

stoked /stōkt/ *adj* **1.** Aus, US delighted or exhilarated (*informal*) ○ *She said she was stoked about the new job.* **2.** N Am in an excited or euphoric state from having taken drugs (*slang*)

stokehold /stók hōld/ *n* **1.** the boiler room of a steamship **2.** a coal bunker for a steamship's boiler

stokehole /stók hōl/ *n* **1.** the opening through which fuel is added to a boiler or furnace **2.** NAUT same as **stokehold** [Mid-17C. Translation of Dutch *stookgat*]

Stoke-on-Trent /stók on trént/ city in Staffordshire, central England. It is a major pottery manufacturing centre. Population: 249,000 (2000).

stoker /stókər/ *n* somebody whose job it is to add fuel to and tend a furnace or boiler, e.g. on a steamship or a steam train [Mid-17C. < Dutch < Middle Dutch *stoken* 'poke with a stick']

Stoker /stókər/, **Bram** (1847–1912) Irish writer. He is best known for the classic vampire story *Dracula* (1897). Full name **Stoker, Abraham**

Stokes-Adams syndrome /stóks áddəmz-/ *n* episodes of temporary dizziness or fainting caused by disruption or extreme slowing of the heartbeat and consequent brief stoppage of blood flow [Early 20C. After William *Stokes* (1804–75) and Robert *Adams* (1791–1875), Irish physicians]

Stokowski /stə kófski/, **Leopold** (1882–1977) British-born US conductor. He brought the Philadelphia Orchestra international recognition as its principal conductor (1912–38). Full name **Stokowski, Leopold Antoni Stanisław Boleslawowicz**

stokvel /stók fel/ *n* S Africa an informal savings society in which members contribute regularly and receive payouts in rotation [< Afrikaans, alteration of English *stock fair* 'livestock market']

STOL /stol, éss tol/ *n* **1.** a flying system that gives an aircraft the ability to take off and land on a very short runway. Full form **short takeoff and landing** **2.** an aircraft fitted with the STOL system

stole[1] /stōl/ past tense of **steal**

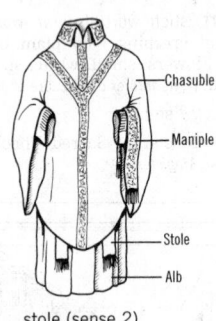

stole (sense 2)

stole[2] /stōl/ *n* **1.** a woman's scarf or shawl, often made of fur or worn as part of evening wear **2.** a long, narrow, and usually embroidered scarf made of silk or linen, worn by various members of the clergy [Pre-12C. Via Latin < Greek *stolē* 'robe, equipment']

stolen past participle of **steal**

Stolen Children *npl* Aus Aboriginal children who, between 1910 and 1970, were taken from their families and placed in state homes or with white foster families, in line with Australian government policy on integration

stolid /stóllid/ *adj* solemn, unemotional, and not easily excited or upset [Late 16C. Directly or via French < Latin *stolidus* 'dense, stupid'] —**stolidity** /stə líddəti/ *n* —**stolidly** *adv* —**stolidness** *n*

SYNONYMS See *impassive*.

stollen /stóllən/ (*plural* same or -**lens**) *n* a rich sweet German fruit bread made with nuts, raisins, and other dried fruits. It is traditionally served at Christmas. [Early 20C. < German < Old High German *stollo* 'post, support']

stolon /stó lon/ *n* **1.** a long stem or shoot that arises from the central rosette of a plant and droops to the ground. It may form new plants where it touches the soil. **2.** a budding of the body wall in simple organisms, especially an extension of some colonial organisms such as hydroids that anchors the colony to a rock or other substrate [Early 17C. < Latin *stolon-*] —**stolonate** /-ət/ *adj* —**stoloniferous** /stólə níffərəss/ *adj*

stoma /stómə/ (*plural* -**mata** /-mətə/) *n* **1.** BOT PLANT PORE a tiny pore in the outer layer (**epidermis**) of a plant leaf or stem that controls the passing of water vapour and other gases into and out of the plant **2.** ZOOL MOUTH OR SIMILAR STRUCTURE a mouth, or an opening that acts as or is shaped like a mouth **3.** SURG SURGICAL OPENING an artificial opening made in an organ of the body, especially an opening in the colon or ileum made via the abdomen [Late 17C. Via modern Latin < Greek, 'mouth'] —**stomal** *adj* —**stomatal** *adj* —**stomatous** *adj*

stomach /stúmmək/ *n* **1.** VERTEBRATES' DIGESTIVE ORGAN an organ resembling a sac in which food is mixed and partially digested. It forms part of the digestive tract of vertebrates and is situated between the oesophagus and the small intestine. **2.** ABDOMEN the

abdomen of a vertebrate (*not used technically*) **3.** COMPARTMENT OF ANIMAL'S STOMACH a digestive chamber in the four-part stomach of ruminant animals (*not used technically*) **4.** INVERTEBRATES' DIGESTIVE ORGAN a digestive organ in some invertebrate animals in which food is mixed, stored, and partially digested **5.** SEAT OF UNPLEASANT FEELINGS the part of the body in which disgust, nausea, and fear are experienced ○ *The very idea makes me sick to my stomach.* **6.** RESISTANCE TO UNPLEASANTNESS the ability to withstand disgust, nausea, or fear ○ *This is not a job for someone with a weak stomach.* **7.** WILLINGNESS TO DO SOMETHING an appetite or willingness to do something or tolerate something ○ *no stomach for a fight* ■ *vt* (**-achs, -aching, -ached**) **1.** TOLERATE SOMETHING to put up with something ○ *I find their gloating hard to stomach.* **2.** EAT FOOD WITHOUT ILL EFFECTS to eat a particular food without ill effects ○ *for those of you who can't stomach seafood* [14C. Via French and Latin < Greek *stomakhos* 'throat, gullet' < *stoma* 'mouth']

stomachache /stúmmək ayk/ *n* a pain in the abdominal region, caused by a minor condition such as indigestion or an infection

stomach-churning *adj* producing feelings of disgust, nausea, or fear

stomach crunch *n* an exercise in which you lie flat on your back with your legs bent and then raise the upper part of your body a few centimetres off the ground without using your hands

stomacher /stúmməkər/ *n* a stiff panel of material, often decorated with embroidery or jewels, worn over the chest and abdomen by women in the 17th and 18th centuries, and earlier by both sexes

stomachic /stə mákik/ *adj* also **stomachical** /stə mákik'l/ associated with the stomach —**stomachically** *adv*

stomach pump *n* the equipment, consisting of a tube, funnel, and bucket, used to flush out the stomach contents of somebody who has swallowed a dangerous substance such as a poison (*informal*)

stomach tooth *n* either of the first canine teeth in the lower jaw of humans, whose appearance is popularly believed to be hastened by stomach upsets in infants

stomach-turning *adj* producing feelings of disgust or nausea

stomata plural of **stoma**

stomatitis /stómə títiss/ *n* inflammation of the mucous tissue lining the mouth [Mid-19C. < Greek *stomat-*, stem of *stoma* 'mouth'] —**stomatitic** /-títtik/ *adj*

stomatology /stómə tólləji/ *n* the branch of medicine or dentistry that is concerned with the study of the mouth and diseases of the mouth [Late 19C. < Greek *stomat-*, stem of *stoma* 'mouth'] —**stomatological** /stómətə lójjik'l/ *adj* —**stomatologist** *n*

stomatopod /stómətə pod, stə máttə-/ *n* a shellfish with abdominal gills and a second pair of claws, e.g. the squilla. Order: Stomatopoda. [Late 19C. < Greek *stomat-*, stem of *stoma* 'mouth']

-stome *suffix* mouth, stoma ○ *peristome* [< Greek *stoma* 'mouth'] —**-stomous** *suffix*

stomodaeum /stómə dee əm/ (*plural* **-daea** /-dee ə/), **stomodeum** (*plural* **-dea**) *n* a depression in the surface of an early embryo that develops into the mouth [Late 19C. < modern Latin < Greek *stoma* 'mouth' + *hodaios* 'on the way, becoming' < *hodos* 'way, road'] —**stomodaeal** *adj*

stomp /stomp/ *vti* (**stomps, stomping, stomped**) WALK WITH HEAVY STEPS to tread heavily and noisily, or bring your feet down heavily and noisily, often in anger ■ *n* **1.** JAZZ DANCE a jazz dance with stamping foot movements **2.** JAZZ MUSIC jazz music accompanying the stomp [Early 19C. Variant of STAMP] —**stomper** *n* —**stompingly** *adv*

stompie /stómpi/ *n S Africa* a cigarette or cigarette end (*informal*) [Mid-20C. < Afrikaans, 'little stump' < *stomp* 'stump']

stomping ground *n* same as **stamping ground** (*informal*)

-stomy *suffix* a surgical operation that creates an artificial opening ○ *gastrostomy* [< Greek *stoma* 'mouth']

stone /stōn/ *n* **1.** HARD NONMETALLIC MATERIAL the hard solid nonmetallic substance that rocks are made of. Use:

building material. **2.** ROCK FRAGMENT a small piece of rock of any shape **3.** SHAPED ROCK FRAGMENT a piece of rock that has been shaped for a particular purpose, e.g. a gravestone or a paving stone (*often used in combination*) **4.** SMALL HARD MASS a small hard mass, e.g. a hailstone (*usually used in combination*) **5.** same as **gemstone 6.** BOT HARD MASS INSIDE FRUIT the hard central part of some fruits e.g. cherries, plums, olives, and peaches, that contains the seed **7.** (*plural* same or **stones**) MEASURE UNIT OF WEIGHT in the United Kingdom, a unit of weight equivalent to 6.35 kg/14 lb. It is used especially for expressing somebody's weight. ○ *He's trying to get down to 12 stone.* **8.** MED MINERAL MASS INSIDE ORGAN a small hard mass of mineral material formed in an organ such as the kidney or gall bladder. Technical name **calculus** (sense 3) **9.** COLOURS LIGHT GREY OR BEIGE a dull light grey or beige colour **10.** SPORTS CURLING BLOCK the shaped and polished mass of granite or iron that is slid along the ice in the game of curling **11.** PRINTING PRINTER'S TABLE a very smooth flat table used for arranging printing type (*dated*) ■ *adj* **1.** OF STONE OR STONEWARE made of stone or stoneware **2.** COLOURS OF THE COLOUR STONE light grey to beige in colour ■ *adv* **1.** EMPHASIZING QUALITY LIKE STONE used to emphasize the degree of a quality associated with stone, e.g. coldness, stillness, or lifelessness **2.** USED FOR EMPHASIS used to emphasize the degree of a quality (*slang*) ○ *stone fine* ○ *stone tired* ■ *vt* (**stones, stoning, stoned**) **1.** THROW STONES AT SOMEBODY to throw stones at somebody or something, especially as a form of punishment, execution, or vandalism **2.** REMOVE STONE FROM FRUIT to remove the hard central part from a fruit such as a plum **3.** US RUB SOMETHING WITH STONE to polish or sharpen something on a stone or with a stone [Old English *stān* < Indo-European] —**stoneless** *adj* ◇ **be carved** or **set** or **cast in (tablets of) stone** to be so firmly established as to make changes impossible or unthinkable ◇ **cast** or **throw the first stone** to be the first person to quarrel with, accuse, or criticize somebody else ◇ **leave no stone unturned** to be very thorough in making a search or in carrying out a task

Stone /stōn/, **Oliver** (b. 1946) US film director. His films deal with contemporary social and political issues, often controversially. He won Academy Awards for best director for *Platoon* (1986) and *Born on the Fourth of July* (1989).

Stone Age *n* the earliest period of human history, in which tools and weapons were made of stone rather than metal. It is divided into the Palaeolithic, Mesolithic, and Neolithic periods. It extends from around 2.5 million years ago to around 2400 BC.

Stone-Age *adj* **1.** dating from the Stone Age, the earliest period of human history **2.** *also* **stone-age** hopelessly behind the times

stone bass /-bass/ *n* a large dark-brown and yellow fish of the perch family. Native to: Atlantic, Mediterranean. Latin name: *Polyprion americanus*. [Because it inhabits rocky ledges and wrecks]

stone-blind *adj* an offensive term meaning completely unable to see —**stone-blindness** *n*

stone bramble *n* a prickly herbaceous plant that produces deep-red berries resembling raspberries. Flowers: white. Native to: Europe, Asia. Latin name: *Rubus saxatilis*. [Because it grows in rocky places]

stone-broke *adj US* same as **stony-broke** (*informal*)

stonecast /stōn kaast/ *n* same as **stone's throw**

stonecat /stōn kat/ (*plural* **-cats** or same) *n* a slender yellowish-brown catfish that inhabits the beds of streams, rivers, and lakes, typically under stones. Native to: North America. Latin name: *Noturus flavus*.

stone cell *n* a short squat plant cell that performs a strengthening function. It occurs in large numbers in fruits such as the quince and the pear.

stonechat /stōn chat/ (*plural* **-chats** or same) *n* a small songbird, the male of which has a black head, brown back, chestnut breast, and white rump. Native to: grassy regions, dry plains of Europe, Asia and Africa. Latin name: *Saxicola torquata*. [Late 18C. Because its call suggests the sound of colliding stones]

stone-cold *adj* completely cold, especially too cold to be palatable ■ *adv* completely and utterly (*informal*) ○ *stone-cold sober*

stone crab *n* a large crab that lays several million eggs and can be a serious pest to oyster beds. Native to: coast of southern United States. Latin name: *Menippe mercenaria*.

stonecrop /stōn krop/ (*plural* **-crops** or same) *n* **1.** an annual or perennial flowering plant with fleshy leaves. Native to: northern temperate regions. Genus: *Sedum*. **2.** a plant related or similar to the stonecrop [Pre-12C. STONE (because the plant grows on rocks) + CROP in the obsolete sense 'flower cluster, ear of grain']

stone curlew *n* a brownish, wading bird with a large head and eyes and thick knee joints, that is active at night. Native to: open dry stony regions worldwide. Family: Burhinidae.

stonecutter /stōn kuttər/ *n* **1.** somebody who cuts and carves stone **2.** a machine that is used to cut stone and concrete, especially a hand-held power tool with a circular blade —**stonecutting** *n*

stoned /stōnd/ *adj* **1.** relaxed, excited, or euphoric from taking illegal drugs, especially cannabis (*slang*) **2.** very intoxicated (*informal*)

stone-dead *adj* definitely or completely lifeless

stone-deaf *adj* an offensive term meaning completely unable to hear

stone-faced *adj* **1.** same as **stony-faced 2.** having a facing of stone

stonefish /stōn fish/ (*plural* **-fishes** or same) *n* a tropical sea fish whose mottled and knobbly body serves as camouflage in its rocky habitat. Genus: *Synanceja*.

stonefly /stōn flī/ (*plural* **-flies** or same) *n* an insect that, in its wingless juvenile stage, lives among stones in rivers and streams. The adults have long antennae and usually two pairs of wings. Both larvae and adults are used as fishing bait. Order: Plecoptera.

stone fruit *n* BOT same as **drupe**

stoneground /stōn grownd/ *adj* ground in the traditional way with millstones rather than with metal rollers ○ *stoneground flour*

stonehearted /stōn haártid/ *adj* same as **stony-hearted**

Stonehenge

Stonehenge /stōn hénj/ prehistoric monument on Salisbury Plain, southern England, consisting of two concentric circles of large standing stones. It was built between 2800 and 1500 BC and is thought to have been an astronomical calendar or a temple to the Sun.

stone lily *n* a fossil of a sea lily

stone marten *n* **1.** a marten that has dark-brown fur with a lighter throat and undersides. Native to: woods of Europe and Asia. Latin name: *Martes foina*. **2.** the fur of the stone marten [Because it inhabits rocky inlets and crevices]

stonemason /stōn mayss'n/ *n* somebody who makes and repairs stone structures or shapes and prepares stone used as a building material —**stonemasonry** *n*

stone parsley *n* a roadside plant with leaves that smell like a mixture of petrol and nutmeg when crushed. Native to: western Europe, Mediterranean. [Translation of Greek *petroselinon* (see PARSLEY)]

stone pine *n* a pine tree with an umbrella-shaped crown that is cultivated for its seeds. Native to: Mediterranean. Latin name: *Pinus pinea*.

stoner /stónər/ *n* a regular smoker of marijuana (*slang*)

stone shoot *n* a strip of loose stones that extends up a steep hillside or mountainside

stone's throw *n* a very short distance ○ *living just a stone's throw from the station*

stonewall /stṓn wáwl/ (**-walls, -walling, -walled**) *v* **1.** *vti* REFUSE TO COOPERATE to create obstructions or refuse to cooperate, especially by avoiding answering questions or providing desired information **2.** *vi* DELIBERATELY CREATE DELAY to create obstructions or employ delaying tactics, especially in order to hinder parliamentary business **3.** *vi* PLAY DEFENSIVELY IN CRICKET in cricket, to play persistently defensive batting strokes —**stonewaller** *n*

stoneware /stṓn wair/ *n* dense opaque nonporous pottery that is fired at a very high temperature

stonewashed /stṓn wosht/ *adj* washed with small pumice pebbles to give a worn faded look ○ *stone-washed jeans*

stonework /stṓn wurk/ *n* **1.** the parts of a building or other structure that are made of stone **2.** the process of building with stone —**stoneworker** *n*

stonewort /stṓn wurt/ (*plural same* or **-worts**) *n* a green alga that grows in fresh or slightly salty water and resembles a plant, having structures resembling leaves arranged on a long structure resembling a stem and jointed branches, often encrusted with lime. Family: Characeae.

stoney *adj* another spelling of **stony**

stonk /stongk/ (*dated slang*) *vt* (**stonks, stonking, stonked**) to subject something such as a building or enemy position to a heavy artillery bombardment ■ *n* a heavy artillery bombardment [Mid-20C. Origin ?]

stonker /stóngkər/ *n* an excellent example of something, often something impressively large or powerful (*slang*) ○ *played a stonker of a shot*

stonkered /stóngkərd/ *adj* (*slang*) **1.** exhausted, defeated, or out of action **2.** extremely drunk [Early 20C. < Scots and N English dialect *stonk* 'game of marbles, marble', origin ?]

stonking /stóngking/ *adj, adv* used to emphasize how good or enjoyable something is (*slang*) ○ *hit a stonking drive straight down the middle* ○ *a stonking good party*

stony /stṓni/ (**-ier, -iest**), **stoney** *adj* **1.** OF OR LIKE STONE made of stone or similar to stone in appearance, texture, or colour **2.** COVERED WITH STONES covered with or having a great many stones **3.** EMOTIONLESS expressing no emotion, especially no friendliness or pity ○ *a stony silence* **4.** same as **stony-broke** (*slang*) —**stonily** *adv* —**stoniness** *n*

stony-broke *adj UK, ANZ, Can* having no money at all (*informal*) US term **stone-broke**

stony coral *n* a coral with a robust external calcium-based skeleton that forms reefs and islands. Order: Scleractinia or Madreporaria.

stony-faced *adj* showing not the slightest emotion, especially no sign of friendliness

stony-hearted /-haártid/ *adj* having or showing no compassion or kindness

stony-iron meteorite *n* a meteorite consisting of metal and stony material

stony meteorite *n* a meteorite that is composed mainly of rock-forming silicate minerals, especially olivine, plagioclase, and pyroxene

stood past participle, past tense of **stand**

USAGE See *sit*.

stooge /stooj/ *n* **1.** COMIC LOSER a comic actor, usually part of a double act, who acts as the butt of most of the jokes **2.** SOMEBODY EXPLOITED somebody who is exploited by others, especially somebody used by criminals in committing their crimes (*slang insult*) **3.** *US* POLICE same as **stool pigeon** (sense 1) (*slang*) ■ *vi* (**stooges, stooging, stooged**) BE TAKEN ADVANTAGE OF to be taken advantage of by another (*informal*) [Early 20C. Origin ?]

stook /stook, stŏŏk/ AGRIC *n* same as **shock**[2] ■ *vt* (**stooks, stooking, stooked**) same as **shock**[2] [14C. Origin ?] —**stooker** *n*

stookie /stŏŏki/ *n Scotland* **1.** a plaster cast on a broken limb **2.** SCULPTURE same as **statue** ○ *stood there like a stookie* [Late 18C. Alteration of STUCCO]

stool /stool/ *n* **1.** SIMPLE SEAT a simple seat with three or four legs and no back or armrests **2.** EXCREMENT a piece of excrement **3.** TOILET a toilet or toilet seat (*slang*) **4.** BOT PLANT BASE the base of a plant, from which shoots or suckers sprout **5.** BOT CLUMP OF SHOOTS a clump of shoots or suckers sprouting from the base of a plant **6.** *US* FIELD SPORTS HUNTER'S DECOY a real or artificial bird used by hunters as a decoy **7.** *W Africa* CHIEF'S THRONE the throne of a tribal chief ■ *vi* (**stools, stooling, stooled**) **1.** SPROUT SHOOTS to sprout shoots or suckers from a stool **2.** *US* EVACUATE BOWELS to evacuate the bowels **3.** FIELD SPORTS BE DECOY OR HUNT WITH DECOY to be a decoy for a hunter of wildfowl, or to hunt wildfowl using decoys **4.** *US* POLICE BE STOOL PIGEON to provide information to law enforcement agencies about criminals (*slang*) [Old English *stōl* 'chair' < Indo-European, 'to stand'] ◇ **fall between two stools 1.** to fail to achieve either of two objectives by hesitating between them and failing to take action, or by trying for both and ending up with neither **2.** to be a possible member of two categories but a true member of neither

stool ball *n* an obsolete game similar to cricket

stoolie /stŏŏli/ *n N Am* POLICE same as **stool pigeon** (sense 1) (*informal*) [Early 20C. Shortening]

stool pigeon *n* **1.** POLICE INFORMER somebody who informs on criminals or their activities to the police (*slang*) **2.** DECOY CRIMINAL a criminal working as a decoy for a gang of criminals, with the job of distracting attention from their activities (*slang*) **3.** FIELD SPORTS HUNTER'S DECOY PIGEON a pigeon, or a dummy of a pigeon, used by a hunter as a decoy [Because hunters' decoys were originally tied to a wooden platform]

stoop[1] /stoop/ *v* (**stoops, stooping, stooped**) **1.** *vti* BEND BODY to bend the top half of the body forwards and downwards **2.** *vi* WALK OR STAND BENT OVER to walk or stand with the head and shoulders bent forwards and downwards **3.** *vi* DO SOMETHING UNETHICAL to act in an unethical or self-degrading way ○ *I never imagined you would stoop so low.* **4.** *vi* CONDESCEND to do something reluctantly and with the attitude of somebody who considers such action unworthy ○*'He could not stoop to love; No lady in the land had power His frozen heart to move.'* (Sir Walter Scott, *Waverley*; 1814) **5.** *vi* SWOOP DOWN to swoop down with wings folded, e.g. when attacking prey (*refers to birds*) ■ *n* **1.** BENT POSTURE a posture in which the head and shoulders are bent forwards and downwards **2.** BIRD'S DOWNWARD SWOOP the downward swoop of a bird of prey [Old English *stūpian* < Germanic] —**stooper** *n* —**stooping** *adj* —**stoopingly** *adv*

CULTURAL NOTE ***She Stoops to Conquer***, a play (1773) by Oliver Goldsmith. An enduringly popular comedy of manners, it is the story of a shy young gentleman, Marlow, who reluctantly travels to the country to woo a young woman. Mistaking her home for an inn, he assumes she is the maid, treats her accordingly, and wins her heart with his frankness.

stoop[2] /stoop/ *n N Am* a small porch at the entrance to a house [Mid-18C. < Dutch *stoep*]

stoop[3] /stoop/ *n* CHR another spelling of **stoup**

stoor *n Scotland* another spelling of **stour**

stop /stop/ *v* (**stops, stopping, stopped**) **1.** *vti* DISCONTINUE SOMETHING to cease doing something, or make somebody cease doing something ○ *She's trying to stop smoking.* **2.** *vti* CEASE MOVING to come to a standstill, or bring something to a standstill ○ *Stop the car!* **3.** *vti* END to come to an end, or bring something to an end ○ *The rain has stopped.* **4.** *vt* PREVENT SOMETHING FROM HAPPENING to cause something not to happen or not to be done ○ *We couldn't stop the roof from caving in.* **5.** *vt* PREVENT SOMEBODY FROM DOING SOMETHING to cause somebody not to do or not to be able to do a particular thing ○ *a way of stopping the children from climbing the fence* **6.** *vi* PAUSE to pause in order to do something before continuing ○ *I urge you to stop and think before deciding.* **7.** *vi* INTERRUPT JOURNEY to interrupt a journey in order to make a brief visit somewhere ○ *Stop at the post office on the way into town.* **8.** *vti* STAY BRIEFLY to stay for a short time (*informal*) ○ *The children's friends like to stop the night.* **9.** *vt* FILL HOLE to fill or block a hole ○ *We need to stop the cracks in the wall.* **10.** *vt* BLOCK SOMETHING to block or plug something such as a pipe or a wound so that nothing can pass through it ○ *Grease has stopped the drain.* **11.** *vt* DEDUCT to deduct money or a payment from somebody's salary ○ *have the cost of breakages stopped from your wages* **12.** *vt* BANKING CANCEL CHEQUE to prevent the honouring of a cheque by an instruction to the bank on which it was to have been drawn **13.** *vt* MUSIC PRESS MUSICAL STRING to press a string on a musical instrument in order to produce a note **14.** *vt* MUSIC COVER HOLE ON INSTRUMENT to use a finger to close a hole on a wind instrument in order to produce a note **15.** *vt* MUSIC PUT HAND INSIDE FRENCH HORN to alter the tone and pitch of a French horn by putting a hand inside the bell **16.** *vt* BOXING KNOCK SOMEBODY OUT to defeat an opponent in boxing by a knockout **17.** *vti* CARDS BLOCK BRIDGE SUIT to block the winning of a suit in bridge **18.** *vt* BE HIT BY SOMETHING to be hit by something, usually a punch or a bullet (*informal*) **19.** *vt* DEFEAT SOMEBODY OR SOMETHING to defeat an opponent or competitor (*informal*) ○ *Nothing's going to stop us now.* ■ *n* **1.** STANDSTILL a complete end or lack of movement **2.** BREAK IN JOURNEY a short break in a journey, e.g. to rest or to visit somebody **3.** PLACE VISITED ON WAY a place visited while on a journey **4.** PAUSE MADE ON ROUTE a place where a bus or a train regularly pauses on its route ○ *Is this your stop?* **5.** BLOCKAGE a blockage or obstruction **6.** PLUG THAT BLOCKS something that is used to block the flow or passage of something, e.g. a plug or a stopper **7.** DEVICE PREVENTING MOVEMENT a device or control that prevents movement (*often used in combination*) ○ *a doorstop* **8.** FULL STOP in punctuation, a full stop (*informal*) **9.** FIN ORDER CANCELLING CHEQUE an order to a bank not to honour a cheque ○ *I had to put a stop on the lost cheque.* **10.** MUSIC STOPPING ON MUSICAL INSTRUMENT an act of stopping a string or a hole on a musical instrument **11.** MUSIC SUBSET OF ORGAN PIPES a subset of organ pipes or harpsichord strings with a common tone colour that can be played in isolation by silencing the remaining pipes or strings **12.** MUSIC ORGAN CONTROL a knob or lever on an organ or harpsichord that isolates a subset of pipes or strings **13.** PHOTOGRAPHY CAMERA'S APERTURE SETTING one of the graded settings for the size of the aperture of a camera lens **14.** PHOTOGRAPHY same as **diaphragm** (sense 3) **15.** NAUT SHORT ROPE a short length of line used to tie up something such as a sail **16.** PHON SPEECH SOUND a consonant sound made by closing the passage of air through the mouth and then suddenly opening it again **17.** ZOOL PART OF ANIMAL'S FACE the area between the nose and the forehead of a cat or a dog **18.** FENCING FENCING COUNTERTHRUST a swift counterthrust made at the time of a fencing opponent's thrust that seeks to make contact first **19.** *Aus* SPORTS BOOT STUD a stud on a football or rugby boot **20.** ARCHIT CARVING a carving that finishes the end of a moulding [Old English *-stoppian* 'block up', via W Germanic < late Latin *stuppare* 'to stuff' < Latin *stuppa* 'plug, stopper' < Greek *stuppē*] —**stoppable** *adj* ◇ **pull out all the stops** to make every possible effort in order to accomplish something ◇ **put a stop to something** to bring something to an end, usually quickly and permanently

stop by *vti* **1.** to interrupt a journey in order to make a brief visit somewhere ○ *Can you stop by the supermarket on your way home?* **2.** to visit a person or place briefly ○ *Stop by any time!*

stop down *vti* to make the aperture of a camera lens smaller

stop off *vi* to interrupt a journey briefly in order to do something or see somebody ○ *We stopped off at the supermarket on the way home.*

stop out *vi* to remain out of the house, or stay out late (*informal*)

stop bath *n* an acid solution in which a negative or print is immersed in order to halt the developing process

stop bit *n* in serial communications, a bit that signals the end of a transmission unit

stopcock /stóp kok/ *n* a valve or tap used to turn on, turn off, or regulate the flow of a fluid in a pipe

stop codon *n* a sequence of three chemical units (**base pairs**) linking complementary strands of DNA or RNA that indicates the end of a protein synthesis. The three stop codons are thymine-adenine-guanine, thymine-adenine-adenine, and thymine-guanine-adenine.

stope /stōp/ *n* an excavation that resembles steps, used especially in the mining of ore ■ *vti* (**stopes, stoping, stoped**) to make stopes in a mine, or extract ore in this way [Mid-18C. Origin ?]

~~stoped~~ incorrect spelling of **stopped**

Stopes /stōps/, **Marie** (1880–1958) Scottish pioneer advocate of birth control and writer. She wrote prolifically promoting scientific methodology of birth control, and established the first birth control clinic in Britain (1921). Full name **Stopes, Marie Charlotte Carmichael**

'An impersonal and scientific knowledge of the structure of our bodies is the surest safeguard against prurient curiosity and lascivious gloating.'
[Marie Stopes, *Married Love*; 1918]

stopgap /stóp gap/ *n* something used as a temporary substitute for something that is needed ■ *adj* used as a temporary substitute for something that is needed ○ *a stopgap spending bill*

stop-go *adj* alternating deliberately between discouragement and encouragement of economic demand so as to control inflation

stoplight /stóp līt/ *n* 1. ROADS same as **traffic light** 2. AUTOMOT same as **brake light**

stop-loss order *n* an order to a stockbroker to stop selling a stock when its price has fallen below a fixed level

stop-off *n* TRAVEL same as **stopover**

stop order *n* an order to a stockbroker to buy or sell a stock when it has risen or fallen to a fixed price

stopover /stóp ōvər/ *n* 1. a usually brief halt on a journey 2. a place where somebody makes a brief halt on a journey

stoppage /stóppij/ *n* 1. STRIKE a strike, especially a brief one 2. DEDUCTION FROM PAY an amount of money deducted from an employee's pay, e.g. tax, national insurance, or pension contributions 3. TIME WHEN PLAY IS HALTED a time during which the play in a game, especially football or rugby, is briefly halted, because of an injury to a player or other situation 4. ACT OF STOPPING the act of stopping the movement of something 5. SITUATION WHERE THINGS ARE STOPPED a situation in which something has been stopped or blocked

stoppage time *n* especially in football or rugby, extra time played at the end of a game to make up for time lost in dealing with injured players or through other interruptions

Sir Tom Stoppard

Stoppard /stóppard/, **Sir Tom** (*b.* 1937) Czech-born British dramatist. He had instant success with *Rosencrantz and Guildenstern are Dead* (1966). Later plays include *Arcadia* (1993). Born **Straussler, Tom**

'Life is a gamble, at terrible odds—if it was a bet, you wouldn't take it.'
[Sir Tom Stoppard, *Rosencrantz and Guildenstern Are Dead*; 1966]

stopper /stóppər/ *n* 1. CORK OR PLUG something that is put into an opening in order to close it 2. SOMEBODY OR SOMETHING THAT STOPS SOMETHING somebody or something that brings something to a stop 3. CARDS CARD THAT PREVENTS TAKING OF SUIT a card held by somebody that will prevent opponents from taking all the tricks in that suit during a hand of bridge ■ *vt* (**-pers, -pering, -pered**) CLOSE SOMETHING WITH STOPPER to close or secure something with a stopper

stopple /stópp'l/ *n* same as **stopper** *n* (sense 1) [15C. < STOP] —**stopple** *vt*

stop press *n* 1. news that is inserted into an edition of a newspaper after printing has begun (*hyphenated before a noun*) 2. a space in a newspaper kept for the insertion of late news

stopstreet /stóp street/ *n* S Africa a street on which there is a junction with a sign requiring motor vehicles to stop before proceeding

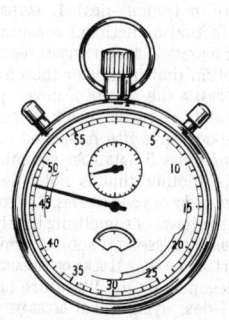

stopwatch

stopwatch /stóp woch/ *n* a special watch that can be started and stopped instantly and is used to measure the amount of time somebody or something takes, e.g. a runner in a race

stop-work meeting *n* Aus a meeting held by workers during working hours to discuss wage claims or strike action

storage /stáwrij/ *n* 1. STORING OR BEING STORED the act of storing something, or the condition of being stored 2. SPACE FOR STORING space in which to store things, especially the amount of such space 3. COMPUT MEDIUM FOR STORING DATA any device or medium used for deposit, retention, and retrieval of computer data, especially a hard disk or floppy disk 4. FIN PRICE FOR STORING the price charged for storing something

storage battery *n* N Am ELEC ENG same as **accumulator** (sense 2)

storage cell *n* ELECTRONICS same as **secondary cell**

storage dump *n* a printout of all the data held in system storage in a computer

storage heater *n* an electrical device that accumulates energy during off-peak times and later releases it as heat

storax /stáw raks/ *n* 1. TREE WITH DROOPING WHITE FLOWERS a deciduous or evergreen tree or bush, some species of which are grown as ornamentals. Flowers: white, drooping in long clusters. Native to: tropical or subtropical regions. Genus: *Styrax*. 2. FRAGRANT GUM RESIN a vanilla-scented gum resin obtained from the tree species, *Styrax officinale* 3. FRAGRANT BALSAM a fragrant liquid balsam obtained from the bark of the Asian liquidambar tree species, *Liquidambar orientalis* [14C. Via Latin < Greek, variant of *sturax*]

store /stawr/ *v* (**stores, storing, stored**) 1. *vt* PUT SOMETHING AWAY to put something away for use in the future 2. *vt* PUT SOMETHING INTO SAFEKEEPING to put or hold something somewhere for safekeeping, e.g. in a warehouse 3. *vi* SURVIVE STORAGE to survive or stay fresh while being kept in storage ○ *Apples will store well in a cool humid building.* 4. *vt* STOCK SOMETHING WITH ITEMS to fill or provide something with other things 5. *vt* COMPUT HOLD DATA to enter or save data or programs into a computer memory ■ *n* 1. PLACE SELLING GOODS a place where goods are offered for retail sale to customers 2. QUANTITY SAVED FOR FUTURE USE a quantity or collection put away for future use ○ *a store of grain in a silo* 3. PLACE WHERE GOODS ARE KEPT a place where goods are kept in quantity, e.g. a warehouse 4. GREAT QUANTITY a great quantity or large collection ○ *a rich store of memories* ○ *a weapon store* 5. ANIMAL BEING FATTENED an animal that is being fattened for sale ■ **stores** *npl* SUPPLIES items or materials needed for something such as a business, expedition, or vessel ■ *adj* US SHOP-BOUGHT purchased from a shop ○ *store bread* [13C. Via Old French *estorer* 'build, supply' < Latin *instaurare*] —**storable** *adj* ◇ **in store** 1. about to happen in the future ○ *She has a surprise in store for you.* 2. in a large amount ○ *He has come back with money in store.* ◇ **set** *or* **lay** *or* **put great store by something** to

consider something to be important, valuable, or worthwhile

store-bought *adj* N Am same as **shop-bought**

store builder *n* a computer program used to create a virtual storefront for a retailer

store card *n* COMM same as **charge card**

storefront /stáwr frunt/ *n* 1. a virtual shop on the World Wide Web providing product information, ordering capability, and provision for secure transfer of payment 2. N Am COMM same as **shopfront** ■ *adj* N Am located on or near the side of a shop where the main entrance is

storehouse /stáwr howss/ (*plural* **-houses** /-howziz/) *n* 1. a place where things are stored 2. an abundant source, collection, or supply ○ *She's a storehouse of information on local history.*

storekeeper /stáwr keepər/ *n* 1. a manager of the supplies or stores of a military unit, ship, or organization 2. N Am same as **shopkeeper**

storeroom /stáwr room, -rōōm/ *n* a room or enclosed space where things are stored

storey /stáwri/ *n* 1. a floor or level in a building 2. a set of rooms, or space, on a particular floor of a building [14C. Shortening of Anglo-Latin *historia* < Latin (see HISTORY)]

SPELLCHECK **storey** or **story**? Do not confuse the spelling of **storey** and **story**, which sound similar. A **storey** is a floor or level of a building, as in *an office block five storeys high, a multistorey car park*; a **story** is a factual or fictional narrative, as in *a news story, a collection of short stories*. Note, however, that the US spelling of **storey** is **story**.

Storey /stáwri/, **David** (*b.* 1933) British novelist and playwright. Many of his works, e.g. *This Sporting Life* (1960), concentrate on ordinary people and draw on his background in northern England. Full name **Storey, David Malcolm**

storeyed /stáwrid/ *adj* having storeys, usually of a particular number (*often used in combination*)

storied[1] /stáwrid/ *adj* 1. decorated with images of scenes from history or legend 2. interesting, famous, or celebrated in stories and books (*literary*) ○ *the storied outlaw Robin Hood* [14C. < STORY[1]]

storied[2] /stáwrid/ *adj* BUILDINGS US spelling of **storeyed**

stork

stork /stawrk/ (*plural* **storks** or **same**) *n* a large wading bird that has a long legs, a long neck, a long straight beak, and often black and white feathers. Family: Ciconiidae. [Old English *storc* < Indo-European, 'stiff']

SPELLCHECK See **stalk**[1].

storksbill /stáwrks bil/ (*plural* **-bills** or **same**) *n* a plant of the geranium family with lobed leaves and fruits with a beak-shaped tip. Flowers: pink or purple, in clusters. Genus: *Erodium*.

storm /stawrm/ *n* 1. VIOLENT WEATHER a disturbance in the air above the Earth, with strong winds and usually also with rain, snow, sleet, or hail and sometimes lightning and thunder 2. HEAVY RAIN OR SNOW a heavy fall of rain, snow, or sleet, often occurring with strong winds 3. RAIN OF OBJECTS a heavy bombardment of solid objects 4. OUTBURST OF FEELING a sudden strong outpouring of feeling in reaction to something, e.g. of protest or laughter ○ *a storm of anger* 5. MIL SUDDEN STRONG ATTACK a sudden strong attack on a defended place or position 6. METEOROL

STRONG WIND a wind of between 88 km/55 mi. and 102 km/63 mi. per hour, classified as force 10 on the Beaufort scale ■ v (**storms, storming, stormed**) **1.** vti **ATTACK VIOLENTLY** to attack or capture a place, especially a well-defended one, suddenly and with great force ○ *stormed the barricades* **2.** vti **BE ANGRY OR SAY SOMETHING ANGRILY** to be violently and noisily angry, or say something in this way **3.** vi **RUSH WITH VIOLENCE OR ANGER** to go somewhere in a rush, violently or angrily ○ *stormed out of the room in a huff* **4.** vi **METEOROL BLOW WITH OR WITHOUT PRECIPITATION** to blow strongly, drop large amounts of rain, snow, or sleet, or do both together [Old English < Indo-European, 'to whirl'] ◇ **a storm in a teacup** a fuss or row over something trivial ◇ **take somebody** *or* **something by storm 1.** to capture a place or overwhelm a body of enemies suddenly and with great force **2.** to make a great and immediate impression on somebody or something

storm beach n an accumulation of coarse sand and stones that is built up by storm action on a shore above the high-water mark

storm belt n a region on the surface of the Earth where there are frequent storms

stormbound /stáwrm bownd/ adj unable to leave, go out, or get in touch with anyone because of a strong storm

storm cellar n a shelter underground used as a refuge during a windstorm

storm centre n **1.** the central region of a cyclonic storm, with a low barometric pressure and relatively calm conditions **2.** a focus of trouble or disturbance

storm cloud n **1.** a large dark cloud that is a sign of approaching heavy rain or a storm **2.** a sign that violence, especially war, is soon to break out

storm-cock n regional BIRDS same as **mistle thrush** [Because it sings even in bad weather]

storm cone n a cone-shaped canvas signal hoisted on a mast as a warning of approaching high winds

storm door n a door added outside the main door of a house to provide additional protection against extreme weather

storm drain n a large drain built to carry away excess water from a road during heavy rain. N Am term **storm sewer**

stormer /stáwrmər/ n somebody or something that is excellent or impressive (slang)

storm glass n UK a glass tube containing a solution that is supposed to indicate weather changes by alterations in its appearance. ANZ, N Am term **weatherglass**

storming /stáwrming/ adj excellent or impressive (informal) ■ n the act of suddenly and violently attacking or capturing a place

storm petrel n a small seabird with black or brown feathers and a white rump. Native to: northern Atlantic, Mediterranean. Family: Hydrobatidae. [Because the bird's appearance was thought to forebode a storm]

stormproof /stáwrm proof/ adj able to withstand the wind, rain, or other elements of a storm, or providing protection from them

storm sewer n N Am same as **storm drain**

storm surge n a rise in sea level above the usual tide level as a hurricane or other intense storm moves over water, causing flooding when the storm comes ashore

storm-tossed adj subjected to or disturbed by storms

storm trooper n **1.** a member of the SA, a private militia of the Nazi Party that used tactics of violence and brutality **2.** a member of a military shock force specially trained to carry out attacks [< storm troop, translation of German *Sturmabteilung*]

storm window n a window added outside an ordinary house window to provide additional protection against extremes of weather

stormy /stáwrmi/ (**-ier, -iest**) adj **1.** affected by or experiencing a storm or frequent storms **2.** dominated by or subject to strong emotions or disturbances —**stormily** adv —**storminess** n

stormy petrel n **1.** BIRDS same as **storm petrel 2.** somebody who causes or brings trouble

Stornoway /stáwrnə way/ town and port on the island of Lewis-with-Harris, in the Outer Hebrides, Scotland. It is the centre of the manufacture of Harris tweed. Population: 5,975 (1991).

Storrier /stórri ər, stáwri ər/, **Tim** (b. 1949) Australian painter, noted for his realist landscapes and surrealist-influenced assemblages

story[1] /stáwri/ n (plural **-ries**) **1.** FACTUAL OR FICTIONAL NARRATIVE a factual or fictional account of an event or series of events **2.** SHORT FICTIONAL PROSE PIECE a work of prose fiction that is shorter than a novel **3.** PLOT OF FICTION OR DRAMA the plot of a novel, play, film, or other fictional narrative work **4.** ACCOUNT OF FACTS what somebody says has happened ○ *changed her story several times* **5.** FALSEHOOD something that one person tells another that is not true (informal) ○ *Don't give me any of your stories.* **6.** MEDIA NEWS REPORT a report in the news of something that has happened **7.** MEDIA SUBJECT FOR REPORT a subject or material for a news report **8.** LITERAT **LEGEND OR ROMANCE** traditional tales and legends, or the literature based on such tales ■ vt (**-ries, -rying, -ried**) DECORATE WITH LEGENDARY SCENES to decorate something with images of scenes from history or legend [13C. Via Anglo-Norman *estorie* < Latin *historia* (see HISTORY)] ◇ **a likely story** (informal ironic) **1.** used to say that you do not believe something **2.** something that is probably untrue ◇ **the same old story** what always happens or is said (disapproving) ◇ **to cut a long story short** to say something in a brief rather than a longer and more detailed way

SPELLCHECK See **storey.**

story[2] /stáwri/ n ARCHIT US spelling of **storey**

storyboard /stáwri bawrd/ n a set of sketches, arranged in sequence on panels, outlining the scenes that will make up something to be filmed, e.g. a film, television show, or advertisement

storybook /stáwri book/ n a book of stories for children ■ adj characteristic of or like something found in children's stories rather than the real world

story line n ARTS same as **story**[1] n (sense 3)

storyteller /stáwri telər/ n **1.** a teller or writer of stories **2.** somebody who tells lies (informal) —**storytelling** n

stoss /stoss/ adj describes a mountain, hill, or slope that faces the direction of an oncoming glacier [Late 19C. < German, 'a thrust, push']

stot[1] /stot, stōt/ (**stots, stotting, stotted**) v Scotland **1.** vti to bounce, or make something bounce **2.** vi to stagger or walk unsteadily [Early 16C. Origin ?]

stot[2] /stot/ n Scotland a bullock [Old English *stot(t)* 'bull', origin ?]

stotin /sto teen/ n a subunit of Slovenian currency. See table at **currency** [< Slovene, 'hundredth']

stotinka /sto tíngkə/ (plural **-ki** /-ki/) n a subunit of Bulgarian currency. See table at **currency** [Late 19C. < Bulgarian, 'hundredth']

stotious /stṓshəss/ adj Ireland, Scotland very drunk (slang) [< STOT[1]]

stoup /stoop/, **stoop** n a basin for holy water in a church [14C. < Old Norse *staup* 'drinking vessel']

stour /stowr, stoor/, **stoor** /stoor/ n Scotland dust, in a deposit or as a cloud [15C. Origin ?] —**stoury** adj

Stourbridge /stówrbrij/ town in central England, noted for glassmaking. Population: 55,624 (1991).

stoush /stowsh/ ANZ (informal) n a fight or dispute ■ vt (**stoushes, stoushing, stoushed**) to fight somebody [Early 20C. Origin ?]

stout /stowt/ adj **1.** THICKSET OR HEAVY thicker and heavier in body than an average person of the same height **2.** COURAGEOUS AND DETERMINED possessing or showing courage and determination **3.** STRONG strong and substantial ○ *stout footwear* ■ n BEVERAGES **DARK STRONG BEER** a strong, very dark, almost black beer made from roasted malted barley [13C. < Anglo-Norman < Germanic] —**stoutly** adv —**stoutness** n

Stout /stowt/, **Sir Robert** (1844–1930) Scottish-born premier of New Zealand. He was premier twice

(1884, 1884–87) before the advent of organized political parties in New Zealand.

stouten /stówt'n/ (**-ens, -ening, -ened**) vti to become stout or stouter, or make somebody or something stout or stouter

stouthearted /stówt haártid/ adj having or showing courage and resolution —**stoutheartedly** adv —**stoutheartedness** n

stove[1] /stōv/ n **1.** APPLIANCE FOR COOKING OR HEATING an appliance that uses electricity, gas, or solid fuel to produce heat for cooking or for heating **2.** HEAT-PRODUCING CHAMBER OR DEVICE a chamber or device that is used to heat or dry something, e.g. a kiln ■ vt (**stoves, stoving, stoved**) INDUST **HEAT SOMETHING IN STOVE** to treat something by heating it in a stove in order to coat it with a surface such as enamel [15C. Probably < Middle Dutch or Middle Low German, 'heated room']

stove[2] /stōv/ past participle, past tense of **stave**

stove enamel n enamel that has been subjected to heat treatment in a stove to make it heatproof

stovepipe /stōv pīp/ n **1.** a pipe used as a chimney for a fuel-burning stove, usually made of sheet steel formed into a tube **2.** CLOTHING same as **stovepipe hat**

stovepipe hat n a tall tube-shaped silk hat for a man

stovepiping /stōv pīping/ n a rigidly vertical management style that discourages lateral lines of responsibility and hinders communication among individual groups within an organization [Early 21C. < the vertical arrangement of a stovepipe]

stovies /stōviz/ npl Scotland a dish of sliced potatoes and onions stewed together, sometimes with a little meat

stow /stō/ (**stows, stowing, stowed**) vt **1.** PUT SOMETHING AWAY to pack something or put something away **2.** FILL SOMETHING WITH TIGHTLY PACKED THINGS to fill something with other things, especially things packed tightly ○ *to stow a boat's hold with cargo* **3.** STORE SOMETHING FOR LATER USE to store something for use in the future **4.** HOLD SOMETHING to be capable of containing something **5.** STOP SOMETHING to stop doing something (slang) ○ *Stow this silly chatter.* [14C. < Old English *stōw* 'place' < Germanic, 'to stand']

stow away vi to hide on a ship or aircraft in the hope of being taken somewhere without having to pay

Stow /stō/, **Randolph** (b. 1935) Australian writer. His poems and novels include *To the Islands* (1958). Full name **Stow, Julian Randolph**

stowage /stō ij/ n **1.** STOWING OF THINGS the loading, packing, or storing of something, or a way of doing this **2.** SITUATION OR ARRANGEMENT OF THINGS PACKED the condition of being stowed, or the arrangement of things stowed **3.** THINGS STOWED something that is stowed somewhere or is to be stowed **4.** PLACE OR SPACE FOR STOWING a place, container, or space for stowing things **5.** FEE FOR STOWING a fee or fees for stowing something

stowaway /stō ə way/ n somebody who hides on a ship or aircraft in the hope of being taken somewhere without paying

Harriet Beecher Stowe

Stowe /stō/, **Harriet Beecher** (1811–96) US writer and abolitionist. She is best known for her antislavery novel *Uncle Tom's Cabin* (1852). Born **Beecher, Harriet Elizabeth**. See Cultural note at **cabin**

'The bitterest tears shed over graves are for words left unsaid and deeds left undone.' [Harriet Beecher Stowe, *Little Foxes*; 1865]

STP *abbr* PHYS standard temperature and pressure

str. *abbr* **1.** *also* **Str.** GEOG strait **2.** stroke

Strabane /strə bán/ town in County Tyrone, Northern Ireland. Population: 11,981 (1991).

strabismus /strə bízməss/ *n* OPHTHALMOL same as **squint** (*technical*) [Late 17C. Via modern Latin < Greek *strabismos* < *strabizein* 'to squint' < *strabos* 'squinting'] —**strabismal** *adj* —**strabismic** *adj* —**strabismical** *adj*

Strabo /stráybō/ (63? BC–AD 24) Greek geographer and historian. His *Geographica* records his observations on his extensive travels throughout the ancient world.

Strachey /stráychi/, **Lytton** (1880–1932) British writer. A member of the Bloomsbury Group, he wrote *Eminent Victorians* (1918) and other biographies known for illuminating the personality of their subjects. Full name **Strachey, Giles Lytton**

Strad /strad/ *n* a Stradivarius violin (*informal*) [Late 19C. Shortening]

straddle /strádd'l/ *v* (**-dles, -dling, -dled**) **1.** *vt* **SIT OR STAND ASTRIDE SOMETHING** to sit or stand so that one leg is on one side and the other leg is on the other side of something or somebody **2.** *vt* **EXTEND TO OTHER SIDE OF SOMETHING** to extend across something or be divided by something and have parts on both sides of it ○ *The city straddles the river.* **3.** *vt* **APPLY TO MORE THAN ONE THING** to exist in, belong to, or apply to more than one situation or category ○ *The rule of the dynasty straddled the end of one century and the beginning of the next.* **4.** *vt* **SPREAD LEGS APART** to spread your legs apart, usually so that they are on both sides of something **5.** *vi* **SIT OR WALK WITH LEGS APART** to sit, stand, or walk with your legs spread apart or on each side of something **6.** *vt* MIL **FIRE SHELLS FOR RANGE** to fire a salvo of artillery shells at a target so that some fall in front of it and some behind it, in order to find the correct range **7.** *vti US* **FAVOUR BOTH SIDES** to appear to favour both sides of an issue, or resist committing to one side or the other ■ *n* **1. POSITION ASTRIDE OR ACROSS SOMETHING** a position in which somebody or something is astride or on both sides of something **2. ACT OF STRADDLING** an act of putting one leg on each side of something **3.** FIN **STOCK TRANSACTION** the simultaneous holding of options to buy and sell a commodity or security at a set price during a specific period of time, ensuring a profit whether the value rises or falls **4.** ATHLETICS **JUMPING TECHNIQUE** a technique used in the high jump, in which the body is held parallel to the bar and the legs straddle it **5.** *US* **NONCOMMITTAL POSITION** a position on an issue that seems to favour both sides or resists committing to one side or the other [Mid-16C. Probably variant of obsolete *striddle* 'keep striding' < earlier form of STRIDE] —**straddler** *n*

Stradivari /stráddi vaári/, **Antonio** (1644–1737) Italian violin maker. The instruments that he produced, including violas and cellos, are among the most highly prized in the world.

Stradivarius /stráddi váiri əss/ *n* a violin or other stringed instrument that was made by the Italian violin maker Antonio Stradivari or his sons [Mid-19C. Latinized form of STRADIVARI]

strafe /straaf, strayf/ *vt* (**strafes, strafing, strafed**) **1. ATTACK SOMETHING WITH GUNFIRE** to attack a position or troops on the ground with machine-gun or cannon fire from a low-flying aircraft **2. PUNISH SOMEBODY** to punish somebody, especially severely (*slang*) ■ *n* **AIR ATTACK** a machine-gun or cannon attack by low-flying aircraft on a ground target [Early 20C. < German *strafen* 'punish'] —**strafer** *n*

Strafford /stráffərd/, **Thomas Wentworth, 1st Earl of** (1593–1641) English soldier and courtier. He was the principal adviser to Charles I of England and lord lieutenant of Ireland. The Long Parliament ordered his execution.

straggle /strágg'l/ *vi* (**-gles, -gling, -gled**) **1. STRAY FROM GROUP** to lag behind, wander away from, or become separated from a group ○ *rounding up cattle that had straggled from the main herd* **2. COME OR GO WITHOUT A PATTERN** to move, come, or go in an irregular or disorganized way, usually in ones or twos ○ *People were still straggling in half an hour after the meeting had started.* **3. BECOME SCATTERED** to be or become spread out irregularly over a wide area ○ *primitive shanties straggling over the dunes* **4. GROW UNTIDILY** to grow or hang in an untidy or irregular way, often in separate disorderly strands or wisps ○ *The roses had been allowed to straggle across the path.* ○ *A few grey wisps straggled from underneath his cap.* ■ *n* **STRAGGLED GROUP OR ARRANGEMENT** a disorganized, scattered, or untidy group or arrangement [15C. Origin ?] —**straggling** *adj* —**straggly** *adj*

straggler /strágg'lər/ *n* somebody or something that straggles, especially a person or animal that lags behind or becomes separated from a group ○ *fell behind to wait for the stragglers*

straight /strayt/ *adj* **1. NOT CURVED** extending or proceeding in one single direction, without bends, curves, irregularities, or deviations **2. LEVEL** level, even, or properly positioned ○ *Your tie isn't straight.* **3. ACCURATE** accurate or correct ○ *Let's get this straight. Did she or did she not say she was coming?* **4. CANDID** making no attempt to deceive or to soften the truth ○ *give a straight answer* ○ *Are you being straight with me?* **5. HONEST** honest, fair, and upright ○ *straight dealings* **6. NEAT AND TIDY** in a neat and orderly state with things properly arranged or cleared away ○ *Make sure the room's straight before the guests arrive.* **7. CONSISTENT** not straying from agreed or published principles or policies ○ *the straight party line* **8. CONSECUTIVE** following one after another, without interruption ○ *The team celebrated its tenth straight win.* **9. NOT DILUTED** not diluted or mixed with any other drink ○ *straight whisky* **10. NOT FUNNY** not intended to be funny or unconventional ○ *playing both straight and comic roles* **11. WITH UNBENT ARM** delivered with the arm unbent ○ *a straight left to the body* **12.** *US* **NOT DISCOUNTED** not sold at a reduced price regardless of how many are bought **13.** same as **heterosexual** (*informal*) **14. CONVENTIONAL** unremarkable or conventional in outlook, style, or way of life (*informal*) ○ *gave up being a rock musician and got a straight job* **15. NOT USING DRUGS** not using or addicted to drugs (*slang*) ■ *adv* **1. WITHOUT BENDING** without bending, curving, or diverging from a course **2. IMMEDIATELY** without delay or detour ○ *She went straight home.* **3. IN LEVEL POSITION** in a level, even, or proper position ○ *Put your hat on straight.* **4. CLEARLY** clearly and correctly or logically ○ *I can't think straight with all this noise going on.* **5. CANDIDLY** without any attempt to deceive or soften the truth ○ *Give it to me straight.* **6. INTO NEAT CONDITION** in or into a neat and orderly condition ○ *We'll have to put the place straight after the party.* **7. WITH NO INTERRUPTION** one after another, without interruption ○ *three nights straight* **8. WITHOUT BEING DILUTED** without being diluted or mixed with any other drink **9. WITHOUT BEING FUNNY** without trying to be funny or unconventional ○ *She decided to play the role straight.* ■ *n* **1. SOMETHING STRAIGHT** something that is straight, e.g. a line **2. FIVE CARDS IN SEQUENCE** in poker, a hand in which the cards form a continuous sequence but are not all of the same suit **3.** *UK, ANZ, Can* **UNBENDING PART OF RACING TRACK** a part of a racing track that does not bend. US term **straightaway** **4.** same as **heterosexual** (*informal*) **5. CONVENTIONAL PERSON** somebody who has a conventional outlook, style, or way of life (*informal*) **6. CIGARETTE WITHOUT ADDED DRUG** an ordinary tobacco-filled cigarette to which no marijuana or other drug has been added (*dated slang*) [14C. Old past participle of STRETCH] —**straightly** *adv* —**straightness** *n* ◇ **go straight** to give up being a criminal and start living within the law (*informal*) ◇ **put** *or* **set somebody straight** to make somebody understand the reality of a situation

USAGE straight or **strait**? Do not confuse ***straight*** with ***strait***, which has a similar pronunciation and spelling but is unrelated in origin. ***Straight*** is an adjective meaning 'not curved', as in *a straight line*; ***strait*** is a noun denoting a narrow body of water or a difficult situation, as in *dire straits*. ***Strait*** was formerly used as an adjective meaning 'narrow, confined' or 'strict', but these senses only survive in forms such as *straitened*, *straitjacket*, and *strait-laced*. *Straitened*, meaning 'restricted', is chiefly used in the phrase *straitened circumstances* and should not be confused with *straightened*, meaning 'made straight'. *Straitjacket* and *strait-laced* are also spelt *straightjacket* and *straight-laced*.

straight-ahead *adj US* showing little variation from what is usual or typical ○ *straight-ahead Italian opera*

straight and narrow *n* the orthodox and law-abiding way to live life (*informal*)

straight angle *n* an angle of 180°

straight-arm *adj* describes a rugby tackle executed with the arm stretched fully out ■ *vt* in rugby football, to push an opponent away with the arm stretched fully out and the hand upturned and stiff

straight arrow *n N Am* somebody who is honest and upright (*informal*) —**straight-arrow** *adj*

straightaway /stráyt ə wáy/ *adv also* **straight away** immediately and without hesitation ■ *n US* **1.** SPORTS same as **straight** *n* (sense 3) **2.** a straight stretch of road

straight chain *n* an open chain of atoms in a molecule that has no side branches

straightedge /stráyt ej/ *n* a rigid strip of wood, metal, or plastic used to draw a straight line or to check for straightness

straighten /stráyt'n/ (**-ens, -ening, -ened**) *vti* to make something straight, or become straight —**straightener** *n*

straighten out *vti* **1.** to make something straight, or become straight ○ *The road straightens out after this next bend.* **2.** to make something clear or satisfactory, or become clear or satisfactory ○ *I want to straighten things out between us.*

straighten up *v* **1.** *vti* to stand up straight, or make somebody stand up straight **2.** *vt* to make something neat and orderly

straight face *n* a serious expression on somebody's face that does not betray the fact that he or she really wants to laugh —**straight-faced** *adj*

straight fight *n* a contest, especially in politics, between only two opponents

straight flush *n* in poker, a hand in which all the cards are of the same suit and form a continuous sequence

straightforward /stráyt fáwrwərd/ *adj* **1. EASY** not difficult to understand or carry out **2. FRANK** truthful and to the point **3. STRAIGHT OR DIRECT** following a straight or direct path —**straightforwardly** *adv* —**straightforwardness** *n*

SYNONYMS See *easy*.

straightjacket *n, vt* another spelling of **straitjacket**

straight-line *adj* **1.** designed to move or transmit motion in a straight line **2.** in accounting, allocating a fixed percentage of the original value of an asset to each year in a given term of years ○ *straight-line depreciation*

straight man *n* a comedian whose role is to say or do things that allow another comedian to deliver a punch line or make witty or humorous comments in response

straight off *adv* right away or at once (*informal*)

straight out *adv* without hesitating or trying to lead up to something gradually

straight-out *adj* (*informal*) **1.** showing directness or bluntness ○ *a straight-out refusal* **2.** *US* complete and unmitigated ○ *a straight-out jerk*

straight razor *n N Am* same as **cutthroat razor**

straight shooter *n N Am* somebody who is honest, frank, and ethical (*informal*)

straight stitch *n* a simple stitch that forms a straight line on the surface of a fabric

straight-talking *adj* direct and straightforward in dealing with others

straight ticket *n US* a ballot cast for all the candidates of the same political party

straight-to-video *adj* released only in video format rather than shown in cinemas

straight up *interj* used to affirm that something is definitely true or, as a question, to ask if something is true (*slang*)

straightway /stráyt way/ *adv* at once and without delay (*archaic*)

strain[1] /strayn/ *v* **(strains, straining, strained) 1.** *vi* MAKE EXTREME EFFORT to have to make an unusually great or even painful physical or mental effort in order to do something ○ *The office strained to complete the work on time.* ○ *strained to hear the speaker* **2.** *vi* PULL VIOLENTLY to pull at or push against something, especially an obstacle or restraint, with great force or violence ○ *straining at the leash* **3.** *vt* MAKE GREAT DEMANDS ON SOMETHING to make something seem barely adequate to meet the demands placed on it ○ *a story that strains credulity* ○ *Taking on more debt would strain our resources to the limit.* **4.** *vti* MAKE SOMETHING LESS CORDIAL to make a relationship less friendly or more difficult, or become less friendly or more difficult ○ *The recent crisis has strained relations between the two countries.* **5.** *vt* INJURE SOMETHING to damage a part of the body through using it too hard or too much **6.** *vti* PULL OR STRETCH TIGHT to pull or stretch something until it is tight, or be pulled or stretched until tight **7.** *vti* PASS SOMETHING THROUGH STRAINER to pass something, or be passed, through a mesh or filter to remove solids or larger particles ○ *Strain the stock and return it to the pan.* **8.** *vt* REMOVE SOMETHING USING STRAINER to separate part of something from the rest using a strainer ○ *to strain lumps from gravy* **9.** *vt* HUG SOMEBODY to hold somebody closely and tightly (*literary*) **10.** *vt* PHYS DEFORM STRUCTURE to deform a body or material by applying an external force to it ■ *n* **1.** STRESS intense demand on body, mind, or resources that can only be met with great effort ○ *under considerable strain* ○ *It's the strain of living with him day after day that's wearing me out.* **2.** DEMAND THAT CAUSES STRESS something that places great demands on somebody or something, or makes something seem barely adequate ○ *unexpected expenses that are a strain on our budget* **3.** GREAT EXERTION a great or extremely taxing exertion or effort ○ *It was a real strain to lift it but we managed it.* **4.** PHYSICAL INJURY an injury to a part of the body caused by excessive use or by a twisting or stretching of muscles or tendons beyond their normal range **5.** ACT OF FILTERING an act of passing something through a strainer **6.** PULLING FORCE a pulling or stretching force exerted on something ○ *the strain on the rope* **7.** PHYS DEFORMATION OF STRUCTURE the deformation of a body or material caused by applying an external force to it [14C. Via Old French *estreindre* 'draw tight' < Latin *stringere* 'draw tight, bind']

strain[2] /strayn/ *n* **1.** LINE OF ANCESTRY a line of ancestry or a group of descendants from a common ancestor **2.** SUBGROUP OF ORGANISM a subgroup of a species of organism distinguished by specific characteristics, sometimes developed by breeders for those characteristics **3.** INHERITED QUALITY OR TRAIT an inherited tendency, character, or trait **4.** TRACE a trace of a particular and often unexpected quality or tone ○ *glimpsed a strain of impatience* **5.** CHARACTER OR MOOD the style, character, mood, or theme of something **6.** MUSIC MUSICAL THEME a musical theme or melody [Old English *strēon* 'offspring', originally 'gain' < Indo-European, 'to spread flat']

strained /straynd/ *adj* **1.** TENSE characterized by tension and covert hostility ○ *relations already strained by trade disputes* **2.** NOT NATURAL not natural or spontaneous but done with effort ○ *a strained smile* **3.** PASSED THROUGH STRAINER having been passed through a strainer to separate out solids or large particles

strainer /stráynər/ *n* a device, usually incorporating a mesh or other filter, for separating solids from liquids or small particles from large

strain gauge *n* a device that measures pressure or stress, using the change of electrical resistance in a wire that is subjected to the same stress as the object being measured

strain hardening *n* the deliberate deformation of a metal to make it resistant to further deformation

straining beam /stráyning beem/, **straining piece** *n* a horizontal beam that connects the tops of two vertical posts **(queen posts)** in a roof truss

strait /strayt/ *n* (*often used in the plural*) **1.** CHANNEL JOINING LARGE BODIES OF WATER a narrow body of water that joins two larger bodies of water **2.** DIFFICULT SITUATION a situation that is difficult or involves hardship ○ *The collapse of the stock market put many brokers in serious financial straits.* ■ *adj* (*archaic*) **1.** NARROW OR CONFINED narrow or with very little room **2.** STRICT OR RIGID very strict or severe [14C. Via Old French *estreit* < Latin *strictus* 'narrow', past participle of *stringere* 'draw tight, bind'] —**straitly** *adv* —**straitness** *n*

USAGE See *straight.*

straitened /stráyt'nd/ *adj* made very difficult, restricted, or narrow ○ *had lost all their money and were living in straitened circumstances*

USAGE See *straight.*

straitjacket /stráyt jakit/, **straightjacket** *n* **1.** CONFINING JACKET-SHAPED GARMENT a jacket-shaped garment with long sleeves that can be tied together, used to restrict the arm movements of somebody who is thought to be dangerous **2.** THING THAT RESTRICTS something that limits somebody's freedom of action or initiative ○ *a bureaucratic straitjacket of regulations* ■ *vt* **(-ets, -eting, -eted) 1.** PUT STRAITJACKET ON SOMEBODY to put somebody into a straitjacket to restrict arm movements **2.** RESTRICT SOMEBODY to limit somebody's freedom of action or initiative

USAGE See *straight.*

strait-laced, straight-laced *adj* prudish, or very strict in morals —**strait-lacedly** /-láyssidli, -láystli/ *adv* —**strait-lacedness** /-láyssidnəss/ *n*

USAGE See *straight.*

strake /strayk/ *n* **1.** a continuous band of wooden planks or metal plates along the hull of a boat or ship **2.** a curved metal plate that is part of a rubber tyre or metal wheel rim [15C. < assumed Old English *straca* < Germanic, 'rigid']

stramash /strə másh/ *n Scotland* an uproar, commotion, or rowdy dispute [Late 18C. Origin ?]

stramonium /strə mṓni əm/ *n* a preparation of dried leaves and flowers of the thorn apple containing alkaloids. Use: formerly, as a medicine. [Mid-17C. < modern Latin]

strand[1] /strand/ *n* LAND AT WATER'S EDGE a strip of land along the edge of a body of water ■ *v* **(strands, stranding, stranded) 1.** *vti* RUN SOMETHING AGROUND to leave or run a ship or sea animal aground, or be left or driven aground **2.** *vt* LEAVE SOMEBODY IN DIFFICULTY to put or leave somebody in a difficult or helpless position (*often passive*) ○ *stranded without any means of getting home* [Old English, origin ?] —**stranded** *adj*

strand[2] /strand/ *n* **1.** SINGLE FILAMENT a single fibre, wire, or thread, especially one of several braided or twisted together to form something such as a rope or cable **2.** LENGTH OF ROPE a length of something such as rope or cotton, made from braided or twisted filaments **3.** HUMAN HAIR OR HAIRS a human hair, or a tress of hair **4.** LENGTH OF TISSUE RESEMBLING THREAD a length of animal, plant, or mineral fibre or tissue that resembles a thread **5.** STRING OF BEADS a length of strung pearls or beads, especially when twisted like a rope **6.** ELEMENT OF WHOLE an element that with others makes up a larger complex whole ■ *vt* **(strands, stranding, stranded)** MAKE SOMETHING BY INTERWEAVING to make something such as a rope or cable by braiding or twisting together fibres or filaments ○ *to strand a rope* [15C. Origin ?]

stranded cotton /strándid-/ *n* an embroidery cotton made up of six strands of thread loosely twisted together

strandline /stránd līn/ *n* a shoreline, especially an earlier shoreline above the present one

strange /straynj/ *adj* **(stranger, strangest) 1.** UNEXPECTED OR EXTRAORDINARY not expected, usual, or ordinary ○ *That's a strange time to hold a wedding.* **2.** UNFAMILIAR not known or experienced previously ○ *There seemed to be a lot of strange faces in the audience.* **3.** HARD TO EXPLAIN difficult to explain or understand ○ *It's strange that they never thought to mention this before.* **4.** UNACCUSTOMED not yet used to or familiar with something ○ *strange to these new surroundings* **5.** ILL AT EASE uncomfortable, embarrassed, or slightly ill ○ *I've been feeling a little strange since I took the medicine.* **6.** EXOTIC from a different place or environment, or of a different kind **7.** RESERVED reserved or distant in manner **8.** PHYS SHOWING QUANTUM CHARACTERISTIC OF STRANGENESS showing or having the quantum characteristic of strangeness ■ *adv* IN UNUSUAL WAY in a strange way (*nonstandard*) [13C. Via Old French *estrange* < Latin *extraneus* 'foreign' < *extra*, form of *exter* 'outside']

strangely /stráynjli/ *adv* **1.** in an unusual or puzzling way ○ *You've been strangely quiet this evening.* **2.** used to indicate that the speaker finds something odd or puzzling ○ *Strangely, they seemed to have no definite plan of action.*

strangeness /stráynjnəss/ *n* **1.** the condition or quality of being strange **2.** a quantum characteristic of some elementary particles that is conserved in strong and electromagnetic, but not weak, interactions and has a value **(strangeness number)** of zero for most particles

strangeness number *n* the value of the quantum characteristic of strangeness, equal to the hypercharge minus the baryon number

strange particle *n* an elementary particle having a strangeness number other than zero [Because such particles' long lifetimes were hard to explain]

strange quark *n* a quark that has an electric charge equal to $-\frac{1}{3}$ that of the electron and a strangeness number of –1

stranger /stráynjər/ *n* **1.** UNFAMILIAR PERSON somebody whom somebody else does not know **2.** NEWCOMER somebody who is new to a place **3.** OUTSIDER somebody who does not belong to a specific organization or group **4.** VISITOR OR GUEST somebody who does not live in a specific house or community but is a visitor or guest **5.** PERSON UNACCUSTOMED TO SOMETHING somebody who is not familiar or acquainted with a particular thing ○ *Being a stranger to hard physical work, he found the job exhausting.* **6.** ALIENATED PERSON somebody who has become distanced or alienated from somebody or something ○ *She is a stranger to her former colleagues.* **7.** PERSON NOT PRIVY TO TRANSACTION somebody who is neither privy nor party to a transaction [14C. < Old French *estrangier* < *estrange* 'foreign' (see STRANGE)]

stranger crime, stranger-on-stranger crime *n* crimes of violence in which the perpetrator is somebody whom the victim does not know

stranger's gallery *n* a gallery from which members of the public may observe the business of a legislature, especially in the British House of Commons

Strangford Lough /strángfərd lókh/ inlet of the sea in County Down, Northern Ireland. Length: 40 km/25 mi.

strangle /stráng g'l/ **(-gles, -gling, -gled)** *v* **1.** *vti* KILL OR DIE BY CHOKING to kill a person or an animal by squeezing the throat and cutting off oxygen to the lungs, or die in this way **2.** *vi* CHOKE to choke or suffocate **3.** *vti* SUPPRESS UTTERANCE to suppress the utterance of a sound, or be suppressed ○ *strangled a sob* **4.** *vti* STIFLE OR BE STIFLED IN DEVELOPMENT to hinder or stop the growth or development of something, or be hindered or stopped ○ *Businesses say the high interest rates are strangling the economy.* [13C. Via Old French *estrangler* < Latin *strangulare* (see STRANGULATE)] —**strangler** *n*

stranglehold /stráng g'l hōld/ *n* **1.** in wrestling, an illegal hold that chokes an opponent **2.** power over something or somebody that is complete and prevents any movement or change

strangles /stráng g'lz/ *n* an infectious disease of horses in which they experience inflammation and abscesses of the mucous membranes of the respiratory tract, causing strangling. It is caused by the bacterium *Streptococcus equi.* (*takes a singular verb*)

strangulate /stráng gyoo layt/ **(-lates, -lating, -lated)** *v* **1.** *vt* to strangle a person or animal **2.** *vti* to constrict an organ or duct of the body, or become constricted, so as to stop the flow of a fluid [Mid-17C. Via Latin *strangulare* < Greek *straggalan* < *straggalē* 'halter, cord'] —**strangulation** /stráng gyoo láysh'n/ *n*

strangury /stráng gyoori/ *n* painful and slow urination caused by spasms that make urine come out drop by drop [14C. Via Latin < Greek *straggouria* < *stragx* 'drop' + *ouron* 'urine']

Stranraer /stran raar/ town and port in Dumfries and Galloway, southwestern Scotland. Population: 11,348 (1991).

a at; aa father; aw all; ay day; ai hair; ə about, item, edible, common, circus; e egg; ee eel; hw when; i it, happy; ī ice; 'l apple; 'm rhythm; 'n fashion; o odd; ō open; oo good; oo pool; ow owl; oy oil; th thin; th this; u up; ur urge;

strap /strap/ *n* **1. FLEXIBLE STRIP USED FOR BINDING** a narrow flexible strip of a material such as leather, plastic, or metal, used to bind or secure something **2. LOOP OF MATERIAL USED AS HANDLE** a loop of flexible material by which something such as a bag can be carried **3. STRIP OF MATERIAL HOLDING UP GARMENT** a thin strip of material that forms part of a garment and passes over the shoulder **4. LOOP TO HOLD ON TO** a hanging loop of material in a bus or train for standing passengers to hold onto for support **5. STROP** a strop for sharpening a cutthroat razor **6. LEATHER STRIP FOR FLOGGING** a long narrow strip of leather used for flogging or beating ■ *vt* **(straps, strapping, strapped) 1. SECURE SOMETHING WITH STRAP** to secure or bind somebody or something with a strap ○ *strapped his son into the back seat* **2.** MED **BANDAGE SOMETHING TIGHTLY** to tie a bandage tightly around an injured body part ○ *They strapped up his leg and carried him off the field.* N Am term **tape 3. FASTEN STRAPS OF SOMETHING** to secure the straps that are used to fasten something ○ *stood up without strapping her shoes* **4. BEAT SOMEBODY WITH STRAP** to beat or flog somebody with a strap **5. SHARPEN RAZOR** to sharpen a cutthroat razor on a strop [Early 17C. Originally a Scottish dialect form of STROP]

straphanger /stráp hangər/ *n* a passenger who stands in a bus or train and holds onto a strap that is suspended from the roof (*informal*)

strap hinge *n* a hinge with a flap fastened to the exposed surface of a door, lid, or gate

strapless /strápləss/ *adj* without shoulder straps or covering

strapline /stráp līn/ *n* a subhead in a piece of print such as a newspaper article

strappado /strə páydō, -paádō/ (*plural* **-does**) *n* **1.** a form of torture in which somebody is hoisted by a rope round the wrists, which are bound behind the back, and then dropped and jerked to a stop before reaching the ground **2.** a device used in strappado [Mid-16C. Alteration of French *(e)strapade* < Italian *strappata* < *strappare*, origin ?]

strapped /strapt/ *adj* in need of money (*informal*) ○ *strapped for cash*

strapper /stráppər/ *n* somebody who is big and powerfully built (*informal*)

strapping /strápping/ *adj* **ROBUST** tall and powerfully built (*informal*) ■ *n* **1. STRAPS** straps in general, or a set of straps **2. MATERIAL FOR STRAPS** material for making straps or for use as straps

strappy /stráppi/ **(-pier, -piest)** *adj* with straps, especially when they are an important part of the look or design of something (*informal*) ○ *strappy sandals*

strap work *n* decorative work in the form of crossing or interlaced bands on the outside of a building, especially in Tudor architecture

Strasberg /stráz burg, stráss-/, **Lee** (1901–82) Austro-Hungarian-born US actor and teacher. Following the theories of Stanislavsky, he developed and taught the influential Method Acting technique. Born **Strassberg, Israel**

Strasbourg /stráz burg/ capital city of Bas-Rhin Department, Alsace Region, northeastern France. It is the site of the headquarters of the European Parliament and the Council of Europe. Population: 264,115 (1999).

strass /strass/ *n* same as **paste**[1] *n* (sense 5) [Early 19C. < German, after Joseph *Strasser*, 18C German jeweller]

Strassman /stráss man/, **Fritz** (1902–80) German chemist. With physical chemist Otto Hahn he was responsible for the discovery of nuclear fission (1938).

strata plural of **stratum**

stratagem /stráttəjəm/ *n* **1. CLEVER SCHEME** a clever ruse or scheme that is designed to deceive others or achieve a goal **2. RUSE FOR DECEIVING ENEMY** a military tactic or manoeuvre that is designed to deceive an enemy **3. USE OF CLEVER SCHEMES** the use of stratagems, or skill in using stratagems [15C. Via French < Greek *stratēgēma* < *stratēgos* 'general' (see STRATEGY)]

~~**stratagy**~~ incorrect spelling of **strategy**

strata title *n Aus* a system of ownership of space within a block of apartments. Titles are issued for each apartment and for common property, which is managed by a committee of unit owners called the body corporate.

strata unit *n Aus* an apartment whose ownership is registered according to strata title

strategic /strə teéjik/, **strategical** /-ik'l/ *adj* **1. TYPICAL OF STRATEGY** relating to, involving, or typical of strategy or a strategy ○ *strategic planning* **2. DONE FOR REASONS OF STRATEGY** necessary to a strategy, or done because a strategy requires it ○ *a strategic retreat* **3. DISPLAYING SOUND STRATEGY** displaying a sound strategy or plan of action ○ *showing strategic timing in selling a stock short* **4.** MIL **DESTROYING ENEMY'S FIGHTING CAPACITY** done with the intention of destroying an enemy's military capability ○ *strategic bombing* **5.** MIL **NECESSARY FOR FIGHTING WAR** necessary for fighting a war, or essential to the military forces fighting a war ○ *strategic metals* ○ *strategic air bases*

strategically /strə teéjikli/ *adv* **1.** as part of, or in a way useful to, a strategy **2.** in a clever or useful way

Strategic Defense Initiative *n* a planned US system of defence against nuclear attack in which incoming missiles would be destroyed by laser weapons mounted in satellites or by antimissile missiles

strategic planning *n* the planning of all the activities of a business to ensure competitive advantage and profitability

Strategic Rail Authority *n* a body set up in 2002 to implement the UK government's strategic plan for the country's railway system, to award franchises to train-operating companies, and to be responsible for consumer protection

strategics /strə teéjiks/ *n* the science or art of military strategy (*takes a singular verb*)

strategist /stráttəjist/ *n* somebody who develops and executes strategy

strategize /stráttə jīz/ **(-gizes, -gizing, -gized)** *vi N Am* to plan or decide on a strategy

strategy /stráttəji/ (*plural* **-gies**) *n* **1. PLANNING IN ANY FIELD** a carefully devised plan of action to achieve a goal, or the art of developing or carrying out such a plan ○ *business strategy* **2.** MIL **PLANNING OF WAR** the science or art of planning and conducting a war or a military campaign **3.** BIOL **ADAPTATION IMPORTANT TO EVOLUTIONARY SUCCESS** in evolutionary theory, a behaviour, structure, or other adaptation that improves viability [Early 19C. Via French *stratégie* < Greek *stratēgia* 'generalship' < *stratēgos* 'general' < *stratos* 'army' + *agein* 'to lead']

strategy game *n* a computer game, e.g. a war game, in which a player makes overall decisions rather than assuming the role of a specific character

Stratford /strátfərd/ city on the Avon River in southeastern Ontario, Canada. It is home to the annual Stratford Festival, founded in 1953 to present Shakespeare's plays and other arts events. Population: 29,676 (2001).

Stratford-upon-Avon /-áyvən/ town in Warwickshire, west-central England. It was the birthplace of William Shakespeare. Population: 111,484 (2001).

strath /strath/ *n Scotland* a river valley that is wide and flat (*often used in placenames*) [Mid-16C. Via Scottish Gaelic < Old Irish *srath*]

Strathclyde /strath klīd/ former administrative region in southwestern Scotland between 1975 and 1996

Strathern /strath úrn/, **Marilyn** (*b.* 1941) British anthropologist. She was noted for her work on gender and identity based on studies of the peoples of Papua New Guinea.

strathspey /strath spáy/ (*plural* **-speys**) *n* **1.** a Scottish dance that is similar to a reel but has a slower tempo **2.** the music for a strathspey [Mid-18C. After *Strathspey*, valley of the River Spey in Scotland]

strati METEOROL plural of **stratus**

strati- *prefix* stratum, layer ○ *stratigraphy* [< STRATUM]

straticulate /strə tíkyŏŏlət, -layt/ *adj* describes a rock formation that is made up of thin layers [Late 19C. < STRATUM, after PARTICULATE] —**straticulation** /strə tíkyŏŏ láysh'n/ *n*

stratification /stráttifi káysh'n/ *n* **1.** the process of stratifying something, or the state of being stratified **2.** a layer, caste, class, or group into which something is stratified [Early 17C. < French < *stratifier* (see STRATIFY)] —**stratificational** *adj*

stratificational grammar *n* a form of grammar in which language is analysed in terms of layers linked to one another by rules

stratified charge engine /strátti fīd-/ *n* an internal-combustion engine with two layers of fuel density within the cylinder. A rich mixture is adjacent to the spark plug whose combustion assists in the ignition of a lean mixture in the remainder of the cylinder.

stratiform /strátti fawrm/ *adj* **1. COMPOSED OF LAYERS** composed of layers, or with a layered appearance or arrangement **2. FORMED AS LAYER** forming or formed as a layer **3.** METEOROL **LIKE STRATUS CLOUD** like or having the form of a stratus cloud [Mid-19C. < STRATUM, STRATUS]

stratify /strátti fī/ **(-fies, -fying, -fied)** *v* **1.** *vti* **FORM INTO LAYERS** to form something into a layer or layers, or become formed into a layer or layers **2.** *vti* SOC SCI **FORM INTO STATUS GROUPS** to form castes, classes, or other groups based on status, or be formed into such groups **3.** *vt* AGRIC **STORE SEEDS IN CHILLED MOIST ENVIRONMENT** to store seeds in chilled moist sand, peat moss, or other material to preserve them [Mid-17C. < French *stratifier* < modern Latin *stratum* (see STRATUM)]

stratigraphic /strátti gráffik/, **stratigraphical** /-gráffik'l/ *adj* relating to stratigraphy —**stratigraphically** *adv*

stratigraphy /strə tíggrəfi/ (*plural* **-phies**) *n* **1. STUDY OF ROCK STRATA** the study of the origin, composition, and development of rock strata **2. DISPOSITION OF ROCK STRATA** the way in which rock strata are arranged, and the chronology of their formation **3.** ARCHAEOL **VERTICAL SECTION THROUGH GROUND** a section cut vertically through the Earth showing its different layers and allowing artefacts to be dated according to the layers in which they are found [Mid-19C. < STRATUM] —**stratigrapher** *n* —**stratigraphist** *n*

stratocumulus /stráytō kyoómyŏŏləss, stráttō-/ (*plural* **-li** /-lī/) *n* a cloud formation in a low-lying extensive layer with large dark round or rolling masses [Late 19C. < STRATUS]

stratopause /stráttō pawz/ *n* the boundary layer between the stratosphere and the mesosphere, at about 50 km/30 mi. above the Earth's surface [Mid-20C. < STRATOSPHERE, after TROPOPAUSE]

stratosphere /stráttə sfeer/ *n* **1.** the region of the Earth's atmosphere between the troposphere and mesosphere, from 10 km/6 mi. to 50 km/30 mi. above the Earth's surface. It has no clouds and is marked by gradual temperature increase. **2.** a very high or the highest level or position ○ *The failure of the harvest is likely to send food prices into the stratosphere.* [Early 20C. < STRATUM]

stratospheric /stráttə sférrik/, **stratospherical** /-sférrik'l/ *adj* **1.** relating or belonging to the stratosphere **2.** very or excessively high —**stratospherically** *adv*

stratovolcano /stráytō vol káynō, stráttō-/ (*plural* **-noes** or **-nos**) *n* a volcano consisting of layers of lava alternating with ash or cinder [Mid-20C. < STRATUM]

stratum /straátəm, stráy-/ (*plural* **-ta** /-tə/ or **-tums**) *n* **1. LEVEL WITHIN SYSTEM** a layer or level within an ordered system ○ *the various strata of meaning within the text* **2. LAYER OF SOCIETY** a social class or level of society consisting of people of similar cultural, economic, or educational status **3.** GEOL same as **bed** *n* (sense 12) **4. LAYER OF ATMOSPHERE OR SEA** a layer of the atmosphere or the sea, regarded as lying between horizontal planes **5. LAYER OF CELLS** a layer of living cells [Late 16C. Via modern Latin < Latin, 'something thrown down' < past participle of *sternere* 'lay or throw down'] —**stratal** *adj*

USAGE The plural of ***stratum*** is *strata*, reflecting the word's Latin history. A variant plural *stratums* exists but is relatively infrequent. People sometimes use the false plurals *stratas* and (after Latin) *stratae*, which treat *strata* as a singular, but these are incorrect: *all strata* [not *stratas* or *stratae*] *of society.*

stratus /stráytəss, straá-/ (*plural* **-ti** /-tī/) *n* a low-lying flat grey cloud formation [Early 19C. < modern Latin < Latin, past participle of *sternere* 'lay or throw down']

Strauss /strowss/, **Johann** (1804–49) Austrian conductor and composer. His compositions include many waltzes and marches. Known as **Johann Strauss the Elder**

Strauss, Johann (1825–99) Austrian composer. The son of Johann Strauss the Elder, he wrote operettas including *Die Fledermaus* (1874) and waltzes and other dance pieces including *The Blue Danube* (1867). Known as **Johann Strauss the Younger**

Strauss, Richard (1864–1949) German conductor and composer. His late romantic symphonic poems and operas such as *Der Rosenkavalier* (1911) develop the ideas of Richard Wagner and are characterized by rich harmonization.

stravaig /strə váyg/, **stravage** *Ireland, N England, Scotland vi* (**-vaigs, -vaiging, -vaiged; -vages, -vaging, -vaged**) to wander about in an aimless manner ■ *n* an aimless ramble [Late 18C. Origin ?]

AKG London

Igor Stravinsky

Stravinsky /strə vínski/, **Igor** (1882–1971) Russian-born US composer. A major figure in 20th-century music, he experimented widely with musical styles and forms and wrote the music for Sergei Diaghilev's ballets *The Firebird* (1910), *Petrushka* (1911), and *The Rite of Spring* (1913). Full name **Stravinsky, Igor Fyodorovich**

> 'Too many pieces of music finish too long after the end.'
> [Attributed to Igor Stravinsky]

straw /straw/ *n* **1.** STALKS OF THRESHED CEREAL CROPS the stalks of threshed cereal crops such as wheat or barley. Use: bedding and food for animals, weaving into objects such as baskets, thatching. **2.** DRIED GRASS STALK a single dried stalk of a cereal crop or grass **3.** ITEM MADE OF STRAW something made of straw, e.g. a hat or basket **4.** THIN TUBE FOR DRINKING a long thin tube used for sucking up a drink **5.** SOMETHING WORTHLESS anything of little or no importance or value **6.** COLOUR a pale brownish-yellow colour ■ *adj* OF STRAW COLOUR of the brownish-yellow colour [Old English *strēaw* < Indo-European, 'spread'] —**strawy** *adj* ◇ **a straw in the wind** a relatively minor incident or thing that gives some indication of what is likely to happen ◇ **clutch** *or* **grasp at straws** to be willing to try anything that may help in a desperate situation ◇ **draw the short straw** to be chosen from a group of people to do a difficult or unpleasant task

strawberry

strawberry /stráwbəri/ (*plural* **-ries**) *n* **1.** a small sweet red fruit containing many achenes resembling seeds **2.** a plant that spreads by means of rooting stems and bears strawberries. Genus: *Fragaria*.

strawberry blonde *adj* describes hair that is very pale in colour with a reddish or pinkish tinge ■ *n* somebody with strawberry blonde hair

strawberry bush *n* a bush or small tree with tiny flowers and scarlet pods and seeds. Native to: eastern North America. Latin name: *Euonymus americanus*.

strawberry mark *n* a raised red birthmark, often found on the scalp or face, containing small blood vessels

strawberry roan *n* a horse that has a coat of reddish hairs mixed with white

strawberry tomato *n* **1.** a round yellow edible fruit produced by a tropical plant and often used in preserves and pickles **2.** a hairy tropical plant of the nightshade family bearing edible yellow fruit. Genus: *Physalis*.

strawberry tree *n* an evergreen tree of the heath family with berries resembling strawberries. Flowers: white or pink. Native to: southern Europe. Latin name: *Arbutus unedo*.

strawboard /straw bawrd/ *n* a coarse cardboard made of straw pulp and used in making packaging materials and book covers

straw colour *n* COLOURS same as straw *n* (sense 6) — **straw-coloured** *adj*

strawflower /straw flowər/ *n* a plant with flower heads that remain colourful when dried. Native to: Australia. Latin name: *Helichrysum bracteatum*.

straw-hat *adj US* describes a theatre that operates only in the summer [< the relatively rustic beginnings of these theatres]

straw man *n* **1.** a straw figure made to resemble a human being **2.** *N Am* same as **man of straw**

straw mushroom *n* a small brown or pale-coloured edible mushroom used in Chinese cookery. It has a delicate flavour and a slightly gelatinous texture. Latin name: *Volvariella volvacea*.

straw poll *n* an unofficial poll or vote used to discover the likely result of an election or the trend of opinion regarding an issue

Strawson /straws'n/, **P. F.** (*b.* 1919) British philosopher associated with the analytic and linguistic philosophy movement. His early work explores the relationships between logic and ordinary language, while his later work is a metaphysical exploration of the structure of human thought and language. Full name **Strawson, Peter Frederick**

straw vote *n* same as **straw poll**

straw wine *n* a sweet wine made from grapes that have been partially dried in the sun, especially on a bed of straw

stray /stray/ *vi* (**strays, straying, strayed**) **1.** WANDER OFF to leave the correct course or wander away from the correct place ○ *The sheep strayed onto the road through the broken fence.* **2.** BECOME SEPARATED FROM GROUP to move away from or become separated from a flock or group **3.** MOVE CASUALLY to move or turn in a casual or abstracted or unconsciously compulsive way towards something ○ *Her eyes strayed again to the window.* **4.** DIGRESS FROM SUBJECT to digress from the main subject, or become diverted from the main or appropriate object of attention ○ *stray from the point* **5.** DEPART FROM ACCEPTED STANDARDS to depart from traditional or accepted standards of behaviour **6.** MEANDER to take an indirect course **7.** WANDER ABOUT AIMLESSLY to roam or wander without a particular aim or destination (*literary*) ○ *stray through the woods* ■ *adj* **1.** LOST OR HOMELESS homeless, lost, or wandering ○ *a stray dog* **2.** SCATTERED OR SEPARATED scattered, separated, or happening accidentally or randomly ○ *stray shots* ■ *n* **1.** SOMEBODY LOST somebody, especially a child, who is lost **2.** HOMELESS ANIMAL a lost or homeless domestic animal ■ **strays** *npl* ELECTRONICS ELECTRICAL INTERFERENCE electrical interference in a radio or television broadcast, causing disruption of a signal [13C. Shortening of Old French *estraier*] —**strayer** *n*

streak /streek/ *n* **1.** THIN STRIPE OF CONTRASTING COLOUR a long thin stripe or band that is a different colour from its background or surroundings **2.** LAYER OF SOMETHING a layer or strip of something **3.** CONTRASTING CHARACTERISTIC a characteristic of somebody or something, especially one that is only occasionally evident or that contrasts with other characteristics ○ *a happy-go-lucky streak* **4.** SHORT PERIOD OR UNBROKEN RUN a short period or unbroken run, especially of good or bad luck ○ *The team is finally having a winning streak.* **5.** RUN IN PUBLIC BY NAKED PERSON a quick run through a public place by somebody with no clothes on, usually as a joke or publicity stunt (*informal*) **6.** METEOROL LIGHTNING a flash of lightning **7.** MINERALS MARK OF MINERAL POWDER the characteristically coloured mark that a mineral makes when scratched on unglazed porcelain **8.** BOT VIRAL PLANT DISEASE a viral disease of plants such as potatoes or tomatoes that produces discoloured markings on stems and leaves **9.** MICROBIOL LINEAR GROWTH OF BACTERIA a linear growth of bacteria on the surface of a culture medium, produced by drawing a contaminated needle across the medium ■ *v* (**streaks, streaking, streaked**) **1.** *vt* MARK SOMETHING WITH STREAKS to mark or cover something with streaks **2.** *vt* LIGHTEN HAIR to lighten strands or sections of hair with a bleach or dye **3.** *vi* BECOME STREAKED to become streaked or form streaks **4.** *vi* DASH OR RUSH to move at great speed **5.** *vi* RUN NAKED IN PUBLIC to run quickly through a public place with no clothes on, usually as a joke or publicity stunt (*informal*) [Old English *strica* < Germanic, 'touch lightly'] —**streaked** *adj* —**streaking** *n*

streaker /streekər/ *n* somebody who runs quickly through a public place with no clothes on, usually as a joke or publicity stunt (*informal*)

streaky /streeki/ (**-ier, -iest**) *adj* **1.** MARKED WITH STREAKS covered or marked with streaks ○ *I cleaned the windows twice but they still looked streaky.* **2.** OCCURRING AS STREAKS occurring in the form of streaks in something else **3.** INCONSISTENT variable and uneven in quality ○ *Her work's a bit streaky.* —**streakily** *adv* —**streakiness** *n*

streaky bacon *n* bacon that consists of alternate layers of meat and fat

stream /streem/ *n* **1.** SMALL RIVER a narrow and shallow river **2.** CONSTANT FLOW a constant flow of liquid or gas **3.** AIR OR WATER CURRENT a current of air or water **4.** CONTINUOUS SERIES a continuous series or flow of people, things, or events **5.** QUICK OR UNBROKEN FLOW a quick or uninterrupted burst, flow, or succession ○ *a stream of questions* **6.** PREVAILING ATTITUDE a general or prevailing attitude, drift, or trend **7.** BEAM OF LIGHT a steady ray or beam of light **8.** EDUC GROUP OF PUPILS OF SIMILAR ABILITY a group or level in which pupils of similar ability are placed and taught together ■ *v* (**streams, streaming, streamed**) **1.** *vi* FLOW IN LARGE QUANTITIES to flow, or appear to flow, continuously or quickly and in large quantities ○ *Blood was streaming from the wound.* ○ *Sunlight streamed through the open window.* **2.** *vi* MOVE IN SAME DIRECTION to move continuously in large numbers in the same direction ○ *Fans streamed onto the pitch at the end of the game.* **3.** *vti* PRODUCE FLOW OF LIQUID to emit or produce liquid in a continuous flow ○ *His eyes streamed tears.* **4.** *vti* FLOAT FREELY to float or trail freely in air, wind, or water, or cause something to do this ○ *an advertising banner streaming behind the plane* **5.** *vti* EDUC PUT PUPILS IN ABILITY GROUPS to place pupils in groups according to their ability **6.** *vt* ONLINE BROADCAST SOMETHING IN REAL TIME to broadcast video, audio etc. material via the Internet or a computer network in real time [Old English *strēam* < Indo-European, 'to flow']

streambed /streem bed/ *n* a channel through which a stream flows or used to flow

streamer /streemər/ *n* **1.** NARROW FLAG a long narrow flag or banner **2.** DECORATIVE PAPER STRIP a long narrow strip of coloured paper or other material that is used for decoration **3.** ASTRON LUMINOUS STREAK IN SKY any one of the luminous streaks that make up the aurora borealis and the aurora australis **4.** MEDIA HEADLINE RUNNING ACROSS FULL PAGE a large headline that extends the entire width of a newspaper page

streaming /streeming/ *n* **1.** UK, ANZ, Can the practice of placing pupils in groups according to ability. US term tracking **2.** BIOL same as cyclosis **3.** ONLINE the playing of sound or video over the Internet or a computer network in real time

streamlet /streemlət/ *n* a small stream

streamline /streem līn/ *vt* (**-lines, -lining, -lined**) **1.** MAKE SOMETHING MORE EFFICIENT to make something such as a

business, organization, or manufacturing process more efficient, especially by simplifying or modernizing it **2. DESIGN OR BUILD WITH SMOOTH SHAPE** to design or build something with a smooth shape so that it moves with minimum resistance through air or water ■ *n* **1. CONTOUR DESIGNED TO MINIMIZE RESISTANCE** a contour of a body, e.g. of a car, boat, or aeroplane, designed to minimize resistance when moving through air or water **2. PHYS LINE IN FLUID** a line in a fluid indicating the direction of the velocity of a particle —**streamlined** *adj* —**streamlining** *n*

streamline flow *n* a flow of fluid in which the particles follow continuous paths and the fluid velocity at a recorded point either remains constant or varies regularly with time

stream of consciousness *n* **1.** a literary style that presents a character's continuous random flow of thoughts as they arise (*hyphenated before a noun*) **2.** the continuous uninterrupted flow of thoughts and feelings through somebody's mind

~~strech~~ incorrect spelling of **stretch**

Streep /streep/, **Meryl** (*b.* 1949) US actor. She won Academy Awards for *Kramer vs. Kramer* (1979) and *Sophie's Choice* (1982). Born **Streep, Mary Louise**

> 'Having wrinkles is at once strange and exciting.'
> [Meryl Streep, *Independent*; 26 March 1994]

street /street/ *n* **1. PUBLIC ROAD IN TOWN** a public road, especially in a town or city, usually lined with buildings **2. BUILDINGS ON STREET** the buildings that line a street **3. PART OF ROAD BETWEEN PAVEMENTS** the part of a road that lies between the pavements and is used by vehicles **4. PEOPLE LIVING IN STREET** the people who live or work in a street **5. URBAN MILIEU** the modern urban environment as a public arena ○ *The word on the street is that Micky knows who did it and is out to get him.* **6. PARTICULAR ENVIRONMENT** the social context or world of a particular group of people ○ *the view of the Conservative street* **7. REPRESENTATIVE GROUP OF PEOPLE** ordinary people considered collectively as representatives of the majority opinion of a particular group ■ *adj* **RELATED TO MODERN URBAN SOCIETY** widely found or used in a modern urban environment or fashionable in modern urban culture, especially among young people or the underworld ○ *Street language has worked its way into the mainstream language.* [Old English *strǣt*, via W Germanic < late Latin *strata* 'paved road' < Latin *sternere* 'pave, throw down'] ◇ **on the street** having nowhere to live ◇ **on the streets** working as a prostitute ◇ **right up somebody's street** exactly suitable or appropriate for somebody ◇ **streets ahead (of somebody or something)** much better in some way than somebody or something ◇ **the man** or **person** or **woman in the street** the average man or person or woman

street Arab, **street arab** *n* an offensive term for a child who has run away from home and lives on the streets (*archaic*) [< the perception of Arabs as nomadic]

streetcar /street kaar/ *n N Am* same as **tram**[1] (sense 1)

street credibility, **street cred** *n* popularity and acceptance among fashionable urban people, especially the young —**street-credible** *adj*

street crime *n* criminal activity occurring in a public place, usually in an urban area, especially theft of personal possessions, carjacking, and the illegal possession or use of firearms

street door *n* the door of a house or other building that opens onto the street

street fashion *n* fashion invented and worn by young people rather than by fashion designers, often associated with popular styles of music and dance or with urban subcultures

street fighter *n* **1.** somebody whose fighting skills were learnt on the streets rather than through formal training as a boxer **2.** somebody who is tough, cunning, and aggressive (*informal*)

street furniture *n* objects that are placed in the street for public use, e.g. pillar boxes, litter bins, benches, and streetlights

streetlight /street līt/, **streetlamp** /-lamp/ *n* a light, normally attached to the top of a tall post and one of a series, that illuminates a road or street at night

street name *n* an informal or colloquial name given to an illegal drug by those who sell or use it ○ *'Smack' has long been used as a street name for heroin.*

Streeton /street'n/, **Sir Arthur** (1867–1943) Australian painter. He pioneered Australian impressionism and was one of the founders of the group of painters known as the Heidelberg School. Full name **Streeton, Sir Arthur Ernest**

streetscape /street skayp/ *n* an artistic portrayal of a street and its activities, especially a busy city street

street-smart *adj* same as **streetwise**

street theatre *n* dramatic entertainment usually performed outdoors, e.g. in a park or shopping precinct

street value *n* the price that something illegal would fetch if sold to a customer

street virus *n* the natural virulent strain of a virus as distinguished from a less virulent strain of the same organism that has been grown or treated in a laboratory

streetwalker /street wawker/ *n* a prostitute who solicits in the streets (*informal*) —**streetwalking** *n*

streetwise /street wīz/ *adj* shrewd and experienced enough to be able to survive in the often difficult and dangerous environment of a modern city (*informal*)

Strehlow /stráylō/, **T. G. H.** (1908–78) Australian anthropologist and linguist. He was the author of pioneering studies of Aboriginal languages, myths, and songs. Full name **Strehlow, Theodor George Henry**

Streisand /strī́ zand/, **Barbra** (*b.* 1942) US singer, actor, and film director. The star of musicals, comedies, and dramas, she won an Academy Award for her acting debut in *Funny Girl* (1968). Born **Streisand, Barbara Joan**

> 'What does it mean when people applaud?...The lack of applause—that I can respond to.'
> [Barbra Streisand, *Life*; 22 May 1964]

strelitzia

strelitzia /stre lítsi ə/ (*plural* **-as** or *same*) *n* a widely cultivated perennial plant. Flowers: showy, often unusual or irregular in shape. Native to: southern Africa. Genus: *Strelitzia*. [Late 18C. After Charlotte of Mecklenburg-*Strelitz* (1744–1818), queen of George III of Great Britain and Ireland]

strength /strength/ *n* **1. PHYSICAL POWER** the physical power to carry out demanding tasks ○ *It took all our strength to lift the heavy table.* **2. EMOTIONAL TOUGHNESS** the necessary qualities required to deal with stressful or painful situations ○ *She showed great strength throughout the trial.* **3. SOURCE OF SUPPORT** a source of strength or support **4. RESISTANCE** the ability to withstand force, pressure, or stress ○ *tensile strength* **5. DEFENSIVE ABILITY** the ability to resist attack **6. ASSET OR QUALITY** a valuable or useful ability, asset, or quality ○ *One of the strengths of this system is its adaptability.* **7. DEGREE OF INTENSITY** the degree of intensity, e.g. of colour, light, smell, or sound **8. FORCE OR EFFECTIVENESS** force, effectiveness, or intensity, e.g. of beliefs, feelings, or expression ○ *It's difficult to recall the strength of purpose which once gripped me.* **9. PERSUASIVE POWER** power to convince or persuade, e.g. by argument or suggestion ○ *the strength of her argument* **10. POTENCY** the potency of something such as an alcoholic drink or a drug **11. NUMBER OF PEOPLE NEEDED** the number of people required to make something such as an army, team, or workforce

complete and enable it to function effectively ○ *at half strength* **12. FIN MAINTENANCE OF PRICES** the tendency of prices to be stable or rise [Old English *strengþu* < Germanic, 'strong'] ◇ **go from strength to strength** to go on from one success or achievement to another and get progressively better ◇ **in strength** in large numbers ◇ **on the strength of something** on the basis of something

strengthen /strength'n/ (**-ens, -ening, -ened**) *vti* to make something stronger or more powerful, or increase in strength or power —**strengthener** *n*

~~strenous~~ incorrect spelling of **strenuous**

~~strenth~~ incorrect spelling of **strength**

strenuous /strénnyoō əss/ *adj* **1.** requiring physical effort, energy, stamina, or strength ○ *strenuous exercise* **2.** active, energetic, or determined ○ *strenuous efforts* [Early 17C. < Latin *strenuus* 'brisk, active'] —**strenuosity** /strénnyoō óssəti/ *n* —**strenuously** *adv* —**strenuousness** *n*

SYNONYMS See **hard**.

strep /strep/ *n* (*informal*) **1.** MICROBIOL same as **streptococcus 2.** MED same as **strep throat** —**strep** *adj*

strept- *prefix* same as **strepto-** (*used before vowels*)

streptavidin /stréptə víddin/ *n* a protein that interacts strongly with biotin and is used in immunological and biochemical assays [Mid-20C. < STREPT- + AVIDIN]

strep throat *n* an acute sore throat caused by the bacterium *Streptococcus pyogenes* and accompanied by fever and inflammation

strepto- *prefix* **1.** streptococcus ○ *streptokinase* **2.** twisted chain ○ *streptococcus* **3.** streptomyces ○ *streptothricin* [< Greek *streptos* 'twisted' < *strephein* 'to turn, twist']

streptobacillus /stréptō bə sílləss/ (*plural* **-li** /-lī/) *n* a rod-shaped bacterium that often causes diseases such as rat-bite fever. Individual cells join to form structures resembling chains. Genus: *Streptobacillus*.

streptocarpus /stréptə kaárpəss/ (*plural* **-puses**) *n* a plant that often has only one large leaf. Flowers: brightly coloured, tubular. Native to: subtropical regions. Genus: *Streptocarpus*. [Early 19C. < modern Latin < Greek *streptos* 'twisted' + *karpos* 'fruit'; because its fruit is spirally twisted]

streptococcus /stréptə kókəss/ (*plural* **-cocci** /-kók sī/) *n* a spherical bacterium that often causes diseases such as scarlet fever or pneumonia. The bacteria link together in pairs or chains. Genus: *Streptococcus*. [Late 19C. < modern Latin < Greek *streptos* 'twisted' + *coccus* 'berry'] —**streptococcal** *adj*

streptodornase /stréptə dáwr nayz, -nayss/ *n* an enzyme derived from streptococci that can liquefy pus [Mid-20C. < STREPTOCOCCUS + contraction of *deoxyribonuclease*]

streptokinase /stréptə kī́ nayz, -nayss/ *n* an enzyme produced by streptococci. Use: dissolving blood clots. [Mid-20C. < streptococcal]

streptolysin /stréptə lī́ssin/ *n* a substance that breaks down red blood cells and is produced by streptococci

streptomyces /stréptə mī́ seez/ (*plural same*) *n* an aerobic soil bacterium. Some streptomyces produce antibiotics. Genus: *Streptomyces*. [Mid-20C. < modern Latin < Greek *strepto-* 'twisted' + *mukēs* 'fungus'; because it forms twisted chains and resembles mould]

streptomycin /stréptə mī́ssin/ *n* an antibiotic produced from the soil bacterium *Streptomyces griseus*. Use: treatment of bacterial infections such as tuberculosis.

Stresemann /stráyze man, shtráyze-/, **Gustav** (1878–1929) German chancellor (1923) and minister of foreign affairs (1923–29). He worked for conciliation after World War I and secured Germany's admission to the League of Nations. He shared a Nobel Peace Prize (1926).

stress /stress/ *n* **1. STRAIN FELT BY SOMEBODY** mental, emotional, or physical strain caused, e.g. by anxiety or overwork. It may cause such symptoms as raised blood pressure or depression. **2. CAUSE OF STRAIN** something that causes stress **3. SPECIAL IMPORTANCE** special emphasis, importance, or significance attached to something **4. EMPHASIS ON SYLLABLE** the emphasis placed

on a sound or syllable by pronouncing it more loudly or forcefully than those surrounding it in the same word or phrase **5. EMPHASIS IN POETRY** the emphasis placed on a syllable or word as part of the rhythm of a poem or line of poetry **6. ACCENT IN MUSIC** the emphasis placed on a note as part of the rhythm of a piece of music, or a mark representing this **7.** PHYS **FORCE DEFORMING BODY** a force or system of forces exerted on a body and resulting in deformation or strain ■ *vt* **(stresses, stressing, stressed) 1. EMPHASIZE SOMETHING** to place emphasis on or attach importance to something **2. PRONOUNCE SOMETHING FORCEFULLY** to pronounce a word or syllable more loudly or forcefully than those surrounding it **3. SUBJECT SOMEBODY OR SOMETHING TO STRAIN** to cause somebody or something to experience mental, emotional, or physical stress [14C. Partly shortening of DISTRESS; partly < Old French *estresse* 'narrowness' < Latin *strictus* 'compressed'] —**stressed** *adj* —**stressor** *n*

SYNONYMS See *worry.*

stress out *vti* to affect somebody with emotional, mental, or physical stress, or be so affected (*informal*)

STRESS *abbr* COMPUT structural engineering system solver

stressed out *adj* unable to relax or function properly as the result of experiencing emotional or mental stress (*informal; hyphenated when used before a noun*)

stress fracture *n* a small fracture of a bone caused by repeated physical strain, sometimes experienced, e.g. by gymnasts, long-distance runners, or marching soldiers

stressful /stréssf'l/ *adj* causing or involving mental or physical stress —**stressfully** *adv* —**stressfulness** *n*

stress management *n* physical and psychological techniques designed to enable people to cope with strain and anxiety

stress mark *n* a mark placed before, on, or after a syllable that is to be stressed when the word containing it is pronounced

stress puppy *n* somebody who complains a lot about being stressed but actually seems to enjoy it (*informal*)

stretch /strech/ *v* **(stretches, stretching, stretched) 1.** *vti* **EXTEND BY FORCE** to lengthen, widen, or extend something, or become lengthened, widened, or extended, especially by force **2.** *vi* **EXPAND AND REGAIN ORIGINAL SHAPE** to be capable of expanding and returning to the original shape afterwards **3.** *vti* **EXTEND EXCESSIVELY** to extend something excessively so that the shape is permanently altered, or be extended in this way ○ *The sleeves of this sweater have stretched.* **4.** *vti* **EXTEND TO FULL LENGTH** to straighten or extend the body or part of it, especially the limbs, to full length ○ *She woke up, yawned, and stretched.* ○ *The cat lay stretched out by the fire.* ○ *stretched his arms* **5.** *vt* **STRAIN BODY PART** to strain a part of the body such as a muscle **6.** *vti* **TAUTEN** to make something taut or tight, or become taut or tight **7.** *vt* **SUSPEND SOMETHING BETWEEN TWO POINTS** to suspend something, or make something reach, between two points **8.** *vi* **EXTEND IN SPACE** to spread out or extend over an area or in a particular direction **9.** *vti* **EXTEND OVER TIME** to last or continue over a period of time, or prolong something **10.** *vt* **MAKE SMALL AMOUNT GO FURTHER** to make limited supplies or resources go further than usual, planned, or expected **11.** *vi* **BE ENOUGH** to be sufficient to allow something ○ *Will the budget stretch to hiring a temporary assistant?* **12.** *vt* **EXCEED LIMIT OR BREAK RULE** to exceed a limit or break a rule that would usually prohibit something **13.** *vt* **PUSH SOMETHING TO LIMIT** to strain or push something to the limit ○ *You're stretching my patience.* **14.** *vt* **PUSH SOMEBODY TO LIMIT OF ABILITY** to cause somebody to make full use of his or her abilities or intellect, e.g. with challenging or demanding work **15.** *vt* **EXAGGERATE SOMETHING** to make something sound better or worse than it really is, especially in order to make it seem more impressive (*informal*) ○ *To call his house a mansion is stretching it a bit.* **16.** *vt* **KNOCK SOMEBODY DOWN** to knock somebody down with a blow (*informal*) ■ *n* **1. STRETCHING EXERCISE** the straightening and extending of a part of the body, e.g. as an exercise **2. EXPANSE** a large expanse of something, especially land or water **3. PERIOD OF TIME** an uninterrupted period of time **4.** CRIME **PRISON TERM** a term of imprisonment (*informal*) **5. ELASTICITY** the ability to expand and return to the original shape afterwards **6. DIFFICULT CHALLENGE** something that is difficult to achieve (*informal*) **7.** SPORTS **STRAIGHT PART OF RACECOURSE** the straight part of a racecourse, especially the final section approaching the finishing line **8. FINAL STAGE** the final stage of an event, task, process, or period of time, especially one that has been difficult or challenging **9.** AUTOMOT **LONG PASSENGER CAR** a limousine that has an extended body (*informal*) ○ *hired a stretch for the wedding* ■ *adj* **1. ELASTIC** made of or being a material that has great elasticity ○ *wore stretch pants for skiing* **2. EXTENDED TO PROVIDE EXTRA SPACE** extended or enlarged in order to provide extra space, e.g. for additional seating ○ *a stretch limousine* [Old English *streccan*, probably < Germanic, 'rigid'] —**stretchability** /stréchə bílləti/ *n* —**stretchable** *adj* ◇ **at a stretch 1.** continuously ○ *worked five hours at a stretch* **2.** with great difficulty or effort ○ *could get there by six at a stretch* ◇ **at full stretch** using all the energy or resources available

stretcher /stréchər/ *n* **1.** MED **DEVICE FOR CARRYING SOMEBODY LYING DOWN** a device consisting of a sheet of material such as canvas stretched over a frame, used to carry somebody in a lying position who is sick, injured, or dead **2.** *ANZ* CAMPING **CAMP BED** a camp bed consisting of a folding tubular metal frame and a canvas covering **3.** ART **FRAME FOR ARTIST'S CANVAS** a wooden frame over which a canvas for an oil painting is stretched **4.** FURNITURE **BAR BRACING FURNITURE LEGS** a bar that joins and braces the legs of a chair, table, or other piece of furniture **5.** CONSTR **STRONG BEAM USED AS BRACE** a strong, usually horizontal beam or bar that is used as a brace in the framework of a structure **6.** CONSTR **STONE WITH LONG EDGE FACING OUT** a brick or stone laid in a wall so that its longer edge forms part of the face of the wall **7.** ROWING **BOARD FOR BRACING ROWER'S FEET** a board fixed across the width of a boat, on which a rower's feet can be braced **8. EXAGGERATED STORY** an exaggerated story, or a lie based partly on the truth (*slang*) ■ *vt* **(stretchers, stretchering, stretchered) CARRY SOMEBODY ON STRETCHER** to carry a sick, injured, or dead person on a stretcher ○ *Their star player was stretchered off in the first half.*

stretcher-bearer *n* somebody who helps carry a stretcher, especially a soldier given the task in wartime

stretch knit *n* knitted fabric that can stretch and return to its original shape afterwards (*hyphenated before a noun*)

stretch mark *n* a mark left on the skin of the abdomen, breasts, buttocks, or thighs after pregnancy or weight loss (*often used in the plural*)

stretchy /stréchi/ **(-ier, -iest)** *adj* capable of being stretched, usually returning to its original shape afterwards, or tending to stretch —**stretchiness** *n*

stretto /stréttō/ (*plural* **-tos** *or* **-ti** /-ti/) *n* **1.** in a fugue or similar musical work, the successive statements of the theme very close together in time **2.** the speeding up of a piece of music at a climactic moment [Mid-18C. Via Italian, 'narrow, tight' < Latin *strictus* (see STRICT)]

streusel /stro͝oz'l, stróyz'l/ *n N Am* a crumbly topping for cakes and pastries made of sugar, flour, butter, cinnamon, and often chopped nuts [Early 20C. < German < *streuen* 'sprinkle']

strew /stroo/ **(strews, strewing, strewed, strewn** /stroon/ *or* **strewed)** *v* (*often passive*) **1.** *vt* to scatter something, especially carelessly or untidily ○ *Clothes were strewn all over the floor.* **2.** *vti* to cover an area with loosely or carelessly scattered objects or material ○ *The retreating army strewed the area with landmines.* ○ *a rock-strewn path* [Old English *strewian* < Indo-European] —**strewer** *n*

strewth /strooth/, **struth** *interj* used to express surprise or irritation (*slang*) [Late 19C. Contraction of *God's truth*, an oath]

stria /strī́ ə/ (*plural* **-ae** /-ee/) *n* **1.** a thin narrow groove or channel in the surface of something, e.g. a decorative feature on a column **2.** ANAT a stripe, streak, or narrow band, e.g. a band of nerve fibres or stretch marks seen in pregnancy **(striae gravidarum) 3.** GEOL same as **striation** (sense 3) [Mid-16C. < Latin, 'furrow, channel']

striate /strī áyt/ *vt* **(-ates, -ating, -ated)** to mark something with parallel grooves, ridges, stripes, or narrow bands ■ *adj* ANAT same as **striated** [Late 17C. < Latin *striat-*, past participle of *striare* < *stria* 'furrow, channel']

striated /strī áytid/ *adj* marked with parallel grooves, ridges, stripes, or narrow bands

striated muscle *n* a muscle or muscle tissue that shows light and dark bands within the muscle fibres

striation /strī áysh'n/ *n* **1. STRIPY PATTERN** a patterning or marking with parallel grooves or narrow bands **2.** ANAT **BANDING OR BAND WITHIN MUSCLE FIBRE** the striped pattern of striated muscle, or any of the light and dark bands that make up this effect **3.** GEOL **NARROW MARK** a narrow groove or scratch on an exposed rock face, caused by abrasion by hard rock fragments embedded in a moving glacier

stricken /stríkən/ past participle of **strike** *v* (senses 22, 26) (*archaic*) ■ *adj* **1. DEEPLY OR BADLY AFFECTED** deeply or very badly affected by something such as grief, misfortune, or trouble (*often used in combination*) ○ *grief-stricken* **2. AFFECTED BY ILLNESS** experiencing severe physical symptoms caused by illness or injury **3. HIT BY MISSILE** injured, struck, or wounded, e.g. by a missile —**strickenly** *adv*

strickle /strík'l/ *n* **1.** MANUF **BOARD FOR LEVELLING OFF EXCESS MATERIAL** a board used to level off excess grain or other material in a container or measuring device **2. SHAPING TOOL** a tool used to shape the surface of a mould ■ *vt* **(-les, -ling, -led)** MANUF **USE STRICKLE ON SOMETHING** to level or shape something with a strickle [Old English *stricel* < Germanic]

~~**strickly**~~ incorrect spelling of **strictly**

strict /strikt/ *adj* **1. SEVERE IN MAINTAINING DISCIPLINE** severe in maintaining discipline, or rigorous in ensuring that rules are obeyed **2. ENFORCED RIGOROUSLY** needing to be closely obeyed ○ *strict guidelines for admission* **3. PRECISE** exact, precise, or narrowly interpreted ○ *a strict interpretation of the statute* **4. FAITHFUL** closely observing rules, principles, or practices ○ *strict party loyalty* **5. ABSOLUTE** complete, utter, or absolute **6.** BOT **GROWING UPRIGHT** growing upwards at or very close to the vertical [15C. < Latin *strictus*, past participle of *stringere* 'draw tight'] —**strictly** *adv* —**strictness** *n*

ORIGIN The Latin word *stringere* 'to draw tight', from which ***strict*** is derived, is also the source of English *constrain, constrict, distress, district, prestige, restrain, restrict, strain*[1], *stress,* and *stringent.*

stricture /stríkchər/ *n* **1. SEVERE CRITICISM** a severe criticism or strongly critical remark (*formal*) **2. LIMIT OR RESTRICTION** a limit or restriction, especially one that seems unfair or too harsh (*formal*) **3.** MED **CONSTRICTION OF BODY PASSAGE** a constriction or narrowing of a body passage [14C. < Latin *strictura* < *strictus* (see STRICT)] —**strictured** *adj*

stridden past participle of **stride**

striddle /strídd'l/ **(-dles, -dling, -dled)** *vi regional* to walk with the legs apart [Mid-16C. Back-formation < obsolete *striddling* 'astride' < STRIDE]

stride /strīd/ *v* **(strides, striding, strode** /strōd/, **stridden** /strídd'n/) **1.** *vi* **WALK WITH LONG STEPS** to walk with long regular steps, often briskly or energetically **2.** *vti* **TAKE LONG STEP OVER SOMETHING** to cross or step over something with a long step **3.** *vti* **STRADDLE SOMETHING** to sit or stand astride something (*archaic or literary*) ■ *n* **1. LONG STEP** a long step, especially one taken briskly or energetically **2. DISTANCE COVERED BY LONG STEP** the distance covered when somebody or something takes a long step **3. ADVANCE TOWARDS IMPROVING SOMETHING** an advance or step towards improving or developing something **4. WAY OF WALKING** a way of walking or running in long regular steps, often taken briskly or energetically **5.** ZOOL **COORDINATED FORWARD MOVEMENT BY ANIMAL** an act of forward motion by a four-legged animal consisting of a coordinated cycle of movements that brings the legs back to their original positions **6.** MUSIC same as **stride piano** ■ **strides** *npl Aus* **TROUSERS** a pair of trousers (*informal*) [Old English *strīdan* 'straddle', probably < Germanic] —**strider** *n* ◇ **get into your stride** to become familiar and at ease with something so that you can do it easily and well ◇ **hit** *or* **reach your stride** *US* same as **get into your stride** ◇ **take something in your stride** to accept something without being unduly upset or worried about it

strident /strī́d'nt/ *adj* **1.** harsh, loud, grating, or shrill ○ *strident tones of voice* **2.** loudly, strongly, or urgently expressed ○ *strident opposition* [Mid-17C. < Latin *strident-*, present participle of *stridere* 'creak'] —**stridence** *n* —**stridency** *n* —**stridently** *adv*

stride piano *n* a style of jazz piano-playing in which the right hand plays the melody while the left hand alternates between playing a single note and a related chord [< STRIDE 'straddle'; from the movements of the left hand]

stridor /strī́ dawr, strī́dər/ *n* **1.** a harsh, grating, or creaking noise **2.** a harsh high-pitched wheezing sound made when breathing in or out, caused by obstruction of the air passages [Mid-17C. < Latin < *stridere* 'to creak']

stridulate /strίddyoǒ layt/ (**-lates, -lating, -lated**) *vi* to make a chirping or grating sound by rubbing parts of the body together, as male crickets and grasshoppers do [Mid-19C. < French *striduler* < Latin *stridere* 'to creak'] —**stridulant** *adj* —**stridulation** /strίddyoǒ láysh'n/ *n* —**stridulator** *n* —**stridulatory** *adj* —**stridulous** *adj*

strife /strīf/ *n* **1.** bitter and sometimes violent conflict, struggle, or rivalry **2.** *ANZ* trouble or difficulty (*informal*) [12C. < Old French *estrif*] —**strifeless** *adj*

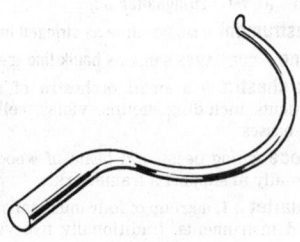

strigil

strigil /strίjjil/ *n* in ancient Greece and Rome, an instrument with a curved blade used to scrape dirt and sweat from the skin after bathing or exercising [Late 16C. < Latin *strigilis*]

strigose /strī́gōss, -gōz/ *adj* **1.** covered with fine scales or short bristles **2.** with thin, closely spaced grooves or ridges [Late 18C. < modern Latin *strigosus* < Latin *striga* 'row, strip']

strike /strīk/ *v* (**strikes, striking, struck** /struk/) **1.** *vti* HIT SOMEBODY OR SOMETHING to hit somebody or something with a hand, tool, weapon, or other object ○ *She was struck on the arm by a piece of falling masonry.* **2.** *vti* DELIVER BLOW to deliver or inflict something such as a blow or punch **3.** *vti* COLLIDE WITH SOMEBODY OR SOMETHING to crash into, knock hard against, or collide with somebody or something ○ *The car swerved and struck a tree.* **4.** *vti* PENETRATE SOMETHING to penetrate or seem to go right through something ○ *The pain struck deep into my shoulder blade.* **5.** *vt* KNOCK SOMETHING AWAY to remove something with a blow ○ *She struck the wasp from the window screen.* **6.** *vti* PRODUCE FIRE to produce fire by friction, or be produced by friction **7.** *vti* LIGHT MATCH to cause a match to light by friction, or be lit by friction ○ *The matches won't strike if they get damp.* **8.** *vt* PRESS KEY TO OPERATE SOMETHING to press a key on something such as a computer keyboard or musical instrument **9.** *vti* INDICATE TIME BY MAKING SOUND to indicate the time by making a sound such as chiming **10.** *vt* MAKE SOMETHING BY STAMPING to make or form something such as a coin by stamping or punching **11.** *vt* PRODUCE MUSICAL SOUND to produce a musical note by pressing a key or keys or by touching a string or strings **12.** *vti* SHINE ON SOMETHING to fall or shine on something ○ *Moonbeams struck the placid water on the lake.* **13.** *vt* BE NOTICED BY SOMEBODY to catch somebody's attention, or be noticed by somebody or something **14.** *vt* BE PERCEIVED BY SOMEBODY to be perceived by or become audible to somebody **15.** *vt* MAKE PARTICULAR IMPRESSION ON SOMEBODY to have a particular effect on or make a particular impression on somebody **16.** *vt* ENTER SOMEBODY'S MIND to enter somebody's mind or occur to somebody, especially suddenly **17.** *vt* AFFECT WITH EMOTION to affect somebody or cause somebody to be affected with an emotion in a deep, painful, or sudden way **18.** *vti* FIND OR DISCOVER SOMETHING to come across, find, or discover something, especially suddenly or unexpectedly **19.** *vti* MIL ATTACK SOMEBODY OR SOMETHING to make a military attack on somebody or something ○ *The enemy struck under cover of darkness.* **20.** *vti* DAMAGE SOMETHING OR SOMEBODY to hit and damage or injure something or somebody **21.** *vi* BITE OR STING SUDDENLY to deliver a sudden fast bite or sting, typically resulting in injury to the one bitten or stung ○ *Suddenly the snake struck.* **22.** (*past participle* **stricken** /strίkən/ or **struck**) *vti* AFFECT SOMEBODY SUDDENLY to affect somebody suddenly or unexpectedly ○ *The illness can strike at any age.* ○ *was stricken with a heart attack* **23.** *vti* HAPPEN SUDDENLY to happen to somebody or something suddenly or unexpectedly ○ *Disaster struck when the volcano suddenly erupted.* **24.** *vi* STOP WORKING AS PROTEST to stop working as a collective form of protest against an employer, often to achieve a specific aim ○ *were striking for a pay increase* **25.** *vt N Am* HR STOP WORKING FOR SOMEBODY to strike against an employer ○ *struck the auto plant* **26.** (*past participle* **stricken** or **struck**) *vt* CROSS OUT to cancel, delete, or cross something out ○ *The judge ordered that the preceding remark be struck from the record.* **27.** *vt* AGREE TO TERMS to agree on the terms of something ○ *struck a deal* **28.** *vt* REACH AGREEMENT to achieve something such as a balance or compromise by careful consideration or calculation **29.** *vt* ADOPT POSE to adopt or assume something such as a pose or attitude **30.** *vti* TAKE BAIT to take or attempt to take a bait (*refers to fish*) ○ *The fish are striking today.* **31.** *vti* BOT GROW ROOTS to send out and establish roots **32.** *vt* DISMANTLE SOMETHING to dismantle something such as a tent or stage set **33.** *vt* LOWER SOMETHING IN RESPECT OR SURRENDER to lower something such as a flag or sail, especially as a sign of respect or surrender **34.** *vt* SAILING LOWER MAST to lower a ship's mast **35.** *vt* SHIPPING LOWER THINGS INTO SHIP'S HOLD to lower something such as cargo into the hold of a ship **36.** *vt* MANUF same as **strickle 37.** *vi US* NAVY ATTEMPT TECHNICAL RATING IN US NAVY to work hard with the aim of achieving a technical rating in the US Navy ■ *n* **1.** HIT OR BLOW a blow delivered with a hand, tool, weapon, or other object **2.** SOUND OF HIT a sound produced by striking somebody or something **3.** WORK STOPPAGE a work stoppage by employees as a protest against an employer, often to achieve a specific aim **4.** REFUSAL TO DO SOMETHING AS PROTEST a refusal to carry out a regular action or activity such as eating or paying rent as a form of protest ○ *a hunger strike* **5.** MIL MILITARY ATTACK a military attack, especially one using aircraft **6.** SUCCESS IN FINDING SOMETHING a success in finding or discovering something, especially a valuable mineral source such as gold or oil **7.** BOWLING KNOCKING DOWN OF ALL BOWLING PINS the knocking down of all the pins with the first ball in a session of tenpin bowling **8.** COINS COINS STRUCK AT SAME TIME the number of coins or medals struck at one time **9.** GEOL DIRECTION OF GEOLOGICAL FORMATION the compass direction of a horizontal line on a sloping rock surface, used to define geological features such as bedding or faults **10.** MANUF same as **strickle** *n* (sense 1) **11.** VET ANIMAL DISEASE CAUSED BY FLIES an animal disease caused by an infestation of flies or fly eggs in open wounds or moist areas of the skin **12.** FISHING PULL ON FISHING LINE BY FISH a pull on a fishing line indicating that a fish has taken the bait **13.** BOT SENDING OUT OF PLANT ROOTS the establishment of roots by a plant cutting or seedling [Old English *strīcan* < Germanic, 'touch lightly'] ◇ **on strike 1.** not working as a form of protest against an employer, often to achieve a specific aim **2.** refusing to undertake usual tasks as a form of protest ◇ **strike it rich** to be extremely lucky or successful, particularly in money matters (*informal*)

strike down *vt* **1.** CAUSE SOMEBODY TO FALL to hit and cause somebody or something to fall **2.** CAUSE SOMEBODY TO BECOME VERY ILL to affect somebody or cause somebody to become seriously ill, especially suddenly **3.** KILL SOMEBODY to cause somebody to die, especially suddenly or unexpectedly

strike off *vt* **1.** PREVENT PROFESSIONAL FROM PRACTISING to prevent somebody such as a doctor or lawyer from continuing to practise his or her profession by removing his or her name from the register of authorized practitioners ○ *The surgeon who performed this operation should be struck off.* **2.** DELETE SOMETHING to cancel or remove something from a list, record, or register by crossing it out ○ *An officer struck off the names of the passengers as they boarded the cruise ship.* **3.** PRINT SOMETHING to print a copy, document, or publication

strike on *vt* to think of something, especially suddenly or by chance

strike out *v* **1.** *vt* DRAW LINE THROUGH SOMETHING to draw a line through written or printed matter in order to cancel or delete it **2.** *vi* SET OUT ENERGETICALLY to set out energetically, especially for a particular destination or in a particular direction ○ *We struck out at sunrise, determined to get there by nightfall.* **3.** *vi* BEGIN SOMETHING to begin doing something, especially independently **4.** *vi* ATTACK SOMEBODY OR SOMETHING to make an attack on somebody or something, either physically or verbally **5.** *vi N Am* FAIL to be unsuccessful (*informal*) ○ *I tried three times to get that job, but struck out completely.*

strike up *v* **1.** *vti* to begin playing or singing something ○ *struck up the band and played a waltz* **2.** *vt* to begin something, or cause something to begin ○ *struck up a friendship*

strike upon *vt* same as **strike on**

strikebound /strī́k bownd/ *adj* closed or unable to operate because people have stopped working as a form of protest

strikebreaker /strī́k braykər/ *n* **1.** a worker who continues on the job while other employees are on strike **2.** somebody hired to do the work of somebody who is on strike

strikebreaking /strī́k brayking/ *n* **1.** the act of working for an employer while other employees are on strike **2.** action intended to break up a workers' strike

strike fault *n* a geological fault with a horizontal line (**strike**) parallel to the rock strata

strike pay *n* money paid by a trade union to members who are on strike

strike price *n UK, ANZ, Can* the price at which the holder of stock options or warrants has the right to buy or sell. US term **striking price**

striker /strī́kər/ *n* **1.** SOMEBODY ON STRIKE somebody who has joined others in ceasing work in protest against working conditions or to compel an employer to accept their demands **2.** SOCCER ATTACKING FOOTBALL PLAYER an attacking player in a football team whose main role is to score goals **3.** DEVICE THAT STRIKES TO TELL TIME a device that strikes to tell the time, e.g. a hammer in a clock or a clapper in a bell **4.** ARMS MECHANISM THAT DRIVES FIRING PIN the mechanical part of a firearm that drives the firing pin forwards

strike-slip fault *n* a geological fault that moves in a direction parallel to its strike

striking /strī́king/ *adj* **1.** CONSPICUOUS conspicuous, marked, or noticeable **2.** ATTRACTIVE OR IMPRESSIVE attracting attention, especially in an impressive or unusual way **3.** HR ON STRIKE not working as a collective form of protest against an employer, often to achieve a specific aim —**strikingly** *adv*

striking distance *n* sufficient closeness to reach or achieve something ○ *within striking distance of the camp*

striking price *n US* FIN same as **strike price**

August Strindberg

Strindberg /strίnd burg/, **August** (1849–1912) Swedish dramatist. Often considered the greatest figure in Swedish literature, he greatly influenced European and US dramatists with his naturalistic novels and

plays, notably *Miss Julie* (1888). Full name **Strindberg, Johan August** —**Strindbergian** /strind búrgi ən/ *adj*

'I loathe people who keep dogs. They are cowards who haven't got the guts to bite people themselves.'
[August Strindberg, *A Madman's Diary*; 1895]

Strine /strīn/, **strine** *n* Australian English, especially a humorous representation in writing of Australian pronunciation, e.g. 'Emma Chisit' for 'How much is it?' (*humorous*) [Mid-20C. Representing supposed Australian pronunciation of AUSTRALIAN]

string /string/ *n* **1.** STRONG THIN CORD a strong thin cord or twine, usually made of twisted fibres, used for fastening, hanging, or tying **2.** SOMETHING LIKE STRING something that resembles string in form or texture **3.** SUCCESSION OF ITEMS a series of similar or connected acts, events, or things **4.** LINE OF THINGS a series of things forming or arranged in a line, usually one behind the other **5.** GROUP OF ASSOCIATED THINGS a group of similar things belonging to, managed by, or connected with a single person or a set of people **6.** SEQUENCE OF SIMILAR ELEMENTS a sequence of items of the same nature, e.g. letters, numbers, symbols, binary digits, sounds, or words **7.** OBJECTS THREADED TOGETHER a set of objects connected with a single thread **8.** MUSIC CORD STRETCHED ACROSS MUSICAL INSTRUMENT a cord made of nylon, wire, or gut that is stretched across a musical instrument and plucked, bowed, or otherwise vibrated to produce sound **9.** RACKET GAMES TIGHT CORD ACROSS SPORTS RACKET a thin cord that is tightly stretched across the face of a sports racket and interwoven with others to form a mesh **10.** ARCHERY CORD ACROSS ARCHER'S BOW in archery, the cord stretched between the ends of a bow **11.** BOT, FOOD PLANT FIBRE a tough chewy fibre in a fruit or vegetable **12.** BUILDINGS same as **stringboard 13.** DESIGN same as **string course 14.** SOMEBODY CHOSEN AND RANKED ON ABILITY a person or group of people chosen, especially for a sports team, and ranked on the basis of ability (*usually used in combination*) ○ *a second-string quarterback* ○ *played first string in the last quarter of the game* **15.** CUE GAMES BILLIARDS HIT DETERMINING PLAYING ORDER in billiards, an act of hitting the cue ball towards the head cushion (**lag**) to determine who will play first **16.** CUE GAMES same as **baulk line** (sense 1) **17.** BOWLS TEN FRAMES OF BOWLING a game of tenpin bowling consisting of ten frames **18.** PHYS, ASTRON HYPOTHETICAL ONE-DIMENSIONAL ENTITY a hypothetical one-dimensional entity that vibrates as it moves through space and is held to be a fundamental component of matter **19.** ZOOL TENDON a tendon or ligament of an animal (*archaic*) ■ **strings** *npl* MUSIC **1.** MUSICIANS PLAYING STRINGED INSTRUMENTS the section of an orchestra consisting of musicians who play instruments with strings **2.** STRINGED INSTRUMENTS OF ORCHESTRA all the instruments of an orchestra or other musical ensemble that have strings, considered as a group ■ *v* (**strings, stringing, strung** /strung/) **1.** *vt* PUT THINGS ON STRING to thread things onto a string **2.** *vt* HANG SOMETHING BETWEEN POINTS to hang or stretch something between two points **3.** *vt* ARRANGE SOMETHING IN LINE to arrange or extend something in a line or series **4.** *vt* PROVIDE SOMETHING WITH STRINGS to provide something such as a sports racket or musical instrument with a string or strings **5.** *vt* FASTEN SOMETHING WITH STRING to bind, fasten, hang, or tie something with a string or strings **6.** *vt* COOK REMOVE FIBRES FROM FOOD to remove the stringy fibres from fruit or vegetables before cooking or eating **7.** *vt* COOK REMOVE CURRANTS to remove currants from their stalks by sliding them off between the prongs of a fork **8.** *vi* BECOME STRINGY to form strings, or become stringy **9.** *vti* CUE GAMES DETERMINE BILLIARDS PLAYING ORDER in billiards, to hit the cue ball towards the head cushion (**lag**) to determine who will play first ■ *adj* MADE OF STRING made of a mesh of string or similar material [Old English *streng* < Germanic, 'stiff'] —**stringed** *adj* —**stringless** *adj* ◇ **have somebody on a string** to be able to control somebody easily ◇ **pull strings** to use influence to try to gain an advantage ◇ **pull the strings** to be in control, although not obviously so ◇ **with no strings (attached)** without any conditions or restrictions being made

string along *v* (*informal*) **1.** *vt* DECEIVE SOMEBODY OVER LONG TIME to deceive or fool somebody over an extended period of time, especially by keeping him or her in a state of false hope **2.** *vi* GO WITH SOMEBODY to ac-

company or stay with somebody, often in a casual manner ○ *She wanted to string along with us when we went to the shops.* **3.** *vi* AGREE WITH SOMEBODY to agree or go along with somebody or somebody's idea or suggestion

string up *vt* **1.** to suspend somebody or something on a string or strings **2.** to kill somebody by hanging (*informal*)

string band *n* a group of musicians who play folk or country music on stringed instruments

string bass /-báyss/ *n* MUSIC same as **double bass**

string bean *n* **1.** FOOD, PLANTS same as **runner bean 2.** *N Am* FOOD, PLANTS same as **French bean** (sense 2) **3.** somebody who is tall and thin (*informal*)

stringboard /string bawrd/ *n* a board that covers the ends of the steps on a staircase [Because the board 'strings' the steps together]

string course *n* a decorative feature on a building in the form of a horizontal band or moulding

stringed instrument /stringd-/ *n* a musical

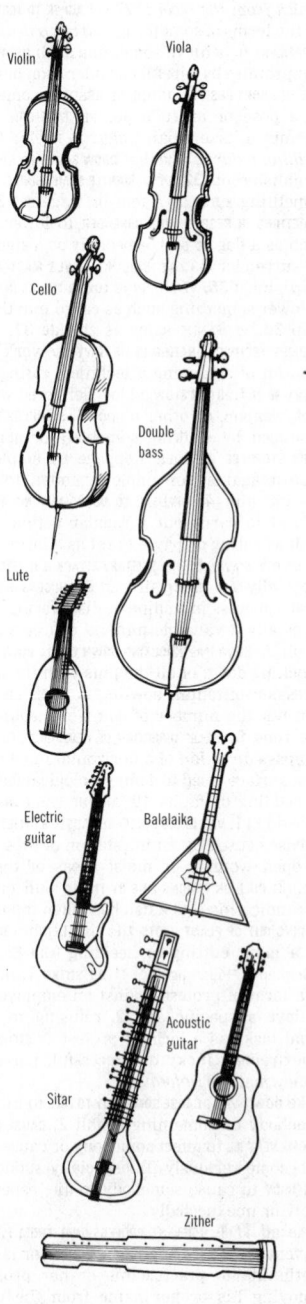

Violin

Viola

Cello

Double bass

Lute

Electric guitar

Balalaika

Acoustic guitar

Sitar

Zither

stringed instruments

instrument in which bowing or plucking causes the vibration of a string or strings tightly stretched across a soundboard, e.g. a violin or guitar

stringendo /strin jéndō/ *adv* at an accelerating tempo (*used as a musical direction*) [Mid-19C. < Italian, present participle of *stringere* 'press, squeeze' < Latin, 'draw tight, bind'] —**stringendo** *adj*

stringent /strínjənt/ *adj* strictly controlled or enforced [Early 17C. < Latin *stringent-*, present participle of *stringere* 'draw tight, bind'] —**stringency** *n* —**stringently** *adv*

stringer /stríngər/ *n* **1.** MEDIA FREELANCE OR PART-TIME JOURNALIST a journalist, often covering a specific geographical area, who works on a freelance or part-time basis for a newspaper or news agency **2.** CONSTR HORIZONTAL TIMBER a heavy horizontal timber used for structural purposes **3.** BUILDINGS same as **stringboard 4.** AEROSP, NAUT AUXILIARY MEMBER OF WING a light auxiliary part parallel with the main structural members of a wing or fuselage, used mainly for bracing and stabilizing **5.** SPORTS PLAYER OF PARTICULAR ABILITY a member of a team who is ranked according to excellence or skill (*usually used in combination*) **6.** GEOL NARROW MINERAL VEIN a narrow or discontinuous linear vein of ore mineral

stringhalt /string hawlt/ *n* a condition of horses marked by sudden lifting of and lameness in the hind legs, caused by muscle spasms [Early 16C. < STRING + HALT²] —**stringhalted** *adj*

string instrument *n* MUSIC same as **stringed instrument**

string line *n* CUE GAMES same as **baulk line** (sense 1)

string orchestra *n* a small orchestra of stringed instruments including violins, violas, cellos, and double basses

stringpiece /stríng peess/ *n* a beam of wood placed horizontally to support a framework

string quartet *n* **1.** a group of four musicians playing stringed instruments, traditionally two violins, a cello, and a viola **2.** a piece of music composed for four stringed instruments, traditionally two violins, a cello, and a viola

string theory *n* a mathematical theory that provides a unified structure to explain the properties and behaviour of elementary particles and fundamental forces

string tie *n* **1.** a narrow necktie made of ribbon, tied in a bow, briefly popular in the 1890s **2.** a narrow thong held by a sliding clip, worn as a necktie, especially by cowboys

string vest *n* a vest knitted or woven with an open mesh

stringy /stríngi/ (**-ier, -iest**) *adj* **1.** FOOD FIBROUS containing strands of fibre and unpleasant to chew **2.** UNATTRACTIVELY THIN unattractively thin, with bones or muscles showing beneath the skin **3.** RESEMBLING PIECES OF STRING looking like pieces of string or hanging in long thin strands ○ *a stringy beard* **4.** FORMING STRANDS forming long sticky threads —**stringiness** *n*

stringy-bark *n Aus* a eucalyptus tree with thick fibrous grey and brown bark

strip¹ /strip/ *v* (**strips, stripping, stripped**) **1.** *vi* GET UNDRESSED to remove your clothes, either completely or to a particular extent **2.** *vt* UNDRESS SOMEBODY to remove somebody's clothes, either completely or to a particular extent **3.** *vi* DO STRIPTEASE to do a striptease, or be a striptease artist **4.** *vt* REMOVE COVERING to take off a covering, or take the covering off something ○ *stripped the paper from the walls* ○ *stripped the walls of paper* **5.** *vt* REMOVE PAINT OR VARNISH FROM SURFACE to remove old paint or varnish from a surface by scraping or burning it or by using a chemical **6.** *vt* REMOVE CONTENTS to remove all the contents from a room, building, or similar place **7.** *vt* REMOVE ALL LEAVES OR PLANTS to remove all the leaves or flowers from a plant, or remove all the plants from an area **8.** *vt* DEPRIVE OF STATUS OR POSSESSIONS to take status or possessions away from somebody ○ *stripped him of his rank* **9.** *vt* TAKE SOMETHING APART to take a machine, engine, or weapon to pieces in order to clean or repair it **10.** *vti* MECH ENG DAMAGE SCREW THREAD OR GEAR TEETH to damage a screw or gearwheel by breaking the thread or teeth, or undergo this damage **11.** *vt* CHEM REMOVE VOLATILE CONTENT to separate one or more components from a solution or mixture, especially

by distillation or evaporation **12.** *vt* PRINTING, PHOTOGRAPHY **MAKE INTO PRINTING PLATE** to put pieces of photographic film or paper together to make a plate for printing ■ *n* **ACT OF STRIPPING** the performance of a striptease [Old English *-strȳpan* < Germanic]

strip off *vi* to take off all your clothes

strip out *vt* to take out parts of a machine for cleaning or repair

strip[2] /strip/ *n* **1. LONG FLAT PIECE** a long flat narrow piece of something **2.** AVIAT same as **airstrip 3.** PUBL same as **comic strip 4.** SPORTS **SPORTS CLOTHES** the distinctive clothes worn by a specific sports team such as a football team **5.** *N Am* COMM **ROAD LINED WITH BUSINESSES** a road lined with stores, shopping centres, restaurants, and other businesses ■ *vt* (**strips, stripping, stripped**) **DIVIDE INTO STRIPS** to cut, tear, or divide something into strips [15C. Probably < Low German *strippe* 'strap, thong'] ◇ **tear a strip off somebody** to rebuke somebody angrily

strip[3] /strip/ (**strips, stripping, stripped**) *vt* to remove the last remaining milk from the udder of a cow or goat by hand after machine-milking [Early 17C. Origin ?]

strip cartoon *n* PUBL same as **comic strip** [< STRIP[2]]

strip club *n* a club or bar where people can watch striptease acts [< STRIP[1]]

strip cropping *n* the growing of different crops in an arrangement of lines or bands to prevent soil erosion [< STRIP[2]]

stripe[1] /strīp/ *n* **1. LONG NARROW BAND** a long narrow band of a different colour, composition, or texture from the surrounding surface or background **2. PATTERN** a pattern of stripes **3.** TEXTILES **FABRIC** a fabric with a pattern of stripes **4.** MIL **INDICATION OF RANK** a narrow band or V-shaped piece of fabric, sewn onto a uniform as a symbol of rank **5.** *US* **TYPE OF PERSON** a recognizable type of person with a specific character or set of opinions ○ *This is a tyrant of a very different stripe.* ○*'...portals of all stripes face a challenging future...'* (*Washington Post*; November 1998) ■ *vt* (**stripes, striping, striped**) **MARK SOMETHING WITH STRIPES** to put a pattern of stripes on something [15C. Probably < Middle Dutch or Middle Low German *strīpe*] —**stripy** *adj*

stripe[2] /strīp/ *n* a blow from a whip, lash, cane, or belt [15C. Probably < Low German or Dutch]

striped /strīpt/ *adj* patterned or marked with stripes [15C. < STRIPE[1]]

striped bass *n* a large game fish with black stripes that travels up rivers to breed. Native to: US coastal waters. Latin name: *Morone saxatilus.*

striped marlin *n* a large game and food fish with dark blue vertical stripes on the sides. Native to: Pacific. Latin name: *Makaira audax.*

striped muscle *n* ANAT same as **striated muscle**

striped skunk *n* a common skunk that has a white cap on its head and white stripes down each side of the spine. Native to: North America. Latin name: *Mephitis mephitis.*

striper /strīpər/ *n* **1.** a member of the armed forces or of a flight or ship's crew whose stripes on the uniform indicate rank or length of service (*slang; usually used in combination*) ○ *a three-striper* **2.** FISH same as **striped bass** [Early 20C. < STRIPE[1]]

strip-grazing *n* a system in which cattle or other livestock are periodically allocated a fresh strip of pasture to graze by the moving of an electrified fence across the field [< STRIP[2]]

strip joint *n* same as **strip club** (*informal*) [< STRIP[1]]

striplight /stríp līt/ *n* **1.** a fluorescent lamp in the form of a long tube, especially on a ceiling **2.** a row of shaded lamps used to light a theatre stage [Early 20C. < STRIP[2]]

stripling /strípling/ *n* a boy in his early teenage years, who has not yet grown to his full size [14C. Probably < STRIP[2]]

strip mall *n N Am* a long building facing a road, divided into separate stores and businesses with parking spaces at the front of each of them [< STRIP[2]]

strip mill *n* an industrial building where steel is rolled into strips [< STRIP[2]]

strip mine *n N Am* a mine where mineral seams near the surface of the ground are exposed by stripping away soil and land [< STRIP[2]] —**strip mining** *n*

strip party *n US* a party for a group of women at which a male stripper performs

stripped-down /strípt-/ *adj* deprived of all but the most essential or simple features [< STRIP[1]]

stripper /strípper/ *n* **1. STRIPTEASE ARTIST** a performer of striptease acts **2. PAINT OR WALLPAPER REMOVER** a tool or substance used for removing paint, varnish, wallpaper, or other substances from a surface **3. SOMEBODY WHO STRIPS SOMETHING** somebody whose job is to strip something [Late 16C. < STRIP[1]]

strip poker *n* a variety of the card game poker in which, at each round, players who lose have to remove an item of their clothing [< STRIP[1]]

strippy /stríppi/ *n* patchwork in which broad strips of fabric are pieced together in vertical bands, then quilted ■ *adj* consisting of strips [Early 19C. < STRIP[2]]

strip-search *vti* to compel somebody to undress completely while searching for concealed drugs, weapons, or contraband [< STRIP[1]] —**strip search** *n*

striptease /stríp teez, stríp tééz/ *n* an entertainment in which the performer slowly undresses in an erotic way, usually with music as an accompaniment [Mid-20C. < STRIP[1]] —**stripteaser** *n*

strive /strīv/ (**strives, striving, strove** /strōv/, **striven** /strívv'n/) *vi* **1. TRY HARD** to try hard to achieve or get something **2. OPPOSE** to fight in opposition to something **3. COMPETE** to compete resolutely against somebody or something [12C. < Old French *estriver* 'contend' < *estrif* 'strife'] —**striver** *n*

SYNONYMS See *try.*

---

strobe /strōb/ *n* **1.** ELECTRONICS same as **strobe light 2.** ELECTRONICS same as **stroboscope 3.** an electronic pulse of short duration used to examine the characteristics of a periodic waveform **4.** the process of viewing vibrations or rotational motion with a stroboscope [Mid-20C. Shortening of STROBOSCOPE]

strobe light *n* a high-intensity flashing beam of light produced by charging a capacitor to a very high voltage then discharging it as a high-intensity flash of light in a tube

strobe lighting *n* the effect produced by strobe lights or by a perforated disc rotating in front of a high-intensity light source, as used in discos

strobila /strōbələ/ (*plural* **-lae** /-lee/) *n* **1.** the segmented body of a tapeworm, usually excluding the head (**scolex**) and neck **2.** a chain of buds that are attached to the body of some jellyfish and that later develop into individual offspring [Mid-19C. Via modern Latin < Greek *strobilē* 'twisted plug of lint', form of *strobilos* (see STROBILUS)]

strobilation /stróbbə láysh'n/ *n* the process of dividing into segments to form reproductive structures such as the buds produced by jellyfish

strobilus /strṓbələss/ (*plural* **-luses** or **-li** /-lī/) *n* **1.** the cone of a coniferous plant, or a similar cone-shaped structure in some lower plants that consists of closely packed fertile leaves bearing spore-producing organs (*technical*) **2.** a cone-shaped structure in flowering plants, e.g. the fruit of the hop [Mid-18C. Via late Latin < Greek *strobilos* 'twisted object, pine cone' < *strobos* 'whirling']

stroboscope /strṓbə skōp/ *n* a flashing lamp of precisely variable periodicity that can be synchronized with the frequency of moving machinery to give the appearance of being stationary. It is often used in conjunction with flash or stop-action photography. [Mid-19C. < Greek *strobos* 'whirling'] —**stroboscopic** /strōbə skóppik, stróbbə-/ *adj*

strobotron /strṓbə tron, -trən/ *n* the triggered gas-discharge tube used as the pulsed light source in a stroboscope [Mid-20C. < STROBOSCOPE]

strode past tense of **stride**

Stroessner /strṓssnər/, **Alfredo** (*b.* 1912) Paraguayan soldier and dictator. As commander in chief of armed forces, he overthrew President Federico Chavez in 1954 and held office until he was overthrown in 1989.

stroganoff /stróggə nof/, **Stroganoff** *adj* cooked in a wine sauce with sour cream ■ *n* FOOD same as **beef stroganoff** [Mid-20C. < French, after Count Pavel Aleksandrovich *Stroganov* (1772–1817), Russian diplomat]

Stroheim ➧ **von Stroheim, Erich**

stroke /strōk/ *n* **1. STOPPAGE OF BLOOD FLOW TO BRAIN** a sudden blockage or rupture of a blood vessel in the brain resulting in, e.g. loss of consciousness, partial loss of movement, or loss of speech. Technical name **cerebrovascular accident 2. SUDDEN OCCURRENCE** a sudden instance or occurrence of something that has a strong or unexpected effect ○ *a stroke of luck* **3. STRIKING OF CLOCK** a single sound made by a clock that is striking ○ *at the stroke of seven* **4. HITTING OF BALL** in racket games or golf, the hitting of a ball or the way in which this is done **5.** SWIMMING **SWIMMING STYLE** a style of swimming, using the arms and legs in a specific way ○ *a difficult swimming stroke* **6.** SWIMMING **SINGLE MOVEMENT IN SWIMMING** a single complete movement of the arms and legs when swimming **7.** ROWING **SINGLE PULL** in rowing, a single movement of the oars through the water **8.** ROWING **ROWER WHO KEEPS TIME** a rower in a racing boat who sets the pace for the crew **9.** ROWING **ROWING STYLE** a particular rowing style **10. SINGLE MOVEMENT IN SERIES** a single movement forming part of a series of movements, e.g. the beat of a wing or the swing of a pendulum ○ *a wing stroke* **11.** MECH ENG **MOVEMENT OF PISTON** a single movement, up or down, of a piston in an engine, or the distance that a piston travels in a single movement **12. HIT** a hit or blow made by the hand, a cane, or a tool **13.** PRINTING same as **slash** *n* (sense 4) **14.** ART **BRUSH OR PEN LINE** a single line or mark made with a brush or pen ○ *a brush stroke* **15.** ART **SINGLE MOVEMENT OF BRUSH OR PEN** a single movement of a brush or pen to make a line or mark **16. CARESSING MOVEMENT** a gentle caressing movement of the hand over fur, hair, or skin **17. ADDITIONAL FEATURE** a small additional feature that has an effect on the style or nature of something ○ *a stroke of sarcasm* **18. VERBAL ENCOURAGEMENT** a usually positive comment or statement, e.g. a compliment made by one person to another ○ *I need all the positive strokes I can get right now.* **19.** PSYCHOL **ELEMENT OF SOCIAL RECOGNITION** in transactional analysis, a unit of social recognition between two or more people that, in its simplest form, can be a one-word greeting such as 'hello' ■ *v* (**strokes, stroking, stroked**) **1.** *vt* **CARESS SOMETHING** to move the hand gently over something as if caressing it ○ *stroked the cat gently* **2.** *vt* **HIT BALL SMOOTHLY** in various sports, to hit or kick a ball smoothly **3.** *vt* **PUSH SOMETHING GENTLY** to push something somewhere gently with a light movement of the hand **4.** *vt* **CROSS SOMETHING OUT** to draw a line through something **5.** *vt* ROWING **SET ROWING PACE** to be the rower who sets the pace for the crew **6.** *vi* ROWING **MOVE OARS** to row at a particular speed or rate of the oars **7.** *vt* **COMPLIMENT SOMEBODY** to behave in an encouraging or solicitous way towards somebody ■ *adj US* **PORNOGRAPHIC** relating to or of the nature of pornography (*slang*) [Old English *strācian* < Indo-European, 'rub, press'] ◇ **different strokes for different folks** used to emphasize that people are all individuals and that what suits one will not necessarily suit another (*dated slang*)

stroke play *n UK, Can* in golf, a way of scoring in which the total number of strokes taken for the round is counted rather than the number of holes won. ANZ, US term **medal play**

stroll /strōl/ *vi* (**strolls, strolling, strolled**) **1. WALK UNHURRIEDLY** to walk in a slow unhurried way, especially for enjoyment **2. PERFORM EFFORTLESSLY** to do, obtain, or achieve something in a casual effortless way ○ *strolled through the exam* ■ *n* **LEISURELY WALK** a slow leisurely walk for pleasure ○ *went for a stroll in the park* [Early 17C. Probably < German *strollen* 'wander', variant of *strolchen* < *Strolch* 'vagabond, fortune teller'] ◇ **stroll on** used as an expression of disbelief or frustration (*informal*)

stroller /strṓlər/ *n* **1.** somebody who is walking in a slow leisurely way for pleasure **2.** *ANZ, N Am* same as **buggy**[1] (sense 1). See illustration on next page

strolling /strṓling/ *adj* going from place to place to earn a living, especially by entertaining ○ *strolling minstrels*

stroma /strṓmə/ (*plural* **-mata** /-mətə/) *n* **1.** the connective tissue that provides the framework of an organ or other anatomical structure rather than

stroller

carrying out its functions **2.** the fluid-filled interior of a chloroplast containing enzymes and other components required for photosynthesis, including the light-trapping components [Mid-19C. Via modern and late Latin < Greek *stroma* 'bed, cushion'] —**stromatic** /strō máttik/ *adj*

stromatolite /strō máttə līt/ *n* a very old fossil formed in sedimentary rock by sea cyanobacteria and consisting of a rounded or columnar calcium-containing mass of many layers [Mid-20C. < late Latin *stromat*-, stem of *stroma* (see STROMA)] —**stromatolitic** /strō máttə líttik/ *adj*

Stromboli /strómbəli/ volcanic island in the Italian Lipari Islands in the Tyrrhenian Sea, north of Sicily. Area: 13 sq. km/5 sq. mi.

Strominger /strómminjər/, **Andrew** (*b.* 1955) US physicist. His work has been influential in merging the study of black holes with that of string theory.

strong /strong/ *adj* **1.** PHYSICALLY POWERFUL having the physical strength needed to exert considerable force, e.g. in lifting, pulling, or pushing something **2.** USING FORCE using great physical force **3.** ROBUST AND STURDY sturdy, well made, and not easily damaged or broken **4.** EMOTIONALLY RESILIENT having the necessary emotional qualities to deal with stress, grief, loss, risk, and other difficulties **5.** HEALTHY AND WELL being in good health, especially after an illness ○ *feeling stronger every day* **6.** THRIVING thriving, developing well, and likely to continue so ○ *a strong economy* **7.** LIKELY TO SUCCEED very likely to succeed, win, or come to be something ○ *a strong candidate for the post.* **8.** CONVINCING supported by facts or good evidence and likely to be correct or effective ○ *a strong argument* **9.** KNOWLEDGEABLE very skilful or knowledgeable in a particular subject or area **10.** EXERTING INFLUENCE influential or authoritative by virtue of having or holding power **11.** EFFECTIVE having a powerful effect ○ *strong painkillers* **12.** FELT POWERFULLY felt or expressed with a powerful effect ○ *She has strong views on the subject.* **13.** DISTINCTIVE bold, clearly defined, and prominent ○ *strong features* **14.** EXTREME unusually severe of its kind ○ *Strong measures were taken to prevent a riot.* **15.** INTENSE IN IMPRESSION having an intense, penetrating, or vivid effect on the senses ○ *a strong smell of garlic* **16.** EASY TO DETECT easy to detect or receive ○ *The signal will be stronger as you get closer.* **17.** CONCENTRATED containing a lot of the main ingredient and not diluted or watery ○ *strong black coffee* **18.** ALCOHOLIC containing much alcohol **19.** FAST MOVING flowing or blowing at high speed ○ *a strong current* **20.** CHEM FULLY IONIZED producing ions freely in solution **21.** MIL WELL DEFENDED well defended and difficult to capture ○ *a strong fortress* **22.** OF PARTICULAR NUMBER having a particular number of members ○ *a force 50,000 strong* **23.** OPTICS WITH HIGH MAGNIFICATION having a powerful magnifying or corrective ability ○ *a strong lens* **24.** COMM WITH HIGH PRICES characterized by high or rising prices ○ *a strong currency* **25.** GRAM WITH CHANGED VOWEL describes an irregular verb that changes the vowel in the stem in its different forms, e.g. 'ring', which has the forms 'rang' and 'rung' [Old English *strang* < Germanic] —**strongly** *adv* ◇ **come on strong** to behave or express something aggressively (*slang*) ◇ **going strong** thriving and doing well

strong-arm (*informal*) *adj* using or involving coercion or physical force ○ *ready to use strong-arm tactics* ■ *vt* to use coercion against somebody to induce cooperation

strongbox /strong boks/ *n* a secure metal box or safe where money or valuables can be kept

strong breeze *n* a wind of between 40 and 50 km/25 and 31 mi. per hour, classified as force six on the Beaufort scale

strong force *n* PHYS same as **strong interaction**

strong gale *n* a wind of between 76 and 87 km/47 and 54 mi. per hour, classified as force nine on the Beaufort scale

stronghold /strong hōld/ *n* **1.** a place that is fortified or that can easily be defended **2.** a place where a particular group, activity, or set of opinions is concentrated

strong interaction *n* a fundamental force between elementary particles that is responsible for binding protons and neutrons together in an atomic nucleus and other interactions between elementary particles (**hadrons**). Mediated by gluons, the interaction is the most powerful force known and is responsible for the particle creation that occurs when high-energy particles collide.

strong language *n* language that expresses something in a forceful way, especially with abusive words or swearing

strongman /strong man/ (*plural* **-men** /-men/) *n* **1.** a man who performs feats of strength, e.g. at a carnival or circus **2.** a powerful, typically dictatorial, leader who rules by force

strong meat *n* behaviour or attitudes that generally upset or offend people and that are acceptable only to a robust minority

strong-minded *adj* **1.** determined and persevering in the face of difficulty **2.** confident, intelligent, and independent in thought —**strong-mindedly** *adv* —**strong-mindedness** *n*

strong point *n* an area for which somebody has a talent ○ *Tact was never his strong point.*

strongpoint /strong poynt/ *n* a fortified place that can be defended

strongroom /strong room, -room/ *n* a reinforced room designed to withstand fire or theft and used for the storage of valuables

strong suit *n* **1.** same as **strong point 2.** in various card games, the suit in which a player or team holds the most cards or the most face cards

strong-willed *adj* determined to prevail in the face of difficulty or opposition

strongwoman /strong woomən/ (*plural* **-women** /-wimin/) *n* a woman who performs feats of strength, e.g. at a carnival or circus, or who competes in weightlifting competitions

strongyle /strónjil/, **strongyl** /strónjəl/ *n* a parasitic nematode worm related to the hookworms that infests the intestinal tract of mammals. Superfamily: Strongyloidea. [Mid-19C. < modern Latin *Strongylus* < Greek *stroggulos* 'round, compact']

strongyloidiasis /strónji loy dī əssiss/ *n* intestinal infestation in mammals by strongyles, producing various severe and sometimes fatal intestinal disorders, especially in individuals with weakened immune systems [Mid-20C. < modern Latin *Strongyloidea*, superfamily name < *Strongylus* (see STRONGYLE)]

strongylosis /strónji lōssiss/ *n* an illness, usually of horses, caused by infection with strongyles

strontia /strónti ə, -shi ə/ *n* CHEM same as **strontium monoxide** [Early 19C. Back-formation < STRONTIAN]

strontian /strónti ən, -shi-/ *n* **1.** MINERALS same as **strontianite 2.** CHEM same as **strontium monoxide 3.** CHEM same as **strontium** [Late 18C. After *Strontian*, parish in W Scotland]

strontianite /strónti ə nīt, -shi-/ *n* a variously coloured strontium carbonate mineral. Use: source of strontium.

strontium /strónti əm, -shi-/ *n* a soft yellow or silvery-white metallic element of the alkaline-earth group, found only in combination with other substances. Source: strontianite, celestite. Use: fireworks, flares, alloys. Symbol **Sr**. See table at **element** [Early 19C. < STRONTIA]

strontium 90 *n* a radioactive isotope of strontium

with a mass number of 90, present in nuclear fallout and assimilated like calcium in bone formation

strontium monoxide *n* a white insoluble solid resembling quicklime. Use: purification of sugar. Formula: SrO.

strontium unit *n* a unit of measurement of the amount of strontium 90 in an organic substance such as soil or bone, in relation to the concentration of calcium in the same substance

Stroop effect /strōop-/ *n* difficulty in identifying the colours in which names of colours are written. For example, if the word 'red' is printed in green ink, people are likely to say 'red' when asked the colour of the printed word. [Mid-20C. After John Ridley *Stroop* 1897–1973, US psychologist]

strop /strop/ *n* **1.** LEATHER STRAP FOR SHARPENING a leather strap used for sharpening a cutthroat razor **2.** STRAP FOR CARGO a strap of leather or rope used for lifting cargo ■ *vt* (**strops, stropping, stropped**) SHARPEN RAZOR to sharpen a cutthroat razor on a strop [14C. < Low German and Dutch, via W Germanic < Latin *stroppus* < Greek *strophos* 'twisted cord'] ◇ **in a strop** in a bad temper or sulk (*informal*)

strophe /strōfi/ *n* **1.** the first type of metrical form in a poem that alternates two contrasting metrical forms **2.** the first of two movements made by the chorus in a classical Greek drama, or the part of an ode sung during this [Early 17C. < Greek *strophē* 'turning'] —**strophic** /stróffik, strōfik/ *adj*

strophoid /strō foyd/ *n* a plane curve symmetrical to the x-axis, generated by a point whose distance from the y-axis along a straight line is equal to the y-intercept [Late 19C. < Greek *strophos* 'twisted cord']

stroppy /stróppi/ (**-pier, -piest**) *adj* bad-tempered and uncooperative (*informal*) [Mid-20C. Origin ?]

stroud /strowd/ *n* a rough woollen fabric [Late 17C. Origin ?]

Stroud /strowd/ town in Gloucestershire, central England. Population: 38,835 (1991).

strove past tense of **strive**

struck /struk/ past participle, past tense of **strike** ■ *adj* US closed temporarily or working at reduced output because of a labour dispute

struck measure *n* a quantity of something such as grain measured by levelling the substance with the top of a container

structural /strúkchərəl/ *adj* **1.** RELATING TO STRUCTURE relating to the way parts are put together or how they work together ○ *made some structural repairs* ○ *a structural reorganization of the company* **2.** USED IN CONSTRUCTION suitable for use in construction ○ *structural fibreglass* **3.** RESULTING FROM STRUCTURE relating to or resulting from the organization or functioning of a political or economic system ○ *gloomy predictions based on lack of structural change in the stock market* **4.** BASIC TO STRUCTURE constituting an important or essential part of a structure **5.** CHEM CAUSED BY ATOMIC ARRANGEMENT relating to or caused by the arrangement of atoms in a molecule **6.** GEOG OF ROCK STRUCTURE relating to or caused by movement of the Earth's surface —**structurally** *adv*

structural formula *n* an expanded chemical formula representing the arrangement of atoms and bonds within a molecule

structural gene *n* a gene that codes for a protein required for the cell's own use

structuralise *vt* another spelling of **structuralize**

structuralism /strúkchərəlizəm/ *n* **1.** SOC SCI a method of sociological analysis based on the notion of human society as a network of interrelations whose patterns and significance can be analysed **2.** LING same as **structural linguistics 3.** PSYCHOL same as **structural psychology** —**structuralist** *n, adj*

structuralize /strúkchərə līz/ (**-izes, -izing, -ized**), **structuralise** (**-ises, -ising, -ised**) *vt* to arrange or organize something so that it has a structure

structural linguistics *n* a branch of linguistics that emphasizes the significance of the interrelations between the elements that constitute a linguistic system (*takes a singular verb*) —**structural linguist** *n*

structural psychology *n* a school of psychology of the early part of the 20th century that sought to

organize the components of subjective experience in a hierarchy from simplest to most complex — **structural psychologist** *n*

structural steel *n* strong steel shaped for use in construction

structure /strúkchər/ *n* 1. SOMETHING BUILT OR ERECTED a building, bridge, framework, or other object that has been put together from many different parts 2. SYSTEM OF PARTS a system or organization made up of interrelated parts functioning as a whole 3. WAY THAT PARTS LINK OR FUNCTION the way in which the different parts of something link or work together, or the fact of being linked together ○ *the structure of local government* ○ *The essay is interesting, but it lacks structure.* 4. BIOL PART OF ORGANISM a part of a body or organism identifiable by its shape and other properties, e.g. tissue or an organ 5. CHEM ARRANGEMENT OF ATOMS the arrangement of atoms in a molecule 6. GEOL COMPONENT PARTS OF ROCKS the physical disposition of a rock mass or its mineral components ■ *vt* (-tures, -turing, -tured) GIVE STRUCTURE TO SOMETHING to organize or arrange something into a whole [15C. Directly or via French < Latin *structura* < *struct-*, past participle of *struere* 'build']

ORIGIN The Latin word *struere* 'to build', from which *structure* is derived, is also the source of the English words *construct*, *construe*, *destroy*, *instruct*, and *obstruct*.

structured /strúkchərd/ *adj* 1. planned, organized, and controlled 2. with a definite shape, form, or pattern ○ *For business wear, suits need a more structured look.*

structured programming *n* a style of computer programming in which a program consists of a hierarchy of simple subroutines

structured query language *n* COMPUT full form of SQL

strudel /stroód'l/ *n* a pastry made with very thin pastry rolled and baked with a filling, usually of chopped apples, raisins, and sugar [Late 19C. < German]

struggle /strúgg'l/ *vi* (-gles, -gling, -gled) 1. TRY TO OVERCOME PROBLEM to make a great effort to deal with a challenge, problem, or difficulty ○ *He was struggling with his maths homework.* 2. MAKE GREAT PHYSICAL EFFORT to make a great physical effort to achieve or obtain something ○ *A rescue party struggled to reach the stranded climbers.* 3. FIGHT BY WRESTLING to fight with somebody by grappling and wrestling 4. WRITHE TO ESCAPE to move and wriggle forcefully in an attempt to escape 5. MOVE WITH DIFFICULTY to move with great effort ○ *so weak I just managed to struggle out of bed* ■ *n* 1. GREAT EFFORT TO OVERCOME DIFFICULTIES a great effort made over a period of time to overcome difficulties or achieve something 2. HARD TASK a strenuous physical or mental effort, or something requiring this 3. FIGHT a prolonged fight or conflict [14C. Origin ?] —**struggler** *n*

struggle for existence *n* the ongoing effort to survive and reproduce in an environment of competing organisms

strum /strum/ *v* (strums, strumming, strummed) 1. *vti* PLAY INSTRUMENT BY BRUSHING STRINGS to play a guitar or other stringed instrument by brushing the strings with the fingers or a pick 2. *vt* PLAY TUNE to play a tune by strumming an instrument ■ *n* SOUND OF STRUMMING the sound of somebody strumming an instrument [Late 18C. An imitation of the sound] —**strummer** *n*

struma /stroómə/ (*plural* -mae /-mee/) *n* 1. BOT a swelling at the base of a moss capsule 2. MED same as **goitre** 3. MED same as **scrofula** (*archaic*) [Mid-16C. Via modern Latin < Latin, 'scrofulous tumour'] —**strumatic** /stroo máttik/ *adj* —**strumose** *adj* —**strumous** *adj*

strumpet /strúmpit/ *n* an offensive term for a prostitute or a woman regarded as too sexually active (*archaic*) [14C. Origin ?]

strung past participle, past tense of **string**

strung out *adj* 1. OVERWROUGHT tired, tense, or overwrought (*informal*) 2. DRUGGED under the influence of a drug, especially a narcotic drug (*slang*) 3. WEAKENED debilitated by long-term drug use (*slang*)

strung up *adj* very tired, tense, and overwrought (*informal*)

strut /strut/ *v* (struts, strutting, strutted) 1. *vi* WALK IN ARROGANT WAY to walk in a stiff or proud way that suggests arrogance or pomposity 2. *vt* PROP SOMETHING WITH PLANKS to support a structure with planks or boards ■ *n* 1. SUPPORTING MEMBER a long rigid plank, board, or other structural member used as a support in building 2. STRUTTING WALK a stiff proud way of walking [Old English *strūtian* 'protrude stiffly' < Indo-European, 'stiff']

struth *interj* another spelling of **strewth** (*slang*)

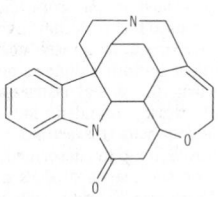

strychnine

strychnine /strík neen, -nin/ *n* a bitter white poisonous alkaloid obtained from nux vomica and related plants. Use: rodenticide, nervous system stimulant. Formula: $C_{21}H_{22}N_2O_2$. [Early 19C. < French < modern Latin *Strychnos* < Latin *strychnon* 'nightshade' < Greek *strukhnos*] —**strychnic** *adj*

Strzelecki /strez léki/, **Paul Edmund de, Sir** (1797–1873) Polish explorer and scientist. During a visit to Australia (1839–43), he explored much of the southeast and named many geographical features including the continent's highest peak, Mt Kosciuszko.

Strzelecki Range range of hills in southern Victoria, Australia. Highest peak: 500 m/1,640 ft.

STS *abbr* GENETICS sequence tagged site

Stuart /styoó ərt/, **Charles Edward** (1720–88) grandson of James II of England and claimant to the British throne. The son of James Francis Edward Stuart, he led the Jacobite uprising in Scotland in 1745 and after its failure lived in exile in Europe. Known as **Bonnie Prince Charlie, the Young Pretender**

Stuart, **James Francis Edward** (1688–1766) son of James II of England and claimant to the British throne. He was supported in his claim to the British throne by France and by the Jacobites in their unsuccessful rising in Scotland (1715). After 1719 he lived in Rome. Known as **the Old Pretender**

Stuart, **John McDouall** (1815–66) British-born Australian explorer. He made the first south-to-north crossing of Australia (1861–62), from Adelaide to Darwin.

stub /stub/ *n* 1. SHORT REMAINING PART a short part of something that is left after the main part has been removed or used 2. SMALL SECTION OF TICKET OR CHEQUE a small detachable section of a ticket, cheque, or voucher, retained as a record of a transaction 3. STUMP OF TREE OR PLANT the stump of a tree or plant 4. SMALL PROJECTION a small projection from a surface ■ *vt* (stubs, stubbing, stubbed) 1. BANG TOE to bang a toe against something accidentally 2. GARDENING DIG SOMETHING UP BY ROOTS to dig up a plant or tree by the roots 3. AGRIC CLEAR LAND OF STUMPS to clear land of tree stumps [Old English *stubb* 'tree stump' < Germanic]

stub out *vt* to put out a cigarette or cigar by pushing the burning end against something

Stubbies /stúbbiz/ *tdmk Aus* a trademark for short heavy-duty shorts

stubble /stúbb'l/ *n* 1. short stalks left in the ground after a grain crop has been harvested 2. the short spiky growth of beard on a man's face when he has not shaved [13C. Via Old French *estuble* < Latin *stupula* 'straw, stalk', alteration of *stipula*] —**stubbly** *adj*

stubborn /stúbbərn/ *adj* 1. UNREASONABLY DETERMINED unreasonably and obstructively determined to persevere or prevail 2. DOGGED carried out in a determined, persistent way ○ *met with stubborn resistance* 3. HARD TO REMOVE difficult to remove or deal

with ○ *a stubborn stain* [14C. Origin ?] —**stubbornly** *adv* —**stubbornness** *n*

~~stubborness~~ incorrect spelling of **stubbornness**

Stubbs /stubz/, **George** (1724–1806) British painter and engraver. He specialized in painting animals, particularly horses.

stubby /stúbbi/ *adj* 1. SHORT AND STOCKY short and stocky in build 2. SHORT AND THICK short and thick, broad, or blunt ○ *stubby fingers* 3. WITH MANY STUBS with projecting stubs or short bristles ■ *n Aus* BEER BOTTLE a small squat bottle of beer (*informal*)

stub nail *n* a short thick nail

STUC *abbr* Scottish Trades Union Congress

stucco /stúkō/ *n* 1. WALL PLASTER plaster used for surfacing interior or exterior walls, often used in association with classical mouldings 2. DECORATIVE PLASTER WORK decorative work moulded from stucco ■ *vt* (-coes or -cos, -coing, -coed) COVER WALL WITH STUCCO to apply a coating of stucco to a wall [Late 16C. < Italian < Germanic] —**stuccoer** /stúkō ər/ *n*

stuck /stuk/ past participle, past tense of **stick**[2] ■ *adj* 1. JAMMED OR CAUGHT jammed, caught, or held in an immovable position ○ *The drawer was stuck fast.* 2. UNABLE TO FIND SOLUTION not able to find a solution or way out of a situation 3. PIERCED pierced by a sharp object

stuckie /stúki/ *n Scotland* BIRDS same as **starling**[1] [Origin ?]

stuck-up *adj* snobbish and conceited (*informal*)

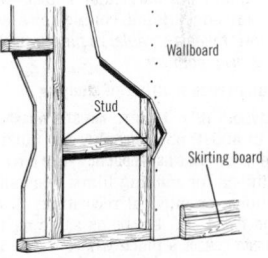

stud (sense 5)

stud[1] /stud/ *n* 1. METAL KNOB a small metal knob, rivet, or nail head that protrudes slightly from a surface, especially for decorative effect 2. JEWELLERY EARRING an earring for pierced ears that has a simple rounded head or is set with a single gemstone 3. CLOTHING COLLAR FASTENER a fastener for collars or dress shirts consisting of a small disc attached to a short rod 4. SPORTS KNOB ON FOOTBALL BOOT one of several knobs fitted to the sole of a football boot or other sports shoe to give a firmer grip on slippery ground 5. CONSTR VERTICAL SUPPORT a vertical length of timber to which material such as lath or plasterboard is attached in constructing a wall 6. HEADLESS BOLT a headless bolt that is smooth in the centre and threaded at each end 7. ENG PROTRUSION ON MACHINE a projecting pin on a machine that serves as a support ■ *vt* (studs, studding, studded) 1. SUPPLY SOMETHING WITH STUDS to fit or decorate something with studs ○ *a studded leather jacket* 2. OCCUR THROUGHOUT SOMETHING to be present or visible throughout something [Old English *studu* < W Germanic] ◇ **studded with** scattered or dotted with something

stud[2] /stud/ *n* 1. BREEDING STALLION a male animal, especially a stallion, used for breeding 2. ESTABLISHMENT WITH STALLIONS a stable or farm where male animals, especially stallions, are kept for breeding 3. GROUP OF STALLIONS a group of male animals, especially stallions, used for breeding 4. SEXUALLY ACTIVE MAN a man considered to be sexually active or good at sex (*informal*) 5. CARDS same as **stud poker** [Old English *stōd* 'standing place' < Germanic] ◇ **at stud** available for breeding with female animals, especially mares

studbook /stúd book/ *n* a book containing a record of the parentage of purebred animals, especially horses or dogs

studdingsail /stúdding sayl, stúnss'l/ *n* an additional sail on an extra yard and boom at either side of a square sail, for use in light winds [Mid-16C. Origin ?]

student /styoōd'nt/ *n* 1. **PERSON STUDYING** somebody who studies at school, college, or university 2. **KNOWLEDGEABLE OR INTERESTED PERSON** somebody who has studied or takes much interest in a particular subject ○ *a student of human foibles* ■ *adj* **IN TRAINING FOR JOB** studying as part of the training for a job or profession ○ *student pilots* [15C. Alteration of Old French *estudiant* < Latin *student-*, present participle of *studere* 'be diligent']

student body *n* the students of a school collectively

student loan *n* a loan taken by a student to pay for educational expenses, usually at a favourable rate of interest that is subsidized by the government

studentship /styoōd'nt ship/ *n* EDUC same as **scholarship** (sense 1)

Student's t-test *n* STATS same as **t-test** [After *Student*, pen name of W. S. Gosset (1876–1937), British statistician]

students' union *n* 1. an organization of students in a college or university that represents students' interests 2. *UK* a building or area at a college or university with a bar and other facilities for the social or recreational activities of students. ANZ, N Am term **student union**

student teacher *n* somebody who is studying and training to become a teacher

student union *n ANZ, N Am* same as **students' union** (sense 2)

studhorse /stúd hawrss/ *n* a stallion used for breeding

studied /stúddid/ *adj* thought about or planned in advance rather than being spontaneous ○ *an air of studied nonchalance*

studies /stúddiz/ *n* a particular subject of study, especially an educational course or academic specialization (*takes a singular or plural verb*) ○ *Women's studies is very popular.*

~~**studing**~~ incorrect spelling of **studying**

studio /styoōdi ō/ *n* 1. ARTS **ARTIST'S WORKPLACE** a place where an artist, photographer, or musician works 2. RECORDING **RECORDING PRODUCTION ROOM** a room or building equipped for making films, television or radio productions, or musical recordings 3. *N Am* same as **studio flat** 4. *US* BUILDINGS same as **studio flat** 5. DANCE **DANCE SCHOOL** a place where dance is taught or can be practised 6. CINEMA **FILM COMPANY** a commercial film production company ■ **studios** *npl* CINEMA **FILM PRODUCTION BUILDINGS** all the buildings connected with a film production company, used for shooting and producing films [Early 19C. Via Italian < Latin *studium* (see STUDY)]

studio apartment *n ANZ, N Am* BUILDINGS same as **studio flat**

studio couch *n* a usually backless sofa that can be converted into a double bed by sliding out a frame from underneath

studio flat *n UK* a small one-roomed flat, perhaps with a separate kitchen and bathroom. N Am term **studio**

studio system *n* the process by which major Hollywood studios made a large number of movies economically and simultaneously from the silent era into the 1950s, using contract actors and controlling every aspect of production

studious /styoōdi əss/ *adj* 1. having a thoughtful nature and a tendency to study 2. careful and painstaking, with considerable attention to detail ○ *a studious investigation* [14C. < Latin *studiosus* < *studium* (see STUDY)] —**studiously** *adv* —**studiousness** *n*

studly /stúdli/ (**-lier, -liest**) *adj* (*slang*) 1. describes a man who is considered sexually attractive 2. impressive or exceptionally good ○ *a player with a studly scoring record*

studmuffin /stúd mufin/ *n US* a man regarded as being physically attractive (*slang*)

stud poker *n* poker in which all but the first card are dealt face up, allowing players to see one another's hands [Mid-19C. Probably shortening of *studhorse poker*, origin ?]

study /stúddi/ *v* (**-ies, -ying, -ied**) 1. *vti* **LEARN ABOUT SOMETHING** to learn about a subject by reading and researching 2. *vti* **TAKE EDUCATIONAL COURSE** to follow a course at college or university 3. *vt* **INVESTIGATE SOMETHING** to discover facts about something by doing research or experiments ○ *a team of researchers studying the effects of sleep deprivation* 4. *vt* **LOOK AT AND CONSIDER SOMETHING** to look at or read something and think about it carefully ○ *He studied the map, frowning.* 5. *vt* THEATRE **LEARN LINES** to learn the lines spoken by a character in a play ■ *n* (*plural* **-ies**) 1. **PROCESS OF LEARNING** the process of learning about a subject by reading, thought, intuition, or research ○ *devoted the afternoons to study* 2. **INVESTIGATION** an investigation or research project designed to discover facts about something 3. **REPORT ON RESEARCH** a work such as a report, thesis, or book that is the result of research or an investigation ○ *published a new study of women in the workplace* 4. **ROOM FOR STUDYING** a room used for work that involves reading, thinking, or writing 5. ARTS **PREPARATORY WORK OF ART** a small drawing or sculpture done as preparation for a larger work 6. MUSIC **INSTRUMENTAL WORK** an instrumental work intended for teaching or practice 7. THEATRE **ACTOR LEARNING LINES** somebody who is learning a role in a play, described in relation to how fast he or she learns ○ *She's a quick study.* [12C. < Old French *estudier* (verb), *estudie* (noun) < Latin *studium* 'zeal, care' < *studere* 'be diligent'] ◇ **in a brown study** deep in thought (*dated*)

study hall *n* 1. *N Am* a schoolroom used for independent study rather than instruction 2. *US* a period during the school day assigned for study rather than classroom instruction

study leave *n* leave of absence from a course of study, granted for the purposes of carrying out additional research

stuff /stuf/ *vt* (**stuffs, stuffing, stuffed**) 1. **FILL SOMETHING** to fill something by pushing things into it ○ *What are you stuffing the cushions with?* 2. **PUSH THINGS INTO CONTAINER** to push things into a container, often hurriedly or forcefully 3. **PUT SOMETHING SOMEWHERE HURRIEDLY** to put something somewhere in a quick careless way ○ *stuffed it under the pillow, out of sight* 4. **EAT TOO MUCH** to eat, or feed somebody, a lot of food 5. **FILL FOOD WITH STUFFING** to put stuffing or filling into food such as pasta, meat, or vegetables 6. **PRESERVE DEAD ANIMAL** to fill a dead animal's skin with material to make it look lifelike and suitable for display 7. *N Am* POL **SUBMIT INVALID VOTES** to put invalid ballots into a ballot box to rig an election 8. **BEAT OPPONENT THOROUGHLY** to beat an opponent or opposing team easily and thoroughly (*informal*) 9. **OFFENSIVE TERM** an offensive term meaning to have sex with a woman (*taboo*) 10. INDUST **TREAT LEATHER** to treat leather with chemicals that preserve and soften it ■ *n* 1. **THINGS** material things generally, especially when unidentified, worthless, or unwanted ○ *What's all this stuff doing in my office?* 2. **WORDS OR ACTION** action, speech, or writing ○ *all that stuff in the news about changing weather patterns* ○ *I really like her stuff.* 3. **POSSESSIONS** personal possessions ○ *called by to collect her stuff* 4. **PERSONAL QUALITIES** personal qualities ○ *She's got the stuff heroes are made of.* 5. **SPECIALITY** something that somebody does uniquely or very well ○ *She knows her stuff.* 6. **FOOLISH WORDS OR ACTION** foolish or blameworthy action, speech, or writing ○ *stuff and nonsense* 7. **DRUGS** a drug, especially heroin (*informal*) 8. same as **money** (sense 1) (*slang*) 9. **WOOLLEN FABRIC** woollen fabric, especially as distinguished from fabric made from other natural fibres (*dated*) [14C. < Old French *estoffer* 'equip' < Germanic] —**stuffer** *n* ◇ **be made of sterner stuff** to be less easily discouraged, frightened, or upset ◇ **do your stuff** to do what is required or expected ◇ **get stuffed** an offensive phrase expressing disagreement or impatience (*slang*) ◇ **not give a stuff** *Aus* to not care less (*informal*) ◇ **strut your stuff** 1. *N Am* to do something impressively, suggesting talent for it or thorough preparation (*slang*) 2. to dance, especially in an expressive way (*informal*) ◇ **stuff it** an offensive phrase used to dismiss something angrily or carelessly (*slang*) ◇ **that's the stuff** used to indicate satisfaction with what has been done or given (*dated*)

stuff up *vti* to make a mess of something (*informal*)

stuffed /stuft/ *adj* 1. **COMPLETELY FULL** completely full, especially after eating too much (*informal*) 2. **WITH FILLING** filled with stuffing or some other filling 3. *Aus* **IN DIFFICULTIES** thwarted, ruined, or broken (*informal*) 4. *Aus* **EXHAUSTED** completely exhausted (*informal*)

stuffed shirt *n* a pompous, formal, or self-important person (*informal*)

stuffing /stúffing/ *n* 1. a mixture of well-flavoured or highly seasoned ingredients used to stuff meat or vegetables 2. feathers, fabric, or artificial fibre used as filling for cushions or pillows ◇ **knock the stuffing out of somebody** (*informal*) 1. to beat or defeat somebody severely 2. to have a sudden weakening effect on somebody

stuffing box *n* an enclosure containing compressed packing that is used to prevent leakage around a moving part such as a piston rod

stuff-up *n Aus* a blunder (*informal*)

stuffy /stúffi/ (**-ier, -iest**) *adj* 1. **AIRLESS** without any fresh air, and often too warm 2. **STRAIT-LACED** very old-fashioned, strict, or conventional 3. **BLOCKED WITH MUCUS** blocked up with mucus, making breathing difficult ○ *a stuffy nose* —**stuffily** *adv* —**stuffiness** *n*

stull /stul/ *n* a supporting timber in a mine or mine-shaft [Late 18C. Origin ?]

stultify /stúlti fī/ (**-fies, -fying, -fied**) *vt* 1. **DIMINISH INTEREST** to dull somebody's interest by being repetitive, tedious, and boring 2. **MAKE SOMEBODY SEEM STUPID** to cause somebody or something to seem unintelligent or silly 3. **RENDER SOMETHING USELESS** to render something useless or ineffectual 4. LAW **PROVE SOMEBODY INCAPABLE OF LEGAL RESPONSIBILITY** to show or allege somebody to be not legally responsible because of a psychiatric disorder or instability [Mid-18C. < late Latin *stultificare* 'make foolish' < Latin *stultus* 'foolish', literally 'immovable'] —**stultification** /stúltifi káysh'n/ *n* —**stultifier** *n*

stum /stum/ *n* WINE same as **must**[2] ■ *vt* (**stums, stumming, stummed**) to ferment wine by adding stum to it while it is in a cask or vat [Mid-17C. < Dutch *stom* 'dumb']

stumble /stúmb'l/ *vi* (**-bles, -bling, -bled**) 1. **TRIP OVER** to trip when walking or running 2. **WALK UNSTEADILY** to walk unsteadily, as if intoxicated 3. **SPEAK OR ACT HESITATINGLY** to speak or act in a halting, confused, or blundering way ○ *spoke the verse without stumbling* 4. **MAKE SLIGHT ERROR** make a minor mistake 5. **MAKE DISCOVERY BY CHANCE** to find or come across something by chance ○ *I stumbled across the note while I was cleaning the cupboard.* ■ *n* 1. **MISTAKE** a mistake or hesitation 2. **ACT OF TRIPPING** an instance of tripping over something [14C. Probably < variant of Old Norse *stumra* 'walk unsteadily' < Germanic] —**stumbler** *n* —**stumblingly** *adv*

SYNONYMS See ***hesitate***.

stumblebum /stúmb'l bum/ *n US* an offensive term for somebody who appears to do things in a blundering unskilful way (*slang insult*)

stumbling block /stúmbling-/ *n* something that stands in the way of achieving a goal or of understanding something [Early 16C. Translation of Greek *proskomma* 'something you stumble against']

stumer /styoōmər/ *n* a forged or fraudulent item, e.g. a banknote (*slang*) [Late 19C. Origin ?]

stumm *adj* another spelling of **shtoom** (*informal*)

stump /stump/ *n* 1. **BASE OF TREE** the base of a tree trunk and its roots after the tree has fallen or been felled 2. **REMAINING SMALL PART** the part of something such as a limb that is left after the main part has been removed 3. CRICKET **PART OF WICKET** in cricket, each of the three upright posts that form part of the wicket 4. ART **CYLINDRICAL DRAWING TOOL** in drawing, a short pointed piece of rolled paper, cork, rubber, or leather, used to shade and soften lines ■ **stumps** *npl* **LEGS** somebody's legs (*slang*) ■ *v* (**stumps, stumping, stumped**) 1. *vt* **BAFFLE SOMEBODY** to baffle somebody by presenting a problem that seems impossible to solve 2. *vt* CRICKET **DISMISS BATSMAN BY TOUCHING STUMPS** to get a batsman out by knocking a bail off the wicket with the ball while the batsman is out of the crease 3. *vi* **WALK HEAVILY** to walk heavily and often angrily 4. *vi US* POL **CAMPAIGN** to campaign for elective office (*informal*) 5. *vt* **CUT TREE TO STUMP** to cut down a tree, leaving a stump 6. *vt* **REMOVE STUMPS** to clear an area of land of tree stumps [13C. < Middle Low German < Germanic] —**stumper** *n* ◇ **on the stump** engaged in making political speeches to win office (*informal*)

stump up *vt* to pay the amount of money that is asked (*informal*) [Originally 'dig up by the roots']

stumpage /stúmpij/ *n US* standing timber, or the amount of money it would bring if felled

stumpwork /stúmp wurk/ *n* raised embroidery with small decorative stitches made over pieces of padding [Early 20C. Because the designs are raised on stumps of wood]

stumpy /stúmpi/ (**-ier, -iest**) *adj* short, thick, and unattractive —**stumpiness** *n*

stun /stun/ (**stuns, stunning, stunned**) *vt* **1. SHOCK SOMEBODY** to shock, upset, or amaze somebody ○ *a tragedy that stunned the nation* **2. MAKE SOMEBODY UNCONSCIOUS** to make a person or animal unconscious for a short time with a blow or drug **3. OVERWHELM SENSE** to overwhelm one of the senses, e.g. with loud noise or very bright light [14C. Via Anglo-Norman *estuner* < assumed Vulgar Latin *extonare* < Latin *tonare* 'to thunder']

stung past participle, past tense of **sting**

stun grenade *n* a nonlethal grenade that creates a loud bang and a bright flash when it explodes and is intended to temporarily disorientate people

stun gun *n* a gun used for stunning animals or people for a short while without causing injury

stunk past participle, past tense of **stink**

stunner /stúnnər/ *n* **1.** an impressive or beautiful person or thing (*informal*) **2.** same as **stun gun**

stunning /stúnning/ *adj* strikingly impressive or attractive in appearance ○ *They looked stunning at the reception.* —**stunningly** *adv*

stunsail /stúnss'l/ *n SAILING* same as **studdingsail** [Mid-18C. Contraction]

stunt[1] /stunt/ *vt* (**stunts, stunting, stunted**) **RESTRICT GROWTH** to restrict the growth of something so that it does not develop to its normal size ■ *n* **1. SOMETHING NOT FULLY DEVELOPED** something that has not grown to its normal size because its growth has been restricted **2. BOT PLANT DISEASE** a plant disease that inhibits growth [Old English, 'unintelligent, dull' < Germanic]

stunt[2] /stunt/ *n* **1. DANGEROUS FEAT** something dangerous that is done as a challenge or to entertain people **2. SOMETHING UNUSUAL DONE FOR ATTENTION** something silly or unusual that is done to attract attention ○ *a publicity stunt* ■ *vi* (**stunts, stunting, stunted**) **PERFORM STUNTS** to perform dangerous feats as a challenge or to entertain people [Late 19C. Origin ?]

stunt double *n* somebody who replaces a film actor in scenes involving potentially dangerous action sequences

stuntman /stúnt man/ (*plural* **-men** /-men/) *n* a man whose job is to take the place of an actor in a scene involving danger or requiring acrobatic skill

stuntperson /stúnt purss'n/ (*plural* **-people** /-peep'l/ or **-persons**) *n* somebody whose job is to take the place of an actor in a scene involving danger or requiring acrobatic skill

stuntwoman /stúnt wŏŏmən/ (*plural* **-women** /-wimin/) *n* a woman whose job is to take the place of an actor in a scene involving danger or requiring acrobatic skill

stupa /stŏŏpə/ *n* a Buddhist shrine, temple, or pagoda that houses a relic or marks the location of an auspicious event [Late 19C. < Sanskrit *stūpah*]

stupe /styoop/ *n* a hot, damp, and sometimes medicated compress used in former times [14C. Via Latin *stuppa* 'tow' < Greek *stuppē*; from the use of tow in making compresses]

stupefacient /styŏŏpi fáysh'nt/ *adj* causing stupor ■ *n* a drug or other agent that causes stupor [Mid-17C. < Latin *stupefacient-*, present participle of *stupefacere* (see STUPEFY)]

stupefaction /styŏŏpi fáksh'n/ *n* **1.** great amazement or astonishment **2.** the inability to think clearly because of boredom, tiredness, or amazement [15C. Via French < medieval Latin *stupefaction-* < Latin *stupefacere* (see STUPEFY)]

stupefy /styŏŏpi fī/ (**-fies, -fying, -fied**) *vt* **1.** to amaze or astonish somebody **2.** to make somebody unable to think clearly because of boredom, tiredness, or amazement [15C. Via French *stupéfier* < Latin *stupefacere* < *stupere* 'be stunned' + *facere* 'make'] —**stupefier** *n* —**stupefyingly** *adv*

stupendous /styoo péndəss/ *adj* impressively large,

excellent, or great in extent or degree ○ *a stupendous achievement* [Mid-17C. < Latin *stupendus*, gerundive of *stupere* 'be stunned'] —**stupendously** *adv* —**stupendousness** *n*

stupid /styóopid/ *adj* **1. REGARDED AS UNINTELLIGENT** regarded as showing a lack of intelligence, perception, or common sense ○ *a stupid mistake* **2. SILLY** irritatingly silly or time-wasting ○ *had us playing stupid games* **3. ADDS EMPHASIS** used to express anger, annoyance, or frustration (*informal*) ○ *I can't get the stupid thing to work!* **4. DAZED** in a dazed state, e.g. from shock, fatigue, or the effects of drugs or alcohol ○ *almost stupid with tiredness* [Mid-16C. < Latin *stupidus* < *stupere* 'be stunned']

stupidity /styoo píddəti/ *n* **1.** lack of intelligence, perception, or common sense **2.** extremely rash or thoughtless behaviour

stupidly /styóopidli/ *adv* **1.** in a way that demonstrates lack of intelligence, perception, or common sense ○ *I had stupidly forgotten to note down the date I mailed it.* **2.** in a way that suggests diminished ability to perceive or reason ○ *He gazed stupidly after her.*

~~stupify~~ incorrect spelling of **stupefy**

stupor /styóopər/ *n* **1.** an acute lack of mental alertness brought on e.g. by shock or lack of sleep **2.** a state of near-unconsciousness induced by e.g. drugs or alcohol [14C. < Latin *stupere* 'be stunned'] —**stuporous** *adj*

sturdy /stúrdi/ (**-dier, -diest**) *adj* **1. WELL MADE** solidly made and likely to withstand prolonged use **2. WITH STRONG BUILD** having a well-developed strong-looking body and limbs **3. RESOLUTE** having or displaying decisiveness or firmness of purpose ○ *sturdy defenders of the right to free speech* [13C. < Old French *estourdir* 'dazed' < Latin *turdus* 'thrush (the bird)'] —**sturdily** *adv* —**sturdiness** *n*

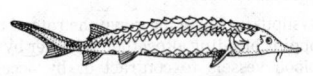

sturgeon

sturgeon /stúrjən/ (*plural* **-geons** or *same*) *n* **1.** a large bottom-feeding fish with a long snout and tough bony-plated skin. Native to: northern rivers, coastal waters. Family: Acipenseridae. **2.** the flesh of a sturgeon as food [13C. < Old French *esturgeon* < Germanic]

Sturluson /stúrlŏŏss'n/, **Snorri** (1179–1241) Icelandic poet and historian. He wrote a history of the kings of Norway and the *Prose Edda*, a repository of Norse myths.

Sturmer /stúrmər/ *n* a pale green English variety of eating apple [Mid-19C. After a village on the border of Essex and Suffolk]

Sturm und Drang /shtŏŏrm ŏŏnt dráng/ *n* **1.** a movement in late 18th-century German literature whose works typically portray the tortured emotions of a central character who violently rejects society **2.** a state of extreme emotional upheaval (*literary*) ○ *films that explore his own personal Sturm und Drang* [Late 18C. < German, 'storm and stress']

Sturt /sturt/, **Charles** (1795–1869) British explorer and administrator. He explored the river system of southeastern Australia (1829–30) and attempted to reach the centre of the continent (1844–46).

Sturt's desert pea *n* a plant of the bean family whose bright red flower is the emblem of South Australia. Native to: Australia. Latin name: *Clianthus formosus*. [Mid-19C. After Charles STURT]

Sturt's desert rose *n* a bush whose pink flower is the emblem of the Northern Territory of Australia.

Native to: Australia. Latin name: *Gossypium sturtianum*. [Mid-20C. After Charles STURT]

stushie /stŏŏshi/, **stishie** /stíshi/ *n Scotland* (*informal*) **1.** a bout or scene of heated discussion or argument **2.** a nervous, anxious, or upset state ○ *She was in a right stushie about the exam.* [Early 19C. Origin ?]

stutter /stúttər/ *v* (**-ters, -tering, -tered**) **1.** *vti* **SPEAK WITH STAMMER** to say something haltingly, repeating sounds frequently when attempting to pronounce them, either from nervousness or as the result of a speech disorder ○ *managed to stutter an apology* **2.** *vi* **SPUTTER** to make repeated short noises ○ *The motor stuttered briefly and then died again.* ■ *n* **1. STAMMERING AS SPEECH DISORDER** a speech disorder that makes somebody repeat speech sounds so that he or she finds difficult to pronounce ○ *has a slight stutter* **2. BURST OF SPUTTERING** a burst of repeated short noises [Early 16C. Alteration of obsolete *stut* < Germanic] —**stutterer** *n* —**stuttering** *adj* —**stutteringly** *adv*

Stuttgart /stŏŏt gaart/ capital of Baden-Württemberg State, in southwestern Germany. Population: 588,482 (1997).

STV *abbr* **1.** Scottish Television **2.** single transferable vote

sty[1] /stī/ *n* (*plural* **sties**) same as **pigsty** ■ *vt* (**sties, stying, stied**) to put or keep a pig in a pigsty [Old English *stī-*, probably form of *stig* 'house, hall']

sty[2] /stī/ (*plural* **sties**), **stye** *n* a temporary swelling on an eyelid at the base of an eyelash [Early 17C. Shortening of obsolete *styany* < *styan* (< Old English *stīgan* 'ascend' < Germanic) + EYE; probably taken as 'sty on eye']

Stygian /stíjji ən/ *adj* **1. PITCH-BLACK** unremittingly dark and frightening, as hell is imagined to be (*literary*) **2. OF STYX** relating to the Styx, the river in Greek mythology that the souls of the dead were ferried across into Hades **3. BINDING** eternally binding, as were promises sworn on the banks of the river Styx in Greek mythology (*literary*) [Mid-16C. < Latin *Stygius* < Greek *Stugios* < *Stux* 'the Styx']

styl- *prefix* same as **stylo-** (*used before vowels*)

stylar /stílər/ *adj* relating to or using a stylus

style /stīl/ *n* **1. DISTINCTIVE FORM** a distinctive and identifiable form in an artistic medium such as music, architecture, or literature ○ *a facade in the neoclassical style* ○ *a different style of jazz* **2. WAY OF DOING SOMETHING** a way of doing something, especially a way regarded as expressing a particular attitude or typifying a particular period (*often used in combination*) ○ *a hands-on management style* ○ *old-style politics* ○ *Confrontation just isn't his style.* **3. WAY OF WRITING OR PERFORMING** the way in which something is written or performed, as distinct from its content **4. FLAIR** impressive flair in the way something is done, especially a quality that suggests a self-confident willingness to exhibit skill or good taste ○ *furnished with impeccable style* **5. FASHION** the prevailing or customary fashion ○ *a look that has gone out of style* **6. CUT OF HAIR OR CLOTHING** a way in which clothes or hair are cut or shaped ○ *dressed in all the latest styles* ○ *That style really suits you.* **7. LUXURIOUSNESS** elegance or lavishness ○ *dining in style* **8. PUBL PUBLISHING CONVENTIONS** a set of conventions for presenting published material, e.g. punctuation and typography **9. BOT FLOWER PART** an extension of a flower's ovary, shaped like a stalk, that supports the stigma **10. ZOOL** same as **stylet** (sense 2) **11. ARTS, HIST** same as **stylus** (sense 3) **12. TITLE** a name or title, especially one that is official or legally correct (*formal*) ■ *vt* (**styles, styling, styled**) **1. SHAPE SOMETHING** to give something a particular shape or design ○ *hair styled in the most up-to-date fashion* **2. CAUSE SOMETHING TO CONFORM** to bring something into conformity with a style **3. NAME SOMEBODY** to give somebody or something a name or title (*formal*) [13C. Via French < Latin *stilus* 'stake, pointed writing instrument, style'] —**styler** *n* ◇ **cramp somebody's style** to restrict what somebody is able to do or would like to do, often by limiting the person's capacity to impress others (*informal*)

SPELLCHECK See *stile*[1].

-style /stīl/ *suffix* with the characteristics of or in the manner of ○ *colonial-style buildings* ○ *moving slowly and stealthily panther-style*

stylebook /stíl boŏk/ n a publisher's guide for presenting material, used by writers and editors

stylee /stíli/ n same as **style** (slang; used in Black English) [Alteration]

stylet /stílət/ n 1. MED WIRE PREVENTING BLOCKAGE IN NEEDLE a fine wire inserted into a catheter or hollow needle to prevent it from becoming blocked when not in use 2. ZOOL PART SHAPED LIKE BRISTLE a thin long organ or appendage shaped like a bristle, e.g. any of the mouthparts of some insects 3. LONG POINTED INSTRUMENT any long thin pointed instrument (formal) [Late 17C. Via French < Italian stiletto (see STILETTO)]

styli plural of **stylus**

styli- prefix same as **stylo-**

styling /stíling/ n 1. the act or an instance of shaping or arranging somebody's hair (often used before a noun) ○ styling mousse 2. an instance of creating something, especially something artistic, in a particular or idiosyncratic way (informal) ○ the zany comedy stylings of the country's favourite stand-up

stylise vt another spelling of **stylize**

stylish /stílish/ adj 1. having confident good taste and appreciation of what is fashionable 2. having or showing impressive skill or accomplishment ○ the most stylish player in the team —**stylishly** adv —**stylishness** n

stylist /stílist/ n 1. HAIR HAIRDRESSER a hairdresser, especially a senior hairdresser in a salon 2. ARTS, LITERAT ACCOMPLISHED ARTIST somebody whose creative work shows a distinctive and accomplished style 3. COMM DESIGNER a designer who is consulted on matters of style, especially somebody responsible for creating a distinctive visual image for a product or company 4. PUBL SOMEBODY WHO PREPARES SCENE FOR PHOTOGRAPH somebody employed to set up scenes to be photographed in a magazine, including supplying any accessories or decorative objects required

stylistic /stí lístik/ adj relating to matters of style, especially in literature and the arts ○ stylistic brilliance compromised by a thinness of content —**stylistically** adv

stylistics /stí lístiks/ n the branch of linguistics that deals with determining which features of written or spoken language characterize specific groups or contexts, especially literary genres or works (takes a singular verb)

stylite /stí līt/ n a Christian ascetic in ancient times who lived alone on top of a tall pillar [Mid-17C. < late Greek stulitēs < Greek stulos 'pillar'] —**stylitic** /stí líttik/ adj

stylize /stí līz/ (-izes, -izing, -ized), **stylise** (-ises, -ising, -ised) vt to design something in a particular artistic style —**stylization** /stí lī záysh'n/ n —**stylized** adj —**stylizer** n

stylo-, **styli-** prefix style, column ○ stylograph [< Latin stylus (see STYLUS)]

stylobate /stílə bayt/ n a continuous raised platform of masonry supporting a row of columns [Mid-16C. Via Latin stylobata < Greek stulobatēs 'column step']

stylograph /stílō graaf, -graf/ n a fountain pen that has a thin hollow tube as its writing point instead of the traditional nib

stylography /stí lóggrəfi/ n the art of drawing or engraving using a stylus —**stylographic** /stílō gráffik/ adj —**stylographically** adv

styloid /stí loyd/ adj describes a bony protuberance (**process**) that is long and thin

stylolite /stílə līt/ n a join between two layers of limestone that in cross-section looks like a row of interlocking pegs —**stylolitic** /stílə líttik/ adj

stylophone /stíləfōn/ n a small battery-operated musical instrument with a surface like a keyboard, played using an electronic pen attached by a wire

stylus (sense 3)

stylus /stíləss/ (plural **-li** /-lī/) n 1. RECORDING RECORD PLAYER NEEDLE the jewel-tipped needle of a record player that rests in the grooves of a record as it revolves and transmits vibrations to the cartridge 2. ELECTRONICS MACHINE TRACING PEN the tracing pen on an electronic device such as a seismograph or polygraph that converts an electrical signal into a written record 3. ART, HIST ENGRAVING TOOL a pointed instrument used for engraving, especially one used in ancient times for writing on clay or wax tablets 4. COMPUT DEVICE FOR TOUCHING SCREEN a pointed device for use on a computer screen that responds to pressure [Early 18C. Alteration of Latin stilus 'stake, pointed writing instrument']

stymie /stími/, **stymy** vt (-mies, -mieing, -mied; -mies, -mying, -mied) 1. HINDER PROGRESS OF SOMEBODY OR SOMETHING to prevent somebody or something from making further progress 2. GOLF BLOCK OPPONENT'S LINE to obstruct the line between a golf opponent's ball and the hole (dated) ■ n (plural -mies) 1. PROBLEM SITUATION a situation in which obstacles hinder progress 2. GOLF OBSTRUCTION OF OPPONENT'S BALL a situation in which one golfer's ball blocks another's (dated) [Mid-19C. Origin ?]

stypsis /stípsiss/ n the use of a styptic substance, or its effect [Late 19C. Via late Latin < Greek stupsis < stuphein 'to contract']

styptic /stíptik/ adj slowing down the rate of bleeding or stopping bleeding altogether, whether by causing the blood vessels to contract or by accelerating clotting ■ n a styptic drug, cream, or lotion [14C. Via late Latin < Greek stuptikos < stuphein 'to contract']

styptic pencil n an astringent substance in solid form in a small cylindrical container that is applied to stop bleeding from small cuts, e.g. after shaving

styrax /stí raks/ n TREES same as **storax** (sense 1) [Mid-16C. Via Latin < Greek sturax]

styrene /stí reen/ n a colourless flammable liquid hydrocarbon. Use: manufacture of synthetic rubber, plastic. Formula: C_8H_8. [Late 19C. < Latin styrax (see STYRAX)]

Styrofoam /stírə fōm/ tdmk a trademark for a light plastic material used to make disposable items, insulation, and packing materials

William Styron

Styron /stírən/, **William** (b. 1925) US writer. His novel The Confessions of Nat Turner (1967) won a Pulitzer Prize. His other works include Sophie's Choice (1979). Full name **Styron, William Clark, Jr.**

'Depression is a wimp of a word for a howling tempest in the brain.'

[William Styron, Darkness Visible; 1990]

STYS abbr speak to you soon (used in e-mails or text messages)

Styx /stiks/ n in Greek mythology, the river across which the souls of the dead were ferried into the underworld [14C. Via Latin < Greek Stux]

SU abbr PHYS strontium unit

Suárez González /swaár ez gon zaál ez/, **Adolfo** (b. 1932) prime minister of Spain (1976–81). He guided the country towards democracy after the death of General Franco.

suave /swaav/ (**suaver**, **suavest**) adj 1. polite and charming, especially in a way that seems affected or insincere 2. well groomed and smartly dressed [Early 16C. Directly or via French < Latin suavis 'sweet, agreeable' < Indo-European] —**suavely** adv —**suaveness** n —**suavity** n

sub /sub/ n 1. SUBSTITUTE a substitute, especially a substitute player in a game (informal) 2. NAVY same as **submarine** n (sense 1) 3. SMALL LOAN a small sum of money borrowed, especially a small advance on wages due (informal) ○ You could ask her for a sub. 4. SUBSCRIPTION FEE a fee paid for membership of an organization (informal) ○ Have you paid your subs for this season? 5. PUBL SUBEDITOR a subeditor on a newspaper or magazine (informal) 6. MIL same as **subaltern** (informal) 7. SUBTITLE a subtitle to a document or printed matter (informal) ■ v (subs, subbing, subbed) (informal) 1. vi REPLACE SOMEBODY to take the place of somebody temporarily, usually in a work situation 2. vti SUBCONTRACT to subcontract work, or work as a subcontractor 3. vt SUBTITLE SOMETHING to add subtitles to something 4. vti SUBEDIT to subedit something, or work as a subeditor 5. vt LEND MONEY to lend somebody a small amount of money, especially as an advance on wages due ○ He could have subbed me a few quid until payday. [Late 17C. Shortening]

sub- prefix 1. under, below, beneath ○ subcutaneous ○ subfloor 2. subordinate, secondary ○ subparagraph 3. less than completely ○ subliterate 4. subdivision ○ subkingdom ○ subcontinent 5. bordering on ○ subequatorial 6. smaller or younger than ○ subcompact ○ subteen 7. nearly, partly, somewhat ○ subfossil 8. containing less than the normal amount of an element ○ suboxide [< Latin sub 'under']

subabdominal adj	**subglacial** adj
subacute adj	**subglacially** adv
subacutely adv	**subhumid** adj
subagency n	**subindex** n
subarid adj	**subindustry** n
subassembly n	**sublethal** adj
subaverage adj	**sublethally** adv
subbasement n	**sublevel** n
subblock n	**sublibrarian** n
subbranch n	**subliterate** adj
subcaste n	**sublot** n
subcategory n	**submaster** n
subchapter n	**submember** n
subchief n	**submetallic** adj
subclan n	**subminimal** adj
subclassification n	**subminimum** adj
subclassify vt	**submolecular** adj
subclause n	**suboceanic** adj
subcollection n	**subofficer** n
subcolony n	**suboptimal** adj
subcommander n	**suborganization** n
subcommission n	**subpar** adj
subcommissioner n	**subparagraph** n
subconference n	**subpart** n
subcouncil n	**subperiosteal** adj
subcranial adj	**subphylar** adj
subdean n	**subphylum** n
subdepartment n	**subpopulation** n
subdesert n	**subprincipal** n
subdialect n	**subproduct** n
subdirector n	**subprofessional** adj
subdiscipline n	**subprogram** n
subdistributor n	**subregion** n
subdistrict n	**subregional** adj
subentry n	**subsample** n
subfile n	**subscale** n
subfreezing adj	**subscience** n
subgenre n	**subsect** n

subsector *n*
subsegment *n*
subsense *n*
subseries *n*
subskill *n*
subspecialist *n*
subspeciality *n*
subspecialization *n*
subspecialize *vi*
substyle *n*
subsurface *adj, n*
subsystem *n*
subteen *n*
subtemperate *adj*
subtheme *n*
subthreshold *adj*
subtopic *n*
subtorrid *adj*
subtribe *n*
subtype *n*
subtypical *adj*
subvariety *n*

subacid /súb ássid/ *adj* **1.** mildly unkind or critical in tone (*literary*) **2.** moderately sour in flavour (*archaic*) —**subacidity** /súbbə síddəti/ *n* —**subacidly** *adv*

subacute sclerosing panencephalitis /-pán en seffə lítiss/ *n* a severe, usually fatal, inflammatory disease of the brain, chiefly affecting children and linked to infection from measles

subadar /sóobə daar/, **subahdar** *n* in the former British Indian army, the chief Indian officer in a company of Indian soldiers [Late 17C. < Urdu, Persian *ṣūbahdār* < *ṣūbah* 'Mughal province' + Persian *-dār* 'holder']

subaerial /súb airi əl/ *adj* formed or situated on or just below the surface of the soil ○ *a plant with subaerial roots*

subalpine /súb ál pīn/ *adj* relating to or growing naturally on the lower slopes of mountains, especially the areas below the tree line

subaltern /súbb'ltərn/ *n* **1.** MIL **JUNIOR OFFICER** an officer in the British Army of a rank below captain, especially a second lieutenant **2. SUBORDINATE PERSON** a person holding a subordinate or inferior position **3.** LOGIC **IMPLIED PROPOSITION** a proposition that is implied by a universal proposition ■ *adj* **1. SUBORDINATE** in a subordinate or inferior position **2.** LOGIC **IMPLIED** in logic, implied as a proposition by a universal proposition [Late 16C. < late Latin *subalternus* < Latin *alternus* 'one after another' (see ALTERNATE)]

subalternate /sub áwltərnət, -ól-/ *adj* **1.** describes a leaf whose leaflets are arranged in semistaggered rows, neither fully alternate nor fully opposite **2.** in a subordinate or inferior position —**subalternation** /sub áwltər náysh'n, sub ól-/ *n*

subantarctic /súb ant áarktik/ *adj* relating to the area between the Antarctic Circle and the South Pole

subapical /súbb áppik'l/ *adj* below or near an apex —**subapically** *adv*

subapostolic /súb apə stóllik/ *adj* belonging to the period in the history of the Christian Church that immediately followed the time of the Apostles

subaqua /súb ákwə/ *adj* relating to or providing facilities for underwater sports such as scuba diving [Mid-20C. < SUB- + Latin *aqua* 'water']

subaquatic /súb ə kwáttik/ *adj* **1.** existing or able to exist partly in water and partly on land **2.** relating or belonging to underwater regions

subaqueous /súb áykwi əss/ *adj* living, found, or formed under water

subarachnoid /súb ə ráknoyd/ *adj* situated beneath the middle of the three membranes (**arachnoids**) that cover the brain and spinal cord

subarctic /súb áarktik/ *adj* **1.** relating to the area bordering the Arctic Circle to the south **2.** similar to the regions that border the Arctic Circle, e.g. in landscape or weather conditions

subatomic /súb ə tómmik/ *adj* **1.** occurring as part of an atom, or smaller than an atom ○ *a subatomic particle* **2.** on a scale smaller than the atom, or involving phenomena at this level

subaudition /súb awdísh'n/ *n* **1.** the act of understanding a word or thought that is implied but not actually expressed in speech or writing **2.** a word, idea, or thought understood by a hearer or reader that is implied but not expressed [Mid-17C. < late Latin *subaudition-* < Latin *audire* 'hear']

subaxillary /súb ak sílləri/ *adj* **1.** located beneath the armpit **2.** growing beneath the axil in plants

subbase /súb bayss/ *n* **1.** a deep layer of large stones that forms the lowest level of a roadbed or of the foundation of a building **2.** the lowest section of any base or foundation, e.g. the bottom part of a pedestal

subbituminous /súb bi tyóominəss/ *adj* describes a type of soft coal that has an intermediate carbon content

subcalibre /sub kállibər/ *adj* describes ammunition whose calibre is smaller than that of the gun from which it is fired. Smaller ammunition is often used for practice because it is cheaper.

subcartilaginous /súb kaarti lájjinəss/ *adj* **1.** lying beneath cartilage or a body part composed of cartilage **2.** made up partly of cartilage

subcelestial /súb sə lésti əl/ *adj* belonging to the earth, not to the heavens or the stars (*literary*)

subcellular /sub séllyoolər/ *adj* **1.** existing inside a cell, or relating to the component parts of cells **2.** on a scale smaller than a cell, or involving phenomena at this level

subclass /súb klaass/ *n* **1.** a smaller group among several into which a main class is divided **2.** BIOL a subdivision of a class in the classification of plants and animals **3.** MATHS same as **subset**

subclavian /sub kláyvi ən/ *adj* located under the collarbone (**clavicle**) [Mid-17C. < modern Latin *subclavius* < Latin *clavis* 'key']

subclinical /sub klínnik'l/ *adj* describes an early stage or mild form of a medical condition, no symptoms of which are detectable —**subclinically** *adv*

subcommittee /súbkəmiti/ *n* a committee set up by and consisting of members of an existing committee to deal with a specific issue

subcompact /súbkəm pákt, sub kóm pakt/ *n N Am* a small car, usually the smallest and lightest model in a manufacturer's range

subconscious /sub kónshəss/ *adj* present in the mind without awareness of it ■ *n* mental activity not directly perceived by the consciousness, from which memories, feelings, or thoughts can influence behaviour without realization of it —**subconsciously** *adv* —**subconsciousness** *n*

subcontinent /sub kóntinənt/ *n* **1.** a large area that is an identifiably separate part of a continent **2.** *also* **Subcontinent** the area encompassing the countries of India, Pakistan, and Bangladesh regarded as a distinct part of South Asia —**subcontinental** /súb konti nént'l/ *adj, n*

subcontract /súb kon trakt/ *n* **SECONDARY CONTRACT** a secondary contract in which the person or company originally hired in turn hires somebody else to do all or part of the work ■ *v* (**-tracts, -tracting, -tracted**) **1.** *vt* **GIVE WORK UNDER SUBCONTRACT** to pass on work to a second person or company under the terms of a subcontract **2.** *vi* **TAKE ON WORK FROM CONTRACTOR** to work on contract with a person or company who is a contractor to somebody else —**subcontractor** *n*

subcontrary /sub kóntrəri/ *adj* describes logical propositions that are related to each other in such a way that both cannot be false at the same time, although both may be true ■ *n* (*plural* **-ies**) a subcontrary logical proposition [Early 17C. < late Latin *subcontrarius*, translation of Greek *hupenantios* 'contrary']

subcortex /sub káwrteks/ (*plural* **-tices** /-ti seez/) *n* the parts of the brain that lie immediately beneath the cerebral cortex —**subcortical** *adj*

subculture /súb kulchər/ *n* **1.** an identifiably separate social group within a larger culture, especially one regarded as existing outside mainstream society **2.** a bacterial culture that is grown from another culture —**subcultural** *adj*

subcutaneous /súbkyoo táyni əss/ *adj* located, living, or made beneath the skin —**subcutaneously** *adv*

subdeacon /sub déekən/ *n* **1.** a member of the Roman Catholic clergy who acts as a deacon's assistant, e.g. by preparing the vessels that are to be used in celebrating Mass **2.** a clergyman ranking just above a lector in an Eastern Church

subdiaconate /súb dī ákənət, -nayt/ *n* the position or term of office of a subdeacon —**subdiaconal** *adj*

subdirectory /súbdi rektəri, -dī-/ (*plural* **-ries**) *n* a directory created within another directory on a magnetic storage device such as a hard disk

subdivide /súbdi vīd/ (**-vides, -viding, -vided**) *v* **1.** *vt* to divide a section, or all the sections, of something into sections that are smaller still **2.** *vi* to be divided, or be able to be divided, into sections that are smaller still —**subdivider** *n*

subdivision /súb divizh'n/ *n* **1.** the dividing of a divided part into units that are smaller still **2.** a section of something that is itself a division of a larger thing —**subdivisional** *adj*

subdomain name /sub də máyn-, -dō-/, **subdomain** *n* **1.** a second level of Internet domain names created by the administrator of the domain **2.** a subdivision of the two-letter country domain names into two- or three-letter organizational subdomains, e.g. 'ac.uk' for United Kingdom academic sites and 'com.au' for Australian commercial sites.

subdominant /sub dómminənt/ *n* **1.** the fourth note in a major or minor musical scale **2.** a musical key, chord, or harmony based on a subdominant

subduct /səb dúkt/ (**-ducts, -ducting, -ducted**) *vi* to be carried under the edge of an adjoining continental or oceanic plate, causing tensions in the Earth's crust that can produce earthquakes or volcanic eruptions [Late 16C. < Latin *subduct-*, past participle of *subducere* 'draw up' (see SUBDUE)] —**subduction** *n*

subdue /səb dyóo/ (**-dues, -duing, -dued**) *vt* **1. BRING SOMEBODY UNDER FORCIBLE CONTROL** to bring a person or group of people under control using force **2. SOFTEN SOMETHING** to soften something, or make something less intense ○ *idealism subdued by experience* **3. REPRESS EMOTIONS** to repress or control feelings ○ *worked hard to subdue her irritation* [14C. Via Old French *souduire* 'seduce' < Latin *subducere* 'draw up' < *ducere* 'to lead'] —**subduable** *adj* —**subduer** *n*

subdued /səb dyóod/ *adj* **1. NOT HARSH** not bright, loud, or intense, or made less bright, loud, or intense ○ *subdued lighting* **2. LOW-SPIRITED** sad or in low spirits **3. QUIET** quiet and restrained ○ *speaking in subdued tones*

subdural /sub dyóorəl/ *adj* beneath the dura mater that covers the brain and spinal cord

subedit /sub éddit/ (**-its, -iting, -ited**) *vt* to read and correct written material before it is published, particularly for newspapers and magazines, under the general supervision of an editor [Mid-19C. Back-formation < SUBEDITOR]

subeditor /sub édditər/ *n* **1.** an assistant editor helping to prepare material for publication **2.** somebody whose job is to read and correct written material before it is published, particularly for newspapers and magazines, under the general supervision of an editor. N Am term **copyreader**

subequatorial /súbekwə táwri əl/ *adj* relating to or situated in the regions that lie just north and south of the equator

suberin /syóobərin/ *n* a waxy waterproof substance found in the cell walls of many plants, especially cork [Early 19C. < French *subérine* < Latin *suber* 'cork']

suberize /syóobə rīz/ (**-izes, -izing, -ized**), **suberise** (**-ises, -ising, -ised**) *vt* to deposit suberin in plant cell walls during their conversion to cork tissue [Late 19C. < Latin *suber* 'cork']

subfamily /súb famli/ (*plural* **-lies**) *n* **1.** a subdivision of a family in the classification of plants and animals **2.** a smaller group of related languages within a language family

subfield /súb feeld/ *n* a mathematical field that is a subset of another field

subfloor /súb flawr/ *n* an underlying layer of rough or unfinished material supporting a finished floor

subflooring /súb flawring/ *n* a subfloor, or the material used to make a subfloor

subfossil /súb foss'l/ *adj* partially fossilized ■ *n* a partially fossilized organism

subframe /súb fraym/ *n* the underlying metal frame on which a vehicle's bodywork is built

subfusc /súb fusk, sub fúsk/ *adj* dark or drab in colour (*literary*) [Mid-18C. < Latin *subfuscus* 'darkish' < *fuscus* 'dark']

subgenus /súb jeenəss, -jenəss/ (*plural* **-genera** /-jénnərə/) *n* a category in the classification of plants and animals that is larger than a species but smaller than a genus

subgrade /súb grayd/ *n* the bed of ground on which

the foundations of a road, railway, or building are laid

subgroup /súb groop/ *n* **1.** a smaller group distinguished in some way from the larger group of which it is a part **2.** a mathematical group whose members are also members of a larger group

subhead /súb hed/, **subheading** /-heding/ *n* a heading or title subordinate to the main one

subhuman /sub hyoōmən/ *adj* **1.** relating to or displaying behaviour that is distastefully inferior in sophistication, moral standards, or intelligence to what is regarded as usual for human beings ○ *a subhuman thug* **2.** at the level of biological development that is considered just below humans

subimago /súb i máygō/ (*plural* **-magoes** or **-magines** /-máyjineez/) *n* a mayfly or related insect in a metamorphic stage in which functional wings are present but not all adult features have developed fully

subinfeudation /súb infyoo dáysh'n/ *n* **1.** in the feudal system, the leasing of a portion of the land held by a feudal lord's servant (**vassal**) to somebody else who became the servant's servant in turn **2.** a portion of land granted to a feudal servant under the terms of subinfeudation —**subinfeudate** /-fyoo dayt/ *vt*

subirrigate /sub írri gayt/ (**-gates, -gating, -gated**) *vt* to irrigate land from below the surface of the ground, e.g. with porous pipes laid underground —**subirrigation** /súb iri gáysh'n/ *n*

subito /sōobitō/ *adv* suddenly or abruptly (*used as a musical direction*) [Early 18C. < Italian < Latin *subire* 'come over']

subj. *abbr* **1.** GRAM subject **2.** subjective **3.** GRAM subjunctive

subjacent /sub jáyss'nt/ *adj* (*formal*) **1.** lying under or just below something **2.** next to something and at a lower level than it ○ *'in the damper tracts of subjacent country and along the river-courses'* (Thomas Hardy, *Jude the Obscure*; 1895) [Late 16C. < Latin *subjacent-*, present participle of *subjacere* 'lie under' < *jacere* 'lie'] —**subjacency** *n* —**subjacently** *adv*

subject *n* /súb jikt/ **1.** TOPIC something that is being discussed, examined, or otherwise dealt with ○ *the subject of our conversation* ○ *On the subject of staff changes, I have some news.* **2.** COURSE OF STUDY a branch of learning that forms a course of study (*often used in the plural*) **3.** PERSON RULED BY ANOTHER somebody who is ruled by a king, queen, or other authority ○ *British subjects* **4.** SOMEBODY TREATED OR ACTED UPON somebody who receives treatment or is the focus of an activity ○ *not an appropriate subject for hypnosis* **5.** ARTS, LITERAT THING REPRESENTED BY ARTIST somebody or something that an artist, writer, or photographer represents in a piece of work ○ *the subject of her latest biography* **6.** GRAM GRAMMATICAL PERFORMER OF ACTION the part of a sentence or utterance, usually a noun, noun phrase, or equivalent, that the rest of the sentence asserts something about and that agrees with the verb. The subject typically performs the action expressed by the verb. 'She' and 'The dog' are the subjects of 'She gave me the book' and 'The dog was found asleep' respectively. **7.** MUSIC MUSICAL THEME the principal theme or melodic phrase that is developed in a musical composition ■ *adj* /súbjikt/ **1.** PRONE TO likely to be affected by something ○ *areas subject to flooding* ○ *a child subject to mood swings* **2.** RULED under the control of somebody or something such as a ruler or a law, and obliged to obey ○ *a subject nation* ○ *not subject to the laws that apply in this country* ■ *adv* **subject to** DEPENDING depending on somebody or something ○ *The plans have been drawn up, subject to your final approval.* ■ *vt* /səb jékt/ (**-jects, -jecting, -jected**) **1.** GIVE SOMEBODY UNPLEASANT EXPERIENCE to cause somebody to undergo something unpleasant ○ *recruits subjected to rigorous physical training* **2.** SUBMIT SOMETHING TO TREATMENT to make something undergo a particular kind of treatment ○ *proposals subjected to detailed scrutiny* **3.** OVERPOWER SOMEBODY to bring a person or group under the power or influence of another person or group ○ *a nation subjected to rule from overseas* [14C. Via French < Latin *subjectus* < *subicere* 'place under' < *jacere* 'lie']

SYNONYMS ***subject, topic, matter, issue, subject matter, theme, burden***

CORE MEANING: what is under discussion

subject something that is being discussed, examined, or otherwise dealt with ○ *I didn't bring up the subject of money with my cousin.* ○ *Restoration of the wreck will be the subject of an exhibition at the Maritime Museum this year.* **topic** something dealt with in a text or in discussion ○ *The paper identified four major topics for consideration.* ○ *the current topic of conversation* **matter** something that is being considered or needs to be dealt with ○ *Readers may have their own views on this matter.* ○ *It may help to hold short family meetings to discuss matters like holidays.* **issue** something for discussion or of general concern ○ *I want to talk to you on the issue of late delivery.* ○ *These are sensitive issues and need to be handled carefully.* **subject matter** the material dealt with in a book, film, discussion, or other medium ○ *Most of the documentation aids are graphic representations of the subject matter.* ○ *a photographer whose subject matter is the narrow streets of lower Manhattan* **theme** the subject of a discourse, discussion, piece of writing, or artistic composition ○ *Death and the passing of time are the principal themes of this book.* **burden** (*literary*) the main or recurring theme in a book, piece of music, speech, or argument ○ *The main burden of the report's criticisms focus on lack of communication.* ○ *Tantalizing unfulfilment is part of the play's emotional burden.*

---

subjection /səb jéksh'n/ *n* **1.** the bringing of a person or people under the control of another, usually by force **2.** the subjecting of somebody to something

subjective /səb jéktiv/ *adj* **1.** NOT IMPARTIAL based on somebody's opinions or feelings rather than on facts or evidence ○ *Of course, that's only my subjective impression.* **2.** PHILOSOPHY EXISTING BY PERCEPTION existing only in the mind and not independently of it **3.** MED OBSERVED ONLY BY PATIENT describes a medical condition that is perceived to exist only by the patient and is not recognizable to anyone else **4.** GRAM RELATING TO SUBJECT OF VERB relating to or forming the subject of a verb —**subjectively** *adv* —**subjectiveness** *n*

subjective idealism *n* a philosophical theory arguing that the external world only exists because it is perceived to exist, and does not have existence of its own

subjectivism /səb jéktivizəm/ *n* **1.** EMPHASIS ON PERSONAL INTERPRETATION emphasis on personal feelings or responses as opposed to external facts or evidence **2.** PHILOSOPHY THEORY OF VALIDITY OF KNOWLEDGE a theory stating that people can only have knowledge of what they experience directly **3.** PHILOSOPHY THEORY OF VALIDITY OF MORAL STANDARDS a theory stating that the only valid moral standard is the one imposed by somebody's own conscience, and therefore that society's moral codes are invalid —**subjectivist** *adj* —**subjectivistic** /səb jékti vístik/ *adj*

subjectivity /súb jek tívvəti/ *n* **1.** interpretation based on personal opinions or feelings rather than on external facts or evidence **2.** concentration on personal, individual responses in artistic expression

subject line *n* a line in an e-mail that indicates the subject of the message

subject matter *n* the matter dealt with in a book, film, discussion, or other medium ○ *contains subject matter unsuitable for children*

SYNONYMS See ***subject.***

---

subjoin /sub jóyn/ (**-joins, -joining, -joined**) *vt* to add something at the end of what has already been written or said (*formal*)

sub judice /súb jōodəssi/ *adj* currently under consideration by a judge or a court of law and therefore not to be commented upon publicly [Early 17C. < Latin, 'under a judge']

subjugate /súbjoo gayt/ (**-gates, -gating, -gated**) *vt* to bring somebody, especially a people or nation, under the control of another, e.g. by military conquest [15C. < Latin *subjugat-*, past participle of *subjugare* < *jugum* 'yoke'] —**subjugable** /súbjəgəb'l/ *adj* —**subjugation** /súbjoo gáysh'n/ *n* —**subjugator** *n*

subjunctive /səb júngktiv/ *n* **1.** GRAMMATICAL MOOD a grammatical mood that expresses doubts, wishes, and possibilities **2.** SUBJUNCTIVE VERB a verb or form in the subjunctive ■ *adj* RELATING TO SUBJUNCTIVE in or relating to the subjunctive [Mid-16C. < late Latin *subjunctivus* < past participle of Latin *subjungere* 'subordinate' < *jungere* 'to join'] —**subjunctively** *adv*

USAGE The subjunctive mood in English is distinguishable from the regular form of verbs (called the *indicative*) only in the third person present singular, which omits the final *-s* (as in *make* rather than *makes*), and in the forms *be* and *were* of the verb *to be*. A typical use of the subjunctive is in clauses introduced by *that* expressing a wish or suggestion: *I suggested that she drop by for a drink before the concert. They demanded that he answer their questions.* The form *were* is used in clauses introduced by *if, as if, as though*, or *supposing*, as in: *If you were to go, you might regret it. It's not as though he were an expert. Supposing I were to meet you outside the theatre.* The subjunctive also occurs in fixed expressions such as *as it were, be that as it may, come what may,* and *far be it from me.*

---

subkingdom /sub kíngdəm/ *n* a category in the classification of plants and animals that is smaller than a kingdom and larger than a phylum

sublease /sub léess/ *n* an arrangement to rent a property from somebody who is already renting it from somebody else ■ *vt* (**-leases, -leasing, -leased**) same as **sublet** —**sublessee** /súb le sée/ *n* —**sublessor** /súb le sáwr/ *n*

sublet /sub lét/ *vti* (**-lets, -letting, -let**) to rent a property to or as a subsidiary tenant ■ *n* a property that is rented from somebody who is renting it from somebody else

sublieutenant /súb lef ténnənt/ *n* the most junior commissioned officer in the Royal Navy and some other navies

sublimate *v* /súbbli mayt/ (**-mates, -mating, -mated**) **1.** *vt* PSYCHOL to channel impulses or energies regarded as unacceptable, especially sexual desires, towards an activity that is more socially acceptable, often a creative activity **2.** *vti* CHEM same as **sublime** *v* (senses 1–2) ■ *n* /súbbli mayt, -mət/ CHEM a chemical substance formed as a result of sublimation [15C. < Latin *sublimat-*, past participle of *sublimare* 'elevate' < *sublimis* 'elevated']

sublimation /súbbli máysh'n/ *n* **1.** the channelling of impulses or energies regarded as unacceptable, especially sexual desires, towards activities regarded as more socially acceptable, often creative activities **2.** a process in which a substance is converted directly from a solid to a gas or from a gas to a solid without an intermediate liquid phase

sublime /sə blím/ *adj* (**-limer, -limest**) **1.** BEAUTIFUL so awe-inspiringly beautiful as to seem almost heavenly ○ *the composer at his most sublime* **2.** MORALLY WORTHY of the highest moral or spiritual value **3.** COMPLETE complete or utter ○ *in sublime ignorance* **4.** EXCELLENT excellent or particularly impressive (*informal*) ○ *a sublime pasta creation* ■ *n* SOMETHING SUBLIME something that is sublime ○ *going from the sublime to the ridiculous* ■ *v* (**-limes, -liming, -limed**) **1.** *vti* CHEM CONVERT SOLID SUBSTANCE TO GAS to convert a substance directly from a solid to a gas or from a gas to a solid without an intermediate liquid phase, or undergo this process **2.** *vti* CHEM CONVERT THEN RECONVERT to convert a solid directly into a gas and then back to a solid again without an intermediate liquid phase, or undergo this process **3.** *vt* MAKE SOMETHING PURE to make something such as an emotion finer or purer [14C. < Latin *sublimis* 'elevated'] —**sublimely** *adv* —**sublimeness** *n* —**sublimity** /sə blímməti/ *n*

Sublime Porte *n* HIST same as **Porte** [Early 17C. < French, 'High Gate', translation of Turkish *Babiâli*, referring to the palace gate where justice was administered]

subliminal /sub límmin'l/ *adj* entering, existing in, or affecting the mind without conscious awareness ○ *subliminal messages* [Late 19C. < SUB- + Latin *limin-* 'threshhold'] —**subliminally** *adv*

subliminal advertising *n* advertising in the form of images flashed onto the screen during a film or television programme that are too brief to be noticed but long enough to be registered subconsciously

sublingual /sub líng gwǝl/ *adj* **1.** situated under the tongue **2.** describes medicines that are administered by being placed under the tongue to dissolve —**sublingually** *adv*

sublittoral /sub líttǝrǝl/ *adj* relating to, living near, or located in the shallow water near a shoreline ■ *n* the area of a sea that lies between the shore and the continental shelf

sublunary /sub loónǝri/ *adj* **1.** relating to or found in the area of space that lies between the Moon and the Earth **2.** belonging to the material world rather than to the spiritual or intellectual world (*archaic or literary*)

subluxation /súb luk sáysh'n/ *n* a partial dislocation of bones that leaves them misaligned but still in some contact with each other

submachine gun /súbmǝ sheén-/ *n* a lightweight portable machine gun fired from the hip or the shoulder. It can fire either in single rounds or continuous bursts.

submandibular /súb man díbbyoõlǝr/ *adj* relating to or located under the lower jaw

submarginal /sub maárjinǝl/ *adj* falling below a necessary minimum, especially the minimum conditions necessary for profitability —**submarginally** *adv*

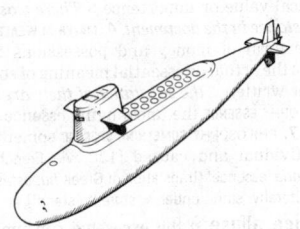

submarine

submarine /súbmǝ reen, súbmǝ reén/ *n* **1.** UNDERWATER BOAT a boat built to operate and travel for long periods under water **2.** *N Am* LONG SANDWICH a sandwich made with a long roll cut horizontally ■ *adj* UNDERWATER taking place or growing under water, especially in the sea ○ *submarine research* —**submariner** /sub márrinǝr/ *n*

submaxillary /súb mak síllǝri/ *adj* ANAT same as **submandibular**

submediant /sub meédi ǝnt/ *n* **1.** the sixth note in a major or minor musical scale **2.** a musical key, chord, or harmony based on a submediant

submerge /sǝb múrj/ (**-merges, -merging, -merged**) *v* **1.** *vt* PLUNGE SOMETHING IN LIQUID to put something into water or some other liquid so that all of it is under the surface **2.** *vi* GO UNDER WATER to go under the surface of water or another liquid **3.** *vt* SUPPRESS SOMETHING to keep something such as feelings or a secret hidden from others [Early 17C. < Latin *submergere* 'dip under' < *mergere* 'dip'] —**submerged** *adj* —**submergence** *n*

submerged tenth /sǝb múrjd-/ *n* the ten per cent of any population that, according to some economic theories, will always remain in poverty

submerse /sǝb múrss/ (**-merses, -mersing, -mersed**) *vt* same as **submerge** (sense 1) [Early 18C. < Latin *submers-*, past participle of *submergere* (see SUBMERGE)] —**submersion** /sub múrsh'n/ *n*

submersible /sǝb múrssǝb'l/ *adj* **1.** FOR UNDERWATER USE designed for use underwater **2.** NOT DAMAGED UNDER WATER capable of being put under water without being damaged ■ *n* UNDERWATER BOAT an underwater vessel, especially a small craft designed for use at deep levels

submicroscopic /súb míkrǝ skóppik/ *adj* too small to be seen with an optical microscope —**submicroscopically** *adv*

subminiature /sub mínnichǝr/ *adj* **1.** SMALLER THAN MINIATURE smaller in size than miniature **2.** SMALLER THAN COMPACT CAMERA describes a camera substantially smaller than a compact camera, using film smaller than the 35mm miniature format ■ *n* VERY SMALL CAMERA a subminiature camera

subminiaturize /sub mínnichǝ ríz/ (**-izes, -izing, -ized**), **subminiaturise** (**-ises, -ising, -ised**) *vt* to manufacture something that is very small in scale —**subminiaturization** /sub mínnichǝ rī záysh'n/ *n*

submission /sǝb mísh'n/ *n* **1.** YIELDING, OR READINESS TO YIELD a willingness to yield or surrender to somebody, or the act of doing so ○ *demanded nothing less than total submission to his authority* **2.** IDEA SUBMITTED something put forward for consideration or approval, e.g. a suggestion, proposal, or plan **3.** ACT OF SUBMITTING SOMETHING the act of submitting or handing in something such as a proposal to be considered or written work to be judged **4.** LAW AGREEMENT TO ARBITRATE an agreement between parties in a dispute to have a contested matter arbitrated **5.** WRESTLING WITHDRAWAL FROM WRESTLING BOUT an acknowledgment by a wrestler that he or she cannot continue a bout because of pain

submissive /sǝb míssiv/ *adj* giving in or tending to give in to the demands or authority of others —**submissively** *adv* —**submissiveness** *n*

submit /sǝb mít/ (**-mits, -mitting, -mitted**) *v* **1.** *vt* PROPOSE OR HAND IN SOMETHING to hand something in or put something forward for consideration, approval, or judgment ○ *Applications must be submitted in triplicate.* **2.** *vi* YIELD to accept somebody else's authority or will, especially reluctantly or under pressure **3.** *vi* AGREE to agree to undergo something ○ *had to submit to intensive questioning* **4.** *vi* DEFER to defer to another's knowledge, judgment, or experience **5.** *vt* ARGUE POINT to state or argue that something is the case (*formal*) [14C. < Latin *submittere* 'send under' < *mittere* 'send'] —**submittable** *adj* —**submittal** *n* —**submitter** *n*

SYNONYMS See *yield.*

submontane /sub món tayn/ *adj* **1.** relating to or found in the foothills or on the lower slopes of a mountain **2.** passing under or through a mountain —**submontanely** *adv*

submucosa /súb myoo kóssǝ/ *n* a layer of loosely meshed microscopic fibres and associated cells occurring beneath a mucous membrane, e.g. in the small intestine [Late 19C. < modern Latin < *mucosa* (see MUCOSA)]

submultiple /sub múltip'l/ *n* a number that can be divided into another an exact number of times and leave no remainder. For example, 7 is a submultiple of 35. ■ *adj* able to be divided into another number an exact number of times without leaving a remainder [Late 17C. < late Latin *submultiplus* < *multiplus* (see MULTIPLE)]

subnormal /sub náwrm'l/ *adj* **1.** with a level of intelligence that is lower than the level regarded as normal **2.** lower or less than normal or average —**subnormality** /súb nawr mállǝti/ *n* —**subnormally** *adv*

subnotebook /sub nót boõk/ *n* a portable personal computer that is smaller and lighter than a notebook

suborbital /sub áwrbit'l/ *adj* **1.** relating to the region below the eye socket (**orbit**) **2.** not designed to make a complete orbit of Earth or another astronomical object

suborder /súb awrdǝr/ *n* a taxonomic category that is a subdivision of an order and usually contains several similar families

subordinary /sub áwrd'nǝri/ (*plural* **-ies**) *n* in heraldry, a small shape or design, e.g. a lozenge, that can appear on a coat of arms and is smaller than the most prominent shape (**ordinary**)

subordinate *adj* /sǝ báwrdinǝt/ **1.** OF LESSER RANK lower than somebody in rank or status **2.** OF LESS IMPORTANCE secondary in importance **3.** GRAM MODIFYING acting as a modifying noun, adjective, or adverb within a sentence ■ *n* /sǝ báwrdinǝt/ SOMEBODY IN JUNIOR POSITION somebody who is lower in rank or status than another ■ *vt* /sǝ báwrdi nayt/ (**-ates, -ating, -ated**) **1.** MAKE SOMETHING SECONDARY to treat something as less important and allow something else to dominate or take priority ○ *had increasingly subordinated her research to the demands of her busy work schedule* **2.** PLACE SOMEBODY IN LOWER RANK to give somebody or regard somebody as having a lower rank or status than another [15C. < medieval Latin *subordinatus*, past participle of *subordinare* 'place below' < Latin *ordinare* (see ORDAIN)] —**subordinately** *adv* —**subordination** /sǝ báwrdi náysh'n/ *n*

subordinate clause *n* a clause that cannot stand alone as a separate sentence since its meaning depends on the meaning of the main clause and simply gives additional information. In the sentence 'We had to run because we were late', the clause 'because we were late' is the subordinate clause and 'We had to run' is the main clause.

subordinate conjunction, **subordinating conjunction** /sǝ báwrdi nayting-/, **subordinator** /sǝ báwrdi naytǝr/ *n* a conjunction that introduces a subordinate clause. It may be either one word such as 'although', 'because', or 'since', or a group of words such as 'in order that' or 'as long as'.

suborn /sǝ báwrn/ (**-orns, -orning, -orned**) *vt* to persuade somebody to commit a crime or other wrongdoing, e.g. to bribe another party to tell lies in court [Early 16C. < Latin *subornare* 'equip secretly' < *ornare* 'equip'] —**subornation** /súbbawr náysh'n/ *n* —**subornative** *adj* —**suborner** *n*

suboscine /sub óss īn, -in/ *adj* relating to, typical of, or belonging to the large subgroup of passerine birds that are not songbirds and are mainly found in America. ◊ **oscine**

suboxide /sub ók sīd/ *n* an oxide containing less oxygen than the normal oxide formed by a specific element

subplot /súb plot/ *n* **1.** a second and less prominent story within a book, play, or film **2.** a division of a plot of land, used especially for crop husbandry experiments

subpoena /sǝ peénǝ, sǝb-/ *n* a written legal order summoning a witness or requiring evidence to be submitted to a court ■ *vt* (**-nas, -naing, -naed**) to summon a witness with a written legal order, or require something to be submitted in evidence to a court [15C. < Latin *sub poena* 'under penalty', first words of the writ] —**subpoenaed** *adj*

subpolar /sub pólǝr/ *adj* **1.** being near the Arctic or the Antarctic polar region **2.** relating to, belonging to, or found in the areas that border the Arctic and Antarctic

sub-post office *n* a small post office offering limited postal services, located inside a larger shop and managed by somebody who is an agent but not an employee

subring /súb ring/ *n* in mathematics, a ring that is a subset of a larger ring

subrogate /súbbrǝ gayt/ (**-gates, -gating, -gated**) *vt* to substitute one person for another, especially in transferring a right or claim [15C. < Latin *subrogat-*, past participle of *subrogare* 'ask for in place of' < *rogare* 'ask, beg']

subrogation /súbbrǝ gáysh'n/ *n* the substitution of one claim for another, especially the transfer of the right to receive payment of a debt to somebody other than the original creditor

sub rosa /sub rózǝ/ *adv* in a secret or private way [Mid-17C. < Latin, 'under the rose' (as an emblem of confidentiality hung above council tables)]

subroutine /súb roo teen/ *n* a sequence of programming statements that performs a single task and can be used repeatedly

sub-Saharan *adj* relating to the area of Africa south of the Sahara desert

subscribe /sǝb skríb/ (**-scribes, -scribing, -scribed**) *v* **1.** *vi* MAKE ADVANCE PAYMENT to agree to pay for and receive or use something over a fixed period of time, e.g. a periodical, series of books, or set of tickets to musical or dramatic performances **2.** *vti* PROMISE TO GIVE MONEY REGULARLY to pledge to make regular donations to something, especially a charity **3.** *vti* GUARANTEE TO INVEST IN SOMETHING to promise to pay for something when it will occur, e.g. the financing of a new business or a new issue of shares **4.** *vi* SUPPORT VIEW to support or believe in a theory or view ○ *those who subscribe to progressive ideals* **5.** *vi* ONLINE PUT NAME ON MAILING LIST to add your name and e-mail address to a mailing list in order to receive

messages from a website automatically, with or without charge **6.** *vt* LAW **SIGN NAME ON LEGAL DOCUMENT** to sign a legal document to indicate agreement or approval of its terms (*formal*) [15C. < Latin *subscribere* 'write underneath' < *scribere* 'write'] —**subscriber** *n*

subscriber trunk dialling *n* a facility to make long-distance telephone calls directly, without the help of an operator (*dated*)

subscript /súb skript/ *n* a character that is printed on a level lower than the rest of the characters on the line, e.g. the '2' in the chemical formula 'H_2O' ■ *adj* printed on a lower level than other characters in a line of type [Early 18C. < Latin *subscript-*, past participle of *subscribere* (see SUBSCRIBE)]

subscription /səb skrípsh'n/ *n* **1. ADVANCE PAYMENT FOR SOMETHING** an agreement to pay for and receive or use something over a fixed period of time, e.g. a periodical, series of books, or set of tickets to musical or dramatic performances ○ *a film channel subscription* **2. MEMBERSHIP FEE** a fee paid for membership in a club or society **3. PLEDGE TO PAY FOR SOMETHING** a promise to pay for something when it will occur, e.g. the financing of a new business or a new issue of shares **4.** LAW **SIGNING OF DOCUMENT OR SIGNATURE** the process of signing a legal document as an indication of approval of its terms, or an approving signature on a document (*formal*) **5. TOTAL AGREEMENT** a full agreement with or approval of something (*literary*) [15C. < Latin *subscription-* < past participle of *subscribere* (see SUBSCRIBE)]

subscription library *n* a library that lends books in return for a regular fee

subsection /súb seksh'n/ *n* any of the smaller parts into which a section may be divided, e.g. in a legal or official document

subsellium /sub sélli əm/ (*plural* **-lia** /-li ə/) *n* CHR, FURNITURE same as **misericord** [Early 18C. < Latin, 'low seat' < *sella* 'seat']

subsequence[1] /súbssikwənss/ *n* something that happens after something else, or the occurrence of something after something else [15C. < SUBSEQUENT]

subsequence[2] /súb seekwənss/ *n* a sequence within another mathematical sequence [Early 20C. < SUB- + SEQUENCE]

subsequent /súbssikwənt/ *adj* later in time or order than something else [15C. Directly or via French < Latin *subsequent-*, present participle of *subsequi* 'follow closely' < *sequi* 'follow']

subsequently /súbs sikwəntli/ *adv* at a later time, and often as a consequence

subsere /súb seer/ *n* a secondary development of a natural plant and animal community after destruction by fire, flood, or human action [Early 20C. < SUB- + SERE[2]]

subserve /səb súrv/ (**-serves, -serving, -served**) *vt* to help to further, promote, or bring something about [Early 17C. < Latin *subservire* 'serve under' < *servire* (see SERVE)]

subservient /səb súrvi ənt/ *adj* **1. TOO EAGER TO OBEY** too submissive or eager to follow the wishes or orders of others **2. OF LESSER IMPORTANCE** in a position of secondary importance **3. INSTRUMENTAL IN SOMETHING** helping to achieve something or bring something about [Mid-17C. < Latin *subservient-*, present participle of *subservire* 'serve under' < *servire* (see SERVE)] —**subservience** *n* —**subserviently** *adv*

subset /súb set/ *n* a mathematical set whose elements are contained in another set

subshell /súb shel/ *n* an orbital within an electron energy level (**shell**)

subshrub /súb shrub/ *n* a low-growing plant with woody stems and main branches and nonwoody tips that die back each year [Mid-19C. Translation of modern Latin *suffrutex* < Latin *frutex* 'shrub'] —**subshrubby** *adj*

subside /səb sīd/ (**-sides, -siding, -sided**) *vi* **1. DIMINISH IN INTENSITY** to become less active or intense **2. DROP TO LOWER LEVEL** to sink to a low or lower level **3. SINK TO BOTTOM** to sink to the bottom of a liquid **4. GRADUALLY SIT OR LIE DOWN** to sink into a sitting or lying position, e.g. out of exhaustion (*formal*) [Mid-17C. < Latin *subsidere* 'settle down' < *sidere* 'settle']

subsidence /səb sīd'nss, súbssidənss/ *n* **1.** the sinking down of land resulting from natural shifts or human activity, frequently causing structural damage to buildings **2.** the waning or lessening of something

subsidiarity /səb síddi árrəti/ *n* **1.** the principle that political power should be exercised by the smallest or least central unit of government **2.** the fact or quality of being subsidiary [Mid-20C. Translation of German *Subsidiarität*]

subsidiary /səb síddi əri/ *adj* **1. OF LESSER IMPORTANCE** having secondary importance, or occupying a subordinate position **2. IN SUPPORTING ROLE** serving to aid, supplement, or support something ■ *n* (*plural* **-aries**) **1. SOMEBODY OR SOMETHING AUXILIARY** somebody or something that occupies a secondary or subordinate position **2. PART OF LARGER COMPANY** a company controlled or owned by a larger one [Mid-16C. < Latin *subsidiarius* < *subsidium* (see SUBSIDY)] —**subsidiarily** *adv*

subsidiary coin *n* a coin that has a lower denomination than that of a standard unit of currency

subsidize /súbssi dīz/ (**-dizes, -dizing, -dized**), **subsidise** (**-dises, -dising, -dised**) *vt* **1.** to contribute money to somebody or something, especially to give a government grant to a private company, organization, or charity to help it to continue to function **2.** to reduce the cost of something by providing a subsidy —**subsidizable** *adj* —**subsidization** /súbssi dī záysh'n/ *n* —**subsidizer** *n*

subsidy /súbssidi/ (*plural* **-dies**) *n* **1. MONEY GIVEN BY GOVERNMENT** a grant or gift of money from a government to a private company, organization, or charity to help it to function **2. HELP WITH EXPENSES** a monetary gift or contribution to somebody or something, especially to pay expenses **3. FORMER PARLIAMENTARY GRANT TO CROWN** a grant of money formerly given by the English Parliament to the Crown [14C. Via Anglo-Norman < Latin *subsidium* 'reserve troops' < *sedere* 'sit']

subsist /səb síst/ (**-sists, -sisting, -sisted**) *v* **1.** *vi* **MANAGE TO LIVE** to remain alive or viable, especially with the help of something **2.** *vt* **MAINTAIN SOMEBODY OR SOMETHING** to support or maintain somebody or something by providing something that is needed, e.g. by supplying troops with food or businesses with capital (*formal*) **3.** *vi* **BE ATTRIBUTABLE TO SOMETHING** to have a particular thing as its reason or origin (*formal*) **4.** *vi* **BE INHERENT** to reside in or consist of a particular thing (*formal*) **5.** *vi* PHILOSOPHY, MATHS **EXIST IN ABSTRACT** to have a timeless conceptual existence (*refers to numbers or mathematical sets*) [Mid-16C. Directly or via French < Latin *subsistere* 'stand up to' < *sistere* (see ASSIST)] —**subsistent** *adj* —**subsister** *n*

subsistence /səb sístənss/ *n* **1. CONDITION OF MANAGING TO STAY ALIVE** the condition of being or managing to stay alive, especially when there is only just enough food or money for survival **2. CONTINUING TO EXIST** the condition of continuing to exist **3.** MATHS, PHILOSOPHY **QUALITY OF ABSTRACT EXISTENCE** the quality that something possesses of existing independently, timelessly, or by virtue of its essence

subsistence allowance *n* **1.** a sum of money given to an employee to cover special expenses incurred in the performance of his or her work **2.** an advance paid to a new employee or soldier to help to meet living costs until wages begin to be paid

subsistence crop *n* a crop grown by a farmer principally to feed his or her family, with little or nothing left over to sell

subsistence farming *n* farming that generates only enough produce to feed the farmer's family, with little or nothing left over to sell —**subsistence farmer** *n*

subsistence level *n* a standard of living that provides barely enough food and money on which to survive

subsistence wage *n* a wage so low that it is barely enough to live on

subsocial /sub sṓsh'l/ *adj* describes insects that associate with others but without any fixed or organized social structure —**subsocially** *adv*

subsoil /súb soyl/ *n* the compacted soil beneath the topsoil ■ *vt* (**-soils, -soiling, -soiled**) to turn, break, or stir the compacted soil beneath the topsoil

subsoiler /súb soylər/ *n* **1.** a farm implement consisting of a frame with long sturdy vertical tines. It is drawn through the soil to break up compacted subsoil in order to improve drainage and aeration. **2.** an operator of a subsoiler

subsolar /sub sṓlər/ *adj* **1.** located directly below the Sun on the Earth's surface when the Sun is at its highest point **2.** located in the equatorial region that lies between the tropics of Cancer and Capricorn

subsong /súb song/ *n* an unstructured song of a bird that is quieter and lower-pitched than full song and is often performed by young adult birds

subsonic /sub sónnik/ *adj* **1.** slower than 1,220 kph/760 mph, the speed at which sound travels in air **2.** flying at speeds slower than the speed of sound, especially not designed to fly above the speed of sound —**subsonically** *adv*

subspecies /súb spee sheez/ (*plural same*) *n* a category used to classify plants and animals whose populations are distinct, e.g. in distribution, appearance, or feeding habits, but can still interbreed —**subspecific** /súb spə síffik/ *adj* —**subspecifically** *adv*

substage /súb stayj/ *n* a component assembly in a microscope that contains the condenser, mirror, or other accessories and is located below the stage

substance /súbstənss/ *n* **1. MATERIAL** a kind of matter or material **2. TANGIBLE PHYSICAL MATTER** physical reality that can be touched and felt **3. PRACTICAL VALUE** real or practical value or importance ○ *There was nothing of substance in the document.* **4. MATERIAL WEALTH** wealth in the form of money and possessions **5. GIST OF MEANING** the actual or essential meaning of something said or written ○ *the substance of their argument* **6.** PHILOSOPHY **ESSENCE** the unchanging essence of something **7.** PHILOSOPHY **SOMETHING SPECIFIC** something that is individual and caused [13C. Via French < Latin *substantia* 'essence' (translation of Greek *hupostasis*) < *substare*, literally 'stand under' < *stare* 'to stand']

substance abuse *n* the excessive consumption or misuse of a substance for the sake of its nontherapeutic effects on the mind or body, especially drugs or alcohol

substance P *n* a peptide found in body tissues, especially nervous tissue, that is involved in the transmission of pain and in inflammation

~~substancial~~ incorrect spelling of **substantial**

substandard /sub stándərd/ *adj* below the expected or required standard of quality

substantial /səb stánsh'l/ *adj* **1. CONSIDERABLE** considerable in amount, extent, value, or importance **2. STURDY** solidly built **3. FILLING** providing a lot of nourishment **4. RICH** wealthy and prosperous **5. REAL AND TANGIBLE** actual and real in a palpable way **6.** PHILOSOPHY **OF SUBSTANCE** consisting of or involving substance ■ *n* **IMPORTANT PART** an important or essential part [14C. Directly or via French < ecclesiastical Latin *substantialis* 'having substance' (translation of Greek *hupostatikos*) < *substare* (see SUBSTANCE)] —**substantiality** /səb stánshi állәti/ *n*

substantialise *vti* another spelling of **substantialize**

substantialism /səb stánsh'l izəm/ *n* the philosophical doctrine that beings or entities of substantial reality underlie all phenomena —**substantialist** *n*

substantialize /səb stánsh'l īz/ (**-izes, -izing, -ized**), **substantialise** (**-ises, -ising, -ised**) *vti* to make something that is imaginary, theoretical, or spiritual become palpable, or become palpable

substantially /səb stánsh'li/ *adv* **1.** in an extensive, substantial, or ample way **2.** in essence

substantiate /səb stánshi ayt/ (**-ates, -ating, -ated**) *vt* **1.** to confirm that something is true or valid **2.** to give something an actual physical existence [Mid-17C. < medieval Latin *substantiat-*, past participle of *substantiare* 'give substance to' < Latin *substantia* (see SUBSTANCE)] —**substantiable** *adj* —**substantiation** /səb stánshi áysh'n/ *n* —**substantiative** *adj* —**substantiator** *n*

substantive *adj* /səb stántiv, súbstəntiv/ **1. WITH PRACTICAL IMPORTANCE** having practical importance, value, or effect ○ *a substantive agreement* **2. SUBSTANTIAL** substantial in amount or quantity ○ *a substantive meal* **3. ESSENTIAL** relating to the substance of something **4. INDEPENDENT** continuing independently **5.**

GRAM **USED LIKE NOUN** relating to or used like a noun **6.** GRAM **EXPRESSING EXISTENCE** expressing existence, as with the verb 'to be' **7.** LAW **RELATING TO LEGAL PRINCIPLES** relating to the essential principles that a court applies in its work, not to the rules of procedure and practice **8.** INDUST **DIRECTLY ATTACHING AS DYE COLOUR** attaching as a colour directly to a material being dyed without the use of a fixing substance **9.** MIL **PERMANENT** describes a rank or appointment that is permanent ■ *n* /súbstəntiv/ GRAM **NOUN** a noun, or a word or group of words used like a noun [15C. Directly or via French < late Latin *substantivus* < Latin *substantia* (see SUBSTANCE)] —**substantival** /súbstən tī́v'l/ *adj* —**substantively** *adv*

substantive right *n* a basic human right that is regarded as existing naturally and indispensably, e.g. the right to life or liberty

substantivize /súbstənti vīz/ (**-vizes, -vizing, -vized**), **substantivise** (**-vises, -vising, -vised**) *vt* to make a word or words function like a noun —**substantivization** /súbstənti vī záysh'n/ *n*

substation /súb staysh'n/ *n* **1.** a branch of a main electrical power station where electrical current is converted, redistributed, or modified in strength **2.** an office, building, or installation that is a branch of something larger, especially one attached to a larger station

substituent /səb stíttyoo ənt/ *n* an atom or group of atoms that replaces another atom or group in a molecule [Late 19C. < Latin *substituent-*, present participle of *substituere* 'set up under' (see SUBSTITUTE)]

substitute /súbsti tyoot/ *v* (**-tutes, -tuting, -tuted**) **1.** *vti* **REPLACE SOMEBODY OR SOMETHING** to put somebody or something in place of another, or take the place of another (*often passive*) **2.** *vt* CHEM **REPLACE ATOM OR ATOMS** to replace an atom or group of atoms in a molecule with another atom or group **3.** *vt* MATHS **REPLACE MATHEMATICAL ELEMENT** to replace one mathematical element with another of equal value ■ *n* **1.** **REPLACEMENT** somebody or something that takes the place of another ○ *Herbal teas can be a pleasant substitute for coffee or tea.* **2.** SPORTS **REPLACEMENT PLAYER** a team member in a game who is ready to replace another on the field **3.** *ANZ, N Am* GRAM same as **pro-form** [15C. < Latin *substitutus*, past participle of *substituere* 'set up under' < *statuere* (see STATUE)] —**substitutable** *adj* —**substituter** *n*

USAGE See *replace*.

substitute teacher *n N Am* EDUC same as **supply teacher**

substitution /súbsti tyóo sh'n/ *n* **1.** **ACT OF REPLACING** the replacement of somebody or something with another, especially one team member with another on the field **2.** **SOMEBODY OR SOMETHING THAT REPLACES** somebody or something that replaces another, especially one team member who replaces another on the field **3.** MATHS **REPLACEMENT OF MATHEMATICAL ELEMENT** the replacement of one mathematical element with another of equal value **4.** LOGIC **REPLACEMENT OF LOGICAL EXPRESSION** the replacement of one logical expression with another, or a replaced logical expression —**substitutional** *adj* —**substitutionally** *adv*

substitutive /súbsti tyootiv/ *adj* acting or usable as a substitute [Early 17C. Partly < SUBSTITUTE, partly < Latin *substitutivus* < past participle of *substituere* (see SUBSTITUTE)] —**substitutively** *adv* —**substitutivity** /súbsti tyoo tívvəti/ *n*

substrate /súb strayt/ *n* **1.** CHEM a substance that is acted upon in a biochemical reaction **2.** ELECTRONICS a single crystal of a semiconductor used as the basis for an integrated circuit or transistor **3.** BIOL same as **substratum** (sense 6) **4.** BIOL same as **medium** *n* (sense 9) [Early 19C. Anglicization of SUBSTRATUM]

substratosphere /sub stráttə sfeer/ *n* the lowest layer of the Earth's atmosphere, at a height of about 20 km/12 mi. above the Earth

substratum /sub straátəm, -stráytəm/ (*plural* **-ta** /-tə/) *n* **1.** **UNDERLYING BASE** an underlying base, layer, or element **2.** AGRIC same as **subsoil** **3.** GEOL same as **bedrock** (sense 2) **4.** PHOTOGRAPHY **BASE FOR EMULSION** a layer of a substance placed on a photographic film or plate as a foundation for an emulsion **5.** LING **SET OF RETAINED INDIGENOUS LINGUISTIC FEATURES** a set of linguistic features retained from the speech of an indigenous culture, especially one that influences the language of a colonizer **6.** BIOL **NONLIVING FOUNDATION FOR GROWING ORGANISM** the nonliving material or base on which an organism lives or grows **7.** PHILOSOPHY **ESSENCE** the essential substance of something [Mid-17C. < modern Latin < form of past participle of Latin *substernere* 'spread underneath' < *sternere* 'lay or throw down'] —**substratal** *adj* —**substrative** *adj*

substructure /súb strukchər/ *n* **1.** the foundation of an erected structure **2.** any underlying structure that supports or gives strength to something —**substructural** /sub strúkchərəl/ *adj*

subsume /səb syóom/ (**-sumes, -suming, -sumed**) *vt* **1.** to include or incorporate something into a larger order, category, or classification **2.** to show that a rule applies to something [Mid-16C. < medieval Latin *subsumere* 'take up so as to include' < Latin *sumere* 'take'] —**subsumable** *adj*

subsumption /səb súmpsh'n/ *n* **1.** the act of subsuming something, or the fact of being subsumed **2.** something that is subsumed [Mid-17C. < medieval Latin *subsumption-* < past participle of *subsumere* (see SUBSUME)] —**subsumptive** *adj*

subtangent /súb tanjənt/ *n* the part of the x-axis in a two-dimensional coordinate system that is included by the ordinate of a specific point on a curve and the tangent at that point

subtenant /súb tenənt/ *n* a renter of a property from a tenant who in turn rents it from the owner —**subtenancy** *n*

subtend /səb ténd/ (**-tends, -tending, -tended**) *vt* **1.** to be opposite and delimit the extent of an angle or side of a geometric figure **2.** to lie underneath something so as to surround or enclose it [Late 16C. < Latin *subtendere* 'stretch underneath' < *tendere* 'stretch, extend']

subterfuge /súbtər fyooj/ *n* a plan, action, or device designed to hide a real objective, or the process of hiding a real objective [Late 16C. Directly or via French < late Latin *subterfugium* < Latin *subterfugere* 'flee secretly' < *fugere* 'flee']

subterminal /sub túrmin'l/ *adj* positioned very near the end of something

subterranean /súb tə ráyni ən/, **subterraneous** /-ni əss/ *adj* **1.** existing or situated below ground level **2.** existing or carried on in secret [Early 17C. < Latin *subterraneus* 'underground' < *terra* 'earth, land'] —**subterraneanly** *adv*

subtext /súb tekst/ *n* an underlying meaning or message —**subtextual** /sub tékschoo əl/ *adj*

subtidal /sub tī́d'l/ *adj* continuously submerged in the area of a tidal estuary system

subtilise *vti* another spelling of **subtilize**

subtilisin /súbti líssin/ *n* a protein-digesting enzyme produced by bacteria. Use: detergents. [Mid-20C. < Latin *subtilis* (see SUBTLE) in modern Latin sense 'subtle']

subtilize /sútt'l īz/ (**-izes, -izing, -ized**), **subtilise** (**-ises, -ising, -ised**) *v* **1.** *vti* to make or use subtle distinctions in discussing something **2.** *vt* to make something increasingly refined —**subtilization** /sútt'l ī záysh'n/ *n* —**subtilizer** *n*

subtitle /súb tīt'l/ *n* **1.** **CAPTION FOR FOREIGN-LANGUAGE FILM** a printed translation of the dialogue in a foreign-language film, usually appearing at the bottom of the screen **2.** **PRINTED WORDS FOR HEARING-IMPAIRED** the printed text of what is being said in a television programme, provided for the hearing-impaired and usually at the bottom of the screen **3.** **CAPTION IN SILENT FILM** a caption for the action or dialogue of a silent film, appearing at intervals as a full-screen panel **4.** **LESSER TITLE** a second and subsidiary title for something such as a book ■ *vt* (**-tles, -tling, -tled**) **1.** **PROVIDE SUBTITLES FOR SOMETHING** to provide subtitles for a film or television programme **2.** **GIVE SUBTITLE TO BOOK** to give a subtitle to something such as a book —**subtitular** /sub tíchŏolər/ *adj*

subtle /sútt'l/ *adj* **1.** **SLIGHT** slight and not obvious **2.** **PLEASANTLY UNDERSTATED** pleasantly delicate and understated **3.** **ABLE TO MAKE REFINED JUDGMENTS** intelligent, experienced, or sensitive enough to make refined judgments and distinctions **4.** **INGENIOUS** cleverly indirect and ingenious [14C. Via Old French *sutil* < Latin *subtilis* 'fine, thin' < *sub tela* 'beneath the weaving'] —**subtleness** *n* —**subtly** *adv*

subtlety /sútt'lti/ (*plural* **-ties**) *n* **1.** the quality or state of being subtle **2.** a distinction that is difficult to make but is important (*often used in the plural*)

~~subtley~~ incorrect spelling of **subtly**

subtopia /sub tṓpi ə/ *n* suburban development, especially when viewed as falling short of the ideals of city planners [Mid-20C. Blend of SUBURB + UTOPIA] —**subtopian** *adj*

subtotal /súb tōt'l/ *n* a sum of part of a set of figures ■ *vt* (**-tals, -talling, -talled**) to calculate the total of part of a set of figures

subtract /səb trákt/ (**-tracts, -tracting, -tracted**) *v* **1.** *vti* to perform the arithmetical calculation of deducting one number or quantity from another **2.** *vt* to withdraw or take away something from a larger unit [Mid-16C. < Latin *subtract-*, past participle of *subtrahere* 'pull away' < *trahere* 'pull'] —**subtracter** *n*

subtraction /səb tráksh'n/ *n* **1.** MATHS **DEDUCTION OF NUMBER** the act or process of deducting one number or quantity from another. Symbol – **2.** **REMOVAL FROM SOMETHING LARGER** a withdrawal or deduction of something from a larger whole **3.** LAW **WITHDRAWAL OF BENEFIT** the withdrawal or withholding of a benefit

subtractive /səb tráktiv/ *adj* **1.** MATHS **ABLE TO SUBTRACT** having the power to subtract one number or quantity from another **2.** MATHS **INDICATING SUBTRACTION** indicating or needing subtraction **3.** PHYS **REMAINING AFTER ABSORPTION BY TINTED FILTERS** describes the colour that remains after all other components of the visible spectrum have been absorbed by tinted filters

subtrahend /súbtrə hend/ *n* a number that is to be deducted from another number [Late 17C. < Latin *subtrahendus*, literally 'be subtracted', form of *subtrahere* 'pull away' < *trahere* 'pull']

subtropical /sub tróppik'l/ *adj* relating to or found in areas between tropical and temperate regions, and experiencing tropical conditions at some times of the year or near-tropical conditions all year round

subtropics /sub tróppiks/ *npl* the area of the Earth adjacent to the tropics

subulate /súbbyŏolət/ *adj* describes a plant part that is long and thin and tapers to a point [Mid-18C. < modern Latin *subulatus* < Latin *subula* 'awl']

subumbrella /súb um brelə/ *n* the inwardly curving underside of a jellyfish

subunit /súb yoonit/ *n* **1.** a unit that forms part of a larger unit **2.** a part of a large molecule or complex that can be dissociated from the whole without rupture of covalent chemical bonds

subunit vaccine *n* a vaccine that creates a bodily immunity to a virus or bacterium from whose DNA the vaccine is made

suburb /súbburb/ *n* a district, especially a residential one, on the edge of a city or large town [14C. Directly or via French < Latin *suburbium* 'near a city' < *urbs* 'city']

suburban /sə búrbən/ *adj* **1.** **RELATING TO SUBURB** relating to, belonging to, or located in a suburb **2.** **RESEMBLING SUBURB** resembling a suburb or its residents **3.** **UNEXCITING AND CONVENTIONAL** characteristic of the undesirable aspects of a suburb or its residents, especially in being dull, conventional, and materialistic

suburbanise *vt* another spelling of **suburbanize**

suburbanite /sə búrbə nīt/ *n* somebody who lives in the suburbs

suburbanize /sə búrbə nīz/ (**-izes, -izing, -ized**), **suburbanise** (**-ises, -ising, -ised**) *vt* to give something the appearance or character of a suburb —**suburbanization** /sə búrbə nī záysh'n/ *n*

suburbia /sə búrbi ə/ *n* suburbs collectively, or the people who live in them

subvention /səb vénsh'n/ *n* (*formal*) **1.** a sum of money given by an official body such as a government, especially to an institution of learning, study, or research **2.** the giving of help or support, especially financial [15C. Via French < late Latin *subvention-* < Latin *subvenire* 'come to somebody's help' < *venire* 'come'] —**subventionary** *adj*

subversion /səb vúrsh'n/ *n* **1.** an action, plan, or activity intended to undermine or overthrow a government or other institution **2.** the destruction or

ruining of something [14C. Directly or via French < late Latin *subversion-* < Latin *subvers-*, past participle of *subvertere* (see SUBVERT)]

subversive /səb vúrssiv/ *adj* intended or likely to undermine or overthrow a government or other institution ■ *n* somebody involved in activities intended to undermine or overthrow a government or other institution [Mid-17C. < medieval Latin *subversivus* < Latin *subvers-* (see SUBVERSION)] —**subversively** *adv* —**subversiveness** *n*

subvert /səb vúrt/ (**-verts, -verting, -verted**) *vt* to undermine or overthrow a government or other institution [14C. Directly or via French < Latin *subvertere* 'turn from below' < *vertere* 'to turn'] —**subverter** *n*

subvirus /súb vīrəss/ *n* an infective agent that is structurally more primitive than a virus, e.g. a prion —**subviral** /sub vīrəl/ *adj*

subvocal /sub vṓk'l/ *adj* mouthed or mentally pictured but not sounded out loud —**subvocally** *adv*

subvocalize /sub vṓkə līz/ (**-izes, -izing, -ized**), **subvocalise** (**-ises, -ising, -ised**) *vti* to mouth words or other speech sounds without saying them out loud —**subvocalization** /sub vṓkə lī záysh'n/ *n*

subway /súb way/ *n* **1.** a passage under a road or railway for pedestrians to get to the other side **2.** *Scotland, N Am* RAIL same as **underground** *n* (sense 1)

subzero /sub zeérō/ *adj* being below zero degrees in temperature

succah *n* JUDAISM another spelling of **sukkah**

~~**succede**~~ incorrect spelling of **succeed**

succeed /sək seéd/ (**-ceeds, -ceeding, -ceeded**) *v* **1.** *vi* ACHIEVE INTENTION to manage to do what is planned or attempted ○ *We succeeded in persuading them to change their decision.* **2.** *vi* GAIN FAME, WEALTH, OR POWER to realize a goal, especially to gain fame, wealth, or power **3.** *vi* MAKE SIGNIFICANT PROGRESS to do well in an activity, making admirable progress or recording impressive achievements ○ *She was one of the first women to succeed in the sciences.* **4.** *vi* PROSPER to thrive or prosper **5.** *vti* BE NEXT AFTER SOMEBODY to be the next person to occupy a post or position after somebody ○ *Mary succeeded him as president over a year ago.* ○ *will succeed to the title* **6.** *vt* FOLLOW SOMETHING IN TIME to come after something in time (*often passive*) **7.** *vi* BE INHERITED BY SOMEBODY to pass to somebody as an inheritance (*formal*) [14C. Directly or via French < Latin *succedere* 'go after' < *cedere* 'give way'] —**succeedable** *adj* —**succeeder** *n*

succentor /sək séntər/ *n* a deputy to a precentor at a church or cathedral [Mid-17C. < late Latin < Latin *succinere* 'sing to' < *canere* 'sing'] —**succentorship** *n*

succès de scandale /syŏŏk sáy də skaan daál/ (*plural same*) *n* something that is successful because it is controversial, e.g. a book, film, or play, or the success that is gained as a result of controversy [< French, 'success of scandal']

succès d'estime /syŏŏk sáy des teém/ (*plural same*) *n* a book, film, or play that is successful with critics but not with the public, or the success that is gained through critical acclaim [< French, 'success of esteem']

succès fou /syŏŏk sáy fóo/ (*plural* **succès fous** /*pronunc. same*/) *n* an overwhelming success [< French, 'mad success']

~~**succesful**~~ incorrect spelling of **successful**

~~**succesive**~~ incorrect spelling of **successive**

success /sək séss/ *n* **1.** ACHIEVEMENT OF INTENTION the achievement of something planned or attempted **2.** ATTAINMENT OF FAME, WEALTH, OR POWER impressive achievement, especially the attainment of fame, wealth, or power **3.** SOMETHING THAT TURNS OUT WELL something that turns out as planned or intended **4.** SOMEBODY SUCCESSFUL somebody who is wealthy, famous, or powerful because of a record of achievement [Mid-16C. < Latin *successus* < past participle of *succedere* (see SUCCEED)]

successful /sək séssf'l/ *adj* **1.** TURNING OUT WELL having the intended result **2.** POPULAR popular and making a lot of money ○ *a successful play* **3.** WITH RECORD OF SIGNIFICANT ACHIEVEMENTS having achieved or gained much, especially wealth, fame, or power —**successfully** *adv* —**successfulness** *n*

succession /sək sésh'n/ *n* **1.** SERIES IN TIME a sequence of people or things coming one after the other in time ○ *rented a succession of dingy flats around town* ○ *a succession of blows* **2.** FOLLOWING ON the following on of one thing after another ○ *three wins in succession* **3.** TAKING UP OF TITLE OR POSITION the assumption of a position or title, the right to take up a position or title, or the order in which a position or title is taken up **4.** ECOL DEVELOPMENT OF PLANT AND ANIMAL COMMUNITY the series of changes that create a fully-fledged plant and animal community, e.g. from the colonization of bare rock to the establishment of a forest [14C. Directly or via French < Latin *succession-* < past participle of *succedere* (see SUCCEED)] —**successional** *adj* —**successionally** *adv*

succession crop *n* a crop that follows another crop as a successive planting, or a crop of a variety with a different rate of growth

succession state *n* a nation created from territory once ruled by another, larger nation

successive /sək séssiv/ *adj* following in an uninterrupted sequence [15C. < medieval Latin *successivus* < Latin *success-*, past participle of *succedere* (see SUCCEED)] —**successively** *adv* —**successiveness** *n*

successor /sək séssər/ *n* somebody or something that follows another and takes up the same position [13C. < Latin < *success-*, past participle of *succedere* (see SUCCEED)] —**successoral** *adj*

success story *n* somebody or something that is very successful

succi ZOOL plural of **succus**

succinate /súksi nayt/ *n* an ester of succinic acid [Late 18C. < SUCCINIC ACID]

succinct /sək síngkt/ *adj* expressed with brevity and clarity, with no wasted words [15C. Directly or via French < Latin *succinctus*, past participle of *succingere* 'encompass from below' < *cingere* 'gird'] —**succinctly** *adv* —**succinctness** *n*

succinic acid /sək sínnik-/ *n* a colourless odourless acid. Source: amber, plant and animal tissues, artificially synthesized. Use: manufacture of lacquers, perfumes, pharmaceuticals. Formula: $C_4H_6O_4$. [< Latin *succinum* 'amber' < *succus* 'juice, moisture, sap']

succinylcholine /súksi nīl kṓ leen/ *n N Am* same as **suxamethonium** [Mid-20C. < SUCCINIC ACID]

succor *n, vt* US spelling of **succour** (*literary*)

succory /súkəri/ *n* PLANTS same as **chicory** (sense 1) [Mid-16C. Alteration of obsolete French *cicorée* (see CHICORY) after Middle Low German *suckerie*, Middle Dutch *sūkerie*]

succotash /súkə tash/ *n* in the United States, sweetcorn and butter beans cooked together, often with tomatoes [Mid-18C. < Narraganset *msiquatash* 'boiled maize and beans']

Succoth *n* JUDAISM another spelling of **Sukkoth**

succour /súkər/ (*literary*) *n* **1.** HELP FOR SOMEBODY OR SOMETHING help or relief for somebody or something in a difficult or unpleasant situation **2.** SOMEBODY OR SOMETHING GIVING HELP somebody or something that provides help or relief ■ *vt* (**-cours, -couring, -coured**) GIVE HELP TO SOMEBODY OR SOMETHING to provide help or relief to somebody or something in a difficult or unpleasant situation [13C. Via Old French *sucurs* < medieval Latin *succursus* < Latin *succurrere* 'run under' < *currere* 'run'] —**succourable** *adj* —**succourer** *n*

succubus /súkyŏŏbəss/ (*plural* **-bi** /-bī/ or **-buses**) *n* in medieval times, a woman demon that was believed to have sexual intercourse with men while they were asleep [14C. < medieval Latin, alteration of late Latin *succuba* 'somebody who lies under another' < Latin *cubare* 'lie down']

succulent /súkyŏŏlənt/ *adj* **1.** JUICY AND TASTY juicy and pleasant to the taste **2.** WITH FLESHY WATER-STORING PARTS describes plants that have thick fleshy leaves and stems that can store water **3.** INTERESTING exciting and interesting (*informal*) ■ *n* SUCCULENT PLANT a plant with thick fleshy leaves and stems that can store water, e.g. a cactus or aloe [Early 17C. Directly or via French < Latin *succulentus* < *succus* 'juice, moisture, sap'] —**succulence** *n* —**succulently** *adv*

succumb /sə kúm/ (**-cumbs, -cumbing, -cumbed**) *vi* **1.** to be unable to resist or oppose something **2.** to die from an illness or injury [15C. Directly or via French < Latin *succumbere* 'lie under' < *cumbere* 'lie'] —**succumber** *n*

SYNONYMS See ***yield.***

succus /súkəss/ (*plural* **-ci** /-sī, -see/) *n* a fluid, especially a secretion, of plant or animal origin [Late 18C. < Latin, 'juice, moisture, sap']

succuss /sə kúss/ (**-cusses, -cussing, -cussed**) *vt* to shake a patient in order to detect the presence of air or fluid in a body cavity, especially the space between the lungs and the chest wall [Mid-19C. < Latin *succuss-* 'shaken', past participle of *succutere* < *sub* 'away' + *quatere*, 'shake'] —**succussion** *n* —**succussive** *adj*

~~**suceed**~~ incorrect spelling of **succeed**

~~**sucessful**~~ incorrect spelling of **successful**

~~**sucessive**~~ incorrect spelling of **successive**

such /such/ *adj* **1.** OF PARTICULAR KIND of the kind mentioned or understood from the context ○ *I've never heard such nonsense.* **2.** SO MUCH to so great an extent or degree ○ *Don't be such a fool.* ■ *adv* VERY extremely or to a great degree ○ *I had never seen such lovely flowers.* ■ *pron* THIS this, or something of this kind ○ *Such was his fate.* [Old English *swilc* < Germanic, 'so formed'] ◇ **such as** used for giving an example ○ *desert plants such as cacti* ◇ **such ... as** used for making comparisons ○ *It wasn't such a good holiday as we thought it would be.* ◇ **such as it is** being what it is and no more

USAGE such ... as or **such ... that?** *We are such stuff as dreams are made on* (Shakespeare, *The Tempest*, Act 4, scene 1, modernized spelling). In sentences of this type, making a comparison, ***such*** is followed by *as* and not by a relative pronoun such as *that* or *who*: *The new law affects only such people as* [not *that*] *are eligible for supplementary benefit.* However, the construction *such ... that* is correctly used to indicate the consequence of a stated circumstance: *The country faces such hardship that it will need a great deal of foreign aid.*

such and such *adj* not specified or named ■ *pron* something that is not specified or named

suchlike /súch līk/ *pron* others of the same kind as those just mentioned (*informal*) ■ *det* similar to the kind just mentioned

suchness /súchnəss/ *n* an essential quality or condition

Suchow ➧ **Suzhou**

suck /suk/ *v* (**sucks, sucking, sucked**) **1.** *vti* DRAW LIQUID OUT WITH MOUTH to draw the liquid out of something with the mouth ○ *The baby sucked on her bottle.* **2.** *vti* MAKE PULLING MOUTH MOVEMENTS ON SOMETHING to hold something in the mouth and make movements with the tongue and lips as if drawing liquid out of it ○ *sucked his thumb* **3.** *vti* MAKE SOMETHING DISSOLVE IN MOUTH to consume something by making it slowly dissolve in the mouth, rolling the tongue around it and making pulling movements with the cheeks and lips ○ *sucking lozenges for a sore throat* **4.** *vt* EXTRACT SOMETHING to draw something out of a container (*often passive*) ○ *Fuel is sucked into the cylinder.* **5.** *vt* PULL SOMETHING IRRESISTIBLY to pull or draw something somewhere with a powerful or irresistible force ○ *The swirling currents suck swimmers under.* **6.** *vi N Am* BE VERY BAD to be very bad or inferior (*slang*) ○ *The movie really sucked, so we walked out.* ■ *n* ACT OF SUCKING SOMETHING an act of sucking something [Old English *sūcan* < Indo-European, 'take liquid'] ◇ **a fair suck of the sauce** *Aus* a fair chance

suck in *v* **1.** *vt* INVOLVE SOMEBODY IN SOMETHING to make somebody become more and more involved in something in a way that he or she is unable to prevent **2.** *vti* BREATHE IN to breathe in sharply, or breathe something in sharply **3.** *vt* DECEIVE SOMEBODY to trick or deceive somebody (*slang*)

suck off *vt* an offensive term meaning to perform fellatio on a man (*slang*)

suck up to *vt* to try to please or win the favour of somebody important by being extremely flattering or helpful (*informal*)

sucker /súkər/ *n* **1.** SOMEBODY EASILY FOOLED an easily fooled or tricked person (*informal*) **2.** SOMEBODY WHO GIVES IN EASILY somebody who has little resistance to and is easily influenced by something (*informal*) ○ *a sucker*

for a pair of big blue eyes **3.** SOMETHING THAT ADHERES BY SUCTION a round, slightly cupped piece of plastic or rubber that when pressed onto a flat surface sticks to it by suction. N Am term **suction cup 4.** MARINE BIOL ORGAN THAT CLINGS BY SUCTION a muscular organ, found on the tentacles of octopuses and similar sea animals, used to cling to or hold things such as prey **5.** ZOOL ORGAN FOR SUCKING IN FOOD the mouth of an animal such as the leech or lamprey that is adapted for sucking in food **6.** BOT SHOOT GROWING FROM ROOT a shoot that grows from the underground root or stem of a plant and is often able to produce its own roots and grow into a new plant **7.** US PERSON OR THING used to refer, usually with emphasis or some degree of irritation, to any person or thing somebody happens to be dealing with (*slang*) ○ *Let's see if we can get this sucker to work.* **8.** ZOOL ANIMAL LIVING ON MOTHER'S MILK a young animal that is still taking milk from its mother, e.g. a young pig or whale **9.** MECH ENG SUCTION PUMP PISTON the piston or piston valve of a suction pump **10.** MECH ENG SUCTION PIPE a pipe through which a liquid is drawn by means of suction **11.** FISH FRESHWATER FISH a bony bottom-feeding freshwater fish with a downward-facing sucking mouth without teeth. Native to: North America. Family: Catostomidae. ■ *v* (**-ers, -ering, -ered**) **1.** *vt* N Am TRICK SOMEBODY to take advantage of somebody's ignorance, innocence, or foolishness to trick him or her (*informal*) ○ *got suckered into the scheme* **2.** *vi* BOT PRODUCE SUCKERS to produce or form suckers on a root or stem (*refers to plants*) **3.** *vt* BOT REMOVE SUCKERS to remove the suckers from a plant

suckerfish /súkər fish/ (*plural same* or **-fishes**) *n* FISH same as **remora**

sucker punch *n* N Am a blow delivered when somebody is not expecting it

sucker-punch *vt* N Am to hit somebody with a sucker punch

sucking /súking/ *adj* still feeding on its mother's milk and not yet weaned ○ *sucking pig*

sucking louse *n* a wingless primitive parasitic insect with mouthparts specially adapted for sucking body fluids, e.g. the head louse and pubic louse that infest human beings. Suborder: Siphunculata.

suckle /súk'l/ (**-les, -ling, -led**) *v* **1.** *vti* to take milk from a mother's breast, teat, or udder, or allow a young child or animal to do this **2.** *vt* to nourish somebody or something (*literary*) [14C. Probably back-formation < SUCKLING] —**suckler** *n*

suckling /súkling/ *n* a human baby or young animal that is still feeding on its mother's milk, e.g. a calf or pig [13C. < SUCK]

sucks /suks/ *interj* used to express disappointment, contempt, or derision (*informal*) ○ *Sucks to her! Who cares what she thinks?*

sucralose /soókrə lōz/ *n* an artificial noncaloric sweetener created from sugar by replacing three hydroxyl groups with three chlorine atoms

sucrase /soó krayz, syoó-/ *n* BIOCHEM same as **invertase** [Early 20C. < SUCROSE + -ASE]

sucre /soó kray/ *n* formerly, the main unit of currency in Ecuador [Late 19C. After Antonio José de SUCRE]

Sucre /soó kray/ judicial capital of Bolivia, located in the centre of the country, southeast of La Paz. Population: 178,426 (1998).

Sucre, Antonio José de (1795–1830) Venezuelan-born South American soldier, nationalist leader, and president of Bolivia (1826–28). After helping to liberate Ecuador, Peru, and Bolivia from Spanish rule, he became Bolivia's first president.

---

sucrose /soó krōss, syoó-/ *n* a disaccharide found naturally in many plants. Use: production of sugar. Formula: $C_{12}H_{22}O_{11}$. [Mid-19C. < French *sucre* 'sugar']

suction /súksh'n/ *n* **1.** the physical force created by a difference in pressure such as that caused by sucking a liquid through a straw **2.** the act or process of sucking [Early 17C. < late Latin *suction-* < past participle of *sugere* 'suck'] —**suctional** *adj*

suction cap *n* same as **sucker** (sense 7)

suction cup *n* N Am same as **sucker** *n* (sense 3)

suction pump *n* a pump that works by means of the suction created when a piston is moved up and down inside a cylinder

suction stop *n* PHON same as **click**[1] *n* (sense 4) (*technical*)

suctorial /suk táwri əl/ *adj* **1.** specially adapted for sucking or for clinging on by suction **2.** having one or more suckers for feeding or for clinging on to something [Mid-19C. < modern Latin *suctorius* < past participle of Latin *sugere* 'suck']

Sudan

Sudan /soo dán/ **1.** largest country in Africa, in the northeast of the continent, south of Egypt. Language: Arabic. Currency: dinar. Capital: Khartoum. Population: 38,114,160 (2003). Area: 2,505,800 sq. km/967,490 sq. mi. Official name **Republic of the Sudan 2.** region of savanna and dry grassland in West Africa, between the Sahara and the tropical forest belt —**Sudanese** /soódə neéz/ *n, adj*

Sudanic /soo dánnik/ *n* GROUP OF LANGUAGES SPOKEN IN SUDAN a group of Chari-Nile languages spoken in Sudan ■ *adj* **1.** OF SUDANIC relating to Sudanic **2.** OF SUDAN relating to Sudan, or to its people or culture

sudatorium /soódə táwri əm, syoódə táwri əm/ (*plural* **-ria** /-ri ə/) *n* a room, especially in an ancient Roman bath-house, in which people are made to sweat by hot air or steam [Mid-18C. < Latin < form of *sudatorius* 'for sweating' < *sudare* 'to sweat']

Sudbury /súdbəri, súdbri/ city in east-central Ontario, Canada, north of Georgian Bay. Population: 103,879 (2001).

sudd /sud/ *n* a floating mass of reeds and weeds that obstructs some tropical rivers, especially the White Nile [Late 19C. < Arabic, 'obstruction' < *sadda* 'obstruct']

sudden /súdd'n/ *adj* done or happening quickly or unexpectedly [13C. Via Anglo-Norman *sudein* < Latin *subitaneus* < *subire* 'go secretly' < *ire* 'go'] —**suddenly** *adv* —**suddenness** *n* ◇ **all of a sudden** in a sudden and unexpected way

sudden death *n* the continuation of play in a tied sports contest until one team or player scores, that team or player being declared the winner

sudden infant death syndrome *n* MED same as **cot death** (*technical*)

sudden oak death *n* a serious disease caused by the fungus *Phytophthora ramorum* that affects many tree species. It has led to the death of various species of oak in California and Oregon, although European species appear to be less at risk.

sudoriferous /soódə ríffərəss, syoódə-/ *adj* producing sweat [Late 16C. < late Latin *sudorifer* 'sudorific' < Latin *sudor* 'sweat']

sudorific /soódə ríffik, syoódə-/ *adj* causing the production of sweat ■ *n* a drug or other agent that causes sweating [Early 17C. < modern Latin *sudorificus* < late Latin *sudorifer* (see SUDORIFEROUS)]

Sudra /soódrə/, **Shudra** /shoódrə/ *n* **1.** the lowest of the four Hindu castes, the members of which were segregated as ritually unclean by the other castes because they performed tasks that were regarded as polluting. There is a wide range of subgroups within the Sudra caste, some being landowners. **2.** a member of the Sudra caste [Mid-17C. < Sanskrit *śūdra*]

suds /sudz/ *npl* (*takes a plural verb*) **1.** BUBBLES a froth of bubbles on the surface of soapy water **2.** SOAPY WATER water with soap or detergent dissolved in it ○ *rinsed the glass in the suds* ■ *n* N Am same as **beer** (sense 1) (*slang; takes a singular verb*) ■ *v* (**sudses, sudsing, sudsed**) N Am **1.** *vt* WASH SOMETHING to rinse or wash something in soapy water **2.** *vi* CREATE FOAM to form suds [Mid-16C. Probably < Middle Dutch *sudse* 'marsh, bog'] —**sudsy** *adj*

sue /syoo, soo/ (**sues, suing, sued**) *v* **1.** *vti* to take legal action against somebody to obtain something, usually compensation for a wrong **2.** *vi* to make a humble, earnest, or begging request for something (*formal*) ○ *sued for peace after the long siege* [12C. Via Anglo-Norman *suer* 'follow' < Latin *sequî*] —**suable** *adj* —**suer** *n*

suede /swayd/ *n* **1.** LEATHER WITH VELVETY SURFACE leather with the flesh side turned outward and rubbed up to make a velvety nap **2.** FABRIC LIKE SUEDE a woven fabric that looks like suede ■ *vti* (**suedes, sueding, sueded**) GIVE SOMETHING VELVETY NAP to give leather or fabric a velvety nap [Mid-17C. < French *gants de Suède* 'gloves of Sweden'] —**sueded** *adj*

suedette /sway dét/ *n* a synthetic fabric with the appearance and texture of suede. Use: clothing, upholstery.

suet /soó it/ *n* a hard white fat found on the kidneys and loins of sheep and cattle. Use: cooking, tallow. [14C. Probably < Anglo-Norman, literally 'small suet' < *sue, seu* 'tallow, suet' < Latin *sebum*] —**suety** *adj*

Suetonius /swee tóni əss/, **Gaius Tranquillus** (69?–140) Roman biographer and historian. His works include biographies of 12 Roman emperors.

suet pudding *n* a sweet or savoury pudding made with suet, usually cooked by boiling or steaming

Suez /soó iz/ port in northeastern Egypt, at the head of the Gulf of Suez and at the southern end of the Suez Canal. Population: 417,000 (1998).

Suez Canal canal in northeastern Egypt, connecting the Mediterranean and the Red Sea. It was opened in 1869. Length: 195 km/121 mi.

Suff. *abbr* Suffolk

suffer /súffər/ (**-fers, -fering, -fered**) *v* **1.** *vti* FEEL PAIN to feel pain or great discomfort in body or mind **2.** *vti* UNDERGO SOMETHING UNPLEASANT to experience or undergo something unpleasant or undesirable **3.** *vti* ENDURE SOMETHING to put up with something painful or unpleasant ○ *She may be rich and famous now, but she certainly suffered for her art when she was younger.* ○ *I do not suffer fools gladly.* **4.** *vi* HAVE ILLNESS to have a disease or a physical or psychological condition ○ *suffers from asthma* **5.** *vi* HAVE A WEAKNESS to have a bad quality, weakness, or flaw ○ *Their whole manifesto suffers from a lack of vision.* **6.** *vi* APPEAR TO BE LESS GOOD to become or appear to be less good ○ *suffers in comparison* **7.** *vi* BE ADVERSELY AFFECTED to be adversely affected by something ○ *The business suffered when the partnership was dissolved.* **8.** *vt* ALLOW SOMETHING to allow something to happen or to be done (*archaic or literary*) ○ *Suffer the little children to come unto me.* [12C. Via Anglo-Norman *suffrir* < Latin *sufferre* 'carry up from underneath, sustain' < *ferre* 'carry'] —**sufferable** *adj* —**sufferer** *n*

~~**sufferage**~~ incorrect spelling of **suffrage**

sufferance /súffərənss/ *n* **1.** TOLERANCE OF SOMETHING PROHIBITED tacit permission for or tolerance of something, because no action is taken to prevent it **2.** ENDURANCE OF DIFFICULTY OR PAIN the capacity to withstand difficulty or pain **3.** PATIENT ENDURANCE the fact of enduring hardship patiently (*archaic*) ◇ **on sufferance** as a result of permission or consent given reluctantly and liable to be withdrawn

suffering /súffəring/ *n* **1.** physical or psychological pain and distress **2.** an experience that is painful or distressing

---

sucrose

suffice /sə físs/ (-fices, -ficing, -ficed) *vti* to be enough for somebody or something [14C. < Old French *suffic-* < Latin *sufficere* 'make up to' < *facere* 'make'] ◇ **suffice it to say that** used to indicate that what you are saying is all that needs to be said on a subject

~~sufficiant~~ incorrect spelling of **sufficient**

sufficiency /sə físh'nssi/ (*plural* -cies) *n* **1.** an amount of something that is enough for somebody or something **2.** the fact or state of being enough

sufficient /sə físh'nt/ *adj* as much as is needed [14C. Directly or via French < Latin *sufficient-*, present participle of *sufficere* (see SUFFICE)] —**sufficiently** *adv*

sufficient reason *n* the philosophical principle that nothing happens by chance and that an explanation must be available for everything

suffix *n* /súffiks/ a letter or group of letters added at the end of a word or word part to form another word, e.g. '-ly' in 'quickly' or '-ing' in 'talking' ■ *vt* /súffiks, sə fíks/ (-fixes, -fixing, -fixed) to add something as a suffix [Early 17C. < modern Latin *suffixum* < form of Latin *suffixus*, past participle of *suffigere* 'fasten underneath' < *figere* 'fix'] —**suffixal** *adj* —**suffixation** /súffik sáysh'n/ *n*

suffocate /súffə kayt/ (-cates, -cating, -cated) *vti* **1.** STOP BREATHING to deprive somebody of air or prevent somebody from breathing, or be unable to breathe **2.** DIE FROM LACK OF AIR to die from lack of air, or kill somebody by stopping him or her from breathing **3.** FEEL, OR MAKE SOMEBODY, TOO WARM to feel uncomfortable through excessive heat and lack of fresh air, or make somebody feel uncomfortable in this way **4.** PREVENT SOMEBODY OR SOMETHING FROM DEVELOPING to confine and restrict somebody or something with adverse effects, or be or feel confined and restricted in development or self-expression [15C. < Latin *suffocat-*, past participle of *suffocare* 'narrow up' < *fauc-* 'throat, narrow entrance'] —**suffocating** *adj* —**suffocatingly** *adv* —**suffocation** /súffə káysh'n/ *n* —**suffocative** *adj*

Suffolk[1] /súffək/ county in East Anglia, eastern England. It is largely agricultural. Ipswich is the county town. Population: 668,553 (2001). Area: 3,800 sq. km/1,467 sq. mi.

Suffolk[2] /súffək/ *n* a large black-faced hornless sheep belonging to a breed that originated in England and is kept for meat [Mid-19C. After SUFFOLK[1]]

Suffolk punch *n* a powerful horse with short legs and a chestnut-brown coat, belonging to a breed that originated in England and is used for pulling loads such as ploughs or carts [< dialect *punch* 'stocky draught horse', shortening of PUNCHINELLO]

suffragan /súffrəgən/ *n* **1.** a Christian bishop appointed to assist the main bishop in a diocese **2.** the Christian bishop of a diocese who is an assistant to the archbishop of the province to which the diocese belongs [14C. Via French < medieval Latin *suffraganeus* 'assisting' < Latin *suffragium* 'support, a vote'] —**suffragan** *adj* —**suffraganship** *n*

suffrage /súffrij/ *n* **1.** RIGHT TO VOTE the right to vote in public elections **2.** ACT OF VOTING a vote or the act of voting (*archaic*) **3.** RELIG SHORT PRAYER a short prayer on behalf of somebody, especially a prayer said as part of a Christian litany [14C. Directly or via French < Latin *suffragium* 'support, a vote']

suffragette /súffrə jét/ *n* a woman campaigning for the right of women to vote in elections, especially one who took part in militant protests in the United Kingdom in the early 20th century —**suffragettism** *n*

suffragist /súffrəjist/ *n* a supporter of the extension of the right to vote to a particular group, especially to women, or to all people above a particular age —**suffragism** *n*

suffuse /sə fyóoz/ (-fuses, -fusing, -fused) *vt* to spread over or through something (*usually passive*) ◇ *A blush suffused his face with colour.* [Late 16C. < Latin *suffus-*, past participle of *suffundere* 'pour from below' < *fundere* 'pour'] —**suffusion** *n* —**suffusive** /sə fyóossiv/ *adj*

Sufi /sóofi/ (*plural* -fis) *n* a Muslim mystic [Mid-17C. < Arabic *ṣūfī* 'woollen'; because of their woollen garments] —**Sufi** *adj* —**Sufic** *adj* —**Sufism** /sóo fístik/ *adj*

~~suficient~~ incorrect spelling of **sufficient**

sugar /shóoggər/ *n* **1.** SWEET-TASTING SUBSTANCE a sweet-tasting substance, usually in the form of tiny hard white or brown grains. Source: sugar cane, sugar beet. Use: sweetener for food, drinks. **2.** PORTION OF SUGAR a spoonful, lump, cube, or other portion of sugar ◇ *likes his coffee black with two sugars* **3.** SWEET CARBOHYDRATE a simple carbohydrate that is sweet-tasting, crystalline, and soluble in water **4.** TERM OF ENDEARMENT used as a term of endearment (*informal*) **5.** WAY OF MAKING SOMETHING MORE AGREEABLE something used as a means of persuasion or to make a difficult or unpleasant thing seem less so **6.** STRONG DRUG a strong drug, e.g. heroin or LSD (*dated slang*) ■ *v* (-ars, -aring, -ared) **1.** *vt* ADD SUGAR TO SOMETHING to add sugar to food or a drink **2.** *vi* MAKE SUGAR to make sugar or form sugar crystals **3.** *vi* MAKE MAPLE SYRUP to boil maple sap to make maple syrup and maple sugar **4.** *vt* TRY TO MAKE SOMETHING MORE AGREEABLE to try to make something more appealing or flattering, or to make something unpleasant seem less so ■ *interj* EXPRESSION OF ANNOYANCE used to express annoyance [13C. Via French and medieval Latin < Arabic *sukkar* < Sanskrit *śarkarā* 'grit, ground sugar'] —**sugared** *adj* —**sugarless** *adj*

sugar apple *n* TREES same as **sweetsop**

sugar beans *npl* S Africa dried beans that are reddish or brown speckled

sugar beet *n* a variety of beet with a large whitish conical root that is an important commercial source of sugar. Latin name: *Beta vulgaris*.

sugarbird /shóoggər burd/ *n* a nectar-eating bird with dull brownish feathers, a long curved beak, and a very long tail. Native to: Africa. Genus: *Promerops*.

sugar bush *n* a wood or group of trees consisting mainly of sugar maples

sugar candy *n* sugar in the form of large crystals, made by suspending a string or stick in a strong sugar solution and allowing crystals to form and grow

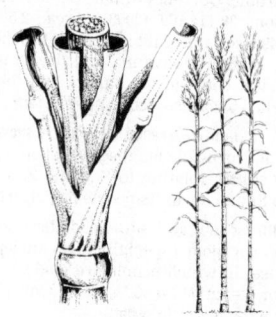

sugar cane

sugar cane *n* a tall tough-stemmed species of grass grown in warm regions throughout the world as a source of sugar, which is obtained from its sweet sap. Latin name: *Saccharum officinarum*. (*hyphenated when used before a noun*)

sugarcoat /shóoggər kṓt/ (-coats, -coating, -coated) *vt* **1.** to enclose something in a hard sugar shell, or coat something with sugar **2.** to make something unpleasant seem less so

sugar daddy *n* a rich man who gives money and gifts to a younger partner in a relationship (*informal*)

sugar diabetes *n* MED same as **diabetes mellitus** (*not in technical use*)

sugar glider *n* an opossum that feeds on flowers, sap, and insects and has flaps of skin attached to its limbs enabling it to glide from tree to tree. Native to: eastern Australia. Latin name: *Petaurus norfolcensis*.

sugar gum *n* a small eucalyptus tree with smooth bark, barrel-shaped fruit, and sweet-tasting leaves. Latin name: *Eucalyptus cladocalyx*.

sugar loaf *n* **1.** a solid cone-shaped mass of refined sugar **2.** something that has a conical shape like a cone of sugar, e.g. a hill

Sugarloaf Mountain

Sugarloaf Mountain /shóoggər lṓf-/ peak on the edge of Rio de Janeiro, Brazil, that provides a panoramic view of the city. Height: 395 m./1,296 ft.

sugar maple *n* a maple tree from whose sweet sap maple sugar and maple syrup are made. Native to: North America. Latin name: *Acer saccharum*.

sugar of lead *n* INDUST same as **lead acetate**

sugar pea *n* a variety of garden pea with an edible thin flat pod. Latin name: *Pisum sativum*.

sugarplum /shóoggər plum/ *n* a small round sweet made of boiled and flavoured sugar

sugar snap, **sugar snap pea** *n* PLANTS, FOOD same as **sugar pea**

sugar soap *n* a strong alkaline mixture of soap and washing soda used, e.g. for stripping paint or for cleaning surfaces before they are painted

sugary /shóoggəri/ *adj* **1.** CONTAINING SUGAR containing a great deal of sugar **2.** LIKE SUGAR looking or tasting like sugar **3.** EXAGGERATEDLY PLEASANT exaggeratedly and often insincerely pleasant or amiable **4.** SENTIMENTAL excessively sentimental —**sugariness** *n*

suggest /sə jést/ (-gests, -gesting, -gested) *vt* **1.** REFER SOMEBODY OR SOMETHING FOR CONSIDERATION to propose somebody or something as a possible choice, plan, or course of action for somebody else to consider ◇ *He couldn't do the job himself but he suggested that John might.* ◇ *Feel free to suggest something else.* **2.** REMIND SOMEBODY OF SOMETHING to remind somebody of something or make somebody think of something ◇ *The sound of the flute is meant to suggest the rippling of a brook.* **3.** IMPLY SOMETHING to imply or hint at something ◇ *I'm not suggesting the deal is off, but we may need to renegotiate.* **4.** INDICATE SOMETHING AS LIKELY to indicate that something is likely ◇ *Declining catches suggest the area is over-fished.* [Early 16C. Back-formation < SUGGESTION] —**suggester** *n*

SYNONYMS See *recommend*.

suggestible /sə jéstəb'l/ *adj* **1.** easily influenced by other people **2.** capable of being suggested —**suggestibility** /sə jéstə bílləti/ *n* —**suggestibly** *adv*

suggestion /sə jéschən/ *n* **1.** IDEA OR PROPOSAL an idea or proposal put forward for consideration ◇ *If I might make a suggestion, why don't we ask Ed to help us?* **2.** SLIGHT TRACE a slight trace, indication, or hint of something ◇ *There is no suggestion of bias in her recommendation.* **3.** ACT OF SUGGESTING the act or process of suggesting something ◇ *He was roused to fury by the mere suggestion of their innocence.* **4.** ABILITY TO CONJURE UP ASSOCIATIONS the ability of words or images to conjure up ideas or feelings, the process by which they do this, or an idea or image conjured up by something **5.** PUTTING IDEAS INTO SOMEBODY'S MIND the deliberate introduction into somebody's mind of an opinion, belief, or instruction, e.g. through hypnosis or advertising, so that it is accepted or acted on as that person's own idea ◇ *The power of suggestion is used in TV commercials to make us want a product.* [14C. Directly or via French < Latin *suggestion-* < *suggerere* 'bring up' < *gerere* 'bring']

suggestive /sə jéstiv/ *adj* **1.** able to conjure up ideas or images in the mind, or able to start a train of thought **2.** implying or hinting at something rude or improper —**suggestively** *adv* —**suggestiveness** *n*

Suharto /sóo haártō/, Mohamed (*b.* 1921) president of Indonesia (1967–98). His authoritarian regime developed a petroleum-based economy. He was forced

to resign as the economy declined and his regime was accused of corruption.

Sui /sway/ *n* a Chinese dynasty lasting from AD 581 to AD 618 that succeeded the Han dynasty, united all of northern China, and reconquered southern China

suicidal /sóo i sīd'l/ *adj* **1. WANTING TO COMMIT SUICIDE** intending or wishing to commit suicide **2. RELATING TO SUICIDE** produced by or involving a wish to commit suicide **3. EXTREMELY DANGEROUS** likely to lead to death, destruction, or ruin, or very much against somebody's own best interests **4. VERY UNHAPPY** deeply unhappy or frustrated (*informal*) —**suicidally** *adv*

suicide /sóo i sīd/ *n* **1. KILLING YOURSELF** the act of deliberately killing yourself **2. SOMEBODY WHO COMMITS SUICIDE** somebody who intentionally kills himself or herself **3. DOING SOMETHING AGAINST OWN BEST INTERESTS** the act of doing something that seems contrary to your own best interests and seems likely to lead to a disaster such as financial ruin or loss of position or reputation ○ *Adopting a policy like that would be political suicide.* [Mid-17C. < modern Latin *suicidium* 'killing of yourself', *suicida* 'somebody who kills himself or herself', both < Latin *sui* 'of yourself']

suicide bomber *n* a person who deliberately allows himself or herself to be killed in the process of attempting to destroy something or kill somebody —**suicide bombing** *n*

suicide pact *n* an agreement between two or more people that they will kill themselves at the same time

suicider /sóo i sīdər/ *n* POL same as **suicide bomber** (*informal*)

suicide terrorist *n* an attacker, e.g. a person wearing concealed explosives, who intends to die while destroying a target [Early 21C.] —**suicide terrorism** *n*

suicide watch *n* the regular checking by prison warders of the cells of prisoners who are thought likely to commit suicide

sui generis /sóo ī jénnəriss/ *adj* unique or occupying a class of its own [< Latin, 'of its own kind']

sui juris /sóo ī jóoriss/ *adj* competent to assume legal responsibility for his or her own affairs [< Latin, 'of its own right']

suint /swint/ *n* the grease found in sheep's wool, formed from dried perspiration [Late 18C. < French < *suer* 'to sweat' < Latin *sudare*]

suit /soot, syoot/ *n* **1. CLOTHES MADE OF SAME MATERIAL** a set of clothes made from the same material, consisting of a jacket and trousers or a skirt, sometimes together with a waistcoat **2. CLOTHES FOR PARTICULAR PURPOSE** a piece of clothing or set of clothes worn for a particular purpose (*often used in combination*) ○ *a diving suit* **3.** CARDS **SET OF PLAYING CARDS** one of the four different sets of 13 playing cards in a pack **4.** LAW **LEGAL PROCEEDINGS** a case brought to a law court **5. PETITION** a petition, especially to somebody in authority (*formal*) **6. BUSINESS EXECUTIVE** a business executive, especially when seen as an anonymous bureaucrat (*slang*) ○ *The hotel was full of suits.* **7. SET OF THINGS** a set of things, especially sails or tools **8. WOOING OF WOMAN** a man's wooing of a woman and attempts to persuade her to marry him (*archaic*) ■ *v* (**suits, suiting, suited**) **1.** *vti* **BE RIGHT** to be appropriate to or the right thing for somebody or something ○ *Choose casual clothes to suit the informal mood.* **2.** *vt* **BE SATISFYING TO SOMEBODY** to be something that a person likes or enjoys ○ *We could meet for lunch if that suits you.* **3.** *vti* **BE CONVENIENT TO SOMEBODY** to be convenient or acceptable to somebody **4.** *vt* **LOOK GOOD ON SOMEBODY** to look good on somebody or go well with something ○ *The colour suits you.* **5.** *vt Scotland* **LOOK GOOD IN SOMETHING** to look good in a particular colour or garment ○ *Emma really suits purple.* **6.** *vt* **MAKE SOMETHING SUITABLE** to adapt something in order to meet requirements or circumstances **7. suit yourself** *vr* **PLEASE YOURSELF** to do what you prefer [13C. < Anglo-Norman *siute* < assumed Vulgar Latin *sequere* 'follow', alteration of Latin *sequi*] ◇ **be somebody's strong suit** to be something at which somebody is particularly good ◇ **follow suit 1.** to do the same as somebody else has done **2.** to play a card of the same suit as the previous player

suit up *vi US* to put on a uniform or a special costume in preparation for an activity, especially a sports event

suitable /sóotəb'l, syóo-/ *adj* of the right type or quality for a particular purpose or occasion —**suitability** /sòotə bíllәti, syòot-/ *n* —**suitableness** *n*

suitably /sóotəbli, syóot-/ *adv* **1.** in a way that is right for a particular purpose or occasion ○ *arrived suitably dressed in a light linen jacket* **2.** to an appropriate or the expected extent ○ *The children were suitably impressed.*

suitcase /sóot kayss, syóot-/ *n* a rectangular case used for carrying clothes and other belongings during travel

suite /sweet/ *n* **1. SET OF MATCHING FURNITURE** a set of matching furniture for a room, e.g. a sofa and two armchairs (**a three-piece suite**) for a lounge **2. SET OF ROOMS** a set of rooms, e.g. in a hotel **3.** MUSIC **SET OF INSTRUMENTAL WORKS PERFORMED TOGETHER** a set of instrumental pieces, especially dances, intended to be performed together **4. PEOPLE WITH VIP** a group of followers, servants, or advisers accompanying somebody important **5.** COMPUT **INTEGRATED SOFTWARE PACKAGE** a collection of integrated application programs functioning as a single program, each of which can incorporate data from the others, eliminating the need for re-entry or transfer of data [Late 17C. Via French < assumed Vulgar Latin *sequere* (see SUIT)]

SPELLCHECK suite or **sweet**? Do not confuse the spelling of ***suite*** and ***sweet***, which sound similar. A ***suite*** is a set of furniture, rooms, musical works, or computer programs, as in *a three-piece suite, the honeymoon suite, Tchaikovsky's Nutcracker Suite.* ***Sweet*** refers to the presence of sugar or the absence of salt or bitterness (*sweet drinks*), and also has approving meanings such as 'pleasant' or 'kind' (*sweet music, a sweet person*); as a noun it denotes 'an item of sweet food'.

suiting /sóoting, syóot-/ *n* material for making suits

suitor /sóotər, syóotər/ *n* **1. MAN WOOING WOMAN** a man who is trying to persuade a woman to marry him (*formal*) **2.** LAW **SOMEBODY WHO BRINGS LAWSUIT** somebody on whose behalf a case is brought to a law court **3.** BUSINESS **SOMEBODY SEEKING TO TAKE OVER BUSINESS** somebody who seeks to buy or take over a business [13C. Via Anglo-Norman *seutor, suitour* < Latin *secutor* 'follower' < *sequi* 'follow']

Sukarno

Sukarno /soo káarnō/ (1901–70) president of Indonesia (1945–67). He led the fight for Indonesia's independence from the Netherlands and became the country's first president.

Sukarnoputri /soo kaárnə póotri/, **Megawati** (*b.* 1947) Indonesian president. After ten years as a member of parliament for the Indonesian Democratic Party, she formed the Indonesian Democratic Party of Struggle in 1996. She was elected vice president in 1999 and president in 2001.

sukiyaki /sóoki yáaki/ *n* a Japanese dish consisting of thin slices of meat, vegetables, and noodles, cooked quickly in a sweet soy sauce [Early 20C. < Japanese, literally 'slice-grill']

sukkah /sóokə/, **succah** *n* a temporary light shelter with a roof of branches built in Jewish homes, gardens, or temples for the festival of Sukkoth [Late 19C. < Hebrew *sukkāh* 'hut']

Sukkoth /sóokəss, -kōt, -kōth, -kōss/, **Succoth, Sukkot** *n* an eight-day Jewish autumn harvest festival. Date: from the eve of the 15th of Tishri. [Late 19C. < Hebrew *sukkōt*, plural of *sukkāh* 'hut']

Sukkur /súkər/ city and district in Sind Province, Pakistan, on the banks of the Indus. Population: 190,551 (1981).

Sulawesi /sóolə wáyssi/ island in Indonesia, in the Malay Archipelago east of Borneo. Population: 13,732,500 (1995). Area: 189,040 sq. km/72,989 sq. mi.

Sulayman I another spelling of **Suleiman I (the Magnificent)**

sulcate /súl kayt/ *adj* marked with lengthways parallel grooves ○ *a sulcate shell/stem* [Mid-18C. < Latin *sulcatus*, past participle of *sulcare* 'furrow' < *sulcus* 'furrow, trench'] —**sulcation** /sul káysh'n/ *n*

sulcus /súlkəss/ (*plural* **-ci** /-sī/) *n* a shallow groove or depression, especially any of those separating the convolutions of the surface of the brain [Mid-17C. < Latin, 'furrow, trench']

Suleiman I (the Magnificent) /sóolli maán, sooli maán, sóol ay maán/, **Sulayman I** (1494–1566) Ottoman sultan. He ruled from 1520 to 1566, extending the Ottoman Empire throughout the Balkans, Southwest Asia, and North Africa, and encouraging artistic and scientific endeavours.

sulfa-, etc. *prefix* another spelling of **sulpha-, etc.** (*technical*)

sulfamethazine /súlfə méthə zeen/ *n N Am* same as **sulphadimidine** [Mid-20C. < *sulfa-* (see SULPHA DRUG)]

sulfur, etc. *n* CHEM another spelling of **sulphur, etc.** (*US, Aus, or technical*)

USAGE See *sulphur.*

sulk /sulk/ *vi* (**sulks, sulking, sulked**) **BE ANGRILY SILENT** to refuse to talk to or associate with others as a show of resentment for a real or imagined grievance ■ *n* **1. BAD-TEMPERED SILENCE** a period, state, or show of resentfulness and refusal to communicate **2. SOMEBODY WHO SULKS** somebody who sulks [Late 18C. Back-formation < SULKY] —**sulker** *n*

sulky /súlki/ *adj* (**-ier, -iest**) in a bad mood and refusing to communicate because of resentment for a real or imagined grievance ■ *n* (*plural* **-ies**) a light open two-wheeled vehicle for one person, pulled by one horse [Mid-18C. Origin ?] —**sulkily** *adv* —**sulkiness** *n*

Sulla /súllə, sóollə/, **Lucius Cornelius** (138–78 BC) Roman general. He successfully led the aristocratic party during the civil war of 88–86 BC and then became dictator of Rome (82–79 BC).

sullage /súllij/ *n* **1.** sewage or any other form of waste or refuse **2.** solid material deposited by flowing water, e.g. by a river [Mid-16C. Origin ?]

sullen /súllən/ *adj* **1. HOSTILELY SILENT** showing bad temper or hostility by a refusal to talk, behave sociably, or cooperate cheerfully **2. CLOUDY AND DULL** dull and grey because of clouds, fog, or haze (*literary*) ○ *sullen prairie skies* **3. SLOW-MOVING** moving slowly (*literary*) ○ *a sullen stream* [14C. < Anglo-Norman *sulein* 'alone' < *sol* 'sole, single' < Latin *solus*] —**sullenly** *adv* —**sullenness** *n*

Sullivan /súllivən/, **Sir Arthur** (1842–1900) British composer. He is best known for his 14 popular comic operas to librettos by Sir William S. Gilbert, including *H.M.S. Pinafore* (1878), *The Pirates of Penzance* (1879), and *The Mikado* (1885). Full name **Sullivan, Sir Arthur Seymour**

Sullivan, Louis (1856–1924) US architect. His tall steel-framed buildings, built mostly in Chicago, were the world's first skyscrapers. Full name **Sullivan, Louis Henri**

Sullom Voe /súlləm vṓ/ inlet on Mainland Island, Shetland Islands, northeastern Scotland. It is home to the principal British oil terminal in the North Sea. Length: 13 km/8 mi.

sully /súlli/ (**-lies, -lying, -lied**) *vt* **1.** to spoil or detract from something, especially somebody's reputation, that has previously been pure and honourable, or become spoiled or tarnished ○ *a reputation sullied by scandal* **2.** to make something dirty (*literary*) [Late 16C. Origin ?] —**sullied** *adj*

sulph- *prefix* sulphur ○ *sulphite* [< SULPHUR]

sulpha-, sulfa- *prefix* drug synthesized from sulphonamide ○ *sulphadimidine*

sulphadiazine /súlfə dī ə zeen/, **sulfadiazine** *n* a sulpha drug. Use: treatment of bacterial infections, es-

pecially in weakened patients. Formula: $C_{10}H_{10}N_4O_2S$. [Mid-20C. < *sulpha-* (see SULPHA DRUG)]

sulphadimidine /súlfə dímmi deen/, **sulfadimidine** *n* a sulphonamide. Use: treatment of bacterial infections. Formula: $C_{12}H_{14}N_4O_2S$. N Am term **sulfamethazine** [Mid-20C. < SULPH- + DI-[1] + *pyrimidine*]

sulpha drug /súlfə-/, **sulfa** *n* a bacteriostatic drug synthesized from sulphonamide. Use: treatment of bacterial infections, but now rarely used because of its toxicity and the resistance of bacteria to it. [< shortening of SULPHANILAMIDE]

sulphanilamide /súlfə níllə mīd/, **sulfanilamide** *n* the first sulpha drug. Use: formerly, treatment of bacterial infections. Formula: $C_6H_8N_2O_2S$. [Mid-20C. < SULPH- + ANILINE]

sulphatase /súlfə tayz, -tayss/ *n* an enzyme that accelerates the decomposition of sulphuric esters

sulphate /súl fayt/ *n* SULPHURIC ACID SALT OR ESTER a salt or ester of sulphuric acid ■ *v* (**-phates, -phating, -phated**) **1.** *vti* MAKE LAYER OF LEAD SULPHATE to make a layer of lead sulphate form on the plates of an accumulator, or become covered with lead sulphate **2.** *vt* TREAT SOMETHING WITH SULPHUR to treat something with sulphur, sulphuric acid, or a sulphate **3.** *vt* CONVERT SOMETHING TO SULPHATE to convert something to a sulphate —**sulphation** /sul fáysh'n/ *n*

sulphide /súl fīd/ *n* a compound in which sulphur is typically combined with one or more electropositive elements or groups

sulphite /súl fīt/ *n* a salt or ester of sulphurous acid —**sulphitic** /sul fíttik/ *adj*

sulphon- *prefix* sulphonic ○ *sulphonyl* [< SULPHONE]

sulphonamide /sul fónnə mīd/ *n* one of a group of compounds responsible for the antibacterial action of sulpha drugs, which work by depriving bacteria of the ability to synthesize folic acid [Late 19C. < SULPHONE]

sulphonate /súlfə nayt/ *n* a salt or ester of sulphonic acid ■ *vt* to treat an organic substance with sulphuric acid [Late 19C. < SULPHONIC] —**sulphonation** /súlfə náysh'n/ *n*

sulphone /súlfōn/ *n* a compound containing the sulphonyl group in which sulphur is attached to two carbon atoms [Late 19C. < German *Sulfon* < *Sulfur* 'sulphur']

sulphonic /sul fónnik/ *adj* relating to, containing, or derived from the acid group SO_2OH [Late 19C. < German *Sulfon* (see SULPHONE)]

sulphonic acid *n* a strong organic acid. Use: manufacture of dyes, drugs.

sulphonium /sul fṓni əm/ *n* an ion or radical containing sulphur with a valency of three [Late 19C. < SULPHUR]

sulphonyl /súlfənil/ *n* the bivalent chemical group SO_2 [Early 20C. < SULPHONIC]

sulphonylurea /súlfə nīl yoo reé ə/ *n* a drug belonging to a group of drugs taken orally that lower blood sugar. Use: treatment of diabetes.

sulphur /súlfər/, **sulfur** *n* **1.** a nonmetallic yellow element that occurs alone in nature or combined in sulphide and sulphate minerals. Use: manufacture of sulphuric acid, matches, fungicides, and gunpowder. Symbol **S**. See table at **element** **2.** a yellowish-green colour [14C. Via Anglo-Norman < Latin *sulfur, sulphur*] —**sulphur** *adj* —**sulphury** *adj*

USAGE sulphur or **sulfur**? In chemistry, the spelling with *-f-* is now the agreed international standard for ***sulfur*** and all related words.

sulphurate /súlfyoo rayt/ (**-rates, -rating, -rated**), **sulfurate** *vt* to treat or combine something with sulphur —**sulphuration** /súlfyoo ráysh'n/ *n*

sulphur bacterium *n* a bacterium that is capable of metabolizing sulphur or inorganic sulphur compounds. Genus: *Thiobacillus*.

sulphur butterfly *n* a butterfly that has yellow or orange wings with black markings. Genus: *Colias*.

sulphur-crested cockatoo *n* a large white cockatoo that lives in large noisy flocks and has a distinctive yellow crest. Native to: northern and eastern Australia, Tasmania. Latin name: *Cacatua galerita*.

sulphur dioxide *n* a colourless pungent toxic gas and air pollutant formed by burning sulphur or fuels containing sulphur. Use: food preservative, fumigant, bleaching agent, manufacture of sulphuric acid.

sulphureous /sul fyoori əs/, **sulfureous** *adj* CHEM same as **sulphurous** —**sulphureously** *adv* —**sulphureousness** *n*

sulphuric /sul fyoorik/, **sulfuric** *adj* relating to or containing sulphur, especially with a valency of six

sulphuric acid *n* a strong colourless oily corrosive acid. Use: batteries, manufacture of fertilizers, explosives, detergents, dyes, chemicals. Formula: H_2SO_4.

sulphurize /súlfyoo rīz/ (**-izes, -izing, -ized**), **sulphurise** (**-ises, -ising, -ised**), **sulfurize**, **sulfurise** *vt* to treat or combine something with sulphur or a sulphur compound —**sulphurization** /súlfyoo rī záysh'n/ *n*

sulphurous /súlfərəss/, **sulfurous** *adj* **1.** CONTAINING SULPHUR relating to or containing sulphur, especially with a valency of four **2.** SIMILAR TO BURNING SULPHUR with the colour or acrid smell of burning sulphur **3.** RELATING TO HELL relating to hell or hellfire (*literary*) **4.** FIERY expressing strong feelings of anger, either physically or in words (*literary*) [15C. < Latin *sulphurosus*, or < SULPHUR] —**sulphurously** *adv* —**sulphurousness** *n*

sulphurous acid *n* a weak colourless acid made by dissolving sulphur dioxide in water. Use: disinfectant, food preservative, bleaching agent. Formula: H_2SO_3.

sulphur pearl *n* a very large bacterium, typically between 0.1 and 0.3 mm in size but sometimes larger, found in sediments off the coast of western Namibia. It uses nitrates as its source of oxygen in oxidizing and breaking down sulphur compounds. Latin name: *Thiomargarita namibiensis*.

sulphur spring *n* a spring with significant amounts of sulphur compounds in the water

sulphur trioxide *n* a toxic, irritating liquid occurring in three forms with different melting points. Use: chemical synthesis.

sulphuryl /súllfyooril/, **sulfuryl** *n* CHEM same as **sulphonyl**

Sulston /súlstən/, **Sir John** (*b.* 1942) British biochemist. As director of the Sanger Centre near Cambridge (1992–2000), he played a pivotal role in the International Human Genome Project. He shared the 2002 Nobel Prize in physiology or medicine with Sydney Brenner and Robert Horvitz.

sultan /súltən/ *n* **1.** the sovereign ruler of an Islamic country, especially formerly the head of the Ottoman Empire **2.** a man who is powerful in some sphere of activity, especially one who behaves in a domineering or tyrannical fashion (*literary*) [Mid-16C. Directly or via French < medieval Latin *sultanus* < Arabic *sulṭān* 'ruler, power' < Aramaic *salīṭa* 'rule'] —**sultanic** /sul tánnik/ *adj* —**sultanship** *n*

sultana /sul taánə/ *n* **1.** a small dried seedless white grape **2.** a wife, mother, sister, daughter, or mistress of a sultan [Late 16C. < Italian, feminine of *sultano* 'sultan' < Arabic *sulṭān* (see SULTAN)]

sultanate /súltənət/ *n* **1.** COUNTRY RULED BY SULTAN a country ruled by a sultan **2.** RANK OF SULTAN the rank or position of sultan **3.** SULTAN'S REIGN the period of a sultan's reign

sultry /súltri/ *adj* **1.** oppressively hot and damp **2.** giving a suggestion of underlying passion and sensuality [Late 16C. < obsolete *sulter* 'swelter'. Origin ?] —**sultrily** *adv* —**sultriness** *n*

Sulu Sea /sóoloo-/ arm of the Pacific Ocean west of the Philippines and northeast of Borneo

sum[1] /sum/ *n* **1.** MONEY an amount of money **2.** ARITHMETICAL CALCULATION a mathematical problem involving adding, subtracting, multiplying, or dividing numbers, especially one given to students to solve **3.** TOTAL the total amount resulting when two or more numbers or quantities are added together **4.** COMBINED TOTAL the combined total amount or quantity of something **5.** MATHS LIMIT OF SUM OF SERIES the limit, as n increases indefinitely, of the sum of the first n terms of an infinite series **6.** GIST the essential point of something that somebody has said or written (*literary*) ■ *vt* (**sums, summing, summed**) ADD UP AMOUNTS to add together two or more amounts to find their total (*formal*) [13C. Via French < Latin *summa* 'sum, substance' < form of *summus* 'highest'] —**summability** /súmmə bílləti/ *n* —**summable** *adj* ◇ **in sum** in short or as a summary

SPELLCHECK See *some*.

ORIGIN The semantic development of ***sum*** from 'highest' to 'sum total' resulted from the Roman practice of counting columns of figures from the bottom upwards, the total being written at the top.

sum up *vti* **1.** SUMMARIZE SOMETHING to present the main points or substance of something concisely **2.** REVIEW EVIDENCE FOR JURY to summarize the main points of a court case for a jury (*refers to a judge*) **3.** BRIEFLY DESCRIBE SOMEBODY OR SOMETHING to describe or evaluate somebody or something concisely

sum[2] /soom/, **som** *n* the main unit of currency in Uzbekistan. See table at **currency** [Late 20C. Via Uzbek *sŭm* < Chuvash *sum, som* 'payment']

sumach /sóo mak, shóo-/, **sumac** *n* **1.** a tree or bush of the cashew family with red hairy fruit, and feathery leaves. Flowers: green, in clusters. Genus: *Rhus*. **2.** the ground dried leaves of one species of sumach. Use: tanning, dyeing. [14C. Directly or via French < medieval Latin *sumac(h)* < Arabic *summāḳ*]

~~**sumary**~~ incorrect spelling of **summary**

Sumatra /soo maátrə/ island in western Indonesia, separated from the Malay Peninsula by the Strait of Malacca. It is the westernmost of the Sunda Islands. Population: 40,830,400 (1995). Area: 473,605 sq. km/182,860 sq. mi. —**Sumatran** *n, adj*

Sumer /sóomər/ ancient country of southern Mesopotamia, in present-day Iraq. Archaeological discoveries reveal the area to have been first settled in the 5th millennium BC. It became prosperous and powerful from about 3000 BC, and fell into decline from about 1760 BC, when it was absorbed into Babylonia and Assyria.

Sumerian /soo meéri ən/ *n* **1.** a member of an ancient people that built the civilization of Sumer **2.** the language of ancient Sumer, unrelated to any other known language. Sumerian is the oldest language preserved in writing, its cuneiform tablets dating from about 3000 BC. —**Sumerian** *adj*

summa /súmmə, sóomə/ (*plural* **-mae** /-mee/) *n* a summary of what is known of a subject, especially a medieval treatise on theology, philosophy, canon law, or alchemy [15C. < Latin (see SUM[1])]

summa cum laude /súmmə kum láwdi, sóomə koom lów day/ *adv, adj US* with the highest level of academic honours at graduation [< Latin, 'with highest praise']

summae plural of **summa**

summand /súmmand, su mánd/ *n* a number or quantity in a sum [Mid-19C. < medieval Latin *summandus* 'for adding', form of *summare* (see SUMMATION)]

summarily /súmmərəli/ *adv* immediately and without discussion or attention to formalities

summarize /súmmə rīz/ (**-rizes, -rizing, -rized**), **summarise** (**-rises, -rising, -rised**) *vti* to give a shortened version of something that has been said or written, stating its main points —**summarist** *n* —**summarizable** *adj* —**summarization** /súmmə rī záysh'n/ *n* —**summarizer** *n*

summary /súmməri/ *n* (*plural* **-ries**) SHORT VERSION CONTAINING GIST OF SOMETHING a shortened version of something that has been said or written, containing only the main points ■ *adj* **1.** IMMEDIATE done immediately and with little discussion or attention to formalities **2.** GIVING ONLY MAIN POINTS shortened and giving only the main points of something **3.** LAW RELATING TO MAGISTRATES' COURTS relating to, dealt with, or given by magistrates' courts operating without the formality of full proceedings [15C. < Latin *summarium* < *summa* (see SUM[1])] —**summariness** *n*

summation /su máysh'n/ *n* **1.** ADDITION the process of adding something up to find a total **2.** TOTAL a total amount or aggregate **3.** SUMMARY OF SOMETHING SAID a summary of something that has been said or written **4.** *US* LAW FINAL ARGUMENT IN COURT the final summing-up of an argument in a court of law [Mid-18C. < modern Latin *summation-* < medieval Latin *summare*

'add' < Latin *summa* (see SUM¹)] —**summational** *adj* —**summative** /súmmətiv/ *adj*

summer¹ /súmmər/ *n* **1.** WARMEST SEASON the warmest season of the year, falling between spring and autumn. It runs from December to February in the southern hemisphere, and from June to August in the northern hemisphere. **2.** WARM WEATHER the warm weather associated with the summer season **3.** PERIOD OF GREAT HAPPINESS a period of greatest happiness, success, or fulfilment in the life of somebody or something **4.** YEAR a year, especially of somebody's age (*literary*) ○ *a man of 70 summers* ■ *v* (**-mers, -mering, -mered**) **1.** *vi* SPEND SUMMER to spend the summer ○ *They summer at the lake.* **2.** *vt* PASTURE ANIMALS FOR SUMMER to keep cattle or other animals on a designated pasture during the summer [Old English *sumor, sumer* < Germanic] —**summery** *adj*

summer² /súmmər/ *n* **1.** a principal horizontal beam in a building used to support floor joists **2.** a stone that lies on top of a pier, column, or wall and supports one or more arches **3.** ARCHIT same as **lintel** [13C. Via Anglo-Norman *sumer*, Old French *som(i)er* 'main beam' < late Latin *sagmarius* 'packhorse' < *sagma* 'pack-saddle' < Greek]

summer camp *n* a place, usually residential, offering outdoor recreational activities and skill development for children during the summer

summer cypress *n Aus, US* a bushy annual plant with narrow light green leaves that turn red in autumn. It spreads rapidly as a weed and is toxic to grazing animals. Native to: Europe and western Asia, naturalized elsewhere. Latin name: *Bassia scoparia.*

summerhouse /súmmər howss/ (*plural* **-houses** /-howziz/) *n* a small building or structure in a garden or park to give seating and shade during the summer

summer pudding *n* a cold pudding consisting of soft fruits such as blackberries, raspberries, and strawberries, cooked together and placed inside a casing of white bread that absorbs their juice

summersault *n, vi* GYMNASTICS another spelling of **somersault**

summer savory *n* PLANTS same as **savory**¹

summer school *n* a course of study held during the summer vacation or holiday, in Britain usually a course of university lectures

summer squash *n* a squash eaten as a vegetable shortly after picking in the summer. Latin name: *Cucurbita pepo melopepo.*

summer time *n* time that is one hour ahead of standard time, used in order to extend the hours of daylight in the evening

summertime /súmmər tīm/ *n* the season of summer

summer tree *n* ARCHIT same as **summer**² (sense 1)

summerwood /súmmər wŏŏd/ *n* wood produced late in a tree's annual growth cycle, which is harder and less porous than early-season growth (**springwood**)

summit /súmmit/ *n* **1.** HIGHEST POINT the highest point or top of something, especially a mountain **2.** POINT OF GREATEST SUCCESS OR INTENSITY the point or time at which something is at its most successful or intense **3.** TOP-LEVEL DIPLOMATIC CONFERENCE a meeting between heads of government or other high-ranking officials to discuss a matter of great importance ■ *vti* (**-mits, -miting, -mited**) CLIMBING REACH TOP OF MOUNTAIN to climb to the summit of a mountain or peak [14C. < Old French *som(m)ete, sumet* 'small top' < *som, sum* 'top' < Latin *summum*, neuter of *summus* 'highest'] —**summital** *adj*

summit conference *n* POL same as **summit** *n* (sense 3)

summiteer /súmmi teer/ *n* a participant in a summit conference

summitry /súmmitri/ *n US* the practice of holding, or deciding matters of international importance through, summit conferences

summon /súmmən/ (**-mons, -moning, -moned**) *v* **1.** *vt* CALL SOMEBODY INTO COURT to order somebody to attend court by serving a summons **2.** *vt* SEND FOR SOMEBODY to send or be a signal for somebody to come ○ *We were summoned to his presence.* **3.** *vt* CONVENE GROUP to call

together a formal or official body ○ *They summoned a meeting to debate the issue.* **4.** *vt* CALL UPON SOMEBODY to request or require somebody to do something ○ *She summoned him to help her.* **5.** *vi* MANAGE TO GET SOMETHING to gather the resources, especially courage or strength, to cope with or do something ○ *trying to summon up the courage to tell him the news* [13C. Via French < Latin *summonere* 'remind secretly' < *sub-* 'under' + *monere* 'warn']

summons /súmmənz/ *n* **1.** COURT ORDER TO DEFENDANT a written order to somebody to attend court to answer a complaint **2.** COURT ORDER TO WITNESS a written order to a witness to attend court **3.** ORDER BY AUTHORITY TO APPEAR an authoritative demand to appear in a specific place at a specific time ■ *vt* (**-monses, -monsing, -monsed**) SERVE SOMEBODY WITH SUMMONS to serve somebody with a summons to attend court [13C. < Old French *somonse*, past participle of *somondre* < Latin *summonere* (see SUMMON)]

sumo

sumo /soʻomō/ *n* traditional Japanese wrestling in which each contestant tries to force the other outside a circle or force him to touch the ground other than with the soles of his feet [Late 19C. < Japanese *sumō*]

sump /sump/ *n* **1.** AUTOMOT LOWEST PART OF CRANKCASE a part located at the bottom of the crankcase of an internal-combustion engine that serves as a lubricating oil reservoir. N Am term **oil pan 2.** RESERVOIR FOR LIQUID a low area into which a liquid drains, e.g. a pit or reservoir **3.** same as **cesspool** (sense 1) **4.** MIN EXTRACT DRAINAGE RESERVOIR IN MINE an area at the bottom of a mineshaft into which water drains and is then pumped away **5.** MIN EXTRACT ADVANCE EXCAVATION an excavation ahead of the main excavation of a mineshaft or tunnel [15C. < Middle Dutch *somp*, Middle Low German *sump*]

sumpter /súmptər/ *n* a packhorse, mule, or other pack animal (*archaic*) [Late 16C. < Old French *sommetier* 'packhorse driver' < late Latin *sagmarius* (see SUMMER²)]

~~**sumptious**~~ incorrect spelling of **sumptuous**

sumptuary /súmptyoo əri/ *adj* **1.** relating to or controlling personal spending **2.** intended to regulate personal behaviour on moral or religious grounds [Early 17C. < Latin *sumptuarius* < *sumptus* 'expense' (see SUMPTUOUS)]

sumptuous /súmptyoo əss/ *adj* **1.** magnificent or grand in appearance **2.** entailing great expense [15C. Via French < Latin *sumptuosus* < *sumptus* 'expense' < past participle of *sumere* 'spend' < *emere* 'take'] —**sumptuously** *adv* —**sumptuousness** *n*

sums /sumz/ *n* simple arithmetical work, especially for schoolchildren, involving addition, subtraction, multiplication, and division (*informal; takes a singular or plural verb*)

sum total *n* **1.** a combined total of separate components ○ *The sum total of his belongings is the clothes on his back.* **2.** a numerical amount obtained by adding sums

sun /sun/ *n* **1.** ASTRON STAR a star or bright astronomical object, especially one around which planets orbit **2.** ASTRON SUN'S RADIATION the light or heat emitted by the Sun **3.** SOMEBODY LIKE SUN somebody or something thought to resemble the Sun in radiance, glory, or warmth, or in being the centre of a society (*literary*) **4.** DAY OR YEAR a day or year (*literary*) ○ *a woman of many suns* ■ *v* (**suns, sunning, sunned**) **1.** sun yourself *vr* WARM OR TAN YOURSELF IN SUNLIGHT to expose your body to the sun's rays for warmth or for a suntan ○ *The*

cat lay sunning herself on the lawn. **2.** *vt* WARM OR DRY SOMETHING IN SUNLIGHT to expose something to the sun's rays for warmth or drying [Old English *sunne* < Indo-European] ◇ **catch the sun** to become a little tanned or sunburnt through exposure to the sun ◇ **everything under the sun** things of all kinds ◇ **take the sun** to go out in the sunshine, especially with the aim of gaining some benefit to your health or wellbeing ◇ **under the sun** in the whole world

SPELLCHECK See **son**.

Sun *n* the star at the centre of our solar system around which Earth and the eight other planets orbit

Sun. *abbr* CALENDAR Sunday

sunbake /sún bayk/ (**-bakes, -baked, -baked**) *vi Aus* same as **sunbathe** —**sunbake** *n* —**sunbaker** *n*

sunbaked /sún baykt/ *adj* **1.** hard and dry from prolonged exposure to the sun **2.** baked by a process of exposure to the sun

sunbath /sún baath/ *n* an act or period of exposing the body to the sun or a sun lamp, especially in order to get a tan

sunbathe /sún bayth/ (**-bathes, -bathing, -bathed**) *vi* to expose the body to sun or a sun lamp, especially in order to get a tan —**sunbathe** *n* —**sunbather** *n*

sunbeam /sún beem/ *n* a ray of light emitted by the Sun —**sunbeamy** *adj*

sun bear *n* a small bear with sleek black fur, a light-coloured muzzle, and a yellowish breast marking. Native to: forests of Southeast Asia. Latin name: *Helarctos malayanus.*

sunbed /sún bed/ *n* **1.** an apparatus resembling a bed with a special canopy that emits rays of ultraviolet light so that the person lying on it develops a suntan. N Am term **tanning bed 2.** FURNITURE same as **sunlounger**

sunbird /sún burd/ *n* a small brightly coloured songbird with a long thin curved beak, which feeds on insects and nectar. Native to: South and Southeast Asia, Africa, Australia. Family: Nectariniidae.

sun-bittern *n* a solitary water bird with mottled brownish feathers and a chestnut marking like a sunburst when its wings are spread. Native to: Central and South America. Latin name: *Eurypyga helius.*

sun blind *n* a blind or awning that shades a room from bright sunlight

sunblock /sún blok/ *n* a substance applied to the skin as a cream or lotion to give complete protection from the sun's ultraviolet rays

sunbonnet /sún bonit/ *n* a bonnet with a wide brim and a flap at the back, worn by babies and, formerly, by women to protect the face and neck from the sun

sunbow /sún bō/ *n* a spectrum of colours similar to a rainbow produced by sunlight refracting through spray, mist, or water vapour, e.g. above a waterfall [After RAINBOW]

sunburn /sún burn/ *n* inflammation and sometimes blistering of the skin caused by overexposure to ultraviolet radiation from the sun ■ *vti* (**-burns, -burning, -burnt** /-burnt/ or **-burned**) to be affected by sunburn, or cause the skin to be affected by sunburn

sunburnt /sún burnt/, **sunburned** /-burnd/ *adj* **1.** affected by sunburn **2.** with a suntan

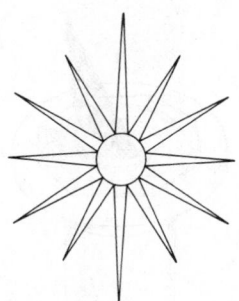

sunburst (sense 2)

sunburst /sún burst/ *n* **1.** SUDDEN BURST OF SUNSHINE a sudden appearance of the sun from behind clouds **2.** SUN-SHAPED DESIGN a design meant to resemble the sun, consisting of a series of rays extending outwards from a central circle. See illustration on previous page **3.** SUN-SHAPED BROOCH a brooch or other ornament designed as a sunburst

Sunbury /súnbri/ town in southern Victoria, Australia, a residential and agricultural centre. Population: 18,533 (1991).

Sunbury-on-Thames /súnbəri on témz, súnbri-/ town in Surrey, southern England. Population: 27,392 (1991).

sundae /sún day, -di/ *n* an ice-cream dessert served with toppings such as whipped cream, fruit, nuts, and flavoured syrup [Late 19C. Alteration of SUNDAY]

Sunda Islands /súndə-/ island group of the Malay Archipelago between the South China Sea and the Indian Ocean. It consists of two groups, the Greater Sunda Islands, which include Sumatra, Java and Borneo, and the Lesser Sunda Islands, which include Bali and Timor.

sun dance *n* an important ceremonial dance of Native North American peoples living on prairies, held annually in honour of the Sun

Sundanese /súndə néez/ (*plural same*) *n* **1.** PEOPLES a member of a people living in the western part of Java, most of whom are Muslims **2.** LANG the Austronesian language of the Sundanese people. Native speakers: 27,000,000. [Late 19C. < Sundanese *Sunda*, western part of Java] —**Sundanese** *adj*

Sunday /sún day, -di/ *n* **1.** 7TH DAY OF WEEK the day of the week after Saturday and before Monday **2.** CHRISTIAN SABBATH DAY in Christian tradition, the day set aside for the Sabbath ■ *adj* **1.** OF SUNDAY relating to or occurring on a Sunday **2.** FOR SPECIAL OCCASIONS worn or used for special occasions **3.** ONLY AT WEEKENDS OR AS HOBBY engaging in an activity only at weekends or as a hobby, and therefore lacking experience, efficiency, or professional skill ○ *These Sunday drivers are a menace on the roads.* [Old English *sunnandæg* 'day of the sun', translation of Latin *dies solis*]

Sunday best *n* somebody's best clothes, traditionally worn on a Sunday to go to church

Sunday punch *n US* **1.** a boxer's most powerful punch, especially a knockout blow **2.** an action that comes as a devastating blow to an opponent or rival

Sundays /sún dayz, -diz/ *adv* every Sunday ■ *npl* special format newspapers published every Sunday ○ *It's in all the Sundays.*

Sunday school *n* a school or class offering children religious education or activities on Sundays

sun deck *n* **1.** an open upper deck on a passenger ship **2.** a balcony, terrace, or platform attached to a building, used for sunbathing. N Am term **deck**

sunder /súndər/ (*-ders, -dering, -dered*) *vti* to separate something into parts, especially by force, or be separated in this way (*literary*) [Old English *sundrian* < *sundor* 'apart' < Indo-European] —**sunderer** *n*

Sunderland /súndərlənd/ city and port in Tyne and Wear, northeastern England. Population: 294,261 (1996).

sundew /sún dyoo/ *n* a plant that produces a rosette of hairy sticky leaves that are used to trap and digest insects. Native to: Australia, New Zealand. Family: Droseraceae. [Translation of Latin *ros solis*; because the drops of juice the plant secretes resemble dew]

sundial /sún dī əl/ *n* an instrument that shows the time of day by the position of a sun-generated shadow cast by a fixed arm (**gnomon**) onto a graduated plate or surface

sun disc *n* an ancient Egyptian Sun god symbol, consisting of a disc with wings and two serpents

sundog /sún dog/ *n* **1.** ASTRON same as **parhelion 2.** a small spectrum of light occasionally visible in the sky at the same altitude as the Sun, either to the left or right of the Sun, and sometimes on both sides simultaneously

sundown /sún down/ *n* the time when the Sun sets

sundowner /sún downər/ *n UK, S Africa* an alcoholic drink taken early in the evening, around sunset (*informal*)

sundrenched /sún drencht/ *adj* describes a place that enjoys a large amount of hot sunshine

sundress /sún dress/ *n* a light sleeveless summer dress with a low bodice that exposes the shoulders, back, and arms to the sun

sun-dried *adj* dried out naturally by the sun, not by applying artificial heat

sundries /súndriz/ *npl* **1.** small miscellaneous items, often of too little value to be mentioned individually **2.** items of food, especially breads or other small extras, that can be ordered in a restaurant as an accompaniment to a meal

sundry /súndri/ *adj* assorted, but considered as a single category or group, usually for the sake of convenience ○ *and other sundry items* [Old English *syndrig* 'separate, distinct' < W Germanic] ◇ **all and sundry** everyone without exception (*takes a plural verb*)

Sundsvall /sóōndz val/ town and port on the Gulf of Bothnia, Sweden, situated about 400 km/250 mi. north of Stockholm. Population: 94,328 (1998).

sunfish /sún fish/ (*plural same* or *-fishes*) *n* **1.** *UK, ANZ, Can* a large brownish-blue sea fish that is nearly oval and has high dorsal and anal fins that it uses like oars for locomotion. Family: Molidae. US term **ocean sunfish 2.** a small to medium-sized spiny-finned freshwater fish, often with iridescent colours. Native to: North America. Family: Centrarchidae.

sunflower /sún flow ər/ *n* **1.** a tall annual plant grown commercially for its edible seeds and the oil extracted from them. Flowers: large heads of yellow petals with a dark centre. Latin name: *Helianthus annuus.* **2.** a plant related to the sunflower. Genus: *Helianthus.* [Mid-16C. Translation of modern Latin *flos solis* and Greek *helianthos*]

sunflower oil *n* oil extracted from sunflower seeds, used in cooking and salad dressings

sung /sung/ past participle of **sing**

Sung /sóōng/, **Song** /song/ *n* a Chinese imperial dynasty that lasted from AD 960–1279, under which science, philosophy, and the arts thrived [Late 17C. < Chinese *Song*]

sungazer /sún gayzər/ *n* a lizard that grows to about 35.6 cm/14 in long and is known for its habit of basking in the sun. Native to: southern Africa. Latin name: *Cordylus giganteus.*

sunglass /sún glaass/ *n* a convex lens used to focus the sun's rays so as to produce heat, especially in order to start a fire ■ **sunglasses** *npl* glasses with tinted or darkened lenses to protect the eyes from sunlight or its glare

sunglow /sún glō/ *n* a pale pink or yellow glow seen in the sky just before sunrise or just after sunset

sun-god *n* **1.** the Sun worshipped as a god **2.** a god that personifies or is seen as controlling the Sun

sungrebe /sún greeb/ *n* a diving bird of the finfoot family that lives along rivers and lakes. Native to: South America. Family: Heliornithidae.

sunhat /sún hat/ *n* a hat with a broad brim, designed to cover the head and shade the face and neck from the sun

suni /sóni/ (*plural -nis* or *same*) *n* a dark brown antelope, growing to only about 355 cm/14 in long, that has small straight horns and a strong musky odour from facial glands. Native to: southern Africa. Latin name: *Neotragus moschatus.* [Late 19C. < Bantu]

sunk /sungk/ past participle, past tense of **sink** ■ *adj* without hope of success (*informal*)

USAGE See *sink*.

sunken /súngkən/ *adj* **1.** SUBMERGED submerged beneath the surface of something ○ *a sunken galleon* **2.** HOLLOW-LOOKING appearing hollow or concave ○ *sunken cheeks* **3.** SUNK LOWER having settled to a lower level **4.** AT LOWER ELEVATION set at a lower level than something adjoining [Old past participle of SINK]

USAGE See *sink*.

sunk fence *n* a ditch containing a fence or wall that separates lands without spoiling the appearance of the landscape

sunlamp /sún lamp/ *n* **1.** a lamp that emits ultraviolet light, used to get a suntan or for therapeutic purposes **2.** a lamp with parabolic mirrors that are directed to focus light, used in cinema photography

sunless /súnləss/ *adj* **1.** deprived of or lacking sunlight **2.** lacking joy or happiness

sunlight /sún līt/ *n* light emitted by the Sun —**sunlit** /súnlit/ *adj*

sun lounge *n UK* a room with large windows designed to receive the maximum amount of sunlight. ANZ, N Am term **sunroom**

sunlounger /sún lownjər/ *n* a light folding chair with an extended section for the legs, used for sunbathing. N Am term **chaise longue**

sunn /sun/ *n* **1.** a strong light plant fibre. Use: rope, sacks. **2.** a thin-branched tropical plant whose inner bark yields sunn. Native to: Asia, Australia. Latin name: *Crotalaria juncea.* [Late 18C. Via Hindi < Sanskrit *śāṇa* 'made of hemp']

Sunna /sóōnə, súnnə/ *n* one of the basic sources of Islamic law, based on Muhammad's words and deeds as recorded in the Hadith. The Sunna complements and often explains the Koran. [Early 18C. < Arabic, 'rule, custom']

Sunni /sóōni, súnni/ (*plural same* or *-nis*) *n* **1.** the largest branch of Islam, which believes in the traditions of the Sunna and accepts the first four caliphs as rightful successors to Muhammad **2.** a member of the Sunni branch of Islam [Late 16C. < Arabic, 'lawful' < *sunna* 'rule, custom']

sunnies /súnniz/ *npl ANZ* CLOTHING same as **sunglasses** (*see* **sunglass**) (*informal*)

Sunnite /sóōnīt, súnn-/ *n* ISLAM same as **Sunni** (sense 2)

sunny /súnni/ (*-nier, -niest*) *adj* **1.** FULL OF SUNSHINE characterized by a lot of sunshine ○ *sunny weather* ○ *a beautiful sunny day* **2.** FULL OF SUNLIGHT bright with or exposed to sunlight ○ *a bright, sunny room* **3.** CHEERFUL characterized by or showing happiness or cheerfulness —**sunnily** *adv* —**sunniness** *n*

sunny-side up *adj* describes a fried egg that is not turned over in cooking and so has a visible yellow yolk uppermost

sun protection factor *n* HEALTH full form of **SPF**

sunquake /sún kwayk/ *n* a violent seismic event on the Sun caused by solar flares

sunrise /sún rīz/ *n* **1.** COMING UP OF SUN the rising of the sun above the eastern horizon each morning **2.** GLOW FROM RISING SUN an atmospheric glow and colouring near the horizon as the Sun rises **3.** TIME SUN RISES the time at which the Sun rises above the horizon in the morning

sunroof /sún roof/ *n* a small panel in the roof of a car that can be raised or slid back to let in air and light

sunroom /sún room, -room/ *n ANZ, N Am* same as **sun lounge**

sunscreen /sún skreen/ *n* a substance applied to the skin as a cream, lotion, or oil to protect it from burning without preventing tanning

sunset /sún set/ *n* **1.** GOING DOWN OF SUN the setting of the Sun below the western horizon in the evening **2.** GLOW FROM SETTING SUN an atmospheric glow and colouring near the horizon as the Sun sets **3.** TIME SUN SETS the time at which the Sun sets below the horizon in the evening **4.** LAST PART the period during which somebody or something is declining, coming to an end, or approaching death

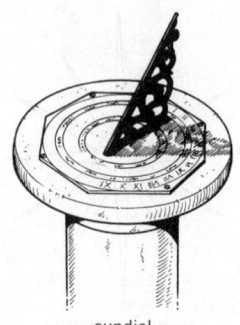

sundial

CULTURAL NOTE *Sunset Boulevard*, a film (1950) by Austrian-born US director Billy Wilder. Wilder uses the story of the relationship between an out-of-favour screenwriter and a faded and eccentric silent-movie star to create one of the cinema's most savage satires on the cynicism and ruthlessness of the Hollywood system. The performances, camerawork, and direction all reinforce the powerful atmosphere of corruption and decay.

sunshade /sún shayd/ *n* something under which somebody is protected from the sun, e.g. an awning or parasol

sunshine /sún shīn/ *n* **1.** DIRECT SUNLIGHT direct rays of the sun, producing heat and light ○ *a ray of sunshine* **2.** SUNNY PLACE a place where the sun's rays are falling ○ *Let's sit in the sunshine.* **3.** SOURCE OF GOOD FEELINGS somebody or something that produces joy, happiness, or other good feelings ○ *bringing a little bit of sunshine into people's lives* **4.** FAMILIAR TERM OF ADDRESS used to address somebody in a cheerful or familiar way (*informal; often ironic*) ○ *Listen, sunshine – you just watch what you're saying – okay?* —**sunshiny** *adj*

Sunshine Coast /sún shīn-/ region in southeastern Queensland, Australia, consisting of the 45 km/28 mi. stretch of coastline between Noosa Heads and Caloundra. It is a popular tourist destination.

sunspot /sún spot/ *n* **1.** any of the relatively cool dark patches that appear in cycles on the Sun's surface and possess a powerful magnetic field **2.** a place that has a warm and sunny climate and is usually popular as a holiday destination (*informal*)

sunstone /sún stōn/ *n* MINERALS same as **aventurine** (sense 2) [Translation of Latin *gemma solis*]

sunstroke /sún strōk/ *n* a condition caused by prolonged and excessive exposure to the sun and characterized by feverishness, faintness, convulsions, and coma. It results when the temperature becomes too extreme to be handled by the body's heat-regulating mechanism. Technical name **insolation**

sunsuit /sún soot, -syoot/ *n* a child's one-piece garment usually consisting of shorts and a bib top with shoulder straps, worn in hot weather

suntan /sún tan/ *n* HEALTH same as **tan**[1] *n* (sense 1) —**suntanned** *adj*

suntrap /sún trap/ *n* a sheltered area with bright sunlight and little or no wind

sunup /sún up/ *n* US METEOROL same as **sunrise** (sense 3)

sunward /súnwərd/ *adj* turned towards or in the direction of the Sun ■ *adv* same as **sunwards**

sunwards /súnnwərdz/ *adv* in the direction of the sun

sunyata /shoónyə taa, soón-/ *n* a tenet of Mahayana Buddhism stating that all things ultimately are 'empty', being neither existent nor nonexistent [Early 20C. < Sanskrit *śūnyatā* 'emptiness']

Sun Yat-sen /soón yat sén/ (1866–1925) Chinese revolutionary leader. He developed his democratic political philosophy during years of foreign travel and returned to China to lead the overthrow of the Manchu dynasty (1911). He led the nationalist Kuomintang Party from 1912 and headed an opposition government in Guangzhou (1917–25), but failed to establish a national republican government.

> 'The foundation of the government of a nation must be built upon the rights of the people, but the administration must be entrusted to experts.'
> [Sun Yat-sen, *The Three Principles of the People*; 1953]

Suomi /soó omi/ Finnish name for **Finland**

sup[1] /sup/ *vti* (**sups, supping, supped**) **1.** SIP LIQUID to drink small amounts of liquid at one time **2.** EAT SOMETHING BY SPOONFUL to eat with a spoon something that is swallowed directly such as soup or porridge ■ *n* SIP OF LIQUID a small amount or mouthful of liquid [Old English *sūpan* < Germanic]

sup[2] /sup/ (**sups, supping, supped**) *vi* to eat your evening meal (*dated*) [14C. < Old French *souper* < *soupe* (see SOUP)] —**sup on**

sup. *abbr* **1.** superior **2.** GRAM superlative **3.** GRAM supine **4.** supplement **5.** supplementary **6.** supply **7.** supra

supari /soópaari/ *n* S Asia broken areca palm nuts, which are chewed with betel leaves, especially after meals, as a digestive aid [Mid-17C. < Hindi *supārī*]

Supdt *abbr* PUBLIC ADMIN Superintendent

super /soópər/ *adj* **1.** EXCELLENT having outstanding or excellent qualities (*informal*) ○ *a super idea* **2.** VERY GREAT exceptionally large or powerful (*informal*) **3.** EXCESSIVE greater than what is normal ■ *adv* ESPECIALLY to or in a high or extreme degree (*informal*) ○ *Everyone has been super helpful.* ■ *n* **1.** POLICE same as **superintendent** (*informal*) **2.** US same as **porter**[2] (sense 3) (*informal*) **3.** same as **supervisor** (*informal*) **4.** US SOMETHING BIGGER OR BETTER something superior in grade or quality or larger in size **5.** ANZ FIN same as **superannuation** (*informal*) **6.** THEATRE same as **supernumerary** (*informal*) **7.** HIGH-OCTANE PETROL high-octane petrol **8.** Aus LEADED PETROL leaded petrol ■ *interj* GREAT! used to express enthusiasm, approval, or agreement (*informal*) [Mid-19C. < SUPER-, or shortening of various words beginning with SUPER-]

super. *abbr* **1.** superfine **2.** superior

super- *prefix* **1.** something larger, stronger, or faster than others of its kind ○ *superstore* **2.** over, above, on ○ *supernatant* ○ *superstructure* **3.** exceeding the usual limits ○ *superheat* **4.** a more inclusive group or category ○ *superclass* **5.** in addition to, over and above ○ *superfetation* **6.** greater in size, quality, number, or degree, superior ○ *superhuman* [< Latin *super* 'over, above' < Indo-European]

superachiever *n*	**supernormally** *adv*
superagent *n*	**superpatriotic** *adj*
superathlete *n*	**superplayer** *n*
superbright *adj*	**superpolite** *adj*
supercar *n*	**superpowerful** *adj*
supercautious *adj*	**superquality** *adj, n*
superchic *adj*	**superrich** *adj, n*
supercivilized *adj*	**superromantic** *adj*
superclean *adj*	**supersale** *n*
supercomfortable *adj*	**supersale** *n*
supercompetitive *adj*	**supersharp** *adj*
superconfident *adj*	**supersize** *adj*
superconservative *adj*	**supersized** *adj*
superconvenient *adj*	**supersleuth** *n*
superdeluxe *adj*	**superslick** *adj*
supereffective *adj*	**supersmart** *adj*
superefficient *adj*	**supersmooth** *adj*
superexpensive *adj*	**supersoft** *adj*
superfast *adj*	**supersophisticated** *adj*
superhigh *adj*	**superspecial** *adj*
superhot *adj*	**superspy** *n*
superintellectual *adj*	**superstrength** *n*
superintelligent *adj*	**superstrong** *adj*
superlarge *adj*	**supersweet** *adj*
superlight *adj*	**superthick** *adj*
superluxurious *adj*	**superthin** *adj*
supermodern *adj*	**supertight** *adj*
supernormal *adj*	**superwide** *adj*
supernormality *n*	

superable /soópərəb'l/ *adj* capable of being overcome [Early 17C. < Latin *superabilis* < *superare* 'overcome' < *super* 'over, above'] —**superability** /soópərə bílləti/ *n* —**superably** *adv*

superabound /soópərə bównd/ (**-bounds, -bounding, -bounded**) *vi* to be too numerous or abundant [14C. < late Latin *superabundare* < Latin *super* 'over, above' + *abundare* (see ABOUND)]

superabundant /soópərə búndənt/ *adj* too numerous or abundant [15C. < late Latin *superabundant-*, present participle of *superabundare* (see SUPERABOUND)] —**superabundance** *n* —**superabundantly** *adv*

superadd /soópər ád/ (**-adds, -adding, -added**) *vt* to add something onto what has already been added [15C. < Latin *superaddere* < *super* 'over, above' *addere* (see ADD)] —**superaddition** /soópərə dísh'n/ *n* —**superadditional** *adj*

superagency /soópər áyjənssi/ (*plural* **-cies**) *n* a large government agency made up of or controlling other agencies

superalloy /soópər álloy/ *n* a heat-resistant alloy with superior mechanical properties, often one used in aerospace applications

superannuant /soópər ányooənt/ *n* Aus somebody who has retired and is receiving a pension

superannuate /soópər ányoo ayt/ (**-ates, -ating, -ated**) *v* **1.** *vti* to become retired with a pension, or retire somebody with a pension **2.** *vt* to reject something or cause something to be rejected because of obsolescence [Mid-17C. Back-formation < SUPERANNUATED]

superannuated /soópər ánnyoo aytid/ *adj* **1.** RETIRED having been retired with a pension **2.** WORN OUT used so much as to be able to offer no more useful service **3.** OUT-OF-DATE no longer in fashion [Mid-17C. < medieval Latin *superannuatus* 'more than a year old' < Latin *super* 'over, above' + *annus* 'year']

superannuation /soópər anyoo aysh'n/ *n* **1.** DEDUCTIONS FOR PENSION SCHEME amounts contributed regularly from an employee's pay towards a pension **2.** RETIREMENT PENSION the pension paid on retirement to a contributing employee **3.** RETIREMENT the process of retiring, or the state of being retired with a pension

superannuitant /soópər ə nyoó itənt/ *n* somebody who has retired and is receiving a pension

superb /soó púrb, syoó-/ *adj* **1.** EXCELLENT of the highest quality **2.** GRAND impressive in size or appearance **3.** SUMPTUOUS rich and sumptuous in appearance or detail [Mid-16C. Via French < Latin *superbus* 'proud, superior' < *super* 'over, above'] —**superbly** *adv* —**superbness** *n*

Super Bowl *tdmk* a trademark for the championship game of the US National Football League, played each year between the champions of the National Football Conference and the American Football Conference

superbug /soópər bug/ *n* a bacterium that has become resistant to the antibiotics normally used to treat it

supercalender /soópər kálləndər/ *n* a machine with an extra large number of rollers to give a glossy finish to paper ■ *vt* (**-ders, -dering, -dered**) to produce a glossy finish on paper using a supercalender

supercargo /soópər kaárgō/ (*plural* **-gos**) *n* an officer who is in charge of the cargo and commercial matters aboard a merchant ship [Late 17C. < alteration of Spanish *sobrecargo* < *sobre-* 'over' + *cargo* (see CARGO)]

supercavitation /soópər kavi táysh'n/ *n* the formation of a large bubble around a fast-moving underwater object such as a submarine or torpedo that greatly reduces the viscous drag of the water —**supercavitating** /soópər kávvi tayting/ *adj* —**supercavity** /soópər kaviti/ *n*

~~**supercede**~~ incorrect spelling of **supersede**

supercentenarian /soópər sent'n áiri ən/ *n* a person who is at least 100 years old

supercharge /soópər chaarj/ (**-charges, -charging, -charged**) *vt* **1.** to charge something such as the atmosphere or a remark with excessive emotion or energy **2.** to increase the power of an internal-combustion engine by means of a supercharger

supercharger /soópər chaarjər/ *n* a device that supplies air to an internal-combustion engine at a pressure greater than the ambient atmospheric pressure in order to increase its power

superciliary /soópər sílli əri/ *adj* **1.** relating to or located in the region of the eyebrow **2.** describes markings above an animal's eye [Mid-18C. < Latin *supercilium* 'eyebrow' (see SUPERCILIOUS)]

supercilious /soópər sílli əss/ *adj* full of contempt and arrogance [Early 16C. < Latin *superciliosus* < *supercilium* 'eyebrow' < *super* 'above' + *cilium* 'eyelid']

superclass /soópər klaass/ *n* a taxonomic category of related organisms of a rank above class

supercluster /soópər klustər/ *n* an association of clusters of galaxies

supercollider /soópər kə līdər/ *n* a very large high-energy particle accelerator

supercolumnar /soópərkə lúmnər/ *adj* having one order of architectural columns above another —**supercolumniation** /soópər kə lúmni aysh'n/ *n*

supercomputer /soópər kəm pyóotər/ *n* a computer with the very highest processing speeds, used for solving complex problems and creating simulations

superconductivity /soópər kon duk tívvəti/ *n* the ability of some metals, alloys, and ceramics to conduct electric current with negligible internal resistance at temperatures near absolute zero and,

in some cases, at higher temperatures —**superconducting** /-kən dúkting/ *adj* —**superconduction** /-kən dúksh'n/ *n* —**superconductive** /-kən dúktiv/ *adj* —**superconductor** /-kən dúktər/ *n*

supercontinent /sóopər kontinənt/ *n* one of the large continental masses believed to have broken into several parts that drifted apart to form the present continents. These land masses included Pangaea, Gondwanaland, and Laurasia.

supercool /sóopər kóol/ *vti* (**-cools, -cooling, -cooled**) to cool a liquid below its freezing point without changing it to a solid, or be cooled in this way ■ *adj* extremely fashionable in attitude or image (*informal*)

supercritical /sóopər kríttik'l/ *adj* **1.** HIGHLY CRITICAL highly critical of something, e.g. a person's work **2.** PHYS SELF-SUSTAINING AS NUCLEAR REACTION describes a nuclear chain reaction that sustains itself explosively because a single transformation produces more than one other transformation **3.** PHYS ABOVE CRITICAL TEMPERATURE AND PRESSURE describes a fluid at temperatures and pressures higher than those at which the liquid and gaseous states of the given substance would have the same density

super-duper /sóopər dóopər/ *adj* exceptionally good, large, or efficient (*humorous; often used ironically*) [Doubling of SUPER]

superego /sóopər eégō/ (*plural* **-gos**) *n* according to Freudian theory, the part of the mind that acts as a conscience to the ego, developing moral standards and rules through contact with parents and society [Early 20C. Translation of German *Über-Ich*]

superelevation /sóopər eli váysh'n/ *n* the distance in height between the inside and outside edges of the bed of a banked road or track

supererogation /sóopər erə gáysh'n/ *n* the performance of work beyond what is required or expected [Early 16C. < late Latin *supererogation-* < *supererogare* 'pay over and above' < Latin *super* 'over, above' + *erogare* 'spend' < *rogare* 'ask, beg']

supererogatory /sóopər i róggətəri/ *adj* **1.** performed to an extent beyond what is required or expected **2.** beyond what is sufficient or necessary, and not wanted —**supererogatorily** *adv*

superfamily /sóopər famli/ (*plural* **-lies**) *n* a taxonomic category of related organisms of a rank above family

superfecundation /sóopər fekən dáysh'n/ *n* **1.** the fertilization of two or more ova at different times during one menstrual cycle by sperm from the same or different males **2.** the fertilization of an unusually large number of ova at the same time

superfetation /sóopər fee táysh'n/ *n* the fertilization of a second ovum after the start of pregnancy, resulting in the presence of two foetuses at different stages of development in the same uterus. It is a regular occurrence in some animal species. [Early 17C. Directly or via French < modern Latin *superfetation-* < *superfetare* 'conceive a second time' < Latin *super* 'over, above' + *foetus* 'offspring']

superficial /sóopər físh'l/ *adj* **1.** NOT PROFOUND concerned with or understanding only the obvious ○ *a superficial knowledge of the subject* **2.** RELATING TO SURFACE relating to, affecting, or located on or near the surface of something ○ *a superficial wound* **3.** WITHOUT DEPTH OF CHARACTER shallow in character or attitude ○ *I find her quite superficial.* **4.** CURSORY swift and not thorough ○ *after a superficial examination of the injury* **5.** ONLY APPARENTLY SO only seeming to be real or the case ○ *The picture bears a superficial resemblance, nothing more.* **6.** INSIGNIFICANT having little significance or substance ○ *superficial changes to the policy* [14C. < Latin *superficies* < *super* 'over, above' + *facies* 'appearance, form, face'] —**superficiality** /-físhi álləti/ *n* —**superficially** *adv*

superficies /sóopər físhi eez/ (*plural same*) *n* **1.** the outer surface or area of something **2.** the outward appearance or form of something [Mid-16C. < Latin (see SUPERFICIAL)]

superfine /sóopər fīn/ *adj* **1.** FINEST IN TEXTURE of extremely fine grain or texture **2.** FINEST IN QUALITY of the highest quality or grade **3.** AFFECTEDLY REFINED excessively refined in manner —**superfineness** *n*

superfluid /sóopər floo id/ *n* a fluid characterized by the absence of viscosity at temperatures near absolute zero. The only known example is liquid helium. ■ *adj* relating to or exhibiting the properties of a superfluid —**superfluidity** /sóopər floo íddəti/ *n*

superfluity /sóopər flóo əti/ (*plural* **-ties**) *n* **1.** an excessive or overabundant supply of something **2.** something beyond what is necessary

superfluous /soo púr floo əss/ *adj* **1.** in excess of what is needed ○ *a lot of superfluous detail* **2.** not essential ○ *superfluous to the discussion* [14C. Directly or via French < Latin *superfluus* < *superfluere* 'overflow' < *super* 'over, above' + *fluere* 'to flow'] —**superfluously** *adv* —**superfluousness** *n*

supergalaxy /sóopər galəksi/ (*plural* **-ies**) *n* ASTRON same as **supercluster**

supergene /sóopər jeen/ *n* a group of genes that lie close together on a chromosome, function as a unit, and are rarely separated

supergerm /sóopər jurm/ *n* MICROBIOL same as **superbug**

supergiant /sóopər jī ənt/ *n* an extremely large brilliant star with a luminosity thousands of times greater than that of the Sun. The stars Rigel and Betelgeuse are supergiants.

superglue /sóopər gloo/ *n* a fast-acting glue that forms a strong bond by polymerization

supergrass /sóopər graass/ *n* somebody who gives information to the police or security forces implicating a large number of criminals or terrorists (*informal*)

supergravity /sóopər grávvəti/ *n* a theory in physics that encompasses all known fundamental interactions and uses hypothetical particles (**gravitons**) to carry the gravitational force. It has largely been supplanted by superstring theory.

supergroup /sóopər groop/ *n* a rock music group whose performers are already famous from having performed individually or in other groups

superhead /sóopər hed/ *n* a very experienced and effective head teacher who is usually appointed either to improve standards in a failing school or to provide overall management and leadership to a group of schools

superheat *vt* /sóopər heét/ (**-heats, -heating, -heated**) **1.** HEAT LIQUID WITHOUT VAPORIZATION to heat a liquid above its pressure-related boiling point without causing it to vaporize **2.** HEAT VAPOUR TO SATURATION to heat a vapour not in contact with its liquid to the point at which a lowering of temperature or increase in pressure will not change it to a liquid **3.** MAKE SOMETHING VERY HOT to heat something to an extremely high temperature ■ *n* /sóopər heet/ HEAT FOR SUPERHEATING the heat used to superheat a vapour —**superheater** *n*

superheavy /sóopər hévvi/ *adj* describes a chemical element having more than 110 protons in the nucleus, and, according to theoretical studies, likely to have special stability

superheavyweight /sóopər hévvi wayt/ *n* **1.** WEIGHT CATEGORY IN AMATEUR BOXING in amateur boxing, a weight category for competitors who weigh more than 91 kg/201 lb **2.** BOXER COMPETING AT SUPERHEAVYWEIGHT an amateur boxer who competes at superheavyweight level **3.** SOMEBODY IN HEAVIEST WEIGHT DIVISION a sportsperson, especially a wrestler or weightlifter, who competes in the heaviest weight division —**superheavyweight** *adj*

superhelix /sóopər heeliks/ (*plural* **-helices** /-heeli seez/) *n* a form of DNA in which the helical molecule is coiled in on itself

superhero /sóopər heerō/ (*plural* **-roes**) *n* a fictional character, e.g. from a cartoon, who has superhuman powers and uses them to fight crime or evil

superheterodyne /sóopər héttərō dīn/ *adj* relating to a method of receiving radio signals in which the incoming signal is mixed with a frequency generated by the receiver. The resulting intermediate frequency is amplified and then decoded. ■ *n* a radio receiver that operates using the superheterodyne method of receiving signals [Early 20C. < SUPERSONIC]

superhigh frequency /sóopərhī-/ *n* a radio frequency between 3,000 and 30,000 megahertz

superhighway /sóopər hī way/ *n* **1.** ONLINE same as **information superhighway 2.** in the United States, a motorway designed for high-speed traffic, with several lanes in each direction

superhuman /sóopər hyóomən/ *adj* **1.** beyond ordinary human capability ○ *made a superhuman effort to move the boulder* **2.** having higher or greater powers than those usually possessed by a human being ○ *a superhuman being* [Early 17C. < late Latin *superhumanus* < Latin *super* 'over, above' + *humanus* 'human'] —**superhumanity** /-hyoo mánnəti/ *n* —**superhumanly** *adv*

superimpose /sóopərim pṓz/ (**-poses, -posing, -posed**) *vt* **1.** to place something such as a transparent image on or over something else, often with the result that both things appear simultaneously, although one may partially obscure the other **2.** to add a feature or element without incorporating it ○ *superimpose one culture on another* —**superimposition** /-impə zísh'n/ *n*

superincumbent /sóopərin kúmbənt/ *adj* lying or resting on or above something [Mid-17C. < Latin *superincumbent-*, present participle of *superincumbere* 'lie on top of' < *super* 'over, above' + *incumbere* (see INCUMBENT)] —**superincumbence** *n* —**superincumbency** *n* —**superincumbently** *adv*

superinduce /sóopərin dyóoss/ (**-duces, -ducing, -duced**) *vt* to introduce somebody or something additional [Mid-16C. < Latin *superinducere* 'bring in upon' < *super* 'over, above' + *inducere* (see INDUCE)] —**superinduction** /-dúksh'n/ *n*

superinfection /sóopərin féksh'n/ *n* an infection that develops during drug treatment for another infection, caused by a different microorganism that is resistant to the treatment used for the first infection —**superinfect** *vt*

superintend /sóopərin ténd/ (**-tends, -tending, -tended**) *vt* to be responsible for and supervise something such as a project or job [Early 17C. Back-formation < SUPERINTENDENT]

~~superintendant~~ incorrect spelling of **superintendent**

superintendent /sóopərin téndənt/ *n* **1.** SOMEBODY IN CHARGE an administrator or manager of something such as an office or organization **2.** HIGH-RANKING POLICE OFFICER in the United Kingdom and Canada, a police officer of a rank above inspector, and in the United States a police officer of high rank, especially the head of a police department **3.** *N Am* same as **porter**[2] (sense 3) ■ *adj* IN CHARGE acting in an administrative or supervisory capacity [Mid-16C. < ecclesiastical Latin *superintendent-*, present participle of *superintendere* 'oversee' < Latin *super* 'over, above' + *intendere* (see INTEND); translation of Greek *episkopos* 'overseer'] —**superintendence** *n* —**superintendency** *n*

superior /soo peéri ər/ *adj* **1.** HIGHER IN QUALITY above average or better than another in quality or grade **2.** BETTER THAN OTHERS surpassing others in something such as intellect, achievement, or ability **3.** HIGHER IN RANK higher in rank, position, or authority than another **4.** CONDESCENDING adopting or showing an attitude of condescension towards others ○ *He gave a superior smile.* **5.** UNCONCERNED above being affected or influenced by something ○ *A player has to be superior to such taunts.* **6.** LARGER greater in number or amount ○ *a quantity superior to our needs* **7.** IN HIGHER LOCATION upper, or situated higher up **8.** PRINTING same as **superscript 9.** BOT ABOVE OTHER FLOWER PARTS describes an ovary of a flower whose stamens, petals, and sepals arise either beside or below it **10.** ANAT NEARER HEAD nearer the head than another body part ■ *n* **1.** SOMEBODY OR SOMETHING HIGHER OR BETTER somebody or something higher in rank, position, authority, or quality than another ○ *Don't argue with your superiors.* **2.** PRINTING same as **superscript 3.** RELIG SOMEBODY IN CHARGE OF RELIGIOUS ORDER the head of a religious order or institution [14C. Via French < Latin, 'higher' < *superus* 'above' < *super*] —**superiority** /soo peéri órrəti/ *n* —**superiorly** *adv*

Superior, Lake /soo peéri ər/ lake in North America. The northernmost and westernmost of the Great Lakes, it is also the world's largest freshwater lake. Area: 82,100 sq. km/31,700 sq. mi. Depth: 406 m/1,333 ft. Length: 560 km/350 mi.

superior conjunction *n* the position of an astronomical object in which it is opposite Earth on the far side of the Sun

superior court *n* in some states of the United States, a court that is higher than an inferior court, but lower than an appellate court

superiority complex *n* an exaggerated sense of being better than other people

superior planet *n* a planet whose distance from the Sun is greater than that of Earth. The superior planets are Mars, Jupiter, Saturn, Uranus, Neptune, and Pluto.

superjacent /so͞opər jáyss'nt/ *adj* lying on or above something [Late 16C. < Latin *superjacent-*, present participle of *superjacere* 'lie above' < *super* 'over, above' < *jacere* 'lie']

superjet /so͞opər jet/ *n* a large supersonic jet plane

superlative /soo púrlətiv/ *adj* **1. EXCELLENT** of the highest quality or degree **2.** GRAM **HIGHEST IN DEGREE OF COMPARISON** expressing the highest degree of grammatical comparison of an adjective or adverb ○ *The superlative form of an adjective or adverb typically has the ending '-est'.* ■ *n* **1.** GRAM **GRAMMATICAL FORM** the grammatical form of an adjective or adverb that expresses the highest degree of comparison ○ *Put 'tiny' into the superlative and you get 'tiniest'.* **2.** GRAM **SUPERLATIVE ADJECTIVE OR ADVERB** a superlative form of an adjective or adverb ○ *the difference between a comparative and a superlative* **3. SOMEBODY OR SOMETHING EXCELLENT** somebody or something of the highest quality **4. EXAGGERATED PRAISE** an exaggerated description or way of referring to somebody or something, usually expressing admiration ○ *heaping superlatives on their performance* [14C. Via French < Latin *superlativus* < past participle of *superferre* 'carry above' < *super* 'over, above' + *ferre* 'carry'] —**superlatively** *adv* —**superlativeness** *n*

superliner /so͞opər līnər/ *n* a large luxurious ocean-going passenger ship

superlunary /so͞opər lo͞onəri/, **superlunar** /-lo͞onər/ *adj* **1.** located beyond the Moon **2.** belonging to a supposed higher world or celestial plane [Early 17C. After SUBLUNARY]

superman /so͞opər man/ (*plural* **-men** /-men/) *n* **1.** a man possessing exceptional or superhuman strength, abilities, or powers **2.** in the philosophy of Nietzsche, an ideal man who, through creativity and integrity, is able to transcend good and evil and is the goal of human evolution [Early 20C. Translation of German *Übermensch*]

CULTURAL NOTE ***Superman***, a comic strip created by US writer Jerry Siegal and drawn by US artist Joseph Shuster that first appeared in 1938. The alter ego of 'mild-mannered reporter' Clark Kent is Superman, an almost invincible crime-fighting superhero in a red cape, who was originally sent to Earth as a child from the doomed planet Krypton. The story has been made into radio shows, musicals, television series, and feature films.

supermarket /so͞opər maarkit/ *n* a large self-service retail store selling food and household goods

supermassive black hole /so͞opər mássiv-/ *n* an extremely large black hole with a mass ranging from a few million to more than several billion solar masses that is believed to be at the centre of many large galaxies

supermax /so͞opər maks/ *n US* describes a prison that is protected or made secure by the most extensive and elaborate security arrangements that are available or in current use

supermodel /so͞opər mod'l/ *n* a fashion model who is extremely well paid and in very high demand by fashion designers and photographers

supernal /soo púrn'l/ *adj* (*literary*) **1.** coming from or located in the sky **2.** suited to or characteristic of the sky [15C. Via French < Latin *supernus* 'heavenly' < *super* 'over, above'] —**supernally** *adv*

supernatant /so͞opər náyt'nt/ *n* the usually clear liquid left above a precipitate or sediment [Mid-17C. < Latin *supernatant-*, present participle of *supernatare* 'float above' < *super* 'over, above' + *natare* (see NATATORY)]

supernatural /so͞opər náchərəl/ *adj* **1. NOT OF NATURAL WORLD** relating to or attributed to phenomena that cannot be explained by natural laws **2. RELATING TO DEITY** relating to or attributed to a deity **3. MAGICAL** relating to or attributed to magic or the occult ■ *n* **1. SUPERNATURAL THINGS** supernatural beings or phenomena **2. WORLD OF SUPERNATURAL THINGS** the realm of supernatural beings or phenomena —**supernaturally** *adv* —**supernaturalness** *n*

supernaturalism /so͞opər náchərəlizəm/ *n* **1.** the quality or condition of being supernatural **2.** the belief that supernatural or divine beings and phenomena intervene in human events —**supernaturalist** *n, adj* —**supernaturalistic** /so͞opər náchərə lístik/ *adj*

supernova /so͞opər nōvə/ (*plural* **-vae** /-vee/ or **-vas**) *n* a catastrophic explosion of a large star in the latter stages of stellar evolution, with a resulting short-lived luminosity from 10 to 100 million times that of the Sun

supernumerary /so͞opər nyo͞omərəri/ *adj* **1. EXTRA** exceeding the usual number **2.** HR **SUBSTITUTING** employed as a substitute or extra worker ■ *n* (*plural* **-ies**) **1. SOMEBODY OR SOMETHING EXTRA** somebody or something in addition to the usual number **2.** THEATRE **ACTOR WITH WALK-ON PART** an actor who appears on stage, but has no lines to speak **3.** HR **SUBSTITUTE EMPLOYEE** somebody employed as a substitute or extra worker [Early 17C. < late Latin *supernumerarius* < Latin *super* 'over, above' + *numerus* 'number']

superorder /so͞opər awrdər/ *n* a taxonomic category of related organisms of a rank above order

superordinate /so͞opər áwrdinət/ *n* **1.** a word whose meaning encompasses the meaning of another more specific word. 'Animal' is a superordinate of 'cat'. **2.** somebody or something of superior rank, status, or class [Early 17C. < SUPER- + SUBORDINATE] —**superordinate** *adj*

superorganism /so͞opər áwrgənizəm/ *n* a group of organisms functioning as a social unit, e.g. an insect colony

superovulation /so͞opər ovjo͞o láysh'n/ *n* increased frequency of ovulation or production of a large number of ova at one time. It is often caused by the administration of gonadotrophin hormones, which are prescribed to induce ovulation in infertility. —**superovulate** /-óvvjo͞o layt/ *vi*

superperson /so͞opər purss'n/ (*plural* **-people** /-peep'l/ or **-persons**) *n* **1.** somebody who succeeds in combining several roles with apparent ease (*informal*) **2.** an imaginary or fictional person with superhuman powers

superphosphate /so͞opər fóssfayt/ *n* a commercially produced fertilizer prepared by treating phosphate mineral deposits with acid, either sulphuric acid, phosphoric acid, or a mixture of the two

superplastic /so͞opər plástik/ *adj* describes alloys that are capable of being easily shaped and moulded at high temperatures without fracturing —**superplasticity** /-pla stíssəti/ *n*

superpose /so͞opər póz/ (**-poses, -posing, -posed**) *vt* **1.** to place or lay one object on top of or above another **2.** to move one geometric figure so that it coincides exactly with another [Early 19C. Probably < French *superposer*, back-formation < *superposition* 'superposing' < Latin *superponere* 'place over' < *super-* 'over, above' + *ponere* 'to place'] —**superposable** *adj* —**superposed** *adj* —**superposition** /-pə zísh'n/ *n*

superpower /so͞opər pow ər/ *n* **1.** an extremely powerful nation with greater political, economic, or military power than most other nations **2.** extremely high electrical or mechanical power —**superpowered** *adj*

supersaturated /so͞opər sáchə raytid/ *adj* **1.** used to describe a chemical solution containing a greater amount of solute than usually possible at a specific temperature and pressure, often as a result of cooling **2.** used to describe a vapour containing more gaseous material than usually possible at a specific temperature and pressure —**supersaturation** /-sachə ráysh'n/ *n*

supersaver /so͞opər sáyvər/ *n* an aeroplane, coach, or train ticket that is cheaper than the usual price and must usually be bought a specific amount of time before the date of travel

superscribe /so͞opər skrīb/ (**-scribes, -scribing, -scribed**) *vt* to write or print something such as a name or address above, outside, or on the surface of something else

superscript /so͞opər skript/ *n* a letter, character, or symbol that is written above, or above and to the right or left of, another character ■ *adj* written or printed as a superscript

superscription /so͞opər skrípsh'n/ *n* **1.** something that is written, printed, or engraved above, outside, or on the surface of something else **2.** the act of writing or printing something above, outside, or on the surface of something else

supersede /so͞opər seéd/ (**-sedes, -seding, -seded**) *vt* **1.** to take the place or position of something that is less efficient, less modern, or less appropriate, or cause something to do this **2.** to succeed somebody or something in a role, office, or function (*formal*) [15C. Via French < Latin *supersedere* 'be superior to' < *super* 'over, above' + *sedere* 'sit'] —**supersedable** *adj* —**supersedence** *n* —**superseder** *n*

USAGE Note that ***supersede*** is correctly spelt *-sede* and not *-cede*. It is derived not from the Latin verb *cedere* 'to go' (as *intercede* and *precede* are) but from *sedere* 'to sit'.

supersensible /so͞opər sénssəb'l/ *adj* above or beyond the perception of the senses —**supersensibly** *adv*

supersensitive /so͞opər sénssətiv/ *adj* MED same as **hypersensitive** —**supersensitively** *adv* —**supersensitivity** /-sénssə tívvəti/ *n*

supersensory /so͞opər sénssəri/ *adj* same as **supersensible**

superserver /so͞opər survər/ *n* an extremely powerful computer that controls a network or networks of other computers

superset /so͞opər set/ *n* in mathematics, a set that contains one or more other sets

supersonic /so͞opər sónnik/ *adj* relating to, produced by, or capable of reaching a speed that is faster than the speed at which sound travels through the air [Early 20C. < SUPER- + Latin *sonus* 'sound'] —**supersonically** *adv*

supersonics /so͞opər sónniks/ *n* the science or study of supersonic motion or phenomena (*takes a singular verb*)

supersonic transport *n* a transport aircraft that travels at supersonic speed

superstar /so͞opər staar/ *n* an extremely famous or successful person, especially in sports or entertainment —**superstardom** *n*

superstate /so͞opər stayt/ *n* a powerful country with a very large geographical area and population, especially one created by the union or federation of a number of nations or states

superstitial /so͞opər stísh'l/ *n* an animated advertisement that pops up on a viewer's screen between page views on the Internet [Late 20C. < SUPER- + INTERSTITIAL]

superstition /so͞opər stísh'n/ *n* **1.** an irrational, but usually deep-seated belief in the magical effects of a specific action or ritual, especially in the likelihood that good or bad luck will result from performing it **2.** irrational and often quasi-religious belief in and reverence for the magical effects of some actions and rituals or the magical powers of some objects [15C. Via French < Latin *superstition-* < *superstes* 'standing over (in awe)' < *super* 'over, above' + *stare* 'to stand']

superstitious /so͞opər stíshəss/ *adj* **1.** convinced that performing or not performing specific actions brings good or bad luck, that some events or phenomena are omens, and, generally, fearfully believing in a supernatural dimension to events **2.** based on a false or irrational belief in, or fear of, the supernatural

superstore /so͞opər stawr/ *n* **1.** a very large supermarket or store offering a wider and more varied range of consumer goods than other stores of the same type **2.** a retail chain or single store that specializes in a range of related products offered at discount prices ○ *a computer superstore*

superstratum /so͞opər straatəm, -straytəm/ (*plural* **-ta** /-tə/) *n* **1.** a layer, especially of rock or sedimentation, on top of another one **2.** the language of an invading or colonizing population in relation to the language of an indigenous population that it changes or influences

superstring /sóopər string/ *n* a hypothetical one-dimensional entity (**string**) of extremely short length, held to be a fundamental component of matter in some theories of elementary particles involving supersymmetry

superstructure /sóopər strukchər/ *n* **1. UPPER PART OF SHIP** the part of a ship above the main deck **2. VISIBLE PART OF BUILDING** the part of a building above its foundations **3. PART DEVELOPED ON BASE** a physical or intellectual structure built on or developed from a fundamental form, base, or concept **4.** POL **INSTITUTIONS ASSOCIATED WITH PARTICULAR ECONOMY** in Marxist theory, the complex of social, legal, and political institutions that are an extension and reflection of the type of economy operating in a particular society —**superstructural** /sóopər strúkchərəl/ *adj*

supersymmetry /sóopər símmətri/ *n* a theory in physics proposing a type of symmetry that would apply to all elementary particles

supertanker /sóopər tangkər/ *n* a very large tanker ship, usually with a capacity of 275,000 tonnes/300,000 tons or more

supertax /sóopər taks/ *n* ECON same as **surtax** *n* (sense 2)

supertitle /sóopər tīt'l/ *n US* THEATRE same as **surtitle** [Late 20C. After SUBTITLE]

supertonic /sóopər tonik/ *n* the note one step above the tonic in a major or minor scale, or the harmony built upon this note

supervene /sóopər véen/ (**-venes, -vening, -vened**) *vi* (*formal*) **1.** to follow or come about unexpectedly, usually interrupting or changing what is going on **2.** to follow immediately after something [Mid-17C. < Latin *supervenire* < *super* 'over, above' + *venire* 'come'] —**supervenience** *n* —**supervenient** *adj* —**supervention** /-vénsh'n/ *n*

supervise /sóopər vīz/ (**-vises, -vising, -vised**) *vti* **1.** to watch over an activity or task being carried out by somebody and ensure that it is performed correctly **2.** to be in charge of a group of people engaged in an activity or task and keep order or ensure that they perform it correctly [Late 16C. < medieval Latin *supervis-*, past participle of *supervidere* 'oversee' < Latin *super* 'over, above' + *videre* 'see'] —**supervision** /sóopər vízh'n/ *n*

~~**superviser**~~ incorrect spelling of **supervisor**

supervision order *n* a court order by which a social worker or probation officer is entrusted with the personal supervision of a child involved in care proceedings

supervisor /sóopər vīzər/ *n* **1. BOSS** somebody whose job is to oversee and guide the work or activities of a group of other people **2.** *N Am* EDUC **MAIN TEACHER OF SUBJECT** a teacher or other school official who oversees the teaching and teachers of a single subject area **3.** EDUC **TUTOR FOR GRADUATE** in some British universities, a teacher assigned to supervise the work of an individual student, especially research done by a postgraduate student —**supervisorship** *n* —**supervisory** /sóopər vīzəri, sóopər vīzəri/ *adj*

USAGE ***Supervisor*** is the only correct spelling of this word. It is sometimes misspelt with an *-er* ending, on the model of many other English words, notably *adviser* (which has a variant spelling in *-or*).

superweed /sóopər weed/ *n* an indestructible or ineradicable weed that could hypothetically evolve as a hybrid of ordinary weeds and genetically modified plants

superwoman /sóopər wòomən/ (*plural* **-women** /-wimin/) *n* **1.** a woman who succeeds in combining several roles such as worker, wife, and mother with apparent ease (*informal*) **2.** an imaginary or fictional woman with superhuman powers

supinate /sóopi nayt, syóo-/ (**-nates, -nating, -nated**) *v* **1.** *vti* **TURN PALM UPWARDS** to turn the hand so that the palm faces upwards, or be turned in this way **2.** *vti* **TURN SOLE UPWARDS** to turn the foot so that the sole is facing upwards, or be turned in this way **3.** *vi* **LIE FACING UPWARDS** to turn the face upwards or lie in a supine position with the face upwards [Mid-19C. < Latin *supinat-*, past participle of *supinare* 'turn backwards' < *supinus* 'lying on the back'] —**supination** /sóopi náysh'n, syóo-/ *n*

supinator /sóopi naytər, syóo-/ *n* a muscle, especially in the forearm, that supinates a hand or foot

supine /sóo pīn, syóo-/ *adj* **1. LYING ON BACK** lying on the back and with the face upwards **2. PALM UPWARDS** having the palm of the hand facing upwards or away from the body **3. FAILING TO ACT** utterly passive or inactive, especially in a situation where a vigorous reaction is called for ■ *n* GRAM **TYPE OF LATIN NOUN** a Latin noun formed from a past participle stem and having only accusative and ablative inflections [15C. < Latin *supinus* 'lying on the back']

~~**supose**~~ incorrect spelling of **suppose**

supper /súppər/ *n* **1. EVENING MEAL** a light meal eaten in the evening **2. MAIN EVENING MEAL** the main meal of the day when taken in the evening **3. SOCIAL EVENT** an evening social event that includes a meal [13C. < Old French *soper* 'eat supper' < *soupe* 'sop, broth' (see SOUP)] ◇ **sing for your supper** to work or do something in exchange for your food and board, or for something that you want

CULTURAL NOTE ***The Last Supper***, a painting (1495–97) by the Italian artist Leonardo da Vinci. Painted directly onto a wall in the monastery of Santa Maria delle Grazie in Milan, it depicts the moment when Jesus Christ declares that one of his companions will betray him. It is noted for its magnificent composition and powerful depiction of the outrage of the disciples, the serenity of Jesus Christ, and the guilt of Judas.

supper club *n* **1.** a group of people who get together periodically to dine in restaurants **2.** *US* a restaurant serving evening meals and sometimes featuring entertainment

suppertime /súppər tīm/ *n* the time at which supper is served or eaten

supplant /sə pláant/ (**-plants, -planting, -planted**) *vt* **1.** to take the place or position of somebody by force or intrigue **2.** to take the place of something, especially something much used, inferior, outmoded, or irrelevant [13C. Directly or via French < Latin *supplantare* 'trip up, overthrow' < *sub-* 'up from beneath' + *planta* 'sole of the foot'] —**supplantation** /súpplaan táysh'n/ *n* —**supplanter** *n*

supple /súpp'l/ (**-pler, -plest**) *adj* **1. FLEXIBLE** flexible and elastic **2. MOVING EASILY** capable of bending, stretching, and moving with ease, fluidity, and grace **3. ADAPTABLE** adaptable and responsive in grappling with problems or dealing with new challenges **4. COMPLIANT** excessively compliant and willing to agree (*literary*) [13C. Via French < Latin *supplex* 'submissive', literally 'bending under' < *-plex* 'fold'] —**supplely** *adv* —**suppleness** *n*

supplejack /súpp'l jak/ (*plural* **-jacks** or *same*) *n* **1.** a woody vine with bluish fruits. Flowers: tiny, white. Native to: southeastern United States. Latin name: *Berchemia scandens*. **2.** a tropical vine whose wood is used for making walking sticks. Native to: Central and South America. Latin name: *Paullinia curvassica*.

supplement *n* /súppliment/ **1. ADDITION** an addition to something to increase its size or make up for a deficiency ○ *a useful supplement to the family income* **2.** PUBL **PUBLICATION** a publication that amplifies or corrects one already published **3.** PUBL **PERIODICAL PART** an additional section included in or sold with a magazine or newspaper, especially an additional section that appears regularly **4.** PHARM **FOOD** a substance with a specific nutritional value taken to make up for a real or supposed deficiency in diet **5.** COMM **EXTRA CHARGE** a charge payable in addition to the basic charge for a special service or under set conditions **6.** MATHS **ANGLE OR ARC** an angle or arc that, when added to another, makes 180° or a semicircle ■ *vt* /súppli ment/ (**-ments, -menting, -mented**) **1. MAKE ADDITION TO SOMETHING** to increase, extend, or improve something by adding something to it ○ *supplemented their diet with vitamins* **2. BE ADDITIONAL PART OF SOMETHING** to be a supplement to something ○ *Her remarks supplemented the report.* [14C. < Latin *supplementum* < *supplere* 'fill out, complete' (see SUPPLY)] —**supplemental** /súppli mént'l/ *adj* —**supplementally** *adv* —**supplementation** /súppli men táysh'n/ *n* —**supplementer** *n*

supplementary /súppli méntəri/ *adj* **1. ADDITIONAL** additional to an existing one or to the usual number or amount **2. COMPLETING** making up for something that is lacking ■ *n* (*plural* **-ries**) **SOMETHING ADDITIONAL** an additional thing, person, or question —**supplementarily** *adv*

supplementary angle *n* an angle that when added to another angle makes up 180°

supplementary benefit *n* in the United Kingdom, an allowance formerly paid weekly by the state to bring a person's or family's income up to what was considered to be a minimum acceptable level

suppletion /sə pléesh'n/ *n* the use of an unrelated word to fill the gap when some inflected or derived forms of a word are missing, as 'was' forms the past tense of 'to be' [14C. Via French < medieval Latin *suppletion-* < past participle of Latin *supplere* (see SUPPLY)] —**suppletive** /sə pléetiv/ *adj*

suppliant /súppli ənt/ *adj* expressing a humble and sincere appeal to somebody who has the power to grant a request (*formal*) ■ *n* same as **supplicant** [15C. < French, present participle of *supplier* 'supplicate' < Latin *supplicare* 'bend under' < *supplex* (see SUPPLE)] —**suppliance** *n* —**suppliantly** *adv*

supplicant /súpplikənt/ *n* somebody who makes a humble and sincere appeal to a person who has the power to grant the request (*formal*) ■ *adj* same as **suppliant** [Late 16C. < Latin *supplicant-*, present participle of *supplicare* (see SUPPLIANT)] —**supplicatory** /súpplikətəri, -káytəri/ *adj*

supplication /súppli káysh'n/ *n* (*formal*) **1.** a humble and sincere appeal to somebody who has the power to grant a request **2.** the addressing of humble and sincere appeals to somebody with the power to grant them —**supplicate** /súppli kayt/ *vti*

~~**suppliment**~~ incorrect spelling of **supplement**

supply /sə plī/ *vt* (**-plies, -plying, -plied**) **1. PROVIDE** to give, sell, or make available something that is wanted or needed by somebody or something ○ *supplied equipment for the expedition* **2. SATISFY NEED** to satisfy a need or requirement (*formal*) **3. MAKE UP FOR LACK** to make up for a deficiency, loss, or lack **4. SERVE AS SUBSTITUTE IN INSTITUTION** to act as a substitute in a place such as a church or school (*formal*) ■ *n* (*plural* **-plies**) **1. AVAILABLE AMOUNT** an amount or quantity of something available for use ○ *a plentiful supply of food and drink* **2. PROVISION** the act or business of giving, selling, or making available something that is wanted or needed by somebody or something, or the system that does this ○ *the supply of electric power to villages in the mountains* **3.** ECON **QUANTITY AVAILABLE IN MARKET** the quantity of a good or service available in a market at a specific time **4. SUBSTITUTE** somebody who acts as a substitute for another, especially in a church (*formal*) **5.** EDUC same as **supply teacher** (*informal*) ■ **supplies** *npl* **NEEDED THINGS** the things, especially food and equipment, that a group of people need to survive and operate, or that are needed to carry out a task or activity ○ *Our supplies were running very low.* [14C. Via Old French *supplier* 'meet a deficiency' < Latin *supplere* 'fill up' < *plere* 'fill'] —**suppliable** *adj* —**supplier** *n* ◇ **in short supply** present or available only in small or insufficient quantities

supply and demand *n* the relationship between the availability of a good or service and the need or desire for it among consumers

supply-side economics *n* economic policies that promote conditions favouring the producers of goods and services (*takes a singular or plural verb*)

supply teacher *n UK* a teacher who takes the place of another temporarily. ANZ term **relief teacher**. N Am term **substitute teacher**

support /sə páwrt/ *vt* (**-ports, -porting, -ported**) **1. KEEP SOMETHING OR SOMEBODY STABLE** to keep something or somebody upright or in place, or prevent something or somebody from falling ○ *Those pillars support the roof.* **2. BEAR WEIGHT** to be strong enough to hold a particular object or weight in place without breaking or giving way ○ *Are you sure the ice is thick enough to support our weight?* **3. SUSTAIN SOMEBODY FINANCIALLY** to provide somebody with money and the other necessities of life over a period of time ○ *She succeeds in supporting her family on what she earns.* **4. GIVE ACTIVE HELP AND ENCOURAGEMENT** to give active help, encouragement, or money to somebody or something ○ *We support the charity through voluntary work.* **5. BE IN FAVOUR OF SOMETHING** to be in

favour of something, e.g. a cause, policy, organization, or sports team and wish to see it succeed ○ *Do you support the committee's policy on membership fees?* **6.** **BE PRESENT AND GIVE ENCOURAGEMENT** to give encouragement to somebody or something by being present at an event ○ *Why not come along on Saturday and support the school team?* **7.** **GIVE ASSISTANCE OR COMFORT** to give assistance or comfort to somebody in difficulty or distress ○ *He supported me throughout the crisis.* **8.** **CORROBORATE STORY** to give something greater credibility by being consistent with it or providing further evidence for it ○ *There is further evidence that supports the defendant's claim.* **9.** **ENABLE SOMETHING TO LIVE** to provide sufficient food and water or the appropriate conditions or facilities to enable people or animals to live or allow something to function ○ *A better irrigation system would enable the area to support a larger population.* **10.** **PROVIDE ASSISTANCE WITH COMPUTER SYSTEM** to provide technical advice and assistance to the users of a product, especially a computing system or package **11.** COMPUT **PERMIT USE OF SOFTWARE OR DEVICES** to be designed to allow something, e.g. a specific type of software, computer device, or programming language, to operate with it ○ *This card cannot support parallel and serial ports.* **12.** ARTS **PLAY SMALL ROLE ALONGSIDE SOMEBODY** to play a subsidiary role alongside an actor with a leading part in a play or film **13.** **TOLERATE SOMETHING** to put up with something unpleasant (*formal*) ○ *The Court will not support such behaviour.* ■ *n* **1.** **SOMETHING THAT SUPPORTS** a means of holding something upright or in place, or of preventing it from falling ○ *If you remove those supports the plank will fall down.* **2.** **REINFORCEMENT TO HOLD THINGS IN PLACE** physical force or reinforcement used to hold things steady or in place ○ *Stakes give the plant extra support.* **3.** **ACTIVE ASSISTANCE OR ENCOURAGEMENT** active assistance and encouragement to, or an approving and encouraging attitude towards, somebody or something ○ *Support for the cause continues to rise.* **4.** **HELP IN CRISIS** practical help or sympathy and encouragement received from others, e.g. friends, family, or charitable organizations, especially during times of crisis and change ○ *Without the support of my family, I would not have survived the ordeal.* **5.** **SUPPORTIVE PERSON OR THING** somebody who or something that provides help, money, encouragement, or comfort **6.** **GROUP OF SUPPORTERS** the supporters of an organization such as a political party, or of an individual person, considered as a group ○ *His support is drawn mainly from the rural areas.* **7.** **TECHNICAL ASSISTANCE** technical assistance and advice offered by the manufacturer or supplier of something, especially a computer device or program, to the user **8.** ARTS **SUPPORTING BANDS OR ENTERTAINERS** the other band or bands, or the other entertainers, appearing in a programme along with the main attraction **9.** CLOTHING **SUPPORTING GARMENT** a garment that supports or protects a part of the body, especially one used by male athletes to protect the genitals [14C. Via French < Latin *supportare* 'bear up' < *portare* 'carry'] —**supportability** /sə páwrtə bílləti/ *n* —**supportable** *adj* —**supportably** *adv* ◇ **in support of** in order to support somebody or something

support area *n* an area with a supply of military material and personnel standing ready for use

supporter /sə páwrtər/ *n* **1.** somebody who supports somebody or something, such as a cause, idea, course of action, or sports team ○ *greeted by a crowd of supporters* **2.** either of a pair of standing figures on either side of a shield in a coat of arms

support group *n* a group of people with a problem or concern in common who meet regularly to discuss it and support one another

support hose *npl N Am* same as **support stockings**

supporting /sə páwrting/ *adj* **1.** accompanying and assisting, but secondary to, the main action or the main participants in something ○ *a supporting role in the contract negotiations* **2.** appearing in the same film, play, or programme as the main star or attraction ○ *supporting acts*

supportive /sə páwrtiv/ *adj* giving support, especially moral or emotional support —**supportiveness** *n*

support level *n* the price at which a security whose price has been falling begins to attract investors again because of its intrinsic worth

support stockings *npl* elasticated stockings that support the veins in the lower legs, used by people with varicose veins or bad circulation. N Am term **support hose**

support system *n* the group of family, friends, colleagues, or professionals available to help a person or organization when required

suppose /sə pṓz/ (**-poses, -posing, -posed**) *v* **1.** *vti* **BELIEVE TO BE TRUE** to believe or imagine something to be the case ○ *I suppose you haven't heard the news.* **2.** *vi* **IMAGINE AS POSSIBLE** to consider or imagine something to be a possibility ○ *Suppose that he doesn't know about your plan.* **3.** *vt* **MAKE SOMETHING A PRECONDITION** to require something as a precondition ○ *Your plan supposes that there are enough presents to go around.* **4.** *vt* **INDICATING TENTATIVENESS** used to indicate real or polite hesitancy when making a statement, suggestion, or request ○ *Well, I suppose I'd better be going.* ○ *I don't suppose you could lend me the £50, could you?* **5.** *vti* **USED TO SHOW RELUCTANT AGREEMENT** used when agreeing to do something, or agreeing that something is the case, to show that you do so reluctantly, uncertainly, or noncommittally ○ *'You know it's the right thing to do, don't you?' 'I suppose so'.* ○ *All right, I suppose I can just about manage it.* [14C. < French *supposer*, alteration of Latin *supponere* (see SUPPOSITION) after French *poser* 'to place'] —**supposable** *adj* —**supposer** *n* ◇ **be supposed to do something 1.** to be expected to do something as the result of a previous agreement or arrangement, or an obligation ○ *You were supposed to wait for me here.* **2.** to be expected to do something as the result of an action or set of conditions ○ *The light's supposed to come on when the tank is empty.* ◇ **be not supposed to do something** to be not allowed or not expected to do something ○ *You weren't supposed to tell anyone that!* ○ *Surely it's not supposed to make a noise like that.*

supposed /sə pṓzd, -pṓzid/ *adj* accepted, at least by some, as correct, real, or having a quality, but on slender or uncertain evidence ○ *Frankly, I'm very dubious about this supposed brilliant idea of his.*

supposedly /sə pṓzidli/ *adv* as some people believe, or as people were led to believe ○ *He was supposedly going to pick us up after work.* ○ *a supposedly instant remedy*

supposing /sə pṓzing/ *conj* imagining or assuming something to be the case ○ *Supposing she comes, will you let her in?*

supposition /súppə zísh'n/ *n* **1.** something that it is suggested might be true, or that is accepted as true on the basis of some evidence but without proof ○ *That seems a reasonable supposition on the basis of his previous behaviour.* **2.** the mental act of supposing something to be the case, or ideas that result from supposing, especially as opposed to ideas based on firm evidence ○ *All this is mere supposition.* [Late 16C. Directly or via French < Latin *supposition-* < *supposit-*, past participle of *supponere* 'place under' < *ponere* 'to place'] —**suppositional** *adj* —**suppositionally** *adv*

suppositious /súppə zíshəss/ *adj* based on supposition rather than firm evidence or proof (*formal*)

supposititious /sə pózzi tíshəss/ *adj* substituted for something else in order to deceive (*formal*) [Early 17C. < Latin *supposititius* < *supposit-* (see SUPPOSITION)] —**supposititiously** *adv*

suppositive /sə pózzitiv/ *adj* expressing or relating to supposition, or introducing a clause expressing a supposition ■ *n* a conjunction that introduces a clause expressing a supposition, e.g. 'if', 'provided that', or 'supposing'

suppository /sə pózzitəri/ (*plural* **-ries**) *n* a medicated mass that melts at body temperature, designed to be inserted into the rectum, vagina, or urethra [14C. < medieval Latin *suppositorium* < Latin *supposit-* (see SUPPOSITION)]

suppress /sə préss/ (**-presses, -pressing, -pressed**) *vt* **1.** **CAUSE TO STOP** to put an end to something, especially something perceived as a threat, by the use of force or a prohibition ○ *suppressed all complaints with a gagging order* **2.** **PREVENT SOMETHING** to prevent something from happening, operating, or becoming apparent, or restrain something and limit its effects ○ *Some slimming drugs are designed to suppress appetite.* ○ *Her voice shook with suppressed anger.* **3.** **STOP SPREAD OR PUBLICATION** to prevent information or evidence from becoming known, or written material from being published ○ *The report was suppressed for political reasons.* **4.** PSYCHOL **RESIST SOMETHING CONSCIOUSLY** to resist thoughts or feelings consciously as they arise, and try to banish them from the mind **5.** ELECTRONICS **DIMINISH OSCILLATION** to reduce unwanted noise or oscillation in a circuit or unwanted frequencies in a signal **6.** BIOL **REDUCE BODILY FUNCTION** to cause the reduction or cessation of a normal bodily function such as menstruation or growth, or undergo such a reduction or cessation **7.** GENETICS **INHIBIT GENE EFFECT** to cancel or reverse the effects of a gene [14C. < Latin *suppress-*, past participle of *supprimere* 'push down' < *premere* 'press'] —**suppresser** *n* —**suppressibility** /sə préssə bílləti/ *n* —**suppressible** *adj*

suppressant /sə préssənt/ *n* a substance, medication, or activity that restrains or limits the effects of something (*often used in combination*) ○ *an appetite suppressant*

suppression /sə présh'n/ *n* **1.** **FORCEFUL PREVENTION** conscious and forceful action to put an end to something, destroy it, or prevent it from becoming known **2.** **STATE OF CONSTRAINT** the state of being forcefully restrained or held back **3.** PSYCHOL **AVOIDANCE OF THOUGHTS AND FEELINGS** conscious avoidance or inhibition of memories, desires, or thoughts **4.** ELECTRONICS **DIMINISHING OF OSCILLATION** reduction of unwanted noise or oscillation in a circuit or of unwanted frequencies in a signal **5.** BIOL **DEVELOPMENTAL FAILURE** the failure of an organ, tissue, or part to develop **6.** PHYSIOL **CESSATION OF BODY FUNCTION** the reduction or stoppage of a normal bodily function such as secretion or excretion **7.** MED **REMOVAL OF SYMPTOMS** the lessening or abolition of a symptom or the outward signs of a disease **8.** GENETICS **REVERSAL OF MUTATION** the cancellation or reversal of the effect of a gene, especially of one genetic mutation by another

suppressive /sə préssiv/ *adj* having the effect of suppressing something —**suppressively** *adv*

suppressor /sə préssər/ *n* **1.** a gene that prevents the expression of another gene **2.** a device that reduces unwanted interference or current in a circuit

suppressor T cell, **suppressor cell** *n* a T cell that diminishes or suppresses the immune response to an antigen of B cells and other T cells

suppurate /súppyŏŏ rayt/ (**-rates, -rating, -rated**) *vi* to produce or discharge pus as a result of an injury or infection [Mid-16C. < Latin *suppurat-*, past participle of *suppurare* < *pus* 'pus'] —**suppuration** *n* —**suppurative** *adj*

supra /sŏŏprə/ *adv* used in formal writing to refer the reader back to something at an earlier point in the same text (*formal*) [Early 16C. < Latin, 'above, beyond']

supra- *prefix* **1.** over, on top of ○ *suprarenal* **2.** transcending ○ *supranational* [< Latin *supra* 'above, beyond']

suprachiasmatic nucleus /sŏŏprə kī az máttik-/ *n* an area in the front part of the hypothalamus, on the underside of the brain, responsible for maintaining the circadian rhythm

supralapsarian /sŏŏprə lap sáiri ən/ *n* in Christianity, somebody who believes that prior to the general fall of humanity God preordained the salvation of some souls [Mid-17C. < SUPRA- + Latin *lapsus* 'sin, falling' (see LAPSE)] —**supralapsarianism** *n*

supraliminal /sŏŏprə límmin'l/ *adj* at or above the threshold of consciousness —**supraliminally** *adv*

supramolecular /sŏŏprə mə lékyŏŏlər/ *adj* **1.** more complex in form than a molecule **2.** composed of more than one molecule

supranational /sŏŏprə násh'nəl/ *adj* not limited by the concerns or boundaries of a single nation —**supranationalism** *n* —**supranationally** *adv*

supraorbital /sŏŏprə áwrbit'l/ *adj* located above the bony socket (**orbit**) of the eye

suprarenal /sŏŏprə reén'l/ *adj* located above the kidneys

suprasegmental /sŏŏprə seg mént'l/ *adj* in phonetics,

connected with features of speech such as pitch and stress that accompany rather than constitute phonemes —**suprasegmentally** adv

supremacist /soō prémmǝssist, syoō-/ n somebody who believes that a group is innately superior to others and therefore is entitled to dominate them (usually used in combination)

supremacy /soō prémmǝssi, syoō-/ n a position of superiority or authority over all others [Mid-16C. < SUPREME, after PRIMACY]

suprematism /soō prémmǝtizǝm, syoō-/ n a school of cubist painting from early 20th-century Russia [Mid-20C. < Russian suprematizm < French suprématie 'supremacy'] —**suprematist** n

supreme /soō preém, syoō-/ adj 1. ABOVE ALL OTHERS greater than or superior to any other, especially above all others in power, authority, rank, status, or skill ○ holding supreme authority ○ In women's long-distance running, she still reigns supreme. 2. HIGHEST IN DEGREE of the greatest or most admirable kind ○ a supreme example of the architect's skill 3. ULTIMATE greater than any that have gone before, or the greatest possible ○ the supreme sacrifice 4. IN HIGHEST DEGREE in the highest degree or of the most unmitigated kind ○ viewed them with supreme contempt [15C. < Latin supremus 'uppermost' < superus 'upper' < super 'over, above'] —**supremely** adv

suprême /soō preém, syoō-, -prém/ n the finest cut from any piece of meat, especially boneless breast of chicken ■ adj served with a suprême sauce ○ chicken suprême [Early 19C. < French, 'supreme']

Supreme Being n RELIG same as **God**

supreme commander n a military commander in charge of all allied forces in a theatre of war or in a coalition such as NATO

Supreme Court n 1. LAW same as **Supreme Court of Judicature** 2. REPLACEMENT FOR LAW LORDS in the United Kingdom, a planned court that will replace the Law Lords operating as a committee of the House of Lords as the highest court in the land 3. HIGHEST COURT in the United States, the highest federal court, consisting of nine justices appointed by the President with the advice and consent of Congress and making decisions solely on constitutional matters 4. HIGHEST STATE COURT the highest appellate court in many states of the United States 5. HIGHEST COURT IN COUNTRY the highest court in a country, or in a state or territory of a federation

Supreme Court of Judicature n the highest national court in England and Wales consisting of two divisions, the High Court of Justice and the Court of Appeal

suprême sauce n a rich sauce made of chicken or veal stock with added cream and egg yolks

Supreme Soviet n the two-chamber national legislature of the former Soviet Union, or a similar legislature in any one of the former Soviet republics

supremo /soō preémō, syoō-/ (plural -mos) n somebody with overriding authority in a particular sphere (informal) [Mid-20C. < Spanish (generalísimo) supremo 'supreme commander']

~~supress~~ incorrect spelling of **suppress**

~~suprise~~ incorrect spelling of **surprise**

supt, Supt abbr superintendent

supvr abbr supervisor

suq n COMM another spelling of **souk**

Suquamish /sǝ kwaámish, skwaámish/ (plural -mishes or same) n 1. a member of a Native North American people who live along the Puget Sound in Washington State 2. the Salish language of the Suquamish people [Mid-19C. < Salish] —**Suquamish** adj

Sur. abbr Suriname

sur- prefix 1. over, above, on top of ○ surprint 2. additional, extra ○ surcharge [Via French < Latin super 'over, above']

sura /soórǝ/ n a chapter of the Koran [Early 17C. < Arabic sūra]

Surabaya /soórǝ bí ǝ/ city on northeastern Java Island, Indonesia. Population: 2,351,303 (1997).

surah /soórǝ/ n a twilled silk or rayon fabric. Use:

women's clothing. [Late 19C. Anglicization of French surat 'Surat', port in W India]

surahi /soō rí, soō raáhi/ (plural -his) n a long-necked clay pot, used in South Asia for storing cold water [Late 17C. < Urdu, Persian ṣurāhī < Arabic ṣurāhiya 'pure wine']

sural /soórǝl, syoō-/ adj relating to the calf of the leg (technical) [Early 17C. < Latin sura 'calf of the leg']

Surat /soō rát, soórǝt/ city, port, and administrative headquarters of Surat District, Gujarat State, western India. Population: 2,811,466 (2001).

surbase /súr bayss/ n an architectural moulding at the top of a base such as a pedestal or baseboard —**surbasement** /sur báyssmǝnt/ n

surbased /sur báyst/ adj describes an arch with a rise of less than half its span [Mid-18C. < French surbaissé 'flattened' < baisser 'to lower' < medieval Latin bassus 'low']

surcease /sur seéss/ vti (-ceases, -ceasing, -ceased) to cease, or bring something to an end (formal) ■ n a cessation, especially a temporary one (literary) [15C. < Anglo-Norman surseser 'refrain' < Latin supersedere (see SUPERSEDE); influenced by CEASE]

surcharge /súr chaarj/ v (-charges, -charging, -charged) 1. vti CHARGE EXTRA to add an additional charge to the amount somebody has to pay 2. vti OVERCHARGE to charge somebody too much for something 3. vt MAKE SOMEBODY RESPONSIBLE FOR REPAYMENT to make somebody repay from personal funds any losses stemming from negligent or intentional mismanagement of a fiduciary responsibility 4. vt RAISE STAMP VALUE to overprint an existing postage stamp so as to increase its face value 5. vt OVERBURDEN SOMEBODY OR SOMETHING to place too great a load on somebody or in or on something, e.g. a ship (literary) ■ n 1. EXTRA CHARGE an excess or extra charge 2. MARK ON STAMP a mark on a postage stamp increasing its face value 3. REIMBURSEMENT OF UNAUTHORIZED EXPENDITURE a repayment that somebody, e.g. a councillor or official, has to make from his or her personal funds for money spent without authorization [15C. < Old French surcharger < charger 'to charge' (see CHARGE)] —**surcharger** n

surcingle /súr sing g'l/ n a broad band fastened around the body of a horse to hold a rug or pack in place [14C. < Old French surcengle, literally 'belt over' < cengle 'belt, girdle' < Latin cingulum (see CINGULUM)]

surcoat

surcoat /súr kōt/ n 1. a short tunic worn over armour in medieval times 2. a short sleeveless garment worn as part of the ceremonial costume of an order of knighthood [14C. < Old French surcote 'overcoat' < cote 'coat']

surd /surd/ n 1. in mathematics, an irrational root or irrational number, or an expression containing one or the other 2. a consonant pronounced without vibration of the vocal cords [Mid-16C. < Latin surdus 'unable to hear or speak']

sure /shoor, shawr/ adj (surer, surest) 1. DEFINITELY TRUE unquestionably true or real and not in doubt ○ One thing is sure, we'll never make the same mistake again! 2. FIRMLY BELIEVING believing strongly and for a good reason, or knowing for a fact, that something is true or the case ○ Are you sure that she understood you? 3. BOUND TO OCCUR inevitably going to do something or to happen, or confidently expected to be going to do something or to happen ○ He's sure to notice that something's missing. 4. CERTAIN TO OBTAIN SOMETHING definitely able to or definitely going to obtain or achieve something ○ Many people book

early in order to be sure of the best seats. 5. VERY CONFIDENT very confident about something, especially personal beliefs or abilities ○ It was her self-confidence that made her so sure of her answer. 6. ALWAYS EFFECTIVE effective, accurate, and reliable at all times ○ His aggressive manner is a sure sign that he is frightened. 7. FIRM AND SECURE firm, secure, and steady ○ The fad had gained a sure hold on every teenager. 8. UNERRING showing both confidence and competence ○ a sure grasp of the complexities of the situation 9. DEPENDABLE able to be safely relied on ○ a sure friend in times of trouble ■ adv (informal) 1. US UNDOUBTEDLY used to give emphasis to something that somebody is saying and to indicate that somebody does not expect anyone to disagree with it ○ This sure tastes good. 2. N Am YES used to indicate emphatic or enthusiastic assent ○ I asked him if he'd like to come and he said, 'Sure!' [14C. Via French < Latin securus (see SECURE)] —**sureness** n ◇ **be sure and do** or **to do something** used to tell somebody to remember to do something ○ Be sure and introduce us. ◇ **for sure** 1. without a doubt, or inevitably (informal) ○ He seems ideal for the job, he'll get it for sure. 2. definitely and precisely ○ He couldn't say for sure what time he'd be home ◇ **make sure (that)** 1. to check that something is the case, or that something has been done as instructed or requested ○ We have to assess our market to try to make sure our products are competitive. 2. to take the necessary action to have something done or make something happen ○ Could you make sure that he's in bed before ten? ◇ **sure enough** as was expected ○ He had a reputation for punctuality, and, sure enough, as the clock struck eight, he appeared. ◇ **sure of yourself** extremely confident ◇ **to be sure** used when admitting or agreeing that something is true, even though it may not agree with most of what you are saying ○ He's charming, to be sure, but I still don't trust his motives.

> **USAGE** The use of **sure** as an intensifying adverb, as in the sentence We sure are glad to see you! is characteristic of informal US usage and has not fully entered British use except as a conscious Americanism. Note that it does not mean the same as surely, which is more judgmental in tone: They surely don't want us to pay for this?

sure-fire adj always successful or effective (informal)

sure-footed adj 1. skilled and confident in moving or climbing, and so unlikely to stumble or fall 2. confident and competent, and so unlikely to err —**sure-footedly** adv —**sure-footedness** n

surely /shoórli, sháwr-/ adv 1. USED TO INVITE RESPONSE used as a means of getting somebody to confirm, deny, agree, or disagree with something being said, by adding in an element of challenging self-assurance or considerable hesitancy ○ Surely you've met before. 2. WITHOUT FAIL definitely or unavoidably ○ slowly but surely 3. N Am WITHOUT DOUBT without a doubt or without fail ○ Did he get his message across? He surely did. 4. Southern US YES used to show ready agreement

sure thing (informal) n something that can be relied on to happen or to be successful ■ adv N Am used to express assent, agreement, or willingness to do something

surety /shoórǝti, sháwr-/ (plural -ties) n 1. LEGAL INSTRUMENT a pledge, bond, or guarantee against loss or damage 2. GUARANTOR somebody who pledges that another's obligations will be met in case of default 3. CERTAINTY the condition or quality of being sure (formal) [14C. Via Old French surete < Latin securitas < securus (see SECURE)] —**suretyship** n

surf /surf/ n 1. FOAMY WAVES the lines of foamy waves that break on a seashore or reef ○ play in the surf ■ v (surfs, surfing, surfed) 1. vi USE SURFBOARD to ride waves on a surfboard 2. vt RIDE WAVES IN PARTICULAR AREA to go surfing in a particular place ○ Have you surfed Waikiki? 3. vti ONLINE VISIT INTERNET SITES to go on the Internet for recreation, education, or entertainment, frequently changing the site [Late 17C. Origin ?] —**surfable** adj —**surfer** n —**surfing** n —**surfy** adj ◇ **surf's up** US used to indicate that it is time to start doing something (slang)

surface /súrfiss/ n (plural -faces) 1. OUTER PART the outermost or uppermost part of a thing, the one that is usually presented to the outside world, and

Popperfoto

surf: a surfer rides a wave at La Jolla Beach, California

can be seen and touched **2.** **UPPER PART OF EARTH, SEA, WATER** the part of the Earth, the sea, or any water that meets the atmosphere **3.** **SOLID FLAT AREA** a solid flat area, e.g. on top of a fitment or piece of furniture, especially an area on which it is suitable to work **4.** **THIN APPLIED OUTER LAYER** a relatively thin outer layer or coating applied to something, usually to give it a smooth finish ○ *a nonstick surface* **5.** **SUPERFICIAL PART** the easily visible or apparent parts or aspects of something or somebody, or those that somebody or something chooses to display to the world, especially when contrasted with the actual reality of the person or thing ○ *This surface of cool composure concealed a passionate heart.* **6.** MATHS **TWO-DIMENSIONAL EXTENT** a flat or curved continuous area definable in two dimensions ○ *the surface of a sphere* ■ *adj* **1.** **USED ON SURFACE** occurring or used on, or relating to, the surface of something ○ *surface lubricants* **2.** **APPARENT** apparent, but not real, deep-seated, or well-founded, or put on for effect or to deceive and not natural or deeply felt ○ *surface affection* ○ *The plan has surface appeal.* **3.** **ON LAND OR SEA** operating or transported over land or sea but not in the air ○ *surface transport* **4.** **NOT SUBMARINE** operating on the surface of the water, as opposed to being submersible ○ *surface ships* ■ *v* (**-faces, -facing, -faced**) **1.** *vi* **COME TO TOP** to come to or appear at the surface, especially of water ○ *She surfaced after a dive of 20 minutes.* **2.** *vi* **APPEAR** to reappear after being hidden or out of reach for a time ○ *She surfaced in Berlin after the war.* **3.** *vi* **BECOME KNOWN** to become apparent or known ○ *The information surfaced during a routine investigation.* **4.** *vt* **GIVE SURFACE TO SOMETHING** to provide something with a surface, especially with a smooth outer layer ○ *surfacing the road* **5.** *vt* **TREAT SURFACE** to treat the surface of something, especially in order to smooth or perfect it **6.** *vi* **WORK NEAR TOP** to mine at or near the Earth's surface **7.** *vi* **WAKE UP OR GET UP** to wake up, or get out of bed (*informal*) ○ *She didn't surface till three o'clock the next afternoon.* [Early 17C. < French < *sur-* 'upon' + *face* (see FACE), after Latin *superficies*] —**surfacer** *n* ◇ **on the surface** to outward appearances or when examined superficially ○ *appears cool and collected on the surface* ◇ **scratch the surface** to deal with only a very small or relatively unimportant part of something

surface-active *adj* having the property of reducing the surface tension of a liquid so that the liquid spreads out, rather than collecting in droplets

surface lift *n* a ski lift that carries skiers uphill while they are standing on their skis

surface mail *n* mail that is transported by sea or land, as opposed to by air

surface noise *n* noise produced as a record player stylus travels over a revolving record, caused by friction, dust, scratches, or static electricity on the record

surface runoff *n* the flow of water over the surface of the ground occurring when rainfall is not absorbed into the soil or evaporated

surface structure *n* in some types of grammar, a representation of the sequence of syntactic elements that constitute an actual phrase or sentence

surface tension *n* the property of liquids that gives their surfaces a slightly elastic quality and enables them to form into separate drops. It is caused by the interaction of molecules at or near the surface that tend to cohere and contract the surface into the smallest possible area. Symbol γ, σ

surface-to-air *adj* launched from a ship or from the ground against a target in the air ○ *surface-to-air missiles*

surface-to-surface *adj* launched from a ship or from the ground against another ship or a target on the ground ○ *a surface-to-surface missile*

surfactant /sur fáktənt/ *n* **1.** an agent that reduces the surface tension of a liquid so that the liquid spreads out, rather than collecting in droplets, e.g. a detergent or a drug **2.** a surface-active lipoprotein substance secreted naturally in the lungs, lack of which causes respiratory problems especially in premature babies [Mid-20C. < SURFACE + ACTIVE]

surf and turf *n Aus, N Am* a meal, menu, or dish including both seafood and meat, especially steak and lobster

surfari /sur fáari/ (*plural* **-ris**) *n* a package holiday or trip specially organized for surfers [Late-20C. Alteration of SAFARI after SURF]

surfbird /súrf burd/ *n* a winter shorebird with dark spotted feathers and a black tail with a white base. Native to: Pacific coasts of North and South America. Latin name: *Aphriza virgata.* [< its being found among wave-washed rocks along the shoreline]

surfboard /súrf bawrd/ *n* a long narrow board, with a rounded or pointed front end, on which a surfer stands while riding waves —**surfboarder** *n* —**surfboarding** *n*

surfboat /súrf bōt/ *n* a light sturdy boat, often with a raised prow and stern and buoyancy chambers, suitable for use in high surf

surf carnival *n* an Australian sports festival held at a beach and involving surfing, swimming, canoeing, and running events

surfcasting /súrf kaasting/ *n* a method of fishing in which a baited line is tossed into the surf from the shore or a boat —**surfcaster** *n*

surf club *n Aus* **1.** an organization of lifesavers **2.** a clubhouse where lifesavers are based, usually with changing rooms, showers, and other facilities that can usually be used by members of the public

surfeit /súrfit/ *n* **1.** **EXCESSIVE NUMBER** an excessive number or quantity of something, especially so much of it that people become sickened, repelled, or bored by it **2.** **OVERINDULGENCE** overindulgence, or a bout of overindulgence, in something, especially food or drink **3.** **DISGUST OR REVULSION** disgust or revulsion resulting from overindulgence (*literary*) ■ *vt* (**-feits, -feiting, -feited**) **GIVE SOMEBODY SURFEIT** to give somebody a surfeit of something [13C. < Old French, past participle of *surfaire* 'overdo' < *faire* 'do' (see AFFAIR)] —**surfeiter** *n*

Surfers Paradise /súrferz párrə dīss/ coastal town in southeastern Queensland, Australia. It is a major tourist resort, and the centre of the Gold Coast region. Population: 4,141 (1991).

surficial /sur físh'l/ *adj* relating to or occurring on a surface, especially the surface of the Earth [Late 19C. Blend of SURFACE + SUPERFICIAL]

surfie /súrfi/ *n ANZ* somebody whose main interest is surfing (*informal*)

surfie chick *n Aus* a woman who associates with surfers (*informal*)

surf-lifesaver *n Aus* somebody, usually a volunteer, who patrols a beach and assists swimmers or surfers who get into difficulties in the water

surf swimming *n ANZ* swimming in the open sea against waves, tides, and currents

surg. *abbr* **1.** surgeon **2.** surgery **3.** surgical

surge /surj/ *vi* (**surges, surging, surged**) **1.** **MOVE LIKE WAVES** to move in or like a wave, rising up and subsiding and sweeping forwards or back ○ *The boat surged in the rising swell.* **2.** **MAKE CONCERTED RUSH** to move in a body, especially to make a sudden concerted rush in a particular direction ○ *The crowd surged towards the exit.* **3.** **INCREASE SUDDENLY** to increase strongly and suddenly **4.** NAUT **SLIP WHILE BEING TURNED** to slip while being turned on a capstan or windlass (*refers to ropes and cables*) ■ *n* **1.** **LARGE MOTION** a powerful rising and falling, or forward rushing movement, like that of the sea **2.** **BURST OF FEELING** a sudden, intense experience of an emotion, especially one that seems to rush through somebody like a wave ○ *a surge of anger* **3.** **SUDDEN INCREASE** a sudden increase in something, often one that is relatively short-lived ○ *a surge in demand* **4.** **POWER INCREASE** a sudden and temporary increase in electrical current or voltage **5.** ASTRON **ENERGETIC SOLAR PROMINENCE** an energetic solar prominence lasting for several minutes, which accompanies a solar flare **6.** NAUT **SLIP OF ROPE** a sudden slipping or slackening of a rope or cable on a boat or ship [Early 16C. < French *surgir* 'rise up', *sourge-*, stem of *sourdre* 'spring up', both < Latin *surgere* 'rise up from below'] —**surger** *n*

surgeon /súrjən/ *n* **1.** a doctor specializing in operations that involve gaining access to the patient's body, e.g. by making incisions into it, in order to correct faults, repair injuries, or treat diseases **2.** a medical officer in the armed services or on board a ship [14C. Via Anglo-Norman < Old French *cirurgien* < *cirurgie* (see SURGERY)]

surgeonfish /súrjən fish/ (*plural same* or **-fishes**) *n* a tropical fish that is often brightly coloured and has spines at the base of its tail that it uses to inflict wounds. Family: Acanthuridae. [< an imagined resemblance of its spines to a surgeon's needle]

surgeon general (*plural* **surgeons general**) *n* **1.** the chief medical officer in many branches of the military service **2.** the cabinet-level chief public health officer of the United States, or the chief public health officer of some individual states. The Surgeon General is roughly the equivalent of the UK Chief Medical Officer.

surgeon's knot *n* a surgical knot of a type that can be relied on to remain tight

surge protector *n* an electrical device designed to protect a computer against the harmful effects of power surges and spikes and sudden outages

surgery /súrjəri/ (*plural* **-ies**) *n* **1.** **MEDICAL PROCEDURES INVOLVING OPERATIONS** medical treatment that involves operations on or manipulations of the patient's body and, usually, cutting the body open to perform these **2.** **BRANCH OF MEDICINE** the branch of medicine that deals with diseases and conditions treated by operation or manipulation, or the range of diseases treated in this way **3.** **SURGEON'S ART OR ACTIVITY** the art or activity of performing surgery **4.** **DOCTOR'S OFFICE** a doctor's, dentist's, or veterinary surgeon's office **5.** **DOCTOR'S CONSULTATION TIME** a time when a doctor, dentist, or veterinary surgeon is available for consultation by patients at a surgery **6.** **POLITICIAN'S OR LAWYER'S CONSULTATION TIME** a time when a Member of Parliament, a councillor, or a professional such as a lawyer is available for consultation by members of the general public **7.** *N Am* **OPERATING ROOM** a hospital or clinic room where surgery is performed [14C. Via Old French *cirurgerie* < Greek *kheirourgia* 'working with the hands' < *kheir* 'hand' + *ergon* 'work']

surgical /súrjik'l/ *adj* **1.** **OF SURGERY** relating to or accomplished by surgery ○ *surgical removal of warts* **2.** **RESULTING FROM SURGERY** as a result of of surgery ○ *surgical scar* **3.** **PRECISE** like surgery in requiring or being characterized by great skill or great precision ○ *surgical strikes* [Late 18C. Alteration (after SURGEON) of French *cirurgical* < *cirurgien* 'surgeon' < *cirurgie* (see SURGERY)] —**surgically** *adv*

surgical boot *n* a specially fitted shoe that compensates for physical malformation. N Am term **corrective shoe**

surgical spirit *n* methylated spirits mixed with castor oil and oil of wintergreen. Use: to prevent bed sores, harden the skin of the feet, and formerly to sterilize the skin before injections and operations. N Am term **rubbing alcohol**

suricate /syoóri kayt/ *n* ZOOL same as **meerkat** [Late 18C. Via French < obsolete Dutch *surikat*]

Suriname /soóri nám, -náamə/ country in northeastern South America, north of Brazil, on the Atlantic Ocean. Language: Dutch. Currency: Suriname guilder. Capital: Paramaribo. Population: 435,449 (2003). Area: 163,265 sq. km/63,037 sq. mi. Official name **Republic of Suriname**. Former name **Dutch Guiana** (until 1948). See map on next page —**Surinamese** /soóri na meéz/ *n, adj*

Suriname

Suriname toad *n* AMPHIB same as **pipa**[1]

surjection /sur jéksh'n/ *n* a mathematical function for which each element of a set is the image of at least one element of another set [Mid-20C. < SUR-, after INJECTION] —**surjective** *adj*

surly /súrli/ (**-lier, -liest**) *adj* bad-tempered, unfriendly, rude, and somewhat threatening ○ *a person with a surly manner* [Late 16C. Alteration of obsolete *sirly* 'lordly, imperious' < SIR] —**surliness** *n*

surmise /sur míz/ *vti* (**-mises, -mising, -mised**) to conclude that something is the case on the basis of only limited evidence or intuitive feeling ■ *n* a conclusion drawn on only limited evidence or intuitive feeling [Early 16C. < Anglo-Norman *surmis*, past participle of *surmettre* 'accuse', literally 'put over' < Latin *mittere* 'send'] —**surmisable** *adj* —**surmiser** *n*

surmount /sur mównt/ (**-mounts, -mounting, -mounted**) *vt* **1.** OVERCOME DIFFICULTY to deal with a difficulty successfully **2.** GET TO TOP OF SOMETHING to get over the top of a physical obstacle (*formal*) **3.** BE PLACED ATOP SOMETHING to be positioned on top of something or rise above it (*formal*) ○ *the statues surmounting the parapet* **4.** PUT SOMETHING ATOP SOMETHING ELSE to place something on top of or above something (*formal*) ○ *surmount the parapet with a row of statues* [14C. < French *surmonter* 'climb over' < *monter* 'mount' (see MOUNT[1])] —**surmountability** /sur mówntə bílləti/ *n* —**surmountable** *adj* —**surmounter** *n*

surname /súr naym/ *n* **1.** SOMEBODY'S FAMILY NAME the name that identifies somebody as belonging to a particular family and that he or she has in common with other members of that family **2.** DESCRIPTIVE ADDITION TO NAME a descriptive addition to somebody's name e.g. 'the Great' in 'Catherine the Great' (*archaic*) ■ *vt* (**-names, -naming, -named**) GIVE SOMEBODY SURNAME to give or transmit a surname to somebody (*usually passive*) [14C. Translation of Old French *surnom*, literally 'name above' < *nom* 'name'] —**surnamer** *n*

~~**suround**~~ incorrect spelling of **surround**

surpass /sur paáss/ (**-passes, -passing, -passed**) *vt* **1.** EXCEED EXPECTATIONS to go beyond what was expected or hoped for, usually by being bigger, better, or greater **2.** DO BETTER THAN SOMEBODY OR SOMETHING to be bigger, greater, better, or worse than somebody or something else **3.** BE BEYOND SOMEBODY'S ABILITY to be beyond somebody's ability to deal with or understand (*formal*) [Mid-16C. < French *surpasser* 'transgress', literally 'pass beyond' < *passer* (see PASS)] —**surpassable** *adj*

surpassing /sur paássing/ *adj* of a quality far superior to others (*literary*) ○ *a view of surpassing beauty* —**surpassingly** *adv*

surplice /súrpliss/ *n* a white ecclesiastical outer garment like a smock, with wide, often flared sleeves, and varying in length [13C. Via Anglo-Norman *surpliz* < medieval Latin *superpellicium* '(vestment worn) over a fur garment' < *pellicium* 'fur coat']

surplus /súrpləss/ *n* **1.** EXCESS AMOUNT an amount remaining after the original purpose has been served or the original requirement met **2.** EXCESS MONEY an amount of money remaining after all liabilities have been met ○ *The government is predicting a trade surplus this year.* **3.** ACCT EXTRA WORTH the amount by which the net worth of a company's assets exceeds the value of its owned stock ■ *adj* ADDITIONAL TO REQUIREMENTS not required to meet existing needs, or left over after these have been met ○ *surplus clothing* ○ *be surplus to requirements* [14C. Via Anglo-Norman < medieval Latin *superplus*, literally 'more beyond' < Latin *plus* 'more']

surplusage /súrplǝssij/ *n* **1.** LAW IRRELEVANT MATTER an irrelevant matter introduced into legal proceedings **2.** VERBIAGE redundant words or arguments (*formal*) **3.** SURPLUS an excess of something (*formal*)

surplus value *n* in Marxist economic theory, the difference between the price of a product produced by labour and the value of labour itself in terms of the wages paid to workers

surprint /súr print/ PRINTING *vt* (**-prints, -printing, -printed**) same as **overprint** ■ *n* same as **overprint** *n* (sense 1)

surprise /sər príz/ *vt* (**-prises, -prising, -prised**) **1.** MAKE SOMEBODY AMAZED to cause somebody to feel sudden wonder or amazement, especially at something unexpected (*often passive*) ○ *I'm surprised that nobody's thought of this before.* ○ *It doesn't really surprise me that nobody accepted the offer.* **2.** CATCH SOMEBODY OR SOMETHING UNAWARES to attack, come upon, or catch somebody or something unexpectedly ○ *I surprised a fox going through the dustbins last night.* **3.** GIVE SOMEBODY SOMETHING UNEXPECTEDLY to make an unexpected gift to somebody ○ *surprised me with flowers* **4.** TRICK SOMEBODY INTO DOING SOMETHING to cause somebody to do something, especially to admit something, unexpected by trickery or deceit ○ *Her boss surprised her into admitting she left work early every day.* ■ *n* **1.** AMAZEMENT a feeling of shock, wonder, or bewilderment produced by an unexpected event ○ *Imagine my surprise when she told me she was already married.* **2.** SOMETHING UNEXPECTED something that produces a feeling of surprise, especially an unexpected event or gift (*often used before a noun*) ○ *He told me he had a surprise for me, but I haven't seen it yet.* ○ *a surprise visit* **3.** ABILITY TO CAUSE SURPRISE the fact of happening unexpectedly or the ability to take somebody unawares ○ *We don't want to lose the element of surprise.* [15C. < French, past participle of *surprendre* 'overtake' < *sur-* 'over' + Latin *prehendere* 'seize'] —**surprised** *adj* —**surpriser** *n* —**surprising** *adj* —**surprisingly** *adv* ◇ **surprise, surprise!** (*informal*) **1.** used when making a surprise announcement or presenting something that is supposed to be a surprise **2.** used ironically to suggest that something is anything but unexpected ○ *Well, surprise, surprise, the weather forecasters got it wrong again.* ◇ **take somebody by surprise** to happen unexpectedly to somebody ○ *Their arrival took everybody by surprise.*

~~**surprize**~~ incorrect spelling of **surprise**

surra /sóorə/ *n* a tropical disease similar to sleeping sickness that affects camels and horses, and occasionally cattle and dogs. It is caused by a protozoan but transmitted by biting flies. [Late 19C. < Marathi *sūra* 'air breathed through the nostrils']

surreal /sə rée əl/ *adj* weirdly unfamiliar, distorted, or disturbing, like the experiences in a dream or the objects or experiences depicted in surrealism ■ *n* the bizarre or unreal qualities associated with surrealism [Mid-20C. Back-formation < SURREALISM] —**surreally** *adv*

surrealism /sə rée əlizəm/ *n* **1.** an early 20th-century movement in art and literature that tried to represent the subconscious mind by creating fantastic imagery and juxtaposing ideas that seem to contradict each other **2.** surreal art or literature [Early 20C. < French *surréalisme* 'beyond realism'] —**surrealist** *n, adj* —**surrealistic** /sə rée ə lístik/ *adj* —**surrealistically** *adv*

surrebuttal /súrri bútt'l/ *n* in a civil court action, an act of giving evidence to support the third reply (**surrebutter**) of the person bringing the action (**plaintiff**) (*archaic*)

surrebutter /súrri búttər/ *n* in a civil court action, the third reply of the person bringing the action (**plaintiff**), in response to the defendant's third statement (**rebutter**) (*archaic*) [Late 16C. < REBUTTER, after SURREJOINDER]

surrejoinder /súrri jóyndər/ *n* in a civil court action, the second reply of the person bringing the action (**plaintiff**), in response to the defendant's second statement (**rejoinder**)

surrender /sə réndər/ *v* (**-ders, -dering, -dered**) **1.** *vi* DECLARE YOURSELF DEFEATED to declare to an opponent that he or she has won so that fighting or conflict can cease **2.** *vt* GIVE UP POSSESSION OF SOMETHING to relinquish possession or control of something because of coercion or force ○ *surrender territory* ○ *surrender your passport* **3.** *vt* GIVE SOMETHING OUT OF COURTESY to give a seat, position, or office to somebody as a courtesy or as a gesture of goodwill **4. surrender yourself** *vr* GIVE SELF UP TO SOMETHING to yield to a strong emotion, influence, or temptation **5.** *vt* LAW ABANDON RIGHTS TO SOMETHING to give up or abandon rights to something, especially to give up a lease before it has expired or an insurance policy before the agreed term ■ *n* **1.** GIVING UP FIGHT an act of declaring defeat at the hands of an opponent ○ *The French demanded an unconditional surrender.* **2.** GIVING UP CONTROL an act of relinquishing control or possession to somebody or something **3.** DELIVERY INTO LEGAL CUSTODY the delivery of a prisoner or fugitive into legal custody **4.** LAW ABANDONMENT OF LEGAL RIGHTS the abandonment of legal rights, especially the giving up of a lease or an insurance policy before it has expired **5.** GIVING SELF UP TO AUTHORITIES an act of willing submission to authorities [15C. < Anglo-Norman, 'give over' < *render* 'give (back)', variant of Old French *rendre* (see RENDER)]

SYNONYMS See ***yield***.

surrender value *n* the amount of money that somebody would receive on terminating a life assurance policy

surreptitious /súrrəp tíshəss/ *adj* done in a concealed or underhand way to escape notice, especially disapproval [15C. < Latin *surreptitius* < *surripere* 'seize secretly', literally 'seize from beneath' < *rapere* 'seize'] —**surreptitiously** *adv* —**surreptitiousness** *n*

SYNONYMS See ***secret***.

surrey /súrri/ (*plural* **-reys**) *n* a late 19th-century horse-drawn four-wheeled carriage with two or four seats, used for short pleasure trips [Late 19C. After SURREY]

Surrey /súrri/ county in southern England. The administrative centre is Kingston-upon-Thames. Population: 1,059,015 (2001). Area: 1,677 sq. km/648 sq. mi.

surrogate *adj* /súrrəgət, -gayt/ SUBSTITUTING FOR SOMEBODY OR SOMETHING taking the place of somebody or something else ■ *n* /súrrəgət, -gayt/ **1.** SOMEBODY AS SUBSTITUTE somebody who acts as a replacement for somebody else **2.** WOMAN WHO GIVES BIRTH FOR ANOTHER a woman who bears a child for a couple, with the intention of handing it over at birth. She is usually either artificially inseminated with the man's sperm or implanted with a fertilized egg from the woman. **3.** PSYCHOL SUBSTITUTE AUTHORITY FIGURE a respected person who replaces a lost or nonexistent parent in somebody's unconscious, e.g. a teacher or older sibling ■ *vt* /súrrə gayt/ (**-gates, -gating, -gated**) APPOINT AS STAND-IN to put somebody in somebody else's place [Mid-16C. < Latin *surrogatus*, past participle of *surrogare* 'ask for in place of' < *rogare* 'ask, beg'] —**surrogacy** /súrrəgəssi/ *n*

surround /sə równd/ *vt* (**-rounds, -rounding, -rounded**) **1.** ENCLOSE SOMETHING to occupy the space all around something **2.** CLOSE OFF MEANS OF ESCAPE to encircle something completely, especially an enemy's military position **3.** BE AROUND SOMEBODY to associate closely with somebody ■ *n* **1.** AREA AROUND an area, border, or frame around a thing or place **2.** SURROUNDINGS the immediate environment of something or somebody (*often pl*) [Early 17C. Via Old French *suronder* 'overflow' < late Latin *superundare* < Latin *unda* 'wave']

surroundings /sə równdingz/ *npl* the immediate environment of somebody or something, including events, circumstances, scenery, conditions, people, and objects

surround sound *n* a system of recording and reproducing sound that uses three or more channels and speakers in order to create the effect of the listener being surrounded by sound sources

sursum corda /súr ssəm káwrdə, -sóom-/ *n* **1.** in the Roman Catholic Church, a short sentence (**versicle**) spoken by a priest during Mass, just before the preface **2.** a cry or exhortation, especially of hope (*literary*) [< late Latin, '(lift) up (your) hearts', the versicle's opening words]

surtax /súr taks/ *n* **1.** ANOTHER TAX a tax that is charged

in addition to other taxes **2.** HIGHER TAX a higher level or levels of tax imposed on individuals and corporations when income or profits exceed a specific amount ■ *vt* (**-taxes, -taxing, -taxed**) CHARGE SOMEBODY SURTAX to charge somebody with an additional or higher tax [Late 19C. < French *surtaxe* 'over tax' < *taxe* 'tax' < *taxer* (see TAX)]

Surtees /súrt eez/, **John** (*b.* 1934) British motorcyclist and motor racing driver. He was the world motorcycling champion at 500 cc (1956, 1958–60) and at 350 cc (1958–60), and Formula One world champion (1964).

surtitle /súr tīt'l/ *n UK, ANZ, Can* a translation of words being spoken in a foreign language during the performance of a play or opera, projected on a screen above the stage (*often used in the pl*) US term **supertitle** —**surtitled** *adj*

~~surveilance~~ incorrect spelling of **surveillance**

surveillance /sur váylənss/ *n* continual observation of a person or group, especially one suspected of doing something illegal [Early 19C. < French < *surveiller* 'watch over' < *veiller* 'keep watch' < Latin *vigilare* (see VIGILANT)] —**surveillant** *adj, n*

survey *vt* /sur váy, súr vay/ (**-veys, -veying, -veyed**) **1.** CONSIDER SOMETHING GENERALLY to look at or consider something in a general or very broad way **2.** LOOK AT SOMETHING CAREFULLY to look at or consider somebody or something closely, especially in order to form an opinion **3.** PLOT MAP OF SOMEWHERE to make a detailed map of an area of land, including its boundaries, area, and elevation, using geometry and trigonometry to measure angles and distances **4.** QUESTION PEOPLE IN POLL to do a statistical study of a sample population by asking questions about age, income, opinions, buying preferences, and other aspects of people's lives **5.** INSPECT BUILDING to inspect a building in order to determine its structural soundness or assess its value ■ *n* /súr vay/ (*plural* **-veys**) **1.** GENERAL VIEW an examination of a subject or situation from a very broad and general perspective **2.** CRITICAL INSPECTION a very detailed, critical examination of something such as a situation or event **3.** ANALYSIS OF POLL SAMPLE a statistical analysis of answers to a poll of a sample of a population, e.g. to determine opinions, preferences, or knowledge **4.** INSPECTION OF BUILDING an inspection of a building to determine its condition and assess its value **5.** REPORT FROM INSPECTING BUILDING a report that results from inspecting the condition and assessing the value of a building **6.** ACT OF MEASURING LAND an act of taking detailed measurements of an area of land **7.** REPORT ON LAND MEASUREMENT a report that shows the results of a survey undertaken to measure an area of land **8.** GROUP DOING SURVEY a team of surveyors working together **9.** AREA SURVEYED an area of land that is being or has been surveyed [15C. Via Anglo-Norman *surveier* < medieval Latin *supervidere* 'oversee' < Latin *videre* 'see'] —**surveyable** *adj*

~~surveyer~~ incorrect spelling of **surveyor**

surveyor /sur váy ər/ *n* **1.** somebody whose occupation is taking accurate measurements of land areas in order to determine boundaries, elevations, and dimensions **2.** somebody whose occupation is inspecting buildings to determine the soundness of their construction or to assess their value **3.** CONSTR same as **quantity surveyor**

surveyor's chain *n* MEASURE same as **chain** *n* (sense 2)

surveyor's level *n* an instrument with a telescope and a spirit level attached, mounted on a tripod and rotating around the vertical axis, used for measuring elevations of land

surveyor's measure *n* a system of measurement that uses the surveyor's chain, about 20 m/22 yd, as its base unit

survival /sur vīv'l/ *n* **1.** the fact of remaining alive or in existence, especially after facing life-threatening danger, or of continuing in a present position or office ○ *The doctor said she had a fifty-fifty chance of survival.* ○ *fighting for her political survival* **2.** a custom, idea, or belief that remains when other similar things have been lost or forgotten

survival bag *n* a protective bag that climbers or hikers get into to protect themselves from exposure

survivalist /sə vīvəlist/ *n* somebody who seeks to survive an impending disaster by hoarding weapons and food, often going off to live alone or with a like-minded group —**survivalism** *n*

survival suit *n* a close-fitting waterproof suit made of insulating and often buoyant material that covers the whole body so that the wearer can survive long periods in cold water

survive /sər vīv/ (**-vives, -viving, -vived**) *v* **1.** *vi* NOT DIE OR DISAPPEAR to remain alive or in existence or able to live or function, especially succeed in staying alive when faced with a life-threatening danger ○ *He was shot three times at close range and survived.* ○ *A fragment of the manuscript still survives.* ○ *How can you survive on £50 a week?* **2.** *vt* LIVE THROUGH SOMETHING to come through a life-threatening experience or a period of difficulty and remain alive, in existence, or in a previous position or life ○ *She survived three assassination attempts.* ○ *The government narrowly survived a vote of no confidence.* **3.** *vt* LIVE LONGER THAN SOMEBODY to remain alive after the death of a particular person ○ *He survived his wife by only three months.* [15C. Via Anglo-Norman *survivre* < Latin *supervivere* 'live beyond' < *vivere* 'to live'] —**survivability** /sər vīvə bílləti/ *n* —**survivable** *adj*

~~surviver~~ incorrect spelling of **survivor**

survivor /sə vīvər/ *n* **1.** SOMEBODY WHO SURVIVES somebody who remains alive despite being exposed to life-threatening danger ○ *There were no survivors from the plane crash.* **2.** SOMEBODY WITH GREAT POWERS OF ENDURANCE somebody who shows a great will to live or a great determination to overcome difficulties and carry on **3.** LAW INHERITOR the one of two or more people having joint interests in property who lives longer than the other or others and is, therefore, entitled to the entire property **4.** PSYCHOL SOMEBODY OVERCOMING TRAUMATIC EXPERIENCE somebody who has been psychologically damaged by a trauma such as rape or an addiction and seeks to overcome its effects

sus[1] /suss/ (*slang*) *n* a state of doubt or misgiving about somebody or something ■ *adj* acting like somebody who has done something wrong or illegal [Mid-20C. Shortening of SUSPICION, SUSPICIOUS]

sus[2] /suss/ *n* somebody who is suspected of a wrongdoing (*slang*) [Mid-20C. Shortening of SUSPECT]

Popperfoto

Jacqueline Susann

Susann /soo zán/, **Jacqueline** (1926–74) US writer. Her first novel, *Valley of the Dolls* (1968), was a best-seller.

Susanna /soo zánnə/ *n* in the Apocrypha, a woman of Babylon who was saved by the prophet Daniel after being falsely accused of adultery

~~susceptable~~ incorrect spelling of **susceptible**

susceptibility /sə séptə bílləti/ *n* **1.** LIKELIHOOD OF BEING AFFECTED the likelihood of being affected, or a tendency to be affected, by a specific thing ○ *susceptibility to colds* **2.** SENSITIVITY the tendency to be affected by strong feelings and emotions **3.** PHYS same as **magnetic susceptibility** ■ **susceptibilities** *npl* FEELINGS somebody's feelings, especially those of somebody who easily becomes upset

susceptible /sə séptəb'l/ *adj* **1.** EASILY AFFECTED easily influenced or affected by something **2.** LIKELY TO BE AFFECTED liable to being affected by something ○ *susceptible to hay fever and other allergies* **3.** EMOTIONAL easily affected emotionally **4.** CAPABLE OF SOMETHING capable or permitting of something (*formal*) ○ *susceptible of several different interpretations* [Early 17C. Directly or via French< late Latin *susceptibilis* < past participle of Latin *suscipere* 'take up' < *capere* 'take'] —**susceptibly** *adv*

susceptive /sə séptiv/ *adj* **1.** easily affected by something **2.** open to new ideas and suggestions [Mid-15C. < Latin *suscept-*, past participle of *suscipere* (see SUSCEPTIBLE)] —**susceptivity** /sússep tívvəti/ *n*

sushi /sóo shee/ *n* small cakes of cold boiled rice, shaped by hand or wrapped in seaweed and topped with pieces of raw or cooked fish, vegetables, or egg [Late 19C. < Japanese]

Susian /sóozi ən/ *n* LANG same as **Elamite** (sense 2) [Mid-16C. < Latin *Susianus* < Greek *Sousa* 'Susa', city in present-day W Iran, where Elamite was spoken] —**Susian** *adj*

sus laws *npl* laws that permit the arrest and prosecution of people suspected of frequenting or loitering in public places for the purpose of committing a crime (*dated informal*)

suslik /sóoss lik/ (*plural* **-liks** or *same*), **souslik** *n* a ground squirrel with large eyes and small ears that lives in dry open areas. Native to: Europe, Asia. Latin name: *Citellus citellus.* [Late 18C. < Russian]

~~suspecious~~ incorrect spelling of **suspicious**

suspect *v* /sə spékt/ (**-pects, -pecting, -pected**) **1.** *vt* BELIEVE SOMEBODY IS GUILTY to believe that somebody may have committed a crime or wrongdoing without having any proof ○ *How can they suspect him of murder?* **2.** *vt* DOUBT SOMETHING to doubt the truth or validity of something ○ *We suspect her reasons for wanting to be friends with us.* **3.** *vt* BELIEVE SOMETHING TO BE SO to think that something is probable or likely ○ *I rather suspect that we haven't heard the last of this business.* **4.** *vti* HAVE SUSPICIONS to be suspicious, or be suspicious about something ■ *n* /súss pekt/ SOMEBODY WHO MIGHT BE GUILTY somebody who is suspected of a wrongdoing ■ *adj* /súss pekt/ **1.** SUSPICIOUS thought or likely to be false or untrustworthy ○ *All his claims about the wealth of his family are rather suspect.* **2.** LIKELY TO CONTAIN SOMETHING ILLEGAL looking likely to contain something dangerous or illegal ○ *inspected the suspect luggage* [14C. < Latin *suspect-*, past participle of *suspicere* 'look up at' < *specere* 'look at'] ◇ **the usual suspects** people, businesses, or organizations frequently mentioned in the context of a particular activity (*informal*)

USAGE suspect or **suspicious**? These two adjectives have overlapping meanings and are sometimes confused. ***Suspicious***, the more frequent and versatile of the two, may describe a person who suspects or somebody or something that causes suspicion: *Her behaviour made us suspicious. There were a couple of suspicious characters standing outside the bank. Her behaviour was suspicious.* ***Suspect*** is chiefly used of things that cause doubt, suspicion, or distrust because they seem likely to be false, illegal, or dangerous: *His claims sounded suspect. The police confiscated a suspect package. The remains of a suspect tuna sandwich were sent away for analysis.*

~~suspence~~ incorrect spelling of **suspense**

suspend /sə spénd/ (**-pends, -pending, -pended**) *v* **1.** *vt* HANG SOMETHING FROM ABOVE to hang something from above, especially so that it can swing freely **2.** *vt* STOP SOMETHING FOR PERIOD to stop something or make something ineffective, usually for a short time **3.** *vt* BAR SOMEBODY FOR PERIOD to bar somebody from a privilege, a position, or an organization, usually when under suspicion of wrongdoing **4.** *vt* POSTPONE SOMETHING to delay or defer action on a decision or a judgment until more of the facts are known **5.** *vt* CHEM DISPERSE SOMETHING IN LIQUID to cause particles to be dispersed in a liquid or gas **6.** *vt* MUSIC SUSTAIN NOTE to hold a note until the next note or chord is sounded, so that they are heard together **7.** *vi* FIN STOP MAKING PAYMENTS to cease payment on something, especially because of an inability to meet financial obligations [13C. Directly or via French < Latin *suspendere* 'hang up' < *pendere* 'hang'] —**suspendibility** /sə spéndə bí lliti/ *n* —**suspendible** *adj* ◇ **be suspended** to hang over or above something as vapour or particles, or be dispersed through something as particles

suspended animation /sə spéndid-/ *n* **1.** the stopping or slowing of the vital functions of an organism for some period of time, especially by freezing **2.** a

state, often caused by asphyxia, in which an organism loses consciousness and stops breathing so that it appears to be dead

suspended sentence *n* a sentence imposed on somebody found guilty of a crime that need not be served as long as the individual commits no other crime during the term of the sentence

suspender /sə spéndər/ *n* **1.** STRAP FOR WOMAN'S STOCKINGS an elastic strap, usually attached to a girdle or belt, with a clamp at one end to hold up a woman's stockings. N Am term **garter 2.** STRAP FOR MAN'S SOCK an elastic strap with a clamp on one end that attaches to and holds up a man's sock **3.** *N Am* ONE OF PAIR OF BRACES a strap, usually made of elastic, worn over the shoulder and with a clip at either end to attach to trousers so that they do not fall down (*usually used in the plural*) **4.** ARCHIT SOMETHING THAT LETS SOMETHING HANG something that allows something else to hang, e.g. one of the cables on a suspension bridge

suspender belt *n* a belt with four elastic straps hanging from it, one down the back and front of each leg, with clamps on the ends to hold up a woman's stockings. N Am term **garter belt**

suspense /sə spénss/ *n* **1.** UNCERTAINTY the state or condition of being unsure or in doubt about something **2.** ENJOYABLE TENSION a feeling of tense excitement about how something such as a mystery novel or film will end **3.** ANXIETY a state of anxiety or intense worry about something [15C. Via Anglo-Norman < Latin *suspensus*, past participle of *suspendere* (see SUSPEND)] —**suspenseful** *adj*

suspense account *n* a financial account in which entries are made temporarily, until it is determined where they belong

suspension /sə spénsh'n/ *n* **1.** TEMPORARY STOP an interruption of something for a period of time **2.** TEMPORARY REMOVAL the temporary removal of somebody from a team, position, school, or organization, especially as punishment **3.** LAW POSTPONEMENT OF SENTENCE a delay in the carrying out of a sentence or the making of a decision or judgment **4.** TRANSP SYSTEM REDUCING VIBRATION OF VEHICLE a system of springs and shock absorbers on a wheeled vehicle that reduces the impact of bumps and uneven running surfaces on the occupants and gives the wheels better contact **5.** FIN END TO REPAYING DEBTS an end to the repayment of financial obligations because of a lack of money **6.** CHEM DISPERSION OF PARTICLES a dispersion of fine solid particles in a liquid or gas, removable by filtration **7.** MUSIC TECHNIQUE FOR CREATING DISSONANCE a technique in which a note of the first chord is held into the second chord, the dissonance created being resolved by moving a step lower in the third chord

suspension bridge *n* a bridge with a roadway that is suspended from cables anchored by towers at either end and often supported by structures at regular intervals

suspension point *n* US each of a series of dots, usually three, used in printed and written material to indicate an omission from text being reproduced or an incomplete phrase (*often used in the plural*)

suspensive /sə spénsiv/ *adj* **1.** STOPPING SOMETHING causing or tending to cause something to stop or be deferred **2.** CAUSING TENSION causing, arousing, or relating to a feeling of doubt or anxious excitement **3.** UNDECIDED ABOUT SOMETHING inclined to delay making a decision or judgment —**suspensively** *adv* —**suspensiveness** *n*

suspensoid /sə spén soyd/ *n* a solution of very fine solid particles dispersed throughout a liquid [Early 20C. < SUSPENSION]

suspensory /sə spénsəri/ *n* (*plural* -**ries**) **1.** ANAT LIGAMENT OR MUSCLE a ligament or muscle from which a structure or part is suspended **2.** MED BANDAGE OR SLING something that holds part of the body in position while it heals, e.g. a bandage or a sling ■ *adj* **1.** TEMPORARILY STOPPING SOMETHING temporarily interrupting or delaying the completion of something **2.** ANAT SUPPORTING providing support for an organ or body part

suspensory ligament *n* a ligament that provides support for an organ or another body part, especially a fibrous membrane that holds the lens of the eye in place

suspicion /sə spísh'n/ *n* **1.** FEELING OF SOMETHING WRONG an unsubstantiated belief that something is the case, especially a belief that something wrong has happened or that somebody may have committed a crime ○ *a sneaking suspicion that she was the one who ate the last biscuit* **2.** MISTRUST OR DOUBTS a feeling of mistrust or doubt, especially because something wrong has happened and has not been explained ○ *an atmosphere of suspicion* **3.** CONDITION OF BEING SUSPECTED the condition of being suspected of something, especially wrongdoing ○ *under suspicion* **4.** SMALL AMOUNT a tiny amount of something such as a colour or flavour ○ *just a suspicion of garlic* [13C. Via French < Latin *suspicion-* < *suspicere* (see SUSPECT)] —**suspicional** *adj*

suspicious /sə spíshəss/ *adj* **1.** AROUSING SUSPICION creating or liable to create suspicion ○ *under suspicious circumstances* **2.** TENDING TO SUSPECT inclined or tending to believe that something is wrong ○ *a suspicious nature* **3.** SUGGESTING DOUBT showing or indicating suspicion ○ *a suspicious look* —**suspiciously** *adv* —**suspiciousness** *n*

USAGE See *suspect*.

suspire /sə spír/ *vi* (-**pires**, -**piring**, -**pired**) **1.** to draw in breath **2.** to give a sigh [15C. < Latin *suspirare* 'breathe up' < *spirare* 'breathe'] —**suspiration** /súspi ráysh'n/ *n*

Susquehanna[1] /súskwi hánnə/ *n* PEOPLES same as **Susquehannock**

Susquehanna[2] /súskwi hánnə/ river that rises in central New York State, flowing across Pennsylvania before emptying into the Chesapeake Bay in Maryland. Length: 719 km/447 mi.

Susquehannock /súskwi hánnək/ (*plural same or* -**nocks**), **Susquehanna** /súskwi hánnə/ (*plural same or* -**nas**) *n* a member of an extinct Native North American people who lived along the Susquehanna River in New York, Pennsylvania, and Maryland [Early 17C. < Algonquian]

suss /sus/ (**susses, sussing, sussed**), **sus** *vt* to discover or understand something such as somebody's motives, a situation, or how to use something (*informal*) ○ *I think I've finally got this camera sussed.* [Mid-20C. Shortening of SUSPECT]

suss out *vt* to get to the bottom of something, or discover what somebody is up to (*informal*)

Sussex /sússiks/ former county of southeastern England. Since 1974 it has been divided into the counties of East Sussex and West Sussex.

Sussex Downs hilly region in southeastern England, forming part of the South Downs. It was designated an Area of Outstanding Natural Beauty in 1966. Area: 983 sq. km/379 sq. mi.

Sussex Drive, 24 Sussex Drive *n* the address of the official residence of the Prime Minister of Canada

Susskind /súss kind/, **Leonard** (*b.* 1940) US physicist. He pioneered the extension of string theory to the problem represented by black holes.

sustain /sə stáyn/ *vt* (-**tains**, -**taining**, -**tained**) **1.** NOURISH SOMEBODY to provide somebody with nourishment or the necessities of life **2.** PROVIDE SOMEBODY WITH MORAL SUPPORT to keep somebody going with emotional or moral support **3.** MAINTAIN SOMETHING to make something continue to exist ○ *sustaining the audience's interest* **4.** BE AFFECTED BY SOMETHING to experience a setback, injury, damage, loss, or defeat ○ *sustained several broken bones* **5.** SUPPORT SOMETHING FROM BELOW to keep something in position by holding it from below ○ *The floor will not sustain the weight of a grand piano.* **6.** WITHSTAND SOMETHING to manage to withstand something and continue in spite of it **7.** LAW VALIDATE SOMETHING to decide that a statement or objection is valid or justified **8.** CONFIRM SOMETHING to confirm that something is true or valid ○ *sustained the lower court's ruling* **9.** KEEP PRETENCE GOING to maintain a pretence successfully ■ *n* MUSIC PROLONGED MUSICAL NOTE a musical note that is prolonged [13C. < Anglo-Norman *sustein-*, stem of *sustenir* < Latin *sustinere* 'hold up' < *tenere* 'hold'] —**sustainment** *n*

sustainable /sə stáynəb'l/ *adj* **1.** able to be maintained **2.** exploiting natural resources without destroying the ecological balance of an area ○ *sustainable agriculture* —**sustainability** /sə stáynə bílliti/ *n* —**sustainably** *adv*

sustainable development *n* economic development maintained within acceptable levels of global resource depletion and environmental pollution ○ *'Sustainable development is the principle which should guide politicians in planning the future...'* (BBC website; April 1999)

sustained yield /sə stáynd-/ *n* **1.** the ongoing supply of a natural resource such as timber by scheduled harvesting **2.** the amount of a natural resource such as timber obtained by scheduled harvesting

sustaining pedal /sə stáyning-/ *n* the right pedal of a piano, used to keep the dampers off the strings so that they can vibrate freely

sustenance /sússtənənss/ *n* **1.** NOURISHMENT something, especially food, that supports life ○ *There isn't much sustenance in a small chocolate bar.* **2.** CONDITION OF BEING PROVIDED FOR the condition of being provided with the necessities of life ○ *'I have hardly a penny in the world – I am staying with my aunt for my bare sustenance.'* (Thomas Hardy, *Far from the Madding Crowd*; 1874) **3.** LIVELIHOOD a means of supporting somebody financially [13C. < Anglo-Norman *sustenance* < *sustenir* (see SUSTAIN)]

sustentacular /súss ten tákyōōlər/ *adj* describes cells or fibres whose only function is to serve as a support [Late 19C. < modern Latin *sustentaculum* 'support' < Latin *sustentare* (see SUSTENTATION)]

sustentation /súss ten táysh'n/ *n* (*formal*) **1.** something that supports or sustains something else **2.** a means of support [14C. Via French < Latin *sustentare* 'keep holding up' < *sustinere* (see SUSTAIN)] —**sustentative** /sústən taytiv, sə sténtətiv/ *adj*

susu *n* FIN another spelling of **sou-sou**

Susu /sóō soo/ (*plural same or* -**sus**) *n* **1.** a member of a people who live in West Africa, mainly in Guinea and Sierra Leone **2.** the Mande language of the Susu people. Native speakers: 700,000. [Late 18C. < Susu] —**Susu** *adj*

susurrate /sússə rayt/ (-**rates**, -**rating**, -**rated**) *vi* to whisper or rustle softly [Early 17C. Back-formation < *susurration* < Latin *susurrare* < *susurrus* 'whisper', an imitation of the sound] —**susurrant** *adj* —**susurration** /sússə ráysh'n/ *n*

susurrus /sússərəss/ *n* a whispering or murmuring sound (*literary*) [15C. < Latin (see SUSURRATE)]

Sutcliffe /sútklif/, **Herbert** (1894–1978) British cricketer. An opening batsman, he played for Yorkshire (1919–45) and for England (1924–35), for whom he formed a highly successful regular opening partnership with Jack Hobbs.

Sutherland /súthərlənd/ former county of northern Scotland. Since 1975 it has been part of Highland council area.

Sutherland, Graham (1903–80) British painter. He is noted for his semiabstract works, portraits, and the design for the tapestry *Christ in Majesty* (1952–58) for Coventry Cathedral. Full name **Sutherland, Graham Vivian**

Dame Joan Sutherland: performing in *Lucia di Lammermoor*

Sutherland, Dame Joan (*b.* 1926) Australian operatic soprano. In a career stretching from 1947 to 1990, she became an opera singer of international renown, noted especially for her coloratura roles in Italian opera.

Sutherland Falls waterfall on the South Island, New Zealand. It is one of the highest in the world. Height: 580 m/1,904 ft.

~~sutle~~ incorrect spelling of **subtle**

Sutlej /súttlij/ river in South Asia, flowing through Tibet, India, and Pakistan. Length: 1,450 km/901 mi.

sutler /súttlər/ *n* somebody who follows an army and sells goods to the soldiers (*archaic*) [Late 16C. < obsolete Dutch *soeteler* < *soetelen* 'befoul, do menial work'] —**sutlership** *n*

sutra /soótrə/ *n* **1.** a short aphoristic summary of the teachings of Hinduism, created to be memorized and later incorporated into Hindu literature **2.** *also* **sutta** /soótta/ a classic religious text of Buddhism, especially one regarded as a discourse of the Buddha [Early 19C. < Sanskrit *sūtram* 'aphorism', literally 'thread']

suttee /súttee, su teé/, **sati** *n* **1.** in South Asia, the now illegal practice of a Hindu widow throwing herself on her husband's funeral pyre **2.** a Hindu widow who throws herself on her husband's funeral pyre [Late 18C. < Sanskrit *satī* 'good woman', feminine present participle of *as-* 'be'] —**sutteeism** *n*

Sutton /sútt'n/, **Henry** (1856–1912) Australian inventor. He was a pioneer of aviation, telecommunications, and colour photography, and in 1885 designed a prototype television.

Sutton Coldfield /-kóld feeld/ town in the West Midlands, in central England, northeast of Birmingham. Population: 106,001 (1991).

suture /soóchər/ *n* **1.** MATERIAL FOR SURGICAL STITCHING a piece of material used to close a wound or connect tissues, e.g. catgut, thread, or wire **2.** SURGICAL SEAM the line formed where a wound has been closed or tissues have been joined **3.** SEAM a seam or line at which two edges have been joined **4.** ANAT IMMOVABLE JOINT a joint, especially in the skull, in which the bones are tightly bound together by fibrous connective tissue so as to prevent movement between them **5.** ZOOL LINE AT POINT OF JUNCTURE a distinguishable line at the junction of adjacent structures, e.g. between the chambers of a mollusc shell or between the exoskeletal plates of an insect **6.** BOT LINE ON SEED POD OR FRUIT a line along which a seed pod or fruit will split to release its seeds ■ *vt* (**-tures, -turing, -tured**) SURG CLOSE WOUND to close a wound by joining the edges [15C. < Latin *sutura* < *sut-*, past participle of *suere* 'sew'] —**sutural** *adj* —**suturally** *adv*

SUV *abbr* N Am sport-utility vehicle

Suva /soóvə/ capital and largest city of Fiji. Situated on the southeastern coast of Viti Levu Island, it is Fiji's main port. Population: 77,366 (2000).

~~suvivor~~ incorrect spelling of **survivor**

Suwannee /soō wónni/ river in the southeastern United States. It rises in southern Georgia and flows 306 km/190 mi. through Florida into the Gulf of Mexico.

suxamethonium /súksə me thóni əm/ *n* an intravenous drug that is an ester of choline with succinic acid. Use: muscle relaxant during surgery. N Am term **succinylcholine** [Mid-20C. Alteration and contraction of *succinylmethylammonium* < *succinyl* < SUCCINIC ACID]

suzerain /soó zə rayn/ *n* a ruler or nation that controls a dependent nation's international affairs but allows it to control its internal affairs [Early 19C. < Old French *suserain*] —**suzerainty** /-rənti/ *n*

Suzhou /soō jó/, **Suchow, Xuzhou** city on the Grand Canal in southern Jiangsu Province, eastern China. It is an important transport and industrial centre. Population: 897,757 (1991).

Suzman /soózmən, soózmən/, **Helen** (*b.* 1917) South African politician. As an MP and cofounder (1959) of the Progressive Party, she campaigned against apartheid and assisted the transition to majority rule in South Africa.

SV *abbr* **1.** El Salvador (*used in Internet addresses*) See table at **domain name 2.** NAUT sailing vessel **3.** side valve **4.** under the word or term

Sv *symbol* MEASURE sievert

SV *abbr* RELIG **1.** Holy Virgin **2.** Your Holiness [Sense 1 Latin *Sancta Virgo*; sense 2 Latin *Sanctitas Vestra*]

s.v.[1] *abbr* **1.** NAUT sailing vessel **2.** side valve

s.v.[2] *abbr* under the word or term [Latin *sub voce*]

SV40 /éss veé fáwrti/ *n* a virus that causes cancer in monkeys and is widely used in genetic and medical research [< abbreviation of *simian virus*]

Svalbard /svál baard/ Norwegian archipelago in the Arctic Ocean. Population: 3,309 (1991). Area: 62,049 sq. km/23,957 sq. mi.

svelte /svelt/ *adj* graceful and slender in figure or contour [Early 19C. Via French < Italian *svelto* 'stretched', past participle of *svellere* 'pluck out' < Latin *vellere* 'pull']

Svengali /sven gaáli/ *n* somebody who controls and manipulates somebody else, usually for evil purposes [Early 20C. After a villainous hypnotist in the novel *Trilby* (1894), by George du Maurier]

Sverdrup Islands /sfáirdrəp-/ island group in Nunavut, Canada, within the Queen Elizabeth Islands, comprising Axel Heiberg, Ellef Ringnes, and Amund Ringnes

SVGA *n* a modified specification for video display controllers used in personal computers. Full form **super video graphics array**

SW *abbr* **1.** MEDIA short wave **2.** COMPASS southwest **3.** COMPASS southwestern

Sw. *abbr* **1.** Sweden **2.** LANG Swedish

swab /swob/ *n* **1.** SMALL STICK WITH COTTON WOOL a small stick, wire, or plastic swab with cotton wool attached to one or both ends, often used to clean wounds, apply medicine, or obtain a specimen of something **2.** MED SPECIMEN a specimen of mucus or another secretion obtained by using a swab **3.** SURG SOFT MATERIAL FOR MOPPING UP BLOOD a small piece of gauze, cotton, or other soft material, used to mop up blood during surgery **4.** MOP a mop used to clean decks or floors **5.** PIECE OF MATERIAL FOR CLEANING GUN a small piece of absorbent material that is used to clean the bore of a firearm **6.** SOMEBODY WHO MOPS somebody who uses a mop to clean, especially on a ship **7.** SOMEBODY WORTHLESS somebody regarded as uncouth or worthless (*archaic slang*) ■ *vt* (**swabs, swabbing, swabbed**) **1.** MOP SOMETHING to clean something such as a floor or deck with a mop **2.** CLEAN SOMETHING UP to clean up something such as a spill **3.** MED CLEAN WOUND WITH SWAB to clean out or apply medicine to a wound with a soft piece of material [Mid-17C. Back-formation < obsolete *swabber* 'deck mop' < obsolete Dutch *zwabben* 'to mop']

swaddle /swódd'l/ (**-dles, -dling, -dled**) *vt* **1.** WRAP SOMEBODY IN SOMETHING to wrap or bandage somebody or something with something **2.** WRAP BABY UP TIGHTLY to wrap a baby tightly in soft material **3.** SMOTHER SOMEBODY OR SOMETHING to restrain somebody or something with a complete wrapping [15C. < form of SWATHE[1]]

swaddling clothes /swódd ling-/, **swaddling bands** *archaic npl* long strips of linen or another soft material, used in some cultures to wrap babies in order to keep them still and calm

Swadeshi /swə dáyshi/ *S Asia adj* describes goods produced within the country of India ■ *n* the practice of favouring domestic products and refusing to buy imported goods as part of the struggle for independence in India [Early 20C. Via Hindi *svadeśī* < Sanskrit *svadeśaḥ* 'your own country']

swag /swag/ *n* **1.** CURTAIN an ornamental drapery or curtain that hangs in a curve between two points **2.** FESTOON an ornamental draping of fruit or flowers **3.** LOOT stolen property (*slang*) **4.** PROPERTY somebody's goods or valuables (*slang*) **5.** *Aus* PACK a pack or rolled-up blanket containing the personal belongings of a wanderer **6.** LURCHING MOVEMENT a lurching or swaying movement ■ *vi* (**swags, swagging, swagged**) MOVE WITH LURCH to move with a lurching or swaying movement [Early 16C. Probably < N Germanic]

swagbelly /swág beli/ *n* a large overhanging stomach (*informal*) —**swagbellied** *adj*

swage /swayj/ *n* **1.** a tool or die used to shape cold metal by hammering or applying pressure **2.** ENG same as **swage block** ■ *vt* (**swages, swaging, swaged**) to bend or shape metal with a swage [14C. < Old French *souage* 'decorative moulding'] —**swager** *n*

swage block *n* a metal block with holes or grooves used to shape cold metal

swagger /swággər/ *vi* (**-gers, -gering, -gered**) **1.** STRUT AROUND to walk in an arrogant or proud way **2.** BRAG to talk boastfully about personal accomplishments

■ *n* ARROGANT WALK an arrogant or proud way of walking or behaving [Early 16C. Probably < SWAG] —**swaggerer** *n* —**swaggeringly** *adv*

swagger stick *n* a short stick often carried by an army officer

swagman /swág man/ (*plural* **-men** /-men/) *n Aus* a tramp or itinerant worker who carries his belongings in a pack or rolled-up blanket (*informal*)

Swahili /swə heéli, swaa-/ (*plural same or* **-lis**) *n* **1.** a member of a people who live mainly along the eastern coasts and islands of eastern and southern Africa **2.** LANG same as **Kiswahili** [Early 19C. Via Kiswahili < Arabic *sawāḥilīy* 'of the coasts' < *sāḥil* 'coast'] —**Swahili** *adj*

swain /swayn/ *n* (*archaic or literary*) **1.** a young man who lives in the country **2.** a man who is somebody's admirer or lover [Late 16C. < Old Norse *sveinn* 'boy, servant' < Germanic, 'your own']

swale /swayl/ *n* a depression between slopes that provides for drainage [Early 16C. Origin ?]

Swaledale /swáyl dayl/ (*plural* **-dales** or *same*) *n* a hardy sheep with long curled horns, a black face, and long fleece, belonging to a breed originating in northern England [Early 20C. After an area in N Yorkshire]

SWALK /swawlk, swolk/ *abbr* sealed with a loving kiss (*sometimes written on the back of an envelope containing a letter to a beloved person*)

swallow[1] /swóllō/ *v* (**-lows, -lowing, -lowed**) **1.** *vti* PASS FOOD DOWN THROAT to take in food or liquid through the mouth and pass it down the throat into the stomach **2.** *vi* GULP to perform the act of swallowing, usually as an emotional response to something ○ *swallowing hard to hold back the tears* **3.** *vt* DESTROY SOMETHING to engulf or destroy something **4.** *vt* SUPPRESS FEELINGS to refrain from expressing thoughts or feelings ○ *Swallow your pride and apologize.* **5.** *vt* BELIEVE SOMETHING to accept something as true without questioning it (*informal*) ○ *They'll never swallow anything so far-fetched.* **6.** *vt* ENDURE SOMETHING to put up with something unpleasant without saying or doing anything to stop it **7.** *vt* RETRACT REMARK to withdraw a statement or remark as false or unjustified **8.** *vt* UTTER WORDS IN UNCLEAR WAY to say words in such a way that you cannot be understood ■ *n* **1.** ACT OF PASSING SOMETHING DOWN THROAT the act of taking something in through the mouth and down the throat **2.** AMOUNT PASSED DOWN THROAT an amount taken into the mouth and passed down the throat [Old English *swelgan* < Indo-European]

swallow

swallow[2] /swóllō/ *n* a small graceful songbird with long pointed wings, a notched or forked tail and rapid flight that migrates annually. Family: Hirundinidae. [Old English *swealwe* < Germanic]

swallow dive *n* a dive performed with the back arched, the legs held together straight, and the arms outstretched. N Am term **swan dive** [< SWALLOW[2]]

swallow hole *n* GEOG same as **sinkhole** (sense 1) [Old English *geswelg* 'deep hole' < Germanic]

swallowtail /swóllō tayl/ (*plural* **-tails** or *same*) *n* **1.** a colourful butterfly distinguished by the small tails that extend from the ends of its hind wings. Family: Papilionidae. **2.** the tail of a swallow or similar bird —**swallow-tailed** *adj*

swallow-tailed coat *n* a man's evening tail coat with a split rounded tail

swallowwort /swóllō wurt/ *n* PLANTS same as **greater celandine**

swam past tense of **swim**

swami /swaámi/ *n* a title of respect for a Hindu saint or religious teacher [Late 18C. Via Hindi < Sanskrit *svāmin*- 'being your own master']

swamp /swomp/ *n* WETLAND an area of land, usually fairly large, that is always wet and is overgrown with various shrubs and trees ▪ *v* (**swamps, swamping, swamped**) **1.** *vt* INUNDATE AREA to submerge an area in water **2.** *vti* NAUT SINK BOAT to cause a boat to fill with water and sink, or become full of water and sink **3.** *vt* OVERBURDEN SOMEBODY to overwhelm somebody by being too much or too many to cope with (*usually passive*) [Early 17C. Origin ?] —**swampy** *adj*

swamp boat *n* a flat-bottomed boat powered by an aeroplane propeller, used to travel in swamps and over shallow water

swamp buggy *n* US a light vehicle used to travel in areas with swamps and shallow lakes

swamp cypress *n* TREES same as **bald cypress**

swamper /swómpər/ *n* **1.** N Am LORRY DRIVER'S ASSISTANT an assistant to a lorry driver **2.** US SWAMP DWELLER OR WORKER somebody who lives or works in a swamp, especially in the southern United States **3.** US SOMEBODY WHO CLEARS SWAMP somebody who clears a swamp of trees and undergrowth or who clears a path through a forest so that logs can be moved **4.** US HELPER IN RESTAURANT somebody who helps in a restaurant

swamp fever *n* **1.** US a disease that is liable to be contracted by people in swampy areas, e.g. malaria or leptospirosis **2.** equine infectious anaemia (*dated*)

swampland /swómp land/ *n* an area of land that is always moist or that contains swamps

swan

swan /swon/ *n* a large graceful water bird with webbed feet, a long slender neck, and usually white feathers. Family: Anatidae. ▪ *vi* (**swans, swanning, swanned**) to wander around in a relaxed way, especially one regarded as irresponsible or selfish (*informal*) [Old English, 'singer' < Indo-European, 'make a sound'] —**swan-like** *adj*

CULTURAL NOTE *Swan Lake*, a ballet (1876) by the Russian composer Peter Ilyich Tchaikovsky. Tchaikovsky's first ballet is the romantic tale of Prince Siegfried, who falls in love with Odette, one of a group of swans he has seen metamorphose into beautiful maidens. When he realizes he has been tricked into declaring his love for another swan-maiden, Siegfried rushes to Odette and the two drown themselves in the Lake of Tears.

Swan /swon/ river in southwestern Western Australia, flowing through the city of Perth. Length: 386 km/240 mi.

swan dive *n* N Am SWIMMING same as **swallow dive**

swank /swangk/ (*informal*) *n* an arrogant, conceited, or pretentious person ▪ *vi* (**swanks, swanking, swanked**) to behave or swagger in an arrogant, conceited, or pretentious way [Early 19C. Origin ?]

swanky /swángki/ *adj* (*informal*) **1.** very stylish and expensive **2.** arrogant, conceited, or pretentious — **swankily** *adv* —**swankiness** *n*

swannery /swónnəri/ (*plural* **-ies**) *n* a place where mute swans gather and breed together

swansdown /swónz down/, **swan's-down** *n* **1.** the soft down feathers of a swan **2.** a soft woollen fabric. Use: baby clothes. **3.** TEXTILES same as **flannelette**

Swansea /swónzi/ city and port in southern Wales, at the mouth of the River Tawe. Population: 223,301 (2001). Welsh name **Abertawe**

swanskin /swón skin/ *n* a cotton or woollen fabric that is very soft to the touch

swansong /swón song/ *n* **1.** a final appearance, performance, or work, as a farewell to a career or profession **2.** a song of legendary beauty said to be sung only once by a swan during its lifetime, when it is dying

swap /swop/, **swop** *vti* (**swaps, swapping, swapped; swops, swopping, swopped**) EXCHANGE SOMETHING to trade or exchange somebody or something for somebody or something else (*informal*) ○ *Let's swap over and you can have my seat.* ▪ *n* **1.** EXCHANGE a trade or exchange of one person or thing for another (*informal*) **2.** SOMEBODY OR SOMETHING EXCHANGED somebody or something that is traded or exchanged for somebody or something else (*informal*) **3.** FIN CONTRACT a contract in which the parties exchange liabilities on outstanding debts, either as a means of managing debt or in the business of trading [14C. Probably an imitation of the sound of hands striking together (to seal an agreement)] —**swappable** *adj*

swap contract *n* a contract that involves a reciprocal exchange of some kind, especially one in which the contracting parties agree to exchange cash flows

swap meet *n* **1.** a gathering that people, especially hobbyists, attend for the purpose of exchanging things **2.** US a flea market where new, used, and sometimes rare or speciality items are sold

swaption /swópsh'n/ *n* an option on a contract giving the holder the right to enter into a swap [Late 20C. Contraction of *swap option*]

swaraj /swə raáj/ *n* S Asia self-government as a political objective in the former British India [Early 20C. Via Hindi *svarāj* < Sanskrit *svarājyam* 'own rule'] — **swarajism** *n* —**swarajist** *n*

sward /swaawrd/ *n* an area of turf or grass ▪ *vti* (**swards, swarding, swarded**) to cover something with turf or grass, or become covered with turf or grass [Old English *sweard* 'hairy skin, rind' < Germanic]

swarf /swaawrf/ *n* **1.** debris, especially from disintegrating satellites, that is in orbit around Earth (*informal*) **2.** the fine metallic shavings removed by grinding or cutting tools [Mid-16C. Origin ?]

swarm¹ /swaawrm/ *n* **1.** GROUP OF INSECTS a large group of insects, especially bees or gnats, in flight **2.** LARGE MASS a large crowd or group of people or animals moving in a confused or disorderly way ▪ *v* (**swarms, swarming, swarmed**) **1.** *vi* FORM FLYING GROUP to form a flying group, especially in order to found a new colony ○ *Do bees swarm often?* **2.** *vi* MOVE IN MASS to move or gather in a large crowd ○ *people swarmed all over the road* **3.** *vi* BE OVERRUN to be overrun with a large mass or group ○ *swarming with people* **4.** *vt* CAUSE SOMETHING TO SWARM to cause something to swarm, or produce a swarm [Old English *swearm* < Germanic, an imitation of the sound of buzzing]

swarm² /swaawrm/ (**swarms, swarming, swarmed**) *vi* to climb up somewhere using the arms and legs [Mid-16C. Origin ?]

swarm cell, **swarm spore** *n* BIOL same as **zoospore**

swart /swaawrt/ *adj* same as **swarthy** (*archaic or literary*) [Old English *sweart* < Indo-European, 'dirty, black']

swarthy /swáwrthi/ (**-ier, -iest**) *adj* having a dark and often weather-beaten complexion [Late 16C. Alteration of obsolete *swarty* < SWART] —**swarthily** *adv* —**swarthiness** *n*

swash /swosh/ *n* **1.** CHANNEL a narrow channel through which tides flow **2.** SANDBAR a sandbar that is washed over by waves **3.** SPLASH the motion or sound of the motion of water splashing or washing over something **4.** same as **swashbuckler** (sense 1) ▪ *v* (**swashes, swashing, swashed**) **1.** *vi* WASH OVER to strike or move with a splashing sound **2.** *vt* SPLASH SOMETHING to throw a liquid at or on something, especially with a splashing sound **3.** *vi* STRUT to move in a swaggering, pretentious way (*dated*) [Early 16C. Prob-

ably an imitation of the sound of splashing liquid or of a blow]

swashbuckler /swósh buklər/ *n* **1.** a bold and swaggering swordsman or adventurer **2.** a play, novel, or film about a swordsman or adventurer [Mid-16C. < SWASH + BUCKLER, from the sound of swords striking shields] —**swashbuckling** *adj*

swash letter /swósh-/ *n* an ornate italic letter with elaborate flourishes and tails [Origin ?]

swastika /swóstikə/ *n* **1.** a Nazi and fascist symbol formed by a Greek cross with the four ends of the arms bent in a clockwise direction **2.** an ancient religious symbol formed by a Greek cross, usually with the four ends of the arms bent at right angles in a clockwise or anticlockwise direction [Late 19C. < Sanskrit *svastikaḥ* 'good-luck sign' < *svasti* 'good luck']

swat¹ /swot/, **swot** *vti* (**swats, swatting, swatted; swots, swotting, swotted**) to strike or slap somebody or something sharply ▪ *n* **1.** a sharp blow or slap **2.** same as **swatter** [Early 17C. Alteration of SQUAT¹ in the obsolete sense 'crush, flatten']

swat² /swot/ *vi, n* another spelling of **swot¹**

SWAT /swot/ *n* US a police unit that is trained in the use of military weapons and tactics. Full form **Special Weapons and Tactics**

swatch /swoch/ *n* a piece cut from a material such as fabric or carpeting, used as a sample [Early 16C. Origin ?]

swath *n* same as **swathe**

swathe¹ /swayth/, **swath** /swoth/ *n* **1.** WIDTH CUT the width cut by a single passage of a scythe or mowing machine **2.** PATH CUT the path through a crop made during a single passage of a scythe or mowing machine **3.** AMOUNT CUT the amount of grass or corn left in the path made by a single passage of a scythe or mowing machine [Old English *swæþ* 'track' < Germanic] ◇ **cut a swathe through something** to destroy or use up a large part of something

swathe² /swayth/ *vt* (**swathes, swathing, swathed**) **1.** WRAP SOMEBODY OR SOMETHING COMPLETELY to wrap somebody or something completely with bandages or a similar covering **2.** ENVELOP SOMEBODY OR SOMETHING to envelop, cover, or hide somebody or something ▪ *n* WRAPPING a bandage, wrapping, or other binding [Old English *swaþian* 'wrap up', origin ?]

swatter /swóttər/, **swotter** *n* a flat meshed flexible piece of metal or plastic attached to a long handle, used to kill insects, especially flies

sway /sway/ *v* (**sways, swaying, swayed**) **1.** *vti* SWING to swing back and forth, or cause something to do this **2.** *vi* LEAN OVER REPEATEDLY to lean or bend to one side or in different directions in turn **3.** *vti* WAVER BETWEEN OPINIONS to go back and forth between two or more opinions, or make somebody do this **4.** *vt* INFLUENCE SOMEBODY to persuade or influence somebody to believe or do something (*usually passive*) ○ *Don't let yourself be swayed.* **5.** *vi* MOVE GRACEFULLY to move back and forth in a graceful way **6.** *vi* STAGGER to move from side to side in a clumsy and unsteady way **7.** *vt* NAUT HOIST SOMETHING to hoist a yard, mast, or other spar (*technical*) ▪ *n* **1.** SWINGING MOTION the act of swinging back and forth **2.** CONTROL OVER SOMEBODY rule or control over a person, group, or area [13C. Probably < N Germanic] —**swayable** *adj* —**swayer** *n* ◇ **hold sway** to have control or influence over a person or place

sway-back *n* an extreme inward or downward curving of the spine in horses and human beings

sway bar *n* US AUTOMOT same as **antiroll bar**

Swazi /swaázi/ (*plural* same or **-zis**) *n* **1.** a member of an African people who live in Swaziland and parts of eastern South Africa **2.** the Bantu language of the Swazi people, an official language of Swaziland. Native speakers: 2 million. [Late 19C. Alteration of Nguni *Mswati*, former Swazi king] —**Swazi** *adj*

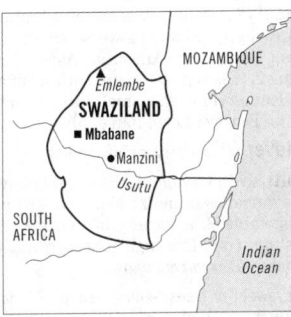

Swaziland

Swaziland /swaázi land/ landlocked country in southern Africa. It became an independent member of the Commonwealth in 1968. Language: Swazi, English. Currency: lilangeni. Capital: Mbabane. Population: 1,161,219 (2003). Area: 17,363 sq. km/6,704 sq. mi. Official name **Kingdom of Swaziland**

swbd *abbr* switchboard

SWbS *abbr* COMPASS southwest by south

SWbW *abbr* COMPASS southwest by west

swear /swair/ *v* (**swears, swearing, swore** /swawr/, **sworn** /swawrn/) **1.** *vti* AFFIRM TRUTH OF SOMETHING to declare solemnly or forcefully that what is said is true, sometimes calling somebody or something thought to be sacred as a witness ○ *She swore on her mother's grave that she had done as she had been asked.* **2.** *vti* SOLEMNLY PROMISE SOMETHING to promise something very solemnly ○ *He swore that he would serve humanity.* **3.** *vi* USE OFFENSIVE WORD OR WORDS to use blasphemous or obscene language, usually as an expression of strong feelings or with the intention of giving offence **4.** *vti* TAKE OATH to make a formal promise in a court of law or when taking up an official position **5.** *vti* DECLARE SOMETHING ON OATH to make a solemn statement under oath, especially in a court of law, or make somebody do this **6.** *vt* MAKE SOMEBODY MAKE PROMISE to cause somebody to make a solemn promise to do something ○ *We were sworn to secrecy.* ■ *n* BURST OF OFFENSIVE LANGUAGE a short spell of using blasphemous or obscene language [Old English *swerian* < Indo-European] —**swearer** *n* ◇ **swear blind** to assert something vehemently ○ *He swore blind he knew nothing about it.*

swear by *vt* **1.** to have great faith or complete confidence in the effectiveness of something or the ability of somebody for a designated purpose or task **2.** to use the name of somebody or something thought to be sacred in order to reinforce a solemn declaration or promise

swear in *vt* to cause somebody to make a formal promise in a court of law or when taking up an official position

swear off *vt* to make a solemn promise to give something up, especially a bad habit

swearword /swáir wurd/ *n* a word or phrase that is considered unacceptable in polite language, especially one that is blasphemous or obscene, used to express strong feelings or give offence

sweat /swet/ *n* **1.** MOISTURE ON SKIN the clear salty liquid that passes to the surface of the skin when somebody is hot or as a result of strenuous activity, fear, anxiety, or illness **2.** STATE OF HAVING SWEAT ON SKIN the production or secretion of sweat, e.g. during strenuous activity or illness, or a state of fear or anxiety that causes this **3.** HARD OR BORING WORK hard, unpleasant, or tedious work **4.** SCI LIQUID EXUDED TO SURFACE drops of liquid that ooze through and collect on the surface of something, e.g. sap on a tree **5.** PHYS MOISTURE CONDENSED ON SURFACE drops of liquid that appear on the surface of something, usually by condensation of water vapour from the surrounding warmer air **6.** HORSERACING RUN BEFORE RACE a run that a horse has before a race, as exercise **7.** EXPERIENCED PERSON an experienced person, especially a soldier (*dated informal*) ■ **sweats** *npl* US CLOTHING TWO-PIECE SPORTS OUTFIT a sweatshirt and tracksuit bottoms made of matching fabric and worn together for sport or casual activities (*informal*) ■ *v* (**sweats, sweating, sweated**) **1.** *vti* PERSPIRE to produce a clear salty liquid on the surface of the skin as a result of

being hot or as a result of strenuous activity, fear, anxiety, or illness **2.** *vt* MAKE SOMEBODY SWEAT to make somebody sweat, e.g. as a medical treatment **3.** *vt* WET OR MARK SOMETHING WITH SWEAT to make something damp or stained with sweat **4.** *vti* COOK SOMETHING IN OWN JUICES to cook something in a pan in its own juices with a small amount of fat or oil until tender, or be cooked in this way **5.** *vt* HEAT SOLDER UNTIL IT MELTS to heat solder until it melts and runs between surfaces to bond them **6.** *vi* WORK HARD to work very hard or overwork (*informal*) **7.** *vt* OVERWORK OR UNDERPAY EMPLOYEES to make somebody work very hard, often in poor conditions or for low wages (*informal*) **8.** *vt* EXTORT INFORMATION FROM SOMEBODY to force somebody to give up information, especially by relentless interrogation or physical violence (*informal*) **9.** *vi* BE UNDER STRESS to be very anxious, impatient, or afraid (*informal*) ○ *He left them sweating in the corridor while he made up his mind.* **10.** *vi* SUFFER FOR WRONGDOING to suffer physically or mentally, especially as a punishment (*informal*) **11.** *vti* SCI EXUDE LIQUID AT SURFACE to produce or form as liquid beads by oozing through the surface of something and collecting there **12.** *vti* SCI FORM OR APPEAR AS MOISTURE to form as moisture on a surface, usually by condensation of water vapour from the surrounding warmer air, or produce moisture in this way **13.** *vti* AGRIC REMOVE MOISTURE FROM SOMETHING to remove moisture from something, or have moisture removed, e.g. when fermenting fruits or tobacco or when curing animal hides [Old English *swāt* < Indo-European] —**sweatless** *adj* ◇ **no sweat 1.** used to say that something can be done with ease and without foreseeable problems (*informal*) ○ *We'll get it there on time. No sweat.* **2.** not requiring effort or difficulty ○ *the no sweat way to learn a language*

sweat off *vt* to get rid of excess weight by sweating, e.g. in a sauna or through strenuous activity

sweat out 1. to relieve the symptoms of an illness by maintaining a raised body temperature, and hence cause profuse sweating **2.** to carry on doing something difficult or put up with something unpleasant until it is over (*informal*)

sweatband /swét band/ *n* **1.** a strip of terry towelling worn around the head or wrists to stop sweat running into the eyes or onto the hands while playing sport **2.** a strip of fabric or leather sewn inside a hat to protect it from damage by sweat

sweatbox /swét boks/ *n* **1.** DEVICE FOR REMOVING WATER FROM HIDES a device in which hides or some fruits are placed to remove water **2.** CONFINED PLACE a very small room, especially a narrow cell where a prisoner is confined for punishment (*informal*) **3.** PLACE WHERE SOMEBODY SWEATS a place where somebody is made to sweat through heat or fear (*informal*)

sweated /swéttid/ *adj* **1.** made to work very hard in poor conditions for low wages **2.** performed or produced by employees who are made to work very hard in poor conditions for low wages

sweater /swéttər/ *n* **1.** CLOTHING same as **jumper²** (sense 1) **2.** somebody who sweats in a particular way **3.** an employer who makes people work very hard in poor conditions for low wages

sweat gland *n* a small tube-shaped gland in the skin of most parts of the body from which sweat is released

sweat lodge *n* a hut, cavern, or building heated by steam from water poured over hot rocks and used, especially by Native Americans, for therapeutic or ritual sweating

sweatpants /swét pants/ *npl* N Am long trousers made of a soft knitted fabric, often with elastic at the waist and ankles, worn casually or for exercising

sweatshirt /swét shurt/ *n* a long-sleeved pullover or zipped jacket made of soft knitted fabric, worn casually or for sport

sweatshop /swét shop/ *n* a small factory or other establishment where employees are made to work very hard in poor conditions for low wages

sweat suit *n* N Am a sweatshirt and tracksuit bottoms made of matching fabric and worn together for sport or casual activities

sweaty /swétti/ (**-ier, -iest**) *adj* **1.** DAMP WITH SWEAT damp with or smelling of sweat **2.** CAUSING SWEAT making somebody sweat **3.** SCI WITH MOISTURE ON SURFACE having

drops of exuded or condensed liquid on the surface —**sweatily** *adv* —**sweatiness** *n*

swede /sweed/ *n* **1.** a large round root with yellowish flesh that is cooked and eaten as a vegetable **2.** a plant that produces swedes. Latin name: *Brassica napus napobrassica*. ▶ N Am term **rutabaga** [Early 19C. < SWEDE; from its introduction (into Scotland) from Sweden]

Swede /sweed/ *n* somebody who comes from Sweden [Early 17C. < Middle Low German or Middle Dutch *Swēde*, probably < Old Norse *Svíar* (plural) 'Swedes' + *þjóð* 'people']

Sweden

Sweden /sweed'n/ country in Scandinavia, in northwestern Europe. Language: Swedish. Currency: krona. Capital: Stockholm. Population: 8,878,085 (2003). Area: 449,964 sq. km/173,732 sq. mi. Official name **Kingdom of Sweden**

Swedenborg /sweed'n bawrg/, **Emanuel** (1688–1772) Swedish scientist and theologian. His theology, deriving from his mystical experiences, was the basis of a religious movement. Born **Swedberg, Emanuel** —**Swedenborgian** /sweed'n báwrji ən, -gi ən/ *n, adj*

Swedish /sweedish/ *n* OFFICIAL LANGUAGE OF SWEDEN the official language of Sweden and an official language of Finland, belonging to the North Germanic branch of the Indo-European family of languages. Native speakers: 8.5 million. ■ *adj* **1.** OF SWEDEN relating to Sweden, or its people or culture **2.** OF SWEDISH relating to the Swedish language [Early 17C. <SWEDEN OR SWEDE]

LANGUAGE HERITAGE See *Scandinavian*.

Swedish glace /-gláss/ *n* a rich creamy frozen dessert that resembles ice cream but contains no dairy products or other ingredients of animal origin

Swedish massage *n* a system of massage employing both active and passive exercising of the muscles and joints

Swedish mile *n* a unit of measure used in Sweden equal to 10 km/6.2 mi

sweeny /sweeni/, **sweeney** *n* atrophy of the shoulder muscles of horses resulting from harness pressure on nerves going to these muscles [Early 19C. Origin ?]

sweep /sweep/ *v* (**sweeps, sweeping, swept** /swept/) **1.** *vti* CLEAN PLACE WITH BRUSH to remove something such as dust, dirt, debris, or snow from the floor or ground with a brush, broom, or similar implement **2.** *vt* CLEAR CHIMNEY to remove soot from the inside of a chimney with a long-handled brush **3.** *vt* MOVE SOMETHING WITH HORIZONTAL STROKE to move something with a long smooth stroke or a quick brushing stroke ○ *I swept the papers off the desk.* **4.** *vti* BRUSH AGAINST GROUND to brush against a horizontal surface such as the floor or the ground **5.** *vi* MOVE WITH SPEED AND FORCE to move quickly, smoothly, and forcefully, often in a large body or group ○ *The crowd swept across the bridge.* **6.** *vi* MOVE WITH DIGNITY to move quickly and smoothly with a proud, majestic, or self-important air ○ *swept angrily out of the room* **7.** *vti* MOVE ACROSS PLACE to move quickly and forcefully across an area ○ *the gales that are sweeping the country* **8.** *vti* SPREAD THROUGH PLACE to pass or spread quickly through a place ○ *The news swept through the city.* **9.** *vt* CARRY SOMEBODY OR SOMETHING ALONG to carry somebody or something quickly and forcefully in the same direction ○ *swept along by the current* **10.** *vt* STRONGLY INFLUENCE SOMEBODY to strongly influence or overwhelm somebody (*often passive*) ○ *We were swept along by their enthusiasm.* **11.** *vti* WIN SOMETHING OVERWHELMINGLY to win something easily and over-

whelmingly, or win all the games in a series or set of games for a championship ○ *watched them sweep to victory* **12.** *vi* **STRETCH OUT IN ARC** to extend in a long smooth graceful curve or a wide circle ○ *plains sweeping down to the coast* **13.** *vti* **EXTEND OVER WIDE AREA** to be directed over a wide range or the entire area of something ○ *Her eyes swept around the room.* **14.** *vti* **SEARCH PLACE FOR SOMETHING** to search a place for something, e.g. an area of water for mines or a room for hidden recording devices **15.** *vti* CRICKET **HIT BALL WITH HORIZONTAL BAT** in cricket, to hit a ball from a half-kneeling position by bringing the bat, held almost horizontally, across the body with a long smooth stroke ■ *n* **1. BOUT OF CLEANING WITH BRUSH** a cleaning of something with a brush, broom, or similar implement **2. BRUSHING STROKE** a quick brushing stroke **3. LONG SMOOTH MOVEMENT** a long smooth curved movement ○ *with a sweep of her arm* **4. LONG SMOOTH CURVE** a long smooth graceful curve ○ *the sweep of the coastline* **5. WIDE EXPANSE** a wide expanse or extent ○ *the sweep of the horizon* **6. CURVED RANGE** the range over which something is directed, usually a wide arc or circle ○ *stay out of the sweep of the searchlights* **7. BROAD RANGE** the broad range or comprehensive nature of something ○ *the sweep of history* **8. SEARCH** a thorough search of a place ○ *a sweep of the neighbourhood* **9. OVERWHELMING VICTORY** an overwhelming or absolute victory ○ *their sweep to power* **10. WINDMILL SAIL** a sail of a windmill **11. POLE FOR LIFTING BUCKET IN WELL** a long pole used as a lever to raise or lower a bucket in a well **12.** GAMBLING same as **sweepstake** (*informal*) **13.** OCCUPATIONS same as **chimney sweep 14.** CRICKET **SHOT WITH BAT HORIZONTAL** in cricket, a shot in which the ball is hit from a half-kneeling position, bringing the bat, held almost horizontally, across the body with a long smooth stroke **15.** BOATING **OAR FOR PROPELLING BOAT** a long oar that is used to propel small boats or sometimes act as a rudder **16.** ELECTRONICS **ELECTRON BEAM MOTION IN CATHODE-RAY TUBE** the steady movement of the electron beam across the fluorescent surface of a cathode ray tube. The motion may be straight, as with television screens, or circular, as with radar screens. ■ **sweeps** *npl US* **TELEVISION RATINGS IN PARTICULAR PERIOD** a periodic survey of television ratings that is used to determine advertising rates, or the period when these ratings are done [13C. Probably < past tense of Old English *swāpan* 'sweep' < Germanic, 'to swing'] —**sweepy** *adj* ◇ **make a clean sweep (of somebody** *or* **something) 1.** to have a complete change by getting rid of everyone or everything unwanted or unnecessary **2.** to win every competition, race, or contest in a series of competitions, races, or contests

sweep away, sweep aside *vt* to remove, dismiss, or destroy something quickly, forcefully, and completely

sweep up *vti* to remove dust, dirt, or debris from the floor or ground with a brush, broom, or similar implement

sweepback /swéep bak/ *n* an aircraft wing that slants backwards towards the tail assembly, forming an acute angle with the fuselage

sweeper /swéepər/ *n* **1. SOMEBODY WHO SWEEPS** somebody whose job involves sweeping something, usually floors or roads **2. SOMETHING THAT SWEEPS** a device or machine, usually fitted with brushes, that sweeps something such as a floor or a road **3.** SPORTS **ROVING DEFENSIVE PLAYER** in football and some other team sports, a defensive player who is not assigned to cover an attacking player, but plays across the pitch in the space between other defenders and the goalkeeper **4.** *S Asia* **INDIAN HOUSE CLEANER** a woman or girl who is employed to clean somebody's house

sweep hand *n* a long hand, mounted concentrically with the minute hand of an analogue watch or clock, that indicates seconds as it sweeps around the same dial as the minute hand

sweeping /swéeping/ *adj* **1. ON LARGE SCALE** wide-ranging and comprehensive, usually affecting a large number of people or things ○ *sweeping reforms* **2. TOO GENERAL** failing to take specific exceptions or details into consideration ○ *a sweeping condemnation of modern youth* **3. OVERWHELMING** complete, overwhelming, or decisive ○ *a sweeping victory* **4. WITH BROAD EXTENT** covering a large area, usually a wide arc or circle ○ *included in her sweeping glance* ■ *n* **ACT OF USING BRUSH** the action of somebody who sweeps with a brush or broom ■ **sweepings** *npl* **THINGS SWEPT UP** dirt and refuse swept up —**sweepingly** *adv* —**sweepingness** *n*

sweep-saw *n* a thin-bladed saw that is held taut in a frame and used for cutting curves

sweep-second hand *n* TIME same as **sweep hand**

sweepstake /swéep stayk/ *n* **1.** a lottery in which the payout is determined by the amount paid in and the winner determined by the outcome of a horse race **2.** the prize offered or won in a sweepstake

sweet /sweet/ *adj* **1. TASTING OR SMELLING OF SUGAR** tasting or smelling of sugar or a similar substance **2. CONTAINING OR RETAINING SUGAR** containing a relatively large amount of sugar, or retaining some natural sugars ○ *sweet cider* **3. NOT SAVOURY** associated with the basic taste sensation that is not bitter, salt, or sour **4. FRESH** not stale, rancid, or soured ○ *sweet water* **5. NOT SALTY** not salty or saline ○ *sweet butter* **6. PLEASING TO SENSES** pleasing to any of the senses ○ *the sweet strains of the violin* **7. SATISFYING** desirable, gratifying, or satisfying ○ *Revenge turned out not to be sweet after all.* **8. KIND** kind, thoughtful, or generous ○ *He's so sweet: he never forgets my birthday.* **9. VERY PLEASING TO LOOK AT** having an appearance that is charming or endearing ○ *a sweet little cottage by the lake* **10. EXCELLENT** excellent or extremely good (*informal*) **11. RESPECTED** dear, respected, or beloved (*archaic*) ○ *Indeed, my sweet lord.* **12.** AGRIC **NOT ACIDIC** describes land that contains no acid or corrosive substances **13.** INDUST **CONTAINING LITTLE OR NO SULPHUR** describes petrol or oil that contains little or no sulphur ○ *rising costs of sweet crude* **14.** *Aus* **OK** satisfactory (*informal*) **15.** *Carib* **GIVING PLEASE** pleasing or delightful ■ *adv* **PLEASANTLY** in a pleasant manner ○ *sing sweet* ■ *n* **1. SHAPED ITEM OF CONFECTIONERY** a small hard, chewy, or soft piece of food made from sugar and other ingredients or flavourings such as chocolate, nuts, fruit, or peppermint. N Am term **candy 2. DESSERT** a course or dish of sweet food served at or near the end of a meal ○ *Would you like a sweet?* **3. SWEET FOOD** an item of sweet food **4.** *US* FOOD same as **sweet potato** (*informal*) **5. SENSATION OF SWEETNESS** a sweet taste or smell ○ *had to take the bitter with the sweet* **6. SOMETHING PLEASANT** a pleasant thing or experience (*literary*) ○ *squander the sweets of life* **7. DEAR** used as a term of endearment ○ *Come to me, my sweet.* **8.** INDUST **SULPHUR-FREE NATURAL GAS OR OIL** a natural gas or crude oil that is essentially free from acidic or odorous sulphur compounds [Old English *swēte* < Indo-European] —**sweetish** *adj* —**sweetly** *adv* —**sweetness** *n* ◇ **be sweet on somebody** to be in love with somebody (*dated informal*) ◇ **keep somebody sweet** to treat somebody with particular kindness or indulgence as a tactic to win favour or secure help or support (*informal*)

SPELLCHECK See ***suite.***

sweet alyssum *n* a widely-cultivated annual plant. Native to: Europe. Flowers: low-growing, fragrant white, pink, purple, in clusters. Latin name: *Lobularia maritima.*

sweet-and-sour *adj* cooked in or served with a sauce that has sugar and vinegar among the ingredients

sweet basil *n* PLANTS same as **basil**

sweet bay *n* **1.** TREES same as **bay**³ (sense 1) **2.** a magnolia bush or tree with yellow-green leaves and red fruit. Flowers: fragrant, white. Native to: eastern United States. Latin name: *Magnolia virginia.*

sweet birch *n* **1.** a hard dark wood **2.** a birch with smooth blackish-brown bark and aromatic stems that yield methyl salicylate. Native to: eastern United States. Latin name: *Betula lenta.*

sweetbread /swéet bred/ *n* the pancreas or thymus of a calf, lamb, or other young animal soaked, fried, and eaten as food

sweetbriar /swéet brīr/ (*plural* **-ars** or *same*), **sweetbrier** (*plural* **-ers** or *same*) *n* a rose that has a long stem with prickles and fragrant leaves. Flowers: rosy pink or white, single. Native to: Europe, Asia. Latin name: *Rosa rubiginosa.*

sweet cherry *n* **1.** a sweet firm-fleshed cherry **2.** a cultivated variety of cherry tree

sweet chestnut *n* TREES same as **chestnut** (sense 2)

sweet cicely /-síssəli/ (*plural same*) *n* **1.** a plant with aromatic fleshy roots. Flowers: small, white, in clusters. Native to: America, Asia. Genus: *Osmorhiza.* **2.** a perennial plant with aromatic compound leaves. Flowers: small, white, in umbels. Native to: Europe. Latin name: *Myrrhis odorata.*

sweet clover *n* PLANTS same as **melilot**

sweetcorn /swéet kawrn/ *n* **1.** the sweet yellow kernels of some varieties of maize plant, cooked and eaten as a vegetable **2.** a variety of maize with yellow kernels that contain a high concentration of sugar. Latin name: *Zea mays rugosa.*

sweeten /swéet'n/ (**-ens, -ening, -ened**) *v* **1.** *vti* **INCREASE IN SWEETNESS** to make something taste sweet or sweeter by adding sugar or another natural or artificial substance, or become sweet or sweeter in flavour **2.** *vt* **IMPROVE TASTE OR SMELL OF SOMETHING** to make something taste or smell more pleasant **3.** *vt* **MAKE SOMETHING MORE DESIRABLE** to make something more attractive, agreeable, or acceptable ○ *sweeten the offer* **4.** *vt* **SOFTEN SOMEBODY** to make somebody kinder, gentler, friendlier, or calmer ○ *might sweeten his temper* **5.** *vt* **PERSUADE SOMEBODY** to persuade somebody by flattery, cajolery, or bribery to accept or agree to something **6.** *vti* INDUST **IMPROVE PROPERTIES OF SOMETHING** to improve a product such as petroleum by making it less corrosive and foul-smelling, or by making its colour more acceptable, or be improved in this way. Petroleum products are sweetened during refining by the removal of sulphides or the conversion of them into disulphides. **7.** *vt US* FIN **INCREASE VALUE OF COLLATERAL** to add securities to collateral so that its value is increased **8.** *vt* CARDS **INCREASE VALUE OF POT** in poker, to add stakes to a pot remaining from a previous deal (*informal*)

sweetener /swéet'nər/ *n* **1.** a natural or artificial substance that is added to food or drink to make it sweet or sweeter, especially a synthetic substance used in place of sugar **2.** something given as a bribe, incentive, or means of persuading somebody to accept or agree to something (*informal*)

sweetening /swéet'ning/ *n* **1.** a substance that makes food or drink sweet or sweeter, especially an artificial additive **2.** the act of making something sweet or sweeter

sweet-eye *n Carib* a loving or flirtatious wink

sweet FA /-ef áy/, **sweet Fanny Adams** /-fánni áddəmz/ *n* nothing at all (*slang*)

sweet fern *n* a bush with aromatic leaves similar to those of a fern. Flowers: small, brownish, in heads. Native to: eastern North America. Latin name: *Comptonia peregrina.*

sweet flag *n* a perennial marsh plant with narrow sword-shaped leaves and an aromatic rootstock. Flowers: tiny, greenish. Latin name: *Acorus calamus.*

sweet gale *n* a bush of the bayberry family that grows in marshy regions and has aromatic lance-shaped leaves. Native to: Europe, Asia, North America. Latin name: *Myrica gale.*

sweet gum *n* **1.** an amber aromatic tree resin **2.** a tree of the witch hazel family that has lobed leaves, hard wood, and round prickly fruit clusters, and is the source of an amber aromatic resin. Native to: North America. Latin name: *Liquidambar styraciflua.*

sweetheart /swéet haart/ *n* **1. AFFECTIONATE TERM OF ADDRESS** used as a term of endearment, usually to a lover or child **2. KIND PERSON** a kind or obliging person ○ *Be a sweetheart and make me a cup of coffee.* **3. BOYFRIEND OR GIRLFRIEND** a boyfriend, girlfriend, or lover (*dated*) **4. SOMETHING CHERISHED** something cherished for its fine qualities and often considered one of a kind

sweetheart agreement *n* **1.** an arrangement arrived at secretly to benefit some at the expense of the rest, especially an industrial agreement between union and management representatives that is not in the workers' best interest **2.** *Aus* in industrial relations, an agreement reached through direct discussions between workers and their employer without recourse to arbitration [< the privileged treatment of one party]

sweetheart neckline *n* on women's clothing, a low-

cut neckline with two curves over the bust, making the bodice look heart-shaped

sweetie /swee'ti/ n **1.** PIECE OF CONFECTIONERY a boiled sweet, toffee, or other piece of confectionery (informal; except in Scotland, usually used by or to children) **2.** TERM OF ENDEARMENT used as a term of endearment (informal) **3.** ENDEARING PERSON OR ANIMAL a likeable or lovable person or animal (informal) **4.** SWEET GRAPEFRUIT a seedless variety of grapefruit with a greenish rind and sweet juicy flesh

sweetie pie n somebody who is lovable or likeable (informal)

sweeting /swee'ting/ n somebody who is loved or cherished (archaic)

sweet marjoram n a herb with aromatic leaves used as a seasoning in cookery and salads. Flowers: small, purple. Native to: Mediterranean. Latin name: Origanum majorana.

sweetmeal /sweet meel/ adj made with wholemeal flour that has been sweetened, usually by adding sugar

sweetmeat /sweet meet/ n a superior type of sweet or confectionery served at the end of a meal or with tea (archaic)

sweetness and light n pleasantness and friendliness or peace and harmony, especially in contrast to normal behaviour or circumstances ○ He has a vile temper, but when he gets his way, he's all sweetness and light.

sweet nothings npl romantic words or phrases

sweet oil n a mild-flavoured oil, e.g. sweet almond oil or grapeseed oil

sweet pea n a widely cultivated climbing plant of the legume family. Flowers: sweet-scented, butterfly-shaped. Native to: Italy. Latin name: Lathyrus odoratus.

sweet pepper n **1.** a bell-shaped red, green, or orange fruit eaten raw or cooked as a vegetable **2.** a plant that produces sweet peppers. Latin name: Capsicum frutescens grossum.

sweet potato n **1.** a fleshy orange root cooked and eaten as a vegetable **2.** a vine that produces sweet potatoes. Flowers: funnel-shaped, purplish. Native to: tropical America. Latin name: Ipomoea batatas.

sweetshop /sweet shop/ n a shop that sells sweets and sometimes other items such as cigarettes or newspapers. N Am term **candy store**

sweet-smelling adj having a pleasant smell

sweetsop /sweet sop/ (plural **-sops** or same) n **1.** a fruit with a hard green rind and a sweet edible pulp **2.** an evergreen bush that produces sweetsops. Native to: tropical America. Latin name: Annona squamosa. [< the sweet pulp of its fruit]

sweet sorghum n PLANTS same as **sorgo**

sweet spot n **1.** the most effective place to hit the ball on a racket, bat, club, or other piece of sports equipment **2.** the price for a product at which the most profit is achieved [< SWEET 'desirable']

sweet sultan (plural **sweet sultans** or same) n a bush with large variously coloured flowers. Native to: eastern Mediterranean region. Latin name: Centaurea moschata.

sweet talk n flattering or pleasing words used to persuade somebody (informal)

sweet-talk vti to use flattering or pleasing words in order to persuade somebody to do something (informal)

sweet tooth n a fondness for sweet food

sweet william /-wíllyəm/ (plural **sweet williams** or same) n a plant widely grown in gardens. Flowers: white, pink, red, or purple, with banded or mottled patterns, in flat clusters. Native to: Europe, Asia. Latin name: Dianthus barbatus.

sweet woodruff n PLANTS same as **woodruff**

swell /swel/ v (**swells, swelling, swelled, swollen** /swólən/ or **swelled**) **1.** vti INCREASE IN SIZE to become, or make something, larger, fuller, or rounder, or expand in size or shape, usually as a result of pressure from within ○ the wind swelled the sails **2.** vi MED BECOME LARGER THAN NORMAL to increase in size temporarily, typically as a result of injury, infection, or other

medical condition ○ My ankles had swelled in the heat. **3.** vti INCREASE IN QUANTITY to increase something in number or amount, usually by adding to it, or increase in this way ○ new members to swell the ranks of the Party **4.** vti INCREASE IN DEGREE to make something stronger or more intense, or become stronger or more intense ○ could feel indignation swelling inside her **5.** vti MUSIC INCREASE AND DECREASE IN LOUDNESS in music, to grow gradually louder and softer in turn, or gradually increase and decrease volume in this way **6.** vti FILL WITH EMOTION to be filled with a strong feeling or emotion, or cause somebody's heart or soul to be filled with a strong feeling or emotion ○ His heart swelled with pride. **7.** vi UNDULATE ON SURFACE to rise and fall on the surface of something in long large waves ■ n **1.** UNDULATION OF SEA SURFACE the rising and falling movement of a large area of the sea as a long wave travels through it without breaking ○ There's quite a swell out there today. **2.** ROUND SHAPE the full, round shape of something **3.** BULGE a bulge or protuberance **4.** INCREASING OF SIZE an increase in size, fullness, or roundness **5.** INCREASING OF NUMBER an increase in number, amount, or degree **6.** PROCESS OF SWELLING the process or an instance of swelling **7.** GENTLE SLOPE a low hill or gentle slope **8.** MUSIC CRESCENDO THEN DIMINUENDO a gradual increase in the loudness of music followed by a gradual decrease, or the sign indicating this **9.** MUSIC same as **swell box** **10.** FASHIONABLE PERSON a fashionably and expensively dressed person (dated informal) **11.** SOMEBODY OF HIGH STATUS a very important person, especially in society or politics (dated informal) ■ adj N Am GOOD very good (dated) ○ did a swell job [Old English swellan < Germanic]

swell box n a device on an organ, usually an enclosed box with pipes, that permits crescendo and diminuendo, a characteristic otherwise lacking on this instrument

swelled head /swéld-/ n ANZ, N Am same as **swollen head**

swellhead /swél hed/ n US somebody regarded as conceited and arrogant (informal) —**swellheaded** /swél héddid/ adj —**swellheadedness** n

swelling /swélling/ n **1.** an increase in size of part of the body, typically as a result of injury, infection, or other medical condition ○ The swelling should go down in a couple of days. **2.** a bulge or protuberance caused by swelling

swelter /swéltər/ vi (**-ters, -tering, -tered**) BE OPPRESSED BY HEAT to feel uncomfortably hot ○ We had been sweltering in a hot car all afternoon. ■ n **1.** UNPLEASANT HEAT excessive or oppressive heat **2.** SENSATION OF HOTNESS an uncomfortable feeling produced by extreme heat [15C. < Old English sweltan 'die' < Germanic, 'to burn']

sweltering /swéltəring/ adj **1.** oppressively hot **2.** feeling uncomfortably hot —**swelteringly** adv

swept past participle, past tense of **sweep**

sweptback /swépt bák/ adj describes a wing that is angled backwards towards the aircraft's tail

sweptwing /swépt wíng/ adj describes an aircraft or missile that has sweptback wings

swerve /swurv/ vti (**swerves, swerving, swerved**) to make a sudden change in direction, often to avoid a collision, or make something change direction suddenly ○ had to swerve the car to avoid a pedestrian ■ n a sudden change in direction [Old English sweorfan 'file, scour, turn aside' < Indo-European, 'to turn'] —**swerver** n

Sweyn I /swayn/ (960?–1014) king of Denmark. He first invaded England in 994, and by 1014 established his rule sufficiently for his son Canute II to become king (1016–35). Known as **Sweyn Forkbeard**

SWG abbr standard wire gauge

swidden /swídd'n/ n a place temporarily cleared for agriculture by cutting back and burning off previous growth [Late 18C. Variant of obsolete swithen 'burn' < Old Norse svíðna 'be singed']

swift

swift /swift/ adj **1.** HAPPENING FAST happening or done very quickly or suddenly ○ issued a swift denial **2.** ACTING FAST acting very quickly or promptly ○ They were swift to respond. **3.** MOVING FAST moving or able to move very quickly ■ adv QUICKLY very quickly ○ a swift-flowing river ■ n **1.** (plural same or **swifts**) BIRDS SMALL BIRD RESEMBLING SWALLOW a small dark bird with long narrow wings, related to the hummingbirds and resembling a swallow. Family: Apodidae. **2.** REPT SMALL FAST LIZARD a small fast-running lizard. Native to: North America. Genera: Sceloporus or Uta. **3.** TEXTILES REEL ON MACHINE the reel on which yarn is placed while it is wound off [Old English, 'quick, moving along a course' < Germanic, 'swing, bend'] —**swiftly** adv —**swiftness** n

Swift /swift/, **Jonathan** (1667–1745) Anglo-Irish author and clergyman. The dean of St Patrick's, Dublin, he was the leading satirist of his age. He wrote A Tale of a Tub (1704) and Gulliver's Travels (1726). See Cultural note at **travel**. Known as **Dean Swift** — **Swiftian** n

'He had been eight years upon a project for extracting sunbeams out of cucumbers, which were to be put into vials hermetically sealed, and let out to warm the air in raw inclement summers.'
[Jonathan Swift, 'A Voyage to Laputa', Gulliver's Travels; 1726]

'We have just enough religion to make us hate, but not enough to make us love one another.'
[Jonathan Swift, Thoughts on Various Subjects; 1711]

'There is nothing in this world constant, but inconstancy.'
[Jonathan Swift, A Critical Essay upon the Faculties of the Mind; 1709]

Swift Current town and railway junction in southwestern Saskatchewan, Canada, 245 km/152 mi. west of Regina. Population: 14,821 (2001).

swift fox n a small fox with large ears. Native to: western North America. Latin name: Vulpes velox.

swiftie /swífti/ n ANZ a trick or deception (informal)

swiftlet /swíftlət/ n a small cave-dwelling swift whose nest is used in making birds' nest soup. Native to: South Asia. Genus: Collocalia.

swig /swig/ (informal) vti (**swigs, swigging, swigged**) to drink something in large gulps ■ n a large gulp of drink [Mid-16C. Origin ?] —**swigger** n

swill /swil/ v (**swills, swilling, swilled**) **1.** vt WASH SOMETHING WITH WATER to wash or rinse something by flooding or filling it with water **2.** vti MOVE LIQUID AROUND IN SOMETHING to make liquid move around or over something, or move in this way ○ He swilled the water around in the bucket. **3.** vti DRINK LOT OF SOMETHING to drink large amounts of something (disapproving) **4.** vt AGRIC FEED ANIMALS WITH WATERY FEED to feed animals, especially pigs, with a watery feed typically containing kitchen waste or food by-products ■ n **1.** AGRIC ANIMAL FEED a watery feed for livestock, especially pigs, typically containing kitchen waste or food by-products **2.** KITCHEN WASTE kitchen waste or general refuse **3.** WASHING OF SOMETHING WITH WATER a wash or rinse using a large amount of water **4.** LARGE DRINK a large drink or mouthful of drink **5.** INFERIOR FOOD OR DRINK inferior or unpleasant food or drink **6.** SLOPPY LIQUID MIXTURE a sloppy liquid mixture or mess

7. NONSENSE talk or writing that is utter nonsense (*informal*) [Old English *swillan* < Indo-European] —**swiller** *n*

swim /swim/ *v* (**swims, swimming, swam** /swam/, **swum** /swum/) **1.** *vi* **MOVE THROUGH WATER** to move or propel yourself unsupported through water using natural means of propulsion such as legs, tails, or fins **2.** *vt* **TRAVEL DISTANCE BY SWIMMING** to cross a particular stretch of water or travel a particular distance by swimming **3.** *vt* **COMPETE IN SWIMMING RACE** to take part as a competitor in a swimming race, especially one of a particular length **4.** *vt* **SWIM WITH PARTICULAR STROKE** to swim using a particular stroke **5.** *vi* **BE DIZZY** to be dizzy or confused ○ *The noise made my head swim.* **6.** *vi* **SEEM TO MOVE OR SPIN** to appear to move, whirl, or sway ○ *words swimming on the page* **7.** *vi* **FLOAT ON SURFACE** to float on the surface of a liquid ○ *oil swimming on the water* **8.** *vi* **BE COVERED IN LIQUID** to be surrounded or covered with a large quantity of liquid ○ *meat swimming in gravy* **9.** *vi* **HAVE PLENTY** to have a large amount of something ○ *not exactly swimming in offers* ■ *n* **1. SPELL OF SWIMMING** a period of time spent swimming, usually for pleasure or exercise ○ *went for her morning swim* **2. SMOOTH MOVEMENT** a smooth gliding movement **3. DIZZINESS** dizziness or confusion ○ *with my head in a swim* **4.** FISHING **PLACE WITH MANY FISH** a place where fish are found in abundance [Old English *swimman* < Germanic] —**swimmable** *adj* —**swimmer** *n* ◇ **be in the swim** to be involved with the latest fashions or trends

swim bladder *n* ZOOL same as **air bladder** (sense 1)

~~**swiming**~~ incorrect spelling of **swimming**

swimmeret /swímmə ret, swímmə rét/ *n* an abdominal appendage of shrimp, lobsters, and some other crustaceans that is adapted for swimming and, in females, for carrying eggs

swimmers /swímmərz/ *npl Aus* same as **swimsuit** (*informal*)

swimmer's itch *n* an inflammation of the skin caused by the larvae of some schistosomes that penetrate the skin and cause itching

swimming /swímming/ *n* the action or activity of making progress unsupported through water using the arms and legs, whether for pleasure, exercise, or sport

swimming bath *n* SWIMMING same as **swimming baths**

swimming baths *n* a building containing a swimming pool for public use (*takes a singular or plural verb*)

swimmingly /swímmingli/ *adv* very smoothly, easily, and successfully ○ *The whole evening went swimmingly.*

swimming pool *n* a water-filled structure in which people can swim, usually set into the ground outdoors or the floor indoors, or a building that houses such a structure

swimming trunks *npl* a piece of clothing worn by men and boys for swimming

swimsuit /swím soot, -syoot/ *n* a piece of clothing worn for swimming, especially a one-piece garment worn by women

swimwear /swím wair/ *n* clothing worn for swimming

Swinburne /swín burn/, **Algernon Charles** (1837–1909) British poet. He wrote two series of *Poems and Ballads* (1866, 1878) and *Tristram of Lyonesse* (1882). He spent his last 30 years in seclusion.

> 'I remember the way we parted, / The day and the way we met; / You hoped we were both broken-hearted, / And knew we should both forget.'
> [Algernon Charles Swinburne, 'An Interlude', *Poems and Ballads: First Series*; 1866]

swindle /swínd'l/ *vt* (**-dles, -dling, -dled**) to obtain something from somebody, especially money, by deception or fraud ○ *I've been swindled!* ■ *n* a transaction in which one person or organization obtains something from another by deception or fraud [Late 18C. Back-formation < *swindler* < German *Schwindler* 'cheat' < *schwindeln* 'be dizzy' < Old High German *swintan* 'vanish'] —**swindler** *n*

swine /swīn/ (*plural same*) *n* **1.** (*plural same* or **swines**) an offensive term that deliberately insults somebody's manner or principles (*insult*) **2.** a pig, boar, or similar animal [Old English *swīn* < Indo-European] —**swinish** *adj* —**swinishly** *adv*

swine fever *n* a very infectious and often fatal viral disease of pigs marked by fever, weakness, lesions, loss of appetite, and diarrhoea

swineherd /swīn hurd/ *n* somebody who tends pigs (*archaic or literary*)

swinepox /swīn poks/ *n* an infectious viral disease of pigs marked by lesions of the skin

swine vesicular disease *n* a mild viral disease in pigs that causes lesions on the feet and in the mouth

swing /swing/ *v* (**swings, swinging, swung** /swung/) **1.** *vti* **MOVE TO AND FRO** to move freely from side to side or backwards and forwards, usually hanging from a fixed point, or make something move in this way **2.** *vti* **PIVOT OR ROTATE** to move or turn in a circle or an arc, usually pivoting around a fixed point, or make something move or turn in this way ○ *The door swung open.* **3.** *vti* **SUSPEND OR HANG SOMETHING** to fix something so that it can swing, or be fixed in this way **4.** *vti* **MOVE IN CURVE** to move in a smooth curve, or make something move in this way ○ *The limousine swung into the drive.* **5.** *vi* **WALK WITH SWAYING MOTION** to walk with a swaying motion in a relaxed or easy manner **6.** *vti* **STRIKE WITH SWEEPING BLOW** to hit or attempt to hit somebody or something with a sweeping blow or stroke ○ *swung wildly at the ball* **7.** *vti* **RIDE ON SWINGING SEAT** to move backwards and forwards on a swinging seat, or make somebody move in such a way by pushing the person or the seat **8.** *vti* **FLUCTUATE OR VACILLATE** to change from one feeling or condition to another, sometimes quickly or suddenly, or make something or somebody change in this way ○ *Their mood swung between elation and gloom.* **9.** *vt* **ARRANGE OR MANIPULATE SOMETHING** to achieve a desired change or result by using influence, persuasion, or other means (*informal*) ○ *swing a deal* **10.** *vi* **BE HANGED FOR SOMETHING** to be hanged as punishment for something (*informal*) **11.** *vi* **SWAP SEXUAL PARTNERS** to have a number of sexual partners, especially by exchanging them within a group (*dated informal*) **12.** *vi* **BE LIVELY** to be lively or animated (*dated informal*) ○ *The party was really swinging by the time we arrived.* **13.** *vi* **BE MODERN AND FASHIONABLE** to be interested in and involved in modern or fashionable trends (*dated informal*) **14.** *vti* MUSIC **PLAY JAZZ** to play a passage or musical work in big-band jazz music, or be played in this way **15.** *vti* CRICKET **BOWL BALL WITH SIDEWAYS CURVE** to bowl a ball in such a way that it moves sideways in the air, or move in this way **16.** *vi* DANCE **DANCE SWING** to dance the swing ■ *n* **1. HANGING SEAT** a seat hung from a frame or branch for somebody to sit on and move backwards and forwards, especially one on which children play **2. SWINGING MOVEMENT** the process of swinging, or a swinging movement ○ *the swing of the pendulum* **3. RANGE OF MOVEMENT** the curve or distance covered by something as it swings **4. SWEEPING STROKE OR BLOW** a sweeping stroke, blow, or punch ○ *took a swing at the ball* **5. WAY OF SWINGING** the manner of movement used to swing a bat or club or bowl a ball ○ *practising her golf swing* **6.** CRICKET **SIDEWAYS MOVEMENT OF BOWLED BALL** the sideways movement through the air of a bowled ball **7.** BOXING **PUNCH FROM SIDE** a wide punch from the side **8. SHIFT OR FLUCTUATION** a sudden or significant change, especially in the way people think or act ○ *frequent mood swings* ○ *a massive swing in popularity towards the younger candidate* **9. UP-AND-DOWN CYCLIC CHANGES** the up-and-down cycles of something such as business profits, economic growth, or share prices **10. STEADY PROGRESSION** a steady progression or advance across territory, or through a process, activity, or phase ○ *took a swing through the south of France* **11.** MUSIC **STYLE OF JAZZ MUSIC** jazz music of the 1930s and 1940s, suitable for dancing and generally played by big bands **12.** DANCE **LIVELY DANCE STYLE** lively dancing for couples involving syncopated steps, spins, and jumps, with one partner often swinging and lifting the other off the ground [Old English *swingan* 'flog, rush' < Germanic, 'violent circulatory movement'] —**swingy** *adj* ◇ **get into the swing of things** to get into the established rhythm or routine ◇ **go with a swing** to be lively and animated ○ *The evening really went with a swing.* ◇ **in full swing** in vigorous progress ◇ **swings and roundabouts** used to indicate that a situation has both advantages and disadvantages, or is sometimes good and sometimes bad

swing around, swing round *vi* **1.** to turn around quickly or suddenly **2.** to change direction quickly or suddenly

swing by *vti US* to visit a person or place briefly on the way to another location (*informal*)

swingboat /swíng bōt/ *n* a boat-shaped carriage with seats in which people swing backwards and forwards for fun, usually at a fairground or amusement park

swing bridge *n* a low movable bridge that pivots horizontally on a pier in midstream and is swung parallel to the stream to allow ships to pass

swing-by *n* a deliberate change in the course of an interplanetary vehicle caused by moving through the gravitational field of an astronomical object, especially that of a planet

swing door *n* a door that can be opened by pushing from either side, especially one that swings shut automatically. N Am term **swinging door**

swinge /swinj/ (**swinges, swingeing** or **swinging, swinged**) *vt* to punish somebody severely, especially by beating or flogging (*literary*) [Old English *swengan* < Germanic]

swingeing /swínjing/ *adj* causing great harm or hardship ○ *swingeing cuts in spending*

swinger /swíngər/ *n* **1.** somebody who or something that swings ○ *caught on the chin by a left-handed swinger* **2.** somebody who lives an unconventional and hedonistic life, especially somebody who exchanges sexual partners with others (*dated informal*)

swinging /swínging/ *adj* **1. LIVELY** lively and animated ○ *a swinging party* **2. FASHIONABLE** spirited and fashionable (*dated*) **3. OFTEN CHANGING SEXUAL PARTNERS** frequently changing or exchanging sexual partners (*dated informal*)

swinging door *n N Am* same as **swing door**

swinging voter *n ANZ* POL same as **floating voter**

swingle /swíng g'l/ *n* a wooden instrument like a knife or paddle used to beat hemp or flax and scrape woody portions out of the material ■ *vt* (**-gles, -gling, -gled**) to beat and scrape hemp or flax with a swingle [15C. < Middle Dutch *swinghel*]

swingletree /swíng g'l tree/ *n UK, Can* a horizontal crossbar by means of which the harness traces of a draught animal are attached to a vehicle or device. ANZ, US term **whiffletree**

swingometer /swing ómmitər/ *n* a device used on television during an election to show the swing of votes from one political party to another [Mid-20C. After BAROMETER]

swing shift *n ANZ, N Am* **1.** a period of work beginning in the afternoon and ending at night. It overlaps between the day shift and the night shift. **2.** a group of employees working on a swing shift ▶ UK term **back shift**

swing voter *n N Am* POL same as **floating voter**

swing-wing *adj* describes an aircraft whose wings are constructed to allow them to move backwards and forwards relative to the fuselage during flight. The rearward configuration improves streamlining at high speeds, while the forward configuration improves lifting qualities during takeoff and landing. ■ *n* an aeroplane with variable-sweep wings

swipe /swīp/ *v* (**swipes, swiping, swiped**) **1.** *vti* **HIT SOMEBODY OR SOMETHING HARD** to strike or attempt to strike somebody or something with a forceful swinging or sweeping blow **2.** *vt* **STEAL SOMETHING** to steal something, often with a snatching movement (*informal*) **3.** *vti* **PUT CARD THROUGH MACHINE** to pass a plastic card on which data has been stored magnetically through an electronic reading device, e.g. to gain access to a building or to initiate a banking transaction, or to be read successfully by such a device ○ *I can't get the card to swipe.* ■ *n* **1. SWINGING BLOW** a forceful swinging or sweeping blow ○ *took a swipe at me but missed* **2. CRITICAL ATTACK** a critical remark or attack (*informal*) **3. PIVOTED POLE** a long pole used as a lever to raise or lower a bucket in a well [Early 19C. Probably variant of SWEEP] —**swiper** *n*

swipe card *n* a plastic card on which data has been stored magnetically that is read and decoded by an electronic device that the card is passed through

swirl /swurl/ *v* (**swirls, swirling, swirled**) **1.** *vti* **TURN WITH CIRCULAR MOTION** to turn around and around with a twisting or spiralling movement, or make something move in this way ○ *caught up in a swirling throng of dancers and musicians* **2.** *vi* **BE DIZZY** to be dizzy or confused ■ *n* **1. CIRCULAR MOTION** a turning, twisting, spiralling movement, or something that moves in this way **2. SPIRAL** a curl, twist, or spiral ○ *a carpet with black swirls on a red background* **3. CONFUSION** dizziness or confusion [15C. Origin ?] —**swirly** *adj*

swish /swish/ *v* (**swishes, swishing, swished**) **1.** *vi* **MAKE, OR MOVE WITH, WHISTLING SOUND** to make the soft smooth whistling or rustling sound of something moving quickly through the air, or move with such a sound **2.** *vt* **MOVE SOMETHING WITH WHISTLING SOUND** to cause something to make or move with a swishing sound ○ *swishing a sword* ■ *n* **STICK** a rod used to beat or flog a person or animal ■ *v* (**swishes, swishing, swished**) *vt* **CUT WITH SWIFT SHARP BLOW** to cut or strike something or somebody with a swift sharp swishing blow ■ *n* **SHARP BLOW** a sharp blow to a person or animal made with a rod ■ *v* (**swishes, swishing, swished**) *vt US* BASKETBALL **SINK BASKETBALL** to throw a basketball through the hoop in such a way that it makes a quiet swishing sound and does not hit the rim ○ *swished a pair of free throws* ■ *n* **1.** *US* BASKETBALL **BASKETBALL SHOT** in basketball, a shot that goes through the hoop with a quiet swishing sound and does not hit the rim **2. SWISHING SOUND** a soft smooth whistling or rustling sound ○ *heard the swish of her skirt* **3. SWISHING MOVEMENT** a movement that makes a swishing sound ○ *the angry swish of its tail* **4.** *US* **OFFENSIVE TERM** an offensive term for a gay man that deliberately insults his manner or behaviour as being more characteristic of a woman (*slang insult*) ■ *adj* **1. ELEGANT** elegant and fashionable (*informal*) ○ *a swish restaurant* **2.** *US* **OFFENSIVE TERM** an offensive term meaning gay and stereotypically effeminate (*insult*) [Mid-18C. Probably an imitation of the sound made when moving through or brushing against something] —**swishy** *adj*

Swiss /swiss/ *n* (*plural same*) **1. SOMEBODY FROM SWITZERLAND** somebody who comes from Switzerland **2. DIALECT SPOKEN IN SWITZERLAND** any dialect of German, French, or Italian spoken in Switzerland ■ *adj* **OF SWITZERLAND** relating to Switzerland, or to its peoples or cultures [Early 16C. < French *Suisse* < Middle High German *Swīz* 'Switzerland']

Swiss ball *n* FITNESS same as **exercise ball**

Swiss chard *n* a variety of beet whose large edible leaves and stems are similar to spinach and are cooked and eaten as a vegetable. Latin name: *Beta vulgaris cicla.*

Swiss cheese plant *n* a houseplant with large perforated leaves. Latin name: *Monstera deliciosa.*

Swiss Guard *n* a group of Swiss-born soldiers employed to protect the pope at the Vatican, or a member of this group

swiss muslin *n* a fine cotton fabric, often with a raised pattern. Use: clothes, curtains.

swiss roll, **Swiss roll** *n* a thin light sponge spread with jam or cream and rolled up into a cylinder before it cools. N Am term **jelly roll**

switch /swich/ *n* **1. BUTTON OR LEVER CONTROLLING ELECTRICAL CIRCUIT** a mechanical or electronic device that opens, closes, or changes the connections in an electrical circuit, e.g. one used to turn a light or machine on or off **2. SUDDEN CHANGE** a quick or sudden change **3. SUBSTITUTION** an exchange or substitution **4. THIN ROD OR CANE** a thin flexible stick, especially one used for punishment **5. BEATING** a blow or beating with a switch or other thin object **6. OPERATION OF SWITCH** the act or process of operating a switch **7.** HAIR **PONYTAIL HAIRPIECE** a hairpiece in the form of a false ponytail **8.** ZOOL **TIP OF ANIMAL'S TAIL** a tuft of hair at the end of the tail of a cow or other animal **9.** CARDS **CARD GAME** a card game in which the suit can be changed during play **10.** TELECOM **ROUTING DEVICE USED IN TELEPHONE EXCHANGES** a device used in a telephone exchange to route transmissions between network nodes **11.** COMPUT **TECHNIQUE FOR CONTROLLING PROGRAM'S LOGIC** in computing, a programmed technique for indicating which alternative path to take at a decision point in a program's logic ■ *v* (**switches, switching, switched**) **1.** *vti* **CHANGE, SHIFT, OR TRANSFER** to change from one time, activity, or situation to another, often quickly or suddenly, or cause somebody or something to make such a change ○ *The dancing class has been switched from Friday afternoon to Saturday morning.* **2.** *vti* **MAKE EXCHANGE OR SUBSTITUTION** to exchange two similar or related things, or put one in the place of the other, sometimes secretly or surreptitiously **3.** *vti* ELEC **CHANGE ELECTRICAL FUNCTION** to make an electrical device do something different by operating a switch to cause current to stop or start flowing or change its path ○ *He switched the radio to a different station.* **4.** *vti* **FLICK OR SWING TO AND FRO** to move quickly from side to side or backwards and forwards, or make something move in this way ○ *The cat switched her tail in annoyance.* **5.** *vt* **BEAT SOMEBODY WITH SWITCH** to beat somebody with a switch, especially as a punishment ■ *adj* **WITH FEET REVERSED** in skateboarding and similar sports, used to describe a stance in which the foot that the rider usually puts nearer the front is nearer the back (*slang*) [Late 16C. Probably < Middle Dutch *swijch* 'twig'] —**switchable** *adj* —**switcher** *n*

switch off *vti* **1. TURN OFF EQUIPMENT** to turn off a piece of electrical equipment, or be turned off **2. STOP PAYING ATTENTION** to stop paying attention, lose interest, or stop thinking about something, or make somebody do this (*informal*) **3.** *US* **TAKE TURNS** to do something one after the other in turns, or occur alternately (*informal*) ○ *We switch off working Saturdays.*

switch on *v* **1.** *vti* to turn on a piece of electrical equipment, or be turned on **2.** *vt* to suddenly and automatically produce something such as a smile, charm, or tears for effect and without sincerity

Switch /swich/ *tdmk* a trademark for a type of debit card

switchback /swích bak/ *n* **1.** LEISURE same as **roller coaster** (sense 1) **2.** *US* **TWISTY ROAD WITH MANY HILLS** a road or track with many steep uphill and downhill slopes and sharp bends **3.** *US* **SHARP BEND ON STEEP SLOPE** a sharp bend on a road or track going steeply uphill or downhill ■ *vi* (**-backs, -backing, -backed**) **BEND SHARPLY** to form or move in sharp turns in alternating directions while going uphill or downhill ○ *The trail climbs and then switchbacks to the summit.*

switchblade /swích blayd/, **switchblade knife** *n N Am* same as **flick knife**

switchboard /swích bawrd/ *n* **1.** a manually operated device for interconnecting telephone lines and routing telephone calls, usually within a telephone exchange or in a workplace, hotel, or other large building **2.** one or more insulating panels containing the electrical devices and instruments such as switches, circuit breakers, fuses, and meters required to operate electrical equipment

switched-on /swícht-/ *adj* **1. AWARE** alert or aware (*informal*) **2. MODERN** modern in outlook or appearance (*dated informal*) **3. DRUGGED** intoxicated by drugs (*dated informal*)

switchgear /swích geer/ *n* a device used solely to open and close electric circuits, especially one used to control a high-current application, e.g. a power and transforming station or an electric motor

switchgrass /swích grass/ *n* a panic grass used for forage and hay. Native to: western North America. Latin name: *Panicum virgatum.* [Mid-19C. Alteration of QUITCH GRASS after SWITCH]

swither /swíthər/ *Scotland vi* (**-ers, -ering, -ered**) to hesitate or be indecisive ■ *n* a state of hesitation or indecision [Early 16C. Origin ?]

Swithin /swíthin, swíthin, swíth'n, swíth'n/, **Swithun** (*d.* 862) English bishop. The greatest of the Anglo-Saxon bishops, he was religious adviser to kings Egbert and Ethelwulf. The weather on his feast day, 15 July, is believed to forecast the next 40 days' weather.

Switz. *abbr* Switzerland

Switzer /swítsər/ *n* a member of the Swiss Guard [Mid-16C. < Middle High German *Switzer* < *Swīz* 'Switzerland']

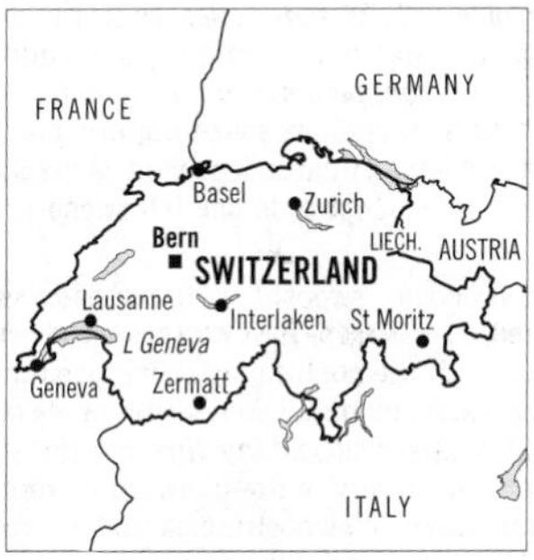

Switzerland

Switzerland /swítsərlənd/ country in west-central Europe. It has been neutral since 1515. Language: German, French, Italian, Romansch. Currency: Swiss Franc. Capital: Bern. Population: 7,318,638 (2003). Area: 41,285 sq. km/15,940 sq. mi. Official name **Swiss Confederation**

swive /swīv/ (**swives, swiving, swived**) *vti* to have sexual intercourse with somebody (*archaic*) [Old English *swīfan* 'to sweep' < Germanic]

swivel /swívv'l/ *v* (**-els, -elling, -elled**) **1.** *vti* **PIVOT OR ROTATE** to turn freely or horizontally in a circle, or make something turn in this way **2.** *vt* **PROVIDE SOMETHING WITH PIVOTING JOINT** to fit, attach, or support something with a joint that allows complete freedom of movement ■ *n* **1. DEVICE ALLOWING PART TO TURN** a joint or fastening that allows a mechanical part attached to it to turn freely **2. SUPPORT ALLOWING SOMETHING TO PIVOT** a pivoting support that allows something such as a gun, chair, or camera to turn from side to side or up and down, sometimes in a full circle **3.** ARMS **PIVOTING GUN** a gun that can be turned from side to side horizontally because of the pivoting mount supporting it [14C. < Old English *swīfan* 'sweep']

swivel chair *n* a chair, generally an office chair, mounted on a central support with a device that enables it to turn horizontally in a circle

swivel-hipped *adj* moving with loosely swinging hips, usually in an exaggerated manner

swivel pin *n* AUTOMOT same as **kingpin** (sense 2)

swiz /swiz/, **swizz** (*informal*) *n* (*plural* **swizzes;** *plural* **swizzes**) **1. DISAPPOINTMENT** a great disappointment, especially something that makes somebody feel cheated **2. SWINDLE** a scheme intended to deceive somebody ■ *vt* (**swizzes, swizzing, swizzed**) **CHEAT SOMEBODY** to swindle or cheat somebody [Early 20C. Shortening of SWIZZLE]

swizzle /swízz'l/ *n* **1.** *US* an iced cocktail, usually containing rum, that is stirred to make it frothy or to frost the glass **2.** same as **swiz** *n* (sense 2) (*informal*) ■ *vt* (**-zles, -zling, -zled**) **1.** to stir a drink with a swizzle stick to mix the ingredients, make it frothy, or reduce its effervescence **2.** same as **swiz** (*informal*) [Early 19C. Origin ?]

swizzle stick *n* a small thin plastic rod used for stirring a drink to mix the ingredients, make it frothy, or reduce its effervescence

swollen past participle of **swell**

swollen head *n* a feeling of conceited self-importance, usually stimulated by personal success or by praise received from others. ANZ, N Am term **swelled head** —**swollen-headed** *adj* —**swollen-headedness** *n*

swoon /swoon/ *vi* (**swoons, swooning, swooned**) **1. FEEL FAINT WITH JOY** to be overwhelmed by happiness, excitement, adoration, or infatuation **2. FALL IN FAINT** to experience a sudden and usually brief loss of consciousness ■ *n* **1. LOSS OF CONSCIOUSNESS** a sudden and usually brief loss of consciousness **2. RAPTURE** a condition of overwhelming happiness, excitement, or infatuation [13C. Shortening of *aswoon* < Old English *geswōgen* 'in a swoon', past participle of assumed *swōgan* 'suffocate'. Origin ?] —**swoony** *adj*

swoop /swoop/ *v* (**swoops, swooping, swooped**) **1.** *vi* **MAKE SWEEPING DESCENT** to descend quickly and suddenly with a sweeping movement, usually from the air **2.** *vi* **POUNCE** to make a sudden swift attack or raid on something or somebody ○ *The police swooped in on*

the terrorists. **3.** *vt* SEIZE SOMETHING QUICKLY OR SUDDENLY to seize or snatch something in a sudden swift movement ○ *shoppers swooping up bargains* ■ **n 1.** SUDDEN DESCENT a sudden sweeping descent **2.** SUDDEN ATTACK a sudden swift attack or raid [Mid-16C. Probably variant of SWEEP] ◇ **at** *or* **in one fell swoop** in a single action

swoosh /swoosh, swŏŏsh/ *v* (**swooshes, swooshing, swooshed**) **1.** *vti* MAKE OR MOVE WITH RUSHING SOUND to make or move with the rushing or swirling sound of fast-moving water, or make something move with such a sound ○ *skiers swooshing through the snow* **2.** *vi* GUSH to flow freely with a swirling motion ■ *n* SWOOSHING SOUND a swooshing sound or movement [Mid-19C. An imitation of the sound]

swop *vti*, *n* another spelling of **swap**

sword

sword /sawrd/ *n* **1.** a hand-held weapon with a long blade that is sharp on one or both edges and sometimes slightly curved **2.** the use of force, violence, or military power ○ *The pen is mightier than the sword.* [Old English *sweord* < Germanic] —**swordless** *adj* ◇ **cross swords (with somebody)** to argue or come into conflict with somebody ◇ **put somebody to the sword** to kill somebody violently, especially in war (*literary*)

sword and sorcery *adj* set in a fantasy place or time with a technology that has not advanced beyond bladed weapons and in which magic is important (*informal*)

sword bayonet *n* a bayonet with a very long blade

swordbearer /sáwrd bairər/ *n* an official who carries a sword that is a symbol of somebody's authority, e.g. a sovereign's sword

swordbill /sáwrd bil/ *n* a hummingbird with a beak longer than its body. Native to: South America. Latin name: *Ensifera ensifera*.

sword cane *n US* same as **swordstick**

sword dance *n* a dance in which swords are used, especially a Highland dance in which somebody dances over swords crossed on the floor

sword fern *n* a fern with long fronds shaped like swords

swordfish

swordfish /sáwrd fish/ (*plural* same *or* **-fishes**) *n* **1.** a large sea fish with an upper jaw that extends into a long point. Latin name: *Xiphias gladius*. **2.** the flesh of a swordfish as food

sword grass *n* a grass with leaves that have very sharp edges

sword knot *n* a decorative ribbon or tassel on the hilt of a sword

sword lily *n* PLANTS same as **gladiolus** (sense 1) [< its sword-shaped leaves]

Sword of Damocles *n* something that threatens to bring imminent disaster [See DAMOCLES]

swordplay /sáwrd play/ *n* fighting with a sword, especially when done with skill

swordsman /sáwrdzmən/ (*plural* **-men** /-mən/) *n* somebody, especially a man, who fights with a sword —**swordsmanship** *n*

swordsperson /sáwrdz purss'n/ (*plural* **-people** /-peep'l/ *or* **-persons**) *n* somebody who fights with a sword

swordstick /sáwrd stik/ *n UK, ANZ, Can* a hollow walking stick or cane whose handle is also the handle of a narrow sword hidden inside the stick. US term **sword cane**

sword-swallower *n* a performer who passes or creates an illusion of passing a sword down his or her throat to its hilt

swordswoman /sáwrdz wŏŏmən/ (*plural* **-women** /-wimin/) *n* a woman who fights with a sword

swordtail /sáwrd tayl/ *n* a small brightly coloured freshwater fish with a long sword-shaped tail, popular as an aquarium fish. Native to: Central America. Latin name: *Xiphophorus helleri*.

swore past tense of **swear**

sworn /swawrn/ past participle of **swear** ■ *adj* **1.** made under oath ○ *a sworn statement* **2.** determined to maintain a particular situation ○ *sworn enemies*

swot¹ /swot/, **swat** (*informal*) *vi* (**swots, swotting, swotted; swats, swatting, swatted**) STUDY VERY HARD to study very hard and intensively, especially for an examination ■ *n* **1.** HARD-WORKING STUDENT an unduly industrious student **2.** PERIOD OF HARD STUDY a period of time spent studying hard, especially for an examination [Mid-19C. Scottish variant of SWEAT]

swot² /swot/ *vti*, *n* another spelling of **swat¹**

SWOT analysis /swót-/ *n* an examination of the strengths, weaknesses, opportunities, and threats connected with an organization, used as a way of evaluating its likelihood of success or developing strategy [Acronym < strengths, weaknesses, opportunities, threats]

swotter *n* another spelling of **swatter**

swotty /swótti/ *adj* given to studying very hard or excessively (*informal*)

SWP *abbr* POL Socialist Workers Party

SWPA *abbr* Southwestern Pacific Area

swum past participle of **swim**

swung past participle, past tense of **swing**

swung dash *n* a character (~) used in printing to represent all or part of a word previously spelt out

sy *abbr* Syria (*used in Internet addresses*) See table at **domain name**

sybarite /síbbə rīt/ *n* somebody devoted to luxury and the gratification of sensual desires [< SYBARITE; because Sybaris had a reputation for luxury and indulgence] —**sybaritic** /síbbə ríttik/ *adj* —**sybaritical** *adj* —**sybaritically** *adv* —**sybaritism** *n*

Sybarite /síbbə rīt/ *n* somebody who was born in or was a citizen of Sybaris, an ancient Greek city in southern Italy [Mid-16C. Via Latin *Sybarita* < Greek *Subaris* 'Sybaris', ancient Greek city in S Italy] —**Sybaritic** /síbbə ríttik/ *adj*

syboe /sī bō/ *n Scotland* same as **spring onion** [Late 16C. < French *ciboule* < Latin *caepa* 'onion']

sycamine /síkə mīn, -meen/ *n* a tree mentioned in the Bible and thought to be the black mulberry [Early 16C. < Greek *sukaminon* < Hebrew *šikmāh*]

sycamore

sycamore /síkə mawr/ (*plural* **-mores** *or* same) *n* **1.** TYPE OF MAPLE TREE a tree of the maple family, naturalized in northern Europe and North America, with five-lobed leaves and two-winged fruits. Native to: central and southern Europe, Asia. Latin name: *Acer pseudoplatanus*. **2.** *US* LARGE SPREADING PLANE TREE a large spreading plane tree with lobed leaves, round spiked fruit clusters, and flaking bark. Native to: central and eastern North America. Latin name: *Platanus occidentalis*. **3.** FIG TREE a fig tree with edible fruit. Native to: Africa, Southwest Asia. Latin name: *Ficus sycomorus*. [14C. Via Old French *sicamor* < Greek *sukomoros* 'fig-mulberry']

syce /sīss/, **saice**, **sice** *n* formerly in India, a groom, stable hand, or other attendant [Mid-17C. Via Persian, Urdu *sā'is* < Arabic < *sūs* 'tend a horse']

~~**sycho**~~ incorrect spelling of **psycho**

syconium /si kṓni əm/ (*plural* **-nia** /-ni ə/) *n* a fleshy fruit in which numerous seeds are borne inside the enlarged hollow tip of the flower stalk, e.g. a fig [Mid-19C. < modern Latin < Greek *sukon* 'fig']

sycophant /síkəfənt, -fant/ *n* a servile or obsequious person who flatters somebody powerful for personal gain [Mid-16C. Via Latin *sycophanta* < Greek *sukophantēs* 'informer' < *sukon* 'fig, obscene gesture' + *-phantes* 'shower' (< *phanein* 'to show')] —**sycophancy** *n* —**sycophantic** /síkə fántik/ *adj* —**sycophantically** *adv*

sycosis /sī kóssiss/ *n* inflammation of hair follicles, especially of the beard, caused by bacterial infection and marked by pustules and encrustations [Late 16C. Via modern Latin < Greek *sukōsis* < *sukon* 'fig']

Sydenham's chorea /sídd'nəmz-/ *n* a neurological disease of children and pregnant women, sometimes following rheumatic fever, in which those affected experience involuntary jerking movements of the body [Late 19C. After Thomas *Sydenham* (1624–89), English physician]

Sydney /sídni/ capital of New South Wales, south-eastern Australia. Population: 3,986,700 (1998).

Sydney blue gum *n* a tall eucalyptus tree with a pale blue-grey peeling trunk. Native to: coasts and adjacent ranges of southern Queensland and New South Wales, Australia. Latin name: *Eucalyptus saligna*.

Sydney Harbour large coastal inlet in eastern New South Wales, Australia, on which the city of Sydney is located. Area: 54 sq. km/20 sq. mi. Also known as **Port Jackson**

Sydney-Hobart yacht race *n* an annual sailing race, first held in 1945, which begins in Sydney, Australia on Boxing Day and ends in Hobart, Tasmania

Sydney Opera House

Sydney Opera House *n* an arts centre in Sydney Harbour, Australia, that was designed by Jörn Utzon and completed in 1973. Its unusual sail-shaped towers make it Australia's best-known building.

Sydneysider /sídni sīdər/ *n* somebody who comes from or lives in Sydney, Australia

syenite /sī ə nīt/ *n* a light-coloured coarse-grained igneous rock consisting mainly of feldspar [Late 18C. < Latin *syenites (lapis)* '(stone of) Syene' (Aswan, Egypt)] —**syenitic** /sī ə níttik/ *adj*

SYHA *abbr* Scottish Youth Hostels Association

~~**sylable**~~ incorrect spelling of **syllable**

~~**sylabus**~~ incorrect spelling of **syllabus**

Sylhet /sil hét/ city and administrative headquarters of Sylhet District, Chittagong Division, in northeastern Bangladesh. Population: 114,284 (1991).

syllabary /síllәbәri/ (*plural* **-ies**) *n* a list or set of written characters in which each character represents a single syllable e.g. the Japanese kana

syllabi EDUC plural of **syllabus**

syllabic /si lábbik/ *adj* **1.** INVOLVING SYLLABLES relating to, involving, or typical of a syllable or syllables **2.** MARKED BY CLEAR ENUNCIATION clearly enunciated with every syllable distinct **3.** BEING SYLLABLE WITHOUT VOWEL describes a consonant that acts as a syllable without a vowel, as does the 'l' in 'bottle' **4.** BASED ON NUMBER OF SYLLABLES describes verse in which the rhythm is set by the number of syllables rather than accents, stresses, or vowel strengths ■ *n* SYLLABIC CONSONANT OR SOUND a syllabic consonant, character, or sound

syllabify /si lábbi fī/ (**-fies, -fying, -fied**), **syllabicate** /si lábbi kayt/ (**-cates, -cating, -cated**) *vt* to break a word down into syllables in speech or writing [Early 20C. Back-formation < *syllabification* < Latin *syllaba* (see SYLLABLE)] —**syllabication** /si lábbi káysh'n/ *n* —**syllabification** /si lábbifi káysh'n/ *n*

syllabism /síllәbizәm/ *n* **1.** the use of characters that stand for individual syllables in writing **2.** the breaking down of words into syllables, in speech or writing

syllable /síllәb'l/ *n* **1.** UNIT OF SPOKEN LANGUAGE a unit of spoken language that consists of one or more vowel sounds alone, a syllabic consonant alone, or any of these with one or more consonant sounds **2.** LETTERS CORRESPONDING TO SPOKEN SYLLABLE one or more letters in a word that roughly correspond to a syllable of spoken language **3.** MENTION the slightest bit of something that is spoken or written (*usually used in negative statements*) ○ *Don't breathe a syllable of this – it's a secret.* ■ *vt* (**-bles, -bling, -bled**) PRONOUNCE SOMETHING CLEARLY to pronounce something in distinct or separate syllables [14C. < Anglo-Norman *sillable*, alteration of Old French *sillabe*, via Latin *syllaba* < Greek *sullabē* < *sullambanein* 'bring together' < *lambanein* 'take']

syllabogram /si lábbō gram/ *n* a written or printed symbol that stands for a single syllable

syllabub /síllә bub/, **sillabub** *n* **1.** a light soft cold dessert made from cream whipped with brandy, wine or sherry, lemon juice, and a little sugar **2.** a drink made of sweetened milk or cream curdled with wine or cider [Mid-16C. Origin ?]

syllabus /síllәbәss/ (*plural* **-bi** /-bī/ or **-buses**) *n* **1.** a summary or list of the main topics of a course of study, text, or lecture **2.** the subjects offered for study by a school, college, or university, or a list of these [Mid-17C. < modern Latin, originally misprint of Latin *sittybas* 'indexes' < Greek *sittuba* 'index, label']

Syllabus, Syllabus of Errors *n* a list of religious doctrines condemned by the Roman Catholic Church as erroneous

syllepsis /si lépsiss/ (*plural* **-lepses** /-lép seez/) *n* **1.** the use of a word that relates to, qualifies, or governs two or more other words but agrees in number, gender, or case with only one of them. 'Neither Fred nor I want to' is an example of syllepsis, where 'want' agrees with 'I' but not 'Fred'. **2.** the use of a word that relates to, qualifies, or governs two or more other words but has a different meaning in relation to each, as in the example 'He picked up his hat and a taxi' [Late 16C. Via late Latin < Greek *sullēpsis* 'a taking together' < *sullambanein* (see SYLLABLE)]

syllogise *vti* PHILOSOPHY another spelling of **syllogize**

syllogism /síllә jizәm/ *n* **1.** LOGICAL ARGUMENT INVOLVING THREE PROPOSITIONS a formal deductive argument made up of a major premise, a minor premise, and a conclusion. An example is, 'All birds have feathers, penguins are birds, therefore penguins have feathers'. **2.** DEDUCTIVE REASONING reasoning from the general to the specific **3.** EXAMPLE OF DEDUCTION an example of deductive reasoning **4.** SPECIOUS ARGUMENT a subtle piece of reasoning, or one that seems true but is actually false or deceptive [14C. Via Latin < Greek *sullogismos* < *sullogizesthai* 'infer' < *logos* 'reason']

syllogistic /síllә jístik/ *adj* relating to, using, or typical of syllogisms [Mid-17C. Via Latin < Greek *sullogistikos* < *sullogizesthai* (see SYLLOGISM)] —**syllogistically** *adv*

syllogize /síllә jīz/ (**-gizes, -gizing, -gized**), **syllogise** (**-gises, -gising, -gised**) *vti* to reason or infer something by means of syllogisms [15C. Via late Latin *syllogizare* < Greek *sullogizesthai* (see SYLLOGISM)] —**syllogizer** *n*

sylph /silf/ *n* **1.** a woman or girl who is slight and graceful **2.** an elemental soulless female being imagined to inhabit the air [Mid-17C. < modern Latin *sylpha*] —**sylphic** *adj* —**sylphish** *adj* —**sylphy** *adj*

sylphlike /sílf līk/ *adj* having a slight and graceful figure

sylvan /sílvәn/, **silvan** *adj* **1.** OF FOREST relating to, typical of, or found in a forest (*literary*) **2.** WOODED covered in or full of trees (*literary*) **3.** RURAL characteristic of the countryside, especially in an idyllic way ■ *n* INHABITANT OF FOREST a person, animal, or spirit that lives in a forest

sylvanite /sílvә nīt/ *n* a mixed telluride mineral containing gold and silver, occurring in long striated crystals [Late 18C. After TRANSYLVANIA]

Sylvanus *n* MYTHOL another spelling of **Silvanus**

sylvatic /sil váttik/ *adj* **1.** affecting wild animals ○ *sylvatic plague* **2.** same as **sylvan** *adj* (senses 1–2)

sylviculture *n* AGRIC another spelling of **silviculture**

sylvite /síl vīt/, **sylvine** /-vīn/ *n* a colourless transparent potassium chloride mineral. Use: source of potassium. [Mid-19C. < modern Latin *(sal digestivus) Sylvii* '(digestive salt) of Sylvius' (François de la Boë Sylvius (1614–72), Flemish chemist)]

sym. *abbr* **1.** symbol **2.** CHEM symmetrical **3.** MUSIC symphony **4.** MED symptom

sym- *prefix* another spelling of **syn-** (*used before b, m, and p*)

symbiogenesis /sím bī ō jénnәssiss/ *n* a hypothetical evolutionary process in which mitochondria and chloroplasts developed from symbiotic organisms within the cell

symbiont /símbi ont, -bī-/ *n* an animal or plant living in close and often mutually beneficial association with another of a different species [Late 19C. < SYM- + Greek *bioun* 'to live' < *bios* 'life'] —**symbiontic** /símbi óntik, -bī-/ *adj* —**symbiontically** *adv*

symbiosis /sím bī óssiss, -bi-/ (*plural* **-oses** /-ósseez/) *n* **1.** a close association of animals or plants of different species that is often, but not always, of mutual benefit **2.** a cooperative, mutually beneficial relationship between two people or groups [Early 17C. Via modern Latin and Greek *sumbiōsis* 'a living together' < *bios* 'life'] —**symbiotic** /sím bī óttik, -bi-/ *adj* —**symbiotical** *adj* —**symbiotically** *adv*

symbiote /símbī ōt/ *n* an organism, person, or thing that exists in or depends on a symbiotic relationship with something or somebody else [Late 19C. Back-formation < *symbiotic*]

~~**symble**~~ incorrect spelling of **symbol**

symbol /símb'l/ *n* **1.** SOMETHING THAT REPRESENTS SOMETHING ELSE something that stands for or represents something else, especially an object representing an abstraction **2.** SIGN WITH SPECIFIC MEANING a written or printed sign or character that represents something in a specific context, e.g. an operation or quantity in mathematics or music **3.** PSYCHOANAL OBJECT REPRESENTING SOMETHING REPRESSED IN UNCONSCIOUS an object or act that represents an impulse or wish in the unconscious mind that has been repressed [15C. Via Latin < Greek *sumbolon* 'mark' < *sumballein* 'compare' < *ballein* 'throw']

SPELLCHECK See *cymbal*.

symbolic /sim bóllik/, **symbolical** /-ik'l/ *adj* **1.** REPRESENTING SOMETHING ELSE acting as a symbol ○ *a gesture symbolic of repentance* **2.** INVOLVING USE OF SYMBOLS characterized by or involving the use of symbols or symbolism ○ *symbolic art* **3.** OF SYMBOLS relating to or typical of symbols —**symbolically** *adv*

symbolic language *n* **1.** an artificially constructed language with many symbols, used for precise formulations, e.g. in symbolic logic or mathematics **2.** a computer programming language that expresses memory addresses and operation codes in symbols recognizable to the programmer rather than in machine language

symbolic logic *n* the branch of formal logic that studies the meaning and relationships of statements through precise mathematical methods and a standardized system of symbols and rules of inference

symbolise *vt* another spelling of **symbolize**

symbolism /símbәlizәm/ *n* **1.** USE OF SYMBOLS the use of symbols to invest things with a representative meaning or to represent something abstract by something concrete **2.** SYSTEM OF SYMBOLS a set or system of symbols **3.** SYMBOLIC MEANING symbolic meaning or quality **4.** ARTS ARTISTIC USE OF SYMBOLS the artistic method of revealing ideas or truths through the use of symbols **5.** *also* **Symbolism** ARTS 19C LITERARY AND ARTISTIC MOVEMENT a 19th-century literary and artistic movement that sought to evoke, rather than describe, ideas or feelings through the use of symbolic images **6.** CHR BELIEF IN SYMBOLIC NATURE OF COMMUNION in Christianity, the belief that the bread and wine used in the Communion are symbols and not literally the flesh and blood of Jesus Christ

symbolist /símbәlist/ *n* **1.** SOMEBODY USING SYMBOLS somebody who uses symbols or symbolism **2.** SOMEBODY SKILLED AT INTERPRETING SYMBOLS somebody skilled in the study or interpretation of symbols **3.** *also* **Symbolist** ARTS SOMEBODY INVOLVED IN 19C ARTISTIC SYMBOLISM a writer or artist involved in or associated with the 19th-century movement of symbolism **4.** CHR SOMEBODY BELIEVING COMMUNION USES SYMBOLS in Christianity, a believer that the bread and wine used in the Communion are symbols and not literally the flesh and blood of Jesus Christ ■ *adj* **1.** OF OR USING SYMBOLS relating to, involving, or using symbols **2.** *also* **Symbolist** ARTS ASSOCIATED WITH 19C ARTISTIC SYMBOLISM involved in, associated with, or typical of the 19th-century movement of symbolism —**symbolistic** /símbә lístik/ *adj* —**symbolistically** *adv*

symbolize /símbә līz/ (**-izes, -izing, -ized**), **symbolise** (**-ises, -ising, -ised**) *v* **1.** *vt* BE SYMBOL OF SOMETHING to serve as a symbol of something **2.** *vt* REPRESENT SOMETHING to represent something by means of a symbol **3.** *vi* USE SYMBOLS to use symbols or symbolism —**symbolization** /símbә lī záysh'n/ *n*

symbology /sim bóllәji/ *n* **1.** the study or interpretation of symbols **2.** the use of symbols to represent things —**symbological** /símbә lójjik'l/ *adj* —**symbologist** *n*

~~**symetrical**~~ incorrect spelling of **symmetrical**

~~**symetry**~~ incorrect spelling of **symmetry**

symmetallism /si métt'lizәm/ *n* a system of coinage in which the unit of currency consists of a combination of two or more metals in fixed relative proportions

symmetrical /si méttrik'l/, **symmetric** /-méttrik/ *adj* **1.** EXHIBITING SYMMETRY in which parts on either side of a central dividing line correspond to each other or are identical to each other **2.** BALANCED relating to or having balanced proportions, especially in two halves of a whole **3.** MATHS WITH PAIRS OF POINTS describes two points that can be joined by a line bisected by a specific point or perpendicular, or a shape that has such pairs of points **4.** MATHS WITH INTERCHANGEABLE TERMS describes an equation or function in which terms or variables may be interchanged without altering its value or form **5.** CHEM WITH SYMMETRICAL MOLECULAR STRUCTURE with atoms or groups that display symmetry about a plane in a chemical structure **6.** ANAT ON OPPOSITE SIDES describes body parts that have the same function but are situated on opposite sides, either of the same organ or the same body —**symmetrically** *adv*

symmetric matrix *n* a square matrix that is identical to the matrix formed by transposing its rows and columns

symmetrize /símmә trīz/ (**-trizes, -trizing, -trized**), **symmetrise** (**-trises, -trising, -trised**) *vt* to give symmetry to something

symmetry /símmәtri/ (*plural* **-tries**) *n* **1.** PROPERTY OF SAMENESS the property of being the same or corresponding on both sides of a central dividing line. See illustration on next page **2.** BALANCED PROPORTIONS harmony or beauty of form that results from balanced proportions **3.** MATHS EXACT CORRESPONDENCE IN POSITION a correspondence in the position of pairs of points of a geometric object that are equally positioned about a point, line, or plane

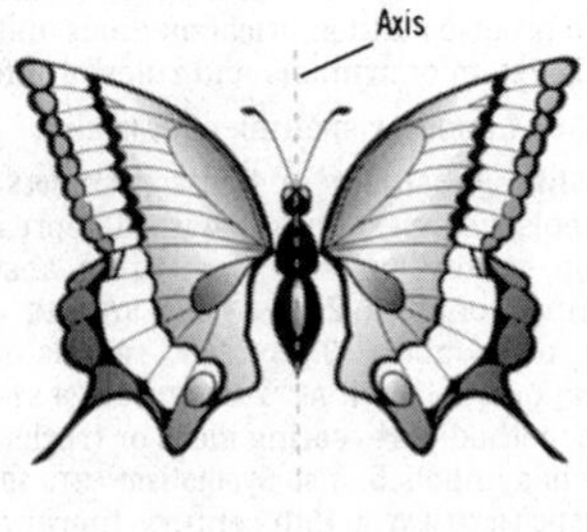

symmetry

that bisects the object **4.** PHYS **STATE OF INVARIANCE** a state of invariance shown by some phenomena when changes of orientation, charge, or parity are made [Mid-16C. Via Latin < Greek *summetria* 'similar measure' < *metron* 'measure']

sympathectomy /símpə théktəmi/ (*plural* **-mies**) *n* formerly, the surgical interruption of a pathway in the sympathetic nervous system by cutting out a nerve segment [Early 20C. < SYMPATHETIC + -ECTOMY]

sympathetic /símpə théttik/ *adj* **1. FEELING OR SHOWING SYMPATHY** showing, having, or resulting from shared feelings, pity, or compassion **2. APPROVING** showing favour, agreement, or approval ○ *was sympathetic to their request* **3. PROVOKING SYMPATHY** provoking sympathy, interest, or compassion ○ *a sympathetic character in a novel* **4. SUITED** agreeably suited to somebody's tastes or mood ○ *a sympathetic environment* **5.** ACOUSTICS **PRODUCED BY OTHER SOUNDS** describes vibrations such as musical tones that are produced in something as a result of similar vibrations at the same frequency from something else **6.** ANAT **OF SYMPATHETIC NERVOUS SYSTEM** relating or belonging to the sympathetic nervous system or to one of its components [Mid-17C. < SYMPATHY after PATHETIC] —**sympathetically** *adv*

sympathetic magic *n* magic based on the belief that somebody or something can be supernaturally affected by something done to an object representing the person or thing

sympathetic nervous system *n* the part of the autonomic nervous system that is active during stress or danger and is involved in regulating pulse and blood pressure, dilating pupils, and changing muscle tone

sympathetic string *n* a string on a musical instrument that vibrates by itself when other strings are bowed or plucked

sympathize /símpə thīz/ (**-thizes, -thizing, -thized**), **sympathise** (**-thises, -thising, -thised**) *vi* **1.** to share the feelings of somebody else or show pity or compassion for another ○ *I can sympathize; the same thing happened to me.* **2.** to share the ideas or ideals of another person or group —**sympathizer** *n*

sympatholytic /símpə thō líttik/ *adj* describes a drug that opposes or blocks the effects of the sympathetic nervous system ■ *n* a drug or agent that acts against the sympathetic nervous system [Mid-20C. < SYMPATHETIC + -LYTE]

sympathomimetic /símpə thō mi méttik/ *adj* describes a drug that stimulates the sympathetic nervous system or produces physiological effects similar to it ■ *n* a drug or agent that stimulates the sympathetic nervous system [Early 20C. < SYMPATHETIC]

sympathy /símpəthi/ (*plural* **-thies**) *n* **1. CAPACITY TO SHARE FEELINGS** the ability to enter into, understand, or share somebody else's feelings **2. FEELINGS CAUSED BY SYMPATHY** the feelings of somebody who enters into or shares another's feelings **3. SORROW FOR ANOTHER'S PAIN** the feeling or expression of pity or sorrow for the pain or distress of somebody else ○ *We extended our sympathies to the widow.* **4. INCLINATION TO FEEL ALIKE** the inclination to think or feel the same as somebody else ○ *A sympathy exists between them.* **5. AGREEMENT** agreement or harmony with something or somebody else ○ *a plan in sympathy with our wishes* **6. ALLEGIANCE OR LOYALTY** allegiance or loyalty to a group or cause (*often used in the plural*) ○ *nationalist sympathies* [Late 16C. Via Latin *sympathia* < Greek *sumpatheia* < *sumpathēs* 'feeling with' < *pathos* 'feeling'] ◇ **come out in sympathy** to go on strike in support of other strikers (*informal*)

sympathy strike *n* a strike by workers demonstrating their support for another group of strikers rather than against their own employer

sympathy vote *n* a vote that people give to somebody for whom they feel pity or affection

sympatric /sim páttrik/ *adj* describes species that occupy roughly the same area of land but do not interbreed [Early 20C. < Greek *patra* 'fatherland' < *patēr* 'father'] —**sympatrically** *adv* —**sympatry** /símpətri/ *n*

symphonic /sim fónnik/ *adj* **1.** relating to, involving, or typical of a musical symphony, or resembling one in form or content **2.** harmonious in sound, colour, or composition —**symphonically** *adv*

symphonic poem *n* an extended piece of music for a symphony orchestra that is based on a literary, artistic, or ideological theme such as a folktale or landscape

symphonist /símfənist/ *n* a composer of symphonies or symphonic works

symphony /símfəni/ (*plural* **-nies**) *n* **1. COMPLEX MUSICAL COMPOSITION** a major work for an orchestra, including wind, string, and percussion instruments, usually composed in four movements, at least one of which is in sonata form **2.** MUSIC same as **symphony orchestra** **3. CONCERT BY SYMPHONY ORCHESTRA** a concert performed by a symphony orchestra **4. HARMONIOUS COMPOSITION OR ARRANGEMENT** something that is harmoniously composed ○ *The colour scheme was a symphony of blues, greens, and yellows.* **5. HARMONY OF SOUNDS OR COLOURS** harmony or agreement of sounds or colours (*archaic*) [13C. Via Latin *symphonia* 'sound of instruments, harmony' < Greek *sumphōnia*, literally 'sounding together' < *phōnē* 'sound']

symphony orchestra *n* a large orchestra that includes wind, string, and percussion instruments and plays symphonies and other works scored for these instruments

symphysis /símfəsiss/ (*plural* **-physes** /-fəseez/) *n* **1.** ANAT **GROWING TOGETHER OF BONES OR PARTS** the natural merging of two or more separate bones or parts of the body **2.** ANAT **JOINT WITH LITTLE MOVEMENT** a joint in which the bones are connected by tough cartilage (**fibrocartilage**) and there is very little movement between them, e.g. between adjacent vertebrae in the spinal column **3.** MED **BONE CONDITION** a condition in which two or more separate bones or parts of the body have merged **4.** BOT **FUSION OF PLANT PARTS** a fusion of two similar organs or parts of a plant **5.** ANAT, BOT **LINE MARKING SYMPHYSIS** a point or line where a symphysis occurs [Late 16C. Via modern Latin < Greek *sumphusis* 'growing together' < *phusis* 'growth'] —**symphyseal** /sim fízzi əl/ *adj* —**symphystic** /sim fístik/ *adj* —**symphytic** /sim fíttik/ *adj*

sympodium /sim pṓdi əm/ (*plural* **-dia** /-di ə/) *n* a main plant stem that develops from a series of lateral branches, often in a zigzag pattern, e.g. the stem of a grapevine [Mid-19C. < modern Latin < Greek *pod-* 'foot'] —**sympodial** *adj* —**sympodially** *adv*

symposia plural of **symposium**

symposiarch /sim pṓzi aark/ *n* a supervisor of a symposium [Early 17C. < Greek *sumposiarkhos* < *sumposion* (see SYMPOSIUM)]

symposiast /sim pṓzi ast/ *n* a participant in a symposium [Mid-17C. < Greek *sumposiazein* 'drink together' < *sumposion* (see SYMPOSIUM)]

symposium /sim pṓzi əm/ (*plural* **-siums** or **-sia** /-zi ə/) *n* **1. FORMAL MEETING FOR DISCUSSION OF SUBJECT** a formal meeting held for the discussion of a subject, during which individual speakers may make presentations **2.** PUBL **PUBLISHED COLLECTION OF OPINIONS** a published collection of opinions or writings on a subject, often in a periodical **3.** ANCIENT HIST **DRINKING PARTY IN ANCIENT GREECE** a drinking party in ancient Greece, usually with music and philosophical conversation [Late 16C. Via Latin < Greek *sumposion* 'drinking party' < *sumpotēs* 'drinker with another' < *potēs* 'drinker'] —**symposiac** *adj*

symptom /símptəm/ *n* **1.** an indication of a disease or other disorder, especially one experienced by the patient, e.g. pain, dizziness, or itching, as opposed to one observed by the doctor (**sign**) ○ *A sore throat and fever were the symptoms of the virus they all had.* **2.** a sign or indication of the existence of something, especially something undesirable ○ *early symptoms of a recession* [Mid-16C. Via late Latin *symptoma* < Greek *sumptōma* 'occurrence' < *sumpiptein* 'fall together' < *piptein* 'fall'] —**symptomless** *adj*

symptomatic /símptə máttik/ *adj* **1. CHARACTERISTIC** typical or indicative of something, especially something undesirable ○ *symptomatic of the breakdown in communication between children and parents* **2.** MED **INDICATING ILLNESS** indicating or typical of a particular illness **3.** MED **OF SYMPTOMS** relating to, affecting, or based on a symptom or symptoms of bodily disorder ○ *Only symptomatic relief is available for the common cold.* [Late 17C. < late Latin *symptomaticus* < *symptoma* (see SYMPTOM)] —**symptomatically** *adv*

symptomatology /símptəmə tólləji/ (*plural* **-gies**) *n* **1.** the study of the relationships between symptoms and diseases **2.** the set of symptoms that are associated with a disease or that affect a patient [Late 18C. < Greek *sumptōmat-*, stem of *sumptōma* (see SYMPTOM)]

symptomize /símptəmīz/ (**-izes, -izing, -ized**), **symptomise** (**-ises, -ising, -ised**) *vt* to be an indication of the existence of something

syn- *prefix* together, together with, united ○ *syncarpous* [< Greek *sun* 'together']

synaeresis *n* CHEM, LING, PHON another spelling of **syneresis**

synaesthesia /sínnəss thee̍zhə/, **synesthesia** *n* **1.** PHYSIOL **SENSATION FELT ELSEWHERE IN BODY** the feeling of sensation in one part of the body when another part is stimulated **2.** PSYCHOL **STIMULATION OF ONE SENSE ALONGSIDE ANOTHER** the evocation of one kind of sense impression when another sense is stimulated, e.g. the sensation of colour when a sound is heard **3.** LITERAT **RHETORICAL DEVICE** in literature, the description of one kind of sense perception using words that describe another kind of sense perception, as in the phrase 'shining metallic words' (*literary*) [Late 19C. < modern Latin < *syn-* (< Greek *sun* 'together') + stem of Greek *aisthēsis* 'sensation', after ANAESTHESIA] —**synaesthetic** /-théttik/ *adj*

synagogue /sínnə gog/ *n* **1.** the place of worship and communal centre of a Jewish congregation **2.** a body of followers of Judaism who worship together [12C. Via French and late Latin *synagoga* < Greek *sunagōgē* 'assembly' < *sunagein* 'bring together' < *agein* 'to lead'] —**synagogal** /sínnə gógg'l/ *adj* —**synagogical** /sínnə gójjik'l/ *adj*

synalepha /sínnə le̍efə/, **synaloepha** *n* the blending of two adjacent vowels into one, e.g. when a word ending in a vowel is immediately followed by a word beginning with a vowel [Mid-16C. Via late Latin < Greek *sunaloiphē* < *sunaleiphein* 'smear together' < *aleiphein* 'to smear']

synapse /sī́ naps, sínnaps/ *n* a junction between two nerve cells, where the club-shaped tip of a nerve fibre almost touches another cell in order to transmit signals ■ *vi* (**-apses, -apsing, -apsed**) to form a synapse between nerve cells [Late 19C. Anglicization of SYNAPSIS]

synapsis /si nápsiss/ (*plural* **-apses** /-apseez/) *n* the pairing of homologous chromosomes from each parent during the initial phase (**prophase**) of cell division [Mid-17C. Via modern Latin < Greek *sunapsis* 'connection' < *haptein* 'join']

synaptic /si náptik/ *adj* **1.** relating to or involving a junction between nerve cells **2.** relating to, involving, or typical of synapsis [Late 19C. < SYNAPSIS or SYNAPSE after Greek *sunaptikos* 'connective']

synaptology /sī́ nap tólləji/ *n* the study of junctions between nerve cells (**synapses**) and synaptic connections in the nervous system

synarthrosis /sín aar thrṓsiss/ (*plural* **-throses** /-thrṓseez/) *n* a rigid joint formed by the union of two bones and connected by fibrous tissue —**synarthrodial** /-thrṓ di əl/ *adj* —**synarthrodially** *adv*

sync /singk/, **synch** (*informal*) *n* **1. SYNCHRONIZATION** the relationship between things that are happening or working at the same time, especially the correspondence of sound and image in a film **2. HARMONY** harmony or agreement ■ *vti* (**syncs, syncing, synced;**

synchs, synching, synched) SYNCHRONIZE to synchronize something, or be synchronized [Early 20C. Shortening]

SPELLCHECK See *sink*.

syncarpous /sin kaárpəss/ *adj* describes the female reproductive parts (**gynoecium**) of a flower in which the carpels are fused —**syncarpy** /sín kaarpi/ *n*

syncategorematic /sín kátəgərə máttik/ *adj* describes an expression that has meaning only in conjunction with another expression [Early 19C. Via medieval Latin *syncategorematicus* < Greek *sugkatēgorēmatikos* 'predicating jointly' < *katēgorein* 'to predicate']

synch *n, vti* same as **sync**

synchondrosis /síng kon drṓsiss/ (*plural* **-droses** /-drṓsseez/) *n* **1.** a joint in which there is slight movement between bones that are held together by cartilage, e.g. between the ribs and the breastbone **2.** a joint in which the cartilage linking two bones in childhood is replaced by bone as development progresses [Late 16C. Via modern Latin < late Greek *sugkhondrōsis* < *khondros* 'cartilage']

synchro /síngkrō/ (*plural* **-chros**) *n* ELEC ENG same as **selsyn** [Mid-20C. Shortening of *synchronizing*]

synchro- *prefix* synchronous, synchronized ○ *synchroscope* [< SYNCHRONOUS]

synchrocyclotron /síngkrō sī́klə tron/ *n* a particle accelerator that compensates for increases in the relativistic mass of accelerated particles and so achieves greater energies by using the synchronizing effects of a frequency-modulated electric field

synchroflash /síngkrō flash/ *n* a mechanism in a camera that opens the shutter at the moment when the light from the flashbulb or electronic flash is brightest

synchromesh /síngkrō mesh/ *n* a gear system in which the speeds of the driving and driven parts are synchronized before they engage so that gear changes are made smoother —**synchromesh** *adj*

synchronal /síngkrən'l/ *adj* happening at the same time [Mid-17C. < late Latin *synchronus* (see SYNCHRONOUS)]

synchronic /sin krónnik/ *adj* relating to something, especially a language, as it exists at a point in time and not historically [Mid-19C. < late Latin *synchronus* (see SYNCHRONOUS)] —**synchronically** *adv*

synchronicity /síngkrə níssəti/ *n* **1.** the coincidence of events that seem related, but are not obviously caused one by the other. The term was first used in this sense in the work of the psychologist Carl Jung. **2.** same as **synchronism** (sense 1)

synchronise *vti* another spelling of **synchronize**

synchronism /síngkrənizəm/ *n* **1.** the simultaneous occurrence of two or more things **2.** an arrangement in chronological order showing historical events that happened or people who were alive around the same time [Late 16C. < Greek *sugkhronismos* < *sugkhronos* (see SYNCHRONOUS)] —**synchronistic** /síngkrə nístik/ *adj* —**synchronistically** *adv*

synchronize /síngkrə nīz/ (**-nizes, -nizing, -nized**), **synchronise** (**-nises, -nising, -nised**) *v* **1.** *vt* MAKE THINGS WORK AT SAME TIME to make something work at the same time or the same rate as something else **2.** *vt* SET WATCHES TO SAME TIME to set timepieces to indicate the same time as each other **3.** *vi* GO TOGETHER to go or work together or in unison **4.** *vi* HAPPEN TOGETHER to happen at the same time **5.** *vt* CINEMA ALIGN SOUND AND IMAGE OF FILM to make the soundtrack of a film match up with the action **6.** *vt* COMPUT UPDATE PARALLEL COMPUTER FILES to copy a file from one computer system or electronic device to another in order to maintain the information on both at the same level [Early 17C. < SYNCHRONISM] —**synchronization** /síngkrə nī záysh'n/ *n*

synchronized sleep /síngkrə nīzd-/ *n* BIOL same as **slow-wave sleep**

synchronized swimming *n* a sport in which swimmers perform coordinated movements in time to music in the manner of a dance

synchronoscope /sing krónnə skōp/ *n* MECH ENG, ELEC ENG same as **synchroscope**

synchronous /síngkrənəss/ *adj* **1.** OCCURRING SIMULTANEOUSLY happening at the same time **2.** WORKING AT SAME RATE working or moving at the same rate **3.** PHYS WITH SAME PERIOD AND PHASE having the same period and phase of oscillation or cyclic movement [Mid-17C. Via late Latin *synchronus* < Greek *sugkhronos* < *khronos* 'time'] —**synchronously** *adv*

synchronous motor *n* an electric motor that operates at a speed directly proportional to the frequency of the applied voltage source

synchronous operation *n* an event that occurs regularly or predictably when triggered by the completion of another process, e.g. the production of a receipt by a cash machine after a transaction is completed

synchronous orbit *n* an orbit that keeps time with the rotation of the orbited object, so that the orbiting body is always directly over the same point on the surface of the orbited body

synchrony /síngkrəni/ (*plural* **-nies**) *n* occurrence at the same time or movement at the same rate, or an example of this phenomenon

synchroscope /síngkrə skōp/ *n* **1.** an instrument that is used to find whether or not two things such as moving machine parts are moving in phase with one another **2.** an instrument used to indicate the difference in frequency between two alternating current supplies

synchrotron /síngkrə tron/ *n* a particle accelerator in which charged particles travelling at near the speed of light are guided round a doughnut-shaped tube by powerful magnets, producing synchrotron radiation

synchrotron radiation *n* short-wave radiation, from infrared to conventional X-rays, produced in a synchrotron. Use: analysis of the structure of proteins, viruses, and inorganic materials such as metals.

syncline /síng klīn/ *n* a fold in a rock formation that is shaped like a basin or trough and contains younger rocks in its core —**synclinal** /sing klī́n'l/ *adj*

syncopate /síngkə payt/ (**-pates, -pating, -pated**) *vt* **1.** to modify a musical rhythm by shifting the accent to a weak beat of the bar **2.** to shorten a word by the loss of one or more sounds or letters from the middle —**syncopator** *n*

syncopation /síngkə páysh'n/ *n* **1.** a rhythmic technique in music in which the accent is shifted to a weak beat of the bar **2.** PHON same as **syncope** (sense 2)

syncope /síngkəpi/ *n* **1.** the action of fainting, or a fainting fit (*technical*) **2.** the shortening of a word by the loss of sounds or letters from its middle [Mid-16C. Via late Latin < Greek *sugkopē* < *sugkoptein* 'cut short' < *koptein* 'to cut'] —**syncopal** *adj* —**syncopic** /sing kóppik/ *adj*

syncretise *vti* PHILOSOPHY, RELIG another spelling of **syncretize**

syncretism /síngkrətizəm/ *n* **1.** the combination of different systems of philosophical or religious belief or practice **2.** the use of a single inflectional form of a word to cover functions previously covered by two separate forms, e.g. 'spun' in English, now used for both the past tense and the past participle although the past tense used to be 'span' [Early 17C. Via modern Latin *syncretismus* < Greek *sugkrētismos* 'union' < *sugkrētizein* 'unite (against a common enemy)'] —**syncretic** /sing kréttik/ *adj* —**syncretist** *n* —**syncretistic** /síngkrə tístik/ *adj*

syncretize /síngkrə tīz/ (**-tizes, -tizing, -tized**), **syncretise** (**-cretises, -cretising, -cretised**) *vti* to combine aspects of different systems of philosophical or religious belief or practice [Late 17C. < Greek *sugkrētizein* 'unite (against a common enemy)'] —**syncretization** /síngkrə tī záysh'n/ *n*

~~**syncronous**~~ incorrect spelling of **synchronous**

syncytium /sin sítti əm/ (*plural* **-tia** /-ti ə/) *n* a mass of cytoplasm within a cell membrane that contains multiple nuclei and is often the result of cellular fusion, e.g. in some slime moulds [Late 19C. < SYN- + Greek *kutos* 'hollow vessel'] —**syncytial** /-sítti əl/ *adj*

synd /sīnd/, **syne** /sīn/ *Scotland vt* (**synds, synding, synded; synes, syning, syned**) to rinse something, usually with water ■ *n* an act of rinsing something [14C. Origin ?]

synd. *abbr* syndicate

syndactyl /sin dáktil/ *adj* having two or more fingers or toes joined together. This may be a natural condition, as in some animals, or congenital, as in people with webbed toes. —**syndactyl** *n* —**syndactylism** *n* —**syndactyly** *n*

syndesis /sin deésiss/ *n* the use in grammar of constructions in which clauses are joined by conjunctions [Early 20C. < German < Greek *desis* 'binding' < *dein* 'bind']

syndesmosis /sín dess mṓsiss/ (*plural* **-moses** /-mṓsseez/) *n* an immovable joint in which the bones are held firmly by fibrous tissue, but are not very close together, e.g. at the lower ends of the tibia and fibula [Late 16C. < Greek *sundesmos* 'ligament' < *sundein* (see SYNDETIC)] —**syndesmotic** /-móttik/ *adj*

syndetic /sin déttik/ *adj* describes a grammatical construction in which two clauses are joined by a conjunction [Early 17C. < Greek *sundetikos* < *sundein* 'bind together' < *dein* 'bind'] —**syndetically** *adv*

syndeton /sin deé t'n/ *n* a grammatical construction in which two clauses are joined by a conjunction [Mid-20C. Back-formation < ASYNDETON]

syndic /síndik/ *n* **1.** somebody appointed to represent an organization such as a corporation or a university in business transactions **2.** a government official, especially a civil magistrate, in some European countries [Early 17C. Via French, 'delegate' < late Latin *syndicus* < Greek *sundikos* 'defendant's advocate' < *dikē* 'judgment'] —**syndical** *adj* —**syndicship** *n*

syndicalism /síndikəlizəm/ *n* **1.** a revolutionary political doctrine that advocates the seizure of the means of production by workers organized in trade unions **2.** a system of government in which workers organized in trade unions control the means of production [Early 20C. < French *syndicalisme* < *syndic* (see SYNDIC)] —**syndical** *adj* —**syndicalist** *adj, n* —**syndicalistic** /síndikə lístik/ *adj*

syndicate *n* /síndikət/ **1.** GROUP OF BUSINESSES an association of businesses jointly contributing capital to a major project **2.** BUSINESS THAT SELLS NEWS MATERIALS a business or agency that sells news stories or photographs to the media **3.** GROUP OF NEWSPAPERS UNDER SAME OWNER a group of newspapers that have the same owner **4.** GROUP OF PEOPLE a group of people who combine to carry out a business, enterprise, or some other common purpose **5.** CRIME ASSOCIATION OF GANGSTERS an association of gangsters that controls an area of organized crime **6.** POL COUNCIL OF SYNDICS a council or body of syndics **7.** POL JURISDICTION OF GOVERNMENT OFFICIAL the office or jurisdiction of a government official, especially a civil magistrate, in some European countries ■ *v* /síndi kayt/ (**-cates, -cating, -cated**) **1.** *vt* SELL SOMETHING FOR MULTIPLE PUBLICATION to sell something such as an article or a cartoon strip for publication in a number of newspapers or magazines simultaneously **2.** *vt US* SELL TV PROGRAMMES TO INDEPENDENT STATIONS to sell television or radio programmes directly to independent stations **3.** *vt* CONTROL SOMETHING AS SYNDICATE to control or manage something as a syndicate **4.** *vi* COME TOGETHER AS SYNDICATE to come together to form a syndicate [Early 17C. Via French < medieval Latin *syndicatus* < late Latin *syndicus* (see SYNDIC)] —**syndication** /síndi káysh'n/ *n*

syndrome /síndrōm/ *n* **1.** a group of signs and symptoms that together are characteristic or indicative of a specific disease or other disorder **2.** a group of things or events that form a recognizable pattern, especially of something undesirable [Mid-16C. Via modern Latin < Greek *sundromē* 'running together' < *dramein* 'run']

syne[1] /sīn/ *Scotland adv* AGO since then ■ *prep* SINCE from a fixed time onward ■ *conj* FROM WHEN from the time that [14C. Contraction of obsolete *sithen* < Old English *siððan* (see SINCE)]

syne[2] /sīn/ *vt, n* same as **synd**

synecdoche /si nékdəki/ *n* a figure of speech in which the word for part of something is used to mean the whole, e.g. 'sail' for 'boat', or vice versa [14C. Via Latin < Greek *sunekdokhē* < *sunekdekhesthai* 'take on a share of' < *ekdekhesthai* 'take'] —**synecdochic** /sínnek dókik/ *adj* —**synecdochical** *adj* —**synecdochically** *adv*

synecology /sínni kólləji/ *n* the branch of ecology that deals with the structure and development of entire ecological communities and the interrelationships of the plants and animals within them —**synecologic**

/sínnikə lójjik/ *adj* —**synecological** *adj* —**synecologically** *adv*

synectics /si néktiks/ *n* an approach to solving problems based on the creative thinking of a group of people from different areas of experience and knowledge (*takes a singular verb*) [Mid-20C. Via late Latin *synecticus* 'producing an effect immediately' < Greek *sunektikos* < *ekhein* 'to hold']

syneresis /si neérəssiss/, **synaeresis** *n* **1. LIQUID SEPARATION IN GEL** the process by which a liquid is separated from a gel owing to further coagulation **2. MERGING OF VOWELS INTO DIPHTHONG** the merging of two vowels into a diphthong **3. MERGING OF VOWELS INTO ONE SYLLABLE** the merging of two vowels into one syllable without making it into a diphthong [Late 16C. Via late Latin < Greek *sunairesis* 'contraction' < *hairein* 'take']

synergism /sínnərjizəm/ *n* **1.** BUSINESS, MED same as **synergy 2.** in Christian theology, the doctrine that the human will and the Holy Spirit work together to bring about spiritual regeneration or salvation [Mid-18C. < SYNERGY] —**synergistic** /sínnər jístik/ *adj* —**synergistically** *adv*

synergist /sínnərjist/ *n* something that works in combination with something else to increase its effect, e.g. a drug that increases the effect of another drug

synergy /sínnərji/ (*plural* **-gies**) *n* **1.** the working together of two or more people, organizations, or things, especially when the result is greater than the sum of their individual effects or capabilities **2.** the phenomenon in which the combined action of two things such as drugs or muscles is greater than the sum of their effects individually. In the case of drugs, the result may be dangerous to the patient. [Mid-17C. Via Latin < Greek *sunergia* < *sunergein* 'work together' < *ergos* 'work'] —**synergetic** /sínnər jéttik/ *adj* —**synergetically** *adv* —**synergic** /si núrjik/ *adj*

synesis /sínnəssiss/ *n* grammatical agreement according to meaning rather than strict syntax, e.g. the use of a plural form of a verb or a plural pronoun with a collective noun. Synesis is shown, e.g., in 'The team are playing badly so we have stopped supporting them', with 'are' and 'them' rather than 'is' and 'it'. [Late 19C. Via modern Latin < Greek *sunesis* 'union' < *sunienai* 'bring together' < *hienai* 'send']

synesthesia *n* PHYSIOL, PSYCHOL, LITERAT another spelling of **synaesthesia**

synfuel /sín fyoo əl/ *n* a liquid fuel synthesized from a nonpetroleum source such as coal, oil shale, or waste plastics. Use: a substitute for a petroleum product. [Late 20C. < SYNTHETIC]

syngamy /síng gəmi/ *n* sexual reproduction through the fusion of gametes [Early 20C. < SYN- + Greek *gamos* 'marriage'] —**syngamic** /sing gámmik/ *adj* —**syngamous** *adj*

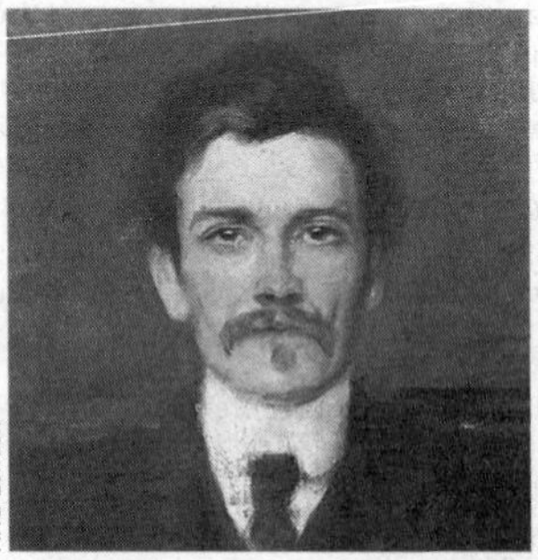

AKG London

J. M. Synge: portrait by John B. Yeats

Synge /sing/, **J. M.** (1871–1909) Irish dramatist. A dominant figure of the Irish Renaissance, he wrote the controversial masterpiece, *The Playboy of the Western World* (1907). Full name **Synge, John Millington**. See Cultural note at **playboy**

> 'In a good play every speech should be as fully flavoured as a nut or apple, and such speeches cannot be written by anyone who works among people who have shut their lips on poetry.'
> [J. M. Synge, *The Playboy of the Western World*; 1907]

syngeneic /sínji neéik, -náyik/ *adj* having an identical or closely similar genetic makeup, especially one that will allow the transplantation of tissue without provoking an immune response [Mid-20C. < Greek *sungeneia* 'kinship' < *genos* 'kind, type'] —**syngeneically** *adv*

syngenesis /sin jénnəssiss/ *n* reproduction involving fusion of male and female genetic material —**syngenetic** /sínjə néttik/ *adj*

synkaryon /sin kárri on/ *n* a cell nucleus formed through the fusion of male and female nuclei [Early 20C. < SYN- + Greek *karuon* 'seed'] —**synkaryonic** /sín kari ónnik/ *adj*

synkinesis /sínki neéssiss, -kī-/, **synkinesia** /sínki neézi ə, -kī-/ *n* the performing of an unintended movement when making a voluntary one —**synkinetic** /-néttik/ *adj*

synod /sínnəd, sínnod/ *n* **1. CHURCH COUNCIL** a special council of church members that holds regular meetings to discuss religious issues **2. PRESBYTERIAN CHURCH COURT** a Presbyterian church court at a level between that of the Presbytery and that of the General Assembly **3. ASSEMBLY OR COUNCIL** an assembly or council held for the discussion of issues (*formal*) [14C. Via late Latin < Greek *sunodos* 'meeting' < *hodos* 'way'] —**synodal** *adj*

synodic /si nóddik/, **synodical** /-ik'l/ *adj* **1.** relating to the alignment of astronomical objects, or the interval between occasions when the same astronomical objects are aligned **2.** relating to or having the character of a church synod —**synodically** *adv*

synodic month *n* ASTRON same as **lunar month** (sense 1)

synoecious /si neéshəss/ *adj* having male and female organs on the same flower or other structure [Mid-19C. < SYN- + Greek *oikos* 'house']

~~synonim~~ incorrect spelling of **synonym**

~~synonomous~~ incorrect spelling of **synonymous**

synonym /sínnənim/ *n* **1. WORD MEANING SAME AS ANOTHER** a word that means the same, or almost the same, as another word in the same language, either in all of its uses or in a specific context. Examples of synonyms in this sense are 'environment' and 'surroundings' and the verbs 'tear' and 'rip'. **2. ALTERNATIVE NAME** a word or expression that is used as another name for something in some styles of speaking or writing or to emphasize a specific aspect or association. Examples include 'Caledonian' and 'Scottish'. **3.** BIOL **REJECTED DUPLICATE TAXONOMIC NAME** a duplicate taxonomic name that has been rejected or replaced [15C. < Latin *synonymum* < Greek *sunōnumos* 'synonymous' < *onuma* 'name'] —**synonymic** /sínnə nímmik/ *adj* —**synonymity** /sínnə nímməti/ *n*

synonymize /si nónni mīz/ (**-mizes, -mizing, -mized**), **synonymise** (**-mises, -mising, -mised**) *vt* to provide an analysis or listing of the synonyms of a word or expression

synonymous /si nónniməss/ *adj* **1.** meaning the same, or almost the same, as another word in the same language, or being an alternative name for somebody or something **2.** having an implication similar to the idea expressed by another word ○ *Andy Warhol is synonymous with pop art.* —**synonymously** *adv* —**synonymousness** *n*

synonymy /si nónnimi/ (*plural* **-mies**) *n* **1. EQUIVALENCE OF MEANING** the state or quality of being synonymous **2. STUDY OF SYNONYMS** the study, classification, and distinguishing of synonyms **3. ANNOTATED LIST OF SYNONYMS** a list or book of synonyms, with emphasis on the discrimination of meanings

synopsis /si nópsiss/ (*plural* **-opses** /-ópseez/) *n* **1.** a condensed version of a text, e.g. a summary of the plot of a book, play, film, or television programme **2.** a concise outline or survey of a subject [Early 17C. Via late Latin < Greek *sunopsis* 'general view' < *opsis* 'view']

synopsize /si nóp sīz/ (**-sizes, -sizing, -sized**), **synopsise** (**-sises, -sising, -sised**) *vt* to summarize or make a synopsis of something

synoptic /si nóptik/ *adj* **1.** constituting a general view of the whole of a subject **2.** METEOROL relating to or showing simultaneous weather conditions over a large area ■ *adj, n* BIBLE another spelling of **Synoptic** [Early 17C. Via modern Latin < Greek *sunoptikos* < *sunopsis* (see SYNOPSIS)] —**synoptical** *adj* —**synoptically** *adv*

Synoptic /si nóptik/ *adj* describes the gospels of Matthew, Mark, and Luke that tell the story of Jesus Christ's life and ministry from a similar point of view and are similar in structure ■ *n* **1.** one of the Synoptic gospels of Matthew, Mark, or Luke **2.** BIBLE same as **synoptist**

synoptist /si nóptist/ *n* an author of one of the Synoptic gospels

synostosis /sín o stóssiss/ (*plural* **-toses** /-tósseez/) *n* the formation of a single bone from the fusion of two adjacent bones —**synostotic** /-stóttik/ *adj*

synovia /sī nóvi ə/ *n* PHYSIOL same as **synovial fluid** [Mid-17C. < modern Latin *sinovia*] —**synovial** /sī nóvi əl/*adj*

synovial fluid *n* a clear viscous fluid that lubricates the linings of joints and the sheaths of tendons

synovitis /sínō vítiss/ *n* inflammation of the synovial membrane of a joint —**synovitic** /-víttik/ *adj*

synsepalous /sin séppələss/ *adj* BOT same as **gamosepalous** [Mid-19C. < SYNTHETIC + SEPAL]

syntactic /sin táktik/, **syntactical** /-ik'l/ *adj* **1.** relating to the rules or patterns of syntax **2.** correctly formed according to the rules or accepted structures of syntax [Early 19C. Via Latin < Greek *suntaktikos* < *suntassein* (see SYNTAX)] —**syntactically** *adv*

syntagma /sin tágmə/ (*plural* **-mata** /-mətə/ or **-mas**), **syntagm** /sín tam/ *n* a linguistic unit made up of sets of phonemes, words, or phrases that are arranged sequentially [Mid-17C. Via late Latin < Greek *suntagma* < *suntassein* (see SYNTAX)]

syntagmatic /sín tag máttik/, **syntagmic** /sin tágmik/ *adj* relating to syntactic units, or to the function and behaviour of a word or phrase within a syntactic unit

syntax /sín taks/ *n* **1. ORGANIZATION OF WORDS IN SENTENCES** the ordering of and relationship between the words and other structural elements in phrases and sentences. The syntax may be of a whole language, a single phrase or sentence, or of an individual speaker. **2. BRANCH OF GRAMMAR** the branch of grammar that studies syntax **3. RULES OF SYNTAX** an exposition of or set of rules for producing grammatical structures according to the syntax of a language **4. RULES GOVERNING PROGRAM STRUCTURE** the rules governing which statements and combinations of statements in a programming language will be acceptable to a compiler for that language **5. RULES FOR DERIVING LOGICAL FORMULAS** the part of logic that gives the rules that define which combinations of expressions in the logical system yield well-formed formulas **6. RULE-BASED ARRANGEMENT** the arrangement of any group of elements in a systematic or rule-based manner [Late 16C. Directly or via French < late Latin < Greek *suntaxis* < *suntassein* 'put in order' < *tassein* 'arrange']

syntaxin /sin táksin/ *n* a cell protein responsible for propelling neurotransmitter chemicals from one neuron to the next

synteny /síntəni/ *n* the occurrence of two or more genes on the same chromosome, whether or not they are linked —**syntenic** /sin ténnik/ *adj*

synth /sinth/ *n* MUSIC same as **synthesizer** (*informal*) [Late 20C. Shortening]

synthesis /sínthəssiss/ (*plural* **-theses** /-thəseez/) *n* **1. RESULT OF COMBINATION** a new unified whole resulting from the combination of different ideas, influences, or objects **2. COMBINING OF VARIOUS COMPONENTS INTO WHOLE** the process of combining different ideas, influences, or objects into a new whole **3.** CHEM **FORMATION OF CHEMICAL COMPOUNDS** the formation of compounds through one or more chemical reactions involving simpler substances **4.** MUSIC **PRODUCING OF SOUND WITH SYNTHESIZER** the production of music or speech using an electronic synthesizer **5.** LING **USE OF INFLECTIONS** the expression of syntactic relationships by means of inflections rather than word order or prepositions and other function words **6.** PHILOSOPHY **IDEA RESOLVING CONTRADICTIONS** in Hegelian philosophy, the new idea that resolves the conflict between the initial proposition (**thesis**) and its negation (**antithesis**) **7.** PHILOSOPHY **DEDUCTIVE REASONING** the process of deductive reasoning from first principles to a conclusion [15C. Via Latin, 'collection' < Greek *sunthesis* < *suntithenai* 'put together' < *tithenai* 'put'] —**synthesist** *n*

synthesise, etc. another spelling of **synthesize**, etc.

synthesis gas *n* a mixture of carbon monoxide and hydrogen derived from the breakdown of carbon- and hydrogen-containing materials. Use: manufacture of ammonia, other chemicals.

synthesize /sínthə sīz/ (**-sizes, -sizing, -sized**), **synthesise** (**-sises, -sising, -sised**) *v* 1. *vti* COMBINE VARIOUS COMPONENTS INTO NEW WHOLE to combine different ideas, influences, or objects into a new whole, or be combined in this way 2. *vt* PRODUCE SUBSTANCE BY CHEMICAL PROCESS to produce a substance or material by chemical or biological synthesis 3. *vt* PRODUCE MUSIC ELECTRONICALLY to produce music using an electronic synthesizer —**synthesization** /sínthə sī záysh'n/ *n*

synthesizer /sínthə sīzər/, **synthesiser** *n* 1. ELECTRONIC MUSICAL INSTRUMENT a device that generates and modifies sounds electronically, especially a musical instrument 2. MANUFACTURER OF SYNTHETIC SUBSTANCES somebody or something involved in the synthesis of substances or materials 3. SOMEBODY WHO COMBINES COMPONENTS somebody who combines ideas, influences, or objects into a new whole

synthespian /sin théspi ən/ *n* a digital image of a person created by a precise full-body scan and used by animators to produce animated characters or films [Late 20C. Blend of SYNTHETIC + THESPIAN]

synthetic /sin théttik/ *adj* 1. MADE BY CHEMICAL PROCESS made artificially by chemical synthesis, especially so as to resemble a natural product 2. INSINCERE not genuine, especially expressed but not genuinely felt ○ *synthetic expressions of sympathy* 3. PHILOSOPHY WITH TRUTH DEPENDING ON FACTS describes a proposition whose truth or falsity is a matter of facts and not merely a matter of the meaning of the words in the sentence 4. LING USING INFLECTIONS TO EXPRESS SYNTAX describes a language that expresses syntactic relationships by means of inflections rather than word order or prepositions and other function words ■ *n* 1. CHEMICALLY PRODUCED SUBSTANCE OR MATERIAL a substance or material produced by chemical processes and not occurring naturally 2. ARTIFICIAL FIBRE a synthetic textile fibre, or an item of clothing made of this (*usually used in the plural*) [Late 17C. Via French or modern Latin < Greek *synthetikos* 'component' < *sunthetos* 'combined' < *suntithenai* (see SYNTHESIS)] — **synthetical** *adj* —**synthetically** *adv*

synthetic resin *n* a resin produced by polymerization of simple molecules, and not obtained directly from plant substances

synthetic rubber *n* a compound synthesized from unsaturated hydrocarbons that resembles rubber

synthetize /sínthə tīz/ (**-tizes, -tizing, -tized**), **synthetise** (**-tises, -tising, -tised**) *vti* same as **synthesize**

syntonic /sin tónnik/ *adj* 1. describes somebody who is emotionally attuned to his or her environment 2. in ego psychology, used to describe behaviour that does not conflict with somebody's basic attitudes and beliefs and, therefore, is not anxiety-provoking (*used in combination*) ○ *ego-syntonic* [Late 19C. < Greek *suntonos* 'attuned' < *sutenein* 'draw tight'] — **syntonically** *adv*

syntype /sín tīp/ *n* a member of a set of specimens that have equal status as the basis for the description of a new species

syphilis /síffəliss/ *n* a serious sexually transmitted disease caused by the spirally twisted bacterium *Treponema pallidum* that affects many body organs and parts, including the genitals, brain, skin, and nervous tissue [Early 18C. < modern Latin, after the person allegedly first affected (according to Girolamo Fracastoro (1483–1553), Veronese physician)] —**syphiloid** *adj*

syphilitic /síffə líttik/ *adj* relating to, caused by, or affected by syphilis ■ *n* an offensive term for somebody who has syphilis [Late 18C. < modern Latin *syphiliticus* < *syphilis* (see SYPHILIS)] —**syphilitically** *adv*

syphiloma /síffə lṓmə/ (*plural* **-mata** /-mətə/ or **-mas**) *n* MED same as **gumma**

syphon *n, vt* another spelling of **siphon**

Syracuse /sírrə kyooz/ 1. capital city and port of Syracuse Province, Sicily, situated about 56 km/35 mi. south of Catania. Population: 126,721 (1999). 2. city in New York State beside Onondaga Lake, west of Utica, and east of Rochester. Population: 145,164 (2002 estimate).

syrah /sírrə/ *n* 1. a typically strong full-bodied red wine made from a variety of black grape grown mainly in France and the United States 2. a black grape variety. Use: to make syrah wine. [Early 19C. Alteration of SHIRAZ]

Syria

Syria /sírri ə/ country in Southwest Asia, bordered by Turkey, Iraq, Jordan, Israel, Lebanon, and the Mediterranean Sea. Capital: Damascus. Population: 17,585,540 (2003). Area: 185,180 sq. km/71,498 sq. mi. Official name **Syrian Arab Republic** —**Syrian** *n, adj*

Syriac /sírri ak/ *n* a form of Aramaic used between the 3rd and 13th centuries that survives in some Eastern Orthodox churches —**Syriac** *adj*

syringa /si ríng gə/ *n* 1. TREES same as **mock orange** (sense 1) 2. a lilac flower or bush. Genus: *Syringa*. [Mid-17C. < modern Latin < Greek *surigx* 'panpipes']

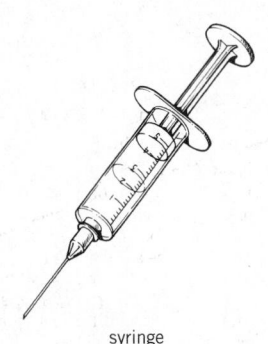
syringe

syringe /si rínj/ *n* 1. INSTRUMENT FOR WITHDRAWING AND EJECTING FLUIDS an instrument consisting of a piston in a small tube, used in conjunction with a hollow needle or tube for the withdrawal and injection of fluids and for cleaning wounds 2. DEVICE FOR PUMPING AND SPRAYING LIQUIDS a device similar to a medical syringe that is used for spraying or extracting fluids by means of pressure or suction ■ *vt* (**-ringes, -ringing, -ringed**) USE SYRINGE ON SOMETHING to clean, spray, or inject something using a syringe [15C. Via medieval Latin *syringa* < Greek *surigx* 'panpipes']

syringes plural of **syrinx**

syringomyelia /si ríng gō mī eéli ə/ *n* a chronic progressive disease of the spinal cord in which tubular fluid-filled cavities form in the nerve tissue, causing sensory disturbances and, eventually, loss of voluntary movement [Late 19C. < SYRINGE + MYEL-] — **syringomyelic** *adj*

syrinx /sírringks/ (*plural* **syrinxes** or **syringes** /si rín jeez/) *n* 1. MUSIC PANPIPES a set of panpipes 2. BIRDS VOCAL ORGAN OF BIRD the vocal organ of a bird, usually situated near the junction between the trachea and bronchi 3. ANCIENT HIST CORRIDOR IN EGYPTIAN TOMB a narrow corridor or gallery in an ancient Egyptian tomb 4. MED CAVITY IN SPINAL CORD any of the tubular fluid-filled cavities formed in the nerve tissue of the spinal cord in cases of syringomyelia [Early 17C. Via Latin < Greek *surinx* 'panpipes'] —**syringeal** /si rínji əl/ *adj*

syrphid /súrfid/ *n* a dipteran fly that hovers and darts, feeds on nectar and pollen, and has coloration mimicking that of a bee or wasp. Family: Syrphidae. [Late 19C. < modern Latin *Syrphidae* < *Syrphus* < Greek *surphos* 'gnat'] —**syrphid** *adj*

Syrtis Major /súrtiss-/ highly conspicuous wedge-shaped dark area on the surface of Mars in the equatorial region, first observed in 1659

syrup /sírrəp/ *n* 1. SWEET LIQUID a liquid made of sugar dissolved in water by heating, widely used in sweet cookery. Syrups vary in density and strength, and can be boiled down to form caramel. 2. FLAVOURED SWEET LIQUID a flavoured thick sweet liquid 3. PHARM PHARMACEUTICAL LIQUID a thick sweet liquid used to convey oral medicines 4. FOOD same as **golden syrup** 5. SENTIMENTALITY excessive sentimentality (*informal*) [14C. Directly or via French < medieval Latin *siropus* < Arabic *šarāb* 'drink']

syrupy /sírrəpi/ (**-ier, -iest**) *adj* 1. resembling syrup in taste, quality, or consistency 2. excessively sentimental in a cloying fashion

SYS *abbr* see you soon (*used in e-mails or text messages*)

sysop /síssop/ *n* a system operator, usually one who runs a bulletin board (*informal*) [Late 20C. Contraction]

syst. *abbr* system

systaltic /si stáltik/ *adj* describes an organ such as the heart that undergoes alternating rhythmic contraction and dilation [Late 17C. Via late Latin < Greek *sustaltikos* < *sustellein* (see SYSTOLE)]

system /sístəm/ *n* 1. COMPLEX WHOLE FORMED FROM RELATED PARTS a combination of related parts organized into a complex whole ○ *a social system* 2. SET OF PRINCIPLES a scheme of ideas or principles by which something is organized ○ *the democratic system* ○ *the metric system* 3. WAY OF PROCEEDING a method or set of procedures for achieving something ○ *I have worked out a system for identifying likely failures.* 4. ORDERLINESS the use or result of careful planning and organization ○ *There doesn't seem to be any system in his working methods.* 5. ESTABLISHED SOCIAL ORGANIZATION the established social order, especially when regarded as oppressive ○ *You can't beat the system.* 6. WHOLE BODY the human or animal body as a unit ○ *foods that are not good for the system* 7. GROUP OF RELATED BODY PARTS a set of organs or structures in the body that have a common function ○ *the nervous system* 8. COMPUT SET OF COMPUTER COMPONENTS an assembly of computer hardware, software, and peripherals functioning together ○ *The system's down again.* 9. ENG ASSEMBLY OF COMPONENTS an assembly of mechanical or electronic components that function together as a unit 10. TRANSP TRANSPORT NETWORK a physical network of roads, railways, and other routes for travel, transport, or communication 11. ASTRON GROUP OF ASTRONOMICAL OBJECTS a group of astronomical objects or other gravitationally linked objects 12. MINERALS MINERAL CLASSIFICATION a division used in the classification of minerals according to their crystal structures 13. GEOL CLASSIFICATION OF ROCKS ACCORDING TO DATE a division of rocks larger than a series but smaller than a stage, used to distinguish formations of a specific era or period 14. SCI ASSEMBLY OF SUBSTANCES IN EQUILIBRIUM an assembly of substances in chemical or physical equilibrium 15. MUSIC GROUP OF MUSICAL STAVES a number of musical staves that are grouped together by a line or brace in a score and are played simultaneously [Early 17C. Directly or via French < late Latin *systema* < Greek *sustēma* < *sunistanai* 'combine' < *histanai* 'set up'] —**systemless** *adj* ◇ **all systems go** used to indicate that everything is functioning and an operation or activity can start (*informal*)

systematic /sístə máttik/, **systematical** /-ik'l/ *adj* 1. DONE METHODICALLY carried out in a methodical and organized manner 2. WELL ORGANIZED habitually using a method or system for organization 3. METHODICAL deliberate and regular in a methodical manner 4. BASED ON SYSTEM constituting, based on, or resembling a system 5. BIOL RELATING TO TAXONOMIC CLASSIFICATION in accordance with a system of taxonomic classification (**systematics**) [Mid-17C. Via late Latin < Greek *sustēmatikos* < *sustēma* (see SYSTEM)] —**systematically** *adv*

systematic desensitization *n* a therapy for phobias and other anxiety disorders in which patients are gradually given longer and longer exposures to the object of their fears

systematics /sístə máttiks/ *n* the study of systems and

classification, especially the science of classifying organisms (*takes a singular verb*)

systematise *vt* another spelling of **systematize**

systematism /sístəmətizəm/ *n* **1.** the practice of classifying information in a systematic manner **2.** adherence to a system

systematist /sístəmətist/ *n* **1. SOMEBODY CONSTRUCTING SYSTEMS** somebody who constructs a system or systems **2.** BIOL **SOMEBODY CLASSIFYING ORGANISMS** somebody who classifies organisms according to a taxonomic system **3. SOMEBODY ADHERING TO SYSTEM** somebody who conforms to a system or method

systematize /sístəmə tīz/ (**-tizes, -tizing, -tized**), **systematise** (**-tises, -tising, -tised**) *vti* to arrange something according to a system, or be arranged according to a system [Mid-18C. < Greek *sustēmat-*, stem of *sustēma* (see SYSTEM)] —**systematization** /sístəmə tī záysh'n/ *n* —**systematizer** *n*

system building *n* building with prefabricated components —**system-built** *adj*

systemic /si stémmik, si steémik/ *adj* **1.** OF SYSTEM relating to or affecting a system as a whole **2.** PHYSIOL **AFFECTING WHOLE BODY** affecting the whole body, as distinct from having a local effect ○ *a systemic infection* **3.** BOT **AFFECTING WHOLE PLANT** describes a herbicide or other chemical that works by spreading through all the tissues of a plant instead of just staying on the surface ■ *n* AGRIC **SYSTEMIC CHEMICAL** a systemic herbicide, pesticide, or other chemical —**systemically** *adv*

systemic circulation *n* the main part of the blood circulation, as distinct from the pulmonary circulation

systemize /sístə mīz/ (**-izes, -izing, -ized**), **systemise** (**-ises, -ising, -ised**) *vt* same as **systematize** —**systemization** /sístə mī záysh'n/ *n* —**systemizer** *n*

system operator *n* somebody who manages an online bulletin board or maintains a computer network

systems analysis *n* the determination of the data-processing requirements of a company, project, procedure, or task, and the designing of computer systems to fulfil them —**systems analyst** *n*

systems engineering *n* the design and implementation of production systems that require the integration of diverse and complex tasks, e.g. motor car assembly lines —**systems engineer** *n*

system software *n* the operating system and utility programs used to operate and maintain a computer system and provide resources for application programs such as word processors and spreadsheets

systole /sístəli/ *n* the contraction of the heart, during which blood is pumped into the arteries [Mid-16C. Via late Latin < Greek *sustolē* < *sustellein* 'contract' < *stellein* 'put'] —**systolic** /si stóllik/ *adj*

syzygy /sízzəji/ (*plural* **-gies**) *n* **1.** CONJUNCTION OF THREE ASTRONOMICAL OBJECTS the straight-line conjunction or opposition of three astronomical objects such as the Sun, Earth, and Moon **2.** PAIR OF CONNECTED THINGS a pair of related things that are either similar or opposite (*formal*) **3.** LITERAT **UNIT OF TWO METRICAL FEET** in classical verse, a metrical unit of two feet [Early 17C. Via late Latin < Greek *suzugia* < *suzugos* 'paired' < *zugon* 'yoke'] —**syzygetic** /sízzə jéttik/ *adj* —**syzygetically** *adv* —**syzygial** /si zíjji əl/ *adj*

SZ *abbr* Swaziland (*used in Internet addresses*) See table at **domain name**

Szczecin /shtshéchin/ capital city and port of Szczecin Province, northwestern Poland. Population: 419,000 (1997). German name **Stettin**

Szechuan, **Szechwan** another spelling of **Sichuan**

Szeged /ségged/ city and river port in southeastern Hungary. Population: 159,133 (1999).

Szell /sel/, **George** (1897–1970) Hungarian-born US conductor. As the musical director of the Cleveland Orchestra from 1946 to 1970, he established the orchestra as one of the finest in the world.

t[1] /tee/ (*plural* **t's**), **T** (*plural* **T's** or **Ts**) *n* **1.** the 20th letter of the English alphabet, representing a consonant sound **2.** a written representation of the letter 't' ◇ **to a T** exactly

t[2] *symbol* **1.** PHYS time **2.** MEASURE troy

t[3] *abbr* **1.** MEASURE tare **2.** MEASURE teaspoon **3.** MEASURE teaspoonful **4.** MUSIC tempo **5.** MUSIC tenor **6.** GRAM tense **7.** MEASURE ton *or* tons **8.** GRAM transitive

T[1] /tee/ (*plural* **T's** or **Ts**) *n* something shaped like a letter 'T'

T[2] *symbol* **1.** PHYS absolute temperature **2.** PHYS kinetic energy **3.** PHYS period **4.** PHYS surface tension **5.** MEASURE temperature **6.** PHYS tesla **7.** CHEM ELEM tritium

T[3] *abbr* **1.** MEASURE tablespoon **2.** MEASURE tablespoonful **3.** TELECOM telephone (number) (*used to contrast with* E (*e-mail address*) *and* F (*fax number*)) **4.** MATHS tera- **5.** Tuesday

T1 *n* a high-capacity telephone line suitable for high-speed digital access to the Internet, handling 24 voice or data channels simultaneously. ◊ **T3**

T3 *n* a high-capacity telephone line handling 672 voice or data channels simultaneously and capable of transferring data at speeds great enough to provide full-screen full-motion video. ◊ **T1**

ta /taa/ *interj* same as **thank you** (*informal*) [Late 18C. Baby-talk alteration of *thank you*]

Ta *symbol* CHEM ELEM tantalum

TA *abbr* **1.** Territorial Army **2.** transactional analysis **3.** TRANSP Transit Authority

tab[1] /tab/ *n* **1.** FLAP FOR HOLDING a small strip, loop, or other attachment to something, used for lifting, moving, hanging, opening, or closing **2.** TAG OR LABEL a small piece of paper, cloth, or plastic attached to something and containing information about the object **3.** CLOTHING FLAP ON GARMENT a small strip or square of fabric attached to a garment for decoration **4.** N Am BEVERAGES same as **ring-pull 5.** RESTAURANT BILL the bill for a meal or drinks in a restaurant or bar (*informal*) **6.** AEROSP AUXILIARY AEROFOIL a small auxiliary aerofoil on a control surface such as an aileron or rudder, used as a stabilizer **7.** MIL STAFF OFFICER'S INSIGNIA the insignia on a staff officer's collar ■ *vt* (**tabs, tabbing, tabbed**) PUT TAB ON SOMETHING to attach a tab to something [Early 17C. Origin ?] ◇ **keep tabs on somebody** *or* **something** to watch somebody *or* something closely (*informal*) ◇ **pick up the tab** to pay the bill (*informal*)

tab[2] /tab/ *n* a key on a computer keyboard, or a device or key on a typewriter, that advances the next character to a predetermined position, used to align lines or columns ■ *vt* (**tabs, tabbing, tabbed**) to move the cursor on a computer screen from one place in a document to another using the tab key [Early 20C. Shortening of TABULATOR]

tab[3] /tab/ *n* a tablet or piece of paper containing a drug, especially one that is illegal (*informal*) [Mid-20C. Shortening of TABLET]

tab[4] /tab/ *n* THEATRE same as **tableau curtain** [Early 20C. Shortening]

TAB[1] /tab/ *n* in Australia and New Zealand, the agency or company that runs legal betting on horseracing, greyhound-racing, and other sporting events, or a branch of this. In Australia the agency has been privatized, but in New Zealand continues to be state-run. Full form **Totalizator Agency Board**

TAB[2] *abbr* MED typhoid-paratyphoid A-paratyphoid B (vaccine)

tab. *abbr* table

tabanca /tə bángkə/ *n* Carib a painful feeling of unrequited love [Late 19C. Probably < Carib]

tabard (sense 3)

tabard /tábbaard/ *n* **1.** SLEEVELESS OVERGARMENT a sleeveless tunic with slits at the sides, worn by women and girls, especially catering staff **2.** HERALD'S COAT an official coat worn by a herald, bearing the sovereign's coat of arms **3.** HIST KNIGHT'S JACKET a sleeveless or short-sleeved garment worn by a knight over his armour [13C. < Old French *tabart*]

tabaret /tábbərit/ *n* a hard-wearing fabric with alternate satin and watered-silk stripes. Use: upholstery. [Late 18C. Probably < TABBY]

Tabasco[1] /tə báskō/ *tdmk* a trademark for a hot-tasting sauce made from peppers, vinegar, and spices

Tabasco[2] /tə báskō/ state in south-central Mexico, on the southern shores of the Gulf of Mexico. Capital: Villahermosa. Population: 1,891,829 (2000). Area: 24,578 sq. km/9,490 sq. mi.

tabbouleh /tə boó lay/ *n* a Southwest Asian salad made with bulgur wheat and finely chopped tomatoes, mint, and parsley [Mid-20C. < Arabic *tabbūla*]

tabby /tábbi/ *n* (*plural* **-bies**) **1.** STRIPED CAT a brown or grey cat with a striped or mottled coat **2.** PET FEMALE CAT a domestic cat, especially a female one **3.** OFFENSIVE TERM an offensive term for a woman who is considered to be gossipy, spiteful, and interfering (*literary insult*) **4.** TEXTILES SILK WITH STRIPED PATTERN watered silk or taffeta with a striped or wavy pattern **5.** TEXTILES PLAIN FABRIC a plain-woven fabric ■ *adj* **1.** HAVING STRIPED COAT describes a cat that has a brown or grey coat with a striped or mottled pattern **2.** STRIPED OR BRINDLED having a striped or wavy pattern **3.** TEXTILES RESEMBLING TABBY resembling or made of tabby [Late 16C. Via French *tabis* < Arabic *'attābī*, after *al-'Attābiyya*, quarter of Baghdad, Iraq]

ORIGIN It was the stripes on the fabric called *tabby* that led to the application of the word to striped or mottled cats. The usage is first recorded in the 1660s.

tabernacle /tábbər nak'l/ *n* **1.** *also* **Tabernacle** BIBLE TENT FOR CARRYING ARK OF COVENANT in the Bible, a portable tent used as a sanctuary for the Ark of the Covenant by the Israelites during the Exodus **2.** *also* **Tabernacle** JUDAISM JEWISH TEMPLE the Jewish Temple, regarded as representing the presence of God **3.** JUDAISM same as **sukkah 4.** RELIG NONCONFORMIST PLACE OF WORSHIP a place of worship, especially in some nonconformist Christian denominations **5.** CHR CONTAINER FOR HOLY BREAD AND WINE a box or case in which the consecrated bread and wine of Communion are kept **6.** ARCHIT NICHE FOR ICON a canopied recess or niche for an icon **7.** NAUT SOCKET FOR MAST a support for the foot of a ship's mast **8.** HUMAN BODY the human body considered as a place temporarily housing the soul or principle of life (*literary*) [13C. Directly or via French < Latin *tabernaculum* 'tent' < *taberna* 'hut'] —**tabernacular** /tábbər nákyoolər/ *adj*

Tabernacles /tábbər nak'lz/ *n* JUDAISM, CALENDAR same as **Sukkoth**

tabes /táy beez/ (*plural same*) *n* **1.** progressive wasting of the body, usually as a result of a chronic disease **2.** MED same as **tabes dorsalis** [Late 16C. < Latin, 'wasting away'] —**tabetic** /tə béttik/ *adj*

tabes dorsalis /-dawr sáyliss/ *n* a disorder of the nervous system characteristic of late-stage syphilis and marked by degeneration of nerve fibres, wasting, pain, and inability to move the leg muscles. Tabes dorsalis is now rare because syphilis can be effectively treated at a much earlier stage. [< late Latin, 'dorsal tabes']

tabi /taábi/ (*plural* **-bis** or *same*) *n* a Japanese sock with a thick sole and a separate section for the big toe [Early 17C. < Japanese]

tab key *n* a key on a computer keyboard that advances the next character to a predetermined position

tabla /tábblə/ *n* a South Asian musical instrument consisting of a pair of small drums played with the hands [Mid-19C. Via Persian and Hindi < Arabic *ṭabl* 'drum']

tablature /tábləchər/ *n* **1.** a musical notation in which the notes themselves are not represented, but rather the hand positions required to play them. It is used especially in early lute and modern popular guitar music. **2.** a tablet or other flat surface that has been engraved or painted [Late 16C. Via French < Italian *tavolatura* < *tavolare* 'set to music' < *tavola* 'table']

table /táyb'l/ *n* **1.** ITEM OF FURNITURE WITH FLAT TOP a piece of furniture with a flat top and one or more legs, used for placing things on or doing things at **2.** PLACE FOR EATING MEALS WHILE SEATED a table at which people sit to eat meals **3.** PLACE FOR BIRDS' FOOD a tall structure with a flat top and one or more legs, placed outdoors for birds to feed from **4.** FLAT SURFACE FOR SPECIFIC PURPOSE a raised flat surface with a nondomestic or office use, e.g. one at which a surgeon operates or one on which a piece of machinery rests **5.** FOOD SERVED the food provided in a household or restaurant in terms of its quality or quantity **6.** PEOPLE SITTING AT TABLE a group of people sitting at a table, especially for a meal ○ *The whole table erupted in laughter.* **7.** ARRANGEMENT OF INFORMATION IN COLUMNS an arrangement of information or data into columns and rows or a condensed list **8.** MATHS same as **multiplication table** (*informal*) **9.** GEOG same as **tableland 10.** ARCHIT BAND OR PANEL ON WALL a band of masonry or a rectangular panel on a wall, either raised or depressed and with ornamentation or inscriptions **11.** FLAT SURFACE OF GEM the upper horizontal surface of a cut gem **12.** SLAB FOR INSCRIPTION a slab of wood, stone, or metal for inscription **13.** BOARD GAMES PART OF BACKGAMMON BOARD either of the two hinged halves of a backgammon

board **14.** MUSIC **FRONT PART OF STRINGED INSTRUMENT** the part of the body of a stringed instrument that acts as a sounding board **15.** ANAT **PLATE OF BONE** a flat layer of bone, especially either of the inner or outer surfaces of the skull that are separated by a more spongy bone (**diploë**) **16. AREA ON PALM** an area on the palm defined by four lines, regarded as significant in palmistry ■ **tables** *npl* ANCIENT HIST **ANCIENT TABLETS INSCRIBED WITH LAWS** tablets on which some ancient Greek, Roman, and Hebrew laws were inscribed, or the laws themselves ■ *vt* (**-bles, -bling, -bled**) **1.** *UK, Can* **PROPOSE SOMETHING** to put forward a bill, motion, or proposal for discussion at a meeting **2.** *N Am* **POSTPONE DISCUSSION OF SOMETHING** to postpone discussion of a bill or motion until a later time **3. ENTER INFORMATION INTO TABLE** to enter information in a tabular form **4. PUT SOMETHING ON TABLE** to place or lay something on a table [Pre-12C. Directly or via French < Latin *tabula* 'board, slab'] —**tableful** *n* ◇ **drink somebody under the table** to continue drinking until after other people present are completely intoxicated ◇ **on the table** put forward for discussion at a meeting ◇ **turn the tables (on somebody)** to reverse a situation and gain the advantage from somebody who had previously held it

tableau /táblō/ (*plural* **-leaux** /-lōz/ or **-leaus**) *n* **1.** a vivid and wide-ranging description or display **2.** a visually dramatic scene or situation that suddenly arises **3.** THEATRE same as **tableau vivant** [Late 17C. Via French < Old French *tablel* 'small table' < *table* (see TABLE)]

tableau curtain *n* either of a pair of stage curtains that are drawn to each side and upwards by a cord

tableau vivant /táblō vee vaáN/ (*plural* **tableaux vivants** /*pronunc. same*/) *n* a representation of a scene by a group in appropriate costume posing silent and motionless [< French, 'living picture']

Table Bay /táyb'l-/ inlet of the Atlantic Ocean, overlooked by Table Mountain, southwestern South Africa. Length: 19 km/12 mi.

tablecloth /táyb'l kloth/ *n* a cloth for covering a table, especially before it is set for a meal

table dancing *n* a type of erotic dancing or striptease performed on a tabletop in front of a customer or small group of customers

table d'hôte /taáb'l dṓt/ *n* a restaurant meal or menu offering a series of courses at a fixed price [Early 17C. < French, 'host's table']

table football *n UK* a game based on football that is played on a table with rows of small model players. The models are attached to metal poles that pass through the sides of the table and are spun and moved from side to side in order to hit the ball. ANZ, N Am term **foosball**

table knife *n* a knife used at table with a fork for cutting food, especially the food of a main course

tableland /táyb'l land/ *n* an extensive elevated region of flat land

table licence *n* a licence authorizing a restaurant to serve alcoholic drinks only with meals

table manners *npl* actions and behaviour considered to be polite or socially correct when eating a meal with other people

table mat *n* a mat placed under hot dishes to protect the table

Table Mountain flat-topped mountain overlooking Cape Town, southwestern South Africa. Height: 1,086 m/3,563 ft.

table sale *n* same as **jumble sale**

table salt *n* fine salt suitable for use on food that has been served out

table soccer *n NZ* LEISURE same as **table football**

tablespoon /táyb'l spoon/ *n* **1. SERVING SPOON** a large serving spoon a size larger than a dessertspoon **2.** *also* **tablespoonful** /táb'l spoonfəl/ **MEASURE BASED ON CAPACITY OF TABLESPOON** a unit of capacity used in recipes, equal to 15 ml/half a fluid ounce or three teaspoons **3.** *also* **tablespoonful AMOUNT HELD BY TABLESPOON** the amount of food or liquid that a tablespoon can hold

tablet /táblət/ *n* **1. PILL** a small solid pill containing a measured medicinal dose, usually intended to be taken orally **2. SMALL FLAT CAKE OF SOMETHING** a measured amount of something compressed and packaged for ease of use **3. INSCRIBED STONE OR WOODEN SLAB** a slab of stone, wood, or metal used for inscription or engraving **4. SHEETS OF PAPER FASTENED TOGETHER** a number of sheets of paper for writing or drawing, fastened together along one edge **5. SHEET OF MATERIAL TO WRITE ON** a thin stiff sheet of wood, slate, or ivory on which somebody writes **6.** ARCHIT same as **table** (sense 10) **7.** *Scotland* FOOD **SWEET CONFECTIONERY** a confectionery similar to fudge made from sugar, butter, and condensed milk **8. PERSONAL COMPUTER** a small thin portable personal computer that relies on a pen instead of a keyboard to input information [14C. < Old French, 'little table' < *table* (see TABLE)]

table talk *n* **1.** informal conversation on subjects considered suitable during a meal **2.** in bridge, the discussion of bidding and strategy across the table with a partner, which is not permitted by the rules

table tennis *n* a game that resembles tennis and is played with small bats and a light hollow ball on a table divided by a net

tabletop /táyb'l top/ *n* the flat upper surface of a table ■ *adj* designed for use on a tabletop or similar surface

tableware /táyb'l wair/ *n* dishes, plates, glasses, cutlery, and other articles used at meals

table wine *n* an unfortified wine for drinking with meals

tabloid /tábbloyd/ *n* **1.** *also* **tabloid newspaper SMALL NEWSPAPER WITH SHORT ARTICLES** a small-format popular newspaper with a simple style, many photographs, and sometimes an emphasis on sensational stories **2. CONDENSED PIECE OF WRITING** a piece of writing, especially a news story, in a condensed form ■ *adj* **SENSATIONALIST** relating to or characteristic of tabloid newspapers, especially in having a popular sensationalist style [Late 19C. < proprietary name for tablets of condensed medicine]

ORIGIN ***Tabloid*** was registered as a proprietary name for a brand of tablet in 1884 by Burroughs, Wellcome, and Company. It was the underlying notion of 'compression' or 'condensation' that led to its application to newspapers of small page size and 'condensed' versions of news stories that emerged at the beginning of the 20th century.

taboo /tə bóo/, **tabu** *adj* **1. SOCIALLY OR CULTURALLY PROHIBITED** forbidden to be used, mentioned, or approached because of social or cultural rather than legal prohibitions **2. UNACCEPTABLE** not acceptable or healthful (*humorous*) ○ *Sweets and fats are strictly taboo.* **3.** RELIG **SACRED AND PROHIBITED** set apart as sacred and at the same time forbidden to be used ■ *n* (*plural* **-boos;** *plural* **-bus**) **1. PROHIBITION** a prohibition or rejection of some types of behaviour or language because they are considered socially unacceptable **2. FORBIDDEN BEHAVIOUR** a subject or behaviour that is forbidden or disapproved of because it is considered socially unacceptable **3.** RELIG **PROHIBITION ON GROUNDS OF BEING SACRED** the practice, especially in some Polynesian societies, of regarding some things, people, or types of behaviour as sacred and therefore forbidden to be used, made contact with, or engaged in ■ *vt* (**-boos, -booing, -booed; -bus, -buing, -bued**) **1. FORBID OR DISCOURAGE SOMETHING** to prohibit or disapprove of some types of behaviour or language because they are considered socially unacceptable **2.** RELIG **PROHIBIT SOMETHING BECAUSE SACRED** to regard some things, people, or types of behaviour as sacred and therefore forbidden to be used, made contact with, or engaged in [Late 18C. < Polynesian *tabu*]

tabor /táybər/, **tabour** *n* a small drum played with one hand while the other hand plays a pipe. Tabors were used especially in the Middle Ages. [13C. < Old French *tabour*] —**taborer** *n*

Tabor, Mount /táybər/ peak in northern Israel, east of Nazareth. In the Bible, it is the site of the transfiguration of Jesus Christ. Height: 588 m/1,929 ft.

Tabora /ta báwrə/ capital city of Tabora Region, west-central Tanzania, situated about 354 km/220 mi. northwest of Dodoma. Population: 960,000 (1995).

taboret /tábbə rét/, **tabouret** *n* **1.** a low solid seat without arms or a back **2.** HANDICRAFT same as **tambour** *n* (sense 1) **3.** a small tabor or tambourine [Mid-17C. < French, 'small tabor']

tabour *n* MUSIC another spelling of **tabor**

Tabriz /tə bréez/ city in northwestern Iran, capital of East Azerbaijan Province. Tabriz has been severely damaged over the centuries by earthquakes. Population: 1,191,043 (1996).

tabu *adj, n, vt* CULTL ANTHROP, RELIG another spelling of **taboo**

tabular /tábbyŏŏlər/ *adj* **1. ARRANGED IN TABLE** arranged in a table or in columns and rows **2. HAVING FLAT SURFACE** having a flat surface that resembles a table **3.** CRYSTALS **BROAD AND FLAT** describes crystals that are broad and flat **4.** GEOL **SPLITTING INTO THIN PLATES** describes rock that is made up of and splits readily into thin horizontal plates **5.** MATHS **COMPUTED USING TABLE** calculated with or making use of a table, e.g. of logarithms [Mid-17C. < Latin *tabularis* < *tabula* 'board, slab'] —**tabularly** *adv*

tabula rasa /tábbyŏŏlə raázə/ (*plural* **tabulae rasae** /tábbyŏŏ lee raázee/) *n* **1.** the mind at birth, regarded as having no innate conceptions **2.** an opportunity to make a clean break or a fresh start [Mid-16C. < Latin, 'scraped table']

tabularize /tábbyŏŏlə rīz/ (**-izes, -izing, -ized**), **tabularise** (**-ises, -ising, -ised**) *vt* same as **tabulate** *v* (sense 1) — **tabularization** /tábbyŏŏlə rī záysh'n/ *n*

tabulate /tábbyŏŏ layt/ *vt* (**-lates, -lating, -lated**) **1. ARRANGE INFORMATION IN TABLE** to arrange information systematically in a table or in columns and rows **2. MAKE SOMETHING FLAT** to give a flat top or upper surface to something (*usually passive*) ■ *adj* **FLAT** with a flat surface that resembles a table [Late 16C. < late Latin *tabulatus* < Latin *tabula* 'board, slab'] —**tabulable** *adj* — **tabulation** /tábbyŏŏ láysh'n/ *n*

tabulator /tábbyŏŏ laytər/ *n* **1.** a person or device that tabulates information **2.** COMPUT same as **tab**[2]

tabun /taa bóon/ *n* an organic phosphorus compound. Use: lethal chemical weapon. Formula: $C_5H_{11}N_2O_2P$. [Mid-20C. < German]

tacamahac /tákəmə hak/, **tacmahack** /tákmə-/ *n* **1.** a resinous tree gum. Use: ointments, incense. **2.** a tree that yields tacamahac resin, especially the balsam poplar [Late 16C. Via obsolete Spanish *tacamahaca* < Nahuatl *tecomahiyac*]

Tacan /ták an/ *n* an aircraft navigation system using UHF signals emitted from a transmitting station to determine distance and bearing [Mid-20C. Acronym < TACTICAL + AIR + NAVIGATION]

tacet /táy set/ *n* a musical direction instructing a musician not to play or sing a passage or phrase [Early 18C. < Latin, '(it is silent' < *tacere* 'be silent']

tach /tak/ *n N Am* same as **tachometer** (*informal*) [Mid-20C. Shortening]

tache *n* another spelling of **tash** (*informal*)

tacheometry /táki ómmətri/ *n* CONSTR same as **tachymetry** —**tacheometric** /táki ə méttrik/ *adj* —**tacheometrical** *adj* —**tacheometrically** *adv*

tachina fly /tákinə-/ *n* a bristly fly whose larvae live as parasites on other insects. They are sometimes used to control harmful insect species. Family: Tachinidae. [< modern Latin *Tachina* < Greek *takhinos* 'swift']

tachinid /tákənid/ *n* INSECTS same as **tachina fly** ■ *adj* relating to the family of insects that the tachina fly belongs to [Late 19C. < modern Latin *Tachinidae* < *Tachina* (see TACHINA FLY)]

tachism /táshizəm/, **tachisme** *n* action painting in which random blotches of colour are used as a method of instinctive expression [Mid-20C. < French *tachisme* < *tache* 'spot'] —**tachist** *n, adj*

tachistoscope /tə kístə skōp/ *n* an instrument for displaying visual images very briefly, used to test perception and memory [Late 19C. < Greek *takhistos* 'swiftest' < *takhus* 'swift'] —**tachistoscopic** /tə kístə skóppik/ *adj* —**tachistoscopically** *adv*

tachogram /tákə gram/ *n* a record in graph form produced by a tachograph

tachograph /tákə graaf, -graf/ *n* an instrument that produces a record of the use and readings of a tachometer, especially one in a commercial vehicle or coach recording speeds and distances travelled. In effect, a tachograph records the hours worked by a driver. [Early 20C. < Greek *takhos* 'speed']

tachometer /ta kómmitər/ n a device used to determine speed of rotation, typically of a vehicle's crankshaft, usually measured in revolutions per minute [Early 19C. < Greek *takhos* 'speed'] —**tachometric** /tákə méttrik/ adj —**tachometrically** adv —**tachometry** n

tachy- prefix accelerated, rapid ○ *tachygraphy* [< Greek *takhus* 'swift']

tachyarrhythmia /táki ə ríthmi ə/ n a medical condition in which the heartbeat is fast and irregular

tachycardia /táki ka̒ardi ə/ n an excessively rapid heartbeat, typically regarded as a heart rate exceeding 100 beats per minute in a resting adult [Late 19C. < TACHY- + Greek *kardia* 'heart'] —**tachycardiac** adj —**tachycardic** adj

tachygraphy /ta kíggrəfi/ n 1. the shorthand system used by the ancient Greeks and Romans 2. the abbreviated cursive writing used in medieval times for Latin and Greek —**tachygrapher** n —**tachygraphic** /táki gráffik/ adj —**tachygraphically** adv —**tachygraphist** n

tachylite /táki līt/, **tachylyte** n black volcanic glass formed by the chilling of basaltic magma [Mid-19C. < German *Tachylyt* < Greek *takhu-* 'quickly', from its rapid decomposition in acids, + *lutos* 'soluble'] —**tachylitic** /táki líttik/ adj

tachymetry /ta kímmətri/ n the measurement of distances, elevations, and directions at speed using a type of theodolite —**tachymeter** n —**tachymetric** /táki méttrik/ adj —**tachymetrically** adv

tachyon /táki on/ n a hypothetical elementary particle that always travels faster than the speed of light

tachypnea n MED US spelling of **tachypnoea**

tachypnoea /tákip neé ə/ n unusually fast breathing, generally considered to be over 20 breaths per minute in a resting adult [Late 19C. < TACHY- + Greek *pnoiē* 'breathing' < *pnein* 'breathe']

tacit /tássit/ adj understood or implied without being stated openly [Early 17C. < Latin *tacitus*, past participle of *tacere* 'be silent'] —**tacitly** adv —**tacitness** n

taciturn /tássi turn/ adj habitually uncommunicative or reserved in speech and manner [Late 18C. Via French *taciturne* < Latin *taciturnus* < *tacitus* (see TACIT)] —**taciturnity** /tássi túrnəti/ n —**taciturnly** adv

SYNONYMS See *silent*.

Tacitus /tássitəss/ (AD 55?–117?) Roman historian. The author of histories of the Roman Empire, he also held various government posts and was famed as an orator. Full name **Tacitus, Gaius Cornelius**

'It is part of human nature to hate the man you have hurt.'
[Tacitus, *De Vita Iulii Agricola (Agricola)*; 98?]

tack[1] /tak/ n 1. SMALL NAIL a small sharp nail with a broad head 2. COURSE OF ACTION a course of action or method of approach intended to achieve something, especially one adopted after another has failed 3. SAILING CHANGE IN DIRECTION OF SAILING a change in the direction of movement of a sailing boat made in order to maximize the benefit from the wind 4. SAILING PART OF ZIGZAG SAILING COURSE a stage or series of stages in the zigzag movement of a sailing boat that is changing direction in order to maximize the benefit from the wind 5. SAILING DIRECTION OF SAILING the direction of movement of a sailing boat in relation to the side from which the wind is blowing, effected by the position of its sails 6. SAILING ROPE HOLDING DOWN SAIL a rope holding down the corner of some sails, or the corner that is held down 7. HANDICRAFT TEMPORARY STITCH a long loose temporary stitch, often used to align seams in preparation for final sewing 8. SLIGHT STICKINESS slight stickiness, e.g. of glue or paint that has not yet dried ■ v (**tacks, tacking, tacked**) 1. vt ATTACH SOMETHING WITH DRAWING PIN to attach something light to a board or wall with a drawing pin 2. vt CONSTR FASTEN SOMETHING WITH TACKS to attach something with small sharp broad-headed nails 3. vi CHANGE APPROACH to take a different course of action or use a different method 4. vt PUT THINGS TOGETHER ARBITRARILY to bring different things together to form an arbitrary or illusory whole 5. vti SAILING CHANGE DIRECTION OF SAILING BOAT to change the direction or course of a sailing boat or ship, or steer a sailing boat or ship on alternate tacks, or be sailed or steered in this

way 6. vt HANDICRAFT to sew something with long loose temporary stitches. N Am term **baste**[3] [14C. < Old N French *taque* 'fastening' < Germanic]
tack on vt to add something to something else either as a supplement or an afterthought

tack[2] /tak/ n saddles, bridles, and other parts of a horse's harness [Late 18C. Shortening of TACKLE]

tack[3] /tak/ n goods that are tasteless and vulgar or cheap and shoddy (*informal*) [Late 20C. Back-formation < TACKY[2]]

tack[4] /tak/ n foodstuff, especially of the poor quality fed to a ship's crew in the days of sailing ships (*slang*) [Late 16C. Origin ?]

tackboard /ták bawrd/ n US same as **noticeboard** (*informal*)

tacket /tákit/ n N England, Scotland a nail or hobnail

tackety boots /tákəti-/ npl Scotland hobnail boots (*informal*)

tackie n S Africa CLOTHING another spelling of **takkie** (*informal*)

tackle /ták'l/ n 1. ATTEMPT TO STOP OPPONENT'S PROGRESS in football, hockey, and some other games, a physical challenge against an opposing player who has the ball. A tackle is made using the foot in football, the stick in hockey, and in rugby and American football by seizing and forcing the opponent to the ground. 2. SPECIALIZED EQUIPMENT the equipment used for a specialized activity such as angling or rock climbing 3. MECH ENG ROPES AND PULLEYS a mechanical arrangement consisting of ropes and pulleys used for lifting heavy weights through increased mechanical advantage 4. SAILING SHIP'S RIGGING the gear and rigging of a sailing ship or boat 5. GENITALS a man's genitals (*slang; sometimes offensive*) 6. AMERICAN FOOTBALL LINEMAN NEXT TO END in American football, a lineman positioned between a guard and an end, or the position of such a player ■ vt (**-les, -ling, -led**) 1. UNDERTAKE PROJECT to undertake or deal with something that requires effort 2. CONFRONT SOMEBODY to open a conversation or discussion on a difficult issue with somebody who would prefer to avoid it ○ *Have you tackled them about paying for it?* 3. SPORTS MAKE TACKLE ON SOMEBODY in football, hockey, and some other games, to make a physical challenge against an opposing player 4. HARNESS ANIMAL to put a harness on an animal, especially a horse [13C. Probably < Low German *takel* 'ship's rigging' < *taken* 'seize'] —**tackler** n

tacksman /táksmən/ n (plural **-men** /-mən/) n Scotland in former times, a leaseholder, especially one who sublet land [Mid-16C. < Scots and N English *tack* 'tenure' < Old Norse *tak* 'hold']

tack welding n the welding of two metals by individual welds at isolated points

tacky[1] /táki/ (**-ier, -iest**) adj slightly sticky to the touch [Late 18C. < TACK[1]] —**tackily** adv —**tackiness** n

tacky[2] /táki/ (**-ier, -iest**) adj (*informal*) 1. perceived as vulgar, lacking in taste, or no longer fashionable 2. appearing to be cheaply made or in need of repair [Early 19C. Origin ?] —**tackily** adv —**tackiness** n

Tacloban /táklō ban/ port and city on Leyte Island in central Philippines. During World War II, US forces landed on beaches south of the city at the start of a campaign to liberate the Philippines. Population: 137,200 (1990).

taco /tákō/ (plural **-cos**) n a crisp fried maize tortilla usually filled with meat, lettuce or cabbage, tomatoes, cheese, and hot sauce [Mid-20C. Via American Spanish < Spanish, 'wad']

Tacoma /tə kốmə/ city in western Washington State, a deep-water port on Commencement Bay, an arm of Puget Sound. Population: 197,553 (2002 estimate).

taconite /tákə nīt/ n a banded iron formation consisting of layers of the iron oxides magnetite and haematite that may be extracted from pulverized rock using a magnet [Early 20C. After *Taconic*, mountain range in New York State]

tact /takt/ n 1. skill in situations in which other people's feelings have to be considered 2. an intuitive sense of what is right or appropriate [Early 17C. Via French < Latin *tactus* '(sense of) touch' < *tangere* 'to touch']

tactful /táktf'l/ adj having or showing concern about

upsetting or offending people —**tactfully** adv —**tactfulness** n

tactic /táktik/ n a method used or a course of action followed in order to achieve an immediate or short-term aim [Mid-17C. Via modern Latin < Greek *taktikos* 'of arrangement' < *taktos* 'arranged' < *tassein* 'arrange']

tactical /táktik'l/ adj 1. OF TACTICS relating to or involving tactics 2. AS MEANS TO END done or made for the purpose of trying to achieve an immediate or short-term aim 3. SHOWING SKILFUL PLANNING showing skilful planning in order to accomplish something 4. MIL WITH LIMITED MILITARY OBJECTIVE used to support limited military operations ○ *tactical forces* 5. MIL FOR SHORT DISTANCE designed to be used over a short distance ○ *tactical weapons* 6. MIL SUPPORTING OTHER MILITARY OBJECTIVE undertaken or for use in support of other military and naval operations ○ *tactical bombing* —**tactically** adv

tactical voting n the act of voting for the second strongest candidate in an election with a view to preventing the strongest candidate from winning

tactics /táktiks/ n the science of organizing and manoeuvring forces in battle to achieve a limited or immediate aim (*takes a singular verb*) ■ npl the art of finding and implementing means to achieve immediate or short-term aims (*takes a plural verb*) —**tactician** /tak tísh'n/ n

tactile /ták tīl/ adj 1. OF TOUCH relating to or used for the sense of touch 2. TANGIBLE capable of being perceived by the sense of touch 3. PLEASANT TO TOUCH pleasing or interesting to the sense of touch 4. HABITUALLY TOUCHING PEOPLE inclined to touch people a lot, e.g. while talking to them 5. ARTS APPARENTLY THREE-DIMENSIONAL giving an illusion of physical solidity and tangibility [Early 17C. Directly or via French < Latin *tactilis* < *tactus* (see TACT)] —**tactilely** adv —**tactility** /tak tílləti/ n

tactile corpuscle, **tactile bud** n a tiny egg-shaped touch receptor that responds to light pressure and is found in the skin of the palms, lips, soles, and other hairless sensitive areas

tactless /táktləss/ adj not concerned about upsetting or offending people, or showing a lack of such concern —**tactlessly** adv —**tactlessness** n

tactual /tákchoo əl/ adj relating to the sense of touch, or imparting the sensation of contact [Mid-17C. < Latin *tactus* (see TACT)] —**tactually** adv

tad /tad/ n a very slight amount or degree of something (*informal*) [Late 19C. Origin ?] ◊ **a tad** somewhat

tadjah /taa ja̒a/ n Carib ISLAM same as **tazia** [Late 20C. Variant]

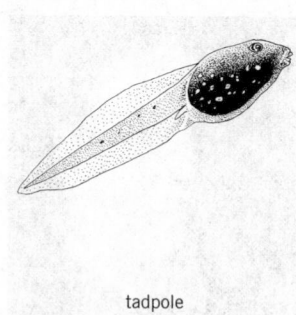
tadpole

tadpole /tád pōl/ n the larva of a frog, toad, or salamander that has a limbless rounded body, gills, and a tail [15C. < earlier forms of TOAD + POLL]

Tadzhik, etc. n, adj PEOPLES, LANG another spelling of **Tajik**, etc.

Tae Bo /tí bố/ n a fitness regime based on exercising to music and performing movements that derive from martial arts such as tae kwon dò [Late 20C. < TAE KWON DO + BOXING]

taedium vitae /teédi əm veé tī/ n the feeling of being weary of or disgusted with life [Mid-18C. < Latin]

Taegu /tí goó/ city in southern South Korea, capital of North Kyongsang Province. It is an important industrial, agricultural, and commercial centre. Population: 2,449,139 (1995).

Taejon /ta jón -jáwn/ city in central South Korea, capital of South Ch'ungch'ong Province. It is a major road and rail junction, industrial and agricultural centre. Population: 1,049,578 (1990).

tae kwon do /tī kwon dố/ *n* a Korean martial art resembling karate but also employing a wide range of kicking moves [Mid-20C. < Korean, 'art of hand and foot fighting']

tael /tayl/ *n* **1.** a varying unit of weight used in East Asia, usually around 38 g/1.75 oz **2.** a silver coin that was a unit of currency in China between 1889 and 1912, equivalent to a tael of silver [Late 16C. Via Portuguese < Malay *tahil*, unit of weight]

taenia /teéni ə/ (*plural* **-niae** /-ni ee/) *n* **1.** ANAT PART SHAPED LIKE RIBBON a body part that resembles a ribbon, especially muscle or nervous tissue **2.** ARCHIT HORIZONTAL BAND IN DORIC ARCHITECTURE in the Doric order of ancient Greek architecture, a narrow band (**fillet**) between the main beam (**architrave**) across the top of the columns and the frieze above **3.** ZOOL PARASITIC TAPEWORM a large parasitic tapeworm. Genus: *Taenia*. **4.** CLOTHING NARROW HEADBAND a fillet or headband worn in ancient Greece [Mid-16C. Via Latin < Greek *tainia* 'band']

taeniacide /teéni ə sīd/ *n* a substance for killing tapeworms

taeniafuge /teéni ə fyóoj/ *n* a drug or other agent that expels tapeworms from the body

taeniasis /tee nī əssiss/ *n* infestation with adult tapeworms, usually following the eating of raw or undercooked meat containing tapeworm larvae

TAFE /tayf/ *n* in Australia, a system of higher education providing instruction in technical subjects. Full form **Technical and Further Education**

taffeta /táffitə/ *n* a stiff lustrous silk or a silky fabric with a slight rib. Use: women's clothes. [14C. Via medieval Latin or Old French *taffetas* < Persian *tāftah* < *tāftan* 'to shine']

taffrail /táf rayl/ *n* **1.** the rail round the stern of a ship **2.** the upper flat and often carved part of a ship's stern [Early 19C. < Dutch *taffereel* 'small table' < *tafel* 'table']

taffy /táffi/ *n* **1.** N Am a chewy confectionery made of sugar or molasses boiled down and pulled until glossy and light in colour **2.** flattery of an insincere kind (*dated informal*) [Early 19C. Probably dialect form of TOFFEE]

Taffy /táffi/ (*plural* **-fies**) *n* an offensive term for a Welsh person (*slang*) [Mid-17C. < the alleged Welsh pronunciation of the forename *David*]

REGIONAL NOTE See **man**.

Bettmann/Corbis
William Howard Taft

Taft /taft/, **William Howard** (1857–1930) 27th president of the United States. A Republican, he was president from 1909 to 1913 and chief justice of the US Supreme Court from 1921 to 1930. See table at **president**

'Well, I have one consolation. No candidate was ever elected ex-president by such a large majority!'
[Attributed to William Howard Taft, referring to his disastrous defeat by Woodrow Wilson in the 1912 presidential election.]

tag[1] /tag/ *n* **1.** LABEL a small piece of cloth, paper, plastic, or other material attached to something as a label or means of identification **2.** TIP AT END OF SHOELACE a plastic or metal tip attached to the end of a shoelace or cord to prevent it from fraying **3.** SMALL LOOSE OR RAGGED PIECE a small piece of a material hanging loosely or raggedly from the main piece **4.** COMPUT CLASSIFYING LABEL FOR DATA a label that describes a piece of data, e.g. to facilitate later retrieval or text formatting **5.** CRIME ELECTRONIC DEVICE WORN BY OFFENDER an electronic device worn, usually on the ankle or wrist, by a convicted offender serving a sentence in the community to allow his or her movements to be monitored **6.** ZOOL TIP OF ANIMAL'S TAIL the tip of an animal's tail, especially if in a contrasting colour with the rest of the tail **7.** AGRIC, ZOOL MATTED LOCK OF WOOL a dirty matted lock of wool or hair in an animal's fleece or coat **8.** FISHING ATTACHMENT TO ARTIFICIAL FLY a piece of usually brightly coloured material tied around the shank of the hook in the body of an artificial fly **9.** LITERAT WELL-KNOWN QUOTATION a well-known or hackneyed quotation, often in Latin, usually intended to add dignity or weight to a speech or piece of writing **10.** LANGUAGE EPITHET a descriptive word or phrase used, especially frequently, about somebody or something **11.** LITERAT ENDING FOR PIECE OF WRITING something ending or added to a piece of writing, e.g. a refrain, the cue line ending an actor's speech, or a final speech addressed to the audience **12.** LING same as **tag question 13.** GRAFFITI ARTIST'S SIGNATURE a signature or identifying symbol used by a graffiti artist ■ *v* (**tags, tagging, tagged**) **1.** *vt* LABEL SOMETHING WITH TAG to attach a tag to something or label something with a tag **2.** *vt* ADD SOMETHING AT END to add an additional piece or section to the end of something, especially a piece of writing ○ *tagged on a couple of extra lines at the end* **3.** *vt* ATTACH EPITHET TO SOMEBODY to give somebody a nickname, or assign a verbal label to somebody **4.** *vt* CRIME ATTACH ELECTRONIC TAG TO OFFENDER to make an offender wear an electronic tag **5.** *vt* US LAW TICKET CAR to attach a ticket to a vehicle to notify the driver that a traffic or parking offence has been committed **6.** *vt* US LAW CHARGE SOMEBODY WITH CRIME to charge somebody with a crime (*often passive*) ○ *He was tagged for theft.* **7.** *vt* ATTACH RHYMES TO TEXT to put unrhymed verse or prose into rhyme **8.** *vt* AGRIC REMOVE TAGS FROM ANIMAL to remove tags from the fleece or coat of an animal **9.** *vti* FOLLOW CLOSELY to follow closely behind somebody [15C. Origin ?]

tag along *vi* to accompany or follow somebody, often when your presence is unwanted

tag[2] /tag/ *n* **1.** LEISURE CHILDREN'S CHASING AND TOUCHING GAME a children's game in which one player is chosen to chase the others and try to touch one of them. Anyone touched becomes 'it' and is then the player who does the chasing. **2.** BASEBALL INSTANCE OF PUTTING RUNNER OUT in baseball, an instance of getting a runner out by touching him or her with the ball before he or she reaches the base **3.** WRESTLING same as **tag wrestling 4.** WRESTLING INSTANCE OF SWITCHING PLACES IN WRESTLING in wrestling, an instance of touching a partner's hand in order to switch places ■ *vt* (**tags, tagging, tagged**) **1.** CATCH PLAYER IN GAME OF TAG in the children's game of tag, to touch a player making that player 'it' **2.** BASEBALL TOUCH RUNNER WITH BALL in baseball, to get a runner out by touching him or her with the ball before he or she reaches the base **3.** WRESTLING TOUCH PARTNER'S HAND IN WRESTLING in tag wrestling, to touch the hand of a partner in order to switch places **4.** Aus MARK OPPONENT in Australian Rules football, to mark an opponent [Mid-18C. Origin ?]

tag up *vi* in baseball, to touch a base before running to the next one after a fly ball is caught

Tagalog /tə gáalog, -gáaləg, -gállog/ (*plural* **-logs** or same) *n* **1.** a member of a people who originally lived in the Manila area of the Philippines **2.** the Austronesian language of the Tagalog people, the basis of Filipino. Native speakers: 17 million. [Early 19C. < Tagalog *tagá* 'native' + *ilog* 'river'] —**Tagalog** *adj*

tag day *n* N Am same as **flag day**

tag end *n* **1.** a loose or detached piece of something **2.** N Am the very last or last remaining part of something

tagetes /ta jeé teez/ *n* a small bushy garden plant with many flowers and strongly aromatic foliage. It is related to marigolds. Flowers: small, yellow to orange. Latin name: *Tagetes*. [Late 18C. < modern Latin *Tagetes* < Latin *Tages*, an Etruscan god]

tagged image file format /tagd-/ *n* COMPUT full form of **TIFF**

tagger /tággər/ *n* a graffiti artist who spray-paints his or her name or symbol on a public structure (*slang*)

taggers /tággərz/ *npl* iron or steel in thin sheets coated with tin [Mid-19C. Perhaps because used to make shoelace tags]

tagine /tə zheén/ *n* **1.** a cooking pot with a high cone-shaped earthenware lid and a cast-iron or earthenware base, used especially for stews in Moroccan cookery and requiring little liquid **2.** a Moroccan stew cooked very slowly in a tagine and consisting usually of meat or poultry combined with fruit [< Arabic *tajin*]

tagliatelle /tállyə télli/ *n* pasta in the form of long narrow ribbons [Late 19C. < Italian < *tagliare* 'cut into strips']

tag line *n* US **1.** the final line of a joke, story, or drama, delivering a humorous or dramatic point **2.** a phrase repeatedly used in connection with a person, organization, or product, especially in publicity

tagma /tágmə/ (*plural* **-mata** /-mətə/) *n* a distinct functional region of the body of an arthropod, e.g. a thorax [Early 20C. < Greek, 'something arranged' < *tag-*, stem of *tassein* 'arrange']

tagmeme /tág meem/ *n* any of the various positions in the structure of a sentence into which a word or phrase of a specific grammatical type can fit [Mid-20C < Greek *tagma* (see TAGMA)] —**tagmemic** /tag meémik/ *adj*

tagmemics /tag meémiks/ *n* a grammatical analysis of language based on the way in which the different elements that make up a sentence are arranged within it (*takes a singular verb*)

Popperfoto
Rabindranath Tagore

Tagore /tə gáwr/, **Rabindranath** (1861–1941) Indian writer. A prolific writer of poetry, plays, short stories, and novels, he revolutionized Bengali poetry by using colloquial language and new verse forms, and translated his own works into English. He was awarded the Nobel Prize in literature (1913).

tag question *n* a short clause added on to a statement to turn it into a question, e.g. 'don't you?' or 'isn't it?', or a statement with a question clause attached. The main function of a tag question is to cue a response from the listener or obtain his or her agreement to the original statement.

tag team *n* a team of two or more wrestlers, only one of whom may wrestle at a time. Wrestlers can change places only after touching hands.

taguan /tág wan/ *n* a large nocturnal flying squirrel that leaps from tree to tree with the help of skin flaps that stretch between its limbs. Native to: Southeast Asia. Latin name: *Petaurista petaurista*. [Early 19C. Probably < local name in the Philippines]

tague *n* Ireland another spelling of **taig** (*slang offensive*)

Tagus /táygəss/ longest river of the Iberian Peninsula, in southwestern Europe. It enters the Atlantic Ocean at Lisbon, Portugal. Length: 1,007 km/626 mi. Portuguese name **Tejo**. Spanish name **Tajo**

tag wrestling *n* a form of wrestling in which wrestlers compete in teams of two or more, taking turns to enter the ring, a touch of hands being required for a changeover

tahini /tə héeni/, **tahina** /-nə/ *n* an oily paste made from crushed sesame seeds. Use: seasoning. [Mid-20C. < Arabic *ṭaḥīnā* < *ṭaḥana* 'grind']

Tahiti /tə héeti/ island of French Polynesia, the largest of the Society Islands, in the southern Pacific Ocean. Population: 115,820 (1998). Area: 1,000 sq. km/400 sq. mi. —**Tahitian** /tə heésh'n/ *n, adj*

Tahoe, Lake /taáhō/ lake in the western United States, situated on the border of Nevada and California. Area: 497 sq. km/192 sq. mi.

tahr /taar/ *n* a cud-chewing animal similar to a goat, with a shaggy coat and curved horns. Native to: mountains in South Asia. Genus: *Hemitragus.* [Mid-19C. < Nepalese *thār*]

tahsil /taa seél/ *n* in parts of South Asia, an administrative district [Mid-19C. Via Urdu and Persian < *taḥṣīl* 'revenue' < Arabic *ḥaṣala* 'collect']

tahsildar /taa seél daar/ *n* in parts of South Asia, a government official in charge of collecting taxes and other revenues in a tahsil [Late 18C. Via Urdu *taḥṣīldār* < Persian, 'revenue-holder' < *taḥṣīl* (see TAHSIL)]

Tai /tī/ *n* a group of tonal languages spoken in Southeast Asia, including Thai and Lao. Tai is sometimes considered to be related to the Sino-Tibetan language family. [Late 17C. Variant of THAI] —**Tai** *adj*

taiaha /tī́ ə haa/ *n NZ* a carved Maori staff, formerly used as a weapon, now carried by speakers at public ceremonies [Mid-19C. < Maori]

tai chi /tī́ cheé/, **T'ai Chi** /tī́ cheé/, **t'ai chi ch'uan** /tī́ cheé chwaán/, **T'ai Chi Ch'uan, Tai Chi Chuan** *n* a Chinese form of physical exercise characterized by a series of very slow and deliberate balletic body movements [Mid 18C. < Chinese, literally 'extreme limit']

taig /tayg/, **tague, teigue** *n N Ireland* an offensive term for a Roman Catholic (*slang*) [Late 20C. < the Irish name *Tadhg*]

taiga /tī́gə/ *n* the subarctic coniferous forests located south of the tundra in North America, northern Europe, and Asia [Late 19C. < Russian]

taihoa /tī́ hō ə/ *NZ interj* used to tell somebody to slow down, wait, or be patient for a short while ■ *n* procrastination [Mid-19C. < Maori]

tail /tayl/ *n* **1.** REAR PART OF ANIMAL'S BODY the flexible rear part, or a movable extension to the rear part, of a vertebrate animal's body that begins above the anus and often contains the terminal vertebrae **2.** LAST PART the rear, last, or lowest part of something ○ *the tail of the procession* **3.** AVIAT REAR OF AIRCRAFT the rear part of an aircraft together with the fin and the tailplane **4.** ARMS REAR OF MISSILE the rear part of a missile or bomb, including structures for controlling the angle of the trajectory **5.** COINS REVERSE OF COIN the reverse side of a coin **6.** ASTRON STREAM OF GAS FROM COMET the luminous stream of gas and dust particles driven by the solar wind from a comet as it approaches and then recedes from the Sun **7.** PEOPLE IN QUEUE a queue of people or things **8.** HAIR LONG PIECE OF HAIR a long lock or braid of hair **9.** PRINTING BOTTOM OF PAGE the bottom of a printed page, or the margin between the bottom of the page and the lowest line of type **10.** CLOTHING LONG PART OF SHIRT the part of a shirt that hangs below the waist and is typically tucked into trousers **11.** CLOTHING LONG PART OF FORMAL COAT either of two long panels at the back of a man's formal coat **12.** SOMEBODY FOLLOWING ANOTHER a secret follower or observer of somebody (*informal*) ○ *The police put a round-the-clock tail on the suspect.* **13.** TRAIL somebody's trail, especially when being followed or pursued (*informal*) **14.** HIST same as **horsetail** (sense 2) **15.** BOTTOM the buttocks (*informal*) **16.** TABOO TERM a highly offensive term meaning a woman's genitals (*taboo*) **17.** *N Am* TABOO TERM a highly offensive term meaning sexual intercourse with a woman (*taboo*) **18.** TABOO TERM a highly offensive term meaning a woman perceived as a potential partner for sexual intercourse (*taboo*) ■ **tails** *npl* **1.** CLOTHING MAN'S FORMAL COAT a formal, usually black coat for a man, cut short at the front and with two long panels at the back **2.** CLOTHING MAN'S EVENING CLOTHES full evening clothes for a man **3.** TAIL OF COIN the reverse side of a coin turned up after a toss ■ *v* (**tails, tailing, tailed**) **1.** *vt* FOLLOW SOMEBODY SECRETLY to follow somebody secretly in order to keep watch on him or her (*informal*) ○ *Someone must have tailed you back to the house.* **2.** *vi* FOLLOW to follow behind somebody or something ○ *She strode out purposefully, leaving the rest of the party to tail along behind.* **3.** *vi* FORM LINE to form a long line when moving, especially a long spread-out line **4.** *vt* VET REMOVE TAIL OF ANIMAL to remove or cut short the tail of an animal **5.** *vt* REMOVE STALK FROM FRUIT to remove the stalk from something such as a piece of fruit **6.** *vt* JOIN THINGS END TO END to join two or more things end to end **7.** *vti* CONSTR BUILD, OR BE BUILT, INTO WALL to build one end of something such as a joist, beam, or brick, into a wall, or be fixed into a wall at one end **8.** *vi* NAUT LIE WITH STERN IN PARTICULAR DIRECTION to lie with the stern pointing in a particular direction when moored (*refers to a boat*) [Old English *tægel* < Germanic] —**tailless** *adj* ◇ **the tail wagging the dog** used for indicating that a situation is ridiculous because something of less importance is in control of something more important (*informal*) ◇ **turn tail** to turn and walk or run away, especially in a cowardly way ◇ **with your tail between your legs** in an abject ashamed manner (*informal*)

SPELLCHECK tail or **tale**? Do not confuse the spelling of ***tail*** and ***tale***, which sound similar. ***Tail*** can be used as a noun, meaning 'the rear part of something, e.g. an animal, aircraft, or comet', or as a verb meaning 'to follow behind': *The dog wagged its tail. She was being tailed by a private detective.* ***Tale*** is only used as a noun, meaning 'a narrative' and also 'an untrue report', as in *traditional folk tales, telling tales out of school.*

SYNONYMS See ***follow.***

tail off, tail away *vi* to grow less, smaller, or fainter, usually gradually

tailback /táyl bak/ *n* a queue of stationary or slow-moving traffic caused by an obstruction ahead

tail beam *n* CONSTR same as **tailpiece** (sense 4)

tailboard /táyl bawrd/ *n* TRANSP same as **tailgate** *n* (sense 1)

tailbone /táyl bōn/ *n* ANAT same as **coccyx**

tail coat *n* a formal, usually black coat for a man, cut short at the front and with two long tails at the back

tail end *n* **1.** the last or hindmost part of something **2.** the buttocks (*informal*)

tailender /tayl éndər/ *n* somebody or something that comes at or towards the end of something (*informal*)

tail fan *n* a fan-shaped structure at the rear end of some crustaceans such as the lobster

tailfin /táyl fin/ *n* the fin attached to the tail of a fish

tailgate /táyl gayt/ *n* **1.** GATE AT BACK OF VEHICLE a gate at the back of a lorry that can be laid flat or dropped down during loading or unloading **2.** REAR DOOR the hinged rear door of a hatchback **3.** *also* **tail gate** GATE IN WATERWAY a gate controlling the flow of water at the lower end of a lock in a waterway ■ *vti* (**-gates, -gating, -gated**) DRIVE CLOSE BEHIND to drive very close behind another vehicle —**tailgater** *n*

tailgate party *n N Am* a social gathering before a sports event held in a car park outside the stadium with vehicles and the adjoining space used for picnicking, barbecuing, and other activities

tail grab *n* in snowboarding, a move in which the back of the board is manoeuvred upwards and grabbed with the hand

tailing /táyling/ *n* the end of something such as a beam that is built into a wall during construction ■ **tailings** *npl* the waste left after something has been processed from rock

tail lamp *n N Am* AUTOMOT same as **rear light**

taille /tīl, tayl/ *n* a tax levied by the French monarch on his subjects before the French Revolution [Mid-16C. < French, 'tax', literally 'a cut']

Tailleferre /tī́ə fáir/, **Germaine** (1892–1983) French composer. She was a member of the Paris-based group of composers known as 'Les Six' and later experimented with polytonality and unusual combinations of voices and instruments, including *Concerto des vaines paroles* (*Concerto of Empty Words*) (1958).

tail light /táyl līt/ *n ANZ, N Am* a red light, usually one of two, mounted at the rear of a vehicle. UK term **rear light**

tailor /táylər/ *n* **1.** CLOTHES MAKER somebody who makes or repairs clothes, especially men's clothes **2.** *Aus* FISH WITH SHARP TEETH a fast-moving aggressive fish with a large strong mouth containing sharp teeth that resemble scissors. Native to: Australia. Latin name: *Pomatomus saltatrix.* ■ *v* (**-lors, -loring, -lored**) **1.** *vti* MAKE CLOTHES to make clothes to meet a particular need or for a particular person **2.** *vt* ADAPT SOMETHING to adapt something to make it suitable for a particular purpose **3.** *vi* WORK AS TAILOR to work as a tailor making or repairing clothes [13C. Via Anglo-Norman *taillour*, Old French, *tailleur* 'cutter' < *taillier* 'to cut' < late Latin *taliare* < Latin *talea* 'twig, cutting']

tailorbird /táylər burd/ *n* a bird of the warbler family that makes a nest by sewing leaves together with plant fibres. Native to: tropical Asia. Genus: *Orthotomus.*

tailored /táylərd/ *adj* **1.** MADE TO FIT NEATLY describes clothes marked by a neat fit with trim lines and a clean and formal or severe look **2.** MADE FOR PARTICULAR PURPOSE made or adapted for a particular purpose **3.** MADE BY TAILOR made individually by a tailor

tailor-made *adj* **1.** IDEAL FOR SOMEBODY OR SOMETHING perfectly suited to somebody or for a purpose **2.** MADE BY TAILOR made by a tailor rather than in a factory ■ *n* **1.** SOMETHING MADE BY TAILOR a garment made by a tailor **2.** MANUFACTURED CIGARETTE a cigarette bought ready-made rather than rolled by hand (*informal*)

tailor's chalk *n* chalk used by tailors to mark out the positions of cuts or alterations on material

tailpiece /táyl peess/ *n* **1.** END something that forms an end or is added at the end of something **2.** PRINTING DECORATION AT BOTTOM OF PAGE a decoration at the bottom of a page, e.g. at the end of a chapter **3.** MUSIC PART OF STRINGED INSTRUMENT a piece of wood or metal at the lower end of a stringed instrument such as a violin, to which the strings are attached **4.** BEAM EMBEDDED IN WALL a beam that has one end embedded in a wall

tailpipe /táyl pīp/ *n N Am* same as **exhaust pipe**

tailplane /táyl playn/ *n* the horizontal part of the tail of an aircraft, designed to give stability

tailrace /táyl rayss/ *n* **1.** a channel that carries away water that has passed through a millwheel or turbine **2.** a channel that carries away mine tailings in water

tail rotor *n* a small rotor on the tail of a helicopter that prevents the helicopter from spinning in the direction opposite to the rotation of the main rotor

tailskid /táyl skid/ *n* **1.** a support or runner on the underside of the tail of an aircraft **2.** a skidding of the rear wheels of a motor vehicle

tailspin /táyl spin/ *n* **1.** a state of great confusion or distress (*informal*) **2.** a rapid and uncontrolled spiral descent of an aircraft

tailstock /táyl stok/ *n* a movable part of a lathe that supports the free end of the workpiece and allows it to rotate freely

tailwind /táyl wind/ *n* a wind that is blowing in the direction in which a ship or aircraft is travelling

Tainan /tī naán/ city in southwestern Taiwan. It is Taiwan's oldest city and former capital. Population: 721,832 (1999).

Taine /ten/, **Hippolyte** (1828–93) French historian and philosopher. An exponent of positivism, he advocated the use of scientific methods in the analysis of literature, history, and human nature. Full name **Taine, Hippolyte Adolphe**

Taino /tī́ nō/ (*plural* **-nos** *or same*) *n* **1.** a member of an extinct Native Central American people who lived on the Caribbean islands of the Greater Antilles and the Bahamas **2.** the Arawak language of the Taino people [Mid-19C. < Taino] —**Taino** *adj*

taint /taynt/ *vt* (**taints, tainting, tainted**) **1.** POLLUTE SOMETHING to pollute or contaminate something with something undesirable or dangerous **2.** CORRUPT SOMEBODY MORALLY to corrupt somebody morally, or detract from somebody's reputation by associating him or her with something reprehensible **3.** FLAVOUR SOMETHING to unintentionally give a scent or flavour of one thing to another **4.** SPOIL SOMETHING to make something such as fruit or vegetables rotten ○ *The peaches are tainted.* ■ *n* **1.** IMPERFECTION DETRACTING FROM QUALITY an

imperfection that detracts from the quality of somebody or something ○ *a taint on her reputation* **2.** **SOMETHING THAT POLLUTES** something that detracts from the purity or cleanliness of something [Late 16C. Partly < Anglo-Norman *teint* 'coloured, dyed' < Latin *tingere* 'moisten, dye', partly < Old French *ataint* 'convicted', past participle of *ateindre* (see ATTAIN)] —**taintless** *adj*

taipan[1] /tī´ pan/ *n* a foreigner in charge of a business or trading operation in China or Hong Kong, especially a powerful business tycoon [Mid-19C. < Chinese (Cantonese) *daaihbāan*]

taipan[2] /tī´ pan/ *n* a large rare highly venomous snake, brown in colour with a lighter brown belly, that can grow to 3.3 m/11 ft in length. Native to: northern Australia. Latin name: *Oxyuranus scutellatus*. [Mid-20C. < Aboriginal]

Taipei /tī´ páy/, **T'aipei** government seat of Taiwan. The largest city on the island, it is regarded by the Taiwanese government as its temporary capital. Population: 2,646,474 (2000).

Taiping /tī´ píng/ *n* a supporter of or participant in a rebellion against the Manchu dynasty in China between 1850 and 1864 [Mid-19C. < Chinese *tài píng* 'great peace']

Taiwan

Taiwan /tī´ waán/ country occupying the island of Taiwan and neighbouring small islands, administered separately since 1949 by a Chinese Nationalist government after its retreat from mainland China. It is claimed as a province by the People's Republic of China. Language: Chinese. Currency: New Taiwan dollar. Administrative capital: Taipei. Population: 22,603,000 (2003). Area: 36,000 sq. km/13,900 sq. mi. —**Taiwanese** /tī´ waa neéz/ *n, adj*

Taiyuan /tī´ ywán, tī´ yoo án/ capital city of Shanxi Province in northern China, southwest of Beijing. Population: 2,100,000 (1995).

taj /taaj/ *n* a tall brimless conical cap, often richly decorated, worn by Muslims as a mark of distinction [Late 19C. Via Arabic < Persian *tāj* 'crown']

tajiah /ta jeé ə/ *n Carib* another spelling of **tadjah**

Tajik /taa jeék/ (*plural* **-jiks** or *same*), **Tadzhik** (*plural* **-dzhiks** or *same*) *n* **1.** somebody who comes from Tajikistan **2.** the official Iranian language of Tajikistan. Native speakers: 4.5 million. [Early 19C. < Persian] —**Tajik** *adj*

Tajiki /taa jeéki/, **Tadzhiki** *n* LANG same as **Tajik** (sense 2) ■ *adj* relating to the Tajik people or their language or culture

Tajikistan /tə jeéki staán/, **Tadzhikistan** country in

Tajikistan

southeastern Central Asia, bordered by Kyrgyzstan, Uzbekistan, China, and Afghanistan. It was part of the Soviet Union until 1991. Language: Tajik. Currency: Tajik rouble. Capital: Dushanbe. Population: 6,863,752 (2003). Area: 143,100 sq. km/55,250 sq. mi. Official name **Republic of Tajikistan**

Taj Mahal

Taj Mahal /taáj mə haál, taázh-/ *n* a white marble mausoleum in Agra, northern India, completed in 1643 in memory of Mumtaz Mahal, the wife of Mughal emperor Shah Jahan. It is considered the greatest example of Mughal architecture.

Tajo /tákhō/ ♦ **Tagus**

taka /taákə/ *n* the main unit of Bangladeshi currency. See table at **currency** [Late 20C. Via Bangla *ţākā* < Sanskrit *ţaṅkaḥ* 'stamped coin']

takahe /taáka hee/ *n* an endangered flightless bird of the gallinule family with a large red beak and sturdy legs. It was thought to be extinct until rediscovered in 1948. Native to: Fiordland area of New Zealand. Latin name: *Notornis mantelli* or *Porphyrio mantelli*. [Mid-19C. < Maori]

Takakkaw Falls /taáka kaw-/ waterfall, located in Yoho National Park, British Columbia. Once considered as Canada's highest waterfall, in the 1980s it was determined that the main drop was only 254 m/833 ft, making it shorter overall than Della Falls, also in British Columbia. Height: 373 m/1,223 ft.

take /tayk/ *v* (**takes, taking, took** /tŏŏk/, **taken** /táykən/) **1.** *vt* CARRY SOMETHING to carry or transport something or somebody from one place to another ○ *I took a notebook with me.* ○ *We decided to take him to the doctor.* **2.** *vt* REMOVE SOMETHING to remove or steal something belonging to somebody else ○ *Did you take my gardening gloves?* ○ *I wish you wouldn't take things without asking.* **3.** *vt* WIN SOMETHING to capture or gain possession of a place, area, or object, or win something in a contest or competition ○ *took the town after a long siege* ○ *took first prize in the competition* **4.** *vt* GET HOLD OF SOMEBODY to get hold of something or somebody using a hand, or receive something into your hand ○ *She took him by the arm and steered him out of the room.* **5.** *vt* SELECT SOMETHING OR SOMEBODY to choose an individual object or person from a number available ○ *Here, take a chocolate.* **6.** *vt* GET INTO OR ONTO SOMETHING to place yourself in something, or start to occupy something ○ *Please take a seat.* **7.** *vt* CLAIM OR ASSUME SOMETHING to obtain something, especially credit, glory, or blame, or accept or maintain that this is deserved ○ *He doesn't mind taking the credit for the party's recent successes.* **8.** *vt* REGULARLY RECEIVE SOMETHING to buy, consume, or perform something as a regular habit ○ *We take the Sunday papers.* ○ *I've stopped taking lunch breaks.* **9.** *vt* LEAD SOMEBODY SOMEWHERE to enable somebody to go towards a particular place or in a particular direction, or go along something that leads to a particular place ○ *Will this road take us to the beach?* ○ *Take the first road on the left.* **10.** *vt* AGREE TO PERFORM SOMETHING to agree to perform or assume the duties associated with something ○ *I decided to take the job.* **11.** *vt* ACCEPT SOMETHING to accept something as valid, true, or satisfactory ○ *The machine refused to take my card.* **12.** *vt* BEAR SOMETHING to endure, deal with, accept, or put up with something, especially when it is unpleasant or unavoidable ○ *She cannot take criticism.* **13.** *vt* REACT TO SOMETHING to behave, feel, or act in response to being told or finding out about something ○ *I don't know how they will take the news.* **14.** *vt* HAVE STRENGTH

TO HOLD SOMETHING UP to be capable of supporting something physically, without collapsing or breaking ○ *Will the shelf take the weight of all those books?* **15.** *vt* TRAVEL BY MEANS OF SOMETHING to use a particular means of transport to make a journey ○ *Let's take a taxi.* **16.** *vt* HAVE ROOM FOR SOMETHING to be capable of containing a particular amount or quantity of something ○ *The tank takes 20 gallons.* **17.** *vt* WRITE SOMETHING to record something in a written form ○ *Do you mind if I take notes?* **18.** *vt* PHOTOGRAPHY CAPTURE SOMETHING ON CAMERA to use a camera to make a photograph ○ *Let's take a few photos to record the event.* **19.** *vt* EDUC STUDY SOMETHING to study something, or teach somebody or something, on a formal basis ○ *We both took French in the sixth form.* ○ *Do you remember that teacher who took us for chemistry?* **20.** *vt* START TO DO SOMETHING to start to perform or occupy something ○ *The new treasurer takes office next month.* **21.** *vt* DO SOMETHING to carry something out ○ *I'll take action on this immediately.* **22.** *vt* TRAVEL OVER OR ROUND SOMETHING to travel over or round something, especially in a vehicle or on a motorcycle or horse and in a particular way ○ *He took the bend too fast.* **23.** *vt* DERIVE FROM SOMETHING OR SOMEBODY to copy or derive something from a particular text or author (*often passive*) ○ *That quote is taken from Shakespeare.* **24.** *vt* CONSIDER SOMETHING to use somebody or something as an example or as a subject for consideration or discussion ○ *Let's take your last point first.* **25.** *vt* REQUIRE PARTICULAR LENGTH OF TIME to need a particular amount of time to be completed or performed ○ *The journey usually takes about three hours.* **26.** *vt* NEED SOMETHING IN ORDER TO FUNCTION to need a particular thing in order to operate ○ *This cassette recorder takes four batteries.* **27.** *vt* REQUIRE SOMETHING FOR SUCCESS to require something, especially a particular quality or characteristic, for something to be achieved ○ *It took a lot of courage to admit that you were wrong.* **28.** *vt* EXPERIENCE EMOTION OR HAVE VIEW to experience a particular emotion, have a particular reaction, or adopt a particular opinion with regard to something ○ *They looked so pathetic that I took pity on them.* **29.** *vt* INTERPRET SOMETHING IN PARTICULAR WAY to interpret, recognize, or understand something, especially somebody's words or actions, in a particular way ○ *I took you to mean that the loan would be approved.* **30.** *vt* ASSUME SOMETHING to make an assumption, usually a mistaken one, about somebody's identity or about the nature of a thing or a situation ○ *I took you for my daughter.* **31.** *vt* CONSUME SOMETHING to swallow or receive something into the body or system ○ *He refuses to take his medicine.* **32.** *vt* EXPOSE BODY TO ELEMENTS to go or sit out in the sun, or expose the body to other elements ○ *She was lying on the beach, taking the sun.* **33.** *vi* WORK OR BE SUCCESSFUL to work or have an effect in the intended way ○ *The perm didn't take because you rinsed out the solution too soon.* **34.** *vi* BOT START TO GROW to start to grow by producing roots ○ *The cutting has taken nicely.* **35.** *vt* MEASURE SOMETHING to measure something in an accurate way using a special instrument or procedure ○ *His temperature was normal when I took it this morning.* **36.** *vi* BECOME ILL to become noticeably or suddenly unwell or more unwell ○ *The whole family took sick and it turned out to be food poisoning.* **37.** *vt* MATHS SUBTRACT NUMBER to subtract a number or quantity from something ○ *Take 19 from 36 and you get 17.* **38.** *vt* ASSUME CHARGE OF SOMETHING to assume control of something as somebody who holds authority or has the attention of others ○ *She took the chair at the meeting.* **39.** *vt* HAVE SEX WITH SOMEBODY to penetrate somebody in an act of sexual intercourse, especially perfunctorily or without the person's consent **40.** *vti* FISHING BITE to bite the hook or fly at the end of an angler's line or the bait containing the hook (*refers to fish*) ○ *The fish just weren't taking that morning.* **41.** *vt* N Am CHEAT SOMEBODY to cheat or swindle somebody, especially out of a particular amount of money (*informal*) ■ *n* **1.** CINEMA CAMERA SHOT a single uninterrupted recording of a piece of the action in a film by a camera. There may be several takes of a particular shot, but only one is eventually used. ○ *This is the 15th take of this scene.* **2.** COMM MONEY OBTAINED IN BUSINESS TRANSACTIONS the amount of money received from customers or clients during a fixed period of time ○ *What was the take last week?* **3.** MUSIC SINGLE UNINTERRUPTED SOUND RECORDING a single un-

interrupted session in which a work or section of a work is recorded by audio recording equipment **4.** FISHING **GRABBING OF BAIT** the action of a fish in picking up or grabbing a bait or lure **5. IMPRESSION** a personal impression or opinion of something (*informal*) ○ *What's your take on his presentation?* [Pre-12C. < Old Norse *taka*] —**takable** *adj* —**taker** *n* ◇ **be taken with somebody** *or* **something** to find somebody or something pleasing or attractive ◇ **on the take** taking or willing to take bribes (*informal*) ◇ **take it 1.** to be able to tolerate a situation, usually one involving hardship, punishment, or criticism **2.** to assume that something is true ○ *I take it that you want some breakfast.* ◇ **take it or leave it 1.** used to indicate that somebody can either accept or refuse something, but cannot alter the conditions **2.** to have no strong feelings about an idea or activity one way or the other ○ *Jogging is okay, I can take it or leave it.*

take after *vt* **1.** to look or behave like somebody else, especially within the same family **2.** to begin to pursue somebody ○ *The dog took after the rabbit.*

take apart *vt* **1. DISMANTLE SOMETHING** to reduce something whole to its individual parts or pieces **2. BEAT SOMEBODY SEVERELY** to give somebody a severe beating or inflict a heavy defeat on somebody (*informal*) **3. CRITICIZE SOMEBODY OR SOMETHING** to criticize somebody or something in a severe and detailed way (*informal*)

take away *vt* **1.** to remove or take somebody or something elsewhere **2.** to subtract a number or quantity

take back *v* **1.** *vt* **WITHDRAW SOMETHING** to withdraw something said or written **2.** *vt* **REGAIN POSSESSION OF SOMETHING** to regain possession of something previously held but lost or given up **3.** *vt* COMM **RETURN SOMETHING BOUGHT AS UNACCEPTABLE** to return unwanted or unsatisfactory goods to the place where they were bought for a refund or exchange **4.** *vt* COMM **ACCEPT GOODS BACK** to accept goods returned as unwanted or unsatisfactory and offer a refund or exchange **5.** *vt* **REACCEPT SOMEBODY** to accept somebody back into a relationship or home **6.** *vt* **REMIND SOMEBODY OF PAST** to remind somebody of an earlier time **7.** *vti* PRINTING **MOVE COPY** to move a portion of text back to the previous line

take down *vt* **1. WRITE SOMETHING DOWN** to make a note of something in writing ○ *take down the names and addresses of the witnesses* **2. DISMANTLE SOMETHING** to dismantle or demolish something **3. HUMILIATE SOMEBODY** to make somebody less arrogant or powerful **4.** WRESTLING **FORCE OPPONENT TO FALL** to force an opponent to the mat during a wrestling match **5. REMOVE ACCUSED FROM DOCK** to remove the accused from the dock to the cells at the end of or during a trial

take for *vt* to think of somebody or something as being of a particular description, often mistakenly ○ *Do you take me for a fool?*

take in *vt* **1. UNDERSTAND SOMETHING** to understand and remember something ○ *Children can't be expected to take in so much new information in one lesson.* **2. ACCEPT SOMETHING AS REAL** to accept something as real or true ○ *The news was such a shock that we still haven't taken it in.* **3. INCLUDE SOMETHING** to include something within the scope of something such as a list or plan ○ *The study takes in the whole postwar period.* **4. DECEIVE SOMEBODY** to deceive or cheat somebody by presenting a false appearance ○ *We were all taken in by her plausible manner.* **5. ACCEPT SOMEBODY AS PAYING GUEST** to accept people as paying guests into a home **6. GIVE SOMEBODY SHELTER** to give somebody shelter in your home **7. GO TO SEE ENTERTAINMENT** to go and see some kind of entertainment or sport ○ *take in a film* **8. WORK ON SOMETHING AT HOME** to do paid work on something at home ○ *takes in ironing twice a week* **9.** HANDICRAFT **MAKE GARMENT NARROWER** to alter a garment to make it narrower

take off *v* **1.** *vt* **HAVE BREAK FROM WORK** to spend a particular amount of time not working ○ *I took a day off for the wedding.* **2.** *vt* **REMOVE GARMENT** to remove something you are wearing **3.** *vt UK* **IMITATE SOMEBODY** to act like somebody, especially to amuse other people (*informal*) **4.** *vt* **STOP SOMETHING OPERATING** to end the operation of something ○ *took off regular boats to the island* **5.** *vt* MATHS **DEDUCT AMOUNT** to deduct an amount from a price or sum **6.** *vi* AVIAT **BEGIN FLYING** to leave the ground and begin flying **7.** *vi* SPORTS **JUMP** to leave the ground at the beginning of a jump ○ *took off from the diving board* **8.** *vi* **DEPART** to leave, especially in a hurry or at short notice (*informal*) **9.** *vi* **SUCCEED** to begin suddenly to be very successful or popular (*informal*)

SYNONYMS See *imitate*.

take on *v* **1.** *vt* **HIRE SOMEBODY** to hire additional people to do work **2.** *vt* **UNDERTAKE TASK** to begin doing something, or accept responsibility for something ○ *I can't take on any more projects at the moment.* **3.** *vt* **ADOPT SOMETHING** to acquire or display a different character ○ *Her voice took on a kindlier tone.* **4.** *vt* **OPPOSE SOMEBODY OR SOMETHING** to oppose somebody or something in a competition or fight ○ *took on the city council* **5.** *vt* TRANSP **TAKE SOMETHING ON BOARD** to have people or things loaded on board a vessel or vehicle **6.** *vi* **BE UPSET** to show extreme feelings, especially grief (*dated informal*) **7.** *vti Carib* **WORRY ABOUT SOMETHING** to pay attention to or worry about somebody or something (*slang*)

take out *v* **1.** *vt* **REMOVE SOMETHING** to remove or extract something from another substance **2.** *vt* **OBTAIN SOMETHING OFFICIALLY** to obtain something such as a permit, mortgage, or insurance by applying for it **3.** *vt* **BRING SOMETHING INTO OPEN** to bring something into the open from a place where it was contained or concealed **4.** *vt* **HAVE SOMEBODY AS COMPANION** to take somebody as a companion or guest to a social event or function **5.** *vt* **DIRECT ANGER AT SUBSTITUTE** to express or relieve a strong feeling such as anger or frustration by directing it against somebody or something that is not the actual cause of it ○ *Don't take it out on me because you didn't get the job.* **6.** *vt* **DESTROY SOMETHING** to destroy, kill, or neutralize somebody or something (*slang*) ○ *took out enemy artillery* **7.** *vt Aus* SPORTS **WIN SOMETHING** to win something, especially a sporting event (*informal*) ○ *They took out this year's premiership.* **8.** *vi US* **BEGIN JOURNEY** to start out on a journey ○ *took out for the frontier*

take over *vti* **1. TAKE CONTROL** to obtain or assume control of something, or gain control of something from somebody else ○ *taken over by a larger company* **2. TAKE SOMEBODY'S PLACE** to begin to do something or operate something in place of somebody else ○ *She takes over when I finish my shift.* **3.** PRINTING **MOVE COPY FORWARD** to move a portion of text forward to the next line

take to *vt* **1. FORM LIKING FOR SOMEBODY** to develop a liking for somebody or something, especially quickly **2. START DOING OR USING SOMETHING** to start doing or using something as a habit, especially for help or consolation ○ *I've taken to checking that all the windows are locked before I leave the house.* **3. ADAPT YOURSELF** to adapt yourself to something, or become comfortable with something new ○ *quickly took to the new procedure* **4. GO TO PLACE** to go to a place, especially for safety ○ *The slightest cough or sneeze would make him take to his bed.* ○ *took to their cars and fled*

take up *vt* **1. LIFT SOMETHING OR SOMEBODY** to lift or raise something or somebody **2. BEGIN DOING SOMETHING REGULARLY** to begin doing something regularly either as an occupation or a hobby **3. BEGIN DOING SOMETHING AGAIN** to begin doing something again after a break ○ *take up where you left off* **4. USE SOMETHING WASTEFULLY** to make use of or occupy something, especially in a wasteful or unwelcome way ○ *took up the whole of the back seat* **5. ACCEPT OFFER** to accept something offered **6. ABSORB SOMETHING** to absorb a liquid **7.** HANDICRAFT **SHORTEN GARMENT** to raise the hem of a garment such as a skirt to make the garment shorter **8.** *US* **PAY OFF DEBT** to pay off a debt such as a mortgage

take up on *vt* **1.** to accept somebody's offer or wager **2.** to argue with somebody on a point

take up with *vt* **1.** to raise a matter for discussion with somebody **2.** to begin associating with a particular person or people

takeaway /táykə way/ *adj* **1. FOR EATING ELSEWHERE** bought ready-cooked and taken away to be eaten elsewhere **2. SELLING FOOD TO TAKE AWAY** selling ready-cooked food to be eaten elsewhere ■ *n* **1. RESTAURANT SELLING FOOD TO TAKE AWAY** a restaurant or shop that sells ready-cooked food for eating elsewhere **2. MEAL TO TAKE AWAY** a meal or food bought ready-cooked for eating elsewhere ▶ N Am term (all senses) **takeout**

take-down *adj* describes a weapon that can be disassembled quickly

take-home pay *n* the amount of pay left to an employee after all deductions such as those for tax have been made

taken past participle of **take**

take-no-prisoners *adj* persistent in an assertive way

takeoff /táyk of/ *n* **1.** AVIAT **BEGINNING OF FLIGHT** the process of leaving the ground and beginning to fly **2.** SPORTS **BEGINNING OF JUMP** the act or point of leaving the ground at the beginning of a jump **3. POINT OF RAPID GROWTH** a point at which substantial success or economic expansion is achieved and the prospect of further success or growth seems assured **4. IMITATION** an imitation of somebody or something, especially for comic effect (*informal*)

takeout /táyk owt/ *N Am* FOOD *adj* same as **takeaway** ■ *n* same as **takeaway**

takeover /táyk ōvər/ *n* **1.** an assumption of control of a company achieved by buying a majority of its shares **2.** the seizure of control of a country or organization by using force

take-up *n* **1.** the degree to which something made available is accepted or used by people **2.** a part of a mechanism onto which something such as tape is wound

Takfiri /tak féeri/ *n* a believer in or follower of Takfir wal Hijira

Takfir wal Hijira /tákfeer wal hə jéerə/ *n* an Islamic ideology that advocates withdrawal into a pure and simple form of life in imitation of Muhammad's withdrawal from Mecca to Medina [< Arabic, 'declaration of apostasy and withdrawal from society']

takin /taá keen/ *n* a large ruminant animal with a heavy build, shaggy coat, and heavy horns that curve back. Native to: mountainous regions of South Asia. Latin name: *Budorcas taxicolor*. [Mid-19C. Probably < Tibeto-Burman]

taking /táyking/ *adj* **1.** displaying a charming or fascinating appeal **2.** infectious (*informal*)

takings /táykingz/ *npl* money received through sales by a business

taki-taki /taáki taaki/ *n* LANG same as **Sranantongo** [Alteration of TALK] —**taki-taki** *adj*

takkie /táki/ *n S Africa* (*informal*) **1.** a rubber tyre **2.** *also* **tackie** a sports shoe often worn with casual clothes. Same as **trainer** [Early 20C. Origin ?]

tala /taálə/ (*plural same* or **-las**) *n* the main unit of Samoan currency. See table at **currency** [Mid-20C. < Polynesian]

talapoin /tállə poyn/ *n* **1.** a small olive-green guenon monkey. Native to: swampy forests in western equatorial Africa. Latin name: *Cercopithecus talapoin* or *Miopithecus talapoin*. **2.** in Myanmar and Thailand, a Buddhist monk [Late 16C. Via French and Portuguese < Mon *tala pói* 'lord of merit']

talaria /tə láiri ə/ *npl* in Greek mythology, winged sandals worn by characters especially by Hermes [Late 16C. < Latin, plural of *talaris* 'of the ankles' < *talus* 'ankle']

Talbot /táwlbət, tól-/, **William Henry Fox** (1800–77) British inventor. A pioneer of photography, he invented the calotype (1841). He later worked on the decipherment of the cuneiform script of Nineveh.

talc /talk/ *n* **1.** same as **talcum powder 2.** a soft mineral consisting of hydrated magnesium silicate. Source: igneous and metamorphic rocks. Use: talcum powder. ■ *vt* (**talcs, talcking** or **talcing, talcked** or **talced**) to put talcum powder on something [Late 16C. Via French *talc* and medieval Latin *talcum* < Persian *ṭalk*] —**talcose** /tál kōss/ *adj* —**talcous** *adj*

talcum powder /tálkəm-/ *n* a powder made from purified talc, often scented, that is applied to the skin to perfume it and absorb moisture [< medieval Latin (see TALC)]

tale /tayl/ *n* **1. NARRATIVE** a narrative or account of events **2. SHORT PIECE OF FICTION** a short piece of fiction, often one of a connected series **3. PIECE OF GOSSIP** an item of gossip, or a malicious rumour **4. FALSEHOOD** a story or report that is untrue [Old English *talu* < Germanic] ◇ **tell tales (out of school)** to report acts of wrongdoing to somebody in authority

SPELLCHECK See *tail*.

CULTURAL NOTE ***The Canterbury Tales***, a collection of stories (1387–1400) by Geoffrey Chaucer. The tales, mainly in verse, are told by a group of pilgrims travelling

to the shrine of St Thomas à Becket in Canterbury. They range from the bawdy 'Miller's Tale' to reworkings of traditional stories, e.g. the 'Nun's Priest's Tale' about Chanticleer the cock. The Prologue sets the scene for the journey and contains colourful descriptions of the pilgrims themselves.

Taleban *npl* ISLAM another spelling of **Taliban**

talebearer /táyl bairər/ *n* somebody who informs against other people or spreads malicious rumours —**talebearing** *n*

talent /tállənt/ *n* **1.** NATURAL ABILITY an unusual natural ability to do something well, especially in artistic areas that can be developed by training **2.** SOMEBODY WITH EXCEPTIONAL ABILITY a person or people with an exceptional ability **3.** POSSIBLE ROMANTIC PARTNERS people considered collectively as possible romantic or sexual partners (*slang*) **4.** MEASURE ANCIENT UNIT an ancient unit of weight and money [14C. Via Old French, 'mental inclination' < Latin *talentum* 'balance, sum of money' < Greek *talanton*] —**talentless** *adj*

SYNONYMS ***talent, gift, aptitude, flair, bent, knack, genius***
CORE MEANING: the natural ability to do something well
talent a natural ability to do something well that can be developed by training ○ *a persuasive speaker with a natural talent for diplomacy* ○ *Our company has a great wealth of underutilized talent.* **gift** a natural ability, especially an artistic ability, or a social skill ○ *Hannah had inherited a gift for music.* ○ *He had the rare gift of speaking only when something needed to be said.* **aptitude** a natural tendency to do something well, especially one that can be further developed ○ *He showed little aptitude for business.* ○ *Depending on the aptitude of the pupils, anything from two to ten topics may be appropriate.* **flair** a natural ability to do something well, especially creative or artistic ability ○ *a new writer-director of visual invention and cinematic flair* ○ *United lacked their usual flair, but remained in control of the match.* **bent** a strong natural inclination or liking for something ○ *The books feature two friends with a bent for detecting crime.* ○ *Technical schools were for pupils who had a practical bent.* **knack** a particular skill, especially one that might be innate or intuitive and therefore difficult to teach ○ *a knack with children* ○ *an obvious knack for sales* **genius** exceptional intellectual or creative ability ○ *He was a man of considerable genius who is not given enough credit for his contribution to science.*

talent contest *n* ARTS same as **talent show**

talented /tálləntid/ *adj* showing an exceptional natural ability to do something

talent scout *n* somebody whose job is to search for people who have exceptional abilities in some field such as entertainment or sport and recruit them for professional work

talent show *n* a public performance made up of acts by amateur entertainers who compete for a prize and are sometimes given professional opportunities

taler *n* COINS another spelling of **thaler**

tales /táy leez/ (*plural* **tales**) *n* a writ used to summon people to court to fill vacancies on a jury ■ *npl* a group of people summoned to court to fill vacancies on a jury (*takes a plural verb*) [15C. < Latin *tales de circumstantibus* 'such of the bystanders', phrase in the writ]

talesman /táy leezmən/ (*plural* **-men** /-mən/) *n* somebody selected from a group to fill a vacant seat in a jury

taleteller /táyl tellər/ *n* **1.** a teller of stories **2.** somebody who informs against other people or spreads malicious rumours —**taletelling** *n*

tali ANAT plural of **talus**[1]

Taliban /tálli ban/, **Taleban** *npl* a strict Islamic group that ruled Afghanistan from 1996 until 2001 [Late 20C. Via Pashto < Persian, 'students']

Taliesin /tal yéssin/ (*fl* AD 6th century) Welsh poet. Possibly mythical, he is claimed as the author of a dozen poems collected in the 13th-century *Book of Taliesin*.

talion /tálli ən/ *n* a punishment that has the same nature as the crime, e.g. the death penalty for murder [15C. Via Anglo-Norman < Latin *talion-*]

talipes /tállə peez/ *n* MED same as **club foot** (*technical*) [Mid-19C. < modern Latin < Latin *talus* 'ankle' + *pes* 'foot']

talipot /tálli pot/ *n* a tall palm tree with very large fan-shaped leaves and a massive inflorescence. Native to: Southeast Asia. Latin name: *Corypha umbraculifera*. [Late 17C. Via Malayalam < Sanskrit *tālīpatra* < *tālī* 'fan palm' + *patra* 'leaf']

talisman /tállizmən/ *n* **1.** an object believed to give magical powers to somebody who carries or wears it, e.g. a stone or jewel **2.** something believed to have magical properties [Mid-17C. Via French or Spanish < Greek *telesma* 'something consecrated' < *telein* 'complete, consecrate' < *telos* 'result'] —**talismanic** /tálliz mánnik/ *adj*

TALISMAN /tállizmən/ *n* a computer system used for buying and selling securities on the London Stock Exchange. Full form **Transfer Accounting Lodgement for Investors and Stock Management**

talk /tawk/ *v* (**talks, talking, talked**) **1.** *vti* EXPRESS SOMETHING BY SPEAKING to speak, or express something using speech ○ *talk nonsense* **2.** *vi* HAVE CONVERSATION ABOUT SOMETHING to address spoken words to somebody, or have a conversation with somebody ○ *talked for an hour* **3.** *vt* DISCUSS SUBJECT to discuss a particular subject ○ *talk business* **4.** *vi* COMMUNICATE to communicate in a way other than by speaking ○ *talk in sign language* **5.** *vti* SPEAK PARTICULAR LANGUAGE to use, or be able to use, a particular language to communicate with people ○ *talks Italian* **6.** *vi* REVEAL INFORMATION to reveal information, especially when being pressured to do so ○ *They interrogated her for hours but she wouldn't talk.* **7.** *vi* GOSSIP to discuss the affairs of others, or spread rumours ○ *People are starting to talk.* **8.** *vi* MAKE SOUNDS LIKE SPEECH to imitate the sounds of speech ○ *The baby is beginning to talk.* **9.** *vi* LECTURE to give a speech or lecture on a subject **10.** *vi* BE ON SPEAKING TERMS to be on sufficiently friendly terms with somebody to be willing or able to have a conversation ○ *They're not talking at the moment.* **11.** *vi* BE PERSUASIVE to have the power to influence or persuade people (*informal*) ○ *Money talks!* **12.** *vt* USED TO CALL ATTENTION used to direct somebody's attention to a particular aspect of something under discussion (*informal*) ○ *We're talking several weeks' work here.* ■ *n* **1.** CONVERSATION a conversation or exchange of ideas or information between two or more people **2.** THINGS SAID the things said by somebody or by a group of people in conversation ○ *The talk after dinner was mostly about politics.* **3.** SPEECH MADE TO AUDIENCE a speech or lecture, given before an audience **4.** GOSSIP ABOUT OTHERS idle or malicious conversation about the affairs of others **5.** EMPTY SPEECH speech about something without any intention of taking action ○ *He's all talk.* **6.** THING TALKED ABOUT a subject of discussion or gossip among a group of people ○ *the talk of the town* **7.** WAY OF SPEAKING a particular way of speaking ■ **talks** *npl* NEGOTIATIONS formal discussions to bring about a resolution to a problem ■ *adj* BROADCAST BROADCASTING TALK involving mainly interviews, discussions, and telephone calls from viewers or listeners ○ *talk radio* [13C. Ultimately < Germanic] —**talker** *n* ◇ **talk about** used to emphasize a comment or statement (*informal*) ○ *Talk about a dream job!* ◇ **walk the talk** to act on what you profess to believe in or value

talk at *vt* to speak to somebody without showing any interest in listening to the person's reply

talk back *vi* to make an impudent reply

talk down *vt* **1.** PREVENT SOMEBODY FROM SPEAKING to prevent somebody from speaking by saying something loudly and ignoring attempts to interrupt **2.** PERSUADE SOMEBODY TO LOWER PRICE to persuade a seller to lower the price of something **3.** TELL SOMEBODY HOW TO LAND AIRCRAFT to give radio guidance to somebody on how to land an aircraft **4.** MAKE SOMETHING SEEM LESS IMPRESSIVE to discuss something in a way that makes it seem less important or successful than it is

talk down to *vt* to speak to somebody in a superior or condescending way

talk into *vt* to persuade somebody to do something by talking to him or her ○ *We talked her into staying for dinner.*

talk out *vt* **1.** to settle a difference of opinion through discussion **2.** to prevent the passage of a piece of legislation, especially a bill in parliament, by prolonging the discussion of it until it is too late to vote on it

talk out of *vt* to dissuade somebody from doing something by talking to him or her ○ *talked him out of buying a car*

talk over *vt* **1.** to discuss something at length or thoroughly **2.** to persuade somebody to agree with an opinion or point of view

talk round *vt* **1.** to persuade somebody to agree with something ○ *She didn't like the idea but we talked her round in the end.* **2.** to talk about matters relating to a topic without discussing the central issue and without coming to any conclusions

talk up *vt* to praise something in the hope of making it popular or successful

talkathon /táwkə thon/ *n UK, ANZ, N Am* a long period of discussion

talkative /táwkətiv/ *adj* tending to talk readily and at length —**talkativeness** *n*

SYNONYMS ***talkative, chatty, gossipy, garrulous, loquacious***
CORE MEANING: talking a lot
talkative tending to talk readily and at length ○ *The normally talkative Italian refused to be drawn on his prospects for the championship.* **chatty** talking freely about unimportant things in a friendly way ○ *That afternoon, the little girl was her usual chatty self, talking about her hamster.* **gossipy** talking with relish about other people and their lives, often unkindly or maliciously ○ *articles ranging from the informative to the gossipy* ○ *a gossipy neighbour* **garrulous** excessively or pointlessly talkative ○ *a garrulous man with a thousand stories to tell to anyone who would listen* **loquacious** tending to talk a great deal ○ *Never loquacious, she was for the moment totally lost for words.* ○ *Her loquacious elder brother was talking enthusiastically about her new business venture.*

talkback /táwk bak/ *n* **1.** a system of communication in a broadcasting studio that enables the staff to speak to each other without the speech being broadcast **2.** *Aus* a radio programme in which listeners telephone the studio and express their opinions

talkboard /táwk bawrd/ *n* an online discussion group on a specific topic, sometimes involving experts who will answer questions

talkie /táwki/ *n* an early film with a soundtrack (*dated*) [Early 20C. Shortening of *talking picture*, after MOVIE]

talking book /táwking-/ *n* a book that has been recorded onto an audio cassette, originally intended for people who cannot see well enough to read

talking head *n* somebody who talks at length into a camera in a television broadcast, usually shown only from the shoulders up, e.g. a newsreader (*informal*)

talking point *n* **1.** INTERESTING ITEM FOR DISCUSSION a topic, or aspect of something, that provokes a lot of discussion **2.** PUBLICITY POINT a claim made about a product in publicity material that is considered particularly interesting or persuasive to potential customers **3.** *N Am* SOMETHING SUPPORTING ARGUMENT something that supports an argument, e.g. a particularly convincing point

talking shop *n* a place where people discuss matters but take no meaningful action, or a group of people who talk prolifically but do nothing (*informal*)

talking-to *n* a scolding given to somebody, especially by somebody in authority (*informal*)

talk radio *n* a broadcast format involving interviews, discussions, and telephone phone-ins

talk show *n ANZ, N Am* a television or radio programme made up mainly of interviews with guests, especially famous people. UK term **chat show**

talky /táwki/ (**-ier, -iest**) *adj* containing too much dialogue and not enough action ○ *a talky and dull film*

tall /tawl/ *adj* **1.** VERY HIGH reaching or having grown to a considerable or above average height ○ *tall trees* **2.** OF PARTICULAR HEIGHT having reached a particular height ○ *five foot tall* **3.** LARGE substantial, demanding, or difficult to deal with ○ *a tall order* **4.** INCREDIBLE exaggerating the events of something beyond the bounds of probability, especially in a boastful way ○ *a tall story* **5.** POMPOUS having an excessively grand or boastful style ○ *tall talk* ■ *adv* PROUDLY in a proud or courageous way ○ *There are times when you must stand tall and defend your beliefs.* [Old English *getæl*

'quick, ready' < Germanic, 'to count'] —**tallish** *adj* —**tallness** *n*

tallage /tállij/ *n* **1. ROYAL TAX** a tax levied by the Norman and Angevin kings of England on royal lands and towns **2. TAX LEVIED BY LORD** in feudal times, a tax levied by a lord on his vassals or tenants ■ *vt* (**-lages, -laging, -laged**) **LEVY TAX ON SOMEBODY OR SOMETHING** to levy a tax, especially a tallage, on somebody or something [13C. < Old French *taillage* < *taillier* 'to cut']

Tallahassee /tállə hássi/ capital of Florida, situated in the northern part of the state. Population: 155,171 (2002 estimate).

tallawah /tálla wa/ *adj* possessing great physical or spiritual strength (*slang; used in Black English*) ○ *Me little, but me tallawah.* [Late 20C. Perhaps alteration of STALWART]

tallboy /táwl boy/ *n* **1.** a high piece of furniture, typically comprising two chests of drawers set one on top of the other or a chest of drawers with a cupboard or hanging space above. N Am term **highboy 2.** a narrow fitting at the top of a chimney to prevent smoke being carried back down

Talleyrand /tálli rand/, **Charles Maurice de** (1754–1838) French politician and diplomat. His long career spanned the French Revolution and the Napoleonic period. As foreign minister, he represented France at the Congress of Vienna (1814–15). Full name **Talleyrand-Périgord, Charles Maurice de**

> 'Mistrust first impulses; they are nearly always good.'
> [Attributed to Charles Maurice de Talleyrand]

Tallinn /tállin, ta lín, -leen/ capital of Estonia, on the Bay of Tallinn, an inlet of the Gulf of Finland, opposite Helsinki, Finland. Population: 408,329 (2000).

tallis *n* JUDAISM same as **tallith**

Tallis /tálliss/, **Thomas** (1510?–85) English composer. He was a major composer of religious choral works.

tallith /tállith/ (*plural* **tallithim** /tálli theem/ or **talliths**), **tallis** /tálliss/ (*plural* **tallisim** /tálli seem/) *n* a four-cornered fringed prayer shawl of white material with a black, blue, or purple stripe, traditionally worn by Jewish men, especially at morning prayers [Early 17C. < Rabbinic Hebrew *ṭallīt* < biblical Hebrew *ṭillel* 'to cover']

tall oil *n* an oily liquid produced as a by-product of a chemical process in the manufacture of wood pulp. Use: making soaps, emulsions. [Early 20C. Partial translation of German *Tallöl* < Swedish *tallolja* < *tall* 'pine' + *olja* 'oil']

tallow /tállō/ *n* **1. FATTY SUBSTANCE** a hard fatty substance extracted from the fat of sheep and cattle. Use: candles, soap. **2. SUBSTANCE MADE FROM VEGETABLE MATTER** a substance similar to tallow, made from vegetable matter ■ *vt* (**-lows, -lowing, -lowed**) **COVER SOMETHING WITH TALLOW** to cover or grease something with tallow [13C. < Low German] —**tallowy** *adj*

tall poppy *n Aus* somebody who, through achievements or wealth, has become a prominent member of society (*informal*)

tall poppy syndrome *n Aus* a tendency among the media and the public to denigrate the achievements of prominent members of society

tall ship *n* a sailing ship with at least two masts, usually square-rigged

tally /tálli/ *v* (**-lies, -lying, -lied**) **1.** *vti* **AGREE** to agree, correspond, or come to the same amount, or cause two or more things to do this **2.** *vt* **COUNT SOMETHING** to count or reckon items **3.** *vt* **REGISTER SOMETHING IN ACCOUNT** to register something in an account of items **4.** *vti* **KEEP SCORE** to keep a record of a score or account **5.** *vt* **PUT LABEL OR TAG ON SOMETHING** to put an identifying label or tag on something ■ *n* (*plural* **-lies**) **1. RECORD OF ITEMS** a record or account of items such as things bought or points scored ○ *keep a tally* **2. SCORE ACHIEVED** the total or current number of things achieved by somebody, especially somebody's score in a game or competition ○ *added to his personal tally of nine goals for the season* **3. IDENTIFYING LABEL OR MARK** something that identifies something, e.g. a label or mark **4. COUNTERPART** something that corresponds to or is the counterpart of something else **5. NOTCHED STICK** formerly, a stick with notches cut into it as a record of something such as loans made or items bought on credit **6. MARK REPRESENTING NUMBER** a mark or marks representing a number, especially a set of four short vertical lines crossed by a diagonal fifth line used for numbering things in fives [15C. Via Anglo-Norman < Latin *talea* 'twig, cutting'] —**tallier** *n*

ORIGIN The Latin word *talea* 'twig, cutting', from which ***tally*** is derived, is also the source of English *detail, entail, retail,* and *tailor.*

tally-ho /tálli hṓ/ *interj* **EXCLAMATION THAT FOX HAS BEEN SIGHTED** used by a participant in a fox hunt to let others know that a fox has been sighted ■ *n* (*plural* **tally-hos**) **1. FOX HUNTER'S CRY** a cry by a participant in a fox hunt to let others know that a fox has been sighted **2.** TRANSP same as **four-in-hand** (sense 1) ■ *vi* (**tally-hos, tally-hoing, tally-hoed**) **SHOUT 'TALLY-HO'** to give a shout of 'tally-ho' [Probably alteration of French *taïaut*]

tallyman /tállimən/ (*plural* **-men** /-mən/) *n* **1.** somebody who records or accounts for something such as items bought on credit or points scored **2.** a travelling sales representative who sells goods to be paid for in instalments

Talmud /tálmood, -məd/ *n* the collection of ancient Jewish writings that forms the basis of Jewish religious law, consisting of the early scriptural interpretations (**Mishnah**) and the later commentaries on them (**Gemara**) [Mid-16C. < post-biblical Hebrew *talmūḏ* 'instruction' < Hebrew *lāmaḏ* 'learn'] —**Talmudic** /tal móodik, -myóodik/ *adj* —**Talmudical** *adj* —**Talmudism** *n* —**Talmudist** *n*

talon /tállən/ *n* **1. HOOKED CLAW** a hooked claw, especially of a bird of prey **2. SOMETHING LIKE CLAW** something that looks like a claw, e.g. a curled human finger **3. PART OF LOCK** the part of a lock that the key presses when turned and that causes the bolt to slide out **4.** ARCHIT same as **ogee** (sense 2) **5.** CARDS **UNDEALT CARDS** in some card games, e.g. piquet, the remainder of the deck of cards after a deal [14C. Via French < assumed Vulgar Latin *talon-* 'heel, spur' < Latin *talus* 'ankle'] —**taloned** *adj*

Talon /tá loN/, **Jean Baptiste, Comte d'Orsainville** (1625?–94) French colonial administrator. As the second-in-command of New France (now Canada) (1665–68 and 1670–72), he promoted agriculture and industry and the immigration to maintain them.

taluk /taa lóok/ (*plural* **-luka** /-lóokə/) *n S Asia* **1.** a subdivision of a district in South Asia **2.** a piece of hereditary land in South Asia [Late 18C. < Urdu, Persian *ta'alluḳ* 'estate' < Arabic *ta'allaḳa* 'be attached']

talus[1] /táyləss/ (*plural* **-li** /-lī/) *n* the bone in the ankle that connects with the lower leg bones to form the ankle joint [Late 16C. < Latin, 'ankle']

talus[2] /táyləss/ (*plural* **-luses**) *n* **1. AREA OF RUBBLE** a sloping area of rock rubble **2. ROCK RUBBLE** rock rubble, e.g. at the base of a cliff **3.** MIL **BASE OF FORTIFICATION** the sloping base of a fortification [Mid-17C. Origin ?]

talweg *n* GEOG another spelling of **thalweg**

tam /tam/ *n* CLOTHING same as **tam-o'-shanter** (*informal*) [Late 19C. Shortening]

TAM /tam/ *abbr* Television Audience Measurement

tamale /tə maáli/ *n* a Mexican dish made by mixing fried chopped meat with peppers and seasonings, rolling the mixture in cornmeal dough, wrapping it in maize husks, and then steaming it [Late 17C. Back-formation < American Spanish *tamales*, plural of *tamal* < Nahuatl *tamalli*]

tamandua /támmən doó ə/, **tamandu** /-doó/ *n* a small tree-living toothless anteater with a long prehensile tail. Native to: Central and South America. Latin name: *Tamandua tetradactyla* or *Tamandua mexicana*. [Early 17C. Via Portuguese < Tupi *tamanduá* 'ant hunter']

Tamar /táymaar/ **1.** river that rises near the northern coast of Devon, southwestern England, and flows south to the English Channel. The Tamar Valley is an Area of Outstanding Natural Beauty. Length: 97 km/60 mi. **2.** river in northern Tasmania, Australia, formed by the confluence of the North and South Esk rivers. Length: 65 km/40 mi.

tamarack /támmə rak/ *n* **1.** the dense wood of a North American larch **2.** a deciduous larch with bluish-green needles and oval cones. Native to: North America. Latin name: *Larix laricina*. [Early 19C. < Canadian French *tamarac* < Algonquian]

tamarau /támmə row/ (*plural* **-raus**), **tamarao** (*plural* **-raos**) *n* a small rare buffalo. Native to: swamps of Mindoro Island, Philippines. Latin name: *Bubalus mindorensis*. [Late 19C. < Tagalog]

tamari /tə maári/ *n* a rich Japanese soy sauce [Late 20C. < Japanese]

tamarillo /támmə rı́llō/ (*plural* **-los**) *n ANZ, US* FOOD same as **tree tomato** [Mid-20C. Alteration of TOMATILLO]

tamarin /támmərin/ *n* a small monkey that has a long tail and is highly vocal. Native to: South America. Genus: *Saguinus*. [Late 18C. Via French < Galibi]

tamarind /támmərind/ *n* **1.** FOOD **FRUIT** a pod containing many seeds within an acid-tasting pulp. Use: preserves, drinks, medicines. **2.** INDUST **WOOD** a very hard reddish wood **3.** TREES **TROPICAL TREE** a tropical evergreen tree that produces tamarinds and yields tamarind wood. Flowers: yellow with red streaks. Latin name: *Tamarindus indica*. [Mid-16C. Via Old French < Arabic *tamr hindī* 'Indian date']

tamarisk /támmərisk/ *n* a tree or bush with leaves resembling scales. Flowers: white to pink, in terminal spikes. Native to: Europe, Asia, Africa. Genus: *Tamarix*. [14C. < late Latin *tamariscus*, variant of Latin *tamarix*]

Tamatave /tamataáv/ former name for **Toamasina**

Tamaulipas /taámow leépəss/ state in northeastern Mexico. Capital: Ciudad Victoria. Population: 2,747,114 (2000). Area: 78,932 sq. km/30,476 sq. mi.

tambac *n* METALL same as **tombac**

tambala /taam baálə/ (*plural same* or **-las**) *n* a subunit of Malawian currency. See table at **currency** [Late 20C. < Chewa, 'cockerel']

Tambo /támbō/, **Oliver** (1917–93) South African political leader. He was leader of the African National Congress (1967–91) and a prominent opponent of apartheid in South Africa. He was in exile from 1960 to 1990.

> 'The need for us to take up arms will never transform us into prisoners of the idea of violence.'
> [Oliver Tambo, *Independent on Sunday*, 25 April 1993]

tambour /tám boor, -bawr/ *n* **1.** HANDICRAFT **EMBROIDERY FRAME** a round frame on which material is stretched while it is being embroidered **2.** HANDICRAFT **EMBROIDERY** embroidery done on a tambour **3.** FURNITURE **FLEXIBLE ROLLING TOP OF DESK** a flexible rolling top of a desk or sliding front of a cabinet, made of thin strips of wood attached to canvas **4.** MUSIC, MIL **DRUM** a drum, especially a side drum **5.** ARCHIT **CIRCULAR WALL** a circular wall, especially one supporting a dome ■ *vti* (**-bours, -bouring, -boured**) HANDICRAFT **EMBROIDER DESIGN USING FRAME** to embroider something using a round frame [15C. Via French < Persian *tabīra* 'drum']

tamboura /tam boórə, -báwrə/, **tanpura** /tan poórə/ *n* a stringed instrument resembling a lute without frets, used in South Asian and Balkan music to produce a harmonic drone [Late 16C. Via Arabic and Persian < Persian *dunbara* 'lamb's tail']

tambourin /támboorin/ *n* **1. DANCE** an 18th-century Provençal dance in a two-beat rhythm, usually accompanied by a drum **2. MUSIC** the music for a tambourin **3. DRUM** a small Provençal drum [Late 18C. < French, 'small drum' < *tambour* (see TAMBOUR)]

tambourine /támbə reén/ *n* a shallow single-headed drum with jingling metallic discs in its frame, held in one hand and played by shaking it or striking it with the free hand [Late 16C. < French, 'small drum' < *tambour* (see TAMBOUR)] —**tambourinist** *n*

tambu-bambu band /támboo bámboo-/ *n Carib* a small band of musicians using bamboo sticks as instruments and parading through the streets during carnival, especially in Trinidad

Tamburlaine ♦ **Tamerlane**

tame /taym/ *adj* (**tamer, tamest**) **1. NO LONGER WILD** changed from a wild or uncultivated state to one suitable for domestic use or life **2. FRIENDLY TOWARDS PEOPLE** describes an animal or bird unafraid of human contact **3. WITHOUT SPIRIT** lacking in spirit or vigour **4. BLAND** lacking in the qualities that make something interesting, e.g. imagination, adventurousness, or

inspiration ○ *a tame rendition of the anthem* **5.** **SLOW-MOVING** describes a river or part of a river with very little current ■ *vt* (**tames, taming, tamed**) **1.** **DOMESTICATE SOMETHING** to make a wild animal or uncultivated land suitable for domestic life or use **2.** **SUBDUE SOMEBODY** to remove the wildness, spirit, or energy from somebody or something **3.** **MODERATE SOMETHING** to make something much less harsh or extreme **4.** **BRING SOMETHING UNDER HUMAN CONTROL** to bring a natural force under human control ○ *a series of dams to tame the raging river* [Old English *tam* < Indo-European, 'constrain'] —**tamable** *adj* —**tamely** *adv* —**tameness** *n* —**tamer** *n*

Tamerlane /támmər layn/, **Tamburlaine** /támbər-/ (1336–1405) Turkic ruler and conqueror. His conquests established an empire that extended from India to the Mediterranean Sea. He died while trying to invade China, and was buried in his capital, Samarkand. Born **Timur**

'It is better to be at the right place with 10 men than absent with 10,000.'
[Attributed to Tamerlane]

Tamil /támmil/ (*plural* **-ils** or *same*) *n* **1.** a member of a Dravidian people who live in southern India and northern Sri Lanka **2.** the Dravidian language of the Tamil people. Native speakers: 50 million. [Mid-18C. < Tamil *Tamil*] —**Tamil** *adj*

LANGUAGE HERITAGE See ***Dravidian***.

Tamil Nadu /támmil naa dóo/ state in southern India. Capital: Chennai. Population: 62,110,839 (2001). Area: 130,058 sq. km/50,216 sq. mi.

Tamil Tiger *n* a member of a movement that seeks to found a separate state for the Tamil people in northeastern Sri Lanka and uses armed resistance and terror tactics against the Sri Lankan authorities

tamis /támmi, -miss/ (*plural same*) *n* COOK same as **tammy**[2] [Early 17C. Via French < medieval Latin *tamisium* < Germanic]

Tammany Hall /támməni-/ *n* a political organization formed as a fraternal society in New York in 1789 but mainly known for political corruption in the early 20th century [Mid-19C. After *Tamanend* (1653?–1750), Delaware leader said to have welcomed William Penn (1682)] —**Tammanyite** *n*

tammar /támmər/ *n* a rabbit-sized wallaby that has a reddish-brown coat with whitish underparts. Native to: southwestern Australia. Latin name: *Wallabia eugenii*. [Mid-19C. < Nyungar *damar*]

Tammuz /támmòoz/ *n* in the Jewish calendar, the fourth month of the religious year, lasting 29 days and falling about the same time as June to July. See table at **calendar** [Mid-16C. Via Hebrew *Tammūz* < Babylonian *Du'uzu*, a deity]

tammy[1] /támmi/ (*plural* **-mies**) *n* CLOTHING same as **tam-o'-shanter** (*informal*) [Late 19C. < TAM]

tammy[2] /támmi/ *n* (*plural* **-mies**) *also* **tammy cloth** a fine strainer made of woollen cloth ■ *vt* (**-mies, -mying, -mied**) to strain something such as a sauce using a tammy [Mid-18C. Probably < French *tamis*]

tam-o'-shanter /támmə shántər/ *n* a brimless Scottish woollen hat, usually with a bobble at the centre of the crown [Mid-19C. < *Tam O' Shanter*, eponymous hero of a poem by Robert BURNS]

tamoxifen /tə móksi fen/ *n* a drug that inhibits the actions of oestrogen. Use: treatment of breast cancer, some types of infertility. Formula: $C_{26}H_{29}NO$. [Late 20C. Shortening of *metamoxifen* < META- + AMINE + OXY- + PHENYL]

tamp /tamp/ *vt* (**tamps, tamping, tamped**) **1.** to pack or push something down, especially by tapping it repeatedly **2.** to pack a substance such as sand or earth into a drill hole above an explosive ■ *n N Am* same as **tamper**[2] (sense 2) [Early 19C. Origin ?]

Tampa /támpə/ seaport in west-central Florida, on Tampa Bay, an arm of the Gulf of Mexico. Population: 315,140 (2002 estimate).

Tampa affair *n Aus* an incident in 2001, when a Norwegian cargo carrier, the MV Tampa, rescued 433 asylum seekers from a sinking ship and attempted to land them on the Australian territory of Christmas Island. The Australian government refused to let the Tampa dock and eventually had the asylum seekers taken to Pacific islands.

tamper[1] /támpər/ (**-pers, -pering, -pered**) *vi* **1.** to interfere with something in a way that damages it or has harmful results **2.** to try to corrupt or influence somebody or affect the outcome of something ○ *tampering with the jury* [Mid-16C. Probably variant of TEMPER] —**tamperer** *n*

tamper[2] /támpər/ *n* **1.** **SOMEBODY OR SOMETHING THAT TAMPS SOMETHING** somebody or something that packs something down with repeated blows **2.** **TAMPING DEVICE** a device for pushing tobacco down into the bowl of a pipe. N Am term **tamp** **3.** ARMS **CASING ON NUCLEAR WEAPON** the casing around the core of a nuclear weapon that reflects neutrons back into the core, slowing the expansion of the nuclear reaction and increasing the weapon's power [Mid-19C. < TAMP]

Tampere /támpər ray, támp e re/ city in southwestern Finland, situated about 169 km/105 mi. northwest of Helsinki. Population: 193,174 (2000).

tamper-proof *adj* designed to be difficult to tamper with

Tampico /tam peékō/ seaport in eastern Mexico, situated on the Pánuco River close to the Gulf of Mexico. Population: 295,442 (2000).

tampion /támpi ən/, **tompion** /tómpi-/ *n* a plug or cover for the muzzle of a gun to keep out moisture and dust when it is not in use [15C. < French *tampon* (see TAMPON)]

tampon /tám pon/ *n* **1.** **PLUG OF MATERIAL USED DURING MENSTRUATION** a cylindrical plug of soft material inserted in the vagina during menstruation to absorb blood **2.** **PAD TO CONTROL BLEEDING** a pad of cotton or other absorbent fabric that is used for plugging wounds or for controlling blood flow in body cavities, especially during surgery ■ *vt* (**-pons, -poning, -poned**) **CONTROL BLOOD FLOW** to use a tampon to plug a wound or to control blood flow in a body cavity, especially during surgery [Mid-19C. < French, 'plug, bung', variant of *tapon* 'piece of cloth to stop a hole' < assumed Frankish *tappo* 'stopper']

tamponade /támpə náyd/ *n* the insertion of a tampon during surgery to check bleeding

tam-tam /tám tam/ *n* a large gong [Mid-19C. Origin ?]

Tamworth[1] /tám wurth/ *n* a reddish-gold pig with a long snout belonging to a hardy breed developed in central England [Mid-19C. After TAMWORTH[2] (sense 1),]

Tamworth[2] /tám wurth, támmwərth/ **1.** market town in Staffordshire, central England. Population: 74,531 (2001). **2.** city in northeastern New South Wales, Australia, an agricultural centre and site of an annual country music festival. Population: 36,952 (2002 estimate).

tan[1] /tan/ *n* **1.** **SUNTAN** the brownish colour that the skin takes on after being exposed to ultraviolet light, especially from the Sun or a sunlamp **2.** **LIGHT BROWN COLOUR** a light brown orange-tinged colour **3.** MANUF same as **tanbark** **4.** CHEM same as **tannin** ■ *v* (**tans, tanning, tanned**) **1.** *vti* **GET OR GIVE SOMEBODY SUNTAN** to give somebody's skin a brownish colour, or take on such a colour **2.** *vt* **CONVERT HIDE TO LEATHER** to convert an animal skin or hide into leather by treating it with something such as tannin **3.** *vt* **BEAT SOMEBODY** to give a beating to somebody (*informal*) ■ *adj* (**tanner, tannest**) **1.** **OF LIGHT BROWN COLOUR** of a light brown orange-tinged colour **2.** *N Am* same as **tanned** **3.** MANUF **OF PROCESS OF TANNING HIDES** relating to or used in the process of tanning animal skins and hides [Pre-12C. < medieval Latin *tannare* 'tan, dye a tawny colour' < *tannum* 'tanbark'] —**tannable** *adj* —**tannish** *adj*

tan[2] /tan/ *abbr* MATHS tangent

Tan /tan/, **Amy** (*b.* 1952) US writer. She came to prominence with her first novel, *The Joy Luck Club* (1989), which deals with the relationships between Chinese-born women and their US-born daughters.

tana /taánə/ *n* **1.** a small lemur with a grey-brown back, whitish underparts, and a dark stripe that runs along the back and encircles each eye. Native to: Madagascar. Latin name: *Phaner furcifer*. **2.** a mainly ground-dwelling tree shrew with a brownish coat that has a black stripe along the back. Native to: Borneo, Sumatra. Genus: *Lyongale*. [Early 19C. Via modern Latin < Malay *tūpai tāna* 'ground-squirrel']

Tana, Lake /taánə/ largest lake in Ethiopia, in the north-central Ethiopian highlands. Area: 2,156 sq. km/832 sq. mi.

Tanabata /taánə baátə/ *n* in Japan, an annual festival during which people write down their wishes and hang them with other decorations on branches of bamboo. Date: 7 July. [Early 20C. < Japanese]

Tanach /taa naákh/, **Tanakh** *n* the sacred book of Judaism consisting of the Torah, Prophets, and Hagiographa [Mid-20C. < Hebrew *tĕnak*, acronym < *tōrāh* 'law' + *nĕbī'īm* 'prophets' + *kĕṯūbīm* 'Hagiographa']

tanager /tánnəjər/ *n* a songbird that is usually fairly small and brightly coloured in bold patterns and has a conical beak. Native to: North and South America, Caribbean. Family: Thraupidae. [Early 17C. < modern Latin *Tanagra* < Tupi *tangará*]

Tanakh *n* JUDAISM another spelling of **Tanach**

Tanami Desert /ta naámi-/ desert in central Australia that extends eastwards from Tennant Creek in the Northern Territory into Western Australia. Area: 184,500 sq. km/71,200 sq. mi.

Tananarive /tánnanə reév/ former name for **Antananarivo**

tanbark /tán baark/ *n* the bark of some trees, especially oak and hemlock, used as a source of tannin

Tancred /táng krid/ (1078–1112) Norman soldier and regent of Antioch (1104–12). He distinguished himself as a military leader at the battles of Nicaea and Dorylaeum (1097) in the First Crusade. He also took part in the capture of Jerusalem (1099).

T & E *abbr* tired and emotional (*informal*)

tandem /tándəm/ *n* **1.** *UK, ANZ, Can* **BICYCLE FOR TWO RIDERS** a bicycle with two saddles and two sets of handlebars and pedals, one behind the other, so that it can be ridden by two people at the same time. US term **tandem bicycle** **2.** **HORSE-DRAWN CARRIAGE** a two-wheeled carriage drawn by two horses harnessed one behind the other **3.** **HORSE TEAM HARNESSED IN SINGLE FILE** a team of two horses harnessed one behind the other **4.** **ARRANGEMENT IN SINGLE FILE** a setup in which two things are arranged one behind the other ■ *adv* **ONE BEHIND ANOTHER** with one behind the other ○ *We'll ride tandem.* ■ *adj* **OF TWO TOGETHER** describes sports activities undertaken by two people together, usually positioned one behind the other, especially when one person is a novice ○ *tandem parachute jumping* [Late 18C. < Latin, 'at length' (< *tam* 'so' + demonstrative suffix *-dem*), humorously interpreted as 'in a straight line'] ◇ **in tandem** **1.** in partnership or cooperation **2.** with one behind the other

tandem bicycle *n US* same as **tandem** *n* (sense 1)

tandoor /tan dóor/ *n* a clay oven used especially in the cuisine of northern South Asia for cooking food quickly at high temperature [Mid-19C. Via Urdu *tandūr*, Persian *tanūr* < Arabic *tannūr* 'oven, furnace']

tandoori /tan dóori/ *adj* **COOKED IN CLAY OVEN** baked or cooked in a tandoor, usually after being marinated in a mixture of yoghurt and spices ■ *n* (*plural* **-is**) (*informal*) **1.** **TANDOORI MEAL** a dish or meal of tandoori food **2.** **INDIAN RESTAURANT** a restaurant that serves South Asian food, especially tandoori dishes ■ *vt* (**-is, -iing, -ied**) **COOK SOMETHING IN TANDOORI STYLE** to cook something in a tandoor, or after marinating the food in the mixture of yoghurt and spices traditionally used for such dishes [Mid-20C. < Persian and Urdu < Urdu *tandūr*, Persian *tanūr* (see TANDOOR)]

tang[1] /tang/ *n* **1.** **STRONG TASTE** a distinctively sharp strong taste **2.** **PUNGENT SMELL** a smell that has a sharp biting quality **3.** **SUGGESTION** a slight hint or flavour of a particular thing ○ *a cake with a tang of lemon* **4.** **SHARP END GOING INTO HANDLE** the sharp part at one end of a chisel, knife blade, or other similar tool that secures it to the handle or shaft [14C. < N Germanic] —**tangy** *adj*

tang[2] /tang/ *n* a loud, often harsh, ringing noise [Early 17C. An imitation of the sound] —**tang** *vti*

Tang /tang/, **T'ang** *n* a wealthy Chinese dynasty that lasted from AD 618 to AD 907 and was renowned for its encouragement and patronage of the arts, especially poetry and ceramics, and the development of printing [Mid-17C. < Chinese *táng*] —**Tang** *adj*

tanga /táng gə/ *n* an undergarment or the lower part of a bikini made of two small triangles of fabric fastened with ties [Early 20C. Via Portuguese, 'triangular loincloth' < Bantu]

Tanga /táng gə/ town in northeastern Tanzania, on the Indian Ocean. Population: 187,634 (1988).

~~tangable~~ incorrect spelling of **tangible**

Tanganyika /táng gən yéèkə/ former country in East Africa, constituting the mainland part of what is now Tanzania —**Tanganyikan** *n*, *adj*

Tanganyika, Lake lake in east-central Africa, with shorelines in Burundi, Tanzania, Zambia, and the Democratic Republic of the Congo. Area: 32,900 sq. km/12,700 sq. mi. Length: 680 km/420 mi.

tangata whenua /tánguttə fénnoo ə/ *npl NZ* the Maori people of an area [Mid-20C. < Maori, 'people of the land']

Tange Kenzo /táng gay kénnzō/ (*b*. 1913) Japanese architect. He is often considered Japan's greatest modern architect. His works include the Peace Centre at Hiroshima (1949).

tangelo /tánjəlō/ (*plural* **-los**) *n* **1.** a citrus fruit with smooth easily peeled skin and sharp-tasting orange flesh **2.** a hybrid between a tangerine tree and a grapefruit tree that produces tangelos [Early 20C. Blend of TANGERINE + POMELO]

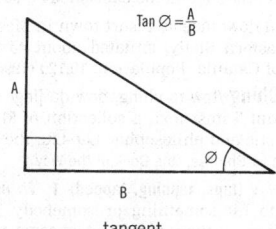

$$\text{Tan} \varnothing = \frac{A}{B}$$

tangent

tangent /tánjənt/ *n* **1.** LINE OR SURFACE THAT TOUCHES ANOTHER a line, curve, or surface that touches another curve or surface but does not cross or intersect it **2.** TRIGONOMETRIC FUNCTION for a given angle in a right-angled triangle, a trigonometric function that is equal to the length of the side opposite the angle divided by the length of the adjacent side **3.** PART OF SURVEY LINE the part of a survey line that is straight **4.** DIGRESSION a change of topic that is not relevant to the subject currently under consideration **5.** MUSIC PART OF CLAVICHORD a part of the clavichord that resembles a small hammer and strikes the strings ■ *adj* **1.** MATHS same as **tangential** (sense 2) **2.** TOUCHING AT ONE POINT touching only at a single point **3.** TOUCHING BUT NOT CROSSING in contact, but not crossing or intersecting **4.** AWAY FROM POINT not relevant to the subject currently under consideration [Late 16C. < Latin *tangent-*, present participle of *tangere* 'touch'] —**tangency** *n* ◇ **go off at** *or* **on a tangent** to change quickly and suddenly to a different subject or line of thought

ORIGIN The Latin word *tangere* 'to touch', from which *tangent* is derived, is also the source of English *attain*, *contact*, *intact*, *tact*, *tangible*, and *tax*, and possibly also of *taste*.

tangent galvanometer *n* a device with a compass needle suspended horizontally in a vertical coil through which a direct current is passed, causing deflection of the needle proportional to the size of the current. It can be used to calculate the strength of the Earth's magnetic field.

tangential /tan jénsh'l/ *adj* **1.** with only slight relevance to the current subject **2.** relating to or involving a tangent —**tangentiality** /tan jénshi álləti/ *n* —**tangentially** *adv*

tangerine /tánjə reén/ *n* **1.** CITRUS FRUIT a citrus fruit with easily peeled orange skin and sweet flesh **2.** CITRUS TREE a citrus tree, widely cultivated in tropical and warm regions, that produces tangerines. Native to: Southeast Asia. Latin name: *Citrus reticulata*. **3.** BRIGHT ORANGE COLOUR a bright orange colour like that of a tangerine [Mid-19C. < TANGERINE] —**tangerine** *adj*

Tangerine /tánjə reén/ *adj* relating to the Moroccan port of Tangier, or its people or culture [Early 18C. Probably after Spanish *Tangerino* 'of or from Tangier']

tangi /túng ee/ (*plural* **-gis**) *n NZ* a Maori funeral ceremony and the feast that accompanies it [Mid-19C. < Maori, 'lament, action of crying']

tangible /tánjəb'l/ *adj* **1.** ABLE TO BE TOUCHED able to be touched or perceived through the sense of touch ○ *a tangible coldness* **2.** ACTUAL capable of being understood and evaluated, and therefore regarded as real ○ *There is no tangible evidence to support this claim.* **3.** ABLE TO BE REALIZED capable of being given a physical existence ○ *tangible financial benefits* ■ *n* SOMETHING TANGIBLE something that has a physical form, especially a financial asset (*often used in the plural*) [Late 16C. Directly or via French < late Latin *tangibilis* 'that may be touched' < Latin *tangere* 'to touch'] —**tangibility** /tánjə bílləti/ *n* —**tangibleness** *n* —**tangibly** *adv*

Tangier /tan jeér/ port city in northern Morocco. Population: 526,215 (1994).

tangle¹ /táng g'l/ *v* (**-gles**, **-gling**, **-gled**) **1.** *vti* BECOME TWISTED to become twisted together into a jumbled mass, or make something become twisted into a jumbled mass **2.** *vt* CATCH AND HOLD SOMETHING to catch and entwine somebody or something in something that is difficult to get out of, e.g. a net or trap. ○ *I got my jacket tangled in the branches.* **3.** *vt* TRAP SOMEBODY IN DIFFICULT SITUATION to trap somebody in a complicated, awkward, or dangerous situation ○ *tangled in a web of controversy* **4.** *vi* COME INTO CONFLICT to become involved in a confrontation or disagreement with somebody, especially somebody powerful or important ○ *Don't tangle with those people.* ■ *n* **1.** JUMBLED MASS a mass of fibres, lines, or other things twisted together **2.** DIFFICULTY a complicated and confused situation or problem **3.** STATE OF MENTAL UPSET a state of mental or emotional confusion or upset **4.** ARGUMENT a confrontation or disagreement with somebody [14C. Origin ?] —**tanglement** *n* —**tangler** *n* —**tangly** *adj*

tangle² /táng g'l/, **tangle weed** *n* a large brown seaweed that grows on shores at or below the level of low tide [Mid-16C. Probably via Norwegian *tángel* < Old Norse *pongull* < *pang* 'bladder wrack']

tango

tango /táng gō/ *n* (*plural* **-gos**) **1.** DANCE OF LATIN AMERICAN ORIGIN a stylized Latin American ballroom dance in 2/4 time in which the steps are marked by glides and sudden pauses **2.** MUSIC the music for a tango ■ *vi* (**-gos**, **-going**, **-goed**) DANCE TANGO to dance a tango [Late 19C. < Argentine Spanish] —**tangoist** *n*

Tango *n* a code word for the letter 'T', used in international radio communications

tangram /tán gram/ *n* a puzzle of Chinese origin that involves putting together seven pieces, usually a square, a parallelogram, and five triangles, to form different shapes [Mid-19C. Origin ?]

Tangshan /táng shán/ city in Hebei Province, northern China, southeast of Beijing. Population: 1,540,000 (1995).

Tanguy /táang geé/, **Yves** (1900–55) French-born US artist. He is known for his surrealist paintings of organic forms in dream landscapes.

Tang Yin /táng yín/ (1470–1523) Chinese painter and poet. One of the most important Ming dynasty artists, he is known for his paintings of landscapes and elegant women.

Tani /taáni/, **Buncho** (1763–1840) Japanese artist. A noted book illustrator, he was responsible for introducing Western style to Japanese painting.

tanist /tánnist/ *n* the heir apparent to a Celtic chieftain, usually a member of the chieftain's own clan and elected during the chieftain's lifetime [Mid-16C. < Irish Gaelic *tánaiste* 'second in excellence or rank']

tanistry /tánnistri/ *n* the process of selecting an heir apparent to a Celtic chieftain while the current chieftain is still alive

taniwha /tún ee faa/ *n NZ* a Maori water spirit that inspires fear [Mid-19C. < Maori]

Tanizaki Junichiro /taán ee zaák ee joòn ee cheér aw/ (1886–1965) Japanese writer. His novels present the conflict between modern Western-influenced realities and traditional values.

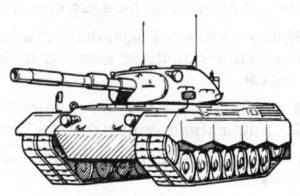

tank (sense 6)

tank /tangk/ *n* **1.** LARGE CONTAINER a large container for storing liquids or gases **2.** AMOUNT HELD BY TANK the amount of liquid or gas that a tank holds ○ *bought a tank of petrol* **3.** CONTAINER FOR FISH a sturdy container with rectangular glass sides, used for keeping live fish or reptiles in **4.** POND OR RESERVOIR a fairly small body of water, especially one used for water storage **5.** *N Am* JAIL prison, or a prison cell (*informal*) **6.** MIL ARMOURED VEHICLE a large armoured combat vehicle with tracks, a rotating turret, and a heavy gun **7.** PHOTOGRAPHY CONTAINER FOR DEVELOPING FILM a lightproof container for developing film, designed so that processing chemicals can be poured in and out without light entering **8.** PHOTOGRAPHY TRAY FOR PROCESSING SHEETS OF FILM a large tray or container for processing a number of sheets of film together ■ *v* (**tanks, tanking, tanked**) **1.** *vt* PUT SOMETHING IN TANK to put or keep something in a tank **2.** *vi* GO FAST to move quickly or heavily, often with great purpose or determination (*informal*) ○ *He tanked up the road to the bus stop.* **3.** *vt* BEAT IN COMPETITION to defeat a person or team heavily in a sport, competition, or election (*informal*) **4.** *vi* *N Am* DROP SHARPLY IN PRICE to drop sharply in price to the point of bottoming out (*slang*) ○ *Tech stocks tanked.* [Early 17C. < Gujarati *tākū*, Marathi *ṭākē* 'pond, cistern'] —**tankful** *n*

tank up *v* **1.** *vti* to fill the fuel tank of a motor vehicle (*informal*) **2.** *vi* to drink enough alcohol to become drunk (*slang*)

tanka¹ /tángkə/ (*plural* **-kas** *or* same) *n* **1.** a five-line Japanese verse form in which the first and third lines have five syllables each and the other lines have seven syllables each **2.** a poem with a tanka verse structure [Late 19C. < Japanese < *tan* 'short' + *ka* 'song']

tanka² /tángkə/ *n* a Tibetan Buddhist painting in a form that can be rolled up, displayed, or carried as a banner [Early 20C. < Tibetan *t'ánka* 'image, painting']

tankage /tángkij/ *n* **1.** TANK CAPACITY the amount that can be held by a tank or tanks **2.** STORAGE IN TANK the storage of something in a tank, or the cost of this **3.** AGRIC FERTILIZER a by-product of the slaughter of livestock consisting of carcass trimmings cooked to reduce moisture and drained of surplus fat. Use: feed supplement, fertilizer.

tankard /tángkərd/ *n* **1.** a large mug with a handle and sometimes a hinged lid, made of glass, pewter, or silver plate, typically used for drinking beer **2.** the amount of liquid that a tankard holds [14C. Origin ?]

tank car *n N Am* RAIL same as **tank wagon**

tanked /tangkt/, **tanked-up** *adj* extremely drunk (*slang*)

tank engine, **tank locomotive** *n* a steam engine that carries its water supply in tanks at the sides of the boiler instead of carrying it in a tender

tanker /tángkər/ *n* a ship, lorry, or aeroplane designed to carry large quantities of liquid or gas

tank farm *n* a site with several large storage tanks, especially ones containing oil

tank farming *n* AGRIC same as **hydroponics**

tankini /tang kéeni/ *n* a woman's swimming costume with a bikini bottom and a brief tank top [Late 20C. Blend of TANK TOP + BIKINI]

tank locomotive *n* RAIL same as **tank engine**

tank top *n* a close-fitting sleeveless, usually knitted garment with a low U-shaped or V-shaped neck [Probably because it resembles a garment worn by the crews of armoured tanks]

tank trap *n* something designed to stop or slow the movement of military tanks, e.g. a concrete block

tank wagon *n* a railway wagon that has a large tank for transporting liquids or gases in bulk. N Am term **tank car**

tannage /tánnij/ *n* 1. the tanning of animal hides or skins 2. an animal skin or hide that has been tanned

tannate /tánnayt/ *n* a salt or ester of tannic acid [Early 19C. < TANNIC]

tanned /tand/ *adj* 1. with a tan from the sun or an artificial source of ultraviolet light. N Am term **tan**[1] 2. prepared by the process of tanning animal skins

tanner[1] /tánnər/ *n* somebody who tans animal skins [Pre-12C. Both < TAN[1] and via Old French *tanere* < medieval Latin *tannator*]

tanner[2] /tánnər/ *n* a sixpence, or the sum of sixpence in predecimal currency (*dated informal*) [Early 19C. Origin ?]

tannery /tánnəri/ (*plural* -**ies**) *n* a building or factory where animal skins and hides are tanned

tannic /tánnik/ *adj* relating to, containing, or derived from tannin [Mid-19C. < French *tannique* < *tanin* (see TANNIN)]

tannic acid *n* CHEM same as **tannin**

tannie /tánni/ *n S Africa* 1. an aunt 2. an older woman (*informal; often used as an affectionate or respectful form of address*) [Mid-20C. < Afrikaans, 'auntie']

tannin /tánnin/ *n* a brownish or yellowish compound found in plants. Use: tanning, dyes, astringents. [Early 19C. < French *tanin* < *tan* 'tanbark' < medieval Latin *tannum*]

tanning /tánning/ *n* 1. BROWNING OF SKIN the browning of skin when it is exposed to the sun or some other ultraviolet light source 2. CONVERSION OF ANIMAL SKIN INTO LEATHER the conversion of animal skins and hides into leather 3. SOUND BEATING a sound beating or whipping

tanning bed *n* N Am same as **sunbed** (sense 1)

Tannoy /tánnoy/ *tdmk* a trademark for a public-address system

tan oak *n* a large evergreen hardwood tree of the beech family whose bark is used for tanning. Native to: California, Oregon. Latin name: *Lithocarpus densiflorus.*

Tanoan /tə nố ən/ *n* a group of Native North American languages spoken mainly in New Mexico and Arizona. Native speakers: 3,000. [Late 19C < Spanish *Tano* 'Tewa'] —**Tanoan** *adj*

tanpura *n* MUSIC same as **tamboura**

tanrec *n* ZOOL same as **tenrec**

tansy /tánzi/ (*plural* -**sies**) *n* 1. an aromatic perennial plant of the daisy family with leaves divided into toothed leaflets. Flowers: yellow, in flat-topped clusters. Use: formerly, in cooking and medicine. Native to: Europe, Asia. Latin name: *Tanacetum vulgare.* 2. a plant similar to the tansy, e.g. ragwort [13C. Origin ?]

Tanta /tántə/ *city* in northeastern Egypt, in the Nile delta, capital of Gharbiyah Governorate. Population: 380,000 (1992).

tantalic /tan tállik/ *adj* relating to or containing tantalum, especially with a valency of five

tantalise *vt* another spelling of **tantalize**

tantalite /tántə līt/ *n* a reddish-black mixed oxide mineral containing tantalum, iron, and manganese. Source: granites, pegmatites. Use: source of tantalum.

tantalize /tántə līz/ (-**lizes**, -**lizing**, -**lized**), **tantalise** (-**lises**, -**lising**, -**lised**) *vt* to tease or torment somebody by letting the person see, but not have, something that is desirable [Late 16C. < Latin *Tantalus* 'Tantalus'] —**tantalization** /tántə līt záysh'n/ *n* —**tantalizer** *n*

tantalizing /tántə līzing/ *adj* 1. tempting but unavailable or unattainable ○ *a really tantalizing offer* 2. causing feelings of excitement, pleasure, or anticipation ○ *tantalizing glimpses of tropical landscapes* —**tantalizingly** *adv*

tantalum /tántələm/ *n* a dense blue-grey metallic element. Use: electronic components, alloys, in plates and pins for orthopaedic surgery. Symbol **Ta**. See table at **element** [Early 19C. Via modern Latin < Latin *Tantalus* 'Tantalus', because of its inability to absorb acid even when it is immersed in it]

tantalus /tántələss/ *n* a lockable stand or case for decanters of alcoholic drinks, especially spirits [Late 19C. < TANTALUS]

Tantalus /tántələss/ *n* in Greek mythology, a king who was condemned to stand in water under a fruit tree. Whenever he tried to drink or eat, the water or fruit receded beyond his reach. [Mid-18C. Via Latin < Greek]

tantamount /tántə mownt/ *adj* equivalent to a particular thing in effect, outcome, or value, especially something unpleasant ○ *an answer that was tantamount to a refusal* [Mid-17C. < Anglo-French *tant amunter* 'amount to as much' < Old French *tant* 'as much' + *amonter* 'to amount']

tantara /tántə raá/ *n* 1. a fanfare or blast on a horn, especially when used to announce something important 2. a sound that resembles a tantara [Mid-16C. An imitation of the sound]

tantie /tánti/, **Tantie** *n Carib* 1. an aunt 2. an older woman [Late 19C. < French Creole, blend of French *tante* + AUNTIE]

tantivy /tan tívvi/ *n* (*plural* -**ies**) 1. HUNTER'S SHOUT a hunting cry, especially one given by a hunter riding a horse at full gallop 2. FAST MOVEMENT a fast ride, especially on a horse going at full gallop ■ *adj* SPEEDY moving very fast, especially when on a horse going at full gallop ■ *interj* USED AS A HUNTING CRY used as a hunting cry, especially by a hunter riding a horse at full gallop [Mid-17C. Probably an imitation of the sound of galloping horses, influenced by TANTARA] —**tantivy** *adv*

tant mieux /taáN myố/ *interj* so much the better [Mid-18C. < French]

tant pis /taáN peé/ *interj* so much the worse [Late 18C. < French]

Tantra /tántrə, tún-/ *n* the sacred books of Tantrism. They were written between the 7th and 17th centuries AD and mostly consist of a dialogue between Shiva and his wife Shakti. [Late 18C. < Sanskrit, 'loom, warp, groundwork, system, doctrine']

Tantrism /tántrizəm, tún-/ *n* a movement in Hinduism and Buddhism, especially a variety based on yoga and intended to release energy through sexual intercourse in which the orgasm is withheld or delayed —**Tantric** *adj* —**Tantrist** *n*

tantrum /tántrəm/ *n* an outburst of anger, especially a childish display of rage or bad temper [Early 18C. Origin ?]

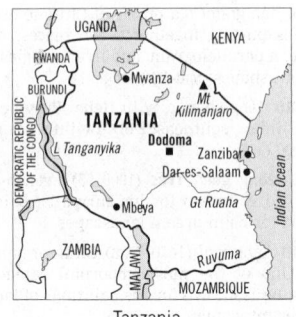

Tanzania

Tanzania /tánzə neé ə/ *country* in East Africa, including the islands of Zanzibar and Pemba. It became an independent member of the Commonwealth, as Tanganyika, in 1961. It changed its name to Tanzania after the union with Zanzibar in 1964. Language: Kiswahili, English. Currency: Tanzanian shilling. Capital: Dodoma. Population: 35,922,454 (2003). Area: 945,100 sq. km/364,900 sq. mi. Official name **United Republic of Tanzania** —**Tanzanian** *n, adj*

Tao /tow, dow/ *n* 1. ULTIMATE REALITY in Taoist philosophy, the ultimate reality in which all things are located or happen 2. *also* **tao** UNIVERSAL ENERGY in Taoist philosophy, the universal energy that makes and maintains everything that exists 3. RELATIONSHIP BETWEEN INDIVIDUAL AND UNIVERSE in Taoist philosophy, the order and wisdom of individual life, and the way that this harmonizes with the universe as a whole [Mid-18C. < Chinese *dào* 'way, path, right way (of life)', reason']

Taoiseach /teéshək/ *n* the prime minister of the Republic of Ireland [Mid-20C. < Irish, 'chief', leader']

Taoism /tów izəm, dów-/ *n* 1. a Chinese philosophy that advocates a simple life and a policy of noninterference with the natural course of things. It was founded in the 6th century BC by the mystic and philosopher Lao-tzu. 2. a popular Chinese religion that seeks harmony and long life through the philosophy of Taoism combined with pantheism and magical practices —**Taoist** *n, adj* —**Taoistic** /tow ístik, dow-/ *adj*

taonga /ta óngə/ *n NZ* a treasure, especially a cultural treasure, that should be cherished [< Maori]

Taormina /towr meénə/ *resort* town in Messina Province, eastern Sicily, situated about 45 km/28 mi. north of Catania. Population: 10,120 (1996).

Tao Te Ching /tów tə ching, dów də jíng/ *n* the most important Taoist text, a collection of 81 poems by the mystic and philosopher Lao-tzu, the founder of Taoism [< Chinese, 'the Book of the Way']

tap[1] /tap/ *v* (**taps**, **tapping**, **tapped**) 1. *vti* HIT SOMETHING LIGHTLY to hit something or somebody lightly, especially more than once 2. *vt* HIT OBJECT AGAINST SOMETHING ELSE to hit an object lightly against something else 3. *vt* MAKE SOUND to produce something such as a noise or rhythm by tapping 4. *vi* MOVE MAKING LIGHT SOUNDS to move making a series of light noises 5. *vi* DO TAP DANCE to perform a tap dance 6. *vt* REINFORCE SHOE to attach a small piece of leather or metal to the toe or heel of a shoe to cover worn parts or to protect against wear 7. *vt* US GIVE POST TO SOMEBODY to select and appoint somebody for a particular role or office (*usually passive*) ○ *tapped her as the publicity chair* ○ *'The coal industry was tapped to lead the way for reform'* (US News & World Report; December 1998) ■ *n* 1. LIGHT BLOW a light blow, especially one that produces a noise 2. SOUND OF BLOW the sound made by a light blow 3. METAL PART ON TAP-DANCING SHOE a metal tip attached to the toe or heel of a tap-dancing shoe so that it can produce sounds 4. TAP-DANCING the performing of tap dancing (*informal*) 5. REINFORCEMENT FOR SHOE a small piece of leather or metal attached to the toe or heel of a shoe to cover a worn part or to protect against wear 6. PHON TOUCH OF TONGUE TO MOUTH TOP the production of a speech sound made when any flexible speech organ hits any hard part of the mouth, e.g. when the tongue is brought into contact with the hard palate [12C. Origin ?] —**tappable** *adj*

tap[2] /tap/ *n* 1. VALVE ON PIPE a valve on a pipe that is operated by a handle and used to draw off or control the flow of liquid, especially from a water supply. N Am term **faucet** 2. BARREL PLUG a stopper in a cask or barrel, used to seal in the contents and also to allow liquid to be drawn off at a controlled rate 3. BEER FROM CASK liquid, especially beer, that has been drawn from a tap in a cask or barrel and is regarded as having particular qualities because of this 4. LEISURE same as **taproom** 5. TELECOM LISTENING DEVICE a device put into a telephone or other telecommunication equipment in order to secretly listen to or record other people's conversations 6. SURG SURGICAL FLUID EXTRACTION a surgical procedure that involves drawing off a body fluid using a hollow needle or tube 7. TOOL FOR SCREW THREADS a tool used to make an internal screw thread 8. *Aus, US* ELEC same as **tapping** 9. FIN SECURITY ON MARKET AT PREDETERMINED PRICE

a government security made available gradually on the stock market when its price reaches a predetermined level ■ *v* (**taps, tapping, tapped**) **1.** *vt* **ATTACH TAP** to attach a tap to something in order to draw off or control the flow of liquid **2.** *vt* **DRAW LIQUID FROM BARREL** to draw off liquid such as wine or beer from a barrel by means of a tap **3.** *vti* **PUT RESOURCE TO USE** to make use of a resource or supply of something (*informal*) ○ *tapped into our capital* **4.** *vt* **BORROW MONEY** to borrow a sum of money from somebody (*informal*) ○ *She tapped me for 20 quid.* **5.** *vt* SURG **DRAW FLUID FROM BODY** to surgically draw off fluid from a part of the body **6.** *vt* FORESTRY **OBTAIN SAP** to cut into a tree in order to draw off sap or resin **7.** *vt* ELEC ENG **GET INTO POWER SUPPLY** to connect to a power supply and divert energy from it, usually illegally **8.** *vt* TELECOM **PLACE LISTENING DEVICE ON PHONE LINE** to fit a device into a telephone or other telecommunication equipment in order to secretly listen to or record other people's conversations **9.** *vt* TELECOM **SECRETLY LISTEN TO PHONE CONVERSATIONS** to secretly listen to or record other people's conversations using a device fitted into a telephone or other telecommunication equipment **10.** *vt* MECH ENG **MAKE INTERNAL SCREW THREAD** to cut an internal screw thread into something [Old English *tæppa* (noun), *tæppian* (verb) < Germanic] —**tappable** *adj* ◇ **on tap** (*informal*) **1.** available for immediate use **2.** on draught

tapa /taápə/ *n* **1.** the inner bark of the paper mulberry tree **2.** a strong fabric made from tapa [Early 19C. < Polynesian]

tapas /táppəss/ *npl* small savoury snacks that are often served as an appetizer along with alcoholic drinks, originally in Spain [Mid-20C. Plural of Spanish *tapa* 'cover, lid']

tap dance *n* a step dance performed by somebody wearing shoes with metal tips to make a rhythmic sound

tap-dance *vi* to perform a dance or dances wearing shoes with metal tips at the toes and heels to make a rhythmic sound —**tap-dancer** *n* —**tap-dancing** *n*

tape /tayp/ *n* **1. LONG NARROW STRIP OF MATERIAL** a long narrow strip of material such as paper, fabric, or plastic used to secure or tie something **2. STRIP OF STICKY MATERIAL** a long strip of plastic or cloth with adhesive on one or both sides, usually on a roll **3. MAGNETIC TAPE** magnetic tape used in cassettes and some computers **4. VIDEO OR AUDIO CASSETTE** a cassette used for audio or video recording or playback ○ *Put the tape in the player.* **5. FINISHING LINE MARKER** a long strip of material that marks the finishing line in a race **6.** same as **tape measure 7.** RECORDING same as **tape recording 8.** MIL same as **stripe**[1] *n* (sense 4) (*informal*) ■ *v* (**tapes, taping, taped**) **1.** *vti* **RECORD SOMETHING** to record something, especially music or a television programme, on magnetic tape **2.** *vt* **FIX SOMETHING** to secure, fasten, or strengthen something using tape **3.** *vt* **MEASURE SOMETHING** to measure something using a tape measure **4.** *vt N Am* MED same as **strap** *v* (sense 2) [Old English *tæppe* 'narrow strip of cloth', origin ?] ◇ **have somebody** *or* **something taped** to have a clear understanding of somebody or something (*informal*)

tape up *vt US* MED same as **strap** *v* (sense 2)

tape deck *n* a piece of electrical equipment that plays and records tapes, especially audio cassettes

tape grass *n* a perennial grass that grows largely submerged in fresh water, forming tufts of long narrow leaves. Flowers: inconspicuous, pinkish-white. Latin name: *Vallisneria spiralis.*

tapeline /táyp līn/ *n* MEASURE same as **tape measure**

tape machine *n* an electronic machine that receives and displays or prints current stock quotations. N Am term **ticker**

tape measure *n* a long roll or strip of fabric, plastic, paper, or thin metal that is marked off in inches or centimetres for measuring the length of something

tapenade /táppə naad, táppə naád/ *n* a paste made from puréed black olives, capers, and anchovies [< French, < Provençal *tapeno* 'caper']

taper /táypər/ *vti* (**-pers, -pering, -pered**) **1. GET OR MAKE NARROWER** to become narrower at one end, especially gradually, or make something do this **2. REDUCE GRADUALLY** to become smaller in size or amount, or less important, especially gradually, or make something do this ○ *Sales of the first album are beginning to taper off.* ■ *n* **1. SLIM CANDLE** a slim candle that is narrower at the top than at the bottom **2. STRIP FOR TRANSFERRING FLAME** a strip of wood or waxed paper used for taking a flame to light something else **3. NARROWING OF SHAPE** a gradual narrowing in the shape of something ○ *a spire with a pronounced taper* **4. DIM LIGHT** a faint source of light, e.g. from a small candle [Pre-12C. Alteration of Latin *papyrus* 'papyrus', whose pith was used for candle wicks] —**tapering** *adj* —**taperingly** *adv*

tape recorder *n* a machine that can record and play audio tapes, especially one with its own speaker —**tape-record** *vt*

tape recording *n* a recording made on magnetic tape, especially an audio recording

taper relief *n* a reduction in capital gains tax due on the disposal of an asset, based on the length of time the asset has been held after 5 April 1998

tapestry /táppistri/ (*plural* **-tries**) *n* **1.** a heavy piece of fabric with a woven pattern or picture. Use: wall hanging, upholstery. **2.** *N Am* HANDICRAFT same as **needlepoint** (sense 1) **3.** something that is considered to be rich, varied, or intricately interwoven ○ *the rich tapestry of life* [14C. < French *tapisserie* < *tapis* 'carpet' < Greek *tapēt-*]

CULTURAL NOTE ***The Bayeux Tapestry***, a large embroidery (1092) found at Bayeux in northern France. A remarkable work of art and an important historical document, it consists of a band of linen measuring 231 ft/70 m by 20 in./50 cm, embroidered with vivid scenes that depict the Norman conquest of England. Its existence was first recorded in 1476 at Bayeux, where it was used to decorate the nave of the cathedral.

---

tapestry moth *n* a moth whose caterpillars eat fabrics made from wool and other natural fibres. The adults are brown with white-tipped forewings and prefer damp conditions. Latin name: *Trichophaga tapetzella.*

tapetum /tə peétəm/ (*plural* **-ta** /-tə/) *n* **1.** a specialized membrane or layer of cells **2.** a layer of cells in the wall of the eye of nocturnal and deep-sea animals that reflects light back onto the retina, enhancing visual sensitivity in dim light. Light reflected by this layer is responsible for the shining eyes of cats seen when they are illuminated at night. [Early 18C. < late Latin < Latin *tapete* < Greek *tapēt-*] —**tapetal** *adj*

tapeworm /táyp wurm/ *n* a flatworm with a long ribbon-shaped segmented body that exists in many varieties and lives mainly as a parasite in the gut of vertebrate animals. Infestation is common among domestic animals, and humans can also become infested, especially by eating undercooked meat containing tapeworm larvae. Class: Cestoda. Technical name **cestode**

taphole /táp hōl/ *n* a hole at the bottom of a furnace for drawing off molten metal or slag

taphonomy /tə fónnəmi/ *n* the scientific study of fossilization [Mid-20C. < Greek *taphos* 'grave'] —**taphonomic** /táffə nómmik/ *adj* —**taphonomist** *n*

taphouse /táp howss/ (*plural* **-houses** /-hówziz/) *n* an inn, bar, public house, or other place serving alcohol (*archaic*)

tap-in *n* **1.** in soccer, a goal scored with minimum effort by a player who is very close to the opposition's goal **2.** in golf, a short putt to put the ball in the hole **3.** BASKETBALL same as **tip-in** (sense 1)

tapioca /táppi ṓkə/ *n* **1.** a milk pudding made from the roots of a cassava plant **2.** a starch obtained from the roots of a cassava plant. Use: puddings, thickener for sauces. [Early 18C. Via Portuguese or Spanish < Tupi *tipioca* < *tipi* 'residue, dregs' + *ok* 'squeeze out']

tapir /táypər, táy peer/ (*plural* **-pirs** or *same*) *n* a nocturnal hoofed forest-dwelling mammal that has short limbs and a fleshy snout and feeds on fruit and vegetation. Native to: Central and South America, Southeast Asia. Family: Tapiridae. [Late 18C. Via Portuguese or Spanish < Tupi *tapira*]

tap-off *n* BASKETBALL same as **tip-off**[2]

tapper[1] /táppər/ *n* somebody or something that draws off or controls the flow of a liquid (*often used in combination*) ○ *a rubber-tapper* [Early 19C. < TAP[1]]

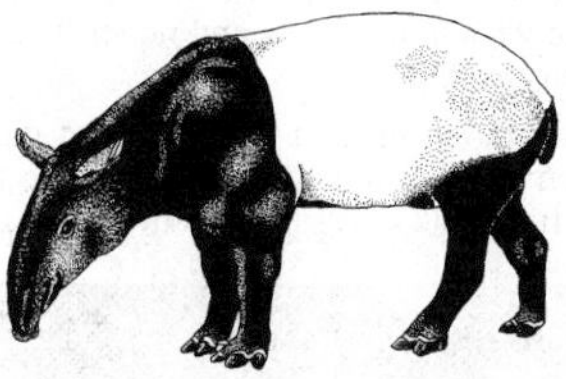

tapir

tapper[2] /táppər/ *n* **1.** somebody or something that hits something or somebody lightly, especially more than once, or that makes a tapping sound **2.** same as **tapster** (*archaic*) [Pre-12C. < TAP[2]]

tappet /táppit/ *n* a lever, arm, or other machine part that transfers motion from a cam to a part such as a valve or push rod [Mid-18C. < TAP[1]]

tapping /tápping/ *n* a point in an electrical circuit where a temporary connection may be made. Aus, US term **tap**[2]

taproom /táp room, -rŏŏm/ *n* a bar in a place such as a hotel or pub

taproot /táp root/ *n* a long tapering root that extends downwards below the stem of some plants and has fine lateral roots. It often serves as a food storage organ, e.g. in the carrot. [Early 17C. < TAP[2]]

taps /taps/ *n* (*takes a singular verb*) **1. SIGNAL FOR LIGHTS OUT** a bugle call or other signal given at the end of the day, especially in a military camp, as an order that lights should be put out **2. SIGNAL AT FUNERAL** a bugle call or other signal given at a funeral or memorial service, especially a military one **3. GUIDE SONG** a song sung by members of the Guide movement at the close of a meeting or around a campfire at the end of the day [Early 19C. < TAP[1], or alteration of *taptoo*, variant of TATTOO[2]]

tapster /tápstər/ *n* somebody who serves drinks in a bar or pub (*archaic*) [Old English *tæpestre*, originally feminine of TAPPER[2]]

tapu /taá poo/ *adj NZ* same as **taboo** *adj* (senses 1–2) [Mid-19C. < Maori]

tap water *n* water that comes out of the tap, from a domestic or commercial water supply

tar[1] /taar/ *n* **1. THICK BLACK LIQUID** a thick black liquid obtained through the destructive distillation of an organic substance such as wood or coal **2. TOBACCO SMOKE RESIDUE** the particulate residue from tobacco smoke ■ *vt* (**tars, tarring, tarred**) **COVER SOMETHING WITH TAR** to coat or cover something, especially a road surface, with tar [Old English *teoru* < Indo-European] —**tarry** *adj* ◇ **tar and feather somebody** to smear tar over somebody and cover the tar with feathers as a form of punishment

tar[2] /taar/ *n* SAILING same as **sailor** (sense 1) (*archaic informal*) [Late 17C. Origin ?]

Tara, Hill of /taárə/ hill in County Meath, Ireland, northwest of Dublin. It was the seat of the Irish kings until about AD 560. Height: 155 m/507 ft.

taradiddle *n* another spelling of **tarradiddle** (*informal*)

tarakihi /tárrə kee/, **terakihi** /térrə-/ *n* an edible fish with a silvery body and a black saddle behind the head. Native to: New Zealand. Latin name: *Nemadactylus macropterus.* [< Maori]

taramasalata /tárrəməssə laátə/ *n* a creamy pink or beige paste made from smoked fish roe. It is usually served in the form of a pâté or dip as an appetizer or snack. [Early 20C. < modern Greek < *taramas* 'preserved roe' (< Turkish *tarama* 'preparation of soft roe or red caviar') + *salata* 'salad']

Taranaki /tárrə náki/ administrative region of New Zealand, located in the southwestern part of the North Island and including the city of New Plymouth. Population: 102,858 (2001). Area: 12,640 sq. km/4,880 sq. mi.

Taranaki, Mount /tárrə náki/ dormant volcano near the

western coast of the North Island, New Zealand. Height: 2,518 m/8,261 ft.

tarantass /taˊarən táss/ n a large Russian horse-drawn carriage with four wheels and no springs [Mid-19C. < Russian *tarantas*]

tarantella /tárrən téllə/ n 1. a whirling dance from southern Italy in 6/8 time 2. the music for a tarantella [Late 18C. < Italian < TARANTO]

Quentin Tarantino

Tarantino /tárrən teˊenō/, **Quentin** (*b.* 1963) US film director and screenwriter. His first film, *Reservoir Dogs* (1992), followed by *Pulp Fiction* (1994), established him as an important but controversial filmmaker. Full name **Tarantino, Quentin Jerome**

'To me, violence is a totally aesthetic subject. Saying you don't like violence in movies is like saying you don't like dance sequences in movies. I do like dance sequences in movies, but if I didn't, it doesn't mean I should stop dance sequences being made.'
[Quentin Tarantino, *True Romance*; 1995]

tarantism /tárrəntizəm/ n a nervous condition characterized by uncontrollable body movements, common in southern Italy between the 15th and 17th centuries and formerly believed to be caused by the bite of the tarantula [Mid-17C. < Italian *tarantismo* < TARANTO]

Taranto /tə rántō/ city, port, and administrative centre of Taranto Province, Apulia Region, southern Italy. Population: 202,033 (2001).

tarantula

tarantula /tə rántyōōlə/ (*plural* -las or -lae /-lee/) n 1. a large spider that has a hairy body and legs and feeds on invertebrates, toads, small reptiles, and young birds. Native to: tropical and subtropical America. Family: Theraphosidae. 2. a wolf spider formerly believed to cause tarantism with its bite. Native to: Europe. Latin name: *Lycosa tarentula*. [Mid-16C. Via medieval Latin < Italian *tarantola* < TARANTO]

Tararua Range /tárrə roˊo ə-/ mountain range in the southern part of the North Island, New Zealand, north of Wellington. Its highest point is Mitre Peak, 1,571 m/5,154 ft.

Tarawa /tə raˊawə, tárrə waa/ atoll in the west-central Pacific Ocean and capital of Kiribati. It was retaken in World War II by US Marines from the Japanese in November 1943. Population: 28,802 (1990). Area: 23 sq. km/9 sq. mi.

taraxacum /tə ráksəkəm/ n 1. a herbal remedy extracted from dandelion roots or leaves. Use: mild laxative, liver tonic, diuretic. 2. a plant such as the dandelion that produces flower heads made up of numerous florets and with seeds attached to whitish hairs. Genus: *Taraxacum*. [Early 18C. Via medieval Latin *altaraxacon* < Arabic, Persian *ṭarakšakūn* 'dandelion, wild endive' < Persian *talk* 'bitter' + *čakūk* 'purslane']

tarboosh /taar boˊosh/, **tarbush**, **tarbouche** n a brimless, usually red, felt hat, similar to a fez, that has a silk tassel and is worn by Muslim men by itself or with a turban [Early 18C. Via Egyptian Arabic *ṭarbūš* < Ottoman Turkish *terpōš*, Turkish *tarbuș* < Persian *sarpūš* < *sar* 'head' + *pūš* 'cover']

tardigrade /taˊardi graydə/ n TINY WATER ANIMAL a tiny invertebrate water animal with a short body and four pairs of stubby legs. Phylum: Tardigrada. ■ adj 1. RELATING TO TARDIGRADES relating to or belonging to the tardigrades 2. SLUGGISH sluggish or slow-moving [Early 17C. Directly or via French < Latin *tardigradus* 'walking slowly' < *tardus* 'slow']

tardis /taˊardiss/, **Tardis** n a room or building that seems to be much larger than it actually is or than it appears to be from the outside [Late 20C. < *Tardis*, time machine used in the British television series *Dr Who*]

tardive dyskinesia /taˊardiv diski neˊezi ə/ n a condition marked by involuntary movements of the tongue and facial muscles, especially after prolonged treatment with phenothiazine tranquillizers or similar drugs [< French *tardif* (see TARDY)]

tardy /taˊardi/ (-dier, -diest) adj 1. later than the expected or usual time 2. slow to move or react (*archaic or literary*) [Mid-16C. < French *tardif* < Latin *tardus* 'slow, sluggish'] —**tardily** adv —**tardiness** n

tare[1] /tair/ n 1. VETCH PLANT a trailing or scrambling vetch plant that has compound leaves with paired leaflets and tendrils. Flowers: bluish or purplish, in spikes. Native to: Europe, North Africa. Genus: *Vicia*. 2. VETCH SEED the seed of a tare or vetch 3. PROBLEMATIC WEED in the Bible, a weed found growing among crops, usually considered to be darnel [13C. Origin ?]

SPELLCHECK tare or tear? Do not confuse the spelling of *tare* and *tear*, which sound similar. There are two words spelt *tare*, one denoting a type of plant, the other the weight of a container, packaging, or vehicle: both are rarely encountered in general usage. The word *tear*, meaning 'to pull apart or rip' and 'to move or act quickly', or as a noun 'a hole or split', is much more common: *Tear it in half. There's a tear in this sheet. They were tearing down the road to catch the bus.*

tare[2] /tair/ n 1. WEIGHT OF PACKAGING the weight of a container or of the packaging used to wrap goods 2. ALLOWANCE FOR WEIGHT OF PACKAGING an allowance for the packaging around goods, deducted from the total weight and not included in transportation costs 3. UNLADEN WEIGHT OF VEHICLE the weight of a motor vehicle without fuel, cargo, passengers, or equipment 4. CONTAINER OF KNOWN WEIGHT a container of known weight that is used as a counterbalance when calculating the net weight of a cargo ■ vt (**tares, taring, tared**) WEIGH PACKAGING to weigh packaging in order to calculate the amount of tare to be deducted from a cargo [15C. Via French, 'waste in goods, deficiency' < Arabic *ṭarh* 'that which is deducted' < *ṭaraḥa* 'reject, subtract']

SPELLCHECK See *tare*[1].

Taree /taa reˊe/ town in eastern New South Wales, Australia, a commercial and manufacturing centre. Population: 16,297 (1991).

targe /taarj/ n a round shield, especially one used by Scottish Highlanders (*archaic*) [Pre-12C. Probably < Old Norse *targa* 'shield'; reinforced by Old French *targe* 'light shield']

target /taˊargit/ n 1. OBJECT AIMED AT IN SHOOTING a round object or surface marked with concentric circles that is aimed at in archery, rifle shooting, and similar sports 2. SOMEBODY OR SOMETHING AIMED AT an area, surface, object, or person aimed at ○ *The bird's bright plumage makes it an easy target.* 3. GOAL a goal or objective towards which effort is directed ○ *Our target is to raise £20,000 for cancer research.* 4. SOMEBODY OR SOMETHING ON RECEIVING END somebody or something that is the focus or object of the behaviour or actions of others ○ *the target of her anger* 5. CIV ENG MARKER FOR TAKING LEVELS a sliding weight on a surveyor's levelling rod that is used to help determine proper levels 6. PHYS SOMETHING HIT BY PARTICLE ACCELERATOR BEAM a substance that is hit by a beam of electrons or other elementary particles or ions from a particle accelerator in order to start a nuclear reaction 7. PHYS SURFACE HIT BY ELECTRONS a surface or electrode, often luminescent, that is hit by an electron beam to produce an output signal, e.g. in an X-ray tube or a television camera tube 8. SMALL SHIELD a small round shield (*archaic*) ■ vt (**-gets, -geting, -geted**) 1. MAKE SOMEBODY OR SOMETHING TARGET to make a person or thing the focus or object of something ○ *a campaign that targets under-35s* 2. AIM SOMETHING to aim something at or direct something towards a person, group, or thing ○ *The missiles were targeted on the enemy capital.* [13C. < TARGE]

targetcast /taˊargit kaast/ (-casts, -casting, -cast or -casted) vi to broadcast a website only to a group of people who are known to be potentially interested, and not to everyone on the Internet [Late 20C. Blend of TARGET + BROADCAST]

target date n the date by which it is expected that something such as a project or piece of work will be completed

target language n 1. TRANSLATION LANGUAGE the language into which a text is to be translated 2. LANGUAGE BEING LEARNED a foreign language that is being learned 3. COMPUT COMPUTER COMPILATION LANGUAGE the machine-readable instructions in which a computer program written in a high-level language is to be compiled

target man n in football, a forward whose role is to receive high passes and crosses, especially in front of the goal

target of opportunity n a military target that is visible or detectable and within range, although no attack on it has been planned or requested

Targum /taˊargəm/ n a translation of part of the Bible in Aramaic [Late 16C. Via Hebrew < Aramaic *targūm* 'interpretation' < *targēm* 'interpret'] —**Targumic** /taar goˊomik/ adj —**Targumist** n

tariff /tárrif/ n 1. DUTY LEVIED ON GOODS a duty levied by a government on imported or exported goods 2. LIST OF LEVIES a list or system of import or export tariffs 3. LIST OF COSTS a list of fees, fares, or other prices charged by a business 4. PRICED MENU a list of the available dishes at a restaurant together with their prices 5. SYSTEM OF CHARGING FOR UTILITIES a system of charging for utility services such as gas and electricity, or a list of such charges ■ vt (-iffs, -iffing, -iffed) SET COST OF SOMETHING to fix a tariff or price on something [Late 16C. Via Italian *tariffa* < Arabic *ta'rif* 'notification, inventory of fees to be paid' < *'arrafa* 'notify']

tariff office n an insurance company that charges premiums according to a schedule established by a group of companies

Tarkington /taˊarkingtən/, **Booth** (1869–1946) US writer. His novels include the Pulitzer Prize-winning *The Magnificent Ambersons* (1918). Full name **Tarkington, Newton Booth**

'There are two things that will be believed of any man whatsoever, and one of them is that he has taken to drink.'
[Booth Tarkington, *Penrod*; 1914]

Tarkovsky /taar kófski/, **Andrei** (1932–86) Russian film director. He is noted for his highly personal and symbolic films such as *Solaris* (1972).

'The goal of all art is...to explain to people the reason for their appearance on this planet; or, if not to explain, at least to pose the question.'
[Andrei Tarkovsky, *Sculpting in Time: Reflections on the Cinema*; 1989]

tarlatan /taˊarlətən/ n an open-weave transparent highly starched cotton muslin. Use: stiffener for collars and other parts of clothes. [Early 18C. < French *tarlatane*]

Tarmac /taˊar mak/ *tdmk* a trademark for a material used for surfacing roads

tarmacadam /taˊar mə káddəm/ n a mixture of broken stone and tar used for surfacing roads

tarn /taarn/ n a small mountain lake, especially one formed by the action of glaciers [14C. < N Germanic]

tarnish /táarnish/ *vti* (**-nishes, -nishing, -nished**) **1.** MAKE OR BECOME DULL AND DISCOLOURED to lose shine and become dull because of oxidation or rust, or make something do this **2.** DAMAGE SOMEBODY'S REPUTATION to damage somebody's reputation or good name, or become damaged ■ *n* **1.** DISCOLORATION the dullness or discoloration of metal affected by oxidation or rust **2.** FILM OF DISCOLORATION ON METAL the film of discoloration that forms on metal **3.** SULLIED CONDITION the damaged condition of somebody's reputation or good name [15C. < French *terniss-*, stem of *ternir* 'make dull'] — **tarnishable** *adj*

taro /táarō/ (*plural* **-ros**) *n* a perennial plant cultivated in tropical regions for its edible starchy tubers and also widely grown as an ornamental plant. Native to: Southeast Asia. Latin name: *Colocasia esculenta*. [Mid-18C. < Polynesian]

tarot

tarot /tárrō/ *n* **1.** a system of fortune-telling using a special pack of 78 cards consisting of 4 suits of 14 cards together with 22 picture cards **2.** *also* **tarot card** a card used in tarot [Late 19C. < French < Italian *tarocchi* plural of *tarocco*]

tarp /taarp/ *n* INDUST same as **tarpaulin** (*informal*) [Early 20C. Shortening]

tarpan /táar pan/ *n* a small grey-brown horse with a short thick neck, erect mane, and a stripe along the back. It is now extinct. Native to: southern Russia, Poland. [Mid-19C. < Turkic]

tarpaper /táar paypər/ *n* a heavy paper coated with tar. Use: waterproofing in building.

tarpaulin /taar páwlin/ *n* **1.** a heavy waterproof material, especially treated canvas, used as a covering and to protect things from moisture **2.** a sheet of tarpaulin [Early 17C. Probably < TAR¹ + PALL² + -ING²]

Tarpeian Rock /taar pée ən-/ *n* a rock on the Capitoline Hill in ancient Rome, from which traitors were hurled to their deaths [Early 17C. After *Tarpeia*, legendary betrayer of the Roman citadel to the Sabines, reputedly buried at the foot of the rock]

tar pit *n* an area where tar or asphalt naturally accumulates, trapping animals and preserving their bones

tarpon /táar pon/ (*plural* same or **-pons**) *n* a sea fish with a streamlined body and thick silvery scales. Native to: tropical and subtropical waters. Genus: *Megalops*. [Late 17C. Probably < Dutch *tarpoen*]

Tarquinius Superbus /taar kwínni əss soo púrbəss/, **Lucius** (*fl* 6th century BC) king of Rome. According to tradition, he was the last of the Etruscan kings of Rome (534–510 BC), and was dethroned after his son raped Lucretia, a Roman matron.

tarradiddle /tárrədid'l/, **taradiddle** *n* (*informal*) **1.** nonsense or idle talk **2.** a small lie [Late 18C. Probably suggesting unintelligible speech]

tarragon /tárrəgən/ *n* a perennial herb with narrow aromatic leaves. Use: flavouring food. Native to: temperate regions of Asia. Latin name: *Artemisia dracunculus*. [Mid-16C. < medieval Latin *tragonia*, *tarchon*]

Tarragona /tárrə gónə/ city, port, and administrative centre of Tarragona Province, northeastern Spain. It has extensive Roman remains. Population: 117,184 (2002).

~~tarrif~~ incorrect spelling of **tariff**

tarry /tárri/ (**-ries, -rying, -ried**) *vi* **1.** REMAIN to stay temporarily at a place **2.** LINGER to delay a departure

tarragon

or arrival, especially in an idle way **3.** WAIT to wait in expectation of somebody or something [13C. Origin ?] —**tarrier** *n*

tarsal /táarss'l/ *adj* **1.** OF TARSUS relating to the group of bones forming the ankle joint (**tarsus**) **2.** OF PART OF EYELID relating to the small section of connective tissue (**tarsus**) along the edge of the eyelid ■ *n* BONE OF ANKLE any of the group of bones forming the ankle joint (**tarsus**) [Early 19C. < TARSUS]

tarsier /táarsi ər/ *n* a small nocturnal animal with large eyes and delicate grasping fingers and toes ending in pads that lives in trees. Native to: Philippines, Indonesia, and neighbouring islands. Genus: *Tarsius*. [Late 18C. < French < *tarse* 'tarsus'; from its long tarsal bones]

tarsometatarsus /táar sō mettə táarssəss/ (*plural* **-tarsi** /-táars sī/) *n* the bone in the lower leg of birds that connects to the toes [Mid-19C. < TARSUS]

tarsus /táarssəss/ (*plural* **tarsi** /táars sī/) *n* **1.** ANKLE BONES the group of bones that form the ankle joint in vertebrates, located between the inner bone of the lower leg (**tibia**) and the main skeleton of the foot (**metatarsus**) **2.** PART OF EYELID the small section of connective tissue along the edge of the eyelid **3.** BIRDS same as **tarsometatarsus 4.** PART OF ARTHROPOD LEG the part of the leg of an arthropod that is farthest from the tibia [Late 17C. Via modern Latin < Greek *tarsos* 'eyelid, flat part of the foot']

Tarsus /táarssəss/ city in southern Turkey, near the Mediterranean Sea. During Roman rule in the 1st century BC it was one of the most prominent cities of Asia Minor. Population: 246,206 (1997).

tart¹ /taart/ *adj* **1.** having a sharp and sour, but usually pleasant, flavour **2.** sharp, cutting, or critical [14C. < Old English *teart* 'painful, severe', origin ?] —**tartly** *adv* —**tartness** *n*

tart up *v* (*informal*) **1.** *vt* IMPROVE APPEARANCE OF PLACE to change the decor of a place in order to improve its appearance **2.** **tart yourself up** *vr* IMPROVE APPEARANCE OF SELF to use makeup, accessories, or different clothing in order to improve your appearance **3.** *vt* DECORATE SOMETHING to improve the appearance of something by decorating it, especially in an excessively ornate way

tart² /taart/ *n* a pie that has no top crust and is usually filled with something sweet such as fruit or custard [14C. < Old French *tarte*]

tart³ /taart/ *n* **1.** an offensive term for a female prostitute or a woman regarded as sexually provocative (*slang*) **2.** somebody who pursues a particular end, e.g. publicity, in a fickle and indiscriminate manner, with little regard for scruple or principle (*slang disapproving*) ○ *He proclaimed himself an unashamed media tart.* [Mid-19C. Probably shortening of SWEETHEART]

tartan¹ /táart'n/ *n* **1.** SCOTTISH WOOL FABRIC a Scottish wool or worsted fabric woven in a wide range of checked or plaid patterns, many of which are associated with specific Scottish clans. The association between clans and tartan has no historical basis and arose in the 19th century. **2.** PATTERN OF TARTAN a pattern of tartan, officially registered and associated with a specific clan, regiment, or other organization **3.** TARTAN GARMENT a piece of clothing made of tartan **4.** TRADITIONAL HIGHLAND DRESS the traditional dress of the Scottish Highlands ○ *wearing the tartan with pride* ■ *adj* same as **Scottish** (*informal*) [15C. Origin ?]

tartan² /táart'n/ *n* a Mediterranean sailing ship with a single mast and a lateen sail [Early 17C. Via French *tartane* < Old Provençal *tartana* 'buzzard']

tartar /táartər/ *n* **1.** a hard deposit of mostly organic material that forms on teeth at the gum line and contributes to dental decay if not regularly removed **2.** a substance consisting mostly of potassium bitartrate that is deposited in wine casks during fermentation [14C. Via medieval Latin *tartarum* < medieval Greek *tartaron*] —**tartarous** *adj*

Tartar /táartər/ *n* **1.** PEOPLES, LANG same as **Tatar 2.** *also* **tartar** somebody regarded as fearsome or ferocious (*sometimes offensive*) [14C. Directly or via French *Tartare* < medieval Latin *Tartarus* < Turkish] —**Tartar** *adj* —**Tartarian** /taar táiri ən/ *adj* —**Tartaric** /taar tárrik/ *adj*

tartare sauce /táartaar-/, **tartar sauce** *n* a mayonnaise mixed with capers and chopped pickles that is served as an accompaniment to fish [< French *Tartare* (see TARTAR)]

tartaric acid

tartaric acid /taar tárrik-/ *n* a white crystalline organic acid. Source: wine vat tartar. Use: foods, beverages, photographic processes. Formula: $(CHOH)_2(COOH)_2$.

tartar sauce *n* FOOD another spelling of **tartare sauce**

tartar steak *n* FOOD same as **steak tartare**

Tartarus /táartərəss/ *n* **1.** in Greek mythology, the lowest part of the underworld, where the worst evildoers were imprisoned **2.** in Greek mythology, Hades or the underworld in general [Mid-16C. Via Latin < Greek *Tartaros*]

Tartary /táartəri/ historical region of eastern Europe and Central Asia. In the Middle Ages, Tartary was the area from western Russia to the Sea of Japan. Later, the Crimea was called European Tartary and Turkestan was called Asian Tartary.

tartlet /táartlət/ *n* a small tart, usually for one person [15C. < French *tartelette*, diminutive of *tarte* 'pie, tart']

tartrate /táar trayt/ *n* a salt or ester of tartaric acid [Late 18C. < French < *tartre* 'tartar']

tartrated /táar traytid/ *adj* in the form of a tartrate

tartrazine /táartrə zeen/ *n* a dye widely used in processed foods to give a yellow colour [Late 19C. < French *tartrate* 'tartrate' + AZO-]

Tartt /taart/, **Donna** (*b.* 1963) US writer. Her novels include *The Secret History* (1992) and *The Little Friend* (2002).

Tartu /táartoo/ city in eastern Estonia, on the River Emajogi. Population: 101,901 (1997).

Tartuffe /taar toof, -tyoof/, **Tartufe** *n* a religious hypocrite [After the main character in Molière's play *Tartuffe* (1664)] —**Tartuffian** *adj*

tarty /táarti/ (**-ier, -iest**) *adj* an offensive term that describes a woman's appearance as vulgar or gaudy (*slang*)

tarweed /táar weed/ *n* a strong-smelling resinous plant. Flowers: yellow, like daisies. Native to: western North America, Chile. Genus: *Madia*.

Tarzan /táarz'n/ *n* a man who is very strong and looks rugged and muscular (*informal*) [Early 20C. After a character raised in the jungle by apes in the stories of Edgar Rice BURROUGHS]

TAS *abbr* true air speed

Tas. *abbr* Tasmania

Taser /táyzər/ *tdmk* a trademark for a nonlethal

weapon that transmits electrical pulses, usually via retractable wires, to contract muscle tissue in order to incapacitate somebody

tash /tash/, **tache** *n* HAIR same as **moustache** (*informal*) [Late 19C. Shortening]

Tashkent /tásh ként/ capital city of Uzbekistan, situated in the eastern part of the country. Population: 2,142,700 (1999).

task /taask/ *n* **1.** JOB ASSIGNED TO SOMEBODY a piece of work that somebody is given to do, usually quite short in duration or with a deadline **2.** JOB TO BE DONE a piece of work or an assignment, especially one that is important or difficult ■ *vt* (**tasks, tasking, tasked**) **1.** ASSIGN WORK TO SOMEBODY to assign a task to somebody ○ *tasked me with writing the letter* **2.** BURDEN SOMEBODY to burden somebody excessively with work or duties [13C. Via Old N French *tasque* 'duty, tax' < medieval Latin *tasca* < Latin *taxare* (see TAX)] ◇ **take somebody to task** to scold or criticize somebody

SYNONYMS See *job*.

taskbar /taask baar/ *n* a bar at the bottom of a computer screen displaying buttons that show, among other things, which programs are currently running

task force *n* **1.** a formation of military units put together on a temporary basis to accomplish a specific mission **2.** a group of people and resources temporarily brought together for a specific purpose

taskmaster /taask maastər/ *n* **1.** somebody who assigns and supervises work, especially in a demanding way **2.** a responsibility or discipline that is very demanding or requires a lot of hard work

taskwork /taask wurk/ *n* unpleasant, demanding, or difficult work

Tasman /tázmən/ administrative region of New Zealand, occupying the northwestern corner of the South Island. Population: 41,352 (2001). Area: 14,538 sq. km/5,613 sq. mi.

Tasman, Mount second highest mountain in New Zealand, located in the Southern Alps in the South Island. Height: 3,498 m/11,476 ft.

Tasman /tázmən, taáss maan/, **Abel** (1603?–59) Dutch navigator. Between 1632 and 1655 he made several expeditions to the Indian and Pacific oceans, reaching Tasmania and New Zealand (1642). Tasmania is named after him. Full name **Tasman, Abel Janszoon**

Tasman Bay bay on the northern coast of the South Island, New Zealand. It extends from Separation Point in the west to Cape Stephens in the east.

Tasman Glacier largest glacier in New Zealand, situated on the eastern side of the Southern Alps in the South Island. Length: 29 km/18 mi.

Tasmania /taz máyni ə/ **1.** island in the Tasman Sea, separated from the southeastern coast of Australia by the Bass Strait. Area: 68,330 sq. km/26,380 sq. mi. **2.** state in southeastern Australia, occupying the island of Tasmania. First settled by the British in 1803, it became a separate colony in 1825. Capital: Hobart. Population: 477,100 (2003). Former name **Van Diemen's Land** (1642–1856) —**Tasmanian** *n, adj*

Tasmanian blue gum /taz máyni ən-/ *n* a large eucalyptus tree that has a thick trunk and small yellow flowers. It is the floral emblem of Tasmania. Native to: Tasmania, Victoria. Latin name: *Eucalyptus globulus.*

Tasmanian devil

Tasmanian devil *n* a burrowing carnivorous marsupial characterized by a black coat with white markings and large powerful jaws. Native to: formerly, all Australia, but now confined to remote regions of Tasmania. Latin name: *Sarcophilus harrisii.*

Tasmanian tiger *n* ZOOL same as **thylacine**

Tasmanian wolf *n* ZOOL same as **thylacine**

Tasman Peninsula peninsula in southeastern Tasmania, Australia. Area: 520 sq. km/200 sq. mi.

Tasman Sea region of the South Pacific Ocean lying between Australia and New Zealand

Tass /tass/ *n* the official news agency of the former Soviet Union [Early 20C. < Russian, acronym < *Telegrafnoe agentsvo Sovetskogo Soyuza* 'Telegraphic Agency of the Soviet Union']

tasse /tass/ *n* ARMS same as **tasset** [Mid-16C. Origin ?]

tassel /táss'l/ *n* **1.** DECORATION MADE OF BUNCHED LOOSE THREADS a bunch of loose parallel threads that are tied together at one end and used as a decoration, e.g. on curtains, cushions, or clothes **2.** AGRIC TUFT AT END OF MAIZE something resembling a tassel, especially the tuft of male flowers at the top of the main stem of a maize plant ■ *v* (**-sels, -selling, -selled**) **1.** *vt* DECORATE SOMETHING WITH TASSELS to decorate something such as a curtain, cushion, or item of clothing with tassels **2.** *vt* REMOVE TASSEL FROM MAIZE to remove the tassel from an ear of maize **3.** *vi* AGRIC PRODUCE TUFT ON MAIZE to produce a tuft of stamens at the end of a flower cluster, especially as seen on an ear of maize [14C. < Old French, 'clasp'] —**tasselly** *adj*

tasset /tássit/ *n* any of a set of overlapping metal plates attached to and hanging below an armoured breastplate in a suit of armour to protect the lower part of the trunk and the thighs [Mid-19C. < French *tassette* < *tasse* 'pouch']

tassie /tássi/ *n* N England, Scotland a small cup, glass, or goblet (*archaic*) [Early 18C. < *tass*, via French *tasse* < Arabic *ṭāsa* 'cup' < Persian *ṭašt* 'bowl']

Tassie /tázzi/, **Tassy** *n* Aus (*informal*) **1.** Tasmania. Same as **Tasmania 2.** a Tasmanian [Late 19C. Shortening and alteration]

taste /tayst/ *n* **1.** SMALL QUANTITY SAMPLED a small quantity of something eaten, drunk, or sampled to assess its effect on the sensory receptors on the surface of the tongue or in the mouth ○ *Can I have a taste of that?* **2.** EXPERIENCE OF SOMETHING a brief sample or experience of something, especially for the first time ○ *a taste of freedom* **3.** LIKING FOR SOMETHING a tendency to like or enjoy something ○ *She has developed a taste for modern art.* **4.** ABILITY TO JUDGE AESTHETICALLY the faculty of making discerning judgments in aesthetic matters ○ *He has good taste.* **5.** SENSE OF SOCIALLY ACCEPTABLE a sense of what is proper or acceptable socially ○ *The remark was in poor taste.* **6.** PHYSIOL SENSE THAT IDENTIFIES FLAVOURS the sense that perceives the distinctive qualities of something such as a food by means of the sensory organs in the mouth (**taste buds**) **7.** PHYSIOL SENSATION STIMULATED IN TASTE BUDS the sensation stimulated in the taste buds when food, drink, or other substances are in contact with them. Sweetness, saltiness, bitterness, and sourness are considered the four basic taste sensations, and all flavours combine these in various ways with the sense of smell. ○ *has a salty taste* **8.** PHYSIOL ASSESSMENT OF TASTE OF SOMETHING an act of putting a small amount of something in the mouth in order to try it or test its flavour ■ *vt* (**tastes, tasting, tasted**) **1.** HAVE PARTICULAR FLAVOUR to have a particular effect on the taste buds ○ *This tastes horrible.* **2.** PHYSIOL DISCERN FLAVOUR OF SOMETHING to discern the flavour of a substance by means of the taste buds **3.** TEST SOMETHING FOR FLAVOUR to put a small amount of food or drink into the mouth in order to try it or to test its flavour ○ *Taste this for salt.* **4.** EXPERIENCE SOMETHING to experience something, especially for the first time or only briefly ○ *He had tasted success.* [13C. < Old French *taster* 'to touch'] —**tastable** *adj*

taste bud *n* a sensory receptor on the surface of the tongue or in the mouth that sends signals to the brain when stimulated by specific chemicals, producing the sense of taste. Taste buds are classified according to the type of substance they respond to: sweet, salty, bitter, or sour.

tasteful /táystf'l/ *adj* **1.** having or showing good aesthetic taste **2.** having a pleasant flavour —**tastefully** *adv* —**tastefulness** *n*

tasteless /táystləss/ *adj* **1.** having little or no flavour **2.** showing a lack of taste or judgment in aesthetic or social matters —**tastelessly** *adv* —**tastelessness** *n*

tastemaker /táyst maykər/ *n* N Am somebody who influences decisions about what is tasteful or stylish, e.g. in fashion or the arts

taster /táystər/ *n* **1.** JUDGE OF FOOD OR DRINK QUALITY a specialist who tastes food or drink to judge its quality **2.** SHORT PREVIEW a sample or short preview of something **3.** FREE SAMPLE OF FOOD a small quantity of food or drink given free as a sample **4.** DEVICE USED FOR TASTING a device or container used for tasting, e.g. a small cup for tasting wine **5.** SOMEBODY TESTING FOR POISON somebody engaged to test an important person's food or drink by sampling it first in case it contains poison

tasty /táysti/ (**-ier, -iest**) *adj* **1.** having a pleasant flavour **2.** attractive or interesting (*informal*) —**tastily** *adv* —**tastiness** *n*

Taswegian /taz wéejən/ *n* Aus a Tasmanian (*informal*) [Mid-20C. < TASMANIA, after GLASWEGIAN]

tat[1] /tat/ *n* **1.** THINGS IN POOR CONDITION articles in very poor condition (*informal*) **2.** TASTELESS THINGS tasteless or very low quality articles (*informal*) **3.** KNOTTED MASS a knotted mass of something, especially hair [Mid-19C. Origin ?]

tat[2] /tat/ (**tats, tatting, tatted**) *vti* to work at tatting, or produce an item by tatting [Late 19C. Back-formation < TATTING]

tat[3] /tat/ *n* Aus same as **tattoo**[1] (*informal*) [Mid-19C. Shortening]

TAT *abbr* thematic apperception test

ta-ta /tə taá/ *interj* used as a childish or familiar way of saying goodbye (*informal*) [Early 19C. Origin ?]

tatami /tə taámi, taa-/ (*plural same* or **-mis**) *n* a straw mat, used especially in Japanese homes as a floor covering [Early 17C. < Japanese]

Tatar /taátər/ *n* **1.** MEMBER OF HISTORICAL CENTRAL ASIAN PEOPLE a member of a people who came from east-central Asia and founded an empire stretching into Serbia, Russia, and Ukraine. The Tatars joined with the Mongols, and their combined empire flourished until the 16th century, when they were defeated by the Russians and the Ottoman Turks. **2.** DESCENDANT OF TATARS a descendant of the Tatars. Most now live in an area of European Russia between the River Volga and the Ural Mountains, with communities in Crimea and Siberia. **3.** TATAR LANGUAGE the Turkic language of the Tatars. Native speakers: 6 million. [Early 17C. < Turkish] —**Tatar** *adj* —**Tatarian** /taa táiri ən/ *adj* —**Tataric** /taa tárrik/ *adj*

Tatarstan /taátər staán/ autonomous republic in the plains of the River Volga, central Russia. Capital: Kazan. Population: 3,743,600 (1994). Area: 68,000 sq. km/26,255 sq. mi.

Tate Britain /táyt-/ *n* a museum in London that houses a collection of British art from 1500 to the present day

Tate Modern /táyt-/ *n* a museum in London that houses a collection of international modern art from 1900 to the present day

tater /táytər/ *n* regional FOOD same as **potato** [Mid-18C. Alteration]

Tati /ta tée/, **Jacques** (1908–82) French actor and film director. He is noted for his wryly humorous films, in several of which he played the lovably bumbling character Monsieur Hulot. Born **Tatischeff, Jacques**

tatie /táyti/ *n* UK regional FOOD same as **potato** [Late 18C. Alteration]

Tatlin /tátlin/, **Vladimir** (1885–1953) Russian sculptor and painter. His abstract sculptures made from different industrial materials led to the foundation of constructivism.

~~tatoo~~ incorrect spelling of **tattoo**

Tatra Mountains /taátrə-, táttrə-/ highest range of the Carpathian Mountains of central Europe, extending along the border between Poland and Slovakia. The highest peak is Gerlachovka, 2,655 m/8,711 ft.

tatter /táttər/ *n* **1.** RAGGED PIECE OF CLOTH a torn or ragged piece of cloth **2.** RUINED STATE a ruined or damaged state (*usually used in the plural*) ○ *The policy was in tatters.* ■ *vti* (**-ters, -tering, -tered**) BECOME OR MAKE RAGGED to become ragged or torn, or make something do this [15C. < Old Norse *totrar* (plural) 'rags']

tatterdemalion /táttərdə máyli ən, -málli-/ *adj* raggedly dressed and unkempt ■ *n* somebody wearing ragged clothes [Early 17C. < TATTERED + ?]

tattered /táttərd/ *adj* **1.** RAGGED ragged or torn to shreds **2.** DRESSED IN RAGS dressed in ragged clothes **3.** SHABBY shabby and run-down

tattersall /táttər sawl/ *n* **1.** a pattern of squares or checks formed by dark lines on a light or brightly coloured background **2.** cloth with a tattersall pattern [Late 19C. After *Tattersall's* horse market, London, from the traditional design of horse blankets]

tattie /tátti/ *n Scotland* FOOD same as **potato** (*informal*) [Late 18C. Alteration]

REGIONAL NOTE **Tattie** is a Scottish form, but Irish men and women often travelled to Scotland as itinerant farm labourers to help harvest potatoes (*tattie howking*) at large farms in autumn, and they tended to pronounce the first element *tatie*. Potatoes have many synonyms, the best known of which are *murphies*, *spuds*, and *taters*.

tattie-bogle /tátti bŏg'l/ *n Scotland* AGRIC same as **scarecrow** (*informal*)

tatting /tátting/ *n* **1.** a form of lace made with a shuttle **2.** the process or craft of making tatting [Mid-19C. Origin ?] —**tatter** *n*

tattle /tátt'l/ *v* (**-tles, -tling, -tled**) **1.** *vi* GOSSIP to gossip about the personal secrets or plans of others **2.** *vti* DISCLOSE SECRET to disclose somebody's personal or private information **3.** *vi* TALK IDLY to talk or chatter idly ■ *n* **1.** SOMEBODY WHO GOSSIPS a gossip or informer **2.** IDLE GOSSIP idle talk, chatter, or gossip [15C. Probably < Middle Flemish *tatelen*, an imitation of the sound]

tattler /táttlər/ *n* **1.** somebody who gossips, reveals secrets, or talks idly **2.** a long-legged shorebird related to the sandpipers and noted for its long migrations. Genus: *Heteroscelus*.

tattletale /tátt'l tayl/ *N Am n* same as **telltale** *n* (sense 1) (*often used by or to children*) ■ *adj* same as **telltale**

tattle-tongue *n* same as **tattler** (sense 1)

tattoo[1] /ta to͞o, tə-/ *n* (*plural* **-toos**) a permanent picture, design, or other marking made on the skin by pricking it and staining it with an indelible dye ■ *vt* (**-toos, -tooing, -tooed**) to mark the skin with a tattoo, or form a tattoo on the skin [Mid-18C. < Polynesian] —**tattooer** *n* —**tattooist** *n*

tattoo[2] /ta to͞o, tə-/ *n* (*plural* **-toos**) **1.** MIL EVENING MILITARY DISPLAY FOR ENTERTAINMENT a military display, often with a variety of items, performed as an entertainment, usually in the evening **2.** CALL TO RETURN TO QUARTERS a bugle or drum call that tells soldiers to return to their quarters in the evening ■ *vti* (**-toos, -tooing, -tooed**) BEAT SOMETHING WITH STEADY RHYTHM to beat a steady rhythm, or beat with a steady rhythm on something such as a drum [Mid-17C. < Dutch *taptoe* 'shut the tap (of the beer barrel)', a signal at closing time in taverns]

tatty /tátti/ (**-tier, -tiest**) *adj* shabby, run-down, or in poor condition [Mid-20C. < TAT[1]] —**tattily** *adv* —**tattiness** *n*

Tatum /táytəm/, **Edward** (1909–75) US geneticist. His work with George W. Beadle on genetic mutations earned them the Nobel Prize in physiology or medicine (1958). Full name **Tatum, Edward Lawrie**

tau /taw, tow/ *n* **1.** the 19th letter of the Greek alphabet, represented in the English alphabet as 't'. See table at **alphabet** **2.** BIOCHEM same as **tau protein** [14C. < Greek]

tau cross *n* a cross shaped like a T

taught past participle, past tense of **teach**

tau neutrino *n* a subatomic particle of the lepton family with no electric charge and a mass less than 69 times that of an electron, created during the decay of a tauon

taunt[1] /tawnt/ *vt* (**taunts, taunting, taunted**) **1.** PROVOKE OR RIDICULE SOMEBODY to provoke, ridicule, or tease somebody in a hurtful or mocking way **2.** TANTALIZE SOMEBODY to tantalize somebody, e.g. by refusing to disclose a secret ■ *n* HURTFUL REMARK a remark intended to provoke, ridicule, or tease somebody in a hurtful or mocking way [Early 16C. < French *tant (pour tant)* 'so much (for so much)' < Latin *tantus* 'so great'] —**taunter** *n* —**taunting** *adj* —**tauntingly** *adv*

taunt[2] /tawnt/ *adj* describes a ship's mast that is taller than average [Early 17C. Origin ?]

Taunton /táwntən/ town and administrative centre of Somerset, southwestern England. Population: 60,300 (1993 estimate).

Taunus /táwnəss, tównəss/ mountain range in west-central Germany, extending northeastwards from the eastern bank of the River Rhine. Highest peak: 880 m/2,887 ft.

tauon /tów on/ *n* an unusually massive subatomic particle of the lepton family with the same charge as an electron, but nearly 3,500 times its mass [Late 20C. < TAU]

taupe /tōp/ *n* a dark brownish-grey colour [Early 20C. Via French < Latin *talpa* 'mole'] —**taupe** *adj*

Taupo /tówpō/ city in the centre of the North Island, New Zealand, on the northern shore of Lake Taupo. It is a commercial centre and tourist resort. Population: 20,310 (2001).

Taupo, Lake largest lake in New Zealand, located in the centre of the North Island. It was formed by an enormous volcanic explosion. Area: 606 sq. km/234 sq. mi.

tau protein *n* a protein that maintains the stability of the microtubules that serve as a transport system within brain cells. It is also implicated in the formation of masses of fibrous protein in the brains of people with Alzheimer's disease.

Tauranga /tów rungə/ city and port in the northern part of the North Island, New Zealand, situated on the Bay of Plenty. Population: 95,694 (2001).

Tauri ZODIAC plural of **Taurus** (sense 3)

taurine[1] /táw rīn/ *adj* relating to or resembling a bull [Early 17C. < Latin *taurinus* < *taurus* 'bull']

taurine[2] /táw reen, -rin/ *n* a crystalline derivative of cysteine found in bile and nerve tissue [Mid-19C. < TAUROCHOLIC ACID]

taurocholic acid /táwrō kolik-/ *n* a bile acid present as a sodium salt in humans that breaks down to produce taurine [Mid-19C. < Greek *tauros* 'bull' + *kholē* 'bile']

tauromachy /taw rómməki/ *n* the activity or skill of bullfighting —**tauromachian** /táwrə máyki ən/ *adj*

Taurus /táwrəss/ *n* **1.** CONSTELLATION IN NORTHERN HEMISPHERE a zodiacal constellation of the northern hemisphere located between Aries and Gemini and containing the bright star Aldebaran, the Pleiades and Hyades, and the Crab Nebula. See illustration at **constellation** **2.** ZODIAC SIGN OF ZODIAC the second sign of the zodiac, represented by a bull and lasting from approximately 20 April to 20 May. Taurus is classified as an earth sign, and its ruling planet is Venus. **3.** (*plural* **Tauruses** or **Tauri** /táwri/) ZODIAC SOMEBODY BORN UNDER TAURUS somebody whose birthday falls between 20 April and 20 May [14C. < Latin *taurus* 'bull'] —**Taurean** /táwri ən, taw rée ən/ *n* —**Taurus** *adj*

TAURUS /táwrəss/ *n* a computerized system used for buying and selling securities on the International Stock Exchange. Full form **Transfer of Automated Registration of Uncertified Stock**

Taurus Mountains /táwrəss-/ mountain range in southern Turkey, parallel to the Mediterranean coast. Its highest peak is Aladag, 3,734 m/12,251 ft.

taut /tawt/ *adj* **1.** STRETCHED TIGHTLY pulled or stretched tightly **2.** PHYSIOL FIRM AND FLEXED flexed and working, as opposed to being in a relaxed state ○ *taut muscles* **3.** STRESSED stressed, tense, or anxious **4.** CONCISE concise and efficient in the use of language or reasoning ○ *taut prose* **5.** NAUT KEPT IN GOOD ORDER trim, tidy, and well run ○ *runs a taut ship* [13C. Origin ?] —**tautly** *adv* —**tautness** *n*

taut- *prefix* same as **tauto-** (*used before vowels*)

tauten /táwt'n/ (**-ens, -ening, -ened**) *vti* to become tightly stretched, or stretch something such as a rope tight

tauto- *prefix* the same, identical ○ *tautomer* [< Greek *tauto* 'the same thing' < *to* 'the' + *auto* 'same']

tautog /taw tóg/ *n* a large dark-coloured edible fish of the wrasse family. Native to: Atlantic coast of North America. Latin name: *Tautoga onitis*. [Mid-17C. < Narraganset *tautauog*]

tautology /taw tólləji/ (*plural* **-gies**) *n* **1.** LINGUISTIC REDUNDANCY the redundant repetition of a meaning in a sentence, using different words **2.** INSTANCE OF LINGUISTIC REDUNDANCY an instance of redundant repetition of a meaning in a sentence, using different words **3.** LOGIC LOGICAL TRUE PROPOSITION a proposition or statement that, in itself, is logically true —**tautological** /táwtə lójjik'l/ *adj* —**tautologically** *adv*

tautomer /táwtəmər/ *n* a compound exhibiting tautomerism [Early 20C. < TAUTO- + ISOMER]

tautomerism /taw tómmərizəm/ *n* the property permitting some compounds to exist as a mixture of two isomers that are interconvertible and thus in equilibrium —**tautomeric** /táwtə mérrik/ *adj*

tautonym /táwtənim/ *n* a species name in which the epithet for the species is the same as that of the genus, e.g. the name of the filarial worm *Loa loa*. This kind of name is used for animal, but not plant species. —**tautonymic** /táwtə nímmik/ *adj* —**tautonymy** /taw tónnəmi/ *n*

tav /taav, taaf/, **taw** *n* the 23rd and final letter of the Hebrew alphabet, represented in the English alphabet as 't'. See table at **alphabet** [Mid-17C. < Hebrew *tāw*]

Tavel /taa vél/ *n* a dry rosé wine from southeastern France [Late 19C. After *Tavel*, France]

Tavener /távvənər/, **John** (*b.* 1944) British composer. He is particularly noted for his choral works, which are often based on religious or spiritual themes. Full name **Tavener, John Kenneth**

tavern /távvərn/ *n* a pub or inn (*archaic*) [13C. Via French *taverne* < Latin *taberna* 'hut, inn']

taverna /tə vúrnə/ *n* **1.** a small restaurant or café in Greece or run by Greeks **2.** a guesthouse in Greece that has a bar [Early 20C. Via modern Greek < Latin *taberna* 'hut, inn']

taverner /távvərnər/ *n* somebody who runs a pub or inn (*archaic*)

Taverner /távvərnər/, **John** (1490?–1545) English composer. His complex and elaborate church music is transitional between the late medieval and the Renaissance styles.

taw[1] /taw/ (**taws, tawing, tawed**) *vt* to whiten animal skins by applying alum or other mineral salts [Old English *tawian* < Germanic, 'make'] —**tawer** *n*

taw[2] /taw/ *n* **1.** MARBLE USED TO HIT OTHERS a fancy marble that is shot at others **2.** LINE FROM WHICH PLAYER SHOOTS MARBLES in a game of marbles, the line from which a player must shoot **3.** GAME PLAYED WITH MARBLES a game of marbles in which the object is to shoot as many marbles as possible out of a circular area where they have been placed [Early 18C. Origin ?]

taw[3] /taav, taaf/ *n* another spelling of **tav**

tawa /táawə/ *n* a tall forest tree of the laurel family with purple fruit. Native to: New Zealand. Latin name: *Beilschmiedia tawa*. [Mid-19C. < Maori]

tawdry /táwdri/ *adj* (**-drier, -driest**) **1.** GAUDY AND OF POOR QUALITY gaudy, cheap in appearance, and of inferior quality **2.** SHABBY BUT WITH PRETENSIONS shabby and worthless, though possibly with a superficial air of grandeur **3.** MEAN-SPIRITED mean-spirited and lacking in human decency ■ *n* CHEAP GAUDY FINERY finery that is gaudy, cheap in appearance, and of inferior quality [Early 17C. Shortening of *tawdry lace*, alteration of *St Audrey's lace*] —**tawdrily** *adv* —**tawdriness** *n*

ORIGIN Anna, Anglo-Saxon king of East Anglia, had a daughter called Etheldreda, who became queen of Northumbria. She had an inordinate fondness in her youth for fine lace neckerchiefs, and when she later developed a fatal tumour of the neck, she regarded it as divine retribution for her former extravagance. After her death in 679 she was canonized and made patron saint of Ely. In the Middle Ages fairs were held in her memory, known as 'St Audrey's fairs' (Audrey is a conflated form of Etheldreda), at which lace neck-

erchiefs were sold. These were often made from cheap gaudy material, and by the 17th century the eroded form **tawdry** was being used generally for 'cheap and gaudy'.

Tawney /táwni/, **R. H.** (1880–1962) Indian-born British economic historian. He is best known for *Religion and the Rise of Capitalism* (1926). Full name **Tawney, Richard Henry**

tawny /táwni/, **tawney** (**-nier, -niest**) *adj* **1.** of an orangey brown colour tinged with gold **2.** describes port wine that has matured for at least ten years in the barrel before bottling and is therefore paler than ruby port [14C. Via Anglo-Norman *tauné* < Old French *tané* < *tan* 'tanbark'] —**tawniness** *n*

tawny frogmouth *n* a common nocturnal insectivorous bird that has a wide mouth resembling that of a frog and brown or grey plumage streaked with black. Native to: Australia. Latin name: *Podargus strigoides*.

tawny owl *n* a common round-headed owl with brown or grey feathers, black eyes, tawny markings, and a hooting call. Native to: woods forests from Europe to China. Latin name: *Strix aluco*.

Tawny Owl *n* formerly, the official name for an assistant to the woman in charge of a group of Brownies

tawse /tawz/, **taws** *Scotland n* a leather strap split at the end, formerly used to punish school pupils with a blow to the palm of the hand ■ *vti* (**tawses, tawsing, tawsed**) to hit a pupil on the hand with a tawse [Early 16C. Plural of *taw* 'lash, whip' < TAW¹]

tax /taks/ *n* **1.** STRAIN a strain or heavy demand **2.** MONEY PAID TO GOVERNMENT an amount of money levied by a government on its citizens and used to run the government, the country, a state, a county, or a municipality **3.** CHARGE PAID BY MEMBERS an amount charged to members of a club or organization to be used for expenses ■ *vt* (**taxes, taxing, taxed**) **1.** CHARGE TAX ON SOMETHING to charge a tax on something such as a company's or person's income **2.** MAKE DEMANDS ON SOMEBODY OR SOMETHING to strain or make heavy demands on somebody or something ○ *You're starting to tax my patience.* **3.** ACCUSE OR CHARGE SOMEBODY to accuse or charge somebody with an offence ○ *She was taxed for failure to appear in court.* **4.** PAY TAX FOR CAR to pay the annual tax required in order to drive a motor vehicle **5.** LAW DETERMINE COSTS OF LITIGATION to determine the costs of litigation and the total amount of costs payable at the end of a trial (*dated*) [13C. Via French < Latin *taxare* 'censure, assess' < *tangere* 'to touch'] —**taxable** *adj*, *n* —**taxer** *n* —**taxless** *adj*

tax- *prefix* same as **taxo-** (*used before vowels*)

taxa ZOOL plural of **taxon**

taxation /tak sáysh'n/ *n* **1.** SYSTEM OF LEVYING TAXES the system whereby taxes are levied on some types of income, earnings, or purchases **2.** MONEY COLLECTED IN TAXES the amount of money raised by collecting taxes **3.** TAX ON SOMETHING an amount levied as a tax on something —**taxational** *adj*

tax avoidance *n* the practice of paying as little tax as possible by claiming all allowable deductions from income

tax break *n* same as **tax relief** (*informal*)

tax-deductible *adj* used to describe an expenditure that can be deducted from taxable income to lower the amount of tax owed by a person or business

tax-deferred *adj* not taxable until a later time, often after retirement

tax disc *n* a small circular official document displayed on a motor vehicle, usually on the inside of the windscreen, showing that the annual road tax has been paid

taxeme /ták seem/ *n* a small linguistic feature, e.g. selection, order, or phonetic modification [Mid-20C. < TAXIS] —**taxemic** /ták se'emik/ *adj*

tax evasion *n* an illegal activity in which a taxpayer seeks to hide taxable income or claim unauthorized tax deductions

tax-exempt *adj* legally exempt from taxation

tax exile *n* somebody who leaves a country in order to avoid paying taxes there

tax file number *n* in Australia, a numerical code used to identify a member of the workforce in dealings with the Australian Taxation Office

tax-free *adj* not subject to taxation

tax haven *n* a country with favourable tax rates

tax holiday *n* a period during which a company is exempt from taxation, e.g. when just starting out in business

taxi /táksi/ *n* (*plural* **-is** or **-ies**) CAR TAKING PAYING PASSENGERS a car, usually with a taximeter, whose driver is paid to transport passengers, typically for short distances ■ *vti* (**-ies, -iing** or **-ying, -ied**) **1.** TRANSPORT SOMEBODY OR BE TRANSPORTED to transport somebody or something, or be transported, especially in a car (*informal*) ○ *taxi the children to school* **2.** AVIAT MOVE AIRCRAFT ON GROUND to make an aircraft move under its own power on the ground, usually before takeoff or after landing, or move on the ground in this way **3.** TRANSP TAKE OR BE TAKEN IN TAXI to transport somebody or something in a taxi, or be transported in a taxi [Early 20C. Shortening of *taximeter cab*]

taxi- *prefix* same as **taxo-**

taxicab /táksi kab/ *n* VEHICLES same as **taxi** [Early 20C. Contraction of *taximeter cab*]

taxidermy /táksi durmi/ *n* the art or skill of preparing, stuffing, and presenting dead animal skins so that they appear lifelike [Early 19C. < Greek *taxis* 'arrangement' (see TAXIS)] —**taxidermal** /táksi dúrm'l/ *adj* —**taxidermist** *n*

taximeter /táksi meetar/ *n* a device installed in a taxi that automatically calculates and displays the fare, which is usually based on time, distance travelled, or a combination of both [Late 19C. < French *taximètre* < *taxe* 'charge, tariff']

taximetrics /táksi metriks/ *n* BIOL same as **numerical taxonomy** (*takes a singular verb*)

tax incentive *n* an incentive in the form of a reduction of, or an exemption from, the tax to which somebody would normally be liable

taxing /táksing/ *adj* placing numerous or severe demands on somebody —**taxingly** *adv*

tax inspector *n* an official whose job is to assess the amount of tax that is payable by a person or organization and ensure the tax is paid

taxiplane /táksi playn/ *n* US an aircraft that is available for hire

taxi rank *n* an area reserved for parked taxis awaiting customers. N Am term **taxi stand**

taxis /táksiss/ *n* **1.** movement of a cell or microorganism towards or away from the source of a stimulus **2.** the manipulating of a displaced body part to return it to its normal position, e.g. in a case of hernia [Late 16C. < Greek, 'order, arrangement' < *tassein* 'arrange']

-taxis *suffix* **1.** movement in response to a stimulus ○ *hydrotaxis* **2.** arrangement, order of parts ○ *phyllotaxis* [< Greek *taxis* (see TAXIS)]

taxi stand *n* N Am ROADS, TRANSP same as **taxi rank**

taxi truck *n* Aus a truck and driver for hire, often used for moving house

taxiway /táksi way/ *n* a path used by aircraft when taxiing to and from a runway or other ground facility

tax loss *n* a transaction that results in a reduced tax liability, even though it may not be associated with an actual cash loss, e.g. the loss associated with depreciation expenses

taxman /táks man/ *n* (*plural* **-men** /-men/) **1.** the taxing authority of a region or nation (*informal*) **2.** somebody who collects taxes

taxo-, taxi- *prefix* order, arrangement ○ *taxonomy* [< Greek *taxis* (see TAXIS)]

Taxol /ták sol/ *tdmk* a trademark for the anticancer drug paclitaxel

taxon /ták son/ (*plural* **taxa** /-sə/) *n* a group to which organisms are assigned according to the principles of taxonomy, including species, genus, family, order, class, and phylum [Early 20C. Back-formation < TAXONOMY]

taxonomy /tak sónnəmi/ (*plural* **-mies**) *n* **1.** GROUPING OF ORGANISMS the science of classifying plants, animals, and microorganisms into increasingly broader categories based on shared features. Traditionally, organisms were grouped by physical resemblances, but in recent times other criteria such as genetic matching have also been used. **2.** PRINCIPLES OF CLASSIFICATION the practice or principles of classification **3.** STUDY OF CLASSIFICATION the study of the rules and practice of classifying living organisms [Early 19C. < French *taxonomie* < Greek *taxis* (see TAXIS)] —**taxonomic** /táksə nómmik/ *adj* —**taxonomically** *adv* —**taxonomist** *n*

taxpayer /táks payər/ *n* somebody who pays tax, especially income tax —**taxpaying** *adj*

tax rate *n* the percentage of income paid in income tax

tax relief *n* tax savings in the form of allowable deductions, e.g. pension contributions, capital gains losses, and business losses

tax return *n* the set of government forms on which earnings and expenses are recorded in order to calculate the tax liability of a person or business

tax shelter *n* an investment activity that tends to reduce income tax liability —**tax-sheltered** *adj*

-taxy *suffix* order, arrangement ○ *epitaxy* [< Greek *-taxia* < *tag-*, stem of *tassein* 'arrange']

tax year *n* a period of twelve months over which income or profits are calculated for purposes of taxation

tay /tay/ *n Ireland* BEVERAGES same as **tea** (senses 1–2) [Mid-17C. Variant]

Tay /tay/ longest river in Scotland, flowing eastwards through Loch Tay and emptying into the North Sea through the Firth of Tay. Length: 190 km/120 mi.

Tay, Firth of /tay/ estuary of the River Tay on the eastern coast of Scotland, an inlet of the North Sea. It is spanned by the Tay Bridge.

tayberry /táybəri, -berri/ (*plural* **-ries**) *n* **1.** a sweet dark red berry that is a cross between a blackberry and a raspberry **2.** a bush that bears tayberries, produced by crossing a blackberry with a raspberry [Late 20C. After the River TAY]

Taylor /táylər/, **Dennis** (*b.* 1949) UK snooker player. He was Irish champion (1982), world champion (1985), and winner of the Rothmans Grand Prix (1984) and Benson & Hedges Masters (1987). Full name **Taylor, Dennis James**

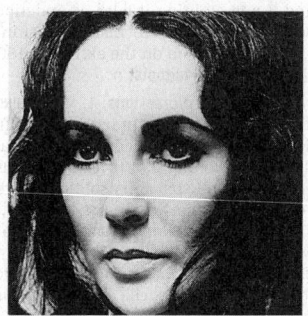

Elizabeth Taylor

Taylor, Dame Elizabeth (*b.* 1932) British-born US film actor. She became a star while still a child, in *National Velvet* (1944) and won Academy Awards for *Butterfield 8* (1960) and *Who's Afraid of Virginia Woolf?* (1966). She has continued to be in the public eye as a celebrity and an activist on behalf of Aids patients. Full name **Taylor, Dame Elizabeth Rosemond**

'Success is a great deodorant.'
[Elizabeth Taylor, *ABC TV*; 6 April 1977]

Taylor, Sir Gordon (1896–1966) Australian aviator. With Charles Kingsford Smith, he completed the first flight from Australia to South America in a single-engine aircraft. Full name **Taylor, Sir Patrick Gordon**

Taylor, Zachary (1784–1850) US military leader and 12th president of the United States. He was a hero of the Mexican War (1846–47) prior to becoming president (1849–50). Known as **Old Rough and Ready**. See table at **president**

Taylor series *n* a basic theorem of calculus relating an approximation of the value of a continuous function at a point to the successive derivatives of the function evaluated at the point [Early 19C. After Brook *Taylor* (1685–1731), English mathematician]

Taymyria /tay míri ə/ autonomous region in north-central Siberia, Russia. Capital: Dudinka. Population: 47,300. Area: 862,100 sq. km/332,859 sq. mi.

tayra /tíra/ *n* an agile weasel similar to the marten, with a brown coat and a buff patch on the throat. Native to: South America. Latin name: *Eira barbara*. [Mid-19C. Via Portuguese or Spanish *taira* < Tupi]

Tay-Sachs disease /táy sáks-/ *n* a genetic disease that principally affects Jews of eastern European ancestry, marked by accumulation of lipids in the brain and nerves and resulting in loss of sight and brain functions [Early 20C. After Warren *Tay* (1843–1927), British ophthalmologist, and Bernard *Sachs* (1858–1944), US neurologist]

tazia /ta zee ə/ *n* a large, decorated, paper and bamboo model of the tomb of either of the martyred grandsons of the prophet Muhammad, paraded during the festival of Muharram [Early 19C. < Arabic *ta'ziya* 'mourning, consolation']

tazza /tátsə/ *n* an ornamental vessel that has a shallow bowl, usually mounted on a pedestal [Early 19C. Via Italian < Arabic *ṭasa* (see TASSIE)]

Tb *symbol* CHEM ELEM terbium

TB *abbr* 1. NAVY torpedo boat 2. *also* **t.b.** ACCT trial balance 3. MED tuberculosis

t.b.a. *abbr* 1. to be agreed 2. to be announced

T-ball *n* a form of baseball played by children in which the ball is not pitched, but is rested on a tee in front of the batter

T-bar *n* 1. SKI TOW FOR TWO PEOPLE a ski tow for two people, shaped like an inverted 'T', in which skiers rest against a horizontal bar on each side of a central shaft 2. T-SHAPED STRAP ON SHOE a T-shaped strap cut from the upper part of a shoe 3. T-SHAPED METAL BAR a metal bar that is T-shaped in cross section

TBC *abbr* ONLINE to be continued

TBD *abbr* 1. to be determined 2. to be discussed

Tbilisi /təbi leéssi/ capital of the Republic of Georgia, in the east-central part of the country, on the River Kura. Population: 1,310,000 (1999).

T-bone steak *n* a large thick sirloin steak containing a T-shaped bone

tbs., tbsp. *abbr* MEASURE tablespoon

tc *abbr* ONLINE Turks and Caicos Islands (*used in Internet addresses*) See table at **domain name**

Tc *symbol* CHEM ELEM technetium

TC *abbr* AUTOMOT twin carburettors

TCCB *abbr* Test and County Cricket Board

TCDD *n* an extremely toxic by-product of herbicide manufacture. Formula: $C_{12}H_4O_2Cl_4$. Full form **tetrachlorodibenzodioxin**

T-cell *n* a white blood cell (**lymphocyte**) that matures in the thymus and is essential for various aspects of immunity, especially in combating viral infections and cancers [< abbreviation of *thymus-derived*]

Peter Ilich Tchaikovsky

Tchaikovsky /chī kófski/, **Peter Ilich** (1840–93) Russian composer. He was a major composer of the romantic era, writing works including symphonies, piano

concertos, and ballet scores such as *Swan Lake* (1876).

T-commerce *n* business conducted by means of interactive television

TCP *tdmk* a trademark for mild antiseptic preparations

TCP/IP *n* a protocol used for transmitting data between computers and as the basis for standard protocols on the Internet. Full form **transmission control protocol/Internet protocol**

TD[1] *abbr* 1. ARMS tank destroyer 2. EDUC technical drawing 3. MIL Territorial Decoration 4. AMERICAN FOOTBALL touchdown

TD[2] *abbr* GOV Member of the Dáil [Irish *Teachta Dála*]

TDD *abbr* telecommunications device for the deaf

TDM *abbr* time-division multiplexing

te /tee/ *n* a syllable that represents the seventh note in a scale when singing solfeggio. In fixed solfeggio it represents the note B. [Mid-19C. Alteration of SI[1]]

Te *symbol* CHEM ELEM tellurium

tea (sense 5)

tea /tee/ *n* 1. DRIED LEAVES OF ASIAN PLANT the dried leaves of an Asian plant, often shredded, used to make a drink by adding boiling water 2. TEA DRINK a drink made with tea, usually served hot but sometimes with ice 3. DRINK MADE BY INFUSION a drink made by the infusion of plant leaves or flowers ○ *drank some herbal tea* 4. DRIED LEAVES OR FLOWERS FOR INFUSION dried plant leaves or flowers, e.g. from herbs, used as the basis of a tea drink ○ *bought a packet of herbal tea* 5. ASIAN EVERGREEN BUSH an evergreen bush with toothed leathery leaves that are dried to make tea. Flowers: fragrant, cup-shaped. Native to: Asia. Latin name: *Camellia sinensis*. 6. EVENING MEAL a meal eaten early in the evening 7. AFTERNOON MEAL a light meal taken in the afternoon, usually consisting of cakes, sandwiches, and tea or other nonalcoholic drinks, or an afternoon social event at which this meal is eaten 8. BREAKFAST in Guyana, the first meal of the day 9. N Am DRUGS same as **marijuana** (*dated slang*) 10. W Africa HOT DRINK a hot drink such as coffee or cocoa [Mid-17C. Probably via Dutch *tee* and Malay *teh* < Chinese (Amoy dialect) *te*]

SPELLCHECK tea or **tee**? Do not confuse the spelling of *tea* and *tee*, which sound similar. *Tea* is a hot drink, a plant used to make it, or a light meal at which it is drunk, as in *a cup of tea, tea leaves, a tea party*. *Tee* can refer to a peg used in golf or to something T-shaped; the golf word *tee* is also used as a verb, as in *teed off at the 18th hole*.

REGIONAL NOTE The names used for meals can reveal a lot about the user's social and regional origins. *Tea* is perhaps the most ambiguous term. It can refer to an optional light snack around 4 p.m. or a meal eaten around 6 p.m. In parts of West Africa, it may refer to any hot drink including coffee or cocoa, and in Guyana it is used to refer to the first meal of the day.

tea bag *n* a small bag made of permeable paper or cloth containing tea leaves that is placed in boiling water to make one serving of tea

tea ball *n* a small perforated metal ball for holding tea leaves that is placed in boiling water to make tea

tea bread *n* a lightly sweetened bread, usually containing dried fruit, that is served sliced and but-

tered. In some recipes, the dried fruit is soaked in tea before being added to the mixture.

tea break *n* a break from work in order to have a drink, usually of tea or coffee

tea caddy *n* a small container, usually with a tight-fitting lid, for holding tea leaves

teacake /teé kayk/ *n* a large round flattened yeast bun made with currants and chopped mixed peel or other fruit, sometimes spiced

tea ceremony *n* a Japanese ritual in which tea is prepared, served, and drunk in a prescribed manner

teach /teech/ (**teaches, teaching, taught** /tawt/) *v* 1. *vt* IMPART KNOWLEDGE TO SOMEBODY to impart knowledge or skill to somebody by instruction or example ○ *taught me how to drive* 2. *vti* GIVE LESSONS IN SUBJECT to give lessons in or provide information about a subject ○ *taught Spanish to them* 3. *vti* GIVE LESSONS TO SOMEBODY to give lessons to a person or animal ○ *teaches the students on Wednesdays* 4. *vt* MAKE SOMEBODY UNDERSTAND SOMETHING to bring understanding of something to somebody, especially through an experience ○ *The episode taught me a lesson I'll never forget.* 5. *vti* TEACH REGULARLY to be a teacher in an institution ○ *teaches college* 6. *vt* ADVOCATE SOMETHING to advocate or preach something ○ *a philosophy that teaches non-violence* [Old English *tǽcan* < Indo-European, 'to show'] —**teachable** *adj*

SYNONYMS *teach, educate, train, instruct, coach, tutor, school, drill*

CORE MEANING: to impart knowledge or skill in something

teach to impart knowledge or skill to somebody by instruction or example ○ *He taught maths at the school for 21 years.* ○ *He taught me a great deal about crosswords, and I taught him how to swim.* **educate** to give knowledge to or develop the abilities of somebody by teaching, in school and elsewhere ○ *dispute over the best way of educating children according to their needs* ○ *The police stress that they want to educate bad drivers as much as prosecute them.* **train** to teach the skills necessary for a task or job by means of instruction, observation, and practice ○ *It is vital that professionals be properly trained to work with volunteers.* ○ *We took on new staff and trained them in skills ranging from bookkeeping to business administration.* **instruct** to teach somebody a subject, methodology, or skill ○ *a manual instructing the user how to run the computer software* ○ *The fire brigade was asked to instruct the officers in the use of the new appliances.* **coach** to give somebody private instruction in a particular subject, prepare somebody for an examination, or teach sporting, artistic, or life skills ○ *On Saturdays I used to coach the local mini rugby team.* ○ *When he's not playing himself, he spends his time coaching promising young players.* **tutor** to give somebody individual tuition in a subject or skill ○ *A blues guitarist of considerable talent, he has been tutoring my son for years.* **school** to train somebody in a skill or area of expertise in a thorough and detailed way ○ *She was schooled in classical drawing in Rome.* ○ *Even before university, he was being schooled to take over the family firm one day.* **drill** to make somebody repeat a sequence of exercises or procedures over and over again in order to learn it ○ *The most common intonation patterns should be drilled early in the series of language lessons.* ○ *The recruits had been drilled in the ideals of patriotism.*

teacher /teéchər/ *n* 1. somebody who teaches, especially as a profession 2. an occurrence, idea, or object from which something may be learnt ○ *Experience is a great teacher.* —**teacherless** *adj* —**teacherly** *adj*

teachers' centre *n* a resource centre where all the teachers in an area can go for materials and assistance

teacher's pet *n* 1. a student who is specially favoured by a teacher and consequently resented by other students (*insult*) 2. a special favourite of somebody in authority

tea chest *n* a large box made of thin wood lined with metal in which tea is packed for transport after drying

teach-in *n* an extended period of speeches, lectures, and discussions, usually held at a college or university as part of a political or social protest

teaching /teeching/ n 1. TEACHER'S PROFESSION the profession or practice of being a teacher 2. SOMETHING TAUGHT something that is taught, e.g. a point of doctrine (often used in the plural) ■ adj 1. FOR TEACHING used for or in teaching 2. THAT TEACHES being a person or establishment that teaches

teaching fellow n a postgraduate student in a university who teaches, especially undergraduates, in return for tuition and usually a small stipend — **teaching fellowship** n

teaching hospital n a hospital that provides supervised practical training for medical students, student nurses, or other healthcare professionals, often in conjunction with a medical school

teaching practice n the part of a student teacher's training that consists of a placement at a school where classroom teaching is undertaken by the student. N Am term **practice teaching**

tea cloth n HOUSEHOLD same as **tea towel**

tea cosy n a soft padded cover for keeping a teapot warm, usually with slits to fit over the handle and spout

teacup /tee kup/ n 1. a small-to-medium-sized cup, usually used with a saucer, especially for serving tea 2. also **teacupful** /tee kup fool/ the amount a teacup holds

tea dance n an afternoon social event at which people dance with partners and tea may be served

tea egg n HOUSEHOLD same as **tea ball**

tea garden n 1. a garden or outdoor restaurant where tea and light refreshments are served to the public 2. a plantation where tea is grown

tea gown n a loose, usually waistless, dress of light thin fabric trimmed with lace, worn by women in the late 19th century for afternoon social occasions at which men would not be present

teahouse /tee howss/ (plural **-houses** /-howziz/) n especially in China or Japan, a restaurant that serves tea and light refreshments

teak /teek/ n 1. INDUST DURABLE WOOD the durable red-brown wood of a South and Southeast Asian tree. Use: furniture, shipbuilding. 2. TREES TALL ASIAN TREE a tall tree valued for its timber. Native to: South Asia, Myanmar, Malay Archipelago. Latin name: *Tectona grandis.* 3. INDUST, TREES WOOD OR TREE LIKE TEAK a wood or tree similar to true teak 4. COLOURS YELLOWISH-BROWN a yellowish-brown colour [Late 17C. Via Portuguese < Tamil or Malayalam *tēkku*] —**teak** adj

teakettle /tee ket'l/ n a kettle used for boiling water for making tea

teakwood /teek wood/ n INDUST same as **teak** (sense 1)

teal /teel/ (plural **teals** or same) n 1. a greenish-blue colour 2. a small freshwater surface-feeding duck with bright iridescent blue or green patches on the wings. Genus: *Anas.* [13C. Origin ?] —**teal** adj

tea lady n a woman employed to make tea during tea breaks, e.g. in a factory or office

tea leaf n 1. a dried leaf or shredded part of the dried leaf of the tea plant, used to make tea 2. a tea leaf, or part of a leaf, after it has been infused (often used in the plural) 3. same as **thief** (slang) [In sense 3 rhyming slang]

team /teem/ n 1. SIDE IN SPORTS COMPETITION a group of people forming one side in a sports competition 2. COOPERATIVELY FUNCTIONING GROUP a number of people organized to function cooperatively as a group 3. ANIMALS WORKED TOGETHER two or more animals worked together, especially to pull a vehicle or agricultural equipment 4. TEAM OF ANIMALS WITH VEHICLE a team of animals and the vehicle harnessed to them 5. GROUPING OF ANIMALS a grouping of animals, e.g. a flock, brood, or herd ■ v (**teams, teaming, teamed**) 1. vti FORM INTO TEAM to form a team, or put people or animals together to form a team ○ Why don't you two team up for the next game? 2. vti PUT SOMETHING WITH COMPLEMENTARY OBJECT to combine something with another object, particularly one that matches or complements it 3. vt N Am TRANSPORT SOMETHING BY TEAM to transport something using a team of animals 4. vi N Am DRIVE TEAM to drive a team of farm animals or a truck [Old English *tēam* < Indo-European, 'to lead']

SPELLCHECK team or **teem**? Do not confuse the spelling of **team** and **teem**, which sound similar. **Team** can be used as a noun or verb, referring to a group of people or animals who work together, as in a team of designers, a team of oxen, teaming up with a former rival. Both words spelt **teem** are only used as verbs, one meaning 'have an extremely large number in a place', the other 'rain very hard' and 'pour out': The river teemed with fish. It's teeming down outside.

tea-maker n 1. a machine that is designed to make tea automatically, usually with a timer so that it turns itself on at the required time 2. HOUSEHOLD same as **tea ball**

team building n activities designed to encourage employees to work cooperatively

team leader n a senior nurse in charge of a ward and of the junior nurses working on the ward

team-mate n a player on the same team as somebody else

tea money n Hong Kong money offered to somebody as a bribe or in return for services provided (informal)

team player n a member of a group who cooperates with other people and who subordinates personal interests in order to achieve a common goal

team spirit n an enthusiastic attitude towards working productively with a team or work group

teamster /teemstər/ n 1. N Am a driver of a lorry that is used commercially for hauling loads 2. a driver of a team of animals used for hauling

Teamster n N Am a member of the Teamsters Union

Teamsters Union n a trade union, the International Brotherhood of Teamsters, Chauffeurs, Warehousemen, and Helpers of America, whose members are mainly lorry drivers

team teaching n an instructional programme involving two or more subjects that are taught in a coordinated way by specialist teachers

teamwork /teem wurk/ n 1. a cooperative effort by a group or team 2. work produced by a group or team

Te Anau /te únnow/ town in the southwestern part of the South Island, New Zealand, on Lake Te Anau. It is a tourist resort and the gateway to the Fiordland region. Population: 1,857 (2001).

Te Anau, Lake second largest lake in New Zealand, located in the southwestern part of the South Island. Area: 344 sq. km/133 sq. mi.

tea party n an afternoon social event at which tea is served

teapot /tee pot/ n a covered container with a spout and handle, used for making and serving tea

teapoy /tee poy/ n 1. a small three-legged ornamental table or stand 2. a small table used to hold a tea caddy and tea service [Early 19C. By folk etymology (after TEA) < Hindi *tipāī*, alteration of Persian *si-pāya* 'three-footed']

tear[1] /tair/ v (**tears, tearing, tore** /tawr/, **torn** /tawrn/) 1. vti PULL OR COME APART to pull something such as paper or cloth into pieces, or come apart or rip ○ She tore open the parcel. 2. vt MAKE HOLE IN SOMETHING to make a hole or opening in something such as a garment, leaving jagged edges ○ tore her skirt on a nail 3. vt CUT SOMETHING UNEVENLY to cut something, especially flesh, leaving jagged edges 4. vt SPRAIN BODY PART to injure a muscle or ligament so that some of the tissue is pulled apart and separated 5. vt SEPARATE SOMETHING BY FORCE to remove or separate something using force 6. vti CAUSE MENTAL PAIN to cause somebody extreme distress or emotional conflict ○ The memory tore at his heart. 7. vt DISRUPT SOMETHING to divide or fragment something ○ an organization that was torn by internal conflict 8. vi MOVE OR ACT QUICKLY OR CARELESSLY to move or act with great or careless speed (informal) ○ tearing down the road ■ n 1. RESULT OF TEARING a hole or split caused by tearing 2. TEARING OF SOMETHING an act of tearing something 3. HURRY a hurry or rush [Old English *teran* < Indo-European, 'to split'] —**tearable** adj —**tearer** n

SPELLCHECK See **tare**[1].

SYNONYMS *tear, rend, rip, split*
CORE MEANING: to pull or come apart by force

tear to pull something such as paper or cloth into pieces, or come apart ○ He tore the paper into little strips. ○ She was always climbing trees and tearing her clothes. **rend** to pull something apart violently, or be pulled apart violently ○ Something exploded with a sound of rending wood and metal and shattering glass. **rip** to roughly tear something apart or off, or become torn in this way ○ She ripped open the envelope. ○ You can't wear those flimsy clothes skateboarding – if you fall off, you'll rip them to shreds. **split** to divide something with a single movement, usually by force and into two parts ○ found him splitting wood to start a fire ○ Split the cake in half horizontally and sandwich it together again with jam.

tear apart vt 1. DESTROY SOMETHING to destroy something by shattering it into pieces 2. FRAGMENT GROUP OF PEOPLE to cause division, separation, or conflict in a group or organization ○ War tore the family apart. 3. DISTRESS SOMEBODY to cause somebody extreme distress or emotional conflict ○ the strain of separation was tearing us apart 4. SEARCH SOMETHING to search a place thoroughly, often causing disruptions and mess ○ The police tore the house apart looking for the weapon.

tear away vr to force or reluctantly persuade yourself or somebody else to leave a place or object ○ tore herself away from the festivities

tear down vt to demolish, destroy, or dismantle something such as a building

tear into vt to attack somebody or something vigorously, either physically or verbally

tear off vt 1. to remove a covering quickly and carelessly ○ He tore off his shirt. 2. to produce something quickly and carelessly

tear up vt to tear something into small pieces, e.g. in order to destroy it

tear[2] /teer/ n 1. DROP OF FLUID FROM EYE a single drop of salty fluid secreted by the lacrimal gland of the eye 2. DROP OF LIQUID a drop of liquid or hardened fluid, especially one with a round base and narrower top ○ tears of rain running down the window ■ **tears** npl 1. EXCESS OF LIQUID IN EYES a greater than usual amount of liquid produced by the eye or eyes, often accompanying intense emotions, or caused by irritation of the eye 2. CRYING weeping accompanied by intense emotion 3. LIQUID BATHING EYE the salty liquid secreted by the lacrimal gland that moistens and protects the surface of the eye and its surrounding tissue ■ vi (**tears, tearing, teared**) PRODUCE TEARS to produce tears, especially in excessive amounts ○ My eyes tear a lot during the hay fever season. [Old English *tēar* < Indo-European] —**tearless** adj

SPELLCHECK tear or **tier**? Do not confuse the spelling of **tear** and **tier**, which sound similar. A **tear** is a drop of fluid secreted by the eye, as in burst into tears. A **tier** is a row or layer one above the other or a level of a hierarchy, as in a two-tier system of taxation.

tearaway /táirə way/ n especially a child or young adult, somebody regarded as reckless, impulsive, and undisciplined

teardown /táir down/ n US 1. a building that is scheduled to be demolished, either because it is in poor condition or in order to build a new structure on its site 2. the process or an instance of tearing something down

teardrop /teer drop/ n 1. PHYSIOL same as **tear**[2] (sense 1) 2. something shaped like a teardrop

tear duct /teer-/ n a passage that conveys tears, especially the duct that drains tears from the inner corner of the eye into the nasal cavity

tearful /teerf'l/ adj 1. crying, about to cry, or feeling like crying, usually because of an emotion such as great sadness 2. sad enough to cause weeping ○ a tearful occasion —**tearfully** adv —**tearfulness** n

tear gas /teer-/ n a chemical agent, delivered by a grenade or other means, that incapacitates somebody by irritating the eyes —**tear-gas** vt

tearing /táiring/ adj violent or frenzied ○ in a tearing hurry

tear-jerker /téer jurkər/ *n* a story or artistic work that is excessively sentimental (*informal*) —**tear-jerking** *adj*

tear-off /táir-/ *adj* produced in a block of paper in sheet form, or perforated, so that individual pieces can be removed easily

tearoom /tée room, -room/ *n* 1. a restaurant or café serving tea and other beverages, and usually cakes and other light refreshments (*often used in the plural*) 2. S Africa a small shop in which some staple groceries, newspapers, and small consumer goods are sold (*dated*)

tea rose *n* a cultivated bushy or climbing rose. Flowers: large, tea-scented, pale pink or yellow. Native to: China. Latin name: *Rosa odorata*.

tear sheet /táir-/ *n* a single page taken from a magazine or other periodical, often used to prove to an advertiser that an advertisement has been published

tearstain /téer stayn/ *n* a mark or track left by tears —**tearstained** *adj*

teary /téeri/ (-**ier**, -**iest**) *adj* 1. WET WITH TEARS wet with or full of tears 2. ABOUT TO CRY seeming to be about to cry 3. CAUSING WEEPING causing or sad enough to cause weeping 4. LIKE TEARS resembling tears —**tearily** *adv* —**teariness** *n*

teary-eyed *adj* 1. with tears in the eyes, especially caused by emotion 2. characterized by weeping, especially when caused by sadness

tease /teez/ *v* (**teases, teasing, teased**) 1. *vti* MAKE FUN OF SOMEBODY to make fun of somebody, either playfully or maliciously 2. *vti* DELIBERATELY ANNOY SOMEBODY to deliberately annoy or irritate a person or an animal 3. *vt* PERSUADE SOMEBODY BY COAXING to urge somebody, especially to do something, by continual coaxing 4. *vt* AROUSE FEELING WITHOUT GIVING SATISFACTION to arouse hope, curiosity, or especially physical desire in somebody with no intention of giving satisfaction 5. *vt* TEXTILES PULL FIBRES APART to pull fibres apart by combing or carding 6. *vt* TEXTILES RAISE NAP BY COMBING to raise the nap on cloth by combing it with a wire brush 7. *vt* BIOL SEPARATE TISSUE to separate the parts of a tissue specimen gently with a needle in preparation for examination under a microscope 8. *vt* ANZ, S Am HAIR MAKE HAIR LOOK THICKER to comb the hair with quick short movements towards the roots so that it stands up away from the head. UK term **backcomb** ■ *n* 1. SOMEBODY WHO TEASES PLAYFULLY somebody who has a tendency to make fun of or annoy others 2. SOMEBODY WHO TEASES SEXUALLY somebody who teases somebody else sexually 3. PROVOCATIVE OPENING REMARK an opening remark or action intended to stimulate curiosity or interest 4. ACT OF TEASING an act of teasing somebody or something [Old English *tǣsan* < W Germanic] —**teasing** *adj* —**teasingly** *adv*

tease out *vt* 1. *also* **tease apart** to gradually separate things that are tangled up, or gradually separate something from an object with which it is entangled 2. to gradually extract something such as the truth or information

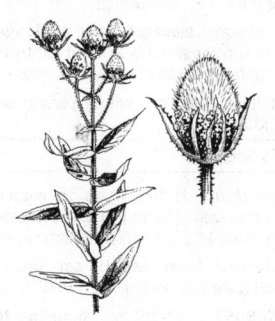

teasel

teasel /tée'z'l/, **teazel**, **teazle** *n* 1. PRICKLY PLANT a prickly plant with flowers covered with hooked leaves (**bracts**). Native to: Europe, Asia. Genus: *Dipsacus*. 2. TEASEL FLOWER HEADS the flower heads of the teasel. Use: formerly, to raise fabric nap in the textile industry. 3. IMPLEMENT USED TO RAISE NAP an industrial implement or device used to raise the nap on fabric [Old English *tǣsel* < W Germanic]

teaser /tée'zər/ *n* 1. TRICKY PROBLEM a tricky or difficult problem or question 2. same as **tease** *n* (sense 1) 3. MARKETING ADVERTISEMENT OFFERING GIFT an advertisement offering something free such as a bonus or gift 4. INDUST IMPLEMENT FOR TEASING WOOL an implement or device for teasing fibres, especially wool

tea service, tea set *n* a set of matching articles used for serving tea, e.g. cups, saucers, and a teapot

teashop /tée shop/ *n* COMM same as **tearoom** (sense 1)

teaspoon /tée spoon/ *n* 1. SMALL SPOON a small spoon, used especially for stirring tea and other beverages and for eating desserts 2. *also* **teaspoonful** /tée spoon fool/ AMOUNT TEASPOON HOLDS the amount of a liquid or solid held by a teaspoon 3. *also* **teaspoonful** ONE-THIRD OF TABLESPOON a standard household measure equal to one-third of a tablespoon or 5 ml

tea strainer *n* a small utensil consisting of a usually round head surrounding a mesh, through which tea is poured to separate the leaves from the liquid

teat /teet/ *n* 1. a protuberance on the breast or udder of a female mammal through which milk is excreted for the nourishment of young 2. a part designed to resemble a nipple or teat on a baby's or baby animal's feeding bottle. N Am term **nipple** [12C. < Old French *tete* < Germanic] —**teated** *adj*

tea table *n* a small table at which tea is served

tea-time *n* 1. the usual time at which tea is served, typically mid- or late afternoon 2. the time at which the evening meal is served

tea towel *n* a cloth for drying dishes and other kitchen items. N Am term **dishtowel**

tea tray *n* a tray intended for carrying a tea service

tea tree *n* a tree or bush from whose leaves an antiseptic oil (**tea tree oil**) is obtained. Use: in cosmetics, lotions. Native to: Australia, New Zealand. Genus: *Leptospermum*.

tea trolley *n* UK, ANZ, Can a small household trolley from which tea can be served. US term **tea wagon**

teazel, **teazle** *n* PLANTS, INDUST another spelling of **teasel**

Tebet *n* JUDAISM, CALENDAR another spelling of **Tevet**

TEC /tek/ *abbr* Training and Enterprise Council

tec. *abbr* technician

tech /tek/ (*informal*) *n* 1. OCCUPATIONS same as **technician** 2. SCI same as **technology** 3. a technical college or institute 4. THEATRE same as **technical rehearsal** ■ *adj* SCI technical or technological ○ *left behind by tech advances* [Early 20C. Shortening]

tech. *abbr* 1. technical 2. technician 3. technology

tech city *n* a town or city where a large number of people are employed in advanced technology industries, especially those connected with computing and electronic engineering

techie /téki/, **tekkie** *n* somebody who is interested in, adept at, or a student of a technology, especially one based on computing or electronics (*informal*) [Mid-20C. < TECHNICAL]

technetium /tek née'shi əm/ *n* a silvery-grey radioactive metallic element. Source: fission products of uranium, made artificially by particle bombardment of molybdenum. Use: as tracer, in corrosion-resistant materials. Symbol **Tc**. See table at **element** [Mid-20C. < modern Latin < Greek *tekhnētos* 'artificial' < *tekhnē* 'art, skill']

technetronic /tékni trónnik/ *adj* associated with or marked by the changes brought about by modern technology and electronics [Mid-20C. Blend of Greek *tekhnē* 'art, skill' + ELECTRONIC]

technic /téknik/ *n* 1. SCI same as **technics** 2. the way in which the basics of something are treated, or skill in handling a technique (*dated*) [Early 17C. < Greek *tekhnikos* (see TECHNICAL)]

technical /téknik'l/ *adj* 1. RELATING TO INDUSTRY OR APPLIED SCIENCE relating to or specializing in industrial techniques or subjects or applied science 2. MECHANICAL relating to the operation of a machine, system, or technique ○ *The Internet connection is down because of a technical fault.* 3. BELONGING TO SPECIALIZED AREA belonging to or involving a specialized subject, field, or profession ○ *a technical glossary* 4. STRICTLY INTERPRETED according to a strict interpretation of

rules or words 5. SKILLED IN PRACTICAL SUBJECTS skilled in practical or scientific subjects 6. EXHIBITING TECHNIQUE exhibiting or deriving from technique or the use of technique ○ *a high level of technical expertise* 7. FIN ANALYSING PRICES AND MARKET INDICATORS describes a type of security analysis based on past prices and volume levels as well as other market indicators 8. CLOTHING HIGH-TECH describes outdoor clothing that has been made using state-of-the-art materials and techniques ○ *Our technical fleece jacket has advanced dual construction.* ■ *n* 1. BASKETBALL same as **technical foul** 2. ARMED PICK-UP TRUCK a civilian pick-up truck equipped with, e.g., a machine gun, rocket-propelled grenade launcher, or antitank gun, used by irregulars or militia in counterinsurgency operations [Early 17C. < Greek *tekhnikos* 'of art or skill' < *tekhnē* 'art, skill']

technical college *n* a further education college in which students study practical rather than academic subjects

technical drawing *n* 1. the technique or practice of drawing objects and plans in a precise and detailed way, especially as taught in school 2. a precise scale drawing of something, usually professionally prepared for architectural, engineering, or industrial purposes, showing dimensions or quantities

technical foul *n* in basketball, a foul against a player or coach for unsporting behaviour or language rather than for physical contact with an opponent

technicality /tékni kálləti/ (*plural* -**ties**) *n* 1. POINT UNDERSTOOD ONLY BY SPECIALISTS a piece of information that is understood by or relevant only to a specialist, e.g. a detail or a term 2. TRIVIAL POINT FROM STRICTLY APPLYING RULES a minor point arising from a rigorous interpretation of laws or rules ○ *a legal technicality* 3. QUALITY OF BEING TECHNICAL the quality or condition of being technical

technical knockout *n* in boxing, a decision that ends a match because one of the participants is too badly injured to continue fighting

technically /téknikli/ *adv* 1. STRICTLY INTERPRETED according to a very strict, even unnecessarily strict, interpretation of rules or regulations ○ *Technically, you shouldn't be here at all.* 2. IN TECHNIQUE as regards a specialized skill or ability in technique 3. TECHNOLOGICALLY as regards the use of technology ○ *technically advanced*

technical rehearsal *n* a rehearsal of a play or other theatrical presentation for the purpose of making sure that lights, sound, and any other technical effects are cued correctly and in working order

technical sergeant *n* a noncommissioned officer in the US Air Force of a rank above staff sergeant

technical support *n* a repair or advice service offered to customers by some computer hardware and software manufacturers, usually by telephone, fax, or e-mail

technician /tek nísh'n/ *n* 1. SPECIALIST IN INDUSTRIAL TECHNIQUES somebody who is skilled in industrial techniques or the practical application of a science 2. LABORATORY EMPLOYEE somebody employed to do practical work in a laboratory 3. SOMEBODY HIGHLY SKILLED somebody who has mastered an artistic, athletic, or other specialized skill at a high level ○ *She's a superb technician who plays with lightning speed.* 4. SOMEBODY SKILLED RATHER THAN EXPERT somebody who has skills but lacks originality or flair

Technicolor /tékni kulər/ *tdmk* a trademark for an early colour process for making films that used three-colour separation negatives and a dye transfer process with three matrices made from the negatives

technics /tékniks/ *n* the science or rules of a field of knowledge, especially a technical one (*takes a singular or plural verb*)

technikon /téknikən/ *n* S Africa a technical college or technical university

~~technique~~ incorrect spelling of **technique**

technique /tek néek/ *n* 1. PROCEDURE OR SKILL REQUIRED the procedure, skill, or art used in a specific task 2. TREATMENT OF BASICS the way in which the basics of something such as an artistic work or a sport are treated 3. SKILL POSSESSED skill or expertise in doing

a specific thing ○ *a pianist with superb technique* **4. SPECIAL ABILITY** a special ability or knack [Early 19C. < French < Greek *tekhnikos* (see TECHNICAL)]

techno /téknō/ *n* electronic dance music characterized by its quick tempo and use of digitally synthesized instruments [Late 20C. Shortening of TECHNOLOGY]

techno- *prefix* technology, technological ○ *technophobia* [Shortening]

technobabble /téknō bab'l/ *n* language in which technical terms are overused

technocracy /tek nókrəssi/ (*plural* **-cies**) *n* **1.** a social system in which scientists, engineers, and technicians have high social standing and political power **2.** a philosophy that advocates the enlistment of a bureaucracy of highly trained engineers, scientists, or technicians to run the government and society

technocrat /téknə krat/ *n* **1.** a bureaucrat who is intensively trained in engineering, economics, or a form of technology **2.** a proponent of government by technicians —**technocratic** /téknə kráttik/ *adj*

technofreak /téknō freek/ *n* a technical expert in, or obsessive enthusiast of, information systems (*informal*)

technol. *abbr* SCI technology

technologize /tek nóllə jīz/ (**-gizes, -gizing, -gized**), **technologise** (**-gises, -gising, -gised**) *vti* to modify or modernize something by introducing technology, or be modified or modernized by the introduction of technology

technology /tek nólləji/ (*plural* **-gies**) *n* **1. APPLICATION OF TOOLS AND METHODS** the study, development, and application of devices, machines, and techniques for manufacturing and productive processes ○ *recent developments in seismographic technology* **2. METHOD OF APPLYING TECHNICAL KNOWLEDGE** a method or methodology that applies technical knowledge or tools ○ *a new technology for accelerating incubation* ○ *'...Maryland-based firm uses database and Internet technology to track a company's consumption of printed goods...'* (*Forbes Global Business and Finance*; November 1998) **3. MACHINES AND SYSTEMS** machines, equipment, and systems considered as a unit ○ *the latest laser technology* **4. CULTL ANTHROP SUM OF PRACTICAL KNOWLEDGE** the sum of a society's or culture's practical knowledge, especially with reference to its material culture [Early 17C. < Greek *tekhnologia* 'systematic treatment' < *tekhnē* 'art, skill'] —**technologic** /téknə lójjik/ *adj* —**technological** *adj* —**technologically** *adv* —**technologist** *n*

technophile /téknō fīl/ *n* a lover of new technology or computerization

technophobe /téknə fōb/ *n* somebody who dislikes new technology or computerization

technophobia /téknō fốbi ə/ *n* fear of or resistance to new technology or computerization

technostructure /téknō strukchər/ *n* a network of controlling technocrats in an organization or society

technothriller /téknō thrilər/ *n* a suspenseful book or film in which the plot turns on seemingly plausible technological wonders

tech wreck *n* the collapse in the share prices of high-tech industries that began in 2000 (*informal*)

techy *adj* another spelling of **tetchy**

~~**tecnical**~~ incorrect spelling of **technical**

~~**tecnique**~~ incorrect spelling of **technique**

tecta ANAT plural of **tectum**

tectonic /tek tónnik/ *adj* **1.** relating to the forces that produce movement and deformation of the Earth's crust **2.** relating to construction and architecture [Mid-17C. Via late Latin < Greek *tektonikos* < *tekton* 'builder, carpenter'] —**tectonically** *adv*

tectonic plate *n* a segment of the Earth's crust that moves relative to other segments and is characterized by volcanic and seismic activity around its margins

tectonics /tek tónniks/ *n* (*takes a singular verb*) **1.** the study of the mechanisms and results of large-scale movement of the Earth's crust, e.g. that producing

mountain ranges and extensive fault systems **2.** the science or practice of building construction

tectrix /téktriks/ (*plural* **-trices** /-tri seez/) *n* BIRDS same as **covert** *n* (sense 3) [Late 19C. < modern Latin < Latin *tect-*, past participle of *tegere* 'to cover'] —**tectricial** /tek trísh'l/ *adj*

tectum /téktəm/ (*plural* **-ta** /-tə/) *n* a part in the body that forms a covering or is arranged like a roof, especially the back upper section of the midbrain [Early 20C. < Latin, 'roof' < *tegere* 'to cover'] —**tectal** *adj*

Tecumseh /tə kúmssə/ (1768?–1813) Shawnee leader. He attempted to form an alliance of Native North American peoples to fight against US expansion into the Midwest. He was killed in battle fighting on the British side in the War of 1812 (1812–14).

> 'Where today are the Pequot? Where are the Narraganset, the Mohican, the Pocanet, and other powerful tribes of our people? They have vanished before the avarice and oppression of the white man, as snow before the summer sun.'
> [Tecumseh. Quoted in *Bury My Heart at Wounded Knee*, Dee Brown; 1970]

ted[1] /ted/ *n* same as **teddy boy** (*informal*) [Mid 20C. Shortening]

ted[2] /ted/ (**teds, tedding, tedded**) *vt* to spread or shake up mown grass in order to dry it when making hay [15C. < Old Norse *teðja* 'spread (manure)']

tedder /téddər/ *n* a machine or person that spreads or shakes up mown grass so that it can dry during hay making

Tedder /téddər/, **Arthur William, 1st Baron** (1890–1967) British air force commander. He played a major role as an RAF commander and strategist during World War II. He was made marshal of the RAF in 1961.

teddy[1] /téddi/ (*plural* **-dies**) *n* same as **teddy bear** [Early 20C. See TEDDY BEAR]

teddy[2] /téddi/ (*plural* **-dies**) *n* a woman's one-piece undergarment serving as both bra and panties [Early 20C. Origin ?]

teddy[3] /téddi/ (*plural* **-dies**) *n* W Country same as **potato** [Early 20C. Alteration]

teddy bear *n* a furry stuffed toy in the shape of a stylized bear cub [Early 20C. After Theodore ('*Teddy*') ROOSEVELT]

ORIGIN President Theodore Roosevelt was fond of bear-hunting. His nickname, 'Teddy', was used in a humorous poem in the *New York Times* about the adventures of two bears. Their names (Teddy B and Teddy G) were then appropriated to two bears in the Bronx Zoo whose popularity caused toy manufacturers to market toy bears as **teddy bears**.

teddy boy *n* **1.** a young man in the United Kingdom in the 1950s and early 1960s who followed the fashion of dressing in Edwardian style with tight narrow trousers, pointed shoes, and long sideboards **2.** any rebellious and tough young man (*dated*) [Mid-20C. Pet form of *Edward*, alluding to EDWARD VII]

teddy girl *n* a teddy boy's woman companion

Te Deum /tay dáy əm, tee deé əm/ *n* **1.** an ancient Christian hymn praising God that is sung or recited at matins in the Roman Catholic Church or at morning prayers in the Church of England **2.** a Christian service of thanksgiving that uses the Te Deum [Pre-12C. < Latin *Te Deum laudamus* 'Thee God, we praise', the first words of the hymn]

tedious /teédi əss/ *adj* boring because of being long, monotonous, or repetitive [15C. Directly or via French < late Latin *taediosus* < Latin *taedium* (see TEDIUM)] —**tediously** *adv* —**tediousness** *n*

tedium /teédi əm/ *n* the quality of being boring, monotonous, too long, or repetitive [Mid-17C. < Latin *taedium* 'weariness, disgust' < *taedere* 'be wearisome']

tee[1] /tee/ *n* **1.** T the letter T **2. T-SHAPED THING** something with the shape or form of a capital 'T', e.g. two pipes joined to form this shape **3.** SPORTS **TARGET** a mark aimed at in curling, quoits, and some other games **4.** N Am CLOTHING same as **T-shirt** (*informal*) [15C. Representing the pronunciation of the name of the letter]

SPELLCHECK See *tea*.

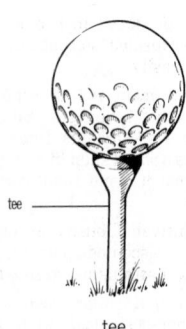

tee

tee

tee[2] /tee/ *n* **1.** GOLF **PEG** in golf, a small wooden or plastic peg with one pointed and one cupped end, inserted in the ground to hold a ball **2.** GOLF **STARTING AREA** an area on a golf course where play for a new hole begins **3.** AMERICAN FOOTBALL, RUGBY **STAND FOR FOOTBALL** a plastic device that supports a football or rugby ball on the ground in a position for kicking **4.** BASEBALL **STAND FOR BASEBALL** a column with a cupped top on a stand that supports a baseball for a hitter in T-ball ■ *vti* (**tees, teeing, teed**) SPORTS **POSITION BALL** to place a ball on a tee ready for striking [Late 17C. Origin ?]

SPELLCHECK See *tea*.

tee off *vi* **1.** to hit the ball from a tee at the start of a hole of golf **2.** to start a new activity (*informal*)

tee[3] /tee/ (**tees, teeing, teed**) [Probably alteration of PEE] **tee off** *vt* US to make somebody angry or annoyed (*informal*)

TEE *abbr* Trans-Europe Express (train)

tee-ball *n* BASEBALL same as **T-ball**

teed off /teéd-/ *adj* N Am angry, especially because of something that somebody has done (*informal*) [Probably alteration of *peed (pissed) off*]

tee-hee /teé heé/, **te-hee** *interj* used to indicate brief, especially mocking or gloating, laughter [14C. An imitation of the sound] —**tee-hee** *vi*

tee-joint *n* CONSTR same as **T-joint**

teem[1] /teem/ (**teems, teeming, teemed**) *vi* to have an extremely large number of people, animals, or things in a place ○ *streets teeming with shoppers* [Old English *tēman* < Germanic]

SPELLCHECK See *team*.

teem[2] /teem/ (**teems, teeming, teemed**) *v* **1.** *vi* to rain very hard **2.** *vt* to pour out or empty something [14C. < Old Norse *tœma* 'to empty' < *tómr* 'empty']

SPELLCHECK See *team*.

teen /teen/ (*informal*) *adj* same as **teenage** ■ *n* same as **teenager** [Early 19C. Shortening]

teenage /teén ayj/, **teenaged** /-ayjd/ *adj* **1.** aged between 13 and 19 ○ *teenage girls* **2.** relating to teenagers ○ *teenage styles* [Early 20C. < THIRTEEN, FOURTEEN, etc]

teenager /teén ayjər/ *n* a young person between the ages of 13 and 19

SYNONYMS See *youth*.

teens /teenz/ *npl* **1.** the years in somebody's life between the ages of 13 and 19 **2.** the numbers ending in '-teen' [Late 16C. < THIRTEEN, FOURTEEN, etc]

teensy /teénzi/ (**-sier, -siest**) *adj* same as **teeny** (*informal*) [Late 19C. Probably < TEENY]

teensy-weensy /-weénzi/ *adj* same as **teeny-weeny** (*informal*) [After TEENY-WEENY]

REGIONAL NOTE See *itsy-bitsy*.

teenth /teenth/ *n* DRUGS same as **sixteenth** (sense 2) (*slang*) [Shortening]

teeny /teéni/ (**-nier, -niest**) *adj* very small (*informal*) [Early 19C. Alteration of TINY, after WEENY]

teenybopper /teéni bopər/ *n* a young teenager, usually a young girl, who follows the latest fads in fashion

and music [Mid-20C. < TEENAGER or TEENS, influenced by TEENY]

teeny-weeny *adj* very small (*informal*)

REGIONAL NOTE See *itsy-bitsy*.

teepee *n* CULTL ANTHROP another spelling of **tepee**

tee-plate *n* CONSTR same as **T-plate**

Tees /teez/ river in northeastern England, flowing into the North Sea at Teesmouth. Length: 128 km/80 mi.

tee shirt *n* CLOTHING same as **T-shirt**

tee-square *n* ART same as **T-square**

Teesside /teéz sīd/ industrial region around the mouth of the River Tees in northeastern England. It includes the city of Middlesbrough.

teeter /teétər/ (**-ters, -tering, -tered**) *vi* **1.** to walk or move unsteadily and as if about to fall ○ *teetering along in her high heels* **2.** to be in a precarious position in which things could imminently go badly wrong ○ *For 24 hours the country teetered on the brink of war.* **3.** *US* same as **seesaw** *v* (senses 2–3) ○ *teetered between wanting to go and not wanting to go* [Mid-19C. Variant of dialect *titter* < Germanic]

teeth ANAT plural of **tooth**

teethe /teeth/ (**teethes, teething, teethed**) *vi* to grow milk teeth [15C. < TEETH]

teether /teéthər/ *n US* an object such as a teething ring on which a baby can bite while teething

teething ring /teéthing-/ *n* a ring of hard rubber or plastic on which a baby can bite when teething

teething troubles *npl* temporary difficulties that arise at the outset of a new activity

teethridge /teéth rij/ *n* ANAT same as **alveolar ridge**

teetotal /tee tōt'l/ *adj* **1.** completely abstaining from alcoholic beverages **2.** complete and absolute [Mid-19C. < initial letter of TOTAL + TOTAL] —**teetotalism** *n* —**teetotaller** *n* —**teetotally** *adv*

teetotum /tee tōtəm/ *n* a top spun with the fingers, formerly used in a game of chance [Early 18C. < Latin *totum* 'all' + its initial letter 'T', inscribed on one side of the toy]

teff /tef/, **tef** *n* an annual grass cultivated for its seed, that is used as a grain. Native to: North Africa. Latin name: *Eragrostis tef.* [Late 18C. < Amharic *ṭēf*]

tefillin /tə fíllin/ *npl* small leather boxes containing Hebrew texts ritually worn by Orthodox Jewish men [Early 17C. < Aramaic *tĕpillīn* 'prayers']

TEFL /téff'l/ *abbr* teaching of English as a foreign language

Teflon /téf lon/ *tdmk* a trademark for polytetrafluoroethylene, a plastic with nonstick properties that is used as a coating, e.g. for cookware

teg /teg/ *n* **1.** a sheep of either sex between weaning and first shearing **2.** *US* a doe that is in the second year of life [Early 16C. Origin ?]

tegmen /tégmən/ (*plural* **-mina** /-mənə/), **tegmentum** /teg méntəm/ (*plural* **-ta** /-tə/) *n* **1.** BOT **INNER LAYER IN SEED** the inner layer of a seed's coat **2.** INSECTS **INSECT FOREWING** the forewing of a primitive insect such as the cockroach **3.** BIOL **COVERING PART** a covering part in a plant or animal [Early 19C. < Latin < *tegere* 'to cover'] —**tegmental** *adj* —**tegminal** *adj*

tegu /ti goó/ (*plural* **-gus** or *same*) *n* a fast-running lizard that grows up to 120 cm/4 ft long. Native to: Central and South America. Genus: *Tupinambis.* [Mid-20C. Shortening of *teguexin* < Nahuatl *tecoixin* 'lizard']

Tegucigalpa /te goóssi gálpə/ capital of Honduras, in the south-central part of the country. Population: 1,037,600 (2000).

tegular /téggyoólər/, **tegulated** /téggyoó laytid/ *adj* relating to or resembling tiles [Early 19C. < Latin *tegula* 'tile' < *tegere* 'to cover'] —**tegularly** *adv*

tegument /téggyoómənt/ *n* the protective outer covering of an organism [15C. < Latin *tegumentum* 'covering' < *tegere* 'to cover'] —**tegumental** /téggyoó mént'l/ *adj* —**tegumentary** /téggyoó méntəri/ *adj*

te-hee *interj, vi* another spelling of **tee-hee**

Tehran /te raán/, **Tehrān** capital of Iran, in the northern part of the country. Population: 11,689,000 (2002).

Teide, Pico de ♦ **Pico de Teide**

te igitur /táy íggitoor/ *n* the first prayer of the Roman Catholic Mass, beginning 'te igitur clementissime Pater', which translates as 'thee, therefore, most merciful Father' [Early 19C. < Latin, 'thee, therefore', its opening words]

teiglach /táyg laakh, tíg-/ *n* a Jewish or German confection made from spiced dough shaped into small balls and simmered in honey, nuts, and spices (*takes a singular or plural verb*) [Early 20C. < Yiddish *teyglekh* < *teyg* 'dough' < Old High German *teic*]

teigue *n Ireland* another spelling of **taig** (*slang offensive*)

teiid /teé id, tí-/ *adj* belonging to a reptile family of large carnivorous lizards with forked tongues, native to Central and South America [Mid-20C. < modern Latin *Teiidae* < Portuguese *teiu* 'lizard' < Tupi *tejú*]

Teilhard de Chardin /táy jaa də shaárdan/, **Pierre** (1881–1955) French priest, palaeontologist, and theologian. He was one of the discoverers of Peking man, and in his major work, *The Phenomenon of Man* (1955), he argued that scientific evolutionary theory is compatible with Christian doctrine.

> 'From an evolutionary point of view, man has stopped moving, if he ever did move.'
> [Pierre Teilhard de Chardin, *The Phenomenon of Man*; 1955]

teind /teend/ *Scotland n* same as **tithe** ■ *vti* (**teinds, teinding, teinded**) to tithe the income or produce [13C. Alteration of TENTH]

Tejo /táyzhō/ ♦ **Tagus**

Te Kanawa /tə kaánəwə, tay-/, **Dame Kiri** (*b.* 1944) New Zealand opera singer. She made her debut as a soprano at Covent Garden in 1970 and went on to perform at major opera houses worldwide. Full name **Te Kanawa, Dame Kiri Janette**

Tekapo, Lake /tékəpō/ lake in the centre of the South Island, New Zealand. Area: 83 sq. km/32 sq. mi.

tekkie *n* COMPUT another spelling of **techie** (*informal*)

Te Kooti /te koóti/ (1830?–93) New Zealand Maori leader. He was the founder of the Ringatu Church, and conducted a guerrilla campaign against the British authorities in New Zealand. Full name **Te Kooti, Arikirangi Te Turuki**

tektite /ték tīt/ *n* a small dark-coloured glassy object, possibly resulting from meteoric impact, found in groups at various locations throughout the world [Early 20C. < Greek *tēktos* 'molten' < *tēkein* 'melt']

tel. *abbr* TELECOM **1.** telegram **2.** telegraph **3.** telegraphic **4.** telephone

tela /teélə/ (*plural* **-lae** /-lee/) *n* a delicate part or tissue in the body with a fine or intricate pattern like a web [Early 20C. < Latin, 'web']

telaesthesia /télliss theézhə, -theézi ə/ *n* the supposed perception of phenomena or events considered beyond the range of normal senses [Late 19C. < TELE- + Greek *aisthēsis* 'perception'] —**telaesthetic** /-théttik/ *adj*

telamon /téllə mon, -mən/ (*plural* **-mones** /-mṓneez/ or **-mons**) *n* ARCHIT same as **atlas** (sense 3) [Early 17C. < Greek, after *Telamon*, Greek mythical hero]

telangiectasia /te lánji ek táyzi ə/, **telangiectasis** /-ek táyssiss/ *n* permanent dilation of the capillaries and small blood vessels, especially in the face and thighs, producing dark red blotches [Mid-19C. < Greek *telos* 'end' + *aggeion* 'vessel' + *ektasis* 'extension'] —**telangiectatic** /-táttik/ *adj*

Tel Aviv-Yafo /tél ə veév yaáfō/, **Tel Aviv-Jaffa** /-jáffə/ city in west-central Israel, on the Mediterranean Sea. It comprises the historical Arab town of Jaffa and modern Tel Aviv. Population: 348,100 (1999).

telco /télkō/ (*plural* **-cos**) *n* a telecommunications company (*informal*) ○ *'Those on the front lines of networking, such as telcos, Internet service providers...'* (*Forbes Global Business and Finance*; November 1998) [Late 20C. Shortening]

telco hotel *n* ONLINE same as **Internet hotel**

tele- *prefix* **1.** distant, operating at a distance ○ *telecommute* **2.** television ○ *telegenic* **3.** telegraph, telephone ○ *telebanking* [< Greek *tēle* 'far away']

telebanking /télli bangking/ *n* a system of transacting business with a bank by telephone

telebridge /télli brij/ *n* a telephone system that enables three or more people to be connected simultaneously ○ *'Group classes are limited to 15 participants and are held on a telebridge.'* (*The Washington Post*; July 1998)

telecast /télli kaast/ *n* a television broadcast ■ *vti* (**-casts, -casting, -cast** or **-casted**) to broadcast a programme on television —**telecaster** *n*

telecom /télli kom/ *n* same as **telecommunication** (*informal*) [Mid-20C. Shortening]

telecommunication /télli kə myoóni káysh'n/ *n* the transmission of encoded sound, pictures, or data over significant distances, using radio signals or electrical or optical lines

telecommunications /télli kə myoóni káysh'nz/ *n* the science and technology of transmitting information electronically by wires or radio signals with integrated encoding and decoding equipment (*takes a singular or plural verb*) ■ *npl* information transmission over communications lines (*takes a plural verb*)

telecommute /télli kə myoót/ (**-mutes, -muting, -muted**) *vi* to engage in teleworking —**telecommuter** *n* —**telecommuting** *n*

telecomputing /télli kəm pyoóting/ *n* the act of sending information to or receiving information from another computer via modem or local area network

telecoms /télli komz/ *n* same as **telecommunications** (*informal; takes a singular or plural verb*) [Contraction]

teleconferencing /télli konfərənssing/ *n* a system of video conferencing that uses a restricted band of frequencies and allows participants to be connected by telephone lines —**teleconference** *n, vi*

teledensity /télli dénssəti/ *n* a measure of telephone availability, expressed as the number of main lines per 100 inhabitants in a country

teledu /télli doo/ (*plural* **-dus** or *same*) *n* a carnivorous animal of the weasel family with a dark coat and a white stripe down its back. Native to: Southeast Asia. Latin name: *Mydaus javanensis.* [Early 19C. < Javanese]

téléférique *n* TRANSP another spelling of **téléphérique**

telefilm /télli film/ *n* a film made for television

teleg. *abbr* TELECOM **1.** telegram **2.** telegraph **3.** telegraphic **4.** telegraphy

telega /te láygə/ *n* a simple four-wheeled Russian cart [Mid-16C. < Russian]

telegenic /télli jénnik/ *adj* pleasant and attractive when viewed on television [Mid-20C. After PHOTOGENIC] —**telegenically** *adv*

telegnosis /téllə nṓssiss, télləg-/ *n* knowledge of phenomena beyond the range of normal sense perception —**telegnostic** /-nóstik/ *adj*

telegram /télli gram/ *n* a message sent by telegraph [Mid-19C. After TELEGRAPH] —**telegrammatic** /télli grə máttik/ *adj* —**telegrammic** /télli grámmik/ *adj*

telegraph /télli graaf, -graf/ *n* **1. LONG-DISTANCE COMMUNICATION THROUGH WIRES** a method of long-distance communication by coded electrical impulses transmitted through wires **2.** TELECOM same as **telegram** ■ *v* (**-graphs, -graphing, -graphed**) **1.** *vti* **SEND SOMETHING BY WIRE** to send a message to somebody by telegraph **2.** *vt* **INDICATE SOMETHING INDIRECTLY** to communicate a thought or feeling indirectly or without words ○ *telegraphed her annoyance with a frown* **3.** *vt* **SHOW INTENTION** to give advance notice of intentions, especially unwittingly, to an audience or opponent ○ *telegraphed the decision in last week's press conference* [Early 18C. < French *télégraphe* 'something that writes far' < *graphe* (see -GRAPH)] —**telegrapher** /ti léggrəfər/ *n* —**telegraphist** /ti léggrəfist/ *n*

telegraphese /télli gra feéz/ *n* language reduced to its essential elements without regard to elegance or grammar, as typically found in telegrams

telegraphic /télli gráffik/ *adj* **1.** concise or elliptical in spoken or written expression **2.** relating to telegraphy or telegrams —**telegraphically** *adv*

telegraph plant *n* a pod-bearing bush with small

leaflets that jerk spasmodically in hot sunshine. Native to: tropical Asia. Latin name: *Desmodium gyrans*.

telegraph pole, **telegraph post** *n* a high wooden pole for supporting telephone wires. N Am term **telephone pole**

telegraphy /ti léggrəfi/ *n* the system, study, or operation of telegraph communications

Telegu *n, adj* LANG, PEOPLES another spelling of **Telugu**

teleimmersion /télli i múrsh'n/ *n* an enhanced teleconferencing technology that uses banks of video cameras linked to computers to enable users in remote locations to collaborate as if they were in the same room

telekinesis /télli ki néessiss, -kī-/ *n* the supposed psychic power to move or change the shape of inanimate objects without the use of physical force —**telekinetic** /-néttik/ *adj* —**telekinetically** *adv*

Telemachus /tə lémməkəss/ *n* in Greek mythology, the son of Odysseus, who waited with his mother, Penelope, for his father's return after the Trojan War

Telemann /táylə man, téllə-/, **Georg Philipp** (1681–1767) German composer. A prolific composer, he bridged the baroque and early classical periods in works that include 40 operas and numerous orchestral suites and chamber pieces.

telemark /télli maark/ *n* a turn in cross-country skiing accomplished by putting the outside ski forwards and turning it slowly inwards [Early 20C. After *Telemark*, region in Norway] —**telemark** *vi*

telemarketing /télli maarkiting/ *n* selling or promoting goods and services by telephone —**telemarketer** *n*

telemark skiing *n* SKIING same as **free-heel skiing**

telematics /télli máttiks/ *n* the study of the processes involved in the long-distance transmission of computer data (*takes a singular verb*) [Late 20C. Blend of TELECOMMUNICATION + INFORMATICS] —**telematic** *adj*

telemedicine /télli medəss'n/ *n* the use of video links, e-mail, telephone, or another telecommunications system to transmit medical information, e.g. in consultations between a doctor and patient or in supervision of medical staff

telementoring /télli méntəring/ *n* the practice of conducting a mentoring relationship remotely, usually by e-mail

telemeter *n* /ti lémmitər, télli méetər/ **1.** REMOTE MEASURING DEVICE a device used to record information about a remote object or event and transmit it to an observer **2.** DEVICE FOR MEASURING DISTANCES DIRECTLY a device used for measuring distances directly that does not use rods or chains across the distance to be measured ■ *vt* /télli méetər/ (**-ters, -tering, -tered**) TRANSMIT DATA to collect and transmit data about a remote object, especially using a satellite —**telemetric** /télli méttrik/ *adj* —**telemetrical** *adj* —**telemetrically** *adv* —**telemetry** /ti lémmətri/ *n*

telencephalon /téllen séffə lon/ *n* the part of the brain that is farthest forward, consisting of the cerebral hemispheres —**telencephalic** /-ensə fállik/ *adj*

teleological /télli ə lójjik'l, téeli-/, **teleologic** /-lójjik/ *adj* relating to the study of ultimate causes in nature or of actions in relation to their ends or utility —**teleologically** *adv*

teleological argument *n* an argument for God's existence from the presence of order, interpreted as design, in the universe

teleology /téeli ólləji/ *n* **1.** STUDY OF CAUSES the study of ultimate causes in nature **2.** APPROACH TO ETHICS an approach to ethics that studies actions in relation to their ends or utility **3.** GOAL-DIRECTED ACTIVITY an activity that tends towards the achievement of a goal [Mid-18C. < modern Latin *teleologia* 'science of ends' < Greek *telos* 'end'] —**teleologism** *n* —**teleologist** *n*

teleoperation /télli oppə ráysh'n/ *n* the operation of systems or equipment in a physically remote location, carried out using specialized electronic communication and robotic engineering —**teleoperator** *n*

teleost /télli ost/, **teleostean** /télli ósti ən/ *n* a bony fish with rayed fins in a suborder that includes most living species, numbering around 20,000, but excluding sturgeons, gars, sharks, rays, and related fish. Subclass: Teleostei. [Mid-19C. < Greek *telos* 'end' + *osteon* 'bone']

telepath /télli path/ *n* somebody who claims to communicate by telepathy

telepathize /tə léppə thīz/ (**-thizes, -thizing, -thized**), **telepathise** (**-thises, -thising, -thised**) *vi* to claim or be believed to communicate by telepathy

telepathy /tə léppəthi/ *n* supposed communication directly from one person's mind to another's without speech, writing, or other signs or symbols —**telepathic** /télli páthik/ *adj* —**telepathically** *adv*

téléphérique /téllifə reék/, **téléférique** *n* TRANSP **1.** same as **cable car 2.** same as **cableway** [Early 20C. < French, 'carrying far' < Greek *pherein* 'carry']

telephone /télli fōn/ *n* **1.** ELECTRONIC COMMUNICATIONS DEVICE an electronic apparatus containing a receiver and transmitter that is connected to a telecommunications system, enabling the user to speak to and hear others with similar equipment **2.** COMMUNICATION USING TELEPHONES a system of communications using telephones ○ *a telephone company* ■ *vti* (**-phones, -phoning, -phoned**) **1.** USE TELEPHONE TO CONTACT SOMEBODY to contact and speak to somebody using the telephone **2.** CONVEY SOMETHING BY TELEPHONE to send a message by telephone ○ *Bob couldn't come to the party and telephoned his regrets.* —**telephoner** *n* —**telephonic** /télli fónnik/ *adj* —**telephonically** *adv*

telephone answering machine *n* TELECOM same as **answering machine**

telephone book *n* N Am TELECOM same as **telephone directory**

telephone box *n* an enclosed or partly enclosed space with a pay telephone in it. N Am term **telephone booth**

telephone directory *n* an alphabetical listing of people or organizations that have telephones, along with their addresses and telephone numbers. N Am term **telephone book**

telephone exchange *n* a centre that houses equipment used for interconnecting telephone lines

telephone pole *n* N Am TELECOM same as **telegraph pole**

telephone tag *n* a situation in which two people repeatedly return each other's telephone calls and leave recorded messages without succeeding in speaking directly to each other (*informal*)

telephonist /tə léffənist/ *n* a telephone switchboard operator

telephony /tə léffəni/ *n* the science, technology, or system of communication by telephone

telephoto /télli fōtō/ *adj* producing a large image of a distant object ■ *n* (*plural* **-tos**) **1.** PHOTOGRAPHY same as **telephoto lens 2.** a photograph taken using a telephoto lens

telephotography /télli fə tóggrəfi/ *n* the photographing of distant objects with the use of special lenses or electronic equipment —**telephotographic** /télli fōtə gráffik/ *adj*

telephoto lens *n* a camera lens that integrates a telescope

teleplay /télli play/ *n* a treatment or script for a play written for presentation on television

teleport /télli pawrt/ (**-ports, -porting, -ported**) *v* **1.** *vt* to move an object supposedly by means of telekinesis **2.** *vi* in science fiction and fantasy, to move instantly from one place to another by futuristic, paranormal, or magical means [Mid-20C. < TELE- + Latin *portare* 'carry'] —**teleportation** /télli pawr táysh'n/ *n*

telepresence /télli prézz'nss/ *n* **1.** the virtual presence of somebody whose actions are transmitted by electronic signals to a physically remote site, e.g. in telesurgery **2.** the experience of being present at a physically remote location

teleprinter /télli printər/ *n* UK, ANZ, Can a piece of equipment for telegraphic communication that uses

a device like a typewriter for data input and output. US term **teletypewriter**

teleprocessing /télli prō sessing/ *n* the use of computer terminals in different locations, connected to a main computer, to process data

TelePrompTer /télli promptər/ *tdmk* a US trademark for a device showing text for somebody speaking on television to read

telerecording /télli ri káwrding/ *n* the recording of a television programme on tape or film as it is being broadcast

telesales /télli saylz/ *n* MARKETING same as **telemarketing**

telescience /télli sī ənss/ *n* the technology of making observations and performing experiments from a great distance

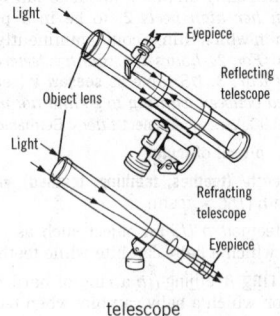

telescope

telescope /télli skōp/ *n* **1.** DEVICE FOR LOOKING AT DISTANT OBJECTS a device for making distant objects appear nearer and larger by means of compound lenses or concave mirrors **2.** ASTRON same as **radio telescope** ■ *v* (**-scopes, -scoping, -scoped**) **1.** *vi* COLLAPSE NEATLY INSIDE ONE ANOTHER to slide neatly one inside another like the sections of a telescope **2.** *vt* CONDENSE SOMETHING to make something shorter in time or length ○ *telescoped his adventure into a one-hour talk* [Mid-17C. < Italian *telescopio* or modern Latin *telescopium*, both literally 'looking far' < Greek *skopein* 'look']

telescopic /télli skóppik/ *adj* **1.** ENLARGING having the ability to make something distant seem nearer or larger ○ *a telescopic lens* **2.** ABLE TO SEE FAR able to see great distances ○ *telescopic vision* **3.** OF TELESCOPES relating to or visible only by using a telescope **4.** COLLAPSIBLE consisting of parts that slide one inside another ○ *a tripod with telescopic legs* —**telescopically** *adv*

telescopic sight *n* a telescope mounted on a rifle and used for sighting, especially on distant targets

Telescopium /téllə skōpi əm/ *n* a constellation of the southern hemisphere [Early 19C. < modern Latin (see TELESCOPE)]

telescopy /tə léskəpi/ *n* the science and technology of making and using telescopes

teleservices /télli survissiz/ *npl* products and services that combine the retail use of the telephone and computers

teleshopping /télli shoping/ *n* the practice or activity of ordering goods advertised on television by phone or computer

telestereoscope /télli stérri ə skōp, -steéri-/ *n* a binocular telescope or telescopic stereoscope adapted to provide a three-dimensional view of distant objects or landscapes

telesthesia /tél es theézhə/ *n* PARAPSYCHOL US spelling of **telaesthesia**

telestich /ti léstik, télli stik/ *n* an acrostic or poem in which the last letters in each line spell a word [Mid-17C. < Greek *telos* 'end' + *stikhos* 'row, line of verse']

Telesto /ti léstō/ *n* a very small natural satellite of Saturn, discovered in 1980. It is irregular in shape with a maximum dimension of 30 km/19 mi., and occupies an intermediate orbit.

telesurgery /télli súrjəree/ *n* surgery carried out by a surgeon who is not physically present at the site of the operation, using specialized electronic communications and robots

teletext /télli tekst/ *n* a system of broadcasting news and other information in written form that can be viewed on specially equipped television sets, superimposed on, or in place of, the picture

telethon /télla thon/ *n* a lengthy television broadcast that combines entertainment with appeals to donate to a charity [Mid-20C. Blend of TELE- + MARATHON]

teletypewriter /télli típ rītər, télli tīp-/ *n US* TELECOM same as **teleprinter**

teleutospore /ti loŏtə spawr/ *n* BIOL same as **teliospore** [Late 19C. < Greek *teleutē* 'completion' < *telos* 'end'] —**teleutosporic** /ti loŏtə spáwrik, -spórrik/ *adj*

televangelist /télli vánjəlist/ *n* a Christian evangelist who broadcasts on television [Late 20C. Blend of TELE-VISION + EVANGELIST] —**televangelism** *n*

televise /télli vīz/ (**-vises, -vising, -vised**) *vt* to broadcast something on television [Early 20C. Back-formation < TELEVISION]

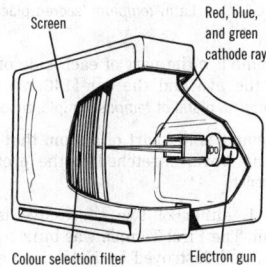

Screen   Red, blue, and green cathode rays

Colour selection filter   Electron gun

television

television /télli vizh'n, -vízh'n/ *n* **1.** *also* **television set** DEVICE FOR RECEIVING IMAGES AND SOUNDS an electronic device for receiving and reproducing the images and sounds of a combined audio and video signal **2.** BROADCAST CONTENT the image, sound, or content of a combined audio and video broadcast ○ *spent the evening watching television* **3.** BROADCASTING INDUSTRY the industry concerned with the making and broadcasting of programmes combining images and sounds ○ *works in television* **4.** VIDEO BROADCASTING SYSTEM a system of capturing images and sounds, broadcasting them via a combined electronic audio and video signal, and reproducing them to be viewed and listened to —**televisual** /télli vízhyoo əl, télla-, -víz-/ *adj*

television tube *n* MEDIA same as **tube** *n* (sense 6)

teleworking /télli wurking/ *n* HR working from home on a computer linked to the workplace via modem —**teleworker** *n*

telex /télleks/ *n* **1.** COMMUNICATIONS SYSTEM a communications system using teleprinters that communicate via telephone lines **2.** MESSAGE a message sent or received by telex ■ *vti* (**-exes, -exing, -exed**) SEND SOMETHING BY TELEX to send a message to somebody by telex [Mid-20C. Blend of TELEPRINTER + EXCHANGE]

telfer, etc. TRANSP another spelling of **telpher, etc.**

Telford /télfərd/ industrial town in Shropshire, west-central England, designated as a new town in 1968. Population: 115,000 (1991).

Telford, Thomas (1757–1834) British civil engineer. He was a pioneer in the building of roads, canals, and bridges, most notably the Menai Suspension Bridge (1826) in Wales.

telia FUNGI plural of **telium**

telic /téllik/ *adj* directed towards a definite end or purpose [Mid-19C. < Greek *telikos* 'final' < *telos* 'end']

teliospore /teéli ə spawr/ *n* a resting spore that develops in rust and smut fungi in the autumn and germinates in the spring [Early 20C. < TELIUM] —**teliosporic** /teéli ə spáwrik, -spórrik/ *adj*

telium /teéli əm, télli-/ (*plural* **-lia** /-li ə/) *n* the spore case of a rust or smut fungus that bears teliospores [Early 20C. < Greek *telos* 'end'] —**telial** *adj*

tell /tel/ (**tells, telling, told** /tōld/) *v* **1.** *vt* INFORM SOMEBODY to inform somebody of something ○ *Who told you?* ○ *Jim told us the news.* **2.** *vt* RELATE EVENTS OR FACTS to give an account in speech or writing of events or facts ○ *tell a story* **3.** *vti* EXPRESS SOMETHING IN WORDS TO SOMEBODY to express thoughts or feelings to somebody in words **4.** *vt* EXPRESS SOMETHING to express a particular thing in speech ○ *tell a lie* **5.** *vt* ORDER SOMEBODY to command or order somebody to do something **6.** *vt* DISTINGUISH ONE FROM OTHER to distinguish two or more people or things ○ *couldn't tell one from the other* **7.** *vt* DISCERN SOMETHING to ascertain or perceive something ○ *couldn't tell whether she was pleased or not* **8.** *vt* REVEAL FUTURE to purport to reveal future events ○ *tell your fortune* **9.** *vi* REVEAL SECRET to reveal secret or damaging information, especially to an authority ○ *Don't worry – I won't tell.* **10.** *vt* COUNT THINGS to count things such as votes cast or beads as part of a prayer ○ *tell a rosary* [Old English *tellan* < Germanic, 'put in order'] —**tellable** *adj* ◇ **all told** altogether, or when everything else is taken into consideration ◇ **tell it like it is** to give a frank and accurate account of something (*informal*) ◇ **tell me about it!** (*informal*) **1.** used to indicate heartfelt agreement **2.** used wryly to indicate to a speaker that you too have had a similar experience to the one being described, usually a negative experience ◇ **there's no telling** it is impossible to ascertain or predict a particular thing ○ *There's no telling how fast the disease will spread.* ◇ **you're telling me!** used to indicate agreement with an observation (*informal*)

tell against *vt* to play a part in determining a negative outcome for somebody ○ *His extreme nervousness told against him in the interview.*

tell apart *vt* to distinguish two or more similar people or things

tell off *vt* to scold or rebuke somebody, especially in anger (*informal*)

tell on *vt* **1.** to have an adverse effect on somebody or something **2.** to report damaging or incriminating information about somebody to an authority

Tell, William *n* ♦ **William Tell**

tell-all *adj* not withholding any information, even what may be considered secret, private, or unsuitable ■ *n* a book or other writing, especially biographical or autobiographical, that withholds no information about its subject

teller /téllər/ *n* **1.** BANK EMPLOYEE an employee in a bank or savings institution who receives and pays out money **2.** COUNTER OF VOTES somebody who counts votes in an election or legislature **3.** SOMEBODY WHO TELLS somebody who tells something ○ *a teller of tales*

Teller /téllər/, **Edward** (1908–2003) Hungarian-born US physicist. He helped construct the first atom bomb (1945) and was the principal architect of the hydrogen bomb, first tested in 1952.

> 'The main purpose of science is simplicity and as we understand more things, everything is becoming simpler.'
> [Edward Teller, *Conversations on the Dark Secrets of Physics*; 1991]

tellin /téllin/ (*plural* **-lins** or *same*) *n* a bivalve sea mollusc that lives in intertidal sand. Genus: *Tellina*. [Early 18C. Via Latin < Greek *tellinē* 'type of shellfish']

telling /télling/ *adj* **1.** very effective or expressive ○ *a telling indictment* **2.** revealing information inadvertently or indirectly ○ *a telling glance* —**tellingly** *adv*

telling-off (*plural* **tellings-off**) *n* a scolding or reprimand for doing something wrong (*informal*)

telltale /tél tayl/ *adj* CLEARLY SHOWING SOMETHING clearly showing or indicating something that is secret or hidden ○ *telltale signs* ■ *n* **1.** SOMEBODY WHO TELLS SECRETS a person, especially a child, who tells others about another person's secrets or bad behaviour **2.** MONITORING DEVICE a device or signal intended to monitor a machine or system **3.** SAILING WIND STRIPS strips of ribbon hung aloft on a sailing boat to show apparent wind direction **4.** RACKET GAMES METAL STRIP a horizontal metal strip across the front wall of a squash or racquetball court, above which the ball must be bounced

tellurate /téllyoo rayt/ *n* a salt or ester of telluric acid [Early 19C. < TELLURIUM]

tellurian /te loŏri ən/ *adj* relating to Earth or life on Earth ■ *n* in science fiction, an inhabitant of Earth [Mid-19C. < Latin *tellus* 'earth']

telluric[1] /te loŏrik/ *adj* **1.** originating or coming from Earth or its atmosphere **2.** GEOG same as **tellurian** [Mid-19C. < Latin *tellus* 'earth']

telluric[2] /te loŏrik/ *adj* relating to or containing tellurium, especially in a high valency [Early 19C. < TEL-LURIUM]

telluric acid *n* a white crystalline inorganic acid. Use: chemical reagent. Formula: H_6TeO_6. [< TEL-LURIC[2]]

telluride /téllyoŏ rīd/ *n* a binary compound of tellurium with an electropositive element or group [Mid-19C. < TELLURIUM]

tellurion /te loŏri on, -lyoŏri ən, -lyoŏri on/ *n* a model that shows how day and night and the seasons result from the Earth's orbit and its tilted axis in relation to the Sun [Mid-19C. < Latin *tellus* 'earth']

tellurise *vt* CHEM another spelling of **tellurize**

tellurium /te loŏri əm/ *n* a semimetallic element that occurs naturally, both in a native state and in mineral ores. Source: refining of copper and lead. Use: alloys, various manufacturing processes. Symbol Te. See table at **element** [Early 19C. < Latin *tellus* 'earth', after URANIUM]

tellurize /téllyoŏ rīz/ (**-izes, -izing, -ized**), **tellurise** (**-ises, -ising, -ised**) *vt* to cause something to combine with tellurium

tellurometer /téllyoŏ rómmitər/ *n* a device that measures distances using the time that microwaves or radio waves take to be transmitted across the distance to be measured [Mid-20C. < Latin *tellus* 'earth']

tellurous /téllyoŏrəss, te loŏrəss/ *adj* relating to or containing tellurium, especially in a low valency [Mid-19C. < TELLURIUM, after FERROUS]

Tellus /télləss/ *n* in Roman mythology, the goddess of the Earth and of fertility [< Latin, 'earth']

telly /télli/ (*plural* **-lies**) *n* MEDIA same as **television** (*informal*) [Mid-20C. Shortening]

Telnet /tél net/ *n* also **TELNET** a terminal emulation program that allows computer users to connect interactively to a server and access remote sites, e.g. on the Internet ■ *vti* (**-nets, -netting, -netted**) to access a remote computer [Late 20C. < TELE- + NETWORK]

telo- *prefix* end, terminal ○ *telophase* [< Greek *telos* 'end']

telocentric /télla séntrik/ *adj* describes a chromosome whose centromere is located at or near one end

telolecithal /télla léssithəl/ *adj* describes reptile, shark, or bird eggs in which the yolk is concentrated at one end [Late 19C. < TELO- + Greek *lekithos* 'egg yolk']

telomerase /télləmə rayz, -rayss/ *n* an enzyme found in cancers that, by re-forming the telomeres at the ends of chromosomes, prevents the shortening that usually limits the number of replications and thus allows cancer growth

telomere /télla meer/ *n* a region of DNA at the end of a chromosome that protects the start of the genetic coding sequence against shortening during successive replications

telophase /télla fayz/ *n* the final stage of cell division, in which daughter cell nuclei form around chromosomes at opposite ends of the dividing mother cell —**telophasic** /télla fáyzik/ *adj*

telpher /télfər/, **telfer** *n* a car or other carrying unit suspended from a cable in a telpherage ■ *vt* (**-phers, -phering, -phered; -fers, -fering, -fered**) to transport somebody or something in a container suspended from cables [Late 19C. Contraction < TELE- + -PHORE] —**telpheric** *adj*

telpherage /télfərij/, **telferage** *n* a transport system in which passengers or goods are carried in containers suspended from cables

telson /télss'n/ *n* the terminal segment of an arthropod or arachnid body, e.g. the stinger of a scorpion [Mid-19C. < Greek, 'limit'] —**telsonic** /tel sónnik/ *adj*

Telstar /tél staar/ *n* a communications satellite used for transmitting television programmes and telephone messages. Two of these were launched by the United States in 1962 and 1963. [Mid-20C. < TELE- + STAR]

Telugu /télla goo/ (*plural same* or **-gus**), **Telegu** *n* **1.** a

Dravidian language of central and southeastern India, especially the state of Andhra Pradesh. Native speakers: over 10 million. **2.** a member of a Telugu-speaking people [Late 18C. < Kannada and Tamil] —**Telugu** *adj*

LANGUAGE HERITAGE See ***Dravidian***.

Tema /téemə/ city in southeastern Ghana, on the Gulf of Guinea, near Accra. Population: 180,600 (1990 estimate).

TEMA *abbr* Telecommunications Engineering and Manufacturing Association

temazepam /tə mázzə pam/ *n* a benzodiazepine drug used for the short-term treatment of insomnia [Late 20C. < *tem-*, origin ? + OXAZEPAM]

temblor /témblər, -blawr/ *n* an earthquake or tremor [Late 19C. < American Spanish, 'trembling' < Vulgar Latin *tremulare* 'tremble']

temerarious /témmə ráiri əss/ *adj* showing a reckless confidence that may be offensive (*literary*) [Mid-16C. < Latin *temerarius* < *temere* 'rashly, blindly']

temerity /tə mérrəti/ *n* reckless confidence that might be offensive [15C. < Latin *temeritas* 'rashness' < *temere* 'rashly, blindly']

temmoku /témmō koo/ *n* a Japanese iron glaze that is black in colour but breaks into rust where the glaze coat is thin [Late 19C. Via Japanese < Chinese *tiān mù* 'eye of heaven']

Temne /témni/ (*plural* **-nes** or *same*) *n* **1.** a member of an African people living in Sierra Leone **2.** the Niger-Congo language of the Temne people. Native speakers: 1 million. [Late 18C. < Temne] —**Temne** *adj*

temp /temp/ *n* a temporary worker, especially one hired from an agency ■ *vi* (**temps, temping, temped**) to do temporary work, especially through an agency ○ *Terry's temping with a bank.* [Early 20C. Shortening of TEMPORARY]

temp. *abbr* **1.** temperance **2.** METEOROL, MICROBIOL temperate **3.** METEOROL temperature **4.** BIOCHEM, ENG, COMPUT template **5.** ANAT temporal **6.** OCCUPATIONS temporary

tempeh /tém pay/, **tempe** *n* fermented soya beans, popular as a health food and in some Asian cuisines [Mid-20C. < Indonesian *tempe*]

temper /témpər/ *n* **1. TENDENCY TO ANGER** a tendency to get angry easily and suddenly ○ *has quite a temper* **2. ANGRY STATE** a state of anger or annoyance ○ *got himself into a terrible temper* **3. EMOTIONAL CONDITION** an emotional condition or predisposition of a particular kind ○ *an even temper* **4. CALM STATE** a state of calm and balance ○ *lost his temper* **5.** METALL **HARDNESS OF METAL** the degree of hardness of a metal **6. ADDITIVE** something added to improve the consistency or strength of something ■ *vt* (**-pers, -pering, -pered**) **1. SOFTEN SOMETHING** to make something less harsh or unacceptable, especially by adding something to it ○ *temper criticism with kindness* **2. MAKE SOMEBODY STRONGER** to make somebody stronger through exposure to hardship ○ *tempered by combat duty* **3. STRENGTHEN MATERIAL** to improve the consistency of something such as glass by heating it or by adding something to it **4. HARDEN METAL** to harden metal by heating it to very high temperatures and then cooling it ○ *temper steel* **5.** MUSIC **TUNE EARLY KEYBOARD INSTRUMENT** to tune a baroque keyboard instrument so that consistent harmonic intervals are achieved throughout its range [Pre-12C. < Latin *temperare* 'mix, restrain yourself' < *tempus* 'time'] —**temperability** /témpərə bílləti/ *n* —**temperable** *adj* —**temperer** *n*

tempera /témpərə/ *n* **1.** a technique of painting with colours made from powdered pigments mixed with water and egg yolk, size, or casein **2.** *US* ART same as **poster paint 3.** a painting done in tempera [Mid-19C. < Italian < Latin *temperare* (see TEMPER)]

temperament /témprəmənt/ *n* **1. QUALITY OF MIND** a prevailing or dominant quality of mind that characterizes somebody **2. MOODINESS** excessive moodiness, irritability, or sensitivity **3.** HIST **MEDIEVAL PHYSIOLOGICAL CLASSIFICATION** in medieval physiology, the quality of mind resulting from various proportions of the four cardinal humours in somebody **4.** MUSIC **NOTE INTERVAL SETTING** the subtle relationship of the pitches of notes of keyboard instruments and the consequences this has for harmony

temperamental /témprə mént'l/ *adj* **1. EASILY UPSET** easily upset or irritated **2. UNPREDICTABLE** unpredictable and erratic in behaviour ○ *a temperamental car* **3. OF TEMPERAMENT** relating to temperament —**temperamentally** *adv*

temperance /témpərənss/ *n* **1.** total abstinence from alcoholic drink **2.** self-restraint in the face of temptation or desire

~~temperary~~ incorrect spelling of **temporary**

temperate /témpərət/ *adj* **1. MILD** mild or restrained in behaviour or attitude **2.** METEOROL **WITHOUT EXTREMES** describes a climate that has a range of temperatures within moderate limits **3.** MICROBIOL **NOT SPREADING** describes viruses that exist in host cells, but do not cause lysis —**temperately** *adv* —**temperateness** *n*

Temperate Zone *n* the parts of Earth that lie between the tropics and the polar circles and generally have hot summers, cold winters, and intermediate autumns and springs

temperature /témprichər/ *n* **1. DEGREE OF HEAT** the degree of heat as an inherent quality of objects expressed as hotness or coldness relative to something else **2. RELATIVE DEGREE OF HEAT** the heat of something measured on a scale such as the Fahrenheit or Celsius scale. Symbol **T, t 3. BODY HEAT** the degree of heat in a living organism **4. FEVER** human body heat in excess of 37.0° C/98.6° F ○ *running a temperature* **5. DEGREE OF EXCITEMENT** the level of excitement or tension in a situation ○ *When the opposition filed in, the temperature in the room went up.* [15C. Directly or via French < Latin *temperatura* < *temperare* (see TEMPER)]

temperature gradient *n* the rate of change in air temperature over distance, especially elevation

temperature-humidity index *n* a measure of ambient humidity relative to heat as it affects human comfort

temperature inversion *n* METEOROL same as **inversion** (sense 3)

tempered /témpərd/ *adj* **1. WITH PARTICULAR TEMPER** having a temper or temperament of a particular type (*usually used in combination*) ○ *even-tempered* **2. WELL PROPORTIONED** having components combined in a balanced and suitable proportion **3.** METALL **HARDENED** hardened through a tempering process ○ *tempered steel* ○ *tempered glass* **4.** MUSIC **TUNED TO TEMPERAMENT** describes a keyboard instrument tuned to a particular temperament, especially equal temperament

~~temperment~~ incorrect spelling of **temperament**

temper tantrum *n* an outburst of anger, especially a childish display of rage or bad temper

~~temperture~~ incorrect spelling of **temperature**

tempest /témpist/ *n* **1.** a severe commotion or disturbance, especially an emotional upheaval **2.** a severe storm with very high winds and often rain, hail, or snow (*literary*) [13C. Via French < Latin *tempestas* < *tempus* 'time']

CULTURAL NOTE *The Tempest*, a play (1611) by William Shakespeare. An elaborate blend of comedy, drama, and fantasy, it is set on an enchanted island where Prospero, rightful duke of Milan, has lived since being usurped by his brother Antonio. Using his magical powers, Prospero conjures up a storm that forces Antonio and his companions onto the island, paving the way for an ingenious reconciliation. The word *sea-change*, meaning a change caused by the sea and, figuratively, a major transformation, comes from Act I, Scene ii of this play: 'Nothing of him that doth fade,/ But doth suffer a sea-change/ Into something rich and strange'.

tempestuous /tem péstyoo əss/ *adj* **1.** frequently turbulent and giving rise to many emotions ○ *a tempestuous relationship* **2.** having or affected by frequent or violent storms ○ *tempestuous seas* —**tempestuously** *adv* —**tempestuousness** *n*

tempi MUSIC plural of **tempo**

Templar /témplər/ *n* **1.** HIST same as **Knight Templar 2.** a barrister or law student with offices in the Temple, London [13C. < the place in Jerusalem (*Temple of Solomon*) where the medieval order had its headquarters]

template /tém playt, -plət/ *n* **1. MASTER** something that serves as a master or pattern from which other similar things can be made **2.** ENG **PATTERN** a mechanical pattern or mould with one or more shapes used to guide the manufacture or drawing of objects with a similar shape **3.** CONSTR **SHORT BEAM** a short beam of metal, wood, or stone, used to distribute weight or pressure in a structure **4.** BIOCHEM **MASTER MOLECULE** a molecule that provides a pattern for the synthesis of other molecules in biochemical reactions **5.** COMPUT **MASTER FILE** a computer file that is used as a master for creating others similar to it [Late 17C. Alteration of TEMPLET, after PLATE]

temple[1] /témp'l/ *n* **1. BUILDING FOR WORSHIP** a building used as a place of worship **2. SPECIAL PLACE** an institution or building considered as a guardian of, or reservation for, a particular activity ○ *a temple of learning* **3. MEETING PLACE** a building where a fraternal order holds meetings and rites **4. HOLY DWELLING** a place where something holy or divine is thought to dwell, e.g. the body of a holy person **5.** *N Am* JUDAISM same as **synagogue 6. MORMON CHURCH** a place of worship for the Church of Jesus Christ of Latter-Day Saints where sacred ordinances such as marriage are executed [Pre-12C. < Latin *templum* 'sacred place, place for worship']

temple[2] /témp'l/ *n* the part of each side of the head between the eye and the ear [14C. Via Old French < Latin *tempora*, plural of *tempus* 'temple, time']

temple[3] /témp'l/ *n* the part of a loom that keeps the cloth being woven stretched to the proper width [15C. < French]

Temple *n* **1.** either of two successive temples in Jerusalem. The First Temple was built by Solomon in 957 BC, and destroyed by Nebuchadnezzar II in 586 BC. The Second Temple was destroyed by the Romans in AD 70. **2.** either of two groups of buildings in Paris and London built on sites that once belonged to the Knights Templar. The London site is now the home of two of the Inns of Court. [< TEMPLE[1]]

Temple /témp'l/, **Shirley** ➧ **Black, Shirley Temple**

templet /témplət/ *n* same as **template** (*archaic*) [< TEMPLE[3]]

tempo /témpō/ (*plural* **-pos** or **-pi** /-pee/) *n* **1.** the speed at which a musical composition or passage is performed **2.** the pace or rate of something ○ *the tempo of urban life* [Mid-17C. Via Italian < Latin *tempus* 'time']

tempolabile /témpō láy bīl/ *adj* changing at an uneven rate [Mid-20C. < Latin *tempus* 'time' + *labilis* < *labi* 'to slip']

temporal[1] /témpərəl/ *adj* **1. RELATING TO TIME** relating to measured time **2. BRIEF** lasting only a short time **3.** RELIG **OF THIS WORLD** relating to life in the world, not to spiritual life **4.** CHR **RELATING TO LAITY** relating to the laity, not to the clergy in the Christian Church **5.** GRAM **RELATING TO TENSES** relating to grammatical tenses or the expression of time in a language [14C. Directly or via French < Latin *temporalis* < *tempus* 'time'] —**temporally** *adv*

temporal[2] /témpərəl/ *adj* relating to or located in the region of the temples on the head [Late 16C. < late Latin *temporalis* < Latin *tempus* 'temple, time']

temporal bone *n* either of a pair of bones that form part of the sides and base of the skull and contain the middle and inner ears [< TEMPORAL[2]]

temporality /témpə rálləti/ *n* the quality or state of being connected with time or the world ■ **temporalities** *npl* the secular property and assets of a church [14C. < late Latin *temporalitas* < Latin *temporalis* (see TEMPORAL[1])]

temporal lobe *n* either of two lobes of the brain, located on the side of each cerebral hemisphere, that contain the auditory centres responsible for hearing [< TEMPORAL[2]]

temporary /témpərəri/ *adj* **1. HAVING LIMITED DURATION** lasting or designed to last for a limited time **2. NOT NEEDED FOR LONG** describes computer files and folders that hold information that is not needed for long and may be deleted automatically ■ *n* (*plural* **-ies**) **WORKER HIRED FOR LIMITED TIME** a paid worker in an office or other workplace taken on for a limited time only [Mid-16C. < Latin *temporarius* < *tempus* 'time'] —**temporarily** *adv* —**temporariness** *n*

SYNONYMS ***temporary, fleeting, passing, transitory, ephemeral, evanescent, short-lived***
CORE MEANING: lasting only a short time
temporary lasting or designed to last for a limited time ○ *The acid caused only temporary injury to the man's eyes.* ○ *In some organizations, temporary jobs offer a step on the way to regular employment.* **fleeting** passing or fading quickly ○ *a fleeting moment of happiness* ○ *Most reviewers predicted the book would enjoy only fleeting success.* **passing** superficial and not long-lasting ○ *This man had no feelings for her other than a passing fancy.* ○ *Who is to say that the views of popular personalities are of anything more than passing interest?* **transitory** not permanent or lasting, but existing only for a short time ○ *transitory peace and stability* ○ *the transitory nature of stardom* **ephemeral** lasting for a short time and leaving no permanent trace ○ *Fashions are ephemeral – new ones regularly drive out the old.* **evanescent** (*literary*) disappearing after a short time and soon forgotten ○ *a shimmering evanescent bubble* ○ *a shifting, changing, fluid evanescent reality* **short-lived** lasting or living for only a short period of time ○ *a short-lived mood disorder which is likely to resolve rapidly without treatment* ○ *The actor has recently been tempted out of his short-lived retirement.* ○ *a short-lived perennial plant*

Temporary Protection Visa *n Aus* a three-year visa granted to an asylum seeker who has arrived unauthorized in Australia but has been recognized as a refugee

temporize /témpə rīz/ (**-rizes, -rizing, -rized**), **temporise** (**-rises, -rising, -rised**) *vi* to use delaying tactics to gain time, especially in order to avoid coming to a decision or committing yourself —**temporizer** *n*

temporomandibular joint /témpərō man díbbyŏŏlər-/ *n* either of the joints connecting the lower part of the jaw (**mandible**) with the temporal bone on each side of the head. Both joints act together when the jaw is moved. [< TEMPORAL[2]]

temporomandibular joint syndrome *n* DENT full form of **TMJ syndrome**

Tempranillo /temprə níllō/ *n* a black grape variety from Spain and Portugal. Use: to make wine. [Late 19C. After a village in N Spain]

~~**temprature**~~ incorrect spelling of **temperature**

tempt /tempt/ (**tempts, tempting, tempted**) *vt* **1.** INCITE DESIRE IN SOMEBODY to cause desire or craving to arise in somebody ○ *I was tempted by that chocolate cake!* **2.** INCITE SOMEBODY TO TRANSGRESSION to persuade or attempt to persuade somebody to do something considered wrong **3.** BE INVITING TO SOMEBODY to be inviting or attractive to somebody ○ *The sightseeing tour tempted us.* **4.** RISK SOMETHING to risk the possible destructive powers of something ○ *tempt fate* [13C. Via Old French *tempter* < Latin *temptare* 'feel, try, test'] —**temptable** *adj*

temptation /temp táysh'n/ *n* **1.** DESIRE FOR SOMETHING BAD a desire or craving for something, especially something considered wrong ○ *yield to temptation* **2.** INCITEMENT OF DESIRE the incitement of desire or craving in somebody **3.** CAUSE OF DESIRE somebody or something that tempts somebody ○ *too many temptations for me here*

tempter /témp tər/ *n* somebody who tempts somebody else to do something considered wrong

Tempter *n* CHR same as **Satan**

tempting /témp ting/ *adj* causing desire or craving to arise in somebody ○ *a tempting offer* —**temptingly** *adv*

temptress /témptriss/ *n* an offensive term for a woman that deliberately insults her sexuality and public behaviour (*dated*)

tempura /témpoorə/ *n* a Japanese dish of vegetables or seafood coated in light batter and deep-fried [Mid-20C. < Japanese]

tempus fugit /témpoos fyoojit/ time flies [Latin]

ten /ten/ *n* **1.** 10 the number 10 **2.** SOMETHING WITH VALUE OF 10 something in a numbered series, e.g. a playing card, with a value of ten ○ *the ten of clubs* ○ *to play the ten* **3.** GROUP OF TEN a group of ten people or objects [Old English *tēn(e)*, *tīen(e)* < Indo-European] ◇ **hang ten** to ride a surfboard with your toes hanging over the front of the board ◇ **ten to one** with overwhelming odds in favour of a particular thing happening or being true (*informal*) ○ *She said it was an accident, but ten to one she's lying.*

tenable /ténnəb'l/ *adj* **1.** WITH REASONABLE SUPPORTING ARGUMENTS justified in a fair or rational way and able to be defended because there is sufficient evidence or reason **2.** ABLE TO BE OCCUPIED capable of being occupied or held, usually by a particular person or for a particular period of time (*formal*) **3.** MIL CAPABLE OF BEING DEFENDED IN BATTLE able to be held successfully against an enemy attack [Late 16C. < French *tenir* 'to hold'] —**tenability** /ténnə bílləti/ *n* —**tenably** *adv*

tenace /ténn ayss/ *n* a combination of two high cards in the same suit that do not form a sequence, e.g. a jack and a king [Mid-17C. Via French < Spanish *tenaza* 'pincers, tongs']

tenacious /tə náyshəss/ *adj* **1.** DETERMINED OR STUBBORN tending to stick firmly to any decision, plan, or opinion without changing or doubting it **2.** TIGHTLY HELD difficult to loosen, shake off, or pull away from ○ *his tenacious grip* **3.** PERSISTENT persisting for a long time and difficult to change, destroy, or get rid of ○ *a tenacious head cold* **4.** ABLE TO REMEMBER MANY THINGS capable of absorbing and retaining a large store of information and of recalling details accurately **5.** STICKY OR CLINGING sticking or clinging to something else, especially a surface ○ *tenacious burrs* **6.** ENG NOT EASILY DISCONNECTED holding together tightly or fused solidly [Early 17C. < Latin *tenac-* 'holding fast' < *tenere* 'to hold'] —**tenaciously** *adv* —**tenaciousness** *n* —**tenacity** /tə nássəti/ *n*

ten-acre block *n NZ* an area of farmland, usually near a city

tenaculum /tə nákyŏŏləm/ (*plural* **-la** /-lə/ or **-lums**) *n* a long-handled instrument with a slender sharp hook, used especially in surgery to grasp and hold arteries or other body parts [Late 17C. < Latin, 'holder' < *tenere* 'to hold']

tenaille /te náyl/ *n* a low outwork in front of the wall between two bastions in a fortification ditch [Late 16C. Via French < Latin *tenacula* 'pincers, forceps']

tena koe /te naá kway/ *interj NZ* a Maori greeting addressed to one person [Mid-19C. < Maori, 'there you are']

tena koutou /teéna kṓtō/, **tena koutou katoa** /-ka tṓ ə/ *interj NZ* a Maori greeting addressed to more than one person [Mid-19C. < Maori, 'there you all are']

tenancy /ténnənssi/ (*plural* **-cies**) *n* **1.** OCCUPATION OF PROPERTY FOR RENT exclusive possession, for a fixed period, of property or land owned by somebody else, in return for an agreed rent. This is usually under the terms of a lease or a similar legal entitlement or agreement. **2.** TIME OF SOMEBODY'S TENANCY a period of time when a piece of property such as a house or farm is legally occupied and used by somebody paying an agreed rent **3.** PLACE LIVED IN BY TENANT a piece of property that somebody is entitled to use or occupy on condition that an agreed rent is paid to the owner [15C. < TENANT]

tenant /ténnənt/ *n* **1.** RENTER OF PROPERTY somebody who rents a building, house, set of rooms, plot of land, or piece of property for a fixed period of time. This arrangement is usually under the terms of a lease or a similar legal entitlement or agreement. **2.** OCCUPIER OF PLACE somebody living in or on a property ■ *vti* (**-ants, -anting, -anted**) PAY RENT TO OCCUPY PROPERTY to live in or on somebody else's property as a tenant [14C. < Anglo-Norman *tenaunt*, Old French *tenant* < *tenir* 'to hold' < Latin *tenere* 'hold, keep'] —**tenantable** *adj* —**tenanted** *adj* —**tenantless** *adj*

ORIGIN The Latin word *tenere* 'to hold, keep', from which ***tenant*** is derived, is also the source of English *abstain, contain, continent*[1], *continue, countenance, detain, maintain, obtain, retain, sustain, tenacious, tenement, tenet, tennis, tenon, tenor,* and *tenure.*

tenant farmer *n* a farmer who rents a farm, smallholding, or agricultural land, and pays the owner in cash or with produce

tenant-in-chief (*plural* **tenants-in-chief**) *n* in a feudal society, a tenant who holds land granted by the sovereign

tenantry /ténnəntri/ *n* **1.** all tenants or tenant farmers, especially all those renting property from a particular landowner (*formal*) **2.** same as **tenancy** (sense 1) (*dated*)

tenants' association *n* an official representative body formed by tenants to negotiate with their landlord, e.g. to ensure that tenants' rights are protected, and to represent the tenants in disputes or when they want improvements made or changes introduced

tenants' charter *n* in the United Kingdom, the legal rights of tenants in new towns, local authorities, and housing associations. These include the right to buy their houses cheaply and to take in lodgers.

tench /tench/ (*plural same* or **tenches**) *n* a freshwater game fish related to the carp, with a heavy greenish body, small scales, and a barbel on each side of its mouth. Native to: Europe, western Asia. Latin name: *Tinca tinca.* [14C. Via Old French *tenche* < late Latin *tinca*]

Ten Commandments *npl* according to the Bible, the ten laws given by God to Moses. They summarize human obligations to each other and to God.

tend[1] /tend/ (**tends, tending, tended**) *vi* **1.** to be generally inclined or likely to react or behave in a particular way, or be in the habit of doing something **2.** to make a gentle steady movement in a particular direction [14C. Via Old French *tendre* 'move towards' < Latin *tendere* 'stretch, extend']

ORIGIN The Latin word *tendere* 'to stretch, extend', from which ***tend*** is derived, is also the source of English *attend, contend, détente, distend, extend, intend, ostensible, portend, pretend, tendency, tender*[1], *tense*[1], and *tent*[1].

tend[2] /tend/ (**tends, tending, tended**) *vt* **1.** to do or provide the things that a person, animal, or plant needs for health, comfort, and welfare **2.** *US* to manage something, especially something that needs constant supervision ○ *tend bar* [12C. Shortening of ATTEND] —**tendance** *n*

~~**tendancy**~~ incorrect spelling of **tendency**

tendencious *adj* another spelling of **tendentious**

tendency /téndənssi/ (*plural* **-cies**) *n* **1.** a way in which somebody or something typically behaves or happens, or is likely to react, behave, or happen **2.** a gradual, but steady progress, development, or shift of opinion in a particular direction [Early 17C. < medieval Latin *tendentia* < Latin *tendere* 'tend, be inclined to']

tendentious /ten dénshəss/, **tendencious** *adj* written or spoken with personal bias in order to promote a cause or support a viewpoint [Early 20C. < TENDENCY] —**tendentiously** *adv* —**tendentiousness** *n*

tender[1] /téndər/ *adj* **1.** PHYSICALLY PAINFUL hurting or unusually sensitive when touched or pressed **2.** WITH GENTLE FEELING showing care, gentleness, and feeling **3.** KIND AND SYMPATHETIC sensitive and caring towards others and often feeling emotions intensely ○ *a tender disposition* **4.** EMOTIONALLY PAINFUL particularly uncomfortable, hurtful, or upsetting to discuss or think about, and so best avoided **5.** PLEASANTLY SOFT FOR EATING soft enough for the teeth to go through easily without much chewing ○ *a tender juicy steak* **6.** YOUNG AND DEFENCELESS vulnerably young, weak, and inexperienced ○ *at a tender age* **7.** FRAGILE so delicate, soft, or weak as to be hurt, crushed, or broken easily ○ *tender flower petals* **8.** BOT, AGRIC NEEDING PROTECTION FROM HARSH WEATHER easily damaged or killed by unsuitable weather or conditions, especially frost and cold ○ *a tender plant* [13C. Via French *tendre* < Latin *tener* 'delicate, tender'] —**tenderly** *adv* —**tenderness** *n*

CULTURAL NOTE ***Tender is the Night***, a novel (1934) by US writer F. Scott Fitzgerald. Set on the French Riviera in the 1930s, it focuses on a group of glamorous US expatriates. Psychologist Richard Diver's attempts to nurse his wife and former patient, Nicole, and his involvement with a visiting woman actor, lead to his mental collapse. A powerful depiction of human frailty, it is also admired for the elegance of its prose.

tender[2] /téndər/ *v* (**-ders, -dering, -dered**) **1.** *vt* OFFER SOMETHING FORMALLY IN WRITING to present something formal or official, in the form of a document ○ *tender a resignation* **2.** *vi* COMM OFFER TO SUPPLY SOMETHING to

offer to undertake a job or supply goods ○ *tender for a contract* **3.** *vt* LAW **OFFER SUM IN SETTLEMENT** to offer to pay money or goods as a way of settling a debt or claim ■ *n* **1.** COMM **FORMAL OFFER TO UNDERTAKE JOB** a formal offer to undertake a job or supply goods ○ *Their tender was accepted because it was the lowest.* **2.** same as **money** ○ *legal tender* **3.** COMM **ACT OF TENDERING** the act of tendering for a contract **4.** LAW **OFFER MADE TO SETTLE SOMETHING** a formal offer to settle legal proceedings on payment of an amount of damages [Mid-16C. Via Old French *tendre* < Latin *tendere* 'hold out, stretch'] —**tenderable** *adj* —**tenderer** *n*

tender[3] /téndər/ *n* **1. SMALL BOAT FERRYING TO LARGE BOAT** a small boat used to go to and from a larger one such as a yacht **2.** RAIL **VEHICLE CARRYING SUPPLIES FOR STEAM ENGINE** the permanently coupled rear part of a large steam locomotive, used for carrying its coal and water **3.** TRANSP **EMERGENCY VEHICLE** a road vehicle that carries tools, specialized equipment, and personnel to assist in an emergency (*usually used in combination*) [15C. Shortening of *attender* (< ATTEND), or < TEND[2]]

tenderfoot /téndər fòot/ (*plural* **-foots** or **-feet** /-feet/) *n* **1.** somebody just starting to do or try something, with little or no previous experience of it (*informal*) **2.** a new member of a Scout troop or Guide company (*dated*)

tenderhearted /téndər haártid/ *adj* quick to feel or show compassion and sympathy for other people —**tenderheartedly** *adv* —**tenderheartedness** *n*

tenderise, etc. *vt* COOK another spelling of **tenderize, etc.**

tenderize /téndə rīz/ (**-izes, -izing, -ized**), **tenderise** (**-ises, -ising, -ised**) *vt* to make meat tender by beating it, soaking it in a marinade, or sprinkling it with a special substance (**tenderizer**) that breaks down its fibres —**tenderization** /téndə rī záysh'n/ *n*

tenderizer /téndə rīzər/, **tenderiser** *n* **1.** a commercial preparation containing enzymes that break down fibrous tissue in meat **2.** a wooden or metal mallet used to pound meat. It has a short handle and a fairly broad head with a hammering surface covered in shallow bumps.

tenderloin /téndər loyn/ *n* a prime cut of lean tender pork or lamb taken from the curve of the ribs at the backbone

tendinitis /téndə nítiss/, **tendonitis** *n* inflammation of a tendon usually occurring after excessive use, as in a sports injury [Early 20C. < modern Latin *tendin-*, stem of *tendo* 'tendon']

tendon /téndən/ *n* an inelastic cord or band of tough white fibrous connective tissue that attaches a muscle to a bone or other part [Mid-16C. Directly and via French < medieval Latin *tendon-*, stem of *tendo*, translation of Greek *tenōn* 'sinew' < *teinein* 'stretch'] —**tendinous** /-dinəss/ *adj*

tendon hammer *n* MED same as **plexor**

tendonitis *n* MED another spelling of **tendinitis**

tendril /téndrəl/ *n* **1.** a modified stem, leaf, or other part of a climbing plant, usually in the form of a thread, that coils around and attaches the plant to supporting objects **2.** a slim, wispy, curling, or winding piece of something, especially hair (*literary*) [Mid-16C. < Middle French *tendrillon* 'little shoot, little cartilage' < *tendron* 'shoot, cartilage' < Old French *tendre* (see TENDER[1])]

Tendulkar /ten dúlkaar/, **Sachin** (*b.* 1973) Indian cricketer. Considered the greatest test batsman of the 1990s, he was the first player to score 10,000 runs in one-day internationals (2001) and by 2002 had scored 30 Test centuries. Full name **Tendulkar, Sachin Ramesh**

Tenebrae /ténnə bray/ *n* in the Roman Catholic Church, the office of matins and lauds for the last three days of Holy Week (*takes a singular or plural verb*) [Mid-17C. < Latin, 'darkness', because candles are extinguished during the service in memory of the darkness at the Crucifixion]

tenebrionid /tə nébbri ənid/ (*plural* **-nids** or *same*) *n* INSECTS same as **darkling beetle** [Early 20C. < modern Latin]

tenebrious *adj* same as **tenebrous**

tenebrism /ténnəbrizəm/, **Tenebrism** *n* a style of painting, popular in 17th-century Naples and Spain and largely associated with Caravaggio, that uses large areas of shadow and dark colours, sometimes with a shaft of light [Mid-20C. < Italian *tenebroso* 'dark'] —**tenebrist** *n*

tenebrous /ténnəbrəss/, **tenebrious** /tə nébbri əss/ *adj* dark, murky, or obscured by shadows (*literary*) [15C. < Old French *tenebrus* < Latin *tenebrae* 'darkness'] —**tenebrosity** /ténnə bróssəti/ *n* —**tenebrousness** *n*

tenement /ténnəmənt/ *n* **1. LARGE MULTIPLE-OCCUPANCY RESIDENTIAL BUILDING** a large residential building in a town, usually of three or more storeys, divided into flats for separate householders, or the section of such a building served by one stair. The dwellings may be owner-occupied or rented. This type of building is characteristic of Scottish urban architecture from an early period, because Scots law allowed for multiple ownership. **2.** *UK, regional* **RENTED ACCOMMODATION IN MULTISTOREY BUILDING** in England and Wales, a room or flat in a multistorey residential building, especially one used by a tenant (*dated*) **3. ITEM OF PROPERTY** a piece of property, e.g. land or houses, held by somebody [14C. Via Old French, 'tenure' < medieval Latin *tenementum* < Latin *tenere* 'to hold']

~~**tenent**~~ incorrect spelling of **tenant**

Tenerife /ténnə réef, ténnə réefay/, **Teneriffe** largest of the Canary Islands, in Santa Cruz de Tenerife Province, Spain. Population: 701,034 (2001). Area: 2,034 sq. km/785 sq. mi.

tenesmus /tə nézməss/ *n* an urgent, painful, and unsuccessful attempt to defecate or urinate [Early 16C. Via medieval Latin < Greek *tēnesmos* < *teinein* 'stretch, strain']

~~**Tenessee**~~ incorrect spelling of **Tennessee**

tenet /ténnit/ *n* an established fundamental belief, especially one relating to religion or politics ○ *a basic tenet of Christianity* [Late 16C. < Latin, 'he or she holds', form of *tenere* 'to hold']

tenfold /tén fōld/ *adj* **1. TIMES TEN** multiplied by ten **2. WITH TEN PARTS** made up of ten parts ■ *adv* **TEN TIMES OVER** to ten times the amount or number, or multiplied by or up to that amount or number

ten-four, 10-4 *interj N Am* used to express affirmation or confirmation [< US police code 'message received']

ten-gallon hat *n* a cowboy hat with a high round uncreased crown and a wide brim

tenge /téngay/ (*plural same*) *n* the main unit of Kazakh currency. See table at **currency** [Late 20C. < Kazakh]

Tennant /ténnənt/, **Kylie** (1912–88) Australian writer. She wrote *The Battlers* (1941), a novel about itinerant workers set during the Depression.

Tennant Creek town in north-central Australia, in the interior of the Northern Territory. Population: 3,003 (2002 estimate).

tenner /ténnər/ *n* (*informal*) **1.** a banknote worth ten pounds sterling, or ten pounds in cash or as a sum **2.** *ANZ* a banknote worth ten Australian or New Zealand dollars, or ten dollars in cash or as a sum

~~**Tennesee**~~ incorrect spelling of **Tennessee**

Tennessee /ténnə sée/ **1.** state in the eastern-central United States, bordered by Kentucky, Virginia, North Carolina, Georgia, Alabama, Mississippi, Arkansas, and Missouri. Capital: Nashville. Population: 5,797,289 (2002 estimate). Area: 109,158 sq. km/42,146 sq. mi. **2.** river of the southeastern United States, formed by the confluence of the Holston and French Broad rivers and flowing into the Ohio River. Length: 1,050 km/652 mi. —**Tennessean** *n, adj*

Tennessee Walking Horse, **Tennessee Walker** *n* a saddle horse with a characteristic fast easy gait, belonging to a breed developed in Tennessee from Standardbred and Morgan stock

Tenniel /ténni əl/, **Sir John** (1820–1914) British illustrator. He contributed more than 2,300 cartoons to *Punch* from 1850 to 1901. His illustrations for *Alice's Adventures in Wonderland* (1865) and *Through the Looking-Glass* (1872) fixed the images of Lewis Carroll's characters for generations of children.

tennis /ténniss/ *n* a game played on a rectangular court by two players or two pairs of players, who use rackets to hit a ball back and forth over a net stretched across a marked-out court [14C. Probably < Old French *tenez* 'hold!', form of *tenir* 'to hold, receive']

tennis ball *n* a white or yellow fuzzy cloth-covered hollow rubber ball about 7.5 cm/3 in in diameter, used in tennis. In lawn tennis the ball is pressurized.

tennis elbow *n* a painful inflammation of the tendon in the outer elbow region caused by excessive and repetitive strain from overuse, e.g. as a result of playing tennis or similar sports. It may be treated with rest, massage, or steroid drugs.

tennis shoe *n* a rubber-soled white canvas shoe with long laces, worn for playing tennis

tennis skirt *n* a short skirt, traditionally white, worn by some women tennis players

Tennyson /ténniss'n/, **Alfred, 1st Baron Tennyson of Freshwater and Aldworth** (1809–92) British poet. His many works include *The Lady of Shalott* (1832), *In Memoriam* (1850), and *The Charge of the Light Brigade* (1854). He was poet laureate (1850–92). Known as **Alfred, Lord Tennyson**. See Cultural note at **brigade** —**Tennysonian** /ténni sṓni ən/ *n, adj*

> 'For words, like Nature, half reveal / And half conceal the Soul within.'
> [Alfred Tennyson, *In Memoriam*; 1850]

> '"Forward the Light Brigade!" / Was there a man dismay'd? / Not tho' the soldier knew / Some one had blunder'd: / Their's not to make reply, / Their's not to reason why, / Their's but to do and die: / Into the valley of Death / Rode the six hundred.'
> [Alfred Tennyson, *The Charge of the Light Brigade, Maud and Other Poems*; 1855]

Tenochtitlán /te nóch tee tlaán/ ancient capital of the Aztecs, in Lake Texcoco, now modern Mexico City. It was founded in 1325 and destroyed by the Spanish in 1521.

tenon /ténnən/ *n* **PROJECTION ON WOOD FOR MAKING JOINT** a projection on one piece of wood that fits into a matching recess (a mortise) on another piece so as to make a joint ■ *vt* (**-ons, -oning, -oned**) **1. MAKE TENON ON WOOD** to make a tenon on a piece of wood **2. JOIN PIECES OF WOOD USING TENON** to join two pieces of wood using a tenon [Early 17C. < Old French, < *tenir* 'to hold'] —**tenoner** *n*

tenon saw *n* a small thin saw with a strong back, used especially for cutting tenons

tenor /ténnər/ *n* **1. HIGH MALE VOICE** the highest natural male singing voice, or a man whose voice is in this register **2. UPPER RANGE INSTRUMENT** an instrument with a range similar to a tenor voice (*often used before a noun*) ○ *a tenor saxophone* **3. WAY SOMETHING IS PROGRESSING** the direction in which something is steadily moving (*formal*) **4. GENERAL NATURE OF SOMETHING** the overall nature, pattern, or meaning of something, especially a written or spoken statement (*formal*) ○ *The general tenor of the reply was positive.* **5.** LAW **EXACT WORDS OF DEED** the exact wording of a document **6.** LAW **EXACT COPY** an exact copy or transcript of a document **7.** FIN **TIME FOR BILL TO BE PAID** the period of time over which cash flows are exchanged with a swap contract [13C. Via Anglo-Norman, Old French < Latin, 'continuous course' < *tenere* 'to hold']

tenor clef *n* a C clef in which middle C is represented by the second highest line on the staff, used in music for the cello, bassoon, and tenor trombone. It was formerly used to notate the tenor voice.

tenor drum *n* a medium-size drum without snares

tenorite /ténnə rīt/ *n* a black copper oxide mineral [Mid-19C. After Michele *Tenore* (1781–1861), president of the Naples Academy of Sciences]

tenosynovitis /ténnō sīnə vítiss/ *n* inflammation of a tendon sheath, usually in the wrist, with swelling and audible creaking on movement. It often results from repetitive movements as in typing or some sports. [Late 19C. < modern Latin < Greek *tenōn* 'tendon']

tenotomy /tə nóttəmi/ (*plural* **-mies**) *n* the surgical cutting of a tendon

tenpin /tén pin/ *n* any of the ten skittles used in tenpin bowling

tenpin bowling *n UK, ANZ, Can* an indoor game in which players try to knock down ten skittles at the far end of a special bowling alley by rolling a heavy ball at them. US term **bowling**

tenpounder /ténn pówndər/ *n US* FISH same as **ladyfish** (sense 1)

tenrec /tén rek/ (*plural* **-recs** or same), **tanrec** /tán-/ *n* a small to medium-sized insect-eating mammal with a long pointed snout. Native to: Madagascar, Comoros. Family: Tenrecidae. [Late 18C. Via French *tanrec* < Malagasy *tàndraka, tràndraka*]

TENS /tens/ *n* a method of treating chronic pain by applying electrodes to the skin and passing small electric currents through sensory nerves and the spinal cord, thus suppressing the transmission of pain signals. Full form **transcutaneous electrical nerve stimulation**

tense[1] /tenss/ *adj* (**tenser, tensest**) **1.** WORRIED AND NERVOUS affected by anxious feelings or mental strain, so that it is impossible to behave in a natural relaxed way **2.** RESTRAINED AND UNNATURAL causing feelings of anxiety, nervousness, and uncertainty, so that natural relaxed talk or behaviour is impossible ○ *a tense wait* **3.** TIGHT AND STIFF stretched or held tight and stiff ○ *tense muscles* **4.** PHON PRONOUNCED WITH TAUT MUSCLES describes a speech sound that is pronounced with muscular effort, is relatively long in duration, and is accurate in articulation ■ *vti* (**tenses, tensing, tensed**) BECOME OR MAKE TENSE to become tense, or make something such as a muscle or part of the body become tense [Late 17C. < Latin *tensus* 'stretched', past participle of *tendere* 'stretch'] —**tensely** *adv* —**tenseness** *n*

tense up *vti* same as **tense**[1] *v*

tense[2] /tenss/ *n* one of the sets of forms of a verb that express the different times at which action takes place relative to the speaker or writer, e.g. the present, past, or future ○ *in the future tense* [14C. Via Old French *tens* 'time' < Latin *tempus*] —**tenseless** *adj*

USAGE Strictly speaking, the English language has only two *tenses*, the present (*go, eat, die*) and the past (*went, ate, died*). All other expressions of time are formed by combining auxiliary verbs with the present participle, past participle, or infinitive, as in the progressive or continuous aspect (*I was going*), the perfect or perfective aspect (*They have eaten*), and the future (*He will die*). They are, however, commonly referred to as tenses.

tensile /tén sīl/ *adj* **1.** relating to or involving tension **2.** capable of being stretched or pulled out of shape [Early 17C. < medieval Latin *tensilis* < Latin *tendere* 'stretch'] —**tensilely** *adv* —**tensileness** *n* —**tensility** /ten sílləti/ *n*

tensile strength *n* the maximum stretching force that a material such as wire can withstand before breaking

tensimeter /ten símmitər/ *n* an instrument used to measure differences in vapour pressure [Early 20C. < TENSION]

tensiometer /ténssi ómmitər/ *n* **1.** INSTRUMENT FOR MEASURING TENSILE STRENGTH an instrument used to measure tensile strength **2.** INSTRUMENT FOR MEASURING SURFACE TENSION an instrument used to measure the surface tension of liquids **3.** GEOL INSTRUMENT FOR MEASURING SOIL MOISTURE an instrument used to measure the moisture content of soils [Early 20C. < TENSION]

tension /ténsh'n/ *n* **1.** ANXIOUS FEELINGS mental worry or emotional strain that makes natural relaxed behaviour impossible **2.** UNEASY FEELING IN RELATIONSHIP a state of wariness, mistrust, controlled hostility, or fear of hostility felt by countries, groups, or people in their dealings with one another (*often used in the plural*) **3.** TAUTNESS the degree to which something such as a wire, string, thread, or muscle is stretched **4.** LITERAT BUILDUP OF SUSPENSE the buildup of suspense in a fictional work, leading to the denouement **5.** LITERAT SENSE OF CONFLICT the way that opposing characters clash or interact in an interesting way with each other in a literary work **6.** HANDICRAFT DEVICE CONTROLLING TIGHTNESS OF THREAD a device on a sewing machine or a loom that regulates how tight the thread is **7.** PHYS PULLING FORCE a force that pulls or stretches something **8.** PHYS STRESS FROM TENSION the stress resulting from a force of tension, or a measure of it **9.** ELEC VOLTAGE voltage or electromotive force (*often used in combination*) ○ *high-tension wires* [Mid-16C. Directly or via French < Latin *tension-* 'stretching' < *tendere* 'stretch'] —**tensional** *adj*

tensity /ténssəti/ *n* the state or quality of being tense

tensive /ténssiv/ *adj* relating to or causing tension [Early 18C. < French *tensif* < Latin *tendere* 'stretch']

tensometer /ten sómmitər/ *n* PHYS same as **tensiometer** (senses 1–2)

tensor /ténssər, -sawr/ *n* **1.** a muscle that tenses or stretches a part of the body **2.** a generalization of a vector that is a mathematical entity specified with respect to a given coordinate system and able to undergo transformation to other coordinate systems [Early 18C. < modern Latin < Latin *tendere* 'stretch'] —**tensorial** /ten sáwri əl/ *adj*

ten-strike *n* BOWLING same as **strike** *n* (sense 7)

tent[1] /tent/ *n* **1.** COLLAPSIBLE SHELTER a collapsible movable shelter consisting of a tough fabric or plastic cover held up by poles and kept in place by ropes and pegs **2.** OBJECT LIKE TENT something that looks like a tent, is constructed in a similar way, or serves a similar purpose ○ *an oxygen tent* ■ *v* (**tents, tenting, tented**) **1.** *vt* COVER SOMETHING AS TENT DOES to form a raised nonrigid cover over something ○ *Tent the roast with aluminium foil.* **2.** *vi* CAMP to live or camp in a tent **3.** *vt* SUPPLY TENT FOR SOMEBODY to accommodate a person or group of people in tents, or provide somebody or something with tents [13C. Via Old French *tente* < Latin *tenta* 'tent' < *tendere* 'stretch']

tent[2] /tent/ *n* a cone-shaped expandable plug of soft material such as gauze used to keep a wound or orifice open ■ *vt* (**tents, tenting, tented**) to open or expand a wound or orifice with a tent [14C. < French *tente* < *tenter* < Latin *temptare* 'feel, try']

tentacle /téntək'l/ *n* **1.** LONG FLEXIBLE ORGAN a long flexible organ around the mouth or on the head of some animals, especially invertebrates such as squid, used in holding, grasping, feeling, or moving **2.** HAIR ON PLANT LEAF a sticky glandular hairy projection from the leaf of an insect-eating plant such as the sundew, whose secretions trap and digest prey **3.** SOMETHING FAR-REACHING something that gradually insinuates its influence or control (*literary; usually used in the plural*) [Mid-18C. < modern Latin *tentaculum* < Latin *temptare* 'feel, try'] —**tentacled** *adj* —**tentacular** /ten tákyoōlər/ *adj*

tentage /tént ij/ *n* tents in general or considered as a group

tentative /téntətiv/ *adj* **1.** said or done in a slow, hesitant, and careful way that reveals a lack of confidence **2.** likely to have changes before becoming final and complete ○ *a tentative draft of the document* [Late 16C. < medieval Latin *tentativus* < Latin *tentare*, variant of *temptare* 'feel, try'] —**tentatively** *adv* —**tentativeness** *n*

tent caterpillar *n* a destructive caterpillar that builds large tent-shaped communal webs in the branches of trees. Genus: *Malacosoma*.

tent dress *n* a wide full dress that hangs loose from the shoulders

tented /téntid/ *adj* **1.** WITH TENT SHAPE constructed or shaped like a tent **2.** CAMPED IN TENTS staying in tents, or supplied with tents as shelter **3.** WITH TENTS covered in tents (*literary*)

tenter /téntər/ *n* a frame on which cloth is held taut during various phases of its manufacture, especially while it dries ■ *vt* (**-ters, -tering, -tered**) to stretch cloth on a tenter [13C. < medieval Latin *tentorium* < Latin *tendere* 'stretch']

tenterhook /téntər hoŏk/ *n* one of the hooks used to hold cloth taut on a frame during manufacture, especially while it dries ◇ **be on tenterhooks** to be anxious or in great suspense

tenth /tenth/ *n* **1.** ONE OF TEN PARTS OF SOMETHING one of ten equal parts of something **2.** ORDINAL NUMBER CORRESPONDING TO 10 the ordinal number assigned to item number 10 in a series **3.** MUSIC MUSICAL INTERVAL a musical interval equal to an octave plus a third [Old English *teogoþa, tēopa* < Germanic; later < TEN] —**tenth** *adj, adv*

tent stitch *n* a short parallel diagonal stitch used to fill in an area in needlepoint or embroidery

tenuis /ténnyoo iss/ (*plural* **-ues** /-yoo eez/) *n* a voiceless stop consonant in classical Greek grammar [Mid-17C. < Latin, 'thin, fine', translation of Greek *psilon* 'bare, smooth']

tenuous /ténnyoo əss/ *adj* **1.** WEAK AND UNCONVINCING not based on anything significant or substantial, and therefore unlikely to stand up to rigorous examination ○ *That's an extremely tenuous argument.* **2.** EXTREMELY DELICATE AND FINE thin and fine, and therefore easily broken (*literary*) **3.** SCI DILUTED thin or diluted in consistency [Late 16C. < Latin *tenuis* 'thin, fine'] —**tenuity** /te nyoō əti/ *n* —**tenuously** *adv* —**tenuousness** *n*

tenure /ténnyər, ténnyoor/ *n* **1.** APPOINTMENT OR PERIOD OF APPOINTMENT the occupation of an official position, or the length of time that an official position is occupied (*formal*) ○ *during her tenure of the presidency* **2.** PROPERTY RIGHTS the rights of a tenant to hold property, or the holding of property as a tenant **3.** *N Am* PERMANENT STATUS the position of having a formal secure appointment until retirement, especially at an institution of higher learning after working there on a temporary or provisional basis [15C. < Old French, 'tenure, estate' < Latin *tenere* 'to hold'] —**tenured** *adj*

tenure-track *adj N Am* guaranteed consideration for tenure in the US and Canadian system of academic employment ○ *offered a tenure-track position at the university*

tenuto /te nyoōtō/ *adv, adj* indicating that a musical note should be held for its full value (*used as a musical direction*) [Mid-18C. < Italian, past participle of *tenere* 'to hold' < Latin]

Tenzing Norgay /ténssing náwrgay/, **Tenzing Norkay** /-náwrkay/ (1914?–86) Nepalese mountaineer. He and Sir Edmund Hillary were the first to reach the summit of Mount Everest (1953).

Tenzin Gyatso /ténssin gyátsō/ (b. 1935) 14th Dalai Lama (1940–). After a Tibetan rebellion against Chinese rule, he fled into exile (1959). He led the nonviolent opposition to continued Chinese rule in Tibet, for which he received the Nobel Peace Prize (1989).

teocalli /tee ō kálli/ (*plural* **-lis**) *n* a temple in ancient Mexico or Central America, or the pyramidal mound on which one was built [Early 17C. Via American Spanish < Nahuatl *teokalli* 'deity's house']

teosinte /táy ō sínti/ *n* a tall annual grass grown for forage, related to, and perhaps the ancestor of, maize. Native to: Mexico, Central America. Latin name: *Zea mexicana*. [Late 19C. Via French *téosinté* < Nahuatl *teocintli*]

Teotihuacán /tay ōtiwə kaán/ ancient city in central Mexico, northeast of Mexico City, now an archaeological site that contains the remains of the earliest city in the western hemisphere (c. 300 BC – AD c. 700)

tepa /téepə/ *n* a soluble crystalline compound. Use: insect sterilization, cancer treatment, textile fireproofing. Formula: $C_6H_{12}N_3OP$. [Mid-20C. Acronym < TRI- + ETHYLENE + PHOSPH- + AMIDE]

tepal /téep'l/ *n* any of the parts that form the outer whorl (**perianth**) of flowers such as the tulip, in which there is no differentiation into petals and sepals [Mid-19C. < French, blend of *sépale* 'sepal' + *pétale* 'petal']

Te Papa Tongarewa /te púppə tóngə ray wə/ *n* a museum in Wellington that contains the New Zealand national collections. It was created in 1998 by combining the collections of the National Museum and National Art Gallery. [Late 20C. < Maori, 'place for us all']

tepary bean /téppəri-/ *n* an annual twining bean grown for its round edible seeds. Native to: southwestern United States, Mexico. Latin name: *Phaseolus acutifolius latifolius*. [Early 20C. Origin ?]

tepee /tee pee/, **teepee, tipi** (*plural* **-pis**) *n* a conical tent built around several long branches or wooden poles that meet and cross at the top. A tepee is traditionally made of animal hide and used as a dwelling by Plains Indians and some other Native North American peoples. See illustration on next page [Mid-18C. < Dakota *típi* 'dwelling' < *tí* 'dwell']

tephra /téffrə/ *n* solid material ejected explosively

tepee

from a volcano, e.g. ash, dust, and boulders [Mid-20C. < Greek, 'ashes']

tepid /téppid/ *adj* **1.** slightly warm ○ *tepid water* **2.** showing little enthusiasm or warmth ○ *tepid applause* [14C. < Latin *tepidus* < *tepere* 'be warm'] —**tepidity** /te píddəti/ *n* —**tepidly** *adv* —**tepidness** *n*

TEPP /tep/ *n* a crystalline compound (**organophosphate**). Use: insecticide, stimulant for nervous system. Formula: $C_8H_{20}O_7P_2$. Full form **tetraethyl pyrophosphate**

Te Puea Herangi /te poó i ə hérrungi/ (1884–1952) New Zealand Maori leader. She was prominent in the revival of Maori culture and the provision of social welfare for Maori.

tequila /ti keélə, te-/ *n* a strong Mexican spirit made by redistilling the fermented juice of the agave plant (**mescal**). It is drunk neat or used as a base for cocktails. [Mid-19C. < Mexican Spanish, after *Tequila*, town in central Mexico]

tequila sunrise *n* a cocktail consisting of tequila combined with orange juice and grenadine

TER *n* in South Australia and Western Australia, a measure on a scale of 0 to 99.95 of a student's performance in the HSC examinations, used to assess eligibility for tertiary courses. Full form **tertiary entrance rank**

ter. *abbr* **1.** GEOG, BUILDINGS terrace **2.** ARMY, ZOOL territorial **3.** GEOG, ZOOL, POL territory

Ter. *abbr* Terrace (*used in addresses*)

ter- *prefix* three, threefold ○ *terpolymer* [< Latin *ter* 'three times' < Indo-European, 'three']

tera- *prefix* **1.** one million million (10^{12}). Symbol **T 2.** in the binary system, a trillion (2^{40}) ○ *terabyte* [< Greek *teras* 'monster']

terabyte /térrə bīt/ *n* **1.** a unit of computer data or storage space equivalent to 1,024 gigabytes **2.** COMPUT one million million bytes

teraflop /térrə flop/ *n* one million million floating-point operations per second, a measure of computer speed [Late 20C. < TERA- + acronym < *floating-point operations per second*]

terahertz /térrə hurts/ (*plural* same) *n* a unit of frequency equal to one million million hertz

terai /tə rí/ *n* a wide-brimmed felt hat with a double crown, once widely worn in the subtropics [Late 19C. After TERAI]

Terai /tə rí/ area of marshy land in the foothills of the Himalaya range in northern India and southern Nepal

terai hat *n* CLOTHING same as **terai**

terakihi *n* FISH another spelling of **tarakihi**

teraph /térrəf/ (*plural* **-aphim** /-əfim/) *n* an image or idol worshipped by ancient Semitic peoples [14C. Originally plural, via late Latin and Greek < Hebrew *tĕrāpīm*]

terato- *prefix* **1.** malformed ○ *teratogen* **2.** tumour ○ *teratoma* [< Greek *terat-*, stem of *teras* 'monster']

teratocarcinoma /térrətō kaarssi nōmə/ (*plural* **-mas** or **-mata** /-mətə/) *n* a malignant teratoma, most often occurring in the testes

teratogen /tə ráttəjən/ *n* an agent that interrupts or alters the normal development of a foetus, with results that are evident at birth, e.g. a chemical, virus, or ionizing radiation —**teratogenesis** /térrətō jénnəssiss/ *n* —**teratogenic** /térrətō jénnik/ *adj*

teratoid /térrə toyd/ *adj* affected by a visible condition caused by the interruption or alteration of normal development

teratology /térrə tólləji/ *n* the scientific study of visible conditions caused by the interruption or alteration of normal development —**teratologic** /térrətə lójjik/ *adj* —**teratologist** *n*

teratoma /térrə tōmə/ (*plural* **-mata** /-mətə/ or **-mas**) *n* a tumour composed of various tissues such as bone, hair, and teeth not normally found together at the site of origin and probably derived from embryonic remnants. They most often occur in the ovary, where they are benign, and in the testis, where they are malignant. —**teratomatous** *adj*

Te Rauparaha /te rówprə haa/ (1768?–1849) New Zealand Maori leader. He led a conquest of much of the southwest of the North Island and the north of the South Island, New Zealand, a territory his people held until the arrival of Europeans.

terbium /túrbi əm/ *n* a silvery-grey metallic element of the rare-earth group. Source: monazite, bastnaesite. Use: lasers, X-rays, television tubes. Symbol **Tb**. See table at **element** [Mid-19C. After *Ytterby*, village in Sweden] —**terbic** *adj*

terce /turss/ *n* in the Roman Catholic Church, the third of the seven separate hours (**canonical hours**) that are set aside for prayer each day [14C. < Old French, variant of *tierce* (see TIERCE)]

Terceira /tər sáyrə, -síirə/ second largest island in the Azores archipelago, in the North Atlantic Ocean. Population: 59,248 (1991). Area: 397 sq. km/153 sq. mi.

tercel /túrss'l/ (*plural* **-cels** or same), **tiercel** /teèrss'l/ *n* a male falcon or hawk used in falconry [14C. < Old French *terçuel* < Latin *tertius* 'third']

tercentenary /túr sen teénəri, -ténnəri/ *n* (*plural* **-ries**) a year, or an exact day, 300 years after an event, usually one of special historic significance ■ *adj* coinciding with the 300th anniversary of an event, and often celebrating or commemorating this [Mid-19C. < Latin *ter* 'three times']

tercet /túrssit, tur sét/ *n* a group of three lines of verse that rhyme with each other or with another group of three [Late 16C. Via French < Italian *terzetto* < Latin *tertius* 'third']

terebinth /térr əbinth/ (*plural* **-binths** or same) *n* a tree of the cashew family that yields turpentine. Native to: Mediterranean. Latin name: *Pistacia terebinthus*. [14C. Directly or via French < Latin *terebinthus* < Greek *terebinthos*]

terebinthine /térrə bín thīn/ *adj* **1.** relating to the terebinth tree **2.** resembling or consisting of turpentine [Early 16C. < Latin *terebinthinus* < *terebinthus* (see TEREBINTH)]

teredo /te reédō/ (*plural* **-dos** or same) *n* MARINE BIOL same as **shipworm** [14C. Via Latin < Greek *terēdōn* < *teirein* 'rub hard, wear away, bore']

Terence /térrənss/ (185–159 BC) Roman playwright. His six surviving comedies, based on Greek originals, are forerunners of the modern comedy of manners. Full name **Publius Terentius Afer**

> 'The quarrels of lovers are the renewal of love.'
> [Terence, *Heauton Timoroumenos*; 2nd century BC]

Teresa (of Ávila) /tə reézə əv ávvilə/, **St** (1515–82) Spanish nun. Famous for the mystical visions she experienced, she was also the founder of the order of the Discalced Carmelites (1562). Born **Cepeda y Ahumada, Teresa de**

> 'Untilled soil, however fertile it may be, will bear thistles and thorns; and so it is with man's mind.'
> [Teresa (of Ávila), 'Maxims for Her Nuns'; 1566?]

Mother Teresa

Express Newspapers

Teresa (of Calcutta) /tə reézə-, -ráyzə-/, **Mother** (1910–97) Albanian-born nun. After 1948 she devoted her life to helping the poor and the sick of Kolkata (formerly Calcutta). She founded the Missionaries of Charity (1950) and opened a shelter for dying people (1952). She won the Nobel Peace Prize (1979). Born **Bojaxhiu, Agnes Gonxha**

> 'The poor are our brothers and sisters...people in the world who need love, who need care, who have to be wanted.'
> [Mother Teresa (of Calcutta), 'Saints Among Us', *Time*; 29 December 1975]

> 'The biggest disease today is not leprosy or tuberculosis, but rather the feeling of being unwanted, uncared for and deserted by everybody.'
> [Mother Teresa (of Calcutta), *Observer*; 3 October 1971]

Tereshkova /térrish kővə/, **Valentina** (*b.* 1937) Soviet cosmonaut. She was the first woman to fly in space (16–19 June 1963).

~~terestrial~~ incorrect spelling of **terrestrial**

terete /té reet/ *adj* describes a plant part that is smooth, cylindrical, and tapering, e.g. a grass stem [Early 17C. < Latin *teret-* 'rounded']

terga ZOOL plural of **tergum**

tergiversate /túrjivər sayt/ (**-sates, -sating, -sated**) *vi* (*formal*) **1.** to make deliberately unclear, ambiguous, or contradictory statements **2.** to change sides or loyalties [Mid-17C. < Latin *tergiversat-*, past participle of *tergiversare* 'turn your back' < *tergum* 'back' + *vertere* 'turn'] —**tergiversant** /-vurs'nt/ *n* —**tergiversator** *n* —**tergiversatory** /túrji vúrssətəri/ *adj*

tergum /túrgəm/ (*plural* **-ga** /-gə/) *n* a thick plate covering the dorsal surface of a body segment of an arthropod, or the movable segments of a barnacle's shell [Early 19C. < Latin, 'back'] —**tergal** *adj*

teriyaki /térri yáki/ *n* a Japanese dish consisting of grilled shellfish or meat brushed with a marinade of soy sauce, sugar, and rice wine [Mid-20C. < Japanese, 'glaze grill']

term /turm/ *n* **1.** NAME OR WORD FOR SOMETHING a word or combination of words, especially one used to mean something very specific or one used in a specialized area of knowledge or work ○ *The correct legal term is 'easement'.* **2.** PERIOD OF TIME SOMETHING LASTS the length of time that something lasts, with a fixed beginning and end, often a period during which a person holds an appointment or office or serves time in prison (*formal*) ○ *during her term of office* **3.** EDUC DIVISION OF ACADEMIC YEAR one of the sections of the academic year during which students attend a school, college, or university and receive regular tuition **4.** LAW, POL PERIOD OF TIME BODY CONTINUES MEETING a length of time over which a political or legal body such as a parliament or court of law regularly assembles and carries out its formal duties **5.** DEADLINE FOR PAYMENT a specific time, especially for making a payment **6.** MED EXPECTED TIME FOR BIRTH OF CHILD the time at the end of a woman's pregnancy when the baby is expected to be born ○ *a pregnancy that came to term* **7.** LOGIC SUBJECT OR PREDICATE OF PROPOSITION in traditional Aristotelian logic, the subject or the predicate of a categorical proposition **8.** LOGIC NAME OR INDIVIDUAL VARIABLE in modern logic, a name or individual variable **9.** MATHS MATHEMATICAL EXPRESSION a mathematical

expression that forms part of a fraction or proportion, is part of a series, or is associated with another by a plus or minus sign **10.** SCULPTURE **SCULPTURED PILLAR** a sculptured pillar, especially one with a bust without arms or an animal portrait on top of a square post **11.** LAW **ESTATE OF LIMITED DURATION** an estate limited to a prescribed period ■ **terms** *npl* **1.** WAY PEOPLE GET ON TOGETHER the treatment given by one person, nation, or power to another, or the opinions or attitudes they have or express towards each other ○ *on good terms with the neighbours* **2.** PARTS THAT MAKE UP AGREEMENT the requirements laid down formally in an agreement or contract, or proposed by one side when negotiating an agreement ○ *the terms of the lease* **3.** LANGUAGE the words that somebody uses, or specifically chooses to use, when speaking or writing ○ *defended his position in robust terms* ■ *vt* (**terms, terming, termed**) USE PARTICULAR WORD FOR SOMETHING to describe or refer to something using a particular name or expression ○ *His followers were termed 'Roundheads'.* [13C. Via French *terme* 'limit of time or space' < Latin *terminus* 'end, boundary, limit'] ◇ **come to terms (with something)** to reach a state of acceptance or of agreement about something ◇ **in no uncertain terms** very forcefully, unambiguously, and bluntly ○ *I told him in no uncertain terms what I thought of his suggestion.* ◇ **in terms of something** in relation to something ◇ **not be on speaking terms (with somebody)** to have had a quarrel or disagreement with somebody, so that neither one will speak to the other

CULTURAL NOTE *For the Term of His Natural Life*, a novel (1874) by Australian writer Marcus Clarke. An epic work set in early 19th-century England and Australia, it tells the story of a young man transported to Australia. He endures the horrors of various penal settlements before drowning during an escape attempt.

term. *abbr* TRANSP, COMPUT terminal

termagant /túrmagant/ *n* an offensive term that deliberately insults a woman's temperament, suggesting a propensity for arguing, criticizing, and quarrelling [13C. Via Old French *Tervagant*, overbearing non-Christian deity in medieval mystery plays < Italian *Trivigante*] —**termagancy** *n*

term assurance *n* life assurance that pays a sum of money only if the person who is covered dies within a specific period of time

-termer *suffix* somebody who serves a term as a political appointee or in prison ○ *a second-termer*

terminable /túrminab'l/ *adj* able to be terminated (*formal*) ○ *The contract is terminable at any time.* [15C. < obsolete *termine* 'terminate', via French < Latin *terminare* (see TERMINATE)] —**terminability** /túrmina bíllati/ *n* —**terminably** *adv*

terminal /túrminal/ *adj* **1.** CAUSING DEATH inevitably, but often gradually, leading to the death of the patient affected ○ *a terminal illness* **2.** DYING affected by a fatal illness or condition that is approaching its final stages ○ *a terminal cancer patient* **3.** RELATING TO DYING PATIENTS for or concerned with patients with terminal conditions ○ *terminal care* **4.** EXTREME extremely intense or overwhelming (*informal humorous*) ○ *terminal boredom* **5.** AT VERY END forming or found at the extreme point or limit of something, or relating to the very end of something **6.** BOT AT END OF STEM positioned at the tip or end of a stem, stalk, or branch **7.** EDUC RELATING TO ACADEMIC TERM taking place during or after an academic term, or every term (*formal*) ■ *n* **1.** TRANSP STATION AT END OF TRANSPORT ROUTE a building or complex containing facilities needed by transport operators and passengers at either end of a travel or shipping route by air, rail, road, or sea **2.** TRANSP same as **terminus** (sense 1) **3.** INDUST ONSHORE INDUSTRIAL SITE FOR OFFSHORE PRODUCTS an industrial installation where raw material is brought onshore and often also processed, e.g. for the offshore gas or oil industry **4.** COMPUT DEVICE LINKED TO COMPUTER a remote input or output device linked to a computer, or a combination of such devices, e.g. a keyboard and video display **5.** ELEC ELECTRICAL CONDUCTOR a conductor attached at the point where electricity enters or leaves a circuit, e.g. on a battery ○ *a battery terminal* **6.** ARCHIT ORNAMENTAL CARVING an ornamental carving or figure at the end of a larger structure [15C. < Latin *terminalis* < *terminus* 'end, boundary, limit']

SYNONYMS See *deadly*.

terminally /túrminali/ *adv* **1.** INEVITABLY LEADING TO DEATH in a way that leads inevitably but often gradually to the death of the patient affected ○ *terminally ill* **2.** EXTREMELY in an extremely intense or overwhelming way (*informal humorous*) ○ *terminally boring* **3.** AT THE END at the tip or end section

terminal moraine *n* a ridge of rock, gravel, and soil across a valley at the end of a glacier or ice field

terminal platform *n* an offshore platform from which gas or petroleum is piped ashore

terminal server *n* a hardware device that links a large number of terminals such as personal computers, printers, and modems to a local or wide area network through a single network connection

terminal tackle *n* the hook or lure attached to the end of a fishing line

terminal velocity *n* the constant speed that a falling object reaches when the downward gravitational force equals the frictional resistance of the medium through which it is falling, usually air

terminate /túrmi nayt/ (**-nates, -nating, -nated**) *v* **1.** *vti* to come to an end, or bring something to an end ○ *terminate a broadcast* **2.** *vt* to murder or assassinate somebody (*slang*) [Late 16C. < Latin *terminat-*, past participle of *terminare* < *terminus* 'end, boundary, limit'] —**terminative** /-nativ/ *adj* —**terminatory** *adj*

terminating decimal /túrmi nayting-/ *n* a decimal fraction with a finite number of digits

termination /túrmi náysh'n/ *n* **1.** ENDING OF SOMETHING the process of bringing something to an end or of being brought to an end, or an instance of this (*formal*) **2.** TIP OR EDGE something that forms the end or final limit of something (*formal*) **3.** FINAL OUTCOME something that happens or is produced as a result of something else (*formal*) **4.** MED ABORTION an induced abortion (*technical*) **5.** LING WORD ENDING a word ending, e.g. a suffix or an inflection [14C. Directly or via French < Latin *termination-* < *terminat-* (see TERMINATE)] —**terminational** *adj*

termination shock *n* the continually shifting boundary of the solar system and the start of interstellar space, where the solar wind abruptly slows down, 8 billion–9.5 billion miles from the Sun

terminator /túrmi naytər/ *n* **1.** SOMEBODY OR SOMETHING THAT TERMINATES SOMETHING somebody or something that puts an end to something (*formal*) **2.** KILLER a killer, especially a hired killer (*slang*) **3.** ASTRON LINE BETWEEN LIGHT AND DARK the boundary between the part of a moon or planet that is illuminated and the part that is dark

terminator gene *n* a gene inserted into genetically modified plants that makes them unable to produce seed after one season

termini plural of **terminus**

terminology /túrmi nólləji/ (*plural* **-gies**) *n* **1.** the expressions and words, or a set of expressions and words, used by people involved in a specialized activity or field of work **2.** the systematic study of names and terms [Early 19C. < German *Terminologie* < medieval Latin *terminus* 'term'] —**terminological** /túrmina lójjik'l/ *adj* —**terminologically** *adv* —**terminologist** *n*

SYNONYMS See *jargon*[1].

terminus /túrmiNəss/ (*plural* **-ni** /-nī/ or **-nuses**) *n* **1.** a town, city, or location at the end or beginning of a fixed transport route such as a railway line or bus route **2.** a point where something stops or reaches its end **3.** SCULPTURE same as **term** (sense 10) [Mid-16C. < Latin, 'end, boundary, limit']

terminus ad quem /túrmiNəss ad kwém/ *n* the aim or finishing point of something [< Latin, 'end to which']

terminus a quo /túrmaNəss aa kwô/ *n* the starting point of something [< Latin, 'end from which']

termitarium: Queensland, Australia

termitarium /túrmi táiri əm/ (*plural* **-ia** /-i ə/) *n* a nest, sometimes extremely large, made by a group of termites

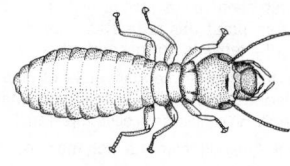
termite

termite /túr mīt/ *n* a light-coloured social insect that forms large colonies. Many species live in warm or tropical regions, feed on wood, and are highly destructive to trees and wooden structures. Order: Isoptera. [Late 18C. < Latin *termit-* 'woodworm'] —**termitic** /tur míttik/ *adj*

termless /túrmləss/ *adj* **1.** having no end or limit (*literary*) **2.** not depending on any terms and conditions (*formal*)

termly /túrmli/ *adj* **1.** taking place once every academic term **2.** for each fixed or agreed time period (*formal*) —**termly** *adv*

term of art *n* a word or phrase with a special meaning, used in a specific field of knowledge

term paper *n N Am* a long essay required of a student during an academic term

terms of trade *npl* the ratio of a nation's export prices to its import prices, used to measure the country's trading position

tern[1] /turn/ (*plural* **terns** or *same*) *n* a seabird, typically white with a black head, related to gulls but with a slenderer body and wings, a pointed beak, and a forked tail. Family: Sternidae. [Late 17C. < N Germanic]

tern[2] /turn/ *n* **1.** a set of three things, especially three numbers that together form a winning combination in a lottery or other gambling game **2.** a schooner with three masts [14C. < French *terne* < Latin *terni* (see TERNARY)]

ternary /túrnəri/ *adj* **1.** THREEFOLD consisting of three things or parts, or arranged in groups of three (*formal*) **2.** MATHS WITH BASE OF 3 describes the number system, or a number belonging to it, that has 3 as its base ○ *a ternary logarithm* **3.** MATHS WITH THREE VARIABLES involving or having three variables **4.** METALL WITH THREE COMPONENTS describes an alloy that consists of three components **5.** CHEM WITH THREE ATOMS OR MOLECULES describes chemical compounds consisting of three active elements, e.g. three atoms, molecules, or radicals [15C. < Latin *ternarius* < *terni* 'three at a time' < *ter* 'three times']

ternary form *n* in musical composition, a three-part form in which the first section is repeated or slightly varied in the last section, following a second, contrasting section

ternary system, **ternary number system** *n* the number system that uses 3 as a basis for counting or

ordering, numbers being expressed as sequences of the digits 0, 1, and 2

ternate /túr nayt/ *adj* describes a compound leaf that is divided into three more or less equal parts [Mid-18C. < modern Latin *ternatus* < medieval Latin *ternare* 'make threefold' < Latin *terni* (see TERNARY)] —**ternately** *adv*

terne /turn/ *n* **1.** an alloy of lead and tin with antimony. Use: coating. **2.** METALL same as **terneplate** [Mid-19C. Probably < French, 'dull, tarnished']

terneplate /túrn playt/ *n* a steel or iron plate coated with terne

Terni /túrni/ capital of Terni Province, Umbria Region, central Italy. Population: 105,018 (2001).

ternion /túrni ən/ *n* a set of three sheets of paper folded once to make 12 pages [Late 16C. < Latin *ternion-* < *ter* 'three times']

terotechnology /teérō tek nóllәji/ *n* a branch of technology that uses managerial and financial expertise as well as engineering skills when installing and running machinery [Late 20C. < Greek *tērein* 'watch over, take care of']

terpene /túr peen/ *n* an aromatic hydrocarbon obtained from plant oils [Late 19C. < German *Terpentin* 'turpentine'] —**terpenic** /tur peénik/ *adj*

terpineol /tur pínni ol/ *n* a derivative of pine oil that has a distinctive lilac smell. Use: perfumery. [Late 19C. < *terpin*, an organic compound < TERPENE]

terpolymer /tur póllimər/ *n* a polymer consisting of three monomers

Terpsichore /turp síkəri/ *n* in Greek mythology, the Muse of choral songs and dance, one of the nine Muses believed to inspire and nurture the arts [< Greek *Terpsikhorē*, literally 'delighting in dance' < *terpein* 'to delight' + *khoros* 'dance']

terpsichorean /túrpsikə reé ən/ (*formal or humorous*) *adj also* **terpsichoreal** /túrpsik reé əl/ relating to or resembling dance ■ *n* a dancer

terr. *abbr* **1.** territorial **2.** territory

Terr. *abbr* Terrace (*used in addresses*)

terra /térrə/ (*plural* **-rae** /-ree/) *n* a light-coloured highland or mountainous area of the Moon or of a planet [Early 17C. Directly or via Italian < Latin, 'earth, land']

terra alba /térrə álbə/ *n* a white substance used in the making of paints and paper, e.g. kaolin or gypsum [< Latin, 'white earth']

terrace /térrəss/ *n* **1.** PORCH OR WALKWAY WITH PILLARS a promenade or portico, usually with columns or a balustrade along the side or sides **2.** STRIP OF AGRICULTURAL LAND ON HILLSIDE a flat, fairly narrow, level strip of ground, bounded by a vertical or steep slope and constructed on a hillside so that the land can be cultivated **3.** FLAT AREA BESIDE BUILDING a paved or grassy area immediately outside and on a level with a building, used for sitting or eating outdoors **4.** ROW OF IDENTICAL HOUSES JOINED TOGETHER a long row of houses built together in the same style, separated only by shared dividing side walls (**party walls**) **5.** BUILDINGS SET ON RAISED GROUND a row of houses facing down from a raised position on or along the top of a piece of sloping ground, or built on a raised bank of ground **6.** *N Am* ROOFTOP PATIO a flat roof used as living space **7.** GEOG AREA OF NATURAL GROUND ALONG COAST a flat raised strip of beach or ground that has been formed naturally along the coast, beside a river or lake, or along the side of a valley by erosion or the changing sea level **8.** CIV ENG CONSTRUCTED BANK OF GROUND a raised bank of ground, artificially constructed ■ **terraces** *npl* FOOTBALL **1.** STANDING AREAS AROUND FOOTBALL PITCHES the broad shallow open-air steps built around football pitches to provide cheap standing areas for spectators, outlawed at larger football grounds in the United Kingdom in the early 1990s **2.** STANDING FOOTBALL SPECTATORS the football spectators standing on the terraces (*informal*) ■ *vt* (**-races, -racing, -raced**) AGRIC FORM TERRACE ON LAND to convert land into a terrace or terraces [Early 16C. < Old French, 'rubble, platform' < Latin *terra* 'earth, land']

terraced house /térrəst-/, **terrace house** *n* a house in a row of similar houses joined side by side and facing the street. N Am term **row house** —**terraced housing** *n*

terracing /térrəssing/ *n* **1.** STRIPS OF AGRICULTURAL LAND IN STEPS a series of level, fairly narrow strips of ground constructed on a hillside that would otherwise be too steep for cultivation **2.** TERRACED AREA OR STRUCTURE something built in shallow, gradually rising steps or tiers, e.g. open-air terraces in a football ground or an area of landscaped garden **3.** TERRACED HOUSES a group of buildings designed or built as a terrace or series of terraces **4.** MAKING OF TERRACES the act or process of creating a terrace or terraces

terracotta /térrə kóttə/ *n* **1.** REDDISH-BROWN POTTERY CLAY unglazed reddish-brown hard-baked clay, often used to make pottery objects **2.** SOMETHING MADE OF TERRACOTTA a work of art or craft modelled in terracotta, or terracotta items generally **3.** BROWNISH-RED COLOUR a reddish-brown colour, like that of terracotta [Early 18C. < Italian, 'baked earth'] —**terracotta** *adj*

terrae ASTRON plural of **terra**

terra firma /térrə fúrmə/ *n* solid ground, in contrast to water or air [< Latin, 'firm land']

terrain /tə ráyn/ (*plural* **-rains** or *same*) *n* **1.** ground or a piece of land seen in terms of its surface features or general physical character, especially for crossing it or using it for military purposes ○ *surveyed the local terrain* **2.** GEOL same as **terrane** ○ *mountainous terrain* [Early 18C. Via French < Latin *terrenum* 'land, ground' < *terrenus* 'of the earth' < *terra* 'earth, land']

terra incognita /térrə in kógnitə/ (*plural* **terrae incognitae** /térree in kógni tee/) *n* **1.** a country or region that is unknown or has not been explored **2.** a subject or area of knowledge that has not been explored and about which nothing is known [< Latin, 'unknown land']

terrane /térrayn/ *n* a section of the Earth's crust that is defined by clear fault boundaries, with stratigraphic and structural properties that distinguish it from adjacent rocks [Early 18C. Via French < Latin *terrenus* (see TERRAIN)]

terra nullius /térrə noólli əss/ *n* in Australia, the idea and legal concept that when the first Europeans arrived in Australia the land was owned by no one and therefore open to settlement. It has been judged not to be legally valid. [< Latin, 'land belonging to no one']

terrapin /térrəpin/ (*plural* **-pins** or *same*) *n* **1.** a turtle with four webbed feet, a shell like that of a tortoise, and a retractable head. Terrapins are usually smaller than tortoises, live in fresh water and on land, and are carnivorous. Family: Emydidae. **2.** a moderate-sized turtle. Native to: brackish water in eastern North America. Latin name: *Malaclemys terrapin*. [Early 17C. Alteration of Virginia Algonquian *torope*]

terraqueous /te ráykwi əss/ *adj* consisting of areas of water and areas of dry land [Mid-17C. < Latin *terra* 'earth, land' + AQUEOUS]

terrarium /tə ráiri əm/ (*plural* **-iums** or **-ia** /-i ə/) *n* **1.** an enclosure that is used for keeping or observing small land animals or reptiles such as lizards in a simulated natural environment **2.** a sealed glass container used for growing ornamental plants that require a high level of humidity [Late 19C. < modern Latin < Latin *terra* 'earth, land', after AQUARIUM]

terrazzo /te rátsō/ *n* mosaic that is made by laying marble or stone chips in mortar and grinding them to a polished level surface. Use: floor or wall coverings. [Early 20C. < Italian, 'terrace']

terrene /te reén/ *adj* (*archaic or literary*) **1.** worldly or earthly as opposed to heavenly or spiritual **2.** consisting of or like earth [14C. Via Anglo-Norman < Latin *terrenus* (see TERRAIN)] —**terrenely** *adv*

terreplein /táir playn/ *n* a raised embankment or platform behind a parapet where heavy guns are positioned [Late 16C. Via French < Italian *terrapieno* < *terrapienare* 'fill with earth' < *terra* 'earth' + *pieno* 'full']

~~terrestial~~ incorrect spelling of **terrestrial**

terrestrial /tə réstri əl/ *adj* **1.** RELATING TO EARTH relating to Earth rather than other planets **2.** BELONGING TO LAND belonging to the land rather than the sea or air **3.** LIVING OR GROWING ON LAND living or growing on land rather than in the sea or the air **4.** BROADCAST BY LAND-BASED TRANSMITTER broadcast by a land-based transmitter rather than by satellite ○ *a terrestrial TV channel* **5.** WORLDLY OR MUNDANE worldly or mundane as opposed to heavenly ■ *n* DWELLER ON PLANET EARTH especially in science fiction, a person or animal who lives on Earth [14C. < Latin *terrestris* < *terra* 'earth, land'] —**terrestrially** *adv*

terrestrial guidance *n* a missile or rocket guidance system in which the missile is programmed with precise details of its flight path, enabling it to follow a predetermined route. Data provided include gravitational field, magnetic field, and atmospheric pressure.

terrestrial link *n* a telecommunications connection that runs on or below the ground

terrestrial planet *n* any of the four planets that are nearest the Sun and are similar in density and composition. The terrestrial planets are Mars, Venus, Mercury, and Earth.

terrestrial radiation *n* electromagnetic radiation in the form of heat emitted by the Earth as it cools down at night, especially when the air is dry and there are no clouds

terrestrial telescope *n* a telescope used for viewing objects on Earth rather than in space. It has an objective and a four-lens eyepiece that give an upright image.

terret /térrit/ *n* **1.** either of two metal rings attached to the driving harness of a horse, through which the reins are passed to prevent them from slipping round the horse's flanks **2.** a metal ring on a dog's collar to which a lead can be attached [Late 15C. < Old French *toret* 'little ring' < *tour* (see TOUR)]

terre verte /táir vúrt/ *n* a greyish-green pigment of powdered glauconite. Use: in paints. [< French, 'green earth']

terrible /térrəb'l/ *adj* **1.** EXTREME very serious or severe ○ *a terrible cold* **2.** VERY UNPLEASANT very unpleasant or harrowing ○ *The past few days have been a terrible time.* **3.** EXTREMELY LOW IN QUALITY of a very low standard or quality ○ *My cooking isn't that great, but it's not terrible.* **4.** ILL OR UNHAPPY unwell, or extremely unhappy ○ *You look terrible. Are you ill?* **5.** TROUBLING causing considerable fear or anxiety ○ *a terrible sight* **6.** FORMIDABLE causing awe or dread ○ *a terrible responsibility* [14C. Via French < Latin *terribilis* < *terrere* 'frighten'] —**terribleness** *n*

terribly /térrəbli/ *adv* **1.** to an extreme degree ○ *I'm terribly pleased that you can come.* **2.** in a way that is extremely difficult or painful ○ *affected terribly by the news*

terricolous /te ríkələss/ *adj* living in or on the soil [Mid-19C. < Latin *terricola* 'earth-dweller' < *terra* 'earth, land']

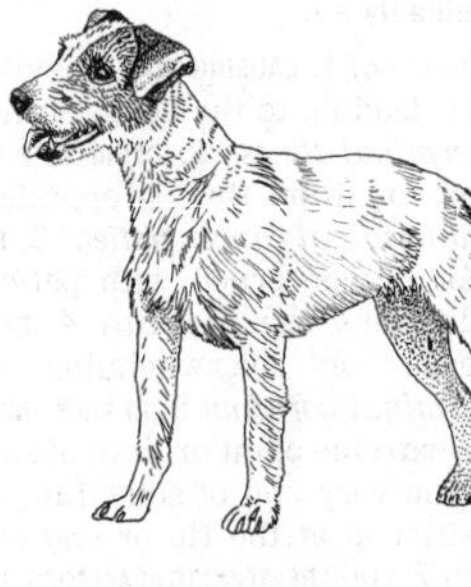

terrier

terrier[1] /térri ər/ *n* a small lively dog belonging to any of the breeds originally developed to hunt animals living in underground burrows, but now common as pets. Examples include the Airedale, cairn, fox, Scottish, and West Highland terriers, and the schnauzer. [15C. < Old French *(chien) terrier* 'terrier (dog)' < Latin *terra* 'earth']

terrier[2] /térri ər/ *n* in English legal history, a land register or survey [15C. Via French < medieval Latin *terrarius* < Latin *terra* 'earth, land']

Terrier /térri ər/ *n* a member of the British Army's Territorial and Volunteer Reserve (*informal*) [Early 20C. < TERRITORIAL, after TERRIER[1]]

terrific /tə ríffik/ *adj* **1.** VERY GREAT very great in size, force, or degree ○ *terrific speed* **2.** VERY GOOD exceptionally good in a way that inspires enthusiasm

(*informal*) 3. **VERY FRIGHTENING** inspiring a sense of terror (*archaic*) [Mid-17C. < Latin *terrificus* 'frightening' < *terrere* 'frighten']

terrifically /tə ríffikli/ *adv* to a very high degree or very great extent

~~terrificly~~ incorrect spelling of **terrifically**

terrify /térri fī/ (**-fies, -fying, -fied**) *vt* **1.** to make somebody feel very frightened or alarmed **2.** to coerce somebody into doing something by using threats ○ *terrified into naming the members* [Late 16C. < Latin *terrificare* < *terrificus* (see TERRIFIC)] —**terrifier** *n* —**terrifying** *adj* —**terrifyingly** *adv*

terrigenous /te ríjjinəss/ *adj* relating to a sediment derived from land erosion that may be formed or deposited on the land or found underwater in shallow ocean areas [Late 17C. < Latin *terrigenus* 'earth-born' < *terra* 'earth, land']

terrine /te réen/ *n* **1.** a coarse pâté or similar cold food cooked and sometimes served in a small dish with a tight-fitting lid **2.** a dish used for cooking terrines **3.** HOUSEHOLD same as **tureen** [Early 18C. < French, form of Old French *terrin* 'earthen' < Latin *terra* 'earth']

territorial /térrə táwri əl/ *adj* **1. RELATING TO OWNED LAND** relating to land or water owned or claimed by an entity, especially a government **2.** ZOOL **ASSERTING OWNERSHIP OF AREA** having a tendency to appropriate an area or territory and to protect that area or territory against intruders of the same species, particularly other males **3. RELATING TO RESERVE ARMY** relating to a reserve army that has been trained for use in emergencies —**territorially** *adv*

Territorial *n* a member of a reserve army that has been trained for use in emergencies, especially the British Army's Territorial and Volunteer Reserve

Territorial Army *n* the British Army's Territorial and Volunteer Reserve, a reserve army established to assist with national defence in emergencies. It was founded between 1907 and 1908.

territorialise *vt* POL another spelling of **territorialize**

territorialism /térrə táwri əlizəm/ *n* **1.** a social system in which the landowners hold or control most of the positions of power and authority **2.** a system of civil government in which the citizens of a territory are penalized unless they adopt the same religion as their civil ruler. Historically it is associated particularly with the Lutheran Church in Germany. —**territorialist** *n*

territoriality /térrə táwri állәti/ *n* **1.** the ranking of a region as a territory **2.** a pattern of animal behaviour marked by the establishment, demarcation, and defence of an area that can support the growth and activity of an animal or group of animals

territorialize /térrə táwri ə līz/ (**-izes, -izing, -ized**), **territorialise** (**-ises, -ising, -ised**) *vt* **1.** to organize something on a territorial basis **2.** to enlarge a country by adding more territory or territories to it —**territorialization** /térrə tawri ə lī záysh'n/ *n*

territorial waters *npl* the area of sea around a country's coast recognized as being under that country's jurisdiction

Territorian /térrə táwri ən/ *n Aus* somebody who comes from the Northern Territory of Australia [Late 19C. < TERRITORY]

territory /térrətəri/ (*plural* **-ries**) *n* **1. LAND** land, or an area of land **2. GOVERNED GEOGRAPHICAL AREA** a geographical area that is owned and controlled by a government or country **3.** *also* **Territory AREA OF COUNTRY WITH SEPARATE GOVERNMENT** an area of a country or empire such as the United States, Canada, or Australia that is not a state or province but has a separate organized government **4. FIELD OF ENQUIRY** a field of knowledge, investigation, or experience **5.** ZOOL **AREA THAT ANIMAL CONSIDERS ITS OWN** an area that an animal considers as its own and that it defends against intruders of the same species **6.** COMM **DISTRICT THAT AGENT COVERS** the district that an agent, especially a sales representative, is responsible for **7.** SPORTS **AREA DEFENDED BY TEAM** the area of a playing field defended by a team [14C. < Latin *territorium* < *terra* 'earth, land'] ◇ **come** *or* **go with the territory** to be an inseparable part of or accompaniment to something else (*informal*)

Territory *n Aus* the Northern Territory, Australia (*informal*)

terror /térrər/ *n* **1. INTENSE FEAR** intense or overwhelming fear **2. TERRORISM** violence or the threat of violence carried out for political purposes **3. SOMETHING CAUSING FEAR** something that causes intense fear, e.g. an event or situation ○ *a rabid dog that became the terror of the neighbourhood* **4. ANNOYING PERSON** an annoying, difficult, or unpleasant person, particularly a naughty child (*informal*) [14C. Via French < Latin < *terrere* 'frighten']

Terror *n* HIST same as **Reign of Terror**

terrorise *vt* another spelling of **terrorize**

terrorism /térrərizəm/ *n* violence or the threat of violence, especially bombing, kidnapping, and assassination, carried out for political purposes

terrorist /térrərist/ *n* somebody who uses violence, especially bombing, kidnapping, and assassination, to intimidate others, often for political purposes — **terroristic** /térrə rístik/ *adj*

terrorize /térrə rīz/ (**-izes, -izing, -ized**), **terrorise** (**-ises, -ising, -ised**) *vt* **1.** to intimidate or coerce somebody with violence or the threat of violence **2.** to fill somebody with feelings of intense fear over a period of time —**terrorization** /térrə rī záysh'n/ *n* —**terrorizer** *n*

terror-stricken, terror-struck *adj* filled with a feeling of intense fear

terry /térri/ (*plural* **-ries**) *n* **1.** *N Am* TEXTILES same as **terry towelling 2.** a square of terry towelling. Use: nondisposable nappy. **3.** an uncut loop of thread in the pile of a fabric that consists of such loops [Late 18C. Origin ?]

Terry /térri/, **Dame Ellen** (1847–1928) British actor. A noted Shakespearean actor, she maintained a stage partnership with Sir Henry Irving that lasted 24 years. Full name **Terry, Dame Ellen Alicia**

> 'What is a diary as a rule? A document useful to the person who keeps it, dull to the contemporary who reads it, invaluable to the student, centuries afterwards, who treasures it!'
> [Dame Ellen Terry, *The Story of My Life*; 1908]

terry towelling *n* a fabric with uncut loops of thread on both sides. Use: towels, bath mats, nappies. N Am term **terry**

terse /turss/ (**terser, tersest**) *adj* **1.** brief and unfriendly, often conveying annoyance **2.** concise and economically phrased [Early 17C. < Latin *tersus* 'wiped off, clean', past participle of *tergere* 'wipe'] —**tersely** *adv* — **terseness** *n*

tertial /túrsh'l/ *adj*, *n* BIRDS same as **tertiary** *adj* (sense 2) [Mid-19C. < Latin *tertius* 'third']

tertian /túrsh'n/ *adj* describes a fever, especially a malarial fever, with symptoms that appear every other day ■ *n* a tertian fever or set of symptoms [14C. < Latin *(febris) tertiana* '(fever) of the third (day)' < *tertius* 'third']

tertiary /túrshəri/ *adj* **1. THIRD** third in degree, order, place, or importance (*formal*) **2.** BIRDS **DESCRIBES BIRD'S INNERMOST FLIGHT FEATHERS** describes the few flight feathers nearest a bird's body on the rear edge of a wing, making up the third row of feathers **3.** CHEM **FORMED BY REPLACEMENT OF ATOMS** relating to or derived by the replacement of three atoms or groups, especially the replacement of the three hydrogen atoms in ammonia with alkyl groups to form amines **4.** CHEM **OF THREE BONDED CARBONS** relating to or containing a carbon atom that has direct bonds to three other carbon atoms ■ *n* (*plural* **-ies**) **1.** BIRDS **BIRD'S INNERMOST FLIGHT FEATHER** a feather on the innermost rear edge of a bird's wing **2.** CHR **MEMBER OF LAY GROUP** in the Roman Catholic Church, a member of a group of the laity associated with a religious order [Mid-16C. < Latin *tertiarius* 'of the third part or rank' < *tertius* 'third']

Tertiary *n* the period of geological time, 65 million to 1.6 million years ago, during which mammals became dominant and modern plants evolved. See table at **geological time** —**Tertiary** *adj*

tertiary care *n* care or treatment provided by an institution specializing in a particular branch of medicine

tertiary colour *n* a colour made by mixing two secondary colours together or by mixing a primary colour with the secondary colour closest to it

tertiary education *n* education at college or university level

tertiary entrance rank *n Aus* EDUC full form of **TER**

tertiary industry *n* the field of industry that provides services such as transport or finance rather than manufacturing or extracting raw materials

tertiary syphilis *n* the final stage of syphilis in which the disease spreads throughout the body, affecting the brain, spinal cord, heart, skin, bones, and joints

tertium quid /túrshi əm kwíd/ *n* an unknown or indefinite thing or factor that is related to but cannot be classified as belonging to either of two other areas or categories [< late Latin, 'some third thing']

Tertullian /tər túlli ən/ (160?–225?) Roman theologian. He was the first important theological writer in Latin, and his often impassioned works greatly influenced his successors.

> 'The blood of the martyrs is the seed of the Church.'
> [Tertullian, *Apologeticus*; 197?]

teruk /te róok/ *adj Malaysia, Singapore* lacking in restraint and liable to cause trouble (*informal*) [Late 20C. < Malay]

tervalent /tur váylənt/ *adj* CHEM same as **trivalent** — **tervalency** *n*

terza rima /táirtsə réemə/ (*plural* **terze rime** /táirt say rée may/) *n* a rhyming verse form of Italian origin consisting of three-line, 11-syllable verses (**tercets**), with the middle line of one verse rhyming with the first and third lines of the next [< Italian, 'third rhyme']

terzetto /tur tséttō/ (*plural* **-tos** or **-ti** /-ti/) *n* a musical trio for instruments or voices [Early 18C. < Italian (see TERCET)]

TE score *n* in Australia, a score awarded on the basis of final secondary school examinations that determines whether or not a student is accepted into some tertiary education institutions. Full form **tertiary entrance score**

TESL /téss'l/ *abbr* teaching of English as a second language

tesla /tésslə/ *n* the derived unit of magnetic flux density in the SI system, equal to a flux of one weber in an area of one square metre. Symbol **T** [Late 19C. After Nikola TESLA]

Tesla /tésslə/, **Nikola** (1856–1943) Croatian-born US electrical engineer. A pioneer of alternating-current systems, he is also credited with many inventions including high-frequency generators (1890) and the tesla coil (1891).

tesla coil *n* a transformer that has an air, rather than iron, core and is used to produce high voltages at high frequencies, e.g. the flyback transformer in a CRT monitor, or ignition coil in a car [After Nikola TESLA]

TESOL /tée sol/ *abbr* EDUC teaching of English to speakers of other languages

TESSA /téssə/, **Tessa** *n* in the United Kingdom, a superseded type of savings account allowing a limited investment without payment of tax on the interest, provided the capital is not withdrawn for five years. Full form **Tax-Exempt Special Savings Account**

tessellate /téssə layt/ (**-lates, -lating, -lated**) *v* **1.** *vt* to construct, pave, or decorate something with small pieces of stone or glass to give a mosaic effect **2.** *vi* to fit together without leaving any spaces (*refers to geometric shapes*) [Late 18C. < Latin *tessellatus* 'made of small square stones' < *tessera* (see TESSERA)] —**tessellation** /téssə láysh'n/ *n*

tessera /téssərə/ (*plural* **-serae** /-seree/) *n* **1.** a small square of stone, tile, or glass used to make a mosaic **2.** a piece of bone or wood that was used in ancient Greece and Rome as a dice, tally, or ticket [Mid-17C. Via Latin < Greek *tesseres*, variant of *tessares* 'four'; from the sides of a square] —**tesseral** *adj*

tesseract /téssə rakt/ *n* the four-dimensional extension of a cube [Late 19C. < Greek *tesseres* (see TESSERA) + *aktis* 'ray']

tessitura /téssi tóòrə/ (*plural* **-ras** or **-re** /-ray/) *n* the pitch range that predominates in a piece of music [Late 19C. Via Italian < Latin *textura* 'web, structure, weaving' (see TEXTURE)]

test[1] /test/ *n* **1.** **EXAMINATION** a series of questions, problems, or practical tasks to gauge somebody's knowledge, ability, or experience **2.** **BASIS FOR EVALUATION** a basis for evaluating or judging something or somebody **3.** **TRIAL RUN-THROUGH OF PROCESS** a trial run-through of a process or on equipment to find out if it works **4.** **DIFFICULT SITUATION** an often difficult situation or event that will provide information about somebody or something **5.** **EXAMINATION OF PART OF BODY** an examination of part of the body or of a body fluid or specimen in order to find something out, e.g. whether it is functioning properly or is infected ○ *an allergy test* ○ *an eye test* **6.** **PROCEDURE TO DETECT PRESENCE OF SOMETHING** a procedure to ascertain the presence of or the properties of a substance ○ *a test for nitrates in drinking water* **7.** CHEM **REACTIVE SUBSTANCE** a substance or a reagent that reacts in a specific way to show the presence of a substance **8.** **RESULT OF PROCEDURE** a result of a procedure to ascertain the presence of a substance ○ *Your test hasn't come back yet.* **9.** CRICKET, RUGBY same as **test match** ■ *v* (**tests, testing, tested**) **1.** *vt* **TRY SOMETHING OUT** to try something out, e.g. by touching, operating, or experiencing it, in order to find out what it is like, how well it works, or what it feels like **2.** *vt* **EVALUATE SOMETHING** to use something on a trial basis in order to evaluate it **3.** *vt* **ASK SOMEBODY QUESTIONS** to ask somebody questions or make somebody do a practical activity in order to gauge knowledge, skill, or experience **4.** *vt* **CARRY OUT MEDICAL TEST** to carry out a test on part of the body or on a bodily specimen **5.** *vti* **EXAMINE SOMETHING TO DETECT PRESENCE** to examine something in order to ascertain the presence of or the properties of a substance ○ *tested the water for bacteria* **6.** *vi* **ACHIEVE PARTICULAR TEST RESULT** to achieve a particular result on a test ○ *She tested positive for rubella immunity.* **7.** *vt* **MAKE DEMANDS ON SOMEBODY** to make considerable demands on somebody, particularly somebody's skills or abilities [14C. Via Old French, 'pot' < Latin *testum* 'earthenware pot'] —**testability** /téstə bíllәti/ *n* —**testable** *adj*

test[2] /test/ *n* the hard outer covering or shell of some invertebrates, e.g. molluscs and crustaceans [Mid-16C. < Latin *testa* 'tile, shell']

Test. *abbr* BIBLE Testament

testa /téstə/ (*plural* **-tae** /-tee/) *n* the protective covering of a seed from a flowering plant [Late 18C. < Latin 'tile, shell']

testaceous /te stáyshəss/ *adj* **1.** made of shell, or having a shell or other hard covering **2.** of a reddish-brown colour like a brick (*technical*)

Test Act *n* an act passed by the English Parliament in 1673 that barred from public office anyone who would not take Anglican Communion or renounce transubstantiation. It was intended to prevent Catholics from occupying civil or military posts, and was repealed in 1828. [< TEST[1] in the archaic sense 'oath']

testae BOT plural of **testa**

testament /téstəmənt/ *n* **1.** **PROOF** something that shows that something else exists or is true ○ *His remarkable recovery is a testament to the doctor's skill.* **2.** **FORMAL STATEMENT OF BELIEFS** a formal statement or speech outlining beliefs (*formal*) **3.** LAW same as **will**[2] *n* (sense 6) (*archaic*) ○ *last will and testament* **4.** JUDCHR **COVENANT BETWEEN GOD AND HUMANKIND** in Judaism and Christianity, a covenant made between God and humankind (*formal*) [13C. < Latin *testamentum* 'legal will' < *testis* 'witness'] —**testamental** /téstə mént'l/ *adj*

ORIGIN The Latin word *testis* 'witness', from which ***testament*** is derived, is also the source of English *attest, contest, detest, intestate, protest, testicle, testify,* and *testimony.*

Testament *n* **1.** either of the two major divisions of the Christian Bible, known as the Old Testament and the New Testament **2.** a printed copy of the New Testament

testamentary /téstə méntəri/ *adj* **1.** bequeathed or set out in a will **2.** relating to a legal will (*formal*)

testate /tés tayt/ *adj* having made a legally valid will ■ *n* somebody who has made a legally valid will [15C. < Latin *testatus*, past participle of *testari* 'bear witness, make your will' < *testis* 'witness'] —**testacy** /téstəssi/ *n*

testator /tes táytər/ *n* somebody, especially a man, who has made a legally valid will [14C. Via Anglo-Norman < Latin < *testari* (see TESTATE)]

testatrix /tes táytriks/ (*plural* **-trices** /-trə seez/) *n* a woman who has made a legally valid will [Late 16C. < late Latin, feminine of Latin *testator* (see TESTATOR)]

test ban *n* an agreement between nations to suspend testing of some or all nuclear weapons [< TEST[1]]

test bed *n* a facility designed and equipped to test engines and machinery under circumstances as close to actual operating conditions as possible [< TEST[1]]

test card *n UK* a geometric pattern usually incorporating areas of different colours, transmitted by a television broadcasting organization to help viewers to tune in their television sets and obtain optimum reception. ANZ, N Am term **test pattern** [< TEST[1]]

test case *n* **1.** an important legal case that establishes a precedent referred to in future cases **2.** an event that provides an opportunity to prove or disprove a hypothesis [< TEST[1]]

testcross /tést kross/ *n* **1.** **GENETIC CROSS TECHNIQUE** a procedure used especially in plant breeding whereby a plant's genetic constitution is inferred by examining the progeny resulting from crossing it with another individual of known genetic makeup **2.** **RESULT OF TESTCROSS** a plant produced by a testcross ■ *vt* (**-crosses, -crossing, -crossed**) **SUBJECT ORGANISM TO TESTCROSS** to subject a plant to a testcross to infer its genetic constitution [Mid-20C. < TEST[1]]

test drive *n* a short drive in a car or other motor vehicle in order to see what it is like, usually with a view to buying it [< TEST[1]] —**test-drive** *vt*

tester[1] /téstər/ *n* **1.** **SOMEBODY WHO TESTS PRODUCTS** somebody whose job it is to try out new products **2.** **SAMPLE OF PRODUCT** a sample of a product, especially a cosmetic **3.** **EQUIPMENT TO CHECK PROPER FUNCTIONING** a piece of equipment that tests if a machine or device is working properly **4.** **SMALL FOOD THERMOMETER** a small thermometer inserted into something that is cooking to determine if it is done **5.** **SOMEBODY WHO CONDUCTS TESTS** somebody who administers or carries out tests ○ *a water tester* [14C. < TEST[1]]

tester[2] /téstər/ *n* a canopy, especially one over a four-poster bed or a pulpit [14C. < medieval Latin *testerium* < Latin *testa* 'tile, shell, (in late Latin) head']

testes ANAT plural of **testis**

testicle /téstik'l/ *n* the male gonad or sperm-producing gland (**testis**) usually with its surrounding membranes, particularly in humans or other higher vertebrates [15C. < Latin *testiculus* 'small testis' < *testis* (see TESTIS)] —**testicular** /te stíkyòòlər/ *adj*

testify /tésti fī/ (**-fies, -fying, -fied**) *vi* **1.** **MAKE DECLARATION UNDER OATH IN COURT** to declare something that can be taken as evidence under oath in a court of law **2.** **AFFIRM SOMETHING FROM EXPERIENCE** to make a factual statement based on personal experience, or declare something to be true from personal experience **3.** **PROVE OR DEMONSTRATE** to be clear evidence of something (*formal*) **4.** CHR **TALK ABOUT EXPERIENCE AS CHRISTIAN** to talk to an audience or group of listeners about personal experience as a Christian [14C. < Latin *testificari* 'make yourself a witness' < *testis* 'witness'] —**testification** /téstifi káysh'n/ *n* —**testifier** *n*

testimonial /tésti mṓni əl/ *n* **1.** **RECOMMENDATION** a favourable report on the qualities and virtues of somebody or something **2.** **TRIBUTE** something given, held, or done in order to honour or thank somebody **3.** **STATEMENT BACKING UP CLAIM** a statement backing up a claim or supporting a fact ■ *adj* **OF TESTIMONY OR TESTIMONIAL** relating to or consisting of testimony or a testimonial

testimony /téstiməni/ (*plural* **-nies**) *n* **1.** **EVIDENCE GIVEN IN COURT** evidence that a witness gives to a court of law. It may take the form of a written or oral statement detailing what the witness has seen or knows about a case. **2.** **PROOF** something that supports a fact or a claim ○ *This win is testimony to the tactical skill of the coach.* **3.** BIBLE **TEN COMMANDMENTS** the Ten Commandments inscribed on two stone tablets, or the Ark of the Covenant in which the tablets were stored **4.** CHR **PUBLIC AVOWAL** a public profession of Christian faith or religious experience [14C. < Latin *testimonium* < *testis* 'witness']

testing /tésting/ *adj* subjecting somebody or something to challenging difficulties ○ *A testing time lies ahead for the new administration.*

testis /téstiss/ (*plural* **testes** /té steez/) *n* either of the paired male reproductive glands, roundish in shape, that produce sperm and male sex hormones, and hang in a small sac (**scrotum**) [Early 18C. < Latin, 'witness', because it 'bears witness' to a man's virility]

test marketing *n* the use of a sample of a larger market to try out a marketing strategy or product [< TEST[1]]

test match *n* any of a series of cricket or rugby matches between two international teams [< TEST[1]]

testosterone /te stóstərōn/ *n* a male steroid hormone produced in the testicles and responsible for the development of secondary sex characteristics. Use: produced synthetically for treatment of androgen deficiency. Formula: $C_{19}H_{28}O_2$. [Mid-20C. < TESTIS + *-sterone* (blend of STEROL + KETONE)]

test paper *n* **1.** a sheet of paper with examination questions, or a student's written answers **2.** a small piece of paper soaked in reagent such as litmus that is used to show the presence of or properties of a substance [< TEST[1]]

test pattern *n ANZ, N Am* same as **test card** [<TEST[1]]

test pilot *n* a pilot who flies new aircraft in order to assess their performance [<TEST[1]]

test-screening *n* a screening of a provisional version of a film to test audience reaction [<TEST[1]]

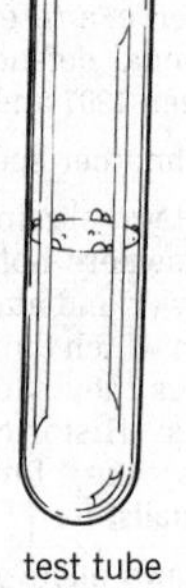

test tube

test tube *n* a small glass tube-shaped container that is closed and rounded at one end and open at the other, used to mix, heat, and store chemicals in laboratories [<TEST[1]]

test-tube *adj* made in a test tube or by other artificial means, rather than occurring or arising naturally

test-tube baby *n* a baby that has been conceived by fertilizing a woman's egg in a laboratory (**in vitro fertilization**) and then inserting it in her womb to develop normally for the remainder of the pregnancy (*informal*)

testudinal /te styóòdinəl/, **testudinary** /-əri/ *adj* resembling a tortoise or the shell of a tortoise

testudo /te styóòdō/ (*plural* **-dines** /-dineez/) *n* a movable shelter against missiles from above, used by the ancient Roman army in siege warfare. It was either a single structure that could be carried or was made by soldiers holding their shields above their heads to form a protective roof. [14C. < Latin, 'tortoise's shell, shelter' < *testa* 'tile, shell']

testy /tésti/ (**-tier, -tiest**) *adj* impatient and easily upset or annoyed [14C. < Anglo-Norman *testif* < Latin *testa* 'tile, shell, (in late Latin) head'] —**testily** *adv* —**testiness** *n*

Tet /tet/ *n* in Vietnam, and in Vietnamese communities, a festival held over three days to mark the lunar New Year [Late 19C. < Vietnamese]

tetanic /te tánnik/ *adj* **1.** relating to tetanus or to the sustained contraction of the muscles that is characteristic of tetanus **2.** capable of producing muscle spasms such as those seen in tetanus [Early 18C. Via Latin < Greek *tetanikos* < *tetanos* (see TETANUS)] —**tetanically** *adv*

tetanize /téttə nīz/ (**-nizes, -nizing, -nized**), **tetanise** (**-nises, -nising, -nised**) *vt* to cause tetanic spasms in a muscle —**tetanization** /téttə nī záysh'n/ *n*

tetanus /téttənəss/ *n* **1.** an acute infectious disease, usually contracted through a penetrating wound, that causes severe muscular spasms and contractions, especially around the neck and jaw. The spasms are caused by a toxin released by the bacterium *Clostridium tetani.* **2.** sustained muscle contraction, e.g. induced by electrical stimulation [14C. Via Latin < Greek *tetanos* 'muscular spasm' < *teinein* 'stretch'] —**tetanal** *adj* —**tetanoid** *adj*

tetany /téttəni/ *n* repeated prolonged contraction of muscles, especially of the face and limbs, caused by low blood calcium arising from, e.g. an underactive parathyroid gland or vitamin D deficiency [Late 19C. Via French, 'intermittent tetanus' < Latin *tetanus* (see TETANUS)]

tetchy /téchi/ (**-ier, -iest**), **techy** *adj* oversensitive and easily upset or annoyed (*informal*) [Late 16C. Probably < *tache* 'blemish, defect' < French] —**tetchily** *adv* —**tetchiness** *n*

tête-à-tête /tét ə tét/ *n* **1.** INTIMATE CONVERSATION FOR TWO a private conversation between two people **2.** TYPE OF SOFA a two-seater sofa shaped like an S, allowing those seated to face each other ■ *adv* INTIMATELY in private with only two people present [< French, 'head-to-head']

tête-bêche /tét bésh/ *adj* describes a pair of stamps, one of which is printed the right way up and the other upside down [< French, '(sleeping) head to foot']

teth /teth, tess, tet/ *n* the ninth letter of the Hebrew alphabet, represented in the English alphabet as 't'. See table at **alphabet** [Early 19C. < Hebrew]

tether /té*th*ər/ *n* a rope or chain attached to an animal and attached to something at the other end, restricting the animal's movement ■ *vt* (**-ers, -ering, -ered**) to tie something, especially an animal, with a rope or chain in order to restrict its movement [14C. < Old Norse *tjóðr* < Germanic, 'fasten'] ◇ **at the end of your tether** having reached the limit of your patience, strength, or endurance

tetherball /té*th*ər bawl/ *n N Am* same as **bumble-puppy** (sense 1)

Tethys /teéthiss, téth-/ *n* **1.** TITAN in Greek mythology, a Titan who was the wife of Oceanus and the mother of thousands of sea and river gods and nymphs **2.** MOON OF SATURN a large natural satellite of Saturn, discovered in 1684. It has a diameter of 1,050 km/651 mi. and is Saturn's ninth most distant satellite, orbiting at a distance of 295,000 km/182,900 mi. **3.** ANCIENT SEA an ancient sea that is thought to have separated Laurasia and Gondwanaland, surviving vestigially today as the Mediterranean [Late 19C. Via Latin < Greek *Tēthus*]

Tetley /téttli/, **Glen** (*b.* 1926) US dancer and choreographer. He danced with internationally known companies including those of Robert Joffrey, Martha Graham, and the American Ballet Theatre, and became associated with the National Ballet of Canada in 1986. His choreography includes *Tagore* (1989).

Teton[1] /teéton, teét'n/ (*plural same* or **-tons**), **Teton Dakota** *n* **1.** a member of a group of Native North American peoples who lived in western parts of the Great Plains, and now live mainly in North and South Dakota. Included in this group are the Oglala, Hunkpapa, and Miniconjou peoples. **2.** the Siouan language of the Teton people. Native speakers: 6,000. [Early 19C. < Dakota *thíthuwa* 'dwellers on the prairie'] —**Teton** *adj*

Teton[2] /teéton, teét'n/ range of the Rocky Mountains in northwestern Wyoming and southwestern Idaho. The highest peak is Grand Teton, 4,197 m/13,770 ft.

Teton Dakota *n, adj* PEOPLES, LANG same as **Teton**[1]

Tétouan /te twaán/, **Tetuán** city in northern Morocco on the Mediterranean Sea, near Tangier. Population: 367,349 (1994).

tetr- *prefix* same as **tetra-** (*used before vowels*)

tetra /téttrə/ (*plural* **-ras** or *same*) *n* a brightly-coloured freshwater fish that lives in tropical regions and is kept as an aquarium fish. Family: Characidae. [Mid-20C. Shortening of modern Latin *Tetragonopterus* < late Latin *tetragonum* (see TETRAGON) + Greek *pteron* 'wing']

tetra- *prefix* four ○ *tetrastich* [< Greek < Indo-European]

tetrabasic /téttrə báyssik/ *adj* describes an acid that contains four atoms of replaceable hydrogen in a molecule —**tetrabasicity** /téttrə bay síssəti/ *n*

tetrabrach /téttrə brak/ *n* a word consisting of four short syllables in Latin or classical Greek literature [Early 20C. < Greek *tetrabrakhus* 'four short' < *brakhus* 'short']

tetracaine /téttrə kayn/ *n* a crystalline compound chemically related to procaine. Use: local anaesthetic. Formula: $C_{15}H_{24}N_2O_2$.

tetrachloride /téttrə kláwr īd/ *n* a compound that has four chlorine atoms in each molecule

tetrachloromethane /téttrə klawrō meé thayn/ *n* CHEM same as **carbon tetrachloride**

tetrachord /téttrə kawrd/ *n* a group of four musical notes, the first and last of which form a perfect fourth, used principally in ancient Greek music —**tetrachordal** *adj*

tetracid /te trássid/ *n* **1.** a base that can react with four molecules of a monobasic acid to form a salt **2.** an alcohol with four OH groups per molecule

tetracyclic /téttrə síklik/ *adj* describes a compound whose molecular structure contains four rings

tetracycline /téttrə sí kleen/ *n* a broad-spectrum antibiotic. Source: bacteria of the genus *Streptomyces*, synthesized from chlortetracycline. Use: treatment of acne, general infections. Formula: $C_{22}H_{24}N_2O_8$. [Mid-20C. < TETRACYCLIC]

tetrad /té trad/ *n* **1.** SERIES OF FOUR a group or series of four things or people **2.** GENETICS GROUP OF FOUR CHROMOSOMES a group of four chromosomes in a diploid cell that is about to undergo the cell division (**meiosis**) that produces sex cells **3.** BIOL GROUP OF FOUR CELLS a group of four cells produced by the division (**meiosis**) of a single parent cell, e.g. as it occurs in the formation of pollen and spores **4.** CHEM ATOM WITH VALENCY OF FOUR an atom or chemical group with a valency of four [Mid-17C. < Greek *tetrad-*, stem of *tetras* 'four']

tetradactyl /téttrə dáktil/ *adj* with four toes or fingers

tetradymite /te tráddi mīt/ *n* a grey metallic sulphide mineral containing tellurium and bismuth. Use: source of tellurium. [Mid-19C. < German *Tetradymit* < Greek *tetradumos* 'fourfold'; from the double twin crystals in which it is usually found]

tetraethyl lead /téttrə eé thīl-/ *n* a colourless, extremely poisonous, oily liquid. Use: petrol antiknock agent now often restricted or banned because it produces air pollution and poisons catalytic converters. Formula: $Pb(C_2H_5)_4$.

tetragon /téttrə gon/ *n* a two-dimensional geometric figure formed of four sides and four angles [Early 17C. < late Latin *tetragonum* < Greek *tetragōnos* 'four-angled' < *gōnos* 'angled'] —**tetragonal** /te trággən'l/ *adj*

tetragram /téttrə gram/ *n* a word that has four letters

Tetragrammaton /téttrə grámmətən/ *n* a four-letter Hebrew name for God revealed to Moses, usually written YHVH or YHWH (Exodus 3:13–14). Orthodox Jews regard this name as too sacred to be pronounced. [14C. < Greek, neuter of *tetragrammatos* 'having four letters' < *gramma* 'letter']

tetrahedra MATHS plural of **tetrahedron**

tetrahedrite /téttrə heé drīt/ *n* a grey to black metallic sulphide mineral containing copper, iron, and antimony. Use: source of copper and other metals. [Mid-19C. Directly < TETRAHEDRON or < Greek *tetraedron*]

tetrahedron /téttrə heédrən/ (*plural* **-drons** or **-dra** /-drə/) *n* a three-dimensional geometric figure formed of four faces [Late 16C. < Greek *tetraedron*, neuter of *tetraedros* 'four-sided' < *hedra* 'face'] —**tetrahedral** /téttrə heédrəl/ *adj* —**tetrahedrally** *adv*

tetrahydrocannabinol /téttrə hídrō kə nábbi nol/ *n* CHEM full form of **THC**

tetrahydroxy /téttrə hī dróksi/ *adj* describes a molecule that has four hydroxyl groups

tetralogy /te trálləji/ (*plural* **-gies**) *n* a series of four related literary, dramatic, artistic, or musical works [Mid-17C. < Greek *tetralogia* 'four dramas' < *-logia* 'discourse']

tetramer /téttrəmər/ *n* a polymer that is formed from four identical monomers —**tetrameric** /téttrə mérrik/ *adj*

tetramerous /te trámmərəss/ *adj* with four parts, or with parts arranged in multiples of four —**tetramerism** *n*

tetrameter /te trámmitər/ *n* **1.** VERSE LINE WITH FOUR FEET a line of verse that has four metrical feet **2.** LINE WITH FOUR PAIRS OF FEET in classical poetry, a line of verse made up of four pairs of feet **3.** VERSE IN TETRAMETER poetry that is written in tetrameters [Early 17C. Via late Latin < Greek *tetrametron*, form of *tetrametros* 'having four measures' < *metron* 'measure']

tetraploid /téttrə ployd/ *adj* possessing four matched sets of chromosomes in the cell nucleus ■ *n* a tetraploid cell, nucleus, or organism —**tetraploidy** *n*

tetrapod /téttrə pod/ *n* **1.** a vertebrate animal that has four limbs or legs **2.** a device comprising four arms projecting from a central point at 120° to each other, making a tripod with the fourth arm projecting vertically upwards [Early 19C. Via modern Latin *tetrapodus* < Greek *tetrapod-* 'four-footed' < *pous* 'foot']

tetrapody /te tráppədi/ (*plural* **-dies**) *n* a line of verse consisting of four feet —**tetrapodic** /téttrə póddik/ *adj*

tetrapterous /te tráptərəss/ *adj* describes insects that have four wings

tetrarch /té traark/ *n* **1.** RULER OF QUARTER OF COUNTRY the ruler of a quarter of a country or province **2.** JOINT RULER one of four joint rulers **3.** SUBORDINATE PRINCE a ruler of a subordinate principality, especially in the eastern provinces of the Roman Empire **4.** PHALANX COMMANDER the commander of a subdivision of a Macedonian phalanx in ancient Greece [Pre-12C. Via late Latin *tetrarcha* < Greek *tetrarkhēs* 'four ruling' < *arkhēs* 'ruler'] —**tetrarchic** /te traárkik/ *adj*

tetrarchy /té traarki/ (*plural* **-chies**), **tetrarchate** /te traar kayt/ *n* **1.** government by four rulers **2.** the rule or domain of one of four joint rulers

tetraspore /téttrə spawr/ *n* an asexual spore that occurs after reproductive cell division (**meiosis**), usually in groups of four, in red algae —**tetrasporic** /téttrə spórrik/ *adj*

tetrastich /téttrə stik/ *n* a poem, verse, or strophe that has four lines [Late 16C. Via Latin *tetrastichon* < Greek *tetrastikhos* 'containing four rows' < *stikhos* 'row, line of verse'] —**tetrastichic** /téttrə stíkik/ *adj*

tetrasyllable /téttrə síllab'l/ *n* a word with four syllables —**tetrasyllabic** /téttrə si lábbik/ *adj*

tetratomic /téttrə tómmik/ *adj* **1.** with four atoms per molecule **2.** with four replaceable atoms or radicals

tetravalent /téttrə váylənt/ *adj* with a valency of four —**tetravalency** *n*

tetri /téttri/ (*plural same*) *n* a subunit of Georgian currency. See table at **currency** [Late 20C. < Georgian]

tetrode /téttrōd/ *n* a four-element electron tube containing an anode, a cathode, a control grid, and an additional electrode or screen grid

tetrodotoxin /te trōdə tóksin/ *n* a potent neurotoxin found in puffers

tetroxide /te tróksīd/, **tetroxid** /-tróksid/ *n* a compound that has four oxygen atoms per molecule [Mid-19C. < TETRA-]

tetryl /téttrīl, -tril/ *n* a yellow crystalline compound. Use: explosives detonator. Formula: $C_7H_5N_5O_8$.

Tetuán another spelling of **Tétouan**

teuchter /tyoó*kh*tər, tyoóktər/ *n Scotland* somebody from the Scottish Highlands (*informal; used in a disrespectful or teasing way by Lowlanders*) [Mid-20C. Origin ?]

Teucrian /tyoókri ən/ *n* same as **Trojan** (sense 1) (*literary*) [< Greek *Teukros* 'Teucer', first king of Troy] —**Teucrian** *adj*

Teut. *abbr* Teutonic

Teutoburg Forest /tóytō burg-/, **Teutoburger Wald** /tóytō burgər vált/ ridge of wooded hills in northwestern Germany, scene of a major Roman defeat by Germans in AD 9

Teuton /tyoó t'n/ *n* **1.** a member of an ancient Germanic

people who originally came from Jutland and invaded Gaul in the 2nd century BC. They were wiped out by the Romans in 102 BC. **2.** somebody from a German-speaking culture, especially from Germany, Switzerland, or Austria (*informal or humorous*) [Early 18C. < Latin *Teutoni* or *Teutones* (plural) 'the Teutons']

Teutonic /tyoo tónnik/ *adj* **1.** describes attributes stereotypically associated with German-speaking cultures or people (*informal or humorous*) **2.** relating to the ancient Teuton people, or their culture — **Teutonically** *adv*

Teutonic Knights, **Teutonic Order** *n* a German religious and military order that was founded as a charitable order in Palestine in 1190 during the Third Crusade but became a military organization operating in Eastern Europe. In the 13th century it conquered Prussia, where it introduced Christianity through killing many of the native inhabitants and colonizing it with Germans.

Teutonise *vti* another spelling of **Teutonize**

Teutonism /tyóotənizəm/ *n* **1.** a German characteristic, custom, or idiom **2.** German society or civilization —**Teutonist** *n*

Teutonize /tyoótə nīz/ (**-izes, -izing, -ized**), **Teutonise** (**-ises, -ising, -ised**) *vti* to become German, or make something German —**Teutonization** /tyoótə nī záysh'n/ *n*

Tevet /te vét/, **Tebet** *n* in the Jewish calendar, the tenth month of the religious year, lasting 29 days and falling about the same time as December to January. See table at **calendar**

Tewa /táywə/ (*plural* **-was** or **same**) *n* **1.** a member of a group of Pueblo peoples who live in northern New Mexico **2.** the Tanoan language of the Tewa people. Native speakers: under 3,000. [Mid-19C. < Tewa *téwa* 'moccasins'] —**Tewa** *adj*

Te Whiti /te fítti/ (1830–1907) New Zealand Maori leader and prophet. He was the leader of passive resistance to European settlement of the Taranaki region of New Zealand. Full name **Te Whiti-o-Rongomai, Erueti**

Tewkesbury /tyóoksbəri/ market town in Gloucestershire, west-central England, with a medieval abbey church. Population: 76,405 (2001).

Tex. *abbr* Texan

Texas /téksəss/ state in the southwestern United States, bordered by Oklahoma, Arkansas, Louisiana, the Gulf of Mexico, Mexico, and New Mexico. Capital: Austin. Population: 21,779,893 (2002 estimate). Area: 692,244 sq. km/267,277 sq. mi. —**Texan** *n, adj*

Texas fever *n* an infectious disease of cattle that is characterized by high fever, anaemia, and severe weight loss, is caused by a protozoan, and is transmitted by tick bites. The discovery in 1893 that ticks transmitted this disease was the first demonstration that arthropods could act as disease vectors.

Texel /téks'l/ *n* a sheep of a breed originally from the Netherlands that has a heavy white fleece and a short neck and is raised for meat and milk production [Mid-20C. After an island off the north coast of the Netherlands]

Tex-Mex /téks méks/ *adj* showing a blend of Texan and Mexican cultures or cuisines [< shortening]

text /tekst/ *n* **1. MAIN BODY OF BOOK** the main body of a book or other printed material, as distinct from the introduction, index, illustrations, and headings **2. WRITTEN MATERIAL** words that have been written down, typed, or printed **3. WRITTEN VERSION OF SOMETHING** a written, typed, or printed version of something such as a speech or a statement ○ *the full text of the President's speech* **4.** COMMUNICATION same as **text message 5.** EDITION one among the extant forms or versions of a written work ○ *compared various texts to arrive at this reading* **6.** ORIGINAL WORDING the original wording of a piece of writing, especially the Bible, as opposed to a translation, summary, or revision **7.** BIBLE PASSAGE a short passage from the Bible that is read aloud and on which a sermon is based **8.** EDUC BOOK FOR STUDY a book or piece of writing that is used for academic study or discussion **9.** EDUC same as **textbook 10.** PRINTING TYPEFACE a style of type that is suitable for printing running text **11.**

COMPUT **WORDS APPEARING ON COMPUTER SCREEN** computer data that represents words, numbers, and other typographical characters, typically stored in ASCII format **12.** LETTERS AND NUMBERS ON PHONE SCREEN alphanumeric characters as they appear on the viewing screen of a mobile phone or pager (*often used before a noun*) ○ *a text message* ■ *vt* SEND TEXT MESSAGE TO SOMEBODY to send a text message to somebody on his or her mobile phone or pager ■ *adj* COMPUT USING WORDS associated with or designed for use with words in written form ○ *a text file* [14C. Via Old French < Latin *textus* 'woven material, literary composition' < past participle of *texere* 'weave']

ORIGIN The Latin word *texere* 'to weave', from which **text** is derived, is also the source of the English words *context, pretext, texture,* and *tissue.*

---

textbook /tékst book/ *n* a book that treats a subject comprehensively and is used by students as a basis for study ■ *adj* typical overall and in detail, and thus a suitable example for study ○ *a textbook case of superpower aggression*

text box *n* a box within a computer dialog box in which characters such as text, dates, or numbers can be typed and edited

text chat *n* a real-time communication between Internet users in which messages are typed via a keyboard

text editor *n* a computer program that permits the creation and editing of stored text

text file *n* a computer file consisting of alphanumeric characters exclusive of transmission characters

textile /téks tīl/ *n* **1.** cloth or fabric that is woven, knitted, or otherwise manufactured **2.** raw material that is used for making fabrics, e.g. fibre or yarn [Early 17C. < Latin *textilis* < past participle of *texere* 'weave']

text index *n* an index of some or all of the words in something such as a computer file or database field, used to aid searching and retrieval

text message *n* a message sent in textual form, especially one designed to appear on the viewing screen of a mobile phone or pager —**text messaging** *n*

text processing *n* the use of a computer to create, store, edit, and print or display text

textual /tékschoo əl/ *adj* **1.** relating to the way a book or piece of writing is written **2.** consisting of words or text [14C. < medieval Latin *textualis* < Latin *textus* (see TEXT)] —**textually** *adv*

textual criticism *n* **1.** the study of a group of manuscripts, especially of the Bible or works of literature, in order to determine which is the original or most authentic one **2.** the critical study of a work of literature involving a detailed analysis of the way in which it was written, e.g. its context, use of language, and principal themes —**textual critic** *n*

textualism /tékschoo əlizəm/ *n* **1.** unswerving adherence to a text, especially a text from the Bible **2.** detailed and critical analysis of a text —**textualist** *n*

textuary /tékschoo əri/ *adj* same as **textual** (*formal*) [Early 17C. < medieval Latin *textuarius* < Latin *textus* (see TEXT)]

texture /tékschər/ *n* **1.** FEEL OF SURFACE the feel and appearance of a surface, especially how rough or smooth it is **2.** STRUCTURE OF SOMETHING the structure of a substance or material such as soil or food, especially how it feels when touched or chewed **3.** ROUGH QUALITY the rough quality of a surface or fabric ○ *a fabric that has plenty of texture* **4.** DISTINCTIVE CHARACTER the typical and distinctive character of something complex ○ *The book captures the texture of 1950s provincial England.* **5.** WAY ARTIST DEPICTS SURFACE the way in which an artist depicts the quality or appearance of a surface **6.** EFFECT OF DIFFERENT COMPONENTS OF MUSIC the effect of the different components of a piece of music such as melody, harmony, rhythm, or the use of different instruments **7.** COMPUT **DETAIL OF GRAPHICS** in computer graphics, surface detail added to images ■ *vt* (**-tures, -turing, -tured**) GIVE ROUGH FEEL TO SURFACE to give a surface a rough and grainy feel [15C. Via French < Latin *textura* 'a weaving' < past participle of *texere* 'weave'] —**textural** *adj* —**texturally** *adv* —**textured** *adj*

textured vegetable protein *n* full form of **TVP**

texturing /tékschəring/ *n* in computer graphics, the adding of surface detail to an image

tg *abbr* Togo (*used in Internet addresses*) See table at **domain name**

TG *abbr* LING transformational grammar

TGAL *abbr* ONLINE think globally, act locally

TGAT /tee gat/ *abbr* EDUC Task Group on Assessment and Testing

TGIF, T.G.I.F. *abbr* Thank God it's Friday *or* Thank goodness it's Friday (*informal*)

TGV *n* in France and some other countries, a very high-speed train [< French, abbreviation of *train (à) grande vitesse* 'high-speed train']

TGWU *abbr* Transport and General Workers' Union

th *abbr* Thailand (*used in Internet addresses*) See table at **domain name**

Th *symbol* CHEM ELEM thorium

Th. *abbr* **1.** BIBLE Thessalonians **2.** CALENDAR Thursday

-th *suffix* **1.** in a series or sequence ○ *tenth* ○ *fortieth* **2.** another spelling of **-eth**[1]

Thackeray /tháke ray/, **William Makepeace** (1811–63) British novelist. Serialization of his novel *Vanity Fair* (1847–48) established him as a major literary figure. He is remembered for his humorous and moralizing portraits of middle- and upper-class life in Britain.

'If a man's character is to be abused, say what you will, there's nobody like a relation to do the business.'
[William Makepeace Thackeray, *Vanity Fair*; 1847–48]

Thaddaeus /tháddi əss/ *n* one of the 12 apostles of Jesus Christ. He is traditionally identified with St Jude (Mark 3:16–19, Matthew 10:2–4).

Thai /tī/ (*plural* **Thais** or **same**) *n* **1.** somebody who comes from Thailand **2.** the official language of Thailand, belonging to the Tai group of languages. Native speakers: 25 million. [Early 19C. < Thai, 'free'] —**Thai** *adj*

Thailand

Thailand /tī land, -lənd/ country in Southeast Asia bordered by Myanmar, Laos, Cambodia, the Gulf of Thailand, Malaysia, and the Andaman Sea. Language: Thai. Currency: baht. Capital: Bangkok. Population: 64,265,276 (2003). Area: 513,115 sq. km/198,115 sq. mi. Official name **Kingdom of Thailand**. Former name **Siam** (until 1939)

Thailand, Gulf of /tī land, -lənd/ wide inlet of the South China Sea separating Vietnam, Cambodia, and eastern Thailand from the Malay Peninsula. Length: 800 km/500 mi.

Thaïs /tháy iss/ (*fl* 4th century BC) Greek courtesan. According to legend, she accompanied Alexander the Great to Persia and persuaded him to raze Persepolis.

thakur /táakoor/ *n* S Asia in northern India, used as a title of respect for a man from a high-ranking family of landowners [Early 19C. Via Hindi < Sanskrit *ṭhakkura* 'chief, lord']

thalamus /thálləməss/ (*plural* **-mi** /-mī/) *n* **1.** either of a pair of egg-shaped masses of grey matter lying beneath each cerebral hemisphere in the brain that relay sensory information to the cerebral cortex. They are concerned with awareness of all the main senses except for smell. **2.** BOT same as **receptacle**

(sense 2) [Late 17C. Via Latin, 'inner chamber' < Greek *thalamos*] —**thalamic** /thə lámmik/ *adj* —**thalamically** *adv*

Thalassa /thə lássə/ *n* a small inner natural satellite of Neptune, discovered in 1989 by the space probe Voyager 2. It is approximately 80 km/50 mi. in diameter.

thalassaemia /thállə seémi ə/ *n* a hereditary form of anaemia, particularly prevalent around the Mediterranean, that is caused by a defect in the synthesis of the red blood pigment haemoglobin [Mid-20C. < Greek *thalassa* 'sea' (from its discovery in Mediterranean countries) + *haima* 'blood'] —**thalassaemic** *adj*

thalassic /thə lássik/ *adj* **1.** living in or growing in the sea **2.** relating to a sea or ocean, especially a smaller inland sea [Mid-19C. < French *thalassique* < Greek *thalassa* 'sea']

thalassocracy /thállə sókrəssi/ (*plural* **-cies**), **thalattocracy** /-tókrəssi/ *n* naval or commercial supremacy over a large area of sea or ocean [Mid-19C. < Greek *thalassokratia* 'authority over the sea' < *thalassa* 'sea'] —**thalassocrat** /thə lássə krat/ *n*

thalassotherapy /thállәssō thérrəpi/ *n* a therapeutic treatment that involves bathing in sea water [Late 19C. < Greek *thalassa* 'sea']

thalattocracy *n* POL same as **thalassocracy**

thaler /taálər/ (*plural same* or **-lers**), **taler** *n* a former silver coin used in Austria, Germany, and Switzerland [Late 18C. < archaic German (now *Taler*)]

Thales (of Miletus) /tháy leez-/ (625?–546? BC) Greek philosopher. He is traditionally regarded as the founder of Greek philosophy.

> 'I will be sufficiently rewarded if when telling it to others you will not claim the discovery as your own, but will say it was mine.'
> [Thales (of Miletus). Quoted in *In Mathematical Circles*, H. Eves; 1969]

Thalia /thə lī́ ə/ *n* **1.** in Greek mythology, the Muse of comedy, one of the nine Muses believed to inspire and nurture the arts **2.** in Greek mythology, one of the three Graces who lived on Mount Olympus and tended the goddess Aphrodite

thalidomide /thə líddə mīd/ *n* a synthetic drug found to cause physical malformations in foetuses when taken by pregnant women. Use: formerly, sedative and hypnotic. [Mid-20C. < *thal* (extracted from PHTHALIC ACID) + *ido* (extracted from *imido-* < IMIDE) + *mide* (extracted from IMIDE)]

thalli BIOL plural of **thallus**

thallic /thállik/ *adj* relating to or containing thallium, especially with a valency of three

thallium /thálli əm/ *n* a soft highly toxic white metallic element. Source: lead and zinc smelting. Use: manufacture of low-melting glass, photocells, infrared detectors. Symbol **Tl**. See table at **element** [Mid-19C. < Greek *thallos* 'green shoot' (because its spectrum is marked by a green band)]

thallophyte /thállə fīt/ *n* a plant that has no stem, roots, or leaves, e.g. algae, lichens, and fungi [Mid-19C. < modern Latin *Thallophyta* < Greek *thallos* 'green shoot' + *phuton* 'plant'] —**thallophytic** /thállə fíttik/ *adj*

thallous /thálləss/ *adj* relating to or containing thallium, especially with a valency of one

thallus /thálləss/ (*plural* **-li** /-lī/ or **-luses**) *n* the body of an organism such as an alga or liverwort that is not differentiated into leaves, stems, and roots [Early 19C. < Greek *thallos* 'green shoot' < *thallein* 'to bloom'] —**thalloid** /thálloyd/ *adj*

thalweg /taál veg/, **talweg** *n* a line connecting the lowest points of successive cross sections through a river channel or valley [Mid-19C. < German < obsolete *Thal* 'valley' (now *Tal*) + *Weg* 'path']

Thames /temz/ major river of southern England. It flows through London before emptying into the North Sea. Length: 338 km/210 mi.

than *stressed* /th̲an/; *unstressed* /th̲ən/ CORE MEANING: used after a comparative adjective or adverb in order to introduce the second element of a comparison ○ (prep) *paying more than £490 a year in fees* ○ (prep) *The hole was no deeper than 12 ft.* ○ (conj) *The risk may be higher than the figures indicate.*

1. *conj* used to introduce a rejected alternative in a contrast between two alternatives, in order to state a preference ○ *more a state of mind than a physical condition* **2.** *prep* in contrast with or in preference to (*informal*) ○ *I'm older than him.* [Old English *þanne, þonne, þænne, þan* < Germanic]

USAGE *Than* (a conjunction and a preposition) and *then* (an adverb and an adjective) are used differently and have different meanings even though they may sound similar when pronounced. Do not confuse them, as in this incorrect usage: *If novels are the force of the tutorial, than* [use *then*] *seven or eight are sufficient. She was the than-president* [use *then-president*] *of the society.* Conversely, do not use *then* when *than* is called for, as in these incorrect usages: *The hole was no deeper then* [use *than*] *12 feet.*

USAGE **than he** or **than him**? Because *than* is a preposition as well as a conjunction, either construction is possible, as is the fuller form *than he is.* The form *than him* is common in conversation and other spoken contexts (*We're older than him*) but is still frowned upon in formal writing, where *We're older than he is* is preferred.

thanatology /thánnə tólləji/ *n* the study of the medical, psychological, and sociological aspects of death and the ways in which people deal with it [Mid-19C. < Greek *thanatos* 'death'] —**thanatological** /thánnətə lójjik'l/ *adj* —**thanatologist** *n*

Thanatos /thánnə toss/ *n* **1.** in Greek mythology, the personification of death and the son of Nyx, goddess of the night. Roman equivalent **Mors 2.** the universal death instinct theorized by Sigmund Freud [Mid-20C. < Greek, 'death']

thane /thayn/ *n* **1.** an Anglo-Saxon nobleman of low rank who held lands in return for military service to a lord **2.** a baron in feudal Scotland, or a hereditary tenant of the Scottish crown [Old English *þegn* < Germanic, 'boy, man'] —**thanage** *n* —**thaneship** *n*

Thanet, Isle of /thánnit/ coastal region in Kent, southeastern England. It was formerly an island.

thank /thangk/ (**thanks, thanking, thanked**) *vt* **1.** to express feelings of gratitude to somebody or be grateful to somebody ○ *We'd like to thank you for a wonderful evening.* ○ *Thank goodness you got here in time.* **2.** to blame somebody or hold somebody responsible for something ○ *You have only yourself to thank for this situation.* [Old English *þancian* < Indo-European] ◇ **I'll thank you to** *or* **not to** used in an ironic or angry way to ask somebody to do or not do something ○ *I'll thank you not to bring any more of your friends round.*

thankful /thángkf'l/ *adj* **1.** feeling or expressing gratitude ○ *We must be thankful for small mercies.* **2.** glad or relieved about something —**thankfulness** *n*

thankfully /thángkf'li/ *adv* **1.** used to express approval or relief about a situation (*informal*) ○ *Thankfully, he didn't fall.* **2.** with feelings or expressions of gratitude ○ *They thankfully accepted her offer of a room for the night.*

USAGE *Thankfully* is used in two ways: as a conventional adverb of manner (*They received the good news thankfully*), and as a sentence adverb (*Thankfully, the news was good*). Some people dislike the second use, although the objection is not as strong as that to *hopefully* used in a corresponding way.

thankless /thángkləss/ *adj* **1.** not likely to be appreciated or rewarded ○ *a thankless task* **2.** not showing or feeling gratitude —**thanklessly** *adv* —**thanklessness** *n*

thank-offering *n* something offered or given to somebody as a sign of gratitude

thanks /thangks/ *interj* USED TO EXPRESS GRATITUDE used to express gratitude to somebody ○ *Goodbye, and thanks!* ■ *npl* **1.** EXPRESSION OF GRATITUDE an expression of gratitude for something ○ *Many thanks for your help yesterday.* **2.** GRATITUDE FOR SOMETHING gratitude or appreciation for something ◇ **no thanks to somebody** *or* **something** despite somebody or something or without somebody's assistance ◇ **thanks a lot** used to express great gratitude (*informal; sometimes used ironically*) ○ *Thanks a lot for coming over.* ○ *You took my glass? Thanks a lot!* ◇ **thanks to somebody** *or* **something** because of somebody or something

thanksgiving /thángks giving/ *n* **1.** PRAYER OF THANKS a prayer that offers thanks to God **2.** GIVING OF THANKS an expression or an act of giving thanks **3.** PUBLIC ACKNOWLEDGMENT OF DIVINE GOODNESS a public acknowledgment or celebration of divine goodness

Thanksgiving Day, Thanksgiving *n* **1.** in the United States, a public holiday marking the feast given in thanks for the harvest by the Pilgrim colonists in 1621. Date: fourth Thursday in November. **2.** in Canada, a public holiday observed as a day of giving thanks for the harvest and other good things received. Date: second Monday in October.

thank you *interj* used to express gratitude to somebody ■ *n* an expression of gratitude to somebody ○ *a big thank-you to all our readers* —**thank-you** *adj*

Thant /thant/, **U** (1909–74) Burmese politician. Following a series of senior government posts, he became secretary-general of the United Nations (1961–71).

thar /th̲aar/ *adv regional* same as **there** (*nonstandard*)

Thar Desert /taar-/ desert in northwestern India, in the state of Rajasthan, extending across the border into Pakistan. Area: 260,000 sq. km/100,000 sq. mi.

Tharp /thaarp/, **Twyla** (*b.* 1941) US dancer and choreographer. Her individual dance style combines ballet, tap, and jazz.

> 'The notion of doing something impossibly new usually turns out to be an illusion.'
> [Twyla Tharp, *Independent*; 8 December 1995]

Tharsis /thaársiss/ *n* an extensive shallow bulge on the surface of Mars in the northern hemisphere about 2000 km/1200 mi. across and 8 km/5 mi. high, supporting several volcanoes

Thásos /táss oss/, **Thassos** /thάss oss/ island in northeastern Greece, in the Aegean Sea, about 8 km/5 mi. from the mainland. Population: 13,111 (1981). Area: 979 sq. km/378 sq. mi.

that *stressed* /th̲at/; *unstressed* /th̲ət/ CORE MEANING: a grammatical word used to indicate somebody or something that has already been mentioned or identified, or something that is understood by both the speaker and hearer ○ (det) *Do you remember that discussion we had?* ○ (det) *Later that week I saw her again.* ○ (pron) *Is that why you're here?* ○ (pron) *Don't touch that!*

1. *det, pron* INDICATING FAMILIAR PERSON OR THING used to refer to somebody or something not described, but familiar to the speaker and hearer and not requiring identification ○ (det) *Did you read that e-mail I sent?* ○ (det) *that woman we met yesterday* ○ (pron) *That was a great year.* **2.** *det, pron* INDICATING DISTANCE FROM SPEAKER indicating somebody or something a distance away from you, or further away from another, referred to as 'this' ○ (det) *You see that girl over there?* ○ (det) *That bag looks more spacious than this one.* ○ (pron) *What's that you're doing?* ○ (pron) *That looks much nicer than this.* **3.** *det* INDICATING TYPE used to characterize a particular type, person, or thing ○ *I really want a sleep that goes on forever.* **4.** *pron* IDENTIFYING SOMEBODY OR SOMETHING used to introduce a clause giving more information to identify the person or thing mentioned ○ *the committee that deals with such matters* ○ *Take the road that forks to the left.* ○ *on the day that he left* **5.** *conj* EXPRESSING COMMENT OR FACT used to introduce a noun clause expressing a comment on a situation or a supposed or real fact ○ *It was clear that she wanted to see the concert.* ○ *The report stated that sales were improving.* **6.** *conj* EXPRESSING RESULT used to introduce a clause expressing result or effect ○ *It made such a noise that we had to cover our ears.* **7.** *conj* EXPRESSING CAUSE used to introduce a clause expressing the cause of a feeling ○ *I feel hurt that you should think such a thing.* ○ *He's sorry that he told her now.* **8.** *conj* EXPRESSING PURPOSE used to introduce a clause expressing purpose (*literary*) ○ *We continue to give, that others may receive and live.* **9.** *conj* EXPRESSING DESIRE OR AMAZEMENT used after an understood but unspoken statement such as 'I wish' or 'If only' to introduce a clause expressing desire, amazement, or indignation (*literary*) ○ *Oh that I had never set eyes on her!* ○ *That you could think such a*

thing! **10.** *adv* TO SPECIFIC DEGREE used to specify the extent of something ○ *I came that close to hitting the car in front.* **11.** *adv* SO VERY used before adjectives to emphasize the quality they are describing (*informal*) ○ *I didn't think she'd be that upset.* **12.** *adv Scotland* same as **so**[1] (senses 8–9) ○ *I was that angry!* [Old English *þæt* < Indo-European] ◇ **that is** in other words, or to be specific ○ *You need a further qualification, that is, a PhD.* ◇ **that's that 1.** used to say that something is finished or dealt with **2.** used to say that something has been settled and there will be no more discussion on it

USAGE that or **who**? For centuries *that* has been used to refer to people as well as things: *the person who* or *that arrived.* Sometimes *that* can be clumsy: *He's the one that did it.* But it is not incorrect, and is occasionally the most appropriate choice of relative pronoun: *anything or anyone that can help* is more elegant than *anything that or anyone who can help.*

USAGE See **what**.

USAGE that or **which**? As relative pronouns, the two words are often interchangeable: *The house that/which stands on the corner is up for sale. The school that/which they go to is several miles away.* When **that** or **which** is the object of a following verb, it can be omitted altogether, as in *The school they go to...* When the relative clause adds information that is additional rather than necessary for identifying the noun it follows, **which** is used and is preceded by a comma: *The largest house, which stands on the corner, is up for sale.* Some usage guides, especially American ones, advocate the use of *that* in defining relative clauses (where the information added is essential to identify the noun it follows) and **which** in nondefining clauses (where the information added is incidental), and this is the practice followed in this dictionary.

thataway /tháttə way/ *adv Can, US regional* in that direction, or over there (*humorous or regional*) ○ *The masked man went thataway, Sheriff.* [Mid-19C. Alteration of *that way*]

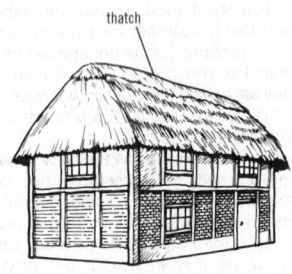

thatch

thatch

thatch /thach/ *n* **1.** PLANT MATERIAL USED FOR ROOF a plant material used as roofing on a house, e.g. straw or rushes **2.** ROOF a roof made of thatch **3.** HAIR ON SOMEBODY'S HEAD the hair on somebody's head, especially when it is thick ○ *The child had an unmistakable thatch of red hair.* **4.** GARDENING LAYER OF DEAD MATERIAL IN GRASS a matted layer of dead plant material that builds up next to the soil at the base of lawn grasses ■ *vti* (**thatches, thatching, thatched**) ROOF BUILDING WITH THATCH to put a roof of thatch on a building, or work at doing this [Old English *þeccan.* < Indo-European 'to cover'] —**thatched** *adj* —**thatcher** *n*

Margaret Thatcher

Thatcher /tháchər/, **Margaret, Baroness Thatcher of Kesteven** (*b.* 1925) British prime minister (1979–90). The leader of the Conservative Party from 1975, and the first woman prime minister of Great Britain, she pursued policies of privatization and economic deregulation. Born **Roberts, Margaret Hilda.** See table at **prime minister**

'We must find ways to starve the terrorist and the hijacker of the oxygen of publicity on which they depend.'
[Margaret Thatcher, *Speech to the American Bar Association, London*; 15 July 1985]

'Remember, George: this is no time to go wobbly.'
[Margaret Thatcher, *to President George H.W. Bush during the Persian Gulf War*, 8 March 1991. Quoted in *The New Yorker*; 7 December 1992]

Thatcherism /tháchərizəm/ *n* the political policies and style of government of Margaret Thatcher, typified by privatization, monetarism, and hostility to trade unions —**Thatcherite** *n, adj*

thatching /tháching/ *n* **1.** the craft or process of constructing or repairing thatched roofs **2.** INDUST same as **thatch** *n* (sense 1)

thaumato- *prefix* miracle ○ *thaumatology* [< Greek *thaumat-*, stem of *thauma* 'marvel, wonder']

thaumatology /tháwmə tólləji/ *n* the study or description of miracles

thaumatrope /tháwmə trōp/ *n* a card with different pictures on either side so that when the card is rapidly twirled, the images appear to combine [Early 19C. < Greek *thauma* 'wonder' + *tropos* 'turning'] —**thaumatropical** /tháwmə tróppik'l/ *adj*

thaumaturge /tháwmə turj/, **thaumaturgist** /tháwmə turjist/ *n* a performer of magic or supposed miracles [Early 18C. Via medieval Latin < Greek *thaumatourgos* < *thauma* 'wonder' + *-ergos* 'working']

thaumaturgy /tháwmə turji/ *n* the performance of miracles or magic —**thaumaturgic** /tháwmə túrjik/ *adj*

thaw /thaw/ *v* (**thaws, thawing, thawed**) **1.** *vti* MELT to melt, or make something melt **2.** *vti* DEFROST to defrost frozen food, or become defrosted ○ *Leave the gateau out to thaw.* **3.** *vi* BECOME LESS COLD to become less cold or numb through exposure to heat ○ *Come and thaw out by the fire.* **4.** *vi* BE WARM ENOUGH TO MELT ICE to be warm enough that snow and ice will melt **5.** *vi* BECOME LESS HOSTILE to become less hostile, tense, or aloof ○ *The atmosphere thawed.* ■ *n* **1.** PROCESS OF THAWING the action or process of thawing **2.** LESSENING OF HOSTILITY a lessening of hostility, tension, or aloofness **3.** WARMER WEATHER a period of weather warm enough to melt snow and ice [Old English *þawian* < Germanic]

Thayer /tháy ər, thair/, **Sylvanus** (1785–1872) US soldier and educator. As the long-term superintendent (1817–33) of the US Military Academy at West Point, he is credited with transforming it into a fully effective institution. Known as **the Father of West Point**

ThB *abbr* EDUC, RELIG Bachelor of Theology [Latin *Theologiae Baccalaureus*]

THC *n* the main active chemical in cannabis. Full form **tetrahydrocannabinol**

ThD *abbr* EDUC, RELIG Doctor of Theology [Latin *Theologiae Doctor*]

the *stressed/emphatic* /thee/; *unstressed; before a vowel* /thi/; *unstressed; before a consonant* /thə/ CORE MEANING: a determiner, the definite article, used before a noun denoting somebody or something that has already been mentioned or identified, or something that is understood by both the speaker and hearer, as distinct from 'a' or 'an' ○ *The film ended with the hero riding off into the desert.* ○ *The food was excellent but the service was poor.* **1.** *det* INDICATING ONE AS DISTINCT FROM ANOTHER used to refer to one in particular of a number of things or people, identified as distinct from all others by the use of a modifier ○ *Put them in the small bag.* ○ *the door on the left* ○ *the girl who answered the phone* ○ *the right to vote* ○ *the points made earlier* **2.** *det* INDICATING GENERIC CLASS used to refer to a person or thing considered generically or universally ○ *Exercise is good for the heart.* ○ *She played the violin.* ○ *The dog is a loyal*

pet. **3.** *det* INDICATING SHARED EXPERIENCE used to refer to objects and concepts associated with the shared experience of a culture, society, or community ○ *go to the hospital* ○ *thinking about the future* ○ *lying in the sun* **4.** *det* ALL PEOPLE OF PARTICULAR TYPE used before adjectives to refer generically to people of a particular type or class ○ *new measures to help the unemployed* ○ *They say the good always die young.* **5.** *det* TITLES AND NAMES used before titles and some names such as placenames ○ *the king of Spain* ○ *the Times newspaper* ○ *the president of the United States* **6.** *det* QUALIFYING NAMES AND TITLES used in names and titles before adjectives and nouns that distinguish somebody from others of the same name or title ○ *Ivan the Terrible* ○ *Henry the Fifth* **7.** *det* INDICATING PARTS OF BODY used instead of a possessive such as 'my' or 'your' to refer to a part of somebody's body ○ *patted him on the head* ○ *took her by the hand* **8.** *det* INDICATING MOST FAMOUS OR IMPORTANT the best, only, or most outstanding ○ *It's the place to be.* **9.** *det* EXPRESSING RATES AND RATIOS used to indicate how many units apply to each or every thing measured ○ *available at £60 the ton* **10.** *det* INDICATING FAMILY RELATIONSHIP used instead of a possessive such as 'your' or 'my' to refer to somebody having a particular family relationship (*informal*) ○ *Give my regards to the family.* ○ *How's the wife?* **11.** *det* PERIOD OF TIME used to refer to a period of time, especially a decade or an era ○ *living in the sixties* **12.** *adv* TO THAT EXTENT used adverbially to emphasize that somebody or something is true to a particular extent (*used before comparatives*) ○ *She looks the better for her holiday.* ○ *the worse for wear* **13.** *adv* BY HOW MUCH OR BY THAT MUCH used adverbially to indicate how one amount or quality changes in relation to another (*used before each of two comparative adjectives or adverbs*) ○ *the cheaper the better* ○ *The more you exercise, the fitter you'll feel.* **14.** *det Scotland* INDICATING FAMILIARITY OF SOMETHING used in various constructions where standard English requires no article, particularly before public institutions, e.g. 'the school' and 'the church', and names of diseases, e.g. 'the mumps' (*informal*) **15.** *det Scotland* INDICATING CLAN CHIEFTAIN used before a surname to indicate the chief of a clan, e.g. 'the MacGregor', or, formerly, with surnames other than Highland ones, e.g. 'Hughie the Graham' **16.** *det Scotland* INDICATING PRESENT TIME ETC. used in various constructions, notably in 'the both' and 'the most', and in 'the day', 'the morn', 'the night', that is today, tomorrow, tonight [Old English *þe*, earlier *se* < Indo-European]

the- *prefix* same as **theo-** (*used before vowels*)

Theano /thee áanō/ (*fl* 5th century BC) Greek philosopher and mathematician. She and her two daughters carried on the Pythagorean School after the death of her husband Pythagoras. She wrote treatises on mathematics, physics, medicine, and child psychology and is credited with writing the treatise on the 'Golden Mean.'

theanthropism /thi ánthrəpizəm/ *n* **1.** the assigning of human characteristics to a god or gods **2.** the Christian doctrine that the human and the divine are united in Jesus Christ [Early 19C. < Greek *theanthrōpos* 'god-man' < *theos* 'god' + *anthrōpos* 'man'] —**theanthropic** /thee ən thróppik/ *adj* —**theanthropist** *n*

thearchy /thee aarki/ (*plural* -**chies**) *n* **1.** RULE BY GOD rule by God, by a god, or by priests **2.** COMMUNITY UNDER DIVINE RULE a community that is ruled by God, by a god, or by priests **3.** HIERARCHY OF GODS a hierarchy or system of gods [Mid-17C. < Greek *thearkhia* < *theos* 'god'] —**thearchic** /thi áarkik/ *adj*

theat. *abbr* ARTS **1.** theatre **2.** theatrical

theater *n* ARTS US spelling of **theatre**

theatre /théertər/ *n* **1.** PLACE FOR PLAYS a building, room, or other setting where plays or other dramatic presentations are performed **2.** PLAYS plays or other dramatic literature **3.** DRAMA AS ART OR PROFESSION dramatic performance as an art, profession, or way of life ○ *She decided to make the theatre her life.* **4.** DRAMATIC QUALITY dramatic or theatrical quality or effectiveness ○ *As a public speaker he has a great sense of theatre.* **5.** MED same as **operating theatre** (*informal*) **6.** ROOM WITH TIERS OF SEATS a room with rising tiers of seats, used for lectures, demonstrations, or assemblies **7.** PLACE OF SIGNIFICANT EVENTS the place or realm where significant actions or events take place

British Information Services

○ *the political theatre* ■ *adj* FOR USE IN THEATRE OF OPERATIONS relating to or for use in a military theatre of operations [14C. Via Old French and Latin < Greek *theatron* < *theasthai* 'to watch']

theatregoer /thée̍tər gō ər/ *n* somebody who goes to the theatre

theatregoing /thée̍ ətər gō ing/ *n* the practice of going to the theatre, especially regularly ■ *adj* attending the theatre, especially regularly ○ *The theatregoing public is being shortchanged by plays of this standard.*

theatre-in-the-round (*plural* **theatres-in-the-round**) *n* **1.** a theatre in which the stage is in the centre with the seats around it on all sides **2.** drama or the style of drama written for performance in a theatre-in-the-round

theatre of cruelty *n* a form of surrealist drama emphasizing that human beings live in a threatening world with precarious moral values

theatre of operations *n* an area where fighting takes place during a war

Theatre of the Absurd *n* a form of drama that represents the absurdity of human life in a meaningless universe by deliberately unrealistic means and by ignoring or distorting conventions of plot and characterization

theatre of war *n* a large area of land, sea, and air in which warfare may take place

theatrical /thi áttrik'l/ *adj* **1.** RELATING TO THEATRE relating to or characteristic of the theatre or dramatic performance **2.** MARKED BY ARTIFICIAL EMOTION full of exaggerated or false emotion ■ *n* ACTOR a professional actor ■ **theatricals, theatrics** /thi áttriks/ *npl* **1.** PERFORMANCES IN THEATRE the performance of plays **2.** EXAGGERATED EMOTIONAL DISPLAY dramatic behaviour —**theatricalism** *n* —**theatricality** /thi áttri kálləti/ *n* —**theatrically** *adv*

thebaine /thée̍bə een, thi báy-/ *n* a poisonous alkaloid that causes convulsions similar to those caused by strychnine. Source: opium. Use: formerly, as medicine. Formula: $C_{19}H_{21}NO_3$. [Mid-19C. < Greek *Thēbai* 'Thebes'; because Upper Egypt was an important source of opium]

thebe /tébbe/ (*plural same*) *n* a subunit of Botswanan currency. See table at **currency** [Late 20C. < Setswana, 'shield']

Thebe /thée̍bee/ *n* a small natural satellite of Jupiter, discovered in 1980. With a diameter of 100 km/60 mi., it is Jupiter's fourth most distant satellite, orbiting at a distance of 222,000 km/138,000 mi. [Mid-18C. Via Latin, a nymph < Greek]

Thebes /theebz/ **1.** city of ancient Greece, in Boeotia, northwest of present-day Athens. A celebrated city in Greek myth, it was the most important city in Boeotia from the beginning of the 6th century BC and was destroyed by Alexander the Great in 335 BC. **2.** capital city of ancient Egypt, situated on both sides of the River Nile, south of present-day Cairo. It first appeared in Egyptian records in the middle of the 3rd millennium BC, and served as the capital of Egypt until 1085 BC. It is across the Nile from the Valley of the Kings, the site of the tombs of the pharaohs. —**Theban** *n, adj*

theca /thée̍kə/ (*plural* **-cae** /-see, -kee/) *n* an enclosing organ, capsule, or sheath, e.g. the spore case of a moss or the horny covering of the pupa of an insect [Early 17C. Via Latin < Greek *thēkē* 'case'] —**thecal** *adj* —**thecate** *adj*

thecodont /thée̍kə dont/ *adj* WITH TEETH IN SOCKETS describes animals whose teeth are set in sockets ■ *n* **1.** EXTINCT PREHISTORIC REPTILE an extinct reptile that lived in the Triassic period, had teeth set in sockets, and was the ancestor of the dinosaur. Order: Thecodontia. **2.** THECODONT REPTILE a reptile with teeth set in sockets [Mid-19C. < Latin *theca* (see THECA)]

thé dansant /táy daaN saáN/ (*plural* **thés dansants** /*pronunc. same*/) *n* same as **tea dance** [< French, 'dancing tea']

thee /thee/ *pron* a form of 'thou' used as the object of a verb or preposition to mean 'you' (*archaic regional*) [Old English *þē*, objective form of *þū* (see THOU[2])]

theft /theft/ *n* the act or crime of stealing somebody else's property [Old English *þēoft* < Germanic]

~~**theif**~~ incorrect spelling of **thief**

theine /thée̍ een, -in/ *n* caffeine, particularly as found in tea [Mid-19C < modern Latin *Thea*, former genus name of the tea plant < Dutch *t(h)ee* (see TEA)]

their /thair/ *det* **1.** belonging to or relating to a specific group of people or things ○ *They have sold their house and moved to London.* **2.** ⚠ belonging to him or her ○ *Everyone should make their own way home.* [12C. < Old Norse *þeirra* 'theirs']

USAGE their, there, or **they're?** Do not confuse these three words, as they have different meanings and spellings, and they function differently. ***Their*** is a possessive determiner: *Their* [not *They're* or *There*] *decisions have been made.* ***There*** can be an adverb or a pronoun, e.g. *Look over there* [not *their* or *they're*] *quickly. There* [not *They're* or *Their*] *are several unanswered questions.* ***They're*** is a contraction of 'they are', as in *They're* [not *There* or *Their*] *sitting in the front row.*

USAGE See *they*.

---

theirs /thairz/ *pron* **1.** belonging to a specific group of people or things ○ *Theirs was the biggest house in the town.* **2.** belonging to an individual person ○ *I have spare copies of the agenda if anyone has forgotten theirs.*

theism /thée̍ izəm/ *n* **1.** belief that one God created and rules humans and the world, not necessarily accompanied by belief in divine revelation such as through the Bible **2.** belief in the existence of a god or gods [Late 17C. < Greek *theos* 'god'] —**theist** *n* —**theistic** /thee ístik/ *adj*—**theistical** *adj*—**theistically** *adv*

them *stressed* /them/; *unstressed* /thəm/ *pron* **1.** OBJECTIVE FORM OF 'THEY' used to refer to a group of people or things other than the speaker or people addressed ○ *I'll put them in a box for you.* **2.** ⚠ HIM OR HER used instead of 'him' or 'her' to refer to a person without specifying gender ○ *If anyone is looking for me, tell them I'll be back soon.* **3.** THOSE a dialect form of 'those' (*nonstandard*) ○ *Give me one of them oranges.* [12C. < Old Norse *þeim*]

USAGE See *they*.

---

thematic /thi máttik/ *adj* **1.** RELATING TO THEME relating to or being a theme **2.** LING RELATING TO WORD STEM relating to the stem of a word **3.** LING LAST BEFORE INFLECTION describes the last part of a word stem before the inflectional ending ○ *a thematic vowel* [Late 17C. < Greek *thematikos* < *thema* 'proposition'] —**thematically** *adv*

thematic apperception test *n* a test for exploring aspects of personality in which somebody is shown pictures of people in various situations and asked to describe what is happening. The presumption is that emotions, prejudices, and other psychological states of the subject will be projected onto the figures in the pictures.

theme /theem/ *n* **1.** SUBJECT OF DISCUSSION OR COMPOSITION the subject of a discourse, discussion, piece of writing, or artistic composition **2.** DISTINCT AND UNIFYING IDEA a distinct, recurring, and unifying quality or idea ○ *Efficiency will be the theme of this organization.* **3.** REPEATED MELODY a melody that is repeated, often with variations, throughout a piece of music ○ *one of the themes of the concerto* **4.** MUSIC IN FILM a song or tune that is played at the beginning or end of, or during, a film or television programme and is identified with it ○ *the theme from 'The Magnificent Seven'* **5.** ESSAY OR WRITTEN EXERCISE a short essay or written exercise for a student **6.** GRAM same as **stem**[1] *n* (sense 6) ■ *adj* WITH DISTINCT SUBJECT with one distinct and recurring subject, principle, or idea ○ *We ate at a Wild West theme restaurant.* ■ *vt* (**themes, theming, themed**) GIVE SOMETHING DISTINCT CHARACTER to give something a single distinct character or subject ○ *The local bar has been themed as an Irish pub.* [13C. Via Old French and Latin < Greek *thema* 'proposition'] —**themed** *adj*

USAGE Like some other verbs formed from nouns that have undergone 'functional shift', ***theme*** has not gained wide acceptance (it is associated with the jargon of commerce and popular culture). It is best to avoid sentences like these: *She worked hard to theme her keynote speech. The party was themed as a Renaissance ball.* Acceptable alternatives are: *She worked hard to develop the theme of her keynote speech. The party theme was a Renaissance ball.* Similarly, it is advisable to avoid using the adjective *themed* alone or in combination with other words, as in *a baroque-themed concert,* where *a concert with a baroque theme* is the safer choice.

SYNONYMS See *subject*.

---

theme park *n* an amusement park in which all of the entertainments and facilities are designed around a specific subject or idea

theme party (*plural* **theme parties**) *n* a party at which a particular subject or idea, e.g. Hollywood movies or the 1960s, determines the way the guests dress and what food, decorations, or games are provided

theme song *n N Am* MUSIC same as **signature tune**

Themistocles /thə místə kleez/ (527?–460? BC) Greek general and political leader. He built up the Athenian navy and led it to victory over the Persians at the battle of Salamis (480 BC), laying the foundations for Athenian domination of Greece.

> 'Athens holds sway over all Greece; I dominate Athens; my wife dominates me; our newborn son dominates her.'
> [Attributed to Themistocles]

~~**themometer**~~ incorrect spelling of **thermometer**

themself /thəm sélf/ *pron* ⚠ used as a reflexive pronoun to refer to somebody whose sex is not indicated (*nonstandard*)

USAGE ***Themself*** is a reflexive pronoun that is sometimes used informally in speech instead of *himself or herself* when the sex of the person is not known or not relevant: *Any member of the party would try to distance themself from this policy.* Its use, however, is not acceptable in standard English and should be avoided.

---

themselves /thəm sélvz/ *pron* **1.** REFLEXIVE OF 'THEY' OR 'THEM' used to refer to a group of people or things when the object of a verb is the same as the subject ○ *They all made themselves at home.* **2.** THEIR NORMAL SELVES their real or normal selves (*usually used in negative statements*) ○ *They haven't been themselves since the accident.* **3.** EMPHASIZING used to emphasize the people or things being referred to ○ *They themselves would rather have gone to a movie.* **4.** HIMSELF OR HERSELF used to refer to an individual person without using 'himself' or 'herself' (*informal*) ○ *Everyone needs to take care of themselves.*

then /then/ CORE MEANING: an adverb used to indicate a particular time in the past or future ○ *We were much happier then.* ○ *Until then, he'll be staying with me.*

1. *adv* INDICATING SPECIFIC TIME indicates a specific time in the past or future ○ *Life was easier then.* **2.** *adv* AFTER THAT after that or subsequently in time, order, or position ○ *Fry the onions and garlic, then the vegetables.* ○ *We went for a walk, then came home.* **3.** *adv* THEREFORE that being the case, or in that case ○ *Then why don't you go back?* **4.** *adv* ON OTHER HAND on the other hand, or at the same time ○ *It was a brave thing to do, but then I would have expected no less of her.* **5.** *adv* IN ADDITION in addition to something else, or besides what has been mentioned ○ *I have to pay the money, then a penalty on top of that!* **6.** *adj* BEING AT THAT TIME being at that time, or existing or belonging to the time mentioned ○ *the then governor* [Old English *þænne* < Indo-European] ◇ **(but) then again** used to introduce a contrasting and additional fact that has to be taken into account ○ *It was a brave thing to do, but then again I would have expected no less of her.* ◇ **then and there** immediately and in that very place ○ *Did you expect me to hand over the money then and there?*

USAGE See *than*.

---

thenar /thée̍ naar/ *n* **1.** PALM OF HAND the palm of the hand (*technical*) **2.** BASE OF THUMB the fleshy area at the base of the thumb ■ *adj* IN PALM OR BALL OF THUMB relating to or in the palm of the hand or the fleshy area at the base of the thumb [Mid-17C. < Greek, 'palm of the hand']

Thénard /táy naar/, **Louis Jacques, Baron** (1777–1857) French chemist. He discovered hydrogen peroxide and potassium peroxide, as well as a pigment used to colour porcelain and known as 'Thénard's blue'. He wrote a once-standard treatise on chemistry.

thence /thenss/ *adv* (*formal or literary*) **1. FROM THERE** from that place ○ *We went by boat to Rotterdam and thence to Amsterdam.* **2. THEREFORE** from that fact, or therefore **3. THEREAFTER** from that time, or thereafter [13C. < obsolete *thenne* < W Germanic]

thenceforth /thénss fáwrth/ *adv* from that time on

thenceforward *adv* from that place or time on or forwards

theo- *prefix* god ○ *theocentric* [< Greek *theos* < Indo-European, 'to shine, sky, heaven']

theobromine /theé ō brő meen, -brő min/ *n* a white alkaloid powder that has effects similar to caffeine. Source: cocoa beans. Use: diuretic, vasodilator, treatment of cardiovascular disorders. Formula: $C_7H_8N_4O_2$. [Mid-19C. < modern Latin *Theobroma*, genus name of the cacao tree, literally 'food of the gods' < Greek *brōma* 'food']

theocentric /theé ō séntrik/ *adj* with God, a god, or gods as the focal point —**theocentricism** *n* —**theocentricity** /-sen tríssəti/ *n* —**theocentrism** *n*

theocracy /thi ókrəssi/ (*plural* -cies) *n* **1.** government by a god or by priests **2.** a community governed by a god or priests [Early 17C. < Greek *theokratia* 'rule of the gods'] —**theocrat** /theé ə krat/ *n* —**theocratic** /theé ə kráttik/ *adj* —**theocratical** *adj* —**theocratically** *adv*

Theocritus /thi ókrətəss/ (310?–250? BC) Greek poet. His graceful lyrics were the foundation of European pastoral poetry.

theodicy /theé óddisi/ (*plural* -cies) *n* argument in defence of God's goodness despite the existence of evil [Late 18C. Anglicization of French *Théodicée*, title of a book by Gottfried LEIBNIZ, literally 'justice of the gods' < Greek *dikē* 'justice'] —**theodicean** /theé óddi seé ən/ *adj*

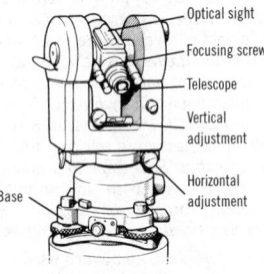

Optical sight
Focusing screw
Telescope
Vertical adjustment
Horizontal adjustment
Base

theodolite

theodolite /thi óddə līt/ *n* an optical instrument consisting of a rotating telescopic sight, used by a surveyor to measure horizontal and vertical angles [Late 16C. < modern Latin *theodelitus*] —**theodolitic** /thi óddə líttik/ *adj*

Theodora /theé ə dáwrə/ (AD 508?–548) Byzantine empress. She was the wife of Justinian I, with whom she shared power (527–48). She acted to save the throne during the Nika riots (532).

Theodorakis /theé ə daw raákiss/, **Mikis** (*b*. 1925) Greek composer. His wide-ranging output includes music for the film *Zorba the Greek* (1965).

Theodore I Lascaris /theé ə dawr láskərəss/ (1174?–1221) Byzantine emperor. During the Crusaders' occupation of Byzantium, he made Nicaea in Asia Minor the centre of a new Byzantine state.

Theodoric /thi óddərik/ (AD 454?–526) king of the Ostrogoths. King from 474, he invaded Italy in 488 and founded the Ostrogothic kingdom there in 493 after conquering the country, making Ravenna the capital and bringing a period of peace. Known as **Theodoric the Great**

'If this man is not faithful to his God, how can he be faithful to me, a mere man?' [Theodoric. Quoted in *Dictionnaire encyclopédique*, Edmond Guérard; 1872]

Theodosius I /theé ə dóssi əss/ (AD 346?–395) Roman emperor. As emperor of both the Eastern (379–95) and Western (392–95) Roman empires, he was the last ruler to unite the empire. He was a champion of Orthodox Christianity. Known as **Theodosius the Great**

Theodosius II /theé ə dóssi əss/ (AD 401–450) Roman emperor. He was the grandson of Theodosius I, and ruled the Eastern Roman Empire from 408 until his death.

theogony /thi óggəni/ (*plural* -nies) *n* the origin and descent of the gods, or an account of this [Early 17C. < Greek *theogonia* 'birth of the gods'] —**theogonic** /theé ə gónnik/ *adj* —**theogonist** *n*

theol. *abbr* RELIG **1.** theologian **2.** theological **3.** theology

theologian /theé ə lőjən/ *n* an expert in, or student of, theology

theological /theé ə lójjik'l/, **theologic** /-lójjik/ *adj* relating to, using, engaged in, or typical of theology —**theologically** *adv*

theological virtues *npl* faith, hope, and charity, the three spiritual graces that, according to Christian theology, are given directly by God

theologize /thi óllə jīz/ (-gizes, -gizing, -gized), **theologise** (-gises, -gising, -gised) *v* **1.** *vt* to give a theological or religious significance to something **2.** *vi* to theorize, speculate, or discourse on religious topics —**theologizer** *n*

theology /thi ólləji/ (*plural* -gies) *n* **1. STUDY OF RELIGION** the study of religion, especially the Christian faith and God's relation to the world **2. RELIGIOUS THEORY** a religious theory, school of thought, or system of belief **3. COURSE OF RELIGIOUS TRAINING** a course of specialized religious training, especially one intended to lead students to a vocation in the Christian Church [14C. Via French and Latin < Greek *theologia* 'study of divine things'] —**theologist** *n*

theomachy /thi ómməki/ (*plural* -chies) *n* a battle among gods or against gods [Late 16C. < Greek *theomakhia* 'fighting of the gods']

theomorphic /theé ə máwrfik/ *adj* in the form or likeness of a deity [Late 19C. < Greek *theomorphos* 'of divine form'] —**theomorphism** *n*

theonomy /thi ónnəmi/ *n* the state of being governed by God, a god, or priests —**theonomous** *adj*

theophany /thi óffəni/ (*plural* -nies) *n* the appearance of a god in a visible form to a human being [Mid-17C. Via medieval Latin < Greek *theophaneia* 'appearance of the gods'] —**theophanic** /theé ə fánnik/ *adj*

Theophilus /theé óffiləss/ *n* a crater on the Moon northwest of Mare Nectaris. It is approximately 100 km/60 mi. in diameter and has a central mountain 2200 m/7200 ft in height.

Theophrastus /theé ə frástəss/ (372?–287 BC) Greek philosopher. Succeeding Aristotle as head of the Lyceum in Athens, he is remembered for an influential treatise on botany and his *Characters*, sketches of personality types.

theophylline /theé ə fílleen, -fíllin, -leen, -lin/ *n* a white crystalline alkaloid. Source: tea leaves or synthetically made. Use: vasodilator, diuretic, treatment of bronchial asthma. Formula: $C_7H_8N_7O_2.H_2O$. [Late 19C. < modern Latin *Thea* (see THEINE) + PHYLLO-]

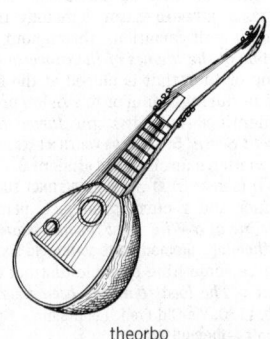

theorbo

theorbo /thi áwr bō/ *n* a stringed instrument from the 17th century similar to the lute except larger and with an extra set of bass strings longer than the main set [Early 17C. Via Italian *tiorba* < Turkish *torba* 'bag'] —**theorbist** *n*

theorem /theé rəm/ *n* **1.** a proposition or formula in mathematics or logic that is provable from a set of axioms and basic assumptions **2.** an idea that is accepted or proposed as true [Mid-16C. Via late Latin < Greek *theōrēma* 'speculation' < *theōrein* 'look at' < *theōros* 'spectator'] —**theorematic** /theérə máttik/ *adj* —**theorematically** *adv* —**theoremic** /theer reémik/ *adj*

theoretical /theer réttik'l/, **theoretic** /-réttik/ *adj* **1. BASED ON THEORY** about, involving, or based on theory **2. DEALING WITH THEORY** dealing with theory or speculation rather than practical applications **3. SPECULATIVE** inclined to or skilled in speculative contemplation or theorizing **4. HYPOTHETICAL** existing only in theory [Early 17C. < late Latin *theoreticus* < Greek *theoretikos* < *theōrētos* 'observable' < *theorein* 'look at']

theoretically /theer réttikli/ *adv* **1. IN THEORY, NOT REALITY** in theory only, not in reality ○ *Time travel is theoretically possible.* **2. IN TERMS OF WHAT IS POSSIBLE** in terms of what is possible in theory ○ *Theoretically speaking, it could be done.* **3. SUPPOSEDLY** supposedly or ideally, but probably not in reality ○ *Can we still win the election? Yes, theoretically.*

theoretician /theerə tísh'n/ *n* somebody who is skilled in considering theories, or is learned in the theoretical aspect of a subject

theoretics /theer réttiks/ *n* the theoretical or speculative aspect of a subject (*takes a singular or plural verb*)

theorise *vi* another spelling of **theorize**

theorist /theé e rīst, theérist/ *n* somebody who holds or expounds a theory

theorize /theé ə rīz, theér īz/ (-rizes, -rizing, -rized), **theorise** (-rises, -rising, -rised) *v* **1.** *vi* to speculate or form a theory about something **2.** *vt* to conceive of something in a theoretical way ○ *Research scientists were able to theorize the existence of the particle before it was actually discovered.* —**theorization** /theé ə rī záysh'n, theér ī-/ *n* —**theorizer** *n*

theory /theéri/ (*plural* -ries) *n* **1. RULES AND TECHNIQUES** the body of rules, ideas, principles, and techniques that applies to a subject, especially when seen as distinct from actual practice ○ *economic theories* ○ *Many coaches have a good grasp of the theory of football but can't motivate players.* **2. SPECULATION** abstract thought or contemplation **3. IDEA FORMED BY SPECULATION** an idea of or belief about something arrived at through speculation or conjecture ○ *She believed in the theory that you catch more flies with honey than with vinegar.* **4. HYPOTHETICAL CIRCUMSTANCES** a set of circumstances or principles that is hypothetical ○ *That's theory, but it may not work out in practice.* **5. SCIENTIFIC PRINCIPLE TO EXPLAIN PHENOMENA** a set of facts, propositions, or principles analysed in their relation to one another and used, especially in science, to explain phenomena [Late 16C. Via late Latin < Greek *theōria* 'contemplation, theory' < *theōros* 'spectator'] ◇ **in theory** under hypothetical or ideal circumstances but perhaps not in reality

theory of games *n* MATHS same as **game theory**

~~theorys~~ incorrect spelling of **theories**

theos. *abbr* RELIG **1.** theosophical **2.** theosophy

theosophy /thi óssəfi/ (*plural* -phies) *n* any religious philosophy based on intuitive insight into the nature of God [Mid-17C. Via medieval Latin < late Greek *theosophia* 'knowledge of the gods'] —**theosophic** /theé ə sóffik/ *adj* —**theosophical** *adj* —**theosophically** *adv* —**theosophism** *n* —**theosophist** *n*

Theosophy *n* the teachings of the Theosophical Society, a religious movement founded in New York in 1875, incorporating chiefly Buddhist and Brahmanic theories such as reincarnation and karma —**Theosophical** *adj* —**Theosophist** *n*

Thera /theérə/ island and tourist centre in the Cyclades group, Greece, north of Crete. Destroyed by a volcanic eruption in 1500 BC, it is sometimes claimed as the origin of the Atlantis legend. Population: 10,000 (1994). Area: 76 sq. km/29 sq. mi.

therap., **therapeut.** *abbr* MED **1.** therapeutic **2.** therapeutics

therapeutic /thérrə pyóotik/ *adj* **1.** relating to, involving, or used in the treatment of disease or disorders **2.** working or done to maintain somebody's health [Mid-16C. < French *therapeutique* or late Latin *therapeutica* < Greek *therapeutēs* 'somebody who treats' < *therapeuein* (see THERAPY)] —**therapeutically** *adv*

therapeutic cloning *n* the use of cloning to produce new body tissues from stem cells, for use in the treatment of disease or injury. ◊ **reproductive cloning**

therapeutic index *n* the ratio of the dose of a drug that causes cell damage to the dose typically needed to effect a cure. Use: indicates relative drug safety.

therapeutics /thérrə pyóotiks/ *n* the branch of medicine that deals with methods of treatment and healing, especially the use of drugs to treat diseases (*takes a singular verb*)

therapist /thérrəpist/ *n* **1.** somebody trained to treat disease, disorders, or injuries, especially somebody who uses methods other than drugs and surgery **2.** *US* a psychoanalyst or a professional from another school of psychotherapy who is trained to treat mental and emotional problems with psychological methods

therapsid /thə rápsid/ *n* an extinct reptile of an order that lived during the Permian and Triassic periods. Many therapsids are thought to be ancestors of the mammals. Order: Therapsida. [Early 20C. < modern Latin *Therapsida* < Greek *thēr* 'wild animal' + *hapsis* 'vault']

therapy /thérrəpi/ (*plural* **-pies**) *n* **1.** treatment of physical, mental, or behavioural disorders that is meant to cure or rehabilitate somebody (*often used in combination*) ○ *radiation therapy* **2.** *N Am* psychoanalysis or techniques from another school of psychotherapy, intended to treat mental and emotional problems with psychological methods [Mid-19C. Via modern Latin < Greek *therapeia* < *therapeuein* 'treat medically' < *theraps* 'attendant']

Theravada /thérrə vaádə/ *n* the doctrines of the Hinayana Buddhists [Late 19C. < Pali, 'doctrine of the elders']

there *stressed* /thair/; *unstressed* /thər/ CORE MEANING: an adverb used to indicate a place, either one that has already been mentioned or is understood, or one indicated by pointing or looking ○ *I don't know how to get there by car.* ○ *May I sit there?*
1. *adv* IN OR TO THAT PLACE used to indicate position in or motion towards a place relatively distant from the speaker **2.** *adv* AT THAT POINT used to refer to a point reached in an activity or process ○ *I suggest we pause there and have coffee.* ○ *And there we end our news bulletin.* **3.** *adv* ON THAT MATTER on that matter, or with respect to that ○ *I can't agree with you there.* **4.** *adv* AT SUCCESSFUL POINT used to indicate that something has reached a final or successful point or stage ○ *We're not the best yet, but we're getting there.* **5.** *adv* USED TO IDENTIFY used to identify somebody or something emphatically ○ *They ran into that house there.* **6.** *pron* INTRODUCING SENTENCE used to introduce a sentence stating that something exists, develops, or can be seen ○ *There's a stain on this sweater.* ○ *There remain several important issues to be discussed.* **7.** *interj* USED TO EXPRESS FEELINGS used to express strong feelings such as anger, satisfaction, relief, finality, or reassurance ○ *There! I told you she would make it.* [Old English *þǣr* < Indo-European] ◇ **be there for somebody** to be ready to give your support, sympathy, or friendship to somebody ◇ **not all there** not fully conscious, rational, or aware of something ◇ **there and then** immediately and in that very place ◇ **there or thereabouts** there or somewhere nearby (*informal*) ◇ **there, there** used to console, soothe, or comfort somebody ○ *There, there. Don't cry.* ◇ **there you are 1.** used when giving somebody something **2.** used to express triumph at having been seen to be right **3.** used to express resignation or sorrow at something that has happened

USAGE When the pronoun ***there*** opens a sentence with a subsequent linking verb like *be, appear,* or *seem,* the verb must agree with the grammatical subject coming *after* the verb: *There is* [not *are*] *a beach nearby. There are* [not *is*] *beaches and hotels nearby. There appear* [not *appears*] *to be mistakes in your essay. There appears* [not *appear*] *to be a mistake in your essay. There's* stands for 'there is'. It should be used only with a singular grammatical subject, as in: *There's a lot still to be done. There's a car in the garage.* It is nonstandard English to say: *There's three cars in the garage. There's a lot of children in the hall.* An easy way to ensure the correct agreement between the verb and the subject is to reorder the words in your sentences mentally without ***there***: *Three cars are in the garage. A lot of children are in the hall.* By contrast, you would never say *Three cars is in the garage. A lot of children is in the hall.* With compound grammatical subjects, ***there*** used with a singular linking verb is acceptable only when the compound subject is regarded not as two separate entities but as a single compound noun, or when two indefinite noun phrases are linked together. Thus it is acceptable to say: *There is/There's food and drink for everybody. There is a pen and a book on the table.* Stylistically, *There is/are* sentences tend to be flat and lacking in emphasis, so it is wise to avoid using them frequently.

USAGE See ***their.***

thereabouts /tháirə bowts, -bówts/, **thereabout** *US* /-bowt/ *adv* near that place, amount, number, or time ○ *We're expecting twenty guests or thereabouts.*

thereafter /tháir aáftər/ *adv* after that time or from that time on ○ *She graduated from college and shortly thereafter found a good job.*

thereat /tháir át/ *adv* (*formal or archaic*) **1.** at that time or place **2.** because of that

thereby /tháir bī́, -bī/ *adv* **1.** by means of or because of that ○ *Interest rates may fall, thereby discouraging investment.* **2.** in connection with or with reference to that ○ *Thereby hangs a tale.*

~~therefor~~ incorrect spelling of **therefore**

therefore /tháir fawr/ *adv* **1.** and so, or because of that ○ *This statement is true; therefore that statement must be false.* **2.** accordingly, or to that purpose ○ *We were forbidden to attend and therefore stayed at home.*

USAGE ***Therefore*** and ***thus*** are both fairly formal words that introduce a statement that is a consequence of the previous statement. They should not be used as empty connectors when what follows them does not derive from what precedes them: *Your mark in the test was 20%; therefore, you have failed.* It is tautologous to use *so therefore*: just ***therefore*** is sufficient. Punctuation around ***therefore*** requires some care. There is no comma between clauses where ***therefore*** is in the second clause, but instead a semicolon or a new sentence: *I had forgotten my key; therefore I could not open the door. She left the library at 4 o'clock. She was therefore not there when the murder took place.*

therefrom /tháir fróm/ *adv* from that place or thing (*archaic or formal*)

therein /tháir ín/ *adv* **1.** in or into that place (*formal*) **2.** in that matter, respect, or detail ○ *Therein lies the problem.*

thereinafter /tháirin aáftər/ *adv* from then on in something, especially a legal document (*formal*)

theremin /thérrə min/ *n* an early electronic musical instrument producing a tremulous sound whose pitch and volume is controlled by the distance between two antennae and the player's hands [Early 20C. After Leo *Theremin* (1896–1993), Russian engineer]

thereof /tháir óv/ *adv* (*formal*) **1.** of or about that ○ *a levy of £50 per annum or part thereof* **2.** from that as a reason or cause

thereon /tháir ón/ *adv* **1.** on the place or surface just mentioned (*formal*) ○ *a metal plate with an inscription thereon* **2.** regarding the point just mentioned (*archaic*) ○ *income and capital expense, including tax thereon*

Theresa of Lisieux /tə reézə əv lee zyő/ (1873–97) French nun. She is the author of *The Story of a Soul* (1898), in which she described the 'little way', the simple path to Christianity. With Joan of Arc, she is a patron saint of France.

thereto /tháir tóo/ *adv* to that thing just mentioned (*formal*)

theretofore /tháirtoo fáwr/ *adv* before or up to that time (*formal*)

thereunder /tháir úndər/ *adv* below that, or after that, especially in a legal document (*formal*)

thereupon /tháirə pón/ *adv* **1.** at that point in time ○ *She was found to have leaked information to a rival firm, and he thereupon insisted on her dismissal.* **2.** upon or concerning that point (*formal*)

therewith /tháir wíth, -wíth/, **therewithal** /tháir with áwl/ *adv* **1.** with that, or as well as that (*formal*) **2.** at that point, or immediately

~~therfore~~ incorrect spelling of **therefore**

therianthropic /theéri ən thróppik/ *adj* describes an imaginary being such as a centaur that is partly human and partly animal [Late 19C. < Greek *thērion* 'small wild animal' + *anthrōpos* 'human being'] —**therianthropism** /theéri ánthrəpizəm/ *n*

theriomorphic /theéri ō máwrfik/ *adj* in the form of an animal, or thought of as being in animal form [Late 19C. < Greek *thērion* 'small wild animal']

therizinosaur /thérri zínnə sawr/ *n* a herbivorous dinosaur that walked relatively upright and had a long neck, long arms and claws, and a short tail [Mid-20C. < modern Latin *Therizinosaurus*, literally 'scythe lizard', from the shape of its claws]

therm /thurm/ *n* a unit of heat equal to 100,000 British thermal units or 1.055 x 10^8 joules [Late 19C. < Greek *thermē* 'heat']

therm. *abbr* PHYS thermometer

therm- *prefix* same as **thermo-** (*used before vowels*)

thermae /thúr mee/ *npl* hot springs or baths, especially the public baths of ancient Rome [Mid-16C. Via Latin < Greek *thermai* < *thermē* 'heat']

thermaesthesia /thúrməss theézi ə/ *n* sensitivity to heat and cold, or to changes in temperature [Late 19C. < modern Latin < Greek *thermē* 'heat' + *aisthēsis* 'perception']

thermal /thúrm'l/ *adj* **1.** PHYS INVOLVING HEAT relating to, affected by, or producing heat ○ *thermal energy* **2.** HOT OR WARM hot or warm, especially because of the presence of hot springs ○ *thermal baths* **3.** MANUF USING HEAT FOR PRODUCTION using heat to produce something **4.** CLOTHING INTENDED FOR BODY WARMTH designed to retain body heat ○ *thermal underwear* ■ *n* METEOROL AIR COLUMN a current of warm air rising through cooler surrounding air ○ *watching hawks ride thermals* ■ **thermals** *npl* THERMAL CLOTHING thermal clothing, especially underwear (*informal*) [Mid-18C. < French < Greek *thermē* 'heat'] —**thermally** *adv*

thermal barrier *n* the problematic heating effect caused by air friction on an aircraft flying at high speed

thermal conductivity *n* the rate at which heat flows through a material between points at different temperatures, measured in watts per metre per degree. Symbol **λ**, *k*

thermal cracking *n* the breaking down of a hydrocarbon using heat

thermal efficiency *n* the work done by a heat engine divided by the thermal energy required to operate it

thermal imaging *n* the use of a device that detects the different levels of infrared energy given off by areas of different temperatures and displays these as a pattern on a screen

thermalize /thúrmə līz/ (**-izes, -izing, -ized**), **thermalise** (**-ises, -ising, -ised**) *vt* to slow neutrons in a nuclear reactor to give them thermal energy and so produce fission —**thermalization** /thúrmə lī záysh'n/ *n*

thermal neutron *n* PHYS same as **slow neutron**

thermal noise *n* noise in an electronic circuit such as an amplifier caused by electrons in conducting elements that are agitated by the absorption of heat

thermal pollution *n* the discharge of water or other liquid that is hot enough to harm wildlife into a natural body of water

thermal printer *n* an output device that produces visible characters by moving heated wires over specially treated heat-sensitive paper

thermal reactor *n* a nuclear reactor in which the chain reaction, and so fission, is brought about mainly by slow neutrons. It contains a moderator to slow down fast neutrons to thermal energies.

thermal shock *n* stress in a material caused by rapid changes in temperature, often resulting in fractures

thermesthesia *n* MED US spelling of **thermaesthesia**

thermic /thúrmik/ *adj* PHYS same as **thermal** *adj* (sense 1) [Mid-19C. < Greek *thermē* 'heat'] —**thermically** *adv*

-thermic *suffix* relating to heat ○ *exothermic* [< Greek *thermē* 'heat']

thermic lance *n* a cutting tool that works by heating steel wool held inside a steel tube

thermion /thúrmi ən, -on/ *n* a positive ion or electron given off by a very hot material such as a hot cathode —**thermionic** /thúrmi ónnik/ *adj*

thermionic current *n* an electric current generated by the flow of electrons leaving a heated cathode and flowing to other electrodes

thermionic emission *n* the emission of electrons or ions from a solid or liquid as a result of its thermal energy

thermionics /thúrmi ónniks/ *n* the branch of electronics that deals with the emission of electrons from hot bodies (*takes a singular verb*)

thermionic valve *n UK, ANZ, Can* an electronic component that consists of an evacuated glass tube containing a heated cathode that emits electrons, an anode that collects the electrons, and other electrodes. US term **thermionic tube**

thermistor /thur místər/ *n* a semiconductor device with a resistance that is very sensitive to temperature, resistance decreasing as the temperature increases [Mid-20C. Contraction of *thermal resistor*]

thermite process /thúrmīt-/ *n* INDUST same as **aluminothermy**

thermo- *prefix* **1.** heat ○ *thermochemistry* **2.** thermoelectricity ○ *thermocouple* [< Greek *thermē* 'heat']

thermobaric /thúrmō bárrik/ *adj* describes a bomb that disperses a cloud of explosive material that then ignites, creating a pressure wave

thermobarometer /thúrmō bə rómmitər/ *n* an instrument that measures both air temperature and pressure

thermocautery /thúrmō káwtəri/ *n* the use of a heated instrument such as a hot wire to destroy tissue, especially in cauterizing wounds

thermochemistry /thúrmō kémmistri/ *n* the branch of chemistry that deals with the relationship between chemical action and heat —**thermochemical** /thúrmō kémmik'l/ *adj*—**thermochemically** *adv*—**thermochemist** *n*

thermocline /thúrmō klīn/ *n* a layer of water, e.g. in a lake, where there is an abrupt change in temperature that separates the warmer surface water from the colder deep water

thermocouple /thúrmō kup'l/ *n* a device for measuring temperature in which two wires of different metals are joined. The potential difference between the wires is a measure of the temperature of something they touch.

thermoduric /thúrmō dyoórik/ *adj* describes a microorganism that is capable of surviving high temperatures or pasteurization [Early 20C. < THERMO- + Latin *durare* 'endure']

thermodynamic /thúrmō dī námmik/, **thermodynamical** /-námmik'l/ *adj* **1.** relating to or involving thermodynamics **2.** obeying or affected by the laws of thermodynamics —**thermodynamically** *adv*

thermodynamics /thúrmō dī námmiks/ *n* the branch of physics that deals with the conversions from one to another of various forms of energy and how these affect temperature, pressure, volume, mechanical action, and work (*takes a singular verb*) ■ *npl* thermodynamic processes or phenomena (*takes a plural verb*) —**thermodynamicist** *n*

thermodynamic temperature *n* PHYS same as **absolute temperature**

thermoelectric /thúrmō i léktrik/, **thermoelectrical** /-léktrik'l/ *adj* involving a direct relationship between temperature of materials and the production of electricity —**thermoelectrically** *adv*

thermoelectricity /thúrmō ilek tríssəti, -éllek-/ *n* electricity produced by maintaining a temperature difference at the point where two different materials come into contact, e.g. in a thermocouple

thermoelectron /thérmō i lék tron/ *n* an electron emitted by a material that is at high temperature

thermoform /thúrmō fawrm/ (**-forms**, **-forming**, **-formed**) *vt* to shape plastic using heat and pressure —**thermoformable** *adj*

thermogenesis /thúrmō jénnəssiss/ *n* the production of heat in a person's or animal's body by physiological processes, especially metabolic processes —**thermogenetic** /-jə néttik/ *adj*

thermogram /thúrmə gram/ *n* **1.** an image or record of the heat radiating from the body, made by thermography **2.** a record of temperatures made by a thermograph

thermograph /thúrmə graaf, -graf/ *n* **1.** an instrument that continuously records temperature readings **2.** a device that shows patterns of heat radiated from a person's or an animal's body, used in diagnostic thermography

thermography /thər móggrəfi/ *n* **1.** the recording of a visual image of the heat that bodies emit as infrared radiation. The technique is used to diagnose disease and tumours, especially breast tumours. **2.** the process of producing a raised image on a printed surface by using heat to fuse a resinous powder and wet ink to the surface —**thermographer** *n* —**thermographic** /thúrmə gráffik/ *adj*—**thermographically** *adv*

thermojunction /thúrmō júngksh'n/ *n* a point at which two dissimilar metals of differing temperatures come into contact, producing a thermoelectric current

thermolabile /thúrmō láy bīl/ *adj* describes substances such as some enzymes that are easily destroyed or altered by heat

thermoluminescence /thúrmō loomi néss'nss/ *n* phosphorescence released by some previously irradiated substances when they are heated. The process is used by geologists and archaeologists to date rocks and pottery. —**thermoluminescent** *adj*

thermolysis /thər mólləssiss/ *n* **1.** loss of body heat, e.g. by sweating **2.** the breaking down of a substance by heat —**thermolytic** /thúrmə líttik/ *adj*

thermomagnetic /thúrmō mag néttik/ *adj* relating to the relationship between heat and magnetism, and especially the effects of heat upon the magnetic properties of a substance

thermometer /thər mómmitər/ *n* an instrument for measuring temperature, e.g. an instrument with a graduated glass tube and a bulb containing mercury or alcohol that rises in the tube when the temperature increases [Mid-17C. < French *thermomètre* < Greek *thermos* 'warm' < *thermē* 'heat' + *-mètre* (see -METER)]

thermometry /thər mómmətri/ *n* temperature measurement and the branch of physics concerned with measuring temperature —**thermometric** /thúrmō méttrik/ *adj* —**thermometrical** *adj* —**thermometrically** *adv*

thermonasty /thúrmə nasti/ *n* the movement of plant parts in response to a change in temperature, e.g. the opening of flowers

thermonuclear /thúrmō nyoókli ər/ *adj* relating to or making use of nuclear fusion ○ *thermonuclear energy* ○ *thermonuclear war*

thermonuclear reaction *n* a reaction in which nuclei of light atoms fuse together producing large amounts of energy. This type of reaction occurs at very high temperatures, e.g. those inside the Sun.

thermoperiodism /thúrmō peéri ədizəm/, **thermoperiodicity** /-peeri ə dísséti/ *n* the response of a plant to cycles of temperature such as the regular cycles of day and night —**thermoperiodic** /thúrmō peeri óddik/ *adj*

thermophile /thúrmə fīl/, **thermophil** /-fil/ *n* an organism that thrives in a warm environment, e.g. a bacterium —**thermophile** *adj*—**thermophilic** /thúrmə fíllik/ *adj*—**thermophilous** /thər móffələss/ *adj*

thermophylous /thúrmō fílləss/ *adj* bearing leaves only in the warmer part of the year

thermopile /thúrmə pīl/ *n* a set of thermocouples, either joined in series for increased voltage or in parallel for increased current, used to measure radiant energy or to convert radiant energy into electric current

thermoplastic /thúrmo plástik/ *n* a substance that becomes soft and pliable when heated, without a change in its intrinsic properties. Polystyrene and polythene are thermoplastics. —**thermoplastic** *adj*—**thermoplasticity** /thúrmō pla stíssəti/ *n*

Thermopylae /thər móppəli/ pass in ancient Greece, northwest of Athens, that controlled entry to central Greece. It was the site of the battle of 480 BC fought by Leonidas I and thousands of his troops, all of whom were killed by the Persian army, led by Xerxes I.

thermoreceptor /thúrmō ri séptər/ *n* a sensory receptor, usually a nerve ending in the skin, that is stimulated by heat or cold

thermoregulation /thúrmo reggyoō láysh'n/ *n* the maintenance of a steady body temperature regardless of changes in the environment —**thermoregulate** /thúrmo réggyoō layt/ *vi* —**thermoregulator** *n*

thermoremanent /thúrmō rémmənənt/ *adj* relating to or being the permanent magnetism that something such as molten rock acquires from the Earth's magnetic field as it cools and hardens

Thermos /thúrməss/ *tdmk* a trademark for an insulated or vacuum container used to hold a liquid and maintain it at a constant temperature

thermoscope /thúrməskōp/ *n* an instrument that measures changes in temperature by their effects on a substance, e.g. the change in volume of a gas —**thermoscopic** /thúrmə skóppik/ *adj* —**thermoscopical** *adj* —**thermoscopically** *adv*

thermosetting /thúrmō seting/ *adj* describes a plastic that sets permanently when heated

thermosphere /thúrmə sfeer/ *n* the region of the atmosphere above the mesosphere in which temperature steadily increases with height, beginning at about 85 km/53 mi. above the Earth's surface

thermostable /thúrmō stáyb'l/ *adj* describes substances such as some toxins that are able to withstand heat without being destroyed or altered —**thermostability** /thúrmō stə bílləti/ *n*

thermostat /thúrmə stat/ *n* **1.** a device that regulates temperature by means of a temperature sensor such as a bimetallic strip. Thermostats are used in

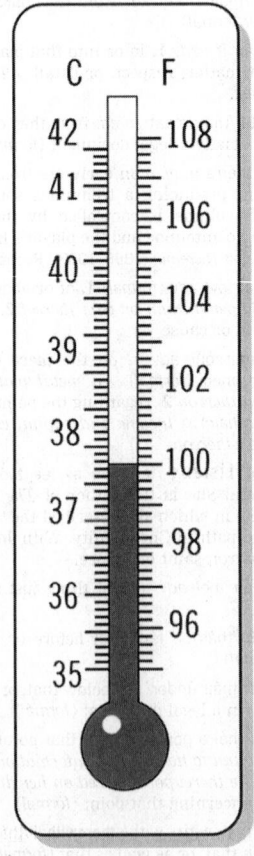

thermometer

vehicle engines and domestic heating systems. **2.** a device that activates a mechanism or system such as a fire alarm or a sprinkler system in response to a change in temperature —**thermostatic** /thúrmə státtik/ *adj* —**thermostatically** *adv*

thermotaxis /thúrmə táksiss/ *n* movement of a living organism towards or away from a heat source —**thermotactic** /thúrmə táktik/ *adj* —**thermotaxic** *adj*

thermotherapy /thúrmō thérrəpi/ (*plural* **-pies**) *n* the use of heat to alleviate pain and stiffness, especially in joints and muscles, and to increase circulation, or a procedure involving this

thermotropism /thúrmō trṓpizəm/ *n* the movement of a plant part towards or away from a source of heat —**thermotropic** /-trṓpik, -tróppik/ *adj*

-thermy *suffix* heat ○ *diathermy* [< modern Latin *-thermia* < Greek *thermē* 'heat']

theropod /theérə pod/ *n* a carnivorous dinosaur with strong hind legs and short front limbs, e.g. a tyrannosaur or megalosaur. Suborder: Theropoda. [Early 20C. < modern Latin *Theropoda* < Greek *thēr* 'wild animal' + *pod-* 'foot'] —**theropodan** /thi róppədən/ *adj*

Theroux /thə roó/, **Paul** (*b.* 1941) US writer. He is known for his travel books such as *The Great Railway Bazaar* (1975) and his novels such as *The Mosquito Coast* (1981). Full name **Theroux, Paul Edward**

> 'Travel is a vanishing act, a solitary trip down a pinched line of geography to oblivion.'
> [Paul Theroux, *The Old Patagonian Express: By Train Through the Americas*; 1979]

~~**thesarus**~~ incorrect spelling of **thesaurus**

thesaurus /thə sáwrəss/ (*plural* **-ri** /-rī/ or **-ruses**) *n* **1. BOOK OF WORD GROUPS** a book that lists words related to each other in meaning, usually giving synonyms and antonyms **2. BOOK OF SUBJECT-RELATED VOCABULARY** a dictionary of words relating to a specific subject **3. TREASURY** a place in which valuable things are stored [Early 19C. Via Latin, 'treasury' < Greek *thēsauros* 'storehouse']

these /t͟heez/ *pron, det* the form of 'this' used before a plural noun or with a multiple referent ○ (pron) *These are the people I was telling you about.* ○ (det) *These delays, along with the paperwork, can be costly for banks.* [Old English *þæs, þās*, plural of *þes* (see THIS)]

theses plural of **thesis**

Theseus /theéssi əss, theésyooss/ *n* in Greek mythology, a hero who performed many brave deeds, including slaying the Minotaur, defeating the Amazons, and descending into Hades to rescue Persephone

thesis /theésiss/ (*plural* **theses** /theésseez/) *n* **1. LENGTHY ACADEMIC PAPER** a dissertation based on original research, especially as work towards an academic degree **2. PROPOSITION** a proposition advanced as an argument **3. STATEMENT** an unproved statement, especially one serving as a premise in an argument **4. ESSAY SUBJECT** a subject for an essay **5.** MUSIC **DOWNBEAT** the downbeat of a bar of music **6.** LITERAT **STRESSED SYLLABLE** a long syllable, on which the stress naturally falls, in classical Greek and Latin poetry **7.** LITERAT **UNSTRESSED SYLLABLE** a short unstressed syllable in modern accentual poetry **8.** PHILOSOPHY **FIRST STAGE OF DIALECTIC** the first of three stages in Hegelian dialectic [14C. Via Latin < Greek, 'proposition, stressed beat']

thespian /théspi ən/ *n* somebody who acts on the stage ■ *adj* relating to the theatre or the profession of acting (*literary*) [Early 19C. < *Thespis*, Greek poet (6C BC), regarded as the father of Greek tragedy]

Thess. *abbr* BIBLE Thessalonians

Thessalonian /théssə lṓni ən/ *n* somebody who came from the ancient Greek city of Thessaloníki [Early 16C. < Latin *Thessalonica*, Greek *Thessalonikē* 'Thessaloníki'] —**Thessalonian** *adj*

Thessalonians /théssə lṓni ənz/ *n* either of two books of the Bible that were originally letters addressed to the Christians of Thessalonica (modern Thessaloníki) and are traditionally attributed to St Paul (*takes a singular verb*) See table at **Bible**

Thessaloníki /théssələ neéki/ capital city of the department of Thessaloníki, northeastern Greece. Population: 383,967 (1991).

Thessaly /théssəli/ region in north-central Greece, consisting mainly of a broad plain. Area: 13,940 sq. km/5,382 sq. mi. —**Thessalian** /the sáyli ən/ *n, adj*

theta /theétə/ *n* the eighth letter of the Greek alphabet, represented in the English alphabet as 'th'. See table at **alphabet** [Early 17C. Via Greek < Phoenician]

theta rhythm, theta wave *n* a pattern of brain waves with a frequency between 4 and 7 Hz seen on an electroencephalogram. The pattern is normal in children under the age of 12 but in adults may be a sign of stress or mental disorder.

Thetford /thétfərd/ town of Saxon origin in Norfolk, eastern England. Population: 20,058 (1991).

thetic /théttik/, **thetical** /théttik'l/ *adj* in classical poetry, relating to or having stress [Late 17C. < Greek *thetikos* < *thetos* 'placed, stressed' < *tithenai* 'to place'] —**thetically** *adv*

theurgy /theé urji/ *n* **1.** RELIG **SUPERNATURAL OR DIVINE INTERVENTION** the supposed intervention of supernatural or divine powers in human affairs **2.** RELIG **PERSUADING SUPERNATURAL TO INTERVENE** the art of trying to secure intervention of supernatural or divine powers in human affairs **3.** PARANORMAL **MAGIC PERFORMED FOR GOOD** magic with the alleged help of benevolent spirits, as practised by neo-Platonists [Mid-16C. Via late Latin < Greek *theourgia* 'ritual, mystery' < *theos* 'god' + *ergon* 'work'] —**theurgic** /thi úrjik/ *adj* —**theurgically** *adv* —**theurgist** *n*

thew /thyoo/ *n* muscle or muscular strength (*archaic; often used in the plural*) [Old English *þēaw* 'custom, habit' < Indo-European, 'to watch'] —**thewy** *adj*

they /t͟hay/ *pron* **1. PEOPLE OR THINGS ALREADY MENTIONED** the people or things already mentioned or identified, or understood by both the speaker and hearer **2. PEOPLE IN GENERAL** used to refer to people in general when making statements about the things people do, think, or say ○ *As people and businesses move to the suburbs, bank branches follow, so they say.* **3.** ⚠ **HE OR SHE** used instead of 'he' or 'she' to refer to a person without specifying gender (*informal*) ○ *A friend phoned the other day and they told me what you had said.* [12C. < Old Norse *þeir*]

USAGE Because English does not have a gender-neutral third person singular pronoun that can be used to refer to people, ***they***, together with the associated words *their* and *them*, is often used in this role and is a revival of an older use that was once well established in English. In more formal contexts, and when the individuality of the subject is significant, it is necessary to use *he or she, his or her*, or *him or her*, but these phrases are too cumbersome to provide a solution in informal conversational usage, e.g. *Everyone taking the test should do the best they can. If anyone asks who I am, tell them that I'm his sister.* A way of avoiding the need to use *he or she* in writing can be to use a plural: *Students taking the test should do the best they can.*

---

they'd /t͟hayd/ *contr* **1.** they had **2.** they would

they'll /t͟hayl/ *contr* **1.** they shall **2.** they will

they're /t͟hair/ *contr* they are

USAGE See ***their***.

---

they've /t͟hayv/ *contr* they have

THI *abbr* PHYS temperature-humidity index

thi- *prefix* same as **thio-** (*used before vowels*)

thiabendazole /thī ə béndəzōl/, **tiabendazole** /tī ə-/ *n* a white compound. Use: treatment of parasitic worm infestations, fungal infections. Formula: $C_{10}H_7N_3S$. [Mid-20C. Contraction of THIAZOLE + BENZENE + IMIDAZOLE]

thiamine /thī ə meen, -əmin/, **thiamin** /-min/ *n* a B vitamin that plays a role in carbohydrate metabolism. Source: grains, meat, yeasts.

thiazide /thī ə zīd/ *n* a compound belonging to a group of compounds that inhibit the reabsorption of sodium and increase the release of calcium by the kidneys, promoting greater water excretion. Use: diuretic, treatment of high blood pressure. [Mid-20C. < *thiadiazine* chemical compound (< THIO- + AZINE) + OXIDE]

thiazine /thī ə zeen/ *n* an organic compound containing a ring composed of four carbon atoms, a sulphur atom, and a nitrogen atom. Use: dyes, tranquillizers.

thiazole /thī ə zōl/, **thiazol** /thīəzol/ *n* **1.** a volatile colourless liquid with a sharp odour. Use: dyes, fungicides. Formula: C_3H_3NS. **2.** a compound derived from thiazole. Use: dyes, fungicides, chemical-reaction accelerators.

thick /thik/ *adj* **1. DEEP OR BROAD** of relatively large extent from surface to surface or side to side ○ *a thick carpet* ○ *The child wrote her name in thick capital letters.* **2. LARGE IN DIAMETER** having a large diameter ○ *a thick cable* **3. IN DEPTH OR BREADTH** having a particular depth or breadth ○ *a wall two feet thick* **4. VISCOUS** having a liquid consistency that is not free-flowing ○ *thick paint* **5. DENSE** composed of many densely packed objects ○ *a thick forest* ○ *thick hair* **6. OF HEAVY FABRIC** made of thick material ○ *thick socks* **7. FILLED** densely covered or filled ○ *The air was thick with mosquitoes.* **8. HARD TO SEE THROUGH** permitting little or no light to enter ○ *a thick mist* **9. PRONOUNCED** readily noticeable or distinct ○ *a thick country accent* **10. NOT CLEAR** not articulating words clearly ○ *a voice thick with emotion* **11. OFFENSIVE TERM** an offensive term meaning regarded as lacking the ability to learn and understand quickly (*informal insult*) **12. FRIENDLY** allied in a close relationship (*informal*) ○ *They seem very thick with each other.* **13. PREVENTING CLEAR THOUGHT** feeling numb and not conducive to clear thought or perception, e.g. because of a cold or a hangover (*informal*) ○ *woke up with a thick head* ■ *adv* **MAKING DEEP LAYER** in a way that produces something deep, broad, or dense ○ *Spread the jam on thick.* ■ *n* **1. MOST ACTIVE PART** the most intense, crowded, or busiest part of something ○ *in the thick of the battle* **2. DENSEST PART** the part of something with the greatest depth, density, or breadth ○ *in the thick of the jungle* [Old English *þicce* < Germanic] —**thickly** *adv* ◇ **be a bit thick** to go beyond what is fair or reasonable (*informal*) ○ *It's a bit thick, expecting me to look after the baby for nothing.* ◇ **thick and fast** in large numbers and with great frequency ◇ **through thick and thin** no matter what might happen

thicken /thíkən/ (**-ens, -ening, -ened**) *v* **1.** *vti* to become thick or thicker, or make something thick or thicker **2.** *vi* to become more complicated or puzzling ○ *The plot thickens.* —**thickener** *n* —**thickening** *n*

thicket /thíkit/ *n* a dense or tangled growth of small trees or bushes

thickfilm technology /thík film-/ *n* a method of fabricating electronic circuitry in which a glaze is printed onto a glass or ceramic support, then wiring and components such as microchips are added

thickhead /thík hed/ *n* an offensive term that deliberately insults somebody's intelligence (*slang insult*) —**thickheaded** /thík héddid/ *adj* —**thickheadedness** *n*

thickie /thíki/, **thicky** (*plural* **-ies**) *n* an offensive term that deliberately insults somebody's intelligence (*slang insult*)

thick-knee *n* a large long-legged shorebird with distinctive enlarged knee joints. Native to: mainly semidesert regions. Family: Burhinidae.

thickness /thíknəss/ *n* **1. THICK QUALITY** the quality or state of being thick **2. DIMENSION** the dimension between two surfaces of an object, especially the shortest dimension as opposed to the width or the length **3. SINGLE LAYER** an individual layer **4. THICK PART** a part of something that is thick

thicko /thíkō/ (*plural* **-os**) *n* an offensive term that deliberately insults somebody's intelligence (*slang insult*)

thickset /thík sét/ *adj* **1.** having a stocky physique **2.** growing closely together ○ *a thickset bed of peonies*

thick-skinned *adj* **1.** not easily offended by criticism or insults **2.** insensitive to other people's feelings or circumstances

thick-witted *adj* an offensive term meaning regarded as unintelligent (*insult*) —**thick-wittedly** *adv* —**thick-wittedness** *n*

thicky *n* another spelling of **thickie** (*slang offensive*)

thief /theef/ (*plural* **thieves** /theevz/) *n* somebody who steals something, especially one who intends to escape notice [Old English *þēof* < Germanic]

Thiele /tḗeli/, **Colin** (*b.* 1920) Australian writer. His volumes of poetry and books for children include *Storm Boy* (1963). Full name **Thiele, Colin Milton**

~~**thier**~~ incorrect spelling of **their**

thieve /theev/ (**thieves, thieving, thieved**) *vti* to steal something, or steal things [Old English *þēofian* < *þēof* (see THIEF)] —**thievery** *n*

thievish /theévish/ *adj* **1.** relating to or characteristic of thieves **2.** given to stealing things [15C. < *thieves*, plural of THIEF] —**thievishly** *adv* —**thievishness** *n*

thigh /thī/ *n* **1.** the top of the leg between the knee and the hip **2.** the part of an animal's leg that corresponds to a human thigh [Old English *þēoh* < Indo-European, 'to swell']

thighbone /thī́bōn/ *n* ANAT same as **femur** (sense 1)

thigmotaxis /thígmo táksiss/ *n* the movement of an entire organism in response to contact with a solid object. ANZ, N Am term **stereotaxis** [Early 20C. < Greek *thigma* 'touch'] —**thigmotactic** *adj* —**thigmotactically** *adv*

thigmotropism /thig móttrəpizəm/ *n* a directional growth movement (**tropism**) of a plant part, especially a tendril, in response to physical contact with a surface [Early 20C. < Greek *thigma* 'touch'] —**thigmotropic** /thígmə trṓpik, -tróppik/ *adj*

thill /thill/ *n* either of the two shafts of a carriage or cart [15C. Origin ?]

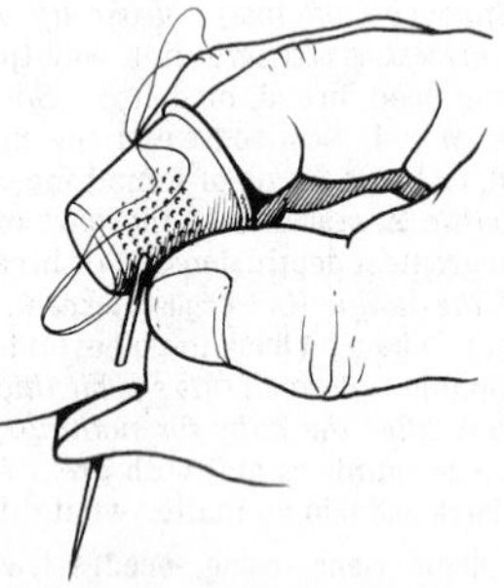

thimble

thimble /thímb'l/ *n* **1.** HANDICRAFT **COVER FOR FINGER WHEN SEWING** a small protective cap for a finger, used to push a needle through fabric **2.** NAUT **RING PROTECTING LOOP FROM WEAR** a metal ring, concave on the outside, that fits into a loop in a rope or an eye in a sail **3.** MECH ENG **METAL SLEEVE** a small metal tube or sleeve used in machinery [Old English *þȳmel* 'leather thumb protector' < *þūma* (see THUMB)]

thimbleberry /thímb'l beri/ (*plural* **-ries**) *n* **1.** a red or dark-purple thimble-shaped raspberry **2.** a bush that produces thimbleberries. Native to: North America. Latin name: *Rubus parviflorus* or *Rubus occidentalis* or *Rubus odoratus*.

thimbleful /thímb'lfŏŏl/ *n* a very small amount of liquid

thimblerig /thímb'lrig/ *n* **1. GUESSING GAME USING TRICKERY** a trick in which a participant guesses which of three cups covers an object after somebody has moved them about, using sleight of hand to change the object's location **2.** *US* **SOMEBODY MOVING CUP** somebody moving the cup in thimblerig ■ *vt* (**-rigs, -rigging, -rigged**) **SWINDLE SOMEBODY** to cheat or swindle somebody —**thimblerigger** *n*

Thimbu ➧ **Thimphu**

thimerosal /thī mérrə sal/ *n N Am* same as **thiomersal** [Mid-20C. Probably contraction of THIO- + MERCURY + SALICYLATE]

Thimphu /thímfoo/, **Thimbu** /-boo/ capital city of Bhutan, situated in the western part of the country at an altitude of 2,368 m/7,770 ft. Population: 22,000 (1999).

thin /thin/ *adj* (**thinner, thinnest**) **1. SHALLOW OR NARROW** of relatively small extent from surface to surface or side to side ○ *A thin layer of snow covered the path.* ○ *Draw a thin line.* **2. OF SMALL DIAMETER** having a small diameter ○ *thin wire* **3. SLIM** having very little body fat **4. SPARSE** composed of few things widely spaced ○ *thin hair* ○ *a thin forest* **5. WATERY** with a free-flowing consistency similar to that of water ○ *a thin soup* ○ *thin paint* **6. LIGHTWEIGHT** made of light or flimsy material ○ *a thin summer dress* ○ *thin cotton socks* **7. EASY TO SEE THROUGH** permitting light to enter or pass through ○ *thin mist* **8. QUIET IN NOISE VOLUME** lacking volume or resonance ○ *a thin sound* **9. UNCONVINCING** lacking credibility or adequacy ○ *a thin excuse* **10.** *US* **WEAK** lacking intensity or colour **11.** PHOTOGRAPHY **LACKING CONTRAST** of a photographic negative, lacking density or contrast ■ *adv* **IN THIN MANNER** in a way that produces something shallow, narrow, or sparse ○ *Spread the paint thin.* ■ *vti* (**thins, thinning, thinned**) **MAKE OR BECOME THINNER** to reduce something in thickness or number, or become reduced in thickness or number ○ *You can thin the paint before you use it.* ○ *The crowd started to thin out in the evening.* [Old English *þynne* < Indo-European, 'stretch'] —**thinly** *adv* —**thinness** *n*

SYNONYMS ***thin, lean, slender, slim, emaciated, scraggy, scrawny, skinny***

CORE MEANING: without much flesh, the opposite of fat

thin having very little body fat ○ *I was surprised at how thin her face had become.* **lean** having no excess body fat and looking muscular and fit ○ *a tall lean runner* **slender** gracefully and attractively thin ○ *A tall, slender model walked down the fashion-show runway.* **slim** slender and well-proportioned ○ *Tall and slim, the ballerina's body had the tautness of an athlete's.* **emaciated** extremely thin, especially because of starvation or illness ○ *Aid officials in the war zone reported seeing seriously undernourished, even emaciated people.* **scraggy** *or* **scrawny** thin and bony ○ *a scraggy neck* ○ *A scraggy old cat lives in the barn.* **skinny** thin, especially in an unappealing or unhealthy way ○ *I think my arms and legs are too skinny.* ○ *A new-born chimpanzee looks like a skinny little thing compared with a human baby.*

thine /th̲īn/ *pron, det* belonging to or associated with you, when 'you' is singular (*archaic; used before a vowel*) ○ (pron) *Thine is the womb where our riches have birth.* ○ (det) *Know thine enemy.* [Old English *þīn*, possessive form of *þū* (see THOU[2])]

thinfilm technology /thín film-/ *n* a method of fabricating electronic circuitry in which a thin layer of semiconductor is applied to a glass or ceramic support, then wiring and passive components such as resistors are added

thing /thing/ *n* **1. OBJECT** an inanimate object ○ *What's that thing over there?* **2. UNSPECIFIED ITEM** an unnamed or unspecified object ○ *I need a few things in town.* **3. OCCURRENCE** something that occurs, or something that is done ○ *The fire was a terrible thing.* **4. WORD OR THOUGHT** a thought or an utterance ○ *Don't say another thing!* **5. DETAIL** a piece of information ○ *You forgot one important thing.* **6. SOMETHING AIMED AT** the objective of an action ○ *The thing is to win.* **7. MATTER OF CONCERN** a matter of responsibility or concern ○ *I have several things to do.* **8. DEED TO BE DONE** an act or deed done or to be done ○ *She promises to do great things.* **9. LIVING BEING** a person or animal, often spoken of affectionately ○ *The poor thing was soaked to the bone.* **10. GARMENT** an article of clothing ○ *This old thing?* **11. SOMETHING THAT CAN BE POSSESSED** an object or right that can be possessed or owned **12. PREFERRED ACTIVITY** a favourite activity or special interest (*informal*) ○ *Golf's not really my thing.* **13. FASHION** the current fashion (*informal*) ○ *When we were young, we considered it the latest thing.* **14. STRONG LIKE OR DISLIKE** a particularly strong feeling of attraction or repulsion (*informal*) ○ *He's got a thing about spiders.* **15. IDEAL** something that is needed or desirable (*informal*) ○ *Iced tea would be just the thing.* ■ **things** *npl* **1. BELONGINGS** personal items owned or carried ○ *You can leave your things in my room.* **2. APPARATUS** equipment for a particular activity ○ *a drawer for all my writing things* **3. AFFAIRS** general matters or circumstances ○ *How are things today?* [Old English *þing* 'assembly' < Germanic, 'time'] ◇ **all** *or* **other things being equal** in a situation in which there is little difference between two or more people or things ○ *Other things being equal, I would choose the cheaper holiday.* ◇ **be on to a good thing** to be in an advantageous or desirable situation ◇ **first things first** do not try to do things in the wrong order, omitting an important basic step ◇ **it comes to the same thing** it has the same result ◇ **make a (big) thing of something** to exaggerate the importance of something and make a fuss about it

ORIGIN The long-lost ancestral meaning of ***thing*** is 'time' (the related Gothic *theihs*, for example, meant 'time'). Its prehistoric Germanic precursor evolved semantically via 'appointed time' to 'judicial or legislative assembly'. This was the meaning it originally had in English, and it survives in other Germanic languages (the Icelandic parliament is known as the *Althing*, literally 'general assembly'). In English, however, the word moved on through 'subject for discussion in such an assembly' to 'subject in general, affair, matter' and finally 'entity, object'.

thingamabob /thíngəmə bob/, **thingumabob** *n* same as **thingamajig** [Mid-18C. Alteration of *thingumbob* < obsolete *thingum* (see THINGUMMY)]

thingamajig /thíngəməjig/, **thingumajig** *n* a word used when the proper word for something is not known or does not come to mind [Early 19C. < obsolete *thingum* (see THINGUMMY)]

thing-in-itself (*plural* **things-in-themselves**) *n* an object that exists even though we have no experience or perception of it [Translation of German *Ding an sich*]

thingness /thíngnəss/ *n* status as a material thing, as distinct from something that is abstract

thingumabob *n* another spelling of **thingamabob**

thingumajig *n* another spelling of **thingamajig**

thingummy /thíngəmi/ (*plural* **-mies**) *n* same as **thingamajig** [Late 18C. Alteration of obsolete *thingum* < THING]

thingy /thíngi/ (*plural* **-ies**) *n* same as **thingamajig**

think /thingk/ *v* (**thinks, thinking, thought** /thawt/ *or* **thunk** *US nonstandard* /thungk/) **1.** *vti* **FORM THOUGHTS** to use the mind to consider ideas and make judgments ○ *Think carefully before you start writing.* **2.** *vt* **HAVE SOMETHING AS OPINION** to believe something, or have something as an opinion ○ *I don't think it will rain today.* ○ *She seems to think she's a good dancer.* **3.** *vti* **HAVE IN MIND** to bring something to mind ○ *I can't think what the date is today.* ○ *I hadn't thought about him for months.* **4.** *vti* **COMPREHEND SOMETHING** to imagine or understand something or the possibility of something ○ *I can't think of letting you leave so soon.* **5.** *vt* **CONCENTRATE ON SOMETHING** to focus the attention on something ○ *He thinks golf day and night.* **6.** *vi* **HAVE REGARD FOR SOMEBODY** to regard somebody with care or concern ○ *You need to think of your family.* **7.** *vt* **VIEW SOMEBODY OR SOMETHING AS SOMETHING** to regard somebody or something in a particular way ○ *Don't think me unkind.* **8.** *vti* **INTEND** to have something as a plan ○ *She thought she'd go out after dinner.* **9.** *vt* **FORESEE SOMETHING** to anticipate something happening ○ *I didn't think he'd actually do it.* ○ *I didn't think you'd be early.* **10.** *vt* **BE HEEDFUL OF SOMETHING** to be attentive or considerate enough to do something ○ *Didn't you think to ask about her mother?* **11.** *vi* **CHOOSE SOMETHING** to make a mental choice ○ *Think of a card and I'll try to guess what it is.* **12.** *vt* **INFLUENCE OUTCOME WITH MIND** to bring something to a particular condition using the mind ○ *Try to think the pain away.* ■ *n* **SPELL OF THINKING** an act of thinking, or a period of time spent thinking (*informal*) ○ *She sat down to have a think.* [Old English *þencan* < Indo-European] —**thinkable** *adj* ◇ **have got another think coming** used to say that somebody is mistaken (*informal*) ○ *If he thinks I'm going to help him he's got another think coming.* ◇ **I don't think** used to indicate that the opposite is true (*informal*) ○ *You can rely on him to be generous – I don't think!* ◇ **not think much of somebody** *or* **something** to regard somebody or something as not being very good ◇ **that's what you think!** used to say that somebody is quite wrong in a belief, assumption, or expectation (*informal*) ○ *"It shouldn't take too long." "That's what you think!"* ◇ **think better of something** to change your mind and decide not to do something ○ *She was about to speak her mind, but then thought better of it.* ◇ **think nothing of something** to regard something as not being unusual ○ *She thinks nothing of working all night to finish a project.* ◇ **think twice** to consider something very carefully ○ *You should think twice about lending them so much money.*

think out *vt* to consider something carefully, taking account of possible problems or consequences ○ *He hadn't really thought the policy out properly.*

think over *vt* to reflect on something ○ *Maybe you'd like to think it over before you sign.*

think through *vt* to consider or reflect on something carefully, especially in order to reach a decision ○ *I needed some time to think it through.*

think up *vt* to invent or devise something ○ *I've thought up an easy way to do it.*

thinker /thíngkər/ *n* **1.** somebody known for being intellectually creative and authoritative, especially in a particular field of study ○ *a leading political thinker* **2.** somebody who thinks deeply about things

CULTURAL NOTE *The Thinker*, a sculpture (1880) by French artist Auguste Rodin. Originally part of a larger work called *The Gates of Hell*, the bronze figure of a naked man hunched in concentration represents Dante pondering his great poem, the *Divine Comedy*. Much reproduced, the statue has become a modern icon.

thinking /thíngking/ *adj* RATIONAL capable of using the mind to reason or reflect ○ *the thinking person's choice* ■ *n* **1.** FORMING OF THOUGHTS use of the mind to form thoughts ○ *There's a lot of thinking to do before we make that decision.* **2.** JUDGMENT opinions or conclusions arrived at ○ *What's your thinking on the political situation?*

thinking cap ◇ **put your thinking cap on** to think carefully about something, especially to find a solution to a problem

think piece *n* an article giving somebody's analysis or opinion of a situation or event, written to provoke thought

think-tank *n* a committee of experts that undertakes research or gives advice, especially to a government

thinner /thínnər/ *n* a liquid such as turpentine that is used to dilute paint or varnish

thin-skinned *adj* **1.** easily offended by criticism or insults **2.** covered in a thin peel or rind

thio- *prefix* containing sulphur ○ *thiophene* [< Greek *theion* 'sulphur']

thiocarbamide /thī ō ka'árbə mīd/ *n* CHEM same as **thiourea**

thiocyanate /thī ō sī ə nayt/ *n* a salt or ester of thiocyanic acid

thiocyanic acid /thī ō sī ánnik-/ *n* an unstable colourless liquid. Use: salts or esters in insecticides. Formula: HSCN.

thiol /thī ol/ *n* an organic compound similar to an alcohol but in which the oxygen atom has been replaced by a sulphur atom. Thiols are liquids with penetrating unpleasant smells.

thiomersal /thī ō múrss'l/ *n* a cream-coloured mercury compound. Use: local antiseptic. Formula: $C_9H_9HgNaO_2S$. N Am term **thimerosal** [Mid-20C. < THIO- + MERCURY + SALICYLATE]

thionic /thī ónnik/ *adj* relating to or containing sulphur [Late 19C. < Greek *theion* 'sulphur']

thionyl /thī ənil/ *n* containing the chemical group SO [Mid-19C. < Greek *theion* 'sulphur']

thiopental sodium /thī ō pént'l-/ *n* a fast-acting barbiturate. Use: general anaesthetic, hypnotic.

thiopentone sodium /thī ō péntōn-/ *n* PHARM former name for **thiopental sodium**

thiophen

thiophen /thī ə fen/, **thiophene** /-feen/ *n* a colourless liquid with a faint odour of benzene. Use: solvent,

manufacture of dyes, resins, pharmaceuticals. Formula: C_4H_4S. [Late 19C. < THIO- + PHENO-]

thioridazine /thī əridáyzeen/ *n* a synthetic compound that is a white or yellow powder. Use: tranquillizer for psychotic patients.

thiosulphate /thī ō súl fayt/ *n* a salt or ester of thiosulphuric acid

thiosulphuric acid /thī ō sul fyoórik-/ *n* an unstable acid known only in the form of salts or esters or in solution. Formula: $H_2S_2O_3$.

thiotepa /thī ō teèpə/ *n* a crystalline compound of tepa that contains sulphur. Use: treatment of malignant tumours.

thiouracil /thī ō yoórəssil/ *n* a compound belonging to a group of bitter-tasting white crystalline compounds. Use: treatment of hyperthyroidism.

thiourea /thī ō yoō reè ə, -joóri ə/ *n* a soluble crystalline substance. Use: manufacture of resins, photographic processes. Formula: $CS(NH_2)_2$.

third /thurd/ *n* **1.** ONE OF THREE PARTS one of three equal parts into which something is or may be divided **2.** ORDINAL NUMBER CORRESPONDING TO 3 item number three in a series **3.** ONE AFTER SECOND IN IMPORTANCE somebody or something ranking next after second in authority or precedence **4.** AUTOMOT VEHICLE GEAR in a motor vehicle, the forward gear between second and fourth **5.** MUSIC MUSICAL INTERVAL in a standard musical scale, the interval between one note and another that lies two notes above or below it. In the scale of C major, C and E form a third. **6.** MUSIC MUSICAL NOTE THIRD AWAY in a standard musical scale, a note that is a third away from another note **7.** MUSIC COMBINED HARMONIC a harmonic of a combination of two tones a third apart **8.** EDUC UNIVERSITY DEGREE the lowest class of honours degree awarded by a British university **9.** BALLET same as **third position** [Old English *þirdda, pridda* < Indo-European, 'three'] —**third** *adj, adv*

CULTURAL NOTE *The Third Man*, a film (1949) by British director Sir Carol Reed. Set in Vienna immediately after World War II, this stylish and gripping film noir recounts US writer Holly Martins' attempts to discover the truth behind the mysterious death of his old friend Harry Lime. It is made particularly memorable by its dramatic war-ravaged setting, innovative lighting and editing, and haunting zither theme.

third class *n* **1.** THIRD IN CLASSIFICATION SYSTEM the next below second in grade or category **2.** EDUC EXAMINATION DIVISION the third highest division in an examination. For British honours degrees, third class is the lowest class. **3.** TRAVEL CHEAPEST ACCOMMODATION formerly, the least expensive and least luxurious accommodation on a ship or train **4.** MAIL MAIL CLASS a class of mail in the United States and Canada for unsealed printed matter —**third-class** *adj, adv*

third degree *n* intensive interrogation, especially when accompanied by rough physical treatment (*informal*) ○ *The interrogators gave the suspects the third degree.* [< the interrogation required to reach the 'third degree', the highest rank in Freemasonry]

SYNONYMS See **question**.

third-degree burn *n* a burn of the most serious kind, in which the skin and the tissues beneath it are severely damaged

third dimension *n* **1.** the added dimension of depth that distinguishes a solid object from one that is two-dimensional or planar **2.** a quality that makes something more vivid —**third-dimensional** *adj*

third estate *n* the third social class, traditionally the commons, in a society divided into estates

third eyelid *n* ZOOL same as **nictitating membrane**

third force *n* a group that mediates between two opposing political groups or parties

thirdhand /thúrd hánd/ *adj, adv* **1.** used by, or after having been used by, two previous owners **2.** from or through two intermediate sources

thirdly /thúrdli/ *adv* used to introduce the third point in an argument or discussion

third man *n* **1.** in cricket, a deep fielder on the off side behind the slips **2.** the position played by a third man

third market *n* a market on the London Stock Exchange trading in the shares of companies such as new or small companies that are not on the main market or the Unlisted Securities Market

third party *n* somebody who is involved in a legal matter but not as a principal party ○ *The signatures need to be witnessed by a third party.* ○ *third-party motor-vehicle insurance*

third person *n* **1.** VERB OR PRONOUN FORM the form of a verb or a pronoun used to refer to somebody or something being spoken about **2.** SET OF GRAMMATICAL FORMS the grammatical set containing the forms indicating the third person **3.** WRITING IN THIRD PERSON a style of writing using forms that are in the third-person, more objective than writing in the first person ○ *Write your account in the third person.*

third-person *adj* **1.** describes verbs or pronouns that designate somebody spoken about. In English, the third-person singular subject pronouns are 'he', 'she', 'it', and 'one', and the third-person plural subject pronoun is 'they'. **2.** displaying the character that a player of a computer game represents on screen from an external viewpoint, rather than through the character's eyes ○ *a third-person action game*

third position *n* in ballet, a position in which the feet are turned outwards with the heel of the front foot touching the instep of the back foot

third rail *n* **1.** a rail from which some electrically powered trains pick up current **2.** *US* an issue or situation that is highly charged, fraught with controversy, or dangerous to deal with ○ *tax hikes as a third rail in US politics*

third-rate *adj* of a low or the lowest quality

third reading *n* the third presentation of a bill to a legislative assembly. In the UK Parliament, it is to discuss a committee's report. In the US Congress, it is the final presentation before a vote.

Third Reich *n* the Nazi regime in Germany between 1933 and 1945

Third Republic *n* the French system of government set up after Napoleon III's reign. It lasted until 1940.

thirdstream /thúrd streem/ *n* music that draws from both classical music and jazz [Mid-20C. After MAINSTREAM] —**third-stream** *adj*

Third Way *n* a centralist political direction or ideology that is neither Socialist nor Conservative, but combines aspects of free-market capitalism with egalitarian social aims

Third World, **third world** *n* the developing nations of Africa, Asia, and Latin America, generally less economically advanced than the industrialized nations but with varied economies. Originally the Third World was contrasted with the First World, the capitalist industrial nations, and the Second World, the industrialized Communist nations. [Translation of French *tiers monde*] —**Third World** *adj*, **Third Worlder** *n*

thirl[1] /thurl/ (**thirls**, **thirling**, **thirled**) *vt regional* **1.** to pierce or drill something **2.** to thrill somebody [Old English *þyrlian* < *þyrel* 'hole' (see THRILL)]

thirl[2] /thurl/ (**thirls**, **thirling**, **thirled**) *vt Scotland* to bind or subject somebody, e.g. to a lease [Mid-16C. Alteration of *thrill*, alteration of THRALL]

Thirlmere, Lake /thúrl meer/ lake in Cumbria, in northwestern England, that serves as a main reservoir for Manchester. Length: 5 km/3 mi.

thirst /thurst/ *n* **1.** NEED FOR LIQUID a desire or need to drink a liquid, or the feeling of dryness in the mouth and throat caused by a need for a liquid **2.** STRONG CRAVING a strong desire for something ○ *a thirst for knowledge* ■ *vi* (**thirsts**, **thirsting**, **thirsted**) **1.** EXPERIENCE THIRST to feel a thirst for a liquid **2.** EXPERIENCE DESIRE to desire something strongly ○ *thirsted for news of home* [Old English *þurst* < Indo-European, 'be dry'] —**thirster** *n*

thirst snake *n* a small nonvenomous snake with long needle-shaped teeth. Native to: Southeast Asia, tropical America. Genus: *Dipsas*.

thirsty /thúrsti/ (**-ier**, **-iest**) *adj* **1.** NEEDING LIQUID feeling the need to drink a liquid ○ *Gardening on a hot morning always makes me thirsty.* **2.** LACKING WATER having insufficient water, especially in the form of

irrigation ○ *The land was thirsty for rain.* **3.** DESIRING having a strong desire or craving ○ *thirsty for companionship* **4.** CAUSING THIRST causing the need to drink a liquid (*informal*) ○ *thirsty work* —**thirstily** *adv* —**thirstiness** *n*

thirteen /thur téen/ *n* **1.** 13 the number 13 **2.** SOMETHING WITH VALUE OF 13 something in a numbered series with a value of 13 **3.** GROUP OF 13 a group of 13 objects or people [Old English *prēotīne* < *prēo* 'three' + *-tīne* 'ten']

Thirteen Colonies *npl* the thirteen British colonies in North America that became the founding states of the United States (1776). They are New Hampshire, Massachusetts, Rhode Island, Connecticut, New York, New Jersey, Pennsylvania, Delaware, Maryland, Virginia, North Carolina, South Carolina, and Georgia.

thirteenth /thúr téenth/ *n* **1.** ONE OF 13 PARTS one of 13 equal parts into which something is or may be divided **2.** ORDINAL NUMBER CORRESPONDING TO 13 item number 13 in a series **3.** MUSICAL NOTE the note an octave and a sixth above the principal note in a musical scale —**thirteenth** *adj, adv*

thirteenth chord *n* a complex musical chord that, in addition to a seventh, also contains the interval of a thirteenth

thirtieth /thúrti əth/ *n* **1.** one of 30 equal parts into which something is or may be divided **2.** item number 30 in a series —**thirtieth** *adj, adv*

thirty /thúrti/ *n* (*plural* **-ties**) **1.** 30 the number 30 **2.** GROUP OF 30 a group of 30 objects or people **3.** SCORE IN TENNIS in a game of tennis, the score awarded to a player with a score of 15 on winning a further point ■ **thirties** *npl* **1.** NUMBERS 30 TO 39 the numbers 30 to 39, particularly as a range of temperature ○ *in the low thirties* **2.** YEARS FROM 30 TO 39 the years from 30 to 39 in a century **3.** PERIOD FROM AGE 30 TO 39 the period of somebody's life from the age of 30 to 39 [Old English *þrītig*, 'twice three'] —**thirty** *adj, pron*

thirty-eight *n* US a handgun with a .38 calibre.

Thirty-nine Articles *npl* the basic teachings and beliefs of the Church of England, written in the 16th century and still the basis of its doctrines

thirty-second note *n* N Am same as **demisemiquaver**

thirtysomething /thúrti sumthing/ *n* somebody who is between 30 and 40 years old (*informal*; *usually used in the plural*) —**thirtysomething** *adj*

thirty-twomo /-toóomō/ (*plural* **thirty-twomos**) *n* a size of book page traditionally created by folding a single sheet of standard-sized printing paper 5 times, giving 32 leaves or 64 pages [Late 18C. Pronunciation of the printers' abbreviation *32mo*]

Thirty Years War *n* a war in Europe between 1618 and 1648, which developed into a struggle for dominance between various powers, notably France, Spain, Sweden, and the Holy Roman Empire. It began as a war between the Catholic Holy Roman Emperor and some of his Protestant German states.

Thiruvananthapuram /theéroo vúnnən thúppoo rum/ port and capital city of Kerala State, southern India. Population: 523,723 (1991). Former name **Trivandrum**

this /thiss/ CORE MEANING: a grammatical word used to indicate somebody or something already mentioned or identified or something understood by both the speaker and hearer ○ (det) *This book is brilliant.* ○ (det) *This holiday – how much is it going to cost?* ○ (pron) *Is this why you've been so happy lately?* ○ (pron) *I first encountered this while travelling abroad.* **1.** *det, pron* CLOSE BY used to indicate somebody or something present or close by, especially as distinct from somebody or something further away, referred to as 'that' ○ (det) *I much prefer this painting to that one.* ○ (pron) *What's this?* **2.** *det, pron* PREVIOUSLY MENTIONED used to indicate somebody or something just mentioned **3.** *det, pron* INDICATING WORDS TO FOLLOW used to indicate a phrase or statement about to be said ○ (det) *All I can say is this one word – no.* ○ (pron) *Hey, listen to this!* **4.** *det, pron* STATED TIME used to refer to a specific time in the past or present ○ (pron) *I expected him back before this.* ○ (det) *At this particular moment she felt she'd never experience such happiness again.* **5.** *det* NOT PREVIOUSLY MENTIONED used to indicate somebody or something not previously mentioned, especially when telling a story

to give a sense of immediacy (*informal*) ○ *Then this woman came running up to me, shouting at the top of her voice.* **6.** *adv* TO THIS DEGREE used to emphasize the degree of a feeling or quality ○ *I was this close to walking out.* [Old English *þis, þes* < Indo-European] ◇ **this and that** miscellaneous unimportant things

Thisbe *n* MYTHOL ♦ **Pyramus and Thisbe**

thistle

thistle /thíss'l/ *n* **1.** a plant with prickly stems and leaves. Flowers: dense, rounded, usually purple, flower heads surrounded by thorny bracts. Genera: *Carduus* or *Cirsium* or *Onopordum*. **2.** the representation of a thistle that is the national emblem of Scotland [Old English *þistel* < Germanic]

thistle butterfly *n* INSECTS same as **painted lady** [Because its larvae live on thistles]

thistledown /thíss'l down/ *n* **1.** the fluffy mass of hairs attached to the seeds of the mature flower head of a thistle **2.** a material or substance that is fine and silky and so resembles thistledown, e.g. a baby's hair or a delicate fabric

thistly /thíss'li/ (**-lier, -liest**) *adj* **1.** full or consisting of thistles **2.** difficult to deal with ○ *thistly problems in economics*

thither /thíthər/, **thitherward** /thíthərwərd/ *adv* to or in the direction of that place (*archaic or formal*) ○ *'I will set thee on thy way to Benares, if thou goest thither, and tell thee what must be known by us.'* (Rudyard Kipling, *Kim*; 1901) [Old English *þider*, alteration (after *hider* 'hither') of *þæder* 'that place' < Germanic]

thixotropic /thíksə tróppik/ *adj* becoming fluid when shaken or stirred and returning to a gel state when allowed to stand [Early 20C. < Greek *thixis* 'touch'] —**thixotropy** /thik sóttrəpi/ *n*

THNQ *abbr* ONLINE thank you (*used in e-mails or text messages*)

tho' /thō/ *adv, conj* same as **though** (*informal*) [Representing the pronunciation]

~~thoght~~ incorrect spelling of **thought**

thole[1] /thōl/ *n* ROWING same as **tholepin** [Old English *þol* < Indo-European, 'stick out']

thole[2] /thōl/ *vt* N England, Scotland to experience or bear something such as pain or grief patiently or uncomplainingly [Old English *þolian* < Indo-European, 'support, lift up']

tholepin /thōl pin/ *n* a small upright wooden peg in the side of a rowing boat, usually provided in pairs to support an oar and act as a pivot when the oar is used

tholos /thō loss/ (*plural* **-loi** /-loy/) *n* an ancient Greek circular domed building, especially a Mycenaean dry-stone tomb [Mid-17C. < Greek]

Thomas /tómməss/ *n*, St (*fl* 1st century AD) one of the 12 apostles of Jesus Christ. His reluctance to recognize Jesus Christ's resurrection until he had

seen and touched his wounds gave rise to the phrase 'doubting Thomas' (John 14:1–7, John 20:19–29).

Thomas (of Erceldoune) /-úrss'l doon/ (1220?–97?) Scottish poet and seer. He was the reputed author of the romance *Sir Tristram*. His prophecies are said to have foretold the English defeat by the Scots at the battle of Bannockburn in 1314. Known as **Thomas the Rhymer**

Popperfoto

Dylan Thomas

Thomas /tómməss/, **Dylan** (1914–53) Welsh poet. His best known work includes the poem 'Fern Hill' and the radio play *Under Milk Wood* (1954). See Cultural note at **milk**

'It is spring, moonless night in the small town, starless and bible-black, the cobble-streets silent and the hunched, courters'-and-rabbits' wood limping invisible down to the sloeblack, slow, black, crowblack, fishingboat-bobbing sea.'
[Dylan Thomas, *Under Milk Wood*; 1954]

Thomas à Kempis /-ə kémpiss/ (1379?–1471) German monk and writer. His most famous work is the devotional treatise *The Imitation of Christ*, written from about 1415 to 1424. Born **Hemerken, Thomas**

Thomism /tōmizəm/ *n* the philosophical and theological doctrines of Thomas Aquinas, which formed the basis of medieval scholasticism [Early 18C. After St *Thomas* AQUINAS] —**Thomist** *n, adj* —**Thomistic** /tō místik/ *adj* —**Thomistical** *adj*

Thompson /tómps'n/ main tributary of the Fraser River in southern British Columbia, Canada. Length: 489 km/304 mi.

Thompson, Benjamin, Count Rumford (1753–1814) US-born British physicist and politician. He is best known for his research into the nature of heat and friction.

Thompson, Daley (*b.* 1958) British athlete. In the decathlon he was Olympic gold medallist (1980 and 1984) and world champion (1983). Born **Thompson, Francis Morgan**

'In my sport you have to peak ten times.'
[Daley Thompson, *Sunday Times*; 11 October 1981]

Thompson, Hunter S. (*b.* 1939) US journalist. An iconoclastic commentator of American culture, his *Fear and Loathing in Las Vegas* (1972) exemplifies the style of writing dubbed 'New Journalism'. Full name **Thompson, Hunter Stockton**

'Mainline gambling is a very heavy business—and Las Vegas makes Reno seem like your friendly neighborhood grocery store. For a loser Vegas is the meanest town on earth.'
[Hunter S. Thompson, *Fear and Loathing in Las Vegas*; 1972]

Thompson, Jack (*b.* 1940) Australian actor. He is noted for his roles in television dramas and films such as *Breaker Morant* (1980). Full name **Thompson, John Payne**

Thompson submachine gun /tómsən-/ *n* a relatively lightweight submachine gun introduced in 1915. It was intended as an infantry weapon. [Early 20C. After the US manufacturing company]

Thomson /tómss'n/ river in southwestern Queensland, Australia. Length: 380 km/236 mi.

Thomson, Sir Joseph John (1856–1940) British physicist.

A pioneer in nuclear physics, he discovered the electron, for which he was awarded the Nobel Prize in Physics (1906), and demonstrated the existence of stable isotopes.

Thomson, Peter (*b.* 1929) Australian golfer. He was the winner of the British Open championship (1954–56, 1958, 1965). Full name **Peter William Thomson**

Thomson effect /tómsən-/ *n* the phenomenon of temperature differences within a conductor or semiconductor causing an electric potential gradient [Late 19C. After William *Thomson* (1st Baron KELVIN)]

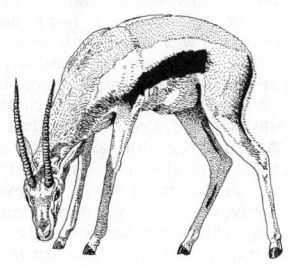

Thomson's gazelle

Thomson's gazelle *n* a small gazelle that has a broad black stripe on its side. Native to: grasslands and dry woodlands of Africa. Latin name: *Gazella thomsoni*. [Late 19C. After Joseph *Thomson*, Scottish explorer (1858–94)]

-thon *suffix* same as **-athon** (used after a vowel) ○ *talkathon* [< MARATHON]

thong /thong/ *n* **1. LONG THIN PIECE OF LEATHER** a thin strip of something, especially leather, used for fastening or supporting things **2. BRAIDED WHIP** a whip made of plaited leather, cord, or some other material **3. LIGHT SANDAL** a light sandal held on by strips of material that join the sole of the sandal at either side of the foot and between the first and second toes **4. BIKINI OR UNDERWEAR BOTTOM** a narrow piece of cloth or leather that goes between the legs and is attached to a band around the hips, worn as a bikini bottom or as underwear [Old English *þwong* < Germanic]

Thor /thawr/ *n* in Norse mythology, the god of thunder and eldest son of Odin. Thursday is named after him.

thoracentesis /tháwrə sen téessiss/ (*plural* **-teses** /-téesseez/) *n* a surgical procedure in which a needle is inserted through the chest wall in order to withdraw fluid, blood, or air [Mid-19C. < THORACO- + Greek *kentēsis* 'pricking' < *kentein* 'to prick']

thoraces ANAT, ZOOL plural of **thorax**

thoracic /thaw rássik/ *adj* involving or located in the chest —**thoracically** *adv*

thoracic duct *n* the main duct of the lymphatic system, which drains lymph from smaller lymph vessels in the trunk and returns it to the bloodstream by emptying into a major vein. In human beings, it ascends in front of the spinal column and discharges into the left subclavian vein at the base of the neck.

thoraco- *prefix* chest, thorax ○ *thoracolumbar* [< Greek *thōrak-*, stem of *thōrax*]

thoracolumbar /tháwrəkō lúmbər/ *adj* **1.** describes the thoracic and lumbar areas of the body **2.** including parts of and behind the vertebral column in the chest and lower back but excluding the pelvis

thoracotomy /tháwrə kóttəmi/ (*plural* **-mies**) *n* a surgical incision made in the chest wall

thorax /tháw raks/ (*plural* **thoraxes** or **thoraces** /tháwrə seez/) *n* **1. UPPER PART OF TORSO** the part of the human body between the neck and abdomen, enclosed by the ribs and containing the heart and lungs **2. UPPER PART OF ANIMAL'S BODY** the area corresponding to the human thorax in other vertebrates **3. PART BETWEEN HEAD AND ABDOMEN** the middle division of the body of an insect, crustacean, or arachnid [14C. Via Latin < Greek *thōrax* 'chest, breastplate']

Thorburn /tháwr burn/, **Archibald** (1860–1935) British

artist. He painted most of the plates for *Coloured Figures of the Birds of the British Isles* (1885–97). His other works include *Observer's Book of British Birds* (1937).

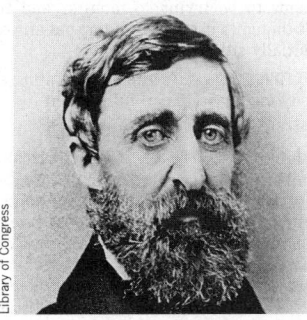

Henry David Thoreau

Thoreau /thaw rố, tháwr ō/, **Henry David** (1817–62) US essayist and philosopher. He was a leading transcendentalist and libertarian. His works include the essay 'Civil Disobedience' (1849) and *Walden* (1854), in which he describes a life lived simply and close to nature. Born **David Henry Thoreau**

> 'The mass of men lead lives of quiet desperation.'
> [Henry David Thoreau, *Walden, or Life in the Woods*; 1854]

thoria /tháwri ə/ *n* CHEM same as **thorium dioxide** [Mid-19C. < THORIUM, after MAGNESIA]

thorianite /tháwri ə nīt/ *n* a rare black radioactive mineral that is an oxide of thorium mixed with rare-earth metals. Use: source of thorium and uranium. [Early 20C. < THORIA + -ITE[1]]

thorite /tháw rīt/ *n* a rare brown, black, or yellow radioactive thorium silicate mineral. Use: source of thorium. [Mid-19C. < THOR]

thorium /tháwri əm/ *n* a soft silvery-white radioactive metallic element. Source: thorite, thorianite. Use: alloys, source of nuclear energy. Symbol **Th**. See table at **element** [Mid-19C. < THOR] —**thoric** *adj*

thorium dioxide *n* an insoluble white powder. Use: catalyst, manufacture of gas mantles, refractories, ceramics, optical glass. Formula: ThO_2.

thorium series *n* one of the natural radioactive decay series that shows how the unstable isotope thorium-232 changes by stages into the stable isotope lead-208

thorn /thawrn/ *n* **1. SHARP POINT ON PLANT STEM** a sharply pointed woody growth projecting from the stem of some trees, bushes, and woody plants **2. PLANT WITH THORNS** a tree, bush, or woody plant that has thorns **3. WOOD OF TREE WITH THORNS** the wood of a tree or bush with thorns **4. RUNIC LETTER** a runic letter used to represent both of the 'th' sounds, as in 'this' and 'thick', in Old English and Middle English. It also represents the voiceless 'th' sound, as in 'thick', in Old Norse and Icelandic and was formerly used as a phonetic symbol. [Old English *þorn* < Germanic] —**thornless** *adj* ◇ **be a thorn in (somebody's) flesh** *or* **side** to be a source of constant irritation to somebody

thorn apple *n* a tall poisonous weed with foul-smelling foliage and spiny capsule fruits. Flowers: large, trumpet-shaped, white or purple. Latin name: *Datura stramonium*. N Am term **jimsonweed**

thornback /tháwrn bak/ (*plural* **-backs** or *same*) *n* a ray with one to three rows of large hooked spines on its back. Latin name: *Raja clavata* or *Platyrhinoidis triseriatis*.

thornbill /tháwrn bil/ (*plural* **-bills** or *same*) *n* **1.** a small songbird with a short sharp beak. Native to: Australia. Family: Acanthizidae. **2.** a hummingbird with a beak that resembles a thorn. Native to: South America. Genera: *Ramphomicron* or *Chalcostigma*.

Dame Sybil Thorndike

Thorndike /tháwrn dīk/, **Dame Sybil** (1882–1976) British actor. A member of the Old Vic Theatre, she played the title role in George Bernard Shaw's *St Joan* more than 2,000 times after he wrote the part for her in 1924. Full name **Thorndike, Dame Agnes Sybil**

Thornhill /tháwrn hil/, **Sir James** (1675–1734) British painter. His work, in the baroque style and executed chiefly for royal and noble patrons, includes decorations for the cupola of St Paul's Cathedral, London.

thorny /tháwrni/ (**-ier, -iest**) *adj* **1.** complicated and difficult to resolve **2.** covered in or full of thorns — **thornily** *adv* —**thorniness** *n*

thorny devil *n* Aus ZOOL same as **moloch**

thoron /tháw ron/ *n* a radioactive isotope of radon with a half-life of 55 seconds, formed by the radioactive decay of thorium [Early 20C. < THORIUM, after RADON]

thorough /thúrrə/ *adj* **1. EXTREMELY CAREFUL** extremely careful to include everything that is needed ○ *She's very thorough in her research methods.* **2. DONE FULLY** complete in every detail and carried out with care ○ *The doctor gave me a thorough examination.* **3. ABSOLUTE** being so to the fullest extent or in the truest sense of the word ○ *a thorough bore* [Old English *þuruh* 'from end to end', variant of *þurh* (see THROUGH)] — **thoroughly** *adv* —**thoroughness** *n*

SYNONYMS See *careful*.

thoroughbass /thúrrə bayss/ *n* MUSIC same as **continuo** [Mid-17C. < THOROUGH 'all the way through']

thoroughbred /thúrrə bred/ *n* **1. PUREBRED ANIMAL** a pure-bred animal, especially a horse **2. ARISTOCRAT** somebody descended from ancestors of high social status ■ *adj* **1. PUREBRED** bred from pure stock **2. OF ARISTOCRATIC FAMILY** descended from ancestors of high social status [Early 18C. < THOROUGH 'all the way through']

Thoroughbred *n* a pure breed of horse descended from English mares and Arab stallions, originally bred in Britain and most often used for racing — **Thoroughbred** *adj*

thoroughfare /thúrrə fair/ *n* **1. PUBLIC ROAD** a public highway that passes through a place ○ *a lorry blocking a busy thoroughfare* **2. MEANS OF ACCESS** a way or passage from one place to another **3. RIGHT OF PASSAGE** the right to go from one place to another along a designated route **4. HEAVILY USED ROUTE** a stretch of road or water, or a pathway between two places, that is used by many people [14C. < THOROUGH 'from end to end' + obsolete *fare* 'way, journey']

thoroughgoing /thúrrə gố ing/ *adj* **1.** carried out in an extremely careful and thorough way ○ *not very thoroughgoing when it comes to housework* **2.** being so to the fullest extent or in the truest sense of the word ○ *a thoroughgoing pragmatist* [Early 19C. < THOROUGH 'all the way through']

thoroughpaced /thúrrə páysst/ *adj* describes a horse that is thoroughly trained so as to be able to perform all paces well

thoroughpin /thúrrə pin/ *n* inflammation and swelling above the hock joint on both sides of a horse's leg, affecting the flexor tendon and causing lameness [Late 18C. < THOROUGH 'all the way through'; from the appearance of the swelling, like a pin passing through the tendon]

thorp /thawrp/, **thorpe** *n* a small village (*archaic*; often used in placenames) [Old English *þorp* < Germanic]

Thorpe /thawrp/, **Ian** (*b.* 1982) Australian swimmer. One of the outstanding freestyle swimmers in the history of the sport, by the age of 20 he had broken 15 world records and won three Olympic gold medals and eight World Championship titles. Full name **Thorpe, Ian James**. Known as **Thorpedo**

those /thōz/ *pron, det* the form of 'that' used before a plural noun or with a multiple referent ○ *Those are the ones I prefer.* ○ *Do you remember those outings to the seaside?* [Old English *þās* (see THESE)]

Thoth /thoth/, **Thot** *n* in Egyptian mythology, the god of the moon, associated with writing and wisdom. He is usually depicted as a man with the head of an ibis, or as a baboon. ◊ **Hermes Trismegistus**

thou[1] /thow/ (*plural* **thous** or *same*) *n* **1.** one thousandth of an inch. A thou is equal to 0.03 mm. **2.** a thousand, especially when referring to money (*informal*) [Mid-19C. Shortening of THOUSAND]

thou[2] /thow/ *pron* **1.** refers to you, the person being addressed or written to (*archaic or regional; used in familiar address to one person*) **2.** *also* **Thou** used to address God, e.g. in prayers and hymns [Old English *þū* < Indo-European]

thoub /thowb/ *n* a white robe worn by Muslim clerics [< Arabic]

though /thō/ *conj* **1.** ALTHOUGH in spite of the fact that ○ *Though she served as president of the student union, she was attracted to journalism rather than politics.* ○ *He didn't receive any special treatment, even though he is a close friend of the chairman.* **2.** AND YET used to introduce added information that restricts the applicability of a previous statement ○ *The weather has improved a lot, though it still doesn't feel like spring.* ■ *adv* **1.** DESPITE BEING used as a link between words, phrases, or clauses, that usually makes one of them function as an admission that partially contradicts the other ○ *Progress, though steady, has been very slow.* ○ *Small though it is, the device produces enormous quantities of heat.* **2.** HOWEVER used in or following a statement that restricts the applicability of the statement that preceded it ○ *It rained all the time. We still enjoyed ourselves, though.* ○ *So they got married. That, though, was not the end of the story.* [Old English *þeah* < Indo-European; partly < Old Norse *þó*]

USAGE See *although*.

thought[1] /thawt/ *n* **1.** THINKING the activity or process of thinking ○ *deep in thought* **2.** IDEA PRODUCED BY MENTAL ACTIVITY an idea, plan, conception, or opinion produced by mental activity ○ *The thought had crossed my mind.* **3.** SET OF IDEAS the intellectual, scientific, and philosophical ideas associated with a particular place, time, or group ○ *medieval religious thought* **4.** REASONING POWER the ability to think and reason ○ *felt incapable of rational thought* **5.** CONSIDERATION the process or an instance of considering somebody or something ○ *I didn't give it another thought.* **6.** INTENTION an intention or desire to do something ○ *I had no thought of offending anybody.* **7.** EXPECTATION an expectation or hope that something will happen ○ *entertained no thoughts of failure* **8.** SMALL AMOUNT a small amount on a comparative scale ○ *Could you be a thought quieter, please?* **9.** COMPASSIONATE CONSIDERATION a feeling of respect, affection, or consideration for somebody or something ○ *no thought for other people* [Old English *þōht* < Germanic] ◇ **perish the thought!** used to indicate, often humorously, that something is too terrible to be thought of

thought[2] /thawt/ past participle, past tense of **think**

thought disorder *n* a disorder affecting the thought processes or the way they are composed or connected, e.g. delusions or an inability to concentrate or think clearly. Thought disorders are a feature of schizophrenia and dementia.

thoughtful /tháwtf'l/ *adj* **1.** CONSIDERATE treating people in a kind and considerate way, especially by anticipating their wants or needs **2.** PENSIVE appearing to be deep in thought **3.** CAREFULLY THOUGHT OUT showing the application of careful thought —**thoughtfully** *adv* —**thoughtfulness** *n*

thoughtless /tháwtləss/ *adj* **1.** INCONSIDERATE showing a lack of consideration for other people or for consequences **2.** DONE WITHOUT THOUGHT showing a lack of planning or forethought **3.** UNABLE TO THINK not having or using the faculty of thought —**thoughtlessly** *adv* —**thoughtlessness** *n*

thought police *n* an oppressive and intrusive group that seems to be trying to monitor and regulate people's thoughts in order to stamp out any original or potentially subversive ideas

thought-provoking *adj* interesting and causing somebody to engage in careful thought

~~**thourough**~~ incorrect spelling of **thorough**

thousand /thówz'nd/ *n* (*plural same* or **-sands**) **1.** 1,000 the number 1,000 **2.** FOURTH DIGIT TO LEFT OF DECIMAL the fourth digit to the left of the decimal point in the decimal number system **3.** LARGE NUMBER a very large number or amount (*informal*) ○ *must have told him a thousand times* ■ **thousands** *npl* VERY MANY a very large but unspecified number ○ *sold thousands of copies* [Old English *þūsend* < Germanic, 'swollen hundred'< Indo-European, 'to swell']

Thousand Guineas, **1,000 Guineas** *n* a flat horse race for fillies run annually since 1814 at Newmarket, England (*takes a singular verb*)

Thousand Island dressing *n* a salmon-pink salad dressing containing mayonnaise, tomato sauce, chopped gherkins, onions, and spices

Thousand Islands /thówz'nd-/ group of more than 1,000 small islands in southeastern Ontario and northern New York State, in the St Lawrence River

thousandth /thówz'nth/ *n* one of a thousand equal parts of something

~~**thousend**~~ incorrect spelling of **thousand**

thp *abbr* MEASURE thrust horsepower

Thrace /thrayss/ region in southeastern Europe, forming part of present-day Greece, Bulgaria, and Turkey. Area: 8,578 sq. km/3,312 sq. mi. —**Thracian** *adj, n*

Thraco-Phrygian /thráykō-/ *n* a branch of the Indo-European family of languages of which all members except for Armenian are now extinct [Early 20C. < *Thracian*] —**Thraco-Phrygian** *adj*

thrall /thrawl/ *n* (*literary*) **1.** DOMINATION a condition of being controlled by a more powerful person or force ○ *Millions are now in thrall to the factitious excitements of reality television.* **2.** SOMEBODY WHOSE LIFE IS CONTROLLED somebody whose life is completely controlled by a more powerful person or a moral or intellectual force **3.** SOMEBODY CONTROLLED BY SOMETHING somebody who is controlled by a particular physical or mental need ○ *a thrall to alcohol* [Pre-12C. < Old Norse *þræll* < Germanic, 'run'] —**thraldom** *n*

thrapple /thrápp'l/ *Scotland n* the human throat or windpipe ■ *vt* (**-ples, -pling, -pled**) to throttle somebody [14C. Origin?]

thrash /thrash/ *v* (**thrashes, thrashing, thrashed**) **1.** *vt* DEFEAT OPPONENT DECISIVELY to defeat a person or team decisively, especially in a sporting competition ○ *The home team got thrashed in the final.* **2.** *vt* BEAT PERSON OR ANIMAL to beat a person or animal violently **3.** *vti* TOSS ABOUT to toss or move the body and limbs about in an uncontrolled or restless way ○ *thrashed around unable to sleep* **4.** *vi* PADDLE WITH LEGS to move the legs up and down in the water while performing a swimming stroke **5.** *vti* AGRIC same as **thresh** *v* (sense 1) **6.** *vti* SAIL BOAT INTO TIDE OR WIND to sail a boat against the direction of the tide or wind ■ *n* **1.** BEATING a blow or beating with a whip or stick **2.** SOCIAL PARTY a party or celebration (*dated informal*) **3.** MUSIC same as **thrash metal** [Late 16C. Variant of THRESH]

SYNONYMS See *defeat*.

thrash out *vt UK, ANZ, Can* to discuss and develop all the possibilities of a situation in order to reach a decision about it. US term **hash out**

thrasher /thráshər/ *n* **1.** a long-tailed brownish bird with a down-curving beak and a speckled breast. Native to: North America. Family: Mimidae. **2.** FISH, AGRIC same as **thresher** (senses 1, 3)

thrashing /thráshing/ *n* **1.** a violent physical beating **2.** a decisive defeat in a sporting competition

thrash metal *n* a very fast, often discordant type of heavy metal music, strongly influenced by punk

thrawn /thrawn/ *adj N England, Scotland* **1.** stubborn and uncooperative or ill-tempered **2.** twisted or crooked (*archaic*) [15C. < an archaic past participle of THROW]

thread /thred/ *n* **1.** FINE TWISTED CORD fine cord made of two or more twisted fibres. Use: sewing, weaving. **2.** PIECE OF THREAD a length of thread **3.** RIDGE ON SCREW the continuous helical ridge on a screw or pipe **4.** VERY THIN STRIP a fine strand of solid material, trickle of liquid, or wisp of gas **5.** FILAMENT OF COBWEB one of the filaments of a spider's web **6.** SOMETHING CONNECTING ELEMENTS a continuous unifying element running through a story, argument, discussion, or series of events **7.** DISCUSSION ON INTERNET a series of messages in an Internet discussion group (**forum**), commenting on or replying to a previous message **8.** HUMAN LIFE the course of human life, believed by the ancient Greeks to be spun, measured out, and cut by the Fates **9.** VEIN OF ORE a thin seam of ore or coal ■ **threads** *npl N Am* CLOTHING same as **clothes** (*slang*) ■ *v* (**threads, threading, threaded**) **1.** *vt* PASS SOMETHING THROUGH HOLE to pass something such as thread, photographic film, magnetic tape, or ribbon through a hole or gap in something else **2.** *vt* STRING BEADS ON THREAD to string beads or pearls on a thread or wire **3.** *vti* GO CAREFULLY to move along carefully, following a winding route ○ *We threaded our way through the crowded streets.* **4.** *vt* INTERSPERSE THINGS to distribute something at intervals in something else ○ *hair threaded with grey* **5.** *vt* MECH ENG PRODUCE SCREW THREAD to produce a thread on a screw or bolt, or within a material into which a bolt or screw may be inserted **6.** *vi* COOK FORM THREAD to form a fine thread when dropped from a spoon (*refers to sugar syrup*) [Old English *þræd* 'twisted cord' < Indo-European, 'to turn, twist'] —**thread-like** *adj* ◇ **lose the thread (of something)** to cease to follow or understand the connection between the parts of a story or argument

threadbare /thréd bair/ *adj* **1.** WORN AWAY TO REVEAL THREADS so heavily used that the soft part of the fabric has been worn away to reveal the threads beneath **2.** OVERUSED SO NO LONGER CONVINCING having been used so often as to be no longer convincing ○ *the same old threadbare excuses* **3.** MEAGRE not large, varied, or substantial enough to be satisfactory ○ *eked out a threadbare existence* **4.** SHABBILY DRESSED wearing worn-out shabby clothes —**threadbareness** *n*

threader /thréddər/ *n* a device for threading a needle, consisting of a loop of extremely fine wire attached to a flat metal disc that is held between the thumb and forefinger

threadfin /thréd fin/ (*plural* **-fins** or *same*) *n* a sea fish with long rays resembling threads on the lower parts of its pectoral fin. Native to: tropical waters. Family: Polynemidae.

thread mark *n* a strand of silk fibres put inside a paper banknote during manufacture to make it more difficult to counterfeit

thread snake *n* a small nonvenomous snake resembling a worm. Native to: Africa, Asia, Central and South America. Genus: *Leptotyphlops*.

thread vein *n* a very slender vein, especially one that is visible through the skin

threadworm /thréd wurm/ *n* a long nematode worm, e.g. a pinworm

thready /thréddi/ (**-ier, -iest**) *adj* **1.** LIKE THREAD resembling thread **2.** HAVING MANY THREADS consisting of or containing many threads, especially loose or visible ones **3.** COOK FORMING THREADS thick and sticky enough to form threads when dropped from a spoon **4.** SOUNDING WEAK sounding thin and lacking in power and tone ○ *thready voice* **5.** MED ONLY JUST PERCEPTIBLE describes a weak and barely perceptible pulse —**threadiness** *n*

threap /threep/ (**threaps, threaping, threaped**), **threep** (**threeps, threeping, threeped**) *vt N England, Scotland* **1.** to scold or criticize somebody harshly **2.** to state something vehemently or persistently, especially something that somebody else has contradicted [Old English *þrēapian*, origin ?] —**threaper** *n*

threat /thret/ *n* **1.** DECLARATION OF INTENT TO CAUSE HARM the expression of an intention to cause harm or pain ○ *The terrorists might carry out their threat to kill the hostages.* **2.** SIGN OF SOMETHING BAD an indication that something unpleasant or dangerous is going to happen ○ *a threat of severe thunderstorms* **3.** SOMEBODY

OR SOMETHING LIKELY TO CAUSE HARM a person, animal, or thing likely to cause harm or pain ○ *The dog is no threat.* [Old English *prēat* 'crowd, menace' < Indo-European, 'press in']

threaten /thrétt'n/ (-ens, -ening, -ened) v 1. *vti* EXPRESS HOSTILE INTENTION TOWARDS SOMEBODY to express an intention to do something that will cause harm, trouble, or inconvenience to somebody else unless that person does what is demanded ○ *They threatened us with legal action.* ○ *She threatened to tell my wife.* 2. *vt* EXPRESS THREAT TO SOMEBODY to express or indicate an intention to harm or kill somebody ○ *He threatened me with a knife.* 3. *vti* BE THREAT TO SOMETHING to be a source of actual or potential harm to something ○ *an injury that could threaten his career* 4. *vti* SIGNIFY SOMETHING BAD HAPPENING to signify that something bad is going to happen, especially that bad weather is going to arrive ○ *Dark clouds threatened rain.* 5. *vi* SUGGEST UNWELCOME CONSEQUENCES to seem likely to result in something unpleasant ○ *The dispute threatened to escalate into all-out war.* [Old English *prēatnian* 'press in on' < *prēat* (see THREAT)] —**threatener** *n*

threatened /thrétt'nd/ *adj* describes an organism or species that is in danger of becoming extinct

threatening /thrétt'ning/ *adj* 1. EXPRESSING THREAT expressing an intention to cause somebody deliberate harm or pain ○ *a threatening gesture* 2. SUGGESTING SEVERE WEATHER likely to bring rain or severe weather ○ *a threatening sky* 3. MAKING SOMEBODY FEEL ANXIOUS OR FEARFUL causing somebody to feel anxious, fearful, and unconfident —**threateningly** *adv*

Thredbo /thrédbō/ ski resort in the Australian Alps, New South Wales, Australia. Population: 2,065 (1991).

three /three/ *n* 1. 3 the number 3 2. SOMETHING WITH VALUE OF 3 something in a numbered series, e.g. a playing card, with a value of 3 ○ *the three of clubs* ○ *to throw a three* 3. GROUP OF THREE a group of three objects or people [Old English *prī*, *prēotīne* < Indo-European]

three-card monte *n* a game in which three cards are dealt face up and then turned face down and moved round. The player must then guess the new position of a particular card.

three-card trick *n* a game in which three cards are dealt face up, and then turned face down and moved round. The player must then guess which is the queen.

three-colour *adj* using, produced by, or relating to a colour printing process in which the print is produced by superimposing separate plates for the colours yellow, magenta, and cyan

three-D, **3-D** *n* a three-dimensional effect ■ *adj* MATHS, ARTS same as **three-dimensional** (senses 1–2) (*informal*)

three-D accelerator *n* computer hardware that improves three-D graphics presentation

three-day event *n* a competition for horses and riders consisting of dressage, cross-country, and show-jumping events, held over a three-day period

three-day measles *n* MED same as **German measles** (*not in technical use*)

three-decker *n* 1. SOMETHING WITH THREE LEVELS a vehicle, building, or other construction with three levels or floors 2. SHIP WITH THREE DECKS a warship with three decks set with guns, or any ship with three decks 3. SANDWICH WITH THREE SLICES OF BREAD a sandwich consisting of two layers of filling between three slices of bread

three-dimensional *adj* 1. WITH THREE DIMENSIONS possessing or appearing to possess the dimensions of height, width, and depth 2. APPEARING TO HAVE DEPTH creating the illusion of depth behind a flat surface 3. BELIEVABLE represented with sufficient complexity to be convincing

three-field system *n* a system of crop rotation that was in operation in western Europe by the 9th century. One-third of land was left fallow, one-third planted in spring grains, and one-third in the season's crops such as barley and vegetables.

threefold /three fōld/ *adj* 1. CONSISTING OF THREE made up of three parts 2. THREE TIMES AS MANY OR MUCH being or

having three times as many or as much ■ *adv* BY THREE TIMES by three times as many or as much

three-four time *n* a time signature in which there are three beats to the bar and each beat is a crotchet. A waltz is in three-four time.

3G *n* a wireless communications technology designed to provide high-speed Internet access and transmission of text, digitized voice, video, and multimedia (*often used before a noun*) Full form **third generation**

Three Kings *n* BIBLE same as **Magi**

Three Kings Islands /three kingz-/ group of uninhabited islands 50 km/31 mi. northwest of the North Island, New Zealand. The islands are a wildlife refuge. Area: 8 sq. km/3 sq. mi.

three-legged race *n* a race in which pairs of runners compete with their adjacent legs bound together

three-line whip *n* a notice, underlined three times for emphasis, issued to members of a political party requiring them to attend and vote in a particular way on a specific motion in the British Parliament

Three Mile Island /three mīl-/ island in the Susquehanna River, near Harrisburg, southeastern Pennsylvania. An accidental release of radioactivity at the nuclear plant on the island in 1979 led to stricter regulation of the US nuclear industry.

three-mile limit *n* the outer limit of a country's territorial waters, three nautical miles from shore

threep *vt* N England, Scotland another spelling of **threap**

threepence /thréppənss, thrúp-/, **thruppence** /thrúppənss, throōp-/ *n* 1. a former British coin worth three old pennies 2. a sum of three pennies, especially old pence (*dated; takes a singular verb*) ○ *a loaf costing threepence*

threepenny /thrépni, thrúp-/, **thruppenny** /thrúpni, throōp-/ *adj* (*dated*) 1. worth or costing three pennies, especially old pence 2. worth or costing very little

threepenny bit *n* a 12-sided former British coin worth three old pennies

three-phase *adj* 1. consisting of three separate phases 2. describes an electrical system or circuit of three alternating voltages that have the same frequency but are separated by one third of a cycle

three-piece *adj* consisting of three matching or coordinated pieces ■ *n* a suit consisting of matching trousers or skirt, waistcoat or blouse, and jacket

three-piece suite *n* a set of living-room furniture consisting of a sofa with two matching armchairs

three-ply *adj* 1. WITH THREE LAYERS consisting of three layers or laminations 2. WITH THREE STRANDS made up of three twisted strands ■ *n* THREE-PLY KNITTING YARN knitting yarn made up of three twisted strands

three-point landing *n* an aircraft landing in which the two main wheels of the landing gear and the nose or tail wheel touch the ground at the same time

three-point turn *n* a turn to reverse the direction of travel of a motor vehicle that involves two forward movements and one reverse movement

three-quarter *adj* 1. BEING THREE QUARTERS OF SOMETHING being three quarters of something measurable or countable, e.g. length, an area, or a time interval ○ *a three-quarter moon* 2. BEING THREE QUARTERS OF FULL LENGTH being three quarters of the full or usual length ○ *a three-quarter coat* 3. ARTS WITH FACE TURNED TO SIDE describes a portrait that shows the subject's face turned slightly to one side ■ *n* RUGBY PLAYER BETWEEN FORWARDS AND BACKS a rugby player in one of four positions between the halfbacks and the full back, or one of these positions

three-quarter binding *n* bookbinding in which the spine and most of the sides of a book are covered in the same material

three-quarter length *adj* 1. describes a sleeve that ends somewhere between the elbow and the wrist 2. describes a coat that ends somewhere between the hips and the knees

three-ring circus *n* N Am 1. a circus in which performances take place simultaneously in three sep-

arate rings 2. a situation full of activity and confusion (*informal*)

three Rs /-aárz/, **3 Rs** *npl* the skills of reading, writing, and arithmetic, considered as the basis of primary education [Presumed to have originated with a toast proposed by Sir William Curtis (1752–1829), illiterate Lord Mayor of London]

threescore /three skáwr/ *adj*, *n* same as **sixty** (*archaic*) ○ *threescore years and ten*

threesome /threéssəm/ *n* 1. GROUP OF THREE a group of three people 2. SEXUAL EXPERIENCE a sexual experience involving three people 3. ACTIVITY FOR THREE a game or activity for three people 4. TYPE OF GOLF GAME a golf game involving three players, one playing one ball and the other two taking alternate shots to play another ball

three-spine stickleback, **three-spined stickleback** *n* a small stickleback of temperate fresh and salt water that has three dorsal spines. Latin name: *Gasterosteus aculeatus.*

three-square *adj* shaped like an equilateral triangle when viewed in cross section

three strikes, **three strikes and you're out** *n* a law that mandates long prison sentences for criminals with three convictions for major offences

three-way *adj* 1. involving three participating people or things 2. providing routes to three different places from one point ○ *a three-way junction*

three-wheeler *n* a vehicle with three wheels, e.g. a small car or a tricycle

Three Wise Men *n* BIBLE same as **Magi**

thremmatology /thrémmə tólləji/ *n* the science of breeding domesticated plants and animals [Late 19C. < Greek *thremmat-* 'nursling']

threnody /thrénnədi/ (*plural* -dies), **threnode** /thrénod/ *n* a song, poem, or speech of lament for the dead [Mid-17C. < Greek *thrēnōidia* < *thrēnos* 'lament' + *ōidē* 'song'] —**threnodial** /thri nṓdi əl/ *adj* —**threnodic** /thri nóddik/ *adj* —**threnodist** *n*

H3C—CH—CH—C—OH with OH, O, NH2 groups

threonine

threonine /three ə nīn/ *n* an amino acid that is a component of proteins and an essential nutrient in the diets of humans and animals. Formula: $C_4H_9NO_5$. [Mid-20C. < *threose*, kind of sugar + -INE]

thresh /thresh/ *v* (threshes, threshing, threshed) 1. *vti* SEPARATE SEEDS FROM PLANT to use a machine, flail, or other implement to separate the seeds of a harvested plant from the straw and chaff, husks, or other residue 2. *vt* EXAMINE EXHAUSTIVELY to examine something such as an issue or a proposal, exhaustively 3. *vti* same as **thrash** *v* (sense 3) 4. *vt* same as **thrash** *v* (sense 2) ■ *n* THRESHING an act of threshing a harvested crop [Old English *perscan* < Indo-European, 'to rub']

thresher /thréshər/ *n* 1. a harvester of a crop with a machine, flail, or other implement 2. AGRIC same as **threshing machine** 3. *also* **thresher shark** a large, widely distributed shark that has a curved elongated upper lobe on the tail with which it agitates or threshes the water. Family: Alopiidae.

threshhold incorrect spelling of **threshold**

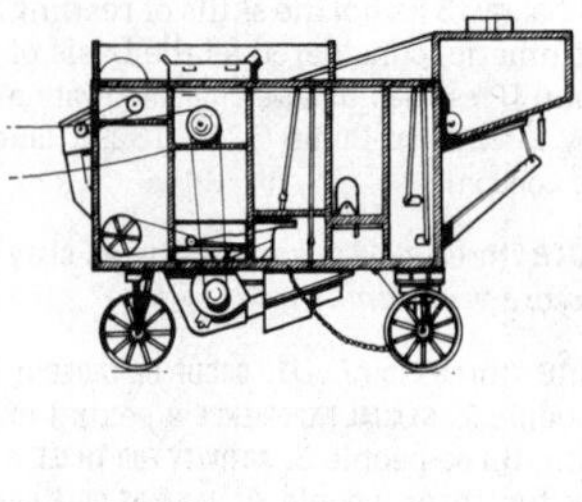

threshing machine

threshing machine *n* a static power-driven agricultural machine formerly used to beat or rub harvested plants in order to separate the seeds from the rest of the plant

threshold /thrésh hōld, -old/ *n* **1. STARTING POINT** the point at which something begins or changes ○ *on the threshold of maturity* **2. LEVEL AT WHICH EFFECT STARTS** the level that must be reached for a psychological or physiological effect to begin or be noticeable ○ *the threshold of consciousness* ○ *her pain threshold* **3. WOOD OR STONE BELOW DOOR** a piece of stone or hardwood that forms the bottom of a doorway **4. ENTRANCE** a doorway or entrance [Old English *þerscold* < Germanic]

threshold agreement *n* an agreement that raises wages in order to compensate for increases in the cost of living

threw past tense of **throw**

thrice /thrīss/ *adv* **1. THREE TIMES** three times over (*archaic or literary*) **2. THREEFOLD** by three times as many or as much (*archaic or literary*) **3. GREATLY** to a high degree (*archaic*) [12C. Alteration of *thries* < Old English *þriga* 'three times' < *þrī* (see THREE)]

thrift /thrift/ *n* **1. PRUDENT USE OF MONEY AND GOODS** the sensible and cautious management of money and goods in order to waste as little as possible and obtain maximum value **2.** *US* BANKING **SAVINGS AND LOAN ASSOCIATION** a savings and loan association or savings bank **3. PLANT WITH PINK OR WHITE FLOWERS** a perennial evergreen plant of the plumbago family. Flowers: dense, round, pink or white. Genus: *Armeria*. **4.** ZOOL **STRONG GROWTH** vigorous and healthy growth of living things such as plants (*formal*) [13C. < Old Norse *þrift* 'prosperity' < *þrífask* (see THRIVE)]

thriftless /thríftləss/ *adj* showing carelessness and wastefulness in the handling of money and other resources —**thriftlessly** *adv* —**thriftlessness** *n*

thrift shop *n N Am* a shop that sells used goods, particularly clothing, usually to benefit charity

thrifty /thrífti/ (**-ier, -iest**) *adj* **1.** managing money and resources in a cautious and sensible way so as to waste as little as possible **2.** prosperous and thriving (*archaic*) —**thriftily** *adv* —**thriftiness** *n*

thrill /thril/ *vti* (**thrills, thrilling, thrilled**) **1. BE OR MAKE SOMEBODY VERY EXCITED** to feel intense excitement, or make somebody experience intense excitement ○ *The children were thrilled by the amusement park.* **2. BE PLEASURABLE** to feel great pleasure, or make somebody feel great pleasure ○ *It thrilled me to see my old friends.* **3. VIBRATE OR CAUSE TO VIBRATE** to vibrate, or make something or somebody quiver or vibrate ■ *n* **1. CAUSE OF GREAT EXCITEMENT** a source or cause of intense excitement, and often pleasure **2. FEELING OF EXCITEMENT** a feeling of intense excitement, which may be experienced as a quivering or trembling sensation **3.** MED **TREMOR ASSOCIATED WITH HEART-VALVE DEFECTS** a slight vibration of the chest wall often associated with some types of heart-valve condition [Old English *þȳrlian* 'go through' < *þȳrel* 'hole' < *þruh* 'through']

thriller /thríllər/ *n* **1.** a book, play, or film that has an exciting plot involving crime, mystery, or espionage **2.** somebody or something that thrills people

thrilling /thrílling/ *adj* **1.** causing intense excitement **2.** characterized by trembling or vibrating —**thrillingly** *adv*

thrips /thrips/ (*plural same*) *n* a tiny sucking insect with four long thin wings fringed with hairs. It feeds on the sap of plants. Order: Thysanoptera. [Late 18C. Via Latin < Greek, 'woodworm']

thrive /thrīv/ (**thrives, thriving, thrived** or **throve** /thrōv/, **thrived** or **thriven** /thrívv'n/) *vi* **1.** to grow vigorously and healthily **2.** to be successful and often profitable [13C. < Old Norse *þrífask* 'grasp for yourself' < *þrífa* 'seize'] —**thriver** *n*

thrive on *vt* to enjoy and be stimulated by something generally considered difficult or undesirable

thro' /throo/, **thro** *prep, adv* same as **through** (*informal or literary*) [15C. Variant]

throat /thrōt/ *n* **1. DIGESTIVE AND BREATHING PASSAGE** the part of the airway and digestive tract between the mouth and both the oesophagus and the windpipe **2. FRONT OF NECK** the front part of the neck of an animal or human being **3. NARROW PART** a narrow part or passage that resembles a human's or animal's throat in shape or function **4. OPENING OF TUBULAR ORGAN OF FLOWER** the opening of a tubular organ of a flower, e.g. of a corolla **5. SORE THROAT** a throat infection (*informal*) [Old English *þrote* < Germanic] —**throated** /thrṓtid/ *adj* ◇ **be at each other's throats** to be constantly quarrelling or fighting ◇ **jump down somebody's throat** to speak angrily and impatiently to somebody ◇ **ram** *or* **force something down somebody's throat** to make repeated and emphatic attempts to get somebody to listen to or accept a view or belief

throatlash /thrṓt lash/, **throatlatch** /-lach/ *n* the strap that passes under a horse's jaw to hold its bridle in place

throat microphone, **throat mike** *informal n* a microphone that is placed in contact with the throat to pick up the vibrations produced by speech

throaty /thrṓti/ (**-ier, -iest**) *adj* **1.** sounding deep and husky **2.** deep or rough in tone, as though having been produced in the throat —**throatily** *adv* —**throatiness** *n*

throb /throb/ *vi* (**throbs, throbbing, throbbed**) **1. BEAT RAPIDLY AND FORCEFULLY** to beat or pulsate in a rapid forceful way ○ *My head is throbbing.* **2. BEAT REGULARLY** to have a regular rhythmic beat ■ *n* **1. SINGLE BEAT** a single beat or pulsation **2. REGULAR BEAT** a regular beat or pulsation [14C. Probably an imitation of pulsating] —**throbbingly** *adv*

throe /thrō/ *n* **PANG** a spasm of pain ■ **throes** *npl* **1. EFFECTS OF PANGS** the effects of severe physical pain **2. EFFECTS OF UPHEAVAL** the effects of an upheaval or struggle [12C. Origin ?] ◇ **in the throes of something** in the process of doing something, usually something difficult or unpleasant

thromb- *prefix* same as **thrombo-** (*used before vowels*)

thrombi MED plural of **thrombus**

thrombin /thrómbin/ *n* an enzyme in blood that causes clotting by catalysing the conversion of fibrinogen to fibrin [Late 19C. < THROMBO-]

thrombo- *prefix* blood clot ○ *thromboplastic* [< Greek *thrombos* 'clot']

thrombocyte /thrómbō sīt/ *n* BIOL same as **platelet** —**thrombocytic** /thrómbō síttik/ *adj*

thrombocytopenia /thrómbō sītō péeni ə/ *n* the state of having fewer than the normal number of blood platelets per unit volume of blood, often associated with haemorrhaging [Early 20C. < THROMBOCYTE] —**thrombocytopenic** *adj*

thromboembolism /thrómbō émbəlizəm/ *n* the blockage of a blood vessel by a blood clot (**thrombus**) that has broken away from its site of origin —**thromboembolic** /thrómbō em bóllik/ *adj* —**thromboembolitic** /thrómbō émbə líttik/ *adj*

thrombokinase /thrómbō kīnayss, -nayz/ *n* BIOCHEM same as **thromboplastin**

thrombolysis /throm bólləssiss/ *n* the breaking down of a blood clot by infusion of an enzyme into the blood —**thrombolytic** /thrómbō líttik/ *adj*

thrombophlebitis /thrómbō fli bītiss/ *n* inflammation of a vein with the formation of a blood clot

thromboplastic /thrómbō plástik/ *adj* causing or increasing blood-clot formation

thromboplastin /thrómbō plástin/ *n* a blood-clotting factor in blood platelets that converts prothrombin to thrombin

thrombose /throm bṓz, thrombṓss/ (**-boses, -bosing, -bosed**) *vti* to affect something such as a coronary artery with thrombosis, or be affected by thrombosis

thrombosis /throm bṓssiss/ (*plural* **-boses** /-bṓs seez/) *n* the formation or presence of one or more blood clots that may partially or completely block an artery or vein [Early 18C. < modern Latin < Greek *thrombos* 'clot'] —**thrombotic** /throm bóttik/ *adj*

thromboxane /throm bók sayn/ *n* a substance in platelets that causes blood clotting and constriction of blood vessels

thrombus /thrómbəss/ (*plural* **-bi** /thróm bī/) *n* a blood clot that forms in a blood vessel and remains at the site of formation [Late 17C. Via modern Latin < Greek *thrombos* 'clot']

throne /thrōn/ *n* **1. CHAIR OF MONARCH OR BISHOP** an ornate chair, often raised on a platform and covered by a canopy, occupied by a monarch or bishop on ceremonial occasions **2. POWER OF ROYAL PERSON** the power, rank, and privileges of a monarch **3. ANGEL OF SEVENTH-HIGHEST ORDER** an angel of the seventh of the nine orders of angels in the traditional Christian hierarchy **4. TOILET** the part of a lavatory on which people sit (*informal humorous*) ■ *vti* (**thrones, throning, throned**) **PUT SOMEBODY ON THRONE** to place somebody on a throne, or be placed on a throne [12C. Via Old French *trone* < Greek *thronos*]

throng /throng/ *n* **CROWD** a large crowd of people or objects (*literary*) ■ *v* (**throngs, thronging, thronged**) **1.** *vt* **CROWD INTO PLACE** to crowd into or fill a place **2.** *vi* **MOVE IN CROWD** to move or gather in a throng **3.** *vt* **CROWD AROUND SOMEBODY** to surround and push against somebody [Old English *geþrang* < Germanic, 'to press, crowd']

throstle /thróss'l/ *n* **1.** a thrush, especially a song thrush (*literary*) **2.** a machine formerly used for the continuous spinning of cotton or wool fibres [Old English *þrostle* < Indo-European]

throttle /thrótt'l/ *n* **1. VALVE CONTROLLING FLUID FLOW** a valve used to control the flow of a fluid, especially the amount of fuel and air entering the cylinders of an internal-combustion engine **2. CONTROL FOR THROTTLE** a pedal or lever for controlling a throttle valve **3.** *regional* **THROAT** a throat, either when regarded as part of the neck or as a digestive or breathing passage ■ *v* (**-tles, -tling, -tled**) **1.** *vt* **KILL PERSON OR ANIMAL BY CHOKING** to kill or injure a person or animal by squeezing the throat **2.** *vt* **SILENCE OR SUPPRESS SOMEBODY OR SOMETHING** to prevent somebody or something from expressing an opinion freely or from engaging in an activity **3.** *vt* **STOP SOMETHING FROM PROGRESSING** to prevent something from continuing or developing ○ *policies that throttle foreign investment* **4.** *vti* **REGULATE FUEL FLOW USING THROTTLE** to regulate the amount of fuel entering an engine using a throttle **5.** *vti* **REGULATE ENGINE SPEED** to regulate the speed of an engine by using a throttle [14C. < THROAT] —**throttler** *n*

through /throo/ CORE MEANING: a grammatical word used to indicate movement from one side or end of something to or past the other side or end

1. *prep, adv* **PASSING ACROSS** passing from one side or end of something to the other ○ *bored a hole through the wall* ○ *trying to find a way through* **2.** *prep, adv* **TRAVELLING ACROSS** travelling across or to various places in a town, country, or area ○ *He spent the summer travelling through Europe.* ○ *We're not stopping long; we're just passing through.* **3.** *prep, adv* **AMONG** in the midst of, or having things or people all around or on either side of ○ *She wandered through the crowds milling around outside the cathedral.* ○ *I'd like to browse through and see if there are any articles that interest me.* **4.** *prep, adv* **PAST BARRIER** past the limitations or difficulties of something such as a barrier or a problem ○ *the problems involved in wading through acres of bureaucracy* ○ *The road has been narrowed to prevent larger vehicles getting through.* **5.** *prep, adv* **FROM BEGINNING TO END** from the beginning until the end or conclusion of ○ *Martin and Johanson's works will be on view through June.* ○ *I can't come I'm afraid; I'm working through.* **6.** *prep, adv* **TO CONCLUSION** to completion, to a usually successful conclusion, or so as to have finished with something ○ *She sailed through the exam.* ○ *They had to twist a few arms to get the proposal through.* ○ *The champion, as expected, is through to the second*

round. **7.** *prep* **VIA** by way or means of ○ *I'll send you a copy through the post.* **8.** *prep* **OVER EXTENT OF** happening or existing over the entire extent of or affecting all of ○ *A flu of epidemic proportions swept through the town.* **9.** *prep* **BECAUSE OF** as a result of ○ *Through his mishandling of our affairs, we'll be lucky to be in credit at all this year.* **10.** *prep N Am* **UP TO** up to and including that time ○ *Museum hours are 2–4 p.m. Tuesdays through Fridays.* **11.** *adv* **THOROUGHLY** completely and in every part ○ *Your clothes are wet through.* **12.** *adv* **ABLE TO SPEAK ON PHONE** so as to establish a telephone connection with somebody ○ *We've been trying to get through all morning but the lines are busy.* ○ *You're through to Ms. Spriggs.* **13.** *adj* **GOING DIRECTLY** going directly without stopping or requiring a change ○ *The through train leaves on the hour.* **14.** *adj* **PASSING THROUGH SOMETHING** proceeding or extending from one side or end of something to the other or through something and beyond it ○ *a through room* ○ *through traffic* [Old English *þurh* < Indo-European, 'pass through'] ◇ **be through with somebody** (*informal*) **1.** to want to have nothing else to do with somebody **2.** to have finished doing something, often something unpleasant, to somebody ○ *When I'm through with him, he really will have a headache!* ◇ **be through with something** to have finished with something (*informal*) ◇ **through and through** completely

through-composed *adj* describes a song with different music for each verse, especially without pauses between the verses, or an opera that is not clearly divided into arias and recitatives

through-other *adj Ireland, Scotland* (*informal*) **1.** in a state of confusion or disorder **2.** in a dishevelled, disorderly, or agitated state —**through other** *adv*

throughout /throo ówt/ *prep, adv* **1.** through or during the whole of ○ *Societies throughout history believed they had reached the frontiers of human accomplishment.* ○ *Throughout, they maintained their dignity.* **2.** happening or existing in all parts of ○ *The group is seeking experts of any age throughout the area.* ○ *The house is carpeted throughout.*

throughput /thróo pòot/ *n* the amount of something such as data or raw material that is processed over a given period [After INPUT and OUTPUT]

throughway /thróo way/, **thruway** *n N Am* ROADS same as **expressway**

throve past tense of **thrive**

throw /thrō/ *vt* (**throws, throwing, threw** /throo/, **thrown** /thrōn/) **1.** **SEND SOMETHING FROM HAND** to propel something through the air by swinging the arm and releasing the object from the hand ○ *throw a brick through a window* **2.** **SEND FORTH SOMETHING INTO AIR** to propel something through or into the air by a mechanical means, or to emit or radiate something **3.** **DROP SOMETHING CARELESSLY** to put or drop something somewhere without paying attention to where it is left ○ *throws magazines all over the place* **4.** **FORCE SOMEBODY OR SOMETHING SOMEWHERE** to put somebody or something forcefully into a particular position or in a particular direction ○ *He was thrown out.* **5.** **PUT SOMEBODY OR SOMETHING IN DIFFERENT CIRCUMSTANCES** to bring somebody or something suddenly or unexpectedly into a particular state, especially an undesirable one ○ *thrown out of a job* ○ *thrown into confusion* **6.** **HURL SOMEBODY TO GROUND** to make a movement that causes somebody, e.g. an opponent in wrestling or judo or a horse rider to fall to the ground **7.** **DISCONCERT SOMEBODY** to take somebody by surprise to the extent that he or she does not know how to react ○ *His unexpected arrival threw me.* **8.** **PROJECT LIGHT** to send out light to illuminate a place, or create a shadow by blocking light **9.** **CAST DOUBT OR SUSPICION** to cause doubt or suspicion in people's minds by saying or doing something **10.** **DIRECT EYES** to direct a look or glance quickly or suddenly ○ *She threw me a warning look.* **11.** **HAVE EXTREME REACTION** to react with a sudden outburst of strong emotion, e.g. anger or ill-temper ○ *throw a tantrum* **12.** **MOVE OPERATING SWITCH OR LEVER** to move something, usually a switch or lever, to make a machine or system operate or to connect up a system **13.** **BUILD SOMETHING HASTILY** to build or erect something hastily ○ *The enemy threw a bridge across the moat.* **14.** **MAKE OBJECT ON POTTER'S WHEEL** to produce a ceramic object by turning clay on a potter's wheel **15.** **TURN MATERIAL ON LATHE** to turn wood or metal on a lathe **16.** **MAKE MATERIAL INTO YARN** to make silk or filaments into thread by twisting or spinning **17.** **DELIVER PUNCH** to deliver a punch or blow with a movement of the arm **18.** **HOST PARTY** to organize and be the host at a party **19.** **LOSE SOMETHING INTENTIONALLY** to lose a fight, race, or contest deliberately, e.g. by not trying or by committing a foul **20.** **PROJECT VOICE** to project a vocal sound so that it seems to be coming from elsewhere **21.** LEISURE **ROLL DICE** to tip or roll dice onto a flat surface to obtain a score, or score a particular number in this way **22.** **GIVE BIRTH TO YOUNG** to give birth to young (*refers especially to cows*) **23.** *Malaysia, Singapore* same as **throw away** (sense 1) ○ *Once you get your new card you can throw the old one.* ■ *n* **1.** **ACT OF THROWING** an act of throwing something such as a ball or missile, or dice in a game **2.** **DISTANCE THROWN** the distance that something is thrown or can be thrown **3.** SPORTS **WAY OF THROWING** an act of being thrown, or a way of throwing an opponent, in wrestling or judo **4.** LEISURE **SCORE THROWN** the score obtained by throwing something such as dice or darts in a game **5.** **EACH** each item or attempt (*informal*) ○ *I didn't buy any – they were ten pounds a throw.* **6.** HOUSEHOLD **COVER FOR FURNITURE** a loose cover used to protect furniture **7.** MECH ENG **MOVEMENT OF MACHINE PART** the maximum movement in a single direction of a machine part driven by a crank, cam, or eccentric **8.** PHYS **DEFLECTION OF MEASURING INSTRUMENT** the distance moved by the tip of the needle of a measuring instrument **9.** GEOL **VERTICAL DISPLACEMENT ALONG GEOLOGICAL FAULT** the vertical displacement up or down produced by movement along a geological fault [Old English *þrāwan* 'twist, hurl' < Indo-European, 'to twist'] —**thrower** *n* ◇ **throw yourself into something** to start doing something with great energy and commitment

---

SYNONYMS ***throw, chuck, fling, hurl, toss, cast***

CORE MEANING: to send something through the air

throw to propel something through the air by swinging the arm and releasing the object from the hand ○ *Fred applauded and threw his hat into the air.* ○ *Police sprayed tear gas when about 500 protesters threw rocks at a passenger train.* **chuck** (*informal*) to throw something, especially in a careless or casual way ○ *He chucked the forms in the bin.* ○ *Then the woman grabbed her bloke's pint and chucked it all over him.* **fling** to throw something or somebody carelessly or forcefully ○ *She flung herself face down on the bed.* ○ *Seb flung aside his pitchfork and climbed down from the loft.* **hurl** to throw something with great force ○ *Rebels fired gunshots and hurled grenades at the police station.* ○ *The elephant seized the boy with its trunk and hurled him to the ground.* **toss** to throw something small or light in a casual or careless way ○ *One of the children tossed a ball high in the air.* ○ *David sat back in his armchair, tossing aside his magazine.* **cast** to throw something to a particular place or into a particular thing, or to throw a fishing line or net ○ *He was cast overboard like so much ballast.*

---

throw away *vt* **1.** **DISCARD SOMETHING** to get rid of something no longer wanted **2.** **WASTE SOMETHING** to fail to take advantage of an opportunity to do something **3.** **SAY SOMETHING IN OFFHAND MANNER** to say a line in a play in a way that makes it seem unimportant, even though it may be crucial to the plot

throw in *vt* **1.** **ADD SOMETHING TO DISCUSSION** to contribute a comment to a conversation or discussion **2.** **ADD SOMETHING AS EXTRA** to add something as an extra, especially another item at no extra cost when selling something **3.** **RETURN BALL INTO PLAY BY HAND** to return a football to the pitch by means of an overhead throw after it has gone out of play ◇ **throw in the towel** *or* **sponge** to admit or accept defeat when something is proving difficult (*informal*)

throw off *vt* **1.** **FREE YOURSELF FROM SOMETHING** to get rid of something troublesome or oppressive **2.** **TAKE CLOTHES OFF HASTILY** to remove an item of clothing in a hurried or careless way **3.** **GIVE OFF SOMETHING** to emit a substance into the air **4.** **ESCAPE FROM SOMEBODY** to elude a pursuer **5.** **SAY SOMETHING IN OFFHAND WAY** to say or write something in a casual manner **6.** **MAKE SOMEBODY FLUSTERED** to confuse or unsettle somebody by doing something unexpected

throw off at *v ANZ* to make harsh or negative judgments about somebody (*informal*)

throw on *vt* to put an item of clothing on in a hurried or careless way

throw out *vt* **1.** **DISCARD SOMETHING** to get rid of something no longer wanted, especially something that has been kept for a while **2.** **EJECT SOMEBODY** to eject somebody forcibly from a place **3.** **DISMISS SOMEBODY** to expel somebody from membership of an organization **4.** **SUGGEST SOMETHING** to make a suggestion, proposal, or hint, especially in an informal way **5.** **REJECT BILL** to reject a bill in Parliament **6.** **REJECT LAWSUIT** to reject a lawsuit so that the defendant does not have to stand trial **7.** **DISCONCERT SOMEBODY** to confuse or unsettle somebody by doing something unexpected **8.** **BUILD PROJECTING CONSTRUCTION** to build something in such a way that it sticks out **9.** **GIVE OFF SOMETHING** to emit a substance into the air **10.** **PUT CRICKET PLAYER OUT** in cricket, to cause a batsman to be run out by throwing the ball and hitting the wicket **11.** **PUT BASEBALL PLAYER OUT** in baseball, to throw the ball to a team-mate who puts the runner out

throw over *vt* to end a romantic or sexual relationship with somebody (*informal*)

throw together *vt* (*informal*) **1.** to make something in a hurry or carelessly **2.** to cause people to meet and become acquainted with each other in a casual or unplanned way

throw up *v* **1.** *vt* **BUILD SOMETHING HASTILY** to erect a building or structure quickly **2.** *vt* **BRING SOMETHING TO NOTICE** to produce or reveal somebody or something, especially unexpectedly or indirectly **3.** *vti* **VOMIT** to vomit the contents of the stomach (*informal*) **4.** *vt* **ABANDON SOMETHING** to give something up, especially something important or valuable (*informal*)

throwaway /thrṓ ə way/ *adj* **1.** **DISPOSABLE** designed to be thrown away after use **2.** **WASTEFUL** tending to discard things too readily ○ *a throwaway society* **3.** **OFFHAND** said or written in an apparently offhand manner ■ *n* **SOMETHING TO BE DISCARDED** an object designed to be thrown away after use

throwback /thrṓ bak/ *n* **1.** **ORGANISM REVERTING TO EARLIER TYPE** an organism with the characteristics of an earlier type **2.** **REVERSION TO EARLIER TYPE** reversion to an earlier ancestral type **3.** **ANIMAL OR PERSON RESEMBLING ANCESTOR** an animal or person bearing a striking resemblance to an ancestor **4.** **ANACHRONISTIC THING** something contemporary that seems to belong to the past

throw-in *n* **1.** **RETURN OF FOOTBALL TO PLAY** an act of returning a football to play from the sideline by propelling it from behind the head with both hands **2.** **RETURN OF BALL FROM OUTFIELD** an act of returning a baseball or cricket ball after it has been hit to the outfield **3.** **RETURN OF BASKETBALL TO PLAY** an act of returning a basketball to play by passing it onto the court

throwing stick /thrṓ ing-/ *n* a device used in many traditional societies for launching a spear or dart

thrown past participle of **throw**

throw pillow *n N Am* same as **scatter cushion**

throw rug *n N Am* HOUSEHOLD same as **scatter rug**

throwster /thrṓstər/ *n* somebody who twists filaments into thread

throw weight *n* the total weight of a missile's payload, including the warhead and guidance system but not the rocket

thru /throo/ *prep, adv, adj N Am* same as **through** (*informal*)

thrum[1] /thrum/ *v* (**thrums, thrumming, thrummed**) **1.** *vti* **STRUM** to strum on a stringed instrument **2.** *vi* **TAP STEADILY** to drum on something, especially with the fingers **3.** *vti* **SAY OR SPEAK MONOTONOUSLY** to say something or talk monotonously ■ *n* **MONOTONOUS BEAT** a low monotonous beating sound [Late 16C. An imitation of the sound] —**thrummer** *n*

thrum[2] /thrum/ *n* **1.** **THREAD END LEFT ON LOOM** an unwoven end or row of ends from warp threads that are left on a loom after the web has been cut off **2.** **FRINGE** a short fringe or thread end ■ **thrums** *npl* **YARN PIECES ADDED TO CANVAS** short pieces of yarn inserted in canvas in order to create a rough surface and prevent chafing or leaks ■ *vt* (**thrums, thrumming, thrummed**) **1.** **ADD FRINGES TO SOMETHING** to put fringes on something **2.** **INSERT YARN PIECES IN CANVAS** to insert pieces of yarn in canvas in order to create a rough surface and prevent chafing or leaks [Old English *þrum* < Indo-European]

thrush

~~thruogh~~ incorrect spelling of **through**

thruppence *npl* MONEY same as **threepence**

thruppenny *adj* MONEY same as **threepenny**

thrush[1] /thrush/ (*plural* **thrushes** or *same*) *n* a small to medium-sized songbird with a slender beak, usually a speckled breast, and an often melodious song. It belongs to the family that includes the song thrush, mistle thrush, and blackbird. Family: Turdidae. [Old English *þrysce* < W Germanic]

thrush[2] /thrush/ *n* 1. FUNGAL DISEASE OF MOUTH a fungal infection of the mouth characterized by white patches 2. FUNGAL INFECTION OF VAGINA a fungal infection of the vagina characterized by a white discharge and itching 3. DISEASE OF HORSE'S HOOF infection of the fleshy part of a horse's foot (**frog**), causing softening of the horn and a foul-smelling discharge [Mid-17C. Origin ?]

thrust /thrust/ *v* (**thrusts, thrusting, thrust**) 1. *vt* PUSH SOMEBODY OR SOMETHING FORCEFULLY to push somebody or something with a single movement of considerable force ○ *He thrust his hands into his pockets.* 2. *vti* FORCE WAY to move with a determined or forceful pushing motion ○ *We thrust our way through the crowd to the bar.* 3. *vti* STRETCH OR EXTEND to stretch or extend something, or be stretched or extended, with a dramatic or forceful effect ○ *towers thrusting skywards* 4. *vt* FORCE SOMEBODY INTO SOMETHING to force somebody to accept or deal with something ○ *He was thrust into the limelight.* 5. *vti* ATTACK BY STABBING to attack somebody with a piercing or stabbing movement with a weapon 6. *vt* INSERT SOMETHING to add or insert material, usually inappropriately, into a context ■ *n* 1. GIST OR AIM OF SOMETHING the chief meaning, direction, or purpose of something ○ *the thrust of her argument* 2. FORCEFUL PUSH a forceful push or shove 3. FORWARD MOVEMENT a forward movement or impetus 4. STABBING ACTION a piercing or stabbing action 5. MILITARY ATTACK a military assault or offensive 6. AEROSP REACTIVE FORCE OF EXPELLED GASES the reactive force of expelled gases such as those generated by a rocket or jet engine 7. ENG FORCE OF PROPELLER a propulsive force produced by a rotating propeller, e.g. on a ship or aircraft 8. GEOL FORCE IN EARTH'S CRUST a force in the Earth's crust that results in recumbent folding of rock strata 9. GEOL same as **thrust fault** 10. CIV ENG FORCE EXERTED BY STRUCTURE the continuous force exerted sideways or downwards by one structure on another, e.g. by an arch on an abutment or a rafter against a wall [12C. < Old Norse *þrýsta*] —**thrustful** *adj*

thrust bearing *n* a bearing designed to withstand axial loading and to prevent movement along the axis of a loaded shaft

thruster /thrústər/ *n* 1. ROCKET THAT CONTROLS ALTITUDE a rocket on a spacecraft or high-altitude aircraft that controls an altitude or flight path 2. MANOEUVRING DEVICE ON OIL-DRILLING VESSEL a jet or propeller on an oil-drilling ship or offshore rig, used to manoeuvre it into position 3. SOMEBODY AGGRESSIVELY AMBITIOUS an aggressive pursuer of personal ambitions 4. SURF-BOARD OR SAILBOARD WITH EXTRA FIN a surfboard or sailboard equipped with one or more extra fins designed to give it greater speed or manoeuvrability 5. FOX HUNTER GETTING TOO FAR FORWARDS a fox hunter who gets too close to the pack during a hunt (*slang*)

thrust fault *n* an inclined fault in which rocks on the lower side of the slope are displaced downwards

thrusting /thrústing/ *adj* tending to pursue ambitions aggressively

thrust stage *n* a stage surrounded on three sides by the audience

thruway *n* N Am ROADS another spelling of **throughway**

Thucydides /thyoo síddi deez/ (460?–400? BC) Athenian historian. A major figure in the development of historical writing, he is known for his *History of the Peloponnesian War*, a conflict in which he himself had fought.

'War, which robs people of the easy supply of their daily wants, is a violent school-master matching most men's tempers to their condition.'
[Thucydides, *History of the Peloponnesian War*; 431–413 BC]

'Happiness depends on being free, and freedom depends on being courageous.'
[Thucydides, *History of the Peloponnesian War*; 431–413 BC]

thud /thud/ *n* 1. DULL HEAVY SOUND a loud dull sound made by a heavy object impacting with a surface 2. DULL HEAVY BLOW a blow that makes a dull heavy sound ■ *vi* (**thuds, thudding, thudded**) MAKE THUD to make a dull heavy sound [Early 16C. Probably < Old English *þyddan* 'thrust']

thug /thug/ *n* 1. somebody, especially a criminal, who is brutal and violent 2. *also* **Thug** a member of a former secret organization of robbers in India, worshippers of the goddess Kali, who strangled their victims [Early 19C. < Hindi *thag* 'swindler, cheat, robber' < Sanskrit *sthagayati* 'covers, conceals'] —**thuggery** *n* —**thuggish** *adj*

thuggee /thu gée/ *n* the method of robbery and murder by strangulation, characteristic of the former thugs of India [Mid-19C. < Hindi *thagī* < *thag* (see THUG)]

thuja /thyoóyə/ (*plural* **-jas** or *same*), **thuya** (*plural* **-yas** or *same*) *n* TREES same as **arbor vitae** [Mid-18C. Via modern Latin *Thuja* < medieval Latin *thuia* 'cedar' < Greek]

thulium /thyoóli əm/ *n* a very rare soft bright silvery-grey metallic element of the lanthanide series. Source: monazite, bastnaesite. Use: X-ray source. Symbol **Tm**. See table at **element** [Late 19C. After *Thule*, most northerly region to the ancients; because first found in Norway]

thumb /thum/ *n* 1. THICKEST DIGIT ON HUMAN HAND the thickest digit of the human hand, located next to the forefinger. It can be moved to face and touch the other fingers so that objects can be grasped. 2. ANIMAL'S DIGIT RESEMBLING HUMAN THUMB a short thick digit in some animals, e.g. in many primates, that is adapted for grasping and corresponds to the human thumb 3. SECTION OF GLOVE FOR THUMB the part of a glove or mitten that covers the thumb 4. ARCHIT same as **ovolo** ■ *v* (**thumbs, thumbing, thumbed**) 1. *vti* HITCH LIFT to obtain or try to obtain a lift by signalling with the thumb to passing drivers 2. *vt* MAKE SOMETHING DIRTY BY USE to soil or cause wear on something, especially a book, by repeated handling (*often passive*) ○ *a well-thumbed book* 3. *vti* FLIP THROUGH PRINTED MATTER to glance through the pages of a book or magazine [Old English *þuma* < Indo-European] —**thumbless** *adj* ◇ **all thumbs** extremely awkward or clumsy ◇ **hold thumbs** S Africa to hope for a good outcome (*informal*) ○ *Cricketing fans will be holding thumbs this week.* ◇ **stick out like a sore thumb** to be completely obvious, or conspicuously out of place ◇ **suck something out of your thumb** S Africa to give an opinion about something without having sufficient information, or to make something up ○ *It is possible he sucked the figure out of his thumb, as it seemed extremely high.* ◇ **twiddle your thumbs** to be idle or unoccupied, especially involuntarily ◇ **under somebody's thumb** under the influence and control of somebody

thumbhole /thúm hōl/ *n* 1. a hole in something such as a bowling ball into which a thumb can be inserted in order to provide a grip 2. a hole in a wind instrument that is covered and uncovered by the thumb to produce notes

thumb index *n* a series of labelled indentations cut into the pages of a book down the edge opposite the binding to allow a particular section to be located quickly —**thumb-index** *vt*

thumb knot *n* same as **overhand knot**

thumbnail /thúm nayl/ *n* 1. NAIL OF THUMB the hard growing plate of keratin on the surface of the tip of the thumb 2. COMPUT MINIATURE GRAPHIC IMAGE a small version of a larger graphic image displayed on a computer monitor so as to save space ■ *adj* CONCISE covering the salient points concisely ○ *a thumbnail sketch*

thumbnut /thúm nut/ *n* CONSTR same as **wing nut**

thumb piano *n* a box-shaped African musical instrument with a row of tuned metal or wooden strips that vibrate when plucked by the thumb

thumbprint /thúm print/ *n* an impression of the fleshy pad near the tip of the thumb, often used to identify people

thumbscrew /thúm skroo/ *n* 1. an instrument of torture used to crush the thumbs 2. a screw with a flat head to be turned with the thumb and forefinger

thumbs-down *n* an indication of disapproval or rejection (*informal*)

thumbstall /thúm stawl/ *n* a sheath of rubber, leather, or fabric used to protect the thumb, e.g. by covering a dressing on an injured thumb

thumbsuck S Africa (*informal*) *n* an opinion or estimate made with little information on which to base it ○ *a thumbsuck figure* ■ *vt* to give an opinion or make a rough estimate about something without having sufficient information ○ *This analysis shows clearly that he is not telling the truth and that he is just thumbsucking his figures.*

thumbs-up *n* an indication of approval or acceptance (*informal*)

thumbtack /thúm tak/ *n* N Am same as **drawing pin**

Thummim /thúmmim/ *n* JUDAISM ♦ **Urim and Thummim** [Mid-16C. < Hebrew *tummīm*, plural of *tōm* 'completeness']

thump /thump/ *v* (**thumps, thumping, thumped**) 1. *vi* PALPITATE OR POUND to beat very fast or loudly because of fear or excitement (*refers to the heart*) 2. *vi* MAKE DULL HEAVY SOUND to make the loud dull sound that a heavy object makes when it impacts with a surface 3. *vti* STRIKE HEAVILY to strike somebody or something heavily with the fist or an object 4. *vt* DEFEAT SOMEBODY CONVINCINGLY to inflict a humiliating defeat upon somebody (*informal; often passive*) ○ *Our team was thumped 9–0.* ■ *n* 1. DULL HEAVY SOUND the loud dull sound made by a heavy object impacting with a surface ○ *I heard a loud thump from next door.* 2. HEAVY BLOW a heavy blow struck with the fist or an object [Mid-16C. An imitation of the sound] —**thumper** *n*

thumping /thúmping/ *adj* 1. LARGE huge, resounding, or impressive (*informal*) ○ *won by a thumping majority* 2. PAINFUL very painful and throbbing ○ *a thumping headache* ■ *adv* VERY extremely or exceptionally (*informal*) ○ *a thumping good read* —**thumpingly** *adv*

Thun /toon/ town in the canton of Bern, central Switzerland. Population: 39,854 (1998).

thunbergia /thun búrji ə/ *n* a widely cultivated ornamental plant of the acanthus family with opposite pairs of simple leaves. Flowers: five-lobed, tubular. Native to: Africa, South Asia. Genus: *Thunbergia*. [Late 18C. < modern Latin *Thunbergia*, after C. P. Thunberg (1743–1822), Swedish botanist]

thunder /thúndər/ *n* 1. LOUD NOISE FOLLOWING LIGHTNING a loud rumbling noise caused by the rapid expansion of air suddenly heated by lightning 2. NOISE RESEMBLING THUNDER a loud deep rumbling noise resembling thunder 3. THREATENING OR VEHEMENT UTTERANCE a manifestation of somebody's anger in an explosion of strong words ■ *v* (**-ders, -dering, -dered**) 1. *vi* MAKE LOUD NOISE FOLLOWING LIGHTNING to make a loud rumbling noise caused by the rapid expansion of air suddenly heated by lightning 2. *vi* RUMBLE LOUDLY LIKE THUNDER to make a loud deep rumbling noise resembling thunder 3. *vti* SHOUT VEHEMENTLY to shout something loudly and angrily [Old English *þunor* (noun), *þunrian* (verb) < Indo-European] ◇ **steal somebody's thunder** to prevent somebody from receiving acclaim for doing something by doing it or something similar first

Thunder Bay /thúndər-/ city in northwestern Ontario, Canada, on Thunder Bay, an arm of Lake Superior. Population: 103,215 (2001).

thunderbird: totem pole, Stanley Park, Vancouver, Canada

thunderbird /thúndər burd/ *n* in Native North American mythology, a bird that produces thunder, used as a stylized symbol on totem poles

thunderbolt /thúndər bōlt/ *n* **1.** FLASH OF LIGHTNING WITH THUNDER a flash of lightning accompanied by a crash of thunder **2.** STARTLING OCCURRENCE a sudden shocking action, occurrence, pronouncement, or piece of news **3.** MYTHOLOGICAL WEAPON WIELDED BY GODS in mythology, a destructive missile hurled to Earth by a god in a flash of lightning **4.** FORMIDABLE PERSON OR THING somebody or something that resembles a thunderbolt in energy or destructive power

thunderbox /thúndər boks/ *n* a toilet, especially a primitive or portable one (*dated informal humorous*)

thunderclap /thúndər klap/ *n* **1.** CRASH OF THUNDER a loud crashing noise produced by thunder **2.** STARTLING OCCURRENCE a sudden shocking occurrence or piece of news **3.** NOISE RESEMBLING THUNDER a sudden loud sound resembling thunder

thundercloud /thúndər klowd/ *n* a large dark cumulonimbus cloud that produces thunder and lightning

thunderhead /thúndər hed/ *n* N Am the upper rounded mass of a cumulonimbus cloud associated with the development of a thunderstorm

thundering /thúndəring/ (*dated informal*) *adj* very great ■ *adv* extremely or exceptionally —**thunderingly** *adv*

thunderous /thúndərəss/ *adj* **1.** resembling thunder in its loudness ○ *thunderous applause* **2.** angry and threatening —**thunderously** *adv*

thunder run *n* formerly, each of two inclined wooden troughs down which iron balls were rolled offstage to simulate thunder as a theatrical sound effect

thunder sheet *n* a large sheet of metal shaken to simulate thunder as a theatrical sound effect

thundershower /thúndər showər/ *n* a shower of rain during a thunderstorm

thunderstone /thúndər stōn/ *n* a naturally occurring long tapering piece of rock, formerly believed to be a thunderbolt

thunderstorm /thúndər stawrm/ *n* a storm with thunder, lightning, heavy rain, and sometimes hail

thunderstruck /thúndər struk/ *adj* so surprised, incredulous, or startled as to be in a state of shock

thundery /thúndəri/ *adj* **1.** causing or indicating the onset of thunder or a thunderstorm **2.** resembling thunder in sound

thunk[1] /thungk/ (*informal*) *n* same as **thud** *n* (sense 1) ■ *vi* (**thunks, thunking, thunked**) to make a thudding sound [Mid-20C. An imitation of the sound]

thunk[2] /thungk/ US past participle, past tense of **think** (*nonstandard*)

Thur. *abbr* CALENDAR Thursday

Thurber /thúrbər/, **James** (1894–1961) US writer and cartoonist. He is known for his humorous and poignant portrayals of the frustrations and absurd situations of modern life. Full name **Thurber, James Grover**

'Then, with that faint fleeting smile playing about his lips, he faced the firing squad; erect and motionless, proud and disdainful, Walter Mitty, the undefeated, inscrutable to the last.'

[James Thurber, 'The Secret Life of Walter Mitty', *My World—And Welcome to It*; 1942]

thurible /thyoório'l/ *n* RELIG same as **censer** [15C. Directly or via French < Latin *t(h)uribulum* < Greek *thuos* 'sacrifice, incense']

thurifer /thyoórifər/ *n* somebody who carries the censer in religious ceremonies [Mid-19C. < late Latin < Greek *thuos* 'sacrifice, incense']

Thurs. *abbr* CALENDAR Thursday

Thursday /thúrz day, -di/ *n* the fourth day of the traditional working week, coming after Wednesday and before Friday [Old English *zzu(n)resdæg* 'day of thunder', translation of late Latin *Jovis dies* 'day of Jupiter (the god of thunder)']

Thursday Island /thúrz day-/ island in the Torres Strait, off the northeastern coast of Australia. Area: 4 sq. km/1 sq. mi.

Thursdays /thúrz dayz, -diz/ *adv* every Thursday

Thurso /thúrssō/ town and seaport on the northern coast of Scotland. It is the northernmost town on the mainland of Great Britain. Population: 8,488 (1991).

thus /thuss/ *adv* (*formal*) **1.** as a result ○ *He did no work at all, and thus was fired.* **2.** in this way ○ *Touch your left knee with your right elbow thus.* [Old English *pus*, origin ?] ◇ **thus far** up to this point ○ *The evidence thus far suggested that he was innocent.*

USAGE See *therefore*.

thusly /thússli/ *adv* US same as **thus** (sense 2) (*humorous*)

Thutmose III /thoot mōsə/ (*d.* 1450 BC) Egyptian pharaoh. He became pharaoh in 1504 BC. Through military conquest, he extended the Egyptian empire eastwards as far as the River Euphrates, and with the vast wealth of his eastern territories erected great temples and other imperial buildings in Egypt.

thuya *n* TREES another spelling of **thuja**

thwack /thwak/ *vt* (**thwacks, thwacking, thwacked**) to strike somebody or something with a flat object such as the flat of the hand ■ *n* a sharp smacking blow with a flat object [Early 16C. An imitation of the sound] —**thwacker** *n*

thwaite /thwayt/ *n* a piece of reclaimed wasteland (*archaic or regional*; *often used in placenames*) [Early 17C. < Old Norse *pveit(i)*]

thwart /thwawrt/ *v* (**thwarts, thwarting, thwarted**) **1.** *vt* FRUSTRATE SOMETHING to prevent somebody or somebody's plan from being successful **2.** *vti* PLACE OR BE PLACED ACROSS to place one thing across another, or be placed across something (*archaic*) ■ *adj* EXTENDING ACROSS situated or extending across something ■ *n* CROSSWISE SEAT IN BOAT a crosswise seat or transverse member on a rowing boat, canoe, or similar small boat ■ *prep, adv* same as **athwart** (*archaic*) [13C. < Old Norse *pvert*] —**thwartedly** /thwáwrtidli/ *adv* —**thwarter** *n*

THX *abbr* ONLINE thanks (*used in e-mails or text messages*)

thy /thī/ *det* belonging or relating to you, the second person singular possessive corresponding to 'thou' (*archaic*) [12C. Shortening of THINE]

Thyestes /thī ést eez/ *n* in Greek mythology, the brother of Atreus and king of Mycenae. After usurping the throne from his brother, he was tricked into eating the flesh of his own sons. —**Thyestean** *adj*

thylacine /thílə seen/ *n* a large carnivorous marsupial that resembles a dog and has brownish fur and black stripes across the back. It was once widespread throughout Australia but is now thought to be extinct. Native to: Tasmania. Latin name: *Thylacinus cynocephalus*. [Mid-19C. < modern Latin *Thylacinus* < Greek *thulakos* 'pouch']

thyme

thyme /tīm/ *n* a small low-growing bush with small aromatic leaves. Use: cooking, source of thymol. Genus: *Thymus*. [15C. Via Old French *thym* < Greek *thumon* < *thuein* 'burn, sacrifice'; from its use as incense] —**thymy** *adj*

SPELLCHECK **thyme** or **time**? Do not confuse the spelling of *thyme* and *time*, which sound similar. *Thyme* is a bush whose leaves are used in cooking. *Time* is a dimension, or the minute or hour as indicated by a clock, and can also be used as a verb: *space and time, asked the time, timed at one hour two minutes.*

thymectomy /thī méktəmi/ (*plural* -**mies**) *n* a surgical operation to remove the thymus gland [Early 20C. < THYMUS]

thymi ANAT *plural* of **thymus**

-thymia *suffix* condition or state of mind ○ *cyclothymia* [Via modern Latin < Greek *thumos* 'mind']

thymic[1] /thī mik/ *adj* relating to the thymus [Mid-17C. < THYMUS]

thymic[2] /tī mik/ *adj* relating to thyme [Mid-19C. < THYME]

thymidine /thī́mi deen/ *n* a nucleoside in DNA, consisting of thymine linked to deoxyribose [Early 20C. < THYMINE + -IDINE]

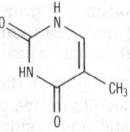

thymine

thymine /thī́ meen/ *n* one of the four nitrogenous bases in DNA in which it pairs with adenine. Formula: $C_5H_6N_2O_2$. Symbol **T** [Late 19C. < THYMIC[1]]

thymocyte /thī́mə sīt/ *n* a small white blood cell (**lymphocyte**) occurring in the thymus that is a precursor of a T-cell

thymol /thī́ mol/ *n* a colourless crystalline phenol with an aromatic odour. Source: thyme oil, synthetically made. Use: fungicide, preservative, vermifuge, perfumes. Formula: $C_{10}H_{14}O$. [Mid-19C. < Greek *thumon* (see THYME)]

thymoma /thī mṓmə/ (*plural* -**mas** or -**mata** /-mətə/) *n* a tumour of the thymus [Early 20C. < Greek *thumos* (see THYMUS)]

thymosin /thī́məssin/ *n* a hormone that influences the development and differentiation of T-cells in the thymus [Mid-20C. < Greek *thumos* (see THYMUS)]

thymus /thī́məss/ (*plural* -**muses** or -**mi** /-mī/), **thymus gland** *n* an organ, located at the base of the neck, that is involved in development of cells of the immune system, particularly T-cells. It is prominent in the young but shrinks after puberty. [Late 16C. Via modern Latin < Greek *thumos* 'warty growth resembling a bunch of thyme' < *thumon* (see THYME)]

thyratron /thíra tron/ n a gas-filled hot-cathode tube that acts as an electronic switch or relay in which a signal applied to the control grid initiates anode current but does not limit it [Early 20C. < Greek *thura* 'door']

thyristor /thī rístar/ n a semiconductor device that has two stable switches used for conductive and nonconductive modes [Mid-20C. Blend of THYRATRON + TRANSISTOR]

thyro- *prefix* thyroid ○ *thyrotropin* [< THYROID]

thyrocalcitonin /thírō kálssi tōnin/ n BIOCHEM same as **calcitonin**

thyroid /thī royd/ n 1. ANAT same as **thyroid gland** 2. ANAT same as **thyroid cartilage** 3. PHARM MEDICINE OBTAINED FROM ANIMAL THYROID GLAND a preparation obtained from the thyroid gland of an animal. Use: treating conditions of the thyroid gland. ■ *adj also* **thyroidal** /thī róyd'l/ 1. OF THYROID GLAND relating to, situated in, or secreted by the thyroid gland 2. OF THYROID CARTILAGE relating to the thyroid cartilage [Early 18C. < obsolete French *thyroide* < Greek *thura* 'door'; from the oblong shape of the cartilage in front of the throat]

thyroid cartilage n the largest cartilage of the larynx, forming the projection called the Adam's apple

thyroidectomy /thī roy déktəmi, thīrə-/ (*plural* **-mies**) n a surgical operation to remove the thyroid gland or part of it

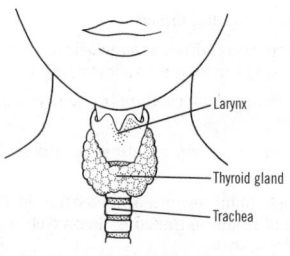

thyroid gland

thyroid gland n an endocrine gland located in the neck of human beings and other vertebrate animals that secretes the hormones responsible for controlling metabolism and growth. Excessive action of the thyroid gland can cause Graves' disease, while underactivity can cause myxoedema.

thyroid hormone n either of the two hormones, thyroxine and triiodothyronine, that are secreted by the thyroid gland and regulate body metabolism and growth

thyroiditis /thī roy dītiss/ n inflammation of the thyroid gland. This may be acute, as a result of bacterial infection, or chronic, as a result of an autoimmune response in which lymphocytes invade the gland.

thyroid-stimulating hormone n BIOCHEM same as **thyrotropin**

thyrotoxicosis /thírō tókssi kōssiss/ n MED same as **hyperthyroidism** (sense 1)

thyrotropin /thírō trōpin/, **thyrotrophin** /-fin/ n a hormone that is secreted by the anterior lobe of the pituitary gland and stimulates the release of hormones by the thyroid gland [Mid-20C. < THYRO- + -TROPIC + -IN]

thyrotropin-releasing hormone n a peptide hormone that is produced by the hypothalamus and controls the release of thyrotropin by the pituitary gland

thyroxine /thī rók seen/, **thyroxin** /-sin/ n the principal hormone secreted by the thyroid gland, which stimulates metabolism and is essential for normal growth and development. A synthetic form is used to treat hypothyroidism. [Early 20C. < THYRO- + OXY- + INDOLE (from a misunderstanding of its chemical structure), altered after -INE]

thyrse /thurss/ n a flower head that consists of numerous branching clusters of individual flowers arising from a single main stem, e.g. in lilacs [Early

17C. Via French < Latin *thyrsus* 'stalk of plant'] —**thyrsoid** *adj*

thyrsus /thúrssəss/ (*plural* **thyrsi** /thúrssī/) n 1. in Greek mythology and art, a staff tipped with a pine cone, carried by the Greek god Dionysus and his followers 2. BOT same as **thyrse** [Late 16C. Via Latin < Greek *thursos* 'stalk of a plant, staff carried by Dionysus']

thysanuran /thíssə nyo̅óorən/ n INSECTS same as **bristletail** [Mid-19C. < modern Latin *Thysanura* < Greek *thusanos* 'tassel, fringe' + *oura* 'tail'] —**thysanurous** *adj*

thyself /thī sélf/ *pron* (*archaic*) 1. the form of 'thy' used to refer to the same person who is being addressed and is the subject of the verb 2. used to emphasize that the person being addressed is also being referred to [Pre-12C. < THEE + SELF (adjective), but interpreted as being < THY + SELF (noun)]

THz *abbr* PHYS, MEASURE terahertz

ti[1] /tee, te/ n US MUSIC same as **te** [Mid-19C. Alteration of SI[1]]

ti[2] /tee/ (*plural* **tis**) n a woody plant with leaves that yield a useful fibre and roots that are used as food or in beverages. Native to: Polynesia, Australia. Genus: *Cordyline*. [Mid-19C. < Tahitian and Maori]

Ti *symbol* CHEM ELEM titanium

TIA *abbr* 1. ONLINE thanks in advance (*used in e-mails or text messages*) 2. MED transient ischaemic attack

tiabendazole PHARM same as **thiabendazole**

Tiananmen Square /tyén an mən-/ n a large square in central Beijing, China, that is a traditional site for festivals, rallies, and demonstrations. In 1989, it was the scene of a prodemocracy demonstration led by students in which hundreds were killed when troops were ordered to clear the square.

Tianjin /tyèn jín/ municipality in northeastern China, near Beijing. It is a major industrial centre and port. Population: 9,420,000 (1995).

Tian Shan ♦ **Tien Shan**

tiara

tiara /ti aárə/ n 1. WOMAN'S JEWELLED CORONET a small jewelled semicircular headdress worn by a woman on formal occasions 2. POPE'S CROWN a headdress consisting of three coronets with an orb and a cross on top, worn by the pope or carried before him on ceremonial occasions 3. PERSIAN KING'S CROWN a high headdress worn by an ancient Persian king [Mid-16C. Directly and via Italian < Latin < Greek *tiara(s)*] —**tiaraed** *adj*

Tiber /tíbər/ river of central Italy. Rising in the Apennines, it flows through Rome and empties into the Tyrrhenian Sea. Length: 406 km/252 mi.

Tiberius /tī beéri əss-/ (42 BC–AD 37) Roman emperor. His reign (AD 14–37) was marked by revolts and conspiracies. Full name **Tiberius Julius Caesar Augustus**

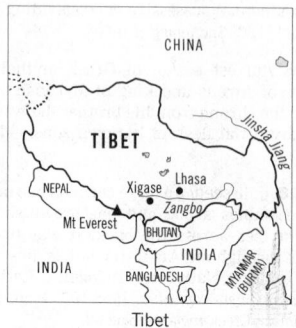

Tibet

Tibet /ti bét/ former independent state in and to the north of the Himalayan range, since 1965 a province-level administrative region of China. With an average elevation of more than 4,000 m/12,000 ft, it is the highest region in the world. Capital: Lhasa. Population: 2,620,000 (2000). Area: 1,222,000 sq. km/471,800 sq. mi. Official name **Tibet Autonomous Region**

Tibetan /ti bétt'n/ n 1. somebody who comes from Tibet 2. the Tibeto-Burman language of Tibet, spoken also in neighbouring parts of China, Nepal, and India. Native speakers: 6 million. —**Tibetan** *adj*

Tibetan Buddhism n BUDDHISM same as **Lamaism**

Tibeto-Burman /ti béttō-/ n a branch of the Sino-Tibetan family of languages that includes Tibetan, Burmese, and many other languages of South and Southeast Asia —**Tibeto-Burman** *adj*

tibia /tíbbi ə/ (*plural* **-iae** /-i ee/ *or* **-ias**) n 1. INNER BONE OF LOWER LEG the inner and larger of the two bones in the lower leg, extending from the knee to the ankle bone alongside the fibula 2. BONE IN ANIMAL'S LEG a bone in the lower leg of vertebrates corresponding to the human tibia 3. PART OF INSECT'S LEG the fourth segment of an insect's leg, between the femur and the tarsus 4. PART OF BIRD'S LEG the lower, often feathered segment of a bird's leg 5. MUSIC ANCIENT WIND INSTRUMENT an ancient flute, originally made from an animal's tibia [Late 17C. < Latin, 'shinbone, pipe'] —**tibial** *adj*

tibiofibular /tíbbi ō fíbbyo̅ōlər/ *adj* relating to the tibia and fibula, the bones of the lower leg

tibiotarsus /tíbbi ō taárssəss/ (*plural* **-tarsi** /-taárssee/) n the main bone of a bird's lower leg, formed by a fusion of the tibia and some of the bones of the tarsus

tic /tik/ n 1. a sudden involuntary spasmodic muscular contraction, especially of facial, neck, or shoulder muscles, which may become more pronounced when somebody is stressed 2. a distinctive behavioural trait or quirk [Early 19C. Via French < Italian *ticchio*]

tic douloureux /-do̅olə ró̄/ n MED same as **trigeminal neuralgia** [< French, 'painful tic']

tich, etc. n another spelling of **titch, etc.** (*informal*)

Ticino /ti cheénō/ river in western Europe, a tributary of the River Po. Length: 248 km/154 mi.

tick[1] /tik/ n 1. RECURRING CLICK a slight quiet recurring clicking sound, especially one made by a clock or watch 2. DEGREE ON SCALE an increment on a scale, especially the smallest amount by which a security may rise or fall in a stock or bond market 3. MOMENT a very short time (*informal*) ○ *I'll be back in a tick.* 4. MARK NOTING ITEM'S STATUS a mark (✓) or electronic signal put beside an item as a record or reminder, or as an indication that something is correct. N Am term **check** ■ *v* (**ticks, ticking, ticked**) 1. *vi* MAKE RECURRING CLICKING SOUND to make a slight quiet recurring clicking sound 2. *vi* REGISTER TAXI FARE BY CLICKING to make a clicking sound while registering the progressive increase of a taxi fare 3. *vt* MARK SOMETHING WITH TICK to put a tick beside an item as a record or reminder, or as an indication that something is correct. N Am term **check** [13C. Origin ?] ◊ **what makes somebody tick** what causes somebody to behave and think in a particular way (*informal*)

tick away, tick by *vi* to pass or elapse at a steady pace (*refers to time*)

tick off *vt* 1. MARK SOMETHING WITH TICK to mark something with a tick, especially an item in a list. N Am term **check off** 2. SCOLD SOMEBODY to tell somebody off for doing something wrong (*informal*) 3. N Am ANNOY SOMEBODY to make somebody angry (*informal*)

tick over *vi* 1. to function slowly without causing a vehicle to move (*refers to a motor-vehicle engine*) 2. to keep going or continue to function without any significant progress or achievement

tick[2] /tik/ n 1. a small wingless bloodsucking insect that lives on the skin of humans and warm-blooded animals and may transmit diseases. Families: Argasidae or Ixodidae. 2. a parasitic fly that lives on the skin of sheep, cattle, horses, and other animals [Old English *ticia* < Germanic]

tick[3] /tik/ n a system of credit for customers, especially an informal system (*dated informal*) ○

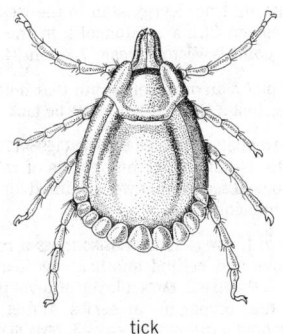

tick

bought it on tick [Mid-17C. Shortening of TICKET 'note of goods received on credit']

tick⁴ /tik/ *n* the cloth case or covering that is filled with cotton, feathers, or other materials to form a pillow or mattress [15C. Via Middle Dutch *tēke* < Greek *thēkē* 'cover, case']

tick-bird *n* a bird that feeds on ticks, e.g. an oxpecker

tick-borne *adj* describes a disease in which the causative microorganism is transmitted by the bite of a tick, e.g. Lyme disease or many forms of encephalitis

ticker /tíkər/ *n* **1.** somebody's heart (*informal*) **2.** a wristwatch or pocket watch (*dated informal*) **3.** N Am FIN same as **tape machine**

ticker tape *n* formerly, a continuous paper ribbon on which a tape machine automatically printed stock quotations

ticker-tape parade *n* in the United States, a parade honouring a visiting celebrity who is showered with shredded paper, formerly ticker tape, from buildings while being driven through the streets

ticket /tíkit/ *n* **1.** PASS FOR ENTERTAINMENT a printed piece of cardboard or paper showing that the holder is entitled to admission to a place of public entertainment or a sports ground **2.** TRAVEL PASS a printed piece of cardboard or paper showing that the holder is entitled to be travelling on a means of transport **3.** NOTIFICATION OF TRAFFIC OFFENCE a printed notice that a traffic or parking offence has been committed and a fine must be paid ○ *a parking ticket* **4.** LABEL OR TAG a small piece of card attached to an article, showing the price or other details **5.** TRANSP QUALIFICATION OF PILOT OR SHIP'S OFFICER a certificate of qualification as a ship's captain or an aircraft pilot **6.** MIL ARMY DISCHARGE a certificate of discharge from the army (*informal*) **7.** PRECISELY WHAT IS NEEDED the right, just, desired, or appropriate thing (*informal*) ○ *A week in France would be just the ticket.* **8.** N Am POL GROUP OF CANDIDATES RUNNING TOGETHER a list of candidates put forward by one party or group in an election **9.** FIN LIST OF STOCK PURCHASERS a list of investors who have purchased securities during a particular period for the purpose of settling accounts ■ *vt* (**-ets**, **-eting**, **-eted**) **1.** ATTACH TICKET TO ARTICLE to attach a ticket to an item, showing the price or other details **2.** ISSUE PASS TO SOMETHING to issue a ticket for admission to something **3.** GIVE PARKING TICKET TO SOMEBODY to issue a motor vehicle or its driver with a ticket for a traffic or parking violation **4.** CATEGORIZE SOMEBODY OR SOMETHING to assign somebody to a particular category, or designate something for a particular purpose [Early 16C. < obsolete French *étiquet* 'ticket, label' < Old French *estiquier* 'to stick'; from the idea of sticking on a label] ◇ **have tickets on yourself** Aus to have an inflated opinion of yourself (*informal*)

ticket day *n* a day on which purchasers of securities during a preceding period are listed so that accounts may be settled

ticket of leave *n* formerly, a permit allowing a convict to leave prison before completion of a sentence, under restrictions (*hyphenated before a noun*) ○ *a ticket-of-leave man*

ticket scalper *n* ANZ, N Am same as **ticket tout**

ticket tout *n* UK somebody who buys tickets for a theatrical or sporting event and sells them on at a profit. ANZ, N Am term **ticket scalper**

tickety-boo /tíkəti bóo/ *adj* UK, Can perfectly fine (*dated informal*)

tickey /tíki/ (*plural* **-eys**) *n* a small silver threepenny coin in use in South Africa between 1806 and 1961 [Late 19C. Origin ?]

tick fever *n* an acute infectious disease transmitted by the bite of a tick, e.g. Rocky Mountain spotted fever or Texas fever

ticking /tíking/ *n* a strong cotton fabric, often twilled. Use: mattress and pillow covers. [Mid-17C. < TICK⁴]

ticking-off (*plural* **tickings-off**) *n* an act of telling somebody off for doing something wrong (*informal*)

tickle /tík'l/ *v* (**-les**, **-ling**, **-led**) **1.** *vt* MAKE SOMEBODY LAUGH AND TWITCH to touch, prod, stroke, or caress lightly a sensitive part of somebody's body, usually so as to produce involuntary laughter and wriggling **2.** *vti* CAUSE ITCHINESS to cause an itchy or scratchy feeling by lightly touching a sensitive part of the body ○ *This feather boa tickles.* **3.** *vi* FEEL ITCHY to experience an itchy or scratchy feeling ○ *My foot tickles.* **4.** *vt* PLEASE OR AMUSE SOMEBODY to make somebody pleased, or appeal to somebody's sense of humour (*often passive*) **5.** *vt* CATCH TROUT WITH HANDS to catch a trout by stroking it gently so that it moves backwards into the hands ■ *n* **1.** TOUCH THAT MAKES SOMEBODY LAUGH a light touch, prod, stroke, or caress applied to a sensitive part of somebody's body, usually so as to produce involuntary laughter and wriggling **2.** ITCHY FEELING an itchy or scratchy feeling caused when a sensitive part of the body is touched lightly by something, especially material **3.** SENSATION LIKE TICKLING an itchy or scratchy sensation similar to that of being tickled by material ○ *have a tickle in my throat* [14C. Probably < TICK¹ 'touch lightly'] ◇ **tickled pink** *or* **silly** *or* **to death** extremely pleased (*informal*) ◇ **tickle somebody's fancy** to please or entertain somebody (*informal*)

tickler /tík'lər/ *n* **1.** ELEC ENG same as **tickler coil** **2.** a difficult, delicate, or puzzling problem or situation (*informal*)

tickler coil *n* a small coil connected in series with a radio vacuum tube's plate circuit and inductively coupled to a coil located in a grid circuit to provide regenerative feedback

tickler file *n* US a file consisting of reminders of matters that must be dealt with

ticklish /tík'lish/ *adj* **1.** SENSITIVE TO TICKLING sensitive to being tickled **2.** PROBLEMATIC requiring careful or delicate handling because of its risk or difficulty **3.** TOUCHY easily irritated, angered, or upset —**ticklishly** *adv* —**ticklishness** *n*

tickly /tík'li/ (**-lier**, **-liest**) *adj* **1.** producing a tickling or itching sensation on the surface of the skin **2.** Scotland same as **ticklish** (sense 1)

tickseed /tík seed/ *n* an annual or perennial plant with opposite-lobed leaves, sometimes grown as an ornamental. Flowers: resembling daisies. Native to: North America. Genus: *Coreopsis*. [Because their seeds resemble the insects]

ticktack /tík tak/, **tictac** *n* **1.** a system of sign language used by bookmakers to convey information at racecourses **2.** a clicking or tapping sound [Mid-16C. An imitation of the sound]

tick-tack-toe, **tic-tac-toe** *n* N Am same as **noughts and crosses** [Probably an imitation of the sound of an earlier game in which players brought pencils down on slates with their eyes closed]

ticktock /tík tok/ *n* the clicking sound made by a clock or watch ■ *vi* (**-tocks**, **-tocking**, **-tocked**) to make a quiet recurring clicking sound (*refers to clocks and watches*) [Mid-19C. An imitation of the sound]

tick trefoil *n* a plant with trifoliate leaves and jointed seed pods that break into segments and cling to fur or clothing. Use: forage. Native to: tropics, subtropics. Genus: *Desmodium*. [Because the joints of the pods stick to things as sticks cling to the fur of animals]

ticky-tacky /tíki táki/, **ticky-tack** N Am (*informal*) *adj* dull, unimaginative, and often of uniform quality or design ■ *n* dull, unimaginative, or inferior materials, or something made from them [Reduplication of TACKY² 'shoddy']

Ticonderoga /tíkondə róˈgə/ village in northeastern New York, on the La Chute River. It is the site of Fort Ticonderoga, an important strategic fortification in the French and Indian War (1754–63)

and the War of American Independence (1775–83). Population: 5,149 (1990).

tictac *n* another spelling of **ticktack**

tic-tac-toe *n* N Am LEISURE another spelling of **tick-tack-toe**

t.i.d. *abbr* PHARM three times a day (*used in doctors' prescriptions*) [Latin *ter in die*]

tidal /tíd'l/ *adj* **1.** OF TIDES relating to or affected by tides **2.** DEPENDENT ON TIDE having a time of departure dependent on the phase of a tide ○ *a tidal ferry* **3.** DEFINED BY TIDE LEVEL changing in character or accessibility according to the level of the tide ○ *a tidal island* **4.** FLUCTUATING not constant but fluctuating between periods of intense activity and periods of little activity —**tidally** *adv*

tidal air *n* the volume of air that passes in and out of the body during normal breathing

tidal basin *n* an artificial basin cut in rock that fills up at high tide

tidal power, **tidal energy** *n* the generation of electricity using the force created by the rise and fall of ocean tides

tidal volume *n* PHYSIOL same as **tidal air**

tidal wave *n* **1.** an enormous and destructive ocean wave caused by extremely strong winds, seaquakes, or earthquakes **2.** a powerful widespread expression or surge of something ○ *a tidal wave of public emotion*

tidbit /tídbit/ *n* N Am same as **titbit**

tiddle /tídd'l/ (*baby talk*) *vi* (**-dles**, **-dling**, **-dled**) same as **urinate** ■ *n* an act of urination [Mid-19C. Alteration of PIDDLE]

tiddler /tídd'lər/ *n* (*informal*) **1.** a very small fish, especially a minnow or a stickleback **2.** somebody or something that is small compared to most others [Late 19C. Probably related to TIDDLY²]

tiddling /tídd'ling/ *n* regional the smallest or weakest piglet in a litter

REGIONAL NOTE See *underling*.

tiddly¹ /tídd'li/ (**-dlier**, **-dliest**) *adj* slightly intoxicated from having drunk a small amount of alcohol (*informal*) [Mid-19C. Origin ?]

tiddly² /tídd'li/ (**-dlier**, **-dliest**) *adj* very small (*informal*) [Mid-19C. Variant of obsolete *tiddy*, origin ?]

tiddlywink /tídd'li wingk/ *n* a plastic counter used in the game of tiddlywinks [Mid-19C. Origin ?]

tiddlywinks /tídd'li wingks/ *n* a game in which players try to flip plastic counters into a cup by pressing them on the side with a larger counter

tide /tíd/ *n* **1.** RISE AND FALL OF SEA the cyclic rise and fall of the sea or another body of water produced by the attraction of the Moon and Sun, occurring about every twelve hours **2.** INFLOW OR OUTFLOW OF WATER the ebb or flow of water at a specific place resulting from the cyclic rise and fall of the sea **3.** GEOG same as **flood tide** (sense 1) **4.** GENERAL TREND something that rises and falls, especially a tendency or trend ○ *the tide of public opinion* **5.** PERIOD OF TIME a period of time or a season (*archaic; usually used in combination*) ○ *Yuletide* **6.** PHYS GRAVITATIONAL STRESS ON SOMETHING a stress caused by gravitational attraction, e.g. in the atmosphere or on an astronomical object **7.** CRUCIAL POINT an extreme or critical point or position ○ *the tide of the illness* ■ *v* (**tides**, **tiding**, **tided**) **1.** *vti* CARRY ALONG ON TIDE to carry somebody or something along on the tide, or be carried along in this way **2.** *vi* EBB AND FLOW to ebb and flow like the tide [Old English *tīd* 'time' < Indo-European, 'to divide'] —**tideless** *adj* ◇ **swim against the tide** to have an opinion or take a stance that is different from or opposite to that taken by most others ◇ **swim with the tide** to follow the opinions and attitudes of other people ◇ **turn the tide** to reverse the way things happen

things together', and is also used as an adjective meaning 'owned by a producer or employer' (*a tied pub, a tied cottage*) or referring to something loaned on specific conditions.

---

tide over *vt* to help somebody through a difficult time, especially with a loan or gift of money

tide gauge *n* a gauge used to measure the level of tidal movement

tideland /tīd land/ *n N Am* land that is covered by water at high tide

tideline /tīd līn/ *n* a line made on a shore by the highest point of a tide

tidemark /tīd maark/ *n* **1. MARK LEFT BY TIDE** a mark made by the highest or lowest point of a tide **2. MARKER INDICATING LEVELS OF TIDES** a marker indicating the highest or lowest point of a tide **3. POINT MARKING RISE OR FALL** a point that somebody or something has reached, risen above, or fallen below **4. RING ROUND BATH** a usually grimy mark left in a bath showing the level of water it contained (*informal*) **5. DIRTY MARK ON BODY** a dirty mark on the skin showing where somebody has stopped washing (*informal*)

tide race *n* a fast tidal current

tide-rip *n* GEOG same as **rip current**

tide table *n* a table showing the expected times and levels of tides

tidewaiter /tīd waytər/ *n* formerly, an officer who boarded incoming ships to enforce customs regulations

tidewater /tīd wawtər/ *n* **1. WATER AFFECTED BY TIDES** water whose movement or level is affected by tides **2. WATER COVERING LAND AT HIGH TIDE** water at high tide covering land that is dry at low tide **3.** *US* **SEACOAST** a coastal region, especially that of eastern Virginia

tideway /tīd way/ *n* **1.** a channel in which a tide runs **2.** a current in a tidal channel

tidings /tīdingz/ *npl* news or information (*literary*) ○ *I bring you glad tidings.* [Old English *tīdung*, alteration of Old Norse *tíðendi* 'events']

tidy /tīdi/ *adj* **(-dier, -diest) 1. NEAT IN APPEARANCE** having a neat orderly appearance **2. METHODICAL** tending to perform tasks in a systematic way **3. CONSIDERABLE** considerable and significant (*informal*) ○ *cost a tidy sum* **4.** *NZ, US* **SATISFACTORY** adequate or satisfactory, especially when circumstances are taken into account (*informal*) ○ *negotiated a tidy redundancy package* ■ *vti* **(-dies, -dying, -died) MAKE SOMETHING OR SOMEBODY TIDY** to make somebody or something neat and orderly ○ *We need to tidy the place up before they arrive.* ■ *n* (*plural* **-dies**) **1. ACT OF MAKING SOMETHING TIDY** an act of making something neat and orderly (*informal*) **2. BOX FOR HOLDING SMALL OBJECTS** a box for holding small objects that would otherwise lie around and look untidy ○ *a desk tidy* **3. SMALL RECEPTACLE FOR WASTE SCRAPS** a small receptacle kept beside or in a kitchen sink for the collection of waste scraps ○ *a sink tidy* **4.** *US* HOUSEHOLD same as **antimacassar** [13C. < TIDE 'time'] —**tidily** *adv* —**tidiness** *n*

tidy-up *n* same as **tidy** *n* (sense 1) (*informal*)

tie /tī/ *v* **(ties, tying, tied) 1.** *vt* **FASTEN SOMETHING WITH ROPE** to fasten things together with a rope, string, or cord ○ *They tied his hands together.* **2.** *vt* **FASTEN SOMETHING BY KNOTTING** to fasten something with a knot or bow ○ *Tie your shoelaces.* **3.** *vi* SPORTS, LEISURE **HAVE EQUAL SCORE** to achieve the same score or place as somebody else in a game, race, or competition **4.** *vt* **MAKE KNOT** to make a knot or bow with rope, string, or cord ○ *All Scouts learn how to tie knots.* **5.** *vt* **CONNECT THINGS** to make a connection or link between people or things **6.** *vt* **RESTRICT** to restrict somebody to particular conditions **7.** *vt* MUSIC **SUSTAIN MUSICAL NOTE** to hold a musical note from one bar to the next, thereby extending its value **8.** *vt* MUSIC **CONNECT NOTES WITH CURVED LINE** in musical notation, to connect two notes with a curved line ■ *n* **1. STRIP OF FABRIC WORN ROUND NECK** a long thin piece of fabric worn round the neck, under a shirt collar, and tied at the front so that the ends hang down **2. CONNECTION** something that links or unites people or things **3. SOMETHING FOR ATTACHING** a long thin piece of material such as rope or wire used to fasten or close something else ○ *ties for bin bags* **4. RESTRICTION** something that restricts or confines somebody or something **5.** SPORTS, LEISURE **EQUAL OUTCOME** an equal score or result in a game, race, or competition **6. MATCH IN KNOCKOUT COMPETITION** a match in a knockout competition, especially in football ○ *a cup tie* **7.** CONSTR **STRENGTHENING BEAM** a connecting, strengthening, or supporting beam or rod **8.** MUSIC **CURVED LINE INDICATING EXTENSION OF NOTES** a curved line shown above or below two musical notes of the same pitch, indicating that they are to be sounded without a break for their combined duration **9.** *N Am* RAIL same as **sleeper** (sense 4) **10.** CIV ENG **SURVEYING MEASUREMENT** either of two measurements on a survey line used to fix the position of a reference point ■ *adj N Am* **MADE EQUAL** having an equal outcome [Old English *tīgan* < Germanic, 'pull'] ◇ **tie one on** *N Am* to get drunk (*informal*)

SPELLCHECK See *tide.*

---

tie down *vt* to prevent somebody from acting freely and make the person confirm something ○ *tied him down to a completion date in January*

tie in *v* **1.** *vi* to be consistent with something **2.** *vti* to fit something in with something else, or fit in with something ○ *I hope to tie in a visit to my sister with my business trip.*

tie up *v* **1.** *vt* **BIND SOMETHING** to fasten or bind something using rope or string **2.** *vti* NAUT **DOCK BOAT, OR BE DOCKED** to moor a boat or ship by securing lines, or be moored in this way **3.** *vt* **OCCUPY SOMEBODY OR SOMETHING** to keep somebody or something busy ○ *I'm going to be tied up all afternoon in meetings.* **4.** *vt* **COMPLETE SOMETHING** to complete the work needed for something **5.** *vti* **STOP** to bring something to a halt, or come to a halt **6.** *vt* FIN **INVEST MONEY WITH RESTRICTIONS** to invest money in such a way that it cannot be used for other purposes ○ *money tied up in a savings account* **7.** *vt* LAW **PLACE RESTRICTIONS ON PROPERTY** to place legal restrictions on the selling or alienation of property

tieback /tī bak/ *n* a length of cord or fabric used to hold a curtain to one side

tie beam *n* a beam that pulls together a structure and stops it spreading outwards, e.g. the bottom horizontal member of a roof truss

tiebreaker /tī braykər/, **tiebreak** /-brayk/ *n* a means of deciding the winner of a game or competition when there is a tie —**tiebreaking** *adj*

tie clip, **tie clasp** *n* an ornamental clasp that holds a tie in place against a shirt

tied /tīd/ *adj* **1. SELLING ONLY OWNER'S PRODUCTS** owned by a producer, especially a brewery, and obliged to sell only its products **2. OWNED BY OCCUPANT'S EMPLOYER** owned by the occupant's employer and lived in only for the duration of the employment **3. LOANED TO BUY LENDER'S GOODS** loaned on condition of being spent only on goods or services supplied by the lender

---

SPELLCHECK See *tide.*

---

tie-dye *vt* to dye designs on cloth by tightly tying portions of it with waxed thread so that the dye only affects the exposed areas ■ *n* a piece of fabric whose designs are made by tie-dyeing (*informal*) —**tie-dyeing** *n*

tief /teef/ (*slang; used in Black English*) *vti* same as **thieve** ■ *n* same as **thief** [Late 18C. Alteration]

tie-in *n* **1. LINK** a link or relationship with something **2. JOINT PROMOTION OF PRODUCTS** an arrangement by which related products are sold, promoted, or marketed together, e.g. a book or toy along with a film **3. RELATED PRODUCT** a product that is sold, promoted, or marketed in close connection with another **4.** *N Am* **SALE REQUIRING DUAL PURCHASES** a sale in which items are advertised or sold with the stipulation that they must be purchased together, or a product sold in this way

~~**tieing**~~ incorrect spelling of **tying**

tie line *n* a telephone line that connects two private exchanges

tiemannite /teemə nīt/ *n* a dark grey mineral compound of mercury and selenium [Mid-19C. < After J. C. W. *Tiemann* (1848–99), German scientist]

Tien Shan /tyén shaán/, **Tian Shan** /tyán-/ mountain range in Central Asia, stretching about 2,400 km/1,500 mi. from Kyrgyzstan in the west through northwestern China to Mongolia in the east. The highest point is Victory Peak, 7,439 m/24,406 ft.

tiepin /tī pin/ *n* an ornamental pin that holds a tie in place against a shirt. N Am term **tie tack**

Tiepolo /tyéppəlō/, **Giovanni Battista** (1696–1770) Italian artist. He is famous for his murals of religious or mythological scenes that were painted for Venetian rococo interiors.

tier /teer/ *n* **1. ROW OF SEATS IN RISING SERIES** a row placed one above and behind another row, e.g. a set of seats in a theatre **2. LAYER** a layer or level placed one above the other in a series (*often used in combination*) ○ *a three-tier cake* **3. LEVEL IN HIERARCHY** a hierarchical level in an organization (*often used in combination*) ■ *vt* **(tiers, tiering, tiered) ARRANGE THINGS IN RISING ROWS** to arrange things in rows rising one above the other [15C. < French *tire* 'rank, sequence, order' < *tirer* 'draw out, elongate'] —**tiered** *adj*

SPELLCHECK See *tear*[2].

---

tierce /teerss, turss/ *n* **1.** CHR same as **terce** **2.** CARDS **THREE CARDS OF SAME SUIT** a sequence of three cards of the same suit **3.** FENCING **PARRYING POSITION** the third of eight positions from which a fencing parry can be made **4.** MEASURE **FORMER MEASURE OF CAPACITY** a former measure of capacity equal to 42 wine gallons [15C. Via French < Latin *tertia*, form of *tertius* 'third']

tiercel *n* BIRDS another spelling of **tercel**

tie rod *n* a metal rod that joins or supports two parts, e.g. one used as a linkage in the steering mechanism of a motor vehicle. Tie rods are also used to keep trusses and arches from spreading.

Tierra del Fuego /ti érrə del fwáygō/ archipelago off the southern tip of South America. Separated from the mainland by the Strait of Magellan, and bordered by the Atlantic, the Antarctic, and the Pacific oceans, the islands belong partly to Argentina and partly to Chile.

tie tack, **tie tac** *n N Am* same as **tiepin**

tie-up *n* **1.** something that connects one thing with another **2.** *N Am* a temporary delay or obstruction, e.g. in the flow of traffic

tif *abbr* a file extension for a TIFF file. Full form **tagged image file format**

tiff /tif/ *n* **1. QUARREL** a minor quarrel **2. ILL HUMOUR** a brief period of bad temper ■ *vi* **(tiffs, tiffing, tiffed) 1. ARGUE** to have a minor quarrel with somebody **2. BE ILL-HUMOURED** to be in a bad temper [Early 18C. Probably suggesting the sound of escaping gas]

TIFF /tif/ *n* a format for a computer file that contains bit-mapped graphics. Full form **tagged image file format**

tiffany /tíffəni/ *n* a fine gauzy fabric [Early 17C. Via Old French *tifanie* < Greek *theophaneia* 'vision of God']

Tiffany /tíffəni/, **Charles Lewis** (1812–1902) US jeweller and retailer. He introduced the British standard of sterling silver in the United States and founded Tiffany and Company (1853).

Tiffany, Louis Comfort (1848–1933) US glassmaker and interior designer. He is known for the stained glass, vases, and lamps produced by his Tiffany Studios. He patented the iridescent glass used in his flowing art nouveau pieces.

TIFF file, **TIF file** *n* a graphic file in a format often used for storing bit-mapped images

tiffin /tíffin/ *n S Asia* **1.** a light midday meal or snack of savouries and sweets **2.** FOOD same as **tiffin-carrier** [Early 19C. Variant of *tiffing* < obsolete *tiff* 'to drink', origin ?]

tiffin-carrier *n S Asia* a carrier consisting of several metal containers stacked one on top of another, used to carry prepared food

tig /tig/ LEISURE *n* same as **tag**[2] *n* (sense 1) ■ *vt* **(tigs, tigging, tigged)** same as **tag**[2] *v* (sense 1) [15C. Variant of TICK[1] 'touch lightly']

tiger

tiger /tígər/ (*plural* **-gers** or *same*) *n* **1.** a carnivorous cat, the largest member of the cat family, that has a tawny coat and black stripes. Native to: Asia. Latin name: *Panthera tigris.* **2.** a fierce, brave, or forceful person [13C. Via Old French *tigre* < Greek *tigris*] —**tigerish** *adj* —**tigerishly** *adv* —**tigerishness** *n* ◇ **ride a tiger** be in a very difficult, precarious, or dangerous position

Tiger *n* FIN same as **TIGR**

tiger beetle *n* a fast-running predatory beetle with strong sharp jaws for digging and brightly coloured patterned wing covers. Native to: warm regions. Family: Cicindelidae. [< its predatory habits]

tiger cat *n* **1.** a small striped or spotted cat, e.g. a margay, serval, or ocelot **2.** a domestic cat with blotched or striped markings resembling those of a tiger **3.** *Aus* ZOOL same as **spotted-tailed quoll**

tigereye /tígər ī/ *n* MINERALS same as **tiger's-eye**

tiger lily *n* **1.** an Asian lily. Flowers: red or orange with dark purple or brown spots. Latin name: *Lilium lancifolium* or *Lilium tigrinium.* **2.** any lily that resembles the Asian tiger lily [< its colouring]

tiger moth *n* a moth that has bold black and yellow or orange markings, especially on its wings. Family: Arctiidae.

tiger nut *n* **1.** the dried tuber of a sedge, used as food, especially in western Africa, and as bait by anglers **2.** the sedge plant that produces tiger nuts. Native to: western Africa. Latin name: *Cyperus esculentus.*

tiger salamander *n* a large black salamander with yellow or green stripes. Native to: North America. Latin name: *Ambystoma tigrinum.* [< its stripes]

tiger's-eye *n* a striped yellow-brown rock composed of bands of quartz and crocidolite. Use: gems.

tiger shark *n* a large striped or spotted shark with a voracious and indiscriminate appetite. Native to: tropics. Latin name: *Galeocerdo cuvieri.*

tiger snake *n* a highly venomous brown and yellow snake. Native to: southeastern Australia, Tasmania. Genus: *Notechis.*

tiger swallowtail *n* a large butterfly with a deeply forked tail and yellow wings with black stripes. Native to: North America. Latin name: *Palilio glaucus* or *Palilio rutilus.*

tight /tīt/ *adj* **1.** SNUG fitting the body very closely ○ *a tight sweater* **2.** TAUT stretched so that there is no slack ○ *pulled the rope tight* **3.** FIXED firmly secured or held ○ *a tight knot* **4.** SEALED sealed against gas or liquid leaks ○ *An airlock must have a tight seal.* **5.** STRICT strictly controlled or administered ○ *Security was tight for the conference.* **6.** CRAMPED lacking sufficient space to move freely ○ *It's going to be tight in the back seat.* **7.** HAVING NO EXTRA TIME allowing no time beyond what is needed to do something ○ *a tight schedule* **8.** HAVING NO EXTRA MONEY allowing no money beyond what is required ○ *working to a tight budget* **9.** MISERLY excessively frugal with money ○ *He's too tight to lend you the money.* **10.** HARD TO GET OUT OF difficult or dangerous to handle ○ *We're in a tight fix now.* **11.** WITH CLOSE RIVALS characterized by well-matched competitors or teams ○ *a tight race* **12.** DRUNK intoxicated with alcohol (*slang*) **13.** WELL DONE arranged or performed with style and precision ○ *a tight performance by the whole team* **14.** SUCCINCT characterized by clear concise expression ○ *tight prose* **15.** *US* INTIMATE having a very close relationship with somebody (*informal*) ○ *He's tight with his boss.* **16.** HARD TO GET characterized by conditions in which demand exceeds supply, often with concomitant rising prices ○ *a tight economy* ■ *adv* FIRMLY in a firm, close, snug, or secure way ○ *hold on tight* [14C. Alteration of obsolete *thight* 'dense, thick' < Old Norse *þéttr* 'watertight, dense'] —**tightly** *adv* —**tightness** *n* ◇ **in a tight spot** *or* **corner** in a difficult or dangerous situation ◇ **sleep tight** used to wish somebody a sound night's sleep

tighten /tīt'n/ (**-ens, -ening, -ened**) *vti* to become tight or tighter, or cause something to become tight or tighter —**tightener** *n*

tight end *n* in American football, a player who lines up near to the tackle

tightfisted /tīt fístid/ *adj* disinclined to spend money —**tightfistedly** *adv* —**tightfistedness** *n*

tight-fitting *adj* **1.** fitting closely to the body ○ *tight-fitting jeans* **2.** fitting closely on to a container so that its contents are not exposed to the air ○ *a tight-fitting lid*

tight head *n* in rugby, the prop forward positioned to the right of the hooker in the front row of the scrum

tightknit /tīt nít/ *adj* **1.** closely united by love, friendship, or common interests ○ *a tightknit community* **2.** arranged or functioning as a well-structured whole

tight-lipped /-lípt/ *adj* **1.** unwilling to communicate ○ *He is remaining tight-lipped in the face of intense press speculation.* **2.** having the lips firmly closed, e.g. in anger or pain

tightrope /tīt rōp/ *n* a rope or wire stretched taut and suspended above the ground, on which somebody walks or performs a balancing act ◇ **walk a tightrope** to have to deal cautiously with a precarious situation, often one involving a choice or compromise

tights /tīts/ *npl* **1.** SHEER ONE-PIECE GARMENT a light tight-fitting sheer covering for a woman's legs that stretches from the toes up to an elastic waistband. N Am term **pantyhose** **2.** THICK ONE-PIECE GARMENT a one-piece close-fitting garment made of opaque coloured material, covering the body from the waist to the feet and worn by women and girls for warmth and casual wear **3.** DANCER'S ONE-PIECE GARMENT a one-piece close-fitting garment covering the body from the neck or waist to the feet, worn especially by men and women dancers and acrobats

tightwad /tīt wod/ *n N Am* somebody who dislikes spending money (*insult*)

Tiglath-pileser I /tíg lath pī léezər/ (*fl* 11th century BC) Assyrian king (1115–1076 BC). He expanded his kingdom by conquering Babylonia and recovering Armenia from invaders.

tiglic acid /tígglik-/ *n* a viscous poisonous colourless liquid. Source: croton oil. Use: pharmaceutical preparations, manufacture of perfumes. Formula: $C_5H_8O_2$. [< modern Latin *(Croton) tiglium*, scientific name of the tree from whose seeds croton oil is obtained]

tigon /tígən/, **tiglon** /tíglən/ *n* the offspring of a male tiger and a female lion [Mid-20C. Blend of TIGER + LION]

TIGR /tígər/, **Tiger** *n* a bond linked to US treasury bonds, profits from which are subject to UK tax when the bond is cashed or redeemed. Full form **Treasury Investment Growth Receipts**

Tigray /tée gray/, **Tigre** region in northeastern Ethiopia, bordering Eritrea. Capital: Mekele. Population: 3,136,267 (1994). Area: 65,786 sq. km/25,400 sq. mi.

tigress /tígrəss/ *n* **1.** a female tiger **2.** a fierce, brave, or passionate woman [Late 16C. < TIGER after French *tigresse* 'tigress']

Tigrinya /ti gréenyə/ *n* a Semitic language of northern Ethiopia. Native speakers: 4 million. [Mid-19C. < Tigrinya] —**Tigrinya** *adj*

Tigris /tígriss/ river in Southwest Asia. It rises in southeastern Turkey, flows through Iraq, and joins the Euphrates to form the Shatt Al-Arab, which empties into the Persian Gulf. Length: 1,900 km/1,180 mi.

Tijuana /ti wáanə/ city in northwestern Mexico, just south of the United States border. It is an industrial and tourist centre. Population: 1,210,820 (2000).

tika /téekə/ *n* RELIG same as **tilak** [Late 19C. < Hindi *tīkā*, Punjabi *tikkā*]

tike *n* another spelling of **tyke**

tiki /téeki/ *n* **1.** a small carved human foetal figure, especially in greenstone, representing an ancestor and worn as an amulet by some Maori and Polynesian peoples **2.** a stone or wooden representation of a Polynesian god [Late 18C. < Maori, 'image']

tikka /téekə/ *adj* a South Asian dish of skewered meat that is marinated and then dry-roasted in an oven [Mid-20C. < Punjabi *ṭikkā*]

til /til/ *n* FOOD same as **sesame** (sense 1) [Mid-19C. < Sanskrit *tila*]

'til *conj, prep* another spelling of **till**[1]

tilak /tíllək/ *n* a decorative or symbolic mark worn by Hindus on the forehead [Late 19C. < Sanskrit *tilaka*]

Tilak /tíllək/, **B. G.** (1856–1920) Indian journalist and political activist. He was a prominent member of the Indian nationalist movement and founder of the Home Rule League (1916). Full name **Tilak, Balwantrao Gangadhar**

tilapia /ti láppi ə, -láy-/ (*plural* **-as** or *same*) *n* a freshwater fish of the cichlid family, introduced and cultivated worldwide. Native to: tropical Africa. Genus: *Tilapia.* [Mid-19C. < modern Latin]

Tilburg /tíl burg/ industrial city in North Brabant Province, southern Netherlands. Population: 193,238 (2000).

tilde /tíldə/ *n* in some languages, a mark (~) placed over a letter to show that the pronunciation is nasalized, e.g. over 'a' or 'o' in Portuguese, or palatalized, e.g. over 'n' in Spanish [Mid-19C. Via Spanish < Latin *titulus* 'heading']

tile /tīl/ *n* **1.** COVERING FOR FLOORS, ROOFS, OR WALLS a thin flat or curved piece of baked, sometimes glazed, clay or synthetic material used to cover roofs, floors, and walls, or for decoration **2.** SHORT PIPE IN DRAIN a short pipe of baked clay, concrete, or plastic used in making a drain **3.** *N Am* HOLLOW BLOCK a hollow block of baked clay, concrete, or gypsum used as a building material for walls or floors **4.** TILES COLLECTIVELY tiles considered collectively **5.** LEISURE PLAYING PIECE a rectangular playing piece in various games such as mahjongg **6.** CLOTHING same as **hat** (*dated informal*) ■ *v* (**tiles, tiling, tiled**) **1.** *vt* LAY TILES ON SOMETHING to cover a surface with tiles **2.** *vt* FIT WITH DRAINAGE TILES to put drainage tiles in something **3.** *vti* COMPUT ARRANGE WINDOWS ON COMPUTER SCREEN to arrange the windows on a computer screen side by side so that all are visible [Pre-12C. < Latin *tegula*] —**tiler** *n* ◇ **on the tiles** in pursuit of drinking and pleasure (*informal*)

tilefish /tīl fish/ (*plural same* or **-fishes**) *n* a long blue deep-water fish with yellow spots on its upper body. Native to: Atlantic coast of North America. Latin name: *Lopholatilus chamaeleonticeps.*

tiling /tīling/ *n* **1.** LAID TILES tiles that have been laid **2.** LAYING OF TILES the laying of tiles on a roof, wall, or floor **3.** TILES tiles collectively

till[1] /til/, **'till, 'til** *conj, prep* same as **until** [Old English *til* 'up to a particular point' < Germanic, 'aim, goal'; sometimes taken as shortening of UNTIL]

USAGE till or **until**? Both words have the same meaning and function (conjunction and preposition), and are largely interchangeable. ***Till*** is more likely to be heard in speech: *Just wait till we get home!* ***Until*** is more usual at the beginning of a sentence: *Until last week there was no one here that we knew.* The spellings *'til* and *'till* reflect the commonly held belief that ***till*** is a shortened form of ***until***, but ***till*** is in fact the older form.

till[2] /til/ *n* **1.** a box, drawer, or tray in which money is kept, e.g. in a cash register **2.** COMM same as **checkout** (sense 1) [15C. Origin ?]

till[3] /til/ (**tills, tilling, tilled**) *vt* to prepare land for the growing of crops by ploughing or harrowing [Old English *tilian* 'cultivate, strive to obtain something' < Germanic, 'aim, purpose'] —**tillable** *adj* —**tiller** *n*

till[4] /til/ *n* sediment of various particle sizes deposited by the direct action of ice [Late 17C. Origin ?]

tillage /tíllij/ *n* **1.** the ploughing or harrowing of land in preparation for growing crops **2.** land that has been tilled [15C. < TILL[3]]

tillandsia /ti lándzi ə/ *n* an epiphytic plant of the pineapple family, e.g. Spanish moss. Native to: tropical or subtropical America. Genus: *Tillandsia*. [Mid-18C. < modern Latin, after Elias *Tillands* (1640–93), Swedish botanist]

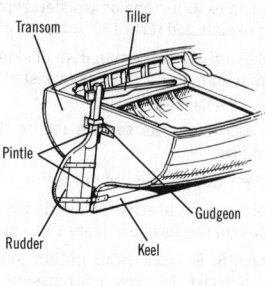

Transom
Tiller
Pintle
Rudder
Gudgeon
Keel

tiller

tiller[1] /tíllər/ *n* the means by which a small boat is steered, consisting of a handle attached to the rudder [14C. < Anglo-Norman *telier* 'weaver's beam' < Latin *tela* 'web']

tiller[2] /tíllər/ *n* a person or machine that ploughs or cultivates the soil [Pre-12C. < TILL[3]]

tiller[3] /tíllər/ *n* a shoot growing from the base of a stem, especially the stem of a grass [Mid-17C. Probably < Old English *telgor* 'extended' < *telga* 'branch']

tillerman /tíllərmən/ (*plural* **-men** /-mən/) *n* a handler of a tiller who steers a boat [Mid-20C. < TILLER[1]]

Tillich /tíllik/, **Paul** (1886–1965) German-born US philosopher and theologian. He emigrated to the United States in 1933. His scholarly and popular books sought to reconcile existential philosophy and contemporary secular culture with Christian faith, and included *The Courage to Be* (1952) and *Systematic Theology* (1951–63). Full name **Tillich, Paul Johannes**

'Religion is the state of being grasped by an ultimate concern... which itself contains the answer to the question of the meaning of our life.'
[Paul Tillich, *Christianity and the Encounter of the World Religions*; 1961]

Tilly /tílli/, **Johann Tserclaes, Count** (1559–1632) Flemish soldier. As a commander of a Catholic extremist league, he won many victories in the Thirty Years War (1618–48), but was eventually defeated and fatally wounded.

tilt[1] /tilt/ *v* (**tilts, tilting, tilted**) **1.** *vti* SLOPE to slant, or cause something to slant ○ *She tilted her head as she listened.* **2.** *vi N Am* HAVE AS PREFERENCE to tend towards favouring a particular opinion, course of action, or side in a dispute ○ *a political party that tilted towards peace not war* **3.** *vi* CRITICIZE to make a spoken or written attack on somebody or something **4.** *vi* STRUGGLE to combat or struggle against somebody or something **5.** *vti* HIST CHARGE WITH LANCE to attack an opponent using a lance **6.** *vi* HIST JOUST WITH SOMEBODY to take part in a joust against somebody **7.** *vi* HIST POINT LANCE to hold a lance ready for combat in a joust **8.** *vt* ENG USE TILT HAMMER ON SOMETHING to work on something using a tilt hammer ■ *n* **1.** ACT OF TILTING an act of tilting or of causing something to tilt **2.** INCLINED SURFACE a slanted surface or position ○ *His hat was at a rakish tilt.* **3.** CRITICISM a spoken or written attack on somebody or something **4.** *US* PREFERENCE a tendency to favour a particular opinion, course of action, or side in a dispute **5.** *Aus* ATTEMPT TO WIN an attempt or campaign to win a competition or contest (*informal*) **6.** HIST ACTIVITY OF JOUST a jousting contest **7.** HIST LANCE THRUST a thrust made with a lance in a jousting contest **8.** ENG same as **tilt hammer** [14C. Probably < assumed Old English *tyltan* 'fall over' < Germanic, 'unsteady'] —**tilter** *n* ◇ (at) full tilt at full speed

tilt[2] /tilt/ *n* a canvas cover or canopy used to cover an otherwise open boat, booth, or trailer of a lorry [15C. < Old English *teld* < W Germanic]

tilth /tilth/ *n* **1.** TILLING OF LAND the ploughing of land in preparation for growing crops **2.** TILLED LAND land under cultivation **3.** CONDITION OF LAND the condition of a piece of tilled land, in terms of its cultivation

history and suitability for crops **4.** DEGREE OF FINENESS OF SOIL the degree of fineness of soil particles in the topmost soil layer [Old English *tilþ(e)* < *tilian* (see TILL[3])]

tilt hammer *n* a heavy drop hammer used to forge metal, pivoted by a lever [< TILT[1]]

tiltyard /tílt yaard/ *n* a place, usually enclosed, where a jousting contest was held [Early 16C. < TILT[1]]

Tim. *abbr* BIBLE Timothy

Timaru /tímməroo/ city on the east-central coast of the South Island, New Zealand. Population: 26,745 (2001).

timbal /tímb'l/, **tymbal** *n* same as **kettledrum** (*archaic*) [Late 17C. < French *timbale*, alteration (after *cymbale* 'cymbal') of obsolete *tamballe* < (influenced by *tambour* 'drum') Spanish *atabal* < Arabic *aṭ -ṭabl* 'the drum']

timbale /tam baál/ *n* **1.** FOOD DISH MADE IN MOULD a dish consisting of a mixture of ingredients, often set with eggs, made in a mould and served hot or cold **2.** HOUSEHOLD COOKING MOULD a small deep or tall mould in which a timbale is cooked ■ **timbales** *npl* MUSIC LATIN AMERICAN DRUMS a pair of cylindrical drums, commonly played in Latin American dance music [Early 19C. < French (see TIMBAL)]

timber /tímbər/ *n* **1.** WOOD CONSTRUCTION MATERIAL wood that has been sawn into boards, planks, or other materials for use in building, woodworking, or cabinetmaking. N Am term **lumber**[1] **2.** GROWING TREES standing trees or their wood **3.** WOODED LAND land covered with trees **4.** CONSTR LARGE WOODEN BUILDING SUPPORT a large piece of wood, usually squared, used in a building, e.g. as a beam **5.** SHIPPING PART OF SHIP'S FRAMEWORK a large piece of wood used in the framework of a wooden ship ■ *adj* WOODEN constructed of wood ■ *interj* WARNING OF FALLING TREE used by a lumberjack to warn others that a tree has been cut and is about to fall ■ *vt* (**-bers, -bering, -bered**) PROVIDE WITH TIMBERS to build, cover, or support something with timbers [Old English, 'a building' < Indo-European, 'build']

timbered /tímbərd/ *adj* **1.** made of timber, or having timbers (*often used in combination*) ○ *a half-timbered house* **2.** covered with growing trees

timberhead /tímbər hed/ *n* the top of a timber of a ship that projects above the deck and is used as a tall post (**bollard**) for securing the ship to a wharf or dock

timber hitch *n* a knot used to tie a rope around a spar or log that is to be hoisted or hauled

timbering /tímbəring/ *n* timber, or objects made of timber

timberland /tímbər land/ *n N Am* an area of wooded land, especially one with trees that have commercial value as timber

timberline /tímbər līn/ *n ANZ, N Am* same as **tree line** (sense 1)

timber rattlesnake *n* a poisonous rattlesnake that is yellowish-brown with wide dark bands and feeds on small mammals. Native to: eastern United States. Latin name: *Crotalus horridus*.

timber wolf *n* ZOOL same as **grey wolf**

timberwork /tímbər wurk/ *n* something constructed of timber, or the timber parts of something

timberyard /tímbər yaard/ *n* a place where timber and other building materials are stored and sold. N Am term **lumberyard**

timbre /támbər, tímbər, táNbrə/ *n* **1.** the quality of a speech sound that comes from its tone rather than its pitch or volume **2.** the quality or colour of tone of an instrument or voice [Mid-19C. Via French, originally 'drum, bell hit with a hammer' < Greek *tumpanon* 'drum']

timbrel /tímbrəl/ *n* in the Bible, a tambourine or small hand drum [Early 16C. Origin ?]

Timbuktu[1] /tímb uk too/, **Timbuctoo** *n* a place that is far away or extremely remote (*informal*) [Mid-19C. After TIMBUKTU[2]]

Timbuktu[2] /tímb uk too/, ♦ **Tombouctou**

time /tīm/ *n* **1.** SYSTEM OF DISTINGUISHING EVENTS a dimension that enables two identical events occurring at the same point in space to be distinguished, measured by the interval between the events. Symbol *t* **2.**

PERIOD WITH LIMITS a limited period during which an action, process, or condition exists or takes place ○ *elapsed time* **3.** also **Time** METHOD OF MEASURING INTERVALS a system for measuring intervals of time ○ *sidereal time* ○ *British Summer Time* **4.** MINUTE OR HOUR the minute, hour, or similar measurement as indicated by a clock ○ *What time is it?* **5.** TIME AS CAUSATIVE FORCE time conceived as a force capable of acting on people and objects ○ *time's ravages* **6.** MOMENT SOMETHING OCCURS a moment or period at which something takes place ○ *at the time of her 90th birthday* **7.** SUITABLE MOMENT a moment or period chosen as appropriate for something to be done or to take place ○ *The times for the games will be announced.* **8.** UNALLOCATED PERIOD a period that is not allocated for a specific purpose ○ *I had time on my hands.* **9.** PERIOD NEEDED a period required, allocated, or taken to complete an activity ○ *How much time?* **10.** PERIOD WITH PARTICULAR QUALITY a period, activity, or occasion that has a particular quality or characteristic (*often used in the plural*) ○ *They've been through some rough times.* ○ *We had an interesting time there.* **11.** APPOINTED MOMENT a designated or customary moment or period at which something is done or takes place ○ *It's time to get up.* **12.** CLOSING TIME the time at which a pub or bar is legally required to close **13.** INTERVAL a limited but unspecified period ○ *We stayed for a time.* **14.** HISTORICAL PERIOD a period in history, often characterized by a particular event or person (*often used in the plural*) ○ *in Shakespeare's time* ○ *ancient times* **15.** THE HERE AND NOW the present as distinguished from the past or future (*often used in the plural*) ○ *technology that is ahead of the times* **16.** GEOL GEOLOGICAL DIVISION a chronological division of geological history **17.** ANTICIPATED MOMENT a moment in which an important event such as a birth or death is expected to happen ○ *He knew his time had come.* **18.** SOMEBODY'S LIFETIME a period during which somebody is alive, especially the most active or productive period in somebody's life ○ *She'd been a well-known athlete in her time.* ○ *We didn't worry about such trifles in my time.* **19.** APPRENTICESHIP PERIOD a period during which somebody is an apprentice ○ *had served his time* **20.** CRIME PRISON TERM a term in prison (*informal*) ○ *serve time for robbery* **21.** MIL MILITARY SERVICE a term of military service **22.** SEASON a period during which particular climatic conditions prevail ○ *the rainy times of the year* **23.** INSTANCE a separate occasion of a recurring event ○ *I told you three times.* **24.** MUSIC TEMPO OF MUSIC the relative speed at which a musical composition is played **25.** MUSIC MUSICAL BEAT the number of beats per bar of a musical composition **26.** PERIOD WORKED the period during a day or week that somebody works ○ *working half time* **27.** PAY RATE a rate of pay ○ *paid double time* **28.** SPORTS PLAYING PERIOD a period of play in a game **29.** *N Am* SPORTS same as **timeout** *n* (sense 1) ■ *v* (**times, timing, timed**) **1.** *vt* MEASURE HOW LONG SOMETHING TAKES to measure or record the duration, speed, or rate of something **2.** *vt* SCHEDULE SOMETHING to plan the moment or occasion for something, especially in order to achieve the best result or effect ○ *time an entrance* **3.** *vt* SET TIME OF SOMETHING to regulate or set the time of something such as a clock or a train's schedule **4.** *vi* STAY IN RHYTHM to keep time to a rhythmic or musical beat [Old English *tīma* 'period of time' < Germanic, 'extend'] ◇ **all in good time** no sooner than is appropriate ◇ **all the time** continuously ◇ **at one time 1.** at a time in the past **2.** simultaneously ◇ **at the same time 1.** simultaneously **2.** nevertheless ◇ **at times** sometimes ◇ **behind the times** out of touch with modern fashions, methods, or attitudes ◇ **bide your time** to wait patiently for the right opportunity ◇ **for old times' sake** in fond memory of the past ○ *We had lunch at the café we used to frequent, for old times' sake.* ◇ **for the time being** for a short period of time starting from now ◇ **from time to time** occasionally ◇ **have no time for somebody** *or* **something** to regard somebody or something with dislike or contempt ◇ **have the time of your life** to have a very enjoyable experience ◇ **in good time 1.** early enough ○ *got there in good time so we could find a parking space* **2.** quickly ◇ **in (less than) no time** in a very short period of time ◇ **in time 1.** early enough ○ *We were in time for the concert.* **2.** after some time has passed ○ *He'll understand in time that you were trying to help him.* **3.** in the correct rhythm ○ *clapping in time to the music* ◇ **in your own time 1.** not during working

hours **2.** at a speed or pace that feels natural and comfortable ◇ **keep time 1.** to show the time accurately **2.** to do something in the correct rhythm, or in the same rhythm as somebody or something else ◇ **live on borrowed time** to enjoy an unexpected extension of life ◇ **make time with somebody** N England, N Am to pursue somebody as a sexual partner (informal) ◇ **mark time 1.** to do something that makes no contribution towards achieving a goal or ambition while awaiting an opportunity to make progress **2.** to continue marching in rhythm without moving forwards ◇ **on time** at the scheduled time ◇ **once upon a time** used at the beginning of fairy tales and children's stories to indicate that something happened a long time ago or in an imaginary world ◇ **pass the time of day (with somebody)** to engage in casual conversation with somebody ◇ **play for time** to delay action or a decision in the hope that conditions will be more favourable later on ◇ **take time out (from)** to take a short break from work or another activity ○ took time out from her studies to travel for a year ◇ **take your time 1.** to take whatever time is necessary **2.** to do something unacceptably slowly ◇ **time after time, time and (time) again** repeatedly ◇ **time out of mind** for an extremely long time ◇ **time was** there was a time in the past ◇ **time will tell** it is impossible to know or judge something until some time in the future ○ Time will tell whether I have made the right decision.

SPELLCHECK see **thyme**

CULTURAL NOTE A Brief History of Time, a book (1988) by physicist Stephen Hawking. This best-selling text aims to describe fundamental concepts in physics in terms that the general reader can understand. It covers a wide range of subjects, from the origin of the universe to the nature of time itself, and explains the theories put forward by other scientists such as Galileo, Newton, and Einstein.

time out vti to fail to respond after a predetermined interval, and thus cause a suspension of activity or a call for intervention from a user, or to cause this to happen to somebody (refers to computers or peripheral devices) ○ '...a dialog box suggested that the server had timed me out.' (Internet Magazine; November 1998)

time and a half n a rate of pay equal to one and a half times the normal rate, usually paid for overtime work

time and motion study n an analysis of the working practices of, e.g. a person, department, or factory, done with the aim of finding ways to increase efficiency

time bomb n **1.** ARMS **BOMB EXPLODING AT FIXED TIME** a bomb with a timing mechanism that allows it to explode at a set time **2.** FUTURE DANGER something that is not dangerous or harmful at the moment but is likely to become so **3.** COMPUT **TIME-TRIGGERED COMPUTER VIRUS** a computer virus either existing independently or included in a larger program that is triggered by date or by the length of time a computer application is used

time capsule n a container of articles representative of the present, placed in a building's foundations or buried for a future generation to find and learn about the period it represents

timecard /tīm kaard/ n a card that an employee has stamped by a time clock when starting and finishing work

time clock n a clock with a mechanism for stamping employees' timecards when they start and finish work

time-consuming adj taking up or wasting a great deal of time

time deposit n a bank deposit from which a withdrawal can be made only after a set period of time or after giving notice

time dilation, time dilatation n the principle that time elapsed is relative to motion, so that time passes more slowly for a system in motion than for one at rest relative to an outside observer. Further, as predicted by Einstein's special theory of relativity, time passes increasingly slowly as the motion relative to the observer approaches the speed of light.

time exposure n **1.** the exposure of photographic film for an unusually long time to achieve a desired effect **2.** a photograph taken by time exposure

time frame n a period of time during which something takes place or is planned to take place ○ What's the time frame for the project?

time fuse n a fuse that can be set to trigger an explosion at a specific time

time-honoured adj respected or continued because of having been the custom for a long time

time immemorial n **1.** time so distant in the past as to be beyond memory or record **2.** the time prior to the keeping of official legal records in England, fixed at 1189, the beginning of Richard I's reign

timekeeper /tīm keepər/ n **1.** SOMEBODY RECORDING TIME ELAPSED a recorder of the timedd elapsed during a sporting event **2.** SOMEBODY RECORDING TIME WORKED a recorder of time worked by employees **3.** SOMEBODY CONSIDERED IN TERMS OF PUNCTUALITY an employee considered in terms of his or her punctuality ○ She's a hard worker and a good timekeeper. **4.** WATCH OR CLOCK an instrument for recording or showing the time, e.g. a watch or clock **5.** WATCH CONSIDERED IN TERMS OF ACCURACY a watch or clock considered in terms of its accuracy —**timekeeping** n

time lag n an amount of time that passes between two connected events

time-lapse photography n a method of filming a slow process such as the opening of a flower by taking a series of single exposures, then showing them at higher speed to simulate continuous action

timeless /tīmləss/ adj **1.** remaining invariable throughout time ○ fiction that has a timeless appeal **2.** having no beginning or end —**timelessly** adv —**timelessness** n

time limit n a period of time within which something must be done or is effective

time line n a linear representation of significant events in a subject area such as the history of art, shown in chronological order

time loan n a loan that has to be repaid by or on a given date

time lock n a lock on a device such as a safe or bank vault with a timing mechanism that allows it to open only at set times

timely /tīmli/ (-lier, -liest) adj happening or done at the right time or an appropriate time ○ a timely intervention —**timeliness** n —**timely** adv

time machine n a fictional or hypothetical machine that can be used to travel backwards or forwards in time

time note n US a legal document that specifies a date for repayment, e.g. a promissory note

time-off n time that somebody spends away from work, study, or other usual duties

Time of Troubles n the period of Russian history between the death of Tsar Ivan IV (1584), when the boyars attempted to regain control of Russia, and the selection of Michael Romanov as tsar in 1613

time-on n Aus in Australian Rules football, a period of time added on at the end of each quarter to make up for time lost through stoppages

timeous /tīməss/ adj Scotland happening or done in good time —**timeously** adv

time out n **1.** N Am a short break or rest from work or other activities ○ took time out from her studies to travel for a year **2.** a brief solitary period of rest and quiet, often imposed upon an overexcited or hyperactive child

timeout /tīm owt/ n **1.** SPORTS **TIME DURING WHICH GAME STOPS** in some games, a break taken to allow players to rest, receive medical treatment, confer, or be substituted **2.** COMPUT **LACK OF COMPUTER RESPONSE** an interruption in the operation of a computer when a device such as a printer or disk drive does not respond to a command in a predetermined amount of time. A timeout usually results in a message to the user giving the option of retrying or cancelling the command. ■ interj **REQUEST FOR BREAK** used to ask for or suggest a break in a game or an activity

timepiece /tīm peess/ n an instrument for recording

or showing the time, especially one that does not strike or chime, e.g. a watch or clock

timer /tīmər/ n **1.** **TIME-SETTING DEVICE** a device that can be preset to start or stop something at a given time or that sounds after a set period of time **2.** **TIME-RECORDING DEVICE** a device for recording, showing, or measuring time, e.g. a stopwatch **3.** **SOMEBODY TRACKING TIME** somebody who measures or records elapsed time **4.** AUTOMOT **DEVICE CONTROLLING IGNITION** a device in an internal-combustion engine that controls the timing of the spark in the cylinders

times /tīmz/ prep used to indicate that a number is to be multiplied by another ○ Three times two is six.

timesaving /tīm sayving/ adj designed to reduce the length of time taken to do something —**timesaver** n

timescale /tīm skayl/ n **1.** a period of time scheduled for something to be completed **2.** a measurement of time relative to the time in which a typical event occurs, e.g. in geological or cosmic time

time series n a sequence of data gathered at uniformly spaced intervals of time

time-served adj having completed an apprenticeship and therefore fully competent to work as a tradesperson

timeserver /tīm survər/ n somebody whose opinions and behaviour change to suit the times and circumstances without regard for principle —**timeserving** n, adj

timeshare /tīm shair/ n **1.** TRAVEL same as **time sharing** (sense 1) **2.** a property, usually an apartment in a resort area, that is jointly owned by people who use it at different times

time sharing n **1.** the joint ownership of a property such as an apartment in a resort area, in which each owner may occupy the property for part of the year **2.** a technique for the concurrent use of a computer by many people working at remote terminals, each apparently operating as the only user of the computer's resources. The apparent simultaneous use is possible because the computer's processing speed is extremely fast in comparison with a person's typing speed at a keyboard. —**time-share** vti

time sheet n a sheet or card on which the hours worked by an employee are recorded

time signature n a sign used in music to show metre, represented by a fraction in which the upper figure shows beats to the bar and the lower figure shows each beat's time value

times sign n MATHS same as **multiplication sign** (informal)

times table n MATHS same as **multiplication table** (informal; often used in combination)

time-stamp n a part of the financial order-routing process in which the time of day is stamped on an order when it is received on the trading floor and when it is completed

time study n INDUST same as **time and motion study**

time switch n an electrical switch that can be set to turn an appliance on or off at a preselected time

timetable /tīm tayb'l/ n a list of the times at which events are to occur, e.g. the arrival and departure times of trains or the times of school classes. N Am term **schedule** ■ vti (-bles, -bling, -bled) to put something in its chronological place in a list of events

time-tested adj N Am proved to be effective over a long period

time trial n a race in which competitors compete individually for the fastest time

time warp n a hypothetical distortion in the continuum of space-time, popular in science fiction, allowing time to stand still or people to travel from one time to another

time-wasting n **1.** the wasting or frittering away of time **2.** in sports, the employment of negative tactics to prevent an opponent from scoring towards the end of a match —**time-waster** n

timework /tīm wurk/ n work paid according to the time it takes, especially by the hour or the day —**timeworker** n

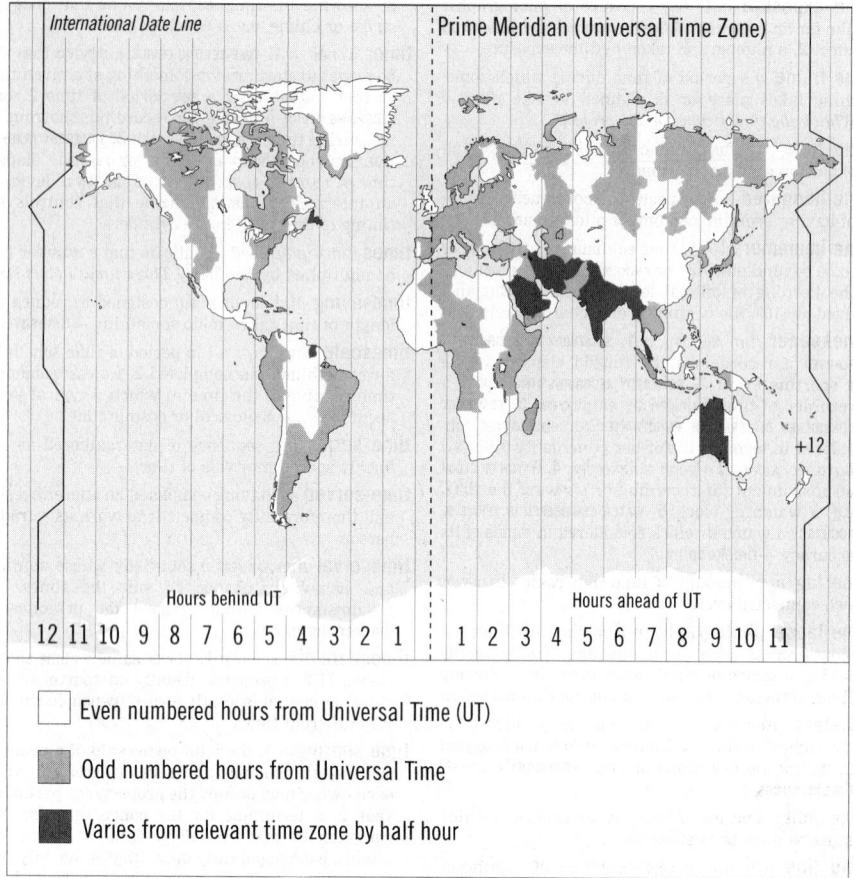

International Date Line   Prime Meridian (Universal Time Zone)

+12

Hours behind UT   Hours ahead of UT

12 11 10 9 8 7 6 5 4 3 2 1   1 2 3 4 5 6 7 8 9 10 11

☐ Even numbered hours from Universal Time (UT)

▨ Odd numbered hours from Universal Time

■ Varies from relevant time zone by half hour

time zone

timeworn /tím wawrn/ *adj* **1.** showing the effects of having been used for a long period of time **2.** having lost effectiveness through overuse ○ *a timeworn phrase*

time zone *n* any of the 24 longitudinal areas into which the world is divided and within which the same standard time is used

timid /tímmid/ *adj* demonstrating a lack of courage or self-assurance [Mid-16C. Directly or via French < Latin *timidus* 'fearful' < *timere* 'to fear'] —**timidity** /ti míddəti/ *n* —**timidly** *adv*

timing /tíming/ *n* **1.** JUDGMENT OF WHEN TO ACT the ability to choose or the choice of the best moment to do or say something, e.g. in performing music or comedy or in sport ○ *a comedian with an immaculate sense of timing* ○ *split-second timing* **2.** RECORDING OF TIME the measurement and recording of the time taken to do something **3.** AUTOMOT ADJUSTMENT OF VALVES OF ENGINE the adjustment of the sequence and relative position of the valves and crankshaft of an automobile engine so that maximum output power is achieved

timing gear *n* the drive in an internal-combustion engine between the crankshaft and the camshaft [Because it causes the valves to open and close at the right time]

Timişoara /tímmi shwaárə/ capital city of Timiş County, western Romania. Population: 332,277 (1997).

timocracy /ti mókrəssi/ (*plural* **-cies**) *n* **1.** government in which the possession of property is a qualification for holding office **2.** a form of government in which honour is the guiding principle [15C. Via French and medieval Latin < Greek *timokratia* < *timē* 'honour, value'] —**timocratic** /tímmə kráttik/ *adj*

Timor /teé mawr/ island in the Malay Archipelago. It is the largest and easternmost of the Lesser Sunda Islands, bordered on the north by the Savu and Banda seas and on the south by the Timor Sea. Population: 3,900,000 (1990). Area: 30,820 sq. km/11,900 sq. mi.

Timor-Leste /teé mawr léstay/ independent nation on the eastern half of the island of Timor in Southeast Asia. Its annexation by Indonesia in 1975 led to protracted internal conflict, and though a plebiscite for independence in 1999 met with Indonesian military intervention, it gained full independence in 2002. Capital: Dili. Population: 997,853 (2003). Area: 14,874 sq. km/5,743 sq. mi. Former name **East Timor**

timorous /tímmərəss/ *adj* showing fear or hesitancy [15C. Via French < medieval Latin *timorosus* < Latin *timere* 'to fear'] —**timorously** *adv* —**timorousness** *n*

Timor Sea /teé mawr-/ arm of the Indian Ocean separating the island of Timor from northern Australia. Area: 450,000 sq. km/174,000 sq. mi.

timothy /tímməthi/ *n* a perennial grass with a cylindrical flower spike, widely cultivated for hay and pasture. Native to: temperate regions. Latin name: *Phleum pratense* [Mid-18C. After *Timothy* Hanson, American farmer who introduced the grass to the Carolinas around 1720]

Timothy /tímməthi/ *n* either of two books of the Bible, originally letters addressed to St Timothy and traditionally attributed to St Paul. They are concerned with the organization of Christian doctrine and codes of Christian behaviour. See table at **Bible**

Timothy, St /tímməthi/ in the Bible, an early Christian missionary, and friend and disciple of St Paul

timothy grass *n* PLANTS same as **timothy**

timpani /tímpəni/, **tympani** *n* a set of two or more kettledrums, usually played as part of an orchestra (*takes a singular or plural verb*) [Late 19C. < Italian, plural of *timpano* 'kettledrum' < Greek *tumpanon* 'drum'] —**timpanist** *n*

timps /timps/ *npl* timpani (*informal*) [Mid-20C. < shortening of TIMPANI]

tin /tin/ *n* **1.** METALLIC ELEMENT a silvery, easily shaped metallic element. Source: oxide ore. Use: alloys such as solder, bronze, and pewter, protective coating for steel. Symbol **Sn**. See table at **element 2.** CONTAINER a sealed container for food or drink, made of thin sheet metal coated with tin or of other thin metal such as aluminium. N Am term **can**[2] **3.** SHEET-METAL CONTAINER a container with a lid, made of thin sheet metal and often decorated **4.** AMOUNT IN TIN the amount that a tin holds ○ *ate a tin of beans* **5.** CORRUGATED IRON corrugated or galvanized iron **6.** same as **money** (*dated informal*) ■ *adj* **1.** MADE OF TIN made from thin sheet metal coated with tin **2.** MADE OF CORRUGATED IRON made of corrugated or galvanized iron ■ *vt* (**tins, tinning, tinned**) **1.** PUT FOOD IN TINS to preserve or seal food in tins. N Am term **can**[2] **2.** COAT SOMETHING WITH TIN to coat or plate something with tin [Old English < Germanic]

tinamou

tinamou /tínni moo/ (*plural* **-mous** or *same*) *n* a short round-bodied ground-dwelling bird. Native to: grassy and jungle areas of Central and South America. Family: Tinamidae. [Late 18C. Via French < Carib *tinamu*]

Tinbergen /tín burgən/, **Jan** (1903–94) Dutch economist. He was a pioneer of econometrics and an economic adviser to the League of Nations Secretariat (1936–38). He shared the first Nobel Prize in economics (1969).

tincal /tíngk'l/ *n* a sodium borate mineral formed by the weathering of borax [Mid-17C. Probably via Portuguese < Persian, Urdu *tinkār* < Sanskrit *ṭankaṇa*]

tin can *n* **1.** a container made of tin or aluminium, especially one used for food **2.** *US* a naval destroyer (*informal*)

tinct /tingkt/ *n* same as **tint** *n* (sense 1) (*archaic*) ■ *vti* (**tincts, tincting, tincted**) same as **tint** *v* (*archaic*) ■ *adj* tinted or coloured (*literary*) [15C. < Latin *tinctus* (see TINT)]

tinct. *abbr* PHARM tincture

tincture /tíngkchər/ *n* **1.** ALCOHOL SOLUTION a solution of a plant extract or chemical in alcohol ○ *tincture of iodine* **2.** TINGE OR COLOUR a tint or slight coloration **3.** TINY AMOUNT OF SOMETHING a hint or small amount of something **4.** HERALDRY HERALDIC COLOUR a colour, metal, or fur used in heraldry ■ *vt* (**-tures, -turing, -tured**) **1.** ADD TINT TO SOMETHING to give something a hint of colour **2.** IMBUE SOMETHING to suffuse something with a quality or property ○ *praise tinctured with criticism* [14C. < Latin *tinctura* 'dyeing' < *tinctus* (see TINT)]

Tindal another spelling of **Tyndale**

tinder /tíndər/ *n* material that is easily combustible and can be used for lighting a fire, e.g. dry sticks [Old English *tynder* < Germanic, 'ignite, kindle']

tinderbox /tíndər boks/ *n* **1.** a person, place, or situation that is likely to become violent **2.** a metal box containing tinder, often fitted with a flint and steel, formerly used for lighting fires

tine /tin/ *n* **1.** a thin pointed projection of a utensil or implement such as a fork or pitchfork **2.** a pointed branch of a deer's antler [Old English *tind* < Germanic] —**tined** *adj*

tinea /tínni ə/ *n* an infection of the skin caused by fungi living as parasites on the outer layer of the skin, nails, or hair [14C. < Latin, 'gnawing worm, moth'] —**tineal** *adj*

tinea barbae /-baárbi/ *n* MED same as **barber's itch** (*technical*) [< Latin, 'tinea of the beard']

tinea pedis /-péddiss/ *n* MED same as **athlete's foot** (*technical*) [< Latin, 'tinea of the foot']

tin ear *n* an inability to perceive differences in musical sounds or subtleties in speech (*informal*)

tineid /tínni id/ *n* a very small moth found worldwide whose larvae either eat fabrics of animal origin or are scavengers. Family: Tineidae. [Mid-19C. < modern Latin *Tineidae* (plural) < Latin *tinea* 'moth']

tinfoil /tín foyl/ *n* **1.** aluminium in a very thin sheet. Use: food wrap. **2.** tin, or an alloy of tin and lead, in a very thin sheet

ting /ting/ *n* a light high-pitched ringing sound, like that of a small bell ■ *vti* (**tings, tinging, tinged**) to produce a light high-pitched ringing sound, or cause something to produce such a sound [Early 17C. An imitation of the sound]

ting-a-ling /tíngə ling/ *n* a tinkling sound resembling that made by a small bell [An imitation of the sound]

tinge /tinj/ *n* **1. SLIGHT ADDED COLOUR** a slight amount of a colour added to something **2. SLIGHT ADDED ELEMENT** a slight amount of something such as an emotion or a flavour ○ *with a tinge of regret in her voice* ■ *vt* (**tinges, tingeing** or **tinging, tinged**) **1. ADD COLOUR TO SOMETHING** to add a slight amount of colour to something **2. MIX IN ELEMENT OF SOMETHING** to mix a slight amount of something with something else (*often passive*) ○ *celebrations tinged with sadness* [15C. < Latin *tingere* 'soak, dye']

tingle /tíng g'l/ *vti* (**-gles, -gling, -gled**) to feel a sensation of stinging, pricking, or vibration, e.g. from cold or a slight electric shock, or cause somebody to feel this ○ *The frost made our faces tingle.* ■ *n* a sensation of stinging, pricking, or vibration [14C. Variant of TINKLE] —**tingler** *n* —**tinglingly** *adv* —**tingly** *adj*

tin god *n* **1.** somebody, often in a position of minor authority, who is regarded as behaving in a self-important overbearing way **2.** somebody or something mistakenly or unjustifiably considered to be worthy of admiration

tin hat *n* a steel helmet (*informal*)

tinhorn /tín hawrn/ *n N Am* somebody relatively insignificant who pretends to be wealthy, influential, or important, especially a gambler (*informal*) [Late 19C. < the horn-shaped metal can used to shake the dice in chuck-a-luck, a gambling game]

tinker /tíngkər/ *n* **1. ACT OF FIDDLING WITH SOMETHING** an act of fiddling with something in an attempt to repair it **2. TRAVELLING POT MENDER** in former times, somebody who travelled from place to place mending metal household items such as pots and pans **3. UNSKILFUL WORKER** a clumsy or unskilful worker, especially at repair work **4. SOMEBODY GOOD AT MANY TASKS** somebody able to do many different kinds of work successfully **5.** *Ireland, Scotland* **ITINERANT** somebody who travels from place to place as a way of life **6. NAUGHTY CHILD** a mischievous or badly-behaved child (*informal*) **7.** FISH **YOUNG MACKEREL** a mackerel that is not fully grown ■ *vi* (**-kers, -kering, -kered**) **1. FIDDLE WITH SOMETHING** to fiddle with something in an attempt to repair it ○ *had been tinkering with the car all morning* **2. HANDLE SOMETHING UNSKILFULLY** to handle something clumsily or unskilfully **3. BE TRAVELLING POT MENDER** in former times, to work as a travelling pot mender [13C. Origin ?] —**tinkerer** *n*

tinker's damn, tinker's cuss *n* the slightest possible amount of care, heed, or value (*informal; used in negative statements*) ○ *This car isn't worth a tinker's damn.* [Probably < the reputation of tinkers for swearing]

tinkle /tíngk'l/ *v* (**-kles, -kling, -kled**) **1.** *vti* **JINGLE LIGHTLY** to make light metallic ringing sounds, or cause something to make light metallic ringing sounds **2.** *vi* same as **urinate** (*informal*) ■ *n* **1. JINGLING SOUND** a series of light metallic ringing sounds **2. URINATION** an act of urinating (*informal*) **3. TELEPHONE CALL** a call on the telephone (*informal*) [14C. < obsolete *tink* 'make a faint metallic sound', origin ?] —**tinkly** *adj*

tin lizzie /-lízzi/ *n* a cheap, old, or dilapidated motor car (*informal*) [< *Tin Lizzie*, nickname for the Model T Ford car]

tinned /tind/ *adj* packed in a tin for storage or sale. N Am term **canned**

tinner /tínnər/ *n* **1.** a worker in a tin mine **2.** INDUST same as **tinsmith 3.** a person or company that packs food into tins

tinnie /tínni/, **tinny** (*plural* **-nies**) *n Aus* (*informal*) **1.** a can of beer **2.** a small aluminium boat, usually with oars or a small engine

tinnitus /tínnitəss/ *n* a continual noise in the ear, e.g. a ringing or roaring, usually caused by damage to the hair cells of the inner ear [Mid-19C. < Latin < *tinnire* 'to ring, tinkle', an imitation of the sound]

tinny[1] /tínni/ (**-nier, -niest**) *adj* **1. HAVING THIN METALLIC SOUND** lacking a full resonant sound ○ *banging out tunes on a tinny old piano* **2. CONSISTING OF TIN** yielding, containing, or having the characteristics of tin **3. TASTING OF METAL** having a metallic taste **4. INFERIOR IN QUALITY** cheaply or shoddily made **5.** *ANZ* same as **lucky** (*informal*) —**tinnily** *adv* —**tinniness** *n*

tinny[2] /tínni/ *n Aus* another spelling of **tinnie** (*informal*)

tin-opener *n* a device for opening tins, especially tins of food. N Am term **can opener**

Tin Pan Alley *n* (*dated*) **1.** a city district in which the business of composing and publishing popular music is carried on **2.** popular music composers and publishers considered collectively [*Tin pan* 'tinny piano', from the cheap pianos associated with music publishers' offices]

tin plate *n* steel or iron in thin sheets coated with tin

tinpot /tín pot/ *adj* inferior in quality or importance (*informal*)

tinsel /tínss'l/ *n* **1. GLITTERING MATERIAL** a thin strip of glittering metal foil, paper, or plastic, used for decoration **2. SOMETHING SHOWY** something worthless that appears glamorous ■ *vt* (**-sels, -selling, -selled**) **1. PUT TINSEL ON SOMETHING** to decorate something with tinsel or other glittering material **2. MAKE SOMETHING SHOWY** to give something a gaudy flashy quality ■ *adj* **1. MADE OF TINSEL** made of or decorated with tinsel **2. GAUDY** appearing glamorous but in fact worthless [15C. < French *étincelé* 'sparkling' (especially with metallic thread), later form of Old French *estincele* 'spark' < Latin *scintilla*] —**tinselly** *adj*

Tinseltown /tíns'l town/ *n* Hollywood and the US film industry regarded as a place of insubstantial glamour (*informal disapproving*)

tinsmith /tín smith/ *n* a maker or repairer of objects made of tin or other easily worked metals

tin snips *npl* shears used for cutting sheet metal

tinstone /tín stōn/ *n* MINERALS same as **cassiterite**

tint /tint/ *n* **1. PALE SHADE** a shade of a colour, especially a pale one **2. COLOUR WITH WHITE ADDED** a colour mixed with white to give low saturation and high lightness **3. TRACE OF COLOUR** a slight amount of a colour **4. HAIR DYE** a dye for the hair **5. SMALL ADDITION** a barely noticeable addition of something **6.** PRINTING **BACKGROUND COLOUR** a pale colour printed as a background onto which another colour is printed **7.** ART **SHADING IN ENGRAVING** a shading effect in engraving, produced by a series of parallel lines ■ *vti* (**tints, tinting, tinted**) **GIVE TINT TO SOMETHING** to colour or shade something with a tint, or acquire a tint [Early 18C. Variant of TINCT < Latin *tinctus*, past participle of *tingere* 'soak, dye'] —**tinter** *n*

Tintagel /tin tájjəl/ coastal town in Cornwall, southwestern England, said to be the birthplace of the legendary King Arthur. Population: 1,800 (1998 estimate).

tintinnabula plural of **tintinnabulum**

tintinnabulation /tínti nabbyōō láysh'n/ *n* the ringing of bells [Mid-19C. < Latin *tintinnabulum* (see TINTINNABULUM)] —**tintinnabular** /tínti nábbyōōlər/ *adj*

tintinnabulum /tínti nábbyōōləm/ (*plural* **-la** /-lə/) *n* a small bell with a high clear ring [Late 16C. < Latin, 'bell' < *tintinnare* 'ring repeatedly' < *tinnire* 'to ring', an imitation of the sound]

Tintoretto /tíntə réttō/ (1518?–94) Italian painter. Based in Venice, he painted large murals in the mannerist style, using free brush strokes and dramatic foreshortened perspectives. Born **Robusti, Jacopo**

> 'Grant me paradise in this world; I'm not so sure I'll reach it in the next.'
> [Attributed to Tintoretto]

tintype /tín tīp/ *n* PHOTOGRAPHY same as **ferrotype**

tinware /tín wair/ *n* objects made of tin plate, especially utensils

tin whistle *n* MUSIC same as **penny whistle**

tinwork /tín wurk/ *n* things made of tin

tinworks /tín wurks/ (*plural same*) *n* a place where tin is smelted and rolled

tiny /tíni/ *adj* (**-nier, -niest**) extremely small ■ *n* (*plural* **-nies**) a very young child (*informal*) [Late 16C. < obsolete *tine* 'very small', origin ?] —**tinily** *adv* —**tininess** *n*

-tion *suffix* action or process, or the result of an action or process ○ *pollution* [Directly or via French < Latin *-tion-*]

tip[1] /tip/ *n* **1. POINTED END** the end of an object, especially a narrow or pointed end ○ *a pencil with a sharp tip* **2. PART ON END** a piece fitted to the end of something else ■ *vt* (**tips, tipping, tipped**) **1. PROVIDE END FOR SOMETHING** to provide something with an end, or form the end of something **2. COVER END OF SOMETHING** to cover or decorate the end of something ○ *shoes with steel-tipped toes* **3. TAKE END OFF SOMETHING** to remove the end from something [15C. Probably < Old Norse *typpi* < Germanic, 'upper extremity'] ◇ **on the tip of somebody's tongue 1.** nearly, but not quite, brought to mind **2.** on the verge of being said but remaining unsaid ◇ **the tip of the iceberg** the small visible or obvious part of a largely unseen problem or difficulty

tip[2] /tip/ *v* (**tips, tipping, tipped**) **1.** *vti* **TILT SOMETHING** to cause something to move from a level or upright position, or be moved in this way ○ *sitting with his chair tipped back* **2.** *vti* **KNOCK SOMETHING OVER** to turn something on its side or upside down, or become turned on the side or upside down ○ *High winds caused the truck to tip over on its side.* **3.** *vt* **POUR SOMETHING OUT** to remove a container's contents by moving it from a level or upright position ○ *tipped the gravel onto the path* **4.** *vti* **DUMP RUBBISH** to dispose of refuse **5.** *vt* **TAKE OFF YOUR HAT** to touch or lift a hat as a greeting ■ *n* **1. ACT OF TIPPING** an act of tipping something **2. TILT** an incline from vertical or horizontal **3. RUBBISH DUMP** a place to dump refuse **4. UNTIDY PLACE** an extremely untidy or dirty place (*informal*) [14C. Origin ?] —**tippable** *adj*

tip[3] /tip/ *n* **1. GRATUITY** a gift of money for a service, especially as an amount above what is owed **2. WARNING OR INFORMATION** an item of advance or confidential information that may give the person who receives it an advantage **3. HELPFUL HINT** a useful suggestion or idea for doing something ○ *cooking tips* ■ *vti* (**tips, tipping, tipped**) **1. GIVE GRATUITY** to give somebody a gift of money in return for a service, especially in addition to what is owed **2. INFORM SOMEBODY** to give somebody advance, inside, or confidential information [Early 17C. Origin ?]

tip off *vt* to give somebody a warning or some useful advance information ○ *The police had been tipped off about the girl's whereabouts.*

tip[4] /tip/ *n* **1. LIGHT HIT** a light glancing blow **2. DEFLECTED BALL** in cricket, a stroke in which the ball glances off the bat ■ *vt* (**tips, tipping, tipped**) **1. HIT SOMEBODY OR SOMETHING LIGHTLY** to strike somebody or something with a light glancing blow **2. DEFLECT CRICKET BALL** in cricket, to hit a ball so that it glances off the bat [15C. Origin ?]

tip and run *n* a variety of cricket in which the batter must run if his or her bat strikes the ball [< TIP[4]]

tip-and-run *adj* striking quickly then withdrawing immediately

tipcart /típ kaart/ *n* a cart whose load is emptied by tilting its body [Late 19C. < TIP[2]]

tipi *n* CULTL ANTHROP another spelling of **tepee**

~~**tipical**~~ incorrect spelling of **typical**

tip-in *n* **1.** in basketball, a goal scored by lightly pushing a rebound into the basket with the fingertips **2.** in hockey, a goal scored at very close range by giving a short stroke with the stick [< TIP[4]]

tip-off[1] *n* a piece of advance information, or a warning given in an effort to help (*informal*) [< TIP[3]]

tip-off[2] *n* in basketball, the start of a period of play in which two players try to tap a jump ball to one of their team-mates [< TIP[4]]

tipper[1] /típpər/ *n* somebody who leaves a tip or gratuity, especially habitually and of a particular kind ○ *a generous tipper* [Late 19C. < TIP[3]]

tipper[2] /típpər/ *n* **1.** somebody or something that tips something over or out **2.** VEHICLES same as **tipper truck** [Mid-19C. < TIP[1]]

Tipperary /típpə ráiri/ former county in Munster Province, southern Republic of Ireland, now divided into the counties of Tipperary North Riding and Tipperary South Riding. Population: 133,535 (2002). Area: 4,225 sq. km/1,643 sq. mi.

tipper truck, **tipper lorry** *n* a lorry built so that the front of the platform carrying the load can be raised to allow the load to slide off

tippet /típpit/ *n* **1.** STOLE WITH HANGING ENDS a stole or cape, often made of fur, with long ends that hang down the front **2.** STOLE OF ANGLICAN CLERGY a long stole worn around the shoulders and over the robes of Anglican clergy during services **3.** HANGING END OF GARMENT a long hanging end worn attached to a sleeve, hood, or cape, worn in medieval times and up to the 16th century **4.** BIRDS same as **ruff**¹ (sense 2) **5.** FISHING PART TO WHICH FLY IS TIED in angling, the thin end section of a leader to which a fly is tied [14C. Probably < TIP¹]

Tippett /típpit/, **Sir Michael** (1905–98) British composer. He is noted for the mystical quality of many of his orchestral, instrumental, and vocal works. Full name **Tippett, Sir Michael Kemp**

Tipp-Ex /típ eks/ *tdmk* a trademark for a correction fluid

tipping point /típping-/ *n* **1.** a defining moment in a series of events at which time a series of significant, often momentous and irreversible reactions occur **2.** the stage during an epidemic when the agent, especially a virus, begins to increase very rapidly in a population [*Tipping* < TIP²]

tipple¹ /típp'l/ *v* (**-ples, -pling, -pled**) **1.** *vi* DRINK ALCOHOL HABITUALLY to drink alcoholic liquor habitually or excessively **2.** *vti* DRINK ALCOHOL REPEATEDLY to drink alcoholic liquor repeatedly a little at a time ■ *n* ALCOHOLIC DRINK a type or drink of alcoholic liquor (*informal*) [Mid-16C. Probably back-formation < *tippler* 'ale seller' < N Germanic]

tipple² /típp'l/ *n* MIN EXTRACT **1.** DEVICE FOR UNLOADING ORE TRUCKS a device for tipping coal or ore trucks to unload them **2.** PLACE FOR UNLOADING ORE a place where ore or coal trucks are unloaded **3.** PLACE FOR SCREENING COAL a place where coal is screened and loaded into trucks or railway goods wagons ■ *vti* (**-ples, -pling, -pled**) N England FALL OR TIP OVER to fall over, or tip something over [Mid-19C. < TIP²]

tippler¹ /típplər/ *n* a habitual drinker of alcoholic beverages [Late 16C. < TIPPLE¹]

tippler² /típplər/ *n* a domestic pigeon of a breed kept for show [Mid-19C. < TIPPLE², because it often turns over backwards in flight]

tipstaff /típ staaf/ (*plural* **-staves** /-stayvz/ *or* **-staffs**) *n* **1.** in former times, a metal-tipped staff carried as a sign of official authority **2.** in former times, a court official who carried a staff, e.g. a bailiff or constable [Mid-16C. Contraction of *tipped staff* < TIP¹]

tipster /típstər/ *n* somebody who provides or sells information to horse-race betters or financial speculators [Mid-19C. < TIP³]

tipsy /típsi/ (**-sier, -siest**) *adj* **1.** slightly drunk **2.** inclined to tilt or tip [Late 16C. < TIP²] —**tipsily** *adv* —**tipsiness** *n*

tipsy cake *n* a sponge cake soaked with alcohol or alcohol-laced syrup

tip-tilted *adj* describes a person's nose that is slightly turned up [< TIP¹]

tiptoe /típ tō/ *vi* (**-toes, -toeing, -toed**) **1.** WALK WITH HEELS RAISED to walk on the toes and the balls of the feet with the heels off the ground **2.** MOVE CAUTIOUSLY to move or proceed quietly or cautiously ■ *n* POSITION WITH HEELS RAISED a standing position in which the heels are raised off the ground and the weight is on the front part of the feet, with the body often also stretched up to gain extra height ○ *walking on tiptoe* ■ *adj* **1.** WALKING ON TOES walking or standing on the toes or balls of the feet **2.** CAUTIOUS proceeding with caution or stealth ■ *adv* ON TIPS OF TOES on the toes or the balls of the feet [14C. < TIP¹]

tiptop /típ tóp/ (*informal*) *adj* OF TOP QUALITY of the highest quality or rank ■ *adv* WELL exceptionally well ■ *n* **1.** SUMMIT the highest point **2.** HIGHEST QUALITY the highest degree of quality or excellence [Early 18C. Doubling of TOP¹, after TIP¹]

tip truck *n* ANZ same as **dumper truck**

tipuna *n* NZ ANTHROP same as **tupuna**

tip-up *adj* designed to tilt upward or fold up [< TIP²]

TIR *abbr* TRANSP international road transport [French *Transports Internationaux Routiers*]

tirade /tī ráyd, ti-/ *n* a long angry speech, usually of criticism or denunciation [Early 19C. < French, 'volley' < *tirer* 'to draw' < assumed Vulgar Latin *tirare*]

tiramisu /tírrə mee soó, -meè soo/ *n* an Italian dessert made with layers of sponge cake soaked in espresso coffee, Marsala, mascarpone cheese, and chocolate [Late 20C. < Italian *tira mi sù* 'pick me up']

Tirana /ti raánə/ capital city of Albania, in the central part of the country, situated 27 km/17 mi. from the Adriatic coast. Population: 343,078 (2001).

tire¹ /tīr/ (**tires, tiring, tired**) *vti* **1.** to make somebody feel in need of rest or sleep, or grow weaker and less energetic and feel a need for rest or sleep **2.** to lose interest in and become bored and impatient with somebody or something, or cause somebody to do this [Old English *tyrian*, origin ?]

tire² /tīr/ *n* a woman's head covering or ornament (*archaic*) [14C. Shortening of ATTIRE]

tire³ /tīr/ *n* TRANSP US spelling of **tyre**

tired /tīrd/ *adj* **1.** NEEDING REST in need of rest or sleep, or weakened and made less active by exertion **2.** NO LONGER INTERESTED having lost patience or interest ○ *grew tired of hearing the same complaints* **3.** OVERUSED no longer new or fresh because of overuse ○ *a tired old slogan* [15C. < TIRE¹] —**tiredly** *adv* —**tiredness** *n* ◇ **tired and emotional** drunk (*humorous*)

tired out *adj* thoroughly tired

Tiree /tī reé/ island of the Inner Hebrides, western Scotland. Population: 950 (1991). Area: 76 sq. km/29 sq. mi.

tireless /tīrləss/ *adj* never slackening or stopping, and apparently immune to tiredness or fatigue [Late 16C. < TIRE¹] —**tirelessly** *adv* —**tirelessness** *n*

Tiresias /tī reési əss/ *n* in Greek mythology, a blind seer from Thebes who often delivered prophecies to Oedipus

tiresome /tīrssəm/ *adj* causing weariness, annoyance, or boredom [Early 16C. < TIRE¹] —**tiresomely** *adv* —**tiresomeness** *n*

Tirgu Mures /túrgoo moŏr esh/ capital city of Mures County in central Romania. Population: 165,534 (1997).

tiring /tīring/ *adj* causing somebody to feel tired, usually because requiring great physical or mental exertion [Late 16C. < TIRE¹]

Tír na n-Óg /teèr na nog/ *n* in Irish legend, a land of eternal youth [Late 19C. < Irish, 'land of the young']

Tirol /ti ról/, **Tyrol** province in western Austria, lying within the Alps. Capital: Innsbruck. Population: 663,603 (1998). Area: 12,647 sq. km/4,883 sq. mi. —**Tirolean** /tírrə leé ən/ *n, adj* —**Tirolese** /tírrə leéz/ *n, adj*

Tiros /tī róss/ (*plural same*) *n* a satellite with infrared and television equipment for transmitting weather data to Earth [Late 20C. Acronym < *television infrared observational satellite*]

Tirso de Molina /teèrss ō day mə leénə/ (1571?–1648) Spanish playwright and theologian. He is the author of several hundred plays, including the comedy *The Trickster of Seville* (1630), which has the first literary presentation of Don Juan. Pseudonym of **Téllez, Gabriel**

Tirthankara /teer tángkərə/ *n* a traditional holy man of Jainism, belonging to a group believed to have attained personal immortality through enlightenment, and by their teaching to have made a path for others to follow [Mid-19C. < Sanskrit *tīrthaṁkarah* 'ford maker' < *tīrtham* 'ford, passage' + *kṛ-* 'make']

Tiruchchirappalli /tírrə chirə púlli, ti roŏchi raápəli/ city in Tiruchchirappalli District, Tamil Nadu State, southern India. Population: 387,223 (1991). Former name **Trichinopoly**

Tirunelveli /tírroŏ nélvəli/ town in Tirunelveli District, Tamil Nadu State, southern India. Population: 431,603 (2001).

Tiryns /tírrinz/ ancient city in Argolis Department in the Peloponnese, southern Greece, situated between Naplion and Mycenae.

'tis /tiz/ *contr* it is (*archaic or literary*)

tisane /ti zán, tee-/, **ptisan** *n* an infusion of leaves or flowers used as a beverage, e.g. a herbal tea [14C. Via French < Greek *ptisanē* 'barley water']

Tisha b'Av /ti shaá bə áv/ *n* in Judaism, a fast on the ninth day of the month of Av to commemorate the destruction of the First and Second Temples [< Hebrew *tišāh bĕāb* 'ninth of Av']

Tishri /tíshri/ (*plural* **-ris**) *n* in the Jewish calendar, the seventh month of the religious year, lasting 30 days and falling about the same time as September to October. See table at **calendar** [Mid-17C. < Hebrew *tišrī*]

Tisiphone /tī síffəni/ *n* in Greek mythology, one of the three Furies. The others were Alecto and Megaera.

Tissot /teéssō/, **Jacques-Joseph** (1836–1902) French painter. He achieved great success with his scenes of fashionable society in London and Paris.

tissue /tíshoo, tíssyoo/ *n* **1.** PIECE OF ABSORBENT PAPER a piece of soft absorbent paper that can be used as a handkerchief, toilet paper, or a towel **2.** INDUST same as **tissue paper 3.** BIOL GROUP OF CELLS IN ORGANISM organic body material in animals and plants made up of large numbers of cells that are similar in form and function and their related intercellular substances. The four basic types of tissue are nerve, muscle, epidermal, and connective. **4.** INTRICATE SERIES an intricate interrelated series of things ○ *a tissue of lies* **5.** TEXTILES GAUZY FABRIC a thin, finely woven fabric with a gauzy texture [14C. < Old French *tissu* < past participle of *tistre* 'weave' < Latin *texere*]

tissue culture *n* **1.** the growth of tissue outside an organism in a nutrient medium, or the techniques involved in this process **2.** the tissue grown in a culture medium

tissue paper *n* a thin soft paper. Use: wrapping and protecting delicate items.

tissue plasminogen activator *n* an anticlotting enzyme that is produced naturally in blood vessel linings and is genetically engineered for use in treating heart attacks, dissolving blood clots, and preventing heart muscle damage

tissue type *n* the chemical characteristics of the body tissue of an organism that determine whether or not the tissue is immunologically compatible with the tissue of another organism

Tisza /tíss aw/ major tributary of the River Danube in eastern Europe. Length: 970 km/600 mi.

tit¹ /tit/ *n* **1.** same as **teat 2.** an offensive term for a woman's breast (*slang*) **3.** a highly offensive term that deliberately insults somebody's intelligence or character (*slang*) [Old English *titt* < Germanic]

tit: great tit

tit² /tit/ *n* a small active songbird with a short beak and strong feet, e.g. a great tit. Native to: northern hemisphere, Africa. Family: Paridae. [Early 18C. Shortening of TITMOUSE]

Tit. *abbr* BIBLE Titus

titan /tít'n/ *n* somebody whose power, achievement, intellect, or physical size is extraordinarily impressive [Early 19C. < TITAN]

Titan /tít'n/ *n* **1.** in Greek mythology, one of the twelve children of Uranus and Gaia, supreme rulers of the universe until they were overthrown by Zeus **2.**

a large natural satellite of Saturn [15C. Via Latin < Greek]

titanate /títə nayt/ *n* a compound that is a salt or an ester of titanic acid

Titania /ti taáni ə/ *n* **1.** in medieval folklore, the wife of Oberon and queen of the fairies **2.** the largest moon of the planet Uranus, the fourth most distant satellite observable from the Earth, orbiting at a distance of 436,000 km/262,000 mi. with a diameter of 1578 km/947 mi. Although it was one of the first two satellites of Uranus to be discovered in 1787, Oberon being the other, Titania is officially designated as Uranus III.

titanic[1] /tī tánnik/ *adj* **1.** having extraordinary physical strength or size **2.** of extraordinary power, scope, or impressiveness [Mid-19C. < TITANIC] —**titanically** *adv*

titanic[2] /tī tánnik/ *adj* relating to or containing titanium, especially with a valency of four [Early 19C. < TITANIUM]

Titanic /tī tánnik/ *adj* relating to or like a mythological Titan [Mid-17C. < Greek *titanikos* < *Titanes*, plural of *Titan* 'Titan']

titanic acid *n* an acid that is the hydrated form of titanium dioxide. Use: for fixing dyes. Formula: H_2TiO_3.

titanic oxide *n* CHEM same as **titanium dioxide**

titaniferous /títəníffərəss/ *adj* yielding or containing titanium [Early 19C. < TITANIUM]

Titanism /títənizəm/ *n* a spirit of defiance of authority, conventional society, and the established order

titanite /títənīt/ *n* MINERALS same as **sphene** [Mid-19C. < TITANIUM]

titanium /tī táyni əm, ti-/ *n* a strong, lightweight, corrosion-resistant silvery metallic element. Source: rutile, ilmenite. Use: manufacture of alloys for aerospace industry. Symbol **Ti**. See table at **element** [Late 18C. < TITAN (sense 2), after URANIUM]

titanium dioxide *n* a white crystalline compound. Source: rutile, ilmenite, other minerals. Use: pigment for durable paints and plastics. Formula: TiO_2.

titanium white *n* **1.** CHEM same as **titanium dioxide 2.** a brilliant white paint pigment consisting primarily of titanium dioxide

titanosaur /tī tánnə sawr/ *n* a huge herbivorous sauropod dinosaur of the Cretaceous and Jurassic periods, found especially in South America. Genus: *Titanosaurus*. [Late 19C. < modern Latin *Titanosaurus* < Greek *Titan* 'Titan' + *sauros* 'lizard']

titanothere /tī tánnə theer/ *n* a large mammal similar to a rhinoceros that lived in North America during the Tertiary Period [Mid-20C. < modern Latin *Titanotherium* < Greek *Titan* 'Titan' + *therion* 'wild beast']

titanous /títənəss/ *adj* relating to or containing titanium with a valency of three [Mid-19C. < TITANIUM]

titarakura /teé tə raa koorə/ (*plural same*) *n NZ* FISH same as **bully**[3] [< Maori]

titbit /tít bit/ *n* **1.** a small, usually bite-sized piece of delicious food **2.** a small piece of interesting information or gossip [Mid-17C. Origin ?]

titch /tich/, **tich** *n* a very small person (*informal*) [Mid-20C. < Little *Tich*, stage name of British comedian Harry Relph (1868–1928), who was very small]

ORIGIN Harry Relph got his nickname *Little Tich*, from his supposed resemblance to the so-called Tichborne claimant. This was the title given to Arthur Orton, who, in an English *cause célèbre* of the 1860s, returned from Australia claiming to be Roger Tichborne, the heir to an English baronetcy who had supposedly been lost at sea.

titchy /títchi/ (**-ier, -iest**), **tichy** *adj* regional very small (*informal*)

REGIONAL NOTE See *itsy-bitsy*.

titer *n* CHEM, BIOCHEM US spelling of **titre**

titfer /títfər/ *n* same as **hat** (*slang*) [Early 20C. Shortening of rhyming slang *tit for tat*]

tit for tat *n* the repayment a wrong or injury suffered by inflicting equivalent harm on the doer

---

(*hyphenated when used before a noun*) ○ *tit-for-tat strikes* [Mid-16C. Origin ?]

tithe /tīth/ *n* **1.** SOMEBODY'S FINANCIAL SUPPORT FOR CHURCH one tenth of somebody's income or produce paid voluntarily or as a tax for the support of a church or its clergy **2.** OBLIGATION OF SUPPORTING CHURCH FINANCIALLY the obligation to pay a tithe to a church or its clergy **3.** ASSESSMENT OR CONTRIBUTION a voluntary contribution or tax payment, especially when it constitutes one tenth of somebody's income **4.** SMALL PART OF SOMETHING one tenth or a small part of something ■ *v* (**tithes, tithing, tithed**) **1.** *vti* PAY ONE TENTH OF INCOME to contribute or pay one tenth of your income or produce, especially to support a church **2.** *vt* COLLECT TENTH OF INCOME OF SOMEBODY to assess or collect the payment of one tenth of the income of somebody [Old English *tēopa* 'tenth, tithe'] —**tithable** *adj* —**tither** *n*

tithe barn *n* formerly, a barn that served as a store for the produce contributed by the parish to the church as a tithe

tithing /tīthing/ *n* **1.** PAYING OF TITHES the assessing or paying of tithes **2.** TEN HOUSEHOLDERS in medieval England, a small district composed of ten householders and their households, each bearing responsibility for the conduct of the others **3.** RURAL DIVISION a rural administrative region in medieval England equal to one tenth of the county division known as a hundred **4.** ONE TENTH one tenth part of something [Old English *tēopung* < TITHE]

titi[1] /teé teé/ (*plural* **-tis**) *n* a tree-dwelling monkey with a round face, thick soft fur, and a long tail. Native to: tropical South America. Genus: *Callicebus*. [Mid-18C. Via Spanish *titi* < Aymara]

titi[2] /teé teé/ (*plural* **-tis**) *n* **1.** an evergreen bush or small tree with glossy leathery leaves. Flowers: fragrant, white or pinkish. Native to: southeastern United States. Latin name: *Cliftonia monophylla*. **2.** a small evergreen tree or bush with leathery leaves and yellow fruit. Native to: southeastern United States, Central and South America. Latin name: *Cyrilla racemiflora*. [Early 19C. Origin ?]

titian /tísh'n/, **Titian** *adj* of a gold-tinged auburn colour ○ *titian hair* [Late 19C. After TITIAN, who used the colour frequently]

AKG London

Titian: self-portrait (1555)

Titian /tísh'n/ (1485?–1576) Italian painter. The foremost Venetian painter of the Renaissance, he painted portraits and religious and mythological scenes that are noted for their rich coloration. Born **Vecellio, Tiziano**

'It is not bright colours but good drawing that makes figures beautiful.'
[Titian. Quoted in *Marvels of the Painter's Art*, Carlo Ridolfi; 1648]

Titicaca, Lake /títti kaá kaa/ lake in east-central South America, extending from southeastern Peru to western Bolivia. It is the largest lake on the continent and the highest navigable lake in the world, about 3,810 m/12,500 ft above sea level. Area: 8,300 sq. km/3,200 sq. mi.

titillate /títti layt/ (**-lates, -lating, -lated**) *v* **1.** *vti* to excite or stimulate somebody pleasurably, usually in a mildly sexual way **2.** *vt* to cause a tingling sensation in somebody by touching him or her lightly [Early 17C. < Latin *titillare* 'tickle'] —**titillating** *adj* —**titillatingly** *adv* —**titillation** /títti láysh'n/ *n* —**titillative** *adj*

USAGE titillate or **titivate**? These two unrelated verbs look and sound similar and are sometimes confused. To **titillate** is to excite or stimulate somebody, usually in a mildly sexual way, whereas to **titivate** is to improve the appearance: *She was accused of titillating her readers with details of the actor's private life. He was titivating himself in front of the mirror.*

titivate /títti vayt/ (**-vates, -vating, -vated**), **tittivate** *vti* to improve the appearance of somebody or something by neatening or adding decoration [Early 19C. Alteration of *tidivate*, origin ?] —**titivation** /títti váysh'n/ *n* —**titivator** *n*

USAGE See *titillate*.

titlark /tít laark/ *n* BIRDS same as **pipit** [Mid-17C. < TIT[2] + LARK[1]]

title /tít'l/ *n* **1.** NAME a name that identifies a book, film, play, painting, musical composition, or other literary or artistic work **2.** DESCRIPTIVE HEADING a descriptive heading for something such as a book chapter, a magazine article, or a speech **3.** PUBL same as **title page 4.** PUBLISHED OR RECORDED WORK a work published or recorded by a company ○ *this spring's new titles* **5.** DESIGNATION ADDED TO NAME a word added to and usually preceding somebody's name to indicate his or her rank, social status, or profession, or as a courtesy, e.g. 'Mr', 'Ms', 'Dr', or 'Lord' **6.** NAME DESCRIBING POSITION a name that describes somebody's job or position in a company or organization ○ *a job title* **7.** CHAMPIONSHIP the status of champion in a sport or competition ○ *a title fight* **8.** LAW RIGHT TO POSSESS PROPERTY a legal right to possess and dispose of property **9.** LAW EVIDENCE OF PROPERTY RIGHTS the evidence of legal right to property **10.** LAW DOCUMENT a document giving the legal right to property **11.** LAW RIGHT OR PROOF OF RIGHT a legitimate right, or something providing proof or justification for a claim **12.** LAW CLAIM BASED ON RIGHT a claim based on a legitimate right **13.** LAW DIVISION a division of a law, statute, or law book **14.** LAW LAW HEADING a heading for a lawsuit or legal action, or one that names a document or statute **15.** CHR REQUIREMENT OF ORDINATION a source of income or office in the church required of a candidate by the Church of England before ordination **16.** CHR ROMAN CATHOLIC CHURCH IN ROME a Roman Catholic church in or near Rome that has a bishop or cardinal as its nominal head ■ **titles** *npl* CINEMA, MEDIA CREDITS OR SUBTITLES ON SCREEN the written presentation on the screen of credits, narration, or subtitles in a film or television programme ■ *vt* (**-tles, -tling, -tled**) **1.** NAME SOMEBODY OR SOMETHING to give a name or title to somebody or something **2.** CALL SOMEBODY BY TITLE to call somebody by a particular title [Pre-12C. Via French < Latin *titulus* 'inscription'] —**titled** *adj*

title bar *n* a horizontal bar at the top of a computer screen that usually shows the names of the program and file that is currently in use

title deed *n* a deed or document that is evidence of somebody's legal right to property

titleholder /tít'l hōldər/ *n* **1.** somebody who holds a sports championship title **2.** somebody who holds a legal title to property —**titleholding** *n*

title page *n* a page at the beginning of a book that gives its title and the name of the author and publisher

title role *n* the role in a play or film that gives the work its name

title track *n* the song or piece of music whose name is used as the title of a particular recording

titmouse /tít mowss/ (*plural* **-mice** /-mīss/) *n* BIRDS same as **tit**[2] [14C. Alteration (influenced by *mouse*) of *titmose* < obsolete *tit* 'something small, runt' + *mose* 'titmouse' (< Old English *māse*)]

Tito /teétō/ (1892–1980) Yugoslav patriot and president of Yugoslavia (1942–77). After leading partisan forces against the Germans in World War II, he established a Communist state independent of the Soviet Union. Known as **Marshal Tito**. Born **Broz, Josip**. See illustration on next page

'I am the only Yugoslav.'
[Attributed to Tito]

Titoism /teétō izəm/ *n* the form of Communism associated with Tito and practised by him in Yugo-

Tito

slavia, especially involving the pursuit of national interests independent of the then Soviet Union and its satellites —**Titoist** n, adj

titrant /títrənt/ n a reagent that is added in titration, e.g. a solution of known concentration [Mid-20C. < TITRATE]

titrate /tī tráyt/ (-trates, -trating, -trated) vt to measure the concentration of a solution by titration [Late 19C. < French titrer < titre (see TITRE)] —**titratable** adj

titration /tī tráysh'n/ n a method of calculating the concentration of a dissolved substance in a known volume of test solution by adding measured quantities of a reagent of known concentration until a reaction occurs

titre /títər, teétər/ n 1. the concentration of a substance in solution as determined by titration 2. the concentration of an antibody in serum [Mid-19C. < French titre 'qualification, quality (of gold or silver alloy)', variant of title (see TITLE)]

titrimetric /títri méttrik/ adj using or calculated by titration [Late 19C. < TITRATION]

titter /títtər/ vi (-ters, -tering, -tered) to laugh quietly or giggle in a self-conscious or nervous way ■ n a quiet self-conscious or nervous laugh or giggle [Early 17C. An imitation of the sound] —**titterer** n —**tittering** n —**titteringly** adv

tittivate vti another spelling of **titivate**

tittle /títt'l/ n 1. a tiny bit of something 2. a small mark used in printing and writing, e.g. an accent, punctuation mark, or diacritical mark [14C. < medieval Latin titulus 'small superscript mark' < Latin, 'title']

tittle-tattle n idle gossip ■ vi (tittle-tattles, tittle-tattling, tittle-tattled) to gossip idly [Early 16C. Doubling of TATTLE] —**tittle-tattler** n

tittup /títtəp/ vi (-tups, -tupping, -tupped) to move in a lively prancing way ■ n a sometimes exaggerated lively prancing movement [Late 17C. Origin ?]

titty /títti/ (plural -ties) n a woman's breast (slang; often considered offensive)

titubation /títtyoŏ báysh'n/ n an unsteady or stumbling gait or a head tremor, often caused by a disorder of the cerebellum [Mid-17C. < Latin titubare 'stagger']

titular /títtyoŏlər/ adj 1. IN NAME ONLY having a particular title, rank, or position, but not possessing the power or exercising the functions usually associated with it 2. WITH TITLE OF RANK holding a title of rank 3. FROM TITLE derived from or figuring in the title of a work such as a book or film 4. CHR FROM INACTIVE SEE bearing the title of a see or monastery that is no longer active ■ n 1. SOMEBODY WITH TITLE OF RANK somebody who holds a title of rank 2. HOLDER OF NOMINAL TITLE somebody who holds a title in name only [Late 16C. < Latin titulus 'title'] —**titularly** adv —**titulary** n

Titus /títəss/ n 1. in the Bible, an early Christian leader and a disciple of St Paul 2. a book of the Bible, originally a letter addressed to Titus and traditionally attributed to St Paul. It contains advice on the organization of the Christian Church. See table at Bible

Titus /títəss/ (AD 39–81) Roman general and emperor. He captured and destroyed Jerusalem in AD 70. As emperor (79–81) he was noted for his leniency and generosity, and he also completed the Colosseum in Rome. Full name **Titus Flavius Sabinus Vespasianus**

Tiv /tiv/ (plural **Tivs** or same) n 1. a member of a people living in West Africa, mainly in southern Nigeria and neighbouring Cameroon 2. the Benue-Congo language of the Tiv people. Native speakers: 1.5 million. [Mid-20C. < Bantu] —**Tiv** adj

TiVo /tee vō/ tdmk a trademark for a type of digital video recorder that automatically records selected television programs each time they are broadcast and stores them on a hard disk

Tivoli /tívvəli/ town in central Italy, near Rome, location of the Renaissance-period Tivoli Gardens and the ruined villa of the emperor Hadrian. Population: 49,342 (2001).

Tiwa /teéwə/ (plural -was or same) n 1. a member of a group of Pueblo peoples who lived in New Mexico and who now live mainly in Texas and northern New Mexico 2. the Tanoan language of the Tiwa people. Native speakers: 5,000. [Early 18C. < Tiwa] —**Tiwa** adj

Tiwi /tí wi/ n an Australian Aboriginal language spoken on Bathurst and Melville islands in the Northern Territory. Native speakers: 2,050. —**Tiwi** adj

Tizard /tíz aard/, Dame Cath (b. 1931) governor general of New Zealand (1990–96). After an extensive career in local government, she became mayor of Auckland in 1983 and the first woman to hold the post of governor general. Full name **Tizard, Dame Catherine Anne**

tizzy /tízzi/, **tizz** /tiz/, **tiz-woz** /tíz woz/ n a nervous agitated or confused state (informal) [Mid-20C. Origin ?]

tj abbr ONLINE Tajikistan (used in Internet addresses) See table at **domain name**

T-joint (plural **T-joints** or **tee-joints**) n a joint in wood or other material forming the letter T

T-junction n a junction where a road joins another road, especially at a right angle, but does not cross it

tk abbr TRANSP truck

TKO abbr BOXING technical knockout

tkt abbr ticket

Tl symbol CHEM ELEM thallium

t.l. abbr INSUR total loss

TLA abbr three-letter acronym

Tlaxcala /tlass káálə, -kállə/ 1. state in east-central Mexico. Capital: Tlaxcala. Population: 962,646 (2000). Area: 4,037 sq. km/1,559 sq. mi. 2. capital city of Tlaxcala State in east-central Mexico. It is the site of the Church of San Francisco, the oldest church in North America (1521). Population: 77,000 (2002).

TLC abbr tender loving care (informal)

Tlemcen /tlem sén/ town in northwestern Algeria. Population: 126,882 (1987).

Tlingit /tlíng git/ (plural -gits or same) n 1. a member of a group of Native North American peoples who lived on coastal southeastern Alaska and who now live mainly there and in British Columbia 2. the Na-Dene language of the Tlingit people. Native speakers: 2,000. [Mid-19C. < Tlingit, 'person'] —**Tlingit** adj

t.l.o. abbr INSUR total loss only

T-lymphocyte n BIOL same as **T-cell**

tm abbr ONLINE Turkmenistan (used in Internet addresses) See table at **domain name**

Tm symbol CHEM ELEM thulium

TM abbr 1. LAW trademark 2. transcendental meditation 3. ONLINE trust me (used in e-mails or text messages)

T-man n a special investigator of the US Department of the Treasury (informal)

tmesis /tmeé siss, meé-, tə meé-/ n the separation of the parts of a word by inserting a word or words between them, as in 'pretty un-bloody-likely' [Mid-16C. < Greek tmēsis 'cutting' < temnein 'cut']

TMJ syndrome n a painful condition involving the temporomandibular joint and the muscles used for chewing, sometimes causing clicking sounds and restricted jaw movement. It is usually associated with a faulty dental bite. Full form **temporomandibular joint syndrome**

TMT abbr FIN technology, media, and telecommunications

tn abbr ONLINE Tunisia (used in Internet addresses) See table at **domain name**

tng abbr training

TNT n a yellow flammable crystalline compound. Use: explosive. Formula: $C_7H_5N_3O_6$. Full form **trinitrotoluene**

TNX abbr ONLINE thanks (used in e-mails or text messages)

to¹ stressed /too/; unstressed /toŏ, tə/ CORE MEANING: a preposition or adverb indicating the direction, destination, or position of somebody or something ○ I met him on his way to school. ○ She climbed all the way to the top. ○ You'll see a supermarket to your left.
1. prep INDICATES DIRECTION indicates the direction or destination of somebody or something ○ He was on his way to the party. ○ You hit the space bar and go to the next screen. **2.** prep INDICATES POSITION indicates the position of somebody or something ○ To the right of the door you will see a noticeboard. **3.** prep FORMS INFINITIVE used before the base form of a verb to make the infinitive of that verb ○ I want to leave now. **4.** prep INDICATES PURPOSE used with the base form of a verb to indicate the intention or purpose of an action ○ The news system is used to distribute information to large groups of people. **5.** prep INDICATES RECIPIENT indicates the recipient of something (used with a noun phrase to form the indirect object) ○ Give it to me. ○ mail sent to another user on the same computer **6.** prep INDICATES DIRECTION OF FEELING OR ACTION indicates who or what a particular feeling or action is directed towards ○ I was very grateful to her for everything she did for me. **7.** prep INDICATES ATTACHMENT indicates that two things are joined together ○ Each triangle consists of three square faces joined to one another along two edges. **8.** prep UNTIL indicates that something goes on until a point in time or until it reaches a fixed amount ○ He shuts the shop on Mondays and opens from Tuesday to Saturday. **9.** prep INDICATES RANGE indicates a range of things or topics ○ Studies have explored everything from pollution to pesticides to genetics to parental occupations to electromagnetic fields and proven nothing. **10.** prep INDICATES RESULT OF CHANGE indicates what somebody or something is changing into or becoming ○ Their excitement soon turned to gloom when they saw what the climb entailed. **11.** prep INDICATES SIMULTANEITY indicates that two things are happening at the same time, especially that a particular sound or music accompanies another action ○ I woke up to the sound of the telephone ringing. **12.** prep INDICATES EQUALITY indicates equality, e.g. of two weights, amounts, or measurements ○ There are 12 inches to the foot. **13.** prep AS COMPARED WITH indicates comparison between two things such as scores in a game ○ The score was 5 to 3 in favour of our team. **14.** prep BEFORE HOUR indicates the number of minutes before the hour ○ It was five to seven before they arrived home. **15.** prep same as at¹ (regional) ○ Where's he to? ○ He's over to the doctor's. **16.** adv SHUT OR ALMOST SHUT indicates that a door is shut, or covering the opening but not completely or firmly shut ○ He pulled the door to after him. **17.** adv CONSCIOUS AGAIN into a state of lucidity and consciousness ○ came to in the recovery room ○ brought the patient to **18.** adv NAUT into the direction from which the wind is blowing ○ turned the yacht to [Old English tō. < Germanic]

SPELLCHECK to, too, or **two?** Do not confuse the spelling of **to, too,** and **two,** which sound similar. **To** has a wide variety of uses, especially as a preposition indicating, among other things, direction or destination (as in flying to New York), position (as in standing to the right), a recipient (as in give it to me), and range (as in from A to B); it also indicates the infinitive of a verb (as in to go). **Too** means 'in addition' or 'more than is desirable': Are you leaving too? It's too cold to go swimming. **Two** is the number 2, as in two boys and four girls.

to² abbr ONLINE Tonga (used in Internet addresses) See table at **domain name**

toad /tōd/ n 1. AMPHIBIAN SIMILAR TO FROG a small squat tailless amphibian distributed nearly worldwide. It is similar to a frog, but has dry warty skin and, except for breeding in water, lives mostly on land.

AKG London

toad

Family: Bufonidae. **2.** AMPHIBIAN RESEMBLING TOAD an amphibian similar to a toad but belonging to a different taxonomic family, e.g. the midwife toad **3.** OFFENSIVE TERM an offensive term for somebody considered loathsome or disgusting [Old English *tādige*, origin ?] —**toadish** *adj*

toadfish /tŏd fish/ (*plural same* or **-fishes**) *n* a scaleless spiny bottom-feeding fish with a broad flattened head and wide mouth. Native to: tropical and temperate seas. Family: Batrachoididae.

toadflax /tŏd flaks/ (*plural* **-flaxes** or *same*) *n* **1.** a common narrow-leaved plant. Flowers: spurred, two-lipped, orange-and-yellow, similar to snap-dragon's. Native to: Europe. Latin name: *Linaria vulgaris*. **2.** a plant related to the common toadflax and similar to it. Flowers: lilac-coloured. Genus: *Linaria*.

toad-in-the-hole *n* a dish consisting of sausages or sausage meat baked in a batter similar to Yorkshire pudding

toadstone /tŏd stōn/ *n* **1.** a dark brownish-grey basalt found in the limestone regions of Derbyshire **2.** a stone or similar object believed to have formed in the head or body of a toad, formerly worn around the neck as a charm against evil and disease

toadstool /tŏd stool/ *n* a poisonous umbrella-shaped fungus with a spore-producing round flat cap on a stalk [14C. Because it resembles a small stool and grows where toads are found]

toady /tŏdi/ *n* (*plural* **-ies**) a self-serving person who behaves in a servile sycophantic manner, fawning on and flattering people with power or influence ■ *vi* (**-ies, -ying, -ied**) to behave in a servile sycophantic manner, fawning on and flattering people with power or influence in order to achieve an advantage [Early 19C. Shortening of *toadeater* 'toady'] —**toadyish** *adj*—**toadyism** *n*

Toamasina /twaảmə seẻnə/ city and major port on the Indian Ocean, in eastern Madagascar, situated about 209 km/130 mi. northeast of Antananarivo. Population: 127,441 (1993). Former name **Tamatave**

to and fro *adv* **1.** backwards and forwards **2.** here and there in movement —**to-and-fro** *adj, n* —**toing and froing** *n*

toast /tōst/ *n* **1.** BREAD BROWNED WITH HEAT sliced bread that has been browned on both sides with heat, in a toaster, under a grill, or in front of an open fire **2.** CALL TO HONOUR SOMEBODY OR SOMETHING a call to a gathering to honour somebody or something by raising glasses and drinking **3.** RAISING OF GLASSES TO HONOUR SOMEBODY an act of raising a glass and drinking in honour of somebody or something **4.** SOMEBODY OR SOMETHING HONOURED somebody or something honoured by a toast **5.** SOMEBODY ADMIRED somebody who is the object of much attention or admiration ○ *the toast of Hollywood* ■ *v* (**toasts, toasting, toasted**) **1.** *vti* HEAT AND BROWN BREAD to heat and brown bread or other food on a grill, in a toaster or in front of an open fire, or become browned in this way **2.** *vt* WARM BODY to warm the body or a part of the body near a source of heat **3.** *vti* DRINK IN HONOUR OF SOMEBODY to drink or propose a drink in honour of somebody or something **4.** *vi* IMPROVISE WORDS TO MUSIC to improvise lyrics to a musical background (*slang; used in Black English*) [14C. Via Old French *toster* 'roast' < Latin *tost-*, past participle of *torrere* 'scorch'] ◇ **be toast** (*informal*) **1.** to be in serious trouble ○ *Do that again and you're toast!* **2.** to be in a nonfunctioning state (*refers to a computer*)

toaster /tōstər/ *n* a small electrical appliance for making toast that works by exposing the bread to heated electrical coils

toastie *n* FOOD another spelling of **toasty**

toastmaster /tōst maastər/ *n* somebody who proposes toasts and introduces speakers at a banquet or reception

toastmistress /tōst mistrəss/ *n* a woman who proposes toasts and introduces speakers at a banquet or reception

toast rack *n* a stand that holds slices of toast on end and separate from each other

toasty /tōsti/ *adj* (**-ier, -iest**) pleasantly warm ■ *n* (*plural* **-ies**) *also* **toastie** a sandwich that has been toasted (*informal*)

Tob. *abbr* BIBLE Tobit

tobacco /tə bákō/ (*plural* **-cos** or **-coes** or *same*) *n* **1.** the dried leaves of a plant of the nightshade family, processed primarily for smoking in cigarettes, cigars, and pipes **2.** a plant of the nightshade family, cultivated for its large leaves that are dried and processed primarily for smoking. Native to: tropical America. Genus: *Nicotiana*. [Late 16C. < Spanish *tabaco*]

tobacco mosaic virus *n* a retrovirus that causes mosaic disease in tobacco and other plants belonging to the nightshade family

tobacconist /tə bákənist/ *n* a person or shop that specializes in selling tobacco products and supplies such as cigarettes, tobacco, and pipes [Mid-17C. < TOBACCO + -IST]

tobacco road *n US* a shabby poverty-stricken rural community [Mid-20C. < the title of a novel by Erskine CALDWELL]

~~tobaco~~ incorrect spelling of **tobacco**

Tobago /tə báygō/ island in the Caribbean, part of Trinidad and Tobago. Population: 50,282 (1990). Area: 300 sq. km/120 sq. mi.

Toba Sojo /tŏbə sŏjŏ/ (1053–1140) Japanese artist and Buddhist high priest. He is noted for his Buddhist icons and humorous paintings.

Tobit /tŏbit/ *n* **1.** in the Bible, a pious Israelite living in Nineveh at the end of the 8th century BC **2.** a book of the Roman Catholic Bible and the Protestant Apocrypha that contains the story of Tobit. See table at **Bible**

toboggan /tə bóggən/ *n* a long narrow sledge without runners, made of strips of wood running length-ways and curled up at the front, used for coasting downhill on snow ■ *vi* (**-gans, -ganing, -ganed**) to ride on a toboggan [Early 19C. Via Canadian French *tabagane* < Mi'kmaq *topaǧan* 'sledge'] —**tobogganer** *n*—**tobogganist** *n*

Tobruk /tə brŏŏk/ city and port in northeastern Libya, on the Mediterranean Sea. British forces were besieged there during World War II. Population: 94,006 (1984).

toby jug /tōbi/, **toby** (*plural* **-bies**), **Toby** *n* a beer mug or jug in the shape of a rotund man wearing a three-cornered hat [Mid-19C. < *Toby* (nickname for *Tobias*), common 19C name for a man or boy)]

TOC /tok/ *n* in the United Kingdom, a train company that has been given a franchise to provide passenger services over specific routes as part of the arrangements by which the national railway system was privatized. Full form **train operating company**

toccata /tə kaátə/ (*plural* **-tas**) *n* a composition for a keyboard instrument written in a free style that includes full chords and elaborate runs and is intended to show off the player's technique [Early 18C. < Italian < feminine past participle of *toccare* 'touch' < assumed Vulgar Latin]

Toc H /tok áych/ *n* an interdenominational association formed in England after World War I to encourage Christian fellowship [Early 20C. < telegraphic code for *TH* 'Talbot House', Belgian recreation centre on which it was modelled]

Tocharian /to kaári ən, tə-/, **Tokharian** *n* **1.** a member of a Central Asian people who lived in the Tarim Basin in western China before being defeated by the Uigurs during the 9th century AD. They are

believed to have spread into China from Eastern Europe. **2.** the extinct language of the Tocharian people. It forms a separate branch of the Indo-European family and shows close resemblances to some western branches of the family. [Early 20C. < Latin *Tochari* < Greek *Tokharoi* 'the Tocharians'] —**Tocharian** *adj*

tocher /tókhər, tókər/ *Scotland* (*literary*) *n* a bride's dowry ■ *vt* (**-ers, -ering, -ered**) to give something as a dowry [15C. < Scottish Gaelic *tochradh*]

tocopherol /to kóffə rol/ *n* one of a group of fat-soluble compounds that make up vitamin E, present in vegetable oils and leafy greens [Mid-20C. < Greek *tokos* 'childbirth' + *pherein* 'to bear']

Tocqueville /tók vil/, **Alexis de** (1805–59) French historian and political writer. After visiting the United States, he wrote the influential *Democracy in America* (1835–40), his most famous work. Full name **de Tocqueville, Alexis Charles Henri Maurice Clérel**

'The French want no one to be their *superior*. The English want *inferiors*. The Frenchman constantly raises his eyes above him with anxiety. The Englishman lowers his beneath him with satisfaction. On either side it is pride, but unerstood in a different way.'
[Alexis de Tocqueville, *Voyage en Angleterre et en Irlande de 1835 (Journeys to England and Ireland*, trs. 1970); 1835]

tocsin /tóksin/ *n* **1.** ALARM an alarm sounded by means of a bell **2.** BELL a bell that sounds an alarm **3.** WARNING a warning signal [Late 16C. Via French < Old Provençal *tocasenh* < *tocar* 'to strike' (< assumed Vulgar Latin *toccare*) + *senh* 'bell' (< Latin *signum* 'signal')]

tod[1] /tod/ *n* **1.** a unit of weight for wool, usually equal to 12.7 kg/28 lb **2.** a mass of foliage, especially ivy **3.** *N England, Scotland* ZOOL same as **fox** *n* (sense 1) [15C. Origin ?]

tod[2] /tod/ [Shortening of *Tod Sloan*, US jockey (1874–1933), rhyming slang for *alone*] ◇ **on your tod** alone (*informal*)

today /tə dáy/ *adv* **1.** ON THIS DAY on or during this day, as distinct from yesterday or tomorrow ○ *She is working today.* **2.** IN PRESENT TIME during the present time or age ○ *Children today have far more sophisticated toys than we ever had.* ■ *n* **1.** THIS DAY this day, as distinct from yesterday or tomorrow **2.** PRESENT AGE the present time or age ○ *the fashions of today* ■ *adj* MODERN modern or of the present day ○ *a today look* [Old English *tō dæge* '(this) day']

Todd /tod/, **Alexander R., Baron Todd of Trumpington** (1907–97) British chemist. For his work on vitamins B₁ and E, he was awarded the Nobel Prize in chemistry (1957). He was the first chancellor of the University of Strathclyde, Scotland. Full name **Todd, Alexander Robertus**

Todd, **Garfield** (1908–2002) New Zealand-born prime minister of Southern Rhodesia (now Zimbabwe; 1953–58). After serving as prime minister, he became a leading spokesperson for the country's independence. He was made a senator by Robert Mugabe (1980), but was later stripped of his passport after criticizing Mugabe's government.

toddle /tódd'l/ *vi* (**-dles, -dling, -dled**) **1.** TAKE SHORT UNSTEADY STEPS to walk with short unsteady steps, as a child does when learning to walk **2.** WALK UNHURRIEDLY to walk at a leisurely pace (*informal*) ■ *n* **1.** UNHURRIED WALK a leisurely walk (*informal*) **2.** UNSTEADY STEPS a gait with short unsteady steps [Late 16C. Origin ?]

toddler /tódd'lər/ *n* a young child who is learning to walk

toddy /tóddi/ (*plural* **-dies**) *n* **1.** a drink made with alcohol, hot water, sugar, and sometimes spices **2.** the sweet sap of a variety of Asian palm tree used as a beverage, either fresh or fermented [Late 18C. Via Hindi *tāṛī* 'palm sap' < Sanskrit *tālaḥ* 'palm', probably < Dravidian]

todger *n* a man's penis (*slang; often considered offensive*)

to-do /tə dŏŏ/ *n* a fuss, especially an angry complaint or protest (*informal*)

tody /tŏdi/ (*plural* **-dies**) *n* a small bird with a short tail, a bright green back, red throat, and a long straight beak. Native to: Caribbean. Family:

Todidae. [Late 18C. Probably via French *todier* < Latin *todus*, a small bird]

toe /tō/ *n* **1.** DIGIT OF HUMAN FOOT one of the digits of the human foot, equivalent to the fingers and thumb of the hand **2.** DIGIT OF VERTEBRATE'S FOOT a part corresponding to the human toe in other vertebrates **3.** FRONT PART OF HOOF the forepart of an animal's hoof **4.** FRONT PART OF SHOE OR SOCK the part of a shoe, boot, sock, or stocking that covers the toes and the front part of the foot **5.** PART RESEMBLING TOES a part that resembles the front part of a foot in form or position ○ *the toe of Italy* **6.** GOLF END OF GOLF CLUB HEAD the end of the head of a golf club **7.** MECH ENG LOWER END OF SHAFT the lower end of a vertical shaft that turns in a bearing **8.** GEOG BASE OF EMBANKMENT the base of an embankment, cliff, wall, or dam ■ *v* (**toes, toeing, toed**) **1.** *vt* TOUCH SOMETHING WITH TOES to touch, kick, reach, or mark something with the toes or the front part of the foot **2.** *vt* GOLF STRIKE GOLF BALL to strike a golf ball with the front part of the head of the club **3.** *vt* DRIVE NAIL AT ANGLE to drive in a nail or spike at an angle **4.** *vt* FASTEN SOMETHING WITH ANGLED NAIL to fasten something with a nail or spike driven in at an angle **5.** *vi* STAND WITH TOES POINTED to stand or move with the toes pointed in a particular direction [Old English *tā* < Indo-European, 'to point'] —**toed** *adj* ◇ **on your toes** alert and ready for action ◇ **tread on somebody's toes** to offend or upset somebody by interfering with something considered to be that person's own responsibility ◇ **turn up your toes** to die (*informal*)

toea /tō i ə, tō aa/ (*plural same* or **-as**) *n* a subunit of Papua New Guinean currency. See table at **currency** [Late 20C. < Motu, 'conical shell', used as currency]

toe and heel *n* a technique used by racing drivers for operating the brake and accelerator simultaneously with the right foot, using the heel for one pedal and the toe for the other

toecap /tō kap/ *n* a metal or leather covering reinforcing the toe of a shoe or boot

toe dance *n* a dance performed on tiptoe ■ *vi* to perform a toe dance —**toe dancer** *n*

TOEFL /tōf'l/ *tdmk* a trademark for a standardized English language test taken by speakers of other languages who are applying to universities in the United States. Full form **Test of English as a Foreign Language**

toehold /tō hōld/ *n* **1.** SMALL ADVANTAGE a small advantage or gain in an endeavour **2.** SMALL RECESS IN ROCK FOR FOOT a small recess or ledge in a rock giving support for the toes **3.** HOLD ON FOOT a wrestling hold in which one competitor holds the foot and twists the leg of the other

toe-in *n* the alignment of a motor vehicle's front wheels so that the front edges are slightly closer together than the rear edges to improve its steering capabilities and reduce tyre wear

toe loop *n* a jump in which an ice skater, skating backwards, takes off from one skate, makes one rotation in the air, and lands on the outer edge of the same skate

toenadering /toŏ naadərəng/ *n* S Africa a getting together or rapprochement between political parties (*informal*) [Early 20C. < Afrikaans < Dutch < *toe* 'to' + *nadering* 'approach']

toenail /tō nayl/ *n* **1.** NAIL ON TOE the nail of a toe **2.** NAIL DRIVEN IN AT ANGLE a nail driven in at an angle, e.g. to join intersecting structural parts **3.** PRINTING same as **bracket** *n* (sense 1) (*slang*) ■ *vt* (**-nails, -nailing, -nailed**) JOIN SOMETHING WITH ANGLED NAILS to join parts of a structure with nails driven in at an angle

toerag /tō rag/ *n* an offensive term that deliberately insults somebody's character or personal value (*insult*)

toe ring *n* a ring worn on the toe, particularly a silver ring worn by married Hindu women

toetoe /tō i tō i, tóy tóy/ *n* **1.** a pampas grass, especially a species native to New Zealand. Genus: *Cortaderia*. **2.** *NZ* FISH same as **bully**[3]

toe-to-toe *adj* involving two people, groups, or organizations in direct opposition to each other ■ *adv* in direct opposition to each other

toey /tō i/ *adj Aus* easily annoyed or irritated (*informal*)

toff /tof/ *n* a rich or upper-class person, especially somebody who is elegantly dressed (*informal*) [Mid-19C. Probably variant of *tuft*, golden plume worn by titled students at Oxford and Cambridge]

toffee /tóffi/ *n* a sweet that can be soft and chewy or hard and brittle, made by boiling brown sugar or treacle with butter and sometimes flavourings or nuts [Early 19C. Variant of TAFFY] ◇ **somebody cannot do something for toffee** used to emphasize somebody's lack of ability or competence (*informal*)

toffee apple *n* a caramel-coated apple mounted on a stick. N Am term **candy apple**

toffee-nosed *adj* behaving in an aloof condescending way (*informal*) [Alteration of TOFF]

toft /toft/ *n* a house with its adjoining buildings and land (*archaic*) [Old English, < Old Norse *topt*]

tofu /tō foo/ *n* a soft food with no distinctive flavour made from soya milk curd pressed into a cake [Late 18C. Via Japanese < Chinese *dòufu* 'fermented beans']

tog /tog/ *vti* (**togs, togging, togged**) DRESS UP to dress up, or dress somebody up, usually in smart clothing (*informal*) ■ *n* MEASURE OF THERMAL INSULATION a measure of the thermal insulation properties of fabrics, quilts, and clothes. It is equal to ten times the temperature difference in Celsius between the two surfaces when the flow of heat across the material is one watt per square metre. ■ **togs** *npl* (*informal*) **1.** GARMENTS clothes of any kind ○ *golf togs* **2.** *Ireland, ANZ* SWIMMING COSTUME clothes for swimming in [Late 18C. Shortening of obsolete slang *togeman* < obsolete French *togue* 'cloak' < Latin *toga* (see 'toga')]

toga /tōgə/ *n* **1.** an outer garment worn by the citizens of ancient Rome, consisting of a semicircular piece of cloth draped around the body **2.** a robe of office [Early 17C. < Latin] —**togaed** *adj*

toga praetexta /tōgə pree tékstə/ (*plural* **togae praetextae** /tō gee pree ték stee/) *n* a toga with a purple border worn in ancient Rome by some magistrates and priests, and by boys before the age of puberty [< Latin, 'bordered toga']

toga virilis /tōgə vi ríliss/ (*plural* **togae viriles** /tō gee vi ríleez/) *n* a white toga worn in ancient Rome by men and by boys from the age of 14 or 15 as a sign of manhood and citizenship [< Latin, 'men's toga']

together /tə géthər/ CORE MEANING: an adverb indicating that people are with one another, or that something is done with another person or other people, or by joint effort ○ *My brother and I always walked to school together.* **1.** *adv* WITH OTHERS in company with others in a group or in a place ○ *We only come together on family occasions.* **2.** *adv* INTERACTING WITH ONE ANOTHER interacting, communicating, or in a relationship with one another ○ *They get on well together.* **3.** *adv* BY JOINT EFFORT cooperating with one another or by joint or combined effort ○ *Let's work together on this one.* **4.** *adv* INTO CONTACT indicates that two or more things are put into contact with one another, or unite to form a single whole ○ *The garment had been sewn together roughly.* **5.** *adv* COLLECTIVELY considered collectively or as a whole ○ *Taken together, these developments add up to a significant change in policy.* **6.** *adv* UNINTERRUPTEDLY without interruption ○ *It has been raining for all of four days together.* **7.** *adv* IN AGREEMENT in or into agreement or harmony ○ *They can't seem to get together on anything.* **8.** *adv* SIMULTANEOUSLY at the same time ○ *They both answered together.* **9.** *adv* IN INTEGRATED COHERENT STRUCTURE in or into a unified structure or a coherent integrated whole ○ *If you understand how something is put together, you will use it better.* **10.** *adv* INTO ORDERLY CONDITION OR STATE into an orderly condition or a stable and effective emotional state (*informal*) ○ *"I'm just trying to get my life together," he said quietly.* **11.** *adv* IN COUPLE indicates that two people are married, having a sexual relationship, or form an established and recognized couple (*informal*) ○ *got back together again after a trial separation* ■ *adj* STABLE AND SELF-CONFIDENT emotionally stable, self-confident, and well-organized (*informal*) ○ *She's a very together person.* [Old English *tōgædere* < *to* 'to' + Germanic, 'joined together'] ◇ **together with** as well as or in addition to

USAGE When **together with** forms an addition to the grammatical subject of a verb, the verb agrees with the grammatical subject. In the following sentence the grammatical subject is *remark*: *This remark, together with earlier comments of the same kind, was not well received.*

togetherness /tə géthərnəss/ *n* a feeling of closeness to others

toggery /tóggəri/ *n* (*informal*) **1.** clothes **2.** *US* a clothes shop [Early 19C. < TOG]

toggle /tógg'l/ *n* **1.** FASTENER ON CLOTHES a small peg sewn on clothes or on a bag, inserted crosswise into a loop or buttonhole and used as a fastener **2.** PEG INSERTED IN LOOP a peg or rod that is inserted crosswise into a loop at the end of a rope, chain, or strap to hold or fasten something **3.** COMPUT KEY FOR SWITCHING BETWEEN OPERATIONS a key or command that switches back and forth between computer operations each time it is used **4.** NAUT PIN INSERTED INTO KNOT a pin inserted into a nautical knot to keep it from coming undone **5.** ENG SOMETHING WITH TOGGLE JOINT a toggle joint or a device with a toggle joint ■ *v* (**-gles, -gling, -gled**) **1.** *vti* COMPUT SWITCH BETWEEN OPERATIONS WITH ONE KEY to switch back and forth between two computer operations using the same key or command **2.** *vt* SUPPLY OR FASTEN SOMETHING WITH TOGGLES to supply or fasten something with a toggle or toggles [Late 18C. Origin ?] —**toggler** *n*

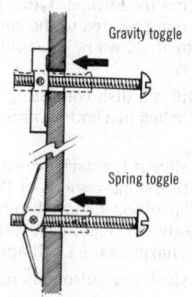

Gravity toggle

Spring toggle

toggle bolt

toggle bolt *n* a threaded bolt that has a nut with spring-loaded hinged wings attached and is used especially for securing things to hollow walls. When the bolt is inserted into a hole in the wall, the wings spread open inside, pressing back against the wall's inner surface and allowing the bolt to be tightened.

toggle iron, **toggle harpoon** *n* a whaling harpoon with a pivoting barb that keeps the whale from freeing itself

toggle joint *n* a device with two arms hinged together so that pressure applied at the pivot point to straighten the device exerts force along the two arms

toggle switch *n* **1.** a small spring-loaded mechanical switch that opens and closes an electrical circuit by manual operation **2.** COMPUT same as **toggle** *n* (sense 3)

Togliatti /to lyátti/ industrial city on the River Volga in southern European Russia. Population: 855,365 (1995).

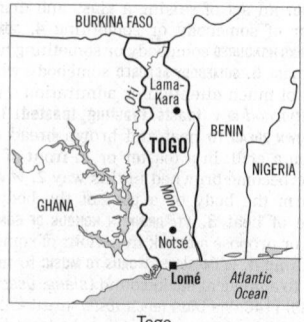

Togo

Togo /tógō/ country in West Africa, bordered by Burkina Faso, Benin, the Gulf of Guinea, and

Ghana. Language: French. Currency: franc. Capital: Lomé. Population: 5,429,299 (2003). Area: 56,785 sq. km/21,925 sq. mi. Official name **Togolese Republic** — **Togolese** /tógə leez/ *n, adj*

Togoland /tógō land/ former German protectorate in western Africa, divided between British and French administration in 1922. British Togoland was incorporated into Ghana (1956) and French Togoland became independent as Togo (1960).

Togrul Beg /tógril bég/ (993?–1063) Turkish Seljuk leader. The founder of the Seljuk dynasty, he conquered most of Iran and Iraq, gaining control of Baghdad in 1055.

toheroa /tó ə rő ə/ (*plural same* or **-as**) *n* **1.** a large edible mollusc with a hinged shell. Native to: New Zealand coasts. Latin name: *Amphidesma ventricosum.* **2.** a greenish soup made from the toheroa [Late 19C. < Maori]

Tohono O'Odham /tōhő nō ő ədəm/ (*plural same* or **Tohono O'Odhams**) *n* PEOPLES, LANG same as **Papago** [Late 20C. < Papago, 'desert people'] —**Tohono O'Odham** *adj*

toil[1] /toyl/ *n* HARD WORK hard exhausting work or effort ■ *vi* (**toils, toiling, toiled**) **1.** WORK HARD to work long and hard **2.** PROGRESS SLOWLY to progress slowly and with difficulty [13C. < Anglo-Norman *toiler* 'drag around' < Latin *tudicula* 'machine for bruising olives' < *tudes* 'hammer'] —**toiler** *n*

SYNONYMS See *work*.

toil[2] /toyl/ *n* a net, snare, or other thing that entraps or entangles (*archaic or literary*; *often used in the plural*) [Early 16C. Via Old French *toile* 'cloth, web' < Latin *tela*]

toile /twaal/ *n* **1.** a sheer cotton or linen fabric **2.** a prototype of a designer garment made up in a cheap fabric so that alterations can be made [Late 18C. Via French < Latin *tela* 'web']

toile de Jouy /-də jwée/ *n* a fabric with a white or light-coloured background and a floral or pastoral print, usually in one colour only. Use: curtains, upholstery. [Mid-18C. < French, after *Jouy*-en-Josas, town near Paris, France]

toilet /tóylət/ *n* **1.** FIXTURE FOR DISPOSING OF BODY WASTE a bowl-shaped fixture with a waste drain and a flushing device connected to a water supply, used for defecating and urinating **2.** ROOM WITH TOILET a room with a toilet and usually a washbasin **3.** WASHING AND DRESSING the process of attending to your personal appearance and making it presentable, e.g. by washing, dressing, shaving, and tidying your hair (*formal*) **4.** MED CLEANSING ASSOCIATED WITH SURGICAL PROCEDURE a cleansing of part of the body after a medical or surgical procedure, often in preparation for applying dressings or bandages [Late 17C. < French *toilette* 'bag for clothing' < Old French *teile* 'cloth' < Latin *tela* 'web']

toilet paper *n* a usually soft absorbent paper, especially in a roll, used for cleaning the body after defecating or urinating

toilet roll *n* a length of toilet paper wound around a cardboard cylinder, or the cardboard cylinder on which the paper is wound

toiletry /tóylətri/ (*plural* **-ries**) *n* a product used in washing or caring for the appearance, e.g. shampoo, deodorant, or soap (*usually used in the plural*)

toilette /twaa lét/ *n* the process of attending to your personal appearance and making it presentable [Mid-16C. < French (see TOILET)]

toilet tissue *n* INDUST same as **toilet paper**

toilet training *n* the process of teaching a young child to control bladder and bowel movements and to use the toilet

toilet water *n* a lightly perfumed liquid used to freshen or scent the skin

toilsome /tóylssəm/ *adj* requiring long hard work (*literary*) —**toilsomely** *adv* —**toilsomeness** *n*

toilworn /tóyl wawrn/ *adj* worn, damaged, or exhausted by hard work

toitoi /tóy toy/ (*plural* **-tois**) *n* PLANTS, FISH same as **toetoe** [Mid-19C. < Maori]

Tojo Hideki /tőjō hee déki/ (1884–1948) Japanese general and prime minister (1941–44). As minister of war (1940–44) and then premier, he led Japan into World War II, resigning after Allied victories in the Pacific. He was tried and hanged for war crimes.

Tokaj /tő káy, to-, -kí/ town in northeastern Hungary. It lies at the heart of a wine-producing region. Population: 5,000 (1989).

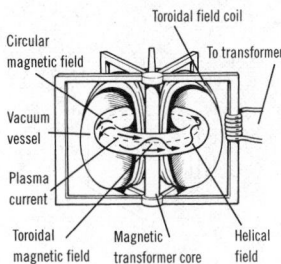

tokamak

tokamak /tókə mak/ *n* an experimental doughnut-shaped nuclear reactor for producing fusion using an electric current and a magnetic field to heat and contain a gaseous plasma [Mid-20C. < Russian, contraction of *toroidal'naya kamera s aksial'nym magnitnym polem* 'toroidal chamber with axial magnetic field']

tokay /tő kay/ *n* a small lizard that has a retractile claw at the tip of each digit. Native to: South and Southeast Asia. Latin name: *Gekko gecko*. [Mid-18C. Via Malay dialect *toke* < Javanese *tekèk*]

Tokay /tő káy, to-, tō kí/ *n* **1.** a sweet wine made from a white grape grown in the area around Tokaj, northeastern Hungary **2.** a large sweet white grape variety. Use: to make Tokay. [Early 18C. After TOKAJ (Tokay)]

toke /tők/ (*slang*) *n* a puff on a cigarette or pipe containing marijuana ■ *vti* (**tokes, toking, toked**) to puff on a cigarette or pipe containing marijuana [Mid-20C. Origin ?]

token /tőkən/ *n* **1.** SOMETHING REPRESENTING SOMETHING ELSE something that represents, expresses, or is a symbol of something else ○ *Please accept this gift as a token of our appreciation.* **2.** DISC USED LIKE MONEY a disc of metal or plastic used instead of money, e.g. in slot machines **3.** KEEPSAKE an object kept in memory of somebody or something **4.** PAPER EXCHANGED FOR GOODS a paper or card certificate that can be exchanged for goods up to the indicated value ○ *a book token for £10* **5.** LING INSTANCE OF EXPRESSION an instance of a word or expression **6.** LING CONCRETE EXAMPLE a written or spoken expression considered as a concrete example ■ *adj* EXISTING AS GESTURE ONLY made, given, or existing merely because expected or required, not because sincere or serving a real purpose ○ *the token student on the committee* [Old English *tācen* < Indo-European 'to point, show']

tokenism /tőkənizəm/ *n* the practice of making only a symbolic effort at something, especially in order to meet the minimum requirements of the law — **tokenistic** /tőkə nístik/ *adj*

Tokharian *n, adj* PEOPLES, LANG another spelling of **Tocharian**

tokoloshe /tóko lósh, -lóshi/ *n* in African folklore, a small mischievous evil spirit or water sprite that takes on human or animal appearance [Mid-19C. < Nguni]

tokonoma /tókə nőmə/ *n* an alcove in the living room of a Japanese house where a decoration such as flowers or an ornament is displayed [Early 18C. < Japanese]

Tokoroa /tókō rő ə/ town in the northwestern part of the North Island, New Zealand, that services the paper and timber mills at nearby Kinleith. Population: 14,427 (2001).

Tok Pisin /tók píssin/ *n* a creole, originating as a pidgin based on English, that is widely spoken in Papua New Guinea. Native speakers: 2 million. [Mid-20C. < Pidgin English, 'talk pidgin'] —**Tok Pisin** *adj*

Tokyo /tóki ō/ capital city of Japan, located on Tokyo Bay on the eastern coast of Honshu Island. Population: 8,025,538 (2002).

tola /tőlə/ *n* a South Asian unit of weight equal to 180 grains troy weight or 11.7 grams [Early 17C. Via Hindi *tolā* < Sanskrit *tulā* 'weight']

tolar /tőlaar/ *n* the main unit of Slovenian currency. See table at **currency** [Via Slovene < German *Taler* 'thaler']

tolbooth /től booth, -booth/ *n Scotland* a town hall or a prison, or a building that performed both functions (*archaic*) [Variant of TOLLBOOTH]

told past participle, past tense of **tell**

tole /tōl/ *n* lacquered or enamelled metal used to make decorative objects, usually brightly painted or gilded or both, or objects made of this kind of decorated metal [Mid-20C. Via French *tôle* 'sheet iron' < Latin *tabula* 'board']

Toledo[1] /to láydō/ (*plural* **-dos**) *n* a sword or sword blade of highly tempered steel, made in Toledo, Spain

Toledo[2] **1.** /to láydō/ historic city in central Spain, the administrative centre of Toledo Province. Population: 70,893 (2002). **2.** /to leédō/ city and major river port in northwestern Ohio, located close to Lake Erie. Population: 309,106 (2002 estimate).

Toledo /to láydō/, **Alejandro** (*b.* 1946) president of Peru (2001–). A centre-left economist who worked for the World Bank before returning to Peru to enter politics, he is the country's first elected president with Native South American roots.

tolerable /tóllərəb'l/ *adj* **1.** not too unpleasant or severe to put up with **2.** moderately good, but not outstanding —**tolerability** /tóllərə bílləti/ *n* —**tolerably** *adv*

tolerance /tóllərənss/ *n* **1.** ACCEPTANCE OF DIFFERENT VIEWS the acceptance of the differing views of other people, e.g. in religious or political matters, and fairness towards the people who hold these different views **2.** TOLERATING OF SOMEBODY OR SOMETHING the act of putting up with somebody or something irritating or otherwise unpleasant **3.** ABILITY TO ENDURE HARDSHIP the ability to put up with harsh or difficult conditions **4.** MED ABILITY TO REMAIN UNAFFECTED the loss of or reduction in the usual response to a drug or other agent as a result of use or exposure over a prolonged period **5.** ENG ALLOWANCE MADE FOR DEVIATION an allowance made for something to deviate in size from a standard, or the limit within which it is allowed to deviate **6.** BIOL ABILITY TO WITHSTAND EXTREMES the ability of an organism to survive in extreme conditions

tolerant /tóllərənt/ *adj* **1.** ACCEPTING DIFFERENT VIEWS accepting the differing views of other people, e.g. in religious or political matters, and treating the people who hold these different views fairly **2.** WITHSTANDING HARSH TREATMENT able to put up with harsh conditions or treatment **3.** MED NOT AFFECTED BY DRUG no longer responding to a drug that has been taken over a prolonged period, or suffering no ill effects from exposure to a harmful substance —**tolerantly** *adv*

tolerate /tóllə rayt/ (**-ates, -ating, -ated**) *vt* **1.** PERMIT SOMETHING to be willing to allow something to happen or exist **2.** ENDURE SOMETHING to withstand the unpleasant effects of something **3.** ACCEPT EXISTENCE OF DIFFERENT VIEWS to recognize other people's right to have different beliefs or practices without attempting to suppress them **4.** MED BE UNAFFECTED BY DRUG to be able to respond to a drug because the body has built up a resistance to it, or suffer no ill effects from being exposed to a harmful substance [Early 16C. < Latin *tolerat-*, past participle of *tolerare* 'bear, endure'] —**tolerative** *adj* —**tolerator** *n*

toleration /tólla ráysh'n/ *n* **1.** official acceptance by a government of religious beliefs and practices that are different from those it upholds **2.** the act of tolerating something

tolidine /tóllə deen/ *n* an isomeric derivative of toluene. Use: manufacture of dyes. Formula: $C_{14}H_{16}N_2$. [Late 19C. < TOLYL + *benzidine*]

Tolkien /tól keen/, **J. R. R.** (1892–1973) South African-born British scholar and writer. A philologist at Oxford University, he wrote *The Hobbit* (1937) and its three-part sequel *The Lord of the Rings* (1954–55). Full name **Tolkien, John Ronald Reuel**

toll[1] /tōl/ *n* **1. FEE FOR USING ROAD** a fee charged for a privilege, usually crossing a bridge or using a road **2. ROADS** same as **tollbooth** (*often used in the plural*) **3. DAMAGE SUSTAINED** the damage done by an accident or disaster in terms of, e.g. people killed, property destroyed, or financial loss ○ *The toll on the environment was significant.* **4. TELECOM CHARGE FOR TELEPHONE CALL** in the United States, a charge for a long-distance telephone call, or, in New Zealand, for a call made to a place outside a free-dialling area **5. FIN FEE FOR SERVICES** a fee charged for services such as transport ■ *vti* (**tolls, tolling, tolled**) **ROADS CHARGE TOLL ON ROAD** to charge a toll for the use of a road or bridge [Pre-12C. Via medieval Latin *toloneum* < Greek *telōnion* 'toll house' < *telos* 'tax']

toll[2] /tōl/ *v* (**tolls, tolling, tolled**) **1.** *vti* **RING SLOWLY AND REPEATEDLY** to ring a bell, repeatedly and with long pauses between each ring, especially to announce a death, or be rung in this way ○*'never send to know for whom the bell tolls; it tolls for thee'* (John Donne, *Devotions*; 1624) **2.** *vt* **ANNOUNCE SOMETHING WITH BELL** to announce something or call somebody with the repeated slow ringing of a bell ○ *bells tolling the death of the king* ■ *n* **ACT OR SOUND OF BELL TOLLING** the act of ringing a bell slowly and repeatedly, or the sound so made [15C. Probably < Old English *-tyllan* 'pull'] —**toller** *n*

tollbooth /tōl booth, -booth/ *n* a booth on a road or bridge where tolls for use of the road or bridge are collected

toll bridge *n* a bridge where a toll is charged for crossing

toll call *n* **1.** *NZ, N Am* a long-distance telephone call charged at a higher rate than a local call **2.** *NZ* a telephone call made to a place outside a free-dialling area, and therefore charged for

Tollens reagent /tóllənz-/ *n* a solution of silver nitrate, ammonia, and sodium bicarbonate. Use: testing for aldehydes. [After Bernhard *Tollens* (1841–1918), German chemist]

Toller /tóllər/, **Ernst** (1893–1939) German playwright. He wrote *Masse Mensch* (1920) and other plays of social protest in the tradition of German expressionism.

toll-free *adj N Am* describes a telephone call that is not charged at a higher rate than a local call —**toll-free** *adv*

tollgate /tōl gayt/ *n* a gate barring the way on a road or bridge where a toll must be paid to proceed

tollhouse /tōl howss/ (*plural* **-houses** /-howziz/) *n* a shelter or kiosk for a toll collector at a tollgate

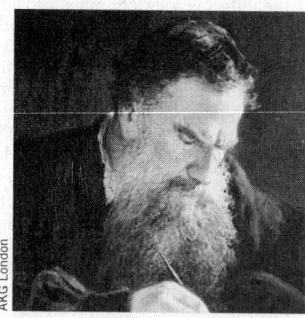
AKG London
Leo Tolstoy

Tolstoy /tólstoy/, **Leo** (1828–1910) Russian writer. He wrote the epic novels *War and Peace* (1865–69) and *Anna Karenina* (1875–77). A profound social thinker and moralist, he was excommunicated from the Russian Orthodox Church for his radical views on Church authority. Full name **Tolstoy, Count Leo Nikolayevich**. See Cultural note at **war**

'There are no conditions of life to which a man cannot get accustomed, especially if he sees them accepted by *everyone* about him.'

[Leo Tolstoy, *Anna Karenina*; 1875–77]

Toltec /tól tek/ (*plural* **Toltecs** or *same*) *n* a member of a Native Central American people who formerly lived in central Mexico and were succeeded by the Aztecs. They dominated the area between the 10th

and the 12th centuries AD, when they were defeated by the Chichimecs, and their lands were later taken over by the Aztecs. [Late 18C. Via Spanish *tolteca* < Nahuatl *toltecatl* 'somebody from Tula', ancient Toltec city] —**Toltec** *adj*

tolu /tə loó, tō-, to-/ *n* an aromatic resin. Source: South American tree. Use: perfumes, cough medicines. [Late 17C. < Spanish *tolú*, after the town of Santiago de *Tolú* in Colombia, from which it was exported]

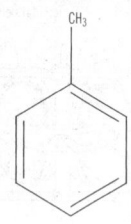
toluene

toluene /tóllyoo een/ *n* a colourless liquid aromatic hydrocarbon resembling benzene, but less flammable. Use: solvent, high-octane fuel, organic synthesis. Formula: C_7H_8. [Late 19C. < TOLU]

toluidine /tol yóo i deen/ *n* a derivative of toluene occurring in three forms. Use: manufacture of dyes. Formula: C_7H_9N.

toluol /tóllyoo ol/ *n* CHEM same as **toluene**

tolyl /tóllil/ *n* a chemical group derived from toluene. Formula: C_7H_7.

tom /tom/ *n* the male of various animals, especially the domestic cat [14C. < the name *Tom* (short for *Thomas*)]

Tom, Dick, and Harry /-hárri/, **Tom, Dick, or Harry** *n* anyone at all

tomahawk

tomahawk /tómmə hawk/ *n* **1. NATIVE N AMERICAN WEAPON** a small axe, formerly used as a weapon by some Native North American peoples **2.** *ANZ* **SMALL AXE** a small short-handled axe ■ *vt* (**-hawks, -hawking, -hawked**) **ATTACK SOMEBODY WITH TOMAHAWK** to attack or kill somebody with a tomahawk [Early 17C. < Virginia Algonquian *tamahaac*]

tomalley /tóm alli, tə málli/ *n* a soft green part of the insides of a cooked lobster, often called the liver, but technically an organ called the hepatopancreas, eaten as a delicacy [Mid-17C. Via French *taumalin* < Carib *taumali*]

toman /tə maán/ *n* **1.** an Iranian coin worth ten rials **2.** a gold coin and former unit of Persian currency [Mid-16C. Via Persian *tūmān* < W Tocharian *tmān*]

tomatillo /tómə teéyō/ (*plural* **-los**) *n* **1.** a purplish sticky edible fruit that grows on a Mexican ground cherry **2.** the ground cherry plant that bears tomatillos. Latin name: *Physalis ixocarpa*. [Early 20C. < Spanish, 'small tomato' < *tomate* (see TOMATO)]

tomato /tə maátō/ (*plural* **-toes**) *n* **1.** a round fruit with bright-red skin and pulpy seedy flesh, eaten cooked or raw as a vegetable **2.** a climbing plant that produces tomatoes and is grown throughout the world, in northern regions usually in greenhouses. Native to: South America. Genus: *Lycopersicon*. [Early 17C. Alteration of Spanish *tomate* < Nahuatl *tomatl*]

tomato

tomb /toom/ *n* **1. GRAVE** a grave or other place for burying a dead person **2. BURIAL CHAMBER** a cave or chamber used for burying a dead person **3. MONUMENT** a monument to a dead person, often built over the place where he or she is buried **4.** same as **death** (*literary*) ○ *go to the tomb unrepentant* **5. HARDENED ENCLOSURE** a hardened enclosure for a closed nuclear reactor, designed to contain radioactive emissions [12C. Via French *tombe* < Greek *tumbos* 'mound, tomb'] —**tombless** *adj*

Tomba /tómba/, **Alberto** (*b.* 1966) Italian skier. In 1988 he won the first of many medals, including Olympic gold medals and World Cups in slalom and giant slalom events.

tombac /tóm bak/, **tambac** /tám-/ *n* an alloy of copper and zinc, often with tin and arsenic, originally used in some Southeast Asian countries to make gongs and bells and now used worldwide to make inexpensive jewellery [Early 17C. Via French < Malay *tembaga* 'copper, brass']

tombola /tom bólə/ *n* a small-scale lottery, often held at a community event, with tickets drawn from a revolving drum turned by hand [Late 19C. Directly or via French < Italian, *tombolare* 'to tumble']

tombolo /tómbələ̄/ (*plural* **-los**) *n* a narrow strip of sand or shingle that links one island to another or to the mainland [Late 19C. Via Italian, 'sand dune' < Latin *tumulus* (see TUMULUS)]

Tombouctou /tóN book toó/, **Timbuktu** /tím buk toó/ city in central Mali, on the southern edge of the Sahara Desert. Population: 36,000 (1998).

tomboy /tóm boy/ *n* a girl who dresses or behaves in a way regarded as boyish, especially a girl who enjoys rough boisterous play [Mid-16C. < the name *Tom* (short for *Thomas*)] —**tomboyish** *adj* —**tomboyishly** *adv* —**tomboyishness** *n*

tombstone /toóm stōn/ *n* an ornamental stone on or at the site of a grave, often with the dead person's name and dates of birth and death engraved on it

Tombstone /toómstōn/ city in southeastern Arizona. Its history as a lawless mining town has made it a popular tourist centre. Population: 1,537 (2002 estimate).

tomcat /tóm kat/ *n* **1. MALE CAT** a male domestic cat **2.** *N Am* **OFFENSIVE TERM** an offensive term for a man who seeks many sexual partners or has casual sex with many partners (*slang*) ■ *vi* (**-cats, -catting, -catted**) *N Am* **OFFENSIVE TERM** an offensive term meaning to seek many sexual partners or have casual sex with many partners (*slang*; refers to men)

tomcod /tóm kod/ *n* either of two small sea fishes of the cod family. Native to: North American Atlantic and northern Pacific waters. Latin name: *Microgradus tomcod* or *Microgradus proximus*.

Tom Collins *n* an alcoholic cocktail consisting of gin, lemon or lime juice, soda water, and sugar [Late 19C. Origin ?]

tome /tōm/ *n* **1.** a book, especially a large heavy book on a serious subject (*formal or humorous*) **2.** a single volume of a book made up of several volumes [Early 16C. Via French < Greek *tomos* 'section, volume']

-tome *suffix* **1.** segment, part ○ *myotome* **2.** cutting instrument ○ *microtome* [Via modern Latin *-tomus* < Greek *tomos* 'cutting, section']

tomentum /tə méntəm/ (*plural* **-ta** /-tə/) *n* a downy covering of tiny hairs on leaves and other plant

parts [Late 17C. < Latin, 'stuffing for a cushion'] —**tomentose** /tə méntōss, tō men-/ adj

tomfool /tóm fóol/ n somebody considered very foolish (dated) [14C. < the name Tom (short for Thomas)] —**tomfool** adj —**tomfoolish** adj

tomfoolery /tom fóoləri/ (plural -**ies**) n (dated) **1.** silly behaviour **2.** a silly action or statement

Tomlinson /tómlinsən/, **Ray** (b. 1941) US computer programmer. He devised the first e-mail program and sent the first e-mail (1971).

~~tommorrow~~ incorrect spelling of **tomorrow**

Tommy /tómmi/ (plural -**mies**), **Tommy Atkins** /-átkinz/ n a private in the British army (dated slang) [Late 19C. < Thomas Atkins, name used on specimen forms in the British army]

tommy bar n a rod used to provide leverage in turning a box spanner [< the name Tommy (short for Thomas)]

Tommy gun n a hand-held machine gun, especially a Thompson submachine gun (informal)

tommyrot /tómmi rot/ n complete nonsense (dated informal) [Late 19C. < the name Tommy (short for Thomas), used for somebody considered foolish]

tommy rough, **tommy ruff** n a fish that is green on the top and silver on its undersides and is related to the Australian salmon. Native to: southern Australia. Latin name: *Arripis georgianus*. [Early 20C. the name Tommy (short for Thomas) meaning 'little'; rough because it is considered inadequate for sport or food]

tomogram /tómə gram/ n an image, especially one of the body, made using tomography [Mid-20C. < TOMOGRAPHY]

tomography /tō móggrəfi/ n the technique of using ultrasound, gamma rays, or X-rays to produce a focused image of the structures across a specific depth within the body, while blurring details at other depths [Mid-20C. < Greek tomos 'cutting, section'] —**tomographic** /tómə gráffik/ adj

tomorrow /tə mórrō/ n **1.** NEXT DAY the day after today **2.** FUTURE a future time, or the future in general ○ the leaders of tomorrow ■ adv **1.** ON NEXT DAY on the day after today **2.** IN FUTURE in the future, or at some time in the future [Old English tō morgenne 'in the morning'] ◇ **like** or **as if there was** or **were no tomorrow** used to emphasize the degree of speed, intensity, or carelessness with which somebody is doing something (informal) ○ He was spending money like there was no tomorrow.

tompion n MIL same as **tampion**

toms /toms/ npl MUSIC same as **tom-tom** [Early 20C. Shortening]

Tomsk /tomsk/ city in southern Siberian Russia, on the River Tom. Population: 605,216 (1995).

Tom Thumb n in English folklore, a character who was no taller than his father's thumb

tomtit /tómtit/ n a bird of the tit family, especially a bluetit (informal) [Early 18C. < name Tom (short for Thomas)]

tom-tom n **1.** DRUM HIT WITH HANDS a drum hit with the hands, especially a drum with a long narrow shell and a small head, first used as a signalling instrument **2.** DEEP-SIDED DRUM IN MODERN DRUM KIT a deep-sided drum that forms part of a modern drum kit, deeper in tone than a snare drum but not as deep as a bass drum **3.** SOUND OF BEATING DRUM the sound of a drum being repeatedly beaten, especially slowly and monotonously [Late 17C. < Telugu ṭamaṭama or Hindi ṭam ṭam, an imitation of the drum's sound]

-tomy suffix cutting, incision ○ lobotomy [Via modern Latin < Greek -tomia < tomos 'cutting, section']

ton[1] /tun/ n **1.** UK UNIT OF WEIGHT in the United Kingdom, an imperial unit of weight, equal to 1,016 kg/2,240 lb **2.** US UNIT OF WEIGHT in the United States, a customary unit of weight, equal to 907 kg/2,000 lb **3.** MEASURE same as **metric ton 4.** MEASURE same as **displacement ton 5.** UNIT MEASURING SHIP'S INTERNAL CAPACITY a unit used to measure the capacity of the inside of a ship, equal to 28.3 cu. m/100 cu. ft **6.** MEASURE same as **freight ton 7.** LARGE AMOUNT OR NUMBER a very large amount of something or a very large number of people or things (informal; often used in the plural) ○ tons of things to do **8.** FIGURE OF HUNDRED a figure of a hundred, especially a hundred miles per hour or a score of a hundred in cricket (slang) [13C. Variant of TUN] ◇ **like a ton of bricks** with great severity, force, or authority (informal) ○ If you're late she'll come down on you like a ton of bricks.

SPELLCHECK See **tonne**.

ton[2] /toN/ n **1.** the current trend in fashion **2.** the group of people who like to stay at the cutting edge of fashion [Mid-18C. < French, 'tone']

tonal /tón'l/ adj **1.** relating to tone or tonality **2.** relating to music written in a harmonic system in which there is a key —**tonally** adv

tonality /tō nálləti/ n **1.** QUALITY OF TONE the quality of tone, especially that of an instrument or voice **2.** MUSIC same as **key**[1] n (sense 12) **3.** MUSIC SYSTEM OF MUSICAL TONES the relationship between the notes and chords of a passage or work that tends to establish a central note or harmony as its focal point **4.** ARRANGEMENT OF COLOURS the scheme connecting the colour tones in a work of art such as a painting

Tonbridge /túnbrij/ town in Kent, southeastern England. Population: 31,600 (2001).

tondo /tóndō/ (plural -**dos**) n a circular painting or relief carving [Late 19C. < Italian, shortening of rotondo 'round' < Latin rotundus (see ROTUND)]

tone /tōn/ n **1.** DISTINCTIVE KIND OF SOUND a sound with a distinctive quality ○ The first bell has a clearer tone. **2.** WAY OF SPEAKING the way somebody says something as an indicator of what that person is feeling or thinking ○ a defiant tone in her voice **3.** GENERAL QUALITY the general quality or character of something as an indicator of the attitude or view of the person who produced it ○ the optimistic tone of the report **4.** MACHINE SOUND a sound, especially one produced by a machine **5.** PREVAILING CHARACTER the characteristic style that something has, particularly in relation to elegance or standing ○ Neon signs lower the tone of the place. **6.** SHADE OF COLOUR a shade of a colour ○ a green with a more vibrant tone **7.** ARTS COMBINATION OF COLOUR AND SHADING the overall blend of colour and light and shade in a painting or photograph **8.** PHYSIOL FIRMNESS OF MUSCLES the natural firmness of muscles, or of the body generally, when not being flexed **9.** PHON INTONATION the way a syllable of a word is spoken in terms of pitch ○ the rising tone signifying a question **10.** MUSIC TIMBRE the quality of a sound that makes it distinctive, e.g. in a voice or musical instrument **11.** MUSIC same as **whole tone 12.** MUSIC PLAINSONG a melody used in singing plainsong, e.g. in psalms **13.** N Am MUSIC same as **note** (sense 8) ■ v (**tones**, **toning**, **toned**) **1.** vi BLEND IN WITH SOMETHING to be similar to something else, especially in colour or brightness, and fit well with it **2.** vti PHOTOGRAPHY CHANGE COLOUR OF PHOTOGRAPH in photography, to develop a monochrome silver negative into a colour image by means of a chemical solution, or be developed in this way **3.** vt PHON SAY SOMETHING WITH PARTICULAR PITCH to say a syllable or word with a particular pitch **4.** PHYSIOL STRENGTHEN MUSCLES to make muscles firmer and stronger [13C. Via French ton < Greek tonos 'tension, tone']

tone down vt **1.** to make something less extreme, usually in order to make it less offensive or controversial **2.** to make something less loud, bright, or intense

tone up vt to make muscles, or the body in general, firmer and stronger

Tone /tōn/, **Wolfe** (1763–98) Irish revolutionary. He was the founder of the Society of United Irishmen in 1791. His efforts on behalf of Irish nationalism resulted in a death sentence. Full name **Tone, Theobald Wolfe**

'Whatever I have said, written, or thought on the subject of Ireland I now reiterate: looking upon the connexion with England to have been her bane I have endeavoured by every means in my power to break that connexion.'
[Wolfe Tone, *Speech at his court martial*; 10 November 1798]

tone arm n a record player's pivoting or sliding arm with a stylus on its end

tone cluster n a group of adjacent notes played together and forming a chord, usually resulting in a dissonant sound

tone colour n MUSIC same as **timbre** (sense 2)

tone control n a control on a radio, record player, or other piece of audio equipment that adjusts the tone it produces, accentuating the higher or lower sound frequencies

tone-deaf adj unable to hear the differences between musical notes —**tone-deafness** n

tone language n a language in which the meaning of a fixed sequence of sounds depends on the pitch in which it is pronounced, different tones identifying different words. Tone languages include the Bantu languages of Africa and Chinese.

toneless /tónləss/ adj **1.** lacking expression in speech **2.** lacking brightness or vitality —**tonelessly** adv —**tonelessness** n

toneme /tó neem/ n a phoneme in a tone language in which the distinctive feature is a tone [Early 20C. After PHONEME] —**tonemic** /tō neemik/ adj

tone poem n MUSIC same as **symphonic poem**

toner /tónər/ n **1.** SKIN COSMETIC a lotion or light astringent used to improve the look or feel of the skin, especially of the face **2.** INK ink in powder or liquid form for a photocopier or computer printer **3.** PHOTOGRAPHIC CHEMICAL a chemical solution used in photograph development

tone row, **tone series** n a sequence of notes that is the basis of a piece of serial music, especially a series of 12 notes

tonetic /tō néttik/ adj relating to a language in which changes in pitch distinguish meaning [Early 20C. After PHONETIC] —**tonetically** adv

tong[1] /tong/ (**tongs**, **tonging**, **tonged**) vt **1.** to lift or move something with tongs **2.** to curl the hair with curling tongs [Mid-19C. < TONGS]

tong[2] /tong/ n a Chinese secret society thought to be involved in criminal activity [Late 19C. < Chinese (Cantonese) t'ông 'hall, meeting place']

tonga /tóng gə/ n in South Asia, a light horse-drawn carriage available for hire [Late 19C. < Hindi ṭagā]

Tonga[1] /tóng gə/ (plural -**gas** or same) n **1.** a member of a people living in south-central Africa, mainly in southwestern Zambia and northwestern Zimbabwe **2.** the Bantu language of the Tonga people. Native speakers: 990,000. [Mid-19C. < Tonga] —**Tonga** adj

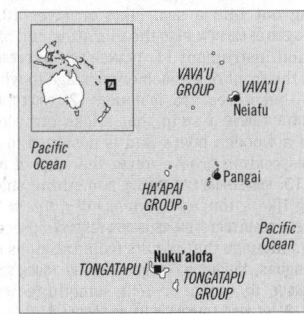

Tonga

Tonga[2] /tóngə/ independent island nation consisting of more than 150 islands in the southern Pacific Ocean. It became an independent member of the Commonwealth in 1970. Language: English, Tongan. Currency: pa'anga. Capital: Nukualofa. Population: 108,141 (2003). Area: 750 sq. km/290 sq. mi. Official name **Kingdom of Tonga**

Tongan /tóngən/ n **1.** somebody who comes from Tonga **2.** the Polynesian language of Tonga. Native speakers: 123,000. [Mid-19C. < TONGA[2]] —**Tongan** adj

Tongariro, Mount /tóngə réerō/ active volcano in New Zealand, in the central part of the North Island. It last erupted in 1926. Height: 1,968 m/6,458 ft.

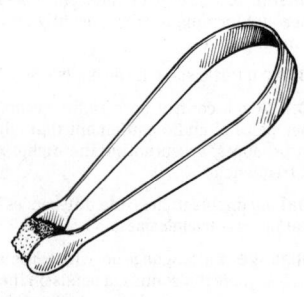

tongs

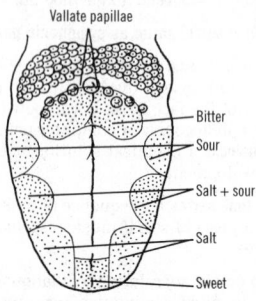

Vallate papillae

— Bitter
— Sour
— Salt + sour
— Salt
— Sweet

tongue: taste-sensitive areas of the human tongue

tongs /tongz/ *npl* **1.** a utensil for handling things that consists of two hinged or sprung arms that press together in a pinching movement around the object to be lifted **2.** HAIR same as **curling tongs** [Old English *tang* < Indo-European, 'to bite']

tongue /tung/ *n* **1.** FLESHY ORGAN INSIDE MOUTH the movable fleshy organ attached to the bottom of the inside of the mouth of humans and most animals, used for tasting, licking, swallowing, and, in humans, speech. Technical name **glossa** (sense 1) **2.** ANIMAL'S TONGUE AS FOOD the tongue of an animal, especially a cow, used as food **3.** LANGUAGE a language or dialect **4.** WAY OF SPEAKING somebody's manner of speaking (*formal*) ○ *She can have a sharp tongue when she's annoyed.* **5.** ABILITY TO SPEAK the power of speech ○ *She was so overwhelmed her tongue deserted her.* **6.** FLAP IN SHOE the middle flap in the opening of a shoe or boot **7.** PIN IN BUCKLE the pivoting pin in a buckle **8.** CLAPPER IN BELL the small swinging hammer inside a bell that hits against the inside of the bell to make the sound **9.** GEOG STRIP OF LAND a narrow strip of land sticking out into a sea, lake, or river **10.** MUSIC VIBRATING END OF MUSICAL REED the vibrating end of a reed in a wind instrument **11.** TRANSP POLE ON CARRIAGE the pole at the front of a coach or carriage to which the horses' harnesses are fastened **12.** PROJECTING STRIP FITTING INTO GROOVE a strip that sticks out along the edge of a wooden board and is designed to fit into a corresponding groove along the edge of another board **13.** SOMETHING LIKE TONGUE something shaped or moving like a tongue ○ *tongues of flame* ■ **tongues** *npl* SPEECH RESULTING FROM RELIGIOUS ECSTASY speech in no known language that results from religious ecstasy ■ *v* (**tongues, tonguing, tongued**) **1.** *vt* TOUCH SOMETHING WITH TONGUE to touch or lick something with the tongue **2.** *vt* KISS SOMEBODY USING TONGUE to kiss somebody with the lips open and the tongue touching the inside of the other person's mouth (*informal*) **3.** *vti* MUSIC USE TONGUE TO ARTICULATE INSTRUMENT'S NOTES to use the tongue to block the flow of air on a wind or brass instrument, thereby separating one note from another **4.** *vt* CUT TONGUE ALONG EDGE OF BOARD to cut a tongue along the edge of a wooden board in order to make one half of a tongue-and-groove joint [Old English *tunge* < Indo-European] —**tongued** *adj* —**tongueless** *adj* ◇ **hold your tongue** to keep silent ◇ **trip off the tongue** to be easy or pleasant to say

SYNONYMS See *language*.

tongue-and-groove joint *n* a joint made between two wooden boards consisting of a projecting strip or tongue along the edge of one board and a groove along the edge of the other

tongue depressor *n* ANZ, N Am MED a wide flat plastic or wooden stick that a doctor uses to hold down the tongue in order to examine the mouth and throat. UK term **spatula**

tongue-in-cheek *adj* spoken with gentle irony and meant as a joke

tongue-lashing *n* a severe scolding

tongue-tie *vt* to make somebody unable to speak, especially because of awe, shyness, or embarrassment ■ *n* the inability to move the tongue with the normal amount of freedom, because the small membrane (**frenulum**) that attaches the tongue to the floor of the mouth is unusually short

tongue-tied *adj* **1.** unable to speak because of awe, shyness, or embarrassment **2.** unable to move the tongue freely because of tongue-tie

tongue twister *n* a word, phrase, or sentence that is difficult to say because of its unusual sequence of sounds, especially an invented sentence such as 'She sells seashells on the seashore'

tongue worm *n* a tongue-shaped parasite with a hooked mouth that infests the lungs or nostrils of mammals, reptiles, and birds. Phylum: Arthropoda.

tonic /tónnik/ *n* **1.** SOMETHING THAT LIFTS SPIRITS something that lifts the spirits or makes somebody feel better generally **2.** MEDICINE PRODUCING SENSE OF WELL-BEING a medicine that purports to make patients feel stronger, more energetic, and generally healthier **3.** BEVERAGES same as **tonic water 4.** MUSIC FIRST NOTE OF SCALE the first note of a musical scale and the harmony built on this note **5.** PHON STRESSED SYLLABLE the syllable that has the main stress in a word ■ *adj* **1.** LIFTING SPIRITS lifting the spirits and creating a feeling of general well-being **2.** BOOSTING ENERGY designed or serving to boost energy and generally create a feeling of strength and health **3.** PHYSIOL RELATING TO MUSCLE TONE relating to or affecting muscular tone or contraction **4.** MUSIC RELATING TO FIRST MUSICAL NOTE relating to or based on the first note of a musical scale **5.** PHON OF STRESSED SYLLABLE relating to or forming the main stressed syllable in a word **6.** LING same as **tonetic** [Mid-17C. Via French *tonique* < Greek *tonikos* 'of stretching' < *tonos* 'tension, tone'] —**tonically** *adv*

tonic accent *n* **1.** a musical accent produced by higher pitch, not by stress **2.** a stress on a syllable created through a change in pitch

tonicity /tō níssəti/ *n* **1.** the state or quality of being tonic **2.** the state or quality of muscles that are slightly contracted or ready to contract

tonic sol-fa *n* a system of using syllables to denote degrees of a musical scale, in which the syllables are movable depending on the key of the piece

tonic water *n* a carbonated drink with a bitter taste, originally and still sometimes containing quinine, drunk on its own as a soft drink or used as an ingredient in cocktails [Because it was originally drunk to stimulate the appetite or digestion]

tonight /tə nít/ *adv* on or during the night or evening of the present day ■ *n* the night or evening of the present day [Old English *tō niht* 'at night']

tonka bean /tóngkə-/ *n* **1.** a fragrant black almond-shaped seed. Use: perfume, scenting tobacco, and snuff. **2.** a leguminous tree that produces tonka beans. Native to: tropical America. Latin name: *Dipteryx odorata*.

Tonkin, Gulf of /tón kin, tóng-/ arm of the South China Sea, on the coast of northeastern Vietnam and southeastern China

Tonle Sap /tón lay sáp/ largest lake in Southeast Asia, in western Cambodia, linked to the Mekong River by the Tonle Sap River. A shallow lake, it swells from 2,600 sq. km/1,000 sq. mi. in the dry season to 10,400 sq. km/4,020 sq. mi. in the monsoon season.

tonnage /túnnij/, **tunnage** *n* **1.** WEIGHT IN TONS weight measured in imperial or metric tons **2.** SHIP'S SIZE the size of a ship measured in tons or cubic feet or metres of seawater displaced **3.** SHIP'S CAPACITY the capacity of a ship measured in cubic feet or metres **4.** WEIGHT OF SHIP'S CARGO the weight of a ship's cargo, measured in tons **5.** DUTY CHARGED ON SHIP'S CARGO the duty charged at a rate per ton on a ship's cargo **6.** SIZE OF FLEET OF SHIPS the size of a fleet of ships such as

a merchant company's fleet or a nation's warships, calculated as the combined weights or carrying capacities of all ships [15C. < TON[1]]

tonne /tun/ *n* MEASURE same as **metric ton** [Late 19C. Via French < medieval Latin *tunna*]

SPELLCHECK tonne, ton, or **tun?** Do not confuse the spelling of *tonne, ton,* and *tun,* which sound similar. A *tonne* is a metric unit equal to 1,000 kilograms. A *ton* is an imperial unit, and differs in value in British and American usage. A *tun* is a large beer or wine cask or a unit of liquid capacity equal to 955 litres/210 gallons.

tonneau /tónnō/ (*plural* **-neaus** /-nōz/ or **-neaux** /-nō/) *n* the back-seat compartment of an open-top vintage car, or a flexible cloth cover protecting it when it is not being used [Late 18C. < French, 'barrel' (because of its shape) < *tonne* (see TONNE)]

tonneau cover *n* a detachable protective cover for the open bed of a pick-up truck or the passenger compartment of a convertible car whose top is down

tonometer /tō nómmitər/ *n* **1.** an instrument, often one fitted with a range of tuning forks, that measures the exact pitch of a sound **2.** an instrument that measures pressure in a part of the body, e.g. the blood vessels, or the eyeball as a test for glaucoma [Early 18C. < Greek *tonos* 'tension, tone'] —**tonometric** /tónnə méttrik, tōnə-/ *adj* —**tonometry** *n*

tonoplast /tónə plast/ *n* the semipermeable membrane separating a fluid-filled internal cavity (**vacuole**) from the surrounding cytoplasm inside a plant cell [Late 19C. < Greek *tonos* 'tension, tone']

tons /tunz/ *adv* to a great degree or extent ○ *The weather's tons better today.* [Early 20C. Plural of TON[1]]

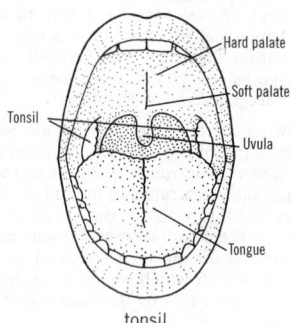

— Hard palate
— Soft palate
Tonsil —
— Uvula
— Tongue

tonsil

tonsil /tónss'l, -sil/ *n* **1.** either of two small oval masses of tissue, one on either side of the back of the mouth, that are important for the body's immune system **2.** a lump of tissue shaped like a tonsil of the mouth, e.g. either of two small lumps in the brain (**tonsils of the cerebellum**) [Late 16C. < Latin *tonsillae* 'tonsils'] —**tonsillar** *adj*

~~tonsilitis~~ incorrect spelling of **tonsillitis**

tonsillectomy /tónssi léktəmi/ (*plural* **-mies**) *n* a surgical operation to remove the tonsils of the mouth

tonsillitis /tónssi lítiss/ *n* inflammation of the tonsils of the mouth, caused either by bacteria or a virus, which makes the throat very sore and can lead to fever and earache —**tonsillitic** /-líttik/ *adj*

tonsorial /ton sáwri əl/ *adj* relating to barbers or their work (*formal or humorous*) [Early 19C. < Latin *tonsorius* < *tonsor* 'barber' < *tondere* 'to clip']

tonsure /tónshər, -syər/ *n* **1.** PARTIALLY SHAVED HEAD a shaved patch on the crown of the head of a priest or monk in some religious orders **2.** SHAVING OF HEAD the shaving of the head, especially to make a shaved patch on the crown of a priest or monk's head ■ *vt* (**-sures, -suring, -sured**) PARTIALLY SHAVE HEAD to shave the crown of the head [14C. Directly or via French < Latin *tonsura* < *tondere* 'to clip']

tontine /tón tīn, -teen, -teén/ *n* an investment or insurance scheme in which contributors pay equal amounts into a common fund and receive equal dividends and benefits from it, with the final surviving contributor receiving everything [Mid-18C. < French, after Lorenzo *Tonti* (1630–95), Neapolitan banker]

tonto /tón tō/ *adj* an offensive term meaning mentally ill (*insult*) [Late 20C. < Spanish]

ton-up (*dated informal*) *adj* **1.** FOND OF RIDING MOTORCYCLES FAST fond of riding motorcycles at high speeds, especially recklessly **2.** CAPABLE OF OVER 100 MPH used to describe a motorcycle travelling at or capable of travelling at over 100 miles per hour ■ *n* SPEED OVER 100 MPH a speed in excess of 100 miles per hour, or a motorcyclist who frequently rides at these speeds

tonus /tṓnəss/ *n* the normal state of a healthy muscle when resting in a state of slight contraction [Late 19C. Via Latin < Greek *tonos* 'tension, tone']

tony /tṓni/ *adj N Am* having an aristocratic, expensive, or stylish presentation (*informal*) [Late 19C. < TONE]

Tony /tṓni/ (*plural* **-nys** or **-nies**) *n* in the United States, an award made annually for achievement in the theatre [Mid-20C. < *Tony*, nickname of Antoinette Perry (1888–1946), US actor and producer]

too /too/ *adv* **1.** AS WELL used to indicate that a person, thing, or aspect of a situation applies in addition to the one just mentioned ○ *You can come too.* **2.** MORE THAN IS DESIRABLE more of an amount or degree of something than is desirable, necessary, or fitting ○ *too flamboyant for my taste* **3.** EXTREMELY used to emphasize a quality ○ *You're too kind.* **4.** VERY used to modify the force of a negative statement in order to sound polite or cautious ○ *didn't look too happy* **5.** *N Am* INDEED used to emphasize the force of a statement or command ○ *You did too!* [Old English *tō* (see TO[1]), in the sense 'in addition, furthermore'] ◇ **too right** used to express emphatic agreement with a statement that has just been made (*informal*) ○ *'So you're leaving?' – 'Too right I am!'*

SPELLCHECK See ***to***[1].

toodle-oo /tood'l ŏo/, **toodle-pip** *interj* same as **goodbye** (*dated informal or humorous*) [Early 20C. Origin ?]

too-hard basket *n Aus* an imaginary receptacle in which one can place materials or issues that are too difficult to deal with or resolve at the present time (*informal*) ○ *We don't have time to resolve that problem; let's put it in the too-hard basket for now.*

took past tense of **take**

tool /tool/ *n* **1.** DEVICE FOR DOING WORK an object designed to do a specific kind of work such as cutting or chopping by directing manually applied force or by means of a motor **2.** MEANS TO END something used as a means of achieving something **3.** SOMETHING USED FOR JOB something used in the course of somebody's everyday work ○ *Words are the poet's tool.* **4.** SOMEBODY MANIPULATED BY ANOTHER somebody who is easily manipulated, especially to carry out unpleasant or dishonest tasks that somebody else is unwilling to do **5.** MECH ENG same as **machine tool** **6.** MECH ENG CUTTING PART OF MACHINE the cutting or shaping part of a power-driven device, e.g. the blade on a lathe **7.** HANDICRAFT BOOKBINDER'S IMPLEMENT an implement that a bookbinder uses to press a design into leather, cloth, or paper **8.** HANDICRAFT STAMPED DESIGN ON BOOK a design pressed into a book cover with a metal tool **9.** GUN a criminal's gun (*slang*) **10.** OFFENSIVE TERM an offensive term for a penis (*slang*) ■ *v* (**tools, tooling, tooled**) **1.** *vt* HANDICRAFT WORK SOMETHING USING HAND TOOLS to cut, shape, or form something, especially to press a design into the cover of a book, using hand tools **2.** *vt* INDUST GIVE SOMEBODY OR SOMETHING TOOLS to equip somebody or something with tools **3.** *vti* AUTOMOT DRIVE CAR to drive a car, especially at high speeds (*slang*) ○ *tooling along at a cool 65* [Old English *tōl* < Germanic, 'to manufacture'] —**tooler** *n*

tool up *vti* **1.** to provide a factory or an industry with the equipment needed for manufacturing ○ *tooled up the automotive industry for the war effort* **2.** to provide a person, company, or organization with the resources or equipment needed to do something ○ *tooled up for the new inventory system*

toolbar /tool baar/ *n* a row of icons on a computer screen that are clicked on to perform frequently used functions

tooled up /toold-/ *adj* (*slang*) **1.** equipped, especially well enough equipped to do a particular job **2.** carrying a gun

tooling /tooling/ *n* **1.** DECORATIVE WORK DONE WITH HAND TOOLS decorative work done with hand tools, especially the carving of stone or the pressing or stamping of designs onto leather ○ *gold tooling* **2.** PROVISION OF INDUSTRIAL MACHINERY the process of providing a factory or an industry with the equipment needed for manufacturing **3.** PROCESS OF WORKING WITH TOOL the process of working with a hand tool or a machine tool

toolkit /tool kit/ *n* **1.** a set of tools, especially for a specific type of work, kept in a special box or bag **2.** a collection of information, resources, and advice for a specific subject area or activity ○ *a best-practice toolkit for housing officials*

toolmaker /tool maykər/ *n* somebody who makes or repairs precision tools, especially the cutting or shaping parts of industrial machines —**toolmaking** *n*

tool pusher *n* somebody who supervises drilling operations on an oil rig (*informal*)

toolroom /tool room, -rŏom/ *n* a room in a machine shop where tools are stored, maintained, or made

tool shed *n* a small outbuilding where tools are kept, especially one in a garden used for storing gardening tools

tool steel *n* a hard steel used to make the cutting or shaping parts of hand tools and power tools

toon[1] /toon/ *n* **1.** a fragrant hard reddish mahogany. Use: furniture, joinery. **2.** a tree of the mahogany family that bears red flowers and yields toon. Native to: Australia, tropical Asia. Latin name: *Cedrela toona*. [Early 19C. Via Hindi *tūn* < Sanskrit *tunnaḥ*]

toon[2] /toon/ *n* **1.** CINEMA same as **cartoon** (sense 1) **2.** a character in a cartoon [Mid-20C. Shortening of CARTOON]

toon[3] /toon/ *n* **1.** *regional* GEOG another spelling of **toun** (sense 1) **2.** CINEMA, PUBL same as **cartoon** (senses 1–2) (*informal*)

toonie /tooni/ *n Can* a coin worth two Canadian dollars [Blend of TWO + LOONIE]

toorie /toori/ *n Scotland* a soft flat cap, with or without a brim, that has a bobble on its top, or the bobble on such a cap (*informal*) [Early 19C. < variant of TOWER[1]]

toot[1] /toot/ *n* a high-pitched hooting sound such as that made by a vehicle's horn or a trumpet or flute ■ *vti* (**toots, tooting, tooted**) to make a short high-pitched hooting sound, or cause something such as a vehicle's horn, a trumpet, or a flute to do this [Early 16C. An imitation of the sound] —**tooter** *n*

toot[2] /toot/ (*slang*) *n* a quantity of an illegal drug, especially cocaine, taken by inhaling through the nose ■ *vti* (**toots, tooting, tooted**) *US* to inhale an illegal drug, especially cocaine, through the nose [Late 17C. Origin ?]

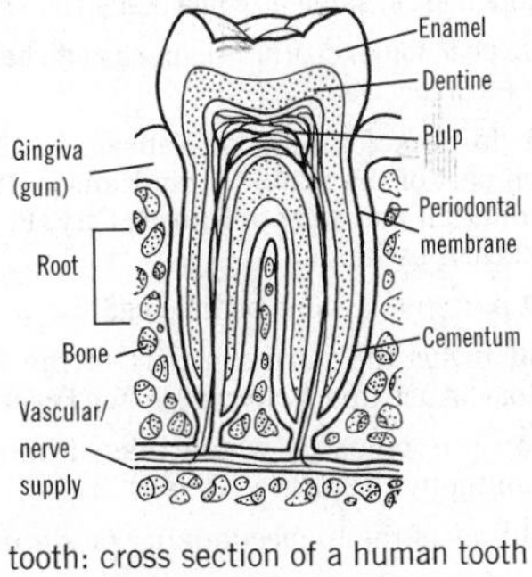

tooth: cross section of a human tooth

tooth /tooth/ *n* (*plural* **teeth** /teeth/) **1.** WHITISH BONY OBJECT IN MOUTH a hard whitish bony object inside a human or vertebrate animal's mouth, used for biting and chewing food **2.** INVERTEBRATE PART RESEMBLING TOOTH a sharp part on an invertebrate made of horny, calcareous, or chitinous material and functioning like or resembling a vertebrate tooth **3.** INDENTATION an object with the shape or function of a tooth, e.g. one of the jagged indentations along the edge of a saw or leaf **4.** PART STICKING OUT ON GEAR WHEEL a part that sticks out from the edge of a gear wheel or sprocket, designed to interlock with a similar part on another wheel **5.** SURFACE ROUGHNESS ALLOWING SUBSTANCE TO ADHERE the roughness of a surface, especially that of paper, that allows paints, glues, and other substances to stick to it **6.** TASTE FOR SOMETHING a liking for the taste of something ○ *a sweet tooth* **7.** SOMETHING DESTRUCTIVE something that has the power to destroy (*usually used in the plural*) ○ *the teeth of the gale* ■ **teeth** *npl* EFFECTIVE POWER the power or ability to accomplish something ○ *Sanctions without teeth won't do any good.* ■ *v* (**tooths, toothing, toothed**) **1.** *vt* PUT TEETH ON SOMETHING to give something teeth, especially to cut teeth into a saw blade or around the edge of a gear wheel or sprocket **2.** *vi* FIT TOGETHER WITH INTERLOCKING TEETH to interlock by means of teeth that fit one set inside the other [Old English *tōþ* < Indo-European] —**toothed** *adj* ◇ **armed to the teeth (with something)** extremely well armed or equipped with something (*informal*) ◇ **cut your teeth (on something)** to learn how to do something and gain experience from it ◇ **get your teeth into something** to start doing something that will be challenging and satisfying ◇ **in the teeth of** against opposition or contradiction from ◇ **kiss teeth** to suck air in noisily through the teeth in order to express displeasure or disagreement (*slang; used in Black English*) ◇ **like pulling teeth** extremely difficult, often because of a lack of co-operation (*informal*) ◇ **set somebody's teeth on edge** to annoy or irritate somebody ◇ **show your teeth** to indicate that you have power and intend to use it ◇ **tooth and nail** very aggressively, or with every available means —**toothed** /tootht/ *adj*

toothache /tooth ayk/ *n* a pain in or around a tooth, especially because the tooth is decaying

toothbrush /tooth brush/ *n* a small brush for cleaning the teeth, with a long handle and a comparatively small head —**toothbrushing** *n*

toothed whale *n* a smallish whale that has teeth and feeds on fish and molluscs. Suborder: Odontoceti.

tooth fairy *n* in children's folklore, a fairy who takes away the milk tooth that a child leaves under the pillow and replaces it with a coin or small gift

toothless /toothləss/ *adj* **1.** lacking teeth, especially because the teeth have decayed and fallen out **2.** lacking power, authority, or a forceful manner

toothless whale *n* a whale without teeth, but with thin horny plates hanging from the upper jaw through which it filters plankton

toothpaste /tooth payst/ *n* a paste brushed onto the teeth to clean them and protect them from decay

toothpick /tooth pik/ *n* a thin pointed stick of wood or plastic used to remove pieces of food from between the teeth

tooth powder *n* a powder that is mixed to a lather with a damp toothbrush and used to clean the teeth and protect them from decay

tooth shell *n* MARINE BIOL same as **tusk shell**

toothsome /toothsəm/ *adj* **1.** having a pleasing smell, taste, or appearance **2.** attractive, especially sexually (*dated informal; sometimes offensive*) —**toothsomely** *adv* —**toothsomeness** *n*

toothwort /tooth wurt/ (*plural* **-worts** or *same*) *n* **1.** a leafless plant that grows on tree roots and has horizontal underground stems (**rhizomes**) covered with scales resembling teeth. Flowers: pinkish. Native to: Europe. Latin name: *Lathraea squamaria*. **2.** a flowering plant with scaly rhizomes. Flowers: showy, pink or purple. Native to: North America. Latin name: *Cardamine bulbifera*.

toothy /toothi/ (**-ier, -iest**) *adj* having or showing a lot of teeth, large teeth, or protruding teeth —**toothily** *adv* —**toothiness** *n*

tootle /toot'l/ (*informal*) *v* (**-tles, -tling, -tled**) **1.** *vi* DRIVE SLOWLY to proceed slowly or aimlessly, especially in a car **2.** *vti* MAKE HOOTING SOUND to make repeated gentle tooting sounds, or cause something to do this ■ *n* **1.** LEISURELY DRIVE a drive at a leisurely pace **2.** REPEATED SOUND a gentle repeated tooting sound [Early 19C. < TOOT[1]]

tootsy /tootsi/ (*plural* **-sies**), **tootsie** *n* a foot or toe (*informal*) [Mid-19C. Alteration of FOOTSIE]

Toowoomba /tə wŏombə/ city in southeastern Queensland, Australia, the commercial centre of the Darling Downs agricultural region. Population: 91,187 (2002 estimate).

top[1] /top/ *n* **1.** HIGHEST PART the highest part or point of something (*often used in combination*) ○ *snow on the mountain tops* **2.** UPPER SURFACE the upper side or surface of something ○ *dust on the top of the cup-*

board **3. LID OR COVER** the part covering and sealing the open upper side of an object, or an opening on the upper side (*often used in combination*) ○ *bottle tops* **4. GARMENT COVERING UPPER BODY** a piece of clothing, especially women's clothing, covering the upper body **5. MOST IMPORTANT POSITION OR PERSON** the most important position or most senior rank, or the person occupying it ○ *at the top of her profession* ○ *He's top of the class.* **6. BEST PART** the best part or section of something ○ *They only take the top of the group.* **7. MOST EXCELLENT LEVEL** the level of highest excellence ○ *not at the top of his game* **8. MOST INTENSE LEVEL** the level of greatest intensity, power, or force ○ *at the top of her voice* **9. FARTHEST END** the farthest end of something such as a road or street **10. BEGINNING OR EARLIEST PART** the beginning or the first or earliest section of something ○ *the top of the programme* **11. CROWN OF HEAD** the crown of the head ○ *from top to toe* **12. PART OF PLANT ABOVE GROUND** the part of a plant that is above the ground ○ *carrot tops* **13. CAR ROOF** the roof of a car, especially a convertible **14.** AUTOMOT same as **top gear** (sense 1) (*informal*) **15.** SPORTS same as **topspin** **16.** SPORTS **STROKE HITTING BALL ABOVE CENTRE** a stroke that puts topspin on a ball by hitting the ball above its centre **17.** CARDS **PLAYER'S BEST CARD OR CARDS** the best card or group of cards in a player's hand **18.** NAUT **PLATFORM ON MAST** a platform around the head of a lower mast on a sailing ship, used to stand on or to support rigging **19.** ACOUSTICS **HIGH-FREQUENCY PART OF SOUND** the high-frequency element of a sound **20.** CHEM **VOLATILE PART OF SOLUTION** the fraction of a volatile solution that is collected first during distillation ■ *adj* **1. UPPERMOST OR HIGHEST** situated at the top, or higher than all others ○ *the top shirt on the pile* **2. LEADING OR MOST SUCCESSFUL** most important, senior, successful, or respected ○ *a convention of top academics* **3. OF BEST QUALITY** of the finest quality available ○ *one of the city's top hotels* **4. MAXIMUM** highest in level or degree ○ *at top speed* **5. EXCELLENT** used to indicate approval (*informal*) ○ *He's a top bloke.* ■ *vt* (**tops, topping, topped**) **1. EXCEED OR BETTER SOMETHING** to do better than something, or be greater than something ○ *profits topping $500 million* **2. OUTRANK ALL OTHERS IN SOMETHING** to be at the head of something such as a list or hierarchy ○ *They've topped the music charts for the fifth week in a row.* **3. ADD TOPPING TO SOMETHING** to put a topping on something (*often passive*) ○ *topped with a layer of melted cheese* **4. CUT TOP OFF SOMETHING** to cut the top off something, especially a vegetable prior to cooking ○ *First top and tail the carrots.* **5. REACH APEX OF SOMETHING** to reach or go over the top of something such as a mountain **6. KILL SOMEBODY** to kill somebody or yourself (*informal*) **7.** SPORTS **PUT TOPSPIN ON BALL** to hit a ball above its centre, putting topspin on it **8.** GOLF **HIT GOLF BALL ABOVE CENTRE** to hit a golf ball too far above its centre, so that it runs along the ground instead of rising into the air **9.** CHEM **DISTIL VOLATILE PART OF SOLUTION** to distil the most volatile part of a solution [Old English *topp* < Germanic, 'tuft, crest'] ◇ **blow your top** to lose your temper and fly into a rage (*informal*) ◇ **off the top of your head** without thinking deeply, checking, or planning something

top off *vt* **1.** to add an impressive or significant finishing touch to something **2.** *US* same as **top up**

top out *vt* to add the final storey or other structural feature to a building under construction, usually as part of an official ceremony

top up *vt* **1. FILL CONTAINER** to fill or refill a container that is partly empty **2. INCREASE SUM BY ADDING MONEY** to give extra money to augment a sum or fund in order to bring it up to a required level **3. GIVE SOMEBODY MORE TO DRINK** to refill somebody's drink, especially when it is not yet finished (*informal*)

top[2] /top/ *n* a toy that spins round on a rounded or pointed base, traditionally a conical wooden toy that is set spinning by pulling a string wrapped round it [Pre-12C. Origin ?]

top- *prefix* same as **topo-** (*used before vowels*)

topaz /tō paz/ *n* **1. TRANSPARENT BROWN GEMSTONE** a usually brown, transparent precious stone. Source: pegmatite. Use: gems. **2. YELLOWISH GEMSTONE** a yellowish gemstone, especially yellow sapphire or a yellow variety of quartz **3. HUMMINGBIRD WITH YELLOWISH THROAT** a vividly coloured hummingbird with a yellowish throat. Native to: South American rainforest. Latin name: *Topaza pella.* **4. YELLOWISH-BROWN COLOUR** a light yellowish-brown colour [13C. Via Old French *topace* < Greek *topazos*] —**topaz** *adj*

topazolite /tō pázzə līt/ *n* a yellowish-green variety of garnet. Use: gems.

top banana *n N Am* the main person in a group (*slang*)

top billing *n* **1.** a performer's status as the star attraction in a show with his or her name appearing first in any list of performers or promotional material **2.** the position of greatest prominence in something

top boot *n* a knee-length boot with a band of differently coloured leather around the top

top brass *n* the highest-ranking officers or officials (*informal*)

top-class *adj* belonging to or characteristic of the highest category of something ○ *a top-class tennis player*

topcoat /tóp kōt/ *n* **1.** a finishing coat of paint, applied over an undercoat **2.** a coat for outdoor wear (*dated*)

top dead-centre *n* the position of a piston in an engine or pump when it is at the top of its stroke

top dog *n* the most important or powerful person, often somebody who has beaten all other competitors (*informal*)

top dollar *n* a very high price (*informal*)

top-down *adj* **1.** having all control in the hands of the people at the most senior levels **2.** starting at the most general level and working towards details or specifics ○ *a top-down approach*

top drawer *n* **1.** the highest level of excellence, or the people at this level **2.** the upper class or highest class in society —**top-drawer** *adj*

top-dress *vt* to spread a thin layer of something on the ground, especially fertilizer on the surface of soil, a growing crop, or a lawn

top dressing *n* **1. SURFACE FERTILIZER** a fertilizer spread thinly on the surface of soil, a growing crop, or a lawn **2. LOOSE GRAVEL AS ROAD SURFACE** loose gravel spread thinly on the surface of a road or path **3. SUPERFICIAL COVERING** a thin or superficial covering, especially a deceptively pleasant facade hiding an unpleasant reality

tope[1] /tōp/ (**topes, toping, toped**) *vti* to drink alcohol heavily and habitually (*archaic or literary*) [Mid-17C. Origin ?]

tope[2] /tōp/ (*plural* **topes** or *same*) *n* a small grey shark with a long snout. Latin name: *Galeorhinus galeus.* [Late 17C. Origin ?]

tope[3] /tōp/ *n* RELIG same as **stupa** [Early 19C. < Hindi *top*]

topee /tō pee/, **topi** *n* CLOTHING same as **pith helmet** [Mid-19C. < Hindi *ṭopī* 'hat']

Topeka /tə péekə/ capital of Kansas, in the northeastern part of the state, on the Kansas River, east of Manhattan and west of Kansas City. Population: 122,103 (2002 estimate).

top end *n* MECH ENG same as **little end**

Top End *n Aus* the northern part of the Northern Territory, Australia (*informal*) —**Top Ender** *n*

toper /tōpər/ *n* somebody who drinks alcohol heavily and habitually (*archaic or literary*)

top-flight *adj* of the highest quality or status

topgallant /top gállənt/ *n* **1.** *also* **topgallant mast** a ship's mast that is taller than a topmast or is an extension of a topmast **2.** *also* **topgallant sail** a sail set on a topgallant mast

top gear *n* **1.** the highest of a motor vehicle's gears, selected for the fastest speed of travel. N Am term **high gear** **2.** the state of greatest intensity, e.g. the fastest working rate or the highest level of enthusiasm (*informal*)

top gun *n N Am* somebody who is the best in his or her field (*informal*)

CULTURAL NOTE ***Top Gun***, a film (1986) by British director Tony Scott. A drama about US Navy fighter pilots in training, it centres on two outstanding pilots in the class competing for the much coveted title of 'Top Gun'. An encounter with enemy aircraft provides them with an opportunity to prove their worth. The film is memorable for its spectacular, high-speed dog-fights. The term 'top gun' promptly moved into the general language.

top-hamper *n* the uppermost sails, spars, and other equipment on a sailing ship, especially when regarded as weight to be minimized or monitored because of the destabilizing effect it can have

top hat *n* a man's tall cylindrical hat with a flat top and a narrow brim. It is usually black, is often made of silk, and is worn as part of formal dress.

top-heavy *adj* **1.** unbalanced or unstable owing to excessive weight at the top **2.** having too many executives or managers in proportion to the number of staff at junior levels —**top-heavily** *adv* —**top-heaviness** *n*

Tophet /tōfət/, **Topheth** *n* according to the Bible, a place of torment and punishment where the wicked are sent after death [14C. < Hebrew *Tōppet*, area near Jerusalem]

tophi MED plural of **tophus**

top-hole *adj UK* first-rate or excellent (*dated informal*) [Late 19C. Probably after TOPNOTCH]

tophus /tōfəss/ (*plural* **-phi** /-fī/) *n* a hard deposit of crystalline uric acid and its salts in cartilage, joints, or skin. It is a characteristic of gout. [Mid-16C. < Latin, 'tufa'] —**tophaceous** /tō fáyshəss/ *adj*

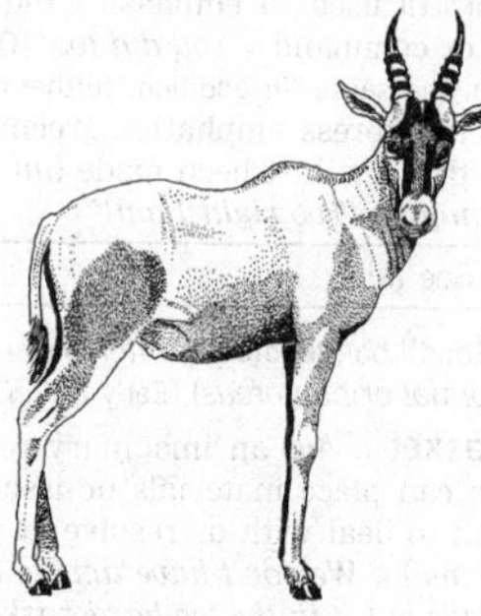

topi

topi[1] /tō pee/ (*plural* **-pis** or *same*) *n* an antelope that has curved horns, a long muzzle, and bluish-black and yellow markings. It is said to be the fastest of all the antelopes. Native to: Africa. Latin name: *Damaliscus lunatus.* [Late 19C. Origin ?]

topi[2] /tō pee/ *n* CLOTHING same as **pith helmet**

topiary /tōpi əri/ (*plural* **-ies**) *n* **1. ART OF SHAPING BUSHES** the art of trimming bushes, hedges, and trees into decorative shapes **2. SHAPED BUSH** a bush, hedge, or tree trimmed into a decorative shape **3. TOPIARY GARDEN** a garden in which topiaries feature prominently [Late 16C. Via French < Latin *topiarius* < Greek *topos* 'place'] —**topiarist** *n*

topic /tóppik/ *n* **1.** something dealt with in a text or in discussion **2.** a class of arguments used as a source of proofs in formal reasoning [15C. < *Topics*, title of Aristotle's treatise on rhetorical commonplaces < Latin *Topica* < Greek *topos* 'place']

SYNONYMS See ***subject***.

TOPIC /tóppik/ *abbr* FIN Teletext Output of Price Information by Computer

topical /tóppik'l/ *adj* **1. OF CURRENT INTEREST** relating to something that is of interest or importance at the moment **2. OF TOPICS** relating to topics or in the form of topics ○ *a topical index* **3. LOCAL** relating to or situated in a specific place or part **4.** MED **APPLIED EXTERNALLY** describes drugs or medications that are applied directly to the surface of the part of the body being treated —**topically** *adv*

topicality /tóppi kálləti/ *n* relevance to something that is of interest or importance at the moment

topic sentence *n* a sentence that states the main idea of a paragraph or larger section of writing, usually placed at or near the beginning

topknot /tóp not/ *n* **1. HAIR DECORATION** a decorative arrangement of hair, or of hairbands or bows, worn on top of the head **2. EUROPEAN FLATFISH** a flatfish, especially a species that has an oval dark-brown body with darker patches. Native to: Europe. Latin

name: *Zeugopterus*. **3. BIRD'S CREST** a small tuft of feathers on the head of some birds such as some types of quail

topless /tópləss/ *adj* **1. WITH NOTHING COVERING BREASTS** wearing no covering over the breasts or upper torso **2. LETTING WOMEN SHOW BREASTS IN PUBLIC** describes a place such as a beach where women expose their breasts in public ○ *a topless beach* **3. WITH NO TOP PART** describes a piece of clothing that has no part covering the upper torso ○ *a topless bathing suit* **4. MISSING TOP** lacking or missing a top —**toplessness** *n*

top-level *adj* **1.** involving the most senior or influential people ○ *top-level negotiations* **2.** at the highest level of influence or authority ○ *a top-level executive*

top-level domain *n* the part of an Internet address that identifies an Internet domain, e.g. edu (education), .com (commercial), or a two-letter country code.

toplofty /tóp lófti/ (**-ier, -iest**) *adj US* haughty, pretentious, or condescending (*informal*) —**toploftily** *adv*

topmast /tóp maast/ *n* a mast that is taller than the lowest mast and is usually the tallest mast on a ship whose sails run fore-and-aft. It is the next tallest after the topgallant mast on a square-rigged ship.

topminnow /tóp minnō/ (*plural* **-nows** or *same*) *n* a small freshwater fish that swims near the surface in warmer waters and has an upturned mouth for catching prey. Guppies and mollies are topminnows. Families: Cyprinodontidae or Poeciliidae or Goodeidae.

topmost /tópmōst/ *adj* highest or uppermost

topnotch /tóp nóch/ *adj* meeting the highest standards of excellence or quality (*informal*) —**topnotcher** *n*

topo /tóppō/ (*plural* **-pos**) *n* a photograph of a mountain that has possible routes for climbing marked on it [Late 20C. Shortening of *topographic*]

topo- *prefix* place, region ○ *topotype* [< Greek *topos* 'place']

top-of-the-range *adj* being the best, most expensive, and most sophisticated available (*not hyphenated after a verb*) ○ *bought the top-of-the-range model*

topog. *abbr* GEOG topography

topography /tə pógrəfi/ (*plural* **-phies**) *n* **1. MAPPING OF SURFACE FEATURES** the study and mapping of the features on the surface of land, including natural features such as mountains and rivers and constructed features such as roads and railways **2. AREA'S FEATURES** the features on the surface of an area of land **3. MAP** a map or chart of an area's topography **4. DESCRIPTION OF STRUCTURE** a study or detailed description of the various features of an object or entity and the relationships between them —**topographer** *n* —**topographic** /tóppə gráffik/ *adj* —**topographical** *adj* —**topographically** *adv*

topoi LITERAT plural of **topos**

topology /tə póllǝji/ *n* **1. STUDY OF GEOMETRIC PROPERTIES** the study of the properties of geometric figures that are independent of size or shape and are not changed by stretching, bending, knotting, or twisting **2. FAMILY OF SUBSETS** the family of all open subsets of a mathematical set, including the set itself and the empty set, which is closed under set union and finite intersection **3. ANATOMY OF BODY PART** the anatomy of a part of the body **4. STUDY LINKING TOPOGRAPHY AND TIME** the study of changes in topography that occur over time and, especially, of how such changes taking place in an area affect the history of that area **5. RELATIONSHIPS BETWEEN LINKED ELEMENTS** the relationships between parts linked together in a system such as a computer network (*formal*) —**topologic** /tóppə lójjik/ *adj* —**topological** *adj* —**topologically** *adv* —**topologist** *n*

Topolski /tə pólski/, **Feliks** (1907–89) Polish-born British artist. He was a British government war artist during World War II and is noted for his scenes of daily life.

toponym /tóppənim/ *n* **1.** a name, e.g. a personal name, that is derived from the name of a place **2.** a name given to a place (*formal*) [Late 19C. < TOPO- after SYNONYM]

toponymy /tə pónnəmi/ *n* the study of the placenames of a region or language —**toponymic** /tóppə nímmik/ *adj* —**toponymical** *adj*

topos /tóppóss/ (*plural* **-poi** /-poy/) *n* a traditional theme, especially one developed in literature or rhetoric [Mid-20C. < Greek, 'place, rhetorical commonplace']

topotype /tóppə tīp/ *n* a biological specimen taken from its typical habitat

-topped *suffix* having a top of a particular kind ○ *flat-topped*

topper /tóppər/ *n* **1. CLOTHING** same as **top hat** (*informal*) **2. SOMEBODY OR SOMETHING DEALING WITH TOPS** a person or machine that removes or adds tops **3. CROWNING COMMENT** a remark or joke that improves on or triumphs over a preceding one (*informal*) **4. PLEASANT PERSON** an outstandingly kind or popular person (*dated informal*) **5. BEST OF KIND** something that surpasses all others of its kind (*dated informal*)

topping /tópping/ *n* **1. GARNISH FOR FOOD** something put on top of food, especially a sauce or garnish **2. FEATHER FOR FISHING FLY** a feather from the crest of a golden pheasant put at the top of a fishing fly ■ *adj UK* **FIRST-RATE** excellent (*dated informal*)

topple /tópp'l/ (**-ples, -pling, -pled**) *v* **1.** *vti* **FALL OR MAKE SOMETHING FALL OVER** to fall forward or tip over, or make something do this **2.** *vi* **TOTTER** to lean or sway precariously, as if about to fall over **3.** *vt* **OVERTHROW SOMEBODY OR SOMETHING** to overthrow somebody or something from a position of authority [Mid-16C. < TOP[1]]

top-quality *adj* of the highest quality (*not hyphenated after a verb*) ○ *top-quality meat*

top quark *n* a quark with an electric charge of +2/3 and zero strangeness and charm

top-ranking *adj* of a senior rank or the highest rank

top-rated *adj* considered highest in quality or rank ○ *the city's ten top-rated restaurants*

top round *n N Am* same as **topside** *adj*

tops /tops/ (*informal*) *adv* at the most ○ *Offer him five hundred, tops.* ■ *n* (*plural same*) the very best person or thing (*usually predicative*) ○ *Thanks, mum, you're the tops.*

TOPS /tóps/ *abbr* Training Opportunities Scheme

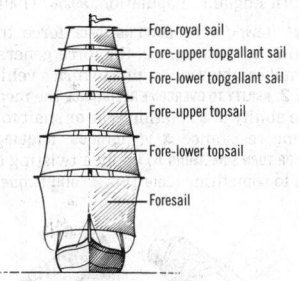

topsail: topsails on a square-rigged ship

topsail /tóp sayl, tópss'l/ *n* a sail set above the lowermost sail on a mast on a square-rigged sailing ship, or above the gaff on a fore-and-aft-rigged ship

top-secret *adj* requiring complete secrecy or containing information that must be kept completely secret, especially because its disclosure would endanger national security

top-shelf *adj* **1.** describes pornographic magazines that are very sexually explicit and are therefore displayed on the top shelf in a shop, out of direct view **2.** *Aus* of the finest quality

topside /tóp sīd/ *n* **1. UPPER SIDE** the uppermost side of something **2. CUT OF BEEF** a lean boneless cut of beef from the outer thigh. N Am term **top round 3. UPPER HULL** the part of a ship's hull that sits above the water ■ *adj* **ON TOPSIDE OF SHIP** relating to or situated on the topside of a ship ■ *adv also* **topsides** /-sīdz/ *US NAUT* **TO SHIP'S DECK** up on or to the deck of a ship

topsoil /tóp soyl/ *n* **TOP LAYER OF SOIL** the upper fertile layer of soil, from which plant roots take nutrients ■ *vt* (**-soils, -soiling, -soiled**) **1. SPREAD LAND WITH TOPSOIL** to spread topsoil onto farming or gardening land to improve fertility **2. REMOVE TOPSOIL FROM LAND** to remove the top layer of soil from farming or gardening land

topspin /tóp spin/ *n* forward spin given to a ball by hitting it on its upper half, making it arc more sharply in the air or bounce higher on impact

topstitch /tóp stich/ *n* a row of stitching on the outer or upper side of a garment, near the seam ■ *vt* (**-stitches, -stitching, -stitched**) to sew a topstitch on a garment —**topstitching** *n*

topsy-turvy /tópsi túrvi/ *adj, adv* **1. UPSIDE DOWN** with the bottom at the top and the top at the bottom **2. IN OR INTO CONFUSION** in or into a confused or chaotic state, especially one in which the natural order or arrangement of things is inverted ■ *n* **DISORDER OR CONFUSION** a state of complete disorder or confusion [Early 16C. Origin ?] —**topsy-turvily** *adv* —**topsy-turviness** *n*

top-up *n* **1.** a refilling of a glass or cup out of which somebody has drunk all or part of the contents **2.** an additional sum of money, especially one that brings a fund up to a required or desirable level (*often used before a noun*) ○ *a top-up loan*

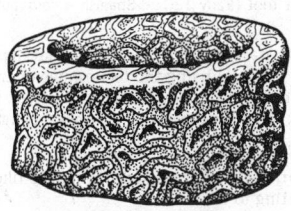

toque

toque /tōk/ *n* **1. BRIMLESS HAT** a close-fitting brimless hat worn by women **2. CHEF'S HAT** a tall white hat worn by chefs **3. HAT WORN IN PAST** a velvet hat with a narrow brim and pouched crown, popular in the 16th century with men and women [Early 16C. < French]

tor /tawr/ *n* a rocky peak of a hill or mountain, specifically one exposed by the weathering of surrounding rock (*often used in placenames*) [Old English *torr*, origin ?]

to raas /tə ráas/ *adv* used as a swearword to add emphasis (*slang; used in Black English*) ○ *him nice to raas*

to raatid /tə ráatid/ *interj* same as **raatid** (*taboo offensive; used in Black English*)

Torah /táwrə/ *n* **1.** the Jewish Pentateuch, or a parchment scroll on which the Pentateuch is written for use in services in synagogues **2.** the collective body of Jewish teaching embodied in the Hebrew Bible and the Talmud [Late 16C. < Hebrew *tōrāh* 'law']

torbernite /táwrbə nīt/ *n* a green mineral containing uranium and copper. Use: source of uranium. [Mid-19C. After *Torbern* Olof Bergman (1735–84), Swedish chemist]

torc *n* JEWELLERY another spelling of **torque**[2]

torch /tawrch/ *n* **1. PORTABLE LIGHT SOURCE** a small handheld lamp usually powered by batteries. N Am term **flashlight 2. BURNING STICK** a stick of wood dipped in wax or with one end wrapped in combustible material, set on fire and carried, especially in former times, as a source of light **3. DEVICE EMITTING FLAME** a portable device that emits an extremely hot flame, e.g. one used in welding or for stripping paint **4. SOURCE OF ENLIGHTENMENT** a source of guidance or enlightenment (*literary*) ■ *vt* (**torches, torching, torched**) **SET SOMETHING ON FIRE** to set fire to something, especially as an act of arson or terrorism (*informal*) [13C. Via French *torche* < Latin *torques* 'torque' < *torquere* 'to twist'] —**torcher** *n* ◇ **carry a torch for somebody** to be in love with somebody, especially when this feeling is secret or unrequited (*informal*)

torchbearer /táwrch bairər/ *n* **1.** somebody who carries a torch, usually in a procession or ceremony **2.** somebody who provides leadership or inspiration

torchère /tawr sháir/ n a tall decorated stand for holding a candle or candelabrum [Early 20C. < French < *torche* (see TORCH)]

torchier /táwrchi ər/, **torchiere** n a tall floor lamp that gives indirect upward lighting [Early 20C. Variant of TORCHÈRE]

torchlight /táwrch līt/ n 1. the light from a torch 2. same as **torch** n (sense 2)

torchon lace /táwrsh'n-/ n lace made from coarse linen or cotton, with a simple open pattern

torch song n a popular sentimental song about un-requited love. Such songs were originally popular in the 1930s. [< the torch as a symbol of unrequited love] —**torch singer** n

torchwood /táwrch wŏŏd/ n 1. a resinous wood once used to make torches 2. a tree yielding torchwood. Native to: Florida, Caribbean. Genus: *Amyris*.

tore[1] /tawr/ past tense of **tear**[1]

tore[2] /tawr/ n ARCHIT same as **torus** (sense 2) [Mid-17C. Via French < Latin *torus* 'bulge']

toreador /tórri ə dawr/ n a bullfighter, especially one on horseback [Early 17C. < Spanish < *torear* 'fight bulls' < *toro* 'bull' (see TORERO)]

torero /to ráirō/ (plural -ros) n a bullfighter, especially one on foot [Early 18C. < Spanish < *toro* 'bull' < Latin *taurus*]

toreutics /tə rŏŏtiks/ n the art of making detailed reliefs in metal using the techniques of embossing and engraving (takes a singular verb) [Mid-19C. < Greek *toreutikos* < *toreus* 'boring tool'] —**toreutic** adj

tori plural of **torus**

toric /tórrik/ adj ring- or doughnut-shaped like a torus, or relating to tori

toric lens n a spectacles lens used to correct the vision of somebody with astigmatism. It is curved in such a way as to have a different focal length along each axis.

torii /táwri ee/ (plural same) n a gateway to a Japanese Shinto temple that has two posts and two cross-pieces [Early 18C. < Japanese, 'bird's perch']

torment vt /tawr mént/ (-ments, -menting, -mented) 1. INFLICT PAIN ON SOMEBODY OR SOMETHING to inflict torture, pain, or anguish on a person or animal 2. TEASE SOMEBODY to tease a person or animal persistently ■ n /táwr ment/ 1. TORTURE severe mental anguish or physical pain 2. CAUSE OF ANGUISH a source of severe mental anguish or physical pain 3. CAUSE OF ANNOYANCE a source of annoyance or anxiety [13C. Via Old French < Latin *tormentum* 'catapult, torment' < *torquere* 'to twist'] —**tormented** adj —**tormentedly** adv —**tormentingly** adv

tormenter n another spelling of **tormentor**

tormentil /táwrməntil/ (plural -tils or same) n a downy plant with an astringent root. Flowers: yellow. Use: medicine, tanning, dyeing. Latin name: *Potentilla erecta*. [14C. < French *tormentille* < Latin *tormentum* (see TORMENT)]

tormentor /tawr méntər/, **tormenter** n 1. CAUSE OF TORMENT a cause of mental anguish, physical pain, annoyance, or anxiety 2. THEATRE CURTAIN MASKING STAGE WINGS a curtain or screen at each side of a theatre stage that hides the wings from the audience 3. CINEMA ECHO-REDUCING DEVICE IN FILMING a panel of sound-absorbent material used to eliminate echo on a film set [13C. < Anglo-Norman *tormentour*, Old French *tormenteor* < Latin *tormentum* (see TORMENT)]

torn /tawrn/ past participle of **tear**[1] ■ adj reluctant or unable to make a choice ○ *torn between her children and her career* ◇ **that's torn it** an expression of annoyance at, or fear of the consequences of, a sudden and unexpected problem (dated informal)

tornado /tawr náydō/ (plural -dos or -does) n 1. COLUMN OF SWIRLING WIND an extremely destructive funnel-shaped rotating column of air that passes in a narrow path over land 2. AFRICAN WINDSTORM a short-lived but severe windstorm, especially one that occurs on the West African coast 3. FRANTIC PERSON OR STATE a state of frenzied activity or intense emotion, or somebody in such a state (informal) [Mid-16C. Probably alteration of Spanish *tronada* 'thunderstorm' < Latin *tonare* 'to thunder'] —**tornadic** /-náddik/ adj

tornament incorrect spelling of **tournament**

toroid /táw royd/ n MATHS same as **torus** (sense 1) —**toroidal** /to róyd'l/ adj

Toronto /tə róntō/ capital city of Ontario Province, Canada, located on the northwestern shore of Lake Ontario. Population: 4,366,508 (2001). —**Torontonian** /tə ron tōnee ən/ n, adj

torose /táwrōz/, **torous** /táwrəss/ adj cylindrical and knotted or bulging [Mid-18C. < Latin *torosus* 'brawny' < *torus* 'bulge'] —**torosity** /taw róssəti/ n

torpedo /tawr peédō/ n (plural -does) 1. SELF-PROPELLED UNDERWATER WEAPON a cylindrical self-propelled missile that is launched from an aircraft, ship, or submarine and travels underwater to hit its target 2. UNDERWATER MINE an underwater explosive mine (dated) 3. US FIREWORK a small gravel-filled firework that explodes when thrown against a hard surface 4. US RAIL RAILWAY DANGER SIGNAL an explosive placed on a railway track that is detonated by a train running over it and serves as a warning of danger ahead 5. US INDUST EXPLOSIVE FOR OIL WELLS an explosive device used to release the oil from an oil well 6. FISH same as **electric ray** ■ vt (-does, -doing, -doed) 1. HIT SHIP WITH TORPEDO to hit or destroy a ship with a torpedo 2. DESTROY SOMETHING to spoil, thwart, or destroy something completely (informal) ○ *threatened to torpedo the agreement* [Early 16C. < Latin, 'numbness' < *torpere* 'be stiff']

torpedo boat n a small light fast boat used to launch torpedoes

torpedo bomber n an aircraft that carries and launches torpedoes

torpedo tube n a tube from which torpedoes are fired from submarines or ships

torpid /táwrpid/ adj 1. SLUGGISH lacking physical or mental energy 2. ZOOL DORMANT describes an animal in a dormant state 3. MED NUMB describes a part of the body that has lost the ability to move or feel [Early 17C. < Latin *torpidus* < *torpere* 'be stiff'] —**torpidity** /tawr píddəti/ n —**torpidly** adv

torpor /táwrpər/ n 1. LACK OF ENERGY lack of mental or physical energy 2. ZOOL DORMANCY the dormant state of an animal 3. MED NUMBNESS absence of the ability to move or feel [13C. < Latin < *torpere* 'be stiff'] —**torporific** /táwrpə riffik/ adj

Torquay /tawr keé/ resort town in Devon, south-western England. Population: 59,587 (1991).

torque[1] /tawrk/ n 1. ROTATING FORCE force that causes twisting or turning, e.g. the force generated by an internal-combustion engine to turn a vehicle's drive shaft 2. ABILITY TO OVERCOME RESISTANCE the measurement of the ability of a rotating gear or shaft to overcome turning resistance ■ vt (torques, torquing, torqued) TWIST OR TURN SOMETHING to apply a twisting or turning force to something [Late 19C. < Latin *torquere* 'to twist']

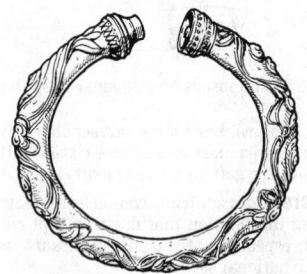

torque

torque[2] /tawrk/, **torc** n a metal collar or armband worn by the ancient Gauls and Britons [Mid-19C. Via French < Latin *torques* (see TORCH)]

torque converter n a hydraulic coupling designed to change the mechanical advantage or torque speed between an input and an output shaft

Torquemada /táwrkwi máadə, táwrkay-/, **Tomás de** (1420–98) Spanish monk. As grand inquisitor for Spain (1487–98), he was notorious for his cruelty. He was largely responsible for the expulsion of the Jews from Spain (1492).

torques /tawrks/ (plural same) n a ring of colour, hair, or feathers around the neck of an animal [Mid-16C. < Latin (see TORCH)]

torque spanner n a spanner with a gauge attached for regulating the amount of torque applied to a bolt. N Am term **torque wrench**

torr /tawr/ (plural same) n a unit of pressure equal to about 133.3 pascals or one millimetre of mercury supported in a column [Mid-20C. After Evangelista TORRICELLI]

Torre del Greco /tórray del grékō/ coastal city near Naples, southern Italy, at the base of Mount Vesuvius. Population: 90,607 (2001).

torrefy /tórri fī/ (-fies, -fying, -fied) vt to subject something, especially an ore or chemical, to intense heat for the purpose of removing excess water [Early 17C. < French *torréfier* < Latin *torrere* 'scorch'] —**torrefaction** /tórri fáksh'n/ n

Torremolinos /tórrimə leén oss/ major seaside resort in Málaga Province, Andalusia Autonomous Region, southern Spain. Population: 37,235 (1998).

Torrens, Lake /tórrənz/ salt lake in South Australia. The second largest lake in Australia, it is often dry at times of low rainfall. Area: 5,800 sq. km/2,200 sq. mi.

Torrens title /tórrənz-/ n in Australia, a system of registering land ownership in which ownership occurs when the document that transfers the property is lodged at the local land office [Mid-19C. After Sir Robert *Torrens* (1814–84), British administrator]

torrent /tórrənt/ n 1. a fast and powerful rush of liquid, especially water 2. a violent or tumultuous flow ○ *resigned amid a torrent of protest* [Late 16C. < Latin *torrent-* 'hot, rushing' < *torrere* 'scorch']

torrential /tə rénsh'l/ adj 1. flowing or falling fast and in great quantities ○ *torrential rain* 2. intense or abundant ○ *torrential outpouring of emotion* —**torrentially** adv

Torreon /tó ray on, tó ray ón/ city in Coahuila State, northern Mexico, on the Nazas River, main city of the agricultural Laguna District. Population: 529,512 (2000).

Torres Strait /tórriss-/ area of sea lying between the northern tip of Cape York, Australia, and the southern coast of Papua New Guinea

Torres Strait Islands group of about 60 Australian islands located in the Torres Strait. Population: 8,905 (1996).

Torricelli /tórri chélli/, **Evangelista** (1608–47) Italian mathematician and physicist. He invented the barometer and defined atmospheric pressure. A unit of pressure, the torr, is named after him.

torrid /tórrid/ adj 1. FULL OF PASSION full of passion, especially sexual passion 2. SCORCHING HOT describes weather that is hot and dry enough to scorch land 3. SCORCHED describes land that has been scorched by extremely hot and dry weather 4. RAPID rapidly moving ○ *predicted a slowing of the economy from its torrid pace* [Late 16C. Directly or via French < Latin *torridus* < *torrere* 'scorch'] —**torridity** /to ríddəti/ n —**torridly** adv —**torridness** n

Torrid Zone n the region of the Earth that lies between the tropics of Cancer and Capricorn

torsade /tawr saád, -sáyd/ n a decorative twist of beads, cord, or fabric [Late 19C. < French < Latin *tors-* (see TORSION)]

Tórshavn /táwrss hown/ administrative headquarters of the Faeroe Islands. It is situated on the island of Streymoy. Population: 14,000 (1990).

torsi plural of **torso**

torsibility /táwrsə billəti/ n the ability to undergo or resist twisting [Mid-19C. < TORSION]

torsion /táwrsh'n/ n 1. SHAPE CAUSED BY TWISTING the distortion caused by applying torque in opposite directions to each end of an object 2. MECHANICAL STRESS the stress placed on an object that has been twisted 3. TWISTING the twisting of something, or a twisted state [15C. Directly or via French < late Latin *torsion-* < Latin *tors-*, past participle of *torquere* 'twist'] —**torsional** adj —**torsionally** adv

torsion balance n an instrument that measures

small electrical or magnetic forces by the degree of twist they produce in a filament

torsion bar *n* a metal bar that acts as a spring when subjected to torsion, e.g. in a motor vehicle's suspension system

torsk /tawrsk/ (*plural* **torsks** or *same*) *n* a soft-finned sea fish of the cod family. Native to: northern coasts. Latin name: *Brosmius brosme.* N Am term **cusk** [Early 18C. Via Norwegian < Old Norse *þorskr*]

torso /táwrssō/ (*plural* **-sos** or **-si** /-see/) *n* **1.** **UPPER BODY** the upper part of the human body, not including the head and arms **2.** **SCULPTURE** a sculpture of a torso, or a broken statue of a human figure with the head, arms, and legs missing **3.** **SOMETHING WITH PARTS MISSING** something that has parts missing, because it has been mutilated or has not been completed (*literary*) [Late 18C. Via Italian, 'trunk of a statue' < Latin *thyrsus* (see THYRSUS)]

tort /tawrt/ *n* in civil law, a wrongful act for which damages can be sought by the injured party [14C. Via Old French < medieval Latin *tortum* < Latin *torquere* 'to twist']

torte /táwrtə, tawrt/ *n* a very rich cake consisting of layers sandwiched together with a cream filling [Mid-18C. Via German < Italian *torta* 'cake' < late Latin, type of bread]

Tortelier /tawr télli ay/, **Paul** (1914–90) French cellist. He had an international career as a solo performer and was also a skilled teacher.

tortellini /táwrtə leéni/ *npl* small filled pasta that is shaped into rings, boiled, and served in a soup or sauce [Mid-20C. < Italian, plural of *tortellino* 'little cake' < *torta* (see TORTE)]

tort-feasor /táwrt feezər/ *n* somebody who commits a tort [Mid-17C. < Old French *tort-fesor* 'wrong-doer']

torticollis /táwrti kólliss/ *n* a twisting of the neck to one side, resulting in the head being tilted. It can be temporary, caused by muscle spasm, or a permanent result of a structural condition such as a short neck muscle. [Early 19C. < modern Latin < Latin *tortus* 'twisted' + *collum* 'neck'] —**torticollar** *adj*

tortilla /tawr teé ə/ *n* **1.** a thin flat Mexican bread, cooked on a hot griddle and eaten folded, with a filling **2.** FOOD same as **Spanish omelette** [Late 17C. < Spanish < *torta* 'cake' < late Latin, type of bread]

tortilla chip *n* a thin crunchy crisp made of maize meal, often served with dips such as salsa and guacamole

tortillon /tawr tíllyən/ *n* ART same as **stump** (sense 4) [Late 19C. < French < *tortiller* 'to twist' < Latin *torquere*]

tortious /táwrshəss/ *adj* involving or constituting a tort in civil law —**tortiously** *adv*

tortoise

tortoise /táwrtəss/ *n* **1.** a slow-moving land-dwelling reptile with a large dome-shaped shell into which it can retract its head and limbs. Family: Testudinidae. **2.** MIL, ANCIENT HIST same as **testudo** **3.** somebody who moves very slowly [15C. Alteration of obsolete *tortuce* < medieval Latin *tortuca*]

tortoise beetle *n* a brightly coloured beetle that has a flat rounded body and whose larvae eat leaves. Subfamily: Cassidinae.

tortoiseshell /táwrtəss shel/ *n* **1.** **OUTER PART OF TURTLE SHELL** the hard mottled outer layer of the shell of a hawksbill turtle. Use: combs, ornaments, jewellery. **2.** **SYNTHETIC TORTOISESHELL** a synthetic substance made to resemble tortoiseshell **3.** **TYPE OF CAT** a domestic cat with black, cream, and brownish markings **4.** **ORANGE-BROWN BUTTERFLY** a butterfly that has jagged orange-brown wings with black markings. Family: Nymphalidae. **5.** REPT same as **hawksbill** ■ *adj* **MOTTLED YELLOW AND BROWN** with mottled yellow and brown markings

Tortola /tawr tṓlə/ largest of the British Virgin Islands in the eastern Caribbean Sea. Capital: Road Town. Population: 10,556 (1996). Area: 54 sq. km/21 sq. mi.

tortoni /tawr tṓni/ *n* rich Italian ice cream often flavoured with sherry or rum and chopped cherries or almonds [Early 20C. Probably after an Italian café-owner of 18C Paris]

tortricid /táwrtrissid/ *n* a small moth whose larvae live in coiled leaves and are often destructive to plants. Family: Tortricidae. [Late 19C. < modern Latin *Tortrix*, genus name < Latin *tortus* 'twisted']

Tortuga Island /tawr tóogə-/ island off northern Haiti, in the Caribbean. Population: 22,880 (1982). Area: 180 sq. km/69 sq. mi.

tortuosity /táwrtyoo óssəti/ (*plural* **-ties**) *n* **1.** the state of being twisted or crooked **2.** a twist or turn

tortuous /táwrtyoo əss/ *adj* **1.** **TWISTING AND WINDING** with many turns or bends **2.** **INTRICATE** extremely complex or intricate **3.** **DEVIOUS** devious or deceitful [14C. Via Anglo-Norman < Latin *tortuosus* < *torquere* 'to twist'] —**tortuously** *adv* —**tortuousness** *n*

USAGE tortuous or **torturous**? Even though both words come ultimately from the same Latin word, meaning 'to twist', their meanings diverge in English. A mountain pass is ***tortuous*** ('with many turns or bends'), and by figurative extension, a legal argument can be ***tortuous*** ('complex or intricate') as well. A severe illness, and by figurative extension a decision, may be ***torturous*** ('causing anguish').

torture /táwrchər/ *vt* (**-tures, -turing, -tured**) **1.** **INFLICT PAIN ON SOMEBODY** to inflict extreme pain or physical punishment on somebody **2.** **CAUSE SOMEBODY ANGUISH** to cause somebody mental or physical anguish ○ *This headache is torturing me.* **3.** **DISTORT SOMETHING** to twist or distort something into an unnatural form ■ *n* **1.** **INFLICTING OF PAIN** infliction of severe physical pain on somebody, e.g. as punishment or to persuade somebody to confess or recant something **2.** **METHODS OF INFLICTING PAIN** the methods used to inflict physical pain on people **3.** **ANGUISH** mental or physical anguish [Mid-16C. Directly or via French < late Latin *tortura* < Latin *tortus* 'twisted' < *torquere* 'to twist'] —**torturer** *n* —**torturingly** *adv*

torturous /táwrchərəss/ *adj* **1.** inflicting or designed to inflict severe physical pain, e.g. as punishment **2.** causing great physical or mental anguish [15C. < Anglo-Norman < Old French *torture* (see TORTURE)] —**torturously** *adv*

USAGE See ***tortuous.***

torula /tórryələ/ (*plural* **-lae** /-lee/ or **-las**) *n* **1.** *also* **torula yeast** an edible yeast that is cultivated for use as a medicine and food additive. Latin name: *Candida utilis.* **2.** a yeast fungus that does not have sexual spores. Many of them grow on dead vegetation and fermented sugars. Genus: *Torula.* [Mid-19C. < modern Latin < Latin *torus* 'bulge']

torus /táwrəss/ (*plural* **-ri** /-rī/) *n* **1.** MATHS **RING-SHAPED SURFACE** a doughnut-shaped geometric surface generated by rotating a circle about a line in the same plane as the circle but not intersecting it **2.** *also* **tore** ARCHIT **MOULDING** a large convex moulding, especially at the base of a classical column **3.** ANAT **RIDGED BODY PART** a body part in the shape of a rounded ridge or bulge, e.g. the bony ridge below an eyebrow **4.** BOT **FLOWER PART** the receptacle of a flower [Mid-16C. < Latin, 'bulge']

Tory /táwri/ *n* (*plural* **-ries**) **1.** **UK CONSERVATIVE** in the United Kingdom, a member of the Conservative Party **2.** **CANADIAN CONSERVATIVE** in Canada, a member of the Progressive Conservative Party **3.** HIST **ENGLISH ROYALIST** a member of an English political party, active from the late 17th century until the 1830s, that supported the social order represented by the monarchy and the Church of England **4.** *also* **tory** **SUPPORTER OF CONSERVATIVE PRINCIPLES** somebody who holds politically conservative views **5.** HIST **AMERICAN SUPPORTER OF BRITAIN** a resident of the American colonies of Great Britain who supported the British Crown during the War of American Independence in the 18th century **6.** HIST **17C IRISH OUTLAW** in 17th-century Ireland, any of the Irish people who became outlaws harrying the English settlers who had displaced and dispossessed them ■ *adj* **1.** **CONSERVATIVE** relating to, belonging to, or supporting any Conservative Party **2.** *also* **tory** **VERY CONSERVATIVE** politically conservative or reactionary [Mid-17C. Via Irish *tóraidhe* 'highwayman' < Old Irish *tóir* 'to chase'] —**Toryism** *n*

ORIGIN In English, ***Tory*** originally denoted an Irish guerrilla, one of a group of Irishmen who in the 1640s were thrown off their property by the British and took to a life of harrying and plundering the British occupiers. In the 1670s, it was applied as a term of abuse to Irish Catholic royalists, and then more generally to supporters of the Catholic James II, and after 1689 it came to be used for the members of the British political party that had at first opposed the removal of James and his replacement with the Protestants William and Mary.

Toscanini /tóskə neeni/, **Arturo** (1867–1957) Italian-born conductor. He was conductor at La Scala opera house, Milan, and the Metropolitan Opera, New York, and also conducted the NBC Symphony Orchestra (1937–57).

> 'Can't you read? The score demands *con amore*, and what are you doing? You are playing it like married men!'
> [Attributed to Arturo Toscanini]

tosh /tosh/ *n* nonsense or foolishness (*informal*) [Mid-19C. Origin ?]

toss /toss/ *v* (**tosses, tossing, tossed**) **1.** *vt* **LIGHTLY THROW SOMETHING** to throw something small or light in a casual or careless way ○ *tossed the letter on the table* **2.** *vt* **THROW SOMEBODY OR SOMETHING OUT** to get rid of somebody or something (*informal*) ○ *tossed them out of her office* ○ *Just toss it; we don't need it.* **3.** *vti* **THROW, OR BE THROWN, REPEATEDLY** to be thrown repeatedly up and down or to and fro, or throw something in this way ○ *tossed by the waves* **4.** *vti* **THROW COIN** to throw a coin upwards, usually spinning it with the thumb on the way, the side it falls on being a way of deciding between two options **5.** *vt* **MIX SOMETHING** to mix something, especially a salad with its dressing, by lifting and turning its parts rather than by stirring **6.** *vt* RIDING **THROW RIDER** to throw the rider off a horse's back **7.** *vt* **THROW SOMEBODY OR SOMETHING UPWARDS** to hurl somebody or something upwards with apparent ease **8.** *vt* **JERK HEAD UPWARDS** to jerk the head upwards, e.g. in a gesture of anger or impatience **9.** *vi* **MOVE RESTLESSLY** to move about restlessly, especially while sleeping **10.** *vi* **MOVE QUICKLY** to move abruptly, e.g. in anger ■ *n* **1.** **THROWING** an act of throwing somebody or something **2.** **DECIDING THROW OF COIN** an act of spinning a coin in the air in order to decide between two options **3.** **HEAD JERK** an abrupt jerk of the head [Early 16C. Origin ?] ◇ **argue the toss** to take part in a prolonged argument, especially in disputing a decision ◇ **not give a toss** not to care in the least (*informal*)

SYNONYMS See ***throw.***

toss off *v* **1.** *vt* **DO SOMETHING QUICKLY** to do something quickly and easily **2.** *vt* **DRINK SOMETHING QUICKLY** to drink something quickly, often in one gulp **3.** *vti* **TABOO TERM** a highly offensive term meaning to masturbate, or masturbate somebody (*taboo*)

tosser /tóssər/ *n* an offensive term for a person, especially a man, regarded as unintelligent or contemptible (*slang*) [Mid-20C. < TOSS OFF]

tosspot /tóss pot/ *n* **1.** an offensive term for somebody regarded as inferior or unintelligent (*slang insult*) **2.** a drunken person (*archaic or literary*)

toss-up *n* **1.** a throw of a coin into the air that decides, by which side it falls on, between two options **2.** an even risk or chance

tostada /to staádə/, **tostado** /to staádō/ *n* a crisply fried Mexican-style tortilla, usually served with several meat and vegetable toppings, grated cheese, and hot sauce [Mid-20C. < Spanish < past participle of *tostar* 'toast']

tot[1] /tot/ *n* **1.** a small child (*informal*) **2.** a small amount of something, especially alcoholic spirit [Early 18C. Origin ?]

tot[2] /tot/ (**tots, totting, totted**) [Mid-18C. Shortening of TOTAL, or < Latin *tot* 'this number, so many']
tot up *v* **1.** *vi* to grow larger in amount or amount to a large total **2.** *vt* to add several amounts together to arrive at a total

total /tṓt'l/ *n* SUM the sum of several amounts added or considered together ■ *adj* **1.** OVERALL with everything added or considered together ○ *the total price* **2.** USED FOR EMPHASIS used to emphasize how good, bad, or complete something is ○ *a total success* ■ *vt* (**-tals, -talling, -talled**) **1.** ADD THINGS TOGETHER to add several amounts together to arrive at a total **2.** AMOUNT TO TOTAL to amount to a particular total when added or considered together ○ *The numbers totalled in the hundreds.* **3.** *N Am* KILL SOMEBODY OR DESTROY SOMETHING to kill, destroy, wreck, or demolish somebody or something (*slang*) [14C. Via French < medieval Latin *totalis* < Latin *totus* 'entire']

total eclipse *n* an eclipse in which the entire surface of an astronomical object such as the Sun or the Moon is obscured

total football *n* a style of football in which players' positions are interchangeable as part of a general method of attack. This playing style was developed by the Dutch national team of the 1970s.

total heat *n* PHYS same as **enthalpy**

total internal reflection *n* the complete reflection of a light ray at the boundary of the medium in which it is travelling, when the angle of incidence exceeds the critical angle

totalisator *n* GAMBLING another spelling of **totalizator** (sense 2)

totalise, etc. *vt* ACCT another spelling of **totalize, etc.**

totaliser /tṓtə līzər/ *n* GAMBLING same as **totalizator** (sense 2)

totalitarian /tō tálli táiri ən/ *adj* relating to or operating a centralized government system in which a single party without opposition rules over political, economic, social, and cultural life [Early 20C. < TOTALITY after AUTHORITARIAN] —**totalitarian** *n* —**totalitarianism** *n*

totality /tō tálləti/ (*plural* **-ties**) *n* **1.** COMPLETENESS the state of being complete or total **2.** TOTAL AMOUNT the sum or total amount of something **3.** ASTRON FULLNESS OF ECLIPSE the stage of an eclipse at which light is completely obscured

totalizator /tṓtə līˈ zaytər/, **totalisator** *n* **1.** GAMBLING same as **tote**[2] **2.** a machine that records bets, odds, and totals, and calculates winnings in the tote betting system [Late 19C. After French *totalisateur*]

totalize /tṓtə līz/ (**-izes, -izing, -ized**), **totalise** (**-ises, -ising, -ised**) *vt* to add several amounts to make a total —**totalization** /tṓtə līˈ záysh'n/ *n*

totalizer /tṓtə līzər/, **totaliser** *n* GAMBLING same as **totalizator** (sense 2)

totally /tṓt'li/ *adv* **1.** in a complete or utter way **2.** used to emphasize how good, bad, or complete something is (*informal*) ○ *I totally hate this!*

total recall *n* the ability to remember accurately in every detail

total reflection *n* PHYS same as **total internal reflection**

totaquine /tṓtə kween/ *n* a mixture of quinine and other alkaloids from cinchona bark. Use: treatment of malaria. [Mid-20C. < modern Latin *totaquina* < Latin *totus* 'whole' + Spanish *quina* 'cinchona bark']

totara /tṓtərə/ *n* a tall coniferous tree that produces dark-red, durable but light wood. Native to: New Zealand. Latin name: *Podocarpus totara*. [Mid-19C. < Maori *tótara*]

tote[1] /tōt/ *vt* (**totes, toting, toted**) (*informal*) **1.** CARRY SOMETHING to carry or haul something, especially something heavy **2.** HAVE SOMETHING ON YOUR PERSON to carry something, especially a gun, on your person ■ *n* **1.** HEAVY LOAD a heavy load that is hauled or carried **2.** SOFT BAG a large soft bag with handles [Late 17C. Origin ?] —**toter** *n*

tote[2] /tōt/ *n* a system of betting on horse races using an electronic machine that totals all bets, deducts management charges and taxes, and determines the final odds and payouts (*informal*) [Late 19C. Shortening of TOTALIZATOR]

---

tote bag *n* CLOTHING same as **tote**[1] *n* (sense 2)

totem /tṓtəm/ *n* **1.** IMPORTANT TRIBAL OBJECT an object, animal, plant, or other natural phenomenon revered as a symbol of a clan or society, and often used in rituals among some peoples **2.** CARVING a carving or other representation of a totem **3.** SYMBOLIC THING something regarded as a symbol, especially something treated with the kind of respect normally reserved for religious icons [Mid-18C. < Ojibwa *nin-doodem* 'my totem'] —**totemic** /tō témmik/ *adj*

totemism /tṓtəmizəm/ *n* **1.** the use of totems as symbols of kinship **2.** the organizing of societies into groups whose members share a common totem —**totemist** *n* —**totemistic** /tṓtə místik/ *adj*

totem pole

totem pole *n* **1.** among some Native North American peoples, a tall wooden pole carved with totems that symbolize family and historical relationships **2.** *N Am* a hierarchy, e.g. in a company or organization (*informal*)

tother /túthər/, **t'other** *adj, pron* the or that other (*informal*) [14C. Contraction of *the other*]

totipalmate /tṓti pál mayt/ *adj* describes birds such as pelicans and cormorants that have all four toes webbed [Late 19C. < Latin *totus* 'whole'] —**totipalmation** /tṓti pal máysh'n/ *n*

totipotent /tō típpətənt/ *adj* describes a cell that is capable of generating new tissue, organs, or individuals, e.g. a fertilized ovum [Early 20C. < Latin *totus* 'whole'] —**totipotency** *n*

tot lot *n* *N Am* a playground for young children (*informal*)

totsiens /tót séens/ *interj* *S Africa* used as a friendly farewell greeting (*informal*) [Mid-20C. < Afrikaans, 'till seeing']

totter /tóttər/ *vi* (**-ters, -tering, -tered**) **1.** WALK UNSTEADILY to move or walk unsteadily **2.** WOBBLE to sway or wobble as if about to fall **3.** BE UNSTABLE to be unstable or on the point of collapse ○ *an economic system tottering on the brink of collapse* ■ *n* WOBBLING GAIT a wavering or wobbling gait [13C. Origin ?] —**totterer** *n* —**tottering** *adj* —**totteringly** *adv* —**tottery** *adj*

tottie /tótti/, **totty** *n* an offensive term that deliberately insults a woman or women collectively regarded only as objects for sexual pleasure (*slang*) ■ *adj* *regional* very small [Early 19C. < TOT[1]]

REGIONAL NOTE See *itsy-bitsy*.

---

totting /tótting/ *n* the salvaging of items from rubbish for reuse or sale [Late 19C. < obsolete *tot* 'bone, rubbish', origin ?]

toucan

---

toucan /tóokən/ (*plural* **-cans** or *same*) *n* a fruit-eating bird with bright feathers and a very large curved beak. Native to: tropical Central and South America. Family: Ramphastidae. [Mid-16C. Via French < Portuguese *tucano* < Tupi *tucan*]

touch /tuch/ *v* (**touches, touching, touched**) **1.** *vti* PUT BODY IN CONTACT WITH SOMETHING to put a part of the body, especially the fingertips, in contact with something so as to feel it **2.** *vti* BE OR PUT SOMETHING IN CONTACT to be in physical contact with an object, or bring something into physical contact with an object ○ *so that the ends are just touching* **3.** *vt* PRESS SOMETHING LIGHTLY to apply the slightest pressure to something ○ *You only have to touch the brake.* **4.** *vt* INTERFERE WITH SOMETHING to interfere with or disturb something by handling it ○ *told the kids not to touch anything on my desk* **5.** *vt* HAVE EFFECT ON SOMEBODY OR SOMETHING to have an effect or influence on somebody or something ○ *events that touched all our lives* **6.** *vt* AFFECT SOMEBODY EMOTIONALLY to affect somebody emotionally, usually arousing gratitude, affection, pity, or compassion ○ *Your concern for my welfare touches me greatly.* **7.** *vt* CONSUME SOMETHING to consume something, especially food or drink, or otherwise make use of something ○ *You've hardly touched your meal.* **8.** *vt* HAVE DEALINGS WITH SOMETHING to have dealings or become involved with something ○ *Don't touch that issue; it's very controversial.* **9.** *vt* MATCH SOMEBODY OR SOMETHING to come close to somebody or something in level of excellence ○ *Others may have more technique, but nobody can touch her style.* **10.** *vt* APPROACH LEVEL to approach or reach a level ○ *profits touching 2 billion* **11.** *vt* APPROACH SOMEBODY FOR MONEY to ask somebody for a loan or gift of money (*informal*) ■ *n* **1.** CONTACT MADE a coming into contact with a part of the body ○ *felt the touch of her hand on my face* **2.** LIGHT STROKE a light pushing or pressing stroke **3.** FEELING SENSE the sense by which the texture, shape, and other qualities of objects are felt through contact with parts of the body, especially the fingertips ○ *the sense of touch* **4.** FELT QUALITIES the particular quality or combination of qualities experienced through the sensation of touch **5.** SMALL AMOUNT a small but noticeable amount ○ *a touch of malice in her voice* **6.** DETAIL a detail that adds to or completes something **7.** DISTINCTIVE STYLE a distinctive style or general facility in doing something ○ *a sure touch* **8.** ATTACK OF ILLNESS a mild attack of an illness or disease ○ *a touch of bronchitis* **9.** COMMUNICATION the fact of getting into communication, or the state of being in communication ○ *I completely lost touch with my brother.* ○ *Keep in touch.* ○ *I'll get in touch with them if I find anything out.* **10.** ACQUIESCING PERSON somebody considered in terms of his or her willingness to do, allow, or give something, usually money (*informal*) ○ *He's always been a soft touch.* **11.** REQUEST FOR MONEY an act of asking for money, or a sum of money given (*informal*) **12.** AREA OUT OF PLAY in some team sports, the area beyond the touchlines in which the ball is out of play **13.** FENCING FENCING SCORE in competitive fencing, a scoring hit delivered to a specific part of an opponent's body [13C. Via Old French *to(u)chier* < assumed Vulgar Latin *toccare* 'to strike'] —**touchable** *adj* —**toucher** *n* ◇ **a touch** somewhat

touch down *v* **1.** *vi* to land in an aircraft or spacecraft **2.** *vt* in rugby, to touch the ball to the ground, either in scoring a try or when behind your own goal line as a way of forcing a restarting of play

touch off *vt* **1.** to make something explode, especially by touching it with a flame or smouldering match **2.** to make something begin, especially something that is difficult to control ○ *touched off a bitter disagreement between them*

touch on, touch upon *v* **1.** to write or talk about something briefly during the course of a discussion ○ *The report only touches on the financial implications.* **2.** to come close to a particular quality, state, or condition ○ *a sympathetic attitude touching on pity*

touch up *vt* **1.** IMPROVE SOMETHING to make slight improvements to something, e.g. with paint ○ *touched up the photograph* **2.** FALSIFY SOMETHING to make changes to something, especially a photograph, so that it is no longer an accurate representation (*disapproving*) **3.** CARESS SOMEBODY to fondle somebody sexually (*slang*)

touch-and-go /adj/ highly uncertain or unpredictable (*not hyphenated after a verb*) ○ *a touch-and-go situation*

touchback /túchbak/ *n* in American football, a play in which the defence recovers and downs a ball that has been kicked or passed into its end zone

touchdown /túch down/ *n* **1. LANDING** a landing made by an aircraft or spacecraft, or the precise moment when it lands **2. TOUCHING BALL ON GROUND** in rugby, a touching of the ball on the ground that scores a try **3. SCORING PLAY** in American football, a scoring of six points achieved by being in possession of the ball behind an opponent's goal line ■ *adj* **OFFERING PHONE AND COMPUTER ACCESS** offering computer and telephone connections and Internet access to visitors and business travellers ○ *touchdown facilities*

touché /tŏŏ shay/ *interj* **1.** a word used to acknowledge that somebody has made an especially witty, penetrating, or cogent remark, usually in retaliation **2.** in fencing, a word used to acknowledge that an opponent has made a scoring hit [Early 20C. < French, past participle of *toucher* 'touch' < Old French *touchier* (see TOUCH)]

touched /tucht/ *adj* **1. AFFECTED EMOTIONALLY** affected emotionally, especially with gratitude, affection, pity, or compassion **2. MODIFIED BY SOMETHING** slightly marked or modified by something ○ *blonde hair touched with grey* **3. OFFENSIVE TERM** an offensive term meaning unable to behave in a reasonable or conventional way

touch football *n* an informal noncompetitive version of American football in which touching replaces tackling

touchhole /túch hōl/ *n* the opening in the breech of an early cannon or gun where a flame or smouldering material was applied to set off the gunpowder

touching /túching/ *adj* causing feelings of warmth, sympathy, and tenderness ■ *prep* concerning or relating to something —**touchingly** *adv* —**touchingness** *n*

SYNONYMS See *moving*.

touch-in-goal *n* the area at each end of a rugby pitch, between the goal line and the dead-ball line, where the ball may be touched down to score a try

touch judge *n* in rugby, either of the two assistant referees whose main task is to decide when and where the ball has gone into touch

touchline /túch līn/ *n* especially in rugby or football, either of the lines that mark the side boundaries of a playing area

touchmark /túch maark/ *n* a mark stamped on something made of pewter that identifies the maker

touch-me-not *n* **1.** a flowering plant with seed pods that burst open if touched when they are ripe. Genus: *Impatiens*. N Am term **jewelweed 2.** *US* PLANTS same as **sensitive plant** (sense 1)

touch pad *n* **1.** an electronic device on which somebody can choose options by touching the display, e.g. an input device in a computer system or a control panel on a microwave oven **2.** a small flat stationary surface on a laptop computer which a user touches to move the cursor

touchpaper /túch paypər/ *n* paper soaked in saltpetre that is lit to set off gunpowder, especially used for the part of a firework that is lit

touch screen *n* an input device that allows a user to choose options and commands on a computer by touching the screen

touchstone /túch stōn/ *n* **1.** a standard by which something is judged **2.** a hard black stone formerly used to test the purity of gold and silver according to the colour of the streak left when the metal was rubbed against it

touch-tone *adj* describes a type of telephone with keys that produce tones when pressed, each of which is decoded as a number at the telephone exchange

touch-type *vi* to type without having to look at the keyboard —**touch-typist** *n*

touch-up *n* **1.** a slight improvement to something such as makeup or paintwork **2.** an alteration, especially one made to cover up or repair a flaw

touchwood /túch wŏŏd/ *n* dry decayed wood that can be used as tinder

touchy /túchi/ (**-ier, -iest**) *adj* **1. EASILY UPSET** liable to become or make somebody angry or upset ○ *a touchy subject* **2. TRICKY** needing care or tact to prevent an undesirable outcome **3. FLAMMABLE** easily catching fire —**touchily** *adv* —**touchiness** *n*

touchy-feely /-feéli/ *adj* (*informal disapproving*) **1.** physically and emotionally demonstrative to an extent that makes some people feel uncomfortable **2.** encouraging open expression of emotions to an extent that makes some people feel uncomfortable

tough /tuf/ *adj* **1. DIFFICULT** physically or mentally challenging ○ *That's a tough question.* ○ *It's a tough climb to the peak.* **2. VERY STRONG** physically or mentally strong and possessing great endurance ○ *Is he tough enough to make the climb?* **3. RESOLUTE** having or showing firm resolve ○ *She's a tough person to negotiate with.* **4. DURABLE** able to withstand much use, strain, or wear without breaking, tearing, or other damage ○ *boots made of tough leather* **5. HARD TO CHEW OR CUT** not easily chewed or cut ○ *This steak is pretty tough.* **6. THREATENING** characterized by antisocial behaviour, crime, and social deprivation ○ *a tough neighbourhood* **7. SEVERE** involving or inflicting severe punishment or strict rules ○ *the police policy of being tough on drink-driving* **8. UNFORTUNATE** not fair or reasonable (*informal*) ○ *It was a tough choice to be offered.* ■ *n* **THUG** an aggressive or antisocial person ■ *adv* **AGGRESSIVELY** in an aggressive way that is intended to be perceived as strength and fearlessness (*informal*) ○ *acting tough* ■ *interj* **BAD LUCK!** used to say that something is unfortunate but cannot be helped and is of no concern to the speaker [Old English *tōh* < Germanic] —**toughly** *adv* ◇ **tough it out** to be strong and resilient during a time of difficulty (*informal*)

SYNONYMS See *hard*.

toughen /túff'n/ (**-ens, -ening, -ened**) *vti* **1. MAKE OR BECOME MORE SEVERE** to become stricter or more severe, or make somebody or something so **2. MAKE OR BECOME STRONGER** to become more resolute, hardier, or physically or emotionally stronger, or make somebody so **3. MAKE OR BECOME TOUGHER** to become less easy to cut or chew or less liable to wear or damage, or make something so —**toughener** *n*

toughie /túffi/ *n* (*informal*) **1.** something that is difficult to deal with **2.** a tough person, especially a child, regarded with some affection or amusement because he or she is rather self-assertive and resilient

tough love *n* a caring but strict attitude adopted towards a friend or loved one with a problem, as distinct from an attitude of indulgence

tough-minded *adj* able to face hardship and misfortunes in a realistic, determined, and unsentimental way —**tough-mindedly** *adv* —**tough-mindedness** *n*

toughness /túffnəss/ *n* **1.** the fact or quality of being tough **2.** the resistance of a metal to breaking under repeated twisting and bending forces, measured in kilojoules

Toulon /too lón/ city, port, and naval base in southeastern France, on the Mediterranean Sea. Population: 160,639 (1999).

Toulouse /too loóz/ capital city of Haute-Garonne Department, Languedoc-Roussillon Region, southern France. Population: 390,350 (1999).

Toulouse-Lautrec /too loóz lō trék/, **Henri de** (1864–1901) French artist. He is noted especially for his portraits, paintings of Paris nightlife, and posters advertising Parisian artists. Full name **de Toulouse-Lautrec, Henri Marie Raymond**

toun /toon/ *n* **1.** *also* **toon** same as **town** (*regional*) **2.** *Scotland* a farm, including all of its buildings and land [Old English *tūn* (see TOWN)]

toupee /too pay/ *n* a wig or partial wig worn to cover a bald area [Early 18C. Alteration of French *toupet* 'tuft of hair' < Germanic, 'topknot']

tour /toor, tawr/ *n* **1. PLEASURE TRIP** a journey visiting several places, usually taken for pleasure **2. PER-**

Henri de Toulouse-Lautrec

FORMING TRIP a long series of performances in different places, e.g. by a rock band or a theatre company ○ *The band are on tour at the moment.* **3. TEAM TRIP** a series of games or tournaments played by the same sports team in different locations **4. BRIEF TRIP TO SEE SOMETHING** a short trip or visit for the purpose of viewing or inspecting something **5. PERIOD OF DUTY** a period of military duty, especially in a specific place or for a fixed length of time ■ *vti* (**tours, touring, toured**) **MAKE TOUR** to take part in a tour [14C. Via Old French < Latin *tornus* 'lathe']

touraco /toórə kō/ (*plural* **-cos**), **turaco** *n* a bird with brightly coloured feathers and a long tail, which is a weak flyer and hops from branch to branch. Native to: Africa. Family: Musophagidae. [Mid-18C. Via French < a W African language]

tour de force /toor də fáwrss, táwr-/ (*plural* **tours de force** /*pronunc. same*/) *n* something done with supreme skill or brilliance [Early 19C. < French, 'feat of strength']

Touré /toor ay/, **Sékou** (1922–84) president of Guinea (1958–84). He campaigned for Guinea's independence from French rule and became the country's first president. Full name **Touré, Ahmed Sékou**

'We, for our part, have a first and indispensable need, that of our dignity. Now, there is no dignity without freedom.... We prefer freedom in poverty to riches in slavery.'
[Sékou Touré. Quoted in *Sékou Touré's Guinea: An Experiment in Nation Building*, Ladipo Adamolekun; 1976]

tourer /toórər, táw-/ *n* a convertible car designed for long-distance leisure driving

Tourette syndrome /toor rét-/, **Tourette's syndrome** *n* a condition in which somebody experiences multiple tics and twitches and utters involuntary vocal grunts and obscene speech [Late 19C. After Gilles de la Tourette (1857–1904), French neurologist]

touring car /toóring-/ *n* a convertible car, popular in the 1920s, designed for long-distance leisure driving

touring company *n* a theatre company that takes part in performing tours rather than performing solely in one venue

tourism /toórizəm, táw-/ *n* **1. TRAVEL FOR PLEASURE** the activity of travelling for pleasure **2. TRAVEL BUSINESS** the business of arranging travel and travel services for people **3. TRAVEL TO OBTAIN SERVICE** travel to benefit from a particular service or activity that is unavailable at home (*usually used in combination*) ○ *health tourism*

tourist /toórist, táw-/ *n* **1. TRAVELLER FOR PLEASURE** a traveller who visits places away from home for pleasure **2. MEMBER OF TOURING TEAM** a member of a sports team that is making a playing tour **3. TRAVELLER FOR PERSONAL ADVANTAGE** somebody who travels in order to take advantage of a particular service or benefit that is not available at home ○ *a health tourist* **4. TRAVEL** same as **tourist class** ■ *adj* **FOR OR OF TOURISTS** provided for or suitable for tourists, e.g. in being cheap or exploitatively priced ■ *adv* **TOURIST CLASS** in tourist class —**touristic** /toor rístik, taw-/ *adj*

tourist class *n* the cheapest class of accommodation on an aircraft or ship

touristed /toóristəd/ *adj* visited by a large number of tourists ○ *one of the world's most touristed cities*

tourist trap *n* a place that is popular with tourists but where, as a result, the prices of goods and services are higher than average

touristy /tóoristi, táw-/ *adj* **1.** relating or appealing to tourists (*informal*) **2.** unpleasantly full of tourists (*informal disapproving*)

tourmaline /tóormə leen, túr-/ *n* a hard, variously coloured crystalline borosilicate mineral. Use: electronics, optics, gems. [Mid-18C. < Sinhalese *tōramalli* 'cornelian'] —**tourmalinic** /tóormə línnik, túr-/ *adj*

Tournai /toor náy/ city in Hainault Province, southwestern Belgium. Population: 67,611 (1999).

tournament /tóornəmənt, táwr-/ *n* **1. SERIES OF GAMES** a sports event made up of a series of games, rounds, or contests **2. MOCK FIGHTING** a sporting contest popular in the Middle Ages in which knights took part in jousting or combat, generally with blunted weapons **3. MILITARY SHOW** a military show with competitions [12C. < Old French *torneiement* 'act of jousting' < *torneier* (see TOURNEY)]

tournedos /tóornə dō/ (*plural same*) *n* a small round cut of fillet steak [Late 19C. < French < *tourner* 'to turn' + *dos* 'back']

~~tournement~~ incorrect spelling of **tournament**

tourney /tóorni, túr-, táwr-/ *n* (*plural* **-neys**) HIST same as **tournament** (sense 2) ■ *vi* (**-neys, -neying, -neyed**) to take part in a medieval tournament [13C. Via Old French *torneier* 'to joust, tilt' < Latin *tornare* 'to turn'] —**tourneyer** *n*

tourniquet /tóorni kay, táwr-/ *n* a tight encircling band applied around an arm or leg in an emergency to stop severe arterial bleeding that cannot be controlled in any other way [Late 17C. < French]

tour of duty *n* MIL same as **tour** *n* (sense 5)

tour operator *n* a person or company that organizes package holidays

tour representative, tour rep *informal n* a representative of a tour operator available to assist its customers at a holiday destination

Tours /toor, toorz/ capital city of Indre-et-Loire Department, Centre Region, west-central France. Population: 132,820 (1999).

tousle /tówz'l/ *vt* (**-sles, -sling, -sled**) to make hair or fur tangled or ruffled ■ *n* a tangled mass of something, especially hair or fur [15C. < obsolete and dialect *touse* 'pull, handle roughly' < Germanic] —**tousled** *adj*

Toussaint L'Ouverture /tóo saN loov air chóor, -tür/, **François Dominique** (1743–1803) Haitian general and independence leader. Born into slavery, he was active in the movement that led to its abolition in Haiti (1791). The effective ruler of Haiti from 1797, he was captured by the French in 1802. Born **Toussaint, François Dominique**

> 'In overthrowing me, you have cut down in San Domingo only the trunk of the tree of liberty. It will spring up again by the roots for they are numerous and deep.'
> [François Dominique Toussaint L'Ouverture, *The Black Jacobins*, C. L. R. James; 1938]

tout /towt/ *v* (**touts, touting, touted**) **1.** *vt* **PRAISE SOMEBODY OR SOMETHING** to praise or recommend somebody or something enthusiastically (*usually passive*) ○ *was touted as the next champion* **2.** *vi* **ATTRACT CUSTOMERS** to try to attract customers or support, especially in an aggressive or persistent way ○ *street traders touting for business* **3.** *vt* **TRY TO SELL SOMETHING** to advertise or offer something for sale ○ *tout merchandise on the Internet* **4.** *vi* **SPY ON RACEHORSES** to spy on racehorses in training to get information to sell to betters **5.** *vti* **SELL INFORMATION ABOUT RACEHORSES** to sell information about racehorses to betters ■ *n* **1. SOMEBODY WHO SELLS INFORMATION ABOUT RACEHORSES** somebody who obtains information about racehorses and sells it to betters **2. AGGRESSIVE SELLER** an aggressive salesperson **3.** BUSINESS same as **ticket tout** [14C. Ultimately < Germanic, 'poke out, project'] —**touter** *n*

tout à fait /tóot aa fáy/ *adv* in a complete or thorough manner [< French]

tout court /tóo kóor/ *adv* without qualification or additional information [< French, 'very short']

tout de suite /tóot sweét/ *adv* as quickly as possible [< French, 'completely in succession']

tout ensemble /tóot on sómb'l/ *adv* all together at the same time, or all in all ■ *n* the total appearance or effect of something [Early 18C. < French, 'all together']

tout le monde /tóo lə móNd/ *n* everyone [< French, 'all the world']

tovarish /tə vaárish/, **tovarich** /tə vaárich/, **tovarisch** /tə vaárish/ *n* a friend or comrade, often used as a term of address, especially in the former Soviet Union [Early 20C. < Russian *tovarishch*]

tow[1] /tō/ *vt* (**tows, towing, towed**) **PULL SOMETHING** to pull something such as a barge or a broken-down car along by a rope or chain attached to it ■ *n* **1. ACT OF PULLING SOMETHING ALONG** the act of pulling something along by a rope or chain attached to it **2. STATE OF BEING PULLED ALONG** the state of being towed by a rope or chain **3. ROPE OR CHAIN** a rope or chain used for towing something **4. SOMETHING THAT TOWS** something that tows something else **5. SOMETHING TOWED** something that is towed [Old English *togian* < Indo-European, 'to lead'] —**towable** *adj* ◇ **have** *or* **take somebody in tow 1.** to have somebody following or accompanying you **2.** *US* to act as a protector or guide for somebody

SYNONYMS See *pull*.

tow[2] /tō/ *n* fibres of flax, hemp, or jute, or of a synthetic material such as rayon [Old English *tow-* < Germanic] —**towy** *adj*

towage /tṓ ij/ *n* **1.** the act or process of towing somebody or something, or the state of being towed **2.** a charge made for towing something

towards /tə wáwrdz/, **toward** /tə wáwrd/ *prep* **1. IN PARTICULAR DIRECTION** used to indicate that somebody or something is moving or facing in the direction of somebody or something else ○ *They headed off towards town.* **2. SHORTLY BEFORE** shortly before a particular time ○ *towards midnight* **3. WITH SPECIFIC AUDIENCE INTENDED** with a particular target group in mind ○ *remarks slanted towards those sitting in the front row* **4. REGARDING** concerning or with regard to ○ *his attitude towards her* **5. CONTRIBUTING TO** as a contribution to or means of achieving something ○ *a grant towards the cost of refurbishment* [Old English *tōweardes*]

USAGE towards or **toward**? In British English, ***towards*** is the usual form of the adverb, but in US English ***toward*** is more common. The same principle applies to *afterwards* and to some other adverbs of direction that end in *-wards*, for example *backwards, upwards*, and *westwards*. The word *forward* is a notable exception, being generally preferred to *forwards* both as adjective and adverb in British English.

towbar /tṓ baar/ *n* a rigid metal bar or frame attached to the back of a vehicle and used for towing other vehicles [Mid-20C. < TOW[1]]

towboat /tṓ bōt/ *n* **1.** same as **tug** *n* (sense 3) **2.** *US* a powerful boat with a broad bow, designed for pushing barges on rivers or canals [Early 19C. < TOW[2]]

tow-coloured *adj* having a pale yellow colour like hemp or flax [< TOW[2]]

towel /tów əl/ *n* a usually rectangular piece of absorbent cloth or paper, used to dry the body or objects such as dishes ■ *vti* (**-els, -elling, -elled**) to use a towel to dry somebody or something [13C. < Old French *toaille* < Germanic, 'to wash']

towelette /tów ə lét/ *n N Am* a small moistened piece of paper or cloth used for cleaning the hands and face

towelling /tów əling/ *n* a soft absorbent, usually looped cotton fabric. Use: towels, bathrobes.

tower[1] /tów ər/ *n* **1. TALL BUILDING** a tall structure, sometimes the upper part or a tall part of a building or structure and sometimes a separate building **2. FORTRESS** a building designed to withstand attack **3. CD STAND** a tall wooden, plastic, or metal case in which to store CDs or videos **4. COMPUTER CASE** a tall slim case for the CPU and drives of a computer ■ *vi* (**-ers, -ering, -ered**) **1. BE TALL** to be very high or tall, or much higher or taller than somebody or something else **2. BE SUPERIOR** to be considerably superior to somebody or something [12C. Via Latin *turris* < Greek] ◇ **a tower of strength** somebody who is reliable and supportive (*informal*)

tower[2] /tṓ ər/ *n* somebody or something that tows something such as a vehicle by a rope or chain [Early 17C. < TOW[1]]

tower block /tów ər-/ *n* a tall modern building, especially a residential one

Tower Bridge /tów ər-/ *n* a bridge across the Thames in London, that has a tower at each end and a roadway that can be raised to allow large ships through. It was opened in 1894.

tower crane /tów ər-/ *n* a crane mounted on top of a very high steel frame, used on a building site

tower house /tów ər-/ *n* a tall fortified house, especially one built in Scotland between the 14th and 16th centuries

towering /tów əring/ *adj* **1. HIGH OR TALL** rising very high or standing very tall **2. OUTSTANDING** of the highest quality or importance **3. INTENSE** characterized by extreme or intense emotion or pain ○ *a towering rage* —**toweringly** *adv*

Tower of Babel /tów ər əv báyb'l/ *n* in the Bible, a tower that people started to build too tall, causing God to show his anger by making them speak different languages, which led to the collapse of the project and ultimately to the scattering of people across the world

Tower of London /tów ər-/ *n* a fortress beside the Thames in London, that now displays the British Crown Jewels. Building began in 1078.

tower of silence /tów ər-/ *n* in Zoroastrianism, an open tower in which the dead are exposed to be eaten by vultures, the bones then being deposited in the centre of the tower

tow-haired *adj* having pale yellow hair [< TOW[2]]

towhead /tṓ hed/ *n* **1.** somebody with pale yellow hair **2.** a head that is covered with pale yellow hair [Late 19C. < TOW[2]] —**towheaded** *adj*

towhee /tów hi, tṓ-/ *n* a large long-tailed sparrow that usually feeds on the ground. Native to: North America. Genera: *Pipilo* or *Chlorura*. [Mid-18C. An imitation of the bird's call]

towkay /tów kay/ *n Malaysia* a term of address meaning 'sir' or 'master' [Mid-19C. < Malay *tauke*]

towline /tṓ līn/ *n* TRANSP same as **towrope** [Early 18C. < TOW[1]]

town /town/ *n* **1. LARGE AREA OF BUILDINGS** a densely populated area with many buildings, larger than a village and smaller than a city **2. URBAN AREA** a large urban area, either a town, a city, or a borough **3.** *N Am* POL **UNIT OF LOCAL GOVERNMENT** in parts of the United States and Canada, a unit of local government that is smaller than a county or city **4. LOCAL TOWN** the nearest large town or city, or the town or city in which somebody lives ○ *moving into town* **5. CENTRE OF SETTLED AREA** the centre of a town or city **6. POPULATION OF SETTLED AREA** the people who live in a town ○ *The whole town's talking about it.* **7. NONACADEMIC POPULATION** the permanent residents of a town that has a university, as opposed to the staff and students of the university ○ *town and gown* **8.** ZOOL **PRAIRIE DOG BURROWS** a group of prairie dog burrows [Old English *tūn* 'yard, buildings within an enclosure' < Germanic] —**townish** *adj* ◇ **go to town (on somebody** *or* **something)** to deal with somebody or something with great enthusiasm or thoroughness (*informal*) ◇ **on the town** spending time enjoying the entertainment available in a town or city, especially if a lot of money is spent (*informal*) ◇ **paint the town red** to go out and celebrate, especially by spending a lot of money on entertainment (*informal*)

town-and-gown *adj* relating to a town that contains a large population of students in higher education, especially Oxford or Cambridge

town clerk *n* **1.** in the United Kingdom, the secretary and chief administrative officer of a town before the reorganization of local government in 1974 **2.** in the United States, a public official responsible for such things as keeping the records of a town and issuing licences

town council *n* the people elected or appointed to govern a town

town crier *n* somebody employed by a town, especially in former times, to make public announcements in the streets

townee n same as **townie**

town gas n gas manufactured from coal for domestic and industrial use

town hall n a building that houses the offices of the local administration and often has a public hall that can be used for meetings

townhall clock /tówn hawl-/ n PLANTS same as **moschatel** [< the plant's flower head of five flowers, one on top and four below, that face different directions]

town house n 1. MODERN HOUSE IN SHORT ROW a modern two- or three-storey house, semidetached or in a row of similar houses and with limited garden space 2. OLD TERRACED HOUSE an old terraced house with three or more storeys in a town or city 3. HOUSE IN TOWN a house in a town or city, especially one that belongs to somebody who also has a house in the country

townie /tówni/, **towny** (plural **-ies**), **townee** /tow neé/ n 1. somebody who lives permanently in a town (informal) 2. a nonacademic resident of a town that has a large proportion of its population studying or teaching at a university in the town

townland /tównlənd/ n Ireland 1. an area of land that is a subdivision of a parish, or an area of land consisting of a town and the region around it 2. a land division, used in postal addresses, averaging about 865 hectares/350 acres

town manager n US an official in charge of the administrative activities of a town

town meeting n 1. MEETING OF INHABITANTS a public meeting involving all of the inhabitants of a town 2. US MEETING OF VOTERS a public meeting involving all of the voters of a town, with the authority to make legislative decisions 3. US TELEVISED GATHERING a television programme centring on an issue of national interest, in which people from a town or region ask questions of debaters or speakers o a televised national town meeting on the role of the military in global peacekeeping

town planning n the organized planning and control of the construction or extension of a town. N Am term **urban planning** —**town planner** n

townscape /tówn skayp/ n 1. a view of a town 2. a painting or photograph of an urban scene

townsfolk /tównz fōk/ npl same as **townspeople**

township /tówn ship/ n 1. URBAN SETTLEMENT FOR BLACK PEOPLE in South Africa during the apartheid era, an urban settlement planned for people classed as Black or of mixed ethnic origin, usually with inferior facilities and services 2. VILLAGE a small town or village 3. PARISH formerly, an English parish or subdivision of a parish 4. N Am SUBDIVISION OF COUNTY a subdivision of a county, often serving as a unit of local government 5. US AREA GOVERNED BY TOWN MEETING in some parts of the United States, an area governed by a town meeting 6. Scotland CROFTING COMMUNITY a small community of crofts in the Highlands and Islands 7. N Am 36 SQUARE MILES an area of surveyed public land equal to 36 sections or 36 square miles

townsman /tównzmən/ (plural **-men** /-mən/) n 1. a man who lives in a town 2. a man who lives in the same town as somebody else

townspeople /tównz peep'l/ npl the people who live in a town

Townsville /tównzvil/ city on the eastern coast of Queensland, Australia. It is a commercial and industrial centre. Population: 93,911 (2002 estimate).

townswoman /tównz wŏŏmən/ (plural **-women** /-wimin/) n 1. a woman who lives in a town 2. a woman who lives in the same town as somebody else

towny n another spelling of **townie**

towpath /tó paath/ (plural **-paths** /-paathz/) n a path beside a canal or river for people or animals to walk along, originally as they pulled a barge or boat [Late 18C. < TOW[1]]

towrope /tó rōp/ n a rope used to tow something such as a boat or a broken-down car [Mid-18C. < TOW[1]]

tow truck n ANZ, US same as **breakdown lorry**

tox. abbr SCI toxicology

tox- prefix same as **toxi-** (used before vowels)

toxaemia /tok seémi ə/ n a condition produced by the presence of bacterial toxins in the blood, usually with tissue or organ damage, fever, and severe intestinal upset [Mid-19C. < TOX- + Greek haima 'blood'] —**toxaemic** adj

toxalbumin /toks álbyŏŏmin, -al byŏŏmin/ n a toxic albumin found in some plants and snake venom

toxaphene /tóksə feen/ n a waxy amber-coloured poisonous compound that smells of pine and is used as an insecticide. Formula: $C_{10}H_{10}Cl_8$. [Mid-20C. < TOXI- + shortening of chlorinated camphene]

toxemia n MED US spelling of **toxaemia**

toxi- prefix poison, poisonous o toxigenic [< TOXIC]

toxic /tóksik/ adj 1. INVOLVING SOMETHING POISONOUS relating to or containing a poison or toxin 2. DEADLY causing serious harm or death ■ n POISONOUS SUBSTANCE a poison or toxin [Mid-17C. Via medieval Latin toxicus 'poisoned' < Greek toxikos 'of the bow' (Greek toxikon pharmakon meant 'poison for smearing arrows')] —**toxically** adv

toxicant /tóksikənt/ n a toxic substance, especially one used as a pesticide

toxicity /tok síssəti/ (plural **-ties**) n 1. the degree to which something is poisonous 2. the state of being poisonous to somebody or something

toxico- prefix poison o toxicogenic [< Greek toxikos (see TOXIC)]

toxicogenic /tóksi kō jénnik/ adj BIOL, MED same as **toxigenic**

toxicology /tóksi kólləji/ n the scientific study of poisons, their effects, and their antidotes —**toxicologic** /tóksikə lójjik/ adj —**toxicological** adj —**toxicologically** adv —**toxicologist** n

toxicosis /tóksi kŏssiss/ (plural **-coses** /-kŏsseez/) n the harmful effects of a poison, including any disease caused by toxins

toxic shock syndrome n an acute, potentially fatal circulatory failure, commonly associated with the use of vaginal tampons, which can create conditions promoting the growth of a toxin-producing staphylococcal bacterium

toxigenic /tóksi jénnik/ adj 1. producing poisonous substances 2. caused or produced by a toxin —**toxigenicity** /tóksi níssəti/ n

toxigenomics /tóksi ji nómiks/ n the study of the way in which known and suspected toxicants act at the genetic level (takes a singular verb)

toxin /tóksin/ n 1. a poison produced by a living organism 2. a substance that accumulates in the body and causes it harm o drinking plenty of water to eliminate toxins [Late 19C. < TOXIC]

toxin-antitoxin n a mixture containing a toxin and slightly less of its antitoxin. Use: formerly, vaccines.

toxocariasis /tóksō kə rí əssiss/ n an infestation of the larvae of a roundworm arising in human beings from worm eggs picked up from contaminated soil or domestic pets [Mid-20C. < alteration of TOXI- + Greek kara 'head']

toxoid /tók soyd/ n a preparation of an inactive toxin that can stimulate antibody production in the toxin. Use: vaccines. [Early 20C. < shortening of TOXIN]

toxophilite /tok sóffi līt/ n an archer or archery enthusiast (humorous) [Late 18C. < Toxophilus, 'lover of the bow', title of a work (1545) by Roger Ascham] —**toxophily** n

toxoplasma /tóksō plázmə/ n a microscopic protozoan organism that lives as a parasite in the organs of vertebrates, especially birds and mammals, and can cause disease. Genus: Toxoplasma. [Early 20C. < alteration of TOXI-] —**toxoplasmic** adj

toxoplasmosis /tóksō plaz mŏssiss/ (plural **-moses** /-mŏsseez/) n a disease of mammals caused by a toxoplasma transmitted to humans via undercooked meat or through contact with infectious animals, especially cats

toy /toy/ n 1. THING TO PLAY WITH something meant to be played with, especially by children 2. REPLICA a replica of a real object, used for playing with or as an ornament 3. SOMETHING ENJOYABLE TO USE a belonging that gives the owner pleasure to use o He showed us his latest toy, a new DVD player. 4. MINIATURE BREED an animal, especially a dog, that is a miniature version of another animal (used before nouns) o a toy poodle 5. SOMETHING UNIMPORTANT something of little

value or importance ■ adj EASILY DISMISSED regarded as irrelevant or of inferior quality (informal) [14C. Origin ?] —**toyer** n

toy with vt 1. PLAY WITH SOMETHING to play or fiddle with something, especially because of a lack of real interest in it or preoccupation with something else 2. THINK ABOUT SOMETHING to consider doing something 3. TREAT SOMEBODY OR SOMETHING CRUELLY to behave in a cruelly insincere or offhand way towards somebody or something 4. TREAT SOMEBODY INSINCERELY to treat somebody in an insincere or flirtatious way, merely for amusement

TOY abbr ONLINE thinking of you (used in e-mails)

toy boy n an offensive term for a young man who is the lover of an older person

toyi-toyi /tóy toyi/ n S Africa a dance with high steps performed by protesters, accompanied by singing and chanting of slogans [Late 20C. < an African language]

Toynbee /tóyn bee/, **Arnold** (1889–1975) British historian. His masterwork, the 12-volume Study of History (1934–61), treated history as a succession of civilizations rather than of nations. Full name **Toynbee, Arnold Joseph**

> 'Civilization is a movement, not a condition; it is a voyage, not a harbour.'
> [Arnold Toynbee, Reader's Digest; October 1958]

toyon /tóy on/ n an evergreen bush with red berries. Flowers: white. Native to: California. Latin name: Heteromeles arbutifolia. [Mid-19C. < Mexican Spanish tollón]

Toyotomi Hideyoshi /tŏyō tōmi híddə yóshi/ (1536–98) Japanese general. He united Japan in 1590 and coordinated two unsuccessful invasions of Korea (1592 and 1597).

toytown /tóy town/ adj small and not to be taken very seriously, especially in comparison with a full-size or fully effective equivalent o a miniature republic with its own toytown capital and parliament

tp[1], **Tp** abbr MIL troop

tp[2] abbr ONLINE Timor Leste (used in Internet addresses) See table at **domain name**

t.p. abbr PUBL title page

TPA abbr BIOL tissue plasminogen activator

TPC abbr BUSINESS Trade Practices Commission

TPI abbr FIN tax and price index

T-plate n a metal plate, shaped like a letter T, used to strengthen a right-angled joint, e.g. between two beams

TPN abbr BIOCHEM triphosphopyridine nucleotide

Tpr abbr POL Trooper

TPV abbr Aus GOV Temporary Protection Visa

TPWS n a safety system that automatically causes the brakes of a train to be applied if it passes a signal set at danger. Full form **Train Protection and Warning System**

TQM abbr BUSINESS total quality management

tr abbr ONLINE Turkey (used in Internet addresses) See table at **domain name**

TR abbr TELECOM transmit-receive

tr. abbr 1. GRAM transitive 2. LANG, BUSINESS translator 3. PRINTING transpose 4. PRINTING transposition 5. FIN treasurer 6. MUSIC trill 7. MIL troop 8. FIN trust 9. FIN trustee

trabeated /tráybi aytid/, **trabeate** /tráybi ət, -ayt/ adj built using horizontal beams instead of arches [Mid-16C. < Latin trab- 'beam'] —**trabeation** /tráybi áysh'n/ n

trabecula /trə békyŏŏlə/ (plural **-lae** /-lee/) n 1. ANAT ROD-SHAPED SUPPORT IN ORGAN a rod-shaped body part that forms an internal support of an organ and divides it into separate chambers 2. ANAT BAR OF BONY TISSUE a thin bar of bony tissue in spongy bone that, with others, forms a mesh whose interconnecting spaces contain bone marrow 3. BOT ROD-SHAPED CELL a rod-shaped cell or structure that bridges a cavity, e.g. between cells [Mid-19C. < Latin, 'small beam' < trab-'beam'] —**trabecular** adj —**trabeculate** adj

trace[1] /trayss/ n 1. REMAINING SIGN a sign that remains to show the former presence of somebody or some-

thing that is no longer there **2. TINY QUANTITY** a tiny amount of something **3. BARELY DETECTABLE AMOUNT** an amount of something that is detectable, but too small to be quantified **4. FOOTPRINT** a footprint or physical sign of the passage of a person or animal **5.** *N Am* **PATH** a path or track left by people or animals regularly passing **6. LINE MARKING SOMETHING** a line made by a recording instrument, e.g. one drawn by a seismograph or one formed on the screen of a cathode ray tube, or the record made in this way **7. DRAWING** a drawing, especially one made using tracing paper **8. ATTEMPT TO FIND SOMEBODY OR SOMETHING** an attempt to find or follow somebody or something **9.** PSYCHOL same as **engram 10.** MATHS **INTERSECTION** the point of intersection of a line or plane with the surface of a coordinate plane **11.** MATHS **SUM OF DIAGONAL ENTRIES** the sum of the diagonal entries of a square matrix **12.** METEOROL **AMOUNT OF PRECIPITATION** an amount of precipitation that is too small to be recorded by instruments, or the record of such an amount ■ *v* **(traces, tracing, traced) 1.** *vt* **FIND SOMEBODY OR SOMETHING** to find out where somebody or something is or who or what somebody or something was **2.** *vti* **FOLLOW OR BE FOLLOWED** to follow or show the course or series of developments of something, or be able to be followed back in time or to a source **3.** *vti* **COPY SOMETHING** to copy writing, a design, or drawing by putting translucent paper on top of it and drawing the visible outlines on this paper **4.** *vt* **DRAW SOMETHING CAREFULLY** to draw or write something with great care **5.** *vt* **DESCRIBE SOMETHING IN OUTLINE** to give an outline or brief description of something **6.** *vt* ARCHIT **PUT TRACERY ON SOMETHING** to decorate something with tracery **7.** *vi* **CARRY OUT SEARCH** to search through something [13C. Via Old French *tracier* 'make your way' < Latin *trahere* 'to pull'] —**traceability** /tráyssə bílləti/ *n* —**traceable** *adj* —**traceableness** *n* —**traceably** *adv* —**traceless** *adj* —**tracelessly** *adv*

ORIGIN See **trace**².

trace² /trayss/ *n* **1. STRAP WITH WHICH HORSE PULLS SOMETHING** either of the two straps or chains connected to a horse's harness by means of which it pulls something such as a cart (*often used in the plural*) **2. BAR TRANSFERRING MOTION** a hinged bar that enables motion to be transferred from one part of a machine to another **3. FLY-TYING THREAD** in angling, a thread or wire for attaching a fly to a line [14C. < Old French *trais*, plural of *trait* 'strap for harnessing' < Latin *tractus* 'drawing' < *trahere* 'to pull'] ◇ **kick over the traces** to reject restrictions and controls and do something unconventional (*informal*)

ORIGIN The Latin word *tractus* 'drawing', from which **trace** is derived, passed into Old French as *trait* 'pulling, draught', hence 'harness-strap'. English *trait* derives from this. The French plural *trais* was borrowed into English in the 14th century as **trace** 'harness strap'. It also formed the basis of a Vulgar Latin verb that evolved into Old French *tracier*, from which English in the 14th century got the verb **trace**. A noun **trace** was also derived from *tracier*, and this too was acquired by English as **trace**, in the 13th century. At first it denoted a 'path' or 'track'; the modern sense 'remaining sign' did not develop until the 17th century.

trace element *n* **1. ELEMENT PRESENT IN TINY AMOUNT** a chemical element present in minute, but detectable amounts in something such as a metal or ore **2. ELEMENT ESSENTIAL FOR HEALTH** an element that is required in minute amounts for normal growth and development and the functioning of vital enzyme systems, e.g. zinc, iodine, or manganese **3. MINUSCULE AMOUNT** a very tiny amount ○ *only a trace element of truth to that statement*

trace fossil *n* a feature in sedimentary rocks that resulted from the activity of an animal, e.g. a worm cast or footprint

tracer /tráyssər/ *n* **1.** ARMS same as **tracer bullet 2. AMMUNITION ACTING AS TRACER BULLETS** ammunition that has been treated to act as tracer bullets ○ *a gun loaded with tracer* **3.** MED, BIOL same as **tracer element 4. INVESTIGATION OR INVESTIGATOR** an investigation into the whereabouts of something missing such as an item of mail or a cargo shipment, or somebody who carries out such an investigation **5. MAKER OF TRACINGS** somebody or something that makes tracings **6. TRACKING DEVICE** a device that gives out a signal that

can be tracked and followed when attached to a vehicle or person

tracer bullet *n* a bullet that has been treated with chemicals to make it leave a glowing or smoky trail as it flies

tracer element *n* a radioactive element used in experiments so that its movements can be monitored

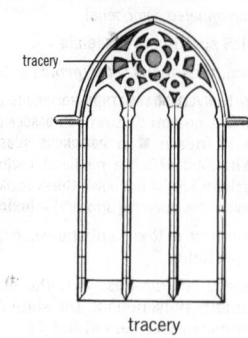

tracery

tracery /tráyssəri/ (*plural* **-ies**) *n* **1.** decorative ribs in windows, especially medieval church windows, and screens **2.** a decorative pattern of interlaced lines, especially one that resembles the form or patterns found in church windows —**traceried** *adj*

trachea /trə keé ə, tráyki ə/ (*plural* **-cheae** /-keé ee/ or **-cheas**) *n* **1.** ANAT same as **windpipe** (*technical*) **2.** ZOOL a tube in insects and related air-breathing invertebrate animals through which air is drawn into the body by the pumping action of the abdominal muscles **3.** BOT a tubular part of water-conducting plant tissue that provides mechanical support and transport of water and nutrients [14C. < medieval Latin < Greek *(artēria) trakheia* 'rough (artery)'] —**tracheal** *adj* —**tracheate** /-ət/ *adj*

tracheid /tráyki id/, **tracheide** *n* a cell in the trachea of conifers and other gymnosperm plants, with bands of lignin thickening the cell walls and adding structural support [Late 19C. < German *Tracheïde* 'something belonging to the trachea'] —**tracheidal** /trə keé id'l, tráyki íd'l/ *adj*

tracheitis /tráyki ítiss/ *n* inflammation of the trachea

tracheo- *prefix* trachea ○ *tracheostomy*

tracheobronchial /tráyki ō bróngki əl/ *adj* relating to or located in both the trachea and the bronchi

tracheole /tráyki ōl/ *n* a fine channel that branches off from an insect's trachea and carries oxygen to its tissues [Early 20C. < TRACHEA]

tracheo-oesophogeal *adj* relating to or located in both the trachea and the oesophagus

tracheophyte /tráyki ō fīt/ *n* a plant that has a system of vascular tissues for conducting water and nutrients through it [Mid-20C. < TRACHEA + Greek *phuton* 'plant']

tracheoscopy /tráki óskəpi/ (*plural* **-pies**) *n* an examination of the inside of the trachea, e.g. using a laryngoscope —**tracheoscopic** /tráki ə skóppik/ *adj*

tracheostomy /tráki óstəmi/ (*plural* **-mies**) *n* **1.** a hole cut in the trachea, e.g. to ensure the airway is unblocked or to suck out secretions **2.** an operation to cut a hole in the trachea

tracheotomy /tráki óttəmi/ (*plural* **-mies**) *n* the making of an incision through the neck into the trachea to assist breathing when the upper airways are blocked

trachoma /trə kṓmə/ *n* a contagious bacterial eye disease in which scar tissue forms inside the eyelid, eventually causing it to curve inwards and the eyelashes to scrape the eye and cause infection [Late 17C. < Greek *trakhōma* 'roughness'] —**trachomatous** /trə kómmətəss, -kṓmə-/ *adj*

trachyte /tráy kīt, trák-/ *n* a fine-grained volcanic rock, characterized by the presence of alkaline feldspar minerals [Early 19C. < Greek *trakhus* 'rough' + -ITE¹] —**trachytoid** /tráki toyd, tráyki-/ *adj*

trachytic /trə kíttik/ *adj* describes igneous rocks in which the crystals are arranged in parallel and show the flow of the molten lava from which they were formed

tracing /tráyssing/ *n* **1.** a copy of something made by putting a sheet of translucent paper on top of it and drawing the visible outlines on this paper **2.** a graphic record made by an instrument such as a seismograph

tracing paper *n* paper through which it is possible to see what is underneath, used for drawing a copy of something underneath

track /trak/ *n* **1. MARK LEFT** a mark left by a moving person, animal, or thing, e.g. a footprint, an animal's paw print, or the mark of a wheel **2. PATH** a path or road, especially one made by the continual passing of people or animals or one specially created for some purpose **3. COURSE OF TRAVEL** the path taken by somebody or something while travelling **4. RAIL STRUCTURE** a rail or pair of parallel rails on which a vehicle, especially a train, runs, along with supporting structures **5. LINE OF ACTION OR THOUGHT** a line of thought or investigation, or a course of action ○ *realized our research was on the wrong track* **6.** SPORTS **RACE COURSE** a course laid out for racing **7.** *N Am* SPORTS same as **athletics** (sense 3) **8.** RECORDING **SEPARATE RECORDING OF MUSIC** a separate piece of music or song on a disc, tape, or record **9.** RECORDING **PATH FOR RECORDING** a separate section of a magnetic tape where the input of a single channel is recorded **10.** RECORDING **RECORDED INPUT** a recording on separate tracks of a magnetic tape that are combined to give a final version, e.g. of a piece of recorded music or a film **11.** RECORDING same as **soundtrack** (sense 1) **12.** COMPUT **SECTION OF COMPUTER DISK** a path on the surface of a storage medium such as a diskette or CD-ROM on which information is recorded and from which recorded information is read. The path is a series of concentric rings on floppy disks and hard files and a spiral on video disks and CD-ROMs. **13.** CINEMA same as **tracking shot 14.** AUTOMOT **TREADS OF TANK OR BULLDOZER** a continuous loop of rubber or metal plates driven by wheels, giving great traction over soft or rough ground, used especially on bulldozers and heavy military vehicles such as tanks **15.** *US* EDUC **COURSE OF STUDY** a course of study tailored to the relative abilities or needs of a student **16.** BUSINESS **CAREER PATH** the course or projected course of a career **17.** MANUF **MOVING ASSEMBLY LINE** a moving belt carrying things along a factory assembly line **18.** HOUSEHOLD **SUPPORTING RAIL** a usually grooved rail along which something moves such as a light fitting or the supporting hooks of a curtain **19.** PHYS **PATH OF PARTICLE** the path taken by a particle of ionizing radiation in a cloud chamber, bubble chamber, or photographic emulsion **20.** ENG **DISTANCE BETWEEN WHEELS** the distance between a pair of wheels, e.g. between the front wheels of a motor vehicle ■ **tracks** *npl* DRUGS **NEEDLE MARKS** marks or scars on the body of a drug user caused by frequent injections (*informal*) ■ *v* **(tracks, tracking, tracked) 1.** *vti* **FOLLOW TRAIL** to follow a trail made by somebody or something, or try to find somebody or something by following a trail left behind **2.** *vti* **FOLLOW PATH** to follow a path through a place **3.** *vt N Am* **MAKE TRACKS WITH MUD ON SOMETHING** to carry something, especially mud, on the shoes or feet and leave it on the surface walked on ○ *tracking mud into the house* **4.** *vt* ELEC ENG **FOLLOW FLIGHT PATH OF SOMETHING** to follow the flight path of a vehicle such as a spacecraft using electronic equipment or radar **5.** *vt* **FOLLOW PROGRESS OF SOMETHING** to follow the progress or development of something **6.** *vti* CINEMA **FILM MOVING OBJECT** to follow and film a moving person or object with a mobile camera **7.** *vi* ENG **ALIGN** to be in alignment or the correct distance apart (*refers to wheels of motor vehicles*) **8.** *vi* RECORDING **FOLLOW GROOVE ON RECORD** to follow the groove on a gramophone record **9.** *vt US* EDUC **ASSIGN SOMEBODY TO COURSE** to assign a student to a course of study tailored to his or her abilities or needs **10.** *vi US* TRAVEL to travel, especially on a long or laborious journey (*informal*) [15C. < French *trac* 'footprint, mark'] —**trackable** *adj* ◇ **cover your tracks** to remove all signs of having been somewhere or done something (*informal*) ◇ **in your tracks** suddenly and immediately, just where somebody or something is or in the middle of what somebody or something is doing (*informal*) ◇ **keep track (of)** to follow, pay attention to, or keep a check on the position or progress of somebody or something ◇ **lose track (of)** to fail to follow or pay attention, or fail to keep an adequate check on the position or progress of somebody or something ◇ **make tracks**

to leave, especially hastily (*informal*) ◇ **off the beaten track** away from the places people usually visit and often difficult to find or get to (*informal*) ○ *The cottage is lovely, but it's a bit off the beaten track.* ◇ **off track** not on the correct or desired path or schedule ◇ **on track** on the correct or desired path or schedule

track down *vt* to find a person, animal, or object by searching or following a trail

trackage /trákij/ *n US* railway tracks collectively

track and field *n N Am* SPORTS same as **athletics** (sense 1)

trackball /trák bawl/ *n* a computer pointing device consisting of a freely rotating ball in a socket with sensors that translate its rotation into movements of an on-screen cursor

tracked /trakt/ *adj* moving on tracks, as a military tank or bulldozer does, or along a fixed track, as a dockside crane does

tracked vehicle *n* a vehicle that is propelled by tracks instead of wheels, e.g. a military tank or a bulldozer

tracker /trákər/ *n* somebody who follows a trail made by another person or an animal, especially in order to guide police, soldiers, or hunters

tracker dog *n* a dog trained to find people who are lost or trying to evade capture by following the trail of their scent

tracker fund *n* an investment fund made up of quantities of all shares listed in a stock market index, whose value automatically follows the market's performance

track event *n* a sports competition that takes place on a running track

trackie daks *npl Aus* another spelling of **trakky daks** (*informal*)

tracking /tráking/ *n* **1.** FOLLOWING OF TRAIL the act or process of following the trail of a person or animal **2.** FUNCTION OF FINDING BEST PICTURE a function on a video player that adjusts the quality of the picture **3.** LEAKING OF CURRENT the leaking of current between two insulated points, e.g. as a result of dampness or dirt **4.** *US* EDUC same as **streaming** (sense 1)

tracking radar *n* a radar system that emits a beam that oscillates about an object being tracked, allowing the system to detect sudden changes of direction

tracking shot *n* a camera shot filmed from a moving dolly, following the movement of somebody or something

tracking station *n* a place from which the movement of something such as a launched missile or a space vehicle can be followed using radar or radio signals

trackless /trákləss/ *adj* **1.** LACKING PATHS containing no trails or paths and therefore extremely isolated **2.** LEAVING NO TRAIL leaving no track or trail **3.** RUNNING WITHOUT RAILS not needing rails on which to run

track light *n* an electric light that can be moved and repositioned anywhere along the length of an electrified track mounted on a wall or ceiling — **track lighting** *n*

trackman /trákmən/ (*plural* **-men** /-mən/) *n US* RAIL same as **platelayer**

track meet *n N Am* an athletics competition in which teams from several places participate in track events

track record *n* **1.** a record of the past performance of a person, organization, or thing (*informal*) **2.** a record set at a specific sports arena, as opposed to a national or international record

track rod *n* the rod that connects the two front wheels of a motor vehicle

track shoe *n* either of a pair of lightweight spiked running shoes

trackside /trák sīd/ *n* the area immediately beside a running track or racetrack

tracksuit /trák soot, -syoot/ *n* a loose-fitting long-sleeved top and matching trousers in knitted nylon or cotton, worn by athletes over their sports clothes and by other people as casual wear

trackwalker /trák wawkər/ *n* somebody employed to inspect railway track

tract[1] /trakt/ *n* **1.** AREA OF LAND OR WATER an unmeasured expanse of land or water, or a measured area, especially of land **2.** GROUP OF ORGANS a system of organs or body parts that work together to provide for the passage of something such as food or bodily waste products **3.** BUNDLE OF NERVES a group of nerve fibres that forms a pathway from one part of the brain or spinal cord to another [15C. < Latin *tractus* 'a drawing out, duration' < *trahere* 'to pull']

tract[2] /trakt/ *n* an anthem sung in some Roman Catholic masses [14C. Via medieval Latin *tractus* < Latin (see TRACT[1])]

tract[3] /trakt/ *n* a pamphlet that sets out a position or an analysis, especially one dealing with a political or religious issue [Pre-12C. < Latin *tractatus* < *tractare* 'to handle' < *trahere* 'to pull']

tractable /tráktəb'l/ *adj* **1.** very easy to control or persuade **2.** very easy to bend or work with [15C. < Latin *tractabilis* < *tractare* (see TRACT[3])] —**tractability** /tráktə bílləti/ *n* —**tractably** *adv*

Tractarianism /trak táiri ənizəm/ *n* CHR same as **Oxford Movement** [Mid-19C. < the tracts distributed] —**Tractarian** *n*, *adj*

tractate /trák tayt/ *n* a treatise or short essay (*formal*) [15C. < Latin *tractatus* (see TRACT[3])]

tract house *n N Am* any of many similar houses built on a tract of land —**tract housing** *n*

tractile /trák tīl/ *adj* able to be stretched into another shape without breaking [Mid-19C. < Latin *tract-*, past participle of *trahere* 'to pull'] —**tractility** /trak tílləti/ *n*

traction /trákshˈn/ *n* **1.** APPLICATION OF WEIGHTS the application of a pulling force for medical purposes, e.g. to reduce a fracture, maintain bone alignment, relieve pain, or prevent spinal injury **2.** FRICTION ALLOWING MOVEMENT the adhesive friction between a moving object and the surface on which it is moving, e.g. between a tyre and the ground, without which the object cannot move **3.** ENG PULLING the act or process of pulling something, especially by means of a motor, or the fact or state of being pulled along **4.** AUTOMOT WAY TO MOVE VEHICLES a means of moving vehicles **5.** WAY TO ACHIEVE PROGRESS a means by which or the degree to which progress can be made [Early 17C. Directly or via French < medieval Latin *traction-* < Latin *tract-*, past participle of *trahere* 'to pull'] —**tractional** *adj*

traction engine *n* a steam-powered road locomotive used for hauling heavy loads by road, as a source of power in fairgrounds, and for ploughing

traction load *n* the coarse-grained fraction of a river's sedimentary load, carried along the riverbed by sliding and rolling

tractive force /tráktiv-/ *n* the force exerted by a tractor or locomotive through a drawbar as it pulls a load

tractor

tractor /tráktər/ *n* **1.** FARM VEHICLE a motor vehicle used for pulling heavy loads, especially on farms, where its large rear wheels enable it to move in fields **2.** FRONT PART OF ARTICULATED LORRY the powered self-contained front section of an articulated lorry, with driving cab, engine, and coupling for trailers **3.** AIRCRAFT WITH PROPELLER IN FRONT an aircraft that has its propeller in front of the engine so that it exerts a pull through the air instead of a pushing force **4.** PROPELLER a propeller at the front of an aircraft engine

5. COMPUT same as **tractor feed** [Late 18C. < Latin *tract-* (see TRACTION)]

ORIGIN The Latin word *trahere* 'to pull, draw', from which *tractor* is derived, is also the source of English *abstract*, *attract*, *contract*, *detract*, *distract*, *extract*, *retract*, *retreat*, *subtract*, *train*, *treat*, *treatise*, and *treaty*.

tractor feed *n* a mechanism for feeding paper into a printer, using toothed wheels to mesh with the perforations in continuous stationery

tractor-trailer *n N Am* a truck for pulling heavy loads, consisting of a tractor attached to a trailer or semitrailer

Barnaby's
Spencer Tracy

Tracy /tráyssi/, **Spencer** (1900–67) US actor. He won Academy Awards for his films *Captains Courageous* (1937) and *Boys Town* (1938).

'There were times my pants were so thin I could sit on a dime and tell if it was heads or tails.'
[Attributed to Spencer Tracy]

trad[1] /trad/ *n* traditional jazz (*informal*) [Mid-20C. Shortening]

trad[2] /trad/ *abbr* traditional

trade /trayd/ *n* **1.** BUYING AND SELLING the activity of buying and selling, or sometimes bartering, goods ○ *a suspension of trade between the two countries* **2.** AREA OF BUSINESS OR INDUSTRY a specific area of business or industry ○ *the book trade* **3.** OCCUPATION a skilled occupation, usually one requiring manual labour ○ *learn a trade* **4.** PEOPLE IN BUSINESS the people who work in a specific area of business or industry ○ *You'll never convince the trade that this tax is fair.* **5.** WORK IN COMMERCE work in commerce as opposed to a profession ○ *graduates going into trade* **6.** CUSTOMERS customers or business generated by customers ○ *losing trade to their competitors* **7.** COMMERCIAL CUSTOMERS customers in business and industry, as opposed to the general public, who purchase products related to their business or industry ○ *This counter is for trade only.* **8.** *N Am* EXCHANGE an exchange of somebody or something for another ○ *If neither of you likes your room, why don't you do a trade?* **9.** METEOROL same as **trade wind** ○ *the southern trades* **10.** PUBL BUSINESS PUBLICATION a publication meant for people in a specific line of business ○ *advertising in all the trades* ■ *v* (**trades, trading, traded**) **1.** *vi* BUY AND SELL GOODS to take part in buying and selling goods for trade **2.** *vt* DEAL IN SOMETHING to buy and sell a particular commodity **3.** *vi US* SHOP OR BUY REGULARLY FROM BUSINESS to shop or buy something regularly at a particular place of business **4.** *vt* EXCHANGE SOMETHING to give and receive something alternately with somebody else ○ *trading punches* **5.** *vti* MAKE EXCHANGE to make an exchange, or exchange somebody or something for another ○ *Each had something the other wanted and they were happy to trade.* [14C. < Middle Low German, 'track'] —**tradable** *adj* —**tradeless** *adj*

trade down *vi* to sell something large or expensive and buy something smaller or less expensive in its place

trade in *vt* to give an old or used item, especially a car, in part payment for a new one

trade on *vt* to take advantage of a personal quality or situation, often unfairly or excessively

trade up *vi* to sell something small or inexpensive and buy something larger and more expensive in its place

trade acceptance *n* a bill of exchange for the amount of a purchase drawn by the seller on the buyer, signed by the buyer, and often specifying the place and date of payment

trade agreement *n* a treaty between two or more countries to regulate trade between them

trade association *n* an organization formed to represent the collective interests of a number of businesses in the same trade

trade book *n* a standard edition of a book, meant for sale to the general public, as opposed to a deluxe or book-club edition

trade cycle *n* the recurrent fluctuation between depression and prosperity in a capitalist economy. N Am term **business cycle**

trade deficit *n* N Am same as **trade gap**

trade discount *n* a reduction in the standard price of something, offered by one business to another, e.g. by a manufacturer to a retailer, especially within the same trade

traded option /tráydəd-/ *n* a stock option that is marketable

trade edition *n* PUBL same as **trade book**

trade fair *n* an occasion when manufacturers and producers can exhibit their products and talk to potential customers

trade gap *n* the difference, measured in monetary value, between a nation's imports and its exports when the imports exceed the exports. N Am term **trade deficit**

~~**tradegy**~~ incorrect spelling of **tragedy**

trade-in *n* 1. a used item that is used as part payment for something new, e.g. a used car 2. a transaction in which an old or used item serves as part payment for something new

trade journal *n* a periodical devoted to news and features relating to a specific trade or profession

trade language *n* a language used between native speakers of different languages to allow them to communicate so that they can trade with each other

trade-last *n* US an exchange in which somebody repeats an overheard compliment to the complimented person if that person will first offer an overheard compliment about the other (*informal*)

trademark /tráyd maark/ *n* 1. COMPANY SYMBOL a name or symbol used to show that a product is made by a specific company and legally registered so that no other manufacturer can use it 2. DISTINCTIVE CHARACTERISTIC a distinctive characteristic associated with a person or group of people ○ *Quick exits are her trademark.* ■ *vt* (**-marks, -marking, -marked**) 1. REGISTER SOMETHING AS TRADEMARK to register a name or symbol as a trademark 2. LABEL PRODUCT WITH TRADEMARK to place a trademark on a product

trade name *n* 1. PRODUCT NAME a name given by a manufacturer to a product or service 2. NAME USED IN TRADE a name for something that is usually known or used only by people working in the trade 3. COMPANY NAME a name under which a company or business operates

trade-off /tráyd of/, **tradeoff** *n* a situation in which somebody is prepared to compromise by giving up all or part of one thing in exchange for another ○ *a trade-off between quality and price*

trade paperback *n* a paperback edition of a book that is superior in production quality to a mass-market paperback edition and is similar to a hardback in size

trade plates *npl* temporary number plates given to a vehicle before it is registered. N Am term **dealer plates**

trader /tráydər/ *n* 1. somebody who buys and sells retail goods 2. somebody who deals in stocks and securities, especially somebody who tries to profit by making frequent deals, each netting a small profit 3. SHIPPING same as **merchant ship**

trade reference *n* a person or company that furnishes a report concerning somebody's credit standing in response to an enquiry by somebody else in the same trade, especially a supplier

trade route *n* a route used by merchant ships or trading vehicles

Tradescant /trə déskənt, tráddə skant/, **John** (1570–1638?) English naturalist. The head gardener to Charles I, he introduced many foreign plants into England and opened an early public museum.

tradescantia /tráddi skánti ə/ (*plural* **-tias** or *same*) *n* a plant grown for its striped leaves and blue, white, or pink flowers. Native to: Americas. Genus: *Tradescantia*. [Early 18C. < modern Latin, after John Tradescant (1570–1638?), English naturalist, or his son]

trade school *n* a school that gives instruction in a specific trade or offers general vocational courses

trade secret *n* 1. a secret formula or technique that is used to make a product, known only to the company that manufactures it 2. a secret (*informal*) ○ *Which shampoo do you use – or is it a trade secret?*

trades holiday *n* Scotland an annual two-week summer holiday taken by many industries and businesses in a town

tradesman /tráydzmən/ (*plural* **-men** /-mən/) *n* 1. a man who works in a skilled trade, especially one related to the building trade such as plumbing or carpentry 2. a man involved in retail trade, especially a shopkeeper (*dated*)

tradesperson /tráydz purss'n/ (*plural* **-persons** or **-people** /-peep'l/) *n* 1. a skilled worker, especially in a trade related to the building trade such as plumbing or carpentry 2. a retail dealer, especially a shopkeeper (*dated*)

trades union *n* POL same as **trade union**

Trades Union Congress *n* an association of British trade unions, to which most of the largest unions belong

tradeswoman /tráydz woomman/ (*plural* **-women** /-wimmin/) *n* a woman who works in a skilled trade, especially one related to the building trade such as plumbing or carpentry

trade union, **trades union** *n* an organized association of people who work in the same trade or profession, formed to represent their interests and help them improve their working conditions. N Am term **labor union** —**trade unionism** *n* —**trade unionist** *n*

trade-weighted index *n* an index reflecting the level of trade between particular nations, e.g. one indicating the value of the dollar in relation to other currencies

trade wind *n* a prevailing tropical wind that blows towards the equator from the northeast in the northern hemisphere or from the southeast in the southern hemisphere. The trade winds are major components of the global weather system. [< *blow trade* 'blow in a constant direction']

~~**tradgedy**~~ incorrect spelling of **tragedy**

trading card /tráyding-/ *n* a card with a picture or information on it that is one of a set designed to be collected

trading estate *n* COMM same as **industrial estate**

trading post *n* 1. especially in former times, a shop in a remote area, where local products can be bartered for supplies 2. a location where a specific security is traded on the floor of a stock exchange

trading stamp *n* a stamp that can be exchanged for goods, given by a shop to customers each time they spend a fixed amount of money

tradition /trə dísh'n/ *n* 1. CUSTOM OR BELIEF a long-established action or pattern of behaviour in a community or group of people, often one that has been handed down from generation to generation 2. BODY OF CUSTOMS a body of long-established customs and beliefs viewed as a set of precedents 3. HANDING DOWN OF CUSTOMS the handing down of patterns of behaviour, practices, and beliefs that are valued by a culture 4. *also* Tradition CHR ACCEPTED UNWRITTEN CHRISTIAN DOCTRINES the body of Christian doctrines that are accepted as the teachings of Jesus Christ and the apostles without written evidence 5. *also* Tradition ISLAM TEACHINGS SUPPLEMENTING KORAN the body of Islamic beliefs and customs that are not written in the Koran, e.g. the words of Muhammad 6. LAW TRANSFER OF OWNERSHIP especially in Roman and Scots law, the formal transfer of ownership of movable property

[14C. Via French < Latin *tradition-* < *tradere* 'hand over, betray' < *trans-* 'across, over' + *dare* 'give'] —**traditionless** *adj*

SYNONYMS See *habit*.

traditional /trə dísh'nəl/ *adj* 1. relating to or based on tradition 2. describes older styles of jazz, usually played by small ensembles featuring clarinet, trumpet, trombone, and rhythm sections. Traditional jazz flourished in New Orleans, Chicago, and Kansas City in the early 20th century. —**traditionality** /trə dísh'n álləti/ *n* —**traditionalize** *vt* —**traditionally** *adv*

traditionalism /trə dísh'nəlizəm/ *n* 1. a deep respect for tradition, especially for cultural or religious practices 2. the idea that all knowledge comes from divine revelation and is passed on by tradition —**traditionalist** *n* —**traditionalistic** /trə dísh'nə lístik/ *adj*

traditional option *n* on the Stock Exchange, an option that cannot be resold after it has been bought

traditional policy *n* a life assurance policy in which premiums are paid into a general fund and benefits are based on actuarial statistics

traditor /trádditər/ (*plural* **traditores** /-táw reez/) *n* an early Christian who betrayed other Christians during the Roman persecutions [14C. < Latin (see TRAITOR)]

traduce /trə dyóoss/ (**-duces, -ducing, -duced**) *vt* to say very critical or disparaging things about somebody or something [Late 16C. < Latin *traducere* 'convert, transfer, scorn, disgrace' < *trans-* 'across, over' + *ducere* 'to lead'] —**traducement** *n* —**traducer** *n* —**traducible** *adj*

traducianism /trə dyóosh'nizəm/ *n* the belief that a child inherits a soul as well as its bodily characteristics from its parents [Mid-18C. < late Latin *traducianus* 'believer in traducianism' < *tradux* 'inheritance, transmission' < *traducere* (see TRADUCE)] —**traducian** *n*, *adj* —**traducianist** *n*, *adj* —**traducianistic** /trə dyóosh'n ístik/ *adj*

Trafalgar, Cape /trə fálgər/ cape in southwestern Spain between Cádiz and the Strait of Gibraltar

traffic /tráffik/ *n* 1. MOVEMENT OF VEHICLES the movement of vehicles on a road or in an area 2. SEA OR AIR TRANSPORT the movement of ships, trains, or aircraft between two places, or the volume of passengers or goods transported by sea, rail, or air 3. BUSINESS OF TRANSPORTATION the business of transporting goods or people 4. TRADE illegal trade in goods such as drugs or weapons 5. COMMUNICATION FLOW OF COMMUNICATIONS the volume or flow of messages carried by a communications system 6. NEGOTIATIONS dealings or negotiations between people (*archaic*) ■ *v* (**-fics, -ficking, -ficked**) 1. *vi* TRADE ILLEGALLY to engage in illegal trading 2. *vt* TRADE SOMETHING to trade or exchange anything ○ *We spent the afternoon trafficking gossip.* [Early 16C. Via obsolete French *trafique* < Old Italian *traffico* < *trafficare* 'carry on trade']

trafficator /tráffi kaytər/ *n* an illuminated signal on either side of an old motor vehicle, raised by the driver to signal a turn [Mid-20C. Blend of TRAFFIC + INDICATOR]

traffic calming *n* the use of obstructions such as speed bumps to force drivers to slow down, especially in residential areas (*hyphenated before a noun*)

traffic circle *n* N Am same as **roundabout** *n* (sense 1)

traffic cone *n* a marker in the shape of a cone, usually made of orange plastic, used to separate lines of traffic during road repairs or to prevent vehicles from entering an area

traffic cop *n* (*informal*) 1. a police officer who supervises traffic 2. NZ POLICE same as **traffic officer**

traffic court *n* a court that deals with people who have committed traffic offences

traffic engineering *n* the design and planning of roads and walkways, considering such factors as pedestrian and vehicular capacity and means for controlling traffic

traffic island *n* a raised area in the centre of a road built to separate lanes of traffic and allow pedestrians to wait safely until they can cross

traffic jam *n* a line of traffic that cannot move or moves very slowly or spasmodically because of

overcrowding or an obstruction —**traffic-jammed** *adj*

trafficker *n* somebody who traffics in something, especially illegal goods such as drugs or weapons

traffic light *n* a signal that uses red, green, and amber lights to control traffic, especially at a junction

traffic officer *n NZ* a member of an official force responsible for enforcing traffic regulations and controlling the flow of traffic

traffic pattern *n* the pattern of routes to which an aircraft is restricted when approaching or circling an airport

traffic signal *n* ROADS same as **traffic light**

traffic warden *n UK* a uniformed public official who enforces parking restrictions on the highway and may also direct traffic

tragacanth /trággə kanth/ *n* **1.** a reddish or white gum extracted from a plant grown in Asia. Use: pills, adhesives, textile printing, stabilizer, thickener for sauces. **2.** a plant from which tragacanth is obtained, especially a spiny Asian plant with white, yellow, or purple flowers. Genus: *Astragalus.* [Late 16C. Via French < Greek *tragakantha* 'goat's thorn' < *tragos* 'goat' + *akantha* 'thorn']

tragedian /trə jeédi ən/ *n* **1.** a playwright who specializes in tragedies **2.** an actor who plays tragic roles

tragedienne /trə jeédi én/ *n* a female actor who plays tragic roles (*dated*) [Mid-19C. < French < *tragédie* (see TRAGEDY)]

tragedy /trájjədi/ (*plural* **-dies**) *n* **1. VERY SAD EVENT** an event in life that evokes feelings of sorrow or grief **2. DISASTROUS EVENT** a disastrous circumstance or event, e.g. serious illness, financial ruin, or fatality **3. TRAGIC PLAY** a serious play with a tragic theme, often involving a heroic struggle and the downfall of the main character **4. TRAGIC PIECE OF LITERATURE** a literary work that deals with a tragic theme **5. TRAGEDIES AS GENRE** the genre of plays or other literary works that deal with tragic themes [14C. Via French *tragédie* < Greek *tragōidia* 'goat's song' < *tragos* 'goat' + *aeidein* 'sing']

tragi ANAT plural of **tragus**

tragic /trájjik/, **tragical** /-ik'l/ *adj* **1.** provoking deep sadness, distress, or grief ○ *a tragic accident* **2.** relating to tragedies as a dramatic genre ○ *a tragic hero* [Mid-16C. Via Latin < Greek *tragikos* 'of tragedy' < *tragos* 'goat'] —**tragically** *adv*

tragic flaw *n* a character flaw that causes the downfall of the protagonist in a tragedy

tragic irony *n* the revealing to an audience of a tragic event or consequence that remains unknown to the character concerned. It is a kind of dramatic irony.

tragicomedy /trájji kómmədi/ (*plural* **-dies**) *n* **1. WORK COMBINING TRAGEDY AND COMEDY** a play or other literary work that combines aspects of tragedy and comedy **2. TRAGICOMIC PLAYS AS GENRE** tragicomic plays or literary works considered as a genre **3. EVENT MIXING TRAGEDY AND COMEDY** an event or situation that has both tragic and comical aspects [Late 16C. Via French *tragicomédie* < late Latin *tragicomoedia* < *tragicus* (see TRAGIC) + *comoedia* (see COMEDY)] —**tragicomic** *adj* —**tragicomical** *adj* —**tragicomically** *adv*

tragopan

tragopan /trággə pan/ *n* a brightly coloured pheasant, the male of which has a bright blue bare throat and fleshy appendages on its head that look like horns. Native to: Asia. Latin name: *Tragopan temminckii.* [Early 17C. Via Latin < Greek, type of hornbill < *tragos* 'goat' + *pan* 'Pan']

tragus /tráygəss/ (*plural* **-gi** /-jī, -gī/) *n* the pointed flap of cartilage that lies above the earlobe and partly covers the entrance to the ear passage [Late 17C. Via modern Latin < Greek *tragos* 'goat, hairy part of the ear'] —**tragal** *adj*

trail /trayl/ *v* (**trails, trailing, trailed**) **1.** *vti* **DRAG SOMETHING, OR BE DRAGGED** to be pulled or dragged along, or pull or drag something along **2.** *vi* **DRAPE** to hang, grow, or float loosely ○ *Her curly hair trailed along her shoulders and down her back.* **3.** *vi* **LAG** to walk slowly, usually from tiredness or boredom **4.** *vt* **FOLLOW SOMEBODY SECRETLY** to follow a person or animal either by staying close but out of sight or by looking for signs of movement left behind such as footprints or scent **5.** *vti* **FALL BEHIND IN SPORTS COMPETITION** to be losing or behind in a race, match, or competition **6.** *vt* CINEMA, MEDIA **SHOW EXCERPT OF IN ADVANCE** to advertise an upcoming film or programme by showing a clip from it **7.** *vt* CERAMICS **DECORATE SOMETHING BY DRIZZLING LIQUID CLAY** to decorate something with liquid clay (**slip**) that is drizzled or sprayed on **8.** *vt* **TOW SOMETHING** to tow something such as a caravan behind a vehicle **9.** *vt* ARMS **CARRY WEAPON IN LOW POSITION** to carry a weapon horizontally or with the butt near to the ground **10.** *vti* **MAKE TRACK** to make a track through a place ■ *n* **1. ROUTE THROUGH COUNTRYSIDE** a route through the countryside that links paths and points of interest ○ *a nature trail* **2. MARKS WHERE SOMEBODY OR SOMETHING MOVED** a sequence of marks left by somebody or something moving along a surface **3. PATH** a path or track, especially one that has been beaten through a wild area **4. SCENT FOLLOWED** a scent or track that is followed in a hunt **5.** ARMS **BOTTOM OF GUN CARRIAGE** the part of a gun carriage that rests on the ground **6.** ENG **DISTANCE FROM STEERING WHEEL** the distance between the centre of a steering wheel and a line intersecting the steering axis and the ground [14C. Via Old French *trailler* 'to tow' < Latin *tragula* 'dragnet, sledge', probably < *trahere* 'to pull']

SPELLCHECK trail or **trial**? Do not confuse the spelling of ***trail*** and ***trial***. ***Trail*** can be used as a verb, meaning 'drag', 'follow secretly', or 'fall behind' (as in *Your coat is trailing on the ground. The police trailed him to a hotel. They trailed the opponents by two goals.*), or as a noun, denoting a path or a track that is followed (as in *a nature trail, a trail of footprints*). ***Trial*** is chiefly used as a noun, referring to a legal process, a test, or a painful experience, as in *trial by jury, a trial of a new drug, trials and tribulations.*

SYNONYMS See ***follow.***

---

trail away, trail off *vi* to become quieter or fainter in sound and gradually fade away

trail bike *n* a lightweight motorcycle for use on rough terrain

trailblazer /tráyl blayzər/ *n* **1.** a pioneer or innovator **2.** somebody who makes a new path through a wilderness —**trailblazing** *adj, n*

trailer /tráylər/ *n* **1. TOWED VEHICLE** a vehicle that is towed by another vehicle, e.g. a small open cart or a platform used for transporting a boat **2. PART OF LORRY** the rear part of an articulated lorry **3.** *N Am* TRANSP same as **caravan** *n* (sense 1) **4. TEMPORARY HOME OR OFFICE** a trailer equipped with facilities for use as a residence or office that is usually left temporarily on a site, e.g. in a campsite **5.** CINEMA, MEDIA **ADVERTISEMENT FOR FILM** an advertisement for a film consisting of extracts from it, shown on television or in a cinema **6.** PHOTOGRAPHY **END OF REEL OF FILM** a blank piece of film at the end of a reel **7. SOMEBODY OR SOMETHING THAT TRAILS** somebody or something that trails, especially somebody who lags behind others **8.** BOT **PLANT** a trailing plant ■ *vt* (**-ers, -ering, -ered**) **1. MOVE SOMETHING BY TRAILER** to transport something using a trailer **2.** CINEMA, MEDIA **ADVERTISE FILM WITH TRAILER** to advertise a film with extracts from it

trailer park *n N Am* an area equipped for mobile homes

trailer sailer *n* a boat that is small enough to be transported on a trailer

trailer tent *n* a large tent that packs into a trailer. When the tent is erected, the trailer's base becomes a raised sleeping or living area.

trailing arbutus /tráyling aar byoōtəss/ *n* a trailing evergreen bush with leathery leaves. Flowers: fragrant, pink-and-white, in clusters. Native to: eastern North America. Latin name: *Epigaea repens.*

trailing edge *n* **1.** the rear edge of a wing, aerofoil, or propeller blade **2.** the part of a pulsed signal during which its amplitude decreases

trail mix *n* a snack containing nuts, dried fruit, and seeds [< its use by walkers]

trail rope *n* **1.** a rope that hangs from a balloon or airship and is used for mooring or as a brake **2.** a long rope attached to the trail of a gun carriage

train /trayn/ *n* **1. LINKED RAILWAY CARRIAGES** a number of railway carriages or trucks pulled by a locomotive (*often used before a noun*) **2. TRAILING PART OF GOWN** a long part at the back of a gown or robe that trails on the ground **3. LONG MOVING LINE** a long moving line of people or animals **4. ENTOURAGE** a retinue or group of followers **5.** MIL **ARMY FOLLOWERS** the people and military vehicles supporting or supplying an army unit **6. SEQUENCE OF EVENTS** a series or sequence of events, actions, or things **7.** MECH ENG **MECHANICAL SERIES** a series of connected wheels or other mechanical parts **8.** ARMS **LINE OF GUNPOWDER** a line of gunpowder or other combustible material **9. SOMETHING DRAGGED BEHIND** something that is pulled or dragged along or that follows something else ■ *v* (**trains, training, trained**) **1.** *vti* **LEARN OR TEACH SKILLS** to learn the skills necessary to do a job, or teach somebody such skills, especially through practical experience **2.** *vt* **DOMESTICATE ANIMAL** to teach an animal to behave in ways acceptable to people, especially by repetition or practice **3.** *vti* **PREPARE FOR SPORTING COMPETITION** to prepare for a sporting competition, or prepare somebody for a sporting competition, usually with a planned programme of appropriate physical exercises **4.** *vt* **MAKE PLANT GROW AS WANTED** to make a plant, bush, or tree grow in a particular way, e.g. by pruning or tying it **5.** *vt* **SHAPE HAIR TO ENCOURAGE PARTICULAR GROWTH** to comb or otherwise arrange hair to encourage it to grow in a particular direction **6.** *vt* **AIM SOMETHING** to aim something such as a weapon or camera at somebody or something ○ *trained her binoculars on the nest* **7.** *vt* **MAKE SOMETHING BETTER** to improve something, especially the mind, with discipline **8.** *vi* **TRAVEL BY TRAIN** to make a journey by train (*informal*) [Mid-15C. < Old French *traïn* 'something that drags or trails behind' < *traïner* 'draw, pull']

SYNONYMS See ***teach.***

---

trainband /tráyn band/ *n* a company of trained civilian militia operating in England and North America between the 16th and the 18th centuries [Mid-17C. Contraction of *trained band*]

trainbearer /tráyn bairər/ *n* an attendant who holds up the train of somebody walking in a procession or other ceremony

trainee /tray neé/ *n* somebody who is being trained to do a job (*often used before a noun*) ○ *a trainee hairdresser* —**traineeship** *n*

trainer /tráynər/ *n* **1. SOMEBODY WHO TRAINS ANIMALS OR PEOPLE** somebody who trains animals or people, especially racehorses or athletes **2. TRAINING APPARATUS** an apparatus or device used in training, especially a simulation cockpit in which pilots train **3. SPORTS SHOE** a shoe designed to be worn during athletic activities or exercising, but worn with casual clothing for any activity. N Am term **athletic shoe**

training /tráyning/ *n* **1.** the process of teaching or learning a skill or job (*often used before a noun*) ○ *a training programme* **2.** the process of improving physical fitness by exercise and diet

Training Agency *n* an organization that provides training and retraining for adults

training college *n* a college that trains people for a specific profession, especially the teaching profession

training shoe *n* CLOTHING same as **trainer** (sense 3)

training wheels *npl ANZ, N Am* a pair of small wheels fitted to the back wheel of a bicycle to help balance it while somebody is learning to ride. UK term **stabilizers** (*see* **stabilizer**)

trainload /tráyn lōd/ *n* the number of people or the amount of cargo that a train can carry ○ *a trainload of tourists*

trainman /tráynmən/ (*plural* **-men** /-mən/) *n* a man who is a member of a train crew, especially a brakeman, who works to assist the conductor

train oil *n* oil from the blubber of a whale or other sea animal. Use: the manufacture of soap and margarine, as a lubricant, in dressing leather. [< Low German *trān* or Middle Dutch *traen* 'train oil']

train operating company *n* RAIL full form of **TOC**

trainspotter /tráyn spotər/ *n* 1. somebody whose hobby is collecting the numbers of railway locomotives 2. somebody who is considered boring because of his or her staid outlook, narrow interests, or unfashionable appearance (*slang insult*)

trainspotting /tráyn spoting/ *n* 1. a hobby that consists of collecting the numbers of railway locomotives 2. the search for a vein that is prominent enough to inject drugs into (*slang*)

traipse /trayps/ *vi* (**traipses, traipsing, traipsed**) to trudge in a weary way (*informal*) ■ *n* a tiring or wearisome walk [Late 16C. Origin ?]

trait /trayt, tray/ *n* 1. INDIVIDUAL CHARACTERISTIC a characteristic or quality that distinguishes somebody 2. INHERITED CHARACTERISTIC a quality or characteristic that is genetically determined 3. INDICATION a hint or trace of something (*literary*) [Late 16C. Via French, 'act of pulling or drawing, line drawn, feature' < Latin *tractus* < *trahere* 'to pull']

traitor /tráytər/ *n* somebody who is disloyal or treacherous [13C. Via French < Latin *traditor* 'betrayer' < *tradere* (see TRADITION)] —**traitorous** *adj*

Trajan /tráyjən/ (AD 53?–117) Roman emperor. Becoming emperor in AD 97, he conducted several military campaigns, notably that in Dacia (modern Romania), commemorated by the carvings on a column in Rome. Full name **Marcus Ulpius Trajanus**

'Anyone who denies that he is a Christian and actually proves this by worshipping our gods is pardoned on repentance, no matter how suspect his past may have been.'
[Trajan. Quoted in *Letters, Trajan with Pliny, The Early Christians*, E. Arnold; 1970]

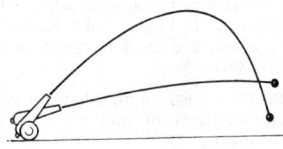

trajectory

trajectory /trə jéktəri/ (*plural* **-ries**) *n* 1. PATH OF FLYING OBJECT the path that a projectile makes through space under the action of given forces such as thrust, wind, and gravity 2. CURVE INTERSECTING AT CONSTANT ANGLE a curve or surface that intersects all of a family of curves or surfaces at a constant angle 3. PATH OF PROCESS OR EVENT the way in which a process or event develops over a period of time [Late 17C. < medieval Latin *trajectorius* 'relating to throwing across' < Latin *trajicere* 'throw across, pass through' < *trans-* 'across, over' + *jacere* 'to throw']

Trajkovski /trī kófski/, **Boris** (1956–2004) president of the Former Yugoslav Republic of Macedonia (1999–2004). Representing the centre-right Internal Macedonian Revolutionary Organisation (VMRO), he was deputy minister of foreign affairs during the Kosovo crisis (1999) and became president later that year.

trakky daks /tráki-/, **trackie daks** *npl* Aus tracksuit trousers (*informal*) [< alteration of TRACK]

Tralee /trə leé/ town and administrative centre of County Kerry, in the southwestern Republic of Ireland. Population: 20,375 (2002).

Tralee Bay inlet of the Atlantic Ocean on the southwestern coast of the Republic of Ireland

tram[1] /tram/ *n* 1. a passenger vehicle that runs along rails on a road. It has an overhead wire from which it draws electricity. N Am term **streetcar** 2. a small vehicle on rails used to carry coal and other materials in a coal mine [Early 16C. Origin ?]

tram[2] /tram/ *n* a fine adjustment that keeps a machine functioning correctly ■ *vt* (**trams, tramming, trammed**) to adjust or align mechanical parts accurately [Late 19C. < *tram-staff* 'straight edge used to adjust a millstone spindle' < *tram* 'instrument for drawing ellipses', shortening of TRAMMEL]

tram[3] /tram/ *n* heavy silk thread. Use: horizontal weave in velvet or silk. [Late 17C. Via French *trame* < Latin *trama* 'woof of a web']

~~**tramatic**~~ incorrect spelling of **traumatic**

tramcar /trám kaar/ *n* TRANSP same as **tram**[1] (sense 1)

tramline /trám līn/ *n* 1. TRAM TRACK a track for a tram 2. TRAM ROUTE the route driven by a tram ■ **tramlines** *npl* 1. MARKINGS ON TENNIS COURT a pair of parallel lines at either side of a tennis court delimiting the singles and doubles courts (*informal*) 2. MARKINGS ON BADMINTON COURT a pair of parallel lines at either side and either end of a badminton court delimiting the singles and doubles courts

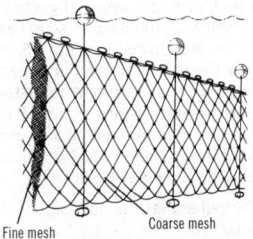

Fine mesh   Coarse mesh

trammel (sense 2)

trammel /trámm'l/ *n* 1. LIMITATION TO FREEDOM something that limits a person's freedom 2. FISHING NET a fishing net consisting of a fine net between two layers of coarse mesh 3. DRAWING INSTRUMENT an instrument used to draw ellipses 4. MECH ENG same as **tram**[2] 5. FIREPLACE HOOK a hook in a fireplace on which a kettle or pot can be hung and raised or lowered ■ *vt* (**-mels, -melling, -melled**) 1. CONFINE SOMEBODY to restrain somebody or something 2. ENSNARE SOMETHING to catch or entangle somebody or something 3. MECH ENG same as **tram**[2] [14C. Via Old French *tramail* < late Latin *tremaculum* < Latin *tres* 'three' + *macula* 'mesh']

tramontana /trámmon taánə/ *n* a cold dry wind that blows down from mountains, especially a north wind that blows into Italy from the Alps [Late 18C. Via Italian, 'north wind' < Latin *transmontanus* 'beyond the mountains' < *trans-* 'across, over' + *mont-* 'mountain']

tramontane /trə món tayn/ *adj* 1. BEYOND MOUNTAINS living or situated on the far side of the mountains, especially the Alps as seen from Italy 2. FOREIGN foreign and uncivilized, originally from an Italian point of view ■ *n* 1. METEOROL same as **tramontana** 2. FOREIGNER somebody from beyond mountains, especially from beyond the Alps as seen from Italy [Late 16C. Via Italian *tramontano* < Latin *transmontanus* (see TRANSMONTANE)]

tramp /tramp/ *n* 1. VAGRANT a homeless person who travels on foot, often begging for a living 2. UK LONG JOURNEY ON FOOT a long and tiring journey on foot 3. SOUND OF FEET the sound of heavy footsteps or horses' hooves 4. HEAVY STEP a heavy step or tread 5. OFFENSIVE TERM an offensive term that deliberately insults a woman who is considered sexually promiscuous or who works as a prostitute 6. METAL PLATE ON BOOT a metal plate that protects the sole of a boot when the wearer is digging 7. PART OF SPADE the part of a spade on which the digger's foot presses ■ *v* (**tramps, tramping, tramped**) 1. *vi* TREAD HEAVILY to tread heavily or noisily 2. *vi* WALK to walk, especially a long way 3. *vt* COVER DISTANCE ON FOOT to traverse an area, especially wearily, or cover a distance in a steady weary way 4. *vt* CRUSH SOMETHING UNDERFOOT to crush something by treading on it 5. *vi* LIVE AS VAGRANT to live or wander about as a vagrant 6. *vi* NZ HIKE to go walking for recreation [14C. < Middle Low German *trampen* 'to stamp'] —**tramper** *n* —**tramping** *n* —**trampish** *adj*

tramping club /trámping-/ *n* NZ an organization of people who go walking together

tramping hut *n* NZ a hut for the use of people walking in the bush

trample /trámp'l/ (**-ples, -pling, -pled**) *vti* 1. to tread heavily, or tread heavily on something or somebody so as to cause damage or injury 2. to behave in an insulting contemptuous way, or treat somebody in a insulting contemptuous way [14C. < TRAMP] —**trampler** *n*

trampoline /trámpə leen/ *n* a strong sheet, usually of canvas, that is stretched tightly on a horizontal frame to which it is connected by springs. It is used for jumping and acrobatics. [Late 18C. < Italian *trampolino* 'springboard' < *trampoli* 'stilts'] —**trampoline** *vi* —**trampolinist** *n*

tramp steamer *n* a merchant ship that carries cargo but does not follow a fixed route

tramway /trám way/ *n* 1. TRANSP same as **tramline** (sense 1) 2. a light-rail system that uses trams, or a company that operates such a system

trance /traanss/ *n* 1. DAZED STATE a state in which somebody is dazed or stunned or in some other way unaware of the environment and unable to respond to stimuli 2. HYPNOTIC STATE a hypnotic or cataleptic state 3. RAPTUROUS STATE a state of rapture or exaltation in which somebody loses consciousness 4. PARAPSYCHOL SPIRITUAL MEDIUM'S STATE the state of apparent semiunconsciousness that a spiritual medium enters into in an attempt to communicate with the dead 5. MUSIC HYPNOTIC ELECTRONIC DANCE MUSIC electronic dance music with a repetitive hypnotic beat ■ *vt* (**trances, trancing, tranced**) ENTRANCE SOMEBODY to put somebody in a trance (*literary*) [14C. < Old French *transe* < *transir* 'be numb with fear' < Latin *transire* (see TRANSIENT)]

tranche /traansh/ *n* a portion or section of something, especially an amount of money [Mid-20C. < French, 'slice' < Old French *trenchier* 'to cut']

trannie /tránni/, **tranny** (*plural* **-nies**) *n* 1. HOUSEHOLD same as **transistor radio** (*informal*) 2. same as **transsexual** (*slang*) 3. same as **transvestite** (*slang*) [Mid-20C. Shortening]

tranquil /trángkwil/ *adj* 1. free of any disturbance or commotion ○ *a tranquil morning* 2. free from or showing no signs of anxiety or agitation [Mid-15C. Via French < Latin *tranquillus*] —**tranquilly** *adv*

tranquility /trang kwílləti/ *n* another spelling of **tranquillity**

tranquilize, etc. *vti* US spelling of **tranquillize, etc.**

tranquillise, etc. *vti* another spelling of **tranquillize, etc.**

tranquilliser *n* MED another spelling of **tranquillizer**

tranquillity /trang kwílləti/, **tranquility** *n* a state of peace and calm [14C. Via French < Latin *tranquillitas* 'quietness' < *tranquillus* 'tranquil']

tranquillize /trángkwi līz/ (**-lizes, -lizing, -lized**), **tranquillise** (**-lises, -lising, -lised**) *v* 1. *vt* MAKE SOMEBODY CALM WITH MEDICINE to use medication to induce calmness in a person or animal 2. *vi* BECOME CALM to become calm or calmer 3. *vi* HAVE CALMING EFFECT to have a calming effect —**tranquillization** /trángkwi līz záysh'n/ *n*

tranquillizer /trángkwi līzər/, **tranquilliser** *n* 1. a medication that reduces anxiety and tension without affecting mental clarity. Use: treatment of anxiety, neuroses, psychoses. 2. anything that renders a person or animal calm

trans. *abbr* 1. BUSINESS transaction 2. LAW transferred 3. GRAM transitive 4. LANGUAGE translated 5. LANGUAGE translation 6. TRANSP transport 7. MATHS transpose 8. MATHS transverse

trans- *prefix* 1. across, on the other side of, beyond ○ *transcontinental* ○ *transfinite* 2. through ○ *transdermal* 3. indicating change, transfer, or

conversion ○ *transliterate* [< Latin *trans* 'across, over, through']

transact /tran zákt, -sákt/ (**-acts, -acting, -acted**) *vti* to conduct or carry out something such as business [Late 16C. Back-formation < TRANSACTION] —**transactor** *n*

transactinide /transs ákti nīd/ *n* an element with an atomic number greater than 103 (*often used before a noun*)

transaction /tran záksh'n, -sák-/ *n* **1. INSTANCE OF DOING BUSINESS** an instance of doing business of some kind, e.g. a purchase made in a shop or a withdrawal of funds from a bank account **2. ACT OF NEGOTIATING** the act of negotiating something or carrying out a business deal **3. INTERACTION** a communication or activity between two or more people that influences and affects all of them (*formal*) **4.** COMPUT **ADDITION TO DATABASE** an action that adds, removes, or changes data in a database or other computer program ■ **transactions** *npl* **PROCEEDINGS** the published records of a learned society [Mid-15C. Via French < late Latin *transactiion-* < Latin *transigere* 'drive through, accomplish' < *agere* 'drive, do'] —**transactional** /tran zákshənəl, -sák-/*adj* —**transactionally** *adv*

transactional analysis *n* a form of psychotherapy that emphasizes the interactions within and between people and classifies these interactions as 'adult', 'parent', or 'child'

transactivation /tránz akti váysh'n, tráns-/ *n* the process whereby an infecting virus activates another virus's genes that are already integrated into the chromosome of the host bacterium, inducing the host cell to replicate the initial virus

transalpine /tranz ál pīn/ *adj* **1. BEYOND ALPS** relating to or found in the area beyond the Alps, especially as seen from Italy **2. CROSSING ALPS** relating to or engaged in crossing the Alps ■ *n* **SOMEBODY FROM BEYOND ALPS** somebody who comes from beyond the Alps, especially as seen from Italy [Late 16C. < Latin *transalpinus* < *Alpes* 'the Alps']

transaminase /tranz ámmi nayz, -nayss/ *n* an enzyme that catalyses the transfer of an amino group in the process of transamination

transamination /tranz ámmi náysh'n/ *n* the formation of one amino acid from another

transatlantic /tránzət lántik/ *adj* **1.** relating to or engaged in crossing the Atlantic **2.** situated on or coming from the other side of the Atlantic

transaxle /tránz aks'l/ *n* a combined front axle and transmission in a motor vehicle with front-wheel drive [Mid-20C. < TRANSMISSION + AXLE]

transboundary /tránz bówndəri/ *adj* crossing or existing across national boundaries

Transcaucasia /tránz kaw káyzhə, -káyzi ə/ region in southeastern Europe, south of the Caucasus Mountains, between the Black and Caspian seas, forming the southern part of Caucasia. It consists of the republics of Georgia, Armenia, and Azerbaijan. Area: 186,100 sq. km/71,853 sq. mi. —**Transcaucasian** *adj*

transceiver /tran seévər/ *n* **1.** a radio transmitter and receiver combined in a single, often portable unit **2.** a device that can receive and transmit data, e.g. a modem [Mid-20C. Blend of TRANSMITTER + RECEIVER]

transcend /tran sénd/ (**-scends, -scending, -scended**) *vt* **1. GO BEYOND LIMIT** to go beyond a limit or range, e.g. of thought or belief **2. SURPASS SOMETHING** to go beyond something in quality or achievement **3. BE INDEPENDENT OF WORLD** to exist above and apart from the material world [14C. Via French < Latin *transcendere* 'climb over or beyond' < *scandere* 'climb, mount']

transcendent /tran séndənt/ *adj* **1. BETTER** superior in quality or achievement **2.** PHILOSOPHY **BEYOND LIMITS OF EXPERIENCE** in Kant's philosophical system, exceeding the limits of experience and therefore unknowable except hypothetically **3.** PHILOSOPHY **BEYOND CATEGORIES** above or outside all known categories **4.** RELIG **INDEPENDENT OF WORLD** existing outside the material universe and so not limited by it —**transcendence** *n* —**transcendent** *n* —**transcendently** *adv*

transcendental /trán sen dént'l/ *adj* **1.** PHILOSOPHY **NOT EXPERIENCED BUT KNOWABLE** independent of human experience of phenomena but within the range of knowledge **2. MYSTICAL** relating to mystical or supernatural experience and therefore beyond the material world **3.** same as **transcendent** (sense 1) **4.** MATHS **NOT ALGEBRAIC** describes a number or function that is not algebraic and is not the root of an algebraic equation ■ *n* MATHS **NUMBER IMPOSSIBLE TO EXPRESS AS INTEGER** a number that cannot be expressed as an integer, e.g. a nonrepeating decimal such as pi [Early 17C. < late Latin *transcendentalis* 'transcending the bounds of all categories' < *transcendere* (see TRANSCEND)] —**transcendentally** *adv*

transcendentalism /trán sen dént'lizəm/ *n* **1.** PHILOSOPHY **EMPHASIZING REASONING** a system of philosophy, especially that of Kant, that regards the processes of reasoning as the key to knowledge of reality **2.** PHILOSOPHY **EMPHASIZING DIVINE** a system of philosophy that emphasizes intuition as a means of knowing a spiritual reality and believes that divinity pervades nature and humanity. It is especially associated with Ralph Waldo Emerson and other New England writers. **3. TRANSCENDENTAL THOUGHT** transcendental thought or language **4. TRANSCENDENTAL NATURE** the state or quality of being transcendental —**transcendentalist** *n, adj*

transcendental meditation *n* a form of meditation in which a mantra is repeated silently. It is based on Hindu traditions.

transcontinental /tránz konti nént'l/ *adj* **1. ACROSS CONTINENT** extending across a continent **2. BEYOND CONTINENT** situated on or coming from the other side of a continent ■ *n* **TRAIN CROSSING CONTINENT** a train or railway that crosses a continent —**transcontinentally** *adv*

transcribe /tran skrīb/ (**-scribes, -scribing, -scribed**) *vt* **1. COPY OUT SOMETHING** to write out an exact copy of something **2. EXPAND SOMETHING IN WRITING** to write something out in full from notes or shorthand **3. TRANSLATE SOMETHING** to translate or transliterate something **4.** PHON **WRITE SOUNDS PHONETICALLY** to write speech sounds phonetically **5.** MUSIC **REARRANGE MUSIC** to arrange a piece of music for a different instrument, voice, or combination **6.** BROADCAST **RECORD SOMETHING FOR LATER BROADCASTING** to record something so that it can be broadcast at a later time **7.** BROADCAST **BROADCAST SOMETHING TRANSCRIBED** to broadcast something that has been transcribed earlier **8.** COMPUT **TRANSFER SOMETHING TO OTHER STORAGE FORMAT** to transfer information from one way of storing it on computer to another, or from a computer to an external storage device **9.** GENETICS **CONVERT CODE FOR TRANSMISSION TO RNA** to convert the genetic code carried by DNA into an equivalent form carried by a molecule of messenger RNA **10.** GENETICS **CONVERT GENETIC CODE INTO DNA MOLECULE** to convert the genetic code carried by the RNA of a retrovirus into a molecule of DNA [Mid-16C. < Latin *transcribere* 'copy, convey' < *scribere* 'write'] —**transcribable** *adj* —**transcriber** *n*

transcript /trán skript/ *n* **1. WRITTEN RECORD** a written record of something, e.g. a copy of the script of a broadcast programme or a record of court proceedings **2.** *N Am* EDUC **STUDENT'S ACADEMIC HISTORY** an official document showing the educational work of a student in a North American school or college **3. COPY** any copy or record **4.** GENETICS **RNA WITH TRANSCRIBED CODE** a molecule of messenger RNA that carries coded genetic information converted from the genetic code held by the DNA during the process of transcription in living cells **5.** GENETICS **DNA CARRYING CODED RETROVIRUS** the DNA that carries the coded information of a retrovirus, converted from the genetic code held by the virus's RNA during transcription following the infection of a living cell [Mid-15C. < Latin *transcriptum* < past participle of *transcribere* (see TRANSCRIBE)]

transcriptase /tran skríp tayz, -tayss/ *n* an enzyme that catalyses the synthesis of messenger RNA from a DNA template during transcription

transcription /tran skrípsh'n/ *n* **1. TRANSCRIBING** the act or process of transcribing something **2. TRANSCRIPT** something that has been transcribed **3.** PHON **PHONETIC REPRESENTATION** a phonetic representation of speech using special symbols **4.** GENETICS **TRANSFER OF GENETIC CODE** the first step in carrying out genetic instructions in living cells, in which the genetic code is transferred from DNA to molecules of messenger RNA, which subsequently direct protein manufacture **5.** GENETICS **TRANSFER OF GENETIC INFORMATION** the first step in the replication of a retrovirus following its infection of a living cell, in which its genetic code is transferred from RNA to a molecule of DNA —**transcriptional** *adj*

transcriptive /tran skríptiv/ *adj* used for transcribing or in the form of a transcript —**transcriptively** *adv*

transcriptome /tran skríp tōm/ *n* the full complement of unique sequenced RNA molecules with coded genetic information (**transcripts**) that an individual produces

transcriptomics /tránskrip tṓmiks/ *n* the scientific classification and analysis of RNA molecules with coded genetic information (**transcripts**) and their formation, structure, and function in an individual (*takes a singular verb*) —**transcriptomic** *adj*

transcultural /tranz kúlchərəl/ *adj* extending across cultures or involving more than one culture

transculturation /tránz kulchə ráysh'n/ *n* the change in a culture brought about by the diffusion within it of aspects from other cultures

transcurrent /tranz kúrrənt/ *adj* running across something, especially perpendicular to an expected direction or flow [Early 17C. < Latin *transcurrent-*, present participle of *transcurrere* 'run across, traverse' < *currere* 'to run']

transcutaneous /tránz kyoō táyni əss/ *adj* MED same as **transdermal**

transcutaneous electrical nerve stimulation *n* MED full form of **TENS**

transdermal /tranz dúrm'l/ *adj* describes something, especially a drug, that is introduced into the body through the skin

transdermal patch *n* a medicated patch applied to the skin. Use: controlled release of medicine into the body.

transduce /tranz dyoōss/ (**-duces, -ducing, -duced**) *vt* **1.** to change one type of energy into another type **2.** to effect the transfer of genetic material from one bacterium to another using a bacteriophage [Mid-20C. Back-formation < TRANSDUCER]

transducer /tranz dyoōssər/ *n* **1.** a device that transforms one type of energy into another, e.g. a microphone, a photoelectric cell, or a car horn **2.** a biological entity that converts energy in one form to another, e.g. the rods and cones of the eye or the hair cells of the ear [Early 20C. < Latin *transducere* 'lead across, transfer' (see TRADUCE)]

transduction /tranz dúksh'n/ *n* **1.** the transfer of genetic material from one bacterium to another using a bacteriophage **2.** the conversion of stimuli detected in receptor cells to electrical impulses that are then transported by the nervous system, as occurs when the ear converts sound waves into nerve impulses —**transductional** *adj*

transect /tran sékt/ *vt* (**-sects, -secting, -sected**) to divide something by running or cutting across it ■ *n* a strip of ground along which ecological measurements, e.g. of the number of organisms, are made at regular intervals [Mid-17C. < TRANS- + INTERSECT] —**transection** *n*

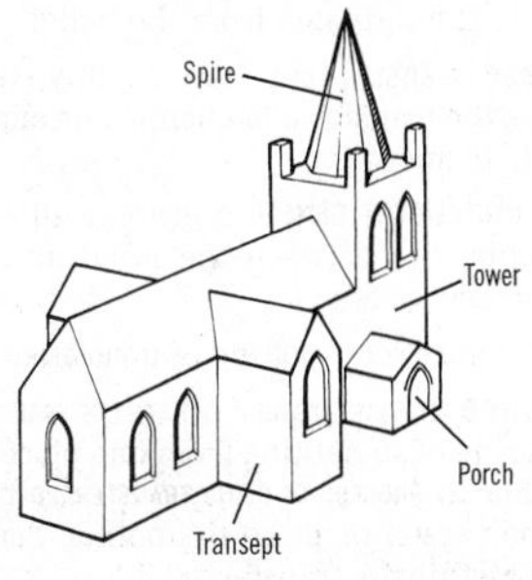

transept

transept /trán sept/ *n* **1.** the part of a cross-shaped church that runs at right angles to the long central part (**nave**) **2.** either of the two arms of a transept [Mid-16C. < modern Latin *transeptum* < Latin *trans-* 'across'

+ *saeptum* 'enclosure, wall, fence'] —**transeptal** /tran sépt'l/ *adj*

transeunt /tránzi ənt/, **transient** *adj* producing effects outside the mind

transf. *abbr* transferred

trans-fatty acid /tránss fátti-/, **trans-fat** /tránss fat/ *n* an unsaturated fat formed during the hydrogenation of vegetable oils to produce margarine. Trans-fatty acids are viewed as a health risk because they raise cholesterol levels.

transfection /transs féksh'n/ *n* the infection of a cell with viral DNA leading to production of the virus in the cell [Mid-20C. < TRANS- + INFECTION] —**transfect** *vt*

transfer *v* /transs fúr/ (**-fers, -ferring, -ferred**) **1.** *vti* **MOVE FROM ONE PLACE TO ANOTHER** to move from one place to another, or cause somebody or something to do so **2.** *vti* **PASS FROM ONE PERSON TO ANOTHER** to pass from one person, group, or organization to another, or cause something to be passed from one person, group, or organization to another ○ *not clear when power will transfer to the new government* **3.** *vti* **START WORKING ELSEWHERE** to employ somebody at a different job or in a different place while working for the same company, or begin employment in such circumstances ○ *transfer to the Chicago branch* **4.** *vti* **START PLAYING FOR DIFFERENT CLUB** especially in professional football, to sign for a different sports club, or sign somebody for a different sports club **5.** *vti* **CHANGE VEHICLES** to change from one vehicle or method of transport to another, or cause somebody to do this **6.** *vt* LAW **CHANGE OWNERSHIP OF SOMETHING** to pass ownership rights in something to somebody else ○ *transfer a deed* **7.** *vt* **PUT IMAGE ON ANOTHER SURFACE** to copy a design or image from a piece of paper onto a different material **8.** *vti* **CHANGE SCHOOLS OR SUBJECTS** to move from one school or university to another, or change from one course to another ■ *n* /tránss fur/ **1. CHANGE OF PLACE** the conveying of somebody or something from one place or position to another **2. DESIGN APPLIED TO SURFACE** an image on a piece of film or paper that is specially designed to be lifted off by heat or pressure and applied permanently to the surface of a material **3. SOMEBODY TRANSFERRED** somebody who is transferred, e.g. a football player moving from one team to another **4.** LAW **CONVEYANCE** the passing of rights or property from one person to another, or a document that conveys rights or property between people **5.** FIN **RECORDING OF SALE** the recording of a change of ownership of shares or bonds in the books of the issuer **6.** *N Am* **TICKET ALLOWING PASSENGER TO TRANSFER** a ticket that allows a passenger to change from one vehicle to another on a journey, or the place where this is done [14C. < Latin *transferre* 'carry across' < *ferre* 'carry'] —**transferee** /tránss fur reé/ *n*

transferable /transs fúrəb'l/, **transferrable** *adj* able to be transferred, especially to somebody else's ownership —**transferability** /transs fúrə bílləti/ *n*

transferable skill *n* a skill that is not limited to a specific academic discipline, area of knowledge, job, or task and is useful in any work situation, e.g. communication or organizational skills

transferable vote *n* a vote that will be given to a voter's second choice if his or her first choice candidate is eliminated from the ballot

transferase /tránssfə rayz, -rayss/ *n* any enzyme that catalyses the transfer of a chemical group from one molecule to another

transfer characteristic *n* a graphic illustration of the relationship between the input and output of an electronic system

~~**transfered**~~ incorrect spelling of **transferred**

transference /tránssfərənss/ *n* **1. ACT OF TRANSFERRING** the transferring of something from one place or person to another **2. PROCESS OF BEING TRANSFERRED** the change from one person or place to another that happens when something is transferred **3.** PSYCHOL **REDIRECTION OF FEELING** in psychoanalysis or other psychotherapy, the process in which somebody unconsciously redirects feelings about something onto a new object, often the analyst or therapist —**transferential** /tránssfə rénsh'l/ *adj*

transfer factor *n* a polypeptide that is produced by white blood cells and can transfer immunity from one cell to another or from one person to another

transfer fee *n* a fee that is paid for a professional footballer or rugby player who is transferred from one club to another before his or her contract has expired

transfer list *n* a list of professional footballers or rugby players who are available to be transferred

transferor /transs fúrər/, **transferrer** *n* somebody who transfers a title, right, or property to somebody else

transfer payment *n* an item of personal income that comes from the state or a financial institution and is not investment income or payment for goods or services

transferrable *adj* another spelling of **transferable**

transferrer *n* LAW another spelling of **transferor**

transferrin /transs férrin/ *n* a serum protein that transports iron to bone marrow for the production of red blood cells [Mid-20C. < TRANS- + Latin *ferrum* 'iron']

transfer RNA *n* RNA that attaches amino acids to protein chains being made at ribosomes

transfiguration /tránss figgə ráysh'n/ *n* **1.** a dramatic change in appearance, especially one that reveals great beauty, spirituality, or magnificence **2.** the transfiguring of somebody or something

Transfiguration *n* **1.** in Christianity, the sudden appearance of radiant light emanating from Jesus Christ, recorded in the Bible as happening on a mountaintop in front of three of his disciples **2.** a Christian festival marking the Transfiguration of Jesus Christ. Date: 6 August or, in the Eastern Orthodox Church, 19 August.

transfigure /transs fíggər/ (**-ures, -uring, -ured**) *vt* to transform the appearance of somebody or something, revealing great beauty, spirituality, or magnificence [14C. < Latin *transfigurare* 'change the shape of' < *figura* 'shape' (see FIGURE)] —**transfigurement** *n*

transfinite /transs fī nīt/ *adj* describes a mathematical entity such as a number, group, or quantity that extends beyond infinity [Early 20C. < German *transfinit* < Latin *trans-* 'across, over' + *finitus* 'finite, limited']

transfinite number *n* a system of cardinal and ordinal numbers, used in the comparison of infinite sets, to which several types of infinity can be assigned concurrently

transfix /transs fíks/ (**-fixes, -fixing, -fixed**) *vt* **1. MAKE SOMEBODY IMMOBILE WITH SHOCK** to shock or terrify somebody so much as to induce a momentary inability to move **2. PIERCE THROUGH SOMEBODY** to pierce somebody or something through with a weapon or other sharp object **3.** MED **CUT COMPLETELY THROUGH LIMB** to cut through a part of the body completely, e.g. when amputating a limb [Late 16C. Directly or via Old French *transfixer* < Latin *transfix-*, past participle of *transfigere* 'pierce, run through' < *figere* 'to fix'] —**transfixion** *n*

transform *v* /transs fáwrm/ (**-forms, -forming, -formed**) **1.** *vt* **CHANGE SOMETHING DRAMATICALLY** to change somebody or something completely, especially improving their appearance or usefulness **2.** *vi* **UNDERGO TOTAL CHANGE** to change completely for the better **3.** *vt* PHYS **CONVERT SOMETHING TO DIFFERENT ENERGY** to convert one form of energy to another **4.** *vt* ELEC ENG **CHANGE ELECTRICAL CURRENT BY TRANSFORMER** to increase or decrease current or voltage by means of a transformer **5.** *vt* MATHS **CHANGE MATHEMATICAL EXPRESSION BY OPERATOR** to change the form of a mathematical expression in keeping with a mathematical rule, especially by the substitution of variables or the change of coordinates **6.** *vt* LING **CHANGE CONSTRUCTION BY LINGUISTIC TRANSFORMATION** to apply transformational rules to a linguistic construction ■ *n* /tránss fawrm/ **1.** LING same as **transformation** (sense 9) **2. RESULT OF MATHEMATICAL TRANSFORMATION** a process or rule by which one mathematical entity such as a line or expression can be derived from another [14C. Directly or via French *transformer* < Latin *transformare* 'form across' < *formare* < *forma* 'mould, shape'] —**transformable** *adj* —**transformative** *adj*

SYNONYMS See *change*.

transformation /tránsfər máysh'n/ *n* **1. COMPLETE CHANGE** a complete change, usually into something with an improved appearance or usefulness **2. TRANSFORMING** the act or process of transforming somebody or something **3.** MATHS **SUBSTITUTION OF VARIABLES** the mathematical conversion of an expression, equation, or function into another equivalent entity, e.g. by the substitution of one set of variables with another **4.** GENETICS **GENETIC CHANGE** a permanent change in the genetic make-up of a cell when it acquires foreign DNA **5.** BIOL **CELL MODIFICATION** the conversion of a normal cell into a malignant cell brought about by the action of a carcinogen or virus **6.** MATHS **CHANGE IN POSITION OF AXIS** a change in the position or direction of the axes of a mathematical coordinate system without changing their relative angles **7.** PHYS **CHANGE IN ATOMIC NUCLEUS** the change of one type of atom to another, resulting from a nuclear reaction **8.** LING **STAGE IN GRAMMATICAL CONVERSION** in transformational grammar, the process of converting one linguistic construction or structure to another, following the rules that convert deep structure to surface structure **9.** LING **STAGE IN GRAMMATICAL CONVERSION** in transformational grammar, a construction or structure generated by using the rules that convert deep structure into surface structure **10.** THEATRE **SUDDEN SET CHANGE** a sudden changing of a stage set that takes place in sight of the audience —**transformational** /tránsfər máysh'nəl/ *adj* —**transformationally** *adv*

USAGE transformation, transmigration, or **transmutation?** ***Transformation*** means 'a complete change, usually into something with an improved appearance or usefulness' (*a transformation of the dingy attic into a sunny loft*). ***Transmutation*** is 'a change, or the process of changing, from one form, substance, nature, or state into another' (*the transmutation of society from industrial to postindustrial; the transmutation of base metals into gold by alchemy*). It is rather close in meaning to ***transformation***. The two senses of ***transmigration*** are not shared by ***transformation*** and ***transmutation***: 'movement from one place to another' (*a huge transmigration of geese from Canada to Florida*), and 'the supposed passage of a dead person's soul into another body' (*transmigration of the soul*). Problems occur when people use ***transmigration*** when either ***transformation*** or ***transmutation*** is the correct choice: *an obvious transformation/transmutation* [not *transmigration*] *in attitude from liberal to conservative.*

transformational grammar *n* grammar that is based on the theory that language has a deep structure and that there are rules that transform the deep structure into the surface structure. It uses transformational rules to describe a language.

transformational rule *n* **1.** in transformational grammar, a rule that generates one stage from another in the conversion of deep structure into surface structure **2.** in logic, a rule for deriving theorems from axioms

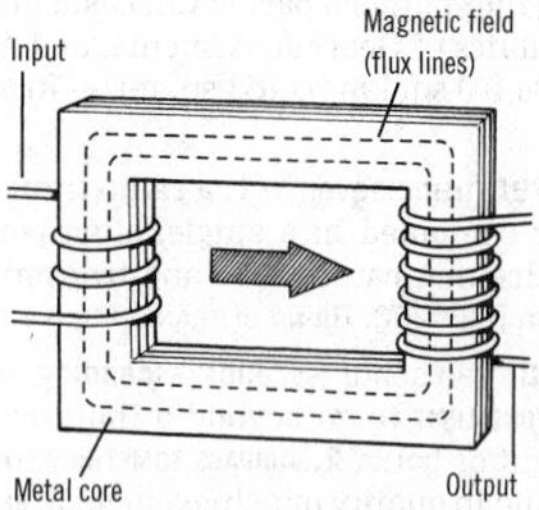

transformer

transformer /transs fáwrmər/ *n* **1.** a device that transfers electrical energy from one alternating circuit to another with a change in voltage, current, phase, or impedance **2.** somebody or something that effects a transformation

transfuse /transs fyóoz/ (**-fuses, -fusing, -fused**) *vt* **1.** MED **GIVE BLOOD TO SOMEBODY** to administer blood obtained from one person into the bloodstream of another person **2.** MED **PUT FLUID INTO SOMEBODY'S BLOODSTREAM** to administer a fluid such as saline or plasma into somebody's bloodstream to replace lost fluid **3. TRANSFER SOMETHING BY POURING** to pour something from one container into another (*formal or technical*)

4. **SPREAD THROUGHOUT SOMETHING** to spread throughout something and affect every part of it [Early 15C. < Latin *transfus-*, past participle of *transfundere* 'decant, transfer' < *fundere* 'pour'] —**transfusable** *adj* —**transfuser** *n* —**transfusive** *adj*

transfusion /transs fyoózh'n/ *n* 1. the transfer of whole blood, blood components, or bone marrow from a healthy donor into the bloodstream of somebody who has lost blood or who has a blood disorder 2. the act or process of transfusing something

transgender /tranz jéndər, transs-/, **transgendered** /trans jéndərd, tranz-/ *adj* relating to transsexuals or transvestites —**transgender** *n*

transgene /tránss jeen, tránz-/ *n* a gene transferred from one organism to another

transgenic /transs jénnik, tranz-/ *adj* 1. describes an animal or plant that contains genes from a different species, transferred using the techniques of genetic modification 2. describes the technique of transferring genetic material from one organism into the DNA of another —**transgenically** *adv* —**transgenesis** /trans jénnəsiss/ *n*

transgress /tranz gréss/ (**-gresses, -gressing, -gressed**) *v* 1. *vt* **BREAK LAW** to break a law, rule, or moral code ○ *transgress the law* 2. *vi* **DO WRONG** to commit a crime or do wrong by disobeying a law, command, or moral code ○ *He transgressed against the organization's code of conduct.* 3. *vt* **OVERSTEP PROPER LIMIT** to go beyond a limit, usually in a blameworthy way ○ *She'd transgressed the bounds of civil behaviour.* [15C. Directly or via French *transgresser* < Latin *transgress-*, past participle of *transgredi* 'step across, go over' < *gradi* 'to step, go'] —**transgressive** /tranz gréssiv/ *adj* —**transgressively** *adv* —**transgressor** *n*

transgression /tranz grésh'n/ *n* 1. **ACTION VIOLATING LAW OR CODE** a crime or any act that violates a law, command, or moral code 2. **COMMISSION OF WRONGS** the committing of acts that violate a law, command, or moral code 3. **OVERSTEPPING LIMIT** an act or the process of overstepping a limit

transgressive fiction *n* a literary genre characterized by graphic exploration of taboo topics, to which the work of writers such as the Marquis de Sade and William Burroughs belongs. It is based on the belief that knowledge is to be found at the very edge of human experience.

tranship *vti* TRANSP another spelling of **transship**

transhumance /transs hyoómənss/ *n* the practice of moving livestock between different grazing lands according to season, especially up to mountain pastures in summer and back down into the valleys in winter [Early 20C. < French < *transhumer* 'go across ground' < Latin *humus* 'ground'] —**transhumant** *adj*

transient /tránzi ənt/ *adj* 1. **SHORT IN DURATION** lasting for only a short time and quickly coming to an end, disappearing, or changing ○ *a transient emotion* ○ *transient sunlight on an otherwise cloudy day* 2. **NOT PERMANENTLY SETTLED IN PLACE** staying in a place for only a short period of time ○ *transient workers* 3. PHILOSOPHY same as **transeunt** ■ *n* 1. **SOMEBODY STAYING BRIEFLY** somebody who stays in a place only briefly, e.g. a migrant labourer or hotel guest 2. ELEC ENG **BRIEF DISTURBANCE IN ELECTRICAL CIRCUIT** an oscillation or brief disturbance in a system, e.g. a sudden pulse of current or voltage in an electrical circuit [Late 16C. Alteration of Latin *transiens* (stem *transeunt-*), present participle of *transire* 'pass away, go across' < *ire* 'go'] —**transience** *n* —**transiency** *n* —**transiently** *adv*

transient ischaemic attack *n* MED same as **ministroke** (*technical*)

transilluminate /tránzi loómi nayt/ (**-nates, -nating, -nated**) *vt* to shine a bright light through a body organ or cavity to detect disease or other anomaly —**transillumination** /tránzi loomi náysh'n/ *n* —**transilluminator** *n*

transistor /tran zístər/ *n* 1. a small low-powered solid-state electronic device consisting of a semiconductor and at least three electrodes, used as an amplifier and rectifier and frequently incorporated into integrated circuit chips 2. HOUSEHOLD same as **transistor radio** [Mid-20C. Blend of TRANSFER + RESISTOR]

transistorize /tran zístə rīz/ (**-izes, -izing, -ized**), **transistorise** (**-ises, -ising, -ised**) *vt* to equip a device or circuit with transistors

transistor radio *n* a small portable radio that uses transistors in its circuits

transit /tránzit/ *n* 1. **ACT OF TRAVELLING ACROSS SOMETHING** the act of travelling or being transported through or across an area, over a distance, or from one place to another ○ *a transit permit* 2. **ROUTE** a particular route or method used in travelling through or across an area 3. *N Am* TRANSP **PUBLIC TRANSPORT** the transportation of passengers by means of a local public transport system ○ *travelled by rapid transit* 4. ASTRON **MOVEMENT OF PLANET ACROSS SUN** the movement of Venus or Mercury across the face of the Sun, or of a moon or its shadow across the face of a planet, as seen from Earth 5. ASTRON **PASSAGE OF STAR ACROSS MERIDIAN** the apparent movement of a star or planet across the meridian from which it is being observed, caused by the Earth's rotation 6. ASTROL **CROSSING OF ZODIAC BY PLANET** the passing of a planet across a specific point on the zodiac 7. **TRANSITION** a transition or passing, e.g. from life to a supposed spiritual existence after death 8. *N Am* CIV ENG same as **transit theodolite** ■ *v* (**-sits, -siting, -sited**) 1. *vti* **PASS THROUGH SOMETHING** to pass through, over, or across something ○ *They transited the area on foot.* 2. *vti* ASTRON **MAKE ASTRONOMICAL TRANSIT** to make a transit across the face of the Sun or a planet, or across a meridian 3. *vt* CIV ENG **REVERSE DIRECTION OF SURVEYING TELESCOPE** to rotate the telescope of a surveying instrument horizontally through 180°, thus reversing its direction [15C. < Latin *transitus* 'passage' < *transire* 'go across' < *ire* 'go'] —**transitable** *adj* ◇ **in transit** in the process of travelling or being transported from one place to another

CULTURAL NOTE ***The Transit of Venus***, a novel (1980) by Australian writer Shirley Hazzard. Set in postwar England and the United States, it tells of the long-term relationship between a British astronomer and an Australian woman.

transit camp *n* a camp set up to accommodate people such as refugees, soldiers, or prisoners of war temporarily, until they can be sent on to a final destination

transit circle *n* an astronomical telescope that moves in a north-south plane so that it can be used to determine the exact time at which a star, planet, or other astronomical object passes directly overhead

transit instrument *n* a telescopic instrument that can move only in the plane of a meridian, used to determine the exact time at which a star, planet, or other astronomical object crosses that meridian

transition /tran zísh'n/ *n* 1. **PROCESS OF CHANGE** a process or period in which something undergoes a change and passes from one state, stage, form, or activity to another 2. MUSIC **MUSICAL PASSAGE** a passage connecting two sections of a musical composition 3. MUSIC **CHANGE OF KEY** a progression from one key to another in a piece of music 4. GRAM **LINKING WORD OR PHRASE** a word, phrase, or passage that links one subject or idea to another in speech or writing 5. PHYS, CHEM **CHANGE BETWEEN PHASES** a change between phases such as solid to liquid or liquid to gas 6. ARCHIT **ARCHITECTURAL STYLE BETWEEN ROMANESQUE AND GOTHIC** a style of architecture in many buildings dating from the 12th century in Western Europe, in which the Romanesque and Gothic styles are combined 7. PHYS **CHANGE IN ATOMIC NUCLEUS** a change in the energy level or state of an atomic nucleus in which a single quantum of electromagnetic radiation is either lost or gained [15C. < Latin *transition-* < *transire* (see TRANSIT)] —**transitional** *adj*

transition element, **transition metal** *n* a metallic element such as copper or gold that has an incomplete penultimate electron shell and variable valencies, and typically forms coloured compounds

transition point *n* 1. the point at which laminar flow in a moving fluid changes to turbulent flow 2. PHYS same as **transition temperature**

transition temperature *n* the temperature at which a substance loses or gains a specific property, especially superconductivity

transitive /tránssətiv/ *adj* 1. GRAM needing or usually taking a direct object ○ *a transitive verb* 2. LOGIC describes a given relation between terms such that if it exists between 'a' and 'b' and between 'b' and 'c', then it also exists between 'a' and 'c'. Typical transitive relationships include 'is greater than', 'is equal to', and 'is similar to'. —**transitively** *adv* —**transitiveness** *n* —**transitivity** /tránssə tívvəti/ *n*

transit lane *n* in Australia, a traffic lane reserved, usually during rush hours, for the exclusive use of some vehicles and private cars carrying a minimum number of passengers

transit lounge *n* a waiting room at an international airport used mainly by passengers transferring from one flight to another without presenting themselves to customs or immigration officials

transitory /tránssətəri/ *adj* not permanent or lasting, but existing only for a short time ○ *a transitory infatuation* —**transitorily** *adv* —**transitoriness** *n*

SYNONYMS See ***temporary***.

transit passenger *n* a passenger at an airport who is there simply to change flights and is therefore not required to go through customs or immigration formalities

transit theodolite *n* a surveying instrument surmounted by a telescope that can be rotated completely around its horizontal axis, used for measuring vertical and horizontal angles. N Am term **transit**

Transkei /tránss kī/ former homeland in South Africa, now part of Eastern Cape Province

transl. *abbr* 1. translated 2. translation 3. translator

translate /transs láyt/ (**-lates, -lating, -lated**) *v* 1. *vti* **TURN WORDS INTO DIFFERENT LANGUAGE** to reproduce a written or spoken text in a different language while retaining the original meaning ○ *Can you translate that phrase?* 2. *vi* **BE CAPABLE OF BEING TRANSLATED** to be capable of being translated, or have an equivalent in another language ○ *The idiom doesn't translate well.* 3. *vt* **CONVERT CODE** to convert computer data to a different form according to an algorithm ○ *translate the program into machine code* 4. *vt* **SAY SOMETHING IN UNDERSTANDABLE TERMS** to say or explain something in terms that are easier to understand ○ *The attendant muttered something vague, which, when translated, meant 'We don't know what happened to your car'.* 5. *vt* **INTERPRET MEANING** to explain the meaning of something not expressed in words, e.g. an action, gesture, or look ○ *I translated his silence as approval.* 6. *vti* **CHANGE FORM OF SOMETHING** to change something from one form or effect into another, or be changed from one form or effect into another ○ *'Microchips controlled by software now translate the flick of a pilot's wrist into the movement of a wing flap.'* (*Discover Magazine*; May 1996) 7. *vt* **MOVE SOMEBODY OR SOMETHING** to move or carry somebody or something from one place to another, usually with a complete change of condition or scene ○ *She was translated from her small country home to a high-rise city apartment.* 8. *vt* CHR **TRANSFER CLERGY** to transfer a member of the clergy to another office, especially a bishop to another see 9. *vt* CHR **MOVE REMAINS OF SAINT** to move the remains or relics of a saint from one place to another 10. *vt* RELIG **CONVEY SOMEBODY TO HEAVEN** to convey somebody to heaven, especially in a way that is believed not to involve death 11. *vt* GENETICS **DECIPHER GENETIC INSTRUCTIONS FOR MAKING PROTEIN** to decipher the genetic message carried by a molecule of messenger RNA and assemble the amino acids of a protein chain according to the instructions 12. *vt* PHYS **MOVE BODY SIDEWAYS IN STRAIGHT LINE** to move a body sideways through space in a direct straight line without rotation [14C. < Latin *translatus*, used as past participle of *transferre* 'carry across' < *ferre* 'carry'] —**translatability** /transs láytə bílləti/ *n* —**translatable** *adj*

translation /transs láysh'n/ *n* 1. **VERSION IN ANOTHER LANGUAGE** a word, phrase, or text in another language that has a meaning equivalent to that of the original 2. **EXPRESSING OF SOMETHING IN DIFFERENT LANGUAGE** the rendering of something written or spoken in one language in words of a different language ○ *It loses a little in translation.* 3. **CHANGE OR TRANSFERENCE** a change in form or state, or transference to a different place, office, or sphere 4. GENETICS **PROCESS DETERMINING AMINO ACID SEQUENCE** the process by which information in messenger RNA directs the sequence of amino acids assembled by a ribosome during protein synthesis 5. PHYS **MOTION IN STRAIGHT LINE** the movement of a body

in a straight line so that every point on the body follows a parallel path and no rotation takes place —**translational** *adj*

translator /transs láytər/ *n* **1.** LANGUAGE **SOMEBODY WHO TRANSLATES** somebody or something that translates, in writing or speech, from one language into another **2.** BROADCAST **TRANSMITTER THAT ALTERS SIGNAL FREQUENCY** a radio transmitter that receives a signal on one frequency and retransmits it on another **3.** COMPUT **COMPUTER CONVERSION PROGRAM** a computer program that converts other programs from one computer language into another

transliterate /transs líttə rayt, tranz-/ (**-ates, -ating, -ated**) *vt* to represent letters or words written in one alphabet using the corresponding letters of another [Mid-19C. < TRANS- + Latin *littera* 'letter of the alphabet'] —**transliteration** /transs líttə ráysh'n, tranz-/ *n* —**transliterator** *n*

translocate /tránss lō káyt/ (**-cates, -cating, -cated**) *vt* to move somebody or something from one place or position to another

translocation /tránss lō káysh'n/ *n* **1. MOVEMENT FROM ONE PLACE TO ANOTHER** movement, or the act of moving something or somebody, from one place or position to another **2.** BOT **MOVEMENT OF FOOD IN PLANTS** the movement of soluble materials within a plant. Common examples are the movement of food materials from the leaves to storage organs, and the movement of dissolved minerals upwards from the roots. **3.** GENETICS **TRANSFER OF PART OF CHROMOSOME** the transfer of part of a chromosome to a new position on the same or on a different chromosome with resultant rearrangement of the genes

translucent /transs lo͞oss'nt/ *adj* **1.** allowing light to pass through, but only diffusely, so that objects on the other side cannot be clearly distinguished ○ *a translucent membrane* **2.** having a glowing appearance, as if light were coming through ○ *translucent skin* [15C. < Latin *translucent-*, present participle of *translucere* 'shine through' < *lucere* 'shine' (see LUCID)] —**translucence** *n* —**translucency** *n* —**translucently** *adv*

translunar /transs lo͞onər/, **translunary** /-lo͞onəri/ *adj* situated or coming from beyond the Moon or its orbit around the Earth

transmarine /tránzmə reén/ *adj* **1.** involving crossing a sea or ocean **2.** situated or coming from across a sea or ocean [Late 16C. < Latin *transmarinus* < *marinus* (see MARINE)]

transmigrate /tránz mī gráyt/ (**-grates, -grating, -grated**) *vi* **1.** to move from one place or country to another **2.** according to some religions, to pass into another body at or after death (*refers to the soul*) [15C. < Latin *transmigrat-*, past participle of *transmigrare* < *migrare* 'migrate'] —**transmigrant** /tranz mígrənt/ *adj, n* —**transmigrative** /tranz mígrətiv/ *adj* —**transmigrator** *n* —**transmigratory** /tranz mígrətəri/ *adj*

transmigration /tránz mī gráysh'n/ *n* **1.** movement by a person or group from one place or country to another **2.** according to some religions, the supposed passage of the dead person's soul into another body at or after death [14C. Directly or via French < late Latin *transmigration-* < Latin *transmigrare* (see TRANSMIGRATE)] —**transmigrational** *adj*

USAGE See *transformation.*

transmissible /tranz míssəb'l/ *adj* able to be transmitted —**transmissibility** /tranz míssə bílləti/ *n*

transmissible spongiform encephalopathy *n* VET full form of **TSE**

transmission /tranz mísh'n/ *n* **1. ACT OF TRANSMITTING** the act or process of transmitting something, especially radio signals, radio or television broadcasts, data, or a disease **2. SOMETHING TRANSMITTED** something transmitted, e.g. a radio signal **3.** BROADCAST **RADIO OR TV BROADCAST** a radio or television broadcast **4.** AUTOMOT **MECHANISM TRANSFERRING POWER TO WHEELS** the mechanical system, including gears and shafts, by which power is transmitted from the engine of a motor vehicle to the drive wheels **5.** *N Am* AUTOMOT same as **gearbox** **6.** PHYS **ABILITY TO LET RADIATION THROUGH** the ability of a material to let incoming radiation pass completely through it [Early 17C. Directly or via French < Latin *transmission-* < *mission-* 'a letting go, release' (see MISSION)] —**transmissive** *adj* —**transmissively** *adv* —**transmissiveness** *n*

transmission line *n* a conductor that carries electricity or other electromagnetic waves, usually over long distances, e.g. a coaxial cable

transmit /tranz mít/ (**-mits, -mitting, -mitted**) *v* **1.** *vt* **SEND SOMETHING** to send something, pass something on, or cause something to spread, from one person, thing, or place to another ○ *The disease is transmitted by droplet infection.* **2.** *vt* **COMMUNICATE INFORMATION** to communicate a message, information, or news ○ *Data was quickly transmitted.* **3.** *vti* TELECOM, MEDIA **SEND SIGNAL** to send a signal by radio waves, satellite, or wire **4.** *vti* BROADCAST **BROADCAST PROGRAMME** to broadcast a radio or television programme **5.** *vt* PHYS **MAKE RADIATION PASS THROUGH SOMETHING** to make heat, sound, light, or other radiation pass or spread through space or a medium **6.** *vt* PHYS **ALLOW RADIATION THROUGH** to allow heat, sound, or light or other radiation to pass through **7.** *vt* MECH ENG **TRANSFER POWER** to transfer power, force, or movement from one part of a mechanism to another [14C. < Latin *transmittere* 'send across' < *mittere* 'send'] —**transmittable** *adj* —**transmittal** *n* —**transmittible** *adj*

transmittance /tranz mítt'nss/ *n* **1.** the act or process of transmitting something **2.** the ability of a material to let incoming radiation pass completely through it, measured as the ratio of incident radiation to transmitted radiation

transmitter /tranz míttər/ *n* **1. AGENT OR MEANS OF TRANSMISSION** somebody or something that transmits something **2.** BROADCAST **PART OF BROADCASTING EQUIPMENT** a piece of broadcasting equipment that generates a radio-frequency wave, modulates it so that it carries a meaningful signal, and sends it out from an antenna **3.** TELECOM **TELEPHONE PART** the part of a telephone that converts sound waves to electrical impulses

transmogrify /tranz móggri fī/ (**-fies, -fying, -fied**) *vt* to change the appearance or form of something, especially in a grotesque or bizarre way (*formal*) [Mid-17C. Origin ?] —**transmogrification** /tranz móggrifi káysh'n/ *n*

transmontane /tranz móntayn/ *adj* GEOG same as **tramontane** ■ *n* PEOPLES same as **tramontane** *n* (sense 2) [15C. < Latin *transmontanus* < *montanus* 'of mountains' < *mont-* 'mountain']

transmundane /tranz mún dayn/ *adj* belonging not to this material world and its concerns, but extending beyond them (*literary*)

transmutation /tránzmyoo táysh'n/ *n* **1. CHANGE** a change, or the process of changing, from one form, substance, nature, or state to another **2.** PHYS **CHANGE OF ONE ELEMENT INTO ANOTHER** the transformation of the atom of one chemical element into the atom of another by disintegration or nuclear bombardment **3.** HIST **CONVERSION TO GOLD** the supposed conversion of base metals into gold or silver by alchemy —**transmutational** *adj*

USAGE See *transformation.*

transmute /tranz myo͞ot/ (**-mutes, -muting, -muted**) *vti* **1. CHANGE** to change something from one form, nature, substance, or state to another, or be changed in this way **2.** PHYS **CHANGE FROM ONE ELEMENT TO ANOTHER** to change one chemical element into another through disintegration or nuclear bombardment, or be changed in this way **3.** HIST **CONVERT BASE METAL TO GOLD** in alchemy, to convert a base metal into gold or silver, or be converted in this way [14C. < Latin *transmutare* 'change thoroughly' < *mutare* 'to change'] —**transmutability** /-myo͞otə bílləti/ *n* —**transmutable** *adj* —**transmutably** *adv* —**transmutative** /-ətiv/ *adj* —**transmuter** *n*

SYNONYMS See *change.*

transnational /tranz násh'nəl/ *adj* not confined to a single nation or state, but including, extending over, or operating within more than one —**transnationally** *adv*

transoceanic /tránz ōshi ánnik/ *adj* **1.** involving crossing an ocean **2.** situated or coming from across an ocean

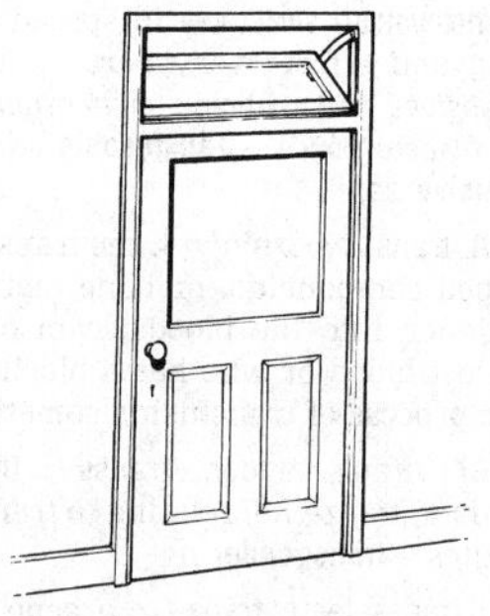

transom

transom /tránssəm/ *n* **1. STRUCTURAL BEAM ABOVE WINDOW** a horizontal beam or stone above a window that supports the structure above **2. CROSSPIECE ABOVE DOOR** a crosspiece over a door or between the top of a door and a window above **3. CROSSBAR THAT DIVIDES WINDOW** a crossbar of wood or stone that divides a window horizontally **4.** *N Am* BUILDINGS same as **fanlight** (sense 2) **5. BEAM FOR STRENGTHENING STERN** a transverse beam for strengthening the stern of a ship **6. PLANKING AT SHIP'S STERN** the planking forming a flat surface across the stern of a ship **7. HORIZONTAL BEAM OF CROSS OR GALLOWS** the horizontal beam of a cross or gallows [14C. Probably alteration of Latin *transtrum* 'crossbeam'] —**transomed** *adj*

transonic /tran sónnik/ *adj* relating to speeds close to the speed of sound or conditions encountered when travelling at those speeds [Mid-20C. < TRANS- + SONIC after SUPERSONIC and ULTRASONIC]

transonic barrier *n* AEROSP same as **sound barrier** (*technical*)

transp. *abbr* **1.** transport **2.** transportation

transpacific /tránzpə síffik/ *adj* **1.** involving crossing the Pacific Ocean **2.** situated or coming from across the Pacific Ocean

transpadane /tránzpə dayn/ *adj* situated on or coming from the northern side of the River Po in northern Italy [Early 17C. < Latin *transpadanus* < *padanus* 'of the Padus (River Po)']

transparency /transs párrənssi/ (*plural* **-cies**) *n* **1.** the quality or state of being transparent **2.** a positive photographic image on a transparent material, especially film or a slide, that can be viewed when light is shone through it. Transparencies are generally viewed using a projector, a light table, or a hand-held viewer. [Late 16C. < medieval Latin *transparentia* < *transparent-* (see TRANSPARENT)]

transparency hood *n* a lid with a light source for a scanner that allows transparencies to be copied

transparent /transs párrənt/ *adj* **1. EASILY SEEN THROUGH** allowing light to pass through with little or no interruption or distortion so that objects on the other side can be clearly seen ○ *transparent plastic* **2. FINE ENOUGH TO SEE THROUGH** thin or fine enough in texture to see through ○ *transparent fabric* **3. OBVIOUS AND EASY TO RECOGNIZE** clearly recognizable as what he, she, or it really is ○ *a transparent motive* **4. FRANK** completely open and frank ○ *She was grateful for the transparent honesty of the reply.* ○ *They were completely transparent about their motives.* **5.** PHYS **LETTING RADIATION THROUGH** allowing electromagnetic radiation of specific wavelengths to pass through [15C. Directly or via French < medieval Latin *transparent-*, present participle of *transparere* 'shine through' < Latin *parere* 'appear'] —**transparently** *adv*

transparent context *n* in logic, an expression in which the truth-value is not changed when any term is replaced by another with the same reference

transpierce /transs peérss/ (**-pierces, -piercing, -pierced**) *vt* to pierce through something (*archaic*)

transpire /tran spír/ (**-spires, -spiring, -spired**) *v* **1.** *vt* **COME TO LIGHT** to become known or be disclosed ○ *It later transpired that they had been furious at what had happened.* **2.** ⚠ *vi* **HAPPEN** to take place ○ *What transpired after they left remains a secret.* **3.** *vti* PHYSIOL **GIVE OFF VAPOUR THROUGH SKIN** to give off water vapour through the pores of the skin **4.** *vti* BOT **LOSE WATER VAPOUR** to lose water vapour from a plant's

surface, especially through minute surface pores **(stomata)** [15C. Directly or via French *transpirer* < medieval Latin *transpirare* 'breathe through' < Latin *spirare* 'breathe'] —**transpirable** *adj* —**transpiration** /tránsspi ráysh'n/ *n* —**transpiratory** *adj*

USAGE The use of ***transpire*** to mean 'happen', as in the sentence *Tell me what transpired at the meeting*, is sometimes criticized, although it has been in common use for several centuries and conveys something of the sense inherent in its uncontroversial meaning 'become known or be disclosed': *It transpired that the police had known about the plan all along.*

transplant *v* /transs plaànt/ (**-plants, -planting, -planted**) **1.** *vt* GARDENING **RELOCATE PLANT** to remove a plant from the place where it is growing and replant it somewhere else **2.** *vi* GARDENING **BE CAPABLE OF BEING MOVED** to be capable of being transplanted ○ *Poppies do not transplant well.* **3.** *vt* **MOVE SOMEBODY TO ANOTHER PLACE** to move somebody or something to another place or position **4.** *vt* SURG **TRANSFER BODY ORGAN** to transfer an organ or tissue from one body to another or from one place in somebody's body to another ■ *n* /tránss plaant/ **1.** SURG **SURGICAL PROCEDURE** a surgical operation or procedure to transplant an organ or tissue **2.** SURG **TRANSPLANTED ORGAN OR TISSUE** an organ or tissue that has been transplanted **3.** GARDENING **TRANSPLANTED PLANT** a plant that has been transplanted [15C. Directly or via French *transplanter* < late Latin *transplantare* 'plant across' < *plantare* 'to plant'] —**transplantable** *adj* —**transplantation** /tránss plaan táysh'n/ *n* —**transplanter** *n*

transpolar /tranz pṓlər/ *adj* crossing or extending across either of the polar regions

transponder /tran spóndər/, **transpondor** *n* **1.** a radio or radar transceiver that automatically transmits a signal of its own when it receives a predetermined signal from elsewhere, used especially for locating and identifying objects **2.** a receiving and transmitting device in a communication or broadcast satellite that relays the signals it receives back to Earth [Mid-20C. < TRANSMIT + RESPOND]

transpontine /tranz pón tīn/ *adj* located on or coming from the other side of a bridge [Mid-19C. < TRANS- + Latin *pont-*, stem of *pons* 'bridge']

transport *vt* /transs páwrt/ (**-ports, -porting, -ported**) **1.** TRANSP **CARRY SOMEBODY OR SOMETHING** to carry somebody or something from one place to another, usually in a vehicle **2. MAKE SOMEBODY IMAGINE BEING ELSEWHERE** to take somebody on a mental or imaginative journey to another place or time ○ *The sounds of the game transported him back to his youth.* **3. AFFECT SOMEBODY WITH STRONG EMOTION** to put somebody in a state of intense or uncontrollable emotion, especially joy ○ *She was transported with joy.* **4.** HIST **SEND SOMEBODY TO PENAL COLONY** to exile somebody to a penal colony ■ *n* /tráns pawrt/ **1.** TRANSP **CONVEYANCE OF SOMEBODY OR SOMETHING** the act or business of carrying somebody or something from one place to another, usually in a vehicle. N Am term **transportation 2.** TRANSP **MEANS OF TRAVELLING** a means of travelling or of carrying somebody or something from one place to another, usually in a vehicle ○ *It'll be quicker by public transport.* N Am term **transportation 3.** MIL, SHIPPING **CRAFT CARRYING PEOPLE OR FREIGHT** a ship or aircraft for carrying passengers, especially military personnel, or freight **4. EXPERIENCE OR DISPLAY OF INTENSE EMOTION** an experience or display of intense and uncontrollable emotion, especially joy (*often used in the plural*) ○ *in transports of delight* **5.** HIST **SOMEBODY SENT TO PENAL COLONY** somebody exiled to a penal colony [14C. Directly or via French *transporter* < Latin *transportare* 'carry across' < *portare* 'carry'] —**transportability** /tránss pawrtə bílləti/ *n* —**transportable** *adj*—**transportive** *adj*

transportation /tránsspawr táysh'n/ *n* **1.** *N Am* TRANSP same as **transport** *n* (senses 1–2) **2.** *US* the fare paid or charge made for travelling in a bus, train, or other public vehicle **3.** HIST exile to a penal colony

transport café *n UK* a roadside café that offers plain and inexpensive meals, used mainly by long-distance lorry drivers. ANZ, N Am term **truck stop**

transporter /transs páwrtər/ *n* **1.** somebody or something that transports something **2.** a large vehicle used to carry heavy loads, often other vehicles

transporter bridge *n* a bridge consisting of a high overarching framework from which a moving platform is suspended on cables. The platform goes back and forth, carrying vehicles across a body of water.

Transport Workers Union, Transport Workers Union of Australia *n* one of Australia's largest and best-known unions, representing workers in the field of transport

transpose /transs pṓz/ *v* (**-poses, -posing, -posed**) **1.** *vt* **REVERSE ORDER OF THINGS** to make two things change places or reverse their usual order, e.g. two letters in a word **2.** *vt* **MOVE SOMETHING TO DIFFERENT POSITION** to move something to a different position, especially in a sequence ○ *transposed that section to the end of the essay* **3.** *vt* **CHANGE SETTING OF SOMETHING** to take something such as a story, incident, or play out of its original setting or time and relocate it in another ○ *transposing the action from Shakespeare's time to the present* **4.** *vti* MUSIC **CHANGE MUSIC TO DIFFERENT KEY** to rewrite or play a musical composition in a key or at a pitch other than the one in which it was originally written or in which it is usually performed **5.** *vt* MATHS **MOVE TERM IN EQUATION** to transfer a term from one side of an equation to the other, reversing its sign ■ *n* MATHS **TYPE OF MATRIX** a matrix created by interchanging the rows and columns of a previously given matrix [14C. < French *transposer*, alteration (by association with *poser* 'to place') of Latin *transponere* < *ponere* 'to place'] —**transposability** /-pṓzə bílləti/ *n* —**transposable** *adj*—**transposal** *n*—**transposer** *n* —**transpositive** /-pózzətiv/ *adj*

transposing instrument /transs pṓzing-/ *n* a musical instrument whose part is written in a different key from the notes it produces when it plays, e.g. a horn or clarinet

transposition /tránsspə zísh'n/ *n* **1. REVERSAL OF ORDER** a reversal or alteration of the positions or order in which things stand **2. ACT OF RECASTING** the placing of something in a different setting, or the recasting of something in a different language, style, or medium **3.** MUSIC **ACT OF CHANGING KEY** the rewriting or playing of a piece of music in a key or at a pitch other than the original or usual one **4.** MATHS **TRANSFER OF TERM IN EQUATION** the transfer of a term from one side of an equation to another and the reversal of its sign —**transpositional** *adj*

transposon /transs pṓ zon/ *n* a segment of DNA that can move to a new position on the same or another chromosome, often modifying the action of neighbouring genes [Late 20C. < TRANSPOSITION]

transputer /tranz pyóotər/ *n* a powerful microchip with the functions of a microprocessor that has its own memory and the capability of parallel processing [Late 20C. Blend of TRANSISTOR + COMPUTER]

transsexual /tranz sékshoo əl/ *n* **1.** somebody who has undergone treatment to change his or her anatomical sex **2.** somebody who identifies himself or herself as a member of the opposite sex —**transsexual** *adj* —**transsexualism** *n*

transship /transs shíp/ (**-ships, -shipping, -shipped**), **tranship** *vti* to transfer goods from one means of transportation to another, or be transferred in this way —**transshipment** *n*

transubstantiate /tránssəb stánshi ayt/ (**-ates, -ating, -ated**) *v* **1.** *vi* in Roman Catholic and Eastern Orthodox doctrine, to undergo a change in substance, from bread and wine to the body and blood of Jesus Christ during Communion **2.** *vti* to change from one substance into another, or change something from one substance into another (*formal*) [15C. < medieval Latin *transubstantiat-*, past participle of *transubstantiare* 'change the substance of thoroughly' < Latin *substantia* (see SUBSTANCE)] —**transubstantial** *adj*—**transubstantially** *adv*

transubstantiation /tránssəb stanshi áysh'n/ *n* **1.** the Roman Catholic and Eastern Orthodox doctrine that the bread and wine of Communion become, in substance, but not appearance, the body and blood of Jesus Christ at consecration **2.** the process by which one substance changes into another (*formal*) —**transubstantiationalist** *n*

transudate /tránss yoo dayt/ *n* a fluid that passes through the pores or interstices of a membrane

transude /tran syóod/ (**-sudes, -suding, -suded**) *vi* to pass through the pores or interstices of a membrane (*refers to a fluid such as sweat*) [Early 17C. < French *transsuder* 'sweat through' < Latin *sudare* 'to sweat'] —**transudation** /trán syoo dáysh'n/ *n* —**transudatory** *adj*

transuranic /tránzyoo ránnik/, **transuranian** /-ráyni ən/, **transuranium** /-ráyni əm/ *adj* having a higher atomic number than uranium

Transvaal /tránz vaal/ independent Afrikaner-dominated territory in South Africa that became a province in the Union of South Africa in 1910. In 1994 the region was divided into the three provinces that are now Gauteng, Limpopoe, and Mpumalanga.

transvalue /tranz vállyoo/ (**-ues, -uing, -ued**) *vt* to re-evaluate something using a different standard, especially one that differs from conventional or accepted standards and results in a very different assessment of the worth of something —**transvaluation** /tránz valyoo áysh'n/ *n* —**transvaluer** *n*

transversal /tranz vúrss'l/ *n* a line that intersects two or more other lines ■ *adj* same as **transverse** —**transversally** *adv*

transverse /tranz vúrss/ *adj* **1. CROSSWISE** lying or extending crosswise or at right angles to something **2.** MATHS **PASSING THROUGH HYPERBOLA FOCI** passing through the foci of a hyperbola ■ *n* **CROSSWISE THING** something that lies or extends crosswise or at right angles to something [14C. < Latin *transversus*, past participle of *transvertere* 'turn across' < *vertere* 'to turn'] —**transversely** *adv*

transverse colon *n* the part of the colon that passes from right to left across the upper abdominal cavity just beneath the liver and stomach

transverse flute *n* a flute with the mouth hole on top of the barrel near one end. The player blows across the hole while holding the flute in a sideways horizontal position. The modern flute used to be known as the transverse flute in order to distinguish it from an end-blown flute such as a recorder.

transverse process *n* either of the two bony projections on the sides of a vertebra

transverse wave *n* a wave that makes the medium through which it travels vibrate in a direction at right angles to the direction of its travel

transvestite /tranz vés tīt/ *n* somebody who adopts the dress and often the behaviour of the opposite sex [Early 20C. < German *Transvestit* 'cross-dresser' < Latin *vestire* 'clothe, dress' (see VEST)] —**transvestism** *n* —**transvestitism** *n*

Transylvania /tránssil váyni ə/ historic region in eastern Europe that now forms the central and northwestern parts of Romania. Area: 62,000 sq. km/24,000 sq. mi. —**Transylvanian** *adj*

Transylvanian Alps /tránssil vayni ən-/ mountain range in the Carpathian Mountains, running east to west through south-central Romania

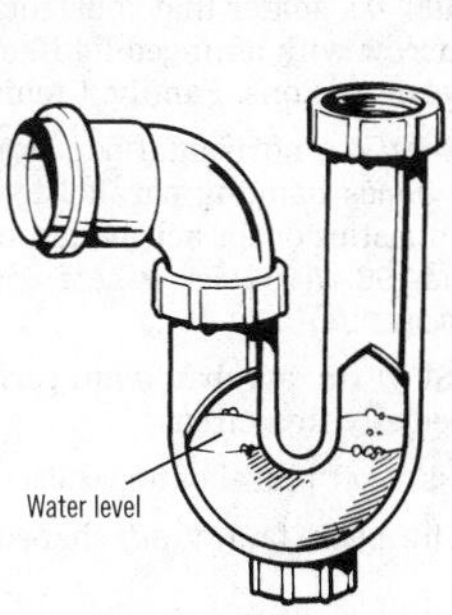

trap (sense 6)

trap[1] /trap/ *n* **1. SOMETHING DESIGNED TO CATCH ANIMALS** a device designed to catch an animal and kill it or prevent it escaping, e.g. a concealed pit or a mechanical device that springs shut **2. SCHEME TO CATCH SOMEBODY OUT** an ambush, scheme, or trick intended to catch somebody unawares and put the person at a disadvantage or in somebody else's power **3. CONFINING SITUATION** a situation from which it is difficult to escape and in which somebody feels confined, restricted, or in somebody else's power ○ *wanted to avoid the trap of being typecast in the same roles* **4.** BUILDINGS same as **trapdoor 5.** ANAT same as **mouth** *n* (sense 1) (*informal*) ○ *If the media ask questions, keep*

your trap shut. **6.** CONSTR **SECTION OF DRAINPIPE BLOCKING GAS** a curved section of a drainpipe that holds a quantity of water to act as a barrier to prevent sewer gas from rising up the pipe **7.** CONSTR **DEVICE PREVENTING PASSAGE OF GAS** a device designed to prevent gas, vapour, or other substances passing through or escaping from something **8.** SPORTS **DEVICE USED IN TRAPSHOOTING** a device that throws clay pigeons into the air for trapshooting **9.** GOLF **GOLFING HAZARD** a hazard, especially a bunker, on a golf course **10.** SPORTS **STARTING STALL FOR GREYHOUND** one of the set of stalls from which greyhounds are released at the start of a race **11.** VEHICLES **CARRIAGE** a light horse-drawn carriage with two wheels ■ **traps** *npl* MUSIC **PERCUSSION INSTRUMENTS** a set of percussion instruments, especially the drum set used in a dance orchestra or jazz band (*informal*) ■ *v* (**traps, trapping, trapped**) **1.** *vt* **CATCH SOMETHING IN TRAP** to catch an animal in a trap so that it is killed or unable to escape **2.** *vi* **SET TRAPS FOR ANIMALS** to set traps for animals, or make a living by catching animals in traps **3.** *vt* **HOLD SOMETHING IN TIGHT GRIP** to catch or hold something in a tight grip or narrow space so that it cannot be moved or is painfully squeezed ○ *I trapped my finger in the door.* **4.** *vt* **PLACE SOMEBODY IN CONFINING SITUATION** to put somebody in a situation from which it is difficult or impossible to escape ○ *They were trapped inside the burning building.* ○ *felt trapped in a dead-end job* **5.** *vt* **TAKE SOMEBODY BY SURPRISE** to put somebody at a disadvantage by means of an ambush, surprise, clever plan, or trick ○ *She was trapped into admitting the truth.* **6.** *vt* SOCCER **CONTROL BALL** to bring a moving ball quickly under control using a part of the body **7.** *vt* CRIME **CATCH OFFENDER** to identify or catch an offender by means of a speed trap or a security device **8.** *vt* **PREVENT AIR FROM ESCAPING** to prevent air, gas, heat, or a fluid from escaping **9.** *vt* CONSTR **EQUIP DRAINPIPE WITH TRAP** to put a trap into a drainpipe [Old English *træppe* (in *coltetræppe*, plant name), *treppe* 'trap, snare' < Germanic] ◇ **have been around the traps** *Aus* to be experienced or knowledgeable (*informal*)

trap² /trap/ *n* a dark fine-grained igneous rock such as basalt. N Am term **traprock** [Late 18C. < Swedish *trapp* < *trappa* 'stair' (from the rock's appearance)]

trap³ /trap/ *n* RIDING same as **trappings** (*archaic*) ■ **traps** *npl* somebody's personal belongings (*informal*) ■ *vt* (**traps, trapping, trapped**) to provide somebody or something with trappings or adornments ○ *They were all trapped out in the gaudiest of clothes.* [14C. Alteration of French *drap* 'cloth' < late Latin *drappus*]

Trapani /trə paáni/ seaport and capital city of Trapani Province, northwestern Sicily. Population: 69,688 (1997).

trapdoor /tráp dawr/ *n* a hatch covering a horizontal or sloping opening in a floor, ceiling, or roof [14C. < TRAP¹]

trapdoor spider *n* a spider that constructs a tubular silk-lined burrow with a hinged lid like a trapdoor. Native to: warm regions. Family: Ctenizidae.

trapeze /trə peéz/ *n* a horizontal bar attached to the ends of two ropes hanging parallel to each other, used for gymnastics or for acrobatics, especially in a circus [Mid-19C. Via French *trapèze* < late Latin *trapezium* (see TRAPEZIUM)]

trapeze artist *n* an acrobat who performs on a trapeze, especially in a circus

trapezia MATHS, ANAT plural of **trapezium**

trapeziform /trə peézi fawrm/ *adj* shaped like a trapezium

trapezii ANAT plural of **trapezius**

trapezium /trə peézi əm/ (*plural* **-ziums** or **-zia** /-zi ə/) *n* **1.** MATHS a quadrilateral that has two parallel sides. N Am term **trapezoid 2.** *N Am* MATHS same as **trapezoid** (sense 1) **3.** ANAT a small bone in the wrist at the base of the thumb [Late 16C. Via late Latin < Greek *trapezion* 'small table' < *trapeza* 'table' < *peza* 'foot'] —**trapezial** *adj*

trapezius /trə peézi əss/ (*plural* **-ziuses** or **-zii** /trə peézi ī/) *n* either of the two large flat triangular muscles that run from the back of the neck and cover each shoulder. They help to move the shoulder blades and draw the head backwards. [Early 18C. < modern Latin < late Latin *trapezium* (see TRAPEZIUM)]

trapezohedron /trə peézō heédrən/ (*plural* **-drons** or **-dra** /-drə/) *n* a crystal with faces that are all trapeziums in shape [Early 19C. < TRAPEZIUM] —**trapezohedral** *adj*

trapezoid /tráppi zoyd/ *n* **1.** MATHS a quadrilateral that has no parallel sides. N Am term **trapezium 2.** *N Am* MATHS same as **trapezium** (sense 1) **3.** ANAT a small bone in the wrist near the metatarsal bone that connects with the index finger —**trapezoidal** /tráppi zóyd'l/ *adj*

trapper /tráppər/ *n* somebody who makes a living by trapping animals for their fur or hides [Mid-18C. < TRAP¹]

trappings /tráppingz/ *npl* **1.** the dress, accessories, insignia, and other outward signs associated with an office, position, or status ○ *the trappings of power* **2.** an ornamental or ceremonial rig for a horse, including a decorated harness, saddle, and cloth covering [14C. < TRAP³]

Trappist /tráppist/ *n* a member of the main reformed branch of the Cistercian order of Christian monks, established in 1664 at La Trappe monastery in Normandy and noted for its vow of silence [Early 19C. < French *trappiste* < *La Trappe*]

traprock /tráp rok/ *n N Am* GEOL same as **trap**² [Early 19C. < TRAP²]

trapshooting /tráp shooting/ *n* the sport of shooting at clay pigeons thrown by a trap [Late 19C. < TRAP¹] —**trapshooter** *n*

trapunto /trə poóntō/ *n* quilting in which only the design, which is outlined with parallel lines of stitches, is padded to give it a raised look [Early 20C. < Italian, past participle of *trapungere* 'embroider' < Latin *pungere* 'to prick']

Traralgon /trə rálgən/ mining town in southeastern Victoria, Australia. Population: 19,699 (1991).

trash /trash/ *n* **1.** **NONSENSE** something spoken or written that is regarded as meaningless, absurd, or very inaccurate **2.** **POOR QUALITY LITERATURE OR ART** literature or art considered worthless or offensive ○ *How can you read such trash?* **3.** *N Am* **DISCARDED MATERIAL** discarded, unwanted, or worthless material or objects **4.** **OFFENSIVE TERM** an offensive term that deliberately insults somebody's social position or morals (*insult*) **5.** AGRIC **TRIMMINGS FROM PLANTS** twigs, branches, or leaves that have fallen or been trimmed from trees and plants **6.** INDUST **SUGAR CANE REFUSE** the dry refuse of sugar cane after it has been crushed for the juice, often used as fuel ■ *vt* (**trashes, trashing, trashed**) **1.** **DESTROY SOMETHING** to destroy, severely damage, or vandalize something deliberately (*informal*) ○*'The storm trashed bridges in Honduras and Central America.'* (*US News & World Report*; December 1998) **2.** **DISCARD SOMETHING** to throw away or discard something (*informal*) **3.** **CRITICIZE SOMEBODY SAVAGELY** to criticize somebody or something savagely, or condemn somebody or something as worthless (*informal*) **4.** AGRIC **REMOVE TWIGS AND BRANCHES** to remove twigs, branches, or leaves from plants **5.** INDUST **STRIP LEAVES FROM SUGAR CANE** to strip the outer leaves from sugar cane [14C. Probably < N Germanic] ◇ **talk trash** *N Am* to try to intimidate somebody, especially a rival or an opponent in a sporting contest, by being boastful or insulting (*slang*)

trash can *n N Am* HOUSEHOLD same as **dustbin** (*informal*)

trash fish *n US* a fish formerly thought of as unfit for human consumption, but now valued for its quality, e.g. skate or monkfish

trashy /tráshi/ (**-ier, -iest**) *adj* of very little worth or merit ○ *a trashy novel* —**trashily** *adv* —**trashiness** *n*

Trasimeno, Lake /trázzi meénō, -máynō/, **Trasimene, Lake** /trázzi meén/ lake in central Italy, and the largest lake in the Italian peninsula. Area: 128 sq. km/49 sq. mi.

trass /trass/ *n* a light-coloured volcanic rock (**tuff**) used in making cement and mortar [Late 18C. Via Dutch *tras* or German *Trass* < Latin *terra* 'earth']

trattoria /tráttə reé ə/ (*plural* **-rias** or **-rie** /-reé ay/) *n* an Italian restaurant, especially one that is simple in style [Early 19C. < Italian < *trattore* 'restaurateur' < Latin *tractare* 'drag, manage' < *trahere* 'pull']

trauchled /traákh'ld, traák'ld/ *adj Scotland* exhausted or overburdened with physical or mental work or with responsibilities and cares [Early 20C. Past participle of *trauchle* 'tire out, trudge', origin ?]

trauma /tráwmə/ (*plural* **-mas** or **-mata** /-mətə/) *n* **1.** an extremely distressing experience that causes severe emotional shock and may have long-lasting psychological effects **2.** a physical injury or wound to the body [Late 17C. < Greek, 'wound']

trauma centre *n* a hospital or a department in a hospital that is specially equipped and staffed to treat patients who have sustained complex, life-threatening injuries such as multiple gunshot wounds or severe internal injuries

traumata PSYCHOL, MED plural of **trauma**

traumatic /traw máttik/ *adj* **1.** **EXTREMELY DISTRESSING** extremely distressing, frightening, or shocking, and sometimes having long-term psychological effects **2.** PSYCHOL **RELATING TO TRAUMA** relating to or caused by psychological trauma **3.** MED **RELATING TO INJURIES** relating to physical injuries or wounds to the body [Mid-17C. Via late Latin < Greek *traumatikos* < *traumat-*, stem of *trauma* 'wound'] —**traumatically** *adv*

traumatise *vt* PSYCHOL, MED another spelling of **traumatize**

traumatism /tráwmətizəm/ *n* the condition resulting from a physical injury or wound or from an emotional shock [Mid-19C. < Greek *traumat-* (see TRAUMATIC)]

traumatize /tráwmə tīz/ (**-tizes, -tizing, -tized**), **traumatise** (**-tises, -tising, -tised**) *vt* **1.** to cause somebody to experience severe emotional shock or distress, often resulting in long-lasting psychological damage **2.** to cause physical injury to somebody or something [Early 20C. < Greek *traumat-* (see TRAUMATIC)] —**traumatization** /tráwmə tī záysh'n/ *n*

traumatology /tráwmə tólləji/ *n* the branch of medicine that deals with serious injuries and wounds and their long-term consequences [Late 19C. < Greek *traumat-* (see TRAUMATIC)] —**traumatologist** *n*

travail /trávvayl/ *n* **1.** **HARD WORK** work, especially work that involves hard physical effort over a long period **2.** MED same as **labour** *n* (sense 5) (*archaic*) ■ *vi* (**-vails, -vailing, -vailed**) **1.** **WORK HARD** to work long and hard (*literary*) **2.** **BE IN LABOUR** to undergo the labour of childbirth (*archaic*) [13C. < French, 'pain', *travailler* 'to toil' < assumed Vulgar Latin *tripalium* 'instrument of torture' < Latin *tripalis* 'having three stakes' < *palus* 'stake']

trave /trayv/ *n* **1.** BUILDINGS same as **crossbeam 2.** BUILDINGS a section of a building formed by crossbeams, e.g. in a ceiling **3.** RIDING a frame to restrain a difficult horse while it is being shod [14C. Via Old French, 'beam' < Latin *trab-*]

travel /trávv'l/ *v* (**-els, -elling, -elled**) **1.** *vi* **GO ON JOURNEY** to go on a journey to a particular place, usually using a form of transport **2.** *vi* **GO FROM PLACE TO PLACE** to go from place to place or visit various places and countries for business or pleasure ○ *We hope to travel more when we retire.* **3.** *vt* **JOURNEY THROUGH AREA** to go on journeys through, around, or within a particular area ○ *They travelled the world.* **4.** *vt* **COVER PARTICULAR DISTANCE** to go or cover a particular distance ○ *travel 10 kilometres* **5.** *vi* **GO AT PARTICULAR SPEED** to move at a particular speed or in a particular way ○ *The train was travelling at 90 mph when it had to stop.* **6.** *vi* **MOVE FAST** to move swiftly (*informal*) **7.** *vi* **MAKE SALES TRIPS** to go from place to place as a salesperson or as part of a business ○ *After five years travelling, she wanted an office job.* **8.** *vi* **REACT TO BEING TRANSPORTED** to be in a particular condition as a result of being transported ○ *Some products do not travel well.* **9.** *vi* **BE TRANSMITTED** to be transmitted or communicated ○ *News travelled fast.* **10.** *vi* **SCAN DURING FILMING** to scan an object or scene in the process of observing or filming it **11.** *vi* MECH ENG **MOVE IN FIXED PATH** to move in a fixed path while operating (*refers to a machine part*) **12.** *vi US* **ASSOCIATE WITH PARTICULAR GROUP** to associate with a particular person or group ○ *They've been travelling with a new crowd.* **13.** *vi* BASKETBALL **TAKE ILLEGAL NUMBER OF STEPS** in basketball or netball, to take more steps while holding the ball than the rules allow ■ *n* **1.** **ACTIVITY OF TRAVELLING** the activity of going on journeys, usually using a form of transport, or visiting different places ○ *air travel* **2.** MECH ENG **TOTAL DISTANCE MECHANICAL PART MOVES** the total distance that a mechanical part such as a piston inside a cylinder moves **3.** *US* **AMOUNT OF TRAFFIC** the amount of traffic at a given place along a route

■ **travels** *npl* **1.** SERIES OF JOURNEYS a series of journeys undertaken by a person or group ○ *She's off on her travels again.* **2.** LITERAT ACCOUNT OF SOMEBODY'S JOURNEYS an account of the journeys undertaken by a person or group ■ *adj* FOR TRAVELLER intended for, accompanying, or used by a traveller ○ *a travel kettle* [14C. Variant of TRAVAIL] —**travellable** *adj*

CULTURAL NOTE ***Gulliver's Travels***, a satire (1726) by Jonathan Swift. It is a four-part account of the adventures of a castaway, ship's surgeon Lemuel Gulliver. First washed ashore in Lilliput, peopled by tiny inhabitants, he subsequently finds himself in Brobdingnag, the kingdom of giants. The third part of the novel deals with his time on the flying island of Laputa and the neighbouring continent, occupied by scientists and philosophers, while the final part takes him to the land of the Houyhnhms, where horses rule with benevolent reason over the brutish human Yahoos. Through the characters and situations encountered by Gulliver in his travels Swift takes every opportunity to satirize the people and practices of his time with varying degrees of humour and bitterness.

travel agency *n* a business that arranges transport, accommodation, and tours for travellers —**travel agent** *n*

travelator *n* TRANSP another spelling of **travolator**

travel bureau *n* TRAVEL same as **travel agency**

travelcard /trávv'l kaard/ *n* a ticket entitling the user to an unlimited number of journeys on a public transport system within a designated area and over a fixed period of time

traveled, etc. *adj* US spelling of **travelled, etc.**

travel insurance *n* insurance to cover the eventualities of a period of travel away from home such as flight delay, loss of luggage, theft of money or belongings, or medical costs

travelled /trávv'ld/ *adj* **1.** having been on many journeys, or having a lot of experience as a traveller **2.** used by many travellers ○ *Keep to the travelled roads.*

traveller /trávv'lər/ *n* **1.** SOMEBODY ON JOURNEY somebody who journeys to a specific place or who uses a specific form of transport **2.** SOMEBODY WHO HAS TRAVELLED somebody who has travelled or travels extensively ○ *an experienced traveller* **3.** OCCUPATIONS same as **travelling salesperson** **4.** MEMBER OF TRAVELLING FOLK a Rom or other person living an itinerant lifestyle **5.** MECH ENG MOVING PART a part of a mechanism that is designed to move in a fixed path **6.** NAUT RING ON ROPE a metal ring that moves freely on a rope, spar, or rod **7.** NAUT ROPE a rope, spar, or rod on which a metal ring moves **8.** PEOPLES same as **Irish Traveller**

traveller's cheque *n* an internationally accepted cheque for a sum in a specific currency that can be exchanged elsewhere for local currency or for goods and is usually guaranteed against loss or theft

traveller's joy *n* a wild climbing plant that has feathery white seed heads. Native to: Europe. Latin name: *Clematis vitalba.*

traveller's tale *n* a fantastic, unlikely, or obviously untrue account of something, as given by a traveller to people who do not travel

travelling /trávv'ling/ *adj* **1.** OF JOURNEYS related to journeys or the activity of making journeys ○ *travelling expenses* **2.** GOING TO DIFFERENT PLACES moving from place to place regularly ○ *a travelling exhibition* **3.** same as **travel** ■ *n* EXTENDED TOURIST TRIP the activity of visiting a number of places or countries as a tourist for an extended period of time, especially as a student or young person ○ *to go travelling for six months*

travelling folk, travelling people *npl* Roma or other itinerant people

travelling salesman *n* a salesman whose work consists of travelling around calling on potential customers within a territory

travelling salesperson *n* a salesperson whose work consists of travelling around calling on potential customers within a territory

travelling saleswoman *n* a saleswoman whose work consists of travelling around calling on potential customers within a territory

travelling wave *n* a wave that continuously carries energy away from its source

travelogue /trávvə log/ *n* a film, video, or piece of writing, or a lecture accompanied by pictures, video or film, about travel, especially to interesting or remote places, or about one person's travels

travel sickness *n UK* a feeling of nausea caused by movement, especially by the movement of the vehicle, train, ship, or aircraft in which somebody is travelling. ANZ, N Am term **motion sickness** —**travel-sick** *adj*

Travers, Mount /trávvərz/ mountain in the north of the South Island, New Zealand, situated in the northern part of the Southern Alps. Height: 2,338 m/7,671 ft.

Travers /trávvərz/, **Ben** (1886–1980) British playwright. He was noted for his farces, which included *Rookery Nook* (1926). Full name **Travers, Benjamin**

traverse /trávvurss, trə vúrss/ *v* (**-verses, -versing, -versed**) **1.** *vt* MOVE ACROSS AREA to travel or move across, over, or through an area or a place ○ *traverse the countryside* **2.** *vti* GO BACK AND FORTH ACROSS SOMETHING to move backwards and forwards across something ○ *Volunteers traversed the field looking for clues.* **3.** *vt* REACH ACROSS SOMETHING to extend or reach across something ○ *the bridge traversing the river* **4.** *vti* CLIMBING MOVE AT ANGLE ACROSS SOMETHING to move at an angle across a rock face while ascending or descending it **5.** *vti* SKIING ZIGZAG DOWN SLOPE to ski in diagonal runs following a zigzag course down a slope **6.** *vti* SWIVEL GUN to swivel something, especially a gun, from side to side on a pivot, or be swivelled in this way **7.** *vi* FENCING SLIDE BLADE TOWARDS OPPONENT'S HILT in fencing, to slide the blade of a sword towards an opponent's hilt while at the same time applying pressure to his or her blade **8.** *vt* THWART SOMEBODY OR SOMETHING to thwart or obstruct somebody or something (*literary*) **9.** *vt* LAW DENY ALLEGATIONS to deny the opposing party's allegations as set out in the pleading in a lawsuit, formally and, usually, in their entirety ■ *n* **1.** MOVEMENT ACROSS AREA a movement or journey across, over, or through something **2.** ROUTE TAKEN a route or way across, over, or through something **3.** CLIMBING MOVEMENT ACROSS ROCK FACE a horizontal or oblique movement across a rock face in climbing **4.** SKIING ZIGZAG SKIING RUN a diagonal zigzag skiing run down a ski slope **5.** CONSTR CROSSBEAM something that is fixed across a gap or lies crosswise, e.g. a structural member of a building **6.** BUILDINGS GALLERY a gallery or loft that crosses from side to side inside a building **7.** BUILDINGS BARRIER WITHIN BUILDING a railing, curtain, screen, or partition forming a barrier within a building **8.** MIL BARRIER ACROSS TRENCH a defensive barrier of earth across a trench **9.** OBSTRUCTION something that thwarts or obstructs somebody or something (*literary*) **10.** MATHS same as **transversal** **11.** ZIGZAG COURSE OF VESSEL the zigzag course of a sailing vessel in contrary winds **12.** MECH ENG LATERAL MOVEMENT OF MACHINE PART the horizontal movement of a machine part such as a lathe or grinding tool as it moves across the work piece **13.** LAW DENIAL OF ALLEGATIONS a formal denial of the opposing party's allegations as set out in their pleading in a lawsuit **14.** CIV ENG SURVEY USING INTERSECTING STRAIGHT LINES a survey made using a series of intersecting straight lines of known length whose angles of intersection are measured for recording on a map or in a table of data ■ *adj* CROSSWISE lying across something [14C. Via French *traverser* < late Latin *tra(ns)versare* < Latin *transversus*, past participle of *transvertere* 'turn across' < *vertere* 'to turn'] —**traversable** *adj* —**traversal** *n* —**traverser** *n*

travertine /trávvərtin/, **travertin** *n* a hard white or light-coloured limestone precipitated in hot springs and caves. Use: facing material in building. [Late 18C. Via Italian *travertino* < Latin *(lapis) tiburtinus* '(stone) of Tibur (Tivoli)']

travesty /trávvəsti/ *n* (*plural* **-ties**) **1.** FALSE REPRESENTATION a distorted or debased version of something ○ *It was a kangaroo court, a travesty of justice.* **2.** ARTS GROTESQUE IMITATION a literary or artistic work, usually meant as a parody, that ridicules something serious by imitating it in a grotesque or distorted manner ■ *vt* (**-ties, -tying, -tied**) MAKE TRAVESTY OF SOMETHING to imitate or ridicule something in a grotesque or distorted manner [Mid-17C. < French *travesti* 'dressed in disguise' < *travestir* 'disguise, ridicule' < Italian *travestire* < Latin *trans-* 'across' + *vestire* 'clothe, dress' (see VEST)]

travois /trə vóy, trávvoy/ (*plural same*) *n* a sledge made of two poles connected by a frame and pulled by an animal, formerly used by Native North Americans of the Great Plains [Mid-19C. < Canadian French variant of French *travail* < Latin *trabs* 'beam']

travolator /trávvə laytər/, **travelator** *n* a moving walkway for pedestrians, e.g. in an airport or shopping precinct [Mid-20C. < TRAVEL, after ESCALATOR]

trawl /trawl/ *n* **1.** FISHERIES same as **trawl net** **2.** FISHERIES same as **trawl line** **3.** SEARCH a search for something, especially information (*informal*) ■ *vti* (**trawls, trawling, trawled**) **1.** SEARCH THROUGH LARGE AMOUNT OF INFORMATION to search for something through a large amount of information or many possibilities **2.** FISHERIES FISH WITH TRAWL to use or put out a trawl to catch fish [Mid-16C. < Middle Dutch *traghelen* 'drag' < *traghel* 'trawl net' < Latin *tragula* < *trahere* 'pull']

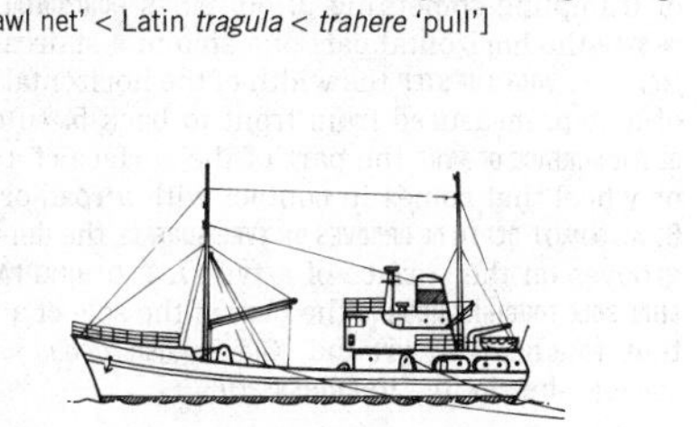

trawler

trawler /tráwlər/ *n* **1.** a boat that is used in trawling for fish **2.** somebody who fishes by trawling —**trawlerman** *n*

trawl line *n* a long fishing line suspended between buoys that has several shorter lines with baited hooks attached

trawl net *n* a large net that is dragged along the sea bottom behind a commercial fishing boat

tray /tray/ *n* **1.** FLAT CARRIER FOR SMALL OBJECTS a flat piece of plastic, wood, or metal with a raised edge, used for carrying or displaying light objects **2.** TRAY AND THINGS IT CARRIES a tray and the objects on it ○ *brought in the tea tray* **3.** CONTAINER IN WHICH TO ORGANIZE THINGS a shallow container, sometimes part of a desk drawer or cabinet, in which to keep items such as stationery or jewellery [Old English *trīg* < Indo-European]

tray-bake *n regional* a cake made in a baking tray and cut up into squares

tray table *n* a small table that folds down from the back of the seat in front of you in a plane or train

treacherous /tréchərəss/ *adj* **1.** betraying or ready to betray somebody's trust, confidence, or faith **2.** involving hidden dangers or hazards ○ *treacherous seas* [14C. < Old French *trecheros* 'deceitfulness' < *trechier* 'cheat, trick'] —**treacherously** *adv* —**treacherousness** *n*

treachery /tréchəri/ (*plural* **-ies**) *n* **1.** betrayal or deceit **2.** an act or instance of betrayal or deceit [12C. < Old French *trecherie* < *trechier* 'cheat, trick']

treacle /treék'l/ *n* **1.** SYRUP FROM SUGAR REFINING a thick brown sticky sweet liquid, produced during the process of refining raw sugar. Use: to make cakes, sweets, puddings. (*often used before a noun*) ○ *treacle toffee* N Am term **molasses** **2.** SOMETHING CLOYING something cloying or excessively sentimental **3.** FORMER ANTIDOTE TO POISON a preparation used in the past as an antidote to poison [14C. Via Old French *triacle*, Latin *theriaca* < Greek *thēriakē (antidotos)* '(antidote to) poisonous animals' < *thērion* 'wild or poisonous animal' < *thēr* 'wild animal']

ORIGIN ***Treacle*** retained its original meaning of 'antidote' when it came into English, but it later gradually broadened out into 'medicine', and the practice of disguising the unpleasant taste of medicine with sugar syrup led in the 17th century to its application to 'syrup'.

treacly /treékli/ *adj* **1.** sticky and sweet like treacle **2.** cloying or excessively sentimental —**treacliness** *n*

tread /tred/ v (**treads, treading, trod** /trod/, **trodden** /tródd'n/ or **trod**) **1.** vi TRAMPLE ON SOMETHING to step or put a foot on something, especially so as to crush or damage it ○ *She trod on his toe.* **2.** vti WALK OR STEP ON SOMETHING to take a step or steps, or walk or step on, across, or along something ○ *Don't tread on the wet concrete.* **3.** vt SPREAD SOMETHING DIRTY BY WALKING to spread something unwanted from the feet or footwear by walking, often grinding it in ○ *food trodden into the carpet* **4.** vt FORM PATH to form something such as a path by trampling or walking **5.** vi ACT IN PARTICULAR WAY to proceed or behave in a particular way ○ *You'll have to tread carefully at the next meeting.* **6.** vi CRUSH SOMEBODY OR SOMETHING to repress or treat somebody or something harshly **7.** vt DO DANCE STEPS to perform the steps of a dance (*dated*) ■ n **1.** WAY OF TREADING a way or sound of walking or stepping ○ *heard the heavy tread of marching feet* **2.** ACT OF TREADING an act of walking or of trampling something **3.** BUILDINGS HORIZONTAL PART OF STEP the horizontal part of a step in a staircase **4.** MEASURE WIDTH OF STEP the width of the horizontal part of a step, measured from front to back **5.** AUTOMOT OUTER SURFACE OF TYRE the part of the surface of a tyre or wheel that comes in contact with a road or rail **6.** AUTOMOT DEPTH OF GROOVES ON TYRE SURFACE the depth of grooves on the surface of a tyre **7.** CLOTHING PART OF SHOE SOLE TOUCHING GROUND the part of the sole of a shoe that touches the ground [Old English *tredan* < Germanic] —**treader** n —**treadless** adj

treadle /trédd'l/ n a lever pushed repeatedly by the foot to provide drive for a machine such as a sewing machine or potter's wheel ■ vti (**-les, -ling, -led**) to operate a treadle, or operate a machine by using a treadle [Old English *tredel* 'step, stair' < *tredan* (see TREAD)] —**treadler** n

treadmill /tréd mil/ n **1.** NEVER-ENDING ROUTINE a monotonous and seemingly endless task, job, or routine **2.** EXERCISE MACHINE a machine with an endless belt on which somebody can walk, jog, or run, used for exercise and stress testing **3.** CYLINDER PROVIDING POWER a continuous belt or series of steps kept moving by people or animals walking on it that is used to provide power to a machine, e.g. to grind grain or raise water from a well

tread separation n the separation of a tyre tread from the rest of the tyre on a moving motor vehicle, often a cause of catastrophic accidents when high speed is a factor

treas. abbr **1.** treasurer **2.** treasury

treason /treéz'n/ n **1.** BETRAYAL OF COUNTRY a violation of the allegiance owed by somebody to his or her own country, e.g. by aiding an enemy **2.** TREACHERY betrayal or disloyalty **3.** ACT OF BETRAYAL an act of betrayal or disloyalty [12C. Via Anglo-Norman *treisoun* 'treacherous handing over, betrayal' < Latin *tradition-* (see TRADITION)]

treasonable /treéz'nəb'l/, **treasonous** /treéz'nəss/ adj punishable as treason —**treasonably** adv

treasure /trézhər/ n **1.** JEWELS AND PRECIOUS OBJECTS wealth, especially in the form of jewels and precious objects, often accumulated or hoarded **2.** SOMETHING VALUABLE something of great value or worth **3.** SOMEBODY HIGHLY VALUED a highly valued or much loved person ○ *an actor considered as one of our national treasures* ■ vt (**-ures, -uring, -ured**) **1.** REGARD SOMEBODY OR SOMETHING AS VALUABLE to prize somebody or something as being of great value or worth ○ *treasured the memory of that day* **2.** ACCUMULATE AND STORE SOMETHING VALUABLE to accumulate and store something regarded as valuable [12C. Via French *trésor* < Latin *thesaurus* < Greek *thēsauros* 'treasure'] —**treasurable** adj

CULTURAL NOTE *Treasure Island*, a novel (1883) by the Scottish writer Robert Louis Stevenson. This classic romance recounts young Jim Hawkins' adventures with a treacherous band of pirates searching for lost treasure on a distant island. The book's most memorable character is the one-legged pirate Long John Silver, who carries a pet parrot given to shrieking 'Pieces of eight!'.

treasure house n **1.** a place or collection in which many valuable things are located **2.** a building in which treasure is kept

treasure hunt n a game in which competitors attempt to solve a series of clues, sometimes leading to a hidden prize

treasurer /trézhərər/ n somebody who manages the finances of an organization such as a club, society, government, or corporation —**treasurership** n

Treasurer n Aus the finance minister in the federal government and in each of the state governments

treasure-trove /-trōv/ n **1.** silver or gold coins or bullion found buried and for which there is no known owner. In the United Kingdom such finds become Crown property. **2.** something discovered that is valuable or the source of something valuable ○ *The new shop is a treasure-trove of antiques.* [Mid-16C. < Anglo-Norman *tresor trove* < Old French *tresor* 'treasure' + *trove*, past participle of *trover* 'find']

treasury /trézhəri/ (*plural* **-ies**) n **1.** STORE OF MONEY the funds or revenues of a government, organization, or corporation, or the place in which they are deposited and disbursed **2.** PLACE FOR THINGS OF VALUE a place in which treasure or other valuable items are stored and preserved **3.** COLLECTION OF VALUABLE THINGS a source or collection of valuable things such as literary or artistic works [13C. < Old French *tresorie* < *tresor* (see TREASURE)]

Treasury n in many countries, the government department in charge of collecting and managing public revenue

Treasury Bench n the front bench to the Speaker's right in the British House of Commons, where members of the government sit

Treasury bill n in the United Kingdom, a financial security issued by the Treasury that is payable to the bearer after a fixed period, usually three months

Treasury bond n an interest-bearing debt security issued by the US government, with an initial life of between ten and thirty years

Treasury note n **1.** an intermediate-term, interest-paying debt instrument issued by the US government, with an initial life of between one and ten years **2.** a currency note issued by the British Treasury in 1914 and valid until 1928

treasury tag n a short length of cord with metal ends that is passed through punched holes in sheets of paper to hold them together

treat /treet/ v (**treats, treating, treated**) **1.** vt REGARD SOMEBODY IN PARTICULAR WAY to behave towards or think of somebody or something in a particular way ○ *They treated us like family.* **2.** vt GIVE MEDICAL AID TO SOMEBODY to give medical aid to somebody, or apply medical techniques to a disease or symptom in order to provide a cure **3.** vt SUBJECT SOMETHING TO PROCESS OR AGENT to subject something to a physical, chemical, or biological process or agent such as a chemical reaction or the application of a coating **4.** vt PAY FOR SOMEBODY to pay for food, drink, entertainment, or gifts for somebody ○ *I'll treat you to lunch at the hotel.* **5.** vt PROVIDE SOMEBODY WITH SOMETHING PLEASURABLE to give somebody or yourself something enjoyable ○ *They treated their mother to breakfast in bed.* **6.** vt DEAL WITH SOMETHING IN PARTICULAR WAY to present or handle a subject, especially in art or literature, in a particular way ○ *treats a delicate subject with great sensitivity* **7.** vi DISCUSS TOPIC to discuss or deal with a topic in writing or speech ○ *a play that treats of greed and revenge* **8.** vi NEGOTIATE TERMS to negotiate, especially in order to reach a settlement (*formal*) ○ *refusing to treat with the enemy* ■ n **1.** ENTERTAINMENT PAID FOR BY SOMEBODY ELSE something that is given to somebody and paid for by somebody else, e.g. food, entertainment, or a gift **2.** ACT OF PAYING FOR SOMEBODY an act of paying for something such as food, entertainment, or a gift, for somebody **3.** SOMETHING ENJOYABLE something enjoyable, especially when a surprise ○ *It's a treat to see a smile on his face again.* [13C. Via Old French *traitier* 'bargain with, negotiate' < Latin *tractare* 'handle' < *trahere* 'pull'] —**treatable** adj —**treater** n ◇ **a treat** in a pleasing or successful way (*informal*) ○ *The woodwork's come up a treat.*

treatise /treétiss, -iz/ n a formal written work that deals with a subject systematically and usually extensively [14C. < Anglo-Norman *tretiz* < Old French *traitier* (see TREAT)]

treatment /treétmənt/ n **1.** PROVISION OF MEDICAL CARE the application of medical care to cure disease, heal injuries, or ease symptoms **2.** MEDICAL REMEDY a remedy, procedure, or technique for curing or alleviating a disease, injury, or condition ○ *a new treatment for asthma* **3.** WAY OF HANDLING SOMEBODY OR SOMETHING the particular way in which somebody or something is dealt with or handled ○ *had pretty rough treatment* **4.** TREATING OF SOMETHING WITH AGENT an act of subjecting something to a physical, chemical, or biological process or agent **5.** USUAL ACTIONS TAKEN the usual way of dealing with a person or situation (*informal*) ○ *As guests of the government we got the full VIP treatment.* **6.** CINEMA SCHEMATIC VERSION OF FILM a schematic version of a film script, generally without dialogue and individual shots, indicating how the story is to be dealt with in a screenplay **7.** ARTS PRESENTATION OF SUBJECT the way of presenting or handling a subject, especially in art or literature

treaty /treéti/ (*plural* **-ties**) n **1.** a formal contract or agreement negotiated between countries or other political entities **2.** an agreement or contract between two or more parties [14C. Via Old French *traité* 'assembly, agreement, treaty' < Latin *tractatus* < *tractare* (see TREAT)]

treaty Indian n Can PEOPLES, POL same as **Status Indian**

treaty port n formerly, a port where foreign trade was allowed by a treaty, especially in China, Japan, and Korea

Trebbiano /trebbi a'anō/ n **1.** a white wine mainly from Italy and France **2.** a white grape variety. Use: to make Trebbiano and other blended wines. [Late 19C. < Italian, after *Trebbia*, river in north-central Italy]

treble /trébb'l/ adj **1.** TRIPLE three times as many or as much **2.** HIGH-PITCHED high-pitched or shrill **3.** OF HIGHEST MUSICAL RANGE relating to or intended for a boy or girl soprano voice or a high-pitched instrument ■ n **1.** HIGH-PITCHED SOUND a high-pitched or shrill sound **2.** SOMETHING TRIPLED something three times as many or as much **3.** MUSIC HIGH-PITCHED INSTRUMENT OR VOICE a treble voice, singer, instrument, or part **4.** RECORDING AUDIO FREQUENCY RANGE the higher audio frequencies electronically reproduced by a radio, recording, or sound system **5.** RECORDING CONTROL FOR HIGH-FREQUENCY AUDIO RESPONSE a control for increasing or decreasing the high-frequency response on a radio or audio amplifier **6.** DARTS RING ON DARTBOARD the narrow inner ring on a dartboard, or a hit landing within this ring, which scores three times the nominal value **7.** SET OF THREE WINS the winning of three major competitions in one season, especially in football **8.** GAMBLING BET ON THREE RACES a bet on three races in which the winnings and stake from each race are placed on the next ■ vti (**-les, -ling, -led**) TRIPLE SOMETHING to become three times as many or as much, or make something become three times as many or as much ○ *Output has trebled over the past year.* [13C. Via French < Latin *triplus* 'triple'] —**trebleness** n —**trebly** adv

treble chance n a way of betting on football pools in which the person betting chooses a number of games as being likely to result in a draw, home win, or away win

treble clef n a clef that puts G above middle C on the second line of the staff, used for soprano and alto voices, high-pitched instruments, and the right hand of keyboard instruments

Treblinka /tre blíngkə/ site of two Nazi concentration camps in eastern Poland, situated about 97 km/60 mi. northeast of Warsaw

trebuchet /trébbyōō shet/, **trebucket** /tree bukit/ n a medieval siege engine with a sling attached to a wooden arm for hurling large stones [14C. < French *trébuchet* < *trébucher* 'overturn']

trecento /tray chéntō/ n the 14th century, used especially in referring to Italian art and literature [Mid-19C. < Italian, shortening of *mil trecento* 'one thousand three hundred'] —**trecentist** n

~~**trecherous**~~ incorrect spelling of **treacherous**

tree /tree/ n **1.** LARGE PERENNIAL WOODY PLANT a woody perennial plant that grows to a height of several metres and typically has a single erect main stem with side branches **2.** PLANT RESEMBLING TREE a large bush or nonwoody plant that resembles a tree, e.g. a palm tree or tree fern **3.** SOMETHING WITH BRANCHES LIKE TREE something that has branches or pegs on which to hang things ○ *a mug tree* **4.** DIAGRAM OF HIERARCHICAL

STRUCTURE a diagram of a hierarchical structure that shows the relationships between components as branches **5.** CONSTR **WOODEN SUPPORT** a wooden beam, bar, or post that supports or is part of a structure **6.** COMPUT **HIERARCHICAL DATA STRUCTURE** a hierarchical data structure in which each element contains data and may be linked by branches to two or more other elements. Every element has only a single predecessor, except for the first, which is called the root and has no predecessor. **7.** CRYSTALS **CRYSTALLINE GROWTH** a branching growth of crystals, particularly of a metal **8.** CRIME same as **gallows** (*archaic*) **9.** CHR **CROSS JESUS CHRIST DIED ON** in Christianity, the cross on which Jesus Christ was crucified (*archaic*) ■ *vt* **(trees, treeing, treed) 1. STRETCH FOOTWEAR ON SHOETREE** to stretch or shape a shoe or boot on a shoetree **2.** *N Am* **PUT SOMEBODY IN DIFFICULT SITUATION** to force somebody into a position of difficulty or disadvantage (*informal*) **3. FORCE SOMEBODY UP TREE** to chase an animal or person up a tree, or force an animal or person to climb a tree [Old English *trēo(w)* < Indo-European, 'oak tree'] —**treeless** *adj* —**treelessness** *n* ◇ **be barking up the wrong tree** to be mistaken, especially as regards the best way to achieve something ◇ **out of your tree** behaving irrationally (*slang*) ◇ **up a tree** *N Am* in a position of difficulty or disadvantage (*informal*)

CULTURAL NOTE ***The Tree of Man***, a novel (1955) by Australian writer Patrick White. The story of a pioneer couple who settle in New South Wales, Australia, it charts the establishment of their farm, the birth of their children, and their gradual estrangement as they search for greater fulfilment in their respective lives.

tree creeper *n* a small forest bird with large claws for climbing tree trunks in search of insects. Family: Certhidae.

tree diagram *n* INFO SCI same as **tree** *n* (sense 4)

tree farm *n* an area where trees are grown commercially for their wood products

tree fern *n* a fern that grows to the height of a tree and has a crown of fronds. Native to: tropics. Family: Cyatheaceae or Marattiaceae.

tree frog *n* a small frog that has long digits with adhesive discs that allow it to climb trees. Native to: America, South Asia, Australia. Family: Hylidae.

tree heath *n* TREES same as **briar**[1] (sense 2)

treehopper /treé hoppər/ *n* a small tree-dwelling insect that feeds on the sap of trees. Many species have grotesque projections on their backs. Family: Membracidae.

tree house *n* a platform, often with a roof and walls, built among the branches of a tree, especially for children to play in

treehugger /treé huggər/ *n* somebody who is regarded as excessively devoted to environmental protection (*informal insult*)

tree kangaroo *n* a kangaroo that has sharp claws and grasping forepaws that allow it to climb trees. Native to: New Guinea, northern Australia. Genus: *Dendrolagus*.

tree line *n* **1.** *UK* the limit of altitude, or northern or southern latitude, beyond which no trees can grow. ANZ, N Am term **timberline 2.** the edge of a wood or forest

tree mallow *n* a tall woody wild or cultivated plant. Flowers: reddish-purple. Native to: rocky coastal areas in Europe and North Africa. Latin name: *Lavatera arborea*.

treen /treen, tree ən/ *n* tableware and other household utensils made of wood ■ *adj* made of wood (*archaic*) [Old English *trēowen* 'made of wood' < TREE]

treenail /treé nayl, trénn'l/, **trenail, trunnel** /trúnn'l/ *n* a large cylindrical peg made of dry wood that expands to give a tight fit when it is wet and is used to fasten timbers together, e.g. in ships

treenware /treén wair/ *n* HOUSEHOLD same as **treen**

tree of heaven *n* a quick-growing deciduous tree that is tolerant of pollution and is often planted in urban areas. Native to: China. Latin name: *Ailanthus altissima* or *Ailanthus glandulosa*.

tree of knowledge *n* in the Bible, the tree that grew in the Garden of Eden and produced the fruit that was forbidden to Adam and Eve (Genesis 2:9, 3)

tree of life *n* in the Bible, the tree that grew in the Garden of Eden and produced a fruit that gave eternal life to somebody who ate it (Genesis 3:22–24)

tree ring *n* BOT same as **growth ring**

tree runner *n* BIRDS same as **sittella**

tree shrew *n* a small insect-eating animal resembling a squirrel with a long snout. Native to: forests of Southeast Asia. Family: Tupaiidae.

tree-sit *n* an extended period of time spent by a protester in a handmade tree house in an effort to prevent tree-felling, e.g. by logging companies —**tree-sitter** *n* —**tree-sitting** *n*

tree snake *n* a slender tree-dwelling snake. Native to: South and Southeast Asia, Malay Archipelago.Family: Colubridae

tree sparrow *n* **1.** a small sparrow that differs from a house sparrow in having a black spot near its ear and a chestnut crown. Native to: Europe, South Asia. Latin name: *Passer montanus*. **2.** a large sparrow with a chestnut cap and a grey breast with a single dark chest spot. Native to: North America. Latin name: *Spizella arborea*.

tree spiking *n N Am* the act of hammering long nails into trees as a form of environmental protest, so as to make it dangerous to cut down the trees using a chain saw

tree surgeon *n* somebody trained in pruning trees or treating diseased or damaged trees, e.g. by cutting off branches or filling cavities —**tree surgery** *n*

tree toad *n* AMPHIB same as **tree frog**

tree tomato *n UK, Can* **1.** the edible red fruit of a plant of the nightshade family **2.** a cultivated bush that produces tree tomatoes. Native to: South America. Latin name: *Cyphomandra betacea* or *Cyphomandra crassifolia*. ▶ ANZ, US term **tamarillo**

treetop /treé top/ *n* the highest branches of a tree

treeware /treé wair/ *n* books and other material printed on paper made from wood pulp

trefoil /tréffoyl/ *n* **1. THREE-LOBED SHAPE OR OBJECT** an object or design with three lobes or connected parts, e.g. an emblem used in heraldry **2.** PLANTS **PLANT WITH THREE-LOBED LEAVES** a plant of the pea family that has three-lobed leaves, especially clover **3.** BOT **THREE-LOBED LEAF OR PART** a leaf or other plant part with three lobes **4.** ARCHIT **ORNAMENT IN SHAPE OF CLOVER LEAF** an architectural ornament or form resembling a clover leaf [14C. Via Anglo-Norman *trifoil* < Latin *trifolium* 'with three leaves' < *folium* 'leaf']

trehala /tri haálə/ *n* an edible sugary substance that comes from the pupal case of an Asian beetle [Mid-19C. Via Turkish *tigale* < Persian *tīgāl*]

trehalase /tri haá layss, -layz/ *n* an enzyme that catalyses the breakdown of trehalose

trehalose /tri haá lōss, -lōz/ *n* a disaccharide found in yeast, lichen, bacteria, and insects

treillage /tráylij/ *n* a trellis or piece of latticework [Late 17C. < French < *treille* < Latin *trichila* 'bower, arbour']

trek /trek/ *vi* **(treks, trekking, trekked) 1. MAKE LONG DIFFICULT JOURNEY** to make a long difficult journey, especially on foot and often over rough or mountainous terrain **2. GO SLOWLY OR LABORIOUSLY** to go somewhere slowly or with difficulty ○ *I had to trek across town to the other bookshop.* **3.** *S Africa* **GO BY OX WAGON** to travel in a wagon pulled by an ox ■ *n* **1. LONG DIFFICULT JOURNEY** a long difficult journey, especially on foot and often over rough or mountainous terrain **2.** *S Africa* **STAGE OF JOURNEY** a journey or stage of a journey, especially a migration by ox wagon [Mid-19C. Via Afrikaans < Dutch *trekken* 'draw, pull, travel'] —**trekker** *n*

CULTURAL NOTE ***Star Trek***, a television series created in 1966 by US writer and producer Gene Roddenberry (1921–91). The adventures of the Starship Enterprise, a 23rd-century spacecraft on a mission 'to boldly go where no man has gone before', initially ran for 79 episodes. The popularity of the series later gave rise to numerous film spinoffs, the follow-up television series *Star Trek: The Next Generation*, *Star Trek: Deep Space Nine*, *Star Trek: Voyager*, and *Enterprise*, and a worldwide network of dedicated fans known as Trekkies.

Trekkie /tréki/ *n* a fan of the science-fiction television series *Star Trek* (*informal*)

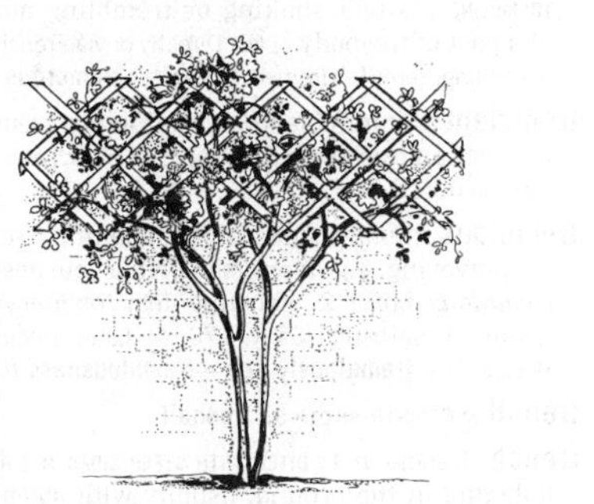

trellis

trellis /trélliss/ *n* **1. LATTICE FOR SUPPORTING PLANT** a lattice of wood, metal, or plastic used to support plants, usually fixed to a wall **2. LATTICEWORK STRUCTURE** a structure made of latticework, especially an arch ■ *vt* **(-lises, -lising, -lised) 1. TRAIN PLANT ON LATTICE** to support or train a plant such as a vine on a trellis **2. MAKE SOMETHING INTO TRELLIS** to interweave pieces of wood, metal, or plastic to make a trellis [14C. Via Old French *trelis* < Latin *trilix* 'three threads' < *licium* 'thread of a warp']

trelliswork /trélliss wurk/ *n* latticework, usually for supporting plants

trematode /trémmətōd, treé-/ *n* a flatworm that lives as a parasite in the liver, gut, lungs, or blood vessels of vertebrates, attaching itself by suckers or hooks and sometimes causing serious disease. Class: Trematoda. [Mid-19C. Via modern Latin *Trematoda* < Greek *trēmatōdēs* 'perforated' (because many have perforated skins) < *trēma* 'hole, orifice']

tremble /trémb'l/ *vi* **(-bles, -bling, -bled) 1. SHAKE SLIGHTLY BUT UNCONTROLLABLY** to shake with slight movements, continuously and uncontrollably, e.g. from fear, cold, or anger **2. VIBRATE** to shake or vibrate as a result of an external force ○ *We felt the house tremble as the train passed.* **3. BE AFRAID** to be afraid or anxious about something ■ *n* **QUIVERING** a shaking, vibration, or quivering [14C. Via Old French *trembler* < medieval Latin *tremulare* 'shake' < Latin *tremulus* 'shaking' < *tremere* 'shake'] —**tremblingly** *adv* —**trembly** *adj*

trembles /trémb'lz/ *n* poisoning in sheep and cattle that have fed on white snakeroot some other poisonous plants. Affected animals tremble and become weak. (*takes a singular verb*)

tremendous /trə méndəss/ *adj* **1.** extremely large, powerful, or great ○ *There was a tremendous clap of thunder.* **2.** extremely good, successful, or impressive ○ *a tremendous improvement* [Mid-17C. < Latin *tremendus* 'fearful' < *tremere* (see 'shake')] —**tremendously** *adv* —**tremendousness** *n*

tremie /trémmi/ *n* a device consisting of a funnel-shaped hopper at the top connected to a large metal pipe with a valve at the bottom, used to spread concrete underwater [Early 20C. Via French, '(mill-)hopper' < Latin *trimodia* 'three-peck measure' < *modius* 'peck']

tremolite /trémmə līt/ *n* a white, grey, or pale green hydrated silicate mineral containing calcium, magnesium, and some iron. Source: metamorphic rocks. Use: substitute for asbestos. [Late 18C. After *Tremola*, valley in Switzerland]

tremolo /trémməlō/ (*plural* **-los**) *n* **1.** the rapid repetition of a tone or the rapid alternation between two tones in singing or playing a musical instrument, which produces a quavering effect **2.** a device in an organ for producing tremolo [Mid-18C. Via Italian < Latin *tremulus* (see TREMBLE)]

tremolo arm *n* a lever attached to the bridge of an electric guitar and used to move the bridge slightly, so as to stretch the strings to alter the pitch of a note

tremor /trémmər/ *n* **1. SHUDDER** a quiver or shudder, e.g. from fear, illness, or nervousness **2. SUDDEN SENSATION** a sudden and usually brief feeling of excitement, nervousness, or anticipation **3. WAVERING SOUND OR LIGHT** a fluctuation in a sound or light **4.** SEISMOL **MINOR EARTHQUAKE** a quivering or vibration

caused by slippage of the Earth's crust at a fault, especially before or after a major earthquake **5.** MED **TREMBLING** a slight shaking or trembling movement of a part of the body [14C. Directly or via French < Latin, 'trembling, terror' < *tremere* 'shake']

tremulant /trémmyŏŏlənt/ *adj* shaking or trembling ■ *n* MUSIC same as **tremolo** (sense 2) [15C. < Latin *tremulus* (see TREMBLE)]

tremulous /trémmyŏŏləss/ *adj* **1.** shaking, trembling, or quavering, e.g. from fear or nervousness ○ *in a tremulous voice* **2.** showing fear or nervousness about something [Early 17C. < Latin *tremulus* (see TREMBLE)] —**tremulously** *adv* —**tremulousness** *n*

trenail *n* CONSTR same as **treenail**

trench /trench/ *n* **1.** DITCH WITH STEEP SIDES a long deep hole dug in the ground, usually with steep or vertical sides **2.** MIL PROTECTION AGAINST ENEMY FIRE a long excavation, often with the excavated earth banked up in front, used as a defence against enemy fire ○ *warfare conducted in the trenches* **3.** OCEANOG VALLEY ON OCEAN FLOOR a long narrow valley on an ocean or sea floor **4.** CLOTHING same as **trench coat** ■ *v* (**trenches, trenching, trenched**) **1.** *vti* DIG TRENCH IN SOMETHING to dig a long deep hole in or through something **2.** *vt* PUT SOMETHING IN TRENCH to place something such as a pipe in a trench **3.** *vt* MIL FORTIFY SOMETHING WITH TRENCHES to fortify a position with trenches as a defence against enemy fire [14C. < Old French *trenche* 'ditch, cutting, slice' < *trenchier* 'to cut' < Latin *truncare* 'cut (off)' < *truncus* 'tree trunk']

trenchant /trénchənt/ *adj* **1.** direct, incisive, and deliberately hurtful ○ *trenchant criticism* **2.** effective and relevant in the pursuit or achievement of a goal ○ *trenchant opinions* [14C. < Old French, 'cutting' < *trenchier* (see TRENCH)] —**trenchancy** *n* —**trenchantly** *adv*

Trenchard /trénch aard, trénchərd/, **Hugh Montague, 1st Viscount** (1873–1956) British air force commander. In World War I he played a central role in the formation of the RAF (1918) and became its first marshal.

trench coat *n* a belted double-breasted raincoat, originally modelled on a military coat of World War I

trencher[1] /trénchər/ *n* formerly, a wooden platter used to serve or cut food (*archaic*) [14C. < Anglo-Norman *trenchour*, Old French *trenchoir* < *trenchier* (see TRENCH)]

trencher[2] /trénchər/ *n* somebody or something that digs trenches, especially a machine that cuts a furrow or ditch in which to lay cables or pipes [Early 17C. < TRENCH]

trencherman /trénchərmən/ (*plural* **-men** /-mən/) *n* a hearty eater

trench fever *n* a contagious illness whose symptoms include fever, headaches, and muscle aches, common among soldiers fighting in trenches in World War I and caused by the bacterium *Rochalimaea quintana*

trench foot *n* a painful condition of the feet caused by prolonged exposure of the feet to cold and wet. It results in loss of sensation, tissue damage, and sometimes gangrene.

trench mortar *n* a small cannon capable of firing shells at high trajectories over short distances, often used in trench warfare

trench mouth *n* MED same as **Vincent's angina**

trench warfare *n* **1.** a form of warfare in which armies conduct attacks on each other from opposing positions in fortified trenches **2.** a long-standing and bitter conflict in which opposing parties continually attack each other

trend /trend/ *n* **1.** TENDENCY a general tendency, movement, or direction ○ *a report documenting recent social trends* **2.** PREVAILING STYLE a current fashion or mode ○ *the latest trends in designer kitchens* ■ *vi* (**trends, trending, trended**) TEND OR MOVE IN PARTICULAR WAY to show a tendency or movement towards something or in a particular direction ○ *public opinion trending towards reunification* [Old English *trendan* 'revolve, turn, turn in a particular direction' < Germanic, 'roundness']

trendoid /trénd oyd/ *n* somebody who slavishly follows

the latest trends or fashions (*informal disapproving*) —**trendoid** *adj*

trendsetter /trénd setər/ *n* somebody or something that starts or popularizes a new trend or fashion —**trendsetting** *adj*

trendy /tréndi/ (*informal*) *adj* (**-ier, -iest**) **1.** CURRENTLY FASHIONABLE relating to or exemplifying the latest fashion ○ *a trendy restaurant* **2.** FOLLOWING LATEST FASHION deliberately reflecting or adopting fashionable, often faddish, ideas or tastes ■ *n* (*plural* **-ies**) SOMEBODY FOLLOWING LATEST FASHION somebody who follows the latest trends or fashions, often slavishly —**trendily** *adv* —**trendiness** *n*

Trent /trent/ third longest river in England. It rises at Biddulph Moor, Staffordshire, and flows into the North Sea via the Humber estuary. Length: 270 km/170 mi.

trente et quarante /traáNt ay ka raáNt/ *n* GAMBLING same as **rouge et noir** [Late 17C. < French, 'thirty and forty' (winning and losing numbers)]

Trenton /tréntən/ capital city of New Jersey, in the west-central part of the state, 45 km/28 mi. northeast of Philadelphia. Population: 85,650 (2002 estimate).

trepan /tri pán/ *n* **1.** SURG EARLY SURGICAL INSTRUMENT an early cylindrical surgical instrument (**trephine**), used especially to cut a hole in the skull **2.** MECH ENG TOOL FOR CUTTING DISC OR CYLINDER a machine tool used to remove a circular disc from a metal sheet or a shallow cylindrical core from a metal ingot or block. The hole is made by removing a concentric ring of material as opposed to disintegrating the material originally within the hole, as with drilling and boring. **3.** MIN EXTRACT ROCK-BORING TOOL a tool for boring holes in rock ■ *vt* (**-pans, -panning, -panned**) **1.** SURG REMOVE CIRCLE OF BONE to remove a circular section from a bone, especially the skull, with a trepan **2.** MECH ENG CUT SOMETHING OUT to cut a disc or cylindrical core from something using a trepan **3.** MIN EXTRACT BORE HOLE IN ROCK to bore a hole in rock using a trepan [14C. Via medieval Latin *trepanum* 'rotary saw' < Greek *trupanon* 'borer' < *trupan* 'pierce' < *trupē* 'hole'] —**trepanation** /tréppə náysh'n/ *n* —**trepanner** *n*

trepang /tri páng/ *n* a large sea cucumber that is eaten in soups, especially in China and Indonesia. Native to: South Pacific, Indian Ocean. Genera: *Holothuria* or *Actinopyga*. [Late 18C. < Malay *teripang*]

trephine /tri feén, -fín/ *n* a cylindrical sharp or sawtooth-edged surgical instrument, used especially to cut a hole in the skull. It is also used in corneal grafting to remove an opaque disc from a cornea so that it can be replaced with a clear disc. ■ *vt* (**-phines, -phining, -phined**) to remove a circular section from a bone, especially the skull, or from corneal tissue with a trephine [Early 17C. < Latin *tres fines* 'three ends', partly after TREPAN] —**trephination** /tréffi náysh'n/ *n*

trepidation /tréppi dáysh'n/ *n* **1.** fear or uneasiness about the future or a future event **2.** an involuntary trembling (*archaic*) [15C. < Latin *trepidation-* < *trepidare* 'startle, be agitated']

treponema /tréppə neémə/ (*plural* **-mas** or **-mata** /-neémətə/), **treponeme** /tréppə neem/ *n* a spirochaete bacterium that lives as a parasite in warm-blooded animals. One species causes syphilis in humans. Genus: *Treponema*. [Early 20C. < modern Latin < Greek *trepein* 'turn' + *nēma* 'thread'] —**treponemal** *adj*

trespass /tréspəss/ *vi* (**-passes, -passing, -passed**) **1.** ENCROACH ON SOMEBODY to intrude on somebody's privacy or time **2.** BREAK MORAL OR SOCIAL LAW to commit a sin or break a social law (*archaic*) **3.** LAW ENTER SOMEBODY ELSE'S LAND UNLAWFULLY to go onto somebody else's land or enter somebody else's property without permission **4.** LAW CAUSE INJURY to cause injury to the person, property, or rights of another ■ *n* **1.** ENCROACHMENT an intrusion into somebody's privacy or time **2.** SIN a sin or act of wrongdoing (*archaic*) **3.** LAW UNLAWFUL ENTRY ONTO SOMEBODY ELSE'S LAND the act or an instance of going onto somebody else's land or entering somebody else's property without permission [14C. < Old French *trespas* 'transgression' < *trespasser* 'pass beyond or across' < medieval Latin *transpassare*] —**trespasser** *n*

tress /tress/ *n* LOCK OF HAIR a lock of long hair, especially a woman's hair ■ **tresses** *npl* HAIR somebody's hair,

especially a woman's long hair ■ *vt* (**tresses, tressing, tressed**) STYLE HAIR IN TRESSES to arrange or style hair in tresses [13C. < Old French *tresse*]

tressure /tréshər, tréss yoor/ *n* an inner border with ornamental fleur-de-lis on a heraldic shield [14C. < Old French *tressour* < *tresse* 'tress'] —**tressured** *adj*

trestle /tréss'l/ *n* **1.** SUPPORTING FRAMEWORK a supporting framework consisting of a horizontal beam held up by a pair of splayed legs at each end **2.** TOWER FOR SUPPORTING BRIDGE a tower with sloping sides braced by horizontal crosspieces that supports a bridge, made of timber, steel, or reinforced concrete **3.** BRIDGE SUPPORTED BY TOWERS a bridge consisting of multiple short spans supported by towers with sloping sides braced by horizontal crosspieces [14C. < Old French *trestel* 'small beam' < Latin *transtrum* 'beam, crossbar']

trestle table

trestle table *n* a table whose top is supported on trestles

trestletree /tréss'l tree/ *n* either of the two horizontal beams fixed to a masthead to support the crosstrees

trestlework /tréss'l wurk/ *n* a system of supporting trestles, e.g. one that supports a bridge

tretinoin /trə tínnō in, trétti noyn/ *n* a drug related chemically to vitamin A. Use: topical treatment of acne and other skin disorders. [Late 20C. < TRANS- + *retinoic (acid)* (< RETINO-)]

trevally /tri válli/ (*plural* **-lies**) *n* a sea fish with a slender body and sharply forked tail. Native to: Australia. Family: Carangidae. [Late 19C. Alteration of *cavalla*]

Trevelyan /trə véllyən/, **G. M.** (1876–1962) British historian. An influential historian, he wrote for both scholarly and popular audiences. His work includes much British history and biographical studies of Giuseppe Garibaldi. Full name **Trevelyan, George Macaulay**

'Disinterested intellectual curiosity is the life blood of real civilisation.'
[G. M. Trevelyan, *English Social History*; 1942]

Trevino /trə veénō/, **Lee** (*b.* 1939) US golfer. He won 27 Professional Golfers' Association titles, including six major tournaments. Full name **Trevino, Lee Buck**

Treviso /tre veézō/ capital city of Treviso Province, Veneto Region, northeastern Italy. Population: 80,144 (2001).

Trevithick /trə víthik/, **Richard** (1771–1833) British engineer and inventor. His steam locomotives, using the high-pressure steam engines that he developed, were the first to carry passengers or freight on a regular basis.

trews /trooz/ *npl* close-fitting trousers, usually made of tartan cloth, worn by some Scottish army regiments [Mid-16C. < Irish *triús* or Gaelic *triubhas* 'close-fitting shorts']

trey /tray/ (*plural* **treys**) *n* a card, or the face of a dice or domino, with three spots [14C. Via Old French *trei(s)* < Latin *tres* 'three']

TRH *abbr* **1.** Their Royal Highnesses **2.** BIOCHEM thyrotropin-releasing hormone

tri- *prefix* three, third ○ *trilateral* [< Latin and Greek, form of Latin *tres*, Greek *treis* 'three' < Indo-European]

triable /trí əb'l/ *adj* **1.** subject to or fit for trial in a

court of law **2.** able to be tried or tested [15C. < Anglo-Norman < Old French *trier* (see TRY)] —**triableness** *n*

triacid /trī ássid/ *adj* **1.** describes a base capable of reacting with three hydrogen atoms or three molecules of a monobasic acid **2.** describes an acid or a salt containing three replaceable hydrogen atoms

triad /trī ad, -əd/ *n* **1.** SET OF 3 a group of three people or things **2.** MUSIC MUSICAL CHORD a musical chord consisting of three notes, especially a chord made up of a tonic, a third, and a fifth **3.** CHEM ATOM WITH VALENCY OF 3 an atom or chemical group with a valency of three **4.** MIL US STRATEGIC MISSILE FORCE a US strategic missile force made up of bombers, land-based ballistic missiles, and submarine-launched ballistic missiles **5.** LITERAT WELSH LITERARY FORM a form of composition in ancient Welsh literature in which subjects or statements are arranged in groups of three [Mid-16C. Via French *triade* or late Latin *triad-* < Greek *triad-* 'three'] —**triadic** /trī áddik/ *adj*

Triad /trī ad/ *n* a Chinese secret society, especially one involved in organized crime [Mid-20C. Said to be from the use of the triangle as a symbol in the early rituals of such societies, with reference to a trinity of heaven, earth, and humankind]

triage /treé aazh, trī ij/ *n* the process of prioritizing sick or injured people for treatment according to the seriousness of the condition or injury [Early 18C. < French < *trier* (see TRY)]

trial /trī əl/ *n* **1.** FORMAL LEGAL PROCESS a formal examination of the facts and law in a civil or criminal action before a court of law in order to determine an issue **2.** USE OF COURT TRIAL the use of a court trial to determine an issue or somebody's guilt or innocence ○ *standing trial for fraud* **3.** TEST a test or experiment to determine the quality, safety, performance, usefulness, or public acceptance of something **4.** PAINFUL EXPERIENCE an instance of trouble or hardship, especially one that tests somebody's ability to endure **5.** SOMEBODY OR SOMETHING TROUBLESOME somebody or something that causes trouble or annoyance to somebody else ○ *He's such a trial!* **6.** PRELIMINARY COMPETITION a sports competition or preliminary test to select candidates for a later competition **7.** EFFORT an earnest attempt to do something (*formal*) ○ *a trial to circle the globe in a hot-air balloon* ■ **trials** *npl* COMPETITION FOR ANIMALS a competition to test the skills of a working animal or one used in sport ○ *sheepdog trials* ■ *adj* **1.** EXPERIMENTAL done as a test or experiment ○ *a trial separation* **2.** LAW OF COURT TRIAL relating to or used in a court trial ○ *a trial judge* ■ *vt* (**-als, -alling, -alled**) TEST SOMETHING to test something, especially under the conditions in which it is intended to be used [Mid-15C. < Anglo-Norman *triallum* < Old French *trier* (see TRY)]

SPELLCHECK See *trail*.

CULTURAL NOTE *The Trial*, a novel (1925) by Austrian (Czech) writer Franz Kafka. It is the story of Josef K, a young bank clerk who is abruptly arrested for an unspecified misdemeanour. After a long, unsuccessful attempt to discover the nature of his crime, Josef is executed. This enigmatic work is seen as a disturbing allegory of the human condition.

trial and error *n* a method of finding a satisfactory solution or means of doing something by experimenting with alternatives and eliminating failures

trial balance *n* a statement used to check that the debits and credits in a double-entry book-keeping ledger are equal

trial balloon *n* a tentative suggestion, proposal, or plan put forward to test opinion or reaction

trial by fire *n* a thorough test of somebody's abilities or character under pressure

trial court *n* a court in which a case is first decided, as opposed to a court of appeal

trial lawyer *n N Am* a lawyer who practises in a trial court as opposed to an appeal court

triallist /trī əlist/ *n* a sports player or competitor who is given a chance to prove worthy of being included in a team for a major competition

trial of strength *n* a contest between two people,

groups, or organizations to decide which is the stronger

trialogue /trī ə log/ *n* discussion involving three people or groups [Mid-16C. Blend of TRI- + DIALOGUE]

trial run *n* a test of something new or untried, especially to assess its performance

triamcinolone /trī am sínnəlon/ *n* a synthetic corticosteroid drug. Use: treatment of skin, oral, and joint inflammations. Formula: $C_{21}H_{27}FO_6$. [Mid-20C. < TRI- + *amyl* + *cinene* + *prednisolone*]

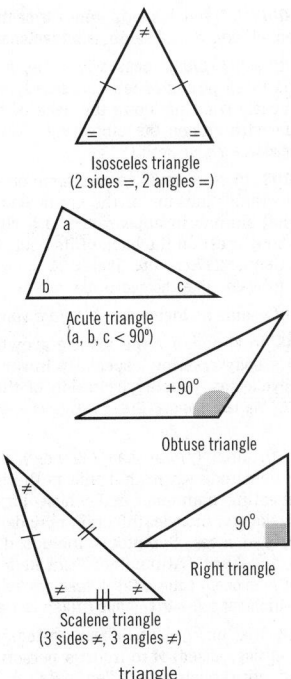

Equilateral triangle
(3 sides =, 3 angles =)

Isosceles triangle
(2 sides =, 2 angles =)

Acute triangle
(a, b, c < 90°)

Obtuse triangle

Right triangle

Scalene triangle
(3 sides ≠, 3 angles ≠)

triangle

triangle /trī ang g'l/ *n* **1.** 3-SIDED FIGURE a two-dimensional geometric figure formed of three sides and three angles. The triangle is a fundamental figure of plane geometry, since it is the polygon with the fewest sides and any other polygon can be subdivided into triangles. **2.** OBJECT WITH 3 SIDES something shaped like a triangle **3.** *N Am* MATHS same as set square **4.** 3-PERSON RELATIONSHIP an emotional or sexual relationship involving three people **5.** MUSIC PERCUSSION INSTRUMENT a metal bar bent into the shape of a triangle with one angle open, used as a percussion instrument [14C. Directly or via French < Latin *triangulum* < *triangulus* 'three-cornered']

triangular /trī áng gyoolər/ *adj* **1.** OF TRIANGLE relating to or in the shape of a triangle **2.** WITH TRIANGULAR BASE having a base in the shape of a triangle **3.** HAVING 3 PARTS consisting of or involving three people or parts [14C. < late Latin *triangularis* < Latin *triangulum* (see TRIANGLE)] —**triangularity** /trī áng gyoo lárrəti/ *n* —**triangularly** *adv*

triangulate *vt* /trī áng gyoo layt/ (**-lates, -lating, -lated**) **1.** MEASURE SOMETHING USING TRIGONOMETRIC RELATIONSHIPS to measure something using the trigonometric relationships between pairs of sides and angles of triangles **2.** SURVEY OR MAP SOMETHING BY TRIANGULATION to survey or map an area by the process of triangulation **3.** SPLIT SOMETHING INTO TRIANGLES to divide a surface into triangles **4.** MAKE SOMETHING TRIANGULAR to make something into the shape of a triangle ■ *adj* /trī áng gyoolit, -layt/ MADE UP OF TRIANGLES shaped like a triangle or made up of triangles [15C. < Latin *triangulum* (see TRIANGLE)] —**triangulately** *adv*

triangulation /trī áng gyoo láysh'n/ *n* **1.** METHOD FOR DETERMINING LOCATION TRIGONOMETRICALLY a navigation technique that uses the trigonometric properties of triangles to determine a location or course by means of compass bearings from two points a known distance apart. Space-age global positioning systems enable people to triangulate their location relative to the known positions of Earth-orbiting satellites. **2.** DIVIDING OF SURVEY AREA INTO TRIANGLES the division of a large area into adjacent triangles for survey purposes using trigonometric relationships to calculate the dimensions of an area bounded by each triangle. One side (**baseline**) and the angles to the third point of each adjacent triangle are measured, and the lengths of the other sides can be calculated from these measurements. **3.** SYSTEM OF TRIANGLES the system of triangles laid out in triangulation

Triangulum /trī áng gyooləm/ *n* a small constellation of the northern hemisphere. See illustration at **constellation**

Triangulum Australe /-o straáyli/ *n* a small constellation of the southern hemisphere. See illustration at **constellation**

triarchy /trī aarki/ (*plural* **-chies**) *n* **1.** a system in which a country is ruled by three leaders **2.** a country ruled by three leaders [Early 17C. < Greek *triarkhia* 'triumvirate', or < TRI- + -ARCH]

Triassic /trī ássik/ *n* the period of geological time, 248 million to 206 million years ago, during which reptiles flourished and dinosaurs and evergreen forests first appeared. See table at **geological time** [Mid-19C. < German *Trias* < Latin, 'three, triad' < Greek] —**Triassic** *adj*

triathlon /trī áthlən, -lon/ *n* an athletics competition in which the contestants compete in three different events and are awarded points for each to find the best all-round athlete. The events are usually swimming, cycling, and running. [Late 20C. < TRI- + Greek *athlon* 'contest'] —**triathlete** *n*

triatomic /trī ə tómmik/ *adj* **1.** containing three atoms in each molecule **2.** having three replaceable atoms or chemical groups —**triatomically** *adv*

triaxial /trī áksi əl/ *adj* having or involving three axes —**triaxiality** /trī áksi álləti/ *n*

triazine /trī ə zeen, trī áy-/ *n* **1.** an organic compound with a six-membered ring containing three carbon and three nitrogen atoms. Formula: $C_3H_3N_3$. **2.** a derivative of a triazine isomer. Use: herbicides, pesticides, dyes.

triazole /trī ə zol, -ə zōl, trī ázzol, -ázzōl/ *n* **1.** an organic compound with a five-membered ring containing two carbon and three nitrogen atoms. Formula: $C_2H_3N_3$. **2.** a derivative of triazole. Use: photocopying.

tribade /tríbbəd/ *n* a lesbian, especially one who takes part in tribadism [Early 17C. Via French or Latin < Greek *tribas* < *tribein* 'rub']

tribadism /tríbbədizəm/ *n* a lesbian practice in which one partner rubs her genitals against the other's

tribalism /tríbbəlizəm/ *n* **1.** the customs, beliefs, and social organization of a tribe or social group **2.** loyalty to a tribe or social group —**tribalist** *n, adj* —**tribalistic** /tríbə lístik/ *adj*

tribasic /trī báyssik/ *adj* **1.** describes an acid containing three replaceable hydrogen atoms and capable of reacting with three hydroxyl ions per molecule **2.** describes a compound that contains three univalent metal atoms or groups in each molecule

tribe /trīb/ *n* **1.** SOCIAL DIVISION OF PEOPLE a society or division of a society whose members have ancestry, customs, beliefs, and leadership in common **2.** FAMILY a large family (*informal humorous*) **3.** GROUP WITH SOMETHING IN COMMON a group of people who have something in common such as an occupation, social background, or political viewpoint ○ *rebelled against the whole tribe of earnest policy makers* **4.** BIOL TAXONOMIC DIVISION a division in the scientific classification of animals and plants, between a subfamily and a genus **5.** ANCIENT HIST ANCIENT ROMAN SOCIAL GROUP one of the three groups, Latins, Sabines, and Etruscans, into which ancient Roman society was divided [13C. Via Old French *tribu* < Latin *tribus* 'one of three ethnic

divisions of the Roman people' < *tri-* 'three'] —**tribal** *adj*—**tribally** *adv*

Tribeca /trī be͞ekə/, **TriBeCa** area of lower Manhattan known for its 19th-century cast-iron buildings, originally built as commercial premises and in the late 20th century renovated into artists' lofts, homes, and shops

tribesman /trībzmən/ (*plural* **-men** /-mən/) *n* a man who is a member of a tribe

tribespeople /trībz peep'l/ *npl* people who are members of a tribe

tribeswoman /trībz wo͝omən/ (*plural* **-women** /-wimin/) *n* a woman who is a member of a tribe

triblet /tríbblət/ *n* a cylindrical or tapered rod used for making ring-shaped and cylindrical items such as rings or nuts or in drawing tubes [Early 17C. < French *triboulet*]

tribo- *prefix* friction ○ *triboelectricity* [< Greek *tribos* 'rubbing' < *tribein* 'rub']

triboelectricity /trībō i lek tríssəti, -éllek-/ *n* an electric charge generated by friction, e.g. by rubbing materials together —**triboelectric** /-léktrik/ *adj*

tribology /trī bólləji/ *n* the science and technology of interacting surfaces in relative motion, including the study of friction, lubrication, and wear —**tribological** /trībə lójjik'l/ *adj*—**tribologist** *n*

triboluminescence /trībō loomi néss'nss/ *n* luminescence caused by friction —**triboluminescent** *adj*

tribomaterial /trībō mə teeri əl/ *n* a material based on carbon, used to control friction and minimize surface wear

tribrach /trī brak, trí-/ *n* a metrical foot of three short syllables [Late 16C. Via Latin *tribrachys* < Greek *tribrakhus* < *tri-* 'three' + *brakhus* 'short'] —**tribrachic** *adj*

tribromoethanol /trī brōmō éthə nol/ *n* a white crystalline organic compound. Use: general anaesthetic. Formula: CBr_3CH_2OH.

tribulation /tríbbyo͞o láysh'n/ *n* **1.** great difficulty, affliction, or distress **2.** something that causes great difficulty, affliction, or distress, e.g. an ordeal ○ *the trials and tribulations of the struggling author* [13C. Via French < ecclesiastical Latin *tribulation-* < Latin *tribulare* 'afflict, press' < *tribulum* 'threshing tool' < *terere* 'rub']

tribunal /trī byo͞on'l, tri-/ *n* **1.** LAW COURT a court of justice **2.** JUDGING BODY a body that is appointed to make a judgment or enquiry ○ *an industrial tribunal* **3.** COURT CONVENED BY GOVERNMENT a court convened, under English law, by the British government to judge or investigate a specific matter **4.** RAISED SEAT a bench or seat on a platform where a judge or magistrate sits [15C. Directly or via Old French < Latin *tribunal* 'platform for magistrates' < *tribunus* (see TRIBUNE[1])]

tribunate /tríbbyo͞onət/ *n* the office, rank, or authority of a tribune in ancient Rome [Mid-16C. < Latin *tribunatus* < *tribunus* (see TRIBUNE[1])]

tribune[1] /tríbbyoon/ *n* **1.** a representative of the common people in the ancient Roman republic, elected annually **2.** a person or institution that defends the rights of the people [14C. Via French < Latin *tribunus* 'magistrate' < *tribus* (see TRIBE)] —**tribunary** *adj*—**tribuneship** *n*

tribune[2] /tríbbyoon/ *n* **1.** PLATFORM a raised platform for a speaker **2.** BISHOP'S THRONE OR SITE OF IT a bishop's throne, or an apse of a Christian basilica containing the throne **3.** CHURCH GALLERY a gallery in a Christian church [Mid-18C. Via French < Italian *tribuna* 'raised platform', alteration of Latin *tribunal* < *tribunus* (see TRIBUNE[1])]

Tribune Group *n* a left-wing group of British Labour Members of Parliament, founded in 1966 (*takes a singular or plural verb*) —**Tribunite** /tríbbyo͞o nīt/ *n, adj*

tributary /tríbbyo͞otəri/ *n* (*plural* **-ies**) **1.** STREAM FEEDING LARGER BODY OF WATER a stream, river, or glacier that joins a larger stream, river, or glacier, or a lake **2.** HIST PAYER OF TRIBUTE formerly, a person or nation that paid a monetary tribute to another ■ *adj* **1.** JOINING LARGER BODY OF WATER flowing into a larger stream, river, or glacier, or into a lake **2.** PAYING TRIBUTE paying tribute in money, goods or praise **3.** HIST PAID AS TRIBUTE paid or owed as a tribute [14C. < Latin *tributarius* 'liable to tax or tribute' < *tributum* (see TRIBUTE)] —**tributarily** *adv*

tribute /tríbbyoot/ *n* **1.** EXPRESSION OF GRATITUDE OR PRAISE something said or given to show gratitude, praise, or admiration **2.** EVIDENCE OF GOOD something that is indicative of a value, benefit, or good quality in somebody or something ○ *The result is a tribute to her powers of persuasion.* **3.** HIST PAYMENT BY ONE RULER TO ANOTHER a payment made by one ruler or state to another as a sign of submission **4.** HIST PAYMENT TO FEUDAL LORD in medieval society, a payment made by a vassal to a lord, or an obligation for such payment [14C. Directly or via French < Latin *tributum* < *tribuere* 'give out among the tribes' < *tribus* (see TRIBE)]

tribute band, **tribute group** *n* a musical group that imitates or performs material made popular by a famous predecessor

tricarboxylic acid cycle /trī kaar bok síllik-/ *n* BIOCHEM same as **Krebs cycle**

trice[1] /trīss/ *n* a very short period of time [15C. < TRICE[2]]

trice[2] /trīss/ (**trices, tricing, triced**) *vt* to haul up or fasten something, especially with a rope [14C. < Middle Dutch *trīsen* 'pull' < *trīse* 'pulley']

tricentenary /trī sen te͞enəri, -tén-/, **tricentennial** /trī sen ténni əl/ *adj, n* TIME same as **tercentenary**

triceps /trī seps/ (*plural* **-cepses** or *same*) *n* a muscle that has three points of anchorage, especially the large muscle running along the back of the upper arm that straightens the elbow [Late 16C. < Latin, 'three-headed' < *caput* 'head']

triceratops /trī sérrə tops/ (*plural same* or **-topses**) *n* a plant-eating dinosaur of the Cretaceous Period, somewhat similar in appearance to a rhinoceros, with a bony crest on the back of its neck and three horns. Genus: *Triceratops.* [Late 19C. < modern Latin < Greek *trikeratos* 'three-horned' + *ōps* 'face']

trich- *prefix* same as **tricho-** (*used before vowels*)

trichiasis /tri kī ə siss/ *n* the inward growth of hair around a body opening, especially inward growth of the eyelashes, causing irritation of the eyeball [Mid-17C. Via late Latin < Greek *trikhiasis* < *trikhian* 'be hairy']

trichina /tri kīnə/ (*plural* **-nae** /-kī nee/) *n* a small slender nematode worm that infests the intestines of meat-eating mammals and whose larvae form cysts in skeletal muscle. Infection may derive from undercooked meat. Symptoms include diarrhoea, nausea, and fever. Latin name: *Trichinella spiralis.* [Mid-19C. < modern Latin < Greek *trikhinos* 'hairy' < *thrix* 'hair'] —**trichinal** *adj*—**trichinous** /tríkənəss/ *adj*

trichinize /tríki nīz/ (**-nizes, -nizing, -nized**), **trichinise** (**-nises, -nising, -nised**) *vt* to infest a person, animal, or meat with trichinae (*often passive*) [Mid-19C. < TRICHINA] —**trichinized** *adj* —**trichinization** /tríki nī záysh'n/ *n*

Trichinopoly /tríchin óppəli/ former name for **Tiruchchirappalli**

trichinosis /tríki nōssiss/ *n* a disease caused by infestation with trichinae and marked by fever, muscle pain, and diarrhoea, often resulting from eating undercooked pork infected with the larvae

trichite /trík īt/ *n* a dark needle-shaped crystal found in volcanic rock —**trichitic** /tri kíttik/ *adj*

trichlorethylene *n* CHEM same as **trichloroethylene**

trichlorfon /trī kláwr fon/, **trichlorphon** *n* a crystalline organic compound. Use: insecticide. Formula: $C_4H_8Cl_3O_4P$. [Mid-20C. < TRI- + CHLORO- + *-fon*, shortening of *phosphonate*]

trichloride /trī kláw rīd/, **trichlorid** /-rid/ *n* a compound with three chloride atoms per molecule

trichloroacetic acid /trī klawrō ə se͞etik-/ *n* a corrosive toxic acid. Use: astringent, antiseptic, herbicide. Formula: $C_2Cl_3HO_2$.

trichloroethane /trī klawrō e͞e thayn/ *n* a volatile colourless nonflammable liquid. Use: industrial solvent. Formula: $C_2H_3Cl_3$.

trichloroethylene /trī klawrō éthə leen/, **trichlorethylene** /-klawr éthə-/ *n* a volatile colourless nonflammable liquid. Use: solvent, degreaser, anaesthetic. Formula: C_2HCl_3.

trichlorphon *n* CHEM another spelling of **trichlorfon**

tricho- *prefix* hair, filament, thread ○ *trichology* [< Greek *trikh-*, stem of *thrix* 'hair']

trichocyst /tríkə sist/ *n* a stinging or grasping organ resembling a thread that protrudes and can be ejected from a minute cavity on the surface of some protozoans, especially ciliates —**trichocystic** /tríkə sístik/ *adj*

trichogyne /tríkə jīn, -jin/ *n* a projection resembling a hair on the female sex organ of some fungi, lichens, and algae that attracts and receives the male sex cell prior to fertilization —**trichogynial** /tríkə jíni əl, -jínni əl/ *adj* —**trichogynic** /tríkə jínik, -jínnik/ *adj*

trichoid /tríkoyd/ *adj* resembling hair

trichology /tri kólləji/ *n* the study and treatment of hair and its diseases —**trichological** /tríkə lójjik'l/ *adj*—**trichologist** *n*

trichome /trīkōm, tríkōm/ *n* **1.** an outgrowth of a plant's outer cell layer (**epidermis**). Trichomes have various shapes and functions, and include root hairs. **2.** a filamentous chain of cells of bacteria or cyanobacteria [Late 19C. < Greek *trikhōma* 'growth of hair' < *thrix* 'hair'] —**trichomic** /tri kómmik/ *adj*

trichomonad /tríkō mónnad/ *n* a flagellated protozoan that lives as a parasite in the digestive and reproductive tracts of humans and animals. Genus: *Trichomonas.* —**trichomonadal** *adj* —**trichomonal** *adj*

trichomoniasis /tríkō mō nī əssiss/ *n* **1.** a sexually transmitted infection, especially of the vagina, marked by persistent discharge and intense itching. It is caused by a protozoan parasite, *Trichomonas vaginalis.* **2.** an infection of animals caused by parasitic protozoans (**trichomonads**). In cattle, this condition can lead to spontaneous abortion or sterility. [Early 20C. < TRICHOMONAD]

trichopteran /trī kóptərən/ *n* INSECTS same as **caddis fly** [Mid-19C. < modern Latin *Trichoptera* < Greek *trikh-* (see TRICHO-) + *ptera*, plural of *pteron* 'wing']

trichotomy /trī kóttə mi/ (*plural* **-mies**) *n* **1.** the division of something into three categories, classes, elements, or parts (*formal*) **2.** in some beliefs, the division of human nature into body, soul, and spirit [Early 17C. < modern Latin *trichotomia* < Greek *trikha* 'in three parts'] —**trichotomic** /tríkə tómmik/ *adj* —**trichotomous** *adj* —**trichotomously** *adv*

trichroism /trī krō izəm/ *n* the property possessed by some crystals of showing three different colours when viewed along each of their three axes [Mid-19C. < Greek *trikhroos* 'three-coloured'] —**trichroic** /trī krṓ ik/ *adj*

trichromat /trīkrō mat, trīkrə-/ *n* somebody who has standard colour vision and is able to perceive red, green, and blue [Early 20C. Back-formation < TRICHROMATIC]

trichromatic /trī krō máttik/, **trichrome** /trī krōm/, **trichromic** /trī krṓmik/ *adj* **1.** 3-COLOUR relating to, involving, or using three colours **2.** COMBINING PRIMARY COLOURS involving the combination of the three primary colours to produce the other colours **3.** RELATING TO STANDARD COLOUR VISION relating to standard colour vision, which is able to perceive red, green, and blue —**trichromatism** /trī krṓmətizəm/ *n*

trichuriasis /tríkyo͞o rī ə siss/ *n* intestinal infection with nematodes of the genus *Trichuris.* It usually produces no symptoms but may cause diarrhoea and bleeding in severely infected children. [Early 20C. < modern Latin *Trichuris* < Greek *trikh* 'hair' + *oura* 'tail']

trick /trik/ *n* **1.** CUNNING DECEPTION a cunning action or plan that is intended to cheat or deceive **2.** PRANK a prank, joke, or mischievous action or plan ○ *played a trick on his sister* **3.** SPECIAL SKILL a special, effective, or ingenious knack, skill, or technique ○ *taught me the tricks of the trade* **4.** SKILFUL ACT DESIGNED TO AMUSE a skilful act or feat designed to amuse or entertain ○ *taught the dog to do tricks* **5.** ACT OF MAGIC an act of magic or illusion, especially one involving sleight of hand, designed to puzzle or entertain ○ *a conjuring trick* **6.** DECEPTIVE EFFECT OF LIGHT an illusion, especially one caused by the light **7.** PECULIAR HABIT a peculiar characteristic, habit, mannerism, or way of behaving ○ *He has this trick of scratching his ear when he's being evasive.* **8.** UNFORESEEN EVENT a strange event or development that was not anticipated or seems unfair or sad ○ *a cruel trick of fate* **9.** CARDS FROM EACH PLAYER IN ROUND the cards played by all the

players participating in one round of a card game and won by an individual player **10.** CARDS **GOOD CARD** a card likely to win a trick, especially in bridge **11.** PERIOD OF DUTY a period of duty, e.g. at the helm of a ship **12.** N Am **PROSTITUTE'S CUSTOMER** a customer of a prostitute (*slang*) **13.** N Am **SEX WITH SOMEBODY FOR MONEY** an individual engagement between a prostitute and a client (*slang*) ■ *vti* (**tricks, tricking, tricked**) CHEAT or deceive somebody ○ *Hundreds of readers were tricked into sending them money.* ■ *adj* **1.** OF TRICKS involving or intended to be used for tricks or trickery ○ *trick photography* **2.** MADE AS IMITATION FOR JOKE made as an imitation of something so that it can be used to play a joke on somebody **3.** N Am MED OCCASIONALLY SYMPTOMATIC displaying symptoms of injury from time to time (*informal*) ○ *a trick ankle* [15C. < Old N French *trique*] ◇ **be unable to take a trick** *Aus* to have a run of back luck (*informal*) ◇ **do the trick** to be effective and do what is needed (*informal*) ◇ **how's tricks?** used as a greeting (*dated informal*) ◇ **never** *or* **not miss a trick** to notice everything that is happening, or any opportunity that is advantageous (*informal*) ◇ **show somebody a trick or two** to demonstrate more skill than somebody else ◇ **up to one's (old) tricks** acting in a characteristically idiosyncratic manner in a way that is disapproved of (*informal*)

trick out, trick up *vt* **1.** to decorate or dress somebody or something up, especially in a fancy or garish way **2.** to modify something such as a vehicle or piece of electronic equipment and add a large number of additional features to it

trick cyclist *n* **1.** somebody who performs stunts on a bicycle or monocycle, especially in a circus **2.** PSYCHIAT same as **psychiatrist** (*dated informal humorous*)

trickery /tríkəri/ (*plural* **-ies**) *n* a trick or prank, especially a trick intended to cheat or deceive, or the use of such tricks

trickle /tríkᵊl/ *v* (**-les, -ling, -led**) **1.** *vti* FLOW SLOWLY IN THIN STREAM to flow slowly in a thin stream or in drops, or cause something to do this ○ *sweat trickled down his face* **2.** *vi* MOVE SLOWLY OR GRADUALLY to move, come, or go slowly or gradually ○ *The crowd trickled slowly away and the park emptied.* ■ *n* **1.** SLOW THIN FLOW a slow thin flow, movement, or stream ○ *a trickle of blood* **2.** ACT OF FLOWING IN THIN STREAM an act of flowing or of causing a liquid to flow in a slow thin stream [14C. Origin ?] —**trickling** *adj* —**tricklingly** *adv* —**trickly** *adj*

trickle charger *n* a small low-current device used to recharge batteries slowly and maintain them in a fully charged state —**trickle charge** *n*

trickle-down theory *n* the economic theory that financial and other benefits received by big businesses gradually spread to benefit the rest of society

trick or treat *n* a Halloween custom in which children call at neighbours' houses and threaten to play a trick on the householder unless they are given a treat such as sweets ■ *interj* used as a greeting by children when they call on a house in order to ask for sweets at Halloween —**trick-or-treat** *vi*

trickster /tríkstər/ *n* somebody who deceives, swindles, or plays tricks

tricksy /tríksi/ *adj* **1.** MISCHIEVOUS mischievous, playful, or inclined to play tricks **2.** NOT STRAIGHTFORWARD intricate, complicated, or overelaborate **3.** GIMMICKY new and ingenious —**tricksiness** *n*

tricky /tríki/ (**-ier, -iest**) *adj* **1.** difficult to do or deal with and requiring skill, caution, or tact ○ *a tricky manoeuvre* ○ *a tricky situation* **2.** likely to cheat or outwit somebody —**trickily** *adv* —**trickiness** *n*

triclad /trī klad/ *n* a flatworm with an intestine that is divided into three sections. Order: Tricladida. [Late 19C. Shortening of modern Latin *Tricladida* < Greek *tri*-'three' + *klados* 'branch']

triclinic /trī klínnik/ *adj* describes a crystal that has three unequal axes, none of which is perpendicular to another

triclinium /tri klínni əm, trī-, tri klín-/ (*plural* **-clinia** /-klínni ə/) *n* **1.** a couch arranged around three sides of a table and used by ancient Romans to recline on at meals **2.** an ancient Roman dining room, especially one containing a triclinium [Mid-17C. Via

Latin < Greek *triklinion* < *triklinos* 'room with three couches' < *klinē* 'couch']

tricolour /tríkələr, trī kulər/ *n* **1.** 3-COLOURED FLAG a flag with three colours **2.** *also* **Tricolour** FRENCH NATIONAL FLAG the French national flag, consisting of three equal vertical bands of blue, white, and red **3.** 3-COLOURED DOG a black, tan, and white dog ■ *adj* **1.** *also* **tricoloured** /trī kulər/ 3-COLOURED involving, or using three colours **2.** *also* **tricoloured** PIEBALD having a coat of black, tan, and white

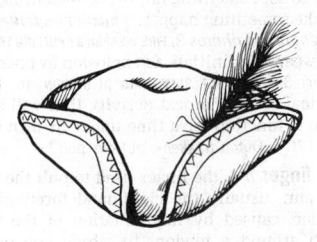

tricorn

tricorn /trī kawrn/, **tricorne** *n* **1.** HAT WITH 3-POINTED BRIM a hat with its brim turned up on three sides, making three points, worn by men in the 18th century **2.** MYTHICAL ANIMAL an imaginary animal with three horns ■ *adj* 3-HORNED having three horns or corners [Mid-18C. Directly or via French *tricorne* < Latin *tricornis* 'three-horned' < *cornu* 'horn']

tricornered /trī kawrnərd/ *adj* having three corners

tricot /tríkō, treèkō/ *n* **1.** a plain close-knit fabric of natural or artificial fibre. Use: underwear. **2.** a soft ribbed fabric of wool or a wool and cotton mix. Use: dresses. [Late 18C. < French *tricoter* 'to knit' < Germanic]

tricotine /tríkə teén, treè-/ *n* a strong woollen fabric woven with a double twill

tricuspid /trī kúss pid/ *adj* *also* **tricuspidal** /trī kúspid'l/ *or* **tricuspidate** /trī kúspi dayt/ having three cusps or points ■ *n* something that has three cusps, e.g. a tooth or leaf

tricuspid valve *n* a heart valve consisting of three flaps that prevents blood from flowing back into the right atrium when the right ventricle contracts

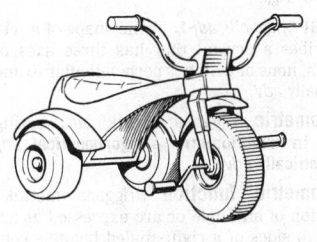

tricycle

tricycle /tríssik'l/ *n* **1.** PEDAL-DRIVEN 3-WHEELED VEHICLE a pedal-driven vehicle with two wheels at the back and one at the front, ridden now especially by young children **2.** MOTOR-DRIVEN 3-WHEELED VEHICLE a motor-driven vehicle with three wheels ■ *vi* (**-cles, -cling, -cled**) RIDE TRICYCLE to ride a tricycle —**tricyclist** *n*

tricyclic /trī síklik/ *adj* having a molecular structure containing three rings ■ *n* PHARM same as **tricyclic antidepressant drug**

tricyclic antidepressant drug *n* a drug belonging to a group of drugs that have a chemical structure based on three linked carbon rings. Use: treatment of depression.

tridactyl /trī dáktil/, **tridactylous** /trī dáktiləss/ *adj* having three claws, fingers, or toes on each limb

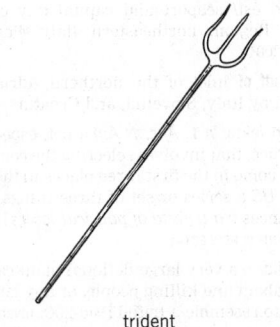

trident

trident /tríd'nt/ *n* **1.** 3-PRONGED SPEAR an instrument, spear, or weapon with three prongs **2.** MYTHOL 3-PRONGED SPEAR OF POSEIDON OR NEPTUNE in classical mythology, the three-pronged spear carried by the Greek sea god, Poseidon, or his Roman equivalent, Neptune ■ *adj* 3-PRONGED having three prongs, points, or teeth [15C. < Latin *trident-*, stem of *tridens* < *dens* 'tooth']

Trident *n* a US-manufactured ballistic missile system fired from nuclear submarines and in service with the US Navy and the British Royal Navy

tridental /trī dént'l/, **tridentate** /trī dén tayt/ *adj* with three points, prongs, or teeth

Tridentine /trī dén tīn, tri-/ *adj* relating to the Council of Trent or its decrees, in which the traditional doctrines of Roman Catholicism were reasserted and the Counter Reformation was begun ■ *n* a Roman Catholic who adheres to doctrines laid down by the Council of Trent, especially in opposition to the reforms of the Second Vatican Council [Mid-16C. < medieval Latin *Tridentinus* < Latin *Tridentum* 'Trent']

tridimensional /trī dī ménsh'nəl, -di-/ *adj* having three dimensions —**tridimensionality** /trī dī ménsh'n álleti, -di-/ *n* —**tridimensionally** *adv*

triduum /tríddyoo əm, trī-/ *n* a period of three days of prayer before a Roman Catholic feast [Early 18C. < Latin < *dies* 'day']

tried /trīd/ past participle, past tense of **try** ■ *adj* (*often used in combination*) **1.** proved through experience or testing to be good, effective, or reliable ○ *using this tried and tested method* **2.** subjected to considerable strain, stress, or worry ○ *the sorely tried teacher of a class of noisy pupils*

triene /trī een/ *n* a chemical compound that has three double bonds

triennia plural of **triennium**

triennial /trī énni əl/ *adj* **1.** HAPPENING EVERY 3 YEARS taking place once every three years **2.** LASTING 3 YEARS lasting for a period of three years ■ *n* **1.** 3RD ANNIVERSARY a third anniversary of an event **2.** 3-YEARLY EVENT an event that takes place every three years **3.** 3-YEAR PERIOD a period of three years [Mid-16C. < Latin *triennis* < *triennium* (see TRIENNIUM)] —**triennially** *adv*

triennium /trī énni əm/ (*plural* **-niums** *or* **-nia** /-ni ə/) *n* a period of three years [Mid-19C. < Latin < *annus* 'year']

trier /trī ər/ *n* **1.** SOMEBODY WHO TRIES somebody or something that tries, e.g. a tester of new things **2.** SOMEBODY WHO PERSEVERES somebody who perseveres in doing something despite limited ability or lack of success **3.** TOOL FOR TESTING MATERIALS a tool or implement designed and used for testing materials, particularly food products, during manufacture

Trier /treer/ city in Rhineland-Palatinate State, southwestern Germany. It lies in the centre of a wine-growing region. Population: 99,602 (1997).

trierarch /trī ə raark/ *n* **1.** the captain of an ancient Greek trireme **2.** in ancient Greece, a citizen commissioned to fit out a trireme for the use of a city-state [Mid-17C. Directly or via Latin < Greek *triērarkhos* 'trireme commander']

trierarchy /trī ə raarki/ (*plural* **-chies**) *n* **1.** SYSTEM FOR SUPPORTING ANCIENT GREEK NAVY in ancient Greece, the system that required citizens to subsidize triremes **2.** OFFICE OF TRIERARCH the authority, office, or position of a trierarch **3.** TRIERARCHS trierarchs as a group [Mid-19C. < Greek *triērarkhia* < *triērarkhos* 'trireme commander']

Trieste /tri ést/ seaport and capital city of Friuli-Venezia Region, northeastern Italy. Population: 211,184 (2001).

Trieste, Gulf of inlet of the northern Adriatic Sea, bordered by Italy, Slovenia, and Croatia

trifecta /trī fékta/ n 1. Aus, N Am a bet, especially on a horse race, that involves selecting the competitors that will come in the first three places in the correct order 2. US a series or set of three things, factors, or influences ○ *a trifecta of political losers* [Late 20C. Blend of TRI- + PERFECTA]

triffid /tríffid/ n a very large fictional plant capable of moving about and killing people, or any large plant thought to resemble a triffid [Mid-20C. Invention]

trifid /trífid/ adj describes a tail or organ that is deeply divided into three parts [Mid-18C. < Latin *trifidus* 'having three clefts' < *findere* 'to split']

trifle /tríf'l/ n 1. COLD DESSERT a cold dessert typically consisting of sponge cake soaked in sherry or fruit juice, spread with jam, jelly, or fruit, and topped with custard, whipped cream, or both 2. SOMETHING TRIVIAL something that has little or no importance, significance, or value ○ *dismissed the complaint as a mere trifle* 3. SMALL QUANTITY a small amount of something ○ *What he'd earned seemed a trifle beside his mountain of debts.* 4. METALL MEDIUM-HARD PEWTER pewter of medium hardness ■ **trifles** npl PEWTER UTENSILS objects or utensils made of trifle [13C. < Old French *trufle*, variant of *truffe* 'deception'] —**trifler** n ◇ a **trifle** slightly or somewhat (formal or humorous) **trifle** with vt to treat or take advantage of somebody or something thoughtlessly ○ *had trifled with her affections*

trifling /trífling/ adj 1. insignificant, trivial, or of little value ○ *trifling matters* 2. concerned with matters of little importance (literary) ○ '*He is not a trifling, silly young man*' (Jane Austen, *Emma*; 1816) —**triflingly** adv

trifocal /trī fók'l/ adj describes a lens that has three different sections, each with a different focal point ■ **trifocals** npl spectacles with trifocal lenses whose three sections correct separately for near, medium, and distant vision

trifold /trī fōld/ adj consisting of three parts

trifoliate /trī fóli ət, -ayt/, **trifoliated** /trī fóli aytid/ adj 1. having three leaves or three parts resembling leaves 2. same as **trifoliolate**

trifoliolate /trī fóli əlit, trī fóli ə layt/ adj 1. describes a compound leaf consisting of three leaflets that arise from the same point, e.g. a clover leaf 2. describes a plant having trifoliolate leaves [Early 19C. < TRI- + medieval Latin *foliolum*, diminutive of Latin *folium* 'leaf']

triforium /trī fáwri əm/ (plural -**ria** /-ri ə/) n an arcaded storey in a church between the nave arches and the clerestory [13C. < Anglo-Latin] —**triforial** adj

triform /trí fawrm/, **triformed** /trí fawrmd/ adj having or consisting of three different forms or parts

trifurcate adj /trí furkət, trí furkit/, **trifurcated** /trí furkaytid/ divided into three branches or forks ■ vi /trī fur kayt/ (-**cates**, -**cating**, -**cated**) to divide into three branches or forks [Early 18C. < Latin *trifurcus* < *furca* 'fork'] —**trifurcation** /trí fur káysh'n/ n

trig[1] /trig/ n trigonometry, especially as a school subject (informal) [Mid-19C. Shortening]

trig[2] /trig/ regional n a brake or supporting block used to stop something from rolling ■ vt (**trigs, trigging, trigged**) to support something or stop something from moving with a block or wedge [Late 16C. Origin ?]

trig[3] /trig/ adj regional neat, smart, tidy, or trim (archaic) [13C. < Old Norse *tryggr* 'true'] —**trig** vt —**trigly** adv —**trigness** n

trig. abbr MATHS 1. trigonometrical 2. trigonometry

trigeminal /trī jémmin'l/ adj relating to or involving a trigeminal nerve ■ n ANAT same as **trigeminal nerve** [Mid-19C. < modern Latin *trigeminus* 'three twins' < Latin *geminus* 'twin']

trigeminal nerve n either of the fifth pair of cranial nerves that provide the jaw, face, and nasal cavity with motor and sensory functions

trigeminal neuralgia n a condition involving recurring sudden sharp pain in the face along the branches of a trigeminal nerve

trigger /tríggər/ n 1. SMALL LEVER THAT FIRES GUN a small lever that is pressed with a finger to fire a gun 2. LEVER THAT OPERATES MECHANISM a small lever or device that is pressed or squeezed to operate a mechanism, e.g. by releasing a spring 3. STIMULUS FOR SOMETHING a stimulus that sets off an action, process, or series of events 4. ENG SIGNAL FOR STARTING OPERATION an automatic or manual pulse or signal for an operation to start ■ vt (-**gers**, -**gering**, -**gered**) 1. MAKE SOMETHING HAPPEN to set something off, bring something about, or make something happen ○ *memories triggered by the sight of old photos* 2. FIRE WEAPON BY PULLING TRIGGER to fire a weapon or initiate an explosion by operating a trigger 3. ENG SET SOMETHING IN MOTION to initiate electrical or mechanical activity that will allow a device to function for a time under its own control [Early 17C. < Dutch *trekker* < *trekken* 'pull']

trigger finger n 1. the finger used to pull the trigger on a gun, usually the right-hand forefinger 2. a disorder, caused by inflammation of the fibrous sheath around a tendon, in which one or more fingers are locked in a bent position and click if forcibly straightened

triggerfish /tríggər fish/ (plural same or -**fishes**) n a sea fish with a thin body and a dorsal fin spine that locks in an erect position as a protection against predators. It is found on coral reefs. Family: Balistidae.

trigger-happy adj (informal) 1. likely or overeager to shoot a firearm without considering the consequences 2. liable to act in a rash or violent way without considering the consequences

triggerman /tríggər man/ (plural -**men** /-men/) n US (informal) 1. somebody who shoots somebody else, usually as part of a gang committing a crime 2. a bodyguard, especially one working for a gangster

triglyceride /trī glíssə rīd/ n an ester formed from a molecule of glycerol and three molecules of fatty acids, considered to have adverse effects on human health when consumed in excessive amounts. Source: animal and plant fats and oils.

triglyph /trí glif/ n in classical architecture, a block carved with three vertical grooves that separates the square panels (**metopes**) in a Doric frieze [Mid-16C. Via Latin < Greek *trigluphos* < *gluphē* 'carving'] —**triglyphic** /trī glíffik/ adj

trigon /trí gon/ n 1. a triangular harp or lyre of ancient Greece and Rome 2. ASTROL same as **triplicity** (sense 3) [Mid-16C. Via Latin *trigonum* < Greek *trigōnon* 'triangle' < *gōnia* 'angle']

trigonal /tríggən'l/ adj 1. in the shape of a triangle 2. describes a crystal that has three axes of equal length, none of which is perpendicular to another — **trigonally** adv

trigonometric /tríggənə méttrik/ adj relating to or used in trigonometry —**trigonometrical** adj —**trigonometrically** adv

trigonometric function /tríggənə méttrik-/ n a function of an angle or arc expressed as a ratio of the two sides of a right-angled triangle containing the angle. The trigonometric functions are sine, cosine, tangent, cotangent, secant, and cosecant.

trigonometry /tríggə nómmətri/ n a branch of mathematics dealing with properties of triangles and their applications, e.g. in surveying [Early 17C. < modern Latin *trigonometria* < Greek *trigonos* 'three-cornered' < *trigōnon* (see TRIGON)]

trigonous /tríggənəss/ adj describes a stem or other plant part that is triangular in cross section

trig point n a land surveyor's reference point on high ground, usually marked by a stone pillar set into the ground [Mid-19C. Shortening of *trigonometric point*]

trigram /trí gram/ n 1. a group of three alphabetical letters 2. each of eight combinations of three solid or broken lines that are joined in pairs to form hexagrams of the I Ching —**trigrammatic** /trígrə máttik/ adj —**trigrammatically** adv

trigraph /trí graaf, -graf/ n a group of three successive letters, especially one representing a single sound

Yang		Yin	
Ch'ien (heaven) NW	K'un (earth) SW	Chen (thunder) E	Sun (wind) SE
K'an (moon) N	Li (sun) S	Ken (mountain) NE	Tui (lake) W

I Ching trigrams

such as 'igh' in 'might' —**trigraphic** /trī gráffik/ adj —**trigraphically** adv

trihalomethane /trī háylō mée thayn/ n a methane-derived compound that contains three halogen atoms, e.g. chloroform, formed especially during the chlorination of drinking water

trihedron /trī heédrən/ (plural -**drons** or -**dra** /-drə/), **trihedral** /-heédrəl/ n a three-dimensional geometric figure formed by the intersection of three planes —**trihedral** adj

triiodothyronine /trī ī ōdō thírə neen/ n an iodine-containing hormone produced by the thyroid gland

trijet /trí jet/ n an aeroplane propelled by three jet engines

trike /trīk/ n CYCLING same as **tricycle** (informal) [Late 19C. Shortening and alteration]

trilateral /trī láttərəl/ adj 1. TRIPARTITE involving three countries or parties 2. 3-SIDED describes a geometric figure that has three sides ■ n 3-SIDED FIGURE a geometrical figure with three sides —**trilaterally** adv

trilateralism /trī láttərəlizəm/ n three-sided relations or discussions between nations, areas, or groups —**trilateralist** n

trilby /trílbi/ (plural -**bies**) n a soft felt hat with a deep crease in the crown and a narrow brim [Late 19C. After *Trilby*, novel by George Du Maurier]

ORIGIN In George Du Maurier's novel, Trilby is an artist's model who falls under the spell of the hypnotist Svengali. In the stage version of the book, the character Trilby wore a soft felt hat with an indented top, and the style soon became fashionable. The novel also dwells on the erotic qualities of Trilby's feet, and for a while in the early 20th century *trilbies* was a slang term for 'feet'.

trilinear /trī línni ər/ adj consisting of, contained by, or involving three lines

trilingual /trī líng gwəl/ adj 1. able to speak or use three languages, especially fluently 2. expressed in or involving three languages —**trilingual** n —**trilingualism** n —**trilingually** adv

triliteral /trī líttərəl/ adj 1. having three alphabetical letters 2. having three consonants —**triliteral** n

AKG London

trilithon

trilithon /trī li thon, trí li-/, **trilith** /trí lith/ n a prehistoric structure consisting of two large vertical stones supporting a horizontal stone laid on top of them [Mid-18C. < Greek < *lithos* 'stone'] —**trilithic** /trī líthik/ adj

trill[1] /tril/ n 1. WARBLING SOUND a high-pitched warbling sound, especially one made by a bird 2. MUSIC MELODIC

ORNAMENT a musical ornament consisting of rapid alternation between two adjacent notes. The interval between the notes of a trill can vary but is usually a semitone or major second. **3.** PHON **SOUND MADE BY VIBRATING VOCAL ORGANS** a sound or consonant made by two vocal organs vibrating rapidly against each other, e.g. the tip of the tongue vibrating against the ridge behind the front teeth ■ *vti* **(trills, trilling, trilled) UTTER SOMETHING WITH TRILL** to play, sing, pronounce, or utter something with a trill or a sound resembling a trill [Mid-17C. < Italian *trillare*]

trill[2] /tril/ **(trills, trilling, trilled)** *vi* to spin or twirl around [14C. Origin ?]

trillion /tríllyən/ (*plural same* or **-lions**) *n* **1. 1 FOLLOWED BY 12 ZEROS** the number equal to 10^{12}, written as 1 followed by 12 zeros **2. 1 FOLLOWED BY 18 ZEROS** the number equal to 10^{18}, written as 1 followed by 18 zeros (*dated*) **3. LARGE NUMBER OF SOMETHING** an exceptionally large but unspecified number or amount of something (*informal; often used in the plural*) ○ *had trillions of fans wanting to meet her* [Late 17C. < French, after *million*] —**trillion** *adj*

USAGE See *billion.*

trillionth /tríllyənth/ *n* one of a trillion equal parts of something —**trillionth** *adj, adv*

trillium /trílli əm/ *n* a plant with a cluster of three leaves at the top of the stem. Flowers: single, large, white, pink, or purple, three-petalled. Native to: North America, South Asia. [Mid-19C. < modern Latin]

trilobate /trī ló bayt/, **trilobated** /trī́lə baytid/, **trilobed** /trī́ lōbd/ *adj* describes a leaf that has three lobes

trilobite /trī́lə bīt/ *n* an extinct Palaeozoic sea arthropod with a flat oval body and a dorsal exoskeleton divided into three vertical sections. Class: Trilobita. [Mid-19C. < modern Latin *Trilobites* < Greek *lobos* 'lobe'] —**trilobitic** /trīlə bíttik/ *adj*

trilocular /trī lókyŏŏlər/ *adj* having or consisting of three cavities, cells, or chambers [Mid-19C. < TRI- + Latin *loculus* 'little place' < *locus* 'place']

trilogy /trílləji/ (*plural* **-gies**) *n* **1.** a group or series of three related works, especially of literature or music **2.** a set of three related things [Mid-17C. < Greek *trilogia* < *logos* 'word']

trim /trim/ *v* **(trims, trimming, trimmed) 1.** *vt* **MAKE SOMETHING TIDY BY CUTTING** to make something tidy by clipping, cutting, or pruning **2.** *vt* **CUT SOMETHING TO REQUIRED SIZE** to reduce something by cutting it to the required shape or size ○ *trimmed the manuscript to 40,000 words* **3.** *vt* **REMOVE EXCESS BY CUTTING** to reduce or remove an excess, by cutting ○ *We had to trim the budget.* **4.** *vt* **DECORATE SOMETHING** to decorate or embellish something ○ *He trimmed the hat with fur.* **5.** *vt* WOODWORK **SHAPE TIMBER** to shape and finish the edges of wood or timber **6.** *vt* CINEMA **EDIT FILM** to cut pieces from a film during editing **7.** *vti* SAILING **CHANGE ARRANGEMENT OF SAILS** to change the position or arrangement of the sails in order to maximize the benefit of the wind **8.** *vti* SHIPPING **CHANGE DISTRIBUTION OF CARGO** to improve, alter, or maintain a vessel's balance by changing the way the ballast or cargo is distributed **9.** *vi* NAUT **BE BALANCED IN WATER** to be or become well balanced in the water (*refers to a vessel*) **10.** *vt* AVIAT **MAKE ADJUSTMENTS TO IMPROVE AIRCRAFT STABILITY** to improve the stability of an aircraft, e.g. by redistributing the load before takeoff or by transferring fuel during flight **11.** *vti* **ALTER OPINION TO SUIT CIRCUMSTANCES** to alter opinions or behaviour to suit the circumstances in order to gain acceptance or personal advantage **12.** *vi* **ADOPT NEUTRAL POSITION** to adopt a neutral position in a dispute between two parties **13.** *vt* **BEAT SOMEBODY THOROUGHLY** to beat or overwhelm somebody completely (*informal*) ○ *got trimmed regularly at tennis by her partner* **14.** *vt* **SCOLD SOMEBODY** to reprimand or scold somebody (*informal*) **15.** *vt* **CHEAT SOMEBODY** to cheat or deceive somebody (*informal*) ■ *adj* **(trimmer, trimmest) 1. FIT** healthy, slim, or in good physical condition ○ *had a trim figure* **2. TIDY** tidy, compact, or in good order ■ *n* **1. ACT OF CUTTING** an act or instance of cutting something in order to make it tidier ○ *gave the hedge a trim* **2. HAIRCUT** a haircut that tidies rather than changes a hairstyle **3. SOMETHING USED AS DECORATION** something used for decoration, e.g. contrasting material attached to a piece of clothing **4.** AUTOMOT **DECORATIVE PARTS OF VEHICLE** the accessories and decorative parts added to the interior or exterior of a vehicle **5.** CONSTR **DECORATIVE ADDITIONS TO BUILDING** the nonstructural decorative additions to a building, especially mouldings around doorways, windows, and walls **6.** *US* COMM **WINDOW DRESSING** the goods, props, and other items placed in a shop window **7. SOMETHING TRIMMED OFF** a piece of something removed by trimming **8.** CINEMA **FILM CUT DURING EDITING** a piece of film eliminated from a shot during editing **9.** AVIAT **ADJUSTMENT OF AIRCRAFT FOR STABILITY** adjustment of the controls of an aircraft to give stability **10.** AVIAT **FLIGHT POSITION** the position of an aircraft in flight relative to the horizon **11.** NAUT **APPEARANCE OF VESSEL** the way a vessel appears when it is fitted out and prepared for sailing **12.** SAILING **RELATION BETWEEN SAIL AND DIRECTION** the relation between the plane of a sail and the direction in which the vessel is pointing **13.** NAUT **POSITION OF VESSEL** the position of a ship or boat, especially with reference to the horizontal and to the difference between the depth in water at the front and back of the vessel **14.** NAUT **BUOYANCY** the relative buoyancy of a submarine [Old English *trymman* 'strengthen'. < Indo-European, 'be solid'] —**trim** *adv* —**trimly** *adv* —**trimness** *n*

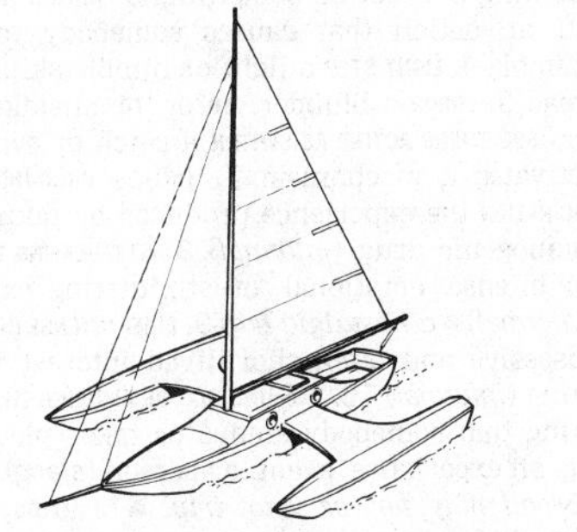

trimaran

trimaran /trī́mə ran, trī́mə rán/ *n* a sailing boat with three hulls arranged side by side [Mid-20C. Blend of TRI- + CATAMARAN]

Trimble /trímb'l/, **David** (*b.* 1944) British politician. He became leader of the Ulster Unionist Party (1995) and played an important role in the peace negotiations that led to the Good Friday peace agreement in Northern Ireland (1998), for which he shared the Nobel Peace Prize (1998). He was first minister of the Northern Irish Assembly (1999–2002) until its suspension. Full name **Trimble, William David**

trimer /trī́mər/ *n* a polymer formed by combining three identical molecules —**trimeric** /trī mérrik/ *adj*

trimerous /trímmərəss/ *adj* **1.** having or consisting of three similar parts or segments **2.** describes a flower with parts arranged in groups of three [Early 19C. < Greek *trimerēs* < *meros* 'part']

trimester /trī méstər/ *n* **1.** a period of three months, especially one of the three three-month periods into which human pregnancy is divided for medical purposes **2.** *N Am* each of the three terms into which the academic year is divided by some North American colleges, schools, and universities [Early 19C. Via French *trimestre* < Latin *trimestris* 'of three months' < *mensis* 'month'] —**trimestral** *adj* —**trimestrial** /-méstri əl/ *adj*

trimeter /trímmitər/ *n* a line of verse consisting of three metrical feet

trimethadione /trī methə dī́ ōn/ *n* a white crystalline bitter-tasting compound with an odour similar to camphor. Use: epileptic anticonvulsant. Formula: $C_6H_9NO_3$. [Contraction of TRI- + METHYL + DI-[1] + -ONE]

trimethoprim /trī méthə prim/ *n* a synthetic drug that kills bacteria. Use: treatment of malaria. Formula: $C_{14}H_{18}N_4O_3$. [Mid-20C. Contraction of TRI- + METHYL + OXY- + PYRIMIDINE]

trimetric /trī méttrik/, **trimetrical** /trī méttrik'l/ *adj* **1.** consisting of one or more trimeters **2.** CRYSTALS same as **orthorhombic**

trimetric projection *n* a geometric projection in which the three axes are measured on different scales and are at arbitrary angles

trimetrogon /trī méttrə gon/ *n* a technique in which three aerial photographs are taken at the same time, one vertical and two at oblique angles, in order to obtain more topographical detail [Mid-20C. < TRI- + *Metrogon*, commercial lens]

trimmer /trímmər/ *n* **1. SOMEBODY OR SOMETHING THAT TRIMS** somebody or something that trims, e.g. a machine for trimming hedges, lawns, or timber **2. SOMEBODY ALTERING OPINION ACCORDING TO CIRCUMSTANCES** somebody who changes his or her opinions or behaviour to suit the circumstances in order to gain acceptance or personal advantage **3.** ELECTRONICS **VARIABLE CAPACITOR** a small variable capacitor used, usually in parallel with a larger capacitor, to adjust overall capacitance **4.** CONSTR **CROSSWISE JOIST** a joist that runs crosswise with the ends of lengthways joists fitted into it **5.** SHIPPING **SOMEBODY WHO STOWS CARGO** somebody who stows cargo on a ship to ensure stability **6.** AEROSP same as **trim tab**

trimming /trímming/ *n* **1. SOMETHING ATTACHED AS DECORATION** a piece of material used as a decoration on clothing or furnishings, e.g. a strip of lace, fur, or braid along the edge of a piece of clothing **2. ACT OF SOMETHING THAT TRIMS** the act of somebody or something that trims **3. BEATING** a thorough defeat or thrashing (*dated informal*) ■ **trimmings** *npl* **1.** COOK **FOOD ACCOMPANYING MAIN DISH** the items of food traditionally served as accompaniments to a main dish **2. EXTRAS** things added to something as accessories or extras **3. PIECES CUT OFF DURING TRIMMING** the parts or pieces cut off when something is trimmed **4.** *UK, regional, NZ* **CHRISTMAS DECORATIONS** decorations put up at Christmas

trimming capacitor *n* ELECTRONICS same as **trimmer** (sense 3)

trimming tab *n* AEROSP same as **trim tab**

trimolecular /trī́mə lékyŏŏlər/ *adj* relating to or consisting of three molecules

trimonthly /trī múnthli/ *adj* occurring or done every three months —**trimonthly** *adv*

trimorph /trī́ mawrf/ *n* **1.** a substance, especially a mineral, that occurs in three distinct crystalline forms **2.** one of the crystalline forms in which a trimorph exists

trimorphism /trī máwrfizəm/ *n* **1.** the property of existing in three different crystalline forms **2.** the adoption of three successive forms during a life cycle, e.g. the forms of larva, pupa, and adult in some insects [Mid-19C. < Greek *trimorphos* < *morphē* 'form'] —**trimorphic** *adj* —**trimorphically** *adv* —**trimorphous** *adj*

trimotor /trī́ mōtər/ *n* a vehicle, typically an aeroplane, with three engines

trim tab *n* an auxiliary flight control surface that enables a pilot to make adjustments during flight to correct any unbalanced condition

Trimurti /tri mŏŏrti/ *n* the Hindu gods Brahma, Vishnu, and Shiva, the creator, preserver, and destroyer respectively, who represent the three forms of the supreme being [Mid-19C. < Sanskrit < *murti* 'form']

trinary /trī́nəri/ *adj* **1.** consisting of three parts **2.** progressing in threes

Tri Nations *adj* used to describe or relating to rugby union competition between the national sides of Australia, New Zealand, and South Africa

Trincomalee /tríngkōmə lée/ town and port in northeastern Sri Lanka. Population: 44,313 (1981).

trine /trīn/ *adj* **1. TRIPLE** consisting of three parts **2.** ASTROL **120° APART AS SEEN FROM EARTH** in astrology, used to describe two astronomical objects separated by an angle of 120° as seen from the Earth ■ *n* **1. GROUP OF 3** a group of three, or something consisting of three parts **2.** ASTROL **ASPECT OF 120° BETWEEN TWO PLANETS** in astrology, an aspect of 120° between two astronomical objects as seen from the Earth [14C. Via French < Latin *trinus*, singular of *trini* 'in threes'] —**trinal** *adj*

Trinidad /trínni dad/ island in the Caribbean, part of Trinidad and Tobago. Population: 1,065,245 (1998). Area: 4,828 sq. km/1,864 sq. mi. —**Trinidadian** /trínni dáddi ən/ *n, adj*

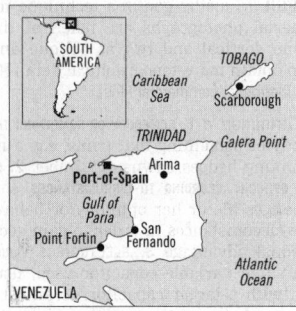

Trinidad and Tobago

Trinidad and Tobago /-tə báygō/ country comprising the two southernmost of the Caribbean Islands, situated off the northeastern coast of Venezuela. It became an independent member of the Commonwealth in 1962. Language: English. Currency: Trinidad and Tobago dollar. Capital: Port-of-Spain. Population: 1,104,209 (2003). Area: 5,128 sq. km/1,980 sq. mi. Official name **Republic of Trinidad and Tobago**

Trinil man /treénil-/ *n* ANTHROP same as **Java man** [Early 20C. After village in Java]

Trinitarian /trínni táiri ən/ *n* somebody who believes in the Christian doctrine of the Trinity —**Trinitarian** *adj* —**Trinitarianism** *n*

trinitrobenzene /trī nītrō bén zeen/ *n* a yellow crystalline compound. Use: explosives. Formula: $C_6H_3(N_3O_2)_3$.

trinitroglycerin /trī nītrō glíssərin/ *n* CHEM same as **nitroglycerine**

trinitrotoluene /trī nītrō tóllyoo een/, **trinitrotoluol** /-tóllyoo ol/ *n* CHEM full form of **TNT**

trinity /trínnəti/ (*plural* **-ties**) *n* **1.** a group of three **2.** the condition of existing as three persons or things [13C. Via French < Latin *trinitas* < *trinus* 'threefold' (see TRINE)]

Trinity *n* **1.** in Christianity, God seen in three ways as the Father, the Son Jesus Christ, and the Holy Spirit **2.** CHR same as **Trinity Sunday 3.** EDUC, LAW same as **Trinity term**

Trinity Brethren *npl* the members of Trinity House

Trinity House *n* an association that licenses maritime pilots and maintains lighthouses and buoys around the coasts of England, Wales, the Channel Islands, and Gibraltar

Trinity Sunday *n* the Sunday that is eight weeks after Easter, when Christians celebrate the doctrine of the Trinity

Trinity term *n* **1.** the term at some universities that begins after Easter **2.** one of the English court terms, beginning in the early summer after Trinity Sunday

Trinitytide /trínnə ti tīd/ *n* the season from Trinity Sunday to Advent

trinket /tríngkit/ *n* **1.** a small object of little value, e.g. an ornament or piece of jewellery **2.** something trivial or unimportant [Mid-16C. Origin ?] —**trinketry** *n*

trinomial /trī nómi əl/ *adj* **1.** MATHS HAVING 3 MATHEMATICAL EXPRESSIONS consisting of three mathematical terms or expressions **2.** BIOL HAVING 3 NAMES relating to or consisting of three taxonomic names, denoting the genus, species, and subspecies or variety of an organism ■ *n* MATHS POLYNOMIAL WITH 3 TERMS a polynomial made up of three terms linked by plus or minus signs [Late 17C. Blend of TRI- + BINOMIAL] —**trinomially** *adv*

trinucleotide /trī nyóokli ə tīd/ *n* a chemical compound consisting of three linked mononucleotides

trio /treé ō/ (*plural* **-os**) *n* **1.** GROUP OF 3 a group or set of three **2.** MUSIC GROUP OF 3 MUSICIANS a group of three musicians who perform together **3.** MUSIC MUSIC FOR 3 MUSICIANS a piece of music composed for a group of three musicians **4.** MUSIC MIDDLE SECTION OF MUSICAL PIECE the middle section of a minuet, march, or other piece of music, composed in a contrasting style and originally written for three instruments **5.** CARDS

SET OF 3 PIQUET CARDS a set of three equal-ranking cards in piquet [Early 18C. < Italian < *tri-* after *duo* 'duet']

triode /trī ōd/ *n* an electron valve that has an anode, a cathode, and a grid that controls electron flow between the two

triol /trī ol/ *n* a chemical compound that has three hydroxyl groups

triolet /treé ə let, trī-, -ōlet, -əlit/ *n* a poem consisting of eight lines with a rhyme scheme of abaaabab in which the first, fourth, and seventh lines are the same, as are the second and eighth lines [Mid-17C. < French, 'small trio']

triose /trī ōz/ *n* a simple sugar containing three carbon atoms

trio sonata *n* a baroque sonata composed for three instruments, usually two violins and one cello or bass viol, with keyboard continuo accompaniment

trioxide /trī ók sīd/ *n* an oxide containing three oxygen atoms per molecule

trip /trip/ *n* **1.** JOURNEY a journey of relatively short duration, especially to a place and back again, usually for a holiday or business meeting **2.** FALL CAUSED BY CATCHING FOOT a fall or stumble caused by catching the foot on something **3.** ACTION THAT CAUSES FALL an action that causes somebody to fall or stumble **4.** LIGHT STEP a light or nimble skip, step, or tread **5.** ERROR a blunder, error, or mistake **6.** ELEC ENG SOMETHING ACTING AS SWITCH a catch or switch that activates a mechanism **7.** DRUGS DRUG-INDUCED HALLUCINATION the experience produced by taking a hallucinogenic drug (*informal*) **8.** STIMULATING EXPERIENCE an intense, emotional, or stimulating experience (*informal*) ○ *a nostalgia trip* **9.** BRIEF INTENSE INTEREST an obsessive and often short-lived interest in something (*informal*) **10.** US UNUSUAL OR AMUSING THING something that somebody enjoys or takes pleasure in, e.g. an experience, event, or person (*slang*) ○ *Living abroad may not be your trip.* ■ *v* (**trips, tripping, tripped**) **1.** *vti* STUMBLE, OR CAUSE SOMEBODY TO STUMBLE to stumble or fall as a result of catching the foot on something, or cause somebody to stumble or fall in this way ○ *She tripped her opponent deliberately.* ○ *I tripped and fell.* **2.** *vi* MOVE WITH RAPID LIGHT STEPS to move, run, walk, or dance with rapid light steps ○ *went tripping off down the road* **3.** *vt* TECH CAUSE DEVICE TO OPERATE to operate, or cause a device or system to operate **4.** *vi* GO ON JOURNEY to go on a journey, tour, or excursion **5.** *vi* DRUGS EXPERIENCE DRUG EFFECTS to experience the effects of a hallucinogenic drug (*informal*) **6.** *vt* NAUT FREE ANCHOR to free an anchor from the sea bed so that it hangs loose on the end of its rope or chain **7.** *vt* NAUT TIP UP YARD to tilt or tip up a yard or mast so that it can be lowered **8.** *vt* NAUT RAISE UPPER MAST to raise one of the upper masts of a sailing ship to remove the bar (**fid**) that supports it so that it can be lowered [14C. < Old French *tripper* < Germanic]

trip up *vti* **1.** to make a mistake, or cause somebody to make a mistake ○ *You're just trying to trip me up with all your questions.* **2.** same as **trip** *v* (sense 1)

tripalmitin /trī pálmitin/ *n* CHEM same as **palmitin**

tripartite /trī paár tīt/ *adj* **1.** INVOLVING 3 PARTIES involving, made between, or ratified by three parties, groups, or nations ○ *a tripartite agreement* **2.** IN 3 PARTS divided into or made up of three parts **3.** BOT WITH 3 LOBES describes a leaf that has three deeply divided lobes —**tripartitely** *adv*

tripartition /trī paar tísh'n/ *n* a division of something into three parts or among three parties

tripe /trīp/ *n* **1.** the stomach lining of a ruminant such as a cow or sheep, used as food **2.** something absurd, untrue, or worthless (*informal*) [14C. < Old French]

trip hammer, **triphammer** /tríp hamər/ *n* a power hammer with a massive head raised by a cam

triphenylmethane /trī feé nīl meé thayn, trī fénnīl-/ *n* a colourless crystalline hydrocarbon. Use: manufacture of dyes. Formula: $CH(C_6H_5)_3$.

triphibian /trī fíbbi ən/ *n* **1.** a craft that can operate on water, on land, and in the air **2.** a competitor in a triathlon ■ *adj* same as **triphibious** [Mid-20C. Blend of TRI- + AMPHIBIAN]

triphibious /trī fíbbi əss/ *adj* operating or occurring in the water, on the land, and in the air [Mid-20C. Blend of TRI- + AMPHIBIOUS]

trip hop *n* a rhythmic dance music that developed from hip-hop in the 1990s. It uses electronic sampling to create a psychedelic effect.

triphosphate /trī fóss fayt/ *n* a salt or ester with three phosphate groups

triphosphopyridine nucleotide /trī fosfō pírri deen-/ *n* BIOCHEM same as **NADP**

triphthong /tríf thong, tríp-/ *n* **1.** a vowel sound composed of three vowels forming a single syllable **2.** LING same as **trigraph** [Mid-16C. Via French *triphtongue* < medieval Greek *triphthongos* < Greek *phthongos* 'sound'] —**triphthongal** /trif thóng g'l, trip-/ *adj*

tripinnate /trī pínnət, -nayt/ *adj* describes a leaf in which the main stalk bears opposite pairs of leaflets that themselves have a similar arrangement of secondary leaflets that are also similarly subdivided —**tripinnately** *adv*

Tripitaka /tríppi taákə/ *n* the collection of long canonical Buddhist texts [Late 19C. < Sanskrit < *piṭaka* 'basket']

tripl. *abbr* triplicate

triplane /trī playn/ *n* an aeroplane with three main wings positioned one above the other

triple /trípp'l/ *adj* **1.** HAVING 3 PARTS consisting of three parts, members, or units **2.** 3 TIMES AS MUCH three times as great, as much, or as many **3.** DONE 3 TIMES done or occurring three times **4.** LITERAT WITH 3 SIMILAR SYLLABLES having three similar or corresponding syllables in a verse **5.** MUSIC WITH 3 BEATS having three musical beats in a bar ○ *music in triple time* ■ *vti* (**-ples, -pling, -pled**) MULTIPLY SOMETHING, OR BE MULTIPLIED, THREEFOLD to become three times as great, as much, or as many, or cause something to become three times as great, as much, or as many ■ *n* **1.** SOMETHING 3 TIMES GREATER a number or amount that is three times greater than another or than usual **2.** BEVERAGES TREBLE MEASURE a measure, usually of spirits, containing three times the amount of a single measure **3.** SET OF 3 a group, series, or set of three things **4.** US HORSERACING same as **trifecta** [14C. Via French or directly < Latin *triplus* < Greek *triplous*]

triple 0 /-ō/, **000** *n* in Australia, the telephone number used to call for police, fire, or ambulance emergency services

triple bond *n* a chemical bond composed of three covalent bonds between two atoms

triple bottom line *n* environmental sustainability and social responsibility used as criteria when judging the overall performance of a company, in addition to purely financial considerations

triple crown, **Triple Crown** *n* **1.** VICTORY IN SPORTS EVENTS victory in all three of a set of major events in some sports **2.** HORSERACING VICTORY in horseracing, victory in the Derby, St Leger, and 2000 Guineas in the same season **3.** VICTORY OVER THREE TEAMS in rugby, victory in the home championships contested between England, Ireland, Scotland, and Wales by one team over the other three in the same season **4.** POPE'S TIARA the tiara that the pope wears as a symbol of the papacy

triple-decker /-dékər/ *n* something with three levels or layers, e.g. a structure or sandwich

Triple Entente *n* an understanding that developed between Britain, France, and tsarist Russia for dealing with their various colonial differences, formalized as a military pact in 1914

triple jump *n* an athletics event in which contestants perform a short run and three consecutive jumps, landing first on one foot, then the opposite foot, and finally both feet, in continuous motion —**triple jumper** *n*

triple measure *n* US MUSIC same as **triple time**

triple point *n* the temperature and pressure at which the solid, liquid, and gaseous phases of a substance exist in equilibrium

triple rhyme *n* a rhyme in which three syllables rhyme with another three, e.g. 'snobbery' and 'robbery'

triple sec *n* a sweet colourless liqueur that is orange-flavoured

triplet /trípplət/ *n* **1.** ONE OF 3 OFFSPRING each of three children or animals that are delivered by the same

mother during one birth **2.** GROUP OF 3 three things that are connected or related to each other in some way **3.** MUSIC GROUP OF 3 NOTES a group of three notes played in the time usually taken by two notes of the same value **4.** LITERAT VERSE OF 3 LINES a poetic stanza of three lines, usually with a single rhyme and sometimes sharing the same metrical pattern **5.** CHEM CHEMICAL UNIT WITH 2 UNPAIRED ELECTRONS an atom, molecule, or radical with two unpaired electrons **6.** PHYS GROUP OF 3 ELEMENTARY PARTICLES a group of three elementary particles with similar characteristics that differ only in their charge **7.** GENETICS same as **codon** [Mid-17C. < TRIPLE, after *doublet*]

tripletail /trípp'l tayl/ *n* a large bony sea fish whose long dorsal, anal, and caudal fins together resemble a three-lobed tail. Native to: mainly tropical waters. Latin name: *Lobotes surinamensis*.

triple-team *vti US* to use three members of a sports team to guard only one opponent, e.g. in basketball or American football —**triple team** *n*

triple time *n* a musical metre or time signature with three beats to the bar ○ *a waltz in triple time*

triple-tonguing *n* production of a rapid series of notes on a wind or brass instrument by alternating tongue movements to repeat a pattern of three articulated sounds —**triple-tongue** *vi*

triple witching hour *n* a time when stock options, stock index futures, and options on such futures all mature at once. Triple witching hours occur quarterly and are usually marked by highly volatile trading.

triplex /tríppleks/ *n N Am* a building divided into three flats on three separate floors, or a single flat that occupies three floors [Early 17C. < Latin, 'threefold']

Triplex /tríppleks/ *tdmk* a trademark for a form of laminated safety glass used for car windows

triplicate *n* /trípplikət/ SOMETHING WITH 3 IDENTICAL PARTS something that has three identical parts to it or that exists in three identical copies ○ *in triplicate* ■ *adj* /trípplikət/ THREEFOLD triple or tripled ■ *v* /tríppli kayt/ (**-cates, -cating, -cated**) **1.** *vt* MAKE 3 COPIES OF SOMETHING to make three identical copies of something, or cause something to be multiplied by three **2.** *vti* MULTIPLY SOMETHING BY 3 to multiply by three, or cause something to be multiplied by three [15C. < Latin *triplicat-*, past participle of *triplicare* 'triple' < *triplex* 'threefold'] —**triplication** /tríppli káysh'n/ *n*

triplicity /tri plíssəti, trī-/ (*plural* **-ties**) *n* **1.** EXISTENCE OF 3 IDENTICAL COPIES the condition of existing in three identical copies **2.** GROUP OF 3 a group or combination of three **3.** ASTROL ZODIACAL DIVISION one of the four groups that the zodiac is traditionally divided into, each separated from the other by 120° and consisting of three astrological signs [14C. < late Latin *triplicitas* < Latin *triplex* 'threefold']

triploblastic /trípplō blástik/ *adj* used to describe a multicellular animal that has three primary germ layers (**ectoderm; endoderm; mesoderm**) during embryonic development [Late 19C. < Greek *triploos* 'threefold' + *-blastos* 'bud']

triploid /trí ployd/ *adj* possessing three representatives of each chromosome ■ *n* a triploid cell, nucleus, or organism —**triploidy** *n*

triply /tríppli/ *adv* threefold or in a triple number, measure, or degree

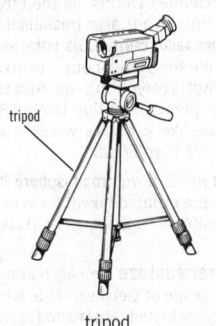

tripod

tripod /trí pod/ *n* **1.** a frame or stand with three legs that are usually collapsible, used for supporting

something such as a camera, compass, theodolite, or other piece of equipment **2.** a piece of furniture with three legs, e.g. a pot, cauldron, stool, or table [Early 17C. < Latin *tripod-*, stem of *tripus* < Greek *tripous* 'three-footed' < *pous* 'foot'] —**tripodal** /tríppəd'l/ *adj*

tripoli /tríppəli/ *n* a light porous siliceous sedimentary rock containing schist or shells of diatoms and used in powdered form for polishing [Early 17C. < French after TRIPOLI]

Tripoli /tríppəli/ **1.** capital city of Libya, situated on the Mediterranean Sea, in the northwestern part of the country. Population: 1,773,000 (1999). **2.** city in northwestern Lebanon, on the Mediterranean Sea. Population: 160,000 (1998).

Tripolitania /tríppəli táyni ə/ ancient region surrounding Tripoli in northwestern Libya. Founded as a Phoenician colony in the 7th century BC, it was captured by the Turks in the 16th century, and occupied by Italy between 1912 and 1941. —**Tripolitanian** *n, adj*

tripos /trí poss/ (*plural* **-poses**) *n* a final honours examination for the BA degree at Cambridge University [Late 16C. Alteration of Latin *tripus* (see TRIPOD)]

tripper /tríppər/ *n* **1.** somebody who takes a journey or outing, especially one for pleasure (*informal*) **2.** *US* somebody who takes a hallucinogenic drug such as LSD (*slang*) **3.** same as **trip** *n* (sense 6)

trippet /tríppit/ *n* a mechanism that strikes another part at regular intervals or is struck by it [15C. < TRIP]

trippingly /tríppingli/ *adv* in a manner that is nimble, lively, or fluent

trippy /tríppi/ (**-pier, -piest**) *adj* accompanied by or producing distorted visual or sound effects similar to those associated with psychedelic drugs, especially LSD (*slang*)

trip switch *n* an electric switch designed to interrupt a circuit, or the power to a machine, quickly

triptane /tríp tayn/ *n* a colourless flammable liquid alkane. Use: antiknock compound in aviation fuel. Formula: C_7H_{17}. [Mid-20C. Contraction of *trimethylbutane*]

triptych /tríptik/ *n* **1.** a painting or carving consisting of three panels, often made as an altarpiece hinged together so that, when the smaller outer panels are folded, the middle part is entirely covered **2.** in ancient times, a set of three writing tablets hinged or tied together [Mid-18C. < Greek *triptukhos* 'threefold' < *ptux* 'fold']

Tripura /tríppoorə/ state in northeastern India. Capital: Agartala. Population: 23,191,168 (2001). Area: 10,486 sq. km/4,050 sq. mi.

tripwire /tríp wīr/ *n* **1.** a wire that activates a device such as a trap, alarm, or camera when it is pulled or disturbed **2.** a concealed length of wire or rope stretched across the ground for an enemy or intruder to trip over

triquetral bone /trī kwéetrəl-, -kwéttrəl-/, **triquetral** *n* a pyramid-shaped bone in the wrist that connects with the inner bone of the forearm (**ulna**) on the side of the little finger [Mid-17C. < Latin *triquetrus* 'three-cornered']

triquetrous /trī kwéetrəss, -kwét-/ *adj* triangular, especially in cross section [Mid-17C. < Latin *triquetrus* 'three-cornered']

triradiate /trī ráydi ət, -ayt/ *adj* having three rays or radiating branches —**triradiately** *adv*

Triratna /tree rátnə/ *n* the three principal components of Buddhism, namely the Buddha or teacher, the teaching, and the priesthood [< Sanskrit, 'three jewels' < *ratna* 'jewel']

trireme /trí reem/ *n* a galley, originally used by the ancient Greeks as a warship and later adopted by the Romans, that had three rows of oars on each side, arranged one above the other [Early 17C. Directly or via French *trirème* < Latin *triremis* 'having three banks of oars' < *remus* 'oar']

trisaccharide /trī sákə rīd/ *n* a sugar that has three linked monosaccharide units

trisect /trī sékt/ (**-sects, -secting, -sected**) *vt* to divide

something into three parts, especially equal parts —**trisection** *n* —**trisector** *n*

trishaw /trí shaw/ *n* TRANSP same as **rickshaw** (sense 2)

triskaidekaphobia /tríss kī dékə fóbi ə/ *n* an irrational or obsessive fear of the number 13 [Early 20C. < Greek *triskaideka* 'thirteen'] —**triskaidekaphobe** /tríss kī dékə fōb/ *n* —**triskaidekaphobic** *adj*

triskelion

triskelion /tri skélli on, trī-/ (*plural* **-ia** /-ļi ə/), **triskele** /trí skeel, tríss-/ *n* a symbol in the form of three bent or curved lines or limbs radiating from a common centre. It is sometimes a representation of three human limbs, as in the emblem of the Isle of Man. [Mid-19C. < modern Latin < Greek *triskelēs* 'three-legged' < *skelos* 'leg']

trismus /trízməss/ *n* a sustained spasm of the jaw muscles, characteristic of the early stages of tetanus [Late 17C. Via modern Latin < Greek *trismos* 'grinding'] —**trismic** *adj*

trisoctahedron /triss óktə heédrən/ (*plural* **-drons** or **-dra** /-drə/) *n* a solid with 24 identical triangular faces, each triplet of which rests on a face of an underlying octahedron [Mid-19C. < Greek *tris* 'thrice'] —**trisoctahedral** *adj*

trisodium /trī sódi əm/ *adj* containing three sodium atoms in a molecule

trisomy /trí sómi/ *n* the genetic condition of having one or more sets of three chromosomes instead of the usual pairs —**trisomic** /trī sómik/ *adj*

Tristan and Iseult /trístən and i soolt, trí stan-/, **Tristram and Isolde** /trístrəm ənd i zóldə, -sóld/ *npl* in medieval legend, a pair of lovers. Tristan was a knight who fell in love with Iseult, his uncle's bride, after drinking a love potion.

Tristan da Cunha /trístən də koonə/ group of volcanic islands in the South Atlantic Ocean, part of the British dependency of St Helena. Population: 313 (1988). Area: 202 sq. km/78 sq. mi.

tristate /trí stayt/ *adj US* relating to or involving three adjacent states of the United States

tristearin /trī steérin/ *n* CHEM same as **stearin** (sense 1)

tristesse /tree stéss/ *n* sadness, sorrow, or melancholy (*archaic or literary*) [14C. Via French < Latin *tristitia* < *tristis* 'sad']

tristful /tristf'l/ *adj* melancholic or mournful (*literary*)

tristich /trístik/ *n* a poem, stanza, refrain, or other division of poetry that consists of three lines [Early 19C. After DISTICH] —**tristichic** /tri stíkik/ *adj*

tristimulus values /trī stímyoōləss-/ *npl* the three values representing the amounts of red, green, and blue light that in combination match a specific colour

Tristram and Isolde *npl* ◆ **Tristan and Iseult**

trisulphide /trī súl fīd/ *n* a sulphide that has three sulphur molecules per atom

trisyllable /trī sílləb'l/ *n* a word of three syllables, e.g. 'enormous' —**trisyllabic** /trí si lábbik/ *adj* —**trisyllabically** *adv*

tritanopia /trítə nōpi ə, trít-/ *n* a rare condition in which perception of blue and green becomes confused as a result of the absence of blue-sensitive pigment in the cone cells of the retina [Early 20C. < Greek *tritos* 'third' + *anōpia* 'blindness'] —**tritanopic** *adj*

trite /trīt/ (**triter, tritest**) *adj* overused and consequently lacking in interest or originality [Mid-16C. < Latin

tritus, past participle of *terere* 'wear out'] —**tritely** *adv* —**triteness** *n*

tritheism /trī́ thi izəm/ *n* belief in three gods, especially the belief or doctrine that the Christian Trinity of Father, Son, and Holy Spirit consists of three distinct divinities —**tritheist** *n* —**tritheistic** /trī́ thi ístik/ *adj*

tritiate /trítti ayt/ (**-ates, -ating, -ated**) *vt* to replace normal hydrogen atoms, or chemically combine something, with tritium —**tritiation** /trítti áysh'n/ *n*

triticale /trítti kaáli, -káyli/ *n* a high-protein high-yielding cereal plant that is a hybrid of wheat and rye [Mid-20C. Blend of modern Latin *Triticum* 'wheat' + *Secale* 'rye']

tritium /trítti əm/ *n* a radioactive isotope of hydrogen occurring naturally in trace amounts and having atomic mass 3 and a half-life of 12.3 years. Although rare in nature, it can be produced artificially and is used in tracers and hydrogen bombs. Symbol **T** [Mid-20C. < modern Latin < Greek *tritos* 'third']

triton[1] /trī́t'n/ *n* a large gastropod sea mollusc with a heavy multicoloured spiral shell. Native to: tropical seas. Family: Cymatiidae. [Late 18C. Via modern Latin < Latin *Triton* 'the god Triton']

triton[2] /trī́ ton/ *n* the nucleus of a tritium atom, consisting of one proton and two neutrons [Mid-20C. < TRITIUM]

Triton /trī́t'n/ *n* **1.** in Greek mythology, a sea god represented as having the tail of a fish and the upper body of a man **2.** the largest moon of the planet Neptune, about 2,700 km/1,680 mi. in diameter, and revolving in a direction counter to that of the planet [Late 16C. Via Latin < Greek *Tritōn* In sense 2 < its dependence on the planet Neptune, like the god Triton's dependence on the sea god Neptune]

tritone /trī́ tōn/ *n* a dissonant musical interval composed of three whole tones

triturate *vt* /tríttyoŏ rayt/ (**-rates, -rating, -rated**) to grind or rub a substance into a fine powder ■ *n* /tríttyoŏrət/ a finely ground powder, especially a drug [Mid-18C. < late Latin *triturat-*, past participle of *triturare* 'thresh' < Latin *terere* 'rub'] —**triturable** *adj* —**triturator** *n*

trituration /tríttyoŏ ráysh'n/ *n* **1. GRINDING OF SOMETHING INTO POWDER** the process of grinding or rubbing a substance into a fine powder **2. BEING FINE POWDER** the condition of having been ground or rubbed into a fine powder **3.** PHARM **POWDERED DRUG MIXTURE** a mixture of powdered drugs prepared pharmaceutically **4.** DENT **MIXING OF AMALGAM** the mixing of an amalgam, usually of silver and mercury, for use in filling cavities in teeth

triumph /trī́ umf/ *n* **1. SUCCESS** an act or occasion of winning, being victorious, or overcoming something **2. JOY ABOUT SUCCESS** the happiness, pride, or feeling of elation that comes from winning, being victorious, or overcoming something **3. OUTSTANDING SUCCESS** something that is notable for its exceptional quality or for being a great achievement ○ *The reviews hailed the new production as a triumph.* **4. ROMAN VICTORY PARADE** in ancient Rome, a procession through the streets of Rome to the Capitoline Hill to mark a general's victory over a foreign army ■ *vi* (**-umphs, -umphing, -umphed**) **1. WIN OR ACHIEVE SUCCESS** to be successful, especially against an adversary or against difficult odds ○ *triumphed over life's setbacks* **2. BECOME EXULTANT** to experience the happiness, pride, or feeling of elation that comes from winning or overcoming something [14C. Via French < Latin *triumphus*]

triumphal /trī úmf'l/ *adj* celebrating or commemorating a victory, usually a military one ○ *a triumphal procession*

USAGE triumphal or **triumphant**? ***Triumphal*** is a neutral word that classifies something as simply commemorating a victory, usually of a military kind: *The band will play a triumphal march.* One march cannot be more ***triumphal*** than another. ***Triumphant*** is a more judgmental word describing the feelings that follow a success, or something outstandingly successful: *The winning team returned home triumphant. She told us of her win with a triumphant look on her face. He made a triumphant comeback.*

triumphal arch *n* a monument, usually in the form of an ornamental free-standing arch spanning a street, built to commemorate something, especially an outstanding military victory

triumphalism /trī úmf'lizəm/ *n* **1.** a display or feeling of often excessive pride in having achieved a victory or having been proved right **2.** the conviction that one belief or set of beliefs, especially religious or political ones, is victorious and far superior to any others —**triumphalist** *n, adj*

triumphant /trī úmfənt/ *adj* **1.** displaying or feeling great pride in having achieved a victory **2.** outstandingly successful or impressive ○ *made a triumphant reappearance in the role he made famous* —**triumphantly** *adv*

USAGE See ***triumphal***.

triumvir /trī úmvər/ (*plural* **-virs** or **-viri** /-vi ree/) *n* **1.** each of the three people who made up a triumvirate, especially in ancient Rome **2.** somebody who shares power with two other people (*formal*) [Late 16C. < Latin, back-formation < *triumviri* 'board of three men' < *trium virum* 'of three men'] —**triumviral** *adj*

triumvirate /trī úmvərət/ *n* **1. ROMAN COMMITTEE OF 3 RULERS** a group of three men who together were responsible for public administration or civil authority in the government system of ancient Rome **2. GROUP OF 3 SHARING AUTHORITY** a group of three people who jointly share some responsibility, authority, or power **3. POSITION OF SHARING POWER** the position of being one of three who exercise power or authority **4. TERM OF OFFICE OF SHARED POWER** the duration of the term of office for somebody who shares power or authority with two others **5. RULE BY GROUP OF 3** government or rule by a group of three [Late 16C. < Latin *triumviratus* < *triumviri* (see TRIUMVIR)]

triune /trī́ yoon/, **Triune** *adj* consisting of or being three in one, e.g. in the Christian Trinity ■ *n* a group consisting of three members, especially the Christian Trinity [Early 17C. < TRI- + Latin *unus* 'one']

triunity /trī yoŏnəti/ (*plural* **-ties**) *n* a group of three

trivalent /trī váylənt/ *adj* **1.** having a chemical valency of three **2.** having three chemical valencies —**trivalency** *n*

Trivandrum /tri vándrəm/ former name for **Thiruvananthapuram**

trivet /trívvit/ *n* **1.** a stand or support, usually metal with three legs, for hot pans and dishes **2.** a device, usually metal with three legs, that fits over the grate of a fire to support a pan or kettle [15C. Probably alteration of Latin *triped-*, stem of *tripes* 'three-footed' < *pes* 'foot']

trivia[1] /trívvi ə/ *n* a collection of insignificant or obscure items, details, or information (*takes a singular or plural verb*) [Early 20C. Latinized back-formation < TRIVIAL]

trivia[2] /trívvi ə/ HIST, EDUC plural of **trivium**

trivial /trívvi əl/ *adj* **1. HAVING LITTLE VALUE** lacking in seriousness, importance, or value **2. COMMONPLACE** lacking any qualities that are unique or interesting **3. CONCERNED WITH TRIVIA** relating to or concerned with trivia **4.** MATHS **WITH ZERO VALUES** describes the simplest possible case mathematically, especially with all mathematical variables equal to zero **5. CONCERNING TRIVIUM** belonging or relating to the trivium [15C. < Latin *trivialis* 'relating to the trivium division of subjects', hence 'commonplace' (because the trivium was considered to incorporate the less important subjects) < *trivium* (see TRIVIUM)] —**trivially** *adv*

ORIGIN Medieval teachers and scholars recognized seven liberal arts: the lower three, grammar, logic, and rhetoric, were known as the *trivium*, and the upper four, arithmetic, astronomy, geometry, and music, were known as the *quadrivium*. The notion of 'less important subjects' led in the 16th century to the use of the derived adjective ***trivial*** for 'commonplace, of little importance'.

trivialise *vt* another spelling of **trivialize**

triviality /trívvi álləti/ (*plural* **-ties**), **trivialism** /-əlizəm/ *n* **1.** the condition or quality of having little importance or seriousness **2.** something that is considered to lack importance or seriousness

trivialize /trívvi ə līz/ (**-izes, -izing, -ized**), **trivialise** (**-ises, -ising, -ised**) *vt* to treat something as, or make it appear, less serious, important, or valuable than it really is —**trivialization** /trívvi ə lī záysh'n/ *n*

trivial name *n* **1.** a common or popular name for a substance that does not describe its exact chemical composition **2.** the noun or adjective that follows the genus name in a taxonomic binomial

Trivial Pursuit *tdmk* a trademark for a board game that tests the players' knowledge of trivia

trivium /trívvi əm/ (*plural* **-ia** /-i ə/) *n* grammar, logic, and rhetoric, three of the seven liberal arts that formed the basis of medieval university study, traditionally considered to be less important than the other four [Early 19C. Via medieval Latin < Latin, 'place where three roads cross']

triweekly /trī weékli/ *adj* **1. APPEARING OR DONE EVERY 3 WEEKS** occurring, published, or performed once every three weeks **2. DONE 3 TIMES WEEKLY** occurring, published, or performed three times each week ■ *adv* **1. EVERY 3 WEEKS** once every three weeks **2. 3 TIMES WEEK** three times each week ■ *n* (*plural* **-lies**) **1. 3-WEEKLY PUBLICATION** a publication that comes out every three weeks **2. PUBLICATION 3 TIMES PER WEEK** a publication that comes out three times each week

-trix *suffix* **1.** a woman who performs a particular function ○ *dominatrix* **2.** a geometric element that performs a particular function ○ *directrix* [< Latin, feminine form of *-tor*]

tRNA *abbr* BIOCHEM transfer RNA

Trobriand Islands /trṓ bri ənd-/ island group of Papua New Guinea in the Solomon Sea, east of New Guinea. Area: 440 sq. km/170 sq. mi.

trocar /trṓ kaar/ *n* a sharply pointed steel rod sheathed with a tight-fitting cylindrical tube (**cannula**), used together to drain or extract fluid from a body cavity. The whole instrument is inserted then the trocar is removed, leaving the cannula in place. [Early 18C. < French *trocart* < *carre*, 'side of an instrument' < Latin *quadrum* 'square']

trochaic /trō káy ik/ LITERAT *adj* relating to, belonging to, or consisting of trochees ■ *n* **1.** same as **trochee** **2.** a poem, or part of a poem, written in trochees —**trochaically** *adv*

trochanter /trō kántər/ *n* **1.** either of two rough knobs on the upper thigh bone (**femur**), where the muscles between the thigh and pelvis are attached in humans and other vertebrates **2.** the second segment from the base of an insect's leg [Early 17C. Via French < Greek *trokhantēr* 'ball on which the hip bone turns in its socket' < *trekhein* 'run']

trochee /trṓki/ *n* a metrical foot of one stressed syllable followed by an unstressed syllable, e.g. the word 'human' [Late 16C. Via Latin *trochaeus* < Greek *trokhaios* 'running' < *trekhein* 'run']

trochlea /trókli ə/ *n* an anatomical part or structure with a grooved surface that resembles a pulley, especially the surface of a bone over which a tendon passes [Late 17C. Via Latin < Greek *trokhileia* 'pulley']

trochlear /trókli ər/ *adj* relating to, situated near, or resembling a trochlea or trochlear nerve

trochlear nerve *n* either of the fourth pair of cranial nerves serving the muscle that is used to rotate the eyeball outward and downward

trochoid /trṓ koyd/ *n* MATHS **CURVE FORMED BY POINT ON RADIUS** a curve formed by a point on the radius of a circle, or on the extended radius, as the circle rolls along a straight line ■ *adj also* **trochoidal** /trō kóyd'l/ **1.** MATHS **ROTATING ABOUT CENTRAL AXIS** rotating, showing rotation, or able to rotate about a central axis **2.** ANAT **RESEMBLING PIVOT** resembling or functioning in the body like a pivot or pulley [Early 18C. < Greek *trokhoeidēs* 'wheel-like' < *trokhos* 'wheel' < *trekhein* 'run'] —**trochoidally** /trō kóyd'li/ *adv*

trochophore /trókə fawr/, **trochosphere** /trókə sfeer/ *n* a free-swimming ciliated larval form of invertebrates such as molluscs and rotifers [Late 19C. < Greek *trokhos* 'wheel']

Trockenbeerenauslese /trókən bairən ówss layzə/ *n* the highest grade of German table wine, made from individually selected shrivelled grapes and typically very sweet [Mid-20C. < German *Trockenbeerenauslese* 'picking out dry grapes']

trod past participle, past tense of **tread**

trodden past participle of **tread**

trog /trog/ (**trogs, trogging, trogged**) *vi* to walk slowly and heavily (*informal*) [Late 20C. Origin ?]

troglodyte /tróggla dīt/ *n* **1.** somebody living in a cave, especially somebody who belonged to a prehistoric cave-dwelling community **2.** a solitary person who lives alone, especially somebody who is antisocial or unconventional [Late 15C. Via Latin *Troglodyta* < Greek *Trōglodutai* 'ones who enter a hole', alteration of *Trōgodutai*, an Ethiopian people] —**troglodytic** /tróggla díttik/ *adj*

trogon /trṓ gon/ *n* a tree-dwelling bird with a short hooked beak, a long tail, and brightly coloured feathers. Native to: tropics, subtropics. Family: Trogonidae. [Late 18C. < modern Latin < Greek *trōgein* 'gnaw', because the bird chews its nest hole out of rotten wood or termites' nests]

troika /tróyka/ *n* **1.** a carriage of Russian origin drawn by three horses harnessed abreast of each other **2.** a team of three horses harnessed abreast of each other **3.** POL same as **triumvirate** (sense 2) [Mid-19C. < Russian < *troe* 'group of three']

troilism /tróylizam/ *n* sexual activity involving three people [Mid-20C. Origin ?] —**troilist** *n*

troilite /tróy līt/ *n* a variety of iron sulphide found in some meteorites [Mid-19C. After Domenico *Troili*, 18C Italian scientist]

Troilus /tróyləss/ *n* in Greek mythology, the son of the Trojan king Priam. He was killed during the Trojan War by the Greek warrior Achilles. In medieval legend he is depicted as the betrayed lover of Cressida.

Trois-Rivières /twaá rívvi áir/ city on the St Lawrence River between Quebec City and Montreal, in southern Quebec Province, Canada. Population: 117,758 (2001).

Trojan /trṓjan/ *n* **1.** somebody who came from ancient Troy **2.** somebody who is determined, strong, or courageous **3.** *also* **trojan** COMPUT same as **Trojan Horse** (sense 3) —**Trojan** *adj*

Trojan Horse *n* **1.** HOLLOW HORSE CONCEALING GREEKS in Greek mythology, a hollow wooden horse that hid Greek soldiers, left at the gates of Troy. The Trojans were convinced it was a gift to Athena and dragged it inside. **2.** *also* **Trojan horse** CONCEALED STRATAGEM somebody or something that is meant to disrupt, undermine, subvert, or destroy an enemy or rival, especially somebody or something that operates while concealed within an organization **3.** *also* **Trojan horse** COMPUT DESTRUCTIVE COMPUTER PROGRAM a computer program containing a hidden function that causes damage to other programs while appearing to perform a valid function

Trojan War *n* the ten-year siege of Troy by the Greeks to recover Helen, the abducted wife of King Menelaus

troll[1] /trōl/ *v* (**trolls, trolling, trolled**) **1.** *vti* DRAG BAITED LINE THROUGH WATER to fish by dragging a baited line through water, or from the back of a boat moving slowly **2.** *vti* TROLL IN ONE AREA to troll a particular area, or for a particular type of fish **3.** *vt* LOOK FOR SOMETHING to attempt to find something (*informal*) ○ *trolled through the job ads* **4.** *vi* AMBLE ALONG to walk casually ○ *We trolled off to see if we could help.* **5.** *vti* WANDER AROUND SEARCHING FOR SOMEBODY to wander round a particular area or place, especially in search of a sexual partner (*slang*) **6.** *vti Scotland, US* ROLL OR CAUSE SOMETHING TO ROLL to roll or rotate, or cause something to roll or rotate **7.** *vi* ONLINE FOOL INTERNET USER INTO RESPONDING to lure other Internet users into sending responses to carefully designed incorrect statements (*informal*) **8.** *vti* SING LOUDLY OR ENTHUSIASTICALLY to sing something loudly and with vigour, or be sung loudly and with vigour, especially in a round, refrain, or chorus (*dated*) ■ *n* **1.** ACTIVITY OF DRAGGING BAITED FISHING LINE the act or process of fishing by trolling **2.** SEARCH MADE an attempt to find something (*informal*) ○ *sat down with the newspaper for a troll through the obituaries* **3.** ONLINE FALSE STATEMENT USED AS INTERNET LURE a carefully worded but incorrect statement that is designed to lure other Internet users into sending responses (*informal*) [14C. Origin ?] —**troller** *n* —**trolling** *n*

troll[2] /trōl, trol/ *n* in Scandinavian legend, a supernatural being depicted as either a dwarf or giant and living in caves or under bridges [Early 17C. Via Swedish or Norwegian < Old Norse, 'demon']

trolley /trólli/ *n* (*plural* **-leys**) **1.** *UK, Can* WHEELED CART PUSHED BY HAND a wheeled cart that is pushed by hand and used for transporting things, especially luggage at an airport or railway station or goods in a supermarket. US term **cart 2.** MED WHEELED HOSPITAL BED a wheeled bed used for taking patients from one part of a hospital to another, e.g. from the ward to the operating theatre. N Am term **gurney 3.** FOOD WHEELED TABLE a small wheeled table used for serving or moving food and drinks **4.** TRANSP same as **trolleybus 5.** ELEC DEVICE COLLECTING POWER FROM OVERHEAD WIRE a device carried at the end of a pole that collects current from an overhead electric wire in order to power a vehicle **6.** VEHICLES WAGON ON RAILS FOR MOVING THINGS a small open cart that runs on rails and carries materials, especially goods in a factory or coal or other minerals in a mine or quarry **7.** INDUST SUSPENDED TRUCK a small cart or basket suspended from an overhead rail and used, especially in factories and mines, for transporting loads ■ *vti* (**-leys, -leying, -leyed**) MOVE BY TROLLEY to travel by or transport something using a wheeled cart on a track or a vehicle powered by electrical current from overhead wires [Early 19C. Probably < TROLL[1] 'roll'] ◇ **be off your trolley** to be mentally ill or intoxicated (*slang*)

trolleybus /trólli buss/ *n* an electric bus that takes its power from overhead wires by means of a trolley on a pole

trolley car *n N Am* TRANSP same as **tram**[1] (sense 1)

trollop /tróllap/ *n* **1.** an offensive term that deliberately insults a woman who is a prostitute or who is reputed to be sexually promiscuous (*dated insult*) **2.** an offensive term that deliberately insults a girl or woman regarded as slovenly or as having untidy habits (*insult*) [Early 17C. Origin ?] —**trollopy** *adj*

Trollope /tróllap/, **Anthony** (1815–82) British novelist. He is best known for two sequences of novels, the Barsetshire novels (1855–67), which have a clerical setting, and the political Palliser novels (1865–80). —**Trollopian** /trólla peé an/ *adj*

> 'Love is like any other luxury. You have no right to it unless you can afford it.'
> [Anthony Trollope, *The Way We Live Now*; 1875]

trombiculiasis /trom bíkyoo lī́ assiss/, **trombidiasis** /trómbi dī́ assiss/ *n* infestation with mite larvae (**chiggers**) that often causes severe rickettsial disease or viral disease [Early 20C. < modern Latin *Trombicula*, genus of mites]

trombone /trom bṓn/ *n* **1.** a brass wind instrument of varying size with a U-shaped slide that is moved to produce different pitches **2.** somebody who plays a trombone [Early 18C. Directly or via French < Italian, 'big trumpet' < *tromba* 'trumpet' < Germanic] —**trombonist** /trom bṓnist/ *n*

trommel /trómm'l/ *n* a rotating sieve for sizing or screening crushed rock or ore [Late 19C. < German *Trommel* 'drum']

trompe /tromp/ *n* a device formerly used for supplying air in a forge by means of a thin column of falling water [Early 19C. < French, 'trumpet']

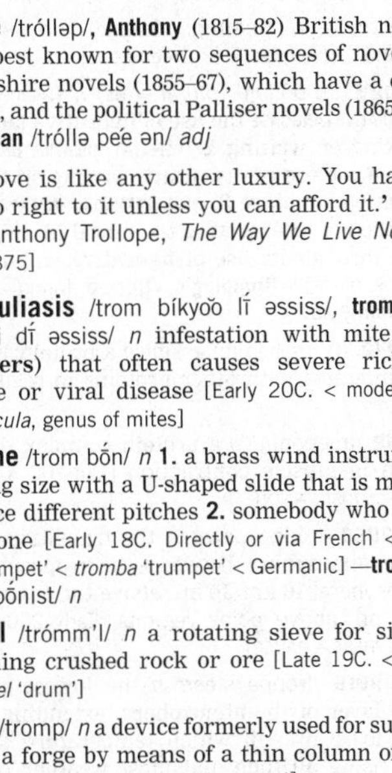

trompe l'oeil: fresco (1561?) by Paolo Veronese at the Villa Barbaro, Maser, Italy

trompe l'oeil /trómp lṓya/ (*plural* **trompe l'oeils** /-lṓya/) *n* **1.** a technique used in realistic paintings to trick the eye, especially through the use of perspective to create an illusion of three-dimensionality **2.** a painting or other artistic object that uses trompe l'oeil [Late 19C. < French, 'deceives the eye']

Tromsø /trómssö/ city and fishing port in northern Norway, located on the offshore island of Tromsøy. Population: 57,485 (1998).

tron /tron/ *n Scotland* formerly, a public weighing machine set up in the marketplace of a burgh for weighing merchandise, now the place or building where the tron stood, particularly in Edinburgh and Glasgow [13C Via Old French *trone* < Latin *trutina* < Greek *trutanē* 'balance']

-tron *suffix* **1.** a device for manipulating atoms or subatomic particles, accelerator ○ *cyclotron* **2.** a vacuum tube ○ *klystron* [< ELECTRON]

trona /trṓna/ *n* a greyish-white or yellowish hydrated sodium carbonate mineral. Source: salt deposits. [Late 18C. < Swedish]

Trondheim /trónd hīm/ city and port in central Norway. It is situated on Trondheim Fjord, which opens into the Norwegian Sea. Population: 150,117 (2001).

Troon /troon/ coastal resort on the Firth of Clyde, southwestern Scotland, known for its golf course. Population: 15,231 (1991).

troop /troop/ *n* **1.** BIG GROUP a large group of similar people, animals, or things **2.** MIL MILITARY UNIT a unit of soldiers that forms a subdivision of a cavalry or armoured cavalry squadron or artillery battery and is about the size of a platoon (*often used before a noun*) ○ *troop movements in the area* **3.** YOUTH ORG SCOUTING UNIT a unit of Guides or Boy Scouts under an adult leader, usually subdivided into several patrols **4.** ZOOL COLLECTIVE NAME FOR SOME ANIMALS a collective name for some animals, especially monkeys and kangaroos ■ **troops** *npl* **1.** MIL MILITARY GROUP a body of soldiers ○ *Order was restored by flooding the area with troops.* **2.** LARGE NUMBER OF PEOPLE OR THINGS a large number of people or things ■ *vi* (**troops, trooping, trooped**) **1.** GO AS LARGE ORDERLY GROUP to move or gather together as a large orderly group **2.** GO AS IF MARCHING to walk somewhere in a deliberate or heavy-footed way, as if marching ○ *After breakfast the family trooped off to church.* [Mid-16C. < French *troupe*] ◇ **troop the colour** to parade a military flag ceremonially along ranks of soldiers

---

USAGE troop or **troupe**? Both these words can be used as nouns denoting a group of people. ***Troop*** is more general, being applied to any large group, and specifically to a military unit. ***Troupe*** is applied only to a group of actors, circus people, or other entertainers. The verb meaning 'to move or gather together as a large orderly group' is spelt ***troop***, not ***troupe***: *We trooped in to speak to the teacher.*

---

trooper /troopar/ *n* **1.** MEMBER OF CAVALRY UNIT a member of a cavalry unit **2.** CAVALRY HORSE a horse in a cavalry unit **3.** same as **troopship** (*informal*) **4.** *US* MOUNTED POLICE OFFICER a member of a mounted police unit **5.** *US* same as **state trooper**

troopship /troop ship/ *n* a ship, sometimes one originally in the merchant navy, used for transporting military personnel

troostite /troost īt/ *n* a greyish or reddish manganese-containing form of the mineral willemite [Mid-19C. After Gerard *Troost* (1776–1850), US geologist]

trop. *abbr* GEOG **1.** tropic **2.** tropical

trop- *prefix* same as **tropo-** (*used before vowels*)

troparion /trō párri on, -páiri-/ *n* a short hymn or stanza sung in Eastern Orthodox services [Mid-19C. < Greek, 'little trope' < *tropos* 'turn']

trope /trōp/ *n* **1.** a word, phrase, expression, or image that is used in a figurative way, usually for rhetorical effect **2.** in the medieval Christian Church, a phrase or text interpolated into the service of the Mass [Mid-16C. Via Latin *tropus* < Greek *tropos* 'turn']

troph- *prefix* same as **tropho-** (*used before vowels*)

trophic /tróffik/ *adj* relating to the nutritive value of food [Late 19C. < Greek *trophikos* < *trophē* (see TROPHO-)] —**trophically** *adv*

-trophic[1] *suffix* needing or pertaining to a particular kind of food or nutrition ○ *autotrophic* [< Greek *trophē* (see TROPHO-)]

-trophic[2] *suffix* same as **-tropic**

trophic cascade *n* in a food web, the cascading effect that a change in the size of one population in the web has on the populations below it

trophic level *n* a stage in a food chain that reflects the number of times energy has been transferred through feeding, e.g. when plants are eaten by animals that are in turn eaten by predators. Plants and plant-eating animals occupy the first two levels, followed by carnivores, usually to a maximum of six levels.

tropho- *prefix* nutrition, feeding ○ *trophoblast* [< Greek *trophē* 'food, nutrition' < *trephein* 'nourish']

trophoblast /trόffə blast/ *n* a thin outer layer **(ectoderm)** that encloses the embryo of mammals, attaches the fertilized ovum to the wall of the womb, and absorbs nutrients —**trophoblastic** /trόffə blástik/ *adj*

trophoderm /trόffə durm/ *n* a trophoblast and its underlying layer **(mesoderm)**

trophozoite /trόffə zṓ īt/ *n* the active or feeding form of a protozoan, especially a parasite, as opposed to the resting or reproductive form

trophy /trṓfi/ *n* (*plural* **-phies**) **1. TOKEN OF VICTORY** a cup, shield, plaque, medal, or other award given in acknowledgment of a victory, success, or some other achievement, especially in a sporting contest **2. HUNTING OR WAR SOUVENIR** a memento that symbolizes victory or success, e.g. the head of an animal killed during a hunting expedition or something taken from an enemy killed in battle **3. MEMENTO OF SUCCESS** something that symbolizes a personal victory or achievement **4.** ANCIENT HIST **GREEK OR ROMAN VICTORY MEMORIAL** in ancient Greece or Rome, a victory memorial in a public place or near a battlefield, originally a display of enemy weapons **5.** ANCIENT HIST **GREEK OR ROMAN BATTLE COMMEMORATION** a representation of a Greek or Roman battle trophy, e.g. on a commemorative medal, plaque, or monument **6.** ARCHIT **DECORATIVE CARVING OF WEAPONS** a decorative casting or carving showing weapons or armour on a square or circular base ■ *adj* **ENHANCING SOMEBODY'S STATUS** describes a romantic or sexual partner apparently chosen by somebody purely to impress others and enhance his or her status ○ *a trophy wife* ○ *a trophy kitchen* [Early 16C. Via French *trophée* < Latin *tropaeum* 'monument to victory' < Greek *tropaion* < *tropē* 'a turning']

-trophy *suffix* **1.** nutrition, food ○ *dystrophy* **2.** growth ○ *hypertrophy* [< Greek *-trophia* < *trophē* (see TROPHO-)]

tropic[1] /tróppik/ *n* **1. LINE OF LATITUDE** a line of latitude on the Earth's globe either 23° 26' north of the equator **(tropic of Cancer)** or 23° 26' south **(tropic of Capricorn) 2.** ASTRON **CIRCLE ON CELESTIAL SPHERE** either of two circles on the celestial sphere that have the same latitudes and mark the limits of the apparent north-and-south movement of the Sun. The tropics lie in the same planes as the tropic of Cancer and the tropic of Capricorn. ■ **tropics, Tropics** *npl* **AREA BETWEEN TROPICS** the area between or near the tropic of Cancer and the tropic of Capricorn [Early 16C. Via Old French *tropique* < Latin *tropicus* < Greek *tropē* 'turn'; from the ancient belief that the sun 'turned back' at the tropics of Cancer and Capricorn] —**tropic** *adj*

CULTURAL NOTE ***Tropic of Cancer***, a novel (1934) by US writer Henry Miller. It is an autobiographical account of a struggling US writer's sojourn in 1930s' Paris. Its focus on the protagonist's erotic encounters gained it notoriety and led to it being banned in both the United States and Britain until the 1960s, but its openness was an inspiration for many contemporary writers.

tropic[2] /trṓ pik/ *adj* relating to or showing tropism [Early 20C. < Greek *tropē* 'turn']

-tropic, **-trophic** *suffix* **1.** turning, changing, or reacting in a particular way ○ *dexiotropic* **2.** attracted to, having an affinity for, or moving towards a particular thing ○ *neurotropic* **3.** acting on something in a particular way ○ *vagotropic* [< Greek *tropē* 'turn' (see TROPIC[1])]

tropical /tróppik'l/ *adj* **1.** relating to or characteristic of the tropics **2.** very hot and often combined with a high degree of humidity —**tropicality** /tróppi kálləti/ *n* —**tropically** *adv*

tropical cyclone *n* a cyclone that develops over tropical oceans and has winds up to hurricane force

tropical fish *n* a fish, usually small and brightly coloured, that occurs naturally in tropical waters but is often kept in aquariums because of its attractive appearance

tropicalize /tróppikə līz/ (**-izes, -izing, -ized**), **tropicalise** (**-ises, -ising, -ised**) *vt* to make or adapt something so that it becomes tropical in character or appearance or can be used under tropical conditions —**tropicalization** *n*

tropical storm *n* a severe storm that develops offshore over tropical seas with less than hurricane force winds but with the ability to develop into a hurricane

tropical year *n* TIME same as **solar year**

tropicbird /tróppik burd/ *n* a seabird with long slender tail feathers, small legs, and white feathers with black markings. Native to: tropics. Family: Phaethontidae.

tropic of Cancer *n* a line of latitude that is about 23° 26' north of the equator [< the constellation that its celestial projection intersects]

tropic of Capricorn *n* a line of latitude that is about 23° 26' south of the equator [< the constellation that its celestial projection intersects]

tropine /trṓ peen, -pin/ *n* a colourless crystalline alkaloid formed by heating atropine with barium hydroxide. Formula: $C_8H_{15}NO$. [Mid-19C. Shortening of ATROPINE]

tropism /trṓpizəm/ *n* the involuntary response of an organism or one of its parts towards or away from a stimulus such as heat or light [Late 19C. < Greek *tropos* 'turning' < *trepein* 'turn'] —**tropismatic** /trṓpiz máttik/ *adj*—**tropistic** /trō pístik/ *adj*—**tropistically** *adv*

tropo- *prefix* **1.** turning, change ○ *tropopause* **2.** tropism ○ *tropotactic* [< Greek *tropē*]

tropology /tro póllәji/ (*plural* **-gies**) *n* **1.** LANGUAGE **USE OF FIGURATIVE LANGUAGE** the use of figurative language in speaking or writing **2.** LITERAT **TREATISE ON FIGURATIVE LANGUAGE** a piece of discursive writing on the use of figurative language **3.** CHR **METHOD OF INTERPRETING BIBLE** a method of interpreting the moral teaching of the Bible through its use of figurative language [Early 16C. < TROPE] —**tropologic** /tróppə lójjik/ *adj* —**tropologically** *adv*

tropomyosin /tróppə mī́ əssin/ *n* a protein in muscle that interacts with other proteins to regulate contraction

troponin /tróppənin/ *n* a protein complex that plays a role in muscle contraction [Mid-20C. Contraction < TROPOMYOSIN + -IN]

tropopause /tróppə pawz/ *n* the transitional region of the atmosphere between the troposphere and stratosphere, 16 km/10 mi. above the equator and 9 km/6 mi. above polar regions [Early 20C. Blend of TROPOSPHERE + PAUSE]

troposphere /tróppə sfeer/ *n* the lowest and most dense layer of the atmosphere, extending 10 to 20 km/6 to 12 mi., in which temperature decreases with rising altitude and most weather occurs —**tropospheric** /tróppə sférrik/ *adj*

tropotaxis /tróppə táksiss/ *n* the movement of an organism towards or away from a stimulus as a result of comparing sensory input received from paired receptors on both sides of the body —**tropotactic** *adj*

-tropous *suffix* turning or growing in a particular way ○ *orthotropous* [< Greek *tropos* 'turning, changing' < *trepein* 'turn']

troppo[1] /tróppō/ *adv* too much (*used in musical directions*) [< Italian]

troppo[2] /tróppō/ *adj Aus* regarded as mentally disturbed or ill (*slang*) ○ *He's been acting very strange – gone a bit troppo, I think.* [Mid-20C. < TROPIC[1]]

-tropy *suffix* the condition of taking a particular molecular form ○ *allotropy* [< Greek *-tropia* < *tropos* (see -TROPOUS)]

trot /trot/ *v* (**trots, trotting, trotted**) **1.** *vti* RIDING **MOVE AT PACE SLOWER THAN CANTERING** to move at a rate that is faster than walking but slower than cantering, and in which diagonal pairs of feet are off the ground alternately, or cause a four-legged animal such as a horse to move in this way **2.** *vi* **MOVE AT JOGGING PACE** to move at a jogging pace that is faster than walking but not as fast as running ○ *The team trotted onto the field.* ■ *n* **1. PACE FASTER THAN WALK** the forward movement of a four-legged animal, especially a horse, in which it trots **2.** RIDING **TROTTING PACE** a ride on a horse in which it trots **3. JOGGING PACE** a jogging pace that is faster than a walk but slower than a run **4.** HORSERACING **TROTTERS' RACE** a race for horses who run in harness **5.** FISHING same as **trotline** ■ **trots** *npl* (*informal*) **1.** MED **DIARRHOEA** a prolonged bout of diarrhoea (*used with 'the'*) **2.** *ANZ* HORSERACING **TROTTER RACE** races for trotting horses [13C. < Old French *troter* < Germanic] ◇ **on the trot 1.** one after the other in succession **2.** *UK, Can* busy, especially doing something that involves walking about a lot

trot out *vt* to bring something out or display something repeatedly, especially in the expectation of gaining admiration or approval (*informal*) ○ *He trots out the same old excuses every time he's late.*

Trot /trot/ *n* a follower of Leon Trotsky (*slang disapproving*) [Mid-20C. Shortening of TROTSKYIST or TROTSKYITE]

troth /trōth/ *n* a solemn pledge, especially the promise to remain faithful exchanged by a bride and groom or an engaged couple (*formal*) [13C. Variant of TRUTH]

trotline /trót līn/ *n* a long fishing line with shorter baited lines attached, used in streams or near the shore [Mid-19C. Origin ?]

Trotsky /trótski/, **Leon** (1879–1940) Russian revolutionary leader. With Lenin he played a major part in the Bolshevik Revolution of 1917 in Russia. He is credited with creating and directing the Red Army, but failed to take power on Lenin's death and was murdered in exile by one of Stalin's agents. Born **Bronstein, Lev Davidovich**

> 'Insurrection is an art, and like all arts it has its laws.'
> [Leon Trotsky, *History of the Russian Revolution*; 1933]

Trotskyism /trótski izəm/ *n* an interpretation of socialism advanced by Leon Trotsky, asserting that fully developed Marxist principles and practices would culminate in a world revolution by the proletariat —**Trotskyist** *n, adj* —**Trotskyite** *n, adj*

trotter /tróttər/ *n* **1.** the foot of an animal, especially that of a pig or sheep, when used as food **2.** somebody or something that trots, especially a horse that has been specially trained to trot in harness

trotting race /trótting-/ *n ANZ* a harness race for trotters

trotyl /trṓtil, -tīl/ *n* the explosive TNT [Early 20C. < TRINITROTOLUENE + -YL]

troubadour /tróōbə dawr, -door/ *n* **1. MEDIEVAL POET OR SINGER** a writer or singer of lyric verses about courtly love, especially in parts of Europe between the 11th and 13th centuries **2. LOVE POET OR SINGER** a writer or singer of love poems or songs **3.** *US* **SINGER** a singer who performs while strolling, especially in a restaurant [Early 18C. Via French < Old Provençal *trobador* < *trobar* 'compose']

trouble /trúbb'l/ *n* **1. CONDITION OF DISTRESS** a condition of distress, anxiety, or danger ○ *When the bills started to come in, we realized we were in serious trouble.* **2. SOMEBODY OR SOMETHING UPSETTING** a source or cause of worry, distress, or concern ○ *This car has been nothing but trouble.* **3. SOURCE OF DIFFICULTY** something that is extremely difficult or presents a problem ○ *Sorry I'm late – I had trouble getting the car to start.* **4. REAL OR APPARENT WEAKNESS** an actual or perceived failing or drawback ○ *Your trouble is that you give up too easily.* **5.** MED **MEDICAL PROBLEMS** an illness or physical condition involving a particular body part that is not functioning as it should ○ *off work with back trouble* **6. EFFORT** the effort or exertion involved in doing something ○ *I hope you like your CD – I went to a lot of trouble to find it.* **7. DISORDER OR UNREST** disorder or unruly behaviour in a public place ○ *crowd trouble* **8. MALFUNCTIONING** a condition in which something mechanical or electronic is not func-

tioning or operating as it should ○ *My car has engine trouble.* ■ *v* (**-bles, -bling, -bled**) **1.** *vt* WORRY OR UPSET SOMEBODY to cause worry, distress, or concern to somebody or something ○ *I'm troubled by the fact that she hasn't been in touch.* **2.** *vt* PHYSICALLY AFFECT SOMEBODY to cause pain or discomfort to somebody or something ○ *My arthritis troubles me from time to time.* **3.** *vt* IMPOSE ON SOMEBODY to put somebody to the inconvenience of doing something ○ *Could I trouble you to open the window?* **4.** *vti* MAKE EFFORT to make an effort to do something or take pains in doing it ○ *He hadn't troubled to check the figures.* **5.** *vt* MAKE SOMETHING ROUGH to agitate or disturb something, especially the surface of water (*often passive*) [13C. Via Old French *troubler* < late Latin *turbidare* < Latin *turbidus* 'confused, muddy'] —**troubler** *n* —**troubling** *adj* —**troublingly** *adv* ◇ **in trouble 1.** discovered in wrongdoing and liable to be punished **2.** pregnant and unmarried (*dated informal; used euphemistically*)

SYNONYMS See *bother*.

troubled /trúbb'ld/ *adj* **1.** ANXIOUS OR UPSET experiencing worry or distress **2.** MARKED BY PROBLEMS characterized by difficulties or adversity ○ *The bill has had a troubled passage through Parliament.* **3.** LACKING INNER CALM experiencing or prone to emotional conflict or psychological difficulties

troublemaker /trúbb'l maykər/ *n* somebody who constantly causes problems —**troublemaking** *n, adj*

Troubles /trúbb'lz/ *npl* the political and civil unrest in Northern Ireland during the period from 1919 to 1923 and after 1969

troubleshoot /trúbb'l shoot/ (**-shoots, -shooting, -shot** /-shot/) *vti* to operate as somebody who finds and eliminates problems

troubleshooting /trúbb'l shooting/ *n* **1.** the act or process of identifying and eliminating problems or faults, especially in electronic or computer equipment **2.** the act or process of mediating in political, industrial, or diplomatic disagreements —**troubleshooter** *n*

troublesome /trúbb'lssəm/ *adj* **1.** causing difficulties or taking a great deal of time ○ *Fixing the bug in the computer program proved more troublesome than I thought.* **2.** producing annoyance, discomfort, or anxiety, especially in a recurrent way ○ *a troublesome knee injury* —**troublesomely** *adv* —**troublesomeness** *n*

trouble spot *n* a place where trouble occurs, especially a place that is notorious for disruption to civil order or a lack of political control

troublous /trúbbləss/ *adj* (*archaic or literary*) **1.** fraught with difficulty or many problems **2.** full of uneasiness or anxiety —**troublously** *adv* —**troublousness** *n*

trough /trof/ *n* **1.** CONTAINER FOR ANIMAL FOOD OR WATER a long low narrow open container that holds feed or water for animals **2.** INDUST INDUSTRIAL CONTAINER a long low narrow open container used in industry, e.g. in washing, kneading, or mixing substances **3.** CHANNEL FOR LIQUID a narrow channel, gully, or gutter in which liquid passes, especially one under the eaves of a roof for catching rainwater **4.** METEOROL AREA OF LOW PRESSURE an elongated area of low atmospheric pressure that may be associated with a front **5.** GEOG SUNKEN AREA a long hollow area in the surface of the ground or the sea bed, or between waves **6.** LOW POINT a low or negative point, especially a temporary one **7.** ECON LOWEST POINT OF ECONOMIC CYCLE the lowest point or period of an economic cycle **8.** PHYS LOW PART OF WAVE OR SIGNAL the low or negative half of the amplitude in the cycle of a periodic wave or alternating signal [Old English *trog* < Indo-European, 'wood, tree']

trounce /trownss/ (**trounces, trouncing, trounced**) *vt* **1.** to defeat an opponent or team convincingly **2.** to beat somebody or something severely (*dated*) [Mid-16C. Origin ?]

SYNONYMS See *defeat*.

troupe /troop/ *n* a group of actors, circus people, or other entertainers, especially one that travels around ■ *vi* (**troupes, trouping, trouped**) to travel as or perform in a troupe of actors or entertainers [Early 19C. < French]

USAGE See *troop*.

trouper /trooper/ *n* **1.** MEMBER OF TROUPE somebody who is a member of a group of travelling entertainers **2.** SOMEBODY RELIABLE AND DEDICATED somebody who is conscientious, dependable, and selfless **3.** VETERAN THEATRICAL PERFORMER somebody who has been involved in the theatre for many years, especially an actor or entertainer

troupial /troopi əl/ *n* a large songbird of the blackbird family with bright black and orange feathers. Native to: South America. Latin name: *Icterus icterus*. [Early 19C. < French *troupiale*, alteration (influenced by *troupe* 'flock') of American Spanish *turpial*]

trouser /trówzər/ *adj* ASSOCIATED WITH TROUSERS belonging to, concerning, suitable for, or part of trousers ○ *a trouser pocket* ■ *n* TROUSERS a pair of trousers, especially one suitable for a smart or formal occasion ■ *vt* (**-sers, -sering, -sered**) TAKE SOMETHING DISHONESTLY to obtain or appropriate money or valuables (*slang; used disapprovingly*) ○ *Contestants battle to trouser huge cash prizes.* [Mid-19C. Back-formation < TROUSERS] —**trousered** *adj*

trousers /trówzərz/ *npl* a garment for the lower body that covers the area from the waist to the ankles and has separate tube-shaped sections for each leg. US term **pants** [Early 17C. < Gaelic *triubhas*] ◇ **be caught with your trousers down** *UK* to be caught in an unprepared or embarrassing position ◇ **wear the trousers** *UK* to be the member of a household who makes the important decisions (*informal*)

trouser suit *n* a woman's suit of matching or coordinating trousers and jacket or top. N Am term **pantsuit**

trousseau /troossō/ (*plural* **-seaus** or **-seaux** /-sōz/) *n* a bride's clothes and linen, especially items such as nightdresses, underwear, and bedclothes, that she has collected during the period of her engagement [Early 19C. < French, 'little bundle' < *trousser* 'truss']

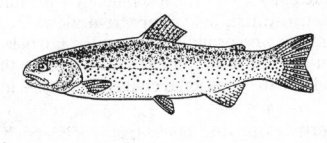

trout

trout /trowt/ (*plural* **trouts** or *same*) *n* **1.** FRESHWATER FISH SIMILAR TO SALMON a freshwater fish that is typically smaller than the related salmon and has a speckled body, small scales, and soft fins. Genus: *Salmo*. **2.** GAME FISH OF SALMON FAMILY a game fish of the salmon family, e.g. the sea trout. Genus: *Salvelinus*. **3.** FISH UNRELATED TO TROUT a fish similar to but unrelated to the trout, e.g. the troutperch **4.** OFFENSIVE TERM an offensive term that deliberately insults a woman's age, appearance, or behaviour (*informal insult*) [Pre-12C. < late Latin *tructa*]

troutperch /trówt purch/ (*plural same*) *n* a small freshwater fish with a spotted body, an adipose fin, and rough scales. Native to: North America. Family: Percopsidae.

trouvaille /troo ví/ *n* something interesting, amusing, or beneficial discovered by chance ○ *The anecdote was one of her many literary trouvailles.* [Mid-19C. < French, 'a find']

trouvère /troo váir/ *n* a poet-musician of northern France during the 12th and 13th centuries who wrote poems and songs of courtly love, as well as narrative and satirical works [Late 18C. Via French < Old French *trovere* < *trover* 'compose' (see TROVER)]

trove /trōv/ *n* **1.** a collection of discovered valuable items **2.** a discovery of great importance or monetary value [Late 19C. Shortening of TREASURE-TROVE]

trover /trōvər/ *n* a common law action to recover goods

that have been wrongly appropriated by somebody else (*archaic*) [Late 16C. < Anglo-Norman < Old French 'to find']

trow /trō/ (**trows, trowing, trowed**) *vti* to think, believe, or suppose that something is the case (*archaic*) [Old English *trēowian*. < Germanic]

Trowbridge /trōbrij/ town and administrative centre of Wiltshire, southwestern England. Population: 29,334 (1991).

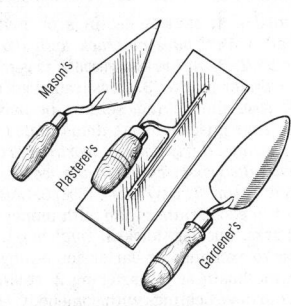

trowel

trowel /trów əl/ *n* **1.** FLAT-BLADED HAND TOOL a small hand tool with a short handle and a flat, usually pointed blade used for spreading, shaping, and smoothing plaster, cement, or mortar **2.** GARDENER'S SHORT-HANDLED TOOL a hand tool with a short handle and a curved tapering blade, used for making holes to put plants and seedlings in and for other light digging work ■ *vt* (**-els, -elling, -elled**) WORK MATERIAL WITH TROWEL to dig, spread, or level something such as earth or mortar using a trowel [14C. Via Old French *troele* < late Latin *truella* 'dipper' < Latin *trua* 'ladle'] —**troweller** *n* ◇ **lay it on with a trowel** to exaggerate, especially in order to flatter somebody (*informal*)

troy /troy/ *adj* measured in or using the troy weight system [14C. Probably < TROYES, which had a fair at which this weight was used]

Troy /troy/ city of ancient Greece on the Aegean sea coast, in present-day Turkey. Site of the ten-year Trojan War described in the epic poems of Homer, the city, also called Ilium, was thought to be purely legendary until ruins were discovered by the archaeologist Heinrich Schliemann in 1870. It is now believed to have been founded during the Bronze Age in 3000 BC.

Troyes /trwaa/ capital of Aube Department, in Champagne, northeastern France. Population: 60,958 (1999).

troy weight *n* a system of weights used for precious metals and gemstones, based on a 12-ounce pound, a 20-pennyweight ounce, and a 24-grain pennyweight

trp *abbr* troop

trs. *abbr* PRINTING transpose

truant /troo ənt/ *n* **1.** SOMEBODY ABSENT FROM SCHOOL somebody who is absent without permission or good reason, especially from school **2.** SHIRKER somebody who avoids work or shirks responsibilities (*dated*) ■ *adj* ABSENT absent without permission ■ *vi* (**-ants, -anting, -anted**) BE ABSENT to be absent without permission, especially from school [14C. < Old French, 'beggar, vagabond', of Celtic origin] —**truancy** *n*

truce /trooss/ *n* **1.** CESSATION IN FIGHTING a cessation of military hostilities that both sides agree to hold to, usually for a fixed period ○ *Both sides called a truce.* **2.** AGREEMENT TO STOP FIGHTING an agreement to suspend military hostilities **3.** AGREED BREAK IN ARGUING an agreed break in a dispute or feud, or the agreement to stop arguing [14C. Variant of earlier *trewes*, the plural of *trewe* 'treaty, pledge' < Old English *trēow* (see TRUE)]

Trucial States /troosh'l-/ former name for **United Arab Emirates** (until 1971)

truck[1] /truk/ *n* **1.** AUTOMOT LARGE GOODS VEHICLE a large vehicle for transporting goods by road **2.** AUTOMOT same as **pick-up truck 3.** CART PUSHED BY HAND a cart or barrow with two or more wheels that is pushed by hand and is used for moving heavy objects **4.** RAIL RAILWAY GOODS WAGON an open railway wagon that carries freight **5.** TRAIN WHEEL UNIT a swivelling frame that the wheels and springs are mounted on at

either end of a railway vehicle **6.** EXTREME SPORTS SKATEBOARD WHEEL UNIT either of a pair of swivelling wheel units on a skateboard **7.** NAUT ROPE GUIDE ON SHIP'S MAST a guide for a ship's ropes, in the form of a disc with holes, fitted horizontally to the top of the mast ■ *v* (**trucks, trucking, trucked**) **1.** *vti* TAKE THINGS BY TRUCK to transport, or transport something, by truck **2.** *vi N Am* DRIVE TRUCK to drive a truck, especially as a job (*informal*) [Early 17C. Origin ?] ◇ **keep on trucking** to carry on with work or life in a cheerful and relaxed way, in spite of problems (*informal*)

truck² /truk/ *n* **1.** DEALINGS dealings or involvement (*informal*) ○ *We'll have no truck with that kind of behaviour.* **2.** *N Am* MARKET PRODUCE vegetables and fruit grown for market **3.** GOODS traded goods of any kind **4.** TRADE the buying, selling, or bartering of goods **5.** STUFF miscellaneous items (*dated informal*) ○*Now I wanted thirty dollars' worth of artist truck, for I was always sketching in the woods.'* (Robert Louis Stevenson, *The Wrecker*; 1896) **6.** PAYMENT IN KIND payment in goods rather than with money (*archaic*) ■ *vti* (**trucks, trucking, trucked**) (*archaic*) **1.** EXCHANGE SOMETHING to exchange or barter something, or take part in the business of bartering **2.** BE INVOLVED WITH SOMEBODY to have dealings with somebody, especially secret or dishonest dealings [12C. < Old French dialect *troquer* 'to barter']

truck bomb *n* a lorry filled with explosives or chemicals that is crashed into a target or detonated beside it, used as a terrorist weapon

trucker¹ /trúkər/ *n* somebody who drives a truck, especially somebody whose job is transporting goods by truck over long distances [Mid-19C. < TRUCK¹]

trucker² /trúkər/ *n N Am* somebody who barters [Mid-16C. < TRUCK²]

truckie /trúki/ *n* somebody who drives a truck (*informal*)

trucking /trúking/ *n* the carrying of freight on roads in trucks

truckle¹ /trúk'l/ (**-les, -ling, -led**) *vi* to behave in a weak or servile way [Early 17C. Shortening of TRUCKLE BED, from the use of such beds by servants] —**truckler** *n*

truckle² /trúk'l/ *n* a small cylindrical cheese [14C. Via Anglo-Norman *trocle* < Greek *trokhileia* 'system of pulleys' < *trokhos* 'wheel']

truckle bed *n* a low bed on casters that can be stowed away under another bed. N Am term **trundle bed** [< TRUCKLE² in sense 'small wheel']

truckload /trúk lōd/ *n* the quantity carried by a truck, or a quantity large enough to fill a truck

truck stop *n ANZ, N Am* a roadside station that sells fuel for trucks and has a restaurant for truck drivers. UK term **transport café**

truculent /trúkyŏŏlənt/ *adj* aggressively or sullenly refusing to accept something or do what is asked [Mid-16C. < Latin *truculentus* < *trux* 'fierce'] —**truculence** *n* —**truculently** *adv*

Trudeau /trŏŏdō/, **Pierre** (1919–2000) prime minister of Canada (1968–79 and 1980–84). A Liberal prime minister, he negotiated the Constitution Act (1982) that granted Canada complete independence from the British parliament. Full name **Trudeau, Pierre Elliott**. See table at **prime minister**

> 'Canada is a country whose main exports are hockey players and cold fronts. Our main imports are baseball players and acid rain.'
> [Pierre Trudeau. Quoted in *Sportswit*, Lee Green; 1984]

> 'Living next to you is in some ways like sleeping with an elephant. No matter how friendly and even-tempered the beast, one is affected by every twitch and grunt.'
> [Pierre Trudeau, *Speech to the National Press Club, Washington, DC*; 25 March 1969]

trudge /truj/ *vti* (**trudges, trudging, trudged**) to walk, or walk a particular path or distance, with slow heavy weary steps ■ *n* a long and exhausting walk [Mid-16C. Origin ?] —**trudger** *n*

true /trŏŏ/ *adj* (**truer, truest**) **1.** REAL OR CORRECT conforming with reality or fact **2.** GENUINE genuine, not pretended, insincere, or artificial **3.** PERSONALLY FAITHFUL showing loyalty to another person ○ *a true friend* **4.** COMMITTED faithful to a cause, purpose, or religious belief ○ *a true believer* **5.** CONFORMING TO STANDARD OR MEASURE conforming to a standard, measure, or pattern ○ *a true fit* **6.** RIGHTFUL conforming to the way things should be by right ○ *returned to the true owners* **7.** MUSIC IN TUNE perfectly in tune ○ *The orchestra maintained true pitch throughout.* **8.** CONFORMING TO INCLUSION CRITERIA meeting the criteria for inclusion in a particular category, in contrast to being given the same name because of superficial resemblance to members of that category ○ *A shooting star is not a true star.* **9.** GEOG IN RELATION TO EARTH'S POLES measured in relation to geographical points on the Earth's surface, rather than to points of magnetic attraction ○ *true north* **10.** PHYS NOT RELATIVE not relative as a value and corrected for all error factors ■ *adv* **1.** IN REAL OR FACTUAL CORRESPONDENCE in a way that corresponds with reality or fact ○ *His explanations just didn't ring true.* **2.** ACCURATELY so as to arrive at the precise position aimed for ○ *The arrow flew straight and true.* **3.** HONESTLY in a frank and open way that seeks to hide nothing ○ *Tell me true.* **4.** CERTAINLY used to admit the validity or accuracy of a statement, often in a discussion or when considering the advantages and disadvantages of something ○ *True, it does rain a lot here.* **5.** AGRIC WITHOUT LOSS OF ANCESTRAL FEATURES without variation from the ancestral form, or producing offspring with the same hereditary characteristics ○ *breed true* ■ *vt* (**trues, truing, trued**) ADJUST POSITION OF SOMETHING to adjust something to make it straight or level or put it in any other required position ■ *n* **1.** ALIGNMENT a correct position, especially a position in relation to the horizontal or vertical ○ *out of true* **2.** REALITY the absolute truth [Old English *trēowe* 'trustworthy' < Indo-European, 'be solid'] —**trueness** *n* ◇ **come true** to happen as hoped or expected ◇ **not true** impossible to believe or accept (*informal*) ◇ **true to life** conforming accurately with reality

true bill *n US* a legal document requesting a criminal trial (**bill of indictment**), formally endorsed by a grand jury and certifying that somebody can be brought to trial

true blue *n* (*informal*) **1.** UK somebody with staunchly loyalist, royalist, or conservative views **2.** Aus an Australian who proudly displays the fairness, egalitarianism, stoicism, and resourcefulness that are considered to be national characteristics —**true-blue** *adj*

true-born *adj* having one's true social position or nationality beyond doubt, because it was established at birth ○ *a true-born Londoner*

true bug *n* INSECTS same as **bug** *n* (sense 1)

true-life *adj* presenting matters, especially human relationships, as they are or have been in reality ○ *a true-life adventure story*

truelove /trŏŏ luv/ *n* somebody who is deeply loved by another

truelove knot, true lovers' knot *n* a complicated bowknot that is difficult to untie, symbolizing lovers' faithfulness

~~truely~~ incorrect spelling of **truly**

Trueman /trŏŏmən/, **Fred** (*b.* 1931) British cricketer. A skilled fast bowler, he took a record 307 test wickets in his career. Full name **Trueman, Frederick Sewards**

true rib *n* a rib that is attached to the breastbone (**sternum**) by cartilage. The seven uppermost ribs in the human body are true ribs.

François Truffaut

Truffaut /trŏŏ fō/, **François** (1932–84) French film director and critic. His first film, the semi-autobiographical *The 400 Blows* (1959), was one of the first films of the French new wave movement. Other films include *Shoot the Pianist* (1960) and *Jules et Jim* (1961).

> 'An actor is never so great as when he reminds you of an animal—falling like a cat, lying like a dog, moving like a fox.'
> [François Truffaut, *The New Yorker*; 20 February 1960]

truffle /trúff'l/ *n* **1.** an underground fungus whose fleshy edible fruiting body is highly valued as a delicacy. Pigs and dogs are often used to sniff out truffles. Genus: *Tuber*. **2.** a rich ball-shaped chocolate with a centre of soft chocolate [Late 16C. Alteration of French *trufe*, via Provençal *trufa* < Latin *tuber* 'swelling']

trug /trug/ *n* a shallow rectangular basket made from curved strips of wood, used especially for carrying garden produce [14C. Origin ?]

Truganini /trŏŏgə neeni/ (1812?–76) Australian Aboriginal. She is said to have been the last full-blooded Aboriginal in Tasmania, Australia.

truism /trŏŏ izəm/ *n* a statement that is so obviously true and so often repeated that people find it trite or meaningless —**truistic** /trŏŏ ístik/ *adj*

Trujillo /trŏŏ hee yō, -heel yō/ city in a coastal desert region of northwestern Peru, founded in 1534. It is situated next to the remains of an important pre-Incan city. Population: 627,553 (1995).

~~truley~~ incorrect spelling of **truly**

trull /trul/ *n* same as **prostitute** *n* (sense 1) (*archaic*) [Early 16C. < Middle High German *trulle*]

truly /trŏŏli/ *adv* **1.** SINCERELY honestly, without affectation or pretence ○ *feel truly sorry* **2.** USED FOR EMPHASIS used to emphasize the extent or degree of something ○ *a truly remarkable achievement* **3.** COMPLETELY to the fullest extent or in the fullest degree ○ *Only she can truly appreciate how happy I feel.* ◇ **yours truly 1.** used as a rather formal way of signing off in a letter **2.** used to refer to yourself (*humorous*) ○ *Doubtless they're expecting yours truly to pick them up from the airport.*

Harry S. Truman

Truman /trŏŏmən/, **Harry S.** (1884–1972) 33rd President of the United States (1945–53). A Democrat, he became President on the death of Franklin D. Roosevelt and continued to pursue his predecessor's welfare policies. In foreign policy, he acted to contain Communism overseas, especially in the Korean War (1950–53). See table at **president**

> 'A politician is a man who understands government, and it takes a politician to run a government. A statesman is a politician who's been dead 10 or 15 years.'
> [Harry S. Truman, *New York World Telegram and Sun*; 12 April 1958]

> 'If you can't stand the heat, get out of the kitchen.'
> [Attributed to Harry S. Truman, *Time*; 28 April 1953]

Trumbull /trúmb'l/, **John** (1750–1831) US lawyer and poet. A Connecticut judge and one of the 'Hartford Wits', he wrote the comic epic *M'Fingal* (1775–82), satirizing British Loyalists during the American War of Independence.

'No man e'er felt the halter draw, / With good opinion of the law.' [John Trumbull, *M'Fingal*; 1775–82]

trumeau /tróo mṓ/ (*plural* **-meaux** /-mṓz/) *n* a pillar or a section of wall that separates two doors or two sections of a door [Late 19C. < French, 'calf of the leg']

trump[1] /trump/ *n* **1. CARD FROM HIGHEST SUIT** in card games, a card from a suit declared to be higher in value than any other suit, or the suit itself **2. KEY RESOURCE** a highly valuable resource or advantage, especially one held in reserve for future use **3. FINE PERSON** an admirable or reliable person (*informal*) ■ *vt* (**trumps, trumping, trumped**) **1. DEFEAT SOMEBODY BY PLAYING TRUMP** in card games, to beat an opponent or an opponent's card by playing a trump **2. OUTDO SOMEBODY** to defeat or outdo a competitor by bringing a valuable resource or advantage into play [Early 16C. Alteration of TRIUMPH]

trump up *vt* to invent false accusations or false evidence in order to incriminate somebody wrongly

trump[2] /trump/ *n* a trumpet, or the sound of a trumpet (*archaic*) [13C. < Old French *trompe* (see TRUMPET)]

trump card *n* CARDS same as **trump**[1] *n* (senses 1–2) ◇ **play your trump card** to make use of a highly valuable resource or advantage that has been held in reserve

trumped-up /trúmpt-/ *adj* false and deliberately invented, usually in order to incriminate somebody wrongly ○ *trumped-up charges*

trumpery /trúmpəri/ (*plural* **-ies**) *n* (*archaic or literary*) **1.** something worthless or useless, often something showy that seems appealing at first glance **2.** empty or ridiculous talk [15C. < French *tromperie* 'trickery' < *tromper* 'deceive']

trumpet /trúmpit/ *n* **1. BRASS INSTRUMENT** a brass musical instrument, either straight or coiled, with three valves and a flared bell. It has a brilliant tone and a middle to high register. **2. SOMETHING SHAPED LIKE TRUMPET** something shaped like the flared bell of a trumpet **3. SOUND OF OR LIKE TRUMPET** a loud high sound made by a trumpet, or a sound such as the call of an elephant **4. PLAYER OF TRUMPET** a player of a trumpet **5.** MED same as **ear trumpet 6. ORGAN STOP** a solo organ stop that imitates the sound of a trumpet ■ *v* (**-pets, -peting, -peted**) **1.** *vti* **ANNOUNCE SOMETHING** to announce something loudly, proudly, or with great ceremony **2.** *vt* **SPEAK IN PRAISE OF SOMETHING** to speak of somebody or something with ostentatious admiration or pride **3.** *vi* **MAKE ELEPHANT'S CALL** to make an elephant's characteristically high-pitched, penetrating call **4.** *vt* **EXPRESS SOMETHING BY TRUMPETING** to convey something with a trumpeting call ○ *The elephant trumpeted a warning.* [14C. < Old French *trompette* 'small horn' < *trompe* 'horn' < Germanic, probably an imitation of the sound of a horn] ◇ **blow your own trumpet** to speak confidently, proudly, or boastfully about your own achievements, qualities, or possessions (*informal*)

trumpet creeper *n* a woody deciduous vine with compound leaves. Flowers: large, red, trumpet-shaped. Native to: North America. Latin name: *Campsis radicans*.

trumpeter /trúmpitər/ *n* **1. TRUMPET PLAYER** a musician who plays the trumpet **2. TROPICAL BIRD WITH LOUD CALL** a medium-sized bird that rarely flies and has long legs, a short bill, dark glossy plumage, and a loud call. Native to: tropical South America. Family: Psophidae. **3. PIGEON** a domestic pigeon with a long ruff, heavily feathered feet, and a loud call

trumpetfish /trúmpit fish/ (*plural* **-fishes** or *same*) *n* a fish with a long body and a tubular snout. Native to: tropical reefs. Family: Aulostomidae.

trumpet flower *n* **1.** a plant with trumpet-shaped flowers, e.g. the trumpet creeper **2.** the flower of a trumpet flower

trumpet vine *n* PLANTS same as **trumpet creeper**

trumps /trumps/ *n* in card games, the suit that is chosen at the outset to be the highest in value (*takes a singular or plural verb*) ○ *Diamonds are trumps.* ◇ **turn up trumps** to prove unexpectedly to be a valuable asset, especially one that plays a decisive role in the success of something

truncate *vt* /trung káyt/ (**-cates, -cating, -cated**) **1. SHORTEN SOMETHING BY REMOVING PART** to shorten something by cutting off or removing a part **2.** MATHS **SHORTEN DECIMAL NUMBER** to restrict the precision of a decimal number by limiting the digits to the right of the decimal point without rounding ■ *adj* /trúng kayt/ **1.** MATHS, CRYSTALS, LITERAT same as **truncated** (senses 2–4) **2.** BOT **NOT POINTED** describes a leaf that has a blunt end, so that it looks as if a part has been cut off [15C. < Latin *truncat-*, past participle of *truncare* 'cut short, mutilate' < *truncus* 'something cut off'] —**truncately** *adv* —**truncation** *n*

truncated /trung káytid/ *adj* **1. WITH END REMOVED** shortened by having a part cut off or removed **2.** MATHS **WITH END REPLACED BY PLANE** describes a geometric figure that has the apex or an end removed and replaced with a plane section, often parallel to the base **3.** CRYSTALS **HAVING INCOMPLETE CORNERS** describes a crystal that lacks the fully formed corners or faces that would be present in a simple form of the crystal **4.** LITERAT **WITH ONE SYLLABLE FEWER** describes a line of poetry that has one syllable fewer in one of its feet than in others in the line

truncheon /trúnchən/ *n* **1. POLICE OFFICER'S STICK** a short heavy stick carried by a police officer **2. SYMBOLIC STICK** a baton carried as a symbol of rank or authority **3. SPEAR SHAFT** the shaft of a spear ■ *vt* (**-cheons, -cheoning, -cheoned**) **HIT SOMEBODY WITH TRUNCHEON** to hit somebody or something with a truncheon [13C. Via Old N French *tronchon* < Latin *truncus* 'something cut off']

trundle /trúnd'l/ *vti* (**-dles, -dling, -dled**) **MOVE HEAVILY ON WHEELS** to move slowly and heavily, especially on wheels or rollers, or move something in this way ■ *n* **1. WHEEL** a small wheel or roller by which something is moved along **2. ROLLING MOVEMENT** a slow heavy movement, especially a rolling movement **3. CART WITH WHEELS** a trolley or cart with small wheels [Mid-16C. Variant of *trendle* 'wheel' < Old English *trendel* 'circle' < Germanic]

trundle bed *n N Am* FURNITURE same as **truckle bed**

trundler /trúndlər/ *n NZ* **1.** a cart for pulling a golf bag along by hand **2.** COMM same as **shopping trolley 3.** same as **buggy**[1] (sense 1)

trunk /trungk/ *n* **1. MAIN STEM OF TREE** the main stem of a tree, excluding branches and roots **2. LARGE TRAVELLING CASE** a large strong travelling case or box with a hinged lid that is bigger, more rigid, and less portable than a suitcase **3. UPPER BODY** the main part of the body of a human being or an animal, excluding the head, neck, and limbs **4. ELEPHANT'S PROBOSCIS** the long muscular proboscis of an elephant, used for grasping, feeding, and drinking **5. MAIN PART** the main part of something that has branches or subsidiary parts leading off it, e.g. a transport network or an electrical or communications network **6.** *N Am* AUTOMOT same as **boot**[1] *n* (sense 2) **7.** ANAT **STEM OF BLOOD VESSEL** the main stem of a blood vessel or nerve, with branches leading off it **8.** NAUT **PART OF CABIN ABOVE DECK** the part of a boat's cabin that sits above the deck **9.** BUILDINGS **DUCT** a duct in a building, e.g. a ventilation duct or a duct carrying electrical wires **10.** ARCHIT **PART OF COLUMN** the shaft of an architectural column, excluding the base and the capital ■ **trunks** *npl* CLOTHING **MEN'S SWIMWEAR** men's shorts worn for sports, especially swimming [15C. Via French *tronc* 'tree trunk, alms box' < Latin *truncus* 'something cut off']

trunk call *n* formerly, a long-distance telephone call (*dated*)

trunkfish /trúngk fish/ (*plural* **-fishes** or *same*) *n* a brightly coloured tropical fish that has a body covered in bony plates. Family: Ostraciidae.

trunk hose *n* short puffed-out breeches worn by men in the late 16th and early 17th centuries. They extended from the waist to the upper or mid thigh.

trunking /trúngking/ *n* **1.** a casing used to anchor, conceal, and protect cables and small pipes **2.** a freight transport system in which bulk deliveries are made to local distribution centres. Individual shops or customers order or collect items from these centres as required.

trunk road *n* a long-distance A road used by high volumes of traffic

trunnel *n* CONSTR same as **treenail**

trunnion /trúnni ən/ *n* either of a pair of pivots, especially the cylindrical knobs on the side of a cannon's barrel that allow it to pivot on the gun carriage [Early 17C. < French *trognon* 'fruit core, tree stump'] —**trunnioned** *adj*

Truro /tróorō/ **1.** city and administrative centre of Cornwall, southwestern England. Population: 17,200 (1994 estimate). **2.** town on Cobequid Bay in central Nova Scotia, Canada. Population: 21,442 (2001).

truss /truss/ *vt* (**trusses, trussing, trussed**) **1. BIND SOMEBODY OR SOMETHING** to tie somebody or something up tightly **2.** COOK **TIE SOMETHING FOR COOKING** to prepare meat for roasting by tying it into a neat shape. Birds such as chickens and turkeys are trussed to keep wings and legs close to the body. **3.** CIV ENG **SUPPORT SOMETHING WITH LOAD-BEARING MEMBERS** to support or strengthen a roof, bridge, or other elevated structure with a network of beams and bars **4.** MED **SUPPORT HERNIA** to support a hernia with a specially designed device ■ *n* **1.** ARCHIT same as **corbel 2.** MED **SUPPORT FOR HERNIA** a device designed to apply pressure to a hernia to stop it enlarging or protruding **3.** BOT **FRUIT CLUSTER** a cluster of flowers or fruit on a single branching stem, e.g. on a tomato plant **4.** NAUT **MAST FITTING** a metal fitting used to attach a ship's beam (**yard**) to a mast **5. BUNDLE** a bundle, especially a bundle of hay of varying weight [12C. < Old French *trousse* < *trousser* 'to truss'] —**trusser** *n*

truss bridge *n* a bridge whose supporting structure consists of a network of beams in a series of triangular sections

trussing /trússing/ *n* a framework of beams arranged in triangular sections and supporting a roof, bridge, or other structure, or the beams themselves

trust /trust/ *n* **1. RELIANCE** confidence in and reliance on good qualities, especially fairness, truth, honour, or ability **2. POSITION OF OBLIGATION** the position of somebody who is expected by others to behave responsibly or honourably ○ *breached the public trust* **3. HOPE FOR FUTURE** hopeful reliance on what will happen in the future **4. CARE** responsibility for taking good care of somebody or something ○ *We put our children in the trust of a good child-minder.* **5.** LAW **HOLDING OF ANOTHER'S PROPERTY** the legal holding and managing of money or property belonging to somebody else, e.g. that of a minor **6.** LAW **ARRANGEMENT TO MANAGE ANOTHER'S PROPERTY** a legal arrangement by which one person (**trustee**) holds and manages money or property belonging to somebody else **7.** COMM **CREDIT** credit given to somebody on purchases made ○ *Let me have it on trust.* ■ *v* (**trusts, trusting, trusted**) **1.** *vti* **RELY ON SOMEBODY OR SOMETHING** to place confidence in somebody or in somebody's good qualities, especially fairness, truth, honour, or ability **2.** *vt* **CONFIDENTLY ALLOW SOMEBODY TO DO SOMETHING** to allow somebody to do something, having confidence that the person will behave responsibly or properly ○ *I trust you to do the right thing.* **3.** *vt* **PLACE SOMETHING IN SOMEBODY'S CARE** to place somebody or something in the care of another person ○ *You could certainly trust him with such an important job.* **4.** *vt* **SUPPOSE SOMETHING** to hope or suppose something ○ *I trust you had a good holiday.* **5.** *vt Carib* **GIVE CREDIT TO SOMEBODY** to give somebody credit on a purchase ○ *wouldn't even trust me a carton of milk* [12C. < Old Norse *traust* 'confidence', *treysta* 'to trust'] —**trustability** /trústə bílləti/ *n* —**trustable** *adj* —**truster** *n* ◇ **take something on trust** to accept something as true or honest without checking that this is the case

trustafarian /trústə fáiri ən/ *n* a young person from an affluent background who is temporarily living in circumstances less comfortable than he or she can expect to enjoy in the future, usually in a bohemian or socially disadvantaged area (*informal humorous*) [Late 20C. Blend of TRUST + RASTAFARIAN]

trust company *n* a bank or other commercial organization that sets up and operates trusts for private individuals and businesses

trustee /tru stée/ *n* **1.** LAW **MANAGER OF ANOTHER'S PROPERTY** somebody who is given the legal authority to manage money or property on behalf of somebody else **2.** FIN **FINANCE MANAGER** a member of a group of people responsible for managing the financial affairs of an institution or organization **3.** POL **COUNTRY SUPERVISING TRUST TERRITORY** a country responsible for administering a trust territory

trusteeship /tru stée ship/ *n* **1.** the status or responsibilities of a trustee, or the period of time for which a trustee holds office **2.** the administration of a country that is not self-governing by a foreign

country under terms laid down by the United Nations

trustful /trústf'l/ *adj* same as **trusting** —**trustfully** *adv* —**trustfulness** *n*

trust fund *n* an investment fund managed on behalf of somebody, particularly a minor, by one or more people given legal authority to do so

trust hotel *n NZ* a hotel operated by elected members of a local community, with profits going to finance community projects

trusting /trústing/ *adj* willing or tending to trust people —**trustingly** *adv* —**trustingness** *n*

trust tavern *n NZ* a bar operated by elected members of a local community, with profits going to finance community projects

trust territory *n* a country that does not have its own government, but is run by a foreign country under terms laid down by the United Nations

trustworthy /trúst wurthi/ *adj* deserving trust, or able to be trusted —**trustworthily** *adv* —**trustworthiness** *n*

trusty /trústi/ *adj* (**-ier**, **-iest**) RELIABLE able to be relied on (*dated or humorous*) ■ *n* (*plural* **-ies**) 1. TRUSTED PERSON somebody who is trusted 2. TRUSTED PRISONER a prisoner regarded by the prison authorities as trustworthy and given special privileges —**trustily** *adv* —**trustiness** *n*

truth /trooth/ *n* 1. SOMETHING FACTUAL the thing that corresponds to fact or reality ○ *If you tell the truth, you have nothing to fear.* ○ *spoke the truth* 2. TRUE QUALITY correspondence to fact or reality 3. TRUE STATEMENT a statement that corresponds to fact or reality ○ *His story was a mixture of truths and untruths.* 4. OBVIOUS FACT something that is so clearly true that it hardly needs to be stated 5. SOMETHING GENERALLY BELIEVED a statement that is generally believed to be true ○ *a religious truth* 6. HONESTY honesty and sincerity ○ *I can say in all truth that I never knew about his crimes.* 7. CONFORMITY adherence to a standard or law 8. LOYALTY faithfulness to a person or a cause (*dated*) 9. ACCURACY accuracy of alignment, setting, position, or shape (*dated*) [Old English *trēowth* 'faithfulness' < *trēow* (see TRUE)] ◇ **be economical with the truth** to tell lies (*euphemistic*)

Truth *n* in Christian Science, God

truth-condition *n* the condition that must apply if a given philosophical proposition is to be true

truth drug *n* a sedative such as thiopentone sodium that is supposed to make the person taking it tell the truth, either by reducing inhibitions or causing hypnosis. N Am term **truth serum**

truthful /trooth f'l/ *adj* 1. telling the truth or tending to tell the truth 2. corresponding to fact or reality —**truthfulness** *n*

truthfully /trooth f'li/ *adv* 1. in a way that corresponds to fact or reality or expresses the truth 2. ⚠ used to reinforce the truth of what has just been said or is about to be said ○ *Truthfully, I did not know she was there.*

USAGE See *sentence adverb*.

truth in sentencing *n Aus* the principal, often enforced with government legislation, that convicted criminals should serve out the full sentence handed down to them by the courts and not be eligible for early parole

truth serum *n N Am* PHARM same as **truth drug**

truth set *n* a set of all the values that make a given mathematical or logic statement true when substituted in the statement

truth table *n* 1. a table used to work out the truth or falsity of a compound statement in logic 2. in electronics and computing, a table used to indicate the value of the output signal from a logic circuit or device for every possible input

truth-value *n* in logic, the truth or falsity of a proposition or of a compound statement consisting of two or more propositions

try /trī/ *v* (**tries**, **trying**, **tried**) 1. ATTEMPT SOMETHING to make an attempt or effort to do something 2. *vt* TEST SOMETHING FOR PURPOSE OF ASSESSMENT to test, sample, or experiment with something in order to assess its usefulness, worth, or quality ○ *You get to try the*

---

software at home. 3. *vt* VEX SOMEBODY to subject somebody or something to great strain ○ *The long wait tried her patience.* 4. *vt* LAW SUBJECT SOMEBODY TO LEGAL TRIAL to carry out the trial in court of somebody accused of a crime or offence 5. *vt* LAW CONDUCT CASE IN COURT to conduct a legal case in court ○ *asked when the case would be tried* 6. *vt* FOOD same as **render** *v* (sense 9) ■ *n* (*plural* **tries**) 1. ATTEMPT MADE an attempt or effort made to do something ○ *a good try* 2. SCORE IN RUGBY in rugby, a score achieved by touching the ball on the ground behind the line of the opposing team's posts (**goal line**). Five points are scored for a try in rugby union, and three points in rugby league. [13C. Via Old French *trier* 'sift out' < assumed Vulgar Latin *triare*]

USAGE try and or **try to**? The two expressions are often interchangeable (*We'll try and come* or *We'll try to come*), although **try and** is rather more informal. In the past tense and in negative and progressive constructions, however, **try to** is needed: *They tried to deliver the parcel on Friday. Are you trying to tell me something?*

SYNONYMS try, attempt, endeavour, strive
CORE MEANING: to make an effort to do something
try to make an attempt or an effort to do something ○ *I tried for years to live with my husband, but it was just impossible.* ○ *I will try to get the report to you by Tuesday.* **attempt** to make an effort to do something, especially without much expectation of success ○ *There are various theories which attempt to explain the phenomenon of dreaming.* ○ *The police became involved after some of the cult's members attempted suicide.* **endeavour** to make a serious and sincere effort to do something ○ *the school at which Dot vainly endeavoured to teach French* ○ *In his writings, he has endeavoured to define patriotism.* **strive** to try hard to achieve or get something ○ *At this hotel we are constantly striving to improve the level of guest services.* ○ *Competing firms must strive to satisfy their customers or they will not prosper.*

try on *vt* to put on an item of clothing in order to test its fit or suitability ◇ **try it on** to behave in an unacceptable way, or make an unjustified claim or request, in order to find out whether this will be allowed or accepted (*informal*)

try out *vi* 1. *N Am* to undergo a competitive test of suitability, especially for a place on a sports team or for a part as an actor ○ *plans to try out for the play* 2. same as **try** *v* (sense 1)

~~**tryed**~~ incorrect spelling of **tried**

trying /trī ing/ *adj* placing great strain on somebody's patience, composure, or good nature, and often physically exhausting as a result —**tryingly** *adv*

trying plane *n* a woodworking plane with a long body, used for planing long surfaces [< *try up* 'to smooth rough-planed wood']

try-on *n* a test of somebody's gullibility or patience (*informal*)

try-out *n US* a trial to test somebody's suitability, especially to play on a sports team or play a role as an actor

trypan blue /tríppən-/ *n* a blue dye used to distinguish live cells from dead cells. Only dead cells turn blue in the presence of trypan blue. [Shortening of TRYPANOSOME]

trypanosome /tríppənə sōm/ *n* a simple microscopic organism (**protozoan**) that lives as a parasite in the blood of some vertebrates, including human beings. It is transmitted by insect bites and causes serious diseases. Genus: *Trypanosoma*. [Early 20C. < modern Latin < Greek *trupanon* 'borer' + *sōma* 'body'] —**trypanosomal** /-sōm'l/ *adj*

trypanosomiasis /tríppənō sō mí əssiss/ *n* a disease caused by infestation with a microscopic organism that lives as a parasite in the blood, especially sleeping sickness

trypsin /trípsin/ *n* a pancreatic enzyme that digests proteins [Late 19C. Probably < Greek *tripsis* 'rubbing', because first obtained by rubbing a pancreas with glycerin] —**tryptic** *adj*

trypsinogen /trip sínnəjən/ *n* an inactive substance secreted in the juices of the pancreas and converted into trypsin in the duodenum

tryptamine /tríptə meen/ *n* an amine formed by the

---

decomposition of tryptophan [Early 20C. < TRYPTOPHAN + -AMINE]

tryptophan

tryptophan /tríptō fan/ *n* an essential amino acid found in proteins such as casein and fibrin. Formula: $C_{11}H_{12}O_2N_2$. [Late 19C. < *tryptic* 'of trypsin' + -PHANE]

trysail /trí sayl/ *n* a strong sail used in stormy weather that is either square or triangular and is set to run parallel to the length of the ship (**fore-and-aft**) [Mid-18C. < *a-try* 'hove to']

try square *n* a woodworking tool used to test and mark out right angles, consisting of a rectangular handle with a thin flat rectangular metal blade fitted perpendicular to it

tryst /trist/ (*archaic or literary*) *n* 1. ARRANGEMENT TO MEET an arrangement to meet, especially one made privately or secretly by lovers 2. SECRET MEETING a secret meeting, or place of meeting, especially between lovers ■ *vi* (**trysts**, **trysting**, **trysted**) MEET OR ARRANGE TO MEET to arrange or attend a meeting with somebody, especially secretly with a lover [14C. < Old French *triste* 'place to lie in wait' < Germanic] —**tryster** *n*

TS, **ts** *abbr* transsexual

TSA *abbr* TRANSP Transportation Safety Administration [Early 21C.]

tsaddik *n* JUDAISM another spelling of **tzaddik**

tsade *n* another spelling of **sadhe**

tsar /zaar/, **czar**, **tzar** *n* 1. RUSSIAN EMPEROR an emperor of Russia, before 1917 2. TYRANT a tyrant or autocrat 3. SOMEBODY IN AUTHORITY somebody given authority, especially for dealing with a particular issue or problem (*informal*) [Mid-16C. Via Russian *tsar'*, Old Slavic *tsĕsarĭ*, and Gothic *kaisar* < Latin *Caesar* (see CAESAR)] —**tsardom** *n*

tsarevitch /zaárə vich/, **czarevitch** *n* the son of a Russian emperor, especially the eldest son [Early 18C. < Russian *tsarevich* < *tsar'* (see TSAR)]

tsarevna /zaa révnə/, **czarevna** *n* 1. the wife of a tsarevitch 2. the daughter of a tsar [Late 19C. < Russian < *tsar'* (see TSAR)]

tsarina /zaa reénə/, **czarina**, **tsaritsa** /-reétsə/, **czaritza** *n* 1. an empress of Russia, before 1917 2. the wife or widow of a tsar [Early 18C. < Italian or Spanish *zarina*, feminine of *zar* < Russian *tsar'* (see TSAR)]

tsarism /zaár izəm/, **czarism**, **tzarism** *n* 1. government by an emperor who has absolute power 2. absolute rule of any kind, especially the cruel abuse of absolute power by a despot —**tsarist** *adj*, *n*

tsaritsa *n* HIST same as **tsarina**

Tsavo National Park /tsaávō-/ national park and game reserve in Kenya, established in 1948. Area: 20,700 sq. km/7,990 sq. mi.

TSE *n* a disease of a group that causes spongy degeneration of the brain and can be transmitted from one species to another, e.g. BSE. Full form **transmissible spongiform encephalopathy**

Tselinograd /tsə línnə grad/ former name for **Astana** (1960–91)

tsessebe /tse sáybi/ *n S Africa* ZOOL same as **sassaby** [Mid-19C. < Setswana *tsessébi*]

Left page

Tunis, Gulf of

...ong goòssik/ *n* a group of Altaic languages ...northern parts of the People's Republic... and Asia of the former Soviet Union. ...eakers: 50,000. —**Tungusic** *adj*

...onik/ *n* **1. LOOSE GARMENT** a loose wide-necked ...that extends to the hip or knee and is ...worn with a belt or gathered at the waist ...ENT WORN IN PAST a knee-length garment worn ...es, a round neck, and a loose body worn by ...ng the Middle Ages **3. CLOTHING, MIL POLICE OR** ...ARY JACKET a close-fitting high-collared jacket ...rn as part of a police or military uniform **4.** ...ORTS DRESS a short belted dress worn by women ...hen playing some sports **5.** ANZ, N Am ANAT same ...s **tunica 6. BOT PAPERY COVERING ON BULB** a dry, often ...brown and papery covering around a bulb or corm ...such as of an onion **7. RELIG** same as **tunicle** [Pre-12C. Directly or via French *tunique* < Latin *tunica*]

tunica /tyòonika/ (*plural* **-cae** /-see/) *n* UK a layer of tissue that covers or lines a body part or organ, especially tubular parts such as the blood vessels. [Late 17C. < Latin, 'tunic']

tunicate /tyòonikat/ *n* **MARINE BIOL SEA ANIMAL** a sac-shaped sea chordate animal that has a tough leathery or rubbery outer coat, e.g. a sea squirt or ascidian. Subphylum: Urochordata. ■ *adj* **1. MARINE BIOL RELATING TO TUNICATES** relating to or classified as a tunicate **2.** also **tunicated** /tyòoni kaytəd/ BOT WITH DRY PAPERY COVERING describes a bulb or corm that has a dry, often brown and papery covering **3.** also **tunicated** ANAT WITH COVERING OF TISSUE describes an organ or body part that is covered or lined with a layer of tissue [Mid-18C. < Latin *tunicatus* 'covered with a tunic']

tunicle /tyòonik'l/ *n* in Christian worship, a short vestment worn over the alb by a subdeacon at a Mass, or under the dalmatic by a bishop or cardinal at other ceremonies [14C. Directly or via Old French < Latin *tunicula* 'small tunic' < *tunica* 'tunic']

tuning /tyòoning/ *n* **1. ADJUSTMENT OF INSTRUMENT** adjustments made to a musical instrument to make it produce the required pitches **2. SET OF PITCHES** the standard range of pitches to which a musical instrument is tuned **3. MUSICAL INTONATION** the degree to which musical instruments or the voices of a choir are adjusted to a norm

tuning fork *n* an instrument with a stem and two prongs that produces a constant pitch when struck, used to tune musical instruments and in acoustics

tuning fork

Tunis /tyòoniss/ capital of Tunisia. Population: 1,897,000 (2000). near the Gulf of Tunis.

Tunis, Gulf of *n* arm of the Mediterranean Sea in northeastern Tunisia

(far-left column, fragments)
...ester of tungstic acid.
...lustrous grey metallic ...melting point. Source: ...high-temperature alloys, ...cutting tools. Symbol **W**. ...8C. < Swedish, 'heavy stone']
...very hard, grey crystalline ...ng tungsten and carbon to- ...re of dies, cutting and abra- ...hine parts.
...andescent electric lamp with ...ngsten ...hard heat-resistant steel con- ...and 20% tungsten, used in tools ...re engineering equipment
...dj relating to or containing tung- ...ith a valency of six ...weak acid of tungsten. Use: manu- ...es, plastics. Formula: H_2WO_4. ...Source: tungsten ores.
...sti/ *n* a rare yellow-green tungsten
...dj relating to or containing ...gstass/ adj with a valency of two
...ng-/ *n* a tree whose large round fruit ...ard seeds that yield tung oil. Native to: ...nus: *Aleurites*. [See TUNG OIL]

Map: SICILY · Bizerte · **Tunis** · Sousse · Mediterranean Sea · Sfax · Gabès · **TUNISIA** · ALGERIA · LIBYA — Tunisia

Main page

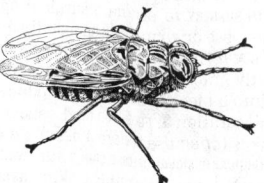
tsetse fly

tsetse fly /tétsi-, tsétsi-/, **tzetze fly** *n* a two-winged biting fly that feeds on the blood of humans and animals and is responsible for transmitting several diseases, including sleeping sickness. Native to: central Africa. Genus: *Glossina*. [Mid-19C. Via Afrikaans < Setswana]

TSH *abbr* BIOCHEM thyroid-stimulating hormone

T-shirt *n* **1.** a collarless usually short-sleeved top without fastenings usually made of cotton and worn for leisure and sports. T-shirts are often printed with designs and slogans. **2.** N Am a man's short-sleeved vest [Early 20C. < its T-shape when spread out]

Tshombe /chómbi/, **Moise** (1919–69) prime minister of the Democratic Republic of the Congo (1964–65). He was president of the secessionist state of Katanga (1960–63), was forced into exile when the secession was crushed, and was recalled to the premiership the following year. Full name **Tshombe, Moise Kapenda**

tshwala /chwaàlà/ *n* S Africa a thick home-brewed beer made from sorghum millet, maize, or other grain that is a traditional drink in South Africa [< Zulu *utshwala*]

tsimmes *n* FOOD another spelling of **tzimmes**

Tsimshian /chímshi ən/ (*plural same* or **-ans**) *n* **1.** a member of a Native North American people who live in coastal southeastern Alaska and British Columbia **2.** the language of the Tsimshian people. Native speakers: 1,500. [Mid-19C. < Tsimshian *čamsián* 'inside the Skeena River'] —**Tsimshian** *adj*

tsitses *npl* JUDAISM another spelling of **tzitzith**

tsk tsk /tisk tísk/ *interj* used in writing to represent a sucking or clicking sound made to express disappointment, disgust, or sympathy [Mid-20C. An imitation of the sound] —**tsk-tsk** *vti*

Tsonga /tsóng gə/ (*plural same* or **-gas**) *n* **1.** a member of a people who live in southern Africa, mainly in Mozambique, Swaziland, and South Africa **2.** the Bantu language of the Tsonga people. Native speakers: 4 million. [Early 20C. < Bantu] —**Tsonga** *adj*

tsotsi /tsótsi/ *n* (*plural* **-sis**) S Africa a young urban criminal, especially one who is a member of a gang (*informal*) [Mid-20C. Origin ?]

Tsotsitaal /tsótsi taal/ *n* S Africa an urban South African speech form originating in township slang, based on Afrikaans and African languages and used among men and boys [*Taal* via Afrikaans < Dutch *taal* 'language']

tsp. *abbr* MEASURE teaspoon

T-square (*plural* **T-squares**) *n* a drawing-board ruler consisting of a rectangular handle with a straight-sided wooden or plastic blade attached perpendicular to it, to form a T shape. The handle sits against the edge of the board.

TSS *abbr* MED toxic shock syndrome

T-strap *n* a style of shoe, usually worn by women or children, with a T-shaped strap cut from the upper part of the shoe

tsunami /tsoo naàmi/ (*plural* **-mis**) *n* a large destructive ocean wave caused by an underwater earthquake or another movement of the Earth's surface [Late 19C. < Japanese, 'harbour wave'] —**tsunamic** *adj*

tsuris /tsoórriss/, **tzuris** *n* problems or difficulties (*informal; takes a singular verb*) [Early 20C. Via Yiddish *tsores* 'troubles' < Hebrew *şārāh* 'trouble']

Tsushima /tsoo sheémə/ island group in the Korea Strait, southwestern Japan. Population: 48,875 (1985). Area: 700 sq. km/270 sq. mi.

tsutsugamushi disease /tsoòtsəgə moòshi-/ *n* MED same as **scrub typhus** [Early 20C. < Japanese, 'disease tick']

Tsvetaeva /tsvi taàyə və/, **Marina** (1892–1941) Russian poet. Many of her poems explore issues of female sexuality and were written while she was living in exile from 1922. She returned to the Soviet Union in 1938 but committed suicide after her husband was executed and her daughter arrested. Full name **Tsvetaeva, Marina Ivanovna**

> 'I won't be seduced by the thought of / my native language, its milky call. / How can it matter in what tongue I / am misunderstood by whoever I meet?'
> [Marina Tsvetaeva, 'Homesickness'; 1934]

Tswana /tswaànə/ (*plural same* or **-nas**) *n* **1.** a member of a people living in southern Africa, mainly in Botswana, where they form the largest ethnic group **2. LANG** same as **Setswana** [Mid-20C. < Bantu] —**Tswana** *adj*

tt *abbr* ONLINE Trinidad and Tobago (*used in Internet addresses*) See table at **domain name**

TT[1] *abbr* **1.** teetotal **2.** BANKING telegraphic transfer **3.** AGRIC tuberculin-tested

TT[2] *n* a series of motorcycle races held every year in the Isle of Man. Full form **Tourist Trophy**

t-test *n* a test of whether a sample of observations comes from a larger sample with a standard distribution of statistical properties

TTL[1] *n* a method of constructing electronic logic circuits. Full form **transistor transistor logic**

TTL[2] *abbr* PHOTOGRAPHY through-the-lens

TTL4N *abbr* ONLINE that's the lot for now (*used in e-mails*)

TU *abbr* POL trade union

Tu. *abbr* CALENDAR Tuesday

tuan /toò aan/ *n* in Malay-speaking countries, a respectful form of address for a man [Early 18C. < Malay]

Tuareg /twaà reg/ (*plural same* or **-regs**) *n* a member of a nomadic people who live in northwestern Africa, mainly in the Sahara and Sahel regions [Early 19C. < Berber] —**Tuareg** *adj*

tuart /toò ərt/ *n* a eucalyptus grown for its very pale durable wood. Native to: Australia. Latin name: *Eucalyptus gomphocephala*. [Mid-19C. < Aboriginal]

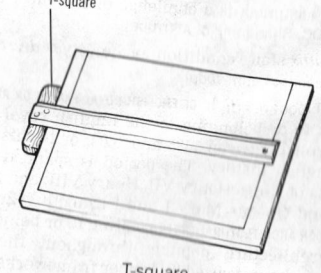
T-square

tuatara /toò ə taàrə/ *n* a large spiny greenish-grey reptile resembling an iguana. Native to: islands off New Zealand. Latin name: *Sphenodon punctatum*. [Late 19C. < Maori, 'with spines on its back']

tub /tub/ *n* **1. LOW OPEN CONTAINER** a low, open, often round container of any size that is used for purposes such as storage and washing **2. ROUND CONTAINER FOR LIQUIDS** a small, often round, plastic or cardboard container for liquid, semiliquid, or soft substances such as ice cream or margarine **3. AMOUNT HELD BY TUB** the contents of a tub **4. HOUSEHOLD** same as **bath** (sense 1) (*informal*) **5. POOR QUALITY BOAT** a slow unreliable boat (*informal*) **6. MIN EXTRACT MINE VEHICLE** an open-top vehicle on rails used to transport coal and other excavated minerals in a mine ■ *v* (**tubs, tubbing, tubbed**) **1.** *vt* STORE SOMETHING IN TUB to store or package something in a tub **2.** *vti* BATHE to wash, or wash something or yourself, in a bath (*informal*) [14C. < Middle Low German or Middle Dutch]

tuba /tyòobə/ *n* a low-pitched brass musical instrument held vertically with the bell pointing upwards and the mouthpiece set horizontally. It has three to five valves. [Mid-19C. Via French or Italian < Latin, 'large war trumpet']

tubal /tyòob'l/ *adj* **1.** relating to or in the form of a tube or tubes **2.** relating to or developing in a fallopian tube

tubal ligation *n* a sterilization technique in which a woman's fallopian tubes are tied to prevent ova entering the uterus. It is usually performed using endoscopic surgery.

tubate /tyòo bayt/ *adj* tubular in shape

tubby /túbbi/ (**-bier, -biest**) *adj* **1. OVERWEIGHT** carrying more body weight than is desirable or advisable (*informal; sometimes considered offensive*) **2. TUB-SHAPED** like a tub in shape **3. MUSIC LACKING RESONANCE** describes a violin or other string instrument that lacks resonance —**tubbiness** *n*

tube /tyoob/ *n* **1. CYLINDER FOR TRANSPORTING OR STORING LIQUIDS** a long hollow cylinder used to transport or store liquids **2. COLLAPSIBLE CONTAINER WITH CAP** a collapsible, generally cylindrical container sealed at one end and closed with a cap at the other. It is used for packaging semiliquid substances such as toothpaste. **3. ANAT CYLINDRICAL BODY ORGAN** a hollow cylindrical organ that transports liquids or gases around the body **4. ANAT** same as **fallopian tube** (*informal; usually used in the plural*) **5. RAIL UNDERGROUND RAILWAY** the underground railway system in London (*informal*) **6. RAIL UNDERGROUND TRAIN** a train on an underground railway system (*informal*) **7. CYCLING** same as **inner tube 8. ELECTRONICS** same as **cathode ray tube 9.** N Am MEDIA same as **television** (sense 1) **10.** Aus CAN OF BEER a can of beer (*informal*) **11.** Scotland OFFENSIVE TERM an offensive term for somebody regarded as foolish or unintelligent **12. BOT CHANNEL IN PLANT** a narrow enclosed channel in a plant, e.g. the organ in a germinating pollen grain that conveys the male gametes to the ovule **13. BOT FLOWER PART** a roughly cylindrical fusion of the petals of a flower such as a daffodil **14. ELECTRONICS** same as **valve** (sense 3) (*informal*) **15. MUSIC BODY OF WIND INSTRUMENT** the hollow cylinder that forms the main body of a wind instrument, through which the player's breath passes **16. SURFING PART OF WAVE** the tunnel formed when a large rolling wave prepares to break ■ *vt* (**tubes, tubing, tubed**) **1. FIT SOMETHING WITH TUBE** to supply or fit something with a tube **2. ENCLOSE SOMETHING IN TUBE** to put something in a tube [Early 17C. Via French < Latin *tubus*]

tubectomy /tyoo béktəmi/ (*plural* **-mies**) *n* the surgical removal of a fallopian tube (*informal*)

tube foot *n* an outgrowth of the body wall of sea invertebrates of the sea urchin family (**echinoderms**), used for feeding, moving around, or performing other functions depending on the species

tubeless tyre /tyòobləss-/ *n* a pneumatic tyre that does not require an inner tube because the casing and wheel rim form an airtight seal

tubenose /tyòob nòz/ *n* **1.** a seabird with large tubular nostrils on the upper beak, e.g. an albatross or petrel. Order: Procellariiformes. **2.** a small sea fish related to the stickleback that has its ribs fused to

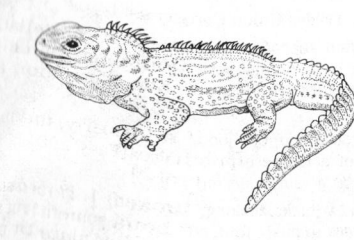
tuatara

lateral bony plates. Native to: eastern Pacific. Latin name: *Aulorhynchus flavidum*. —**tubenose** *adj*

tube pan *n N Am* a round cooking pan with a hollow cylinder or cone in the middle, used for baking or moulding foods in a ring shape

tuber /tyoóbər/ *n* 1. a fleshy swollen part of a root such as a dahlia root or of an underground stem such as a potato that stores food over winter and produces new growth in spring. A stem tuber has buds, popularly called eyes, unlike a root tuber. 2. a small raised area or swelling on the body [Mid-17C. < Latin, 'swelling']

tubercle /tyoóbərk'l/ *n* 1. a small raised area on a plant or animal part 2. a small rounded swelling on the skin or on a mucous membrane, caused by a disease, especially a nodule in the lungs that is the characteristic symptom of tuberculosis [Late 16C. < Latin *tuberculum* 'small swelling' < *tuber* 'swelling']

tubercle bacillus *n* a rod-shaped bacterium that causes tuberculosis. Latin name: *Mycobacterium tuberculosis*.

tubercular /tyoó búrkyoólər/ *adj* 1. OF TUBERCULOSIS relating to, characteristic of, or affected by tuberculosis 2. CAUSED BY TUBERCLE BACILLUS caused by the tubercle bacillus ○ *tubercular meningitis* 3. NODULE-SHAPED taking the form of a small rounded swelling or nodule [Late 18C. < Latin *tuberculum* (see TUBERCLE)]

tuberculate /tyoó búrkyoólət/ *adj* covered with small rounded swellings or nodules (**tubercles**) [Late 18C. < Latin *tuberculum* (see TUBERCLE)] —**tuberculately** *adv*—**tuberculation** /tyoó búrkyoó láysh'n/ *n*

tuberculin /tyoó búrkyoólin/ *n* a sterile liquid obtained from cultures of the tubercle bacillus and used in a scratch test to establish whether somebody has or has had tuberculosis [Late 19C. < Latin *tuberculum* (see TUBERCLE)]

tuberculin-tested *adj* describes a dairy herd that has been certified as not having tuberculosis or to describe milk from such a herd

tuberculosis /tyoó búrkyoó lóssiss/ *n* an infectious disease that causes small rounded swellings (**tubercles**) to form on mucous membranes, especially a disease (**pulmonary tuberculosis**) that affects the lungs [Mid-19C. < Latin *tuberculum* (see TUBERCLE)] —**tuberculoid** /tyoó búrkyoó loyd/ *adj*

tuberculous /tyoó búrkyoóləss/ *adj* MED same as **tubercular**

tuberose

tuberose[1] /tyoób róz, tyoóbə rōz/ *n* a perennial agave with blade-shaped leaves. Flowers: fragrant, white, in spikes. Native to: Mexico. Latin name: *Polianthes tuberosa*. [Mid-17C. < modern Latin *tuberosa* < Latin *tuberosus* < *tuber* 'swelling']

tuberose[2] /tyoóbə róss/ *adj* BOT, MED same as **tuberous**

tuberosity /tyoóbə róssəti/ (*plural* -**ties**) *n* a rounded protuberance, especially at a point on a bone where muscles or ligaments are attached

tuberous /tyoóbərəss/ *adj* 1. relating to tubers or in the form of tubers 2. producing or covered with knobbly growths [Mid-17C. < Latin *tuberosus* (see TUBEROSE[1])]

tube top *n N Am* a short strapless stretchy top for women

tube worm *n* a worm that builds itself a tube-shaped shelter that sticks out of the soil

tubifex /tyoóbi feks/ *n* a thin reddish freshwater worm that builds a tube-shaped shelter in the sand of

riverbeds and is used as food for aquarium fish. Genus: *Tubifex*. [Mid-20C. < modern Latin < Latin *tubus* 'tube' + *-fex* 'maker']

tubing /tyoóbing/ *n* 1. a system or series of tubes 2. the hollow cylindrical material that tubes are made of 3. HANDICRAFT same as **piping** *n* (sense 2)

Tübingen /toóbingən/ university city in Baden-Württemberg State, southwestern Germany. Population: 82,260 (1997).

Harriet Tubman

Tubman, Harriet (1830–1913) US abolitionist. Escaping from slavery in about 1849, she helped other slaves escape to freedom along the clandestine route known as the Underground Railroad.

'Dere's *two* things I've got a *right* to, and dese are, Death or Liberty—one or tother I mean to have.'
[Harriet Tubman. Quoted in *Scenes in the Life of Harriet Tubman*, Sarah Bradford; 1869]

Tubman, William (1895–1971) president of Liberia (1943–71). During his presidency, he introduced policies of national unification, social reform, and economic development. Full name **Tubman, William Vacanarat Shadrach**

tubocurarine /tyoóbō kyoó raárin/ *n* 1. a toxic alkaloid that is the active constituent of curare. Use: muscle relaxant. 2. the hydrochloride salt of tubocurarine [Late 19C. < TUBE (because shipped in bamboo tubes) + CURARE]

tuboplasty /tyoóbō plasti/ (*plural* -**ties**) *n* the surgical repair of one or both fallopian tubes, especially when these have been cut and tied for contraceptive reasons

tub-thump *vi* to speak out in favour of somebody or something in a passionate or aggressive way (*informal*)

tub-thumper *n* a passionate or aggressive public speaker (*informal*) —**tub-thumping** *adj, n*

tubular /tyoóbyoólər/ *adj* 1. shaped like a tube 2. having a tube or tubes [Late 17C. < Latin *tubulus* (see TUBULE)]

tubular bells *npl* a set of tuned metal tubes, usually arranged in a scale and hung from a frame, that are struck with a mallet

tubulate /tyoóbyoólət/ *adj* same as **tubular** [Mid-18C. < Latin *tubulatus* < *tubulus* (see TUBULE)]

tubule /tyoób yool/ *n* a very small tubular part in a plant or animal [Late 17C. < Latin *tubulus* 'small tube' < *tubus* 'tube']

tubulin /tyoóbyoólin/ *n* a globular protein found in microscopic filamentous tubes (**microtubules**) in cells

tubulous /tyoóbyoóləss/ *adj* same as **tubular**

TUC *abbr* Trades Union Congress

Tucana /too kaánə/ *n* a small faint constellation of the southern hemisphere containing much of the smaller Magellanic Cloud. See illustration at constellation

tuchun /too chóon, doo jóon/ *n* formerly, the military leader of a Chinese province [Early 20C. < Chinese *dūjūn* < *dū* 'govern' + *jūn* 'military']

tuck[1] /tuk/ *v* (**tucks, tucking, tucked**) 1. *vt* FOLD SOMETHING INTO POSITION to push, fold, or bend something such as a flap of material into a particular place or position 2. *vti* DRAW SOMETHING TOGETHER to pull or draw some-

thing together, or be pulled or drawn together 3. *vt* HANDICRAFT SEW FOLD to sew a fold into fabric, e.g. to reduce its length or for decoration 4. *vt* SURG TIGHTEN SKIN WITH SURGERY to perform a surgical operation to remove loose or wrinkled skin, usually for cosmetic reasons ■ *n* 1. TUCKED PART a part that is tucked safely or neatly into position 2. HANDICRAFT PLEAT a fold sewn into a piece of fabric, e.g. to reduce its length or for decoration 3. FOOD FOOD food, especially sweets and cakes (*often used before a noun*) ○ *tuck box* 4. SURG SURGICAL REMOVAL OF LOOSE SKIN a surgical operation to remove loose or wrinkled skin, especially for cosmetic reasons 5. SPORTS BODY POSITION a compact body position, adopted in sports such as diving, with the knees drawn up to the chest, the hands round the shins, and the chin held on the chest 6. NAUT PART OF SHIP'S STERN the part of a ship's hull where the side planks or plates join the spar or spars forming the stern [15C. Probably < Middle Dutch *tucken* 'draw up']

tuck away *vt* 1. to put something in a safe or secluded place 2. to eat large quantities of food heartily or hungrily (*informal*)

tuck in *v* 1. *vt* to make somebody, especially a child, comfortable in bed by tucking the bedclothes snugly around the body 2. *also* **tuck into** *vi* to eat hungrily (*informal*)

tuck up *vt* same as **tuck in** (sense 1)

tuck[2] /tuk/ *n* a beating of a drum or a blast on a trumpet as a flourish [15C. Via Old French *toquer* 'to strike' < assumed Vulgar Latin *toccare*]

tuckahoe /túkəhō/ *n* 1. a plant of the arum family with arrow-shaped leaves and edible roots. Use: formerly, as food by Native North Americans. 2. a large edible fungus that grows underground on the roots of trees. Native to: southern United States. Latin name: *Poria cocos*. [Early 17C. < Virginia Algonquian *tockawhoughe*]

tucker[1] /túkər/ *n* 1. HANDICRAFT an attachment for a sewing machine, used to sew tucks 2. CLOTHING a detachable lace or linen cover for the neck and chest, formerly worn by women under a low-cut dress 3. ANZ same as **food** (*informal*; *often used before a noun*) [13C. < TUCK[1]]

tucker[2] /túkər/ (-**ers**, -**ering**, -**ered**) *vt N Am* to tire a person or animal out completely (*informal*) [Mid-19C. Origin ?]

tucker out *vt* same as **tucker**[2]

Tucker /túkər/, **Albert** (1914–99) Australian painter. He was a pioneer of expressionism and surrealism in Australia.

tucket /túkit/ *n* a fanfare played on a trumpet (*archaic*) [Late 16C. < TUCK[2]]

tuck-in *n* a large and delicious meal (*dated informal*)

tuck-point *vt* to finish a wall by sealing the facing joints between the bricks or stones with a thin line of putty or very fine lime-based mortar

tuck shop *n* a small shop, especially one in or near a school, selling sweets, drinks, and snacks

tucotuco /tookō tookō/ (*plural* -**cos**) *n* a rodent that digs complex systems of burrows. Native to: South America. Latin name: *Ctenomys talarum*. [Mid-19C. An imitation of its call]

Tucson /too son/ city in southern Arizona, on the Santa Cruz River. Population: 503,151 (2002 estimate).

Tucumán /tookoo man, tookoo mán/ province in northern Argentina. Its capital is San Miguel de Tucumán. Population: 1,265,322 (1999). Area: 22,524 sq. km/8,697 sq. mi.

'tude /tood/ *n* an arrogant or assertive manner or stance assumed as a challenge or for effect (*slang*) [Late 20C. Shortening of ATTITUDE]

-tude *suffix* state, condition, or quality ○ *decrepitude* [Via French < Latin *-tudo*]

Tudor /tyoódər/ *adj* 1. OF ENGLISH ROYAL FAMILY OR REIGN relating to or belonging to the English royal family that ruled between 1485 and 1603, or to this period of English history. The period is spanned by the reigns of Kings Henry VII, Henry VIII, and Edward VI, and Queens Mary I and Elizabeth I. 2. RELATING TO TUDOR ARCHITECTURAL STYLE relating to or being a style of architecture popular throughout the Tudor period characterized by timber frameworks, visible

---

from the outside, filled in with plaster ... MEMBER OF TUDOR FAMILY a member of the ... family [Mid-18C. Named after the Tudor ... (d.1461), father of Henry VII]

Tue., Tues. *abbr* CALENDAR Tuesday

Tuesday /tyóoz day, -di/ *n* the second day ... traditional working week, coming after ... and before Wednesday [Old English *Tiwesdæg* ... < TIW, Germanic god of war (translation of Latin ... 'Mars' day')]

Tuesdays /tyóoz dayz, -diz/ *adv* every Tuesday

tufa /tyóofə/ *n* a porous rock formed from deposits of calcium carbonate and found near mineral springs. Use: as medium on which to grow alpine plants ... [Late 18C. Via obsolete Italian < late Latin *tofus* 'porous rock'] —**tufaceous** /tyoo fáyshəss/ *adj*

tuff /tuf/ *n* a rock made up of very small volcanic fragments compacted together [Mid-16C. Via French ... < Latin *tofus*] —**tuffaceous** /tu fáyshəss/ *adj*

tuffet /túffit/ *n* 1. a small mound or clump of grass 2. a low seat or stool [Mid-16C. Via French < TUFT]

tuft /tuft/ *n* 1. BUNCH OF FIBRES OR GRASS a small bunch of hair, grass, feathers, or fibres held or growing together at the base 2. CLUMP OF PLANTS a bunch or clump of plants or trees 3. BUNCH OF THREADS a small clump UPHOLSTERY a group of threads drawn through fabric and tied to secure it to material beneath ■ *v* (**tufts, tufting, tufted**) 1. *vti* FORM INTO TUFTS to grow in tufts, or form something into tufts 2. *vt* HANDICRAFT SEW TUFTS IN SOMETHING to sew tufts in fabric, either for decoration or to secure one surface to another [14C. Alteration of Old French *toffe*] —**tufted** *adj*—**tufty** *adj*

Tu Fu /doó foó/ (712–770) Chinese poet. He is often considered to be the greatest of all Chinese poets.

tug /tug/ *v* (**tugs, tugging, tugged**) 1. *vti* PULL SHARPLY AT SOMEBODY OR SOMETHING to pull at or drag somebody or something with a sharp forceful movement 2. *vt* TOW SHIP to tow a ship with a tugboat 3. *vi* MAKE LABORIOUS EFFORT to work hard or struggle to do something ■ *n* 1. SHARP PULL a sharp forceful pull ○ *gave it a tug* 2. STRUGGLE OR CONTEST a struggle or strenuous contest between opposing forces or people 3. UK, Can BOAT USED FOR TOWING SHIPS a small powerful boat used to tow ships and barges. ANZ, US term **tugboat** 4. VEHICLE THAT PULLS ANOTHER a land, sea, air, or space vehicle that is used to pull another 5. CHAIN OR STRAP FOR PULLING a chain, rope, or strap that is used for pulling or hauling something [13C. Ultimately < Indo-European 'pull'] —**tugger** *n*

tugboat /túg bōt/ *n* ANZ, US same as **tug** *n* (sense 3)

Tugela /too gáylə/ river in eastern South Africa, flowing into the Indian Ocean. Length: 502 km/312 mi.

Tugela Falls /too gáylə-/ series of waterfalls on the River Tugela, KwaZulu-Natal Province, South Africa. Height: 948 m/3,110 ft.

tug of love *n* a struggle between divorced parents over custody of a child (*informal*)

tug of war *n* 1. an athletic contest in which two teams pull at opposite ends of a rope, each team being the one who drags the other a set distance 2. a struggle between two evenly matched people, groups, or influences

tugrik /tóogreek/ (*plural* same or -**griks**) *n* the main unit of Mongolian currency. See table at **currency**. [Mid-20C. < Mongolian *dughurik* 'round thing']

tui /too i/ (*plural* -**is**) *n* a bird with iridescent dark blue-green feathers, white tufts at the throat, and white spots on the wings. Native to: New Zealand. Latin name: *Prosthemadera novaeseelandiae*. [Mid-19C. < Maori]

Tuileries Gardens /tweelări-/ formal gardens beside the River Seine, central Paris, formerly belonging to a royal palace. Area: 0.25 sq. km/0.1 sq. mi.

tuition /tyoo ísh'n/ *n* 1. instruction, especially when given individually or in a small group 2. a sum charged for instruction at a school or university [15C. Via French < Latin *tuition-* 'support' < *tueri* 'protect'] —**tuitional** *adj*

tulip /tyoó-/ ... from ... large, ... oured. ... French ... shape of ...

tulip tree /tyoó-/ ... nolia family ... shaped flowers ... America, Ch... *lipifera* or Li...

tulipwood /tyoó-/ ... tulip tree, or th... in making woo...

tulle /tyool/ ... or rayon fabric ... dresses, ve...

Tulsa /túl... Ark...

tundish /tún... into which molt... as **tunnel** *n* (sense 1)

tundra /túndrə/ *n* a ... plain between the ice cap and ... North America, Europe, and Asia in ... manently frozen subsoil [Late 18C. Via Russian ... *tundar*]

tune /tyoon/ *n* 1. SIMPLE MELODY a series of musical ... that make a simple melody 2. SONG a melodious song ... or short piece of music ■ *v* (**tunes, tuning, tuned**) 1. *vt* ADJUST INSTRUMENT FOR PITCH to adjust a musical ...

Tuileries Gardens ...

tumbledown /túmb'l... and falling dow...

tumble drier *n* HOU... dryer

> **LANGUAGE HERITAGE** *Tupi-Guarani* Much of English is made up of words from other languages, and the Tupi-Guarani group of South American languages is a small but significant contributor in this respect. Names of unfamiliar animals and birds reached English relatively soon after Europeans discovered the New World (usually via Portuguese, Spanish, or sometimes French): the *agouti* and the *toucan* in the mid-16th century, the *capybara*, *eyra*, *jaguar*, and *tanager* in the early 17th, followed later by, for example, *cougar*, *jabiru*, *piranha*, and *tapir*. Foodstuffs were adopted: *manioc* (mid-16th century), *cashew* (late 16th), *cayenne pepper*, and *tapioca*, for example. Valuable products and their sources became known and used, for instance *ipecacuanha* (a plant from whose dried roots an emetic is made, early 17th century), *jacaranda* (a tree with a valuable wood), and *jaborandi* (a bush whose dried leaves yield the drug pilocarpine). Tupi also gave us (via Portuguese) the sound of the *maraca* (early 17th century).

Tunisia /tyoo nízzi ə/ country in North Africa, bordered by the Mediterranean Sea, Libya, and Algeria. Language: Arabic. Currency: Tunisian dinar. Capital: Tunis. Population: 9,924,742 (2003). Area: 164,418 sq. km/63,482 sq. mi. Official name **Republic of Tunisia**. See map on previous page — **Tunisian** *n*, *adj*

tunnage *n* MEASURE, SHIPPING another spelling of **tonnage**

tunnel /túnn'l/ *n* **1.** PASSAGEWAY UNDER OBSTRUCTION a long passage that allows pedestrians or vehicles to proceed under or through an obstruction such as a river, mountain, or congested area **2.** ANIMAL'S UNDERGROUND PASSAGE an underground passage or system of passages dug by a burrowing animal **3.** PART OF MINE a corridor or working area in a mine **4.** PASSAGE a passage, channel, or route through or under something ■ *v* (-nels, -nelling, -nelled) **1.** *vti* MAKE TUNNEL to make, burrow, or excavate a tunnel under or through something **2.** *vt* MAKE SOMETHING LIKE TUNNEL to produce or dig something that resembles or is shaped like a tunnel [15C. < Old French *tonel* 'small barrel' < medieval Latin *tunna* 'cask'] —**tunneller** *n*

tunnel disease *n* MED same as **ancylostomiasis** [Because caused by tunnel worms]

tunnel effect *n* a quantum mechanical effect in which elementary particles can pass through barriers that would be impossible under the laws of classical mechanics by apparently disappearing and reappearing on the other side, as through a tunnel

tunnelling /túnn'ling/ *n* **1.** the digging, excavation, or construction of a tunnel **2.** in quantum mechanics, the phenomenon of elementary particles passing through barriers by apparently disappearing and reappearing on the other side, as through a tunnel

tunnel vault *n* ARCHIT same as **barrel vault**

tunnel vision *n* **1.** a condition in which peripheral vision is lost or severely limited, so that only objects directly in line with the eyes can be seen **2.** a very limited viewpoint or conception of things

tunny /túnni/ (*plural same* or *-nies*) *n* FISH same as **tuna**[1] (sense 1) [Mid-16C. Via French *thon* and Latin *thunnus* < Greek *thunnos*]

tup /tup/ *n* **1.** MECH ENG HEAD OF HAMMER the head of a power hammer or a mechanism resembling a hammer **2.** N England, Scotland RAM a male sheep used for breeding ■ *vt* (tups, tupping, tupped) AGRIC MATE WITH EWE to copulate with a ewe [14C. Origin ?]

tupek /toópək/, **tupik** /-pik/ *n* a tent made of animal skins, used in the summer by the Inuit in the Arctic [Mid-19C. < Inuit *tupiq*]

tupelo /toópəlō/ (*plural -los*) *n* **1.** the soft pale wood of a deciduous tree **2.** a deciduous tree that grows in swamps and on river banks and yields tupelo. Native to: North America, Asia. Genus: *Nyssa*. [Mid-18C. < Creek '*topilwa* 'swamp tree']

Tupi /toó pee/ (*plural same* or *-pis*) *n* **1.** a member of a group of Native South American peoples who live in the Amazon valley **2.** the Tupi-Guarani language of the Tupi people. Native speakers: 3,000. [Mid-19C. < Tupi, 'comrade'] —**Tupi** *adj*

Tupian /toópi ən/ *n* **1.** LANG same as **Tupi** (sense 2) **2.** a family of South American languages that includes Tupi-Guarani —**Tupian** *adj*

Tupi-Guarani *n* a Native South American language family whose principal members are Tupi and Guarani. It is itself a branch of the Andean-Equatorial family of languages. —**Tupi-Guarani** *adj*

tupik *n* CULTL ANTHROP another spelling of **tupek**

tuppence, etc. MONEY same as **twopence, etc.**

tupuna /toó poónə/ (*plural same*), **tipuna** /ti-/ *n* NZ an ancestor or grandparent [< Maori]

tuque /took/ *n* Can a cylindrical stocking cap of double-thickness wool or synthetic yarn [Late 19C. Via Canadian French < French *toque* 'toque']

tu quoque /toó kwō kway/ *interj* used when accused of a crime to accuse the accuser of the same crime [Late 17C. < Latin, 'you too']

Tur. *abbr* **1.** Turkey **2.** Turkish

turaco *n* BIRDS another spelling of **touraco**

Turanian /tyoó ráyni ən/ *n* **1.** URAL-ALTAIC SPEAKER a member of any of the peoples who speak a Ural-Altaic language **2.** OLD LANGUAGE GROUPING a formerly accepted grouping of Asian languages roughly corresponding to the Altaic family with others added (*dated*) ■ *adj* RELATING TO ANCIENT TURKESTAN relating to ancient Turkestan, or to its people or culture [Late 18C. < Persian *Turān* 'Turkestan']

turban /túrbən/ *n* **1.** a man's headdress that consists of a long piece of fabric wrapped around the head or around a small cap, completely covering the hair, worn especially by some Sikhs and Muslims **2.** a woman's hat that is similar in shape to a man's turban [Mid-16C. Via obsolete French *turbant*, Italian *turbante* < Turkish *tülbend* < Persian *dulband*] —**turbaned** *adj*

turbary /túrbəri/ *n* an area of land where turf or peat may be cut or dug [14C. < Anglo-Norman *turberie* < French *tourbe* 'turf' < Germanic]

turbellarian /túrbi láiri ən/ *n* a free-living flatworm that inhabits wet soil, freshwater, and sea environments, e.g. a planarian. Class: Turbellaria. [Late 19C. < modern Latin *Turbellaria* < Latin *turbella* 'small commotion'] —**turbellarian** *adj*

turbid /túrbid/ *adj* **1.** MUDDY opaque and muddy as when particles and sediment are stirred up **2.** FOGGY dense and cloudy or dark **3.** CONFUSED confused and muddled ○ *turbid thought processes* [Early 17C. < Latin *turbidus* 'troubled' < *turba* 'disorder'] —**turbidity** /tur bíddəti/ *n* —**turbidly** *adv* —**turbidness** *n*

USAGE turbid or **turgid**? The two words are unrelated in form but can both describe water in their literal meanings (either 'opaque and muddy' in the case of *turbid* or 'swollen and overflowing' in the case of *turgid*), and can both describe literary styles in their figurative meanings. *Turgid* is the more common and means 'pompous and overcomplicated' (as in *turgid prose*), whereas *turbid* means 'confused and muddled'.

turbidimeter /túrbi dímmitər/ *n* an instrument that determines the amount of material in suspension in a liquid or gas by measuring the decrease in light transmittance through the fluid —**turbidimetric** /túrbidi méttrik/ *adj* —**turbidimetrically** *adv* —**turbidimetry** *n*

turbidite /túrbi dīt/ *n* a sedimentary deposit laid down by a turbidity current, e.g. on the ocean floor at the bottom of the continental shelf

turbidity current *n* a rapidly moving current containing dispersed sediments, sometimes started off by seismic shocks or slumping

turbinate /túrbinət, -nayt/, **turbinal** /-n'l/ *adj* **1.** SPIRAL IN SHAPE having a shape like a spiral or scroll **2.** ANAT SHAPED LIKE SCROLL describes any of the three scroll-shaped bones found on the walls of the nasal passages of mammals **3.** ZOOL SHAPED LIKE INVERTED CONE describes a mollusc shell that spirals and is shaped like an inverted cone ■ *n* **1.** ANAT TURBINATE BONE a turbinate bone in the nasal passage of mammals **2.** ZOOL MOLLUSC SHELL a turbinate mollusc shell [Mid-17C.

< Latin *turbinatus* < Latin *turbin-* 'spiral, spinning top'] — **turbination** /túrbi náysh'n/ *n*

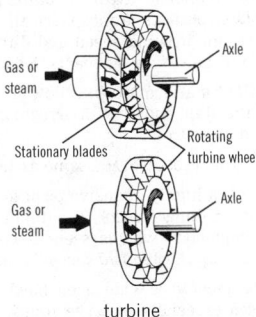

Gas or steam — Axle — Stationary blades — Rotating turbine wheel — Gas or steam — Axle

turbine

turbine /túrb īn, -bin/ *n* a machine in which a moving fluid such as steam acts on the blades of a rotor to produce rotational motion that can be transformed to electrical or mechanical power [Mid-19C. Via French < Latin *turbin-* 'spiral, spinning top']

turbit /túrbit/ *n* a domestic pigeon of a breed with a ruffed neck and breast [Late 17C. Origin ?]

turbo[1] /túrbō/ (*plural -bos*) *n* ENG **1.** same as **turbine 2.** same as **turbocharger**

turbo[2] /túrbō/ (*plural -bos*) *n* a gastropod mollusc that has a whorled spiral shell. Genus: *Turbo*. [Mid-17C. < Latin, 'spiral, spinning top']

turbo- *prefix* **1.** using the principle of a turbine, or driven by a turbine ○ *turbocharger* **2.** turbojet ○ *turboprop* [< TURBINE]

turbocharge /túrbō chaarjə/ (-charges, -charging, -charged) *vt* **1.** to equip an engine with a turbocharger, usually to increase its power **2.** to increase the power, speed, or performance of something (*informal*) ○ *resources to turbocharge your career* —**turbocharged** *adj*

turbocharger /túrbō chaarjər/ *n* a specialized turbine driven by the exhaust gases of an engine that supplies air under pressure to the engine for combustion [Mid-20C. Contraction of TURBOSUPERCHARGER]

turbo-electric *adj* using or relating to an electric generator driven by a turbine

turbofan /túrbō fan/ *n* UK, ANZ, Can **1.** a jet engine in which fans driven by a turbine force air into the exhaust gases, thereby increasing the propelling thrust of the engine **2.** a jet aircraft that has turbofan engines ► US term **fanjet**

turbogenerator /túrbō jénnə raytər/ *n* a machine used to generate electricity in which steam from coal, oil, or gas is used to drive the turbine

turbojet /túrbō jet/ *n* **1.** a jet engine with a gas turbine that uses exhaust gases to provide the propulsive thrust for an aircraft **2.** an aircraft powered by turbojet

turboprop /túrbō prop/ *n* **1.** a turbojet engine that powers a propeller **2.** an aircraft whose propellers are driven by a gas turbine

turboramjet /túrbō rám jet/ *n* **1.** a turbojet engine in which forward motion is achieved by compression of the fuel **2.** an aircraft powered by a turboramjet

turbosupercharger /túrbō soópər chaarjər/ *n* ENG same as **turbocharger**

turbot /túrbət/ (*plural same* or *-bots*) *n* **1.** EUROPEAN FLATFISH a flatfish that is almost circular with bony tubercles on its body and both eyes on the left side. Native to: Europe. Latin name: *Scophthalmus maximus*. **2.** TURBOT AS FOOD the flesh of a turbot as food **3.** FLATFISH a flatfish in the same family as the European turbot, e.g. the spotted turbot of the Pacific. Family: Pleuronectidae. [13C. Via Old French < Old Swedish *törnbut* 'thorn-flatfish'; from the bony tubercles on its back]

turbulence /túrbyoōlənss/, **turbulency** /-lənssi/ *n* **1.** UNREST a state of confusion characterized by unpredictability and uncontrolled change **2.** METEOROL INSTABILITY IN ATMOSPHERE an instability in the atmosphere that disrupts the flow of the wind, causing gusty, unpredictable air currents **3.** PHYS EDDIES eddies or secondary motion within a moving fluid

turbulent /túrbyŏŏlənt/ adj 1. MOVING VIOLENTLY full of violent motion and agitation ○ *turbulent rapids* 2. CHAOTIC AND RESTLESS marked by disturbances, changes, and unrest ○ *a turbulent year in politics* 3. METEOROL ATMOSPHERICALLY UNSTABLE atmospherically unstable, with variations in wind speed and direction [15C. < Latin *turbulentus* < *turba* 'disorder'] —**turbulently** adv

turbulent flow n a form of fluid flow in which particles of the fluid move with irregular local velocities and pressures

Turcoman n, adj PEOPLES, LANG same as **Turkmen**

turd /turd/ n 1. a highly offensive term for a piece of excrement or dung (*taboo*) 2. a highly offensive term for somebody who is seen as contemptible (*taboo insult*) [Old English *tord* < Indo-European]

tureen /tyŏŏ reen/ n a wide deep bowl with a lid that is used especially to serve soups, stews, and casseroles [Mid-18C. Alteration of TERRINE]

turf /turf/ n (*plural* **turfs** or **turves** /turvz/) 1. DENSE LAYER OF GRASS a dense thick even cover of grass and roots in the top layer of soil 2. ARTIFICIAL GRASS artificial grass such as that used on surfaces for playing sport 3. PIECE OF SOIL WITH GRASS a piece of soil with grass growing in it, put down to form lawns and new grassed surfaces 4. PEAT FOR FUEL peat when sold for fuel 5. AREA OF EXPERTISE an area in which somebody feels confident or has authority or expertise (*informal*) 6. TERRITORY a territory or geographical area (*informal*) 7. GANG TERRITORY an area or territory that a gang claims to be its own (*informal*) 8. HORSE-RACING horseracing as a sport or industry 9. HORSE-RACING TRACK a track where horses are raced ■ vt (**turfs, turfing, turfed**) COVER SOMETHING WITH TURF to cover an area with pieces of turf [Old English, < Indo-European] —**turfy** adj

turf out vt to eject somebody from a place or organization (*informal*)

turf accountant n same as **bookmaker** (sense 1)

Ivan Turgenev

Popperfoto

Turgenev /tur gáy nyef/, **Ivan** (1818–83) Russian writer. His best-known works include the play *A Month in the Country* (1850) and the novel *Fathers and Sons* (1862). Full name **Turgenev, Ivan Sergeyevich**. See Cultural note at **father**

'Nature is not a temple, but a workshop,
and man's the workman in it.'
[Ivan Turgenev, *Fathers and Sons*; 1862]

turgescent /tur jéss'nt/ adj swollen or becoming swollen, usually as a result of an accumulation of blood or other fluids [Early 18C. < Latin *turgescent*, present participle of *turgescere* 'begin to swell' < *turgere* 'swell'] —**turgescence** n —**turgescency** n

turgid /túrjid/ adj 1. POMPOUS AND OVERCOMPLICATED pompous, boring, and overcomplicated ○ *a turgid speech* 2. OVERFLOWING swollen and overflowing 3. MED DISTENDED swollen or distended by a build-up of fluid [Early 17C. < Latin *turgidus* < *turgere* 'swell'] —**turgidity** /tur jíddəti/ n —**turgidly** adv

USAGE See **turbid**.

turgor /túrgər/ n the normal rigid state of plant cells, caused by outward pressure of the water content of each cell on its membrane [Late 19C. < late Latin < Latin *turgere* 'swell']

Turin /tyoor rín/ capital of Turin Province, Piedmont Region, northwestern Italy. Population: 865,263 (2001).

Turing /tyŏŏring/, **Alan** (1912–54) British mathematician. He was a major figure in the theoretical development of the computer. During World War II, he worked as a British government cryptographer and helped to break the code of the German Enigma machine. Full name **Turing, Alan Mathison**

Turing machine n a mathematical model of a hypothetical computer that can modify its instructions and read from, write on, or erase a potentially infinite tape. It was instrumental in the evolution of computer theory.

Turing test n a test in artificial intelligence in which a human interrogator attempts to determine whether an unseen entity is human or a computer

turion /tyoʻori ən/ n 1. a bud that breaks off from an water plant and lies submerged and dormant until the following spring, when it produces a new plantlet that floats to the surface 2. a shoot from an underground root or stem, e.g. in asparagus [Early 18C. Via French < Latin *turion*- 'young sprig']

Turk /turk/ n 1. SOMEBODY FROM TURKEY somebody who comes from Turkey 2. MEMBER OF TURKISH ETHNIC GROUP a member of the Turkish-speaking ethnic group in Turkey, or, formerly, in the Ottoman Empire 3. TURKIC SPEAKER a member of a people speaking a Turkic language 4. OFFENSIVE TERM an offensive term for a Muslim (*archaic*) [14C. Via French *Turc*, medieval Latin *Turcus* < Turkish *Türk*]

Turk. abbr 1. Turkey 2. Turkish

Turkana, Lake /tur kaána/ lake in northwestern Kenya, bordering Ethiopia at its northern end. Area: 7,100 sq. km/2,700 sq. mi. Former name **Rudolf, Lake**

Turkestan /túrki stán, -staán/, **Turkistan** mountainous region of central Asia that stretches from the Caspian Sea to the Gobi Desert. It is divided into three sections, Russian or Western Turkestan, which includes Kazakhstan, Kyrgyzstan, and Uzbekistan, Chinese or Eastern Turkestan, made up of the Xinjiang Uygor Autonomous Region of China, and Afghan Turkestan, consisting of the northeastern part of Afghanistan.

turkey

turkey /túrki/ (*plural* **-keys**) n 1. LARGE N AMERICAN BIRD a large bird with a bare wattled head and neck and brownish feathers. Kept for: meat. Native to: North America. Latin name: *Meleagris gallopavo*. 2. TURKEY MEAT the meat of the turkey used for food 3. LARGE CENTRAL AMERICAN BIRD a large bird similar to the North American turkey. Native to: Central America. Latin name: *Agriocharis ocellata*. 4. *N Am* FAILURE something that fails or flops, especially a bad play or film (*slang*) 5. *US* OFFENSIVE TERM an offensive term that deliberately insults somebody regarded as unintelligent, incompetent, or socially inept (*slang*) 6. THREE CONSECUTIVE BOWLING STRIKES in bowling, three strikes in a row (*informal*) [Mid-16C. < the N American bird's resemblance to the guinea fowl, imported through Turkish territory] ◇ **talk turkey** *N Am* to talk honestly and bluntly (*informal*)

Turkey /túrki/ country in southeastern Europe and Southwest Asia, bordered by Greece, the Black Sea, Georgia, Armenia, Iran, Iraq, Syria, the Mediterranean Sea, the Aegean Sea, and Bulgaria. Language: Turkish. Currency: Turkish lira. Capital: Ankara. Population: 68,109,469 (2003). Area: 779,452 sq. km/300,948 sq. mi. Official name **Republic of Turkey**

Turkey

turkey buzzard n *N Am* BIRDS same as **turkey vulture**

Turkey carpet n a handwoven woollen carpet with rich colours and a deep pile

turkey cock n 1. a male turkey, especially when fully grown 2. a person regarded as arrogant or conceited (*insult*)

Turkey red adj of the vibrant red colour produced using alizarin as a dye [Late 18C. < fabrics made in the Ottoman Empire] —**Turkey red** n

turkey shoot n *US* 1. a marksmanship contest in which rifles are fired at moving targets 2. something that is easily accomplished (*slang*)

turkey trot n a round dance to ragtime music in which dancers walk springily and make movements with their upper body

turkey vulture n a blackish-brown vulture with a bare wrinkled red head and neck. Native to: Americas. Latin name: *Cathartes aura*.

Turkic /túrkik/ n a subgroup of the Altaic family of languages spoken in western and central Asia, including Turkish, Azeri, Kazakh, Kyrgyz, Tatar, Uigur, and Uzbek ■ adj relating to Turkic languages, to the region where they are spoken, or to the peoples who speak them

Turkish /túrkish/ adj 1. OF TURKEY relating to Turkey, or to its people or culture 2. OF LANGUAGE OF TURKEY relating to the language of Turkey ■ n OFFICIAL LANGUAGE OF TURKEY the Turkic language that is the official language of Turkey, also spoken in Cyprus and several European countries. Native speakers: 50 million. See panel on next page —**Turkishness** n

Turkish bath n 1. a bath in which the bather sweats freely in hot air or steam, followed by a shower and often a massage 2. a commercial establishment where somebody can have a Turkish bath

Turkish coffee n a strong coffee, usually sweetened, made by simmering finely ground coffee and serving the liquid with the grounds

Turkish delight n a sweet made with flavoured gelatin, cut into cubes and dusted with icing sugar

Turkish tobacco n an aromatic dark tobacco grown in southeastern Europe and Turkey

Turkish towel n a large coarse-fibred cotton towel

Turkistan ♦ **Turkestan**

Turkmen /túrk men/ (*plural same* or **-mens**), **Turkoman** /túrkəmən/ (*plural* **-mans**), **Turcoman** n 1. a member of an originally nomadic Turkic-speaking people who now live mainly in Turkmenistan and Afghanistan 2. the Turkic official language of Turkmenistan. Native speakers: 4 million. [Early 20C. Via Persian *turkmān* < Turkish *türkmen*] —**Turkmen** adj

Turkmenistan /turk ménni staán/ country in southwestern Central Asia, bordered by Kazakhstan, Uzbekistan, Afghanistan, Iran, and the Caspian Sea. Language: Turkmen. Currency: manat. Capital: Ashgabat. Population: 4,775,544 (2003). Area: 488,100 sq. km/188,500 sq. mi. Official name **Republic of Turkmenistan**. See map on next page

Turkoman n, adj PEOPLES, LANG same as **Turkmen**

Turks and Caicos Islands /túrks ənd káykəss-/ British dependency consisting of two island groups in the northern Caribbean, southeast of the Bahamas and north of Hispaniola. Capital: Cockburn Town. Population: 18,122 (2001). Area: 430 sq. km/166 sq. mi.

LANGUAGE HERITAGE ***Turkish*** Much of English is made up of words from other languages, and some are from Turkish. Though relatively few purely Turkish words have moved directly into English, many words have migrated through Turkish on their way into the language, especially from Arabic and Persian, or have set out from Turkish and found their way by a more circuitous route. A typical example would be Turkish *ordu*, 'camp, army', which is represented in English as both ***horde*** and ***Urdu***. The former arrived in the mid-16th century, either directly or via French and German from Polish *horda*, which is from the Turkish word. ***Urdu*** came later, in the late 18th century, via Persian and Urdu *(zabān i) urdū* '(language of the) camp', from the same Turkish *ordū* 'camp'. Turkish *tülbend*, 'turban', represents a significant stage in the development of both ***turban*** and ***tulip***, as it is the source of the words from which ***turban*** was borrowed in the mid-16th century (French *turbant* and Italian *turbante*), and also of the French *tulipe*, from which ***tulip*** was adopted later in the same century, though the Turkish itself goes back further to Persian *dulband*.

Turkish naturally played a part in the migration of words relating to Eastern culture or society: for example, ***bazaar***, immediately from Italian in the late 16th century, but with the Italian via Turkish from Persian *bazaar* 'market'; ***divan***, adopted at much the same time via French or Italian from Turkish *dīvān*, itself from Persian; ***fez***, early 19th century via French from Turkish *fes*; ***harem***, mid-17th century, via Turkish from Arabic *ḥaram* 'prohibited (place), women's quarters'; ***minaret***, late 17th century from French from Turkish *minārī* from Arabic *manāra* 'lighthouse, minaret'; ***yashmak***, mid-19th century directly from Turkish *yaşmak*. Some of the most familiar migrants from Turkish relate to food and drink: ***baklava*** in the mid-17th century; ***bulgur*** wheat, a relative newcomer, mid-20th century via Turkish from Persian *bulgūr* 'bruised grain'; ***caviar***, mid-16th century via French and Italian from Turkish *havyar* (from Persian dialect *khāvyār*); ***coffee***, late 16th century via Turkish *kahve* from Arabic (the Turkish word is also the source, through French, of ***café***); ***doner kebab***, also fairly new, from Turkish *döner kebap* 'rotating kebab'; ***meze***, 'assortment of snacks or light dishes', early 20th century from Turkish, from Persian *maza* 'taste, relish'; ***pilau***, early 17th century from Turkish *pilâv*, 'cooked rice'; ***sherbet***, early 17th century via Turkish *şerbet* and Persian *šerbet* from Arabic *šarbat* 'drink' (the Turkish is also the source, through French and Italian, of ***sorbet***); and ***yoghurt***, early 17th century. Some other words, all from the early 17th century, whose Turkish origins may be less apparent are ***jackal***, via Turkish from Persian *šagāl*, ***kiosk***, via French from Turkish *köşk* 'villa' from Persian *kūšk* 'villa, palace', and ***theorbo***, 'stringed instrument like a large lute', via Italian *tiorba* from Turkish *torba* 'bag'.

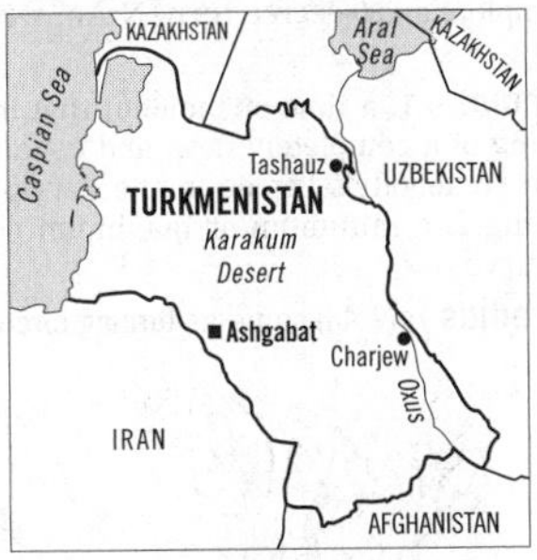

Turkmenistan

Turk's-cap lily *n* either of two lilies that have bright nodding flowers with petals that bend sharply backwards. Latin name: *Lilium martagon* or *Lilium superbum*.

Turk's-head *n* a knot shaped like a turban, made by weaving a smaller rope around a larger rope or spar

turmeric /túrmərik/ *n* **1.** a yellow spice made from the dried rhizomes of an Asian plant. Use: cooking, yellow dye. **2.** a tropical Asian plant of the ginger family with yellow flowers and rhizomes that are dried to produce turmeric. Latin name: *Curcuma longa*. [Mid-16C. < French *terre-mérite* 'worthy earth']

turmeric paper *n* a strip of test paper impregnated with turmeric. Use: turns brown in the presence of alkalis and red-brown in the presence of boric acid.

turmoil /túr moyl/ *n* **1.** a state of great confusion, commotion, or disturbance **2.** a disruptive event that causes confusion, commotion, or disturbance ○ *a leader untroubled by the nation's turmoils* [Early 16C. Origin ?]

turn /turn/ *v* (**turns, turning, turned**) **1.** *vti* **MOVE TO FACE DIFFERENT DIRECTION** to move to face in a different direction or towards a particular location, or move something so that it does this ○ *She turned to see what was happening.* ○ *turning his eyes skywards* **2.** *vti* **MOVE ROUND AXIS** to move around an axis or point in a particular direction, or move something in this way ○ *Turn the handle to the left.* **3.** *vt* **USE CONTROL TO OPERATE SOMETHING** to control something such as a machine or an appliance or some aspect of its performance by moving a knob, switch, or slider to a different setting ○ *Turn the heat to high.* **4.** *vti* **CHANGE DIRECTION OF VEHICLE** to go in a different direction when moving or travelling, or make a vehicle change direction ○ *Turn left at the crossroads.* **5.** *vt* **GO AROUND SOMETHING** to change direction and go round something ○ *to turn a corner* **6.** *vi* **FOLLOW DIFFERENT COURSE** to change direction and follow a different course ○ *The path turns uphill.* **7.** *vti* **MOVE PAGE OVER** to move a page so that the other side, or another page, can be read or looked at ○ *turned the pages* **8.** *vti* **CHANGE** to change or be transformed into somebody or something different, or change or transform somebody or something into somebody or something different ○ *turned into a butterfly* **9.** *vti* **CHANGE COLOUR** to change colour, or cause something to change colour **10.** *vti* **ALTER FOCUS OF SOMETHING** to direct the focus of something towards something else, or be focused on something ○ *Her thoughts turned to the past.* **11.** *vi* **START DOING SOMETHING DIFFERENT** to start doing something new or different, especially as a way of solving a problem or improving a situation **12.** *vi* **CONSULT SOMEBODY** to seek or appeal for help from somebody ○ *He turned to his mother for advice.* **13.** *vi* **CHANGE IN WEATHER** to change to become a different temperature or type of weather ○ *It's turned cold again.* **14.** *vti* **MAKE SOMEBODY FEEL SLIGHTLY SICK** to be sufficiently unpleasant or upsetting to make somebody feel nauseous, or respond with feelings of nausea ○ *violence that turned my stomach* **15.** *vt* GYMNASTICS **PERFORM CARTWHEEL** to rotate the body to perform a physical action such as a cartwheel or somersault **16.** *vt* **TWIST ANKLE** to injure the ankle or wrist by twisting or spraining it ○ *She turned her ankle getting off the bus.* **17.** *vt* **SEARCH SOMETHING EXTENSIVELY** to search a place extremely thoroughly ○ *They turned the house upside down looking for the ticket.* **18.** *vt* **PASS TIME OR AGE** to pass a particular age, time, or speed ○ *She's just turned sixty.* **19.** *vi* **BECOME SOUR** to become sour (*refers to milk*) **20.** *vi* **START TO EBB OR FLOW** to reach high tide and start to ebb, or reach low tide and start to rise ○ *The tide has turned.* **21.** *vt* WOODWORK, METALL **SHAPE SOMETHING ON LATHE** to shape or cut something on a lathe **22.** *vt* **FORM SOMETHING INTO ROUND SHAPE** to shape clay or a pot into a rounded form with the hands or with tools **23.** *vt* **EARN MONEY** to earn or achieve a monetary gain ○ *The business should turn a profit in this financial year.* **24.** *vti* **CHANGE ALLEGIANCE** to cause a change in somebody's allegiance, or undergo a change of allegiance ○ *a diplomat who turned spy* **25.** *vt* **SAY OR WRITE SOMETHING WELL** to give a distinctive or pleasing form to something said or written **26.** *vt* GARDENING, AGRIC **DIG UP LOWER LEVELS OF SOIL** to dig soil so as to bring lower layers up to the surface **27.** *vt* MIL **PASS ROUND ENEMY** to pass round an enemy in order to attack from the flank or rear **28.** *vti* CRICKET **SPIN, OR MAKE BALL SPIN** to spin, or make a cricket ball spin **29.** *vt* **BLUNT WEAPON** to blunt the edge of a weapon (*archaic*) ■ *n* **1.** **OPPORTUNITY** a time when somebody gets an opportunity to do something or somebody is asked to do something, especially when this is rotated among other people ○ *It's your turn to do the washing up.* **2.** **CHANGE OF DIRECTION** a change of direction in something such as a road or the plot of a book ○ *Slow down for the turn in the road ahead.* **3.** *N Am* ROADS same as **turning** (sense 1) **4.** **MOVEMENT OF ROTATION** a full or partial rotation ○ *Give the screw a few more turns.* **5.** **PARTICULAR INCLINATION** a particular inclination or tendency ○ *an academic turn of mind* **6.** **SUDDEN SCARE** a sudden shock or scare ○ *It gave me quite a turn.* **7.** **SPELL OF ILLNESS** a short period of feeling unwell or faint ○ *She had a nasty turn but she's OK now.* **8.** **END OF TIME PERIOD** the point at which one period of time ends and another begins ○ *at the turn of the century* **9.** **GOOD OR BAD DEED** a deed that helps or harms another person ○ *a good turn* **10.** **SHORT OUTING** a short walk, excursion, or dance (*dated*) ○ *They took a turn around the park.* **11.** MUSIC **MELODIC EMBELLISHMENT** a melodic embellishment that is played around a given note, using one note above and one note below the principal note **12.** THEATRE **INDIVIDUAL THEATRICAL PERFORMANCE** a short theatrical solo performance, e.g. in a cabaret or variety show **13.** FIN **STOCK MARKET TRANSACTION** a stock market transaction that includes both a sale and a purchase **14.** MIL **ADVANCE PASSING ROUND ENEMY** a military advance that passes around an enemy in order to attack from the flank or rear [Pre-12C. < Latin *tornare* 'turn on a lathe' < *tornus* 'lathe' < Greek *tornos*] —**turnable** *adj* ◇ **at every turn** everywhere, or at every significant moment ◇ **a turn of phrase** a particular way of expressing yourself ◇ **a turn of speed** the ability to move fast for a short period or the act of doing so ◇ **by turns** one after the other, alternately ◇ **in turn** in a regular order, one after the other ◇ **on the turn 1.** on the point of going sour **2.** on the point of changing **3.** at high or low tide and just about to ebb or return ◇ **out of turn 1.** not in a regular or correct order **2.** in an inappropriate way, or at an inappropriate time ◇ **to a turn** perfectly ○ *meat done to a turn* ◇ **turn of phrase** a particular way of expressing yourself ○ *a memorable turn of phrase*

turn against *vt* to stop approving or being friendly and show definite disapproval or unfriendliness instead, or make somebody change his or her attitude in this way

turn away *v* **1.** *vti* **TURN TO FACE SOMEWHERE ELSE** to change position so as to face away from somebody or something, or move somebody or something so as to face in another direction **2.** *vt* **REFUSE ADMISSION TO SOMEBODY** to send somebody away, refusing to see, entertain, or accommodate him or her **3.** *vt* **REFUSE TO ACCEPT SOMETHING** to refuse to listen to somebody or to what somebody wants to say or offer **4.** *vi* **GIVE SOMETHING UP** to reject something as unworthy or undesirable ○ *to turn away from a life of sin*

turn back *v* **1.** *vti* to stop and return in the direction you have come from, or stop people or vehicles and make them return in the direction they have come from **2.** *vt* to fold something over and down ○ *turned back the top sheet on the bed*

turn down *vt* **1.** **REJECT SOMETHING** to reject or refuse something such as an offer or application **2.** **REDUCE VOLUME OR INTENSITY** to make something less powerful, bright, loud, or hot, especially by moving a knob, switch, or slider **3.** **FOLD SOMETHING DOWNWARDS** to fold something or the top part of something towards the bottom, so that a double layer is formed

turn in *v* **1.** *vt* **RETURN SOMETHING AFTER USE** to give something back to its owner or to whoever is responsible for it ○ *Turn in your key at reception before leaving.* **2.** *vt* **SUBMIT SOMETHING** to hand in or send in something such as work assigned in school **3.** *vt* **TAKE SOMEBODY TO POLICE** to hand over somebody or something to the police or other authorities **4.** *vt* **PRODUCE RESULT** to achieve a particular outcome ○ *turned in a creditable performance* **5.** *vti* **FOLD INWARDS** to arrange something so that it bends or points inwards, or be arranged in this way **6.** *vi* **GO TO BED** to go to bed at the end of the day (*informal*)

turn into *v* **1.** *vti* to change or develop into a different form ○ *The caterpillar will turn into a butterfly.* **2.** *vt* to start travelling on a new route, or enter a new place by changing direction ○ *turned into the drive*

turn off *v* **1.** *vt* **STOP SOMETHING OPERATING** to make a machine or appliance stop working, or something stop flowing, by operating a control **2.** *vt* **SET SOMETHING TO OFF POSITION** to move a device such as a button, knob, or lever so that a machine stops working or something stops flowing **3.** *vti* **GO IN NEW DIRECTION** to split off from a road or path and head a different way, or take a road or path that goes in a new direction **4.** *vti* **DIMINISH ENTHUSIASM** to diminish or

destroy somebody's interest or excitement, or stop being interested or excited (*informal*) **5.** *vt* **PREVENT AROUSAL** to prevent or stop somebody from becoming sexually interested or aroused (*informal*)

turn on *v* **1.** *vt* **START SOMETHING OPERATING** to make a machine or appliance operate, or make something start flowing, by operating a control **2.** *vt* **SET SOMETHING TO ON POSITION** to move a device such as a button, knob, or lever so that a machine starts working or something starts flowing **3.** *vt* **ADOPT CALCULATED BEHAVIOUR** to display a particular behaviour or emotion in a way that people find calculated, irritating, or insincere ○ *He'll really turn on the charm if he thinks he's losing the sale.* **4.** *vt* **REACT AGGRESSIVELY TO SOMEBODY** to react aggressively or violently to somebody **5.** *vt* **MAKE SOMEBODY EXCITED** to interest or excite somebody greatly (*informal*) **6.** *vt* **AROUSE SOMEBODY** to make somebody feel sexually excited (*informal*) **7.** *vti* **TAKE ILLEGAL DRUGS** to take drugs, especially a hallucinogenic drug, or cause somebody to take a hallucinogen or similar drug (*informal*)

turn out *v* **1.** *vt* **SWITCH LIGHT OFF** to make an electric light go out by operating its power switch **2.** *vi* **COME TO EVENT** to come to a place, especially for a special event or public occasion ○ *Hardly anybody turned out for the reunion.* **3.** *vt* **MAKE SOMEBODY LEAVE** to force somebody to leave a room, building, or residence **4.** *vi* **HAPPEN IN PARTICULAR WAY** to happen or result in a particular way, often in a way that was not expected ○ *turned out to be a nice day* **5.** *vt* **MAKE SOMETHING** to create or produce something, especially in a consistent way or by mass production ○ *turning out 400 cars a week* **6.** *vt* **DRESS SOMEBODY UP** to clothe yourself or somebody else in a particular way (*often passive*) **7.** *vti* MIL **SIGNAL GROUP TO ASSEMBLE** to call an organized group of people, usually soldiers, to assemble for duty or for a military parade **8.** *vt* **EMPTY CONTENTS** to take out the contents of a pocket or bag, usually to check or reorganize what is there **9.** *vti* **FOLD OUTWARDS** to be arranged so as to bend or point outwards, or arrange something in this way **10.** *vi* **GET UP** to get out of bed (*informal*)

turn over *v* **1.** *vti* **TURN SOMETHING OTHER WAY UP** to alter the position of the body or of an object, bringing the underside uppermost, or move so that the underside is uppermost **2.** *vt* **THINK ABOUT SOMETHING** to give something slow and careful thought, considering different aspects or possibilities **3.** *vt* **GIVE SOMETHING TO SOMEBODY ELSE** to hand something over to the police or other authorities, especially when required to do so **4.** *vt* **DELEGATE SOMETHING** to give the responsibility for something to somebody else ○ *turned over some duties to her assistant* **5.** *vt* **PUT SOMEBODY UNDER SOMEBODY'S RESPONSIBILITY** to transfer the responsibility for somebody to another person or authority ○ *The principal turned him over to his parents.* **6.** *vt* **ROB PLACE** to break into a building or premises and steal anything thought to be valuable (*slang; often used in the passive*) **7.** *vti* **START ENGINE, OR BE STARTED** to start an engine or motor, or be started ○ *couldn't get the engine to turn over* **8.** *vt* FIN **HAVE SALES AMOUNTING TO SOMETHING** to have sales or other business transactions totalling a particular amount ○ *The firm turns over several million a month.* **9.** *vti* COMM **SELL AND RESTOCK GOODS** to sell and restock all items for sale, or be sold and restocked ○ *The produce usually turns over in 10 days.*

turn round *v* **1.** *vti* **TURN SOMETHING TO FACE OTHER WAY** to alter the position of the body or an object so that it faces the opposite direction, or move to face the opposite direction **2.** *vt* **COMPLETE ALL NECESSARY PROCEDURES** to carry out all the necessary procedures between receiving an order or task and shipping the order or completing the task ○ *How long will it take you to turn this work round?* **3.** *vt* **PREPARE VEHICLE BETWEEN JOURNEYS** to prepare an aircraft for its next flight or a ship for its next sailing **4.** *vt* **IMPROVE SOMETHING SIGNIFICANTLY** to cause a significant improvement in something, especially in the profits made by a company or organization ○ *moves to turn the debt round*

turn to *vi* to set to work, especially vigorously (*dated*)

turn up *v* **1.** *vt* **INCREASE SOMETHING** to make something louder, brighter, hotter, or more powerful, especially by operating its control **2.** *vti* **UNFOLD UPWARDS** to unfold something so that it stands up instead of lying in a flat double layer, or be capable of unfolding in this way **3.** *vt* **SHORTEN GARMENT** to fold and sew the bottom edge of a garment or piece of fabric, so as to shorten it **4.** *vi* **BE FOUND** to reappear or be rediscovered after being lost or in an unknown place, often in a surprising or unexpected way ○ *It'll turn up sooner or later.* **5.** *vt* **FIND SOMETHING BY SEARCHING** to uncover something that was hidden or previously unknown by investigating, hunting, or digging ○ *He didn't expect to turn up such an interesting story.* **6.** *vi* **ARRIVE** to come or appear somewhere, especially in a casual or unplanned way ○ *She just turned up yesterday.* **7.** *vi* **HAPPEN** to take place luckily or unexpectedly to settle matters or put things right ○ *They manage to get along somehow...something always seems to turn up.*

turnabout /túrn ə bowt/ *n* **1.** a shift from one situation, opinion, policy, or attitude to another that is the complete opposite **2.** the act of turning to face in the opposite direction

turnaround /túrn ə rownd/ *n* same as **turnround**

turn-based *adj* describes a computer game in which the action stops while a player makes his or her move, as opposed to continuing in real time ○ *You can choose from turn-based or real-time combat and readily toggle between the two.*

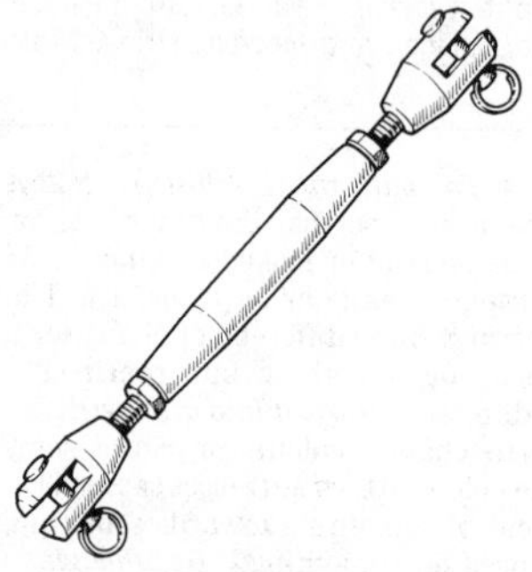

turnbuckle

turnbuckle /túrn buk'l/ *n* a device to tighten or loosen rope or wire, consisting of a tube through which the rope or wire is threaded and held so that the tension can be adjusted

turncoat /túrn kōt/ *n* somebody who abandons or betrays a group or cause and joins its opponents

turndown /túrn down/ *adj* **FOLDED DOWN** folded down or over from the top ■ *n* **1.** ECON same as **downturn** **2.** *US* **REJECTION** a rejection of something such as an offer or application **3.** *US* **SOMEBODY REJECTED** somebody who has been turned down or rejected for something ○ *a credit card turndown* **4.** *US* **SOMETHING FOLDED DOWN** something that is folded down or over from the top

turned-on *adj* **1.** **SEXUALLY EXCITED** sexually aroused or excited (*informal*) **2.** **UP-TO-DATE** aware of or involved in the most modern trends in culture and fashion (*dated informal*) **3.** **HIGH ON DRUGS** under the influence of a drug such as cannabis or LSD, or familiar with its effects as a result of having taken it (*dated informal*)

turner /túrnər/ *n* **1.** somebody whose job involves operating a lathe **2.** somebody or something that turns or that is used for turning something else, e.g. a device for turning food while it is cooking ○ *a pancake turner*

Turner /túrnər/, **J. M. W.** (1775–1851) British painter and watercolourist. His powerful landscape and seascape paintings used colour to explore the effects of light, and influenced the French impressionists. His works include *Hannibal and his Army Crossing the Alps* (1812) and *Rain, Steam, and Speed* (1844). Full name **Turner, Joseph Mallord William**

'My business is to paint not what I know, but what I see.'
[Attributed to J. M. W. Turner]

Turner, John Napier (*b.* 1929) Canadian prime minister (1984). He was a Liberal member of the Canadian parliament (1962–75) and leader of the Liberal Party (1984–90). See table at **prime minister**

Turner, Lana (1920–95) US actor. She is known for her roles in such Hollywood films as *The Postman Always Rings Twice* (1946) and *The Bad and the Beautiful* (1952). Born **Turner, Julia Jean Mildred Frances**

Turner, Ted (*b.* 1938) US business executive and philanthropist. He built his broadcasting system into an international media empire. Full name **Turner, Robert Edward III**

Turner's syndrome *n* a genetic disorder affecting women in which only one X chromosome per cell is present, instead of two, resulting in underdeveloped ovaries and underdevelopment of the womb, vagina, and breasts [Mid-20C. After Henry Hubert *Turner* (1892–1970), US physician]

turnery /túrnəri/ (*plural* **-ies**) *n* **1.** **WORK ON LATHE** the technique, art, or skill of forming and contouring using a lathe **2.** **ARTICLES TURNED ON LATHE** articles that have been made or turned on a lathe **3.** **WORKSHOP** a room or building where lathes are used

turning /túrning/ *n* **1.** **JUNCTION** a road or path that joins the main road or the road that is being travelled. N Am term **turn** **2.** **PROCESS OF MAKING TURN** the act or process of executing a turn **3.** **DEVIATION** a deviation from a straight or planned course **4.** HANDICRAFT **FABRIC THAT FORMS HEM** the amount of fabric that will be turned back to form a hem at the edge of a piece of sewing **5.** MANUF same as **turnery** (sense 1) ■ **turnings** *npl* MANUF **WASTE MATERIAL FROM LATHE** the waste material produced when something is turned on a lathe

turning circle *n* the smallest circle in which a vehicle can complete a 360-degree turn. N Am term **turning radius**

turning point *n* **1.** a time or incident that marks the beginning of a completely new, and usually better, stage in somebody's life or in the development of something **2.** a minimum or maximum point on a plane curve

turning radius *n N Am* same as **turning circle**

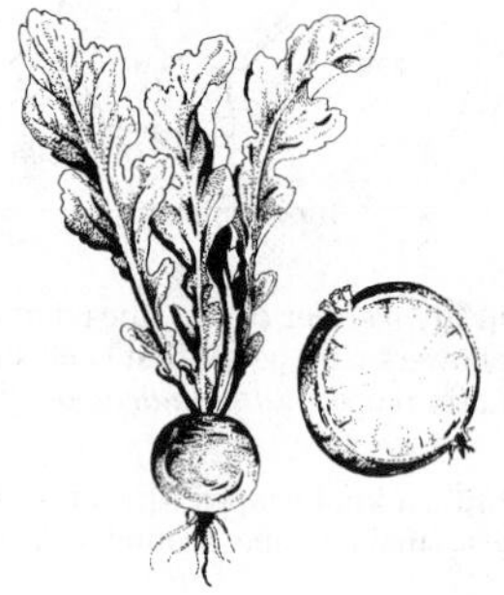

turnip

turnip /túrnip/ *n* **1.** a white rounded fleshy root that is cooked and eaten as a vegetable **2.** a plant that produces turnips. Latin name: *Brassica rapa*. [Mid-16C. < *tur-* (origin ?) + NEEP]

turnip moth *n* a brownish moth whose caterpillar feeds on the stem base and roots of turnips, carrots, and similar plants. Native to: Europe, Asia, Africa. Latin name: *Agrotis segetum*.

turnkey /túrn kee/ *adj* complete and ready to use upon delivery or installation ○ *a turnkey operation* ■ *n* (*plural* **-keys**) a keeper of keys, especially in a jail (*archaic*)

turn-off *n* **1.** **ROAD BRANCHING OFF MAIN ROAD** a road that branches off a main road, **2.** **ROAD JUNCTION** a junction formed by two roads, especially a larger and a smaller one **3.** **ACT OF TURNING OFF** the act or process of turning off **4.** **SOMETHING DISGUSTING OR OFF-PUTTING** somebody or something that causes a complete loss of interest, enthusiasm, or sexual arousal (*informal*)

turn-on *n* somebody or something that causes sexual arousal (*informal*)

turnout /túrn owt/ *n* **1.** **ATTENDANCE** the number of people who attend or take part in an event ○ *expecting a huge turnout for the carnival this weekend* **2.** POL **NUMBER OF VOTERS** the number or proportion of voters who register their vote in an election **3.** BUSINESS **AMOUNT OF WORK PRODUCED** the total quantity or amount produced, e.g. by a particular company or manufacturing process **4.** CLOTHING **OUTFIT** the clothes or equipment somebody is wearing ○ *a smart turnout*

5. *US* ROADS WIDENED PART OF STREET a section where a narrow roadway is broader, allowing vehicles to pass each other, pull over, or park **6.** BALLET OUTWARD ROTATION OF DANCER'S LEGS the outward rotating movement from the hip sockets of a classical ballet dancer's legs

turnover /túrn ōvər/ *n* **1.** ACCT AMOUNT OF BUSINESS the amount of business transacted over a given period of time, especially when expressed as gross revenue **2.** COMM THROUGHPUT OF STOCK the rate at which business stock is sold and replaced **3.** FIN NUMBER OF SHARES SOLD the number of shares sold on a stock exchange within a particular period of time **4.** HR CHANGE IN EMPLOYEES the number of employees in an organization who leave and are replaced over a given period ○ *job dissatisfaction that results in high turnover* **5.** *N Am* SPORTS LOSS OF POSSESSION in basketball and football, a loss of possession of the ball resulting from error or violation of rules **6.** FOOD FILLED PASTRY a filled pastry made by folding a square or circle of pastry in half over a filling to form a semicircle or triangle **7.** ACT OF TURNING OVER an act or process of turning something over ○ *a turnover in leadership* ■ *adj* ABLE TO BE FOLDED OVER designed to be turned or folded over

turnpike /túrn pīk/ *n* **1.** TOLL ROAD in the United States, a motorway on which a toll is charged. Drivers usually receive a ticket when they start their journey and pay a fee at the end that depends on the length of journey. **2.** ROAD BARRIER a gate formerly used to bar the way onto a section of road or a bridge until a toll had been paid **3.** ROAD WITH TURNPIKE in former times, a road that travellers were allowed to use only after paying a toll at the turnpike [14C. < TURN + PIKE[5]]

turnround /túrn rownd/, **turnaround** /-ə rownd/ *n* **1.** TIME TAKEN TO DO ENTIRE JOB the time it takes to carry out all the necessary procedures between receiving an order or task and the shipment of the order or completion of the task **2.** PREPARATION OF VEHICLE BETWEEN JOURNEYS the process of unloading and reloading, refuelling, and checking an aircraft, ship, or vehicle between journeys **3.** BIG IMPROVEMENT a dramatic improvement in a bad or unsatisfactory situation **4.** *N Am* PLACE FOR TURNING CAR ROUND a circular or curved driveway or section of road where vehicles can turn round

turnsole /túrnsōl/ *n* **1.** a purple dye obtained from a Mediterranean plant **2.** an annual plant that yields turnsole. Native to: Mediterranean. Latin name: *Chrozophora tinctoria*. [14C. Via Old French *tournesole* < Old Italian *tornasole* < *tornare* 'turn' + *sol* 'sun']

turnstile /túrn stīl/ *n* a mechanical barrier designed to let people pass through a narrow opening one at a time between revolving bars

turnstone /túrn stōn/ *n* a shorebird with mottled black or tortoiseshell markings. Native to: Arctic coast, migrating south. Genus: *Arenaria*. [Late 17C. Because it turns over stones to find food]

turntable /túrn tayb'l/ *n* **1.** RECORD PLAYER DECK a record player deck, especially without the amplifier and speakers, and as distinct from a separate tape player, CD player, or tuner **2.** REVOLVING PLATFORM ON RECORD PLAYER the flat round revolving plate on which the record rests on a record player **3.** ROTATING PLATFORM a rotating platform for turning round a vehicle such as a railway locomotive so that it is facing the opposite way

turntable ladder *n* an extending ladder mounted on a rotating platform on the back of a fire engine. N Am term **aerial ladder**

turn-up *n* **1.** *UK* FOLD AT BOTTOM OF TROUSER LEG a fold of material that is turned up at the bottom of a trouser leg. ANZ, N Am term **cuff 2.** SOMETHING SURPRISING an unexpected, unlikely, or unusual event (*informal*) ○ *That's a turn-up for the books!* ■ *adj* FOR TURNING UP designed to be folded or turned up

turpentine /túrpən tīn/ *n* **1.** PAINT THINNER a colourless petroleum-based liquid used as a thinner for paint and varnish **2.** SUBSTANCE FROM PINE TREES a viscous substance obtained from coniferous trees. Use: manufacture of paint solvent. **3.** STICKY SUBSTANCE FROM TEREBINTH TREE a brownish-yellow sticky mixture of essential oil and resin that comes from the terebinth tree **4.** LIQUID FROM TURPENTINE a colourless, flammable,

strong-smelling essential oil distilled from turpentine. Use: paint solvent, in medicine. ■ *vt* (**-tines, -tining, -tined**) **1.** TREAT SOMETHING WITH TURPENTINE to treat or thin something with turpentine **2.** EXTRACT TURPENTINE FROM SOMETHING to extract turpentine from trees [14C. Via Old French *terbentine* 'terebinth resin' < Greek *terebinthos* 'terebinth tree']

turpentine tree *n* **1.** a tree that yields turpentine, e.g. the terebinth **2.** a tree of the eucalyptus family that yields a viscous resin and is often planted as a shade tree. Native to: Australia. Genus: *Syncarpia*.

turpeth /túrpith/ (*plural* **-peths** or *same*) *n* **1.** a plant belonging to the bindweed family whose roots are turpeths. Native to: Asia. Latin name: *Operculina turpethum*. **2.** the root of an Asian plant. Use: formerly, as a laxative. [14C. Via medieval Latin *turbithum* < Persian *turbid* < Sanskrit *tripuṭín* 'castor-oil plant']

Turpin /túrpin/, **Dick** (1706–39) British bandit. His exploits, including an alleged swift ride from London to York on his horse, Black Bess, were later romanticized. Full name **Turpin, Richard.** Known as **the King of the Road**

turpitude /túrpi tyood/ *n* extreme immorality or wickedness (*formal*) [15C. Directly or via French < Latin *turpitudo* < *turpis* 'repulsive']

turps /turps/ *n* (*informal*) **1.** same as **turpentine** *n* (sense 4) **2.** *Aus* beer or other alcoholic drink [Early 19C. Shortening]

turquoise /túr kwoyz, -kwaaz/ *n* **1.** a greenish-blue semiprecious stone that is a form of aluminium copper phosphate. Source: igneous rocks. Use: gems. **2.** a bright greenish-blue colour [15C. < Old French (*pierre*) *turqueise* 'Turkish (stone)'; because first found in Turkestan] —**turquoise** *adj*

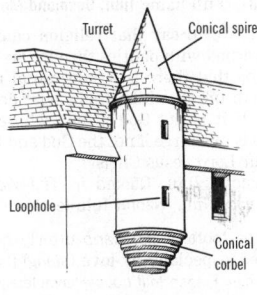

turret

turret /túrrit/ *n* **1.** SMALL TOWER a small rounded tower that projects from a wall or corner of a large building such as a castle **2.** ARMS DOME CONTAINING GUN a rotating armoured structure on a ship or tank, or a dome projecting from the fuselage of an aircraft, containing one or more guns and a gun crew **3.** MECH ENG PART OF LATHE a device on a lathe that holds a range of tools [14C. < Old French *tourete* 'small tower' < *tour* 'tower' < Latin *turris*]

turreted /túritid/ *adj* **1.** constructed or designed to include turrets **2.** shaped like a long pointed spiral

turret lathe *n* *N Am* same as **capstan lathe**

turtle

turtle[1] /túrt'l/ *n* **1.** WATER-DWELLING REPTILE a large turtle with limbs shaped like paddles that is usually found in tropical and subtropical seas. Family: Cheloniidae or Dermochelyidae. N Am term **sea turtle 2.** *US* WATER- OR LAND-DWELLING REPTILE a water- or land-

dwelling reptile with a body protected by a bony shell, e.g. a tortoise or terrapin **3.** TURTLE MEAT the flesh of an edible type of turtle, tortoise, or terrapin used as food [Mid-16C. Origin ?] ◇ **turn turtle** to turn upside down

turtle[2] /túrt'l/ *n* same as **turtledove** (*archaic*) [Pre-12C. < Latin *turtur*, an imitation of its call]

turtleback /túrt'l bak/ *n* an arched cover for protecting the deck of a ship in heavy seas

turtledove /túrt'l duv/ *n* a slender dove with black-and-chestnut upper parts, a pink breast, and a black-and-white neck, noted for its purring call. Native to: Europe, migrating to Africa. Latin name: *Streptopelia turtur*. [13C. < TURTLE[2]]

turtlehead /túrt'l hed/ (*plural* **-heads** or *same*) *n* a perennial plant found near running water. Flowers: white, purplish, greenish, or yellowish. Native to: eastern North America. Genus: *Chelone*. [Mid-19C. < the shape of its flowers]

turtleneck /túrt'l nek/ *n* CLOTHING **1.** a high tight-fitting round collar on a garment such as a sweater **2.** a sweater with a turtleneck **3.** *N Am* same as **polo neck** (sense 1) ▶ N Am term **mock turtle**

turves plural of **turf**

Tuscan /túskən/ *adj* **1.** OF TUSCANY relating to the Italian region of Tuscany, or its people or culture **2.** OF STYLE OF ARCHITECTURE relating to a classical order of architecture characterized by plain bases and capitals and unfluted columns ■ *n* **1.** SOMEBODY FROM TUSCANY somebody who comes from Tuscany **2.** STANDARD ITALIAN the standard and literary form of Italian, principally based on the dialect of Florence [14C. Via Old French *tuscan*, Italian *toscano* < Latin *Tuscanus* < *Tuscus* 'Etruscan']

Tuscany /túskəni/ region in northern Italy, a centre of culture during the Renaissance period. Capital: Florence. Population: 3,536,392 (2000). Area: 22,993 sq. km/8,878 sq. mi.

Tuscarora /túskə ráwrə/ (*plural* **-ras** or *same*) *n* a member of an Iroquois people who lived in North Carolina and who now live mainly in New York State and Ontario. In 1722 the Tuscarora joined the Iroquois Confederacy, which then became known as the Six Nations. [Mid-17C. < Iroquois, 'hemp gatherer']

tusche /toosh/ *n* a thick black liquid that is used as a drawing medium in lithography and as a protective coating (**resist**) in silk-screen printing and etching [Late 19C. < German, a back-formation < *tuschen* 'draw in ink', via French *toucher* < Old French *touchier* (see TOUCH)]

tush[1] /toosh/ *n* somebody's buttocks or bottom (*informal*) [Mid-20C. Alteration of Yiddish *tokhes*]

tush[2] /tush/ *interj* an expression of mild disapproval or disdain (*archaic*) [Mid-16C. Natural exclamation]

tusk /tusk/ *n* **1.** ENLARGED TOOTH an enlarged pointed front tooth that projects from the mouth in animals such as the elephant, walrus, and wild boar and is often used for fighting **2.** TENON JOINT in joinery, a form of tenon that has a short projecting part to make it stronger ■ *vti* (**tusks, tusking, tusked**) JAB TUSK INTO SOMEBODY OR SOMETHING to use a tusk or tusks to attack, dig at, or stab somebody or something [Old English *tūsc, tux* < Indo-European, 'tooth'] —**tusked** *adj*

tusker /túskər/ *n* a wild boar, elephant, or other animal with large tusks (*informal*)

tusk shell *n* **1.** an invertebrate sea animal that lives partly buried in sand and has a slender, tapering, and often curved shell that is open at both ends. Order: Scaphopoda. **2.** the tapering shell of an invertebrate sea animal ▶ US term **tooth shell**

tussah /tússə/ (*plural* **-sahs** or *same*) *n* ANZ, N Am **1.** TEXTILES same as **tussore** (senses 1–2) **2.** INSECTS same as **tussore** (sense 1) [Late 16C. < Hindi *tasar*, probably < Sanskrit *tasara* 'shuttle']

Tussaud /tə sáwd, tóoss ō/, **Madame** (1760–1850) Swiss wax-modeller. She made death masks in Paris of victims of the French Revolution, which she exhibited in Great Britain, and founded Madame Tussaud's Exhibition in London (1835). Born **Grosholtz, Marie**

tussis /tússiss/ *n* a cough or coughing (*technical*) [< Latin] —**tussal** *adj* —**tussive** *adj*

tussle /túss'l/ *vi* (**-sles, -sling, -sled**) to have a vigorous

physical or verbal struggle with somebody ■ *n* a vigorous physical or verbal struggle [15C. Probably < N English dialect *touse* 'pull about']

tussock /tússək/ *n* **1.** a small thick clump of growing vegetation, usually coarse grass **2.** *ANZ* PLANTS same as **tussock grass** [Mid-16C. Origin ?] —**tussocky** *adj*

tussock grass *n* a grass that grows in clumps. Native to: New Zealand, Australia.

tussock moth *n* a moth whose caterpillars are covered in tufts of brightly coloured hair. Some are pests of crops and shade trees. Family: Lymantriidae.

tussore /tússər/ (*plural* **-sores** or *same*) *n UK* **1.** SILK FABRIC a coarse brownish or yellowish silk fabric with an attractive uneven surface, woven from the silk of the silkworm of an Asian moth **2.** SILK THREAD the silk thread produced by the silkworm of an Asian moth **3.** SILKWORM the silkworm of an Asian moth, from which a coarse silk is obtained. Latin name: *Antheraea paphia*. ▶ ANZ, N Am term **tussah** [Late 19C. Alteration of TUSSAH]

tut /tut/, **tut-tut** /tut tút/ *interj* a clicking sound made with the tongue, or a spoken imitation of this sound, used as an expression of annoyance or disapproval, sometimes ironically ■ *vi* (**tuts, tutting, tutted; tut-tuts, tut-tutting, tut-tutted**) to make a clicking sound with the tongue to express annoyance or dissatisfaction [Early 16C. Natural exclamation]

Tutankhamen

Tutankhamen /tootən kaʹamən/, **Tutankhamun** /-kaa moon/ (1343–1325 BC) Egyptian pharaoh. His sumptuously decorated tomb was discovered almost intact in 1922.

tutee /tyoo teʹe/ *n* the student of a tutor [Early 20C. < TUTOR + -EE]

tutelage /tyooʹtəlij/ *n* **1.** TEACHING instruction and guidance provided by somebody such as a tutor ○ *Under her tutelage, he became a first-rate sailor.* **2.** SUPERVISION BY TUTOR the condition of being supervised or protected by a tutor or guardian **3.** CONDITION OF BEING TUTOR the condition of being a tutor or guardian [Early 17C. < Latin *tutela* 'guardianship' < *tut-*, past participle of *tueri* 'watch over']

tutelary /tyooʹtələri/, **tutelar** /tyooʹtələr/ *adj* (*formal or literary*) **1.** ACTING AS PROTECTOR acting in the role of a protector or guardian ○ *tutelary saints* **2.** OF GUARDIAN relating to or belonging to a guardian ■ *n* (*plural* **-ies**; *plural* **-lars**) GUARDING PRESENCE a tutelary being or person, especially a saint or deity (*literary*) [Early 17C. < Latin *tutelarius* < *tutela* (see TUTELAGE)]

tutor /tyooʹtər/ *n* **1.** TEACHER a teacher who instructs an individual pupil or a small group of pupils **2.** BRITISH UNIVERSITY TEACHER an academic who is responsible for teaching and advising an allocated group of students **3.** US LOW-RANKING US UNIVERSITY TEACHER in some US universities, a teacher of a rank below instructor **4.** GUARDIAN OF PUPIL in Scottish law, somebody who is the guardian of a pupil (*formal*) ■ *v* (**-tors, -toring, -tored**) **1.** *vti* ACT AS TUTOR to give somebody individual tuition in a subject or skill **2.** *vi US* RECEIVE PRIVATE TUITION to study under a tutor [14C. Via Anglo-Norman < Latin, 'guardian' < *tut-* (see TUTELAGE)] — **tutorage** *n* —**tutorship** *n*

SYNONYMS See *teach*.

tutorial /tyoo táwri əl/ *n* **1.** LESSON WITH TUTOR a teaching session spent individually or in a small group under the direction of a tutor **2.** LESSON FROM BOOK a chapter of a book or manual, or a section of a computer program, designed to provide instruction or training using exercises and assignments ■ *adj* RELATING TO TUTOR relating to or belonging to a tutor, or to the role and responsibilities of a tutor

tutsan /túts'n/ (*plural* **-sans** or *same*) *n* a woodland plant with large stalkless leaves and small rounded red fruits that turn black when ripe. Flowers: yellow. Native to: Europe, Asia. Latin name: *Hypericum androsaemum*. [14C. < French *toute-saine* < *toute* 'all' + *saine* 'healthy']

Tutsi /tootsi/ (*plural same* or **-sis**) *n* a member of an African people living in Rwanda and Burundi [Mid-20C. < Bantu] —**Tutsi** *adj*

tutti /tootti/ *n* the part of a concerto or other orchestral composition in which all the musicians play, as opposed to a solo section [Early 18C. Via Italian < Latin *totus* 'entire']

tutti-frutti /tooti frooti/ (*plural* **tutti-fruttis**) *n* an ice cream, dessert, or type of confectionery containing a variety of chopped, usually dried or candied fruit [Mid-19C. < Italian, 'all fruits']

tut-tut *interj, vi* same as **tut**

tutu[1] /tootoo/ *n* a ballet dancer's skirt that is very short and made of layers of stiffened net so that it stands out from the body [Early 20C. < French, baby-talk alteration of *cucu* < *cul* 'buttocks' < Latin *culus*]

tutu[2] /tootoo/ (*plural* **-tus** or *same*) *n* a tree with poisonous sap and seeds. Native to: New Zealand. Latin name: *Coriaria arborea*. [Mid-19C. < Maori]

Tutu /tootoo/, **Desmond** (*b.* 1931) South African archbishop and political activist. A leader of the anti-apartheid movement, he was the first Black bishop of Johannesburg (1984) and archbishop of Cape Town (1986–96). He was awarded the Nobel Peace Prize (1984). Full name **Tutu, Desmond Mpilo**

'If we are to say that religion cannot be concerned with politics then we are really saying that there is a substantial part of human life in which God's writ does not run. If it is not God's, then whose is it? Who is in charge if not the God and Father of our Lord Jesus Christ?'
[Desmond Tutu. Quoted in *The Words of Desmond Tutu*, Naomi Tutu (ed.); 1989]

tutulbay /too toolbay/ *adj Carib* utterly confused or bewildered, especially by love (*slang*) [Late 20C. Via French Creole< French *tout troublé* 'completely upset']

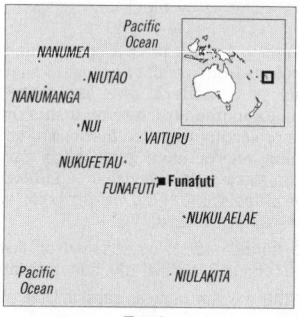

Tuvalu

Tuvalu /too vaʹaloo/ country consisting of coral islands in the western Pacific Ocean. Fiji and Samoa, each about 1,050 km/650 mi. away, are the islands' nearest neighbours. It became an independent member of the Commonwealth in 1978. Language: English, Tuvaluan. Currency: Australian dollar. Capital: Funafuti. Population: 11,305 (2003). Area: 26 sq. km/10 sq. mi. Former name **Ellice Islands** (until 1975) —**Tuvaluan** *n, adj*

Tuwhare /too fúrray/, **Hone** (*b.* 1922) New Zealand poet. He is the author of *No Ordinary Sun* (1964).

tu-whit tu-whoo /tə wít tə woo/ *interj* used to represent the sound of an owl hooting (*informal*) [Late 16C. An imitation of the sound]

tux /tuks/ *n N Am* CLOTHING same as **tuxedo** (*informal*) [Early 20C. Shortening]

tuxedo /tuk seʹedō/ (*plural* **-dos**) *n N Am* **1.** CLOTHING same as **dinner jacket 2.** a formal set of clothing for a man including a tuxedo jacket and matching trousers, usually with a band of silk down each leg, dress shirt, bow tie, and cummerbund [Late 19C. After *Tuxedo* Park, town in New York]

tuyère /twee air/, **twyer** /twī ə/ *n* an opening in the refractory lining and shell of a furnace through which air is forced in order to promote combustion [Late 18C. < French < *tuyau* 'pipe']

Tuzla /toozzlə/ city in northeastern Bosnia and Herzegovina. Before the Bosnian-Croatian-Serbian War Tuzla was a major road and rail junction and mining centre, during the war it became a Bosnian government stronghold and a major United Nations-run refugee centre. Population: 121,717 (1991).

tv *abbr* ONLINE Tuvalu (*used in Internet addresses*) See table at **domain name**

TV[1] *n* same as **television** (*informal*) [Mid-20C. Abbreviation]

TV[2] *n* same as **transvestite** (*informal*) [Mid-20C. Abbreviation]

TV dinner *n* a precooked frozen or chilled meal that can be reheated in the oven or microwave and eaten straight from the tray or dish, especially while watching television

TVEI *abbr* technical and vocational initiative

Tver /tvair/ city in western Russia, at the confluence of the Volga and Tvertsa rivers. Population: 479,610 (1995). Former name **Kalinin** (1933–90)

TVP *n* a high-protein product made from processed soya beans that are formed into chunks or minced and flavoured to taste like meat. Full form **textured vegetable protein**

TVR *abbr* television rating

TVRO *n* an aerial used for receiving television signals from a broadcasting satellite. Full form **television receive only**

tw *abbr* ONLINE Taiwan (*used in Internet addresses*) See table at **domain name**

twa /twaw/ *n Scotland* same as **two** (*nonstandard*) [Variant]

twaddle /twódd'l/ *n* nonsensical or pretentious speech or writing (*informal*) ■ *vi* (**-dles, -dling, -dled**) to speak or write twaddle (*dated informal*) [Late 18C. Origin ?] —**twaddler** *n*

twain /twayn/ *npl* two people or things (*archaic or literary*) ○ *'Oh, East is East, and West is West, and never the twain shall meet.'* (Rudyard Kipling, *The Ballad of East and West*) [Old English *twēgen* < Germanic, 'two']

Mark Twain

Twain /twayn/, **Mark** (1835–1910) US writer. He wrote humorous travel books and the classic stories *The Adventures of Tom Sawyer* (1876) and *The Adventures of Huckleberry Finn* (1884). Born **Clemens, Samuel Langhorne**

'That's always the way; it don't make no difference whether you do right or wrong, a person's conscience ain't got no sense, and it just goes for him *anyway*.'
[Mark Twain, *The Adventures of Huckleberry Finn*; 1884]

'All say, "How hard it is that we have to die"—a strange complaint to come from the mouths of people who have had to live.'
[Mark Twain, *Pudd'nhead Wilson*; 1894]

'Man is the Only Animal that Blushes, Or has to.'
[Mark Twain, *Following the Equator*; 1897]

twang /twang/ *n* **1.** SOUND OF TIGHT STRING VIBRATING the sharp resonating noise made when something such as a tight string on an instrument is plucked or released **2.** NASAL SOUND a nasal quality of voice associated with various accents ○ *a Texas twang* ■ *vti* (**twangs, twanging, twanged**) **1.** VIBRATE WITH TWANG to produce a twang, or make something do this **2.** MUSIC STRUM SOMETHING CARELESSLY to play a stringed instrument, or a tune on a stringed instrument, in a rough amateur style **3.** MOVE WITH TWANG to move, spring, or be released suddenly with a twang, or move something do this ○ *The lid of the box twanged shut.* **4.** LANGUAGE SPEAK WITH TWANG to speak or say something with a twang [Mid-16C. An imitation of the sound] —**twangy** *adj*

'twas /twoz/ *contr* it was (*archaic or literary*)

twat /twat/ *n* **1.** a highly offensive term for a woman's vagina or genital area (*taboo*) **2.** a highly offensive term for somebody regarded as unintelligent, worthless, or detestable (*taboo insult*) [Mid-17C. Origin ?]

twayblade /twáy blayd/ *n* an orchid that has only two leaves, arranged opposite each other, at the base. Genera: *Listera* or *Liparis* or *Ophrys*. [Late 16C. < obsolete variant of TWAIN]

tweak /tweek/ *vt* (**tweaks, tweaking, tweaked**) **1.** TWIST SOMETHING QUICKLY to take hold of something between the finger and thumb and twist it sharply **2.** PINCH SOMEBODY AFFECTIONATELY to pinch somebody gently and usually affectionately or playfully ○ *tweaked the baby on the cheek* **3.** ADJUST SOMETHING SLIGHTLY to make a slight adjustment or change to something, especially in order to improve it or fix it (*informal*) ○ *tweaked the controls* **4.** US TEASE SOMEBODY to tease somebody, either playfully or maliciously ■ *n* **1.** SHARP PINCH a sharp pinch or twist with the finger and thumb **2.** SLIGHT ADJUSTMENT a slight adjustment or change to something, especially in order to improve it or fix it (*informal*) **3.** US TEASING REMARK a teasing remark or action [Early 17C. Probably variant of obsolete *twick* < Old English *twiccian* < Germanic]

twee /twee/ *adj* dainty or pretty in an overdone and affected way ○ *Those frilly curtains are a bit twee for my taste.* [Early 20C. Baby-talk alteration of SWEET] —**tweely** *adv* —**tweeness** *n*

tweed /tweed/ *n* a fairly rough, thick woollen fabric often made with several different shades of wool to give it a distinctive flecked appearance. Use: warm clothing. ■ **tweeds** *npl* a tweed suit or outfit [Mid-19C. Alteration of *tweel*, Scottish variant of TWILL, after the river TWEED]

ORIGIN Early accounts date the coinage of **tweed** to 1831, and ascribe it to the London cloth merchant James Locke (although Locke himself in his book *Tweed and Don* (1860) does not make any such claim). The term was in general use by 1850, and it was registered as a trademark.

Tweed /tweed/ river of southern Scotland and northeastern England, flowing into the North Sea at Berwick-upon-Tweed. Its lower course runs along the Scottish-English border. Length: 160 km/97 mi.

tweedy /tweedi/ (**-ier, -iest**) *adj* **1.** made of or resembling tweed **2.** showing a liking for the attitudes and outdoor lifestyle traditionally associated with the upper classes, especially activities such as hunting and shooting (*informal*) —**tweediness** *n*

'tween /tween/ *prep, adv* same as **between** (*archaic or literary*) [13C. Shortening]

tweet /tweet/ *n* a light high-pitched note, especially one sung by a small bird ■ *vi* (**tweets, tweeting, tweeted**) to make the light high-pitched sound of a small bird [Mid-19C. An imitation of the sound]

tweeter /tweetər/ *n* a loudspeaker used to reproduce high-frequency sounds, e.g. in a hi-fi system

tweeze /tweez/ (**tweezes, tweezing, tweezed**) *vt N Am* to pull out or manipulate something using tweezers [Mid-20C. Back-formation < TWEEZERS]

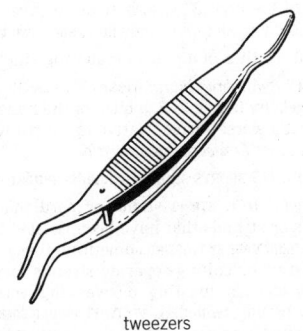
tweezers

tweezers /tweezərz/ *npl* a metal tool consisting of two narrow slightly curved arms joined at one end, used for extracting or holding small objects [Mid-17C. Alteration of obsolete *tweeze* 'tweezer case' < French *étuis*, plural of *étui* (see ÉTUI)]

twelfth /twelfth/ *n* one of twelve equal parts of something [Old English *twelfta.* < Germanic, 'twelve'] —**twelfth** *adj, adv*

Twelfth Day *n* CHR same as **Epiphany**

twelfth man *n* a reserve player in a cricket team

Twelfth Night *n* **1.** the Christian feast of the Epiphany. Date: 6 January. **2.** 5 January, the day before Epiphany in the Christian calendar, or the evening of that day. It was formerly a time of special celebration at the end of the Christmas season.

CULTURAL NOTE *Twelfth Night* a play (1600?) by William Shakespeare. A comedy set in Illyria, it tells of the shipwrecked Viola, who disguises herself as a young man called Cesario and enters the service of Orsino. Orsino loves Olivia, who falls in love with Cesario, while Viola herself is attracted to Orsino. The reappearance of Viola's twin brother Sebastian ultimately brings a happy conclusion to the complicated plot, which also features the colourful characters Malvolio, Sir Andrew Aguecheek, and Sir Toby Belch. The saying 'some men are born great, some achieve greatness, and some have greatness thrust upon them' comes from this play.

~~**twelth**~~ incorrect spelling of **twelfth**

twelve /twelv/ *n* **1.** 12 the number 12 **2.** SOMETHING WITH VALUE OF 12 something in a numbered series with a value of twelve **3.** GROUP OF 12 a group of twelve people or objects **4.** 12 UK FILM RATING in the United Kingdom, a rating given to films and videos considered unsuitable for children under the age of twelve [Old English *twelf* < Germanic, 'two left', that is 'two left beyond ten'] —**twelve** *adj, pron*

12A *tdmk* in the United Kingdom, a rating given to a film considered unsuitable for children under the age of twelve to see in a cinema unless accompanied by an adult

Twelve Apostles, **Twelve** *n* according to the Bible, eleven of the twelve followers originally chosen by Jesus Christ, together with Matthias, who was chosen to replace Judas

twelve-inch *n* a record that is 30.5 cm/12 in. in diameter and played at 45 rpm, usually containing a single, often extended track (*informal*)

twelve-mile limit *n* an offshore boundary 12 miles from a country's coast, claimed by some countries as marking the territorial limit of their jurisdiction in order to safeguard fishing rights and limit the approach of foreign vessels

twelvemo /twélvmō/ (*plural* **-mos**) *n* PRINTING same as **duodecimo** [Early 18C. Pronunciation of the printers' abbreviation *12mo*]

twelvemonth /twélv munth/ *n* a calendar year (*archaic*)

twelve-step programme *n* a programme for recovery from addiction, based on the methods of Alcoholics Anonymous and involving self-improvement techniques

Twelve Tables *n* the earliest code of Roman law on civil, criminal, and religious matters, dating back to 451–450 BC

~~**twelveth**~~ incorrect spelling of **twelfth**

twelve-tone *adj* relating to or using compositional techniques based on strict sequences of notes selected from the 12 notes of the chromatic scale

twelve-tone row *n* MUSIC same as **tone row**

twentieth /twénti əth/ *n* one of twenty equal parts of something [Old English *twentigoþa* < Germanic, 'twenty'] —**twentieth** *adj, adv*

twenty /twénti/ *n* (*plural* **-ties**) **1.** 20 the number 20 **2.** GROUP OF 20 a group of twenty people or objects **3.** £20 NOTE a banknote worth twenty pounds (*informal*) ■ **twenties** *npl* **1.** NUMBERS 20 TO 29 the numbers 20 to 29, particularly as a range of temperature ○ *in the low twenties* **2.** YEARS FROM 20 TO 29 the years from 20 to 29 in a century ○ *in the late twenties* **3.** PERIOD FROM AGE 20 TO 29 the period of somebody's life from the age of 20 to 29 ○ *when I was in my twenties* [Old English *twentig* < Germanic, 'twice ten'] —**twenty** *adj, pron*

twenty-first *n* somebody's 21st birthday, formerly marking the person's legal coming of age

24/7 /twénti fawr sévv'n/ (*informal*) *adv* constantly or around the clock ○ *now open 24/7* ■ *adj* occurring, happening, or appearing 24 hours a day, 7 days a week

twenty-one *n* CARDS same as **pontoon**[2]

twenty questions *n* a game in which one player thinks of an object and others try to work out what it is by asking questions that can be answered only with 'yes' or 'no'

twenty-six counties *npl* the counties of the Republic of Ireland

twentysomething /twénti sumthing/ *n* somebody who is between 20 and 30 years old (*informal; usually used in the plural*) —**twentysomething** *adj*

twenty-twenty, **20/20** *adj* describes standard vision or eyesight [< the figures denoting standard eyesight at a distance of 20 feet]

.22 *n* a gun or rifle that uses a bullet with a diameter of .22 in., usually used for killing small game

'twere /twur/ *contr* it were (*archaic or literary*) [Early 17C. Contraction]

twerp /twurp/, **twirp** *n* an offensive term that deliberately insults somebody's seriousness or importance (*informal insult*) [Late 19C. Origin ?]

Twi /twee/ (*plural same* or **Twis**) *n* **1.** a member of an African people who live in southern Ghana **2.** the language of the Twi people, a dialect of Akan. Native speakers: 1,400,000. [Late 19C. < Kwa] —**Twi** *adj*

twibill /twíbil/ *n* **1.** a large pick (**mattock**) with one blade shaped like an axe and one blade like an adze **2.** a double-edged battleaxe, formerly used as a weapon [Old English *twibil* < *twi-* 'two' + *bill* 'bladed weapon']

twice /twīss/ *adv* **1.** on two occasions, or in two instances **2.** double in amount or degree [Old English *twige* < Indo-European]

twice-laid *adj* describes ropes or cables that are made from previously used rope

Twickenham /twíkənəm/ residential district in west London, the site of a rugby football stadium used for international matches

twiddle /twídd'l/ *vti* (**-dles, -dling, -dled**) **1.** TURN SOMETHING BACK AND FORTH to turn something round or back and forth repeatedly ○ *twiddling the dial on the radio to get a better reception* **2.** TWIST OR TURN SOMETHING ABSENT-MINDEDLY to keep twisting something or turning it round in a bored or absent-minded way ○ *sat twiddling his pencil and staring out of the window* ■ *n* **1.** TWISTING ACTION a to-and-fro turning or twisting action **2.** LITTLE PIECE OF EXTRA DECORATION a small extra twist or curve added to something for ornamentation, e.g. a small flourish on a letter of script, or a musical ornament such as a mordent or trill [Mid-16C. Origin ?] —**twiddler** *n* —**twiddly** *adj*

twig[1] /twig/ *n* **1.** a small branch or shoot, especially one from a tree or bush **2.** a structure that resembles a branch, e.g. a minute offshoot of a nerve or blood vessel [Old English *twigge* 'forked branch' < Germanic] —**twiglet** *n*

twig[2] /twig/ *vti* (**twigs, twigging, twigged**) to understand

or realize something (*informal*) ○ *finally twigged what was going on* [Mid-18C. Origin ?]

twiggy /twíggi/ (**-gier, -giest**) *adj* **1.** covered in twigs ○ *a twiggy shrub* **2.** very thin or fragile ○ *twiggy legs*

twilight /twí līt/ *n* **1.** TIME AFTER SUNSET OR BEFORE DAWN the time of day just after sunset or before dawn, when the Sun is below the horizon **2.** HALF-LIGHT the faint diffuse light that occurs at twilight **3.** PERIOD OF OFFICIAL TWILIGHT the period during which the Sun is at a specific angle below the horizon. The angle is 6° for civil twilight, 12° for nautical twilight, and 18° for astronomical twilight. **4.** FINAL PERIOD the time when something is declining or approaching its end, especially in a gentle or peaceful way ○ *the twilight of the empire* **5.** same as **twilight zone** (sense 1) ■ *adj* OUTSIDE ORDINARY SOCIETY existing or operating beyond the laws and morals of ordinary society ○ *the twilight world of prostitution* [15C. < archaic twi- 'two, half' < Germanic]

Twilight of the Gods *n* **1.** same as **Götterdämmerung** (sense 1) **2.** same as **Ragnarök** [Translation of German *Götterdämmerung*]

twilight sleep *n* a state of partial consciousness in which awareness of pain is diminished or abolished, formerly induced during childbirth by injecting morphine and scopolamine

twilight war *n* a period of ominous inactivity that occurs during a war or leads up to a war

twilight zone *n* **1.** STATE OF UNCERTAINTY an ambiguous or unsettled state or condition, especially between two opposing conditions such as life and death or reality and fantasy **2.** RUN-DOWN AREA a neglected or run-down area, especially one on the edge of a city or town between the business centre and residential areas **3.** LOWEST PART OF SEA WITH LIGHT the lowest layer of the sea that natural light can reach

CULTURAL NOTE *The Twilight Zone*, a television series (1959–65) created by US writer Rod Serling. These dramatized fictional tales were the first adult television programmes to present paranormal events in a serious and believable way. Staple topics included time travel, accidental journeys, premonitions, and encounters with the dead and with aliens. The series inspired a film, *Twilight Zone—The Movie* (1983), and was revived sporadically from 1985–87, and run in syndication 1987–88. The expression *twilight zone* has long had the meaning 'the lowest layer of the sea that natural light can reach'. The show, however, popularized another pre-existing meaning, 'an ambiguous or unsettled state between two opposing conditions such as life and death or reality and fantasy'.

twilit /twílit/ *adj* lit by twilight or a similar kind of half-light, especially so as to create a feeling of mystery [Mid-19C. Past participle of earlier *twilight*, verb]

twill /twil/ *n* **1.** STRONG FABRIC a strong woven material with diagonal ridges or ribs across its surface **2.** TEXTILE WEAVE the weave used to produce twill ■ *vt* (**twills, twilling, twilled**) WEAVE TWILL to weave fabric with diagonal ridges or ribs across its surface [14C. < N English dialect variant of Old English *twilic* 'having two threads']

'twill /twil/ *contr* it will (*archaic or literary*)

twin /twin/ *n* **1.** EITHER OF TWO OFFSPRING BORN TOGETHER either of two people or animals born to the same mother at the same time. Fraternal twins arise from different egg cells and are equivalent to ordinary siblings, while identical twins are derived from the same egg cell and are genetically identical. (*often used before a noun*) ○ *twin boys* **2.** EITHER OF TWO SIMILAR THINGS somebody or something similar to or unusually closely associated with another **3.** TOWN LINKED WITH ANOTHER either of a pair of towns in two different countries with cultural and administrative links (*often used before a noun*) ○ *twin towns* **4.** CHEM COMPOUND CRYSTAL a compound crystal consisting of two mirror-image crystals that share a common plane ■ *adj* DOUBLE describes two identical things that operate together ○ *the streamlined twin hulls of a racing catamaran* ■ *v* (**twins, twinning, twinned**) **1.** *vti* PAIR PEOPLE OR THINGS to group people or things in pairs, or link people or things very closely, or be paired or closely grouped **2.** *vt* LINK UP TOWN WITH ANOTHER to create a cultural and administrative link in one town or city with another town or city in a

different country **3.** *vi* HAVE TWINS to give birth to twins [Old English *twinn* < Indo-European, 'two by two']

twin bed *n* either of a pair of matching single beds

twinberry /twínbəri/ (*plural* **-ries**) *n* **1.** PLANTS same as **partridgeberry** (sense 2) **2.** a bush of the honeysuckle family. Flowers: purple. Native to: North America. Latin name: *Lonicera involucrata*.

twin bill *n US* SPORTS same as **double-header**

twine /twīn/ *n* **1.** STRING string or cord made from threads or strands that have been twisted together **2.** SOMETHING MADE BY TWISTING something that is formed by twisting or coiling separate strands together **3.** TWISTING ACTION a twisting or weaving action ■ *v* (**twines, twining, twined**) **1.** *vti* TWIST AROUND SOMETHING to grow, wind, or twist around or together, or make something grow, wind, or twist around something else ○ *the ivy twining around the old oak tree* **2.** *vi* HAVE WINDING COURSE to take or follow a winding route (*literary*) **3.** *vt* WEAVE SOMETHING to make something by weaving or twisting separate strands together [Old English *twīn* 'double thread'. < Germanic] —**twiner** *n* —**twiny** *adj*

twin-engined, **twin-engine** *adj* powered by two engines ○ *a twin-engined plane*

twinflower /twín flow ər/ *n* a creeping plant of the honeysuckle family with opposite oval leaves. Flowers: pinkish-white, bell-shaped, in pairs. Native to: North America. Latin name: *Linnaea borealis*.

twinge /twinj/ *n* **1.** BRIEF PAIN a sudden brief stab of pain **2.** BRIEF UNCOMFORTABLE EMOTION a sudden brief uncomfortable pang of an emotion such as guilt or fear ■ *vti* (**twinges, twingeing, twinged**) FEEL TWINGE to feel a twinge of pain or emotion, or make somebody feel this [Old English *twengan* 'pinch' < Germanic]

twinkle /twíngk'l/ *vi* (**-kles, -kling, -kled**) **1.** SHINE WITH FLICKER to give out or reflect a bright but unsteady light, especially from a small or distant source **2.** SHINE WITH AMUSEMENT to be bright because of a feeling such as amusement, delight, or mischief (*refers to people's eyes*) ■ *n* **1.** FLICKERING SHINE a bright unsteady light, especially one that is small or seen from a distance **2.** BRIGHTNESS IN SOMEBODY'S EYES a brightness in somebody's eyes, caused by a feeling such as amusement, delight, or mischief **3.** same as **twinkling** [Old English *twinclian* 'keep blinking' < *twincan* 'blink' < Germanic] —**twinkler** *n* —**twinkly** *adj*

twinkling /twíngkling/ *n* MOMENT an instant of time ■ *adj* **1.** FLICKERING giving out or reflecting light brightly but unsteadily, especially from a small or distant source **2.** SHINING WITH AMUSEMENT shining because of a feeling such as amusement, delight, or mischief (*refers to people's eyes*) ◇ **in the twinkling of an eye** very quickly or very soon

twin-lens reflex *n* a camera that has two forward-facing lenses, one for focusing through and one for taking pictures

twinned /twind/ *adj* **1.** EXISTING AS MATCHING PAIR linked together as or like a couple **2.** SHARING CULTURAL LINK describes towns or cities in different countries that share cultural and administrative links **3.** CRYSTALS SYMMETRICAL describes a compound crystal consisting of two mirror-image crystals that share a common plane

twin room *n* a hotel room with twin beds

Twins /twinz/ *n* ASTRON, ZODIAC same as **Gemini** (senses 1–2)

twin-screw *adj* describes a ship that has two propellers

twinset /twín set/ *n* a woman's matching short-sleeved jumper and cardigan designed to be worn together

twin-tip *n* a ski with turned-up points front and back, fatter and softer than a typical downhill ski, designed so that the wearer can move forwards and backwards on a slope and perform complex moves while engaging in the sport of freeskiing [Late 20C.]

twin-tipped *adj* describes skis, snowboards, or similar pieces of sports equipment that are the same at both ends, e.g. that are rounded or upturned at front and rear

twin town *n* a town or city that has special cultural and administrative links with another town or city in a different country. Towns that are twinned

often display the names of their counterparts on boundary signs.

twin-tub *n* a washing machine with two separate compartments, one for washing and the other for spin-drying

twirl /twurl/ *v* (**twirls, twirling, twirled**) **1.** *vti* SPIN ROUND QUICKLY to turn lightly and rapidly round in a circle, or make something do this ○ *twirled his partner around the dance floor* **2.** *vt* FIDDLE WITH SOMETHING to fiddle with something by turning or spinning it between the fingers **3.** *vi* TURN AND FACE OTHER WAY to turn round suddenly to face somebody or face the other way ○ *She twirled round, her eyes blazing.* ■ *n* **1.** QUICK SPINNING MOVEMENT a quick turning or spinning movement, e.g. when somebody is dancing or modelling clothes **2.** SPIRAL a twisting or spiral shape, pattern, or line, especially something used for decoration [Late 16C. Probably alteration of *tirl*, variant of TRILL², after WHIRL] —**twirler** *n* —**twirly** *adj*

twirp *n* another spelling of **twerp**

twist /twist/ *v* (**twists, twisting, twisted**) **1.** *vti* MAKE ENDS TURN IN OPPOSITE DIRECTIONS to make one part or end of something turn in the opposite direction to the other, or turn in this way ○ *I twisted my handkerchief into a knot.* **2.** *vti* DISTORT SOMETHING to distort the shape or position of something, or become distorted ○ *His face was twisted in a grimace of disgust.* **3.** *vti* WIND SOMETHING to wind something round something else or wind things together, or be wound ○ *constantly twisting her hair round her fingers* **4.** *vt* INJURE PART OF BODY to injure part of the body by turning or moving it out of position ○ *I've twisted my ankle.* **5.** *vti* ROTATE SOMETHING to rotate something, or be rotated ○ *The lid just twists and comes off.* **6.** *vt* DISTORT MEANING OF SOMETHING to distort the meaning of something deliberately ○ *keeps twisting what I'm saying to make it sound as if I agree* **7.** *vt* AFFECT SOMETHING ADVERSELY to distort somebody's mind or outlook **8.** *vi* CONSTANTLY CHANGE DIRECTION to change direction constantly instead of continuing in a direct or straight line **9.** *vi* SQUIRM to squirm or wriggle ○ *a child twisting restlessly in her chair* **10.** *vi* DANCE to dance the twist **11.** *vt* CHEAT SOMEBODY to cheat somebody, especially by getting money from that person by fraudulent means (*informal*) ■ *n* **1.** TWISTING MOVEMENT the action or movement performed when somebody twists something ○ *a twist of the screw* **2.** UNEXPECTED DEVELOPMENT an unexpected development in a narrative or a sequence of events ○ *The story had a strange twist.* **3.** BEND a bend in something such as a road or river ○ *a road full of twists and turns* **4.** PAINFUL WRENCH a painful wrench or pull in a wrist, ankle, or another body part **5.** 1960S' DANCE a 1960s dance that involved moving the hips from side to side **6.** SOMETHING SHAPED BY BEING TWISTED something that has been shaped, split, or gathered together by being twisted ○ *a twist of paper* **7.** LENGTH OF YARN OR THREAD a length of yarn or thread whose strands have been twisted together **8.** SLICE OF LEMON a thin slice of lemon, lime, or another peel that is cut and twisted and added to a drink **9.** BREAD OR ROLL a roll or loaf of bread made by twisting pieces of dough **10.** CIGAR a cigar made from three cigars twisted together **11.** CHEWING TOBACCO tobacco leaves twisted into a roll from which pieces can be cut off and chewed **12.** FORCE CAUSING STRESS a force that causes stress or strain by twisting **13.** SPIN GIVEN TO BALL spin imparted to a hit or thrown ball **14.** ROTATION OF BODY a complete turn of the body around a vertical axis, e.g. in gymnastics or diving **15.** DISTORTION a contortion or distortion in the shape of something **16.** QUIRK OF CHARACTER an eccentricity or strange personal characteristic [Mid-16C. < Old English, 'something split in two, twisted yarn' < Germanic] —**twistable** *adj* —**twisting** *adj* —**twistingly** *adv* —**twisty** *adj* ◇ **be** or **go round the twist** an offensive term meaning to be or become mentally ill (*informal*)

CULTURAL NOTE *Oliver Twist*, a novel (1837–39) by Charles Dickens. It tells the tale of an abandoned child who runs away from his workhouse home to London, where he falls in with a band of criminals led by Fagin and his young assistant, a streetwise pickpocket called the Artful Dodger. The novel inspired a musical, *Oliver!* (1960) and several films, most notably David Lean's 1948 adaptation.

twist drill *n* a drill bit with one or more helical grooves along its axis to expel cuttings or swarf

twisted /twístid/ *adj* **1.** SUBJECTED TO TWISTING having one part or end turned in the opposite direction to the other ○ *twisted strands of fibre* **2.** DISTORTED IN SHAPE severely distorted in shape or form ○ *The force of the blast reduced the car to a heap of twisted metal.* **3.** CORRUPT morally unacceptable ○ *What kind of twisted mind could think up a thing like that?* **4.** BADLY AFFECTED BY EXPERIENCES badly affected by unpleasant experiences or constant disappointment (*informal*) ○ *The experience left her bitter and twisted.*

twister /twístər/ *n* **1.** SPORTS BALL WITH TWIST a ball that has been thrown or hit with a twist **2.** SOMEBODY OR SOMETHING THAT TWISTS a person or device that twists **3.** CHEAT somebody who cheats or misleads others (*dated informal insult*) **4.** *N Am* TORNADO a tornado, cyclone, or whirlwind (*informal*)

twist grip *n* a control mounted in one of the handlebars of a motorcycle or bicycle, allowing the rider to change gear or accelerate by twisting the grip

twistor /twíst awr/ *n* any of the solutions to the equations of twistor theory that manifest themselves as matter or energy

twistor theory *n* a mathematical theory of space-time that uses four complex numbers to define the three spatial dimensions plus time, rather than the conventional four real numbers, and has applications in relativity, integrable systems, and differential and integral geometry

twist-tie *n* a piece of wire sealed in a paper or plastic strip, used as a fastener, especially for a plastic bag

twit /twit/ *n* an offensive term that deliberately insults somebody's commonsense or consideration for others (*informal insult*) ■ *vt* (**twits, twitting, twitted**) to make fun of or criticize somebody in a playful friendly way (*dated*) [Mid-16C. Shortening of Old English *ætwītan* 'find fault' < *æt-* 'at' + *wītan* 'reproach' < Germanic]

twitch /twich/ *v* (**twitches, twitching, twitched**) **1.** *vi* JERK SLIGHTLY to move with a slight jerk, either once or repeatedly ○ *His eyebrow twitches when he's nervous.* **2.** *vt* PULL SOMETHING LIGHTLY AND QUICKLY to give something a sudden light tug or jerk **3.** *vi* HURT SHARPLY to hurt with a sharp or sudden pain ■ *n* **1.** JERKY MOVEMENT a slight jerky movement **2.** MUSCLE CONTRACTION a brief rapid contraction of a muscle **3.** FEELING OF DISCOMFORT a sharp or sudden feeling of physical or emotional pain **4.** VET HORSE RESTRAINT a restraint used on a horse during a veterinary procedure, consisting of a cord loop that can be pulled tight around the animal's upper lip [12C. Origin ?]

twitcher /twíchər/ *n* **1.** a person, animal, or thing that twitches **2.** a birdwatcher who will go to extreme lengths to spot rare birds (*informal*)

twitch grass *n* PLANTS same as **couch grass** [Alteration of QUITCH GRASS]

twitchy /twíchi/ (**-ier, -iest**) *adj* **1.** nervous and jittery (*informal*) **2.** twitching frequently

twite /twīt/ *n* a bird of the finch family with streaked brown feathers, the male of which has a pink rump. Native to: northern Europe. Latin name: *Acanthis flavirostris*. [Mid-16C. An imitation of the bird's call]

twitter[1] /twíttər/ *v* (**-ters, -tering, -tered**) **1.** *vi* CHIRP to sing in a succession of light high-pitched chirping sounds (*refers to birds*) **2.** *vi* CHATTER to chatter or giggle in an overexcited or nervous way **3.** *vti* USE SMALL HIGH VOICE to sing or say something in a light shaky high-pitched voice **4.** *vi* TREMBLE to quiver or move about nervously and quickly ■ *n* **1.** REPETITIVE HIGH-PITCHED SONG a continuous string of light high-pitched sounds made by a small bird or animal **2.** HIGH-PITCHED CHATTERING the light high-pitched sound of chattering or laughter **3.** EXCITEMENT a state of great agitation or excitement ○ *all of a twitter* [14C. An imitation of birds chirping] —**twitterer** *n* —**twittery** *adj*

twitter[2] /twíttər/ *n* somebody who makes fun of or criticizes somebody in a playful friendly way (*dated*) [Late 16C. < TWIT]

'twixt /twikst/ *prep* same as **between** (*archaic*) [14C. Shortening of BETWIXT]

twizzle /twízz'l/ (*informal*) *vt* (**-zles, -zling, -zled**) to twirl or twist something vigorously ■ *n* a vigorous twirl or twist [Late 18C. Probably alteration of TWIST or TWIRL]

two /too/ *n* (*plural* **twos**) **1.** **2** the number 2 **2.** SOMETHING WITH VALUE OF 2 something in a numbered series, e.g. a playing card, with a value of 2 ○ *the two of clubs* **3.** GROUP OF TWO a group of two people or objects ○ *arrived in twos and threes* ■ *prep* **2** ONLINE same as **to**[1] (*used in e-mails and text messages*) ○ *up 2 U* ■ *adv* **2** ONLINE same as **too** (*used in e-mails and text messages*) ○ *me 2* ■ *symbol* **2** TO-, -TO-, OR -TO used to replace 'to' within words (*used in e-mails and text messages*) ○ *2day* [Old English *twā* < Indo-European] — **two** *adj, pron* ◇ **it takes two to tango** used to indicate that both of the people involved in an awkward or unpleasant situation are responsible or to blame, not just one ◇ **put two and two together** to work something out from the available evidence ◇ **that makes two of us** used to indicate agreement with something expressed or acknowledgment of something shared

SPELLCHECK See ***to***[1].

2,4-D /tóo fawr dée/ *n* a white crystalline compound. Use: weedkiller. Formula: $C_8H_6Cl_2O_3$. [Mid-20C. *D* < DI-[1]]

2,4,5-T /too fawr fīv tée/ *n* an insoluble crystalline compound. Use: chemical weedkiller, plant hormone. Formula: $C_8H_5Cl_3O_3$. [Mid-20C. *T* < TRI-]

two-bit *adj N Am* of very low quality or importance (*informal*)

two-by-four, 2 x 4 *n N Am* INDUST same as **four-by-two**

twoc /twok/, **twock** (*slang*) *vt* (**twocs, twoccing, twocced; twocks, twocking, twocked**) to steal a car, often only temporarily for the purpose of joyriding ■ *n* the theft of a car, often only temporarily for the purpose of joyriding [Late 20C. Acronym < *taken without owner's consent*] —**twoccer** *n*

two cents worth *n N Am* an opinion, when expressed assertively as one of several ○ *just had to add her two cents worth*

twock *vt, n* CRIME another spelling of **twoc**

two-cycle *adj N Am* ENG same as **two-stroke**

two-dimensional *adj* **1.** HAVING LENGTH AND WIDTH describes a figure that has length and width but no depth, e.g. a geometrical figure on a single plane **2.** DONE ON FLAT SURFACE describes works of art such as paintings and drawings that exist on a flat surface, as opposed to art forms such as sculpture that also have depth **3.** HAVING NO DEPTH OF CHARACTER lacking the emotional or psychological depth that creates the impression of realism ○ *a two-dimensional character* —**two-dimensionality** *n* —**two-dimensionally** *adv*

two-edged *adj* **1.** having two sharp edges for cutting in opposite directions **2.** having two effects, one positive and one negative, especially two possible and opposite interpretations or meanings

two-faced *adj* **1.** insincere in dealings with people, especially by being outwardly friendly, but secretly disloyal **2.** having two faces or surfaces —**two-facedly** /-fáyssidli/ *adv*

twofer /tóofər/ *n US* (*informal*) **1.** DISCOUNT ENTITLEMENT a coupon entitling somebody to buy two items for the price of one, especially tickets for a play **2.** PAIR OF ITEMS SOLD AT DISCOUNT a set of two items sold together for exactly or approximately the price of each item sold singly **3.** DEAL OFFERING ADDED BENEFIT an offer or a situation in which a single expense or effort yields a benefit additional to the intended return [Late 19C. Alteration of *two for (one)*]

two-fisted /-fístid/ *adj N Am* characterized by energy, enthusiasm, assertiveness, or aggression (*informal*)

twofold /tóo fōld/ *adj* **1.** DOUBLE twice as much or as many **2.** HAVING TWO PARTS consisting of two parts ■ *adv* DOUBLY by the same amount over again

two-four time *n* a rhythm with two crotchet beats to the bar

two-handed *adj* **1.** USING TWO HANDS using or requiring the use of two hands **2.** DESIGNED FOR TWO designed for two people, especially for two players or operators **3.** AMBIDEXTROUS able to use either the left or right hand with equal skill **4.** WITH TWO HANDS having two hands —**two-handedly** *adv*

two-hander *n* a play written for and performed by two actors

two-master *n* a sailing ship with two masts

two one, 2.1 *n* in the United Kingdom and Australia, an undergraduate university degree awarded for the second-highest level of academic achievement

two-pack *n* a set of two identical products packaged together and sold as one

twopence /túppənss/, **tuppence** *n* **1.** the value of two pence, especially two pennies in the predecimal UK monetary system **2.** the least amount (*used in negative statements*) ○ *I don't care twopence what they think.*

twopenny /túppəni/, **tuppenny** *adj* **1.** costing or worth twopence **2.** inexpensive and of the poorest quality

two-phase *adj* describes an electrical system in which there are two alternating voltages of the same frequency, with a phase difference of 90° between them

two-piece *adj* consisting of two parts or pieces, especially pieces of clothing ■ *n* a suit consisting of two garments, e.g. a bikini

two-ply *adj* consisting of two layers or strands

two-pot screamer *n Aus* somebody who becomes drunk very easily (*informal*)

two-seater *n* **1.** a vehicle with seats for two people, especially a sports car **2.** a seat for two people, especially a sofa

two-shot *n* a film or television shot in which two people more or less fill the screen

two-sided *adj* **1.** HAVING TWO CONTESTING SIDES consisting of two contesting sides, e.g. two groups opposing each other or two equally valid opinions **2.** USING TWO SIDES OF PAGE using both sides of a sheet of paper **3.** HAVING TWO SURFACES having two sides or surfaces

twosome /tóossəm/ *n* **1.** a pair of people, especially two golfers paired to play together, a couple on a date together, or a team consisting of two players **2.** GOLF same as **single** *n* (sense 5)

two-spot *n* **1.** a game piece with two marks on it, e.g. a playing card or a domino **2.** *US* a two-dollar bill (*informal*)

two-step *n* **1.** BALLROOM DANCE a ballroom dance in 2/4 time with sliding steps **2.** DANCE MUSIC the music for a two-step ■ *vi* DANCE DANCE TWO-STEP to dance the two-step

two-stroke *adj* describes an internal-combustion engine in which the piston makes two movements, usually one upwards and one downwards, in each power cycle. N Am term **two-cycle**

two-tailed pasha *n* a butterfly that has brownish wings with an orange border. Native to: southern Europe. Latin name: *Charaxes jasius*.

two-tier *adj* having two levels, especially two levels of administration or two standards of treatment or privilege

two-time *vt* (*informal*) **1.** to be unfaithful to a romantic or sexual partner **2.** to deceive or betray a partner in an undertaking —**two-timer** *n*

two-toed sloth *n* a mainly nocturnal sloth with two digits on each forefoot. Native to: Central and South America. Latin name: *Choloepus didactylus*.

two-tone *adj* **1.** consisting of two colours or two shades of the same colour ○ *two-tone shoes* **2.** consisting of two sounds with different frequencies ○ *a two-tone siren*

two two, 2.2 *n* in the United Kingdom and Australia, an undergraduate university degree awarded for the third-highest level of academic achievement

'twould /twŏŏd/ *contr* it would (*archaic or literary*)

two-up *n Aus* an Australian gambling game in which bets are placed on how two tossed coins will land

two-way *adj* **1.** MOVING IN BOTH DIRECTIONS moving in opposite directions or allowing for movement in opposite directions ○ *a two-way street* **2.** INVOLVING TWO CONTESTANTS involving two people or teams ○ *a two-way race* **3.** ABLE TO TRANSMIT AND RECEIVE able both to transmit and to receive radio signals ○ *two-way radio* **4.** RECIPROCAL requiring cooperation between two people or groups **5.** WORKING IN DIFFERENT WAYS able to operate or be operated in either of two ways

two-way mirror *n* a sheet of glass that is a mirror on one side and can be seen through from the other.

Such mirrors are installed, e.g., in police stations to allow witnesses to identify suspects without themselves being seen. N Am term **one-way mirror**

two-wheeler *n* a vehicle with two wheels, especially a bicycle

TWU *abbr Aus* Transport Workers' Union

twyer *n* ENG same as **tuyère**

TX *abbr* ONLINE thanks (*used in e-mails or text messages*)

txt *abbr* a file extension for a text file. Full form **text**

TY *abbr* ONLINE thank you (*used in e-mails*)

Tycho /tíkō/ *n* a crater on the south of the Moon that is the centre of the Moon's most extensive ray system. It is 84 km/52 mi. in diameter, 4500 m/14,750 ft high, and is surrounded by terraced walls.

tycoon /tī kōon/ *n* **1.** an amasser of great wealth and power, especially in business **2.** same as **shogun** (*archaic*) [Mid-19C. < Japanese *taikun* 'great lord, shogun' < Chinese *dà* 'great' + *jūn* 'prince']

tyiyn /ti yeén/ (*plural same* or **-iyns**) *n* a subunit of Kyrgyz currency. See table at **currency** [Late 20C. < Kyrgyz]

tyke /tīk/, **tike** *n* **1.** MONGREL a dog of mixed breed **2.** NAUGHTY CHILD a little child, especially one who is naughty or mischievous (*informal*) **3.** *regional* PERSON FROM YORKSHIRE somebody who was born or lives in Yorkshire **4.** BOOR a man regarded as having coarse manners (*dated insult*) [14C. < Old Norse *tík* 'bitch']

tylectomy /tī léktəmi/ (*plural* **-mies**) *n* MED same as **lumpectomy** [Late 20C. < Greek *tulos* 'lump']

Tyler, **Anne** (*b.* 1941) US writer. Her novels include *Dinner at the Homesick Restaurant* (1982) and *The Accidental Tourist* (1985).

> 'I write because I want more than one life; I insist on a wider selection. It's greed, plain and simple.'
> [Anne Tyler, *Civilization*; 1995]

Tyler, **John** (1790–1862) 10th president of the United States. He was William Henry Harrison's vice president, and set a controversial historical precedent by assuming the presidency after Harrison's death. As president (1841–45), his greatest achievement was the annexation of Texas (1844). See table at **president**

Tyler, **Wat** (*d.* 1381) English revolutionary leader. The leader of the Peasants' Revolt of 1381, he secured concessions from Richard II but was killed during negotiations.

> 'No man should be a serf, nor do homage or any manner of service to any lord, but should give fourpence rent for an acre of land, and that no one should work for any man but as his own will, and on terms of a regular covenant.'
> [Attributed to Wat Tyler. Quoted in *Anonimalle Chronicle*; 14th century]

tylosis /tī lốssiss/, **tylose** /tílōss/ (*plural* **tyloses** /-seez/) *n* **1.** a callus or thickening, especially of the eyelids **2.** a sac that forms in the water-conducting vessels of the older wood of a tree, often in response to drought or disease. Tyloses may cause blockage, and often fill with resins, gums, or pigments that may help to preserve, strengthen, or colour the wood or provide a source of dyes. [Late 19C. Via modern Latin < Greek *tulōsis* 'formation of a callus or lump' < *tulē* 'callus, swelling']

tymbal *n* MUSIC another spelling of **timbal**

tympan /tímpən/ *n* **1.** PRINTING a piece of padding that fits between the impression cylinder of a printing press and the paper to be printed so as to ensure a uniform image **2.** ARCHIT same as **tympanum** (sense 1) **3.** ACOUSTICS a membrane or diaphragm that vibrates to produce or transmit sound, e.g. the skin on a drum or the diaphragm in a telephone receiver [Pre-12C. < Latin *tympanum* 'drum' (see TYMPANUM)]

tympana plural of **tympanum**

tympani MUSIC another spelling of **timpani**

tympanic /tim pánnik/ *adj* relating to a tympanum

tympanic bone *n* the part of the temporal bone that supports and partly surrounds the auditory canal

tympanic membrane *n* ANAT same as **eardrum** (*technical*)

tympanites /tímpə nī teez/ *n* swelling of the abdominal wall caused by gas trapped in the intestines or peritoneal cavity [14C. Via late Latin < Greek *tumpanitēs* < *tumpanon* 'drum'] —**tympanitic** /-níttik/ *adj*

tympanitis /tímpə nītis/ *n* inflammation of the eardrum [Mid-19C. < TYMPANUM]

tympanoplasty /tímpə nō plasti/ (*plural* **-ties**) *n* the surgical repair or reconstruction of the eardrum, usually in order to close a perforation [Mid-20C. < TYMPANUM]

tympanum

tympanum /tímpənəm/ (*plural* **-nums** or **-na** /-nə/) *n* **1.** ARCHIT RECESSED SPACE a recess, especially the recessed space between the top of a door or window and the arch above it, or between the cornices forming a classical triangular gable (**pediment**) **2.** ANAT EAR PART the eardrum or the cavity of the middle ear (*technical*) **3.** INSECTS INSECT ORGAN a vibrating membrane in some insects that serves as a hearing organ **4.** ACOUSTICS same as **tympan** (sense 3) [Early 16C. Via Latin < Greek *tumpanon* 'drum']

tympany /tímpəni/ *n* MED same as **tympanites** [15C. < Greek *tumpanias* < *tumpanon* 'drum']

Tyndale /tínd'l/, **Tindal**, **William** (1492?–1536) English religious reformer. His translation of the Bible into English laid the foundations of the Authorized Version (1611), but he was condemned for heresy and executed by the Church authorities.

Tyndall effect /tínd'l-/ *n* the scattering of light by minute particles in its path, such as dust in the air [Early 20C. After John *Tyndall* (1820–93), British physicist]

tyndallimetry /tínd'l ímmətri/ *n* the measurement of the concentration of suspended particles in a liquid by gauging the amount of light they scatter [See TYNDALL EFFECT]

Tyne /tīn/ river in northeastern England, formed by the union of the North Tyne and South Tyne rivers. It flows through Newcastle upon Tyne shortly before reaching the North Sea. Length: 48 km/30 mi.

Tynemouth /tín mowth, tínməth/ town at the mouth of the River Tyne, northeastern England. Population: 17,422 (1991).

Tyneside /tín sīd/ industrial and shipbuilding region along both banks of the lower River Tyne, northeastern England

typ. *abbr* PRINTING **1.** typographer **2.** typographical **3.** typography

type /tīp/ *n* **1.** CATEGORY OR KIND a group made up of individuals or items that have strongly marked and readily defined similarities ○ *What type of decoration did you have in mind?* ○ *People of that type never stay in a job for long.* **2.** PERSON OR THING somebody or something regarded as belonging to a group or category by virtue of having the main qualities associated with it ○ *They sent me a new type of keyboard to try out.* **3.** PARTICULAR KIND OF PERSON a person regarded as having a particular temperament or characteristics (*informal*) ○ *a gathering of bookish types* **4.** SOMEBODY WHO APPEALS somebody with the qualities that appeal to somebody else (*informal*) ○ *He's really not my type.* **5.** PRINTED CHARACTERS printed words, letters, or symbols as they appear on a page ○ *headings in italic type* **6.** PRINTING BLOCKS the set of small metal blocks used in printing, especially formerly, each of which has a raised figure that is the mirror image of a number or letter on one of its

sides ○ *set up the type* **7.** INDIVIDUAL PRINTING BLOCK an individual piece of type bearing a single character **8.** TEMPLATE something used as a pattern or template for making other things of the same kind **9.** BIOL REPRESENTATIVE ORGANISM a plant or animal that most fully represents its genus and whose attributes are used to define the genus as a whole and, usually, give it its name **10.** BIOL REPRESENTATIVE GENUS OR SPECIES a genus or species of plant or animal whose attributes serve as the defining characteristics for the next higher level of taxonomic classification **11.** LING LINGUISTIC UNIT a letter, word, or other linguistic unit regarded as representing all units that are forms of it, as distinct from an individual form (**token**) **12.** PHILOSOPHY GENERAL EXPRESSION an expression regarded not as a physical object but as an abstract pattern that individual expressions can conform to **13.** CHR SIGN OF SOMETHING TO COME an event, figure, or sign taken as foreshadowing something in the future ■ *v* (**types**, **typing**, **typed**) **1.** *vti* KEY WORDS ON KEYBOARD to key words using a computer keyboard, word processor, or typewriter **2.** *vt* CLASSIFY SOMETHING to classify something, especially blood, according to its type **3.** *vt* TYPECAST SOMEBODY to characterize somebody as being a person who plays a particular kind of role **4.** *vt* CHR FORESHADOW SOMETHING to foreshadow a future event or fact [15C. Via Latin *typus* < Greek *tupos* 'blow, impression'] —**typal** *adj*

USAGE See **kind**[2].

SYNONYMS *type, kind, sort, category, class, species, genre*

CORE MEANING: a group having a common quality or qualities

type a group made up of individuals or items that have strongly marked and readily defined similarities ○ *Certain types of bacteria can build up resistance to disinfectants.* ○ *The reactor was the same type as the one that exploded at Chernobyl in 1986.* **kind** or **sort** a group of individuals or items connected by shared characteristics ○ *comparing soils of different kinds* ○ *the kind of music you might have danced to in the 1600s* ○ *leisure activities of various sorts* ○ *What sort of things will you be painting?* **category** a group or set of things, people, or actions that are classified together because of common characteristics ○ *The available courses are broken into two main categories, full-time and part-time.* ○ *People who fall into none of these official categories can still contribute.* **class** a group into which things with at least one characteristic in common are organized ○ *other classes of drugs used in the treatment of cardiac arrest patients* ○ *They swept to eight golds and 11 medals in the 12 weight classes at the world championships.* **species** a type of something ○ *a species of formal public oration rarely heard nowadays* **genre** one of the categories, based on form, style, or subject matter, into which artistic works of all kinds can be divided. ○ *dramatic scenarios that parody genres such as the thriller and the spy novel* ○ *The club promises to feature quality music of all genres.*

type A *n* an anxious, hard-working person who has a strong drive to succeed and finds it hard to delegate or share tasks with colleagues (*often used before a noun*) ○ *type A behaviour*

type B *n* a patient and friendly person (*often used before a noun*) ○ *a type B personality*

typebar /típ baar/ *n* a lever operated by a typewriter key. Each typebar has one or more printing blocks on the end that print characters on the paper.

typecase /típ kayss/ *n* a tray or box for storing printer's type

typecast /típ kaast/ (**-casts**, **-casting**, **-cast**) *vt* **1.** to give an actor a series of parts of the same type, to the extent that the performer becomes associated with that kind of role and is overlooked for others **2.** to give an actor a part that suits his or her physical or emotional type —**typecaster** *n*

typeface /típ fayss/ *n* **1.** a style of printed character, e.g. roman or bold **2.** the side of a printing block that has the shape of the printed character on it

type founder *n* a manufacturer of metal printing type —**type foundry** *n*

type genus *n* the genus within a family or other higher taxonomic category that is most typical of it and usually bears the same name

type-high *adj* as high as the standard height of a block of printer's type, 23.3 mm/0.9186 in

type I error *n* in statistics, the error of rejection of a null hypothesis when it is true

type II error *n* in statistics, the failure to reject a false null hypothesis

type locality *n* a place where a rock formation or other geological feature was first found and described, and after which it is named

type metal *n* the alloy from which printing type is made, consisting mostly of lead, antimony, and tin

typescript /tīp skript/ *n* a typewritten document or other text [Late 19C. < TYPE + MANUSCRIPT]

typeset /tīp set/ (**-sets, -setting, -set**) *vt* to prepare text for printing, either by the use of computers or by arranging blocks of type manually

typesetter /tīp setər/ *n* **1.** somebody who sets type for printing **2.** a mechanical or electronic device that prepares text for printing —**typesetting** *n*

type-site *n* an archaeological site that is thought to typify a culture and that gives the culture its name

type species *n* a species of plant or animal that is most typical of its genus and bears the same name or a related name

type specimen *n* an individual plant or animal that serves as the basis for the description of its species. Its name is usually taken as the name of the species.

type style *n* PRINTING same as **typeface** (sense 1)

typewrite /tīp rīt/ (**-writes, -writing, -wrote** /-rōt/, **-written** /-rit'n/) *vti* to type something using a typewriter [Late 19C. Back-formation < TYPEWRITER]

typewriter

typewriter /tīp rītər/ *n* **1.** an electrical or mechanical device with keys that are pressed to print letters or other characters one by one on a sheet of paper inserted into the machine **2.** a printing typeface that looks like characters produced by a typewriter

typewriting /tīp rīting/ *n* **1.** the process or skill of using a typewriter **2.** text produced on a typewriter

typewritten past participle of **typewrite**

typewrote past tense of **typewrite**

typhlitis /ti flītiss/ *n* inflammation of the entrance to the large intestine (**caecum**) [Mid-19C. < Greek *tuphlon* 'caecum' < *tuphlos* 'sightless'] —**typhlitic** /ti flíttik/ *adj*

typhlology /ti flólləji/ *n* the scientific study of sightlessness [Late 19C. < Greek *tuphlos* 'blind']

Typhoeus /tī fée əss/ *n* in Greek mythology, a monster with a hundred dragon heads who fought with Zeus and was thrown down into the ground under Mount Etna —**Typhoean** *adj*

typhoid /tī foyd/, **typhoid fever** *n* a serious and sometimes fatal bacterial infection of the digestive system, caused by ingesting food or water contaminated with the bacillus *Salmonella typhi*. It causes fever, severe abdominal pain, and sometimes intestinal bleeding. ■ *adj* relating to typhoid or typhus —**typhoidal** /tī fóyd'l/ *adj*

Typhoid Mary *n* **1.** an offensive term for somebody who spreads a disease or is held to be responsible for spreading it **2.** an offensive term for somebody who spreads something undesirable such as pessimism or bad news, and is generally avoided (*insult*) [Early 20C. Nickname of *Mary* Mallon (d. 1938), Irish-born cook in the United States who was found to be a typhoid carrier]

typhoon /tī fóon/ *n* a violent tropical storm in the western Pacific and Indian oceans [Late 16C. Partly < Chinese (Cantonese) *taaî fung* 'big wind', partly via Portuguese *tufão* < Urdu *ṭūfān* < Arabic < Greek *tuphōn* 'whirlwind, hurricane'] —**typhonic** /tī fónnik/ *adj*

typhus /tīfəss/, **typhus fever** *n* an infectious disease that causes fever, severe headaches, a rash, and often delirium. It is spread by ticks and fleas carried by rodents. [Late 18C. < Greek *tuphos* 'smoke, stupor' < *tuphein* 'to smoke'] —**typhous** *adj*

typical /típpik'l/ *adj* **1.** REPRESENTATIVE having all or most of the characteristics shared by others of the same kind and therefore suitable as an example of it ○ *a typical small Midwestern town* ○ *typical of life in Victorian England* **2.** CHARACTERISTIC characteristic of an individual person or thing ○ *He evaded the question with typical dexterity.* **3.** AS BAD OR ANNOYING AS USUAL in accordance with your worst expectations (*informal*) ○ *That's just typical! There's never a cab when you want one.* **4.** BIOL RESEMBLING OTHERS IN TAXONOMIC GROUP describes an organism, species, or genus that has most of the characteristics that identify the larger taxonomic group to which it belongs [Early 17C. < medieval Latin *typicalis* < late Latin *typicus* < Greek *tupikos* < *tupos* 'blow, impression'] —**typicality** /típpi kálləti/ *n*

typically /típpikli/ *adv* **1.** IN USUAL WAY with all or many of the usual or expected characteristics ○ *a typically Mediterranean vista* **2.** AS A RULE in most cases or on most occasions ○ *Political action committees are typically formed by interest groups to raise money for political causes.* **3.** CHARACTERISTICALLY as is to be expected, especially annoyingly expected, of a particular person or thing ○ *The car, typically, refused to start.*

typify /típpi fī/ (**-fies, -fying, -fied**) *vt* **1.** to have all or most of the characteristics of a particular type of person or thing and therefore be a suitable example of it ○ *a community that typifies small-town America* **2.** to be a symbolic representation of something [Mid-17C. < Latin *typus* (see TYPE)] —**typification** /típpifi káysh'n/ *n* —**typifier** *n*

typist /tīpist/ *n* somebody who produces documents using a typewriter or computer keyboard

typo /tīpō/ (*plural* **-pos**) *n* PRINTING same as **typographical error** (*informal*) [Early 19C. Shortening]

typo., **typog.** *abbr* PRINTING **1.** typographer **2.** typographical **3.** typography

typographical /tīpə gráffik'l/, **typographic** /tīpə gráffik/ *adj* **1.** relating to the appearance of printed characters on the page **2.** relating to the activity of preparing texts for printing

typographical error *n* a printing error that results from striking the wrong key on a keyboard, e.g. a misspelt word

typography /tī póggrəfi/ *n* **1.** the appearance of printed characters on the page **2.** the activity or business of preparing texts for printing [Early 17C. Via French < modern Latin *typographia* < Greek *tupos* 'blow, impression'] —**typographer** *n*

typology /tī pólləji/ *n* **1.** CLASSIFICATION OF TYPES the study or systematic classification of types **2.** LANGUAGE STUDY the study of syntactic and morphological similarities in languages without regard to their history **3.** STUDY OF RELIGIOUS TEXTS the study of religious texts for the purpose of identifying episodes in them that appear to prophesy later events [Mid-19C. < Greek *typos* 'blow, impression'] —**typologic** /tīpə lójjik/ *adj* —**typological** /tīpə lójji-k'l/ *adj* —**typologically** *adv* —**typologist** *n*

typw. *abbr* **1.** typewriter **2.** typewritten

tyramine /tīrəmin/ *n* an amine, found in some foods and formed from the breakdown of the amino acid tyrosine, that has the effect of simulating sympathetic nervous system action. Formula: $C_8H_{11}NO$. [Early 20C. Blend of TYROSINE + AMINE]

tyrannical /ti ránnik'l/, **tyrannic** /ti ránnik/ *adj* **1.** ruling with absolute power over a population cruelly kept submissive and fearful **2.** cruelly or irrationally insisting on complete obedience and giving harsh punishment to those who disobey [Mid-16C. < French *tyrannique* < Greek *turannikos* < *turannos* 'tyrant'] —**tyrannically** *adv*

tyrannicide /ti ránni sīd/ *n* **1.** the killing of a tyrant **2.** the killer of a tyrant [Mid-17C. < Latin *tyrannicidium* 'tyrant-killing', *tyrannicida* 'tyrant-killer' < *tyrannus* (see TYRANT) + *caedere* 'kill' (see -CIDE)] —**tyrannicidal** /ti ránni sīd'l/ *adj*

tyrannize /tírrə nīz/ (**-nizes, -nizing, -nized**), **tyrannise** (**-nises, -nising, -nised**) *vti* **1.** to govern a people or community with extreme cruelty and harshness **2.** to treat somebody in a cruelly unfair way [15C. < French *tyranniser* < Old French *tyrant* (see TYRANT)] —**tyrannizer** *n*

tyrannosaur /ti ránnə sawr/, **tyrannosaurus** /-əss/, **tyrannosaurus rex** /-réks/ *n* a large fierce flesh-eating dinosaur that walked on powerful hind legs and had small front legs. It lived during the Cretaceous Period and was the largest carnivore. [Early 20C. < modern Latin *Tyrannosaurus* < Greek *turannos* 'tyrant' + *sauros* 'lizard']

tyranny /tírrəni/ (*plural* **-nies**) *n* **1.** CRUEL USE OF POWER cruelty and injustice in the exercise of power or authority over others **2.** OPPRESSIVE GOVERNMENT oppressive government by one or more people who exercise absolute power cruelly and unjustly **3.** STATE RULED BY TYRANT a country or state under the power of an oppressive ruler **4.** CRUEL ACT a cruel or oppressive act, especially one committed by a person wielding great power **5.** OPPRESSIVE EFFECT a controlling influence over somebody's life or actions that is felt to be harsh and unrelenting ○ *glad to be free for a while from the tyranny of books and book learning* [14C. Via French < late Latin *tyrannia* < Latin *tyrannus* 'tyrant'] —**tyrannous** *adj*

CULTURAL NOTE ***The Tyranny of Distance***, a book (1966) by Australian writer Geoffrey Blainey. A historical account of the way in which distance both within Australia and between Australia and the United Kingdom influenced the formation of the nation. The phrase is now part of the Australian English language.

tyrant /tīrənt/ *n* **1.** ABSOLUTE RULER an absolute ruler who exercises power cruelly and unjustly **2.** AUTHORITARIAN PERSON an unjust and oppressive exerciser of authority **3.** ANCIENT GREEK RULER in ancient Greece, a ruler who took control of a state without legal sanction and governed with absolute power [13C. Via Old French < Latin *tyrannus* < Greek *turannos*]

tyrant-flycatcher *n* BIRDS same as **flycatcher** (sense 2) [Translation of modern Latin *Tyrannidae*, family name]

~~**tyrany**~~ incorrect spelling of **tyranny**

tyre /tīr/ *n* **1.** RUBBER EDGING FOR WHEEL a hollow band of rubber, often reinforced with fibres of other material, fitted around the outer edge of a vehicle's wheel and filled with compressed air **2.** SOLID RUBBER EDGING a solid band of rubber fitted to a wheel's edge, e.g. on prams and children's bicycles **3.** METAL EDGING a band of metal fitted for reinforcement to the rims of wheels on various vehicles such as handcarts and railway carriages

Tyre /tīr/ town in southern Lebanon, on the Mediterranean Sea. It was the most important city of ancient Phoenicia. Population: 120,000 (1988). —**Tyrian** /tírri ən/ *adj*

Tyree, Mount /tī rée/ peak in the Ellsworth Mountains, the second highest mountain in Antarctica, first climbed in 1966. Height: 4,965 m/16,290 ft.

Tyrian purple *n* **1.** a deep purple dye extracted from molluscs **2.** a rich crimson-purple colour —**Tyrian purple** *adj*

tyro /tīrō/ (*plural* **-ros** /-rōz/) *n* somebody who is just beginning to learn something [Early 17C. Via medieval Latin, 'squire' < Latin *tiro* 'young soldier, recruit'] —**tyronic** /tī rónnik/ *adj*

SYNONYMS See ***beginner***.

tyrocidine /tīrō sīdeen/, **tyrocidin** /-sīdin/ *n* an antibiotic polypeptide that is the main constituent of the antibiotic tyrothricin. Source: the soil bacillus *Bacillus brevis*. [Mid-20C. Contraction of TYROTHRICIN + GRAMICIDIN + -INE]

Tyrol another spelling of **Tirol**

Tyrolienne /ti rōli én/ *n* **1.** a lively folk dance of Tirolese origin **2.** the music for a Tyrolienne [Late 19C. < French *tyrolienne*, feminine of *tyrolien* 'Tirolean']

Tyrone /tī rōn/ historic county in western Northern Ireland, now divided into four local government districts. It was the largest of the six counties of Northern Ireland.

tyropitta /ti róppitə/ *n* a Greek cheese pie usually made with filo pastry [Late 20C. < modern Greek *turopēta* 'cheese pie']

tyrosinase /tī róssə nayz/ *n* a copper-containing enzyme involved in the production of dopa from tyrosine [Late 19C. < TYROSINE]

tyrosine

tyrosine /tī́rō seen/ *n* an amino acid that is the precursor of adrenaline, thyroxine, and melanin. Formula: $C_9H_{11}NO_3$. [Mid-19C. < Greek *turos* 'cheese']

tyrothricin /tī́rō thrī́ssin/ *n* an antibiotic drug made from tyrocidine and gramicidin. Use: against grampositive bacteria in local infections. [Mid-20C. < modern Latin *Tyrothric-* < Greek *turos* 'cheese' + *thrix* 'hair']

~~tyrrany~~ incorrect spelling of **tyranny**

Tyrrhenian Sea /ti re̊eni ən-/ arm of the Mediterranean Sea, partially enclosed by the Italian Peninsula and the islands of Corsica, Sardinia, and Sicily. Area: 155,000 sq. km/59,800 sq. mi.

Tyson /tī́ss'n/, **Mike** (*b.* 1966) US boxer. He is the youngest heavyweight fighter to win a world title (1986). Born **Tyson, Michael Gerald**

> 'I'm just a normal guy with heart.'
> [Mike Tyson, *Mike Tyson: Money, Myth and Betrayal*, Monteith Illingworth; 1992]

tz *abbr* ONLINE Tanzania (*used in Internet addresses*) See table at **domain name**

tzaddik /tsaʹadik/ (*plural* **-dikim** /tsaʹadi keʹem/), **tsaddik**, **zaddik** (*plural* **-dikim**) *n* **1.** in Judaism, a righteous man **2.** same as **rebbe** [Late 19C. < Hebrew *ṣaddīq* 'righteous']

tzar *n* POL another spelling of **tsar**

Tzara /tsaʹarə/, **Tristan** (1896–1963) Romanian-born French essayist and poet. A cofounder of the Dada movement, he wrote *Sept Manifestes Dada* (*Seven Dada Manifestos*) (1924).

tzarism *n* POL another spelling of **tsarism**

tzatziki /sat seʹeki, tsat-/ *n* a dip of Greek origin made from yogurt, chopped cucumber, mint, and garlic [Mid-20C. Via modern Greek *tsatsiki* < Turkish *cacik*]

tzetze fly *n* INSECTS another spelling of **tsetse fly**

tzigane /tsi gaʹan, si/ *n* a member of a Roma people, especially one from Hungary [Mid-18C. Via French < Hungarian *czigany*] —**tzigane** *adj*

tzimmes /tsímməss/ (*plural same*), **tsimmes** *n* **1.** a stew of meat, vegetables, and dried fruits, baked in a casserole **2.** *US* a confused, muddled, or agitated state (*slang*) [Late 19C. < Yiddish *tsimes*]

tzitzith /tsítsiss/, **tzitzit**, **tzitzes**, **tsitses** *npl* the fringes on the corners of a Jewish prayer shawl (**tallis**), a reminder to Jews of God's commandments (Numbers 15:38) [Late 17C. < Hebrew *ṣīṣīt*]

tzuris *n* another spelling of **tsuris**

Uu

u /yoo/ (*plural* **u's**), **U** (*plural* **U's** or **Us**) *n* **1**. the 21st letter of the English alphabet, representing a vowel sound **2**. a written representation of the letter 'u'

U[1] /yoo/, **u** *pron* a written form of 'you' (*informal*) [Because the letter *U* and *you* are pronounced the same]

U[2] /yoo/ (*plural* **U's** or **Us**) *n* **1**. something shaped like a letter 'U' **2**. in the United Kingdom, film classification for films that can be seen by everybody, regardless of age. Full form **universal**

U[3] /oo/ *n* a title of respect for a man used in Myanmar, equivalent to 'Mr' [Mid-20C. < Burmese]

U[4] *symbol* **1**. PHYS internal energy **2**. *also* Ⓤ JUDAISM kosher certification **3**. ELEC potential difference **4**. CHEM ELEM uranium

U[5] *abbr* **1**. united **2**. EDUC university **3**. EDUC unsatisfactory

u., **U.** *abbr* **1**. uncle **2**. unit **3**. upper

ua *abbr* ONLINE Ukraine (*used in Internet addresses*) See table at **domain name**

UAE *abbr* United Arab Emirates

UAI *n* in New South Wales and the Australian Capital Territory, Australia, a rank between 0 and 100, awarded on the basis of performance in HSC examinations, that is used to assess eligibility for tertiary courses. Full form **Universities Admission Index**

uakari /wə kaˈari/ (*plural same*) *n* a short-tailed monkey that lives high in the forest canopy, seldom coming down onto the ground. Native to: South America. Genus: *Cacajao*. [Mid-19C. < Tupi]

UAM *abbr* underwater-to-air missile

U&Es *npl* blood tests of the body's chemistry used to determine the general health of a patient and, specifically, kidney and lung function, effects of medications, and state of hydration. Full form **urea and electrolytes**

UART /yoo aart/ *abbr* COMPUT universal asynchronous receiver/transmitter

UAV *n* an uncrewed aerial vehicle that can fly over combat zones and staging areas, dropping supplies to troops, releasing bombs, and carrying out reconnaissance on enemy forces [Late 20C. Acronym < *uncrewed aerial vehicle*]

Ubangi /yoo báng gi/ river in central Africa. The chief tributary of the River Congo, it is formed by the confluence of the Bomu and Uele rivers. Length: 1,130 km/700 mi.

Ubangi-Shari /yoo báng gi shaˈari/ former name for **Central African Republic** (until 1958)

U-bend *n* a U-shaped section of water pipe inserted in a waste system, e.g. beneath a basin, to trap water and so prevent the backflow of noxious vapours

uber- *prefix* exceptional of his or her kind (*slang*) ○ *uberchef* ○ *ubermodel* [< German *über* 'over, above, higher', after ÜBERMENSCH]

uberchef /óóbər shef/ *n* a chef who is considered to be outstandingly talented and successful (*slang*)

Übermensch /óóbər mensh, yóóbər-/ (*plural* **-menschen** /-mensh'n/) *n* a superior kind of human being, especially in Nietzschean philosophy or Nazi ideology [Late 19C. < German, back-formation < *übermenschlich* 'superhuman']

ubermodel /óóbər modd'l/ *n* a fashion model who is regarded as being among the most successful and well-known in the industry (*slang*)

ubiety /yoo bíˈəti/ *n* the condition of existing in a specific place (*literary*) [Late 17C. < medieval Latin *ubietas* < Latin *ubi* 'where']

ubiquinone /yoo bíkwinōn/ *n* an electron transporter in energy-producing reactions that take place in mitochondria [Mid-20C. Blend of UBIQUITOUS + QUINONE]

ubiquitarianism /yoo bíkwi táiri ənizəm/ *n* the Christian belief, held particularly by the Lutheran Church, that Jesus Christ is present in all places and at all times, not just in Communion —**ubiquitarian** *n*, *adj*

ubiquitin /yoo bíkwitin/ *n* a heat-stable protein found in most cellular organisms (eukaryotes) that is involved in many cell processes such as DNA repair and removing metabolic wastes

ubiquitous /yoo bíkwitəss/ *adj* present everywhere at once, or seeming to be [Mid-19C. < modern Latin *ubiquitas* 'presence everywhere' < Latin *ubique* 'everywhere' < *ubi* 'where'] —**ubiquitously** *adv* —**ubiquitousness** *n* —**ubiquity** *n*

ubi supra /úbi soˈoprə/ *adv* where mentioned above [Latin, 'where above']

U-boat *n* a German submarine, especially one used during World Wars I and II [Early 20C. Partial translation of German *U-Boot*, shortening of *Unterseeboot* 'undersea boat']

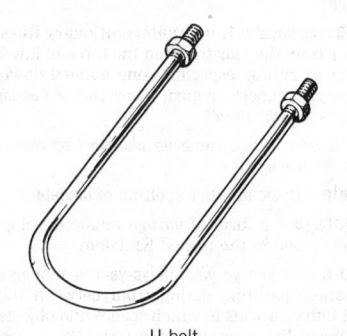
U-bolt

U-bolt *n* a U-shaped bolt, threaded at the two ends

ubuntu /oo bŏontoo/ *n* S Africa humanity, compassion, and goodness, regarded as fundamental to the way Africans approach life [Late 20C. < Xhosa]

Uc *tdmk* in the United Kingdom, a rating given to a video that is particularly suitable for preschool children

u.c. *abbr* PRINTING uppercase

UCAS /yoo kass/ *n* the central organization that processes applications for full-time undergraduate courses at UK universities and colleges. Full form **Universities and Colleges Admissions Service**

UCATT /yoo kat/ *abbr* Union of Construction, Allied Trades, and Technicians

UCAV /yoo kav/ *n* an attack aircraft, typically miniaturized, pilotless, and controlled by targeting and weapons systems based both on the ground and in the air. Full form **unmanned combat aerial vehicle**

Ucayali /oo kaa yaˈali/ river in eastern Peru, formed by the confluence of the Apurímac and Urubamba rivers. It is one of the headwaters of the River Amazon. Length: 1,900 km/1,200 mi.

UCC *abbr* United Church of Christ

UCCA /úkə/ *abbr* EDUC Universities Central Council on Admissions. Now called **UCAS**

UCE, **uce** *abbr* ONLINE unsolicited commercial e-mail

UCLA *abbr* University of California at Los Angeles

UDA *abbr* POL Ulster Defence Association

Udaipur /yoo dīpoor, yoo dīpoor/ city and administrative headquarters of Udaipur District, Rajasthan State, northwestern India. Population: 308,571 (1991).

udder /úddər/ *n* a bag-shaped structure containing two or more milk-secreting glands, each with its own teat, found in mammals such as cows, sheep, and goats [Old English *ūder* < Indo-European]

UDI *abbr* POL unilateral declaration of independence

Udjung Pandang /oojŏong pan dáng/, **Ujungpandang** city and port on the Makassar Strait, southwestern Sulawesi, Indonesia. Population: 944,372 (1990). Former name **Makassar**

UDM *abbr* Union of Democratic Mineworkers

Udmurt /óod moort/ (*plural same* or **-murts**) *n* **1**. a member of a people who live mainly in Udmurtia in central Russia **2**. the Finno-Ugric language of the Udmurt people. Native speakers: 500,000. [Mid-20C. Via Russian < Udmurt *Ud murt*, < *Ud*, name of a region + *murt* 'man'] —**Udmurt** *adj*

Udmurtia /óod moˈorti ə/ autonomous republic in eastern European Russia between Tatarstan and Bashkortostan. Capital: Izhevsk. Population: 1,640,700 (1994). Area: 42,100 sq. km/16,300 sq. mi.

udo /óodō/ (*plural* **udos**) *n* a perennial plant of the ginseng family whose tender shoots are cooked and eaten as a vegetable. Native to: South Asia. Latin name: *Aralia cordata*. [Late 20C. < Japanese]

udometer /yoo dómmitər/ *n* a gauge that measures rainfall (*technical*) [Early 19C. < French *udomètre* < Latin *udus* 'wet' + *mètre* 'meter']

udon /óo don/ *n* in Japanese cooking, pasta in the form of thick wheat strips [Early 20C. < Japanese]

UDR *abbr* POL Ulster Defence Regiment

UE *abbr* LEISURE urban exploration

UEFA /yoo áyfə/ *abbr* Union of European Football Associations

Ufa /oo faˈa/ industrial city in southeastern European Russia, situated at the confluence of the Ufa and Belaya rivers, on the western slopes of the Ural Mountains. Population: 1,473,912 (1995).

Uffington /úffingtən/ village in Oxfordshire, south-central England. A large figure of a white horse cut in the chalk hill nearby is believed to date from the Iron Age. Population: 748 (1991).

Uffizi /oo fítsi/ *n* a museum in Florence that contains one of the world's finest collections of Italian paintings. It is located in 16th-century buildings first used to house the Medici family's art collection, the nucleus of the museum's present holdings. [Mid-19C. < Italian, 'offices', because built to house the administrative centre of the Florentine state]

UFO /yoo ef ō, yóofō/ (*plural* **UFOs**) *n* a flying object that cannot be identified and is thought by some to be an alien spacecraft [Mid-20C. Acronym < *unidentified flying object*]

ufology /yoo fólləji/ *n* the study of UFOs, especially the investigation of recorded sightings of them

ug *abbr* ONLINE Uganda (*used in Internet addresses*) See table at **domain name**

Uganda

Uganda /yoo gándə/ country in East Africa. It became a member of the Commonwealth in 1962 and a republic in 1967. Language: English. Currency: Uganda shilling. Capital: Kampala. Population: 25,632,794 (2003). Area: 241,038 sq. km/93,065 sq. mi. Official name **Republic of Uganda** —**Ugandan** *n*, *adj*

Ugaritic /óogə ríttik/ *n* an extinct Semitic language of the region that is now northern Syria, closely related to Hebrew and Phoenician [Mid-20C. < *Ugarit*, ancient city in N Syria] —**Ugaritic** *adj*

UGC *abbr* University Grants Committee

Ugg boot *n* ▸ **Ugh boot**

ugh /ug, òokh, u/ *interj* used as the written form of a grunting exclamation of disgust, strain, or horror [Mid-19C. Representing an involuntary utterance]

Ugh boot /úg-/ *tdmk Aus* a trademark for a sheepskin boot with a fleecy lining

uglify /úggli fī/ (-**fies, -fying, -fied**) *vt* to make somebody or something physically unappealing —**uglification** /úgglifi káysh'n/ *n* —**uglifier** *n*

ugly /úggli/ (-**lier, -liest**) *adj* **1.** UNATTRACTIVE lacking appealing physical features, especially facial ones ○ *one of the ugliest cities in Europe* ○ *He was an exceedingly ugly man, and the painter didn't attempt to disguise the fact.* **2.** POTENTIALLY VIOLENT having the potential to result in violence or hostility ○ *an ugly mood* **3.** UNPLEASANT generally unpleasant or objectionable, or morally repulsive ○ *a dull ugly afternoon* ○ *Ugly rumours have been circulating about her private life.* [13C. < Old Norse *uggligr* 'frightful' < *uggr* 'fear'] —**uglily** *adv* —**ugliness** *n*

SYNONYMS See *unattractive*.

ugly American *n* a loud, boorish, nationalistic American, especially one travelling abroad, who is regarded as conforming to a stereotype that gives Americans a bad reputation

ugly Australian *n Aus* an Australian whose behaviour, especially when overseas, is thought to conform to a negative national stereotype of an ignorant, uncultivated person with a tendency towards drunkenness and boorishness (*informal*)

ugly duckling *n* **1.** somebody or something originally considered ordinary but whose true beauty or value is later revealed or appreciated **2.** somebody or something regarded as physically unappealing in comparison to others [< *The Ugly Duckling*, children's story by Hans Christian Andersen in which a cygnet raised by a duck is considered ugly until it grows into a beautiful swan]

Ugrian /yoógri ən/ *n* a member of a group of peoples, including the Magyars and Voguls, who live in Hungary and parts of Siberia [Mid-19C. < Russian *Ugry* 'Hungarians' < Turkic] —**Ugrian** *adj*

Ugric /yoógrik/ *n* a branch of the Finno-Ugric family of languages that includes Hungarian [Mid-19C. < Russian *Ugry* 'Hungarians' (see UGRIAN)] —**Ugric** *adj*

uh /u/ *interj* used as the written form of a grunting exclamation used to express surprise or request something to be said again [Early 17C. Representing an inarticulate sound]

UHF *n* any or all radio frequencies between 300 and 3000 megahertz, typically used for television transmission. Full form **ultrahigh frequency**

uh-huh /u hú/ *interj* used as the written form of a grunting exclamation made to express agreement

or to answer affirmatively [Representing an inarticulate sound]

uh-oh /ú ō/ *interj* used as the written form of a grunting exclamation made to express apprehension [Representing an articulate sound]

UHT *adj* sterilized and having a long shelf-life as a result of being heated to a very high temperature. Full form **ultra heat treated**

uh-uh /u ú, ú u/ *interj* used as the written form of a grunting exclamation made to express disagreement or to answer in the negative [Representing an inarticulate sound]

uhuru /oo hóoroo/ *n* freedom or national independence, especially for the people of eastern Africa [Mid-20C. < Kiswahili]

UI *abbr* COMPUT user interface

U-ie /yoo í/ (*plural* **U-ies**) *n* same as **U-turn** (*informal*) [Late 20C. Shortening and alteration of U-TURN]

Uigur /wéegər, -goor/ (*plural same* or -**gurs**), **Uighur** *n* **1.** a member of a people who live in western China, mainly in northwestern Xinjiang Uygur Autonomous Region **2.** the Turkic language of the Uigur people. Native speakers: 7 million. [Mid-18C. < E Turkic] —**Uigur** *adj* —**Uigurian** /wee goóri ən/ *adj* —**Uiguric** /wee goórik/ *adj*

uilleann pipes /óoli ən-/ *npl* Irish bagpipes played by squeezing the bellows under the arm [Early 20C. < Irish *píob uilleann* 'elbow pipe' < *uille* 'elbow' < Old Irish *uilind*]

uintaite /yoo íntə īt/ *n* a bitumen mined in the Uinta mountains in Utah in the United States. Use: manufacturing industries. [Late 19C. < the *Uinta* mountains]

uitlander /áyt landər/, **Uitlander** *n S Africa* a foreigner, especially a British person resident in the former Transvaal or Orange Free State [Late 19C. < Afrikaans < Middle Dutch *uteland* 'foreign country']

Ujungpandang another spelling of **Udjung Pandang**

uk *abbr* ONLINE United Kingdom (*used in Internet addresses*) See table at **domain name**

UK *abbr* United Kingdom

UKAEA *abbr* United Kingdom Atomic Energy Authority

ukase /yoo káyz/ *n* **1.** in pre-Revolutionary Russia, an order from the tsar that had the force of law **2.** any order or ruling, especially one handed down by a self-styled expert or guru [Early 18C. < Russian *ukaz* 'edict' < *ukazat* 'show']

uke /yook/ *n* MUSIC same as **ukulele** (*informal*) [Early 20C. Shortening]

ukelele *n* MUSIC another spelling of **ukulele**

UK garage *n* a form of garage music developed by bands based in the United Kingdom

ukiyo-e /yoó kee yō yáy/, **ukiyo-ye** *n* a movement in Japanese painting dating from between the 17th and 19th centuries in which scenes and objects from ordinary life were depicted [Late 19C. < Japanese, 'transitory-world picture']

Ukraine

Ukraine /yoo kráyn/ country in eastern Europe, south of Russia, with a coastline on the Black Sea. Language: Ukrainian. Currency: hryvnia. Capital: Kiev. Population: 48,055,439 (2003). Area: 603,700 sq. km/233,100 sq. mi.

Ukrainian /yoo kráyni ən/ *n* **1.** somebody who comes from Ukraine **2.** a Balto-Slavic language, the official language of the Ukraine, also spoken in Poland and

the Czech Republic. Native speakers: 45 million. —**Ukrainian** *adj*

ukulele /yoókə láyli/, **ukelele** *n* an instrument like a small guitar with four strings [Late 19C. < Hawaiian 'ukulele 'jumping flea']

Ulaanbaatar /oó laan báatər/, **Ulan Bator** capital city of the Republic of Mongolia, situated in the north-central part of the country, on the River Tuul. Population: 791,000 (2000).

ulama /oólimə/, **ulema** *npl* a body of Islamic scholars who have jurisdiction over legal and social matters for the people of Islam ■ *n* a member of the ulama [Late 17C. Via Turkish *'ulemā* < Arabic *'ulamā* 'learned men']

Ulan Bator another spelling of **Ulaanbaatar**

Ulan-Ude /oo laán oo dáy/ port city in southern Siberian Russia, located at the confluence of the Uda and Selenge rivers. Population: 410,359 (1995).

Ulbricht /óol brikht/, **Walter** (1893–1973) president of East Germany (1960–73). He was the cofounder and secretary of the Socialist Unity Party (1950–71) and served as deputy premier (1949–50) before becoming head of state in 1960.

ulcer /úlssər/ *n* **1.** INTERNAL SORE a slow-healing sore on the surface of a mucous membrane, especially the membrane lining the stomach or other part of the digestive tract **2.** EXTERNAL SORE a suppurating sore on the skin that does not heal and results in the destruction of tissue **3.** BAD INFLUENCE a corrupting or debilitating influence [14C. < Latin *ulcer-*, stem of *ulcus* 'a sore'] —**ulcerous** *adj*

ulcerate /úlssə rayt/ (-**ates, -ating, -ated**) *vti* to cause the formation of an ulcer or ulcers, or undergo the formation of an ulcer or ulcers —**ulceration** /úlssə ráysh'n/ *n* —**ulcerative** /-raytiv, -rətiv/ *adj*

ulcerative colitis *n* inflammation of the walls of the bowel accompanied by the formation of ulcers. The condition can result in permanent bowel damage.

ulcerative gingivitis *n* painful inflammation of the gums accompanied by the formation of ulcers. The condition is associated with bacterial infection and malnutrition.

-ule *suffix* small one, miniature ○ *lobule* [Via French < Latin -*ulus*]

ulema *npl* ISLAM another spelling of **ulama**

-ulent *suffix* having a great deal of something ○ *flocculent* [< Latin -*ulentus*]

ullage /úllij/ *n* (*formal*) **1.** the amount or volume by which a container, especially one for liquids, is short of being full **2.** the amount of liquid lost from a container through evaporation or leakage [15C. < Anglo-Norman *ulliage* < Old French *ouillier* 'fill a barrel to the bunghole' < *oeil* 'eye, bunghole' < Latin *oculus* 'eye']

Ullswater /úlz wawtər/ second largest lake in England, in the Lake District, northwestern England. Area: 8 sq. km/3 sq. mi.

Ulm /óolm/, **Charles** (1898–1934) Australian aviator. He flew as copilot with Charles Kingsford Smith on several flights, including the first crossing of the Pacific in 1928. Full name **Ulm, Charles Thomas Philippe**

ulna /úlnə/ (*plural* -**nae** /-nee/ or -**nas**) *n* **1.** the longer of the two bones in the human forearm, situated on the inner side **2.** a bone in the lower forelimb of vertebrate animals, roughly corresponding to the human ulna [Mid-16C. < Latin, 'elbow, forearm'] —**ulnar** /úlnər/ *adj*

ulnar nerve *n* a major nerve of the arm that runs down the inner side of the upper arm and is situated just under the skin at the elbow

ulotrichous /yoo lóttrikəss/ *adj* having hair that is naturally tightly curled, or belonging to a group of people with this kind of hair [Mid-19C. < Greek *oulos* 'crisp, curly' + *trikh-*, stem of *thrix* 'hair']

ulster /úlstər/ *n* a man's long heavy double-breasted overcoat [Mid-19C. After ULSTER]

Ulster /úlstər/ **1.** historic province in the north of Ireland comprising nine counties, including the six that make up Northern Ireland **2.** an informal name for Northern Ireland —**Ulsterman** *n* —**Ulsterwoman** *n*

Ulster Unionist Party *n* a Northern Ireland political party, formed in 1920. It is the largest and most moderate of the parties committed to the main-

tenance of the union between the UK and Northern Ireland.

ult. *abbr* **1.** ultimate **2.** ultimo

ulterior /ul tééri ər/ *adj* **1. UNDERLYING** existing in addition to, or being other than, what is apparent or assumed ○ *ulterior intent* **2. LYING OUTSIDE** lying beyond or outside a point or area **3. HAPPENING IN FUTURE** happening or expected in the future [Mid-17C. < Latin, 'further' < assumed *ulter* 'beyond'] —**ulteriorly** *adv*

ulterior motive *n* a second and underlying motive, usually a selfish or dishonourable one

ultima /últimə/ *n* the final syllable of a word [Early 20C. < Latin, form of *ultimus* (see ULTIMATE)]

ultimata plural of **ultimatum**

ultimate /últimət/ *adj* **1. FINAL** coming or attained at the end of a series of stages, and often constituting the culmination of something ○ *our ultimate destination* ○ *Their ultimate aim is to introduce a new system of government.* **2. GREATEST** greatest, most nearly perfect, or highest in quality ○ *the ultimate home entertainment system* **3. FUNDAMENTAL** existing as an underlying reality, when all other things are disregarded ○ *the ultimate truth* **4. FARTHEST AWAY** outermost or most remote ■ *n* **GREATEST THING** the greatest or most nearly perfect thing ○ *seats that were the ultimate in passenger comfort* [Mid-17C. < late Latin *ultimatus*, past participle of *ultimare* 'be at an end' < Latin *ultimus* 'last, final' < assumed *ulter* 'beyond'] —**ultimacy** *n*

ultimately /últimətli/ *adv* **1.** in the end, as the culmination of a process or event ○ *I ultimately decided not to take part.* **2.** most importantly, when all things are considered ○ *She believes that human beings are ultimately good.*

ultima Thule /-thyóoli/ *n* (*literary*) **1.** a distant or very remote place **2.** an ultimate or distant goal [Late 18C. < Latin, 'farthest Thule', the northernmost part of the inhabited world]

ultimatum /últi máytəm/ (*plural* **-tums** or **-ta** /-tə/) *n* a demand accompanied by a threat to inflict some penalty if the demand is not met [Mid-18C. < modern Latin < Latin *ultimatus* (see ULTIMATE)]

ultimo /últimō/ *adj* used in formal correspondence to refer to the previous month (*dated formal*) ○ *your letter of the 20th ultimo* [Late 16C. < Latin *ultimo (mense)* 'in the last (month)' < *ultimus* (see ULTIMATE)]

ultimogeniture /últimō jénnichər/ *n* the principle of inheritance or succession by the youngest son [Late 19C. < Latin *ultimus* 'last', after *primogeniture*]

ultra /últrə/ *adj* **1. EXTREME** exceeding or going beyond all other of the same kind **2. HOLDING EXTREMIST VIEWS** holding extremist views, especially in religious or political matters **3. EXCELLENT** excellent or superior (*slang*) ■ *n* **EXTREMIST** somebody with extremist views, especially in religious or political matters [Late 19C. Via French < Latin, 'beyond']

ultra- *prefix* **1.** more than normal, excessively, completely ○ *ultrasophisticated* **2.** outside the range of ○ *ultrasound* [< Latin *ultra* 'beyond' < Indo-European]

ultracareful *adj*
ultracasual *adj*
ultracautious *adj*
ultrachic *adj*
ultraclean *adj*
ultracold *adj*
ultracompact *adj*
ultraconservative *adj, n*
ultracontemporary *adj*
ultraconvenient *adj*
ultracool *adj*
ultracritical *adj*
ultradense *adj*
ultradry *adj*
ultraefficient *adj*
ultraexclusive *adj*
ultrafamiliar *adj*
ultrafast *adj*
ultrafastidious *adj*
ultrafine *adj*
ultraglamorous *adj*
ultraheavy *adj*
ultrahigh *adj*
ultrahip *adj*
ultrahot *adj*
ultraliberal *adj*
ultralow *adj*
ultramilitant *adj, n*
ultraminiature *adj*
ultrapatriot *n*
ultrapatriotic *adj*
ultrapowerful *adj*
ultrapractical *adj*
ultraprecise *adj*
ultraprofessional *adj*
ultrarapid *adj*
ultrarare *adj*
ultrarealistic *adj*
ultrareliable *adj*
ultrareligious *adj*
ultrarespectable *adj*
ultrarevolutionary *adj*
ultrarich *adj*
ultraroyalist *n*
ultrasafe *adj*
ultrasensitive *adj*
ultrasharp *adj*
ultrasmart *adj*
ultrasmooth *adj*
ultrasoft *adj*
ultrasophisticated *adj*
ultrastable *adj*
ultrathin *adj*
ultraviolent *adj*

ultrabasic /últrə báyssik/ *adj* describes igneous rock that is high in iron and magnesium and contains no free quartz ■ *n* a rock of ultrabasic composition

ultracentrifuge /últrə séntri fyooj/ *n* a centrifuge for separating microscopic or submicroscopic particles by using a force many times greater than gravity ■ *vt* (**-fuges, -fuging, -fuged**) to subject something to the action of an ultracentrifuge —**ultracentrifugal** /últrə séntri fyóog'l/ *adj* —**ultracentrifugally** *adv* —**ultracentrifugation** /últrə séntrifyoo gáysh'n/ *n*

ultrafiche /últrə feesh/ *n* **1.** a sheet of microfilm of similar size to a microfiche but with a much greater number of documents on it **2.** a device for viewing ultrafiches that has much greater magnification than a microfiche

ultrafilter /últrə fíltər/ *n* a filter for separating extremely small particles from a solution or colloid

ultrafiltrate /últrə fíl trayt/ *n* the material that is not filtered out and remains in the liquid phase after ultrafiltration

ultrafiltration /últrə fil tráysh'n/ *n* a filtration process that uses a porous membrane to isolate and remove particles such as bacteria and viruses. The process is used for water purification and in the pharmaceutical industry.

ultra-heat-treated *adj* FOOD INDUST full form of **UHT**

ultrahigh frequency /últrə hī-/ *n* MEDIA full form of **UHF**

ultraism /últrə izəm/ *n* religious or political extremism —**ultraist** *n* —**ultraistic** /-ístik/ *adj*

ultralarge crude carrier /últrə laarj-/ *n* a very large oil tanker, larger than a supertanker, that has a capacity greater than 400,000 tons

ultralight /últrə līt/ *adj* extremely light in weight ■ *n* a small single-seat or two-seat aircraft, sometimes resembling a hang-glider, constructed of lightweight materials, powered by a small motor, and flown chiefly for recreation

ultramafic /últrə máffik/ *adj* describes a dark igneous rock, over 90% of whose content consists of ferromagnesian minerals, including olivine and pyroxenes ■ *n* a rock of ultramafic composition

ultramarine /últrəmə réen/ *n* **1. BLUE PIGMENT** a deep blue pigment or dye, especially one made from lapis lazuli **2. DEEP BLUE COLOUR** a brilliant deep blue colour ■ *adj* **1. DEEP BLUE** ultramarine blue in colour **2. BEYOND SEA** coming from or lying beyond the sea (*literary*) [Late 16C. < medieval Latin *ultramarinus* 'beyond the sea']

ultramicrometer /últrə mī krómmitər/ *n* a measuring device designed to measure spaces and thicknesses more minute than those measurable using a standard micrometer

ultramicroscope /últrə míkrəskōp/ *n* a microscope that uses scattered light to make submicroscopic objects visible

ultramicroscopic /últrə mīkrə skóppik/ *adj* **1.** SCI same as **submicroscopic 2.** involving the use of an ultramicroscope

ultramodern /últrə móddərn/ *adj* more modern than anything comparable, especially in using the very latest designs or making use of the most advanced technology —**ultramodernism** *n* —**ultramodernist** *n*

ultramontane /últrə món tayn/ *adj* **1. BEYOND MOUNTAINS** coming from or lying beyond mountains, especially beyond the Alps as viewed from ancient Rome **2.** CHR **SUPPORTING POPE** supporting the power and authority of the pope within the Roman Catholic Church ■ *n* **1. DWELLER BEYOND MOUNTAINS** somebody who lives beyond mountains, especially beyond the Alps as viewed from ancient Rome **2.** CHR **PAPAL SUPPORTER** a supporter of the power and authority of the pope in the Roman Catholic Church [Late 16C. < medieval Latin *ultramontanus* 'beyond the mountains']

ultramontanism /últrə móntənizəm/ *n* in the Roman Catholic Church, the policy of investing all power and authority in the pope

ultramundane /últrə mun dáyn/ *adj* (*literary*) **1.** coming from or lying beyond Earth or its solar system **2.** belonging or relating to heaven or to the realm of the spirit, and not to the physical world [Mid-16C. < Latin *ultramundanus* 'beyond the world' < *ultra* 'beyond' + *mundus* 'world']

ultranationalism /últrə násh'nəlizəm/ *n* nationalism that is so extreme as to be detrimental to international interests or cooperation —**ultranationalist** /últrə násh'nəlist/ *n* —**ultranationalistic** /-násh'nə lístik/ *adj*

ultrashort /últrə sháwrt/ *adj* **1.** describes wavelengths that are shorter than 10 metres **2.** extremely short in length or duration

ultrasonic /últrə sónnik/ *adj* describes sound waves that have frequencies above the upper limit of the normal range of human hearing, which is about 20 kilohertz —**ultrasonically** *adv*

ultrasonics /últrə sónniks/ *n* the study of sound waves that have frequencies above the upper limit of the normal range of human hearing, which is about 20 kilohertz (*takes a singular verb*)

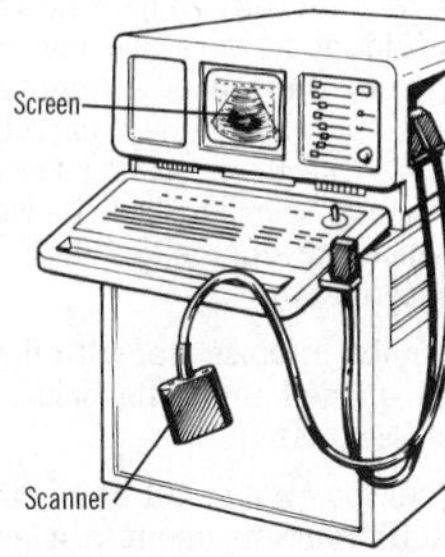

ultrasonic testing

ultrasonic testing *n* the scanning of surfaces with high-frequency sound waves in order to gauge their integrity and check for flaws or to measure the thickness of materials

ultrasonic welding *n* the bonding of two components by bombarding them with ultrasonic waves to cause vibrations between them

ultrasonogram /últrə sṓnə gram/ *n* a picture made with ultrasound for the purpose of medical examination or diagnosis

ultrasonography /últrə sə nóggrəfi/ *n* the use of ultrasound to make images of objects or features that cannot be seen, especially for the purpose of medical examination or diagnosis —**ultrasonographic** /últrə sṓnə gráffik/ *adj*

ultrasound /últrə sownd/ *n* **1.** sound of a frequency above the upper limit of the normal range of human hearing, which is about 20 kilohertz **2.** a technique that uses high-frequency sound waves for medical diagnosis and treatment, e.g. to create images of internal organs, to treat deep tissue disorders, and to break up kidney stones **3.** MED same as **ultrasound scan**

ultrasound scan *n* a medical examination of an internal body part, especially a foetus in the womb, using ultrasound technology

ultrastructure /últrə strúkchər/ *n* the minute structure of an organic substance or object that becomes evident only under electron microscopy —**ultrastructural** *adj*

ultraviolet /últrə vī ələt/ *adj* relating to or producing electromagnetic radiation of wavelengths from about 5 to about 400 nanometres, beyond the violet end of the visible light spectrum ■ *n* radiation with ultraviolet wavelengths. Radiation of this kind is a component of sunlight and is the light that makes exposed skin become darker.

ultra vires /últrə vī reez/ *adj, adv* beyond the legal capacity of a person, company, or other legal entity [< Latin, 'beyond the powers']

ultravirus /últrə vīrəss/ *n* a virus small enough to pass through an ultrafilter —**ultraviral** *adj*

ulu /oo lóo/ *adj Malaysia, Singapore* rural and not economically or technologically advanced (*informal*) [< Malay *(h)ulu* 'the interior', literally 'head']

ululate /yóolyoo layt/ (**-lates, -lating, -lated**) *vi* to howl or wail, in grief or in jubilation [Early 17C. < Latin *ululare*, an imitation of the sound] —**ululation** /yóolyoo láysh'n/ *n*

Uluru /óolə roo/ largest individual rock mass in the world, located in the south of the Northern Territory, Australia. Height: 868 m/2,848 ft. Former name **Ayers Rock**

Ulverstone /úlvərstən/ town situated on the northern coast of Tasmania, Australia, at the mouth of the River Leven. Population: 9,935 (1991).

Ulysses /yoo lísseez, yoóli seez/ n the name used by the Romans for the Greek hero Odysseus [Early 17C. < Latin] —**Ulyssean** /yoo líssi ən/ adj

um /um/ interj a word used in writing to represent the kind of grunting sound that people make when they hesitate in speaking [Early 17C. Representing an inarticulate sound]

Umayyad /oo mí yad/, **Omayyad** n the family that dominated the politics and commercial economy of Mecca and later established a dynasty as rulers (**caliphs**) of Islam [Mid-18C. < Umayya, cousin of Muhammad's grandfather] —**Umayyad** adj

umbel /úmb'l/ n an umbrella-shaped flower head in which the individual flowers are borne on short stems arising from the top of a main stem. It is typical of plants such as parsley, carrot, dill, and fennel. [Late 16C. Directly or via Old French umbelle < Latin umbella 'parasol' < umbra 'shade'] —**umbellar** /um béllər/ adj —**umbellate** /úmbələt, -layt/ adj —**umbellated** /úmbə láytid/ adj

umbelliferous /úmbə líffərəss/ adj with flower heads shaped like an opened umbrella [Mid-17C. < Latin umbella 'parasol' (see UMBEL)]

umbellule /um béllyool/ n a small umbel that is part of, and has a similar arrangement to, a larger umbel [Late 18C. < modern Latin umbellula 'little umbel' < Latin umbella (see UMBEL)]

umber /úmbər/ n 1. PIGMENT pigment or dye made from soil that contains oxides of iron and manganese 2. SOIL USED FOR PIGMENTS AND DYES a soil that yields umber. It is dark yellowish-brown in its natural state (**raw umber**), and dark reddish-brown when roasted (**burnt umber**). ■ adj BROWN coloured any shade of brown produced by umber pigment ■ vt (**-bers, -bering, -bered**) PAINT WITH UMBER to paint or dye something with umber, or colour something dark brown [Mid-16C. Via French terre d'ombre or Italian terra di ombre < Latin umbra 'shadow']

Umberto I /oóm búrtō/ (1844–1900) king of Italy. During his reign (1878–1900), he sought to consolidate Italy as a unified country.

Umberto II (1904–83) king of Italy. He abdicated in 1946, a month after becoming king, when Italians voted in a referendum to establish a republic.

umbilical /um bíllik'l/ adj 1. OF UMBILICAL CORD relating to or situated in the umbilical cord, the navel, or the area of the abdomen that surrounds the navel 2. RESEMBLING NAVEL resembling a navel (**umbilicus**) in appearance 3. PROVIDING LIFELINE providing a link to something essential, e.g. to supplies or services in wartime, or connecting an astronaut working outside a spacecraft to the spacecraft ■ n ANAT same as **umbilical cord** (sense 1) [Mid-16C. < obsolete French, 'navel' < Latin umbilicus (see UMBILICUS)]

umbilical cord n 1. the flexible, often spirally twisted tube that connects the abdomen of a foetus to the mother's placenta in the womb, and through which nutrients are delivered and waste expelled 2. a cable, tube, or pipe attaching somebody or something to an essential supply, e.g. the tube that connects a deep-sea diver to an oxygen supply on a ship

umbilicate /um bíllikət/, **umbilicated** /um bílli kaytid/ adj 1. with a mark, depression, or perforation that resembles a navel 2. shaped like a navel [Late 17C. < UMBILICUS] —**umbilication** /um bílli káysh'n/ n

umbilicus /um bíllikəss, úmbi líkəss/ (plural **-ci** /-sī/) n 1. ANAT same as **navel** (technical) 2. a dip or hollow that resembles a navel, e.g. the hollow at each end of the shaft of a feather [Late 17C. < Latin < Indo-European]

umbo /úmbō/ (plural **-bones** /um bố neez/ or **-bos**) n 1. BUMP ON PLANT OR ANIMAL PART a small protuberance on a plant or animal part, e.g. the hump on the caps of some mushrooms, or the bump just above the hinge of a bivalve shell 2. SMALL HOLLOW IN EARDRUM a small hollow in the centre of the outer surface of the eardrum, at the point where the malleus joins it on the inside 3. KNOB ON SHIELD a knob at the centre of a round shield, especially a Saxon shield [Early 18C. < Latin, 'shield boss'] —**umbonal** /um bốn'l/ adj —**umbonate** /úmbənət/ adj

umbra /úmbrə/ (plural **-brae** /-bree/ or **-bras**) n 1. PHYS COMPLETE SHADOW an area of complete shadow caused by light from all points of a source being prevented from reaching the area, usually by an opaque object 2. ASTRON DARKEST PART ON MOON OR EARTH the darkest portion of the shadow cast by an astronomical object during an eclipse, especially that cast on Earth during a solar eclipse 3. ASTRON DARK PART OF SUNSPOT the inner, darker area of a sunspot [Late 16C. < Latin, 'shadow'] —**umbral** adj

umbrage /úmbrij/ n 1. resentment or annoyance arising from some offence ○ took umbrage 2. something that gives shade, e.g. a tree (literary) [15C. < Old French < Latin umbra 'shadow']

ORIGIN The Latin word umbra 'shadow', from which *umbrage* is derived, is also the source of English *adumbrate, penumbra, sombre, sombrero*, and *umbrella*.

umbrageous /um bráyjəss/ adj 1. easily offended or likely to become irritated 2. providing shade and coolness (literary) —**umbrageously** adv

umbrella /um bréllə/ n 1. COLLAPSIBLE CANOPY THAT PROTECTS FROM WEATHER a round collapsible canopy of plastic or waterproof material on a frame at the top of a handle, held in the hand to protect somebody from rain, snow, or sun 2. SUPPORT OR AUTHORITY something that gives support, protection, or authority ○ under the umbrella of the United Nations 3. OBJECT LIKE UMBRELLA an object that looks like an open umbrella, or that collapses like an umbrella, e.g. the folding paper decoration sometimes served in cocktails 4. ZOOL JELLYFISH'S BODY the rounded body of a jellyfish 5. MIL AIRCRAFT FLYING OVERHEAD FOR PROTECTION a group of aircraft patrolling the sky above a place where troops are carrying out operations, to give them protection 6. MIL SHIELD OF GUNFIRE gunfire used to suppress enemy fire and thus shield friendly forces making a movement or attack 7. US MIL same as **parachute** n (sense 1) (slang) ■ adj 1. UNIFYING MEMBER ORGANIZATIONS acting to coordinate or protect a number of member organizations or bodies 2. INCLUDING SEVERAL THINGS including or containing a number of things ○ an umbrella term for a variety of plants [Early 17C. Via Italian ombrella < late Latin umbrella, alteration of Latin umbella 'parasol' (see UMBEL) after umbra 'shadow']

umbrella bird

umbrella bird n a bird of the cotinga family with a large umbrella-shaped crest and a long feathered wattle. Native to: Central and South America. Genus: *Cephalopterus*.

umbrella pine n TREES same as **stone pine**

umbrella plant n a plant of the sedge family that has thin leaves radiating from the top of long stems. Native to: Africa. Latin name: *Cyperus alternifolius*.

umbrella stand n an upright stand or rack for holding walking sticks and folded umbrellas

umbrella tree n 1. a magnolia tree with large leaves clustered around the ends of the branches. Native to: southeastern United States. Latin name: *Magnolia fraseri* or *Magnolia tripetala*. 2. a bush or tree with umbrella-shaped clusters of leaves. Flowers: red, clustered on long spikes. Native to: Australia. Latin name: *Schefflera actinophylla*.

Umbria /úmbri ə/ agricultural region in central Italy, west of the Apennines. Population: 835,488 (2001). Area: 8,456 sq. km/3,265 sq. mi.

Umbrian /úmbri ən/ n 1. somebody who comes from Umbria 2. an extinct Italic language of ancient southern Italy —**Umbrian** adj

Umbriel /úmbri əl/ n a large natural satellite of the planet Uranus, discovered in 1851 [After a sprite in the poem 'The Rape of the Lock' by Alexander POPE]

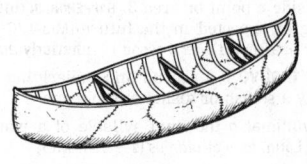

umiak

umiak /oómi ak/ n a large Inuit boat made of animal skins stretched across a wooden frame, larger and more open than a kayak and traditionally paddled by women [Mid-18C. < Inuit umiaq]

UMIST /yoómist/ abbr University of Manchester Institute of Science and Technology

umlaut /oóm lowt/ n 1. CHANGE IN VOWEL SOUND in Germanic languages, a change in the way a vowel is pronounced, caused by the influence of another vowel in a syllable immediately after it 2. ACCENT OVER VOWEL in Germanic languages, the mark (¨) that is placed above a vowel to show that it is pronounced differently from the way the vowel is usually pronounced. See table at diacritic ■ v (-lauts, -lauting, -lauted) 1. vti CHANGE VOWEL SOUND to change a vowel sound because of other vowel sounds close to it, or be changed in this way 2. vt MARK VOWEL WITH TWO DOTS to write or print a vowel with an umlaut above it [Mid-19C. < German < um- 'about, change' + Laut 'sound']

umma /oómə/, **ummah** n within Islam, the community of the faithful that transcended long-established tribal boundaries to create a degree of political unity [Late 19C. < Arabic, 'people, community']

umpire /úm pīr/ n 1. OFFICIAL ENFORCING SPORT'S RULES an official who supervises play and enforces the rules of the game in some sports, e.g. cricket and baseball 2. SOMEBODY SETTLING DISPUTE somebody called in to settle a dispute ■ vti (-pires, -piring, -pired) 1. SUPERVISE PLAY IN SPORT to supervise play in a game or sport and enforce the rules 2. SETTLE DISPUTE to give a ruling on a dispute as an impartial arbitrator [Late 16C. By false division < noumper < Old French nonper < non 'not' + per 'pair']

umpteen /úmp teén/ det a large but unspecified number of (informal) [Early 20C. Humorous formation after thirteen, fourteen, etc] —**umpteenth** det

umrah /oómraa/ n a lesser form of pilgrimage to Mecca that is not obligatory for Muslims, unlike the hajj, and that can be performed at any time of year [Early 19C. < Arabic 'umra]

Umtata /um taátə/ town in Eastern Cape Province, South Africa. Population: 67,000 (1995 estimate).

umunna /oó moónə/ n W Africa a social grouping consisting of a person's extended family [< Ibo]

un /ən/, 'n/, 'un pron a spelling of the pronoun 'one' intended to reflect the way it is sometimes pronounced in informal speech (informal) [Early 19C. Alteration of ONE]

UN abbr POL United Nations

un- prefix 1. not ○ unavoidable 2. opposite of, lack of ○ unrest 3. to do the opposite of, reverse ○ uninstall 4. to deprive of, remove something from ○ unfrock 5. to release from ○ unchain 6. completely ○ unloose [Old English < Indo-European]

USAGE un- or non-? Many adjectives formed with **un-** have special (usually unfavourable) meanings, for example *uncooperative* and *unprofessional*. In these cases neutral equivalents that mean simply 'not …' are formed by means of **non-**, for example *noncooperative*, *nonprofessional*.

unabashed adj	**unacademic** adj
unabashedly adv	**unaccented** adj
unabbreviated adj	**unacceptability** n
unabridged adj	**unacceptable** adj
unabsorbed adj	**unacceptably** adv
unabsorbent adj	**unaccepted** adj

unaccepting *adj*
unaccommodating *adj*
unaccommodatingly *adv*
unaccomplished *adj*
unaccounted *adj*
unaccredited *adj*
unachievable *adj*
unachievably *adv*
unacknowledged *adj*
unadaptable *adj*
unadapted *adj*
unaddicted *adj*
unaddressed *adj*
unadjacent *adj*
unadjusted *adj*
unadmired *adj*
unadmitted *adj*
unadorned *adj*
unadventurous *adj*
unadvertised *adj*
unadvisable *adj*
unaesthetic *adj*
unaffected *adj*
unaffectedly *adv*
unaffectedness *n*
unaffecting *adj*
unaffectionate *adj*
unaffiliated *adj*
unaffordable *adj*
unafraid *adj*
unaggressive *adj*
unaided *adj, adv*
unaligned *adj*
unalike *adj*
unalive *adj*
unalleviated *adj*
unallied *adj*
unallocated *adj*
unallowable *adj*
unalluring *adj*
unalterable *adj*
unalterably *adv*
unaltered *adj*
unamazed *adj*
unambitious *adj*
unambivalent *adj*
unambivalently *adv*
unamenable *adj*
unamended *adj*
unamiable *adj*
unamplified *adj*
unamused *adj*
unamusing *adj*
unanalysable *adj*
unanchored *adj*
unannounced *adj*
unanswered *adj*
unanticipated *adj*
unapologetic *adj*
unapologetically *adv*
unapparent *adj*
unappeasable *adj*
unappeased *adj*
unappetizing *adj*
unapplied *adj*
unappreciated *adj*
unappreciative *adj*
unapprehended *adj*
unappropriated *adj*
unapproved *adj*
unarable *adj*
unarm *vt*
unarmoured *adj*
unaroused *adj*
unarresting *adj*
unarrestingly *adv*
unarticulated *adj*
unartistic *adj*
unartistically *adv*
unascertainable *adj*
unascertained *adj*
unassertive *adj*
unassertiveness *n*
unassignable *adj*
unassigned *adj*
unassimilated *adj*
unassisted *adj*
unassociated *adj*
unassuaged *adj*
unathletic *adj*
unatoned *adj*

unattainable *adj*
unattested *adj*
unattributable *adj*
unattributed *adj*
unaudited *adj*
unauthentic *adj*
unauthenticated *adj*
unauthorized *adj*
unautomated *adj*
unavailability *n*
unavailable *adj*
unavenged *adj*
unavowed *adj*
unbaited *adj*
unbaked *adj*
unban *vt*
unbaptized *adj*
unbated *adj*
unbeautiful *adj*
unbeautifully *adv*
unbefitting *adj*
unbefittingly *adv*
unbefittingness *n*
unbeholden *adj*
unbeloved *adj*
unbiddable *adj*
unbleached *adj*
unblemished *adj*
unblended *adj*
unbonded *adj*
unbookish *adj*
unbordered *adj*
unbought *adj*
unbranched *adj*
unbranded *adj*
unbreachable *adj*
unbreakable *adj*
unbreathable *adj*
unbribable *adj*
unbridgeable *adj*
unbruised *adj*
unbrushed *adj*
unbuckle *vti*
unbudgeted *adj*
unbuildable *adj*
unbuilt *adj*
unburied *adj*
unburnable *adj*
unburnt *adj*
unbusinesslike *adj*
uncaged *adj*
uncandid *adj*
uncanonical *adj*
uncanonically *adv*
uncarbonated *adj*
uncaring *adj*
uncarpeted *adj*
uncashed *adj*
uncastrated *adj*
uncatchable *adj*
uncaught *adj*
uncaused *adj*
uncelebrated *adj*
uncensored *adj*
uncensured *adj*
uncertified *adj*
unchallengeable *adj*
unchallenged *adj*
unchallenging *adj*
unchangeability *n*
unchangeable *adj*
unchangeableness *n*
unchangeably *adv*
unchanged *adj*
unchanging *adj*
unchannelled *adj*
unchaperoned *adj*
uncharacteristic *adj*
uncharacteristically *adv*
uncharged *adj*
uncharismatic *adj*
uncharitable *adj*
uncharitableness *n*
uncharitably *adv*
unchaste *adj*
unchastely *adv*
unchasteness *n*
unchic *adj*
unchivalrous *adj*
unchosen *adj*
unchronicled *adj*

uncinematic *adj*
uncirculated *adj*
uncircumcised *adj*
uncircumcision *n*
unclaimed *adj*
unclarified *adj*
unclassifiable *adj*
uncleaned *adj*
unclear *adj*
uncleared *adj*
unclearly *adv*
unclearness *n*
unclench *vti*
unclouded *adj*
uncoagulated *adj*
uncoated *adj*
uncollected *adj*
uncolonized *adj*
uncoloured *adj*
uncombed *adj*
uncombined *adj*
uncomely *adj*
uncompanionable *adj*
uncompensated *adj*
uncompetitive *adj*
uncomplaining *adj*
uncomplainingly *adv*
uncompleted *adj*
uncomplexed *adj*
uncomplimentary *adj*
uncompounded *adj*
uncomprehending *adj*
uncomprehendingly *adv*
unconcealed *adj*
unconceivable *adj*
unconceivably *adv*
unconcluded *adj*
uncondescending *adj*
unconfessed *adj*
unconfident *adj*
unconfidently *adv*
unconfirmed *adj*
unconfused *adj*
uncongenial *adj*
unconjecturable *adj*
unconquerable *adj*
unconquerably *adv*
unconquered *adj*
unconsecrated *adj*
unconsenting *adj*
unconsolidated *adj*
unconstrained *adj*
unconstrainedly *adv*
unconstricted *adj*
unconstructive *adj*
unconsulted *adj*
unconsummated *adj*
uncontaminated *adj*
uncontentious *adj*
uncontested *adj*
uncontestedly *adv*
uncontradicted *adj*
uncontrived *adj*
uncontrolled *adj*
uncontrolledly *adv*
uncontroversial *adj*
uncontroversially *adv*
unconverted *adj*
unconvinced *adj*
unconvincing *adj*
unconvincingly *adv*
unconvincingness *n*
uncooked *adj*
uncooperative *adj*
uncooperatively *adv*
uncooperativeness *n*
uncopiable *adj*
uncorrectable *adj*
uncorrected *adj*
uncorroborated *adj*
uncorrupted *adj*
uncourageous *adj*
uncrease *vt*
uncreased *adj*
uncreated *adj*
uncreative *adj*
uncreatively *adv*
uncreativeness *n*
uncropped *adj*
uncrowded *adj*
uncrowdedness *n*

uncrushable *adj*
uncrushed *adj*
uncrystallized *adj*
unculled *adj*
uncultivated *adj*
uncultured *adj*
uncurbed *adj*
uncured *adj*
uncurtailed *adj*
uncurtained *adj*
uncustomary *adj*
uncuttable *adj*
undamaged *adj*
undamaging *adj*
undated *adj*
undauntable *adj*
undealt *adj*
undecayed *adj*
undeceivable *adj*
undeceivably *adv*
undecipherable *adj*
undeciphered *adj*
undecorated *adj*
undefeatable *adj*
undefeated *adj*
undefended *adj*
undefiled *adj*
undefinable *adj*
undefinably *adv*
undefined *adj*
undeformed *adj*
undeliverable *adj*
undelivered *adj*
undeluded *adj*
undemanding *adj*
undemarcated *adj*
undemonstrated *adj*
undenied *adj*
undenominational *adj*
undented *adj*
undependability *n*
undependable *adj*
undependably *adv*
undesigned *adj*
undesignedly *adv*
undesired *adj*
undesirous *adj*
undestroyed *adj*
undetailed *adj*
undetectable *adj*
undetected *adj*
undeterred *adj*
undeveloped *adj*
undiagnosed *adj*
undifferentiated *adj*
undigestible *adj*
undignified *adj*
undiluted *adj*
undiminished *adj*
undiminishing *adj*
undimmed *adj*
undiscerning *adj*
undiscerningly *adv*
undischarged *adj*
undisciplined *adj*
undisclosed *adj*
undiscoverable *adj*
undiscovered *adj*
undiscriminating *adj*
undiscussed *adj*
undismayed *adj*
undisputable *adj*
undisputed *adj*
undissolved *adj*
undistorted *adj*
undividable *adj*
undivided *adj*
undocumented *adj*
undomesticated *adj*
undoubting *adj*
undrained *adj*
undramatic *adj*
undraped *adj*
undrawn *adj*
undrinkable *adj*
undyed *adj*
undynamic *adj*
uneatable *adj*
uneaten *adj*
unedifying *adj*
unelaborate *adj*

unelected *adj*
unembarrassed *adj*
unembellished *adj*
unembroidered *adj*
unemphatic *adj*
unemphatically *adv*
unenclosed *adj*
unencumbered *adj*
unendowed *adj*
unenforceability *n*
unenforceable *adj*
unenforced *adj*
unengaged *adj*
unenjoyable *adj*
unenlightened *adj*
unenlightening *adj*
unenlightenment *n*
unentered *adj*
unenterprising *adj*
unenterprisingly *adv*
unenthusiastic *adj*
unenthusiastically *adv*
unenvied *adj*
unequipped *adj*
unerasable *adj*
uneroded *adj*
unerotic *adj*
unerupted *adj*
unescorted *adj*
unestablished *adj*
unevangelical *adj*
unexamined *adj*
unexciting *adj*
unexecuted *adj*
unexercised *adj*
unexhausted *adj*
unexpired *adj*
unexplainable *adj*
unexplained *adj*
unexploited *adj*
unexplored *adj*
unexposed *adj*
unexpressive *adj*
unextraordinary *adj*
unfaceted *adj*
unfading *adj*
unfadingly *adv*
unfarmed *adj*
unfatherliness *n*
unfatherly *adj*
unfathomed *adj*
unfavoured *adj*
unfazed *adj*
unfeathered *adj*
unfed *adj*
unfederated *adj*
unfeigned *adj*
unfelt *adj*
unfeminine *adj*
unfemininity *n*
unfenced *adj*
unfermented *adj*
unfertile *adj*
unfertilized *adj*
unfilled *adj*
unfiltered *adj*
unfired *adj*
unflashy *adj*
unflavoured *adj*
unflawed *adj*
unfluctuating *adj*
unflustered *adj*
unfluted *adj*
unforceful *adj*
unfordable *adj*
unforested *adj*
unforgiven *adj*
unforgotten *adj*
unformulated *adj*
unfortified *adj*
unfound *adj*
unframed *adj*
unfree *adj*
unfretted *adj*
unfulfilling *adj*
unfunded *adj*
unfunniness *n*
unfurrowed *adj*
unfused *adj*
unfussily *adv*
unfussy *adj*

ungainsayable *adj*
ungallant *adj*
ungallantly *adv*
ungarnished *adj*
ungelded *adj*
ungenerous *adj*
ungenerously *adv*
ungenerousness *n*
ungenial *adj*
ungenteel *adj*
ungentle *adj*
ungentlemanliness *n*
ungentlemanly *adj*
ungifted *adj*
unglamorous *adj*
unglazed *adj*
ungraceful *adj*
ungracefully *adv*
ungracefulness *n*
ungraded *adj*
ungratified *adj*
ungreased *adj*
unguessable *adj*
unguided *adj*
unhampered *adj*
unhardened *adj*
unharmful *adj*
unharmonious *adj*
unhatched *adj*
unhealed *adj*
unhealthful *adj*
unheeding *adj*
unheedingly *adv*
unhemmed *adj*
unheralded *adj*
unheroic *adj*
unheroically *adv*
unhewn *adj*
unhip *adj*
unhonoured *adj*
unhopeful *adj*
unhoused *adj*
unhuman *adj*
unhyphenated *adj*
unideal *adj*
unidealized *adj*
unidentifiable *adj*
unidiomatic *adj*
unignorable *adj*
unilluminated *adj*
unilluminating *adj*
unillustrated *adj*
unimagined *adj*
unimpassioned *adj*
unimposing *adj*
unimposingly *adv*
unimpressionable *adj*
unimpressive *adj*
unindented *adj*
unindicted *adj*
unindustrialized *adj*
uninfected *adj*
uninflamed *adj*
uninflated *adj*
uninflected *adj*
uninfluenced *adj*
uninfluential *adj*
uninsulated *adj*
unintellectual *adj*
unintended *adj*
uninterest *n*
uninterpreted *adj*
unintimidated *adj*
uninventive *adj*
uninventively *adv*
uninventiveness *n*
uninvestigated *adj*
unironed *adj*
unirrigated *adj*
unissued *adj*
unjaded *adj*
unjam *vti*
unjoined *adj*
unkillable *adj*
unknot *vti*
unknowledgeable *adj*
unlabelled *adj*
unladen *adj*
unladylike *adj*
unlaid *adj*
unlamented *adj*

unlatch *vti*
unleased *adj*
unliberated *adj*
unlighted *adj*
unlikable *adj*
unlined *adj*
unlink *vti*
unlit *adj*
unlockable *adj*
unlocked *adj*
unlovable *adj*
unloved *adj*
unloving *adj*
unlovingly *adv*
unlovingness *n*
unmailed *adj*
unmanaged *adj*
unmapped *adj*
unmarketable *adj*
unmaterialistic *adj*
unmatured *adj*
unmeasurable *adj*
unmechanized *adj*
unmelodic *adj*
unmelodious *adj*
unmelodiously *adv*
unmelted *adj*
unmemorable *adj*
unmemorably *adv*
unmentioned *adj*
unmerchantable *adj*
unmerited *adj*
unmethodical *adj*
unmethodically *adv*
unmilitary *adj*
unmindful *adj*
unmindfully *adv*
unmindfulness *n*
unmined *adj*
unmissable *adj*
unmixed *adj*
unmodernized *adj*
unmodifiable *adj*
unmodified *adj*
unmolested *adj*
unmotivated *adj*
unmoulded *adj*
unmounted *adj*
unmourned *adj*
unmovable *adj*
unmown *adj*
unmuffle *vt*
unmutilated *adj*
unnavigable *adj*
unnavigated *adj*
unneeded *adj*
unneighbourliness *n*
unneighbourly *adj*
unneutral *adj*
unnoticeable *adj*
unnoticeably *adv*
unobjectionable *adj*
unobjectionably *adv*
unobscured *adj*
unobservable *adj*
unobservant *adj*
unobservantly *adv*
unobserved *adj*
unobstructed *adj*
unobtainability *n*
unobtainable *adj*
unoffended *adj*
unoffending *adj*
unoiled *adj*
unopen *adj*
unopenable *adj*
unopened *adj*
unoriginal *adj*
unoriginality *n*
unoriginally *adv*
unornamental *adj*
unornamented *adj*
unostentatious *adj*
unostentatiously *adv*
unostentatiousness *n*
unowned *adj*
unpackaged *adj*
unpainted *adj*
unpasteurized *adj*
unpatented *adj*
unpatriotic *adj*

unpatronizing *adj*
unpatronizingly *adv*
unpatterned *adj*
unpaved *adj*
unpeeled *adj*
unpenalized *adj*
unpeopled *adj*
unperceived *adj*
unperceptive *adj*
unperceptively *adv*
unperceptiveness *n*
unperfected *adj*
unperforated *adj*
unperformable *adj*
unperformed *adj*
unperfumed *adj*
unpersuadable *adj*
unpersuaded *adj*
unpersuasive *adj*
unpersuasively *adv*
unpicked *adj*
unpicturesque *adj*
unpigmented *adj*
unpitied *adj*
unplanted *adj*
unplayable *adj*
unplayed *adj*
unpleasing *adj*
unpledged *adj*
unploughed *adj*
unplucked *adj*
unplundered *adj*
unpointed *adj*
unpolarized *adj*
unpolished *adj*
unpolitical *adj*
unpollinated *adj*
unpolluted *adj*
unpopulated *adj*
unposed *adj*
unpowered *adj*
unpractical *adj*
unpredicted *adj*
unprejudiced *adj*
unprescribed *adj*
unpressed *adj*
unpressurized *adj*
unpresumptuous *adj*
unpriced *adj*
unprimed *adj*
unprinted *adj*
unproblematic *adj*
unprocessed *adj*
unproclaimed *adj*
unprocurable *adj*
unprofessed *adj*
unprogressive *adj*
unpropitious *adj*
unpropitiously *adv*
unprosperous *adj*
unprotesting *adj*
unproud *adj*
unprovable *adj*
unproved *adj*
unproven *adj*
unprovoked *adj*
unpruned *adj*
unpublicized *adj*
unpublished *adj*
unpunctual *adj*
unpunctuality *n*
unpunctually *adv*
unpunctuated *adj*
unpunishable *adj*
unpunished *adj*
unpurified *adj*
unqualifiable *adj*
unquantifiability *n*
unquantifiable *adj*
unquelled *adj*
unquenchable *adj*
unquenchably *adv*
unquenched *adj*
unquotable *adj*
unreachability *n*
unreachable *adj*
unreachableness *n*
unreachably *adv*
unreached *adj*
unreactive *adj*
unrealism *n*

unrealistic *adj*
unrealistically *adv*
unrealizable *adj*
unrealized *adj*
unreceptive *adj*
unreceptively *adv*
unreceptiveness *n*
unreciprocal *adj*
unreciprocated *adj*
unrecognizability *n*
unrecognizable *adj*
unrecognizably *adv*
unrecognized *adj*
unrecompensed *adj*
unreconciled *adj*
unrecordable *adj*
unrecorded *adj*
unrectifiable *adj*
unrectified *adj*
unredeemable *adj*
unredeemably *adv*
unredeemed *adj*
unredressed *adj*
unreformed *adj*
unregistered *adj*
unregulated *adj*
unrehearsed *adj*
unrelated *adj*
unrelatedly *adv*
unrelatedness *n*
unrelaxed *adj*
unrelieved *adj*
unreligious *adj*
unremedied *adj*
unremembered *adj*
unremorseful *adj*
unremorsefully *adv*
unremovable *adj*
unrenewable *adj*
unrenewed *adj*
unrepealed *adj*
unrepeated *adj*
unrepentant *adj*
unreported *adj*
unrepresentative *adj*
unrepresentativeness *n*
unrepresented *adj*
unreproved *adj*
unrequested *adj*
unresearched *adj*
unresentful *adj*
unresistant *adj*
unresisted *adj*
unresisting *adj*
unresistingly *adv*
unresolvable *adj*
unresolved *adj*
unresonant *adj*
unresponsive *adj*
unresponsively *adv*
unresponsiveness *n*
unrestful *adj*
unrestraint *n*
unrestricted *adj*
unrestrictedly *adv*
unreturnable *adj*
unreturned *adj*
unrevealed *adj*
unrevealing *adj*
unrevised *adj*
unrevoked *adj*
unrewarded *adj*
unrewarding *adj*
unrhymed *adj*
unrhythmic *adj*
unrhythmical *adj*
unrhythmically *adv*
unridable *adj*
unrig *vt*
unripened *adj*
unrisen *adj*
unromantic *adj*
unromantically *adv*
unroofed *adj*
unroyal *adj*
unruptured *adj*
unrushed *adj*
unsafe *adj*
unsafely *adv*
unsafeness *n*
unsaleable *adj*

unsalted *adj*
unsanctified *adj*
unsanctioned *adj*
unsanitary *adj*
unsatisfied *adj*
unsatisfying *adj*
unsatisfyingly *adv*
unscarred *adj*
unscented *adj*
unscheduled *adj*
unscholarly *adj*
unsearched *adj*
unseasoned *adj*
unseaworthy *adj*
unseeing *adj*
unseeingly *adv*
unsegmented *adj*
unsegregated *adj*
unselect *adj*
unselected *adj*
unselective *adj*
unselectively *adv*
unselfconscious *adj*
unselfconsciously *adv*
unselfconsciousness *n*
unsent *adj*
unsentimental *adj*
unseparated *adj*
unserious *adj*
unserviceable *adj*
unserviceableness *n*
unsewn *adj*
unsexy *adj*
unshaded *adj*
unshaken *adj*
unshaking *adj*
unshapeliness *n*
unshapely *adj*
unshared *adj*
unshaved *adj*
unshaven *adj*
unshed *adj*
unshell *vt*
unsheltered *adj*
unshielded *adj*
unshockability *n*
unshockable *adj*
unshorn *adj*
unsifted *adj*
unsinkable *adj*
unskimmed *adj*
unslakable *adj*
unsmoked *adj*
unsoiled *adj*
unsoldierly *adj*
unsolvability *n*
unsolvable *adj*
unsolved *adj*
unsorted *adj*
unsoured *adj*
unsown *adj*
unspecifiable *adj*
unspecific *adj*
unspecified *adj*
unspectacular *adj*
unspiritual *adj*
unspontaneous *adj*
unsporting *adj*
unsportingly *adv*
unsportingness *n*
unspun *adj*
unstained *adj*
unstartling *adj*
unstated *adj*
unsteadfast *adj*
unsterile *adj*
unstiffened *adj*
unstimulating *adj*
unstinted *adj*
unstipulated *adj*
unstrap *vt*
unstuffy *adj*
unstylish *adj*
unsubdued *adj*
unsubjugated *adj*
unsubtle *adj*
unsuccess *n*
unsuggestive *adj*
unsuited *adj*
unsullied *adj*
unsummoned *adj*

unsupervised *adj*
unsupported *adj*
unsuppressed *adj*
unsurfaced *adj*
unsurmountable *adj*
unsurpassable *adj*
unsurpassed *adj*
unsurprised *adj*
unsusceptible *adj*
unsuspicious *adj*
unsustainability *n*
unsustainable *adj*
unsustainably *adv*
unswathe *vt*
unswayed *adj*
unsweetened *adj*
unsymmetrical *adj*
unsymmetrically *adv*
unsympathetic *adj*
unsystematic *adj*
unsystematically *adv*
untainted *adj*
untaken *adj*
untalented *adj*
untamable *adj*
untamed *adj*
untanned *adj*
untarnished *adj*
untasted *adj*
untaxed *adj*
unteachable *adj*
untempered *adj*
untenanted *adj*
untended *adj*
untested *adj*
unthanked *adj*
unthankful *adj*
unthankfully *adv*
unthankfulness *n*
unthemed *adj*
unthreatened *adj*
unthrone *vt*
untilled *adj*
untinged *adj*
untoasted *adj*
untraceable *adj*
untraceably *adv*
untraced *adj*
untraditional *adj*
untrained *adj*
untranslatable *adj*
untranslated *adj*
untransportable *adj*
untreatable *adj*
untreatably *adv*
untreated *adj*

untrendy *adj*
untrimmed *adj*
untrodden *adj*
untrusting *adj*
untrustworthily *adv*
untrustworthiness *n*
untrustworthy *adj*
unturned *adj*
untwine *vt*
untwist *vti*
untypical *adj*
untypically *adv*
unusable *adj*
unutilized *adj*
unuttered *adj*
unvaccinated *adj*
unvanquished *adj*
unvaried *adj*
unvarying *adj*
unvaryingly *adv*
unventilated *adj*
unverifiable *adj*
unverified *adj*
unversed *adj*
unviability *n*
unviable *adj*
unvisited *adj*
unwanted *adj*
unwarlike *adj*
unwarmed *adj*
unwatched *adj*
unwatchful *adj*
unwaxed *adj*
unweaned *adj*
unweary *adj*
unweathered *adj*
unwed *adj*
unweighted *adj*
unwelcome *adj*
unwelcomely *adv*
unwelcomeness *n*
unwelcoming *adj*
unwelcomingly *adv*
unwetted *adj*
unwhipped *adj*
unwilled *adj*
unwinnable *adj*
unwithered *adj*
unwitnessed *adj*
unworked *adj*
unworried *adj*
unworriedly *adv*
unwounded *adj*
unwoven *adj*
unwritable *adj*
unyeasted *adj*

unabated /únnə báytid/ *adj* still as forceful or intense as before —**unabatedly** *adv*

unable /un áyb'l/ *adj* not able to do something

unaccommodated /únnə kómmə daytid/ *adj* (*formal*) **1.** not adapted to or for something ○ *unaccommodated to the dryness of the desert* **2.** lacking accommodation, equipment, or supplies

unaccompanied /únnə kúmpənid/ *adj, adv* **1.** alone, especially when a companion would be expected **2.** playing or singing alone, without any other instruments or voices

unaccountable /únnə kówntəb'l/ *adj* **1.** not answerable or responsible to anyone **2.** impossible to explain or give a reason for —**unaccountability** /-kowntə bílləti/ *n*

unaccountably /únnə kówntəbli/ *adv* for some unknown and usually puzzling reason

unaccounted-for /únnə kówntid-/ *adj* **1.** missing or absent, for unknown reasons **2.** not explained or understood

unaccustomed /únnə kústəmd/ *adj* **1.** not used or accustomed to something **2.** not usual or known before

una corda /oónə káwrdə/ *adj, adv* in piano music, using only one string per pitch, achieved by depressing the soft pedal. The effect is a reduction in volume and a change in the quality of the tone. [< Italian, 'one string']

unacquainted /únnə kwáyntid/ *adj* **1.** having no knowledge of something **2.** unknown to somebody or to each other

unadopted /únnə dóptid/ *adj* **1.** not adopted by new parents **2.** describes a road that is not maintained or repaired by a local authority

unadulterated /únnə dúltə raytid/ *adj* **1.** not mixed or diluted with something else **2.** free from any element that would spoil or detract from it ○ *unadulterated joy*

unadvised /únnəd vízd/ *adj* **1.** done without being carefully considered **2.** without asking the advice of others —**unadvisedly** *adv*

Unaipon /oo ní pon/, **David** (1872–1967) Australian writer and inventor. He was the author of *Native Legends* (1929), the first book by an Aboriginal writer to be published in Australia. He also designed agricultural machinery.

unaired /un áird/ *adj* **1.** not broadcast on radio or television **2.** not exposed to the air in order to be dried, have damp removed, be cooled, or be ventilated

Unalaska /únnə láskə/ island in southwestern Alaska, between the Bering Sea and the Pacific Ocean. It is the most important and second largest of the Aleutian Islands. Population: 4,580 (2002 estimate). Area: 1,287 sq. km/800 sq. mi.

unalienable /un áyli ənəb'l/ *adj* same as **inalienable**

unallowed /únnə lówd/ *adj* **1.** not allowed because illegal, forbidden, or invalid **2.** not allowed as a deduction, e.g. against tax

unalloyed /únnə lóyd/ *adj* **1.** containing no impurities, and not mixed or alloyed with other metals **2.** not mixed with anything else, especially anything that would dilute it or any other feeling that would diminish it ○ *unalloyed pleasure*

unambiguous /ún am bíggyoo əss/ *adj* completely clear in meaning or intention and unable to be misunderstood —**unambiguously** *adv*

un-American *adj* **1.** at odds with the customs, traditions, or ways of the people of the United States ○ *It's practically un-American not to like apple pie.* **2.** unpatriotic or disloyal to the United States

unaneled /únnə néeld/ *adj* in the Roman Catholic Church, not having received the last rites given to people who are dying or very ill (*archaic*) [Early 17C. < UN- + *aneled*, past participle of obsolete *anele* 'anoint' < Old English *ele* 'oil' < Latin *oleum*]

unanimous /yoo nánnimǝss/ *adj* **1.** shared or taken as a view by all of the people concerned, with nobody disagreeing **2.** with all members in agreement with each other ○ *Board members were unanimous in their rejection of the proposed merger.* [Early 17C. < Latin *unanimus* < *unus* 'one' + *animus* 'mind'] —**unanimity** /yóonə nímməti/ *n* —**unanimously** *adv*

unanswerable /un áanssərəb'l/ *adj* **1.** impossible to answer or solve **2.** so clearly true that nobody could contradict or deny it —**unanswerability** /un áansərə bílliti/ *n* —**unanswerably** *adv*

unappealable /únnə péeləb'l/ *adj* describes a case or judgment that is not open to appeal —**unappealably** *adv*

unappealing /únnə péeling/ *adj* not attractive or likely to be enjoyable —**unappealingly** *adv*

unapprised /únnə prízd/ *adj* not informed or given notice about something

unapproachable /únnə próchəb'l/ *adj* **1.** TOO UNFRIENDLY TO APPROACH OR CONTACT characterized by a formal, unfriendly, or hostile manner that discourages communication **2.** INACCESSIBLE difficult to get to **3.** UNRIVALLED so excellent that nothing or nobody else is nearly as good —**unapproachability** /-próchə bílləti/ *n* —**unapproachably** *adv*

unapt /un ápt/ *adj* **1.** lacking the qualities suitable for or appropriate to a context **2.** not likely or liable to do something (*formal*) ○ *unapt to cause any problems* —**unaptly** *adv* —**unaptness** *n*

unarchive /un áar kív/ (**-chives, -chiving, -chived**) *vt* to retrieve a computer file from archive storage

unarguable /un áargyoo əb'l/ *adj* **1.** so clearly true or correct that nobody can argue with it or deny it **2.** not sound or convincing enough to be put forward as an argument —**unarguably** *adv*

unarmed /un áarmd/ *adj* **1.** WITHOUT WEAPONS not carrying or using weapons **2.** BIOL WITH NO OBVIOUS MEANS OF SELF-DEFENCE with no horns, claws, shells, thorns, prickles, or other means of self-protection **3.** MIL UNABLE TO FIRE used to describe a missile or projectile whose fuse or firing mechanism has been disabled

unarranged /únnə ráynjd/ *adj* **1.** not put in order or relative position **2.** not brought about by agreement or planning

unary /yóonəri/ *adj* describes a mathematical operation that is applied to only one member of a set at a time, e.g. squaring a number [Early 20C. < Latin *unus* 'one']

unashamed /únnə sháymd/ *adj* **1.** not ashamed or embarrassed, and not feeling the need to apologize to others **2.** not limited, restrained, or avoided out of a feeling of shame or embarrassment —**unashamedly** /-sháymidli/ *adv* —**unashamedness** /-sháymidnəss/ *n*

unasked /un áaskt/ *adj* **1.** NOT ASKED not having been asked **2.** NOT INVITED coming to a gathering without an invitation **3.** *also* **unasked-for** NOT ASKED FOR providing something such as assistance that has not been asked for

unaspirated /un áspi raytid/ *adj* describes a letter 'h' at the beginning of a word that is not pronounced when the word is spoken, as in 'hour' or 'honour'

unaspiring /únnə spíring/ *adj* not aspiring to attain a goal

unassailable /únnə sáyləb'l/ *adj* **1.** so sound or well established that it cannot be challenged or overtaken ○ *an unassailable lead* **2.** so strong or impregnable that it cannot be successfully attacked —**unassailability** /únnə sáylə bílləti/ *n* —**unassailably** *adv*

unassuming /únnə syóoming/ *adj* acting in a way that does not assume superiority —**unassumingly** *adv* —**unassumingness** *n*

unattached /únnə tácht/ *adj* **1.** WITHOUT SPOUSE OR PARTNER not married and not in a long-term romantic or sexual relationship **2.** NOT JOINED not joined or attached, especially to other or larger organizations or bodies **3.** LAW NOT SEIZED FOR SECURITY describes property that is not taken away from its owner for security under the orders of a court of law

unattended /únnə téndid/ *adj* **1.** WITH NO ONE THERE with no one present to listen, watch, or participate **2.** NOT CARED FOR not looked after or seen to **3.** NOT ESCORTED not accompanied or escorted (*formal*) **4.** NOT HEEDED not listened to or heeded (*formal*) **5.** NOT HAVING SOMETHING AS CONSEQUENCE not accompanied by something, or not having something as a result or consequence (*formal*)

unattractive /únnə tráktiv/ *adj* **1.** not having a beautiful, pleasing, or desirable appearance **2.** not having any obvious advantages or interesting aspects ○ *nothing but unattractive prospects* —**unattractively** *adv* —**unattractiveness** *n*

SYNONYMS ***unattractive, unsightly, ugly, hideous, homely, plain***

CORE MEANING: not pleasant to look at

unattractive not having a beautiful, pleasing, or desirable appearance ○ *an unattractive combination of colours* ○ *Some find him physically unattractive, but his sense of humour is charming.* **unsightly** not pleasant to look at, or spoiling the appearance of something ○ *unsightly yellow teeth* ○ *an unsightly construction that will mar a beautiful view* **ugly** lacking appealing physical features, especially facial ones ○ *Isn't everyone afraid of getting old and ugly?* ○ *an ugly shape* **hideous** extremely unpleasant to look at ○ *a hideous monster* ○ *It's time to get rid of that hideous orange carpet.* **homely** *NAm* plain or less than pleasing in appearance ○ *a homely, awkward giant of a man* ○ *Next to her swanlike grace, I'm homely by comparison.* **plain** not pretty or good-looking ○ *a plain woman* ○ *She had a longish, plain face with a straight nose and a small mouth.*

~~unatural~~ incorrect spelling of **unnatural**

unau /yóo now/ (*plural* **unaus** or *same*) *n* ZOOL same as **two-toed sloth** [Late 18C. Via French < Tupi *unáu*]

un-Australian *adj Aus* contrary to what are seen as the characteristically Australian traditions of fairness and egalitarianism

unavailing /únnə váyling/ *adj* done but failing to achieve the desired result —**unavailingly** *adv*

unavoidable /únnə vóydəb'l/ *adj* unable to be avoided —**unavoidability** /únnə vóydə bílləti/ *n* —**unavoidably** *adv*

unaware /únnə wáir/ *adj* **1.** not conscious or aware of something **2.** lacking important information or analysis ○ *a politically unaware generation* ■ *adv* same as **unawares** —**unawarely** *adv* —**unawareness** *n*

unawares /únnə wáirz/ *adv* **1.** without any warning or anticipation ○ *His question caught me unawares.* ○ *You took me completely unawares.* **2.** without planning or intending to do something ○ *He took the wrong coat, unawares.* [Mid-16C. < UNAWARE + -*s*, adverbial suffix]

unb. *abbr* PUBL unbound

unbacked /un bákt/ *adj* **1.** NOT SUPPORTED OR BACKED having no support or backing, especially financial backing **2.** FURNITURE WITHOUT BACK describes a chair that has been made without a back **3.** RIDING NEVER RIDDEN describes a horse that has never been ridden ○ *an unbacked mare* **4.** GAMBLING NOT BET ON describes a horse that has had no bets placed on its performance

unbalance /un bállənss/ *vt* (**-ances, -ancing, -anced**) **1.** KNOCK SOMETHING OFF BALANCE to make something lose its balance or equilibrium **2.** MAKE SOMEBODY PSYCHOLOGICALLY UNSTABLE to make somebody psychologically or emotionally unstable ■ *n* STATE OF INSTABILITY the state of being unstable and out of balance —**unbalanceable** *adj*

unbalanced /un bállənst/ *adj* **1.** PSYCHOLOGICALLY UNSTABLE unable to make sound judgments **2.** ONE-SIDED done or provided from only one perspective ○ *unbalanced reporting* **3.** WITHOUT EQUILIBRIUM lacking the proper distribution of weight or forces that would provide balance **4.** ACCT HAVING UNEQUAL DEBITS AND CREDITS in which the totalled debits and credits are not equal

unbar /un báar/ (**-bars, -barring, -barred**) *vt* **1.** to unlock or open a door or gate **2.** to remove the bars or obstructions from something

unbd *abbr* PUBL unbound

unbearable /un báirəb'l/ *adj* difficult, unpleasant, or impossible to bear or tolerate —**unbearableness** *n* —**unbearably** *adv*

unbeatable /un béetəb'l/ *adj* too good or favourable to be beaten or surpassed —**unbeatably** *adv*

unbeaten /un béet'n/ *adj* **1.** UNDEFEATED never having been defeated or outdone **2.** COOK NOT WHIPPED OR POUNDED not subjected to pounding, whipping, or beating as part of preparation for cooking or eating ○ *unbeaten eggs* **3.** ROADS NOT TRAVELLED not made smooth from pedestrian or vehicular traffic ○ *an unbeaten path* **4.** CRICKET NOT OUT without being got out

unbecoming /únbi kúmming/ *adj* **1.** unsuitable or unattractive on the wearer **2.** not suitable, especially as not conforming with accepted attitudes or behaviour —**unbecomingly** *adv* —**unbecomingness** *n*

unbeknown /únbi nón/, **unbeknownst** /-nónst/ *adj* **1.** WITHOUT SOMEBODY KNOWING happening without a particular person knowing about it **2.** NOT KNOWN TO SOMEBODY not known or familiar to somebody ■ *adv* WITHOUT BEING SEEN without being noticed or seen by anybody ○ *slipped away unbeknownst* [Mid-17C. < UN- + *beknown*, past participle of obsolete *beknow* 'know thoroughly' < KNOW]

unbelief /únbi léef/ *n* lack of religious or political belief

unbelievable /únbi léevəb'l/ *adj* **1.** too unrealistic or improbable to be believed **2.** used to emphasize that something is very great, or very good, bad, or impressive ○ *reacted with unbelievable agility* —**unbelievability** /únbi leevə bílliti/ *n* —**unbelievably** *adv*

unbeliever /únbi léevər/ *n* somebody who does not believe in an established religious faith or in conventional beliefs

unbelieving /únbi léeving/ *adj* **1.** lacking belief or expressing disbelief about something **2.** with no religious faith or doctrinal beliefs —**unbelievingly** *adv*

unbelt /un bélt/ (**-belts, -belting, -belted**) *vt* **1.** to unfasten the belt on a garment **2.** to remove somebody or something from a supporting or restraining belt

unbend /un bénd/ (**-bends, -bending, -bent** /-bént/) *v* **1.** *vti* MAKE SOMEBODY RELAXED to make somebody become more informal, relaxed, or friendly, or become more informal, relaxed, or friendly **2.** *vti* MAKE SOMETHING STRAIGHT to make something become straight, or become straight, after being bent, twisted, or flexed **3.** *vt* NAUT UNFASTEN SAIL OR ROPE to free a sail, rope, or mooring line that was fastened —**unbendable** *adj*

unbending /un bénding/ *adj* **1.** RESOLUTE not willing to change opinions, beliefs, or attitudes **2.** STRICTLY OBSERVED strictly applied or observed **3.** ALOOF formal or unfriendly in manner or behaviour —**unbendingly** *adv* —**unbendingness** *n*

unbeneficial /ún benni físh'l/ *adj* not advantageous or profitable

unbent /un bént/ past participle, past tense of **unbend** ▪ *adj* **1.** not forced into submitting or giving in **2.** not bent or twisted

unbiased /un bí əst/, **unbiassed** *adj* **1.** fair and impartial rather than biased or prejudiced **2.** in statistics, with an expected value that is equal to the parameter being estimated —**unbiasedly** *adv*

unbiblical /un bíbblik'l/ *adj* opposed or in contrast to the teachings of the Bible, or not present or approved in biblical teaching

unbidden /un bídd'n/ *adj, adv* (*literary*) **1.** not wished for or willed **2.** not asked for or invited

unbigoted /un bíggətid/ *adj* having none of the characteristics of a bigot or of bigotry

unbind /un bínd/ (**-binds, -binding, -bound** /-bównd/) *vt* (*literary*) **1.** to free somebody from something restraining or restricting such as a duty or obligation **2.** to untie a person or animal

unblessed /un blést/ *adj* **1.** WITHOUT BLESSING not given a blessing **2.** UNFORTUNATE unfortunate or wretched (*literary*) **3.** REGARDED AS EVIL in some religions, regarded as behaving in unrighteous ways (*literary*)

unblinking /un blíngking/ *adj* **1.** failing or unable to close and open the eyes in quick succession **2.** showing no emotion, reluctance, or hesitation —**unblinkingly** *adv*

unblock /un blók/ (**-blocks, -blocking, -blocked**) *vt* **1.** REMOVE BLOCKAGE FROM SOMETHING to remove an obstruction from something in order to allow free access to it or a passage through it **2.** REMOVE OBSTRUCTION to remove something that is causing an obstruction **3.** RESTART PROCESS to remove an obstacle to the progress of something

unblushing /un blúshing/ *adj* feeling or showing no shame or embarrassment —**unblushingly** *adv*

unbolt /un bólt/ (**-bolts, -bolting, -bolted**) *vt* to pull back the bolt or bolts on a door or gate, so that it can be opened

unbolted /un bóltid/ *adj* **1.** not fitted with bolts, or with bolts not fastened **2.** describes flour or grain that has not had the coarse particles sifted from the fine ones

unborn /un báwrn/ *adj* **1.** not yet born, but usually already conceived and gestating ○ *behaviour that could benefit the unborn child* **2.** not thought of or begun yet (*literary*)

unbosom /un boōzzəm/ (**-oms, -oming, -omed**) *v* (*literary*) **1.** *vti* to express something previously suppressed or hidden **2. unbosom yourself** *vr* to reveal the thoughts, feelings, or secrets you have been keeping inside yourself ○ *unbosomed himself to us*

unbothered /un bóthərd/ *adj* not worried or disturbed by anything or anybody

unbound /ún bównd/ past participle, past tense of **unbind** ▪ *adj* **1.** WITHOUT COVER not fastened inside a permanent cover **2.** UNRESTRICTED without restraints or fetters **3.** SCI NOT IN CHEMICAL COMBINATION free from chemical or physical combination **4.** LING CONSTITUTING WORD used to describe a morpheme that can form a word on its own without any added affixes

unbounded /un bówndid/ *adj* **1.** not controlled or restrained in any way **2.** not subject to limits, boundaries, or restrictions —**unboundedly** *adv* —**unboundedness** *n*

unbowed /un bówd/ *adj* **1.** having refused to submit or admit defeat **2.** remaining in an erect position, not bent or bowed

unbrace /un bráyss/ (**-braces, -bracing, -braced**) *vt* to make something less tense or strained (*literary*)

unbred /un bréd/ *adj* **1.** NOT TRAINED not given training or instruction (*literary*) **2.** NOT WELL BRED lacking refinement or breeding (*literary*) **3.** AGRIC NOT YET MATED not yet mated with another animal

unbridle /un bríd'l/ (**-dles, -dling, -dled**) *vt* **1.** to take away the limits, controls, or restraints that apply to something **2.** to take the bridle from a horse

unbridled /un bríd'ld/ *adj* **1.** freely and openly expressed **2.** not fitted with a bridle

un-British *adj* at odds with the customs, traditions, or ways of the people of Great Britain

unbroken /un brókən/ *adj* **1.** WITHOUT GAPS with no gaps or pauses **2.** ONGOING continued without interruption **3.** UNDEFEATED not beaten or subdued **4.** UNTAMED not yet having submitted to human control ○ *an unbroken horse* **5.** NOT FRAGMENTED remaining intact or in one piece **6.** NOT VIOLATED having remained viable or in force —**unbrokenly** *adv* —**unbrokenness** *n*

unbundle /un búnd'l/ (**-dles, -dling, -dled**) *vt* to sell or charge for related products and services separately, rather than as a unit

unburden /un búrd'n/ (**-dens, -dening, -dened**) *v* **1. unburden yourself** *vr* to relieve yourself of something that has been worrying you by telling somebody about it (*formal*) **2.** *vt* to remove a load from a person or animal (*literary*)

unbutton /un bútt'n/ (**-tons, -toning, -toned**) *v* **1.** *vt* to undo a garment by unfastening the buttons **2.** *vi* to relax and become more talkative (*informal*)

uncalculated /un kálkyoō laytid/ *adj* done or accepted without careful consideration of the possible results

uncalculating /un kálkyoō layting/ *adj* not having or showing a determination to gain the greatest personal advantage —**uncalculatingly** *adv*

uncalled-for /un káwld-/ *adj* beyond what is necessary or expected, especially in being unjustifiably unkind or impolite

uncanny /un kánni/ (**-nier, -niest**) *adj* **1.** too strange or unlikely to seem merely natural or human **2.** unexpectedly accurate or precise ○ *an uncanny resemblance to the president* —**uncannily** *adv* —**uncanniness** *n*

uncanvassed /un kánvəst/ *adj* **1.** UNASKED not canvassed for orders, opinions, or votes **2.** NOT FULLY CONSIDERED not debated or discussed thoroughly **3.** NOT PROPERLY EXAMINED not examined in detail, e.g. to confirm validity

uncap /un káp/ (**-caps, -capping, -capped**) *vt* **1.** to remove an upper limit or restriction from something **2.** to remove the cap from a container

uncared-for /un káird-/ *adj* neglected and allowed to deteriorate

uncategorized /un káttigə rīzd/, **uncategorised** *adj* not placed into a category

unceasing /un seéssing/ *adj* continuing without stopping, pausing, or diminishing —**unceasingly** *adv*

unceremonious /ún seri móni əss/ *adj* **1.** sudden and rather rude, with no concern for politeness or good manners **2.** done without formality or ceremony —**unceremoniously** *adv* —**unceremoniousness** *n*

uncertain /un súrt'n/ *adj* **1.** WITHOUT KNOWLEDGE lacking clear knowledge or a definite opinion **2.** NOT KNOWN OR SETTLED not yet known, or remaining undecided **3.** CHANGEABLE likely to change, and therefore not reliable or stable **4.** LACKING SELF-ASSURANCE lacking self-assurance or confidence —**uncertainly** *adv*

SYNONYMS See *doubtful*.

uncertainty /un súrt'nti/ (*plural* **-ties**) *n* **1.** the quality or state of being uncertain **2.** something that nobody can predict or guarantee (*often used in the plural*) ○ *economic uncertainties*

uncertainty principle *n* a principle in quantum mechanics holding that it is impossible to determine both the position and momentum of a particle at the same time

unchain /un cháyn/ (**-chains, -chaining, -chained**) *vt* **1.** to take off the chain or chains holding a person or animal **2.** to take away the limits, controls, or restraints that apply to something or somebody

uncharted /un cháartid/ *adj* **1.** not surveyed or recorded on a map **2.** not previously encountered, experienced, or investigated

unchartered /un cháartərd/ *adj* not officially authorized or permitted

unchecked /un chékt/ *adj* **1.** not limited or controlled, especially when restraint or control is required **2.** remaining unverified or untested, especially for problems or imperfections

unchristian /ún krístyən/ *adj* **1.** unkind or selfish, and

therefore against Christian principles and teachings **2.** not belonging to the Christian Church

unchurch /un chúrch/ (**-churches, -churching, -churched**) *vt* **1.** to expel somebody from a church **2.** to remove the status of being a church from a building

unci ANAT plural of **uncus**

uncial

uncial /únssi əl/ *n* **1.** STYLE OF LETTER USED IN MANUSCRIPTS a letter of the kind used in Greek and Latin manuscripts written between the 3rd and 9th centuries that resembles a modern capital letter but is more rounded **2.** MANUSCRIPT IN UNCIALS a manuscript written in uncials ▪ *adj* WRITTEN IN UNCIALS relating to or written in uncials [Mid-17C. < late Latin *unciales (litterae)* 'inch-high (letters)' < Latin *uncia* 'twelfth part, inch'] —**uncially** *adv*

unciform /únssi fawrm/ *adj* shaped like a hook ▪ *n* ANAT same as **hamate** [Mid-18C. < Latin *uncus* 'hook']

uncinariasis /únssinə rí əssiss/ *n* infestation of the intestines with hookworms [Early 20C. < modern Latin *Uncinaria*, genus of hookworms < Latin *uncus* 'hook']

uncinate /únssinət/ *adj* shaped like a hook at the end [Mid-18C. < Latin *uncinatus* < *uncus* 'hook']

uncinus /un sínəss/ (*plural* **-ni** /-nī/) *n* **1.** a small hooked body part, e.g. the hook-shaped tooth of a gastropod or a chitinous hook on the body of an annelid **2.** a cirrus cloud that is curled in a hook shape at one of its elongated ends [Mid-19C. < Latin < *uncus* 'hook']

uncivil /un sívv'l/ *adj* behaving in a way that is seen as hostile or indifferent —**uncivility** /únssi vílləti/ *n* —**uncivilly** *adv*

uncivilized /un sívvə līzd/, **uncivilised** *adj* **1.** NOT CULTURALLY ADVANCED existing in a condition or behaving in ways that are thought to be socially or culturally undeveloped **2.** REMOTE far from civilized or settled areas **3.** NOT POLITE, REFINED, OR COMFORTABLE unacceptable or unbecoming to educated, cultured people used to refinement and comfort (*humorous*) —**uncivilizedly** /-līzidli/ *adv*

unclad /un klád/ *adj* not wearing any clothes

unclasp /un klaásp/ (**-clasps, -clasping, -clasped**) *vt* **1.** to separate hands previously held together **2.** to unfasten the clasp holding something closed

unclassified /un klássi fīd/ *adj* **1.** NOT ARRANGED SYSTEMATICALLY not arranged or grouped systematically **2.** NOT SECRET remaining open for examination by anyone who wishes access **3.** NOT FOR MAIN TRAFFIC not classed as a motorway, an A-road, or a B-road

uncle /úngk'l/ *n* **1.** the brother of somebody's mother or father, or the husband of somebody's aunt (*capitalized before a name*) **2.** a parent's male friend (*capitalized before a name*) SAME as **pawnbroker** (*dated slang*) [13C. Via Old French *oncle* < Latin *avunculus* 'maternal uncle']

unclean /un kleén/ *adj* **1.** DIRTY dirty or insanitary **2.** UNCHASTE sinful, especially involving or guilty of committing a sexual sin **3.** RELIG RELIGIOUSLY OR RITUALLY IMPURE not pure according to religious rules or rituals —**uncleanness** *n*

SYNONYMS See *dirty*.

uncleanly /un klénnli/ *adj* same as **unclean** (*formal or literary*) ▪ *adv* in a way that is not clean —**uncleanliness** *n*

Uncle Sam /-sám/ *n* **1.** a personification of the government of the United States, shown as a tall thin white man with a white beard, wearing red and white striped trousers, a blue tail coat, and a

stovepipe hat with a band of stars **2.** the United States or the American people [19C. Invented < *US*, abbreviation of *United States*]

Uncle Tom /-tóm/ *n* a highly offensive term for a Black man who is thought to be too solicitous of or subservient to white people (*taboo*) [Mid-19C. After a character in Harriet Beecher Stowe's novel *Uncle Tom's Cabin*] —**Uncle Tomism** *n*

uncloak /un klṓk/ (**-cloaks, -cloaking, -cloaked**) *vt* to reveal the identity or true nature of somebody or something

unclog /un klóg/ (**-clogs, -clogging, -clogged**) *vt* to remove a blockage from something such as a pipe

unclose /un klṓz/ (**-closes, -closing, -closed**) *vti* **1.** to make something open rather than closed, or become open rather than closed **2.** to reveal something, or be revealed

unclosed /un klṓzd/ *adj* not in a closed condition

unclothe /un klṓth/ (**-clothes, -clothing, -clothed**) *vt* to remove the clothes or covering from somebody or something —**unclothed** *adj*

unclutter /un klúttər/ (**-ters, -tering, -tered**) *vt* **1.** to remove the clutter from a place **2.** to remove the complexities, disorganization, or undue busyness from something ○ *Unclutter your life!*

uncluttered /un klúttərd/ *adj* not having an excessive amount of objects or details and therefore not appearing untidy, obstructed, or cramped

unco[1] /úngkō/ *Scotland adv* very or extremely ■ *adj* unusual or unfamiliar [15C. Variant of UNCOUTH]

unco[2] /úngkō/ *adj Aus* an offensive term used to tease somebody who is regarded as clumsy or inept at sports and games (*informal*) [Late 20C. Shortening of UNCOORDINATED]

uncoil /un kóyl/ (**-coils, -coiling, -coiled**) *vti* to release something from a coiled or wound position, or be released from a coiled or wound position

uncomfortable /un kúmftəb'l/ *adj* **1.** feeling a lack of or not providing physical comfort **2.** feeling or making others feel awkward and ill at ease —**uncomfortableness** *n* —**uncomfortably** *adv*

uncomfy /un kúmfi/ *adj* same as **uncomfortable** (*informal*)

uncommercial /únkə múrsh'l/ *adj* **1.** NOT CONCERNED WITH COMMERCE OR BUSINESS not involved in commerce, especially not operated or organized for profit **2.** AGAINST BUSINESS PRINCIPLES OR PRACTICES contrary to the way things are usually done in commerce or business **3.** UNPROFITABLE unappealing to consumers and so not likely to turn a profit

uncommitted /únkə míttid/ *adj* **1.** not dedicated to a principle, cause, or organization **2.** not pledged to any cause, purpose, or course of action ○ *uncommitted funds*

uncommon /un kómmən/ *adj* **1.** appearing or happening infrequently **2.** used to emphasize the great extent of something ○ *showing uncommon wisdom* —**uncommonness** *n*

uncommonly /un kómmənli/ *adv* **1.** not frequently **2.** to a degree or extent that is unusual or rare

uncommunicative /únkə myoónikətiv/ *adj* not willing to say much, especially not to reveal information, or tending not to say much —**uncommunicatively** *adv* —**uncommunicativeness** *n*

SYNONYMS See ***silent***.

---

uncomplicated /un kómpli kaytid/ *adj* readily understood, or easy to deal with —**uncomplicatedness** *n*

SYNONYMS See ***easy***.

---

uncompromising /un kómprə mīzing/ *adj* feeling or showing no willingness to compromise or back down —**uncompromisingly** *adv* —**uncompromisingness** *n*

unconcern /únkən súrn/ *n* lack of concern or interest, especially where concern would be expected or thought appropriate

unconcerned /únkən súrnd/ *adj* **1.** not worried or anxious, especially when this seems unexpected or unnatural **2.** lacking concern or interest or unwilling to become involved in something —**unconcernedly** /-súrnidli/ *adv*

unconditional /únkən dísh'nəl/ *adj* complete or guaranteed, with no conditions, limitations, or provisos attached ○ *unconditional love* —**unconditionality** /-dishə nálləti/ *n* —**unconditionally** *adv*

unconditioned /únkən dísh'nd/ *adj* **1.** without any conditions or limits restricting or affecting it **2.** arising spontaneously and not as a result of learning or conditioning ○ *an unconditioned reflex*

unconditioned stimulus *n* a stimulus that evokes a reflexive response without prior conditioning or learning

unconfined /ún kən fīnd/ *adj* **1.** not enclosed or kept within limits or boundaries ○ *in an unconfined space* **2.** expressed naturally and uninhibitedly ○ *Let joy be unconfined!*

unconformable /únkən fáwrməb'l/ *adj* **1.** unwilling or unable to follow conventional social customs **2.** describes a layer of rock that lies directly on a much older stratum, indicating a period of erosion —**unconformability** /-fawrmə bílləti/ *n* —**unconformably** *adv*

unconformity /únkən fáwrməti/ (*plural* **-formities**) *n* **1.** LACK OF CONFORMITY behaviour or thinking that refuses to follow conventional social prescriptions **2.** GEOL BREAK IN CONTINUITY IN SEDIMENTARY ROCKS a break in the continuity of sedimentary rocks resulting from erosion or cessation of deposition **3.** GEOL SURFACE BETWEEN MISMATCHED STRATA the contact surface between two unconformable strata, often marked by angular discordance

unconnected /únkə néktid/ *adj* not related or connected to something else or each other ○ *The two incidents are entirely unconnected.* —**unconnectedly** *adv* —**unconnectedness** *n*

unconscionable /un kónsh'nəb'l/ *adj* **1.** shocking and morally unacceptable **2.** far beyond what is considered reasonable —**unconscionably** *adv*

unconscious /un kónshəss/ *adj* **1.** EXPERIENCING LOSS OF SENSES unable to see, hear, or otherwise sense what is going on, usually temporarily and often as a result of an accident or injury **2.** UNAWARE not aware of something **3.** UNINTENTIONAL not intended, or not realized or recognized ○ *unconscious irony* ■ *n* PSYCHOL, PSYCHOANAL MIND'S HIDDEN PART the part of the mind containing memories, thoughts, feelings, and ideas that the person is not generally aware of but that manifest themselves in dreams and dissociated acts —**unconsciously** *adv* —**unconsciousness** *n*

unconsidered /únkən síddərd/ *adj* done without being properly thought about beforehand

~~**unconsious**~~ incorrect spelling of **unconscious**

unconstitutional /ún konsti tyoósh'nəl/ *adj* not allowed by or against the principles set down in a constitution, especially a nation's written constitution —**unconstitutionality** /-tyoosh'n álləti/ *n* —**unconstitutionally** *adv*

uncontrollable /únkən trṓləb'l/ *adj* **1.** too strongly felt to be suppressed **2.** too unruly or wild to discipline or control —**uncontrollability** /-trōlə bílləti/ *n* —**uncontrollably** *adv*

unconventional /únkən vénsh'nəl/ *adj* different from what is regarded as normal or standard —**unconventionality** /-venshə nálləti/ *n* —**unconventionally** *adv*

uncool /ún kóol/ *adj* **1.** not suitably relaxed, casual, or self-assured, especially in the opinion of young people (*informal*) **2.** unfashionable, undesirable, or unacceptable, especially in the opinion of young people (*slang*)

uncoordinated /ún kō áwrdi naytid/ *adj* **1.** awkward when moving or doing something, as if different parts of the body were not acting in harmony **2.** with no organization or proper cooperation between people or groups —**uncoordinatedly** *adv*

uncork /un káwrk/ (**-corks, -corking, -corked**) *vt* **1.** to open a bottle of something, especially wine, by taking out its cork **2.** to release something that has been restrained or repressed, e.g. a strong emotion

uncountable /un kówntəb'l/ *adj* **1.** too various or great in number to be counted **2.** used to describe a noun that does not refer to a single object

uncounted /un kówntid/ *adj* **1.** too numerous to be counted **2.** not, or not yet, subjected to a count

uncount noun /ún kownt-/ *n* GRAM same as **mass noun**

uncouple /un kúpp'l/ (**-ples, -pling, -pled**) *v* **1.** *vti* to separate two things or one thing from another by undoing a fastening that connects them, or be separated in this way **2.** *vt* to let loose something that has been restrained

uncouth /un koóth/ *adj* **1.** behaving in an ill-mannered or unrefined way **2.** clumsy and ungraceful [Old English *uncūþ* 'unknown' < *cūþ* 'known', past participle of *cunnan* 'know' (see CAN[2])] —**uncouthly** *adv* —**uncouthness** *n*

uncovenanted /un kúvvənəntid/ *adj* not bound, sanctioned, or guaranteed by a covenant

uncover /un kúvvər/ (**-ers, -ering, -ered**) *v* **1.** *vt* TAKE COVER OFF SOMETHING to remove a covering from something **2.** *vt* EXPOSE SOMETHING to find, find out about, or reveal something secret or previously hidden ○ *uncover the truth about somebody* **3.** *vti* TAKE OFF YOUR HAT to take off a hat or other head covering (*dated*)

uncovered /un kúvvərd/ *adj* **1.** WITH NO COVERING without any covering or protection **2.** WITH HEAD BARE with a hat or other head covering removed, usually as a sign of respect (*dated*) **3.** INSUR NOT INSURED not protected by insurance or guaranteed by some security

uncrewed /un kroód/ *adj* not having any personnel, especially not having a pilot or crew

uncritical /un kríttik'l/ *adj* accepting or approving something without analysing or questioning it or discriminating between good and bad —**uncritically** *adv*

uncross /un króss/ (**-crosses, -crossing, -crossed**) *vt* to straighten something out from a crossed position ○ *She sat crossing and uncrossing her arms impatiently.*

uncrowned /un krównd/ *adj* **1.** possessing power, status, or wide respect but without an official title or recognition **2.** with royal rank but not yet crowned

unction /úngksh'n/ *n* **1.** ANOINTING WITH OIL the rubbing or sprinkling of oil on somebody as part of a religious ceremony **2.** SUBSTANCE USED IN RITE an oil, ointment, or salve used in religious rites **3.** REAL OR PRETENDED EARNESTNESS real or pretended earnestness or fervour, especially with regard to spiritual matters and especially when expressed in suitably solemn language **4.** FLATTERING EFFORTS TO CHARM excessively ingratiating efforts to charm or convince somebody **5.** SOMETHING SOOTHING something that soothes or comforts somebody [14C. < Latin *unction-* < *unguere* 'smear, anoint']

unctuous /úngkchoo əss/ *adj* **1.** attempting to charm or convince somebody in an unpleasantly suave, smug, or smooth way **2.** resembling or containing oil, fat, or grease [14C. < medieval Latin *unctuosus* < Latin *unctus* 'anointing' < *unguere* 'smear, anoint'] —**unctuosity** /úngkchoo óssəti/ *n* —**unctuously** *adv* —**unctuousness** *n*

uncurl /un kúrl/ (**-curls, -curling, -curled**) *vti* to straighten something that was previously wound in a curl, coil, or spiral, or become unwound or straight

uncus /úngkəss/ (*plural* **-ci** /-sī/) *n* a body part shaped like a hook [Early 19C. Via modern Latin < Latin, 'hook']

uncut /un kút/ *adj* **1.** NOT CUT with no part removed or divided by cutting **2.** COMPLETE not abridged, shortened, or censored **3.** NOT FACETED describes a gemstone in its original shape, before facets have been cut ○ *uncut diamonds* **4.** PUBL WITH UNSEPARATED PAGES with the edges of the pages not yet trimmed to separate them **5.** DRUGS NOT ADULTERATED in a pure and unadulterated form (*informal*)

undamped /un dámpt/ *adj* **1.** not subdued or discouraged **2.** describes a scientific instrument or system that is allowed to oscillate unchecked

undaunted /un dáwntid/ *adj* not afraid or deterred by the prospect of defeat, loss, or failure —**undauntedly** *adv* —**undauntedness** *n*

undead /un déd/ *npl* in fiction, especially vampire stories, people or other beings who are technically dead but still exist, move, and interact with the living in a physical form —**undead** *adj*

undecagon /un dékəgən/ *n* a two-dimensional geometric figure formed of eleven sides and eleven angles [Early 18C. < Latin *undecim* 'eleven' + -GON, after DECAGON]

undeceive /úndi seév/ (**-ceives, -ceiving, -ceived**) *vt* to tell the truth to somebody who has been misled (*often passive*) —**undeceiver** *n*

undecided /úndi sīdid/ *adj* **1.** NOT HAVING DECIDED not yet having made a choice or decision **2.** NOT FINALIZED not yet settled or resolved ■ *n* SOMEBODY WITHOUT MIND MADE

UP somebody who has not yet made a decision or choice about something ○ *She was counted among the undecideds.* —**undecidedly** *adv*

undeclared /úndi kláird/ *adj* **1.** NOT STATED not stated clearly or announced officially **2.** FIN NOT REVEALED AS DUTIABLE OR TAXABLE not notified to customs or tax authorities **3.** *N Am* EDUC NOT YET DECIDED ON MAJOR SUBJECT describes students who have not yet chosen or notified the subject in which they wish to specialize at university or college

undelete /úndi léet/ (-letes, -leting, -leted) *vt* to reinstate text or a file that has been deleted on a computer

undemocratic /ún demmə kráttik/ *adj* not in accordance with or not practising democracy —**undemocratically** *adv*

undemonstrative /úndi mónstrətiv/ *adj* tending not to show emotions openly —**undemonstratively** *adv* —**undemonstrativeness** *n*

undeniable /úndi nī́ əb'l/ *adj* **1.** BEYOND QUESTION unquestionably true or real and beyond dispute **2.** UNABLE TO BE REFUSED not able to be refused because of its importance or impact **3.** INDISPUTABLY WORTHY with worth, merit, or quality that cannot be doubted ○ *a person of undeniable character* —**undeniably** *adv*

under /úndər/ CORE MEANING: a grammatical word used to express the concept of being beneath or below something, e.g. in location, size, age, or price ○ (prep) *Johnny had the book hidden under his tunic.* ○ (prep) *The machine is under a foot high and will fit on to any work surface.* ○ (prep) *This toy should not be given to children under three years old.* ○ (prep) *It's the best meal you can get for under £5.* ○ (adv) *For one week only, kids five and under eat free.* **1.** *prep* BELOW at or to a lower level than something that rests on top or covers and protects ○ *They were sheltering under a huge umbrella.* **2.** *prep* INSIDE inside something that forms a covering outer layer or has an upper surface ○ *He had two sweaters on under his jacket.* ○ *under the water* **3.** *prep* LESS THAN fewer in number than something, or less than something, e.g. in age, quantity, size, or price ○ *We should be finished in under a month.* ○ *There were under a hundred people at the meeting.* **4.** *prep* SUBORDINATE TO lower in rank or status than somebody or something ○ *I was under him in the company hierarchy.* **5.** *prep* SUBJECT TO subject to the control or authority of somebody or something ○ *under existing legislation* ○ *working under a new boss* **6.** *prep* DURING RULE OF during the rule of a person or government ○ *The crime rate had in fact gone down under the new mayor.* **7.** *prep* GIVEN THE EXISTENCE OF while something, especially conditions or circumstances, exists ○ *impossible under these conditions* **8.** *prep* IN THE PROCESS OF used to indicate that somebody or something is going through a particular process or experience ○ *under scrutiny* ○ *under construction* **9.** *prep* USING NAME using a particular name, especially an assumed one ○ *travelling under a false name* **10.** *prep* CLASSIFIED WITHIN classified as or in something ○ *filed under 'Miscellaneous'* **11.** *prep* PLANTED WITH planted with a particular crop ○ *a field under rye* **12.** *prep* POWERED BY powered or driven by something ○ *under sail* **13.** *prep* IN SIGN OF ZODIAC during a period in which the Sun is in a particular position in the zodiac ○ *born under Aries* **14.** *adv* BELOW SURFACE OR POINT at or to a point at a lower level, especially one below a surface or covering, or passing through at a lower level ○ *watched from the lifeboats as the ship went under* ○ *lifted the wire and crawled under* **15.** *adv* FEWER OR LESS fewer or less than a previously given figure ○ *Employers with 50 employees or under are exempt.* **16.** *adv, adj* SUBSERVIENT in or into a position of submissiveness or subservience (*informal*) ○ *keeping the masses under* **17.** *adv, adj* UNCONSCIOUS in or into a state of unconsciousness or hypnosis (*informal*) ○ *felt myself going under* [Old English < Indo-European]

under- *prefix* **1.** too little, less than usual ○ *underachiever* ○ *underpay* **2.** below, underneath ○ *underpants* ○ *underscore* **3.** subordinate, of lower rank ○ *undersecretary*

underactive *adj*	**undercook** *vt*
underactivity *n*	**undercrewed** *adj*
underappreciated *adj*	**undereat** *vi*
underbake *vt*	**undereducated** *adj*
underbooked *adj*	**underemphasis** *n*
underbudgeted *adj*	**underemphasize** *vt*
underconsumption *n*	**underendow** *vt*

underendowment *n*	**underproduction** *n*
underexercise *vi*	**underprovided** *adj*
underfinanced *adj*	**underpublicized** *adj*
underfund *vt*	**underqualified** *adj*
underfunding *n*	**underreact** *vi*
underinflated *adj*	**underripe** *adj*
underinvestment *n*	**underserved** *adj*
underlayer *n*	**understaff** *vt*
undermanned *adj*	**understock** *v*
undermodulation *n*	**undersubscribe** *vt*
underorganized *adj*	**undersubscribed** *adj*
underpay *vt*	**undersupply** *vt, n*
underpayment *n*	**undertrain** *vt*
underpopulated *adj*	**underuse** *n, vt*
underpopulation *n*	**underused** *adj*
underpowered *adj*	**underutilization** *n*
underproduce *vt*	**underutilized** *adj*

underachieve /úndər ə chéev/ (-chieves, -chieving, -chieved) *vi* to fail to fulfil your potential or somebody's expectations —**underachievement** *n*

underachiever /úndər ə chéevər/ *n* somebody who or something that performs less well than might be expected, especially a student whose academic results are poor, given his or her intelligence and aptitude

underact /úndər ákt/ (-acts, -acting, -acted) *v* **1.** *vti* to fail to play a dramatic role with enough power or conviction **2.** *vt* to play a role in an understated way deliberately, for dramatic effect

underage /úndər áyj/ *adj* **1.** below the legal or required age for something **2.** carried on by people who are below the age at which something is legally permitted ○ *underage driving*

underarm /úndər aarm/ *adj* **1.** KEEPING ARM BELOW SHOULDER HEIGHT carried out with the arm kept below shoulder height and usually close to the body ○ *an underarm throw* **2.** BELOW ARM below the arm or for use under the arm, especially in the armpit ○ *an underarm deodorant* **3.** FROM WRIST TO ARMPIT relating to the area along the underside of the arm from armpit to wrist ■ *adv* WITH ARM LOW with the arm kept below shoulder height ○ *bowl underarm* ■ *n* AREA JUST BELOW ARM the area below the arm on the body or on a garment, especially the armpit

underbelly /úndər belli/ (*plural* -lies) *n* **1.** LOWEST PART OF ANIMAL'S BELLY the underside of an animal, normally the part of the belly that is closest to the ground **2.** LOWER SURFACE the underside of an object, especially an aircraft **3.** WEAK POINT a weak or vulnerable part of something ○ *the soft underbelly of the regime*

underbid /úndər bíd/ (-bids, -bidding, -bid) **1.** *vti* OFFER LESS to offer a lower price than somebody else in competitive bidding **2.** *vi* MAKE TOO LOW BID to make a very low bid or too low a bid to obtain something **3.** *vti* BID LESS THAN VALUE OF CARDS to bid less than the full value of a hand in cards ■ *n* VERY LOW BID a bid that is lower than somebody else's, or too low to obtain something —**underbidder** *n*

underbite /úndər bīt/ *n* a dental condition in which the lower incisor teeth overlap the upper

underbody /úndər boddi/ (*plural* -ies) *n* the underside of the body of a motor vehicle or of an animal

underbred /úndər bréd/ *adj* **1.** not bred from pure stock **2.** not brought up well or well-mannered —**underbreeding** /-bréeding/ *n*

underbrush /úndər brush/ *n N Am* FORESTRY same as **undergrowth** (sense 1)

undercapitalize /úndər káppit'l īz/ (-izes, -izing, -ized), **undercapitalise** (-ises, -ising, -ised) *vti* to fail to supply an organization, especially a business, with enough capital to operate efficiently (*often passive*) —**undercapitalization** /úndər kappit'l ī záysh'n/ *n*

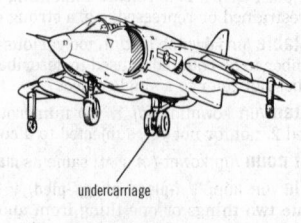

undercarriage

undercarriage

undercarriage /úndər karij/ *n* **1.** the supporting framework underneath a vehicle, to which wheels, tracks, or other means of locomotion are attached **2.** the framework of struts and wheels on which an aircraft runs when it moves on the ground

undercharge *v* /úndər cháarj/ (-charges, -charging, -charged) **1.** *vti* NOT CHARGE SOMEBODY ENOUGH to charge somebody too low a price for something **2.** *vt* INSERT INSUFFICIENT CHARGE IN SOMETHING to put an inadequate charge in a firearm ■ *n* /úndər chaarj/ EXCESSIVELY LOW PRICE a price charged that is too low

underclass /úndər klaass/ *n* a social class consisting of people so underprivileged that they are seen as being excluded from mainstream society

underclay /úndər klay/ *n* a layer of fine-grained sedimentary clay found beneath a coal seam, containing the fossilized roots of the plants that became the coal

underclothes /úndər klō̄thz/ *npl* CLOTHING same as **underwear**

underclothing /úndər klō̄thing/ *n* CLOTHING same as **underwear**

undercoat /úndər kōt/ *n* **1.** COAT BENEATH FINAL PAINT COAT a coat of paint or emulsion applied to a surface before a top coat is applied **2.** PAINT TO BE COVERED paint or emulsion designed to be used as an undercoat **3.** ZOOL SHORT HAIRS UNDER ANIMAL'S COAT a dense layer of short hairs, fur, or wool beneath the longer growth of an animal's outer coat ■ *vt* (-coats, -coating, -coated) **1.** PAINT SOMETHING WITH UNDERCOAT to apply an undercoat to a surface **2.** *N Am* AUTOMOT same as **underseal**

undercoating /úndər kōting/ *n N Am* same as **underseal**

undercool /úndər kōol/ (-cools, -cooling, -cooled) *vti* CHEM, PHYS same as **supercool** *v*

undercover /úndər kúvvər/ *adj* engaged in or involving the secret gathering of information, especially by somebody who disguises himself or herself as a member of the group whose activities are being investigated ○ *an undercover police officer* —**undercover** *adv*

undercroft /úndər kroft/ *n* an underground room, especially the crypt of a church

undercurrent /úndər kurrənt/ *n* **1.** a current in a body of water or air that flows beneath another current or the surface **2.** a feeling, opinion, force, or tendency felt to be present in a person or group, but not openly shown or expressed and often differing markedly from any outwardly expressed reaction ○ *an undercurrent of resentment*

undercut *v* /úndər kút/ (-cuts, -cutting, -cut) **1.** *vt* BUSINESS CHARGE LOWER AMOUNT THAN SOMEBODY to charge less for something than somebody else **2.** *vt* REDUCE SOMETHING'S FORCE to undermine something or detract from its force (*often passive*) **3.** *vt* CUT LOWER PART OF SOMETHING to cut away or cut into the lower part of something, especially in a way that leaves a portion overhanging **4.** *vti* SPORTS HIT BALL WITH BACKSPIN to hit a ball with a downward oblique stroke so that it has backspin, e.g. in golf or tennis ■ *n* /úndər kut/ **1.** CUT MADE IN LOWER PART a cut made below another cut or into the lower part of something **2.** SOMETHING CUT AWAY a piece of material that has been cut away from the lower part of something **3.** SPORTS STROKE WITH BACKSPIN a stroke that gives backspin to a ball **4.** *N Am* FORESTRY NOTCH IN TREE TRUNK a notch cut in a tree that is being felled that helps it make a clean break and directs its fall

underdaks /úndər daks/ *npl Aus* underpants, especially men's underpants (*informal*)

underdeveloped /úndər di vélləpt/ *adj* **1.** NOT FULLY GROWN not grown to a full or normal extent **2.** WITHOUT MEANS FOR ECONOMIC GROWTH lacking the technology and capital to make efficient use of available resources **3.** NOT DEVELOPED ENOUGH describes a photograph, negative, or film that was inadequately developed during processing, usually through being taken out of the developer too soon, and lacks contrast as a result —**underdevelopment** *n*

underdog /úndər dog/ *n* **1.** somebody who is expected to lose a fight or contest **2.** somebody who is unsuccessful

underdone /úndər dún/ *adj* **1.** not cooked as thoroughly as intended or required **2.** cooked only lightly or partially to achieve a desired flavour or texture

underdrain *vt* /úndər dráyn/ (**-drains, -draining, -drained**) to equip an area, especially cultivated land, with a system of underground drains ■ *n* /úndər drayn/ an underground drain or system of drains on agricultural land —**underdrainage** /úndər draynij/ *n*

underdress *vi* /úndər dréss/ (**-dresses, -dressing, -dressed**) to dress less fully or formally than an occasion or circumstance demands, e.g. in cold weather or for a social event (*often passive*) ■ *n* /úndər dress/ a garment or set of garments worn beneath others, especially if designed to be seen when worn

underemployed /úndər im plóyd/ *adj* **1.** not having enough work to do, or not being used to full capacity in a job **2.** working part-time but preferring full-time employment —**underemployment** *n*

underestimate *v* /úndər ésti mayt/ (**-mates, -mating, -mated**) **1.** *vti* MAKE TOO LOW ESTIMATE to make an estimate of something that is too low ○ *We underestimated the time it would take.* **2.** *vt* MISJUDGE WORTH OF SOMEBODY OR SOMETHING to judge people or things as being inferior to their real value or ability ○ *Don't underestimate her – she's tougher than she looks.* ■ *n* /úndər éstimət/ TOO LOW ESTIMATE an estimate that is too low, or a judgment that is too unfavourable to somebody or something —**underestimation** /úndər esti máysh'n/ *n*

underexpose /úndər ik spṓz/ (**-poses, -posing, -posed**) *vt* **1.** to expose photographic film to light for too short a time, or expose it to inadequate light **2.** to fail to give somebody or something enough publicity —**underexposure** *n*

underfeed /úndər féed/ (**-feeds, -feeding, -fed** /-féd/) *vt* **1.** to fail to give a person or animal enough to eat **2.** to fuel something such as an engine or a furnace from underneath

underfelt /úndər felt/ *n* a layer of felt or other material put down on a floor before a carpet is laid to give better insulation and wear

underfloor /úndər fláwr/ *adj* located beneath the flooring of a room or building ○ *underfloor heating*

underflow /úndərflō/ *n* **1.** the inability of a location in computer memory to handle data of an excessively small magnitude **2.** a computer error caused by underflow

underfoot /úndər fóot/ *adv* **1.** BENEATH FEET under the feet of a person or animal, on the ground, or between the feet and the ground ○ *It was muddy underfoot.* **2.** IN SOMEBODY'S WAY creating an obstacle or obstruction **3.** WITH ARROGANT DISREGARD OR DESTRUCTIVE INTENT in a way that shows an arrogant or callous disregard or an intention to destroy ○ *trampled underfoot the feelings of everyone who worked for them*

underfur /úndər fur/ *n* ZOOL same as **undercoat** *n* (sense 3)

undergarment /úndər gaarmənt/ *n* a piece of clothing worn beneath outer clothes, especially next to the skin, and not normally seen in public

undergird /úndər gúrd/ (**-girds, -girding, -girded** or **-girt** /-gúrt/) *vt* **1.** to support or secure something from below, e.g. by means of ropes passed underneath it **2.** to provide something with support or reinforcement of any kind

underglaze /úndər glayz/ *adj* describes decoration or pigment applied to a piece of pottery before the glaze is put on ■ *n* something, especially a decoration or pigment, that is applied to a piece of pottery before the glaze is put on

undergo /úndər gṓ/ (**-goes, -going, -went** /-wént/, **-gone** /-gón/) *vt* to experience or endure something, or have something happen to you ○ *You'll be obliged to undergo a thorough medical examination.* ○ *The city underwent a period of great change.*

undergrad /úndər grad/ *n* EDUC same as **undergraduate** (*informal; often used before nouns*) ○ *undergrad humour* [Early 19C. Shortening]

undergraduate /úndər grájjoo ət/ *n* a student at university or college who is studying for a first degree (*often used before a noun*) ○ *undergraduate courses*

underground *adj* /úndər grownd/ **1.** BENEATH EARTH'S SURFACE located, happening, or operating beneath the surface of the Earth **2.** COVERT concealed and done in secret **3.** CONTRARY TO PREVAILING CULTURE separate from a prevailing social or artistic environment, and often exercising a subversive influence ○ *The story had been circulating in the underground press.* ■ *n* /úndər grownd/ **1.** RAIL RAILWAY RUNNING BELOW GROUND a railway system that runs below ground (*often used before nouns*) N Am term **subway 2.** RESISTANCE MOVEMENT a secret movement that aims to overthrow a government or fight against an occupying enemy **3.** MOVEMENT CONTRARY TO PREVAILING CULTURE a movement or group that is separate from the prevailing social or artistic environment and often exerts a subversive influence ■ *adv* /úndər grównd/ **1.** BELOW GROUND below the surface of the ground **2.** SECRETLY in secret or in hiding

Underground Railroad *n* a secret organization that helped slaves flee from the southern United States to Canada or other places of safety prior to the abolition of slavery

undergrown /úndər grōn, úndər grṓn/ *adj* **1.** not grown to the expected size **2.** having or covered with undergrowth

undergrowth /úndər grōth/ *n* **1.** bushes, small trees, or other vegetation growing beneath the trees in a forest **2.** growth that is less than expected **3.** ZOOL same as **undercoat** *n* (sense 3)

underhand /úndər hánd, úndər hand/ *adj* **1.** done secretively and dishonestly or with the intention to deceive or cheat somebody **2.** *N Am* SPORTS same as **underarm** *adj* (sense 1) ■ *adv* **1.** in a secretive and dishonest way **2.** *N Am* same as **underarm**

underhanded /úndər hándid/ *adj, adv* same as **underhand** *adj* (sense 1), *adv* (sense 1) —**underhandedly** *adv* —**underhandedness** *n*

underhung /úndər húng/ *adj* **1.** describes a lower jaw that projects beyond the upper jaw **2.** running on a rail or track situated underneath ○ *underhung sliding doors*

underinsure /úndərin shóor/ (**-sures, -suring, -sured**) *vt* to take out insufficient insurance to cover the value of something (*often passive*)

underlain past participle of **underlie**

underlay[1] *vt* /úndər láy/ (**-lays, -laying, -laid** /-láyd/) PROVIDE WITH SOMETHING UNDERNEATH to lay something underneath something else (*often passive*) ■ *n* /úndər lay/ **1.** LAYER BENEATH CARPET a layer of cushioning and insulating material put down on a floor before a carpet is laid **2.** SUPPORT FOR SOMETHING something laid beneath something else as a base, support, or foundation —**underlaid** *adj*

USAGE underlay or **underlie**? Unlike the root words *lay* and *lie*, both verbs are transitive (i.e. take an object). The more common word is ***underlie***, and this has a wider range of meanings including the figurative meaning 'be the basis or cause of something': *This trend underlies all the social changes of recent times.* The primary meaning of ***underlay*** is 'to lay something underneath something else' (*We underlaid the carpet with felt*), and in this meaning it also acts as a noun (with the stress on the first syllable).

underlay[2] past tense of **underlie**

underlet /úndər lét/ (**-lets, -letting, -let**) *v* **1.** *vt* to let a property for less than its full value **2.** *vti* COMM same as **sublet**

underlie /úndər lī́/ (**-lies, -lying, -lay** /-láy/, **-lain** /-láyn/) *vt* **1.** LIE BENEATH SOMETHING to lie or be put under something else **2.** BE FOUNDATION OF SOMETHING to be the basis or cause of something ○ *the assumptions that underlie this argument* **3.** FIN HAVE FINANCIAL PRIORITY OVER SOMETHING to take priority over other financial rights or securities ○ *This claim underlies yours.*

USAGE See *underlay*[1].

underline *vt* /úndər lī́n/ (**-lines, -lining, -lined**) **1.** PUT LINE BELOW SOMETHING to draw or type a line under something **2.** EMPHASIZE SOMETHING to give emphasis or extra force or prominence to something, or make something appear more important or urgent ○ *The mistake underlines the need for individuals to take responsibility for their own actions.* ■ *n* /úndər līn/ **1.** LINE BENEATH SOMETHING a line drawn or typed under something **2.** PRINTING CAPTION UNDER ILLUSTRATION a caption placed below an illustration —**underliner** *n*

underlinen /úndər linnin/ *n* underwear, especially when made of linen (*archaic*)

underling /úndərling/ *n* **1.** a servant or subordinate, especially one regarded as of little worth or importance **2.** *regional* a young or baby pig

REGIONAL NOTE As well as having its standard meaning, the noun ***underling*** is one of the many words used in rural dialects for a weak piglet or for the weakest of the litter. Others include *cad, crit, dack, dawl, dwindler, harry, joey, little dawling, nestle-draf, nisgal, nuzzle-tripe, piggy-whidden, rackling, runt, tiddling,* and *whidden*.

underlip /úndər lip/ *n* the lower lip of a person or animal

underlying /úndər lī́ ing/ *adj* **1.** LYING UNDERNEATH positioned beneath something else ○ *the underlying rock strata* **2.** HIDDEN AND SIGNIFICANT present and important but not immediately obvious ○ *the underlying reasons for his odd behaviour* **3.** ESSENTIAL basic or fundamental to something ○ *at odds with the underlying ideology of the party* **4.** FIN FINANCIALLY MOST IMPORTANT describes financial obligations or assets that take priority over others

undermentioned /úndər mensh'nd/ *adj* named or listed below, or later in a document (*formal*)

undermine /úndər mī́n/ (**-mines, -mining, -mined**) *vt* **1.** ERODE SOMETHING to weaken something by removing or wearing away material from its base or from beneath it ○ *The chalk cliffs are being gradually undermined by the waves.* **2.** WEAKEN SOMETHING GRADUALLY to diminish or weaken something gradually ○ *undermined her confidence* **3.** SUBVERT SOMEBODY OR SOMETHING to weaken, discredit, or destroy somebody or something by covert and malicious action ○ *The leaked memos undermined the government's credibility.* **4.** TUNNEL UNDER SOMETHING to dig a tunnel underneath something, especially a fortification, in order to plant explosives or make it collapse

undermost /úndər mōst/ *adj* lowest or last in position, status, or level ■ *adv* in the lowest or last place

underneath /úndər néeth/ CORE MEANING: a grammatical word indicating that something is below or beneath another thing, and may be covered by it ○ (adv) *I lifted up the pile of clothes, and underneath, on the floor, was a dark red stain.* ○ (prep) *I left the key underneath the doormat.*

1. *prep, adv* BENEATH SOMETHING below or beneath something, and perhaps covered by it ○ (prep) *found old paint layers underneath the surface* ○ (adv) *I was wearing a dressing gown and had nothing on underneath.* **2.** *prep, adv* UNDERLYING SOMETHING underlying something that is shown on the surface or openly expressed ○ (prep) *Underneath her confident exterior she was a very shy person.* ○ (adv) *There must be deeper problems underneath.* **3.** *adv, adj* ON LOWER PART OF SOMETHING on the bottom of something or the part that faces towards the ground ○ (adv) *brown with white feathers underneath* ○ (adj) *The underneath part is hard to reach.* **4.** *n* LOWER PART the bottom part of something or the part that faces towards the ground [Old English *underneoþan* < UNDER + *neoþan* 'beneath']

undernourish /úndər núrrish/ (**-ishes, -ishing, -ished**) *vt* to fail to supply somebody with enough food or other resources to provide for proper development (*often passive*) —**undernourishment** *n*

underpants /úndər pants/ *npl* briefs or shorts worn as underclothes

underpart /úndər paart/ *n* **1.** the lower part or underside of an animal or object (*often used in the plural*) **2.** a lesser or subordinate role, e.g. in a play

underpass /úndər paass/ *n* **1.** a part of a road that crosses under another road or a railway line **2.** a tunnel for pedestrians beneath a road or railway

underperform /úndər pər fáwrm/ (**-forms, -forming, -formed**) *vi* to do less well than expected or than something or somebody else ○ *underperforming investments* —**underperformance** *n* —**underperformer** *n*

underpin /úndər pín/ (**-pins, -pinning, -pinned**) *vt* **1.** to support a weakened wall or structure by propping it up from below **2.** to act as a support or foundation for something (*often passive*) ○ *the hard facts that underpin these assumptions*

underpinning /úndər pining/ *n* **1.** a structure built to support a weakened wall or building **2.** something that supports or acts as a foundation for something (*often used in the plural*)

underplay /úndər pláy/ (**-plays, -playing, -played**) *v* **1.** *vt* NOT EMPHASIZE SOMETHING ENOUGH to present something as less important than it actually is, sometimes as a deliberate tactic ○ *I don't wish to underplay the*

internal conflicts within the organization. **2.** *vti* ACT ROLE SUBTLY to act a role in a deliberately restrained or subtle way **3.** *vi* PLAY LOWER CARD to play a lower card while holding a higher one

underplot /úndər plot/ *n* a secondary plot in a play, novel, or other work of fiction

underprice /úndər prīss/ (**-prices, -pricing, -priced**) *vt* to put a price on something for sale that is less than its actual value

underprivileged /úndər prívvəlijd/ (*often used euphemistically*) *adj* deprived of many of the rights and privileges enjoyed by most people in society, usually as a result of poverty ■ *npl* underprivileged people considered as a social group

underproof /úndər próof/ *adj* describes an alcoholic drink that contains less alcohol than is standard or than is legally required

underprop /úndər próp/ (**-props, -propping, -propped**) *vt* to prop something up from underneath —**underpropper** *n*

underquote /úndər kwṓt/ (**-quotes, -quoting, -quoted**) *v* **1.** *vti* to offer something for sale at a lower price than the market value **2.** *vt* to quote a lower price than a competitor in tendering for a job

underrate /úndər ráyt/ (**-rates, -rating, -rated**) *vt* to judge the value, degree, or worth of somebody or something to be less than it really is ○ *a greatly underrated writer*

underreport /úndər ri páwrt/ (**-ports, -porting, -ported**) *vt* to declare or report a number or amount to be smaller than is actually the case

underrepresent /úndər réppri zént/ (**-sents, -senting, -sented**) *vt* **1.** to contain a disproportionately small number of representatives of something such as a population group (*often passive*) ○ *addressing the problem of women being underrepresented in government* **2.** to present something as smaller, less widespread, or less important than it actually is —**underrepresentation** /úndər reppri zen táysh'n/ *n*

underrun *v* /úndər rún/ (**-runs, -running, -ran** /-rán/, **-run**) **1.** *vt* MOVE UNDER to run, pass, or go under something **2.** *vti* NAUT PASS SOMETHING OVER BOAT FOR INSPECTION to haul something in, e.g. a net or cable, and pass it over the deck of a boat so that it can be inspected or repaired, or be hauled in in this way ■ *n* /únder run/ **1.** LOWER-THAN-ESTIMATED COST a cost or expense that is less than anticipated **2.** LOWER-THAN-REQUIRED PRODUCTION RUN a production run of a manufactured or printed item that is less than the quantity ordered **3.** SHORTFALL OF PRODUCTION RUN the amount by which a production run of a manufactured or printed item falls short of the quantity ordered

undersaturated /úndər sáchə raytid/ *adj* describes igneous rock that contains low levels of combined silica and no free silica

underscore *vt* /úndər skáwr/ (**-scores, -scoring, -scored**) **1.** DRAW LINE BELOW SOMETHING to draw or incise a line under something **2.** EMPHASIZE SOMETHING to give emphasis or extra force to something ■ *n* /úndər skawr/ **1.** LINE BENEATH SOMETHING a line drawn or incised under something **2.** BACKGROUND MUSIC a piece of background music accompanying action or dialogue in a film

undersea *adj* /úndər see/ existing, carried out, or designed for use below the surface of the sea ■ *adv* /úndər seé/ in or into the area below the surface of the sea

underseal *n* /úndər seel/ a coating applied to the underside of a motor vehicle to retard rust and corrosion. N Am term **undercoating** ■ *vt* /úndər seél/ (**-seals, -sealing, -sealed**) to apply an underseal to the underside of a motor vehicle. N Am term **undercoat**

underseas /úndər seéz/ *adv* OCEANOG same as **undersea**

undersecretary /úndər sékritəri/ (*plural* **-ies**) *n* **1.** a secretary who ranks just below a chief secretary in a government or bureaucratic organization **2.** a government minister who is subordinate to the secretary of state for a government department —**undersecretariat** /úndər sekri táiri ət/ *n* —**undersecretaryship** *n*

undersell /úndər sél/ (**-sells, -selling, -sold** /-sṓld/) *vt* **1.** SELL SOMETHING BELOW PROPER VALUE to sell something at a price below its full or usual value **2.** SELL MORE CHEAPLY THAN SOMEBODY to sell something more cheaply than a competitor **3.** ADVERTISE SOMETHING WITH TOO LITTLE ENTHUSIASM to present the merits of something or somebody with too little enthusiasm or conviction or in too restrained or understated a way —**underseller** *n*

underset *n* /úndər set/ **1.** OCEAN UNDERCURRENT an ocean undercurrent that runs in a direction contrary to the direction of the surface waves **2.** UNDERLYING ORE a vein of ore lying beneath another layer ■ *vt* /úndər sét/ (**-sets, -setting, -set**) PROVIDE PROP FOR to support something from below

undersexed /úndər sékst/ *adj* having less sex drive or less interest in sex than some other people

undershirt /úndər shurt/ *n N Am* CLOTHING same as **vest** *n* (sense 1)

undershoot /úndər shóot/ (**-shoots, -shooting, -shot** /-shót/) *vti* **1.** to land an aircraft short of a landing area ○ *The pilot undershot the runway.* **2.** to shoot something such as an arrow so that it lands short of the target

undershorts /úndər shawrts/ *npl N Am* shorts or briefs worn as underclothes by men and boys

undershot /úndər shot/ *adj* **1.** MED same as **underhung** (sense 1) **2.** describes a device, especially a water wheel, that is driven by water flowing beneath it

undershrub /úndər shrub/ *n* BOT same as **subshrub**

underside /úndər sīd/ *n* **1.** the lower side or bottom of something **2.** an aspect of something that is undesirable or unpleasant and usually hidden

undersigned /úndər sīnd/ (*formal*) *n* somebody whose signature appears on the document being read ■ *adj* whose signature is written, or whose signatures are written, below

undersized /úndər sīzd/ *adj* smaller than the prevailing or preferred size

underskirt /úndər skurt/ *n* a skirt worn under another skirt

underslung /úndər slúng/ *adj* **1.** suspended or supported from above, like a motor vehicle chassis that is suspended from the axles **2.** built close to the ground with a low centre of gravity

undersoil /úndər soyl/ *n* AGRIC same as **subsoil**

undersold COMM past participle, past tense of **undersell**

underspend /úndər spénd/ (**-spends, -spending, -spent** /-spént/) *vi* to spend less money than is required or expected —**underspend** /úndər spend/ *n*

understand /úndər stánd/ (**-stands, -standing, -stood** /-stóod/) *v* **1.** *vti* GRASP MEANING OF SOMETHING to know or be able to explain to yourself the nature of somebody or something, or the meaning or cause of something ○ *I can't understand what all the fuss is about.* **2.** *vti* COME TO KNOW SOMETHING to realize or become aware of something ○ *finally understood the urgency of the situation* **3.** *vt* KNOW MEANING OF WORDS IN LANGUAGE to recognize and be able to translate the words of a foreign language ○ *understands Spanish* **4.** *vti* KNOW AND SYMPATHIZE to recognize somebody's character or somebody's situation, especially in a sympathetic, tolerant, or empathetic way ○ *It's such a relief to find someone who understands.* **5.** *vt* TAKE SOMETHING AS MEANT to interpret something in a particular way, or to infer or deduce a particular meaning from something ○ *understood it as a peaceful gesture* **6.** *vt* TAKE SOMETHING AS SETTLED to believe something to be agreed, settled, or firmly communicated ○ *The bank was given to understand that you would repay the loan in six months.* **7.** *vt* KNOW SOMETHING BY LEARNING OR HEARING to gather or assume something on the basis of having heard or been told it ○ *He is, I understand, expected later.* **8.** *vt* LING INFER IMPLICIT MEANING to assume information or a meaning that is implied but not expressed directly (*usually passive*) [Old English *understandan* < UNDER + *standan* (see STAND)]

understandable /úndər stándəb'l/ *adj* **1.** having a meaning or nature that can be understood ○ *Try to make it understandable to a nonspecialist.* **2.** able to be accepted as normal, reasonable, or forgivable ○ *Under the circumstances it was a perfectly understandable reaction.* —**understandability** /úndər stándə bíllati/ *n* —**understandably** *adv*

understanding /úndər stánding/ *n* **1.** ABILITY TO GRASP MEANING the ability to perceive and explain the meaning or the nature of somebody or something ○ *Surely even someone with a very limited understanding could see the logic in that.* **2.** KNOWLEDGE OF SOMETHING knowledge of a particular subject, area, or situation ○ *gaining a better understanding of industrial processes* **3.** INTERPRETATION OF SOMETHING somebody's interpretation of something, or a belief or opinion based on an interpretation of or inference from something ○ *It was my understanding that the costs would be shared equally.* **4.** MUTUAL COMPREHENSION an agreement, often an unofficial or unspoken one ○ *I'm sure we can come to an understanding about this.* **5.** KNOWLEDGE OF ANOTHER'S NATURE a sympathetic, empathetic, or tolerant recognition of somebody else's nature or situation ○ *I thought you of all people would show a little understanding.* ■ *adj* SYMPATHETICALLY AWARE sympathetic, empathetic, or tolerant in recognizing somebody's or something's character and situation ○ *fortunate in having understanding parents* —**understandingly** *adv*

understate /úndər stáyt/ (**-states, -stating, -stated**) *vt* **1.** to express something in a deliberately less dramatic, emphatic, or emotional way than it seems to warrant, often to increase its actual impact or for the sake of irony **2.** to describe something as being smaller in quantity or number than it really is ○ *understate the cost*

understated /úndər stáytid/ *adj* achieving its effect through restraint, subtlety, and good taste ○ *understated elegance*

understatement /úndər staytmənt, úndər stáytmənt/ *n* **1.** a statement, or a way of expressing yourself, that is deliberately less forceful or dramatic than the subject would seem to justify or require **2.** a statement that underrepresents or underreports something

understeer *vi* /úndər steér/ (**-steers, -steering, -steered**) to turn less sharply than the turning of a steering wheel would lead the driver to expect ■ *n* /úndər steer/ a motor vehicle's tendency to turn less sharply than expected

understood /úndər stóod/ past participle, past tense of **understand** ■ *adj* agreed, assumed, or implied, especially without being openly or officially expressed

understorey /úndər stawri/ (*plural* **-reys**) *n* a layer of small trees and bushes below the level of the taller trees in a forest

understrapper /úndər strapər/ *n* same as **subordinate** (*dated formal or humorous*) [Early 18C. < *strapper* 'somebody who straps or harnesses horses']

understrength /úndər stréngth/ *adj* having inadequate strength, especially less than the usual or desirable number of personnel

understudy /úndər studi/ *n* (*plural* **-ies**) **1.** SUBSTITUTE ACTOR an actor who learns the role of another actor in order to be able to act as a replacement if necessary **2.** TRAINED SUBSTITUTE a trained replacement or substitute for somebody ■ *vti* (**-ies, -ying, -ied**) BE SUBSTITUTE ACTOR to learn the role of another actor in order to be able to replace him or her if necessary

undertake /úndər táyk/ (**-takes, -taking, -took** /-tóok/, **-taken** /-táykən/) *v* **1.** *vti* to make a commitment to do something ○ *undertook to find out the cost of flights* **2.** *vt* to begin to do something or to set out on something ○ *They were prepared to undertake the work at the formerly agreed price.*

undertaker /úndər taykər/ *n* **1.** *UK, ANZ, Can* somebody whose profession is to prepare the dead for burial or cremation and to arrange funerals. US term **funeral director 2.** somebody who sets about doing a task

undertaking /úndər táyking/ *n* **1.** TASK a task or project ○ *It was a colossal undertaking.* **2.** PLEDGE TO DO SOMETHING a promise or agreement to do something ○ *She gave an undertaking to keep it for a year.* **3.** FUNERAL BUSINESS the business of preparing the dead for burial or cremation and arranging funerals

under-the-counter *adj* sold or obtained clandestinely or illegally (*not hyphenated after a verb*)

under-the-table *adj* done or organized clandestinely and often illegally (*not hyphenated after a verb*)

underthings /úndər thingz/ *npl* underwear, especially women's underwear

underthrust /úndər thrust/ *n* a reverse fault in which a lower layer of rock is driven underneath a higher, relatively passive layer

undertime /úndər tīm/ *n* time spent by employees during working hours on non-work-related activities, such as shopping or personal appointments [Late 20C. Modelled on OVERTIME] —**undertime** *vi*

undertint /úndər tint/ *n* a slight or subtle tint

undertone /úndər tōn/ *n* **1.** LOW TONE a quiet, subdued, or background tone, especially of the voice ○ *He spoke in an undertone.* **2.** UNDERLYING QUALITY OR ELEMENT something that is suggested or implied rather than stated openly ○ *undertones of menace* **3.** MUTED COLOUR a subdued colour

undertow /úndər tō/ *n* **1.** the seaward pull of water away from a shore after a wave has broken **2.** an underlying tendency or force that runs in the opposite direction to the apparent one ○ *an undertow of dissatisfaction*

undertrick /úndər trik/ *n* in bridge, a trick short of the number declared by a player

undertrump /úndər trúmp/ (**-trumps, -trumping, -trumped**) *vi* in cards, to play a trump that is lower than a trump that has already been played in a hand

undervalue /úndər vállyoo/ (**-ues, -uing, -ued**) *vt* **1.** to hold too low an opinion of something or somebody **2.** to judge the value of something or somebody as being lower than it really is ○ *buy up stock that is undervalued* —**undervaluation** /úndər vallyoo áysh'n/ *n* —**undervaluer** *n*

underwater *adj* /úndər wawtər/ **1.** BELOW WATER SURFACE existing, carried out, or designed for use below the surface of water **2.** NAUT UNDER SHIP'S WATER LINE below the water line in a ship or boat ■ *adv* /úndər wáwtər/ BELOW WATER SURFACE in or to a place below the surface of a body of water ■ *n* WATER UNDERNEATH SURFACE the water beneath the surface of a river, lake, or sea

under way, **underway** /úndər wáy/ *adj, adv* in motion or progress ○ *not long before the project was under way*

USAGE under way or **underway**? Although the form ***underway*** is often seen, and has long been in use, ***under way*** is still widely preferred. The only exception to this is the adjectival use that precedes the noun: *The submarine received underway servicing.*

underwear /úndər wair/ *n* clothes worn beneath outer clothes, usually next to the skin, and not normally seen in public

under weigh *adj, adv* NAUT same as **under way**

underweight /úndər wáyt/ *adj* weighing less than is normal or required

underwent past tense of **undergo**

underwhelm /úndər wélm/ (**-whelms, -whelming, -whelmed**) *vt* to fail notably to impress or excite somebody (*humorous*) [Mid-20C. After OVERWHELM] —**underwhelming** *adj*

underwing /úndər wing/ *n* **1.** HIND WING OF INSECT a hind wing of an insect such as a beetle, especially when covered by a forewing while the insect is not in flight **2.** MOTH WITH BRIGHT WINGS a moth that has brightly coloured hind wings that become visible only in flight. Genus: *Catocala.* **3.** LOWER SIDE OF BIRD'S WING the underside of a bird's wing

underwire /úndər wīr/ *n* **1.** a brassiere with wire sewn into the lining under each cup to provide support **2.** a wire sewn into the lining under each cup of a brassiere to provide support —**underwired** *adj*

underwood /úndər wŏŏd/ *n* ECOL same as **undergrowth** (sense 1)

underworld /úndər wurld/ *n* **1.** the part of society that lives by crime (*often used before a noun*) ○ *an underworld shooting* **2.** in classical mythology, the place beneath the ground where the souls of the dead go

underwrite /úndər rīt, úndər rīt/ (**-writes, -writing, -wrote** /-rōt, -rōt/, **-written** /-rítt'n, -ritt'n/) *v* **1.** *vti* SUBSIDIZE SOMETHING to agree to provide funds for something and to cover any losses ○ *The tour was underwritten by an electronics company.* **2.** *vti* ISSUE INSURANCE to insure somebody or something by accepting liability for designated losses, or to be in the business of doing this **3.** *vti* AGREE TO BUY UNSOLD SECURITIES to guarantee the sale of an issue of securities at a fixed price **4.** *vt* LEND SUPPORT TO SOMEBODY OR SOMETHING to give support to somebody or something, especially by signing a document **5.** *vt* WRITE BENEATH OTHER WRITING to write something, or add a signature, underneath other written matter [15C. After Latin *subscribere* 'write underneath, sign']

underwriter /úndər rītər/ *n* **1.** INSURER COVERING LIABILITIES a person, firm, or organization that issues insurance and accepts liability for designated risks **2.** SOMEBODY ASSESSING RISKS ON INSURANCE somebody employed by an insurance company to assess risks and fix premiums **3.** GUARANTOR OF SECURITIES ISSUE a person or organization that agrees to buy at a fixed price any unsold part of an issue of securities

undescended /úndi séndid/ *adj* describes a testicle that has remained in the inguinal canal and has not descended into the scrotum

undeserved /úndi zúrvd/ *adj* unfairly awarded or unfairly endured, or not merited on the basis of the facts ○ *undeserved punishment* —**undeservedly** /-vidli/ *adv*

undeserving /ún di zúrving/ *adj* unworthy of receiving benefits or rewards

undesirable /úndi zīrəb'l/ *adj* not wanted, liked, or approved of ■ *n* somebody or something regarded as undesirable —**undesirability** /úndi zīrə bílləti/ *n* —**undesirably** *adv*

undetermined /úndi túrmind/ *adj* **1.** not resolved, decided, or fixed **2.** unknown or undiscovered

undeviating /un déevi ayting/ *adj* not turning or changing, especially remaining constant or true to somebody or something ○ *undeviating loyalty* —**undeviatingly** *adv*

undid past tense of **undo**

undies /úndiz/ *npl* underclothes, especially women's underclothes (*informal*) [Late 19C. Shortening]

undigested /ún dī jéstid, -di-/ *adj* **1.** not having undergone the process of digestion **2.** not fully analysed, considered, or understood

undine /ún deen/ *n* a female spirit that lives in water, especially one that could become human by bearing the child of a human male [Early 19C. < modern Latin *undina* < Latin *unda* 'wave']

undiplomatic /ún diplə máttik/ *adj* lacking in tact and diplomacy —**undiplomatically** *adv*

undirected /úndi réktid, ún dī-/ *adj* **1.** without a purpose or object **2.** not marked with an address in the proper way

undisguised /úndiss gīzd/ *adj* expressed fully and openly —**undisguisedly** /-gīzidli/ *adv*

undisposed /úndi spōzd/ *adj* **1.** not resolved or dealt with **2.** not prepared or inclined to do something

undissociated /úndi sōshi aytid, -sōssi-/ *adj* describes a molecule not broken down into simpler molecules, atoms, or ions

undistinguished /úndi stíng gwisht/ *adj* **1.** MEDIOCRE not very good or ever rising above the ordinary ○ *an undistinguished career* **2.** COMMONPLACE not at all striking or likely to stand out from others ○ *undistinguished appearance* **3.** NOT MADE SEPARATE not differentiated from others

undistributed /úndi stríbbyŏŏtid/ *adj* **1.** not paid out as a dividend to shareholders, but invested back into the business ○ *undistributed profits* **2.** used to describe a term that does not refer to all members of the class it designates. The term 'dogs' is undistributed in the statement 'Some dogs are unfriendly'.

undisturbed /ún di stúrbd/ *adj* not interrupted or disrupted by anybody or anything

undo /un dóo/ (**-does** /-dúz/, **-doing**, **-did** /-díd/, **-done** /-dún/) *v* **1.** *vti* UNFASTEN to open, unfasten, untie, or unwrap something, or become unfastened, untied, or unwrapped ○ *I can't undo this button.* **2.** *vt* NULLIFY SOMETHING to cancel or reverse the effect of an action ○ *What's done can't be undone.* **3.** *vt* REVERSE EFFECT OF COMPUTER COMMAND to cancel the effect of the last command or action done on a computer, restoring the material being worked on to its previous condition **4.** *vt* RUIN SOMEBODY to bring somebody or something to ruin or disaster (*literary*)

undock /un dók/ (**-docks, -docking, -docked**) *vti* to detach something, or become detached, from a space station or another spacecraft in space

undoing /un dóo ing/ *n* **1.** ACT OF BRINGING TO RUIN the ruin, downfall, or destruction of somebody or something, or something that causes this ○ *Pride was our undoing.* **2.** ACT OF UNFASTENING the opening, unfastening, untying, or unwrapping of something **3.** ACT OF NULLIFYING SOMETHING'S EFFECT the cancelling or reversing of the effect of an action

undone /un dún/ past participle of **undo** ■ *adj* **1.** UNCOMPLETED not yet done or completed **2.** UNFASTENED not tied or fastened **3.** BROUGHT TO RUIN ruined, destroyed, or brought to the brink of collapse (*formal or humorous*)

undoubted /un dówtid/ *adj* not subject to doubt or dispute ○ *an undoubted success*

undoubtedly /un dówtidli/ *adv* without any doubt or question

~~**undoubtly**~~ incorrect spelling of **undoubtedly**

undraw /un dráw/ (**-draws, -drawing, -drew** /-dróo/, **-drawn** /-dráwn/) *vt* to draw something such as a curtain back or open

undreamed-of /un dréemd ov/, **undreamt-of** /-drémt-/ *adj* impossible to imagine in advance, usually through being too wonderful or too unlikely

undress *v* /un dréss/ (**-dresses, -dressing, -dressed**) **1.** *vti* TAKE CLOTHES OFF to remove the clothes from your own or somebody else's body **2.** *vt* TAKE DRESSING OFF to remove a dressing from a wound **3.** *vt* REMOVE ORNAMENTATION to strip something of its decoration ■ *n* **1.** CONDITION OF HAVING NO CLOTHES ON a condition of nakedness or of being scantily clothed **2.** INFORMAL CLOTHING informal attire or an everyday uniform ■ *adj* /ún dress/ INFORMAL worn on occasions when full or formal dress is not required, or for which informal clothing can be worn ○ *an undress uniform*

undressed /un drést/ *adj* **1.** WITHOUT CLOTHES not wearing any or many clothes, or having just removed clothes **2.** UNTREATED not processed or treated in some way ○ *undressed leather* **3.** NOT READY FOR TABLE not fully prepared for cooking or eating **4.** WITHOUT DRESSING not covered with a dressing or sauce **5.** INFORMALLY DRESSED appropriately but not formally dressed for an event or occasion **6.** WITHOUT BANDAGE without a dressing or bandage ○ *an undressed wound*

SYNONYMS See *naked.*

undue /ún dyóo/ *adj* **1.** going beyond the limits of what is proper, normal, justified, or permitted ○ *using undue force to disperse the crowd* **2.** not owed or payable at present

undulant /úndyŏŏlənt/ *adj* resembling waves in motion or form (*formal*) [Early 19C. < UNDULATE]

undulant fever *n* brucellosis as it affects humans

undulate *v* /úndyŏŏ layt/ (**-lates, -lating, -lated**) **1.** *vti* MOVE SINUOUSLY LIKE WAVES to move in waves or in a movement resembling waves, or cause something to move in this way **2.** *vi* GO UP AND DOWN GRACEFULLY to rise and fall gracefully in volume or pitch ■ *adj* /úndyŏŏlət, -layt/ *also* **undulated** /úndyŏŏ láytid/ WAVY IN APPEARANCE with a wavy appearance, edge, or markings [Mid-17C. < Latin *undulatus* 'wavy' < *unda* 'wave'] —**undulation** /úndyŏŏ láysh'n/ *n* —**undulatory** /úndyŏŏlətəri/ *adj*

ORIGIN The Latin word *unda* 'wave', from which ***undulate*** is derived, is also the source of English *abound, inundation, redundant, sound*[3], and *surround.*

unduly /un dyóoli/ *adv* to a very great extent, or to an excessive, improper, or unjustifiable degree ○ *We were not unduly concerned.*

undutiful /un dyóotif'l/ *adj* **1.** lacking a sense of moral or legal obligation **2.** unwilling to fulfil moral or legal obligations —**undutifully** *adv* —**undutifulness** *n*

undying /un dī ing/ *adj* describes an emotion that does not diminish but continues forever —**undyingly** *adv*

unearned /un úrnd/ *adj* **1.** not acquired by labour or service ○ *unearned income* **2.** not deserved ○ *unearned criticism*

unearned increment *n* an increase in property value resulting from factors other than labour or improvements made by the owner

unearth /un úrth/ (**-earths, -earthing, -earthed**) *vt* **1.** DIG SOMETHING UP to bring something up out of the ground **2.** DISCLOSE SOMETHING to discover or disclose something, especially after an investigation **3.** FIND SOMETHING LOST to find something that has been lost or hidden

unearthly /un úrthli/ *adj* **1.** NOT FROM THIS WORLD not being or seeming to be from this world **2.** EERIE looking or sounding so strange as to be frightening **3.** UNREASONABLE completely inappropriate or unreasonable (*informal*) ○ *at this unearthly hour* **4.** PERFECT embodying perfection (*literary*) —**unearthliness** *n*

unease /un éez/ *n* a feeling of anxiety, awkwardness, or discomfort

SYNONYMS See *worry.*

uneasy /un éezi/ (**-ier, -iest**) *adj* **1.** ANXIOUS anxious or afraid ○ *I always feel slightly uneasy until I know they're safely home.* **2.** NOT GUARANTEED TO ENDURE not sufficiently well established for people to be confident that it will endure ○ *an uneasy truce* **3.** ILL AT EASE awkward or lacking confidence ○ *felt uneasy with strangers* **4.** RESTLESS not restful or not allowing somebody to rest properly ○ *an uneasy sleep* —**uneasily** *adv* —**uneasiness** *n*

~~**unecessary**~~ incorrect spelling of **unnecessary**

uneconomic /ún eekə nómmik, -ekə-/ *adj* **1.** not making or not likely to make a profit **2.** *also* **uneconomical** /ún eekə nómmik'l, -ekə nómmik'l/ not efficient or worth the expense —**uneconomically** *adv*

unedited /un édditid/ *adj* **1.** not corrected or revised **2.** not adapted for a specific audience, purpose, or medium

uneducated /un éddyŏŏ kaytid/ *adj* lacking the learning that is usually acquired in schools

unelectable /únni léktəb'l/ *adj* certain to be defeated as a candidate for public office, e.g. because of extreme positions on controversial issues

unemotional /únni mṓsh'nəl/ *adj* **1.** showing little or no feeling **2.** involving reason or intellect rather than feelings —**unemotionally** *adv*

unemployable /únnim plóy əb'l/ *adj* lacking the skills, education, or ability to get a job

unemployed /únnim plóyd/ *adj* **1.** JOBLESS not in paid employment **2.** NOT IN USE not being used ■ *npl* JOBLESS PEOPLE people who are out of work

unemployment /únnim plóymənt/ *n* **1.** the condition of having no job **2.** the number of people who are unemployed in an area, often given as a percentage of the total labour force

unemployment benefit *n* a regular payment made by the government to somebody who is out of work

unending /un énding/ *adj* continuing or seeming to continue forever, especially when an end would be welcome

un-English /un íng glish/ *adj* **1.** not characteristic of the English **2.** not considered standard English usage

unentangle /ún in táng g'l/ (**-gles, -gling, -gled**) *vt* **1.** FREE SOMETHING FROM TANGLES to free things that are knotted or tied **2.** STRAIGHTEN OUT SOMETHING COMPLEX to clarify or resolve something that is intricate or puzzling **3.** FREE SOMEBODY FROM BAD SITUATION to release another person, or yourself from a confused, complicated, or undesired situation

unenviable /un énvee əb'l/ *adj* not pleasant, easy, or likely to be wished for ○ *had the unenviable task of breaking the bad news* —**unenviably** *adv*

unequal /un éekwəl/ *adj* **1.** NOT MEASURABLY SAME not measurably the same, e.g. in size or number **2.** NOT OF SAME SOCIAL POSITION not of the same status, rank, or position in society **3.** UNEVENLY MATCHED not evenly matched in competition **4.** VARIABLE uneven or variable in quality or character **5.** ASYMMETRICAL not evenly balanced **6.** UNABLE TO DO SOMETHING having less than the required ability to do something ○ *unequal to the task* ■ *n* SOMEBODY NOT EQUAL TO ANOTHER somebody or something not equal to another —**unequally** *adv*

unequalled /un éekwəld/ *adj* having no equal or parallel among people or things of the same kind

unequivocal /únni kwívvək'l/ *adj* allowing for no doubt or misinterpretation —**unequivocally** *adv*

unerring /un úr ing/ *adj* unfailingly accurate or correct —**unerringly** *adv*

UNESCO /yoo néskō/, **Unesco** *n* a United Nations agency that promotes international collaboration on culture, education, and science. Full form **United Nations Educational, Scientific, and Cultural Organization**

unessential /únni sénsh'l/ *adj* not absolutely needed ■ *n* something that is not absolutely needed

unethical /un éthik'l/ *adj* not conforming to agreed standards of moral conduct, especially within a particular profession ○ *unethical business practices* —**unethicality** /un éthi kálləti/ *n* —**unethically** *adv* —**unethicalness** *n*

uneven /un éev'n/ *adj* **1.** NOT LEVEL having a surface that is not level or smooth **2.** VARYING varying and inconsistent, e.g. in quality, thoroughness, or duration **3.** NOT PARALLEL not straight or parallel **4.** NOT FAIRLY MATCHED not fairly matched in competition **5.** ODD not divisible by two **6.** NOT SAME SIZE unequal in number or measurement to another —**unevenly** *adv* —**unevenness** *n*

uneventful /únni véntf'l/ *adj* not marked by any unusual or momentous occurrence —**uneventfully** *adv* —**uneventfulness** *n*

unexampled /únnig záamp'ld/ *adj* having no similar case or occurrence

unexceptionable /únnik sépsh'nəb'l/ *adj* good enough to provide no reason for criticism or objection —**unexceptionability** /únnik sépsh'nə bílləti/ *n* —**unexceptionableness** *n* —**unexceptionably** *adv*

USAGE See *unexceptional.*

unexceptional /únnik sépsh'nəl/ *adj* **1.** not special or unusual **2.** allowing no exception —**unexceptionally** *adv*

USAGE unexceptional or **unexceptionable**? The distinction in meaning corresponds to that between the positive forms *exceptional* and *exceptionable.* Something is described as ***unexceptional*** when it is not special or unusual, even perhaps a little dull: *Her performance got a good review, but I thought it was unexceptional.* ***Unexceptionable*** comes close to this in meaning, but its strict meaning is 'good enough to provide no reason for criticism or objection': *Their behaviour has been unexceptionable so far.*

unexcited /únnik sītid/ *adj* **1.** not emotionally aroused **2.** describes particles that remain at the lowest energy level —**unexcitedly** *adv*

unexpected /únnik spéktid/ *adj* coming as a surprise —**unexpectedly** *adv* —**unexpectedness** *n*

unexperienced /únnik speeri ənst/ *adj* **1.** not known or undergone before **2.** lacking experience

unexploded /ún ik splṓdid/ *adj* having failed to explode but still capable of exploding ○ *an unexploded bomb*

unexpressed /únnik sprést/ *adj* **1.** not spoken or made known **2.** describes a gene that does not have an observable effect on the organism that carries it

unexpurgated /un ékspər gaytid/ *adj* not edited to remove words or passages considered offensive or unsuitable

unfailing /un fáyling/ *adj* **1.** LIMITLESS never used up or exhausted **2.** ALWAYS RELIABLE able to be relied on at all times ○ *unfailing good humour* **3.** ALWAYS ACCURATE totally accurate and without fault ○ *an unfailing eye for symmetry and beauty* —**unfailingly** *adv* —**unfailingness** *n*

unfair /un fáir/ *adj* **1.** not equal or just **2.** not ethical in business dealings —**unfairly** *adv* —**unfairness** *n*

unfaithful /un fáythf'l/ *adj* **1.** ADULTEROUS engaging in sexual relations with somebody other than a spouse or partner **2.** UNTRUE TO COMMITMENTS untrue to commitments, duties, beliefs, or ideals **3.** NOT LIKE ORIGINAL not true to the original —**unfaithfully** *adv* —**unfaithfulness** *n*

unfaltering /un fáwltəring, -fóltə-/ *adj* strong, steady, and not becoming weaker —**unfalteringly** *adv*

unfamiliar /únfə mílli ər/ *adj* **1.** not previously known or recognized **2.** having no previous knowledge or experience ○ *unfamiliar with the software* —**unfamiliarity** /únfə mílli árrəti/ *n* —**unfamiliarly** *adv*

unfashionable /un fásh'nəb'l/ *adj* **1.** not in the current style **2.** not socially approved of ○ *an unfashionable suburb* —**unfashionableness** *n* —**unfashionably** *adv*

unfasten /un fáass'n/ (**-tens, -tening, -tened**) *vti* to undo or open something by moving or loosening things that are holding it together, e.g. the buttons of a garment, or be undone or opened in this way

unfathomable /un fáthəməb'l/ *adj* **1.** too deep to be measured ○ *unfathomable ocean depths* **2.** impossible to understand because of being very mysterious or complicated —**unfathomability** /un fáthəmə bílləti/ *n* —**unfathomableness** *n* —**unfathomably** *adv*

unfavourable /un fáyvərəb'l/ *adj* **1.** expressing disapproval or opposition **2.** unlikely to be beneficial —**unfavourableness** *n* —**unfavourably** *adv*

unfeasible /un féezəb'l/ *adj* impractical as a goal, or not easily carried out —**unfeasibility** /un féezə bílləti/ *n* —**unfeasibly** *adv*

unfeeling /un féeling/ *adj* **1.** having or expressing no sympathy for somebody else's feelings **2.** unable to experience physical sensation —**unfeelingly** *adv* —**unfeelingness** *n*

unfetter /un féttər/ (**-ters, -tering, -tered**) *vt* **1.** to release somebody or something from fetters **2.** to allow somebody to act without restraint

unfettered /un féttərd/ *adj* not subject to limits or restrictions

unfinished /un fínnisht/ *adj* **1.** NOT COMPLETED not completed satisfactorily **2.** NOT FINALLY TREATED not finally processed or treated with dye, varnish, paint, or bleach **3.** TEXTILES WITH SLIGHT NAP woven with a slight nap

unfit /un fít/ *adj* **1.** UNSUITABLE unsuitable for a particular purpose **2.** UNQUALIFIED lacking the necessary skills or qualifications to perform a particular task adequately **3.** NOT HEALTHY not physically or mentally healthy —**unfitly** *adv* —**unfitness** *n*

unfitted /un fíttid/ *adj* **1.** not suited or adapted for a particular purpose **2.** describes furniture that is not fitted

unfitting /un fítting/ *adj* not suitable or appropriate for somebody or something —**unfittingly** *adv*

unfix /un fíks/ (**-fixes, -fixing, -fixed**) *vt* **1.** to loosen or detach something **2.** to upset the certainty or stability of something

unflagging /un flágging/ *adj* remaining strong and unchanging —**unflaggingly** *adv*

unflappable /un fláppəb'l/ *adj* able to maintain composure under all circumstances —**unflappability** /un fláppə bílləti/ *n* —**unflappably** *adv*

unflattering /un fláttəring/ *adj* showing or depicting somebody or something in an uncomplimentary or unfavourable way

unfledged /un fléjd/ *adj* **1.** describes a young bird that has not yet developed the feathers required for flight **2.** young and inexperienced

unflinching /un flínching/ *adj* strong and unhesitating —**unflinchingly** *adv*

unfocused /un fṓkəst/, **unfocussed** *adj* **1.** not adjusted for a clear image **2.** lacking a clear purpose or objective

unfold /un fṓld/ (**-folds, -folding, -folded**) *v* **1.** *vti* OPEN OUT to open something and spread it out, or open and spread out **2.** *vti* MAKE SOMETHING UNDERSTOOD to make something clear and understood by gradual exposure, or become clear and understood in this way **3.** *vi* DEVELOP to develop or expand over time ○ *His talent unfolded as he grew older.*

unforced /un fáwrst/ *adj* **1.** spontaneous and natural ○ *unforced laughter* **2.** not resulting from compulsion, irresistible pressure, or an opponent's superior skill ○ *made an unforced error and lost the point*

unforeseeable /un fawr sée əb'l/ *adj* not able to be predicted or planned for in advance —**unforeseeably** *adv*

unforeseen /ún fawr séen/ *adj* not expected or anticipated

unforgettable /únfər géttəb'l/ *adj* remarkable in a way that cannot be forgotten —**unforgettably** *adv*

unforgivable /únfər gívvəb'l/ *adj* so bad as to be impossible to forgive —**unforgivably** *adv*

unforgiving /únfər gívving/ *adj* **1.** unwilling or unable to forgive **2.** providing little or no margin for mistakes or weakness ○ *The sea is an unforgiving environment.* —**unforgivingly** *adv*

unformatted /un fáwr matid/ *adj* describes computer disks that are not formatted into the sectors that are required in order to allow data to be saved and stored

unformed /un fáwrmd/ *adj* **1.** WITH NO REAL SHAPE lacking a coherent shape or structure ○ *the unformed restless desire in her mind* **2.** UNDEVELOPED not yet fully developed **3.** NOT CREATED not yet created

unforthcoming /ún fawrth kúmming/ *adj* **1.** UNINFORMATIVE reluctant to talk or to reveal information **2.** UNAVAILABLE not ready when required or requested **3.** FAILING TO HAPPEN not happening despite being expected

unfortunate /un fáwrchənət/ *adj* **1.** UNLUCKY never experiencing good luck **2.** INVOLVING BAD LUCK ac-

companied by or bringing bad luck **3.** INAPPROPRIATE not appropriate to a given situation ○ *The unfortunate comment was an example of his lack of social polish.* ■ *n* POOR PERSON somebody who has bad luck or inadequate resources

unfortunately /un fáwrchənətli/ *adv* **1.** used when somebody wishes something were not true ○ *I didn't get there before he left, unfortunately.* **2.** in a way that is inappropriate to a given situation ○ *an unfortunately worded critique*

unfounded /un fówndid/ *adj* **1.** not supported by evidence or facts ○ *unfounded allegations* **2.** not yet established

unfreeze /un fréez/ (**-freezes, -freezing, -froze** /-frṓz/, **-frozen** /-frṓz'n/) *vt* to remove controls or restrictions on something such as wages, prices, or rents

unfrequented /únfri kwéntid/ *adj* not often visited, especially by tourists or travellers

unfriendly /un fréndli/ *adj* **1.** behaving in an obviously cold or hostile way **2.** not beneficial or advantageous ○ *was faced with an array of unfriendly choices* —**unfriendliness** *n*

unfrock /un frók/ (**-frocks, -frocking, -frocked**) *vt* **1.** RELIG REMOVE ORDAINED PERSON FROM OFFICE to remove an ordained person from office and duties as a punishment for doing something considered immoral or heretical **2.** TAKE AWAY RIGHT FROM SOMEBODY to take away from somebody the right to practise a profession **3.** REMOVE SOMEBODY FROM POSITION to remove somebody from an honorary or privileged position

unfroze past tense of **unfreeze**

unfrozen past participle of **unfreeze**

unfruitful /un fróotf'l/ *adj* **1.** not having a successful outcome **2.** not bearing fruit or offspring (*literary*) —**unfruitfully** *adv* —**unfruitfulness** *n*

unfulfilled /ún fool fíld/ *adj* **1.** NOT REALIZED not developed or made use of adequately or to the fullest possible extent **2.** LAW NOT FULLY CARRIED OUT not carried out fully or in accordance with the original requirements or stipulations **3.** NOT SATISFIED not satisfied, especially by not having fully realized ambitions or potential —**unfulfilment** *n*

unfunny /un fúnni/ *adj* not amusing, especially when intended to be so —**unfunnily** *adv*

unfurl /un fúrl/ (**-furls, -furling, -furled**) *vti* to unroll or spread out something, or be unrolled or spread out

unfurnished /un fúrnisht/ *adj* not furnished, or available to be rented without furniture ○ *an unfurnished flat*

ungainly /un gáynli/ *adj* **1.** LACKING GRACE lacking grace in moving **2.** AWKWARD awkward to handle **3.** GANGLING having an awkward long-limbed appearance [Early 17C. < obsolete *gain* 'straight, convenient' < Old Norse *gegn*]

Ungava /oong gaávə/ region in northeastern Canada, situated east of Hudson Bay and North of the Eastmain River. Area: 912,000 sq. km/352,100 sq. mi.

Ungava Bay bay in northeastern Quebec, Canada, opening into Hudson Strait

unglued /ún glóod/ *adj* **1.** having become separated or detached **2.** *N Am* having lost your composure or temper (*informal*)

ungodly /un góddli/ *adj* **1.** NOT REVERING GOD not devoted to or obeying God **2.** WICKED behaving in a way thought to violate moral strictures **3.** UNREASONABLE not meeting standards for reasonableness (*informal*) ○ *at this ungodly hour* —**ungodliness** *n*

ungovernable /un gúvvərnəb'l/ *adj* incapable of being governed or restrained —**ungovernably** *adv*

ungracious /un gráyshəss/ *adj* **1.** inconsistent with good manners **2.** unpleasant or difficult —**ungraciously** *adv* —**ungraciousness** *n*

ungrammatical /ún grə máttik'l/ *adj* not conforming to the accepted rules of grammar —**ungrammatically** *adv*

ungraspable /un graáspəb'l/ *adj* **1.** impossible to catch hold of and retain a grip on ○ *icy deck ropes that were ungraspable* **2.** so complex, difficult, or high-level as to be impossible to understand, reach, or explain ○ *an ungraspable mystery*

ungrateful /un gráytf'l/ *adj* **1.** not thankful or appreciative **2.** unpleasant or unrewarding —**ungratefully** *adv* —**ungratefulness** *n*

ungrudging /un grújjing/ *adj* feeling or showing no reluctance or reservations ○ *offered ungrudging support* —**ungrudgingly** *adv*

ungual /úng gwəl/ *adj* **1.** relating to or affecting the fingernails or toenails **2.** relating to, occurring in, or supporting a nail, claw, or hoof [Mid-19C. < Latin *unguis* 'nail, claw']

unguarded /un gaárdid/ *adj* **1.** UNPROTECTED lacking a guard or protection **2.** NATURAL free from pretence or guile **3.** NOT WARY showing a lack of thought or care —**unguardedly** *adv* —**unguardedness** *n*

unguent /úng gwənt/ *n* a healing or soothing ointment [15C. < Latin *unguentum* < *unguere* 'smear, anoint']

unguis /úng gwiss/ (*plural* **-gues** /-gweez/) *n* **1.** a nail, claw, hook, or hoof on a digit or foot of an animal **2.** the claw-shaped base of some petals [Early 18C. < Latin, 'nail, claw']

ungulate /úng gyoo layt, -lət/ *adj* **1.** WITH HOOFS having hoofs **2.** SHAPED LIKE HOOF resembling a hoof in shape or function ■ *n* HOOFED MAMMAL a mammal with hoofs, e.g. the horse, rhinoceros, pig, giraffe, deer, or camel [Early 19C. < late Latin *ungulatus* < Latin *ungula* 'hoof, claw' < *unguis* 'nail, claw']

unguligrade /úng gyóoli grayd/ *adj* describes a mammal that walks on hoofs [Mid-19C. < Latin *ungula* 'hoof' (see UNGULATE)]

unhallowed /un hállōd/ *adj* **1.** NOT CONSECRATED not consecrated or blessed **2.** IRREVERENT lacking religious reverence **3.** NOT ACCEPTABLE TO RELIGION not conforming to the standards of a religion

unhand /un hánd/ (**-hands, -handing, -handed**) *vt* to let somebody go by releasing a grasp (*archaic or humorous*)

unhandy /un hándi/ (**-ier, -iest**) *adj* **1.** NOT SKILLED WITH HANDS not skilled at working with the hands or with tools **2.** INCONVENIENTLY LOCATED situated in an inconvenient location **3.** DIFFICULT TO USE not easy to use or handle

unhappily /un háppili/ *adv* **1.** in a way that expresses or is characterized by unhappiness **2.** used to express a wish that something were not true ○ *Unhappily, she was never able to go there.*

unhappy /un háppi/ (**-pier, -piest**) *adj* **1.** SAD not cheerful or joyful **2.** DISPLEASED not pleased or satisfied with somebody or something **3.** UNFORTUNATE not bringing good luck **4.** INAPPROPRIATE done without proper thought or inappropriate in a specific context ○ *an unhappy choice of words* —**unhappiness** *n*

unharmed /un haármd/ *adj* not hurt or damaged in any way

unharness /un haárnəss/ (**-nesses, -nessing, -nessed**) *vt* **1.** RIDING REMOVE HARNESS FROM HORSE to remove the harness from a horse **2.** RELEASE ENERGY OR PASSIONS to release energy or passions from restraints **3.** ARMS TAKE ARMOUR OFF SOMEBODY to remove the armour from somebody (*archaic*)

UNHCR *abbr* United Nations High Commission for Refugees

unhealthy /un hélthi/ (**-ier, -iest**) *adj* **1.** SICK affected by ill health **2.** BAD FOR HEALTH not good for the health **3.** SYMPTOMATIC OF ILL HEALTH showing the symptoms of or resulting from ill health **4.** HARMFUL TO CHARACTER harmful to the character of somebody or something **5.** CORRUPT morally corrupt or unwholesome **6.** RISKY involving unnecessary risks (*informal*) —**unhealthily** *adv* —**unhealthiness** *n*

unheard /un húrd/ *adj* **1.** not perceived by the ear **2.** not listened to or given a hearing ○ *unheard testimony*

unheard-of *adj* **1.** UNKNOWN not previously known **2.** UNPRECEDENTED never having happened before **3.** OFFENSIVE extremely offensive or rude

unheated /un héetid/ *adj* not supplied or fitted with any form of heating

unheeded /un héedid/ *adj* not listened to or given serious attention ○ *My warnings went unheeded.*

unhelpful /un hélpf'l/ *adj* not providing or willing to provide help —**unhelpfully** *adv* —**unhelpfulness** *n*

unhesitating /un hézzi tayting/ *adj* without pause, indecision, or change —**unhesitatingly** *adv*

unhindered /un híndərd/ *adj* not obstructed by any obstacles or difficulties ○ *allowed them to carry on with the work unhindered*

unhinge /un hínj/ (**-hinges, -hinging, -hinged**) *vt* **1.** REMOVE SOMETHING FROM HINGES to remove something from its hinges **2.** REMOVE HINGES FROM SOMETHING to remove the hinges of something **3.** DISLOCATE SOMETHING to dislodge or detach something **4.** DISRUPT SOMETHING to throw something into confusion **5.** MAKE SOMEBODY PSYCHOLOGICALLY UNSTABLE to cause somebody to become emotionally or mentally unstable

unhitch /un hích/ (**-hitches, -hitching, -hitched**) *vt* to unfasten something that is connected to something else

unholy /un hṓli/ (**-lier, -liest**) *adj* **1.** NOT BLESSED not blessed or consecrated by a church ritual **2.** DEFYING RELIGIOUS PRECEPTS deliberately defiant of specific religious precepts **3.** EXTREME extremely bad or awful (*used for emphasis*) ○ *This place is an unholy mess!* —**unholiness** *n*

unhook /un hóok/ (**-hooks, -hooking, -hooked**) *vt* **1.** to unfasten the hooks of something **2.** to remove something from a hook

unhoped-for /un hṓpt-/ *adj* not expected or anticipated ○ *an unhoped-for victory*

unhorse /un háwrss/ (**-horses, -horsing, -horsed**) *vt* **1.** to knock or throw somebody from a horse **2.** to bring somebody down from a high office or position

unhurried /un húrrid/ *adj* done in a relaxed and deliberate way —**unhurriedly** *adv*

unhurt /un húrt/ *adj* having met with no injury or harm ○ *The driver escaped unhurt from the accident.*

unhygienic /ún hī jéenik/ *adj* not clean, sanitary, or healthy

uni /yóoni/ *n* EDUC same as **university** (*informal*) [Late 19C. Shortening]

uni- *prefix* one, single ○ *unicellular* [< Latin < *unus* 'one'. < Indo-European]

Uniat /yóoni at/, **Uniate** /-ət, -ayt/ *n* a member of one of the Eastern Christian Churches that recognize papal supremacy, but keep their own liturgy, language, and canon law ■ *adj* relating to the Uniat Churches [Mid-19C. < Russian *uniyat*, Polish *uniat* < *unia* 'union' (of the Roman Catholic and Greek churches) < Latin *union-* (see UNION)]

uniaxial /yóoni áksi əl/ *adj* **1.** describes a crystal or mineral that has one direction, parallel to the principal axis, along which single refraction occurs **2.** describes a plant with an unbranched main stem —**uniaxially** *adv*

unicameral /yóoni kámmərəl/ *adj* having only one legislative chamber [Mid-19C. < UNI- + Latin *camera* 'chamber' (see CAMERA)] —**unicameralism** *n* —**unicameralist** *n* —**unicamerally** *adv*

unicast /yóoni kast/ *n* a transmission from a single computing terminal to one other terminal

UNICEF /yóoni sef/, **Unicef** *n* a United Nations agency that works for the protection and survival of children around the world. Full form **United Nations Children's Fund**

unicellular /yóoni séllyoolər/ *adj* consisting of a single cell —**unicellularity** /-sellyoo lárrəti/ *n*

unicity /yóoni sitti/ (*plural* **-ies**) *n S Africa* a metropolitan area which consists of a major city and its surrounding municipalities, and has a unified system of government and administration

unicolour /yóoni kúllər/ *adj* composed of or containing only one colour

unicorn

unicorn /yóoni kawrn/ *n* **1.** a mythical animal usually depicted as a white horse with a single straight spiralled horn growing from its forehead **2.** in the

Bible, a horned animal now believed to be a rhinoceros or aurochs [13C. Via French < Latin *unicornis* 'one-horned' < *cornu* 'horn']

unicostate /yoʻoni kóst ayt/ *adj* describes a leaf with one main rib

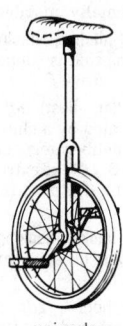

unicycle

unicycle /yoʻoni síkˈl/ *n* a pedal-powered vehicle that has a single wheel with a seat mounted on a frame above it [Mid-19C. After BICYCLE] —**unicyclist** *n*

unidentified /ún ī dénti fīd/ *adj* **1.** unable to be recognized or given a name **2.** unwilling to be associated with or held responsible for something

unidirectional /yoʻoni di réksh'nəl, -dī-/ *adj* thinking, moving, or operating in only one direction

UNIDO /yoo neʻedō/, **Unido** *abbr* United Nations Industrial Development Organization

unifactorial /yoʻoni fak táwri əl/ *adj* describes an inherited characteristic dependent on a single gene

unification /yoʻonifi káysh'n/ *n* **1.** the act or process of uniting or joining together **2.** a result of uniting or joining together

Unification Church *n* a religious denomination founded in 1954 by the South Korean industrialist Sun Myung Moon

unified /yoʻoni fīd/ *adj* brought together to form a single unit or entity

unified field theory *n* a single theory capable of defining the nature of the interrelationships among nuclear, electromagnetic, and gravitational forces

unifoliate /yoʻoni fóli ət/ *adj* having a single leaf or leaf-shaped part

uniform /yoʻoni fawrm/ *n* **1.** DISTINCTIVE SET OF CLOTHES a distinctive set of clothes worn to identify somebody's occupation, affiliation, or status **2.** COMPLETE OUTFIT a single outfit of identifying clothes **3.** IDENTIFYING LOOK a distinctive style or other feature that identifies somebody as a member of a group ■ *adj* **1.** UNCHANGING always the same in quality, degree, character, or manner **2.** CONSISTENT conforming to one standard or rule **3.** RESEMBLING ANOTHER OR OTHERS being the same as another or others **4.** UNVARYING IN DESIGN unvarying in colour, texture, or design ■ *vt* (-forms, -forming, -formed) **1.** PROVIDE SOMEBODY WITH UNIFORMS to provide a person or group with a uniform or uniforms **2.** MAKE SOMETHING UNVARYING OR SAME to make something homogeneous, unvarying, or consistent [Mid-16C. Directly or via French < Latin *uniformis* 'having one form' < *forma* 'shape'] —**uniformed** *adj* —**uniformity** /yoʻoni fáwrməti/ *n* —**uniformly** *adv*

Uniform *n* a code word for the letter 'U', used in international radio communications

uniformitarianism /yoʻoni fawrmi táiri ənizəm/ *n* the theory that the same geological processes occurred in the past as occur today, and that geological formations and structures can be interpreted by observing present-day actions —**uniformitarian** *adj, n*

Uniform Resource Locator *n* ONLINE full form of **URL**

unify /yoʻoni fī/ (-fies, -fying, -fied) *vt* to bring people or things together to form a single unit or entity [Early 16C. Via French *unifier* < Latin *unificare* 'make one'] —**unifiable** *adj* —**unifier** *n* —**unifying** *adj*

unilateral /yoʻoni láttərəl/ *adj* **1.** DECIDED BY ONE PARTY decided or acted on by only one involved party or nation irrespective of what the others do **2.** ACCOUNTING FOR ONE SIDE ONLY taking into account only one side of a subject **3.** BINDING ONLY ONE PARTY binding or at the insistence of only one party to a contract, obligation, or agreement **4.** MED AFFECTING ONLY ONE SIDE affecting or involving only one side of the body,

only one of a pair of organs, or only one side of an organ **5.** BOT HAVING PARTS ON ONLY ONE SIDE having parts that are arranged on only one side of a stem or other axis **6.** WITH ONE SIDE having only one side **7.** SOCIOL THROUGH ONE PARENT ONLY tracing lineage through one parent only ■ *n* WAR CORRESPONDENT WORKING ALONE a war correspondent who chooses to work independently rather than being attached officially to a military unit —**unilaterally** *adv*

unilateralism /yoʻoni láttərəlizəm/ *n* a foreign policy that takes little or no regard of the views of other nations, including allies, or the implementation of such a policy —**unilateralist** *n*

unilineal /yoʻoni línni əl/ *adj* SOCIOL same as **unilateral** *adj* (sense 7)

unilinear /yoʻoni línni ər/ *adj* developing or evolving progressively through defined stages from primitive to advanced and excluding any variation on this course

unilingual /yoʻoni líng gwəl/ *adj* using or knowing only one language

uniliteral /yoʻoni lítterəl/ *adj* having only a single letter ○ *The pronoun 'I' is uniliteral.*

unilocular /yoʻoni lókyoōlər/ *adj* having a single loculus, cell, or cavity

unimaginable /únni májjinəbˈl/ *adj* impossible to imagine —**unimaginably** *adv*

unimaginative /únni májjinətiv/ *adj* **1.** unable to think of new or interesting ideas, plans, or situations **2.** boring and ordinary, and showing no evidence of any new or interesting ideas —**unimaginatively** *adv* —**unimaginativeness** *n*

unimpaired /únnim páird/ *adj* not adversely affected by anything unpleasant, dangerous, or different that happens

unimpeachable /únnim péechəbˈl/ *adj* **1.** impossible to discredit or challenge **2.** so good as to be beyond reproach —**unimpeachably** *adv*

unimpeded /únnim peédid/ *adj* not obstructed, blocked, or held back by anything —**unimpededly** *adv*

unimportant /únnim páwrtˈnt/ *adj* of little or no significance —**unimportance** *n* —**unimportantly** *adv*

unimpressed /únnim prést/ *adj* not favourably impressed by somebody or something

unimproved /únnim proóvd/ *adj* **1.** NOT MADE BETTER not made better or not developed **2.** WITHOUT IMPROVEMENTS describes land that is not modified in a way that would increase value, e.g. by cultivation or the addition of buildings, landscaping, or services ○ *an unimproved plot* **3.** NOT GETTING HEALTHIER not showing improvement in health ○ *Her condition remains unimproved.*

unincorporated /únnin káwrpə raytid/ *adj* **1.** *N Am* not organized into a corporation or municipality **2.** not included as a part of something else

uninformative /únnin fáwrmətiv/ *adj* not providing adequate information —**uninformatively** *adv*

uninformed /únnin fáwrmd/ *adj* lacking facts or knowledge about something

uninhabitable /únnin hábbitəbˈl/ *adj* unfit as a habitation, especially for human beings —**uninhabitability** /-habbitə bílləti/ *n*

uninhabited /únnin hábbitid/ *adj* lacking all human habitation

uninhibited /únnin híbbitid/ *adj* **1.** expressing feelings or views without restraint **2.** not subject to social or other constraints —**uninhibitedly** *adv* —**uninhibitedness** *n*

uninitiate /únni níshi ət/ *adj* having no experience

uninitiated /únni níshi aytid/ *adj* having no experience or knowledge of something ■ *npl* people who have no experience or knowledge of something

uninjured /un ínjərd/ *adj* having sustained no injuries

uninspired /únnin spírd/ *adj* lacking originality or distinction

uninspiring /únnin spíring/ *adj* not arousing interest, enthusiasm, or excitement —**uninspiringly** *adv*

uninstall /únnin stáwl/ (-stalls, -stalling, -stalled) *vt* to remove a piece of software from a computer

uninstructed /únnin strúktid/ *adj* **1.** not educated or informed **2.** natural or instinctive and not acquired by teaching or instruction

uninsurable /únnin shoórəbˈl, -sháwr-/ *adj* considered too great a risk to cover by insurance —**uninsurability** /-shoorə bílləti, -shawrə-/ *n*

uninsured /únnin shoórd, -sháwrd/ *adj* not covered by insurance ■ *n* somebody who is not covered by insurance

unintelligent /únnin téllijənt/ *adj* **1.** lacking or showing a lack of intelligence **2.** not having a mind or the ability to think and reason —**unintelligence** *n* —**unintelligently** *adv*

unintelligible /únnin téllijəbˈl/ *adj* difficult or impossible to understand —**unintelligibility** /-tellijə bílləti/ *n* —**unintelligibly** *adv*

unintentional /únnin ténsh'nəl/ *adj* not on purpose or by plan —**unintentionally** *adv*

uninterested /un íntrəstid/ *adj* having or showing no interest in somebody or something —**uninterestedly** *adv* —**uninterestedness** *n*

USAGE See *disinterested*.

uninteresting /un íntrəsting/ *adj* having no interesting qualities —**uninterestingly** *adv* —**uninterestingness** *n*

uninterrupted /únnintə rúptid/ *adj* **1.** having no interruptions or breaks **2.** free from obstructions ○ *an uninterrupted view* —**uninterruptedly** *adv*

uninterruptible power supply /únnintə rúptibˈl-/ *n* a piece of electrical equipment with internal batteries that provides a continuing source of power for a short period of time during a power failure to a computer or electrical appliance that is plugged into it

uninucleate /yoʻoni nyoókli ət/ *adj* describes a cell that has a single nucleus

uninvited /únnin vítid/ *adj* not invited or welcome

uninviting /únnin víting/ *adj* not appealing or pleasant —**uninvitingly** *adv*

uninvolved /únnin vólvd/ *adj* **1.** not connected with or participating in something **2.** not participating in a romantic or sexual relationship with somebody

union /yoʻonyən/ *n* **1.** ACT OF JOINING TOGETHER the act of joining together people or things to form a whole **2.** RESULT OF JOINING TOGETHER a result of joining together people or things **3.** AGREEMENT agreement or unity of interests or opinions **4.** MARRIAGE the state of being married **5.** SEX sexual intercourse **6.** POLITICAL ALLIANCE an alliance formed by the joining of people or organizations for a common political purpose **7.** COMM same as **trade union 8.** PARISHES UNITED TO AID POOR in 19th-century Great Britain, a number of parishes that worked together to administer relief to the poor **9.** WORKHOUSE in 19th-century Great Britain, a workhouse supported by parishes working together to aid the poor **10.** MATHS SET OF MATHEMATICAL ELEMENTS the smallest set that consists of all the elements of any or all of two or more given sets and no other elements. An element is counted only once even if it occurs in more than one of the given sets. **11.** *also* **Union** EDUC same as **students' union 12.** CONSTR COUPLING a coupling for parts such as pipes and pipe fittings **13.** TEXTILES FABRIC OF DIFFERENT YARNS a fabric made of two or more different yarns, e.g. cotton and linen **14.** *Aus* RUGBY same as **rugby union** (*informal*) [15C. Directly or via French < Latin *union-* 'oneness' < *unus* 'one']

Union *n* **1.** UNION OF BRITAIN AND NORTHERN IRELAND the union of Great Britain and Northern Ireland since 1920 **2.** NORTHERN SIDE IN US CIVIL WAR the side of the northern states in the American Civil War, or its armed forces. The northern states favoured preservation of the nation as a union of states whereas the southern states declared their secession from that union. **3.** UNITED STATES the United States of America

union card *n* a card signifying membership of a trade union

union catalogue *n* a library catalogue combining the materials in more than one library or in branches of the same library

Union flag *n* same as **Union Jack**

unionise *vti* HR another spelling of **unionize**

unionism /yoʻonyənizəm/ *n* **1.** the principles or policies of trade unions **2.** the advocacy of forming and joining trade unions —**unionist** *n, adj*

Unionism *n* **1.** SUPPORT FOR UNION WITH NORTHERN IRELAND support or advocacy since 1920 for the union between Northern Ireland and Great Britain **2.**

SUPPORT FOR IRELAND'S UNION WITH BRITAIN support or advocacy before 1920 for the union of all Ireland and Great Britain **3. LOYALTY TO FEDERAL UNION** loyalty to the federal union during the Civil War in the United States —**Unionist** *n, adj*

unionize /yóonyə nīz/ (**-izes, -izing, -ized**), **unionise** (**-ises, -ising, -ised**) *vti* to organize workers into a trade union, or be organized into a trade union —**unionization** /yóonyə nī záysh'n/ *n* —**unionizer** *n*

Union Jack *n* the flag of the United Kingdom, which combines the flags of England, Scotland, and Ireland

Union of Utrecht *n* a treaty signed at Utrecht in 1579 between the northern provinces of the Netherlands in which they agreed to act as allies in the event of war against Spain

union shop *n* a place of employment where a contract between the employer and a trade union requires employees to be or become members of the union within a specific time

Union Territory, **union territory** *n* a territory in India ruled directly by the central government

uniparous /yoo níppərəss/ *adj* **1.** having given birth to only one child **2.** producing a single offspring at each birth

unipersonal /yóoni púrss'nəl/ *adj* **1.** existing or manifested in the form of only one person **2.** describes a word existing as an inflected form in only one person, especially the third person singular

uniplanar /yóoni pláynər/ *adj* in mathematics, occurring or located in a single plane

unipod /yóoni pod/ *n* a one-legged stand, e.g. for a camera [Mid-20C. After TRIPOD]

unipolar /yóoni pṓlər/ *adj* **1.** PHYS **HAVING SINGLE POLE** operating by means of, having, or produced by a single electric or magnetic pole **2.** BIOL **BRANCHING OUT AT ONLY ONE END** describes a neuron that branches out at only one end **3.** PHYS **WITH ONE POLARITY** describes a transistor that has carriers with only one polarity —**unipolarity** /yóonipō lárrəti/ *n*

unipotent /yóoni pṓt'nt/ *adj* describes an embryonic cell that is capable of developing into only one type of cell or tissue

~~**uniqe**~~ incorrect spelling of **unique**

unique /yoo néek/ *adj* **1. ONLY ONE** being the only one of a kind **2.** ⚠ **SPECIAL** different from others in a way that makes somebody or something special and worthy of note ○ *a unique marketing opportunity* **3. LIMITED TO SOMEBODY OR SOMETHING** limited to a particular person or thing ○ *concerns that are unique to resettled refugees* [Early 17C. Via French < Latin *unicus* < *unus* 'one'] —**uniquely** *adv* —**uniqueness** *n*

USAGE The use of ***unique*** in its sense 'worthy of note' is common in marketing and advertising (*Don't miss this unique offer*), as well as in conversation. Many dictionaries and usage guides argue that ***unique*** is an absolute concept and, as such, cannot be used with qualifying words such as *very* and *rather*, but in many cases this stricture seems a pedantic objection to what is a linguistic rather than a philosophical convention. It is, however, best avoided in formal writing.

unique selling point, **unique selling proposition** *n* MARKETING full form of **USP**

uniseptate /yóoni sép tayt/ *adj* having a single separating wall or membrane [Mid-19C. < UNI- + SEPTUM]

uniserial /yóoni séeri əl/, **uniseriate** /-ayt/ *adj* arranged in or consisting of a single row or series

unisex /yóoni seks/ *adj* **1.** designed or suitable for people of either gender ○ *unisex fashions* **2.** not distinctly of either the male or the female gender

unisexual /yóoni sékshoo əl/ *adj* **1.** related to or limited to one gender **2.** having either only male or only female reproductive organs —**unisexuality** /-sekshoo állәti/ *n* —**unisexually** *adv*

unison /yóoniss'n/ *n* **1.** two or more notes sharing the same pitch **2.** the performance of two or more parts at the same pitch or an octave apart [Late 16C. Via French < late Latin *unisonus* 'having the same sound' < *sonus* 'sound'] ◇ **in unison 1.** in perfect agreement or harmony **2.** at the same time as somebody or something else

UNISON /yóoniss'n/ *n* the largest trade union in the United Kingdom, for public service employees

unit /yóonit/ *n* **1. ONE PERSON, THING, OR GROUP** a single person, thing, or group, usually regarded as a whole part of something larger ○ *the family unit* **2. DISCRETE PART** an individual or discrete part or element into which something can be divided, especially for analysis **3. GROUP WITH PARTICULAR FUNCTION** a group of people with a particular function who are part of a larger organization ○ *the cancer research unit* **4.** MIL **GROUP OF MILITARY PERSONNEL** a group of military personnel organized as a subdivision of a larger body **5. COMPONENT OR ASSEMBLY OF COMPONENTS** a component or assembly of components that performs a specific function ○ *a kitchen unit* **6.** *Aus, NZ, N Am* **RESIDENCE** each of a number of similar residences within a building or development **7.** *ANZ* **SET OF ROOMS** a set of rooms on one floor, as in a flat or apartment **8.** EDUC **PART OF ACADEMIC COURSE** a part of an academic course that focuses on a specific theme **9.** MEASURE **MEASUREMENT** a standard measurement whose multiples are used in determining quantity, e.g. an inch, degree, calorie, volt, or hour **10.** MED **DRUG AMOUNT** an amount of an enzyme, hormone, drug, or other agent that produces a given effect, often as specified by an internationally agreed standard **11.** MED **MEASURE OF ALCOHOL INTAKE** a measure of alcohol intake used in monitoring the effects of alcohol on the body. One unit is roughly equivalent to the alcohol in half a pint of beer, one glass of wine, or a single measure of spirits. **12.** MATHS **NATURAL NUMBER** the lowest positive natural number **13.** MATHS **NUMBER LESS THAN TEN** the first digit to the left of the decimal point in decimal notation, representing a whole number less than ten **14.** MATHS **SET WITH SINGLE NUMBER** a set containing a single number [Late 16C. < Latin *unus* 'one', after *digit*]

unitard /yóoni taard/ *n* a one-piece stretchable garment with or without sleeves that covers the body from the neck to the feet [Mid-20C. < UNI- + LEOTARD]

unitarian /yóoni táiri ən/ *n* **1.** somebody who supports unity or a unitary system **2.** somebody who believes that God is one being **3.** CHR another spelling of **Unitarian** (sense 2) —**unitarianism** *n*

Unitarian /yóoni táiri ən/ *n* **1.** a member of a Christian Church that rejects the doctrine of the Trinity and stresses individual conscience **2.** a Christian who does not believe in the doctrine of the Trinity — **Unitarian** *adj*

Unitarianism /yóoni táiri ənizəm/ *n* a religious doctrine that rejects the Christian doctrine of the Trinity, the divinity of Jesus Christ, and formal dogma, but stresses reason and individual conscience in belief and practice

unitary /yóonitəri/ *adj* **1. RELATING TO UNIT** relating to or consisting of a unit **2. CHARACTERIZED BY UNITY** based on or characterized by unity **3. EXISTING AS UNIT** undivided and existing as a unit **4.** POL **OF CENTRALIZED GOVERNMENT** relating to or based on a system of government in which authority is centralized —**unitarily** *adv*

unitary authority *n* an administrative body responsible for the provision of all local government services in its area

unitary council *n* PUBLIC ADMIN same as **Unitary Authority**

unit cell *n* the smallest structural unit of a crystal that has all its symmetry and by repetition in three dimensions makes up its full lattice

unit cost *n* the cost of producing a single item

unite /yoo nít/ (**unites, uniting, united**) *v* **1.** *vti* **BRING THINGS TOGETHER** to bring things together to form or act as a unit, or be brought together in this way **2.** *vti* **UNIFY PEOPLE** to unify people by a common interest or concern, or become unified in this way **3.** *vti* **MARRY OR GET MARRIED** to join a couple in marriage, or be joined in marriage **4.** *vti* **ADHERE** to adhere, or cause things to adhere **5.** *vt* **COMBINE QUALITIES** to combine qualities or traits [15C. < Latin *unit-*, past participle of *unire* 'make one' < *unus* 'one'] —**uniter** *n*

united /yoo nítid/ *adj* **1. COMBINED INTO ONE** combined into or made one **2. BY OR FROM UNION** formed by or resulting from the union of two or more persons or things **3. HARMONIOUS** in agreement or harmony —**unitedly** *adv*

United Arab Emirates /yoo nítid-/ federation of seven independent states, Abu Dhabi, Ajmān, Dubai, al Fujayrah, Ra's al Khaymah, Sharjah, and Umm al-Qaiwain, located along the southern coast of the Persian Gulf. Language: Arabic. Currency: dirham. Capital: Abu Dhabi. Population: 2,484,818 (2003). Area: 83,600 sq. km/32,300 sq. mi. Former name **Trucial States** (until 1971)

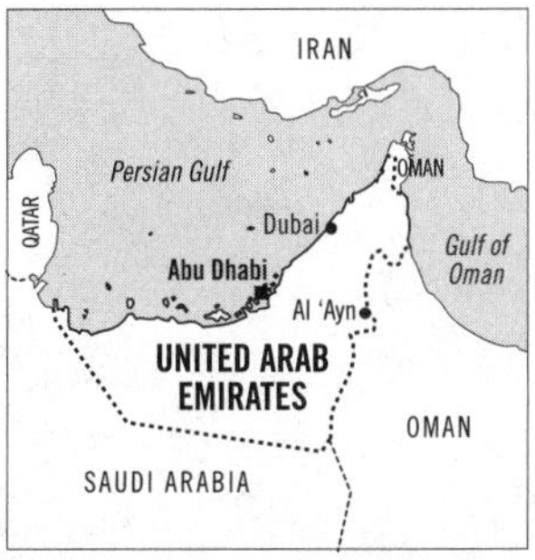

United Arab Emirates

United Arab Republic former independent union between Egypt and Syria, founded in 1958. It was disbanded when Syria left the union in 1961, although Egypt retained the name until 1971.

United Kingdom country in northwestern Europe, comprising the historic kingdoms of England and Scotland, the principality of Wales, and the province of Northern Ireland. Language: English. Currency: pound sterling. Capital: London. Population: 60,094,648 (2003). Area: 244,110 sq. km/94,251 sq. mi. Official name **United Kingdom of Great Britain and Northern Ireland**. See map on next page

United Nations *n* (*takes a singular or plural verb*) **1.** an organization of nations that was formed in 1945 to promote peace, security, and international co-operation **2.** an alliance of nations that pledged in January 1942 to defeat the Axis powers in World War II

United States country in central North America, consisting of 50 states. Language: English. Currency: dollar. Capital: Washington, DC. Population: 290,342,550 (2001). Area: 9,629,047 sq. km/3,717,796 sq. mi. Official name **United States of America**. See map on next page

unitise *vti* another spelling of **unitize**

unitive /yóonitiv/ *adj* **1.** having the ability to unite or promoting unity **2.** characterized by union or unity [Early 16C. < late Latin *unitivus* < Latin *unit-* (see UNITE)]

unitize /yóoni tīz/ (**-izes, -izing, -ized**), **unitise** (**-ises, -ising, -ised**) *v* **1.** *vti* **MAKE ONE** to form into a single unit, or make something into a single unit ○ *a container for unitizing loose items* **2.** *vt* **DIVIDE SOMETHING INTO UNITS** to separate something into units **3.** *vt* FIN **CONVERT TRUST** to convert an investment trust into a unit trust —**unitization** /yóoni tī záysh'n/ *n*

unit of account *n* **1.** the way money is used to keep financial accounts **2.** FIN same as **money of account** **3.** the official currency of a nation

unit operation *n* an operation that is common to the chemical process industries, e.g. mixing, filtration, chemical reaction, or distillation. The study of unit operations is the basis of chemical engineering.

unit price *n* the price of goods per item or measure, e.g. per pound or dozen

unit trust *n* a trust company that manages investments for investors with holdings in the form of units representing a fraction of the value of the investments that are issued by and bought back by the managers. N Am term **mutual fund**

unity /yóonəti/ (*plural* **-ties**) *n* **1. CONDITION OF BEING ONE** the state or condition of being one **2. COMBINATION INTO ONE** the combining or joining of separate things or entities to form one **3. SOMETHING WHOLE** something whole or complete formed by combining or joining separate things or entities **4. HARMONY** harmony of opinion, interest, or feeling **5. SINGLENESS AMONG INDIVIDUALS** singleness or constancy among individuals or groups **6.** ARTS **AESTHETIC ARRANGEMENT OF ARTISTIC ELEMENTS** the arranging of separate components in a literary or artistic work to create an overall aesthetic impression **7.** ARTS **AESTHETIC IMPRESSION** the overall aesthetic impression produced by the arrangement of components in an artistic or literary work **8.** THEATRE **PRINCIPLE OF DRAMATIC STRUCTURE** one of the three principles of dramatic structure derived from Aristotle's *Poetics*. These state that the action of a play should be limited to one plot (**unity of action**), one day (**unity of time**), and one location (**unity of place**). **9.** MATHS **NUMBER ONE** a number by which a given element of a

United Kingdom

United States

mathematical system can be multiplied with the result being equal to the value of the given element **10.** MATHS same as **identity element** [13C. Via French *unite* < Latin *unitas* < *unus* 'one']

univ. *abbr* university

univalent /yoòni váylənt, yoo nívvələnt/ *adj* **1.** CHEM same as **monovalent** (sense 1) **2.** describes a chromosome that remains unpaired during the cell division (**meiosis**) that precedes sex cell formation —**univalency** *n*

univalve /yoòni valv/ *adj* **1.** WITH SINGLE-PIECE SHELL having a shell that is a single piece or valve ○ *a univalve gastropod* **2.** MADE OF SINGLE PIECE describes a shell that is made of a single piece ■ *n* MOLLUSC a mollusc or shell that is univalve

universal /yoòni vúrss'l/ *adj* **1.** RELATING TO WHOLE WORLD relating to, affecting, or accepted by the whole world **2.** RELATING TO UNIVERSE relating to the universe or everything **3.** RELATING TO THOSE IN PARTICULAR GROUP relating to, affecting, or including everyone in a group or situation **4.** USED BY EVERYONE used or understood by everyone **5.** APPLICABLE TO ALL applicable to all situations or purposes ○ *a universal solution* **6.** PRESENT EVERYWHERE present or prevalent everywhere **7.** KNOWLEDGEABLE knowledgeable about or encompassing extensive skills, interests, activities, or subjects **8.** ADAPTABLE TO DIFFERENT SIZES adaptable to many uses or sizes **9.** LOGIC AFFIRMING OR DENYING EVERY MEMBER relating to a proposition that is true or false of every member of a class or group ■ *n* **1.** COMMON CHARACTERISTIC a characteristic or behaviour pattern common to everyone or all the people in a particular group or situation **2.** LOGIC PROPOSITION APPLYING TO ALL MEMBERS a proposition that is true or false for all members of a class or group **3.** PHILOSOPHY GENERAL TERM OR CONCEPT a general term or concept, or the thing that it denotes **4.** PHILOSOPHY UNCHANGING METAPHYSICAL ENTITY a metaphysical entity that remains unchanged in character through a series of changing relations **5.** PHILOSOPHY PLATONIC IDEA OR ARISTOTELIAN FORM a Platonic idea or Aristotelian form **6.** LING GRAMMATICAL CHARACTERISTIC COMMON TO ALL LANGUAGES an actual or possible characteristic common to the grammatical description of all human languages —**universality** /yoòni vur sálləti/ *n* —**universally** *adv*

SYNONYMS See **widespread**.

universal beam *n* a strong steel beam suitable as a support, used either vertically or horizontally

universal class *n* MATHS same as **universal set**

universal coupling *n* ENG same as **universal joint**

universal donor *n* somebody with group O blood who can potentially donate blood to anyone, regardless of the recipient's blood group

universal grammar *n* the set of actual or possible rules that form the grammatical description of all human languages

universal indicator *n* a solution that undergoes several colour changes over a wide range of pH values

universalise *vt* another spelling of **universalize**

universalism /yoòni vúrss'lizəm/ *n* **1.** COMPREHENSIVE RANGE a comprehensive range of knowledge, interests, or activities **2.** UNIVERSAL FEATURE a universal characteristic or feature **3.** PRINCIPLE OF WELFARE SERVICES the principle that welfare services should be publicly funded and available to all strictly on the basis of need —**universalist** *n* —**universalistic** /yoòni vurssə lístik/ *adj*

Universalism *n* in Christianity, the doctrine of salvation for all people —**Universalist** *n*

universalize /yoòni vúrssə līz/ (**-izes, -izing, -ized**), **universalise** (**-ises, -ising, -ised**) *vt* **1.** to make something universal in use or distribution, often within a particular field **2.** to generalize a theory, proposition, or idea so that it applies to all people, instances, or situations —**universalizability** /-vurssə līzə bílləti/ *n* —**universalization** /-vurssə līz záysh'n/ *n*

universal joint, **universal coupling** *n* a coupling device between two rotating shafts in line with each other that permits rotation in three planes. See illustration on next page

universal motor *n* an electric motor that runs with a relatively constant output speed on either alternating or direct current

Universal Product Code *n* N Am a bar code con-

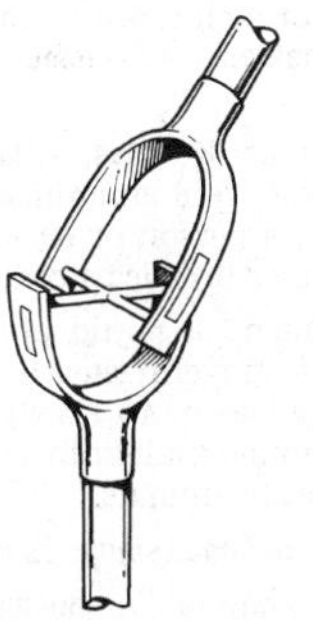
universal joint

taining a unique 12-digit number that identifies a commercial product

universal quantifier *n* a word that performs the same function in symbolic, mathematical, or predicate logic, e.g. 'all' and 'every' in English and the logical operator or constant

universal recipient *n* a member of the AB blood group who can receive transfusions of blood from any ABO group

Universal Resource Locator *n* ONLINE same as **URL** (*dated*)

universal serial bus *n* COMPUT full form of **USB**

universal set *n* a mathematical set that contains all of the possible elements and all of the subsets relevant to the solution of a specific problem

Universal Time, Universal Time Coordinated *n* **1.** same as **Greenwich Mean Time** **2.** an internationally accepted standard for calculating time based on International Atomic Time

universe /yóoni vurss/ *n* **1.** ALL MATTER AND ENERGY IN SPACE the totality of all matter and energy that exists in the vastness of space, whether known to human beings or not **2.** HUMANITY AND ITS HISTORY the human race or the totality of human experience **3.** SPHERE OF PERSON OR THING a sphere of activity that is centred on and includes everything associated with a person, place, or thing **4.** LOGIC same as **universe of discourse** **5.** STATS same as **population** (sense 6) [14C. Directly or via French < Latin *universum* 'the whole world' < *universus* 'whole', < *versus*, past participle of *vertere* 'turn']

universe of discourse *n* in logic, all of a set of objects implied by a specific discussion

Universities and Colleges Admissions Service *n* EDUC full form of **UCAS**

university /yóoni vúrssəti/ (*plural* **-ties**) *n* **1.** UNDERGRADUATE AND POSTGRADUATE EDUCATIONAL INSTITUTION an institution of higher education comprising departments offering courses of undergraduate and postgraduate study in many subjects **2.** BUILDINGS HOUSING UNIVERSITY the buildings, other facilities, and grounds of a university **3.** STUDENTS AND STAFF the students, teachers, and administrative and other staff of a university [14C. Via French *université* < Latin *universitas* 'the whole, society, guild' < *universus* (see UNIVERSE)]

univocal /yóoni vṓk'l/ *adj* having only one meaning ■ *n* a word or term with only one meaning [Mid-16C. < late Latin *univocus* 'having one voice' < *vox* 'voice'] —**univocally** *adv*

UNIX /yóoniks/, **Unix** *tdmk* a trademark for a widely used computer operating system, developed in 1969 at AT&T Bell Laboratories, that can support multitasking in a multiuser environment

unjoint /un jóynt/ (**-joints, -jointing, -jointed**) *vt* to cut off or dislocate something at a joint —**unjointed** *adj*

unjust /un júst/ *adj* contrary to what is right, just, or fair, or lacking fairness or justice —**unjustly** *adv* —**unjustness** *n*

unjustifiable /un jústi fī əb'l/ *adj* incapable of being shown to be or defended as being fair, reasonable, or correct —**unjustifiability** /un jústi fī əbílləti/ *n* —**unjustifiably** *adv*

unjustified /un jústi fīd/ *adj* **1.** HAVING NO ACCEPTABLE JUSTIFICATION shown to have no good or just reason or explanation **2.** NOT HAVING STRAIGHT VERTICAL MARGIN not arranged evenly in such a way that the ends of the lines on a page form a straight vertical line parallel to the margin **3.** NOT PRONOUNCED TO BE RIGHTEOUS not having been made or declared righteous

unkempt /un kémpt/ *adj* **1.** NEEDING GROOMING tangled and matted and in need of combing or grooming **2.** UNTIDY AND NEGLECTED untidy or disorderly as a result of neglect **3.** UNPOLISHED lacking in polish or elegance [14C. < UN- + *kempt*, past participle of *kemb* 'comb' < Old English *cemban* < Germanic] —**unkemptness** *n*

unkennel /un kénn'l/ (**-nels, -nelling, -nelled**) *vt* **1.** RELEASE DOG FROM KENNEL to let a dog out of a kennel **2.** FORCE ANIMAL OUT OF LAIR to make an animal leave its den or lair **3.** MAKE SOMETHING KNOWN to reveal something secret or hidden

unkind /un kīnd/ *adj* **1.** lacking kindness, sympathy, or consideration, or resulting from such a lack **2.** severe, harsh, or inclement —**unkindness** *n*

unkindly /un kīndli/ *adv* in an unkind manner or without showing kindness ■ *adj* lacking in kindliness —**unkindliness** *n*

unkink /un kíngk/ (**-kinks, -kinking, -kinked**) *v* **1.** *vti* to remove a kink or kinks from something, or have a kink or kinks removed **2.** *vi N Am* to become loose or relaxed

unknit /un nít/ (**-knits, -knitting, -knitted** or **-knit**) *vti* **1.** to unravel something, or become unravelled **2.** to allow the eyebrows to move back to a natural position from a position of being drawn together, or be moved apart in this way

unknowable /un nṓ əb'l/ *adj* impossible to know, often because of being beyond human experience or understanding ■ *n* something that cannot be known —**unknowability** /un nṓ ə bílləti/ *n* —**unknowableness** *n* —**unknowably** *adv*

unknowing /un nṓ ing/ *adj* **1.** unwitting or lacking awareness **2.** not intended —**unknowingly** *adv*

unknown /ún nṓn/ *adj* **1.** NOT KNOWN not forming part of somebody's knowledge or of knowledge in general ○ *an unknown assailant* **2.** NOT IDENTIFIED undetermined or undiscovered ○ *Unknown to her family, she left town.* **3.** NOT WIDELY KNOWN not known to, or recognized by, many people ○ *An unknown actress was starring in the play.* ■ *n* **1.** SOMEBODY OR SOMETHING NOT KNOWN somebody or something that is not part of a person's knowledge or of knowledge in general **2.** SOMEBODY OR SOMETHING NOT WIDELY KNOWN somebody or something that is not known or recognized by many people **3.** MATHS VARIABLE TO BE DETERMINED a variable in an equation whose values are solutions of the equation

unknown quantity (*plural* **unknown quantities**) *n* something or somebody whose nature, behaviour, or importance is uncertain and unpredictable

Unknown Soldier *n* an unidentified soldier killed in battle and selected for burial with national honours to represent all those who died fighting for their country but remain unidentified

unlaboured /un láybərd/ *adj* **1.** DONE WITHOUT EFFORT done or produced without toil, effort, or difficulty **2.** NATURAL AND UNSTUDIED exhibiting a naturalness and ease of accomplishment **3.** UNCULTIVATED describes agricultural land that is not being ploughed or cultivated

unlace /un láyss/ (**-laces, -lacing, -laced**) *vt* **1.** to loosen or untie the laces of a shoe, piece of clothing, or other item **2.** to remove the shoes or clothes from somebody by undoing the laces

unlade /un láyd/ (**-lades, -lading, -laded, -laded** or **-laden** /-láyd'n/) *vt* **1.** to empty a ship or vehicle by removing its cargo **2.** to remove the cargo from a ship or vehicle

unlash /un lásh/ (**-lashes, -lashing, -lashed**) *vt* to release something by loosening or untying the ropes or other lashing holding or restraining it

unlawful /un láwf'l/ *adj* **1.** not permitted by the law **2.** contrary to religious precepts, ethical standards, or the conventions of society —**unlawfully** *adv* —**unlawfulness** *n*

SYNONYMS ***unlawful, illegal, illicit, wrongful, nonlegal***
CORE MEANING: not in accordance with laws or rules
unlawful not permitted by the law ○ *Possessing a knife was not per se an unlawful act.* ○ *This amendment makes it unlawful for employers to have different compulsory retirement ages for men and women.* **illegal** contravening a specific law, especially a criminal law ○ *drug smuggling and other illegal activities* ○ *Under the new law, refugees whose appeals failed would be declared illegal immigrants.* **illicit** not permitted by the law and considered morally wrong or unacceptable ○ *illicit weapons and drugs* ○ *The divorce papers cited her numerous illicit affairs.* **wrongful** not fair, just, or legal, but not punishable by criminal law ○ *the wrongful use of confidential information* ○ *awarded damages for wrongful arrest* **nonlegal** not established under the law, or by common law or legislation ○ *nonlegal sanctions*

unlawful assembly *n* a gathering of people that is not sanctioned by law and is therefore illegal, e.g. a march or picket that is not in compliance with the Public Order Acts

unlawful combatant *n US* somebody who undertakes military-style operations but does not belong to a country's regular armed forces, is not commanded by somebody responsible for subordinates, and does not follow the rules of war

unlay /un láy/ (**-lays, -laying, -laid** /-láyd/) *vti* to separate the strands of a rope by untwisting them, or become separated in this way

unlead /un léd/ (**-leads, -leading, -leaded**) *vt* in traditional hot-metal printing, to take out the leading or leads separating lines of type

unleaded /un léddid/ *adj* **1.** FREE OF TETRAETHYL LEAD not containing tetraethyl lead as an antiknock additive and consequently less harmful to the environment ○ *unleaded petrol* **2.** PRINTING NOT SEPARATED BY LEADS describes lines of type that are not separated by leads ■ *n* UNLEADED PETROL petrol that does not contain tetraethyl lead as an antiknock additive

unlearn /un lúrn/ (**-learns, -learning, -learnt** /-lúrnt/ or **-learned** /-lúrnd/) *vt* **1.** to rid the mind of the knowledge or memory of something **2.** to break the habit or end the practice of something

unlearned /un lúrnid/ *adj* **1.** LACKING EDUCATION not having received an education or schooling **2.** DISPLAYING LACK OF EDUCATION showing or resulting from a lack of education **3.** UNSKILLED OR UNFAMILIAR lacking a knowledge of, skills in, or familiarity with, a particular field **4.** *also* **unlearnt** /-lúrnt/ NATURAL OR UNSTUDIED possessed or known without having been practised, studied, or taught —**unlearnedly** *adv*

unleash /un léesh/ (**-leashes, -leashing, -leashed**) *vt* **1.** to allow something, especially something previously held in check, to have its full effect **2.** to set a person or animal free from a leash or other form of restraint or confinement

unleavened /un lévv'nd/ *adj* made without yeast or other raising agent

unless /un léss/ *conj* except under the circumstances that ○ *I won't go unless the weather improves.* [15C. < obsolete *on less than* 'on a lower condition, except']

unlettered /un léttərd/ *adj* **1.** NOT WELL-EDUCATED lacking a good education or the knowledge and understanding that such an education can provide **2.** ILLITERATE unable to read and write **3.** NOT HAVING ANY LETTERING not containing or inscribed with any lettering

unlicensed /un līss'nst/ *adj* **1.** HAVING NO LICENCE lacking a required official licence, especially an official licence to sell alcohol **2.** UNSANCTIONED done without authorization or permission **3.** WITHOUT ETHICAL INHIBITIONS lacking ethical or religious constraints

unlike /un līk/ *prep* **1.** DISSIMILAR TO having qualities and characteristics dissimilar to or different from somebody or something ○ *It's unlike anything we've ever seen before.* **2.** IN CONTRAST TO used to indicate a contrast between two things, people, or situations ○ *Unlike the previous government, we intend to fulfil our manifesto promises.* **3.** ATYPICAL OF used to indicate that somebody's words or actions are not characteristic of him or her ○ *It was so unlike her to speak like that.* ■ *adj* NOT ALIKE dissimilar to each other ○ *The boys are very unlike in appearance.* —**unlikeness** *n*

unlikely /un līkli/ (**-lier, -liest**) *adj* **1.** IMPROBABLE not likely to occur **2.** NOT BELIEVABLE not likely to be true or be believed **3.** INCONGRUOUS not suitable or appropriate **4.** PROBABLY NOT SUCCESSFUL not likely to meet with success —**unlikelihood** *n* —**unlikeliness** *n*

unlimber /un límbər/ (**-bers, -bering, -bered**) *vti* **1.** to prepare something for action or use **2.** to remove a piece of field artillery from its gun carriage and prepare it for use

unlimited /un límmitid/ *adj* **1.** NOT RESTRICTED without limits, restrictions, or controls **2.** INFINITE lacking or appearing to lack a boundary or end **3.** COMPLETE OR TOTAL not subject to qualification or exception **4.**

COMM NOT LIMITED IN MONEY PAYABLE describes a financial liability that is not limited in the amount of money that the members of a company are required to pay out if the company ceases to trade **5.** COMM NOT HAVING MEMBERS WITH LIMITED LIABILITY describes a company in which each of the members is financially liable for his or her full share of the company's debts if the company ceases to trade —**unlimitedly** *adv* —**unlimitedness** *n*

unlisted /un lístid/ *adj* **1.** *ANZ, N Am* NOT PUBLICLY AVAILABLE not included in a telephone directory available to the public. UK term **ex-directory 2.** NOT LISTED ON STOCK EXCHANGE not registered on a physical stock exchange and consequently not available for trading on that exchange **3.** NOT ON LIST not included on a list

unlisted securities market *n* the London market trading in shares that are not included on the official Stock Exchange list

unlivable /un lívvəb'l/ *adj* not fit for somebody to live in

unlive /un lív/ (**-lives, -living, -lived**) *vt* to reverse or undo the effects of an experience, action, or period of life

unload /un lṓd/ (**-loads, -loading, -loaded**) *vti* **1.** REMOVE CARGO FROM CARRIER to take the load off a ship, lorry, or pack animal **2.** DISCHARGE to discharge passengers or cargo **3.** REMOVE CHARGE FROM GUN to remove a charge or cartridge from a gun **4.** TAKE FILM OUT OF CAMERA to remove a roll of film from a camera **5.** SHARE TROUBLES to find an outlet for worries or negative feelings by sharing them with somebody else **6.** SELL ON SOMETHING UNWANTED to get rid of something, especially by selling a large quantity of it **7.** TRANSFER SOMETHING UNWANTED to pass work, responsibility, or a problem on to somebody else

unlock /un lók/ (**-locks, -locking, -locked**) *v* **1.** *vti* OPEN OR BECOME OPEN AFTER LOCKING to open a lock or something locked, or to become open after being locked **2.** *vt* GIVE ACCESS TO SOMETHING to provide access to something previously unavailable **3.** *vt* MAKE USABLE WITH OTHER SYSTEMS to program a mobile phone so that it can be used with more than one service provider **4.** *vti* RELEASE EMOTION to release or unleash a pent-up feeling or emotion, or be released or unleashed **5.** *vti* REVEAL SOMETHING, OR BE REVEALED to expose or explain something, or be exposed or explained

unlooked-for /un lo͝okt-/ *adj* not hoped for or expected

unloose /un lo͞oss/ (**-looses, -loosing, -loosed**), **unloosen** /-lo͞oss'n/ (**-ens, -ening, -ened**) *vt* **1.** UNFASTEN SOMETHING to untie or undo something, especially a knot **2.** FREE SOMEBODY FROM RESTRAINT to release somebody or something from restraint or confinement **3.** MAKE SOMETHING LOOSER to relax the tightness of something **4.** MAKE SOMETHING LESS INTENSE to reduce the intensity of something

unlovely /un lúvvli/ (**-lier, -liest**) *adj* **1.** not beautiful or pleasing to look at **2.** not producing pleasure or delight —**unloveliness** *n*

unlucky /un lúki/ (**-ier, -iest**) *adj* **1.** HAVING BAD LUCK not experiencing good luck **2.** FULL OF MISFORTUNE OR FAILURE full of bad luck or failure **3.** BRINGING MISFORTUNE causing or heralding misfortune **4.** DISAPPOINTING producing disappointment or regret —**unluckily** *adv* —**unluckiness** *n*

unmade /un máyd/ past participle, past tense of **unmake** ■ *adj* **1.** not restored to a tidy state after being slept in ○ *an unmade bed* **2.** ROADS same as **unmetalled**

unmake /un máyk/ (**-makes, -making, -made** /-máyd/) *vt* **1.** UNDO SOMETHING to undo the effects of something **2.** CHANGE SOMETHING COMPLETELY to make a fundamental change or changes in something **3.** REMOVE SOMEBODY FROM POWER to remove somebody from office or a position of authority

unman /un mán/ (**-mans, -manning, -manned**) *vt* **1.** to cause somebody to lose a quality or qualities traditionally attributed to men, especially courage (*literary*) **2.** to deprive a man or boy of the ability to have intercourse or father children

unmanageable /un mánnijəb'l/ *adj* difficult or impossible to deal with —**unmanageability** /un mánnijə bíllәti/ *n* —**unmanageably** *adv*

unmanly /un mánnli/ (**-lier, -liest**) *adj* not typical of or appropriate for a man, according to traditional perceptions of masculinity —**unmanliness** *n*

unmanned /un mánd/ *adj* AEROSP same as **uncrewed** (*sometimes considered offensive*)

unmannered /un mánnərd/ *adj* **1.** lacking good manners, or displaying such a lack **2.** having an easy unaffected manner —**unmanneredly** *adv*

unmannerly /un mánnərli/ *adj* lacking good manners, or displaying such a lack ■ *adv* in a rude or discourteous manner —**unmannerliness** *n*

unmarked /un ma̋arkt/ *adj* **1.** WITHOUT MARK not bearing any mark **2.** LACKING IDENTIFYING MARKINGS lacking identifying letters, numbers, or symbols ○ *an unmarked police car* **3.** LACKING DISTINGUISHING QUALITY having no distinguishing quality or character **4.** UNSEEN not seen or spotted **5.** LING WITHOUT DISTINCTIVE LINGUISTIC FEATURE not having an extra or less usual distinctive linguistic feature

unmarried /un márrid/ *adj* not joined to another person by marriage ■ *n* somebody who is not married

unmask /un ma̋ask/ (**-masks, -masking, -masked**) *vti* **1.** to reveal the true nature or identity of somebody or something, or reveal your own true nature or identity **2.** to remove a mask, or remove a mask from somebody

unmatched /ún mácht/ *adj* **1.** not matching, especially not belonging to a matching pair **2.** having no equal or rival

unmeaning /un meéning/ *adj* **1.** MEANINGLESS lacking meaning or significance **2.** UNINTENTIONAL not intended or deliberate **3.** UNINTELLIGENT blank and devoid of intelligence ○ *an unmeaning stare* —**unmeaningly** *adv*

unmeasured /un mézhərd/ *adj* **1.** NOT MEASURED not determined by measuring **2.** NOT RESTRAINED unrestrained, incautious, or ill-considered **3.** MUSIC NOT DIVIDED INTO BARS not marked with bar lines and therefore with no set rhythm

unmechanical /únmi kánnik'l/ *adj* lacking the skill to work with tools and machinery —**unmechanically** *adv*

unmentionable /un ménsh'nəb'l/ *adj* not to be mentioned or discussed, especially in polite conversation ■ *n* something that should not be mentioned or discussed, especially in polite conversation ■ **unmentionables** *npl* CLOTHING same as **underwear** (*dated or humorous*) —**unmentionableness** *n* —**unmentionably** *adv*

unmerciful /un múrssif'l/ *adj* **1.** displaying no mercy, or characterized by a lack of mercy **2.** going beyond what is reasonable —**unmercifully** *adv* —**unmercifulness** *n*

unmet /ún mét/ *adj* not satisfactorily fulfilled

unmetalled /ún mét'ld/ *adj* not covered with a durable road surfacing material

unmetered /un meétərd/ *adj* **1.** not measured using a meter **2.** describes Internet service that is available at a flat rate, typically by the month, rather than by connection time

unmistakable /únmi stáykəb'l/, **unmistakeable** *adj* easily recognized or understood —**unmistakability** /únmi staykə bíllәti/ *n* —**unmistakably** *adv*

~~**unmistakeable**~~ incorrect spelling of **unmistakable**

unmitigated /un mítti gaytid/ *adj* **1.** not lessened or eased in any way **2.** absolute and unqualified —**unmitigatedly** *adv*

unmoor /un mo͝or, un máwr/ (**-moors, -mooring, -moored**) *v* **1.** *vti* to free a ship or boat from its moorings, or be freed from moorings **2.** *vt* to leave a ship or boat moored by only one of its anchors

unmoral /un mórrəl/ *adj* **1.** lacking a moral sense, or displaying such a lack **2.** not subject to morality or ethics —**unmorality** /únmə rállәti/ *n* —**unmorally** *adv*

unmould /un mṓld/ (**-moulds, -moulding, -moulded**) *vt* to remove something from a mould

unmoved /un mo͞ovd/ *adj* having or showing no emotional reaction to something when it would usually be expected

SYNONYMS See *impassive.*

UNMOVIC /ún mō vik/ *abbr* INTERNAT REL United Nations Monitoring, Verification, and Inspection Commission

unmoving /un mo͞oving/ *adj* **1.** not in motion ○ *unmoving vehicles* **2.** failing to arouse deep emotions ○ *an unmoving story*

unmusical /un myo͞ozik'l/ *adj* **1.** lacking melodic qualities and consequently unpleasant to hear **2.** having no ability for, or no interest in, music —**unmusically** *adv* —**unmusicalness** *n* —**unmusicality** /un myo͞ozi kállәti/ *n*

unmuzzle /un múzz'l/ (**-zles, -zling, -zled**) *vt* **1.** to remove a muzzle from an animal, especially a dog **2.** to restore to a person or organization the right to say, publish, or broadcast something

unmyelinated /un mī́ əli naytid/ *adj* describes a nerve fibre that lacks a myelin sheath. Such fibres transmit nerve impulses more slowly than myelinated ones, and are found mainly in worms, insects, and other invertebrate animals.

unna *pron* same as **oonu** (*slang; used in Black English*)

unnameable /un náyməb'l/, **unnamable** *adj* incapable of being named, especially too terrible to name

unnamed /ún náymd/ *adj* **1.** having a name but not identified by it **2.** not yet assigned a name

unnatural /un náchərəl/ *adj* **1.** CONTRARY TO EXPECTED BEHAVIOUR contrary to habit, custom, or practice ○ *an unnatural tense silence between them* **2.** NOT CONFORMING TO CONVENTIONS behaving in ways that contradict conventional assumptions about what constitutes normal or acceptable human behaviour **3.** ARTIFICIAL affected, artificial, contrived, or strained ○ *an unnatural festive atmosphere* **4.** CONTRARY TO LAWS OF NATURE contrary to the physical laws of nature —**unnaturally** *adv* —**unnaturalness** *n*

unnecessary /un néssəssəri/ *adj* **1.** gratuitous, unjustified, and hurtful **2.** not essential, needed, or required —**unnecessarily** *adv*

unnerve /un núrv/ (**-nerves, -nerving, -nerved**) *vt* **1.** to deprive somebody of courage, resolve, or self-confidence **2.** to cause somebody to feel nervous —**unnerving** *adj* —**unnervingly** *adv*

unnoticed /un nṓtist/ *adv* without being seen or spotted by anybody —**unnoticed** *adj*

unnu *pron* another spelling of **oonu** (*slang; used in Black English*)

unnumbered /un númbərd/ *adj* **1.** not given an identifying number **2.** too many to be counted

UNO *abbr* United Nations Organization

unobtrusive /únnəb tro͞ossiv/ *adj* not conspicuous, blatant, or assertive —**unobtrusively** *adv* —**unobtrusiveness** *n*

unoccupied /un ókyo͞o pīd/ *adj* **1.** NOT IN USE not being used by anybody **2.** NOT DOING ANYTHING not doing anything, or anything important **3.** NOT INHABITED not lived in by anybody **4.** NOT UNDER FOREIGN MILITARY RULE not under the control or military rule of a foreign country

SYNONYMS See *vacant.*

unofficial /únnə físh'l/ *adj* **1.** UNAUTHORIZED not authorized or sanctioned by the proper authority **2.** NOT ACTING OFFICIALLY not acting or employed in an official capacity or position **3.** NOT DONE OR MADE OFFICIALLY not done or made by somebody acting in an official capacity **4.** LACKING UNION APPROVAL not ratified by the trade union to which the strikers belong ○ *an unofficial strike* **5.** NOT ON LIST OF APPROVED DRUGS not included on an official list of medicinal drugs —**unofficially** *adv*

unopposed /únnə pṓzd/ *adj, adv* **1.** MEETING WITH NO OPPOSITION not fought, objected to, or resisted **2.** HAVING NO OPPONENT unchallenged by an official opponent in an election or competition ■ *adv* **1.** WITH NO OPPOSITION without being fought, objected to, or resisted **2.** WITH NO OPPONENT without being challenged by an official opponent in an election or competition

unorganized /un áwrgə nīzd/, **unorganised** *adj* **1.** NOT DONE IN ORGANIZED WAY not arranged or done in an orderly or systematic way **2.** NOT ACTING IN ORGANIZED WAY not acting, thinking, or working in an orderly or systematic manner **3.** NOT UNIONIZED not part of a trade union **4.** NOT LIVING lacking the characteristics of a living organism

unorthodox /un áwrthə doks/ *adj* **1.** failing to follow conventional or traditional beliefs or practices **2.** not practising or conforming to the accepted or established form of a religion —**unorthodoxly** *adv* —**unorthodoxy** *n*

unp. *abbr* PUBL unpaged

unpack /un pák/ (**-packs, -packing, -packed**) *v* **1.** *vt* TAKE CONTENTS FROM SOMETHING to take the contents out of something ○ *Unpack your suitcase later.* **2.** *vti* TAKE OUT PACKED THINGS to remove something that has been

packed from its container or packaging ○ *I had to unpack and repack all my belongings.* **3.** *vt* **REMOVE BURDEN FROM SOMEBODY OR SOMETHING** to take a pack or other burden from a person or animal that has been carrying it **4.** *vt* COMPUT same as **unzip 5.** *vt* **REVEAL WHAT IS HIDDEN IN** to reveal what is hidden, buried, or encoded within something

unpaged /un páyjd/, **unpaginated** /un pájji naytid/ *adj* not marked with page numbers

unpaid /ún páyd/ *adj* **1. NOT YET SETTLED** awaiting payment or settlement ○ *unpaid bills* **2. HAVING NOT YET RECEIVED PAYMENT** not yet in receipt of payment for work done **3. WORKING FOR NO PAY** working without wages or a salary ○ *unpaid volunteers* **4. NOT PAYING MONEY** not paying wages or a salary ○ *unpaid overtime*

unpaired /ún páird/ *adj* **1.** not being one of a pair **2.** characterized by a lack of pairs

unpalatable /un pállətəb'l/ *adj* **1.** not pleasant, agreeable, or acceptable **2.** having an unpleasant taste —**unpalatability** /un pállәti bíllәti/ *n* —**unpalatably** *adv*

unparalleled /un párrә leld/ *adj* not equalled, matched, or paralleled in kind or quality ○ *an unparalleled opportunity*

unpardonable /un paárd'nəb'l/ *adj* **1.** impossible to pardon **2.** so bad as to merit no forgiveness

unparliamentary /ún paarlə méntəri/ *adj* not acceptable according to parliamentary procedure

unpeg /un pég/ (**-pegs, -pegging, -pegged**) *vt* **1. TAKE PEG FROM SOMETHING** to take a peg or pegs from something **2. RELEASE SOMETHING BY REMOVING PEG** to release something by removing a peg or pegs **3. STOP FIXING LEVEL OF SOMETHING** to allow something, especially prices or wages, to fluctuate freely by removing the restrictions holding them at a fixed level

unperson /ún purss'n/ *n* somebody whose existence is not acknowledged officially, especially a public figure whose existence is, for political or ideological reasons, unrecognized by a totalitarian government and the news media it controls

unperturbed /únpər túrbd/ *adj* not worried, concerned, or upset —**unperturbedly** *adv*

unphonetic /ún fə néttik/ *adj* using a system of writing that does not represent or correspond to the sounds of human speech

unpick /un pík/ (**-picks, -picking, -picked**) *vt* to undo something by pulling out a thread or threads

unpin /un pín/ (**-pins, -pinning, -pinned**) *vt* **1.** to take a pin or pins from something **2.** to release or unfasten something by removing a pin or pins

unpitched /un pícht/ *adj* describes a musical instrument such as a drum, tambourine, or gong that is not set to a particular pitch or key

unplaced /un pláyst/ *adj* **1.** failing to finish first, second, or third in a race **2.** not assigned a specific place or position

unplanned /un plánd/ *adj* **1. NOT INTENDED** not happening according to a plan **2. LACKING PLAN** not following or structured according to an overall plan **3. DONE SPONTANEOUSLY** accomplished without any advance planning

unpleasant /un plézz'nt/ *adj* **1.** not pleasing, enjoyable, or agreeable **2.** unfriendly and nasty to somebody —**unpleasantly** *adv*

unpleasantness /un plézz'ntnəss/ *n* **1. UNPLEASANT CONDITION OR QUALITY** the condition or quality of being unpleasant **2. UNPLEASANT EXPERIENCES OR EVENTS** experiences or events that are not pleasing or enjoyable **3. UNFRIENDLINESS** an unfriendly and nasty attitude or behaviour **4. UNPLEASANT SITUATION** a situation that is not pleasing or enjoyable **5. DISAGREEMENT** an argument or disagreement

unpleasantry /un plézz'ntri/ (*plural* **-ries**) *n* **1. UNFRIENDLINESS** hostility towards somebody **2. UNPLEASANT REMARK OR ACTION** a nasty remark or action (*often used in the plural*) **3. NASTY SITUATION** a situation that is disconcerting or unpleasant (*often used in the plural*)

unplug /un plúg/ (**-plugs, -plugging, -plugged**) *vt* **1. DISCONNECT ELECTRICAL APPLIANCE** to disconnect an electrical appliance by pulling its plug out of a socket **2. PULL PLUG OUT OF ELECTRIC SOCKET** to disconnect an electric plug or wire by pulling it out of a socket **3. TAKE STOPPER FROM SOMETHING** to remove a stopper, cork, or other plug from something **4. REMOVE BLOCKAGE FROM SOMETHING** to remove a blockage, clog, or other obstruction from something

unplugged /ún plúgd/ *adv* without the use of amplified musical instruments, especially guitars ■ *adj* performed without the use of amplified musical instruments, especially guitars

unplumbed /un plúmd/ *adj* **1. NOT FULLY EXAMINED** not thoroughly understood or investigated **2. NOT CHECKED FOR VERTICALITY** not checked for verticality with a plumb line **3. NOT MEASURED FOR DEPTH** not measured with a plumb line to determine depth **4. LACKING PLUMBING** having no plumbing or sanitation installed

unpolled /un pṓld/ *adj* **1. NOT INVITED TO PARTICIPATE IN POLL** not invited to participate in a survey of public opinion **2. NOT VOTING** not having cast a vote at an election **3.** *US* **NOT ON ELECTORAL ROLL** not included in a list of electors

unpopular /un póppyŏŏlər/ *adj* not liked by, approved of, or acceptable to a person, a group of people, or the general public —**unpopularity** /ún popyŏŏ lárrəti/ *n* —**unpopularly** *adv*

unpractised /un práktist/ *adj* **1. UNTRAINED OR INEXPERIENCED** lacking in training or experience **2. NOT DONE FREQUENTLY** not done or not commonly done **3. NOT REHEARSED** not prepared and tried out beforehand

unprecedented /un préssi dentid/ *adj* having no earlier parallel or equivalent

unpredictable /únpri díktəb'l/ *adj* not easily foreseen or predicted —**unpredictability** /únpri díktə bílləti/ *n* —**unpredictably** *adv*

unpremeditated /ún pree méddi taytid/ *adj* done without advance planning or thought —**unpremeditatedly** *adv*

unprepared /únpri páird/ *adj* **1. UNREADY** not ready for something or not expecting something to happen **2. NOT MADE READY** not having been prepared as required or expected **3. IMPROVISED** done without any preparation —**unpreparedly** /-páiridli/ *adv* —**unpreparedness** /-páiridnəss/ *n*

unprepossessing /ún preepə zéssing/ *adj* not producing a favourable impression —**unprepossessingly** *adv*

unpretending /únpri ténding/ *adj* not pretentious or affected

unpretentious /únpri ténshəss/ *adj* not putting on a false or showy display of importance, wealth, or knowledge —**unpretentiously** *adv* —**unpretentiousness** *n*

unprincipled /un prínssip'ld/ *adj* lacking, or resulting from a lack of, moral or ethical principles

unprintable /un príntəb'l/ *adj* not fit for publication, usually because of being obscene, libellous, or otherwise illegal or offensive

unproductive /únprə dúktiv/ *adj* **1.** not producing useful results, decisions, or achievements **2.** not producing much work or output —**unproductively** *adv* —**unproductiveness** *n* —**unproductivity** /un próddukt ívvəti/ *n*

unprofessional /únprə fésh'nəl/ *adj* **1. CONTRARY TO PROFESSIONAL STANDARDS** contrary to the expected standards of a profession **2. AMATEURISH** unworthy of a professional **3. NOT BELONGING TO PROFESSION** not having membership of a profession —**unprofessionalism** *n* —**unprofessionally** *adv*

unprofitable /un próffitəb'l/ *adj* **1.** not producing a profit **2.** not producing a desirable result or having a useful purpose —**unprofitability** /un próffitə bílləti/ *n* —**unprofitably** *adv*

UNPROFOR /ún prō fawr/ *abbr* United Nations Protection Force

unpromising /un prómmissing/ *adj* **1.** not likely to prove successful **2.** not favourable —**unpromisingly** *adv*

unprompted /un prómptid/ *adj* said or done without any encouragement or help

unpronounceable /únprə nównssəb'l/ *adj* very difficult or impossible to pronounce

unpronounced /únprə nównst/ *adj* **1.** not clear or easy to notice **2.** not sounded or pronounced

unprotected /únprə téktid/ *adj* **1. HAVING NO PROTECTION FROM HARM** having no protection against harm or damage ○ *With that insurance policy you're still unprotected against accidental damage.* **2. LACKING SAFETY PRECAUTIONS** not provided with something to prevent accident or injury ○ *an unprotected fire* **3. PERFORMED WITHOUT CONDOM** performed without the use of a condom ○ *unprotected sex* **4.** COMPUT **NOT LOCKED AGAINST UNAUTHORIZED CHANGES** not locked against changes by unauthorized users ○ *an unprotected computer network*

unprovided /únprə vídid/ *adj* **1.** not supplied or furnished with something **2.** not ready for something —**unprovidedly** *adv* ◇ **unprovided for** not provided with money or the means to live adequately

unpublishable /un púbblishəb'l/ *adj* not fit or feasible to publish, usually because of poor quality or expected poor sales

unputdownable /ún pŏŏt dównəb'l/ *adj* so interesting, entertaining, or exciting that the reader cannot stop reading (*informal*)

unqualified /un kwólli fīd/ *adj* **1. LACKING REQUIRED QUALIFICATIONS** having no academic, professional, or vocational qualifications **2. GIVEN WITHOUT RESERVATION** not limited or modified by any condition or reservation **3. TOTAL** complete and absolute ○ *an unqualified success* —**unqualifiedly** *adv*

unquestionable /un kwéschənəb'l/ *adj* **1.** impossible to doubt, question, or dispute **2.** acknowledged as not subject to doubt or open to question —**unquestionability** /un kwéschənə bílləti/ *n* —**unquestionably** *adv*

unquestioned /un kwéschənd/ *adj* **1.** not open to questioning, doubt, or dispute **2.** not asked a question or questions

unquestioning /un kwéschəning/ *adj* not asking questions, expressing doubt, or hesitating because of questions or doubts —**unquestioningly** *adv*

unquiet /un kwī́ ət/ *adj* **1. NOISY OR TURBULENT** full of noise or unrest **2. ANXIOUS** unsettled or restless, especially in thought or feeling ■ *n* **1. NOISE OR UNREST** a state of noisiness or unrest **2. ANXIETY** restlessness or uneasiness —**unquietly** *adv* —**unquietness** *n*

unquote /un kwṓt/ *adv* used when speaking to indicate where the end of a quotation falls ○ *He said, quote, You're fired, unquote.*

unquoted /un kwṓtid/ *adj* not listed or quoted on a stock exchange

unraised /ún ráyzd/ *adj* **1.** made without yeast and therefore fairly flat and firm in consistency **2.** not moved, lifted, or increased to a raised position or level

unravel /un rávv'l/ (**-els, -elling, -elled**) *v* **1.** *vti* **UNDO KNITTED STRANDS, OR BECOME UNDONE** to undo the knitted or woven yarn, thread, or other strands of something, or become undone by having the strands come apart **2.** *vti* **BECOME OR MAKE SOMETHING UNDERSTANDABLE** to make the complexities of something clear and understandable, or become clear and understandable **3.** *vti* **DISENTANGLE OR BECOME DISENTANGLED** to separate something out from a tangle or other mass, or become disentangled or separated out **4.** *vi* **START TO FAIL** to begin to fail or come to an end

unread /un réd/ *adj* **1. NOT READ** not read, especially by a usual or intended reader **2. NOT WELL READ** having read very little and consequently lacking knowledge acquired from reading **3. LACKING KNOWLEDGE OF SUBJECT** not acquainted with a particular subject through reading

unreadable /un reédəb'l/ *adj* **1. NOT ENJOYABLE TO READ** impossible to read through being boring, badly written, or intellectually difficult **2. ILLEGIBLE** consisting of letters, words, or symbols that are difficult to identify **3. IMPOSSIBLE TO INTERPRET** impossible to interpret or make sense of ○ *his unreadable face* —**unreadability** /ún reedə bílləti/ *n* —**unreadably** *adv*

unready /un réddi/ *adj* **1. UNAVAILABLE** not available or prepared for use **2. NOT PREPARED TO DO SOMETHING** not prepared or available to do something or to act **3. LACKING MENTAL ALERTNESS** lacking or displaying a lack of mental alertness or quickness —**unreadily** *adv* —**unreadiness** *n*

unreal /un reél, un reé əl/ *adj* **1. NOT EXISTING** having no substance, reality, or existence **2. FALSE** not true or genuine **3. IMAGINARY** imaginary or dreamlike **4. EXCELLENT** excellent or extremely good (*informal*) **5. INCREDIBLE** difficult to believe (*informal*) —**unreally** *adv*

unreality /únri álləti/ (*plural* **-ties**) *n* **1. UNREAL QUALITY** an unreal or seemingly unreal state or quality **2. UNREAL THING** something that is not real, genuine, or true, or that lacks substance **3. INABILITY TO FACE REALITY** an inability to accept reality

unreason /un reéz'n/ *n* lack of reason or rationality

unreasonable /un reéz'nəb'l/ *adj* **1.** not acting with or subject to reason **2.** going beyond accepted or

reasonable limits —**unreasonableness** *n* —**unreasonably** *adv*

unreasonable behaviour *n* behaviour that is considered unacceptable in a marital relationship and constitutes grounds for divorce

unreasoned /un réez'nd/ *adj* not resulting from sound reasoning

unreasoning /un réez'ning/ *adj* not guided by sound judgment or reasoning —**unreasoningly** *adv*

unreckonable /un rékənəb'l/ *adj* impossible to calculate

unreconstructed /ún reekən strúktid/ *adj* **1.** retaining outdated beliefs, views, or practices **2.** not rebuilt, restored, or recreated

unreel /un réel/ (**-reels, -reeling, -reeled**) *vti* to unwind something from a reel, or become unwound from it

unreeve /un réev/ (**-reeves, -reeving, -rove** /-rṓv/, **-reeved** or **-rove**) *vti* to pull out a rope or cable from a block or thimble on a ship, or be pulled out from a block or thimble

unrefined /únri fínd/ *adj* **1.** not processed to remove impurities or unwanted substances **2.** not in accord with socially acceptable manners and tastes

unreflecting /únri flékting/ *adj* showing or resulting from a lack of deep or serious thinking —**unreflectingly** *adv*

unreflective /únri fléktiv/ *adj* not thinking or reflecting or resulting from a tendency to not think or reflect —**unreflectively** *adv*

unregenerate /únri jénnərət/ *adj* **1. NOT REFORMED** not reborn spiritually and not repentant **2. VIOLATING SOCIAL OR MORAL STRUCTURES** behaving in a way regarded as violating social or moral structures **3. CLINGING TO OUTDATED BELIEFS** retaining outdated beliefs, views, or practices **4. STUBBORN** unyielding or stubborn —**unregeneracy** *n* —**unregenerately** *adv*

unrelenting /únri lénting/ *adj* **1.** unyielding or unswerving in determination or resolve **2.** not weakening, easing up, or otherwise diminishing in strength, speed, or effort —**unrelentingly** *adv* —**unrelentingness** *n*

unreliable /únri lí əb'l/ *adj* not able to be relied on or trusted —**unreliability** /-lī ə bílləti/ *n* —**unreliably** *adv*

unremarkable /únri máarkəb'l/ *adj* not worthy of special notice or attention because of being ordinary or common

unremarked /únri máarkt/ *adj* not noticed or observed

unremitting /únri mítting/ *adj* continuing, persisting, or recurring without diminishing or ceasing —**unremittingly** *adv* —**unremittingness** *n*

unrepeatable /únri péetəb'l/ *adj* **1.** too offensive or shocking for the hearer to wish to repeat ○ *His answer was unrepeatable!* **2.** not able to be done or made again ○ *an unrepeatable performance*

unrequited /únri kwítid/ *adj* **1.** not felt in response, or not returned in the same way or to the same degree **2.** not avenged —**unrequitedly** *adv*

unreserve /únri zúrv/ *n* a lack of reserve in showing and expressing feelings or opinions

unreserved /únri zúrvd/ *adj* **1. NOT RESERVED FOR SPECIFIC USE** not set aside or retained for a specific person or group of people to use **2. GIVEN WITHOUT QUALIFICATION** not limited or modified by any condition or reservation **3. FRANK OR OPEN** not cautious, restrained, or reticent —**unreservedly** /-zúrvidli/ *adv* —**unreservedness** /-zúrvidnəss/ *n*

unrest /un rést/ *n* **1.** social or political discontent or protest that disrupts the established order **2.** a disturbed, unsettled, or uneasy mental or emotional state

unrestrained /únri stráynd/ *adj* **1.** not subject to control, restriction, or restraint **2.** natural and uninhibited —**unrestrainedly** /-stráynidli/ *adv* —**unrestrainedness** /-stráynidnəss/ *n*

unriddle /un rídd'l/ (**-dles, -dling, -dled**) *vt* to find a solution or explanation for something

unrifled /un ríf'ld/ *adj* having no spiral grooves (**rifling**) cut on the inside of the barrel

unrighteous /un ríchəss/ *adj* **1.** sinful or evil **2.** not just, fair, or right —**unrighteously** *adv* —**unrighteousness** *n*

unrip /un ríp/ (**-rips, -ripping, -ripped**) *vt* **1.** to open something by ripping **2.** to reveal or divulge something (*archaic*)

unripe /un ríp/ (**-riper, -ripest**) *adj* **1.** not yet ripe or mature **2.** not yet complete or fully developed —**unripeness** *n*

unrivalled /un rív'ld/ *adj* having no rival or equal

unroll /un rṓl/ (**-rolls, -rolling, -rolled**) *vti* **1.** to unwind, uncoil, or open up something that is rolled up, or become unwound, uncoiled, or opened up **2.** to disclose something gradually and smoothly, or become disclosed in this way

unround /un równd/ (**-rounds, -rounding, -rounded**) *vt* to pronounce a sound with the lips kept flat —**unround** *adj*

unrove NAUT past participle, past tense of **unreeve**

UNRRA, **Unrra** *abbr* United Nations Relief and Rehabilitation Administration

unruffled /un rúff'ld/ *adj* **1.** calm and poised, especially in a crisis **2.** having a smooth surface, especially in having no ripples

unruly /un róoli/ (**-lier, -liest**) *adj* difficult to control, manage, discipline, or govern [15C. < archaic *ruly* 'disciplined, observing rules' < RULE] —**unruliness** *n*

SYNONYMS ***unruly, intractable, recalcitrant, obstreperous, wilful, wild, wayward***

CORE MEANING: not submitting to control

unruly difficult to control, manage, discipline, or govern ○ *Police tried to subdue the more unruly elements of the crowd.* ○ *an unruly student who disrupts and unsettles the class* **intractable** stubbornly refusing to be controlled or submit to discipline ○ *Barbara had made up her mind, and she is intractable once she has an idea.* ○ *the problem created by intractable people who refuse to eat the right food to ameliorate their condition* **recalcitrant** stubbornly resisting the authority of another person or group ○ *an armed force sufficient to enforce the law on recalcitrant individuals* ○ *When she spoke, it was in the voice that she reserved for very recalcitrant children.* **obstreperous** noisily and aggressively boisterous ○ *an incident between a shop assistant and an obstreperous customer* **wilful** stubbornly determined to act on a desire, regardless of the opinions or advice of others ○ *a wilful refusal to answer these specific questions* ○ *the challenge of bringing up a wilful child* **wild** showing a disregard for rules or restraint ○ *We were young, inexperienced, and inclined to be rather wild.* **wayward** disobedient and uncontrollable ○ *The boy's mother found it hard to keep track of her other sometimes wayward children.*

UNRWA, **Unrwa** *abbr* United Nations Relief and Works Agency

unsaddle /un sádd'l/ (**-dles, -dling, -dled**) *v* **1.** *vti* to take a saddle from a horse **2.** *vt* to throw a rider from a saddle

unsaddling enclosure /un sáddling-/ *n* an enclosure at a racecourse where the horses are brought after a race to have their saddles removed. Prizes are sometimes presented there.

unsaid /un séd/ past participle, past tense of **unsay** ■ *adj* not spoken of or discussed, although thought about

unsatisfactory /ún satiss fáktəri/ *adj* not adequate, acceptable, or satisfying —**unsatisfactorily** *adv* —**unsatisfactoriness** *n*

unsaturate /un sáchərət/ *n* an unsaturated chemical compound

unsaturated /un sáchə raytid/ *adj* **1. ABLE TO CONTINUE TO DISSOLVE** able to dissolve more of a substance **2. ABLE TO FORM MORE CARBON BONDS** having or able to form double and triple carbon bonds **3.** FOOD **HAVING MOLECULES WITH DOUBLE BONDS** describes fats with a high proportion of fatty acid molecules with double bonds, that create less cholesterol in the body than saturated fats and are regarded as more healthy in the diet

unsavoury /un sáyvəri/ *adj* **1. DISTASTEFUL** not pleasant or agreeable **2. IMMORAL** morally unacceptable **3. UNAPPETIZING** tasting or smelling unappetizing —**unsavourily** *adv* —**unsavouriness** *n*

unsay /un sáy/ (**-says** /-séz/, **-saying, -said** /-séd/) *vt* to take back something said so that it is as if it has never been said

unsayable /un sáy əb'l/ *adj* difficult or impossible to say or speak about

unscathed /un skáythd/ *adj* not hurt, damaged, or harmed in any way

unschooled /un skóold/ *adj* **1.** not educated or trained **2.** innate and not acquired by education or training

unscientific /ún sī ən tíffik/ *adj* **1.** not following or compatible with the methods and principles of science **2.** not possessing knowledge about science and its methods and principles —**unscientifically** *adv*

unscramble /un skrámb'l/ (**-bles, -bling, -bled**) *vt* **1.** to restore order to something jumbled or confused **2.** to make a message understandable by undoing the effects of scrambling, especially electronic scrambling —**unscrambler** *n*

unscrew /un skróo/ (**-screws, -screwing, -screwed**) *vti* **1. REMOVE OR LOOSEN SCREWS OF SOMETHING** to remove or loosen a screw or screws holding something in place, or have a screw or screws removed or loosened **2. OPEN SOMETHING BY REMOVING THREADED LID** to open something by turning and removing a threaded lid or cap, or be opened in this way **3. TURN TO REMOVE OR ADJUST SOMETHING** to remove or adjust something by rotating, or be removed or adjusted by rotating

unscripted /un skríptid/ *adj* **1.** not having a script that was written or agreed on in advance **2.** not planned or expected

unscrupulous /un skróopyooləss/ *adj* not restrained by moral or ethical principles —**unscrupulously** *adv* —**unscrupulousness** *n*

unseal /un séel/ (**-seals, -sealing, -sealed**) *vt* **1.** to break or remove the seal of something, or to open something by breaking a seal or closure **2.** to free something from constraint or restriction —**unsealable** *adj*

unsealed road /únseeld-/ *n ANZ* a dirt road that has no tar or bitumen surface

unseam /un séem/ (**-seams, -seaming, -seamed**) *vt* to unpick a seam or seams of something

unsearchable /un súrchəb'l/ *adj* not capable of being searched or investigated —**unsearchableness** *n* —**unsearchably** *adv*

unseasonable /un séez'nəb'l/ *adj* **1.** not usual or appropriate for the time of year **2.** not occurring at the right time or at a good time —**unseasonableness** *n* —**unseasonably** *adv*

unseat /un séet/ (**-seats, -seating, -seated**) *vt* **1.** to remove somebody from office or a position, especially by means of an election **2.** to eject somebody from a seat, especially a saddle

unsecured /únssi kyóord, -kyáwrd/ *adj* **1. LACKING SECURITY** not protected against financial loss **2. NOT MADE SECURE** not fastened, held in place, or otherwise made secure **3. UNPROTECTED FROM BUGGING** not protected against electronic eavesdropping

unseeded /un séedid/ *adj* not assigned a position in a draw arranged so that the best players or teams can, in theory, avoid meeting until the later rounds

unseemly /un séemli/ *adj* **1. NOT IN GOOD TASTE** contrary to accepted standards of good taste or appropriate behaviour **2. INCONVENIENT** occurring at an inconvenient time or place ■ *adv* **IN UNSEEMLY MANNER** in an improper or inappropriate manner —**unseemliness** *n*

unseen /ún séen/ *adj* **1. NOT SEEN** not observed, noticed, watched, or examined **2. DONE WITHOUT PRACTICE** done or comprehended without previous study or practice **3. TRANSLATED AT SIGHT** translated without preparation, especially in a test or examination ■ *n* **UNSEEN TRANSLATION** a text for translation without preparation, especially in a test or examination

unselfish /un sélfish/ *adj* putting the general good or the needs or interests of others first —**unselfishly** *adv* —**unselfishness** *n*

unsell /un sél/ (**-sells, -selling, -sold** /-sṓld/) *vt US* to convince somebody that something is false or worthless

unset /un sét/ *adj* **1. NOT HARDENED** not hardened or firm **2. NOT READY** not prepared or made ready **3. NOT MOUNTED** not mounted in a jewellery setting

unsettle /un sétt'l/ (**-tles, -tling, -tled**) *vt* **1.** to make somebody ill at ease or insecure **2.** to disrupt the orderly, fixed, or established state of something —**unsettlement** *n*

unsettled /un sétt'ld/ *adj* **1. NOT DECIDED** not resolved, determined, or decided ○ *an unsettled issue* **2. CHANGEABLE** changing frequently within a given period of time ○ *unsettled weather* **3. LACKING ORDER OR STABILITY** characterized by a lack of order or stability ○ *an unsettled political climate* **4. NOT LEGALLY RESOLVED** not

resolved as required by law ○ *an unsettled lawsuit* **5.** UNCERTAIN not sure, or full of doubt ○ *He was unsettled about his future at the firm.* **6.** MOVING not being in a condition or position of rest ○ *unsettled sediment in the water* **7.** UNINHABITED not yet inhabited or colonized ○ *unsettled territory* **8.** UNPAID not paid or fulfilled ○ *unsettled debts* **9.** ITINERANT not regular or fixed ○ *an unsettled lifestyle* —**unsettledness** *n*

unsettling /un séttling/ *adj* producing a feeling of unease or insecurity

unsex /un séks/ (**-sexes, -sexing, -sexed**) *vt* **1.** to strip away from somebody the qualities stereotypically associated with his or her sex ○ *'Come, you spirits / That tend on mortal thoughts, unsex me here'* (William Shakespeare, *Macbeth*; c. 1605) **2.** to deprive somebody of the ability to have sex

UNSF *abbr* United Nations Special Fund for Economic Development

unshackle /un shák'l/ (**-les, -ling, -led**) *vt* **1.** to release somebody from restrictions or constraints **2.** to release somebody from shackles

unshakable /un sháykəb'l/, **unshakeable** *adj* not subject to doubt or uncertainty —**unshakably** *adv*

unshaped /un sháypt/, **unshapen** /-sháyp'n/ *adj* **1.** not yet shaped, formed, or finished **2.** having a final or finished form or state that is imperfect

unsheathe /un shee̱th/ (**-sheathes, -sheathing, -sheathed**) *vt* to remove a sword from a sheath

unshift /un shíft/ (**-shifts, -shifting, -shifted**) *vi* to release the depressed shift key on the keyboard of a computer or typewriter

unship /un shíp/ (**-ships, -shipping, -shipped**) *vti* **1.** to unload something from a ship, or be unloaded **2.** to move something out of its usual position on a ship, or be moved out of the usual position on a ship

unshod /un shód/ *adj* not wearing shoes or horseshoes

unshriven /un shrívv'n/ *adj* not having confessed sins to a priest and been given absolution

unsighted /un sītid/ *adj* **1.** UNDETECTED not seen or noticed **2.** NOT FITTED WITH SIGHT FOR AIMING not fitted with a sight or sights to help with aiming **3.** WITHOUT CLEAR VIEW not having a clear view, e.g. because of an obstruction

unsightly /un sītli/ *adj* not pleasant to look at, or spoiling the appearance of something ○ *an unsightly addition to the building* —**unsightliness** *n*

SYNONYMS See *unattractive*.

unsigned /un sīnd/ *adj* **1.** LACKING SIGNATURE having no signature **2.** NOT SIGNED TO PLAY FOR TEAM not having signed a contract to join a sports team as a player **3.** MATHS, COMPUT LACKING PLUS OR MINUS SIGN having no plus or minus sign, or having no digit in binary notation representing a positive or negative value

unskilful /un skílf'l/ *adj* lacking or done without skill or expertise —**unskilfully** *adv* —**unskilfulness** *n*

unskilled /ún skíld/ *adj* **1.** NOT REQUIRING SPECIAL SKILLS not requiring special training, education, or skill **2.** LACKING SKILL lacking skill or the basic or proper skills **3.** LACKING TRAINING lacking the skills acquired through technical training or higher education **4.** DONE WITHOUT SKILL done without skill, or displaying a lack of the basic or proper skills

unslaked lime /ún sláykt-/ *n* CHEM same as **calcium hydroxide**

unsling /un slíng/ (**-slings, -slinging, -slung** /-slúng/) *vt* **1.** REMOVE SOMETHING SLUNG to remove something that has been slung, especially over the shoulder or shoulders **2.** REMOVE SOMETHING FROM SLING to take something out of a sling **3.** NAUT REMOVE SUPPORTING ROPES FROM SOMETHING to remove the supporting ropes or chains (**slings**) from something

unsmiling /un smīling/ *adj* looking serious and showing no signs of pleasure, amusement, or approval ○ *his grim unsmiling manner*

unsnag /un snág/ (**-snags, -snagging, -snagged**) *vt* **1.** to free something caught on an obstruction **2.** to remove a difficulty or difficulties impeding the progress or development of something

unsnap /un snáp/ (**-snaps, -snapping, -snapped**) *vt* to release or open something by unfastening a press stud or press studs

unsnarl /un snaárl/ (**-snarls, -snarling, -snarled**) *vt* to free something from a snarl or snarls

unsociable /un sṓshəb'l/ *adj* **1.** not liking or seeking the company of other people **2.** not favouring or encouraging social interaction —**unsociability** /ún sṑshə bílləti/ *n* —**unsociableness** *n* —**unsociably** *adv*

USAGE unsociable or **antisocial**? These words can both refer to somebody who avoids the company of others, but ***unsociable*** is less strong in force than ***antisocial***, which often indicates behaviour or attitudes that are hostile or indifferent to other people.

unsocial /un sṓsh'l/ *adj* **1.** PREFERRING OWN COMPANY not liking or seeking the company of other people **2.** CHARACTERISTIC OF UNSOCIAL PERSON characterized or caused by a dislike of the company of other people **3.** ANTISOCIAL annoying, inconsiderate, or indifferent to the needs of others **4.** OUTSIDE USUAL WORKING HOURS relating to or done at a time outside usual working hours —**unsocially** *adv*

unsold /ún sṓld/ COMM past participle, past tense of **unsell** ■ *adj* not bought by anybody

unsolicited /únssə líssitid/ *adj* given, sent, or received without being requested

unsophisticated /únssə físti kaytid/ *adj* **1.** naive, inexperienced, and not wise in the ways of the world **2.** simple and lacking in refinements —**unsophisticatedly** *adv* —**unsophisticatedness** *n* —**unsophistication** /únssə fisti káysh'n/ *n*

unsought /un sáwt/ *adj* not looked for or asked for

unsound /un sównd/ *adj* **1.** NOT RELIABLE not based on reliable facts, information, or reasoning ○ *an unsound conclusion* **2.** UNHEALTHY not in a healthy physical or psychological state **3.** NOT SOLID OR FIRM in a structurally poor or dangerous state ○ *unsound foundations* **4.** FINANCIALLY INSECURE not safe or secure financially ○ *an unsound investment* **5.** DISTURBED AND NOT RESTFUL characterized by periods of restlessness ○ *unsound sleep* —**unsoundly** *adv* —**unsoundness** *n*

unsparing /un spáiring/ *adj* **1.** not frugal or stingy with something **2.** harsh or without mercy —**unsparingly** *adv* —**unsparingness** *n*

unspeakable /un speékəb'l/ *adj* **1.** EXTREMELY BAD OR AWFUL so bad or awful as to be impossible to describe in words **2.** NOT DESCRIBABLE IN WORDS incapable of being described in words **3.** NOT TO BE SPOKEN OF not allowed to be spoken of, mentioned, or talked about —**unspeakableness** *n* —**unspeakably** *adv*

unspecialized /un spéshə līzd/, **unspecialised** *adj* **1.** not having a special use or purpose **2.** not concerned or involved with just one specialized area of knowledge or skill

unspoiled /ún spóyld/, **unspoilt** /-spóylt/ *adj* **1.** UNCHANGED BY DEVELOPMENT not changed for the worse by modern civilization, industry, or tourism **2.** NOT DAMAGED not damaged or physically harmed **3.** UNFLAWED not lessened or diminished by flaws or imperfections **4.** NOT RUINED IN CHARACTER not ruined in character as a result of success, wealth, or being overindulged

unspoken /un spṓkən/ *adj* not uttered or talked about, although thought about

unsportsmanlike /un spáwrtsmən līk/ *adj* being or acting contrary to fair play or the rules and spirit of a sport or of sport in general

unspotted /un spóttid/ *adj* **1.** NOT SPOTTED OR STAINED not soiled with spots or stains **2.** MORALLY UNBLEMISHED not marred by moral or ethical lapses or failures **3.** UNOBSERVED not seen or observed

unsprung /un sprúng/ *adj* having no springs or having the springs removed

unstable /un stáyb'l/ *adj* **1.** NOT FIXED not firm, solid, or fixed ○ *unstable ground* **2.** LIKELY TO FALL OR COLLAPSE likely to fall, collapse, or sway ○ *unstable scaffolding* **3.** LACKING EMOTIONAL OR PSYCHOLOGICAL STABILITY lacking, or resulting from a lack of, emotional control or psychological stability ○ *unstable behaviour* **4.** CHANGEABLE apt to change ○ *unstable weather* **5.** UNSTEADY IN PURPOSE OR INTENT unsteady or unsure in purpose or intent ○ *political support that is unstable* **6.** PHYS HAVING SHORT HALF-LIFE having a brief existence or half-life **7.** PHYS SUBJECT TO SPONTANEOUS CHANGE describes a particle that is subject to spontaneous change such as radioactive decay —**unstableness** *n* —**unstably** *adv*

unsteady /un stéddi/ *adj* **1.** NOT FIXED not firm, solid, or fixed **2.** TOTTERING staggering or tottering in walking **3.** LIKELY TO MOVE likely to move or shift position ○ *an unsteady ladder* **4.** CHANGEABLE subject to large and frequent changes ○ *unsteady financial markets* **5.** IRREGULAR IN RHYTHM irregular in movement, rhythm, or pitch ○ *a voice that is unsteady* **6.** NOT CONSTANT OR RELIABLE not constant in purpose or actions ■ *vt* (**-ies, -ying, -ied**) MAKE SOMETHING UNSTEADY to cause something to become unsteady —**unsteadily** *adv* —**unsteadiness** *n*

unsteel /un steél/ (**-steels, -steeling, -steeled**) *vt* to soften or weaken somebody's harsh attitude or firm resolve

unstep /un stép/ (**-steps, -stepping, -stepped**) *vt* to take a mast out of its step or socket

unstick /un stík/ *v* (**-sticks, -sticking, -stuck** /-stúk/) **1.** *vt* MAKE SOMETHING STOP STICKING to cause something to stop sticking **2.** *vti* TAKE OFF FROM GROUND to cause an aircraft to take off, or take off in an aircraft (*informal*) ■ *n* TAKEOFF a takeoff in an aircraft (*informal*)

unstinting /un stínting/ *adj* given or giving generously —**unstintingly** *adv*

unstop /un stóp/ (**-stops, -stopping, -stopped**) *vt* **1.** TAKE STOPPER FROM SOMETHING to remove a stopper from something **2.** UNBLOCK SOMETHING to remove a blockage from something **3.** MUSIC PULL OUT STOPS OF ORGAN to pull out the stops of an organ

unstoppable /un stóppəb'l/ *adj* not capable of being halted, or not easily halted —**unstoppably** *adv*

unstopped /un stópt/ *adj* **1.** NOT BLOCKED OR STOPPERED not blocked, closed, or stoppered **2.** NOT HALTED able to continue without being halted **3.** PHON ARTICULATED WITH VOCAL ORGANS PARTLY OPEN articulated without a complete closure of the vocal organs

unstrained /un stráynd/ *adj* **1.** not put through a strainer to remove lumps **2.** not subjected to strain

unstratified /un strátti fīd/ *adj* **1.** not arranged in or forming layers or strata **2.** not arranged in or forming social classes, grades, or ranks

unstreamed /ún streémd/ *adj* not split into groups on the basis of ability or educational achievement

unstressed /un strést/ *adj* **1.** not accented or emphasized in pronunciation **2.** not subjected to physical, psychological, or emotional pressure

unstriated /un strī aytid/ *adj* lacking transverse striations

unstring /un stríng/ (**-strings, -stringing, -strung** /-strúng/) *vt* **1.** REMOVE STRINGS OF SOMETHING to remove or loosen a string or strings of something **2.** REMOVE SOMETHING FROM STRING to remove something from a string or wire **3.** UPSET SOMEBODY to make somebody upset or nervous

unstructured /un strúkchərd/ *adj* **1.** NOT ORGANIZED INTO HIERARCHY not organized into a hierarchy or similar system **2.** NOT ORDERED OR CONVENTIONALLY ARRANGED not forced to conform to a specific order or arrangement, especially a conventional one **3.** CLOTHING LOOSE AND FLOWING not tailored to fit tightly, but flowing freely

unstrung /un strúng/ past participle, past tense of **unstring** ■ *adj* **1.** UPSET upset or nervous **2.** LACKING STRINGS having a string or strings missing, removed, or loosened **3.** NOT ON STRING not threaded on a string or wire

unstuck /un stúk/ past participle, past tense of **unstick** ■ *adj* freed from being stuck or adhering to something ◇ **come unstuck** to fail or experience a setback (*informal*)

unstudied /un stúddid/ *adj* **1.** NATURAL natural or casual in manner **2.** NOT LEARNED THROUGH STUDYING not acquired through studying or training **3.** NOT KNOWLEDGEABLE lacking the knowledge and understanding of a particular field that is acquired through studying or training

unsubscribe /únsəb scríb/ *vi* to end a subscription to or registration with something, especially an e-mail mailing list

unsubstantial /únssəb stánsh'l/ *adj* **1.** IMMATERIAL not having physical substance **2.** FLIMSY not strong or firm **3.** NOT TRUE OR BASED ON FACT having no basis in truth or fact —**unsubstantiality** /-stanshi álləti/ *n* —**unsubstantially** *adv*

unsubstantiated /únssəb stánshi aytid/ *adj* not proven factually

unsuccessful /únssək sésf'l/ *adj* **1.** NOT RESULTING IN SUCCESS not resulting in success or turning out favourably **2.** NOT ACHIEVING SUCCESS not achieving an intended aim or goal **3.** LACKING RECORD OF SIGNIFICANT ACHIEVEMENTS not having achieved or gained wealth, fame, or power —**unsuccessfully** *adv* —**unsuccessfulness** *n*

unsuitable /un sóotəb'l/ *adj* not appropriate or becoming —**unsuitability** /un sóotə bílləti/ *n* —**unsuitableness** *n* —**unsuitably** *adv*

unsung /un súng/ *adj* **1.** not given the praise or honour that is due **2.** not sung or not to be sung

unsupportable /únssə páwrtəb'l/ *adj* **1. INDEFENSIBLE** impossible to defend or excuse **2. INTOLERABLE** impossible to tolerate or endure **3. IMPOSSIBLE TO SUPPORT PHYSICALLY** impossible to support physically in order to prevent collapse

unsure /un shóor, -sháwr/ *adj* **1. UNCERTAIN** lacking clear knowledge or a definite opinion **2. NOT CONFIDENT** lacking in confidence **3. NOT FIXED OR SECURE** not firm or secure **4. UNRELIABLE** not trustworthy or reliable —**unsurely** *adv* —**unsureness** *n*

SYNONYMS See ***doubtful***.

unsurprising /únssər prízing/ *adj* not causing surprise, usually because not unexpected —**unsurprisingly** *adv*

unsuspected /únssə spéktid/ *adj* **1.** not known or believed to exist **2.** not under suspicion of having done something —**unsuspectedly** *adv*

unsuspecting /únssə spékting/ *adj* not suspicious of somebody or something —**unsuspectingly** *adv*

unswerving /un swúrving/ *adj* **1.** firm and unchanging in intent or purpose **2.** not turning to the side or otherwise altering the direction of movement —**unswervingly** *adv*

untangle /un táng g'l/ (**-gles, -gling, -gled**) *vt* **1. REMOVE TANGLES FROM SOMETHING** to undo the tangles in something such as yarn or hair **2. STRAIGHTEN OUT SOMETHING COMPLEX** to clarify or resolve something that is intricate or puzzling **3. FREE SOMEBODY FROM BAD SITUATION** to remove somebody from a difficult or complicated situation

untapped /ún tápt/ *adj* **1.** not yet in use, but available ○ *untapped talents* **2.** not yet opened or tapped

untaught /un táwt/ *adj* **1.** ignorant or lacking a formal education **2.** arising from innate or natural talent or ability, not from instruction

unteach /un téech/ (**-teaches, -teaching, -taught** /-táwt/) *vt US* **1.** to cause somebody to forget something previously learned **2.** to reverse somebody's opinion or belief about something previously learned

untenable /un ténnəb'l/ *adj* lacking the qualities such as sound reasoning or high ground that make defence possible ○ *an untenable position* —**untenability** /un ténnə bílləti/ *n* —**untenableness** *n* —**untenably** *adv*

untether /un té<u>th</u>ər/ (**-ers, -ering, -ered**) *vt* **1.** to free a person or animal from a restraining rope or other tie **2.** to give vent to something such as an emotion after keeping it suppressed —**untethered** *adj*

unthink /un thíngk/ (**-thinks, -thinking, -thought** /-tháwt/) *vt* **1.** to stop thinking about something **2.** to change a view or opinion about something

unthinkable /un thíngkəb'l/ *adj* **1. OUT OF QUESTION** too strange or extreme even to be considered **2. INCONCEIVABLE** impossible even to conceive of **3. UNLIKELY TO HAPPEN** highly unlikely to happen or succeed **4. TERRIBLE** extremely frightening or unpleasant —**unthinkability** /un thíngkə bílləti/ *n* —**unthinkably** *adv*

unthinking /un thíngking/ *adj* **1. INCONSIDERATE** not thoughtful or considerate of other people **2. HEEDLESS** not giving proper consideration to the possible effects or consequences of what is said or done **3. UNAWARE** unable or unwilling to think deeply about things —**unthinkingly** *adv* —**unthinkingness** *n*

unthought past participle, past tense of **unthink**

unthread /un thréd/ (**-threads, -threading, -threaded**) *vt* to remove the thread or threads from something

untidy /un tídi/ *adj* (**-dier, -diest**) **1. NOT NEAT** not neat or tidy **2. DISORDERED** not properly organized or ordered ■ *vt* (**-dies, -dying, -died**) **MESS SOMETHING UP** to mess up something that was tidy —**untidily** *adv* —**untidiness** *n*

untie /un tí/ (**-ties, -tying, -tied**) *v* **1.** *vti* to loosen or unfasten a knot or similar fastening in something such as a string, ribbon, or rope, or be loosened or unfastened **2.** *vt* to release or free somebody or something that is tied up

until /ən tíl, un tíl/ *conj, prep* **1.** up to a time or event, but not afterwards ○ (conj) *I lived with my grandparents until I was ten.* ○ (prep) *from the late 1980s until 1994* **2.** before a time or event (*used in negative statements*) ○ (conj) *She agreed not to write about the case until a verdict was reached.* ○ (prep) *He did not open his mail until Monday.* [12C. < assumed Old Norse *und* 'till' + TILL[1]]

USAGE See ***till***[1].

~~**untill**~~ incorrect spelling of **until**

untimely /un tímli/ *adj* **1. OCCURRING AT BAD TIME** happening or done at a bad or inconvenient time ○ *an untimely decision* **2. PREMATURE** happening before the expected time ○ *his untimely death* ■ *adv* (*archaic*) **1. AT INAPPROPRIATE TIME** at a bad or inconvenient time **2. PREMATURELY** earlier than wanted or expected —**untimeliness** *n*

untiring /un tíring/ *adj* **1.** not becoming weary or exhausted **2.** continuing in spite of difficulty or frustration ○ *her untiring efforts* —**untiringly** *adv*

untitled /un tít'ld/ *adj* **1. UNNAMED** not having a name or title **2. NOT BELONGING TO NOBILITY** possessing no aristocratic title **3. WITHOUT PROPER CLAIM** having no legitimate right or claim

unto *stressed* /úntoo/; *unstressed* /úntóo/ *prep* (*archaic*) **1.** used to indicate that something is said, given, or done to somebody ○ *the elders of Gilead said unto Jephthah* ○ *and they said unto God* **2.** used to indicate that something continues until a particular time ○ *faithful unto death* [13C. < UNTIL, with TO[1] replacing TILL[1]]

untold /ún tóld/ *adj* **1.** too great or numerous to be properly described or counted **2.** not having been revealed or related

untouchable /un túchəb'l/ *adj* **1. NOT TO BE TOUCHED** not able or allowed to be touched **2. OUT OF REACH** completely out of reach **3. ABOVE CRITICISM** too well known or important to be investigated or criticized **4. DISAGREEABLE TO TOUCH** unpleasant or disagreeable to touch ■ *n also* **Untouchable OFFENSIVE TERM** an offensive term for a member of the hereditary Hindu class that was formerly segregated and regarded as ritually unclean by the four castes, and performed tasks that were considered polluting. Gandhi's alternative term (**Harijan**) meaning 'children of God' has also been rejected by many in favour of a term (**Dalit**) meaning 'the oppressed'. —**untouchability** /un túchə bílləti/ *n* —**untouchably** *adv*

untouched /un túcht/ *adj* **1. UNINJURED** not injured, damaged, or harmed **2. NOT TOUCHED** not touched or handled **3. UNEATEN** not eaten or consumed **4. UNALTERED** not changed or altered **5. EMOTIONALLY UNAFFECTED** emotionally unaffected by something **6. NOT MENTIONED** omitted from mention or discussion

untoward /úntə wáwrd/ *adj* **1. INAPPROPRIATE** not appropriate or fitting ○ *untoward rudeness* **2. UNEXPECTED** unusual or unexpected ○ *an untoward piece of luck* **3. CAUSING MISFORTUNE** causing misfortune or disadvantage ○ *several untoward events* —**untowardly** *adv* —**untowardness** *n*

untrammelled /un trámm'ld/ *adj* not restricted or restrained

untravelled /un trávv'ld/ *adj* **1.** not having wide knowledge or experience of the world **2.** never or rarely travelled along ○ *an untravelled path*

untried /ún tríd/ *adj* **1.** not tried, tested, or proved **2.** not tried in a court of law

untroubled /un trúbb'ld/ *adj* **1.** not bothered, uneasy, or distracted by something **2.** tranquil and without disturbances ○ *untroubled sleep*

untrue /un tróo/ *adj* **1. WRONG OR FALSE** not in accordance with the facts or what is known **2. UNFAITHFUL** not faithful or loyal to somebody **3. NOT PRECISE** not precise or accurate according to a standard or measure —**untruly** *adv*

untruth /un tróoth/ *n* **1.** something that is presented as being true, but is actually false ○ *accused of telling untruths* **2.** a lack of truth, especially as a result of lying

SYNONYMS See ***lie***[2].

untruthful /un tróothf'l/ *adj* **1.** not in accordance with the facts or what is known **2.** lying or failing to tell the truth —**untruthfully** *adv* —**untruthfulness** *n*

untutored /un tyóotərd/ *adj* **1.** not formally educated or trained **2.** lacking any awareness of or interest in what is socially acceptable behaviour

unu *pron* another spelling of **oonu** (*slang; used in Black English*)

ununbium /ún un bée əm/ *n* a highly unstable radioactive chemical element, produced artificially by nuclear fusion, with an atomic number of 112. Symbol **Uub**. See table at **element** [Late 20C. < Latin *unus* 'one' (repeated) + *bi* 'two' (see BI-), representing 112, its atomic number]

ununhexium /ún un héksi əm/ *n* a highly unstable, artificially produced radioactive chemical element with an atomic number of 116. Symbol **Uuh**. See table at **element** [Late 20C. < Latin *unus* 'one' (repeated) + Greek *hex* 'six', representing 116, its atomic number]

ununnilium /ún un ílli əm/ *n* former name for **darmstadtium**. See table at **element** [Late 20C. < Latin *unus* 'one' (repeated) + *nil* 'nothing', representing 110, its atomic number]

ununpentium /ún un pénti əm/ *n* a highly unstable radioactive chemical element with an atomic number of 115, reported to have been produced artificially by bombarding americium with calcium atoms. Symbol **Uup**. See table at **element** [Late 20C. < Latin *unus* 'one' (repeated) + Greek *pente* 'five', representing 115, its atomic number]

ununquadium /ún un kwáydi əm/ *n* a highly unstable radioactive chemical element, produced artificially by nuclear fusion, with an atomic number of 114. Symbol **Uuq**. See table at **element** [Late 20C. < Latin *unus* 'one' (repeated) + shortening of *quadri-* 'four' (see QUADRI-), representing 114, its atomic number]

ununtrium /ún un trée əm/ *n* a highly unstable radioactive chemical element with an atomic number of 113, reported to have been produced artificially by bombarding americium with calcium atoms. Symbol **Uut**. See table at **element** [Late 20C. < Latin *unus* 'one' (repeated) + *tri-* 'three' (see TRI-), representing 113, its atomic number]

unununium /ún un únni əm/ *n* a highly unstable radioactive chemical element, produced artificially by nuclear fusion, with an atomic number of 111. Symbol **Uuu**. See table at **element** [Late 20C. < Latin *unus* 'one' (repeated), representing 111, its atomic number]

unused /un yóozd, -yóost/ *adj* **1. NOT USED** never having been used ○ *unused matches* **2. NOT IN USE** not being put to use ○ *unused land* **3. UNFAMILIAR** not familiar with or accustomed to something ○ *Our dog is unused to city traffic.*

unusual /un yóo<u>zh</u>oo əl/ *adj* **1.** remarkable or out of the ordinary **2.** not common or familiar —**unusually** *adv* —**unusualness** *n*

unutterable /un úttərəb'l/ *adj* producing such an intense emotional reaction as to be impossible to express or describe ○ *scenes of unutterable sadness* —**unutterably** *adv*

unvalued /un vállyood/ *adj* **1. NOT VALUED** not regarded as valuable, especially when true value is being overlooked **2. NOT APPRAISED** not assigned a value **3. PRICELESS** so valuable as to have no price in monetary terms (*archaic*)

unvalved /un válvd/ *adj* describes a brass musical instrument that has no valves to extend the range of notes it can play

unvarnished /un vaárnisht/ *adj* **1.** said or presented without any attempt to disguise the truth ○ *the unvarnished facts* **2.** having no protective or decorative coat of varnish

unveil /un váyl/ (**-veils, -veiling, -veiled**) *v* **1.** *vt* **EXPOSE SOMETHING SECRET** to reveal something that has been hidden or kept secret **2.** *vt* **TAKE COVERING OFF SOMETHING** to remove a veil or other covering from something, especially somebody's face or a plaque, monument, or work of art during a formal ceremony of inauguration **3.** *vi* **TAKE OFF VEIL** to remove a veil from your face

unveiling /un váyling/ *n* **1.** the formal removal of a covering that has hidden a plaque, monument, or work of art during a formal ceremony of inauguration **2.** the revelation of something that has been hidden or kept secret

unvoice /un vóyss/ (**-voices, -voicing, -voiced**) *vt* PHON same as **devoice**

unvoiced /un vóyst/ *adj* **1.** not spoken or explicitly stated **2.** pronounced without vibration of the vocal chords

unwaged /un wáyjd/ *adj* not in formal paid employment

unwarrantable /un wórrəntəb'l/ *adj* unable to be justified or condoned —**unwarrantably** *adv*

unwarranted /un wórrəntid/ *adj* **1.** not authorized **2.** not justified or deserved —**unwarrantedly** *adv*

unwary /un wáiri/ *adj* failing to be alert and cautious —**unwarily** *adv* —**unwariness** *n*

unwashed /ún wósht/ *adj* not having been washed ◇ **the great unwashed** an offensive term for the mass of ordinary people

unwatchable /un wóchəb'l/ *adj* too bad to be worth watching, or too unpleasant and distressing to watch

unwavering /un wáyvəring/ *adj* firm in view or purpose and unable to be swayed or diverted from it —**unwaveringly** *adv*

unwearied /un wéerid/ *adj* **1.** performing a task or promoting a cause without ceasing **2.** not tired, e.g. from working or playing —**unweariedly** *adv*

unwell /un wél/ *adj* not in good health

unwept /un wépt/ *adj* **1.** held back and not allowed to flow from the eyes ○ *unwept tears* **2.** not cried over as a loss (*literary*)

unwholesome /un hólssəm/ *adj* **1.** UNHEALTHY harmful to health ○ *unwholesome eating habits* **2.** REGARDED AS HARMFUL TO MORALS regarded as being harmful to character or morals **3.** LOOKING UNHEALTHY unhealthy in appearance ○ *an unwholesome pallor* —**unwholesomely** *adv* —**unwholesomeness** *n*

~~unwieldly~~ incorrect spelling of **unwieldy**

unwieldy /un wéeldi/ *adj* **1.** hard to handle because of being large, heavy, or awkward **2.** too complex or extensive to be manageable —**unwieldily** *adv* —**unwieldiness** *n*

USAGE ***Unwieldy*** is often incorrectly spelt and pronounced *unwieldly*, as if it were formed with the common adjectival ending *-ly*.

unwilling /un willing/ *adj* **1.** not willing to do something ○ *unwilling to participate* **2.** given reluctantly or grudgingly ○ *unwilling assistance* —**unwillingly** *adv* —**unwillingness** *n*

SYNONYMS ***unwilling, reluctant, disinclined, averse, hesitant, loath***

CORE MEANING: lacking the desire to do something

unwilling not willing to do something ○ *The authorities seem unable or unwilling to take tough action.* ○ *The Minister of Transport said he had no intention of forcing the new Bill on an unwilling House of Commons.* **reluctant** showing no enthusiasm for doing something ○ *Most elderly people value their independence and are often reluctant to accept help.* **disinclined** without a strong motivation to do something ○ *a weapon of last resort that the government is disinclined to use* ○ *The obvious lack of consensus made us disinclined to pursue the matter further.* **averse** (*formal*) strongly opposed to or disliking something ○ *Neither country is averse to using the desperate plight of millions to arouse resentment of the West.* ○ *not averse to marriage* **hesitant** slow to do or say something because of indecision or lack of confidence ○ *Throughout the first set, both players looked tense and were hesitant to attack.* ○ *hesitant about getting involved* **loath** unwilling or reluctant to do something ○ *Today's Hollywood producers are notoriously loath to take chances on newcomers.*

unwind /un wínd/ (**-winds, -winding, -wound** /-wównd/) *v* **1.** *vti* UNCOIL to undo something such as tape or cable by winding, or come undone in this way **2.** *vt* UNTANGLE SOMETHING to remove or undo the tangles in something **3.** *vti* RELAX to relieve somebody of tension or worry, or obtain relief from tension or worry ○ *It's sometimes hard to unwind at the end of a busy day.* —**unwindable** *adj*

unwinking /un wíngking/ *adj* never closing the eyes or becoming distracted

unwire /un wír/ (**-wires, -wiring, -wired**) *vti* to stop using hard-wired landline technology in, e.g. a business environment and adopt wireless communication technology ○ *needed to unwire the office system for higher performance ratings* [Early 21C.]

unwisdom /un wízdəm/ *n* a lack of wisdom, judgment, or good sense

unwise /un wíz/ (**-wiser, -wisest**) *adj* lacking wisdom, judgment, or good sense —**unwisely** *adv*

unwish /un wísh/ (**-wishes, -wishing, -wished**) *vt* **1.** to undo or take back a wish **2.** to want something not to be or not to happen

unwitting /un witting/ *adj* **1.** unaware of what is happening in a situation **2.** said or done unintentionally [Old English *unwitende* < present participle of *witan* 'become aware of, learn' < Germanic] —**unwittingly** *adv*

unwonted /un wóntid/ *adj* unexpected or unusual —**unwontedly** *adv* —**unwontedness** *n*

unworkable /un wúrkəb'l/ *adj* **1.** NOT PRACTICAL too complicated or ambitious to be accomplished or established **2.** INDUST NOT ABLE TO BE WORKED unable to be cut, shaped, or otherwise fashioned **3.** AGRIC IMPOSSIBLE TO FARM so hard or rocky as to be impossible to farm —**unworkability** /un wúrkə bílləti/ *n* —**unworkableness** *n* —**unworkably** *adv*

unworldly /un wúrldli/ *adj* **1.** NOT MATERIALISTIC not interested in money or material goods **2.** INEXPERIENCED lacking experience of the world **3.** NOT OF THIS WORLD not concerned with or part of the material world —**unworldliness** *n*

unworn /un wáwrn/ *adj* **1.** not previously or recently worn ○ *an unworn shirt* **2.** in good condition, and not worn out or ruined ○ *unworn tyres*

unworthy /un wúrthi/ *adj* **1.** UNDESERVING not deserving something, e.g. a benefit, privilege, or compliment ○ *They proved themselves unworthy of our trust.* **2.** BENEATH SOMEBODY lower than somebody's usual standards of behaviour ○ *Such conduct is unworthy of you.* **3.** WITHOUT VALUE lacking value or merit **4.** VILE bad or unpleasant and wholly undeserved —**unworthily** *adv* —**unworthiness** *n*

unwound past participle, past tense of **unwind**

unwrap /un ráp/ (**-wraps, -wrapping, -wrapped**) *vti* to take off the wrapping from something, or have the wrapping removed

unwritten /un rítt'n/ *adj* **1.** generally accepted and understood, even though not formally recorded in writing ○ *unwritten law* **2.** remaining unprinted or not written down

unyielding /un yéelding/ *adj* **1.** not giving in to persuasion, pressure, or force **2.** hard, rigid, or inflexible —**unyieldingly** *adv* —**unyieldingness** *n*

unyoke /un yók/ (**-yokes, -yoking, -yoked**) *vt* **1.** UNTIE SOMETHING to release an animal such as a horse from a yoke **2.** DISCONNECT SOMETHING to separate two or more connected things **3.** FREE SOMEBODY to set somebody free (*archaic or literary*)

unzip /un zíp/ (**-zips, -zipping, -zipped**) *v* **1.** *vti* to open or unfasten something such as clothing or luggage by means of a zip, or become open or unfastened by this means **2.** *vt* to decompress a computer file that has been compressed

up /up/ *prep, adv* **1.** AT HIGHER LEVEL in, at, or to a higher level or position ○ (adv) *Put your hand up if you know the answer.* ○ (prep) *We climbed up the hill.* ○ (adv) *Prices are going up all the time.* ○ (prep) *I went up the ladder as far as the first-floor window.* **2.** ALONG in the same direction or way ○ (prep) *Go up the road until you come to a school.* ○ (adv) *You'll find her house up at the top of the road* ■ *adv* **1.** INDICATING COMPLETION used to indicate thoroughness or the completion of an action ○ *I tore up all the photographs.* ○ *drew up a contract* **2.** UPRIGHT in or to an upright position from a lower or prone position ○ *sitting up in bed* **3.** COMING OUT coming through or out of some medium ○ *The whales came up for air.* **4.** OUT in a way that detaches or removes ○ *Pulling up weeds isn't easy.* ○ *We drew up water from the well.* **5.** RISING ABOVE rising, or seeming to rise, above or over something ○ *When does the moon come up?* **6.** INTO CONSIDERATION so as to be discussed or mentioned ○ *The subject just didn't come up.* **7.** IN NORTHERLY POSITION towards or in a northerly position relative to the speaker ○ *Our cousins live up in Scotland.* **8.** TO HIGHER VALUE to or at a higher amount or price ○ *The interest rate is going up again.* **9.** TO GREATER INTENSITY with or to more intensity or higher pitch or volume ○ *His voice goes up when he's nervous.* ○ *Let's turn up the volume.* **10.** NEAR so as to move towards or closer to the speaker ○ *She ran up to me and gave me a big hug.* ○ *They came up to the door and knocked.* ■ *adv, n* AHEAD to the better or ahead ○ (adv) *Our team is up by two.* ○ (n) *Sales are on the up this month.* ■ *adj* **1.** INCREASED more than before ○ *Your grades are up this term.* **2.** OUT OF BED awake and out of bed ○ *She was already up when I called.* **3.** FACING UPWARDS having the face or top side upwards **4.** RAISED UPWARDS in a raised or lifted position ○ *The switch is in the up position.* **5.** GOING HIGHER OR NORTH located in or moving towards a higher or northern direction ○ *Take the up escalator.* ○ *The train is waiting at the up platform.* **6.** CHEERFUL happy and feeling good ○ *We've been so up since hearing the news.* **7.** HAPPENING going on (*informal*) ○ *What's up with you these days?* **8.** BEING CONSIDERED approaching a deadline for an action ○ *The contract is up for renewal.* **9.** NOMINATED FOR SOMETHING in the running for an office or professional achievement ○ *I hear she's up for a promotion.* **10.** ON TRIAL charged with an offence or called into a court of law ○ *The accused is up for first-degree murder.* **11.** OVER at an end or finished ○ *Your time is up.* **12.** HAVING KNOWLEDGE possessing up-to-date or accurate information ○ *I'm not up on the latest gossip.* ○ *He's well up with recent developments in the field.* **13.** FUNCTIONING able to operate or function ○ *Is the computer up?* **14.** BASEBALL BATTING taking a turn at bat in baseball ○ *Who's up first in this inning?* ■ *n* **1.** UPWARD SLOPE something that gradually rises from a base point ○ *Let's try to avoid the ups on our hike today.* **2.** SOURCE OF GOOD FEELING something that causes excitement or a feeling of euphoria (*informal*) ○ *The news was a real up for her.* ■ *v* (**ups, upping, upped**) (*informal*) **1.** *vt* RAISE SOMETHING to raise or increase something ○ *The insurance company has upped our premiums again.* **2.** *vt* PROMOTE SOMEBODY OR SOMETHING to promote or raise somebody or something to a higher level or position (*usually passive*) ○ *He was upped to manager last week.* **3.** *vi* ACT SUDDENLY to act suddenly or impulsively ○ *She just upped and left.* ○ *He upped and bought a new car without shopping around.* [Old English *up* 'upward', *uppe* 'on high' < Indo-European] ◇ **be up for something** to be ready or eager to do something (*informal*) ◇ **be up to somebody** to be the duty, responsibility, or job of somebody ◇ **be up to something 1.** to be able to undertake or endure ○ *I don't think I'm up to the journey.* **2.** to be engaged in or doing something, especially something reprehensible (*informal*) ○ *What have you been up to?* ◇ **it is all up with somebody** *or* **something** used to indicate that somebody *or* something is bound to fail, be destroyed, or get into trouble or danger (*informal*) ◇ **on the up and up 1.** making very good progress (*informal*) **2.** honest or legitimate (*dated informal*) ◇ **up against it** facing difficulty or danger ◇ **up and about** out of bed and moving around after being asleep or ill ◇ **ups and downs** changes of fortune or alternating spells of good and bad experiences ◇ **up to 1.** as many as, or as long as ○ *anything up to 25 miles a day* **2.** until ○ *up to now* ◇ **up yours** an offensive phrase indicating anger, contempt, or strong disagreement ◇ **what's up?** (*informal*) **1.** what is the matter? **2.** what is happening?

USAGE See ***back***.

UP *abbr* Uttar Pradesh

up. *abbr* upper

Upanayana /óopə nī ə nə/ *n S Asia* a rite of passage into adulthood for Hindi boys that can involve ear-piercing, head-shaving, and being doused with milk [Early 19C. < Sanskrit < *upa* 'towards' + *nayana* 'leading']

up-and-coming *adj* successful or improving, and showing signs of continuing to do so

up-and-down *adj* (*not hyphenated after a verb*) **1.** GOING UP AND DOWN moving alternately upwards and downwards **2.** VARIABLE uneven or readily changing **3.** VERTICAL in a vertical position or direction ○ *up-and-down stripes*

Upanishad /oo púnnishad, oo pánnə shad/ *n* a sacred Sanskrit text belonging to a set that forms the basis for Hindu philosophy and doctrine. They date from 400 BC and represent the last stage in the tradition of the Vedas, the most ancient of Hindu scriptures. [Early 19C. < Sanskrit *upaniṣad* 'a sitting down near (something)' < *upa* 'near' + *ni-ṣad* 'sit down'] —**Upanishadic** /oo púnni sháddik, -pánnə-/ *adj*

upas /yóopəss/ (*plural* **upases** or *same*) *n* **1.** a tree with white bark and poisonous sap. Native to: Southeast Asia. Latin name: *Antiaria toxicaria*. **2.** a poison made from the sap of the upas. Use: tipping arrows. [Late 18C. < Malay *(pohun) upas* 'poison (tree)']

upbeat /úp beet/ *adj* OPTIMISTIC full of optimism or cheerfulness (*informal*) ■ *n* **1.** IMPROVEMENT an increase in happiness, prosperity, or favourable activity **2.** MUSIC UNACCENTED BEAT an unaccented beat in music, especially one that ends a bar **3.** MUSIC GESTURE OF BATON the upward movement of a conductor's baton that indicates an upbeat

upbow /úp bō/ *n* the movement of the bow across the strings of an instrument in which the tip of the bow moves away from the instrument

upbraid /up bráyd/ (**-braids, -braiding, -braided**) *vt* to criticize or scold somebody in a harsh manner [Old

English *upbrēdan*, origin ?] —**upbraider** *n* —**upbraidingly** *adv*

upbringing /úp bringing/ *n* the way in which somebody has been brought up, or trained and educated early in life

upbuild /up bíld/ (-builds, -building, -built /-bílt/) *vt* to build up, develop, or enlarge something

upcast /up ka̋ast/ *adj* CAST UPWARDS thrown, propelled, or looking upwards ■ *n* 1. SOMETHING THROWN UP material that has been thrown up 2. MIN EXTRACT VENTILATION SHAFT a ventilation shaft in a mine that brings air up

upchuck /úp chuk/ (-chucks, -chucking, -chucked) *vti* N Am to vomit the contents of the stomach (*slang*)

upcoming /úp kumming/ *adj* about to happen or coming soon

upcountry *adj* /úp kuntri/ COMING FROM INTERIOR coming from, associated with, or located in an inland region of a country ■ *n* /úp kuntri/ INLAND AREA an inland region of a country ■ *adv* /up kúntri/ TOWARDS INTERIOR in or towards the inland region of a country

update *vt* /up dáyt/ (-dates, -dating, -dated) to provide somebody or something with the most recent information or with more recent information than was previously available ○ *The website is updated once a month.* ■ *n* /úp dayt/ the latest available information or more recent information —**updatable** *adj*

updater /úp daytər/ *n* a computer program that automatically updates data or another program

Popperfoto

John Updike

Updike /úp dīk/, **John** (*b.* 1932) US writer. He is best known for the novel *Rabbit, Run* (1960) and its sequels, two of which won Pulitzer Prizes. Full name **Updike, John Hoyer**

'Truth should not be forced; it should simply manifest itself, like a woman who has in her privacy reflected and coolly decided to bestow herself upon a certain man.'
[John Updike, *Self-Consciousness: Memoirs*; 1989]

updraught /úp draaft/ *n* a current of air that is moving upwards

upend /up énd/ (-ends, -ending, -ended) *vti* to stand or turn something up so that it is standing or resting on one end, or be turned over onto one end

up-front /up frúnt/, **upfront** *adj* (*informal*) 1. frank or straightforward 2. paid in advance —**up front** *adv* —**up-frontness** *n*

upgrade *v* /up gráyd/ (-grades, -grading, -graded) 1. *vti* IMPROVE QUALITY OF SOMETHING to improve the quality, standard, or performance of something, especially by incorporating new advances ○ *upgrade a computer* 2. *vti* EXCHANGE SOMETHING FOR SOMETHING BETTER to exchange something for another of better quality ○ *upgrade a seat on a flight* 3. *vt* HR PROMOTE SOMEBODY to promote somebody, or increase the status of somebody's job or position 4. *vt* AGRIC IMPROVE LIVESTOCK to improve the quality of livestock by breeding with superior animals in order to introduce desirable traits into the offspring ■ *n* /úp grayd/ 1. IMPROVEMENT OF SOMETHING an improvement in the quality or performance of something such as computer hardware or software 2. SOMETHING THAT IMPROVES something that improves the performance or quality of something else, or something that has better performance or qualities 3. TRAVEL MOVE TO BETTER TRAVEL CLASS a move to a higher class of travel than that purchased 4. *N Am* UPWARD SLOPE an upward slope or incline —**upgradable** *adj*

upgrowth /úp grōth/ *n* the process of growing upwards, or the result of this process

Upham /úppəm/, **Charles** (1908–94) New Zealand soldier. He fought in World War II, becoming the only combat soldier ever to win the Victoria Cross and Bar. Full name **Upham, Charles Hazlitt**

upheaval /up he̋ev'l/ *n* 1. a strong or sudden change in political, social, or living conditions 2. a sudden raising of part of the Earth's crust

upheave /up he̋ev/ (-heaves, -heaving, -heaved or -hove /-hōv/, -heaved) *vti* to lift something forcefully from underneath, or rise or be thrust upwards

uphill *adv* /up híl/ 1. UP SLOPE up a slope or towards the top of a hill 2. WITH DIFFICULTY against great resistance or in spite of difficulty ■ *adj* /úp hil/ 1. SLOPING UP sloping upwards 2. ON HIGHER GROUND located farther up a slope or hill 3. DIFFICULT requiring a lot of effort ○ *an uphill struggle*

uphold /up hōld/ (-holds, -holding, -held /-héld/) *vt* 1. to maintain or defend something, especially laws or principles, in the face of hostility 2. to provide somebody with moral support, or inspire somebody with confidence —**upholder** *n*

upholster /up hōlstər/ (-sters, -stering, -stered) *vt* to fit a piece of furniture such as a chair or couch with stuffing, cushions, fabric and other materials [Mid-19C. Back-formation < UPHOLSTERY] —**upholsterer** *n*

upholstery /up hōlstəri/ *n* 1. the stuffing, cushions, fabric and other materials used to upholster furniture such as chairs and couches ○ *upholstery fabric* 2. the craft, trade, or business of upholstering furniture [Mid-17C. < obsolete *upholster* 'upholsterer' < UPHOLD]

~~upholstry~~ incorrect spelling of **upholstery**

UPI *abbr* MEDIA United Press International

upkeep /úp keep/ *n* 1. the maintenance of somebody or something in proper condition or operation 2. the financial cost of providing maintenance for somebody or something

upland /úpplənd, úp land/ *n* 1. HIGH LAND land that has a high elevation, or a region of such land 2. INLAND REGION a region that lies in the interior of a country ■ *adj* HIGH OR INLAND relating to, located in, or native to a region that is at a high elevation or lies in the interior of a country

upland cotton *n* 1. the woolly fibre of a Central American cotton plant, or fabric made from it 2. a low, multibranched cotton plant commercially grown as an annual. Native to: Central America. Latin name: *Gossypium hirsutum.*

uplift *vt* /up líft/ (-lifts, -lifting, -lifted) 1. SPIRITUALLY LIFT SOMEBODY to help somebody attain a higher intellectual, moral, or spiritual level, or improve the living conditions of somebody 2. RAISE SPIRITS OF SOMEBODY to make somebody feel happier 3. PHYSICALLY LIFT SOMETHING to raise or lift somebody or something 4. *Scotland, NZ* COLLECT SOMEBODY to pick up passengers or baggage ■ *n* /úp lift/ 1. SOMETHING IMPROVING something that elevates somebody intellectually, morally, or spiritually, or improves somebody's living conditions 2. LIFTING UP the lifting up of something, or the result of doing this 3. GEOL UPWARD MOVEMENT OF EARTH'S CRUST the slow upward movement of large parts of stable areas of the Earth's crust —**uplifter** *n*

uplifting /up lífting/ *adj* raising somebody's intellectual, moral, or spiritual level

uplighter /úp lītər/ *n* a lamp or lampshade that directs the light upwards

uplink /úp lingk/ *n* a transmitter on the ground that sends radio or other signals to an aircraft or communications satellite ■ *vti* (-links, -linking, -linked) to transmit a radio or other signal from a ground transmitter to an aircraft or communications satellite

upload /úp lōd/ (-loads, -loading, -loaded) *vti* to transfer data or programs, usually from a peripheral computer to a central, often remote, computer

upmarket /up ma̋arkit/ *adj* intended or designed for wealthy discriminating consumers ■ *adv* towards a higher and more expensive standard that appeals to wealthy, discriminating consumers ○ *The hotel seems to have gone upmarket.*

upmost /úp mōst/ *adj* same as **uppermost** *adv*

upon /ə pón/ CORE MEANING: means the same as 'on',

but is more formal ○ *He stretched out his legs upon the sofa.* ○ *She climbed upon her father's knee.*
prep 1. ON SURFACE on or onto the surface of something (*formal*) ○ *The great beast bounced to a halt upon the parapet.* 2. ONE AFTER ANOTHER used between two occurrences of the same noun to indicate a large amount or number of that noun ○ *They claimed that the report contained 'innuendo upon innuendo'.* 3. FOLLOWED BY used to indicate that one event is followed immediately by another event ○ *Upon finding the relevant text, they store it in their own electronic files.* 4. ABOUT TO HAPPEN used to indicate that an event is imminent ○ *The holidays are upon us again.* [12C. < UP + ON; after Old Norse *upp á*]

upper /úppər/ *adj* 1. HIGHER located above another part of something ○ *the upper deck* ○ *a muscle in the upper arm* 2. MORE IMPORTANT higher in social position or rank, or greater in importance ○ *upper management* 3. MORE DISTANT lying farther inland, upstream, or to the north ○ *the upper reaches of the river* 4. GEOL LATER later in a particular geological formation, period, or system ○ *Upper Jurassic clay formations* 5. MATHS INDICATING MATHEMATICAL LIMIT indicating a limit or bound of a set of numbers equal to or greater than every member of the set ■ *n* 1. SOMEBODY OR SOMETHING ABOVE the higher of two people or objects 2. CLOTHING PART OF SHOE the part of a boot or shoe that covers the upper surface of the foot 3. DRUGS STIMULANT a drug that has a stimulating effect, e.g. an amphetamine (*informal*) ■ **uppers** *npl* UPPER TEETH the teeth of the upper jaw or of a top set of dentures (*informal*) ◇ **be on your uppers** to be very short of money (*informal*)

upper atmosphere *n* the part of the Earth's atmosphere above the troposphere, especially at heights unreachable by balloon

upper bound *n* in mathematics, a number that is greater than or equal to all the members of a set

Upper Canada /úppər-/ former British province in Canada, corresponding to present-day southern Ontario

Upper Carboniferous *n* GEOL same as **Pennsylvanian** (sense 2) —**Upper Carboniferous** *adj*

uppercase /úppər kayss, úppər káyss/ *n* CAPITAL LETTERS capital letters used in writing, typing, typesetting, or printing ○ *printed in uppercase* ■ *adj* IN CAPITAL LETTERS relating to or written or printed in capital letters ■ *vt* (-cases, -casing, -cased) CAPITALIZE SOMETHING to write, type, typeset, or print something in capital letters [Mid-18C. Because types for capital letters were kept in the upper of two type cases]

upper chamber *n* GOV same as **upper house**

upper circle *n* the gallery of seats at the top of a theatre, above the dress circle

upper class *n* the highest social class, or the people in it, e.g. the aristocracy and the very wealthy (*often used in the plural*) —**upper-class** *adj*

upperclassman /úppər klaássmən/ (*plural* -men /-mən/) *n* a student who belongs to the junior or senior class of an American high school, college, or university

upper crust *n* SOC SCI same as **upper class** (*informal*)

uppercut /úppər kut/ *n* a swinging upward blow in which the fist is aimed at an opponent's chin ■ *vt* (-cuts, -cutting, -cut) to hit or attempt to hit an opponent with an uppercut

upper hand *n* the controlling position in a situation

upper house *n* the house in a two-house legislature that is smaller and less representative of the general population, e.g. the House of Lords in the United Kingdom

Upper Hutt /-hút/ city in the southern part of the North Island, New Zealand, 32 km/20 mi. north of Wellington. Population: 34,527 (2001).

uppermost /úppər mōst/ *adj* highest in position, rank, or level ■ *adv* in, at, or towards the highest position, rank, or level

Upper Palaeolithic *n* the latest of the three periods of the Palaeolithic era, about 40,000 to 14,000 years ago, during which modern human beings first appeared —**Upper Palaeolithic** *adj*

upper respiratory *adj* relating to or affecting any of the air passages or associated structures that connect the lungs with the exterior, including the nasal passages, trachea, and bronchi

upper school *n* the senior students in a secondary school, particularly those in Year 10 and above

Upper Volta former name for **Burkina Faso**

upper works *npl* the parts of a ship above the water line when it is fully loaded

uppity /úppəti/ *adj* **1.** behaving in a way that is considered presumptuous and more suited to somebody belonging a higher social class or position (*informal*) **2.** having a stubborn inflexible personality (*dated informal*) [Late 19C. Fancifully < UP] —**uppityness** *n*

Uppsala /úp saalə/ city in eastern central Sweden, location of the country's oldest university. Population: 187,302 (1998).

up quark *n* a quark with an electric charge of +2/3 and zero strangeness and charm

upraise /up ráyz/ (**-raises, -raising, -raised**) *vt* to raise something or cause something to rise such as hands, prayers, or voices (*literary*)

uprate /up ráyt/ (**-rates, -rating, -rated**) *vt* to increase the value, price, rank, or size of something

upright /úp rīt/ *adj* **1.** ERECT standing vertically or straight upwards **2.** RIGHTEOUS behaving in a moral or honourable manner ■ *adv* ERECTLY vertically or straight upwards rather than at an angle ■ *n* **1.** VERTICAL SUPPORT something that stands upright, e.g. a stake or post **2.** MUSIC same as **upright piano** —**uprightly** *adv* —**uprightness** *n*

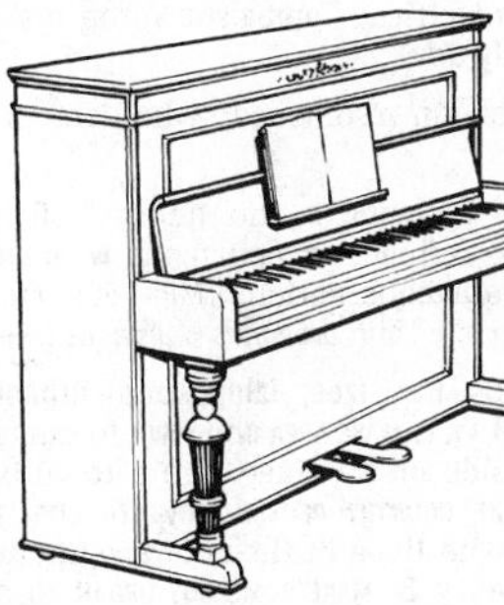

upright piano

upright piano *n* a piano with a rectangular upright case in which the strings are mounted vertically and a keyboard at right angles to the case

uprise *vi* /up rīz/ (**-rises, -rising, -rose** /-rṓz/, **-risen** /-rízz'n/) (*literary or archaic*) **1.** RISE UP to stand or get up **2.** MOVE UPWARDS to stand, go, or move in an upward direction ■ *n* /úp rīz/ UPWARD SLOPE an upward slope or incline

uprising /úp rīzing/ *n* an act of rebellion or revolt against an authority

upriver /up rívvər/ *adv, adj* towards or closer to the source of a river

uproar /úp rawr/ *n* a loud or noisy disturbance [Early 16C. By folk etymology < Middle Low German *uprōr* or Dutch *oproer* 'stirring up']

uproarious /up ráwri əss/ *adj* **1.** TUMULTUOUS characterized by noisy confusion **2.** HILARIOUS extremely funny and causing loud laughter **3.** VERY LOUD loud and boisterous —**uproariously** *adv* —**uproariousness** *n*

uproot /up rṓot/ (**-roots, -rooting, -rooted**) *vt* **1.** PULL PLANT FROM SOIL to pull a plant and its roots from the soil **2.** DISPLACE SOMEBODY OR SOMETHING to displace somebody or something from a home or habitual environment ○ *I don't want to uproot the children until they've finished school.* **3.** REMOVE OR DESTROY SOMETHING to remove or destroy something completely ○ *a plan to uproot terrorism* —**uprooter** *n*

uprose past tense of **uprise**

uprush /úp rush/ *n* a sudden upward rush of something

UPS *abbr* ELEC uninterruptible power supply

upsadaisy *interj* same as **upsy-daisy**

upscale /úp skáyl/ *adj, adv N Am* same as **upmarket**

upset *adj* /up sét/ **1.** DISTRESSED unhappy, disappointed, or emotionally distressed because of something that has happened **2.** DIGESTING POORLY affected by indigestion or nausea ○ *an upset stomach* **3.** OVERTURNED overturned or spilled ○ *an upset dinghy* ■ *v* /up sét/ (**-sets, -setting, -set**) **1.** *vt* DISTRESS SOMEBODY to make somebody feel unhappy, disappointed, or emotionally distressed **2.** *vt* DISTURB ORDER OF SOMETHING to disrupt the usual order or course of something ○ *upset our routine* **3.** *vti* TURN SOMETHING OVER to knock or tip something over accidentally, usually scattering its contents, or be knocked or tipped over in this way **4.** *vt* MAKE SOMEBODY FEEL SICK to make somebody feel sick, or cause a disorder of the digestive system ○ *Spicy foods upset my stomach.* **5.** *vt* DEFEAT SOMEBODY UNEXPECTEDLY to defeat somebody unexpectedly, e.g. in a sports contest or an election **6.** *vt* METALL THICKEN RIVET END to make a heated bolt, rivet, or bar shorter and thicker by hammering one end ■ *n* /úp set/ **1.** UNEXPECTED RESULT an unexpected result, e.g. in a sports contest or an election **2.** STOMACH ILLNESS a mild illness of the stomach **3.** UNHAPPY EXPERIENCE an unhappy experience **4.** DRAMATIC CHANGE an unexpected problem that causes distress or a change of plans **5.** METALL TOOL a hammering tool used to make a heated bolt, rivet, or bar shorter and thicker at one end **6.** METALL RIVET a bolt, rivet, or bar that has been heated and then hammered to make it shorter and thicker at one end —**upsetter** *n*

upset price *n Scotland, N Am* the lowest sale price at which something can be sold or auctioned

upsetting /up sétting/ *adj* emotionally distressing or disturbing —**upsettingly** *adv*

upshift /úp shift/ (**-shifts, -shifting, -shifted**) *vi N Am* AUTOMOT same as **change up**

upshot /úp shot/ *n* the end result of something [Mid-16C. Originally 'final shot (in archery)']

upside /úp sīd/ *n* **1.** POSITIVE SIDE the most favourable or positive aspect of a situation or event **2.** UPPER SIDE the upper side or part of something **3.** *US* FIN INCREASE IN VALUE an increase in business profits or stock prices

upside down *adv* **1.** turned so that the part that should be higher is lower or the side that should be underneath is on top **2.** in or into total confusion or great disorder ○ *We turned the house upside down looking for the keys.* —**upside-down** *adj*

upside-down cake *n* a sponge cake baked with a layer of fruit at the bottom and then inverted before it is served so that the caramelized fruit is on top

upsilon /úpsi lon, up sīlən/ *n* the 20th letter of the Greek alphabet, represented in the English alphabet as 'y' or 'u'. See table at **alphabet** [Mid-17C. < Greek *u psilon* 'simple u' (to distinguish it from the diphthong *oi*) < *psilon*, form of *psilos* 'simple']

upskilling /úp skilling/ *n* the process of increasing or improving the skills of members of a workforce, usually through additional training —**upskill** *vti*

upslope /úp slōp/ *n* **1.** ASCENDING SLOPE a slope considered as being angled upwards **2.** METEOROL COOLING OF RISING AIR the even cooling of air as it rises and expands ■ *adj* **1.** SITUATED ON ASCENDING SLOPE situated on, happening on, or caused by an ascending slope **2.** METEOROL FORMED BY COOLING OF RISING AIR describes fog formed by the even cooling of air as it rises and expands ■ *adv* TOWARDS HIGHER POINT ON SLOPE at or towards a higher point on a slope

upspeak /úp speek/ *n* LING same as **uptalk**

upstage /up stáyj/ *vt* (**-stages, -staging, -staged**) **1.** OUTDO SOMEBODY ELSE to divert attention from somebody else to yourself by being more impressive or noticeable **2.** THEATRE TURN ACTOR AWAY FROM AUDIENCE to move towards the back of the stage in order to force another actor to turn his or her back to the audience ■ *adv* THEATRE TOWARDS REAR OF STAGE in, at, or towards the rear part of a stage ■ *adj* THEATRE LOCATED AT REAR OF STAGE relating to or located in or at the rear part of a stage ■ *n* THEATRE BACK OF STAGE the rear part of the stage —**upstager** *n*

upstairs /up stáirz/ *adv* **1.** TO HIGHER FLOOR to, towards, or on an upper floor or level in a building or structure **2.** MENTALLY in the mind or brain (*humorous*) ○ *not a lot happening upstairs* **3.** TO HIGHER JOB to a higher level or job in an organization or hierarchy (*informal*) ■ *n* **1.** UPPER FLOOR an upper floor or the part of a building above the ground floor (*often used before a noun*) ○ *an upstairs bathroom* **2.** OWNERS OF WEALTHY HOUSEHOLD used to refer collectively to wealthy householders, as opposed to the servants who lived downstairs (*archaic informal*) ◇ **kick somebody upstairs** to promote somebody to a rank or position that is officially superior, but in fact carries less power and opportunity for influence (*informal*)

upstanding /up stánding/ *adj* **1.** honest and socially responsible **2.** in an erect position (*archaic*) ◇ **be upstanding** to stand in response to a formal request, particularly for a toast or prayer, or in a court of law (*formal*)

upstart /úp staart/ *n* somebody who is newly wealthy, powerful, or famous, but is regarded as not deserving to be so

upstate /úp stayt/ *US adj* NORTHERN relating to or living in the northern part of a state ■ *adv* NORTHWARD in, to, or towards the northern part of a state ■ *n* NORTHERN AREA the northern part of a state

upstream /up stréem, úp streem/ *adv* **1.** TOWARDS SOURCE in or towards the source of a river or stream **2.** GENETICS IN OPPOSITE DIRECTION TO TRANSCRIPTION in a direction along a strand of a DNA molecule counter to that in which transcription takes place ■ *adj* LOCATED NEARER SOURCE located farther towards the source of a river or stream

upstretched /úp strécht/ *adj* stretched or raised upwards

upstroke /úp strōk/ *n* **1.** an upward or rising movement of a pen or brush, or the mark it makes **2.** the upward movement of a piston in a reciprocating engine

upsucking /úp suking/ *n* sycophantic behaviour (*slang*)

upsurge /úp surj/ *n* a rapid increase in something

upsweep *n* /úp sweep/ **1.** UPWARD SWEEP an upward or curving line or motion **2.** *US* HAIRSTYLE a hairstyle in which the hair is swept upward from the neck ■ *vti* /up swéep/ (**-sweeps, -sweeping, -swept** /-swépt/) MOVE UPWARDS to sweep, curve, or brush something upwards, or be swept, curved, or brushed upwards

upswing /úp swing/ *n* an increase or improvement, e.g. in business profits

upsy-daisy /úpsi-/, **upsadaisy** /úpsə dáyzi/ *interj* used to reassure a child who is being lifted or who has fallen or stumbled (*baby talk*) [Mid-19C. Alteration of *up-a-daisy* < UP + *a-day*, expressing surprise]

uptake /úp tayk/ *n* **1.** the process of physically absorbing something into a living organism **2.** a passage that draws up smoke or air, e.g. a pipe or chimney **3.** MIN EXTRACT same as **upcast** *n* (sense 2) ◇ **be quick** *or* **slow on the uptake** to be quick or slow to understand things or realize what is happening (*informal*)

uptalk /úp tawk/ *n* the tendency to end sentences with an upward intonation, making a statement sound like a question

uptempo *n* /úp tempō/ a fast or lively musical tempo ■ *adj* /up témpō/ fast-paced, lively, or exciting

upthrow /úp thrō/ *n* the upward movement of one block of rock over another in a low-angle fault

upthrust /úp thrust/ *n* **1.** UPWARD PUSH an upward push or thrust **2.** ROCK MOVING UPWARDS a block of rock that has moved upwards in a low-angle fault ■ *adj* RAISED UP raised or lifted up

uptick /úp tik/ *n N Am* a small increase in something, especially in stock or bond prices

uptight /up tīt/ *adj* (*informal*) **1.** tense as a result of anger, fear, or annoyance in a way that is difficult to control **2.** unable or unwilling to show emotion

uptime /úp tīm/ *n* the time during which a computer or other machine is operating or ready for use

up-to-date *adj* (*not hyphenated after a verb*) **1.** WITH LATEST KNOWLEDGE including or possessing knowledge of the latest information **2.** CURRENT extending up to or reflecting the current time **3.** FASHIONABLE familiar with or knowledgeable about current fashions, styles, or ideas

up-to-the-minute *adj* including or relating to the most recent events or things

uptown *adv* /up tówn/ *N Am* TOWARDS UPPER PART OF CITY to, towards, or in the upper or northern part of a city ■ *n* /úp town/ *N Am* UPPER PART OF CITY the upper or northern part of a city ■ *adj* /úp town/ (*informal*) **1.** *US* CONDESCENDING pretentious or condescending in behaviour or attitudes **2.** *N Am* FASHIONABLE of the latest fashion or style

uptrend /úp trend/ *n* an upward improving trend, especially in business or an economy

upturn *v* /up túrn/ (**-turns, -turning, -turned**) **1.** *vti* TURN OVER to turn over, up, or upside down, or make something do this **2.** *vt* TURN FACE UPWARDS to turn something such as a face or gaze upwards (*usually passive*) ■ *n* /úp turn/ IMPROVEMENT an improvement in the economy or in business conditions

upward /úppwərd/ *adj* **1.** going or directed towards a higher level or position ○ *a steep upward climb* **2.**

increasing or becoming better ○ *an upward trend* ■ *adv* same as **upwards** —**upwardly** *adv*

upwardly mobile *adj* able or desiring to move to a higher social class or to acquire greater wealth, power or status ■ *npl* those who can or desire to move to a higher social class or acquire greater wealth, power or status

upward mobility *n* the ability or desire to move to a higher social class and acquire greater wealth, power, or status

upwards /úppwərdz/ *adv* **1.** TOWARDS HIGHER LEVEL in, to, or towards a higher place, level, or position ○ *She's working her way upwards through the company hierarchy.* ○ *Keep going upwards and you'll soon see the house.* **2.** TOWARDS INTERIOR OR SOURCE towards the interior of a place, or towards an origin or source ○ *The hikers left the path and headed upwards along the river.* **3.** TOWARDS GREATER AMOUNT towards a larger amount, degree, or position ○ *Sales have gone steadily upwards during the last quarter.* ◇ **upwards of** more than

upwelling /up wélling/ *n* **1.** ACT OF RISING TO SURFACE an act of rising up from inside the Earth or the body **2.** SURGE a steady surge of something such as an emotion **3.** RISING OF WATER TO SURFACE a process in which cold nutrient-rich water rises to the surface from the ocean depths

upwind /up wínd/ *adv, adj* **1.** against or into the wind **2.** on the side towards which the wind is blowing

Ur /ur/ ancient city of Mesopotamia, in the southeastern part of present-day Iraq. It was a major city-state of the Sumerian civilization by 2800 BC.

ur-[1] *prefix* same as **uro-**[1] (used before vowels)

ur-[2] *prefix* same as **uro-**[2] (used before vowels)

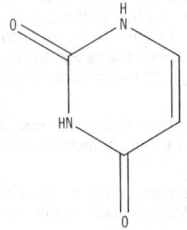

uracil

uracil /yóorə sil/ *n* a pyrimidine base, one of the four bases in RNA in which it pairs with thymine. Symbol U [Late 19C. Origin ?]

uraemia /yoo reémi ə/ *n* a form of blood poisoning caused by the accumulation in the blood of products that are normally eliminated in the urine [Mid-19C. < modern Latin < Greek *ouron* 'urine' + *haima* 'blood'] —**uraemic** *adj*

uraeus

Barnaby's

uraeus /yoo reé əss/ *n* the sacred serpent found on the headdresses of Egyptian rulers and divinities, representing sovereignty [Mid-19C. Via modern Latin < Greek *ouraios* 'cobra']

Ural /yóorəl/ river of southern Russia and north-western Kazakhstan, rising in the southern Ural Mountains and flowing southwards into the Caspian Sea. Length: 2,428 km/1,509 mi.

Ural-Altaic *n* a hypothetical language group formerly proposed by scholars as containing the Uralic and Altaic language families —**Ural-Altaic** *adj*

Uralic /yoo rállik/ *n* a family of languages spoken in northern and central Europe and western Siberia, including the branches Finno-Ugric and Samoyed —**Uralic** *adj*

uralite /yóorə lít/ *n* a fibrous blue-green mixture of amphibole minerals. Source: metamorphosed pyroxenes. [Mid-19C. < German *Uralit* < *Ural* 'Ural Mountains']

Ural Mountains /yóorəl-/, **Urals** /yóorəlz/ mountain system running from northern Russia southwards to the Kirgiz Steppe in Kazakhstan. It is the traditional dividing line between Asia and Europe. Its highest peak is Mount Narodnaya, 1,894 m/6,214 ft. Length: 2,400 km/1,490 mi.

uran- *prefix* uranium ○ *uranous* [< URANIUM]

uranalysis *n* MED same as **urinalysis**

Urania /yoo ráyni ə/ *n* in Greek mythology, the Muse of astronomy, one of the nine Muses believed to inspire and nurture the arts

uranic /yoo ránnik/ *adj* relating to or containing uranium, especially with a high valency [Mid-19C. < Latin *uranus* < Greek *ouranos* 'the heavens']

uraninite /yoo ránni nīt/ *n* a black uranium oxide mineral containing thorium, radium, and lead. Use: source of uranium. [Late 19C. < German *Uranin* < modern Latin *uranium* (see URANIUM)]

uranite /yóorə nīt/ *n* a mineral that contains uranium [Late 19C. < URANIUM] —**uranitic** /yóorə níttik/ *adj*

uranium /yoo ráyni əm/ *n* a heavy silvery-white radioactive metallic element occurring in three isotopes. Source: uraninite, pitchblende. Use: in one isotope, as fuel in nuclear reactors and weapons. Symbol U. See table at element [Late 18C. < modern Latin < *Uranus* the planet (discovered eight years before the element was identified)]

uranium 235 /-too thurti fív/ *n* a uranium isotope with a mass number of 235 that readily undergoes fission when bombarded with neutrons. Use: nuclear energy source.

uranium 238 /-too thurti áyt/ *n* the most abundant stable isotope of uranium, with a mass number of 238

uranium-lead dating /-led-/ *n* the determination of the age of a uranium-containing mineral by measuring the level of lead isotope produced by the radioactive decay of uranium, which occurs at a known rate

uranography /yóorə nóggrəfi/ *n* the branch of astronomy that deals with making maps of the constellations [Mid-17C. < Greek *ouranographia* 'science of the skies'] —**uranographer** *n* —**uranographic** /yóorənə gráffik/ *adj* —**uranographist** *n*

uranous /yóorənəss/ *adj* relating to or containing uranium, especially with a low valency

Uranus /yóorənəss, yoo ráynəss/ *n* **1.** the seventh smallest planet in the solar system and the seventh planet from the Sun **2.** in Greek mythology, the ruler of the heavens, husband of Gaia, and father of the Titans. He was dethroned by his son Cronus. [Via Latin < Greek *Ouranos*]

uranyl /yóorənil/ *adj* relating to a chemical group containing uranium and oxygen. Formula: UO₂. [Mid-19C. < URANIUM]

urase *n* BIOCHEM same as **urease**

urate /yóor ayt, yáwr-/ *n* a salt of uric acid —**uratic** /yoo ráttik, yaw-/ *adj*

urban /úrbən/ *adj* relating to or belonging to a city [Early 17C. < Latin *urbanus* < *urbs* 'city']

USAGE urban or **urbane**? Though ultimately from the same Latin form, these words differ in meaning in English. **Urban** refers generally to cities (as in *the stress of urban life*); **urbane** means 'sophisticated' (as in *an urbane manner, He was very urbane.*).

Urban II /úrbən/ (1040?–99) pope (1088–99). The sermon he preached to the Council of Clermont (1095) led to the First Crusade against the Seljuk Turks. Born **Odo of Lagery**

Urban VIII (1568–1644) pope (1623–44). His reign was marked by diplomatic activity, reform of church affairs, and lavish artistic and architectural patronage. Born **Barberini, Maffeo**

urban adventure *n* LEISURE same as **urban exploration**

urban blues *n* blues music that has a stronger beat than country blues, often played with electric instruments and featuring songs about life in the city (takes a singular verb)

urban cowgirl *n* a woman who wears fashionable clothing that is influenced by the western United States, e.g. fringed skirts and cowboy-style hats and boots

urbane /ur báyn/ (**-baner, -banest**) *adj* showing sophistication, refinement, or courtesy [Mid-16C. Directly or via Old French *urbaine* 'urban' < Latin *urbanus* (see URBAN)] —**urbanely** *adv* —**urbaneness** *n*

USAGE See **urban**.

urban exploration *n* the recreational activity of secretly exploring urban sites closed to the public, e.g. road and rail tunnels and abandoned buildings

urban guerrilla *n* somebody who lives in a city and carries out violent acts there in order to further a political cause

urbanise *vt* SOCIOL another spelling of **urbanize**

urbanism /úrbənizəm/ *n* **1.** the typical way of life of people who live in a city or town **2.** the study of life in cities and towns

urbanist /úrbənist/ *n* a specialist in city planning and the study of cities —**urbanistic** /úrbə nístik/ *adj* —**urbanistically** *adv*

urbanite /úrbə nīt/ *n* somebody who lives in a city or town

urbanity /ur bánnəti/ *n* the quality of being sophisticated, refined, or courteous ■ **urbanities** *npl* polite or courteous actions [Mid-16C. Directly or via French *urbanité* < Latin *urbanitas* < *urbanus* (see URBAN)]

urbanize /úrbə nīz/ (**-izes, -izing, -ized**), **urbanise** (**-ises, -ising, -ised**) *vt* **1.** MAKE AREA INTO TOWN to make an area of countryside or a village into a town or part of one **2.** MAKE COUNTRY PERSON MOVE TO CITY to make somebody who lives in the countryside migrate to a town or city **3.** MAKE SOMEBODY URBAN to accustom somebody to living in a town or city —**urbanization** /úrbə nī záysh'n/ *n*

urban myth, **urban legend** *n* a bizarre untrue story that circulates in a society through being presented as something that actually happened, usually to a friend or relative of somebody the speaker knows

urban planning *n* N Am PUBLIC ADMIN same as **town planning** —**urban planner** *n*

urban renewal *n* the redevelopment of urban areas that have become run down or impoverished, by demolishing or renovating old buildings or building new ones

urban sprawl *n* the expansion of an urban area into areas of countryside that surround it

urban warrior *n* somebody who copes successfully with the stresses and pace of modern urban living (slang)

urbi et orbi /úrbi et áwrbi/ *adv* a phrase used in a papal blessing, meaning 'to the city (of Rome) and to the world' [< Latin]

URC *abbr* United Reformed Church

urceolate /úrssi ələt, -layt/ *adj* shaped like an urn or pitcher, with a swollen middle and narrowing top [Mid-18C. < Latin *urceolus* 'little pitcher' < *urceus* 'pitcher']

urchin /úrchin/ *n* **1.** a mischievous child, especially a young one who is unkempt in appearance **2.** MARINE BIOL same as **sea urchin** **3.** ZOOL same as **hedgehog** (archaic or regional) [13C. Via Old N French *herichon* < Latin *(h)ericius* 'hedgehog']

REGIONAL NOTE See **hedgehog**.

Urdu /óordoo, úrdoo/ *n* the Indic official language of Pakistan, spoken also in Bangladesh and India. It belongs to the Indic group of Indo-European languages and shares basic grammar and vocabulary with Hindi. Native speakers: 40 million. [Late 18C. Via Persian and Urdu (*zabān i) urdū* '(language of the) camp' < Turkish *ordū* 'camp'] —**Urdu** *adj*

LANGUAGE HERITAGE See **Persian**.

-ure *suffix* **1.** process or condition, or something resulting from an action ○ *erasure* **2.** office or function, or a body performing a particular function ○ *prefecture* ○ *legislature* [Via Old French < Latin *-ura*]

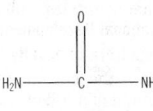

urea

urea /yoo reé ə, yoóri ə/ *n* a nitrogenous compound found in the urine of mammals, produced through protein decomposition. It is also produced synthetically. Use: fertilizers, feeds, manufacture of resins. Formula: $CO(NH_2)_2$. [Early 19C. < modern Latin, alteration of French *urée* < Old French *urine* (see URINE)] —**ureal** *adj*

urea-formaldehyde resin *n* a resin made from urea and formaldehyde. Use: making electrical fittings and in cavity insulation.

urease /yoóri ayss, -ayz/, **urase** /yoó rayss/ *n* an enzyme in some bacteria and seeds that breaks down urea to produce carbon dioxide and ammonia [Late 19C. < UREA + -ASE]

urediniospore /yoóri dínni ə spawr/ *n* FUNGI same as **uredospore** [Early 20C. < Latin *uredin-*, stem of *uredo* (see UREDO)]

uredinium /yoóri dínni əm/ (*plural* **-ia** /-i ə/), **uredium** /yoórí di əm/ (*plural* **-dia** /-di ə/) *n* a reddish or black mass of spores produced on a plant by a rust fungus [Early 20C. < Latin *uredin-*, stem of *uredo* (see UREDO)]

uredo /yoó reédō/ *n* MED same as **urticaria** [Early 18C. < Latin < *urere* 'to burn']

uredosorus /yoó reédō sáwrəss/ (*plural* **-sori** /-sáwrī/) *n* FUNGI same as **uredinium** [Early 20C. < UREDO]

uredospore /yoó reédō spawr/ *n* a reddish unicellular spore that develops in the uredinia of rust fungi

ureide /yoóri īd/ *n* an acyl derivative of urea

uremia *n* MED US spelling of **uraemia**

ureotelic /yoóri ə téllik/ *adj* producing nitrogen-containing waste in the form of urea [Early 20C. < UREA] —**ureotelism** *n*

ureter /yoó reétər, yoóritər/ *n* either of a pair of ducts that carry urine from the kidneys to the bladder in mammals or to the common cavity for wastes (**cloaca**) in lower vertebrate animals [Late 16C. Via modern Latin < Greek *ourētēr* < *ourein* 'urinate' < *ouron* 'urine'] —**ureteral** /yoó reétərəl/ *adj* —**ureteric** /yoóri térrik/ *adj*

urethane /yoóri thayn/, **urethan** /yoóri thán/ *n* **1.** a colourless odourless crystalline compound, the ethyl ester of carbamic acid. Use: solvents, pesticides, pharmaceuticals. Formula: $C_3H_7NO_3$. **2.** an ester of carbamic acid other than the ethyl ester **3.** CHEM same as **polyurethane** [Mid-19C. < modern Latin *urea* (see UREA) + ETHANE]

urethra /yoó reéthrə/ (*plural* **-thras** or **-thrae** /-three/) *n* the tube in mammals that carries urine from the bladder out of the body and in the male also carries semen during ejaculation [Mid-17C. Via late Latin < Greek *ourēthra* < Greek *ourein* 'urinate' (see URETER)] —**urethral** *adj*

urethritis /yoóri thrítiss/ *n* inflammation of the urethra, usually caused by infection [Early 19C. < URETHRA] —**urethritic** /-thríttik/ *adj*

urethroscope /yoó reéthrə skōp/ *n* a medical instrument for examining the inside of the urethra, consisting of a fine flexible tube fitted with lenses and a light [Mid-19C. < URETHRA] —**urethroscopic** /yoó reéthrə skóppik/ *adj* —**urethroscopy** /yoóri thróskəpi/ *n*

uretic /yoó réttik/ *adj* relating to, involving, or found in urine [Mid-19C. Via late Latin < Greek *ourētikos* < *ourein* 'urinate' (see URETER)]

Urey /yoóri/, **Harold C.** (1893–1981) US chemist. He discovered the isotope deuterium (**heavy hydrogen**), for which he won the Nobel Prize in chemistry (1934). Full name **Urey, Harold Clayton**

urge /urj/ *vt* (**urges, urging, urged**) **1.** ADVISE SOMEBODY

STRONGLY to advise somebody strongly to do something ○ *urged his firm to reconsider* **2.** ADVOCATE SOMETHING EARNESTLY to recommend or advise something earnestly and with persistence ○ *urging restraint* **3.** ENCOURAGE SOMEBODY OR SOMETHING to encourage, drive, or force somebody or something to do something ○ *could hear the crowd urging her on* ■ *n* STRONG NEED a strong need, wish, or impulse to do something ○ *the urge to travel* [Mid-16C. < Latin *urgere* 'push, press, compel'] —**urger** *n*

urgent /úrjənt/ *adj* **1.** calling for immediate action or attention **2.** showing earnestness or the desire for something to be done quickly [15C. Via French < Latin *urgent-*, present participle of *urgere* 'push, press, compel'] —**urgency** *n* —**urgently** *adv*

urgent care centre *n* a treatment centre for patients with less serious medical problems, staffed by doctors, registered nurses, pharmacists, and other care providers

-urgy *suffix* technique or art of working with something ○ *metallurgy* [Via modern Latin *-urgia* < Greek *-ourgos* 'working' < *ergon* 'work']

-uria *suffix* **1.** the condition of having a particular substance in the urine ○ *aciduria* **2.** the condition of having a particular kind of urine ○ *polyuria* [< modern Latin < Greek *ouron* 'urine']

Uriah /yoó rí ə/ *n* in the Bible, a Hittite officer deliberately killed in battle to allow King David to marry his wife, Bathsheba (2 Samuel 11:2–16)

Uribe /oō reébay/, **Alvaro** (*b.* 1952) president of Colombia (2002–). A former member of the Liberal Party, he became president as an independent candidate, promising a tough military response to the country's armed rebel groups. Full name **Uribe Velez, Alvaro**

uric /yoórik/ *adj* relating to, involving, or found in urine [Late 18C. < French *urine* (see URINE)]

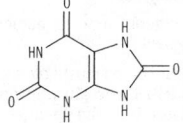

uric acid

uric acid *n* a slightly soluble compound in urine and blood, made in the breakdown of nitrogenous waste. Crystals of uric acid accumulate in the joints of people affected by gout. Formula: $C_5H_4N_4O_3$.

uridine /yoóri deen/ *n* a nucleoside, consisting of uracil and ribose, that plays a role in the metabolism of carbohydrates [Early 20C. < URACIL + -IDINE]

Urim and Thummim /yoórim ənd thúmmim/ *npl* oracles on the breastplate of the high priest of ancient Israel [Hebrew *'ūrīm* and *tummīm*]

urin- *prefix* same as **urino-** (used before vowels)

urinal /yoó rín'l, yoórin'l/ *n* **1.** RECEPTACLE FOR MEN TO URINATE INTO a receptacle that is fixed to a wall and plumbed in, used for men to urinate into **2.** PLACE WITH URINALS a room or building in which there are urinals **3.** PORTABLE CONTAINER FOR URINE a container used to transport urine [13C. Via French < late Latin *urinalis* 'urinary' < *urina* 'urine']

urinalysis /yoóri nálləssiss/ (*plural* **-yses** /-ə seez/), **uranalysis** /yoórə nálləssiss/ *n* the analysis of the physical, chemical, and microbiological properties of urine, carried out to help diagnose disease, monitor treatment, or detect the presence of a specific substance [Late 19C. Blend of URINE + ANALYSIS]

urinary /yoórinəri/ *adj* relating to, involving, or affecting urine or the organs that form and discharge urine [Late 16C. < Latin *urina* 'urine']

urinary bladder *n* an expanding muscular sac in mammals and some other vertebrates in which urine collects before it is discharged from the body through the urethra

urinate /yoóri nayt/ (**-nates, -nating, -nated**) *vi* to

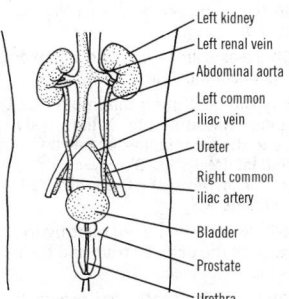

urinary: human male urinary system

Left kidney
Left renal vein
Abdominal aorta
Left common iliac vein
Ureter
Right common iliac artery
Bladder
Prostate
Urethra

discharge urine from the body [Late 16C. < medieval Latin *urinat-* past participle of *urinare* < Latin *urina* 'urine'] —**urination** /yoóri náysh'n/ *n* —**urinative** *adj* —**urinator** *n*

urine /yoórin/ *n* the yellowish liquid containing waste products that is excreted by the kidneys and discharged through the urethra. In birds and reptiles it is semisolid. [14C. Directly or via French < Latin *urina*] —**urinous** *adj*

uriniferous /yoóri nífferəss/ *adj* describes a tube that carries urine, especially the tubules of the kidneys [Mid-18C. < URINE]

urino- *prefix* urine, urinary ○ *urinometer* [< Latin *urina* 'urine']

urinogenital /yoórinō jénnit'l/ *adj* ANAT same as **urogenital**

urinometer /yoóri nómmitər/ *n* a hydrometer for measuring the specific gravity of urine

URL *n* an address identifying the location of a file on the Internet, consisting of the protocol, the computer on which the file is located, and the file's location on that computer. Full form **Uniform Resource Locator**

Urmia, Lake /úrmi ə/ large salt lake in northwestern Iran. Area: 4,700 sq. km/1,800 sq. mi.

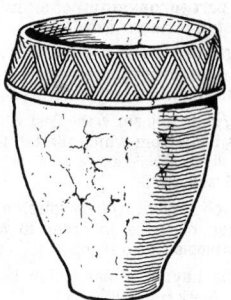

urn (sense 3)

urn /urn/ *n* **1.** VESSEL FOR HOT DRINKS a closed vessel in which a hot drink, especially tea or coffee, is made in a large quantity and poured out through a tap **2.** VASE FOR SOMEBODY'S ASHES a sealed vase in which the ashes of somebody who has died and been cremated are kept **3.** ORNAMENTAL VASE an ornamental vase that may have a foot or a pedestal **4.** BOT SPORE-PRODUCING PART OF MOSS CAPSULE the part of a moss capsule where spores are produced [14C. < Latin *urna*]

CULTURAL NOTE *Ode on a Grecian Urn*, a poem (1819) by John Keats. It describes the poet's reaction to a Greek vase decorated with reliefs of joyful rural scenes. The urn becomes a symbol of the contrast between the permanence of art and the transience of human life, and inspires the poem's famous proclamation 'Beauty is truth, truth beauty'.

uro-[1] *prefix* **1.** urine, urinary tract ○ *uroscopy* ○ *urolithiasis* **2.** urea ○ *urease* [< Greek *ouron* 'urine']

uro-[2] *prefix* tail ○ *uropod* [< Greek *oura*]

urochord /yoórō kawrd/ *n* **1.** a flexible skeletal rod (**notochord**) that supports the posterior part of the body in some sea animals such as sea squirts **2.** MARINE BIOL same as **tunicate** [Late 19C. < URO-[2] + CHORD[2]] —**urochordal** /yoórō káwrd'l/ *adj*

urochordate /yoórō káwr dayt/ *n* MARINE BIOL same as

tunicate [Late 19C. < URO-[1] + CHORD[1] + -ATE] —**urochordate** *adj*

urochrome /yóorō krōm/ *n* a yellow pigment that gives urine its normal colour

urodele /yóorō deel/ *n* an amphibian that has a tail throughout its adult life, a long body, and short limbs, e.g. the salamander or newt. Order: Caudata or Urodela. [Mid-19C. Directly or via French *urodèle* < modern Latin *Urodela*, < Greek *oura* 'tail' + *dēlos* 'visible'] —**urodele** *adj*

urogenital /yóorō jénnit'l/ *adj* relating to or involving the organs of the urinary tract and the reproductive organs [Mid-19C. < URO-[1] + GENITAL]

urogenous /yoo rójjənəss/ *adj* producing, obtained from, or formed in urine

urogram /yóorō gram/ *n* an X-ray picture of the urinary tract or a part of it

urography /yoo róggrəfi/ *n* X-ray photography of all or part of the urinary tract. It is performed after a patient has been given an opaque substance that highlights the various structures, in order to locate and diagnose urinary disorders. —**urographic** /yóorō gráffik/ *adj*

urokinase /yóorō kī nayz, -nayss/ *n* an enzyme, produced by the kidneys, that catalyses the conversion of plasminogen to plasmin. Use: medicinally, to dissolve blood clots.

urol. *abbr* MED **1.** urological **2.** urology

urolith /yóorōlith/ *n* a stony mass (**calculus**) in the urinary tract —**urolithic** /yóorō líthik/ *adj*

urolithiasis /yóorōli thī́ əssiss/ *n* the formation or presence of stony masses in the urinary tract, or the medical condition resulting from this

urology /yoo rólləji/ *n* the branch of medicine that deals with the study and treatment of disorders of the urinary tract in women and the urogenital system in men —**urologic** /yóorō lójjik/ *adj* —**urological** *adj* —**urologist** *n*

uropod /yóorō pod/ *n* either of a pair of flat appendages on the last abdominal segment of a crustacean such as a lobster or shrimp [Late 19C. < URO-[2]] —**uropodal** /yoo róppəd'l/ *adj*

uropygial /yóorō píjji əl/ *adj* relating to the fleshy hindmost part (**uropygium**) of a bird's body from which the tail feathers grow

uropygial gland *n* a gland in the skin at the base of the tail of most birds that secretes an oil used while preening to condition and waterproof the feathers

uropygium /yóorō píjji əm/ *n* the fleshy hindmost part of a bird's body from which the tail feathers grow [Late 18C. Via medieval Latin < Greek *ouropugion* < *oura* 'tail' + *pugē* 'buttocks']

uroscopy /yoo róskəpi/ (*plural* **-pies**) *n* the medical examination of urine in order to make a diagnosis —**uroscopic** /yóorō skóppik/ *adj* —**uroscopist** *n*

-urous *suffix* having a particular kind of tail ○ *anurous* [< Greek *oura* 'tail']

Urquhart /úrkət/, **Sir Thomas** (1611?–60) Scottish writer and soldier. A fighter for the Royalist cause in the English Civil War, he also wrote on a wide range of subjects and translated Rabelais.

urrin /úrrin/ *n regional* same as **earwig** [Origin ?]

REGIONAL NOTE See *earwig*.

Ursa Major /úrssə-/ *n* a prominent constellation of the northern hemisphere containing the Plough. See illustration at **constellation**

Ursa Minor *n* a small constellation of the northern hemisphere containing the star Polaris. See illustration at **constellation**

ursine /úr sīn/ *adj* **1.** relating to or typical of a bear, or belonging to the bear family **2.** having the characteristics usually associated with a bear [Mid-16C. < Latin *ursinus* < *ursus* 'a bear']

Ursuline /úrssyoo līn/ *n* a member of a Roman Catholic order of nuns founded by St Angela Merici in Brescia, Italy, in the 16th century and dedicated to teaching [Late 17C. < *Ursula*, patron saint of the order's founder] —**Ursuline** *adj*

urticaceous /úrti káyshəss/ *adj* describes a plant that belongs to the nettle family [Mid-19C. < Latin *urtica* 'nettle' < *urere* 'to burn']

urticaria /úrti káiri ə/ *n* a skin rash, usually occurring as an allergic reaction, that is marked by itching and small pale or red swellings, and often lasts for a few days (*technical*) [Late 18C. < modern Latin < Latin *urtica* 'nettle'] —**urticarial** *adj* —**urticarious** *adj*

urticate /úrti kayt/ *vi* (**-cates, -cating, -cated**) to be affected by or cause urticaria ■ *adj* producing weals and itching [Mid-19C. < medieval Latin *urticat-* past participle of *urticare* 'sting' < Latin *urtica* 'nettle'] —**urticant** *adj, n*

urtication /úrti káysh'n/ *n* **1.** the process by which somebody develops urticaria **2.** an intensely itchy or burning sensation

Uru. *abbr* Uruguay

BRAZIL
Salto
Uruguay
Paysandú
Negro
URUGUAY
Mercedes
Montevideo
Rio de La Plata
ARGENTINA
Atlantic Ocean

Uruguay

Uruguay /yóorə gwī/ **1.** country in southeastern South America, south of Brazil, bordering the Atlantic Ocean. Language: Spanish. Currency: Uruguayan peso. Capital: Montevideo. Population: 3,413,329 (2003). Area: 176,215 sq. km/68,037 sq. mi. Official name **Oriental Republic of Uruguay 2.** river in southeastern South America, rising in southern Brazil and entering the Atlantic Ocean through the River Plate. Length: 1,600 km/990 mi. —**Uruguayan** /yóorə gwī́ ən/ *n, adj*

Urumqi /oo róomchi/ capital city of Xinjiang Uygur Autonomous Region, northwestern China. Population: 1,310,000 (1995).

urus /yóorəss/ *n* ZOOL same as **aurochs** [Early 17C. Via Latin < Greek *ouros*]

urushiol /oo róoshi ol, oo róoshi ol/ *n* an oily poisonous irritant found in the resin and on the leaves and stems of poison ivy, the lacquer tree, and some related plants [Early 20C. < Japanese *urushi* 'lacquer' + -OL[1]]

us[1] /uss, əss/ *pron* **1.** SELF AND OTHER OR OTHERS a pronoun used to refer to both yourself and another person or other people (*used after a verb or preposition*) ○ *He told us to go away.* ○ *This problem affects all of us.* **2.** ROYAL US used by a king or queen, or the editor of a newspaper, to mean 'me' (*formal*) ○ *It gives us great pleasure to declare this building open.* **3.** ME used by a person to refer to himself or herself (*informal*) ○ *Give us a look, then!* **4.** *regional* same as **ourselves** (sense 1) (*informal; used after a verb as the indirect object*) ○ *We'd better find us a place to sleep.* ■ *det regional* same as **our** (sense 1) (*regional*) [Old English *ūs* < Germanic]

REGIONAL NOTE In parts of northern England, ***us*** is used as both a pronoun (*They met us at the station.*) and as a possessive adjective (*We sat down to have us tea when the phone rang.*). This parallels the widespread use of *me* as an adjective, as in *Where's me book?*, although this is normally regarded as a mispronunciation of *my.*

us[2] *abbr* United States (*used in Internet addresses*) See table at **domain name**

US *abbr* United States

u.s. *abbr* **1.** ubi supra **2.** ut supra

U/S *abbr* unserviceable

USA *abbr* United States of America

usable /yóozəb'l/, **useable** *adj* capable of being used —**usability** /yóozə bílləti/ *n* —**usably** *adv*

USAF *abbr* United States Air Force

usage /yóossij, yóoz-/ *n* **1.** ACT OR WAY OF USING SOMETHING the act of using something, the way something is used, or the extent to which something is used **2.** ACCEPTED PRACTICE a customary and generally accepted practice or procedure **3.** LANGUAGE WAY LANGUAGE IS USED the way in which words and phrases are used in speech or writing **4.** LANGUAGE EXAMPLE OF LANGUAGE USE an example of a specific use of language **5.** TREATMENT the handling or treatment of something [13C. < Old French < Latin *usus* (see USE)]

USAID /yoo ess áyd/ *n* a US government agency that provides humanitarian aid and assistance for development to other countries. Full form **United States Agency for International Development**

~~usally~~ incorrect spelling of **usually**

usance /yóoz'nss/ *n* the customary length of time allowed for payment of a bill of exchange in foreign commerce [14C. < Old French < assumed Vulgar Latin *usare* 'keep on using' < Latin *uti* 'to use']

USB *n* an external interface standard designed for communication between a computer and attached low- to mid-speed peripheral devices such as printers, scanners, and keyboards. Full form **universal serial bus**

USDAW /úz daw/ *abbr* Union of Shop, Distributive, and Allied Workers

use *v* /yooz/ (**uses, using, used**) **1.** *vt* EMPLOY SOMETHING FOR PURPOSE to put something into action or service for some purpose ○ *use a hammer* **2.** *vt* DO SOMETHING HABITUALLY to do something habitually ○ *use common sense* **3.** *vt* CONSUME SOMETHING to expend or consume something, often until none is left ○ *All of the space on the disk has been used.* **4.** *vt* MANIPULATE OR EXPLOIT SOMEBODY to exploit or manipulate somebody as a means to an end ○ *the type of person who uses others* **5.** *vti* DRUGS CONSUME DRUGS OR ALCOHOL REGULARLY to consume something regularly, especially drugs or alcohol **6.** *vt* TREAT SOMEBODY IN PARTICULAR WAY to behave towards somebody or something in a particular way ○ *used his employees poorly* **7.** *vt* BENEFIT FROM SOMETHING to benefit or get satisfaction from something ○ *I could use a good night's sleep.* ■ *modal v* /yooss/ USED used after 'did' in the past tense instead of 'used' ○ *Did you use to go there too?* ○ *I didn't use to eat much fruit.* ■ *n* /yooss/ **1.** ACT OF USING SOMETHING the act of using something for a purpose ○ *skilled in the use of computers* **2.** STATE OF BEING USED the state or fact of being used for something ○ *no longer in use* **3.** WAY OF USING SOMETHING a way of using something ○ *We admired the artist's use of colour.* **4.** RIGHT TO USE SOMETHING the right to use something, or the benefit of using something ○ *He was denied use of the car as a punishment.* **5.** ABILITY TO USE SOMETHING the power or ability to use something ○ *She lost the use of her left eye.* **6.** PURPOSE the purpose of something ○ *Put your education to good use.* **7.** USEFULNESS the quality of being useful ○ *These empty boxes will be of use when we move.* **8.** NEED TO USE SOMETHING the occasion or need to use something ○ *We may have use for these things later.* **9.** LAW BENEFIT OF PROPERTY the benefit or profit of property held by one person for another **10.** LAW LEGAL ENJOYMENT OF PROPERTY the legal enjoyment of property, especially by occupying it **11.** RELIG MODIFIED LOCAL LITURGY a modified liturgical form or observance practised in a particular church or religious order [13C. Via Old French *user* 'to use' < Latin *usus*, past participle of *uti*] ◇ **have no use for somebody or something 1.** to have no need or purpose for somebody or something **2.** to have no liking or respect for somebody or something (*informal*) ◇ **make use of somebody** to exploit or manipulate somebody as a means to an end ◇ **make use of something** to use something that is readily available, especially in a sensible or economical way ◇ **what's the use?** used to suggest that doing something is pointless (*informal*)

USAGE See ***utilize.***

SYNONYMS ***use, employ, make use of, utilize***

CORE MEANING: to put something to use

use to put something into action or service for some purpose ○ *In photography, different lenses are used for different purposes.* ○ *When talking about computers we use the word 'hardware' to describe the actual machine and its accessories.* **employ** to make use of something such as a tool or a resource in a particular way ○ *the high-pressure selling techniques sometimes employed by door-to-door salespeople* ○ *There are seven base metals that are commonly employed in the making of coins and artefacts.* **make use of** to use something that is readily available, especially in a sensible or economical way ○ *A split-level bedroom makes maximum use of space.* ○ *All members of staff are encouraged to make use of this facility.* **utilize** to make use of something, or find a practical or effective use for something ○ *Karate is a method of fighting which utilizes all parts of the body as deadly weapons.* ○ *We need to ensure that the country's varied and rich reserves are utilized in the most efficient way.*

use up *vt* to expend or consume something, usually until none is left

useable *adj* another spelling of **usable**

~~**useage**~~ incorrect spelling of **usage**

use-by date *n* a date displayed on food and other perishable products, after which they should not be used or consumed

used[1] /yoozd/ *adj* **1.** formerly owned by somebody else ○ *bought a used car* **2.** already put to use or expended ○ *a used match*

used[2] /yoósst-/ *modal v* used in the past tense to say that somebody or something habitually or usually did something ○ *We used to eat out more often.* ○ *He used not to be so grumpy.* ◊ **use** ■ *adj* accustomed to or familiar with somebody or something ○ *We're not used to this weather.*

useful /yoósf'l/ *adj* **1.** capable of being put to use or serving a purpose **2.** having value or benefit, or bringing an advantage —**usefully** *adv* —**usefulness** *n*

~~**usefull**~~ incorrect spelling of **useful**

~~**useing**~~ incorrect spelling of **using**

useless /yoóssləss/ *adj* **1. UNUSABLE** not able to be used **2. UNSUCCESSFUL** unsuccessful, or unlikely to be worthwhile **3. INEPT** not able to do something properly (*informal*) —**uselessly** *adv* —**uselessness** *n*

Usenet /yoóz net/ *n* a worldwide system that uses the Internet and other networks to distribute articles of news or information

user /yoózər/ *n* **1. PERSON OR THING THAT USES** somebody or something that uses something ○ *computer users* **2. EXPLOITER** somebody who exploits or manipulates others as a means to an end (*informal*) **3. DRUG TAKER** somebody who takes illegal drugs (*informal*) **4.** LAW **EXERCISE OF RIGHT** the exercise of a right to do or use something

user-friendly *adj* easy to operate, understand, or deal with ○ *user-friendly software* —**user-friendliness** *n*

user group *n* a group of people with common interests in an aspect of computer hardware or software who share information among themselves and with the hardware manufacturer or software developer

userID /yoózər ī deé/ *n* an identification name or password used to allow an individual user access to a computer system

user interface *n* the part of the design of a computer or other device or program that accepts commands from and returns information to the user

username /yoózər naym/ *n* a unique identifier composed of alphanumeric characters, used as a means of initial identification to gain access to a computer system or Internet Service Provider

~~**usful**~~ incorrect spelling of **useful**

USGS *abbr* GEOL United States Geological Survey

usher /úshər/ *n* **1. SOMEBODY WHO SEATS PEOPLE** somebody who escorts people to their seats in a place such as a theatre or church **2. DOORKEEPER** somebody who is in charge of the door of a court, hall, or chamber **3. COURT OFFICIAL** in England and Wales, an official in a law court who keeps order **4. OFFICER WALKING BEFORE SOMEBODY OF RANK** an officer who walks in front of people of rank in a procession or who introduces strangers at formal events ■ *v* (**-ers, -ering, -ered**) **1.** *vt* **ESCORT OR SEAT SOMEBODY** to escort somebody to or from a place or seat **2.** *vi* **ACT AS USHER** to act as an usher [14C. Via Anglo-Norman *usser* < Latin *ostarius* 'doorkeeper' < *ostium* 'door']

SYNONYMS See *guide.*

usher in *vt* to introduce or lead up to something

usherette /úshə rét/ *n* a woman or girl who escorts people to their seats in a theatre or cinema, (*dated*)

Usk /usk/ river in southeastern Wales. It rises in Brecon Beacons National Park and flows to the Severn Estuary at Newport. Length: 97 km/60 mi.

USM *abbr* **1.** ARMS underwater-to-surface missile **2.** FIN unlisted securities market

USN *abbr* United States Navy

usnea /ússni ə, úzni ə/ (*plural* **-neae** /-ni ee/ or **-neas**) *n* a common lichen with a hanging body in which the root, stem, and leaf are not distinguished. Genus: *Usnea*. [Late 16C. Via modern and medieval Latin < Arabic, Persian *ušna* 'moss, lichen']

USO *abbr* United Service Organizations

USP *n* a characteristic of a product that makes it different from all similar products (*used in advertisements and marketing*) Full form **unique selling point**

usquebaugh /úskwi baw/ *n Ireland, Scotland* Scotch or Irish whisky (*archaic or literary*) [Late 16C. < Gaelic *uisge beatha* 'water of life']

USS *abbr* **1.** United States Senate **2.** United States Ship

USSR *abbr* HIST Union of Soviet Socialist Republics

ustad /oō staád/ *n S Asia* somebody who is expert in an art or skill, especially music [Early 20C. < Urdu, Persian *ustād*]

AKG London

Sir Peter Ustinov

Ustinov /yoósti nof/, **Sir Peter** (1921–2004) British writer, director, and actor. A noted raconteur and mimic, he wrote or directed many plays and films. He won Academy Awards for supporting actor in *Spartacus* (1960) and *Topkapi* (1964). Full name **Ustinov, Sir Peter Alexander**

> 'Parents are the bones on which children sharpen their teeth.'
> [Sir Peter Ustinov, *Dear Me*; 1977]

usu. *abbr* usually

usual /yoózhoo əl/ *adj* **TYPICAL OR NORMAL** characteristic or expected of somebody or something ■ *n* **1. ORDINARY WAY** the ordinary, normal, or customary way of things **2. WHAT SOMEBODY CUSTOMARILY HAS** what somebody customarily has, especially a drink in a bar (*informal*) [14C. Directly or via Old French *usuel* < late Latin *usualis* < Latin *usus* (see USE)] —**usually** *adv* —**usualness** *n* ◇ **as usual** in the customary way

SYNONYMS ***usual, customary, habitual, routine, wonted***

CORE MEANING: often done

usual characteristic or expected of somebody or something ○ *He made his way home by his usual route.* ○ *Mother responded in the usual way, with a long-suffering sigh.* **customary** conforming to what is usual or normal ○ *When a new pope was elected, it was customary for him to give presents to the chief citizens.* ○ *done with customary formality* **habitual** done frequently and predictably ○ *He addressed the meeting with his habitual frankness.* **routine** regular or standard, even predictable and monotonous ○ *They found a fault in the fuel supply during a routine check.* ○ *nurses who are engaged in routine work on the wards* **wonted** (*literary*) usual or typical ○ *Briefly overcome with emotion, she soon resumed her wonted composure.*

~~**usualy**~~ incorrect spelling of **usually**

usufruct /yoózyoō frukt, yoóss-/ *n* the legal right to use and enjoy the advantages or profits of another person's property [Early 17C. < Latin *usufructus*, variant of *ususfructus* 'use (and) enjoyment' < *usus* (see USE) + *fructus* 'enjoyment']

usufructuary /yoózyoō frúktyoo əri, yoóss-/ (*plural* **-ies**) *n* somebody who is entitled by usufruct to the use of somebody else's property —**usufructuary** *adj*

usurp /yoo zúrp/ (**usurps, usurping, usurped**) *vti* to use something without the right to do so [14C. Via French < Latin *usurpare* 'seize for use' <, perhaps, *usus* 'use' (see USE) + *rapere* 'seize'] —**usurpation** /yoō zur páysh'n/ *n* —**usurpative** *adj* —**usurper** *n* —**usurpingly** *adv*

usury /yoózhəri/ (*plural* **-ries**) *n* **1.** the lending of money at an exorbitant rate of interest **2.** an exorbitant rate of interest [14C. Via assumed Anglo-Norman *usurie* < Latin *usura* 'use of money lent, interest' < *usus* 'use'] —**usurer** *n* —**usurious** /yoo zhoóri əss/ *adj* —**usuriously** *adv*

USW *abbr* MEDIA ultrashort wave

ut /ut, oot/ *n* the note C, equivalent to 'doh' in the solmization system [14C. < Latin, syllable sung to this note in a hymn]

UT *abbr* Universal Time

Utah /yoō̆t aa, -aw/ state in the western United States, bordered by Idaho, Wyoming, Colorado, Arizona, and Nevada. Capital: Salt Lake City. Population: 2,233,169 (2000). Area: 219,900 sq. km/84,904 sq. mi. —**Utahan** *n, adj*

Utamaro /oōtə maárō/ (1753–1806) Japanese artist. He was noted for his delicate portraits of women in teahouses, shops, and brothels. Full name **Kitagawa Utamaro**

UTC *n* Greenwich Mean Time. Full form **Universal Time Coordinated**

ut dict. /út díkt/ *abbr* as directed (*used on prescriptions*) [Latin *ut dictum*]

ute /yoot/ *n ANZ* a pick-up truck (*informal*) [Mid-20C. Shortening of UTILITY]

Ute /yoot, yoóti/ (*plural same* or **Utes**) *n* **1.** a member of a Native North American people who mainly live in Colorado, Utah, and New Mexico **2.** the Uto-Aztecan language of the Ute people. Native speakers: 2,500. [Early 19C. < Spanish *Yuta*, Native American language] —**Ute** *adj*

ute muster *n Aus* a social event centred on a display of decorated or customized utes

utensil /yoo ténss'l/ *n* a tool or container, especially one used in a kitchen [14C. Via Old French *utensile* < Latin *utensilis* 'usable' < *uti* 'to use']

uteri ANAT, ZOOL plural of **uterus**

uterine /yoótə rīn/ *adj* **1.** relating to, in, or affecting the womb **2.** related by having the same mother but a different father ○ *a uterine brother* [15C. < late Latin *uterinus* 'from the same womb' < Latin *uterus* 'womb']

uterus /yoótərəss/ (*plural* **uteruses** or **uteri** /yoótə rī/) *n* **1.** a hollow muscular organ in the pelvic cavity of female mammals, in which the embryo is nourished and develops before birth (*technical*) **2.** a structure in some animals that is similar to the mammalian womb, in which eggs or young develop [17C. < Latin, 'belly, womb']

UTI *abbr* MED urinary tract infection

util. *abbr* utility

utilise *vt* another spelling of **utilize**

utilitarian /yoo tílli táiri ən/ *adj* **1. BELIEVING VALUE LIES IN USEFULNESS** relating to, characteristic of, or advocating the doctrine that value is measured in terms of usefulness **2. PRACTICAL** designed primarily for practical use rather than beauty ■ *n* **BELIEVER IN UTILITARIANISM** a believer in the doctrine of utilitarianism

utilitarianism /yoo tílli táiri ənizəm/ *n* **1. ETHICAL DOCTRINE OF GREATEST GOOD** the ethical doctrine that the greatest happiness of the greatest number should be the criterion of the virtue of action **2. DOCTRINE BASED ON VALUE OF USEFULNESS** the doctrine that the value of an action or an object lies in usefulness **3. UTILITARIAN QUALITY** the quality of being designed primarily for practical use rather than beauty

utility /yoo tílləti/ *n* (*plural* **-ties**) **1.** UTIL same as **public utility 2. SERVICE PROVIDED BY PUBLIC UTILITY** a service such as electricity, gas, or water that is provided by a public utility **3. USEFULNESS** the quality or state of being useful for something **4. SOMETHING USEFUL** something that serves a useful purpose **5. COMPUTER PROGRAM PERFORMING ROUTINE TASKS** a computer program that performs routine tasks and supports operations, as distinct from an applications program **6.** ECON **SATISFACTION DERIVED FROM CONSUMPTION** in economic theory, the amount of satisfaction or pleasure that somebody gains from consuming a commodity, product, or service **7.** *Aus* VEHICLES same as **pick-up truck** ■ *adj* **1. INTENDED FOR PRACTICAL USE** designed or intended for practical use rather than for show or appearance **2.** THEATRE **ABLE TO PERFORM ANY SMALL ROLE** able to perform any small role in a theatre production ○ *a utility actor* **3. ABLE TO PLAY SEVERAL POSITIONS** in some sports, able to substitute for other players in several different positions **4.** *ANZ, N Am* **DESIGNED FOR STRENGTH** built or designed for performing tasks that require strength and versatility ○ *a utility truck* **5.** *US* AGRIC **RAISED FOR FARM USE** grown or raised to be used on a farm ○ *utility livestock* **6.** *N Am* AGRIC **OF LOWEST GRADE** classified as the lowest grade of beef **7.** CLOTHING **FOR EVERYDAY WEAR** describes garments designed for functional use or casual wear, rather

than elegance or fashion [14C. Via French < Latin *utilitas* < *utilis* 'usable' < *uti* 'to use']

utility program *n* COMP same as **utility** *n* (sense 1)

utility room *n* a room in a house where there are large domestic appliances such as a washing machine or boiler, and where many household tasks are done

utility truck *n Aus* VEHICLES same as **pick-up truck**

utility vehicle *n* VEHICLES **1.** *N Am* same as **sport-utility vehicle 2.** *NZ* same as **pick-up truck**

utilize /yóoti līz/ (-izes, -izing, -ized), **utilise** (-ises, -ising, -ised) *vt* to make use of something, or find a practical or effective use for something [Early 19C. < French *utiliser* < Latin *utilis* (see UTILITY)] —**utilizable** *adj* —**utilization** /yóoti līzáysh'n/ *n* —**utilizer** *n*

USAGE **utilize** or **use**? *Utilize* means 'to make use of something, or find a practical use for something' and so means something more specific than *use*. *Utilize* is more common in technical contexts: *The device utilizes a special plug-in connection.* It can also refer to using things in unusual or unintended ways, as a more formal equivalent of 'make use of': *When the fan belt broke they had to utilize a leather belt.* In business jargon and in other contexts, **utilize** is often found when the meaning intended is simply 'use', and this should be avoided: *Successful applicants will be able to utilize their skills and experience in this field.*

SYNONYMS See *use*.

uti possidetis /yóo tī póssi deétiss/ *n* the principle in international law that land and property captured by belligerent parties in war remain their property unless a treaty rules otherwise (*formal*) [< late Latin, 'as you possess']

utmost /útmōst/ *adj* **1.** OF GREATEST DEGREE of the greatest degree, number, or amount **2.** AT EXTREMITY at the most distant point or extremity ▪ *n* GREATEST DEGREE OR AMOUNT the greatest degree, number, or amount of something, especially the greatest effort that somebody is capable of ○ *I did my utmost to persuade her.* [Old English *ūt(e)mest* < OUT + -MOST]

Uto-Aztecan /yóotō áz tekən/ *n* **1.** a family of Native American languages, including Ute and Nahuatl, spoken in the western United States and in Mexico **2.** a member of a people who speak a Uto-Aztecan language [< UTE] —**Uto-Aztecan** *adj*

utopia /yoo tốpi ə/, **Utopia** *n* an ideal and perfect place or state where everyone lives in harmony and everything is for the best [Mid-16C. < modern Latin, literally 'noplace', first used in Sir Thomas More's *Utopia* (1516) < Greek *ou* 'not' + *topos* 'place']

CULTURAL NOTE *Utopia*, a philosophical treatise (1516) by English writer and statesman Sir Thomas More. It contrasts the moral decadence and disunity of contemporary Christian Europe with the tolerance and prosperity of More's imaginary ideal state of Utopia, which is run on secular, communist principles. The term *utopia* has spawned a number of derivatives, for example *utopian*, *utopianism*, and *utopianist*.

utopian /yoo tốpi ən/, **Utopian** *adj* **1.** IDEAL belonging to or characteristic of an ideal perfect state or place **2.** ADMIRABLE BUT IMPRACTICABLE admirable but impracticable in real life **3.** IMPRACTICALLY IDEALISTIC tending to deal in admirable but impracticable ideas ▪ *n* PROPOSER OF UTOPIAN REFORMS a proposer or advocate of visionary but impractical social or political reforms

utopianism /yoo tốpi ənizəm/, **Utopianism** *n* **1.** the principles, views, or aims of a utopian **2.** the belief that an ideal society can be achieved —**utopianist** *n*

utopian socialism *n* a form of socialism based on the belief that a socialist society can be brought about by peacefully persuading those in power to accept it

Utrecht /yóot rekt, -rekht, yoo trékt, -trékht/ historic university city in the central Netherlands. Population: 234,323 (2000).

utricle /yóotrik'l/, **utriculus** /yoo trí kyóoləss/ (*plural* **-li** /-lī/) *n* **1.** the larger of two fluid-filled sacs in the labyrinth of the inner ear, into which the semicircular canals open **2.** the bladder-shaped fruit of some plants [Mid-18C. Directly or via French *utricule* < Latin *utriculus* 'little leather bottle' < *uter* 'leather bottle'] —**utricular** /yoo tríkyóolər/ *adj* —**utriculate** /yoo tríkyoo layt/ *adj*

Utrillo /oo trí llō/, **Maurice** (1883–1955) French artist. The most frequent subject of his paintings was the Parisian urban landscape. His early works show the influence of the impressionist school, whereas later pieces show his interest in the techniques of cubism.

ut supra /út sóoprə/ *adv* as above [< Latin]

Uttaranchal /óottə raán chaal/ state in northern India. Capital: Dehra Dun. Population: 8,479,562 (2001). Area: 56,000 sq. km/21,620 sq. mi.

Uttar Pradesh /óottər prə désh/ state in northern India. Capital: Lucknow. Population: 166,052,859 (2001). Area: 231,256 sq. km/89,288 sq. mi.

utter[1] /úttər/ (-ters, -tering, -tered) *vt* **1.** SAY SOMETHING to say or pronounce something **2.** EMIT SOMETHING AS VOCAL SOUND to emit something as a sound made by the voice ○ *uttered a low growl* **3.** PUBLISH SOMETHING to publish something, e.g. in a book or newspaper ○ *You would not dare to utter this nonsense in print.* **4.** LAW PUT SOMETHING INTO CIRCULATION to put something into circulation, especially counterfeit money or a forgery, in the pretence that it is genuine (*formal*) [14C. < Middle Dutch *ūteren* 'drive out, announce, speak' < Old Low German *ūt* 'out'] —**utterable** *adj* —**utterer** *n*

utter[2] /úttər/ *adj* at the most extreme point or of the highest degree ○ *utter chaos* ○ *utter nonsense* [Old English *ūtera* 'farther out' < OUT]

utterance /úttərənss/ *n* **1.** SOMETHING SAID something said or emitted as a vocal sound **2.** EXPRESSION the expression of something, especially in speech or vocal sound **3.** WAY OF SPEAKING a style or way of speaking **4.** ACT OF SAYING the act of saying something ◇ **give utterance** to express something, especially in speech

utterly /úttərli/ *adv* in an extreme or complete way

uttermost /úttərmōst/ *adj*, *n* same as **utmost**

utu /óo too/ *n NZ* in the Maori culture, satisfaction or reward [Early 19C. < Maori]

U-turn *n* **1.** a turn in the shape of a 'U' made by a vehicle seeking to reverse direction **2.** a complete reversal in opinion, actions, or policy

Utzon /óot zon/, **Jørn** (*b.* 1918) Danish architect. He is best known for designing the Sydney Opera House in Australia.

UU *abbr* **1.** POL Ulster Unionist **2.** RELIG Unitarian Universalist

UV *abbr* PHYS ultraviolet

UVA *n* ultraviolet radiation, especially from the Sun, with a relatively long wavelength

uvarovite /oo vaárə vīt/ *n* a bright emerald-green garnet containing calcium and chromium. Use: gems. [Mid-19C. < Count Sergei Semenovich *Uvarov* (1785–1855), Russian statesman]

UVB *n* ultraviolet radiation, especially from the Sun, with a relatively short wavelength

uvea /yóovi ə/ *n* the middle of the three layers of the eyeball, made up of the choroid, ciliary body, and iris surrounding the lens [Early 16C. Via medieval Latin < Latin *uva* 'grape'] —**uveal** *adj* —**uveous** *adj*

uveitis /yóovi ítiss/ *n* inflammation of the uvea of the eye

UVF *abbr* Ulster Volunteer Force

UV Index *n* a scale used to indicate the intensity of the Sun's ultraviolet rays

uvula /yóovyóoolə/ (*plural* **-las** or **-lae** /-lee/) *n* a small fleshy 'V'-shaped extension of the soft palate that hangs above the tongue at the entrance to the throat [14C. < late Latin, 'little grape' < Latin *uva* 'grape'; from its shape]

uvular /yóovyóoolər/ *adj* **1.** INVOLVING UVULA relating to or involving the uvula **2.** PHON PRONOUNCED VIBRATING UVULA describes a speech sound pronounced with vibration of the uvula ▪ *n* UVULAR SOUND a uvular consonant —**uvularly** *adv*

uvulitis /yóovyoo lítiss/ *n* inflammation of the uvula

UW *abbr* INSUR **1.** underwriter **2.** underwritten

UWIST /yóo wist/ *abbr* University of Wales Institute of Science and Technology

ux. *abbr* wife [Latin *uxor*]

UXB *abbr* unexploded bomb

uxorial /uk sáwri əl/ *adj* relating to, involving, or characteristic of a wife [Early 19C. < Latin *uxor* 'wife'] —**uxorially** *adv*

uxoricide /uk sáwri sīd/ *n* **1.** murder of a wife by her husband **2.** a man who murders his wife [Mid-19C. < Latin *uxor* 'wife'] —**uxoricidal** /uk sáwri sīd'l/ *adj*

uxorious /uk sáwri əss/ *adj* describes a man who is excessively devoted to or submissive to his wife [Late 16C. < Latin *uxoriosus* < *uxor* 'wife'] —**uxoriously** *adv* —**uxoriousness** *n*

uy *abbr* ONLINE Uruguay (*used in Internet addresses*) See table at **domain name**

uz *abbr* ONLINE Uzbekistan (*used in Internet addresses*) See table at **domain name**

Uzbek /óoz bek, úz-/ (*plural* same or **-beks**) *n* **1.** a member of a people who live mainly in Uzbekistan and in neighbouring regions **2.** a Turkic language spoken in Uzbekistan and Central Asia. Native speakers: 16 million. [Early 17C. Directly or via Persian or Russian *uzbek* < Turkish, Uzbek *özbek*] —**Uzbek** *adj*

Uzbekistan

Uzbekistan /óoz béki staán, uz-/ country in Central Asia. It was part of the Soviet Union from 1924 to 1991. Language: Uzbek. Currency: som. Capital: Tashkent. Population: 25,981,647 (2003). Area: 447,400 sq. km/172,700 sq. mi. Official name **Republic of Uzbekistan**

Uzi /óozi/ *n* a 9 mm compact submachine gun [Mid-20C. After *Uziel* Gal, its Israeli designer]

V v

v¹ /vee/ (*plural* **v's**), **V** (*plural* **V's** or **Vs**) *n* **1. 22ND LETTER OF ENGLISH ALPHABET** the 22nd letter of the English alphabet, representing a consonant sound **2. LETTER 'V' WRITTEN** a written representation of the letter 'v' **3. ROMAN NUMERAL FOR 5** the Roman numeral for 5

v², **V** *symbol* PHYS **1.** instantaneous potential difference **2.** instantaneous voltage **3.** specific volume

v³ *abbr* **1.** PHYS vacuum **2.** MATHS vector **3.** MED vein **4.** PHYS velocity component **5.** PHYS velocity speed **6.** MED ventilator **7.** ANAT, BOT ventral **8.** GRAM verb **9.** GRAM verbal **10.** verse **11.** PRINTING verso **12.** versus **13.** vertical **14.** very **15.** via **16.** CHR vicarage **17.** victory **18.** vide **19.** MUSIC violin **20.** MED virus **21.** METEOROL (abnormally good) visibility **22.** MED vision **23.** GRAM vocative **24.** MUSIC voice **25.** GEOG volcano **26.** MEASURE voltage **27.** LING vowel

V¹ /vee/ (*plural* **V's** or **Vs**) *n* something shaped like a letter 'V'

V² *symbol* **1.** PHYS electric potential **2.** PHYS electromotive force **3.** PHYS potential **4.** PHYS potential efficiency **5.** PHYS potential energy **6.** CHEM ELEM vanadium **7.** MEASURE volt **8.** MEASURE volume

V³ *abbr* **1.** PHYS vacuum **2.** BIOCHEM valine **3.** MED variable region **4.** MONEY vatu **5.** MATHS vector **6.** MED vein **7.** CHR Venerable (*used in titles*) **8.** MED ventilator **9.** BOT, ANAT ventral **10.** GRAM verb **11.** GRAM verbal **12.** verse **13.** version **14.** PRINTING verso **15.** versus **16.** vertical **17.** Very (*used in titles*) **18.** CHR vespers **19.** via **20.** CHEM vibrational quantum number **21.** CHR vicar **22.** CHR vicarage **23.** vice **24.** victory **25.** vide **26.** village **27.** MUSIC violin **28.** MED virus **29.** Viscount **30.** Viscountess **31.** METEOROL (abnormally good) visibility **32.** MED vision **33.** GRAM vocative **34.** MUSIC voice **35.** GEOG volcano **36.** MEASURE volt **37.** MEASURE voltage **38.** PHYS voltmeter **39.** Volunteer **40.** Volunteers **41.** LING vowel

v. *abbr* PUBL volume

V-1 /vee wún/ (*plural* **V-1's**) *n* a German robot bomb used in World War II, mainly against England [Abbreviation of German *Vergeltungswaffe eins* 'reprisal weapon one']

V-2 /vee too/ (*plural* **V-2's**) *n* a German liquid-fuelled ballistic missile used in the latter part of World War II, mainly against London [Abbreviation of German *Vergeltungswaffe zwei* 'reprisal weapon two']

V6 /vee síks/ (*plural* **V6's**) *n* an internal-combustion engine with six cylinders arranged in a 'V' shape

V8 /vee áyt/ (*plural* **V8's**) *n* an internal-combustion engine with eight cylinders arranged in a 'V' shape

va *abbr* **1.** ONLINE Vatican City (*used in Internet addresses*) See table at **domain name 2.** GRAM verb active **3.** GRAM verbal adjective **4.** MUSIC viola

VA *abbr* **1.** ECON value-added **2.** COMM value analysis **3.** MED ventricular arrhythmia **4.** CHR vicar apostolic **5.** NAVY Vice Admiral **6.** (Royal Order of) Victoria and Albert **7.** Virginia **8.** visual acuity **9.** visual aid **10.** MEASURE volt-ampere **11.** MIL Volunteer Artillery

V/A *abbr* voucher attached

Vaal /vaal/ river in northeastern South Africa, a tributary of the River Orange. Length: 1,160 km/720 mi.

Vaasa /va'ass aa/ capital of Vaasa Province, western Finland. Population: 56,658 (2000).

vac¹ /vak/ *n* same as **vacation** *n* (sense 2) [Early 18C. Shortening]

vac² /vak/ *n* same as **vacuum cleaner** [Late 20C. Shortening]

vac³ /vak/ *abbr* **1.** vacancy **2.** vacant **3.** PHYS vacuum

vacancy /váykǝnsi/ (*plural* **-cies**) *n* **1. VACANT OFFICE OR POSITION** an office, position, or tenancy that is unfilled or unoccupied **2. MENTAL INACTIVITY** mental inactivity or lack of thought or intelligence **3. VACANT STATE** the state of being vacant **4.** PHYS **EMPTY SITE IN CRYSTAL** an empty site, normally containing an atom or ion, in a crystal [Late 16C. < VACANT or < late Latin *vacantia* < Latin *vacant-* (see VACANT)]

vacant /váykǝnt/ *adj* **1. WITHOUT OCCUPANT** with no occupant or contents, often temporarily ○ *There were several vacant seats on the bus.* **2. UNOCCUPIED BY INCUMBENT OR OFFICIAL** not occupied by an incumbent, official, or possessor, often temporarily ○ *The post remains vacant.* **3. LACKING EXPRESSION** showing no signs of thought, intelligence, or expression ○ *a vacant stare* **4. FREE FROM ACTIVITY** free from activity, business, or work ○ *a vacant afternoon* [13C. Via Old French < Latin *vacant-*, present participle of *vacare* 'be empty'] —**vacantly** *adv*

SYNONYMS *vacant, unoccupied, empty, void*
CORE MEANING: lacking contents or occupants

vacant with no occupant or contents, often temporarily ○ *posts left vacant by teachers* ○ *In this part of the country, there is a plentiful supply of vacant land and public support for development.* **unoccupied** not being used or lived in by anybody ○ *The building was unoccupied at the time of the incident.* ○ *Across the room, Oliver's desk was unoccupied.* **empty** not containing or holding anything, or unoccupied or uninhabited ○ *He took a last gulp and placed the empty glass down on the bar.* ○ *Cinemas showing the film were almost empty.* **void** having no contents, or not occupied ○ *void spaces between the particles*

vacant possession *n* ownership of a house whose previous occupants have already moved out

vacate /vǝ káyt, vay-/ (**-cates, -cating, -cated**) *vt* **1. GIVE UP OCCUPANCY OF SOMETHING** to relinquish the possession or occupancy of something ○ *vacate the premises* **2. EMPTY SOMETHING OF OCCUPANTS** to empty something of incumbents or occupants **3. RESIGN FROM SOMETHING** to withdraw from or surrender possession of an office or post ○ *vacate a legislative seat* **4.** LAW **MAKE SOMETHING INVALID** to make something legally void [Mid-17C. < Latin *vacat-*, past participle of *vacare* 'be empty'] —**vacatable** *adj*

vacation /vǝ káysh'n/ *n* **1.** N Am same as **holiday** *n* (sense 2) **2.** a scheduled period during which the activities of law courts, universities, or other regular businesses are suspended **3.** an act or an instance or vacating something ■ *vi* (**-tions, -tioning, -tioned**) N Am LEISURE same as **holiday** [14C. Directly or via French < Latin *vacation-* < *vacat-* (see VACATE)]

vacationer /vǝ káysh'nǝr/, **vacationist** /vǝ káysh'nist/ *n* N Am same as **holidaymaker**

vaccinate /váksi nayt/ (**-nates, -nating, -nated**) *vt* to inoculate a person or animal with a vaccine to produce immunity to a disease —**vaccination** /váksi náysh'n/ *n* —**vaccinator** *n* —**vaccinatory** /-nǝtǝri/ *adj*

vaccine /vák seen/ *n* **1.** a preparation containing weakened or dead microbes of the kind that cause a disease, administered to stimulate the immune system to produce antibodies against that disease **2.** a software program that protects a system against a computer virus [Late 18C. < Latin *vaccinus* 'of a cow' < *vacca* 'cow', because originally the cowpox virus used to prevent smallpox] —**vaccinal** *adj*

ORIGIN *Vaccine* was used by the British physician Edward Jenner at the end of the 18th century in the terms *vaccine disease*, meaning 'cowpox', and hence *vaccine inoculation*, meaning the technique he developed of preventing smallpox by injecting people with cowpox virus. There is no evidence of the use of **vaccine** as a noun to denote the inoculated material until the 1840s.

vaccinee /váksi nee/ *n* somebody who is vaccinated [Late 19C. < VACCINATE]

vaccinia /vak sínni ǝ/ *n* a skin eruption in reaction to inoculation with the weakened cowpox virus that was once used to vaccinate people against smallpox [Early 19C. < modern Latin < Latin *vaccinus* (see VACCINE)] —**vaccinial** *adj*

~~vaccum~~ incorrect spelling of **vacuum**

vacherin /vásh raN, vash ráN/ *n* a soft cheese from France or Switzerland [Mid-20C. < French]

vacillate /vássi layt/ (**-lates, -lating, -lated**) *vi* **1.** to be indecisive or irresolute, changing between one opinion and another **2.** to sway from side to side [Late 16C. < Latin *vacillat-*, past participle of *vaccillare* 'sway, totter'] —**vacillant** *adj* —**vacillation** /vássi láysh'n/ *n* —**vacillator** *n*

SYNONYMS See *hesitate*.

vacua PHYS plural of **vacuum**

vacuity /va kyóo ǝti/ (*plural* **-ties**) *n* **1. LACK OF IDEAS** a lack of intelligent or serious content **2. EMPTINESS** the condition or quality of being empty of all contents (*formal*) **3. EMPTY SPACE** an empty area or space (*formal*) **4. MEANINGLESS STATE OR THING** a thing or condition that is inane or devoid of any meaningful content (*formal*) ○ *legislative vacuity* [Mid-16C. Directly or via French *vacuité* < Latin *vacuitas* < *vacuus* 'empty']

vacuolar membrane /vákyoo ṓlǝr-/ *n* a membrane containing fluid in the cytoplasm of a cell

vacuolate /vákyoo ǝlǝt, -layt/, **vacuolated** /-laytid/ *adj* having small holes —**vacuolation** /vákyoo ǝ láysh'n/ *n*

vacuole /vákyoo ōl/ *n* **1.** a membrane-bound compartment containing fluid that is found in the cytoplasm of a cell **2.** a small cavity in tissue [Mid-19C. < French, 'little empty (space)' < Latin *vacuus* 'empty'] —**vacuolar** /vákyoo ṓlǝr/ *adj*

vacuous /vákyoo ǝss/ *adj* **1. INANE** lacking ideas or intelligence, or showing such a lack ○ *a vacuous remark* **2. IDLE** lacking attention, concentration, or serious thought ○ *a vacuous stare* **3. LACKING CONTENT** having no content or substance (*archaic*) [Mid-17C. < Latin *vacuus* 'empty'] —**vacuously** *adv* —**vacuousness** *n*

vacuum /vákyoo ǝm, vákyoo̅m/ *n* (*plural* **-uums** or **-ua** /-yoo ǝ/) **1.** PHYS **SPACE EMPTY OF MATTER** a space completely empty of matter but not achievable in practice on Earth **2.** PHYS **SPACE WITH ALL GAS REMOVED** a space from which all air or gas has been extracted **3. EMPTINESS CAUSED BY ABSENCE** an emptiness caused by somebody or something's absence or removal ○ *Her death left a vacuum in his life.* **4. ISOLATION FROM OUTSIDE WORLD** isolation from external influences ○ *You can't live in a vacuum.* **5.** (*plural* **vacuums**) HOUSEHOLD same as **vacuum cleaner** ■ *vti* (**-uums, -uuming, -uumed**) CLEAN SOMETHING USING VACUUM CLEANER to clean an area or object using a vacuum cleaner [Mid-16C. < modern Latin < neuter of Latin *vacuus* 'empty']

vacuum bottle *n* US same as **vacuum flask**

vacuum brake *n* a train or vehicle brake system in which a reservoir-maintained vacuum, under the control of the driver, operates the brake cylinder

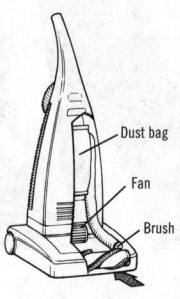

Dust bag

Fan

Brush

vacuum cleaner

vacuum cleaner *n* an electrical appliance that cleans surfaces such as carpets and upholstery by sucking dirt and other material into a bag or cylinder

vacuum distillation *n* a process of distilling liquid at low pressure so that it boils at a lower boiling point

vacuum drying *n* the removal of liquid from a solution or mixture at reduced air pressure so that it dries at a lower temperature than it would at full pressure

vacuum flask *n* a flask with double walls, usually of silvered glass, separated by an airless space, used to hold liquids and maintain them at constant high or low temperatures. US term **vacuum bottle**

vacuum forming *n* 1. the process of shaping sheets of heated thermoplastic by placing them in a mould and removing air by suction 2. a method of shaping plastic by applying suction to heated sheets held above a mould

vacuum gauge *n* an instrument that measures pressures below atmospheric pressure

vacuum-packed *adj* packed in an airtight container or package under low pressure in order to prevent the contents from spoiling or corroding

vacuum pan *n* a device with a vacuum pump that removes moisture quickly by boiling a substance at a low temperature under reduced pressure

vacuum pump *n* 1. a device that creates a partial vacuum 2. ENG same as **pulsometer**

vacuum tube *n* N Am same as **valve** (sense 3)

vada *n* S Asia FOOD another spelling of **wada**

vade mecum /vaˈadi máykəm/ *n* 1. a guidebook, handbook, or manual, especially one carried around or designed to be carried around constantly and referred to often 2. an object that a person carries constantly because it is useful [Early 17C. < Latin, 'go with me']

Vadodara /vəˈdṓdərə/ industrial city in Gujarat State, western India. Population: 1,492,398 (2001).

vadose /váy dṓss/ *adj* describes water in the unsaturated zone of the Earth's crust that is above the level of ground water, or relating to such water [Late 19C. < Latin *vadosus* < *vadum* 'shallow piece of water']

vadose zone *n* the unsaturated zone between the ground surface and the water table through which ground water can percolate

Vaduz /fa dṓots/ capital of Liechtenstein, on the River Rhine. Population: 4,927 (2001).

Vafa /vaˈafə/, **Cumrun** (*b*. 1960) Iranian physicist. A professor of physics at Harvard University, he made important advances in string theory as a unified description of gravity and other forces.

vag- *prefix* same as **vago-** (*used before vowels*)

vagabond /vággə bond/ *n* 1. HOMELESS WANDERER a wanderer who has no permanent place to live 2. BEGGAR a beggar for food or money ■ *adj* 1. OF VAGABONDS relating to or characteristic of a vagabond 2. UNPREDICTABLE wayward or capricious by nature ■ *vi* (-bonds, -bonding, -bonded) BE VAGABOND to wander from place to place [15C. Via French < Latin *vagabundus* < *vagari* 'wander'] —**vagabondage** *n* —**vagabondism** *n*

vagal /váyg'l/ *adj* relating to the tenth pair of cranial nerves (**vagi**) —**vagally** *adv*

vagary /váygəri/ (*plural* -**ries**) *n* an unpredictable or eccentric change, action, or idea ○ *the vagaries of the weather* [Late 16C. < Latin *vagari* 'wander'] —**vagarious** /və gáiri əss/ *adj*

vagi ANAT plural of **vagus**

vagile /vájjīl/ *adj* able to move around within a specific environment [Early 20C. < VAGUS] —**vagility** /və jílləti/ *n*

vagina /və jínə/ (*plural* -**nas** or -**nae** /-nee/) *n* 1. in female mammals, a lubricated muscular tube that connects the cervix of the womb to the vulva 2. a plant or animal part that forms a sheath, e.g. that formed by a leaf around a stem [Late 17C. < Latin, 'sheath, scabbard'] —**vaginal** *adj* —**vaginally** *adv*

vaginate /vájji nət, -nayt/, **vaginated** /-naytid/ *adj* having, forming, or resembling a sheath

vaginectomy /vájji néktəmi/ (*plural* -**mies**) *n* 1. surgical removal of all or part of the vagina 2. surgical removal of all or part of the smooth moist membrane that encloses the testis and epididymis

vaginismus /vájji nízməss/ *n* a painful and often prolonged contraction of the vagina in response to touching of the vulva or vagina [Mid-19C. < modern Latin < VAGINA]

vaginitis /vájji nítiss/ *n* inflammation of the vagina

vago- *prefix* vagus ○ *vagotomy* [< VAGUS]

vagotomy /və góttəmi/ (*plural* -**mies**) *n* the surgical cutting of the tenth pair of cranial nerves (**vagi**) or any of their branches, performed to control duodenal ulcers by decreasing acid secretion of the stomach

vagotonia /váygə tṓni ə/ *n* a pathological condition in which overactivity of the tenth pair of cranial nerves (**vagi**) affects bodily functions controlled by these nerves, e.g. those in blood vessels and the gut [Early 20C. < VAGO- + Greek *tonos* 'stretching, tension'] —**vagotonic** /-tónnik/ *adj*

vagotropic /váygə tróppik, -trṓpik/ *adj* describes a drug that has an effect on the tenth pair of cranial nerves (**vagi**)

vagrant /váygrənt/ *n* 1. HOMELESS WANDERER a wanderer who has no permanent place to live 2. WANDERER somebody who never stays in one place for long 3. LAW SOMEBODY ILLEGALLY LIVING ON STREETS somebody guilty of the legal offence of living on the streets and, in some jurisdictions, begging 4. BIRDS BIRD OFF USUAL MIGRATION ROUTE a migratory bird that deviates from its usual migration route ■ *adj* 1. HOMELESS wandering from one place to another and having no permanent place to live 2. WANDERING never staying in one place for long 3. WAYWARD wayward or capricious in nature 4. RANDOM acting or done in a random way ○ *a vagrant breeze* 5. BOT GROWING IN UNCONTROLLED WAY describes plants that grow in a lush uncontrolled way [15C. < Anglo-Norman *varagarant*] —**vagrancy** *n* —**vagrantly** *adv* —**vagrantness** *n*

vague /vayg/ (**vaguer**, **vaguest**) *adj* 1. NOT EXPLICIT not clear in meaning or intention ○ *a vague proposal* 2. NOT DISTINCTLY SEEN not having a clear or perceptible form ○ *a vague form in the shadows* 3. NOT CLEARLY PERCEIVED IN MIND not clearly felt, understood, or recalled ○ *I have a vague recollection of it.* 4. UNCLEAR IN THINKING unclear or incoherent in thinking or expression ○ *made vague mutterings in his sleep* 5. UNVERIFIED not properly validated or having no clear or identifiable source ○ *vague allegations* [Mid-16C. Directly or via French < Latin *vagus* 'wandering, inconstant'] —**vaguely** *adv* —**vagueness** *n*

vagus /váygəss/ (*plural* -**gi** /-jī, -gī/), **vagus nerve** *n* either of the tenth pair of cranial nerves that carry sensory and motor neurons serving the heart, lungs, stomach, intestines, and various other organs [Mid-19C. < Latin *vagus* 'wandering, inconstant']

vaidya /vídi ə/ *n* S Asia an Ayurvedic Hindu physician [Mid-20C. < Hindi < *vaidy* 'expert on Ayurvedic medicine']

vain /vayn/ *adj* 1. EXCESSIVELY PROUD excessively proud, especially of personal appearance 2. UNSUCCESSFUL failing to have or unlikely to have the intended or desired result ○ *a vain attempt to escape* 3. EMPTY OF SUBSTANCE devoid of meaning or substance [14C. Via Old French < Latin *vanus* 'without substance'] —**vainly** *adv* —**vainness** *n* ◇ **in vain** 1. fruitlessly, pointlessly, or unsuccessfully ○ *We searched in vain for a solution.* 2. in a disrespectful or blasphemous way

SPELLCHECK **vain**, **vane**, or **vein**? Do not confuse the spelling of **vain**, **vane**, and **vein**, which sound similar. *Vain* is an adjective meaning 'excessively proud', 'unsuccessful', or 'devoid of meaning', as in *a vain man*, *a vain hope*, *vain threats*; it is also used in the phrase *in vain*, as in *trying in vain to reach them*. *Vane* is a noun denoting a flat rotating blade or the flat part of a feather; a *weather vane* indicates the direction of the wind. *Vein* is chiefly used as a noun, denoting a blood vessel, a similar structure in a leaf or an insect's wing, a layer of ore in rock, or a streak in something such as marble, wood, or cheese.

vainglorious /vayn gláwri əss/ *adj* excessively proud or boastful (*literary*) —**vaingloriously** *adv* —**vaingloriousness** *n*

vainglory /vayn gláwri/ (*plural* -**ries**) *n* (*literary*) 1. excessive pride in or boastfulness about personal abilities or achievements 2. an excessive display of something in order to draw attention to it [12C. Via French < Latin *vana gloria* 'empty glory']

vair /vair/ *n* 1. fur used as a trimming on medieval robes 2. a blue-and-white fur used on heraldic shields [14C. Via French < Latin *varius* 'speckled, changeable']

vairy /váiri/ *n* SW England same as **weasel** *n* (sense 1) (*regional*)

Vaisakha /vīss aakə/ *n* in the Hindu calendar, the second month of the year, lasting 31 days and falling about the same time as April to May. See table at **calendar**

Vaishnava /víshnəvə/ *n* a member of a group devoted to the worship of the Hindu god Vishnu or one of his incarnations [Late 18C. < Sanskrit *vaiṣnava* 'relating to Vishnu'] —**Vaishnavism** *n*

Vaisya /víssyə, vísh-/, **Vaishya** *n* 1. the third of the four Hindu castes, the members of which were traditionally merchants and farmers 2. a member of the Vaisya caste [Mid-17C. < Sanskrit *vaiśya* 'farm labourer, tradesman']

Vajpayee /vaj páy ee/, **Atal Bihari** (*b*. 1924) Indian prime minister. He was the first leader of the Hindu nationalist party Bharatiya Janata Party (1980). He was briefly prime minister (1996) but was forced to resign due to lack of support from other parties. He was prime minister of a coalition government (1998–2004).

vakil /vaa keél/, **vakeel**, **wakil** *n* S Asia a lawyer or legal representative in a court of law [Early 17C. Via Persian and Urdu *wakīl*, Turkish *vakīl* < Arabic *wakīl*]

val. *abbr* 1. GEOL valley 2. FIN valuation 3. COMM value

Valais Alps /vaa láy-/ ◆ **Pennine Alps**

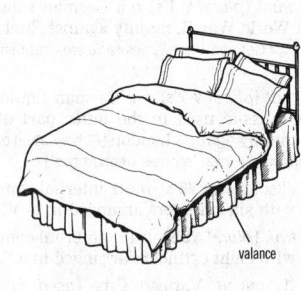

valance

valance

valance /vállənss/, **valence** *n* 1. a plain, pleated, or gathered fabric cover that hangs from a shelf or from the base of a bed to the floor 2. a short decorative piece of drapery or wood hung across a window to cover the rod from which curtains hang [15C. Origin ?] —**valanced** *adj*

vale[1] /vayl/ *n* a valley or dale, often one that has a stream running through it (*often used in placenames*) [14C. Via French < Latin *valles* 'valley'] ◇ **vale of tears** the world considered as a place full of sadness or unhappiness

SPELLCHECK **vale** or **veil**? Do not confuse the spelling of **vale** and **veil**, which sound similar. The word **vale**, meaning 'valley', is chiefly found in place names (as in *the Vale of Evesham*) or in the phrase *vale of tears*. **Veil**

is a noun or verb referring to a covering for the face or something that conceals in a similar way, as in *a bride's veil, a veil of mist, veiled in secrecy*.

vale[2] /vaá lay/ *interj* A Latin expression of farewell ■ *n* an act of saying farewell or adieu [Mid-16C. < Latin, 'be well!', form of *valere* 'be strong or well']

valediction /válli díksh'n/ *n* (*formal*) **1.** the act of saying goodbye or an instance of leave-taking **2.** a statement, speech, or letter of farewell [Mid-17C. < Latin *valedicere* 'say goodbye', after BENEDICTION]

valedictorian /vállidik táwri ən/ *n* in the United States and Canada, a student in a graduating class who is highest in academic ranking and is usually required to give a valedictory address at the graduation ceremony

valedictory /válli díktəri/ *n* (*plural* **-ries**) **1.** a statement or speech of farewell (*formal*) **2.** N Am EDUC same as **valedictory address** ■ *adj* performing the function of saying farewell (*formal*)

valedictory address *n* N Am a speech delivered at graduation, usually by the graduating student with the highest academic ranking

valence[1] *n* CHEM, IMMUNOL same as **valency**

valence[2] *n* HOUSEHOLD another spelling of **valance**

Valencia /və lénshi ə, -si ə/ **1.** capital of the autonomous region of Valencia in eastern Spain. The city was founded in Roman times. Population: 761,871 (2002). **2.** city in northern Venezuela, on the River Cabriales. Population: 1,034,033 (1992 estimate).

Valenciennes[1] /vállənssi én/ *n* a fine cotton lace made with bobbins in a floral design, originally made of linen [Early 18C. After VALENCIENNES[2]]

Valenciennes[2] /vállənssi én, va laaNss yen/ city in the Nord-Pas-de-Calais Region of northern France and administrative centre of the Nord Department. Population: 41,278 (1999).

valency /váylənssi/ (*plural* **-cies**), **valence** /-lənss/ *n* **1.** COMBINING POWER OF ATOMS the combining power of atoms or groups measured by the number of electrons the atom or group will receive, give up, or share in forming a compound **2.** COMBINING ANTIGENIC DETERMINANTS the number of different antigenic determinants with which a single antibody molecule can combine **3.** COMBINING POWER OF VERB the ability of a verb to combine grammatically with noun phrases in a given clause [Mid-19C. < Latin *valentia* 'power, competence' < *valere* 'be powerful']

valency electron *n* an electron in an outer shell of an atom that can be lost to or shared with another atom to form a molecule

valency shell *n* the outer electron shell of an atom, containing one or more electrons (**valency electrons**) that are available to form bonds with other atoms to create molecules

Valens /váyl enz/ (328?–378) Roman emperor. The brother of Valentinian I, he ruled the eastern half of the empire from 364 until his death in battle against the Visigoths.

-valent *suffix* having a particular valency or valencies ○ *divalent* [< VALENCY]

valentine /vállən tīn/ *n* **1.** a greeting card or gift sent, traditionally anonymously, to somebody on Valentine's Day as a token of love **2.** the person to whom somebody sends a card or gift on Valentine's Day as a token of love [15C. After VALENTINE]

Valentine /vállən tīn/, **St** (*d.* AD 269?) Roman priest and martyr. He is thought to have been killed during the persecution of Christians by Emperor Claudius II.

Valentine's Day *n* the Christian feast day of St Valentine and the traditional day for sending a romantic card or gift, especially anonymously, to somebody you love. Date: 14 February.

Valentinian I /vállən tínni ən/ (321–375) Roman emperor. As the emperor of the western half of the empire from 364, he was militarily successful and promoted education and medical care.

Valentinian II (371?–392) Roman emperor. After periods of regency and exile, he gained power over the western empire in 388, but was murdered four years later.

Valentinian III (419–455) Roman emperor. He ruled the western empire at a time when much of it was overrun by invaders.

Rudolph Valentino

Valentino /vállən teenō/, **Rudolph** (1895–1926) Italian-born US actor. His passionate roles in silent films made him a romantic screen idol. Born **d'Antonguolla, Rodolpho Guglielmi di Valentina**

Valera ♦ De Valera, Eamon

valerian /və leéri ən/ *n* (*plural* **-ans** or *same*) *n* **1.** PLANTS PLANT WITH MEDICINAL ROOT a herbaceous perennial plant. Flowers: small, sweet-smelling, white or pinkish. Native to: Europe, Asia. Genus: *Valeriana*. **2.** FLOWERING PLANT a bushy perennial plant. Flowers: red, pink, or white. Native to: Mediterranean. Latin name: *Centranthus ruber*. **3.** MED SEDATIVE MADE FROM VALERIAN a herbal medicine made from the dried roots of valerian. Use: mild sedative, tranquillizer. [15C. Via French < medieval Latin *valeriana*, after *Valeria*, Roman province]

Valerian /və leéri ən/ (*d.* 260?) Roman emperor. Reigning from 253, he had to contend with repeated invasions and died in captivity after defeat by the Persians.

valeric acid /və leérik-/ *n* a pungent colourless liquid. Use: flavourings, perfumes, pharmaceuticals. Formula: $C_5H_{10}O_2$. [< VALERIAN]

Valéry /valle reé/, **Paul** (1871–1945) French poet and critic. He was considered to be one of France's greatest 20th-century poets and his prolific early output was followed by a 20-year silence, during which he worked mainly on mathematics and philosophical meditations. His later work was heavily influenced by the symbolists. Full name **Valéry, Paul Ambroise**

> 'God made everything out of nothing. But the nothingness shows through.'
> [Paul Valéry, *Mauvaises pensées et autres* (*Wicked and Other Thoughts*); 1942]

valet /vállit, vállay/ *n* **1.** MALE SERVANT a male personal servant of a man, whose duties include looking after his employer's clothes and providing his meals **2.** MALE HOTEL OR PASSENGER SHIP EMPLOYEE a male employee whose duties include cleaning the clothes of hotel guests or passengers on ships **3.** SOMEBODY PERFORMING CAR PARKING SERVICE somebody employed to park the cars of people arriving at a hotel, restaurant, or airport and bring the cars back for them on departure ■ *v* (**-ets, -eting, -eted**) **1.** *vti* WORK AS VALET to work as a valet or provide valet services to somebody **2.** *vt* CLEAN CAR to clean somebody's car in return for payment [15C. < French < assumed medieval Latin *vassus* 'servant to a knight']

valeta *n* DANCE another spelling of **veleta**

valet de chambre /vállay də shaáNbrə/ (*plural* **valets de chambre** /*pronunc. same*/) *n* OCCUPATIONS same as **valet** *n* (sense 1) [French, 'valet of the room']

valet parking *n* a service provided by some hotels, restaurants, and airports whereby an employee parks people's cars for them on arrival and brings the cars back for them on departure

valetudinarian /válli tyoóodi náiri ən/, **valetudinary** /válli tyoóodinəri/ (*plural* **-ies**) *n* **1.** SOMEBODY WITH POOR HEALTH somebody who has persistent ill health **2.** SOMEBODY OBSESSED WITH HEALTH somebody who is excessively concerned with his or her own health ■ *adj* **1.** OF VALETUDINARIAN relating to or being a valetudinarian **2.** OF POOR HEALTH relating to, characterized by, or arising from poor health **3.** TRYING TO BE HEALTHIER trying

to recover or improve health [Late 16C. < Latin *valetudinarius* 'in ill health' < *valetudo* 'state of health' < *valere* 'be well'] —**valetudinarianism** *n*

~~**valey**~~ incorrect spelling of **valley**

valgus /válgəss/ *adj* describes a condition in which a body part such as the knee or foot is bent or twisted outwards away from the midline of the body ■ *n* the position or state in which a bone or body part is bent or twisted outwards away from the midline of the body [Early 19C. < Latin, 'knock-kneed'] —**valgoid** *adj*

Valhalla /val hállə/, **Walhalla**, **Walhall** /val háll/ *n* in Norse mythology, the great hall where the souls of heroes killed in battle spend eternity [Late 17C. Via modern Latin < Old Norse *valhall* 'hall of the slain' < *valr* 'those slain in battle']

valiant /válli ənt/ *adj* **1.** COURAGEOUS brave and steadfast ○ *a valiant warrior* **2.** DONE COURAGEOUSLY characterized by or performed with bravery but often ending in failure ○ *a valiant attempt at rescue* ■ *n* SOMEBODY COURAGEOUS a brave and steadfast person [14C. Via Old French < Latin *valent-*, present participle of *valere* 'be strong'] —**valiance** *n* —**valiancy** *n* —**valiantly** *adv*

valid /vállid/ *adj* **1.** UNEXPIRED usable or acceptable until a fixed expiry date or under specific conditions of use ○ *a valid passport* **2.** JUSTIFIABLE reasonable or justifiable in the circumstances ○ *That's a valid question.* **3.** EFFECTIVE bringing about the results or ends intended ○ *regards the test as a valid measure of student performance* **4.** LAW LEGALLY BINDING having binding force in law **5.** LAW LEGALLY ACCEPTABLE acceptable under law **6.** LOGIC LOGICAL having premises from which the conclusion follows logically ○ *It's a perfectly valid argument.* [Late 16C. Directly or via French < Latin *validus* 'strong' < *valere* 'be strong'] —**validity** /və líddəti/ *n* —**validly** *adv*

SYNONYMS **valid, cogent, convincing, reasonable, sound**

CORE MEANING: worthy of acceptance or credence

valid reasonable or justifiable in the circumstances ○ *Mrs Smith raises a valid point in her letter.* ○ *We are required to notify all other parties unless there is a valid reason why such notice should not be given.* **cogent** forceful and convincing to the intellect and reason ○ *a cogent analysis of the situation* ○ *How cogent his arguments are is questionable.* **convincing** likely to overcome doubts and win the support of those who hear it ○ *Your explanation is not wholly convincing.* ○ *He requires convincing evidence before he will adopt this theory.* **reasonable** acceptable and according to common sense ○ *must show reasonable grounds for his actions* ○ *It seemed like a reasonable assumption at the time.* **sound** based on good sense and acceptable reasoning and worthy of approval ○ *We trust that these decisions are based on sound business sense.* ○ *Our expert offers some sound advice on minimizing the dangers of climbing in the Alps.*

validate /válli dayt/ (**-dates, -dating, -dated**) *vt* **1.** CONFIRM TRUTHFULNESS OF SOMETHING to confirm or establish the truthfulness or soundness of something **2.** LAW MAKE SOMETHING LEGAL to declare or render something legal or binding ○ *validate a passport* **3.** REGISTER SOMETHING FORMALLY to register something formally and have its use officially sanctioned **4.** MAKE SOMEBODY FEEL VALUED to make somebody feel valued as a person, or feel that his or her ideas or opinions are worthwhile [Mid-17C. < Latin *validare* 'render legally valid' < *validus* (see VALID)] —**validation** /válli dáysh'n/ *n* —**validatory** /-dətəri/ *adj*

$$H_3C-\overset{\displaystyle |}{\underset{\displaystyle CH_3}{CH}}-\overset{\displaystyle |}{\underset{\displaystyle NH_2}{CH}}-\overset{\displaystyle O}{\overset{\displaystyle \|}{C}}-OH$$

valine

valine /váy leen, vál-/ *n* an essential amino acid, required for normal growth. Formula: $C_5H_{11}NO_2$. See illustration on previous page [Early 20C. < VALERIC ACID]

valise /və léez/ *n* a small piece of luggage (*dated*) [Early 20C. Via French < Italian *valigia*]

Valium /válli əm/ *tdmk* a trademark for diazepam, a tranquillizer

Valkyrie /válkəri, val keéri/, **Walkyrie**, **Valkyr** /vál keer/ *n* in Norse mythology, one of the twelve handmaids of Odin who ride their horses over the field of battle and escort the souls of slain heroes to Valhalla [Mid-18C. < Old Norse *Valkyrja* 'chooser of the slain' < *valr* 'those slain in battle'] —**Valkyrian** /val keéri ən/ *adj*

valla ANCIENT HIST, BUILDINGS plural of **vallum**

Valladolid /válldə líd/ capital of Valladolid Province, northern Spain. It was the capital of Spain before Madrid. Population: 318,576 (2002).

vallate /vállayt/ (**-lates, -lating, -lated**) *vt* to plan or build earthworks to defend a position [Late 19C. Back-formation < VALLATION]

vallate papillae *npl* large papillae forming a line near the back of the tongue and containing taste buds

vallation /va láysh'n/ *n* **1.** a defensive fortification or embankment made of earth **2.** the planning or building of defensive fortifications or embankments made of earth [Mid-17C. < Latin *vallation-* < *vallare* 'protect' < *vallum* SEE VALLUM]

vallecula /və lékyōōlə/ (*plural* **-lae** /-lee/) *n* a shallow groove, depression, or furrow in an animal or plant body, e.g. that between the hemispheres of the cerebellum in the brain [Mid-19C. < Latin *vallicula* < *valles* 'valley'] —**vallecular** *adj* —**valleculate** *adj*

Valle d'Aosta /vállay daa óstə/ region in northern Italy, on the border with France and Switzerland. It contains the Alpine peaks of the Matterhorn and Mont Blanc. Population: 120,343 (2000). Area: 3,264 sq. km/1,260 sq. mi.

Valles Marineris /válless márri náiriss/ system of valleys and canyons in the equatorial region of Mars, 4,000 km/2,500 mi. long, up to 240 km/150 mi. wide, and 6.5 km/4 mi. deep

Valletta /və léttə/ capital and chief port of Malta. Population: 7,048 (2000).

valley /válli/ (*plural* **-leys**) *n* **1.** LOW-LYING AREA a long low area of land, often with a river or stream running through it, that is surrounded by higher ground **2.** LOW-LYING LAND AROUND RIVER a large area of low-lying land around a river and its tributaries **3.** VALLEY-SHAPED HOLLOW a long sunken area or groove shaped like a valley **4.** ARCHIT ANGLE BETWEEN ROOF SLOPES the angle formed where two slopes of a roof meet [13C. Via Old French *valee* < Latin *valles* 'valley'] —**valleyed** *adj*

valley fever *n* MED same as **coccidioidomycosis** [After the San Joaquin *Valley*, California]

Valley Forge /válli fawrj/ historic site in Pennsylvania, northwest of Philadelphia on the Schuylkill River. During the winter of 1777–78, George Washington and 12,000 troops of the Continental Army endured a season of intense deprivation and demoralization that came to be seen as the bleakest period of the War of American Independence.

Valley of the Kings gorge on the western bank of the River Nile, southern Egypt. It was the burial site of pharaohs of the New Kingdom (1570–1070 BC).

Vallis Alpes /válliss ál pez/ valley on the Moon northeast of mare imbrium, orientated approximately from west to east and cutting across Montes Alpes

vallum /válləm/ (*plural* **-lums** or **-la** /-lə/) *n* an ancient Roman fortification or embankment, built for defence [Early 17C. < Latin < *vallus* 'palisade, stake']

Valois /vállwaa/, **Dame Ninette de** (1898–2001) Irish-born British dancer and choreographer. She founded the Sadler's Wells Ballet (1931) which became the Royal Ballet in 1956. Born **Stannus, Edris**

> 'Ladies and gentleman, it takes more than one to make a ballet.'
> [Dame Ninette de Valois, *New Yorker*; 1950]

valonia /və lóni ə/ *n* the dried acorn cups and unripe acorns of an oak. Use: tanning, inks, dyes. [Early 18C. Via Italian < Greek *balanos* 'acorn']

Dame Ninette de Valois
(credit: Hulton-Deutsch Collection/Corbis)

valor *n* US spelling of **valour**

valorize /vállə ríz/ (**-izes, -izing, -ized**), **valorise** (**-ises, -ising, -ised**) *vt* to set and maintain the price of a commodity at an artificially high level through government action [Early 20C. Via Portuguese *valorizar* < *valor* 'value' < late Latin (see VALOUR)] —**valorization** *n*

valorous /vállərəss/ *adj* having or showing courage, especially in war or battle —**valorously** *adv*

valour /vállər/ *n* courage, especially that shown in war or battle [Late 16C. Via Italian *valore* < Latin *valor* < *valere* 'be strong']

Valparaiso /válpə rízō/, **Valparaíso** /bálpara eéssō/ capital of Valparaiso Region in central Chile. Population: 293,800 (1998).

Valpolicella /vál polli chéllə/ *n* a light red wine from northwestern Italy [Early 20C. After a district]

valproate /válprō ayt/, **valproic acid** /val prṓ ik-/ *n* a synthetic crystalline compound with anticonvulsant properties. Use: treatment of epilepsy. [Late 20C. < *valproic acid* (< VALERIC ACID + PROPYL)]

Valsalva manoeuvre /val sálvə-/ *n* **1.** the action of attempting to breathe out when the mouth is closed and the nostrils are held shut, thereby forcing air into the middle ear via the Eustachian tubes **2.** the action of attempting to breathe out against a closed glottis, which increases pressure in the thoracic cavity and hinders the return of venous blood to the heart [After Antonio Maria *Valsalva* (1666–1723), Italian anatomist]

valse /valss/ *n* a waltz, especially one of French origin [Late 18C. Via French < German *Walzer* (see WALTZ)]

valuable /vállyoob'l, -yoo əb'l/ *adj* **1.** WORTH GREAT DEAL OF MONEY having significant monetary value **2.** USEFUL having great importance or usefulness ○ *a valuable insight* **3.** HELD DEAR cherished or esteemed because of personal qualities **4.** RARE highly prized because of being in short or limited supply **5.** ABLE TO BE VALUED capable of being assigned a value ■ *n* VALUABLE ITEM a possession, especially a piece of jewellery, that has significant monetary value (*often used in the plural*) —**valuably** *adv*

valuable consideration *n* in English contract law, something given or undertaken as part of an agreement between two parties that has some objective value and so makes the agreement a valid contract. For example, in the sale of a car, valuable consideration is the money paid to the person selling the car.

valuate /vállyoo ayt/ (**-ates, -ating, -ated**) *vt* to determine the price or cost of something

valuation /vállyoo áysh'n/ *n* **1.** APPRAISAL OF COST the act of determining the value or price of something, especially property **2.** PRICE the price of something established by appraisal of its quality, condition, and desirability, or of the cost of replacement **3.** ESTIMATE OF IMPORTANCE an estimate of the importance or usefulness of something —**valuational** *adj* —**valuationally** *adv*

valuator /vállyoo aytər/ *n* somebody who assesses the value of objects such as jewellery or works of art

~~valuble~~ incorrect spelling of **valuable**

value /vállyoo/ *n* **1.** MONETARY WORTH an amount expressed in money or another medium of exchange that is thought to be a fair exchange for something **2.** FULL RECOVERED WORTH the adequate or satisfactory return on or recompense for something ○ *It's value*

for money. **3.** WORTH OR IMPORTANCE the worth, importance, or usefulness of something to somebody ○ *a ring with great sentimental value* **4.** LING MEANING the exact meaning or significance of a word **5.** MATHS NUMERICAL QUANTITY a numerical quantity assigned to a mathematical symbol **6.** MUSIC LENGTH OF NOTE in music, the length of time that a note or pause is held **7.** ART SHADE OF COLOUR in painting and drawing, the lightness or darkness of a colour **8.** PHON SOUND REPRESENTED the quality or tone of a speech sound that a letter or written character represents ■ **values** *npl* PRINCIPLES OR STANDARDS the accepted principles or standards of a person or a group ■ *vt* (**-ues, -uing, -ued**) **1.** ESTIMATE VALUE OF SOMETHING to estimate or determine the value of something **2.** RATE SOMETHING to rate something according to its perceived worth, importance, or usefulness **3.** REGARD SOMEBODY OR SOMETHING HIGHLY to regard somebody or something as important or useful ○ *I value her as a friend.* [14C. < Old French < *valoir* 'be worth' < Latin *valere* 'be powerful'] —**valuer** *n*

value added *n* **1.** the difference between the gross profit of a commercial enterprise and its costs paid to other businesses **2.** the amount by which the value of a product increases as it proceeds through the various stages of its manufacture and distribution —**value-added** *adj*

value-added network *n* ONLINE full form of **VAN**

value-added tax *n* FIN full form of **VAT**

value date *n* in the calculation of exchange rates, the date on which a transaction is judged to have occurred

valued policy *n* an insurance policy in which the amount payable for a valid claim is established when the policy is issued and is independent of the value of a loss subsequently incurred

value-free *adj* not affected by or based on value judgments

value judgment *n* a judgment of the worth, appropriateness, or importance of somebody or something made on the basis of personal beliefs, opinions, or prejudices rather than facts

valueless /vállyooləss/ *adj* having no value —**valuelessness** *n*

value system *n* a set of personal principles and standards

valuta /və lóotə/ *n* the value of one nation's currency in terms of its exchange rate with another currency [Late 19C. < Italian, 'value']

valval, **valvar** *adj* ANAT same as **valvular**

valvate /vál vayt/ *adj* **1.** EQUIPPED WITH VALVES having valves or parts similar to valves **2.** BOT NOT OVERLAPPING IN BUD describes sepals or petals that touch but do not overlap in the bud **3.** BOT TAKING PLACE BY MEANS OF VALVES describes the splitting open of the seed capsules of the iris or lily that takes place by means of valves [Early 19C. < Latin *valvatus* 'having folding doors' < *valva* 'leaf of a folding door']

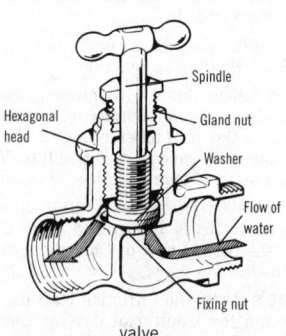

Spindle
Gland nut
Hexagonal head
Washer
Flow of water
Fixing nut
valve

valve /valv/ *n* **1.** ENG DEVICE THAT CONTROLS LIQUID FLOW a device that controls the movement of liquids or gases through pipes or other passages by opening or closing ports and channels **2.** MUSIC PART ON BRASS INSTRUMENT a device in some brass instruments that diverts air down tubes of varying length, thereby altering the pitch **3.** ELECTRONICS ELECTRON TUBE PRODUCING AMPLIFICATION an electron tube that is either evacuated or filled with low-pressure gas and in

which electrons are pulled from the cathode by an applied anode voltage. It is used to produce amplification, oscillation, or other effects. US term **vacuum tube 4.** ANAT CLOSABLE FLAP IN ORGAN a membranous structure in a hollow organ or vessel such as the heart or a vein that prevents the return flow of fluid passing through it by folding or closing **5.** BOT PART OF SEED POD a segment of the wall of a seed pod or other fruit that splits apart to reveal the contents **6.** BOT ANTHER FLAP a flap that acts like a lid in some types of anther **7.** BOT PART OF CELL WALL either of the two parts of the silica-impregnated cell wall of a type of alga (**diatom**) that fit together like the lid and base of a box **8.** ZOOL SEPARABLE PART OF SHELL a hinged part of the shell of a brachiopod or some molluscs **9.** ZOOL SINGLE-UNIT SHELL the single-unit shell of a snail and some other molluscs [15C. < Latin *valva* 'leaf of a folding door'] —**valved** *adj* —**valveless** *adj*

valve gear *n* a mechanical device that controls the valves of a reciprocating engine

valve-in-head engine *n* UK MECH ENG an internal-combustion engine with its inlet and exhaust valves in the cylinder head, not in the engine block. ANZ, N Am term **overhead-valve engine**

valvelet /válvlət/ *n* ANAT same as **valvule**

valve spring *n* **1.** a spiral spring that holds a valve closed in the cylinder head of an internal-combustion engine **2.** a spring that closes an opened valve

valvula /válvyŏŏlə/ (*plural* **-lae** /-lee/) *n* BIOL, ANAT same as **valvule** [Early 17C. < modern Latin < Latin *valva* 'leaf of a folding door']

valvular /válvyŏŏlər/, **valval** /válvəl/, **valvar** /válvər/ *adj* **1.** relating to, having, or acting like a valve or set of valves **2.** involving or affecting a valve or set of valves

valvule /vál vyool/ *n* a small valve or a part that functions or looks like one [Mid-18C. Variant of VALVULA]

valvulitis /válvyŏŏ lítiss/ *n* inflammation of a valve in the body, especially one in the heart, often caused by rheumatic fever

valvuloplasty /válvyŏŏlō plasti/ (*plural* **-ties**) *n* plastic surgery performed to repair a valve in the body, especially one in the heart [Mid-20C. < VALVULE]

vambrace /vám brayss/ *n* a piece of armour formerly worn over the forearm as protection [14C. Via Anglo-Norman *vauntbras* < Old French *avantbras* < *avant* 'before' + *bras* 'arm']

vamoose /va mŏŏss, və-/ (**-mooses, -moosing, -moosed**) *vi* to leave in a hurried way (*slang*) [Mid-19C. < Spanish *vamos* 'let us go']

vamp[1] /vamp/ (*sometimes considered offensive*) *n* SEDUCTIVE WOMAN a woman who is believed to use her sexual attractiveness for the seduction and manipulation of others ■ *v* (**vamps, vamping, vamped**) **1.** *vti* SEDUCE SOMEBODY to seduce and manipulate somebody by appearing to offer sexual intercourse **2.** *vi* ACT LIKE VAMP to act like or play the role of a vamp [Early 20C. Shortening of VAMPIRE] —**vampish** *adj* —**vampishly** *adv* —**vampy** *adj*

vamp[2] /vamp/ *n* **1.** SOMETHING PATCHED UP something repaired so as to appear new **2.** REHASHING OF SOMETHING a reworking of something already used or available, especially a book or article **3.** CLOTHING UPPER PART OF SHOE the upper part of a shoe that covers the front part of the foot **4.** MUSIC IMPROVISED MUSICAL INTRODUCTION an improvised musical introduction or accompaniment that is repeated as necessary until the entry of the solo line ■ *v* (**vamps, vamping, vamped**) **1.** *vt* CLOTHING PUT VAMP ON SHOE to put a vamp on a shoe **2.** *vti* MUSIC IMPROVISE MUSICAL INTRODUCTION OR ACCOMPANIMENT to improvise a musical introduction or accompaniment for a solo line [14C. Shortening of Old French *avantpié* < *avant* 'before' + *pié* 'foot'] —**vamper** *n* —**vampish** *adj*

vamp up *vt* **1.** to rework or renovate something **2.** to make something up or improvise something

vampire /vám pīr/ *n* **1.** BLOODSUCKING EVIL SPIRIT in European folklore, a dead person believed to rise each night from the grave and suck blood from the living for sustenance **2.** PREDATORY PERSON somebody who preys on other people for financial or emotional gain **3.** ZOOL same as **vampire bat 4.** THEATRE TRAP DOOR a trap door on the floor of a stage (*technical*) [Mid-

18C. Via French or German < Serbo-Croatian *vampir*] —**vampiric** /vam pírrik/ *adj* —**vampirical** *adj* —**vampirish** *adj*

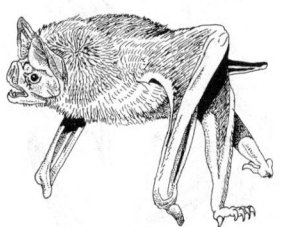

vampire bat

vampire bat *n* a bat that bites the skin of birds or other mammals and laps the blood. Native to: tropical and subtropical Central and South America. Family: Desmodontidae.

vampirism /vám pīrizəm/ *n* **1.** BELIEF IN VAMPIRES the belief that some corpses can leave their graves at night and suck the blood of living people **2.** STATE OF BEING VAMPIRE the supposed state or practices of a vampire **3.** FINANCIAL OR EMOTIONAL EXPLOITATION the act of preying on other people for financial or emotional gain

van[1] /van/ *n* **1.** a motor vehicle that has rear or side doors or sliding side panels and is chiefly used for transporting goods **2.** RAIL a closed railway wagon for goods, or the section of the carriage for the guard, luggage, parcels, or mail **3.** TRANSP same as **caravan** *n* (sense 1) [Early 19C. Shortening of CARAVAN]

van[2] /van/ *n* **1.** same as **vanguard** (sense 1) (*informal*) **2.** MIL same as **vanguard** (sense 2) [Early 17C. Shortening]

van[3] /van/ *n* in tennis, the point scored after deuce (*informal*) [Early 20C. Shortening of ADVANTAGE] ◇ **van in** or **out** in tennis, the score of advantage in favour of or against the server

van[4] /van/ *n* **1.** a device used for winnowing grain (*archaic*) **2.** a bird's wing (*archaic or literary*) [15C. Variant of FAN[1]]

van[5], **Van** see also under surname

Van /van/ city in eastern Turkey, the capital of Van Province. It lies on the eastern shore of Lake Van, about 80 km/50 mi. west of the Turkish-Iranian border. Population: 219,319 (1997).

Van, Lake saltwater lake in eastern Turkey, between the sources of the Euphrates and Tigris rivers, at an altitude of 1,720 m/5,643 ft. Area: 3,763 sq. km/1,453 sq. mi.

VAN /van/ *n* a computer network that enables private companies to exchange information with other registered subscribers. Full form **value-added network**

van. *abbr* vanilla

vanadate /vánnə dayt/ *n* a salt or ester of vanadium [Mid-19C. < VANADIUM]

vanadic /və náddik, -náyd-/ *adj* relating to or containing vanadium, especially with a high valency [Mid-19C. < VANADIUM]

vanadinite /və náddi nīt/ *n* a rare brown, red, or yellow mineral. Source: lead minerals. Use: source of vanadium. [Mid-19C. < VANADIUM]

vanadium /və náydi əm/ *n* a poisonous silvery white metallic element. Source: carnotite, vanadinite. Use: manufacture of tough steel alloys, catalyst. Symbol **V**. See table at **element** [Mid-19C. < modern Latin < Old Norse *Vanadis*, Scandinavian goddess]

vanadium pentoxide *n* a yellow or red crystalline compound. Use: catalyst, manufacture of glass. Formula: V_2O_5.

vanadium steel *n* a low-alloy steel containing the element vanadium for added strength

vanadous /vánnədəss/ *adj* relating to or containing vanadium, especially with a low valency [Mid-19C. < VANADIUM]

Van Allen /van állən/, **James** (*b.* 1914) US physicist. A pioneer in high altitude and space research, he discovered (1958) two radiation belts that encircle the Earth. Full name **Van Allen, James Alfred**

Van Allen belt, **Van Allen radiation belt** *n* either of two belts surrounding Earth and containing charged particles held there by the Earth's magnetic field

vanaspati /və náspəti/ *n* a hydrogenated vegetable oil commonly used in South Asian cooking instead of butter [Mid-20C. < Sanskrit *vanas-pati* 'lord of the plants']

Vanbrugh /vánbrə/, **Sir John** (1664–1726) English playwright and architect. After achieving great popular success with his comedies *The Relapse* (1696) and *The Provok'd Wife* (1697), he became equally renowned as an architect, designing Castle Howard in northern England (1699–1726) and Blenheim Palace, near Oxford (1705–20).

> 'The want of a thing is perplexing enough, but the possession of it is intolerable.'
> [Sir John Vanbrugh, *The Confederacy*; 1705]

Van Buren /van byŏŏrən/, **Martin** (1782–1862) 8th president of the United States (1837–41). During his presidency, he supported the war against the Seminoles in Florida but opposed the annexation of Texas. Known as **Little Magician, Red Fox of Kinderhook**. See table at **president**

> 'I tread in the footsteps of illustrious men, whose superiors it is our happiness to believe are not found on the executive calendar of any country'
> [Martin Van Buren, *Inaugural presidential address*; 4 March 1837]

vancomycin /vangkə míssin/ *n* an antibiotic that is effective against some bacteria that are resistant to other antibiotics. Strains of bacteria resistant to vancomycin have now developed. [Mid-20C. < *vanco-*, origin?]

vancomycin intermediate Staphylococcus aureus *n* MICROBIOL full form of **VISA**

vancomycin resistant Staphylococcus aureus *n* MICROBIOL full form of **VRSA**

Vancouver /van kŏŏvər/ city and port in southwestern British Columbia, Canada, opposite Vancouver Island. Population: 545,671 (2001).

Vancouver, Mount peak of St Elias Range in southwestern Yukon Territory, Canada. Height: 4,828 m/15,840 ft.

Vancouver, George (1757–98) British naval officer and explorer. He sailed with Captain James Cook and later was the first European to circumnavigate Vancouver Island, during a surveying expedition.

Vancouver Island island off the southwestern coast of British Columbia, Canada. It is the largest island off western North America. Population: 702,000. Area: 31,285 sq. km/12,079 sq. mi.

vanda /vándə/ (*plural* **-das** or *same*) *n* an orchid with strap-shaped leaves. Flowers: flattened with a spur on the lip. Native to: East Asia, Australia. Genus: *Vanda*. [Early 19C. Via modern Latin < Sanskrit *vandā*]

V and A, V & A *abbr* Victoria and Albert Museum

vandal /vánd'l/ *n* somebody who intentionally defaces or destroys somebody else's property [Mid-16C. < Latin *Vandalus* 'Vandal' < Germanic] —**vandalish** /vánd'lish/ *adj*

Vandal *n* a member of an ancient Germanic people who came from Jutland, conquering Gaul, Spain, Rome, and parts of North Africa during the 3rd and 4th centuries AD, before being defeated at Carthage in 533 [Old English *Wendlas* (plural) 'Vandals' < Germanic] —**Vandalic** /van dállik/ *adj*

vandalise *vt* CRIME another spelling of **vandalize**

vandalism /vánd'lizəm/ *n* the malicious and deliberate defacement or destruction of somebody else's property —**vandalistic** /vándə lístik/ *adj*

vandalize /vándə līz/ (**-izes, -izing, -ized**), **vandalise** (**-ises, -ising, -ised**) *vt* to deface, destroy, or otherwise damage private or public property maliciously and deliberately —**vandalization** *n*

vanda orchid *n* PLANTS same as **vanda**

van de Graaff generator /van də gra̱af-/ *n* an electrostatic machine that produces electrical discharges at extremely high voltages, used in particle accelerators and for testing electrical insulators. The electric charge from a source of direct current accumulates on a high-speed belt inside an insulated metal sphere filled with Freon™

or nitrogen gas under high pressure. [After R. J. *van de Graaff* (1901–67), US physicist]

Van der Hum /van dər hoŏm/ *n* S Africa a tangerine-flavoured liqueur [Mid-19C. Probably < a personal name]

van der Post, **Sir Laurens** (1906–96) South African writer, farmer, and explorer. His many books include *The Lost World of the Kalahari* (1958) and *The Heart of the Hunter* (1961), which brought international attention to the Kalahari and the Bushmen.

'Human beings are perhaps never more frightening than when they are convinced beyond doubt that they are right.'
[Laurens van der Post, *The Lost World of the Kalahari*; 1958]

van der Waals' equation /van dər waàlz-/ *n* a modified equation of state describing the physical behaviour of gases that takes into account the volumes of molecules and the interactions between them. It explains the difference in behaviour between a real gas and an ideal gas that obeys the gas laws. [After Johannes *van der Waals* (1837–1923), Dutch physicist]

van der Waals' force *n* a weak attractive force between atoms or molecules resulting from the positioning of the electrons within the interacting particles [See VAN DER WAALS' EQUATION]

Van Diemen's Land /van deèmənz-/ former name for Tasmania (1642–1856)

Vandyke /van dík/ *n* **1.** HAIR same as **Vandyke beard 2.** CLOTHING same as **Vandyke collar 3.** a V-shape forming part of a decorative border on material or clothing **4.** a decorative border on material or clothing made up of V-shaped points [Mid-18C. After Sir Anthony *van DYCK*] —**vandyked** *adj*

Vandyke beard *n* a short, neatly trimmed, pointed beard

Vandyke brown *n* a deep rich brown colour or pigment —**Vandyke brown** *adj*

Vandyke collar *n* a large white collar of linen or lace that has a deeply indented edge

Vandyke stitch *n* a V-shaped variation of cross stitch, used as a filling stitch to form a solid decoration

vane /vayn/ *n* **1.** ENG ROTATING BLADE a flat blade mounted as part of a set in a circle so as to rotate under the action of wind or liquid. Windmill sails and turbine blades are examples. **2.** METEOROL same as **weather vane 3.** ARMS STABILIZER ON MISSILE a stabilizing or guiding blade on a missile **4.** BIRDS BLADE OF BIRD'S FEATHER the flat part of a feather, consisting of interlocking rows of barbs. Each feather has two vanes, one on each side. **5.** PART OF LEVELLING ROD the moving part on a levelling rod **6.** COMPASS COMPASS OR QUADRANT SIGHT a sight on a compass or quadrant [15C. Variant of *fane* 'temple'] —**vaned** *adj*

SPELLCHECK See *vain*.

Vänern, Lake /vénnərn, váynərn/ largest lake in Sweden, situated in the southwest of the country. Area: 5,584 sq. km/2,156 sq. mi.

vang /vang/ *n* a guy rope forming part of a pair that extend from a gaff to the deck of a boat [Mid-18C. Variant of FANG]

van Gogh /van gókh, -góf/, **Vincent** (1853–90) Dutch painter. His highly expressive canvases are characterized by their bright colours and vigorous brushstrokes. Among his best-known works is *Starry Night* (1889). Full name **van Gogh, Vincent Willem**

'The Mediterranean has the colour of mackerel, changeable I mean. You don't always know if it is green or violet, you can't even say it's blue, because the next moment the changing reflection has taken on a tint of rose or grey.'
[Vincent van Gogh, *The Letters of Vincent Van Gogh*, M. Roskill (ed.); 1927]

vanguard /ván gaard/ *n* **1.** the leading position of a movement, field, or cultural trend, or the people who are foremost in a movement, field, or cultural trend **2.** the military divisions of an army or navy that lead the advance into battle [15C. Shortening of French *avant-garde* < *avant* 'before' + *garde* 'guard'] —**vanguardism** *n* —**vanguardist** *n*

Vanhanen /vánhənən/, **Matti** (*b.* 1955) prime minister of Finland (2003–). A member of the Centre Party, he entered parliament in 1991 and was briefly minister of defence before becoming prime minister.

vanilla

vanilla /və níllə/ *n* **1.** also **vanilla bean** VANILLA POD the long narrow fleshy seed pod of a tropical climbing orchid. Use: food flavouring. **2.** VANILLA EXTRACT a substance with a mild taste extracted from vanilla seed pods or produced artificially. Use: food flavouring, perfumes. **3.** CLIMBING PLANT a climbing plant of the orchid family that produces seed pods from which vanilla is extracted. Native to: tropical America. Genus: *Vanilla*. ■ *adj* **1.** FLAVOURED WITH VANILLA flavoured or scented with vanilla, or having a flavour or scent of vanilla **2.** PLAIN OR DULL lacking outstanding or interesting characteristics (*slang*) ○ *a vanilla rendition of the concerto* **3.** COMPUT OF BASIC SOFTWARE OR HARDWARE relating to the most basic version of a hardware device or software program that does not have the refinements of the full-featured version (*slang*) [Mid-17C. < Spanish *vainilla* 'small sheath' < *vaina* 'sheath' < Latin *vagina*]

vanillic /və níllik/ *adj* resembling, containing, or derived from vanilla or vanillin

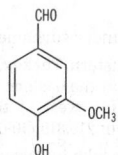

vanillin

vanillin /və níllin/ *n* a white aldehyde obtained from vanilla or prepared synthetically. Use: food flavourings, perfumes. Formula: $C_8H_8O_3$.

Vanir /vaàn eer/ *npl* in Norse mythology, a race of peace-loving gods [< Old Norse]

vanish /vánnish/ (**-ishes, -ishing, -ished**) *vi* **1.** DISAPPEAR SUDDENLY to disappear suddenly or inexplicably **2.** STOP EXISTING to cease to exist **3.** MATHS BECOME ZERO to assume or be given the value of zero (*refers to a function or variable*) [14C. < Old French *esvaniss-* < *esvanir* < Latin *evanescere* 'die out, pass away' < *vanus* 'empty'] —**vanisher** *n* —**vanishingly** *adv* —**vanishment** *n*

vanishing point /vánnishing-/ *n* **1.** a point in a drawing or painting at which parallel lines seem to meet as represented in perspective **2.** a point at which something disappears or ceases to exist

Vanitory /vánnitəri/ *tdmk* a trademark for a vanity unit

vanity /vánnəti/ (*plural* **-ties**) *n* **1.** EXCESSIVE PRIDE excessive pride, especially in personal appearance ○ *She is entirely free of personal vanity.* **2.** SOMETHING SOMEBODY IS VAIN ABOUT an instance or source of excessive pride **3.** FUTILITY the state or fact of being futile, worthless, or empty of significance **4.** SOMETHING FUTILE something that is considered futile, worthless, or empty of significance **5.** *N Am* FURNITURE same as **dressing table 6.** *NZ, N Am* CABINET HOLDING SINK a cabinet that holds a sink and its

plumbing, usually with drawers or shelves under the sink for storage **7.** *US* COSMETICS same as **vanity case** [13C. Via French < Latin *vanitas* < *vanus* 'empty']

vanity case, vanity bag *n* a small case or bag for carrying cosmetics and toiletries

Vanity Fair, vanity fair *n* a place, especially a very large city or the world in general, considered to be frivolous and full of idle worthless amusements (*literary*) [Coined by John BUNYAN in his *Pilgrim's Progress* (1678)]

CULTURAL NOTE *Vanity Fair*, a novel (1847–48) by William Makepeace Thackeray. Thackeray's first major novel, it is a story of English society at the time of the Napoleonic Wars. The central characters are the penniless orphan Becky Sharp and Amelia Sedley, the daughter of a rich merchant. The fortunes in life and love of the two young women remain in distinct contrast throughout the complex plot, as Amelia descends into poverty and widowhood while the sharp-witted and unscrupulous Becky enjoys an extravagant lifestyle with a series of lovers.

vanity plate *n N Am* a number plate for a motor vehicle for which the owner has paid extra to be able to choose its numbers and letters

vanity publisher, vanity press *n* a publishing house that publishes an author's work in return for payment from the author. Vanity publishers do not typically market or distribute their publications. —**vanity publishing** *n*

vanity table *n N Am* FURNITURE same as **dressing table**

vanity unit *n* a cabinet that holds a hand basin and its plumbing, usually with storage space, drawers, or shelves underneath

vank /vangk/ (**vanks, vanking, vanked**) *vt* to destroy or get rid of something (*slang; used in Black English*) [Shortening of VANQUISH]

vanload /ván lōd/ *n* the amount of goods or passengers that a van can transport at one time

vanpool /ván pool/ *n N Am* an arrangement by which a number of people travel together to and from work in a shared van ■ *vi* (**-pools, -pooling, -pooled**) to commute in a shared van

vanquish /vángkwish/ (**-quishes, -quishing, -quished**) *vt* **1.** DEFEAT SOMEBODY IN BATTLE to defeat an opponent or opposing army in a battle or fight **2.** DEFEAT SOMEBODY IN COMPETITION to prove convincingly superior to somebody in a contest, competition, or argument **3.** OVERCOME EMOTION to overcome, suppress, or subdue an emotion, feeling, or idea [14C. < Old French *venquis*, form of *veintre* < Latin *vincere* 'conquer'] —**vanquishable** *adj* —**vanquisher** *n* —**vanquishment** *n*

SYNONYMS See *defeat*.

vantage /vaàntij/ *n* **1.** a position that provides an advantage **2.** superiority in a contest or competition **3.** same as **vantage point** (sense 1) [14C. < Old French *avantage* (see ADVANTAGE)] —**vantageless** *adj*

vantage ground *n* a position of superiority over somebody

vantage point *n* **1.** a position or location that provides a broad view or perspective of something **2.** a personal point of view

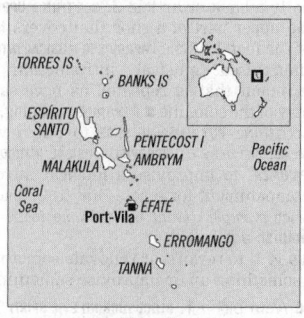

Vanuatu

Vanuatu /vánnoo aàtoo/ country in the southwestern Pacific Ocean, comprising approximately 80 islands. It became an independent member of the Commonwealth in 1980. Language: English, French.

Currency: vatu. Capital: Port-Vila. Population: 199,414 (2003). Area: 12,190 sq. km/4,707 sq. mi. Official name **Republic of Vanuatu**. Former name **New Hebrides** (until 1980) —**Vanuatan** *adj, n*

Van Vleck /van vlék/, **John Hasbrouck** (1899–1980) US physicist. He shared the 1977 Nobel Prize in physics for his contributions to the study of semiconductors.

vanward /vánnwərd/ *adj* in or at the vanguard of something ■ *adv* to or towards the vanguard of something

vapid /váppid/ *adj* **1.** lacking interest or liveliness **2.** lacking strength, taste, or flavour [Mid-17C. < Latin *vapidus* 'insipid'] —**vapidity** /və píddəti/ *n* —**vapidly** *adv* —**vapidness** *n*

vapor *n, vti* PHYS, CHEM US spelling of **vapour**

vaporescence /váypə réss'nss/ *n* the formation or creation of vapour —**vaporescent** *adj*

vaporetto /váppə réttō/ (*plural* **-ti** /-ti/ or **-tos**) *n* a motorboat for transporting passengers along the canals in Venice [Early 20C. < Italian, 'small steamboat' < *vapore* 'steam' < Latin *vapor* (see VAPOUR)]

vaporific /váypə ríffik/ *adj* **1.** PRODUCING VAPOUR producing, causing, or becoming vapour **2.** BEING VAPOUR being, containing, or resembling vapour **3.** PHYS VOLATILE capable of changing easily from a liquid or solid state into vapour

vaporise, etc. *vti* another spelling of **vaporize, etc.**

vaporize /váypə rīz/ (**-izes, -izing, -ized**), **vaporise** (**-ises, -ising, -ised**) *vti* **1.** CHANGE INTO VAPOUR to change into vapour, or cause something to change into vapour **2.** VANISH OR MAKE VANISH to vanish, or cause somebody or something to vanish **3.** ANNIHILATE OR BE ANNIHILATED to destroy somebody or something so completely that the person or object is turned into a gas or vapour, or be destroyed in this way —**vaporizable** *adj* —**vaporization** /váypə rī záysh'n/ *n*

vaporizer /váypə rīzər/, **vaporiser** *n* something used to produce a vapour, especially a device used to vaporize a medication so that it can be inhaled

vaporous /váypərəss/ *adj* **1.** BEING VAPOUR being, containing, or resembling vapour **2.** PRODUCING VAPOUR producing, causing, or becoming vapour **3.** VOLATILE capable of changing easily from a liquid or solid state into vapour **4.** UNSUBSTANTIAL lacking material existence or permanence **5.** FANCIFUL of a fanciful, ridiculous, or implausible nature **6.** OBSCURED BY VAPOUR made hard to see because of being obscured by mist or vapour —**vaporosity** /váypə róssəti/ *n* —**vaporously** *adv* —**vaporousness** *n*

vapour /váypər/ *n* **1.** PHYS MOISTURE PARTICLES moisture or another type of matter visible in the air as mist, clouds, fumes, or smoke **2.** PHYS GASEOUS SUBSTANCE a gaseous substance at a temperature lower than that at which it can be liquefied or solidified by an appropriate increase in pressure alone **3.** PHYS GASEOUS STATE OF SUBSTANCE the gaseous state of a liquid or solid at a temperature below its boiling point **4.** CHEM VAPORIZED SUBSTANCE a substance prepared for military, industrial, or medical use in vaporized form **5.** ENG GAS AND AIR MIXTURE a combination of air with a gaseous substance such as that of air and petrol in an internal-combustion engine ■ **vapours** *npl* LOW SPIRITS a bout of low spirits or sadness (*literary; usually used ironically*) ■ *v* (**vapours, vapouring, vapoured**) **1.** *vti* EVAPORATE to change into a vapour, or cause something to change into a vapour **2.** *vi* EMIT VAPOUR to give off or send up vapour **3.** *vi* BRAG to talk boastfully [14C. Directly or via Old French < Latin *vapor* 'steam, heat'] —**vapourability** /váypərə bílləti/ *n* —**vapourable** *adj* —**vapourer** /váypərər/ *n* —**vapoury** *adj*

vapour barrier *n* a protective layer of material used in building to keep out moisture

vapour density *n* the density of a gas or vapour in relation to that of hydrogen

vapourer moth *n* a tussock moth that lives in hedges and trees. The female has only vestigial wings and lays her eggs on the cocoon from which she emerged. Latin name: *Orgyia antiqua*.

vapour lock *n* a bubble of vaporized petrol that blocks the normal flow of fuel in the line that supplies the carburettor of an internal-combustion engine

vapour pressure, **vapour tension** *n* the pressure exerted by a vapour, particularly a vapour in contact with its liquid form

vapour trail *n* a visible trail of condensed vapour left by an aircraft flying at high altitude

vapourware /váypər wair/ *n* new software that has been announced or advertised but has not yet been, and may never be, produced [Late 20C. After SOFTWARE]

vaquero /va káirō/ (*plural* **-ros**) *n* same as **cowboy** (sense 1) [Early 19C. < Spanish < *vaca* 'cow']

var *abbr* MEASURE volt-ampere reactive

VAR[1] /vaar/ *n* a retail seller of computers who adds products to computers produced by manufacturers or performs services such as product integration or customization before selling the computers to customers. Full form **value-added reseller**

VAR[2] *abbr* **1.** NAVIG visual aural range **2.** ELEC volt-ampere reactive

var. *abbr* **1.** variable **2.** variant **3.** variation **4.** variety

vara /vaarə/ *n* a unit of length used in Spain, Portugal, and Latin America that can be from 80 cm/32 in to 108 cm/43 in in length [Late 17C. Via Spanish, 'rod, yardstick' < Latin, 'forked pole, trestle' < *varus* 'bent']

varactor /váir aktər/ *n* a semiconductor diode with a capacitance that varies according to the voltage applied to it, used to regulate the frequency of electronic circuits in amplifiers [Mid-20C. Blend of VARIABLE + REACTOR]

Varanasi /və raanəssi/, **Vārānasi** city in Uttar Pradesh State, northern India, on the River Ganges. It was a centre of Hindu learning and is an important place of pilgrimage for Hindus. Population: 1,100,748 (2001). Former name **Benares**

Varangian /və ránji ən/ *n* a member of a Scandinavian people who invaded and settled in Russia between the 8th and the 11th centuries [Late 18C. < medieval Latin *Varangus* < medieval Greek *baraggos* < Old Norse *Væringi* < *vár* 'pledge'] —**Varangian** *adj*

Varangian Guard *n* **1.** the body of Scandinavian soldiers who were the Byzantine emperor's bodyguard in the 10th and 11th centuries **2.** a Scandinavian soldier in the Varangian Guard

Vardon /vaard'n/, **Harry** (1870–1937) British golfer. He won the British Open championship six times between 1896 and 1914, and the US Open in 1900.

varec /várrek/ *n* PLANTS same as **kelp** [Late 17C. < French]

~~**vareity**~~ incorrect spelling of **variety**

AKG London

Mario Vargas Llosa

Vargas Llosa /vaargəss lóssə/, **Mario** (*b.* 1936) Peruvian writer and critic. Many of his works deal with issues of social change and political corruption. Full name **Vargas Llosa, Jorge Mario Pedro**

> 'Since it is impossible to know what's really happening, we Peruvians lie, invent, dream...Because of these strange circumstances, Peruvian life, a life in which so few actually do read, has become literary.'
> [Mario Vargas Llosa, *The Real Life of Alejandro Mayta*, 1984]

vari- *prefix* same as **vario-** (*used before vowels*)

variable /váiri əb'l/ *adj* **1.** ABLE TO CHANGE able or liable to change, especially suddenly and unpredictably **2.** INCONSISTENT inconsistent or uneven in quality or performance **3.** FICKLE inconstant and capricious in nature or character **4.** METEOROL LIKELY TO BLOW DIFFERENTLY describes a wind that is likely to change direction or intensity **5.** ELECTRONICS HAVING VARYING RESISTANCE describes an electrical device that has a resistance that varies **6.** BIOL DIFFERING FROM SPECIES NORM describes a species that tends to differ in some characteristic from a recognized or known type **7.** MATHS HAVING NO FIXED NUMERICAL VALUE not having a fixed numerical value ■ *n* **1.** SOMETHING THAT CAN VARY something capable of changing or varying **2.** MATHS SYMBOL FOR UNSPECIFIED QUANTITY a symbol that represents an unspecified or unknown quantity, e.g. 'a', 'b', or 'x' **3.** MATHS RANGE OF VALUES a range of values, any one of which is a solution to an algebraic expression **4.** LOGIC LOGIC SYMBOL a symbol, especially 'x', 'y', or 'z', that is used usually in connection with quantifiers to represent individuals in a universe of discourse **5.** ASTRON same as **variable star** **6.** METEOROL VARIABLE WIND a wind that is likely to change in direction or intensity ■ **variables** *npl* METEOROL REGION OF VARIABLE WINDS a region where variable winds are likely to be encountered [14C. Via French < Latin *variabilis* < *variare* (see VARY)] —**variability** /váiri ə bílləti/ *n* —**variableness** *n* —**variably** *adv*

variable cost *n* a cost that varies directly in relation to output

variable-geometry *adj* describes an aircraft with wings that are hinged so that in flight they can move backwards or forwards. The wings are swept back to give low drag in supersonic flight and are moved forwards for takeoff and landing.

variable-rate mortgage *n* a mortgage on which interest is payable at a rate that changes, usually in accordance with market interest rates. N Am term **adjustable-rate mortgage**

variable star *n* a star whose brightness changes at regular or irregular intervals

variable-sweep *adj* AVIAT same as **variable-geometry**

variance /váiri ənss/ *n* **1.** CHANGE IN SOMETHING a change that occurs in something **2.** DIFFERENCE BETWEEN THINGS a difference between two or more things **3.** DISAGREEMENT a difference of opinion or attitude **4.** LAW DISCREPANCY IN SOMETHING a discrepancy between two statements, documents, or steps in a legal proceeding **5.** ACCT DIFFERENCE IN COST a difference between actual costs and the usual costs of production **6.** STATS SQUARE OF STANDARD DEVIATION a statistical measure of the spread or variation of a group of numbers in a sample, equal to the square of the standard deviation. Other measures are the ratio of the squared standard deviation to the sample size (**population variance**), and the ratio of the squared standard deviation to the sample size minus one (**sample variance**). **7.** *N Am* LAW LEGAL DISPENSATION a dispensation to ignore a rule or law ○ *a zoning variance* [14C. Via Old French < Latin *variantia* < *variare* (see VARY)]

variant /váiri ənt/ *adj* **1.** DIFFERING SLIGHTLY having or showing a difference from the norm ○ *variant pronunciations of common words* **2.** CHANGEABLE tending or likely to change ■ *n* **1.** SLIGHTLY DIFFERENT FORM something that differs slightly from the norm **2.** LING DIFFERENT FORM OR SPELLING OF WORD a form or spelling of a word or phrase that differs from the standard one **3.** STATS same as **random variable** [14C. French, < *varier* 'vary' < Latin *variare* (see VARY)]

variant CJD *n* a form of Creutzfeldt-Jakob disease that has a much shorter incubation period than previously recognized types but is clinically identical. It first appeared in the late 1980s. Full form **variant Creutzfeldt-Jakob disease**

variate /váiri ət, -ayt/ *n* STATS same as **random variable** [Late 19C. < Latin *variatus*, past participle of *variare* (see VARY)]

variation /váiri áysh'n/ *n* **1.** ACT OF VARYING the act or a result of varying **2.** STATE OF DIFFERING the state or fact of differing, e.g. from a former state or value, from others of the same type, or from a standard **3.** DEGREE OF DIFFERENCE the degree to which something differs, e.g. from a former state or value, from others of the same type, or from a standard ○ *There is a variation of several marks in the exam results.* **4.** SOMETHING DIFFERING SLIGHTLY something that differs slightly from the norm **5.** MUSIC ALTERED VERSION OF MUSICAL THEME an altered version of an original musical theme or melody, such that the rhythm or harmony is varied or melodic embellishment is added. Variations are often found in sets, where a theme is followed by

several variations. **6.** MUSIC **REPETITION OF MUSICAL THEME** the repetition of a musical theme with modifications of melody, rhythm, or harmony **7.** MATHS **MATHEMATICAL FUNCTION** a mathematical function that relates the values of one variable to those of other variables **8.** BIOL **BIOLOGICAL DEVIATION** a significant deviation from the normal biological form, function, or structure **9.** BIOL **LIVING ORGANISM THAT DIFFERS** a living organism that differs from the normal form for its kind **10.** BALLET **SOLO DANCE** a dance performed by a single dancer **11.** ASTRON **CHANGE IN ORBIT** a change in or deviation from the average motion or orbit of an astronomical object **12.** ASTRON **TERM IN EQUATION DESCRIBING MOON'S MOTION** a term representing the gravitational attraction of the Sun on the Earth-Moon system in the mathematical equation for the Moon's motion **13.** PHYS same as **magnetic declination** [14C. Directly or via French < Latin *variation-* < *variare* (see VARY)] —**variational** *adj* —**variationally** *adv*

~~**variaty**~~ incorrect spelling of **variety**

varic- *prefix* same as **varico-** (*used before vowels*)

varicella /várri séllə/ *n* MED same as **chickenpox** (*technical*) [Late 18C. < modern Latin, 'lesser smallpox' < late Latin *variola* (see VARIOLA)] —**varicellar** *adj* —**varicellous** *adj*

varicella-zoster virus *n* a herpes virus that is responsible for chickenpox and shingles

varices MED, MARINE BIOL plural of **varix**

varico- *prefix* varix, varicose vein ○ *varicotomy* [< Latin *varic-*, stem of *varix*]

varicocele /várrikō seel/ *n* a swelling of the veins in the spermatic cord of the scrotum. It may cause only slight discomfort but can affect fertility, so that surgical correction is required.

varicoloured /váiri kullərd/ *adj* consisting of or having many colours

varicose /várrikōss/, **varicosed** /várrikōst/ *adj* **1.** MED **SWOLLEN** swollen, knotted, or distended to a greater extent than normal **2.** MED **WITH VARICOSE VEINS** affected with or having varicose veins **3.** MED **PRODUCING SWELLING** relating to or producing swelling **4.** ZOOL **RIDGED LIKE GASTROPOD SHELL** resembling a small longitudinal ridge (**varix**) on the shell of some gastropods [15C. < Latin *varicosus* < *varix* 'dilated vein, varicose vein']

varicoses MED, ZOOL plural of **varicosis**

varicose vein *n* a vein that has become swollen and knotted as a result of faulty valves ■ **varicose veins** *npl* a condition in which the surface veins, especially of the legs, become knotted and swollen, as a result of flaws in the valves of the affected veins. The tendency to develop the condition may be inherited, while other causes include injury, inflammation, or thrombosis.

varicosis /várri kṓssiss/ (*plural* **-coses** /-kṓ sees/) *n* **1.** a condition in which a vein or veins become swollen or knotted **2.** the formation of small longitudinal ridges on the surface of a gastropod shell

varicosity /várri kóssəti/ (*plural* **-ties**) *n* MED **1.** the state of being swollen or knotted **2.** same as **varicose vein** (*technical*) **3.** the condition of suffering from or having swollen or enlarged veins

varicotomy /várri kóttəmi/ (*plural* **-mies**) *n* a surgical incision into a swollen vein, usually performed to treat varicose veins

varied /váirid/ *adj* **1. DIVERSE** showing or characterized by many different forms or kinds **2. CHANGED** having undergone change or alteration **3. MULTICOLOURED** consisting of or having many colours —**variedly** *adv* —**variedness** *n*

variegate /váiri gayt/ (**-gates, -gating, -gated**) *vt* **1.** to change the way something looks, especially by adding different colours **2.** to add variety to something [Mid-17C. < Latin *variegare* 'make varied' < *varius* 'diverse'] —**variegation** /váiri gáysh'n/ *n* —**variegator** *n*

variegated /váiri gaytid/ *adj* **1. HAVING PATCHES OF DIFFERENT COLOURS** marked with or containing patches of different colours **2. HAVING PATCHES OF LIGHTER COLOUR** marked with or containing patches of lighter colour ○ *variegated leaves* **3. DIVERSE** showing or characterized by many different forms or kinds

varietal /və rī́ ət'l/ *adj* **1. TYPICAL OF BIOLOGICAL VARIETY** relating to, typical of, or being a variety of something, especially a biological variety **2. MADE FROM SINGLE GRAPE VARIETY** describes wine made entirely or principally from a single variety of grape ■ *n* **WINE MADE FROM SINGLE GRAPE VARIETY** a wine that is made entirely or principally from a single variety of grape, and is usually known by the name of the grape variety —**varietally** *adv*

variety /və rī́ əti/ (*plural* **-ties**) *n* **1. QUALITY OF BEING VARIED** the quality of being varied or diversified ○ *It's easy to get bored if there's no variety in your work.* **2. SPECIFIC TYPE** a specific type or kind within a general group ○ *a new variety* **3. COLLECTION OF VARIED THINGS** a collection of varied things, often belonging to the same general group **4.** THEATRE **ENTERTAINMENT MADE UP OF DIFFERENT ACTS** entertainment made up of a number of different types of act **5.** BOT **SUBDIVISION OF SPECIES** a taxonomic category of related organisms, especially plants, of a rank below a species. Varieties of a species generally have distinguishing characteristics such as a flower colour and may arise naturally or through deliberate plant breeding. [Mid-16C. Via French < Latin *varietas* < *varius* 'variegated, diverse']

variety meat *n US* **1.** meat taken from a slaughtered animal other than flesh removed from the skeleton, especially organ meat **2.** meat that is processed, e.g. sausage

variety show *n* a theatrical show made up of a number of short performances of different kinds, such as singing, comic sketches, dancing, and magic acts

varifocal /váiri fṓk'l/ *adj* describes composite spectacle lenses with varying focal length that allow different focusing distances for near, far, and intermediate vision ■ **varifocals** *npl* spectacles with composite lenses for distant, intermediate, and near vision

variform /váiri fawrm/ *adj* existing in different shapes or forms [Mid-17C. < VARIOUS] —**variformly** *adv*

~~**varigated**~~ incorrect spelling of **variegated**

vario- *prefix* variation, variance, difference ○ *variolite* [< Latin *varius* 'variegated, diverse']

variola /və rī́ ələ/ *n* MED same as **smallpox** (*technical*) [Early 19C. < late Latin, 'pustule' < Latin *varius* 'variegated, diverse'] —**varioloid** /váiri ə loyd/ *adj, n*

variolate *adj* /váiri ələt/ with a pitted or scarred appearance, like the skin of somebody who has had smallpox ■ *vt* /váiri ə layt/ (**-lates, -lating, -lated**) to inoculate somebody with the smallpox virus (*dated*) —**variolation** /váiri ə láysh'n/ *n*

variole /váiri ōl/ *n* a small rounded mass that causes the pock-marked surface in the rock variolite [Early 19C. < late Latin *variola* (see VARIOLA)]

variolite /váiri ə līt/ *n* a rock that has a pock-marked surface caused by rounded fibrous crystalline masses that are embedded in it [Late 18C. < VARIOLA] —**variolitic** /váiri ə líttik/ *adj*

variolous /və rī́ ələss/ *adj* relating to, like, or affected by smallpox

variometer /váiri ómmitər/ *n* **1.** an instrument used to measure magnetic fields, especially variations in the Earth's magnetic field **2.** an instrument used to measure the rate of climb of an aircraft such as a glider

variorum /váiri áwrəm/ *adj* **1. CONTAINING VARIOUS ANNOTATIONS** having commentary or notes written by various editors or scholars **2. HAVING DIFFERENT VERSIONS OF TEXT** containing different versions or readings of a text ■ *n* **VARIORUM EDITION** an edition of a text with commentary or notes written by various editors or scholars, or with various different versions or readings [Early 18C. < Latin genitive plural of *varius* 'variegated, diverse', in *editio cum notis variorum* 'edition with notes of various (commentators)']

various /váiri əss/ *det* **ASSORTED** many different ○ *after various attempts* ■ *pron* **DIFFERENT EXAMPLES** different examples of something (*nonstandard*) ○ *I've already spoken to various of the witnesses.* ■ *adj* **1. OF DIFFERENT KINDS** of different kinds or categories ○ *declined the invitation for various reasons* **2. INDIVIDUAL** individual or separate ○ *The various arguments all have their strong and weak points.* **3. BEING ASSORTMENT** being an assortment or variety [Mid-16C. < Latin *varius* 'variegated, diverse'] —**variously** *adv* —**variousness** *n*

varisized /váiri sīzd/ *adj US* being or consisting of different sizes

varistor /və rístər/ *n* a two-element semiconductor with nonlinear resistance in which the resistance drops as the applied voltage increases. Varistors are often used as a safety device to short-circuit transient high voltages in electronic circuits. [Mid-20C. < VARIABLE + RESISTOR]

varix /váiriks/ (*plural* **-ices** /váiri seez/) *n* **1.** a swollen or knotted bodily vessel, especially a vein **2.** a ridge along the length of the shell of a gastropod mollusc [14C. < Latin, 'dilated vein, varicose vein'] —**variceal** /várri sée əl/ *adj*

varlet /vaárlət/ *n* (*archaic*) **1.** a rogue or rascal **2.** a servant or attendant [15C. < Old French, variant of *valet* (see VALET)]

varmint /vaármint/ *n* a person or an animal regarded as troublesome, unpleasant, or despicable (*regional; offensive when used of people*) [Mid-16C. Variant of VERMIN]

varna /vaárnə/ *n* a social caste in Hindu society. The four castes are the priests (**Brahmins**), warriors (**Kshatriyas**), merchants (**Vaisyas**), and workers (**Sudras**), with, below these, the untouchables (**Dalits**). [Mid-19C. < Sanskrit, 'colour, cover, class, sort']

Varna /vaárnə/ city, port, and tourist centre in eastern Bulgaria, on the Black Sea. Population: 301,421 (1996).

varnish /vaárnish/ *n* **1. TRANSPARENT RESIN SOLUTION** a solution of a resin in oil or spirits, applied to a surface to give it a protective gloss **2. SMOOTH COATING OF VARNISH** a coating of varnish, applied to something to give it a protective gloss **3. SUPERFICIALLY ATTRACTIVE MANNER OR APPEARANCE** a superficially or deceptively attractive manner or appearance ■ *vt* (**-nishes, -nishing, -nished**) **1. APPLY VARNISH TO SOMETHING** to coat something with varnish **2. GIVE SOMETHING SMOOTH SURFACE** to give something a smooth and usually glossy surface **3. MAKE SOMETHING SUPERFICIALLY ATTRACTIVE** to make something superficially or deceptively attractive [14C. Via Old French *vernis* < medieval Latin *vernicium* 'sandarac' < Greek *Berenīkē* 'Berenice', city in Cyrenaica] —**varnisher** *n*

Varro /várrō/, **Marcus Terentius** (116–27 BC) Roman scholar. He was one of the most learned Romans of his day, and the author of more than 70 known works on a variety of subjects from farming to the Latin language. Little of his work survives.

varsity /vaárssəti/ (*plural* **-ties**) *n* EDUC same as **university** (*dated*) [Mid-19C. Dialectal variant of *versity*, shortening of UNIVERSITY]

Varuna /várrŏŏnə/ *n* in Hinduism, the all-seeing creator god, who uses the sun as his eye and acts as a life-sustaining force, ever-present in all he has created [< Sanskrit, 'wise one, seer']

varus /váirəss/ *adj* used to describe a condition in which a body part such as the foot is turned or displaced inwards towards the midline of the body or limb (*technical*) [Late 18C. < Latin, 'bent, crooked']

varve /vaarv/ *n* a layer or series of layers of sediment deposited annually in a still body of water, e.g. by a glacier. Varves can be counted back to date a specific layer. [Early 20C. < Swedish *varv* 'layer, turn']

vary /váiri/ (**-ies, -ying, -ied**) *v* **1.** *vti* **UNDERGO CHANGE OR CHANGE SOMETHING** to change within a range of possibilities, or in connection with something else, or make something undergo such a change **2.** *vi* **BE DIFFERENT** to be different **3.** *vt* **GIVE VARIETY TO SOMETHING** to give variety or diversity to something [14C. Via Old French *varier* < Latin *variare* < *varius* 'variegated, diverse'] —**varying** *adj* —**varyingly** *adv*

SYNONYMS See ***change***.

vas /vass, vaass/ (*plural* **vasa** /váyzə, vaázə/) *n* a vessel or duct in the body of a person or animal [Mid-17C. < Latin, 'vessel'] —**vasal** /váyss'l, váyz'l/ *adj*

vas- *prefix* same as **vaso-** (*used before vowels*)

vasa ANAT plural of **vas**

Vasarély /vassə ráyli/, **Victor** (1908–97) Hungarian-born French painter, sculptor, and graphic artist. He was the creator of Op Art and one of the most important artists in the movement.

vascula BOT plural of **vasculum**

vascular /váskyŏŏlər/ *adj* relating to fluid-carrying vessels, e.g. blood vessels in animals or the sap-carrying vessels in plants [Mid-17C. < modern Latin *vascularis* < Latin *vasculum* (see VASCULUM)] —**vascularity** /váskyŏŏ lárrəti/ *n* —**vascularly** *adv*

vascular bundle *n* a strand of plant tissue containing the xylem and phloem vessels, responsible for conducting sap through the stems and branches of a plant. They are most prominent in annual and young plants, and in perennial and woody plants they become part of an inner cylinder of vascular tissue.

vascular cylinder *n* BOT same as **stele** (sense 2)

vascularization /váskyŏŏlə rī záysh'n/, **vascularisation** *n* the development of vessels, especially blood vessels, in an organism or tissue

vascular plant *n* any plant that possesses specialized sap-conducting tissues, particularly phloem and xylem. Vascular plants include all flowering plants and conifers, as well as ferns, club mosses, and horsetails, but not mosses and liverworts.

vascular tissue *n* plant tissue that is specialized for conducting sap. It comprises phloem, which conveys chiefly dissolved sugars, and xylem, which conveys water and dissolved minerals.

vasculature /váskyŏŏləchər/ *n* the arrangement of blood vessels in the body or in an organ or tissue

vasculitis /váskyŏŏ lítiss/ *n* inflammation of a blood vessel or lymph vessel

vasculum /váskyŏŏləm/ (*plural* **-la** /-lə/ or **-lums**) *n* a small box or case used by botanists in the field for storing collected plants or other specimens [Mid-19C. < Latin, 'little vessel' < *vas* 'vessel']

vas deferens /váss déffə renz, vaáss-/ (*plural* **vasa deferentia** /váyzə defə rénshə, vaázə-/) *n* either of a pair of ducts that carry sperm from the testes to the urethra during ejaculation. Contraction of its thick muscular wall propels sperm rapidly through the duct, which forms part of the spermatic cord. [Late 19C. < Latin, 'carrying-away vessel']

vase /vaaz/ *n* an open container, usually tall and rounded, used for displaying cut flowers or as an ornament [Mid-16C. Via French < Latin *vas* 'vessel']

vasectomize /və séktə mīz/ (**-mizes, -mizing, -mized**), **vasectomise** (**-mises, -mising, -mised**) *vt* to perform a vasectomy on somebody

vasectomy /və séktəmi/ (*plural* **-mies**) *n* a surgical operation in which the vas deferens from each testis is cut and tied to prevent transfer of sperm during ejaculation. It is the most common form of male sterilization. [Late 19C. < VAS DEFERENS]

Vaseline /vássə leen/ *tdmk* a trademark for petroleum jelly

vaso- *prefix* **1.** blood vessels, vascular ○ *vasodilation* **2.** vas deferens ○ *vasectomy* [< Latin *vas* 'vessel']

vasoactive /váyzō áktiv/ *adj* making blood vessels contract or dilate —**vasoactivity** /váyzō aktívvəti/ *n*

vasoconstriction /váyzō kən stríksh'n/ *n* narrowing of the blood vessels with consequent reduction in blood flow or increased blood pressure

vasoconstrictor /váyzō kən stríktər/ *n* an agent that narrows the blood vessels, which in turn increases resistance to blood flow and raises blood pressure, e.g. a nerve or hormone. Vasoconstrictors such as the hormone adrenaline and various drugs are used medically to maintain or raise blood pressure in circulatory disorders or during surgery, or to counteract shock. ■ *adj* causing narrowing of the blood vessels —**vasoconstrictive** *adj*

vasodilation /váyzō dī láysh'n/, **vasodilatation** /váyzō dīla táysh'n/ *n* widening of the blood vessels, especially the arteries, leading to increased blood flow or reduced blood pressure

vasodilator /váyzō dī láytər/ *n* an agent that widens the blood vessels, which in turn decreases resistance to blood flow and lowers blood pressure, e.g. a nerve or hormone. Drugs that act as vasodilators are used medically to treat high blood pressure and various other circulatory disorders. ■ *adj* causing widening of the blood vessels —**vasodilatory** *adj*

vasoinhibitor /váyzō in híbbitər/ *n* something that depresses or stops the activity of the nerves that control widening or narrowing of the blood vessels —**vasoinhibitory** *adj*

vasomotor /váyzō mótər/ *adj* causing or influencing changes in the diameter of blood vessels

vasopressin /váyzō préssin/ *n* a hormone produced by the pituitary gland that causes narrowing of the arteries and raises blood pressure. It also reduces the volume of urine excreted by the kidneys.

vasopressor /váyzō préssər/ *adj* causing or promoting the narrowing of blood vessels, which in turn raises blood pressure ■ *n* something that has the effect of raising blood pressure

vasospasm /váyzō spázzəm/ *n* sustained contraction of the muscular walls of the blood vessels with a resultant reduction in blood flow. In Raynaud's disease there is vasospasm of the arteries of the fingers, which causes cold or numb fingers. —**vasospastic** /-spástik/ *adj*

vasovagal /váyzō váyg'l/ *adj* relating to or involving the influence of the vagus nerve on circulation. Stimulation of the vagus reduces heart rate and, consequently, the amount of blood being pumped by the heart.

vassal /váss'l/ *n* **1.** somebody who gave loyalty and homage to a feudal lord and received the right to occupy the lord's land and be protected by him **2.** a person, nation, or group that is dependent on or subordinate to another [14C. Via French < medieval Latin *vassallus* < *vassus* 'servant' < Celtic, 'young man, squire'] —**vassal** *adj*

vassalage /váss'lij/ *n* **1.** the dependent condition of being somebody's vassal **2.** a condition of being dependent on or subordinate to somebody or something else (*literary*)

vast /vaast/ *adj* very great in number, size, amount, extent, or degree ■ *n* the immense expanse of space (*literary*) [Late 16C. < Latin *vastus* 'immense, empty'] —**vastidity** /va stíddəti/ *n* —**vastitude** *n* —**vastity** *n*

vastly /vaástli/ *adv* to a very great extent or degree

vastness /vaástnəss/ *n* **1.** the state or quality of being vast **2.** an immense expanse or area of space (*literary*)

vat /vat/ *n* **1.** LARGE CONTAINER FOR LIQUID a large container used to hold or store liquid **2.** PREPARATION OF DYE a preparation of weakly coloured soluble dye (**vat dye**) ■ *vt* (**vats, vatting, vatted**) TREAT OR PUT IN VAT to treat, store, or put something in a vat [12C. Alteration of *fat* < Old English *fæt* 'vessel' < Germanic]

VAT /veé ay teé, vat/ *n* a tax on the increased value of a product or service added at each stage of its production or distribution, paid by the consumer. Full form **value-added tax** —**VATable** /vátteb'l/ *adj*

Vat. *abbr* Vatican

vat dye *n* a dye that is made insoluble and fixed by oxidation after being taken up by fibres —**vat-dyed** *adj*

vatic /váttik/ *adj* relating to, involving, or characteristic of a prophet (*formal*) [Early 17C. < Latin *vates* 'prophet, seer']

Vatican /váttikən/ *n* **1.** the palace in the Vatican City that is used as the official residence of the pope and the administrative centre of the papacy **2.** the authority and jurisdiction of the pope [Mid-16C. < Latin (*mons*) *Vaticanus* 'Vatican (hill)']

Vatican City

Vatican City world's smallest independent nation and headquarters of the Roman Catholic Church.

Language: Italian, Latin. Currency: euro. Population: 1000 (2001). Area: 44 hectares/110 acres. Official name **State of Vatican City**

Vaticanism /váttikənizəm/ *n* the policies and authority of the pope, especially the idea of absolute papal authority

vaticinate /və tíssi nayt/ (**-nates, -nating, -nated**) *vti* same as **prophesy** (*formal*) [Early 17C. < Latin *vaticinari* < *vates* 'prophet, seer' + *canere* 'sing'] —**vaticinal** *adj* —**vaticination** /váttissi náysh'n/ *n* —**vaticinator** *n*

VATman /vát man/ (*plural* **-men**) /-men/, **vatman** *n* an official of the customs and excise department whose job it is to assess or collect VAT (*informal*)

vatu /vaá too/ (*plural same*) *n* a unit of currency in Vanuatu. See table at **currency** [< Bislama]

Vauban /vō baáN/, **Sébastien le Prestre de** (1633–1707) French marshal of France. He was a specialist in sieges and fortifications during the reign of Louis XIV. He directed the sieges of Mons (1691) and Namur (1692).

vaudeville /váwdəvil/ *n* **1.** ANZ, N Am THEATRE, MUSIC a type of entertainment popular in the late 19th and early 20th centuries consisting of a variety of singing, dancing, and comic acts. UK term **music hall 2.** COMIC PLAY WITH SONGS a comic play with songs and dances **3.** MUSIC SATIRICAL POPULAR SONG a satirical popular song of the type performed in cabarets in the 19th and 20th centuries **4.** MUSIC OPERATIC SONG a song used as a finale in an opera, with each verse sung by a different character, all joining in a refrain [Mid-18C. < Old French *vaudevire*, shortening of *chanson du Vau de Vire* 'song of the Valley of Vire', region of Normandy noted for satirical folksongs] —**vaudevillian** /váwdə vílli ən/ *adj, n*

ORIGIN In 15th-century France there was a fashion for songs from the valley of the Vire, in the Calvados region of Normandy (particularly popular, apparently, were the satirical songs composed by a local fuller, Olivier Basselin). The geographical connection had been lost by the time English acquired the word, and the element *-vire* had been replaced with *-ville* 'town'. The semantic transition from 'popular song' to 'light theatrical entertainment' is not recorded until the early 19th century.

Vaudreuil /vō drö i/, **Pierre de Rigaud de Vaudreuil de Cavagnal, Marquis de** (1698–1778) French soldier and colonial administrator. He was governor of New France (now Canada) from 1755 to 1760, when he was forced to surrender to British forces during the Seven Years' War.

Sarah Vaughan

Vaughan /vawn/, **Sarah** (1924–90) US jazz singer. Performing with Earl Hines, Billy Eckstine, Count Basie, and other leading jazz musicians, she was known for her complex harmonization and vocal improvisation. Full name **Vaughan, Sarah Lois**

Vaughan Williams /-wíllyəmz/, **Ralph** (1872–1958) British composer. He developed a British national style of music from choral tradition and folk song. His works include nine symphonies and many choral pieces. See illustration on next page

vault[1] /vawlt, volt/ *n* **1.** STRENGTHENED ROOM FOR VALUABLES a strengthened room or compartment used for the safe storage of valuables, especially one in a bank **2.** ARCHED CEILING an arched structure of stone, brick, wood, or plaster that forms a ceiling or roof. See illustration on next page **3.** ROOM WITH ARCHED CEILING a room, especially an underground room, with an arched ceiling **4.** BURIAL CHAMBER a burial chamber,

Ralph Vaughan Williams

usually underground **5.** SOMETHING ARCHING OVERHEAD something that arches overhead, especially the sky (*literary*) ○ *the great vault of the sky* **6.** ANAT ARCHED PART OF BODY a part of the body with an arched shape ■ *v* (**vaults, vaulting, vaulted**) **1.** *vi* FORM VAULT to arch or curve like a vault **2.** *vt* ARCHIT PUT ARCHED STRUCTURE OVER SOMETHING to cover a building with an arched ceiling or roof **3.** *vt* ARCHIT BUILD SOMETHING AS VAULT to build something in the shape of a vault [14C. < Old French *vaute* < assumed Vulgar Latin *volvita* 'turn, vault' < Latin *voluta*, feminine past participle of *volvere* 'turn, roll'] —**vaulted** *adj*

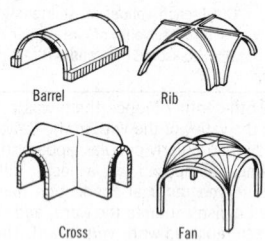

Barrel   Rib

Cross   Fan

vault¹ (sense 2)

vault² /vawlt, volt/ *v* (**vaults, vaulting, vaulted**) **1.** *vti* SPRING OVER OBJECT to leap or spring over something, especially by pushing on it with the hands or using a pole **2.** *vi* MOVE WITH BOUND to move with a leap or bound **3.** *vi* RISE SUDDENLY TO PROMINENCE to arrive somewhere or achieve something suddenly ○ *She vaulted to fame with the publication of her first novel.* **4.** *vti* RIDING same as **curvet** ■ *n* **1.** ACT OF VAULTING an act of vaulting **2.** RIDING same as **curvet** [Mid-16C. Via Old French *volter* < assumed Vulgar Latin *volvitare* 'roll repeatedly' < Latin *volvere* 'turn, roll'] —**vaulter** *n*

vaulting¹ /váwlting, vólt-/ *n* the structural use of brick, stone, or reinforced concrete to form a ceiling or roof over a space [15C. < VAULT¹]

vaulting² /váwlting, vólt-/ *adj* aspiring or confident, especially in an excessive way (*literary*) ○ *vaulting ambition* [Late 16C. < VAULT²]

vaulting horse *n* a piece of gymnastic equipment with four legs and a solid leather-covered oblong body, used for exercises and especially for vaulting over

vaunt /vawnt/ *v* (**vaunts, vaunting, vaunted**) **1.** *vt* BE BOASTFUL ABOUT SOMETHING to boast or act boastfully about something such as achievements or possessions **2.** *vi* BOAST to boast or brag (*literary*) ■ *n* BOASTFUL STATEMENT OR DISPLAY a boast, or display of boasting [14C. Via Old French *vanter* < late Latin *vanitare* 'be vain' < *vanus* 'empty'] —**vaunter** *n* —**vauntingly** *adv*

vaunted /váwntid/ *adj* boasted about or praised in an ostentatious way ○ *their vaunted home and car*

vav /vaw/, **waw** /waw/ *n* the sixth letter in the Hebrew alphabet, represented in the English alphabet as 'v' or 'w'. See table at **alphabet** [Early 19C. < Hebrew *wāw* 'hook']

vavasor /vávvə sawr/, **vavasour** *n* a feudal lord or knight who has power over vassals but is himself a vassal of a more powerful lord [14C. Via French < medieval Latin *vavassor*]

vb *abbr* LING **1.** verb **2.** verbal

VBAC /veé bak/ *n* a vaginal delivery of a baby by a woman whose first baby was delivered by Caesarean section. Full form **vaginal birth after Caesarean (delivery)**

VC *abbr* ONLINE St Vincent and the Grenadines (*used in Internet addresses*) See table at **domain name**

VC *abbr* **1.** FIN, BUSINESS venture capital **2.** FIN venture capitalist **3.** vice chairman **4.** vice chancellor **5.** POL vice consul **6.** MIL Victoria Cross **7.** PEOPLES Vietcong

vCJD *abbr* MED variant CJD

VCR *abbr* visual control room (*on an airfield*)

VCT *abbr* venture capital trust

vd *abbr* **1.** PHYS vapour density **2.** various dates **3.** void

VD *abbr* **1.** MED venereal disease **2.** Volunteer Decoration

VDC *abbr* Aus Volunteer Defence Corps

VDR *abbr* **1.** videodisk recorder **2.** videodisk recording

VDRL *abbr* venereal disease research laboratory

VDSL *abbr* TELECOM, ONLINE **1.** Very-High-Bit-Rate Digital Subscriber Line **2.** Very-High-Data-Rate Digital Subscriber Line

VDT *abbr* video display terminal

VDU *abbr* visual display unit

ve *abbr* ONLINE Venezuela (*used in Internet addresses*) See table at **domain name**

've /əv, v/ *contr* have

USAGE See *of*.

veal /veel/ *n* **1.** meat from a calf **2.** AGRIC same as **veal calf** [14C. Via Anglo-Norman, Old French *veel* < Latin *vitellus*, diminutive of *vitulus* 'calf']

veal calf *n* a calf reared for veal

vealer /veélər/ *n* ANZ, N Am AGRIC same as **veal calf**

vector /véktər/ *n* **1.** MATHS QUANTITY WITH DIRECTION AND MAGNITUDE a quantity that has both direction and magnitude, e.g. force or velocity, usually represented by an arrow **2.** MATHS ITEM IN SET OF VECTORS an element of a vector space **3.** AVIAT COURSE OF AIRCRAFT the course taken by an aircraft or a missile **4.** BIOL DISEASE-TRANSMITTING ORGANISM an organism such as a mosquito or tick that transmits disease-causing microorganisms from an infected person or animal to another **5.** GENETICS GENE TRANSFER AGENT an agent such as a plasmid or bacteriophage that is used in genetic modification to transfer a segment of foreign DNA into a bacterium or other cell. The foreign DNA is spliced into the vector's DNA, which contains the genes necessary for switching on replication and transcription of the foreign DNA in its new setting. **6.** COMPUT COMPUTER ARRAY in computing, an array of any length, but only one dimension ■ *vt* (**-tors, -toring, -tored**) AVIAT **1.** DIRECT AIRCRAFT BY RADIO to direct an aircraft or pilot by radio, often from the ground **2.** CHANGE THRUST DIRECTION OF AIRCRAFT ENGINE to change the direction of the thrust of an aircraft engine as a means of steering the aircraft [Early 18C. < Latin, 'carrier' < *vectus*, past participle of *vehere* 'carry'] —**vectorial** /vek táwri əl/ *adj* —**vectorially** *adv*

vector graphics *npl* COMPUT same as **object-oriented graphics**

vector product *n* the result of multiplying two vectors. It is perpendicular to the vectors and its magnitude equals the product of their magnitudes multiplied by the sine of the included angle.

vector space *n* a mathematical set of vectors associated with a field of scalars comprising a commutative group under addition and in which multiplication of a vector and a scalar is a vector

vector sum *n* the result of adding two vectors, obtained graphically as the directed diagonal of the parallelogram whose sides are the given vectors

Veda /váydə, veédə/ *n* any or all of the collections of Aryan hymns, originally transmitted orally, but written down in sacred books from the 6th century BC [Mid-18C. < Sanskrit, 'knowledge, sacred book' < Indo-European, 'know'] —**Vedic** /ví dáy ik/ *adj*

Vedaism /váydə izəm/ *n* HINDUISM same as **Vedism**

Vedanta /vi daántə/ *n* one of the six philosophical schools of Hinduism [Late 18C. < Sanskrit *vedānta*

< *veda* (see VEDA) + *anta* 'end'] —**Vedantic** *adj* —**Vedantism** *n* —**Vedantist** *n*

V-E Day *n* the day after the German surrender, designated by the Allies to mark their victory in Europe in World War II. Date: 8 May 1945.

Vedda /véddə/ (*plural same* or **-das**), **Veddah** (*plural same* or **-dahs**) *n* a member of an indigenous forest people of Sri Lanka [Late 17C. < Sinhalese *vaddā* 'hunter'] —**Veddoid** *adj*

vedette /vi dét/ *n* **1.** a mounted soldier positioned ahead of a force of soldiers to serve as a scout **2.** *also* **vedette boat** a small fast boat that serves as a scout for a seaborne force [Mid-17C. Via French < Italian *vedetta*, alteration (after *vedere* 'see') of *veletta* < Spanish *vela* 'watch' < Latin *vigilare* (see VIGILANT)]

Vedic /váydik, veédik/ *adj* **1.** RELIG OF VEDAS relating to the Vedas **2.** HINDUISM OF CULTURE THAT PRODUCED VEDAS relating to the Hindu culture that produced the Vedas **3.** LANG IN ANCIENT SANSKRIT relating to the ancient form of Sanskrit in which the Vedas are written ■ *n* LANG ANCIENT SANSKRIT the ancient form of Sanskrit in which the Vedas are written

Vedism /váydizəm, veédizəm/ *n* the Hindu religious theory and practice contained in, or based on, the Vedas

vee /vee/ *n* the letter 'V', or something with a similar shape [Late 19C. < the pronunciation of the letter's name]

veena /veénə/, **vina** *n* a South Asian musical instrument with seven strings that has a long fretted fingerboard with resonating gourds at both ends and is played by plucking [Late 18C. < Sanskrit *vīnā*]

veep /veep/ *n* N Am same as **vice-president** (*slang*) [Mid-20C. < VP]

veer¹ /veer/ *v* (**veers, veering, veered**) **1.** *vti* CHANGE DIRECTION SUDDENLY to change direction, especially suddenly, or make something do this **2.** *vi* CHANGE FROM ONE OPINION TO ANOTHER to change from one opinion or state of mind to another, especially suddenly or radically **3.** *vi* METEOROL MOVE CLOCKWISE to shift in a clockwise direction (*refers to winds*) **4.** *vti* NAUT, SAILING SAIL AWAY FROM WIND to change course in a sailing vessel away from the wind, or make a vessel do this ■ *n* CHANGE IN DIRECTION a change in direction or course [Late 16C. < French *virer* 'turn']

veer² /veer/ (**veers, veering, veered**) *vt* to let out a cable or chain, or make it go slack [15C. < Middle Dutch *vieren* 'let out']

veery /veéri/ (*plural* **-ries**) *n* a woodland thrush with tawny upper parts and a spotted breast. Native to: eastern United States. Latin name: *Catharus fuscescens*. [Mid-19C. Origin ?]

veg¹ /vej/ (*plural same*) *n* vegetables, or a vegetable (*informal*) [Mid-20C. Shortening]

veg² /vej/ (**vegges, vegging, vegged**) *vi* same as **veg out** (*informal*) [Late 20C. < VEGETATE]

veg out *vi* to relax, be idle, or loaf, e.g. while watching television (*informal*)

Vega /váygə/ *n* the brightest star in the constellation Lyra and one of the brightest in the northern hemisphere

Vega /váygə/ ♦ **Lope de Vega**

vegan /veégən/ *n* somebody who does not eat meat, fish, dairy products, or eggs ■ *adj* not eating or including meat, fish, dairy products, or eggs [Mid-20C. Contraction of VEGETARIAN] —**veganism** *n*

Vegeburger /véjji burgər/ *tdmk* a trademark for a veggieburger

Vegemite /véjji mīt/ *tdmk* ANZ a trademark for a savoury yeast extract that is eaten as a spread

vegetable /véjtəb'l/ *n* **1.** EDIBLE PLANT a plant with edible parts, especially leafy or fleshy parts that are used mainly for soups or salads, or to accompany main courses **2.** FRUIT EATEN AS VEGETABLE a plant product that is strictly a fruit but is eaten as, and popularly believed to be, a vegetable, e.g. the tomato **3.** PLANTS PLANT a member of the plant kingdom **4.** OFFENSIVE TERM an offensive term for somebody in whom the usual mental or physical functions are severely reduced or absent, often as a result of injury to the brain **5.** SOMEBODY INACTIVE somebody regarded as lacking in vitality, alertness, or drive (*insult*) ■ *adj* CONSISTING OF VEGETABLES consisting of, made from, using, or resembling vegetables [14C. Via Old French < medieval

Latin *vegetabilis* 'animating, able to grow' < Latin *vegetare* (see VEGETATE)]

vegetable ivory *n* **1.** a hard pale material like ivory, used to make decorative items and accessories. It comes from the endosperm of a South American palm nut **(ivory nut)**. **2.** TREES same as **ivory nut**

vegetable marrow *n* FOOD, PLANTS same as **marrow** (senses 1–2)

vegetable oil *n* an oil that has been extracted from a plant or the seeds of a plant, e.g. olive oil, sunflower oil, sesame oil, or rapeseed oil

vegetable oyster *n* FOOD same as **salsify**

vegetable sheep *n* a plant of the daisy family that has dense foliage and white flowers that make it resemble sheep from a distance. Native to: New Zealand uplands. Genus: *Raoulia*.

vegetable wax *n* a waxy material that forms part of the thin film covering the surfaces of most plants and helps reduce their loss of water through evaporation. It is obtained commercially from some palms such as the carnauba.

vegetal /véjjit'l/ *adj* **1.** relating to plants **2.** BIOL same as **vegetative** (sense 2) [14C. < medieval Latin *vegetalis* < Latin *vegetare* (see VEGETATE)]

vegetal pole *n* the end of an animal egg that contains the greatest concentration of yolk, lying opposite to the animal pole

vegetarian /véjjə táiri ən/ *n* somebody who eats vegetables, fruits, grains, seeds, and usually eggs and dairy products, but not meat or fish ■ *adj* eating or including vegetables, fruits, grains, seeds, and usually eggs and dairy products, but not meat or fish [Mid-19C. < VEGETABLE] —**vegetarianism** *n*

vegetate /véjjə tayt/ (**-tates, -tating, -tated**) *vi* **1.** BEHAVE IN DULL OR INACTIVE WAY to live or behave in a dull, inactive, or undemanding way **2.** BOT DEVELOP LIKE PLANT to grow or sprout like a plant **3.** MED PRODUCE FLESHY OUTGROWTHS to grow or spread, especially by producing fleshy outgrowths (*refers to warts or polyps*) [Early 17C. < Latin *vegetat-*, past participle of *vegetare* 'grow' < *vegere* 'quicken']

vegetation /véjjə táysh'n/ *n* **1.** PLANTS IN GENERAL plants in general or the mass of plants growing in a particular place **2.** VEGETATING the process of vegetating **3.** MED OUTGROWTH an outgrowth from a body part, e.g. on the membranes surrounding the heart —**vegetational** *adj*

vegetative /véjjətətiv/ *adj* **1.** OF PLANTS relating to or typical of vegetation, plants, or plant growth **2.** INVOLVING GROWTH, NOT SEXUAL REPRODUCTION relating to, involving, or typical of the growth and maintenance of an organism, rather than its sexual reproduction **3.** REPRODUCING ASEXUALLY describes reproduction, especially in plants, in which new individuals develop asexually from specialized structures such as bulbs, rhizomes, or runners rather than from specialized sex cells **4.** HAVING SEDENTARY LIFESTYLE leading a physically or mentally inactive life **5.** MED RELATING TO PERSISTENT COMA characterized by the reduction or absence of the usual mental or physical functions, often as a result of injury to the brain —**vegetatively** *adv* —**vegetativeness** *n*

vegetative nervous system *n* the part of the body's nervous system that controls involuntary functions such as the beating of the heart

veggie /véjji/, **vegie** *n* FOOD (*informal*) **1.** same as **vegetarian** **2.** *N Am* same as **vegetable** [Mid-20C. Shortening] —**veggie** *adj*

veggieburger /véjji burgər/ *n* a flat cake made from vegetables, grains, or legumes, often served in the same way as a hamburger

vegie *n* FOOD another spelling of **veggie** (*informal*)

~~**vegtable**~~ incorrect spelling of **vegetable**

vehement /veé əmənt/ *adj* **1.** expressed with or showing conviction or intense feeling **2.** done with vigour or force [15C. Via Old French < Latin *vehement-* 'forceful, violent'] —**vehemence** *n* —**vehemently** *adv*

~~**vehical**~~ incorrect spelling of **vehicle**

vehicle /veé ik'l/ *n* **1.** MEANS OF LAND TRANSPORT a usually wheeled conveyance used on land for carrying people or goods **2.** STRUCTURE FOR TRANSPORT IN SPACE a powered structure, device, or rocket used to transport a payload or another craft through space **3.** COMMUNICATION MEDIUM a medium for communicating, expressing, or accomplishing something **4.** ARTS PERFORMANCE FOR PARTICULAR PERFORMER a film, play, show, or other performance designed or used to show off the talents of a particular performer **5.** ART MIXTURE FOR PAINT PIGMENT a substance such as linseed oil or an acrylic vinyl polymer in which a pigment is mixed for painting **6.** PHARM SUBSTANCE BLENDED WITH DRUG an inactive substance with which a drug is blended to make it easier to apply, administer, or take [Early 17C. Via French *véhicule* < Latin *vehiculum* < *vehere* 'carry']

vehicle registration document *n* AUTOMOT same as **registration document**

vehicular /vi hík yoōlər/ *adj* relating to, involving, or for use by vehicles, especially motor vehicles [Early 17C. < late Latin *vehicularis* < Latin *vehiculum* (see VEHICLE)]

veil /vayl/ *n* **1.** FACE COVERING WORN BY WOMEN a length of fabric, usually sheer, worn by women over the head and face as a concealment or for protection **2.** NETTING ATTACHED TO WOMAN'S HAT a piece of netting or other sheer fabric attached to a woman's hat and covering the eyes **3.** NUN'S HEADDRESS a part of a nun's headdress covering the sides and back of the head **4.** NUN'S VOWS OR LIFE the vows that a nun takes, or the life that she leads **5.** MEANS OF CONCEALMENT something that hides, disguises, or obscures something, or separates one thing from another **6.** BOT MEMBRANE COVERING YOUNG MUSHROOM a thin membrane that covers the cap and stalk of an immature mushroom **7.** ANAT same as **caul** (sense 1) **8.** CHR same as **humeral veil** ■ *v* (**veils, veiling, veiled**) **1.** *vt* COVER SOMETHING WITH VEIL to cover something such as somebody's face with a veil **2.** *vt* HIDE SOMETHING to hide or disguise something, or separate one thing from another **3.** *vi* WEAR VEIL to put on or wear a veil [12C. Via Old French *veile* < Latin *vela* 'covering', plural of *velum* 'sail'] —**veiler** *n* ◇ **draw a veil over something** to ignore something deliberately or refrain from mentioning it, in order to be discreet ◇ **take the veil** to become a nun (*literary*)

SPELLCHECK See *vale*[1].

Veil /vīl/, **Simone** (*b.* 1927) French government official and politician. A lawyer and campaigner for women's rights, she was the French minister of health (1974–79) and president of the European Parliament (1979–82).

veiled /vayld/ *adj* **1.** not open or direct, but disguised or suggested **2.** covered with or wearing a veil —**veiledly** /váylidli/ *adv*

veiling /váyling/ *n* **1.** fabric used for veils **2.** a veil

vein /vayn/ *n* **1.** VESSEL CARRYING BLOOD TO HEART a blood vessel that carries blood to the heart **2.** BLOOD VESSEL a vessel that carries blood around the body (*not in technical use*) **3.** INSECTS SUPPORTING STRUCTURE IN INSECT WING a hollow supporting structure in the wing of an insect that carries blood vessels, nerves, and air tubes supplying the wing **4.** BOT SAP-CONDUCTING LEAF STRAND a distinct strand of tissue in a leaf that contains the sap-conducting vessels. It comprises one of several bundles of vessels and associated tissues **(vascular bundles)** and forms part of a network, arranged in a characteristic pattern. **5.** GEOL LAYER OF MINERAL a layer of a mineral in rock, especially an ore or a metal **6.** GEOL FISSURE FILLED WITH MATERIAL a fissure, crack, or channel in rock or ice that has been filled with a crystallized mixture of minerals **7.** STREAK OF DIFFERENT COLOUR a streak of different colour or material within a substance such as marble, wood, or cheese **8.** PARTICULAR QUALITY a particular recurrent quality or characteristic **9.** DISPOSITION a disposition, tone, or mood ○ *continued his speech in a more light-hearted vein* ■ *vt* (**veins, veining, veined**) **1.** STREAK SOMETHING to streak or suffuse something of one colour or material with another ○ *green marble veined with white* **2.** FORM VEINS IN SOMETHING to form veins, streaks, or layers in something [13C. Via Old French *veine* < Latin *vena* 'blood vessel, vein of metal, mine'] —**veinal** *adj* —**veined** *adj* —**veiny** *adj*

SPELLCHECK See *vain*.

veining /váyning/ *n* a distribution or pattern of veins or streaks

veinlet /váynlət/ *n* a small vein

veinstone /váyn stōn/ *n* MIN EXTRACT same as **gangue**

vel. *abbr* **1.** vellum **2.** PHYS velocity

vela BIOL plural of **velum**

Vela /veélə/ *n* a constellation of the southern hemisphere. See illustration at **constellation** [Mid-19C. Latin, literally 'sails', from the shape of the constellation]

velamen /və láy men/ (*plural* **-lamina** /-lámminə/) *n* a spongy absorbent and protective layer that covers the aerial roots of some plants such as tree-dwelling orchids [Late 19C. < Latin, 'covering' < *velare* 'to cover' < *velum* 'sail']

velar /veélər/ *adj* **1.** WITH TONGUE NEAR SOFT PALATE pronounced with the back of the tongue close to, or in contact with, the soft palate **2.** OF VELUM relating to, involving, or typical of a velum ■ *n* PHON VELAR CONSONANT a consonant pronounced with the back of the tongue close to, or in contact with, the soft palate [Early 18C. < modern Latin *velaris* < Latin *velum* 'sail']

velaria ANCIENT HIST plural of **velarium**

velarise *vt* PHON another spelling of **velarize**

velarium /vi láiri əm/ (*plural* **-ia** /-i ə/) *n* in ancient Rome, a large awning used in amphitheatres to shade the audience [Mid-19C. < Latin, 'awning, curtain' < *velum* 'sail']

velarize /veélə rīz/ (**-izes, -izing, -ized**), **velarise** (**-ises, -ising, -ised**) *vt* to pronounce a speech sound by bringing the back of the tongue close to or against the soft palate —**velarization** /veélə rī záysh'n/ *n*

velate /veélət, -layt/ *adj* having or covered by a velum [Mid-19C. < VELUM]

Velázquez /vi láskwez, ve láthketh/, **Diego** (1599–1660) Spanish painter. Court painter to Philip IV, he is noted for his portraits, kitchen scenes, and interior schemes. *Las Meninas* (1656) is considered to be his masterpiece. Full name **Velázquez, Diego Rodríguez de Silva y**

Velcro /vélkrō/ *tdmk* a trademark for a fastener consisting of two strips, one with a dense layer of tiny nylon hooks and the other of loops that interlock with them. Use: outerwear, athletic shoes, luggage.

veld /felt/, **veldt** /velt/ *n* an area of open grassland, especially in southern Africa [Early 19C. Via Afrikaans < Dutch, 'field']

Velde /véldə/, **Henry van de** (1863–1957) Belgian architect. He was the most influential architect of the Art Nouveau style. After designing integrated buildings and furniture in Belgium, France, and Germany, he founded the Weimar School of Arts and Crafts (1907), which later became the Bauhaus.

veldskoen /vélt skoōn/ *n S Africa* a shoe or boot made of rough hide [Early 19C. < Afrikaans, by folk etymology (after *veld* 'veld') < *velskoen* 'skin shoe' < *vel* 'skin']

veldt *n* GEOG another spelling of **veld**

veleta /və leétə/, **valeta** *n* a ballroom dance in triple time in which partners sometimes dance side by side and sometimes do a quick waltz [Early 20C. < Spanish, literally 'weather vane']

velites /veéli teez/ *npl* in ancient Rome, lightly armed foot soldiers [Early 17C. < Latin, plural of *veles* 'light-armed soldier, skirmisher']

velleity /ve leé əti/ (*plural* **-ties**) *n* **1.** volition or desire at its weakest level (*literary*) **2.** a vague wish or desire [Early 17C. < medieval Latin *velleitas-* < Latin *velle* 'to wish']

vellum /vélləm/ *n* **1.** ANIMAL SKIN PARCHMENT high quality parchment made from calfskin, kidskin, or lambskin **2.** VELLUM MANUSCRIPT a manuscript written or printed on vellum **3.** PAPER RESEMBLING VELLUM an off-white heavy paper resembling vellum [15C. < French *vélin* 'of a calf' < Old French *veel* 'calf' (see VEAL)] —**vellum** *adj*

veloce /ve lóchi/ *adv* to be played or performed rapidly (*used as a musical direction*) [Early 19C. Via Italian < Latin *veloc-* 'quick, swift'] —**veloce** *adj*

velocimeter /véllə símmitər, veélō-/ *n* an instrument used to measure the speed of a fluid or sound

velocipede /və lóssi peed/ *n* an early form of bicycle or tricycle, including those that had pedals attached to the front wheel or were propelled by pushing the feet along the ground [Early 19C. < French *vélocipède* 'bicycle' < Latin *veloc-* 'quick, swift' + *ped-* 'foot'] —**velocipedist** *n*

velociraptor /və lóssi raptər/ *n* a small two-legged carnivorous dinosaur

velocity /və lóssəti/ (*plural* **-ties**) *n* **1.** the speed at which something moves or happens **2.** the rate of change in the position of an object as it moves in a particular direction [Mid-16C. < Latin *velocitas-< veloc-* 'quick, swift']

velocity of circulation *n* the rate at which money circulates throughout an economy during a particular period, usually a year

velodrome /véllədrōm/ *n* a stadium that has a banked track for bicycle races [Late 19C. < French *vélodrome* < *vélocipède* (see VELOCIPEDE) + -DROME < Greek *dromos* (see -DROME)]

velours /və loŏr/, **velour** *n* a fabric with a thick pile, similar to velvet. Use: upholstery, clothing. [Early 18C. Via Old French *velous* < Latin *villosus* 'shaggy' < *villus* 'shaggy hair, wool']

velouté /və loŏ tay/ *n* a creamy white sauce based on chicken, veal, or fish stock that is often used on poultry or vegetables [Mid-19C. < French, 'velvety' < Old French *vellute* < *velous* (see VELOURS)]

velum /veeləm/ (*plural* **-la** /-lə/) *n* **1.** a thin layer of tissue that covers or separates something **2.** ANAT same as **soft palate 3.** BOT same as **veil** *n* (sense 6) [Late 18C. < Latin, 'sail, covering']

velutinous /və loŏtinəss/ *adj* densely covered with short soft hairs [Early 19C. < modern Latin *velutinus* 'velvety' < medieval Latin *velutum* 'velvet' < *villutus* (see VELVET)]

velvet /vélvit/ *n* **1.** FABRIC WITH SOFT LUSTROUS PILE a cotton, silk, or nylon fabric with a dense, soft, usually lustrous pile and a plain underside **2.** SOMETHING LIKE VELVET something that is smooth and soft like velvet **3.** ZOOL FURRY COVERING ON DEER ANTLERS the furry layer that covers the growing antlers of deer and is sloughed off when the antlers stop growing and harden ■ *adj* **1.** MADE OF VELVET made of or covered with velvet **2.** LIKE VELVET like velvet, especially in being or looking soft, smooth, or lustrous [14C. < Old French *veluotte* < *velu* 'shaggy (cloth)' < medieval Latin *villutus* < Latin *villus* 'shaggy hair, wool']

velvet ant *n* a wasp whose body is covered in soft hair. The female is generally wingless and has a potent sting. Family: Mutillidae.

velveteen /vélvə teen/ *n* a brushed fabric with a soft pile like velvet [Late 18C. < VELVET + variant of -INE]

velvet glove *n* kind, careful, or gentle treatment, often disguising strength or determination

velvet shank *n* an edible mushroom that grows in clusters on hardwood trees and has a yellow cap and a velvety dark brown stalk. Native to: Europe, North Africa. Latin name: *Flammulina velutipes.*

velvety /vélvəti/ *adj* **1.** soft and smooth in a way that suggests the feel of velvet **2.** smooth and mellow

Ven. *abbr* **1.** CHR Venerable **2.** Venezuela

ven- *prefix* same as **veno-** (*used before vowels*)

vena /veenə/ (*plural* **-nae** /-nee/) *n* ANAT same as **vein** *n* (sense 1) (*technical*) [14C. < Latin]

vena cava /veenə kávvə/ (*plural* **venae cavae** /veë nee káy vee/) *n* either of two major veins that carry circulating blood into the right atrium of the heart. One carries blood returning from the upper body and head (**superior vena cava**) and the other brings that from below the chest (**inferior vena cava**). [Late 16C. < Latin, 'hollow vein']—**vena-caval** *adj*

venal /veen'l/ *adj* **1.** OPEN TO BRIBERY open to persuasion by corrupt means, especially bribery **2.** CORRUPT characterized by corruption **3.** ABLE TO BE BOUGHT able to be obtained for a price [Mid-17C. < Latin *venalis* < *venum* 'something for sale']—**venality** /vee nálləti/ *n*—**venally** *adv*

USAGE venal or **venial**? The two words are derived from entirely different Latin roots: **venal** comes from *venum* meaning 'something for sale' and **venial** from *venia* meaning 'forgiveness'. *Venal*, meaning 'open to or characterized by corruption', describes people as well as processes and organizations: *The political system is so venal that bribery is commonplace.* *Venial*, meaning 'easily forgiven', is used in connection with minor faults or transgressions: *He was inclined to be thoughtless, but that was a venial fault in one so young.* In Roman Catholic theology, a *venial sin* is one that does not

deprive the soul of divine grace, as opposed to a *mortal sin,* which does.

venation /vee náysh'n/ *n* **1.** the pattern formed by the network of veins in an insect's wing or in a leaf **2.** all the veins making up a network [Mid-17C. < Latin *vena* 'vein']—**venational** *adj*

vend /vend/ (**vends, vending, vended**) *v* **1.** *vt* to sell something from a vending machine **2.** *vti* to sell something, especially in the street, or make a living doing this [Early 17C. Directly or via French *vendre* < Latin *vendere* 'sell']

Venda[1] /véndə/ (*plural same* or **-das**) *n* **1.** a member of a people who live in northern South Africa and southern Zimbabwe **2.** a Bantu language spoken mainly in northern South Africa. Native speakers: 750,000. [Early 20C. < Bantu]—**Venda** *adj*

Venda[2] /véndə/ former homeland in South Africa. Abolished in 1994, it is now part of Limpopo Province.

vendace /vén dayss/ (*plural* **-daces** or *same*) *n* a white-fish with a streamlined body and protruding lower jaw. Native to: freshwater lakes of northwestern Europe, Russia. Genus: *Coregonus.* [Late 17C. Probably < Old French *vendoise* < Celtic]

vendee /vén dee/ *n* somebody who buys something

vender *n* COMM another spelling of **vendor**

vendetta /ven déttə/ *n* **1.** a prolonged bitter feud or quarrel **2.** a feud between families started by the killing of a member of one family that is then avenged by the killing of a member of the other family [Mid-19C. Via Italian < Latin *vindicta* 'vengeance']

vendible /véndəb'l/ *adj* suitable or fit to be sold ■ *n* something that can be sold or is available for sale— **vendibility** /véndə billəti/ *n*—**vendibleness** *n*

vending machine /vénding-/ *n* a machine from which items such as packaged food or drinks can be bought by inserting money

Vendôme /vaN dốm/, **Louis Joseph, Duc de** (1654–1712) French soldier. He commanded forces in a number of battles during the War of the Spanish Succession (1701–14).

vendor /véndər/, **vender** *n* **1.** somebody who sells something **2.** COMM same as **vending machine**

vendue /vén dyoo/ *n* US a public sale or auction [Late 17C. Via Dutch *vendu* < French *vendue,* form of *vendre* 'sell' (see VEND)]

veneer /və neer/ *n* **1.** THIN LAYER AS SURFACE a thin layer of a material bonded to the surface of a less attractive or inferior material **2.** DECEPTIVE APPEARANCE a superficial appearance or show put on to please or impress others ○ *a thin veneer of civility* **3.** OUTER LAYER an outer layer applied to a surface for decoration or protection, e.g. a facing of stone on a brick building **4.** LAYER OF PLYWOOD a thin layer of wood that is glued together with others to make plywood ■ *vt* (**-neers, -neering, -neered**) **1.** FIX VENEER TO SOMETHING to bond or apply a veneer to a surface **2.** HIDE SOMETHING BEHIND DECEPTIVELY PLEASANT APPEARANCE to hide or disguise something behind a deceptively pleasant or impressive appearance **3.** GLUE LAYERS OF WOOD to glue layers of wood together to make plywood [Early 18C. < German *Fournier* 'inlay, veneer' < French *fournir* 'furnish, provide']—**veneerer** *n*

venepuncture *n* MED another spelling of **venipuncture**

venerable /vénnərəb'l/ *adj* **1.** WORTHY OF RESPECT worthy of respect as a result of great age, wisdom, remarkable achievements, or similar qualities **2.** RELIG REVERED revered for qualities such as great age or holiness **3.** ANCIENT extremely old **4.** CHR USED AS TITLE BEFORE CANONIZATION used by the Roman Catholic Church to describe somebody who has died and attained the first of the three degrees of canonization **5.** CHR USED AS ARCHDEACON'S TITLE used in the Church of England as a title for an archdeacon [15C. Directly or via French < Latin *venerabilis* < *venerari* (see VENERATE)]—**venerability** /vénnərə billəti/ *n*—**venerably** *adv*

venerate /vénnə rayt/ (**-ates, -ating, -ated**) *vt* **1.** to regard somebody with profound respect or reverence **2.** to honour somebody or something as sacred or special [Early 17C. < Latin *venerat-,* past participle of *venerari* < *vener-,* stem of *venus* 'love, desire']—**venerator** *n*

veneration /vénnə ráysh'n/ *n* **1.** FEELING OF RESPECT feel-

ings of deep respect or awe **2.** EXPRESSING OF RESPECT the expression of profound respect or reverence for somebody or something **3.** CONDITION OF BEING RESPECTED the condition of being respected or revered —**venerational** *adj*

SYNONYMS See *regard*.

venereal /və neeri əl/ *adj* **1.** PASSED ON THROUGH SEX describes an infection or disease that is caught or transmitted through sexual intercourse **2.** ASSOCIATED WITH SEXUALLY TRANSMITTED DISEASE associated with, symptomatic of, or infected with a sexually transmitted disease **3.** GENITAL affecting or originating in the genitals **4.** ABOUT SEX relating to sex acts or sexual desire (*archaic or literary*) [15C. < Latin *venereus* < *vener-,* stem of *venus* 'love, desire']

venereal disease *n* MED same as **sexually transmitted infection** (*dated*)

venereology /və neeri ólləji/ *n* the branch of medicine involving the study and treatment of sexually transmitted diseases [Late 19C. < VENEREAL]—**venereological** /və neeri ə lójjik'l/ *adj*—**venereologist** *n*

venery[1] /vénnəri, veen-/ *n* the pursuit of or indulgence in sexual pleasure (*archaic*) [15C. < medieval Latin *veneria* < Latin *vener-,* stem of *venus* 'love, desire']

venery[2] /vénnəri, veen-/ *n* the sport or practice of hunting, or the animals hunted (*archaic*) [14C. Via French *vénerie* < *venari* 'to hunt']

venesection /vénni seksh'n/ *n* SURG same as **phlebotomy** [Mid-17C. < medieval Latin *venae sectio* 'cutting of a vein']

Veneti /ve nétti/ *npl* an ancient people who lived in northeastern Italy and neighbouring areas from about the 10th century BC. The Veneti allied themselves with the Romans during the 1st century BC. [Early 17C. < Latin]

Venetian /və neesh'n/ *adj* relating to the Italian city of Venice, or its people or culture ■ *n* somebody who comes from Venice [15C. < Old French *Venicien* < Latin *Venetia* 'Venice']

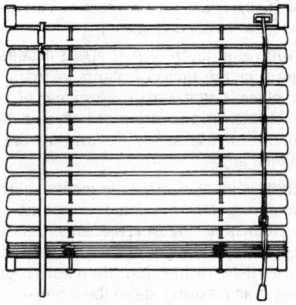

Venetian blind

Venetian blind, venetian blind *n* a window blind consisting of narrow horizontal slats whose angle can be adjusted to let in more or less light

Venetian glass *n* delicate glassware, often with colourful ornamentation, made in or around Venice, especially at Murano

Venetian red *n* **1.** a dark red pigment. Source: haematite, synthetic iron oxide. **2.** a strong reddish-brown colour —**Venetian red** *adj*

Venetic /və néttik/ *n* the extinct language spoken in northwestern Italy by the Veneti people —**Venetic** *adj*

Venez. *abbr* Venezuela

Venezuela

Venezuela /vénnə zwáylə/ country in northeastern South America, north of Brazil, on the Caribbean Sea and the Atlantic Ocean. Language: Spanish. Currency: bolivar. Capital: Caracas. Population: 24,654,694 (2003). Area: 912,050 sq. km/352,144 sq. mi. Official name **Republic of Venezuela**. See map on previous page —**Venezuelan** n, adj

Venezuela, Gulf of inlet of the Caribbean Sea in northwestern Venezuela. It is connected to Lake Maracaibo to the south by a narrow strait.

~~vengance~~ incorrect spelling of **vengeance**

vengeance /vénjənss/ n punishment that is inflicted in return for a wrong [13C. Via French < Latin *vindicare* 'avenge' (see VINDICATE)] ◇ **with a vengeance** in an extreme or intense manner

vengeful /vénjf'l/ adj 1. having or showing a strong desire for revenge 2. serving the purpose of revenge or resulting from somebody's desire for revenge —**vengefully** adv —**vengefulness** n

V-engine n an internal-combustion engine with cylinders arranged in two rows to form a V-shaped angle

veni- prefix same as **veno-**

venial /véeni əl/ adj easily forgiven or excused [13C. Via French < late Latin *venialis* < Latin *venia* 'forgiveness'] —**veniality** /véeni álləti/ n —**venially** adv

USAGE See **venal**.

venial sin n in the Roman Catholic Church, a sin that does not deprive the soul of divine grace, either because it was not serious or because it was committed without intent or without understanding its seriousness

Venice /vénniss/ historic city and seaport in northeastern Italy, built on islands in a lagoon on the coast of the Adriatic Sea. Population: 271,073 (2001).

venipuncture /vénni pungkchər, véeni-/, **venepuncture** n the puncturing of a vein for any medical purpose, e.g. to take blood, to feed somebody intravenously, or to administer a drug

venire /vi níri/, **venire facias** /-fáyshi ass/ n in the United States, and formerly in the United Kingdom, a judicial writ ordering the summoning of jurors [Mid-17C. < medieval Latin *venire facias* 'you should cause to come']

venireman /vi nírimən/ (plural **-men** /-mən/) n a citizen summoned for jury duty under a venire

venison /vénniss'n, -z'n/ n the meat of a deer used as food [13C. Via Old French < Latin *venation-* 'hunting' < *venari* 'to hunt']

Venite /vi níti/ n 1. the 95th Psalm from the Bible, sung as an invitation to morning prayer 2. a musical setting of the 95th Psalm [13C. Latin, 'come ye', the first word of the psalm]

Venlo /vénnlō/ city in Limburg Province, in the southeastern Netherlands. Population: 64,775 (2000).

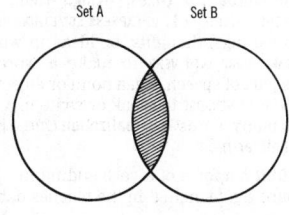

Venn diagram

Venn diagram /vén-/ n a mathematical diagram representing sets as circles, with their relationships to each other expressed through their overlapping positions, so that all possible relationships between the sets are shown [Early 20C. After John *Venn* (1834–1923), British logician]

vennel /vénn'l/ n Scotland an alley or narrow lane between buildings [15C. Via French < medieval Latin *venella* 'little vein' < Latin *vena* 'vein']

veno-, **veni-** prefix vein, venous ◦ *venogram* [< Latin *vena* 'vein']

venogram /véenə gram/ n an X-ray photograph of a vein or network of veins, taken after injecting a substance that absorbs X-rays and so makes the veins visible

venography /vi nóggrəfi/ n the examination of somebody's veins by taking an X-ray photograph (**venogram**) after injecting a substance that absorbs X-rays

venom /vénnəm/ n 1. a poisonous fluid produced by an animal and injected into prey or attackers by a bite or sting. Venoms are produced by a wide range of animals, including snakes, scorpions, spiders, and fish. 2. malice, spite, or vicious hostility [13C. Via Old French *venim* < Latin *venenum* 'poison'] —**venomous** adj

venose /véenōss/ adj describes something such as an insect's wing or the leaf of a plant that contains veins, especially many branched veins [Mid-17C. < Latin *venosus* < *vena* 'vein']

venosity /vi nóssəti/ n 1. EXCESSIVE AMOUNT OF BLOOD an excessive amount of blood in the veins, an organ, or other body part 2. HIGH NUMBER OF VEINS an unusually large number of veins in an organ or other body part 3. QUALITY OF VENOUS BLOOD the deoxygenated state of venous blood 4. VEINED CONDITION the presence or possession of veins, especially many branched veins

venous /véenəss/ adj 1. OF VEINS relating to or involving the veins 2. RELATING TO BLOOD IN VEINS describes blood in the veins, which is returning to the heart, as opposed to blood in the arteries, which is leaving the heart 3. WITH VEINS containing or full of veins [Early 17C. < Latin *vena* 'vein'] —**venously** adv

vent[1] /vent/ n 1. OPENING FOR AIR a small opening that allows fresh air to enter or lets air, gas, smoke, or steam to escape 2. RELEASE OF STRONG FEELINGS a release or expression of strong feelings or emotions, or a chance to do this ◦ *gave vent to his anger* 3. GEOL OPENING IN EARTH'S CRUST an opening in the Earth's crust from which gases or volcanic material escape 4. ZOOL OPENING IN ANIMAL'S BODY the external opening through which all waste material and eggs pass in fish, amphibians, reptiles, birds, and primitive mammals 5. ARMS OPENING IN GUN BREECH a small opening in the breech of an old muzzle-loading gun through which the charge is ignited ■ vt (**vents, venting, vented**) 1. RELEASE EMOTIONS to release or forcefully express strong feelings or emotions ◦ *She vented her frustration on her family.* 2. LET OUT AIR to let out stale air, gas, smoke, or steam through a vent 3. MAKE VENT FOR SOMETHING to provide a vent for something [14C. Via Old French *esventer* 'let out air' < assumed Vulgar Latin *exventare* < Latin *ventus* 'wind'] —**ventless** adj

vent[2] /vent/ n a vertical slit at the bottom of a seam in a jacket or other garment that provides room for movement ■ vt (**vents, venting, vented**) to put a vent in a jacket or other garment [15C. Old French *fente* 'slit' < Latin *findere* 'to split'] —**vented** adj —**ventless** adj

ventage /véntij/ n 1. a finger hole in a recorder or other wind instrument 2. a small opening or vent [Early 17C. < VENT[1]]

ventail /vént ayl/ n a movable covering for the neck or lower face on a medieval helmet [14C. < Old French < Latin *ventus* 'wind']

venter /véntər/ n 1. ANAT, ZOOL BELLY OF ANIMAL WITH BACKBONE the abdomen of a vertebrate 2. ZOOL BODY PART RESEMBLING ABDOMEN the part of the body in invertebrates that corresponds to the abdomen in vertebrates 3. ANAT SOFT PART OF MUSCLE the soft fleshy area that forms the main part of a muscle 4. ANAT HOLLOW OR CAVITY a hollow or cavity, e.g. on a bone 5. BOT FEMALE PLANT PART in plants such as mosses and ferns, the swollen lower part of the female sex organ (**archegonium**) where the ovum develops 6. LAW WOMB a woman's womb (technical) [Mid-16C. Directly or via French *ventre* < Latin *venter* 'stomach, abdomen']

ventifact /vénti fakt/ n a rock, stone, or pebble that has been shaped, cut, or polished by wind-blown sand [Early 20C. < Latin *ventus* 'wind', after *artifact*, variant of ARTEFACT]

ventilate /vénti layt/ (**-lates, -lating, -lated**) vt 1. PROVIDE ROOM WITH FRESH AIR to provide a room or other enclosed space with fresh air or a current of air 2. PROVIDE ENCLOSED SPACE WITH VENT to provide an enclosed space with a vent or other means of letting fresh air in and stale air out 3. EXPOSE SOMETHING TO MOVING AIR to expose something to moving fresh air, e.g. in order to dry, cool, or preserve it 4. PUBLICLY EXAMINE SOMETHING to state, examine, or discuss publicly something such as an opinion, question, or grievance 5. PHYSIOL SUPPLY OXYGEN TO BLOOD to oxygenate or aerate the blood through the blood vessels of the lungs [15C. < Latin *ventilat-*, past participle of *ventilare* 'to fan' < *ventilus* 'fan' < *ventus* 'wind']

ventilation /vénti láysh'n/ n 1. CIRCULATION OF AIR the movement or circulation of fresh air 2. MEANS OF SUPPLYING FRESH AIR the means of supplying fresh air to an enclosed space, e.g. an opening or equipment installed in a building 3. PUBLIC DISCUSSION the public announcement, examination, or discussion of something such as an opinion, question, or grievance

ventilator /vénti laytər/ n 1. a machine that keeps air moving in and out of the lungs of a patient who cannot breathe unaided 2. a device that circulates fresh air in an enclosed space

ventilatory /véntilətəri, -laytəri/ adj relating to or used for breathing or for oxygenating the blood

ventr- prefix same as **ventro-** (used before vowels)

ventrad /vén trad/ adv towards the ventral surface or side

ventral /véntrəl/ adj 1. ZOOL OF LOWER BODY AT FRONT located on or affecting the lower surface of an animal's body, or the front of the human body ◦ *ventral fin* 2. ANAT OF OR CLOSE TO ABDOMEN relating to or situated in, on, or near the abdomen 3. BOT FACING STEM describes the upper side of a leaf or other surface that faces towards the stem ■ n FISH same as **ventral fin** [Mid-18C. < Latin *ventr-* 'stomach, abdomen'] —**ventrally** adv

ventral fin n a fin on the underside of a fish, especially a pelvic fin or anal fin

ventral root n the spinal nerve root emerging from the lower surface of the spinal cord in animals and from the front surface in humans and mammals, consisting of motor nerve fibres

ventricle /véntrik'l/ n 1. PHYSIOL HEART CHAMBER either of the two lower chambers of the heart that receive blood from the upper chambers (**atria**) and pump it into the arteries by contraction of their thick muscular walls 2. PHYSIOL BRAIN CAVITY a cavity in the brain that is an enlargement of the central canal of the spinal cord and contains cerebrospinal fluid 3. HOLLOW IN BODY PART a small cavity or chamber in the body or in an organ [14C. < Latin *ventriculus* (see VENTRICULUS)]

ventricose /véntrikōss/ adj 1. describes a body part or plant part that is swollen, distended, or protruding on one side 2. corpulent and fleshy, especially around the middle of the body (formal) [Mid-18C. < modern Latin *ventricosus* < Latin *venter* 'stomach, abdomen'] —**ventricosity** /véntri kóssəti/ n

ventricular /ven tríkyŏŏlər/ adj relating to, involving, or affecting a ventricle or a ventriculus

ventricular fibrillation n an often fatal heartbeat irregularity in which the muscle fibres of the ventricles work without coordination and cause a loss of effective pumping action of the heart

ventriculus /ven tríkyŏŏləss/ n (plural **-li** /-lī/) n 1. the part of an insect's gut where digestion takes place 2. the part of a bird's stomach where digestion takes place [Early 18C. < Latin, 'little stomach' < *venter* 'stomach, abdomen']

ventriloquise vi ARTS another spelling of **ventriloquize**

ventriloquism /ven tríllәkwizәm/, **ventriloquy** /-kwi/ n the art or skill of producing vocal sounds that seem to come from somewhere other than the speaker [Late 18C. < modern Latin *ventriloquium* 'speaking from the stomach' < Latin *venter* 'stomach, abdomen' + *loqui* 'speak'] —**ventriloquial** /véntri lṓkwi əl/ adj

ventriloquist /ven tríllәkwist/ n somebody who engages in ventriloquism, especially a performer who makes a puppet or doll appear to speak —**ventriloquism** n

ventriloquize /ven tríllə kwīz/ (**-quizes, -quizing, -quized**), **ventriloquise** (**-quises, -quising, -quised**) vi to produce vocal sounds that seem to come from somewhere other than the speaker

ventriloquy *n* ARTS same as **ventriloquism**

Ventris /véntriss/, **Michael** (1922–56) British linguist. He is known for his decipherment of the Linear B script of ancient Crete, revealing it to be a form of Greek. Full name **Ventris, Michael George Francis**

ventro- *prefix* ventral, having to do with the stomach or abdomen ○ *ventromedial* [< Latin *venter* 'stomach, abdomen']

ventrodorsal /véntrō dáwrss'l/ *adj* ANAT same as **dorsoventral** (sense 1) —**ventrodorsally** *adv*

ventrolateral /véntrō láttərəl/ *adj* relating to or extending between the ventral and lateral surfaces of something such as an animal or organ —**ventrolaterally** *adv*

ventromedial /véntrō meédi əl/ *adj* located near or facing the middle of a ventral surface of something such as an animal or organ —**ventromedially** *adv*

venture /vénchər/ *n* **1.** NEW BUSINESS ENTERPRISE a business enterprise that involves risk, but could lead to profit **2.** RISKY PROJECT a risky or daring undertaking that has no guarantee of success **3.** MONEY RISKED the money or property risked in a business venture ■ *v* (**-tures, -turing, -tured**) **1.** *vi* MAKE DANGEROUS TRIP to make a trip that is unpleasant or dangerous ○ *I ventured out into the storm to close the barn doors.* **2.** *vt* RISK DANGERS OF SOMETHING to undertake the risks or dangers of a particular task or project **3.** *vt* MAKE SUGGESTION to offer or express something tentatively at the risk of being contradicted, embarrassed, or ignored ○ *ventured a suggestion* **4.** *vi* DARE TO DO SOMETHING to presume or dare to do something **5.** *vt* FIN PUT MONEY AT RISK to expose money or property to risk [15C. Shortening of ADVENTURE] —**venturer** *n* ◇ **nothing ventured, nothing gained** if you take no risks, you will achieve nothing

venture capital *n* money used for investment in enterprises that involve high risk, but offer the possibility of large profits —**venture capitalist** *n*

Venture Scout, **Venturer** /vénchərər/ *n* formerly, a young person aged between 16 and 20 who was a member of the senior branch of the Scouts. ◊ **Explorer**

venturesome /vénchərssəm/ *adj* (*formal*) **1.** willing to take risks or have new experiences **2.** involving risk or danger —**venturesomely** *adv* —**venturesomeness** *n*

venturi /ven tyóori/ (*plural* **-ris**) *n* **1.** a constriction in a tube designed to cause a pressure drop when a liquid or gas flows through it **2.** a restricted air inlet in a carburettor that produces a drop in pressure, causing fuel vapour to be drawn out of the carburettor bowl [Late 19C. After Giovanni Battista Venturi (1746–1822), Italian physicist]

Venturi /ven tyóori/, **Robert** (*b.* 1925) US architect. He led a reaction as both theorist and practitioner against modernist architecture, and is regarded as the founder of postmodernism. He won the Pritzker Prize in 1991. He worked in partnership with his wife, Denise Scott Brown (*b.* 1931). Full name **Venturi, Robert Charles**

> 'In iconographic terms, the cathedral is a decorated shed.'
> [Robert Venturi, 'Historical and Other Precedents', *Learning from Las Vegas*; 1972]

venturi tube, **Venturi tube** *n* a tube containing a constriction (**venturi**) that is placed in a fluid to measure its rate of flow. The measurement is based on the pressure drop in the fluid as it travels from one end of the tube to the other.

venturous /vénchərəss/ *adj* same as **venturesome** (sense 1)

venue /vénnyoo/ *n* **1.** SCENE a scene or setting in which something takes place **2.** PLACE WHERE EVENT IS HELD a place where an event such as a sports competition or a concert is held, especially one where such events are often held **3.** LAW SCENE OF CRIME the place at which a crime takes place or a cause of action arises **4.** LAW PLACE OF TRIAL a county or other area from which a jury is selected and in which a trial is held [Mid-16C. < Old French, past participle of *venir* 'come' < Latin *venire*]

venule /vénnyool/ *n* **1.** a small blood vessel, especially one that transfers blood from the capillaries to the veins **2.** a small branching vein in a leaf or an insect's wing [Mid-19C. < Latin *venula* 'small vein' < *vena* 'vein'] —**venular** *adj*

Venus /veénəss/ *n* **1.** in Roman mythology, the goddess of love and beauty. Greek equivalent **Aphrodite 2.** the fourth smallest planet in the solar system and the second planet from the Sun, seen from Earth as a bright morning or evening star [Pre-12C. < Latin < *venus* 'love, desire'] —**Venusian** /və nyóozi ən/ *adj, n*

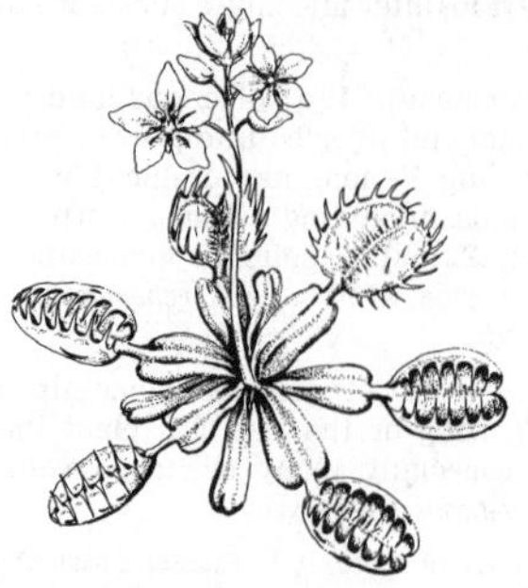

Venus flytrap

Venus flytrap, **Venus's flytrap** *n* an insect-eating plant that has leaves ending in hinged lobes that spring shut to entrap insects. Native to: North and South Carolina. Latin name: *Dionaea muscipula.*

Venushair *n* PLANTS same as **Venus's-hair**

Venus's flower basket *n* a deep-sea sponge with a skeleton of glassy slender pointed structures (**spicules**) that intersect to form a geometrically patterned surface. Native to: western Pacific and Indian oceans. Genus: *Euplectella.*

Venus's flytrap *n* PLANTS same as **Venus flytrap**

Venus's girdle *n* a ctenophore that lives in warm seas and has a long almost transparent belt-shaped body with rows of cilia along the top and bottom edges. Latin name: *Cestum veneris.*

Venus's-hair /veénəss hair/, **Venushair** *n* a delicate fan-shaped maidenhair fern that is widely grown as an ornamental plant. Native to: southern United States and tropical America. Latin name: *Adiantium capillus-veneris.*

Venus shell *n* a common sea mollusc that has a hinged shell with rounded ribbed patterning on it. Family: Veneridae.

Venus's looking-glass *n* an annual plant with hairy oval leaves that grows on cultivated and bare land. Flowers: purple. Native to: Europe, Asia, North Africa. Latin name: *Legousia hybrida.*

ver. *abbr* **1.** LITERAT, MUSIC verse **2.** LITERAT, BIBLE version

veracity /və rássəti/ (*plural* **-ties**) *n* **1.** TRUTH the truth, accuracy, or precision of something ○ *They questioned the veracity of our claims.* **2.** TRUTHFULNESS the truthfulness or honesty of somebody **3.** TRUE STATEMENT a truth or true statement [Early 17C. Directly or via French < medieval Latin *veracitas* < Latin *verax* 'truthful' < *verus* 'true'] —**veracious** /və ráyshəss/ *adj*

Veracruz /veérə króoz, vérrə-/ city and port in eastern Mexico, located on the Gulf of Mexico. Population: 457,377 (2000).

veranda /və rándə/, **verandah** *n* **1.** a porch, usually roofed and sometimes partly enclosed, that extends along an outside wall of a building **2.** *ANZ* a canopy sheltering a walkway along a shopping street [Early 18C. Via Hindi *varaṇḍā* < Portuguese *varanda* 'railing, balcony'] —**verandaed** *adj*

verapamil /vi ráppəmil/ *n* a synthetic compound that inhibits the movement of calcium ions across membranes. Use: treatment of angina pectoris, hypertension, irregular heartbeat. [Mid-20C. < *v(al)er(ic)* + *am(ino-)* + *(nitr)il(e)* (with inserted 'p'), its chemical name]

veratridine /vi ráttri deen/ *n* a poisonous yellowish-white substance obtained from sabadilla seeds. Use: insecticides. Formula: $C_{36}H_{51}NO_{11}$. [Early 20C. < Latin *veratrum* 'hellebore']

veratrine /vérrə treen, -trin/, **veratrin** /-trin/ *n* a poisonous mixture of alkaloids including veratridine. Use: formerly, to relieve inflammation. [Early 19C. < Latin *veratrum* 'hellebore']

verb /vurb/ *n* **1.** a word used to show that an action is taking place or to indicate the existence of a state or condition, or the part of speech to which such a word belongs **2.** the part of a clause or sentence that includes the verb, but excludes the subject of the verb [14C. Via Old French < Latin *verbum* 'word']

verbal /vúrb'l/ *adj* **1.** USING WORDS AS OPPOSED TO PICTURES using words or language, especially as opposed to pictorial representation ○ *a verbal picture of the scene outside* **2.** USING WORDS AS OPPOSED TO ACTION relating to or consisting of words, as opposed to physical action or confrontation ○ *verbal protest* **3.** ORAL AS OPPOSED TO WRITTEN relating to or consisting of spoken words, as opposed to written words ○ *They made a verbal agreement.* **4.** RELATING TO WORDS ALONE relating to words alone, as opposed to their meaning ○ *a purely verbal distinction* **5.** INVOLVING SKILL WITH WORDS involving skill in the use and understanding of words and language ○ *verbal dexterity* **6.** GRAM RELATING TO VERBS relating to or derived from a verb or verbs in general **7.** GRAM FORMING VERBS used to form verbs ■ *n* **1.** GRAM WORD FORMED FROM VERB a word formed from a verb, especially one used as a noun or an adjective, e.g. a gerund or participle **2.** ADMISSION OF GUILT an admission of guilt upon being arrested for a crime (*slang*) ■ *vt* (**-bals, -balling, -balled**) MAKE SOMEBODY SOUND GUILTY to make somebody sound guilty during police testimony in court by referring to an admission of guilt allegedly given earlier (*slang*) [15C. Via Old French < late Latin *verbalis* < Latin *verbum* 'word'] —**verbally** *adv*

SYNONYMS ***verbal, spoken, oral***

CORE MEANING: expressed in words

verbal using words, especially spoken words, as opposed to pictures or physical action ○ *a stream of verbal abuse* ○ *the sort of eye contact that transmits messages more effectively than any verbal communication* **spoken** expressed with the voice ○ *the development of pupils' understanding of the spoken word* ○ *Written language is sometimes viewed as more 'correct' than spoken language.* **oral** expressed in spoken form as distinct from written form ○ *Assessment is by written essays and an oral examination.* ○ *The local commissioner has the power to take written and oral evidence from witnesses.* ○ *The committee's findings relied on oral histories and genealogical records.*

---

verbal adjective *n* a verb participle ending in -ing or -ed that is used as an adjective

verbalise *vti* LANGUAGE another spelling of **verbalize**

verbalism /vúrbəlizəm/ *n* **1.** PHRASE something expressed in words **2.** LONG-WINDED EXPRESSION a wordy expression that has little meaning or relevance **3.** USE OF TOO MANY WORDS the uncritical or undisciplined use of words, especially without any attempt to analyse their meaning or value **4.** *US* WAY SOMETHING IS EXPRESSED the manner in which something is expressed or communicated

verbalist /vúrbəlist/ *n* **1.** somebody who is skilled in the use of words and language **2.** somebody who concentrates on words or language rather than on facts, feelings, or ideas —**verbalistic** /vúrbə lístik/ *adj*

verbalize /vúrbə līz/ (**-izes, -izing, -ized**), **verbalise** (**-ises, -ising, -ised**) *v* **1.** *vt* EXPRESS SOMETHING IN WORDS to express feelings, thoughts, or ideas in words **2.** *vt* GRAM MAKE WORD INTO VERB to make a word that is another part of speech, e.g. a noun or adjective, into a verb **3.** *vi* BE VERBOSE to speak or write in a way that uses too many words —**verbalization** /vúrbə lī záysh'n/ *n* —**verbalizer** *n*

verbal noun *n* a form of a verb ending in '-ing' used as a noun, e.g. 'dancing' in 'he teaches dancing'

verbatim /vur báytim/ *adj* corresponding word for word with something else ■ *adv* repeated, written down, or copied word for word [15C. < medieval Latin < Latin *verbum* 'word']

verbena /vur beénə/ *n* a common ornamental herbaceous plant. Flowers: colourful, in clusters. Native to: North and South America. Genus: *Verbena.* [Mid-16C. < Latin]

verbiage /vúrbi ij/ *n* **1.** an excess of words that add little or nothing to the meaning **2.** the style of language in which something is expressed ○ *bureaucratic verbiage* [Early 18C. < French < Latin *verbum* 'word']

verbid /vúrbid/ *n* LING same as **verbal** *n* (sense 1)

verbigerate /vur bíjji rayt/ (**-ates, -ating, -ated**) *vi* to repeat the same words or phrases obsessively as a symptom of a psychiatric disorder [Late 19C. < Latin *verbigerat-*, past participle of *verbigerare* 'chat' < *verbum* 'word' + *gerare* 'keep carrying on'] —**verbigeration** /vur bíjjə ráysh'n/ *n*

verbose /vur bṓss/ *adj* expressed in or using too many words [Late 17C. < Latin *verbosus* < Latin *verbum* 'word'] —**verbosely** *adv* —**verbosity** /-bóssiti/ *n*

SYNONYMS See ***wordy.***

verboten /fər bṓt'n, vər-/ *adj* forbidden or prohibited [Early 20C. < German]

verb phrase *n* a grammatical construction that includes a verb and any direct and indirect objects and modifiers linked to it, but excludes the subject of the verb

Vercingetorix /vúrssin jéttəriks/ (*d.* 46 BC) Gaulish leader. He led a revolt of Gallic tribes against Roman rule, but was eventually captured by Julius Caesar in 52 BC.

verdant /vúrd'nt/ *adj* **1. WITH LUSH GREEN GROWTH** green with vegetation or foliage **2. GREEN** green in colour **3. NAIVE** lacking experience or sophistication (*literary*) [Late 16C. < Old French *verdeant* 'becoming green' < Latin *viridis* 'green'] —**verdancy** *n* —**verdantly** *adv*

verd antique /vúrd an téek/, **verde antique** *n* **1.** a dark-green mottled or veined variety of serpentine marble that is used in decoration **2.** a green marble or stone that resembles verd antique **3.** CHEM same as **verdigris** (sense 1) [< obsolete French, 'antique green']

Verde, Cape /vurd/ **1.** ➧ **Cape Vert 2.** ➧ **Cape Verde**

verde antique *n* MINERALS, CHEM another spelling of **verd antique**

verderer /vúrdərər/ *n* a judicial official in charge of maintaining the royal forests in medieval England [Mid-16C. < Anglo-Norman < Latin *viridis* 'green']

Verdi /váirdi/, **Giuseppe** (1813–1901) Italian composer. He was one of the greatest operatic composers of all time. His works include *Rigoletto* (1851), *La Traviata* (1853), *Aïda* (1871), *Otello* (1887), and *Falstaff* (1893). Full name **Verdi, Giuseppe Fortunino Francesco**

> 'Our mistake, you see, was to write interminable large operas, which had to fill an entire evening...And now along comes someone with a one- or two-act opera without all that pompous nonsense...that was a happy reform.'
> [Attributed to Giuseppe Verdi]

verdict /vúrdikt/ *n* **1.** the finding of a jury on the matter that has been submitted to it in a trial **2.** a judgment, opinion, or conclusion about something ○ *Power companies are being asked for their verdict on wind power as an energy source.* [13C. < Anglo-Norman *verdit* 'true speech' < *ver* 'true' + *dit* 'speech, saying']

verdigris /vúrdi gree, -greess/ *n* **1.** a green or greenish-blue deposit (**patina**) of copper carbonates on copper, brass, and bronze that is caused by atmospheric corrosion **2.** a green or greenish-blue poisonous powder formed by the action of acetic acid on copper and consisting of one or more basic copper acetates. Use: paint pigment, fungicide. [14C. < Old French *vert de Grece* 'green of Greece']

verditer /vúrditər/ *n* either of two basic copper carbonates, of which one is blue and the other green. Use: pigments. [Early 16C. < Old French *verd de terre* 'green of the earth']

Verdun /vur dún/ town in northeastern France. One of the longest and bloodiest battles of World War I was fought around the town during 1916. Population: 19,624 (1999).

verdure /vúrjər/ *n* **1. VIVID GREEN OF PLANTS** the green colour associated with lush vegetation **2. VEGETATION** extremely lush vegetation **3. FRESHNESS** a fresh, healthy, or flourishing condition (*literary*) [14C. < French < Latin *viridis* 'green'] —**verdured** *adj* —**verdureless** *adj* —**verdurous** *adj* —**verdurousness** *n*

Vereeniging /fə réeniking/ industrial city in Gauteng Province, South Africa. Population: 71,255 (1991).

verge^{1} /vurj/ *n* **1. POINT BEYOND WHICH SOMETHING HAPPENS** the point beyond which something happens or begins ○ *He was on the verge of tears.* **2. BOUNDARY** a line, belt, or strip that acts as a boundary or edge **3. EDGE** the edge, rim, or margin of something **4.** ROADS **ROADSIDE BORDER** a narrow border that runs alongside a road **5.** ARCHIT **ROOF EDGE** the edge of a sloping roof where it extends beyond the gable **6. CLOCK SPINDLE** the spindle of a balance wheel in early clock and watch mechanisms **7.** HIST **AREA AROUND ROYAL COURT** an area around the English royal court that was under the jurisdiction of the Lord High Steward **8.** HIST **ROD HELD BY TENANT** a rod held by a feudal tenant when swearing an oath of loyalty to his or her lord **9. ROD AS SYMBOL OF OFFICE** a rod or staff carried as a symbol of authority or an emblem of office [14C. Via French, 'rod' (symbolizing office) < Latin *virga*]

verge on (**verges on, verging on, verged on**), **verge upon** *vt* **1.** to border on or be on the edge of a particular place or area ○ *Their property verged on ours.* **2.** to approach or come close to a particular quality or condition ○ *The whole performance verged on the ridiculous.*

verge^{2} /vurj/ (**verges, verging, verged**) *vi* **1. MOVE IN PARTICULAR DIRECTION** to move or lean in a particular direction or towards a particular condition **2. CHANGE GRADUALLY** to change gradually from one thing to another (*literary*) **3. SINK FROM VIEW** to descend towards the horizon (*literary*) [Early 17C. < Latin *vergere* 'to bend, incline']

vergence /vúrjənss/ *n* the inward or outward turning of both eyes when they are focusing on an object [Early 20C. Back-formation < CONVERGENCE and DIVERGENCE]

verger /vúrjər/ *n* **1.** a church official in the Church of England who carries the staff of office (**verge**) in front of somebody such as a bishop or dean during ceremonies and processions **2.** a church official who acts as a caretaker and attendant and looks after the inside of a church, usually including the furnishings and the vestments [15C. < Anglo-Norman < Old French *verge* 'rod of office' (see VERGE^{1})]

Vergil another spelling of **Virgil**

verglas /váir glaa/ *n* a thin coating of ice found on rock or exposed ground [Early 19C. < French < *verre* 'glass' + *glas* 'ice']

Verhofstadt /vər hóf stat/, **Guy** (*b.* 1953) prime minister of Belgium (1999–). He became leader of a newly merged party, VLD, Flemish Liberals and Democrats (1992), and prime minister of a coalition comprising six parties.

veridical /və ríddik'l/ *adj* (*formal*) **1.** telling the truth **2.** corresponding to facts or to reality, and therefore genuine or real [Mid-17C. < Latin *veridicus* 'truth-speaking' < *verus* 'true' + *dicere* 'say'] —**veridicality** /və ríddi kálləti/ *n* —**veridically** *adv*

verification /vérrifi káysh'n/ *n* **1. ESTABLISHMENT OF TRUTH** the establishment of the truth or correctness of something by investigation or evidence **2. EVIDENCE** the evidence that proves something is true or correct **3.** LAW **CONFIRMATION OF PROCEDURES** in international law, the process of confirming that procedures laid down in an agreement such as a weapons limitation treaty are being followed **4.** LAW **AFFIDAVIT** in law, an affidavit swearing to the truth of a pleading **5.** LAW **CONFIRMATORY EVIDENCE** evidence or testimony that confirms something —**verificative** /vérrifi kaytiv/ *adj*

verificationism /vérrifi káysh'nizəm/ *n* the view that every meaningful proposition is capable of being shown to be true or false

verification principle *n* the principle that a proposition or sentence is meaningful only if it is possible to establish whether it is true or false by experience or observation

verify /vérri fī/ (**-fies, -fying, -fied**) *vt* **1. PROVE SOMETHING** to prove that something is true **2. CHECK WHETHER SOMETHING IS TRUE** to check whether or not something is true by examination, investigation, or comparison **3.** LAW **SWEAR SOMETHING UNDER OATH** in law, to swear or affirm under oath that something is true **4.** LAW **ATTEST TO TRUTH BY AFFIDAVIT** in law, to support the truth of a pleading by affidavit [14C. Via French *verifier* < medieval Latin *verificare* 'make true' < Latin *verus* 'true' + *facere* 'make'] —**verifiability** /vérri fī ə bílləti/ *n* —**verifiable** *adj* —**verifiably** *adv* —**verifier** *n*

verily /vérrili/ *adv* in truth (*archaic*) ○ *Verily, he has admitted it.* [13C. < VERY 'true']

verisimilar /vérri símmilər/ *adj* appearing to be true or real (*archaic*) [Late 17C. < Latin *verisimilis* 'like the truth' < *verus* 'true' + *similis* 'like'] —**verisimilarly** *adv*

verisimilitude /vérrissi mílli tyood/ *n* (*formal*) **1.** the appearance of being true or real **2.** something that only appears to be true or real, e.g. a statement that is not supported by evidence [Early 17C. < Latin *verisimilitudo* < *verisimilis* (see VERISIMILAR)] —**verisimilitudinous** /vérrissi mílli tyoōdinəss/ *adj*

verism /véerizəm/ *n* strict realism or naturalism in art and literature [Late 19C. < Latin *verus* or Italian *vero* 'true'] —**verist** *n* —**veristic** /veer rístik/ *adj*

verismo /ve rízmō/ *n* a late 19th-century movement in Italian opera that advocated the use of themes drawn from real life and naturalistic portrayal of characters and events. Puccini was one of the principal members of this movement. [Early 20C. < Italian, 'verism']

veritable /vérritəb'l/ *adj* used to emphasize a figurative concept ○ *The business is a veritable gold mine.* [15C. < French < Latin *veritas* 'truth' (see VERITY)] —**veritably** *adv*

verity /vérrəti/ (*plural* **-ties**) *n* (*formal*) **1.** the quality of being true or real **2.** something that is true, especially a statement or principle that is accepted as a fact [14C. Via French < Latin *veritas* < *verus* 'true']

verjuice /vúr jooss/ *n* **1.** an acid liquid made from crab apples or other sour or unripe fruit. Use: formerly, in cooking or as a condiment instead of vinegar. **2.** sourness of temper, attitude, or expression [14C. < Old French *vertjus* < *verd* 'green' + *jus* 'juice']

verkrampte /fər krámptə/ *n S Africa* somebody regarded as bigoted, narrow-minded, or reactionary (*insult*) [Mid-20C. < Afrikaans, 'cramped, narrow']

Verlaine /vair lén/, **Paul** (1844–96) French poet. He wrote *Songs Without Words* (1874) while in prison for shooting his friend Arthur Rimbaud. His later symbolist verse influenced the development of French poetry. Full name **Verlaine, Paul Marie**

> 'The drawn-out sobs of the violins of autumn wound my heart with a monotonous languor.'
> [Paul Verlaine, 'Chanson d'Automne (Song of Autumn)', *Poèmes Saturniens (Saturnine Poems)*; 1866]

verlan /ver láN/ *n* a form of French slang, used commonly in some ethnic working-class French districts and among young people, that involves reversing the order of syllables [20C. < French, reversal of syllables of *l'envers* 'reverse side']

verligte /fər lí<u>kh</u>tə/ *n S Africa* somebody who is liberal, enlightened, or progressive [Mid-20C. < Afrikaans, 'enlightened']

Vermeer /vər méer, -máir/, **Jan** (1632–75) Dutch artist. A major painter of the Dutch Golden Age, he painted domestic interiors of great serenity. Only 35 of his paintings survive.

vermeil /vúr mayl/ *n* **1.** gilded silver, bronze, or copper **2.** COLOURS same as **vermilion** (*literary*) [14C. Via Old French < late Latin *vermiculus*, kermes insect from which red dye was made (see VERMICULAR)] —**vermeil** *adj*

vermi- *prefix* worm ○ *vermivorous* [< Latin *vermis* 'worm' < Indo-European]

vermicelli /vúrmi chélli/ *n* **1.** pasta in long fine threads **2.** short thin strands of chocolate that are used to decorate cakes [Mid-17C. < Italian, 'little worms' < Latin *vermis* 'worm']

vermicide /vúrmi sīd/ *n* **1.** a substance used to kill worms **2.** a chemical substance that expels parasitic worms from the small intestine —**vermicidal** /vúrmi sīd'l/ *adj*

vermicomposter /vúrmi kompostər/ *n* a container in which specially bred worms are used to convert organic matter into compost

vermicomposting /vúrmi komposting/ *n* GARDENING same as **vermiculture**

vermicular /vur míkyoōlər/ *adj* **1.** in wavy lines like the movements, shape, or tracks of worms **2.** relating to worms [Late 17C. < medieval Latin *vermicularis* < Latin

vermiculus 'little worm' < *vermis* 'worm'] —**vermicularly** *adv*

vermiculate /vur míkyo͝o layt/ *vt* (**-lates, -lating, -lated**) DECORATE SOMETHING WITH WAVY LINES to decorate something with wavy lines or patterns (*formal*) ■ *adj* **1.** WITH WAVY LINES with wavy lines like the movements, shape, or tracks of a worm **2.** SINUOUS with many twists and turns (*formal*) **3.** LOOKING WORM-EATEN with a worm-eaten appearance (*literary*) [Early 17C. < Latin *vermiculat-*, past participle of *vermiculari* 'be full of worms' < *vermiculus* (see VERMICULAR)]

vermiculation /vur míkyo͝o láysh'n/ *n* **1.** MOVEMENT IN WAVES movement in waves, e.g. the muscular contractions of the intestines (**peristalsis**) **2.** WAVY DECORATION decorative wavy lines, patterns, or carvings **3.** WORM INFESTATION infestation by worms, or the resulting worm-eaten condition

vermiculite /vur míkyo͝o līt/ *n* a hydrous silicate of aluminium, magnesium, or iron. Source: altered basic rocks. Use: insulation, lubricant, growing medium in horticulture. [Early 19C. < Latin *vermiculus* 'little worm' (see VERMICULAR), because of the way flakes of it expand and writhe in long shapes when heated]

vermiculture /vúrmi kulchər/ *n* the use of specially bred worms to convert organic matter into compost

vermiform /vúrmi fawrm/ *adj* resembling a worm in shape

vermiform appendix, **vermiform process** *n* same as **appendix** (sense 1)

vermifuge /vúrmi fyooj/ *n* a drug or other substance that causes worms or other parasites to be expelled from the intestines —**vermifugal** /vúrmi fyo͞og'l/ *adj*

vermilion /vər mílli ən/, **vermillion** *n* **1.** a bright red pigment made from mercuric sulphide or synthetically **2.** a bright red colour, sometimes tinged with orange [13C. < Old French *vermeillon* < *vermeil* (see VERMEIL)] —**vermilion** *adj*

vermin /vúrmin/ *n* **1.** small animals or insects that harm people, livestock, property, or crops and are difficult to control, e.g. rats, weasels, fleas, or cockroaches **2.** an offensive term for a person or group considered to be extremely unpleasant or undesirable [13C. Via Old French < assumed Vulgar Latin *verminum* 'noxious life forms' < Latin *vermis* 'worm']

vermination /vúrmi náysh'n/ *n* the spreading of or infestation with vermin, especially parasites

verminous /vúrminəss/ *adj* **1.** OF VERMIN relating to or infested with vermin **2.** CAUSED BY VERMIN caused by vermin or parasitic worms **3.** DISGUSTING extremely unpleasant or offensive —**verminously** *adv* —**verminousness** *n*

vermis /vúrmiss/ *n* the middle lobe of the brain that connects the two hemispheres of the cerebellum [Late 19C. < Latin, 'worm']

vermivorous /vur mívvərəss/ *adj* used to describe birds or other animals that feed on worms

Vermont /vər mónt/ state in the northeastern United States, bordered by Canada, New Hampshire, Massachusetts, and New York State. Capital: Montpelier. Population: 616,592 (2002 estimate). Area: 24,903 sq. km/9,615 sq. mi. —**Vermonter** *n*

vermouth /vúrməth, vər mo͞oth/ *n* a wine flavoured with aromatic herbs [Early 19C. Via French < German *Wermut* 'wormwood', with which it was originally flavoured]

vernacular /vər nákyo͝olər/ *n* **1.** ORDINARY LANGUAGE the everyday language of the people in a country or region, as distinct from official or formal language **2.** SPOKEN LANGUAGE the common spoken language of a people, as distinct from formal written or literary language **3.** LANGUAGE OF GROUP the distinctive vocabulary or language of a profession, group, or class **4.** BIOL COMMON NAME a common name of a plant, animal, or other organism, as distinct from its scientific name **5.** ARCHIT ORDINARY BUILDING STYLE the local architecture of a place or people, especially the architectural style that is used for ordinary houses as opposed to large official or commercial buildings [Early 17C. < Latin *vernaculus* 'native' < *verna* 'native-born slave'] —**vernacular** *adj* —**vernacularly** *adv*

vernacularise *vt* LANG another spelling of **vernacularize**

vernacularism /vər nákyo͝olərizəm/ *n* **1.** a word or phrase from the everyday language of a country or region, as distinct from official or formal language **2.** the use of everyday language, as distinct from official or formal language

vernacularize /vər nákyo͝olə rīz/ (**-izes, -izing, -ized**), **vernacularise** (**-ises, -ising, -ised**) *vt* to make a word or phrase part of ordinary everyday language

vernal /vúrn'l/ *adj* **1.** appearing or happening in the season of spring **2.** having the freshness or energy associated with youth (*literary*) [Mid-16C. < Latin *vernalis* < *vernus* 'of the spring' < *ver* 'spring']

vernal equinox *n* **1.** the time when the Sun crosses the celestial equator and day and night are of equal length, marking the beginning of spring. In the northern hemisphere this occurs around 21 March, in the southern hemisphere around 23 September. **2.** the point on the celestial sphere where the path of the Sun (**ecliptic**) crosses the celestial equator, in the constellation Pisces

vernal grass *n* an early-blooming grass that smells like new-mown hay when crushed. Native to: Europe, Asia. Genus: *Anthoxanthum*.

vernalize /vúrnə līz/ (**-izes, -izing, -ized**), **vernalise** (**-ises, -ising, -ised**) *vt* to expose plant seeds or seedlings to artificially cold temperatures in order to promote subsequent development and flowering —**vernalization** /vúrnə lī záysh'n/ *n*

vernation /vur náysh'n/ *n* the way that young leaves are arranged in a bud [Late 18C. < modern Latin *vernation-* < Latin *vernare* 'grow in the spring' < *vernus* (see VERNAL)]

Verne /vurn/, **Jules** (1828–1905) French writer. His novels, which include *20,000 Leagues Under the Sea* (1870) and *Around the World in Eighty Days* (1873), anticipated later scientific developments.

> 'An Englishman does not joke about such an important matter as a bet.'
> [Jules Verne, *Around the World in Eighty Days*; 1873]

vernicle /vúrnik'l/ *n* CHR same as **veronica**[2] [14C. < Old French *vernicle*, variant of *veronique* < medieval Latin *veronica* (see VERONICA[2])]

vernier /vúrni ər/ *n* **1.** SMALL SCALE FOR PRECISE READINGS a small movable graduated scale parallel to a larger graduated scale, calibrated to obtain more precise readings from the larger scale **2.** DEVICE FOR MAKING FINE ADJUSTMENTS an auxiliary device used to make fine adjustments to a precision instrument ■ *adj* WITH VERNIER relating to or fitted with a vernier [Mid-18C. After Pierre *Vernier* (1580–1637), French mathematician]

vernier rocket *n* AEROSP same as **thruster** (sense 2) [Mid-20C. See VERNIER]

vernissage /vúrni sa͞azh/ *n* a private showing or preview before the public opening of an art exhibition [Early 20C. < French, 'varnishing', because originally the day before a public exhibition, when exhibitors varnished paintings after they were in place]

Vernon /vúrnən/ city in southern British Columbia, Canada. Population: 39,995 (2001).

Verny /vúrni/ former name for **Almaty** (1855–1921)

Verona /və rṓnə/ capital city of Verona Province, Veneto Region, northern Italy. Population: 253,208 (2001). —**Veronese** /vérrō ne͞ez/ *n, adj*

Veronal /vérrən'l/ *tdmk* a trademark for barbitone, formerly prescribed as a sedative

Veronese /vérrō náyzi/, **Paolo** (1528–88) Italian artist. A painter of the Venetian school, he made dramatic use of colour and perspective in his large-scale religious and secular compositions. Born **Caliari, Paolo**

veronica[1] /və rónnikə/ *n* a perennial or annual plant or bush of the figwort family, e.g. the speedwell. Flowers: small, typically blue, in clusters. Genus: *Veronica*. [Early 16C. < modern Latin]

veronica[2] /və rónnikə/ *n* **1.** IMPRESSION OF JESUS CHRIST'S FACE the impression of Jesus Christ's face believed by some to have been miraculously left on the cloth with which Saint Veronica wiped it on his way to his crucifixion **2.** CLOTH THAT WIPED JESUS CHRIST'S FACE the cloth with which Saint Veronica is said to have wiped Jesus Christ's face on his way to his crucifixion **3.** CLOTH WITH JESUS CHRIST'S FACE a cloth bearing a representation of Jesus Christ's face, sometimes worn by pilgrims [Late 17C. < medieval Latin, perhaps alteration (after the saint Veronica) of *vera iconica* 'true image']

veronica[3] /və rónnikə/ *n* in bullfighting, a move in which the bullfighter stands in place and slowly swings the cape away from the bull as it charges [Mid-19C. < Spanish *verónica*, after Saint *Veronica*; from the gesture involved in wiping Jesus Christ's face]

verruca /və ro͞okə/ (*plural* **-cas** or **-cae** /-see, -kee/) *n* **1.** a wart that grows on the foot, usually on the sole **2.** a wart-shaped growth or projection on a plant or the skin of an animal [Mid-16C. < Latin, 'wart']

verrucose /vérrookōss/, **verrucous** /vérrookəss, ve ro͞okəss/ *adj* covered with warts or similar growths or projections [Late 17C. < Latin *verrucosus* < *verruca* 'wart'] —**verrucosity** /vérroo kóssəti/ *n*

vers *abbr* MATHS versed sine

Versailles /vair sī/ *n* a large and elaborately decorated palace near Paris, built for Louis XIV in the mid-17th century. It is now a museum. The Treaty of Versailles was signed there in 1919, ending World War I.

versant /vúrss'nt/ *n* **1.** the slope of a mountain or mountain range **2.** the slope of a large area of land [Mid-19C. < French, present participle of *verser* 'turn over' < Latin *versare* (see VERSATILE)]

versatile /vúrssə tīl/ *adj* **1.** WITH MANY USES able or meant to be used in many different ways **2.** MOVING EASILY BETWEEN TASKS able to move easily from one subject, task, or skill to another **3.** CHANGEABLE subject to rapid or unpredictable change **4.** ZOOL FREE-MOVING describes a body part or joint that can turn or move freely in more than one direction, e.g. an insect's antenna **5.** BOT ATTACHED LOOSELY describes an anther that is attached to the filament by a small area, allowing it to move more freely [Early 17C. < Latin *versatilis* < *versat-*, past participle of *versare* 'keep turning or changing' < *vertere* 'to turn'] —**versatilely** *adv* —**versatility** /vúrssə tílləti/ *n*

vers de société /váir də sóssyə táy/ *n* verse or poetry written in a light witty sophisticated style [< French, 'society verse']

verse /vurss/ *n* **1.** GROUP OF LINES a section of a poem or song consisting of a number of lines arranged together to form a single unit **2.** BIBLE NUMBERED DIVISION OF BIBLE CHAPTER a numbered subdivision into which each chapter of the Bible is divided **3.** LITERAT POETRY poetry, as distinct from prose **4.** LITERAT BAD POETRY poetry that is trivial in content or inferior in quality ○ *It's not poetry at all, it's just verse.* **5.** LITERAT SHORT POEM a poem, especially a short one **6.** LITERAT LINE OF POEM a single line of a poem, arranged rhythmically in metrical feet ■ *vt* (**verses, versing, versed**) VERSIFY PROSE CONTENT to turn something from prose into poetry (*archaic*) [Pre-12C. Directly and via Old French *vers* < Latin *versus* 'turning (of a plough), furrow, line' < *vertere* 'to turn']

ORIGIN The Latin word *vertere* 'to turn', from which ***verse*** is derived, is also the source of the English words *adverse, advertise, controversy, converse*[1] ('to talk'), *convert, divert, inverse, obverse, pervert, prose, reverse, subvert, universe, versatile, version, versus, vertebra, vertical*, and *vertigo*.

versed /vurst/ *n* very knowledgeable about or skilled in something ○ *well versed in the art of flattery* [Early 17C. Directly or via French *versé* < Latin *versatus*, past participle of *versari* 'occupy yourself with' < *versare* (see VERSATILE)]

versed cosine *n* a trigonometric function equal to one minus the sine of an angle [After VERSED SINE]

versed sine *n* a trigonometric function equal to one minus the cosine of an angle [Translation of modern Latin *sinus versus* 'turned sine']

verset /vúrssit/ *n* a short verse, especially one from a sacred book [Early 17C. < French, 'short verse' < *vers* 'line' (see VERSE)]

versicle /vúrssik'l/ *n* **1.** a short sentence spoken or chanted by the minister during a liturgical service and responded to by the congregation or choir **2.** a short verse (*literary or archaic*) [14C. < Latin *versiculus* 'short verse' < *versus* 'line' (see VERSE)] —**versicular** /vur síkyo͝olər/ *adj*

versicolour /vúrssi kullər/, **versicoloured** /vúrssi kullərd/ *adj* **1.** having various colours **2.** varying or changing

in colour [Early 17C. < Latin *versicolor* < *versus*, past participle of *vertere* 'turn, change' + *color* 'colour']

versification /vúrssifi káysh'n/ *n* **1.** ART OF VERSE-WRITING the art or practice of writing verse **2.** METRICAL FORM the metrical form or structure of a poem **3.** TURNING PROSE INTO VERSE the conversion of prose into verse, or the recounting of something in verse **4.** VERSION IN POETRY a poetic or metrical version of a prose work

versify /vúrssi fī/ (**-fies**, **-fying**, **-fied**) *v* **1.** *vt* CHANGE PROSE INTO POETRY to turn prose into verse, e.g. by introducing rhyme and a metrical structure **2.** *vt* TELL STORY IN POETRY to recount something in verse **3.** *vi* WRITE POETRY to compose verse [14C. Via Latin *versificare* 'make verses' < *versus* 'line' (see VERSE)] —**versifier** *n*

versine /vúrsīn/ *n* MATHS same as **versed sine**

version /vúrsh'n, vúrzh'n/ *n* **1.** ACCOUNT OF SOMETHING an account of something, given from a specific point of view **2.** SPECIFIC VARIETY a form or variety of something that is different from others or from the original ○ *a later version of the text* **3.** ADAPTATION OF SOMETHING an adaptation of something for another medium, e.g. a book made into a play or film **4.** TRANSLATION OF SOMETHING a translation of something into another language **5.** *also* Version BIBLE TRANSLATION a particular translation of the Bible **6.** MED MANIPULATION OF FOETUS the manipulation of a foetus to change its position in the womb, e.g. so that it can be delivered safely **7.** MED TILTED CONDITION OF ORGAN a condition in which an internal organ, especially the womb, is tilted or turned ■ *vt* COMPUT IDENTIFY PREVIOUS VERSIONS OF DATA to attach versioning information to data, especially for diagnostic or security purposes [Late 16C. Via French < Latin *version-* < *vers-*, past participle of *vertere* 'turn'] —**versional** *adj*

versioning /vúrsh'ning, vúrzh'ning/ *n* the storage and management of previous versions of data, especially for security or diagnostic purposes

vers libre /váir leébrə/ *n* LITERAT same as **free verse** [< French]

verso /vúrssō/ (*plural* **-sos**) *n* **1.** PUBL the back of a page or other printed sheet **2.** PUBL any left-hand page of a book, usually printed with an even page number **3.** COINS same as **reverse** *n* (sense 6) [Mid-19C. < Latin *verso (folio)* '(with the page) turned' < *versus*, past participle of *vertere* 'turn']

verst /vurst/ *n* a Russian measure of length equal to 1.07 km/0.66 mi [Mid-16C. Via French *verste* or German *Werst* < Russian *versta* 'line']

versus /vúrssəss/ *prep* **1.** against, especially in a competition or court case ○ *the United States versus Canada* **2.** as opposed to or contrasted with ○ *such considerations as money versus job satisfaction* [15C. < medieval Latin, 'against' < past participle of Latin *vertere* 'turn']

vert /vurt/ *n* **1.** HERALDRY GREEN COLOUR in heraldry, the colour green **2.** LAW RIGHT TO CUT WOOD OR VEGETATION formerly, the right to cut living wood or green vegetation in a forest **3.** HIST WOOD OR VEGETATION formerly, living wood or green vegetation in a forest [15C. Via Old French, 'green' < Latin *viridis*] —**vert** *adj*

Vert, Cape /vair/ ▸ **Cape Vert**

vert. *abbr* vertical

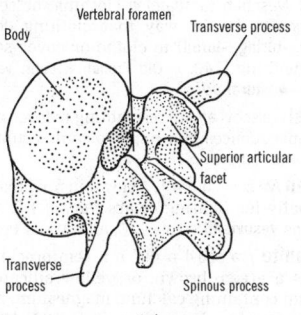

vertebra

vertebra /vúrtibrə/ (*plural* **-brae** /-bray, -bree/ or **-bras**) *n* a bone of the spinal column, typically consisting of a thick body, a bony arch enclosing a hole for the spinal cord, and stubby projections that connect

with adjacent bones [Early 17C. < Latin < *vertere* 'to turn'] —**vertebral** *adj* —**vertebrally** *adv*

vertebral canal *n* ANAT same as **spinal canal**

vertebral column *n* ANAT same as **spinal column**

vertebrate /vúrtibrət/ *n* an animal with a segmented spinal column and a well-developed brain, e.g. a mammal, bird, reptile, amphibian, or fish [Early 19C. < Latin *vertebratus* 'having joints' < *vertebra* (see VERTEBRA)] —**vertebrate** *adj*

~~**verternarian**~~ incorrect spelling of **veterinarian**

vertex /vúrt eks/ (*plural* **-texes** or **-tices** /-ti seez/) *n* **1.** APEX the highest point of something **2.** ANAT TOP OF HEAD the highest point of a body part, especially the top or crown of the head **3.** MATHS POINT OPPOSITE BASE the point of a geometrical figure that is opposite the base **4.** MATHS POINT WHERE SIDES OF ANGLE MEET the point where two sides of a plane figure or an angle intersect **5.** MATHS POINT WHERE PLANES OF SOLID MEET the point where three or more planes of a solid figure intersect **6.** ASTRON POINT TOWARDS WHICH STARS MOVE a point on the celestial sphere towards which or from which a group of stars appears to move [Late 16C. < Latin, 'whirl, spiral of hair at the top of the head' < *vertere* 'to turn']

vertical /vúrtik'l/ *adj* **1.** AT RIGHT ANGLE TO HORIZON positioned at a right angle to the horizon **2.** UPRIGHT in an upright position, or running lengthways up or down **3.** OVERHEAD at the vertex or directly overhead **4.** ECON INVOLVING ALL STAGES OF PRODUCTION relating to or involving all the consecutive stages in the production of goods, from design to sale **5.** ANAT AT TOP OF HEAD at or relating to the highest point of a body part, especially the top or crown of the head **6.** MADE UP OF MANY LEVELS involving or made up of successive or many levels ○ *a vertical management structure* ■ *n* **1.** SOMETHING VERTICAL a vertical structure, line, surface, or part **2.** VERTICAL POSITION a position that is upright or at a right angle to the horizon [Mid-16C. Directly or via French < late Latin *verticalis* 'overhead' < Latin *vertex* (see VERTEX)] —**verticality** /vúrti kálləti/ *n* —**vertically** *adv*

vertical angle *n* either of a pair of equal angles formed on opposite sides of the point at which two lines intersect

vertical circle *n* a great circle on the celestial sphere whose plane is perpendicular to the horizon and passes through the zenith and the nadir

vertical mobility *n* the movement of people or groups in society either upwards or downwards in terms of class or status

vertical stabilizer *n* AEROSP same as **fin** *n* (sense 4)

vertices ANAT, MATHS, ASTRON plural of **vertex**

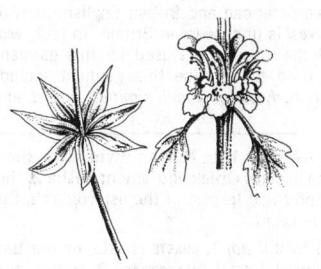

verticil: two types of verticil

verticil /vúrtissil/ *n* a circular arrangement of similar parts around a central point [Early 18C. < Latin *verticillus* 'whorl of a spindle']

verticillaster /vúrtissi lástər/ *n* a flower cluster that looks like a whorl of flowers but actually consists of two crowded clusters (**cymes**) arising opposite each other, as in dead nettles and many mints [Mid-19C. < Latin *verticillus* 'whorl of a spindle'] —**verticillastrate** *adj*

verticillate /vur tíssilət/ *adj* arranged in whorls, or forming a whorl —**verticillately** *adv* —**verticillation** /vur tíssi láysh'n/ *n*

vertigines HEALTH plural of **vertigo**

vertiginous /vur tíjjinəss/ *adj* **1.** DIZZYING causing dizziness, especially because of being very high or

exposed ○ *the mountain's vertiginous summit* **2.** SUFFERING FROM VERTIGO relating to or suffering from the whirling or tilting sensation of vertigo **3.** ROTARY whirling or spinning on an axis **4.** FICKLE tending to change frequently or suddenly (*formal*) —**vertiginously** *adv*

vertigo /vúrtigō/ (*plural* **-tigoes** or **-tigos** or **-tigines** /-tíjji neez/) *n* **1.** a condition in which somebody feels a sensation of whirling or tilting that causes a loss of balance **2.** an instance or episode of vertigo [15C. < Latin (stem *vertigin-*), 'whirling about, giddiness' < *vertere* 'to turn']

CULTURAL NOTE *Vertigo*, a film (1958) by British director Alfred Hitchcock. One of Hitchcock's most highly regarded films, it is both a typically suspenseful thriller and a powerful study of obsession. When former policeman Scottie Fergusson is asked to shadow a friend's wife, he first falls in love with her and then, after her suicide, becomes infatuated with a woman who appears to be her double.

vertu *n* ARTS another spelling of **virtu**

Vertumnus /vur túmnəss/ *n* in Roman mythology, the god of gardens

vervain /vúr vayn/ *n* a herbaceous plant that grows wild in temperate regions. Flowers: small, blue, white, or purple. Genus: *Verbena*. [14C. Via French *verveine* < Latin *verbena* 'verbena']

verve /vurv/ *n* **1.** enthusiasm, energy, or spirit, especially in the expression of artistic ideas **2.** lively vigorous spirit [Late 17C. Via French, 'vigour, fanciful expression' < Latin *verba* 'whimsical words', plural of *verbum* 'word']

vervet

vervet /vúrvit/, **vervet monkey** *n* an African monkey that lives in large groups in savanna woodlands and has a long tail and black face, hands, and feet. Latin name: *Cercopithecus aethiops*. [Late 19C. < French]

Verwoerd /fər voórt/, **Hendrik** (1901–66) Dutch-born prime minister of South Africa (1958–66). During his premiership, he introduced apartheid legislation and outlawed the opposition African National Congress. Full name **Verwoerd, Hendrik Frensch**

very /vérri/ CORE MEANING: an adverb that is used in front of adjectives and adverbs to emphasize their meaning ○ *That is a very, very strong argument.* ○ *Let me very briefly give you some examples.* **1.** *adv* GIVES EMPHASIS used to give emphasis to adjectives or adverbs that can be graded ○ *I think buying a dog is something we want to be very careful about.* ○ *Someone had copied her style very accurately.* **2.** *adj* EXTREME indicates an extreme position or extreme point in time ○ *They moved to the very back of the set, smiling at the technicians.* **3.** *adj* RIGHT exactly the right or appropriate person or thing, or exactly the same person or thing ○ *Hello! The very person I wanted to see!* ○ *He died this very day in 1986.* **4.** *adj* EMPHASIZES IMPORTANCE used before nouns to emphasize seriousness or importance ○ *An event like this can't help but shake the boxing world to its very foundation.* [13C. Via Old French *verrai* < Latin *verax* 'truthful' < *verus* 'true'] ◇ **very much so** an emphatic way of saying yes to something or indicating that it is true or correct ○ *'He was a good man, brave and honest.' 'Yes, very much so.'* ◇ **very well** indicates that somebody agrees to do something or accepts what somebody has said

very high frequency *n* the radio frequency band

between 30 and 300 megahertz, reserved for the transmission of television and FM radio signals

Very light /véeri-/ *n* a coloured flare fired from a pistol, used as a signal [Early 20C. After Edward W. *Very* (1847–1910), US naval officer]

very low frequency *n* the radio frequency band between 3 and 30 kilohertz

Very pistol /véeri-/ *n* a pistol used for firing coloured flares [Early 20C. See VERY LIGHT]

Very Reverend *n* the title of a dean and some other religious officials

vesica /véssikə/ (*plural* **-cae** /-see/) *n* **1.** a bladder, especially the urinary bladder (*technical*) **2.** a pointed oval shape used in medieval art and sculpture, especially to enclose a figure of Jesus Christ or the Virgin Mary [Mid-17C. < Latin, 'bladder, blister']

vesical /véssik'l/ *adj* occurring in or relating to a bladder, especially the urinary bladder ○ *vesical veins*

vesicant /véssikənt/, **vesicatory** /véssi káytəri/ *n* (*plural* **-ries**) a substance that causes blisters, especially a substance such as mustard gas used in chemical warfare ■ *adj* causing blisters to form

vesicate /véssi kayt/ (**-cates, -cating, -cated**) *vti* to cause blisters, or be affected by blisters —**vesication** /véssi káysh'n/ *n*

vesicatory *n* CHEM same as **vesicant**

vesicle /véssik'l/ *n* **1.** MED **FLUID-FILLED CYST** a small sac or hollow organ in the body, especially one containing fluid **2.** MED **FLUID-FILLED BLISTER** a very small blister filled with clear fluid (**serum**) **3.** GEOL **SPHERICAL CAVITY WITHIN ROCK** a bubble-shaped cavity in an igneous rock, formed by the expansion of gases trapped in lava and often later filled with minerals deposited from percolating solutions **4.** BOT **CAVITY IN WATER PLANT** a cavity filled with air in a seaweed or water plant [Late 16C. Directly or via French *vésicule* < Latin *vesicula* 'small vesica' < *vesica* 'bladder, blister']

vesicular /və síkyŏŏlər/ *adj* resembling, having, or made up of vesicles —**vesicularly** *adv*

vesiculate *vti* /və síkyŏŏ layt/ (**-lates, -lating, -lated**) to form blisters or vesicles in something, or take on the form of a blister or vesicle ■ *adj* /və síkyŏŏlət/ having or resembling blisters or vesicles —**vesiculation** /və síkyŏŏ láysh'n/ *n*

Vespasian /ve spáyzh'n/ (AD 9–79) Roman emperor. His reign (69–79) saw the destruction of Jerusalem and the construction of the Colosseum. Born **Vespasianus, Titus Flavius Sabinus**

> 'Dear me, I believe I am becoming a god. An emperor ought at least to die on his feet.'
> [Vespasian. Quoted in 'Vespasian, Afterwards Deified', *Lives of the Caesars*, Suetonius; 121?]

vesper /véspər/ *n* **1.** a bell rung in the evening, e.g. to summon worshippers to vespers **2.** same as **evening** *n* (sense 1) (*archaic or literary*) ■ *adj* relating to the evening or vespers [14C. < Latin, 'evening, evening star']

Vesper *n* Venus when seen as a bright star in the evening sky

vesperal /véspərəl/ *n* **1.** a book that contains the prayers and hymns used at vespers **2.** a covering for an altar cloth

vesper bell *n* RELIG same as **vesper** *n* (sense 1)

vespers /véspərz/, **Vespers** *n* (*takes a singular or plural verb*) **1.** an evening church service, particularly evensong **2.** in the Roman Catholic Church, the sixth of the seven separate hours (**canonical hours**) that are set aside for prayer each day, or a service held on Sundays and holy days at this time [14C. Via Old French *vespres* (plural) < Latin *vespera* (singular) 'evening' < *vesper* 'evening, evening star']

vespertilionid /véspər tílli ənid/ *n* an insect-eating long-tailed bat. Family: Vespertilionidae. [Late 19C. < modern Latin *Vespertilionidae* < Latin *vespertilio* 'bat' < *vesper* 'evening']

vespertine /véspər tīn/ *adj* **1.** BOT **OPENING IN EVENING** describes a flower that opens in the evening **2.** ZOOL **ACTIVE IN EVENING** describes an animal that tends to be most active in the evening **3.** ASTRON **APPEARING IN EVENING** describes an astronomical object that appears or sets in the evening

vespiary /véspi əri/ (*plural* **-ies**) *n* a nest or colony of social wasps or hornets [Early 19C. < Latin *vespa* 'wasp', after APIARY]

vespid /véspid/ *n* an insect of the family that includes wasps and hornets. Family: Vespidae. ■ *adj* belonging or related to the family of insects that includes wasps and hornets [Early 20C. < Latin *vespa* 'wasp']

vespine /vés pīn/ *adj* relating to or resembling wasps [Mid-19C. < Latin *vespa* 'wasp']

Vespucci /ve spóochi/, **Amerigo** (1454–1512) Italian explorer. He claimed to be the first European to reach the mainland of the Americas (1497–98). America is named after him.

> 'These new regions of America which we found and explored with the fleet...we may rightly call a New World...a continent more densely peopled and abounding in animals than our Europe or Asia or Africa.'
> [Amerigo Vespucci, *Letter to Lorenzo de' Medici*; 1503]

vessel /véss'l/ *n* **1.** **RECEPTACLE** a hollow receptacle, especially one that is used as a container for liquids **2.** **LARGE WATERCRAFT** a ship or large boat **3.** **AIRSHIP** a flying craft, especially an airship **4.** ANAT **TUBULAR STRUCTURE CONDUCTING BODY FLUID** a duct that carries fluid, especially blood or lymph, around the body **5.** BOT **TUBE CONDUCTING WATER IN PLANT** a tube found in most flowering plants and some ferns that carries water and dissolved minerals through the plant, forming part of the sap-conducting tissue (**xylem**) **6.** **SOMEBODY WHO EMBODIES QUALITY** somebody seen as the recipient or embodiment of a quality (*literary*) [14C. Via Anglo-Norman < Latin *vascellum* 'small dish or vase, ship' < *vas* 'dish, vase']

vest /vest/ *n* **1.** **SLEEVELESS UNDERGARMENT** a sleeveless garment worn on the upper part of the body, under the clothes. N Am term **undershirt 2.** *Aus, N Am* CLOTHING same as **waistcoat** (sense 1) ■ *v* (**vests, vesting, vested**) **1.** *vt* **CONFER POWER ON SOMEBODY OR SOMETHING** to bestow a power on somebody or something (*usually passive*) ○ *The governor was vested with powers.* **2.** *vti* **CONFER RIGHTS, OR EXIST AS RIGHT** to settle or confer property, power, or rights on somebody, or be a part of somebody's property, power, or rights ○ *Sovereignty vests in the state.* ○ *by the authority vested in me* **3.** *vti* **CLOTHE SOMEBODY, OR PUT ON CLOTHES** to clothe somebody, or put on clothes, especially vestments [15C. < Old French *vestu*, past participle of *vestir* 'clothe' < Latin *vestire* < *vestis* 'clothing, garment']

REGIONAL NOTE People commenting on differences between American and British English often point out that a ***vest*** is underwear in Britain. In fact, ***vest*** is only one of the many words used for this garment. Other words used to describe this garment include *body-flannen*, *body-sark*, *flannel*, *simmet*, *singlet*, and *undersark*.

Vesta /véstə/ *n* **1.** in Roman mythology, the goddess of the hearth. Greek equivalent **Hestia 2.** the brightest and third largest of the asteroids that orbit the Sun [< Latin]

vestal /vést'l/ *adj* **1.** **CHASTE** chaste, or not having experienced sexual intercourse **2.** MYTHOL **OF VESTA** relating to the Roman goddess Vesta ■ *n* **1.** **VIRGIN** a woman who is a virgin (*literary*) **2.** same as **nun**[1] (sense 1) (*literary*) **3.** RELIG, ANCIENT HIST same as **vestal virgin**

vestal virgin *n* in ancient Rome, a celibate woman who tended the sacred fire in the temple of Vesta. There were originally four, and later six vestal virgins, who were vowed to 30 years of service.

vested /véstid/ *adj* **1.** having an unquestionable right to the possession of property or a privilege **2.** wearing clothes, especially religious vestments

vested interest *n* **1.** **SPECIAL INTEREST** a special concern in maintaining or promoting an issue or situation for reasons of private gain **2.** **PERSON OR GROUP HAVING SPECIAL INTEREST** a person or group with a vested interest in maintaining or promoting something (*often used in the plural*) **3.** LAW **RIGHT TO POSSESS SOMETHING** a right to the present or future possession of property

vestee *n* a decorative, detachable piece of material that is worn under a man's jacket and is intended to look like a waistcoat

vestiary /vésti əri/ *n* (*plural* **-ies**) a dressing room or storeroom for clothes ■ *adj* relating to clothes (*formal*) [13C. Via Old French *vestiarie* < Latin *vestiarium* 'clothes chest, wardrobe', later 'vestry' < *vestis* 'clothing, garment']

vestibular /ve stíbbyŏŏlər/ *adj* relating to a vestibule

vestibular nerve *n* a branch of the acoustic nerve that carries nerve impulses from the semicircular canals and other organs in the inner ear, conveying information about posture and balance

vestibule /vésti byool/ *n* **1.** **ENTRANCE HALL** a small room or hall between an outer door and the main part of a building **2.** ANAT **BODY CAVITY** a cavity or space in the body that serves as the entrance to another cavity or canal, e.g. the part of the mouth between the teeth and lips **3.** ANAT **MIDDLE CAVITY OF INNER EAR** the middle cavity of the inner ear between the cochlea and the semicircular canals [Early 17C. Directly or via French < Latin *vestibulum*]

vestibulocochlear nerve /ve stíbbyŏŏ lō kókli ər-/ *n* either of the eighth pair of cranial nerves, critical to the sense of hearing [< Latin *vestibulum* 'entrance']

vestige /véstij/ *n* **1.** **TRACE OF SOMETHING GONE** a trace or sign of something that is no longer present **2.** **SMALL AMOUNT** the slightest amount ○ *There wasn't a vestige of truth in what she wrote.* **3.** BIOL **RUDIMENTARY BODY PART** an organ or part of the body that is now rudimentary and no longer functions, but was formerly fully developed [Early 17C. Via French < Latin *vestigium* 'sole of the foot, footprint, trace']

vestigial /ve stíjji əl/ *adj* **1.** remaining after nearly all the rest has disappeared or dwindled ○ *a vestigial stirring of passion* **2.** having become degenerate or functionless in the course of time ○ *the vestigial muscles of the ear* —**vestigially** *adv*

vestment /véstmənt/ *n* **1.** a garment, especially a robe worn to show rank or office **2.** a ceremonial robe worn by members of the clergy during a religious ceremony [13C. Via Old French *vestiment* < Latin *vestimentum* < *vestire* (see VEST)] —**vestmental** /vest mént'l/ *adj* —**vestmented** *adj*

vest-pocket *adj N Am* small enough to fit into the pocket of a waistcoat ○ *a vest-pocket edition*

vestry /véstri/ (*plural* **-tries**) *n* **1.** **ROOM FOR VESTMENTS** a room attached to a church, where vestments or sacred objects are kept **2.** **MEETING ROOM** a room in a church where meetings or classes are held **3.** **CHURCH COMMITTEE** in the Anglican Church, a committee of parishioners elected by the congregation to manage the temporal affairs of the parish **4.** **MEETING OF CHURCH MEMBERS** in the Anglican Church, a meeting of church members or their representatives [14C. < Anglo-Norman variant of Old French *vestiarie* (see VESTIARY)] —**vestral** *adj*

vestryman /véstrimən/ (*plural* **-men** /-mən/) *n* somebody, especially a man, who is a member of a church vestry

vestryperson /véstri purss'n/ *n* a member of a church vestry

vestrywoman /véstri wŏŏmən/ (*plural* **-women** /-wimin/) *n* a woman who is a member of a church vestry

vesture /véschər/ (*archaic*) *n* clothing, or something that covers in the way that clothing does ■ *vt* (**-tures, -turing, -tured**) to clothe or cover somebody or something [14C. < Old French < Latin *vestire* (see VEST)] —**vestural** *adj*

Vesuvial /və sóovi əl/ *adj* resembling in force or degree the consequences of a huge volcanic eruption ○ *in a Vesuvial rage*

vesuvian /və sóovi ən/ *n* **1.** a slow-burning match used especially for lighting cigars (*archaic*) **2.** MINERALS same as **vesuvianite** [Late 17C. After Mount VESUVIUS]

vesuvianite /və sóovi ə nīt/ *n* a semiprecious stone that is a green, brown, or yellow silicate of aluminium containing calcium, magnesium, and iron. Source: marble. Use: gems. [Late 19C. After MOUNT VESUVIUS]

Vesuvius, Mount /və sóovi əss/ active volcano overlooking the Bay of Naples, southern Italy. An eruption in AD 79 destroyed the Roman cities of Pompeii and Herculaneum. Height: 1,277 m/4,190 ft.

vet[1] /vet/ *n* same as **veterinary surgeon** ■ *vt* (**vets, vetting, vetted**) **1. CHECK UP ON SOMEBODY OR SOMETHING** to subject somebody or something to a careful examination or scrutiny, especially when this involves determining suitability for something **2.** VET **EXAMINE ANIMAL** to examine or treat an animal **3. STERILIZE ANIMAL** to sterilize an animal by castrating or spaying (*informal*) [Mid-19C. Shortening of VETERINARY or VETERINARIAN]

vet[2] /vet/ *n N Am* a former member of the armed forces, especially in a particular conflict (*informal*) ○ *Vietnam vets* [Mid-19C. Shortening of VETERAN]

vet. *abbr* **1.** MIL veteran **2.** VET veterinarian **3.** VET veterinary

vetch /vech/ (*plural* **vetches** or *same*) *n* **1.** a leguminous plant with small flowers. Use: silage, fodder. Genus: *Vicia*. **2.** a plant related to or similar to vetch, e.g. the kidney vetch [14C. Via Old N French *veche* < Latin *vicia*]

vetchling /véchling/ *n* a creeping wild plant that is related to vetch. Genus: *Lathyrus*.

veteran /véttərən/ *n* **1. SOMEBODY WITH EXPERIENCE** somebody who is considerably experienced in something **2.** MIL **EXPERIENCED SOLDIER** a long-serving member of the military who has had much active service ○ *a veteran of three foreign wars* **3.** *N Am* MIL **SOMEBODY FORMERLY IN ARMED FORCES** a former member of the armed forces [Early 16C. Directly or via French *vétéran* < Latin *veteranus* < *vetus* 'old'] —**veteran** *adj*

veteran car *n* a car made before 1919 or, strictly, one made before 1905

Veterans Day *n* in the United States, a public holiday honouring former members of the armed forces. Date: 11 November.

veterinarian /vèttəri náiri ən/ *n N Am* same as **veterinary surgeon** [Mid-17C. < Latin *veterinarius* (see VETERINARY)]

veterinary /véttərinəri, véttri-, véttənri/ *adj* relating to diseases of animals and their treatment [Late 18C. < Latin *veterinarius* < *veterinus* 'relating to (mature) cattle' < *veter-*, stem of *vetus* 'old']

veterinary medicine, veterinary science *n* the branch of medicine dealing with the health of animals and the diagnosis and treatment of their diseases and injuries

veterinary surgeon *n* somebody who is trained and qualified in the medical treatment of animals. N Am term **veterinarian**

~~**vetinary**~~ incorrect spelling of **veterinary**

vetiver /véttivər/ *n* **1.** a tall grass, the leaves of which are used to make screens and fans. Native to: South Asia. Latin name: *Vetiveria zizanioides*. **2.** the roots of the vetiver, which produce an oil that is used to make perfume [Mid-19C. Via French *vétiver* < Tamil *vettivēr* < *vēr* 'root']

veto /vee̍tō/ *n* (*plural* **-toes**) **1. RIGHT TO REJECT** the right to reject something such as a piece of legislation proposed by somebody else **2. EXERCISE OF RIGHT TO REJECT MEASURES** the exercise of the right to reject something, especially a political measure **3. PROHIBITION** an order prohibiting something ○ *put her veto on it* ■ *vt* (**-toes, -toing, -toed**) **1. REJECT SOMETHING** to reject something such as a measure or government bill by veto **2. PROHIBIT SOMETHING** to refuse to consent to or approve something ○ *My teacher vetoed the idea.* [Early 17C. < Latin, 'I forbid'] —**vetoer** *n*

vex /veks/ (**vexes, vexing, vexed**) *vt* **1. ANNOY SOMEBODY** to make somebody slightly annoyed or upset, especially over a relatively unimportant matter **2. AGITATE SOMEBODY** to cause somebody anxiety or distress (*archaic*) **3. CONFOUND SOMEBODY** to confuse or puzzle somebody [15C. Via French *vexer* < Latin *vexare* 'shake, disturb'] —**vexingly** *adv*

SYNONYMS See *annoy*.

vexation /vek sáysh'n/ *n* **1. STATE OF BEING VEXED** the state of being provoked to slight annoyance, anxiety, or distress **2. ACT OF VEXING** the act of provoking somebody to irritability or anxiety **3. SOMETHING THAT VEXES** something that provokes irritability or anxiety

vexatious /vek sáyshəss/ *adj* **1.** provoking irritation or anxiety by causing trouble **2.** describes legal proceedings put forward on insufficient grounds and with the intention of causing annoyance to the defendant —**vexatiously** *adv* —**vexatiousness** *n*

vexed /vekst/ *adj* **1.** provoked to slight annoyance, anxiety or distress **2.** being the subject of much debate ○ *a vexed issue such as global warming* ○ *the vexed question of the next budget* —**vexedly** /véksidli/ *adv* —**vexedness** *n*

vexilla ANCIENT HIST plural of **vexillum**

vexillology /véksi lólləji/ *n* the study of flags —**vexillologic** /véksilə lójjik/ *adj* —**vexillological** *adj* —**vexillologist** *n*

vexillum /vek síll əm/ (*plural* **-la** /-lə/) *n* in ancient Rome, a military standard, or the troops serving under a separate standard [Early 18C. < Latin, 'flag, banner' < *vex-*, a stem of *vehere* 'carry']

VF *abbr* **1.** MEDIA video frequency **2.** TELECOM voice frequency

VFR *abbr* AEROSP visual flight rules

VFT *abbr* RAIL very fast train

vg *abbr* **1.** very good **2.** ONLINE British Virgin Islands (*used in Internet addresses*) See table at **domain name**

VG *abbr* CHR Vicar General

VGA *n* a specification for video display controllers used in personal computers. Full form **video graphics array**

VHF, vhf *abbr* COMMUNICATION very high frequency

VHS *n* a system for recording television programmes in the home. Full form **Video Home System**

vi[1] *abbr* vide infra

vi[2] *abbr* ONLINE Virgin Islands of the United States (*used in Internet addresses*) See table at **domain name**

VI, V.I. *abbr* Vancouver Island

via /vī ə, vée ə/ *prep* **1.** by way of or through ○ *Can you come home via the post office?* **2.** using the means or agency of ○ *removed the obstruction via surgery* [Early 17C. < Latin, 'by way of', form of *via* 'way, road']

viable /vī əb'l/ *adj* **1. PRACTICABLE OR WORTHWHILE** able to be done or worth doing ○ *a viable proposition* **2.** BIOL **ABLE TO GROW** able to germinate or develop normally **3.** MED **ABLE TO SURVIVE OUTSIDE WOMB** describes a foetus that can survive outside the womb [Early 19C. < French *vie*, < Latin *vita* 'life'] —**viability** /vī ə bílləti/ *n* —**viably** *adv*

USAGE The word *viable* was originally restricted to the senses of 'able to grow' and 'able to survive', as in *a viable foetus*. However, its extended sense of 'able to be done or worth doing', as in *viable alternatives*, is well established in the language.

Via Dolorosa /vée ə dóllə róssə/ *n* **1.** the route taken by Jesus Christ to Calvary to be crucified **2.** *also* **via dolorosa** a difficult or distressing experience or series of events [< Latin, 'sorrowful way']

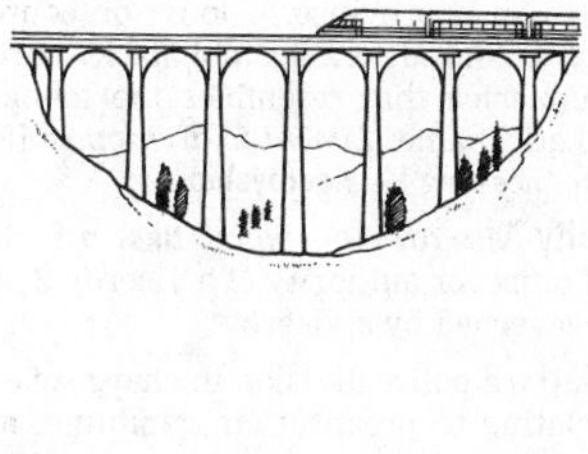

viaduct

viaduct /vī ə dukt/ *n* a bridge that consists of a series of short masonry or concrete arched spans supported on towers [Early 19C. < Latin *via* 'way, road', after AQUEDUCT]

Viagra /vī ággrə/ *tdmk* a trademark for sildenafil citrate, an enzyme-inhibiting drug. Use: treatment of male impotence.

vial /vī əl/ *n* a small glass bottle, especially one for medicines [14C. Alteration of PHIAL]

via media /vī ə mée di ə/ *n* a middle course or choice between extreme possibilities [< Latin]

viand /vī ənd, vée-/ *n* (*formal*) **1.** a store or collection of food, especially the food that makes up a meal or a feast (*often used in the plural*) **2.** an item of food [14C. Via French *viande* 'food' (now 'meat') < Latin *vivenda* 'things for living' < *vivere* 'to live']

viaticum /vī áttikəm, vi-/ (*plural* **-ca** /-kə/ or **-cums**) *n* **1.** Communion given to somebody who is dying or in danger of dying **2.** provisions or money for a journey (*literary*) [Mid-16C. < Latin, 'provision for a journey' < *via* 'way, road']

vibe /vīb/ *n* a particular kind of feeling or ambience (*slang; often used in the plural*) ○ *The new decor has a kind of 50s vibe to it.* [Mid-20C. Shortening of VIBRATION]

vibes /vībz/ (*plural same*) *n* same as **vibraphone** (*slang*) [Shortening]

vibist /víbist/ *n* somebody who plays the vibraphone (*slang*)

Viborg /vée bawrg/ capital city of Viborg County, north-central Jutland, Denmark. Population: 31,239 (1996).

Vibram /víbrəm/ *tdmk* a trademark for a brand of hard-wearing moulded rubber sole with a deep tread, used in footwear such as walking boots

vibrant /víbrənt/ *adj* **1. ENERGETIC** full of liveliness or energy **2. PULSATING WITH ENERGY** seeming to quiver or pulsate with energy or activity **3. RESONANT** having a full rich sound that tends to continue for some time **4. BRIGHT** dazzling or radiantly bright **5. VIBRATING** vibrating very rapidly [Mid-16C. < Latin *vibrant-*, past participle of *vibrare* 'shake'] —**vibrancy** *n* —**vibrantly** *adv*

vibraphone /víbrə fōn/ *n* a percussion instrument with electrically driven resonators beneath a set of metal bars that are struck with small mallets or sometimes played with a bow, causing vibration [Early 20C. < VIBRATE] —**vibraphonist** *n*

vibrate /vī bráyt/ (**-brates, -brating, -brated**) *v* **1.** *vti* **MAKE SMALL MOVEMENTS RAPIDLY** to shake or move to and fro rapidly, or make something move in this way ○ *Passing trains make the whole room vibrate.* **2.** *vti* PHYS **OSCILLATE** to oscillate with a continuing periodic change relative to a fixed reference point, or make something oscillate in this way **3.** *vi* **RESONATE** to make a full rich sound that tends to continue for some time **4.** *vi* **THRILL** to experience a rush of emotion in response to something [Early 17C. < Latin *vibrat-*, past participle of *vibrare* 'shake'] —**vibratory** /vī bráytəri, víbrətəri/ *adj*

vibratile /víbrə tīl/ *adj* **1.** showing vibration **2.** capable of vibrating, or operating by means of vibration [Early 19C. Alteration of *vibratory* after PULSATILE] —**vibratility** /víbrə tílləti/ *n*

vibration /vī bráysh'n/ *n* **1. INSTANCE OF VIBRATING** an instance of shaking or moving to and fro very rapidly **2. PROCESS OF VIBRATING** the process of moving or being moved to and fro very rapidly **3.** PHYS **REPETITIVE PERIODIC OSCILLATION** a continuing periodic oscillation relative to a fixed reference point, or a single complete oscillation **4. ATMOSPHERE OF PLACE** the atmosphere or aura given off by a place or situation (*informal; often used in the plural*) **5. FEELING COMMUNICATED SUBCONSCIOUSLY** a feeling communicated from one person to another (*informal; often used in the plural*) —**vibrational** *adj*

vibrato /vi bráatō/ (*plural* **-tos**) *n* **1.** a throbbing effect in the playing of a stringed or wind instrument, made by rapidly varying the pitch **2.** a throbbing effect in singing, produced by rapidly varying the breath pressure or the pitch [Mid-19C. < Italian, 'vibrated']

vibrator /vī bráytər/ *n* **1. VIBRATING DEVICE** an electric device that vibrates, e.g. one used to give a massage or as a sexual aid **2. SOMETHING THAT VIBRATES** something that vibrates or makes something vibrate **3.** ELEC ENG **DEVICE CONVERTING DIRECT TO ALTERNATING CURRENT** an electromechanical device, often used in bells and buzzers, that interrupts a direct current to convert it into an alternating current

vibrio /víbbri ō/ (*plural* **-os** or **-ones** /víbbri óneez/) *n* a bacterium shaped like a comma or like the letter S. Genus: *Vibrio*. [Mid-19C. < modern Latin < Latin *vibrare* 'shake'] —**vibrioid** /víbbri oyd/ *adj*

vibrissa /vī bríssə/ (*plural* **-sae** /-see/) *n* **1.** a mammal's hair or whisker, usually on the face or limbs, that vibrates when touched, stimulating nervous tissue in the animal's skin **2.** a feather that is like a bristle,

near the beak of an insect-eating bird [Late 17C. < Latin < *vibrare* 'shake'] —**vibrissal** *adj*

vibronic /vī brónnik/ *adj* relating to the electronic and vibrational energy states of elementary particles and atoms [Mid-20C. < *vibrational* + ELECTRONIC]

vibrotron /víbrə tron/ *n* a triode valve in which the anode can be vibrated by an external force

viburnum /vī búrnəm/ (*plural* **-nums** or *same*) *n* a bush or small tree with flat or rounded flower clusters, e.g. the guelder rose. Flowers: white, sometimes tinged with pink. Genus: *Viburnum*. [Mid-18C. Via modern Latin < Latin, 'wayfaring tree']

vic. *abbr* RELIG vicar

Vic. *abbr* Victoria

vicar /víkər/ *n* **1. ANGLICAN PRIEST** a priest in the Church of England who is in charge of a parish. Vicars, unlike rectors, were not formerly entitled to receive the tithes, which went to a religious house, chapter, or lay person, and were paid a stipend. **2. MEMBER OF ANGLICAN CLERGY** a member of the Anglican clergy who acts in place of a rector or bishop at Communion **3. ROMAN CATHOLIC PRIEST** a Roman Catholic priest who represents or deputizes for a bishop **4. CHOIR MEMBER** a cleric or member of a choir who sings parts of a cathedral service in the Church of England **5.** *US* **EPISCOPAL CHURCH CLERIC** a cleric in the Episcopal Church who is in charge of a chapel [14C. Via Anglo-Norman *vicare* < Latin *vicarius* 'substitute' < *vic-* 'change, place'; because the vicar acted as a substitute for the rector] —**vicarly** *adj* —**vicarship** *n*

vicarage /víkərij/ *n* **1.** the residence of a vicar **2.** the office or duties of a vicar

vicar apostolic (*plural* **vicars apostolic**) *n* a titular bishop or missionary in the Roman Catholic Church

vicarate *n* CHR same as **vicariate**

vicar general (*plural* **vicars general**) *n* **1.** a priest acting as an assistant to a Roman Catholic bishop **2.** a lay official assisting an Anglican bishop with administrative or judicial duties

vicarial /vi káiri əl, vī-/ *adj* **1.** being or acting as a vicar **2.** relating to a vicar **3.** same as **vicarious** (sense 3)

vicariate /vi káiri ət, vī-/, **vicarate** /víkərət/ *n* **1.** the office or authority of a vicar **2.** the district that falls under the care of a vicar

vicarious /vi káiri əss, vī-/ *adj* **1. EXPERIENCED THROUGH ANOTHER BY IMAGINING** experienced through somebody else rather than at first hand, by using sympathy or the power of the imagination ○ *vicarious pleasure* **2. ENDURED FOR SOMEBODY ELSE** done or endured by somebody as a substitute for somebody else ○ *vicarious suffering* **3. DELEGATED** delegated to somebody else or performing a function that has been delegated ○ *vicarious authority* **4.** MED **IN UNEXPECTED PART OF BODY** occurring in a part of the body remote from the usual site, e.g. menstrual bleeding in the breasts, nose, or sweat glands [Mid-17C. < Latin *vicarius* (see VICAR)] —**vicariously** *adv* —**vicariousness** *n*

Vicar of Christ *n* in Roman Catholicism, the pope

vice[1] /vīss/ *n* **1. IMMORAL HABIT** an immoral or wicked habit or characteristic ○ *Lying is the least of her vices.* **2. DEPRAVITY** immoral conduct **3. PROSTITUTION, GAMBLING, AND DRUGS** criminal activity connected with prostitution and other sexual offences, gambling, and illegal drugs (*often used before a noun*) **4. MILD FAILING IN CHARACTER** a mild failing or flaw in somebody's behaviour or character **5. FAULT IN ANIMAL** a fault or undesirable habit in a horse or other domestic animal [13C. Via French < Latin *vitium*]

vice[2] /vīssi/ *prep* in place of or instead of somebody or something [Late 18C. < Latin *vice* 'in place of' < *vic-* 'change, place']

vice[3] /vīss/ *n* a tool with two jaws that can be closed by a lever or screw, used to hold an object immobile so that it can be worked on ■ *vt* (**vices, vicing, viced**) to hold something tightly in a vice [13C. Via Old French *vis* 'screw' < Latin *vitis* 'vine'] —**vice-like** *adj*

vice-admiral *n* an officer in the British and Canadian navies and US Navy or Coast Guard of a rank above rear admiral —**vice-admiralty** *n*

vice chair *n* somebody who takes the place of a chairperson in his or her absence

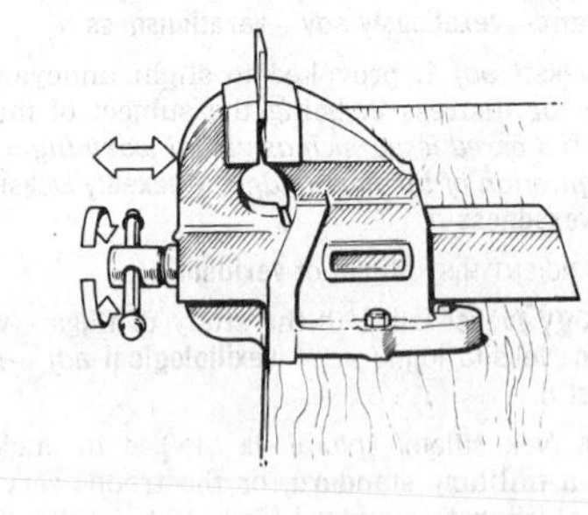

vice

vice chairman *n* somebody, especially a man, who takes the place of a chairperson in his or her absence

vice chairperson *n* same as **vice chair**

vice chairwoman *n* a woman who takes the place of a chairperson, especially a woman, in his or her absence

vice chancellor *n* **1. ASSISTANT CHANCELLOR OF UNIVERSITY** a deputy or assistant chancellor in a university, often the person in charge of administration **2. DEPUTY CHANCELLOR** a deputy for the chancellor of a state **3. JUDGE** a US judge ranking below a chancellor, or an English judge who runs the Chancery Division of the High Court —**vice-chancellorship** *n*

vice consul *n* an officer who acts as the deputy for the official representing a country's commercial interest in an overseas country —**vice-consular** *adj*

vicegerent /vīss jérrənt, -jeér-/ *n* a deputy appointed to act on the authority of a ruler or magistrate, especially in administrative duties [Mid-16C. < medieval Latin, 'deputy' < Latin *gerent-*, present participle of *gerere* 'carry on'] —**vicegeral** *adj* —**vicegerency** *n*

vicenary /víssinəri/ *adj* **1.** being or relating to the number 20 **2.** using 20 as a basis for counting or ordering [Early 17C. < Latin *vicenarius* < *viginti* 'twenty']

vicennial /vi sénni əl/ *adj* lasting for or occurring every 20 years [Mid-18C. < Latin *vicennium* 'period of twenty years' < *vic-*, stem of *vicies* 'twenty times']

Vicenza /vi chéntsə/ capital of Vicenza Province, Veneto Region, northern Italy. Population: 107,223 (2001).

vice-president *n* an official of a rank below a president, who can take the place of the president's place if necessary —**vice-presidency** *n* —**vice-presidential** *adj*

viceregal /vīss reég'l/ *adj* **1.** relating to a viceroy **2.** *ANZ, Can* relating to a governor general —**viceregally** *adv*

viceregent /vīss reéjənt/ *n* a deputy for the regent of a country —**viceregency** *n*

vicereine /vīss ráyn/ *n* a viceroy who is a woman, or the wife of a viceroy [Early 19C. < French, 'vice-queen']

viceroy /vīss roy/ *n* **1.** a governor who represents a sovereign in a province, colony, or country **2.** a brightly coloured orange-and-black butterfly of North America that resembles the monarch butterfly. Latin name: *Limenitis archippus*. [Early 16C. < French, 'vice-king'] —**viceroyship** *n*

viceroyalty /vīss róy əlti/ (*plural* **-ties**) *n* **1.** the office, term of office, or authority of a viceroy **2.** a district that is governed by a viceroy

vice squad *n* a police division in charge of enforcing laws relating to prostitution, gambling, and drug abuse

vice versa /vīss vúrssə, vīssi-/ *adv* the other way round [< Latin, 'the position being reversed']

Vichy[1] /veéshi/ *n* same as **Vichy water** [Mid-19C. < VICHY[2]]

Vichy[2] /veéshi/ city in central France, the site of important mineral springs. It was the seat of a French government that collaborated with the Germans during World War II. Population: 26,528 (1999).

vichyssoise /veéshi swaáz, víshi-/ *n* a creamy soup made from leeks, potatoes, and onions, often served chilled [Mid-20C. Shortening of French *crème vichyssoise glacée* 'iced cream soup from Vichy']

Vichy water *n* a natural sparkling mineral water from Vichy, France, or a similar sparkling water

vicinage /víssinij/ *n* **1.** a neighbourhood, or the people living in it (*archaic*) **2.** *N Am* the area immediately surrounding a place [14C. < Old French *vis(e)nage*, < Latin *vicinus* (see VICINITY)]

vicinal /víssin'l/ *adj* **1. NEIGHBOURING** adjacent or neighbouring **2. LOCAL** relating to or restricted to a local area **3.** CHEM **BEING CONSECUTIVE POSITIONS ON CARBON CHAIN** relating to two or more adjacent positions on a carbon ring or chain [Early 17C. Directly or via French < Latin *vicinalis* < *vicinus* (see VICINITY)]

vicinity /vi sínnəti/ (*plural* **-ties**) *n* (*formal*) **1.** a neighbourhood, or the area surrounding a particular place ○ *The fire threatened to spread, and all the houses in the vicinity had to be evacuated.* **2.** the fact of being close either in space or relationship [Mid-16C. < Latin *vicinitas* < *vicinus* 'neighbour' < *vicus* 'village, homestead'] ◇ **in the vicinity of 1.** close to, neighbouring, or surrounding **2.** roughly or approximately

vicious /víshəss/ *adj* **1. FEROCIOUS AND VIOLENT** carried out with intense violence and an apparent desire to inflict serious harm, or acting in an aggressive, cruel, and violent way ○ *a vicious attack* ○ *Her husband's a vicious brute.* **2. DANGEROUS AND AGGRESSIVE** aggressive and liable to attack or bite ○ *a vicious dog* **3. MALICIOUS** intended to cause somebody mental anguish or to defame somebody **4. SEVERE** extremely severe or powerful and damaging in its effects ○ *a vicious frost* **5. GOING FROM BAD TO WORSE** involving a chain of cause and effect or action and reaction in which things get progressively worse ○ *a vicious spiral* **6. UNSOUND** incorrect or showing faulty logic **7. WICKED AND IMMORAL** displaying or given to immoral behaviour (*formal*) [14C. < VICE[1]] —**viciously** *adv* —**viciousness** *n*

vicious circle, **vicious cycle** *n* **1. SITUATION WORSENED BY ATTEMPTED SOLUTIONS** a situation in which attempts to solve one problem lead to further problems that only make the original position worse **2.** LOGIC **REASONING BASED ON UNPROVEN ASSUMPTION** a form of reasoning that bases a conclusion on a statement assumed to be true but not proven independently **3.** MED **LINKING OF TWO DISEASES** a situation in which two diseases or conditions are linked so that each leads to or aggravates the other

USAGE vicious circle or **vicious cycle**? Until quite recently the invariable choice was ***vicious circle***. Perhaps influenced by such phrases as *the cycle of welfare dependency*, the use of the variant ***vicious cycle*** has been gaining ground and is now seen in virtually indistinguishable contexts.

vicissitude /vī sissi tyood, vi-/ *n* the fact of being variable (*literary*) ■ **vicissitudes** *npl* unexpected changes, especially in somebody's fortunes [Mid-16C. Directly or via French < Latin *vicissitudo* < *vicissim* 'by turns' < *vic-* (see VICAR)] —**vicissitudinary** /vī síssi tyoōdinəri, vi-/ *adj* —**vicissitudinous** /-tyoōdinəss/ *adj*

vicomte /veé koNt/ *n* a French nobleman who is equal in rank to a British viscount [Mid-19C. Via French < Old French *vi(s)conte* (see VISCOUNT)]

vicomtesse /veé koN téss/ *n* a French noblewoman who is equal in rank to a British viscountess [Late 18C. < French < *vicomte* (see VICOMTE)]

victim /víktim/ *n* **1. SOMEBODY HURT OR KILLED** somebody who is hurt or killed by somebody or something, especially in a crime, accident, or disaster ○ *a murder victim* **2. SOMEBODY OR SOMETHING HARMED** somebody who or something that is adversely affected by an action or circumstance ○ *a victim of her own success* **3. SOMEBODY DUPED** somebody who is tricked or exploited **4. LIVING BEING USED FOR SACRIFICE** a live human or animal used as a sacrifice or in a religious rite **5. HELPLESS PERSON** somebody who experiences misfortune and feels helpless to remedy it [15C. < Latin *victima* 'animal offered as a sacrifice'] ◇ **fall victim to somebody** *or* **something** to be affected, harmed, or deceived by somebody *or* something

victimize /vikti mīz/ (**-izes, -izing, -ized**), **victimise** (**-ises, -ising, -ised**) *vt* **1.** to single somebody out unfairly for punishment or ill treatment **2.** to cause somebody to become a victim —**victimization** /vikti mī záysh'n/ *n* —**victimizer** *n*

victimless crime /víktimləss-/ *n* an illegal act in which there is no obvious injured party, e.g. loitering

victor /víktər/ *n* a winner in a contest or battle [14C. Directly or via Anglo-Norman < Latin < *vic-* past participle of *vincere* 'conquer']

Victor /víktər/ *n* a code word used for the letter 'v' in telecommunications

Victor Emmanuel I /víktər i mánnyoŏ əl/ (1759–1824) king of Sardinia. His family possessions in northern Italy were occupied by French forces for much of his reign. He abdicated in 1821 following an uprising.

Victor Emmanuel II /víktər i mánnyoo əl/ (1820–78) king of Sardinia (1849–61) and king of Italy (1861–78). He became the first king of a united Italy and, in the course of his reign, established the Italian capital in Rome after it was annexed in 1870.

victoria /vik táwri ə/ *n* **1.** RED-AND-YELLOW PLUM a large red-and-yellow variety of plum **2.** HORSE-DRAWN CARRIAGE WITH FOLDING HOOD a horse-drawn carriage with four wheels and a folding hood, accommodating two passengers **3.** WATER LILY a giant water lily. Flowers: fragrant, red or white. Native to: South America. Genus: *Victoria*. [Mid-19C. After Queen VICTORIA]

Victoria /vik táwri ə/ **1.** river in the northwestern part of the Northern Territory, Australia. Length: 640 km/398 mi. **2.** state in southeastern Australia. Capital: Melbourne. Population: 4,917,400 (2003). Area: 227,600 sq. km/87,880 sq. mi. **3.** capital city of British Columbia, Canada, on the southern tip of Vancouver Island. Population: 288,346 (2001). **4.** capital city of the Republic of Seychelles, situated on the northeastern coast of Mahé Island. Population: 30,000 (2001). **5.** capital city of the Hong Kong Special Administrative Region, situated on the north coast of Hong Kong Island. Population: 1,183,621 (2000).

Victoria (1819–1901) queen of the United Kingdom. She reigned longer than any other British monarch (1837–1901), and was empress of India (1876–1901).

> 'Please understand that there is no one depressed in *this* house; we are not interested in the possibilities of defeat; they do not exist.'
> [Victoria. Quoted in *Life of Robert, Marquis of Salisbury*, Gwendolen Cecil; 1931]

Victoria, Lake largest lake in Africa, with shorelines in Tanzania, Uganda, and Kenya. Area: 69,490 sq. km/26,830 sq. mi.

Victoria Cross *n* a decoration in the form of a bronze cross, given to members of British and Commonwealth armed forces for conspicuous bravery. It was instituted by Queen Victoria in 1856.

Victoria Day *n* in Canada, a statutory holiday marking the birthday of Queen Victoria. Date: 24 May or preceding Monday.

Victoria Falls

Barnaby's

Victoria Falls waterfall on the River Zambezi in south-central Africa, on the border between Zambia and Zimbabwe. Height: 108 m/355 ft.

Victoria Land region of Antarctica, west of Ross Sea and east of Wilkes Land

Victorian /vik táwri ən/ *adj* **1.** CHARACTERISTIC OF TIME OF QUEEN VICTORIA relating to, belonging to, or characteristic of the reign of Queen Victoria **2.** CONVENTIONAL, HYPOCRITICAL, OR PRUDISH characterized by attitudes commonly considered to be prevalent during the Victorian era, especially prudery or conventionalism **3.** ARCHITECTURALLY ELABORATE in, or typical of, the elaborate style of architecture popular in Victorian Britain **4.** FROM VICTORIA relating to or coming from the state of Victoria in Australia, or the cities of Victoria in Canada or the Seychelles ■ *n* **1.** SOMEBODY LIVING IN VICTORIA'S REIGN somebody who lived in the reign of Queen Victoria **2.** SOMEBODY FROM VICTORIA somebody who comes from the state of Victoria in Australia, or the cities of Victoria in Canada or the Seychelles **3.** *US* VICTORIAN HOUSE a house in Victorian architectural style —**Victorianism** *n*

Victoriana /vik táwri áənə/ *npl* collectable objects dating from the time of Queen Victoria

Victoria Nile section of the upper River Nile in Uganda, between lakes Victoria and Albert

Victoria Peak mountain on Hong Kong Island, overlooking Hong Kong Harbour. Height: 554 m/1,818 ft.

victoria plum *n* FOOD same as **victoria** (sense 1)

victorious /vik táwri əss/ *adj* **1.** having won something such as a contest or a battle **2.** resulting in victory, or characteristic of victors, victory, or the joy of winning —**victoriously** *adv* —**victoriousness** *n*

victory /víktəri/ (*plural* -**ries**) *n* **1.** success in a contest against an enemy or opponent, or a particular contest or battle that is won **2.** success in overcoming a difficult situation or an obstacle ○ *Being able to get out of bed was a small victory in her struggle against the illness.* [14C. Via Anglo-Norman *victorie* < Latin *victoria* < *victor* (see VICTOR)]

victory roll *n* an airborne rolling manoeuvre carried out by a pilot of an aircraft as a sign of victory or celebration

victual /vítt'l/ *v* (*archaic or formal*) **1.** *vt* to provide something or somebody, e.g. a ship or its crew, with a supply of food **2.** *vi* to collect a store of food [14C. < Old French *vitaillier* < *vitaille* (see VICTUALS)]

victualler /vítt'lər/ *n* (*archaic or formal*) **1.** SUPPLIER OF PROVISIONS somebody who supplies food or other provisions **2.** INNKEEPER an innkeeper, especially one licensed to sell spirits **3.** SHIP CARRYING STORES a ship carrying food or other provisions

victuals /vítt'lz/ *npl* food or other provisions (*archaic or humorous*) [14C. Via Old French *vitaille* < Latin *victualia* (which later influenced the English spelling) < *victus* 'livelihood, food' < *vivere* 'to live']

vicuña

vicuña /vi kyóonə, -koónyə/, **vicuna** *n* **1.** a tawny-coloured mammal with a silky fleece, related to the llama. Native to: Andes. Latin name: *Vicugna vicugna*. **2.** cloth made from the wool of the vicuña, or an imitation of it [Early 17C. Via Spanish < Quechua *wikúña*]

vid /vid/ *n* same as **video cassette** (*informal*) [Late 20C. Shortening]

Vidal /vi dáal/, **Gore** (*b.* 1925) US writer. His novels, critical works, and essays are often sharply critical of US politics and culture. They include *The City and the Pillar* (1948) and the fictionalized study *Lincoln* (1984). Full name **Vidal, Eugene Luther Gore**

> 'Unless drastic reforms are made, we must accept the fact that every four years the United States will be up for sale, and the richest man or family will buy it.'
> [Gore Vidal, *Reflections upon a Sinking Ship*; 1969]

vidarabine /vī dárrə been/ *n* an antiviral drug. Use: treatment of herpes, chickenpox, shingles, hepatitis B. [Late 20C. Probably < VIRUS + -*d*- for euphony + ARABINOSE]

vidclip /víd klip/ *n* a short excerpt from a film or television production, used for news or promotion (*informal*) [Late 20C. Shortening of *video clip*]

vide /vídi, vée day/ *vt* a word used to refer a reader to another place in a text, or tell a musician to skip to a place farther ahead in the score (*used only as a command*) [Mid-16C. < Latin, 'see!', form of *videre* 'see']

vide infra a term used to refer a reader to a place farther on in a text [< Latin, 'see below!']

videlicet /vi déeli set/ *adv* full form of **viz** [15C. < Latin < *vide* stem of *videre* 'to see' + *licet* 'it is permissible']

video /víddi ō/ *n* (*plural* -**os**) **1.** VISUAL PART OF TELEVISION the visual part of a television broadcast **2.** SOMETHING RECORDED ONTO VIDEOTAPE something that has been recorded on videotape, especially a feature film or a short promotional film made to accompany a newly issued pop record ○ *a video of my brother's wedding* **3.** VIDEO CASSETTE videotape, or a video cassette (*informal*) ○ *now available to rent or buy on video* **4.** COMPUT IMAGES ON COMPUTER SCREEN the text and graphics images that appear on a computer screen **5.** same as **video recorder** (*informal*) **6.** IMAGE REPRODUCTION INDUSTRY the industry of recording and broadcasting visual information and entertainment, especially that which can be viewed on a television ○ *a star of stage, screen, and video* ■ *adj* **1.** RELATING TO VISUAL IMAGE REPRODUCTION relating to the recording or broadcasting of visual information or entertainment by means of videotape or television **2.** RELATING TO VIDEO FREQUENCIES relating to or using video frequencies ■ *vt* (-**os**, -**oing**, -**oed**) RECORD SOMETHING ON VIDEO to record something on videotape [Mid-20C. < Latin *videre* 'to see', after AUDIO]

video adapter *n* COMPUT same as **graphics card**

video arcade *n* a place where people pay to play video games

video blog *n* a weblog that uses video as a means of communication, e.g. to conduct an interview or illustrate a story (*informal*)

video camera *n* a camera that records onto videotape

video card *n* COMPUT same as **graphics card**

video cassette *n* a flat rectangular plastic cassette containing two tape reels and a magnetic videotape

video cassette recorder *n* HOUSEHOLD full form of **VCR**

video conferencing *n* the holding of meetings in which the participants are in different places but are connected by audio and video links —**video conference** *n*

videodisk /víddi ō disk/, **videodisc** *n* an optical disk that can store full-motion video and audio

video display terminal *n* a device used to display data from and enter data into a computer, consisting of a visual display such as a cathode-ray tube and a keyboard, mouse, or touch-screen

video frequency *n* a frequency in the range of signals used to carry the image and synchronizing pulses in a television broadcasting system. Video frequencies range from the very high to the ultra high in the United States and are found in two ultra high bands in Europe.

video game *n* an electronic or computerized game, usually controlled by a microprocessor, played by making images move on a computer or television screen or, for hand-held games, on a liquid-crystal display

videography /víddi óggrəfi/ *n* N Am the art or practice of using a video camera to make films or programmes —**videographer** *n*

video jockey *n* somebody who plays videos, especially music videos, on television

video nasty *n* a film on videotape that contains explicitly violent or pornographic scenes (*informal*)

videophile /víddi ō fīl/ *n* somebody who enjoys watching or making video recordings

videophone /víddi ō fōn/ *n* a communications device that can transmit and receive both video and audio signals using a camera, receiver, and screen

video recorder *n* a tape recorder that can record and play video cassettes through a standard television receiver

videotape /víddi ō tayp/ *n* magnetic tape on which pictures and sound can be recorded ■ *vt* (**-tapes, -taping, -taped**) to make a recording of something on videotape

video tape recorder *n* a tape recorder that can record and play back images and sound using magnetic tape

videotext /víddi ō tekst/ *n* a communications service linked to an adapted television receiver or video display terminal by telephone or cable television lines to allow access to pages of information. Systems can be one-way, allowing only for the display of selected information, or on-line or interactive, allowing for two-way communication.

video vérité /-vérri tay/ *n* the use in video documentaries of the realistic unrehearsed portrayal of people and situations [After CINÉMA VÉRITÉ]

vide supra /veédi soópra, vídi-/ *vi* a term used to refer a reader to an earlier place in a text [< Latin, 'see above!']

vidette *n* ARMY another spelling of **vedette** (sense 1)

vidicon /víddi kon/ *n* a light-sensitive television camera tube in which an image is stored on a photoconductive plate as an electric charge pattern that is scanned by an electron beam and transmitted. These tubes have been replaced by more reliable solid-state television cameras using semiconductor charge-coupled devices. [Mid-20C. < VIDEO + ICONOSCOPE]

~~vidio~~ incorrect spelling of **video**

Vidor /veéd awr/, **King** (1894–1982) US film director. His films spanned the period from the silent era to the television age. Full name **Vidor, King Wallis**

   'Marriage isn't a word...it's a *sentence*!'
   [King Vidor, *The Crowd*; 1928]

vie /ví/ (**vies, vying, vied**) *vi* to strive for superiority or compete with somebody or something [Mid-16C. Shortening of obsolete *envie* < Old French *envier* 'raise the bid (at cards), challenge' < Latin *invitare* 'entertain, feast'] —**vier** *n*

~~viel~~ incorrect spelling of **veil**

Vienna /vi énna/ capital city of Austria, located in the east of the country, on the River Danube. Population: 1,562,482 (2001). —**Viennese** /veé a neéz/ *n, adj*

Vienna circle *n* the leading school of logical positivists of the 1920s and 1930s [Because based at Vienna University]

Vienna sausage *n* a small spicy sausage like a frankfurter, often served as a snack or hors d'oeuvre

Vientiane /vyén tyaán/ capital city of Laos, in the central part of the country, on the Mekong River. Population: 640,000 (2000).

Vieques, Isla de /vee áy kayss/ island of Puerto Rico off the eastern coast of the main island, used until May of 2003 as a bombing test range by the US Navy. Area: 135 sq. km/52 sq. mi. Population: 8,602 (1990). Official name **Isla de Vieques**

Viet. *abbr* **1.** Vietnam **2.** PEOPLES, LANG Vietnamese

Vietcong /vyet kóng/ (*plural same*), **Viet Cong** *n* a member or supporter of the Communist-led armed forces of the National Liberation Front of South Vietnam that fought to unite the country with North Vietnam between 1954 and 1976 [Mid-20C. < Vietnamese *Viêt-công*, shortening of *Viêt-Nam Công Sam* 'Vietnamese Communist']

Vietminh /vyét mín/ (*plural same*), **Viet Minh** *n* a member or supporter of the Vietnamese armed forces led by Ho Chi Minh that resisted and defeated first the Japanese and then the French between 1941 and 1954. The Vietminh operated from a base in southern China during World War II and employed guerrilla tactics similar to the Maoists in China. [Mid-20C. < Vietnamese *Viêt Minh*, shortening of *Viêt-Nam Dôc-Lâp Dông-Minh* 'Vietnam Independence Federation']

Vietnam

Vietnam /vyet nám/ country in Southeast Asia, on the South China Sea, south of China and east of Cambodia and Laos. Language: Vietnamese. Currency: new dong. Capital: Hanoi. Population: 81,624,716 (2003). Area: 331,690 sq. km/128,066 sq. mi. Official name **Socialist Republic of Vietnam**

Vietnamese /vyétna meéz/ *adj* **1.** OF VIETNAM relating to Vietnam, or its people or culture **2.** OF VIETNAMESE LANGUAGE relating to the official language of Vietnam ■ *n* (*plural same*) **1.** SOMEBODY FROM VIETNAM somebody who comes from Vietnam **2.** OFFICIAL LANGUAGE OF VIETNAM the Austro-Asiatic official language of Vietnam. Native speakers: 60 million.

Vietnamese potbellied pig *n* ZOOL same as **potbellied pig**

Vietnam War *n* a conflict in which the Communist forces of North Vietnam and guerrillas in South Vietnam fought against the non-Communist forces of South Vietnam and the United States. It began in 1954 and ended in 1975 in a Communist victory.

vieux jeu /vyúr zhúr, vyô zhô/ *adj* no longer fashionable [< French, 'old game']

view /vyoo/ *n* **1.** RANGE OF VISION the range or extent of somebody's ability to see something ○ *As we rounded the bend the mountains came into view.* **2.** SCENE a scene or an area that can be seen, especially one that is pleasing or impressive ○ *We have a wonderful view of the sea from our balcony.* **3.** OPINION somebody's opinion or judgment on something or particular way of interpreting or thinking about something (*often used in the plural*) ○ *His superiors took the view that he had made an error.* ○ *a person with strong political views* **4.** ACT OF LOOKING AT SOMETHING an act of looking at or inspecting something **5.** PERSPECTIVE a particular position or angle from which something is seen ○ *a bird's eye view* **6.** PICTORIAL REPRESENTATION a painting, drawing, or photograph of a scene or building **7.** SURVEY a general survey of a subject ■ *v* (**views, viewing, viewed**) **1.** *vt* REGARD SOMETHING IN PARTICULAR WAY to have a particular opinion of or attitude to somebody or something, or interpret something in a particular way ○ *She viewed his motives with suspicion.* ○ *The committee views this proposal as an attempt to undermine its authority.* **2.** *vt* OBSERVE SOMETHING to see or look at something, especially from a particular angle or location or using a particular device ○ *viewed from above* ○ *viewed the specimen through a microscope* **3.** *vt* INSPECT SOMETHING to make an inspection or examination of something, often with the intention of buying it ○ *The prospective buyers have arranged to view the house tomorrow morning.* **4.** *vti* WATCH TELEVISION to watch television, or watch something on television **5.** *vt* REVIEW SOMETHING to make a mental survey of something or of a range of things [15C. < Old French *vêue*, past participle of *vêoir* 'see' < Latin *videre*] —**viewless** *adj* ◇ **in view of something** because of something, or bearing something in mind ◇ **on view** put somewhere so as to be seen ◇ **take a dim view of somebody** *or* **something** to consider somebody or something with disapproval ◇ **with a view to something** with the aim, intention, or hope of doing or achieving something

CULTURAL NOTE *A Room with a View*, a novel (1908) by E. M. Forster. It describes how a young Englishwoman's visit to Italy and her encounter there with a young unconventional expatriate encourage her to rebel against the emotionally stifling conventions of her upper-class background. It was made into a film by Ismail Merchant and James Ivory in 1985.

viewable /vyoó ab'l/ *adj* **1.** able to be seen or inspected **2.** of a good enough standard, or in a good enough condition, to be watched

viewdata /vyoó dayta/ *n* an interactive information system in which text and graphic data stored in a central computer are transmitted over telephone lines to be displayed on a modified home television receiver. Typical applications include airline and theatre reservations, financial transactions, and access to news reports of current events.

viewer /vyoó ar/ *n* **1.** SPECTATOR somebody who watches something such as television, a film, or an event **2.** OPTICAL DEVICE an optical device for illuminating and magnifying a photographic transparency, videotape, or motion picture film **3.** SOMEBODY WHO MAKES FORMAL INSPECTION somebody appointed, especially by a court, to inspect something such as property —**viewership** *n*

viewfinder /vyoó fīndər/ *n* a device on a camera that lets the user see what is being photographed

view halloo *interj* used during a fox hunt as a shout to signal that the fox has been seen breaking cover ■ *n* a shout of 'view halloo!'

viewing /vyoó ing/ *n* **1.** ACT OF LOOKING the act or an act of looking at, seeing, or inspecting something, or an opportunity to look at or inspect something **2.** WATCHING TELEVISION the act of watching television programmes **3.** TV SHOWS COLLECTIVELY television programmes considered collectively or with respect to their nature or quality

viewpoint /vyoó poynt/ *n* **1.** a personal perspective from which somebody considers something **2.** a place or position from which people can look at something

viewscreen /vyoó skreen/ *n* the screen on a digital camera on which the user can view the image he or she has just recorded

VIF *abbr* variable import fee

vigesimal /vī jéssim'l/ *adj* based on or reckoned in units of the number twenty [Mid-17C. < Latin *vigesimus*, variant of *vicesimus* 'twentieth' < *viginti* 'twenty']

vigia /vi jeé a/ *n* something marked on a chart as a hazard to navigation, although its existence, position, and nature are unconfirmed [Mid-19C. < Portuguese, 'lookout' < Latin *vigilia* (see VIGIL)]

vigil /víjjil/ *n* **1.** NIGHT WATCH a period spent in doing something through the night, e.g. watching, guarding, or praying **2.** FESTIVAL EVE the eve of some festivals and holy days, spent in prayer ■ **vigils** *npl* RELIGIOUS SERVICES AT NIGHT religious services or prayers at night, especially on the eve of a festival or holy day [13C. Via Old French *vigile* < medieval Latin *vigilia* 'eve of a holy day' < Latin, 'watchfulness' < *vigil* 'awake, alert']

vigilance /víjjilanss/ *n* the condition of being watchful and alert, especially to danger

vigilance committee *n* US a group of people who pursue and punish suspected or alleged criminals without having the legal authority to do so

vigilant /víjjilant/ *adj* watchful and alert, especially to guard against danger, difficulties, or errors [15C. < Latin *vigilant-*, present participle of *vigilare* 'keep awake' < *vigil* 'awake, alert'] —**vigilantly** *adv*

SYNONYMS See *cautious*.

vigilante /víjji lánti/ *n* **1.** somebody who punishes lawbreakers personally rather than relying on the legal authorities **2.** US a member of a vigilance committee [Mid-19C. < Spanish, 'watchman' < Latin *vigilant-* (see VIGILANT)] —**vigilantism** *n*

vign *abbr* ARCHIT vignette

Vigneaud ♦ du Vigneaud, Vincent

vigneron /veényə ron, -roN/ *n* a grower of grapes for use in making wine [15C. < French < *vigne* (see VINE)]

vignette /vin yét/ *n* **1.** SHORT ESSAY a short descriptive piece of literary writing **2.** BRIEF SCENE a brief scene from a film or play **3.** DESIGN ON BOOK PAGE a small decorative design printed at the beginning or end of a book or chapter of a book, or in the margin of a page **4.** UNBORDERED PICTURE a painting, drawing, or photograph that has no border but is gradually faded into its background at the edges **5.** ARCHITECTURAL ORNAMENTATION a carved architectural decoration in the form of tendrils and leaves ■ *vt*

(**-gnettes, -gnetting, -gnetted**) **1.** **FINISH PICTURE OFF BY SOFTENING EDGES** to finish a painting, drawing, or photograph by gradually fading it into its background at the edges rather than giving it a border **2.** **DESCRIBE SOMETHING BRIEFLY** to describe something in a brief but elegant way [Mid-18C. < French, 'small vine' (from such decorations in margins in early books) < *vigne* (see VINE)] —**vignetter** *n* —**vignettist** *n*

Vignola /vin yṓlə/, **Giacomo da** (1507–73) Italian architect. His work and writings influenced the development of the baroque style in architecture. Born **Barozzi, Giacomo**

Vigo /veégō/ city and port in the autonomous region of Galicia, northwestern Spain, on the Atlantic Ocean. Population: 288,324 (2002).

vigor *n* US spelling of **vigour**

vigorish /víggərish/ *n US* (*slang*) **1.** any additional payment that somebody is forced to make, e.g. a bribe or interest paid to a usurer **2.** a sum of money that a bookmaker or gambling establishment charges a customer for accepting a bet [Early 20C. Origin ?]

vigoroso /viggə rṓssō/ *adv* to be played with intensity and liveliness (*used as a musical direction*) [Early 18C. < Italian, 'vigorous' < medieval Latin *vigorosus* < Latin *vigor* (see VIGOUR)] —**vigoroso** *adj*

vigorous /víggərəss/ *adj* **1.** extremely strong and active, physically or mentally **2.** displaying or using great energy ○ *vigorous exercise* —**vigorously** *adv* —**vigorousness** *n*

vigour /víggər/ *n* **1.** **VITALITY** great physical or mental strength and energy **2.** **INTENSITY** intensity or forcefulness in the way something is done **3.** **ABILITY TO GROW** the ability of plants or animals to survive, grow, and thrive **4.** *US* **LEGAL VALIDITY** legal validity or force [14C. Via Old French < Latin *vigor* 'liveliness, energy' < *vigere* 'be lively']

Vijayawada /veéj ī ə waádə/ city in Krishna District, Andhra Pradesh State, southern India. Population: 1,011,152 (2001).

Viking /vīking/ *n* **1.** a member of a Scandinavian people who carried out seaborne raids of northwestern Europe between the 8th and 11th centuries AD, often settling in the areas they invaded, as in Britain. They usually came in longships and raided mainly coastal regions. **2.** LANG same as **Old Norse** **3.** either of two identical highly instrumented uncrewed US space probes to Mars, launched in 1975. The probes' orbiters photographed the surface of Mars and its satellites and mapped water vapour and surface temperature variations while the landers transmitted colour pictures and meteorological and soil data. [Early 19C. < Old Norse *víkingr*, either < *vík* 'creek, inlet' or < Old English *wīc* 'camp']

vil. *abbr* village

~~**vilage**~~ incorrect spelling of **village**

vile /vīl/ (**viler, vilest**) *adj* **1.** **DISGUSTING** causing disgust or abhorrence ○ *vile smell* **2.** **WICKED** despicable or shameful ○ *vile crimes* **3.** **VERY UNPLEASANT** extremely unpleasant to experience ○ *vile weather* **4.** **WORTHLESS** of little or no worth (*archaic*) [13C. Via French < Latin *vilis* 'of little value, cheap, base'] —**vilely** *adv* —**vileness** *n*

SYNONYMS See *mean*[2].

vilify /vílli fī/ (**-fies, -fying, -fied**) *vt* to make malicious and abusive statements about somebody [15C. < late Latin *vilificare* 'hold cheap' < Latin *vilis* 'worthless'] —**vilification** /víllifi káysh'n/ *n* —**vilifier** *n*

SYNONYMS See *malign*.

vilipend /vílli pend/ (**-pends, -pending, -pended**) *vt* (*literary*) **1.** to treat or view somebody with contempt **2.** to make malicious or contemptuous statements about somebody [15C. Via Old French *vilipender* < Latin *vilipendere* 'consider base' < *vilis* 'base, cheap']

vill *abbr* village

villa /víllə/ *n* **1.** **HOLIDAY HOME** a house rented for a holiday, especially one rented abroad **2.** **EXPENSIVE HOUSE** a large luxurious house in the country **3.** **HOUSE IN RESIDENTIAL AREA** a detached or semidetached house in a residential area built in the late 19th or early 20th century (*dated*) **4.** *NZ* **SUBURBAN HOME** a detached suburban house built in the late 19th or early 20th century usually with a veranda and bay window **5.** *Aus* BUILDINGS same as **villa home** **6.** **ROMAN HOUSE** in ancient Rome or one of its colonies, a country house with living quarters, farm buildings, and a courtyard [Early 17C. Via Italian < Latin, 'country home, farm']

villa-flotilla *n* a holiday in which a period spent ashore in a hotel, villa, or apartment is followed by a period spent afloat on a sailing boat

village /víllij/ *n* **1.** **RURAL COMMUNITY** a group of houses and other buildings in a rural area, smaller than a town but larger than a hamlet **2.** **INHABITANTS OF VILLAGE** all of the people who live in a village **3.** **TEMPORARY COMMUNITY** a place where people live temporarily as a community, e.g. an apartment complex for the use of athletes taking part in the Olympic Games **4.** **ANIMAL DWELLINGS** a group of bird or animal dwellings [14C. Via French < Latin *villaticum* 'farmstead' < *villa* 'country home, farm'] —**villager** *n*

village college *n* in Cambridgeshire, an educational centre, with recreational facilities, available to the whole community

Villahermosa /veé ə hair mṓssə/ city and capital of Tabasco State, southeastern Mexico. Population: 536,498 (2000). Former name **San Juan Bautista**

villa home *n Aus* a modern suburban home built on a small plot of land and usually separated from a neighbouring house by its garage

villain /víllən/ *n* **1.** **EVIL CHARACTER** an evil character in a novel, film, play, or other story, especially one who is the main enemy of the hero **2.** **CONTEMPTIBLE PERSON** any person regarded as evil or otherwise contemptible **3.** **CAUSE OF PROBLEM** somebody or something that causes a specific problem ○ *A virus is the villain responsible for the rapidly spreading epidemic.* **4.** **MISCHIEVOUS PERSON** somebody who is mischievous or troublesome (*humorous*) **5.** same as **criminal** (*slang*) **6.** HIST same as **villein** [14C. Via Old French *vilein* 'feudal serf' < medieval Latin *villanus* 'farmhand' < Latin *villa* 'country home, farm']

villainage /víllənij/ *n* HIST same as **villeinage**

villainess /víllə ness/ *n* **1.** an evil woman character in a novel, film, play, or other story, especially one who is the main enemy of the hero **2.** any woman regarded as evil or otherwise contemptible

villainous /víllənəss/ *adj* **1.** characteristic of an evil or contemptible person **2.** obnoxious or unpleasant —**villainously** *adv* —**villainousness** *n*

villainy /vílləni/ *n* **1.** **EVIL CONDUCT** behaviour characteristic of an evil or contemptible person **2.** **STATE OF BEING EVIL** the state of being evil or contemptible **3.** (*plural* **villainies**) **EVIL ACT** an evil, immoral, or criminal act

Villa-Lobos /víllə lṓb oss/, **Heitor** (1887–1959) Brazilian composer. His prolific output was much influenced by popular Brazilian and Native South American music. His work includes the nine suites entitled *Bachianas brasileiras* (1930–45).

~~**villan**~~ incorrect spelling of **villain**

villanelle /víllə nél/ *n* a 19-line poem, originally French, that uses only two rhymes and consists of five three-line stanzas and a final quatrain. The first and third lines of the first stanza are alternately repeated as a refrain that closes the following stanzas, and are joined as a final couplet of the quatrain. [Late 16C. Via French < Italian *villanella* 'old rustic (Italian) song' < *villano* 'peasant' < medieval Latin *villanus* (see VILLAIN)]

Villanovan /víllə nṓv'n/ *adj* belonging to or characteristic of an early Iron Age culture that existed near Bologna, Italy, in which bronze was used and also, in a simple way, iron ■ *n* a member of the Villanovan culture [Early 20C. After *Villanova*, town in NE Italy]

Villarrica /vilə ríkə/ city in southern Paraguay. Population: 21,203 (1982).

~~**villege**~~ incorrect spelling of **village**

villein /víllən, víllayn/ (*plural* **-leins** or **-lains**) *n* a feudal serf who had the status of a freeman except in relation to his lord, to whom he owed dues and services in exchange for land [14C. Variant of VILLAIN]

villeinage /víllənij/ *n* **1.** the status of being a villein in feudal society **2.** the form of feudal tenure by which a villein held land

villi BIOL plural of **villus**

villiform /vílli fawrm/ *adj* in the form of or resembling a minute projection (**villus**) [Mid-19C. < VILLUS]

Villon /veé yoN/, **François** (1431?–63?) French poet. He wrote lyric poetry notable for its fresh interpretation of medieval verse forms and its frank expression of feeling. He was repeatedly arrested for criminal acts, and nothing is known of him after he was banished from Paris in 1463. Born **Montcorbier, François de,** *or* **Loges, François des**

> 'I know everything except myself.'
> [François Villon, 'Ballade of Small Talk'; 1460?]

villose *adj* BIOL same as **villous** [Early 18C. < Latin *villosus* (see VILLOUS)]

villosity /vi lóssəti/ (*plural* **-ties**) *n* BIOL **1.** **HAIRINESS** the condition of being covered in long shaggy hairs **2.** **BEING COVERED WITH PROJECTIONS** the state of being covered with minute projections **3.** **COATING OF PROJECTIONS** a surface or coating of very fine projections resembling hairs **4.** **PART RESEMBLING HAIR** a fine projection that resembles a hair [Late 18C. < Latin *villosus* (see VILLOUS)]

villous /vílləss/ *adj* **1.** covered with long shaggy hairs **2.** relating to, resembling, or covered with minute projections [14C. < Latin *villosus* 'shaggy' < *villus* 'shaggy hair'] —**villously** *adv*

villus /vílləss/ (*plural* **-li** /-lī/) *n* **1.** a vascular protuberance growing out from some mucous membranes, e.g. from that of the small intestine of some vertebrates or from the chorion that surrounds an embryo **2.** a fine part resembling a hair, growing from the surface of a plant [Early 18C. < Latin, 'shaggy hair']

Vilnius /vílni əss/ capital city of Lithuania, situated in the southeast of the country, near the border with Belarus. Population: 577,970 (2000).

vim /vim/ *n* exuberant vitality and energy (*informal*) [Mid-19C. Probably < Latin, form of *vis* 'power, strength']

vin. *abbr* FOOD vinegar

vin- *prefix* same as **vini-** (*used before vowels*)

vina *n* MUSIC another spelling of **veena**

vinaceous /vī náyshəss/ *adj* **1.** of the nature of or containing wine **2.** of the colour of red wine [Late 17C. < Latin *vinaceus* < *vinum* 'wine']

~~**vinagrette**~~ incorrect spelling of **vinaigrette**

vinaigrette /vinnay grét, vínni-/ *n* **1.** a salad dressing made with vinegar, oil, salt, pepper, and sometimes other seasonings **2.** a small bottle or box with a perforated cap, used to hold aromatic substances such as smelling salts or vinegar [Late 17C. < French, 'little vinegar' < *vinaigre* < Old French *vyn egre* (see VINEGAR)]

vinasse /vi náss/ *n* the residue left in a still after the distillation of an alcoholic beverage, especially brandy. It is used as a fertilizer and is a source of potassium salts. [Via French < Provençal *vinassa* < Latin *vinaceus* (see VINACEOUS)]

vinblastine /vin blás teen/ *n* an alkaloid drug from the Madagascar periwinkle. Use: cancer treatment. Formula: $C_{46}H_{58}N_4O_9$. [Mid-20C. < modern Latin *Vinca* (see VINCA) + LEUCOBLAST]

vinca /víngkə/ *n* PLANTS same as **periwinkle**[2] [Mid-19C. < modern Latin *Vinca* < late Latin *pervinca* (see PERIWINKLE[2])]

Vincennes /vin sénz, vaN sénn/ town in north-central France, near Paris. It is the site of a medieval castle that was used as a royal residence until 1740. Population: 42,651 (1990).

Vincent de Paul /vínssənt də páwl, vaaN saN də páwl/, **St** (1581–1660) French priest. He was the founder of the Congregation of the Mission (1625), also called the Vincentians.

> 'Mental disease is no different to bodily disease and Christianity demanded of the humane and powerful to protect, and the skilful to relieve, the one as well as the other.'
> [St Vincent de Paul. Quoted in *The Life and Works of St. Vincent de Paul*, Père Coste; 1934]

Vincentian /vin sénsh'n/ *n* a member of the Congregation of the Mission, a Roman Catholic order of missionary priests founded by St Vincent de Paul [Mid-19C. After St VINCENT DE PAUL] —**Vincentian** *adj*

Vincent's angina, **Vincent's infection** *n* a painful mouth inflammation with ulcers and gum damage. Two organisms that are normally present cause the condition only when somebody has a vitamin B deficiency or an immune deficiency. [Early 20C. After Jean Hyacinthe *Vincent* (1862–1950), French physician]

Vinci ◆ **Leonardo da Vinci**

vincible /vínssəb'l/ *adj* able to be defeated or conquered (*literary*) [Mid-16C. < Latin *vincibilis* < *vincere* 'conquer'] —**vincibility** /vínssə bílləti/ *n*

vincristine /vin krís teen/ *n* an alkaloid drug similar to vinblastine. It works by blocking cell division (**mitosis**) and is highly toxic. Use: cancer treatment. Formula: $C_{46}H_{56}N_4O_{10}$. [Mid-20C. < modern Latin *Vinca* (see VINCA) + Latin *crista* 'crest']

vinculum /víngkyŏŏləm/ (*plural* **-la** /-lə/) *n* **1.** a horizontal line above two or more members of a compound mathematical expression, used to show that the expression is to be treated as a single term. Parentheses, brackets, and braces are used more frequently for this purpose than is the vinculum. **2.** a band of tissue, especially a ligament [Mid-17C. < Latin, 'fetter, bond' < *vincire* 'tie, fasten']

vindaloo /víndə lóo/ *n* a very hot curry sauce made with coriander, red chilli, ginger, and other spices, or a dish cooked in this [Late 19C. Via Konkani *vindalu* < Portuguese *vinho de alho*, a wine and garlic sauce, literally 'wine of garlic']

vin de garde /ván də gaárd/ (*plural* **vins de garde** /*pronunc. same*/) *n* a wine that improves with ageing [< French, 'wine for keeping']

vin de pays /ván də páy ee/ (*plural* **vins de pays** /*pronunc. same*/), **vin du pays** /-dŏŏ-/ (*plural* **vins du pays** /-dŏŏ-/) *n* a French wine with the third highest grade of classification, which guarantees its origin [< French, 'wine of (the) region']

vin d'honneur /ván do núr/ *n* wine that is served in honour of a guest, e.g. at a celebratory dinner [< French, literally 'wine of honour']

vindicate /víndi kayt/ (**-cates, -cating, -cated**) *vt* **1.** SHOW SOMEBODY TO BE BLAMELESS to clear somebody or something of blame, guilt, suspicion, or doubt **2.** JUSTIFY SOMEBODY OR SOMETHING to show that somebody or something is justified or correct **3.** UPHOLD SOMETHING to defend or maintain something such as a cause or rights [Mid-16C. < Latin *vindicat-*, past participle of *vindicare* 'claim, set free, avenge' < *vindic-* 'avenger'] —**vindicable** *adj* —**vindicator** *n* —**vindicatory** /-kətəri, -kaytəri/ *adj*

vindication /víndi káysh'n/ *n* **1.** the act of vindicating somebody or something, or the condition of being vindicated **2.** evidence or an argument used to vindicate somebody or something

vindictive /vin díktiv/ *adj* **1.** VENGEFUL looking for revenge or done through a desire for revenge **2.** SPITEFUL feeling, showing, or done through a desire to hurt somebody **3.** LAW MEANT TO PUNISH describes damages awarded by a court that are set higher than the amount necessary to compensate the victim, in order to punish the defendant [Early 17C. < Latin *vindicta* 'revenge'] —**vindictively** *adv* —**vindictiveness** *n*

vine /vīn/ *n* **1.** CLIMBING PLANT a plant that supports itself by climbing, twining, or creeping along a surface **2.** STEM the weak flexible stem of a vine **3.** PLANTS same as **grapevine** (sense 1) **4.** GRAPEVINES grapevines considered collectively [13C. Via French < Latin *vinea* 'vine, vineyard' < *vinum* 'wine'] —**viny** *adj*

vinedresser /vīn dressər/ *n* somebody who tends and prunes grapevines

vinegar /vínnigər/ *n* **1.** SOUR-TASTING LIQUID a sour-tasting liquid that is used to flavour and preserve foods. It is a dilute acetic acid made by fermenting beer, wine, or cider. **2.** ILL TEMPER sourness or ill-tempered behaviour or speech **3.** *N Am* VITALITY exuberant energy and enthusiasm [13C. < Old French *vyn egre* 'sour wine' < Latin *vinum acre*] —**vinegarish** *adj*

vinegar eel, **vinegar worm** *n* a very small nematode worm that feeds on bacteria that cause fermentation, especially in vinegar. Latin name: *Anguillula aceti*.

~~vinegarette~~ incorrect spelling of **vinaigrette**

vinegary /vínnigəri/ *adj* **1.** with a sour taste or smell like vinegar **2.** showing an unpleasant irritable disposition

vinery /vīnəri/ (*plural* **-ies**) *n* an area or building, especially a greenhouse, in which grapevines are grown

vine weevil *n* a black flightless weevil that produces adult females only and has creamy-white larvae that destroy the roots of many different plants. Latin name: *Otiorhycus sulcatus*.

vineyard /vínnyərd, -yaard/ *n* a piece of land where grapevines are grown

vingt-et-un /vánt ay ÚN/ *n* CARDS same as **pontoon**[2] [Late 18C. < French, 'twenty-one']

vinho verde /vínnyō vúrdi/ *n* a light dry typically white wine from northern Portugal [Mid-20C. < Portuguese, 'green wine' (referring to its youthfulness)]

vini- *prefix* wine, grapes ○ *viniculture* [< Latin *vinum*]

viniculture /vínni kulchər/ *n* AGRIC same as **viticulture** —**vinicultural** /vínni kúlchrəl/ *adj* —**viniculturist** /vínni kúlchrist/ *n*

vinify /vínni fī/ (**-fies, -fying, -fied**) *vt* to ferment grape juice, or another liquid, into wine —**vinification** /vínnifi káysh'n/ *n*

Vinland /vínnlənd/ part of North America, now northern Newfoundland, first seen by the Norse voyager Bjarni Herjólfsson during a voyage from Iceland to Greenland in about AD 986. The Icelandic explorer Leif Ericson explored the Newfoundland and Labrador coasts several years later.

vino /véenō/ *n* wine, especially cheap wine (*informal*) [Late 19C. < Italian, 'wine']

vin ordinaire /ván awrdi náir/ *n* cheap table wine, especially from France [Early 19C. < French, 'ordinary wine']

vinosity /vī nóssəti/ *n* the distinctive and essential character of wine, including qualities such as body, colour, and taste

vinous /vīnəss/ *adj* **1.** relating to, typical of, or containing wine **2.** tending to drink a lot of wine, or caused by wine-drinking [Mid-17C. < Latin *vinum* 'wine'] —**vinously** *adv* —**vinousness** *n*

Vinson Massif /vínss'n máss eef/ highest mountain in Antarctica, in the central Ellsworth Mountains. Height: 4,897 m/16,066 ft.

vintage /víntij/ *n* **1.** WINE PRODUCTION YEAR the year in which the grapes used in making a specific wine were harvested **2.** WINE FROM PARTICULAR YEAR wine made from a particular harvest of grapes **3.** GRAPE HARVESTING the harvesting of grapes for wine **4.** PERIOD the period of time when something appeared or began, or when somebody was born or flourished **5.** GROUP SHARING CHARACTERISTICS a group of people or things that are similar or belong to the same period of time (*informal*) ■ *adj* **1.** GOOD FOR WINE produced from or characterized by a good harvest of grapes for winemaking, so that the wine does not have to be improved by blending with wine from another harvest ○ *a vintage year* **2.** OF BEST representing what is best or most characteristic of somebody or something ○ *a vintage performance* **3.** CLASSIC recognized as being of high quality and lasting appeal ○ *a series of vintage Laurel and Hardy comedies* **4.** OUT OF DATE no longer fashionable or modern ■ *vt* (**-tages, -taging, -taged**) **1.** GATHER GRAPES to harvest grapes to make wine **2.** MAKE WINE to make wine from harvested grapes [14C. Alteration (influenced by VINTNER) of *vendage* < Old French *vendange* < Latin *vindemia* 'grape-gathering' < *vinum* 'wine' + *demere* 'take away'] —**vintager** *n*

vintage car *n* an old car, especially one built between 1919 and 1930

vintage year *n* **1.** a year in which the wine that is made is of excellent quality **2.** a year of extraordinary accomplishment or success

vintner /víntnər/ *n* a dealer in wines [15C. Via Old French *vinetier* < medieval Latin *vinetarius* < Latin *vinetum* 'vineyard' < *vinum* 'wine']

vinyl /vīn'l/ *n* **1.** CHEMICAL GROUP a univalent unsaturated chemical group or radical that is formed when one hydrogen atom is removed from ethylene. Formula: CH_2CH. **2.** COMPOUND USED IN PLASTICS a reactive compound that contains the vinyl group, usually in polymerized form. Use: plastics. **3.** PLASTIC MATERIAL a plastic material, made from a vinyl polymer **4.** PLASTIC RECORDS gramophone records made of a vinyl polymer, as opposed to compact discs [Mid-19C. < VINI- + -YL] —**vinyl** *adj* —**vinylic** /vī níllik/ *adj*

vinyl chloride *n* a colourless carcinogenic explosive flammable gas. Use: manufacture of polyvinyl chloride, adhesives, organic chemicals. Formula: CH_2:CHCl.

vinylidene /vī nílli deen/ *n* a bivalent chemical group or radical, made when two hydrogen atoms are removed from one carbon atom of ethylene. Formula: CH_2:C.

vinyl polymer, **vinyl resin** *n* an odourless tasteless thermoplastic material made by polymerizing compounds containing vinyl groups, e.g. PVC

Viognier /vee ón yáy/ *n* **1.** a typically dry white wine made from a variety of grape originally grown mainly in the Rhône valley of France but now cultivated elsewhere **2.** a white grape variety. Use: to make Viognier.

viol /vī əl/ *n* **1.** a member of a family of stringed instruments popular during the 16th and 17th centuries. Viols have a fretted fingerboard, a flat-backed body, six strings, and are played with a curved bow. They were the precursors of the violin family. **2.** MUSIC same as **viola da gamba** [15C. Via Old French *viole* < Old Provençal *viola*]

viola[1] /vi ólə/ *n* **1.** a stringed instrument slightly larger and lower in pitch than a violin. It is held under the chin and played with a bow. The viola is tuned an octave above the cello and is the alto of the violin family. **2.** MUSIC same as **viola da gamba** [Late 18C. Via Italian < Old Provençal]

viola[2] /vī ələ/ *n* a plant related to violets and pansies, especially one with small, white, yellow, or purple flowers. Genus: *Viola*. [15C. < Latin, 'violet']

violaceous /vī ə láyshəss/ *adj* relating to, belonging to, or typical of the family of plants that includes violets and pansies [Mid-17C. < Latin *violaceus* 'violet-coloured' < *viola* 'violet']

viola da braccio /vi ólə də bráchō/ (*plural* **violas da braccio**) *n* an old stringed instrument of the viol family, held against the shoulder when played [Mid-19C. < Italian, 'viol for (the) arm']

viola da gamba /vi ólə də gámbə/ (*plural* **violas da gamba**) *n* an old stringed bass instrument of the viol family, with a range similar to a cello [Late 16C. < Italian, 'viol for (the) leg']

viola d'amore /vi ólə da máwri/ (*plural* **violas d'amore**) *n* a fretless stringed instrument of the viol family with six or seven strings and a second set of strings that are not played but are made to vibrate by the first set (**sympathetic strings**) [Late 17C. < Italian, 'viol of love']

~~violance~~ incorrect spelling of **violence**

violate /vī ə layt/ (**-lates, -lating, -lated**) *vt* **1.** DISREGARD SOMETHING to act contrary to something such as a law, contract, or agreement, especially in a way that produces significant effects **2.** DISTURB SOMETHING to disturb or interrupt something in a rude or violent way **3.** DEFILE SOMETHING to treat something sacred with a lack of respect **4.** RAPE SOMEBODY to rape or sexually assault somebody (*formal*) [15C. < Latin *violatus*, past participle of *violare* 'treat with violence, injure'] —**violable** *adj* —**violative** *adj* —**violator** *n*

violation /vī ə láysh'n/ *n* **1.** the act or an example of violating somebody or something **2.** a crime or infringement of a law

violence /vī ələnss/ *n* **1.** PHYSICAL FORCE the use of physical force to injure somebody or damage something ○ *threats of violence* **2.** DESTRUCTIVE FORCE extreme, destructive, or uncontrollable force, especially of natural events ○ *the violence of the storm* **3.** FERVOUR intensity of feeling or expression ○ *the violence of her response to our suggestion* **4.** LAW ILLEGAL FORCE the illegal use of unjustified force, or the intimidating effect created by the threat of this ○ *robbery with violence* ◇ **do violence to something** to violate, harm, or damage something

violent /vī ələnt/ *adj* **1.** USING PHYSICAL FORCE using physical force to injure somebody or damage something

○ *violent crime* **2.** EMOTIONALLY INTENSE showing emotional intensity or strong feeling ○ *his violent objections to the plan* **3.** SHOWING DESTRUCTIVE FORCE showing extreme, destructive, or uncontrollable force ○ *a violent thunderstorm* **4.** INTENSE very intense or severe ○ *a violent headache* ○ *violent passion* **5.** CAUSED BY FORCE caused by force rather than natural causes ○ *met a violent death* [14C. < Latin *violentus* 'forcible, vehement'] —**violently** *adv*

violent storm *n* a storm that causes widespread damage with winds of force 11 on the Beaufort scale, reaching speeds of 103–117 kph/64–72 mph

violet

violet /ví əlet/ *n* **1.** FLOWERING PLANT a low-growing perennial plant. Flowers: irregular, usually purplish-blue. Genus: *Viola*. **2.** PLANT RESEMBLING VIOLET a plant that looks like a violet but is not necessarily related to it, e.g. an African violet **3.** PURPLISH-BLUE COLOUR a deep purplish-blue colour [14C. < Old French *violete*, diminutive of *viole* < Latin *viola* 'violet'] —**violet** *adj*

violin /vī ə lín/ *n* **1.** a wooden musical instrument with four strings and an unfretted fingerboard, held under the player's chin and played with a bow. The violin has the highest range in the family of stringed instruments to which it gives its name. **2.** a musician who plays a violin, especially in an orchestra [Late 16C. < Italian *violino*, diminutive of *viola* (see VIOLA¹)] —**violinist** *n*

violist¹ /vi ólist/ *n* N Am somebody who plays the viola [Late 20C. < VIOLA¹]

violist² /vī əlist/ *n* somebody who plays the viol [Mid-17C. < VIOL]

violoncello /vī ələn chéllō/ (*plural* **-los**) *n* MUSIC same as **cello** (*formal*) [Early 18C. < Italian, diminutive of *violone* (see VIOLONE)]

violone /vī əlōn/ *n* the double-bass viol, larger and with a deeper range than the viola da gamba [Early 18C. < Italian, 'large viola' < *viola* (see VIOLA¹)]

VIP *abbr* **1.** MED vasoactive intestinal peptide **2.** very important person

vipassana /vi pássənə/, **Vipassana** *n* Theravada Buddhist meditation that aims at concentrating the mind on the body

viper

viper /vípər/ *n* **1.** POISONOUS SNAKE a snake with hollow fangs that it uses to inject venom into its victim when it bites. Native to: Europe, Asia, Africa. Family: Viperidae. **2.** REPT same as **adder**² **3.** POISONOUS SNAKE NOT OF VIPER FAMILY a poisonous snake belonging to a family other than the vipers proper, e.g. the horned viper **4.** ZOOL same as **pit viper 5.** OFFENSIVE TERM an offensive term for somebody who is considered to be malicious, treacherous, or ungrateful

(*offensive literary*) [Early 16C. Via Old French *vipere* < Latin *vipera* 'snake', contraction of assumed *vivipera* 'live-bearing' (from the ancient belief that snakes bore live young) < *vivus* 'alive'] —**viperous** *adj*

viperish /vípərish/ *adj* **1.** malicious or spiteful **2.** characteristic of or resembling a viper —**viperishly** *adv*

viper's bugloss *n* a widely naturalized weed with rough foliage. Flowers: blue, tubular, in spikes. Native to: Europe, Asia. Latin name: *Echium vulgare*.

VIR *abbr* Victoria Empress and Queen [Latin *Victoria Imperatrix Regina*]

Vir. *abbr* **1.** LITERAT Virgil **2.** ASTRON Virgo

vir- *prefix* same as **viro-** (*used before vowels*)

viraemia /vī reèmi ə/ *n* the presence of viruses in the bloodstream [Mid-20C. < modern Latin < VIRUS] —**viraemic** *adj*

virago /vi raàgō/ (*plural* **-goes** or **-gos**) *n* **1.** an offensive term that deliberately insults a woman by implying that her temperament or behaviour is violent **2.** a woman who is strong and brave (*archaic*) [Pre-12C. < Latin *vir* 'man, husband'] —**viraginous** /vi rájjənəss/ *adj*

viral /vírəl/ *adj* **1.** CAUSED BY VIRUS relating to, typical of, or caused by a virus **2.** OF UNWANTED FORWARDED E-MAIL of or using unsolicited e-mails that are forwarded spontaneously from one user to another ■ *n* MESSAGE INTENDED TO BE SPREAD an e-mail message, usually in the form of advertising, that contains elements that make recipients want to forward it to others (*informal*) —**virally** *adv*

viral load *n* the amount of HIV in a person's blood, usually measured by a test that determines the number of copies of HIV in one millilitre of blood

viral marketing *n* **1.** the distribution over the Internet of a service that becomes so immediately desirable that it leads to an enormous growth in traffic **2.** a form of marketing in which an organization's customers, wittingly or unwittingly, act as advertisers for its products by spreading knowledge of them by word of mouth [< the idea of a virus spreading rapidly]

viral pneumonia *n* an infection of the lungs caused by a virus

Virchow /vúrkō/, **Rudolf** (1821–1902) German pathologist and anthropologist. His textbook on cellular pathology (1850) was the foundation text of the field. He also published significant works in anthropology and archaeology. Full name **Virchow, Rudolf Carl**

'As long as vitalism and spiritualism are open questions so long will the gateway of science be open to mysticism.'
[Rudolf Virchow. Quoted in *Bulletin of the New York Academy of Medicine*, F. H. Garrison; 1928]

virelay /vírrə lay/ *n* an old French verse form consisting of short lines arranged in stanzas with two rhymes, the end rhyme being repeated in the first line of the next stanza [14C. < French *virelai*]

virement /vírmənt, veèr maaN/ *n* an authorized transfer of funds from one use to another [Early 20C. < French, 'turning, transfer' < *virer* 'turn, veer']

viremia *n* MED US spelling of **viraemia**

Viren /veéran/, **Lasse** (*b.* 1949) Finnish athlete. An Olympic gold medallist in the 5,000 and 10,000 metres (1972 and 1976), he set several world records in both events. Full name **Viren, Lasse Artturi**

vireo /vírri ō/ (*plural* **-os**) *n* a small songbird with greyish or greenish feathers that eats insects. Native to: Americas. Genus: *Vireo*. [Mid-19C. Via modern Latin < Latin, a bird (probably the greenfinch) < *virere* 'be green']

virescent /vī réss'nt/ *adj* **1.** being or becoming green **2.** used to describe plant parts that are not normally green but are turned green by disease [Early 19C. < Latin *virescent-*, present participle of *virescere* 'become green'] —**virescence** *n*

virga /vúrgə/ *n* vertical trails of rain, snow, or ice from the underside of a cloud that evaporate before reaching the ground [Mid-20C. < Latin, 'rod, staff, twig']

virgate¹ /vúrgət/ *adj* describes plant parts that are

long and thin like a rod (*technical*) [Early 19C. < Latin *virgatus* < *virga* 'rod, staff']

virgate² /vúrgət/ *n* an old English land measure thought to be the equivalent of about 12 hectares/30 acres [Mid-17C. < medieval Latin *virgata* < Latin *virga* 'rod']

Virgil /vúrjil/, **Vergil** (70–19 BC) Roman poet. Regarded as the finest Latin poet of his age, he wrote pastoral verse before composing his great mythological epic *The Aeneid*, which tells the story of the seven-year wanderings of Aeneas after the fall of Troy. Full name **Publius Vergilius Maro** —**Virgilian** /vur jílli ən/ *adj*

'I sing of arms and the man....'
[Virgil, *The Aeneid*; 19 BC]

'Do not trust the horse, Trojans. Whatever it is, I / fear the Greeks even when they bring gifts.'
[Virgil, *The Aeneid*; 19 BC]

virgin /vúrjin/ *n* **1.** SOMEBODY WHO HAS NEVER HAD SEX somebody who has never had sexual intercourse **2.** RELIG RELIGIOUS WOMAN COMMITTED TO CHASTITY a woman who has taken a vow of chastity for religious reasons **3.** ZOOL FEMALE ANIMAL a female animal that has never copulated **4.** INSECTS FEMALE INSECT a female insect that produces fertile eggs without the help of a male ■ *adj* **1.** OF VIRGIN relating to or characteristic of a virgin **2.** PURE in a pure, natural, or clean state ○ *virgin snow* **3.** ENVIRON NOT TOUCHED BY HUMANS describes a natural area that has never been explored or exploited by humans **4.** OCCURRING FOR FIRST TIME happening or carried out first or for the first time **5.** FOOD FROM FIRST PRESSING describes vegetable oils that come from the first pressing of fruit, leaves, or seeds without the use of heat **6.** METALL PRODUCED DIRECTLY FROM ORE describes metals produced directly from an ore, not from scrap metal **7.** MINERALS UNALLOYED found in a pure unmixed state **8.** PHYS NEVER HAVING COLLIDED describes a neutron that has never been in a collision and therefore retains the energy with which it started [12C. Via Old French *virgine* < Latin *virgin-*, stem of *virgo* 'maiden']

Virgin /vúrjin/ *n* **1.** CHR same as **Virgin Mary 2.** ZODIAC, ASTRON same as **Virgo**

virginal¹ /vúrjin'l/ *adj* **1.** CHASTE relating to, characteristic of, or appropriate for somebody, especially a woman, who has never had sexual intercourse **2.** LIVING CHASTELY living in a state of virginity **3.** PURE not corrupted or spoiled in any way [15C. Directly or via French < Latin *virginalis* < *virgin-* (see VIRGIN)] —**virginally** *adv*

virginal² /vúrjin'l/ *n* a smaller, often legless, oblong version of the harpsichord, popular in the 16th and 17th centuries [Early 16C. Directly or via French < Latin *virginalis* < *virgin-* (see VIRGIN)] —**virginalist** *n*

Virgin Birth *n* in Christianity, the doctrine that Jesus Christ was born as the son of God, not of a human father, and that his mother was a virgin

Virginia¹ /vər jínni ə/, **virginia** *n* tobacco of a type originally grown in the US state of Virginia [Early 17C. < VIRGINIA²]

Virginia² /vər jínni ə/ state in the eastern United States, bordered by Maryland, the Atlantic Ocean, North Carolina, Tennessee, Kentucky, and West Virginia. Capital: Richmond. Population: 7,293,542 (2002 estimate). Area: 109,624 sq. km/42,326 sq. mi. Official name **Commonwealth of Virginia** —**Virginian** *n*, *adj*

Virginia Beach largest city in Virginia, situated in the southeastern part of the state, on the Atlantic Ocean and the Chesapeake Bay, near the border with North Carolina. Population: 433,934 (2002 estimate).

Virginia creeper *n* a climbing plant with leaves made up of five leaflets and bluish-black berries. Latin name: *Parthenocissus quinquefolia*.

Virginia reel *n* a US country dance in which a caller instructs couples facing each other in long rows

Virginia stock *n* a low-growing plant. Flowers: white, pink, four-petalled, sweet-scented. Native to: Mediterranean. Latin name: *Malcomia maritima*.

Virgin Islands, British /vúrjin-/ ◆ **British Virgin Islands**

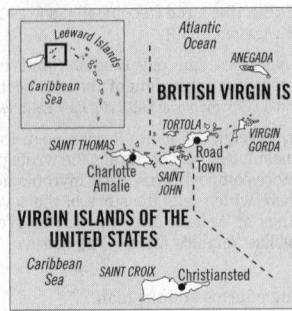

Virgin Islands of the United States and British Virgin Islands

Virgin Islands of the United States unincorporated external territory of the United States in the eastern Caribbean Sea, consisting of three main islands and over 60 smaller islands and islets. Capital: Charlotte Amalie. Population: 122,211 (2001). Area: 347 sq. km/134 sq. mi.

virginity /vər jínnəti/ *n* 1. the state of being a virgin 2. the state of being untouched, unexplored, or unspoiled

Virgin Mary *n* in Christianity, Mary, the mother of Jesus Christ

Virgin Queen *n* Elizabeth I, queen of England

virgin's bower *n* a clematis that produces silky glistening seeds. Flowers: small, white, in clusters. Native to: eastern North America. Latin name: *Clematis virginiana*.

virgin soil *n* 1. soil that has not yet been used for cultivation 2. something that has not been used, developed, or exploited, or somebody who does not have experience of something

virgin wool *n* wool that has not already been used to make something

Virgo /vúrgō/ (*plural* **-gos**) *n* 1. ZODIAC SIXTH SIGN OF ZODIAC the sixth sign of the zodiac, represented by a virgin and lasting from approximately 23 August to 22 September. Virgo is classified as an earth sign and its ruling planet is Mercury. 2. ASTROL SOMEBODY BORN UNDER VIRGO somebody whose birthday falls between 23 August and 22 September 3. ASTRON CONSTELLATION ON CELESTIAL EQUATOR a zodiacal constellation on the celestial equator. The Virgo cluster, which lies near the north galactic pole about 16 billion light-years from the Earth, contains about 3,000 galaxies. See illustration at **constellation** [Pre-12C. < Latin, 'maiden'] —**Virgo** *adj* —**Virgoan** /vur gṓ ən/ *n, adj*

virgo intacta /vúrgō intáktə/ *n* a girl or woman whose hymen remains unbroken [< Latin, 'intact virgin']

virgulate /vúrgyōōlət/ *adj* shaped like a rod (*technical*) [Mid-19C. < Latin *virgula*, diminutive of *virga* 'rod, staff, twig']

virgule /vúr gyool/ *n* US PRINTING same as **solidus** (sense 1) (*technical*) [Mid-19C. Via French, 'comma, little rod' < Latin *virgula* (see VIRGULATE)]

viricide /vírə sīd/, **virucide** *n* a drug or other agent that neutralizes or destroys a virus or viruses [Mid-20C. < VIRUS] —**viricidal** /vírə sīd'l/ *adj*

viridescent /vírri déss'nt/ *adj* green or becoming green [Mid-19C. < late Latin *viridescent-*, present participle of *viridescere* 'become green' < Latin *viridis* 'green'] —**viridescence** *n*

viridian /vi ríddi ən/ *n* 1. a green pigment made from a hydrated chromic oxide 2. a bluish-green colour [Late 19C. < Latin *viridis* 'green'] —**viridian** *adj*

viridity /vi ríddəti/ *n* (*literary*) 1. the state of being green 2. the state of being inexperienced [15C. < Latin *viridis* 'green']

virile /vírrīl/ *adj* 1. MASCULINE relating to or having the characteristics of an adult male 2. FORCEFUL showing energy, power, and forcefulness 3. SEXUALLY POTENT able to carry out the male sexual function [15C. < Latin *virilis* < *vir* 'man, husband']

virilism /vírrəlizəm/ *n* the development of male secondary sex characteristics culturally considered to be unusual in a woman, e.g. body hair or a deep voice

virility /və rílləti/ *n* the state of being male, having male characteristics, or male sexual potency

virilocal /vírri lṓk'l/ *adj* describes a form of marriage or the custom where, after the wedding, the bride moves to her new husband's family home [Mid-20C. < Latin *virilis* 'of a man' (see VIRILE)]

virion /vírri ən/ *n* the form taken by a virus when it is outside living cells and capable of causing infection. It consists of a core of DNA or RNA surrounded by a protein coat, sometimes covered by an outer envelope. [Mid-20C. < French < *virien* 'viral' + -ON[1]]

viro- *prefix* virus, viral ○ *virology* [< VIRUS]

viroid /vír oyd/ *n* an infectious RNA particle that resembles a virus, but is smaller. It causes diseases in plants. [Mid-20C. < VIRUS]

virology /vī rólləji/ *n* the branch of science and medicine that deals with the study of viruses and the diseases caused by them —**virologic** /vírə lójjik/ *adj*—**virological** *adj*—**virologically** *adv*—**virologist** *n*

virtu /vur tóo/, **vertu** *n* 1. a love of or taste for fine-art objects or curios 2. fine-art objects or curios [Early 18C. < Italian, 'virtue']

virtual /vúrchoo əl/ *adj* 1. BEING SOMETHING IN PRACTICE being something in effect even if not in reality or not conforming to the generally accepted definition of the term 2. GENERATED BY COMPUTER simulated by a computer for reasons of economics, convenience, or performance 3. PHYS HYPOTHETICAL describes a particle whose existence is suggested to explain observed phenomena, but is not proved or directly observable [14C. < medieval Latin *virtualis* < Latin *virtus* (see VIRTUE)]

virtual assistant *n* somebody who uses a computer and phone links to work from a distance as a personal assistant to somebody else ○*'There are many reasons why home-based business owners are hiring virtual assistants.'* (*Washington Post*; December 1998)

virtual community *n* a group of people communicating with each other via the Internet ○ *'… an interactive virtual community where local residents can do anything from look for local work to book seats at the local cinema.'* (*BBC website*; April 1999)

virtual disk *n* random-access memory used as a disk drive

virtual focus *n* the point from which divergent reflected or refracted light rays seem to originate

virtual image *n* an image from which reflected or refracted light rays appear to diverge. It cannot be projected onto a screen or photographic emulsion.

virtuality /vúrchoo álləti/ *n* 1. the inherent ability or potential to come into existence 2. COMPUT same as **virtual reality**

virtually /vúrchoo əli/ *adv* almost, but not quite ○ *At that time he was virtually unknown as a writer.*

virtual machine *n* a program running on a computer that creates a self-contained operating environment and presents the appearance to the user of a different computer. A virtual machine simulates at a minimum the instruction set of the computer it emulates.

virtual memory *n* a technique for creating the illusion that a computer has more memory than it really has by swapping blocks or pages of data between memory and external storage

virtual private network *n* COMPUT full form of **VPN**

virtual reality *n* 1. a technique by which a computer simulates a three-dimensional physical environment using visual and auditory stimuli with and within which somebody can interact to affect what happens in the simulation 2. a computer-generated environment that simulates three-dimensional reality

Virtual Reality Modelling Language *n* COMPUT full form of **VRML**

virtual storage *n* COMPUT same as **virtual memory**

~~**virtualy**~~ incorrect spelling of **virtually**

virtue /vúrchoo/ *n* 1. GOODNESS the quality of being morally good or righteous ○ *a paragon of virtue* 2. GOOD QUALITY a quality that is morally good ○ *Patience is a virtue.* 3. ADMIRABLE QUALITY a quality that is good or admirable, but not necessarily in terms of morality 4. CHASTITY the moral quality of being chaste, especially in a woman 5. WORTH the worth, advantage, or beneficial quality of something ○ *knew the virtue of thrift* 6. CHR ANGEL OF FIFTH HIGHEST ORDER in the traditional Christian hierarchy, an angel of the fifth of the nine orders of angels [12C. Via Old French *vertu* < Latin *virtus* 'manliness, excellence, worth' < *vir* 'man, husband'] —**virtueless** *adj* ◇ **by** or **in virtue of** because of, through the power of, or by the authority of something ◇ **make a virtue of necessity** to do something with good grace, when you are obliged to do it anyway

virtuosi ARTS plural of **virtuoso**

virtuosity /vúrchoo ósseti/ *n* 1. great skill or technique shown by somebody who excels at doing something, especially performing music 2. interest in, or knowledge and appreciation of, fine-art objects

virtuoso /vúrchoo ṓssō/ (*plural* **-sos** or **-si** /-si/) *n* 1. EXCEPTIONAL PERFORMER a musician who shows exceptional ability, technique, or artistry 2. TALENTED PERSON somebody who shows exceptional technique or ability in something 3. CONNOISSEUR somebody who is knowledgeable and cultivated in appreciating the fine arts [Early 17C. < Italian, 'skilful, versed' < late Latin *virtuosus* 'good' < Latin *virtus* (see VIRTUE)] —**virtuosic** /-óssik/ *adj*

virtuous /vúrchoo əss/ *adj* 1. having or showing moral goodness or righteousness 2. not having sexual intercourse with anyone except a partner in marriage, especially a husband —**virtuously** *adv* —**virtuousness** *n*

virtuous circle *n* a chain or cycle of events, the opposite of a vicious circle, in which one event with a beneficial outcome brings about further events with increasingly beneficial outcomes

virucide *n* PHARM another spelling of **viricide**

virulent /vírrōōlənt, vírryōō-/ *adj* 1. extremely poisonous, infectious, or damaging to organisms 2. showing great bitterness, malice, or hostility ○ *virulent criticism* [14C. < Latin *virulentus* 'poisonous' < *virus* 'poison, venom'] —**virulence** *n* —**virulently** *adv*

viruliferous /vírrōō lífferəss, vírryōō-/ *adj* describes an organism that contains or carries a virus [Mid-20C. < VIRULENT]

virus /vírəss/ *n* 1. SUBMICROSCOPIC PARASITE a submicroscopic parasitic particle of a nucleic acid surrounded by protein that can only replicate within a host cell. Viruses are not considered to be independent living organisms. 2. VIRAL DISEASE a disease caused by a virus 3. DISRUPTIVE COMPUTER PROGRAM a short computer program, hidden within another, that makes copies of itself and spreads them, disrupting the operation of a computer that receives one. A virus may be transmitted on diskettes and through networks, on-line services, and the Internet. ◊ **Trojan Horse** (sense 3), **worm** *v* (sense 1) 4. SOMETHING THAT CORRUPTS something that has a corrupting or poisonous effect, especially on the mind [Late 16C. < Latin, 'poison, venom, medicinal liquid']

Vis. *abbr* 1. Viscount 2. Viscountess

visa /vée zə/ *n* 1. PASSPORT INSERTION an official endorsement in a passport authorizing the bearer to enter or leave, and travel in or through, a specific country or region 2. AUTHORIZATION a mark of official authorization ■ *vt* (**-sas**, **-saing**, **-saed**) 1. SUPPLY DOCUMENT WITH VISA to insert a visa in a passport or other document 2. GIVE SOMEBODY VISA to provide somebody with a visa [Mid-19C. Via French < Latin *visa* 'things seen' < past participle of *videre* 'see']

VISA *n* a strain of a common infection-causing bacterium that shows some resistance to treatment by the antibiotic vancomycin. Full form **vancomycin intermediate Staphylococcus aureus**

~~**visable**~~ incorrect spelling of **visible**

visage /vízzij/ *n* (*literary*) 1. somebody's face or facial expression 2. the appearance or look of something [13C. < Old French < *vis* 'face, appearance' < Latin *visus* past participle of *videre* 'see']

visagiste /vée zaa zhéest/ *n* a specialist in applying facial makeup [Mid-20C. < French < *visage* (see VISAGE)]

vis-à-vis /vée zə vée/ *prep* 1. REGARDING in relation to 2. OPPOSITE opposite to or face to face with ■ *adv* FACE TO FACE face to face, or opposite each other ■ *n* (*plural* same) 1. SOMEBODY OR SOMETHING FACING somebody or

something that is face to face with another person or thing **2.** COUNTERPART somebody who is the counterpart of somebody else **3.** HORSE-DRAWN CARRIAGE a horse-drawn carriage in which people sit facing each other [Mid-18C. < French, 'face to face' < Old French *vis* (see VISAGE)]

Visayan /vi saá yən, bi-/ *n* **1.** a member of a people of the central and southern islands of the Philippines **2.** the Austronesian language of the Visayan people. Native speakers: 15,000,000. [Early 20C. < a language of the central Philippines] —**Visayan** *adj*

Visby /vízbi/ port on the western coast of the island of Gotland, Sweden. It was an important member of the Hanseatic League in the Middle Ages. Population: 20,986 (1994).

visc *abbr* viscosity

Visc. *abbr* **1.** Viscount **2.** Viscountess

visc- *prefix* same as **visco-** (*used before vowels*)

viscacha /vi skaáchə/, **vizcacha** *n* a burrowing gregarious rodent with black and white markings on its face, related to and resembling the chinchilla. Native to: South America. Latin name: *Lagostomus maximus*. [Early 17C. Via Spanish < Quechua *(h)uiscacha*]

viscera /víssərə/ *npl* the internal organs of the body, especially those of the abdomen such as the intestines [Early 18C. < Latin, 'internal organs, entrails']

visceral /víssərəl/ *adj* **1.** INSTINCTUAL proceeding from instinct rather than from reasoned thinking **2.** EMOTIONAL characterized by or showing basic emotions **3.** ANAT OF INTERNAL ORGANS relating to or affecting one or more internal organs of the body —**viscerally** *adv*

visceromotor /víssərō mōtər/ *adj* relating to the nervous control of gut movements, especially to disorders of bowel movement

viscid /víssid/ *adj* **1.** thick and sticky in consistency **2.** describes a leaf or other plant part that is covered with a sticky substance [Mid-17C. < late Latin *viscidus* < Latin *viscum* (see VISCOUS)] —**viscidity** /vi síddəti/ *n* —**viscidly** *adv* —**viscidness** *n*

visco- *prefix* viscosity ○ *viscoelastic* [< VISCOUS]

viscoelastic /vískō i lástik/ *adj* describes asphalt and many polymers that exhibit both viscous and elastic properties —**viscoelasticity** /vískō ée la stíssəti/ *n*

viscometer /vi skómmitər/ (*plural* **-cometers** or **-cosimeters**) *n* an instrument used to measure the viscosity of a substance —**viscometric** /vískō méttrik/ *adj* —**viscometrical** *adj* —**viscometry** *n*

Visconti /vi skónti/, **Luchino** (1906–76) Italian film and theatre director. He is noted for his neorealist films and literary adaptations. He also directed plays, ballets, and operas. Full name **Visconti, Don Luchino, Conte di Modrone**

viscose /vískōss/ *n* **1.** a rayon with a soft silky feel, made from a cellulose solution **2.** a cellulose solution of thick consistency. Use: rayon manufacture. [Late 19C. < late Latin *viscosus* (see VISCOUS)]

viscosimeter /vísk ō símmitər/ *n* PHYS same as **viscometer** —**viscosimetric** *adj* —**viscosimetrical** *adj* —**viscosimetry** *n*

viscosity /vi skóssəti/ (*plural* **-ties**) *n* **1.** THICKNESS AND STICKINESS a thick and sticky consistency or quality **2.** PHYS PROPERTY OF FLUID THAT RESISTS FLOWING the property of a fluid or semifluid that causes it to resist flowing **3.** PHYS MEASURE OF SUBSTANCE'S RESISTANCE TO MOTION a measure of the resistance of a substance to motion under an applied force

viscosity index *n* an arbitrary scale for lubricating oils that is used to indicate how much the viscosity of the oil varies according to its temperature

viscount /vī kownt/ *n* **1.** BRITISH NOBLEMAN a British nobleman of a rank above baron **2.** COUNT'S SON OR YOUNGER BROTHER in European countries other than the United Kingdom, especially France, somebody whose father or elder brother is a count **3.** COUNT'S REPRESENTATIVE in medieval Europe, somebody acting for or representing a count [14C. Via Anglo-Norman *viscounte*, Old French *vi(s)conte* < medieval Latin *vicecomes* < Latin *vice* 'in place of' (see VICE[2]) + *comes* 'companion'] —**viscountcy** *n* —**viscounty** *n*

viscountess /vī kowntəss/ *n* **1.** a woman who holds a rank equivalent to viscount **2.** the wife or widow of a viscount

viscous /vískəss/ *adj* **1.** thick and sticky, reluctant to flow, and difficult to stir **2.** describes a fluid that has a relatively high resistance to flow [14C. < late Latin *viscosus* 'sticky' < Latin *viscum* 'mistletoe, birdlime made from mistletoe berries'] —**viscously** *adv* —**viscousness** *n*

Visct. *abbr* **1.** Viscount **2.** Viscountess

viscus /vískəss/ *n* ANAT singular of **viscera**

vise *n, vt* MECH ENG US spelling of **vice**[3]

Vishakhapatnam /vi shaákə pútnəm/ city and port on the Bay of Bengal, in Andhra Pradesh State, southeastern India. Population: 1,329,472 (2001).

Vishnu /víshnoo/ *n* in Hinduism, a god called the Preserver, the second member of the triad that includes Brahma the Creator and Shiva the Destroyer [Mid-17C. < Sanskrit *Viṣṇu*]

visibility /vízzə bílləti/ *n* **1.** ABILITY TO BE SEEN the fact of being able to be seen **2.** DISTANCE IT IS POSSIBLE TO SEE the distance it is possible to see under the prevailing atmospheric or weather conditions **3.** CLEAR VIEW the ability to provide somebody, especially the driver of a vehicle, with a good view of what is around him or her, or the view obtained from a fixed position **4.** PUBLIC PROMINENCE the degree to which somebody or something is easily noticed by and catches the attention of the public or a group of people ○ *the comparatively low visibility of the board of directors*

visible /vízzəb'l/ *adj* **1.** ABLE TO BE SEEN capable of being seen by, or perceptible to, the human eye ○ *the visible spectrum* **2.** IN SIGHT in somebody's sight at a particular time ○ *The building became visible again as soon as she turned the corner.* **3.** OBVIOUS easily noticeable ○ *the very visible results of the recent floods* **4.** DETECTABLE capable of being discovered by means of the mental faculties ○ *no visible prospect of a solution to the problem* **5.** OFTEN SEEN PUBLICLY frequently in the public eye ○ *the company's very visible head of public relations* **6.** DESIGNED TO KEEP SOMETHING IN VIEW designed to keep information or an item in view or able to be readily brought to view ○ *a visible index* **7.** ECON CONSISTING OF ACTUAL GOODS relating to or in the form of goods imported or exported, as opposed to other types of transaction that affect a country's balance of trade ○ *visible exports* [14C. < Latin *visibilis* < *vis-*, past participle of *videre* 'see'] —**visibleness** *n* —**visibly** *adv*

visible radiation *n* radiation that falls within the range of wavelengths that can be detected by the human eye, e.g. sunlight

visible speech *n* **1.** a set of phonetic symbols intended to represent the position of the lips, tongue, and other speech organs in creating sounds **2.** a visual representation of speech using a spectrograph that disperses radiation into a spectrum and photographs it

Visigoth /vízzi goth/ *n* a member of an ancient Germanic people who conquered parts of the Roman Empire during the 5th century. They destroyed Rome in 410 and took over parts of Spain and southern France, where they established a powerful kingdom that lasted until the beginning of the 8th century. [Mid-16C. < late Latin *Visigothi* 'Visigoths'] —**Visigothic** /vízzi góthik/ *adj*

vision /vízh'n/ *n* **1.** EYESIGHT the ability to see **2.** MENTAL PICTURE an image or concept in the imagination ○ *visions of power and wealth* **3.** PARAPSYCHOL SOMETHING SEEN IN DREAM OR TRANCE an image or series of images seen in a dream or trance, often interpreted as having religious, revelatory, or prophetic significance **4.** FAR-SIGHTEDNESS the ability to anticipate possible future events and developments **5.** BROADCAST TELEVISION PICTURE the picture on a television screen **6.** SOMEBODY OR SOMETHING BEAUTIFUL a beautiful or pleasing sight [13C. < Latin *vision-* < *vis-* (see VISIBLE)] —**visional** *adj* —**visionally** *adv* —**visionless** *adj*

visionary /vízh'nəri/ *adj* **1.** FULL OF FORESIGHT characterized by unusually acute foresight and imagination **2.** IMAGINARY produced by, resulting from, or originating in the imagination **3.** INCAPABLE OF BEING REALIZED so idealistic or unrealistic as to be unrealizable in practice **4.** GIVEN TO DREAMINESS tending by nature to be dreamy or to have impractical schemes and ideas **5.** RELATING TO MYSTICAL VISIONS relating to or seen in a mystical vision **6.** PARAPSYCHOL HAVING VISIONS given to seeing mystical visions ■ *n* (*plural* **-ies**) **1.** SOMEBODY WITH MUCH FORESIGHT somebody of unusually acute foresight and imagination **2.** PARAPSYCHOL SOMEBODY WHO HAS VISIONS somebody who has mystical visions **3.** DREAMER somebody who daydreams or indulges in impractical schemes and ideas —**visionariness** *n*

vision mixer *n* **1.** a technician who mixes and combines the different camera shots during the production of a television programme or film **2.** a piece of equipment used by a vision mixer in television or film production

vision quest *n* a personal spiritual search undertaken by an adolescent Native North American boy in order to learn by means of a trance or vision the identity of his guardian spirit

visit /vízzit/ *v* (**-its, -iting, -ited**) **1.** *vti* GO TO SEE SOMEBODY to go to see and spend time with somebody, especially as an act of affection or friendship ○ *Nobody visited him in hospital.* **2.** *vt* STAY WITH SOMEBODY to go to stay with somebody for a time as a guest in his or her home ○ *I'm going to visit my family during the holidays.* **3.** *vti* GO TO SEE PLACE to go to see or stay at a place for a time, e.g. as a tourist **4.** *vt* GO TO INSPECT PLACE to go to a place as an official inspector **5.** *vt* ONLINE GO TO WEBSITE to view a website **6.** *vt* INFLICT SOMETHING ON SOMEBODY to inflict something unpleasant such as punishment or vengeance on somebody (*literary or formal*) ○ *visited them with plagues* **7.** *vi* N Am CHAT WITH SOMEBODY to engage in amiable or casual conversation with somebody ■ *n* **1.** SOCIAL CALL a trip to see somebody and a period of time spent in his or her company **2.** EXTENDED STAY IN PLACE an extended temporary stay in a place, e.g. as somebody's guest or as a tourist **3.** OFFICIAL INSPECTION an official call paid for the purpose of inspection ○ *a visit to the ship by the admiral* **4.** LAW BOARDING OF SHIP the boarding of a ship on the high seas to carry out a search for contraband **5.** N Am CONVERSATION an amiable or casual conversation [12C. Directly or via French < Latin *visitare* 'go to see', < *visare* 'to view' < *vis-* (see VISIBLE)] —**visitable** *adj*

visitant /vízzitənt/ *n* **1.** same as **visitor** (sense 1) (*archaic*) **2.** PARANORMAL a being thought to visit from the spirit world ■ *adj* paying a visit to somebody or something

visitation /vízzi táysh'n/ *n* **1.** OFFICIAL VISIT an official visit for inspection or examination **2.** SOCIAL VISIT a social visit to somebody's home, especially if it is unwelcome or lasts too long (*humorous*) **3.** RELIG PUNISHMENT FROM GOD a punishment or, sometimes, a benefit received, especially one believed to be sent by God **4.** PARAPSYCHOL APPEARANCE FROM SPIRIT WORLD a supposed appearance made by a supernatural being **5.** US LAW RIGHT OF PARENTAL ACCESS the right of a divorced parent to have access to a child for a set period of time, or a period of time with the child granted by this right —**visitational** *adj*

Visitation *n* **1.** according to the Bible, the visit made by the Virgin Mary after the Annunciation to her cousin Elizabeth **2.** a Christian festival celebrating the Visitation of the Virgin Mary to Elizabeth. Date: 2 July.

visiting card /vízziting-/ *n* a small card bearing somebody's name and sometimes address, presented, especially in former times, when visiting or left behind when calling and finding that somebody is out. N Am term **calling card**

visiting fireman *n* N Am an important visitor who is entertained lavishly and impressively (*informal*)

visiting hours *npl* the period of time during which patients in a hospital may have visitors

visiting professor *n* a professor from one university who teaches at another for a term or academic year

visiting teacher *n* US EDUC same as **home teacher**

visitor /vízzitər/ *n* **1.** SOMEBODY VISITING somebody who visits a person or place **2.** BIRDS MIGRATORY BIRD APPEARING TEMPORARILY a migratory bird that regularly spends a season or part of a season in a place **3.** ONLINE WEBSITE VIEWER an Internet user who views a website ■ **visitors** *npl* SPORTS AWAY TEAM an away team that travels to an opponent's stadium or sports field to play

visitor centre *n* a building offering information and services to visitors in a city or at a historical or archaeological site, park, or nature reserve

visitors' book *n* a book in which visitors, e.g. to a house, guesthouse, hotel, or art gallery, write their names, their home addresses, and often their comments on the visit

visitorship /vízzitər ship/ *n* the total number of tourists visiting a specific place

visitor's passport *n* a one-year British passport, phased out in 1995, that permitted the holder to visit some countries for periods of up to three months

visna /víssnə/ *n* a chronic progressive pneumonia of sheep and goats [Mid-20C. < Old Norse, 'wither']

visor

visor /vízər/, **vizor** *n* **1.** TRANSPARENT FRONT OF HELMET a hinged front part of a helmet, made of transparent or tinted plastic and designed to protect the face or eyes, especially on helmets worn by motorcyclists or welders **2.** FLAP OVER WINDSCREEN FOR GLARE a flap mounted above the windscreen inside a car used to shield the eyes from glare **3.** EYESHADE a shade for the eyes attached to a band worn around the head **4.** *N Am* CAP PEAK the peak of a cap **5.** FRONT OF MEDIEVAL HELMET a hinged metal front part of a medieval helmet in a suit of armour, designed to protect the face and fitted with slits for the eyes to see through [13C. < Anglo-Norman *viser* < French *vis* (see VISAGE)] — **visored** *adj*

vista /vístə/ *n* **1.** SCENIC VIEW a scenic or panoramic view **2.** VIEW SEEN THROUGH NARROW OPENING a view seen through a long narrow opening, e.g. between rows of trees or buildings **3.** MENTAL PICTURE a mental picture covering a wide range of objects or a long succession of events in the past or future ○ *open up vistas of expansion into hitherto untapped markets* [Mid-17C. < Italian, 'view' < past participle of *vedere* 'see' < Latin *videre*]

Vistula /vístyŏŏlə/ longest river of Poland, flowing northwards from the Carpathian Mountains in the southwest of the country, through Cracow, Warsaw, and Torun, before emptying into the Baltic Sea at the Gulf of Gdansk. Length: 1,090 km/675 mi. Polish name **Wisła**

visual /vízhoo əl, vízzyoo-/ *adj* **1.** OF VISION relating to vision or sight **2.** VISIBLE able or intended to be seen by the eyes, especially as opposed to being registered by one of the other senses or by a machine ○ *visual humour* **3.** PERCEPTIBLE BY MIND'S EYE able to be perceived as a picture in the mind rather than as an abstract idea ○ *a visual memory* **4.** DONE BY SIGHT ONLY describes direction-finding done by sight only and without the use of scientific instruments or equipment ○ *visual navigation* ○ *made a visual landing* ■ *n* MARKETING PIECE OF ILLUSTRATIVE MATERIAL a photograph, picture, chart, or graph that displays information or promotional material in a way that appeals to the eye [15C. < late Latin *visualis* < Latin *visus* 'sight' < past participle of *videre* 'see'] — **visually** /vízhoo əli/ *adv* — **visualness** *n*

visual acuity *n* acuteness of vision as determined by a comparison with the normal ability to identify letters at a distance of 6 m/20 ft

visual aid *n* something that is looked at as a complement to a lesson or presentation, e.g. a model, chart, or film

visual arts *npl* arts that are perceived by sight, e.g. painting or sculpture

visual binary *n* a star that can be seen to be a double star either with the naked eye or when viewed through a telescope

visual display unit *n* a device used to display data from a computer, e.g. a cathode ray tube

visual field *n* OPTICS same as **field of vision**

visualize /vízhoo ə līz, vízzyoo-/ (-izes, -izing, -ized), **visualise** (-ises, -ising, -ised) *v* **1.** *vti* IMAGINE SOMETHING to form a visual image of something in the mind **2.** *vti* PSYCHOL CREATE POSITIVE MENTAL PICTURE OF SOMETHING to create a vivid positive mental picture of something such as a desired outcome to a problem, in order to promote a sense of wellbeing **3.** *vt* MED MAKE IMAGE OF INTERNAL ORGANS to produce an image of an internal organ or other part of the body by using X-rays or other means such as magnetic resonance imaging — **visualization** /vízhoo ə lī záysh'n, vízzyoo-/ *n* — **visualizer** *n*

visually impaired *adj* having reduced vision, especially having eyesight so poor that it interferes with the ability to perform day-to-day activities effectively

visual-motor coordination *n* the coordination of the body's visual and motor systems, as occurs when somebody reaches out for something that is being looked at

visual purple *n* BIOL same as **rhodopsin**

visuomotor /vízhoo ō mōtər, vízzyoo-/ *adj* relating to or involving body motor processes that are linked to vision, e.g. the coordination of movements

vital /vít'l/ *adj* **1.** CRUCIAL extremely important and necessary, or indispensable to the survival or continuing effectiveness of something **2.** NEEDED FOR LIFE required for the continuation of life ○ *vital body organs* **3.** LIVELY full of animation or vigour **4.** OF LIFE relating to life ○ *vital records of a population* [14C. < Latin *vitalis* < *vita* 'life'] — **vitalness** *n*

SYNONYMS See *necessary*.

vital capacity *n* a measure of the air that can be exhaled from the lungs after maximum inhalation

vital force *n* **1.** FORCEFUL VITALIZING PERSON OR THING somebody or something infusing vitality or strength into somebody or something else ○ *She was the vital force behind passage of the law.* **2.** ANIMATING SOUL OR SPIRIT the animating or vitalizing spirit, soul, or source of energy believed by some to be inherent in living beings **3.** NATURAL FORCE FOR HEALTH in alternative medicine, the natural mechanism or force that keeps somebody healthy and that, when weakened, makes the person susceptible to illness

vitalism /vít'lizəm/ *n* a doctrine that maintains that life and the functions of a living organism depend on a nonmaterial force or principle separate from physical and chemical processes — **vitalistic** /vítə lístik/ *adj* — **vitalistically** *adv*

vitality /vī tálləti/ *n* **1.** LIVELINESS abundant physical and mental energy, usually combined with a wholehearted and joyous approach to situations and activities **2.** DURABILITY the ability of something to live and grow or to continue in existence **3.** PHILOSOPHY VITAL PRINCIPLE the nonmaterial force that, according to vitalism, distinguishes the living from the nonliving

vitalize /vítə līz/ (-izes, -izing, -ized), **vitalise** (-ises, -ising, -ised) *vt* **1.** to cause somebody or something to live **2.** to make somebody or something lively — **vitalization** /vítə lī záysh'n/ *n* — **vitalizer** *n*

vitally /vítəli/ *adv* extremely or indispensably

vitals /vít'lz/ *npl* **1.** PHYSIOL ORGANS ESSENTIAL TO LIFE the internal organs of the body that are essential to life, especially the stomach and intestines **2.** MED same as **vital signs** (*informal*) **3.** GENITALS the genitals, especially those of a man (*humorous*) **4.** ESSENTIALS the essential parts of something [Early 17C. < Latin *vitalia* 'vital things' < form of *vitalis* (see VITAL)]

vital signs *npl* the signs that indicate life, e.g. pulse, body temperature, breathing, and blood pressure

vital staining *n* the process of using a substance that colours only live cells in order to study the fate of cells in embryonic development

vital statistics *npl* **1.** statistics of human births, deaths, marriages, and health **2.** the measurements of a woman's bust, waist, and hips (*dated informal*)

vitamin /víttəmin, vítə-/ *n* an organic substance essential in small quantities to the metabolism in most animals. Vitamins are found in minute

quantities in food, in some cases are produced by the body, and are also produced synthetically. [Early 20C. < German *Vitamine* < Latin *vita* 'life' + AMINE] — **vitaminic** /víttə mínnik, vítə-/ *adj*

ORIGIN *Vitamins* were originally *vitamines*: the Polish-born biochemist Casimir Funk who introduced them to the world in 1912 believed that they were amino acids and so formed the name from Latin *vita* 'life' and *amine*. It was soon discovered that Funk's belief was mistaken, and alternative names were suggested, but in 1920 it was successfully proposed that the *-e* be dropped to avoid confusion, and the form **vitamin** was born.

vitamin A, **vitamin A**$_1$ *n* a fat-soluble vitamin found in some vegetables, fish, milk, and eggs, important for vision. Vitamin A is important to the health of the outer layer of cells in the skin and organs. A deficiency leads to roughening of the skin and night blindness.

vitamin A$_2$ *n* a form of vitamin A obtained from fish liver

vitamin B *n* BIOCHEM **1.** same as **vitamin B complex 2.** same as **thiamine**

vitamin B$_1$ *n* BIOCHEM same as **thiamine**

vitamin B$_2$ *n* BIOCHEM same as **riboflavin**

vitamin B$_6$ *n* BIOCHEM same as **pyridoxine**

vitamin B$_{12}$ *n* a water-soluble vitamin obtained only from fish and other animal products, important for blood formation. A deficiency of it causes pernicious anaemia.

vitamin B complex *n* a group of water-soluble coenzyme vitamins found in many foods

vitamin C *n* a water-soluble vitamin found in fruits and leafy vegetables or made synthetically and used as an antioxidant. Lack of vitamin C causes scurvy.

vitamin D *n* a fat-soluble vitamin that occurs in fish-liver oils and eggs, essential for the formation of bones and teeth. Lack of vitamin D causes rickets.

vitamin D$_2$ *n* a form of vitamin D made by plants

vitamin D$_3$ *n* a form of vitamin D formed by the action of sunlight on the skin

vitamin E *n* a mixture of fat-soluble vitamins found in seed oils, essential for reproduction

vitamin G *n US* BIOCHEM same as **riboflavin**

vitamin H *n US* BIOCHEM same as **biotin**

vitamin K *n* a fat-soluble vitamin essential for blood clotting

vitamin K$_1$ *n* a form of vitamin K found in green vegetables

vitamin K$_2$ *n* a form of vitamin K found in fish

vitamin P *n* BIOCHEM same as **bioflavonoid**

vitelli BIOL plural of **vitellus**

vitellin /vi téllin/ *n* a protein in egg yolk [Mid-19C. < *vitellus*]

vitelline /vi tél īn, -téllin/ *adj* **1.** relating to egg yolk **2.** of the yellow colour of egg yolk [< medieval Latin *vitellinus* < Latin *vitellus* 'egg yolk']

vitelline membrane *n* the membrane that encloses a fertilized egg

vitellus /vi télləs/ (*plural* -luses or -li /-lī/) *n* the yolk of an egg (*technical*) [Early 18C. < Latin, 'egg yolk']

vitiate /víshi ayt/ (-ates, -ating, -ated) *vt* (*formal*) **1.** MAKE SOMETHING INEFFECTIVE to destroy or drastically reduce the effectiveness of something, or make it invalid **2.** MAKE SOMETHING FAULTY to cause something to become faulty **3.** DEBASE SOMETHING to degrade something morally [Mid-16C. < Latin *vitiare* < *vitium* 'fault, vice'] — **vitiable** *adj* — **vitiation** /víshi áysh'n/ *n* — **vitiator** *n*

viticulture /vítti kulchər/ *n* the science or practice of growing grapevines, especially for winemaking [Late 19C. < Latin *vitis* 'vine'] — **viticultural** /vítti kúlchərəl/ *adj* — **viticulturally** *adv* — **viticulturist** /vítti kúlchərist/ *n*

vitiligo /vítti lígō/ *n* a skin disorder in which smooth whitish patches appear on the skin [Late 16C. < Latin, 'skin eruption']

Vitoria /vi táwri ə/ capital city of the Basque Country in northern Spain. Population: 221,270 (2002).

Vitória /vi táwri ə/ island city and capital of Espírito

Santo State, eastern Brazil. Population: 265,874 (1996).

vitr- *prefix* same as **vitri-** (*used before vowels*)

vitrain /víttrayn/ *n* a narrow glassy band found in bituminous coal [Early 20C. < VITREOUS + -*ain* after FUSAIN]

vitrectomy /vi tréktəmi/ (*plural* **-mies**) *n* a surgical operation to remove some or all of the vitreous humour of the eye

vitreous /víttri əss/ *adj* **1.** SIMILAR TO GLASS having the characteristics or appearance of glass **2.** OF GLASS relating to, consisting of, or derived from glass **3.** MED OF VITREOUS HUMOUR relating to the vitreous humour of the eye [Mid-17C. < Latin *vitreus* < *vitrum* 'glass'] —**vitreosity** /víttri óssəti/ *n* —**vitreousness** *n*

vitreous body *n* the transparent gel that fills the main cavity of the eye between the lens and the retina

vitreous enamel *n* an opaque glassy coating applied to steel or other metals through firing

vitreous humour *n* the fluid component of the gel (**vitreous body**) that fills the main cavity of the eye between the lens and the retina

vitreous silica *n* glass made solely from silica

vitrescent /vi tréss'nt/ *adj* capable of being made into glass [Mid-18C. < Latin *vitrum* 'glass']

vitri- *prefix* glass ○ *vitrify* [< Latin *vitrum*]

vitric /víttrik/ *adj* having the characteristics or appearance of glass [Early 20C. < Latin *vitrum* 'glass']

vitrification /víttrifi káysh'n/ *n* **1.** the process of converting materials to glass **2.** in pottery, the point at which a pot loses its porosity during a firing

vitriform /víttri fawrm/ *adj* having the form or appearance of glass [Late 18C. < Latin *vitrum* 'glass']

vitrify /víttri fī/ (**-fies, -fying, -fied**) *vti* to become changed into glass, or change materials into glass [Late 16C. < French *vitrifier* or directly < Latin *vitrum* 'glass'] —**vitrifiability** /víttri fī ə bílləti/ *n* —**vitrifiable** *adj*

vitrine /víttreen/ *n* a cabinet or case with glass walls for displaying specimens or art objects [Late 19C. < French < *vitre* 'glass' < Latin *vitrum* 'glass']

vitriol /víttri əl/ *n* **1.** extreme bitterness and hatred towards somebody or something, or an expression of this feeling in speech or writing **2.** a glassy metallic sulphate such as that of copper or iron **3.** CHEM same as **sulphuric acid** (*archaic or literary*) [14C. < medieval Latin *vitriolum* < Latin *vitrum* 'glass']

vitriolic /víttri óllik/ *adj* **1.** filled with or expressing extreme bitterness and hatred towards somebody or something **2.** CHEM resembling a glassy metallic sulphate —**vitriolically** *adv*

Vitruvius /vi troóvi əss/ (*fl* 1st century BC) Roman architect and engineer. His book *De Architectura* provides valuable information about architecture and engineering in classical times. Full name **Vitruvius Pollio, Marcus**

> 'Pictures should not be given approbation which are not likenesses of reality; even if they are refined creations executed with artistic skill.'
> [Vitruvius, *Vitruvius, The Ten Books on Architecture*; 1960 (tr. M. H. Morgan)]

vitta /víttə/ (*plural* **-tae** /-tee/) *n* **1.** a tube or cavity containing oil in the carpels of the family of plants that includes carrot, parsley, and celery **2.** a stripe or band of colour on the body of an animal [Late 17C. < Latin, 'headband'] —**vittate** *adj*

vittles /vítt'lz/ *npl* food or other provisions (*dated*) [Variant of VICTUALS]

vituline /víttyoŏ līn, -lin/ *adj* relating to or resembling a calf or veal (*technical*) [Mid-17C. < Latin *vitulinus* < *vitulus* 'calf']

vituperate /vī tyoŏpə rayt, vi-/ (**-ates, -ating, -ated**) *vti* to attack somebody in violently abusive or harshly critical language [Mid-16C. < Latin *vituperare* < *vitium* 'fault, vice' + *parare* 'make ready'] —**vituperative** /-rətiv/ *adj* —**vituperator** *n* —**vituperatory** /-rətəri/ *adj*

vituperation /vī tyoŏpə ráysh'n, vi-/ *n* **1.** an outburst of violently abusive or harshly critical language **2.** the use of violent abuse or extremely harsh criticism

viva[1] /véévə/ *interj* used to express enthusiastic support for somebody ○ *Viva the president!* [Mid-17C. < Italian, 'may he, she, or it live', form of *vivere* 'to live' < Latin]

viva[2] /vīvə/ *n* an examination, especially one taken as part of a university degree, in which a student is asked and answers questions in a spoken interview instead of on paper ■ *vt* (**-vas, -vaing, -vaed**) to examine a student orally [Late 19C. Shortening of VIVA VOCE]

vivace /vi vaáchi/ *adv* in a lively and spirited manner (*used as a musical direction*) ■ *n* a piece of music, or a section of a piece, played vivace [Late 17C. < Italian, 'lively' < Latin *vivac-* (see VIVACIOUS)] —**vivace** *adj*

vivacious /vi váyshəss/ *adj* exhibiting or characterized by liveliness and high-spiritedness [Mid-17C. < Latin *vivac-* 'lively, long-lived' < *vivus* (see VIVID)] —**vivaciously** *adv* —**vivaciousness** *n*

vivacity /vi vássəti/ *n* liveliness and high-spiritedness

Vivaldi /vi váldi/, **Antonio** (1678–1741) Italian composer. His music epitomizes the Italian baroque style, his concertos being particularly influential on later composers. Full name **Vivaldi, Antonio Lucio**

vivandière /vée vaaN dyáir/ *n* in former times, a woman who followed an army and sold food and drink to the soldiers [Late 16C. < French, feminine of *vivandier* < late Latin *vivenda* (see VIAND)]

vivarium /vī váiri əm/ (*plural* **-ia** /-i ə/ or **-iums**) *n* a transparent enclosure in which small animals are kept so that their behaviour can be studied [Early 17C. < Latin, 'game preserve, fishpond' < form of *vivarius* 'of living things' < *vivus* (see VIVID)]

viva voce /vīvə vóchi/ *n* EDUC same as **viva**[2] ■ *adv* by word of mouth (*formal*) [Mid-16C. < medieval Latin, 'with the living voice']

vivax malaria /vī vaks-/, **vivax** *n* a form of malaria marked by convulsions that occur every 48 hours and caused by the parasite *Plasmodium vivax* [< modern Latin *vivax* taxonomic name < Latin, 'long lived']

viverrid /vī vérrid/ *n* a civet, mongoose, or other similar small carnivorous mammal with a long slender body. Family: Viverridae. [Early 20C. < modern Latin *Viverridae* (plural) < *Viverra* (singular) < Latin, 'ferret'] —**viverrid** *adj*

vivid /vívvid/ *adj* **1.** VERY BRIGHT strikingly bright or intense in colour **2.** GRAPHIC producing strong and distinct mental images **3.** INVENTIVE active and inventive ○ *a vivid imagination* **4.** EXTREMELY CLEAR AND FRESH characterized by striking clarity, distinctness, or truth to life when perceived either by the eye or the mind ○ *a vivid image* **5.** LIVELY characterized by spirit and animation [Mid-17C. < Latin *vividus* < *vivus* 'alive' < *vivere* 'to live'] —**vividly** *adv* —**vividness** *n*

vivify /vívvi fī/ (**-fies, -fying, -fied**) *vt* **1.** to cause somebody or something to come to life **2.** to give liveliness or vividness to something [14C. Via French *vivifier* < late Latin *vivificare* 'make alive' < Latin *vivus* (see VIVID)] —**vivification** /vívvifi káysh'n/ *n* —**vivifier** *n*

viviparous /vi víppərəss/ *adj* **1.** ZOOL BEARING LIVE YOUNG bearing live young, not eggs **2.** BOT PRODUCING PLANTLETS describes a plant that produces plantlets or bulbils from the flower stem, e.g. the spider plant **3.** BOT PRODUCING SEEDLINGS ON PLANT describes a plant with seeds that germinate and develop into seedlings before being shed from the parent plant, e.g. a mangrove [Mid-17C. < Latin *viviparus* 'bringing forth alive' < *vivus* (see VIVID)] —**viviparously** *adv*

vivisect /vívvi sekt/ (**-sects, -secting, -sected**) *vti* to perform operations on living animals that involve cutting into their bodies in order to gain knowledge of pathological or physiological processes [Mid-19C. Back-formation < VIVISECTION] —**vivisective** /vívvi sektiv, -séktiv/ *adj* —**vivisector** *n*

vivisection /vívvi séksh'n/ *n* the practice of operating on living animals in order to gain knowledge of pathological or physiological processes [Early 18C. < Latin *vivus* (see VIVID) after DISSECTION] —**vivisectional** *adj* —**vivisectionally** *adv* —**vivisectionist** *n*

vivisectorium /vívvi sek táwri əm/ (*plural* **-riums** or **-ria** /-ri ə/) *n* an establishment where vivisection is practised [Late 20C. < VIVISECTION after EMPORIUM]

vivo /véévō/ *adv* in a lively and energetic manner (*used*

as a musical direction) [Mid-18C. Via Italian < Latin *vivus* (see VIVID)] —**vivo** *adj*

vixen /víks'n/ *n* **1.** a female fox **2.** an offensive term that deliberately insults a woman regarded as vindictive and bad-tempered (*insult*) [15C. Variant of *vixen* < Old English *fyxe*, feminine of *fox* (see FOX)] —**vixenish** *adj* —**vixenly** *adj*, *adv*

viz /viz/ *adv* namely. Full form **videlicet**

vizcacha *n* ZOOL another spelling of **viscacha**

vizier /vi zeér/ *n* in some Islamic countries and especially in the former Ottoman Empire, a high-ranking government officer [Mid-16C. Via French or Spanish *visir* < Turkish *vezir* < Arabic *wazīr* 'vizier', earlier 'helper, assistant'] —**vizierate** *n* —**vizierial** *adj* —**viziership** *n*

vizor *n* CLOTHING, AUTOMOT, HIST another spelling of **visor**

vizsla

vizsla /vízhlə/ *n* a medium-sized hunting dog with a short smooth reddish coat, belonging to a Hungarian breed [Mid-20C. Origin ?]

VJ *abbr* video jockey

V-J day *n* the day of the Japanese surrender in World War II. Date: 15 August 1945. [Abbreviation of *victory over Japan*]

vl *abbr* variant reading [Latin *varia lectio*]

VL *abbr* Vulgar Latin

Vlach /vlaak/ *n* **1.** a member of a southeastern European people who in the 13th century founded the principalities of Walachia and Moldavia, later merged to become Romania. Vlachs now live mainly in the mountainous regions of the Balkans, the Former Yugoslav Republic of Macedonia, Albania, or northern Greece. **2.** a language of the Romance family that is spoken in southeastern Europe, especially by the Vlach people. Native speakers: 300,000. [Mid-19C. < Bulgarian and Serbo-Croatian < Germanic, 'foreign'] —**Vlach** *adj*

Vladimir /vláddi meer, vi dée meer/ city and capital of Vladimir Oblast in western Russia. Population: 349,899 (1995).

Vladivostok /vláddi vóstok/ city and major port in southeastern Russia, on Golden Horn Bay, an inlet of the Sea of Japan. It is the eastern terminus of the Trans-Siberian Railway. Population: 640,672 (1995).

Vlaminck /vlá mingk/, **Maurice de** (1876–1958) French painter. Greatly influenced by the work of van Gogh, he was a leading light of the Fauvist movement. The bright colours and strong contrasts of his early works give way to a more subdued palette in his later landscapes.

> 'Painting was an abscess which drained off the evil in me. Without a gift for painting I would have gone to the bad...What I could only have achieved in a social context by throwing a bomb...I have tried to express in art.'
> [Maurice de Vlaminck. Quoted in *Fauvism*, Joseph Émile Muller; 1967]

VLCC *abbr* INDUST very large crude carrier

VLDL *abbr* MED very low density lipoprotein

vlei /flay, vlay/ (*plural* **vleis**) *n* S Africa a stretch of low-lying ground that is either permanently marshy or is flooded in the rainy season to form a shallow lake [Late 18C. Via Afrikaans < Dutch *wallei* 'valley']

VLF, **vlf** *abbr* MEDIA very low frequency

VLSI *adj* made using technology that allows hundreds of thousands of components to exist on a single microchip. Full form **very large-scale integration**

v-mail /veé mayl/, **vmail** *n* an e-mail message with a video clip as an attachment [Late 20C. < v for VIDEO after E-MAIL]

VMD *abbr* EDUC Doctor of Veterinary Medicine

vn *abbr* Vietnam (*used in Internet addresses*) See table at **domain name**

V neck *n* **1.** a neckline shaped like a letter 'V' (*hyphenated before a noun*) **2.** a garment, especially a sweater or T-shirt, with a V-shaped neckline —**V-necked** *adj*

VO *abbr* **1.** Royal Victorian Order **2.** verbal order **3.** very old (*used on labels for bottles of brandy, whisky, or port*) **4.** voiceover

vo. *abbr* PRINTING verso

VOC *abbr* CHEM volatile organic compound

voc. *abbr* GRAM vocative

vocab /vő kab/ *n* LANGUAGE same as **vocabulary** (sense 3) (*informal*) [Early 20C. Shortening]

vocable /vőkəb'l/ *n* a single word considered only as a grouping of sounds or letters, not in terms of its meaning (*dated formal*) ■ *adj* capable of being pronounced or spoken (*formal*) [Mid-16C. Directly or via French < Latin *vocabulum* 'name' < *vocare* 'call, name'] —**vocably** *adv*

vocabulary /vō kábbyŏŏləri/ (*plural* **-ies**) *n* **1.** WORDS OF LANGUAGE all the words used in a language as a whole **2.** WORDS OF SUBJECT AREA the set of words associated with a subject or area of activity, or used by an individual person ○ *the vocabulary of international diplomacy* ○ *The course encourages students to develop a wide scientific vocabulary.* **3.** LIST OF WORDS an alphabetical list of words and phrases supplied with definitions or translations **4.** ARTS RANGE OF EXPRESSIVE TECHNIQUES a repertoire of expressive forms or techniques used by an artist or in an art form [Mid-16C. < medieval Latin *vocabularium* 'of words' < Latin *vocabulum* (see VOCABLE)]

SYNONYMS See ***language*** and ***jargon***[1].

vocal /vők'l/ *adj* **1.** UTTERED uttered with the voice **2.** OF VOICE relating to the voice **3.** HAVING VOICE having a voice or using a voice to produce speech or sound **4.** OUTSPOKEN using frank, forthright, or insistent speech ○ *vocal objections* **5.** MUSIC OF OR FOR SINGING composed or arranged for singing, or relating to the art or techniques of singing **6.** NOISY WITH VOICES full of the sound of voices ○ *vocal enthusiasm* **7.** PHON same as **vocalic** ■ *n* **1.** SUNG PART the sung part of a piece of pop music or jazz **2.** MUSIC POP OR JAZZ SONG a song in the pop or jazz style [14C. < Latin *vocalis* < *voc-*, stem of *vox* 'voice'] —**vocality** /vō kálləti/ *n* —**vocally** *adv*

vocal cords *npl* a pair of fibrous sheets of tissue that span the cavity of the larynx and produce sounds by vibrating

vocal folds *npl* a pair of folds in the wall of the larynx situated just above the vocal cords

vocalic /vō kállik/ *adj* **1.** relating to or containing vowels **2.** used or acting as a vowel —**vocalically** *adv*

vocalise[1] /vőkə līz/ *vti* LING, MUSIC another spelling of **vocalize**

vocalise[2] /vőkə leéz/ *n* **1.** a voice training exercise in which a singer sings using only vowel sounds, especially one single vowel sound **2.** a passage or composition for performance in which a singer sings only vowel sounds, especially one single vowel sound [Late 19C. < French < *vocaliser* 'vocalize']

vocalism /vőkəlizəm/ *n* **1.** USE OF VOICE the use of the voice in producing speech, singing, or other sounds **2.** MUSIC ART OF SINGING the art or technique of singing **3.** PHON VOWELS OF LANGUAGE the range of vowels used in a language **4.** PHON VOWEL a vowel sound

vocalist /vőkəlist/ *n* a singer, especially of pop music or jazz —**vocalistic** /vőkə lístik/ *adj*

vocalize /vőkə līz/ (**-izes, -izing, -ized**), **vocalise** (**-ises, -ising, -ised**) *v* **1.** *vti* EXPRESS SOMETHING WITH VOICE to use the voice to express something **2.** *vt* ARTICULATE SOMETHING to use words to express something ○ *vocalized their concerns* **3.** *vti* PHON TRANSFORM INTO VOWEL to transform a consonant into a vowel sound in speaking, or be transformed into a vowel **4.** *vt* PHON same as **voice** *v* (sense 2) **5.** *vt* LING same as **vowelize** **6.** *vi* MUSIC SING WITHOUT WORDS to sing without words, using only one or more vowel sounds, especially as a vocal exercise to warm up the voice —**vocalization** /vőkə lī záysh'n/ *n* —**vocalizer** *n*

vocal score *n* the score of a vocal work, especially an opera, that gives the vocal parts in full with the orchestral parts transcribed for piano

vocal tic *n* a sudden noise or shout produced involuntarily, especially as a symptom of Tourette's syndrome or a similar neurological condition

vocat. *abbr* GRAM vocative

vocation /vō káysh'n/ *n* **1.** somebody's work, job, or profession, especially a type of work demanding special commitment **2.** a strong feeling of being destined or called to undertake a specific type of work, especially a sense of being chosen by God for religious work or a religious life [15C. < Latin *vocation-* < *vocat-*, past participle of *vocare* 'call, name']

ORIGIN The Latin word *vocare* 'to call, name', from which ***vocation*** is derived, is also the source of the English words *advocate, convoke, evoke, invoke, provoke, revoke, vocable, vocabulary, vocative*, and *vouch*.

vocational /vō káysh'nəl/ *adj* **1.** relating to education designed to provide the necessary skills for a specific job or career **2.** relating to somebody's vocation —**vocationally** *adv*

vocational guidance *n* guidance in the form of interviews and tests to see which job or career would best suit somebody's individual abilities and personality

vocationalism /vō káysh'nəlizəm/ *n* an emphasis on vocational training in education

vocative /vókətiv/ *n* **1.** GRAMMATICAL CASE OF SOMEBODY ADDRESSED a grammatical case that indicates that somebody or something is being directly addressed by the speaker. In Julius Caesar's dying words to Brutus 'et tu, Brute', 'Brute' is in the vocative. **2.** WORD IN VOCATIVE a word or form in the vocative case ■ *adj* INDICATING SOMEBODY OR SOMETHING ADDRESSED in or relating to the vocative [15C. < Latin *vocativus* < *vocat-* (see VOCATION)] —**vocatively** *adv*

vociferate /vō síffə rayt/ (**-ates, -ating, -ated**) *vti* to shout something out loudly [Late 16C. < Latin *vociferari* 'carry voice' < *voc-* (see VOCAL) + *ferre* 'carry'] —**vociferant** *adj* —**vociferation** /vō síffə ráysh'n/ *n* —**vociferator** *n*

vociferous /vō sífférəss/ *adj* **1.** shouting in a noisy and determined way **2.** characterized by noisy and determined shouting [Early 17C. < Latin *vociferari* (see VOCIFERATE)] —**vociferously** *adv* —**vociferousness** *n*

vocoder /vō kődər/ *n* an electronic device or computer program that converts speech into digital form and resynthesizes it at a later time or after transmission as artificial speech [Mid-20C. < VOICE + CODE]

vodka /vódkə/ *n* a colourless distilled spirit originally from Russia that is made from a grain such as rye or wheat or from potatoes [Early 19C. < Russian, 'small water' < *voda* 'water']

vodkatini /vódkə teéni/ *n* a cocktail consisting of vodka mixed with dry vermouth and ice, often served in a frosted glass [Late 20C. Blend of VODKA + MARTINI]

vodoun /vō dóon/, **vodun** *n* RELIG same as **voodoo** *n* (sense 1) [Late 19C. < Fon *vodū* 'fetish']

voe /vō/ *n* in Orkney and Shetland, a small bay [Late 17C. < Norwegian *våg*, Icelandic *vogur* 'bay, inlet']

voetsak /fŏŏt sak, vŏŏt-/ *interj S Africa* used to tell somebody to go away (*slang*) [Mid-19C. < Afrikaans *voertsek* < Dutch *voort zeg ik* 'be off, I say']

voetstoots /fŏŏt stóots, vŏŏt-/ *adv S Africa* with the seller having no responsibility for any faults in the item sold or for any other problems arising from the sale [Late 20C. < Afrikaans] —**voetstoots** *adj*

Vogel /vőg'l/, **Sir Julius** (1835–99) British-born premier of New Zealand. He was leader of the opposition (1865–68) before serving twice as prime minister (1873–75 and 1876). He also founded New Zealand's first daily newspaper, the *Otago Daily Times* (1861).

vogue[1] /vōg/ *n* **1.** PREVAILING FASHION the prevailing fashion at a particular time **2.** POPULARITY the state of being widely popular and fashionable at a particular time ○ *in vogue* ■ *adj* FASHIONABLE currently popular or fashionable [Late 16C. < French, literally 'rowing' < *voguer* 'to row']

vogue[2] /vōg/ (**vogues, voguing** or **vogueing, vogued**) *vi* to dance by imitating the poses struck by fashion models [Late 20C. After *Vogue*, fashion magazine] —**voguing** *n*

voguish /vőgish/ *adj* **1.** elegantly fashionable and stylish in appearance **2.** enjoying brief or sudden popularity —**voguishly** *adv* —**voguishness** *n*

Vogul /vőgŏŏl/ (*plural same* or **-guls**) *n* a member of a people who live along the western tributaries of the River Ob and the central and northern Ural Mountains in Russia [Late 18C. < Russian *vogul*] —**Vogul** *adj*

voice /voyss/ *n* **1.** SOUND MADE USING VOCAL ORGANS the sound produced by using the vocal organs, especially the sound used in speech **2.** SOUND OF SINGING the musical sound produced in singing **3.** ABILITY TO USE VOICE the ability to produce vocal sounds for speaking or singing ○ *have a good voice* **4.** SOUND LIKE HUMAN VOICE a sound similar to a human voice ○ *listening to the voice of the wind* **5.** RIGHT TO STATE OPINION a right to express an opinion ○ *sections of society that feel they have no voice* **6.** EXPRESSED OPINION an expressed opinion or desire ○ *hear the voice of the people* **7.** REPRESENTATIVE EXPRESSION a medium of communication or expression for somebody or something ○ *the voice of reason* **8.** MUSIC SINGER a singer taking a part in a musical composition **9.** MUSIC SINGING PART a sung part in a musical composition **10.** PHON VIBRATION OF VOCAL CORDS IN SPEAKING the passing of air across the vocal cords so as to create audible vibrations **11.** GRAM FORM OF VERB the form of a verb that indicates the relation of the subject to the verb. In the active voice, the subject performs the action, as in 'I hit him', while in the passive voice the subject suffers the effect of the action, as in 'he was hit'. ■ *v* (**voices, voicing, voiced**) **1.** *vt* UTTER SOMETHING to express a sentiment or opinion verbally **2.** *vt* PHON PRONOUNCE SOMETHING USING VOCAL CORDS to pronounce a consonant or vowel by passing air across the vocal cords so as to create audible vibrations **3.** *vt* MUSIC REGULATE TONE OF ORGAN to regulate the tone of an organ pipe in order to produce the desired sound **4.** MEDIA DO VOICEOVER FOR to provide the voiceover for a character in a cartoon or a radio or television advertisement [13C. Via Old French *vois* < Latin *vox*] —**voicer** *n* ◇ **be in (good) voice** to be singing well or speaking well ◇ **with one voice** simultaneously or unanimously

voice-activated *adj* operated by the user's spoken commands, rather than by physical input

voice box *n* ANAT same as **larynx**

voiced /voyst/ *adj* **1.** having or conducted in a voice of a particular kind (*often used in combination*) ○ *a low-voiced conversation* **2.** describes a consonant or vowel pronounced by passing air across the vocal cords to create audible vibrations, as is the 's' sound in the word 'his' —**voicedness** *n*

voiceful /vóysf'l/ *adj* having a loud or ringing voice (*literary*) —**voicefulness** *n*

voiceless /vóyssləss/ *adj* **1.** SAYING NOTHING maintaining a silence **2.** HAVING NO SAY having no vote or influence ○ *the voiceless people in a dictatorship* **3.** HAVING NO VOICE not endowed with a voice **4.** PHON PRONOUNCED WITHOUT VIBRATION OF VOCAL CORDS describes a consonant or vowel pronounced without passing air across the vocal cords and creating audible vibrations, as is the 's' sound in the word 'hiss' —**voicelessly** *adv* —**voicelessness** *n*

voicemail /vóyss mayl/ *n* an electronic communications system that stores digitized recordings of telephone messages for later playback (*hyphenated before a noun*)

voiceover /vóyss ōvər/ *n* the voice of, or the words spoken by, an unseen narrator, commentator, or character in a film or television programme

voice over Internet protocol *n* ONLINE full form of **VoIP**

voice-over-the-Net *adj* describes voice communication using VoIP technology

voiceprint /vóyss print/ *n* a representation in graph form of the frequencies that make up somebody's voice [Mid-20C. < VOICE + FINGERPRINT]

voiceprint identification *n* the use of the sound frequencies of speech as a method of identifying somebody

voice recognition *n* **1.** COMPUT same as **speech recognition 2.** a computer function that enables the machine to recognize the voice of a person speaking into a microphone attached to it

voice vote *n* a vote taken in a parliament or other legislative body in which voters cry out 'aye' or 'no', or 'yea' and 'nay', with the louder cry winning the vote

voice writing *n US* the process of recording proceedings by voice by speaking into a device that silences and records the spoken words for subsequent transcription by hand or voice-recognition software —**voicewriter** *n*

void /voyd/ *adj* **1.** NOT LEGALLY VALID having no legal force ○ *declared the will null and void* **2.** DEVOID totally lacking in something (*formal*) ○ *a personality void of all compassion* **3.** NOT CONTAINING ANYTHING having no contents **4.** VACANT not occupied **5.** POINTLESS ineffective or useless **6.** CARDS HAVING NO CARDS IN SUIT lacking any cards in a particular suit in a hand dealt in a card game ■ *n* **1.** EMPTY SPACE a large empty space **2.** PRIVATION a state of loss or privation **3.** FEELING OF LOSS a feeling of loneliness and emptiness **4.** GAP a gap or opening **5.** CARDS LACK OF CARDS IN SUIT a complete lack of cards in a particular suit in a hand dealt in a card game ○ *a void in spades* ■ *v* (**voids, voiding, voided**) **1.** *vt* MAKE SOMETHING LEGALLY INVALID to deprive something of legal force **2.** *vt* EMPTY CONTENTS OF SOMETHING to empty out the contents of something, or empty something of its contents **3.** *vti* EMPTY BOWELS OR BLADDER to empty the bowels or bladder [13C. < Old French *voide* 'empty' < assumed Vulgar Latin *vocitus*, alteration of Latin *vocivus*] —**voidable** *adj* —**voider** *n* —**voidness** *n*

SYNONYMS See *vacant*.

voidance /vóyd'nss/ *n* **1.** INVALIDATION OF CONTRACT the act of depriving a contract of legal force **2.** ACT OF EMPTYING the act of voiding or emptying something **3.** VACANCY the situation of having no incumbent or occupant, e.g. no bishop in a diocese

void deck *n* in Malaysia and Singapore, the empty ground floor of a block of flats, used for social events by people living in the block

voided /vóydid/ *adj* **1.** having been deprived of legal force **2.** in heraldry, having the centre and a narrow surrounding area removed or left empty

voilà /vwa laá/ *interj* used to bring somebody's attention to something, especially in order to elicit appreciation or approval [Mid-18C. < French *voi* 'see!' + *là* 'there']

voile /voyl/ *n* a crisp lightweight translucent fabric made from cotton, synthetic fibres, or wool [Late 19C. < French, 'veil' < Latin *vela* (see VEIL)]

VoIP /voyp/ *n* a technology that enables voice messages to be sent via the Internet, often simultaneously with data in text or other forms. Full form **voice over Internet protocol**

voir dire /vwaar deér/ *n* the preliminary examination of a witness or juror to determine his or her competence to give or hear evidence [Late 17C. < Law French < Old French *voir* 'truth' + *dire* 'speak']

voix céleste /vwaá sə lést/ *n* an organ stop that gives a light wavering otherworldly quality to the notes played [Late 19C. < French < *voix* 'voice' + *céleste* 'heavenly']

vol. *abbr* **1.** GEOG volcano **2.** MEASURE volume **3.** volunteer

Volans /vó lanz/ *n* a small constellation of the southern hemisphere. See illustration at **constellation** [Mid-20C. Shortening of modern Latin *Piscis Volans* 'flying fish', earlier name of the constellation]

volant /vólənt/ *adj* **1.** ABLE TO FLY flying or having the power of flight **2.** NIMBLE moving quickly, lightly, and easily (*literary*) **3.** HERALDRY HAVING WINGS SPREAD in heraldry, having the wings outspread as in flight [Early 16C. < French, present participle of *voler* 'fly' < Latin *volare*]

Volapük /vóllə pook, vólə-/ *n* a synthetic language based on English and German, invented by Johann

---

MAJOR VOLCANOES OF THE WORLD

Cotopaxi *Ecuador*
Elevation [19,347 ft / 5,897 m]
World's highest active volcano

Mauna Loa *Hawaii*
Elevation [13,680 ft / 4,170 m]
Major eruption 1984

Erebus *Antarctica*
Elevation [12,448 ft / 3,794 m]
Major eruptions 1970s

Cameroon *Cameroon*
Elevation [13,435 ft / 4,095 m]
Major eruption 1982

Etna *Italy*
Elevation [10,902 ft / 3,323 m]
Over 90 recorded eruptions

Ruapehu *New Zealand*
Elevation [9,177 ft / 2,797 m]
Major eruptions 1995, 1996

St Helens *United States*
Elevation [8,365 ft / 2,550 m]
Major eruption 1980

Vesuvius *Italy*
Elevation [4,190 ft / 1,277 m]
Major eruption 79 AD —
destroying Roman Pompeii

Soufriere Hills *Montserrat*
Elevation [3,002 ft / 915 m]
Major eruption 1997 —
much of island left uninhabitable

Krakatau *Indonesia*
Elevation [2,667 ft / 813 m]
Major eruption 1883 —
tidal waves from eruption estimated
to have caused over 30,000 deaths

Martin Schleyer in 1880 [Late 19C. < *vol*, alteration of WORLD + *pük* 'speech', alteration of SPEAK] —**Volapük** *adj*

volar /vólər/ *adj* relating to the palm of the hand or the sole of the foot [Early 19C. < *vola* 'hollow of the hand or foot' < Latin, 'sole, palm']

volatile /vóllə tīl/ *adj* **1.** UNSTABLE AND POTENTIALLY DANGEROUS apt to become suddenly violent or dangerous **2.** UNPREDICTABLE OR FICKLE changeable in mood, temper, or desire **3.** CHANGING SUDDENLY characterized by or prone to sudden change **4.** SHORT-LIVED continuing for only a short time **5.** CHEM PRONE TO EVAPORATION evaporating at a relatively low temperature **6.** COMPUT LOSING DATA WHEN POWER IS OFF describes a computer memory that does not store data when the power is turned off ■ *n* CHEM VOLATILE SUBSTANCE a substance that evaporates at a relatively low temperature [Late 16C. < Latin *volatilis* < *volat*-, past participle of *volare* 'fly'] —**volatilely** *adv* —**volatility** /vóllə tílləti/ *n*

volatile organic compound *n* an organic compound that evaporates at a relatively low temperature and contributes to air pollution, e.g. ethylene, propylene, benzene, or styrene

volatilize /və látti līz/ (**-izes, -izing, -ized**), **volatilise** (**-ises, -ising, -ised**) *vti* to change into a vapour, or cause a solid or liquid to be changed into a vapour —**volatilizable** *adj* —**volatilization** /və látti lī záysh'n/ *n* —**volatilizer** *n*

vol-au-vent /vólō vaaN/ *n* a small light pastry shell traditionally filled with meat or fish in a sauce [< French, literally 'flight in the wind']

volcanic /vol kánnik/ *adj* **1.** OF VOLCANOES relating to or originating from a volcano **2.** CONSISTING OF VOLCANOES characterized by or made up of volcanoes **3.** SUDDEN AND VIOLENT characterized by sudden violent outbursts ○ *a volcanic temper* [Late 18C. < French *volcanique* < *volan* 'volcano'] —**volcanically** *adv*

volcanic arc *n* GEOG same as **island arc**

volcanic bomb *n* a lump of lava ejected from a volcano that has acquired a characteristic form as a result of its solidification while travelling through the air

volcanic cone *n* a cone-shaped mass of material that has built up around the crater of a volcano

---

volcanic dust *n* fine particles of ash that are suspended in the atmosphere after a volcanic eruption

volcanic glass *n* natural glass formed when molten lava from a volcano cools too quickly to crystallize

volcanicity /vólkə níssəti/ *n* the tendency or likelihood of a volcano or group of volcanoes to erupt [Mid-19C. < French *volcanicité* < *volcan* 'volcano']

volcanic plug, **volcanic neck** *n* a massive cylindrical formation of solidified lava that once blocked the vent of a volcano, now exposed after erosion of softer surrounding material

volcanise *vt* GEOL another spelling of **volcanize**

volcanism /vólkənizəm/ *n* the processes involved in the formation of volcanoes, and in the transfer of magma and volatile material from the interior of the Earth to its surface [Mid-19C. < French *volcanisme* < *volcan* 'volcano']

volcanize /vólkə nīz/ (**-nizes, -nizing, -nized**), **volcanise** (**-nises, -nising, -nised**) *vt* to cause something to change as a result of volcanic activity —**volcanization** /vólkə nī záysh'n/ *n*

volcano /vol káynō/ (*plural* **-noes** or **-nos**) *n* **1.** a naturally occurring opening in the surface of the Earth through which molten, gaseous, and solid material is ejected **2.** a mountain created by the deposition and accumulation of materials ejected from a vent in a central crater [Early 17C. Via Italian < Latin *Volcanus, Vulcanus* 'Vulcan'] —**volcanian** *adj*

CULTURAL NOTE *Under the Volcano*, a novel (1947) by Malcolm Lowry. Set in Mexico on the annual Day of the Dead, it describes the last hours of British consul Geoffrey Firman, who, depressed by the failure of his marriage and the onset of war, slowly drinks himself to death. A harrowing psychological study, it can also be read as an allegory of the disintegration of Western values.

volcanology /vólkə nólləji/ *n* the scientific study of volcanoes, including their formation, signs of an eruption, and other aspects of volcanic activity —**volcanologic** /vólkənə lójjik/ *adj* —**volcanological** *adj* —**volcanologist** *n*

vole

vole[1] /vōl/ (*plural* **voles** or *same*) *n* a small rodent similar to a mouse but with a shorter tail and legs and a stocky body. Native to: North America, Europe, Asia. Genus: *Microtus*. [Early 19C. < Norwegian *voll mus* 'field mouse']

vole[2] /vōl/ *n* in a card game such as bridge, a taking of all the tricks in a single hand [Late 17C. < French, probably < *voler* 'to fly' < Latin *volare*]

Volga /vólgə/ longest river of Europe, in western Russia. It rises northwest of Moscow and flows southeast and south before emptying into the Caspian Sea. Length: 3,700 km/2,300 mi.

Volgograd /vólgə grad/ industrial and port city in southwestern Russia on the River Volga. It is an important rail junction and inland port. In World War II, the city was subjected to a long siege by German forces that proved to be one of the turning points of the war. Population: 1,260,171 (1995). Former name **Stalingrad** (1925–61)

volitant /vóllitənt/ *adj* **1.** flying, or capable of flight **2.** moving about rapidly or constantly [Early 17C. < Latin *volitare* 'keep on flying' < *volare* 'to fly']

volition /vō lísh'n/ *n* **1.** CHOOSING the act of exercising the will **2.** ABILITY TO CHOOSE the ability to make conscious choices or decisions **3.** CHOICE MADE the result of ex-

---

ercising the will **4.** PHILOSOPHY **ACT OF WILL** an act of will distinguished from the intended physical movement it causes [Early 17C. Directly or via French < Latin *volition-* < *vol-* (see VOLUNTARY)] —**volitional** *adj* —**volitionally** *adv* —**volitionary** *adj*

volitive /vóllətiv/ *adj* **1.** relating to or beginning in the will **2.** GRAM same as **desiderative** (sense 2) [15C. < medieval Latin *volitivus* < Latin *volition-* (see VOLITION)]

volk /folk/ *n S Africa* a people or nation, especially the nation of Afrikaners [Late 19C. Via Afrikaans < Dutch, 'nation, people']

Völkerwanderung /fólkər vandəróong, fólkər vaandəróong/ *n* a movement of peoples, especially the migration of Germanic and Slavic peoples into southern and western Europe between the 2nd and 11th centuries [Mid-20C. < German, 'migration of nations']

Volkslied /fólks leet/ (*plural* **-lieder** /-leedər/) *n* a traditional German folk song [Mid-19C. < German, 'people's song']

volley /vólli/ *n* **1.** SIMULTANEOUS EXPRESSION OF SOMETHING a simultaneous rapid expression of something such as curses or protests **2.** MISSILES FIRED a discharge of missiles or other projectiles fired simultaneously **3.** FIRING OF WEAPONS a simultaneous discharge of several weapons, especially firearms **4.** SWING AT BALL in tennis or football, a swing, kick, or hit at a ball before it touches the ground **5.** MIN EXTRACT **MULTIPLE ROCK BLASTING** a simultaneous blasting of several sections of rock ■ *v* (**-leys, -leying, -leyed**) **1.** *vti* STRIKE BALL BEFORE IT LANDS to hit or kick a ball before it reaches the ground, e.g. in tennis or football **2.** *vti* FIRE SIMULTANEOUSLY to fire weapons simultaneously, or be fired simultaneously **3.** *vti* SAY RAPIDLY to say something forcefully or loudly and rapidly, or be spoken forcefully or loudly and rapidly **4.** *vi* MOVE RAPIDLY to move rapidly or loudly [Late 16C. < French *volée* < Latin *volare* 'to fly'] —**volleyer** *n*

volleyball: players jump to block a smash

volleyball /vólli bawl/ *n* **1.** a sport in which two teams hit a large ball over a high net using their hands, played on a rectangular court **2.** a large, usually white inflated ball used to play volleyball —**volleyballer** *n*

volost /vó lost/ *n* **1.** in the former Soviet Union, a rural elected council **2.** in tsarist Russia, a peasant community made up of several villages [Late 19C. < Russian]

volplane /vól playn/ *vi* (**-planes, -planing, -planed**) **1.** GLIDE TO GROUND to glide towards the ground in an aeroplane with the engine turned off **2.** MOVE BY GLIDING to travel or move by gliding ■ *n* ACT OF GLIDING a glide towards the ground in an aircraft with the engine turned off [Early 20C. < French *vol plané* 'planed flight']

vols. *abbr* volumes

Volsci /vólski/ *npl* an ancient people who lived in Latium, a region of central Italy that was taken over by the Romans during the 5th and 4th centuries BC —**Volscian** *adj, n*

volt[1] /vōlt/ *n* the unit of electromotive force and electric potential difference equal to the difference between two points in a circuit carrying one ampere of current and dissipating one watt of power. Symbol V [Late 19C. After Alessandro VOLTA]

volt[2] /volt/, **volte** *n* **1.** in dressage, a circular movement executed by a horse **2.** in fencing, a sudden leap made to elude an opponent's thrust [Late 16C. Via French *volte* < Italian *volta* (see VOLTA)]

volta /vóltə/ (*plural* **-te** /-tay/) *n* **1.** ITALIAN DANCE a fast Italian dance of the 16th and 17th centuries **2.** VOLTA MUSIC the music for a volta **3.** ONE PLAYING OF MUSICAL PASSAGE a single playing of a passage of music that may then be repeated [Late 16C. < Italian, 'a turn' < *volgere* 'to turn' < Latin *volvere* 'to roll']

Volta /vóltə/ river in southeastern Ghana, formed by the confluence of the Black Volta and White Volta rivers and emptying into the Atlantic Ocean. Length: 1,500 km/930 mi.

Volta, Alessandro, Count (1745–1827) Italian physicist. He developed the first electric battery (1800).

voltage /vóltij/ *n* electric potential expressed in volts

voltage divider *n* a resistor or series of resistors used to provide various voltages that are fractions of the source voltage

voltaic /vol táy ik/ *adj* relating to or denoting direct electric current produced by chemical action [Early 19C. < After Alessandro VOLTA]

Voltaic /vol táy ik/ *adj* **1.** relating to Burkina-Faso, or to its people or culture **2.** relating to the Gur group of languages, spoken chiefly in Burkina-Faso and Ghana [Mid-20C. < the River VOLTA]

voltaic battery *n* an electric battery made up of one or more primary cells

voltaic cell *n* ELEC same as **primary cell**

voltaic couple *n* two different metals immersed in an electrolyte that produce a potential difference by chemical action

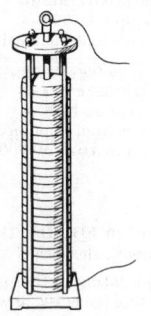

voltaic pile

voltaic pile *n* a source of electricity consisting of a stack of dissimilar metal discs separated by a porous material soaked in electrolyte that functions as a battery

Voltaire /vol táir/ (1694–1778) French writer and philosopher. A leading figure in the Enlightenment, he produced a range of literary works embodying his radical spirit and religious ideas. They include *Philosophical Letters* (1734), *Candide* (1759), and the *Dictionnaire philosophique* (*Philosophical Dictionary*) (1764). Born **Arouet, François Marie**

'In this best of possible worlds...all is for the best.'
[Voltaire, *Candide*; 1759]

'If God did not exist, it would be necessary to invent Him.'
[Voltaire, 'À l'auteur du livre des trois Imposteurs' (To the Author of The Three Impostors)', *Épîtres* (Epistles); 1769]

voltaism /vóltə izəm/ *n* PHYS same as **galvanism** (sense 1)

volte[1] /volt/ *n* RIDING, FENCING another spelling of **volt**[2]

volte[2] /vóltay/ DANCE, MUSIC plural of **volta**

volte-face /vólt faáss/ *n* **1.** a sudden reversal in opinion or policy **2.** a change in position so as to be facing the opposite direction [Early 19C. Via French < Italian *voltafaccia* 'turn of the face']

voltmeter /vólt meetər/ *n* an instrument calibrated in volts that measures the electromotive force or potential difference between two points in a circuit

voluble /vóllyoob'l/ *adj* **1.** talking easily and at length, or involving lengthy talking **2.** twining or twisting [14C. Directly or via French < Latin *volubilis* < *volvere* 'to roll'] —**volubility** /vóllyoo bílləti/ *n* —**volubleness** *n* —**volubly** *adv*

volume /vóllyoom/ *n* **1.** SPACE INSIDE OBJECT the size of a three-dimensional space enclosed within or occupied by an object. Symbol **V 2.** AMOUNT the total amount of something **3.** LOUDNESS the loudness of a sound **4.** SOUND CONTROL the knob or button on a radio, television, or audio player that controls loudness **5.** BOOK a bound collection of printed or written pages **6.** BOOK OF SET a single book that belongs to a set of books **7.** PUBL CONSECUTIVE MAGAZINE ISSUES a set of issues of a periodical spanning one calendar year **8.** HIST SCROLL a roll of parchment or papyrus **9.** THICKNESS the thick quality or appearance of somebody's hair ○ *Apply to roots for added volume.* ■ *adj* INVOLVING LARGE QUANTITIES using or involving large amounts or quantities ○ *offering volume discounts on carpeting* [14C. Via Old French < Latin *volumen* 'roll, scroll, book' < *volvere* 'to roll'] ◇ **speak volumes** to be highly expressive or significant

volumed /vóllyoomd/ *adj* **1.** published in a series or set of a number of books (*usually used in combination*) ○ *a three-volumed set* **2.** forming or rolling in a rounded mass (*literary*)

volumeter /vo lyoómitər/ *n* an instrument used to measure the volume of a solid, liquid, or gas

volumetric /vóllyoo méttrik/ *adj* relating to volume, or using measurement by volume —**volumetrically** *adv*

volumetric analysis *n* **1.** an analysis of liquids using measured volumes of standard chemical reagents **2.** an analysis of gas by volume

voluminous /və loóminəss/ *adj* **1.** LARGE having great size, capacity, or fullness ○ *a voluminous cloak* **2.** EXTREMELY LONG very lengthy and taking up many pages or books ○ *a voluminous report* **3.** PROLIFIC producing a large amount of creative work ○ *a voluminous writer* [Early 17C. < late Latin *voluminosus* 'with many coils' < Latin *volumen* (see VOLUME)] —**voluminosity** /və loómi nóssəti/ *n* —**voluminously** *adv* —**voluminousness** *n*

voluntarism /vólləntərizəm/ *n* **1.** PHILOSOPHICAL THEORY the philosophical theory that regards the will rather than the intellect as the essential principle of humankind or the cosmos **2.** RELIANCE ON VOLUNTARY CONTRIBUTIONS the use of or dependence on voluntary contributions rather than government funds to keep an institution such as a school or church in existence **3.** NO INTERFERENCE the belief that no level of government or law should interfere in the process of collective bargaining or the organization of trade unions —**voluntarist** *n* —**voluntaristic** /vólləntə rístik/ *adj*

voluntary /vólləntəri/ *adj* **1.** OF FREE WILL arising, acting, or resulting from somebody's own choice or decision rather than because of external pressure or force **2.** WITHOUT PAY performing, working, or done without financial reward ○ *voluntary work* **3.** USING VOLUNTEERS composed of, functioning with or requiring volunteers ○ *voluntary organizations* **4.** NOT PART OF GOVERNMENT not part of statutory provision such as that of social services, and usually maintained at least in part by private charitable donations rather than by government or other official support ○ *Many organizations in the voluntary sector receive some state funding.* **5.** HAVING WILL having the capacity required to make conscious choices or decisions **6.** LAW WITHOUT LEGAL OBLIGATION not involving legal obligation, coercion, or persuasion ○ *a voluntary agreement* **7.** LAW DONE ON PURPOSE performed or carried out with intention rather than by accident ○ *voluntary manslaughter* **8.** LAW GIVEN WITHOUT PAYMENT IN RETURN done or given freely with no promise of money or other recompense ■ *n* (*plural* **-ies**) **1.** SHORT COMPOSITION a short musical composition, often played on a solo instrument, that introduces a longer work **2.** MUSIC CHURCH MUSIC a piece of music or improvisation for the organ, played before, during, or at the end of a church service [14C. < Latin *voluntarius* < *voluntas* 'will, choice' < *vol-*, stem of *velle* 'to wish'] —**voluntarily** /vólləntərəli, -térrəli/ *adv* —**voluntariness** *n*

voluntary arrangement *n* a procedure in which a failing business can make arrangements with its creditors to resolve its financial problems, often after a court order

voluntaryism /vólləntəri izəm/ *n* PUBLIC ADMIN same as **voluntarism** (sense 2) —**voluntaryist** *n*

voluntary muscle *n* a muscle, usually made up of striated fibres, that is consciously controlled

volunteer /vóllən teér/ *n* **1.** SOMEBODY WHO WORKS FOR NOTHING somebody who works without being paid **2.** SOMEBODY ACTING VOLUNTARILY somebody who does something voluntarily, especially something undesirable **3.** VOLUNTARY RECRUIT TO ARMED FORCES somebody who has freely offered to serve in the armed services **4.** BOT CULTIVATED PLANT GROWING NATURALLY a cultivated plant, especially a crop plant, that grows without having been intentionally sown or planted **5.** LAW SOMEBODY ACTING WITHOUT LEGAL OBLIGATION a participant in something who is not legally bound to participate and does not expect to be paid **6.** LAW SOMEBODY GIVEN PROPERTY a recipient of property who does not have to pay for it or give anything in return ■ *v* (**-teers, -teering, -teered**) **1.** *vti* OFFER FREE HELP to do charitable or helpful work without receiving pay for it ○ *volunteers his time* ○ *Many companies now encourage their staff to volunteer.* **2.** *vti* DO SOMETHING BY CHOICE to perform, or offer to perform, work of your own free will ○ *volunteered to work the night shift* **3.** *vt* TELL SOMETHING WITHOUT BEING ASKED to tell somebody something or give information without being asked ○ *volunteering information* **4.** *vt* OFFER SOMEBODY ELSE'S HELP to suggest somebody else as a helper (*informal*) ○ *volunteered her secretary for a few days* **5.** *vi* OFFER TO DO MILITARY SERVICE to offer to serve in one of the armed services without being required by law to join [Late 16C. Via French *volontaire* < Latin *voluntarius* (see VOLUNTARY)]

volunteer army *n* an army that relies on recruiting people who enlist voluntarily, rather than conscripting recruits by law

volunteerism /vóllən teérizəm/ *n N Am* the practice of using volunteer workers, especially in community service or educational organizations and programs

volunteer vacation *n US* a holiday during which somebody does volunteer work such as cleaning up the environment or housing construction and repair

~~**voluptious**~~ incorrect spelling of **voluptuous**

voluptuary /və lúpchoo əri/ (*plural* **-ies**) *n* somebody whose life is devoted to enjoying luxury and the pleasures of the senses [Early 17C. < Latin *voluptuarius* < *voluptas* 'pleasure']

voluptuous /və lúpchoo əss/ *adj* **1.** sensual in appearance, or providing sensual pleasure **2.** inclined or devoted to a life of sensual pleasure [14C. Directly or via French *voluptueux* < Latin *voluptuosus* < *voluptas* 'pleasure'] —**voluptuously** *adv* —**voluptuousness** *n*

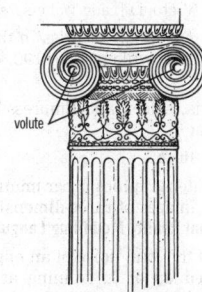

volute (sense 2)

volute /və loʻot, vóllyoot/ *n* **1.** SPIRAL SHAPE a spiral form or structure, e.g. the whorl in the shell of a snail **2.** ARCHIT DECORATIVE SCROLL a carved spiral decoration, usually on an Ionic capital **3.** MARINE BIOL TROPICAL MOLLUSC a gastropod mollusc with a colourful spiral shell. Native to: tropical waters. Family: Volutidae. ■ *adj* SPIRALLING moving in or following a spiral path [Mid-16C. Directly or via French < Latin *voluta*, feminine past participle of *volvere* 'to roll']

ORIGIN The Latin word *volvere* 'to roll', from which *volute* is derived, is also the source of the English words *convolute*, *convolvulus*, *devolution*, *evolution*, *involve*, *revolt*, *revolution*, *revolve*, *vault*[1], *voluble*, and *volume*.

volutin /vóllyoʻotin/ *n* an easily stained substance found in the cytoplasm of some bacterial and fungal cells that serves to store phosphates for the energy needs of the cell [Early 20C. < modern Latin *Spirillum*

volutans 'rolling spirillum', bacterium in which first found < Latin *volutare* 'wallow']

volution /və loʻosh'n/ *n* **1.** a shape that coils, twists, or turns around a centre **2.** a spiral segment of a gastropod's shell [15C. < late Latin *volution-* < Latin *volvere* 'to roll']

volva /vólvə/ (*plural* **-vae** /-vee/ or **-vas**) *n* a cup-shaped structure that encircles the base of the stalk of some mushrooms [Mid-18C. < modern Latin < Latin *volvere* 'to roll'] —**volvate** *adj*

volvox /vól voks/ *n* freshwater green algae that form communities made up of hollow multicellular spheres. Genus: *Volvox*. [Late 18C. < modern Latin < Latin *volvere* 'to roll']

volvulus /vólvyoʻoləss/ (*plural* **-li** /-lī, -lee/) *n* a twisting of the digestive tract that leads to partial or complete obstruction and a reduction in blood supply [Late 17C. < medieval Latin < Latin *volvere* 'to roll']

vomer /vóʻmər/ *n* a thin plate of bone that forms part of the septum dividing the nasal passages inside the nose [Early 18C. < Latin, 'ploughshare'; because of its shape] —**vomerine** /-rīn/ *adj*

vomit /vómmit/ *vti* (**-its, -iting, -ited**) **1.** THROW UP STOMACH CONTENTS to expel the contents of the stomach through the mouth as a result of a series of involuntary spasms of the stomach muscles **2.** GUSH FORTH to send something out in a forceful stream, or be ejected forcefully ○ *to vomit curses* ■ *n* **1.** EXPELLED STOMACH CONTENTS the stomach contents expelled through the mouth. Technical name **vomitus 2.** ACT OF VOMITING the act of expelling the stomach contents through the mouth [15C. Directly or via Anglo-French < Latin *vomitus*, past participle of *vomere* 'eject, vomit'] —**vomiter** *n*

vomitory /vómmitəri/ *n* (*plural* **-ries**) **1.** OPENING an opening through which matter is ejected (*formal*) **2.** BUILDINGS, ANCIENT HIST ANCIENT ROMAN PASSAGEWAY a passageway, usually in an ancient Roman amphitheatre or stadium, connecting a tier of seats with an outside entrance ■ *adj also* **vomitive** /vómmitiv/ MED CAUSING VOMITING causing the vomiting of stomach contents (*dated*) [Early 17C. < Latin *vomitorius* < *vomitus* (see VOMIT)]

vomitus /vómmitəss/ *n* vomited contents of the stomach (*technical*) [Early 20C. < Latin (see VOMIT)]

von, Von see also under surname

von Braun /von bŕown/, **Wernher** (1912–77) German engineer. He developed the V-2 rocket for Germany during World War II. After 1945, he worked in the United States developing the launch vehicle used in the Moon landing programme.

'Everything in space obeys the laws of physics. If you know these laws and obey them, space will treat you kindly. And don't tell me that man doesn't belong out there. Man belongs wherever he wants to go; and he'll do plenty well when he gets there.'
[Wernher von Braun, *Time*; 17 February 1958]

Vo Nguyen Giap /vó əng goʻo yen jáp/ (b. 1912) Vietnamese military leader. In Vietnam, he led Communist fighters against the Japanese (1945), the French (1954), and the United States (1964–73).

Vonnegut /vónni gut/, **Kurt** (b. 1922) US writer. He is known for his satirical novels, including *Slaughterhouse Five* (1969). Full name **Vonnegut, Jr, Kurt**. See Cultural note at **slaughterhouse**

'Beware of the man who works hard to learn something, learns it, and finds himself no wiser than before, Bokonon tells us. He is full of murderous resentment of people who are ignorant without having come by their ignorance the hard way.'
[Kurt Vonnegut, *Cat's Cradle*; 1963]

'A flaw in the human character is that everybody wants to build and nobody wants to do maintenance.'
[Kurt Vonnegut, *Hocus Pocus*; 1969]

von Neumann /von nóymən/, **John** (1903–57) Hungarian-born US mathematician. He developed game theory and quantum mechanics and was a pioneer

in computer theory and design. Born **János von Neumann**

'In mathematics you don't understand things. You just get used to them.'
[John von Neumann. Quoted in *The Dancing Wu Li Masters*, Gary Zukav; 1979]

von Sternberg /von stúrn burg/, **Josef** (1894–1969) Austrian-born US film director. His interest in visual style is a notable element in his films, most notably *The Blue Angel* (1930). Born **Sternberg, Jonas**

'The only way to succeed is to make people hate you. That way, they remember you.'
[Josef von Sternberg, *Fun in a Chinese Laundry*; 1965]

von Stroheim /von strő hīm/, **Erich** (1885–1957) Austrian-born US actor and film director. In Hollywood after 1914, he directed films of unparalleled realism and psychological intensity, including his masterpiece, *Greed* (1925). Born **Stroheim, Erich Oswald**

voodoo /voʻodoo/ *n* (*plural* **-doos**) **1.** CARIBBEAN RELIGION a religion practised throughout Caribbean countries, especially Haiti, that is a combination of Roman Catholic rituals and animistic beliefs, involving magic and communication with ancestors **2.** PRACTITIONER OF VOODOO a practitioner, priest, or priestess of voodoo **3.** SUPPOSED MAGIC CHARM a charm, spell, or fetish regarded by those who practise voodoo as having magical powers ■ *vt* (**-doos, -dooing, -dooed**) CAST SPELL ON SOMEBODY to cast a voodoo spell on somebody [Early 19C. Via Louisiana French *voudou* < Fon *vodū* 'fetish']

voodooism /voʻodoo izəm/ *n* **1.** the practices and beliefs of voodoo **2.** an attempt to control or affect the world using magic or sorcery —**voodooist** *n* —**voodooistic** /-ístik/ *adj*

voop /voop/ *n Carib* in cricket, a wild uncontrolled swing at the ball by a batsman [Late 20C. Probably < an imitation of the sound of the bat passing through the air] —**voop** *vi*

voorkamer /foʻor kaamər/ *n S Africa* the front room of a house, especially of a Cape Dutch house or farmhouse [Late 18C. Via Afrikaans < Dutch, 'front room']

Voortrekker /foʻor trekər/ *n S Africa* a member of a band of Afrikaner pioneers who, in the early 19th century, left the British-ruled Cape for the eastern Cape and the interior of South Africa [Late 19C. Via Afrikaans < Dutch, 'before-trekker']

VOR *abbr* very-high-frequency omnidirectional radio range

voracious /və ráyshəss/ *adj* **1.** desiring or consuming food in great quantities ○ *a voracious appetite* **2.** unusually eager or enthusiastic about an activity ○ *a voracious reader* [Mid-17C. < Latin *vorac-* < *vorare* 'devour'] —**voraciously** *adv* —**voraciousness** *n* —**voracity** /və rássəti/ *n*

Vorlage /fáwr laagə/, **vorlage** *n* a skiing position in which a skier leans forward from the ankle but keeps his or her heels on the skis [Mid-20C. < German, 'forward position']

Voronezh /və rónnezh/ city and capital of Voronezh Oblast in western Russia. Population: 1,084,734 (1995).

-vorous *suffix* eating, having a particular kind of food ○ *herbivorous* [< Latin *-vorus* < *vorare* 'to swallow']

Vorster /fáwrstər/, **John** (1915–83) South African politician. During his premiership (1966–78) and presidency (1978–79), he reinforced the apartheid legislation introduced by his predecessor and mentor, Hendrik Verwoerd. His career ended after he was implicated in a financial scandal. Born **Vorster, Balthazar Johannes**

'As far as criticism is concerned, we don't resent that unless it is absolutely biased, as it is in most cases.'
[John Vorster, *Observer*; 9 November 1969]

vortal /váwrt'l/ *n* a portal website devoted to one specific industry that enables business-to-business e-commerce transactions by bringing together businesses at different points in the supply chain [Late 20C. Blend of VERTICAL + PORTAL]

vortex /váwr teks/ (*plural* **-texes** or **-tices** /-ti seez/) *n* **1.** a whirling mass of something, especially water or air, that draws everything near it towards its centre

2. a situation or feeling that seems to swamp or engulf everything else [Mid-17C. < Latin, variant of *vertex* (see VERTEX)]

vortical /váwrtik'l/, **vorticose** /váwrti kōss/ *adj* relating to or moving in a vortex [Mid-17C. < Latin *vortic-*, stem of *vortex* (see VORTEX)] —**vortically** *adv*

vorticella /váwrti séllə/ (*plural* **-lae** /-lee/) *n* an underwater protozoan with a bell-shaped body. It is usually attached to something such as a plant by a slender stalk. Genus: *Vorticella*. [Late 18C. < modern Latin, 'little vortex' < Latin *vortic-* (see VORTICAL)]

vortices plural of **vortex**

vorticism /váwrtissizəm/ *n* a short-lived early-20th-century British movement in art and literature that used abstract forms to express concern about the future and the machine age [Early 20C. < Latin *vortic-* (see VORTICAL)] —**vorticist** *n*

vorticity /vawr tíssəti/ *n* the state of a fluid moving in a vortex [Late 19C. < Latin *vortic-* (see VORTICAL)]

vorticose *adj* PHYS same as **vortical**

Vosges /vōzh/ mountain range in northeastern France. Length: 190 km/120 mi. Highest peak: Grand Ballon 1424 m/4,672 ft.

Vostok /vóstok/ *n* a spacecraft of a type launched by the former Soviet Union. Seven were launched, beginning in April 1961. [Mid-20C. < Russian]

votary /vōtəri/ (*plural* **-ries**), **votarist** /-rist/ *n* **1.** somebody who has sworn to dedicate his or her life to religious worship or service **2.** a dedicated follower of something such as a religion or cause [Mid-16C. < Latin *vot-*, past participle of *vovere* 'vow']

vote /vōt/ *n* **1.** FORMAL CHOICE FOR OR AGAINST SOMETHING a formal indication of somebody's choice or opinion, especially in an election or referendum **2.** ACT OF CHOOSING the act of making a choice or of stating a preference to determine the outcome of something **3.** BALLOTS CAST the total number of ballots cast by eligible voters ○ *They got 83 per cent of the vote.* **4.** SUFFRAGE the right to express opinions and preferences by casting a ballot ○ *Women struggled for many years to get the vote.* **5.** MEANS OF EXPRESSING VOTE the ticket, ballot, or other method by which somebody expresses a vote **6.** RESULT OF BALLOTING the outcome of an election or referendum ○ *Yesterday's vote indicates that people are tired of being lied to.* **7.** OPINION EXPRESSED the preference of a group of people as indicated by a ballot ○ *the youth vote* **8.** PROPOSAL a proposal to be voted for or against, usually by a committee ■ *v* (**votes, voting, voted**) **1.** *vti* INDICATE FORMAL PREFERENCE to express an opinion or preference in an election or referendum ○ *How did you vote in the last election?* **2.** *vt* VOTE FOR OR AGAINST SOMEBODY to decide the outcome of an election by voting for or against somebody ○ *was voted out of office* **3.** *vt* VOTE TO MAKE SOMETHING AVAILABLE to create something or make something available by casting a vote ○ *refused to vote additional funds for the new building* **4.** *vt* DECLARE WINNER BY VOTING to declare somebody to be the winner of a competition by voting ○ *He was voted 'Waiter of the Year'.* **5.** *vt* SHOW OPINION ON SOMETHING to express agreement on something with regard to its degree of success (*informal*) ○ *The meal was voted a great success.* **6.** *vt* SUGGEST SOMETHING to make a suggestion ○ *I vote that we eat out.* [13C. < Latin *votum* 'vow' < *vovere* 'to vow', later 'desire'] —**votable** *adj*

vote down *vt* to defeat a proposal or candidate in a vote

vote bank *n S Asia* a group of voters whose votes can be won by offering policies that meet their special interests related to religion or caste

vote-bank politics *n S Asia* the practice of putting forward policies designed to appeal to a specific group of voters in order to gain or keep their support (*disapproving*)

vote-catcher *n* POL same as **vote-winner**

voteless /vōtləss/ *adj* without the right to choose or express a political opinion

vote of confidence *n* **1.** a vote in which voters express their continuing approval of the leadership of a party or policy **2.** a formal or informal expression of continuing support for somebody or something

vote of no confidence *n* in a parliamentary system, a vote originating with an opposition party that censures an act or policy of the government in power and, if passed, requires that the government resign

vote of thanks *n* a formal expression of thanks to somebody, proposed as a motion at a meeting

voter /vōtər/ *n* somebody who votes or is eligible to vote

vote-winner *n* a policy or strategy that will attract a high proportion of votes

voting booth *n US* same as **polling booth**

votive /vōtiv/ *adj* **1.** given, done, or offered in fulfilment of an oath or vow ○ *a votive offering* **2.** showing or symbolizing a wish or desire ○ *a votive prayer* [Late 16C. < Latin *votivus* < *votum* (see VOTE)] —**votively** *adv* —**votiveness** *n*

Votyak /vót yak/ (*plural same* or **-yaks**) *n* **1.** a member of a Finnish people living in east-central European Russia, especially in the Udmurt Autonomous Region **2.** LANG same as **Udmurt** (sense 2) [Mid-19C. < Russian] —**Votyak** *adj*

vou. *abbr* voucher

vouch /vowch/ (**vouches, vouching, vouched**) *vt* in English law, to summon somebody to court to prove ownership of land (*archaic*) [14C. Via French *voucher* 'summon' < Latin *vocare* 'to call']

vouch for *vt* **1.** to give an assurance that somebody will behave well or appropriately **2.** to guarantee that something such as a document or statement is accurate or genuine

vouchee /vów chée/ *n* somebody for whom another person vouches

voucher /vówchər/ *n* **1.** SUBSTITUTE FOR MONEY WHEN BUYING SOMETHING a card, token, or other document that can be exchanged for goods and services in place of money **2.** DOCUMENTARY EVIDENCE a document that provides supporting evidence for a claim, e.g. a receipt proving that a purchase was made **3.** GUARANTOR somebody or something that guarantees something or provides proof of something **4.** LAW CREDENTIALS FOR UK RESIDENCE a document that entitles a British national born outside the United Kingdom to live in Britain

vouchsafe /vówch sáyf/ (**-safes, -safing, -safed**) *vt* to promise, give, or allow something (*formal*)

voussoir /voo swaár/ *n* a wedge-shaped brick or stone used to form the curved parts of an arch or vault [14C. < French < Latin *volvere* 'to roll']

Vouvray /vóo vray/ *n* a still or sparkling white wine from west-central France [Late 19C. After a village in Indre-et-Loire, France]

vow /vow/ *n* SOLEMN PLEDGE a solemn promise to perform an act, carry out an activity, or behave in a given way ■ **vows** *npl* RELIGIOUS PROMISE a solemn promise to join a religious order and live in accordance with its rules ■ *v* (**vows, vowing, vowed**) **1.** *vt* PLEDGE SOMETHING to promise something solemnly and seriously **2.** *vti* DEDICATE SOMEBODY to promise somebody to a pledge or task, or to somebody such as a deity **3.** *vt* ASSERT SOMETHING to assert or declare something [13C. Via Old French *vou* < Latin *votum* (see VOTE)] —**vower** *n*

vowel /vów əl/ *n* **1.** a speech sound produced by the passage of air through the vocal tract, with relatively little obstruction **2.** a letter of the alphabet that represents a vowel. In English, the vowels are 'a', 'e', 'i', 'o', 'u', and sometimes 'y'. [14C. Via Old French *vouel* < Latin *vocalis* (see VOCAL)]

vowel gradation *n* LING same as **ablaut**

vowelize /vów ə līz/ (**-izes, -izing, -ized**), **vowelise** (**-ises, -ising, -ised**) *vt* to mark the vowel points in a Hebrew or Arabic text —**vowelization** /vów ə lī záysh'n/ *n*

vowel mutation *n* LING same as **umlaut** *n* (sense 1)

vowel point *n* a diacritical mark placed above or below a consonant to show a preceding or following vowel, used especially in languages such as Arabic and Hebrew that lack symbols for vowel sounds

vox angelica /vóks an jéllikə/ *n* a quiet organ stop, usually with vibrato, that enriches the tone of other quiet stops [< Latin, 'angelic voice']

voxel /vóksəl/ *n* the smallest unit of three-dimensional space in a computer image, equivalent to a three-dimensional pixel [Blend of VOLUME + PIXEL]

vox humana /vóks hyoo maánə/ *n* an organ reed stop that produces a tone resembling the human voice [< Latin, 'human voice']

vox pop /vóks póp/ *n* the impromptu opinions of ordinary members of the public as gathered by a radio or television interviewer (*hyphenated when used before a noun*) [Shortening of VOX POPULI]

vox populi /vóks póppyòò lī/ *n* popular public opinion ○ *Let's see if we can detect the vox populi.* [< Latin, 'voice of the people']

voyage /vóy ij/ *n* **1.** LONG TRIP a long journey, especially one by sea or through space **2.** EVENTS DURING JOURNEY the events that take place during an exploratory trip, regarded as a story (*literary*) **3.** NARRATIVE a story of an exploratory trip ■ *vti* (**-ages, -aging, -aged**) TRAVEL to make a long journey to or through a place [13C. Via Old French *voiage* < Latin *viaticus* 'of a road or journey' < *via* 'road']

voyager /vóyijər/ *n* somebody who makes a long journey to or through a place

Voyager *n* the name of two US spacecraft, Voyager 1 and Voyager 2, designed for exploring the outer planets of the solar system without a crew, launched in 1977

voyageur /vóy ə júr/ *n Can* a boatman, woodsman, trapper, or explorer formerly hired by fur companies to carry furs and supplies from one remote station to another, especially in Canada and the northwestern United States [Late 18C. < French, 'voyager']

voyeur /vwī yúr/ *n* **1.** somebody who gains pleasure from watching, especially secretly, other people's bodies or the sexual acts in which they participate **2.** a fascinated observer of distressing, sordid, or scandalous events [Early 20C. < French, 'somebody who sees' < *voir* 'see' < Latin *videre*] —**voyeurism** *n* —**voyeuristic** /vwī yur rístik/ *adj* —**voyeuristically** *adv*

Voysey /vóyzi/, **Charles** (1857–1941) British architect and designer. A member of the Arts and Crafts movement, he designed furniture, wallpapers, textiles, tiles, and country houses. Full name **Voysey, Charles Francis Annesley**

VP *abbr* **1.** GRAM verb phrase **2.** vice president

VPL *abbr* visible panty line

VPN *n* a network that provides remote offices or users with secure access to their organization's network using the Internet or other public telecommunications system. Full form **virtual private network**

vr *abbr* GRAM verb reflexive

VR[1] *abbr* **1.** variant reading **2.** COMPUT virtual reality **3.** MIL Volunteer Reserve

VR[2] *abbr* Queen Victoria [Latin *Victoria Regina*]

vraisemblance /vráy saaN blaáNss/ *n* the quality of seeming to be true or likely [Early 19C. < French, 'true appearance']

VRI *abbr* Victoria, Queen and Empress [Latin *Victoria Regina et Imperatrix*]

Vries ➧ **De Vries, Hugo**

VRML *n* a computer-graphics programming language used to create images of three-dimensional scenes. Full form **Virtual Reality Modelling Language**

vroom /vroom/ *n* the loud noise of an engine when it is being revved up or is running at high speed (*informal*) ■ *vi* (**vrooms, vrooming, vroomed**) to move noisily at high speed [Mid-20C. An imitation of the sound]

VRSA *n* a strain of a common infection-causing bacterium that has become resistant to treatment by the antibiotic vancomycin and is therefore a hazard in places such as hospitals. Full form **vancomycin-resistant Staphylococcus aureus**

vs *abbr* versus

v.s. *abbr* vide supra

V-shaped *adj* having the shape of a 'V'

V-sign *n* **1.** a hand sign that indicates victory, approval, or solidarity, made by holding up the index and middle fingers so that they form a 'V' with the palm facing outwards **2.** a hand sign that indicates contempt, anger, or abuse, made by holding up the index and middle fingers so that they form a V with the palm facing inwards

VSO[1] *n* an organization that sends volunteers to

work and teach in developing countries. Full form **Voluntary Service Overseas**

VSO[2] *adj* used to indicate that brandy or port is between 12 and 17 years old. Full form **very superior old**

VSOP *adj* used to indicate that brandy or port is between 20 and 25 years old. Full form **very special old pale, very superior old pale**

vss. *abbr* **1.** verses **2.** versions

V/STOL[1] /veé stol/ *abbr* vertical and short takeoff and landing

V/STOL[2] /veé stol/ *n* **1.** a system used by some aircraft that enables them to take off and land vertically or using a short runway. Full form **vertical/short takeoff and landing 2.** an aircraft capable of taking off and landing vertically or using a short runway

vt *abbr* GRAM verb transitive

VT *abbr* **1.** PHYS vacuum tube **2.** variable time **3.** Vermont

VTOL /veé tol/ (*plural* **VTOLs**) *n* **1.** a system used by some aircraft that enables them to take off and land vertically. Full form **vertical takeoff and landing 2.** an aircraft capable of vertical takeoff and landing

VTR *abbr* HOUSEHOLD video tape recorder

vu *abbr* Vanuatu (*used in Internet addresses*) See table at **domain name**

vug /vug/ *n* a small hole in a rock or vein that often contains a mineral lining that differs from that of the surrounding matrix [Early 19C. < Cornish *vooga*] — **vuggy** *adj*

Vuillard /vweé aar/, **Édouard** (1868–1940) French painter. He designed theatre sets and textiles in addition to the intricately patterned paintings of domestic interiors for which he is best known. Full name **Vuillard, Jean Édouard**

Vul. *abbr* BIBLE Vulgate

Vulcan /vúlkən/ *n* in Roman mythology, the god of fire. Greek equivalent **Hephaestus** —**Vulcanian** /vul káyni ən/ *adj*

vulcanian /vul káyni ən/ *adj* **1.** relating to or caused by a type of explosive volcanic eruption resulting when the pressure of gases trapped in viscous magma is sufficient to blow off overlying solidified material **2.** relating to or consisting of metalworking or metal craft

vulcanicity /vúlkə níssəti/ *n* GEOL same as **volcanicity** [Late 18C. < French *vulcanicité*, variant of *volcanicité* (see VOLCANICITY)]

vulcanise *vt* INDUST another spelling of **vulcanize**

vulcanism *n* GEOL another spelling of **volcanism**

vulcanite /vúlkə nīt/ *n* a hard rubber produced by vulcanizing natural rubber with large amounts of sulphur [Mid-19C. After VULCAN]

vulcanize /vúlkə nīz/ (**-nizes, -nizing, -nized**), **vulcanise** (**-nises, -nising, -nised**) *vt* to strengthen a material such as rubber by combining it with sulphur and other additives and then applying heat and pres-

sure —**vulcanizable** *adj* —**vulcanization** /vúlkə nī záysh'n/ *n* —**vulcanizer** *n*

vulcanology /vúlkə nólləji/ *n* GEOL same as **volcanology** [Mid-19C. < French *vulcanique*, variant of *volcanique* (see VOLCANIC)] —**vulcanologic** /vúlkənə lójjik/ *adj* —**vulcanological** *adj* —**vulcanologist** *n*

vulg. *abbr* **1.** vulgar **2.** vulgarly

Vulg. *abbr* BIBLE Vulgate

vulgar /vúlgər/ *adj* **1.** CRUDE OR INDECENT crude or obscene, particularly with regard to sex or bodily functions ○ *vulgar language* **2.** TASTELESS OR OSTENTATIOUS showing a lack of taste or reasonable moderation **3.** LACKING REFINEMENT lacking in courtesy and manners **4.** LANGUAGE OF ORDINARY PEOPLE'S LANGUAGE relating to a form of a language spoken by people generally **5.** OF ORDINARY PEOPLE relating to the majority of people (*archaic*) ■ *npl* ORDINARY PEOPLE ordinary people in society regarded as a group (*disapproving*) ○ *She believes that fine food and wine are beyond the taste of the vulgar.* [14C. < Latin *vulgaris* < *vulgus* 'the common people'] —**vulgarly** *adv*

vulgar fraction *n* MATHS same as **simple fraction**

vulgarian /vul gáiri ən/ *n* somebody who is a wealthy but lacks taste or a sense of reasonable moderation

vulgarise *vt* another spelling of **vulgarize**

vulgarism /vúlgərizəm/ *n* **1.** a crude or indecent word or phrase **2.** a word or phrase from the language spoken by people generally, as contrasted with a more formal or refined usage **3.** same as **vulgarity**

vulgarity /vul gárrəti/ (*plural* **-ties**) *n* **1.** a vulgar state or way of behaving **2.** a crude or tasteless joke, remark, or act

vulgarize /vúlgə rīz/ (**-izes, -izing, -ized**), **vulgarise** (**-ises, -ising, -ised**) *vt* **1.** to make something less refined or lower in quality **2.** to present or treat something in a way that makes it accessible to ordinary people —**vulgarization** /vúlgə rī záysh'n/ *n* —**vulgarizer** *n*

Vulgar Latin *n* the form of Latin that was the common spoken language of the western Roman Empire

vulgate /vúl gayt/ *n* **1.** the everyday informal use of a language **2.** a text generally accepted among experts as being the best or most accurate version [Early 16C. < Latin *vulgatus*, past participle of *vulgare* 'make public or common' < *vulgus* 'the common people']

Vulgate /vúl gayt/ *n* a Latin version of the Bible, produced by Saint Jerome in the 4th century [Early 17C. < Latin *vulgata editio* 'edition made public, edition for ordinary people' < *vulgatus* (see VULGATE)]

vulnerable /vúlnərəb'l/ *adj* **1.** WITHOUT ADEQUATE PROTECTION open to physical or emotional harm **2.** EXTREMELY SUSCEPTIBLE easily persuadable or liable to give in to temptation **3.** PHYSICALLY OR PSYCHOLOGICALLY WEAK unable to resist illness, debility, or failure **4.** MIL OPEN TO ATTACK exposed to an attack or possible damage **5.** CARDS LIABLE TO INCREASED STAKES in bridge, liable to higher penalties as well as bonuses after winning one game of a rubber [Early 17C. < late Latin *vulnerabilis* < Latin *vulnerare* 'to wound' < *vulnus* 'wound, injury'] —**vulnerability** /vúlnərə bílləti/ *n* —**vulnerableness** *n* —**vulnerably** *adv*

vulnerary /vúlnərəri/ (*archaic*) *adj* capable of or used for treating and healing wounds ■ *n* (*plural* **-ies**) a drug or other agent used in treating and healing wounds [Late 16C. < Latin *vulnerarius* < *vulnus* 'wound, injury']

Vulpecula /vul pékyoolə/ *n* a constellation of the northern hemisphere [< Latin, diminutive of *vulpes* 'fox']

vulpine /vúl pīn/ *adj* **1.** typical of or resembling a fox **2.** having or displaying a trait such as cunning that is commonly associated with foxes [Early 17C. < Latin *vulpes* 'fox']

vulture

vulture /vúlchər/ *n* **1.** a large bird of prey with usually dark feathers and broad wings that feeds on carrion. Native to: Europe, Asia, Africa, the Americas. Family: Accipitridae or Cathartidae. **2.** somebody who waits for the chance to exploit somebody else when that person is vulnerable [14C. Via French < Latin *vultur*]

vulturine /vúlchə rīn/ *adj* **1.** typical of or resembling a vulture **2.** *also* **vulturous** /vúlchərəss/ having a trait such as opportunism or greed that is commonly associated with vultures

vulva /vúlvə/ (*plural* **-vae** /-vee/ or **-vas**) *n* the external female genitals. These include the clitoris and the two pairs of fleshy folds, the labia majora and labia minora, that surround the opening of the vagina. [14C. < Latin, variant of *volva* 'womb' < *volvere* 'to roll'] —**vulval** *adj* —**vulvar** *adj* —**vulviform** *adj*

vulvectomy /vul véktəmi/ (*plural* **-mies**) *n* the surgical removal of all or part of a woman's external genitals

vulvitis /vul vítiss/ *n* painful swelling and redness of the vulva

vulvovaginitis /vúlvō vajji nítiss/ *n* painful swelling and redness of the vulva and vagina

vv *abbr* vice versa

vv. *abbr* **1.** verses **2.** MUSIC (first and second) violins **3.** volumes

VW *abbr* very worshipful

VX, VX gas *n* a deadly human-made nerve agent that is odourless and tasteless and occurs as an amber oily liquid that evaporates slowly [Mid-20C. < code letters, *V* indicating that it is very persistent]

Vyatka /vyátkə/ former name for **Kirov** (1780–1934)

Ww

w¹ /dúbb'lyoo/ (*plural* **w's**), **W** (*plural* **W's** or **Ws**) *n* **1.** the 23rd letter of the English alphabet, representing a consonant or sometimes a vowel **2.** a written representation of the letter 'w'

w² *abbr* **1.** TIME week **2.** CRICKET wicket *or* wickets **3.** CRICKET wide *or* wides **4.** MEASURE width **5.** wife **6.** with

W¹ /dúbb'l yoo/ (*plural* **W's** or **Ws**) *n* something shaped like a letter 'W'

W² *symbol* **1.** CHEM ELEM tungsten **2.** ELEC watt **3.** PHYS weight **4.** PHYS work

W³ /dúbb'l yoo/ *abbr* **1.** Wales **2.** warden **3.** COMMUNICATION web (address) **4.** Wednesday **5.** Welsh **6.** W. West **7.** Western **8.** women's (*used of clothing sizes*)

w/ *abbr* with

W3 *abbr* ONLINE World Wide Web

W3C *n* a consortium of organizations, programmers, developers, industry executives, and users that seeks to guide the future development of the World Wide Web and ensure that all web technologies are compatible with one another. Full form **World Wide Web Consortium**

W8 *abbr* wait (*used in e-mails or text messages*)

W8ING *abbr* waiting (*used in e-mails or text messages*)

WA *abbr* **1.** Washington (State) **2.** Western Australia **3.** INSUR with average

WAAAF¹ /waf/ (*plural* **WAAAFs**) *n* a member of the former Women's Auxiliary Australian Air Force

WAAAF² /waf/ *abbr* HIST Women's Auxiliary Australian Air Force

WAAC¹ /wak/ (*plural* **WAACs**), **Waac** (*plural* **Waacs**) *n* a member of the former British Women's Army Auxiliary Corps

WAAC² /wak/ *abbr* HIST Women's Army Auxiliary Corps

WAAF¹ /waf/ (*plural* **WAAFs**), **Waaf** (*plural* **Waafs**) *n* a member of the former Women's Auxiliary Air Force or, loosely, of the Women's Auxiliary Australian Air Force [Mid-20C. Acronym]

WAAF² /waf/ *abbr* HIST Women's Auxiliary Air Force

Waal /waal/ largest and southernmost of the three branches of the River Rhine in the Netherlands. Length: 84 km/52 mi.

wabbit /wábbit/ *adj Scotland* tired, weak, or feeling slightly ill [Late 19C. Origin ?]

WACA /wákə/ *n Aus* a cricket ground in Perth, Western Australia (*informal*) Full form **West Australian Cricket Association**

wack /wak/, **wacker** /wákər/ *n regional* used to address a friend ■ *adj* in snowboarding, bad or unlucky (*slang*) [Mid-20C. Origin ?]

wacko /wákō/ (*plural* **-os** or **-oes**), **whacko** *n* an offensive term that deliberately insults somebody regarded as unconventional, unpredictable, or unusual (*informal*) [Late 20C. < WACKY]

wacky /wáki/ (**-ier, -iest**), **whacky** *adj* (*informal*) **1.** an offensive term meaning unconventional, unpredictable, or unusual **2.** entertainingly silly [Mid-19C. Probably < *out of whack* 'out of order'] —**wackily** *adv* —**wackiness** *n*

Waco /wáykō/ city on the Brazos River in central Texas. In 1993, 84 people were killed when federal agents stormed the compound of a religious group just outside the city. Population: 115,749 (2002 estimate).

wad /wod/ *n* **1.** PIECE OF SOFT MATERIAL a small rounded mass of soft material, usually used to pack or stuff something ○ *The vase was carefully packed in wads of cotton.* **2.** BUNDLE a roll or small bundle of paper money ○ *a wad of notes* **3.** LUMP OF COMPRESSED MATERIAL a rounded compressed lump of something soft, especially tobacco or gum for chewing **4.** ARMS POWDER PLUG a plug of material such as paper or cloth used to hold the powder charge in a muzzle-loading gun or cannon **5.** ARMS DISC IN SHOTGUN CARTRIDGE a disc made of felt or paper, used to hold the powder or shot in a shotgun cartridge **6.** *N Am* LOT OF MONEY a large amount of money (*informal*) **7.** *US* LARGE QUANTITY a large number or amount of people or things (*informal*) ○ *She has wads of friends.* **8.** MINERALS MINERAL MIXTURE IN BOGGY GROUND a fine-grained mixture of hydrated barium manganese oxide and other hydrated oxide minerals. Source: poorly drained boggy ground. **9.** AGRIC PART OF HAY OR STRAW BALE a segment of a bale of hay or straw **10.** MIL BREAD ROLL a small bread roll (*slang*) ■ *v* (**wads, wadding, wadded**) **1.** *vti* COMPRESS TIGHTLY to compress something into a small mass, or be compressed in this way ○ *He wadded up the speeding ticket and threw it away.* **2.** *vt* PUT WADDING INTO SOMETHING to stuff or plug something with wadding ○ *She wadded her ears so she wouldn't hear the noise.* **3.** *vt* ARMS KEEP CHARGE IN PLACE to hold a charge of powder or shot in place **4.** *vt* ARMS INSERT WADDING INTO GUN to insert a piece of wadding into a gun [Mid-16C. Origin ?] —**wadder** *n*

wada /vúddə/, **vada** *n S Asia* a fried lentil ball eaten as a snack, especially in southern India [< Hindi *vaḍā*]

waddie *n* another spelling of **waddy**

wadding /wódding/ *n* **1.** SOFT PROTECTIVE MATERIAL soft material used to protect something, especially in packaging **2.** ARMS GUN WADS material used to hold powder or shot in a gun or cartridge **3.** TEXTILES PADDING MATERIAL USED IN SEWING a bonded fibre material produced in different thicknesses. Use: interlining, patchwork quilt padding.

Waddington /wóddingtən/, **C. H.** (1905–75) British embryologist and geneticist. He was the author of *Principles of Embryology* (1956) and popular books on biology, and contributed to evolutionary theory. Full name **Waddington, Conrad Hal**

waddle /wódd'l/ *vi* (**-dles, -dling, -dled**) to walk with short steps while causing the body to tilt slightly from one side to the other, especially because of having short legs and being overweight ■ *n* a way of walking, taking short steps with the body tilting slightly from one side to the other with each step [Late 16C. < WADE] —**waddler** *n* —**waddly** *adj*

waddy /wóddi/ (*plural* **-dies**), **waddie** *n* in traditional Aboriginal society, a heavy wooden club used as a weapon [Late 19C. Origin ?]

wade /wayd/ *v* (**wades, wading, waded**) **1.** *vti* WALK IN WATER to walk against the pressure of water or mud **2.** *vi* READ THROUGH SOMETHING WITH DIFFICULTY to read through something with difficulty, especially because it is very long or boring ○ *wading through a tome on Greek philosophy* ■ *n* WALK TAKEN IN WATER an act or instance of walking against the pressure of water or mud [Old English *wadan* < Indo-European, 'go'] —**wadable** *adj*

wade in *v* **1.** *vi* to interrupt forcefully or with determination **2.** *vti* to intervene in a situation in an attempt to help or restore order

Wade /wayd/, **Virginia** (*b.* 1945) British tennis player. She won the US Open (1968), Italian Open (1971), French Open (1972), Australian Open (1972), and Wimbledon (1977). Full name **Wade, Sarah Virginia**

wader /wáydər/ *n* **1.** a person or animal that wades through something **2.** BIRDS same as **wading bird** ■ **waders** *npl* waterproof boots or combined boots and trousers that reach to the hips or chest, worn as protection while fishing

wadi /wóddi/ (*plural* **-dis** or **-dies**), **wady** (*plural* **-dies**) *n* **1.** a steep-sided watercourse in dry regions of North Africa and southern Asia through which water flows only after heavy rainfall **2.** an oasis, especially in North Africa [Early 17C. < Arabic *wādī* 'valley, river bed']

wading bird /wáyding-/ *n* a long-legged bird such as a crane, heron, or stork that walks in water and hunts for food such as fish, frogs, invertebrates, carrion, or algae

wading pool *n Aus, N Am* SWIMMING same as **paddling pool**

wadmal /wódməl/ *n* a dense coarse woollen fabric once made in Orkney and Shetland. Use: outer garments. [14C. < Old Norse *vaðmál* 'cloth measure']

Wad Medani /waád mi daáni/ capital city of El Gezira Province, central Sudan. Population: 218,714 (1993).

wady *n* GEOG another spelling of **wadi**

Wafd /woft/ *n* an Egyptian nationalist party that emerged after an Egyptian delegation was refused a hearing at the Versailles Treaty negotiations following World War I. Negotiations eventually led to limited Egyptian independence beginning in 1922. [Early 20C. < Arabic, 'delegation', shortening of *al-wafd, al-misrî* 'the Egyptian delegation']

wafer /wáyfər/ *n* **1.** THIN CRISP BISCUIT a thin, crisp, and sometimes sweetened biscuit, usually in a rectangular, fan, or cone shape, often eaten with ice cream **2.** DISC OF ADHESIVE MATERIAL a small thin disc of adhesive material, used to seal a letter or formal document **3.** CHR BREAD DISC IN CHRISTIAN COMMUNION SERVICE a very thin disc of unleavened bread used to represent the body of Jesus Christ in the Christian Communion **4.** ELECTRONICS same as **chip** *n* (sense 5) ■ *vt* (**-fers, -fering, -fered**) FASTEN SOMETHING WITH WAFER to fasten something such as a letter or formal document with a wafer [14C. Via Anglo-Norman *wafre*, variant of French *gaufre* < Middle Low German *wāfel* < Germanic]

wafer-thin *adj* extremely thin or narrow

waffle¹ /wóff'l/ (*informal*) *vi* (**-fles, -fling, -fled**) to speak or write at length without saying anything important or interesting ■ *n* speech or writing that is lengthy and does not contain anything important or interesting [Late 17C. < *waff* 'yelp or bark', an imitation of the sound] —**waffly** *adj*

waffle² /wóff'l/ *n* a thick light pancake, crisp on the outside, that is baked in a waffle iron to give a pattern of indentations on both sides [Mid-18C. < Dutch *wafel* 'wafer']

waffle iron *n* an appliance used to bake waffles that has hinged indented plates that press a grid design into both sides of the waffle as it cooks

waft /woft, waaft/ *vti* (**wafts, wafting, wafted**) FLOAT GENTLY to float gently through the air, or move something gently through the air ■ *n* **1.** SOMETHING CARRIED THROUGH AIR something carried on the air or by a breeze, e.g. a scent **2.** WAVING MOTION a gentle waving or fluttering motion **3.** LIGHT BREEZE a brief gentle gust of air [Early

16C. Back-formation < *wafter* 'armed ship used to guard a convoy' < Dutch *wachter* < *wachten* 'to guard']

wag[1] /wag/ *v* (**wags, wagging, wagged**) **1.** *vti* MOVE SOMETHING RAPIDLY TO AND FRO to move part of the body to and fro, or move to and fro ○ *The dog wagged its tail.* **2.** *vi* GOSSIP to gossip about somebody or something, especially disapprovingly ○ *Tongues are wagging.* ■ *n* MOTION GOING TO AND FRO a motion that goes to and fro rapidly [Old English *wagian* 'move backwards and forwards' < Germanic]

wag[2] /wag/ *vti* (**wags, wagging, wagged**) to be absent from school without permission (*slang*) ■ *n* a humorous or witty person (*dated*) [Mid-16C. Origin ? Originally an affectionate term for a mischievous boy] —**waggery** *n* —**waggish** *adj* —**waggishly** *adv* —**waggishness** *n*

wage /wayj/ *n* a sum of money paid to a worker in exchange for services, especially for work performed on an hourly, daily, weekly, or piece-rate basis (*often used in the plural*) ■ *vt* (**wages, waging, waged**) to engage in war or in a serious fight to achieve an end ○ *wage war* [14C. < Anglo-Norman or Old N French < Germanic, 'pledge'] —**wageless** *adj* —**wagelessness** *n*

SYNONYMS **wage, salary, pay, fee, remuneration, emolument, honorarium, stipend**

CORE MEANING: money given for work done

wage a sum of money paid to a worker in exchange for services, especially for work performed on an hourly, daily, weekly, or piece-rate basis ○ *on a low wage* ○ *The club pays my wages weekly.* **salary** a fixed annual sum, paid at regular intervals, usually monthly, to an employee, especially for professional or clerical work ○ *teachers' salaries* ○ *The successful candidate was to be paid an annual salary approaching £1 million.* **pay** money that is given in return for work or services provided, especially in the form of a salary or wages ○ *a month-long strike for better pay and conditions* ○ *'Equal pay for equal work' was the battle cry of the feminist movement.* **fee** a payment for professional services ○ *Such lawyers charged high fees and served only the elite.* ○ *The expert's fees are to be borne equally by the parties concerned.* **remuneration** a payment or reward for goods or services or for losses sustained or inconvenience caused ○ *a review body to advise the Government on the proper remuneration for teachers* ○ *a need to investigate the levels of remuneration paid to those who work in children's homes* **emolument** (*formal*) a payment for work done ○ *Unfortunately, his fame was accompanied by only a small emolument.* **honorarium** an amount of money paid to somebody, especially a professional person, for providing a service such as giving a lecture ○ *Group members receive a small honorarium on the principle that their time is valued.* ○ *It was revealed yesterday that the company was giving a monthly honorarium to all four men.* **stipend** a fixed amount of money paid at regular intervals as a salary or to cover living expenses, especially one paid to a member of the clergy ○ *The priest's yearly stipend was barely sufficient to live on.*

---

wage curve *n* a graphic representation showing the relationship between the average wage rate in a region or industry and the unemployment rate in that region or industry

waged /wayjd/ *adj* working and in receipt of a wage

wage differential *n* a difference in wages between workers with different skills working in the same industry or workers with similar skills working in different industries or regions

wage earner *n* **1.** somebody in a family or household who is earning a wage or salary **2.** somebody who works by the hour, day, or week for wages and not for a fixed salary

wage incentive *n* an additional sum of money paid to a worker in order to improve that person's productivity

wage packet *n* a wage or salary that is paid to somebody

wager /wáyjər/ *n* **1.** BET ON OUTCOME an agreement between two people that whoever loses a bet on an uncertain outcome will pay the other a specific amount or another form of compensation **2.** AMOUNT BET a sum of money, piece of property, or other compensation to be paid to the person who wins a bet **3.** HIST PLEDGE in former times, a pledge to engage in combat, especially in order to establish guilt or

innocence by single combat ■ *vt* (**-gers, -gering, -gered**) BET MONEY to risk or bet money or property on the outcome of a game, event, or uncertain situation [14C. < Anglo-Norman *wageure* < *wagier* 'to pledge' < *wage* 'pledge'] —**wagerer** *n*

wages /wáyjiz/ *n* a just reward or recompense for something (*literary; takes a singular verb*) ○ *the wages of sin*

wage scale *n* a scale of the different wages paid to employees who are performing different jobs within a single company or industry

wage slave *n* somebody who depends completely on earning money from work in order to live (*informal*)

Wagga Wagga /wóggə wóggə/ city in southern New South Wales, Australia. Population: 57,131 (2002 estimate).

waggle /wágg'l/ *vti* (**-gles, -gling, -gled**) to move rapidly back and forth, or make something do this ■ *n* a rapid motion back and forth [Late 16C. < WAG[1]] —**waggly** *adj*

waggon, etc. another spelling of **wagon, etc.**

Richard Wagner

Wagner /vaágnər/, **Richard** (1813–83) German composer. He developed both the form and content of opera, notably in his opera cycle *The Ring of the Nibelung* (1852–76), and was a major influence on orchestral composers of the late romantic period. Full name **Wagner, Wilhelm Richard** —**Wagnerian** /vaag neéri ən/ *adj, n*

> 'It is a truth for ever, that where the speech of man stops short there Music's reign begins.'
> [Richard Wagner, 'A Happy Evening'; 1841]

Wagner /wágnər/, **Robert F.** (1877–1953) German-born US politician. He took the lead in passing progressive legislation while representing New York in the US Senate (1927–49). Full name **Wagner, Robert Ferdinand**

wagon /wággən/, **waggon** *n* **1.** WHEELED VEHICLE FOR CARRYING LOADS a rectangular vehicle that is used to carry heavy loads and is pulled by an animal or tractor or is motor-powered **2.** RAILWAY GOODS TRUCK a railway truck for goods, particularly an open one **3.** US DELIVERY VEHICLE a van used to sell or deliver something **4.** N Am POLICE TRANSPORT VEHICLE a van used by the police to transport suspects or criminals **5.** N Am CHILD'S FOUR-WHEELED CART a low four-wheeled cart with a long handle that a child can use to pull the cart or to control the direction of the front wheels **6.** N Am SERVING CART a four-wheeled rectangular cart used to display or serve food or drink [15C. < Dutch *wagen* < Germanic] —**wagoner** *n* ◇ **be off the wagon** to resume drinking alcohol after a period of abstinence ◇ **be on the wagon** to abstain from drinking alcohol

wagonette /wággə nét/, **waggonette** *n* a light four-wheeled horse-drawn vehicle with two lengthways seats facing each other behind a crosswise driver's seat

wagon-lit /vággon leé/ (*plural* **wagon-lits** /-leéz/ or **wagons-lits** /vággon leé/) *n* **1.** a sleeping car on a European railway **2.** an individual compartment in a railway sleeping car [< French < *wagon* 'railway coach' + *lit* 'bed']

wagonload /wággən lōd/, **waggonload** *n* the amount that a wagon holds

wagon train *n* a line of two or more animal-drawn wagons travelling cross-country and carrying people, food supplies, or goods

wagon vault *n* ARCHIT same as **barrel vault**

Wagram /vaág ram/ village in northeastern Austria. It was the site of the Battle of Wagram in which Napoleon's army defeated the Austrians in July 1809.

wagtail /wág tayl/ *n* a songbird with a long tail that bobs up and down when it walks and especially when it lands. Native to: Europe, Asia, Africa. Family: Motacillidae.

Wag the Dog syndrome *n* US a situation in which a US president uses military attacks on other nations as a diversionary tactic to deflect intense public and media scrutiny from a personal scandal (*slang*) [Late 20C. *Wag the Dog* < a film title]

wah /waa/ *interj* S Asia used to express admiration or appreciation (*usually repeated*) [Mid-20C. < Hindi]

wahey /wə háy/ *interj* an exclamation usually expressing delight or triumph (*informal*) [Late 20C. Emphatic extension of HEY]

Wahhabi /wə haábi/ (*plural* **-bis**), **Wahabi** *n* a member of a very conservative Islamic group that rejects any innovation that occurred after the 3rd century of Islam. It flourishes primarily in Arabia. [Early 19C. < Arabic *wahhābī*, after Muhammad ibn bd-al-*Wahhāb* (1703–92), its founder] —**Wahhabism** *n*

wahine /waa heéni/ *n* **1.** NZ, Hawaii a Hawaiian or Maori woman or wife **2.** Hawaii a young woman surfer (*informal*) [Late 18C. < Hawaiian or Maori]

wahoo /waá hoo, waa hoó/ (*plural* **-hoos**) *n* a large fast-swimming fish of the mackerel family that weighs up to 54.4 kg/120 lb. Native to: tropical seas. Latin name: *Acanthocybium solanderi.* [Early 20C. Origin ?]

wah-wah /waá waa/, **wa-wa** *n* **1.** WAVERING SOUND OF WIND INSTRUMENT the wavering sound made by alternately covering and uncovering the bell of a brass instrument **2.** ELECTRONIC SOUND a sound resembling a wah-wah, created for electronic instruments **3.** ELECTRONIC DEVICE an electronic device that is attached to a musical instrument and produces a wah-wah sound [Early 20C. An imitation of the sound]

wah-wah pedal *n* a foot pedal attached to an electronic musical instrument, used to create a wavering sound

waiata /wí aatə/ *n* NZ a Maori song [< Maori]

waif /wayf/ *n* **1.** ABANDONED CHILD a homeless or friendless person, especially an abandoned child **2.** STRAY ANIMAL a stray animal whose owner is unknown **3.** THIN YOUNG PERSON somebody, usually a young person, with a thin fragile appearance who looks in need of care **4.** UNCLAIMED ITEM an item that has been found whose owner is unknown (*literary*) **5.** PIECE OF UNCLAIMED PROPERTY a piece of property that, if shown to be ownerless and left unclaimed, becomes the property of the Crown or the lord of the manor [14C. < Anglo-Norman *weyf*, earlier *gwayf* 'lost property' < N Germanic] —**waif-like** *adj*

Waiheke Island /wī heéki-/ island in the Hauraki Gulf off the northeastern coast of the North Island, New Zealand. Population: 7,137 (2001). Area: 93 sq. km/36 sq. mi.

Waikaremoana /wī kúrrəmō aanə/ lake in the eastern part of the North Island, New Zealand. Area: 54 sq. km/21 sq. mi.

Waikato[1] /wī kaatō/ administrative region in the northern part of the North Island, New Zealand. Population: 357,726 (2001). Area: 34,892 sq. km/13,472 sq. mi.

Waikato[2] longest river in New Zealand. It rises in Lake Taupo in the centre of the North Island and empties into the Tasman Sea south of Waiuku. Length: 425 km/264 mi.

Waikiki /wí kee kee/ beach resort northeast of Honolulu, Oahu Island, Hawaii

wail /wayl/ *v* (**wails, wailing, wailed**) **1.** *vti* MAKE MOURNFUL CRY to express pain, grief, or misery in a long mournful high-pitched cry or in words uttered in a mournful way ○ *He could only wail when he heard the news.* **2.** *vi* MAKE LONG HIGH-PITCHED NOISE to make a long loud high-pitched sound ○ *The sirens wailed.* **3.** *vt* LAMENT SOMEBODY OR SOMETHING to express grief over somebody or something (*archaic*) ■ *n* **1.** LONG MOURNFUL SOUND a long mournful high-pitched cry or sound **2.** PROTEST a loud plaintive expression of protest, resentment, or disappointment [13C. < Old Norse *vei* 'woe'] —**wailer** *n* —**wailful** *adj* —**wailfully** *adv*

SPELLCHECK wail, wale, or **whale**? Do not confuse the spelling of ***wail***, ***wale***, and ***whale***, which sound similar. ***Wail*** is a noun or verb denoting a long loud high-pitched sound, as in *the wail of a siren, wailing children*. The word ***wale***, which is less frequently encountered in general usage, denotes a raised mark on the skin caused by a blow or a ridge (for example on fabric). A ***whale*** is a large sea mammal or something similarly impressive, as in *having a whale of a time*.

Wailing Wall *n* JUDAISM same as **Western Wall**

wain /wayn/ *n* a farm wagon or cart (*archaic or literary*) [Old English *wæ(g)n* < Germanic]

wainscot /wáynskət, wáyn skot/ *n* **1.** WOODEN PANELS LINING ROOM a lining for the walls of a room, especially one made of wood panelling **2.** LOWER PART OF WALL OF ROOM the lower part of the wall of a room, especially when it is panelled in wood or finished differently from the upper part **3.** OAK PANELLING a fine grade of oak used as wall panelling ■ *vt* (**-scots, -scoting** or **-scotting, -scoted** or **-scotted**) COVER WALL WITH PANELLING to cover a wall, especially with wood panelling [14C. < Middle Dutch *waghenscote* or Middle Low German *wagenschot* 'wagon-boarding']

wainscoting /wáynskəting, wáyn skotting/, **wainscotting** *n* **1.** the material, especially wood, used to cover a wall **2.** CONSTR same as **wainscot** *n* (sense 1)

wainwright /wáyn rīt/ *n* somebody who makes and repairs wagons

Wairarapa, Lake /wī raa raápə/ lake in the southern part of the North Island, New Zealand. Area: 80 sq. km/50 sq. mi.

Wairau /wīr ow/ river in the northern part of the South Island, New Zealand. It rises in the Southern Alps and empties into the Cook Strait near Blenheim. Length: 169 km/105 mi.

waist /wayst/ *n* **1.** BODY AREA BETWEEN RIBS AND HIPS the part of the human trunk between the rib cage and the hips, usually narrower than the rest of the trunk **2.** PART OF CLOTHING the part of a garment that fits around the waist of the body **3.** NARROW PART the narrow middle part of something, e.g. the middle of a violin **4.** NAUT MIDDLE OF SHIP the middle part of a ship or of a ship's deck between the raised sections at the bow and stern **5.** AVIAT MIDDLE OF AEROPLANE the middle section of an aircraft's fuselage **6.** INSECTS MIDDLE OF INSECT the narrow part of an insect's body between the thorax and the abdomen [14C. Origin ?] —**waisted** *adj* —**waistless** *adj*

SPELLCHECK waist or **waste**? Do not confuse the spelling of ***waist*** and ***waste***, which sound similar. ***Waist*** is only used as a noun, denoting the narrow part of the body between the rib cage and the hips, or a part of a garment that fits around it. ***Waste*** can be used as a noun, denoting a failure to use something wisely or unwanted or unusable remains (as in *a waste of money, industrial waste*), or as a verb, meaning 'fail to make use of something' or 'become gradually weaker or thinner': *You're wasting your time. They were wasting away from malnutrition.*

waistband /wáyst band/ *n* a band of fabric that circles the waist at the top of a garment such as a skirt or pair of trousers

waistcloth /wáyst kloth/ *n* CLOTHING same as **loincloth** (*archaic*)

waistcoat /wáyss kōt, wáyst-/ *n* **1.** a man's or woman's sleeveless and collarless waist-length garment, usually with buttons down the front, worn over a shirt and traditionally worn by men under a suit jacket **2.** a man's sleeveless garment reaching to the hips or knees, worn under a doublet in the 16th century —**waistcoated** *adj*

waistline /wáyst līn/ *n* **1.** the measurement round the narrowest part of the waist **2.** the level, usually near the waist, where the bodice and skirt of a dress meet ○ *a low waistline*

wait /wayt/ *v* (**waits, waiting, waited**) **1.** *vi* DO NOTHING EXPECTING SOMETHING TO HAPPEN to stay in one place or do nothing for a period of time until something happens or in the expectation or hope that something will happen ○ *I'll wait for you here until noon.* **2.** *vi* STOP SO SOMEBODY CAN CATCH UP to stop or slow down in order to allow somebody else to catch up ○ *Wait for me!* **3.** *vi* BE HOPING FOR SOMETHING to be hoping for something or on the lookout for something ○ *He is waiting for a job opportunity.* **4.** *vi* BE DELAYED OR IGNORED FOR NOW to be postponed or put off until later ○ *Fame would just have to wait.* **5.** *vi* BE READY OR AVAILABLE to be ready or available for somebody to take or use ○ *Your mail is waiting for you.* **6.** *vt* DELAY SOMETHING to delay something, especially a meal, because somebody is expected to arrive soon (*informal*) ○ *We waited dinner for you.* **7.** *vi* BE WAITER to work as a waiter ○ *She waits at the local restaurant.* ■ *n* TIME SPENT WAITING a period of time spent while expecting something to happen ○ *The wait seemed like forever.* ■ **waits** *npl* BAND OF MUSICIANS a band of musicians who play and sing Christmas carols in the streets (*archaic*) [12C. Via Old N French *waitier* 'spy, prepare to ambush' < Frankish] ◇ **lie in wait for somebody** *or* **something** to be waiting to catch or attack somebody or something

SPELLCHECK wait or **weight**? Do not confuse the spelling of ***wait*** and ***weight***, which sound similar. ***Wait*** refers to a period of time before doing something or before something happens: *Wait until it stops raining. We had a long wait for the train.* ***Weight*** refers to heaviness, importance, or arranging something so that it either favours or disadvantages a particular person or group, as in *the weight of the suitcase, weighted it down with a stone, opinions that carry little weight, weighted in their favour.*

USAGE See ***await***.

CULTURAL NOTE ***Waiting for Godot***, a play (1954) by Samuel Beckett. A classic drama of the theatre of the absurd, it has two main characters, the tramps Estragon and Vladimir. They indulge in idle conversation and games while waiting for Godot, who they hope will give some meaning to their futile existence. Godot does not arrive, and the tramps decide to go, but they do not leave the stage.

wait on *v* **1.** *vt* SERVE SOMEBODY BY BRINGING REQUESTED ITEMS to go and get the things that somebody asks for, usually continuously for a period of time ○ *It's nice to be waited on for a change.* **2.** *vt* SERVE SOMEBODY AT TABLE to bring food and drink to somebody sitting at a table, usually in a restaurant **3.** *vt* SERVE RETAIL CUSTOMER to attend to the purchasing needs of a customer **4.** *vi* WAIT FOR SOMEBODY OR SOMETHING to wait for somebody or something (*informal; usually used as a command*) **5.** *vt* VISIT SOMEBODY to pay a formal visit to somebody (*archaic*)

wait out *vt* to stay in one place or do nothing until something ends ○ *We decided to wait out the storm.*

wait up *vi* **1.** to delay going to bed to await an event or somebody's arrival ○ *I'll be home late; don't wait up.* **2.** *N Am* to wait for somebody or something (*informal; usually used as a command*) ○ *Wait up! I won't be a minute.*

wait upon *vt* same as **wait on** (senses 1–3, 5)

Waitaki /wī táki/ river in the southeastern part of the South Island, New Zealand. It rises in Lake Benmore and empties into the Pacific Ocean near the town of Waitaki. Length: 209 km/130 mi.

Waitangi /wī túngi/ historic site in the northern part of the North Island, New Zealand. A treaty between the Maori people and the British government was signed there in February 1840.

Waitangi Day *n* in New Zealand, a national day and public holiday marking the signing of the Treaty of Waitangi in 1840 by Maori chiefs and representatives of the British government. Date: 6 February.

Waitemata Harbour /wītə máttə-/ arm of the Pacific Ocean on the northeastern coast of the North Island, New Zealand. Auckland is situated on part of it.

waiter /wáytər/ *n* **1.** SOMEBODY WHO SERVES AT TABLES somebody employed to bring food and drink to people, usually in a restaurant **2.** TRAY a tray for carrying dishes or serving food **3.** MESSENGER a messenger at the London Stock Exchange or Lloyd's [14C. Via Anglo-Norman, 'attendant, watchman' < Old N French, or directly < WAIT]

waiting game /wáyting-/ *n* a tactic whereby somebody delays taking any action or making a move in a contest or negotiation, hoping that his or her position will improve with the passage of time

waiting list *n* a list of people waiting for something that is not immediately available such as a hospital bed, a place in a school, or an out-of-stock product

waiting room *n* a room in which people may wait, e.g. for a doctor's appointment or a train

Waitomo Caves /wī tómō-/ limestone cave system in the western part of the North Island, New Zealand, noted for its large colonies of glowworms

waitperson /wáyt purss'n/ (*plural* **-people** /-peep'l/ or **-persons**) *n N Am* OCCUPATIONS same as **waiter** (sense 1)

waitress /wáytrəss/ *n* a woman employed to bring food or drink to people, usually in a restaurant

waitron /wáytrən/ *n US* OCCUPATIONS same as **waiter** (sense 1) (*slang*) [Late 20C. Blend of WAITER or WAITRESS and AUTOMATON, suggesting mechanical repetitive work]

waitstaff /wáyt staaf/ *n US* the waiters and waitresses in a café or restaurant

wait state *n* a period of time during which a central processing unit in a computer sits idle while a slower component such as a memory or bus functions

waive /wayv/ (**waives, waiving, waived**) *vt* **1.** SURRENDER CLAIM to give something up voluntarily, especially a right or claim ○ *She waived her right to remain silent.* **2.** NOT ENFORCE SOMETHING to refrain from enforcing or applying something ○ *They decided to waive the restrictions.* **3.** TEMPORARILY DELAY SOMETHING to put off something for a time [13C. < Anglo-Norman *weyver* 'make a waif of, abandon' < *weyf* (see WAIF)]

SPELLCHECK waive or **wave**? Do not confuse the spelling of ***waive*** and ***wave***, which sound similar. ***Waive*** is a verb meaning 'surrender or refrain from enforcing something': *She waived her right to remain silent. They decided to waive the restrictions.* The related noun is spelt *waiver*. ***Wave*** is a noun and verb with various meanings, usually involving ridge-shaped or undulating motion, as in *the waves of the sea, radio waves, waved goodbye.* The noun *waver* is unrelated to ***wave***: it corresponds to the verb *waver* meaning 'go back and forth between possibilities'.

waiver /wáyvər/ *n* **1.** the voluntary surrender of a right or claim **2.** a document or formal statement giving up a right or claim, or an action indicating an intention to waive something

SPELLCHECK See ***waive***.

Wajda /vīdə/, **Andrzej** (*b.* 1926) Polish film director. Much of his work focuses on Poland during and after World War II and on Polish nationalism of the 1970s and 1980s.

wakame /waa kaámi/ (*plural* **-mes** or *same*) *n* an edible brown seaweed. Use: dried, in Japanese and Chinese cooking. Native to: coasts of Japan, China, and Korea. Latin name: *Undaria pinnatifida*. [Mid-20C. < Japanese]

Wakashan /waa káshən/ *n* a family of languages spoken by Native North American peoples in British Columbia and Washington State. Native speakers: 3,000. [Late 19C. < Nootka *waukash* 'good'] —**Wakashan** *adj*

Wakatipu /waákə típpoo/ lake in the southwestern part of the South Island, New Zealand. The town of Queenstown is located on its northern shore. Area: 293 sq. km/113 sq. mi.

Wakayama /wákə yaámə/ port and capital city of Wakayama Prefecture, southwest of Osaka, Japan. Population: 391,008 (2002).

wake[1] /wayk/ *v* (**wakes, waking, woke** /wōk/, **woken** /wókən/) **1.** *vti* STOP SLEEPING to come back to a conscious state after sleeping, or make somebody do this ○ *I woke suddenly at dawn.* **2.** *vti* STOP BEING INACTIVE to become alert and active after being inactive, in a daydream, or preoccupied, or make somebody do this **3.** *vti* REALIZE OR MAKE SOMEBODY REALIZE SOMETHING to become aware of something, or make somebody aware ○ *Their pleas woke us to the situation.* **4.** *vi* WATCH OVER CORPSE to hold a vigil over the body of somebody who has died **5.** *vi* STAY AWAKE to be or remain awake ○ *'Fled is that music — Do I wake or sleep?'* (John Keats, *Ode to a Nightingale*; 1819) **6.** *vti* KEEP WATCH to keep watch over somebody or something (*archaic*) ■ *n* **1.** WATCH KEPT OVER CORPSE a vigil held over a corpse before burial or cremation **2.** FESTIVE GATHERING ASSOCIATED WITH DEATH a social gathering held after a funeral or, in Ireland, often after the death but before the funeral. Traditionally people drink and talk about the dead person, and there is a happy jovial atmosphere. **3.** *regional* CHR CHURCH FESTIVAL a festival for the patron saint of a parish church, or a festival held to commemorate the dedi-

cation of a parish church [Old English *wacan* 'become awake' < Indo-European, 'be active or lively'] —**waker** *n*

USAGE See ***awake***.

CULTURAL NOTE *Finnegans Wake*, a novel (1939) by the Irish writer James Joyce. Joyce's last novel recounts a single night in the life of a Dublin publican, Humphrey Chimpden Earwicker, and his family. An extraordinary multilayered work consisting chiefly of extended interior monologues, it is crammed with multilingual puns, poetry, and literary and historical allusions that emphasize the universal and cyclic nature of human experience.

wake up *v* **1.** *vti* same as **wake**[1] *v* (senses 1–3) **2.** *vt* to make something look more interesting or attractive

wake[2] /wayk/ *n* **1. TRACK IN WATER** the track left in water by a vessel or another body moving through it **2. DISTURBED AIR BEHIND VEHICLE** the stream of turbulence in the air left by an aircraft or land vehicle passing through it **3. POSITION BEHIND SOMEBODY** the position or area behind somebody or something that is moving ahead fast ○ *left the rest of the field trailing in her wake* **4. AFTEREFFECTS** the aftermath or aftereffects of a dramatic event or powerful thing ○ *The bomb left destruction in its wake.* [15C. Via Middle Low German < Old Norse *vok* 'hole in ice (made by a boat)'] ◇ **in the wake of something** immediately after and usually as a result of something

wakeboarding /wáyk bawrding/ *n* a water sport in which somebody riding a single board is pulled behind a motor boat and performs jumps while crisscrossing the wake of the boat [Late 20C. After SKATEBOARDING] —**wakeboard** *vi* —**wakeboarder** *n*

Wakefield /wáyk feeld/ city in West Yorkshire, northern England, on the River Calder. Population: 315,172 (2001).

Wakefield, Edward Gibbon (1796–1862) British-born New Zealand social theorist. He formulated the programme of selling Crown lands in the British colonies to encourage colonization. Pieces of land bought under this programme became known as 'Wakefield settlements'.

wakeful /wáykf'l/ *adj* **1. NOT SLEEPING** unable to sleep **2. SLEEPLESS** passed without sleep ○ *a wakeful night* **3. ALERT** awake, especially while watching or guarding something ○ *promised to remain wakeful* —**wakefully** *adv* —**wakefulness** *n*

wakeless /wáykləss/ *adj* uninterrupted by waking, or spent in uninterrupted sleep

waken /wáykən/ (**-ens, -ening, -ened**) *vti* to become conscious, active, or aware after sleeping, being inactive, or being unaware, or make a person or animal do this —**wakener** *n*

USAGE See ***awake***.

wake-robin (*plural* **wake-robins** or *same*) *n* **1.** a member of a group of early-blooming arums such as the arrow arum. Native to: North America. **2.** PLANTS same as **cuckoopint**

wakes /wayks/ *n regional* an annual one- or two-week holiday, originally to celebrate a parish church festival in the industrial areas of northern England, when the local factories shut down (*takes a singular or plural verb*)

wake-up call *n* **1.** a telephone call or a personal visit made to awaken somebody, especially a telephone call from or arranged by hotel staff made at an agreed time to awaken a guest **2.** a frightening experience that is interpreted as a sign that a major change is needed in the way somebody lives or conducts business

wakil LAW another spelling of **vakil**

Wal. *abbr* LANG Walloon

Walachia /wo láyki ə/, **Wallachia** former region in southeastern Europe, in present-day southern Romania. Founded as a principality towards the end of the 13th century, it was ruled by Turkey from 1387 until it joined Moldavia to form Romania in 1861. —**Walachian** *n, adj*

Walbri *n, adj* LANG same as **Warlpiri**

Walcott /wáwlkət/, **Derek** (*b.* 1930) St Lucian writer. His Caribbean-based novels and plays are characterized by a vivid use of language. He won the Nobel Prize in literature (1992).

> 'I who have cursed / The drunken officer of British rule, how choose / Between this Africa and the English tongue I love? / Betray them both, or give back what they give? / How can I face such slaughter and be cool? / How can I turn from Africa and live?'
> [Derek Walcott, 'A Far Cry From Africa', *In a Green Night*; 1962]

Waldemar I /vaáldə maár/ (1131–82) king of Denmark. Having gained sole control of the Danish throne (1157–82), he established a dynastic rule in Denmark. Known as **Waldemar the Great**

Waldemar II (1170–1241) king of Denmark. He was the son of Waldemar I. As king (1202–41), he extended Danish territory and instituted legal and administrative reforms. Known as **Waldemar the Conqueror**

Waldenses /wawl dénseez, wol-/ *npl* the members of a small Christian denomination, originating in southern France, that broke with the Roman Catholic Church in the 12th century and experienced much persecution. In the 16th century the Waldenses joined the Reformation and adopted Calvinist doctrines. [Mid-16C. < medieval Latin < *Waldensis*, variant of Peter *Valdes* (d. 1205), who founded the movement] —**Waldensian** *adj*

waldgrave /wáwld grayv, wóld-/ *n* in medieval Germany, an officer with jurisdiction over a royal forest [Early 20C. < German *Waldgraf* 'forest count']

Waldheim /wáwld hīm, vaált-/, **Kurt** (*b.* 1918) secretary general of the United Nations (1972–81) and president of Austria (1986–92). During his presidency it was alleged he had been complicit in Nazi war crimes.

Waldorf salad /wáwl dawrf-, wól-/ *n* a salad made of diced raw apples, celery, and walnuts with a mayonnaise dressing [Early 20C. After the *Waldorf-Astoria Hotel* in New York, USA]

Waldorf School /wáwl dawrf-, wól-/ *n* a school belonging to a movement that emphasizes a holistic approach to education and a broad curriculum linked to knowledge of child development. The movement is based on the ideas of Rudolph Steiner. [After the *Waldorf* cigarette factory in Stuttgart, Germany, whose chief executive initiated such a school for its workers' children in 1919]

waldrapp /wáwld rap/ *n* an ibis with a red head and mainly dark green feathers. Native to: Morocco. Latin name: *Geronticus eremita*.

waldsterben /vált shtairbən, wáwld-/ *n* widespread disease and death of trees, thought to be the result of atmospheric pollution. It was first identified in Central Europe in the 1970s. [Late 20C. < German, 'forest dying']

wale /wayl/ *n* **1. SKIN WELT** a raised red swollen mark on the skin made by a blow, especially with a whip **2.** TEXTILES **RIDGE ON FABRIC** a ridge on the surface of a woven fabric such as corduroy **3.** TEXTILES **WEAVE OF FABRIC** the weave or texture of a fabric with ribs **4.** HANDICRAFT **VERTICAL ROW OF KNITTING** a vertical row of stitches in knitting **5.** NAUT **WOOD FORMING SIDES OF SHIP** a strong horizontal plank forming part of the side of a wooden ship ■ *vt* (**wales, waling, waled**) **1. RAISE WELT ON SKIN** to raise a red swollen mark on the skin by striking a blow, especially with a whip **2.** TEXTILES **WEAVE RIDGED FABRIC** to weave fabric with ridges [Old English *walu* 'ridge' < Germanic]

SPELLCHECK See ***wail***.

Wales /waylz/ principality in Great Britain, part of the United Kingdom. Once a separate kingdom, it was united with England in 1536. It voted in 1997 to have its own assembly, and as a result has a degree of self-government. Capital: Cardiff. Population: 2,903,085 (2001). Area: 20,760 sq. km/8,015 sq. mi.

Wałęsa /və wénssə/, **Lech** (*b.* 1943) trade unionist and president of Poland (1990–95). At the head of Solidarity after 1980, he led Poland's independent trade union movement and was instrumental in ending Communist rule there. He was awarded the Nobel Peace Prize (1983).

> 'SOLIDARITY was born at that precise moment when the shipyard strike evolved from a local success in the shipyard, to a strike in support of other factories and business enterprises, large and small, in need of our protection.'
> [Lech Wałęsa, 'The Strike and the August Agreements', *A Path of Hope*; 1987]

Wales Office *n* a UK government department responsible for representing Welsh interests within the government of the United Kingdom. Welsh name **Swyddfa Cymru**

Walhalla, Walhall *n* MYTHOL same as **Valhalla**

walk /wawk/ *v* (**walks, walking, walked**) **1.** *vi* **MOVE ON FOOT** to move or travel on legs and feet, alternately putting one foot a comfortable distance in front of, or sometimes behind, the other, and usually proceeding at a moderate pace. When walking, as opposed to running, one of the feet is always in contact with the ground, the one being put down as or before the other is lifted. ○ *a toddler just learning to walk* **2.** *vt* **TRAVEL THROUGH PLACE ON FOOT** to travel along or through something on foot ○ *walking the coastal path* **3.** *vt* **TAKE ANIMAL FOR EXERCISE BY WALKING** to take an animal for exercise by walking, usually a dog on a lead ○ *walked the dog* **4.** *vt* **WALK WITH SOMEBODY TO PLACE** to accompany somebody on foot as far as a particular place such as a home or car ○ *I'll walk you home.* **5.** *vt* **CAUSE SOMEBODY TO WALK** to help or force somebody to walk by holding and pushing from behind ○ *We kept walking him till he was able to stand on his own.* **6.** *vti* **MOVE LARGE OBJECT BY ROCKING** to move something in a way that suggests walking, e.g. by pivoting a large heavy object alternately on its corners and swinging the other side forwards, or be moved in this way ○ *The wardrobe's too heavy to lift; we'll have to walk it into the bedroom.* **7.** *vt* **MEASURE SOMETHING BY WALKING** to measure or inspect something by walking over or along it, especially the boundaries of an area or piece of property ○ *walk the west property line* **8.** *vti* **HAUNT PLACE** to haunt a place as a ghost ○ *She walks the tower.* **9.** *vi* **BE STOLEN** to disappear or be stolen (*informal*) ○ *The petty cash seems to have walked.* **10.** *vi US* **GO ON STRIKE** to take strike action (*informal*) ○ *threatened to walk* **11.** *vi US* **LEAVE IN PROTEST** to leave a job, event, or meeting in order to express disagreement (*informal*) ○ *I'd better get an apology or I'm walking!* **12.** *vi N Am* **BE FREED FROM JAIL OR ACQUITTED** to be released from prison or found innocent of a crime (*informal*) ○ *I couldn't believe they walked after what they did!* **13.** *vi* **LIVE IN PARTICULAR WAY** to conduct your life in a particular way (*archaic*) ○ *walk with God* **14.** *vi* CRICKET **ACKNOWLEDGE BEING OUT BY LEAVING WICKET** in cricket, to leave the wicket without waiting to be given out by the umpire **15.** *vti* BASEBALL **GO TO FIRST BASE** in baseball, to proceed to first base after four deliveries from the pitcher, none of which was in the strike zone or swung at, or allow the batter to do this **16.** *vi* BASKETBALL **TAKE STEPS ILLEGALLY** in basketball, to take more than two steps without dribbling while holding the ball, in contravention of the rules ■ *n* **1. JOURNEY MADE ON FOOT** a journey made on foot, especially for pleasure or exercise ○ *a walk in the woods* **2. DISTANCE OR TIME OF FOOT JOURNEY** the distance travelled or the time it takes to go somewhere on foot ○ *a four-mile walk* ○ *a ten-minute walk from home* **3. WAY OF WALKING** somebody's characteristic way of walking ○ *She's got a graceful walk.* **4. PLACE FOR PEDESTRIANS** a place designed or set aside for the use of people on foot **5. ROUTE FOR PEOPLE WALKING** a route or path for travellers on foot ○ *The miners' trail is an easy scenic walk.* **6. ROUTE** a regular route taken by a street vendor or delivery person **7. MARCH** a procession or march **8. RACE** a race in which the competitors walk a particular distance as quickly as possible **9. AREA FOR ANIMALS** an enclosed area for exercising or pasturing domestic animals such as horses **10. ROWS OF TREES** a plantation of widely spaced trees or shrubs **11. SPACE BETWEEN ROWS** the space between rows of widely spaced trees or shrubs **12.** *US* **SOMETHING VERY EASY** something that is very easy to do (*informal*) ○ *We'll certainly beat them. It'll be a walk.* **13.** RIDING **SLOW GAIT OF HORSE** a relatively slow-paced way of moving for a horse or other four-legged animal, in which two feet are always on the ground ○ *The mare started at a walk before breaking into a trot.* **14.** BASKETBALL **ILLEGAL MOVEMENT WHILE HOLDING BALL** in basketball, the taking of more than two steps without dribbling while holding the ball, in contravention of the rules **15. FOREST** a section of a forest controlled by a single keeper (*archaic*) [Old English *wealcan* 'roll, toss', *wealcian* 'roll up' < Germanic] —**walkable** *adj* ◇ **walk it** to gain victory or success easily (*informal*) ◇ **walk all over somebody 1.** to ignore the rights or feelings of somebody **2.** to defeat some-

body easily ◇ **walk tall** to feel and display self-confidence and pride in your achievements

walk away *vi* **1.** ABANDON PROBLEM to avoid becoming or refuse to become involved in a situation or problem **2.** HAVE MINOR INJURIES to survive an accident uninjured or with only minor injuries and be able to walk from the scene **3.** WIN SOMETHING to win or achieve something ○ *She walked away with the first prize.* **4.** DEFEAT SOMEBODY to defeat or outdo another person or team easily

walk in on *vt* to interrupt or intrude on somebody or something by entering a place without warning ○ *She walked in on them in the middle of an argument.*

walk off *v* **1.** *vi* to leave a place abruptly ○ *She walked off without a word.* **2.** *vt* to get rid of something such as an injury or feeling of sickness by walking

walk off with *vt* (*informal*) **1.** to steal something ○ *walked off with all the jewels* **2.** to win something effortlessly

walk out *vi* **1.** LEAVE WITHOUT EXPLANATION to leave, especially in anger or protest, without explanation **2.** GO ON STRIKE to take strike action **3.** LEAVE to leave, abandoning a spouse, partner, or family permanently

walk out on *vt* to abandon a spouse, partner, or family permanently (*informal*) ○ *My wife walked out on me last summer.*

walk through *vt* **1.** ARTS REHEARSE OR PERFORM PLAY PERFUNCTORILY to rehearse something in a simple unelaborate way, without props or costumes, mainly practising basic moves and positions, or perform something in a perfunctory uncommitted way that resembles a rehearsal **2.** MEDIA REHEARSE PROGRAMME WITHOUT CAMERAS to rehearse a television programme without cameras **3.** GIVE SOMEBODY STEP-BY-STEP EXPLANATION to go through the various stages of something with somebody in advance in order to make it familiar and understandable ○ *They walked their client through the whole cross-examination procedure.*

walkabout /wáwkə bowt/ *n* **1.** PUBLIC WALK an informal walk among the people by royalty or a celebrity **2.** *Aus* JOURNEY THROUGH BUSH an extended journey on foot through a remote area made by an Australian Aboriginal wishing to experience or return to a traditional way of life and to traditional beliefs **3.** *Aus* WALK a walking trip ◇ **go walkabout** (*informal*) **1.** to be stolen **2.** *Aus* to go for an extended journey on foot through a remote area in order to experience or return to a traditional Australian Aboriginal way of life and beliefs **3.** *Aus* to leave your normal surroundings

CULTURAL NOTE *Walkabout*, a film (1970) by British director Nicholas Roeg. Set in 1960s Australia, it tells the story of two British children who are left to fend for themselves in the outback when their father commits suicide. They are befriended by a young Aboriginal boy who teaches them to cope with and appreciate the seemingly harsh environment.

walker /wáwkər/ *n* **1.** somebody who walks, especially for exercise or in races **2.** *N Am* same as **baby walker** **3.** a lightweight waist-high framework, usually with four legs and rubber feet, used to help somebody who cannot walk without support

Corbis/Bettmann

Alice Walker

Walker /wáwkər/, **Alice** (*b.* 1944) US writer. Her novels, including the Pulitzer Prize-winning *The Color Purple* (1982), are concerned largely with the experience of African American women. Full name **Walker, Alice Malsenior**. See Cultural note at **purple**

'People think pleasing God is all God cares about. But any fool living in the world can see it always trying to please us back.'

[Alice Walker, *The Color Purple*; 1982]

'Expect nothing. Live frugally / on surprise.'
[Alice Walker, 'Expect Nothing'; 1973]

Walker, John (*b.* 1952) New Zealand athlete. He won the 1,500 metres at the 1976 Olympic Games and was the first person to run a mile in less than 3 minutes 50 seconds (1975). Full name **Walker, John George**

walkies /wáwkiz/ (*informal*) *interj* an indication to a dog that you are going to take it for a walk ■ *n* a walk for or with a dog ◇ **go walkies** (*informal*) **1.** to go for a walk with a dog **2.** to disappear, become lost, or be stolen

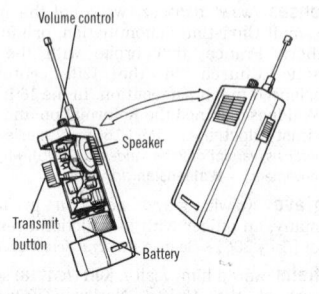

Volume control

Speaker

Transmit button

Battery

walkie-talkie

walkie-talkie /wáwki táwki/, **walky-talky** (*plural* **walky-talkies**) *n* a hand-held battery-operated radio transmitter and receiver often used by emergency personnel to communicate with one another [Mid-20C. Playful variant of WALK + TALK]

walk-in *adj* large and spacious enough to enter ○ *a walk-in cupboard*

walking /wáwking/ *adj* **1.** ABLE TO WALK capable of walking **2.** FOR WALKING used or designed for the purpose of walking ○ *walking shoes* **3.** OF WALKING involving travelling on foot ○ *a walking tour* ◇ a **walking dictionary** *or* **encyclopedia** somebody who is very knowledgeable

walking bass *n* a bass musical accompaniment, usually consisting of small steps or intervals up and down the scale in 4/4 time

walking boot *n* **1.** a heavy boot worn to support the ankle when hiking or trekking over rough terrain **2.** a lightweight rigid knee-length boot with a reinforced sole and straps that fasten around the leg. Use: support after a sprain or fracture.

walking catfish *n* a freshwater catfish with special organs that enable it to breathe on land for short periods while it moves to another body of water. Native to: tropical Asia. Latin name: *Clarius batrachus.*

walking delegate *n* **1.** *US* a trade union representative appointed to visit local unions and their employers to ensure compliance with contracts and sometimes to represent the local union in negotiations **2.** *NZ* a representative of a trade union delegated from among on-site members to deal promptly with disputes

walking fern, **walking leaf** *n* a fern whose long arching fronds take root at the tip and sprout new plants. Native to: eastern North America. Latin name: *Camptosorus rhizophyllus.*

walking papers *npl N Am* official notification that somebody has been fired from a job or dismissed from military service (*informal*)

walking stick *n* **1.** a cane or stick used to assist in walking **2.** *US* a long brown or green insect that resembles a twig, especially a North American species that feeds on leaves. Latin name: *Diapheromera femorata.*

walking wounded *npl* **1.** casualties of war, terrorism, or disaster who are able to walk despite their injuries **2.** people who continue to be affected by great emotional pain experienced during their lives

Walkman /wáwkmən/ *tdmk* a trademark for a small portable cassette player with earphones

walk of life *n* somebody's occupation or social or economic class ○ *people from all walks of life*

walk-on *n* **1.** a small part, usually a nonspeaking one, in a stage or film production **2.** an actor who has a small part, usually a nonspeaking one, in a stage or film production

walkout /wáwk owt/ *n* **1.** an organized strike by employees in which workers walk out of the building or off the premises **2.** a departure in protest or anger about something

walkover /wáwk ōvər/ *n* **1.** an easy victory or one that is obtained without a contest, e.g. because the opposing side did not turn up (*informal*) **2.** a horse race in which only one horse is entered

walk-through *n* **1.** an early play rehearsal without props or costumes, or a television rehearsal without cameras, usually held to practise basic moves and positions **2.** a set of instructions on how to use a piece of software or complete a computer game, including advice on how to proceed if problems are encountered

walk-up *n N Am* **1.** a building of several storeys without a lift (*informal*) **2.** a flat in a building of several storeys without a lift

walkway /wáwk way/ *n* **1.** a specially constructed path for pedestrians **2.** a passage above ground level designed for pedestrian use such as one connecting buildings or passing over a roadway

Walkyrie *n* MYTHOL another spelling of **Valkyrie**

walky-talky *n* COMMUNICATION another spelling of **walkie-talkie**

wall /wawl/ *n* **1.** FLAT SIDE OF BUILDING OR ROOM a vertical structure forming an inside partition or an outside surface of a building **2.** STANDING STRUCTURE THAT SURROUNDS OR BLOCKS a narrow upright structure, usually built of stone, wood, plaster, or brick, that acts as a boundary or keeps something in or out ○ *a garden wall* **3.** DEFENSIVE STRUCTURE a structure of earth or stone built for defensive purposes **4.** PHYSICAL OR PSYCHOLOGICAL OBSTACLE something similar to a wall in appearance or impenetrability ○ *met with a wall of reporters* **5.** SOMETHING THAT PREVENTS COMMUNICATION an obstacle to understanding or communication between people **6.** CLIMBING ROCK FACE a vertical or nearly vertical rock face ○ *a sheer wall of granite* **7.** CIV ENG BARRIER TO FLOODING a structure built as a barrier to flooding **8.** ANAT BODY MEMBRANE OR LINING a membrane or lining enclosing or bounding an organ, blood vessel, or cavity of the body ○ *the uterine wall* **9.** BIOL RIGID COVERING FOR SOME CELLS a rigid covering over the outer membranes of plant cells and of some prokaryotic animal cells **10.** FOOTBALL LINE OF DEFENSIVE PLAYERS in football, a line of defensive players who must stand at least ten yards from a free kick and who try to block a shot on goal ■ *vt* (**walls, walling, walled**) **1.** SURROUND SOMETHING WITH WALLS to fortify or surround somebody or something with a wall ○ *They walled in the back garden.* **2.** SEPARATE SOMETHING WITH WALLS to put up a wall to separate one area from another **3.** CLOSE SOMETHING WITH WALL to close an opening with a wall ○ *wall up the passage* **4.** TRAP OR BURY SOMEBODY BEHIND WALL to seal somebody or something in a space with a wall [Pre-12C. < Latin *vallum* 'rampart' < *vallus* 'stake'] —**walled** *adj* ◇ **be climbing the wall** *or* **walls** to be extremely bored or frustrated (*informal*) ◇ **drive somebody up the wall** to annoy or irritate somebody to an extreme degree (*informal*) ◇ **go to the wall** to be destroyed or ruined, especially financially (*informal*) ◇ **hit a brick wall** to encounter an insurmountable difficulty or obstacle ◇ **hit the wall** to reach a point at which no more can be done or achieved, e.g. a state of total exhaustion during a marathon run (*informal*)

walla *n* another spelling of **wallah** (*dated informal*)

Wallabies /wóllǝbiz/ *npl* the Australian rugby union team (*informal*)

wallaby /wóllǝbi/ (*plural* **-bies**) *n* a marsupial that resembles a small kangaroo. Native to: Australia, New Guinea. Family: Macropodidae. See illustration on next page [Early 19C. < Dharuk *walabi*, *waliba*]

wallaby grass *n* PLANTS same as **danthonia**

wallaby track *n Aus* a route traditionally taken by itinerant workers seeking seasonal employment (*informal*)

Wallace /wólliss/, **Alfred Russel** (1823–1913) British naturalist. He formulated a theory of natural selection independently of Charles Darwin, and his recognition of the distinctions between the fauna of

wallaby

Asia and Australia led him to define Wallace's line.

'Why do some die and some live?...The answer was clearly, that on the whole the best fitted live...This self-acting process would necessarily *improve the race...the fittest would survive.*'
[Alfred Russel Wallace, *My Life: A Record of Events and Opinions*; 1905]

Edgar Wallace

Wallace, Edgar (1875–1932) British writer. He wrote more than 170 popular crime novels and thrillers, beginning with *The Four Just Men* (1905). Full name **Wallace, Richard Horatio Edgar**

'What is a highbrow? It is a man who has found something more interesting than women.'
[Edgar Wallace, *Interview, New York Times*; 24 January 1932]

Wallace, Sir William (1272?–1305) Scottish patriot. He led a rebellion against the English (1297), but was defeated by Edward I (1298). He was later captured and executed.

Wallace's line /wóllissiz-/ *n* a hypothetical boundary separating the southwestern Pacific into two biogeographical regions with distinctive types of wildlife. The line runs between Bali and Lombok in the Indonesian island chain and north through the Makassar Strait, passing south of the Philippines. [Mid-19C. After Alfred Russel WALLACE]

Wallachia another spelling of **Walachia**

wallah /wólla/, **walla** *n* somebody in charge of something or associated with a particular service or occupation (*dated informal*) ○ *a legal wallah* [Late 18C. Via Hindi -*vālā* '(somebody) responsible for something or some duty' < Sanskrit *pālaka* 'keeper']

wallaroo /wòlla róo/ (*plural* **-roos** or *same*) *n* a large and sturdy kangaroo. Native to: rocky upland areas of Australia. Latin name: *Macropus robustus* or *Macropus bernardus*. [Early 19C. < Dharuk *walāru*]

Wallasey /wóllassi/ town on the Wirral Peninsula, northwestern England. Population: 60,895 (2001).

wall bars *npl* a series of horizontal bars attached to a wall and used for exercise

wallboard /wáwl bawrd/ *n* BUILDINGS same as **plasterboard**

wallchart /wáwl chaart/ *n* a chart designed to be displayed on a wall to provide information or aid in instruction

wallcovering *n* something such as wallpaper used as a decorative covering for a wall

wallcreeper *n* a songbird with a long slender beak and black wings with scarlet markings. Native to:

mountains of Europe and Asia. Latin name: *Tichodroma muraria*.

walled garden *n* **1.** a garden surrounded on all sides by a high wall **2.** a browsing environment for viewing websites that provides a means of controlling the information and websites that a user is able to access. It may either protect users such as children from unsuitable information or direct users to specific, often paid content supported by an Internet service provider.

Wallenberg /vaálan bérg, waálan burg/, **Raoul** (1912–47?) Swedish diplomat. While based as a diplomat in Budapest during World War II, he worked to protect persecuted Jews in Hungary. He was captured by the Soviets, and his fate remains unknown.

Waller /wóllar/, **Fats** (1904–43) US singer, pianist, and composer. He wrote and performed many jazz classics such as 'Ain't Misbehavin'' (1929). Born **Waller, Thomas Wright**

'Jazz isn't *what* you do, it's *how* you do it.'
[Fats Waller. Quoted in *The Jazz Book*, Joachim E. Berendt; 1983]

wallet /wóllit/ *n* **1.** POCKET-SIZED FOLDED CASE FOR MONEY a small flat folding case, usually made of leather or plastic, that holds paper money and credit cards and is usually carried in a pocket or handbag **2.** FOLDER a folder for holding items such as papers, photographs, or maps **3.** SOFTWARE PROGRAM FOR ONLINE PURCHASES a software program used to carry out transactions for purchases made on the Internet (*used in e-commerce*) **4.** KNAPSACK a bag or knapsack for carrying articles on a trip (*archaic*) [14C. Probably via Anglo-Norman, 'travelling pack' < Germanic, 'roll']

walleye /wáwl ī/ (*plural same* or **-eyes**) *n* **1.** EYE THAT APPEARS WHITE an eye with a white or streaked iris that gives the appearance of a pale ring round the pupil **2.** WHITE IN CORNEA an eye with an opaque white cornea, or the condition that causes this opacity **3.** SQUINT a squint (**strabismus**) in which one or both eyes turn outwards **4.** FRESHWATER FISH OF N AMERICA a large predatory freshwater fish with large eyes that is related to the perch. Native to: northeastern North America. Latin name: *Stizostedion vitreum*. [Early 16C. Back-formation < WALLEYED]

walleyed /wáwl īd/ *adj* **1.** affected by walleye **2.** having bulging or staring eyes [14C. < N Germanic, 'speckle-eyed']

walleyed pike *n* FISH same as **walleye** (sense 4)

walleyed pollack *n* a fish of the cod family resembling a pollack. Native to: northern Pacific. Latin name: *Theragra chalcogramma*.

wallflower /wáwl flow ər/ *n* **1.** SPRING-FLOWERING GARDEN PLANT a common spring-blooming garden plant with rather woody erect stems. Flowers: fragrant, yellow, orange, or brownish, clustered at top of stem. Genera: *Cheiranthus* or *Erysimum*. **2.** PLANT WITH FRAGRANT COLOURFUL FLOWERS a wild plant often found growing on walls, rocks, and cliffs. Flowers: fragrant, colourful. Native to: southern Europe. Latin name: *Cheiranthus cheiri*. **3.** SOMEBODY UNNOTICED AT SOCIAL EVENT a shy or retiring person who remains unnoticed at social events, especially a woman without a dance partner (*informal*)

wall fruit *n* **1.** a fruit of a tree or bush that has been trained to grow against a wall **2.** a fruit-bearing tree or bush that has been trained to grow against a wall

wall game *n* a variant on association football unique to Eton College in which a ball is moved along a wall in a field by two teams using hands and feet

wall hanging *n* a tapestry or other large flat object hung on a wall as a decoration

wallies /wálliz/ *npl Scotland* a set of false teeth (*informal humorous*) [Plural of WALLY², 'made of china']

Wallis, Sir Barnes (1887–1979) British aeronautical engineer. He designed the Wellington bomber and the 'bouncing bombs' that destroyed two dams in a raid on Germany during World War II. Full name **Wallis, Sir Barnes Neville**

Wallis and Futuna Islands /-fə tyóonə-/ island group situated in the southwestern Pacific Ocean, northeast of Fiji. It is an overseas territory of France. Capital: Mata Utu. Population: 15,734 (2003). Area: 274 sq. km/106 sq. mi.

wall knot *n* a bulky knot made at the end of a rope by unwinding the strands and tying them together

wall lizard *n* a lizard that can be found on walls and rocks. Family: Lacertidae.

wall mustard *n* PLANTS same as **wall rocket**

wall of death *n* an attraction at a fairground in which a motorcyclist rides round the inside wall of a large cylinder

wall of sound *n* a recorded musical effect on pop records achieved by overdubbing or layering many different instruments around a pop tune

Walloon /wo lóon/ *n* **1.** a member of a French-speaking people living in southern Belgium, mainly in the autonomous region of Wallonia, and in neighbouring parts of France **2.** a dialect of French spoken in southern Belgium and neighbouring parts of France [Mid-16C. Via French *Wallon* < medieval Latin *wallo(n)*- 'foreigner' < Germanic] —**Walloon** *adj*

wallop /wólləp/ *vt* (**-lops, -loping, -loped**) (*informal*) **1.** BEAT SOMEBODY to give somebody a sound physical beating **2.** HIT SOMEBODY OR SOMETHING VERY HARD to strike somebody or something with great force ○ *She can really wallop the ball.* **3.** DEFEAT SOMEBODY DECISIVELY to defeat a person or team decisively ■ *n* **1.** HARD HIT a powerful blow (*informal*) **2.** ABILITY TO HIT HARD the ability to strike a powerful blow (*informal*) ○ *He's got a wallop that could make him heavyweight champion.* **3.** ABILITY TO IMPRESS the ability to create a powerful impression on others (*informal*) ○ *The play's final revelations pack the emotional wallop of the most sublime of Shakespearean comedies.* **4.** BEVERAGES same as **beer** (*dated slang*) [14C. < Old French *waloper*, variant of *galoper* 'gallop, run well' < Germanic]

walloping /wólləping/ (*informal*) *n* **1.** BEATING a sound physical beating **2.** DECISIVE DEFEAT a decisive defeat or victory ■ *adj* BIG very large or impressive ○ *The angler came back with a walloping catch.* ■ *adv* ADDS EMPHASIS used to emphasize the size or extent of something ○ *a walloping big lie*

wallow /wóllō/ *vi* (**-lows, -lowing, -lowed**) **1.** ROLL IN SOMETHING to lie down and roll around in something ○ *pigs wallowing in mud* **2.** INDULGE IN SOMETHING EXCESSIVELY to take pleasure or be immersed in something in a self-indulgent way ○ *wallowed in memories of the long-gone glory days* **3.** HAVE HUGE AMOUNT OF SOMETHING to have an ample or excessive supply of something ○ *a family wallowing in money* **4.** WALK WITH DIFFICULTY to move clumsily or with difficulty ■ *n* **1.** ACT OF WALLOWING an instance of wallowing in something such as mud, emotion, or material luxury **2.** ZOOL PLACE WHERE ANIMALS ROLL a muddy, wet, or dusty place used by animals for rolling around in **3.** ZOOL DEPRESSION FORMED BY ANIMAL a sunken area in the ground made by a rolling animal [Old English *wealwian* 'to roll' < Indo-European] —**wallower** *n*

wallpaper /wáwl paypər/ *n* **1.** PAPER TO DECORATE WALLS paper, usually printed with a pattern, that is pasted on walls and sometimes ceilings as a covering and decoration **2.** BACKGROUND PATTERN FOR SCREEN the background pattern for a computer screen, composed of graphics **3.** SOMETHING BLAND AND DULL something that is so bland and unexciting that it serves as a hardly noticed background (*informal*) ■ *vti* (**-pers, -pering, -pered**) PUT WALLPAPER ON SOMETHING to cover a surface with wallpaper

wall pass *n* in football, a movement in which one player passes the ball to another and runs forward to receive the return

wall pepper *n* a stonecrop with creeping stems and leaves with a peppery taste. Flowers: yellow. Native to: Europe, Asia. Latin name: *Sedum acre*.

wall plate *n* a horizontal structural member placed along the top of a wall to support the ends of beams, joists, or trusses

wall plug *n* a receptacle in a wall, connected to an electric circuit, into which appliances can be plugged

wall rock *n* the rock that surrounds a vein, mineral deposit, or fault

wall rocket *n* a cruciferous plant that grows on walls and waste ground. Flowers: yellow. Native to: Europe. Latin name: *Diplotaxis muralis* or *Diplotaxis tenuifolia*.

wall rue *n* a small delicate fern that grows in fan-shaped clusters on walls or in rocky crevices. Latin name: *Asplenium ruta-muraria*.

Wallsend /wáwlz end/ town in northeastern England, near Newcastle upon Tyne. It marks one end of Hadrian's Wall. Population: 45,280 (1991).

Wall Street /wáwl-/ *n* **1.** the street in Manhattan, New York City, where the New York Stock Exchange and many major financial institutions of the United States are located **2.** the US financial market, especially as represented by the publicly owned companies comprising the stock markets

wall-to-wall *adj* **1. FROM ONE WALL TO ANOTHER** completely covering a floor ○ *wall-to-wall carpeting* **2. FILLING SOMETHING COMPLETELY** completely filling, covering, or pervading something (*informal*) ○ *fed up with wall-to-wall pop music* **3. ALL-INCLUSIVE** including everyone or everything (*informal*) ○ *wall-to-wall insurance coverage*

wally[1] /wólli/ (*plural* **-lies**) *n* an offensive term that deliberately insults somebody's intelligence or common sense (*slang*) [Mid-20C. Origin ?]

wally[2] /wálli/ *adj Scotland* **1. CHINA** made of china **2. TILED** lined with ceramic tiles **3. SPLENDID** splendid or excellent [15C. Origin ?]

walnut /wáwl nut/ *n* **1. EDIBLE NUT** a deeply wrinkled nut that is enclosed in a hard shell and a thick leathery husk **2. VALUABLE WOOD** a hard dark-brown wood. Use: cabinetwork, panelling, veneers. (*often used before a noun*) **3. TREE VALUED FOR NUTS AND WOOD** a deciduous tree with fragrant compound leaves and drooping catkins, grown worldwide for its shade, wood, and walnuts. Genus: *Juglans*. **4. DARK-BROWN COLOUR** a dark brown colour like that of walnut wood [14C. < Old English *wealhnutu* 'foreign nut', < *wealh* 'foreign, Welsh, Celtic'] —**walnut** *adj*

ORIGIN The prehistoric Germanic peoples regarded the ***walnut*** as the 'foreign nut' because it did not originally grow in northern Europe, but was introduced from Gaul and Italy, the lands of the Celts and the Romans (the Germans' own native nut was the hazel).

Walpole /wáwlpōl, wól-/, **Horace** (1717–97) British writer. The son of Sir Robert Walpole, he wrote one of the first Gothic novels *The Castle of Otranto* (1764) and engaged in extensive and celebrated literary correspondence.

> 'This world is a comedy to those who think, a tragedy to those who feel.'
> [Horace Walpole, *Letter to Anne, Countess of Upper Ossory*; 16 August 1776]

Walpole, Robert, 1st Earl of Orford (1676–1745) English political leader. He became a Whig MP in 1701. From 1721 to 1742 he wielded considerable political power as chief minister to George I and George II. Although he himself repudiated the title, which did not become official until much later, he is regarded as Britain's first prime minister.

> 'Anything but history, for history must be false.'
> [Robert Walpole, *Walpoliana*; 1781]

Walpurgis Night /val póorgiss-/ *n* **1.** in German folklore, the witches' feast night on the Brocken in the Harz Mountains. Date: 30 April. **2.** a nightmarish situation [Early 19C. Translation of German *Walpurgisnacht*, after *Walpurga*, 8C Anglo-Saxon saint]

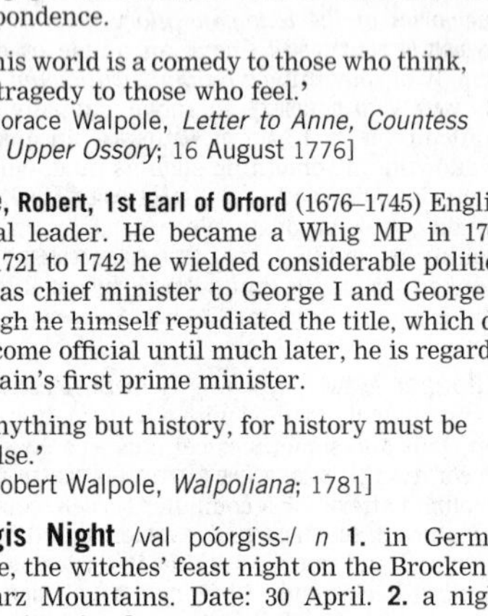

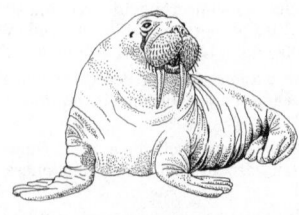

walrus

walrus /wáwlrəss, wóll-/ (*plural* **-ruses** or *same*) *n* a large sea mammal related to seals and sea lions, with tough wrinkled skin, large tusks, and bristly whiskers. Native to: Arctic. Latin name: *Odobenus rosmarus*. [Early 18C. < Dutch *walrus, walros* 'whale-horse' < *walvis(ch)* 'whale']

walrus moustache *n* a thick drooping moustache resembling a walrus's whiskers

Walsall /wáwl sawl, wól-/ industrial town near Birmingham, in central England. Population: 174,739 (1991).

Walsingham /wáwlsingəm, wóls-/ village in Norfolk, eastern England. For hundreds of years the Shrine of Our Lady of Walsingham has been a Christian pilgrimage centre.

Walter /vàltər/, **Bruno** (1876–1962) German-born US conductor. He was best known for his interpretations of the music of Mozart, Bruckner, and Mahler. Born **Schlesinger, Bruno Walter**

Walter /wáwltər/, **John** (1739–1812) British newspaper publisher. He founded the London-based *Daily Universal Register* (1785), which in 1788 was retitled *The Times*. It is the oldest newspaper still in publication.

Walter Mitty /wáwltər mítti, wóltər-/ (*plural* **Walter Mitties**) *n* somebody with a very ordinary dull life who daydreams about having great adventures and success [Mid-20C. After the hero of 'The Secret Life of Walter Mitty', a 1939 short story by James Thurber] —**Walter Mittyish** *adj*

Walters /wáwltərz/, **Barbara** (*b.* 1931) US television journalist and presenter. As a reporter and host of television news magazines and celebrity interview shows, she established a reputation for eliciting candid answers to difficult questions from public figures.

Waltham Forest /wáwlthəm-, wólth-/ residential borough in northeastern London, England. Population: 218,341 (2001).

Walton /wáwlt'n/, **Ernest T. S.** (1903–95) Irish physicist. He helped develop a particle accelerator, which led to the first artificial nuclear reaction. He shared the Nobel Prize in physics (1951). Full name **Walton, Ernest Thomas Sinton**

Walton, Izaak (1593–1683) English writer. He is remembered for his book on fishing and the charms of pastoral life, *The Compleat Angler* (1653).

> 'No man can lose what he never had.'
> [Izaak Walton, *The Compleat Angler*; 1653]

Walton, Sir William (1902–83) British composer. He wrote orchestral works, an opera, and film scores, including the music for Laurence Olivier's adaptations of Shakespeare's plays. Full name **Walton, Sir William Turner**

waltz /wawlss, wolss, wawlts/ *n* (*plural* **waltzes**) **1. DANCE FOR COUPLES IN TRIPLE TIME** a ballroom dance in triple time in which a couple turn continuously while moving round **2. MUSIC FOR WALTZ** the music for a waltz **3. SOMETHING EASY** something that can be accomplished effortlessly (*informal*) ■ *v* (**waltzes, waltzing, waltzed**) **1.** *vti* **DANCE WALTZ** to dance a waltz, or lead somebody in a waltz ○ *waltzed me round the room* **2.** *vi* **MOVE WITH SELF-CONFIDENCE** to move quickly with ease and self-assurance (*informal*) ○ *She just waltzed right in and demanded more money.* **3.** *vi* **SUCCEED EASILY** to achieve success effortlessly in an activity [Late 18C. < German *Walzer* < *walzen* 'waltz, roll, revolve'] ◇ **waltz Matilda** *Aus* to wander around looking for work carrying your belongings in a pack (*dated slang*)

CULTURAL NOTE ***Waltzing Matilda***, a song (1895) with lyrics by Australian writer A. B. Paterson. Set in late nineteenth-century Australia, it is a ballad about an itinerant worker who is arrested for stealing sheep. Rather than go to jail, he drowns himself in a water hole. A song that evokes the rugged rebellious spirit of early Australia, it is now regarded as an unofficial national anthem.

Walvis Bay /wáwlviss-/ town and port in western Namibia, on the Atlantic coast. It was a former enclave of South Africa until 1994. Population: 50,000 (1997).

wamble /wómb'l/ (**-bles, -bling, -bled**) *vi regional* to twist the body [14C. Origin ?]

wame /waym/ *n Scotland* the belly, abdomen, or womb [15C. Variant of WOMB]

Wampanoag /wómpə nṓ ag/ (*plural same* or **-ags**) *n* a member of an Algonquian people who lived in Rhode Island and Massachusetts [Late 17C. < Narraganset, 'easterners'] —**Wampanoag** *adj*

wampum /wómpəm/ *n* small polished beads made from shells, threaded on string, and used by some Native North Americans as decoration, for ceremonial purposes, or in former times for money [Mid-17C. Shortening of *wampumpeag* < Massachuset, 'white strings']

wan /won/ *adj* (**wanner, wannest**) **1. PALE** unhealthily pale, especially from illness or grief **2. INDICATIVE OF LOW SPIRITS** suggesting ill health or unhappiness ○ *He gave me a wan look.* **3. FAINT** lacking brightness ○ *a wan star* ■ *vti* (**wans, wanning, wanned**) **MAKE OR BECOME PALE OR ILL** to become pale or unhealthy, or make somebody or something do this (*literary*) [Old English *wann* 'dark, dusky, grey', origin ?] —**wanly** *adv* —**wanness** *n*

WAN /wan/ *abbr* **1.** West Africa Nigeria (*international vehicle registration*) **2.** COMPUT wide area network

Wanaka /wə naákə/ town in the southern part of the South Island, New Zealand, situated at the southern end of Lake Wanaka. It is a tourist resort. Population: 3,330 (2001).

Wanaka, Lake lake in the southern part of the South Island, New Zealand. Area: 194 sq. km/75 sq. mi.

wand /wond/ *n* **1. ROD WITH SUPPOSED MAGICAL POWERS** a thin rod believed to possess magical powers, used by supposed magicians, wizards, and supernatural beings **2. STAFF SHOWING AUTHORITY** a thin staff carried as a symbol of office **3. VACUUM CLEANER PART** an attachment between the hose and cleaning tool of a vacuum cleaner that resembles a pipe **4.** COMPUT **BAR-CODE SCANNER** a hand-held optical scanning device used to read and enter bar-code information into a computer **5.** MUSIC same as **baton** [12C. < Old Norse *vondr* 'straight flexible stick' < Germanic, 'to turn']

wander /wóndər/ *v* (**-ders, -dering, -dered**) **1.** *vti* **TRAVEL WITHOUT DESTINATION** to move from place to place, either without a purpose or without a known destination ○ *They wander the countryside looking for work.* **2.** *vi* **MEANDER** to follow a winding course ○ *The river wandered through the meadows.* **3.** *vi* **STROLL SOMEWHERE** to go somewhere at a leisurely pace **4.** *vi* **LEAVE FIXED PATH** to stray from a place, path, or course ○ *Don't wander far from home.* **5.** *vi* **DAYDREAM** to lose the ability to concentrate or pay attention ○ *My mind was wandering.* **6.** *vi* **FAIL TO THINK OR SPEAK CLEARLY** to lose the ability to think, speak, or write in an organized and coherent way ■ *n* **AIMLESS STROLL** an act of moving from place to place in an aimless or leisurely way [Old English *wandrian* < Germanic, 'to turn'] —**wanderer** *n* —**wandering** *adj* —**wanderingly** *adv*

SPELLCHECK **wander** or **wonder**? Do not confuse the spelling of ***wander*** and ***wonder***, which sound similar. ***Wander*** means 'move from place to place without a purpose or destination' or 'stray': *We wandered along the beach. Try not to let your thoughts wander.* ***Wonder*** is a noun denoting 'amazed admiration or awe' or 'something marvellous' (as in *a feeling of wonder, one of the wonders of the world, no wonder he doesn't trust her*), and also a verb meaning 'speculate about something' (as in *I wonder how much it costs.*).

wandering Jew *n* a trailing plant widely grown as a houseplant for its variegated foliage. Flowers: white, rose-red. Native to: tropical America. Latin name: *Tradescantia fluminensis* or *Tradescantia albiflora* or *Zebrina pendula*.

Wandering Jew *n* in medieval legend, a Jewish man who was condemned to remain alive and wandering the world until Judgment Day for having mocked Jesus Christ on the day of the Crucifixion

wanderlust /wóndər lust/ *n* a strong desire to travel [Early 20C. < German, 'desire to travel']

wane /wayn/ *vi* (**wanes, waning, waned**) **1. SHOW LESS LIGHTED AREA** to show a decreasing illuminated surface between a full moon and new moon **2. GET SMALLER OR LESS** to decrease gradually in intensity or power ○ *His interest was waning.* **3. FINISH** to draw to a close ○ *Winter is waning at last.* ■ *n* **1. LESSENING IN INTENSITY** a gradual lessening of power or intensity **2. TIME DURING WANING OF MOON** the period during which the Moon's visible illuminated surface is decreasing in size **3. PERIOD OF LESSENING** a period of gradual decrease **4. END OF PERIOD** the conclusion of a time or season ○ *the wane of summer* **5.** WOODWORK **IRREGULARITY ON PLANK EDGE** a flawed edge left on a rough-sawn plank [Old English *wanian* 'lessen' < Germanic, 'lacking'] ◇ **be on the wane** to be decreasing or passing out of fashion

Wanganui /wóngə nóo i/ **1.** river in the southwestern part of the North Island, New Zealand. It rises on Mount Tongariro and flows southwards through the city of Wanganui to the Cook Strait. Length: 290

km/180 mi. **2.** city and port in the southwestern part of the North Island, New Zealand, situated on the Wanganui River. Population: 39,423 (2001).

Wangaratta /wáng gə rάttə/ city in northern Victoria, Australia. It is a centre for agriculture and textile production. Population: 26,683 (2002 estimate).

wangle /wáng g'l/ (*informal*) *vt* (**-gles, -gling, -gled**) **1. GET SOMETHING DEVIOUSLY** to get something using indirect and sometimes deceitful methods ○ *I'm trying to wangle some time off work.* **2. FALSIFY ACCOUNTS** to manipulate accounts or records, usually deceitfully ■ *n* **DEVIOUS METHOD** an indirect and sometimes deceitful means of accomplishing something [Late 19C. Origin ?] —**wangler** *n*

wank /wangk/ (*taboo*) *vti* (**wanks, wanking, wanked**) a highly offensive term meaning to masturbate, or masturbate somebody ■ *n* **1.** a highly offensive term for an act of masturbation **2.** a highly offensive term for self-indulgent, pretentious, or arrogant behaviour [Mid-20C. Origin ?]

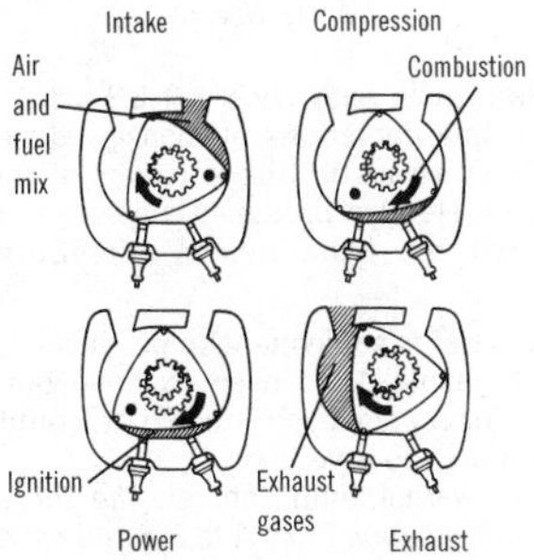

Wankel engine

Wankel engine /wángk'l-, váng-/ *n* an internal-combustion engine in which an approximately triangular rotor inside an elliptical combustion chamber replaces the pistons of a conventional engine, thus reducing the number of moving parts [Mid-20C. After Felix *Wankel* (1902–88), German engineer]

wanker /wángkər/ *n* **1.** a highly offensive term for somebody who masturbates (*taboo*) **2.** a highly offensive term for somebody considered unpleasant, self-indulgent, pretentious, or arrogant (*insult*)

wanna /wónnə/ *contr* want to (*nonstandard*) ○ *I wanna go!*

wannabe /wónnə bee/ *n* somebody who tries to be like somebody else or to belong to a specific group (*informal disapproving*) [Late 20C. Alteration of *want to be*]

want /wont/ *vt* (**wants, wanting, wanted**) **1. DESIRE SOMETHING** to feel a need or desire for something ○ *We want a new car.* **2. WISH SOMETHING DONE** to desire to do something or that something should be done ○ *I don't want you being late.* ○ *He wants his steak well done.* **3. MISS SOMETHING** to feel the lack of something ○ *After a week on the road, I want my own bed.* **4. WISH SOMEBODY TO BE PRESENT** to wish to see or speak to somebody ○ *He's wanted on the phone.* ○ *Someone wants you at the door.* **5. SEEK SOMEBODY AS CRIME SUSPECT** to seek somebody in connection with a crime (*usually passive*) ○ *wanted for two felonies* **6. SHOULD** used to indicate that something is desirable or advisable (*informal*) ○ *You want to see a doctor about that.* **7. NEED SOMETHING** to have a need for something (*informal*) ○ *What that kid wants is some discipline!* ○ *The cupboards want cleaning.* **8. DESIRE SOMEBODY SEXUALLY** to feel sexual desire for somebody (*informal*) ■ *n* **1. NEED** something that somebody desires or needs (*usually used in the plural*) ○ *All your wants can be easily supplied.* **2. LACK OF SOMETHING** an absence or scarcity of something ○ *no want of snow for the skiers this winter* ○ *If we fail, it won't be for want of trying.* **3. POVERTY** the state of being poor ○ *Freedom from want is a fundamental human right.* [12C. < Old Norse *vanta* 'be lacking' < Germanic, 'lacking'] —**wanter** *n*

SYNONYMS ***want, desire, wish, long, yearn, covet, crave***

CORE MEANING: to seek to have, do, or achieve something

want to feel a need or desire for something ○ *What do you want for your birthday?* ○ *All I really wanted was to buy a house and settle down.* **desire** to want something very strongly ○ *He had everything that a man could desire – looks, talent, wealth.* ○ *She needed to conquer her phobia if she was to lead the normal happy life she so desired.* **wish** to have a strong feeling of wanting something to happen or wanting to have something. ○ *We wished there was more time to arrange everything.* ○ *'I do wish we could help her somehow,' sighed Christine.* **long** to have a strong desire for a person, place, or thing, especially somebody or something unattainable or not within immediate reach ○ *We've all been longing to see him.* ○ *She'd been longing for peace and quiet so that she could finish her book.* **yearn** to have a strong desire for somebody or something, especially when the desire is tinged with sadness ○ *peoples who yearn for freedom, democracy, equality, and human rights* ○ *Ever since he had been in football he had yearned for a chance to play in the World Cup.* **covet** to have a strong desire to possess something that belongs to somebody else, or (*formal*) to want to have something very much ○ *This is his third failure to win the post he so covets.* **crave** to have a strong desire for something ○ *She openly craves publicity.* ○ *Will craved fame and fortune.*

want for *vt* to experience the lack of something ○ *The family wants for nothing.*

want in *vi* to wish to be included in something, especially a business deal (*informal*) ○ *Do you want in?*

want out *vi* to wish to be excluded from or to leave something, especially a business deal (*informal*) ○ *We want out before we get into trouble.*

want ad *n N Am* a classified advertisement in a newspaper or magazine (*informal*)

wanted /wóntid/ *adj* sought as a suspect in a crime

wanting /wónting/ *adj* **1. INADEQUATE** lacking something necessary **2. UNSATISFACTORY** not meeting expectations or requirements ○ *found wanting in the area of security* ■ *prep* **SHORT OF** missing something necessary ○ *a chair wanting one leg*

wanton /wóntən/ *adj* **1. SEXUALLY INDISCRIMINATE** lacking restraint or inhibition, especially in sexual behaviour **2. RANDOM** lacking reason or provocation ○ *wanton violence and destruction* **3. DESIRING TO DO HARM** done out of a desire to cause harm **4. EXCESSIVE** unrestrained, heedless of reasonable limits, or characterized by greed and extravagance ○ *wanton indulgence* **5. UNRULY** lacking discipline **6. LUSH** growing luxuriantly (*archaic*) **7. PLAYFUL** engaged in play that is carefree (*archaic*) ■ *n* **SOMEBODY WITHOUT SEXUAL RESTRAINT** a lascivious or sexually uninhibited person ■ *vi* (**-tons, -toning, -toned**) **BE WANTON** to behave in a wanton manner (*archaic*) [14C. < Old English *wan-* 'un-' + *togen* 'disciplined' < *tēon* 'train, discipline, pull'] —**wantonly** *adv* —**wantonness** *n*

WAP /wap/, **Wap** *n* a standard protocol for the transmission of electronic data between hand-held narrowband devices such as mobile phones and pagers and other sources of digital information such as the Internet. Full form **wireless application protocol**

wapentake /wóppən tayk/ *n* a historical subdivision of some counties in northern and central England, equivalent to the hundred in other counties [Pre-12C. < Old Norse *vápnatak* 'weapon-taking']

wapiti /wóppiti/ (*plural* **-tis** or *same*) *n* a large deer that has tall branched antlers and lives in herds. Native to: mountains of western North America. Latin name: *Cervus elaphus.* [Early 19C. < Shawnee *wapiti* 'white rump']

war /wawr/ *n* **1. ARMED FIGHTING BETWEEN GROUPS** a period of hostile relations between countries, states, or factions that leads to fighting between armed forces, especially in land, air, or sea battles ○ *The two countries are at war.* **2. PERIOD OF ARMED FIGHTING** a period of armed conflict between countries or groups ○ *during the Vietnam War* **3. METHODS OF WARFARE** the techniques or the study of the techniques of armed conflict **4. CONFLICT** a serious struggle, argument, or conflict between people ○ *The candidates are at war.* **5. SERIOUS EFFORT TO END SOMETHING** an effort to combat or eradicate something harmful ○ *a war against drugs* ■ *vi* (**wars, warring, warred**) **1. MAKE WAR** to engage in an armed conflict with somebody **2. BE IN STRUGGLE** to be involved in a serious struggle, argument, or conflict with somebody or an effort to combat or eradicate something harmful [12C. Via Old N French *werre*, Old French *guerre* < Germanic, 'strife, confusion']

CULTURAL NOTE ***War and Peace***, a novel (1865–69) by the Russian writer Leo Tolstoy. This monumental work is set in Russia during and after the Napoleonic Wars (1805–14). Though it focuses on five fictional families, the story incorporates historical accounts and philosophical essays to create an extraordinarily comprehensive portrait of Russian society that touches on almost every aspect of human experience, from love and happiness to grief and war.

SYNONYMS See ***fight***.

war. *abbr* warrant

War. *abbr* Warwickshire

waragi /wa̋ərəgi/ *n* a Ugandan alcoholic drink made from bananas [Early 20C. < Kiswahili *wargi*]

~~**waranty**~~ incorrect spelling of **warranty**

waratah /wórrə tа́ə, -taa/ (*plural* **-tahs** or *same*) *n* a bush that is the emblem of New South Wales, Australia. Flowers: large, dark red, globular. Native to: New South Wales. Latin name: *Telopea speciosissima.* [Late 18C. < Dharuk *warrada*]

war baby *n* a baby born or conceived during a war

Warbeck /wáwr bek/, **Perkin** (1474?–99) Flemish royal pretender. Posing as Richard, duke of York, the murdered son of Edward IV, he challenged Henry VII's right to the English throne, but was captured and hanged.

War Between the States *n US* HIST same as **Civil War** (sense 1)

warble[1] /wáwrb'l/ *vti* (**-bles, -bling, -bled**) **1. SING WITH CHANGING NOTES** to sing with trills and often changing notes (*refers to birds*) **2. SING SOMETHING** to sing in a quavering or trilling way, or express something in such song ○ *warble a tune* ■ *n* **1. SINGING WITH OFTEN CHANGING NOTES** singing with trills or other vocal modulations **2. TRILLING SOUND** a sound with trills or quavers [14C. < Old N French *werbler* 'sing with trills' < Frankish, 'whirl, trill']

warble[2] /wáwrb'l/ *n* **1. SWELLING IN HORSES AND CATTLE** a swelling under the skin, usually on the back, of horses and cattle, caused by the warble fly maggot **2. WARBLE FLY OR ITS LARVA** the warble fly, or the maggot of the warble fly **3. LUMP ON HORSE'S BACK FROM SADDLE** a hard lump of tissue on the back of a riding horse, caused by the rubbing of the saddle [Late 16C. Origin ?]

warble fly *n* a large hairy fly, the larvae of which form painful swellings under the skin of cattle and horses. Family: Oestridae.

warbler /wáwrblər/ *n* **1. BIRD RELATED TO THRUSH** a songbird that is related to the thrush. Native to: Europe, Asia. Family: Sylviidae. **2. SMALL INSECT-EATING BIRD** a small songbird of the wood warbler family that eats insects and is often brightly coloured. Native to: North and South America. Family: Parulidae. **3. SOMEBODY WHO SINGS** somebody who sings, especially in a quavering or trilling way

warblog /wáwr blog/ *n* a weblog concerned with terrorism, war, and conflict, often with a pro-military stance [Late 20C. After WEBLOG] —**warblogger** *n*

war bride *n* a woman who meets and marries a serviceman during wartime, especially one from another country

warchalking /wáwr chawking/ *n* the act of scrawling symbols on pavements or building walls that indicate to others the presence of unprotected private or corporate high-speed Internet connections, for use in obtaining free access (*slang*) —**warchalker** *n*

war chest *n* an amount of funds collected to pay for a war or something such as a political campaign

war clouds *npl* signs of impending war

war correspondent *n* a journalist reporting from a war

war crime *n* a crime committed during wartime that is in violation of international agreements concerning the conventions of war, e.g. the mistreatment of prisoners or genocide (*often used in the plural*) —**war criminal** *n*

war cry *n* MIL same as **battle cry** (sense 1)

ward /wawrd/ *n* **1. ROOM IN HOSPITAL** a room in a hospital, especially one for several patients being given similar treatment **2. CITY DIVISION** an administrative or electoral division of an area such as a city, town, or county **3. PRISON DIVISION** a division in a prison **4.** LAW **SOMEBODY UNDER OFFICIAL CARE** somebody, especially a child or young person, who is under the care of a guardian or a court **5.** BUILDINGS **AREA IN CASTLE** an open area within the walls of a castle **6.** LAW **CUSTODY** a state of official custody or protection (*archaic*) **7.** **DEFENCE MOVEMENT** a movement or stance used as a

means of protection, e.g. in fencing **8. RIDGE IN KEY OR LOCK** a ridge or groove in a key or a lock that makes one fit the other ■ *vt* (**wards, warding, warded**) **PROTECT SOMEBODY OR SOMETHING** to guard or protect somebody or something (*archaic*) [Old English *weard* < Germanic, 'be on guard']

ward off *vt* **1.** to parry or repel a blow or attack **2.** to keep away or avert something bad

Ward /wawrd/, **Frederick** (1835–70) Australian bushranger. As an outlaw, he was renowned for his nonviolent chivalrous attitude. Known as **Captain Thunderbolt**

Ward, Sir Joseph (1856–1930) Australian-born prime minister of New Zealand (1906–12 and 1928–30). After serving as a Liberal prime minister, he was again elected to the premiership in 1928 as the leader of the United Party. See table at **prime minister**. Full name **Ward, Joseph George**

Ward, Russell (1914–95) Australian historian. He wrote *The Australian Legend* (1958), a study of the Australian ideals of freedom, egalitarianism, and comradeship. Full name **Ward, Russell Braddock**

-ward *suffix* **1.** moving in a particular direction or directed towards a particular place ○ *earthward* **2.** lying or occurring in a particular direction ○ *rightward* ○ *windward* **3.** same as **-wards** [Old English *-weard* < Germanic, 'to turn']

USAGE See *towards*.

war dance *n* a dance performed as a ceremony before a battle or to celebrate victory, e.g. by Native North Americans

warded /wáwrdid/ *adj* describes keys or locks that have ridges or grooves

warden[1] /wáwrd'n/ *n* **1. SOMEBODY IN CHARGE OF BUILDING** somebody who is in charge of a building **2. SOMEBODY IN CHARGE OF INSTITUTION** somebody who is in charge of an institution such as a college or school **3. OFFICIAL CONCERNED WITH REGULATIONS** an official who makes sure that regulations are enforced, e.g. a traffic warden or air-raid warden ○ *game warden* **4.** *N Am* **CRIME** same as **governor** (sense 3) **5. CHR** same as **churchwarden** (sense 1) [12C. < Anglo-Norman *wardein* < Germanic, 'be on guard'] —**wardenry** *n* —**wardenship** *n*

warden[2] /wáwrd'n/ *n* a pear used especially in cooking [14C. Origin ?]

warder /wáwrdər/ *n* a prison officer [14C. < Anglo-Norman < Old N French *warder* 'to guard', variant of French *garder*]

ward heeler *n* *N Am* somebody who does minor tasks for a local or city politician (*informal*)

ward manager *n* a nurse in charge of a ward in a hospital

wardmote /wáwrdmōt/ *n* a meeting of the people who live in a ward (*archaic*) [14C. < WARD + MOOT]

ward of court *n* somebody, especially a minor, who is under the protection of a court or a court-appointed guardian

wardriving /wáwr drīving/ *n* the act of driving around an area in search of an unprotected wireless network in order to take advantage of a high-speed Internet connection belonging to somebody else and avoid paying a fee (*slang*)

wardrobe /wáwrdrōb/ *n* **1. PLACE FOR CLOTHES** a large cupboard with a rail or shelves for clothes and shoes **2. CLOTHES COLLECTION** all the clothes that belong to somebody **3. CLOTHES FOR PARTICULAR PURPOSE** a collection of clothes for a particular season or purpose **4. THEATRE COSTUMES** the costumes used by a theatrical company **5. PLACE FOR COSTUMES** a place in a theatre where costumes are kept **6. ROYAL DEPARTMENT** the department in a royal or noble household in charge of robes and jewels [14C. < Old N French *warderobe*, variant of French *garderobe* < French *garder* 'to guard' + *robe* 'robe']

wardrobe mistress *n* the woman in charge of the costumes in a theatre or on a film set

wardrobe trunk *n* a large upright trunk with a rail on which clothes can be hung

wardroom /wáwrd room, -room/ *n* **1.** a room on a warship used by all the officers except the captain **2.** the officers on a ship who can use the wardroom

-wards *suffix* in a particular direction or towards a particular place ○ *northwards* [Old English *weardes* < Germanic, inflected form of source of -WARD]

USAGE See *towards*.

wardship /wáwrdship/ *n* the state of being in the care of a guardian appointed by parents or a court

ward sister *n* a woman who is a ward manager in a hospital (*dated*)

ware[1] /wair/ *n* **1. SIMILAR THINGS** similar things, or things that are made of the same material (*usually used in combination*) ○ *glassware* **2. CERAMICS** ceramic articles of a particular kind or made by a particular manufacturer (*often used in combination*) ○ *delftware* ■ **wares** *npl* **1. THINGS FOR SALE** articles offered for sale **2. MARKETABLE SKILLS** skills or talents offered as a service or a commodity [Old English *waru*]

SPELLCHECK ware, wear, were, or **where?** Do not confuse the spelling of *ware, wear, were,* and *where,* which sound similar. *Ware* (referring to similar things, or things made of the same material) is not to be confused with *wear* (referring to clothing) in compound words such as *software, tableware, footwear,* and *knitwear*. *Were* is the past tense of *are* (as in *We were all young once*), and *where* is used to ask about or indicate the place that somebody or something is in, at, going to, or coming from: *Where were you last night? They still live in the town where they were born.*

ware[2] /wair/ (*archaic*) *vti* (**wares, wared, waring**) same as **beware** ■ *adj* wary or prudent [Old English *warian* < Germanic, 'be on guard']

warehouse *n* /wáir howss/ (*plural* **-houses** /-howziz/) **1. STORAGE BUILDING** a large building in which goods, raw materials, or commodities are stored **2. BIG SHOP** a large store or shop, especially one where goods are sold wholesale ■ *vt* /wáir howz, -howss/ (**-houses** /-howziz/, **-housing** /-howzing/, **-housed** /-howzd/) **STORE SOMETHING IN WAREHOUSE** to store goods, raw materials, or commodities in a warehouse

warehouseman /wáir howssmən/ *n* (*plural* **-men** /-mən/) *n* somebody, especially a man, who works in or owns a warehouse

warehouseperson /wáir howss purss'n/ *n* somebody who works in or owns a warehouse

warehousing /wáir howzing/ *n* the accumulation of a security in the hope that demand will push the price up as a result of the reduced supply on the open market

warez /wairz/ *n* a commercial game or application that has been stripped of its copy protection and made available on the Internet by software pirates (*slang*) [Late 20C. Respelling of *wares*, the *-z* suffix being typically used to indicate the plural of terms for pirated software]

warf incorrect spelling of **wharf**

warfare /wáwr fair/ *n* **1.** the act or fact of engaging in a war **2.** conflict or struggle ○ *economic warfare*

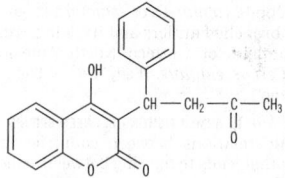

warfarin

warfarin /wáwrfərin/ *n* a colourless crystalline compound. Use: rodenticide, anticoagulant in medicine. Formula: $C_{19}H_{16}O_4$. [Mid-20C. < initial letters of *Wisconsin Alumni Research Foundation* + COUMARIN]

warfighter /wáwr fītər/ *n* a member of the armed forces

warfighting /wáwr fīting/ *n* armed combat between the armed forces of nations engaged in war

war game *n* **1.** a military exercise that simulates battle conditions **2.** a game in which models of soldiers, battlefields, and equipment are used to refight historical battles —**war gaming** *n*

war-game (**war-games, war-gaming, war-gamed**) *v* **1.** *vi* to take part in a war game **2.** *vt US* to try out a

military operation or strategy using simulation —**war-gamer** *n*

warhead /wáwr hed/ *n* the part of a bomb, ballistic or guided missile, rocket, or torpedo that contains the biological, chemical, explosive, incendiary, or nuclear material intended to damage the enemy

Andy Warhol

Warhol /wáwrhōl/, **Andy** (1928–87) US artist. His stylized multiple depictions of mass-produced objects and celebrities made him a leader of the pop art movement. He also produced a series of films that reproduced the banalities of life. Born **Wahola, Andrew**

'An artist is someone who produces things that people don't need to have but that he—for *some reason*—thinks it would be a good idea to give them.'
[Andy Warhol, 'Atmosphere', *The Philosophy of Andy Warhol: From A to B and Back Again*; 1975]

'In the future everybody will be world-famous for 15 minutes.'
[Andy Warhol, *Andy Warhol*; 1968]

warhorse /wáwr hawrss/ *n* **1. HORSE IN BATTLE** a horse ridden in battle **2. SURVIVOR OF CONFLICT** somebody who has taken part in and survived many conflicts (*informal*) **3. STANDARD WORK** a play or a piece of music that is familiar and hackneyed because of too frequent performance (*informal*)

Waring /wáiring/, **Marilyn** (b. 1952) New Zealand politician and writer. She was a National Party MP from 1975 to 1984 and wrote *If Women Counted* (1988). Full name **Waring, Marilyn Joy**

War in Iraq *n* the invasion of Iraq in 2003 by forces led by the United States, the United Kingdom, Spain, and some other nations, during which Saddam Hussein and his Baath Party were overthrown

warison /wárriss'n/ *n* a note played on a bugle as a sign for soldiers to attack [13C < Old French, variant of *garison* 'provision' (see GARRISON)]

Warks *abbr* Warwickshire

Warlbiri *n, adj* LANG another spelling of **Warlpiri**

warlike /wáwr līk/ *adj* **1. HOSTILE** hostile and inclined to fight **2. RELATING TO WAR** relating to war or warfare **3. RELATING TO WARRIORS** relating to the armed forces or military

warlock /wáwr lok/ *n* a man who is supposed to be a sorcerer or wizard [Old English *wærloga* 'oath-breaker' < *wær* 'oath, pledge' + *-loga* 'liar' < Indo-European, 'true']

Warlock /wáwr lok/, **Peter** (1894–1930) British composer and musicologist. He is noted for his songs and choral works, editions of Elizabethan and Jacobean music, and a biography of Frederick Delius. Pseudonym of **Heseltine, Philip Arnold**

warlord /wáwr lawrd/ *n* a military leader, especially a powerful one, operating outside the control of government —**warlordism** *n*

Warlpiri /wáalrbri/, **Warlbiri, Walbri** /wáalbri/ *n* an Australian Aboriginal language spoken in the central-western Northern Territory. Native speakers: 2,490. [< an Aboriginal language] —**Warlpiri** *adj*

warm /wawrm/ *adj* **1. FAIRLY HOT** moderately or comfortably hot ○ *a warm climate* **2. PROVIDING WARMTH** providing warmth or protection against cold ○ *a warm scarf* **3. WITH TOO MUCH HEAT** having or feeling an undesirable amount of heat, from exertion or ambient temperature **4. FRIENDLY** showing or feeling kindness and friendliness ○ *a warm person* **5. PASSIONATE** showing passion or liveliness ○ *a warm*

debate **6.** ENTHUSIASTIC OR ARDENT showing or feeling great enthusiasm ○ *Warm congratulations!* **7.** QUICK TO ANGER excitable or easily angered **8.** SUGGESTING WARMTH having a colour suggesting warmth, especially yellow or red **9.** PHYSIOL HEATED BY METABOLISM giving off the heat that arises naturally in warm-blooded animals **10.** FIELD SPORTS FRESH describes a scent in hunting that is fresh and strong **11.** CLOSE close to the hidden object in a game or to guessing a secret (*informal*) ○ *You're getting warm.* **12.** UNCOMFORTABLE uncomfortable because of danger (*informal*) ■ *v* (**warms, warming, warmed**) **1.** *vti* MAKE SOMETHING OR BECOME WARM to increase the temperature of something to a desirable or comfortable level, or become warm **2.** *vt* MAKE SOMEBODY HAPPY to make somebody or something cheerful or happy ○ *were warmed by the presence of all their children* **3.** *vi* BECOME ENTHUSIASTIC to become enthusiastic about something ○ *warmed to the idea of buying a new car* **4.** *vi* BECOME FRIENDLY to become fond of somebody ○ *She warmed to him.* **5.** *vt regional* BEAT BODY PART to beat or cane a part of somebody's body ■ *n* (*informal*) **1.** WARM PLACE a warm environment **2.** ACT OF WARMING an act of making somebody or something warm or becoming warm ○ *Have a warm by the fire.* [Old English *wearm* < Indo-European] —**warmer** *n* —**warmish** *adj* —**warmness** *n*

warm down *vi* to gradually return to the body's usual level of activity after strenuous physical exertion (*informal*)

warm over *vt N Am* **1.** COOK same as **reheat** **2.** to suggest something again, without having greatly altered it

warm up *v* **1.** *vi* PREPARE FOR EXERCISE to prepare for physical exercise by stretching or practising **2.** *vi* PREPARE FOR SOMETHING to prepare for something that is going to happen **3.** *vti* GET WARM to become warm or warmer, or make something become warm or warmer **4.** *vti* GET TO OPERATING TEMPERATURE to run something such as an engine to bring it to a temperature at which it works efficiently, or reach this condition **5.** *vti* GET ANIMATED to become enthusiastic, animated, or eager, or make somebody enthusiastic, animated, or eager

war machine *n* the combined military resources with which a country can fight a war

warm-blooded *adj* **1.** maintaining a nearly constant body temperature, usually higher than and independent of the environment **2.** passionate, impetuous, and enthusiastic —**warm-bloodedness** *n*

warmboot /wáwrm boot/ (**-boots, -booting, -booted**) *vt* to restart a computer without switching it off, e.g. by pressing the control, Alt, and delete keys together

warm front *n* the gently sloping advancing edge of a warm air mass that displaces colder air, bringing a temperature increase and heavy rain where the front makes contact with the ground

warm fuzzies *npl* a warm feeling of contentment and wellbeing (*informal*)

warm-hearted *adj* having or showing a kind and sympathetic nature —**warm-heartedly** *adv* —**warm-heartedness** *n*

warming pan /wáwrming-/ *n* in former times, a long-handled metal pan that was filled with hot coals and placed in a bed to warm it

warmly /wáwrmli/ *adv* **1.** with enthusiasm, fondness, or passion **2.** in a way that will keep somebody warm ○ *dressed warmly*

warmonger /wáwr mung gər/ *n* somebody who is eager for war or tries to start a war —**warmongering** *n*

warm sector *n* a wedge of warm air within the low-pressure region between the cold front and warm front of a storm

warmth /wawrmth/ *n* **1.** WARM STATE the feeling, quality, or state of being warm **2.** AFFECTION affection and kindness **3.** AMOUNT OF HEAT a moderate amount of heat present in something **4.** EXCITEMENT strong emotion, especially anger or zeal **5.** EFFECT OF COLOUR the effect gained from using colours such as red and yellow

warm-up, **warmup** /wáwrm up/ *n* an exercise or a period spent exercising before a contest or event

warn /wawrn/ (**warns, warning, warned**) *v* **1.** *vti* TELL SOMEBODY OF RISK to tell somebody about something that might cause injury or harm **2.** *vt* TELL SOMEBODY IN ADVANCE to tell somebody about something in advance **3.** *vt* ADVISE SOMEBODY AGAINST SOMETHING to advise somebody against a potentially risky or damaging course of action ○ *The doctor warned him against travelling.* ○ *were warned against complacency* [Old English *war(e)nian* < Germanic, 'be cautious'] —**warner** *n*

SPELLCHECK warn or **worn**? Do not confuse the spelling of ***warn*** and ***worn***, which sound similar. ***Warn*** is a verb meaning 'tell somebody about something that may cause injury or harm': *I warned them not to set sail.* ***Worn*** is the past participle of the verb *wear* or an adjective derived from this, as in *clothes that are worn for comfort rather than fashion, worn down by rubbing, worn out after a hard day's work.*

warn off *vt* **1.** to tell somebody to leave or keep away from a place, usually in an authoritative or forceful manner ○ *Sightseers were warned off by security guards.* **2.** to advise somebody to avoid something, usually in an authoritative manner ○ *warned customers off buying cheap imitations*

Warne /wawrn/, **Shane** (*b.* 1969) Australian cricketer. Regarded as one of the best spin bowlers of all time, he has taken more than 500 Test wickets, but has been followed by controversy and in 2003–4 served a year-long suspension from cricket for drug abuse. Full name **Warne, Shane Keith**

warning /wáwrning/ *n* **1.** SIGN OF SOMETHING BAD COMING a threat or a sign that something bad is going to happen **2.** ADVICE TO BE CAREFUL a piece of advice given to somebody to be careful or to stop doing something ○ *If you're late again, you'll get a written warning.* ■ *adj* MEANT TO WARN intended to warn somebody —**warningly** *adv*

warning coloration *n* markings on an animal warning predators that it is poisonous or dangerous. Many insects and amphibians have warning coloration.

warning shot *n* a shot fired deliberately off target as a warning to somebody to stop doing something

war of nerves *n* a conflict in which psychological tactics are used against an opponent

War on Terror *n* the US response to the 11 September 2001 attacks by Islamic terrorists on the World Trade Center, the Pentagon, and other targets

warp /wawrp/ *v* (**warps, warping, warped**) **1.** *vti* GET TWISTED to become twisted or out of shape, or make something become twisted or out of shape ○ *warped wood* **2.** *vti* DEVIATE FROM COURSE to make something deviate from its usual or correct course, or deviate from a usual or correct course ○ *Funny how the thought of huge profits can warp your judgment.* **3.** *vti* NAUT MOVE SHIP BY PULLING ON ROPES to move a ship by pulling on ropes fastened to a dock or fixed buoy, or be moved in this way **4.** *vt* TEXTILES ARRANGE THREADS to arrange threads to form the warp in a loom ■ *n* **1.** DISTORTION a twist or distortion in something, e.g. in wood that curls when dried **2.** PERVERSION a deviation or perversion of mind or character **3.** TEXTILES THREADS RUNNING LENGTHWAYS the threads that run lengthways on a loom or in a piece of fabric **4.** NAUT ROPE FOR TOWING a rope used to warp a vessel [Old English *weorpan* < Germanic, 'to throw'] —**warpage** *n* —**warper** *n*

war paint *n* **1.** paint used to decorate the body before a battle, e.g. that used in former times by some Native North American peoples **2.** COSMETICS same as **makeup** (sense 1) (*informal*)

warpath /wáwr paath/ *n* in former times, a route taken by Native North Americans on the way to war ◇ **on the warpath** angry and in the mood for a confrontation (*informal*)

warplane /wáwr playn/ *n* an aircraft used in war

Warr ➧ **De la Warr, Thomas West**

warrant /wórrənt/ *n* **1.** AUTHORIZATION something that authorizes somebody to do something **2.** WRITTEN AUTHORIZATION a written authorization or certifying document **3.** DOCUMENT AUTHORIZING POLICE TO DO SOMETHING a document that gives police specific rights or powers such as the right to search or arrest somebody **4.** FIN OPTION TO BUY STOCK a document authorizing a stockholder to buy shares from a company at a later date and at a specific price **5.** MIL WARRANT OFFICER'S CERTIFICATE a warrant officer's certificate of appointment ■ *vt* (**-rants, -ranting, -ranted**) **1.** SERVE AS REASON FOR SOMETHING to serve as a justifiable reason to do, believe, or think something **2.** GUARANTEE SOMETHING to guarantee something such as the truth or dependability of somebody or something **3.** AUTHORIZE SOMEBODY to give authority to somebody **4.** LAW GUARANTEE TITLE to guarantee the title to property [12C. < Old N French *warant*, variant of Old French *guarant* < Germanic, 'be on guard'] —**warranter** *n*

warrantable /wórrəntəb'l/ *adj* able to be justified or permitted —**warrantability** /wórrəntə bílləti/ *n* —**warrantably** *adv*

warrant card *n* an official card carried by a police officer as proof of his or her identity and authorization

warrantee /wórrən tée/ *n* somebody to whom a warrant is given or a warranty is made

warrant officer *n* an officer in the armed services of a rank between a commissioned and a non-commissioned officer

warrantor /wórrən tawr/ *n* somebody who gives a warranty to somebody else

warrant sale *n Scotland* the enforced sale of a debtor's belongings in order to raise money to pay off the debts

warranty /wórrənti/ (*plural* **-ties**) *n* **1.** GUARANTEE a guarantee on purchased goods that they are of the quality represented and will be replaced or repaired if found to be faulty **2.** LAW INSURED PERSON'S UNDERTAKING a condition in an insurance contract in which the insured person guarantees that something is the case **3.** LAW GUARANTEE OF TITLE a covenant guaranteeing the security of the title to property being sold **4.** JUSTIFICATION a justification or authorization for an action

warren /wórrən/ *n* **1.** RABBIT HABITAT a group of connected burrows where rabbits live and breed **2.** RABBITS IN WARREN a group of rabbits living in a warren **3.** CROWDED BUILDING OR AREA an area or building that is crowded or has a complicated layout **4.** AREA FOR GAME ANIMALS a piece of ground where game animals are kept and bred [14C. < Anglo-Norman *warenne* 'enclosed area for breeding game']

Warren /wórrən/, **Earl** (1891–1974) chief justice of the US Supreme Court (1953–69). As Supreme Court chief justice he presided over a liberal court that desegregated public schools and articulated the rights of criminal suspects.

> 'We conclude that in the field of public education the doctrine of "separate but equal" has no place. Separate educational facilities are inherently unequal.'
> [Earl Warren, *Opinion in Brown v. Board of Education of Topeka, 347 US 483*; 1954]

> 'The freedom to marry has long been recognized as one of the vital personal rights essential to the orderly pursuit of happiness by free men.'
> [Earl Warren, *Unanimous opinion striking down a Virginia law prohibiting interracial marriages, Loving v. Virginia*; 12 June 1967]

warrener /wórrənər/ *n* a gamekeeper, or the keeper of a rabbit warren

~~**warrent**~~ incorrect spelling of **warrant**

Warrington /wórringtən/ town in Cheshire, northwestern England. Population: 181,080 (2001).

warrior /wórri ər/ *n* **1.** somebody who takes part in or is experienced in warfare **2.** somebody who takes part in a struggle or conflict [13C. < Old N French *werreior* < *werre* 'war' (see WAR)]

Warrnambool /wáwrnəm bool/ city in southwestern Victoria, Australia. It is a commercial and industrial centre. Population: 30,115 (2002 estimate).

Warrumbungle Range /wórrəm búng g'l-/ range of volcanic peaks in northern New South Wales, Australia

Warsaw /wáwr saw/ capital city of Poland, located in the centre of the country, on the River Vistula. Population: 1,618,468 (1999).

warship /wáwr ship/ *n* an armoured ship that is equipped with weapons and is used in war

wart /wawrt/ *n* **1.** a small benign rough lump that grows, usually, on the hands, feet, or genitals, caused by a virus **2.** a growth on a plant that looks like a wart [Old English *wearte* < Indo-European, 'raised spot'] —**warted** *adj* —**warty** *adj* ◇ **warts and all** including any flaws, faults, or disadvantages (*hyphenated when used before a noun*)

wart hog

wart hog *n* a wild pig that has tusks, a coarse mane, and warty growths on its face. Native to: Africa south of the Sahara. Latin name: *Phacochoerus aethiopicus.*

wartime /wáwr tīm/ *n* the period during which a war is being fought

war-torn *adj* disrupted by war, especially war between different groups from one country

Warwick /wórrik/ **1.** /wórrik/ town and administrative centre of Warwickshire, central England. Warwick Castle, a large medieval fortification, is located there. Population: 125,931 (2001). **2.** /wáwr wik/ town in southeastern Queensland, Australia. It is an agricultural centre. Population: 21,387 (2002 estimate).

Warwickshire /wórrikshər/ county in central England. It is largely agricultural with some light industry. Warwick is the administrative centre. Population: 505,860 (2001). Area: 1,981 sq. km/765 sq. mi.

war widow *n* a woman whose husband was killed in a war, especially while serving as a member of a country's armed forces

wary /wáiri/ (**-ier, -iest**) *adj* **1.** cautious and alert for problems ○ *wary of hidden rocks in the water* **2.** showing watchfulness or suspicion ○ *a wary approach* [15C. < WARE²] —**warily** *adv* —**wariness** *n*

SYNONYMS See *cautious.*

was *stressed* /woz/; *unstressed* /wəz/ past tense of **be**¹ (*used with I, he, she, it, and singular nouns*) [Old English *wæs*, form of *wesan* 'be' < Indo-European, 'stay, dwell']

wasabi /wə sáabi/ (*plural* **-bis** *or* same) *n* **1.** a strong-tasting green powder or paste from a plant root. Use: condiment in Japanese cooking. **2.** a plant whose root is ground to make wasabi powder or paste. Native to: Asia. Latin name: *Eutrema wasabi.* [Early 20C. < Japanese]

Wasatch Range /wáw sach-/ mountain range in the western United States, forming part of the Rocky Mountain system, in southeastern Idaho and central Utah. Its highest point is Mount Timpanogos (3,662 km/12,008 ft).

wash /wosh/ *v* (**washes, washing, washed**) **1.** *vt* CLEAN SOMETHING to clean something with water, usually with added soap or detergent ○ *He washed his hair.* **2.** *vti* CLEAN YOURSELF to clean yourself, especially your hands or face, with soap and water ○ *went upstairs to wash before supper* **3.** *vi* WASH CLOTHES to clean clothes in soap and water or in a washing machine ○ *spent the morning washing* **4.** *vi* BE WASHABLE to be capable of being washed without fading or being damaged (*refers to garments or fabrics*) ○ *curtains that wash well* **5.** *vti* LICK SOMETHING CLEAN to clean something by licking ○ *The cat washed her kittens.* **6.** *vti* REMOVE SOMETHING BY WASHING to remove something with water and usually with soap, or be removed in this way ○ *couldn't get the stain to wash out* **7.** *vt* MOISTEN SOMETHING to wet or moisten something (*literary*) ○ *lashes washed with tears* **8.** *vt* FLOW OVER SOMETHING to flow over the surface of something ○ *washed by the tides* **9.** *vt* ERODE SOMETHING WITH WATER to erode something by the action of water **10.** *vt* MOVE SOMETHING ON WATER to carry something along or away on water, or in a way that resembles the action of water ○ *A huge wave washed her over the side.* ○ *He was washed along by the huge crowd.* **11.** *vt* PURIFY SOMETHING to remove something corrupting ○ *the power to wash away sins* **12.** *vt* MIN EXTRACT SEPARATE SOMETHING BY WASHING to separate something such as

precious stones or valuable minerals by sifting earth or gravel through water **13.** *vt* APPLY THIN COATING TO SOMETHING to brush a thin coating or layer over something **14.** *vi* BE CONVINCING to be convincing or believable (*informal*) ○ *That story won't wash with her.* **15.** *vt* CHEM PUT GAS THROUGH LIQUID to pass a gas or vapour through a liquid to remove contaminants ■ *n* **1.** ACT OF WASHING the act or process of washing somebody or something **2.** QUANTITY OF CLOTHES a quantity of clothes that have been or are to be washed **3.** SKIN TREATMENT a lotion, antiseptic, or cosmetic that is applied to the skin **4.** MANUF THIN LIQUID COATING a thin or weak liquid, especially one used to rinse or coat something **5.** ART LAYER OF COLOUR a thin layer of colour applied with a brush **6.** ART PAINTING TECHNIQUE the technique of using washes in painting **7.** ART same as **wash drawing 8.** FLOW OF WATER the flow of water against a surface, or the sound made by this **9.** SURGE OF DISTURBED WATER OR AIR the surge of disturbed water, air, or other fluid caused by something such as an oar, propeller, or jet engine moving through the fluid **10.** AGRIC REMOVAL OF SOIL the removal of soil by the action of flowing water **11.** GEOL SEDIMENT alluvial material carried and left by the movement of water. When washed down the side of a mountain, the sediment forms fans and cone-shaped deposits. **12.** GEOG LAND PERIODICALLY COVERED BY WATER land that is periodically covered by a sea or river, e.g. by a tide **13.** MIN EXTRACT ORE material from which precious stones and valuable minerals can be extracted by washing, e.g. gravel **14.** AGRIC same as **swill** *n* (sense 1) **15.** BEVERAGES FERMENTED MALT the liquor from fermented malt before it is distilled **16.** *Southwest US* DRY STREAM BED the dry bed of a stream that flows only after heavy rains, often found at the bottom of a canyon [Old English *wæscan* < Germanic]

wash down *vt* **1.** to wash something thoroughly and completely ○ *had to wash down the kitchen walls afterwards* **2.** to follow something drunk or eaten with another drink ○ *washed down the cake with a glass of milk*

wash out *v* **1.** *vt* CLEAN INSIDE OF SOMETHING to clean something by washing the inside of it **2.** *vti* REMOVE SOMETHING BY WASHING to come out by washing, or get something out by washing **3.** *vt* CANCEL SOMETHING to cancel an event because of rain **4.** *vti* MOVE SOMETHING AWAY ON WATER to carry away something on water, or be carried away on water ○ *washed out to sea* **5.** *vti* WEAR SOMETHING AWAY to wear something away by water, or be worn away by water

wash over *vt* **1.** FLOW OVER SOMETHING to flow over and cover something **2.** FILL SOMEBODY WITH EMOTION to well up in and affect somebody emotionally ○ *A wave of homesickness washed over him.* **3.** FAIL TO AFFECT SOMEBODY DEEPLY to fail to make an impression on somebody

wash up *v* **1.** *vti* WASH DISHES to wash the dishes after a meal **2.** *vi* N Am WASH FACE AND HANDS to wash your face and hands **3.** *vti* ARRIVE BY WATER to deposit something on the shore as a result of tidal or wave action, or be deposited in this way ○ *Look what the tide washed up!*

Wash /wosh/ shallow inlet of the North Sea, on the eastern coast of England, between Lincolnshire and Norfolk. Area: 855 sq. km/330 sq. mi.

washable /wóshəb'l/ *adj* capable of being washed without being damaged —**washability** /wóshə bílləti/ *n*

wash-and-wear *adj* easily washed and dried and needing little or no ironing

washbasin /wósh bayss'n/ *n* a bowl or basin for washing the face and hands or small articles

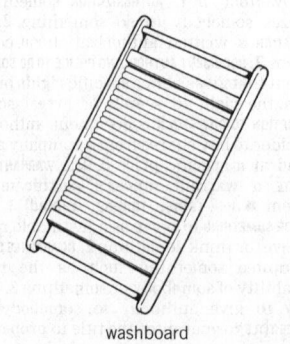

washboard

washboard /wósh bawrd/ *n* **1.** RIDGED BOARD a board with a corrugated surface on which clothes that are being washed can be rubbed to help get them clean **2.** MUSICAL INSTRUMENT a board resembling a washboard, used as a musical instrument to produce a scratching sound **3.** NAUT PROTECTIVE FEATURE ON BOAT a thin plank on the gunwale of a boat to stop water from splashing over the side ■ *adj* MUSCULAR describes a stomach that is flat with well-defined muscles

washbowl /wósh bowl/ *n* HOUSEHOLD same as **washbasin**

washcloth /wósh kloth/ *n* US HOUSEHOLD same as **facecloth**

washday /wósh day/ *n* a day when clothes are washed, especially the same day each week

wash drawing *n* a drawing made in ink to which a wash of colour is applied, or a painting made using washes

washed-out *adj* (*not hyphenated after a verb*) **1.** faded or lacking colour **2.** exhausted or lacking vitality and strength

washed-up *adj* no longer likely to continue or succeed (*informal; not hyphenated after a verb*)

washer /wóshər/ *n* **1.** SMALL RING a small disc or ring used to keep a screw or bolt secure or prevent leakage at a joint **2.** WASHING APPLIANCE an appliance used for washing, especially a washing machine **3.** SOMEBODY WASHING SOMETHING somebody who washes something **4.** Aus HOUSEHOLD CLOTH FOR WASHING a small cloth used in washing the face and hands (*informal*) Same as **facecloth**

washer-dryer *n* a machine that both washes and dries clothes

washer-up (*plural* **washers-up**) *n* somebody who is employed to wash dishes (*informal*)

washerwoman /wóshər wŏomən/ (*plural* **-women** /-wimin/), **washwoman** /wósh wŏomən/ *n* a woman employed to wash clothes

washery /wóshəri/ (*plural* **-ies**) *n* a place where something such as coal or wool is washed

wash house *n* a building where laundry or other washing is done

washing /wóshing/ *n* **1.** CLOTHES FOR WASHING clothes that are to be washed, are being washed, or have just been washed **2.** DOING OF LAUNDRY the act or process of washing clothes **3.** MANUF THIN COAT a thin coat of something ○ *a washing of silver* **4.** LIQUID USED FOR WASHING the liquid that has been used to wash something (*often used in the plural*)

washing machine *n* a machine for washing clothes, usually an electric one

washing powder *n* detergent in powder form, used for washing clothes. N Am term **laundry detergent**

washing soda *n* a crystalline form of sodium carbonate. Use: washing and cleaning.

Washington /wóshingtən/ **1.** state in the northwestern United States, bordered by British Columbia, Idaho, Oregon, and the Pacific Ocean. Capital: Olympia. Population: 6,068,996 (2002 estimate). Area: 182,949 sq. km/70,637 sq. mi. **2.** town in northeastern England. It is the location of Washington Old Hall, the ancestral home of George Washington. Population: 61,500 (1996). —**Washingtonian** /wóshing tōni ən/ *n, adj*

Washington, DC capital city of the United States. The city of Washington has the same boundaries as the District of Columbia, a federal territory established in 1790 as the site of the new nation's permanent capital. Located at the confluence of the Potomac and Anacostia rivers, it is bordered by Maryland and Virginia. Population: 570,898 (2002 estimate).

Washington, Booker T. (1856–1915) US educator. As the first principal of Alabama's Tuskegee Institute (1881–1915), he urged African Americans to attempt to gain advancement through educational attainments. Full name **Washington, Booker Taliaferro**

> 'When freedom came, the slaves were almost as well fitted to begin life anew as the master, except in the matter of book learning and ownership of property. The slave owner and his sons had mastered no special industry.'

[Booker T. Washington, *Up from Slavery*; 1901]

Washington, Denzel (*b.* 1954) US actor. His films include *Malcolm X* (1992) and *Training Day* (2001), for which he won the Academy Award for best actor.

George Washington

Library of Congress

Washington, George (1732–99) 1st president of the United States (1789–97). Commander in chief of the American forces during the American War of Independence (1775–83) and president of the second Constitutional Convention, he was the first president of the newly independent United States. See table at **president**

> 'Discipline is the soul of an army. It makes small numbers formidable; procures success to the weak, and esteem to all.'
> [George Washington, *Letter of Instructions to the Captains of the Virginia Regiments*; 29 July 1759]

> 'The preservation of the sacred fire of liberty, and the destiny of the republican model of government, are justly considered as deeply, perhaps as finally staked, on the experiment entrusted to the hands of the American people.'
> [George Washington, *First inaugural address*; 30 April 1789]

washing-up *n* **1.** the cleaning of dishes, cutlery, and other items used for cooking and eating **2.** the items that need to be washed after a meal

washing-up liquid *n* detergent in liquid form, used for washing dishes. N Am term **dishwashing liquid**

wash-off *adj* removable by washing or by the use of water with soap or a detergent

washout /wósh owt/ *n* **1.** FAILURE a complete failure or fiasco (*informal*) **2.** INEFFECTUAL PERSON somebody regarded as lacking in competence or effectiveness (*informal insult*) **3.** GEOL EROSION CAUSED BY RUNNING WATER erosion caused by running water, e.g. during a flash flood **4.** GEOL CHANNEL WASHED OUT a hole or channel made by floodwater

washroom /wósh room, -room/ *n* a room, especially in a public place, with a toilet and washing facilities

wash sale *n* US **1.** the illegal practice of buying and selling a stock almost simultaneously in order to give the impression that the stock is being actively traded **2.** the repurchase of stock sold within 30 days of the time it was sold. Capital losses on such a sale are not tax deductible

washstand /wósh stand/ *n* a stand on which a basin

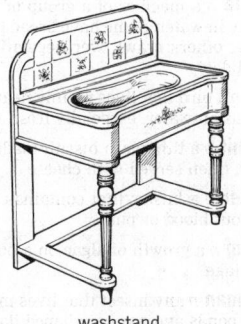

washstand

and jug can be placed for washing the face and hands

washtub /wósh tub/ *n* a large container in which clothes can be washed

wash-up *n* **1.** Aus FINAL PHASE the final phase or summing up of a process (*informal*) ○ *In the wash-up on TV after the election, the senator admitted that government policy was out of step with the public.* **2.** Aus OUTCOME the outcome of a process or series of events **3.** Wales SINK a kitchen sink (*informal*)

washwoman *n* OCCUPATIONS same as **washerwoman**

washy /wóshi/ (**-ier, -iest**) *adj* **1.** WEAK watery or weak **2.** PALE faint or faded **3.** NOT FORCEFUL lacking intensity or vitality —**washily** *adv* —**washiness** *n*

wasn't /wózz'nt/ *contr* was not

wasp

wasp /wosp/ *n* a slender black-and-yellow-striped social stinging insect that typically has well-developed wings, biting mouthparts, and a narrow stalk connecting the abdomen and thorax. Families: Vespidae or Sphecidae. [Old English *wæsp* < Indo-European, 'to weave']

Wasp /wosp/, **WASP** *n* N Am an offensive term for a white person who has a Protestant Anglo-Saxon background and is viewed as belonging to the dominant and most powerful level of US society (*informal insult*) [Mid-20C. Acronym < White Anglo-Saxon Protestant]

waspish /wóspish/, **waspy** /wóspi/ (**-ier, -iest**) *adj* **1.** OF WASPS like a wasp, or relating to wasps **2.** EASILY IRRITATED easily irritated or annoyed **3.** SPITEFUL showing spite or bad temper —**waspishly** *adv* —**waspishness** *n*

wasp waist *n* a very slender waist, or one that is corseted to make it appear slender —**wasp-waisted** *adj*

waspy *adj* same as **waspish**

wassail /wóssayl/ (*archaic*) *n* **1.** FESTIVE SALUTATION a salutation or drinking toast made during festivities **2.** FESTIVE OCCASION a festive occasion at which people drink a great deal **3.** ALCOHOLIC DRINK an alcoholic drink, usually mulled wine or ale, drunk on a festive occasion **4.** DRINKING OR CHRISTMAS SONG a drinking song or a song sung at Christmas ■ *v* (**-sails, -sailing, -sailed**) **1.** *vi* DRINK IN CELEBRATION to celebrate by drinking alcohol **2.** *vi regional* SING CHRISTMAS SONGS to go from house to house at Christmas, singing carols and greeting people **3.** *vt* TOAST SOMEBODY to drink to somebody's health [12C. < Old Norse *ves heill* 'be healthy', *heill* < Germanic] —**wassailer** *n*

Wassermann test /wássərmən-, vássər-/, **Wassermann reaction** *n* a test for syphilis infection, based on determining the presence in a blood sample of antibodies to the syphilis bacterium [After August Paul Wassermann (1866–1925), German bacteriologist]

wast /wost, wəst/ 2nd person singular past of **be**[1] (*archaic*)

wastage /wáystij/ *n* **1.** AMOUNT WASTED an amount that is lost or wasted **2.** LOSS loss caused when something is used, is worn, decays, or leaks **3.** REDUCTION IN NUMBERS the reduction in numbers of people working in a place because of deaths and resignations, rather than from redundancies

waste /wayst/ *n* **1.** ACT OF WASTING a failure to use something wisely, properly, fully, or to good effect ○ *a complete waste of money* **2.** UNWANTED MATERIAL unwanted or unusable items, remains, or by-products, or household rubbish ○ *chemical waste* **3.** EXCREMENT the undigested remainder of food expelled from the body as excrement **4.** USED OR CONTAMINATED WATER used

or contaminated water from domestic, industrial, or mining applications **5.** ROCK ASSOCIATED WITH MINERAL enclosing rock mined with a mineral, or ore with insufficient mineral content to justify further processing **6.** WILD AREA an uncultivated, desolate, or wild area (*often used in the plural*) ○ *the frozen wastes of Antarctica* **7.** DESTROYED AREA a place or region that has been destroyed or ruined **8.** LAW PROPERTY DEPRECIATION loss of value in a property or estate caused by damage done by the tenant ■ *v* (**wastes, wasting, wasted**) **1.** *vt* USE SOMETHING CARELESSLY to use something or use something up carelessly, extravagantly, or ineffectively ○ *She wasted the whole morning daydreaming.* ○ *Don't waste your arguments on her; she's already made up her mind!* **2.** *vt* FAIL TO USE SOMETHING to fail to make use of something such as an opportunity **3.** *vt* NOT EXPLOIT POTENTIAL OF SOMEBODY to fail to make full use of the abilities or talents possessed by somebody (*usually passive*) ○ *You're wasted as a nurse, you should have been a doctor.* **4.** *vti* GET WEAKER OR MORE ILL to become gradually weaker or thinner, e.g. as a result of disease, or make somebody become gradually weaker or thinner ○ *children wasting away from malnutrition* ○ *a body wasted by illness* **5.** *vt* DESTROY SOMETHING to ravage or devastate something **6.** *vt* KILL SOMEBODY to kill or murder somebody (*slang*) ■ *adj* **1.** NOT NEEDED useless or not needed **2.** UNPRODUCTIVE unproductive, uninhabited, or uncultivated ○ *waste ground* **3.** EXCRETED expelled from the body as indigestible ○ *waste matter* **4.** FOR WASTE used to carry off or store waste [12C. Via Old N French < Latin *vastus* 'empty'] —**wastable** *adj* ◇ **be wasted on somebody** to be directed at somebody who is unable or unwilling to understand or heed it ○ *I'm afraid all her good advice was wasted on me.* ◇ **go to waste** to be unused or underutilized and therefore discarded or lost ○ *This pie will just go to waste if we don't eat it.* ○ *Don't let your talent go to waste.* ◇ **lay something (to) waste** to destroy or devastate something

SPELLCHECK See *waist*.

wastebasket /wáyst baaskit/ *n* N Am HOUSEHOLD, COMM same as **wastepaper basket**

wasted /wáystid/ *adj* **1.** USED TO NO PURPOSE used without achieving any purpose or in an extravagant or careless manner ○ *wasted efforts* **2.** NOT USED not used or exploited when available ○ *a wasted opportunity* **3.** VERY THIN emaciated or shrunken as a result of disease **4.** EXHAUSTED exhausted from exertion (*slang*) **5.** INTOXICATED under the influence of drink or drugs (*slang*)

waste disposal, **waste disposal unit** *n* UK an electrical device, fitted in a kitchen sink, that grinds up food so that it can go into the waste pipe. ANZ, N Am term **garbage disposal**

wasteful /wáystf'l/ *adj* **1.** using resources unwisely **2.** causing waste or devastation —**wastefully** *adv* —**wastefulness** *n*

waste heat recovery *n* the reclaiming of otherwise wasted heat from furnaces, kilns, engines, or similar sources, for use in another process, e.g. preheating air or water

wasteland /wáyst land, -lənd/ *n* **1.** an area of land that is desolate or barren and not used **2.** an environment that is thought to be spiritually or intellectually barren ○ *the wasteland of daytime TV*

CULTURAL NOTE *The Waste Land*, a poem by US-born British poet T. S. Eliot (1922). One of the 20th century's major poetic works, it portrays the disintegration of Western values, the soullessness of modern society, and humankind's desperate search for salvation. It consists of five seemingly disconnected sections made up of fragmented verses written in a variety of styles but linked by imagery, symbols, and diverse literary and historical references.

wastelot /wáyst lot/ *n* Can an area of wasteland in a city

waste management *n* activities that deal with waste before and after it is produced, including its minimization, transfer, storage, separation, recovery, recycling, and final disposal

wastepaper /wáyst páypər/ *n* paper that is not needed and has been thrown away

wastepaper basket, **wastepaper bin** *n* a small container for rubbish, especially paper. N Am term **wastebasket**

waste pipe *n* a pipe that carries excess or used fluids from a container such as a sink or bathtub

waste product *n* a useless or unwanted by-product of a process

waster /wáystər/ *n* **1.** WASTEFUL PERSON OR THING somebody or something that wastes something, especially somebody who is careless with money or resources **2.** RUINED OBJECT an object that has been spoiled during manufacture, especially a ceramic piece **3.** LAZY PERSON somebody regarded as lazy or worthless (*informal insult*)

wastewater /wáyst wawtər/ *n* water that has been used ○ *a wastewater treatment plant*

wasteweir /wáyst weer/ *n* GEOG same as **spillway**

wasting /wáysting/ *adj* gradually taking away strength and energy and emaciating the body ○ *a wasting disease* —**wastingly** *adv*

wasting asset *n* an asset, especially a natural resource such as a mine, that cannot be renewed and that loses its value over time

wastrel /wáystrəl/ *n* somebody regarded as wasteful, spendthrift, or lazy (*insult*) [Late 16C. < WASTE + *-rel*, ending indicating 'little' or a derogatory sense]

Wastwater /wóst wawtər/ lake in the Lake District, northwestern England. With a maximum depth of 79 m/258 ft, it is the deepest lake in England. Area: 4 sq. km/2 sq. mi.

wat /wot/ *n* a Buddhist monastery or temple in Thailand, Cambodia, or Laos [Mid-19C. Via Thai < Sanskrit *vāta* 'enclosure']

watch /woch/ *v* (**watches, watching, watched**) **1.** *vti* OBSERVE to look at and keep your attention on something or somebody over a period of time ○ *Are you coming to watch the game?* ○ *I watched him as he walked off down the street.* ○ *Would you mind doing that again? I wasn't watching.* **2.** *vi* KEEP LOOKOUT to keep a lookout for something that might appear or happen ○ *Your job is to watch for anyone coming.* **3.** *vti* MONITOR SOMETHING OR SOMEBODY to keep something or somebody under observation as a protective measure, to gather information, or to exert control ○ *Can you watch the baby while I go upstairs?* **4.** *vt* EXERCISE CARE ABOUT SOMETHING to be careful about something (*often used as a command*) ○ *Watch your language!* ○ *Watch where you're going!* **5.** *vi* KEEP VIGIL to stay awake and keep a vigil ■ *n* **1.** PERSONAL CLOCK a small clock worn on the wrist or carried in a pocket **2.** TIME SPENT OBSERVING a period of time spent observing something closely **3.** PEOPLE WATCHING a person or group that guards or observes something, especially at night ○ *posted a watch around the house, day and night* **4.** GUARD'S DUTY the period during which a guard is on duty **5.** DUTY ON SHIP a fixed period of a day spent on duty on board a ship **6.** PERSON'S PERIOD IN CHARGE a period when a particular person is in charge of something (*informal*) ○ *didn't want anything going wrong on his watch* **7.** CREW ON DUTY the members of a ship's crew who are on duty at a particular time **8.** DIVISION OF NIGHT one of the periods of time into which the night was formerly divided [Assumed Old English *wæccan* 'keep watch, be awake' < Germanic] —**watcher** *n* ◇ **be on the watch for somebody** or **something** to look out for somebody or something ◇ **watch it** to be careful (*informal*)

watch out *vi* **1.** to be careful, alert, or wary **2.** to look and wait for somebody or something

watch over *vt* to look after, supervise, or guard somebody or something

watchable /wóchəb'l/ *adj* **1.** capable of being observed **2.** interesting and enjoyable to watch ○ *a very watchable detective series* —**watchability** /wóchə bílləti/ *n*

watchband /wóch band/ *n* N Am same as **watchstrap**

watch cap *n* a dark-blue close-fitting knitted woollen cap worn in cold weather, especially by sailors

watchcase /wóch kayss/ *n* the protective casing for a watch mechanism

watchdog /wóch dog/ *n* **1.** same as **guard dog 2.** a person or organization guarding against illegal practices, unacceptable standards, or inefficiency ○ *a government watchdog* ■ *vti* (**-dogs, -dogging, -dogged**) to act as a watchdog on something

watch fire *n* a fire kept burning at night either as a signal or for the comfort of somebody keeping watch

watchful /wóchf'l/ *adj* **1.** carefully observant or alert ○ *watchful for signs of recovery* **2.** not asleep (*archaic*) —**watchfully** *adv* —**watchfulness** *n*

watch glass *n* **1.** a piece of glass or plastic fitted to a watch to cover and protect its face. N Am term **crystal 2.** a shallow round glass dish used to evaporate liquids or to cover something

watchmaker /wóch maykər/ *n* a maker or repairer of watches

watchman /wóchmən/ (*plural* **-men** /-mən/) *n* somebody, especially a man, employed to patrol or guard buildings or an area

watch night *n* **1.** the last night of the year, marked in some churches by a service that spans the midnight transition from the old year to the new one. Date: night of 31 December. **2.** the night before Christmas Day, marked in some churches by a service that spans midnight. Date: night of 24 December.

watchperson /wóch purss'n/ *n* somebody employed to patrol or guard buildings or an area

watch pocket *n* a small pocket for a watch in a waistcoat or trousers

watchstrap /wóch strap/ *n* a strap for a wristwatch. N Am term **watchband**

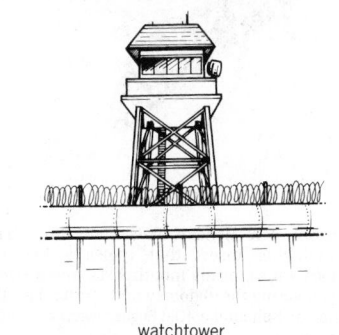

watchtower

watchtower /wóch tow ər/ *n* a high tower in which sentries keep watch for the approach of an enemy

watchwoman /wóch woomən/ (*plural* **-women** /-wimin/) *n* a woman employed to patrol or guard buildings or an area

watchword /wóch wurd/ *n* **1.** a word or slogan that encapsulates a mode of action, a set of beliefs, or membership of a group **2.** a word or phrase that somebody has to say to prove a right to be in a place with restricted access

water /wáwtər/ *n* **1.** LIQUID OF RAIN AND RIVERS the clear colourless liquid, odourless and tasteless when pure, that occurs as rain, snow, and ice, forms rivers, lakes, and seas, and is essential for life. Naturally occurring water picks up colour and taste from substances in its environment. Formula: H_2O. **2.** AREA OF WATER an area or body of water, e.g. a river, stream, lake, or sea ○ *We went down to the water to feed the ducks.* **3.** SURFACE OF WATER the surface of a body of water ○ *swim under water* **4.** ELEMENT in ancient and medieval philosophy, water as one of the four elements **5.** TRANSPORT OVER WATER transport by ship, boat, or some other means of travel over or through water ○ *can only get there by water* **6.** WATER SUPPLY a supply of water to a house, town, or region ○ *Our water's been turned off.* **7.** WATERING the action of giving water to a plant **8.** SOLUTION OF SUBSTANCE IN WATER a solution of a particular chemical or substance in water ○ *lavender water* **9.** BODY FLUID any watery fluid present in or secreted by the body, e.g. urine, sweat, saliva, or tears **10.** WAVY PATTERN a lustrous wavy pattern on the surface of some fabrics such as silk **11.** BRIGHTNESS the quality of brightness of a gem ■ **waters** *npl* **1.** FLUID SURROUNDING FOETUS the amniotic fluid that surrounds the foetus in the womb ○ *Her waters have broken.* **2.** PARTICULAR AREA OF SEA a particular region of sea, e.g. that belonging to a specific nation ○ *territorial waters* **3.** WATER CONTAINING MINERALS naturally occurring water containing minerals, e.g. that found at a spa and used for health reasons ○ *take the waters* ■ *v* (**-ters, -tering, -tered**) **1.** *vt* SPRINKLE OR SOAK SOMETHING WITH WATER to sprinkle, wet, or soak something with water **2.** *vt* IRRIGATE LAND to take water to crops or fields **3.** *vti* GIVE OR GET WATER to give drinking water to an animal, or get or take water as an animal does **4.** *vi* FILL WITH TEARS WHEN IRRITATED to fill with tears, especially because of irritation (*refers to eyes*) **5.** *vi* PRODUCE SALIVA to produce saliva, particularly in pleasant anticipation of food

(*refers to the mouth*) **6.** *vi* NAUT TAKE ON WATER SUPPLY to take on a supply of water **7.** *vt* TEXTILES GIVE FABRIC WAVY SHEEN to give a lustrous wavy pattern to fabric, especially silk [Old English *wæter* < Indo-European, 'water'] —**waterer** *n* ◇ **be dead in the water** to have no chance of success or survival ◇ **be water under the bridge** to be something that is in the past and that cannot be altered ◇ **clear (blue) water** a clearly perceptible difference or distance between two things, e.g. between two political parties and their policies ◇ **hold water** to be well-founded, or stand up under scrutiny ◇ **in deep water** in a difficult or complicated situation ◇ **in hot water** in trouble because of having done something wrong ◇ **muddy the waters** to cause confusion or trouble ◇ **pour** *or* **throw cold water on** *or* **onto** *or* **over something** to discourage a plan or idea by showing a lack of interest in it or rejecting it as impractical ◇ **throw water** W Africa to offer somebody a bribe ◇ **tread water 1.** to keep afloat without moving forwards, by moving the legs and arms **2.** to make no progress but manage to keep a situation the same for a period of time ◇ **water off a duck's back** words or actions that have absolutely no effect on the attitude or behaviour of the person to whom they are said or done

---

CULTURAL NOTE *Water Music*, an orchestral suite (1717) by German-born British composer George Frederick Handel. It consists of three separate suites for strings and wind instruments. The exact circumstances of its composition are not known, but it was first performed to accompany a royal barge trip along the Thames from Whitehall to Chelsea on 17 July 1717.

---

water down *vt* **1.** to weaken or dilute something by adding water to it **2.** to moderate or attenuate something in order to make it less difficult, offensive, or controversial ○ *The producers want to water down her original script.* —**watered-down** *adj*

waterage /wáwtərij/ *n* **1.** the carrying of passengers or cargo by water **2.** money paid for the carrying of passengers or cargo by water

water arum *n* a water plant cultivated for its glossy heart-shaped leaves and large white funnel-shaped cone surrounding the flower spike. Native to: northern temperate regions. Latin name: *Calla palustris*.

water bag *n* **1.** a bag made of leather, canvas, or similar material used for carrying water **2.** ANAT, MED same as **amnion** (sense 2)

water ballet *n* the performance of dance movements in water

water bear *n* ZOOL same as **tardigrade**

Water Bearer *n* ZODIAC same as **Aquarius** (sense 2)

water bed *n* a bed with a special mattress filled with water

water beetle

water beetle *n* a member of a group of beetles that live mainly in water. Some have broad hind legs for swimming; others crawl over vegetation. Family: Hydrophilidae.

water bird *n* a bird that lives mainly near and wades in or swims on water, especially fresh water

water biscuit *n* a thin plain biscuit made from flour and water, often served with cheese

water blister *n* a blister that contains clear watery fluid without blood or pus

water bloom *n* a growth of algae on a body of water such as a lake

water boatman *n* any insect that lives mainly at the bottom of ponds and has oar-shaped flattened hind

legs used for swimming. Most water boatmen are good fliers. Family: Corixidae.

waterborne /wáwtər bawrn/ *adj* **1.** travelling on or transported by water ○ *a waterborne vessel* **2.** transmitted or transported by water, as some infectious agents are

water brash *n* the sudden filling of the mouth with acidic juices from the stomach, usually accompanied by heartburn and often resulting from indigestion. It is common in pregnancy but may also be an indication of a disorder of the digestive tract.

waterbuck /wáwtər buk/ (*plural* **-bucks** or *same*) *n* a large antelope with a shaggy dark-grey or reddish coat, found in grassland and woodland near open water. Native to: southern Africa. Latin name: *Kobus ellipsiprymnus.*

water buffalo *n* **1.** LARGE ASIAN BUFFALO a large buffalo with a grey-black coat and long backward-curving horns that is domesticated in many countries. Kept for: haulage, milk. Native to: Southeast Asia. Latin name: *Bubalus bubalis.* **2.** *US* MIL AMPHIBIOUS TANK an amphibious tank, especially one used in World War II **3.** *US* MIL DRINKING WATER CONTAINER a water storage container hauled by truck into an operational area without potable water

water bug *n* an insect that lives in water, e.g. the water boatman or pond skater

waterbus /wáwtər buss/ *n* a boat carrying passengers in a regular service across or along a river or lake

water butt *n* a large barrel for collecting rainwater, usually from a drainpipe

water caltrop *n* PLANTS same as **water chestnut** (sense 3)

water cannon *n* an apparatus, usually mounted on a lorry, that produces a jet of high-pressure water and is used to disperse crowds

Water Carrier *n* ZODIAC same as **Aquarius** (sense 2)

water chestnut *n* **1.** CRUNCHY NUT-SHAPED CORM a round white crunchy stem base (**corm**) of a Chinese water plant, often used in Asian cooking. Water chestnuts are sometimes used in food manufacture to add crunchiness to processed foods. **2.** CHINESE PLANT WITH EDIBLE STEM a Chinese water plant that produces water chestnuts. Latin name: *Eleocharis tuberosa.* **3.** WATER PLANT an annual water plant that forms rosettes of diamond-shaped floating leaves, has feathery underwater leaves, and bears hard spiny dark-grey fruit containing edible seeds. Native to: Europe, Asia. Latin name: *Trapa natans.*

water chinquapin *n* a water plant with shield-shaped leaves and edible seeds. Flowers: fragrant, cup-shaped, pale yellow. Native to: North America. Latin name: *Nelumbo lutea.*

water clock *n* TIME same as **clepsydra**

water closet *n* **1.** a small room fitted with a toilet and, often, a washbasin **2.** a flush toilet (*archaic*)

watercolour /wáwtər kulər/ *n* **1.** PAINTING a painting created with pigments mixed with water rather than oil **2.** PIGMENT MIXED WITH WATER an individual painting pigment mixed with water for use rather than oil, or such pigments collectively (*often used in the plural*) **3.** METHOD OF PAINTING the art or technique of painting with pigments mixed with water rather than oil —**watercolourist** *n*

water-cool *vt* to cool an engine or machine by means of water, typically by circulating water in a water jacket or by pipes —**water-cooled** *adj*

water cooler *n* a device that dispenses cooled drinking water and often serves as a focal point in a workplace where colleagues meet and gossip ■ *adj N Am* popular enough to be the subject of everyday conversation, especially between colleagues around the water cooler in the workplace (*informal*) ○ *water cooler TV*

watercourse /wáwtər kawrss/ *n* **1.** a natural or artificial channel through which water flows **2.** the water of a river or stream that flows along a watercourse

watercraft /wáwtər kraaft/ (*plural same*) *n* **1.** skill in swimming, handling boats, or other water-related activities **2.** a vessel used for travelling on water (*formal*)

watercress

watercress /wáwtər kress/ *n* a perennial water plant, widely cultivated for its peppery-flavoured leaves and stems, used in salads. Native to: Europe, Asia. Latin name: *Nasturtium officinale.*

water cure *n* a session of treatment by hydrotherapy or hydropathy

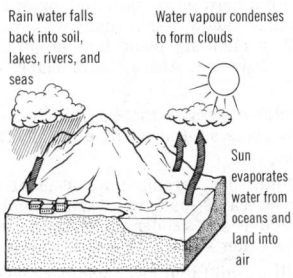

Rain water falls back into soil, lakes, rivers, and seas

Water vapour condenses to form clouds

Sun evaporates water from oceans and land into air

water cycle

water cycle *n* the constant circulation of water between atmosphere, land, and sea by evaporation, precipitation, and percolation through soils and rocks

water diviner *n* somebody who dowses for water, especially underground water, usually by using divining rods. US term **dowser**

water dog *n* **1.** a dog that likes water, especially one trained to hunt or retrieve game in water **2.** somebody who likes being in, on, or near water, e.g. a keen sailor or swimmer (*informal*)

water dropwort *n* **1.** a perennial plant of the carrot family that grows alongside watercourses and has a hollow grooved stem and compound leaves. Flowers: small, white, in flat-topped clusters. Latin name: *Oenanthe fistulosa.* **2.** any plant related to water dropwort

waterfall /wáwtər fawl/ *n* a vertical stream of water that occurs where a river or stream falls over the edge of a steep place

water feature *n* a small fountain or pond, used for aesthetic effect in landscape gardening

water fern *n* PLANTS same as **mosquito fern**

water filter *n* an appliance or fitting for removing unwanted matter from water, especially bacteria or harmful chemicals from drinking water

water flea *n* a tiny crustacean that swims with rapid jerky movements, using its large forked antennae. Suborder: Cladocera.

Waterford /wáwtərfərd/ **1.** county in Munster Province, in the southern part of the Republic of Ireland. Population: 94,680 (2002). Area: 1,838 sq. km/710 sq. mi. **2.** city and administrative centre of County Waterford, Republic of Ireland. Population: 44,000 (1996).

waterfowl /wáwtər fowl/ *n* (*plural same* or **-fowls**) a bird that lives on freshwater lakes and streams ■ *npl* swimming game birds such as ducks, considered as a group

waterfront /wáwtər frunt/ *n* **1.** the part of a town that lies alongside a body of water **2.** land beside an area of water

water gap *n* a deep valley through a mountain ridge, in which water flows

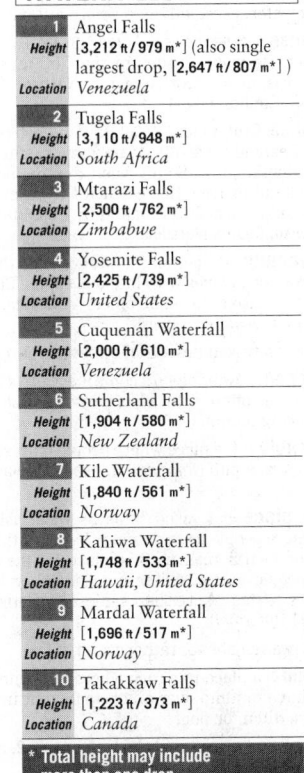

WORLD'S HIGHEST WATERFALLS

	Name	Height	Location
1	Angel Falls	[3,212 ft / 979 m*] (also single largest drop, [2,647 ft / 807 m*])	Venezuela
2	Tugela Falls	[3,110 ft / 948 m*]	South Africa
3	Mtarazi Falls	[2,500 ft / 762 m*]	Zimbabwe
4	Yosemite Falls	[2,425 ft / 739 m*]	United States
5	Cuquenán Waterfall	[2,000 ft / 610 m*]	Venezuela
6	Sutherland Falls	[1,904 ft / 580 m*]	New Zealand
7	Kile Waterfall	[1,840 ft / 561 m*]	Norway
8	Kahiwa Waterfall	[1,748 ft / 533 m*]	Hawaii, United States
9	Mardal Waterfall	[1,696 ft / 517 m*]	Norway
10	Takakkaw Falls	[1,223 ft / 373 m*]	Canada

*** Total height may include more than one drop**

water gas *n* a toxic mixture of carbon monoxide and methane generated by passing air and steam over hot glowing coals. Use: fuel for heating, lighting, and power.

water gate *n* **1.** CIV ENG same as **floodgate 2.** a gate that gives access to an area of water

Watergate /wáwtər gayt/ *n* **1.** a political scandal stemming from a break-in by Republican operatives at the 1972 US Democratic National Committee headquarters, which were in the Watergate complex in Washington, DC. The scandal led to the resignation of President Nixon and the conviction and imprisonment of a number of his closest aides. **2.** a public scandal involving politicians or officials abusing power, especially if a cover-up is also attempted

water gauge *n* a device that indicates the quantity or level of water in a tank, boiler feed, reservoir, or stream

water glass *n* **1.** DRINKING GLASS a drinking glass, especially for water **2.** THICK CHEMICAL SOLUTION an extremely viscous solution of sodium silicate. Use: cement, waterproofing and fireproofing agent, egg preservative. **3.** GLASS GAUGE a water gauge consisting of a glass tube **4.** DEVICE FOR EXAMINING UNDERWATER OBJECTS an instrument used for looking at objects under the water's surface, e.g. an open box or tube with a glass bottom

water gum *n* **1.** a tree with dark glossy leaves and a dense crown that grows near water in rain forests. Latin name: *Tristaniopsis laurina.* Native to: Australia. **2.** a deciduous tree that is a species of tupelo. Native to: southeastern United States. Latin name: *Nyssa aquatica.*

water gun *n US* same as **water pistol**

water hammer *n* a hammering or stuttering sound in a pipeline that sometimes accompanies a sudden and significant change in the flow rate of the fluid through the pipeline

water hemlock *n* any of various poisonous highly scented plants found in marshy areas. Flowers: small, white, in dense flat-topped clusters. Native to: northern hemisphere. Genus: *Cicuta.*

zh vision. In foreign words: kh German Ba*ch*; aN French v*in*; aaN French bl*anc*; ö German sch*ö*n, French f*eu*; oN French b*on*; õN French *un*; ü as in French r*ue*. Stress marks: ˈ as in secret /seékrət/, academic /ákə démmik/

water hen *n* a bird that lives near water, e.g. a rail or a coot. Family: Rallidae.

water hole *n* a natural hollow in the ground containing water, especially one where animals drink

Waterhouse /wáwter howss/, **Alfred** (1830–1905) British architect. He was a leader in the Gothic Revival. Among his major works is the Natural History Museum, London (1881).

Waterhouse, George (1824–1906) British-born premier of New Zealand (1872–73). After a successful career as a businessman in South Australia, he moved to New Zealand in 1869. He resigned the premiership in 1873 and returned to England in 1888. Full name **Waterhouse, George Marsden**

water hyacinth *n* a perennial water plant that has glossy rounded leaves with bulbous stalks. Flowers: lilac-blue. Native to: subtropical America. Latin name: *Eichhornia crassipes*.

water ice *n* a frozen dessert of sweet flavoured ice

watering can /wáwtering-/ *n* a container with a handle and a spout, often with a perforated nozzle, used for watering plants

watering hole *n* 1. a place where people meet socially to drink, e.g. a pub (*informal*) 2. GEOG same as **water hole**

watering place *n* 1. GEOG same as **water hole** 2. a place where people go to drink or bathe in the local water for health reasons 3. a place by the sea to which people go for swimming and other leisure activities (*dated*) 4. LEISURE same as **watering hole** (sense 1) (*informal*)

waterish /wáwterish/ *adj* rather watery

water jump *n* a place in a race where the runners or horses have to jump over an obstacle that includes a stream, ditch, or pool

waterless /wáwterless/ *adj* 1. lacking water 2. able to be made or used without water

water level *n* 1. the level of the surface of a body of water 2. NAUT same as **water line** (sense 1) 3. GEOL same as **water table** (sense 1)

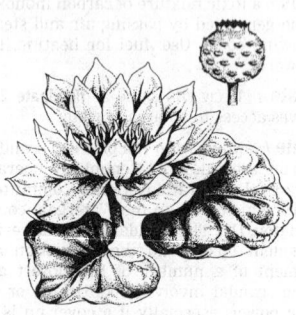

water lily

water lily *n* a perennial water plant with rounded leaves that float on the water. Flowers: cup-shaped, often fragrant. Family: Nymphaeaceae.

CULTURAL NOTE *Water Lilies*, the title of a number of paintings (1899–1925) by French artist Claude Monet. In his later years, Monet retired to his house at Giverny near Paris, where he painted numerous studies of the water lilies in his garden pond. While tending towards abstraction, many of these works, for example the enormous panels now in the Orangerie in Paris, succeed brilliantly in capturing the evanescent quality of natural phenomena.

water line *n* 1. a line on a ship's hull indicating the level to which the ship can sink into the water under various conditions 2. the line to which a body of water rises or reaches

waterlogged /wáwter logd/ *adj* 1. having absorbed so much water as to become spongy or marshy and difficult to walk or play on ○ *a waterlogged pitch* 2. filled with water and therefore hard to steer ○ *a waterlogged boat* —**waterlog** *vt* —**waterlogging** *n*

Waterloo /wáwter loō/ town in central Belgium, about 16 km/10 mi. south of Brussels. It was the site of the Battle of Waterloo on 18 June 1815, where Napoleon was decisively defeated by British and Prussian forces. Population: 28,111 (1995). ◇ **meet your Waterloo** to be decisively defeated or overcome

water louse *n* any freshwater crustacean related to the woodlouse. Genus: *Asellu*.

water main *n* a large underground pipe supplying water

waterman /wáwtermən/ (*plural* **-men** /-mən/) *n* somebody who works on or hires out boats

watermark /wáwter maark/ *n* 1. HIDDEN MARK IN PAPER a design or mark in paper that can be seen when the paper is held up to the light, or the metal tool used to make such a design 2. NAUT same as **water line** (sense 1) 3. LINE LEFT BY WATER a line showing where the edge or surface of water has been 4. COMPUT EMBEDDED PATTERN IN DATA FILE a pattern of bits digitally embedded in a data file, used in detecting unauthorized copies ■ *vt* (**-marks, -marking, -marked**) 1. PUT WATERMARK OR PATTERN IN PAPER to put a watermark into paper while it is being made, or impress a pattern as a watermark 2. COMPUT EMBED IDENTIFYING PATTERN IN DATA FILE to embed a pattern of bits in a data file for identification and detection of unauthorized copies

water meadow *n* a meadow that is often flooded by a stream or river

watermelon /wáwter melən/ *n* 1. a large oval or round fruit with a hard green skin and sweet and juicy pink, red, or yellow flesh, usually with many black seeds 2. a climbing plant that produces watermelons. Native to: Africa. Latin name: *Citrullus lanatus*.

water meter *n* a device that records the amount of water that passes through a pipe, usually for billing purposes

water milfoil *n* a perennial water plant that has submerged leaves made up of many feathery segments and bears slender spikes of tiny flowers above the water surface. Genus: *Myriophyllum*.

water mill *n* a mill that has machinery powered by moving water

water mint *n* a perennial plant of swampy areas with toothed hairy leaves and a hairy stem, that emits a strong scent when crushed. Flowers: lilac-pink, in whorls. Latin name: *Mentha aquatica*.

water moccasin *n* 1. a venomous snake belonging to the pit viper family that has an olive to brownish back and indistinct black bars and lives partly on land, partly in water. Native to: southern United States. Latin name: *Agkistrodon piscivorus*. 2. a snake that resembles the venomous water moccasin but is harmless. Genus: *Nerodia*.

water mould *n* a fungus that inhabits fresh or brackish water and feeds mainly on dead organic material but is sometimes parasitic on fish, plants, and other living organisms. Order: Saprolegniales.

water nymph *n* 1. in folklore and classical mythology, a nymph that lives in water 2. a water plant, e.g. a water lily

water of crystallization *n* water molecules incorporated in a crystalline substance that are typically necessary for its properties and structure

water of hydration *n* water molecules incorporated in a substance that can be removed without affecting its essential chemical composition

water on the brain *n* MED same as **hydrocephalus**

water on the knee *n* the accumulation of watery fluid in or around the knee indicating disease or injury of the knee joint

water opossum *n* ZOOL same as **yapok**

water ouzel *n* BIRDS same as **dipper** (sense 2)

water park *n* a leisure area or theme park with water-based facilities such as slides with flowing water

water pennywort *n* a creeping plant that grows in water or moist places. Genus: *Hydrocotyle*.

water pepper *n* an annual plant widely distributed in damp places that has lance-shaped leaves and a hot peppery taste. Flowers: inconspicuous, pink or greenish, in slender spikes. Latin name: *Polygonum hydropiper*.

water pipe *n* 1. a pipe for transporting water from one place to another 2. a pipe for smoking tobacco or marijuana that incorporates a water container through which the smoke is drawn and cooled

water pistol *n* a toy pistol that squirts out water

water plantain *n* a perennial plant found in water or wet places, with a rosette of pointed oval leaves. Flowers: pinkish or white, in branching heads. Genus: *Alisma*.

water polo *n* a game played in a swimming pool by two teams of seven players whose object is to score by sending a large ball into the opposing team's goal

water power *n* energy contained in moving water, or derived from the weight of standing water, used to drive machinery or to generate electricity through the use of hydraulic turbines

waterproof /wáwter proof/ *adj* IMPERVIOUS TO WATER treated or constructed so as to be impenetrable or unaffected by water ■ *n* 1. ITEM OF WATERPROOF CLOTHING an item of waterproof clothing, e.g. a plastic cape 2. TEXTILE IMPERVIOUS TO WATER a textile that has been made or treated so as to be impenetrable by water ■ *vt* (**-proofs, -proofing, -proofed**) MAKE SOMETHING WATERPROOF to make something such as a surface or an item of clothing impenetrable by water —**waterproofness** *n*

water purslane *n* a creeping annual plant growing in moist places with fleshy rounded leaves. Flowers: small, purplish, growing at leaf base. Latin name: *Lythrum portula*.

water rat *n* 1. ZOOL same as **water vole** 2. a large amphibious rat with broad paddle-shaped hind feet for swimming. Native to: Australia, New Guinea, Philippines. Subfamily: Hydromyinae. 3. *N Am* ZOOL same as **muskrat** (sense 1) 4. *US* a criminal, loafer, or hooligan who often frequents waterfront areas (*slang*)

water-repellent, water-resistant *adj* treated or constructed so as to prevent water being absorbed or passing through

water right *n* 1. the right to use a water source, especially for irrigation (*often used in the plural*) 2. the right to sail on specific rivers, lakes, or seas

Waters /wáwterz/, **Muddy** (1915–83) US guitarist and singer. He was a country blues singer who originated the Chicago blues style in the 1950s, and was a leading figure in the revival of folk-blues music in the 1960s. Born **Morganfield, McKinley**

'All my life I was having trouble with women…Then after I quit having trouble with them, I could feel in my heart that somebody would always have trouble with them, so I kept writing those blues.'
[Muddy Waters. Quoted in *All You Need is Love*, Tony Palmer; 1977]

water sapphire *n* a blue precious stone that is a variety of cordierite. Source: river gravel. Use: gems.

waterscape /wáwter skayp/ *n* a view or picture of an expanse of water

water scorpion *n* an insect that lives in water and uses a long tubular siphon for breathing. It catches prey with its front pair of legs. Family: Nepidae.

water seal *n* water that lies in a waste pipe and forms a seal that prevents the escape of unpleasant smells

watershed /wáwter shed/ *n* 1. LINE BETWEEN CATCHMENT AREAS the boundary separating the catchment basins of different rivers. N Am term **divide** 2. REGION DRAINING INTO RIVER OR OCEAN the land area that drains into a particular lake, river, or ocean 3. TURNING POINT an important period, time, event, or factor that marks a change or division ○ *Becoming a mother was a watershed in her life*. [Early 19C. Anglicization of German *Wasserscheide* 'water divide']

water shield *n* 1. a perennial water plant with floating leaves that are purple underneath and covered in a layer of clear jelly. Flowers: purple. Latin name: *Brasenia schreberi*. 2. a water plant with roundish floating leaves or finely divided needle-shaped submerged leaves. Genus: *Cabomba*. [Because the leaves are shaped like shields]

water shrew *n* a shrew that lives in or near water

water-sick *adj* describes land that has been made unproductive by excessive irrigation

waterside /wáwter sīd/ *n* land alongside an area of water ■ *adj* living or working beside an area of water

watersider /wáwtər sīdər/ *n ANZ* somebody who works on wharves loading and unloading ships

water sign *n* each of the three signs of the zodiac, Pisces, Cancer, and Scorpio, traditionally associated with emotional sensitivity

water skater *n* INSECTS same as **pond-skater**

waterski

waterski /wáwtər skee/ *n* **water-ski, water ski** a ski designed for skiing over water ■ *vi* (**-skis, -skiing, -skied**) to ski over water while being towed by a boat —**waterskier** *n* —**waterskiing** *n*

water slide *n* a slide with water flowing down it at a swimming pool or an amusement park

water snake *n* **1.** a snake that lives in or near water **2.** a nonvenomous snake that lives in marshes and other wet places. Native to: North America, Europe, Southeast Asia. Genus: *Natrix*.

water softener *n* **1.** a device that removes or reduces hardness in water, usually by means of ion-exchange resins **2.** a substance used to reduce water hardness, e.g. by precipitating out the minerals causing the hardness

water soldier *n* a perennial water plant that produces a semi-submerged rosette of toothed lance-shaped leaves. Flowers: white and prominent. Native to: Europe. Latin name: *Stratiotes aloides*.

water-soluble *adj* capable of being dissolved completely by water

water spaniel *n* a dog with a thick curly water-resistant coat, belonging to a breed developed for retrieving game from water

water spider *n* a spider that lives underwater in a bell-shaped web that it spins among vegetation and fills with air bubbles transported from the surface in its body hairs. Native to: Europe, Asia. Latin name: *Argyroneta aquatica*.

water splash *n* a section of road where a stream flows across it

water sports *npl* **1.** sports carried out on or in water **2.** an offensive term for sexual activity in which urine or the act of urination provides gratification (*slang*)

waterspout /wáwtər spowt/ *n* **1.** a funnel-shaped tornado, sometimes hundreds of metres wide, extending from the surface of the sea or a lake to the cloud base and caused by violent circulation of air **2.** a hole or spout through which water flows, e.g. from the gutter of a building

water sprite *n* in folklore and classical mythology, a sprite that lives in water

water stick insect *n* a water insect with a long slender body and a long siphon used for breathing underwater that waits in vegetation for prey it catches by using its front legs. Although winged, it has poorly developed flight muscles and cannot fly. Native to: Europe. Latin name: *Ranatra linearis*.

water strider, water skipper *n ANZ, N Am* an insect that walks on water with long legs and feeds on dead insects. Family: Gerridae. UK term **pond-skater**

water supply *n* **1.** the water distributed to a town, community, or region **2.** the source or delivery system supplying water to an area, e.g. reservoirs, pipes, or purification plants

water system *n* **1.** a river with all its tributaries **2.** a system for delivering water to a group of users or a town or region

water table *n* **1.** the upper surface of ground water, below which pores in the rocks are filled with water

2. a moulding or band that projects from a wall and is intended to divert rainwater

water taxi *n* a motorboat used to ferry passengers between destinations separated by water for a fare

waterthrush *n* a small songbird of the wood warbler family with markings similar to a thrush, found near streams, ponds, and swampy ground. Native to: North America. Genus: *Seiurus*.

watertight /wáwtər tīt/ *adj* **1.** not allowing water to pass in, out, or through **2.** without loopholes or flaws ○ *a watertight argument*

water torture *n* a form of torture in which water is used, especially one in which water is dripped steadily onto somebody's forehead

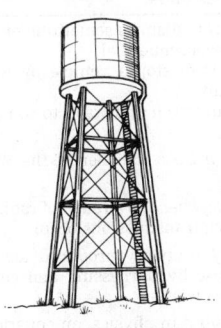

water tower

water tower *n* **1.** a tower for water storage where the prevailing water pressure is not sufficient for either firefighting or general distribution **2.** a firefighting apparatus for lifting hoses to high levels

water vapour *n* water in vapour form, but usually below boiling point

water-vascular system *n* a system of water-filled vessels connecting the tube feet of echinoderms such as starfish

water vole *n* an amphibious vole that lives near rivers and streams, often burrowing into the banks. Native to: Europe, Asia. Genus: *Arvicola*.

waterway /wáwtər way/ *n* **1.** a navigable channel used by boats or ships, e.g. a river or canal **2.** a drain for water at the edge of the deck of a boat

waterweed /wáwtər weed/ *n ANZ, N Am* same as **pondweed** (sense 2)

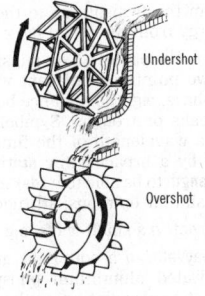

Undershot

Overshot

water wheel

water wheel *n* **1.** a simple wheel driven by water flowing or falling onto vanes or into buckets on the edges of the wheel, used to power machinery **2.** a wheel with buckets fixed to its rim, used for lifting water

water wings *npl* a pair of air-filled supports that fit closely around the upper arms of a swimmer, especially a child learning to swim

water witch *n* PARANORMAL same as **water diviner**

waterworks /wáwtər wurks/ *n* (*plural same*) **1.** SYSTEM FOR SUPPLYING WATER the entire system of treating, storing, supplying, and managing the distribution networks of pumps and pipes that provide water to a community or region (*takes a singular or plural verb*) **2.** COMPONENT OF WATER SYSTEM a single component of a waterworks system, e.g. a pumping station ■ *npl* **3.** FOUNTAINS a display of fountains, cascades, and other mechanically driven water-moving devices, or the equipment that produces such a display **4.** URINARY

SYSTEM the bodily system involved in excreting urine (*informal*) **3.** TEARS a display of crying (*informal*)

waterworn /wáwtər wawrn/ *adj* smoothed or eroded by the action of water

watery /wáwtəri/ *adj* **1.** RELATING TO OR CONTAINING WATER relating to, containing, soaked with, or like water **2.** HAVING EXCESSIVE WATER containing too much water ○ *watery coffee* **3.** FILLED WITH TEARS filled with tears, either from emotion or physical irritation ○ *watery eyes* **4.** LACKING FORCE lacking the usual full force and appearing thin or weak ○ *A watery sun hung in the autumn sky.* **5.** WEAK lacking strength or sincerity ○ *a watery smile* **6.** FULL OF FLUID discharging, secreting, or filled with a watery fluid ○ *watery blister* —**wateriness** *n*

Watford /wótfərd/ town in Hertfordshire, south-central England. Population: 79,726 (2001).

Watson /wóts'n/, **Chris** (1867–1941) Chilean-born prime minister of Australia (1904). He was involved in the labour movement during the 1890s and became the leader of the Labour Party in 1901. He was Australia's first Labour prime minister. Full name **Watson, John Christian**. See table at **prime minister**

Watson, James D. (*b.* 1928) US biochemist. He worked with Francis Crick and Maurice Wilkins in exploring the structure of the DNA molecule, for which they shared the Nobel Prize in physiology and medicine (1962). Full name **Watson, James Dewey**

'Biology has at least 50 more interesting years.'
[James D. Watson, *Remark*; 31 December 1984]

Watson-Crick model *n* the three-dimensional double-helix model of the DNA molecule proposed by James Watson and Francis Crick in 1953 [Mid-20C. After J. D. WATSON and F. H. C. CRICK]

watt /wot/ *n* the international (**SI**) unit of power equal to the power produced by a current of one ampere acting across a potential difference of one volt. Symbol **W** [Late 19C. After James WATT]

Watt /wot/, **James** (1736–1819) British inventor. He improved the steam engine and, in partnership with Matthew Boulton, developed a pumping engine and rotative engine. The SI unit of power is named after him.

wattage /wóttij/ *n* electrical power measured in watts

Watteau /wóttō/, **Jean-Antoine** (1684–1721) French painter. His festive rural scenes and figures from the commedia dell'arte epitomize French rococo painting.

watt-hour *n* a unit of electrical energy equal to that of one watt operating for one hour

wattle /wótt'l/ *n* **1.** STAKES INTERWOVEN WITH BRANCHES stakes or poles interwoven with branches and twigs, used for walls, fences, and roofs **2.** MATERIAL FOR WATTLE material used to make wattle, e.g. branches or stakes **3.** SKIN HANGING FROM ANIMAL'S THROAT a loose, often highly coloured fold of bare skin hanging from the throat or cheek of birds and lizards. It is used in courtship and other displays. **4.** AUSTRALIAN ACACIA TREE a drought-resistant tree or bush, often planted for shade or ornament, whose feathery-looking leaves are sometimes replaced by flattened green leaf stalks in maturity. Native to: Australia. Genus: *Acacia*. ■ *vt* (**-tles, -tling, -tled**) **1.** MAKE SOMETHING FROM WATTLE to construct something from wattle **2.** WEAVE BRANCHES INTO WATTLE to weave branches or twigs into wattle [Old English *watul*, origin ?] —**wattled** *adj*

wattle and daub *n* building material consisting of wattle covered with mud or clay, often containing lime, dung, or straw (*hyphenated before a noun*)

wattlebird /wótt'l burd/ *n* a slender-bodied grey-brown or olive-brown bird with a long beak, a brush-tipped tongue for lapping nectar, and wattles on the cheeks. Native to: Australia. Genus: *Anthochaera*.

wattmeter /wót meetər/ *n* an instrument designed to measure the magnitude of the power in an electric circuit. It may be scaled in watts, kilowatts, or megawatts.

Watts /wots/, **George Frederick** (1817–1904) British painter and sculptor. He painted portraits of well-known contemporary figures and grandly allegorical paintings.

Popperfoto

Evelyn Waugh

Waugh /waw/, **Evelyn** (1903–66) British novelist. His early novels satirizing high society gave way to the more serious later work such as *Brideshead Revisited* (1945) that reflected his preoccupation with Roman Catholicism. Full name **Waugh, Evelyn Arthur St John**. See Cultural note at **handful**

'You never find an Englishman among the underdogs–except in England, of course.'
[Evelyn Waugh, *The Loved One*; 1948]

Waugh, Mark (*b.* 1965) Australian cricketer, twin brother of Steve. An outstanding batsman, he scored more than 8,000 Test runs, registering an average of over 41. Full name **Waugh, Mark Edward**

Waugh, Steve (*b.* 1965) Australian cricketer, twin brother of Mark. He has scored more than 9,000 Test runs, serving as captain of the Australian test team (1999–January 2004). Full name **Waugh, Stephen Roger**

waul /wawl/, **wawl** *vi* (**wauls, wauling, wauled; wawls, wawling, wawled**) to cry out shrilly like a cat or baby ■ *n* a shrill cry, like that of a cat or baby [Early 16C. An imitation of the sound]

waulk /wawk/ (**waulks, waulking, waulked**) *vt Scotland* to make cloth such as tweed thicker and more felted by soaking and beating it [15C. < Dutch or Low German *walken*]

waulking song /wáwking-/ *n Scotland* a Gaelic work-song traditionally sung while fulling cloth

waur /wawr/ *adj, adv Scotland* same as **worse** [Late 18C. Scots dialect variant of WAR]

wav /wav/ *abbr* a file extension for a sound file. Full form **waveform**

wave /wayv/ *n* **1.** LARGE RIPPLE ON LIQUID OR SEA a raised ridge-shaped formation moving across the surface of a liquid, especially the sea, or a sea wave curling over and falling as it reaches the shore **2.** UNDULATING MOTION a movement through, or over the surface of or along the edge of something that is similar in its appearance or effects to a wave ○ *The wind made waves across the field of grain.* **3.** ACT OF WAVING HAND an instance of moving the hand or arm as a signal or greeting **4.** LINE CURVING IN ALTERNATING DIRECTIONS a line, shape, surface, or pattern that curves in one direction and then another, especially one with repeated curves **5.** SURGE IN ACTIVITY a sudden occurrence of or increase in a particular phenomenon or activity ○ *a crime wave* ○ *a wave of strikes* **6.** BURST OF FEELING a sudden and often overwhelming experience of a particular feeling ○ *a wave of sorrow* ○ *Relief came over me in waves.* **7.** INCOMING GROUP a large number or body of people working together or doing the same thing at the same time ○ *a wave of immigrants* ○ *attack in waves* **8.** LOOSE CURVE IN HAIR a soft, usually large curve or ripple in the hair where the lie of the hair changes direction, either naturally or after setting **9.** RIPPLED PATTERN a rippled pattern in material such as silk **10.** PHYS OSCILLATION OF ENERGY an oscillation that travels through a medium by transferring energy from one particle or point to another without causing any permanent displacement of the medium ○ *sound waves* **11.** *N Am* LEISURE same as **Mexican wave** ■ **waves** *npl* SEA the waves of the sea, or the sea itself ■ *v* (**waves, waving, waved**) **1.** *vti* MOVE HAND REPEATEDLY AS SIGNAL to move the hand or arm from side to side or up and down as a greeting, farewell, or signal **2.** *vti* MOVE SOMETHING REPEATEDLY IN AIR to move from side to side or up and down, or cause something such as a flag to move from side to side or up and down ○ *The flag waved in the wind.* **3.** *vt* DIRECT SOMEBODY OR SOMETHING BY WAVING to direct somebody or something by waving a hand, arm, or object ○ *The police waved the traffic around the procession.* **4.** *vti* MAKE INTO OR BE IN UNDULATIONS to make something into swells, ridges, or swirls, or be in the form of swells, ridges, or swirls ○ *a field of grain waving in the wind* **5.** *vti* BE OR MAKE SLIGHTLY CURLED to be slightly curled, or make hair slightly curled **6.** *vt* GIVE MATERIAL RIPPLED PATTERN to create a rippled pattern in a fabric such as silk [Old English *wafian* < Germanic, 'move back and forth'] ◇ **catch a wave** to find or launch yourself onto a wave of the type that can be enjoyably ridden on a surfboard (*slang*) ◇ **make waves** to cause a disturbance or trouble, e.g. by suggesting or introducing changes or making criticisms

SPELLCHECK See *waive*.

wave aside *vt* to dismiss something or somebody as trivial or inconsequential

wave down *vt* to stop a vehicle by waving to the driver to halt

wave off *vt* to watch and wave to somebody who is leaving

Wave /wayv/ *n US* a member of the WAVES [Back-formation]

waveband /wáyv band/ *n* a range of radio frequencies within which transmissions occur

wave energy *n* energy produced for domestic or industrial use by harnessing and converting the energy of sea waves

wave equation *n* in physics, an equation, usually a partial differential equation, that defines the propagation of a wave through a medium. The form of the equation is determined by the medium, the method by which the wave is transmitted, and the circumstance of its propagation.

wave file *n* a computer file containing a digitized representation of sound waves

waveform /wáyv fawrm/ *n* in physics, the profile or shape of a wave, especially the graphic representation of one of its characteristics such as frequency or amplitude relative to time

wavefront /wáyv frunt/ *n* in physics, a line or surface that joins points of the same phase in a wave travelling through a medium

wave function *n* in quantum physics, an equation that shows how a wave's amplitude varies in space and time

waveguide /wáyv gīd/ *n* in electronics, a transmission line consisting of a hollow metal conductor used as a path to convey microwave energy along its length. It is used in radar systems to convey transmitted energy from the transmitter to the aerial and received energy from the aerial back to the receiver.

wavelength /wáyv length/ *n* **1.** in physics, the distance between two points on adjacent waves that have the same phase, e.g. the distance between two consecutive peaks or troughs. Symbol λ **2.** in broadcasting, the wavelength of the fundamental radio wave used by a broadcasting station ◇ **be on the same wavelength** to be able to understand each other, or to have similar opinions, attitudes, or tastes

wavelet /wáyvlət/ *n* a small wave, e.g. a ripple

wavellite /wáyvəlīt/ *n* a soft light grey, yellow, or brown hydrated aluminium phosphate mineral, forming clusters of radiating crystals. Source: slates and shales. [Early 19C. After William *Wavell* (d. 1829), British physician]

wave mechanics *n* a form of quantum theory in which happenings on the atomic scale are explained in terms of interactions between systems of waves, represented by wave functions (*takes a singular verb*)

wavemeter /wáyv meetər/ *n* an instrument for measuring wavelengths

wave number *n* in physics, the number of waves in a given unit distance. Wave number is the reciprocal of wavelength. Symbol σ

waveoff /wáyv of/ *n* a signal or instruction to an aircraft that it is not to land

wave-particle duality *n* a fundamental concept of quantum theory holding that energy sometimes behaves like particles and sometimes behaves like waves, so that descriptions of energy as one or the other are inadequate

wave pool *n* a public swimming pool equipped with a device to produce waves

wave power *n* INDUST same as **wave energy**

waver /wáyvər/ *vi* (**-vers, -vering, -vered**) **1.** FLUCTUATE BETWEEN POSSIBILITIES to go back and forth between possibilities, or be indecisive in making a choice **2.** BEGIN TO CHANGE OPINION to become unsure or begin to change from a previous opinion **3.** MOVE IN DIFFERENT DIRECTIONS to move one way and then another in an irregular pattern **4.** FLUCTUATE, ESPECIALLY IN TONE to vary or fluctuate, e.g. as the voice does from emotion **5.** FLICKER to go on and off, especially when burning unsteadily (*refers to lights or flames*) ■ *n* ACT OF WAVERING an instance or act of wavering [14C. < Old Norse *vafra*] —**waverer** *n* —**waveringly** *adv*

SPELLCHECK See *waive*.

SYNONYMS See *hesitate*.

WAVES /wayvz/ *npl* the women's branch of the US Naval Reserve that was organized in World War II. It no longer exists as a separate entity. Full form **Women Accepted for Volunteer Emergency Service**

wave theory *n* the theory that the behaviour of light or any other electromagnetic radiation can be explained by assuming that it travels in waves

wave train *n* in physics, a series of similar waves produced at equal intervals and travelling in the same direction

wavy /wáyvi/ (**-ier, -iest**) *adj* **1.** REPEATEDLY CURVING forming a series of smooth curves that go in one direction and then another **2.** HAVING SOFT CURVES having loose open waves ○ *wavy hair* **3.** CONTAINING WAVES full of waves or having a surface covered by waves **4.** MOVING LIKE WAVE moving with an up-and-down or side-to-side motion **5.** WAVERING wavering or changeable —**wavily** *adv* —**waviness** *n*

waw *n* same as **vav**

wa-wa /wáwaw/ *n* MUSIC another spelling of **wah-wah**

wawl *vi*, *n* another spelling of **waul**

wax¹ /waks/ *n* **1.** INDUST NATURALLY-OCCURRING GREASY SUBSTANCE a mouldable substance of animal, plant, or mineral origin that feels slightly greasy or oily to the touch **2.** HOUSEHOLD PREPARATION FOR POLISHING a preparation containing wax used for polishing floors, cars, and other surfaces **3.** INDUST same as **beeswax** (sense 2) **4.** MED same as **earwax 5.** INDUST RESINOUS MIXTURE USED IN SHOEMAKING a resinous mixture rubbed onto thread used in shoemaking **6.** SOMEBODY OR SOMETHING EASILY MOULDED somebody or something that is easily moulded, shaped, or manipulated **7.** RECORDING, MUSIC same as **record** *n* (sense 10) (*dated informal*) ■ *vt* (**waxes, waxing, waxed**) **1.** POLISH SOMETHING WITH WAX to coat or polish something such as a floor or car with wax **2.** COSMETICS REMOVE HAIR WITH WAX to remove unwanted hair from the skin using heated wax that is left to dry and then removed [Old English *wæx* < Germanic] —**waxer** *n*

wax² /waks/ (**waxes, waxing, waxed**) *vi* **1.** to show a gradually increasing illuminated surface, as does the Moon between its new and full phases **2.** to increase in size, power, or intensity (*literary*) **3.** same as **become** (*literary*) ○ *waxed lyrical* [Old English *weaxan* < Indo-European, 'to increase']

wax³ /waks/ *n* a fit of temper or anger (*dated informal*) [Mid-19C. Origin ?]

wax bean *n N Am* a variety of string bean that is yellow

waxbill /wáks bil/ *n* a small brightly-coloured bird of the finch family with a conical beak. Waxbills feed on seeds and insects and build roofed nests of grass. Native to: Africa, Arabia. Genus: *Estrilda*.

wax cap *n* a mushroom with a cap that has waxy gills. Family: Hygrophoraceae.

waxcloth /wáks kloth/ *n* TEXTILES same as **oilcloth**

waxed jacket /wákst-/ *n* a jacket for outdoor use made from fabric that has been coated with wax to repel moisture

waxed paper *n* HOUSEHOLD same as **greaseproof paper**

waxen /wáks'n/ *adj* **1.** LIKE WAX resembling wax in texture and appearance **2.** MADE OF WAX covered with, permeated with, or made of wax **3.** PALE AND UNHEALTHY-LOOKING lacking the rosy glow of life or health ○ *a waxen complexion* **4.** EASY TO SHAPE easily shaped, changed, or manipulated [Pre-12C. Old past participle of WAX¹]

wax flower *n* a plant that has waxy flowers, especially a hoya

waxhead /wáks hed/, **waxie** /wáksi/ *n Aus* an enthusiastic surfer (*informal*)

wax insect *n* a scale insect that secretes wax. Superfamily: Coccoidea.

wax light *n* a candle or taper made of wax

wax moth *n* a small brownish moth whose larvae develop inside beehives, feeding on the wax of the honeycombs and often damaging the honey and the honey bee larvae. Latin name: *Galleria mellonella.*

wax museum *n* same as **waxworks** (sense 2) (*dated*)

wax myrtle *n* TREES same as **bayberry** (sense 2)

wax palm *n* TREES same as **carnauba** (sense 1)

wax paper *n N Am* HOUSEHOLD same as **greaseproof paper**

waxwing /wáks wing/ *n* a bird with a crest, buff-brown feathers, and waxy-looking red tips on the edges of the wings. Native to: northern regions. Genus: *Bombycilla.*

waxwork /wáks wurk/ *n* **1.** WAX MODEL a realistic model, usually of a famous person, made from wax **2.** WAX OBJECT an object made of wax, especially an ornament **3.** ART OF USING WAX FOR MODELLING the art of using wax as a modelling or expressive medium

waxworks /wáks wurks/ (*plural same*) *n* **1.** an exhibition, usually in a museum, of lifelike wax models, usually of famous people **2.** a museum containing a waxworks

waxy /wáksi/ (**-ier, -iest**) *adj* **1.** LIKE WAX resembling wax in texture, appearance, or pliability **2.** COVERED WITH WAX covered with, containing a lot of, or made of wax **3.** MED HAVING HARD DEPOSITS LIKE WAX containing deposits of a hard substance resembling wax (**amyloid**) resulting from tissue degeneration [15C. < WAX¹] —**waxiness** *n*

way /way/ *n* **1.** MANNER OR METHOD a means, manner, or method of doing something ○ *I'll do it my way.* **2.** RESPECT a feature, aspect, or example of something ○ *In some ways, they're very similar.* **3.** PATH a path or physical means of getting from one place to another ○ *The way out is through here.* **4.** DOOR OR OPENING a door or opening leading or providing access to or from somewhere ○ *came in the front way* **5.** JOURNEY OR ROUTE a journey or the route followed or to be followed ○ *on my way home* **6.** PROGRESS THROUGH LIFE progress or a path through life and its experiences or difficulties **7.** *also* **Way** STREET a street, usually a small or narrow one (*often used in placenames*) **8.** DIRECTION a direction, e.g. left, right, up, or down **9.** MANNER OF PLACING the manner in which something is placed, packed, or arranged, or the direction it faces **10.** SPACE FOR ACTION path, room, territory, or space allowing movement, progress, or action ○ *got out of the way* **11.** AREA an area or district, e.g. around somebody's home (*informal*) ○ *out our way* **12.** DISTANCE a distance away in space or time ○ *a long way off* **13.** AMOUNT the extent or amount to which somebody does something or to which something happens ○ *He's fallen for her in a big way.* **14.** PART OF SOMETHING each of a particular number of parts into which something divides or is split ○ *split the money four ways* **15.** CONDITION the state or condition of somebody or something, especially with regard to health or finances ○ *He's in a bad way.* **16.** PREFERENCE something that somebody wants to do or to happen ○ *always wants his own way* **17.** CHARACTERISTIC ASPECT OF BEHAVIOUR a usual, characteristic, or distinctive activity or style of behaviour ○ *her irritating ways* **18.** TRADITION OR CUSTOM the customary practice of a person or group ○ *the way of the Sufi* **19.** TYPICAL OCCURRENCE the usual occurrence or pattern of events ○ *It's always the way when you're in a hurry.* **20.** MECH ENG GUIDE OR SUPPORT a surface used to guide or provide support for moving parts of a machine tool such as a lathe (*often used in the plural*) **21.** NAUT MOVEMENT THROUGH WATER movement or speed of a ship through water ○ *The vessel now had some way on.* ■ *adv* **1.** VERY MUCH to a considerable degree or at a considerable distance (*informal*) ○ *way out of our price range* **2.** VERY extremely (*slang*) ○ *That's way cool!* [Old English *weg* < Indo-European, 'to go'] ◇ **by the way** used to introduce something that is not strictly part of the subject at hand ◇ **by way of something 1.** as a means of or for the purpose of something **2.** via a particular place or route ◇ **every which way** *N Am* **1.** in all directions **2.** in every way possible (*informal*) ◇ **get into the way of doing something** to get into the habit of doing something ◇ **give way 1.** to give in or give precedence to somebody else **2.** to become useless, break, or otherwise fail, especially under weight or pressure or from age or wear **3.** TRANSP to slow down or stop in order to let another vehicle pass ◇ **give way to somebody** *or* **something** to be replaced or superseded by somebody or something ○ *The rain gave way to patchy sunshine.* ◇ **give way to something** to be overcome by an emotion that you have been trying to resist ◇ **go out of your way to do something** to make an exceptional effort or take exceptional steps in order to do something ◇ **have a way with somebody** *or* **something** to be good at dealing with somebody or something ◇ **have it both ways** to have the benefits of opposing situations or actions ◇ **in a way** from a certain point of view ◇ **(in) the worst way** *N Am* very much, very badly, or very intensely ◇ **make way (for somebody** *or* **something)** to move aside in order to make room for somebody or something ◇ **make your way 1.** to go somewhere, especially when getting there requires overcoming some obstacle, e.g. finding the route or some transport **2.** to become successful ◇ **nine ways from Sunday** *US* in every possible way and to the greatest extent (*informal*) ○ *The potential cross-examination questions were covered nine ways from Sunday during pretrial preps.* ◇ **no way** used as an emphatic negative (*informal*) ◇ **out of the way** in a remote location ◇ **pay your way** to pay your share of expenses ◇ **see your way (clear) to doing something** to be willing and able to oblige somebody by doing something ○ *If you could see your way clear to lending me another £50, I'd be grateful.* ◇ **there are no two ways about it** there is no room for dispute ◇ **way to go** *N Am* used to congratulate somebody on something that he or she has done (*informal*)

SPELLCHECK way, weigh, or **whey**? Do not confuse the spelling of *way, weigh,* and *whey,* which sound similar. *Way* is a noun in frequent use, with meanings including 'means, manner, or method', 'journey or route', and 'direction', as in *a different way to do it, on the way home, going the wrong way. Weigh* is a verb meaning 'find out the weight of something', 'be of a particular weight', or 'consider or evaluate something', as in *weigh the ingredients, weighs five kilograms, weigh up the pros and cons. Whey* is a much less usual noun denoting the watery liquid that separates from the solid part of milk, as in *curds and whey.*

waybill /wáy bil/ *n* a document that gives information about goods being shipped or carried

wayfarer /wáy fairər/ *n* a traveller, especially somebody who makes a journey on foot (*literary*) — **wayfaring** *n, adj*

wayfaring tree *n* a bush with red berries that turn black as they ripen. Flowers: white, in flat-topped clusters. Native to: Europe, western Asia. Latin name: *Viburnum lantana.*

Wayland /wáylənd/, **Wayland Smith, Wayland the Smith** *n* in northern European folklore, a magical smith who was the king of the elves [< Old Norse *Völundr*]

waylay /way láy/ (**-lays, -laying, -laid** /-láyd/) *vt* **1.** to lie in wait for somebody, especially as part of an attack or ambush **2.** to stop or accost somebody, e.g. in order to talk —**waylayer** *n*

wayleave /wáy leev/ *n* the right of way over somebody else's property, for which payment is usually made

waymark /wáy maark/ *n also* **waymarker** /-maarkər/ a signpost or other marker used to guide travellers, especially walkers ■ *vt* (**-marks, -marking, -marked**) to mark out a path with waymarks

Wayne /wayn/, **John** (1907–79) US actor. He starred as the rugged hero in numerous westerns, including *True Grit* (1969), for which he won an Academy Award. Born **Morrison, Marion Michael.** Known as **the Duke**

'Courage is being scared to death and saddling up anyway.'
[John Wayne. Quoted in *Never Let Them See You Cry,* Edna Buchanan; 1992]

John Wayne

way of life *n* **1.** the habits and behaviour that characterize a person or group of people ○ *had an increasingly sedentary way of life* **2.** something commonly used, done, or experienced by a person or group of people ○ *Smart cards are a way of life for most of us.*

Way of the Cross *n* a series of pictures representing Jesus Christ's progress on the road to Calvary, according to the Bible

way-out *adj* **1.** unusual, peculiar, or unconventional (*informal*) **2.** excellent or exciting (*dated informal*)

waypoint /wáy poynt/ *n* a point on a journey or route where a traveller can stop or change course

ways /wayz/ *n* **1.** the tracks a ship slides down to be launched (*takes a singular or plural verb*) **2.** *N Am* a distance travelled or to be travelled (*informal; takes a singular or plural verb*) ○ *The next gas station is quite a ways from here.*

-ways *suffix* in a particular direction or position ○ *edgeways* [Old English *weges,* form of *weg* 'way', of (such a) way']

ways and means *npl* **1.** methods of accomplishing or achieving something, especially finding a way of paying for something **2.** methods used by a government to raise money, e.g. legislation

Ways and Means *n* in the United States, a legislative committee in charge of methods of raising money for government

wayside /wáy sīd/ *n* the side of a road or path ■ *adj* situated at the side of a road or path ◇ **fall by the wayside** to fail to continue or complete something ○ *Several students fell by the wayside after the first few weeks.*

way station *n US* **1.** a station between the major stations on a railway **2.** a point or stopping place on a route or process

wayward /wáywərd/ *adj* **1.** disobedient and uncontrollable **2.** behaving in an erratic, apparently perverse, or unpredictable manner [14C. Alteration of *awayward*] —**waywardly** *adv* —**waywardness** *n*

SYNONYMS See *unruly.*

wayworn /wáy wawrn/ *adj* worn out or weary from travelling

wayzgoose /wáyz gooss/ *n* formerly, an annual outing for people working at a printing house [Mid-18C. Alteration of *waygoose,* origin ?]

wazzock /wázzək/ *n* an offensive term that deliberately insults somebody's intelligence or common sense (*slang insult*) [Late 20C. Origin ?]

wb *abbr* **1.** water ballast **2.** waybill **3.** westbound

Wb *symbol* MEASURE weber

WB *abbr* **1.** water ballast **2.** waybill **3.** westbound

w.b. *abbr* waybill

W/B *abbr* waybill

WBA *abbr* World Boxing Association

WBC *abbr* **1.** BIOL white blood cell **2.** BOXING World Boxing Council

WbN *abbr* COMPASS west by north

W boson *n* PHYS same as **W particle**

WbS *abbr* COMPASS west by south

WC¹ *n* HOUSEHOLD full form **water closet**

WC² *abbr* **1.** GEOG West Central (London) **2.** ONLINE who cares (*used in e-mails or text messages*)

w.c. *abbr* without charge

WCC *abbr* World Council of Churches

wd *abbr* **1.** HEALTH SERVICES ward **2.** COMM warranted **3.** wood **4.** word

WD *abbr* MIL War Department

w/d *abbr* COMM warranted

WDA *abbr* **1.** POL Welsh Development Agency **2.** ACCT writing-down allowance

WDM, **wdm** *abbr* wavelength division multiplex

wdth *abbr* width

WDV *abbr* ACCT written-down value

WDYT *abbr* what do you think (*used in e-mails or text messages*)

we *stressed* /wee/; *unstressed* /wi/ *pron* **1.** REFERS TO SPEAKER AND OTHERS used to refer to the speaker or writer and at least one other person (*first person plural personal pronoun, used as the subject of a verb*) ○ *We are going on holiday.* ○ *We all want our children to have a better future.* **2.** REFERS TO PEOPLE IN GENERAL used to refer to all people or to people in general, including the speaker or writer ○ *We're getting closer to the election.* **3.** USED INSTEAD OF 'I' used by a writer or speaker to include the listener or speaker in what is being said, especially to talk about how a book or talk is organized or by a monarch as the people's symbolic head ○ *We will now consider the causes of the war.* **4.** USED INSTEAD OF 'YOU' used sarcastically or condescendingly by a speaker ○ *And how are we today?* [Old English *wē* < Indo-European]

WEA *abbr* Workers' Educational Association

weak /week/ *adj* **1.** NOT STRONG OR FIT not physically fit or mentally strong **2.** EASILY DEFEATED easily overcome or defeated **3.** LACKING STRENGTH OF CHARACTER not having strength of character **4.** NOT INTENSE not powerful or intense ○ *weak winter sunshine* **5.** LACKING SKILLS OR ABILITIES not having particular skills or abilities ○ *weak in maths* **6.** WATERY OR TASTELESS watery or lacking flavour ○ *weak coffee* **7.** NOT WORKING TO FULL CAPACITY not working as well as usual or desirable **8.** UNCONVINCING not persuasive or convincing ○ *a weak excuse* **9.** NOT STRONG POLITICALLY not politically strong or powerful ○ *a weak country* **10.** LITERAT UNSTRESSED describes a syllable or word that is not stressed or accented **11.** LITERAT HAVING ACCENT ON UNSTRESSED SYLLABLE describes verse that has the accent on a syllable that is usually unstressed **12.** GRAM CHARACTERIZED BY REGULAR INFLECTIONAL ENDINGS describes a verb whose forms are characterized by regular inflectional endings, not by vowel changes **13.** FIN CHARACTERIZED BY FALLING PRICES falling in price, or characterized by falling prices ○ *a weak market* **14.** PHOTOGRAPHY LACKING IN CONTRAST not having much contrast between tones [13C. < Old Norse *veikr* 'pliant' < Germanic]

SPELLCHECK weak or **week**? Do not confuse the spelling of ***weak*** and ***week***, which sound similar. ***Weak*** is an adjective meaning 'not strong', as in *weak legs, weak tea, a weak argument.* ***Week*** is a noun denoting a period of seven days, as in *three weeks ago.*

SYNONYMS ***weak, feeble, frail, infirm, debilitated, decrepit, enervated***

CORE MEANING: lacking physical strength or energy

weak not physically fit or mentally strong ○ *He felt too weak to climb the stairs.* ○ *He's a weak man who can't resist the chance of what seems like easy money.* **feeble** lacking physical or mental strength or health ○ *Her father grew bent and feeble, but still walked his dog every day.* ○ *feeble, incompetent people who were easily persuaded by her promises* **frail** in a physically weakened state and vulnerable to injury ○ *a slight old man with the light, frail bones of a child* ○ *He looked frail but happy as he descended the hospital steps.* **infirm** lacking strength and vitality, especially because of sickness or age ○ *elderly and infirm people* ○ *Their aunt was becoming increasingly infirm and was unable to visit them this year.* **debilitated** with reduced strength or energy as a result of illness or physical exertion ○ *feeling thoroughly debilitated after his operation* ○ *Rescuers found the pair in a half-frozen and debilitated condition.* **decrepit** (*informal*) with strength lessened by the effects of age ○ *The president wasn't always the decrepit old man of his last years in office.* **enervated** weakened or exhausted physically, mentally, or morally ○ *The intense heat made us feel faint and enervated.* ○ *She's been enervated by her long ordeal.*

weaken /weékən/ (**-ens, -ening, -ened**) *vti* to make somebody or something weak or weaker, or become weak or weaker —**weakener** *n*

weaker sex /weékər-/ *n* an offensive term for women considered as a group (*dated*)

weakfish /weék fish/ (*plural same* or **-fishes**) *n* FISH same as **sea trout** (sense 2) [Late 18C. < obsolete Dutch *weekvisch* 'soft fish' < *week* 'soft' + *visch* 'fish']

weak interaction, **weak force** *n* the fundamental interaction between elementary particles that is mediated by the W and Z particles. It is involved in radioactive decay, which occurs by electron production, and particle decay. One of the four fundamental interactions, it is only effective at distances of less than 10^{-15} m and is a million million times weaker than the strong interaction.

weak-kneed /-neéd/ *adj* easily persuaded or intimidated (*informal*)

weakling /weékling/ *n* somebody who lacks physical strength or a strong character

weakly /weékli/ *adj* (**-lier, -liest**) sickly or delicate ■ *adv* with little strength or force ○ *She nodded weakly.* —**weakliness** *n*

weak-minded *adj* **1.** easily persuaded or convinced (*disapproving*) **2.** an offensive term meaning of low intelligence —**weak-mindedness** *n*

weakness /weéknəss/ *n* **1.** LACK OF STRENGTH OR DETERMINATION lack of strength, power, or determination **2.** WEAK POINT a weak point in the structure or arrangement of something ○ *Unfortunately, the escape plan had a serious weakness.* **3.** CHARACTER FLAW a feature of somebody's character regarded as unfavourable **4.** FONDNESS a strong liking for something ○ *a weakness for chocolate* **5.** OBJECT OF DESIRE an irresistible object of desire ○ *My weakness is adventure stories.*

SYNONYMS See *flaw*[1].

weak sister *n N Am* **1.** an offensive term for somebody regarded as a weak or unreliable member or component of a group (*insult*) **2.** an offensive term for somebody regarded as timid or cowardly

weak-willed *adj* not having a strong will

weal[1] /weel/, **wheal** *n* **1.** a raised or reddened area on the skin, caused by being hit with something **2.** a short-lived raised area on the skin, often red and itchy, caused by something such as a nettle or insect sting or by exposure to an allergen [Early 19C. Alteration of WALE]

weal[2] /weel/ *n* a general state of wellbeing, prosperity, and happiness (*literary*) [Old English *wela* < Indo-European, 'to wish']

Weald /weeld/ once-wooded region in Kent and East Sussex, southeastern England. It was the centre of England's iron industry in medieval times. Area: 1,300 sq. km/500 sq. mi.

wealth /welth/ *n* **1.** LARGE AMOUNT OF MONEY a large amount of money or possessions **2.** STATE OF HAVING MUCH MONEY the state of having plenty of money or possessions ○ *came from a background of great wealth* **3.** ABUNDANCE OF SOMETHING an abundance or great quantity of something ○ *quoted a wealth of statistics to prove the point* **4.** ECON VALUE OF ASSETS the value of assets owned by a person or a community ○ *need to determine the college's wealth* [13C. < WEAL[2]]

CULTURAL NOTE ***The Wealth of Nations***, a philosophical treatise (1776) by Scottish economist and philosopher Adam Smith. One of the earliest and most comprehensive analyses of economic systems, it began as a study of the relationship between human nature and social evolution. Smith's assertion that the natural outcome of this evolution is an economy based on open markets and driven by competition inspired many modern-day laissez-faire capitalist philosophies.

wealth tax *n* a tax levied on financial assets above a fixed level

wealthy /wélthi/ (**-ier, -iest**) *adj* **1.** having a large amount of money or possessions **2.** enjoying an abundance or great quantity of something —**wealthily** *adv*

wean[1] /ween/ (**weans, weaning, weaned**) *v* **1.** *vti* STOP FEEDING BABY WITH MOTHER'S MILK to start feeding a baby or young animal food other than its mother's milk **2.** *vt* STOP SOMEBODY HAVING SOMETHING to cause somebody to go without something that has become a habit or that is much liked ○ *She had weaned herself away from watching all the soaps on TV.* **3.** *vt* ACCUSTOM SOMEBODY TO SOMETHING FROM CHILDHOOD to accustom somebody to something from an early age ○ *children weaned on computer games and videos* [Old English *wenian* 'accustom' < Germanic]

wean[2] /wayn, ween/ *n regional* a child, especially a young one [Late 17C. Contraction of *wee ane*; *ane* a dialect form of ONE]

weaner /weénər/ *n* **1.** a young animal that has recently been weaned, especially a pig **2.** somebody who weans animals, or something used in weaning animals

weanling /weénling/ *n* a child or young animal that has just been weaned ■ *adj* newly weaned ○ *a weanling lamb*

weapon /wéppən/ *n* **1.** DEVICE DESIGNED TO INJURE OR KILL a device designed to inflict injury or death on an opponent **2.** SOMETHING USED TO GAIN ADVANTAGE something used as a way of getting an advantage in a situation ○ *A teacher's best weapon can be humour.* **3.** ZOOL ANIMAL'S PROTECTIVE PART an animal part used for defence or attack, e.g. claws ■ *vt* (**-ons, -oning, -oned**) GIVE ARMS TO SOMEBODY to provide somebody with weapons [Old English *wǣpen* < Germanic] —**weaponed** *adj* —**weaponless** *adj*

weaponeer /wéppə neér/ *n* **1.** somebody who prepares a nuclear weapon for detonation **2.** somebody who designs nuclear weapons

weaponize /wéppə nīz/ (**-izes, -izing, -ized**), **weaponise** (**-ises, -ising, -ised**) *vt* to process chemical, nuclear, or biological material so that it can be deployed as a weapon or integrated into a weapon —**weaponization** /wéppənī záysh'n/ *n*

weapon of mass destruction *n* a weapon, usually nuclear, biological, or chemical, that causes overwhelming devastation and loss of life

weaponry /wéppənri/ *n* **1.** all the weapons possessed by a person, group, or nation **2.** techniques for producing weapons

weapons-grade *adj* describes plutonium, uranium, or other material in a form suitable for manufacturing weapons

weapons system, **weapon system** *n* a weapon consisting of two or more major components, e.g. a missile and its ground-based radar guidance

wear[1] /wair/ *v* (**wears, wearing, wore** /wawr/, **worn** /wawrn/) **1.** *vt* HAVE SOMETHING ON BODY to have something on all or part of the body as clothing, jewellery, protection, or for another purpose, e.g. to aid sight or hearing, either temporarily or habitually **2.** *vt Malaysia, Singapore* PUT SOMETHING ON to put on a piece of clothing **3.** *vt* DISPLAY FACIAL EXPRESSION to display, show, or present an expression or physical manifestation of an emotion on the face ○ *wearing a smile* **4.** *vti* DAMAGE SOMETHING BY USING OR RUBBING to damage or alter something by using or rubbing it, or be damaged or altered in this way ○ *The lettering had been worn away by years of use.* **5.** *vti* PRODUCE SOMETHING BY USING OR RUBBING to produce something, especially a hole, through continued use, pressure, or friction, or be produced in this way ○ *had worn a hole in his sweater* **6.** *vti* RUB OFF to rub something off or away, or be rubbed off or away **7.** *vti* TIRE OUT to tire somebody out, or become tired out **8.** *vi* MAINTAIN SAME CONDITION to last in the same, especially good condition with much use or through time ○ *The carpet's wearing well.* **9.** *vti* PASS SLOWLY to pass time slowly, or be passed slowly ○ *as the evening wore on* **10.** *vt* ACCEPT OR TOLERATE SOMETHING to accept or put up with something (*informal*) ○ *She'll never wear that idea.* **11.** *vt* NAUT FLY FLAG to fly a particular flag or colours as a ship's identification ■ *n* **1.** ACT OF WEARING the act of wearing something, or the condition of being worn **2.** DAMAGE FROM BEING USED damage or deterioration that results from being used **3.** ABILITY TO LAST the ability to last without deteriorating **4.** CLOTHING CLOTHING OF PARTICULAR KIND clothing, especially clothing of a particular kind (*often used in combination*) ○ *children's wear* [Old English *werian* < Germanic] —**wearer** *n* ◇ **the worse for wear 1.** in a poor condition because of much use **2.** looking or feeling unwell, especially because of being tired or of having drunk too much alcohol ◇ **wear thin 1.** to weaken or fail ○ *My patience is wearing rather thin.* **2.** to become unacceptable or implausible because of excessive use ○ *That excuse is beginning to wear a bit thin.* **3.** to become thinner or disappear because of abrasion or heavy use

SPELLCHECK See *ware*[1].

wear down *vti* **1.** to overcome or weaken somebody or something by a gradual process, or be overcome or weakened in this way **2.** to rub or use something so much that it becomes thinner or disappears, or be rubbed or used in this way

wear off *vi* to lose effectiveness or strength gradually

wear out *v* **1.** *vti* to use something heavily or for a

long time until it is no longer useful, or be used in this way **2.** *vt* to tire somebody out

wear² /wair/ (**wears, wearing, wore** /wawr/, **worn** /wawrn/) *vti* to bring a ship about by turning the stern to windward, or come about in this way [Early 17C. Origin ?]

Wear /weer/ river in County Durham, northern England. It flows past the city of Durham and empties into the North Sea at Sunderland. Length: 107 km/67 mi.

-wear *suffix* clothing of a particular kind or for a particular context or activity ○ *swimwear*

wearable /wáirəb'l/ *adj* suitable and in a condition to be worn ■ *n* COMPUT same as **wearable computer** (*often used in the plural*) —**wearability** /wáirə bílləti/ *n*

wearable computer *n* a battery-powered computer small enough to be worn on the body —**wearable computing** *n*

wear and tear /-táir/ *n* damage caused by using something over a period of time

weariful /wéereef'l/ *adj* **1.** tedious and causing annoyance or fatigue **2.** tired and weary

weariless /wéereeləss/ *adj* not feeling or showing tiredness

wearing /wáiring/ *adj* **1.** tiring or tedious ○ *found the long journey very wearing* **2.** made or designed to be worn ○ *wearing apparel* —**wearingly** *adv*

wearing course *n* the upper layer of an asphalt or bitumen carriageway

wearisome /wéerissəm/ *adj* physically or mentally tiring and tedious ○ *a wearisome task* —**wearisomely** *adv* —**wearisomeness** *n*

wearproof /wáir proof/ *adj* able to withstand ordinary wear or use

weary /wéeri/ *adj* (**-rier, -riest**) **1.** TIRED tired, especially in having run out of strength, patience, or endurance **2.** TIRING tiring or exhausting **3.** SHOWING TIREDNESS showing or characterized by tiredness ■ *vti* (**-ries, -rying, -ried**) BECOME OR MAKE SOMEBODY TIRED to become tired or impatient, or make somebody do this [Old English *wērig* < Germanic] —**wearily** *adv* —**weariness** *n* —**wearying** *adj* —**wearyingly** *adv*

weasel

weasel /wéez'l/ *n* (*plural* **-sels** or same) **1.** SMALL ANIMAL WITH LONG BODY a small carnivorous animal with a long body and tail, short legs, and brown fur that in northern species may turn white in winter. Genus: *Mustela*. **2.** SOMEBODY SLY a sly or underhand person (*informal insult*) ■ *vi* (**-sels, -selling, -selled**) *N Am* BE EVASIVE to be evasive or try to mislead [Old English *wesule* < Germanic] —**weaselly** *adj*

weasel out *vi* to try to get out of an obligation or commitment, especially in a cowardly way (*informal*)

weasel words *npl* deliberately misleading or ambiguous language (*informal*) —**weasel-worded** *adj*

weather /wéthər/ *n* **1.** STATE OF ATMOSPHERE the state of the atmosphere with regard to temperature, cloudiness, rainfall, wind, and other meteorological conditions **2.** BAD WEATHER adverse weather, e.g. a storm, or the effects of this ○ *protection from the weather* ■ *adj* **1.** METEOROL USED IN WEATHER FORECASTING relating to or used in weather forecasting **2.** NAUT WINDWARD towards the wind ■ *v* (**-ers, -ering, -ered**) **1.** *vti* EXPOSE SOMETHING TO WEATHER to expose something to the weather, or be exposed to it **2.** *vti* CHANGE BECAUSE OF EXPOSURE TO WEATHER to change colour or become worn because of prolonged exposure to the weather, or make something do this **3.** *vi* ENDURE EFFECTS OF WEATHER to endure the damaging effects of the weather **4.** *vt*

○	Clear sky (night)		Sleet shower (night)
	Sunny		Sleet shower (day)
	Partly cloudy (night)		Sleet
	Sunny intervals		Hail shower (night)
	Dust		Hail shower (day)
	Mist		Hail
	Fog		
	Medium-level cloud		Light snow shower (night)
	Low-level cloud		Light snow shower (day)
	Light rain shower (night)		Heavy snow shower (night)
	Light rain shower (day)		Heavy snow shower (day)
	Drizzle		Heavy snow
	Light rain		Thundery shower (night)
	Heavy rain shower (night)		Thundery shower (day)
	Heavy rain shower (day)		Thunderstorm
	Heavy rain		Tropical storm

© Crown copyright

weather symbols

SURVIVE CRISIS to come safely through a crisis or difficult time **5.** *vt* NAUT SAIL WINDWARD OF SOMETHING to sail on the windward side of something **6.** *vt* CONSTR SLANT SOMETHING TO KEEP OFF RAIN to give a slope to something such as a roof to keep off rain [Old English *weder* < Indo-European, 'to blow'] —**weatherer** *n* ◇ **make heavy weather of something** to make a task that is fairly easy to do seem more difficult than it is ◇ **under the weather** slightly unwell

---

SPELLCHECK **weather, wether,** or **whether**? Do not confuse the spelling of *weather, wether,* and *whether,* which sound similar. *Weather* is a noun referring to meteorological conditions such as rain, sunshine, wind, or clouds (as in *stormy weather, the weather forecast*) or a verb meaning 'expose something to the weather' or 'come safely through a difficult time' (as in *weathered timber, weather the storm*). The word **wether,** which is not frequently encountered in general usage, denotes a castrated sheep or goat. *Whether* introduces an alternative or indirect question: *whether you want to or not; Ask her whether she wants some coffee.*

---

weather balloon *n* a balloon used to carry meteorological instruments

weather-beaten *adj* damaged, worn, or marked by exposure to the weather ○ *a weather-beaten face*

weatherboard /wéthər bawrd/ *n* **1.** BOARD ON BOTTOM OF DOOR a sloping piece of wood fitted to the bottom of a door to allow rain to run off **2.** GROOVED BOARD FOR CLADDING a grooved piece of timber used as part of a series of overlapping horizontal pieces forming cladding for walls or roofs **3.** WINDWARD SIDE the windward side of a ship **4.** ANZ BUILDINGS same as **weatherboard house** ■ *vt* (**-boards, -boarding, -boarded**) COVER SOMETHING WITH WEATHERBOARDS to fit a building with weatherboards

weatherboard house *n* ANZ a house clad with weatherboarding in horizontal overlapping planks of wood

weatherboarding /wéthər bawrding/ *n* weatherboards collectively

weatherbound /wéthər bownd/ *adj* delayed or kept from functioning by bad weather ○ *a weatherbound plane*

weather bureau *n* ANZ, US METEOROL same as **weather centre**

weathercast /wéthər kaast/ *n* US METEOROL same as **weather forecast** [Mid-19C. Contraction of WEATHER FORECAST]

weather centre *n* UK, Can an agency that collects meteorological information and provides weather forecasts. ANZ, US term **weather bureau**

weather chart *n* METEOROL same as **weather map**

---

weathercock /wéthər kòk/ *n* **1.** WEATHER VANE a weather vane shaped like a farmyard cock **2.** SOMEBODY FICKLE somebody who changes opinion or allegiance frequently ■ *vi* (**-cocks, -cocking, -cocked**) TURN IN DIRECTION OF WIND to tend to turn in the direction of the wind (*refers to aircraft*)

weather deck *n* US an open deck on a ship

weathered /wéthərd/ *adj* **1.** WORN BY EXPOSURE TO WEATHER worn, damaged, or seasoned by exposure to the weather **2.** GIVEN WEATHERED APPEARANCE given an artificial appearance of having been exposed to weather **3.** GEOL ERODED BY WEATHER describes rocks that have been eroded or changed by the action of the weather **4.** CONSTR WITH SLOPING SURFACE having a sloping surface so that rain can run off ○ *a weathered roof*

weather eye *n* **1.** the eye of somebody trained to watch for changes in the weather **2.** alertness or watchfulness, especially an alertness to change (*informal*) ◇ **keep a weather eye open, keep a weather eye on something** to be alert and watchful for any change or development in something

weather forecast *n* a radio or television broadcast announcing weather conditions —**weather forecaster** *n* —**weather forecasting** *n*

weatherglass /wéthər glaass/ *n* **1.** an instrument used to indicate changes in atmospheric conditions, e.g. a barometer **2.** ANZ, N Am METEOROL same as **storm glass**

weathering /wéthəring/ *n* **1.** the effect of prolonged exposure to the weather on, e.g. a building **2.** the disintegration and decomposition of rocks and minerals by natural processes such as the action of frost or percolating ground water

weatherly /wéthərli/ *adj* capable of sailing close to the wind

weatherman /wéthər man/ (*plural* **-men** /-men/) *n* a man who works as a professional weather forecaster

weather map *n* a map or chart showing the meteorological conditions over a large area

weatherperson /wéthər purss'n/ (*plural* **-persons** or **-people** /-peep'l/) *n* somebody who works as a professional weather forecaster

weatherproof /wéthər proof/ *adj* able to withstand exposure to rain or bad weather ■ *vt* (**-proofs, -proofing, -proofed**) to make something able to withstand exposure to rain or bad weather

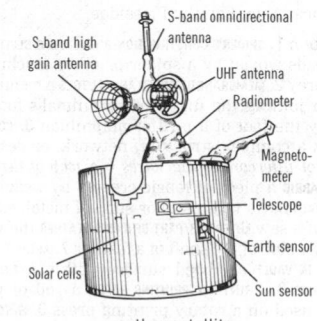

weather satellite

weather satellite *n* a satellite that records cloud distribution and temperature to help in predicting weather patterns

weather ship *n* a ship that collects meteorological information

weather station *n* an observation post where meteorological conditions are observed and recorded

weather strip *n* a thin piece of material fitted around a door or window to stop wind, rain, and cold from coming through

weatherstrip /wéthər strip/ (**-strips, -stripping, -stripped**) *vt* to put a weather strip around a door or window

weather stripping *n* CONSTR same as **weather strip**

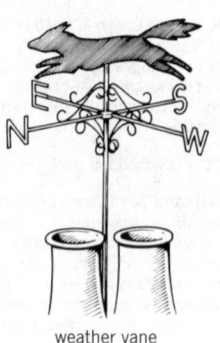

weather vane

weather vane *n* a device, usually mounted on a roof, that turns to point in the direction that the wind is blowing

weather window *n* a period of time in which weather conditions are suitable for an activity

weather-wise *adj* **1.** good at predicting what the weather will be **2.** good at predicting what public opinion will be

weatherwoman /wéthər woomən/ (*plural* **-women** /-wimin/) *n* a woman who works as a professional weather forecaster

weatherworn /wéthər wawrn/ *adj* worn or damaged by exposure to the weather

weave[1] /weev/ *v* (**weaves, weaving, wove** /wōv/ or **weaved, woven** /wṓv'n/ or **weaved**) **1.** *vti* MAKE CLOTH to make cloth by interlacing threads vertically and horizontally, especially on a loom **2.** *vt* MAKE SOMETHING BY INTERLACING STRANDS to make something by interlacing strands or strips of any material **3.** *vti* ZOOL SPIN WEB to spin something such as a spider's web **4.** *vt* CONSTRUCT STORY to construct something such as a story by combining separate parts **5.** *vt* INTRODUCE PARTS INTO SOMETHING LARGER to introduce separate parts into something larger ○ *weaving new characters into the plot* ■ *n* WAY IN WHICH SOMETHING IS WOVEN the way in which something is woven and the pattern formed by it ○ *a fabric with an open weave* [Old English *wefan* < Germanic] ◇ **get weaving** to hurry and start doing something (*dated informal; often used as a command*)

weave[2] /weev/ (**weaves, weaving, weaved**) *vi* to move forwards on a zigzag course [Late 16C. Origin ?]

weaver /weevər/ *n* **1.** somebody who weaves, especially professionally **2.** BIRDS same as **weaverbird**

weaverbird /weevər burd/, **weaver finch** *n* a gregarious finch known for its communal woven nest. Native to: Africa, Asia. Family: Ploceidae.

web /web/ *n* **1.** SPIDER'S CONSTRUCTION a delicate structure of threads woven by a spider or other arachnid to catch prey **2.** MEMBRANE BETWEEN ANIMAL TOES a membrane of skin joining the digits of an animal's foot, especially the foot of a bird or amphibian **3.** COMPLEX NETWORK a complex structure, network, or design ○ *a web of interconnecting wires* ○ *a web of deceit* **4.** WOVEN FABRIC a piece of fabric created by weaving **5.** THIN METAL PLATE a thin plate or strip of metal, e.g. the blade of a saw **6.** BIRDS PART OF BIRD'S FEATHER the vanes on either side of the shaft of a feather **7.** ARCHIT RIBBED SURFACE IN VAULT a ribbed surface within a vaulted structure **8.** PRINTING PRINTING PAPER a roll of paper that is used on a rotary printing press **9.** *also* **Web** ONLINE same as **World Wide Web** (*informal*) ■ *vi* (**webs, webbing, webbed**) FORM WEB to form or produce a web [Old English, < Indo-European, 'weave']

Webb /web/, **Sir Aston** (1849–1930) British architect. He was the designer of Admiralty Arch and the eastern facade of Buckingham Palace in London.

webbed /webd/ *adj* **1.** JOINED BY SKIN MEMBRANE joined by a membrane or membranes of skin ○ *webbed feet* **2.** HAVING WEB formed of, covered by, or connected with a web **3.** DESIGNED FOR INTERNET USE optimized for use on the Internet, e.g. by minimizing the loading time of webpages

webbing /wébbing/ *n* **1.** STRONG COARSE FABRIC a strong coarse fabric. Use: belts, harnesses, upholstery support. **2.** SKIN OF FOOT the membrane of skin joining the digits of an animal's foot, especially the foot of a bird or amphibian **3.** SOMETHING FORMING WEB something that forms a web

web browser *n* a program used for displaying and viewing pages on the World Wide Web

web bug *n* a minute inclusion in a webpage or e-mail message designed to record information about the person reading it

Webby /wébbi/ (*plural* **-bys**) *n* an annual award made by the International Academy of Digital Arts and Sciences for the best Internet website (*informal*)

webcam /wéb kam/, **Webcam** *n* a video camera recording pictures that are broadcast live on the Internet [Late 20C. < WEB + CAMERA]

webcast /wéb kaast/, **Webcast** *n* a broadcast made on the World Wide Web ○ '...*they spent $5 million promoting the live Webcast of their Spring Fashion Show ...*' (*The New York Times*; April 1999) [Late 20C. < WEB + BROADCAST]

webcasting /wéb kaasting/, **Webcasting** *n* the use of the World Wide Web as a medium for broadcasting information [Late 20C. < WEB + BROADCASTING]

web crawler *n* a program used to search through pages on the World Wide Web for documents containing a specific word, phrase, or topic

web designer *n* somebody who designs websites

web-enable *vt* to make an electronic device or a software application capable of accessing the Internet

weber /váybər/ *n* the SI unit of magnetic flux, equal to 1 joule per ampere or 1 volt-second. Symbol **Wb** [Late 19C. After Wilhelm Eduard *Weber* (1804–91), German physicist]

Weber /váybər/, **Carl Maria von** (1786–1826) German composer. His orchestral works and operas were important for the growth of early romanticism. Full name **Weber, Carl Maria Friedrich Ernst von**

Weber, Max (1864–1920) German economist and sociologist. He was a major influence in modern sociological theory and the author of *The Protestant Ethic and the Spirit of Capitalism* (1904–05).

Webern /váybərn/, **Anton** (1883–1945) Austrian composer. He extended the 12-tone system of Arnold Schoenberg and influenced a generation of post-World War II composers. Full name **Webern, Anton Friedrich Wilhelm von**

web farm *n* E-COMMERCE same as **web server farm**

web folio *n* a collection of webpages with an underlying defining theme, e.g. the pages of an electronic book or the electronic images of an artist's portfolio

webfoot /wéb foot/ (*plural* **-feet** /-feet/) *n* **1.** a foot that has the toes joined by a membrane of skin **2.** an animal with webbed feet —**web-footed** /wéb foottid/ *adj*

webhead /wéb hed/, **Webhead** *n* a frequent user of the World Wide Web (*slang*)

web hosting *n* the business of supplying server space for storage of websites on the Internet, and sometimes the provision of ancillary services such as website creation

webisode /wébbi sōd/, **Webisode** *n* an episode, preview, or promotion of a film, television programme, or music video on a website (*slang*) [Late 20C. Blend of WEB + EPISODE]

webliography /wébbli óggrəfi/ (*plural* **-phies**), **Webliography** *n* **1.** a list of documents available on the World Wide Web **2.** a list or catalogue of all the web-based material relating to a specific subject [Late 20C. Blend of WEB + BIBLIOGRAPHY]

weblish /wébblish/, **Weblish** *n* the form of English used globally online, with characteristic features such as the omission of apostrophes and capital letters, the use of abbreviations, and the rapid absorption of new words [Late 20C. Blend of WEB + ENGLISH]

weblog /wéb log/, **Web log** *n* a frequently updated personal journal chronicling links at a website, intended for public viewing

webmaster /wéb maastər/, **Webmaster** *n* somebody who creates, organizes, or updates information on a website

webmeister /wéb mīstər/, **Webmeister** *n* ONLINE same as **webmaster** (*informal*)

web member *n* a brace that links the top and bottom flanges of a lattice girder or truss

web offset *n* offset printing carried out on a web press

webpage /wéb payj/, **Web page** *n* a computer file, encoded in HyperText Markup Language (**HTML**) and containing text, graphics files, and sound files, that is accessible through the World Wide Web

webphone /wéb fōn/, **Webphone** *n* a phone that uses the Internet to make connections and carry voice messages

web press *n* a printing press that is fed paper from a large roll

web ring *n* a series of interlinked websites that are visited one after the other until the first is reached again

web server *n* a program that serves up webpages when requested by a client, e.g. a web browser

web server farm *n* a business with a group of interconnected servers engaged in web hosting

website /wéb sīt/, **Web site** *n* a computer program that runs a web server that provides access to a group of related webpages

web spinner *n* an insect that spins a web, especially one with glands that produce silk for constructing a web. Order: Embioptera.

Webster /wébstər/, **John** (1578?–1632?) English playwright. His plays *The White Devil* (1612?) and *The Duchess of Malfi* (1614?) are outstanding examples of the revenge tragedy.

'We think caged birds sing, when indeed they cry.'
[John Webster, *The White Devil*; 1612]

Webster, Noah (1758–1843) US lexicographer. He is known for institutionalizing the differences between American and English grammar, pronunciation, and spelling in his *American Dictionary of the English Language* (1828).

'This Dictionary, like all others of the kind, must be left, in some degree, imperfect; for what individual is competent to trace the source, and define in all their various applications, popular, scientific, and technical, seventy or eighty thousand words!'
[Noah Webster. Author's Preface, *An American Dictionary of the English Language*; 1828]

web storefront *n* US a virtual shop on the Internet providing information about the retailer, a product catalogue, and secure payment facilities

web-toed /-tōd/ *adj* having a membrane of skin tissue between the toes

webwheel /wéb weel/ *n* a wheel with no spokes but a web or plate instead, or a wheel with the centre formed from one piece

webworm /wéb wurm/ (*plural* **-worms** or *same*) *n* N Am a caterpillar, especially a tiger moth caterpillar, that spins a web in which it feeds or rests

webzine /wéb zeen/, **Webzine** *n* ONLINE same as **e-zine**

wed /wed/ (**weds, wedding, wedded** or **wed**) *v* **1.** *vt* MARRY SOMEBODY to marry somebody (*formal or literary*) ○ *wanted to wed a princess* **2.** *vi* GET MARRIED to become united in marriage ○ *They wed in April.* **3.** *vt* JOIN COUPLE IN MARRIAGE to join two people in marriage **4.** *vt* UNITE THINGS to bring two things together or regard them as linked ○ *The two concepts had become wedded in his mind.* [Old English *weddian* < Indo-European, 'pledge']

we'd /weed/ *contr* **1.** we had **2.** we would

Wed. *abbr* Wednesday

wedded /wéddid/ *adj* **1.** MARRIED united in marriage **2.** OF MARRIAGE relating to marriage ○ *wedded bliss* **3.** COMMITTED TO SOMETHING strongly attached or committed to something ○ *wedded to the idea of reform*

Weddell Sea /wédd'l-/ arm of the South Atlantic Ocean, south of Cape Horn and the Falkland Islands

wedding /wédding/ *n* **1.** MARRIAGE CEREMONY a ceremony in which two people get married (*often used before a noun*) ○ *Their rabbi will perform the wedding service.* **2.** ACT OF MARRYING the act or an instance of marrying somebody (*often used before a noun*) ○ *a wedding veil* **3.** WEDDING ANNIVERSARY the anniversary of a marriage (*used in combination*) ○ *a silver wedding* **4.** UNITING OF TWO THINGS the bringing together of two things ○ *the wedding of form and function*

wedding band *n* N Am JEWELLERY same as **wedding ring**

wedding breakfast *n* a celebratory meal served after a wedding ceremony

wedding cake *n* a cake, often a fruit cake, decorated with icing, usually white, and arranged in tiers, served at a wedding reception

wedding-cake *adj* characterized by an extremely ornate style of architecture

wedding dress *n* a dress worn by a bride at her wedding

wedding march *n* a piece of music in march time played during a marriage ceremony, usually when the bride enters the church

wedding ring *n* a ring, usually a gold band, worn on the third finger of the left hand by somebody who is married

Wedekind /váydə kint/, **Frank** (1864–1918) German playwright. His work, often dealing with sexual themes, anticipates expressionism and the theatre of the absurd. Full name **Wedekind, Benjamin Franklin**

~~**Wedensday**~~ incorrect spelling of **Wednesday**

wedge

wedge /wej/ *n* **1.** TAPERING BLOCK a solid block that is thick at one end and thin at the other, used to secure or separate two objects **2.** WEDGE-SHAPED OBJECT an object that has a wedge shape ○ *a wedge of cake* **3.** SOMETHING ACTING AS WEDGE something that acts as a wedge, e.g. by causing division ○ *drove a wedge between the two families* **4.** CLOTHING same as **wedge heel 5.** GOLF GOLF CLUB a golf club with a markedly slanted head, used to hit the ball along a high arcing trajectory **6.** STROKE IN CUNEIFORM WRITING a wedge-shaped stroke used in cuneiform writing ■ *v* (**wedges, wedging, wedged**) **1.** *vt* SECURE SOMETHING WITH WEDGE to secure or tighten something with a wedge **2.** *vti* SQUEEZE to squeeze or pack something into a small space, or be squeezed or packed in this way ○ *Hundreds of people were wedged into the room.* **3.** *vt* FORCE SOMETHING APART WITH WEDGE to force something apart or open with a wedge [Old English *wecg* < Germanic, probably < Indo-European, 'ploughshare, wedge'] —**wedgy** *adj*

wedge heel *n* **1.** a shoe heel shaped like a wedge, forming a solid extension of the sole so that there is no gap under the instep **2.** a shoe with a wedge heel

wedge-tailed eagle *n* a large eagle with dark brown or black plumage and tail feathers in the form of a wedge. Native to: Australia. Latin name: *Aquila audax.*

wedgie /wéjji/, **wedgy** (*plural* -**gies**) *n* **1.** a wedge heel (*informal*) **2.** an uncomfortable intrusion of clothing, usually underpants, up into the crack between the buttocks (*slang*)

Wedgwood /wéj wood/, **Josiah** (1730–95) British potter. He developed a distinctive pottery inspired by ancient Greek ware, and established a highly successful pottery business.

Wedgwood blue *adj* pale grey-blue in colour [Early 20C. After Josiah WEDGWOOD] —**Wedgwood blue** *n*

wedgy *n Aus* another spelling of **wedgie**

wedlock /wéd lok/ *n* the state of being married [12C. < *wedlac* 'action of pledging' < *wed* 'pledge', after LOCK[1]] ◊ **born** or **conceived out of wedlock** born to or conceived by parents who are not married (*formal*)

Wednesday /wénz day, -di/ *n* the third day of the traditional working week, coming after Tuesday and before Thursday [Old English *wōdnesdæg* 'Woden's day' < WODEN + *dæg* 'day', translation of Latin *Mercurii dies* 'Mercury's day']

Wednesdays /wénz dayz, -diz/ *adv* every Wednesday ○ *Wednesdays I leave a little early.*

~~**Wednsday**~~ incorrect spelling of **Wednesday**

wee[1] /wee/ *adj* very small ■ *n Scotland* a brief period of time ○ *bide a wee* [Old English *wēg* 'weight']

wee[2] /wee/ (*informal or baby talk*) *n* **1.** same as **urine 2.** an act or instance of urinating ■ *vi* (**wees, weeing, weed**) same as **urinate** [Mid-20C. An imitation of the sound of urinating]

weed[1] /weed/ *n* **1.** UNWANTED PLANT a plant, especially a wild plant, growing where it is not wanted **2.** UNWANTED PLANTS weeds in general (*often used before a noun*) ○ *weed control* **3.** PLANT GROWING IN WATER a plant that grows in water, especially seaweed **4.** TOBACCO tobacco or cigarettes (*slang*) **5.** MARIJUANA marijuana for smoking as a drug (*slang*) **6.** WEAK PERSON a weak or strikingly thin person (*informal*) **7.** INFERIOR ANIMAL an inferior animal, especially a horse that cannot be bred ■ *v* (**weeds, weeding, weeded**) **1.** *vt* REMOVE WEEDS FROM GROUND to clear an area of weeds ○ *to weed the garden* **2.** *vi* PULL UP WEEDS to pull up and remove weeds ○ *spent several hours weeding* [Old English *wēod* < Germanic] —**weeder** *n*

weed out *vt* to separate out or remove somebody or something undesirable or unwanted ○ *a test to weed out unsuitable candidates*

weed[2] /weed/ *n* something worn as a sign of mourning, especially a black band or sleeve or hat ■ **weeds** *npl* the black clothes once traditionally worn by widows (*archaic or literary*) [Old English *wǣd* < Germanic, 'garment']

weedkiller /wéed kilər/ *n* a chemical that kills plants by attacking the root, leaf, or vascular system

weedy /wéedi/ (-**ier**, -**iest**) *adj* **1.** FULL OF WEEDS filled with or containing many weeds ○ *a weedy patch of ground* **2.** LIKE WEED resembling or having the characteristics of a weed ○ *weedy plants* **3.** THIN considered strikingly thin and weak-looking **4.** WEAK physically or morally weak (*informal*) —**weedily** *adv* —**weediness** *n*

WEEE /wee/, **WEE** *n* an EC directive governing the disposal of electrical and electronic equipment such as household appliances, tools, and computers. Full form **waste electric and electronic equipment**

Wee Free *n Scotland* a member of the Free Kirk, a body that broke away from the Free Church of Scotland in 1900 (*informal; sometimes offensive*) [Early 20C. Because it was a minority body of the Free Church of Scotland]

wee hours *npl* same as **wee small hours**

week /week/ *n* **1.** 7-DAY PERIOD a period of seven consecutive days **2.** CALENDAR WEEK a period of seven days beginning from a specific day, usually Sunday ○ *the middle of the week* **3.** WORKING WEEK the days of the week or the time every week during which somebody usually works ○ *goes to bed early during the week* **4.** SPECIAL WEEK a week containing a particular holiday or dedicated to a particular cause ○ *Easter week* ■ *adv* ONE WEEK AFTER PARTICULAR DAY one week after or before a particular day ○ *arranged to meet on Thursday week* [Old English *wice* < Germanic, 'series, succession']

SPELLCHECK See **weak**.

weekday /wéek day/ *n* a day of the week other than Sunday, or, sometimes, other than Saturday or Sunday ○ *only open on weekdays*

weekend /wéek énd/ *n* the end of the week, from Friday evening until Sunday evening ■ *vi* (-**ends**, -**ending**, -**ended**) to spend a weekend or weekends in a particular place

weekend bag *n* a bag or small suitcase used to carry clothes and other items needed for a short trip or holiday

weekend break *n* a short holiday away from home lasting for a weekend

weekender /wéek éndər/ *n* **1.** somebody spending a weekend somewhere, especially on a regular basis **2.** *Aus* a holiday house (*informal*)

weekends /wéek éndz/ *adv* at or during the weekend (*informal*)

weeklong /wéek lóng/ *adj* lasting for a whole week

weekly /wéekli/ *adj* **1.** HAPPENING ONCE EACH WEEK happening, produced, or done once a week or every week **2.** CALCULATED BY WEEK worked out by the week ○ *weekly pay* ■ *adv* **1.** ONCE EACH WEEK once each week ○ *does the shopping weekly* **2.** EVERY WEEK every single

week **3.** BY WEEK by the week ○ *paid weekly* ■ *n* (*plural* -**lies**) SOMETHING PUBLISHED ONCE EACH WEEK a newspaper or magazine published once a week

weeknight /wéek nīt/ *n* the evening or night of a weekday ○ *I'm not letting you go out on a weeknight.*

ween /ween/ (**weens, weening, weened**) *vti* to think, believe, or suppose something (*archaic*) [Old English *wēnan* < Indo-European, 'to desire']

weenie /wéeni/ *n N Am* **1.** an offensive term for somebody regarded as weak or insignificant (*slang insult*) **2.** an offensive term for a penis (*slang*)

weeny /wéeni/ (-**nier**, -**niest**), **weensy** /wéenzi/ (-**sier**, -**siest**) *adj* very small (*informal*) [Late 18C. < WEE[1] after *tiny*]

weeny-bopper *n* a child, especially a young girl, who is keen on pop music and the latest fashions (*informal*) [After TEENYBOPPER]

weep /weep/ *v* (**weeps, weeping, wept** /wept/) **1.** *vti* CRY to shed tears, especially as a sign of sorrow for something or somebody ○ *They walked behind the coffin, weeping silently.* ○ *It's no use weeping over him, that won't bring him back.* ○ *weep bitter tears* **2.** *vt* EXPRESS SOMETHING WHILE WEEPING to say something while crying or express something by crying tears **3.** *vti* LEAK FLUID to leak, drip, or ooze drops of liquid ○ *The area around the wound was inflamed and weeping.* **4.** *vt* MOURN SOMEBODY to lament or cry tears for somebody or something (*literary*) ■ *n* SPELL OF CRYING a period of time spent crying ○ *When they'd had a little weep, they both felt better.* [Old English *wēpan* < Germanic]

weeper /wéepər/ *n* **1.** SOMEBODY WHO WEEPS somebody who weeps **2.** SIGN OF MOURNING something that is worn as a sign of mourning, e.g. a black armband or a veil **3.** CONSTR HOLE FOR WATER TO ESCAPE a hole in a wall or foundation that allows accumulated water to escape **4.** *US* CINEMA, LITERAT same as **weepie** (*informal*) ■ **weepers** *npl* SIDEBURNS long sideburns (*informal*)

weepie /wéepi/, **weepy** (*plural* -**ies**) *n* a film, play, or book that tends to move people to tears, especially one that is blatantly sentimental in tone (*informal*)

weeping /wéeping/ *adj* **1.** WITH DROOPING BRANCHES having slender drooping branches **2.** CRYING shedding tears **3.** LEAKING FLUID leaking, dripping, or oozing drops of liquid —**weepingly** *adv*

weeping fig, **weeping ivy** *n* a small fig tree with glossy leaves, often grown as a houseplant. Latin name: *Ficus benjamina.*

weeping willow

weeping willow *n* a popular ornamental willow tree with long drooping branches and narrow leaves. Native to: China. Latin name: *Salix babylonica.*

weepy /wéepi/ (*informal*) *adj* (-**ier**, -**iest**) **1.** weeping frequently, or feeling sad and liable to weep **2.** tending to make people cry ■ *n* (*plural* -**ies**) CINEMA, THEATRE another spelling of **weepie** —**weepily** *adv* —**weepiness** *n*

wee small hours *npl* the early hours of the morning, especially those just after midnight

weever /wéevər/, **weeverfish** /wéevər fish/ (*plural* -**fishes** or *same*) *n* a small sea fish with a venomous spine on each gill cover and several on its back. Family: Trachinidae. [Early 17C. Probably < Old N French *wivre* (see WYVERN)]

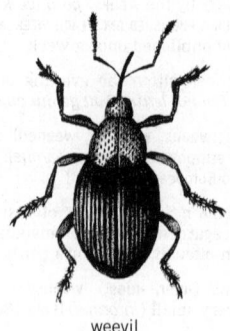

weevil

weevil /weev'l/ n 1. DESTRUCTIVE BEETLE WITH SNOUT a member of a family of beetles that have an elongated downward-curving snout (**rostrum**). Many weevils are pests, destroying plants and grain. Family: Curculionidae. 2. PEA OR BEAN PEST a beetle whose larvae live in the seeds of peas and beans. Family: Bruchidae or Lariidae. 3. BEETLE RESEMBLING WEEVIL a beetle similar to a weevil, especially in being likely to eat stored grain. Family: Rhynchophora. [Old English *wifel* 'beetle' < Indo-European, 'move quickly'] —**weevily** *adj*

wee-wee (*informal or baby talk*) n 1. an act or instance of urinating 2. same as **urine** ■ *vi* (**wee-wees, wee-weeing, wee-weed**) same as **urinate** [Doubling of WEE²]

weft /weft/ n 1. HORIZONTAL THREADS the horizontal threads of a woven fabric or a tapestry 2. YARN FOR WEFT yarn used for the weft 3. SOMETHING WOVEN a piece of woven fabric [Old English, < Indo-European, 'weave']

Wegener /váygənər/, **Alfred** (1880–1930) German meteorologist. His *Origin of Continents and Oceans* (1915) introduced the theory of continental drift.

Wehrmacht /váir maakht, -maakt/ n the German armed forces, especially the army between 1935 and 1945 [Mid-20C. < German, 'defence force']

weigela /wī jeelə, wi geelə/ n a deciduous bush. Flowers: bell-shaped, pink, white, or red. Native to: Asia. Genus: *Weigela*. [Mid-19C. < modern Latin *Weigela*, after Christian E. *Weigel* (1748–1831), German physician]

weigh /way/ (**weighs, weighing, weighed**) v 1. *vt* FIND WEIGHT OF SOMETHING to find out the weight of somebody or something ○ *He weighed himself regularly.* 2. *vi* BE PARTICULAR WEIGHT to be of a particular weight ○ *The baby weighed seven pounds three ounces at birth.* 3. *vt* MEASURE BY WEIGHT to measure or distribute something by weight ○ *weighed out a kilo of onions* 4. *vt* EVALUATE to consider or evaluate something, especially so as to be able to come to a decision or choice ○ *had to weigh all possible options* 5. *vi* HAVE IMPORTANCE to have importance or be influential ○ *Her advice weighs heavily with him.* 6. *vt* GUESS WEIGHT OF to hold something in the hand in order to assess its weight 7. *vi* BE BURDENSOME to be burdensome, oppressive, or worrying to somebody ○ *The problem weighed heavily on my mind.* 8. *vt* NAUT RAISE ANCHOR to raise the anchor of a vessel [Old English *wegan* 'weigh, carry' < Indo-European, 'carry'] —**weighable** *adj* —**weigher** *n*

SPELLCHECK See *way*.

weigh against *vt* 1. to assess the relative importance of one thing in relation to another ○ *had to weigh the added costs against the gain in speed* 2. to have a negative part in influencing a decision with regard to somebody or something ○ *Her lack of experience weighed against her in the final selection.* **weigh down** *vt* 1. to be oppressive or burdensome to somebody ○ *weighed down by grief* ○ *weighed down with extra paperwork* 2. to press or pull somebody or something down by being heavy ○ *trees weighed down with fruit* **weigh in** *vi* 1. BE WEIGHED FOR RACE OR CONTEST to be weighed before or after a boxing match, a horse race, or a similar contest 2. HAVE BAGGAGE WEIGHED to have baggage weighed before a flight 3. CONTRIBUTE COMMENT to contribute or produce something such as an argument or comment, especially in an assertive way (*informal*) ○ *Then Sarah weighed in with some candid observations on Melanie's dress sense.* **weigh up** *vt* 1. to consider something carefully, especially so as to come to a decision or choice ○

weighing up the pros and cons 2. to judge the qualities or character of somebody or something (*informal*) ○ *The two boys weighed each other up.*

weighbridge /wáy brij/ n a weighing machine for vehicles, consisting of a metal plate set into a road

weigh-in /wáy in/ n the weighing of the competitors before or after a boxing match or a race

weight /wayt/ n 1. HEAVINESS the quality of heaviness in things, determined by their mass or quantity of matter as acted on by the force of gravity, that counteracts efforts to lift or move them ○ *Just feel the weight of it!* 2. AMOUNT SOMEBODY OR SOMETHING WEIGHS the heaviness of a particular object or person, especially as measured by a particular system of weight ○ *She'll have to watch her weight.* 3. SYSTEM FOR MEASURING HEAVINESS a system of standard measures of weight ○ *troy weight* 4. UNIT OF WEIGHT a unit used as a measure of weight 5. WEIGHTED COUNTER USED ON SCALES an object of known weight, usually one of a set, placed on one side of a pair of scales to counterbalance another object that is being weighed 6. HEAVY OBJECT a heavy object used to hold something down 7. OBJECT USED IN WEIGHTLIFTING a heavy object, often a bar with a heavy metal disc at each end, used in weightlifting or for exercise (*often used in the plural*) 8. HEAVY LOAD a heavy load to carry ○ *had to put the trunk down since it was too heavy a weight* 9. MENTAL BURDEN a mental or moral burden or load ○ *That's a weight off my mind.* 10. IMPORTANCE importance, or power to influence or persuade ○ *a motion that did not carry much weight with the judge* 11. GREATER PART the preponderance or greater part of something ○ *the weight of exculpatory evidence* 12. PRINTING HEAVINESS OF TYPEFACE the heaviness or thickness of a typeface 13. TEXTILES THICKNESS OF CLOTH the heaviness or thickness of cloth (*often used in combination*) 14. PHYS FORCE CAUSED BY GRAVITY the vertical force experienced by a mass because of gravity. Symbol *W* ■ *vt* (**weights, weighting, weighted**) 1. MAKE SOMETHING HEAVIER to add weight or weights to something 2. KEEP SOMETHING IN PLACE WITH WEIGHTS to hold something in position by placing a heavy object on it ○ *weighted the papers down with an ashtray to stop them blowing away* 3. SLANT SOMETHING IN SOMEBODY'S FAVOUR to arrange something in such a way that it either favours or disadvantages a specific person or group (*often passive*) ○ *The criteria governing the choice of candidate were heavily weighted in her favour.* 4. GIVE ADDITIONAL IMPORTANCE TO SOMETHING to assign additional importance to something, e.g. a test or part of one 5. TEXTILES INCREASE DENSITY OF FABRIC to treat fabric so as to increase its density 6. HORSE-RACING ASSIGN HORSE HANDICAP WEIGHT to assign a handicap weight to a horse [Old English *wiht* < Indo-European] — **weighter** *n* ◇ **be worth its** *or* **your weight in gold** to be extremely valuable ◇ **gain** *or* **lose weight** ◇ **pull your weight** to do your fair share of work or take your fair share of responsibility ◇ **punch above your weight** to succeed at something that seems to others to be beyond your capabilities (*informal*) ◇ **throw your weight around** *or* **about** to be domineering (*informal*)

SPELLCHECK See *wait*.

weighted /wáytid/ *adj* adjusted by the addition of a statistical value

weighting /wáyting/ n additional pay given in special cases, e.g. to somebody who has to live in a place where the cost of living is higher ○ *The job carries an inner London weighting.*

weightless /wáytləss/ *adj* having no weight, especially by virtue of being in an atmosphere in which there is no gravitational pull —**weightlessly** *adv* —**weightlessness** *n*

weightlifting /wáyt lifting/ n the sport of lifting heavy weights, either for exercise or in competition —**weightlifter** *n*

weight training *n* physical training using weights to strengthen the muscles

weighty /wáyti/ (*-ier, -iest*) *adj* 1. HEAVY weighing a great deal 2. IMPORTANT of an important or serious nature ○ *discussing weighty matters* 3. INFLUENTIAL able to exert influence 4. OPPRESSIVE oppressive or burdensome ○ *a weighty responsibility* —**weightily** *adv* —**weightiness** *n*

Weil /vīl/, **Simone** (1909–43) French philosopher and mystic. Her major writings, reflecting her Christian mysticism, were published posthumously and include *Waiting for God* (1950).

'The word "revolution" is a word for which you kill, for which you die, for which you send the labouring masses to their death, but which does not possess any content.' [Simone Weil, 'Reflections Concerning the Causes of Liberty and Social Oppression', *Oppression and Liberty*; 1958]

~~weild~~ incorrect spelling of **wield**

Weill /vīl/, **Kurt** (1900–50) German-born US composer. His work, including *The Threepenny Opera* (1928) which he wrote with Bertolt Brecht, was banned by the Nazis. After settling in the United States (1935) he wrote successful Broadway musicals. Full name **Weill, Kurt Julian**

'Musical theater is the highest, the most expressive and the most imaginative form of theater...a composer who has a talent and a passion for the theater can express himself completely in this branch of musical creativeness.' [Kurt Weill. Quoted in *American Composers*, David Ewen; 1982]

Weil's disease /vīlz-/ n a severe form of leptospirosis, usually resulting from contact with the urine of infected animals such as rats. Symptoms include jaundice, anaemia, haemorrhaging, fever, and meningitis. [Late 19C. After H. Adolf *Weil* (1848–1916), German physician]

Weimar /vīm aar/ city in Thuringia State, east-central Germany, southwest of Leipzig. It was a major cultural centre in the 18th and 19th centuries. Population: 62,233 (1997).

Weimaraner

Weimaraner /vīmə raanər, wīmə-, -raánər/ n a large hunting dog with a short-haired silver-grey coat, belonging to a breed originating in Germany [Mid-20C. After WEIMAR]

Weimar Republic *n* the government of Germany between 1919 and 1933, so named because the National Assembly met in Weimar in 1919 to establish a new republic and draw up a constitution

Weiner /weénər/, **Lawrence** (*b.* 1942) US conceptual artist. He has been a central figure of conceptual art since the 1960s. Many of his installations consist solely of words in a nondescript lettering painted on walls.

weir /weer/ n 1. a dam built across a river to regulate the flow of water, divert it, or change its level 2. a fence placed in a stream to catch fish [Old English *wer* < Indo-European, 'cover']

Weir /weer/, **Peter** (*b.* 1944) Australian film director. After achieving international success with the Australian-made *Picnic at Hanging Rock* (1975), he established himself as a leading Hollywood director. Full name **Weir, Peter Lindsay**

weird /weerd/ *adj* 1. ODD strange or unusual 2. SUPERNATURAL belonging to or suggesting the supernatural 3. OF FATE relating to or influenced by fate (*archaic*) ■ *n* Scotland FATE fate or destiny (*archaic*) [Old English *wyrd* 'fate' < Indo-European, 'turn'] —**weirdly** *adv* —**weirdness** *n* ◇ **dree your own weird** Scotland to live your own life, accepting or making your own destiny

weirdie /weérdi/, **weirdy** (*plural* -ies) n an offensive term for somebody who is regarded as strange or unconventional (*slang*)

weirdo /weérdō/ (*plural* -os) n an offensive term for somebody who behaves in a way regarded as strange or unconventional, especially somebody whose sexual tastes or habits are regarded as unusual (*slang*)

weird sisters, Weird Sisters *npl* **1.** MYTHOL same as **Fates 2.** the three witches in Shakespeare's play *Macbeth* [*Weird* in the meaning of 'having the power to control fates']

weirdy *n* another spelling of **weirdie** (*slang offensive*)

Weismann /vīssmən/, **August** (1834–1914) German biologist. He was the first to propose that genetic variability results from the recombination of chromosomes during reproduction. Full name **Weissman, August Friedrich Leopold**

Weismannism /vīssmənizəm/ *n* the principle that the inherited characteristics of any organism are determined solely by material (**germplasm**) contained in the male and female sex cells from which the organism develops. This theory excludes any role for the body cells in inheritance and rules out the inheritance of characteristics acquired during an organism's lifetime. It remains a fundamental tenet of modern genetics. [Late 19C. After August WEISMANN]

Weizmann /vītsmən/, **Chaim** (1874–1952) Russian-born chemist and first president of Israel (1949–52). He helped to secure the Balfour Declaration (1917) which committed Britain to Zionism and was president of the World Zionist Organization (1921–29). Full name **Weizmann, Chaim Azriel**

weka /wáykə/ *n* a fast-running flightless bird of the rail family with mainly brown and black feathers. Native to: scrubland and forest margins of New Zealand. Latin name: *Gallirallus australis.* [Mid-19C. < Maori, an imitation of bird's call]

welch *vi* another spelling of **welsh** (*sometimes offensive*)

Welch /welch/, **Jack** (*b.* 1936) US business executive. He introduced new management techniques as chairman and chief executive officer of General Electric (1981–2001), and helped it to grow into the world's largest company. Full name **Welch, John Francis, Jr**

> 'People always overestimate how complex business is. This isn't rocket science; we've chosen one of the world's more simple professions.'
> [Jack Welch, *Harvard Business Review*, September-October 1989]

welcome /wélkəm/ *adj* **1.** ADMITTED GLADLY received, especially into somebody's home, or entertained gladly ○ *a welcome guest* ○ *She's no longer welcome in this house.* **2.** EAGERLY AND DELIGHTEDLY ACCEPTED accepted or anticipated with delight and eagerness, often because it answers a need ○ *It was a welcome break after two solid weeks of writing.* **3.** FREELY INVITED OR PERMITTED freely and willingly invited or permitted ○ *You're welcome to stay for dinner.* **4.** WITH NOTHING EXPECTED IN RETURN used to respond to expressions of thanks and indicate that something such as a courtesy, favour, or gift was gladly done or given ○ *'Thank you for giving me a lift.' 'You're very welcome, it was no trouble.'* ■ *n* **1.** GREETING a greeting or reception, especially a friendly or celebratory one, given to somebody who arrives or is being met ○ *gave a warm welcome to their guests* **2.** REACTION a positive response or reaction to something, or a response of the kind specified ○ *Local authorities have extended a cautious welcome to the new proposals.* ■ *vt* (**-comes, -coming, -comed**) **1.** RECEIVE SOMEBODY IN FRIENDLY WAY to greet, receive, or entertain somebody, especially in a friendly way ○ *There was nobody there to welcome us when we arrived.* **2.** ACCEPT SOMETHING WITH PLEASURE to accept or receive something with pleasure ○ *We welcome any feedback from our customers.* ■ *interj* USED AS GREETING used to express a friendly or courteous greeting to somebody who has just arrived or is a stranger [Old English *wilcuma* 'welcome guest' (influenced by WELL² and either Old Norse *velkominn* or Old French *bien venu*)] —**welcomely** *adv* —**welcomeness** *n* —**welcomer** *n* ◇ **be welcome to something** used to indicate that the speaker is happy for somebody to have something (*often used ironically*) ◇ **make somebody welcome** to show that you are pleased to see somebody or treat somebody hospitably ◇ **wear out** *or* **outstay** *or* **overstay your welcome** to stay longer than is polite or accept somebody's hospitality for too long

welcome mat *n* a doormat, especially one with the word 'welcome' on it ◇ **put out** *or* **roll out the welcome mat for somebody** *N Am* to make somebody feel very welcome (*informal*)

welcome page *n* ONLINE same as **homepage** (sense 1)

welcome swallow *n* a swallow with a long forked tail, glossy dark-blue back and wings, grey underparts, and a reddish throat. Native to: southern and eastern Australia. Latin name: *Hirundo neoxena.*

welcoming /wélkəming/ *adj* providing a warm and friendly greeting ○ *a welcoming smile* —**welcomingly** *adv*

weld¹ /weld/ *v* (**welds, welding, welded**) **1.** *vti* FUSE MATERIAL BY HEATING to join together pieces or parts of some material by heating them and hammering or using other pressure to make them fuse, or be joined in this way ○ *to weld two pieces of iron together* **2.** *vt* MAKE SOMETHING BY WELDING to construct or repair something by welding separate pieces or parts together ○ *to weld a metal sculpture* **3.** *vti* FORM ASSOCIATION OR BECOME ASSOCIATED to form a union or a close association, or become joined in a union or a close association ○ *weld an alliance* ■ *n* **1.** JOINT FORMED BY FUSION a joint where pieces or parts have been fused together **2.** FUSION OF PARTS the union or fusion of parts or pieces [Late 16C. Alteration of WELL¹ (verb) in the obsolete meaning of 'liquefy by heating'; influenced by its past participle *welled*] —**weldability** /wéldə bíllәti/ *n* —**weldable** *adj* —**welder** *n*

weld² /weld/ *n* **1.** PLANTS same as **dyer's rocket 2.** a yellow dye extracted from the dyer's rocket plant. Use: colourant for wool and other fabrics. [14C. Ultimately < Germanic]

Weld /weld/, **Frederick Aloysius** (1823–91) British-born premier of New Zealand (1864–65). He was responsible for introducing Maori representation and the removal of British troops from New Zealand.

welfare /wél fair/ *n* **1.** WELLBEING somebody's state or condition with respect to whether he or she is healthy, safe, happy, or prospering ○ *concerned about the welfare of prisoners held in solitary confinement* **2.** WORK TO IMPROVE PEOPLE'S WELFARE efforts, especially on the part of government and institutions, to ensure that the physical, social, and financial conditions under which people live are satisfactory **3.** *N Am* AID TO PEOPLE IN NEED financial aid and other benefits for people who are unemployed, below a specific income level, or otherwise requiring assistance, especially when provided by a government agency or programme ■ *adj* **1.** AIDING PEOPLE IN NEED concerning or designed to aid people who are poor, unemployed, or in need of assistance in some other way ○ *a welfare agency* **2.** *N Am* RECEIVING GOVERNMENT AID OWING TO NEED receiving government financial aid or benefits because of income level, unemployment, or other conditions that create a need for assistance ○ *welfare clients* [14C. Contraction of *well fare*]

welfare state *n* **1.** a political system in which a government assumes the primary responsibility for assuring the basic health, education, and financial wellbeing of all its citizens through programmes and direct assistance **2.** a nation whose government assumes primary responsibility for the social welfare of its citizens

welfare work *n US* the efforts of an organization, community, or agency to improve the living conditions and economic status of its socially disadvantaged members, residents, or citizens —**welfare worker** *n*

welfarism /wél fairizəm/ *n* the policies, practices, and beliefs that characterize the welfare state (*disapproving*) —**welfarist** *n*

welkin /wélkin/ *n* the sky, heaven, or the upper air (*archaic or literary*) [Old English *weolcen, wolc(e)n* 'cloud, firmament' < Germanic]

Welkom /wélkəm, vélk-/ town in Free State, central South Africa. It is the centre of a gold-mining region. Population: 68,111 (1991).

well¹ /wel/ *n* **1.** HOLE MADE TO DRAW UP FLUIDS a hole or shaft that is dug or drilled into the ground in order to obtain water, brine, petroleum, or natural gas ○ *an oil well* ○ *get their water from a well* **2.** SOURCE OF SOMETHING a source providing a freely and abundantly available supply of something ○ *a well of information* **3.** CONTAINER FOR LIQUID a container or sunken area for holding ink or another liquid ○ *a well on a cutting board* **4.** VERTICAL PASSAGE IN BUILDING a vertical space within or enclosed by a building, often used as a passageway for stairs or lifts or for air and light **5.** SPACE IN CENTRE OF COURTROOM the open space in the centre of a courtroom **6.** ENCLOSURE FOR SHIP'S PUMPS an enclosed area in the hold of a ship in which the pumps are located **7.** SHIPBOARD CONTAINER FOR FISH a compartment in a fishing boat in which freshly caught fish are held **8.** ENCLOSING COMPARTMENT a compartment that encloses or is used to store something temporarily such as the retracted wheels of an aircraft in flight **9.** SPRING OF WATER a place where water comes out of the ground as a natural spring or forms a natural pool (*often used in placenames*) ■ *v* (**wells, welling, welled**) **1.** *vti* RISE OR BRING TO SURFACE to rise or flow to the surface from inside the ground or the body, or cause something to do this ○ *Tears welled up in his eyes.* ○ *The fountain welled a stream of clear water into the basin below.* **2.** *vi* GROW STRONGER to surge from within or grow stronger so as to threaten to burst forth ○ *Fear welled up inside me.* [Old English *wella* 'spring of water', *wellan* 'boil' < Indo-European, 'turn']

well

well² /wel/ (**better** /béttər/, **best** /best/) CORE MEANING: a grammatical word indicating that something is satisfactory or is performed in a satisfactory way ○ *She did very well in her test.*

1. *adv* PLEASINGLY OR DESIRABLY in an efficient, satisfying, or otherwise desirable way (*often used in combination*) ○ *I thought the party went very well.* **2.** *adv* ETHICALLY OR PROPERLY in an ethical, proper, or courteous way ○ *He always treated the children very well.* **3.** *adv* SKILFULLY OR EXPERTLY with proficiency, skill, or expertise (*often used in combination*) ○ *She plays tennis really well.* **4.** *adv* JUSTLY AND APPROPRIATELY with justice and good reason ○ *I could not very well refuse her request.* **5.** *adv* COMFORTABLY in ease and comfort (*often used in combination*) ○ *I just want to be rich enough to live well.* **6.** *adv* ADVANTAGEOUSLY in a way that promotes somebody's advantage and wellbeing (*often used in combination*) ○ *She married well.* **7.** *adv* CONDUCIVE TO GOOD HEALTH in a way that promotes health and physical wellbeing (*often used in combination*) ○ *Both mother and baby are doing well.* **8.** *adv* CONSIDERABLY to a considerable extent, distance, or degree (*often used in combination*) ○ *I was well prepared for the exams.* **9.** *adv* FULLY AND THOROUGHLY in a complete and thorough way (*often used in combination*) ○ *Stir the mixture well, then turn it out onto a baking sheet.* **10.** *adv* WITH CERTAINTY with no doubt whatever about something ○ *As you well know, I will not tolerate any laziness.* **11.** *adv* FAMILIARLY AND INTIMATELY in a familiar and intimate way ○ *I knew them well when they were students.* **12.** *adv* GOOD-NATUREDLY taking something in a tolerant or good-humoured way ○ *I teased him but he took it well.* **13.** *adv* VERY very or completely (*slang*) ○ *He was well drunk last night.* **14.** *adj* IN GOOD HEALTH mentally and physically healthy ○ *I don't feel very well.* ○ *There's a well baby clinic every Wednesday.* **15.** *adj* PROPER OR APPROPRIATE suitable, proper, or appropriate in the circumstances ○ *It is as well that you apologized to her.* **16.** *adj* HIGHLY SATISFACTORY in a good, pleasing, or satisfying condition ○ *Is everything well with you?* **17.** *interj* EXPRESSING EMOTION expresses surprise, agreement, indignation, disapproval, or some other emotion ○ *Well! You've finally come back!* **18.** *interj* INTRODUCING OR RESUMING introduces a comment or statement, or resumes a conversation ○ *Well, it looks as if we'll be waiting a while.* [Old English *wel(l)* < Indo-European, 'to wish'] ◇ **as well** in addition to something ○ *The members were mostly young couples, but there were several grandparents as well.* ◇ **as well as** to an equal degree or extent ○ *Banking, as well as other businesses, will take the demographics into consideration.* ◇ **be as well to do something** to be advisable or sensible to do something ○ *It would be as well to look at all the building societies before investing your savings.* ◇ **be well** *US* used to wish somebody well on parting (*informal*) ◇ **be well out of**

something to be fortunate in having escaped from a difficult or unhappy situation (*informal*) ○ *You're well out of it – they weren't treating you very nicely in that job.* ◇ **go well** *S Africa* used as a friendly way of saying goodbye to somebody who is leaving ◇ **stay well** *S Africa* used as a friendly way of saying goodbye to somebody who is staying behind ◇ **that's** or **it's (just) as well** used to indicate that something is fortunate ○ *It's just as well that she's going to be a bit late, because we're not quite ready.* ◇ **well and good** indicating qualified approval ○ *If he wants to come with us, well and good, but he'll have to pay his share.* ◇ **well done**

USAGE *As well* is spelt as two words: *You know as well* [not *aswell*] *as I do that the information is wrong.*

USAGE See *good*.

REGIONAL NOTE In the standard language, 'very' modifies adjectives such as 'happy', 'kind', and 'thoughtful', whereas *well* modifies adjectives formed from verbs. Thus we have *very happy* but *well dressed, very kind* but *well mannered*. There is a growing tendency, thought to have started in Liverpool, for *well* to be used in phrases where 'very' is traditional, for example *well happy* and *well annoyed*.

well-accepted *adj*	well-intended *adj*
well-accustomed *adj*	well-judged *adj*
well-acquainted *adj*	well-justified *adj*
well-acted *adj*	well-liked *adj*
well-adapted *adj*	well-lit *adj*
well-adjusted *adj*	well-loved *adj*
well-administered *adj*	well-maintained *adj*
well-advertised *adj*	well-managed *adj*
well-aimed *adj*	well-manicured *adj*
well-aired *adj*	well-marked *adj*
well-argued *adj*	well-matched *adj*
well-armed *adj*	well-merited *adj*
well-arranged *adj*	well-mixed *adj*
well-assorted *adj*	well-motivated *adj*
well-attended *adj*	well-nourished *adj*
well-attested *adj*	well-organized *adj*
well-authenticated *adj*	well-paid *adj*
well-aware *adj*	well-placed *adj*
well-behaved *adj*	well-planned *adj*
well-beloved *adj, n*	well-played *adj*
well-blessed *adj*	well-pleased *adj*
well-calculated *adj*	well-practised *adj*
well-clothed *adj*	well-prepared *adj*
well-concealed *adj*	well-presented *adj*
well-conditioned *adj*	well-produced *adj*
well-conducted *adj*	well-proportioned *adj*
well-considered *adj*	well-protected *adj*
well-constructed *adj*	well-provided *adj*
well-controlled *adj*	well-publicized *adj*
well-cooked *adj*	well-qualified *adj*
well-coordinated *adj*	well-reasoned *adj*
well-covered *adj*	well-received *adj*
well-cultivated *adj*	well-recommended *adj*
well-cut *adj*	well-regarded *adj*
well-defended *adj*	well-regulated *adj*
well-defined *adj*	well-rehearsed *adj*
well-demonstrated *adj*	well-remembered *adj*
well-described *adj*	well-represented *adj*
well-deserved *adj*	well-researched *adj*
well-designed *adj*	well-respected *adj*
well-developed *adj*	well-rested *adj*
well-disciplined *adj*	well-rewarded *adj*
well-disguised *adj*	well-run *adj*
well-documented *adj*	well-satisfied *adj*
well-drained *adj*	well-schooled *adj*
well-dressed *adj*	well-seasoned *adj*
well-drilled *adj*	well-secured *adj*
well-educated *adj*	well-shaped *adj*
well-equipped *adj*	well-situated *adj*
well-established *adj*	well-spaced *adj*
well-expressed *adj*	well-spent *adj*
well-favoured *adj*	well-stocked *adj*
well-filled *adj*	well-struck *adj*
well-financed *adj*	well-structured *adj*
well-finished *adj*	well-suited *adj*
well-fitted *adj*	well-supplied *adj*
well-fortified *adj*	well-supported *adj*
well-fought *adj*	well-taught *adj*
well-furnished *adj*	well-tended *adj*
well-governed *adj*	well-timbered *adj*
well-grown *adj*	well-timed *adj*
well-guarded *adj*	well-trained *adj*
well-hidden *adj*	well-travelled *adj*
well-honed *adj*	well-treated *adj*
well-illustrated *adj*	well-trodden *adj*
well-integrated *adj*	well-understood *adj*

well-upholstered *adj*	well-worked *adj*
well-used *adj*	well-written *adj*
well-versed *adj*	well-wrought *adj*

we'll /weel, wil/ *contr* **1.** we shall **2.** we will

well-advised *adj* acting with or showing good sense (*not hyphenated after a verb*) ○ *You would be well advised to leave before the storm hits.*

well-affected *adj* favourably disposed towards somebody (*formal*)

Welland Canal /wélland-/, **Welland Ship Canal** canal system in Ontario, Canada, linking Lake Ontario and Lake Erie. It is part of the St Lawrence Seaway, and bypasses Niagara Falls. Length: 44 km/28 mi.

well-appointed *adj* equipped, furnished, or arranged with whatever is necessary or desired (*not hyphenated after a verb*)

well-balanced *adj* (*not hyphenated after a verb*) **1.** organized, conducted, or constructed so that all the parts are appropriately and sensibly proportioned or coordinated ○ *a well-balanced diet* **2.** psychologically or emotionally stable

wellbeing /wél beé ing/ *n* a good, healthy, or comfortable state

wellborn /wél báwrn/ *adj* born into an aristocratic, highly respected, or wealthy family ■ *npl* people who are born in aristocratic, highly respected, or wealthy families

well-bred *adj* (*not hyphenated after a verb*) **1.** possessing or displaying good manners or other marks of a good upbringing **2.** born from a good breed or of good stock

well-built *adj* (*not hyphenated after a verb*) **1.** having a sturdy and strong physique **2.** of strong or sound construction

well-chosen *adj* selected carefully so as to be suitable or appropriate (*not hyphenated after a verb*)

well-connected *adj* having relatives, friends, or acquaintances in important or influential positions who can provide help when necessary (*not hyphenated after a verb*)

well-disposed *adj* feeling or inclined to be approving, friendly, kindly, or sympathetic and potentially helpful (*not hyphenated after a verb*) ○ *She seemed well disposed towards us.*

well-done *adj* (*not hyphenated after a verb*) **1.** carried out or performed correctly, properly, or skilfully **2.** cooked right through to the centre

well dressing *n* in England, the practice of decorating a well with flowers at Whitsuntide in a traditional ancient ceremony

well-earned *adj* fully deserved, especially as a result of hard work or effort (*not hyphenated after a verb*) ○ *sat down for a well-earned rest*

well-endowed *adj* **1.** AFFLUENT provided with substantial property, a sizable income, or a good source of income (*not hyphenated after a verb*) **2.** NATURALLY EXCELLENT talented or capable as a result of a natural gift (*not hyphenated after a verb*) **3.** OFFENSIVE TERM an offensive term meaning having a large penis or large breasts (*slang*)

Orson Welles

Welles /welz/, **Orson** (1915–85) US actor and director. He starred in and directed *Citizen Kane* (1941), which garnered enormous critical respect. His other movies include *Touch of Evil* (1958) and *The Trial* (1962), but Hollywood's mistrust of his maverick talents prevented him from producing more than a handful of films. Full name **Welles, George Orson**

'There are only two emotions in a plane: boredom and terror.'
[Orson Welles, *Interview*, *Times*; 6 May 1985]

welfare incorrect spelling of **welfare**

well-fed *adj* (*not hyphenated after a verb*) **1.** having a diet that provides proper nourishment **2.** overweight, especially as a result of having eaten a great deal of good or rich food

well-formed *adj* fully conforming to the rules of grammar and syntax in a language (*not hyphenated after a verb*)

well-found *adj* properly and fully fitted out or equipped (*not hyphenated after a verb*)

well-founded *adj* based on sound reasons, information, or evidence or on undisputable facts (*not hyphenated after a verb*)

well-groomed *adj* (*not hyphenated after a verb*) **1.** clean, neat, and well-dressed **2.** carefully cleaned, brushed, or tended

well-grounded *adj* (*not hyphenated after a verb*) **1.** encompassing or thoroughly familiar with the essential details or knowledge of a subject **2.** same as **well-founded**

well-handled /-hánd'ld/ *adj* (*not hyphenated after a verb*) **1.** managed or conducted properly and efficiently **2.** handled many times or by many people, especially showing wear or other signs of having been handled in this way

wellhead /wél hed/ *n* **1.** SOURCE OF SPRING OR STREAM the place where a spring emerges from the earth or a stream begins **2.** SOURCE OF SOMETHING a principal or primary source of something **3.** STRUCTURE ON TOP OF WELL a structure or enclosure at the upper end of a water, oil, or natural-gas well, e.g. one containing pipes and pumping equipment

well-heeled *adj* having a large income or substantial property (*informal*; *not hyphenated after a verb*)

SPELLCHECK See *heal*.

well-hung *adj* (*not hyphenated after a verb*) **1.** OFFENSIVE TERM an offensive term meaning having a large penis or a large penis and testicles (*slang*) **2.** HANGING AS DESIRED OR REQUIRED suspended or attached so as to hang in a way that is desired or required **3.** HUNG FOR PROPER TIME hung up long enough to mature and be good to eat ○ *He liked his venison well hung.*

wellie /wélli/, **wellie boot**, **welly** (*plural* -**ies**), **welly boot** *n* CLOTHING same as **wellington boot** (sense 1) (*informal*) [Mid-20C. Shortening and alteration] ◇ **give it some wellie** to put some effort into doing something (*usually used as a command*)

well-informed *adj* having a broad and detailed knowledge, either of things in general, or of a specific subject, or of recent events and developments (*not hyphenated after a verb*)

Wellingborough /wéllingbərə/ town in Northamptonshire, central England. Population: 41,602 (1991).

wellington /wéllingtən/ *n* CLOTHING same as **wellington boot**

Wellington /wéllingtən/ **1.** capital city of New Zealand, built around a deep harbour at the southern end of the North Island. Population: 162,981 (2001). **2.** administrative region of New Zealand, occupying the southern tip of the North Island and including the city of Wellington. Population: 423,765 (2001). Area: 15,821 sq. km/6,109 sq. mi.

Wellington, Mount mountain near Hobart in southern Tasmania, Australia. Height: 1,270 m/4,167 ft.

Wellington, Arthur Wellesley, 1st Duke of (1769–1852) British general and prime minister (1828–30). He led the British forces that helped defeat Napoleon at the Battle of Waterloo (1815).

'I always say that, next to a battle lost, the greatest misery is a battle gained.'
[Arthur Wellesley Wellington. Quoted in *Recollections by Samuel Rogers*, William Sharpe; 1859]

wellington boot *n* **1.** a loose waterproof rubber boot extending to the knee or just below it and worn in wet weather or muddy conditions **2.** a leather boot that reaches to the top of or above the knee in the front but is cut lower in the back [Early 19C. After the 1st Duke of WELLINGTON]

wellingtonia /wélling tṓni ə/ (*plural* -**as** or *same*) *n*

TREES same as **giant sequoia** [Mid-19C. < modern Latin, after the 1st Duke of WELLINGTON]

well-intentioned *adj* intended to be helpful or useful in some way, but producing a negative effect or result (*not hyphenated after a verb*)

well-kept *adj* (*not hyphenated after a verb*) **1.** carefully maintained or looked after **2.** not revealed to anyone or to only a few people ○ *a well-kept secret*

well-knit *adj* (*not hyphenated after a verb*) **1.** BOUND BY CLOSE TIES bound or joined together by close relationships or ties **2.** FIRMLY CONSTRUCTED constructed or produced in such a way that the parts are firmly joined together or are integrated well **3.** COMPACT IN PHYSIQUE with a compact and strong physique

well-known *adj* (*not hyphenated after a verb*) **1.** known to many people **2.** fully known or understood

well-made *adj* (*not hyphenated after a verb*) **1.** STRONGLY CONSTRUCTED built or constructed strongly or skilfully **2.** WITH STRONG PHYSIQUE with a strong and sturdy physique **3.** SKILFULLY DEVISED skilfully contrived or executed **4.** WELL-PLOTTED skilfully plotted or structured, though often considered to be unadventurous in subject matter or treatment ○ *a well-made play*

well-man *adj* monitoring men's health and advising men on ways to prevent illness

well-mannered *adj* behaving with politeness and courtesy (*not hyphenated after a verb*)

well-meaning *adj* trying to be helpful or useful in some way, but often producing a negative effect or result (*not hyphenated after a verb*)

well-meant *adj* arising from a desire to be helpful or useful, but often producing a negative effect or result (*not hyphenated after a verb*)

wellness /wélnəss/ *n US* physical wellbeing, especially when maintained or achieved through good diet and regular exercise

well-nigh *adv* nearly or almost ○ *well-nigh impossible*

well-off (**better-off, best-off**) *adj* **1.** FAIRLY WEALTHY having a good income or enough money to live comfortably (*not hyphenated after a verb*) ○ *They were well off, certainly, but not millionaires.* **2.** FAVOURABLY PLACED in a good or favourable situation or circumstances ○ *It's not a good idea to change jobs, you're better off where you are.* **3.** WITH PLENTY having a good supply of something ○ *well off for fuel right now*

well-oiled *adj* (*not hyphenated after a verb*) **1.** functioning, operating, or carried out efficiently **2.** having drunk too much alcohol (*informal*)

well-ordered *adj* (*not hyphenated after a verb*) **1.** arranged or organized so that things are in the proper place or run smoothly **2.** in mathematics, having the property that every subset with members has an element that precedes all other elements in that subset

well-padded *adj* having a greater body weight than is desirable or advisable (*informal; not hyphenated after a verb*)

well-preserved *adj* in good condition or maintaining a good appearance or good health in spite of advanced age (*not hyphenated after a verb*)

well-read /-réd/ *adj* knowing much about many things or a particular field from having read widely and thoroughly (*not hyphenated after a verb*)

well-rounded *adj* (*not hyphenated after a verb*) **1.** WITH EXPERIENCE IN MANY AREAS having abilities, experience, or achievements in a wide and balanced variety of fields **2.** COMPREHENSIVE AND VARIED encompassing or including a wide, desirable, and balanced variety of subjects or activities **3.** SHAPELY having a rounded or otherwise pleasingly shaped body

Wells /welz/ city in Somerset, southwestern England. It is known for its medieval cathedral. Population: 9,763 (1991).

Wells, H. G. (1866–1946) British writer. A prolific writer of history and science books, he is remembered for his science fiction novels, including *The Time Machine* (1895), *The War of the Worlds* (1898), and *The Shape of Things to Come* (1933). Full name **Wells, Herbert George**

> 'Moral indignation is jealousy with a halo.'
> [H. G. Wells, *The Wife of Sir Isaac Harman*; 1914]

Wells, Ida B. (1862–1931) US teacher, journalist, and reformer. She campaigned against lynching in the 1890s and served as secretary of the National Afro-American Council (1898–1902). She became the founder and president of the Negro Fellowship League in 1910. Full name **Wells-Barnett, Ida Bell**

well-set *adj* (*not hyphenated after a verb*) **1.** strong and solid in physique **2.** solidly established or fixed

well-spoken *adj* (*not hyphenated after a verb*) **1.** speaking clearly, articulately, and with an accent that is regarded as the product of a good education **2.** selected or expressed appropriately

wellspring /wél spring/ *n* **1.** a source of a spring or stream **2.** a plentiful source or supply of something ○ *a wellspring of artistic talent*

well-stacked *adj* an offensive term meaning having large breasts (*slang*)

well-taken *adj* (*not hyphenated after a verb*) **1.** performed or executed skilfully or effectively ○ *a well-taken penalty kick* **2.** based on sound reasons, information, or evidence ○ *The point is well taken.*

well-tempered *adj* tuned so as to permit playing in any key (*not hyphenated after a verb*)

well-thought-of *adj* regarded with respect or esteem or enjoying a good reputation (*not hyphenated after a verb*)

well-thought-out *adj* carefully and skilfully planned (*not hyphenated after a verb*)

well-thumbed *adj* with pages that show signs of having been turned many times (*not hyphenated when used after a verb*)

well-to-do *adj* having a good income or enough money to live comfortably

well-tried *adj* thoroughly tested or used and so known from experience to be reliable (*not hyphenated after a verb*) ○ *a well-tried publishing formula*

well-turned *adj* (*not hyphenated after a verb*) **1.** GRACEFULLY OR ATTRACTIVELY SHAPED having a graceful or attractive shape ○ *a well-turned ankle* **2.** SKILFULLY STATED skilfully expressed or worded ○ *a well-turned phrase* **3.** MANUFACTURED WITH GRACEFUL SHAPE turned on a lathe or formed so as to have a pleasing, graceful shape

well-wisher *n* somebody who wishes success or good luck to another or good will towards somebody or something —**well-wishing** *adj, n*

well-woman *adj* monitoring women's health and advising women on ways to prevent illness

well-worn *adj* (*not hyphenated after a verb*) **1.** showing signs of wear as a result of much use **2.** trite or hackneyed as result of being used too often in speech or writing

welly *n* CLOTHING another spelling of **wellie** (*informal*)

wels /velss/ (*plural same*) *n* a large freshwater catfish. Native to: central and eastern Europe. Latin name: *Silurus glanis*. [Late 19C. < German]

welsh /welsh/ (**welshes, welshing, welshed**), **welch** (**welches, welching, welched**) *vi* an offensive term meaning to fail to fulfil or honour an obligation entered into or incurred [Mid-19C. Probably < WELSH] —**welsher** *n*

Welsh /welsh/ *npl* the people of Wales ■ *n* a Celtic language spoken in Wales. Native speakers: 50,000. [Old English *Wēlisc, Wælisc*. < *W(e)alh* 'Briton, Celt, Welshman' ('foreigner'), via Germanic 'foreign'. < Latin *Volcae* 'Celtic people of southern Gaul'] —**Welsh** *adj*

Welsh Assembly GOV ➧ **National Assembly for Wales**

Welsh cob *n* a horse with a strong neck, powerful shoulders, and compact body, used as a saddle and harness horse. It is descended from the Welsh mountain pony.

Welsh corgi *n* BREED same as **corgi**

Welsh dresser *n* a sideboard with cupboards and drawers in the lower part and open shelves in the top part

Welsh English *n* the variety of English spoken in Wales. See panel on next page

Welsh harp *n* a harp with three rows of strings that allow the production of a chromatic scale

Welshman /wélshmən/ (*plural* **-men** /-mən/) *n* a man who comes from Wales [Old English]

Welshman's button *n* a caddis fly used by anglers as bait. Latin name: *Sericostoma personatum*.

Welsh Mountain, **Welsh Mountain sheep** *n* a hardy small-bodied sheep belonging to a breed that has a grey-white face and legs, and a fleece that often contains red fibres. Native to: Wales. [Late 19C. < its having originated in high areas of Wales]

Welsh mountain pony *n* a pony of a breed that has tiny pointed ears and a compact body. Native to: Wales.

Welsh Mountain sheep *n* BREED same as **Welsh Mountain**

Welsh pony *n* a pony belonging to a breed developed from crosses between Welsh cobs and Welsh mountain ponies, slightly larger than the latter. It is used for jumping and riding.

Welsh poppy *n* a poppy that forms branching tufts of deeply divided compound leaves. Flowers: yellow, on a long slender stem. Native to: western Europe. Latin name: *Meconopsis cambrica*.

Welsh rarebit /-ráir bit/, **Welsh rabbit** *n* a dish made of hard cheese melted with seasoning, then spread on toast and grilled until bubbling and golden

Welsh springer spaniel *n* a spaniel with a thick silky coat that is chiefly white with large reddish patches, belonging to a breed that is smaller than the English springer spaniel

Welsh terrier *n* a wire-haired terrier that has a long thick, typically black-and-tan coat, belonging to a breed originally developed for hunting

Welshwoman /wélsh wŏŏmən/ (*plural* **-women** /-wímin/) *n* a woman who comes from Wales

welt /welt/ *n* **1.** RIDGE ON SKIN a raised ridge or bump on the skin caused by a lash from a whip, a scratch, or a similar blow **2.** LASH FROM A WHIP CAUSING RIDGE a lash from a whip or a similar blow that causes a raised ridge or bump on the skin **3.** STRIP SEWN INTO SHOE a strip of leather or other material that is sewn into a shoe or boot between the upper and the sole in order to strengthen the seam **4.** REINFORCEMENT FOR SEAM a folded strip of cloth, sometimes wrapped around a cord, that is sewn into a seam in a garment or pillow as a reinforcement or decoration ■ *vt* (**welts, welting, welted**) **1.** BEAT SOMEBODY SEVERELY to beat or hit somebody severely, especially with a whip or switch **2.** RAISE SMALL RIDGES ON SKIN to cause raised ridges or bumps on the skin as a result of a lash from a whip or switch **3.** STITCH SOMETHING REINFORCING OR DECORATIVE to stitch or supply something with a strip of material as a reinforcement or decoration [15C. Origin ?]

Weltanschauung /vélt an show ŏŏng/ (*plural* **-ungen** /-ŏŏngən/) *n* PHILOSOPHY same as **world view** [Mid-19C. < German, 'world view' < *Welt* 'world' + *Anschauung* 'view']

welter /wéltər/ *n* **1.** CONFUSED MASS a confused or jumbled mass of something **2.** CONFUSED CONDITION a state of confusion or chaos or a disorderly or chaotic situation **3.** SURGING MOTION OF WATER a surging, rolling, or heaving motion made by the sea or waves **4.** BOXING same as **welterweight** (*informal*) ■ *vi* (**-ters, -tering, -tered**) **1.** WALLOW IN SOMETHING to wallow or roll around in something **2.** LIE DRENCHED WITH LIQUID to lie soaked or bathed in water, blood, or some other liquid **3.** BE COMPLETELY IMMERSED IN SOMETHING to be completely or deeply involved, absorbed, or entangled in something **4.** SURGE OR ROLL IN WATER to surge, roll, or heave in the sea or waves [14C. < Middle Dutch or Middle Low German *welteren* 'roll']

welterweight /wéltər wayt/ *n* BOXING **1.** WEIGHT CATEGORY IN PROFESSIONAL BOXING in professional boxing, a weight category for competitors who weigh between 61 kg/135 lb and 66.5 kg/147 lb **2.** WEIGHT CATEGORY IN AMATEUR BOXING in amateur boxing, a weight category for competitors who weigh between 61 kg/135 lb and 66.5 kg/147 lb **3.** BOXER AT WELTERWEIGHT LEVEL a professional or amateur boxer who competes at welterweight **4.** BOXER BETWEEN LIGHTWEIGHT AND MIDDLEWEIGHT a sports contestant ranked by body weight between a lightweight and a middleweight [Early 19C. < *welter* 'heavyweight rider or boxer', origin ?]

Weltschmerz /vélt shmairts/, **weltschmerz** *n* sadness felt at the imperfect state of the world, especially at

WORLD ENGLISH *Welsh English* is the variety of English used in Wales, where it is the majority language, coexisting with Welsh, the surviving Celtic language with the largest number of speakers but a minority language in its homeland. *Welsh English* has three main influences: the Welsh language (mainly in the northern counties, often referred to as 'Welsh Wales'; dialects in neighbouring counties of England; and school and the media. The Welsh are often said to have a singsong accent, perhaps because of their use of a rise-fall tone at the end of sentences (rather than a simple fall), and because of their full vowels and stress on usually weak syllables such as the 'den' in *garden*. *Welsh English* tends not to pronounce *r* in words such as *art*, *door*, and *worker*. Two sounds from Welsh are common, especially in names: the 'll' of *Llangollen*, pronounced as /hl/, and the 'ch' in *bach* (dear), pronounced as /kh/. Native speakers of English in South Wales, like some dialect speakers in England, generally do not pronounce an initial 'h' (as in *hat* and *home*), whereas residents of North Wales do, because it occurs in Welsh. A general influence from Welsh is notable in such usages as *Coming back soon she is* for *She's coming back soon* and *there* in exclamations such as *There's kind he is!* for *How kind he is!* The catch-all question tag *isn't it?* has long been common, as in *They'll be here soon, isn't it?* (as opposed to standard *won't they?*). Words from Welsh include: *eisteddfod* 'cultural festival' (plural eisteddfodau); and *iechyd da* ('good health', often rendered as 'yachy da').

---

the behaviour of human beings [Late 19C. < German < *Welt* 'world' + *Schmerz* 'pain']

CORBIS/Philip Gould

Eudora Welty

Welty /wéltee/, **Eudora** (1909–2001) US writer. Her novels, set in her native Mississippi, include the Pulitzer Prize-winning *The Optimist's Daughter* (1969).

> 'Fiction has, and must keep, a private address.'
> [Eudora Welty, *The Eye of the Story*; 1977]

welwitschia /wel wíchi ə/ (*plural* **-as** or *same*) *n* a desert plant that produces two large strap-shaped leaves from the base of a short trunk and scarlet cones in which flowers develop. Native to: southern Africa. Latin name: *Welwitschia mirabilis*. [Mid-19C. < modern Latin, after Friedrich *Welwitsch* (1806–72), Austrian botanist]

Welwyn Garden City /wéllin-/ town in Hertfordshire, southeastern England, founded in 1920 as part of the garden city movement, and designated as a new town in 1948. Population: 42,087 (1991).

Wemba-Wemba /wémbə wémbə/ *n* an Australian Aboriginal language of New South Wales, now almost extinct [< an Aboriginal language] —**Wemba-Wemba** *adj*

wen[1] /wen/ *n* **1.** a cyst containing material secreted by a sebaceous gland of the skin, usually on the scalp or genitals. It may grow to an appreciable size and become infected. **2.** a very large overpopulated city [Old English *wen(n)*, origin ?]

wen[2] /wen/ *n* same as **wynn**

Wenceslas /wénsəsləss/, **Wenceslaus** (1361–1419) Holy Roman Emperor and king of Germany (1378–1400) and, as Wenceslas IV, king of Bohemia (1378–1419). A weak ruler, he was deposed by the German Electors and imprisoned by his own relatives in Bohemia.

Wenceslas, **Wenceslaus**, **St** (907?–929) duke of Bohemia. He encouraged Bohemia's conversion to Christianity during his reign (925?–929), but was murdered by his brother. He is the patron saint of the Czech Republic. Known as **Good King Wenceslas**

wench /wench/ *n* **1.** SERVANT GIRL formerly, a girl or young woman who worked at a paid job, usually as a servant or on a farm (*archaic*) **2.** OFFENSIVE TERM an offensive term for a prostitute or a woman who is regarded as sexually promiscuous **3.** OFFENSIVE TERM an offensive term for a young woman ■ *vi* (**wenches, wenching, wenched**) OFFENSIVE TERM an offensive term meaning to engage in sex with prostitutes or with women considered to be promiscuous [13C. Shortening of obsolete *wenchel* 'child, enslaved labourer, prostitute' < Old English *wencel* 'child' < Germanic, 'to falter'] —**wencher** *n*

wend /wend/ (**wends, wending, wended**) *vti* to proceed along a course or route ○ *The boat wended its way through the reefs.* [Old English *wendan* 'turn, proceed' < Germanic, 'turn']

Wend /wend/ *n* a member of a Slavic people who lived in northeastern Germany in medieval times [Late 18C. < German *Wende*]

wendigo /wéndi gō/ (*plural* **-gos** or **-goes**), **windigo** /wíndi gō/ *n Can* in Cree and Algonquian folklore, a demonic being who eats people or possesses them and turns them into cannibals [Early 18C. < Ojibwa *wintiko*]

Wendish /wéndish/ *n* a Slavic language spoken in eastern Germany. Native speakers: 100,000. —**Wendish** *adj*

Wendy house /wéndi-/ *n UK* a model house that is large enough for small children to go inside and play in. Aus term **cubbyhouse**. NZ, N Am term **playhouse** [Mid-20C. After the house built around the character *Wendy* in the play *Peter Pan* (1904) by J. M. Barrie]

Wen Jiabao /wén jyaá bów/ (1942–) Chinese premier (2003–). A former geologist, he was vice-premier (1998–2003), when he was involved in agricultural reform.

wenge /wéng gay/ *n* the dark brown wood of an African tree. Use: veneer for furniture. Latin name: *Millettia laurentii*. [Mid-20C. < a Congolese language]

Wensleydale /wénzli dayl/ *n* **1.** a white crumbly hard English cheese with a slightly tangy flavour **2.** a sheep with a blue-grey head and ears and dark mottled legs, belonging to a breed originating in northern England and kept for its wool [Late 19C. After a valley in N Yorkshire]

went past tense of **go**[1]

wentletrap /wént'l trap/ *n* a sea gastropod mollusc with a spiral prominently ribbed shell that is typically white but is sometimes tinged with brown. Family: Epitoniidae. [Mid-18C. < Dutch *wenteltrap* 'winding stair', from the appearance of the shells]

Wentworth /wént wurth/, **W. C.** (1793–1872) Australian explorer and politician. He was a leader, with Gregory Blaxland and William Lawson, of the first crossing of the Blue Mountains in New South Wales, Australia (1813). He established the newspaper *The Australian* (1824–48) to promote self-government. Full name **Wentworth, William Charles**

wept past participle, past tense of **weep**

were *stressed* /wur/; *unstressed* /wər/ past tense of **be**[1] [Old English *wæron* (plural past indicative), *wæren* (plural past subjunctive), and *wære* (2nd person singular past indicative and singular past subjunctive), forms of *wesan* 'be' (see WAS)]

SPELLCHECK See *ware*[1].

REGIONAL NOTE In the north of England, *I were sat* is the usual equivalent of the standard language's *I was sitting*. *Were* regularly follows 'I', 'he', and 'she', whereas *was* tends to be used with 'you', 'we', and 'they', as in *You was stood where?* This usage is still strong, even in urban areas.

we're /weer/ *contr* we are

weregild *n* LAW, HIST another spelling of **wergild**

weren't /wurnt/ *contr* were not

werewolf /wáir woolf, weer-/ (*plural* **-wolves** /-woolvz/), **werwolf** *n* somebody believed to have been transformed into a wolf, or to be able to change into a wolf and then back into a human being [Old English

werewulf < *were-* 'man' + *wulf* 'wolf' < Indo-European, 'man']

Wergaia /wur gí ə/ *n* an Aboriginal language of South Australia and western Victoria [Late 19C. < an Aboriginal language] —**Wergaia** *adj*

wergild /wúr gild/, **weregild**, **wergeld** /-geld/ *n* in Anglo-Saxon and Germanic law, the amount of compensation paid to the relatives of somebody slain, calculated on the basis of the person's rank in society [Old English *wergeld* < *wer* 'man' + *gield* 'payment' < Germanic]

wernerite /wúrnə rīt/ *n* MINERALS same as **scapolite** [Early 19C. After Abraham Gottlob *Werner* (1750–1817), German mineralogist]

Wernicke-Korsakoff syndrome /váirnikə káwrssə kof-/ *n* a form of brain damage occurring in long-term alcoholics that results from severe nutritional deficiencies [Mid-20C. After Karl *Wernicke* (1848–1905), German neurologist, and Sergei Sergeevich *Korsakov* (1854–1900), Russian psychiatrist]

wersh /wursh/ *adj Scotland* **1.** bitter or sour-tasting **2.** having little or no taste or flavour [Probably contraction of obsolete (except for dialect) *wearish*]

wert past tense of **be**[1] (*archaic*)

werwolf *n* another spelling of **werewolf**

Weser /váyzər/ river in northwestern Germany. Formed by the confluence of the Werr and Fulda rivers, it flows northwestwards through Lower Saxony and empties into the North Sea near Bremerhaven. Length: 439 km/273 mi.

weskit /wéskit/ *n* CLOTHING same as **waistcoat** (sense 1) (*archaic*) [Mid-19C. Alteration]

Wesley /wézzli/, **Charles** (1707–88) British religious leader. He cofounded Methodism with his brother John in 1739 and wrote many hymns.

Wesley, John (1703–91) British religious leader. He cofounded Methodism with his brother Charles in 1739, and thereafter preached tirelessly to huge crowds and published hymns and other religious works for mass distribution.

> 'Beware you be not swallowed up in books! An ounce of love is worth a pound of knowledge.'
> [John Wesley. Quoted in *Life of Wesley*, R. Southey; 1820]

Wesleyan /wézzli ən/ *adj* based on, consisting of, or resembling the teachings, practices, and beliefs of the Christian preacher John Wesley and his brother Charles, or of Methodism ■ *n* a follower of the Christian preacher John Wesley and his brother Charles, or a believer in their teachings or those of Methodism —**Wesleyanism** *n*

Wessex /wéssiks/ former Anglo-Saxon kingdom in southern England

west /west/ *n* **1.** DIRECTION IN WHICH SUN SETS the direction that lies directly ahead of somebody facing the setting Sun or that is located towards the left-hand side of a conventional map of the world **2.** COMPASS POINT OPPOSITE EAST the compass point that lies directly opposite east **3.** AREA IN WEST the part of an area, region, or country that is situated in or towards the west **4.** POSITION EQUIVALENT TO WEST the position equivalent to west in any diagram consisting of four points at 90-degree intervals ■ *adj* **1.** IN WEST situated in, facing, or coming from the west of a place, region, or country **2.** BLOWING FROM WEST describes a wind that blows from the west ○ *a west wind* ■ *adv* TOWARDS WEST in or towards the west [Old English < Indo-European, 'evening, night'] ◇ **go west** to die, disappear, or be destroyed (*informal*)

West *n* **1.** EUROPE AND AMERICAS the countries of Europe and North and South America (*often used with 'the'*) **2.** COUNTRIES WITH GRAECO-ROMAN AND CHRISTIAN TRADITIONS the countries of the world, especially in Europe and North and South America, whose culture and society are most influenced by traditions rooted in Greek and Roman culture and in Christianity **3.** NON-COMMUNIST COUNTRIES IN COLD WAR the non-Communist countries of Europe and North and South America during the Cold War **4.** W UNITED STATES the part of the United States west of the Mississippi River or west of the Allegheny Mountains, especially during early phases of the country's history

West /west/, **Benjamin** (1738–1820) US artist. His historical and portrait paintings include *The Death of General Wolfe* (1771).

Mae West

West, Mae (1892–1980) US actor and comedian. She was known for her irreverent wit and disdain for conventional morals. Her films include *She Done Him Wrong* (1933), *I'm No Angel* (1933), and *Klondike Annie* (1936).

> 'Too much of a good thing can be wonderful.'
> [Mae West, *The Wit and Wisdom of Mae West*; 1967]

West, Morris (1916–99) Australian novelist. He wrote *The Shoes of the Fisherman* (1963). Full name **West, Morris Langlo**

West, Nathanael (1903–40) US writer. His four novels, which include *The Day of the Locust* (1939), satirize contemporary society. Born **Weinstein, Nathan Wallenstein**

> 'The Miss Lonelyhearts are the priests of twentieth-century America.'
> [Nathanael West, *Miss Lonelyhearts*; 1933]

West, Dame Rebecca (1892–1983) British writer. She wrote noted studies of the Nuremberg war crimes trials, *Black Lamb and Grey Falcon* (1941), a study of Yugoslavia and Nazism, and novels including *The Thinking Reed* (1936). Born **Fairfield, Cicily Isabel**

> 'But there are other things than dissipation that thicken the features. Tears, for example.'
> [Dame Rebecca West, 'Serbia', *Black Lamb and Grey Falcon*; 1941]

West Africa /wést-/ region in sub-Saharan western Africa including Ghana and Nigeria —**West African** adj, n

West Australian n somebody who comes from the state of Western Australia ■ adj relating to or coming from the state of Western Australia

West Bank

West Bank territory in Southwest Asia on the western bank of the River Jordan, bordered by Israel and Jordan. Once part of Palestine, it was annexed by Jordan in 1950 and occupied by Israel in 1967. As a result of peace agreements between 1993 and 1997 some of it was transferred to Palestinian National Authority administration, with further negotiations under way. Population: 2,237,194 (2003). Area: 6,080 sq. km/2,350 sq. mi.

West Bengal former name for **Bangla**[2]

West Berlin western part of the city of Berlin. It was officially part of West Germany between 1945 and 1990, when the rest of the city was designated East German territory. —**West Berliner** n

westbound /wést bownd/ adj leading, going, or travelling towards the west

West Bromwich /-brómmich, -brómmij/ industrial town in west-central England, near Birmingham. Population: 146,386 (1991).

west by north n the direction or compass point midway between west and west-northwest —**west by north** adj, adv

west by south n the direction or compass point midway between west and west-southwest —**west by south** adj, adv

West Coast 1. administrative region of New Zealand, occupying the western coast of the South Island. Population: 30,330 (2001). Area: 36,116 sq. km/13,944 sq. mi. **2.** region comprising the coastal areas of California, Oregon, and Washington on the Pacific coast of the United States

West Country southwestern part of England, comprising the counties of Cornwall, Devon, and Somerset

West Dunbartonshire /-dun baárt'nshər/ council area in west-central Scotland, on Loch Lomond and the Clyde estuary. Population: 96,005 (2001). Area: 162 sq. km/63 sq. mi.

West End n the western part of central London and its commercial and entertainment centre

wester /wéstər/ n a wind that blows from the west, especially one blowing ahead of or with a storm ■ vi (**-ers, -ering, -ered**) to move, or appear to move, across the sky to the west (refers to the Sun, Moon, or other astronomical objects)

westerly /wéstərli/ adj **1. IN WEST** situated in or towards the west **2. BLOWING FROM WEST** describes a wind that blows from the west ■ n (plural **-lies**) **WIND FROM WEST** a wind that blows from the west ■ adv **1. FROM WEST** coming from the west **2. TOWARDS WEST** moving towards the west

western /wéstərn/ adj **1. IN WEST** situated in the west of a region or country **2. FACING WEST** situated in or facing the west ○ The house has a western aspect. **3. COMING FROM WEST** blowing from the west ○ a western wind **4. WEST OF PRIME MERIDIAN** lying west of the prime meridian **5. OF WEST** characteristic of or native to the west of a region or country **6.** also **Western** another spelling of **Western** ■ n **COWBOY FILM OR NOVEL** a film, novel, or radio or television programme set in the western United States, usually during the late 19th century [Old English westerne < WEST + a suffix denoting direction]

Western, western adj **1. INFLUENCED BY GRAECO-ROMAN AND CHRISTIAN TRADITIONS** found in or characteristic of countries, especially in Europe and North and South America, whose culture and society are greatly influenced by traditions rooted in Greek and Roman culture and in Christianity **2. OF NON-COMMUNIST COUNTRIES IN COLD WAR** found in or belonging to the non-Communist countries of Europe and North and South America during the Cold War **3. CHARACTERISTIC OF AMERICAN WEST** found in or relating to the part of the United States west of the Mississippi River or west of the Allegheny Mountains, especially during early phases of the country's history **4. FOUND IN EUROPE AND AMERICAS** located in or relating to Europe and North and South America **5. CHR CATHOLIC AND PROTESTANT** based on, consisting of, or resembling the teachings, practices, and beliefs of Roman Catholicism and Protestantism, as opposed to those of the Eastern Orthodox Church ■ n LITERAT, CINEMA, MEDIA another spelling of **western**

Western Australia /wéstərn-/ state occupying the western part of Australia. Founded as a British colony in 1829, it is the largest state in Australia. Capital: Perth. Population: 1,527,400 (2003). Area: 2,525,500 sq. km/975,100 sq. mi.

Western blotting, Western blot n a technique that analyses mixtures of proteins by separating them and then binding them to specific antibodies [After SOUTHERN BLOT]

Western Cape province in South Africa, in the southwestern part of the country. Capital: Cape Town. Population: 4,524,316 (2001). Area: 129,370 sq. km/49,950 sq. mi.

Western Church n the Christian Church as found in or influenced by that of Europe, especially the Roman Catholic Church

westerner /wéstərnər/, **Westerner** n **1.** somebody who comes from Europe or the Americas or from a country that is culturally aligned with Europe and, particularly, North America **2.** somebody who comes from the western part of a country or region

Western European Time n the standard time in the time zone centred on 0° longitude (**the prime meridian**), which includes the United Kingdom. It is the same time as Universal Time.

Western European Union n an association of European countries, inaugurated in 1955, whose main function is to coordinate defence, economic, and social policy

Western Front n the battle line between the French and British armies and the German armies in western Europe during World War I. It extended from Belgium to the Swiss border.

Western Ghats /-gaáts/ mountain range in southern India, forming the western edge of the Deccan plateau. The highest peak is Doda Betta, 2,637 m/8,652 ft.

western grey kangaroo n a large grey kangaroo. Native to: scrubland of southern and western Australia. Latin name: *Macropus fuliginosus*.

western hemisphere n the half of the Earth that is to the west of the Greenwich meridian, including North and South America and portions of western Europe and Africa

western hemlock n a coniferous tree with drooping foliage, widely grown for ornament and timber. Native to: western North America. Latin name: *Tsuga heterophylla*.

Western Isles council area in the Outer Hebrides, western Scotland. Population: 29,600 (1991). Area: 2,901 sq. km/1,120 sq. mi.

westernism /wéstərnizəm/, **Westernism** n **1.** a custom or practice characteristic of the countries of Europe and North and South America **2.** a word or idiom chiefly used in the western part of a country or region, especially the western United States

westernize /wéstər nīz/ (**-izes, -izing, -ized**), **westernise** (**-ises, -ising, -ised**), **Westernize, Westernise** v **1.** vti to adopt the customs, practices, or beliefs of the people of Europe or North and South America, or cause a person, country, or culture to adopt the customs, practices, or beliefs of the people of Europe or North and South America **2.** vt to change a law, custom, practice, or belief so that it resembles or is replaced by its European or North American counterpart —**westernization** /wéstər nī záysh'n/ n

Western meadowlark n BIRDS a meadowlark with a yellow throat and black V on the breast and a sharply pointed beak. Native to: central and western United States and Canada. Latin name: *Sturnella neglecta*.

westernmost /wéstərn mōst/ adj situated farthest west

western red cedar n **1.** the wood of the red cedar tree of western North America **2.** TREES same as **red cedar** (sense 2)

western roll n a high jump in which the body is half-turned over the bar

Western saddle n a large and heavy saddle for a horse with a raised pommel. It was originally used on ranches in the western and southwestern United States. N Am term **stock saddle**

Western Sahara region in northwestern Africa formerly ruled by Spain. It was partitioned between Morocco and Mauritania in 1976 and fully occupied by Morocco in 1979. While currently under United Nations mediation, the territory is disputed between Morocco and internal independence movements. Area: 252,120 sq. km/97,344 sq. mi. Former name **Spanish Sahara**

Western Samoa former name for **Samoa**

western sandwich n N Am a sandwich with a filling of an omelette made with diced ham, green pepper, and onion

Western Standard Time n the standard time in the time zone centred on longitude 120° W, which includes the whole of Western Australia. It is seven to nine hours ahead of Universal Time.

western swing n country and western music played on guitars, steel guitars, fiddles, and other instruments and incorporating aspects of swing music

Western Wall n a wall in Jerusalem believed to be part of the Second Temple, destroyed in AD 70 by the Romans. It is used by some Jews as a place for prayer and lamentation.

West Germanic *n* **1.** a subgroup of Germanic languages that consists of English, German, Yiddish, Dutch, Flemish, Afrikaans, and Frisian **2.** the language that is the ancestor of modern languages belonging to West Germanic —**West Germanic** *adj*

West Germany former republic of western Europe from 1945 to 1990, formed from the territories of Germany occupied by the British, French, and US forces at the end of World War II. In 1990 it was reunited with East Germany. Area: 248,577 sq. km/95,976 sq. mi. Official name **Federal Republic of Germany** —**West German** *n, adj*

West Goth *n* PEOPLES, HIST same as **Visigoth**

West Highland terrier, **West Highland white terrier** *n* a small hardy terrier with a pure white long-haired coat, belonging to a breed originally developed for hunting small animals but now kept as a pet [< its having originated in the western Highlands of Scotland]

westie /wésti/ *n* BREEDS same as **West Highland terrier**

Westie /wésti/ *n Aus* (*informal*) **1.** an offensive term for somebody from the western suburbs of Sydney, Australia, traditionally regarded as unsophisticated **2.** an offensive term for somebody from the outer suburbs of any city who is regarded as unsophisticated and unfashionable

West Indies /-ín deez/ former name for the islands of the Caribbean, now used only in specific contexts, such as the West Indies cricket team —**West Indian** *adj, n*

westing /wésting/ *n* **1.** the distance due west between two points on a course heading in a westwards direction **2.** travel or progress in a westwards direction

West Irian /-írri ən/ former name for **Irian Jaya**

West Lothian council area and historic county in central Scotland, on the Firth of Forth. Population: 143,972 (2001). Area: 425 sq. km/164 sq. mi.

West Lothian question *n* the question of the justice of allowing Westminster MPs representing Scottish constituencies to vote on issues affecting England and other parts of the UK. Non-Scottish MPs cannot vote on equivalent Scottish issues that are dealt with by the Scottish Assembly. [< the name (at the time of proposed Scottish devolution) of the constituency whose MP raised the question]

Westm. *abbr* Westminster

Westmeath /wést méeth/ county in Leinster Province, in the central part of the Republic of Ireland. The administrative centre is Mullingar. Population: 63,314 (2002). Area: 1,763 sq. km/681 sq. mi.

Westminster[1] /wéstminstər/ borough in central London, England. Many notable buildings including the Houses of Parliament, Buckingham Palace, and Westminster Abbey are located there. Population: 181,286 (2001). Official name **City of Westminster**

Westminster[2] /wéstminstər/ *n* the British parliament or parliamentary system (*often used before a noun*)

Westminster Abbey *n* a large Gothic church in London, originally a Benedictine abbey, in which British monarchs are traditionally crowned

Westmorland /wést mòorlənd/ former county in northwestern England on the Scottish border, now part of Cumbria

West New Guinea former name for **Irian Jaya**

West Nile fever, **West Nile disease**, **West Nile encephalitis** *n* a mosquito-borne viral infection affecting birds, horses, and humans that causes fever, rash, headache, muscle pain, enlarged lymph nodes, and, in some cases, inflammation of the brain [Because first identified in the West Nile district of Uganda]

West Nile virus *n* **1.** a virus, carried by mosquitoes, that causes West Nile fever **2.** MED same as **West Nile fever**

west-northwest *n* the direction or compass point midway between west and northwest ■ *adj, adv* in, from, facing, or towards the west-northwest —**west-northwesterly** *adj, adv*

Edward Weston: photographed in 1923 by Tina Modotti

Weston /wést'n/, **Edward** (1886–1958) US photographer. His sharp, semiabstract photographs often magnify details of natural objects.

Weston standard cell *n* a portable, highly accurate, voltage source used as a standard for calibration purposes [Early 20C. After Edward *Weston* (1850–1936), British-born electrical engineer]

Weston-super-Mare /wést'n sòopər máir/ resort town on the coast of Somerset, southwestern England. Population: 69,372 (1991).

West Pakistan one of the two areas that made up Pakistan following the partition of British India in 1947, comprising the provinces of Baluchistan, North-West Frontier Province, Punjab, and Sind. It became the Islamic Republic of Pakistan in 1971 after East Pakistan seceded to become the independent nation of Bangladesh.

Westphalia /west fáyli ə/ former province in northeastern Germany, in the present-day state of North-Rhine Westphalia. The Peace of Westphalia, signed at Münster and Osnabrück in 1648, marked the end of the Thirty Years' War. —**Westphalian** *n, adj*

Westphalian ham *n* German ham that is cured and eaten raw, very thinly sliced

West Point *n* the site of the US Military Academy, on the Hudson River in New York State, or the Academy itself

Westport /wést pawrt/ town on the northwestern coast of the South Island, New Zealand. It is the commercial centre of a coal-mining region. Population: 3,783 (2001).

West Riding /-ríding/ former county in Northern England, abolished in 1974, and a historic division of Yorkshire

West Saxon *n* **1.** a dialect of Old English used in Wessex during Anglo-Saxon times as the main literary dialect **2.** somebody who came from Wessex during Anglo-Saxon times —**West Saxon** *adj*

west-southwest *n* the direction or compass point midway between west and southwest ■ *adj, adv* in, from, facing, or towards the west-southwest —**west-southwesterly** *adj, adv*

West Sussex county in southeastern England, formed in 1974 from the former county of Sussex. Chichester is the administrative centre. Population: 753,614 (2001). Area: 1,989 sq. km/768 sq. mi.

West Virginia state in the eastern United States, bordered by Ohio, Pennsylvania, Maryland, Virginia, and Kentucky. Capital: Charleston. Population: 1,801,873 (2002 estimate). Area: 62,758 sq. km/24,231 sq. mi. —**West Virginian** *n, adj*

westward /wéstwərd/ *adj* towards or in the west ■ *n* a direction towards or a point in the west ■ *adv* same as **westwards** —**westwardly** *adv, adj*

USAGE **westward** or **westwards**? *Westward* is the only form available for the adjective: *In a westward direction.* *Westwards* is commonly used as well as *westward* for the adverb: *The ship was moving slowly westward/westwards.*

westwards /wéstwərdz/ *adv* in a westerly direction

USAGE See **westward**.

West Wing *n US* the US president's senior staff and advisers [Because the Oval Office is located in the West Wing of the White House]

Vivienne Westwood

Westwood /wést wòod/, **Vivienne** (b. 1941) British fashion designer. She was a pioneer of punk fashion in the late 1970s and is known for her unconventional clothing designs.

> 'What I do is restricted by the cloth and the human body. My job is to make that cloth give expression to the body.'
> [Vivienne Westwood, *Times*; 16 November 1992]

wet /wet/ *adj* **1.** SOAKED WITH WATER covered, soaked, or dampened with water or some other liquid **2.** NOT YET DRY not completely dry **3.** NOT YET SET not yet firm or solidified ○ *wet cement* **4.** RAINY, SHOWERY, MISTY, OR FOGGY characterized by rain, showers, mist, or fog ○ *a wet weekend* **5.** WITH RAINY WEATHER subject to frequent heavy rain, showers, mist, or fog ○ *a wet climate* **6.** USING OR DONE WITH LIQUID using or done in water or another liquid **7.** OFFENSIVE TERM an offensive term used to indicate somebody regarded as weak and lacking resolution or decisiveness (*informal insult*) **8.** *N Am* ALLOWING SALES OF ALCOHOL allowing the legal manufacture, storage, transportation, and sale of alcoholic beverages (*informal*) ○ *a wet town* **9.** *US* FAVOURING SALES OF ALCOHOL favouring the legal manufacture, storage, transportation, and sale of alcoholic beverages (*informal*) ○ *a wet representative* ■ *n* **1.** LIQUID OR MOISTURE water or another liquid, or moisture from it **2.** RAINY OR DAMP WEATHER rainy, showery, misty, or foggy weather ○ *Come in out of the wet.* **3.** WET GROUND a wet area or surface **4.** OFFENSIVE TERM an offensive term for somebody regarded as weak, irresolute, or indecisive (*informal insult*) **5.** LIBERAL CONSERVATIVE a Conservative politician whose policies some other Conservatives consider not to be sufficiently pure or doctrinaire (*informal*) **6.** *US* SUPPORTER OF LEGAL SALES OF ALCOHOL a supporter of the legal manufacture, storage, transportation, and sale of alcoholic beverages (*informal*) **7.** also **Wet** *Aus* METEOROL **N AUSTRALIAN RAINY SEASON** in northern Australia, the rainy season lasting from December to March ■ *v* (**wets, wetting, wet** or **wetted**) **1.** *vti* MAKE OR BECOME WET to become damp or soaked with water or some other liquid, or cause something to become damp or soaked **2.** *vt* MAKE WET BY URINATING to cause something to be damp or soaked with urine **3.** *vt* MAKE TEA to make tea with boiling water (*regional*) [Old English *wǣt, wǣta* (noun), *wǣt* (adjective), and *wǣtan* (verb) < Indo-European, 'water, wet'] —**wetly** *adv* —**wetness** *n* —**wettable** *adj* —**wettish** *adj* ◇ **all wet** *N Am* completely mistaken or wrong (*slang*)

SPELLCHECK **wet** or **whet**? Do not confuse the spelling of *wet* and *whet*, which sound similar. *Wet* is chiefly used as an adjective, meaning 'not dry' (as in *a wet towel*, *wet paint*, *wet weather*); as a verb it usually means 'make something wet': *I wetted my handkerchief and wiped the dirt from my face.* *Whet* is chiefly used as a verb, meaning 'stimulate' or 'sharpen', as in *recipes to whet your appetite,whet the blade on a stone.*

SYNONYMS **wet, damp, moist, dank, humid, sodden, saturated, soaking, sopping**

CORE MEANING: not dry

wet covered, soaked, or dampened with water or some other liquid ○ *a wet sponge* ○ *It can be dangerous driving on wet roads.* **damp** slightly wet, especially undesirably so ○ *The mattress was too damp to sleep on.* **moist** slightly wet, especially pleasantly so ○ *rich moist gardening soil* **dank** unpleasantly damp and cold ○ *Inside the hut, the walls were cold, dank, and rather slimy.* **humid** with a relatively high level of moisture in the air ○ *the humid swamps of Florida* ○ *unpleasantly hot and humid weather* **sodden** extremely

wet and heavy with retained moisture ○ *Emergency workers watched warily over the weak and sodden dike.* **saturated** soaked with moisture. ○ *There is no indication that farmers would be able to get into the saturated fields even if the weather is becoming drier.* **soaking** very wet, especially because of being rained on ○ *He came in from the downpour with soaking clothes and shoes.* ○ *I'm soaking – there's never a cab to be had when it's raining.* **sopping** (*informal*) thoroughly and unpleasantly wet ○ *a tangle of sopping hair*

WET *abbr* Western European Time

weta /wéttə/ *n* a heavy-bodied wingless insect of nocturnal habit that is a relative of grasshoppers and locusts. There are over 100 species. Native to: New Zealand. Genus: *Deinacrida* or *Hemideina*. [Mid-19C. < Maori]

wetback /wét bak/ *n N Am* a highly offensive term for a Mexican person recently arrived in the United States, especially somebody who has entered the country illegally to work as a labourer (*taboo*) [Early 20C. < Mexican immigrants having waded or swum across the Rio Grande to enter the United States]

wet bar *n N Am* a small bar equipped with a sink in a house or hotel room, used for mixing alcoholic drinks

wet blanket *n* somebody who spoils or diminishes other people's enthusiasm or enjoyment (*informal*) [< the use of wet blankets to smother small fires]

wet-bulb thermometer *n* a thermometer that records the temperature at which pure water must be evaporated to saturate a given volume of air

wet cell *n* a primary cell that contains a free-flowing electrolyte

wet dream *n* a dream that has sexual content and leads to the ejaculation of semen (*sometimes offensive*)

wet fish *n* fresh fish for sale, as distinguished from frozen or cooked fish

wet fly *n* a fishing lure resembling a fly that slips beneath the surface of the water after it is cast

wether /wéthər/ *n* a male sheep or goat that has been castrated before becoming sexually mature [Old English *weþer* < Germanic]

SPELLCHECK See *weather.*

wetland /wétlənd/ *n* a marsh, swamp, or other area of land where the soil near the surface is saturated or covered with water, especially one that forms a habitat for wildlife (*often used in the plural*)

wet look *n* **1.** a glossy finish on a material that gives an appearance of wetness **2.** a glossy sheen given to the hair by the use of a special hair gel that gives an appearance of wetness —**wet-look** *adj*

wet nurse *n* a woman who breast-feeds and takes care of another woman's baby

wet-nurse *vt* **1.** to breast-feed and take care of another woman's baby **2.** to bestow excessive care or attention on somebody (*informal*)

wet pack *n* a piece or pieces of material dampened with hot or cold water and wrapped around a patient's body for therapeutic purposes

wet rot *n* rot that affects moist or wet timber, caused by fungi and characterized by brown discoloration of the wood

wet steam *n* steam that is under low pressure and contains water droplets

wet suit *n* a tight-fitting garment worn by a diver, made of foam neoprene rubber or a similar material. It traps a thin insulating layer of water near the skin.

wetting agent /wétting-/ *n* a chemical agent that allows a liquid to spread more easily across or into a surface by lowering the liquid's surface tension

wetware /wétwair/ *n* the human brain or human thought processes, regarded as data-processing devices comparable with, or in contrast to, computer systems

WEU *abbr* Western European Union

we've /weev, wiv/ *contr* we have

Wewak /wé wak/ coastal town on northern New Guinea island, Papua New Guinea. Population: 23,224 (1990).

Wexford /wéksfərd/ **1.** county in Leinster Province, in the southeastern part of the Republic of Ireland. Population: 104,371 (2002). Area: 2,351 sq. km/908 sq. mi. **2.** town, port, and administrative centre of County Wexford, in the Republic of Ireland. Population: 16,000 (1996).

Weyden /wáydən/, **Rogier van der** (1399?–1464) Flemish painter. His predominantly religious oeuvre, characterized by elegant, flowing lines and the use of cold colours, influenced other European painters of the 15th century.

Weymouth /wáyməth/ resort town and ferry port on the coast of Dorset, England. Population: 46,065 (1991).

wf, w.f. *abbr* **1.** Wallis and Futuna Islands (*used in Internet addresses*) See table at **domain name 2.** PRINTING wrong font

WFD *abbr Aus* Work for the Dole

wff *abbr* LOGIC well-formed formula

WFTU *abbr* World Federation of Trade Unions

wg, WG *abbr* **1.** water gauge **2.** wire gauge

WG *abbr* (Windward Islands) Grenada (*international vehicle registration*)

Wg Cdr *abbr* AIR FORCE Wing Commander

W. Glam. *abbr* West Glamorgan

Wh *abbr* watt-hour

wh. *abbr* white

whack /wak/ *v* (**whacks, whacking, whacked**) **1.** *vti* HIT SOMEBODY WITH LOUD SHARP BLOW to hit somebody or something with a swift sharp blow that produces a loud noise **2.** *vt* PLACE SOMETHING CASUALLY AND QUICKLY to put or place something somewhere casually and quickly (*informal*) **3.** *vti* CUT OR CHOP SOMETHING to cut or chop something with a swift sharp blow **4.** *vt US* same as **murder** (*informal*) ■ *n* **1.** LOUD SHARP BLOW a swift sharp blow that produces a loud noise **2.** LOUD SOUND OF SHARP BLOW the loud sound made by a swift sharp blow **3.** ATTEMPT AT SOMETHING an attempt at doing something (*informal*) ○ *That looks like fun – can I take a whack at it?* **4.** SHARE OF SOMETHING a share or portion of something, especially one deserved or due (*informal*) **5.** COST the amount that something costs (*informal*) [Early 18C. Probably an imitation of the sound] —**whacker** *n* ◇ **out of whack** *ANZ, N Am* not working properly, especially because of being out of order or alignment (*informal*)

whack off *vti* a highly offensive term meaning to masturbate, or masturbate somebody (*taboo*)

whacked /wakt/ *adj* **1.** *UK, Can* very tired or exhausted (*informal*) **2.** *N Am* relaxed, excited, or euphoric as a result of taking drugs, especially marijuana (*slang*)

whacked-out *adj* **1.** very tired after physical or mental exertion (*informal*) **2.** *US* same as **whacked** (sense 2) (*slang*)

whacking /wáking/ (*informal*) *adj* very large or impressive ■ *adv* to an extreme degree

whacko *n* same as **wacko** (*slang offensive*)

whacky *adj* same as **wacky** (*informal*)

whakapapa /fúkə puppə/ (*plural same*) *n NZ* in Maori culture, the genealogy of a person or family [Mid-20C. < Maori]

Whakatane /fúkə taá nay/ coastal town in the northeastern part of the North Island, New Zealand. It is a commercial centre for agriculture and timber from the surrounding region. Population: 17,778 (2001).

whale[1] /wayl/ *n* **1.** BIG SEA MAMMAL a large sea mammal that breathes through a blowhole on the top of its head and has front flippers, no hind limbs, and a flat horizontal tail. Its body is insulated by a thick layer of fatty blubber beneath the skin, and many species live in social groups, communicating by sound. Order: Cetacea. **2.** IMPRESSIVE EXAMPLE OF SOMETHING an impressive, very large, or very enjoyable example of something (*informal*) ○ *a whale of a party* ■ *vi* (**whales, whaling, whaled**) HUNT WHALES to hunt for and kill whales [Old English *hwæl* < Germanic]

SPELLCHECK See *wail.*

whale[2] /wayl/ (**whales, whaling, whaled**) *vt* **1.** to beat somebody severely as a punishment **2.** *N Am* to defeat somebody soundly or completely (*informal*) [Late 18C. Origin ?]

whaleback /wáyl bak/ *n* **1.** something large and rounded like the back of a whale, e.g. an ocean wave or a small hill **2.** a cargo vessel with a rounded bow and arched upper deck designed to allow the water from waves breaking on it to run off more easily

whaleboat /wáyl bōt/ *n* a long, narrow, easily manoeuvred boat with a pointed bow and stern, originally rowed in pursuit of whales, but now often powered and used as a lifeboat

whalebone /wáyl bōn/ *n* **1.** MARINE BIOL same as **baleen 2.** a piece or strip of a hard elastic material found in some whales. Use: formerly, corset stays, whips.

whalebone whale *n* MARINE BIOL same as **baleen whale**

whale catcher *n* a boat with a harpoon launcher mounted in its bow, used for pursuing and catching whales

Whale Island /wayl-/ uninhabited volcanic island in the Bay of Plenty off the northeastern coast of the North Island, New Zealand. Area: 4 sq. km/2 sq. mi.

whale oil *n* a yellowish oil manufactured by rendering the blubber of whales. Use: formerly, lamp fuel, soap, candles.

whaler /wáylər/ *n* **1.** same as **whaleboat 2.** a ship used for hunting whales or processing killed whales **3.** somebody who hunts or harpoons whales, or who processes killed whales

whale shark *n* the largest of all sharks, with a white-spotted dark body up to 15 m/50 ft in length. Native to: warm oceanic waters. Latin name: *Rhincodon typus*.

whaling /wáyling/ *n* the activity or industry of hunting and processing whales

wham /wam/ (*informal*) *n* **1.** FORCEFUL BLOW a solid forceful blow or impact **2.** SOUND OF FORCEFUL BLOW the loud noise produced by a solid forceful blow or impact ■ *vti* (**whams, whamming, whammed**) HIT SOMETHING WITH LOUD NOISE to hit or crash into somebody or something forcefully with a loud noise ○ *The car whammed into the brick wall.* ■ *interj* INDICATES SOUND OF BLOW used to imitate the loud sound of a forceful blow or impact ■ *adv* SUDDENLY AND FORCEFULLY with a startling or jarring suddenness ○ *I ran wham right into my ex-husband.* [Early 20C. An imitation of the sound]

whammy /wámmi/ (*plural* **-mies**) *n* (*informal*) **1.** a jinx or hex on somebody or something **2.** something with unpleasant or damaging consequences [Mid-20C. Origin ?]

whanau /faán ow/ (*plural same*) *n NZ* **1.** somebody's family (*informal*) **2.** a Maori extended family or group of extended families living in the same area [Mid-20C. < Maori]

whang[1] /wang/ *n* **1.** RESOUNDING BLOW a heavy blow that resounds loudly when it hits something **2.** SOUND OF RESOUNDING BLOW the loud sound produced by a heavy blow when it hits something ■ *vti* (**whangs, whanging, whanged**) HIT WITH RESOUNDING SOUND to hit something heavily and produce a loud resounding sound [Early 19C. An imitation of the sound]

whang[2] /wang/ *n* **1.** THONG a thong, especially one made from leather **2.** UNTANNED ANIMAL HIDE untanned hide from cattle or other animals **3.** *US* OFFENSIVE TERM an offensive term for a penis (*slang*) ■ *vt* (**whangs, whanging, whanged**) HIT SOMEBODY SEVERELY to beat, whip, or thrash somebody severely [Early 16C. Alteration of *thwang*, a variant of THONG]

Whangarei /faángə ráy/ coastal town in the northern part of the North Island, New Zealand. It is a commercial and tourist centre. Population: 46,047 (2001).

whangee /wang eé/ *n* **1.** a walking stick or cane made from a piece of bamboo **2.** a bamboo plant whose stems are used to make whangees. Native to: China. Genus: *Phyllostachys*. [Late 18C. < Chinese *huang* 'bamboo sprouts too old for eating']

whap *n, vt* another spelling of **whop**

whare /wáwrri/ *n NZ* **1.** a house or building for domestic or communal use **2.** a simple or makeshift hut on a beach or in the bush on newly occupied land [Early 19C. < Maori]

wharf /wawrf/ *n* (*plural* **wharves** /wawrvz/ or **wharfs**) LANDING PLACE FOR SHIPS a structure built alongside or out into the water as a landing place for boats and ships, sometimes with a protective covering or enclosure ■ *v* (**wharfs, wharfing, wharfed**) **1.** *vti* MOOR BOAT AT WHARF to moor a vessel at a wharf, or be moored there **2.** *vt* UNLOAD OR STORE CARGO ON WHARF to

zh vision. In foreign words: kh German Bach; aN French vin; aaN French blanc; ö German schön, French feu; oN French bon; öN French un; ü as in French rue. Stress marks: ´ as in secret /seékrət/, academic /ákə démmik/

unload cargo onto or store it on a wharf **3.** vt **EQUIP PLACE WITH WHARF** to provide a place with a wharf or wharves [Old English *hwearf* 'embankment, wharf' < Germanic, 'turn']

wharfage /wáwrfij/ n **1. USE OF WHARF** the use of a wharf or wharves **2. FEE TO USE WHARF** a fee that is paid for the use of a wharf or wharves **3. WHARVES** wharves collectively, especially the wharves in a particular location

wharfie /wáwrfi/ n Aus a worker at a dock or wharf (*informal*)

wharfinger /wáwrfinjər/ n somebody who owns or supervises the running of a wharf or group of wharves [Mid-16C. Alteration of obsolete *wharfager*]

Edith Wharton
AKG London

Wharton /wáwrt'n/, **Edith** (1862–1937) US writer. She is best known for her novels, particularly the Pulitzer Prize-winning *The Age of Innocence* (1920). Born **Jones, Edith Newbold**. See Cultural note at **innocence**

'The worst of doing one's duty was that it apparently unfitted one for doing anything else.'
[Edith Wharton, *The Age of Innocence*; 1920]

wharve /wawrv/ n a wheel or similar part on a spindle that operates as a pulley on a spinning machine or as a flywheel on a spinning wheel [Old English *hweorfa* < *hweorfan* 'turn' < Germanic]

wharves NAUT plural of **wharf**

what /wot/ CORE MEANING: a grammatical word used in direct and indirect questions to request information, e.g. about the identity or nature of somebody, or about the purpose of something ○ (det) *What time will you be back?* ○ (det) *I'm not sure what kind of sauce goes best with this dish.* ○ (pron) *What are they doing?* ○ (pron) *Do you know what she does for a living?*
1. det, pron **REQUESTS INFORMATION** used to request information, e.g. about the identity or nature of somebody or something ○ *What time is it?* ○ *What are they doing?* **2.** det, pron **THAT WHICH** the person or persons who, or the thing or things that ○ (det) *We spent what money we did have.* ○ (pron) *picking their way through what remained of the house* **3.** det **EMPHASIZING REACTION** used in exclamations to emphasize a reaction or opinion ○ *What fantastic news!* ○ *What a miserable day it's been.* **4.** adv **HOW** in what respect or to what degree ○ *What does it matter now that they've gone?* **5.** adv **AT GUESS** used to indicate a guess or approximation of an amount or value ○ *It must be, what, ten years since we first met.* **6.** interj **EXCLAMATION** used as an exclamation when expressing an emotion such as surprise, anger, or disappointment ○ *The plane will be delayed by two hours. –What?* [Old English *hwæt* < Indo-European] ◇ **give somebody what for** to scold or punish somebody severely (*informal*) ◇ **what about ... 1.** used to suggest that somebody or something be taken into consideration ○ *What about all the money we've already paid then?* **2.** used to suggest that somebody might like to do something ○ *What about going on a fishing trip?* ◇ **what for** used to ask the reason for or the purpose of something ◇ **what have you** other things similar to those just mentioned ◇ **what if 1.** used to make a suggestion about a possible course of action **2.** used to ask what might or would happen in a given situation ◇ **what of it?** used to suggest that something is not important ◇ **what's what** the true facts or actual situation (*informal*) ◇ **what with** used to introduce the reason or reasons for something ○ *I didn't get there until ten, what with all the traffic and setting out late.*

USAGE As a pronoun, the word *what* means 'the thing that', as in *This is much nicer than what he gave me last Christmas. Remember what I told you.* Beware of adding *what* where it is not needed: *It was a lot more difficult than* [not *than what*] *I thought it would be.* Another common error is the use of *what* in place of *that, which,* or *who: This is the book that* [not *what*] *I told you about. The woman who* [not *what*] *owns the dog is out at work all day.*

whatchamacallit /wóchəmə kawlit/ n something whose name is forgotten or is not known (*informal*) [Early 20C. < a pronunciation of *what you may call it*]

whatever /wot évvər/ CORE MEANING: a grammatical word used to refer to everything of a particular type, without limitation ○ (pron) *Feel free to say whatever you like.* ○ (det) *He lost whatever interest he may have had in it.*
1. pron, adj **NO MATTER WHAT** used to indicate that something is the case in all circumstances ○ (pron) *She always seems to succeed, whatever she does.* ○ (adj) *Whatever problem you come up with they'll deal with.* **2.** pron also **what ever** EMPHATIC '**WHAT**' an emphatic form of 'what' used to express an emotion such as surprise or perplexity ○ *Whatever is the matter now?* **3.** adv **OF ANY KIND** used for emphasis ○ *I can see no reason whatever why you shouldn't go.* **4.** adv **EXPRESSING MILD DISAGREEMENT** used to indicate that the speaker disagrees with what has just been said, but is not prepared to argue (*informal*) ○ *OK, if that's what you think, whatever.* ◇ **or whatever** used to refer generally to something else of the same kind ○ *any tool such as a hoe, fork, spade, or whatever*

USAGE whatever or **what ever?** *Whatever*, written as one word, is a relative pronoun used in statements or commands: *I'll have whatever you're having. I don't want it, whatever it is.* It is also spelt as one word as an adverb used to reinforce negative statements: *I've no desire whatever to find out. What ever* is sometimes written as two words when each word retains its separate meaning and the expression is equivalent to *what on earth*, usually in questions: *What ever are they doing?*

what-if n a situation, difficulty, or obstacle that could arise in the future (*informal*)

whatnot /wót not/ n **1. SOMETHING SAME OR SIMILAR** something of the same or a similar kind **2.** FURNITURE **SET OF SHELVES** a set of light shelves for displaying small ornamental items **3. SOMETHING UNIMPORTANT** something nondescript, trivial, or unimportant

what's /wots/ contr **1.** what does **2.** what has **3.** what is

whatshername /wótsər naym/ pron a woman or girl whose name has been forgotten or is not known (*informal*)

whatshisname /wótsiz naym/ pron a man or boy whose name has been forgotten or is not known (*informal*)

whatsit /wótsit/ n something whose name is not known or has been forgotten (*informal*) [Contraction of *what-is-it*]

whatsitsname /wótsits naym/ pron something whose name is not known or has been forgotten (*informal*)

whatsoever /wót sō évvər/ adv used to emphasize a negative statement, after words such as 'none', 'no one', and 'anyone' ○ *'Did you have any doubts?' – 'None whatsoever'.* ■ pron, det same as **whatever** (*archaic*)

whaup /wawp/ n Scotland BIRDS same as **curlew** [Mid-16C. An imitation of the sound of its cry]

wheal n MED **1.** another spelling of **weal**[1] **2.** US spelling of **weal**[1] (sense 2)

wheat /weet/ n **1. EDIBLE GRAIN** a grain harvested in temperate regions from a widely cultivated annual grass. Use: making flour for bread, pasta, and other foods. **2. CEREAL PLANT** an annual grass of a genus that includes types cultivated for their grain for making flour. The numerous varieties of cultivated wheat belong to three main species: bread wheat, durum or hard wheat, and emmer. Native to: southwestern Asia. Genus: *Triticum.* **3. PALE YELLOW COLOUR** a pale yellow colour [Old English *hwǣte* 'that which is white' < Indo-European, 'white'] —**wheat** adj

wheatear /weét eer/ n a small thrush with a white rump and black face. Native to: Europe, Asia, Africa, North America. Genus: *Oenanthe.* [Late 16C.

Back-formation < *wheatears*, probably by folk etymology < WHEAT + EAR[1]]

wheaten /weét'n/ adj **1.** made from or with wheat or milled wheat flour **2.** pale yellow in colour —**wheaten** n

wheaten terrier n a terrier with a soft, wavy, pale gold coat and a docked tail, belonging to a medium-sized breed that originated in Ireland

wheat germ n the embryonic centre of the wheat grain, rich in B vitamins, that is milled finely and sometimes toasted, and is used for sprinkling over cereals or in cooking

wheatgrass /weét graass/ n wheat grains sprouted to a height of around 17 cm/7 in., cut, and pulped to produce a highly nutritious juice that is drunk in very small quantities

wheatish /weétish/ adj S Asia light creamy brown, or having a light-brown complexion

wheatmeal /weét meel/ n wheat flour that has had some of the bran and germ removed

wheat rust n **1.** a disease of wheat caused by various fungi and marked by blackish, brownish, or yellowish streaks on the leaves and stems **2.** a fungus that causes rust in wheat

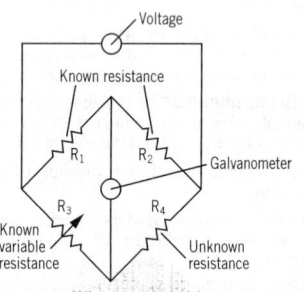
Wheatstone bridge

Wheatstone bridge /weétstən-/ n a device consisting of an electrical circuit, three known resistances, and a galvanometer, used for measuring an unknown resistance [Late 19C. After Sir Charles Wheatstone (1802–75), British physicist who popularized it]

wheatworm /weét wurm/ n (plural **-worms** or same) n a small nematode worm that lives as a parasite on and is destructive to wheat. Latin name: *Anguina tritici.*

whee /wee/ interj used to express exhilarating or unrestrained joy, pleasure, or excitement [Early 20C. Natural exclamation]

wheech /hweekh/ (**wheechs, wheeching, wheeched**) vt Scotland to take something or put something somewhere with a swift and energetic movement [Probably to suggest quick movement]

wheedle /weéd'l/ (**-dles, -dling, -dled**) v **1.** vti to coax or try to persuade somebody to do something using flattery, guile, or other indirect means **2.** vt to obtain something from somebody by coaxing, persuasion, flattery, guile, or other indirect means [Mid-17C. Origin ?] —**wheedler** n —**wheedlingly** adv

wheel /weel/ n **1. ROTATING ROUND PART** a ring or disc that revolves or is turned by a central shaft or pin, sometimes with a central hub that has radiating spokes attached to a circular rim (*often used in combination*) ○ *a wagon wheel* **2. SOMETHING RESEMBLING WHEEL** something that resembles a wheel in shape, form, or function **3.** MECH ENG **ROUND MACHINE PART THAT TURNS ANOTHER** a rotating circular part of a mechanism, often with projections on the outer edge, used to turn another part **4.** AUTOMOT same as **steering wheel** ○ *He fell asleep at the wheel.* **5.** HANDICRAFT same as **spinning wheel 6.** FURNITURE **CASTOR** a small rotating or swivelling circular part fitted to the base of something such as a piece of furniture or luggage to make it easier to move **7.** CERAMICS same as **potter's wheel** (*informal*) **8. ROTATING FIREWORK** a flat round or coiled firework that spins as it burns (*often used in combination*) **9. WHEEL OF FORTUNE** an imaginary wheel said to be spun by fate **10.** GAMBLING **ROUND FRAME SPUN IN GAMBLING** a circular device that is spun in games of chance such as roulette in order to determine who wins in a random way **11.** HIST **MEDIEVAL TORTURE DEVICE** a medieval instrument of torture in the form of a large wheel to which the

victim was tied. The outstretched arms and legs of the victim were usually broken with a metal bar. **12.** **TURN** a turn or revolution **13.** **MOVEMENT IN CIRCLE** a turning, spinning, pivoting, or circular movement **14.** MIL **MILITARY FORMATION** a military formation in which the inner unit remains in one place, as a pivot, while the outer units change direction and make an arc around it. It is used in marching performances by a troop of soldiers and displays by a fleet of ships. **15.** LITERAT **SET OF RHYMING LINES** a group of rhyming lines that end a stanza of verse. They are usually shorter than the other lines and often occur in a group of four. ■ **wheels** *npl* **1.** **CAR** a car, especially for personal use (*slang*) **2.** **DRIVING FORCE OR WORKINGS** the system or influences controlling the way something functions or operates ○ *the wheels of justice* ■ *v* (**wheels, wheeling, wheeled**) **1.** *vt* **MOVE ON WHEELS** to push something that has wheels ○ *wheeled her bicycle up the steep hill* **2.** *vt* **TRANSPORT SOMEBODY IN WHEELED OBJECT** to move or carry somebody or something in a conveyance with wheels such as a trolley or wheelchair ○ *wheeled the patient out of the room* **3.** *vi* **TURN QUICKLY** to move quickly in a circle **4.** *vi* **MAKE CIRCULAR MOVEMENT** to do something with a circular or curving movement ○ *Her arms wheeled frantically in the air as she tried to signal for help.* **5.** *vi* **MOVE SMOOTHLY** to move smoothly and easily ○ *He wheeled through the gathering, making all his appointed stops.* **6.** *vt* **PROVIDE SOMETHING WITH WHEELS** to fit something with a wheel or wheels [Old English *hwēol* < Indo-European, 'go round'] —**wheeled** *adj* —**wheelless** *adj* ◇ **reinvent the wheel 1.** to waste time recreating something that already exists in a perfectly usable and acceptable form **2.** to produce a new version of something very basic and familiar ◇ **wheel and deal** to use complex, skilful and sometimes slightly dishonest negotiating techniques in order to secure something (*informal*)

wheel about, wheel around *vi* **1.** to turn round quickly or suddenly **2.** to reverse or radically change an opinion, position, practice, or belief

wheel in *vi* to approach or enter a place quickly and confidently (*informal*)

wheel out *v* **1.** *vt* to present somebody or use something readily or repeatedly **2.** *vi* to leave a place quickly (*informal*)

wheel round *vi* same as **wheel about**

wheel and axle *n* a simple machine, often used to raise or lower loads, usually consisting of a cylindrical drum and wheel mounted on the same axle with ropes wound around each

wheelarch /wéel aarch/ *n* a semicircular cavity in the body of a vehicle that fits over a wheel. Aus, US term **wheel well**

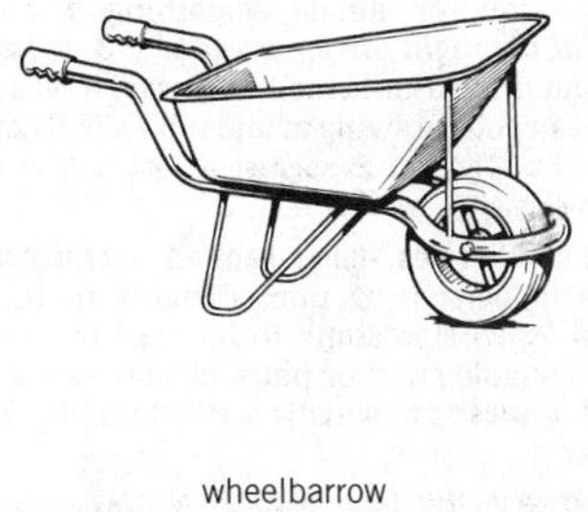

wheelbarrow

wheelbarrow /wéel barō/ *n* a small cart used to transport things, usually in the form of an open container with a single wheel at the front and two handles at the back ■ *vt* (**-rows, -rowing, -rowed**) to move or transport something in a wheelbarrow

wheelbase /wéel bayss/ *n* the distance between the front axle and the rear axle of a motor vehicle, usually measured in inches. It determines how sharply the vehicle can turn in a given direction.

wheel bug *n* a large and powerful insect belonging to the assassin bug family that preys on other insects and has an outgrowth on its back resembling a gear. Latin name: *Arilus cristatus.*

wheelchair /wéel chair/ *n* a chair with two small wheels at the front and two large wheels at the sides, used as a way of moving around by somebody who cannot walk. Wheelchairs may be propelled by turning the large wheels, by somebody pushing from behind, or by a small motor.

wheelchair housing *n UK, Can* houses and flats designed or adapted for people who use wheelchairs to enable them to move around easily

wheel clamp *n* a metal device fitted over the wheel of an illegally parked car to immobilize it until a fine is paid. US term **Denver boot** —**wheel-clamp** *vt*

wheeler /wéelər/ *n* **1.** **WHEELED VEHICLE** a vehicle that has a particular number of wheels (*used in combination*) ○ *He hauled it in a ten-wheeler.* **2.** **SOMEBODY WHO WHEELS** somebody or something that wheels or pushes something with wheels **3.** **MAKER AND REPAIRER OF WHEELS** somebody who makes and repairs wheels, especially the wheels of carriages or wagons

Wheeler /wéelər/, **Sir Mortimer** (1890–1976) British archaeologist. He was noted for his excavations in the Indus Valley and for his scientific approach to archaeological investigation. Full name **Wheeler, Robert Eric Mortimer**

wheeler-dealer *n* an adroit negotiator who uses complex or sometimes dishonest techniques to obtain what he or she wants, especially in business or politics (*informal*) —**wheeler-dealing** *n*

wheel horse *n N Am* a steady, diligent, and reliable worker, especially in a political organization

wheelhouse /wéel howss/ (*plural* **-houses** /-howziz/) *n* NAUT same as **pilot house**

wheelie /wéeli/ *n* a manoeuvre performed on a moving or stationary bicycle or motorcycle in which the rider raises the front wheel off the ground and balances on the back wheel (*informal*)

wheelie bin *n* a large rubbish bin that has wheels on its base so that it can be manoeuvred easily (*informal*)

wheel lock *n* in some old firearms, a firing mechanism in which a steel spring-wound wheel strikes sparks from a piece of iron pyrite

wheelman /wéelmən/ (*plural* **-men** /-mən/), **wheelsman** /wéelzmən/ *n N Am* NAUT same as **helmsman** (sense 1)

wheel of fortune, Wheel of Fortune *n* an imaginary revolving wheel said to determine random changes in the course of somebody's life, used as a symbol of the inconstancy of fortune

wheelsman *n N Am* NAUT same as **helmsman** (sense 1)

wheelspin /wéel spin/ *n* the rapid revolving of a vehicle's wheels without sufficient contact with the ground to produce forward or backward motion

wheels up *adj* airborne after having taken off from a runway ◇ **go wheels up** to take off from a runway and become airborne

wheel-thrown *adj* made by being turned on a potter's wheel

wheel well *n Aus, US* AUTOMOT same as **wheelarch**

wheelwork /wéel wurk/ *n* an arrangement of interlocking wheels or gears within a machine or other device, e.g. the gear train in a mechanical timepiece

wheelwright /wéel rīt/ *n* somebody who makes and repairs wheels, especially the wheels of carriages and wagons

wheen /hween/ *n Scotland* a considerable amount or number [14C. Representing Old English *hwēne* 'somewhat', form of *hwōn* 'a few']

wheesht *vti, n Scotland* same as **whisht**

wheeze /weez/ *v* (**wheezes, wheezing, wheezed**) **1.** *vi* **BREATHE WITH AUDIBLE HOARSE WHISTLING SOUND** to breathe with an audible whistling sound and with difficulty, usually because of a respiratory disorder such as asthma **2.** *vt* **SAY SOMETHING WITH HOARSE WHISTLING SOUND** to say or express something while breathing with an audible whistling sound and with difficulty **3.** *vi* **MAKE WHISTLING OR PUFFING SOUND** to make a noisy whistling or puffing sound that resembles wheezing ○ *The old locomotive wheezed and puffed up the steep slope.* ■ *n* **1.** **NOISY BREATHING SOUND** noisy and difficult breathing, or the hoarse whistling sound of this **2.** **CLEVER IDEA** a good idea or clever plan (*dated informal*) **3.** **OFTEN REPEATED JOKE** a hackneyed story, joke, or saying (*informal*) [15C. Origin ?] —**wheezer** *n* —**wheezily** *adv* —**wheeziness** *n* —**wheezy** *adj*

whelk[1] /welk/ (*plural same or* **whelks**) *n* an invertebrate sea animal with a conical spiralling shell. Some kinds of whelk are edible. Family: Buccinidae. [Old English *weoloc*, altered perhaps by association with WHELK[2]]

whelk[2] /welk/ *n* a raised spot or mark on the skin, e.g. a pimple, boil, or weal [Old English *hwylca* 'pustule, tumour'] —**whelky** *adj*

whelm /welm/ (**whelms, whelming, whelmed**) *vt* (*literary*) **1.** to engulf or submerge something in water **2.** to overpower or overburden somebody or something [14C. Probably alteration of Old English *āhwylfan* 'cover over, submerge', influenced by *helmian* 'to cover']

whelp /welp/ *n* **1.** **YOUNG ANIMAL** a young animal, especially the young of carnivorous mammals such as wolves, lions, bears, and dogs **2.** **CHILD** a child or young person **3.** **RUDE YOUNG MAN** a boy or young man regarded as showing inappropriate boldness or lack of deference (*insult*) **4.** NAUT **RIDGE ON CAPSTAN OR WINDLASS** a projection on the barrel of a capstan or windlass **5.** MECH ENG **TOOTH ON WHEEL** a tooth on a sprocket wheel ■ *vti* (**whelps, whelping, whelped**) **BEAR YOUNG** to give birth to young, especially baby carnivores [Old English *hwelp* < Germanic]

when /wen/ CORE MEANING: an adverb used to ask at what time or at what point something happens ○ *When can we expect you?* ○ *When should you use your rearview mirror?*

1. *conj* **WHILE** at or during the time that ○ *When I was a child, I lived in the country.* **2.** *conj* **AS SOON AS** as soon as somebody does something or something happens ○ *Call me when you get home.* **3.** *conj* **AT SOME POINT** at some point during an activity, event, or circumstance ○ *We got him when he was still a pup.* **4.** *conj* **EACH TIME THAT** each time that something happens ○ *When a train goes by, the whole house shakes.* **5.** *conj* **IF** considering the fact that ○ *Why walk when you can ride?* **6.** *conj* **ALTHOUGH** in spite of the fact that ○ *They think I'm really easygoing, when in fact I'm not.* **7.** *adv* **AT OR DURING WHICH TIME** used to indicate a time at or during which something happens ○ *When did it happen?* ○ *Since when has that been a problem?* ○ *He remembered a time when he could run a mile without any difficulty.* **8.** *n* **UNSPECIFIED TIME PERIOD** used to refer to the time that something happened or will happen (*often used in the plural*) ○ *We're having trouble determining the whens and hows of the thing.* [Old English *hwonne, hwænne* < Indo-European]

USAGE See *if.*

whenas /wen áz/ *conj* (*archaic*) **1.** **WHENEVER** at such time as **2.** **WHILE** at or during the time that **3.** **ALTHOUGH** in spite of the fact that

whence /wenss/ *adv* **1.** **AS RESULT** from which cause or origin (*formal*) ○ *You have treated her badly, whence her anger.* **2.** **FROM WHERE** from what place or source (*archaic or literary*) ○ *Can we know whence comes this good luck?* **3.** **FROM WHICH PLACE** from the place or thing previously referred to (*archaic or literary*) ○ *that envy whence comes hate* [13C. < *whennes* 'of or from when']

USAGE whence or **from whence**? Both uses now sound old-fashioned or literary in tone, but ***from whence***, as an attempt to bring the form up to date, fits rather better in the structures of modern English. In everyday English, however, the word can normally be avoided altogether: *They did not know from whence they came* can easily be recast as *They did not know where they came from.*

whencesoever /wénssō évvər/ *adv, conj* from whatever cause, origin, or source (*archaic*) ○ *accept the gifts whencesoever they come*

whene'er /wen áir/ *adv, conj* same as **whenever** (*literary*)

whenever /wen évvər/ *conj* **1.** **NO MATTER WHEN** at whatever time that ○ *Whenever you need me I'll be there.* **2.** **EACH TIME THAT** each and every time that ○ *Whenever you're around, the dog growls.* ■ *adv* (*informal*) **1.** **WHEN INDEED** used as an emphatic form of 'when' ○ *Whenever will you learn?* **2.** **SOMETIME** at another time

USAGE whenever or **when ever**? ***Whenever*** is written as one word when it is a conjunction (*Come whenever you can*), or an adverb used informally: *I'll do it at the weekend or whenever.* In questions in which *ever* is a reinforcing word, the two words are usually written separately: *When ever did I say that?*

whensoever /wén sō évvər/ *adv, conj* used as an intensive form of 'whenever' (*formal*)

whenua /fe noò ə/ *n NZ* same as **land** *n* (senses 1–5) [< Maori]

when-we *n S Africa* an offensive term for a South African who has migrated from or emigrated to Australia, New Zealand, Canada, or the United

Kingdom (*informal insult*) [Because such an immigrant stereotypically uses phrases beginning with 'When we', for example 'When we were in Kenya']

where /wair/ CORE MEANING: an adverb used to ask a question about the place that somebody or something is in, at, coming from, or going to ○ *Where are my keys?* ○ *Where are you going?* ○ *'Guess where I've been'. – 'Where?'*
1. *adv, rel adv* **IN OR TO PLACE** used to indicate the place in which something is located or happens ○ *I want to live where it's warm.* ○ *Nobody really knew where she had gone.* ○ *They went to the beach, where they spent the afternoon.* **2.** *adv* **WHAT PURPOSE** used to ask a question about the purpose or goal of something ○ *Where will all your hard work get you?* ○ *Where do you want to be after five years in this job?* **3.** *adv, rel adv* **IN SITUATION IN WHICH** in a or any situation in which ○ *Where there's life, there's hope.* ○ *They're at a stage where they can now talk about their problems.* **4.** *n* **UNKNOWN PLACE** used to refer to an unspecified place or event (*usually used in the plural*) ○ *Let us know the wheres and whens of your itinerary.* [Old English *hwær, hwar* < Indo-European]

SPELLCHECK See ***ware***[1].

USAGE It is best to avoid usages in which ***where*** follows nouns that are unrelated to the ideas of place and space: *This is a case where we must confer with a specialist. This is a situation where the accountants are wrong.* In formal writing, *in which* would be more appropriate than ***where*** in both these sentences. The preposition *from* is needed with ***where*** when the context involves a point of origin: *Where did that cat come from? From where we sit, we can see the stage clearly.* In formal writing, the redundant, dangling use of *at* with ***where*** should also be avoided. Thus: *He doesn't know where the car is* not *He doesn't know where the car is at.* The preposition *to* is superfluous with ***where*** when ***where*** is used in contexts involving destination. Thus: *Where are you going?* not *Where are you going to?*

whereabouts /wáir ə bowts/ *adv* in, at, or near what location ○ *Do you know whereabouts the hotel is?* ○ *I've forgotten whereabouts I parked the car.* ■ *n* the approximate place where somebody or something is (*takes a singular or plural verb*) ○ *Could you give us any information regarding the whereabouts of your brother?*

whereafter /wair áaftər/ *rel adv* after which time or event (*formal*) ○ *She left, whereafter he also departed.*

whereas /wair áz/ *conj* **1. WHILE IN CONTRAST** while on the other hand ○ *She was saving money, whereas you were living in the fast lane.* **2. BECAUSE** for the reason that (*formal*) ○ *Whereas you've proven your worth, you're welcome to join the team.* **3. CONNECTS SERIES OF CLAUSES** used to introduce each clause in a series (*formal*)

whereat /wair át/ (*archaic*) *rel adv* towards or at which place ■ *conj* because or as a consequence of which

whereby /wair bī/ *rel adv* by means of or through which ○ *the invention whereby he made his millions*

where'er /wair áir/ *adv, rel adv* same as **wherever** (*literary*)

~~**whereever**~~ incorrect spelling of **wherever**

wherefore /wáir fawr/ *n* **REASON** a reason or purpose for something ○ *I don't want to know the whys or the wherefores of your decision.* ■ *adv* **BECAUSE OF WHICH** for which reason (*archaic*) ■ *rel adv* **FOR WHAT REASON** for what reason or purpose (*archaic*)

wherefrom /wair fróm/ *adv* from what place or origin (*archaic*) ○ *Do we know wherefrom this stranger comes?*

wherein /wair ín/ *adv* **HOW** in what way or respect (*formal*) ○ *Wherein did I misspeak myself?* ■ *rel adv* (*archaic*) **1. WHERE** in which place ○ *the country wherein they dwelled* **2. DURING WHICH** during the time that ○ *the years wherein we were ignorant and happy*

whereof /wair óv/ *adv* of or about what person or thing (*formal*) ○ *Do you know whereof you speak?*

whereon /wair ón/ *rel pron* on which thing or place (*archaic or formal*) ○ *the couch whereon she lay*

wheresoever /wáir sō évvər/ *adv, conj* used as an emphatic form of 'wherever' (*formal*)

whereto /wair to͞o/, **whereunto** /-ún too/ *adv* where or to which (*archaic or formal*) ○ *the place whereto you've brought me*

whereupon /wáir ə pón/ *conj* at which time or as a result of ○ *The rain began to come down hard, whereupon we ran for the house.* ■ *rel pron* on or upon which (*archaic or formal*) ○ *the pillow whereupon she laid her head*

wherever /wair évvər/ *conj* **1. TO ANY PLACE** in, at, or to any place ○ *I'll go wherever you go.* **2. EVERY TIME OR PLACE THAT** on every occasion or in every place that ○ *Take exercise wherever possible.* ○ *I crossed the fields wherever there was a gate.* ■ *adv* **1. NO MATTER WHERE** at or in an indefinite place ○ *I'll sleep on the couch, the floor, wherever.* **2. AT UNKNOWN PLACE** to, in, or at an unknown or unidentified place or position **3.** *also* **where ever WHERE INDEED** used as an emphatic form of 'where' ○ *Where ever have my glasses gone?*

USAGE wherever or **where ever**? ***Wherever*** is written as one word when it is a conjunction (*You can go wherever you like*), or an adverb used informally: *I'll stop in Paris or wherever.* In questions in which *ever* is a reinforcing word, the two words are usually written separately: *Where ever did they go?*

wherewith /wair wi<u>th</u>/ *rel adv* with or by means of which (*archaic*) ○ *the tool wherewith the deed was done*

wherewithal /wáir wi<u>th</u> awl/ *n* the money or resources required for a purpose

wherry /wérri/ (*plural* **-ries**) *n* **1.** a small light rowing boat used in inland waters **2.** a small barge, once used for commercial purposes in parts of England, now used largely for pleasure cruises [15C. Origin ?] —**wherryman** *n*

whet /wet/ *vt* (**whets, whetting, whetted**) **1. STIMULATE SOMETHING** to make a feeling, sense, or desire more keen or intense ○ *The thought of easy money whetted my enthusiasm for the undertaking.* **2. SHARPEN TOOL OR WEAPON** to sharpen the cutting edge or blade of a tool or weapon, usually by rubbing it on a stone ■ *n* **1. SHARPENING OR INTENSIFYING OF SOMETHING** an act of sharpening, intensifying, or stimulating something **2. SHARPENING BLOCK** something that sharpens a cutting edge **3. SOMETHING THAT STIMULATES SENSES** something that stimulates a feeling, sense, or desire, especially a small amount that makes somebody want more (*informal*) [Old English *hwettan* 'sharpen' < Germanic, 'sharp'] —**whetter** *n*

SPELLCHECK See ***wet***.

whether /wé<u>th</u>ər/ *conj* **1. INTRODUCES ALTERNATIVES** used to indicate alternatives in an indirect question or a clause following a verb that expresses or implies doubt or the possibility of choice ○ *We should try to meet them whether it's raining or not.* **2. INTRODUCES INDIRECT QUESTION** used to introduce an indirect question ○ *I wonder whether it's worth the effort.* **3. EITHER** used to introduce doubt regarding two equal possibilities ○ *She said she'd get here whether by car or by train.* [Old English *hwæþer, hweþer* < Indo-European] ◇ **whether or no** whatever the circumstances might be (*archaic*)

SPELLCHECK See ***weather***.

whetstone /wét stōn/ *n* **1.** a stone used to sharpen the cutting edge or blade of a tool or weapon by rubbing **2.** something that makes a feeling, sense, or desire more keen or intense

whew /fyoo, hyoo/ *interj* used to express great relief, surprise, or discomfort [15C. Natural exclamation]

whey /way/ *n* the watery liquid that separates from the solid part of milk when it turns sour or when enzymes are added in cheese making [Old English *hwæg, hweg* < Germanic] —**wheyey** *adj*

SPELLCHECK See ***way***.

wheyface /wáy fayss/ *n* **1.** a very pale face (*informal*) **2.** somebody whose face is regarded as too pale (*insult*) —**wheyfaced** *adj*

whf *abbr* wharf

which /wich/ CORE MEANING: used to ask for something to be identified from a known larger group or range of possibilities ○ (det) *Which part of it don't you understand?* ○ (pron) *Which would you like?* ○ (pron) *Which of the colours do you prefer?* ○ (adj) *At which stage do we start to cut our losses?*
1. *det, pron* **ASKS QUESTION** asks for something to be identified from a known group or range ○ *Which hat should I wear?* **2.** *det, pron* **ONE FROM KNOWN SET** one of a range of things or possibilities specified or implied by the immediate context ○ (det) *I can't decide which activity would be the most fun.* ○ (pron) *He decided which to buy and paid the money.* **3.** *det, pron* same as **whichever** ○ (det) *Use which method best suits you.* ○ (pron) *Take which you prefer.* **4.** *pron* **INTRODUCES RELATIVE CLAUSE** used to introduce a clause that provides additional information about something previously mentioned ○ *The cabin, which we bought last spring, sits high on the dunes.* ○ *A success for which she is to be congratulated.* **5.** *pron* **THAT** used to introduce a relative clause that provides necessary information about its antecedent ○ *Please return the money which I loaned to you.* **6.** *pron* **REFERS BACK TO PHRASE OR SENTENCE** used to refer back to an entire verb phrase or sentence ○ *Swimming after eating, which I've told you not to do, can be very dangerous.* [Old English *hwilc* 'of what form, like what' < Germanic]

SPELLCHECK which or **witch**? Do not confuse the spelling of ***which*** and ***witch***, which sound similar. The word ***which*** is used to ask about or identify one or more of a larger group (as in *decide which car to use, Which are your children?*) or to introduce additional information: *The house, which was built in the 18th century, is now in ruins.* A ***witch*** is a person, especially a woman, with supposed magical powers.

USAGE See ***that*** and ***what***.

whichever /wich évvər/ *det, pron* used to refer to any one or any number of items in a class ○ (det) *Whichever job you take, starting out will be hard.* ○ (pron) *I'll buy whichever you think best.*

whichsoever /wíchssō évvər/ *pron, det* same as **whichever** (*archaic*)

whicker /wíkər/ (**-ers, -ering, -ered**) *vi* to neigh softly [Mid-17C. An imitation of the sound] —**whicker** *n*

whidah *n* BIRDS another spelling of **whydah**

whidden /wídd'n/ *n regional* the smallest or weakest piglet in a litter [Origin ?]

REGIONAL NOTE See ***underling***.

whiff /wif/ *n* **1. SLIGHT OR BRIEF ODOUR** a faint smell of something, pleasant or unpleasant, usually perceived briefly ○ *a whiff of disinfectant* **2. BAD SMELL** an unpleasant smell **3. TRACE OF SOMETHING** a slight sign or trace of something ○ *a whiff of corruption* **4. GENTLE GUST OR PUFF** a short light gust, puff, or breath of wind or smoke **5. SNIFF OF SOMETHING** a sniff, smell, or brief inhalation of something ○ *took one whiff of the concoction and started coughing* **6.** NAUT **SMALL SKIFF** a narrow skiff for one rower **7.** GOLF **COMPLETE MISS** in golf, a swing that completely misses the ball ■ *v* (**whiffs, whiffing, whiffed**) **1.** *vti* **WAFT OR PUFF** to come in short light gusts or puffs, or send something out in short light gusts or puffs ○ *The smoke whiffed and curled around the room.* **2.** *vt* **SNIFF SOMETHING** to sniff, smell, or inhale something ○ *The hyena whiffed the night air for predators.* **3.** *vi* **SMELL BAD** to have an unpleasant smell (*informal*) **4.** *vi* GOLF **FAIL TO HIT BALL** in golf, to swing at and miss a ball completely [Late 16C. Thought to suggest a light puff of wind that carries a smell] —**whiffer** *n*

whiffle /wíff'l/ (**-fles, -fling, -fled**) *v* **1.** *vi* **BEHAVE ERRATICALLY** to be indecisive or unpredictable in thought or action **2.** *vti* **BLOW GENTLY** to blow or move in short light variable gusts or puffs, or make something do this **3.** *vi* **WHISTLE** to whistle softly [Late 17C. < WHIFF] —**whiffler** *n*

whiffletree /wíff'l tree/ *n ANZ, N Am* AGRIC same as **swingletree** [Mid-19C. Variant of WHIPPLETREE]

whiffy /wíffi/ (**-ier, -iest**) *adj* having an unpleasant smell (*informal*)

Whig /wig/ *n* **1. MEMBER OF FORMER BRITISH POLITICAL PARTY** a member of a reforming British political party that supported the aristocracy and later the business community, finally becoming the core of the Liberal Party **2. CONSERVATIVE IN BRITISH LIBERAL PARTY** a conservative member of the Liberal Party in the United Kingdom **3. SUPPORTER OF FREE ENTERPRISE** an opponent of government intervention in commerce and the economy **4.** *US* **SUPPORTER OF WAR AGAINST BRITISH** a supporter of the American side against the British in the American War of Independence **5.** *US* **MEMBER OF 19C US POLITICAL PARTY** a member of a 19th-century US political party that favoured a loose interpretation of the Constitution and opposed the Democratic Party **6.** *Scotland* **SCOTTISH PRESBYTERIAN** a 17th-century Presbyterian in Scotland [Mid-17C. Shortening of ob-

solete Scots dialect *whiggamaire* 'horse driver'] —**Whiggery** *n* —**Whiggish** *adj* —**Whiggishly** *adv* —**Whiggishness** *n* —**Whiggism** *n*

ORIGIN The Scots word ***Whig*** seems originally to have been used as a contemptuous term for a country dweller, but by the middle of the 17th century it was being applied to Presbyterian supporters in Scotland. It was later adopted as a name for those who opposed the succession of the Catholic King James II, and by 1689 it had established itself as the title of one of the two main British political parties, opposed to the Tories.

whigmaleerie /hwígmə léeri/ *n Scotland* a fanciful ornament or trinket [Mid-18C. Origin ?]

while /wīl/ *conj* **1.** AT OR DURING SAME TIME at or during the same time that ○ *We can talk while I fix supper.* **2.** EVEN THOUGH in spite of the fact that ○ *While I admire your tenacity, I cannot support your aims.* **3.** BUT IN CONTRAST but on the contrary ○ *An older car would be cheaper to buy while a newer one might be more reliable.* **4.** *Scotland* same as **until** ■ *n* PERIOD OF TIME a period of time or an interval ○ *It's been a while since I saw her.* [Old English *hwīl* 'period of time' < Indo-European, 'rest, period of rest'] ◇ **once in a while** very occasionally ◇ **worth somebody's while 1.** deserving somebody's time, money, or support **2.** rewarding in terms of money or advantage

SPELLCHECK while or **wile**? Do not confuse the spelling of ***while*** and ***wile***, which sound similar. ***While*** indicates a time or an additional consideration: *took it while I was not looking, While I applaud the motive, the result might be disastrous.* ***Wile***, or more often the plural ***wiles***, refers to cunning behaviour.

USAGE while or **whilst**? In all the main meanings ***while*** and ***whilst*** are interchangeable, but ***whilst*** is used more in the north of Great Britain than in the south. Some people dislike the use of ***while*** to mean 'even though', as in *While we agree with some of what you say, we do not accept your conclusions.*

while away (whiles away, whiling away, whiled away) *vt* to pass time in an idle, leisurely, and usually pleasant way

whiles /wīlz/ (*archaic*) *adv* at some times ■ *conj* same as **while**

whilom /wīləm/ (*archaic*) *adv* same as **formerly** ■ *adj* same as **former**[1] *adj* (sense 1) ○ *his whilom friend* [Old English *hwīlom*, form of *hwīl* (see WHILE)]

whilst /wīlst/ *conj* same as **while** [15C. < WHILES]

USAGE See ***while***.

whim /wim/ *n* **1.** a sudden thought, idea, or desire, especially one based on impulse rather than reason or necessity **2.** a winch used to lift ore or water from a mine, drawn by a horse [Mid-17C. Origin ?]

whimberry /wímbəri/ (*plural* **-ries**) *n Wales* FOOD same as **bilberry** (*informal*) [Mid-19C. Alteration of *wineberry*]

whimbrel /wímbrəl/ (*plural same* or **-brels**) *n* a large shorebird with a long downward-curving beak, related to the curlew. Latin name: *Numenius phaeopus.* [Mid-16C. < obsolete dialect *whimp* 'whimper' (with reference to the bird's cry), or < WHIMPER]

~~whimp~~ incorrect spelling of **wimp**

whimper /wímpər/ *v* (**-pers, -pering, -pered**) **1.** *vi* SOB SOFTLY to make repeated weak plaintive crying or whining sounds of pain, distress, or fear **2.** *vt* SAY SOMETHING PLAINTIVELY to say something in a plaintive crying or whining voice **3.** *vi* COMPLAIN PEEVISHLY to complain in a weak, whining, or irritated manner ■ *n* **1.** WHINE a weak plaintive cry or whine **2.** COMPLAINT a weak, whining, or irritated complaint [Early 16C. < *whimp* 'whimper', an imitation of the sound] —**whimperingly** *adv*

whimsey *adj* another spelling of **whimsy**

whimsical /wímzik'l/ *adj* **1.** FANCIFUL imaginative and impulsive **2.** AMUSING slightly odd or playfully humorous, especially in an endearing way ○ *He gave me that whimsical smile of his.* **3.** ERRATIC OR UNPREDICTABLE behaving in a way that is impossible to predict ○ *She distrusted his whimsical nature.* [Mid-17C. < WHIMSY] —**whimsicality** /wímzi kálləti/ *n* —**whimsically** *adv* —**whimsicalness** *n*

whimsy /wímzi/ (*plural* **-sies**), **whimsey** (*plural* **-seys**) *n* **1.** the quality of being slightly odd or playfully humorous, especially in an endearing way ○ *There's a touch of whimsy about the old cottage.* **2.** an idea that has no immediately obvious reason to exist ○ *We can't always be catering to their whimsies.* [Early 17C. Probably based on WHIM-WHAM, perhaps after words like *dropsy*]

whim-wham *n* a quaint, odd, or fanciful object, e.g. an ornament, toy, or device (*archaic*) ○ *some whim-wham he bought somewhere* [Origin ?]

whin[1] /win/ (*plural same* or **whins**) *n* PLANTS same as **gorse** [15C. Probably < a N Germanic word related to Old Danish *hvinegræs* 'rough grass']

whin[2] /win/ *n* MINERALS same as **whinstone** [13C. Origin ?]

whinchat /wín chat/ (*plural same* or **-chats**) *n* a small songbird of the thrush family with mottled brown and white feathers and a streaky reddish-brown breast. Native to: Asia, Europe. Latin name: *Saxicola rubetra.* [Late 17C. < WHIN[2] + CHAT 'warbler']

whine /wīn/ *v* (**whines, whining, whined**) **1.** *vi* COMPLAIN PEEVISHLY to complain in an unreasonable, repeated, or irritating way **2.** *vi* MAKE HIGH SORROWFUL SOUND to cry, moan, or plead with a long, plaintive, high-pitched sound **3.** *vt* UTTER SOMETHING IN WHINING VOICE to say something in a plaintive high-pitched voice **4.** *vi* MAKE HIGH-PITCHED SOUND to make a continuous high-pitched sound ○ *The wind whined and moaned through the trees.* ■ *n* **1.** HIGH-PITCHED CRY a long, plaintive, high-pitched cry **2.** PEEVISH COMPLAINT a complaint or protest, especially one made repeatedly in an annoyingly plaintive voice **3.** CONTINUOUS HIGH-PITCHED SOUND a long or continuous high-pitched sound ○ *The whine of the jet engines woke me up.* [Old English *hwīnan* '(of an arrow) to whistle through the air', of imitative origin] —**whiner** *n* —**whiningly** *adv* —**whiny** *adj*

SPELLCHECK whine or **wine**? Do not confuse the spelling of ***whine*** and ***wine***, which sound similar. ***Whine*** is a noun and verb referring to a long plaintive high-pitched sound or a peevish complaint, as in *the whine of the engines, customers whining about poor service.* ***Wine*** is a noun denoting an alcoholic drink made from grapes or other fruit; it is occasionally used as a verb in the phrase *wine and dine.*

SYNONYMS See ***complain***.

whinge /winj/ (*informal*) *vi* (**whinges, whingeing, whinged**) **1.** COMPLAIN PEEVISHLY to complain annoyingly or continuously about something relatively unimportant **2.** MAKE IRRITATING SORROWFUL SOUND to cry or whimper annoyingly or continuously ■ *n* PEEVISH COMPLAINT an irritable, peevish complaint about something relatively unimportant [Old English *hwinsian* 'whine', an imitation of the sound of a whining dog] —**whinger** *n* —**whingy** *adj*

whingeing Pom /wínjing-/ *n Aus* an offensive term for a British person, especially one perceived as constantly complaining, usually about life in Australia (*informal insult*)

whinny /wínni/ *v* (**-nies, -nying, -nied**) **1.** *vi* NEIGH to neigh softly **2.** *vi* MAKE SOUND LIKE NEIGHING HORSE to make a neighing sound, especially when laughing **3.** *vt* UTTER SOMETHING WITH NEIGHING SOUND to say or express something with a sound like a neighing horse ■ *n* (*plural* **-nies**) NEIGHING SOUND a soft neigh, or a sound like a neighing horse [Mid-16C. An imitation of the sound]

whinstone /wín stōn/ *n* a hard, dark, fine-grained rock, e.g. basalt or chert [Early 16C. < WHIN[2]]

whip /wip/ *v* (**whips, whipping, whipped**) **1.** *vt* LASH SOMEBODY OR SOMETHING to strike a person or animal repeatedly with a flexible rod, length of rope, thin strip of leather attached to a handle, or something similar, especially as a punishment **2.** *vti* STRIKE AGAINST SOMETHING SHARPLY to strike somebody or something very hard, sharply, or repeatedly ○ *The icy rain whipped our faces.* **3.** *vt* CRITICIZE SOMEBODY SEVERELY to criticize or reproach somebody very strongly or severely **4.** *vti* MOVE RAPIDLY to move very quickly, forcefully, or suddenly, or make something do this ○ *She whipped around guiltily as I came in.* **5.** *vt* DO SOMETHING WITH RAPID ACTION to do something very quickly, suddenly, or forcefully ○ *She whipped out her camera and took a photo.* **6.** *vt* BIND END OF ROPE to wind thread, cord, or twine around the end of a rope or cable to keep it from fraying **7.** *vt* DEFEAT SOMEBODY to defeat, overcome, or outdo somebody (*informal*) **8.** *vt* COOK BEAT LIQUID UNTIL STIFF to make food such as batter or cream stiff and creamy by adding air to it with short quick movements, using a fork, whisk, or electric beater **9.** *vt* NAUT LIFT SOMETHING BY ROPE AND PULLEY to lift something by means of a device consisting of a rope passed through a single pulley **10.** *vt* HANDICRAFT SEW SOMETHING IN WHIPSTITCH to sew the edge of a piece of fabric using whipstitch **11.** *vt* SPIN TOP to make a top start to spin **12.** *vt* STEAL to steal something or remove something (*informal*) ■ *n* **1.** INSTRUMENT FOR INFLICTING PAIN a flexible rod, length of rope, or thin strip of leather attached to a handle, used to strike people or animals repeatedly **2.** LASHING STROKE OR BLOW a stroke or blow with a whip or something similar ○ *a whip across the face* **3.** SOMETHING RESEMBLING WHIP something that resembles a whip in form, motion, or flexibility **4.** SOMEBODY WHO USES WHIP somebody who is experienced or skilled in using a whip, e.g. the driver of a horse-drawn carriage **5.** POL SOMEBODY IN CHARGE OF PARTY DISCIPLINE an elected representative in a legislative body such as Parliament or the US Congress who has special responsibility for ensuring discipline and attendance among his or her party's members **6.** POL CALL FOR PARTY SOLIDARITY a call issued to a political party's elected members to ensure they attend for an important vote and vote the party line **7.** POL WEEKLY LEGISLATIVE AGENDA in Parliament, a weekly agenda sent to a party's members that indicates which items are routine, important, or urgent **8.** FOOD SWEET DISH a light creamy dessert made from whipped cream with added sweetening and flavouring **9.** NAUT HOISTING APPARATUS a device that consists of a rope, a pulley, and a snatch block. Use: raising heavy cargo. **10.** MUSIC FLEXIBLE PERCUSSION INSTRUMENT a percussion instrument with two flexible strips of wood attached in the shape of a V that make a loud clapping sound when they are waved in the air **11.** FIELD SPORTS same as **whipper-in** **12.** INDUST WINDMILL VANE a sail or arm of a windmill **13.** LEISURE FAIRGROUND AMUSEMENT a ride at an amusement park with small cars that travel with sudden rapid jerking movements round a track **14.** WRESTLING WRESTLING THROW in wrestling, a throw in which an opponent is seized by an outstretched arm and thrown to the floor **15.** *US* LONG FLEXIBLE BRANCH a long, slender, flexible branch of some trees such as willows ○ *furniture made of willow whips* [13C. Probably < Middle Low German or Middle Dutch *wippen* 'swing', < Germanic, 'move quickly'] ◇ **crack the whip** a game in which children join hands in a line and pull each other around sharply

whip in *v* **1.** *vi* to keep a pack of hounds under control **2.** *vt* to keep the members of a political party in line with the party's aims

whip through *vt* to do something very quickly (*informal*)

whip up *vt* **1.** EXCITE SOMEBODY OR SOMETHING to arouse or provoke a strong feeling or reaction in a group of people **2.** MAKE SOMETHING RISE UP to stir or disturb something with force so that it rises or flies up **3.** PREPARE SOMETHING RAPIDLY to make something quickly, especially an impromptu meal (*informal*)

whipbird /wíp burd/ *n* a bird that has a long tail and prominent crest and emits a loud whistling sound that ends with a sound like that of a whip being cracked. Native to: Australia. Latin name: *Psophodes olivaceus* or *Psophodes nigrogularis.*

whipcord /wíp kawrd/ *n* **1.** a strong cotton or woollen fabric woven with diagonal ribs **2.** a tough twisted cord used for whips

whip graft *n* a way of grafting two plants by inserting the cut end of a scion into a similar cut in a rootstock and tying them securely together until they join

whip hand *n* **1.** the most powerful or advantageous position in a situation ○ *She has the whip hand.* **2.** the hand that holds a whip, especially when driving horses

whiplash /wíp lash/ *n* **1.** MED INJURY TO NECK an injury to the muscles, ligaments, vertebrae, or nerves of the neck caused when the head is suddenly thrown forward and then sharply back **2.** FLEXIBLE PART OF WHIP the flexible part of a whip **3.** LASHING BLOW a stroke or blow from a whip **4.** LASHING MOVEMENT OR IMPACT something that resembles a stroke or blow from a whip in motion, speed, or force

whipper-in /wíppər-/ (*plural* **whippers-in**) *n* somebody who assists to a fox hunter in controlling a pack of hounds

whippersnapper /wíppər snapər/ *n* an impudent and unimportant person, especially somebody who is young (*dated*) [Late 17C. Origin ?]

whipper snipper /wíppər-/ *n Aus* a machine for trimming the edges of lawns

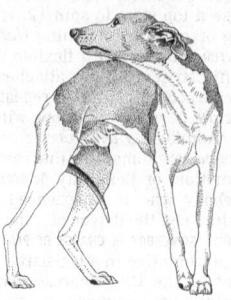

whippet

whippet /wíppit/ *n* a fast slender short-haired dog belonging to a breed that resembles, but is smaller than, a greyhound [Mid-16C. < WHIP]

whipping /wípping/ *n* **1.** PUNISHMENT a beating, spanking, or flogging with a whip or something similar **2.** BINDING CORD thread, cord, or twine wound round the end of a rope or cable to keep it from fraying **3.** DEFEAT a convincing defeat (*informal*) ○ *Didn't they give us a whipping in that last game?*

whipping boy *n* somebody who gets the blame or punishment for the mistakes or wrongdoings of more important people [Originally, this referred to a boy raised and educated with a prince. If the prince misbehaved, the boy would be punished in his place]

whipping cream *n* a heavy cream containing a high proportion of butterfat, which causes it to stiffen when whipped

whippletree /wípp'l tree/ *n* AGRIC same as **swingletree** [Mid-18C. < WHIP]

whippoorwill /wíppərwil/ *n* a nocturnal bird of the nightjar family, with spotted dark feathers and a distinctive song. Native to: North America. Latin name: *Caprimulgus vociferus.* [An imitation of its call]

whip-round *n* an informal and often impromptu collection of money within a group of people for a specific purpose, often buying a present for somebody (*informal*)

whipsaw /wíp saw/ *n* a saw with a flexible blade, e.g. a band saw ■ *vt* (**-saws, -sawing, -sawed** or **-sawn** /-sawn/) to saw something with a whipsaw

whip scorpion *n* a terrestrial invertebrate related to the scorpion, but with a whip-shaped appendage at the end of its abdomen. Native to: tropics, subtropics. Order: Uropygi.

whip snake *n* a nonpoisonous snake that can pursue its prey at a fast speed. Native to: North America, Asia, Europe, Africa. Genus: *Coluber.*

whipstall /wíp stawl/ *n* a manoeuvre in a small aircraft in which it goes into a vertical climb, pauses briefly, and then drops towards the earth, nose first

whipstitch /wíp stich/ *n* a small stitch that passes over the edge of a piece of fabric, used to finish the edge or baste two pieces of fabric together ■ *vt* (**-stitches, -stitching, -stitched**) to sew the edge of a piece of fabric using a whipstitch

whipstock /wíp stok/ *n* the handle of a whip

whiptail /wíp tayl/ *n* a lizard with a long thin tail. Native to: South America, Mexico. Genus: *Cnemidophorus.*

whipworm /wíp wurm/ *n* a nematode worm found in human intestines. Its presence usually produces no symptoms, but a severe infection with this parasite can cause diarrhoea. Latin name: *Trichuris trichiura.*

whir *vti, n* another spelling of **whirr**

whirl /wurl/ *v* (**whirls, whirling, whirled**) **1.** *vti* TURN OR SPIN RAPIDLY to turn or spin very quickly, or make something do this **2.** *vti* MOVE WHILE TURNING QUICKLY to move along while turning or spinning very quickly, or make something do this ○ *The dancers whirled round the floor.* **3.** *vi* FEEL DIZZY OR CONFUSED to seem to spin with dizziness, confusion, or excitement ○ *So much information at one time made my head whirl.* **4.** *vti* MOVE VERY FAST to move very quickly on a straight or curved course, or make something do this ○ *Cars whirled past on the highway.* ■ *n* **1.** SPINNING MOTION a rapid turning or spinning movement ○ *The whirl of the top was mesmerizing.* **2.** SOMETHING THAT WHIRLS something that moves or is moved with a rapid circular or spiral motion ○ *Whirls of dust filled the air.* **3.** SENSATION OF SPINNING a spinning sensation caused, e.g. by dizziness, confusion, or excitement ○ *So much good luck had my head in a whirl.* **4.** QUICK SUCCESSION OF EVENTS the bustling activity of an endless series of events or engagements ○ *the whirl and bustle of a large city* **5.** BRIEF TRIP OR RIDE a short trip, ride, or dance (*informal*) ○ *Let's go for a whirl in my new car.* [13C. Probably < Old Norse *hvirfla* < Indo-European, 'turn around'] —**whirler** *n* —**whirly** *adj* ◇ **give something a whirl** to have a try at something (*informal*)

whirlabout /wúrl ə bowt/ *n* a turn, spin, or revolution

whirligig /wúrligig/ *n* **1.** SPINNING TOY a toy that spins or turns very quickly **2.** MERRY-GO-ROUND a merry-go-round or carousel **3.** SOMETHING THAT WHIRLS something that revolves rapidly or changes continuously ○ *Her life's a whirligig since she took over the business.* **4.** INSECTS same as **whirligig beetle** [15C. < *whirling* or *whirly* + *gig* 'spinning top']

whirligig beetle *n* an insect with a smooth oval flattened body, usually seen spinning around in groups on the surface of calm fresh water. Family: Gyrinidae.

whirling dervish /wúrling-/ *n* **1.** somebody who busily does many things in quick succession **2.** a member of an ascetic Muslim religious group known for very energetic whirling

whirlpool /wúrl pool/ *n* **1.** a spiralling current of water in a stream or river **2.** something that has or seems to have the action, motion, or power of a whirlpool ○ *a whirlpool of despair* **3.** US HOUSEHOLD same as **whirlpool bath**

whirlpool bath *n* a bath or outdoor pool with powerful underwater jets that keep the water constantly moving or swirling around the body. It is sometimes used in physical therapy. US term **whirlpool**

whirlwind /wúrl wind/ *n* **1.** SOMETHING HAPPENING OR CHANGING SWIFTLY something that happens very quickly, or a rapid succession of events (*often used before a noun*) ○ *a whirlwind romance* ○ *a whirlwind visit* **2.** SOMETHING VERY DESTRUCTIVE something that has a terrible destructive force ○ *swept up in the whirlwind of war* **3.** METEOROL SPINNING COLUMN OF AIR a column of air rotating rapidly round a core of low pressure [14C. < Old Norse *hvirfilwindr*]

whirlybird /wúrli burd/ *n* AVIAT same as **helicopter** (*informal*)

whirr /wur/, **whir** *vti* (**whirrs, whirring, whirred; whirs, whirring, whirred**) to make a continuous soft buzzing or humming sound, usually by vibrating or turning very quickly, or make something do this ■ *n* a continuous soft buzzing or humming sound like that of something vibrating or turning very quickly [14C. Probably < N Germanic]

whish /wish/ *v* (**whishes, whishing, whished**) **1.** *vi* MAKE OR MOVE WITH RUSHING SOUND to make a soft whistling or rushing sound, or move with such a sound ○ *Water whished along the boat as we rowed upstream.* **2.** *vt* MOVE SOMETHING WITH WHISHING SOUND to make something move with a whishing sound ○ *The dog whished its tail.* ■ *n* WHISHING SOUND OR MOVEMENT a soft whistling or rushing sound, or a movement that makes such a sound ○ *the whish of the windscreen wipers* ■ *adv* WITH WHISHING SOUND moving or falling with a whishing sound ○ *Whish, the branch came down.* [Early 16C. An imitation of the sound]

whisht /hwisht/, **whist** /hwist/, **wheesht** /hweesht/ *Scotland interj* CALL FOR SILENCE used to command a person or a group to be silent ■ *vti* (**whishts, whishting, whishted; whists, whisting, whisted; wheeshts, wheeshting, wheeshted**) BE SILENT to silence somebody or something, or become or remain silent ■ *n* SILENCE the state or condition of being silent [Mid-16C. An imitation of the sound made by someone calling for silence]

whisk /wisk/ *n* **1.** UTENSIL FOR WHIPPING LIQUIDS a kitchen utensil, formed of curved or coiled wires attached to a handle or a bundle of twigs or stalks, used to whip soft or liquid substances **2.** BRUSHING MOVEMENT a quick light brushing or sweeping movement ○ *He wiped the table with a whisk of his hand.* **3.** BRUSH a bundle of twigs, straw, or grass attached to a handle used to sweep things ■ *v* (**whisks, whisking, whisked**) **1.** *vt* WHIP LIQUID WITH WHISK to whip a soft or liquid substance with a fork, whisk, or other utensil **2.** *vt*

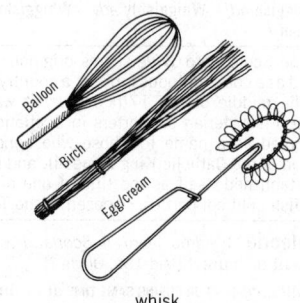

whisk

BRUSH SOMETHING AWAY LIGHTLY to remove something with a quick light brushing or sweeping movement ○ *He whisked the crumbs from the table.* **3.** *vt* MOVE SOMETHING WITH SWEEPING MOTION to move something or put something somewhere with a quick light sweeping motion **4.** *vti* MOVE QUICKLY to move somewhere quickly or suddenly, or make somebody or something do this ○ *They whisked her off to hospital.* [14C. < Germanic]

whisker /wískər/ *n* **1.** HAIR ON SOMEBODY'S FACE a short stiff hair growing on somebody's face, especially on the cheeks, chin, or upper lip **2.** HAIR NEAR ANIMAL'S MOUTH a long stiff hair growing near the mouth of some mammals such as cats, mice, and rabbits **3.** SMALL MARGIN a very small amount or margin ○ *We came within a whisker of losing everything.* **4.** *also* **whisker boom** NAUT LIGHT POLE a light pole used for extending the corners of a sail **5.** CHEM THIN CRYSTAL a strong thin hair-shaped crystal of a metal or mineral ■ **whiskers** *npl* SOMEBODY'S FACIAL HAIR a short growth of hair growing on somebody's cheeks, chin, or upper lip [15C. < WHISK] —**whiskered** *adj* —**whiskery** *adj*

whiskey /wíski/ *n Ireland, US* another spelling of **whisky**

whiskey jack *n N Am* BIRDS same as **grey jay** [< *whiskey john*, by folk etymology < Cree *wiskatjan*]

whisk fern *n* a simple plant with slender branching stems and tiny scale-shaped leaves that reproduces by means of spores. Native to: tropical and subtropical regions. Latin name: *Psilotum nudum.*

whisky /wíski/ (*plural* **-kies**) *n* **1.** an alcoholic drink made from a fermented grain such as barley or rye and sometimes aged or blended **2.** a drink or measure of whisky [Early 18C. < Scottish Gaelic *usquebea, usque beatha* 'water of life' < *usque* 'water' and *bethu* 'life']

USAGE **whiskey** or **whisky**? *Whisky* is the spelling used for the Scottish drink and in British English generally; *whiskey* is used for the drink produced in Ireland and in American English generally.

Whisky *n* a code word for the letter 'W', used in international radio communications

whisky mac *n* a drink made of whisky and ginger wine

whisper /wíspər/ *v* (**-pers, -pering, -pered**) **1.** *vti* BREATHE WORDS VOICELESSLY to speak or say something very softly, without using the vocal cords **2.** *vti* SPEAK OR SUGGEST SOMETHING SECRETLY to speak or say something in a confidential or furtive manner, e.g. in order to reveal a secret or conspire with somebody ○ *Whisper so that no one else hears.* **3.** *vi* RUSTLE SOFTLY to make a soft rustling sound ■ *n* **1.** VERY LOW VOICE a soft speaking sound that uses the breath but not the vocal cords ○ *She spoke in a whisper.* **2.** SOMETHING SAID IN SOFT VOICE something said in a whisper **3.** RUMOUR a rumour expressed confidentially or furtively ○ *There have been whispers of a romance.* **4.** RUSTLING SOUND a soft rustling sound **5.** FAINT HINT a hint or trace of something ○ *a whisper of interest* [Old English *hwisprian* < Germanic] —**whisperer** *n*

whispering campaign /wíspəring-/ *n* a concerted effort to spread scandalous rumours in order to damage or destroy the reputation of a person or group

whispering gallery *n* a space or gallery beneath a dome or vault with acoustic properties that enable a faint sound made at one point to travel round the entire circumference and be audible at any point on it

whist[1] /wist/ *n* a card game in which two pairs of people try to take a majority of the tricks and the trump suit is determined by the last card dealt. Whist is a forerunner of bridge. [Mid-17C. Origin ?]

whist[2] *interj, vti, n* same as **whisht**

whist drive *n* a card party at which the winning players of each hand of whist move to different tables and play the losers of the preceding hand

whistle /wíss'l/ *v* (**-tles, -tling, -tled**) **1.** *vi* MAKE SHRILL SOUND THROUGH PURSED LIPS to make a shrill or musical sound by forcing the breath through a small gap between the lips or the teeth **2.** *vi* PRODUCE SHRILL SOUND to produce a shrill sound or signal by forcing steam or air through a narrow opening (*refers to trains, kettles, etc.*) ○ *heard the train whistle as it came round the bend* **3.** *vi* EMIT SHRILL CALL to make a shrill call or cry (*refers to birds and animals*) **4.** *vi* MOVE WITH SHRILL SOUND to move at great speed through the air, making a shrill sound ○ *traffic whistling by* **5.** *vt* MAKE MUSICAL SOUND BY WHISTLING to produce music or give a signal by whistling ○ *whistling a tune* **6.** *vti* ISSUE CALL OR ORDER BY WHISTLING to summon, order, or signal to a person or animal by whistling ■ *n* **1.** DEVICE PRODUCING SHRILL SOUND a device or instrument that produces a shrill or musical sound when air or breath is forced through it **2.** WHISTLING SOUND a sound or signal made by a person, animal, or object whistling ○ *He let out a low whistle.* **3.** ACT OF WHISTLING an act of whistling [Old English *hwistlian* < Germanic, 'whistle, hiss'] ◇ **blow the whistle (on somebody** *or* **something)** to report somebody for doing something wrong or illegal, or reveal something wrong or illegal that is being done, especially within an organization (*informal*) ◇ **wet your whistle** to have a drink, especially of alcohol (*informal*)

whistle for *vt* to expect something that is not going to happen or be given (*informal*)

whistle up *vt* to summon a person or animal by making a whistling call

whistle-blower *n* somebody who exposes wrongdoing, especially within an organization (*informal*) [< the idea of a police officer sounding the alarm when witnessing a crime] —**whistle-blowing** *n*

whistler /wísslər/ *n* **1.** WHISTLING PERSON OR OBJECT somebody or something that whistles **2.** MEDIA RADIO DISTURBANCE an interference signal in a radio receiver, resembling a whistling sound of decreasing pitch and caused by lightning or other electromagnetic disturbance **3.** BIRDS WHISTLING SONGBIRD an often brightly coloured songbird with a particularly melodious whistling call. Native to: Indonesia, New Guinea, Australia, western Pacific. Family: Pachycephalidae. **4.** VET HORSE WITH RESPIRATORY PROBLEM a horse with a respiratory condition that causes it to make a whistling noise when it breathes in

AKG London

James McNeill Whistler

Whistler /wísslər/, **James McNeill** (1834–1903) US artist. Influenced by both European and Japanese art, he was renowned for his etchings, subtle landscapes, and portraits such as the one popularly known as *Whistler's Mother* (1871). Full name **Whistler, James Abbott McNeill**

> 'As music is the poetry of sound so painting is the poetry of sight, and the subject matter has nothing to do with harmony of sound or colour.'
> [James McNeill Whistler, *The Gentle Art of Making Enemies*; 1890]

whistle stop *n* **1.** SHORT CAMPAIGN STOP a brief stop by a political candidate in a small town during an election campaign **2.** *N Am* SMALL RAILWAY STATION a town or railway station where trains stop only when signalled to do so **3.** *N Am* SMALL TOWN a small town or community (*slang*)

whistle-stop *adj* conducted very rapidly with frequent brief stops in order to make public appearances or deliver election speeches ○ *a whistle-stop tour of the state* ■ *vi* to make a series of brief stops in small towns as part of a political campaign

whistling duck /wíssling-/ *n* a long-legged duck with an upright stance and often a whistling call. Native to: tropical wetlands. Genus: *Dendrocygna*.

whit /wit/ *n* the smallest imaginable degree or amount ○ *I don't care a whit whether they succeed or fail.* [15C. Alteration of WIGHT]

Whit /wit/ CHR, CALENDAR *adj* same as **Whitsun** ■ *n* same as **Whitsuntide** [Mid-16C. Shortening of *Whitsun* or *Whit Sunday*]

Whitaker /wíttəkər/, **Sir Frederick** (1812–91) British-born premier of New Zealand. He was New Zealand's first attorney general and held the premiership twice (1863–64, 1882–83) before the advent of organized political parties.

Whitby /wítbi/ fishing port and tourist resort in North Yorkshire, northern England. Population: 14,000 (1994).

white /wīt/ *adj* (**whiter, whitest**) **1.** SNOW-COLOURED having the colour of fresh snow or milk, as a result of the reflection of nearly all light from visible wavelengths **2.** WITHOUT COLOUR lacking colour or hue **3.** *also* **White** PALE-SKINNED relating to or belonging to a people with naturally pale skin, especially one of European ancestry **4.** COMPARATIVELY LIGHT light in colour in comparison with others of the same kind ○ *white cabbage* **5.** WINE MADE FROM WHITE GRAPES describes wine made from pale-skinned grapes **6.** LACKING PIGMENT describes hair that has lost most or all of its pigment, usually as a result of aging **7.** HAVING VERY PALE COMPLEXION unusually pale in the face, e.g. from fright or shock **8.** ZOOL, BOT HAVING WHITE PARTS OR COLOURINGS describes plants or animals with light or white parts or colourings ○ *white bass* **9.** FOOD INDUST WITHOUT BRAN OR GERM describes flour that has had the bran and wheat germ removed **10.** COOK MADE FROM WHITE FLOUR made using white flour **11.** BEVERAGES SERVED WITH MILK served with milk added ○ *white coffee* **12.** UNMARKED BY WRITING not written on or printed on **13.** PURE unblemished, especially in character **14.** WEARING WHITE dressed in white, or characterized by the wearing of white **15.** INCANDESCENT heated to such a high degree that the substance turns white in colour **16.** HAVING SNOW accompanied or characterized by the presence of snow **17.** MUSIC LACKING TONAL WARMTH relating to a pure musical tone that lacks warmth, colour, and resonance **18.** *also* **White** HIST, POL POLITICALLY CONSERVATIVE conservative or royalist in political outlook ■ *n* **1.** COLOURS COLOUR OF SNOW the colour of fresh snow or milk **2.** ART WHITE PAINT a paint or dye that is or is near to the colour of fresh snow **3.** WHITE FABRIC OR AREA a white substance or fabric, or the part of something that is white, e.g. an unprinted area on a page **4.** WHITE THING a white object, especially the white cue ball in snooker **5.** *also* **White** PALE-SKINNED PERSON a member of a people with pale skin, especially one of European ancestry **6.** FOOD PART OF EGG the transparent liquid that surrounds the yolk of an egg and turns white when the egg is cooked **7.** ANAT PART OF EYE the part of the eyeball surrounding the iris **8.** BOARD GAMES GAME PIECE OR PLAYER a white or light-coloured piece or set of pieces in a game such as chess or draughts, or the player using them **9.** INSECTS BUTTERFLY a butterfly that is predominantly white in colour. Family: Pieridae. **10.** ARCHERY PART OF TARGET the white outermost ring of an archery target, or a shot that lands in it ■ *npl* **1.** WHITE LAUNDRY white or light-coloured laundry, usually washed separately from coloured laundry items **2.** SPORTS CLOTHES white or off-white sports clothing, especially as worn by tennis players or cricketers **3.** *US* WHITE DRESS MILITARY UNIFORM the white dress uniform of a military service, e.g. that of the US Navy or Coast Guard **4.** MED same as **leucorrhoea** (*informal*) ■ *v* (**whites, whiting, whited**) **1.** *vt* LEAVE BLANK SPACES IN SOMETHING to put or leave blank spaces in something, especially something printed **2.** *vti* WHITEN to become white, or cause something to become white (*archaic*) [Old English *hwīt* < Indo-European, 'shine'] —**whiteness** *n* —**whitish** *adj*

white out *v* **1.** *vt* to cover a mistake in written, printed, or typed material using white correction fluid **2.** *vi* to lose visibility in daylight because of snow or fog

White /wīt/, **Patrick** (1912–90) British-born Australian writer. His works, mainly set in Australia, include plays, poems, short stories, and novels. He won a Nobel Prize in literature (1973). Full name **White, Patrick Victor Martindale**. See Cultural note at **tree**

> '"I dunno," Arthur said. "I forget what I was taught. I only remember what I've learnt."'
> [Patrick White, *The Solid Mandala*; 1966]

white admiral *n* **1.** a butterfly that has brown wings with white marks. Native to: Europe, Asia. Latin name: *Limenitis camilla*. **2.** a butterfly that has bluish-black wings with a large white band on them. Native to: North America. Latin name: *Limenitis arthemis*.

white alkali *n* a whitish deposit of mineral salts that is sometimes seen on the surface of very alkaline soils

white ant *n* INSECTS same as **termite**

white-ant (**white-ants, white-anting, white-anted**) *vt Aus* to destroy or undermine something from within (*informal*) [Early 20C. < the methods of the Australian termite]

white area *n* an area of land not yet subject to planning proposals or limitations [< The idea of its not being coded in any particular colour on planning maps]

white ash *n* **1.** the strong resilient wood of an ash tree whose leaves have a pale silvery underside. Use: oars. **2.** an ash tree that has leaves with a pale silvery underside and yields white ash. Native to: North America. Latin name: *Fraxinus americana*. [< the pale colour of the undersides of its leaves]

White Australia Policy *n* the policy of limiting the number of non-white people migrating to Australia, embodied in the Immigration Restriction Act of 1901 and officially abandoned in 1945. Some restrictions remained in place for some time afterwards.

whitebait /wīt bayt/ (*plural same*) *n* **1.** a small young fish fried and eaten whole, especially a young herring **2.** a small sea fish that swims into brackish or fresh water to spawn. Native to: Australia, New Zealand. Latin name: *Galaxias attenuatus*. [Mid-18C. *White* < the silvery colour of most of the fish]

white bass *n* an edible silvery freshwater fish of the bass family. Native to: Great Lakes, Mississippi valley. Latin name: *Morone chrysops*.

whitebeam /wīt beem/ *n* a deciduous tree whose leaves have pale hairy undersides. Native to: Europe, Asia. Latin name: *Sorbus aria*. [Early 18C. < the white undersides of its leaves]

white belt *n* **1.** the belt worn by a beginner in a martial art such as karate or judo **2.** a beginner in a martial art such as karate or judo who wears a white belt

white blood cell *n* an unpigmented large cell in blood that helps protect the body against infection and also plays a role in inflammation and allergic reactions

whiteboard /wīt bawrd/ *n* a board with a white plastic surface that is written on with erasable marker pens, used in teaching and in giving presentations [Mid-20C. < WHITE, after *blackboard*]

white book *n* in some countries, an official government report published in a white binding

Whiteboy /wīt boy/ *n* in the mid-18th century, a member of a secret organization of Irish farmers fighting for agrarian reform [Mid-18C. *White* < the white shirts they wore]

white bread *n* bread made from flour that has had the bran and wheat germ removed

white-bread *adj* **1.** bland, conventional, and unimaginative **2.** *N Am* relating to, belonging to, or considered characteristic of white middle-class North America (*informal*)

white bryony *n* a climbing plant with lobed leaves and reddish-black berries. Native to: Europe, Asia, North Africa. Genus: *Bryonia*. [< its greenish-white flowers]

whitecap /wīt kap/ *n* the white crest of a breaking wave

white cedar *n* **1.** a light-coloured highly durable wood from either of two coniferous trees. Use: building boats, telegraph poles. **2.** a coniferous tree that has leaves resembling scales and yields white cedar. Native to: eastern North America. Latin name:

Chamaecyparis thyoides or *Thuja occidentalis*. [< the light colour of their wood]

white cell *n* PHYSIOL same as **white blood cell**

white chip *n* **1.** a betting chip with the lowest possible value **2.** something of little value

white chocolate *n* a cream-coloured confection containing the same ingredients as chocolate but lacking cocoa powder

white Christmas *n* a Christmas when there is snow, especially on Christmas day

white clover *n* a perennial plant grown with grass as pasture for livestock. Flowers: small, white, attractive to honey bees. Native to: Europe, Asia, naturalized in North America. Latin name: *Trifolium repens*.

white coal *n* flowing water considered as a source of hydroelectric power

white-collar *adj* relating to jobs that are usually salaried and do not involve manual labour [< the white shirts traditionally worn by people in such jobs]

white-collar crime *n* theft, fraud, embezzlement, or some other nonviolent lawbreaking act perpetrated by a salaried employee or senior manager of a company or organization

white corpuscle *n* PHYSIOL same as **white blood cell**

white currant *n* **1.** a greenish-white berry, usually eaten raw **2.** a variety of the redcurrant bush that produces white currants. Latin name: *Ribes sativum*.

whitedamp /wít damp/ *n* a mixture of poisonous gases that collects in coalmines [After BLACKDAMP]

whited sepulchre /wítid-/ *n* a hypocrite, especially somebody who is falsely righteous or pious [< the Bible (Matthew 23:27), which compares such people to whitewashed tombs]

white dwarf *n* a small, dim, extremely dense star that has collapsed on itself and is in the final stages of its evolution [< its colour]

white elephant *n* **1.** SOMETHING COSTLY TO MAINTAIN an expensive and often rare or valuable possession whose upkeep is a considerable financial burden **2.** POSSESSION OF QUESTIONABLE VALUE something with a questionable or at least very limited value **3.** CONSPICUOUS FAILED VENTURE a much publicized or keenly anticipated venture that proves to be a spectacular flop **4.** DISCARDED OBJECT an unwanted object of possible use to somebody else (*hyphenated before a noun*) **5.** ALBINO ELEPHANT a rare albino Indian elephant regarded as sacred in parts of South and Southeast Asia [In sense 1 and related senses < the reputed practice of the King of Siam (Thailand) of giving a white elephant to troublesome courtiers, who would be ruined by the cost of keeping it]

White Ensign *n* the flag of the British Royal Navy, showing a red cross on a white background with the Union Jack in the upper corner nearest the hoist

white-eye *n* a small green or greenish-brown songbird with a ring of white feathers round the eye. Native to: tropical and subtropical regions. Family: Zosteropidae.

whiteface /wít fayss/ *n* white makeup for the face, particularly as used by clowns

white-faced *adj* **1.** having an unusually pale face **2.** having white markings on the face, especially as a distinguishing feature between similar species

white-faced heron *n* a medium-sized heron that has grey plumage, yellow legs, and a white face. Native to: Australia. Latin name: *Ardea novaehollandiae*.

white feather ◇ **show the white feather** to behave in a cowardly way (*dated*)

white fish *n* an edible sea fish with whitish flesh such as the cod, hake, or whiting, as distinct from a flat fish such as the plaice and an oily fish such as the mackerel

whitefish /wít fish/ (*plural* **-fishes** /-fish/ or *same*) *n* **1.** a freshwater fish with large scales and a small mouth. Native to: North America. Family: Coregonidae. **2.** the pale flesh of a whitefish eaten as food

white flag *n* a white cloth or improvised flag waved as an international sign of truce or surrender

white flight *n* the movement of white people that sometimes occurs from neighbourhoods where members of other groups are settling, especially because of racism

white flour *n* flour from which most of the bran and wheat germ has been removed. It is whitish and much lighter in texture than wholemeal flour.

whitefly /wít flī/ (*plural* **-flies** or *same*) *n* a minute insect with a white waxy coating on the body. Many species suck the sap from garden and house plants. Family: Aleyrodidae.

white-footed mouse *n* a mouse with small white feet and undersides. Native to: North and Central America. Latin name: *Peromyscus leucopus*.

white fox *n* the arctic fox in its white winter coat. Its coat is dark grey in summer.

white friar, White Friar *n* a member of the Carmelite order of monks [< the white habits of the monks]

white frost *n* METEOROL same as **hoar frost**

white gold *n* a silvery-looking gold alloy that contains gold mixed with palladium, nickel, or sometimes zinc and is usually used in jewellery

white goods *npl* **1.** household goods made of fabric, e.g. bed linen, towels, and tablecloths **2.** large household appliances typically finished with white enamel, e.g. refrigerators, cookers, and dishwashers

white gum *n* a eucalyptus tree with a whitish bark. Native to: Australia. Genus: *Eucalyptus*.

white-haired *adj* having hair that has become white with advanced age

Whitehall /wít hawl/ *n* **1.** CENTRAL LONDON STREET a street in central London, between Trafalgar Square and the Houses of Parliament, containing the main offices of the British civil service **2.** BRITISH GOVERNMENT a collective term for the administration and civil service departments of the British government, many of which are located in Whitehall **3.** TRINIDADIAN PRIME MINISTER'S RESIDENCE the official residence of the prime minister of Trinidad

Whitehaven /wít hayv'n/ town and fishing port in Cumbria, northwestern England. Population: 26,542 (1991).

whitehead /wít hed/ *n* a small pimple with a whitish top formed when a sebaceous gland becomes blocked. Technical name **milium** [Mid-20C. After *blackhead*]

Whitehead /wít hed/, **Alfred North** (1861–1947) British mathematician and philosopher. He wrote *Principia Mathematica* (1910–13) with Bertrand Russell.

> 'Civilization advances by extending the number of important operations which we can perform without thinking about them.'
> [Alfred North Whitehead, *An Introduction to Mathematics*; 1948]

white-headed *adj* **1.** having white markings on the feathers, hair, or fur of the head, especially as a distinguishing feature between similar species **2.** favoured over others and considered blessed by luck

white heat *n* **1.** an extremely high degree of heat characterized by the emission of white light **2.** a state of intense excitement or activity

white hole *n* a hypothetical region in space from which stars, light, and other forms of energy emerge explosively [After *black hole*]

white horse *n* **1.** same as **whitecap 2.** the outline of a horse carved in prehistoric times in exposed chalk on a hillside. There are many examples in southern England. [In the sense of 'whitecap', from its imagined resemblance to a horse's head and flowing mane]

Whitehorse /wít hawrss/ capital city of the Yukon Territory, Canada, located on the Yukon River, just off the Alaska Highway. Population: 16,843 (2001).

white-hot *adj* **1.** so hot that white light is emitted **2.** characterized by intense excitement or activity

White House, Washington, DC

White House *n* **1.** OFFICIAL RESIDENCE OF US PRESIDENT the large white mansion in Washington, DC that is the official residence of the president of the United States **2.** EXECUTIVE BRANCH OF US GOVERNMENT the executive branch of the US government **3.** RUSSIAN PARLIAMENT BUILDING the Russian parliament building in central Moscow

white hunter *n* especially formerly in Africa, a white man hunting big game professionally or working as a safari guide

White Island /wít-/ uninhabited volcanic island in the Bay of Plenty, off the northeastern coast of the North Island, New Zealand. Area: 3 sq. km/1 sq. mi.

white knight *n* **1.** somebody who rescues a person or situation from disaster **2.** a person or organization that rescues a company, especially from an undesirable takeover

white-knuckle *adj* causing or characterized by fear, apprehension, nervousness, or uncertainty [< the appearance of nervously clenched fists]

white-knuckle ride *n* **1.** a situation, experience, or encounter that causes fear, anxiety, or uncertainty **2.** a frightening or exhilarating fairground ride, especially a roller coaster

white lady *n* a cocktail made with gin, Cointreau, and lemon juice

white lead *n* **1.** lead carbonate in the form of a poisonous heavy white powder. Use: pigment in paints and in putty. Formula: $2PbCO_3.Pb(OH)_2$. **2.** putty made from white lead suspended in boiled linseed oil

white leather *n* a soft leather treated with salt and alum for a white finish

Whiteley /wítli/, **Brett** (1939–92) Australian artist. His works include sculpture, prints, and photography, but he is best known for expressionistic landscape paintings and portraits.

white lie *n* a lie not intended to harm, but told in order to avoid distress or embarrassment

SYNONYMS See *lie²*.

white light *n* light that contains all the wavelengths from red to violet at approximately equal intensity, e.g. sunlight

white lightning *n* Can, Southern US BEVERAGES same as **moonshine** (sense 1) [*White* because it is usually colourless]

white line *n* a usually broken line of white paint along the middle or edge of a road, used to mark the edge of a road or to separate lanes of traffic, especially those moving in opposite directions

white list *n* **1.** a list of people, organizations, or items deemed acceptable **2.** a list of e-mail addresses, e.g. from friends or customers, to which somebody wants to permit access. ◊ **blacklist** [After *blacklist*] — **white-listed** *adj*

whitely /wítli/ *adv* showing a face pale with anger, fear, or shock

white magic *n* supposed magic practised for good purposes or to counteract evil [After *black magic*]

white mahogany *n* US INDUST same as **primavera¹** (sense 1)

white man's burden *n* the supposed responsibility of Europeans and their descendants to impose their allegedly advanced civilization on the non-white original inhabitants of the territories they colonized

white marlin *n* a large sea fish with a light-coloured belly. It is one of the smaller species of marlin. Native to: western Atlantic. Latin name: *Tetrapturus albidus.*

white matter *n* the whitish nerve tissue of the brain and spinal cord, consisting mostly of myelinated nerve fibres

white meat *n* light-coloured meat, especially chicken, turkey, or pork

white metal *n* a light-coloured alloy, especially one with a high tin or lead content such as pewter or babbitt

white mica *n* MINERALS same as **muscovite**

white mulberry *n* **1.** the edible berry of a Chinese mulberry tree **2.** a mulberry tree that produces white mulberries. Native to: China. Latin name: *Morus alba.*

whiten /wīt'n/ (**-ens, -ening, -ened**) *vti* to become white or lighter in colour, or make something do this

whitener /wīt'nər/ *n* **1.** a substance such as bleach used to colour something white or enhance its whiteness **2.** a substance added to tea or coffee as a substitute for milk, usually in powder form and lower in calories or with a longer shelf life than milk

White Nile /wīt-/ section of the river Nile from near the Sudan-Uganda border to its junction with the Blue Nile at Khartoum. Length: 2,084 km/1,295 mi.

white noise *n* low-volume electrical or radio noise of equal intensity over a wide range of frequencies [By analogy with white light, which contains light from the whole range of visible frequencies]

white oak *n* an oak tree with evenly lobed hairless leaves and pale wood. Native to: eastern North America. Latin name: *Quercus alba.*

whiteout /wīt owt/ *n* **1.** an atmospheric condition in which low clouds merge with a snow-covered landscape, greatly restricting visibility, so that only darker objects are discernible **2.** a blizzard that is so severe it reduces visibility almost to zero [Mid-20C. After BLACKOUT]

white paper *n* **1.** in many countries, an official report setting out government policy on an issue to be voted on by the country's parliament or congress **2.** an official, authoritative, or heavily researched report on a topic, e.g. a report produced by a group of journalists [Because such reports are customarily printed as white pamphlets]

white pepper *n* a light-coloured pepper made from peppercorns that have had their dark husk removed

white perch *n* a silver-coloured edible fish that is a variety of sea bass. Native to: western Atlantic, freshwater streams of eastern North America. Latin name: *Morone americana.*

white pine *n* **1.** SOFT DURABLE PINE WOOD the soft durable wood of a North American pine tree (*hyphenated before a noun*) **2.** N AMERICAN PINE TREE a fast-growing pine tree that is grown for its soft durable wood. Native to: eastern North America. Latin name: *Pinus strobus.* **3.** PINE SIMILAR TO WHITE PINE a pine that resembles the white pine, particularly in having five-needle clusters [< its light-coloured wood]

white poplar *n* **1.** the straight-grained wood of a poplar tree that has white woolly leaves (*hyphenated before a noun*) **2.** a poplar tree that has white woolly leaves and yieldswhite poplar. Native to: Europe, Asia. Latin name: *Populus alba.*

white potato *n* **1.** a potato with whitish flesh **2.** a plant whose tubers are white potatoes

white pudding *n* a sausage made from light-coloured offal such as brain and sweetbreads and bound with oatmeal or a similar starchy ingredient, but not mixed with blood

white rat *n* an albino strain of brown rat, used widely in scientific research. Latin name: *Rattus norvegicus.*

white rice *n* a rice that has had both the outer husk and the bran layer removed

white room *n* SCI same as **clean room**

White Russian *n* **1.** PEOPLES same as **Belarusian** (sense 1) **2.** an opponent of the Bolsheviks during the Civil War (1918–21) that followed the 1917 Russian Revolution **3.** a cocktail made from vodka, coffee liqueur, and cream

white sale *n* a sale of household linen

white sapphire *n* a colourless precious stone that is a variety of corundum. Use: gems.

white sauce *n* a pale milk sauce, thickened with butter and flour or cornflour, and variously seasoned or flavoured

White Sea arm of the Barents Sea, forming an indentation in the coast of northwestern Russia and partly enclosed on the north by the Kola Peninsula. Area: 90,000 sq. km/30,000 sq. mi.

white shark *n* FISH same as **great white shark**

white sheep *n* BREED same as **Dall sheep**

white slave *n* a white girl or woman sold into prostitution against her will —**white slaver** *n* —**white slavery** *n*

whitesmith /wīt smith/ *n* **1.** somebody who makes or repairs objects made from white metals **2.** somebody whose job is polishing forged metal articles [14C. After BLACKSMITH]

white snakeroot *n* a poisonous plant with heart-shaped leaves. Flowers: small, white, in clusters. Native to: eastern North America. Latin name: *Eupatorium rugosum.*

white space *n* an area of a page or other printed surface where no text or pictures appear

white spirit *n* a colourless liquid derived from petroleum and used like turpentine, e.g. to clean paint-brushes or to thin paint

white spruce *n* **1.** the soft wood of a North American spruce tree **2.** a spruce tree that has short blue-grey needles and whitish shoots and yields a white spruce. Native to: northern North America. Latin name: *Picea glauca.* [< its silvery-brown bark]

white squall *n* a violent tropical or subtropical storm that stirs up the surface of the sea into whitecaps, but is limited to a very localized area, often with no storm clouds present

white stick *n* a white-coloured walking stick used by a visually-impaired person to detect obstacles in his or her path

white supremacy *n* the view that white people are supposedly genetically and culturally superior to all other people or races and should therefore rule over them —**white supremacist** *n*

white-tailed deer, **whitetail** /wīt tayl/ *n* a deer with a greyish or reddish-brown coat and a tail that is white on the underside. Native to: North America. Latin name: *Odocoileus virginianus.*

whitethorn /wīt thawrn/ *n* TREES same as **hawthorn** [13C. *White* < the fact that its bark is lighter in colour than the blackthorn's]

whitethroat /wīt thrōt/ *n* a small songbird with a white throat. Native to: Europe, Asia, North Africa. Genus: *Sylvia.*

white tie *n* **1.** a white bow tie worn as part of a man's formal evening dress **2.** a man's full formal evening clothes, consisting of a black suit with a tail coat and a white bow tie —**white-tie** *adj*

white trash *n* N Am an offensive term for a white person or group of white people considered as possessing the stereotypical characteristics of members of a lower-income group in society (*slang*; *takes a singular or plural verb*)

white vitriol *n* CHEM same as **zinc sulphate**

whitewall /wīt wawl/, **whitewall tyre** *n* a vehicle tyre with a band of white on the outside sidewall

whitewash /wīt wosh/ *n* **1.** COVER-UP a coordinated attempt to hide unpleasant facts, especially in a political context (*informal*) **2.** WHITE PAINTING SOLUTION lime suspended in water, often with glue or sizing, and used like paint for whitening walls **3.** THOROUGH DEFEAT a resounding defeat, especially one in which the losing player or team does not score (*informal*) ■ *v* (**-washes, -washing, -washed**) **1.** *vti* HIDE TRUTH ABOUT SOMETHING to conceal the unpleasant facts about something **2.** *vt* PAINT SOMETHING WITH WHITEWASH to paint something, usually a wall, with whitewash **3.** *vt* DEFEAT SOMEBODY DECISIVELY to defeat an opposing player or team resoundingly, especially by preventing the player or team from scoring —**whitewasher** *n*

white water *n* **1.** fast-flowing water with a foamy choppy surface **2.** lighter-coloured sea water visible in shallow areas

whitewater rafting /wīt wawtər-/ *n* the outdoor leisure pursuit of floating on a raft down a fast-flowing river

white wedding *n* a wedding for which the bride wears a traditional white dress, often taking place in church

white whale *n* a small white fish-eating whale with a bulbous head. Native to: Arctic waters. Latin name: *Delphinapterus leucas.*

white witch *n* a witch whose supposed magic is designed to do good or to counteract evil [*White* because such a witch practises supposed white magic]

whitewood /wīt wood/ *n* **1.** the pale wood of some deciduous trees **2.** a deciduous tree whose wood is pale in colour, e.g. the tulip tree, cottonwood, or basswood

whitey /wīti/ (*plural* **-eys**), **whity** (*plural* **-ies**) *n* an offensive term for a white person (*slang*)

whither /wīthər/ (*literary or archaic*) *adv*, *rel adv* to what place ■ *adv* to what state, condition, outcome, or degree ○ *a debate entitled 'Whither capitalism?'* [Old English *hwider* < Germanic]

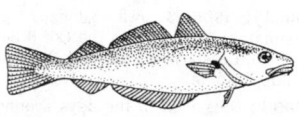

whiting

whiting[1] /wīting/ (*plural same*) *n* **1.** EUROPEAN FISH a small edible sea fish with a silvery underside, related to the cod, commercially important throughout Europe. Native to: Europe. Latin name: *Merlangus merlangus.* **2.** PACIFIC AND ATLANTIC FISH a commercially important fish that is similar to the European whiting, e.g. the silver hake. Native to: Pacific and Atlantic oceans. Genera: *Merluccius* or *Menticirrhus.* **3.** FOOD WHITING AS FOOD the white flesh of the whiting as food [15C. < Dutch *wijting*, < *wijt* 'white']

whiting[2] /wīting/ *n* pure powdered chalk used as an ingredient in various commercial preparations such as putty and whitewash [15C. < WHITE]

Whitlam /wītləm/, **Gough** (*b.* 1916) prime minister of Australia (1972–75). He became leader of the Labor Party in 1967 and introduced a wide-ranging reform programme during his premiership. His government was controversially dismissed by the governor general, Sir John Kerr. Full name **Whitlam, Edward Gough**. See table at **prime minister**

Whitley Council /wītli-/ *n* a consultative committee or organization consisting of representatives from the management and staff of a company or industry, set up to discuss industrial relations, working conditions, and other work-related issues [Early 20C. After J. H. *Whitley* (1866–1935), British politician]

whitlow /wītlō/ *n* a pus-filled infection on the skin at the side of a fingernail or toenail [14C. Alteration of earlier *whitflawe* < WHITE + FLAW[1]]

Walt Whitman

Whitman /wítmən/, **Walt** (1819–92) US poet and essayist. He is known for his free verse, best exemplified in the stylistically revolutionary collection *Leaves of Grass* (1855–91). Born **Whitman, Walter**. See Cultural note at **grass**. See illustration on previous page

> 'No one will ever get at my verses who insists upon viewing them as a literary performance.'
> [Walt Whitman, *'A Backward Glance O'er Travel'd Roads'*; 1888]

Whit Monday *n* formerly, a public holiday in England, Ireland, and Wales. Date: the Monday after Pentecost. [After WHIT SUNDAY]

Whitney /wítnee/, **Eli** (1765–1825) US inventor. His cotton gin, a machine for separating the seeds from the fibre of the cotton plant, revolutionized the cotton industry.

Whitstable /wítstəb'l/ town and fishing port in Kent, southeastern England. It is famous for its oysters. Population: 28,907 (1991).

Whitsun /wíts'n/ *n* CALENDAR, CHR same as **Whitsuntide** ■ *adj* relating to or happening on Whitsuntide or Whit Sunday [13C. Back-formation < WHIT SUNDAY, understood as 'Whitsun day']

Whit Sunday *n* CALENDAR, CHR same as **Pentecost** (sense 1) [Old English *hwīta sunnandæg* 'white Sunday', because of the white robes the priests wear on this day]

Whitsunday Islands /wít sunday-/ group of approximately 70 islands in the Coral Sea, off the coast of southeastern Queensland, Australia. Area: 98 sq. km/38 sq. mi.

Whitsuntide /wíts'n tīd/ *n* the days around and including the Christian festival of Pentecost [13C. < WHITSUN + TIDE in obsolete sense of 'period of time']

Whittington /wíttingtən/, **Dick** (1358?–1423) English merchant and Lord Mayor of London (1397–98, 1406–07, 1419–20). The legend of his beginnings as an orphaned country boy who went to London with his cat is a popular source of English folk tales and pantomimes.

whittle /wítt'l/ (**-tles, -tling, -tled**) *vti* to carve something out of wood, usually something small enough to hold in the hand, by cutting away small pieces of wood [Mid-16C. < *whyttel* 'knife', variant of *thwitel*, 'tool for paring' < Old English *þwītan* 'pare, cut'] —**whittler** *n*
whittle away *vt* to deplete something by using or spending a little of it at a time
whittle down *vt* to reduce or diminish something gradually by taking away a little of it at a time

Whittle /wítt'l/, **Sir Frank** (1907–96) British engineer. He invented and developed the turbojet engine (1936), first used to power British fighter aircraft during World War II.

whittlings /wíttlingz/ *npl* pieces of wood that have been whittled off a larger piece and discarded

Whitworth screw thread /wít wurth-/ *n* the thread form used in the United Kingdom for all screws, produced in a series of standard sizes. It has a 55° flank angle and a rounded top and foot. [Late 19C. After Sir Joseph Whitworth (d. 1887), English inventor]

whity *n* another spelling of **whitey** (*slang; offensive*)

whiz /wiz/, **whizz** *v* (**whizzes, whizzing, whizzed**) **1.** *vi* HUM to make a humming, hissing, or buzzing noise **2.** *vti* MOVE WITH HUMMING NOISE to move swiftly with a humming, hissing, or buzzing noise, or make something do this ○ *bullets whizzing past* **3.** *vi* MOVE QUICKLY to move or travel somewhere rapidly ○ *whizzed down to the shops* **4.** *vt* PROCESS SOMETHING IN FOOD MIXER to blend or liquidize something using a food mixer or food processor (*informal*) **5.** *vi* OFFENSIVE TERM an offensive term meaning to urinate (*slang*) ■ *n* (*plural* **whizzes**) **1.** HUMMING SOUND a humming, hissing, or buzzing sound **2.** FAST MOVEMENT a fast movement, often accompanied by a humming, hissing, or buzzing sound **3.** EXPERT somebody who is very skilled at something (*informal*) ○ *a computer whiz* **4.** AMPHETAMINES amphetamine drugs taken for non-medical reasons (*slang*) **5.** OFFENSIVE TERM an offensive term for an act of urinating (*slang*) [Mid-16C. An imitation of the sound]

whiz-bang (*informal*) *n* **1.** SOMEBODY OR SOMETHING EXCELLENT somebody or something that is outstandingly successful or effective, loud, or fast **2.** ARMS, HIST ARTILLERY SHELL a lightweight artillery shell used in World War I ■ *adj* EXCELLENT, FAST, OR LOUD outstandingly successful or effective, loud, or fast ○ *a whiz-bang presentation*

whiz kid *n* a young and exceptionally talented and successful person in a field of activity (*informal*)

whizz, etc. *vti, n* another spelling of **whiz, etc.**

whizzo /wízzō, hwízzō/ (*humorous or dated*) *adj* ingeniously clever ○ *a whizzo plan* ■ *interj* excellent

who /hoo/ *pron* **1.** used to introduce a question asking about the name or identity of a person or people ○ *Who's that at the door?* ○ *Who did you see there?* **2.** used to introduce a relative clause giving information about a person or people ○ *meals for people who are too busy to cook* [Old English *hwā* < Indo-European, 'who, what']

USAGE **who** or **whom**? **Whom** has fallen into disuse in everyday speech, with **who** taking its place. *Do you remember whom you saw?* is more usually expressed as *Do you remember who you saw?*, and **whom** is omitted when it is associated with a preposition: *the man I was talking to* rather than *the man to whom I was talking*. However in formal contexts, **whom** is still preferred by careful writers. Note that **whom** is incorrect in sentences such as *The woman who we thought was dead is still alive*: **who** is the subject of *was*, not the object of *thought* (*We thought that she was dead...*).

USAGE See **that**.

WHO *abbr* World Health Organization

whoa /wō/ *interj* used to order an animal or, humorously, a person, to stop [Mid-19C. Variant of HO[2]]

who'd /hood/ *contr* **1.** who had **2.** who would

whodunit /hoo dúnnit/, **whodunnit** *n* a novel, film, or play centring on the solving of a crime, usually a murder [Mid-20C. Alteration of 'who done it?']

whoever /hoo évvər/ *pron* **1.** INTRODUCES EMPHATIC QUESTION used to introduce an emphatic question indicating surprise or disbelief ○ *Whoever would do such a thing?* **2.** ANY PERSON WHO used to indicate a person or people whose identity is not known ○ *Whoever takes over from her will have difficult decisions to make.* **3.** NO MATTER WHO used to indicate a person or people whose identity is not important ○ *You can bring whoever you like to the party.*

whole /hōl/ *adj* **1.** ENTIRE complete, including all parts or aspects, with nothing left out **2.** UNDIVIDED not divided into parts or not regarded as consisting of separate parts **3.** RELATING TO DURATION OR EXTENT relating to or representing the full duration or extent of something ○ *stayed up the whole night* **4.** UNBROKEN not damaged or broken ○ *not a single item of furniture left whole* **5.** UNIMPAIRED not wounded, impaired, or incapacitated ○ *no longer a whole man* **6.** HEALED OR HEALTHY healed or restored to health physically or psychologically ○ *made him whole again* **7.** HAVING PARENTS IN COMMON having both parents in common with your siblings ○ *a whole sister* **8.** NOT FRACTIONAL containing no vulgar or decimal fractions ■ *adv* **1.** AS SINGLE PIECE in a single piece ○ *Many snakes swallow their food whole.* **2.** COMPLETELY completely and in every way (*informal*) ○ *a whole different approach* ■ *n* **1.** SOMETHING COMPLETE something that is complete and has no parts missing **2.** SINGLE ENTITY OR UNIT something regarded as a single and complete unit or entity, as opposed to a set of components [Old English *hāl* < Indo-European, 'sound, propitious'] —**wholeness** *n* ◇ **as a whole** as a single and complete entity ◇ **on the whole 1.** as a rule or in general **2.** taking all relevant factors into account

SPELLCHECK See **hole**.

ORIGIN The prehistoric Germanic word from which **whole** is derived, is also the source of English *hale*[1], *hallow*, *heal*, *health*, and *holy*.

whole cloth *n* N Am complete fiction or fabrication ○ *an explanation made out of whole cloth* [< the underlying meaning 'cut from new material, in any shape you please']

whole enchilada *n* N Am the entirety of something (*slang*)

wholefood /hōl food/ *n* food that has undergone very little processing and has been grown or produced without the use of synthetic pesticides or fertilizers

whole gale *n* a wind of between 87 km/55 mi. and 102 km/63 mi. per hour, classified as force ten on the Beaufort scale and capable of causing considerable structural damage

wholegrain /hōl grayn/ *adj* describes food containing whole unprocessed grains of something ○ *wholegrain muffins* ○ *wholegrain mustard*

wholehearted /hōl haártid/ *adj* characterized by unreserved enthusiasm, passion, or commitment —**wholeheartedly** *adv* —**wholeheartedness** *n*

whole hog *adv* in every way or to the fullest extent (*informal*) [Origin ?]

~~**wholely**~~ incorrect spelling of **wholly**

wholemeal /hōl meel/ *adj* **1.** not having had the bran and wheat germ taken out **2.** made using wholemeal flour ▶ N Am term **whole-wheat**

whole milk *n* cow's milk from which no fat has been removed

whole note *n* N Am MUSIC same as **semibreve** [*Whole* < because it lasts for one full bar in common time]

whole number *n* a positive or negative number, including zero, that does not contain a vulgar or decimal fraction

whole rest *n* N Am same as **semibreve rest**

wholesale /hōl sayl/ *n* SALE OF GOODS TO RETAILERS the business of buying goods in large quantities and selling them especially to retailers for resale ■ *adj* **1.** OF TRADE IN QUANTITY relating to the wholesale business **2.** DONE ON LARGE SCALE done on a large scale and indiscriminately ○ *wholesale destruction* ■ *adv* **1.** IN BULK in large quantities, especially for resale by retailers ○ *Buy wholesale and save yourself money.* **2.** INDISCRIMINATELY as a whole, without exercising judgment or taking individual cases into account ■ *vti* (**-sales, -saling, -saled**) BUY AND SELL GOODS WHOLESALE to buy goods in large quantities and sell them especially to retailers for resale [15C. < the phrase 'by whole sale', that is, sold in a single lot for redistribution at retail] —**wholesaler** *n*

wholesome /hōlssəm/ *adj* **1.** HEALTH-GIVING beneficial to physical health, usually by virtue of being fresh and naturally produced **2.** MORALLY BENEFICIAL leading to or promoting improved moral wellbeing **3.** SENSIBLE based on openness, honesty, and common sense **4.** HEALTHY AND FIT having a fit healthy appearance that suggests clean living —**wholesomely** *adv* —**wholesomeness** *n*

whole step *n* US MUSIC same as **whole tone**

whole tone *n* UK, Can a musical interval consisting of two semitones, e.g. between the notes D and E or A and B. US term **whole step**

whole-tone scale *n* a musical scale that begins on any of two notes that are a semitone apart and goes up or down in whole notes for one octave

whole-wheat *adj* N Am same as **wholemeal**

who'll /hool/ *contr* **1.** who shall **2.** who will

wholly /hōl li/ *adv* **1.** totally and in every way or to the fullest extent **2.** solely and to the exclusion of all other things

whom /hoom/ *pron* (*formal*) **1.** used to introduce a question asking about the name or identity of a person or people ○ *Whom did you expect to see?* **2.** used to introduce a relative clause giving information about a person or people ○ *Birch and her colleagues studied 162 infants, none of whom were born prematurely.* [Old English *hwǣm* < Germanic]

USAGE See **who**.

whomever /hoom évvər/ *pron* a formal word for 'whoever' when used as the object of a verb or preposition

whomp /womp/ *v* (**whomps, whomping, whomped**) **1.** *vti* N Am STRIKE SOMEBODY OR SOMETHING to hit somebody or something with great force, especially noisily **2.** *vt* US DEFEAT SOMEBODY RESOUNDINGLY to subject somebody to a crushing defeat (*informal*) ■ *n* N Am BLOW OR NOISE OF BLOW a heavy blow, or the loud deep sound it makes [Early 20C. An imitation of the sound]
whomp up *vt* US to arouse, incite, or stir up interest or enthusiasm (*dated*)

whomsoever /hoom sō évvər/ *pron* an emphatic form of 'whomever' (*formal*)

whoop /woop, hoop/ *v* (**whoops, whooping, whooped**) **1.** *vi* CRY OUT IN EXCITEMENT OR JOY to make a loud howling cry of excitement or joy **2.** *vt* EXCLAIM SOMETHING to exclaim something loudly and with great excitement **3.** *vt* URGE OR DRIVE SOMEBODY FORWARD to urge, chase, or drive a person or animal forward with a whooping call **4.** *vi* MED WHEEZE to breathe in with the

sharp wheezing sound associated with whooping cough ■ *n* **1.** EXCITED OR JOYFUL CRY a loud howling cry of excitement or joy **2.** BATTLE CRY a cry uttered before a battle or hunt, by a warrior, soldier, or hunter **3.** CALL MADE BY BIRD OR ANIMAL a loud call or hoot, e.g. from a bird or animal **4.** MED WHEEZING SOUND a sharply wheezing inhalation associated with whooping cough [14C. An imitation of the sound] ◇ **whoop it up** (*informal*) **1.** to have fun or celebrate in an extravagant or noisy way **2.** *N Am* to express and try to arouse enthusiasm for somebody or something

whoop-de-do /wŏŏp di dŏŏ/, **whoop-de-doo** (*informal*) *n* (*plural* **whoop-de-dos**; *plural* **whoop-de-doos**) **1.** *N Am* PARTY a large-scale party or celebration that is lively or noisy **2.** *US* PUBLICITY noisy activity meant to attract attention ○ *the whoop-de-do surrounding the film's release* **3.** *N Am* FUSS a noisy public commotion or outcry ■ *interj N Am* EXPRESSING EXCITEMENT used to express excitement (*often used ironically*) [Mid-20C. Expressive alteration of WHOOP]

whoopee /wŏŏ pée/ *interj* used to express great and sudden excitement (*informal*; *often used ironically*) [Mid-19C. Alteration of WHOOP] ◇ **make whoopee** /wŏŏppi/ (*dated informal*) **1.** to engage in sexual activity **2.** to celebrate noisily and exuberantly

whoopee cushion /wŏŏppi-/ *n* a practical joker's toy in the form of an inflatable cushion with a small opening, designed to make a noise resembling flatulence when somebody sits on it

whooper /hŏŏpər, wŏŏ-/ *n* BIRDS **1.** same as **whooping crane 2.** same as **whooper swan**

whooper swan *n* a large white swan with a yellow and black beak, straight neck, and loud whooping cry in flight. Native to: Europe, Asia. Latin name: *Cygnus cygnus*.

whoopie pie *n US* a cake consisting of two layers with a moist filling [< variant of WHOOPEE]

whooping cough /hŏŏping-/ *n* an infectious bacterial disease that causes violent coughing spasms followed by sharp, shrill inhalations. It mainly affects children. Latin name: *Bordetella pertussis*. Technical name **pertussis**

whooping crane /hŏŏping-/ *n* a large white crane with black wing tips that makes a loud whooping cry in flight. It is now an endangered species. Native to: North America. Latin name: *Grus americana*.

whoops /woops/, **whoops-a-daisy** *interj* used to express surprise, concern, or embarrassment at making a mistake or having a slight accident (*informal*) [Mid-20C. Origin ?]

whoosh /wŏŏsh/, **woosh** *n* **1.** NOISE OF RUSHING AIR OR WATER the sound made by rushing air or water **2.** SWIFT MOTION OR RUSH a swift motion, spurt, or rush ■ *vi* (**whooshes, whooshing, whooshed; wooshes, wooshing, wooshed**) **1.** MAKE RUSHING SOUND to make the sound of rushing air or water **2.** MOVE FAST to move rapidly, with a whooshing sound ○ *whooshed into the room* [Mid-19C. An imitation of the sound]

whop /wop/, **whap** *vt* (**whops, whopping, whopped; whaps, whapping, whapped**) (*informal*) **1.** HIT SOMEBODY OR SOMETHING to strike somebody or something forcefully **2.** DEFEAT SOMEBODY DECISIVELY to subject an opponent to a crushing defeat ■ *n* BLOW OR NOISE OF BLOW a heavy blow or the loud dull sound it makes [14C. Variant of *wap* 'strike, slap', also 'a blow', origin ?]

whopper /wóppər/ *n* (*informal*) **1.** something that is much bigger than others of its kind **2.** a blatant and outrageous lie [Late 18C. < WHOPPING]

whopping /wópping/ (*informal*) *adj* very big or great ■ *adv* extremely [Early 18C. < WHOP]

whore /hawr/ *n* (*insult*) **1.** an offensive term for a prostitute **2.** an offensive term for somebody regarded as being sexually indiscriminate **3.** an offensive term for somebody who is regarded as willing to set aside principles or personal integrity in order to obtain something, usually for selfish motives ■ *vi* (**whores, whoring, whored**) **1.** an offensive term meaning to be a regular customer of prostitutes **2.** an offensive term meaning to work as a prostitute [Old English *hōre* < Indo-European, 'to desire'] —**whoredom** *n*

whore after *vt* an offensive term meaning to pursue something desperately, making whatever sacrifices of principles or personal integrity are necessary

whorehouse /háwr howss/ (*plural* **-houses** /-howziz/) *n* an offensive term for a brothel or other place of prostitution

whoremonger /háwr mung gər/ *n* an offensive term for a sexually indiscriminate man, especially one who frequents prostitutes (*archaic*) —**whoremongery** *n*

whoreson /háwrss'n/ *n* an offensive term for a man regarded as dishonest, treacherous, or otherwise disreputable (*archaic insult*) ■ *adj* an offensive term meaning contemptible or loathsome (*archaic*) [14C. Translation of Anglo-Norman *fiz a putain*]

Whorf hypothesis /wáwrf-/ *n* PSYCHOL same as **Sapir-Whorf hypothesis**

whorish /háwrish/ *adj* **1.** an offensive term meaning characteristic of the behaviour stereotypically ascribed to prostitutes **2.** an offensive term meaning relating to prostitutes or prostitution —**whorishly** *adv* —**whorishness** *n*

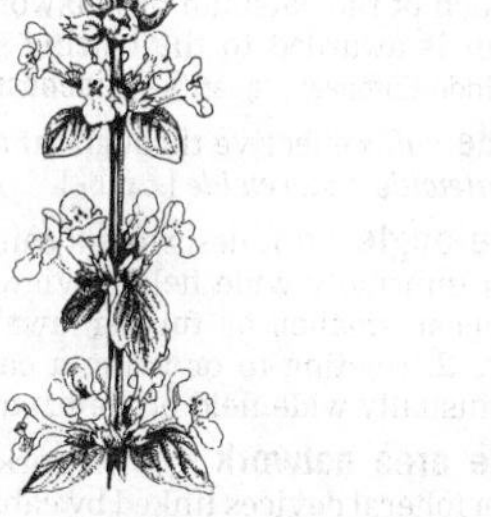

whorl (sense 3)

whorl /wurl/ *n* **1.** SOMETHING SPIRAL-SHAPED something in the shape of a spiral, coil, or curl **2.** ANAT, CRIME PATTERN ON FINGER a series of concentric circular or elliptical ridges in the pattern of lines on the gripping surface of a finger or thumb, or this shape seen in a fingerprint **3.** BOT CIRCLE OF PLANT PARTS a circular arrangement of three or more leaves, petals, or other plant parts arising at the same level on a stem or other axis, like spokes on a wheel **4.** ZOOL SPIRAL IN SHELL a turn or coil in a mollusc's shell [15C. Alteration of WHIRL] —**whorled** *adj*

whortleberry /wúrt'lbəri/ (*plural* **-ries**) *n* **1.** EDIBLE BERRY a small sweet edible blue-black fruit **2.** PLANT WITH EDIBLE BERRIES a low-growing plant found in heath and mountainous areas that produces whortleberries. Flowers: greenish-pink. Native to: Europe. Latin name: *Vaccinium myrtillus*. **3.** PLANT RELATED TO WHORTLEBERRY a plant related to the whortleberry that has edible berries, e.g. the blueberry [Late 16C. Dialect variant of *hurtleberry*, origin?]

who's /hooz/ *contr* **1.** who has **2.** who is

USAGE whose or **who's**? ***Who's*** is a contraction of *who is* or *who has*: *She's the one who's* [not *whose*] *coming to dinner next week. Who's* [not *Whose*] *got my pen?* ***Whose*** means 'of whom' or 'of which' and indicates or asks about belonging: *These are the children whose* [not *who's*] *father we saw yesterday. Whose* [not *Who's*] *coat is that?*

whose /hooz/ *pron, det* a grammatical word used to talk or ask about the person or thing something belongs to ○ *Whose are these boots?* ○ *'It wasn't my idea'. – 'Well, whose was it then?'* ○ *a theatre whose doors will always be open to such a talented performer* ○ *Whose car shall we use?* ○ *He wanted to know whose the scarf was.* [Old English *hwæs*, genitive of the pronouns *hwa* (masculine) 'who' and *hwæt* (neuter) 'what'. Influenced in Middle English by *who* and *whom*]

USAGE See ***who's***.

USAGE Some people dislike the use of ***whose*** to mean 'of which' (as in *There was a church whose steeple had been struck by lightning.*), but it is a well-established use and the alternatives are usually awkward.

whosoever /hŏŏ sō évvər/ *pron* an emphatic form of 'whoever' (*formal*)

Who's Who *tdmk* a trademark for a reference work giving brief biographical sketches of notable people

wh- question *n* a question that starts with *who, what, where, when, why,* or *how*. It cannot be answered by 'yes' or 'no'.

whs. *abbr* COMM warehouse

whsle *abbr* COMM wholesale

whump /wump/ *n* the sound of a dull thump or muffled explosion ■ *vti* (**whumps, whumping, whumped**) to make the sound of a dull thump or muffled explosion, or hit somebody or something with such a sound [Late 19C. An imitation of the sound]

whup /wup, wŏŏp/ (**whups, whupping, whupped**) *vt* **1.** *US* to subject an opponent to a crushing defeat (*informal*) **2.** *Southern US* to beat somebody with a whip [Late 19C. Dialect variant of WHIP]

why /wī/ CORE MEANING: an adverb used to ask or talk about the reason, purpose, or cause of something ○ *Why didn't you call?* ○ *I wish you'd tell me why you're so unhappy.* ○ *He couldn't say why he'd done it.* ○ *It seems clear to me why.*

1. *adv* ASKING REASON for what reason ○ *Why didn't you call?* **2.** ⚠ *adv, rel adv* BECAUSE OF for or on account of which ○ *There's no reason why you shouldn't go.* **3.** *interj* EXCLAMATION an exclamation used to express surprise, shock, or indignation ○ *Why, John, how could you!* **4.** *n* REASON a reason or purpose for something ○ *the whys and wherefores of the case* [Old English *hwȳ*, instrumental case form of *hwæt* 'what'] ◇ **why not** used to express agreement with a suggestion or proposed course of action ○ *'Would you like another coffee?' – 'Why not?'*

USAGE Since people disagree as to whether *reason why* is redundant, the safest course is to avoid using it in formal writing: *The reason the experiment failed is that our test procedures were flawed*, rather than *The reason why the experiment failed is that our test procedures were flawed.*

Whyalla /wī állə/ city and port on the Spencer Gulf in South Australia. It is a centre of iron and steel production. Population: 21,903 (2002 estimate).

whydah /wíddə/ (*plural same* or **-ahs**), **whidah** *n* a songbird, the male of which has long black tail feathers during the breeding season. Native to: Africa. Genus: *Vidua*. [Late 18C. After *Ouidah*, W African town]

whys and wherefores *n* all the reasons and explanations for something ○ *Without going into all the whys and wherefores, let's just say the wedding's off.*

WI *abbr* **1.** West Indian **2.** West Indies **3.** Women's Institute

Wicca /wíkə/ *n* a religious practice involving nature-worship and witchcraft [Mid-20C. Revival of Old English *wicca* 'wizard'] —**Wiccan** *n, adj*

Wichita[1] /wíchi taw/ (*plural same* or **-tas**) *n* a member of a Native North American people who lived in Kansas, Oklahoma, and Texas, and now live mainly in Oklahoma [Mid-19C. < Caddo] —**Wichita** *adj*

Wichita[2] /wíchi taw/ city in south-central Kansas, on the Arkansas River, southwest of Emporia. Population: 355,126 (2002 estimate).

wick /wik/ *n* **1.** MATERIAL HOLDING FUEL THAT BURNS a string or piece of fabric that uses capillary action to draw the fuel to the flame in a candle, oil lamp, or cigarette lighter **2.** MED MATERIAL THAT DRAWS UP LIQUID any piece of material that draws liquid up by capillary action, e.g. a strip of gauze put into a wound to drain it ■ *vti* (**wicks, wicking, wicked**) MOVE LIQUID BY CAPILLARY ACTION to take in or transfer liquid by capillary action, or be taken in or transferred in this way [Old English *wēoc*, origin ?] ◇ **get on somebody's wick** to annoy or irritate somebody greatly (*slang*)

Wick /wik/ town and port near the northeastern tip of Scotland. Population: 7,681 (1991).

wicked /wíkid/ *adj* **1.** EVIL very wrong or very bad **2.** MISCHIEVOUS playfully mischievous without intending to upset people seriously ○ *a wicked sense of humour* **3.** NASTY expressing very unpleasant things to people ○ *She has a really wicked tongue sometimes!* **4.** DANGEROUS capable of causing harm to somebody ○ *a knife with a wicked blade* **5.** DISGUSTING tasting or smelling disgusting and repulsive **6.** DISTRESSING causing discomfort, distress, or disappointment (*informal*) ○ *I've got a wicked headache.* **7.** VERY GOOD very impressive or very skilful (*slang*) ○ *What do you think of the car, then? Pretty wicked, eh?* ■ *adv US* VERY extremely (*slang*) ○ *It was wicked good!* ■ *npl* BAD PEOPLE people who do very bad things [13C. Related to Old English *wicca* 'sorcerer' (see WITCH)] —**wickedly** *adv* —**wickedness** *n*

wicker /wíkər/, **wickerwork** /wíkər wurk/ *n* **1.** objects made of twigs, canes, or reeds, e.g. baskets **2.** twigs, canes, or reeds woven together to make such things

as baskets or chairs [14C. < N Germanic < Indo-European, 'bend']

wickerwork /wíkər wurk/ n 1. same as **wicker** (sense 1) 2. objects made by weaving together thin twigs, canes, or reeds, e.g. baskets and chairs

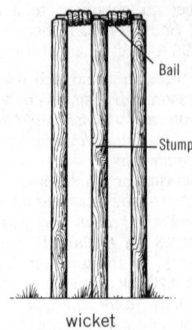

wicket

wicket /wíkit/ n 1. UPRIGHT STICKS DEFENDED BY CRICKET BATSMAN in cricket, either of two sets of three upright sticks (**stumps**) on which are balanced two shorter sticks (**bails**) and in front of which the batsman or batswoman stands 2. PART OF CRICKET PITCH the part of a cricket pitch between the two sets of stumps, which are placed 20 m/22 yd apart 3. TURN OF BATTING in cricket, a batsman's or batswoman's turn of batting, or that of a pair of batsmen or batswomen ○ a fifth-wicket partnership between Crawley and Hussein 4. ENDING OF TURN OF BATTING in cricket, the ending of somebody's turn of batting, effected, e.g. by knocking down the stumps or catching the ball 5. SMALL DOOR OR GATE a small door or gate, especially one close to or forming part of a larger one 6. GATE CONTROLLING WATER FLOW a gate used to control the flow of water at a lock or water wheel 7. US SMALL OPENING FOR COMMUNICATION a small opening or window in a wall or door through which people can communicate. Wickets are often fitted with glass, a grating, or a sliding panel. 8. N Am CROQUET HOOP a hoop through which the ball is hit in croquet [13C. < Old N French wiket < Germanic < Indo-European, 'bend']

wicketkeeper /wíkit keepər/ n in cricket, the player positioned behind the wicket to catch the ball or knock the bails off the stumps —**wicketkeeping** n

wicket maiden n in cricket, an over in which no runs are conceded and at least one wicket is taken by the bowler

wicking /wíking/ n material used to make wicks

wickiup /wíki up/, **wikiup** n a hut made by Native North Americans of the southwestern United States by covering a framework of arched poles with mats of bark, grass, or branches [Mid-19C. < Fox wikiyapi]

Wicklow /wíklō/ 1. county in Leinster Province in the southeastern part of the Republic of Ireland. Population: 102,683 (2002). Area: 2,025 sq. km/782 sq. mi. 2. town and administrative centre of County Wicklow in the Republic of Ireland. Population: 6,215 (1991).

Wicklow Mountains mountain range in County Wicklow, on the eastern coast of the Republic of Ireland. The highest peak is Lugnaquill, 926 m/3,039 ft.

Wicliff ♦ **Wycliffe, John**

widdershins /wíddərshinz/, **withershins** /wíthər-/ adv Scotland (literary) 1. anticlockwise or in a direction opposite to that of the apparent movement of the Sun 2. in the direction that is contrary to the natural course [Early 16C. Alteration of Middle Low German weddersinnes < Middle High German widersinnes < wider 'against, opposite' + sin 'sense, direction']

widdle /wídd'l/ (informal; usually used by children) vi (-dles, -dling, -dled) same as **urinate** ■ n an act or instance of urinating [Mid-20C. Alteration of PIDDLE]

wide /wīd/ adj (**wider, widest**) 1. WITH SIDES OR EDGES FAR APART having a relatively large distance or space between one side or edge and the other 2. BEING PARTICULAR DISTANCE APART having a particular distance between one side or edge and the other ○ three inches wide 3. OPENED TO GREAT EXTENT opened to a great extent or as far as possible ○ staring at him with wide eyes 4. WITH MANY TYPES OR CHOICES including many varieties, offering many choices, or having a large range ○ a wide selection of cheeses 5. INVOLVING MANY PEOPLE from, involving, or given to many people ○ wide support for the plan 6. LARGE IN SCOPE with a large scope ○ a very wide gap between living standards here and in developing countries 7. NOT HITTING TARGET going some distance away from the intended, expected, or correct place 8. GOING BEYOND DETAILS looking beyond the issue towards the more general aspects of something rather than the details ○ We need to look at the wider implications of these proposals. 9. FITTING LOOSELY not fitting tightly round the body 10. CLEVER AND UNSCRUPULOUS shrewd and slightly dishonest or unscrupulous (slang) ○ There's some pretty wide characters in this game. 11. PHON same as **lax** (sense 4) ■ adv (**wider, widest**) 1. TO GREAT EXTENT to a great extent or as much as possible ○ Stand with your legs wide apart. 2. OVER LARGE AREA over an extensive area ○ scattered far and wide 3. TO SIDE OF TARGET to one side of the intended target ○ A few shots were fired but they all went wide. ■ n BALL BOWLED BEYOND BATSMAN'S REACH in cricket, a ball bowled beyond the reach of the batsman or batswoman, for which one run is awarded to the batting side [Old English wīd < Indo-European, 'apart'] —**wideness** n —**widish** adj

-wide suffix effective throughout a particular place ○ statewide ○ storewide [< WIDE]

wide-angle adj 1. describes a camera lens that gives an unusually wide field of view by making things appear smaller or further away than they really are 2. relating to or using a camera lens with an unusually wide field of view ○ a wide-angle shot

wide area network n a network of computers and peripheral devices linked by cable and satellite over a broad geographical area

wide-awake adj 1. FULLY AWAKE completely awake and alert (not hyphenated after a verb) 2. ALERT very aware of surroundings and watching for advantageous possibilities (informal) ○ a wide-awake young go-getter ■ n also **wide-awake hat** FELT HAT a soft felt hat with a wide brim and a low crown —**wide-awakeness** n

wide ball n CRICKET same as **wide**

widebody /wíd bóddi/ n a commercial jet aircraft with a fuselage wide enough to accommodate three rows of seats and two aisles

wide-body, **wide-bodied** adj describes a jet airliner with a fuselage wide enough to have three sets of passenger seats in a row, separated by two long aisles

wide boy n a shrewd and rather unscrupulous man who makes his money in dishonest ways (informal)

wide brown land n Aus Australia (informal) [< phrase in 'My Country', poem by Dorothea Mackeller]

wide-eyed adj 1. with eyes that are wide open, e.g. in amazement or fear 2. lacking experience, wisdom, or common sense and therefore easily fooled by other people

widely /wídli/ adv 1. BY MANY PEOPLE by a large number of people ○ It is not widely known that he was once an acrobat. 2. OVER LARGE RANGE so as to cover an extensive range ○ The conversation ranged widely, from politics to bee-keeping. 3. GREATLY to a great degree ○ widely different examples of this phenomenon 4. OVER LARGE AREA over an extensive area ○ She is very widely travelled. 5. WITH SPACE BETWEEN with a relatively large distance between ○ Plant them fairly widely apart. 6. MAKING SOMETHING SPREAD OR OPEN WIDE in such a way as to make something open or spread as much as possible or to a great extent ○ smiling a little too widely

wide-mouthed adj 1. with a mouth that is notably wider than average 2. with the mouth open wide, e.g. in surprise

widen /wíd'n/ (-ens, -ening, -ened) vti to become wider, or make something wider —**widener** n

wide-open adj (not hyphenated after a verb) 1. OPEN TO GREAT EXTENT open to a great extent, or as much as possible ○ The door was wide open. 2. UNPREDICTABLE not as yet decided or even predictable in outcome ○ The match is still wide open. 3. VULNERABLE TO ATTACK unprotected and therefore able to be attacked easily 4. US WITHOUT LAWS OR LAW-ENFORCEMENT with few laws regulating such things as prostitution, gambling, or the sale of alcohol, or not stringently enforcing the laws that do exist (informal)

wide-ranging adj 1. dealing with a great variety of matters 2. affecting a large number of people or things ○ a decision that has wide-ranging implications

wide receiver n in American football, a player who positions himself to the side of the offensive formation, and whose role is to catch long passes from the quarterback

wide-screen adj 1. describes a type of film projection in which the image is substantially wider than it is tall 2. describes a television whose screen is noticeably wider than average —**wide screen** n

widespread /wíd spred/ adj 1. existing or happening in many places, or affecting many people 2. spread or extending far apart ○ with arms widespread

SYNONYMS *widespread, prevalent, rife, epidemic, universal*

CORE MEANING: occurring in many situations

widespread existing or happening in many places, or affecting many people ○ This semi-desert antelope was once widespread in North Africa. ○ The report claims that drugs in sports are becoming a much more widespread problem. **prevalent** occurring, accepted or practised, commonly or widely ○ the prevalent public mood ○ Depression is the most prevalent of all psychiatric disorders. **rife** extremely widespread, or occurring over a wide area, in great numbers, or very frequently ○ Prostitution is rife in the area. ○ Wall Street at the time was rife with insider trading scandals. **epidemic** spreading more quickly and more extensively than would usually be expected ○ Bribery in the country was reported to have reached epidemic proportions. **universal** applicable to all situations or purposes ○ His suggestions met with almost universal derision. ○ Divorce has become an almost universal feature of modern life.

widgeon n BIRDS another spelling of **wigeon**

widget /wíjjit/ n 1. a little device or mechanism, especially one whose name is unknown or forgotten (humorous) 2. a hypothetical manufactured object, considered to represent the typical product of a manufacturer [Early 20C. Origin ?]

Widnes /wídniss/ town near Liverpool, northwestern England, on the River Mersey. Population: 57,162 (1991).

widow /wíddō/ n 1. WOMAN WHOSE HUSBAND HAS DIED a woman whose husband has died, especially when she has not remarried 2. WOMAN LEFT BEHIND a woman whose partner regularly goes away from her to take part in a particular activity (only used in combination) ○ a golf widow 3. PRINTING SHORT FINAL LINE OF PARAGRAPH a short line at the end of a paragraph, especially when occurring as the top line of a page or column of text. The text is usually altered so that this is removed. 4. CARDS EXTRA HAND OF CARDS an extra hand of cards dealt out in some card games ■ vt (-ows, -owing, -owed) MAKE SOMEBODY WIDOW OR WIDOWER to cause somebody to become a widow or widower (usually passive) [Old English widuwe < Indo-European, 'to separate'] —**widowhood** n

widowbird /wíddōburd/ (plural -birds or same) n BIRDS same as **whydah** [Late 18C. Alteration]

widower /wíddō ər/ n a man whose wife has died, especially when he has not remarried —**widowerhood** n

widowmaker /wíddō maykər/ n something that is so dangerous that it might kill anyone who uses it or tries it

widow's benefit n a sum of money paid weekly to a widow under the National Insurance scheme in the United Kingdom

widow's cruse n a source that provides an unending supply of something [< the biblical story of the widow's cruse of oil that supplies Elijah during a famine (I Kings 17:8–16)]

widow's mite n a contribution that, although small, is generous because it comes from somebody who has very little to give [< the poor widow's contribution of two copper coins to the treasury in the Bible (Mark 12:42)]

widow's peak n a V-shaped hairline across the top of somebody's forehead behind which the hair grows [< the superstition that this feature portends early widowhood]

widow's walk n a walkway with a rail around it on the rooftop of a house, especially one that was used to keep watch for incoming ships [Because, while pacing along it, wives commonly looked for signs of their husbands returning from sea]

widow's weeds *npl* the black clothes once traditionally worn by widows (*archaic or literary*)

width /width, witth/ *n* **1.** DISTANCE ACROSS the distance from one side or edge of something to the other **2.** STATE OF BEING WIDE the fact of being wide, or how wide something is **3.** SWIMMING SIDE TO SIDE DISTANCE OF POOL the distance from one side of a swimming pool to the other ○ *Learners begin by swimming widths rather than lengths.* **4.** HANDICRAFT MATERIAL OF FULL WIDTH a piece of material of its full width

widthwise /width wīz, witth-/, **widthways** /-wayz/ *adv* from one side or edge to the other

~~wiegh~~ incorrect spelling of **weigh**

~~wieght~~ incorrect spelling of **weight**

Wieland /vee lant/, **Christoph Martin** (1733–1813) German writer. He wrote both the first German play in blank verse and the first psychological novel.

> 'A single moment can change all.'
> [Christoph Martin Wieland, *Oberon*; 1780]

wield /weeld/ (**wields, wielding, wielded**) *vt* **1.** to have and be able to use something, especially power or authority ○ *the immense economic power wielded by large companies* **2.** to hold and use a weapon or tool [Old English *wielden* 'rule', variant of *wealden* < Indo-European, 'be strong'] —**wieldable** *adj* —**wielder** *n*

wieldy /weeldi/ (**-ier, -iest**) *adj* easily handled or used, or easy enough to manage

wiener /weenər/ *n* FOOD same as **frankfurter** [Late 19C. Shortening of WIENERWURST]

Wiener /weenər/, **Norbert** (1894–1964) US mathematician. His work on the mathematics and theories underlying communication and electronic machines founded the science of cybernetics.

> 'The world of the future will be an ever more demanding struggle against the limits of our intelligence, not a comfortable hammock in which we can lie down to be waited upon by our robot slaves.'
> [Norbert Wiener, *God and Golem, Inc.*; 1964]

Wiener schnitzel /veenər shnits'l/ *n* a thin slice of veal coated in egg and breadcrumbs and fried [< German *Wiener* 'of Vienna']

wienerwurst /weenər wurst/ *n* FOOD same as **frankfurter** [Late 19C. < German < *Wiener* 'of Vienna' + *Wurst* 'sausage']

~~wier~~ incorrect spelling of **weir**

~~wierd~~ incorrect spelling of **weird**

Wiesbaden /veess baad'n/ industrial city and spa resort in west-central Germany. It is the capital city of Hesse State. Population: 266,081 (1997).

Wieschaus /wee showss, vee-/, **Eric F.** (*b.* 1947) US geneticist. He shared the Nobel Prize in physiology or medicine (1995) with Christiane Nüsslein-Volhard and Edward B. Lewis for his research into embryonic development.

Wiesel /weez'l/, **Elie** (*b.* 1928) Romanian-born US writer. He survived the Holocaust, and after settling in the United States in 1956 devoted himself to writing and speaking about it. His first book *And the World Remained Silent* (1956), abridged as *Night* (1958), is regarded as one of the most important works in the Holocaust literary canon. He won a Nobel Peace Prize (1986). Full name **Wiesel, Eliezer**

> 'No one is as capable of gratitude as one who has emerged from the kingdom of the night....'
> [Elie Wiesel, *On accepting the Nobel Peace Prize, New York Times*; 11 December 1986]

> 'Take sides. Neutrality helps the oppressor, never the victim. Silence encourages the tormentor, never the tormented.'
> [Elie Wiesel, *On accepting the Nobel Peace Prize, New York Times*; 11 December 1986]

Wiesenthal /veez'n taal/, **Simon** (*b.* 1908) Polish-born Austrian war-crimes investigator. He founded the Jewish Documentation Centre, Linz (1947) and Vienna (1961), and is thought to have tracked down about 1,000 Nazi war criminals.

wife /wīf/ (*plural* **wives** /wīvz/) *n* **1.** the woman to whom a man is married **2.** *regional* a woman, especially a mature or married one (*archaic*) [Old English *wīf* 'woman, wife', origin ?] —**wifehood** *n*

wifely /wīfli/ (**-lier, -liest**) *adj* showing the attitudes or behaviour stereotypically expected of a wife — **wifeliness** *n*

Wi-Fi /wī fī/ *tdmk* a certification trademark assuring the interoperability of wireless local area network products

wig[1] /wig/ *n* **1.** a covering of hair or something resembling hair worn on the head for adornment, ceremony, or to cover baldness **2.** same as **toupee** (*informal*) [Late 17C. Shortening of PERIWIG] —**wigged** *adj*

wig[2] /wig/ (**wigs, wigging, wigged**) *vt UK* to speak sternly to somebody who has done something wrong (*dated informal*) [Early 19C < WIG[1]]

wigan /wiggən/ *n* a tough fabric used for stiffening clothes [Mid-19C. After the town in Lancashire where the material was first made]

Wigan /wiggən/ industrial town near Manchester, northwestern England. Population: 301,415 (2001).

wigeon /wijjən/ (*plural* **-geons** or *same*), **wdgeon** *n* **1.** a freshwater duck with a white patch on each wing. Native to: Europe, Asia. Latin name: *Anas penelope*. **2.** a freshwater duck, the male of which has a white crown. Native to: North America. Latin name: *Anas americana*. [Early 16C. Origin ?]

wigged-out /wigd-/ *adj US* experiencing an extreme emotional or psychological state such as nervousness or anxiety (*slang*) ○ *wigged-out from staying up all night*

wigging /wigging/ *n* a severe scolding (*dated informal*)

wiggle /wigg'l/ *vti* (**-gles, -gling, -gled**) MAKE SMALL MOVEMENTS to move from side to side in small quick movements, or make something move in this way ■ *n* **1.** INSTANCE OF WIGGLING a small quick side-to-side movement **2.** WAVY LINE a line with irregular curves in it [13C. < Low German or Dutch *wiggelen* < Germanic] —**wiggler** *n*

wiggle room *n* freedom or latitude, e.g., in making decisions or achieving an aim ○ *The terms of the contract leave little wiggle room.*

wiggly /wigg'li/ (**-glier, -gliest**) *adj* **1.** moving from side to side with small quick movements, or able to be moved in this way (*informal*) **2.** with many irregular curves ○ *a wiggly line*

wight /wīt/ *n* a living being, especially a human being (*archaic*) [Old English *wiht* < Germanic]

Wight, Isle of /wīt/ ◆ **Isle of Wight**

wiglet /wigglət/ *n* a small hairpiece for a woman, worn as an addition to a hairstyle rather than to cover the head

wigmaker /wig maykər/ *n* a professional maker of wigs

wigwag /wig wag/ *vti* (**-wags, -wagging, -wagged**) **1.** MOVE FROM SIDE TO SIDE to wave or swing from side to side in an arc about a fixed point, or make something such as a flag move in this way **2.** NAUT SIGNAL BY WAVING SOMETHING to send a message by waving something such as an arm or a flag ■ *n NAUT* **1.** PROCESS OF WIGWAGGING the method of communicating by waving an arm or a flag **2.** MESSAGE SENT BY WIGWAGGING a message communicated by the moving of arms or flags [Late 16C. Reduplication of WAG[1]] — **wigwagger** *n*

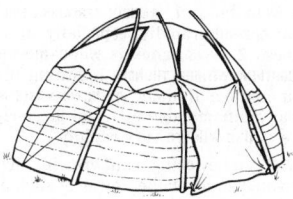

wigwam

wigwam /wig wam/ *n* **1.** a Native North American hut made by covering a conical or dome-shaped framework of poles with woven rush mats or sheets of bark. Wigwams were used by the Algonquian-speaking Native North Americans of the northeastern United States. **2.** a light tent in the shape of

a wigwam for a child to play in [Early 17C. < Abenaki *wikewam* 'house']

Wik /wik/ *n* a judgment passed by the High Court of Australia in 1996, ruling that the granting of a pastoral lease did not necessarily extinguish all native title rights to land [After an Aboriginal people of the central eastern areas of the Gulf of Carpentaria, Australia, in whose favour the court ruled]

wikiup *n* BUILDINGS another spelling of **wickiup**

wikiwiki /wiki wiki/ *adv* Hawaii quickly [< Hawaiian]

Wilberforce /wilbər fawrss/, **William** (1759–1833) British politician and political reformer. His campaign to end the slave trade resulted in its abolition in the Atlantic in 1807, and in the Slave Abolition Act of 1833.

> 'They charge me with fanaticism. If to be feelingly alive to the sufferings of my fellow-creatures is to be a fanatic, I am one of the most incurable fanatics ever permitted to be at large.'
> [William Wilberforce, *Speech in Parliament*; 19 June 1816]

wilco /wilkō/ *interj* used to indicate that you understand what has just been said in a radio message and will do what is necessary [Mid-20C. Blend and shortening of *will comply*]

Wilcoxon test /wil kóks'n-/ *n* a statistical test of the equality of similar or matched groups of data to determine whether they differ significantly from one another, without any assumptions about the underlying distribution patterns [Mid-20C. After Frank Wilcoxon (1892–1965), Irish statistician]

wild /wīld/ *adj* **1.** NOT TAME OR DOMESTICATED not kept as a pet or used for display, work, or experimentation, but living freely in a natural habitat **2.** NOT CULTIVATED growing in a natural state rather than being cultivated in fields, parks, or gardens ○ *wild strawberries* **3.** PRODUCED BY WILD ANIMALS produced by animals living freely rather than by domesticated animals ○ *wild honey* **4.** REMOTE AND BARREN describes territory that is not inhabited or able to be inhabited by humans because of being remote and barren **5.** ENTHUSIASTIC OR EAGER feeling enthusiastic or eager or showing enthusiasm or eagerness ○ *I'm not wild about the idea.* **6.** OVERWHELMED BY EMOTION overwhelmed by or showing a strong emotion such as anger, grief, or desire ○ *wild with grief* **7.** STORMY rough and stormy, with a strong wind ○ *wild winds and seas* **8.** UNRULY lively and showing a disregard for rules ○ *The kids next door are really wild.* **9.** UNRESTRAINED marked by a lack of restraint or prudence, especially in things considered to be vices ○ *a really wild party* **10.** UNTIDY not neat or well-groomed ○ *His hair was wild.* **11.** NOT CAREFULLY THOUGHT OUT not based on rational thought, evidence, or probability ○ *I just made a wild guess.* **12.** OFFENSIVE TERM an offensive term meaning supposedly culturally inferior **13.** UNCONVENTIONAL unconventional, exciting, and slightly irrational (*informal*) ○ *a wild idea* **14.** EXCELLENT very good or admirable (*dated slang*) ○ *Hey, man, that's really wild!* **15.** POORLY AIMED not carefully aimed ○ *throwing wild punches* **16.** CARDS WITH VALUE ASSIGNED BY PLAYER describes a playing card that has any value that the player using it wishes to give it ○ *Jokers are wild.* ■ *adv* **1.** IN UNCULTIVATED WAY in a natural state rather than being cultivated in fields, parks, or gardens ○ *flowers that grow wild in the fields* **2.** IN UNCONTROLLED WAY in an uncontrolled, unpredictable, or unplanned way ○ *He just lets his kids run wild.* **3.** *Ireland* EXTREMELY to an extreme degree (*informal*) ○ *That was wild stupid.* ■ *n* UNDOMESTICATED STATE the natural, free state of an undomesticated animal ○ *Most people have never actually seen a panda in the wild.* ■ **wilds** *npl* UNINHABITED AREA an area that is completely uninhabited or only very sparsely populated because it is remote and barren ○ *They live somewhere out in the wilds.* [Old English *wilde* < Indo-European, 'wild, woods'] —**wildish** *adj* —**wildness** *n*

SYNONYMS See *unruly*.

Wild /wīld/, **Jonathan** (1682?–1725) English criminal. He gained widespread notoriety in England as the organizer of a gang that both stole and sold goods. He was eventually hanged.

wild boar *n* a wild pig with a coat ranging from pale grey to black, dense bristles, a thin body, and small tusks. Native to: Europe, Asia. Latin name: *Sus scrofa*.

wild card *n* **1.** SOMEBODY OR SOMETHING UNPREDICTABLE somebody or something that is important to a plan or course of action but whose behaviour cannot be predicted (*informal*) **2.** EXTRA PLAYER OR TEAM IN COMPETITION an extra player or team selected to take part in a competition although not technically qualified to do so **3.** CARDS CARD OF NO FIXED VALUE in card games, a card that can have whatever value its player assigns it **4.** COMPUT COMPUTER SYMBOL REPRESENTING ANY CHARACTER a symbol that can be used to represent any character that may appear in the same position in a computer search argument. A single character is usually represented by ? and multiple characters by *.

wildcat

wildcat /wíld kat/ *n* (*plural* **-cats** or *same*) **1.** UNDOMESTICATED CAT a wild cat that resembles the domestic tabby but is heavier and has a bushy tail. Native to: Europe, Asia, Africa. Latin name: *Felis sylvestris*. **2.** N Am MEDIUM-SIZED WILD FELINE any medium-sized wild feline, e.g. the lynx or caracal **3.** QUICK-TEMPERED PERSON an easily angered person **4.** INDUST EXPLORATORY OIL OR GAS WELL an exploratory or speculative well drilled in an area not yet known to be productive of oil or gas **5.** N Am COMM FINANCIALLY UNSOUND BUSINESS a financially unsound business ■ *adj* N Am NOT FINANCIALLY SAFE practising unethical or financially risky business methods, or characteristic of such methods ○ *wildcat stocks* ■ *vti* (**-cats**, **-catting**, **-catted**) US DRILL EXPLORATORY WELL to drill an exploratory well in, or take samples in, an area not yet known to have any reserves of what is being sought, especially oil or gas

wildcat strike *n* a sudden strike not authorized by the trade union that the strikers belong to

wildcatter /wíld katər/ *n* N Am **1.** PROSPECTOR a prospector for oil in areas not yet known to be productive **2.** UNETHICAL BUSINESSPERSON a developer or promoter of risky or fraudulent business ventures **3.** WILDCAT STRIKE PARTICIPANT a participant in a sudden strike not authorized by the trade union that he or she belongs to

wild cherry *n* a tree, ancestral to cultivated sweet cherries, that flowers in spring before the leaves emerge and bears clusters of red berries. Flowers: white. Native to: Europe, western Asia, North Africa. Latin name: *Prunus avium*.

wild child *n* a reckless, impulsive, and undisciplined person, usually a young adult (*informal*)

wild dog *n* any wild member of the dog family, especially the dingo, the African hunting dog, or the dhole

AKG London
Oscar Wilde

Wilde /wíld/, **Oscar** (1854–1900) Irish writer. His works include the plays *Lady Windermere's Fan* (1892) and *The Importance of Being Earnest* (1895) and the novel *The Picture of Dorian Gray* (1891). His flamboyance and legendary wit made him a leading figure in society, but he was convicted of sodomy and sentenced to two years' hard labour in 1895. Full name **Wilde, Oscar Fingal O'Flahertie Wills**

'To lose one parent, Mr. Worthing, may be regarded as a misfortune; to lose both looks like carelessness.'
[Oscar Wilde, *The Importance of Being Earnest*; 1895]

'I can resist everything except temptation.'
[Oscar Wilde, *Lady Windermere's Fan*; 1892]

wildebeest /vílde beest, wílde-/ (*plural* **-beests** or *same*) *n* ZOOL same as **gnu** [Early 19C. < Afrikaans, 'wild beast']

wilder /wíldər/ (**-ders**, **-dering**, **-dered**) *vti* (*archaic*) **1.** to go astray, or lead somebody or something astray **2.** to become confused by a number of complex options, or confuse somebody in this way [Early 17C. Origin ?] —**wilderment** *n*

Wilder /wíldər/, **Billy** (1906–2002) Austrian-born US film director. At home in a wide variety of film genres, he made several Hollywood classics, including *Sunset Boulevard* (1950) and *Some Like It Hot* (1959). Born **Wilder, Samuel**

'An audience is never wrong. An individual member of it may be an imbecile, but a thousand imbeciles together in the dark—that's critical genius.'
[Billy Wilder, *Arena* (BBC Television); 24 January 1992]

Wilder, Thornton (1897–1975) US writer. His Pulitzer-Prize-winning works include the novel *The Bridge of San Luis Rey* (1927) and the play *Our Town* (1938). Full name **Wilder, Thornton Niven**

'The best part of married life is the fights. The rest is merely so-so.'
[Thornton Wilder, *The Matchmaker*; 1954]

wilderness /wíldərnəss/ *n* **1.** NATURAL UNCULTIVATED LAND a mostly uninhabited area of land in its natural uncultivated state, sometimes deliberately preserved like this, e.g. a forest or mountainous region **2.** BARREN AREA an area that is empty or barren ○ *in the vast wilderness of outer space* **3.** DELIBERATELY UNCULTIVATED LAND a piece of land that is deliberately not cultivated but is left to grow wild, e.g. in a garden **4.** LOSS OF INFLUENCE the state of being without power or influence for a time after having been in a position of leadership or authority, especially in politics **5.** UNCOMFORTABLE SITUATION a place, situation, or multitude of people or things that makes somebody feel confused, overwhelmed, or desolate ○ *the wilderness of the big city* [Old English *wilddēornes* < *wilddēor* 'wild beast' < *wilde* 'wild' + *dēor* 'animal'] ◇ **be (a voice) crying in the wilderness** to be giving advice or suggestions that are very unlikely to be followed

wilderness area *n* US a protected area set aside for preservation in as natural a state as possible, with restrictions on most human activity except for non-motorized forms of outdoor recreation ○ *backpacking in the wilderness areas*

wild-eyed *adj* **1.** with eyes that are wide and glaring because of fear, anger, or a psychological disorder **2.** marked by or advocating ideas that are so extreme and far-fetched as to be completely impracticable

wildfire /wíld fīr/ *n* **1.** RAPIDLY SPREADING FIRE a fierce fire that spreads rapidly, especially in an area of wilderness **2.** PHYS same as **will-o'-the-wisp** (sense 1) **3.** LIGHTNING WITHOUT THUNDER lightning that occurs without audible thunder **4.** INFLAMMABLE MATERIAL AS WEAPON any inflammable material formerly used in warfare ◇ **like wildfire** very rapidly

wild flower *n* a flowering plant growing in a natural, uncultivated state, or the flower of such a plant

wildfowl /wíld fowl/ (*plural same*) *n* a bird that is hunted for food or sport, e.g. a duck or a goose — **wildfowler** *n* —**wildfowling** *n*

Wild Geese *n, npl* Irish Jacobites who left Ireland for Europe after the fall of James II at the end of the 17th century, especially those who joined the French army [Mid-19C. Because of their flight to the European continent]

wild ginger *n* a herb with two heart-shaped leaves and an aromatic root. Flowers: single, reddish-brown. Native to: North America. Latin name: *Asarum canadense*.

wild-goose chase *n* a futile search for something that there is no chance of finding, especially because it does not exist [Originally of an irregular course, like the patterned flight of wild geese]

wild hyacinth *n* PLANTS same as **bluebell** (sense 1)

wilding /wílding/ *n* **1.** WILD PLANT OR TREE a plant that grows wild, or one that has escaped from cultivation, especially a wild crab-apple tree **2.** FRUIT the fruit of a plant that grows wild or that has escaped from cultivation, especially a wild crab apple **3.** WILD ANIMAL a wild animal ■ *adj* UNCULTIVATED uncultivated or undomesticated

wildland /wíld land/ *n* land that is in a natural uncultivated state, especially when it forms a habitat for wildlife (*often used in the plural*)

wildlife /wíld līf/ *n* wild animals, birds, and other living things, sometimes including vegetation, living in a natural undomesticated state

wildlife park *n* LEISURE same as **safari park**

wildling /wíldling/ *n* BIOL same as **wilding**

wildly /wíldli/ *adv* **1.** WITH ENTHUSIASM in a very enthusiastic way ○ *cheering wildly* **2.** WITHOUT CAREFUL THOUGHT not considering something carefully **3.** VERY to a great extent (*informal*) ○ *not wildly enthusiastic about the idea* **4.** IN WAY THAT SHOWS FEAR in an uncontrolled way that betrays fear or anxiety, and often with eyes that are wide and staring ○ *looking wildly in all directions* **5.** STRONGLY in a fierce and rough way ○ *The wind blew wildly through the trees.*

wild man *n* a man who has extreme or radical opinions, especially in politics

wild mustard *n* PLANTS same as **charlock**

wild oat *n* a weedy annual grass of temperate regions that resembles cultivated oats. Latin name: *Avena fatua*. ◇ **sow your wild oats** to behave in an uncontrolled way, especially sexually, while young

wild pansy *n* a plant of the violet family. Flowers: blue, violet, and yellow. Native to: Europe, Asia. Latin name: *Viola tricolor*.

wild pitch *n* a baseball pitch that a catcher could not have caught and that results in a runner advancing to the next base

wild rice *n* **1.** the dark grain of a grass, traditionally used as food by Native Americans **2.** a tall perennial grass that grows in water and produces edible seeds. Native to: North America. Latin name: *Zizania aquatica*.

wild rose *n* any wild-growing rose, e.g. the dog rose and sweetbriar

wild rubber *n* rubber obtained from uncultivated rubber trees

wild silk *n* **1.** silk fibre obtained from wild silkworms **2.** fabric woven from the silk of wild silkworms, or an imitation of this made with short silk fibres

wild type *n* the form of an organism, strain, or gene that results from natural breeding, as distinct from mutant forms or those resulting from selective breeding

wild water *n* same as **white water** (sense 1)

Wild West *n* the western United States in the second half of the 19th century, regarded as a place of lawlessness

Wild West show *n* a North American form of entertainment involving the demonstration of skills associated with the Wild West, e.g. shooting, riding, and roping cattle, especially performed by people dressed as cowboys

wildwood /wíld wŏŏd/ *n* natural uncultivated woodland (*archaic or literary*)

wile /wíl/ *n* CUNNING STRATEGY a trick or cunning ruse ■ **wiles** *npl* CUNNING BEHAVIOUR cunning behaviour intended to persuade somebody to do something, especially in the form of insincere charm or flattery ■ *vt* (**wiles, wiling, wiled**) PERSUADE SOMEBODY BY WILES to trick or entice somebody into doing or not doing something (*dated*) [12C. Origin ?]

SPELLCHECK See *while*.

Wilfrid /wílfrid/, **Wilfrith** /wílfrith/, **St** (634–709?) English prelate. At the Synod of Whitby (664), he successfully argued for the replacement of Celtic forms

of worship with Roman ones in the English Church.

wilful /ˈwɪlfʊl/ *adj* **1.** done deliberately, especially with the intention of harming somebody or in spite of knowing that it will harm somebody **2.** stubbornly determined to act on a desire, regardless of the opinions or advice of others —**wilfully** *adv* —**wilfulness** *n*

SYNONYMS See *unruly*.

Wilhelm /ˈwɪl helm/ highest mountain in Papua New Guinea. Height: 4,509 m/14,793 ft.

Wilhelm I /ˈvɪl helm/ (1797–1888) king of Prussia. He became the first emperor of Germany in 1871, and is noted for the repression of the later part of his reign.

Wilhelm II (1859–1941) emperor of Germany. A grandson of Queen Victoria, he succeeded his grandfather Wilhelm I in 1888 and presided over a rise in German militarism. After defeat in World War I he went into exile.

Wilhelmina /wɪl hel ˈmiːnə/ (1880–1962) queen of the Netherlands. In the course of her reign (1890–1948) she supported Dutch neutrality during World War I and established a government in exile in England during World War II. Full name **Wilhelmina Helena Pauline Maria**

Wilhelmshaven /ˈvɪl helmz haːvən, -helms haːfən/ city and port in northwestern Germany. It was formerly an important naval base. Population: 91,230 (1997).

Wilkes /wɪlks/, **John** (1725–97) British political leader and reformer. An MP from 1757, he was imprisoned for libel after publishing an attack on a speech by George III. On his release he campaigned for political reforms and supported the patriots during the War of American Independence.

'The chapter of accidents is the longest chapter in the book.'
[John Wilkes. Quoted in *The Doctor*, Robert Southey; 1847]

Wilkins /ˈwɪlkɪnz/, **Maurice** (*b.* 1916) New Zealand-born British biophysicist. He worked with James D. Watson and Francis H. Crick in exploring the structure of DNA, for which they shared the Nobel Prize in physiology or medicine (1962). Full name **Wilkins, Maurice Hugh Frederick**

will[1] /wɪl/ CORE MEANING: a modal verb used to indicate future time ○ *Delegates from all over Europe will attend the forum.* ○ *Will you ever be able to forgive him?* ○ *Your suit will be ready for collection tomorrow.*
modal v **1.** RESOLUTION indicating intent, purpose, or determination ○ *I will be staying with Jean when I come to England.* ○ *I will study harder for these exams.* **2.** POLITE QUESTIONS used in questions to make polite invitations or offers ○ *Will you sit down, please?* ○ *Will you have more coffee?* **3.** REQUESTS used in questions to make requests ○ *Will you take the washing out for me please?* ○ *Phone the garage, will you?* **4.** COMMANDS used when ordering somebody to do something ○ *You will do exactly as I say.* **5.** CUSTOMARY BEHAVIOUR used to indicate the way that something usually happens or the way that somebody usually does something ○ *The wetter the road conditions, the harder it will be for a vehicle to stop.* ○ *When they're out together they will shop till they drop!* **6.** WILLINGNESS used to indicate that somebody is willing to do something ○ *I will mail your letters for you.* ○ *I will not tolerate this kind of behaviour.* **7.** ABILITY used to indicate the ability or capacity of something ○ *That wardrobe will not fit in your bedroom.* ○ *The truck will carry loads of up to 10 tons.* **8.** EXPECTATION used to express surmise or likelihood ○ *That will be them at the door now.* ○ *He will have left the country by now.* **9.** INCLINATION used to indicate the inevitability of something happening or being true ○ *She will stay up till all hours in front of the TV.* **10.** *Scotland* POLITE WAY OF ASKING SOMETHING used in statements to avoid the impoliteness of a question (*informal*) ○ *This will be your brother.*
[Old English *wyllan* < Indo-European]

USAGE See *shall*.

will[2] /wɪl/ *n* **1.** PART OF MIND THAT MAKES DECISIONS the part of the mind with which somebody consciously decides things **2.** POWER TO DECIDE the power to make decisions ○ *This lawn mower seems to have a will of its own!* **3.** PROCESS OF MAKING DECISIONS the use of the mind to

make decisions about things ○ *It's a matter of will as much as opportunity.* **4.** DETERMINATION the determination to do something ○ *She has lots of ability but she lacks the will to succeed.* **5.** DESIRE OR INCLINATION a desire or inclination to do something **6.** ATTITUDE TOWARDS SOMEBODY ELSE the attitude or feelings somebody has towards somebody or something ○ *I bear you no ill will.* **7.** SOMETHING THAT SOMEBODY WANTS TO HAPPEN what a person or group, especially one in authority, wants to happen (*formal*) ○ *It was her will that he should never be told the truth.* **8.** LAW STATEMENT OF DISTRIBUTION OF DECEASED'S PROPERTY a statement of what somebody wants to happen to his or her property after he or she dies, or a legal document containing this statement ■ *vt* (**wills, willing, willed**) **1.** TRY TO CAUSE SOMETHING WANTS to try to make something happen by the power of the mind ○ *He willed himself to stay awake.* ○ *Her parents were watching her run, willing her on.* **2.** LAW LEAVE SOMEBODY SOMETHING IN WILL to give something officially to somebody by declaring it in a will **3.** WANT OR DECIDE SOMETHING to want something to happen or to decide that something will happen (*archaic or formal*) ○ *It shall be as God wills.* [Old English *willa* (noun), *wyllan* (verb), and *willian* (verb < noun) < Indo-European, 'to will, wish'] —**willable** *adj* —**willer** *n* ◇ **at will** when somebody wishes (*formal*) ○ *They are free to come and go at will.* ◇ **with a will** with energy and enthusiasm ○ *He set about the task with a will.* ◇ **with the best will in the world** used to indicate that somebody cannot do something however much he or she wishes or tries to do it ○ *With the best will in the world we won't be able to supervise her all the time.*

Willadsen /ˈwɪladsᵊn/, **Steen** (*b.* 1944) Danish geneticist. He was responsible for the first cloning of a mammal from embryo cells.

willemite /ˈwɪlə maɪt/ *n* a colourless fluorescent brown, green, or red zinc sulphate mineral [Mid-19C. After *Willem* I (1772–1843), king of the Netherlands]

Willemstad /ˈwɪləm staːt/ capital and port of the Netherlands Antilles, on southern Curaçao. Population: 125,000 (1985).

willet /ˈwɪlɪt/ *n* a large grey shorebird with a long straight beak, long legs, and a distinctive black and white wing pattern. Native to: North America. Latin name: *Catoptrophorus semipalmatus.* [Mid-19C. An imitation of its call]

willful *adj* US spelling of **wilful**

William /ˈwɪljəm/, **Prince** (*b.* 1982) He is the first child of Prince Charles and Diana, Princess of Wales. Full name **Prince William Arthur Philip Louis**

William I (1028?–87) king of England. A Norman, he invaded England and defeated Harold II at the Battle of Hastings (1066), subsequently imposing a new ruling aristocracy on England. The *Domesday Book* was compiled during his reign. Known as **William the Conqueror**

'By the splendour of God I have taken possession of my realm; the earth of England is in my two hands.'
[Attributed to William I]

William I (1533–84) prince of Orange. He led the Dutch rebellion against the imperial rule of Philip II that culminated in the Pacification of Ghent (1576) and the Union of Utrecht (1579). Known as **William the Silent**

William II (1056?–1100) king of England. The son and successor of William I, he seized territory in Normandy and Scotland. He was killed, probably accidentally, while hunting in the New Forest. Known as **William Rufus**

William II (1859–1941) emperor of Germany and king of Prussia. His foreign policy during his reign (1888–1918), especially his support of Austro-Hungarian activities in the Balkans, intensified the tensions that led to the start of World War I. He lived in the Netherlands from the end of the war until his death in 1941. Full name **Friedrich Wilhelm Viktor Albert.** Known as **Kaiser Wilhelm**

William III (1650–1702) king of England, Scotland, and Ireland. Dutch-born, he was the grandson of Charles I and the husband of James II's daughter, Mary. He and Mary replaced James II on the English throne after the Revolution of 1689. Known as **William of Orange**

'There is one certain means by which I can

be sure never to see my country's ruin; I will die in the last ditch.'
[William III. Quoted in *History of England*, David Hume; 1757]

William IV (1765–1837) king of the United Kingdom. He succeeded his brother George IV on the throne after a 50-year naval career, and during his reign (1830–37) was the last monarch to exercise the royal prerogative. Known as **the Sailor King**

William (of Malmesbury) /-ˈmɑːmzbəri/ (1090?–1143?) English monk and chronicler. He wrote histories of the kings of England from Saxon times to 1142 and of the bishops of England to 1123.

'Belching from daily excess he came hiccuping to the war.'
[William (of Malmesbury), *Gesta Regum*; 1135–40]

Williams /ˈwɪljəmz/ (*plural same*), **Williams pear** *n UK* a cultivated variety of pear with juicy white flesh and yellow skin. Aus, N Am term **Bartlett** [Early 19C. After *William's* Nursery of Middlesex]

Williams /ˈwɪljəmz/, **Emlyn** (1905–87) British playwright, novelist, and actor. He wrote *Night Must Fall* (1935) and autobiographical works. He acted in his own plays and appeared in films. Full name **Williams, George Emlyn**

Williams, Eric (1911–81) Trinidadian politician and historian. Having led his country to independence from the United Kingdom, he then became its first prime minister (1962–81). He wrote *Capitalism and Slavery* (1944).

Williams, Fred (1927–82) Australian painter. He is noted for his semiabstract paintings of the Australian landscape. Full name **Williams, Frederick Ronald**

Williams, Hank (1923–53) US musician. He developed a wide audience for country music through his recordings and performances on radio and at the Grand Ole Opry. His songs include 'Your Cheatin' Heart'. Born **Williams, Hiram**

'You got to have smelt a lot of mule manure before you can sing like a hillbilly.'
[Hank Williams. Quoted in *Look*; 13 July 1971]

Williams, John (*b.* 1941) Australian-born British classical guitarist. His solo and orchestral work contributed much to the popularization of the classical guitar. Full name **Williams, John Christopher**

Williams, J. P. R. (*b.* 1949) Welsh Rugby Union footballer. He played on the Welsh national rugby team in 55 matches. Full name **Williams, John Peter Rhys**

Williams, Robin (*b.* 1952) US comedian and actor. Originally known for his standup comedy, he went on to perform both comic and serious roles in Hollywood films, and won an Academy Award for *Good Will Hunting* (1997).

'[Psychotherapy is] open-heart surgery in installments.'
[Robin Williams, *New York Times*; 25 January 1988]

Williams, Rowan, archbishop of Canterbury (*b.* 1950) British cleric. He was archbishop of Wales (2000–02) before being appointed archbishop of Canterbury (2002).

Williams, Serena (*b.* 1981) US tennis player. She and her sister Venus Williams came to dominate international women's tennis after 1999.

Williams, Shirley, Baroness Williams of Crosby (*b.* 1930) British politician. She held various ministerial posts in the Labour governments of the 1970s before cofounding the Social Democratic Party in 1981. She served as the party's president from 1982 to 1988. Born **Brittain, Shirley Vivien Teresa**

'The British civil service...is a beautifully designed and effective braking mechanism.'
[Shirley Williams, *Speech, Royal Institute of Public Administration*; 11 February 1980]

Tennessee Williams

Williams, Tennessee (1911–83) US playwright. His plays are largely set in the American South, and he won Pulitzer Prizes for *A Streetcar Named Desire* (1947) and *Cat on a Hot Tin Roof* (1955). Born **Williams, Thomas Lanier**. See Cultural note at **roof**

> 'A vacuum is a hell of a lot better than some of the stuff that nature replaces it with.'
> [Tennessee Williams, *Cat on a Hot Tin Roof*; 1955]

> 'Humanity is just a work in progress.'
> [Tennessee Williams, *Camino Real*; 1953]

Williams, Venus (*b.* 1980) US tennis player. She has recorded the fastest ever women's service, and with her sister Serena Williams came to dominate international women's tennis after 1999.

Williams, William Carlos (1883–1963) US writer and physician. While practising medicine (1910–51), he produced poetry and novels concerned with everyday American life, including the epic poem *Paterson* (1946–58).

> 'Minds like beds always made up, / (more stony than a shore) / unwilling or unable.'
> [William Carlos Williams, *Paterson*; 1946–58]

> 'A cool of books / will sometimes lead the mind to libraries / of a hot afternoon, if books can be found / cool to the sense to lead the mind away.'
> [William Carlos Williams, *Paterson*; 1946–58]

Williamsburg /wílyəmz burg/ city in southeastern Virginia. The central part of the city has been restored along colonial lines and is an important tourist centre. Population: 11,693 (2002 estimate).

Williamson /wílyəms'n/, **David** (*b.* 1942) Australian playwright. He wrote *The Removalists* (1971). His screenplays include *Gallipoli* (1981). Full name **Williamson, David Keith**

Williamson, Henry (1895–1977) British novelist. He wrote nature stories and novels, including *Tarka the Otter* (1927).

Williams pear *n* FOOD, PLANTS same as **Williams**

William Tell *n* in Swiss legend, a patriot who liberated Switzerland from Austrian rule in the 14th century. He was forced by the Austrian governor to shoot an arrow through an apple on his son's head and later killed the governor.

willie *n* another spelling of **willy** (*informal offensive*)

willies /wíliz/ *npl* an uncomfortable, anxious, or fearful feeling (*informal*) [Late 19C. Origin ?]

willing /wíling/ *adj* **1.** READY TO DO SOMETHING VOLUNTARILY ready to do something without being forced to **2.** HELPFUL cooperative and enthusiastic **3.** OFFERED VOLUNTARILY offered or given by somebody readily and enthusiastically —**willingly** *adv* —**willingness** *n*

willing horse *n* a hard and willing worker

Willis /wíliss/, **Norman** (*b.* 1933) British trade union leader. As secretary general of the Trades Union Congress (1984–93), he was noted for his moderation in negotiating industrial disputes. Full name **Willis, Norman David**

williwaw /wíli waw/ *n N Am* a violent gust of cold wind that blows down from a mountainous region

to the coast and out to sea, especially in the Straits of Magellan and in Alaska [Mid-19C. Origin ?]

will-o'-the-wisp /wíll ə thə wísp/ *n* **1.** a phosphorescent light sometimes seen at night over marshy ground, caused by the spontaneous combustion of gases given off by rotting organic matter **2.** somebody or something that is misleading or elusive, e.g. a false hope [< *Will*, shortening of the first name *William*, + OF + THE + WISP]

willow /wíllō/ *n* **1.** TREE WITH LONG FLEXIBLE BRANCHES a tree or bush with long flexible branches, narrow leaves, and catkins containing small flowers without petals. Some species are valued for their wood, twigs, and tanbark. Genus: *Salix*. **2.** WILLOW WOOD the wood of a willow tree **3.** CRICKET BAT a cricket bat (*informal*) **4.** INDUST MACHINE WITH SPIKES a machine with a revolving spiked cylinder inside a box that is also fitted with spikes. Use: cleaning or loosening fibrous materials such as cotton, wool, or rags. [Old English *welig* < Germanic] —**willowish** *adj*

CULTURAL NOTE *The Wind in the Willows*, a children's story (1908) by British writer Kenneth Grahame. Originally written as a bedtime story for Grahame's son, it recounts the mishaps that befall four animals – Mole, Ratty, Toad, and Badger – when they venture outside their natural habitats. Much-loved by children, the tales are also enjoyed by adults as entertaining allegories of human behaviour.

willow goldfinch *n* BIRDS same as **American goldfinch**

willow grouse *n* a plump ground bird of the grouse family that turns from mottled brown to white in the winter. Native to: Arctic regions. Latin name: *Lagopus lagopus*. US term **willow ptarmigan**

willowherb /wíllō hurb/ *n* PLANTS same as **rosebay willowherb**

willow pattern *n* a pattern used to decorate china, usually blue on a white background, featuring a Chinese landscape with a willow tree, pagoda-style buildings, a bridge, and two swallows. The willow pattern was created for Thomas Turner in about 1799 by Thomas Minton, who later founded his own pottery firm in Stoke-on-Trent. (*hyphenated before a noun*)

willow ptarmigan *n US* same as **willow grouse**

willow tit *n* a black-capped member of the tit family whose numbers are in steep decline. Native to: forest and scrub in northern Europe and Asia. Latin name: *Parus montanus*.

willowware

willowware /wíllō wair/ *n* china decorated with the willow pattern

willowy /wíllō i/ (**-ier, -iest**) *adj* **1.** GRACEFUL describes somebody who is slim, graceful, and elegant, partly because of being tall **2.** FLEXIBLE able to be bent easily, and springing back into place **3.** COVERED BY WILLOWS covered or shaded by willow trees

willpower /wil pow ər/ *n* a combination of determination and self-discipline that enables somebody to do something despite the difficulties involved

Wills /wilz/, **Helen Newington** (1905–98) US tennis player. She won the US women's singles title seven times between 1923 and 1931, and was eight times Wimbledon singles champion. Also known as **Moody, Helen Wills**

Wills, William (1834–61) British-born Australian surveyor and explorer. He was second in command to Robert Burke on an ill-fated expedition to northern

Australia (1860–61), during which both died. Full name **Wills, William John**

willy /wílli/ (*plural* **-lies**), **willie** *n* an offensive term for a penis (*informal*) [Early 20C. < shortening of the first name *William*]

willy-nilly /wílli nílli/ *adv* **1.** WITHOUT WANTING TO whether or not somebody wants it to happen ○ *He won't be rushed willy-nilly into a quick decision.* **2.** HAPHAZARDLY in a disorganized or unplanned way ○ *Totally confused by now, I handed out the invitations willy-nilly.* ■ *adj* **1.** HAPPENING WITHOUT CHOICE happening or existing without plan or choice **2.** HAPHAZARD lacking direction or organization [Early 17C. < *will I, nill I* 'whether I wish it or do not wish it']

willy wagtail *n* a small insect-eating bird of the fantail family that is black with white underparts and frequently wags its wide tail. It is often found in urban areas. Native to: Australia. Latin name: *Rhipidura leucophrys*. [< form of *William*]

willy-willy *n Aus* a spiralling wind or dust storm [Late 19C. < Aboriginal]

Wilmut /wílmət/, **Ian** (*b.* 1944) British embryologist. With Keith Campbell, he was responsible for the first successful cloning of a mammal from adult cells.

Wilson /wílss'n/, **Alexander** (1766–1813) British-born US ornithologist. He conducted the first major studies of North American birds and wrote and illustrated *American Ornithology* (1808–13).

Wilson, Sir Angus (1913–91) British writer. He wrote short stories and novels including *Anglo-Saxon Attitudes* (1956) and *The Old Men at the Zoo* (1961). Full name **Wilson, Sir Angus Frank Johnstone**

Wilson, August (*b.* 1945) US playwright. He won Pulitzer prizes for his plays *Fences* (1985) and *The Piano Lesson* (1987) which portray the lives of African Americans.

> 'You all line up at the door with your hands out. I give you the lint from my pockets. I give you my sweat and my blood. I ain't got no tears. I done spent them.'
> [August Wilson, *Fences*; 1985]

Wilson, Edmund (1895–1972) US literary critic. One of the leading essayists of his generation, he wrote critical studies across a broad spectrum of literature and social thought, including a volume on the American Civil War, *Patriotic Gore* (1962).

> 'The taking over by the state of the means of production and the dictatorship in the interests of the proletariat can by themselves never guarantee the happiness of anybody but the dictators themselves...Lenin and Trotsky...founded a dictatorship which perpetuated itself as an autocracy.'
> [Edmund Wilson, 'Old Antichrist's Sayings', *Letters on Literature and Politics 1912–72*; 1977]

Harold Wilson

Wilson, Harold, Baron Wilson of Rievaulx (1916–95) British prime minister (1964–70 and 1974–76). During his premierships, he sought to bolster Britain's economy and introduced the first antiracist legislation. See table at **prime minister**. Full name **Wilson, James Harold**

> 'Everybody should have an equal chance – but they shouldn't have a flying start.'
> [Harold Wilson, *Observer*; 1963]

Wilson, Henry (1812–75) vice president of the United States (1873–75). He joined the Republican Party (1856) because of its opposition to slavery and became Ulysses S. Grant's vice president in 1873. Born **Colbath, Jeremiah Jones**

Wilson, Robert (1936–2002) US astrophysicist. He and coresearcher Arno Penzias discovered background radiation in the Milky Way, which supported the 'big bang' theory. They shared the Nobel Prize in physics (1978). Full name **Wilson, Robert Woodrow**

Library of Congress

Woodrow Wilson

Wilson, Woodrow (1856–1924) 28th president of the United States (1913–21). A Democratic president, he brought the United States into World War I in 1917 and negotiated the peace treaty in 1918, making the League of Nations a part of the treaty. He was awarded the Nobel Peace Prize (1919). Full name **Wilson, Thomas Woodrow**. See table at **president** — **Wilsonian** /wil sóni ən/ adj

'A general association of nations must be formed under specific covenants for the purpose of affording mutual guarantees of political independence and territorial integrity to great and small states alike.' [Woodrow Wilson, *Speech to Congress*, 'Fourteen Points'; 8 January 1918]

'The world must be made safe for democracy.' [Woodrow Wilson, *Speech to Congress*; 2 April 1917]

Wilson's disease n a rare hereditary disease resulting from an inability to metabolize copper and marked by cirrhosis of the liver, damage to other organs, and psychiatric disorder [Early 20C. After S. A. Kinnier *Wilson* (1878–1937), British neurologist]

Wilson's Promontory /wílss'nz-/ peninsula in southeastern Victoria, Australia. It is the most southerly point on the Australian mainland.

wilt[1] /wilt/ v (**wilts, wilting, wilted**) 1. vti DROOP OR SHRIVEL to droop or shrivel through lack of water, too much heat, or disease, or make a plant droop or shrivel 2. vi BECOME WEAK to become weak and tired, e.g. because of heat 3. vti LOSE SPIRIT to lose confidence, composure, or enthusiasm, or make somebody do this ■ n 1. DROOPING OR SHRIVELLING the drooping of plants or shrivelling of leaves because of a lack of water, too much heat, or disease 2. PLANT DISEASE a plant disease caused by fungi, bacteria, or viruses that make plants droop and leaves shrivel 3. ACT OF WILTING an instance of wilting or the condition of having wilted [Late 17C. Origin ?]

wilt[2] /wilt/ vti 2nd person singular present of **will**[1] (archaic)

Wilton /wíltən/ n carpet with a thick velvety pile [Late 18C. After a town in Wiltshire]

Wilts abbr Wiltshire

Wiltshire /wíltshər/ county in southwestern England. Trowbridge is the administrative centre. Population: 432,973 (2001). Area: 3,486 sq. km/1,344 sq. mi.

wily /wíli/ (**-lier, -liest**) adj skilled at using clever tricks to deceive people —**wilily** adv —**wiliness** n

wimble /wímb'l/ n a hand-held tool used for boring holes ■ vt (**-bles, -bling, -bled**) to bore a hole with a wimble [13C. < Anglo-Norman, probably < Middle Dutch wimmel 'augur']

Wimbledon /wímb'ldən/ southern suburb of London, England. It is the home of the All England Lawn Tennis Club, the site of annual international tennis championships.

wimp /wimp/ n an offensive term that deliberately insults somebody regarded as weak, timid, unassertive, or ineffectual (informal insult) [Early 20C. Origin ?] —**wimpish** adj —**wimpy** adj

wimp out (**wimps out, wimping out, wimped out**) vi to fail to do or finish doing something because of fear or a weakness of character (slang)

WIMP[1] /wimp/ n a graphical user interface for computers, designed to make them more user-friendly, that includes windows, icons, mice, and pull-down menus. Full form **windows, icons, mice, and pull-down menus**

WIMP[2] /wimp/ n a hypothetical nonbaryonic subatomic particle that has been proposed as a possible form of dark matter. Full form **weakly interacting massive particle**

wimple /wímp'l/ n 1. WOMAN'S HEAD COVERING a cloth covering for a woman's head and neck. The wimple was common in medieval Europe and it is still worn by some orders of nuns. 2. FOLD IN CLOTH a fold or pleat in a piece of cloth ■ v (**-ples, -pling, -pled**) 1. vi RIPPLE to form small undulating waves 2. vt DRESS SOMEBODY IN WIMPLE to put a wimple on somebody (archaic) [Old English wimpel < Germanic]

win /win/ v (**wins, winning, won** /wun/) 1. vti ACHIEVE VICTORY to beat any or every opponent or enemy in a competition or fight 2. vt GET SOMETHING FOR DEFEATING OTHERS to get something as a prize by beating other competitors ○ proud of the cups he had won for swimming 3. vt MAKE SOMEBODY SUCCEED IN GETTING SOMETHING to be the reason that somebody is first in something or receives something as a prize ○ Their attacking play won them the game. ○ That photo is sure to win you a prize. 4. vt GAIN SOMETHING to gain something such as respect or friendship, e.g. because of something done or said or an ability shown, or to make somebody do this ○ His attitude won him few friends in the company. 5. vt GET SOMETHING to obtain something by hard work (literary) ○ winning his livelihood by the sweat of his brow 6. vt REACH PLACE WITH EFFORT to arrive somewhere by great effort or with difficulty (literary) 7. vt CAPTURE SOMETHING USING FORCE to capture something such as a city using force (formal) 8. vt GAIN SUPPORT to persuade somebody to do something or agree to something, or to gain somebody's sympathy or support 9. vt EARN LOVE OF SOMEBODY to persuade somebody to love or marry you 10. vt MIN EXTRACT GET SOMETHING BY MINING to mine coal, oil, or ore from a source 11. vt MIN EXTRACT PREPARE LODE FOR MINING to discover a source of coal, oil, or ore and prepare it for mining 12. vt MIN EXTRACT EXTRACT SOMETHING FROM ORE to extract a metal or mineral from its ore ■ n 1. VICTORY success in a competition, game, or bet ○ The team has had six wins in a row. 2. AMOUNT OF MONEY WON the amount of money won, e.g. in a bet [Old English winnan < Indo-European, 'to desire'] —**winnable** adj ◇ **some you win, some you lose** used to indicate philosophically or humorously that in life everyone has some successes and some failures

win out, win through vi to be successful or dominant after a struggle

win over vt to persuade somebody to agree with you, support you, or give you permission

wince /winss/ vi (**winces, wincing, winced**) 1. MAKE PAINED EXPRESSION to make an expression of pain with the face because of seeing or thinking of something unpleasant or embarrassing 2. MOVE BODY BACK SLIGHTLY to make an involuntary movement away from something because of pain or fear ■ n 1. EXPRESSION OF PAIN a facial expression of pain or fear 2. EXPRESSION OF DISPLEASURE OR EMBARRASSMENT a facial reaction to seeing or thinking of something unpleasant or embarrassing 3. SLIGHT MOVEMENT AWAY a slight movement away from something because of pain or fear [13C. < Anglo-Norman, variant of Old French guencir 'turn aside' < Germanic] —**wincer** n

SYNONYMS See *recoil*.

wincey /wínssi/ n a cloth made of linen and wool [Early 19C. Probably variant of *woolsey* in LINSEY-WOOLSEY]

winceyette /wínssi ét/ n cloth made of cotton that has a raised surface, used especially for nightclothes

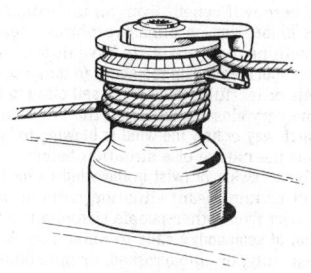

winch

winch /winch/ n 1. LIFTING MACHINE a machine for lifting loads by means of a rope or chain that is wound round a cylinder turned by an engine or by hand 2. CRANK OR HANDLE the handle used to turn a machine ■ vt (**winches, winching, winched**) MOVE SOMETHING WITH WINCH to lift or pull something by means of a winch [Old English wince < Germanic] —**wincher** n —**winchman** n

winchester /wínchistər/ n a large bottle with a short narrow neck. Use: carrying or storing liquid chemicals. [Early 18C. After WINCHESTER, where standards for liquid and dry measures were once kept]

Winchester /wínchistər/ city in Hampshire, southern England. It was the capital of the Anglo-Saxon kingdom of Wessex. Population: 102,222 (2001).

Winchester rifle /wínchistər-/ tdmk a trademark for a rifle first produced in the late 19th century that can fire several shots before it has to be reloaded

Winckelmann /vínk'l man/, **Johann Joachim** (1717–68) German archaeologist and art historian. He made the first scientific reports on the excavations at Pompeii and Herculaneum, and his theories concerning Greek art and aesthetics influenced many writers and philosophers.

wind[1] /wind/ n 1. MOVING AIR air moving across the surface of the planet or through the atmosphere at a speed fast enough to be noticed 2. AIR MOVED ARTIFICIALLY air that is being made to move by a device such as a fan 3. SOCIAL OR ECONOMIC FORCE a force or movement bringing something such as change or destruction ○ the winds of change 4. BREATH the breath of normal breathing and talking 5. POWER TO BREATHE the power to breathe, especially when making an effort such as running 6. IDLE TALK talk that is empty and meaningless 7. HINTING INFORMATION news that brings information of something intended to be secret ○ If wind of this gets out, we've had it. 8. DIRECTION OF WIND the direction from which the wind blows (literary) 9. ASTRON FLOW OF PARTICLES INTO SPACE a flow of particles ejected into space from the surface of the Sun or a star 10. MUSIC MUSICAL INSTRUMENTS a group of musical instruments that requires a flow of air to produce a sound, including both woodwind and brass instruments ○ the wind section of the orchestra 11. PHYSIOL STOMACH GAS gas that builds up in the stomach and intestines while food is being digested 12. FIELD SPORTS AIR CARRYING SCENT the air on which a scent such as that of a hunter is carried ■ **winds** npl MUSIC PLAYERS OF WIND INSTRUMENTS the musicians in an ensemble, especially an orchestra, who play wind instruments ■ v (**winds, winding, winded**) 1. vt MAKE SOMEBODY SHORT OF BREATH to make somebody temporarily unable to breathe properly, e.g. because of too much exertion or by a blow to the abdomen 2. vt MAKE BABY RELEASE STOMACH GAS to help a baby bring up gas from its stomach, e.g. by patting and rubbing its back 3. vt LET HORSE REST to allow a horse to rest after exertion 4. vt EXPOSE SOMETHING TO WIND to expose something to the wind, e.g. in order to dry it 5. vti SMELL SOMEBODY OR SOMETHING to get a scent of somebody or something in the air 6. vt PURSUE ANIMAL BY SCENT to pursue an animal in a hunt by following its scent [Old English, < Indo-European, 'to blow'] —**winded** adj ◇ **be in the wind** to be about to happen or be likely to happen ◇ **break wind** to pass intestinal gas through the anus ◇ **get the wind up** to become nervous or fearful (informal) ◇ **get your** or **a second wind** to recover your natural breathing pattern, and your usual energy levels, after a period of breathlessness and great effort ◇ **get wind of something** to hear indirectly about something ◇ **it's**

an ill wind (that blows nobody any good) somebody somewhere will benefit from an unfortunate event ◇ **piss in the wind** an offensive phrase meaning to do something that is likely to have little or no effect (*slang*) ◇ **put the wind up somebody** to make somebody nervous or fearful (*informal*) ◇ **sail close to the wind** to come very close to breaking the law or a rule ◇ **see which way** *or* **how the wind is blowing** to wait and find out the nature of a situation before making a decision ◇ **swing** *or* **twist in the wind** to be left in a difficult or unpleasant situation without any help or support from other people (*informal*) ◇ **take the wind out of somebody's sails** to make somebody feel deflated, silly, or embarrassed, or put somebody at a disadvantage

CULTURAL NOTE ***Gone With the Wind***, a film (1939) by US director Victor Fleming and producer David O. Selznick. Based on Margaret Mitchell's popular novel (1936), this idealized portrait of the American South focuses on the relationship between dashing rake Rhett Butler (Clark Gable) and resourceful, prewar plantation belle and formidable postwar southern woman Scarlett O'Hara (Vivien Leigh).

wind[2] /wīnd/ *v* (**winds, winding, wound** /wownd/) **1.** *vti* GO ALONG PATH WITH BENDS to move along a course with many bends and twists in it ○ *The river winds lazily through the valley.* ○ *The procession wound its way slowly up the hill.* **2.** *vi* FOLLOW SPIRAL PATH to go in a spiral path ○ *smoke winding slowly up into the air* **3.** *vti* GO OR PUT SOMETHING ROUND to go round something in a coil or coils, or wrap something round something else in a coil or coils ○ *winding the thread onto the bobbin* **4.** *vt* WRAP SOMETHING WITH COILS to cover or decorate something by wrapping something else round it in coils ○ *She wound the injured arm with a scarf.* **5.** *vt* MOVE SOMETHING UP OR DOWN to move or lift something by turning a handle or pressing a button ○ *wound the window up* **6.** *vti* MOVE SOMETHING BACKWARD OR FORWARD to move something such as film or tape forwards or backwards by turning a handle or pressing a button, or be moved in this way **7.** *vt* MAKE SOMETHING REVOLVE to turn something such as a crank with a circular motion **8.** *vt* MAKE CLOCKWORK MECHANISM WORK to turn a key or handle in a clock or clockwork device in order to make the mechanism operate, usually by means of a spring that tightens on being wound ■ *n* **1.** CURVE OR BEND a bend or twist in something such as a river or a path **2.** ACT OF WINDING SOMETHING the act of winding something such as a clock or motor **3.** TURN IN WINDING SOMETHING a single turn in the process of winding something [Old English *windan* < Germanic]

wind down *v* **1.** *vi* RELAX to relax after a period of feeling stressed or tense **2.** *vti* STEADILY REDUCE WORK to reduce gradually the amount of work done before stopping completely, or bring a business or activity gradually to an end **3.** *vi* GO MORE SLOWLY to operate more and more slowly and then stop because the spring by which a mechanism works is losing or has lost its tension

wind up *v* **1.** *vt* CLOSE BUSINESS DOWN to close down a business, bringing trading to an end **2.** *vt* FINISH ACTIVITY to conclude something or to bring an activity to an end **3.** *vi* END UP to come to be in a particular place or situation as a result of, or at the end of, a series of earlier events (*informal*) **4.** *vt* LIE TO SOMEBODY AS JOKE to tease or trick somebody by telling him or her things that are not true (*informal*) ○ *You're winding me up, aren't you?* **5.** *vt* MAKE SOMEBODY TENSE to make somebody nervous or irritated, usually deliberately (*informal; often passive*)

wind[3] /wīnd/ (**winds, winding, winded** or **wound** /wownd/) *v* **1.** *vti* to blow a horn or bugle to create a sound **2.** *vt* to make a signal by blowing a horn [14C. < WIND[1]]

windage /wíndij/ *n* **1.** DEFLECTION CAUSED BY WIND the amount of deflection the wind will produce in a projectile **2.** ALLOWANCE MADE FOR WIND DEFLECTION the amount of adjustment needed in the aim of a projectile to counter wind deflection **3.** ARMS DIFFERENCE BETWEEN BORE AND PROJECTILE the amount by which the bore of a gun is larger than the bullet or shell it fires, so that gases can escape **4.** NAUT PART OF SHIP ABOVE WATER the part of a ship's body that is above the water and consequently causes wind resistance **5.** MECH ENG FRICTION BETWEEN AIR AND MOVING PARTS the friction between air and the moving parts of a machine, which tends to slow the machine

windbag /wínd bag/ *n* **1.** a talkative person who is thought to have little of interest or value to say (*informal insult*) **2.** the bag in a set of bagpipes into which air is forced by the player's lungs or a set of bellows and from which it flows to produce sound

windball cricket /wínd bawl-/ *n* a form of cricket played with a wooden bat and a tennis ball. It is popular especially in the Caribbean, in Trinidad.

wind-bell /wínd-/ *n* a light bell that rings when the wind moves it

windblast /wínd blaast/ *n* the harmful effect of air friction on a pilot who has ejected from an aircraft travelling at high speed

windblown /wínd blōn/ *adj* **1.** blown about by the wind ○ *They came back from their walk looking a bit windblown.* **2.** growing in a shape caused by the action of the prevailing winds

wind-borne /wínd-/ *adj* carried or dispersed by the wind

windbound /wínd bownd/ *adj* unable to sail because the wind is blowing in the wrong direction

windbreak /wínd brayk/ *n* **1.** something that breaks the force of the prevailing wind, e.g. a wall or hedge **2.** same as **windshield** (sense 1)

windbreaker /wínd braykər/ *n US* CLOTHING same as **windcheater**

wind-broken /wínd-/ *adj* describes a horse that has impaired breathing, e.g. because of heaves

windburn /wínd burn/ *n* redness and inflammation of the skin caused by exposure to harsh wind — **windburnt** *adj*

windcheater /wínd cheetər/ *n* a warm windproof outer jacket with tight-fitting neck, cuffs, and waistband, and sometimes with a hood. US term **windbreaker**

wind chest /wínd-/ *n* a compartment in a pipe organ that stores wind from the bellows under pressure before it goes to the pipes

wind-chill factor /wínd-/, **wind-chill** *n* the combined effect on exposed skin of air temperature and wind speed, usually given as an equivalent temperature in calm conditions

wind chime /wínd-/ *n* a musical decoration consisting of objects such as beads or metal tubes suspended on strings so that they will make a pleasant noise when moved by the wind

wind cone /wínd kōn/ *n* AVIAT same as **windsock**

winder /wīndər/ *n* **1.** SOMETHING THAT WINDS UP a key, knob, or other device that is used to wind up a spring-powered mechanism such as a clock **2.** SOMEBODY OR SOMETHING THAT WINDS SOMETHING a person or device that winds something such as thread or textiles around a spool, cone, or tube **3.** OBJECT FOR WINDING SOMETHING AROUND a spool or bobbin around which something such as thread is wound **4.** HOISTING MECHANISM OR OPERATOR a mechanism for hoisting or lowering a cage in a mineshaft, or an operator of such a mechanism **5.** STEP IN SPIRAL STAIRCASE a step in a spiral staircase or at the turn of a staircase that is narrower at the inside

Windermere, Lake /wíndər meer/ largest lake in England, in the Lake District in the northwest of the country. Area: 16 sq. km/6 sq. mi.

windfall /wínd fawl/ *n* **1.** something good that is received unexpectedly, especially a sum of money **2.** something that the wind has blown down, especially a piece of ripe fruit blown off a tree

wind farm /wínd-/ *n* an area of land with a large number of electricity-generating windmills or wind turbines

windflaw /wínd flaw/ *n* METEOROL same as **flaw**[2] (sense 1)

windflower /wínd flowər/ *n* PLANTS same as **anemone** (sense 1)

windgall /wínd gawl/ *n* a fluid-filled swelling around the fetlock joint of a horse, usually not associated with loss of function or lameness

wind gap /wínd-/ *n* a shallow pass or gap in a mountain ridge, often originally a water gap

wind gauge /wínd-/ *n* **1.** METEOROL same as **anemometer** **2.** an attachment to the sight on a musket or rifle showing how much the aim should be adjusted to allow for the effect of the wind on the bullet

wind harp /wínd-/ *n* MUSIC same as **aeolian harp**

Windhoek /wínd hòok, wínt-, vínt-/ capital city of Namibia, located in the centre of the country. Population: 202,000 (1999).

windhover /wínd hovər/ *n regional* same as **kestrel** [Late 17C. < its habit of hovering in the air]

windigo *n Can* same as **wendigo**

winding /wīnding/ *adj* **1.** TWISTING AND CURVING made up of many consecutive curves or twists **2.** SPIRALLING arranged or moving in a spiral ■ *n* **1.** SOMETHING WOUND something wound or coiled round an object **2.** SINGLE COIL a single turn of something coiled or wound around an object **3.** ACT OF COILING the act or process of coiling something **4.** CURVING COURSE the bending or curving course that something follows **5.** ELEC ENG WIRE COIL CARRYING ELECTRICITY a wire coil designed to have an electric current passing through it, forming part of numerous electrical devices such as electric motors and transformers —**windingly** *adv*

winding drum *n* a revolving drum with a wire rope coiled round it that acts as the lifting mechanism of a hoist or winch

winding sheet *n* a sheet that a corpse is wrapped in before it is buried

wind instrument /wínd-/ *n* a musical instrument played by causing air to vibrate by blowing into or across a tube, e.g. a trumpet or flute

windjammer /wínd jamər/ *n* **1.** a large sailing ship, especially a large and fast merchant ship **2.** CLOTHING same as **windcheater** (*dated*)

windlass /wíndləss/ *n* a device that uses a rope or cable wound round a revolving drum to pull and lift things, especially the mechanism on a ship to raise and lower the anchor ■ *vt* (**-lasses, -lassing, -lassed**) to raise or pull something using a windlass [14C. Alteration of Old Norse *vindáss* < *vinda* 'wind' + *áss* 'pole']

windlestraw /wínd'l straw/ *n* **1.** DRY GRASS STALK a thin dry stalk of grass **2.** *regional* THIN PERSON somebody who is regarded as unhealthily thin (*archaic or literary*) **3.** *regional* WEAK-WILLED PERSON somebody who is regarded as lacking in strength of character (*archaic or literary*) [Old English *windelstrēaw* < *windan* 'wind' + *strēaw* 'straw']

wind machine /wínd-/ *n* **1.** a device used to simulate the sound or effects of wind, e.g. a machine used backstage in a theatre **2.** a machine that creates a strong current of air, e.g. a device that produces warm air to protect crops from frost

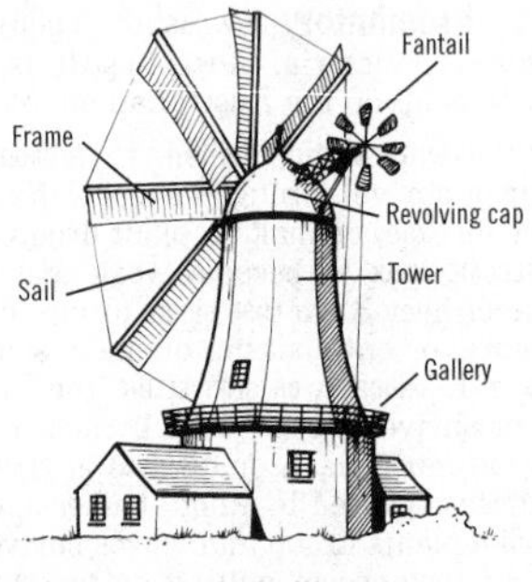

windmill

windmill /wínd mil/ *n* **1.** BUILDING WITH REVOLVING BLADES a building with a set of wind-driven revolving sails or blades fitted to the side of its roof that drive a grinding machine inside **2.** REVOLVING BLADES OR GRINDING MECHANISM the set of revolving sails or blades on a windmill, or the grinding mechanism inside the building **3.** DEVICE HARNESSING WIND POWER a building or device fitted with a set of revolving blades designed to harness the power of the wind, e.g. to pump water or generate electricity **4.** CHILD'S TOY WITH SPINNING BLADES a child's toy consisting of a stick with a set of plastic or paper blades fitted to it, which spin round when the wind blows them. N Am term **pinwheel** ■ *v* (**-mills, -milling, -milled**) **1.** *vti* SPIN LIKE WINDMILL to spin or turn like the sails of a windmill, or be spun or turned in this way **2.** *vi* ROTATE UNPOWERED to rotate solely by wind force and with no engine power ◇ **tilt at windmills** to struggle against imagined enemies or opponents

window /wíndō/ *n* **1.** GLASS-COVERED OPENING IN BUILDING an opening in a wall of a building, usually with an inner frame of wood or metal with glass fitted to it, to let in light or, when opened, air **2.** GLASS-COVERED OPENING IN VEHICLE a glass-covered opening designed to let in light or, when opened, air, e.g. in a vehicle **3.** BUILDINGS same as **windowpane 4.** DISPLAY IN SHOP WINDOW the area immediately behind a large window in the wall of a shop, where goods are put on display **5.** OPENING WHERE SOMETHING IS DISPENSED an opening above a counter where somebody provides information, goods, or services to customers **6.** OPENING SIMILAR TO WINDOW an opening that makes it possible to see something behind or underneath, e.g. the opening on some envelopes **7.** PERIOD OF AVAILABLE TIME a period of time available for a particular activity or during which conditions are right for something to take place **8.** OPPORTUNITY TO EXPERIENCE SOMETHING an opportunity to see or experience something **9.** COMPUT SECTION ON COMPUTER SCREEN a rectangular frame on a computer screen in which images output by application programs can be displayed, moved around, or resized **10.** PHYS PART OF ELECTROMAGNETIC SPECTRUM the range of the electromagnetic spectrum that a given medium will allow to pass through it **11.** AIR FORCE same as **chaff**[1] (sense 3) [Pre-12C. < Old Norse *vindauga* < *vindr* 'wind' + *auga* 'eye'] ◇ **go out of the window** to be lost for good (*informal*)

window box *n* **1.** a box in which plants can be grown or displayed on a window ledge **2.** either of the spaces in the sides of the frame of a sash window that conceal the weights, ropes, and pulleys that raise and lower the window's separate sections

window dressing *n* **1.** the arrangement of a display of goods for sale in a shop window **2.** a deceptively appealing presentation of something, intended to conceal flaws —**window dresser** *n*

window envelope *n* an envelope with a transparent panel at the front through which the address of the recipient, printed or written on the material inside, can be seen

window of opportunity *n* a brief opportunity to do something, especially something that will be beneficial or profitable in some way

windowpane /wíndō payn/ *n* a sheet of glass that forms part of a window

window seat *n* **1.** an indoor seat fixed to a wall under a window, especially a window that is set into a recess **2.** a seat by a window in an aeroplane, train, or bus

window-shop *vi* to look at goods displayed in shop windows without a serious intention of buying anything —**window-shopper** *n* —**window-shopping** *n*

windowsill /wíndō sil/ *n* the shelf on the bottom edge of a window, either a projecting part of the window frame or the bottom of the wall recess that the window fits into

window tax *n* a tax on windows that was levied between 1691 and 1851, the avoidance of which accounts for the blocked-up windows in some old houses

windpipe /wínd pīp/ *n* the tube in air-breathing vertebrates that conducts air from the throat to the bronchi, strengthened by incomplete rings of cartilage. Technical name **trachea**

wind-pollinated /wínd-/ *adj* pollinated by pollen that is carried to the plant by the wind

wind power /wínd-/ *n* **1.** electricity produced by windmills or wind turbines **2.** the force of the wind harnessed by windmills and wind turbines for conversion into electricity

windproof /wínd proof/ *adj* resisting the force of the wind

wind rose /wínd rōz/ *n* a circular diagram indicating the range of wind speeds and directions for a location over a given time period

windrow /wíndrō/ *n* **1.** ROW OF DRYING HAY a long thin pile of cut hay or grain designed to catch the wind and dry quickly **2.** PILE BLOWN TOGETHER BY WIND a long thin pile of things, especially leaves or snow, heaped up by the wind ■ *vt* (**-rows**, **-rowing**, **-rowed**) GATHER HAY INTO WINDROWS to gather cut grass, hay, or other crop material into windrows for drying —**windrower** *n*

windsail /wínd sayl/; *nautical* /wíndss'l, wínss'l/ *n* **1.** a tube or funnel of sailcloth rigged over a companionway or hatch to catch breezes and provide ventilation for a ship **2.** a sail on a windmill

wind scale /wínd-/ *n* a scale for measuring the strength of a wind, e.g. the beaufort scale

windscreen /wínd skreen/ *n* **1.** the piece of glass or plastic that forms the front window of a motor vehicle. N Am term **windshield 2.** *US* same as **windshield** (sense 1)

windscreen wiper *n* a motorized device consisting of a rubber blade attached to a metal arm that is fixed just below a vehicle's windscreen, used for wiping rain and snow off the windscreen

wind shake /wínd-/ *n* a crack between the growth rings of a tree, thought to be caused when the tree bends violently in the wind

wind shear /wínd-/ *n* the amount by which the speed of the wind varies at different altitudes, often causing difficulties for aircraft

windshield /wínd sheeld/ *n* **1.** a screen used to protect from the wind people such as sunbathers on a beach or plants in a garden. US term **windscreen 2.** *N Am* AUTOMOT same as **windscreen** (sense 1)

windsock /wínd sok/ *n* a fabric tube or cone attached at one end to the top of a pole, so that it blows like a flag to show which way the wind is blowing

Windsor[1] /wínzər/ **1.** town in southern England, on the River Thames. Windsor Castle, located in the town, has been a royal residence for over 900 years. Population: 30,832 (1991). **2.** town in southeastern New South Wales, Australia. Founded in 1810, it is one of Australia's oldest settlements. Population: 5,364 (1991). **3.** city in southern Ontario, Canada, on the border opposite Detroit, Michigan. It is Canada's southernmost city. Population: 263,204 (2001).

Windsor[2] *n* the royal house of the United Kingdom from 1917, when George V changed the family name to Windsor

Duke and Duchess of Windsor

Windsor, Duke of title granted to Edward VIII after his abdication from the British throne in 1936 and subsequent marriage to Wallis Simpson in June 1937

Windsor chair *n* a wooden chair that traditionally has a back formed of spindles, a saddle-shaped seat, and splayed legs [Mid-18C. After WINDSOR[1] in England]

Windsor knot *n* a large triangular knot in a man's tie, made by putting an extra turn on each side of the loop that lies beneath the knot [Mid-20C. Probably after the Duke of WINDSOR]

Windsor tie *n* a broad necktie loosely knotted with a double bow

windstorm /wínd stawrm/ *n* a storm consisting of very strong winds and little or no rain or other precipitation

wind-sucking /wínd-/ *n* the habit some horses have of biting the edge of a stall or fence while gulping air or sucking in air by moving their head and neck —**wind-sucker** *n*

windsurf /wínd surf/ (**-surfs**, **-surfing**, **-surfed**) *vi* to ride and steer a sailboard fitted with a movable sail —**windsurfer** *n*

Windsurfer /wínd surfər/ *tdmk* a trademark for a type of sailboard

windsurfing

windsurfing /wínd surfing/ *n* the sport of riding and steering a sailboard

windswept /wínd swept/ *adj* **1.** EXPOSED TO WIND exposed to the wind and usually very windy **2.** DISHEVELLED dishevelled in appearance as a result of exposure to the wind **3.** FASHIONED TO LOOK WINDBLOWN fashioned so as to look blown by the wind ○ *a windswept hairstyle*

wind tee /wínd-/ *n* a T-shaped weather vane at an airfield that shows which way the wind is blowing

wind tunnel /wínd-/ *n* a tunnel-shaped chamber through which air can be passed at a known speed in order to test the aerodynamic properties of an object such as an aircraft or car placed inside it

wind turbine *n* a turbine with vanes that are rotated by the wind to generate electricity, usually similar in appearance to a giant aircraft propeller and mounted on a tall slim tower

wind-up /wínd-/ *adj* OPERATED BY TURNING HANDLE made to work by turning a handle or key that winds an internal spring ■ *n* **1.** ENDING OF SOMETHING the bringing to a close of an activity such as a meeting, discussion, or electoral campaign, or closing down a business **2.** TEASE an act of teasing, especially a lie told as a joke (*informal*)

windward /wíndwərd/ *adj* FACING WIND facing the wind, or on the side of something, especially a boat, that is facing the wind ■ *adv* INTO WIND towards the direction the wind is blowing from ■ *n* PLACE FACING WIND a place or direction facing, towards, or exposed to the direction the wind is blowing from

Windward Islands /wíndwərd-/ group of islands in the eastern Caribbean Sea, at the southern end of the Lesser Antilles. It includes Martinique and the independent island states of Barbados, Dominica, St Lucia, Grenada, and St Vincent and the Grenadines. Area: 3,657 sq. km/1,412 sq. mi.

windway /wínd way/ *n* an opening or passage allowing air through, e.g. a ventilation shaft in a mine

windy /wíndi/ (**-ier**, **-iest**) *adj* **1.** WITH WIND BLOWING with strong winds blowing ○ *a windy day* **2.** WHERE WINDS BLOW where strong winds tend to blow ○ *a high and windy hill* **3.** FULL OF EMPTY WORDS full of long and important-sounding though largely meaningless words designed to impress people (*informal*) **4.** FLATULENT suffering from flatulence (*informal*) **5.** NERVOUS nervous or frightened (*dated informal*) —**windily** *adv* —**windiness** *n*

wine /wīn/ *n* **1.** ALCOHOL FERMENTED FROM GRAPES an alcoholic drink made by fermenting the juice of grapes **2.** ALCOHOL FERMENTED FROM OTHER FRUIT an alcoholic drink made by fermenting the juice or an infusion of another fruit, a flower, or a vegetable ○ *dandelion wine* **3.** SOMETHING STIMULATING OR INTOXICATING something that has a stimulating or intoxicating effect resembling that of wine (*literary*) **4.** DARK PURPLISH-RED COLOUR a dark purplish-red colour, like that of red wine [Old English *wīn* < Latin *vinum* < Indo-European] —**wine** *adj* ◇ **wine and dine** (**wining and dining, wines and dines, wined and dined**) to enjoy, be treated, or treat somebody to an expensive meal out

SPELLCHECK See *whine*.

wine bar *n* a bar that specializes in serving wine, although other drinks may also be served

wine cellar *n* **1.** a dark cool room used for storing wine, especially in a cellar **2.** a stock of wine

wine cooler *n* **1.** a container filled with ice or a refrigerator and used to keep one or more bottles of

wine cool **2.** a mixture of wine and fruit juice, sometimes with carbonated water, sold in bottles

wine gallon *n* an obsolete British unit of capacity equal to 3.79 litres/231 cubic inches, which is smaller than the imperial gallon but exactly equal to the standard US gallon

wineglass /wín glaass/ *n* **1.** a glass suitable for drinking wine, with a bowl mounted on a stem and usually a rounded base **2.** the amount of liquid that the average wineglass will hold, around 0.11 litres/4 fluid ounces, used as a measure in recipes

wine grower *n* a grower of grapes for making wine, especially the owner or manager of a vineyard who also oversees the winemaking

winemaking /wín mayking/ *n* the art or business of producing wine, from the growing of the grapes to the finished product —**winemaker** *n*

Wine of Origin *n* a certification for South African wine that guarantees its origin

winepress /wín press/ *n* a piece of winemaking equipment that squeezes the juice from grapes

winery /wínəri/ (*plural* **-ies**) *n* ANZ, N Am a place where wine is made

wineskin /wín skin/ *n* a container for wine made from the skin of a sheep or goat sewn into a bag

wine tasting *n* **1.** the sampling of a variety of wines, either as a preliminary to buying wine or as instruction in the appreciation of wine **2.** a gathering of people to sample, learn about, and enjoy drinking a variety of wines

winey /wíni/, **winy** *adj* like wine in taste or appearance

Winfrey /wínfri/, **Oprah** (b. 1954) US talk show host and actor. Hosting *The Oprah Winfrey Show* from 1985, she pioneered television programmes in which people publicly discuss their intimate problems. Full name **Winfrey, Oprah Gail**

'I am the product of every other black woman before me who has done or said anything worthwhile. Recognizing that I am a part of history is what allows me to soar.'
[Oprah Winfrey. Quoted in *I Dream a World: Portraits of Black Women Who Changed America*, Brian Lanker; 1989]

wing /wing/ *n* **1.** BIRD'S LIMB FOR FLYING either of a bird's feather-covered limbs that are typically used for flying **2.** INSECT'S OR BAT'S LIMB FOR FLYING a large membrane-covered limb on an insect or a bat that is used for flying. Many insects have two pairs of wings. **3.** AIRCRAFT STRUCTURE either of the large flat surfaces sticking out from the sides of an aircraft's body that provide the main source of lift **4.** FLAT PROJECTING PART either of a pair of flat parts that stick out from the main body of something, e.g. the outgrowths of a wind-dispersed seed case or the ends of an old-fashioned collar **5.** PART OF BUILDING PROJECTING FROM MIDDLE one of the parts of a building that project from the main part **6.** LONGER SIDE OF SPORTS FIELD in some sports, either of the longer sides of the field of play, at right angles to the sides where the goals are **7.** ATTACKING PLAYER ON SIDE OF FIELD in some team sports such as football and hockey, an attacking player who plays down one side of the field **8.** ATTACKING FIELD POSITION in some sports, the position played by a wing **9.** FOOTBALL same as **wingman** (sense 2) **10.** SUBSIDIARY GROUP a group attached and subordinate to a parent organization **11.** POL SUBDIVISION OF POLITICAL GROUP a faction within a political party or movement, especially either of two broad factions, one more conservative, the other more liberal **12.** AUTOMOT CORNER OF CAR any of the corner parts of the body of a motor vehicle that surround each wheel. N Am term **fender 13.** AIR FORCE AIR FORCE UNIT an air force unit that is larger than a group but smaller than a division **14.** MIL PART OF MILITARY FORMATION the left or right part of a large military formation such as a field army or a fleet **15.** THEATRE SCENERY PIECE AT SIDE OF STAGE a piece of scenery at the side of the stage ■ **wings** *npl* **1.** THEATRE SIDE OF THEATRE STAGE the areas of a theatre to the sides of the stage, unseen by the audience **2.** AVIAT QUALIFIED PILOT'S BADGE a badge with a design in the shape of wings, worn by a trained and qualified pilot ■ *v* (**wings, winging, winged**) **1.** *vti* MOVE SWIFTLY to move or travel somewhere swiftly, or send something with great speed **2.** *vt* THROW SOMETHING to throw or propel something **3.** *vt* WOUND BIRD BY HITTING

WING to wound a bird superficially by hitting it on its wing **4.** *vt* WOUND OR DAMAGE SOMEBODY SUPERFICIALLY to wound somebody superficially, especially in the arm or leg, or cause only superficial damage to something **5.** *vt* THEATRE PREPARE PERFORMANCE AT LAST MINUTE to prepare a performance as a last-minute replacement actor, learning the lines in the wings immediately before going on, or perform a part without having thoroughly learned or prepared it [12C. < N Germanic < Indo-European, 'to blow'] ◇ **be (waiting) in the wings** to be ready and prepared to do something, or available for use when needed ◇ **on the wing** flying or in flight (*refers to birds*) ◇ **take somebody under your wing** to look after or protect somebody ◇ **wing it** to improvise (*informal*) ◇ **with wings** to be taken away rather than consumed on the premises (*informal*) ○ *one cappuccino with wings*

wingback /wíng bak/ *n* **1.** in football, an essentially defensive player who also makes attacking runs and who plays close to the touchlines on either side of the defence **2.** the position played by a wingback

wing-bar *n* a short white band on the wing of a bird, visible when the wing is folded

wing-case *n* INSECTS same as **elytron**

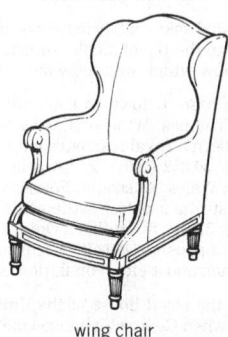

wing chair

wing chair *n* an armchair with a high back and large side panels

wing collar *n* a high stiff collar on a man's shirt, worn with the points at the upper corner turned down over the tie as part of formal dress

wing commander *n* a commissioned officer in the Royal Air Force of a rank above squadron leader and below group captain

wing covert *n* BIRDS same as **covert** *n* (sense 3)

wingding /wíng ding/ *n* N Am a party or celebration, especially a noisy and boisterous one (*dated*) [Early 20C. Origin ?]

winged /wingd/ *adj* **1.** CAPABLE OF FLIGHT able to fly because of having wings **2.** WITH PARTICULAR WINGS having wings of a particular kind ○ *broad-winged* **3.** /wingd, wíngid/ MOVING SWIFTLY moving swiftly in a manner resembling flying (*literary*) **4.** /wingd, wíngid/ FLYING moving using or as if using wings (*literary*)

winger /wíngər/ *n* SPORTS same as **wing** (sense 7)

wingless /wínglǝss/ *adj* used to describe insects without wings or having only very small wings that are not used for flying

wingman /wíng man/ (*plural* **-men** /-men/) *n* **1.** a pilot who flies in a position behind, and to the side of, the leader of a flying formation **2.** in Australian Rules football, either of two players playing in positions on either side of the centre circle

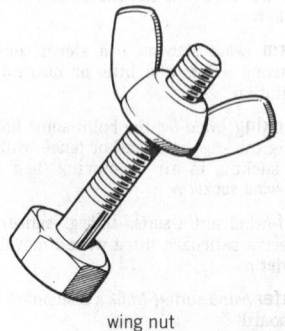

wing nut

wing nut *n* a nut that has flat projections on its sides for the fingers to grip

wingover /wíng ōvər/ *n* a flying manoeuvre to turn an aircraft in which the pilot puts the aircraft into a steep banking climb to a near stall and then allows the nose to fall

wingspan /wíng span/, **wingspread** /-spred/ *n* **1.** the distance from tip to tip of an aircraft's wings **2.** the distance from tip to tip of the outstretched wings of a bird or insect

wing tip *n* **1.** the tip of the wing of a bird, insect, or aircraft that is the point farthest away from the centre of its body **2.** N Am CLOTHING same as **brogue**[2] (sense 1)

wink /wingk/ *v* (**winks, winking, winked**) **1.** *vti* GESTURE BY CLOSING ONE EYE BRIEFLY to close one eye briefly, usually to show that something just done or said is a joke or a secret **2.** *vi* SHINE INTERMITTENTLY to shine intermittently or faintly ■ *n* **1.** BRIEF CLOSING OF ONE EYE a brief closing of one eye as a gesture, greeting, or signal **2.** TWINKLING LIGHT a twinkling or faintly flashing light **3.** SHORT TIME the briefest period of time [Old English *wincian* 'close your eyes' < Germanic, 'move from side to side' < Indo-European] ◇ **not sleep a wink, not get a wink of sleep** to be unable to sleep ◇ **tip somebody the wink** to give somebody information privately or confidentially (*informal*)

wink at *vt* to pretend not to notice an offence or wrongdoing (*informal*)

winker /wíngkər/ *n* **1.** SOMEBODY WHO WINKS somebody or something that winks **2.** FLASHING LIGHT a light that winks or flashes, especially an indicator on a motor vehicle **3.** US EYE OR PART OF EYE an eye, or a part of the eye such as an eyelid or eyelash (*informal*) ■ **winkers** *npl* BLINKERS a racehorse's blinkers

winkle /wíngk'l/ *n* a small edible mollusc with a spiral shell. Native to: coastal waters. Genus: *Littorina*. [Late 16C. Shortening of PERIWINKLE[1]]

winkle out (**winkles out, winkling out, winkled out**) *vt* to extract something such as information with difficulty [< the practice of extracting molluscs from their shells]

winkle-pickers *npl* shoes with narrow pointed toes, popular in the 1950s (*informal*) [Because the shoe's pointed toe resembles a pin used for removing winkles from their shells]

Winnebago[1] /wínni báygō/ (*plural* same or **-gos** or **-goes**) *n* **1.** a member of a Siouan people who lived in Wisconsin and Illinois, and now live mainly in Wisconsin and Nebraska **2.** the Siouan language of the Winnebago people. Native speakers: 250. [Mid-18C. < Algonquian *wi:nepye:ko:ha* 'person of the dirty water'] —**Winnebago** *adj*

Winnebago[2] /wínni báygō/ *tdmk* a trademark for a large motor vehicle with cooking and sleeping facilities

Winnebago, Lake /wínni báy gō/ lake in eastern Wisconsin, forming part of the course of the Fox River. Area: 534 sq. km/206 sq. mi.

winner /wínnər/ *n* **1.** SOMEBODY OR SOMETHING WINNING COMPETITION somebody or something that wins a competition or contest **2.** SOMEBODY OR SOMETHING SUCCESSFUL somebody or something that is or seems likely to become very successful or popular **3.** WINNING SHOT in some sports, a shot that wins a point

winner's enclosure, **winner's circle** *n* an enclosure at a racecourse where the winning horses are unsaddled and prizes awarded to owners, trainers, and jockeys

winning /wínning/ *adj* **1.** VICTORIOUS victorious or bringing victory **2.** CHARMING very charming, to the extent that people are won over ■ *n* VICTORY the act of earning a victory or succeeding in a competition ■ **winnings** *npl* MONEY WON money or other valuables that are won, especially from gambling —**winningly** *adv*

winningest /wínningist/ *adj* N Am winning the highest number of victories or prizes, or the most prize money (*informal*) ○ *a list of the all-time winningest baseball coaches*

winning gallery *n* an opening in a side wall of a real tennis court into which the ball is hit from the other side of the net in order to win a point

winning post *n* the post that marks the finish line on a racecourse

Winnipeg /wínni peg/ capital city of Manitoba, Canada, located in the southern part of the province. Population: 626,685 (2001).

Winnipeg, Lake freshwater lake in central Manitoba, Canada. Depth: 18 m/60 ft. Area: 24,390 sq. km/9,417 sq. mi.

winnow /wínnō/ *v* (**-nows, -nowing, -nowed**) **1.** *vti* **REMOVE CHAFF FROM GRAIN** to separate grain from its husks (**chaff**) by tossing it in the air or blowing air through it **2.** *vt* **EXAMINE SOMETHING TO REMOVE BAD PARTS** to examine something in order to remove the bad, unusable, or undesirable parts ■ *n* **1. DEVICE FOR WINNOWING** a device used to winnow grain **2. PROCESS OF WINNOWING** the process of separating grain from chaff [Old English *windwian* < *wind* 'wind'] —**winnower** *n*

wino /wínō/ (*plural* **-os**) *n* an offensive term for somebody who is addicted to alcohol, especially wine, and is usually also homeless (*informal insult*)

winsome /wínssəm/ *adj* charming, especially because of a naive, innocent quality [Old English *wynsum* 'pleasant' < *wynn* 'joy' < Indo-European, 'to desire'] —**winsomely** *adv* —**winsomeness** *n*

Winston /wínst'n/, **Lord Robert** (*b.* 1940) British fertility expert and broadcaster. A professor of fertility studies, he is internationally renowned for his work in reproductive medicine and has presented several television programmes about medical science.

Winston-Salem /wínstən-/ city in northern North Carolina, an important centre of manufacturing and tobacco production. Population: 188,934 (2002 estimate).

winter /wíntər/ *n* **1. YEAR'S COLDEST SEASON** the coldest season of the year, which runs in the northern hemisphere from around November or December to February or March and in the southern hemisphere from June to August **2. CLOSING PERIOD OR PERIOD OF INACTIVITY** a period in which something is declining, inactive, or ending **3. YEAR** one of a number of years, especially a great number (*literary*) ○ *a man of many winters* ■ *v* (**-ters, -tering, -tered**) **1.** *vi* **SPEND WINTER SOMEWHERE** to spend the winter in a particular place, especially away from home **2.** *vt* **KEEP SOMETHING SOMEWHERE IN WINTER** to keep something, especially farm animals, in a particular place during the winter [Old English, < Indo-European, 'wet']

winter aconite *n* a low-growing plant with a single yellow flower that blooms in winter or early spring. Native to: Europe, Asia. Latin name: *Eranthis hyemalis.*

winterberry /wíntərbəri/ (*plural* **-ries** or *same*) *n* a deciduous holly with bright red berries and leaves that turn black in the autumn. Native to: eastern North America. Latin name: *Ilex verticillata.*

winterbourne /wíntər bawrn/ *n* a stream that flows only or mostly in winter, after heavy rains

winter cherry *n* **1.** a small plant with round red fruit, often grown as a pot plant. Latin name: *Solanum capsicastrum.* **2.** *US* PLANTS same as **Chinese lantern** (sense 2) **3.** the fruit of the winter cherry

wintercress /wíntər kress/ *n* a bitter-tasting plant of the mustard family. Flowers: yellow. Genus: *Barbarea.*

winterfeed /wíntər feed/ (**-feeds, -feeding, -fed** /-fed/) *vt* to feed livestock in winter, e.g. on hay or silage, when there is little or no grazing

winter flounder *n* a reddish-brown flounder that is a popular food fish in winter. Native to: northwestern Atlantic. Latin name: *Pseudopleuronectes americanus.*

winter garden *n* **1.** a garden planted with evergreens and other plants that give colour and interest in winter **2.** a greenhouse or conservatory where plants are kept or grown during the winter

wintergreen /wíntər green/ (*plural* **-greens** or *same*) *n* **1.** a low-growing evergreen bush with red berries and fragrant leathery leaves from which an oil (**oil of wintergreen**) is distilled. Native to: eastern North America. Latin name: *Gaultheria procumbens.* **2.** same as **oil of wintergreen** [Mid-16C. Translation of Dutch *wintergroen*]

winter heliotrope *n* a creeping winter-flowering perennial plant. Flowers: lilac-coloured, vanilla-scented. Latin name: *Petasites fragrans.*

winterize /wíntə rīz/ (**-izes, -izing, -ized**), **winterise** (**-ises, -ising, -ised**) *vt N Am* to prepare something, especially a house or a car, to withstand cold winter conditions —**winterization** /wíntə rī záysh'n/ *n*

winter jasmine *n* a variety of jasmine that has yellow flowers in winter. Native to: China. Latin name: *Jasminum nudiflorum.*

winter moth *n* a brown moth with no wings in the female whose larvae crawl with a series of looping movements. Latin name: *Operophtera brumata.*

Winter Olympics, Winter Olympic Games *n* an international gathering for athletes competing in a variety of winter sports, taking place every four years (*takes a singular or plural verb*)

winter sports *npl* sports performed on snow and ice, e.g. skiing and ice skating

winter squash *n N Am* a slow-maturing squash that grows on long trailing vines, has a tough skin, and stores well

wintertide /wíntər tīd/ *n* same as **wintertime** (*archaic or literary*)

wintertime /wíntər tīm/ *n* the season of winter

winterweight /wíntər wayt/ *adj* made of thick heavy fabric and designed to protect somebody or something from cold weather

winter wheat *n* a variety of wheat planted in autumn, left in the ground over winter, and harvested the following spring or early summer

wintery *adj* another spelling of **wintry**

Winthrop /wín throp/, **John** (1587–1649) English-born American colonial governor. For most of the years between 1629 and 1649, he presided over the Massachusetts Bay Colony, exerting a decisive influence in shaping it as a Puritan commonwealth.

Winton /wíntən/, **Tim** (*b.* 1960) Australian writer. His numerous novels and short stories include the prize-winning *Cloudstreet* (1991). Full name **Winton, Timothy John**

wintry /wíntri/ (**-trier, -triest**), **wintery** (**-ier, -iest**) *adj* **1.** relating to or typical of winter, especially in being cold **2.** cheerless or unfriendly ○ *She gave him a wintry smile.* —**wintrily** *adv* —**wintriness** *n*

win-win *adj* describes a situation in which all parties benefit in some way (*informal*)

winy /wīni/ (**-ier, -iest**) *adj* another spelling of **winey**

winze /winz/ *n* a steeply inclined or vertical shaft between levels in a mine [Mid-18C. Alteration of obsolete *winds*, origin ?]

wipe /wīp/ *v* (**wipes, wiping, wiped**) **1.** *vt* **RUB SOMETHING WITH LIGHT STROKES** to rub something with long light strokes with a soft material, or rub something lightly on a soft material ○ *wiped their hands on the towel* **2.** *vti* **REMOVE OR BE REMOVED BY RUBBING** to remove something such as dirt with long light rubbing strokes, usually with a soft material, or be removed in this way ○ *The mark wiped off easily.* **3.** *vt* **REMOVE RECORDING FROM TAPE** to remove recorded material from an audiotape or video tape **4.** *vt* **REMOVE SOMETHING** to remove something or get rid of it as if by wiping ○ *wiped it from my memory* **5.** *vt* **APPLY SOMETHING WITH LIGHT RUBBING** to apply something, especially a liquid or cream, by rubbing it on lightly, e.g. with a cloth or the hand ■ *n* **1. LIGHT RUBBING STROKE** one or more long light rubbing strokes **2. DISPOSABLE CLEANING CLOTH** a soft disposable cloth or tissue soaked with a cleansing liquid, used for cleaning something such as the skin ○ *Remember rubbish bags, wipes, and paper napkins when you go on a picnic.* **3.** CINEMA, MEDIA **ONE PICTURE PUSHING OTHER OFF SCREEN** a cinematic scene-changing device in which one picture appears to push the other off the screen, often used to move from scene to scene [Old English *wīpian* < Indo-European, 'move back and forth']

wipe out *v* **1.** *vt* **DESTROY SOMETHING IN LARGE NUMBERS** to destroy large numbers of things or kill large numbers of people, especially suddenly and violently (*informal*) **2.** *vt* **TIRE SOMEBODY** to make somebody feel thoroughly exhausted (*informal*) **3.** *vi* **FALL FROM SURFBOARD** to fall from a surfboard, either because of losing control or because of being knocked off by a wave, or fall or crash in some other sport (*informal*) **4.** *vt* **MURDER SOMEBODY** to murder or assassinate somebody (*slang*)

wiped out /wīpt-/ *adj* thoroughly exhausted (*slang*)

wipeout /wīp owt/ *n* (*informal*) **1. FALL IN SURFING** a fall from a surfboard, or a fall or crash in other sports such as skiing and cycling **2. FAILURE OR DEFEAT** a total failure or a crushing defeat **3.** MEDIA **RECEIVING OF RADIO SIGNAL MASKING OTHERS** the receiving of a radio signal that is so strong it makes receiving other signals impossible

wiper /wīpər/ *n* **1.** AUTOMOT same as **windscreen wiper** **2. SOMEBODY WHO WIPES** somebody or something that wipes **3. SOMETHING USED FOR WIPING** something such as a cloth or sponge that is used for wiping **4.** MECH ENG **CAM PROJECTING FROM SHAFT** a cam that projects from a rotating shaft and is designed to move, dislodge, or lift another component **5.** ELEC ENG **ELECTRICAL DEVICE MOVING CONDUCTING ARM** an electrical device in which a conducting arm may be rotated or moved over a row of contacts, e.g. a selector

WIPO /wīpō/, **Wipo** *abbr* World Intellectual Property Organization

Wiradhuri /wi rájjəri/, **Wiradjuri** *n* an Australian Aboriginal language of New South Wales and southern Queensland, now extinct [Late 19C. < an Aboriginal language < Wiradhuri *wirai* 'no'] —**Wiradhuri** *adj*

wire /wīr/ *n* **1. STRAND OF METAL** metal in the form of thin flexible strands, or a single strand of it **2. METAL STRAND CARRYING ELECTRIC CURRENT** a strand of metal, usually copper, that is encased in plastic or another insulating material and is used to carry an electric current **3. MESH STRUCTURE** a mesh made of strands of metal, or a structure made of the mesh, e.g. a fence **4.** *US* **END OR FINISH** the end of something, or the time when something ends (*informal*) ○ *writing in their exam books right down to the wire* **5.** *US* **ELECTRONIC LISTENING DEVICE** a slimline electronic listening device concealed in somebody's clothes (*slang*) **6.** TELECOM **CABLE PROVIDING TELECOMMUNICATIONS LINK** a cable that provides a telecommunications link **7.** TELECOM **TELEGRAM OR TELEGRAPH** a telegram, or the telegraph system ■ *v* (**wires, wiring, wired**) **1.** *vt* **FASTEN SOMETHING WITH WIRE** to use wire to fasten or secure something **2.** *vti* **EQUIP PLACE WITH ELECTRICAL WIRES** to install a system of electrical wires in a building or an area **3.** *vt* **CONNECT ELECTRICAL EQUIPMENT** to connect a piece of electrical equipment to a power source or to another piece of equipment **4.** *vt* **SEND TELEGRAM** to send a telegram to somebody, or send something to somebody by means of a telegram **5.** *vt* **PROVIDE PLACE WITH NECESSARY EQUIPMENT** to provide a place with the equipment, especially electrical or electronic equipment, needed to give it a particular facility or capability (*informal*) **6.** *vt US* **FIT SOMEBODY WITH LISTENING DEVICE** to fit somebody or a place with a concealed electronic listening device (*slang*) **7.** *vt* PHYSIOL **DETERMINE FUNCTION WITH PHYSIOLOGICAL STRUCTURE** to control a function in the body by means of a neurological or physiological structure or process ○ *This is learned behaviour; it's not wired into the genes.* [Old English *wīr* 'metal thread' < Indo-European, 'twist'] ◇ **down to the wire** to the very last minute ◇ **go to the wire** to risk your reputation, job, or life in order to help somebody (*informal*) ◇ **have** *or* **get your wires crossed** to have a misunderstanding

wire brush *n* a brush with short stiff wires instead of bristles

wire cloth *n* a flexible mesh of soft fine wires woven closely together, used to make strainers and some types of screening

wired /wīrd/ *adj* **1. SUPPORTED BY WIRE** supported or strengthened by wire **2. EQUIPPED FOR INTERNET** having computer equipment that allows use of the Internet (*informal*) ○ *'Ireland has seen Dublin go wired.'* (*Newsweek*; November 1998) **3.** *N Am* **FITTED WITH LISTENING DEVICES** fitted with one or more concealed electronic listening devices (*slang*) **4. NERVY** full of nervous energy or excitement, especially because under the influence of drugs (*slang*)

wiredraw /wīr draw/ (**-draws, -drawing, -drew** /-droo/, **-drawn** /-drawn/) *vt* **1.** to reduce the diameter of a wire by pulling it through successively smaller dies **2.** to spin something out to great lengths, over-refining it and treating it with excessive subtlety [Late 16C. Back-formation < *wiredrawer* 'somebody skilled in drawing metal into threads']

wire entanglement *n* a barrier of barbed wire used to keep enemy troops back

wire fraud *n* in the United States, the crime of using interstate telecommunications wires to obtain money or some other benefit by deliberate deception

wirefree /wír free/ *adj* describes telephone systems that do not use electrical wires in order to operate ○*Today, more than 1.7 million people subscribe to our wirefree services.'* (*Marketing Week*; December 1998)

wire gauge *n* **1.** a gauge used to measure the thickness of wire or sheet metal **2.** a standard system of sizes for measuring wire

wire gauze *n* a fine mesh of thin wires woven closely together

wire glass *n* glass reinforced with a sheet of wire mesh embedded in it

wire grass *n* a coarse grass with tough wiry roots

wire-haired /wír háird/ *adj* having a coat of coarse stiff hair

wireless /wírləss/ *n* **1.** RADIO a radio or a radio set (*dated*) **2.** TELECOM same as **wireless telegraphy** ■ *adj* **1.** WITHOUT WIRES lacking wires **2.** USING RADIO SIGNALS using radio signals rather than wires **3.** USING MOBILE PHONE TECHNOLOGY describes communications systems and devices that make use of mobile phone technology ○ *wireless networks* ○ *wireless headphones* —**wirelessly** *adv*

wireless local area network *n* a local area network that uses high-frequency radio signals to communicate between computers over relatively short distances

wireless markup language *n* a standardized system for tagging text files, based on XML, that specifies the interfaces of narrowband wireless devices

wireless telegraphy *n* a system that sends telegrams using radio signals rather than wires

wireline /wír līn/ *adj* operating or transmitting by means of a connecting wire, as opposed to using a wireless system

wireman /wírmən/ (*plural* **-men** /-mən/) *n US* **1.** somebody, especially a man, who installs or repairs electrical or telecommunications cables **2.** an expert at installing and operating electronic listening devices (*slang*)

wire netting *n* mesh made of medium to thick wire that is stronger, is less flexible, and has larger spaces than wire gauze

wireperson /wír purss'n/ (*plural* **-people** /-peep'l/ or **-persons**) *n* same as **wirer** (sense 1)

wirer /wírər/ *n* **1.** an electrician who installs and maintains electrical circuits and wiring systems **2.** somebody who snares animals (*informal*)

wire recorder *n* an early type of magnetic recorder that used stainless steel wire instead of magnetic tape to record sound

wire rope *n* strong thick rope made of plaited strands of wire

wire service *n* *N Am* a news agency that sends out syndicated news items to various media by means of wire or satellite

wiretap /wír tap/ *vti* (**-taps, -tapping, -tapped**) **1.** TAP TELEPHONE LINE to make a wire connection to a telephone line in order to listen in secret to somebody's conversations **2.** LISTEN IN SECRET TO TELEPHONE COMMUNICATIONS to listen in secret to somebody's conversations on a telephone line by means of a wire connection ■ *n* **1.** SECRET CONNECTION TO TELEPHONE LINE a connection made to a telephone line in order to listen secretly to somebody's conversations **2.** INSTALLATION OR USE OF WIRETAP the act of installing or using a wiretap —**wiretapper** *n*

wire wheel *n* **1.** a motor vehicle wheel that has wire spokes connecting the hub to the rim **2.** a disc of coarse wires designed to be attached to a power tool and used for rubbing down metal

wirework /wír wurk/ *n* **1.** LAYOUT OF WIRES an arrangement or system of wires **2.** SOMETHING MADE OF WIRE something made by shaping or weaving wire **3.** TIGHTROPE ACROBATICS acrobatics performed on a tightrope

wireworks /wír wurks/ *n* a factory where wire is made, or where wire articles are made

wireworm /wír wurm/ *n* the long thin hard-bodied larva of various kinds of beetle that feeds on plant roots and is a serious agricultural pest

wiring /wíring/ *n* **1.** INSTALLATION OF ELECTRICAL WIRES the act or process of installing a system of electrical wires **2.** SYSTEM OF ELECTRICAL WIRES a network of electrical

wires **3.** PHYSIOLOGICAL STRUCTURE DETERMINING FUNCTION a neurological or physiological structure or process that controls a function in the body ○ *A certain degree of anxiety may simply be built into our wiring.*

wirra /wírrə/ *interj Ireland* used to express concern, sorrow, confusion, or annoyance [Early 19C. < Irish *a Mhuira* 'oh, Mary!']

Wirral /wírrəl/ peninsula in northwestern England, between the rivers Dee and Mersey. Population: 312,293 (2001). Area: 218 sq. km/84 sq. mi.

wiry /wíri/ (**-ier, -iest**) *adj* **1.** SLIM BUT STRONG slim but muscular and strong **2.** COARSE stiff and coarse like wire ○ *a dog with wiry hair* **3.** PRODUCED BY VIBRATING WIRES produced by or sounding as though produced by vibrating wires —**wirily** *adv* —**wiriness** *n*

wis /wiss/ (**wisses, wissing, wissed** or **wist** /wist/) *vti* to know, think, or suppose something (*archaic*) [Old English *wissian*]

Wisbech /wíz beech/ town in Cambridgeshire, eastern England. Population: 24,981 (1991).

Wisconsin /wi skónssin/ state of the north-central United States, bordered by Lake Superior, Michigan, Lake Michigan, Illinois, Iowa, and Minnesota. Capital: Madison. Population: 5,441,196 (2002 estimate). Area: 169,642 sq. km/65,499 sq. mi. —**Wisconsinite** *n*

Wisd. *abbr* BIBLE Wisdom of Solomon

Wisden /wízdən/, **John** (1826–84) British cricketer. A notable player himself, in 1864 he founded *Wisden's Cricketer's Almanack*, an annual review of cricket.

wisdom /wízdəm/ *n* **1.** GOOD SENSE the ability to make sensible decisions and judgments based on personal knowledge and experience **2.** WISE DECISION good sense shown in a way of thinking, judgment, or action **3.** ACCUMULATED LEARNING accumulated knowledge of life or of a sphere of activity that has been gained through experience **4.** OPINION WIDELY HELD an opinion that almost everyone seems to share or express **5.** SAYINGS ancient teachings or sayings [Old English *wīsdōm* < *wīs* (see WISE[1])]

SYNONYMS See *knowledge*.

Wisdom literature *n* a speculative or didactic form of religious writing, exemplified by the books of Job, Proverbs, and Ecclesiastes in the Bible, and the Wisdom of Solomon and Ecclesiasticus in the Apocrypha

Wisdom of Jesus, the Son of Sirach *n* BIBLE same as **Ecclesiasticus**

Wisdom of Solomon *n* a book of the Roman Catholic Bible and Protestant Apocrypha that expounds Jewish doctrines in the terminology of Greek philosophy. It was probably written in the 1st century BC. See table at **Bible**

wisdom tooth *n* one of the four teeth at the back of either side of the upper and lower jaw of human beings. They are the last teeth to come through. [Translation of Latin *dens sapientiae*]

Wisdom writings *npl* works of Wisdom literature

wise[1] /wīz/ (**wiser, wisest**) *adj* **1.** KNOWING MUCH FROM EXPERIENCE able to make sensible decisions and judgments on the basis of personal knowledge and experience **2.** SENSIBLE showing good sense or good judgment **3.** LEARNED knowledgeable about many subjects **4.** SHREWD capable of achieving some purpose or goal by cunning [Old English *wīs* < Indo-European, 'see, know'] —**wisely** *adv* ◇ **be** *or* **get wise (to something)** to be or become aware of something, usually something dishonest or secret (*informal*) ◇ **put somebody wise (to something)** to let somebody know about something, or give somebody information about something (*informal*)

wise up (**wises up, wising up, wised up**) *vti* to become aware or informed, or make somebody aware or informed (*informal*)

wise[2] /wīz/ *n* a way or manner (*archaic*) [Old English *wīse* < Germanic, 'shape, form, something seen']

-wise *suffix* **1.** in a particular manner or direction ○ *clockwise* **2.** ⚠ with regard to, with respect to (*informal*) ○ *salary-wise* [Old English *-wīsan* < *wīse* 'manner' (see WISE[2])]

USAGE Many critics object to words ending in the suffix *-wise* when the meaning is 'with regard to, with respect to', as in these controversial examples: *moneywise*, *timewise*, and *politicswise*, as in *Politicswise, this has*

been an exciting year. The use of words ending in *-wise* is acceptable when the meaning of the suffix is 'in a particular manner or direction', as in *clockwise*, *anticlockwise*, and *lengthwise*.

wiseacre /wíz aykər/ *n* somebody who speaks with irritating authority or self-assurance, especially when not truly knowledgeable (*informal*) [Late 16C. Alteration of Middle Dutch *wijssegger* 'soothsayer']

wisecrack /wíz krak/ (*informal*) *n* a flippant or sarcastic remark ■ *vi* (**-cracks, -cracking, -cracked**) to make flippant or sarcastic remarks —**wisecracker** *n*

wise guy *n* **1.** *N Am* somebody inclined to make impudent or sarcastic remarks (*informal*) **2.** *also* **wiseguy** /wíz gī/ *US* a member of the Mafia (*slang*)

wise man *n* **1.** LEARNED MAN a scholar or a very learned man **2.** ONE OF MAGI in the Bible, a Magi who came with two others to pay homage to the infant Jesus Christ **3.** SPECIAL ADVISER a man chosen as a special senior adviser to a government or other authority (*informal*) **4.** ANCIENT PRACTITIONER OF OCCULT ARTS a man who, in ancient times, practised any of the occult arts such as magic or astrology (*archaic*)

wisent /weéz'nt/ *n* a bison with a head that is smaller and higher than that of the North American bison. Native to: Europe. Latin name: *Bison bonasus*. [Mid-19C. Via German < Old High German *wisunt* < Indo-European]

wisewoman /wíz woֹomən/ (*plural* **-women** /-wimin/) *n* a woman who is skilled in the art of using herbs to heal people and ease the pains of childbirth

wish /wish/ *v* (**wishes, wishing, wished**) **1.** *vt* HAVE STRONG DESIRE to have a strong feeling of wanting something to happen or wanting to have something ○ *I wish she'd say yes.* ○ *What do you wish for?* **2.** *vt* WANT SOMETHING to want something or want to do something ○ *Stay longer, if you wish.* **3.** *vti* EXPRESS DESIRE to express or feel a desire that something is true or will come to pass ○ *They wished me a safe journey.* ○ *We only wish for peace.* **4.** *vt* REGRET SOMETHING used for expressing regret about something ○ *I wish I'd never mentioned it.* **5.** *vt* GREET SOMEBODY to greet somebody in a particular way ○ *She wished me good afternoon as I left.* ■ *n* **1.** A DESIRE a desire to do or have something ○ *I had no wish to offend you.* **2.** SOMETHING WISHED something that is desired ○ *He finally got his wish.* **3.** HOPE a hope for somebody's welfare or health (*usually plural*) ○ *Give him our best wishes.* **4.** POLITE REQUEST a polite request (*formal; often plural*) ○ *They honoured our wishes and changed the date of the meeting.* [Old English *wýscan* < Indo-European, 'to desire'] —**wisher** *n*

SYNONYMS See *want*.

wish on *vt* to wish that something, usually something unpleasant, would happen to somebody ○ *I wouldn't wish that on my worst enemy.*

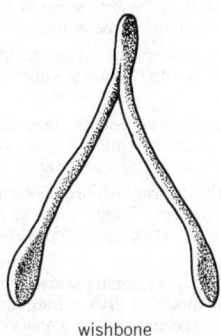

wishbone

wishbone /wísh bōn/ *n* **1.** the V-shaped bone found between the breasts of a chicken or other bird. Technical name **furcula 2.** a Y-shaped component connecting the wheels to the frame in a vehicle or aircraft suspension, the single end usually attaching to the wheel and the double end to the frame [Mid-19C. < a tradition of pulling the bone from a cooked bird between two people to break it, the person left with the larger part then making a wish]

wishbone boom *n* the boom on a sailboard that a windsurfer holds on to. It has two curving arms, one on either side of the sail, joined at the ends.

wishful /wíshf'l/ *adj* wishing for something, or expressing a wish or longing —**wishfully** *adv* —**wishfulness** *n*

wish fulfilment *n* in psychoanalytic theory, the process by which unconscious desires are realized in the imagination, mainly through dreams and fantasies

wishful thinking *n* the unrealistic belief that something that is wished for is actually true or will be realized

wishing well *n* a well or representation of a well, supposed to grant the wish of somebody who makes a wish while dropping a coin into the well

wish list *n* an often informal list of things somebody would like to have or would like to happen

wish-wash *n* (*informal*) **1.** an unpleasantly weak or tasteless drink **2.** uninteresting and uninspiring talk or writing [Late 18C. Doubling of WASH, in the sense 'thin, weak']

wishy-washy /wíshi woshi, wíshi wóshi/ *adj* (*informal*) **1.** changeable or fluctuating in character, especially unable to make firm decisions or develop clear opinions **2.** weak, lacking taste, or unattractively pale [Late 17C. Doubling of *washy* 'thin, watery' < WASH] —**wishy-washily** *adv* —**wishy-washiness** *n*

Wisła /víssw ə/ Polish name for **Vistula**

wisp /wisp/ *n* **1.** SOMETHING RESEMBLING THREAD something that is thin and delicate like thread, especially a lock of hair, a piece of straw, or a streak of smoke **2.** SOMEBODY SLENDER AND DELICATE somebody or something that is slender and delicate ○ *a wisp of a child* **3.** SOMETHING INSUBSTANTIAL something that is vague and fleeting ○ *a wisp of a memory* **4.** BUNDLE a bundle of something, especially a bundle of hay or straw ■ *v* (**wisps, wisping, wisped**) **1.** *vt* BUNDLE UP STRAW OR HAY to make a handful of straw or hay into a bundle **2.** *vi* MOVE LIKE WISP to float like something delicate or faint [14C. Origin ?] —**wispily** *adv* —**wispiness** *n* —**wispy** *adj*

wist[1] past participle, past tense of **wis** (*archaic*)

wist[2] past participle, past tense of **wit**[2] (*archaic*)

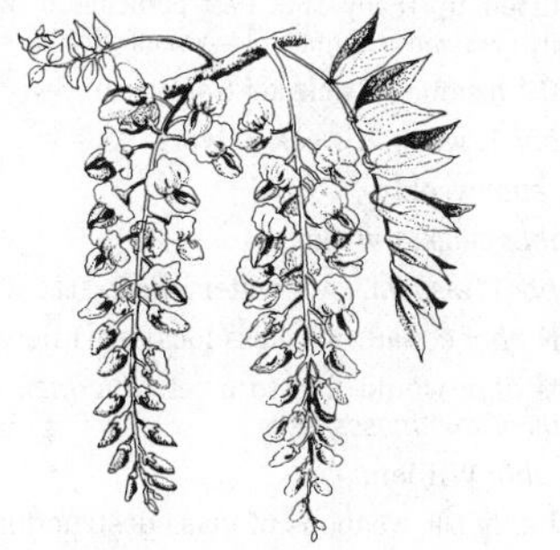

wisteria

wisteria /wi stéeri ə/ (*plural* **-as** or *same*) *n* a deciduous climbing bush. Flowers: blue, pink, or white, hanging in clusters. Native to: North America, Asia. Genus: *Wisteria*. [Early 19C. < modern Latin, after Caspar *Wistar* (1761–1818), US anatomist]

wistful /wístf'l/ *adj* deep in sad thoughts, especially thoughts of something yearned for or lost, or expressing this sad yearning [Early 17C. < obsolete *wistly* 'intently'] —**wistfully** *adv* —**wistfulness** *n*

wit[1] /wit/ *n* **1.** INGENIOUS HUMOUR the apt, clever, and often humorous association of words or ideas, or a capacity for it **2.** SPEECH OR WRITING SHOWING WIT speech or writing that shows an apt, clever, and often humorous association of words **3.** WITTY PERSON somebody known for using wit **4.** INTELLIGENCE mental acumen, intelligence, or reasoning power **5.** *regional* COMMON SENSE knowledge, information, or common sense ■ **wits** *npl* SHREWDNESS mental acumen, shrewdness, or reasoning power [Old English *wit* 'mind, understanding' < Indo-European, 'see, know'] —**witted** *adj* ◇ **be at your wits' end** to be in despair as to how to cope with something ◇ **live by your wits** to use cunning and ingenuity in order to survive ◇ **pit your wits against somebody** to compete with somebody in an intellectual exercise ◇ **scare** *or* **frighten somebody out of his** *or* **her wits** to fill somebody with sudden terror

wit[2] /wit/ (**wits** or **wot** /wot/, **witting**, **wist** /wist/) *vti* to know or become aware of something (*archaic*) [Old English *witan* < Germanic] ◇ **to wit** that is to say

witan /witt'n/ *n* in Anglo-Saxon England, an assembly of the king's counsellors [Early 19C. Revival of Old English, 'counsellors' < *wita* 'counsellor, person who knows']

Witbank /wít bank/ town in Mpumalanga Province, northeastern South Africa. Population: 83,400 (1998).

witblits /vítblits/ *n S Africa* illegally distilled alcoholic liquor, usually made from grapes [Mid-20C. < Afrikaans, 'white lightning']

witch /wich/ *n* **1.** SOMEBODY WITH ALLEGED MAGIC POWERS somebody, especially a woman, who is supposed to have magical or wonder-working powers that are most often used malevolently **2.** FOLLOWER OF NATURE RELIGION a follower of Wicca, a pre-Christian natural religion **3.** OFFENSIVE TERM an offensive term that deliberately insults a woman regarded as ugly, vicious, or malicious (*insult*) **4.** SEDUCTIVE WOMAN a woman who is regarded as alluring or seductive (*informal*; *sometimes offensive*) ■ *vt* (**witches, witching, witched**) AFFECT SOMETHING USING WITCHCRAFT to cause or change something by use of the supposedly magical powers of witchcraft [Old English *wicce* 'witch' and *wicca* 'wizard']

SPELLCHECK See *which*.

witchcraft /wích kraaft/ *n* **1.** EXERCISE OF ALLEGEDLY MAGICAL POWERS the art of using allegedly magical powers **2.** ALLEGED EFFECT OF MAGICAL POWERS the alleged effect or influence of magical powers **3.** SEDUCTIVE CHARM alluring or seductive charm or influence (*informal*)

witch doctor *n* **1.** in tribal societies, somebody who practises healing, divining, or other magical powers **2.** in some African cultures, somebody who detects or identifies supposed witches

witch elm *n* TREES another spelling of **wych elm**

witchery /wíchəri/ *n* **1.** the practice of witchcraft or magic (*dated or literary*) **2.** charm or influence that has a bewitching quality or effect

witches' brew *n* **1.** a malevolent or diabolical mixture of different things ○ *an article that was a witches' brew of spite and innuendo* **2.** a potion concocted by a witch

witches' broom *n* a tufted growth of shoots on a tree or woody plant, usually caused by parasitic fungi. The fungi usually responsible are of the genus *Taphrina*.

witches' butter *n* FUNGI same as **jelly fungus**

witches' Sabbath *n* an assembly to celebrate Wicca rites

witchetty grub /wíchiti-/ *n* the wood-eating larva of a number of species of Australian moth, used as food by Aboriginal people and people who live in the bush [Mid-19C. Probably < Australian Aboriginal words meaning 'climb' or 'hooked stick' and 'grub']

witch grass *n* **1.** a grass with creeping roots. Native to: North America. Latin name: *Panicum capillare*. **2.** PLANTS same as **couch grass** [Probably alteration of QUITCH GRASS]

witch hazel, **wych hazel** *n* **1.** a tree or bush that has toothed egg-shaped leaves and blooms in autumn or winter. Flowers: small, yellow with strap-shaped petals. Genus: *Hamamelis*. **2.** a mixture of water, alcohol, and extract from the bark and dried leaves of the witch hazel. Use: astringent, embrocation. [< Old English *wice* (see WYCH ELM)]

witch-hunt *n* **1.** an intensive systematic campaign directed against those who have done something wrong or who hold different views **2.** a persecution of people believed to be witches —**witch-hunter** *n*

witching /wíching/ *adj* **1.** suitable for or resembling witchcraft (*archaic*) **2.** same as **bewitching** (*literary*) ■ *n* witchcraft or sorcery (*archaic*)

witching hour *n* midnight, said to be the time when witches allegedly appear

witchweed /wích weed/ *n* a parasitic weed. Flowers: small, red. Native to: South Africa, introduced into the southern United States. Genus: *Striga*. [Probably < alteration of 1st element of QUITCH GRASS]

witenagemot /wíttənəgi mōt/ *n* HIST same as **witan** [Old English *witena gemōt* 'assembly of wise men' < *wita* 'counselor' + *gemōt* 'assembly']

Wite-Out /wít owt/ *tdmk* a trademark for a white fluid used to cover up mistakes in writing, typing, or printing

with /wi*th*/ *prep* **1.** IN COMPANY OF used to indicate that somebody is accompanying or is in the company of another person or people, or that something is accompanying something else ○ *at the theme park with their children* ○ *Do you still want me to go with you?* **2.** USED TOGETHER used together or at the same time ○ *ordered tea with cream* **3.** INVOLVING involving that person or people ○ *He organized the meeting together with the head of his department.* **4.** AGAINST in opposition to ○ *students competing with one another for a limited number of spaces* **5.** BY MEANS OF by the means of or using a particular object, substance, or system ○ *After 18 months, all the rats treated with the altered virus were healthy.* **6.** ON ONE'S PERSON carrying or having in one's possession ○ *He came into the office with a box full of files.* **7.** HAVING having as a possession, attribute, or feature ○ *The film is in French with English subtitles.* **8.** BECAUSE OF in a particular condition as a result of something ○ *I felt heartsick and faint with anxiety.* **9.** ON OR IN used to indicate that something has a substance or things on or in it ○ *brightly painted walls covered with photographs of Italy* **10.** CONCERNING used to indicate the person or thing that a state, quality, or action relates to or affects ○ *not happy with the service provided* **11.** IN THIS WAY used to indicate the way something is done, or the degree to which it is done ○ *sitting with her head on his shoulder* **12.** ACCOMPANIED BY used to indicate the feeling, gesture, sound, or facial expression that accompanies or causes an action ○ *walks with a limp* **13.** IN LIGHT OF in the light of or given the situation mentioned ○ *With all the problems you have, the last thing you need is a lawsuit.* **14.** IN SPITE OF in spite of the situation mentioned ○ *With all his charm and good breeding, he's not a man to be trusted.* **15.** AT TIME OF at the same time as ○ *He woke with the alarm and hurriedly dressed.* **16.** FOLLOWING DIRECTION OF in the same direction as ○ *They were to sail with the tide the next day.* **17.** ACCORDING TO used to indicate that something happens or is true according to something else ○ *how much the risk of death increases with age* **18.** AFTER following on from ○ *With a final wave goodbye she turned the corner.* [Old English *wiþ* 'with, against' < Indo-European, 'apart'] ◇ **be with it 1.** to be fashionable or up to date with fashion (*informal dated*) **2.** to be able to understand what is going on in a situation (*informal*) ◇ **be with somebody 1.** to understand somebody **2.** to approve of or support somebody ○ *Are you with us or not?* **3.** to be an established sexual or romantic partner of somebody ◇ **with that** immediately after saying or doing something specified ○ *With that, she turned to go.*

withal /wi*th* áwl/ (*archaic*) *adv* **1.** along with the rest or in addition **2.** in spite of that ■ *prep* same as **with** (*used after its object*) ○ *all the better to see you withal* [12C. < WITH + ALL]

withdraw /wi*th* dráw/ (**-draws, -drawing, -drew** /-droo/, **-drawn** /-dráwn/) *v* **1.** *vt* REMOVE SOMETHING to remove or take back something that was previously provided or in place **2.** *vt* RETRACT STATEMENT to deny the truth or validity of something that was previously stated **3.** *vi* MIL RETREAT FROM POSITION to retreat or retire from a position, especially during a battle **4.** *vt* BANKING TAKE MONEY FROM ACCOUNT to take money out of an account —**withdrawable** *adj* —**withdrawer** *n*

withdrawal /wi*th* dráw əl/ *n* **1.** TAKING MONEY FROM BANK the act of taking money from a bank or building society account, or the amount of money taken out **2.** TAKING SOMETHING AWAY the act or condition of taking something away or no longer taking part in something **3.** DRUGS PERIOD OF FIGHTING ADDICTION a period during which somebody addicted to a drug or other addictive substance stops taking it, causing the person to experience painful or uncomfortable symptoms **4.** MIL RETREAT OF ARMY retreat or retirement of an army or other military force from an area in which it was fighting

withdrawing room /wi*th* dráwing-/ *n* same as **drawing room** (*archaic*)

withdrawn /wi*th* dráwn/ past participle of **withdraw** ■ *adj* **1.** not friendly or sociable but quiet and thoughtful, especially to an unusual or worrying degree **2.** removed from circulation, competition, or activity

withdrew past tense of **withdraw**

withe /with, wi*th*/ *n* **1.** FLEXIBLE STEM a strong flexible twig or stem used to bind something **2.** FLEXIBLE TOOL HANDLE a shock-absorbing flexible handle for a tool ■ *vt* (**withes, withing, withed**) BIND SOMETHING WITH WITHES

to bind something with strong flexible twigs or stems [Old English *wippe* < Indo-European, 'twist, bend']

wither /withər/ (-ers, -ering, -ered) v 1. *vti* SHRIVEL to shrivel or dry up as part of the process of dying, or make something, especially a plant or part of a plant, shrivel in this way 2. *vi* FADE AWAY to fade or lose freshness or vitality 3. *vti* BECOME OR MAKE SOMEBODY LESS CONFIDENT to make somebody feel embarrassed, foolish, or incapable of activity as the object of scorn or contempt, or lose confidence in the face of somebody's scorn [14C. Probably variant of WEATHER 'expose to the elements'] —**withered** *adj* —**witherer** *n*

withering /withəring/ *adj* expressing scorn or contempt with the intention of causing somebody to feel embarrassed or foolish ○*When he assumed this attitude in the courtroom, ears were always pricked up, as it usually foretold a flood of withering sarcasm.'* (Willa Cather, *The Troll Garden*; 1905) —**witheringly** *adv*

witherite /withə rīt/ *n* a rare greyish-white barium carbonate mineral. Source: lead ores. Use: source of barium. [Late 18C. After William *Withering* (1741–99), British scientist]

withers /withərz/ *npl* the ridge between the shoulder bones of a horse, sheep, ox, or similar four-legged animal, forming the highest part of its back [Early 16C. Probably < Old English *wiper* 'against']

withershins *adv* Scotland another spelling of **widdershins** (*literary*)

withhold /with hōld/ (-holds, -holding, -held /-héld/) v 1. *vti* to refuse to do or give something until something else is done 2. *vt* to collect or deduct tax from a salary —**withholder** *n*

withholding tax /with hólding-/ *n* 1. tax deducted at source from dividends paid to nonresidents of a country 2. *US* part of an employee's wage or salary withheld and remitted to the government by an employer in payment of taxes

within /with ín/ *prep, adv* 1. INSIDE PLACE used to indicate that somebody or something is inside or enclosed by a place, area, or object ○ (prep) *goods manufactured within a country* ○ (prep) *A natural pool lay within a copse of young trees.* ○ (adv) *The door was locked from within.* 2. INSIDE ORGANIZATION happening inside an organization, system, or society ○ (prep) *keeping companies within a given industry technologically competitive* ○ (adv) *Much of our Internet development activity is coming from within.* 3. INSIDE YOURSELF inside the body or mind ○ (adv) *Her new-found happiness was from within.* ○ (prep) *He needed to find the strength within him to carry on.* ■ *prep* 1. INSIDE LIMITS OF inside the limits or rules of ○ *Try to keep within your budget and avoid overspending.* 2. NOT BEYOND not beyond the scope, experience, range, time, or distance of ○ *regulations requiring that all accidents be reported within 48 hours* ■ *adv* same as **indoors** (*literary*) [Old English *wipinnan* 'on the inside' < WITH + *innan* 'from within']

USAGE See *inside*.

with-it *adj* fashionable and modern in dress and behaviour (*dated informal*)

~~**withold**~~ incorrect spelling of **withhold**

without /with ówt/ *prep* 1. NOT HAVING used to indicate that somebody or something does not have the thing mentioned ○ *left without proper tools to finish the job* 2. NOT ACCOMPANIED BY not with somebody, or not having the involvement of somebody ○ *We can't really make any decisions without him.* 3. LACKING lacking a feeling of ○ *The accused committed perjury without remorse.* 4. NOT HAPPENING used to indicate that something does not happen or occur ○ *The bill was passed without a dissenting vote.* ■ *prep, adv* OUTSIDE on, at, or to the outside of somewhere (*archaic or literary*) ○ (prep) *Without the town the air was fresher.* ○ (adv) *She knocked and waited without.* ■ *conj* same as **unless** (*nonstandard*) [Old English *wipūtan* 'on the outside of', < WITH + *ūtan* 'from the outside'] ◇ **be** *or* **do without** to manage in spite of not having something considered necessary or desirable ○ *a form of power he could not buy or do without*

withstand /with stánd/ (-stands, -standing, -stood /-stóod/) *vti* to be strong enough to stand up to somebody or remain unchanged by something such as extremes of heat or pressure —**withstander** *n*

withy /withi/ *n* (*plural* -ies) 1. CONSTR same as **withe** *n* (sense 1) 2. TREES a willow tree, especially an osier

■ *adj* tough and pliable, like withes (*dated*) [Old English *wīpig* 'willow' < Indo-European, 'twist, bend']

witless /wíttləss/ *adj* lacking intelligence or common sense ○ *a witless comment* —**witlessly** *adv* —**witlessness** *n*

witling /wíttling/ *n* somebody who wishes to be witty (*archaic*)

witness /wítnəss/ *n* 1. SOMEBODY WHO SEES OCCURRENCE somebody who gives evidence after seeing or hearing something 2. SIGNATORY OF DOCUMENT somebody who signs a document to show that it, or another signature, is genuine 3. SOMEBODY WHO TESTIFIES TO CHRISTIAN BELIEFS somebody who publicly states his or her strong Christian beliefs 4. *N Am* PUBLIC STATEMENT OF CHRISTIAN BELIEFS a public statement of strong personal Christian beliefs ■ *v* (-nesses, -nessing, -nessed) 1. *vt* SEE SOMETHING HAPPEN to see something happen, especially a crime or an accident 2. *vt* COUNTERSIGN DOCUMENT to affirm the authenticity of a document or a signature on a document by signing it 3. *vt* EXPERIENCE IMPORTANT EVENTS to experience important events or changes, or be the time in which they occur 4. *vt* BE SIGN OF SOMETHING to be a sign or proof of something that is happening 5. *vi* SPEAK PUBLICLY ABOUT RELIGIOUS BELIEFS to talk in public about strong personal Christian beliefs [Old English *witnes* < *wit* (see WIT[1])] —**witnessable** *adj* —**witnesser** *n* ◇ **bear witness (to something)** to prove or be evidence that something is true or that something happened

witness box *n* the enclosed place in a courtroom where witnesses give evidence. US term **witness stand**

Witt ♦ **De Witt, Jan**

Wittenberg /vítt'n burg/ city in east-central Germany where Martin Luther began his campaign for the reform of the Roman Catholic Church in 1517. Population: 53,400 (1989).

witter /wíttər/ (-ters, -tering, -tered) *vi* to chatter or babble at undue length (*informal*) [Early 19C. Origin ?]

wittering /wíttəring/ *n* continuous pointless chatter (*informal*)

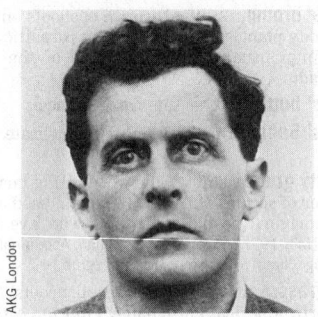
Ludwig Wittgenstein

Wittgenstein /vítgən stīn/, **Ludwig** (1889–1951) Austrian-born British philosopher. He is considered one of the most important thinkers of the 20th century. His *Tractatus Logico-philosophicus* (1921) and *Philosophical Investigations* (1953) represent distinct phases in his work in analytic and linguistic philosophy. Full name **Wittgenstein, Ludwig Josef Johann**

'The world is everything that is the case.'
[Ludwig Wittgenstein, *Tractatus Logico-philosophicus*; 1921]

'Philosophy is a battle against the bewitchment of our intelligence by means of language.'
[Ludwig Wittgenstein, *Philosophical Investigations*; 1953]

witticism /wíttissizəm/ *n* a witty or clever remark [Late 17C. Blend of WITTY + CRITICISM]

witting /wítting/ *adj* (*formal*) 1. done deliberately or intentionally 2. responsible and fully aware —**wittingly** *adv*

witty /wítti/ (-tier, -tiest) *adj* 1. using words in an apt, clever, and amusing way 2. strikingly clever, stylish, or original in design or execution —**wittily** *adv* —**wittiness** *n*

SYNONYMS See *funny*.

Witwatersrand /wit wáwtərz rand/ rocky ridge in northeastern South Africa. Commonly known as 'the Rand', it is the most productive gold-mining area in the world. Johannesburg is located near its centre. Length: 100 km/60 mi.

wive /wīv/ (**wives, wiving, wived**) v (*archaic*) 1. *vti* to marry a woman 2. *vt* to supply somebody with a wife [Old English *wīfian* < *wīf* 'woman, wife']

wivern *n* HERALDRY another spelling of **wyvern**

wives plural of **wife**

wiz /wiz/ (*plural* **wizzes**) *n* same as **whiz** *n* (sense 3) (*informal*) [Early 20C. Partly shortening of WIZARD; partly variant of WHIZ]

wizard /wízzərd/ *n* 1. MALE WITCH a man who is supposed to have magical or wonder-working powers 2. SOMEBODY EXCELLING somebody who is extremely skilled in or knowledgeable about something (*informal*) ■ *adj* UK VERY GOOD AT SOMETHING extremely proficient or adept at something (*dated*) [15C. < WISE[1]] —**wizardly** *adj*

CULTURAL NOTE *The Wizard of Oz*, a film (1939) by US producer David O. Selznick and director Victor Fleming. This enchanting musical, based on a novel by L. Frank Baum (1900), tells the story of Dorothy, a young Kansas girl who dreams she is transported to the magical world of Oz, a utopian place without disease, poverty, or political discussion 'except in the outlying districts'. Evading the Wicked Witch of the West, she sets off along the yellow brick road in search of the mysterious Wizard. The words *Oz* (a magical, unreal, even bizarre place or situation), *Wicked Witch of the West* (evil person), and *munchkin* (from the elflike Munchkins in the movie, now meaning also an elflike person, a young child, or a minor government official) have established a place in the English language.

wizardry /wízzərdri/ *n* 1. the art, activities, or alleged accomplishments of a wizard 2. extreme skill, ability, or accomplishment

wizened /wízz'nd/ *adj* looking wrinkled, shrivelled, or dried up [Early 16C. Past participle of *wizen* < Old English *wisnian* < Germanic] —**wizen** *adj, vi*

wiz kid *n* same as **whiz kid** (*informal*)

wk *abbr* 1. weak 2. week 3. work

wkly *abbr* weekly

wkt *abbr* CRICKET wicket

WL *abbr* 1. *also* **w.l.** NAUT water line 2. ELEC wavelength

WLAN *abbr* COMPUT wireless local area network

WLTM *abbr* would like to meet (*informal; used in e-mails or text messages*)

Wm. *abbr* William

WMD *abbr* MIL weapons of mass destruction

wmk. *abbr* watermark

WML *abbr* COMPUT wireless markup language

WMO *abbr* World Meteorological Organization

WNF *abbr* MED West Nile fever

WNV *abbr* MED West Nile virus

WNW *abbr* COMPASS west-northwest

WO, W.O. *abbr* 1. HIST War Office 2. MIL warrant officer 3. MIL wireless operator

w/o *abbr* without

woad /wōd/ *n* 1. a blue dye obtained from the leaves of a European plant. Use: formerly, body paint. 2. a plant formerly cultivated for woad. Native to: Europe. Latin name: *Isatis tinctoria*. [Old English *wād* < Germanic]

w.o.b. *abbr* INSUR washed overboard

wobbegong /wóbbi gong/ (*plural* **-gongs** *or* same) *n* a carpet shark with wide jaws and sharp teeth that lives at the bottom of the ocean and feeds mainly on crustaceans, small fish, and molluscs. Native to: Australia. Genus: *Orectolobus*. [Mid-19C. < an Aboriginal language]

wobble /wóbb'l/ *v* (-bles, -bling, -bled) 1. *vti* MOVE FROM SIDE TO SIDE to move in a swaying, shaking, or trembling way, or cause something to move in a swaying, shaking, or trembling way 2. *vi* QUAVER to vary uncertainly in pitch or volume ○ *a voice wobbling with emotion* 3. *vi* BE UNABLE TO DECIDE to be unable or unwilling to reach a decision ■ *n* WOBBLING

EFFECT a wobbling movement or sound [Mid-17C. Probably < Low German *wabbeln* < Germanic] —**wobbler** *n* —**wobblingly** *adv*

wobble board *n Aus* a makeshift musical instrument made of a sheet of fibreboard that is flexed repeatedly to create a deep, rhythmic sound

wobbler syndrome *n* a condition in horses and dogs characterized by an unsteady gait and sometimes falling, as a result of a misalignment of vertebrae in the neck, which press on the spinal cord

wobbly /wóbbli/ (**-blier, -bliest**) *adj* **1. UNSTEADY** moving unsteadily from side to side **2. FEELING WEAK** feeling weak and unable to keep balanced (*informal*) **3. WISHY-WASHY** unable or unwilling to make firm decisions and stand by them in the face of opposition (*informal*) ○ *a wobbly leader with a vacillating foreign policy* [Mid-19C. < WOBBLE] —**wobbliness** *n* ◇ **throw** or **chuck a wobbly** to become very angry or frightened suddenly (*informal*)

Wobbly /wóbbli/ (*plural* **-blies**) *n US* a member of the Industrial Workers of the World (*informal*) [Early 20C. Origin ?]

P. G. Wodehouse

Wodehouse /wood howss/, **P. G.** (1881–1975) British writer. He wrote over 100 novels, many of which feature the fictional characters Bertie Wooster and his 'gentleman's gentleman', Jeeves. He became a US citizen in 1955. Full name **Wodehouse, Sir Pelham Grenville**

> 'Fate was quietly slipping the lead into the boxing glove.'
> [P. G. Wodehouse, *Very Good, Jeeves*; 1930]

> 'Has anyone ever seen a dramatic critic in the daytime? Of course not. They come out after dark, up to no good.'
> [P. G. Wodehouse, *New York Mirror*; 27 May 1955]

Woden /wód'n/ *n* in Anglo-Saxon mythology, the equivalent of the Norse god Odin

wodge /woj/ *n* a large lump or chunk of something (*informal*) ○ *They caught him stuffing wodges of banknotes into his pockets.* [Mid-19C. Blend of WAD + WEDGE]

woe /wō/ *n* **1.** a serious affliction or misfortune **2.** grief or distress resulting from a serious affliction or misfortune [Old English *wā* < Germanic < Indo-European] ◇ **woe betide somebody** used as a threat to indicate that somebody is going to regret something or be punished in some way ○ *Woe betide him if he turns up late for work again.* ◇ **woe is me** used to indicate that the speaker is in distress or feels unhappy or unfortunate (*literary or humorous*)

woebegone /wó bi gon/ *adj* feeling or looking distressed or sorrowful [13C. < WOE + *begon* 'beset' (< Old English *gān*)]

woeful /wófl/ *adj* **1. UNHAPPY** feeling or expressing great distress or sorrow **2. CAUSING GRIEF** bringing or causing great distress or sorrow **3. PATHETICALLY BAD** pitifully or regrettably bad —**woefully** *adv* —**woefulness** *n*

wog[1] /wog/ *n* a highly offensive term for a member of any people who have dark skin (*taboo insult*) [Early 20C. Probably shortening of GOLLIWOG]

wog[2] /wog/ *n Aus* influenza or a similar illness (*informal*) [Mid-20C. Origin ?]

woggle /wóggʼl/ *n* the thin ring of leather through which a Scout's neckerchief is drawn and secured [Mid-20C. Origin ?]

Wöhler /vólər, vö́lər/, **Friedrich** (1800–82) German chemist. His work on urea (1828) proved that organic processes can be synthesized in the laboratory. He also isolated aluminium and beryllium.

wok

wok /wok/ *n* a large thin metal pan with a curved base, used for stir-frying, steaming, and braising food, especially in Chinese and other East Asian styles of cooking [Mid-20C. < Chinese (Cantonese)]

woke past tense of **wake**[1]

woken past participle of **wake**[1]

Woking /wóking/ town in Surrey, southeastern England. Population: 89,840 (2001).

Wokingham /wókingəm/ town in southern England, west of London. Population: 150,229 (2001).

wold /wōld/ *n* upland or rolling country, especially when treeless [Old English *wald*, *weald* 'forest' < Indo-European, 'wild']

Wolds /wōldz/ range of chalk hills in eastern England. It is divided by the Humber estuary into the Yorkshire Wolds and the Lincolnshire Wolds.

wolf

wolf /woolf/ *n* (*plural* **wolves** /woolvz/) **1. CARNIVORE THAT HUNTS IN PACKS** any one of several predatory animals that are related to the dog and hunt in packs, especially the grey wolf. Native to: North America, Europe, Asia. Genus: *Canis*. **2. ANIMAL RESEMBLING WOLF** an animal that resembles a wolf but is not of the dog family, e.g. the Tasmanian wolf **3. FUR OF WOLF** the fur of the wolf **4. OFFENSIVE TERM** an offensive term for somebody who is regarded as greedy and cruel **5. LOTHARIO** a sexually aggressive or predatory man (*informal*) **6. INSECTS DESTRUCTIVE LARVA** the destructive larva of several moths and beetles that sometimes infests granaries **7.** **MUSIC DISCORD** an unpleasant discord produced on a string or keyboard instrument (*often used before a noun*) ■ *vt* (**wolfs, wolfing, wolfed**) **EAT SOMETHING QUICKLY AND GREEDILY** eat food quickly and greedily or in gulps [Old English *wulf* < Indo-European] ◇ **a wolf in sheep's clothing** somebody who looks harmless or pleasant but is in fact dangerous or unpleasant ◇ **cry wolf** to give a false alarm or cry for help too many times, so that when help is really needed, no one will give it ◇ **keep the wolf from the door** to be enough to prevent hunger or starvation ◇ **throw somebody to the wolves** to abandon somebody to be destroyed by enemies in order to save yourself

Wolf *n* ASTRON same as **Lupus**

Wolf /volf/, **Hugo** (1860–1903) Austrian composer. He wrote nearly 300 songs exploring a wide range of themes and moods. Full name **Wolf, Hugo Philipp Jakob**

Wolf Cub *n* formerly, a Cub Scout

wolf dog *n* **1.** a dog that is used to hunt wolves **2.** an offspring of a wolf and a dog

James Wolfe

Wolfe /woolf/, **James** (1727–59) British general. The second in command of British troops in North America, he is most famous for his capture of Quebec (1759) from the French in the Seven Years' War (1756–63). He was fatally wounded in the attack.

Wolfe, Thomas (1900–38) US writer. His novels, including *Look Homeward, Angel* (1929) and *You Can't Go Home Again* (1940), are heavily autobiographical. Full name **Wolfe, Thomas Clayton**

> 'Which of us has known his brother? Which of us has looked into his father's heart? Which of us has not remained forever prison-pent? Which of us is not forever a stranger and alone?'
> [Thomas Wolfe. Foreword, *Look Homeward, Angel*; 1929]

Wolfe, Tom (*b.* 1930) US journalist and writer. A leading proponent of New Journalism, he is the author of *The Right Stuff* (1979) and *Bonfire of the Vanities* (1987). He established his reputation as a satirist of American society with his first collection of essays entitled *The Kandy-Colored Flake Streamline Baby* (1964). Full name **Wolfe, Thomas Kennerly Jr**

> 'He was learning for himself the truth of the saying, "A liberal is a conservative who has been arrested".'
> [Tom Wolfe, *The Bonfire of the Vanities*; 1987]

> 'Status is an influence at every level...all part of what I call plutography: depicting the acts of the rich.'
> [Tom Wolfe, *Time*; 13 February 1989]

wolfer *n* FIELD SPORTS same as **wolver**

wolffish /woolf fish/ (*plural same* or **-fishes**) *n* a large fish with sharp teeth and no pelvic fins. Native to: northern Atlantic. Genus: *Anarhichas*. [< its voracious appetite]

wolfhound /woolf hownd/ *n* a large dog belonging to a breed originally developed to hunt wolves

wolfish /woolfish/ *adj* resembling or characteristic of a wolf —**wolfishly** *adv*

Wolfit /wúlfit/, **Sir Donald** (1902–68) British actor and manager. He was noted for his interpretation of Shakespearean characters and, with his own company, his productions of Shakespeare's plays.

wolf pack *n* **1.** a group of wolves that hunt together **2.** a group of submarines, especially German ones, that engaged in hunting and attacking enemy convoys during World War II

wolfram /woolfrəm/ *n* CHEM ELEM same as **tungsten** (*archaic*) [Mid-18C. < German, 'wolframite' < *Wolf* 'wolf' + German dialect *Rahm* 'soot, dirt']

wolframite /woolfrə mīt/ *n* a brownish-black crystalline mineral consisting of iron manganese tungstate. Use: source of tungsten. [Mid-19C. < German (see WOLFRAM)]

wolfsbane /woolfs bayn/ (*plural* **-banes** or *same*) *n* a wild or cultivated poisonous plant. Flowers: yellow or purplish-blue. Use: medicines. Genus: *Aconitum*. [Mid-16C. Translation of Greek *lukoktonon* 'wolf-killer', from the poison found in the plants]

Wolfsburg /woolfs burg, vólfs bóork/ industrial city in

Lower Saxony State, north-central Germany. Population: 126,965 (1997).

wolf spider *n* a ground spider that hunts its prey rather than using a web. Family: Lycosidae.

wolf whistle *n* a whistle given to signal sexual interest in or admiration of somebody —**wolf-whistle** *vti*

wollastonite /wóllǝstǝ nīt/ *n* a fibrous grey-white calcium silicate mineral. Source: metamorphosed limestone. [Early 19C. After William Hyde *Wollaston* (1766–1828), British physicist]

Wollongong /woōllǝng gong/ coastal city in eastern New South Wales, Australia. It is an industrial centre and the site of a university. Population: 191,254 (2002 estimate).

Wollstonecraft /woōlstǝn kraaft/, **Mary** (1759–97) British feminist. Her work *A Vindication of the Rights of Woman* (1792), advocating the equality of the sexes, is an important early document of modern feminism.

> 'Till women are more rationally educated, the progress in human virtue and improvement in knowledge must receive continual checks.'
> [Mary Wollstonecraft, *A Vindication of the Rights of Women*; 1792]

Wolof /wól of/ (*plural same* or **-lofs**) *n* **1.** a member of a people who live in West Africa, mainly in Senegal but also in Gambia and Mauritania **2.** a Niger-Congo language spoken in Senegal and the Gambia. Native speakers: 2 million. [Early 19C. < *Wolof*] —**Wolof** *adj*

Wolsey /woōlzi/, **Thomas** (1475–1530) English clergyman and political leader. As Henry VIII's Lord Chancellor (1515–29), he exercised great power both in England and abroad. He was impeached for failing to secure Henry's divorce from Catherine of Aragon. Known as **Cardinal Wolsey**

> 'Had I but served God as diligently as I have served the king, he would not have given me over in my grey hairs.'
> [Thomas Wolsey. Quoted in *Negotiations of Thomas Wolsey*, George Cavendish; 1641]

wolver /woōlvǝr/, **wolfer** *n* somebody who hunts wolves

Wolverhampton /woōlvǝr hámptǝn/ industrial city in west-central England. Population: 236,582 (2001).

wolverine /woōlvǝ reen/ (*plural* **-ines** or *same*) *n* a strong dark-furred, usually solitary carnivore of the weasel family. Native to: forests of northern Europe, Asia, North America. Latin name: *Gulo gulo*. [Late 16C. Probably < WOLF]

wolves plural of **wolf**

woman /woōmmǝn/ (*plural* **women** /wímmin/) *n* **1.** FEMALE ADULT an adult female human being **2.** WOMEN AS GROUP women collectively or in general **3.** FEMININITY feminine qualities or feelings **4.** DOMESTIC EMPLOYEE a woman who is a domestic employee (*sometimes offensive*) **5.** WIFE OR GIRLFRIEND a wife, female lover, or girlfriend (*informal*; *sometimes offensive*) [Old English *wimman*, variant of *wīfman*, < *wīf* 'woman, wife' + *man* 'person'] ◇ **to a woman** used to indicate that every one of a group of women does or thinks something, without any exceptions

USAGE See **girl** and *person*.

CULTURAL NOTE *Little Women*, a novel (1868–69) by US writer Louisa May Alcott. An abidingly popular family saga set in 1860s New England, it recounts the emotional and intellectual development of four sisters – Meg, Jo, Beth, and Amy – as they progress through adolescence to adulthood. It was followed by two sequels, *Little Men* (1871) and *Jo's Boys* (1886).

womanfully /woōmmǝnfǝli/ *adv* in a way that shows or is characteristic of womanly spirit or energy [Early 19C. After *manfully*]

womanhood /woōmmǝnhoōd/ *n* **1.** the state or condition of being a woman **2.** women in general, or as a group

womanise *vti* another spelling of **womanize** (*disapproving*)

womanish /woōmmǝnish/ *adj* an offensive term meaning having qualities stereotypically attributed to women such as weakness or fussiness —**womanishly** *adv* —**womanishness** *n*

womanist /woōmmǝnist/ *adj* having a respect for and a belief in the abilities and talents of women [Late 20C. After *humanist*]

womanize /woōmmǝ nīz/ (**-izes, -izing, -ized**), **womanise** (**-ises, -ising, -ised**) *vi* to be constantly in search of casual sex with women (*disapproving*; *refers to men*) —**womanizer** *n*

womankind /woōmmǝn kīnd/, **womenkind** /wímmin-/ *n* women collectively or in general

womanly /woōmmǝnli/ *adj* having positive characteristics or qualities, especially warmth, calmness, and competence, attributed to mature women —**womanliness** *n*

woman of the hour (*plural* **women of the hour**) *n* a woman, often a public figure, who is currently publicly admired because of her accomplishments or actions ○ *Because of her bravery in enemy captivity the army nurse was the woman of the hour.*

woman of the house *n* a woman who is in charge of or who is the primary woman of a household

woman of the world (*plural* **women of the world**) *n* a socially experienced and sophisticated woman

womanpower /woōmmǝn powǝr/ *n* **1.** women as part of the workforce in society **2.** the influence and impact of women in society [Early 20C. After MANPOWER]

woman suffrage *n* POL same as **women's suffrage**

woman-to-woman *adj* **1.** marked by directness and candour between women **2.** in sports such as women's football, hockey, or basketball, having each defender of one team mark a corresponding attacker of the other team —**woman-to-woman** *adv*

womb /woōm/ *n* **1.** UTERUS OF WOMAN a uterus, especially a woman's (*not in technical use*) **2.** PLACE OF ORIGIN a place where something is conceived and nurtured **3.** PLACE OF SECURITY a place that offers protection and shelter, or a state of mind that provides comfort [Old English *wamb* < Germanic]

wombat

wombat /wóm bat/ *n* a burrowing marsupial that is short, robust, covered in dense wiry hair, and has a stumpy tail and wide blunt snout. Native to: Australia. Latin name: *Vombatus ursinus* or *Lasiorhinus latifrons*. [Late 18C. < Dharuk *wambaty*]

womblike /woōm līk/ *adj* resembling a womb, especially in being reassuring, all-enclosing, and giving a feeling of security

women plural of **woman**

womenfolk /wímmin fōk/ *npl* women collectively, or a particular group of women, especially those belonging to the same family or society (*dated*)

womenkind *n* same as **womankind**

Women's Army Auxiliary Corps *n* a women's branch of the UK armed forces between 1917 and 1918 established to replace men in technical and administrative roles and free them for combat

Women's Auxiliary Air Force *n* a women's branch of the UK armed forces between 1939 and 1948 established to give technical and administrative support to flying crew

Women's Auxiliary Australian Air Force *n* a women's branch of the Australian armed forces between 1941 and 1947 established to give technical and administrative support to flying crew

Women's Institute *n* a worldwide organization of affiliated groups of women, especially in rural areas, who hold regular meetings for social and cultural activities, or a group belonging to this

women's lib *n* SOC SCI same as **women's liberation** (*informal*) —**women's libber** *n*

women's liberation *n* a political movement intended to free women from oppression, or the act of a woman's freeing herself

women's movement *n* a movement seeking to promote and improve the position of women in society

women's refuge *n* a place where women and children can stay after leaving home to escape domestic violence. N Am term **women's shelter**

women's room *n* N Am a public toilet for women and girls to use

Women's Royal Voluntary Service *n* a British service run by women that provides support for people in need

women's shelter *n* N Am same as **women's refuge**

women's studies *n* a course of study examining the historical, economic, and cultural roles and achievements of women (*takes a singular or plural verb*)

women's suffrage *n* the right of women to vote in elections

womenswear /wímminz wair/ *n* clothing and accessories for women

womera *n* ARMS another spelling of **woomera**

won[1] /won/ (*plural same*) *n* the main unit of currency in North and South Korea. See table at **currency** [Mid-20C. < Korean *wǎn*]

won[2] /wun/ past participle, past tense of **win**

wonder /wúndǝr/ *n* **1.** AMAZED ADMIRATION amazed admiration or awe, especially at something very beautiful or new **2.** SOMETHING MARVELLOUS a miracle or other cause of intense admiration or awe ▪ *adj* EXTRAORDINARILY GOOD exciting admiration or amazement by virtue of being outstandingly good, effective, or unusual ▪ *v* (**-ders, -dering, -dered**) **1.** *vti* SPECULATE ABOUT SOMETHING to speculate or be curious to know about something **2.** *vi* BE AMAZED to be in a state of amazed admiration or awe [Old English *wundor* < Germanic] —**wonderer** *n* ◇ **no** *or* **small** *or* **little wonder** used to indicate that something is not surprising ◇ **wonders (will) never cease** used, often ironically, to express astonishment or incredulity ○ *I hear he managed to get to work on time today – wonders will never cease!* ◇ **work** *or* **perform** *or* **do wonders** to achieve remarkable results or be very effective in solving a problem

SPELLCHECK See *wander*.

Wonder /wúndǝr/, **Stevie** (*b.* 1950) US singer and songwriter. He released his first album at age 13, began an international career, and won numerous Grammy awards for a succession of recordings of Motown rhythm and blues. Born **Judkins, Steveland**

> 'Pride is like a perfume. When it is worn, it radiates a sense of self the world reacts to.'
> [Stevie Wonder, *Essence*; January 1975]

wonder drug *n* MED same as **miracle drug**

wonderful /wúndǝrf'l/ *adj* **1.** of a quality that excites admiration or amazement **2.** suiting somebody perfectly —**wonderfully** *adv* —**wonderfulness** *n*

wonderland /wúndǝr land/ *n* a land where wonderful things happen or exist

CULTURAL NOTE *Alice's Adventures in Wonderland*, a children's story (1865) by Lewis Carroll. This extraordinarily inventive and immensely popular tale was based on stories that the author made up to entertain his friends' children. A girl called Alice dreams that she falls down a rabbit hole into a surreal world inhabited by eccentric characters including the Mad Hatter, the March Hare, and the King and Queen of Hearts. The expressions 'Curiouser and curiouser!' and 'Oh my fur and whiskers!' are direct quotations from this book. The often-used expressions 'grin like a Cheshire cat', 'wild as a March hare', and 'mad as a hatter' have associations with characters in the book.

wonderment /wúndǝrmǝnt/ *n* **1.** amazed admiration or awe **2.** puzzled surprise

wonderwork /wúndǝr wurk/ *n* something made or done that arouses amazed admiration or awe —**wonderworker** *n*

wondrous /wúndrəss/ (*literary*) *adj* so good or admirable as to inspire wonder or awe ■ *adv* wondrously or extraordinarily [15C. Alteration (influenced by MARVELLOUS) of obsolete *wonders* < WONDER] —**wondrously** *adv* —**wondrousness** *n*

wonga-wonga /wóng gə wóng gə/ (*plural* **wonga-wongas** or *same*) *n* a climbing bush that has pale cream or brown tubular flowers with red throats. Native to: Australia. Latin name: *Pandorea pandorana*. [Early 19C. < an Aboriginal language]

wonk /wongk/ *n* **1.** an expert in matters of policy, especially in government, the economy, or diplomacy (*informal*) ○ *The dinner conversation was dominated by deep discussions among the government's policy wonks.* **2.** *N Am* a student who works unduly hard or long (*informal disapproving*) [Early 20C. Origin ?]

wonky[1] /wóngki/ *adj* (**-kier, -kiest**), *adv* (*informal*) **1.** not to be relied on to be steady or secure or to function correctly **2.** not straight or level [Early 20C. Origin ?] —**wonkily** *adv* —**wonkiness** *n*

wonky[2] /wóngki/ (**-ier, -iest**) *adj US* (*informal disapproving*) **1.** expert in matters of policy, especially in government, the economy, or diplomacy ○ *a wonky Vice President who delved deep into economic policies* **2.** studying too hard or too much [< WONK] —**wonkiness** *n*

wont /wōnt/ *adj* **ACCUSTOMED TO SOMETHING** accustomed or likely to do something (*formal*) ○ *He is wont to be rather quick of temper when tired.* ■ *n* **SOMEBODY'S CUSTOM** a habit or custom followed by a person or group of people (*formal*) ○ *She arrived late and left early, as is her wont.* ■ *vti* (**wonts, wonting, wont** or **wonted**) **BE ACCUSTOMED** to have the habit of doing something, or give somebody the habit of doing something (*archaic*) [12C. < past participle of Old English *wunian* 'be accustomed']

SYNONYMS See ***habit***.

won't /wōnt/ *contr* will not

wonted /wṓntid/ *adj* usual or typical (*literary*) —**wontedly** *adv* —**wontedness** *n*

SYNONYMS See ***usual***.

won ton /wón tón/ *n* **1.** in Chinese cookery, a small dumpling made from a square of noodle dough with a little filling in the middle, boiled in soup or deep-fried **2.** *also* **won ton soup** Chinese soup with boiled small dumplings in it [Mid-20C. < Chinese (Cantonese) *wān t'ān*]

woo /woo/ (**woos, wooing, wooed**) *vti* **1.** to seek the affection or love of a woman in order to marry her (*literary*) **2.** to try to please somebody in order to gain something, especially acceptance, fame, or approval [Old English *wōgian*, origin ?] —**wooingly** *adv*

wood /wŏŏd/ *n* **1. SUBSTANCE OF TREES** a hard fibrous substance that chiefly composes trees and bushes and is found beneath their bark **2. FUEL OR BUILDING MATERIAL** wood from trees, cut and dried for use as a fuel or a building material or in other areas of craft and manufacture **3. AREA WITH TREES** an area of land covered by trees or bushes. A wood is usually smaller than a forest. **4. GOLF CLUB** a golf club with a head formerly made of wood, but now usually made of stainless steel or titanium **5.** BOWLS same as **bowl**[2] *n* (sense 1) ■ **woods** *npl* **1. FORESTED AREA** a forested or wooded area or region **2. WOODWIND** the woodwind instruments or players of an orchestra ■ *adj* **1. OF WOOD** made of or used for wood **2. AMONG TREES** located or living in a forested area ■ *vt* (**woods, wooding, wooded**) **COVER AREA WITH TREES** to cover an area of land with trees [Old English *wudu* < Germanic] —**wooded** *adj* ◇ **not see the wood for the trees** used to indicate that somebody is too concerned with the details to appreciate the general nature of a situation or problem ◇ **out of the woods** out of danger or difficulty (*informal*) ◇ **touch wood** used, whether you are actually touching wood or not, to try to avoid the bad luck that is supposed to come from being too confident or hopeful

SPELLCHECK wood or **would**? Do not confuse the spelling of ***wood*** and ***would***, which sound similar. ***Wood*** refers to the hard substance that chiefly composes trees, or to an area covered by trees, as in *boats made of wood, a path through the wood.* ***Would*** indicates a conditional statement or introduces a polite request: *I would write to her if I knew her address. Would you close the door, please.*

CULTURAL NOTE ***Stopping by Woods on a Snowy Evening***, a poem (1923) by US poet Robert Frost. In this much-anthologized poem, the narrator pauses on horseback, drawn into the dark beauty of the woods in snow. He lingers, attracted by the quiet, the solitude, and, according to many critics, the prospect of death, while yet considering the practical obligations of society. It ends with the famous lines, 'But I have promises to keep, / And miles to go before I sleep, / And miles to go before I sleep'.

ORIGIN The ancestral meaning of ***wood*** is probably 'collection of trees, forest'. The meanings 'tree' (now obsolete) and 'substance from which trees are made' are secondary developments. It has been suggested that the word ***wood*** may go back to an Indo-European source meaning 'separate', in which case it would originally have denoted a 'separated' or 'remote' piece of territory, near the outer edge or borders of known land. Since such remote, uninhabited areas were usually wooded, the word came to denote 'forest'.

Wood /wŏŏd/, **Sir Henry** (1869–1944) British conductor. In 1895 he initiated what are now known as the Henry Wood Promenade Concerts. He was a noted champion of contemporary music. Full name **Wood, Henry Joseph**

Wood (the Elder), John (1704?–54) British architect and town planner. His most notable work is his early Georgian terraces in central Bath, England.

Wood (the Younger), John (1728–81) British architect and town planner. The son of John Wood the Elder, he designed the classical Georgian Assembly Rooms (1771) and Royal Crescent (1775) in Bath, England.

wood alcohol *n* CHEM same as **methanol**

wood anemone *n* a spring-flowering anemone that grows in shady places. Flowers: single, white to crimson. Native to: North America, Europe. Latin name: *Anemone quinquefolia* or *Anemone nemorosa*.

wood ant *n* a large reddish ant that builds huge domed colonies of wood chips. Native to: Europe. Latin name: *Formica rufa*.

wood avens *n* PLANTS same as **herb bennet**

wood betony *n* a plant related to lousewort that grows in woods and clearings. Flowers: yellow, red, or both. Native to: eastern North America. Latin name: *Pedicularis canadensis*.

woodbine /wŏŏd bīn/ (*plural* **-bines** or *same*) *n* a honeysuckle with fragrant yellow flowers. Native to: Europe, Asia, North Africa. Latin name: *Lonicera periclymenum*. [Old English *wudubinde*, < *wudu* 'wood' + *bindan* 'bind'; because the plant grows around trees]

woodblock /wŏŏd blok/ *n* **1.** HANDICRAFT same as **woodcut** (sense 1) **2.** MUSIC a hollow block of wood used as a percussion instrument in an orchestra or band **3.** CONSTR a small flat piece of wood laid in a pattern with others to make a floor surface

woodborer /wŏŏd bawrər/ *n* a medium sized moth with a stocky body that, as a large fleshy larva, bores into wood, causing considerable damage. Family: Cossidae.

Wood Buffalo National Park /wŏŏd búffəlō-/ national park and nature reserve in central Canada, on the Alberta-Northwest Territories border, established in 1922. Area: 44,807 sq. km/17,300 sq. mi.

woodcarving /wŏŏd kaarving/ *n* **1.** the art of carving wood **2.** a decorative object carved from wood

woodchat /wŏŏd chat/ (*plural* **-chats** or *same*), **woodchat shrike** *n* a songbird of the shrike family with black and white feathers and a reddish-brown crown. Native to: Europe, North Africa. Latin name: *Lanius senator*.

woodchop /wŏŏd chop/ *n* in Australia, a wood-chopping competition held at country fairs

woodchopper /wŏŏd chopər/ *n* somebody who chops wood, especially somebody who chops down trees

woodchuck /wŏŏd chuk/ (*plural* **-chucks** or *same*) *n* a heavy-set short-legged marmot with brownish fur streaked with grey. Native to: northern North America. Latin name: *Marmota monax*. [Late 17C. By folk etymology < Algonquian]

wood coal *n* INDUST **1.** same as **brown coal 2.** same as **charcoal** (sense 1)

woodcock /wŏŏd kok/ (*plural* **-cocks** or *same*) *n* a medium-sized ground-dwelling game bird related to the snipe, with short legs and rounded wings, a stocky body and a long beak. Native to: North America, Europe, Asia. Genus: *Scolopax*.

woodcraft /wŏŏd kraaft/ *n* **1.** skill in travelling, living, or working in woods or forests **2.** *N Am* skill in carving or making objects from wood —**woodcrafter** *n* —**woodcraftsman** *n*

woodcreeper /wŏŏd kreepər/ (*plural* **-ers** or *same*) *n* a brown bird that clings to tree trunks with its short strong legs and probes for insects with its long beak. Native to: forests of Central and South America. Family: Dendrocolaptidae.

woodcut /wŏŏd kut/ *n* **1.** a block of wood carved with a picture or design from which prints are made **2.** a print made by pressing a woodcut into a colouring substance and then onto paper

woodcutter /wŏŏd kutər/ *n* **1.** somebody who cuts down trees **2.** somebody who makes and prints from woodcuts

wood duck *n* a crested duck that nests in tree cavities near water, the male of which has black, chestnut, green, purple, and white feathers. Native to: North America. Latin name: *Aix sponsa*.

wooden /wŏŏdd'n/ *adj* **1. MADE OF WOOD** made or consisting of wood **2. UNGAINLY** lacking flexibility, relaxation, and grace ○ *a ballet dancer with wooden movements* **3. INEXPRESSIVE** lacking animation, emotion, or responsiveness ○ *a wooden prose style* **4. DULL IN SOUND** making a dull unresonant sound ○ *spoke in a toneless, wooden voice* —**woodenly** *adv* —**woodenness** *n*

wood engraving *n* **1.** the art or process of engraving a picture or design with a burin on a block of wood **2.** an engraving made with a burin on a block of wood, or a print made from such an engraving —**wood engraver** *n*

woodenhead /wŏŏdd'n hed/ *n* an offensive term for a person considered to be unintelligent (*informal insult*) —**woodenheaded** /wŏŏdd'n héddid/ *adj* —**woodenheadedly** *adv* —**woodenheadedness** *n*

Wooden Horse *n* MYTHOL same as **Trojan Horse** (sense 1)

wooden spoon *n* a prize awarded for being last in a race or competition

woodenware /wŏŏdd'n wair/ *n* dishes or utensils made from wood

woodfree /wŏŏd free/ *adj* describes paper made from wood pulp that has been chemically treated to remove impurities

wood frog *n* a frog that lives in woodland and is light brown with darker markings on the head. Native to: eastern North America. Latin name: *Rana sylvatica*.

woodgrain /wŏŏd grayn/ *n* a material or finish that imitates the natural grain of wood

woodgrouse /wŏŏd growss/ *n* BIRDS same as **capercaillie**

wood hedgehog *n* a pale buff fungus that has a spiny underside to the cap and is found in broad-leaved woodland. Latin name: *Hydnum repandum*.

wood hoopoe /-hoo poo, -pō/ *n* a bird that has dark glossy feathers, a long tail, and a slender curved beak. Native to: tropical Africa. Genus: *Phoeniculus*.

wood hyacinth *n* PLANTS same as **bluebell** (sense 1)

woodie *n US* another spelling of **woody** (*slang offensive*)

woodland /wŏŏddlənd/, **woodlands** *n* land that is covered with trees, shrubs, or bushes —**woodland** *adj* —**woodlander** *n*

woodland burial *n* a ecologically sound funeral and burial using biodegradable burial products such as caskets and shrouds, with burial taking place in a natural wooded setting, usually without headstones

woodlark /wŏŏd laark/ (*plural* **-larks** or *same*) *n* a small lark noted for its song in flight. Native to: Europe, Asia. Latin name: *Lullula arborea*.

woodlouse /wŏŏd lowss/ (*plural* **-lice** /-līss/) *n* a small land-dwelling crustacean that lives in damp woody places and is capable of rolling into a ball. Genera: *Oniscus* or *Porcellio*.

woodman *n* same as **woodsman**

wood mouse *n* a small mouse. Native to: woodlands in western and central Europe and North Africa. Latin name: *Adopdemus sylvaticus*.

woodnote /wŏŏd nōt/ n a natural musical note, call, or song, e.g. that made by a wild bird (*literary*)

wood nymph n 1. MYTHOL **WOODLAND NYMPH** a nymph that lives in woodland, e.g. a dryad 2. INSECTS **BUTTERFLY** a brown butterfly, especially one with a broad yellow band and black-and-white eyespots on each front wing. Family: Satyridae. 3. *also* **woodnymph** /wŏŏd nimf/ BIRDS **HUMMINGBIRD** a tropical hummingbird. Native to: Central and South America. Genus: *Thalurania*.

wood opal n wood impregnated and fossilized by silica, preserving the grain

wood owl n BIRDS same as **tawny owl**

woodpecker

woodpecker /wŏŏd pekər/ n a bird with boldly-patterned feathers, a stiff tail used in climbing or clinging to tree trunks, and a hard beak for hammering into wood to extract insects or create a nest hole. Family: Picidae.

wood pigeon n a large pigeon that has a white patch on each side of the neck and lives in parks, fields, and woodland. Latin name: *Columba palumbus*.

woodpile /wŏŏd pīl/ n a heap or stack of firewood

wood pitch n the sticky residue left after wood tar has been distilled

woodprint /wŏŏd print/ n HANDICRAFT same as **woodcut** (sense 1)

wood pulp n wood that has been mechanically and chemically broken down for use in making paper and paper products

wood rat n ZOOL same as **pack rat**

Woodroffe, Mount /wŏŏd rof/ mountain in South Australia, the highest peak in the state. Height: 1,440 m/4,724 ft.

woodruff /wŏŏd ruf/ (*plural* **-ruffs** *or same*) n a plant with sweet-scented flowers. Use: perfumery, flavouring for wines and liqueurs. Genera: *Asperula* or *Galium*. [Old English *wudurofe*, < *wudu* 'wood' + *rofe*, origin ?]

Woodruff key n a self-aligning key that is semicircular in cross-section, designed to fit into the recess of a shaft [Late 19C. After the *Woodruff* Manufacturing Co. in Hartford, Connecticut]

woodrush /wŏŏd rush/ n a plant with flat leaves fringed with hairs. Native to: cold and temperate areas of the northern hemisphere. Genus: *Luzula*.

Express Newspapers

Tiger Woods

Woods /wŏŏdz/, **Tiger** (*b.* 1975) US golfer. At 21, he became the youngest player ever to win the US Masters championship (1997). Born **Woods, Eldrick**

wood sage n a downy aromatic plant. Native to:

woods and heaths of Europe. Latin name: *Teucrium scordonia*.

woodscrew /wŏŏd skroo/ n a tapered metal screw that can be driven into wood by a screwdriver

woodshed /wŏŏd shed/ n an outbuilding or connected room in which firewood and tools are stored

woodsia /wŏŏdzi ə/ (*plural* **-as** *or same*) n a small fern that has wiry fronds. Native to: northern, often mountainous regions. Genus: *Woodsia*. [Mid-19C. < modern Latin, after Joseph *Woods* (1776–1864), British botanist]

woodsman /wŏŏdzmən/ (*plural* **-men** /-mən/), **woodman** /wŏŏdmən/ n somebody who is skilled at living, working, or travelling in the woods

wood sorrel n a herb with a creeping stem and heart-shaped leaves. Flowers: white, with coloured veins. Genus: *Oxalis*.

wood spirit n CHEM same as **methanol**

Woodstock /wŏŏd stok/ 1. town in Oxfordshire, England. Blenheim Palace, home of the Dukes of Marlborough, is located there. Population: 2,898 (1991). 2. town in New York State. It is best known for a rock music festival in 1969, although the site of the festival was moved beforehand to nearby Bethel. Population: 6,261 (2002 estimate).

wood sugar n CHEM same as **xylose**

woodswallow /wŏŏd swollō/ n a medium-sized, long-winged bird with a black-tipped beak that feeds on insects while on the wing. Native to: Asia, Australia. Genus: *Artamus*.

woodsy /wŏŏdzi/ (**-ier, -iest**) adj N Am relating to or reminiscent of the woods (*informal*)

wood tar n a black viscous tar produced as a by-product in the destructive distillation of wood, used as a protective coating for rope and timber

wood tick n a tick that transmits the pathogenic microorganism that causes Rocky Mountain spotted fever. Native to: western North America. Genus: *Dermacentor*.

wood vinegar n CHEM same as **pyroligneous acid**

wood warbler n 1. a small yellowish-green songbird that lives in woods. Native to: Europe. Latin name: *Phylloscopus sibilatrix*. 2. a small, insect-eating, often brightly coloured songbird. Native to: North and South America. Family: Parulidae.

Woodward /wŏŏdwərd/, **Robert B.** (1917–79) US chemist. He is noted for his work in chemical synthesis, especially quinine (1944), cholesterol (1951), and cortisone (1951). He won the Nobel Prize in chemistry (1965). Full name **Woodward, Robert Burns**

Woodward, Roger (*b.* 1944) Australian pianist. He is noted for his renditions of works by Beethoven and Chopin. Full name **Woodward, Roger Robert**

wood wasp n same as **horntail**

woodwind /wŏŏd wind/ n MUSICAL INSTRUMENT a wind musical instrument that produces sound by vibration of mouthpiece reeds, e.g. the bassoon, clarinet, oboe, or saxophone, or by passage of air over the mouthpiece, e.g. the flute ■ npl 1. MUSICAL INSTRUMENTS wind instruments belonging to the family that includes the flute, clarinet, oboe, and bassoon, instruments originally made of wood 2. PLAYERS IN ORCHESTRA the players of woodwind instruments in an orchestra, considered collectively —**woodwind** adj

woodwork /wŏŏd wurk/ n 1. SKILL OF MAKING WOODEN ITEMS the skill or craft of making items out of wood. US term **woodworking** 2. ITEMS MADE FROM WOOD items or components made from wood, especially the interior parts of a building, e.g. the frames of windows, staircases, and doors 3. FRAME OF FOOTBALL GOAL the goalposts and crossbar of a football goal (*informal*) —**woodworker** n ◇ **crawl** *or* **come out of the woodwork** to appear suddenly and unexpectedly in large numbers (*slang*)

woodworking /wŏŏd wurking/ n US same as **woodwork** (sense 1) ■ adj relating to woodwork, or used in making things from wood

woodworm /wŏŏd wurm/ n 1. a worm or insect larva that bores into and weakens wood, e.g. in joists or stairs inside a building 2. the damaged condition of wood from its infestation by wood-boring insects, especially larvae

woody /wŏŏdi/ adj (**-ier, -iest**) 1. HAVING MANY TREES containing or covered with many trees 2. RELATING TO

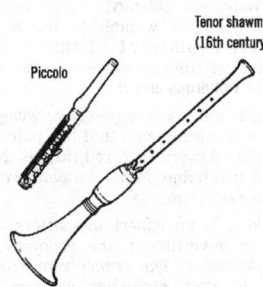

Piccolo

Tenor shawm (16th century)

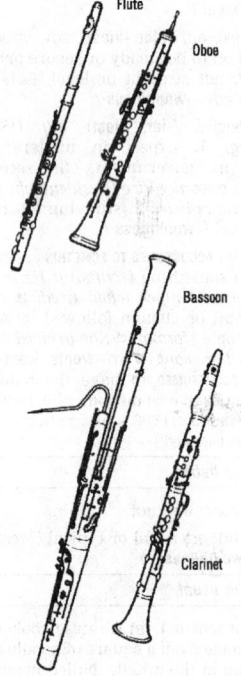

Flute

Oboe

Bassoon

Clarinet

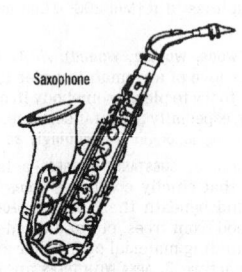

Saxophone

woodwind: woodwind instruments

WOOD relating to, typical of, or situated in the wood 3. MADE OF WOOD made of or containing wood or a material resembling wood 4. RESEMBLING WOOD resembling wood in some way, e.g. in appearance, texture, or smell ■ n (*plural* **-ies**) *also* **woodie** US OFFENSIVE TERM an offensive term for an erect penis (*slang*)

woodyard /wŏŏd yaard/ n a place where wood is cut and stored

woody nightshade n UK, ANZ, Can a woody plant with poisonous red fruits resembling berries. Flowers: purple. Native to: Europe, Asia. Genus: *Solanum dulcamara*. US term **bittersweet**

woof[1] /wŏŏf/ n SOUND OF BARKING DOG the sound made by a dog when it barks ■ interj REPRESENTATION OR IMITATION OF BARKING a representation or imitation of the sound made by a barking dog ■ vi (**woofs, woofing, woofed**) MAKE BARKING SOUND to produce a woof [Early 19C. An imitation of the sound]

woof[2] /woof/ n 1. HANDICRAFT same as **weft** (sense 1) 2. a woven fabric, or its texture [Old English *owef* 'weave on' < *wefan* 'weave' < Indo-European]

woofer /wŏŏffər, wŏŏfər/ n a loudspeaker used to reproduce low-frequency sounds [Mid-20C. As a metaphor < WOOF[1]]

wool /wŏŏl/ n **1.** SHEEP'S HAIR the short curly overlapping hair of sheep and some other animals such as the llama and the alpaca **2.** YARN USED TO MAKE CLOTHES yarn spun from the wool of sheep or other animals. Use: knitting, weaving. **3.** WOOLEN MATERIAL material knitted or woven using wool **4.** INSECTS HAIR OF INSECT LARVA the furry hair of some insect larvae such as caterpillars (informal) **5.** BOT HAIRS GROWING ON PLANT a mass of soft hairs that grows on some plants ■ adj MADE FROM WOOL knitted or woven using wool [Old English wull < Indo-European]—**woolled** adj ◇ **pull the wool over somebody's eyes** to deceive or trick somebody

wool clip n the annual wool yield of a farm, district, or country

woolen adj, n TEXTILES US spelling of **woollen**

Virginia Woolf

Corbis/Bettmann

Woolf /wŏŏlf/, **Virginia** (1882–1941) British novelist and critic. The psychological depth of her stream-of-consciousness technique and the poetic language of novels such as *To the Lighthouse* (1927) profoundly influenced the 20th-century English novel. Born **Stephen, Virginia Adeline**

> 'If we didn't live venturously, plucking the wild goat by the beard, and trembling over precipices, we should never be depressed, I've no doubt; but already should be faded, fatalistic and aged.'
> [Virginia Woolf, *A Writer's Diary*, Leonard Woolf, ed.; 1953]

wool fat n PHARM same as **lanolin**

woolgathering /wŏŏl gathəring/ n daydreaming or absent-mindedness [Mid-16C. Originally 'gathering the bits of wool torn from sheep by bushes']—**woolgather** vi—**woolgatherer** n

wool grease n a fatty wax that coats the fibres of sheep's wool and yields lanolin

woolgrower /wŏŏl grō ər/ n somebody who keeps sheep in order to sell their wool—**woolgrowing** n

woollen /wŏŏllən/ adj **1.** MADE FROM WOOL knitted or woven using wool **2.** OF WOOL PRODUCTION relating to the production of wool or items made from wool ■ n WOOLLEN GARMENT a garment made from wool, especially a sweater or cardigan

Woolley /wŏŏlli/, **Sir Leonard** (1880–1960) British archaeologist. He excavated the royal cemetery and ziggurat at Ur and other sites in Egypt and the Near East. Full name **Woolley, Sir Charles Leonard**

woolly /wŏŏlli/ adj (-**lier**, -**liest**) **1.** MADE OF WOOL knitted or woven using wool **2.** CONFUSED confused, vague, and lacking focus ○ *woolly thinking* **3.** US UNCIVILIZED AND UNRULY rough and boisterous in a way that is reminiscent of the frontier days of the American West (informal) **4.** INSECTS COVERED WITH INSECT HAIR describes an insect larva such as a caterpillar that is covered with furry hair resembling wool **5.** BOT COVERED WITH PLANT HAIRS describes a stem, leaf, or other plant part that is covered with long, soft, white hairs ■ n (plural -**lies**) CLOTHING same as **woollen** (informal)—**woollily** adv—**woolliness** n

woolly aphid n a tiny insect that secretes a waxy substance in long filaments that give it a woolly appearance. Family: Aphididae.

woolly bear n the caterpillar of various moths, especially the tiger moth, that has a coat of dense woolly hairs

woollybutt /wŏŏlli but/ (plural -**butts** or same) n a eucalyptus tree that has loose stringy bark hanging in strips at the base of the trunk. Native to: Australia. Genus: *Eucalyptus*.

woolly-headed adj **1.** confused, vague, and lacking focus **2.** having thick curly hair that looks or feels like wool

woolly mammoth n an extinct mammoth with a shaggy coat that lived during the Ice Age. Native to: cold regions of North America, Europe, and Asia. Genus: *Mammuthus primigenius*.

Woolner /wŏŏlnər/, **Thomas** (1825–92) British sculptor and poet. A founder of the Pre-Raphaelite Brotherhood, he is best known for his portrait sculptures of leading intellectuals, poets, and scientists, including Wordsworth, Tennyson, Gladstone, and Darwin.

woolpack /wŏŏl pak/ n **1.** the coarse material, usually jute or canvas, used to wrap a bale of wool **2.** a package in which a bale of raw wool is transported

woolsack /wŏŏl sak/ n a sack for holding wool

Woolsack n the seat traditionally stuffed with wool from which the Lord Chancellor presides over the House of Lords

woolshed /wŏŏl shed/ n ANZ a building or group of buildings in which sheep are sheared and their wool is prepared and packed for market

wool sorter n somebody who sorts wool into different grades

wool-sorter's disease n pulmonary anthrax resulting from the inhalation of spores of an anthrax bacterium that contaminates wool

wool stapler n **1.** somebody who deals in wool **2.** OCCUPATIONS same as **wool sorter**

Woolwich /wŏŏllij, -ich/ district of London, England, located on the southern bank of the River Thames. The Thames Barrier, designed to prevent London from being flooded, was completed there in 1982.

Woolworth /wŏŏlwərth/, **Frank W.** (1852–1919) US retailer. In 1879 he opened what was to prove the first of a chain of more than 1,000 shops across the United States and Britain. Full name **Woolworth, Frank Winfield**

wooly adj, n TEXTILES US spelling of **woolly**

woomera /wŏŏmmərə, wŏŏm-/, **woomerah, womera** n a wooden stick with a notch at one end, used by Australian Aboriginals to launch a spear. The stick provides extra leverage and force. [Early 19C. < Dharuk]

Woop Woop /wŏŏp wŏŏp/ n Aus a remote town or area that is regarded as lacking the facilities and sophistication of the city (informal humorous) [Early 20C. Mock Australian Aboriginal]

woosh n, vi another spelling of **whoosh**

Wootton /wŭtt'n/, **Barbara Frances, Baroness Wootton of Abinger** (1897–1988) British social scientist. Her writings include *Testament for Social Science* (1950), a pioneering study of the nature of social science. Born **Adam, Barbara Frances**

woozy /wŏŏzi/ (-**ier**, -**iest**) adj **1.** weak and unsteady or dizzy **2.** confused or unable to think clearly [Late 19C. Origin ?]—**woozily** adv—**wooziness** n

wop /wop/ n a highly offensive term for an Italian person (taboo) [Early 20C. < Italian dialect *guappo* 'tough, bold' < Spanish *guapo* 'dandy']

wop-wops /wóp wops/ n NZ a rural or isolated region (informal)

Worcester /wŏŏstər/ **1.** city and administrative centre of Worcestershire, west-central England. Population: 93,353 (2001). **2.** city in central Massachusetts, west of Boston. Population: 174,962 (2002 estimate).

Worcester china, **Worcester porcelain**, **Worcester** n a fine china made in Worcester since 1751, or the articles made from this china

Worcester sauce n a thin pungent table sauce flavoured with soya, tamarind, and spices, originally made in Worcestershire. ANZ, N Am term **Worcestershire sauce**

Worcestershire /wŏŏstərshər/ county of west-central England. It was abolished in 1974, but restored as an administrative county in 1998. Area: 1735 sq. km/670 sq. mi.

Worcestershire sauce n FOOD same as **Worcester sauce**

Worcs. abbr Worcestershire

word /wurd/ n **1.** MEANINGFUL UNIT OF LANGUAGE SOUNDS a meaningful sound or combination of sounds that is a unit of language or its representation in a text **2.** BRIEF UTTERANCE a brief comment, announcement, discussion, or conversation ○ *Could I have a word with you in my office, please?* **3.** INFORMATION information or news about somebody or something ○ *Is there any word on your daughter?* **4.** RUMOUR rumour or gossip ○ *The word is that she's leaving the company.* **5.** PROMISE a promise, assurance, or guarantee ○ *I give you my word.* **6.** COMMAND a command, order, or authorization ○ *He gave the word to attack.* **7.** PASSWORD a password or verbal signal ○ *Don't let anyone in unless they give the word.* **8.** COMPUT FIXED NUMBER OF PROCESSED BITS a number of bits processed as a single unit by a computer, e.g. 32, 48, or 64 ■ **words** npl **1.** ANGRY TALK angry or quarrelsome speech ○ *had words with him over the shoddy merchandise he sold us* **2.** TEXT OF SONG the text or lyrics of a song, musical, or opera ■ vt (**words, wording, worded**) PHRASE SOMETHING to express something in words [Old English < Indo-European]—**worded** adj ◇ **a man of his word, a woman of her word** somebody who keeps his or her promise ◇ **bandy words (with somebody)** to have an argument or discussion with somebody, often one that is unnecessary or a waste of time ◇ **be as good as your word** to do as promised ◇ **eat your words** to admit humbly that you were wrong or mistaken (informal) ◇ **get a word in edgeways** to succeed in speaking when other people are talking nonstop (usually used in negative statements) ◇ **in a word** briefly or very concisely expressed ◇ **my word** used to express surprise or astonishment (dated) ◇ **put in** or **say a good word for somebody** to speak well of or recommend somebody ◇ **put something into words** to express something such as a feeling or emotion clearly ◇ **put words in somebody's mouth** to say that somebody has said something when in fact he or she did not say it ◇ **the ... word** used after a letter of the alphabet to indicate a word beginning with that letter that you wish to avoid saying but that can be understood from the context ○ *the F word*

Word n **1.** in Christian theology, the divine rational principle as epitomized by Jesus Christ **2.** in Christianity, the Bible or Scriptures, considered as revealing divine truth

wordage /wúrdij/ n **1.** NUMBER OF WORDS the number of words in a text **2.** WORDS COLLECTIVELY words considered as a group **3.** WORDINESS the use of too many words to express something **4.** WORDING OF SOMETHING the choice of words made by a writer or speaker

word association n a method of assessing somebody's mental state or personality by asking the person to respond with the first word that comes to mind when a given word is heard

word blindness n MED same as **alexia**—**word-blind** adj

wordbook /wúrd bŏŏk/ n a dictionary, vocabulary, or lexicon

wordbreak /wúrd brayk/ n the point in a word where it can be divided if there is insufficient room at the end of a line for the entire word

word class n a category of words that have the same form or function, e.g. parts of speech

word count n the calculation of the number of words in a piece of text, or the result of such a calculation

word deafness n the loss of the capacity to understand spoken words, especially when caused by a cerebral lesion—**word-deaf** adj

word finder n a book that lists words according to meaning or subject, designed to help users find the word that best expresses the meaning they want to convey

word for word adv **1.** in exactly the same words as originally used **2.** by translating each word used in a spoken or written piece of foreign language individually—**word-for-word** adj

word game n **1.** a game in which players have to construct, find, or change the form of words **2.** a piece of disingenuous language intended to mislead, misrepresent, conceal, or put a spin on a usually awkward situation or issue (slang; often used in the plural) ○ *Please stop the word games and give me a truthful answer.*

word-hoard n the total number of words that somebody is able to use or understand

wording /wúrding/ *n* the choice of words made by a writer or speaker

wordless /wúrdləss/ *adj* **1.** communicating without the use of speech **2.** incapable of speech, especially temporarily —**wordlessly** *adv* —**wordlessness** *n*

Word of God *n* CHR same as **Word** (sense 2)

word of honour *n* a solemn promise or undertaking to do something

word of mouth *n* communication using the spoken word —**word-of-mouth** *adj*

word-perfect *adj* **1.** memorized, spoken, or sung with total accuracy. N Am term **letter-perfect 2.** accurate in every detail

word picture *n* a vivid description of something in words

wordplay /wúrd play/ *n* the witty, subtle, or ingenious use of words, e.g. in taking advantage of their multiple meanings

word processing *n* the creation, retrieval, modification, storage, and printing of text using a computer or other electronic equipment (*hyphenated before a noun*)

word processor *n* **1.** MACHINE FOR MANIPULATING TEXT a piece of electronic equipment that has a keyboard and video display unit and is used to create, retrieve, modify, store, and print text. It is usually not as advanced as a personal computer. **2.** COMPUTER PROGRAM FOR MANIPULATING TEXT a computer program that is used to create, retrieve, modify, store, and print text **3.** SOMEBODY PROCESSING WORDS somebody who does word processing

wordsmith /wúrd smith/ *n* somebody who uses words skilfully, e.g. a professional writer or journalist

word square *n* a puzzle consisting of a square grid to be constructed of words that read the same vertically and horizontally

word stress *n* the placing of stress on the syllables of a word, or an instance of this

Wordsworth /wúrdz wurth/, **Dorothy** (1771–1855) British writer. She was the sister and companion of William Wordsworth. Her journals, which are literary documents in their own right, shed valuable light on her brother's life and work.

> 'But as we went along there were more and yet more and at last under the boughs of the trees, we saw that there was a long belt of them along the shore, about the breadth of a country turnpike road. I never saw daffodils so beautiful they grew among the mossy stones about and about them, some rested their heads upon these stones as on a pillow for weariness and the rest tossed and reeled and danced and seemed as if they verily laughed with the wind that blew upon them over the lake.'
> [Dorothy Wordsworth, *The Grasmere Journals*; 15 April 1802]

Wordsworth, William (1770–1850) British poet. *Lyrical Ballads* (1798), written with Samuel Taylor Coleridge, was the seminal work of English romantic poetry. His greatest work is the autobiographical epic *The Prelude* (1850). See Cultural note at **prelude** —**Wordsworthian** /wúrdz wúrthi ən/ *adj*

> 'I wandered lonely as a cloud / That floats on high o'er vales and hills, / When all at once I saw a crowd, / A host, of golden daffodils.'
> [William Wordsworth, 'I Wandered Lonely as a Cloud', *Poems in Two Volumes*; 1807]

> 'Poetry is the spontaneous overflow of powerful feelings: it takes its origin from emotion recollected in tranquillity.'
> [William Wordsworth, *Lyrical Ballads (2nd ed.)*; 1800]

> 'Our birth is but a sleep and a forgetting: / The Soul that rises with us, our life's Star, / Hath had elsewhere its setting, / And cometh from afar: / Not in entire forgetfulness, / And not in utter nakedness, / But trailing clouds of glory do we come / From God, who is our home.'
> [William Wordsworth, 'Ode: Intimations of Immortality from Recollections of Early Childhood', *Poems in Two Volumes*; 1807]

word wrap, word wrapping *n* a feature of word-processing programs in which a word that exceeds a preset line length is moved automatically to the next line

wordy /wúrdi/ (**-ier, -iest**) *adj* **1.** using an excessive number of words in writing or speech **2.** relating to or consisting of words —**wordily** *adv* —**wordiness** *n*

SYNONYMS ***wordy, verbose, long-winded, rambling, prolix, diffuse***

CORE MEANING: not concisely expressed

wordy using an excessive number of words in writing or speech ○ *I need a clear concise summary of the relevant material rather than an exhaustive and wordy report.* ○ *He has played some of the theatre's wordiest parts, including Prospero and King Lear.* **verbose** expressed in or using too many words ○ *His memoirs, at 1088 pages, are as long and verbose as his political speeches.* ○ *a verbose and self-pitying excuse* **long-winded** tediously wordy in speech or writing ○ *a very long-winded question* ○ *The records were infuriatingly terse about important things, and long-winded about trivial ones.* **rambling** continuing for too long and with many changes of subject ○ *a rambling 15-page letter* ○ *He told a series of long, rambling stories to which he forgot the punch lines.* **prolix** tiresomely wordy ○ *His lengthy and prolix instructions are no help at all.* **diffuse** lacking organization and conciseness, especially in writing or speech ○ *Section 4 of the 1938 Act has been described as being turgid and diffuse.*

wore past tense of **wear**[1]

work /wurk/ *n* **1.** PAID JOB paid employment at a job ○ *people looking for work* **2.** DUTIES OF JOB the duties or activities that are part of a job or occupation ○ *Much of my work involves talking on the phone.* **3.** SOMEBODY'S PLACE OF EMPLOYMENT the place where somebody is employed ○ *spends all her time at work* **4.** TIME SPENT AT PLACE OF EMPLOYMENT the time that somebody spends carrying out his or her job ○ *I'll meet you after work.* **5.** PURPOSEFUL EFFORT the physical or mental effort directed at doing or making something ○ *It was a lot of work, but it was worth it.* **6.** FUNCTION the function of completing a process or carrying out a task ○ *Computers have taken over the work of filing.* **7.** SOMETHING DONE OR MADE something that has been done or made as part of a job or as a result of effort or activity requiring skill (*often used in combination*) ○ *Your work is not satisfactory.* **8.** SOMETHING MANUFACTURED something that has been or is in the process of being worked on or manufactured **9.** ARTISTIC OR INTELLECTUAL CREATION an artistic or intellectual composition, e.g. a book, treatise, painting, sculpture, film, or piece of music (*often used in the plural*) **10.** PHYS MEANS FOR ENERGY TRANSFER the transfer of energy, measured as the product of the force applied to a body and the distance moved by that body in the direction of the force. Symbol *W* ■ *v* (**works, working, worked**) **1.** *vi* HAVE JOB to have a paid job **2.** *vti* EXERT EFFORT to exert physical or mental effort in order to do, make, or accomplish something, or make somebody do this ○ *worked without a break till evening* ○ *He works his staff hard.* **3.** *vti* FUNCTION to function or operate, or make something do this ○ *The television doesn't work.* ○ *Do you know how to work the burglar alarm?* **4.** *vi* BE SUCCESSFUL to be effective or achieve a desired result ○ *Our relationship just isn't working.* **5.** *vti* WORK IN SPECIFIC PLACE to carry on an operation or activity in a particular place or area ○ *You'll be working the southern region.* **6.** *vi* EXERT INFLUENCE to produce results or exert an influence ○ *Everything seemed to be working against them.* **7.** *vti* SHAPE SOMETHING to shape, bend, form, or forge a material, or be shaped, bent, formed, or forged ○ *worked the malleable metal* **8.** *vt* CULTIVATE LAND to cultivate land in order to grow crops on it **9.** *vt* ACHIEVE SOMETHING to effect something or bring something about ○ *Attention to detail can work wonders.* **10.** *vti* ATTAIN PARTICULAR CONDITION to attain a particular condition slowly or gradually, or cause something to do this ○ *The screw worked itself loose.* **11.** *vti* MOVE SLOWLY AND WITH EFFORT to move or progress slowly and with effort, or make something do this ○ *He worked his way through the crowd.* **12.** *vt* N Am SOLVE MATHEMATICAL PROBLEM to solve a mathematical problem or puzzle **13.** *vti* EXERCISE to move or exercise a muscle or part of the body, or be moved or exercised **14.** *vt* PROVOKE EMOTIONAL RESPONSE IN SOMEBODY to arouse or stir up emotions in somebody ○ *worked the crowd into a frenzy* **15.** *vt* CHARM SOMEBODY to use charm and personal influence on somebody in order to attain popularity or acclaim ○ *a politician who really knew how to work a crowd* **16.** *vt* ARRANGE SOMETHING to arrange or exploit something in order to gain an advantage (*informal*) ○ *He managed to work it so that he got every other Friday off.* **17.** *vti* FERMENT to ferment, or make something ferment **18.** *vt* HANDICRAFT MAKE SOMETHING IN NEEDLEWORK to make or decorate something by hand in needlework or embroidery **19.** *vi* MECH ENG MOVE LOOSELY to move in a loose way that results in friction and wear (*refers to machinery*) **20.** *vi* NAUT STRAIN SLIGHTLY IN ROUGH WATER to give slightly in rough water so that the joints move slightly and the fastenings become looser (*refers to boats*) **21.** *vi* SAILING SAIL INTO WIND to sail against the wind [Old English *weorc* < Indo-European] ◇ **at work 1.** engaged in employment **2.** in operation ◇ **have your work cut out (for you)** to be faced with a difficult task ◇ **make short work of somebody** *or* **something** to dispose of or deal with somebody or something very quickly ◇ **work to rule** *UK, ANZ, US* to take part in a labour protest in which workers make a point of adhering strictly to the rules of the workplace so that work will slow down

USAGE See ***wrought.***

SYNONYMS ***work, labour, toil, drudgery***

CORE MEANING: sustained effort required to achieve something

work the physical or mental effort directed at doing or making something, or the function of completing a process or carrying out a task ○ *You will have general managers to coordinate your work.* ○ *Most installation programs will do all the work for you.* **labour** work done using the strength of the body ○ *Antony did casual manual labour in his vacations.* ○ *A group spent the day cleaning up the beach, and the results of their labour was a skip full of rubbish.* **toil** hard exhausting work or effort ○ *His rough hands bore testimony to a life of toil.* **drudgery** exhausting, boring, unpleasant work ○ *the drudgery of filing, coding, and organizing reams of documents*

work back *vi Aus* to stay on late at work, with or without payment

work in *vt* **1.** to add something gradually while blending it with another substance **2.** to arrange a time or place for somebody or something in a particular situation ○ *I'll see if I can work you in on Friday.*

work off *vt* **1.** to pay back a debt by doing work instead of paying the money owed **2.** to use up or get rid of something by the effort of working ○ *worked off the extra fat*

work on, work upon *vt* **1.** AFFECT SOMEBODY OR SOMETHING to influence or attempt to influence somebody or something ○ *He's been working on her to change her decision.* **2.** MAKE OR FIX SOMETHING to spend time making, improving, or fixing something **3.** USE SOMETHING AS BASIS to use something as a starting point for further investigation or enquiry ○ *We've nothing to work on in this case.*

work out *v* **1.** *vt* SOLVE OR CALCULATE SOMETHING to solve a problem or find an answer to a question by reasoning or calculation **2.** *vt* RESOLVE DIFFICULTY to resolve differences or find a way of dealing with a difficulty **3.** *vt* THINK SOMETHING UP to devise something, especially a course of action **4.** *vt* COMPREHEND SOMEBODY OR SOMETHING to understand somebody or something fully **5.** *vi* EXERCISE to train or take part in strenuous physical exercise as a way of keeping fit ○ *How do you find the time for working out?* **6.** *vi* END SATISFACTORILY to have a satisfactory or successful result **7.** *vi* END IN PARTICULAR WAY to have a particular result **8.** *vi* MAKE TOTAL to come to a particular amount ○ *That works out at £100 each.* **9.** *vt* ACHIEVE SOMETHING BY EFFORT to succeed in doing something after working long and hard at it **10.** *vt* same as **work off** (sense 1) **11.** *vt* EXHAUST MINE BY EXTRACTION to extract all the valuable material from a mine or deposit

SYNONYMS See ***deduce.***

work over *vt* **1.** GIVE SOMEBODY BEATING to give somebody a severe beating or physical punishment (*informal*) **2.** REDO SOMETHING to do something again **3.** EXAMINE SOMETHING THOROUGHLY to work at or examine something thoroughly and in detail

work through *vt* to deal with an emotional problem by thinking about it often until it is understood or its impact is lessened

work up *v* **1.** *vt* EXCITE EMOTIONS IN SOMEBODY to arouse or stir up emotions in somebody **2.** *vt* CREATE SOMETHING to create something or cause it to grow ○ *working up a sweat* **3.** *vt* IMPROVE SOMETHING to develop, refine,

a at; aa father; aw all; ay day; ai hair; ə about, item, edible, common, circus; e egg; ee eel; hw when; i it, happy; ī ice; 'l apple; 'm rhythm; 'n fashion; o odd; ō open; ŏŏ good; oo pool; ow owl; oy oil; th thin; th this; u up; ur urge;

or improve something **4.** *vi* BECOME MORE INTENSE to grow or develop in intensity **5.** *vt* MED EXAMINE PATIENT THOROUGHLY to subject a patient to a thorough diagnostic examination
work upon *vt* same as **work on**
work up to *vt* to gradually reach a particular level by effort

workable /wúrkəb'l/ *adj* **1.** able to be accomplished or carried out ○ *The plan is not workable.* **2.** capable of being operated, handled, or shaped ○ *workable steel* —**workability** /wúrkə bílləti/ *n* —**workably** *adv*

workaday /wúrkə day/ *adj* **1.** ordinary or forming part of the experience of most people **2.** suitable for work or for a working day [Mid-16C. Origin ?]

workaholic /wúrkə hóllik/ *n* somebody who has a compulsive need to work hard and for very long hours (*informal*) —**workaholism** *n*

workaround /wúrkə rownd/ *n* a technique that enables somebody to overcome a fault in a computer program or system without actually putting the fault or defect right

workbag /wúrk bag/ *n* a bag for holding materials and tools for work, especially sewing or knitting

workbasket /wúrk baaskit/ *n* a basket for holding materials and tools for work, especially sewing or knitting

workbench /wúrk bench/ *n* a table or surface on which work is done, e.g. by a carpenter or mechanic

workboat /wúrk bōt/ *n* a boat used solely for work, e.g. for fishing or transporting cargo

workbook /wúrk bo͝ok/ *n* **1.** STUDENT'S EXERCISE BOOK a book of exercises and questions for students, usually with spaces for answers to be written in **2.** INSTRUCTION BOOK a book of instructions on how to do or operate something **3.** RECORD OF WORK a book in which a record is kept of work done or to be done

work camp *n* **1.** a camp where volunteers, especially young people or members of a religious organization, work on a project of benefit to the community **2.** a camp in which prisoners are forced to work

workday /wúrk day/ *n N Am* **1.** same as **working day 2.** same as **working day** (sense 2) ■ *adj US* same as **workaday**

worked /wurkt/ *adj* produced, decorated, or treated with craft and skill

worked up *adj* full of anger or another strong emotion (*informal*)

worker /wúrkər/ *n* **1.** PERSON OR THING THAT WORKS a person, animal, or device that is engaged in or used for a task of some kind **2.** EMPLOYEE an employee of a person, company, or organization **3.** MEMBER OF WORKING CLASS a member of the working class, especially a factory employee or manual labourer **4.** INSECTS INSECT THAT WORKS a member of a colony of social insects, especially sterile females, that carry out all the work such as gathering food or feeding larvae

worker participation *n* the involvement of ordinary employees in making decisions at all levels in a business

worker-priest *n* a Roman Catholic priest who also has a secular job

workers' compensation *n* **1.** in the United States, a form of insurance required from employers that provides money as compensation for workers who are injured at work or contract an occupational disease **2.** in the United States, money paid as compensation to a worker who is injured at work or contracts an occupational disease

workers' cooperative *n* a business that is owned jointly by those who work in it

Workers' Revolutionary Party *n* a Marxist political party in the United Kingdom

work ethic *n* a dedication to work, or belief in the moral value of hard work ○ *hasn't got much of a work ethic*

work experience *n* time spent by a student doing a job in an ordinary work environment in order to give him or her experience of employment

workfare /wúrk fair/ *n* a government scheme that obliges unemployed people to do community work or attend training schemes in return for benefit payments [Mid-20C. Blend of WORK + WELFARE]

workflow /wúrkflō/ *n* the progress or rate of progress of work done by a business, department, or person

workforce /wúrk fawrss/ *n* **1.** all of the workers employed in a company or industry **2.** all of the people who are employed or able to work, e.g. in a country

Work for the Dole *n Aus* an Australian federal government scheme providing unemployed people with work experience

work function *n* the minimum energy needed to remove an electron from within a solid to a point outside its surface in a vacuum. Symbol Φ

work-harden *vt* to increase the hardness or strength of a metal by subjecting it to compression, tension, or another mechanical process

workhorse /wúrk hawrss/ *n* **1.** HORSE USED FOR HEAVY WORK a horse used for heavy work such as hauling **2.** HARD-WORKING PERSON somebody who works hard and diligently, often assuming extra duties (*informal*) **3.** RELIABLE TOOL OR MACHINE something that performs well over long periods, e.g. a machine

workhouse /wúrk howss/ (*plural* **-houses** /-howziz/) *n* formerly, a publicly run institution in Britain and Ireland in which people living in poverty were given food and accommodation in return for unpaid work

work-in *n* a form of industrial action in which the workers of a business that is threatened with closure occupy the premises, but continue to work

working /wúrking/ *adj* **1.** FUNCTIONING capable of being used or operated **2.** WORN AT WORK suitable for use while at work **3.** HAVING PAID JOB engaged in doing paid work **4.** SPENT AT WORK taken up with work ○ *all his working life* **5.** GIVEN OVER TO WORK spent doing work at a time when work is not normally done ○ *a working lunch* **6.** ADEQUATE good enough for a purpose, though not perfect or complete ○ *a working knowledge of Italian* **7.** PROVIDING BASIS usable as a basis for further work ○ *a working theory* ■ *n* **1.** PROCESS OF SHAPING SOMETHING the shaping, bending, forming, or forging of a material **2.** JERKING MOTION the convulsive involuntary motion of a part of the body, caused by excitement or tension (*formal*) ■ **workings** *npl* **1.** FUNCTIONING OF SOMETHING the operation of something, or the way in which it operates ○ *the workings of the government* **2.** MECHANISM INSIDE DEVICE the internal mechanism of a device **3.** PARTS OF MINE BEING WORKED the parts of a mine or quarry in which work is carried on

working capital *n* **1.** the money that a business has available for use **2.** the amount of current assets that remains after current liabilities are deducted

working class *n* **1.** the part of society made up of people who work for hourly wages, not salaries, especially manual or industrial labourers (*often used in the plural*) **2.** in Marxist theory, the proletariat or revolutionary class

working-class *adj* relating to or belonging to the part of society made up of people who work for hourly wages, not salaries, especially manual or industrial labourers ○ *a working-class neighbourhood*

working day *n* **1.** a day on which people work, usually, but not always, a weekday **2.** the part of a day during which somebody works ▶ N Am term **workday**

working dog *n* a dog that is kept in order to do work such as herding, guarding, or guiding. Among breeds of working dog are the collie, Doberman pinscher, Alsatian, and husky.

working drawing *n* a detailed scale drawing of something, used as a guide in building or manufacturing

working girl *n* (*informal*) **1.** a young woman who works for a living **2.** a woman who is a prostitute

working group *n US* same as **working party**

working hours *npl* the part of the day during which most people usually work and shops and offices are open

working man *n* a man who works for wages, especially at manual labour

working memory *n* the contents of somebody's consciousness at the present moment

working paper *n* a document created as a basis for discussion rather than as an authoritative text

working party *n* a group of people appointed to study and report back on a subject. US term **working group**

working storage *n* the amount of storage in a computer's memory that is assigned for data stored only while a program is running

working substance *n* a substance, especially a fluid, that undergoes changes in form or degree that are used to operate something such as an engine

working title *n* the provisional title by which a project, especially a film or novel, is known while it is still being worked on

Workington /wúrkingtən/ town and port in Cumbria, northwestern England. Population: 25,579 (1991).

working week *n* the amount of hours or days worked in a week. N Am term **workweek**

working woman *n* a woman who works for wages, not a salary, especially in a manual job

work in progress *n* an incomplete ongoing piece of work, especially an artistic work

workless /wúrkləss/ *adj* having no work or employment —**worklessness** *n*

workload /wúrk lōd/ *n* **1.** the amount of work assigned to a person or group to do in a specific period **2.** the amount of work that a machine does or can do in a specific period

workman /wúrkmən/ (*plural* **-men** /-mən/) *n* **1.** a man who works for wages, not a salary, especially at a manual job **2.** a man described or judged according to his skill or diligence as a worker ○ *a tidy workman*

workmanlike /wúrkmən līk/, **workmanly** /-li/ *adj* done in a way that is thorough and satisfactory, but not imaginative or exciting

workmanship /wúrkmənship/ *n* **1.** ART OR SKILL OF WORKER the skill or craft of a worker or artisan **2.** QUALITY OF SKILL the level of skill used in making or doing something **3.** PRODUCT OR RESULT OF WORKER'S SKILL the product or result of the skill of a worker or artisan

workmate /wúrk mayt/ *n* somebody who works with or in the same place as another

work of art *n* **1.** a piece of fine art, e.g. a painting or sculpture **2.** something made or done exceptionally well ○ *The second goal was an absolute work of art.*

workout /wúrk owt/ *n* **1.** a session of strenuous physical exercise or of practising physical skills as a way of keeping fit or as practice for a game or athletics competition **2.** a tough practical test of the capability or performance of a person, animal, or device

workpeople /wúrk peep'l/ *npl* people who work for wages, not a salary, especially in manual jobs

workpiece /wúrk peess/ *n* something that has been, or is in the process of being, worked on or manufactured

workplace /wúrk playss/ *n* the place where somebody works, e.g. a factory or office

work print *n* a print of a film used in various stages of editing and as a guide in cutting the original negative from which the final commercial prints are made

work rage *n* feelings of violent anger experienced by people as a result of stress or frustration at work and often leading to outbursts of violent or destructive behaviour

work release *n N Am* a system of allowing prisoners to take on paid work outside prison while serving their sentences

workroom /wúrk room, -ro͝om/ *n* a room in which work is done, especially one equipped for manual work

works /wurks/ *n* (*plural same*) PLACE FOR INDUSTRIAL PRODUCTION a place where industrial work, especially manufacturing, is done ○ *an engineering works* ■ *npl* **1.** INNER MECHANISM the interior moving parts of a mechanism ○ *The works of the clock are rusty.* **2.** ACTS deeds or actions **3.** EVERYTHING all things that are available (*informal*) ○ *a hot dog with the works* **4.** SYRINGE FOR INJECTING NARCOTICS a syringe used to inject narcotics (*slang*) **5.** *US* BAD BEATING a severe beating or punishment (*slang*) ◇ **in the works** being prepared or worked on

works council, **works committee** *n* a group of representatives of employers and employees in a company who meet to discuss matters of common interest relating to the running of the business

worksheet /wúrk sheet/ *n* **1. SHEET OF QUESTIONS FOR STUDENTS** a sheet of questions or tasks for students on a recent lesson **2. SHEET RECORDING WORK** a sheet of paper used for keeping a record of work done or scheduled **3. SHEET FOR DRAFT** a sheet of paper used for making a rough draft or preliminary notes

workshop /wúrk shop/ *n* **1.** a place where manual work is done, especially manufacturing or repairing **2.** a group of people working on a creative project, discussing a topic, or studying a subject ○ *a songwriting workshop*

workshy /wúrk shī/ *adj* lazy and unwilling to work [Early 20C. Translation of German *arbeitsscheu*]

work song *n* a song sung by people working, usually with a repetitive rhythm that guides the rhythm of the work being done

Worksop /wúrk sop/ town in Nottinghamshire, east-central England. Population: 37,247 (1991).

workspace /wúrk spayss/ *n* an area set aside for an individual worker or a business

workstation /wúrk staysh'n/ *n* **1. WORKING AREA** a small area in a workplace assigned to one worker, especially a desk with a computer **2. TERMINAL OF NETWORK OR MAINFRAME** a computer terminal, usually connected to a network in a business environment, that runs application programs and serves as an access point to the network **3. POWERFUL SPECIALIZED COMPUTER** a powerful stand-alone computer, often with a high-resolution display, used for computer-aided design and other complex and specialized applications

work stoppage *n* an occasion when a group of employees stop work, often as a protest or as a bargaining tool

work-study *n* an investigation into the most efficient way of doing a job ■ *adj N Am* combining an academic programme with paid employment in which a student gains practical experience in the workplace

work surface *n* same as **worktop**

worktable /wúrk tayb'l/ *n* a table at which work such as writing or drawing is done

worktop /wúrk top/ *n* a rigid flat surface on which work is done, especially the flat top fitted onto kitchen units, used when preparing food. US term **work surface**

work-to-rule *n UK, ANZ, US* a labour protest in which workers make a point of adhering strictly to the rules of the workplace so that work will slow down

workup /wúrk up/ *n* a complete diagnostic medical examination

workwear /wúrk wair/ *n* clothes worn at work, especially at manual work

workweek /wúrk week/ *n N Am* same as **working week**

workwoman /wúrk wŏŏmən/ (*plural* **-women** /-wimin/) *n* SOC SCI same as **working woman**

world /wurld/ *n* **1. PLANET EARTH** the planet Earth **2. EARTH AND EVERYTHING ON IT** the Earth, including all of its inhabitants and the things upon it **3. HUMAN RACE** all of the human inhabitants of Earth ○ *Soon, the world would know the truth.* **4. SOCIETY** human society ○ *in the eyes of the world* **5. PART OF EARTH** a particular part of the Earth, considered in terms of time or space ○ *the western world* **6. AREA OF ACTIVITY** a particular area of human activity and the people involved in it ○ *the world of fashion* **7. UNIVERSE** all the galaxies that are known or thought to exist in space **8. DOMAIN** a sphere, realm, or domain ○ *the world of reptiles* **9. INHABITED BODY** an astronomical body considered to be inhabited, e.g. a planet ○ *the alien worlds of science fiction* **10. EVERYTHING IN SOMEBODY'S LIFE** all that relates to or makes up somebody's life ○ *Her entire world collapsed.* **11. CONDITION OF EXISTENCE** a condition or state of existence ○ *the world of tomorrow* **12. GREAT DEAL OR AMOUNT** a very large amount, degree, or distance ○ *They're still worlds apart.* **13. SECULAR EXISTENCE** secular life and its ways ○ *a woman of the world* ■ *adj* **1. OF ENTIRE WORLD** relating to the entire world ○ *the world champions* **2. EXERTING INFLUENCE GLOBALLY** exerting influence over the whole of the world ○ *a world figure* **3. AFFECTING WHOLE WORLD** involving or affecting the whole of the Earth ○ *a world crisis* [Old English *woruld* 'human existence, age, Earth' < Germanic, 'age of man'] ◇ **come down in the world** to have less money or power than previously ◇ **for all the world** exactly and in every detail ◇ **have the best of both worlds** to have the advantage of the best features of two different situations ◇ **in the world** used to add intensity to a question, often indicating surprise or disbelief on the part of the questioner ○ *What in the world have you done?* ◇ **it's a small world** used to express surprise at a coincidence such as unexpectedly meeting somebody you know in a distant place ◇ **not for the world** no matter what happens ○ *Not for the world would I think of doing such a thing.* ◇ **out of this world** extraordinarily good (*informal*) ◇ **the world is your oyster** there are limitless opportunities available for you to be successful ◇ **think the world of somebody** to be extremely fond of somebody

World Bank *n* a specialized agency of the United Nations, established in 1944, that guarantees loans to member nations for the purpose of reconstruction and development. Official name **International Bank for Reconstruction and Development**

world-beating *adj* surpassing all others in a particular field —**world-beater** *n*

world-class *adj* ranked among the best or most prominent in the world ○ *a world-class downhill racer*

World Council of Churches *n* an international ecumenical organization, founded in 1948, that links Protestant and Eastern churches from around the world for the purpose of coordinated and cooperative action in religious and secular areas

World Court *n* LAW same as **International Court of Justice**

World Cup *n* a sports tournament, especially in football, contested by the national teams of qualifying countries, held every four years in a different country of a different continent

world economy *n* the economy of the world, considered as an international exchange of goods and services

World English *n* the English language in all its varieties as it is spoken and written throughout the world

world-famous *adj* renowned throughout the world

World Health Organization *n* a specialized agency of the United Nations that helps countries to improve their health services and coordinates international action against diseases

World Heritage Site *n* an area or structure designated by UNESCO as being of global significance and conserved by a country that has signed a United Nations convention pledging its protection

world language *n* **1.** a language that is used in many countries, e.g. English, Spanish, or Arabic **2.** a language created for international use, e.g. Esperanto or Interlingua

world leader *n* **1.** the leader of a politically and economically powerful country **2.** a company, organization, or country that is the biggest or best in a particular field

world line *n* the path of a particle in time and space, which is straight if the particle moves in a uniform way

worldling /wúrldling/ *n* somebody more interested in everyday material things than in spiritual matters

worldly /wúrldli/ *adj* **1. BELONGING TO PHYSICAL WORLD** relating to everyday material existence ○ *all my worldly goods* **2. MATERIALISTIC** much more interested in everyday materialistic concerns than in the spiritual side of life **3. EXPERIENCED IN LIFE** experienced in and knowledgeable about human society and its ways —**worldliness** *n*

worldly-minded *adj* same as **worldly** (senses 2–3)

worldly-wise *adj* same as **worldly** (sense 3)

world music *n* popular music from or influenced by countries outside the Western world and its traditions

world power *n* a country or alliance of countries powerful enough to influence events on a global scale

World Series *tdmk* a trademark for a series of baseball games played in the United States, between the winners of the American League and the National League to decide the major leagues championship

world's fair *n* an exhibition of commercial and cultural products from many different countries

world-shaking, **world-shattering** *adj* same as **earth-shattering**

world soul *n* in some beliefs, a spirit that animates the world in the same way that the human soul is believed to animate the body

World Trade Center *n* a complex of buildings containing two skyscrapers in New York City, destroyed with great loss of life in a terrorist attack using two hijacked aircraft on 11 September 2001. The complex was completed in 1972, and the twin towers, 110 storeys high, were at one time the tallest in the world.

World Trade Organization *n* an international organization founded in 1995 to promote and regulate trade between countries. It was created to replace GATT.

world view, **worldview** /wúrld vyoo/ *n* a comprehensive and usually personal conception or view of humanity, the world, or life [Translation of German *Weltanschauung*]

world war *n* a war involving a number of countries on each side, with fighting spread over much of the world

World War I *n* a war fought mainly in Europe from 1914 to 1918, in which an alliance including Great Britain, France, Russia, Italy, and the United States defeated the alliance of Germany, Austria-Hungary, Turkey, and Bulgaria

World War II *n* a war fought in Europe, Africa, and Asia from 1939 to 1945, in which an alliance including Great Britain, France, the Soviet Union, and the United States defeated the alliance of Germany, Italy, and Japan

world-weary *adj* tired of or bored with life —**world-weariness** *n*

worldwide /wúrld wīd/ *adj* affecting or found throughout the entire world ■ *adv* all over the world

World Wide Web *n* a system for accessing, manipulating, and downloading a very large set of hypertext-linked documents and other files located on computers connected through the Internet

World Wide Web Consortium *n* ONLINE full form of **W3C**

worm /wurm/ *n* **1. LONG CYLINDRICAL INVERTEBRATE** an invertebrate that has a slender, soft, cylindrical or flat body and no apparent appendages, especially an annelid, nematode, or flatworm (*often used in combination*) **2. INSECT LARVA** the larva of an insect, e.g. a caterpillar, grub, or maggot **3. ANIMAL LOOKING OR MOVING LIKE WORM** an animal that looks or moves like a worm, e.g. the shipworm or the slowworm **4. OFFENSIVE TERM** an offensive term for somebody regarded as contemptible, especially because of behaving in a grovelling way (*insult*) **5. SOMETHING THAT TORMENTS** something that torments, undermines, or corrupts somebody from within ○ *a worm of discontent* **6. SPIRAL CONDENSER IN STILL** a spiral pipe in a still in which alcohol condenses **7.** COMPUT **INVASIVE COMPUTER PROGRAM** a computer program that invades computers on a network, replicates itself to prevent deletion, interferes with the host computer's operation, and often carries a virus **8.** MECH ENG **THREADED SHAFT** a shaft with a helical thread that is the part of a gear that meshes with a toothed wheel ■ *v* (**worms, worming, wormed**) **1.** *vt* **PROCEED DEVIOUSLY** to make your way or advance yourself deviously or obsequiously ○ *wormed her way out of trouble* **2.** *vt* **OBTAIN SOMETHING DEVIOUSLY** to obtain something from somebody by devious or underhanded means ○ *They wormed his secret out of him.* **3.** *vt* VET, MED **TREAT SOMEBODY FOR PARASITIC WORMS** to treat a person or animal in order to prevent or remove an infestation of parasitic worms **4.** *vi* **MOVE LIKE WORM** to move in a slow, slithering way **5.** *vt* **WIND YARN ROUND ROPE** to wind yarn round a rope so as to give it a smooth surface **6.** *vi* **SEARCH FOR WORMS** to search for worms, especially for use as fishing bait [Old English *wurm* < Indo-European] —**wormer** *n* —**wormish** *adj*

WORM /wurm/ *n* a computer storage medium, usually optical, in which data cannot be changed after it is stored but can be read. Full form **write once read many (times)**

worm burner *n* (*slang*) **1.** a shot in golf or football that travels close to the surface of the ground **2.** a sailboarding manoeuvre that involves swinging the mast through 360 degrees while balancing on the tail of the board

wormcast /wúrm kaast/ *n* a small spiral mound of

earth or sand that has been excreted by a burrowing earthworm or lugworm

worm-eaten *adj* **1.** EATEN INTO BY WORMS weakened by burrowing worms **2.** DECAYED affected by decay or rot **3.** DILAPIDATED old or worn out

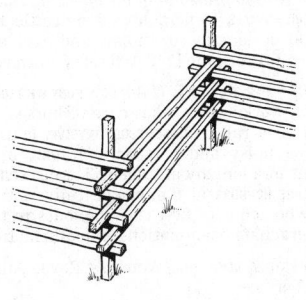

worm fence

worm fence *n* a fence consisting of crossed poles that support interlocking rails in a zigzag pattern

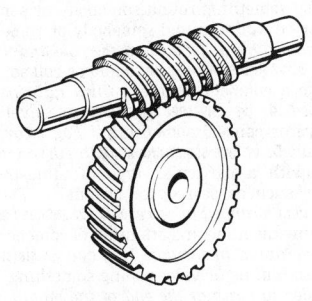

worm gear

worm gear *n* **1.** a gear consisting of a shaft with a helical thread that meshes with a toothed wheel to transfer rotary motion between two shafts at right angles to one another **2.** MECH ENG same as **worm wheel**

worm grass *n* PLANTS same as **pinkroot** (sense 2)

wormhole /wúrm hōl/ *n* **1.** a hole made by a burrowing worm, e.g. in wood **2.** a hypothetical passage in space-time connecting widely separated parts of the universe —**wormholed** *adj*

worm lizard *n* REPT same as **amphisbaena** (sense 1)

worms /wurmz/ *n* an infestation of parasites, especially pinworms or tapeworms, affecting the intestines or other parts of a person's or animal's body (*takes a singular verb*)

Worms /wurmz, vawrmz/ historic city in Rhineland-Palatinate State, southwestern Germany. Population: 79,521 (1997).

wormseed /wúrm seed/ *n* a plant whose seeds or other parts are used as a treatment for infestation by parasitic worms

worm's-eye view *n* a view of somebody or something from a lower or inferior position

worm snake *n* a small nonvenomous snake with vestigial eyes. Native to: central and eastern United States. Genus: *Carphophis*.

worm wheel *n* the toothed wheel that meshes with the threaded shaft in a worm gear

wormwood /wúrm woŏd/ *n* **1.** a plant that yields a bitter extract. Use: flavouring for absinthe, formerly, medicine for intestinal worms. Genus: *Artemisia*. **2.** something that causes somebody to feel bitter (*literary*) ○ *Her ingratitude was wormwood to him.* [14C. By folk etymology < Old English *wermod*, by association with WORM, because the plant was used as medicine for intestinal worms]

wormy /wúrmi/ *adj* **1.** full of or eaten into by worms **2.** resembling or characteristic of a worm —**worminess** *n*

worn /wawrn/ past participle of **wear**[1] ■ *adj* **1.** SHOWING EFFECTS OF WEAR weakened or frayed by use **2.** SHOWING EFFECTS OF FATIGUE showing the effects of fatigue, worry, illness, or age **3.** HACKNEYED used so much as to have lost meaning ○ *trite, worn phrases* —**wornness** *n*

SPELLCHECK See *warn.*

worn-out *adj* (*not hyphenated after a verb*) **1.** DAMAGED OR WEAKENED BY LONG USE so damaged or affected by prolonged use as to be no longer usable **2.** EXHAUSTED very tired **3.** OUTDATED no longer relevant, useful, or fashionable

worrisome /wúrrissəm/ *adj* **1.** causing worry, anxiety, or distress **2.** having a tendency to worry —**worrisomely** *adv*

worrit /wúrrit/ *v* (**-rits, -riting, -rited**) *vti regional* same as **worry** *v* (senses 1–2)

worry /wúrri/ *v* (**-ries, -rying, -ried**) **1.** *vti* BE OR MAKE ANXIOUS to feel anxious about something unpleasant that may have happened or may happen, or make somebody do this **2.** *vt* ANNOY SOMEBODY to annoy somebody by making insistent demands or complaints **3.** *vt* TRY TO BITE ANIMAL to try to wound or kill an animal by biting it ○ *a dog suspected of worrying sheep* **4.** *vt* same as **worry at** (sense 1) **5.** *vi* PROCEED DESPITE PROBLEMS to proceed persistently despite problems or obstacles **6.** *vt* TOUCH SOMETHING REPEATEDLY to touch, move, or interfere with something repeatedly ○ *Stop worrying that button or it'll come off.* ■ *n* (*plural* **-ries**) **1.** ANXIOUSNESS a troubled unsettled feeling **2.** CAUSE OF ANXIETY something that causes anxiety or concern **3.** PERIOD OF ANXIETY a period spent feeling anxious or concerned [Old English *wyrgan* 'strangle'] —**worried** *adj* —**worriedly** *adv* —**worriedness** *n* —**worrier** *n* —**worrying** *adj* —**worryingly** *adv* ◇ **not to worry** used to tell somebody that something is not important and need not be a cause of concern (*informal*) ○ *Not to worry. We'll do better next time.* ◇ **no worries** used to say that something is no trouble or is not worth mentioning (*informal*)

SYNONYMS *worry, unease, care, anxiety, angst, stress*
CORE MEANING: a troubled state of mind
worry a troubled unsettled feeling ○ *I was beside myself with worry.* ○ *Unemployment was his major source of worry.* **unease** a feeling of anxiety, awkwardness, or discomfort ○ *The announcement provoked considerable unease among UN officials.* ○ *There was a silence, laden with unease.* **care** (*literary or formal*) a troubled state of mind arising from worry or concern ○ *worn down with care and grief* **anxiety** nervousness or agitation, often about something that is going to happen ○ *Although she has been teaching for eight years, she always feels a twinge of anxiety at the beginning of a new term.* **angst** any feeling of dread or anxiety ○ *suffering from loneliness, insecurity and general teenage angst* **stress** mental, emotional, or physical strain caused, for example by anxiety or overwork ○ *a class in breathing techniques to help control the stress of everyday life*

worry at *vt* **1.** to shake or tear at something with the teeth ○ *a dog worrying a bone* **2.** to think about a problem repeatedly in an effort to find a solution

worry beads *npl* a string of beads for fingering or playing with when feeling tense

worryguts /wúrri guts/ (*plural same*) *n* somebody who tends to worry needlessly (*informal*) Aus, US term **worrywart**

wors /vawrss/ *n* S Africa FOOD same as **boerewors** (*informal*)

worse /wurss/ comparative of **bad, badly, ill** ■ *adj* **1.** LESS GOOD THAN SOMETHING ELSE less good in quality or effect than before or than somebody or something else ○ *did a worse job on the decorating than the previous workers* **2.** MORE SEVERE more severe than before or than something else of the same kind ○ *Her fever is worse this morning.* **3.** SICKER more ill than before ○ *The patient is worse today.* ■ *adv* TO WORSE DEGREE to a degree worse than before ■ *n* SOMETHING WORSE somebody or something that is worse than another ○ *Of the two of them, this one's the worse.* [Old English *wyrsa* < Germanic] ◇ **be none the worse for something** to experience no harm or ill effects from something ◇ **if worse comes to worst** if the situation reaches an intolerable state

worsen /wúrss'n/ (**-ens, -ening, -ened**) *vti* to become worse, or cause something to become worse

worser /wúrssər/ comparative of **bad** (*nonstandard*)

worship /wúrship/ *v* (**-ships, -shipping, -shipped**) **1.** *vti* TREAT SOMEBODY OR SOMETHING AS DEITY to treat somebody or something as divine and show respect by engaging in acts of prayer and devotion **2.** *vi* TAKE

PART IN RELIGIOUS SERVICE to take part in a religious service **3.** *vt* LOVE SOMEBODY DEEPLY to love, admire, or respect somebody or something greatly and perhaps excessively or unquestioningly ■ *n* **1.** RELIGIOUS ADORATION the adoration, devotion, and respect given to a deity **2.** RELIGIOUS RITES the rites or services through which people show their adoration, devotion, and respect for a deity **3.** GREAT DEVOTION great or excessive love, admiration, and respect felt for somebody or something [Old English *weortscipe* 'condition of worth' < *weorth* 'worth'] —**worshipper** *n* —**worshippingly** *adv*

Worship *n* UK, Can a title of respect for a mayor, magistrate, or other similar dignitary ○ *His Worship, the Mayor*

~~worshiped~~ incorrect spelling of **worshipped**

worshipful /wúrshipf'l/ *adj* **1.** showing or expressing deep reverence and devotion **2.** *also* **Worshipful** used as the honouring adjective in the titles of some dignitaries such as mayors, and of the ancient guild companies of the City of London —**worshipfully** *adv* —**worshipfulness** *n*

worst /wurst/ superlative of **bad, badly, ill** ■ *adj* LEAST GOOD least good, most unpleasant, or most unfavourable ○ *your worst enemy* ○ *My worst forebodings were soon realized.* ■ *adv* LEAST WELL in the least good, most unpleasant, or most unfavourable way ■ *n* LEAST GOOD THING the least good, least pleasant, or least favourable aspect or part of something, or the worst thing that could happen or be done ○ *fear the worst* ○ *The worst was over.* ■ *vt* (**worsts, worsting, worsted**) DEFEAT SOMEBODY to get the better of or defeat an opponent ○ *We were worsted by the visiting team.* [Old English *wyrsta* < Indo-European, 'confuse'] ◇ **get the worst of it** to be defeated, or get the least benefit from something

worst case *n* the least desirable, most disastrous situation or result that can be envisaged (*hyphenated before a noun*) ○ *the worst-case scenario*

worsted /woŏstid/ *n* **1.** smooth closely-woven woollen cloth without a nap, made from tightly twisted yarn **2.** the tightly twisted yarn, made from long-fibred wool, from which worsted cloth is made [13C. After the village of *Worstead* in Norfolk.]

wort[1] /wurt/ *n* a medicinal plant. This word survives mainly in plant names such as 'liverwort' and 'woundwort'. (*usually used in combination*) [Old English *wyrt* < Indo-European, 'branch, root']

wort[2] /wurt/ *n* a sugary liquid produced from crushed malted grain and water, to which yeast and hops are added in the brewing of beer [Old English *wyrt* < Germanic]

worth /wurth/ *n* **1.** VALUE IN MONEY the value of something, especially in terms of money ○ *The necklace has little real worth, but it means a lot to me.* **2.** AMOUNT EQUALLING GIVEN VALUE the amount of something that can be bought for a particular sum of money or that will last for a particular length of time ○ *twenty pounds' worth of petrol* **3.** MORAL OR SOCIAL VALUE the goodness, usefulness, or importance of something or somebody, irrespective of financial value or wealth ○ *A diploma from that place has little worth.* **4.** WEALTH the wealth of a person, group, organization, or other entity ■ *adj* **1.** EQUAL TO PARTICULAR AMOUNT equalling in value to a particular amount ○ *How much is it worth?* ○ *a painting worth thousands* **2.** IMPORTANT ENOUGH TO JUSTIFY SOMETHING important, large, or good enough to justify something ○ *His friendship is not worth having.* [Old English *weorp* < Indo-European, 'turn'] ◇ **for all you are worth** as fast, energetically, or enthusiastically as possible ◇ **for what it's worth** used to suggest that what you say may not be true or of much value ○ *Here's my opinion on the issue, for what it's worth.*

Worthing /wúrthing/ seaside resort in West Sussex, southeastern England. Population: 97,568 (2001).

worthless /wúrthləss/ *adj* **1.** having no financial or other value or usefulness **2.** having no good, attractive, or admirable qualities at all —**worthlessly** *adv* —**worthlessness** *n*

worthwhile /wúrth wīl/ *adj* rewarding or beneficial enough to justify the time taken or the effort made [Mid-17C. Shortening of *worth the while*] —**worthwhileness** *n*

USAGE *Worthwhile* is now usually written as one word, and the traditional rule that it should be written as two

words after a verb (*It seemed worth while* but *It was a worthwhile thing to do*) is largely disappearing.

worthy /wúrthi/ *adj* (**-thier, -thiest**) **1.** DESERVING fully deserving something, usually as a suitable reward for merit or importance ○ *That remark is not worthy of a reply.* **2.** RESPECTABLE morally upright, good, and deserving respect ○ *a worthy person* **3.** GOOD BUT DULL having good qualities, good intentions, or the best of motives, but being boring and pedestrian ○ *a worthy attempt at playing the concerto* ■ *n* (*plural* **-thies**) SOMEBODY GOOD OR MORAL a good, morally upright, or reputable person (*often ironic*) ○ *colonial governors and other 18th-century worthies* —**worthily** *adv* —**worthiness** *n*

wot[1] /wot/ *pron, det, adv* another spelling of **what** (*humorous or informal*) ○ *Wot they done then?*

wot[2] /wot/ **1.** 1st person singular present of **wit**[2] **2.** 3rd person singular present of **wit**[2] (*archaic*)

Wotan /vō taan, -tan/ *n* in Germanic mythology, the supreme god and the god of war. He corresponds to Odin in Norse mythology.

wotcher /wóchər/, **wotcha** /wóchə/ *interj* same as **hello** (*slang*) [Late 19C. Contraction of *what cheer*]

would *stressed* /wŏŏd/; *unstressed* /wəd/ CORE MEANING: used to express the sense of 'will' in reported speech or when referring to an event that has not happened yet ○ *Susan didn't think she would pass.* ○ *It would be wrong to suggest otherwise.*

modal v **1.** USED WITH 'IF' CLAUSES used in stating what will or suggesting what might happen under the circumstances described in the conditional clause ○ *You would know him if you saw him.* ○ *My mother would be annoyed if I were late.* **2.** POLITE REQUEST used in making polite requests or offers ○ *Would you mind closing the window?* ○ *Would you like more coffee?* **3.** HABITUAL ACTION used to indicate that a past action was habitual ○ *Every Sunday we would drive out to Henley.* ◇ **would that** used to introduce a strong desire or wish, usually one that is not expected to be fulfilled (*formal*) ○ *Would that we had never met.*

SPELLCHECK See ***wood***.

USAGE See ***should***.

would-be *adj* desiring or aspiring to do or be something ○ *a would-be poet* ■ *n* somebody who is hoping or trying to become something or achieve the status of something (*informal*) ○ *The reception was attended by all the major candidates for office and other would-bes.*

wouldn't /wŏŏdd'nt/ *contr* would not

wouldst /wŏŏdsst, wŏŏtsst/ 2nd person singular past of **will**[1] (*archaic*)

would've /wŏŏddəv/ *contr* would have (*informal*)

USAGE See ***of***.

Woulfe bottle /wŏŏlf-/ *n* a container with more than one neck. Use: bubbling gases through liquids. [After Peter *Woulfe* (1727?–1803), English chemist]

wound[1] /woond/ *n* **1.** INJURY TO BODY an injury in which the skin, tissue, or an organ is broken by some external force such as a blow or surgical incision, with damage to the underlying tissue **2.** EMOTIONAL INJURY a lasting emotional or psychological injury ○ *still recovering from the wounds of a bitter divorce* ■ *vti* (**wounds, wounding, wounded**) **1.** INJURE to cause a wound in the body of somebody or something, especially using a knife, gun, or other weapon ○ *He was wounded in the leg.* **2.** CAUSE EMOTIONAL WOUND to cause somebody emotional or psychological distress by saying or doing something ○ *cutting remarks intended to wound* [Old English *wund* < Indo-European, 'to beat'] —**woundable** *adj* —**wounded** *adj* —**wounder** *n* —**wounding** *adj* —**woundingly** *adv* —**woundless** *adj*

SYNONYMS See ***harm***.

wound[2] /wownd/ past participle, past tense of **wind**[3]

Wounded Knee /woondid née/ village in South Dakota. In 1890 it was the site of a massacre of Native North Americans in which between 150 and 370 Sioux people were killed, most of them unarmed.

wound up /wównd-/ *adj* extremely tense, nervous, and agitated (*informal*) ○ *a litigator who is really wound up the night before trial*

woundwort /woond wurt/ (*plural* **-worts** or *same*) *n* **1.** betony or a related plant of the mint family. Use: formerly, to treat wounds. Genus: *Stachys*. **2.** any plant formerly used to treat wounds

wove HANDICRAFT past tense of **weave**[1]

woven /wṓv'n/ HANDICRAFT past participle of **weave**[1] ■ *adj* made or manufactured by the process of weaving ○ *woven synthetic textiles*

wove paper *n* paper made using a roller with a fine mesh that leaves a faint mesh imprint

wow[1] /wow/ (*informal*) *interj* EXPRESSING SURPRISE used to express surprise, admiration, wonder, or pleasure ■ *vt* (**wows, wowing, wowed**) IMPRESS SOMEBODY GREATLY to impress or delight somebody greatly ○ *The acrobats wowed the audience with their daring moves.* ■ *n* GREAT SUCCESS a great success or an object of great admiration [Early 16C. Natural exclamation]

wow[2] /wow/ *n* a distortion in recorded sound in the form of slow fluctuations in the pitch of long notes, caused by variations in the speed of the reproducing or recording equipment [Mid-20C. An imitation of the acoustic effect]

WOW *abbr* INDUST waiting on weather

wowser /wówzər/ *n ANZ* (*informal*) **1.** somebody who disapproves of activities such as drinking and dancing **2.** somebody regarded as spoiling other people's fun [Late 19C. Origin ?]

WP *abbr* **1.** weather permitting **2.** LAW without prejudice **3.** word processing **4.** word processor

WPA *abbr* HIST Work Projects Administration

W particle *n* an elementary particle with a relatively large mass and a positive or negative charge, believed to mediate weak interactions between other particles in which the charges on the particles change

WPB, w.p.b. *abbr* wastepaper basket

WPC *abbr* woman police constable

WPGA *abbr* Women's Professional Golfers' Association

WPI *abbr* FIN wholesale price index

wpm *abbr* MEASURE words per minute

wpn *abbr* ARMS weapon

Wraac /rak/ *n Aus* a member of the Women's Royal Australian Army Corps

WRAAC /rak/ *abbr Aus* Women's Royal Australian Army Corps

WRAAF /raf/ *abbr Aus* Women's Royal Australian Air Force

WRAC /rak/ *abbr* Women's Royal Army Corps

wrack[1] /rak/ *n* **1.** SEA VEGETATION seaweed floating in the sea or growing on the shoreline **2.** BROWN SEAWEED any brown seaweed, e.g. bladder wrack. Family: Fucaceae. **3.** WRECKED SHIP a wrecked ship, especially one driven onto the shore (*archaic*) **4.** WRECKAGE wreckage, or a piece of wreckage (*archaic*) ■ *vti* (**wracks, wracking, wracked**) WRECK OR BE WRECKED to wreck something, or be wrecked (*archaic*) [14C. < Dutch *wrak* 'wreck']

SPELLCHECK See ***rack***[1].

wrack[2] /rak/ *n* another spelling of **rack**[6]

SPELLCHECK See ***rack***[1].

WRAF /raf/ *abbr* Women's Royal Air Force

Wragge /rag/, **Clement** (1852–1922) British-born Australian meteorologist. He set up many of Australia's earliest meteorological observatories and introduced the practice of giving names to tropical storms. Full name **Wragge, Clement Lindley**

wraith /rayth/ *n* **1.** the supposed ghost of a dead person, or any ghostly and insubstantial apparition **2.** a vision of a person still alive, said to appear as a premonition of that person's death [Early 16C. Origin ?]

Wran /ran/ *n Aus* a member of the Women's Royal Australian Naval Service

Wrangel Island /ráng g'l-/ island in the Arctic Ocean, northeastern Russia, between the East Siberian Sea and the Chukchi Sea. Area: 4,662 sq. km/1,800 sq. mi.

Wrangell Mountains /ráng g'l-/ mountain range in southeastern Alaska, near the border with the Yukon Territory, Canada. The highest peak is Mount Blackburn, 4,996 m/16,390 ft.

wrangle /ráng g'l/ *v* (**-gles, -gling, -gled**) **1.** *vi* ARGUE PERSISTENTLY to argue persistently and angrily ○ *wrangled for hours over the wording of the agreement* **2.** *vt* GET SOMETHING BY PERSISTENT ARGUMENT to obtain something or persuade somebody by arguing persistently (*informal*) ○ *managed to wrangle a commitment to peace out of the opposing side* **3.** *vt N Am* HERD ANIMALS to herd horses or cattle ■ *n* LONG ARGUMENT a lengthy or noisy and bad-tempered argument or dispute [14C. Ultimately < Germanic]

wrangler /ráng glər/ *n* **1.** *N Am* SOMEBODY WHO LOOKS AFTER HORSES a worker who takes care of horses kept for riding on a ranch **2.** SOMEBODY INVOLVED IN LENGTHY ARGUMENT a noisy and persistent arguer, or a participant in a lengthy argument **3.** MATHS STUDENT WITH FIRST CLASS HONOURS at Cambridge University, somebody who achieves first class honours in the final undergraduate examinations in mathematics

WRANS /ranz/ *abbr Aus* Women's Royal Australian Naval Service

wrap /rap/ *v* (**wrapping, wraps, wrapped**) **1.** *vt* COVER SOMETHING UP to cover something up by winding or folding a pliable material such as cloth or paper around it ○ *The package was wrapped in plain brown paper.* **2.** *vti* COIL AROUND SOMETHING to wind, fold, or clasp something round somebody or something else, or be wound round somebody or something ○ *He wrapped his arms around the pole and wouldn't let go.* **3.** *vt* FOLD SOMETHING UP to fold or roll something up into a compact bundle ○ *linen napkins neatly wrapped* **4.** *vt* ENVELOP SOMETHING to envelop and obscure or conceal something ○ *Fog wrapped the harbour.* **5.** *vt* GIVE SOMETHING AURA to surround something with a particular type of atmosphere or quality such as secrecy or scandal ○ *The whole affair was wrapped in secrecy.* **6.** *vt* ENGROSS SOMEBODY to occupy the mind and attention of somebody fully ○ *was wrapped in thought* **7.** *vi* CINEMA FINISH FILMING to finish filming or video-taping something ○ *We're scheduled to wrap at the end of the month.* **8.** *vi N Am* FINISH to come to an end ○ *'The government's antitrust case ... was supposed to wrap by the end of the year.'* (*Newsweek*; November 1998) **9.** *vti* COMPUT TAKE SOMETHING OVER TO NEXT LINE to take a word or piece of text over to the next line automatically on reaching the margin, or be taken over in this way **10.** *also* **rap** *vt Aus* PRAISE SOMEBODY to sing somebody's praises ■ *n* **1.** OUTER GARMENT an outer garment to be wrapped or folded around the wearer, e.g. a shawl, cloak, or coat **2.** INDUST MATERIAL FOR WRAPPING material, or a piece of material, used to wrap something **3.** CINEMA COMPLETION OF FILMING the completion of filming or video-taping something ○ *All right, everybody, that's a wrap!* **4.** FOOD FILLED TORTILLA SANDWICH a sandwich consisting of fillings enclosed in a tortilla ○ *a ham and cheese wrap* **5.** *Aus* PIECE OF PRAISE a praising comment or assessment of something (*informal*) ■ *adj* CLOTHING same as **wraparound** *adj* (sense 1) [14C. Origin ?] ◇ **keep something under wraps** to keep something secret ○ *Our new product is being kept under wraps for the moment.*

SPELLCHECK See ***rap***[1].

wrap up *v* **1.** *vt* COVER SOMETHING WITH MATERIAL to cover something completely with material such as paper, plastic, or foil **2.** *vi* DON WARM CLOTHES to put on warm clothes for protection from the cold, wind, or rain ○ *Wrap up well, it's freezing outside.* **3.** *vt* COMPLETE SOMETHING to complete something or bring it to an end (*informal*) ○ *We'll wrap up the editing phase of the project next week.* **4.** *vt US* SUMMARIZE SOMETHING to give a short final summary of something such as the news **5.** *vi* BE SILENT to stop talking and be silent (*informal; usually used as a command*) **6.** *vt Aus* PRAISE SOMEBODY to sing somebody's praises (*informal*) ◇ **wrapped up in somebody** *or* **something** completely absorbed by or preoccupied with somebody or something ○ *She is completely wrapped up in her career.*

wraparound /ráp ə rownd/ *adj* **1.** *also* **wrapround** /ráp rownd/ *or* **wrapover** /ráp ōvər/ DESIGNED FOR WRAPPING AROUND BODY designed to be worn wrapped around the body and tied in position with one edge overlapping the other, rather than fastened with buttons or a zip **2.** CURVING AROUND SIDES curving around the sides of whatever it is fitted to ○ *a wraparound porch* ■ *n* **1.** *also* **wrapround** *or* **wrapover** WRAPAROUND GARMENT a wraparound skirt or other piece of clothing **2.** WRAPAROUND FITMENT a fitment that is shaped to curve around the sides of something **3.** COMPUT COMPUTER FUNCTION AUTOMATICALLY STARTING NEW LINE a function of a

computer program or visual display unit that makes text automatically begin a new line as soon as the last character space in the previous line is filled **4.** PUBL **PAPER STRIP AROUND BOOK'S DUST COVER** a strip of paper fastened around the dust cover of a book, e.g. to announce a price reduction **5.** PRINTING **PLATE FOR ATTACHING TO PRESS CYLINDER** a plate of flexible material that can be attached to the cylinder of a rotary press

wrapped /rapt/ *adj Aus* extremely pleased (*informal*) [Mid-20C. Blend of *wrapped (up in)* + RAPT]

wrapper /rápper/ *n* **1.** **MATERIAL WRAPPED AROUND SOMETHING** the paper, plastic, or other material wrapped around something that is sold **2.** PUBL same as **dust jacket 3.** **PAPER AROUND MAGAZINE OR NEWSPAPER** a piece of paper wrapped around a magazine or newspaper sent by post **4.** **TOBACCO LEAF FORMING OUTSIDE OF CIGAR** a tobacco leaf wrapped around a cigar to form its outer skin **5.** *US* **LOOSE LOUNGING GARMENT** a garment that wraps loosely around the body, e.g. a dressing gown

wrapping /rápping/ *n* the paper, plastic, or other material used to wrap something

wrapping paper *n* specially decorated paper used for wrapping gifts

wraparound *n, adj* CLOTHING same as **wraparound**

wrap-up *n* **1.** *US* a short summary at the end of something such as a news bulletin **2.** *Aus* a praising comment or assessment of something (*informal*)

wrasse /rass/ (*plural* **wrasses** or *same*) *n* a fish with protruding lips and well-developed canine teeth. Native to: temperate and tropical seas. Family: Labridae. [Late 17C. < Cornish *wrah* 'old woman']

wrath /roth/ *n* **1.** **GREAT ANGER** strong anger, often with a desire for revenge **2.** **DIVINE RETRIBUTION** in some beliefs, God's punishment for sin **3.** **VENGEANCE** the vengeance, punishment, or destruction wreaked by somebody in anger (*literary*) [Old English *wrǣþþu* < *wrāþ* 'angry'] —**wrathful** *adj* —**wrathless** *adj*

SYNONYMS See *anger.*

Wrath, Cape /roth/ the most northwesterly point of mainland Scotland

Wray /ray/, **Fay** (*b.* 1907) Canadian-born US actor. She starred in several films of the early sound era, most notably *King Kong* (1933). Full name **Wray, Vina Fay**

wreak /reek/ (**wreaks, wreaking, wreaked**) *vt* **1.** **CAUSE DESTRUCTION** to cause havoc or destruction ○ *a storm that wreaked vast destruction* **2.** **INFLICT REVENGE** to inflict revenge or punishment on somebody **3.** **EXPRESS ANGER OR HATRED** to express anger, hatred, or another violent emotion in action against somebody (*literary*) [Old English *wrecan* 'drive out' < Indo-European] —**wreaker** *n*

SPELLCHECK See *reek.*

USAGE See *wrought.*

wreath /reeth/ (*plural* **wreaths** /reethz, reeths/) *n* **1.** **CIRCULAR ARRANGEMENT OF FLOWERS** a circular arrangement of flowers or greenery placed as a memorial on a grave, hung up as a decoration, or put on somebody's head as a sign of honour **2.** **REPRESENTATION OF WREATH** a representation of a circular arrangement of flowers, vines, or other things, e.g. in a carving or on a coat of arms **3.** **CIRCULAR SHAPE** a hollow circular shape formed by something such as smoke [Old English *wriþa* < *wrīþan* (see WRITHE)] —**wreathless** *adj*

SPELLCHECK **wreath** or **wreathe**? Do not confuse the spelling of **wreath** and **wreathe**. **Wreath** is a noun, meaning 'a circular arrangement of flowers or greenery' or 'a hollow circular shape', as in *lay a wreath at the base of the monument, wreaths of smoke.* **Wreathe** is a verb, meaning 'encircle', 'intertwine', or 'coil': *Mist wreathes the mountains in the early morning.*

wreathe /reeth/ (**wreathes, wreathing, wreathed**) *v* **1.** *vt* **PUT WREATH ON OR AROUND SOMETHING** to encircle, surround, or cover something with a wreath or wreaths or a similar type of decoration **2.** *vt* **MAKE SOMETHING INTO WREATH BY INTERTWINING** to make things into a wreath by twisting and intertwining them **3.** *vti* **WRITHE OR COIL** to move in coils, curves, or spirals, or cause something to move in coils, curves, or spirals [Mid-16C. Partly < WREATH, partly back-formation < *wrethen* 'twisted', obsolete past participle of WRITHE]

SPELLCHECK See *wreath.*

wreck /rek/ *vt* (**wrecks, wrecking, wrecked**) **1.** **DESTROY OR DAMAGE SOMETHING** to destroy something completely or damage it beyond repair **2.** **DESTROY SHIP** to cause a ship to sink or run aground and be destroyed ■ *n* **1.** **DESTRUCTION OF SHIP** the sinking or destruction at sea of a ship from accidental causes **2.** **BADLY DAMAGED SHIP** a very badly damaged or sunken ship **3.** **REMAINS OF SOMETHING DESTROYED** something that has been totally destroyed, or its shattered remains **4.** **SOMETHING BADLY DAMAGED** something that is in very poor condition, damaged, or dilapidated **5.** **SOMEBODY LOOKING OR FEELING TERRIBLE** somebody who is physically or emotionally exhausted or broken down **6.** **DESTRUCTION** the ruin or destruction of something **7.** **CARGO FROM WRECKED SHIP** cargo or other goods that are washed ashore after a shipwreck **8.** *N Am* same as **crash**[1] *n* (sense 1) [13C. Via Anglo-Norman *wrec* < N Germanic]

wreckage /rékij/ *n* **1.** the broken pieces left after something has been extremely badly damaged or destroyed **2.** the ruin or destruction of something (*formal*)

wrecked /rekt/ *adj* **1.** very tired or exhausted (*informal*) **2.** in an intoxicated or drugged state (*slang*)

wrecker /rékər/ *n* **1.** **DESTROYER OR SPOILER** somebody who destroys or spoils something, especially deliberately, maliciously, or with pleasure **2.** *N Am* **SOMEBODY DEMOLISHING BUILDINGS OR DISMANTLING CARS** somebody whose job is to demolish buildings or dismantle old cars for salvage **3.** *N Am* AUTOMOT same as **breakdown lorry 4.** **SOMEBODY LURING SHIPS TO DESTRUCTION** in former times, somebody who lured ships onto rocks in order to steal the cargo or other goods on board

wrecker's ball *n N Am* CONSTR same as **wrecking ball**

wreckfish /rék fish/ (*plural same* or **-fishes**) *n* FISH same as **stone bass** [Late 19C. < its habit of following wreckage]

wrecking ball *n* a heavy ball attached by a cable to a crane and swung to knock down parts of buildings that are being demolished

wrecking bar *n* a short crowbar forked at one end and bent at the other to provide leverage

Wrekin /réekin/ hill in Shropshire, west-central England, near the River Severn. Height: 407 m/1,335 ft.

wren

wren /ren/ *n* **1.** a small songbird with a slender down-turned beak, usually brown feathers, and a short upright tail. Native to: Europe, Asia, North and South America. Family: Troglodytidae. **2.** BIRDS same as **fairy wren** [Old English *wrenna*]

Wren /ren/ *n* a member of the former Women's Royal Naval Service [Early 20C. < WRNS]

Sir Christopher Wren: portrait medal by G. D. Gaab

Wren /ren/, **Sir Christopher** (1632–1723) English architect, scientist, and mathematician. The founder of the English baroque style, he designed St Paul's Cathedral, London (1675–1710) and some 50 other London churches as well as residences and public buildings. He was also a noted mathematician and inventor, and a founding member of the Royal Society.

'Architecture has its political use; public buildings being the ornament of a country; it establishes a nation, draws people and commerce; makes the people love their native country.'
[Sir Christopher Wren, *Parentalia*; 1750]

wrench /rench/ *v* (**wrenches, wrenching, wrenched**) **1.** *vti* **PULL AND TWIST SOMETHING AWAY** to pull something away forcefully, often using a twisting movement **2.** *vt* **INJURE SOMETHING BY TWISTING** to injure part of the body by twisting it suddenly and forcibly **3.** *vt* **DISTRESS SOMEBODY** to make somebody feel very sad or distressed **4.** *vt* **SKEW MEANING OR FUNCTION** to distort something in order to make it mean or appear to be something different ■ *n* **1.** **FORCEFUL TWISTING PULL** a forceful twisting pull at something, especially to free it **2.** **ADJUSTABLE SPANNER** a spanner, especially a large one, with adjustable jaws **3.** *N Am* CONSTR same as **spanner 4.** **SADNESS AND LOSS ON PARTING** a difficult parting from a person or place, or the feelings of sadness and loss that accompany such a parting ○ *Leaving New York was a terrible wrench after having lived there for 30 years.* **5.** **SURGE OF EMOTION** a sudden surge of emotion such as pity or empathy ○ *the wrench we felt when viewing film footage of the flood's devastation* **6.** **SPRAIN CAUSED BY TWISTING** a sprain caused by a sudden forceful twisting movement of a part of the body [Old English *wrencan* < Indo-European, 'to turn']

wrest /rest/ *vt* (**wrests, wresting, wrested**) **1.** **GAIN CONTROL OR POWER** to take something such as control or power from somebody in the face of opposition or resistance **2.** **PULL SOMETHING AWAY FORCIBLY** to seize something away forcibly **3.** **GET SOMETHING WITH EFFORT** to get or extract something with an effort or struggle **4.** **ALTER SOMETHING'S MEANING** to change or twist the meaning of something ■ *n* **FORCEFUL PULL** a sharp wrench or pull at something [Old English *wrǣstan* < Germanic] —**wrester** *n*

wrestle /réss'l/ *v* (**-tles, -tling, -tled**) **1.** *vti* **FIGHT BY GRIPPING AND PUSHING** to fight somebody using special holds and moves in an attempt to force his or her shoulders onto a mat **2.** *vti* **HAVE STRUGGLING FIGHT** to fight with somebody by gripping and pushing rather than hitting **3.** *vi* **HAVE DIFFICULTY** to struggle to deal with something difficult or intractable ○ *I spent the evening wrestling with my accounts.* **4.** *vti* **MANOEUVRE SOMETHING AWKWARD** to struggle to lift or move something ○ *We wrestled the trunk down the hall.* ■ *n* **1.** **FIGHT BETWEEN WRESTLERS** a wrestling match, or a fight in which people wrestle rather than hit each other **2.** **DIFFICULT STRUGGLE** a struggle to deal with something difficult or intractable [Old English. < *wrǣstan* (see WREST)] —**wrestler** *n*

wrestling /réssling/ *n* **1.** a sport in which two contestants fight by gripping each other using special holds, each trying to force the other's shoulders onto a mat **2.** the action of having a struggling fight with somebody

wretch /rech/ *n* **1.** **SOMEBODY WHO IS PITIED** a troubled or distressed person who evokes pity in others **2.** **ANNOYING PERSON** somebody who causes mild irritation or annoyance (*humorous*) **3.** **DESPICABLE PERSON** somebody viewed with contempt or disapproval (*informal*) [Old English *wrecca* < W Germanic]

SPELLCHECK See *retch.*

wretched /réchid/ *adj* **1.** **UNHAPPY OR ILL** feeling very unhappy or ill **2.** **APPEARING MISERABLE OR DEPRIVED** in a state of great hardship, deprivation, and hopelessness and arousing sympathy in others ○ *living in wretched conditions* **3.** **INADEQUATE OR OF LOW QUALITY** seriously inadequate or of very low quality **4.** **IRRITATING** provoking irritation or anger ○ *The wretched car won't start!* —**wretchedly** *adv* —**wretchedness** *n*

Wrexham /réksəm/ town in northeastern Wales, near the border with England. Population: 128,416 (2001).

wrick *vt, n* MED another spelling of **rick**[2]

wriggle /rígg'l/ *v* (**-gles, -gling, -gled**) **1.** *vti* TWIST AND TURN to make small quick twisting and turning movements with the body, or cause the body to move in this way **2.** *vi* MOVE WHILE TWISTING AND TURNING to move by making quick twisting and turning movements ○ *managed to wriggle out of the sleeping bag* ■ *n* **1.** TWISTING OR TURNING MOVEMENT a small quick twisting or turning movement **2.** TWISTING PASSAGE OR COURSE a twisting passage or line [14C. Probably < Middle Low German *wriggelen* < *wriggen* 'to turn'] —**wriggler** *n* —**wriggly** *adj*

wriggle out of *vt* to avoid doing something or suffering the consequences of something by making excuses or using deception

Wright /rīt/, **Billy** (1924–94) British footballer. As captain of England, he was the first player to win more than 100 caps. His club was Wolverhampton Wanderers. Born **Wright, William Ambrose**

Library of Congress

Frank Lloyd Wright

Wright, Frank Lloyd (1867–1959) US architect. The clean lines of his designs, his use of new materials, and his consideration of the environment around his buildings made him one of the most influential modern architects. Fallingwater (1937), a house that extends over a waterfall in Bear Run, Pennsylvania, is one of his best known designs.

> 'No house should be ever on a hill or on anything. It should be of the hill, belonging to it, so hill and house could live together each the happier for the other.'
> [Frank Lloyd Wright, *Autobiography*; 1932]

Wright, Joseph (1734–97) British painter. His genre scenes and portraits show the striking effects of light. Known as **Joseph Wright of Derby**

Wright, Joseph (1855–1930) British philologist. He wrote books on philology and was editor of the *English Dialect Dictionary* (1896–1905).

Wright, Judith (1915–2000) Australian poet. Her works display concern for the environment and sympathy with Australia's Aboriginals. Full name **Wright, Judith Arundell**

Wright, Peter (1916–95) British intelligence officer. He worked for MI5 (1955–76). The British government failed to suppress publication of his autobiography *Spy Catcher* (1987).

Library of Congress

Wilbur (right) and Orville Wright

Wright Brothers /rīt brŭthərz/ US inventors and aviation pioneers. Wilbur (1867–1912) and Orville (1871–1948) made the first successful flight of a powered aircraft at Kitty Hawk, North Carolina (1903).

> 'The airplane stays up because it doesn't have the time to fall.'
> [Attributed to Wright Brothers]

wring /ring/ *vt* (**wrings, wringing, wrung** /rung/) **1.** TWIST AND COMPRESS SOMETHING to twist and compress something in order to force liquid out of it ○ *Wring the towel out and hang it up to dry.* **2.** FORCE OUT LIQUID BY TWISTING to force liquid out of something by twisting and compressing it **3.** EXTRACT SOMETHING WITH DIFFICULTY to extract something from somebody with great difficulty ○ *finally managed to wring an answer out of him* **4.** TWIST SOMETHING FORCIBLY AND PAINFULLY to twist something such as an animal's neck forcefully, usually causing pain or death **5.** CAUSE DISTRESS to cause somebody emotional pain and distress ■ *n* TWIST GIVEN TO WET MATERIAL a twist or squeeze given to wet material in order to force out water or other liquid [Old English *wringen* < Germanic]

SPELLCHECK See *ring*[1].

wringer /ríngər/ *n N Am* same as **mangle**[2] ◇ **put somebody through the wringer** to subject somebody to a very difficult or stressful experience (*informal*)

wringing wet /rínging-/ *adj* extremely wet

wrinkle /ríngk'l/ *n* **1.** FACIAL LINE FROM AGEING a line or crease between small folds of skin that forms on the face as a result of ageing or exposure to the sun **2.** SMALL FOLD IN MATERIAL a small untidy or unintentional fold in cloth or paper **3.** PROBLEM something that causes trouble or inconvenience ○ *We need to iron out the wrinkles in the plan before implementing it.* **4.** NEW FEATURE an ingenious trick, method of doing something, or feature of something (*informal*) ○ *We've added a couple of new wrinkles to the policy.* ■ *vti* (**-kles, -kling, -kled**) **1.** MAKE OR GET SMALL UNTIDY FOLDS to make small untidy or unintentional folds in something, or come to have untidy folds ○ *This fabric wrinkles easily.* **2.** MAKE OR GET LINES ON SKIN to develop lines in the skin as a result of ageing or exposure to the sun, or to cause such lines to develop **3.** CONTRACT PART OF FACE to tighten the muscles in part of the face so that it contracts or creases, or be tightened in this way ○ *wrinkled her nose* [14C. Origin ?] —**wrinkled** *adj*

wrinkly /ríngkli/ *adj* (**-klier, -kliest**) covered with wrinkles ■ *n* (*plural* **-klies**) an offensive and condescending term for somebody of advanced age (*slang offensive*)

wrist /rist/ *n* **1.** the lower end of the forearm or the joint between the forearm and the hand together with the tissue surrounding it **2.** the part of a sleeve or glove that covers the wrist [Old English, < Germanic]

wristband /ríst band/ *n* **1.** ABSORBENT BAND WORN ROUND WRIST an absorbent band of material worn round the wrist to keep sweat from running onto the hand **2.** WATCH STRAP the strap of a wristwatch **3.** IDENTIFICATION BAND WORN ROUND WRIST an identification band worn round the wrist, e.g. when in hospital **4.** CLOTHING PART OF SOMETHING COVERING WRIST a band of material that fits over the wrist, e.g. at the end of a long sleeve or on a glove

wrist-drop *n* inability to move the muscles that raise the wrist and move the fingers, caused by damage to or compression of the radial nerve

wristlet /rístlət/ *n* a close-fitting band of material worn round the wrist, especially a decorative one that is attached to the top of a glove or the end of a sleeve

wristlock /ríst lok/ *n* a hold in wrestling in which the wrist is held and twisted, rendering an opponent helpless

wrist pin *n* MECH ENG *N Am* same as **gudgeon pin**

wrist support, wrist rest *n* a long rectangular pad in front of a keyboard on which a keyboarder's wrists can rest, designed to help prevent repetitive strain injury

wristwatch /ríst woch/ *n* a watch on a band that is worn round the wrist

wristy /rísti/ (**-ier, -iest**) *adj* using a lot of wrist movement when hitting a ball

writ[1] /rit/ *n* a written court order demanding that the addressee do or stop doing whatever is specified in the order [Old English, 'something written' < *wrītan* (see WRITE)]

writ[2] /rit/ past participle, past tense of **write** (*archaic*)

write /rīt/ (**writes, writing, wrote** /rōt/, **written** /rítt'n/) *v* **1.** *vti* PUT WORDS ON PAPER to put words, letters, numbers, or musical notation on a surface using a pen, pencil, or similar instrument **2.** *vti* CREATE BOOK, POEM, OR MUSIC to create or compose something for others to read or listen to such as a letter or note, an article, a poem, or a piece of music **3.** *vt* SPELL SOMETHING to spell a word or words ○ *two words that are written the same but mean different things* **4.** *vti* COMPOSE AND SEND LETTER to compose and send a letter to somebody ○ *I wrote her a long letter.* **5.** *vi* COMPOSE MATERIAL FOR PUBLICATION to create books, poems, or newspaper articles for publication, often as part of a job ○ *writes for a newspaper* **6.** *vt* FILL IN FORM to fill in the details on a form such as a cheque, prescription, or other document and, usually, sign it ○ *I'll write you a cheque.* **7.** *vt* EXPRESS SOMETHING IN WORDS to express something in a letter, book, or article ○ *He wrote that he would be home on Tuesday.* **8.** *vi* WORK AS WRITING TOOL to function as a writing instrument, or function in a particular way ○ *There's something wrong with this pen: it won't write.* **9.** *vti* USE CURSIVE SCRIPT to employ a cursive script when setting down words **10.** *vt* DISPLAY SOMETHING to reveal or exhibit something clearly ○ *She had glee written all over her face.* **11.** *vt* INSUR same as **underwrite** (sense 3) **12.** *vt* PREDETERMINE SOMETHING to ordain or prophesy what will happen in the future (*usually passive*) ○ *It is written in the stars.* **13.** *vt* COMPUT STORE COMPUTER DATA to transfer data to a storage medium such as a magnetic or optical disc or tape **14.** *vt* COMPUT DISPLAY SOMETHING ON SCREEN to display text or images on a computer monitor [Old English *wrītan* 'score, draw, write' < Germanic, 'to tear']

SPELLCHECK See *right*.

ORIGIN The notion underlying ***write*** is of 'cutting' or 'scratching' (it is related to German *reissen* 'to tear'). The earliest form of writing involved cutting marks on hard materials such as stone and wood, and the same word was carried over when the technique of writing moved on to pen and ink.

write away *vt* to send off an order for goods of some kind to a distant supplier ○ *wrote away for new upholstery materials*

write down *vt* **1.** RECORD SOMETHING IN WORDS to record something in writing, usually so that the information is not lost or forgotten ○ *I wrote down her address.* **2.** OVERSIMPLIFY SOMETHING FOR UNSOPHISTICATED AUDIENCE to write something in excessively simplified language for the benefit of an audience considered to be unsophisticated, inexperienced, or unintelligent **3.** WRITE DISPARAGINGLY ABOUT SOMEBODY to write slightingly or disparagingly about somebody **4.** REDUCE ENTERED VALUE OF SOMETHING to reduce the price or value of something, especially the value of an asset as entered in the accounts of a business

write in *v* **1.** *vt* WRITE DETAILS IN FORM to write additional words into a text or document ○ *wrote in all the personal health data required* **2.** *vi* WRITE TO ORGANIZATION to send a letter to an organization **3.** *vt N Am* ADD NAME TO BALLOT to add somebody's name to a ballot paper in an election in order to vote for that person

write off *v* **1.** *vi* WRITE TO ORGANIZATION to send a letter to an organization, usually in order to obtain something from it ○ *I wrote off for a brochure.* **2.** *vt* DECIDE SOMEBODY OR SOMETHING IS WORTHLESS to dismiss somebody or something as worthless or unsuccessful and not worth continued attention (*informal*) **3.** *vt* DAMAGE VEHICLE TOO BADLY TO REPAIR to damage a vehicle so badly that it is not economic to repair it **4.** *vt* REDUCE VALUE OF SOMETHING to reduce the estimated value of an asset for accounting purposes **5.** *vt* REMOVE BAD DEBT OR VALUELESS ASSET to remove a debt considered irrecoverable or an asset with no value from the accounts of a business

write out *v* **1.** *vt* WRITE SOMETHING IN COMPLETE FORM to write something in its complete form ○ *write out your name* **2.** *vt* EXPRESS SOMETHING IN WRITING to express something in written form **3.** *vt* REMOVE SOMEBODY FROM SERIES to remove a regular character from a radio or television series ○ *He's been written out of the show.* **4. write yourself out** *vr* WRITE TO POINT OF EXHAUSTION to write so much that your ideas or stamina are exhausted ○ *By midnight I was written out after 12 hours at the keyboard.*

write up *vt* **1.** WRITE SOMETHING FROM EARLIER NOTES to write a report or account of something from notes made earlier **2.** WRITE REVIEW OF SOMETHING to write a review of something such as a new play or book **3.** UPDATE JOURNAL OR DIARY to bring something such as a journal or log up to date by writing additional entries **4.** *US* REPORT SOMEBODY FOR UNLAWFUL ACT to report somebody in writing for violating a law or rule ○ *wrote the motorist up for illegal parking* **5.** *US* OVERVALUE ASSETS to overvalue corporate assets

write-down *n* a reduction in the value of an asset as entered in the books of a business

write-in *n N Am* **1.** a vote cast in an election by adding somebody's name to the ballot paper **2.** a candidate added to a ballot paper by a voter

~~writeing~~ incorrect spelling of **writing**

~~writen~~ incorrect spelling of **written**

write-off *n* **1.** VEHICLE DAMAGED BEYOND REPAIR a vehicle that is so badly damaged that it is not economic to repair it ○ *Nobody was injured but the car was a write-off.* **2.** REDUCTION IN VALUE a reduction in the estimated value of an asset **3.** SOMETHING REDUCED IN VALUE an asset that has had its estimated value reduced **4.** AMOUNT OF REDUCTION IN VALUE the monetary amount by which something such as a corporate asset has been reduced in value

write-protected *adj* describes computer storage space that cannot be altered or erased

writer /rítər/ *n* **1.** SOMEBODY WHO WRITES AS PROFESSION somebody who writes books or articles professionally **2.** PERSON WHO WROTE DOCUMENT the person who wrote a specific text or document **3.** SOMEBODY WHO CAN WRITE somebody who can write, who writes well, or who enjoys writing

writer's block *n* an inability on the part of a writer to start a new piece of writing or continue an existing one

writer's cramp *n* a muscular spasm that results from a prolonged period of writing and affects the muscles of the forearm, hand, and fingers, causing temporary cramping and pain

Writer to the Signet (*plural* **Writers to the Signet**) *n* in Scotland, a member of an ancient society of solicitors who have the exclusive power to prepare crown writs [Originally a clerk who prepared writs for the royal signet]

write-up *n* **1.** a written account of material, especially a published review of a new play, book, or film **2.** *US* a deliberate overvaluation of company assets

writhe /rīth/ *v* (**writhes, writhing, writhed**) **1.** *vi* TWIST OR SQUIRM to make violent twisting and rolling movements with the body, especially as a result of severe pain ○ *writhing in agony* **2.** *vti* MOVE IN TWISTING WAY to move in a twisting squirming way, or cause the body to move in this way **3.** *vi* EXPERIENCE STRONG EMOTION to feel a strong emotion, especially embarrassment or shame, and experience internal stress as a result of it ■ *n* WRITHING MOVEMENT a twisting or squirming movement [Old English *wrīþan* < Germanic] —**writher** *n*

writing /ríting/ *n* **1.** WORDS WRITTEN DOWN words or other symbols such as hieroglyphics written down as a means of communication **2.** WRITTEN MATERIAL written material, especially considered as the product of a writer's skill **3.** ACTIVITY OF CREATING BOOKS the activity of creating written works, especially as a job **4.** same as **handwriting** (sense 2) ■ **writings** *npl* ALL AUTHOR'S WRITTEN OUTPUT all the publications and written work of a writer ○ *Churchill's writings on the war* ◇ **see the writing on the wall** to foresee the decline or demise of something or somebody ○ *She should have seen the writing on the wall when her boss suggested a change of career.*

writing case *n* a portable case with compartments for holding paper, pens, and other materials for writing

writing desk *n* **1.** a desk with a surface for writing on and compartments for holding paper, envelopes, and other writing materials **2.** a portable case used for carrying writing materials, often with a hard surface for writing

writing paper *n* paper of a quality good enough to write on with ink

Writings /rítingz/ *npl* BIBLE same as **Hagiographa**

written past participle of **write**

Written Law *n* JUDAISM same as **Torah** (sense 2)

~~writting~~ incorrect spelling of **writing**

WRNS *abbr* HIST Women's Royal Naval Service

wrnt *abbr* LAW warrant

Wroclaw /vrót slaaf, -swaaf/ city and port in southwestern Poland, on the River Oder. Population: 639,400 (1997).

wrong /rong/ *adj* **1.** INCORRECT not correct or accurate ○ *That's the wrong answer.* **2.** MISTAKEN holding an incorrect opinion about a person, thing, or matter ○ *I thought it would be fun, but I was wrong.* **3.** NOT MEANT not the intended or desired one ○ *It was sent to the wrong address.* **4.** NOT IN NORMAL STATE not in the normal satisfactory state ○ *What's wrong with you today?* **5.** NOT CONFORMING TO ACCEPTED STANDARDS not in accordance with law, morality, or with people's sense of what is acceptable behaviour ○ *It's wrong to steal.* **6.** UNSUITABLE unsuitable, or showing poor judgment on the part of the person who chooses, does, or says it ○ *It's the wrong time of year to be planting seeds.* **7.** NOT WORKING not functioning properly ○ *Something's wrong with the TV.* **8.** NOT VISIBLE describes the side of a fabric or garment that is not intended to be seen ○ *I always iron knitted garments on the wrong side.* **9.** REVERSED OR INVERTED opposite to the normal, proper, or intended side, way, or direction ○ *This picture is the wrong way up.* ■ *adv* **1.** INCORRECTLY incorrectly or in a way that leads to failure or a different result from the one intended ○ *You've spelt that wrong.* **2.** IN WRONG DIRECTION in a direction that is different from or opposite to the right or intended direction ■ *n* **1.** ACTION NOT CONSIDERED MORAL an action or situation that does not conform to ideas of morality or justice **2.** UNACCEPTABLE BEHAVIOUR behaviour that is morally or socially unacceptable ○ *Children have to be taught the difference between right and wrong.* **3.** LAW same as **tort** **4.** LAW INFRINGEMENT OF SOMEBODY'S LEGAL RIGHTS an infringement, abridgment, or violation of another party's rights under the law ■ *vt* (**wrongs, wronging, wronged**) **1.** TREAT SOMEBODY UNJUSTLY to judge or treat somebody unjustly ○ *He felt he had been wronged.* **2.** DISCREDIT SOMEBODY to discredit somebody by saying malicious but untrue things about him or her [Old English *wrange* 'wrongful act'. The adjective *wrang* probably existed in Old English, but is not found before the 12C] —**wronger** *n* —**wrongly** *adv* —**wrongness** *n* ◇ **get somebody wrong** to misunderstand somebody ○ *Don't get me wrong: I'm very grateful for your help.* ◇ **get something wrong 1.** to make a mistake in an answer or calculation **2.** to misunderstand something ◇ **go wrong 1.** to go badly or not according to plan **2.** to make a mistake **3.** to fail to conform to ideas of morality or justice ◇ **in the wrong 1.** at fault for something **2.** mistaken ◇ **two wrongs don't make a right** an act of retaliation cannot be justified

wrongdoing /róng doo ing/ *n* behaviour or an action that fails to conform to standards of law or morality —**wrongdoer** *n*

wrong-foot *vt* **1.** to put somebody at a disadvantage or in an embarrassing position by doing or saying something unexpected **2.** in sport, to cause an opponent to anticipate wrongly the direction in which you are going to move or hit, kick, or pass a ball

wrongful /róngf'l/ *adj* not fair, just, or legal, but not punishable by criminal law ○ *wrongful dismissal* —**wrongfully** *adv* —**wrongfulness** *n*

SYNONYMS See ***unlawful***.

wrong-headed *adj* **1.** completely contrary to reason or good sense ○ *a wrong-headed notion* **2.** obstinately sticking to a false belief, opinion, or course of action —**wrong-headedly** *adv* —**wrong-headedness** *n*

wrong number *n* an incorrectly dialled telephone number that connects the caller with the wrong person

wrong'un /róngən/ *n* (*informal*) **1.** somebody regarded as having a bad character or criminal tendencies **2.** CRICKET same as **googly** [Late 19C. Contraction of *wrong one*]

wrote past tense of **write**

wroth /rōth, roth/ *adj* extremely angry (*archaic or literary*) [Old English *wrāþ* < Germanic]

wrought /rawt/ past participle, past tense of **work** (*archaic*) ■ *adj* **1.** made in a skilful or decorative way (*often used in combination*) ○ *a delicately wrought ebony screen* **2.** describes decorative metalwork shaped by hammering and welding

USAGE ***Wrought*** is an old past tense and past participle not of *wreak* (for which the past tense is *wreaked*) but of *work*: it is the equivalent of modern *worked*. ***Wrought*** survives mainly as an adjective in a few, rather specialized contexts such as *wrought iron*; it is seen also in the set phrase *What hath God wrought* (used by Samuel Morse in the first successful test of the telegraph). *Wrought havoc* is not correct; it should be *wreaked havoc*.

wrought iron

wrought iron *n* a highly refined form of iron that is easy to shape but is strong and fairly resistant to rust. Use: decorative metalwork. —**wrought-iron** *adj*

wrought-up *adj* tensely nervous, agitated, or excited

WRP *abbr* POL Worker's Revolutionary Party

WRT *abbr* POL (*used in e-mails or text messages*) **1.** with regard to **2.** with respect to

wrung past participle, past tense of **wring**

WRVS *abbr* Women's Royal Voluntary Service

wry /rī/ (**wrier** or **wryer, wriest** or **wryest**) *adj* **1.** AMUSING AND IRONIC combining or expressing a mixture of mild amusement and irony ○ *a wry remark* **2.** CHARACTERIZED BY IRONIC ACCEPTANCE characterized by or showing a slightly ironic acceptance of something that is not particularly pleasant or desirable ○ *a wry grin* **3.** TWISTED out of shape or twisted to one side [Old English *wrīgian* 'to turn' < Indo-European] —**wryly** *adv* —**wryness** *n*

wrybill /rī bil/ *n* a shorebird of the plover family whose beak is bent to one side allowing it to search for food beneath pebbles. Native to: New Zealand. Latin name: *Anarhynchus frontalis.*

wryneck /rī nek/ *n* **1.** a bird of the woodpecker family that has mottled grey-brown feathers and a short sharp beak, eats insects and lives in holes, but does not drill into trees. Native to: Europe, Asia. Latin name: *Jynx torquilla* or *Jynx ruficollis.* **2.** MED same as **torticollis**

ws *abbr* ONLINE Samoa (*used in Internet addresses*) See table at **domain name**

WSW *abbr* COMPASS west-southwest

wt *abbr* MEASURE weight

WTA *abbr* **1.** Women's Tennis Association **2.** World Tennis Association

WTC *abbr US* World Trade Center

WTO *abbr* COMM World Trade Organization

Wu /woo/ *n* a group of Chinese dialects spoken mainly in the Jiangsu and Zhejiang provinces of China, the colloquial language of Shanghai. Native speakers: 90 million. [Early 20C. < Chinese *wú*] —**Wu** *adj*

Wuhan /wóo hán/ capital city of Hubei Province, central China. Population: 4,250,000 (1995).

wulfenite /wóolfə nīt/ *n* an orange, yellow, or brown mineral consisting of lead molybdenum. Use: source of molybdenum. [Mid-19C. After F. X. von *Wulfen* (1728–1805), Austrian scientist]

wunderkind /wúndər kind, vóondər kint/ (*plural* **-kinds** or **-kinder** /-kindər/) *n* **1.** somebody who is extremely successful at a young age **2.** a child who is unusually talented at something [Late 19C. < German, 'wonder child']

Wundt /vóont/, **Wilhelm** (1832–1920) German psychologist. His work established psychology as an independent science. Full name **Wundt, Wilhelm Max**

Wuppertal /vóoppər taal/ city in North Rhine-Westphalia State, northwestern Germany. It is situated about 32 km/20 mi. east of Düsseldorf. Population: 383,776 (1997).

Wurlitzer /wúrlitsər/ *tdmk* **1.** a trademark for an electric organ **2.** a trademark for a jukebox

wurst /wurst, woorst, voorst/ *n* **1.** a sausage made in Germany and Austria, especially a large sausage intended to be sliced and eaten cold **2.** *US* sausage of any kind [Mid-19C. < German *Wurst* 'sausage' < Indo-European, 'confuse']

Würzburg /vúrts burg, vúrts berk/ city in northeastern Bavaria State, southern Germany. Population: 127,946 (1997).

wushu /woo shoo/, **wu shu** *n* Chinese martial arts considered collectively [Late 20C. < Chinese *wŭ shù* 'military technique']

wuss /wooss/ *n* an offensive term that deliberately insults somebody regarded as weak or ineffectual (*slang insult*) [Late 20C. Origin ?] —**wussy** *adj*

wuthering /wúthəring/ *adj N England* **1.** describes a wind that blows strongly and makes a loud roaring sound **2.** subject to persistent blustery or noisy winds [Late 18C. < obsolete *wuther* 'to rush']

WV *abbr* West Virginia

WWF *abbr* **1.** ENVIRON World Wide Fund for Nature **2.** WRESTLING World Wrestling Federation

WWI *abbr* HIST World War One

WWII *abbr* HIST World War Two

WWW *abbr* ONLINE World Wide Web

Wyandot /wí ən dot/ (*plural same* or **-dots**), **Wyandotte** (*plural same* or **-dottes**) *n* a member of an Iroquois people who lived west of Lake Huron, and now live mainly in Oklahoma [Mid-18C. Via French *Ouendat* < Huron *Wendat*]

Wyatt /wí ət/, **James** (1746–1813) British architect. He is noted for his restoration of English cathedrals. His work in the Gothic Revival style is exemplified by Fonthill Abbey, Wiltshire (1807).

Wyatt, Sir Thomas (1503–42) English courtier and poet. His service at Henry VIII's court included diplomatic missions. His poems, published in 1557, introduced Italian verse forms into England.

> 'Now is this song both sung and past: / My lute, be still, for I have done.'
> [Sir Thomas Wyatt, 'My Lute Awake!'; 1542?]

wych elm /wích-/, **witch elm** *n* an elm with prominently tipped leaves and clusters of winged green fruit. Latin name: *Ulmus glabra*. [Old English *wice* < Indo-European, 'bend, be pliant']

Wycherley /wíchər li/, **William** (1640?–1716) English playwright. His comedies include *The Country Wife* (1675) and *The Plain Dealer* (1677).

> 'A man without money needs no more fear a crowd of lawyers than a crowd of pickpockets.'
> [William Wycherley, *The Plain Dealer*; 1677]

wych hazel *n* TREES another spelling of **witch hazel**

Wycliffe /wíklif/, **Wyclif, Wiclif, John** (1330?–84) English philosopher and religious reformer. He supervised the first English translation of the Bible, published posthumously in 1388. He rejected the doctrine of transubstantiation and denounced abuses in the Roman Catholic Church, anticipating the Protestant Reformation. —**Wycliffite** *n, adj*

wye /wí/ *n* **1.** the letter 'Y' **2.** something shaped like the letter 'Y' [Mid-19C. Probably representing the letter's pronunciation]

Wye /wí/ *n* river of southwestern Wales and western England. It flows into the estuary of the River Severn. Length: 209 km/130 mi.

Popperfoto
Andrew Wyeth (right)

Wyeth /wí əth/, **Andrew** (*b.* 1917) US artist. The son of N. C. Wyeth, he typically depicted rural scenes with a strong emotional charge in paintings such as *Christina's World* (1948). Full name **Wyeth, Andrew Newell**

Wyeth, N. C. (1882–1945) US artist. A leading illustrator and muralist, he produced illustrations for many children's classics, notably *Treasure Island* (1924). Full name **Wyeth, Newell Convers**

Wykeham /wíkəm/, **William of** (1324–1404) English cleric and politician. He was bishop of Winchester (1367) and lord chancellor of England (1367–71, 1389–91). He founded New College, Oxford (1379) and Winchester College (1382).

Wykehamist /wíkəmist/ *n* a pupil or former pupil of Winchester College, an English public school founded in 1382 by William of Wykeham [Mid-18C. After William of WYKEHAM]

wyn *n* another spelling of **wynn**

wynd /wīnd/ *n N England* a narrow lane in a town [15C. Probably < WIND²]

wynn /win/, **wyn, wen** /wen/ *n* a runic letter used in Old and early Middle English, representing a 'w' sound [Old English *wyn* 'joy'. Runes were named using words beginning with their sound]

Wyoming /wī óming/ state in the northwestern United States, bordered by Montana, South Dakota, Nebraska, Colorado, Utah, and Idaho. Capital: Cheyenne. Population: 498,703 (2002 estimate). Area: 253,347 sq. km/97,818 sq. mi. —**Wyomingite** *n*

WYSIWYG /wízzi wig/ *adj* describes a technology that enables the user to see an image of text and graphics on a computer display exactly as it will appear when printed [Late 20C. Acronym < *what you see is what you get*]

wyvern

wyvern /wívərn, -urn/, **wivern** *n* in heraldry, a mythical being depicted as having two legs, a dragon's head, wings, and a long tail [Late 16th C. Via Old French *wivre* < Latin *vipera* 'snake']

x[1] /eks/, **X** n (plural **x's**; plural **X's** or **Xs**) **1. 24TH LETTER OF ENGLISH ALPHABET** the 24th letter of the English alphabet, representing a consonant sound **2. LETTER 'X' WRITTEN** a written representation of the letter 'x' **3. 'X' INDICATING SOMETHING** an x-shaped mark used for indicating a vote, showing that something is incorrect, representing a kiss, or representing a signature by somebody who cannot write **4. ROMAN NUMERAL** the Roman numeral for 10 ■ vt (**x-es** or **x'es, x-ing** or **x'ing, x-ed** or **x'ed; X-es** or **X'es, X-ing** or **X'ing, X-ed** or **X'ed**) **MARK SOMETHING WITH 'X'** to mark or sign something with an 'x'

x out, X out vt US to cross something out

x[2] symbol **1. SYMBOL USED TO REPRESENT UNKNOWN** a letter 'x' or an 'x'-shaped mark used to represent something or somebody unknown or unspecified **2.** by (used in dimensions) **3. TELECOM, BUSINESS** extension **4. MATHS** multiplied by **5. MATHS** an algebraic variable **6. MATHS** a Cartesian coordinate along the x-axis **7. CARDS** a card that is not an honour **8. COMM** ex

X[1] /eks/ (plural **X's** or **Xs**) n **1.** something shaped like a letter 'X' **2.** a censorship classification used in the United Kingdom until 1982 for films that could not be shown publicly to anyone under 18 and until 1990 in the United States for films considered unsuitable for under-17s

X[2] symbol PHYS, ELECTRONICS reactance

Xanadu /zánnə doo, zánnə doó/ (plural **-dus**) n a beautiful idyllic place [Mid-20C. After the residence of KUBLAI KHAN in Samuel Taylor Coleridge's poem Kubla Khan (1816)]

xanth- prefix same as **xantho-** (used before vowels)

xanthan gum /zánthən-/ n a natural gum with a high molecular weight. Source: bacterial fermentation of glucose. Use: food stabilizer. [Mid-20C. < modern Latin Xanthomonas, a bacterium < Greek xanthos 'yellow' + late Latin monas(stem monad-): see MONAD]]

xanthate /zán thayt/ n a salt or ester of xanthic acid. Use: extraction of metals, manufacture of rayon. [Mid-19C. < XANTHIC ACID]

xanthene /zán theen/ n a yellow crystalline compound. Use: fungicide, basis of some organic dyes. Formula: $CH_2(C_6H_4)_2O$.

xanthic acid /zánthik-/ n an unstable organic sulphur-containing acid. Formula: ROC(S)SH where R is an organic group.

xanthine

xanthine /zán theen, -thīn/ n **1.** a yellow-white crystalline compound, the precursor of uric acid, found in blood, urine, and some plants. Formula: $C_5H_4N_4O_2$. **2.** a derivative of xanthine, e.g. caffeine, theophylline, or theobromine

xantho- prefix **1.** yellow ○ xanthophyll **2.** xanthic acid ○ xanthate [< Greek xanthos 'yellow']

xanthoma /zan thṓmə/ (plural **-mas** or **-mata** /-mətə/) n a yellow lipid-filled lesion on the skin, especially on the eyelids, that indicates a disorder of fat metabolism —**xanthomatous** adj

xanthomatosis /zánthōmə tṓssiss/ n the presence of multiple xanthomas on the skin

xanthone /zán thōn/ n a colourless crystalline compound. Use: basis of some yellow dyes. Formula: $C_{13}H_8O_2$.

xanthophyll /zánthōfil/ n a yellow or brown oxygenated carotenoid pigment that colours autumn leaves —**xanthophyllic** /zánthō fíllik/ adj

Xanthus /zánthəss/ ancient capital city of Lycia in southern Asia Minor, in present-day southwestern Turkey. It was destroyed by the Persians in 546 BC and again by the Romans in 42 BC. The remains of the city and numerous artworks were discovered by Sir Charles Fellows in 1838. —**Xanthian** n, adj

Xavier /závvi ər, záyvi ər/, **St Francis** (1506–52) Spanish missionary. He helped St Ignatius Loyola to found the Society of Jesus and established missions in India, Japan, and parts of Southeast Asia. Known as **the Apostle of the Indies**

x-axis n **1.** the horizontal axis in a two-dimensional coordinate system **2.** an axis in the three-dimensional Cartesian coordinate system, conventionally the horizontal one

X-certificate adj containing explicitly sexual or violent material or unsuitable for children, as in the former UK classification for cinema films. Aus, N Am term **X-rated**

X chromosome n a chromosome present in both sexes that plays a role in determining the sex of an individual. Female mammals carry two X chromosomes and males carry one.

x-coordinate n the position of a point in space with reference to the x-axis in the Cartesian coordinate system, defined in conjunction with the y- and z-coordinates

XD abbr FIN ex dividend

xdiv abbr FIN ex dividend

Xe symbol CHEM ELEM xenon

xebec /zeébek, záy-/, **zebec** n a small Mediterranean ship with three masts rigged with both square and triangular sails [Mid-18C. Via French chebec < Arabic šabbāk]

xen- prefix same as **xeno-** (used before vowels)

Xenakis /ze naákis/, **Iannis** (1922–2001) Romanian-born Greek composer. Originally an engineer and architect, he used mathematical ideas in his 'stochastic music'.

xenia /zeéni ə, zénni ə/ n the effect of genes carried by pollen on the food storage tissue (**endosperm**) of the pollinated seed [Late 19C. Via modern Latin < Greek, 'hospitality' < xenos 'stranger, foreigner']

xeno- prefix foreign, strange, different ○ xenophile ○ xenolith [Via modern Latin < Greek xenos 'stranger, foreigner']

xenobiotic /zénnō bī óttik, zeénō-/ adj describes a chemical compound such as a drug or pesticide

that is foreign to the body of a living organism —**xenobiotic** n

Xenocrates /ze nókrə teez/ (396–314 BC) Greek philosopher. A student of Plato, he is considered the first philosopher to have drawn the distinction between mind, body, and soul.

xenocryst /zénnōkrist/ n a crystal in an igneous rock introduced from an external source and not crystallized from the magma [Late 19C. < XENO- + CRYSTAL]

xenodiagnosis /zénnō dī əg nṓssiss/ (plural **-noses** /-nṓ seez/) n the diagnosis of a parasitic infection by allowing a noninfected disease-carrying organism such as a mosquito to feed on an infected person's blood and then examining the organism for infection —**xenodiagnostic** /-nóstik/ adj

xenogeneic /zénnōjə náy ik/ adj coming from or derived from a different species [Mid-20C. After SYNGENEIC]

xenogenesis /zénnō jénnəssiss/ n **1.** the supposed production of offspring completely different from both parents **2.** the existence in the life cycle of an organism of two or more alternating forms or reproductive modes, e.g. sexual and asexual cycles —**xenogenetic** /zénnōjə néttik/ adj

xenograft /zénnō graaft/ n MED same as **heterograft**

xenolith /zénnōlith/ n a fragment of rock that is different in origin from the igneous rock in which it occurs —**xenolithic** /zénnō líthik/ adj

xenon /zee'on, zén-/ n a heavy colourless odourless gaseous element that is relatively inert. Source: in minute quantities in air. Use: electronic tubes, specialized lamps. Symbol **Xe**. See table at **element** [Late 19C. < Greek xenon, neuter of xenos 'stranger, foreigner']

Xenophanes /ze nóffə neez/ (fl late 6th–early 5th century BC) Greek philosopher and poet. He ridiculed the polytheistic beliefs of earlier Greek poets and is considered the founder of the Eleatic school of philosophy.

'But if cattle and horses or lions had hands…horses would draw the forms of the gods like horses, and cattle like cattle.' [Xenophanes. Quoted in The Presocratic Philosophers, G. S. Kirk, J. E. Raven, and M. Schofield; 1983]

xenophile /zénnō fīl/ n somebody who likes the people, customs, and culture of other countries, or things from abroad —**xenophilia** /zénnō fílli ə/ n —**xenophilous** /ze nóffiləss/ adj

xenophobia /zénnə fṓbi ə/ n an intense fear or dislike of foreign people, their customs and culture, or foreign things —**xenophobe** /zénnəfōb/ n —**xenophobic** adj

Xenophon /zénnəfən/ (430?–355? BC) Greek historian and soldier. A pupil of Socrates, he participated in the attack on Persia by Cyrus the Younger (401 BC) and led a 10,000-strong Greek force back to safety on the Black Sea, an episode he described in his Anabasis.

xenopus /zénnəpəss/ (plural same or **-pi** /-pī/) n a water frog. Native to: southern Africa. Genus: Xenopus. [Late 19C. < modern Latin < Greek xeno- 'stranger, foreigner' + pous 'foot']

xenotransplant vt /zénnō transs pláant/ (**-plants, -planting, -planted**) **TRANSPLANT SOMETHING TO DIFFERENT**

SPECIES to transfer a tissue or organ between members of different species ■ *n* /zénnō tránss plaant/ **1. OPERATION TRANSPLANTING TISSUE TO DIFFERENT SPECIES** a surgical operation in which a tissue or organ is transferred between members of different species **2. SOMETHING TRANSPLANTED TO DIFFERENT SPECIES** a tissue or organ that is transferred between members of different species —**xenotransplantation** /zénnō transs plaan táysh'n/ *n*

xer- *prefix* same as **xero-** (*used before vowels*)

xeric /zeérik/ *adj* relating to or living in a dry habitat —**xerically** *adv*

Xeriscape /zeérə skayp, zérrə-/ *tdmk US* a trademark for a method of landscaping that emphasizes water conservation in its use of drought-resistant plants

xero- *prefix* dry, dryness ○ *xerothermic* [< Greek *xēros* 'dry']

xeroderma /zeérō dúrmə/, **xerodermia** /-dúrmi ə/ *n* a mild form of the hereditary disorder ichthyosis, marked by discoloured dry hard scaly skin —**xerodermatic** /-dur máttik/ *adj* —**xerodermatous** *adj*

xeroderma pigmentosum /-píg mən tṓssəm/ *n* a rare and often fatal hereditary condition beginning in infancy in which the skin and eyes are damaged by sunlight. It results in freckles, discoloured patches, and skin cancers.

xerodermia *n MED* same as **xeroderma**

xerography /zeer róggrəfi/ *n* a method of photocopying in which an image is formed by attracting a resinous powder to an electrostatically charged plate, and is then transferred to paper and fixed by heating —**xerographer** *n* —**xerographic** /zeérō gráffik/ *adj* —**xerographically** *adv*

xeromorphic /zeérō máwrfik/ *adj* describes plants or plant parts that are adapted for survival in dry conditions, e.g. spiny leaves that reduce surface area and therefore water loss

xerophilous /zeer róffiləss/ *adj* thriving in or adapted for a hot dry habitat —**xerophile** /zeérō fīl/ *n* —**xerophily** *n*

xerophthalmia /zeér of thálmi ə/ *n* an eye disease caused by vitamin A deficiency, marked by dryness and ulceration of the conjunctiva and cornea. If untreated, it may cause blindness. —**xerophthalmic** *adj*

xerophyte /zeérə fīt/ *n* a plant that is adapted for a dry habitat, e.g. a cactus —**xerophytic** /zeérō fíttik/ *adj* —**xerophytism** *n*

xeroradiography /zeérō ráydi óggrəfi/ *n* a high-definition X-ray photography in which the image is first made on a specially coated metal plate and then transferred to paper. It is often used in screening for breast cancer.

xerosis /zeer rṓssiss/ *n* excessive dryness of the skin and mucous membranes of the eye, caused by thickening of the membranes —**xerotic** /-róttik/ *adj*

xerostomia /zeérō stṓmi ə/ *n* a lack of saliva in the mouth, caused by disease, poisoning, or some drugs

xerothermic /zeérō thúrmik/ *adj* very hot and having little rainfall ○ *a xerothermic climate*

Xerox /zeér roks/ *tdmk* a trademark for a photocopying process that uses xerography

Xerxes I /zúrk seez/ (519?–465 BC) king of Persia. As king (486–465 BC), he led a huge army into Greece (480 BC), defeating the Greeks at Thermopylae and burning Athens, but his fleet was defeated at Salamis. He was assassinated by his palace guard. Known as **Xerxes the Great**

> 'I am moved to pity, when I think of the brevity of human life, seeing that of all this host of men not one will still be alive in a hundred years' time.'
> [Xerxes I, *Remark*; 480? BC]

x-height *n* the height of the lower-case letter 'x' in a typeface, used as a measure of the height of the main body of all lower-case letters in that typeface

Xhosa /kṓssə, káwssə/ (*plural same* or **-sas**), **Xosa** *n* **1.** a member of a Bantu-speaking people of South Africa **2.** the Bantu language of the Xhosa people. Native speakers: 7 million. [Early 19C. < Nguni] —**Xhosa** *adj* —**Xhosan** *adj*

xi /zī, sī, ksī, ksee/ (*plural* **xis**) *n* the 14th letter of the Greek alphabet, represented in the English alphabet as 'x'. See table at **alphabet**

Xiamen /shyaá mén/ city and seaport on Xiamen Island in Fujian Province, southeastern China. It lies in the Taiwan Strait, west of Taiwan. Population: 357,290 (1991).

Xi'an /shyaan/ capital city of Shaanxi Province in eastern China. One of China's oldest cities, it is home to some major archaeological sites, including one found to contain a vast army of life-size soldiers made of terracotta, known as 'The Terracotta Warriors'. Population: 2,970,000 (1995).

Xiangtan /shyáng tán, syáng-/ city in southern China, in Hunan Province. It is an inland port and industrial centre on the River Xiang. Population: 525,448 (1991).

xi hyperon *n* a neutral or negatively charged elementary particle present in cosmic rays and in high-energy collisions in particle accelerators

Xi Jiang /shee jyáng/ river in southern China that rises in Yunnan Province and flows east to the South China Sea. Length: 2,100 km/1,300 mi.

Xingu /shíng goó/ river in northwestern Brazil. It flows north through the states of Mato Grosso and Pará and empties into the Amazon delta. Length: 1,980 km/1,230 mi.

Xining /shee níng/ capital city of Qinghai Province, in western China, northeast of Lanzhou. Population: 777,983 (1991).

Xinjiang Uygur /shín jyáng weéegər/ autonomous region in northwestern China. With one sixth of China's land, it is the country's largest region. Capital: Urumqi. Population: 16,890,000 (1997). Area: 1,646,800 sq. km/635,833 sq. mi.

xi-particle *n PHYS* same as **xi hyperon**

xiphisternum /zíffi stúrnəm/ (*plural* **-na** /-nə/) *n* the third and lowest segment of the breastbone (**sternum**) in humans. It consists of a flat plate of cartilage that gradually changes into bone during life.

xiphoid /zíffoyd/ *adj* **1.** shaped like a sword **2.** relating to the xiphisternum ■ *n ANAT* same as **xiphisternum**

xiphoid process *n ANAT* same as **xiphisternum**

Xizang /shee dzáng/ Chinese name for **Tibet**

XL *abbr* extra large (*clothing size*)

Xmas /kríssməss, éksməss/ *n CHR, CALENDAR* same as **Christmas** (*informal*) [Mid-16C. *X* represents the Greek letter *chi*, in *Khristos* 'Christ']

XML *n* a programming language designed for web documents that allows for the creation of customized tags for individual information fields. Full form **Extensible Markup Language**

Xmodem /éks mō dem/ *n* a file transfer protocol for asynchronous communications in which data is sent in 128-byte blocks

Xn *abbr CHR* Christian

Xnty *abbr CHR* Christianity

xoanon /zṓ ə non/ (*plural* **-ana** /-ənə/) *n* an image of a god that has been carved out of wood [Early 18C. < Greek, 'carved statue']

Xochimilco /kóchi mílkō/ city in south-central Mexico. It is a suburb of Mexico City and is famous for its precolonial canals and floating gardens. Population: 356,833 (2000).

Xosa *n, adj PEOPLES, LANG* another spelling of **Xhosa**

X-radiation *n* **1.** exposure to or medical treatment by X-rays **2.** radiation in the form of X-rays

X-rated *adj* **1.** containing explicit sex scenes or descriptions of sex (*informal*) **2.** *Aus, N Am CINEMA* same as **X-certificate**

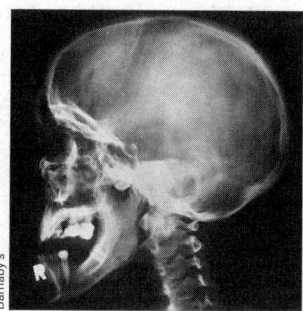

X-ray: image of a human skull

Barnaby's

X-ray, X ray, x-ray, x ray *n* **1. ELECTROMAGNETIC RADIATION** a high-energy electromagnetic radiation that can penetrate solids and ionize gas. It has a wavelength between 0.01 and 10 nanometres, which is between gamma rays and ultraviolet light. **2. PHOTOGRAPHIC IMAGE USING X-RAYS** an image produced on photographic film by X-rays passing through objects or parts of the body, often used in medicine and science as a diagnostic tool **3. COMMUNICATION CODE WORD FOR LETTER 'X'** a code word for the letter 'X', used in international radio communications ■ *vt* (**X-rays, X-raying, X-rayed**) **1. PHOTOGRAPH SOMETHING USING X-RAYS** to expose something such as a part of the body to X-rays in order to obtain a photographic image of it **2. EXAMINE SOMETHING WITH X-RAYS** to examine something, e.g. luggage or freight, using X-rays [Late 19C. Translation of German *X-Strahl*, *X* signifying 'unknown']

X-ray astronomy *n* the branch of astronomy in which the properties of astronomical objects are determined using the X-rays they emit

X-ray crystallography *n* the study of crystal structures using the diffraction patterns produced by scattered X-rays

X-ray diffraction *n* the diffraction of X-rays produced by the atoms within a crystal, used to determine information about the crystal's structure

X-ray star, X-ray source *n* an astronomical object that emits X-rays in addition to other types of radiation

X-ray therapy *n* the medical application of X-rays in treating illnesses such as cancer

X-ray tube *n* an evacuated tube in which a stream of high-energy electrons is made to strike a metal target to produce X-rays

XS *abbr* extra small (*clothing size*)

Xt. *abbr CHR* Christ

Xtian *abbr CHR* Christian

xtn *abbr TELECOM, BUSINESS* extension

Xty *abbr CHR* Christianity

xu /soo/ (*plural same*) *n* a subunit of Vietnamese currency. See table at **currency** [Mid-20C. Via Vietnamese < French *sou* (see **SOU**)]

Xuzhou /shoó zhṓ/ another spelling of **Suzhou**

xyl- *prefix* same as **xylo-** (*used before vowels*)

xylan /zī lan/ *n* a polysaccharide (**pentosan**) found in plant cell walls and woody tissue

xylem /zīləm, -lem/ *n* the woody supportive plant tissue that carries water and dissolved minerals from the roots through the stem and leaves [Late 19C. Via German < Greek *xulon* 'wood']

CH₃ | 1,4-Xylene

CH₃ | 1,3-Xylene   CH₃ | 1,2-Xylene

xylene

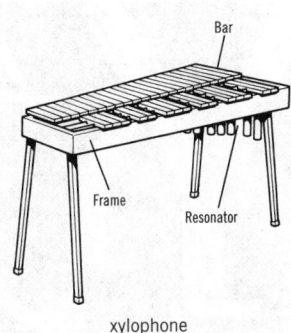

xylophone

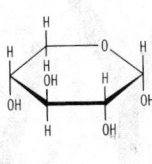

xylose

xylene /zī leen/ *n* a flammable volatile colourless liquid hydrocarbon in three forms. Source: petroleum, natural gas, coal tar. Use: solvents, manufacture of aviation fuel, resins, and dyes. Formula: C_8H_{10}. See illustration on previous page

xylidine /zíli deen, zíli dīn, zílli-/ *n* a toxic amine in six forms derived from xylene. Use: manufacture of dyes, organic synthesis. Formula: $C_8H_{11}N$.

xylo- *prefix* **1.** wood ○ *xylograph* **2.** xylene ○ *xylidine* [< Greek *xulon* 'wood']

xylogenous /zī lójjənəss/ *adj* adapted to or living in or on wood

xylograph /zílə graaf, -graf/ *n* **1.** WOOD ENGRAVING an engraving made on wood **2.** PRINT FROM WOOD ENGRAVING a print made from an engraving made on wood ■ *vt* (**-graphs, -graphing, -graphed**) MAKE XYLOGRAPH to take a print from an engraving made on wood —**xylographer** /zī lóggrəfər/ *n* —**xylographic** /zílə gráffik/ *adj* —**xylographical** *adj* —**xylography** /zī lóggrəfi/ *n*

xyloid /zí loyd/ *adj* relating to or resembling wood

xylol /zí lol/ *n* CHEM same as **xylene**

xylophagous /zī lóffəgəss/ *adj* feeding on or living in wood —**xylophage** /zílō fayj/ *n*

xylophone /zíləfōn/ *n* a musical instrument with a row of wooden bars of different lengths that are laid out like a keyboard and produce a tone when struck with a mallet —**xylophonist** /zī lóffənist/ *n*

xylose /zí lōz, -lōss/ *n* a sugar with five carbon atoms in each molecule, found in the cell walls of many plants. As it cannot be broken down in humans, it does not increase blood sugar levels, so is used in sugar-free foods for people with diabetes or a need to control their weight. Formula: $C_5H_{10}O_5$.

xystus /zístəss/ (*plural* **-tuses**), **xyst** /zist/ *n* **1.** in ancient Greece, a long walkway with a roof supported by pillars, used for athletics **2.** in ancient Rome, a covered or open path in a garden, lined with trees or pillars [Mid-17C. Via Latin < Greek *xustos* 'covered colonnade', literally 'smooth' (from its polished floor) < *xuein* 'to scrape']

y[1] /wī/ (*plural* **y's**), **Y** (*plural* **Y's** or **Ys**) *n* **1.** the 25th letter of the English alphabet, representing a consonant sound or sometimes a vowel **2.** a written representation of the letter 'y'

y[2] *symbol* **1.** MATHS an algebraic variable **2.** MATHS a Cartesian coordinate along the y-axis **3.** MATHS y-axis **4.** MEASURE yocto-

y[3] *abbr* year

Y[1] /wī/ (*plural* **Y's** or **Ys**) *n* **1.** something shaped like a letter 'Y' **2.** a YMCA or YWCA hostel (*informal*)

Y[2] *symbol* **1.** ELEC admittance **2.** MATHS an unknown factor **3.** MEASURE yotta- **4.** CHEM ELEM yttrium

Y[3] *abbr* MONEY **1.** yen **2.** yuan

-y[1], **-ey** *suffix* **1.** consisting of or characterized by ○ *muddy* **2.** somewhat, like ○ *chilly* ○ *wintry* **3.** tending towards ○ *sleepy* [Old English *-ig* < Germanic]

-y[2] *suffix* **1.** a condition, state, or quality ○ *infamy* **2.** an activity ○ *chandlery* **3.** the place where an activity is carried on, or the result or product of an activity ○ *colliery* ○ *laundry* **4.** a body or group ○ *soldiery* [Via Old French *-ie* < Latin *-ia*]

-y[3] *suffix* same as **-ie**

Y2K *n* used to refer to the year 2000, especially with regard to the millennium bug and its anticipated damaging effects on software ○ *Y2K-compliant software* [Abbreviation]

yaar /yaar/ *n* S Asia used as a familiar or affectionate form of address, especially among young people (*informal*) [Via Hindi < Arabic *yar*]

yabber /yábbər/ (*informal*) *vti* (**-bers, -bering, -bered**) to talk a lot or say something rapidly, often so that it is incomprehensible ■ *n* rapid speech that is often incomprehensible [Mid-19C. < an Aboriginal language]

yabby /yábbi/ (*plural* **-bies** or *same*), **yabbie** *n* Aus a small freshwater crayfish. Native to: Australia. Genus: *Cherax*. [Late 19C. < Wembawemba *yabij*]

ya-boo *interj* another spelling of **yah-boo** (*informal*)

YAC /yak/ *abbr* GENETICS, BIOTECH yeast artificial chromosome

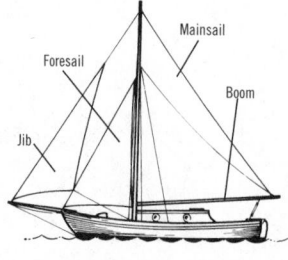

yacht

yacht /yot/ *n* **1.** SAILING BOAT a sailing boat, often one that has living quarters and is used for cruising or racing **2.** MOTORBOAT FOR CRUISING a large motorboat used for cruising ■ *vi* (**yachts, yachting, yachted**) SAIL IN YACHT to sail in a yacht for leisure or sport [Mid-16C. < obsolete Dutch *jaghte*, shortening of *jaghtschip* 'chasing ship']

yachtie /yótti/ *n* somebody who owns a yacht or enjoys sailing, cruising, or racing in yachts (*informal*)

yachting /yótting/ *n* the sport or pastime of sailing a yacht

yachtsman /yótsmən/ (*plural* **-men** /-mən/) *n* somebody, especially a man, who owns or sails a yacht — **yachtsmanship** *n*

yachtsperson /yóts púrss'n/ (*plural* **-people** /-peep'l/ or **-persons**) *n* somebody who owns or sails a yacht

yachtswoman /yóts wŏŏmən/ (*plural* **-women** /-wimin/) *n* a woman who owns or sails a yacht

yack *vi, n* ZOOL another spelling of **yak**[2] (*informal*)

yacker *n* ANZ another spelling of **yakka** (*informal*)

yackety-yak /yákəti yák/ *v* (**yackety-yaks, yackety-yakking, yackety-yakked**), *n* same as **yak**[2] (*informal*) [Mid-20C. An imitation of the sound]

yadda yadda yadda /yáddə yaddə yáddə/, **yada yada yada** *n* US boring trite superficial unending talk (*slang*) ○ *just a lot of yadda yadda yadda on the talk shows tonight* [Late 20C. Origin ?]

YAG /yag/ *n* a synthetic mineral containing yttrium, aluminium, and garnet. Use: infrared lasers, gems. [Mid-20C. Acronym < *yttrium, aluminium, garnet*]

Yagara /yaágərə/ *n* an Australian Aboriginal language of Queensland, now extinct [< an Aboriginal language] —**Yagara** *adj*

Yagi aerial /yaági-/ *n* a directional radio or television aerial consisting of several components arranged in line [Mid-20C. After Hidetsugu *Yagi* (1886–1976), Japanese electrical engineer]

yah[1] /yaa/ *interj* used to express derision or defiance [Early 17C. Natural exclamation]

yah[2] /yaa/ *adv* same as **yes** (*informal; especially parodying affected upper-class accents*) ○ *Okay, yah, super.* [Mid-19C. Representing a pronunciation]

yah-boo /yaá bŏŏ/, **yah-boo sucks, ya-boo, ya-boo sucks** *interj* used to express defiance, disrespect, or derision (*informal; usually used by children*)

yah-boo politics *npl* politics in which parties automatically and unthinkingly criticize and reject any idea put forward by an opposing party, regardless of its merits (*informal*)

yahoo[1] /yaa hŏŏ, yə-, yaá hoo/ (*plural* **-hoos**) *n* somebody who is regarded as unruly, crude, or brutish (*informal insult*) [Early 18C. After the *Yahoos* in Jonathan Swift's *Gulliver's Travels* (1726)] —**yahooism** *n*

yahoo[2] /yə hŏŏ/ (*informal*) *interj* used to express enthusiasm, approval, or celebration ○ *Yahoo! Let's go!* ■ *n* (*plural* **-hoos**) a cry of enthusiasm, approval, or celebration [Late 20C. Natural exclamation]

Yahrzeit /yáwrt sīt/ *n* in Judaism, the anniversary of somebody's death, celebrated by near relatives with the lighting of a memorial candle and the saying of the Kaddish [Mid-19C. < Yiddish *yortsayt* 'year's time']

Yahveh, etc. *n* JUD-CHR same as **Yahweh, etc.**

Yahweh /yaá way/, **Jahweh, Yahveh** /-vay/, **Jahveh** *n* a name of God, expanded from the four letters YHWH (**Tetragrammaton**) that form the name of God in Hebrew [Late 19C. < Hebrew]

Yahwism /yaáwizəm/, **Yahvism** /yaáv-/ *n* the use of the four letters YHWH (**Tetragrammaton**) to represent the name of God or to worship God

Yahwist /yaáwist/, **Yahvist** /yaáv-/ *n* the unknown writer of the parts of the Bible in which the set of four letters YHWH (**Tetragrammaton**) is used to refer to God

Yahwistic /yaa wístik/, **Yahvistic** /-vístik/ *adj* relating to Yahweh, Yahwism, or the Yahwist

yak

yak[1] /yak/ (*plural* **yaks** or *same*) *n* a large long-haired ox that has long curved horns and is found both wild and domesticated. Native to: Tibetan highlands. Latin name: *Bos grunniens*. [Late 18C. < Tibetan *gyag*]

yak[2] /yak/, **yack** (*informal*) *vi* (**yaks, yakking, yakked; yacks, yacking, yacked**) to talk continuously, usually about unimportant matters ■ *n* continuous talking, usually about unimportant matters, or an instance of this [Mid-20C. An imitation of the sound]

Yakama /yákəmə/ (*plural same* or **-mas**) *n* **1.** a member of a Native North American people of south-central Washington State **2.** the Penutian language of the Yakama people. Native speakers: 3,000. [Mid-19C. < Sahaptin] —**Yakama** *adj*

yakitori /yáki táwri/ *n* a dish of Japanese origin consisting of small pieces of grilled chicken that are basted on skewers with a sauce of soya, stock, sugar, and mirin [Mid-20C. < Japanese, 'grilling fowl']

yakka /yákə/, **yakker** /yákər/, **yacker** *n* ANZ same as **work** *n* (sense 5) (*informal*) ○ *hard yakka* [Late 19C. Origin ?]

Yakut /ya kŏŏt/ (*plural same* or **-kuts**) *n* **1.** a member of a people who live in northeastern Siberia, mainly in the Russian republic of Sakha **2.** the Turkic language of the Yakut people. Native speakers: 300,000. [Mid-18C. Via Russian < Yakut] —**Yakut** *adj*

Yakutsk /ya kŏŏtsk/ capital city of the autonomous region of Sakha, northeastern Russia. Population: 240,743 (1995).

yakuza /yə kŏŏzə/ (*plural same*) *n* **1.** a Japanese criminal organization involved in illegal activities such as drug-dealing, extortion, and prostitution **2.** a member of the yakuza [Mid-20C. < Japanese, 'gambler' < *ya* 'eight' + *ku* 'nine' + *-za* 'three', the worst hand in a card game]

Yale lock /yáyl-/ *tdmk* a trademark for a cylindrical lock that is operated using a flat serrated key

y'all *pron* Southern US same as **you-all**

Yallourn /yál awrn/ town in southern Victoria, Australia. It is a major coal-mining centre. Population: 15,512 (1996).

Yalta /yáltə, yóltə/ resort city in Crimea Region, southern Ukraine. Situated on the Black Sea, it was the site of a conference in 1945 between Joseph Stalin,

Yalu /yaa loo/ river in East Asia, forming most of the boundary between North Korea and China. Length: 790 km/490 mi.

Franklin Roosevelt, and Winston Churchill that determined the administration of Germany after World War II. Population: 115,548 (1993).

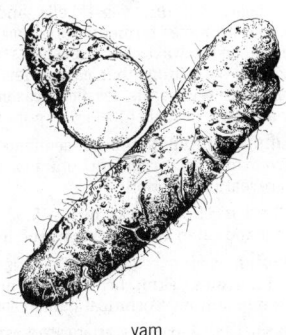

yam

yam /yam/ *n* **1.** a vine root that resembles a large white floury potato and is eaten cooked as a vegetable **2.** a tropical plant that produces yams. Genus: *Dioscorea*. [Late 16C. Via Portuguese *inhame* or Spanish *iñame* < a W African language]

yamen /yaámən, yaá men/ *n* in the Chinese Empire, the home or office of a mandarin or other public official [Early 19C. < Chinese *yámen* < *yá* 'office' + *mén* 'gate']

Yamim Nora'im /yaa mím nawr aa ím/ *npl* in Judaism, the period of repentance lasting from Rosh Hashanah to Yom Kippur [< Hebrew, 'Days of Awe']

yammer /yámmər/ (*informal*) *vi* (**-mers, -mering, -mered**) **1.** TALK LOUDLY AND AT LENGTH to talk, chat, or chatter noisily and continuously **2.** WHINE to whine or complain persistently about something **3.** HOWL OR WAIL to make repeated howling sounds of pain or distress ■ *n* **1.** NOISY CHATTERING noisy continuous talk, chat, or chattering **2.** COMPLAINT a whine or complaint [15C. Probably < Middle Dutch *jammeren* 'mourn'] —**yammerer** *n*

Yamoussoukro /yámmoo soókrō/ capital city of Côte d'Ivoire, in the central part of the country. Population: 120,000 (1990).

Yamuna /yúmmoönə/ river in northern India flowing south through Delhi into the River Ganges at Allahabad. Length: 1,400 km/870 mi. Former name **Jumna**

Yan'an /yán án/ city in northern Shaanxi Province, northeastern China. The terminus of the Long March, Yan'an was used by Communist forces as a base between 1936 and 1949. Population: 113,277 (1991).

yang /yang/, **Yang** *n* in Chinese philosophy, the principle of light, heat, motivation, and masculinity that is the counterpart to yin and is thought to exist along with yin in all things [Late 17C. < Chinese *yáng* 'sun, positive']

Yangon /yang gón/ capital city of Myanmar, in the south of the country. Population: 4,196,000 (2000). Former name **Rangoon** (until 1989)

Yangtze /yáng tsee, -see/, **Yangzi** longest river in China. It rises in the Kunlun Mountains, and flows southwards and then eastwards to enter the East China Sea directly north of Shanghai. Length: 6,300 km/3,900 mi.

yank /yangk/ *v* (**yanks, yanking, yanked**) **1.** *vti* PULL SOMEBODY OR SOMETHING SHARPLY to pull somebody or something suddenly and sharply **2.** *vt* REMOVE SOMEBODY OR SOMETHING SWIFTLY to remove somebody or something suddenly and quickly ■ *n* SHARP PULL a sudden sharp pull or jerk [Early 19C. Origin ?]

SYNONYMS See *pull*.

Yank /yangk/ *n* somebody who is from the United States (*informal; sometimes offensive*) [Late18C. Shortening of YANKEE]

Yankee /yángki/ *n* **1.** PEOPLES same as **Yank** (*informal*) **2.** *US* SOMEBODY FROM NORTHERN US STATE somebody who comes from a Northern state of the United States, especially a soldier fighting on the side of the Union

during the American Civil War (*offensive in some contexts*) **3.** *US* SOMEBODY FROM NEW ENGLAND somebody who comes from one of the states of New England (*offensive in some contexts*) **4.** CODE WORD FOR LETTER 'Y' a code word for the letter 'Y', used in international radio communications [Mid-18C. Origin ?] —**Yankeedom** *n*

Yankee Doodle /-doód'l/ *n* **1.** a song first popular during the War of American Independence **2.** PEOPLES same as **Yank** (*informal*)

Yankeeism /yángki izəm/ *n* something such as an expression that is considered characteristic of Yankees

yanqui /yángki/ (*plural* **-quis**) *n* an offensive term used by some Latin Americans to refer disparagingly to an English-speaking US citizen [Early 20C. Spanish-style spelling of YANKEE]

Yao /yow/ (*plural same*) *n* **1.** PEOPLES a member of a people who live in the mountains of southern People's Republic of China **2.** LANG the language of the Yao people, belonging to the Miao-Yao group of languages. Native speakers: 1 million. [Mid-19C. < Chinese, literally, 'precious jade'] —**Yao** *adj*

Yaoundé /yaa oónd ay/ capital city of Cameroon, in the southwestern part of the country. Population: 1,000,000 (1997).

yap /yap/ *vi* (**yaps, yapping, yapped**) **1.** MAKE HIGH BARKING SOUND to make a short loud high-pitched barking noise **2.** CHATTER ANNOYINGLY to talk annoyingly about trivial things, often in a loud or high-pitched voice (*informal*) ■ *n* **1.** SHORT HIGH-PITCHED BARK a short loud high-pitched bark **2.** TRIVIAL CONVERSATION a trivial or meaningless conversation (*informal*) **3.** ANAT same as **mouth** *n* (senses 1–2) (*slang*) [Early 19C. An imitation of a dog's bark] —**yapper** *n* —**yappy** *adj*

Yap /yap/ group of islands, islets, and atolls in the western Pacific Ocean. Part of the Caroline Islands, the group is one of the states of Micronesia. Population: 10,886 (1991). Area: 119 sq. km/46 sq. mi.

yapok /yáppok/ (*plural* **-poks** or *same*) *n* an amphibious nocturnal opossum that has dense fur, webbed hind feet, a long tail, and feeds on water organisms such as shrimp. Native to: Central and South America. Latin name: *Chironectes minimus*. [Early 19C. After the River *Oyapok*, which forms the border between N Brazil and French Guiana]

Yaqui /yáki/ (*plural same* or **-quis**) *n* **1.** a member of a Native North American people of Arizona and Sonora, and a state in northwestern Mexico **2.** the Uto-Aztecan language of the Yaqui people. Native speakers: 20,000. [Early 19C. Via Spanish < Yaqui *Hiaki*] —**Yaqui** *adj*

yarborough /yaárbərə/ *n* in bridge or whist, a hand consisting of 13 cards, each of which has a value lower than nine [Late 19C. After Charles Anderson Worsley (1809–97), 2nd Earl of *Yarborough*]

yard[1] /yaárd/ *n* **1.** UNIT OF LENGTH a unit of length equal to 0.9144 m/3 ft **2.** MEASURE same as **yardstick** (sense 1) **3.** SPAR SUPPORTING SAIL a long spar that supports the head of a square sail, lugsail, or lateen **4.** A BILLION one billion in foreign-exchange currency (*slang*) ○ *a yard of yen* [Old English *gerd* 'rod' < W Germanic] ◇ **the whole nine yards** *N Am* the totality or full extent of something (*informal*)

yard[2] /yaárd/ *n* **1.** ENCLOSED PAVED PIECE OF LAND an area of ground that is usually paved and enclosed, and is next to or surrounded by a building or buildings ○ *a prison yard* **2.** AREA USED FOR BUSINESS OR ACTIVITY an area of ground, sometimes with associated buildings, used for a particular purpose (*often used in combination*) ○ *a builder's yard* **3.** *N Am* same as **garden** *n* (sense 1) **4.** RAILWAY STORAGE AREA an area of railway tracks used for storing rolling stock or locomotives and for making up trains **5.** LIVESTOCK ENCLOSURE an enclosed area of land for livestock **6.** *N Am* WINTER GRAZING AREA an area of land where deer, moose, or other animals graze in winter **7.** HOME a house or flat (*used in Black English*) ■ *vt* (**yards, yarding, yarded**) KEEP LIVESTOCK IN YARD to put or keep livestock in a yard [Old English *geard* 'enclosure, garden']

Yard *n* POLICE same as **Scotland Yard** (*informal*) [< YARD[2]]

yardage[1] /yaárdij/ *n* measurement in yards, or an amount measured in yards [Late 19C. < YARD[1]]

yardage[2] /yaárdij/ *n* **1.** the use of a livestock yard for storing animals before transporting them **2.** a fee charged for storing livestock in a yard [Mid-19C. < YARD[2]]

yardarm /yaárd aarm/ *n* an end of the yard used to support a sail [15C. < YARD[1]]

yardbird /yaárd burd/ *n US* **1.** SOLDIER ASSIGNED MENIAL DUTIES a soldier who is assigned menial tasks or is confined to a limited area, usually as a punishment (*informal*) **2.** INEPT RECRUIT an untrained and inept military recruit (*dated informal*) **3.** CONVICT a convict or prisoner (*dated informal*) [Mid-19C. < YARD[2], after JAILBIRD]

yard goods *npl* COMM same as **piece goods** [< YARD[1]]

yard grass *n* a coarse annual grass with ground-hugging leaves and grouped spikes that grows widely as a weed. Latin name: *Eleusine indica*. [< YARD[2]]

Yardie /yaárdi/ *n* **1.** a member of a criminal syndicate that originated in Jamaica **2.** *Carib* somebody who lives in a building with a shared yard [Late 20C. < YARD[2] in the Jamaican sense 'house, home']

yard-long bean *n* the long thin edible pod produced by a type of cowpea. Native to: South Asia. Latin name: *Vigna unguiculata sesquipedalis*. [Because it reaches up to a yard (nearly a metre) in length]

yardman /yaárdmən/ (*plural* **-men** /-mən/) *n* **1.** somebody, especially a man, who works in a yard, especially a railway yard or a timberyard **2.** *US* somebody, especially a man, employed to look after a lawn or garden [Early 19C. < YARD[2]]

yard of ale *n* **1.** a long narrow drinking glass, sometimes shaped like a horn, approximately one yard long and holding two to three pints of beer **2.** the contents of a yard of ale [< YARD[1]]

yardperson /yaárd purss'n/ (*plural* **-people** /-peep'l/) *n* **1.** somebody who works in a yard, especially a railway yard or a timberyard **2.** *US* somebody employed to look after a lawn or garden [Late 20C. < YARD[2]]

yard sale *n N Am* a sale at which personal possessions and household items are sold, usually held in the garden of somebody's house [< YARD[2]]

yardstick /yaárd stik/ *n* **1.** a measuring stick one yard long, usually marked in feet and inches **2.** a standard used to judge the quality, value, or success of something [Early 19C. < YARD[1]]

yare /yair/ *adj* **1.** EASY TO HANDLE describes a ship that is easy to handle and responsive **2.** READY ready or prepared (*archaic*) **3.** QUICK quick or lively (*archaic*) ■ *adv* QUICKLY quickly or nimbly (*archaic*) [Old English *gearo* 'ready' < Germanic] —**yarely** *adv*

yarmulke /yaármoölkə/, **yarmulka**, **yarmulkah** *n* a small round cap worn by Jewish men and boys. Orthodox Jews wear the yarmulke at all times, while others wear it for prayer or on ceremonial occasions only. [Mid-20C. Via Yiddish < Polish *jarmułka*]

yarn /yaarn/ *n* **1.** STRAND OF FIBRE a continuous twisted strand of wool, cotton, or synthetic fibre. Use: knitting, weaving. **2.** STRAND OF GLASS OR METAL a continuous strand of a material such as glass or metal **3.** LONG STORY a long or involved tale, especially one that relates exciting or incredible events (*informal*) ■ *vi* (**yarns, yarning, yarned**) TELL STORY to relate a long tale full of incredible events (*informal*) [Old English *gearn* < Indo-European, 'entrail']

yarn-dyed *adj* dyed in the form of yarn before being woven or knitted

Yaroslavl /yaárə slaav'l, yaárə slaáv'l/ city and capital of Yaroslavl Oblast, central European Russia. It is situated on the River Volga. Population: 763,175 (1995).

Yarra /yárrə/ river in southern Victoria, Australia. Length: 250 km/155 mi.

Yarralumla /yárrə lúmlə/ *n* the official residence of the Australian governor general in Canberra

yarrow /yárrō/ (*plural* **-rows** or *same*) *n* a plant of the daisy family with leaves like ferns. Flowers: usually white, in broad flat clusters. Native to: Europe, Asia. Latin name: *Achillea millefolium*. [Old English *gearwe* < W Germanic]

yashmak /yásh mak/, **yashmac** *n* a veil covering the

face except for the eyes worn by some Muslim women in public [Mid-19C. < Turkish *yaşmak*]

yaso /yaássō/, **ya so, yah so** *adv* same as **here** (*slang*; *used in Black English*) [Perhaps representing a pronunciation of HERE + SO[1]]

yataghan /yáttəgən/, **yatagan, ataghan** /áttəgən/ *n* a Turkish sword with no handle guard and a single-edged blade that curves inwards then outwards [Early 19C. < Turkish *yatağan*]

yatra /yáttrə/ *n* a holy pilgrimage for Hindus [Early 19C. < Sanskrit *yātrā* < *yā* 'undertake a trip']

yatter /yáttər/ (*informal*) *vi* (**-ters, -tering, -tered**) to talk continuously, especially about trivial things ■ *n* continuous talk, especially about trivial things, or an instance of this [Mid-19C. An imitation of the sound]

yaup *vi, n US* another spelling of **yawp**

yautia /yáwti ə/ (*plural* **-as** or *same*) *n* **1.** a brown starchy tuber, cooked and eaten as a vegetable **2.** a plant of the arum family that produces yautias. Native to: Caribbean. Genus: *Xanthosoma*. [Early 20C. Via Spanish < Taino]

yaw /yaw/ *vti* (**yaws, yawing, yawed**) **1.** GO OR PUT SHIP OFF COURSE to deviate from a straight course, or make a boat or ship do this **2.** TURN AROUND VERTICAL AXIS to turn around the vertical axis, or make an aircraft do this **3.** ZIGZAG to move unsteadily on a zigzag course, or make somebody or something do this ■ *n* **1.** DEVIATION FROM COURSE the deviation of a boat or ship from a straight course **2.** MOVEMENT ABOUT VERTICAL AXIS the movement of an aircraft about its vertical axis [Mid-16C. Origin ?]

yawl /yawl/ *n* **1.** a sailing vessel rigged fore-and-aft with a large mainmast and a smaller mizzenmast towards the stern **2.** a small boat kept on a ship, rowed by four or six people [Mid-17C. < Dutch *jol*]

Yawm Arafat /yawm árrə fat/, **Yom Arafat** *n* an Islamic festival during which people on the hajj gather at the plain of Arafat near Mecca and Muslims elsewhere remember them in prayer. Date: 9th day of Dhu al-Hijjah.

yawn /yawn/ *v* (**yawns, yawning, yawned**) **1.** *vi* OPEN MOUTH WIDE to open the mouth wide and take a long deep breath, usually involuntarily, because of tiredness or boredom **2.** *vt* SAY SOMETHING WHILE YAWNING to say something while yawning, or in a tired or bored voice **3.** *vi* GAPE to open wide or be a wide open space in front of somebody or something ■ *n* **1.** ACT OF YAWNING an involuntary response to tiredness or boredom in which the mouth is opened wide and a long deep breath is taken **2.** SOMEBODY OR SOMETHING BORING a boring person, thing, or event (*informal*) [Old English *ginian*] —**yawning** *adj* —**yawningly** *adv*

yawner /yáwnər/ *n* **1.** somebody who yawns **2.** same as **yawn** *n* (sense 2) (*informal*)

yawp /yawp/, **yaup** *N Am* (*informal*) *vi* (**yawps, yawping, yawped; yaups, yauping, yauped**) **1.** TALK COARSELY to talk or complain loudly, coarsely, and sometimes meaninglessly **2.** UTTER YELP to utter a sharp loud yelp ■ *n* **1.** COARSE TALK loud, coarse, and sometimes meaningless talk **2.** YELP a sharp loud yelp [14C. Origin ?] —**yawper** *n*

yaws /yawz/ *n* an infectious tropical disease marked initially by red skin eruptions and later by joint pains. It mainly affects children and is caused by the bacterium *Treponema pertenue*. (*takes a singular or plural verb*) [Late 17C. < Carib *yaya*]

y-axis *n* **1.** the vertical axis in a two-dimensional coordinate system such as a graph **2.** one of the axes in the three-dimensional Cartesian coordinate system, conventionally the vertical one

Yb *symbol* CHEM ELEM ytterbium

YC *abbr* POL Young Conservative

Y chromosome *n* the sex chromosome that determines the male sex in humans and other mammals. The body cells of males each possess one Y chromosome paired with one X chromosome.

yclept /i klépt/ *adj* called by the name of (*archaic or humorous*) [Old English *geclipod*, past participle of *geclipian* 'to call']

yd *abbr* MEASURE yard

YDT *abbr* TIME Yukon Daylight Time

ye[1] /yee/; *unstressed* /yi/ *pron* plural of **thou**[2] (*archaic or regional*) [Old English *gē*]

ye[2] *abbr* Yemen (*used in Internet addresses*) See table at **domain name**

yea /yay/ (*archaic*) *adv, n* same as **yes** ■ *adv* same as **indeed** (sense 1) ○ *'Yea, though I walk through the valley of the shadow of death, I will fear no evil'* (*Psalm 23, King James Bible*) [Old English *gēa* 'yes' < Germanic]

Yeager /yáygər/, **Chuck** (*b.* 1923) US aviator. He was the first person to fly faster than the speed of sound. Full name **Yeager, Charles Elwood**

yeah /yaa, yair/ *adv, interj* **1.** same as **yes** (*informal*) **2.** used to express scepticism about what somebody has just said (*informal*) ○ *Yeah, yeah, I've heard that before!* [Early 20C. Variant of YEA]

year /yeer, yur/ *n* **1.** TWELVE-MONTH PERIOD FROM JANUARY 1 a period of 365 days (or 366 in a leap year), measured from 1 January to 31 December **2.** TWELVE-MONTH PERIOD FROM ANY DATE a period of 365 or 366 days, measured exactly or approximately from any date ○ *The company's financial year ends on 31 July.* **3.** SOLAR YEAR the time it takes Earth to orbit the Sun, approximately 365.25 days **4.** TIME OF PLANET'S ORBIT AROUND SUN the time taken for a planet to orbit the Sun once **5.** PERIOD OF PARTICULAR ACTIVITY the time occupied by a particular activity within a twelve-month period ○ *academic year* **6.** AGE BAND IN SCHOOL OR COLLEGE a group of students, usually of approximately the same age, who start school or college at the same time and study together in one or more classes ○ *in my year at university* ■ **years** *npl* **1.** LONG TIME a very long time (*informal*) ○ *It's years since I last saw him.* ○ *We haven't been back for years.* **2.** AGE age, especially advanced age ○ *a man of his years* **3.** TIME IN GENERAL time in the past, present, or future ○ *in years to come* **4.** PARTICULAR PERIOD OF TIME a particular period of time, usually in the past ○ *her early years* [Old English *gēar* < Indo-European] ◇ **since the year dot** since an extremely long time ago (*informal*) ◇ **year in, year out** in a regular or repeated way over a long period of time, especially when this is seen as monotonous (*informal*)

yearbook /yeer book, yúr-/ *n* **1.** a book published annually containing details of events in the previous year, usually within a particular organization or field of interest **2.** in the United States, a book compiled by members of a graduating class of a high school or college, commemorating their school year and usually including photographs of the students

year-end *n* the end of a financial year or calendar year ■ *adj* occurring or done at the end of a financial year or calendar year

yearling /yeerling, yúr-/ *n* **1.** YOUNG ANIMAL an animal between one and two years of age, e.g. a calf or deer **2.** YEAR-OLD RACEHORSE a racehorse that is one year old, as reckoned from 1 January in the year after it was born **3.** BOND MATURING IN ONE YEAR a bond that comes to term after one year

yearlong /yeer lóng, yúr-/ *adj* lasting for a year or continuing throughout a year

yearly /yeerli, yúrli/ *adj* **1.** ANNUAL happening, done, appearing, or published once a year or every year **2.** RELATING TO ONE YEAR relating to or lasting for a period of twelve months ■ *adv* **1.** ANNUALLY once every year **2.** PER YEAR during a period of a year ■ *n* (*plural* **-lies** /yeerliz/) ANNUAL EVENT OR ISSUE something that happens or appears once a year, especially an annual publication

yearn /yurn/ (**yearns, yearning, yearned**) *vi* **1.** to have a strong desire for somebody or something, especially when the desire is tinged with sadness **2.** to feel affection, tenderness, or compassion [Old English *giernan* < Indo-European, 'to want'] —**yearner** *n*

SYNONYMS See **want**.

yearning /yúrning/ *n* a strong desire, often tinged with sadness —**yearningly** *adv*

year of grace, **year of our Lord** *n* a year of the Christian era

year out *n* EDUC same as **gap year**

year-round *adj* existing, continuing, or operating throughout the year ■ *adv* throughout the year

yea-sayer *n US* **1.** somebody who is always confident and optimistic **2.** somebody who always agrees submissively with a superior

yeast /yeest/ *n* **1.** SMALL SINGLE-CELLED FUNGUS a small single-celled fungus that ferments sugars and other carbohydrates and reproduces by budding. Genus: *Saccharomyces*. **2.** PREPARATION OF YEAST CELLS a commercial preparation of yeast cells. Use: brewing, baking, food supplement. **3.** FROTH the yellowish froth that forms on the surface of a fermenting liquid such as beer, contains yeast cells and carbon dioxide, and promotes fermentation **4.** FOAM a foam or froth, e.g. on sea waves **5.** CAUSE OF UNREST OR ACTIVITY somebody or something that causes ferment, activity, or unrest ■ *vi* (**yeasts, yeasting, yeasted**) FERMENT to ferment, froth, or foam [Old English *gist* < Germanic]

yeast artificial chromosome *n* a sequence of DNA taken from another organism and inserted in a yeast to reveal its function

yeast extract *n* a thick sticky brown food obtained from yeast and eaten as a spread or used in cooking

yeast infection *n* an overgrowth of a fungus in the vagina, intestines, skin, or mouth, causing irritation and swelling. Technical name **candidiasis**

yeasty /yeesti/ (**-ier, -iest**) *adj* **1.** RELATING TO YEAST relating to, containing, or tasting or smelling of yeast **2.** CAUSING FERMENTATION fermenting, or causing fermentation **3.** FROTHY full of foam or froth **4.** RESTLESS marked by or causing agitation or restlessness **5.** ENERGETIC full of vitality, productivity, or creativity **6.** FRIVOLOUS light and frivolous —**yeastily** *adv* —**yeastiness** *n*

Barnaby's

William Butler Yeats

Yeats /yayts/, **W. B.** (1865–1939) Irish poet and dramatist. A leader of the Irish Renaissance, he is considered to be one of the greatest poets of the 20th century. His poetry incorporates a complex personal mythology and includes 'The Wild Swans at Coole' (1919) and 'The Second Coming' (1922). He wrote plays for Dublin's Abbey Theatre, which he cofounded. He won the Nobel Prize in literature (1923). Full name **Yeats, William Butler**

'All changed, changed utterly: / A terrible beauty is born.'
[W. B. Yeats, 'Easter 1916', *Michael Robartes and the Dancer*; 1921]

'Things fall apart; the centre cannot hold; / Mere anarchy is loosed upon the world, / The blood-dimmed tide is loosed, and everywhere / The ceremony of innocence is drowned; / The best lack all conviction, while the worst / Are full of passionate intensity.'
[W. B. Yeats, 'The Second Coming', *Michael Robartes and the Dancer*; 1921]

yech /yekh, yek/ *interj US* used to express disgust (*informal*) [Mid-20C. Natural exclamation]

yegg /yeg/ *n N Am* a burglar, especially a safebreaker (*slang*) [Early 20C. Origin ?]

~~yeild~~ incorrect spelling of **yield**

Yekaterinburg /ye káttə reén burg/ industrial city in central Russia, on the River Iset, on the eastern slopes of the Ural Mountains. Population: 1,398,774 (1995).

Yekaterinodar /ya káttə reénə daar/ former name for **Krasnodar**

yell /yel/ *vti* (**yells, yelling, yelled**) SHOUT LOUDLY to shout or scream something, or speak in a very loud voice ○ *Stop yelling at me!* ■ *n* **1.** LOUD CRY a loud shout, scream, or cry **2.** *N Am* CHEER OF SUPPORT a rhythmic word or phrase chanted by a group of people to give

support or encouragement [Old English *giellan* < Indo-European, 'to call'] —**yeller** *n*

Yell /yel/ second largest of the Shetland Islands, Scotland. Population: 1,075 (1991). Area: 210 sq. km/81 sq. mi.

yellow /yéllō/ *adj* **1.** OF COLOUR OF BUTTER having or being near the colour of butter or ripe lemons **2.** COWARDLY cowardly or afraid (*insult*) **3.** SENSATIONALIST using scandalous or sensational material, often greatly exaggerating or distorting the truth ○ *yellow journalism* **4.** OFFENSIVE TERM a highly offensive term meaning from or born in East or Southeast Asia (*dated taboo*) ■ *n* **1.** YELLOW COLOUR a colour that lies between orange and green on the visible spectrum, e.g. that of butter or ripe lemons. It is one of the three primary colours of pigment. Yellow is also one of the three primary colours used in printing and photographic processing. **2.** YELLOW PIGMENT a yellow pigment or dye ○ *using a bright yellow to complement the green* **3.** YELLOW FABRIC yellow clothing or fabric ○ *dressed in yellow* **4.** YELLOW THING a yellow object, especially the yellow ball in snooker **5.** *US regional* EGG YOLK the yolk of an egg ■ *vti* (**-lows, -lowing, -lowed**) BECOME YELLOW to become, or make something, yellow or yellowish, especially as a result of age [Old English *geolu* < Indo-European, 'to shine'] —**yellowish** *adj* —**yellowly** *adv* —**yellowness** *n* —**yellowy** *adj*

yellow-bellied *adj* **1.** cowardly or afraid (*informal insult*) **2.** describes organisms having a yellow underside

yellow-belly *n* an offensive term that deliberately insults somebody's courage (*informal insult*)

yellow bile *n* MED, HIST same as **choler** (sense 2)

yellow brain fungus *n* FUNGI same as **jelly fungus**

yellow-breasted chat *n* a songbird with a bright yellow breast and white marks over the eyes. Native to: North America. Latin name: *Icteria virens*.

yellow cake *n* the concentrated semirefined oxide of uranium ore

yellow card *n* in football, a card shown by the referee to a player guilty of serious or persistent foul play as an indication that the player has been cautioned

yellow-dog contract *n* *US* an illegal employment contract in which the employee agrees not to join a trade union

yellow fever *n* an infectious, often fatal viral disease of warm climates, transmitted by mosquitoes and marked by high fever, haemorrhaging, vomiting of blood, liver damage, and jaundice

yellowfin tuna /yéllōfin-/, **yellowfin** (*plural* **-fins** or *same*) *n* a small tuna with yellowish anal and dorsal fins. Native to: warm regions. Latin name: *Thunnus albacares*.

yellow flag *n* **1.** NAUT same as **quarantine flag 2.** a signal in motor racing advising caution on the racetrack and prohibiting the passing of another vehicle

yellow-green alga *n* an alga that lives in soil and other moist environments and contains brown and bright yellow pigments that mask the chlorophyll. Division: *Chrysophyta*.

yellowhammer /yéllō hamər/ *n* a songbird of the bunting family, the male of which has a bright yellow head, neck, and breast. Native to: Europe. Latin name: *Emberiza citrinella*. [Mid-16C. < HAMMER, origin ?]

yellow jack *n* **1.** MED same as **yellow fever** (*archaic*) **2.** NAUT same as **quarantine flag 3. yellow jack** (*plural* **yellow jacks** or *same*) FISH a large yellowish food fish. Native to: Atlantic coast of North, South, and Central America. Latin name: *Caranx bartholomaei*.

yellow jacket *n* *N Am* a social wasp with black-and-yellow bands on its body that nests in the ground or in the hollows of trees, and can sting repeatedly. Family: Vespidae.

yellow jersey *n* in the Tour de France, the jersey awarded to the cyclist with the fastest elapsed time at a completed stage of the race

yellow journalism *n* a style of journalism that makes unscrupulous use of scandalous, lurid, or sensationalist stories to attract readers [Late 19C. After

the *Yellow Kid* cartoons, in yellow ink, in the sensationalistic *New York World*]

Yellowknife /yéllō nīf/ capital city of the Northwest Territories, Canada. It is situated on the northern shore of the Great Slave Lake. Population: 16,055 (2001).

yellowlegs /yéllō legz/ (*plural same*) *n* a large shorebird of the sandpiper family with bright yellow legs, mottled brown feathers, and white underparts. Native to: Americas. Latin name: *Tringa melanoleuca* or *Tringa flavipes*.

yellow line *n* in the United Kingdom, a line painted in yellow at the edge of a road, indicating that parking is allowed only for limited periods or at specific times

yellow ochre *n* a yellow-brown pigment containing iron. Use: artists' colours.

Yellow Pages *tdmk* a trademark for a telephone directory printed on yellow paper and containing names, addresses, and telephone numbers of businesses and other organizations listed according to the products or services offered

yellow peril *n* a highly offensive term referring to the perceived threat to Western nations posed by the nations of East Asia, especially China (*dated taboo*)

yellow pine *n* a strong yellowish pine wood

yellow poplar *n* **1.** TREES same as **tulip tree 2.** INDUST same as **tulipwood**

yellow press *n* collectively, the newspapers that make unscrupulous use of scandalous, lurid, or sensationalized stories to attract readers

yellow rain *n* a fungal toxin that occurs as a form of precipitation in Southeast Asia. It has been attributed by different sections of the scientific community to residue from chemical warfare or to the excrement of wild honeybees.

yellow rattle *n* a plant with yellow flowers whose seeds rattle in their pouches when they are shaken. Native to: Europe, North America. Latin name: *Rhinanthus minor*.

Yellow River /yéllō-/ ▸ **Huang He**

yellows /yéllōz/ *n* a plant disease marked by a yellowing of foliage that may be caused by a mineral deficiency, virus, or some other infectious agent (*takes a singular verb*)

Yellow Sea arm of the Pacific Ocean bordered on the west and north by China and on the east by the Korean Peninsula. It merges with the East China Sea to the south. Chinese name **Huang Hai**

yellow spot *n* OPHTHALMOL same as **macula** (sense 2)

Yellowstone /yéllō stōn/ river in the western United States, rising in northwestern Wyoming, and flowing into the Missouri River in North Dakota. Length: 1,110 km/692 mi.

Yellowstone National Park world's first national park, established in 1872 in parts of Wyoming, Montana, and Idaho. It is noted for its geysers, hot springs, and the Yellowstone Falls. Area: 8,983 sq. km/3,468 sq. mi.

yellowtail /yéllō tayl/ (*plural* **-tails** or *same*) *n* **1.** a sea game fish with a yellowish tail. Native to: coastal waters of California and Mexico. Latin name: *Seriola lalandei*. **2.** a small greenish fish with silver underparts and a yellow tail and fins that is commonly used as bait. Native to: southern Australian and New Zealand waters. Latin name: *Trachurus novaezelandiae*.

yellowthroat /yéllō thrōt/ *n* a small songbird of the warbler family that nests in dense undergrowth and has a yellow breast and throat, a black mask, and a brownish back. Native to: North America. Latin name: *Geothlypis trichas*.

yellowweed /yéllō weed/ *n* a yellow-flowered plant, e.g. the ragwort or the goldenrod

yellowwood /yéllō wŏŏd/ (*plural* **-woods** or *same*) *n* **1.** YELLOWISH WOOD OF N AMERICAN TREE the yellowish wood of a leguminous North American tree. Use: source of yellow dye. **2.** YELLOWISH WOOD OF S AFRICAN TREE the yellowish wood of a southern African coniferous tree **3.** N AMERICAN TREE a leguminous tree that yields yellowwood. Native to: southern United States. Latin name: *Cladastris lutea*. **4.** S AFRICAN TREE a con-

iferous tree that yields yellowwood. Native to: southern Africa. Latin name: *Podocarpus falcatus*.

yellowwort /yéllō wurt/ (*plural* **-worts** or *same*) *n* a perennial plant that has grey waxy foliage and is usually found on chalky turf. Flowers: yellow. Latin name: *Blackstonia perfoliata*.

yellow-yite /yéllō yīt/ (*plural* **yellow-yites** or *same*) *n* *Scotland* BIRDS same as **yellowhammer** [Early 19C. Origin ?]

yelp /yelp/ *v* (**yelps, yelping, yelped**) **1.** *vi* BARK OR CRY SHARPLY to utter a short sharp high-pitched bark or cry, usually of pain **2.** *vt* UTTER SOMETHING WITH YELPING SOUND to say something in a sharp high-pitched voice ■ *n* SHORT BARK OR CRY a short high-pitched bark or cry [Old English *gielpan* 'to boast' < Indo-European, 'to call'] —**yelper** *n*

Yeltsin /yéltsin/, **Boris** (b. 1931) Russian president (1991–99). He was the first democratically elected Russian president, and was instrumental in planning the country's transition from Communism to a market economy. Full name **Yeltsin, Boris Nikolayevich**

> 'Europe has not yet freed itself from the heritage of the Cold War and is in danger of plunging into a Cold Peace.'
> [Boris Yeltsin, *Independent*; 6 December 1994]

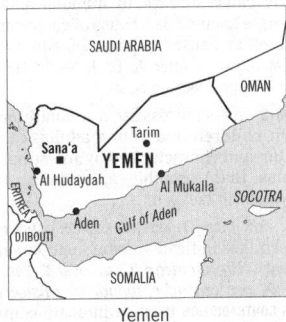

Yemen

Yemen /yémmən/ country on the Arabian peninsula, in Southwest Asia, on the Red Sea. The country was created in 1990 by the unification of the Yemen Arab Republic, or North Yemen, and the People's Democratic Republic of Yemen, or South Yemen. Language: Arabic. Currency: Yemeni riyal. Capital: Sana'a. Population: 19,349,881 (2003). Area: 527,970 sq. km/203,850 sq. mi. Official name **Republic of Yemen** —**Yemeni** *n, adj*

yen[1] /yen/ (*plural same*) *n* the main unit of currency in Japan, worth 100 sen. See table at **currency** [Late 19C. Via Japanese *en* < Chinese *yuán* 'round']

yen[2] /yen/ *n* a strong yearning for something ■ *vi* (**yens, yenning, yenned**) to have a strong yearning for something [Early 20C. Probably < Chinese (Cantonese) *yăn*]

Yenisey /yénni sáy/ river in central Siberian Russia. It is formed in the Sayan Mountains in southern Siberia by the union of the Greater Yenisey and the Little Yenisey, and flows northwards into the Kara Sea. Length: 4,090 km/2,540 mi.

yenta /yéntə/, **yente** *N Am* somebody, often a woman, known as a meddler or a gossip (*slang; sometimes offensive*) [Mid-20C. Via Yiddish *yente* < woman's name *Yente* < Latin *gentilis* 'of the same family']

yeoman /yṓmən/ *n* (*plural* **-men** /-mən/). **1.** NAVY SIGNALS OFFICER a noncommissioned or petty officer in the Royal Navy or the Marines who is in charge of signals **2.** FARMER WITH SMALL FREEHOLD a member of a former class of English commoners who owned and cultivated their own land **3.** SHERIFF'S ASSISTANT formerly, an assistant to a sheriff or other official **4.** ATTENDANT TO NOBILITY OR ROYALTY formerly, a servant or minor official employed in a royal or noble household **5.** MIL same as **yeoman of the guard** ■ *adj* PERFORMED DILIGENTLY characterized by loyalty, diligence, and reliability ○ *performed yeoman service in completing the task on time* [13C. Origin ?]

yeomanly /yṓmənli/ *adj* **1.** RELATING TO YEOMAN relating to or characteristic of a yeoman or yeomen **2.** STAUNCH

AND DEPENDABLE dependable, loyal, and brave (*archaic or literary*) ■ *adv* BRAVELY in a brave and loyal way

yeoman of the guard (*plural* **yeomen of the guard**) *n* a member of a British royal guard who perform ceremonial duties, especially as guards of the Tower of London

yeomanry /yṓmənri/ *n* **1.** in England in former times, a class of commoners who owned and cultivated their own land **2.** a British cavalry force, organized as a home guard in 1761, that became part of the Territorial Army in 1907

Yeovil /yṓvil/ town in Somerset, southwestern England. Population: 35,000 (1993 estimate).

yep /yep/ *adv, interj* same as **yes** (*informal*) [Late19C. Alteration]

YER *abbr* BANKING yearly effective rate

yerba /yáirbə, yúr-/, **yerba maté** *n* BEVERAGES, TREES same as **maté** [Early 19C. < Spanish, 'herb']

Yerevan /yérrə vaán/ capital and largest city of Armenia, on the River Hrazdan, in the west of the country. Population: 1,250,000 (2000).

Yerkish /yúrkish/ *n* an artificial language of visual symbols created for experimental communication between chimpanzees and humans [Late 20C. After Robert Mearns *Yerkes* (1876–1956), US psychobiologist] —**Yerkish** *adj*

yersinia /yur sínni ə/ *n* a Gram-negative bacterium that may cause disease in humans and animals. One of these bacteria is a cause of gastric infections, while another causes bubonic plague. Genus: *Yersinia.* [Mid-20C. < After A. E. J. *Yersin* (1863–1943), Swiss-born French bacteriologist]

yersiniosis /yur sínni ṓssiss/ *n* a condition, mainly found in children and young adults, caused by a bacterium and characterized by intestinal pain and symptoms that resemble appendicitis [Late 20C. < YERSINIA, which causes it]

yes /yess/ *adv, interj* **1.** ASSENT INDICATOR used, especially in speech, to indicate assent, agreement, or affirmation ○ *'Do you mean it's all over?' 'Yes, I suppose I do'.* ○ *97 per cent of respondents answered yes.* **2.** INDICATES CONTRADICTION used to indicate contradiction in response to a negative proposition ○ *'He won't believe you'. 'Oh yes he will'.* **3.** MARK OF ATTENTION used to indicate that somebody is ready to give his or her attention to somebody who has asked for it ○ *'Doctor?' 'Yes?'* **4.** ACCEPTANCE used to accept an offer or a request ○ *'Would you like some tea?' 'Yes, please'.* ■ *n* (*plural* **yeses** or **yesses**) **1.** AFFIRMATIVE RESPONSE an affirmative response to a question ○ *Was that a yes or a no?* **2.** AFFIRMATIVE VOTER somebody who votes in the affirmative ○ *The yeses have 65 per cent and the noes 35 per cent, so the motion is carried.* ■ *interj* EXCLAMATION OF JUBILATION used as a loud exclamation to express triumph, jubilation, or extreme excitement and pleasure (*informal*) ○ *Our team won the championship--yes!!!* [Old English *gēse* < *gēa* (see YEA) + *sīe* 'may it be (so)', form of the verb *to be*] ◇ **say yes** to express agreement or consent

yeshiva /yə shéevə/ (*plural* **-vas** or **-vot** /-vot/ or **-voth**), **yeshivah** (*plural* **-vahs** or **-vot** or **-voth**) *n* **1.** a seminary for orthodox Jewish, usually unmarried, men where they study the primary source of Jewish law, the Talmud **2.** a secondary school for Jewish students with a curriculum including religious and cultural, as well as academic, studies [Mid-19C. < Hebrew *yĕšībāh* < *yāšab* 'sit']

yes man, **yes-man** *n* somebody, especially a man, who enthusiastically and uncritically agrees with the ideas and views of a superior

yes/no question *n* a question that can be answered with 'yes' or 'no' and that in English begins with an actual or implied verb

yessir /yéssər/, **yessiree** /yés sə rée/ *interj* used, often ironically or humorously, to express submissive assent or obedience (*informal*) [Early 20C. Representing a casual pronunciation of *yes, sir*]

yester- *prefix* used to refer to a time in the past denoted by the suffix ○ *yestermorning* [Old English *geostran* < Germanic]

yesterday /yéstərday, -di/ *n* **1.** DAY BEFORE TODAY the day before this one **2.** PAST a time in the past ■ *adv* **1.** ON PREVIOUS DAY on the day before today **2.** IN PAST at a time in the past

yesterevening /yéstər eevning/ (*archaic or literary*) *adv* yesterday in the evening ■ *n* the evening of yesterday

yestermorning /yéstər mawrning/ (*archaic or literary*) *adv* yesterday in the morning ■ *n* the morning of yesterday

yesternight /yéstər nīt/ (*archaic or literary*) *adv* yesterday in the night ■ *n* the night of yesterday

yesteryear /yéstər yeer, -yur/ *n* **1.** the not very recent past **2.** the year before this one (*literary*)

yet /yet/ *adv* **1.** SO FAR up to now or a particular time in the past or future (*often used with a negative or interrogative*) ○ *The information had not yet been analysed.* ○ *Have you finished eating yet?* ○ *This study is the most comprehensive yet.* **2.** NOW now, as opposed to later (*often used with a negative*) ○ *I can't come over just yet.* **3.** EVEN even or still (*often used with a comparative*) ○ *This spurred her on to yet greater efforts.* ○ *Yet again, we find the same reluctance to act.* **4.** IN SPITE OF EVERYTHING used to stress that it remains possible that something will happen or that you are still determined to do something despite present difficulties ○ *We'll solve this problem yet.* **5.** FOR LONGER used to indicate that something will go on happening for a particular length of time ○ *It will take hours yet for the space telescope photos to arrive on Earth and be processed.* **6.** NEVER UP TO NOW used to indicate that somebody has not done something up to now ○ *The largest hotel in the town, the Queen's Head, has yet to welcome a member of the royal family.* ■ *conj* NEVERTHELESS however or nevertheless ○ *Her problems are increasing, yet she keeps smiling.* [Old English *gīet*, origin ?]

USAGE *Did she go yet?* In the simple past tense ***yet*** is not used in this way in British English; the perfect tense (*Has she gone yet?*) is used. The simple past is usual, however, in American English. In some meanings, ***yet*** and *still* are largely interchangeable: *This has still to be decided* or *This has yet to be decided.*

yeti /yétti/ (*plural* **-tis**) *n* a mysterious hairy humanoid animal said to live in the Himalaya range [Mid-20C. Origin ?]

yettie /yétti/ *n* a young, technologically knowledgeable entrepreneur who is involved in e-commerce and who typically buys and sells technology shares (*slang*) [Late 20C. Acronym < *young, entrepreneurial, tech(nology)-based*, after YUPPIE and similar words]

Yevtushenko /yévtə shéngkō/, **Yevgeny Aleksandrovich** (*b.* 1933) Russian poet. His works such as *Zima Junction* (1956) and *Babi Yar* (1961) were critical of the former Soviet Union during its post-Stalinist years, and, although officially condemned by the Soviets, were widely read in both his own country and the West.

> 'Over Babi Yar / There are no memorials. / The steep hillside like a rough inscription.'
> [Yevgeny Aleksandrovich Yevtushenko, *Babi Yar*; 1961]

yew

yew /yoo/ *n* **1.** WOOD the fine-grained wood of a poisonous evergreen tree. Use: cabinetmaking and, especially formerly, making bows. **2.** EVERGREEN TREE an evergreen tree or bush that has flat dark-green needles and scarlet fruits (**arils**) that resemble berries. Most parts of the tree are considered poisonous. Genus: *Taxus.* **3.** YEW BOW an archer's bow made of yew wood [Old English *īw* < Germanic]

Yezidi /yézzidi/ *n* a member of a Kurdish religious group founded by an Muslim mystic in the 12th century but incorporating Iranian myth and tradition. The group has been declared as heretical by orthodox Muslims and has been the object of intense persecution. [Early 19C. Origin ?] —**Yezidism** *n*

Y-fronts *tdmk* a trademark for men's or boys' underpants that have an opening at the front with seams in the shape of an inverted Y

Yggdrasil /ígdrə sil/, **Ygdrasil** *n* in Norse mythology, the great ash tree that overshadows the world, binding together earth, heaven, and hell [< Old Norse]

YHA *abbr* Youth Hostels Association

YHWH, **YHVH**, **JHVH**, **JHWH** *n* the transliteration of the four letters (**Tetragrammaton**) representing the name of God in the Bible. This transliteration was only ever pronounced by the high priest in the Temple.

Yi /yee/ *n* a Korean dynasty that ruled Korea from 1392, following a period of Mongol invasions, until 1910, and that restored aristocratic dominance and Chinese influence

yid /yid/ *n* a highly offensive term for a Jew (*taboo insult*) [Late 19C. Via Yiddish < Middle High German *jüde* 'Jew' (see YIDDISH)]

Yiddish /yíddish/ *n* a language derived from a medieval German dialect and written in Hebrew script, spoken by some Jews in Europe, Israel, and North and South America. It reflects the influence of Hebrew, Aramaic, and other languages, especially Slavonic languages. See panel on next page [Late 19C. Via Yiddish *yidish (daytsh)* 'Jewish (German)' < Middle High German *jüdisch diutsch* < *jüde* 'Jewish person' < Latin *Judaeus* (see JEW)] —**Yiddish** *adj*

yield /yeeld/ *v* (**yields, yielding, yielded**) **1.** *vt* PRODUCE SOMETHING to produce something naturally or as a result of cultivation ○ *The field yields a good crop.* **2.** *vt* GIVE SOMETHING AS RESULT to produce something as the result of work, activity, or calculation ○ *The research has yielded some interesting results.* **3.** *vt* FIN GIVE PROFIT to gain an amount as a return on an investment ○ *bonds that yield 9 per cent* **4.** *vi* NOT BE FIRM OR SOLID to move or bend under pressure or when force is applied ○ *The window was painted shut and wouldn't yield.* **5.** *vi* STOP RESISTING to stop opposing or resisting and agree to somebody's demands or requests ○ *She refused to yield despite our pleas.* **6.** *vi* SURRENDER to admit defeat and surrender ○ *The commander finally yielded after a long siege.* **7.** *vt* PASS SOMETHING ON TO SOMEBODY to give something up to somebody else or allow somebody else to take it over ○ *He eventually yielded control of the company to his daughter.* **8.** *vi* BE REPLACED BY SOMETHING to be replaced by something else ○ *Older houses and gardens were gradually yielding to modern purpose-built flats.* **9.** *vi N Am* ROADS LET ANOTHER PASS to slow down or stop in order to let another vehicle pass ○ *yield to traffic on the right* ■ *n* **1.** AMOUNT PRODUCED the amount of something, especially a crop, produced by cultivation or labour ○ *Yields per acre were slightly lower than last year.* **2.** RETURN ON INVESTMENT a return on an investment in the form of interest or dividends ○ *The yield on the account was disappointing.* **3.** PRODUCT FROM CHEMICAL REACTION the quantity of product resulting from a chemical reaction or process, often expressed as a percentage of the amount that is theoretically obtainable **4.** EXPLOSIVE FORCE the amount of energy released in a nuclear explosion expressed as the amount of TNT that would have the same explosive force [Old English *geldan* 'pay' < Germanic] —**yieldable** *adj* —**yielder** *n*

SYNONYMS ***yield, capitulate, submit, succumb, surrender, give in***

CORE MEANING: to stop resisting

yield to stop opposing or resisting and agree to somebody's demands or requests ○ *The government would not yield to public pressure.* **capitulate** to accept an argument, request, pressure, or something unavoidable ○ *We cannot afford the gains we have made to be lost by capitulating to the demands of special interest groups.* **submit** to accept somebody else's authority or will, especially reluctantly or under pressure ○ *We don't intend to submit meekly to the proposed changes.* **succumb** to be unable to resist or oppose something ○ *For all her good intentions, she soon succumbed to the temptation of another cigarette.* **sur-**

LANGUAGE HERITAGE *Yiddish* Much of English is made up of words from other languages, and Yiddish is an important contributor in this respect, especially in North America, making English all the more richly textured and colourful. Words migrating into English directly from Yiddish alone are, for example, *mazuma*, *shlemiel*, and *tush*. Many others came into English via Yiddish but have other ancestral roots, for example *bagel* (from Old High German), *chutzpah* (from Aramaic), and *yenta* (from Latin). And the word *Yiddish* itself is an émigré from Middle High German and Latin. Yiddish words derived from Hebrew include, for example, *matzo*, *maven*, and *schmooze*.

Yiddish has also given English two colourful affixes. The first is the suffix *-nik*, 'somebody associated with or characterized by', for example *peacenik*, *beatnik*, and *refusenik*, along with creative forms such as 'noshnik', 'Freudnik', 'nogoodnik', and 'allrightnik'. Yiddish acquired this form from Russian, and some early words containing it may be derived from that language, but its creativity stems from Yiddish use. The second is *schm-* or *shm-*, 'somebody or something purported or purporting to be genuine, real, or of the expected high quality but really not'. This prefix creates hyphenated rhyming compounds by replacing the initial consonants or consonant clusters in English words, yielding, for example, 'doctor-schmoctor', 'fancy-schmancy', or by preceding initial vowels ('Elvis-Schmelvis', 'opera-shmopera').

In some instances Yiddish has fused with English to yield familiar compounds like *gefilte fish* and *matzo balls*. What is more, certain English – especially American English – grammatical constructions and idioms are traceable to Yiddish constructions, for example 'Be well', a loose translation of Yiddish *zay gezunt*. Other English expressions originally associated with Yiddish speakers are these verb commands, a good many opening with *so*: 'So stop it already!' 'So sit'. 'Enjoy'. 'Go know'. 'Get lost!' 'Eat your heart out'. Others are inversions, for example, 'He is a boy is all'. 'A fashion model she is not'. Still others are rhetorical questions opening with 'What's to' followed by a verb, for example, 'What's to like?' 'What's not to like?' 'What's to forgive?' See also *Hebrew*.

render to declare to an opponent that he or she has won so that fighting or conflict can cease ○ *Still the enemy refused to surrender.* **give in** to accept demands or conditions ○ *Governments can't be seen to give in to terrorist threats.*

yield up *vt* to reveal something formerly hidden or secret

yielding /yeélding/ *adj* **1.** SOFT AND BENDING inclined to give or bend under pressure **2.** COMPLIANT tending to obey others **3.** PRODUCING productive of a good or bad yield or crop —**yieldingly** *adv*

yikes /yīks/ *interj* used when suddenly startled (*informal*) [Late 20C. Origin ?]

yin /yin/ *n* the principle of darkness, negativity, and femininity in Chinese philosophy that is the counterpart of yang. The dual, opposite, and complementary principles of yin and yang are thought to exist in varying proportions in all things. [Late 17C. < Chinese *yīn* 'shade, feminine, moon']

Yinchuan /yín chwaán/ capital city of Ningxia Hui Autonomous Region in north-central China. Population: 337,855 (1991).

Yinglish /yíng glish/ *n* a type of English influenced by Yiddish words and syntax, spoken by early Jewish immigrants to the United States [Mid-20C. Blend of YIDDISH + ENGLISH] —**Yinglish** *adj*

yip /yip/ *vi* (**yips, yipping, yipped**) to give a high-pitched bark ■ *n* a high-pitched bark [Early 20C. An imitation of the sound]

yipe /yīp/ *interj* US used to express fear or alarm (*informal*) [Mid-20C. Origin ?]

yippee *interj* used to express joy and excitement (*usually used by children*) [Early 20C. A natural exclamation]

yips /yips/ *npl* nervousness that impairs the performance of a sportsman or sportswoman, especially a golfer [Mid-20C. Origin ?]

yissus /yíssəss/ *interj* S Africa used to express astonishment, disbelief, or annoyance (*informal*) [Representing an Afrikaans pronunciation of *Jesus*]

Yizkor /yíz kawr/ *n* in Judaism, a memorial prayer for deceased relatives recited in synagogues on festivals and Yom Kippur [Mid-20C. < Hebrew *yizkōr* 'may He remember']

-yl *suffix* a group of atoms forming a radical ○ *carbonyl* [Via French *-yle* < Greek *hulē* 'wood, organic matter']

ylang-ylang /eé lang eé lang/, **ilang-ilang** *n* a tree with flowers that yield a fragrant oil used in perfumery. Native to: tropical Asia, northern Australia. Latin name: *Cananga odorata*. [Late 19C. < Tagalog *ilang-ilang*]

ylem /íləm/ *n* hypothetical matter that, according to the big bang theory of the origin of the universe, was the substance from which the chemical elements were formed [Mid-20C. < medieval Latin *hylem* 'universal matter' < Greek *hulē* 'wood, matter']

Y-level *n* a rotatable level mounted on a Y-shaped frame, used in surveying

YMCA[1] *n* a building or other centre where social, sports, or educational facilities are provided by the YMCA for its members

YMCA[2] *abbr* Young Men's Christian Association

YMHA *abbr* Young Men's Hebrew Association

Ymir /eé meer/ *n* in Norse mythology, the forefather of all the giants. Ymir was killed by Odin and his brothers, and the world was formed from his body, the sky from his skull, and the water from his blood.

Ymodem /wī mō dem/ *n* a variation of the Xmodem file transfer protocol in which data is sent in 1-kilobyte blocks

yo /yō/ *interj* used as a greeting or to get somebody's attention (*informal*) [15C. Natural exclamation]

yob /yob/, **yobbo** /yóbbō/ (*plural* **-bos**) *n* a young hooligan (*slang*) [Mid-19C. Backward spelling of BOY] —**yobbery** *n* —**yobbish** *adj*

YOB *abbr* year of birth

yobbo *n* same as **yob**

yocto- *prefix* indicates 10^{-24} in measurements ○ *yoctojoule* [Late 20C. Modelled on OCTO-]

yod /yod/, **yodh** *n* the tenth letter of the Hebrew alphabet, represented in the English alphabet as 'y'. See table at **alphabet** [Mid-18C. < Hebrew *yōd*]

yodel /yṓd'l/, **yodle** *vi* (**-dels, -delling, -delled; -dles, -dling, -dled**) to sing, changing rapidly between a normal and falsetto voice. It is a feature of Alpine folk music and of some US country and western music. ■ *n* a song or passage that features yodelling [Early 19C. < German *jodeln* an imitation of the sound] —**yodeller** *n*

yodh *n* another spelling of **yod**

yodle *vi, n* MUSIC another spelling of **yodel**

yoga: half spinal twist position

Tony Arruza/Corbis

yoga /yṓgə/ *n* **1.** a Hindu discipline that promotes spiritual unity with a supreme being through a system of postures and rituals **2.** a system or set of breathing exercises and postures derived from or based on Hindu yoga [Late 18C. < Sanskrit *yogaḥ* 'union']

Yogalates /yṓgə laátayz/ *tdmk* a trademark for a holistic form of exercise that combines the breathing techniques of yoga with the body movements of Pilates

yogh /yog/ *n* a letter ʒ used in Middle English, usually represented in modern English as 'gh' or 'y' [13C. Origin ?]

yoghurt /yóggərt, yṓgərt/, **yogurt**, **yoghourt** *n* milk fermented by bacteria to give a tangy or slightly sour flavour and a lightly set or thick and creamy consistency. It is sometimes sweetened and flavoured, usually with fruit. [Early 17C. < Turkish *yoğurt*]

yogi /yṓgi/ (*plural* **-gis**), **yogin** /yṓgin/ *n* S Asia **1.** somebody who has mastered yoga **2.** a guru or other spiritual teacher of religion [Early 17C. < Sanskrit *yogī* < *yogaḥ* 'yoga']

yogurt *n* FOOD another spelling of **yoghurt**

Yogyakarta /yóggyə kaártə/ city in southwestern Indonesia, on the island of Java. Population: 477,073 (1997).

yo-heave-ho *interj* formerly used by sailors as a rhythmic accompaniment to hauling work

YOI *abbr* young offender institution

yoicks /yoyks/ *interj* used to encourage hounds in a foxhunt [Mid-18C. Origin ?]

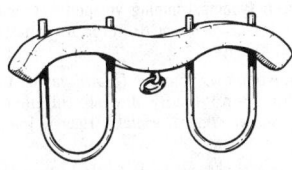
yoke

yoke /yōk/ *n* **1.** ANIMAL HARNESS a wooden frame for harnessing two draught animals to whatever they had to pull **2.** JOINED ANIMALS two animals joined by a yoke ○ *a yoke of oxen* **3.** FRAME FOR CARRYING LOADS a frame designed to fit across somebody's shoulders with balanced loads suspended at each end **4.** CLOTHING FITTED PART OF GARMENT the fitted part of a garment, usually around the shoulders or waist, from which an unfitted part is suspended **5.** RESTRICTIVE BURDEN something that is felt to be oppressive and restrictive ○ *throw off the tyrant's yoke* **6.** BOND KEEPING PEOPLE CLOSE a bond or tie that keeps people together ○ *the yoke of marriage* **7.** CROSSED SPEARS an archway made of crossed spears under which defeated enemies of the ancient Romans were forced to march **8.** NAUT RUDDER CROSSBAR a crossbar fitted to the top of a rudder and connected to the front of a boat by ropes or cables for steering **9.** ELECTRONICS CATHODE RAY DEVICE a device fitted to the neck of a cathode ray tube to control the scanning motion of the electron beam **10.** RECORDING EQUIPMENT FOR MULTITRACK RECORDING equipment for recording or reproducing sounds or music on more than one track simultaneously, by joining together two or more magnetic recording heads **11.** AVIAT AIRCRAFT PART the handle of the steering mechanism for an aeroplane's ailerons **12.** Ireland, N Ireland WHATSIT OR THINGUMABOB a gadget or implement whose proper name is not known ○ *I need a yoke to fix this screw in.* ■ *vt* (**yokes, yoking, yoked**) **1.** FIT ANIMALS WITH YOKE to put a yoke on two draught animals **2.** CONNECT ANIMAL TO VEHICLE to connect a draught animal to a plough or vehicle **3.** LINK THINGS TOGETHER to join or link two things forcibly or surprisingly ○ *Foxhunters were yoked together with farmers on the issue.* [Old English *geoc* < Indo-European, 'join']

SPELLCHECK Do not confuse the spelling of *yoke* and *yolk*, which sound similar. *Yoke* refers to a frame for pulling or carrying a load, or something oppressive or restrictive: *put the yoke on the oxen, the yoke of tyranny, yoked them to the plough.* The *yolk* is the yellow portion of an egg.

yokel /yṓk'l/ *n* an offensive term that deliberately insults a country dweller by suggesting that he or she lacks the sophistication, education, or other

qualities thought characteristic of city dwellers (*insult*) [Early 19C. Origin ?] —**yokelish** *adj*

Yokohama /yṓkō haʹaməʹ/ capital city and port of Kanagawa Prefecture, in southeastern Honshu Island, Japan. Population: 3,433,612 (2002).

yolk /yōk/ *n* **1.** the round yellow portion of a bird's or reptile's egg, containing protein and fats that provide nourishment for the developing young. The eggs of mammals, whose embryos absorb nutrients from the mother, contain very little yolk. **2.** a greasy substance from the skin of sheep that collects in wool [Old English *geol(o)ca < geolu* (see YELLOW)] —**yolky** *adj*

SPELLCHECK See *yoke*.

yolk sac *n* a thin membrane surrounding the embryo in birds, fish, reptiles, and mammals. In birds, fish, and reptiles, it encloses the yolk.

Yolngu *n* **1.** a member of an Australian Aboriginal people of eastern Arnhem Land **2.** a group of Australian Aboriginal languages spoken in eastern Arnhem Land

Yom Arafat another spelling of **Yawm Arafat**

Yom Kippur /yom kíppər, -ki pŏŏrʹ/ *n* the holiest day of the Jewish year, on which Jews fast and say prayers of penitence. Date: 10th day of Tishri. [< Hebrew *Yōm Kippūr* 'day of atonement']

yomp /yomp/ (**yomps, yomping, yomped**) *vi* to walk while heavily laden or over difficult terrain (*informal*) [Late 20C. Origin ?]

yom tov /yóm tóv, yómtəv/ (*plural* **yamim tovim** /yaa meʹem to veʹem/) *n* any Jewish religious festival [Directly and via Yiddish *yontef* < Hebrew *yōm ṭōb* 'good day']

yon /yon/ *adv* OVER THERE in or to that place over there (*literary*) ○ *wandered hither and yon* ■ *det* N England, Scotland THAT OR THOSE located in that place over there ■ *pron* N England, Scotland THAT ONE OR THOSE ONES the one or ones in that place over there (*takes a singular or plural verb*) [Partly shortening of YONDER, partly < Old English *geon* 'that one']

REGIONAL NOTE *Yon* and *yonder* were once widely used in English. There was thus a tripartite system where *this book* meant 'the book close to the speaker', *that book* meant 'the one close to the listener', and *yon book* meant 'the one close to neither speaker nor listener'. Some dialect speakers linked these words even more closely by combining both and pronouncing **yon** as 'thon' and **yonder** as 'thonder'.

yond /yond/ (*archaic or literary*) *adv* in or to that place over there ■ *det* located in that place over there [Old English *geond, geondan* < Indo-European, 'that one']

yonder /yóndər/ *n* THE DISTANCE the far distance (*informal*) ○ *set off into the blue yonder* ■ *adv* regional OVER THERE in or to that place over there ■ *det* regional THAT OR THOSE located in that place over there ■ *pron* regional THAT ONE OR THOSE ONES the one or ones in that place over there (*takes a singular or plural verb*)

REGIONAL NOTE See *yon*.

yoni /yóni/ (*plural* **-nis**) *n* in Hinduism, a representation of the female genitals regarded as a manifestation of the feminine principle [Late 18C. < Sanskrit *yoniḥ* 'womb']

Yonkers /yóngkərz/ *n* city in southeastern New York State, on the Hudson River. It is a northern suburb of New York City. Population: 197,234 (2002 estimate).

yonks /yongks/ *n* a very long time (*informal*) [Mid-20C. Origin ?]

yoo-hoo /yŏŏ hooʹ/ *interj* used to get somebody's attention, especially when the speaker is at a distance ■ *vti* (**yoo-hoos, yoo-hooing, yoo-hooed**) to say or shout 'yoo-hoo' to somebody [Early 20C. Natural exclamation]

yore /yawr/ [Old English *geāra*, origin ?] ◇ **of yore** in the far distant past (*literary*) ○ *in days of yore*

york /yawrk/ (**yorks, yorking, yorked**) *vt* in cricket, to get a batsman out or to attempt to get a batsman out by bowling a ball so that it pitches immediately under the bat [Late 19C. Back-formation < YORKER]

York[1] /yawrk/ *n* the branch of the Plantagenet dynasty that ruled England from 1461 to 1485. It was named

after its founder, Edmund of Langley, 1st Duke of York (1341–1402).

York[2] /yawrk/ city in North Yorkshire, northern England. Originally a Celtic settlement, under the Romans it became an important regional centre. Population: 181,094 (2001).

Yorke Peninsula /yáwrk-/ peninsula in South Australia, situated between the Gulf of St Vincent and the Spencer Gulf

yorker /yáwrkər/ *n* a ball bowled in cricket so that it pitches on the ground immediately under the bat [Probably after the city of YORK[2]]

yorkie /yáwrki/, **Yorkie** *n* BREED same as **Yorkshire terrier** (*informal*) [Early 19C. Shortening]

Yorkist /yáwrkist/ *n* a supporter or member of the House of York during the Wars of the Roses and when it ruled England from 1461 to 1485

York rite *n* a masonic ceremony that confers different degrees at different levels of the membership [Late 19C. After YORK[2]]

Yorks. *abbr* Yorkshire

Yorkshire /yáwrkshər/ former county in northern England, historically divided into East, North, and West Ridings. The largest traditional county in England, it is now divided into the counties of North Yorkshire, West Yorkshire, South Yorkshire, and the East Riding of Yorkshire.

Yorkshire Dales area of wild moorlands divided by fertile valleys in the mid-Pennines, northern England

Yorkshire Dales National Park national park, in northern England, established in 1954. Area: 1,769 sq. km/683 sq. mi.

Yorkshire fog *n* a common grass of the British Isles that has downy leaves and white or pink flower heads. Latin name: *Holcus lanatus*.

Yorkshireman /yáwrkshərmən/ (*plural* **-men** /-mən/) *n* a man who comes from Yorkshire

Yorkshire pudding *n* a flour-based batter pudding that is traditionally served with roast beef. It was originally served with gravy before roast meat with the intention of satisfying appetites so that a small amount of meat would go a long way.

Yorkshire terrier

Yorkshire terrier *n* a very small long-haired terrier with a long silky brown-and-grey coat

Yorkshirewoman /yáwrkshər wŏŏmən/ (*plural* **-women** /-wimin/) *n* a woman who comes from Yorkshire

Yorkton /yáwrktən/ town in Saskatchewan, Canada, northeast of Regina. Population: 15,107 (2001).

Yorktown /yáwrk town/ *n* historic site in southeastern Virginia, situated on the York River near Chesapeake Bay. It was the site of the final battle of the American War of Independence and of Cornwallis's surrender to George Washington on 19 October 1781.

Yoruba /yórrŏŏbə/ (*plural same* or **-bas**) *n* **1.** MEMBER OF W AFRICAN PEOPLE a member of a West African people living mostly in Nigeria **2.** W AFRICAN LANGUAGE a Niger-Congo language spoken in southwestern Nigeria, Benin, and Togo. Native speakers: 20 million. **3.** REGION OF CITY-STATES IN NIGERIA a region of city-states that developed in northern Nigeria around AD 1200, notable for the population's animistic religion and their artistic work, in particular wood and bronze pieces [Mid-19C. < Yoruba] —**Yoruba** *adj* —**Yoruban** *adj*

Yosemite Falls /yə sémməti-, yō-/ waterfall in the Yosemite National Park, California. Consisting of

the Upper Yosemite Falls and the Lower Yosemite Falls, it is one of the highest waterfalls in the world, with a total drop of 739 m/2,425 ft.

Yosemite National Park national park in central California in the Sierra Nevada, established in 1890. It is noted for its giant sequoia trees and waterfalls. Area: 3,081 sq. km/1,189 sq. mi.

yotta- *prefix* indicates 10^{24} in measurements ○ *yotta-byte* [Late 20C. Probably < Italian *otto* 'eight']

you *stressed* /yoo/; *unstressed* /yŏŏ/; /yə/ *pron* **1.** PERSON BEING ADDRESSED refers to the person or people being addressed or written to ○ *I'm fine – how about you?* **2.** PERSON OR PEOPLE UNSPECIFIED refers to an unspecified person or people in general ○ *You have to see it to believe it.* ○ *You mix all the dry ingredients together in a bowl.* **3.** THOSE BEING REFERRED TO used to refer to the person you are talking to, as well as other people of the same type or class (*used before a pl*) ○ *Isn't it time you kids were in bed?* **4.** PERSONALITY OF PERSON ADDRESSED refers to the personality of the person addressed or something's suitability to express it (*informal*) ○ *Don't buy that suit – it's not really you!* **5.** US same as **yourself** (sense 1) (*informal; used as an indirect object*) ○ *You'll have to get you a job.* [Old English *īow < gē* (see YE[1])]

USAGE See *yourself*.

you-all, **y'all** /yawl/ *pron* Southern US used to address more than one person (*informal*)

you-beaut *adj* Aus exceptional or outstanding (*informal*)

you'd /yood/ *contr* **1.** you had **2.** you would

you'll /yool/ *contr* **1.** you shall **2.** you will

young /yung/ *adj* (**younger, youngest**) **1.** NOT VERY OLD having lived or been in existence a relatively short time ○ *a young person* **2.** OF YOUTH relating to somebody's youth ○ *my younger days* **3.** YOUTHFUL looking or behaving like a young or younger person ○ *very young for her age* **4.** FOR YOUNG PEOPLE designed for or appropriate to young people ○ *young fashions* **5.** RECENTLY BEGUN recently begun or in an early stage ○ *The night is still young.* **6.** GEOL NOT SIGNIFICANTLY ERODED in a relatively early stage of landscape formation and therefore steep and largely uneroded ■ *npl* **1.** OFFSPRING offspring, especially when still completely dependent on parents ○ *watching her young* **2.** YOUNG PEOPLE young people in general ○ *a club for the young* [Old English *geong* < Indo-European, 'youth, vigour'] —**youngish** *adj* ◇ **in your younger days** when you were younger than you are now ◇ **the Younger** used after a person's name to indicate that he or she is the second-born person of that name ○ *Pitt the Younger*

Young /yung/, **Arthur** (1741–1820) British agriculturist and writer. He is known for his books describing his travels in England, Ireland, and France.

Young, Brigham (1801–77) US religious leader. He succeeded Joseph Smith as the leader of the Church of Jesus Christ of Latter-Day Saints (1844–77). He organized the church members' migration from Illinois to Utah (1846–47), where he founded Salt Lake City.

> 'I am here to answer. I shall be on hand to answer when I am called upon, for all the counsel and for all the instruction that I have given to this people.'
> [Brigham Young. Quoted in *Journal of Discourses*, John A. Widtsoe (ed.); 1954]

Young, Cy (1867–1955) US baseball player. He was the first player in major league history to pitch a perfect game (1904), and an annual award for the best major league pitcher was established in his honour. Born **Young, Denton True**

Young, Nat (*b.* 1947) Australian surfer. He was the winner of the world amateur championship (1966), the world pro-am championship (1970), and the world professional longboard championship (1986–87, 1989). Born **Young, Robert**

Young, Thomas (1773–1829) British physicist and Egyptologist. He was noted for his work in optics, in particular his discovery of the phenomenon of interference. He helped decipher the Egyptian hieroglyphics on the Rosetta stone.

youngberry /yúngbəri/ (*plural* **-ries**) *n* **1.** a large, sweet, dark-purple fruit, a hybrid of the blackberry and

dewberry **2.** the trailing bramble that produces youngberries. Native to: southwestern United States. [Early 20C. After B. M. *Young*, US horticulturist]

young blood *n* fresh, new, and vigorous ideas or people

Younger Edda *n* LITERAT same as **Edda** (sense 2)

young fogy *n* a young person whose ideas and outlook are old-fashioned and conservative (*disapproving*)

young fustic *n* TREES same as **fustic** (sense 3)

Young Ireland *n* a movement of Irish nationalists in the 1840s who were prepared to use violence to achieve their ends —**Young Irelander** *n*

young lady *n* **1.** used to refer to or address a girl or young woman, often in annoyance or exasperation **2.** a man's or boy's girlfriend (*dated*)

youngling /yúngling/ *n* a young person or a young animal

young man *n* **1.** used to refer to or address a boy or young man, often in annoyance or exasperation **2.** a girl's or woman's boyfriend (*dated*)

young offender *n* in the United Kingdom, somebody under 18 who has committed a criminal act. US term **youthful offender**

young offender institution, **young offenders institution** *n* in the United Kingdom, a place where somebody between the ages of 14 and 20 can be detained to serve a court sentence or while on remand accused of a crime

Young Pretender ♦ **Stuart, Charles Edward**

youngster /yúngstər/ *n* **1.** CHILD a child or young person **2.** YOUNGEST IN GROUP somebody who is younger than other people in a group or category ○ *All you youngsters in your 40s don't think too seriously about retirement.* **3.** YOUNG HORSE a young horse

SYNONYMS See *youth.*

Young Turk *n* **1.** a member of a liberal pro-democratic Turkish nationalist movement in the early 20th century that brought about a short-lived revolution in 1908 **2.** a young person, especially one of a group, who attempts to wrest control of an organization from an older, established, more conservative group

young'un /yúngən/ *n* an infant or child (*informal*)

younker /yúngkər/ *n* (*archaic*) **1.** a young man **2.** same as **child** (sense 1) **3.** a young nobleman [Early 16C. < Middle Dutch *jonckher* < *jonc* 'young' + *hēre* 'lord']

your *stressed* /yawr, yoor/; *unstressed* /yər/ *det* **1.** BELONGING TO PERSON SPOKEN TO refers to something that belongs to or relates to the person who is being spoken to ○ *What's your phone number?* **2.** BELONGING OR RELATING TO SOMEBODY refers to something that belongs or relates to an unspecified person or people in general ○ *The house is on your left as you come down the road.* **3.** INDICATES TYPICALITY refers to somebody or something as a typical example of a familiar type (*informal*) ○ *your typical local park* [Old English *ēower* < *gē* (see YE[1])]

SPELLCHECK **your** or **you're**? Do not confuse the spelling of *your* and *you're*, which sound similar. The word *your* indicates possession: *Your* [not *You're*] *e-mail password must be protected.* **You're** is a contraction of 'you are': *You're* [not *Your*] *protecting your e-mail password, aren't you?*

Popperfoto

Marguerite Yourcenar

Yourcenar /yoórsə naar/, **Marguerite** (1903–87) Belgian-born French and US writer. Many of her works,

including *Memoirs of Hadrian* (1951), follow historical themes. Pseudonym of **Crayencour, Marguerite de**

> 'A man who reads, who thinks, or who calculates, belongs to the species and not to the sex; in his better moments, he even escapes being human.'
> [Marguerite Yourcenar, *Memoirs of Hadrian*; 1951]

you're *stressed* /yoor, yawr/; *unstressed* /yər/ *contr* you are

SPELLCHECK See *your.*

yours /yawrz, yoorz/ *pron* **1.** refers to something that belongs or relates to the person or people being addressed ○ *I'm taking my tea through to the sitting-room – shall I take yours as well?* **2.** also **Yours** used at the end of letters before somebody signs his or her name ○ *Sincerely yours, Marcia Klein*

yourself /yawr sélf, yoor-, yər-/ *pron* **1.** SOMEBODY BEING ADDRESSED refers to the person or people being addressed or written to ○ *Be careful not to hurt yourself.* **2.** MAKING REFERENCE TO SOMEBODY SPOKEN TO refers emphatically or politely to the person or people being addressed or written to ○ *'Consider', he replied, 'how you yourself really feel about such things'.* **3.** YOUR NORMAL SELF your normal or usual self ○ *You are not yourself tonight.*

USAGE The primary uses of *yourself* are as a reflexive pronoun (*Don't hurt yourself*) and as a reinforcing pronoun (*Can you do it yourself?*). In formal writing it should not be used as an alternative for *you* in sentences of the type: *That's up to you* [not *up to yourself*].

yours truly *pron* me, myself, or I (*informal*) ○ *Of course, everyone's going to be there except yours truly.*

yous /yooz/, **youse** *pron regional* used to address more than one person (*nonstandard*) [Late 19C. < YOU]

youth /yooth/ *n* **1.** TIME WHEN SOMEBODY IS YOUNG the period of human life between childhood and maturity **2.** TIME OF BEING YOUNG the state of being young **3.** YOUNG MAN a boy or young man in his teens or early twenties **4.** EARLY STAGE an early stage of something **5.** GEOL EROSION STAGE the first stage in landscape formation in which fast-flowing streams travel down steep mountain valleys ■ *npl* YOUNG PEOPLE young people in general [Old English *geoguþ* < Germanic]

SYNONYMS **youth, child, kid, teenager, youngster**
CORE MEANING: somebody who is young

youth a boy or young man in his teens or early twenties ○ *youths who regularly attend rock concerts* **child** a young person between birth and the onset of puberty ○ *In these early years, children grow and learn within their families.* **kid** (*informal*) a child or young person ○ *a happily married bank manager with four lovely kids* **teenager** somebody between the ages of 13 and 19 ○ *the problems and pressures facing teenagers today* **youngster** a child or young person, or somebody who is younger than others mentioned or present ○ *a club for youngsters aged between 6 and 11* ○ *veterans in their 70s and 80s, with a few youngsters in their 60s*

youth-centric *adj* specifically focused on and directed towards the interests of young people ○ *a youth-centric website*

youth club *n* a centre that provides organized activities for young people during their leisure time

Youth Court *n* in Canada, a provincial court with jurisdiction over all cases involving offenders under the age of 18

youth custody *n* in the United Kingdom, a custodial sentence of four to eighteen months for an offender aged 15 to 21

youth custody centre *n* formerly in the United Kingdom, a penal institution for young offenders. It has been replaced by the young offender institution.

youthful /yoóthf'l/ *adj* **1.** LIKE YOUTH characteristic of or possessing youth **2.** VIGOROUS vigorous and energetic **3.** NOT FULLY DEVELOPED in early development and not yet mature **4.** GEOL MILDLY ERODED steep, rugged, and relatively uneroded **5.** GEOG NEAR SOURCE describes a fast-flowing stream close to its source —**youthfully** *adv* —**youthfulness** *n*

youthful offender *n* US same as **young offender**

youth hostel *n* an establishment offering cheap accommodation for travellers, especially young travellers

Youth Training Scheme *n* in the United Kingdom, a former government scheme providing work-related training courses and work experience for jobless school-leavers

yout'man /yoótmən/ (*plural* **yout'men** /-mən/) *n* a young man or a boy (*slang; used in Black English*)

you've /yoov/ *contr* you have

yow /yow/ *interj* used to express pain, surprise, or alarm (*informal*) [Mid-19C. Natural exclamation]

yowl /yowl/ *vi* (**yowls**, **yowling**, **yowled**) to cry out mournfully or as an expression of pain ■ *n* a long mournful wail [12C. Probably an imitation of the sound] —**yowler** *n*

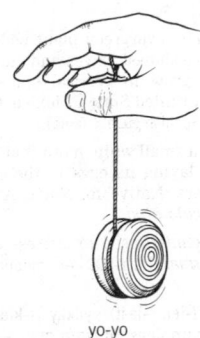
yo-yo

yo-yo /yō yō/ *n* (*plural* **yo-yos**) **1.** TOY WITH STRING WOUND ON SPOOL a toy consisting of a long string wound onto a spool that is dropped and raised repeatedly using the force of gravity and momentum to unwind and rewind the string **2.** FLUCTUATING THING something that repeatedly goes up and down or fluctuates between one extreme and another **3.** *N Am* OFFENSIVE TERM an offensive term that deliberately insults a person's intelligence or judgment (*slang insult*) ■ *vi* (**yo-yos**, **yo-yoing**, **yo-yoed**) FLUCTUATE to fluctuate between two extremes or directions [Early 20C. Origin ?]

yo-yo dieting *n* a situation in which somebody repeatedly loses weight through dieting and then regains the weight that he or she has lost

Ypres /eéprə/ town in southwestern Belgium, in West Flanders Province, near the border of France. During World War I, the town was the site of several major battles and was almost completely destroyed. Population: 35,409 (1995).

Ypsilanti /ípsə lánti/, **Alexander, Prince** (1792–1828) Greek soldier. In 1821 he led an unsuccessful rebellion against the Turks in the Greek War of Independence.

yr *abbr* **1.** year **2.** younger **3.** your

Yrs *abbr* Yours (*used at the end of a letter*)

YST *abbr* Yukon Standard Time

yt *abbr* Mayotte (*used in Internet addresses*) See table at **domain name**

YT *abbr* Yukon Territory

YTD *abbr* year to date

YTS *abbr* Youth Training Scheme

ytterbia /i túrbi ə/ *n* CHEM same as **ytterbium oxide** [Late 19C. After *Ytterby* (see YTTERBIUM)]

ytterbium /i túrbi əm/ *n* a soft silvery metal of the lanthanide group of rare-earth elements. Source: monazite, bastnaesite. Use: strengthening steel, in laser devices and portable X-ray units. Symbol Yb. See table at **element** [Late 19C. After *Ytterby*, a Swedish quarry] —**ytterbic** *adj*

ytterbium oxide *n* a colourless oxide of ytterbium. Use: alloys, ceramics. Formula: Yb_2O_3.

yttria /íttri ə/ *n* CHEM same as **yttrium oxide** [Early 19C. After *Ytterby*, a Swedish quarry]

yttriferous /i tríffərəss/ *adj* yielding or containing yttrium

yttrium /íttri əm/ *n* a silvery-grey metallic element. Source: uranium, rare-earth ores. Use: superconducting alloys, permanent magnets. Symbol Y. See table at **element** [Early 19C. < YTTRIA] —**yttric** *adj*

yttrium metal *n* a metal in the group that includes yttrium and related rare-earth elements such as holmium, erbium, thulium, ytterbium, and lutetium

yttrium oxide *n* a yellowish powder. Use: optical glass, ceramics, lasers, microwave components. Formula: Y_2O_3.

yu *abbr* Yugoslavia (*used in Internet addresses*)

yuan /yoo án/ (*plural same*) *n* the main unit of currency in China, worth 10 jiao. See table at **currency** [Early 20C. < Chinese *yuán* 'round']

Yucatán /yoo͞kə taán/ **1.** peninsula in Central America consisting of three Mexican states, Belize, and part of northern Guatemala. Area: 181,300 sq. km/70,000 sq. mi. **2.** state in southeastern Mexico on the northern coast of the Yucatán Peninsula. Capital: Mérida. Population: 1,686,500 (2000). Area: 43,257 sq. km/ 16,700 sq. mi.

yucca /yúkə/ *n* an evergreen plant widely grown for its sharp lance-shaped leaves and clusters of white flowers that grow in vertical spikes. Native to: southwestern United States, Mexico. Genus: *Yucca*. [Mid-16C. Via Spanish *yuca* < Taino]

yucca moth *n* a small white moth that pollinates the yucca plant, laying its eggs in the ovaries of the yucca's flowers. Native to: North America. Latin name: *Tegeticula alba*.

yuck /yuk/, **yuk** *interj* used to express disgust or revulsion (*informal*) [Mid-20C. An imitation of the sound of vomiting]

yucky /yúki/ (**-ier, -iest**), **yukky** (**-kier, -kiest**) *adj* disgusting or unpleasant (*informal*) —**yuckiness** *n*

Yug. *abbr* Yugoslavia

yuga /yoogə/ *n* in Hinduism, any of the four stages in each cycle of history, each worse than the one before [Late 18C. < Sanskrit *yugam* 'yoke, era']

Yugo. *abbr* Yugoslavia

Yugoslavia /yoogō slaávi ə/ former name for **Serbia and Montenegro** —**Yugoslav** /yoogō slaav/ *n*, *adj* —**Yugoslavian** *adj*, *n*

yuk /yuk/ *interj* another spelling of **yuck** (*informal*)

yukata /yoo káttə/ (*plural same* or **-tas**) *n* a light cotton kimono, worn especially as a dressing gown or housecoat [Early 19C. < Japanese < *yu* 'hot water' + *kata(bira)* 'light kimono']

yukky *adj* another spelling of **yucky** (*informal*)

Yukon /yoo͞k on/ river in North America, flowing through Canada and Alaska and into the Bering Sea. Length: 3,190 km/1,980 mi.

Yukon Territory territory in northwestern Canada. It was the site of the Klondike gold rush between 1896 and 1899. Capital: Whitehorse. Population: 28,674 (2001). Area: 482,443 sq. km/186,272 sq. mi.

Yukon Time *n* the time observed in the Yukon Territory and in a section of more or less equivalent longitude extending southwards from there, being nine hours behind Universal Coordinated Time

Yule /yool/, **yule** *n* Christmas day or the Christmas season (*archaic or literary*) [Old English *gēol* 'mid-winter festival, Christmas' < Germanic]

yule log *n* a large log traditionally placed on the hearth fire on Christmas Eve

Yuletide /yool tīd/ *n* the Christmas season (*archaic or literary*)

Yuma /yoomə/ *n* a member of a Native North American people of southwestern Arizona and neighbouring areas [Early 19C. < Pima *yumī*] —**Yuma** *adj*

Yuman /yoomən/ *n* a family of languages spoken in the southwestern United States and in northern Mexico. Native speakers: 4,000. —**Yuman** *adj*

yum cha /yoom chá/ *n* a Chinese meal that consists of small servings of food selected from a display on a trolley, traditionally served with tea

yummy /yúmmi/ (**-mier, -miest**) *adj* very appealing to taste or smell (*informal*) [Late 19C. < *yum*, an imitation of the sound of smacking the lips] —**yumminess** *n*

Yunnan /yoo nán/ province in southern China, on the southwestern border of the country. Capital: Kunming. Population: 40,420,000 (1997). Area: 394,000 sq. km/152,124 sq. mi.

Yun Shouping /yŭn shō píng/ (1633–90) Chinese artist. He is known for his landscapes and flower paintings.

yup /yup/ *adv* same as **yes** (*informal*) [Early 20C. Representing a casual pronunciation of YES]

Yupik /yoopik/ (*plural same* or **-piks**) *n* **1.** a member of an aboriginal people of western Alaska and parts of coastal Siberia, related to the Inuit of the Canadian Arctic and Greenland **2.** the group of Eskimo-Aleut languages spoken by the Yupik people. Native

speakers: 3,000. [Mid-20C. < Alaskan Yupik *Yup'ik* 'real person'] —**Yupik** *adj*

yuppie /yúppi/ *n* a young educated city-dwelling professional, especially when regarded as materialistic (*disapproving*) [Late 20C. < *y(oung) u(rban) p(rofessional)*, after HIPPIE]

yuppie flu, **yuppie disease** *n* MED same as **chronic fatigue syndrome** (*informal*)

yuppify /yúppi fī/ (**-fies, -fying, -fied**) *vt* to cause an area to be increasingly populated by young educated city-dwelling professionals or to modify something with the values ascribed to yuppies (*disapproving*) —**yuppification** /yúppifi káysh'n/ *n*

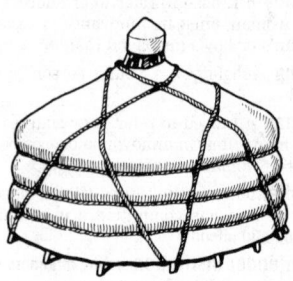

yurt

yurt /yurt/ *n* **1.** a collapsible circular tent of felt and skins stretched over a pole frame, originally used by Central Asian nomadic peoples and now used more widely **2.** a circular structure with a tight, fitted roofing material, used especially by highway departments to store road salt and sand for winterstorm use [Late 18C. Via Russian *yurta* < Turkic *jurt*]

Yuwaalaraay /yoo waálə rī/ *n* an extinct Australian Aboriginal language of New South Wales, now being revived —**Yuwaalaraay** *adj*

yuzu /yoo zoo/ *n* a citrus fruit about the size of a mandarin, with a rough skin and very sour flesh, mainly used for its peel [< Japanese]

YWCA[1] *abbr* Young Women's Christian Association

YWCA[2] *n* a building or other centre where social, sports, or educational facilities are provided by the YWCA for its members

YWHA *abbr* Young Women's Hebrew Association

Zz

z¹ /zed/, **Z** n (plural **z's**; plural **Z's** or **Zs**) **1.** 26TH LETTER OF ENGLISH ALPHABET the 26th and final letter of the English alphabet, representing a consonant sound **2.** LETTER 'Z' WRITTEN a written representation of the letter 'z' ■ **z's** npl SLEEP sleep, from the traditional transcription of the sound of snoring (informal) ○ *I need to catch some z's.*

REGIONAL NOTE Words beginning with *z* are rare in British dialects. Indeed, the letter is often pronounced 'a-zed', and words such as *zip* and *zoo* are often pronounced 'azip' and 'azoo'. The exception to this generalization is southwestern England, where we find *zart* used as an oath, and *zawster* and *zichel* used for 'seamstress' and 'suchlike'.

z² symbol **1.** MATHS an algebraic variable **2.** CHEM atomic number **3.** MATHS a Cartesian coordinate along the z-axis **4.** MEASURE zepto- **5.** MEASURE zetta-

z³ abbr **1.** MONEY zaïre **2.** GEOG zone

Z¹ /zed/ (plural **Z's** or **Zs**) n something shaped like a letter 'Z'

Z² abbr GEOG zone

Z³ symbol **1.** CHEM atomic number **2.** PHYS impedance **3.** MEASURE zetta-

za abbr South Africa (used in Internet addresses) See table at **domain name**

Zaanstad /zaan shtát/ city in North Holland Province, western Netherlands. Population: 135,621 (2000).

zabaglione /zább'l yŏni, zábba lyŏni/ n a dessert made of egg yolks, sugar, and Marsala wine beaten over hot water until pale and foamy. It is served hot with sponge finger biscuits. [Late 19C. < Italian]

Zacatecas /zákə táykəss/ capital city of Zacatecas State in central Mexico. It is an important mining centre. Population: 125,258 (2000).

Zacharias /zákə rí əss/ n in Christian tradition, the father of John the Baptist

zaddik n JUDAISM another spelling of **tzaddik**

zaffer /záffər/, **zaffre** n an impure form of cobalt oxide. Use: blue colouring agent in enamels and glass. [Mid-17C. Via Italian *zaffera* < French *safre*]

zaftig /záftig/ adj with a full-figured body [Mid-20C. Via Yiddish < Middle High German *saftec* 'juicy' < *saft* 'juice']

zag /zag/ n a direction or segment of a course running opposite to a zig ■ vi (**zags, zagging, zagged**) to change direction quickly [Late 18C. < ZIGZAG]

Zagreb /zá'a greb/ capital city of Croatia, situated in the north of the country, approximately 25 km/15 mi. from the border with Slovenia. Population: 682,598 (2001).

Zagros Mountains /zág ross-/ mountain range in southwestern Iran, extending from the borders with Turkey and Azerbaijan in the north to the Persian Gulf in the south. The highest peak is Zard Kuh, 4,548 m/14,921 ft. Length: 1,600 km/1,000 mi.

Zaharias /zə hárri əss/, **Babe Didrikson** (1913–56) US athlete. She excelled in basketball, swimming, athletics, and golf. She won two gold medals, in javelin and 80-metre hurdles, at the summer Olympics (1932). In golf, she also won the US Open three times (1948, 1950, and 1954). Born **Didrikson, Mildred**

Zaharoff /zə khá'arəf/, **Sir Basil** (1849–1936) Turkish-born French arms dealer. He was an Allied agent during World War I, and established chairs at a number of major European universities. Born **Zacharias, Basileios**

zaibatsu /zī bátsoo/ (plural same) n a large industrial combine created in Japan in the 1890s, usually by a single family, as part of the process of industrialization [Mid-20C. < Japanese < *zai* 'wealth' + *batsu* 'clique']

zaikai /zī kí/ n the business and financial community of Japan [Mid-20C. < Japanese *zai* 'wealth' + *kai* 'world']

zaïre /zī e'er/ (plural same or **-ïres**) n a former unit of currency in the Democratic Republic of Congo [Mid-20C. After *Zaire*, local name for the Congo River]

Zaire /zī e'er, zaa-/ **1.** former name for **Congo, Democratic Republic of the 2.** former name for **Congo** —**Zairean** /zī e'eri ən/ adj, n

zakat /zə ka'at/ n a tax that goes to charity, obligatory for all Muslims, set traditionally at 2.5 per cent of somebody's annual income and capital [Early 19C. Via Persian and Urdu *zakā(t)* or Turkish *zekāt* < Arabic *zakā(t)* 'the giving of alms']

Zakinthos /zákin thoss, zə kínthoss/, **Zakynthos** most southerly of the Ionian Islands, in southwestern Greece. Population: 38,680 (2001). Area: 401 sq. km/155 sq. mi.

zakuski /zə kŏoski/ npl blinis and breads of various kinds with savoury toppings, especially caviar, served in Russia with vodka. Traditionally, zakuski are an alternative to the first course of a meal, but they sometimes provide a pretheatre supper, followed by the main meal after the show. [Late 19C. < Russian, plural of *zakuska* 'hors d'oeuvre']

Zakynthos /zákin thoss, zə kínthəss/ another spelling of **Zakinthos**

Zambezi /zam bee'zi/ river in southern Africa, flowing through Zambia, Angola, Botswana, Zimbabwe, and Mozambique, and into the Indian Ocean. Length: 2,650 km/1,650 mi.

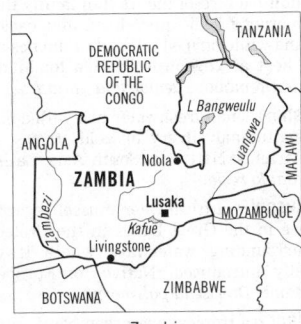

Zambia

Zambia /zámbi ə/ country in south-central Africa. It became an independent member of the Commonwealth in 1964. Language: English. Currency: kwacha. Capital: Lusaka. Population: 10,307,333 (2003). Area: 752,614 sq. km/290,586 sq. mi. Official name **Republic of Zambia**. Former name **Northern Rhodesia** (until 1964) —**Zambian** n, adj

Zamboni /zam bóni/ tdmk N Am a trademark for a machine that resurfaces the ice on hockey and skating rinks

zamia /záymi ə/ n a small tropical tree (**cycad**) that resembles a palm tree, with a short thick trunk, spiky leaves, and upright woody cones that contain seeds. It is a modern representative of a group of trees that are largely extinct. Genus: *Zamia*. [Early 19C. < modern Latin, misreading of Latin *azaniae* 'pine cones']

zamindar /zə meén daar/, **zemindar** n in South Asia, somebody who has traditionally owned land [Late 17C. Via Urdu < Persian *zamīndār* < *zamīn* 'land' + *dār* ''holder']

zamindari /zə meén da'ari/ (plural **-is**), **zemindary** (plural **-ies**) n in South Asia, the system of traditional land ownership, or the area of land owned [Mid-18C. Via Urdu < Persian *zamīndārī* < *zamīndār* (see ZAMINDAR)]

zanana n ISLAM, TRANSP another spelling of **zenana**

zander /zándər/ (plural same or **-ders**) n a freshwater fish of the perch family, harvested for food. Native to: central Europe. Latin name: *Stizostedion lucioperca*. [Mid-19C. Via German < Low German *sandāt*]

zang /zang/ npl in traditional Chinese medicine, the five organs, the heart, lungs, kidneys, liver, and spleen, that control the yin-yang bodily balance and the main body functions [< Chinese]

Zantac /zán tak/ tdmk a trademark for the drug ranitidine. Use: to treat peptic ulcers.

Zante /zántay/ ♦ **Zakinthos**

ZANU /zá'a noo/, **Zanu** n a nationalist political party that helped bring about majority rule in Zimbabwe, it merged with opposition party ZAPU in 1988 to form ZANU-PF. Full form **Zimbabwe African National Union**

ZANU-PF n a major political party in Zimbabwe, formed in 1988 by a merger between ZANU and ZAPU. Full form **Zimbabwe African National Union-Patriotic Front**

zany /záyni/ adj (**-nier, -niest**) AMUSINGLY UNCONVENTIONAL entertainingly strange or amusingly unusual ■ n (plural **-nies**) **1.** CLOWN a fool, buffoon, or clown **2.** STOCK CHARACTER a stock character in Renaissance comedies who mimicked other characters [Late 16C. Via French *zani* < Italian dialect *Zanni*, variant of *Gianni*, pet form of *Giovanni*, character in the commedia dell'arte who tried to mimic the clown] —**zanily** adv —**zaniness** n —**zanism** n

Zanzibar /zánzi baar/ island of Tanzania, in the Indian Ocean, approximately 35 km/22 mi. off the eastern coast of Africa. Population: 456,934 (1995). Area: 1,660 sq. km/641 sq. mi. —**Zanzibari** adj, n

zap /zap/ (informal) v (**zaps, zapping, zapped**) **1.** vt DESTROY SOMEBODY OR SOMETHING to kill or finish somebody or something off with sudden force **2.** vti CHANGE TV CHANNELS USING REMOTE CONTROL to change channels on a television set using a remote control device, especially to change channels rapidly **3.** vi MOVE QUICKLY to move about or accomplish something very rapidly **4.** vt COOK SOMETHING IN MICROWAVE to cook something in a microwave oven ○ *I'll just zap this for a minute and then we can eat.* **5.** vt Malaysia, Singapore PHOTOCOPY SOMETHING to make a photocopy of something ■ n **1.** ENERGY energy and excitement **2.** TIME IN MICROWAVE a short period of time in a microwave oven ■ interj EXPRESSION OF FORCEFUL ACTION used especially in comic books to indicate sudden and violent force [Early 20C. An imitation of the sound of a lightning strike or electric sparks]

Zapata /saa pá'ataa, zə pá'atə/, **Emiliano** (1879–1919) Mexican revolutionary. He took part in a number of uprisings, and redistributed land among the Native Central Americans in southern Mexico.

---

zh vision. In foreign words: kh German Ba*ch*; aN French *vin*; aaN French *blanc*; ŏ German sch*ön*, French *feu*; oN French *bon*; ŏN French *un*; û as in French *rue*. Stress marks: ´ as in se**cret** /seékrət/, **academic** /ákə démmik/

Zapata moustache *n* a thick moustache that curves down around the edges of the mouth

zapateado /záppə tay áadō/ (*plural* **-dos**), **zapateo** /záppə táy ō/ (*plural* **-os**) *n* a Spanish or Latin American dance involving rhythmic tapping of the feet [Mid-19C. < Spanish *zapatear* 'tap with the shoe' < *zapato* 'shoe']

Zapatero /záppə táirō/, **José Luis** (*b.* 1960) Spanish politician. He was Spain's youngest member of parliament (1986) and went on to become leader of the Socialist Party (2000). He became prime minister following the general election of 2004. Full name **Zapatero, José Luis Rodríguez**

Zapopan /zaápō pan/ city in southwestern Mexico near Guadalajara. Population: 1,001,021 (2000).

Zaporizhzhya /záppə rizhyə/ city in southeastern Ukraine. It is situated about 217 km/135 mi. west of Donets'k. Population: 863,000 (1998).

Zapotec /zápə tek/ (*plural same* or **-tecs**) *n* **1.** a member of a Native Central American people who founded a Mesoamerican civilization in the region of Oaxaca, Mexico, between the 7th century BC and the 11th century AD, and now live in the highlands of the same region **2.** the Oto-Manguean language of the Zapotec people. Native speakers: 500,000. [Late 18C. Via Spanish *zapoteco* < Nahuatl *tzapotecatl* 'person from the place of the sapodilla'] —**Zapotecan** *adj*

zapper /záppər/ *n* (*informal*) **1.** a remote control for a television or video recorder **2.** *US* a device that attracts and electrocutes insects

zappy /záppi/ (**-pier**, **-piest**) *adj* lively and forcefully impressive (*informal*)

ZAPU /záppoo/, **Zapu** *n* a nationalist political party that helped bring about majority rule in Zimbabwe, it merged with ZANU in 1988 to form ZANU-PF. Full form **Zimbabwe African People's Union**

Zaragoza /sárrə góssə/ capital of Zaragoza Province in the autonomous region of Aragon, northeastern Spain. Population: 620,419 (2002).

Zarathustra /zárrə thoóstrə/ ♦ **Zoroaster**

zaratite /zárrə tīt/ *n* an amorphous green mineral consisting of hydrated nickel carbonate [Mid-19C. < Spanish *zaratita* < the surname *Zarate*]

zareba /zə reébə/ *n* an outdoor enclosure, especially one made of thorn bushes and used as protection around a campsite or village in various parts of North Africa [Mid-19C. < Arabic *zariba* 'cattle pen']

zarf /zaarf/ *n* a metal frame for holding a cup, used in Southwest Asia [Mid-19C. < Arabic *zarf* 'vessel']

zari /zaári/ *n* *S Asia* gold brocade used to decorate clothes [Mid-20C. Via Urdu < Persian *zari* < *zar* 'gold']

Zaria /zaári ə/ city in Kaduna State, north-central Nigeria. Population: 369,800 (1995).

zart /zaart/ *interj* *SW England* a mild expression of surprise or annoyance [Alteration of *God's heart*]

REGIONAL NOTE See *z*[1].

zarzuela /zaar zwáylə/ *n* Spanish musical theatre, usually comic, combining dialogue, music, and dance [Late 19C. < Spanish]

Zátopek /záttəpek/, **Emil** (1922–2000) Czech athlete. He was the Olympic gold medallist in the 10,000 metres (1948 and 1952), 5,000 metres (1952), and marathon (1952).

zawster /záwstər/ *n* *SW England* same as **seamstress** [Variant of obsolete *sewster*]

REGIONAL NOTE See *z*[1].

zax /zaks/ *n* a tool similar to a hatchet used for cutting and shaping slate [Mid-17C. Representing Old English *seax* 'knife' < Indo-European]

z-axis *n* one of the axes of the Cartesian coordinate system that provides a reference in three-dimensional space

zayin /záayin/ *n* the seventh letter of the Hebrew alphabet, represented in the English alphabet as 'z'. See table at **alphabet** [Early 19C. < Hebrew, 'weapon']

zazen /zaá zen/ *n* a form of meditation in Zen, practised sitting in a prescribed position [Early 18C. < Japanese, 'sitting Zen']

Z boson *n* PHYS same as **Z particle**

Z chart *n* a chart used in business and industry to illustrate production data

z-coordinate *n* one of three numbers that provide a reference to a position in three-dimensional space, conventionally the vertical one

zeal /zeel/ *n* energetic and unflagging enthusiasm, especially for a cause or idea [14C. Via late Latin *zelus* < Greek *zēlos* 'eager rivalry']

Zealand /zeéland/ ♦ **Sjælland**

zealot /zéllət/ *n* a zealous supporter of a cause, especially a religious cause [Mid-16C. Via late Latin < Greek *zēlotēs* < *zēloun* 'be jealous' < *zēlos* 'eager rivalry'] —**zealotry** *n*

Zealot *n* a member of a group of Jewish rebels who attempted the military overthrow of Roman rule in Palestine in the 1st and 2nd centuries AD

zealous /zélləss/ *adj* actively and unreservedly enthusiastic [Early 16C. < medieval Latin *zelosus* < *zelus* (see ZEAL)] —**zealously** *adv* —**zealousness** *n*

zeatin /zeé ətin/ *n* a naturally occurring growth promoter found in many plants, first isolated from kernels of Indian corn [Mid-20C. < modern Latin *Zea* (see ZEIN) + -IN]

zebec *n* another spelling of **xebec**

Zebedee /zébbəddi/ *n* in the Bible, a fisherman, and the father of the apostles James and John (Matthew 4:21)

zebra

zebra /zébbrə, zeébrə/ *n* an animal resembling a horse that has a black-and-white or brown-and-white striped hide. Native to: Africa. Genus: *Equus*. [Early 17C. < Italian, Spanish, or Portuguese, originally 'wild ass'] —**zebraic** /zi bráy ik/ *adj* —**zebrine** /-rīn/ *adj* —**zebroid** /-royd/ *adj*

zebra crossing *n* a pedestrian crossing marked by white stripes in the road, at which drivers of vehicles must stop if a pedestrian is waiting to cross

zebra finch *n* a bird of the waxbill family that has a reddish-orange beak, grey head and back, and a black-and-white striped tail. Zebra finches are commonly kept as cagebirds. Native to: inland Australia. Latin name: *Taeniopygia guttata*.

zebra fish *n* a small freshwater fish with a blue body and longitudinal silvery or gold stripes, popular for aquariums. Native to: South Asia. Latin name: *Brachydanio rerio*.

zebra mussel *n* a freshwater mussel regarded as a nuisance in the Great Lakes in the United States and surrounding waterways where it was accidentally introduced. Native to: Europe, Asia. Latin name: *Dreissena polymorpha*.

zebra plant *n* a tropical evergreen plant with green-and-purple striped leaves. Native to: South America. Latin name: *Calathea zebrina*.

zebrawood /zébbrə wŏŏd, zeébrə-/ *n* **1.** STRIPED WOOD wood in two distinct colour bands, from any of various tropical trees. Use: furniture. **2.** HARDWOOD TREE WITH STRIPED WOOD a tropical hardwood tree producing zebrawood. Latin name: *Connarus guianensis*. **3.** TREE WITH STRIPED WOOD a tropical tree that produces zebrawood

zebu /zeé boo/ (*plural same* or **-bus**) *n* a domesticated ox of East and South Asia with a humped back, curving horns, floppy ears, and a large dewlap. Latin name: *Bos indicus*. [Late 18C. < French *zébu*]

zecchino /ze keénō/ (*plural* **-ni** /-nee/ or **-nos**) *n* MONEY

same as **sequin** (sense 2) [Early 17C. < Italian (see SEQUIN)]

Zechariah /zékə rí ə/ *n* **1.** in the Bible, a Hebrew priest and prophet of the 6th century BC **2.** a book of the Bible that contains the prophecies traditionally attributed to Zechariah, including his visions of the rebuilding of the Temple in a restored Jerusalem. See table at **Bible**

zechin /zékin/ *n* MONEY same as **sequin** (sense 2) [Late 16C. < Italian *zecchino* (see SEQUIN)]

zed /zed/ *n* a written representation of the sound of the letter 'Z'. N Am term **zee** [15C. Via French *zède* < Greek *zēta* (see ZETA)]

Zedekiah /zéddi kī ə/ *n* in the Bible, the last king of Judah (597–586 BC). After rebelling against Nebuchadnezzar II, he was imprisoned in Babylon, where he died in captivity (2 Kings 24–25, 2 Chronicles 36).

zedoary /zéddō əri/ (*plural* **-ies**) *n* **1.** an aromatic powder obtained from crushing the dried roots of a South Asian tree **2.** a plant with starchy aromatic rhizomes that yield zedoary. Use: as a condiment, in cosmetics, perfume, medicinally as a stimulant. Flowers: yellow. Native to: South Asia. Latin name: *Curcuma zedoaria*. [15C. < medieval Latin *zedoarium* < Persian *zadwār*]

zedonk /zeé dónk, zé-/ *n* the offspring of a male zebra and a female donkey [Late 20C. < ZEBRA + DONKEY]

zee /zee/ *n* *N Am* same as **zed** [Late 17C. Alteration of Latin *zeta* (< Greek *zēta*: see ZETA) after *b*, *p*, etc.]

Zeebrugge /záy brŏŏgə, zeé-/ port in northwestern Belgium, in northwestern Flanders Province. Population: 4,500 (1996).

Zeeland /zeéland/ province in the southwestern Netherlands. Population: 371,686 (2000). Area: 1,792 sq. km/692 sq. mi.

Zeeman /zeémən/, **Pieter** (1865–1943) Dutch physicist. He discovered the zeeman effect, which confirmed the electromagnetic theory of light, and was awarded the Nobel Prize in physics (1902).

Zeeman effect /zeémən-/ *n* the splitting of single lines in a spectrum into two, three, or more polarized lines when the source of the spectrum is placed in a magnetic field

Franco Zeffirelli

Zeffirelli /zéffə rélli/, **Franco** (*b.* 1923) Italian film, stage, and opera director. His films include versions of Shakespeare and adaptations of operas.

Zeil /zīl/ highest mountain in the Northern Territory of Australia. Height: 1,510 m/4,954 ft.

zein /zeé in/ *n* a powder of proteins obtained from corn, with various applications in industry and manufacturing [Early 19C. < modern Latin *Zea* via Latin *zea* 'emmer' < Greek *zeia*, kind of wheat]

Zeiss /tsīss, zīss/, **Carl** (1816–88) German manufacturer. In partnership with Ernst Karl Abbe, he produced high-quality optical instruments, notably cameras and microscopes.

Zeitgeist /zīt gīst, tsīt-/, **zeitgeist** *n* the ideas prevalent in a period and place, particularly as expressed in literature, philosophy, and religion [Mid-19C. < German, 'spirit of the time']

zelkova /zélkəvə/ *n* a tree of the elm family cultivated for its resistance to Dutch elm disease. Native to: Asia. Genus: *Zelkova*. [Late 19C. Via modern Latin < a Caucasian language]

zemindar another spelling of **zamindar**

zemstvo /zémst vō/ (*plural* **-stvos**) *n* an elected provincial legislature that existed in Russia between 1864 and 1917 [Mid-19C. < Russian < obsolete *zem* 'land']

Zen /zen/ *n* a major school of Buddhism originating in 12th-century China that emphasizes enlightenment through meditation and insight [Early 18C. Via Japanese *zen* and Chinese *chán* < Sanskrit *dhyānam* 'meditation']

zenana /zə naánə/, **zanana** *n* **1.** in parts of northern South Asia, an area reserved for women in some trains and waiting rooms in railway stations **2.** in Muslim households in parts of South and Southwest Asia, the area of the house reserved for women and girls [Mid-18C. < Persian, Urdu *zanānah* < *zan* 'woman']

Zen Buddhism *n* BUDDHISM same as **Zen**

Zend /zend/ *n* **1.** RELIG same as **Zend-Avesta** **2.** LANG same as **Avesta** —**Zend** *adj*

Zend-Avesta *n* the canonical writings of Zoroastrianism, preserved in the Pahlavi language [Mid-17C. Via French < Persian *zand-awastā* 'Avesta with interpretation']

zener diode /zénnər-/ *n* a semiconductor used as a voltage regulator because of its ability to maintain a constant voltage during fluctuating current conditions [Mid-20C. After Clarence M. *Zener* (1905–93), US physicist]

Zenica /zénnitsə/ city in central Bosnia and Herzegovina. Before the Bosnian-Croatian-Serbian War, Zenica was a major centre for heavy industry. Population: 145,577 (1991).

zenith /zénnith/ *n* **1.** HIGHEST POINT the high point or climax of something **2.** POINT STRAIGHT UP the point of the celestial sphere that is directly over the observer and 90 degrees from all points on that person's horizon **3.** HIGHEST POINT OF ASTRONOMICAL OBJECT the highest point reached by an astronomical object [14C. Via Old French and medieval Latin < Arabic *samt (ar-ra's)* 'path (over the head)'] —**zenithal** /zénnith'l/ *adj*

zenithal projection *n* a map projection of the Earth onto a plane tangential to a point on the surface of the Earth such as the North Pole or the equator

Zeno of Citium /zeénō uv sìshee əm/ (*fl* late 4th-early 3rd century BC) Greek philosopher. He founded a school of philosophy, stoicism, in Athens in about 300 BC.

> 'The reason why we have two ears and one mouth is that we may listen the more and talk the less.'
> [Zeno of Citium. Quoted in 'Zeno', *Lives of the Philosophers*; Diogenes; 3rd century BC]

Zeno of Elea /-eéli ə/ (*fl* 5th century BC) Greek mathematician and philosopher. The paradoxes for which his philosophy is known were designed to discredit the information conveyed by the senses. Aristotle regarded him as the inventor of dialectical reasoning.

zeolite /zeé ə līt/ *n* one of a large group of amorphous hydrated aluminium silicate minerals containing various other elements. Source: weathered igneous rocks, hydrothermal veins. Use: water purification. [Late 18C. < Greek *zein* 'to boil'] —**zeolitic** /zeé ə líttik/ *adj*

Zepa /zé paa/ town in eastern Bosnia and Herzegovina, overrun by Bosnian Serb forces during the Bosnian-Croatian-Serbian War. Population: 15,000 (1995).

Zephaniah /zéffə nī ə/ *n* **1.** in the Bible, a minor Hebrew prophet of the 7th century BC **2.** a book in the Bible, traditionally attributed to Zephaniah. It urges repentance by the people of Judah, and predicts a day of judgment. See table at **Bible**

zephyr /zéffər/ *n* **1.** a light warming breeze **2.** a delicate, usually woollen fabric or garment [Pre-12C. Via Latin < Greek *zephuros* 'west wind']

zephyr lily *n* a plant that grows from clump-forming bulbs and has narrow grassy leaves. Flowers: funnel-shaped, colourful. Native to: tropical America. Genus: *Zephyranthes*.

Zephyrus /zéffərəss/ *n* in Greek mythology, the god who personified the west wind and was always mild and gentle in character

zeppelin /zéppəlin/ *n* a rigid cylindrical airship consisting of a covered frame and a suspended compartment for engines and passengers [Early 20C. After Count Ferdinand von *Zeppelin* (1838–1917), German inventor]

zepto- *prefix* indicates 10^{-21} in measurements ○ *zeptosecond* [Late 20C. After SEPTI-]

zeptosecond /zéptō sekənd/ *n* a unit of time equal to one-sextillionth of a second

Zermatt /tsúr mat, tsur mát/ town and ski resort in Valais Canton, southwestern Switzerland. Population: 4,225 (1996).

zero /zeérō/ *n* (*plural* **-ros** or **-roes**) **1.** SYMBOL 0 the numerical symbol 0, representing the absence of any quantity or magnitude **2.** NUMBER WITH VALUE OF 0 the number that, when added to another number, results in that number, e.g. 0 + 4 = 4 **3.** STARTING POINT FOR VALUES ON GAUGE the starting or centre point for values on a counter, scale, or gauge ○ *Set the counter to zero.* **4.** LOW TEMPERATURE the temperature indicated by 0 on a thermometer scale, especially that corresponding to the freezing point of water on the Celsius scale ○ *It got down to zero last night.* **5.** LOW POINT the lowest possible point or degree ○ *Her spirits are at zero.* **6.** NOTHING nothing or nil ○ *They beat us five zero.* **7.** *US* FAILURE somebody who is regarded as a complete failure (*informal insult*) **8.** LING ABSTRACT REALIZATION OF MORPHEME a variant form of a morpheme (**allomorph**) that is purely abstract and does not exist in any physical phonetic form. An example of a zero allomorph in English is the plural marker of 'sheep'. **9.** ARMS SETTING ON GUN SIGHT a setting on a gun sight indicating the centre of a target ■ *vt* (**-roes, -roing, -roed**) SET SOMETHING TO ZERO to set an instrument, gauge, counter, or similar measuring device to zero ■ *adj* **1.** NIL having no quantity or magnitude ○ *zero inflation* **2.** MINIMAL very small in amount or extent (*informal*) ○ *Our chances of winning are zero.* ○ *had zero confidence* **3.** METEOROL WITH LIMITED VISIBILITY describes a level of visibility limited to 15 m/50 ft vertically or 50 m/165 ft horizontally **4.** LING LACKING USUAL EXPRESSION OF FEATURE characterized by the absence of a form or feature that exists elsewhere in the same linguistic context, e.g. an inflection or vowel change [Early 17C. Via French and Italian < Arabic *ṣifr* 'emptiness']

zero in *vi* **1.** to identify something precisely and concentrate all efforts on dealing with it ○ *The report zeroed in on the weaknesses in the current policy.* **2.** to find the precise position of a target and move towards it or aim a weapon at it, threateningly or inexorably [< the technique of setting a gun sight exactly on a target by cancelling out the effects of elevation and wind deflection]

zero out *vt* **1.** ELIMINATE SOMETHING to eliminate something or reduce it to zero ○ *That round zeroes out your score.* **2.** CUT OFF FUNDING FOR SOMETHING to cut off funding for a project or activity so that it cannot go forward ○ *zeroing out after-school programs* **3.** SET SOMETHING TO ZERO to set something such as a gauge or counter to zero

zero-base, **zero-based** *adj* relating to a budget or budgeting that considers each item on its merits without reference to previous practice or expenditure

zero-coupon *adj* not paying interest but sold at a discount and redeemable at maturity ○ *a zero-coupon bond*

zero-defect *adj* with no flaws or errors

zerofill /zeérō fil/ (**-fills, -filling, -filled**) *vti* in computing, to fill empty storage space with zeros

zero gravity *n* a condition of apparent weightlessness resulting from the centrifugal force on an object counterbalancing the gravitational force attracting it

zero grazing *n* a system of feeding cattle or other livestock in which freshly cut forage is brought daily to animals that are permanently housed instead of being allowed to graze

zero growth *n* no increase in the growth or development of something, especially when an increase might have been expected and where any increase is measured as a percentage ○ *predictions of zero growth in the economy*

zero hour *n* **1.** the time set for the start of a military operation **2.** the time or date when something important is due to happen

zeroize /zeérō īz/ (**-izes, -izing, -ized**), **zeroise** (**-ises, -ising, -ised**) *vti* COMPUT same as **zerofill**

zero option *n* an offer to limit the number of short-range nuclear missiles or remove them altogether if an opposing side agrees to do the same

zero population growth *n* a situation in which the number of new births is no greater than the number of people dying, so that the overall population size remains the same

zero-rate *vt* to charge goods or services at a zero rate of value-added tax —**zero-rated** *adj* —**zero rating** *n*

zero-sum *adj* relating to a situation in which a gain by one side or person requires any other side or person involved in it to sustain a corresponding loss

zeroth /zeér ōth/ *adj* preceding number one in a series

zero tolerance *n* the absence of any leniency or exception in the enforcement of a law, rule, or regulation, especially a law against antisocial behaviour

zero-zero *adj* describes flying conditions in which cloud is so thick and low that the pilot can see nothing ahead and nothing above or below the aircraft [Shortening of *zero ceiling, zero visibility*]

zero-zero option *n* MIL same as **double-zero option**

zest /zest/ *n* **1.** HEARTY ENJOYMENT lively enjoyment and enthusiasm ○ *zest for life* **2.** EXCITING AND ENJOYABLE QUALITY an exciting or interesting aspect of something that makes it particularly enjoyable **3.** COOK CITRUS PEEL USED AS FLAVOURING the thin outer rind of the peel of a citrus fruit that is cut, scraped, or grated to yield a sharp fruity flavouring for foods and drinks **4.** PIQUANT FLAVOUR a pleasantly sharp flavour ■ *vt* (**zests, zesting, zested**) **1.** COOK GRATE SKIN OF CITRUS FRUIT to cut, grate, or scrape the rind of a citrus fruit for use as a flavouring in foods and drinks **2.** MAKE SOMETHING MORE STIMULATING AND ENJOYABLE to make an experience more enjoyable by adding excitement or interest to it [15C. < French] —**zestful** *adj* —**zesty** *adj*

zester /zéstər/ *n* a small utensil with a row of tiny sharpened holes or edges at its tip for cutting strips of zest from oranges, lemons, or other citrus fruits

zeta /zeétə/ *n* the sixth letter of the Greek alphabet, written in the English alphabet as 'z'. See table at **alphabet** [Early 18C. < Greek *zēta*, of Phoenician origin]

Zethus /zeéthəss/ *n* in Greek mythology, a son of Zeus and Antiope and the twin of Amphion. The brothers became joint kings of Thebes.

zetta- *prefix* indicates 10^{21} in measurements ○ *zettabyte* [Late 20C. Probably < Italian *sette* 'seven']

zettabyte /zéttə bīt/ *n* a unit of computer memory or disk storage space equal to one sextillion bytes

zeugma /zyoógmə, zoóg-/ *n* a figure of speech in which an adjective or verb is used with two nouns but is appropriate to only one of them or has a different sense with each, as in 'During the race he broke the record and his leg' [Late 16C. Via Latin < Greek, 'joining'] —**zeugmatic** /zyoog máttik, zoog-/ *adj* —**zeugmatically** *adv*

Zeus /zyooss/ *n* in Greek mythology, the god of the sky, ruler of the Olympian gods, and spiritual father of gods and mortals. Roman equivalent **Jupiter** (sense 1)

Zhangjiakou /jáng jyaá kō/ city in northeastern China in Hebei Province, situated at one of the gates of the Great Wall of China. Population: 673,901 (1991).

Zhang Zhidong /jáng jee túng/ (1837–1909) Chinese reformer and provincial governor. A modernizer at the end of the Manchu dynasty, he held several provincial governorships (1884–1907) and reformed the Chinese educational system.

Zhao Mengfu /jów məng foó/ (1254–1322) Chinese artist. He is known for his realistic animal pictures and for his expressive landscapes and studies of bamboo.

Zhejiang /jé jáng/ province in eastern China, on the East China Sea. Capital: Hangzhou. Population: 43,430,000 (1997). Area: 102,000 sq. km/39,382 sq. mi.

Zhenghe expeditions /júng húr-/ *npl* a series of seven overseas trade expeditions under the Ming emperor

Yonglo between 1405 and 1423 that were the last Chinese attempt to create a worldwide trading empire [After *Zhenghe*, court eunuch who led them]

Zhengzhou /júng jṓ/ capital of Henan Province, eastern China, on the Huang He between Taiyuan and Wuhan. Population: 1,990,000 (1995).

zho *n* ZOOL another spelling of **dzo**

Zhou /jṓ/ *n* a Chinese dynasty that ruled between the 12th and the 3rd centuries BC, during which China was divided into feudal states and the religions of Confucianism and Taoism arose [Late 18C. < Chinese *zhōu*]

Zhou Enlai /jṓ ən líi/ (1898–1976) premier of the People's Republic of China (1949–75). He became the first premier of Communist China and also served as the country's foreign minister (1949–58). Towards the end of his premiership, he increased contact with Japan and the United States.

Zia /zeé ə/, **Khaleda** (*b.* 1945) prime minister of Bangladesh (1991–96, 2001–). The widow of the murdered military ruler Zia ur-Rahman and leader of the Bangladesh Nationalist Party, she came to power in 1991 after a series of coups and assassinations. She was re-elected in 2001.

Zia ul-Haq /zeé ə oõl haák/, **Muhammad** (1924–88) Pakistani general and national leader. He overthrew Prime Minister Zulfikar Ali Bhutto (1977), and as president of Pakistan (1978–88) imposed martial law and introduced the Islamic legal code. He approved Bhutto's execution (1979) over international protests.

zibeline /zíbbə līn/, **zibelline** *n* a thick soft fabric with a long nap, made of wool, especially mohair or alpaca, or of the hair of another animal such as a camel [Late 16C. Via French < Italian *zibellino* 'sable' < Slavic]

zibet /zíbbit/ *n* a species of civet that is eaten in China. Native to: Southeast Asia. Latin name: *Viverra zibetha*. [Late 16C. Via medieval Latin *zibethum* or Italian *zibetto* < Arabic *zabād* 'musky perfume obtained from civets']

zichel /zíchəl/ *pron* SW England same as **suchlike** [Alteration]

REGIONAL NOTE See **z**[1].

---

zidovudine /zī dṓvyŏŏ deen/ *n* an antiviral drug. Use: Aids treatment. [Late 20C. < AZIDE + *-vudine*, INN stem]

Florenz Ziegfeld

Ziegfeld /zíg feld/, **Florenz** (1869–1932) US theatre producer. He launched the Ziegfeld Follies, an annual musical revue (1907), and produced extravagant musicals in New York.

zig /zig/ *n* a sharp line, direction, movement, or course that forms part of a zigzag ■ *vi* (**zigs, zigging, zigged**) to move in a sharp line, direction, movement, or course that forms part of a zigzag [Mid-20C. < ZIGZAG]

ziggurat /zíggŏŏ rat/ *n* an ancient Mesopotamian pyramid-shaped tower with a square base, rising in storeys of ever-decreasing size, with a terrace at each storey and a temple at the very top [Late 19C. < Assyrian *ziqquratu* 'pinnacle']

zigzag /zíg zag/ *n* **1.** LINE TAKING ALTERNATING TURNS a line going at an angle first one way, then sharply the opposite way, then back the first way, and so on, like the outline of a saw's teeth **2.** SOMETHING REPEATEDLY SWITCHING DIRECTIONS SHARPLY something that follows a sharply alternating line or course, e.g. a road with sharp bends alternating right and left ■ *adv* IN SHARPLY

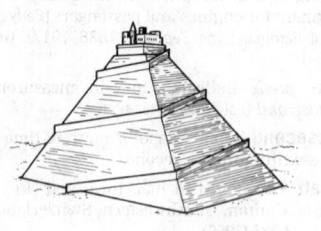
ziggurat

ALTERNATING DIRECTIONS along a sharply alternating line or course ■ *v* (**-zags, -zagging, -zagged**) **1.** *vti* PROCEED IN SHARPLY ALTERNATING PATH to follow a sharply alternating line or course, or cause something to move in this way ○ *They zigzagged across the field, dodging enemy bullets.* **2.** *vt* HANDICRAFT MAKE SHARPLY ALTERNATING PATTERN to make a pattern of sharply alternating lines or directions on something, e.g. with herringbone stitches [Early 18C. Via French < German *Zickzack*]

zigzag fence *n* Northeast US a fence made of split rails each resting on and set at angles to the next, forming a zigzag

zila /zíllə, zíllaa/, **zilla** *n* in South Asia, an administrative district [Early 19C. Via Persian and Urdu < Arabic *ḍila*' 'division']

zila parishad /-púrrishəd/ *n* a local council that governs an administrative district in South Asia

zilch /zilch/ *pron* zero or nothing at all (*informal*) ○ *They take all the profits and we're left with zilch.* [Mid-20C. Origin ?]

zill /zil/ *n* either of a pair of tiny cymbals that belly dancers hold in their fingers and play in time to their dancing [< Turkish *zil* 'cymbals']

zilla *n* PUBLIC ADMIN another spelling of **zila**

zillion /zíllyən/ *n* a number of people or a quantity of things so huge it cannot be counted or determined (*informal*) ○ *Zillions preferred the new model to the old one.* [Mid-20C. After MILLION and BILLION, with *z* representing the last in a series] —**zillion** *det*

zillionaire /zílyə náir/ *n* an extremely wealthy person (*informal*) [Mid-20C. After MILLIONAIRE]

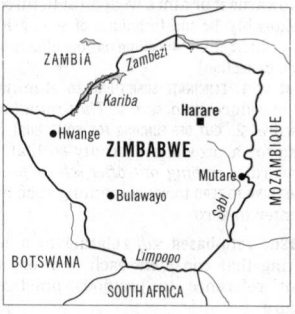
Zimbabwe

Zimbabwe /zim baábwi, -way/ country in southern Africa. Language: English. Currency: Zimbabwe dollar. Capital: Harare. Population: 12,576,742 (2003). Area: 390,759 sq. km/150,873 sq. mi. Official name Republic of Zimbabwe. Former name **Rhodesia** (1964–79), **Southern Rhodesia** (1923–64) —**Zimbabwean** *n, adj*

Zimmer /zímmər/ *tdmk* a trademark for a lightweight metal tubular frame with four rubber-tipped legs, designed to support somebody who needs help in walking

zinc /zingk/ *n* **1.** BLUISH METALLIC ELEMENT a bluish-white metallic element. Source: calamine, sphalerite, franklinite. Use: in alloys such as brass and nickel-silver, as a protective corrosion-resistant coating for other metals, especially steel and iron. Symbol Zn. See table at **element 2.** GALVANIZED IRON corrugated iron with a protective zinc coating (*informal*) ■ *vt* (**zincs, zincing** or **zincking, zinced** or **zincked**) COAT SOMETHING WITH ZINC to cover a metal, especially iron or steel, with a protective corrosion-resistant

coating of zinc [Mid-17C. < German *Zink*] —**zincic** *adj* —**zincky** *adj* —**zincoid** *adj*

zincate /zíng kayt/ *n* a salt derived from zinc hydroxide

zinc blende *n* MINERALS same as **sphalerite**

zinc chloride *n* a poisonous soluble salt. Use: wood preservative, antiseptic, catalyst. Formula: $ZnCl_2$.

zinc hydroxide *n* a colourless crystalline compound. Use: in chemical synthesis, as an absorbent.

zinciferous /zing kíffərəss/ *adj* containing or yielding zinc, especially as an ore

zincite /zíngk īt/ *n* a reddish-orange zinc oxide mineral

zinckenite *n* MINERALS another spelling of **zinkenite**

zinco /zíngkō/ (*plural* **-cos**) *n* PRINTING same as **zincograph** (*informal*) [Late 19C. Shortening]

zincograph /zíngkə graaf, -graf/ *n* **1.** a printing plate made of zinc that has the design to be printed etched into its surface **2.** a print taken from a zincograph —**zincography** /zing kóggrəfi/ *n*

zinc ointment *n* an antiseptic ointment containing zinc oxide in a base of petroleum jelly or lanolin. Use: treatment of skin disorders.

zinc oxide *n* an odourless water-insoluble white powder. Use: pigment, astringent, antiseptic. Formula: ZnO.

zinc sulphate *n* a colourless crystalline powder. Use: pigment, emetic, wood preservative, crop spray. Formula: $ZnSO_4$.

zinc sulphide *n* a crystalline white or yellowish powder. Use: pigment, phosphor on X-ray and television screens. Formula: ZnS.

zinc white *n* zinc oxide used as a white pigment in paint

zindabad /zíndə bad/ *S Asia interj* expresses loud approval, acclaim, or enthusiasm ■ *n* a loud shout of approval, acclaim, or enthusiasm [Mid-20C. < Urdu, 'may … live']

Zinder /zíndər/ city in south-central Niger. Situated about 113 km/70 mi. north of the border with Nigeria, it was Niger's capital until 1926. Population: 120,900 (1988).

zine /zeen/ *n* a self-published paper, Internet magazine, or other periodical, issued at irregular intervals with and usually appealing to a specialist readership (*informal*) [Mid-20C. Shortening of MAGAZINE]

Zinfandel /zínfən del/ *n* **1.** a typically light fruity red or rosé wine made from a black variety of grape grown mainly in California, United States **2.** a black grape variety. Use: to make Zinfandel. [Mid-19C. Origin ?]

zing /zing/ *n* **1.** LIVELY AND EXCITING QUALITY a lively exciting aspect of something that makes it particularly enjoyable (*informal*) ○ *The rhythm guitar gives the tune extra zing.* **2.** SHARP SINGING SOUND a short high-pitched humming or buzzing sound, e.g. the sound of a bullet whizzing through the air ■ *v* (**zings, zinging, zinged**) (*informal*) **1.** *vi* MAKE HUMMING NOISE to make or move with a short high-pitched humming or buzzing noise **2.** *vi* SPEED to move very quickly ○ *kids zinging by on skates* **3.** *vi* BE LIVELY to be very energetic and animated ○ *The production zings with energy.* **4.** *vt* N Am ATTACK SOMEBODY WITH WORDS to criticize somebody sharply, especially in a swift and clever way [Early 20C. An imitation of the sound] —**zingy** *adj*

zinger /zíngər/ *n* N Am (*informal*) **1.** CLEVER REMARK SKILFULLY DELIVERED a remark delivered with great skill and speed, especially a sharp and perfectly timed witticism or criticism **2.** SHOCKING AND UNEXPECTED HAPPENING a shocking and unexpected turn of events, e.g. an abrupt shift in the plot of a film, play, or book **3.** SOMEBODY OR SOMETHING ENERGETIC AND SURPRISING an energetic person or thing that produces startling results

zinjanthropus /zin jánthrəpəss/ (*plural* **-pi** /-pī/ or **-puses**) *n* a hominid fossil found in 1959 at Olduvai Gorge in East Africa. Originally classified as a distinct genus and species, it is now recognized as an australopithecine. [Mid-20C. < modern Latin < medieval Arabic *Zinj* 'East Africa' + Greek *anthrōpos* 'person'] —**zinjanthropine** *adj, n*

~~**zink**~~ incorrect spelling of **zinc**

zinkenite /zíngkən īt/, **zinckenite** n a dark-grey lead antimony sulphide mineral [Mid-19C. After J. K. L. Zincken (1790–1862), German mineralogist]

zinnia

zinnia /zínni ə/ (plural **-as** or same) n a plant of the daisy family with large colourful flowers that is widely grown as a garden plant. Native to: Mexico. Genus: Zinnia. [Mid-18C. < modern Latin, after J. G. Zinn (1727–59), German botanist]

Zinzendorf /tsíntsən dawrf/, **Nikolaus Ludwig, Graf von** (1700–60) German religious reformer. A founder and leader of the Moravian Church, he established Moravian congregations in Europe and North America.

Zion /zí ən/ n 1. one of the hills of Jerusalem, in biblical times emblematic of the house or household of God and later by extension the Jews and their religion 2. in Christian belief, the place where God lives and is worshipped on Earth or in the kingdom of heaven [Pre-12C. Via late Latin and Greek < Hebrew ṣīyôn]

Zionism /zí ənizəm/ n a worldwide movement, originating in the 19th century, that sought to establish and develop a Jewish nation in Palestine. Since 1948 its function has been to support the state of Israel.

Zionist /zí ənist/ n 1. a supporter of Zionism 2. S Africa a member of an independent Christian church in South Africa that incorporates traditional African beliefs and forms of worship —**Zionist** adj —**Zionistic** /zí ə nístik/ adj

zip[1] /zip/ n 1. FASTENER WITH INTERLOCKING TEETH a fastener for clothes, bags, or other items, consisting of two rows of interlocking metal or plastic teeth with an attached sliding tab pulled to open or close the fastener. US term **zipper** 2. BRIEF HISSING SOUND a brief sibilant sound, e.g. the sound of a bullet whizzing through the air 3. LIVELY AND EXCITING QUALITY a lively exciting aspect of something that makes it particularly enjoyable (informal) ■ v (**zips, zipping, zipped**) 1. vti FASTEN WITH ZIP to fasten something with a zip, or be fastened with a zip 2. vt COMPUT COMPRESS FILE to compress a computer file for storage or transmission 3. vi MAKE OR MOVE WITH HISSING SOUND to make or move with a rapid sibilant sound (informal) 4. vti GO OR MOVE VERY FAST to go somewhere very fast, or move something somewhere very fast (informal) [Late 19C. An imitation of the sound]

zip[2] /zip/ abbr a file extension for a zip file

zip code n US MAIL same as **postcode**

ZIP drive tdmk a trademark for a piece of computer equipment that compresses large computer files for easier storage or faster transmission

zip fastener n CLOTHING same as **zip**[1] n (sense 1)

zip file n a computer file with the extension .zip containing data that has been compressed for storage or transmission.

zip gun n N Am a homemade pistol, especially one that uses a spring or a rubber band as the firing mechanism (slang)

zipless /zíppləss/ adj 1. not fitted with a zip, or not fastened using a zip 2. passionate and lasting only a short time [Late 20C. In the sense 'passionate' from the idea of clothes coming off without the awkward undoing of zips]

zipper /zíppər/ n same as **zip**[1] n (sense 1) ■ vti (**-pers, -pering, -pered**) N Am to fasten or unfasten a zip fastener, or become fastened or unfastened in this way

zippered /zíppərd/ adj N Am same as **zip-up**

zippy /zíppi/ (**-pier, -piest**) adj (informal) 1. showing or having spirit or energy 2. with good acceleration

zip-up adj fitted with, or fastened using, a zip. N Am term **zippered**

zircalloy /zúrk álloy, zúrkə loy/, **zircaloy** n an alloy of zirconium with tin, chromium, and nickel that is resistant to heat and corrosion, making it a useful material in the nuclear power industry

zircon /zúr kon/ n a very hard zirconium silicate mineral. Use: source of zirconium, gems. [Late 18C. < German Zirkon]

zirconia /zur kṓni ə/ n CHEM same as **zirconium oxide**

zirconium /zur kṓni əm/ n 1. a greyish-white, corrosion-resistant, metallic element. Source: zircon, zirconia. Use: coating fuel rods in nuclear reactors. Symbol **Zr**. See table at **element** 2. the mineral zircon used as a gemstone, often as a substitute diamond — **zirconic** /-kónnik/ adj

zirconium oxide n a heavy water-insoluble white powder. Use: pigment, abrasive, manufacture of heat-resistant materials and ceramics. Formula: ZrO_2.

zit /zit/ n a pimple on the skin (slang) [Mid-20C. Origin ?] —**zitty** adj

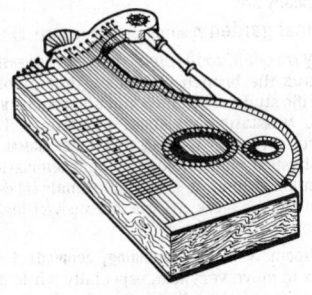

zither

zither /zíthər/ n a musical instrument consisting of a flat shallow sound box with metal strings stretched across it that are plucked [Mid-19C. Via German < Latin cithara (see CITHARA)] —**zitherist** n

ziti /zée tee/ n pasta in the form of medium-sized tubes, longer and thicker than macaroni [Mid-19C. < Italian, plural of zito 'boy']

zizz /ziz/ (informal) n a brief sleep ■ vi (**zizzes, zizzing, zizzed**) to have a brief sleep [Mid-20C. < ZZZ]

Zl abbr MONEY zloty

Z line n a narrow dark line across striated muscle fibres that marks the boundaries between adjacent segments [< abbreviation of German Zwischenscheibe 'intervening disc']

zloty /zlótti/ (plural **-ties** or same) n the main unit of currency in Poland, worth 100 groszy. See table at **currency** [Early 20C. < Polish złoty 'golden' < złoto 'gold']

zm abbr Zambia (used in Internet addresses) See table at **domain name**

Zmodem /zéd mō dem/ n a variation of the Ymodem file transfer protocol in which data is sent in 512-byte blocks without waiting for acknowledgment from the recipient between blocks

Zn symbol CHEM ELEM zinc

zo /zō/ n ZOOL another spelling of **dzo**

zo- prefix same as **zoo-** (used before vowels)

zoarium /zō áiri əm/ (plural **-iums** or **-ia** /-i ə/) n a collection of distinct organisms that together form a compound organism [Late 19C. < Greek zōion 'animal' (see -ZOON)]

zod. abbr zodiac

zodiac /zṓdi ak/ n 1. ASTROLOGICALLY SIGNIFICANT PART OF SKY a narrow band in the sky in which the movements of the major planets, Sun, and Moon take place, astrologically divided into twelve sections named after the major constellations 2. ASTROLOGER'S CHART a chart linking twelve constellations to twelve divisions of the year, used as the astrologer's main tool for analysing character and predicting the future 3. RECURRING SET a set of things or a sequence of events

that repeats itself cyclically (literary) [14C. Via French and Latin < Greek zōidiakos kuklos 'circle of animal figures' < zōidion 'small animal' < zōion (see -ZOON)] —**zodiacal** /zō dī ək'l/ adj

zodiacal constellation n a constellation that a sign of the zodiac is named after

zodiacal light n a faint glow in the sky, seen before sunrise to the east and after sunset to the west, and caused by small particles reflected in sunlight

Zog I /zōg/ (1895–1961) king of Albania. He was prime minister (1922–24) and president (1925–28) of Albania before proclaiming himself king (1928). He fled when the Italians invaded during World War II (1939), and abdicated in 1946.

Zohar /zō haar/ n a 13th-century Jewish mystical text that is the primary text of Kabbalistic writings [Late 17C. < Hebrew zōhar 'light, splendour']

-zoic suffix 1. relating to a particular geological era ○ Mesozoic 2. having a particular kind of animal existence ○ epizoic [< Greek zōē 'life' < Indo-European, 'to live']

zoisite /zóy sīt/ n a grey or green hydrated calcium aluminosilicate mineral. Source: metamorphic rocks. [Early 19C. After Baron Sigismund Zois von Edelstein (1747–1819), Slovenian scholar]

zol /zol/ n S Africa (slang) 1. same as **cannabis** (sense 1) 2. a hand-rolled cannabis cigarette [Mid-20C. Origin ?]

Émile Zola

Zola /zṓlə/, **Émile** (1840–1902) French novelist. One of the leading French novelists of the 19th century, he employed a scientifically based technique of naturalism in his epic 20-novel cycle Les Rougon-Macquart (1871–93). He is also known for 'J'Accuse' (1898), a defence of Alfred Dreyfus. Full name **Zola, Émile Édouard Charles Antoine**

'One forges one's style on the terrible anvil of daily deadlines.'
[Emile Zola, Le Figaro; 1881]

Zollverein /zólfə rīn, tsól-/ n 1. a customs union formed in the 19th century by a number of German states to establish uniform import tariffs from other countries and free trade among themselves 2. a customs union formed to establish uniform import tariffs [Mid-19C. < German, 'tariff union']

zombie /zómbi/, **zombi** n 1. OFFENSIVE TERM an offensive term for a person considered to lack energy, enthusiasm, or the ability to think independently (insult) 2. DEAD BODY GIVEN LIFE BY VOODOO in voodoo, a dead body supposedly brought back to life again without a soul 3. VOODOO SPIRIT REVIVING DEAD BODY in voodoo, a spirit that supposedly brings a dead body back to life again 4. RELIG SNAKE GOD OF VOODOO in Caribbean, Brazilian, and West African voodoo religions, a snake god 5. BEVERAGES STRONG RUM COCKTAIL a very strong alcoholic cocktail made with various kinds of rum 6. HIST ARMY CONSCRIPT ASSIGNED FOR HOME DEFENCE in Canada, a conscripted soldier assigned to home defence during World War II (slang) 7. COMPUT PROGRAM ALLOWING REMOTE CONTROL a hidden software program that is installed on another computer by means of a virus, allowing it to be accessed remotely and used to access or attack another computer 8. COMPUT REMOTELY CONTROLLED COMPUTER a computer that has been infected with a zombie [Early 19C. Via Caribbean Creole < Kimbundu n-zumbi 'ghost, snake god'] —**zombiism** n

zombie drone n COMPUT same as **zombie** (senses 7–8) (slang)

zombify /zómbi fī/ (**-fies, -fying, -fied**) *vt* to convert somebody into a zombie

zonal /zṓn'l/, **zonary** /zṓnəri/ *adj* **1.** relating to a zone or zones **2.** divided up into zones —**zonally** *adv*

zonal soil *n* soil whose nature is established by the action of the climate and vegetation of the area in which it is found

zona pellucida /zṓnə pə lo͞ossidə/ *n* a thick transparent envelope that surrounds a developing ovum, allowing only one sperm cell through to fertilize the ovum [< modern Latin, 'transparent band']

zonary *adj* same as **zonal**

zonate /zṓ nayt/, **zonated** /zō náytid/ *adj* **1.** divided up into zones **2.** distinguished by zones, e.g. of colour or texture —**zonation** /zō náysh'n/ *n*

zone /zōn/ *n* **1. SEPARATE AREA WITH PARTICULAR FUNCTION** an area regarded as separate or kept separate, especially one with a particular use or function ○ *a loading zone* **2. SUBSECTION OF PARTICULAR AREA** one of the smaller, usually named or numbered sections that an area is divided into, e.g. those of a transport network or a sports field **3.** METEOROL **HORIZONTAL CLIMATIC BAND AROUND EARTH** one of the five horizontal belts across the Earth's surface, separated by the Arctic Circle, the Tropic of Cancer, the Tropic of Capricorn, and the Antarctic Circle, that marks out a climatic region. The zones are called the North Frigid Zone, the North Temperate Zone, the South Frigid Zone, the South Temperate Zone, and the Torrid Zone. **4.** TIME same as **time zone 5.** ECOL **AREA WITH DISTINCT PLANTS AND ANIMALS** an area with characteristic types of organism determined largely by its environment, e.g. a belt of vegetation on a mountain **6.** GEOL **UNIT OF ROCK FORMATION WITH FOSSILS** a unit of a rock formation characterized by its fossil content **7.** MATHS **PART OF SPHERE** the portion of a sphere included between two parallel planes meeting the sphere, one of which may be tangent to the sphere or both of which may intersect it ■ *v* (**zones, zoning, zoned**) **1.** *vt* **SPLIT AREA INTO ZONES** to divide an area into zones **2.** *vti* **DESIGNATE AREA FOR SOMETHING** to declare officially that an area is to be used for a particular purpose, or be developed in a particular way (*often passive*) ○ *The canal areas have been zoned for leisure and recreation.* [15C. Via French and Latin < Greek *zōnē* 'belt, girdle'] —**zoning** *n* ◇ **in the zone** *US* performing an action, especially playing a sport, extremely well with intense focus (*informal*)

zone out *vi US* to lose focus or concentration or fall asleep (*slang*)

zone melting *n* METALL same as **zone refining**

zone of saturation *n* an area of soil or rock below the level of the water table where all the voids are filled with water

zone refining *n* a technique for greatly purifying metals in which a molten area is made to pass along an otherwise solid bar so that impurities become concentrated at one end

zonetime /zṓn tīm/ *n* the standard time that exists throughout a time zone

zonk /zongk/ (**zonks, zonking, zonked**) *vti* to lose consciousness or become stupefied from exhaustion or an intake of alcohol or narcotic drugs, or make somebody do this (*slang*) [Early 20C. An imitation of the sound of a heavy blow]

zonked /zongkt/, **zonked out** *adj* **1.** exhausted to the point of hardly being able to function (*informal*) **2.** unconscious, stupefied, or sleeping, especially as a result of the effects of alcohol or a drug (*slang*)

zonule /zónnyool/ *n* **1.** a small zone, band, or belt **2.** a set of fibres attaching the ciliary body in the eye to the lens —**zonular** *adj*

zoo /zoo/ (*plural* **zoos**) *n* **1.** a park where live wild animals from different parts of the world are kept in cages or enclosures for people to come and see, and where they are bred and studied by scientists **2.** a place characterized as being full of noisy obstreperous people creating confusion and disorder (*informal*) [Mid-19C. Shortening of ZOOLOGICAL GARDEN]

zoo- *prefix* **1.** animal, animal kingdom ○ *zoology* **2.** motile organism ○ *zoospore* [< Greek *zōion* (see -ZOON)]

zooflagellate /zṓ ə flájələt/ *n* a colourless protozoan that ingests organic matter, is often parasitic, and has one or more flagella

zoogeography /zṓ ə ji óggrəfi/ *n* the scientific study of the areas where different animals live and the causes and effects of such distribution, especially distributions on a large or global scale —**zoogeographer** *n* —**zoogeographic** /zṓ ə jee ə gráffik/ *adj*

zoogloea /zṓ ə glée ə/ (*plural* **-as** or **-ae** /-ee/), **zooglea** *n* a colony of microbes embedded in a gelatinous matrix [Late 19C. < modern Latin, < Greek *zōion* 'animal' + *gloios* 'glutinous substance'] —**zoogloeal** *adj*

zoography /zō óggrəfi/ *n* a branch of zoology that deals with describing animals and their habitats — **zoographer** *n* —**zoographic** /zṓ ə gráffik/ *adj*

zooid /zṓ oyd/ *n* an individual invertebrate animal that reproduces nonsexually by budding or splitting, especially one that lives in a colony in which each member is joined to others by living material, e.g. a coral [Mid-19C. < ZOO- + -OID] —**zooidal** *adj*

zookeeper /zo͞o keepər/ *n* somebody whose job is looking after the animals in a zoo

zool. *abbr* **1.** zoological **2.** zoology

zoolatry /zō óllətri/ *n* **1.** in some ancient cultures, the worshipping of animals **2.** an excessive devotion to animals, especially domestic pets (*humorous*) — **zoolater** *n* —**zoolatrous** *adj*

zoological /zṓ ə lójjik'l, zo͞o-/ *adj* **1.** relating to the scientific study of animals **2.** relating to animals — **zoologically** *adv*

zoological garden *n* same as **zoo** (sense 1) (*dated*)

zoology /zō ólləji, zoo-/ (*plural* **-gies**) *n* **1. SCIENTIFIC STUDY OF ANIMALS** the branch of biology that involves the scientific study of animals and all aspects of animal life **2. ANIMALS LIVING IN REGION** the animal life of a particular region **3. CHARACTERISTICS OF ANIMAL OR GROUP** the physical and biological characteristics of a particular animal or group of animals [Mid-17C. Via modern Latin < Greek *zōologia* 'the study of life' < *zōion* (see -ZOON)] —**zoologist** *n*

zoom /zoom/ *v* (**zooms, zooming, zoomed**) **1.** *vi* **MOVE SPEEDILY** to move very fast, especially while emitting a loud low-pitched buzzing noise **2.** *vi* **MAKE LOUD BUZZING NOISE** to emit a loud low-pitched buzzing or humming noise **3.** *vi* **INCREASE SUDDENLY** to rise or increase suddenly and significantly **4.** *vi* **SIMULATE MOVEMENT WITH CAMERA LENS** to simulate movement towards or away from an object with a camera lens that allows various focal lengths **5.** *vti* AVIAT **CARRY OUT STEEP CLIMB IN AIRCRAFT** to make an aircraft climb rapidly at a very steep angle, or be piloted in this way ■ *n* **1. LOUD BUZZING NOISE** a loud low-pitched buzzing noise, especially one caused by rapid movement **2.** PHOTOGRAPHY, CINEMA same as **zoom lens 3.** PHOTOGRAPHY, CINEMA **SHOT WITH ZOOM LENS** a shot in which a zoom lens is used to make the object in focus appear to move closer or farther away while the camera itself stays still [Late 19C. An imitation of a buzzing sound]

zoom in *vi* to make an object appear bigger or closer, or to decrease the area in view, by use of a zoom lens or a graphic imaging device

zoom out *vi* to make an object appear smaller or farther away, or to increase the area in view, by use of a zoom lens or a graphic imaging device

zoometry /zō ómmətri/ *n* the branch of zoology that deals with the sizes and proportions of animals — **zoometric** /zṓ ə méttrik/ *adj* —**zoometrist** *n*

zoom lens *n* a camera lens assembly with adjustable focal lengths, facilitating transitions between long shots and close-ups

zoomorphism /zṓ ə máwrfizəm/ *n* **1.** the attribution of animal forms or characteristics to gods **2.** the use of animal figures in art and design, or of animal symbols in literature —**zoomorphic** *adj*

-zoon *suffix* animal, zooid ○ *epizoon* [Via modern Latin < Greek *zōion* 'living being, animal' < Indo-European, 'to live']

zoonosis /zṓ ə nṓssiss, zō ónnəssiss/ (*plural* **-onoses** /-nósseez/) *n* a disease that can be transmitted from vertebrate animals to humans, e.g. rabies, anthrax, or ringworm [Late 19C. < ZOO- + Greek *nosos* 'disease'] — **zoonotic** /zṓ ə nóttik/ *adj*

zoophagous /zō óffəgəss/ *adj* feeding on animals

zoophilia /zṓ ə filli ə/ *n* a sexual attraction to animals

zoophilic /zṓ ə fillik/ *adj* ZOOL same as **zoophilous**

zoophilism /zō óffilizəm/ *n* a strong affinity for animals and a devotion to protecting or rescuing them from human activities such as vivisection that exploit or endanger them

zoophilous /zō óffiləss/ *adj* **1.** very fond of animals **2.** using the actions of animals other than insects in pollinating a plant

zoophobia /zṓ ə fṓbi ə/ *n* an unusually intense fear of animals —**zoophobe** /zṓ əfōb/ *n* —**zoophobous** /zō óffəbəss/ *adj*

zoophyte /zṓ ə fīt/ *n* an invertebrate animal that looks like a plant, e.g. a sea anemone, coral, or sponge [Early 17C. Via modern Latin < Greek *zōiophuton* 'animal-plant' < *zōion* 'animal' + *phuton* 'plant'] —**zoophytic** /zṓ ə fittik/ *adj*

zooplankton /zṓ ə plángktən/ *n* plankton that is made up of microscopic animals such as protozoans

zooplasty /zṓ ə plasti/ *n* the surgical transplantation of an animal organ such as a pig's heart into a human body —**zooplastic** /zṓ ə plástik/ *adj*

zoosperm /zṓ ə spurm/ *n* BIOL same as **spermatozoon** — **zoospermatic** /zṓ ə spur máttik/ *adj*

zoosporangium /zṓ əspə ránji əm/ (*plural* **-gia** /-ji ə/) *n* an organ of a fungus or plant that produces spores that can swim —**zoosporangial** *adj*

zoospore /zṓ ə spawr/ *n* a spore of some algae and fungi that is capable of independent movement — **zoosporal** /zṓ ə spáwrəl/ *adj* —**zoosporic** /zṓ ə spórrik/ *adj*

zoosterol /zō óstə rol/ *n* a sterol produced by an animal

zootomy /zō óttəmi/ *n* **1.** the study of the anatomy of animals, especially comparative anatomy **2.** the dissection of animals [Mid-17C. < ZOO-, after ANATOMY] —**zootomic** /zṓ ə tómmik/ *adj* —**zootomically** *adv* —**zootomist** *n*

zootoxin /zṓ ə tóksin/ *n* a poisonous substance produced by an animal, e.g. snake venom —**zootoxic** *adj*

zoot suit /zo͞ot-/ *n* a man's suit, popular in the 1940s, that had a long jacket heavily padded at the shoulders and baggy high-waisted trousers tapering to narrow bottoms [Mid-20C. Rhyming formation] —**zoot suiter** *n*

zoo TV *n* a genre of television programme that encourages emotional and often uncontrolled reactions from the participants, featuring debates or personal disclosures in front of live audiences (*slang*)

zooxanthella /zṓ əzən théllə/ (*plural* **-lae** /-li/) *n* a microscopic yellow-green alga that lives symbiotically within the cells of some sea invertebrates, especially corals [Late 19C. < modern Latin, 'small yellow animal' < Greek *zōion* 'animal' + *xanthos* 'yellow']

zorbing /záwrbing/ *n NZ* the activity of rolling down a hill while strapped inside an extremely large plastic ball [Late 20C. After the company that invented the sport]

zori /záwri, zórri/ (*plural same* or **-ris**) *n* a simple Japanese sandal with a flat sole and a single thong, originally made of straw but now also made of rubber or felt [Early 19C. < Japanese *sō* 'grass, straw' (< Middle Chinese *tsaw*) + *ri* 'sole' (< Middle Chinese *li*)]

zorilla /zo rillə/, **zorille** /zórril/, **zoril** *n* a carnivorous mammal of the weasel family that looks like a skunk and has long black-and-white fur. Native to: Africa. Latin name: *Ictonyx striatus*. [Late 18C. Via French and modern Latin < Spanish *zorilla* 'little fox' < *zorro* 'fox']

Zoroaster /zórrō ástər/, **Zarathustra** /zárrə tho͞ostrə/ (630?–550? BC) Persian prophet. He founded Zoroastrianism, a religion based on revelations he received from Ahura Mazda, the 'Lord Wisdom'.

Zoroastrianism /zórrō ástri ənizəm/ *n* an ancient religion founded by the Persian prophet Zoroaster, the principal belief of which is in a supreme deity and a cosmic contest between two spirits, one good and one evil —**Zoroastrian** *n, adj*

zoster /zóstər/ *n* **1.** MED same as **shingles** (*technical*) **2.** a belt worn by men, especially soldiers, in ancient Greece [Early 18C. Via Latin < Greek *zōstēr* 'girdle']

Zouave /zoo aáv/ *n* **1.** a member of a former French infantry unit composed of Algerian soldiers, noted for their colourful uniforms and precision drill **2.** a member of an army unit whose uniforms imitate

those of the French Zouaves, especially such a soldier on the Union side during the US Civil War [Mid-19C. Via French < Kabyle *Zouaoua*, tribe in Algeria]

zouk /zook/ *n* a style of dance music originating in Guadeloupe and Martinique and played with guitars and synthesizers, combining a strong fast disco beat and Caribbean rhythms [Late 20C. Via French < French Creole of the Antilles]

zounds /zowndz/ *interj* a mild expression of surprise or annoyance (*archaic*) [Late 16C. Contraction of *by God's wounds!*]

Zovirax /zóvi raks, zō ví raks/ *tdmk* a trademark for an antiviral drug. Use: treatment of herpes infections.

zoysia /zóyssi ə/ *n* a low-growing grass plant often used for lawns. Native to: Asia. Genus: *Zoysia*. [Mid-20C. < modern Latin, after Carl von *Zoys* zu Laubach (1756–1800?), Austrian botanist]

Z particle *n* a short-lived electrically neutral elementary particle considered to mediate the weak interaction between other elementary particles

ZPG *abbr* zero population growth

Zr *symbol* CHEM ELEM zirconium

zucchetto /zoo kéttō/ (*plural* **-tos**) *n* a small round skullcap worn by members of the Roman Catholic clergy, the colour of which depends on the rank of the person wearing it [Mid-19C. Alteration of Italian *zucchetta* 'small head' < *zucca* 'gourd, head' (see ZUCCHINI)]

zucchini /zoo keéni/ (*plural same* or **-nis**) *n* ANZ, N Am FOOD, PLANTS a small summer squash that is shaped like a cucumber with a smooth thin dark-green or yellow skin and is eaten cooked as a vegetable. UK term **courgette** [Early 20C. < Italian, plural of *zucchino* 'courgette' < *zucca* 'gourd' < late Latin *cucutia*, variant of Latin *cucurbita*]

~~zuchini~~ incorrect spelling of **zucchini**

zugzwang /zoóg zwang/ *n* a chess situation in which a player is forced into making a disadvantageous move, especially one that involves the loss of a piece ■ *vt* (**-zwangs, -zwanging, -zwanged**) to force a chess opponent into a disadvantageous situation, especially one that involves the loss of one of the opponent's pieces [Early 20C. < German, 'being forced to move']

Zuider Zee /zídər zeé/ former inlet of the North Sea in the northern Netherlands. After completion of the IJsselmeer Dam in 1932, parts of it were drained, and the remainder now forms the IJsselmeer.

Zukerman /zoókər man/, **Pinchas** (*b.* 1948) Israeli-born US violinist and conductor. His performance of both the classical repertoire and 20th-century works established his reputation as one of the outstanding violinists of his generation.

Zulu /zoóloo/ (*plural same* or **-lus**) *n* **1.** MEMBER OF S AFRICAN PEOPLE a member of a people of South Africa who live mainly in northern KwaZulu-Natal Province **2.** S AFRICAN LANGUAGE a Bantu language spoken in eastern South Africa, closely related to Xhosa. Native speakers: 8 million. **3.** COMMUNICATION CODE WORD FOR LETTER 'Z' a code word for the letter 'Z', used in international radio communications [Early 19C. < Zulu *umzulu*] —**Zulu** *adj*

Zululand /zoóloo land/ historic region in South Africa. Now incorporated into KwaZulu-Natal Province, it is the homeland of the Zulu people.

Zulu time *n* TIME same as **Greenwich Mean Time**

Zuni /zoóni/ (*plural same* or **-nis**), **Zuñi** /zoónyi/ (*plural same* or **-ñis**) *n* **1.** a member of a Pueblo people of western New Mexico **2.** the language of the Zuni people, unrelated to other languages. Native speakers: 5,000. [Mid-19C. < American Spanish < Keresan] —**Zuni** *adj*

Zurich /zyoórik, zoórik/, **Zürich** largest city in Switz-

erland, in the north of the country. It is the capital of Zurich Canton and an important financial, commercial, and manufacturing centre. Population: 337,900 (2001).

Zurich, Lake lake in northern Switzerland. Area: 88 sq. km/34 sq. mi.

zw *abbr* ONLINE Zimbabwe (*used in Internet addresses*) See table at **domain name**

Zwickau /zwík ow, tsvík ow/ city in Saxony, eastern Germany. Population: 104,921 (1997).

zwieback /zweé bak/ *n* a piece of bread, sliced and baked again until crisp and dry [Late 19C. < German, 'twice-bake']

Zwingli /zwíng gli, zwíngli/, **Huldreich** (1484–1531) Swiss religious reformer. Using his own translations of the Christian Scriptures, he questioned many Roman Catholic practices, held that the Communion wafer and wine were only symbolic of Christ's body and blood, and became the leader of the Reformation in Switzerland.

Zwinglian /zwíng gli ən, zwíngli ən/ *adj* relating to the life, works, or beliefs of the Swiss Protestant theologian Huldreich Zwingli ■ *n* a follower of Huldreich Zwingli or his beliefs —**Zwinglianism** *n*

zwitterion /zwíttər ī ən, tsvíttər-/ *n* an ion that has both a negative and a positive pole [Early 20C. < German, 'hybrid ion']

Zwolle /zwóllə/ capital city of Overijssel Province, in the north-central Netherlands. Population: 105,819 (2000).

Zworykin /zwáwrikin/, **Vladimir** (1889–1982) Russian-born US inventor. He was largely responsible for the development of the television camera and television tube during the 1920s and 1930s. Full name **Zworykin, Vladimir Kosma**

zydeco /zídikō/ *n* a style of dance music originating in Louisiana that is usually played on accordion, guitar, and violin and combines traditional French melodies with Caribbean and blues influences [Mid-20C. Probably < Louisiana creole *Les haricots (sont pas salés)* 'the beans (are not salted)', a well-known dance tune]

zyg- *prefix* same as **zygo-** (*used before vowels*)

zygo- *prefix* **1.** yoke, pair ○ *zygomorphic* **2.** union, reproduction ○ *zygogenesis* [< Greek *zugon* 'yoke, pair' < Indo-European, 'join']

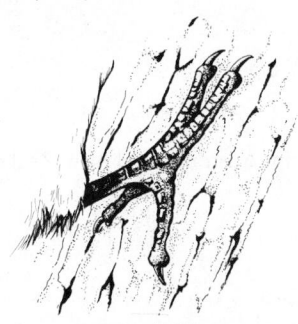

zygodactyl

zygodactyl /zígō dáktil/, **zygodactylous** /zígo dáktiləss/ *adj* describes the feet of birds in which the second and third toes face forwards and the first and fourth toes face backwards. ◊ **heterodactylous** ■ *n* a bird that has two pairs of toes facing in different directions, such as a woodpecker —**zygodactylism** *n*

zygogenesis /zígō jénnəssiss/ *n* reproduction involving the fusion of male and female nuclei —**zygogenetic** /zígōjə néttik/ *adj*

zygoma /zī gōmə/ (*plural* **-mata** /-mətə/) *n* ANAT **1.** same as **cheekbone** (*technical*) **2.** same as **zygomatic arch** **3.** same as **zygomatic process** [Late 17C. < Greek *zugōma* 'joining' < *zugoun* 'to join'] —**zygomatic** /zígə máttik/ *adj*

zygomatic arch *n* a slender bar of bone connecting the cheekbone with the temporal bone on the side of the skull

zygomatic bone *n* ANAT same as **cheekbone** (*technical*)

zygomatic process *n* a bony projection that forms part of the zygomatic arch and is joined to the cheekbone

zygomorphic /zígō máwrfik/ *adj* producing identical halves only when divided along a vertical axis —**zygomorphism** *n* —**zygomorphy** /zígō mawrfi/ *n*

zygosis /zī góssiss/ *n* BIOL same as **conjugation** (sense 6) [Late 19C. < Greek *zugōsis* < *zugoun* 'to join'] —**zygose** /zígōss/ *adj*

zygosity /zī góssəti/ *n* a characterization of a genetic trait, zygote, or embryo, e.g. whether twins have resulted from the division of one zygote or from two different zygotes (*often used in combination*) [Mid-20C. < ZYGOSIS]

zygospore /zígō spawr/ *n* a thick-walled sexual spore formed from the union of two gametes in some fungi and green algae —**zygosporic** /zígō spórrik/ *adj*

zygote /zígōt/ *n* an ovum that has been fertilized by a spermatozoon [Late 19C. < Greek *zugōtos* 'joined' < *zugoun* 'to join'] —**zygotic** /zī góttik/ *adj* —**zygotically** *adv*

zygotene /zígə teen/ *n* a stage of the first meiotic cell division in which homologous chromosomes are paired [Early 20C. < French *zygotène* < *zygo-* 'zygo-' + *-tène* 'ribbon' (< Latin *taenia*)]

-zygous *suffix* having a particular kind of zygotic constitution ○ *hemizygous* [< Greek *zugos* 'yoked, paired', < *zugon* (see ZYGO-)]

zym- *prefix* same as **zymo-** (*used before vowels*)

zymase /zím ayss, -ayz/ *n* an enzyme or enzyme complex obtained from yeast that ferments sugars [Late 19C. < Greek *zumē* 'leaven' (see ZYMO-)]

zymo- *prefix* **1.** fermentation ○ *zymology* **2.** enzyme ○ *zymogen* [Via modern Latin < Greek *zumē* 'leaven' < Indo-European, 'to mix']

zymogen /zímmǝjən/ *n* BIOCHEM same as **proenzyme**

zymogenesis /zímō jénnǝssiss/ *n* the transformation of a zymogen into an enzyme

zymogenic /zímō jénnik/, **zymogenetic** /zímmǝjə néttik/, **zymogenous** /zī mójjənəss/ *adj* **1.** relating to a zymogen **2.** causing or producing fermentation

zymology /zī mólləji/ *n* the study of fermentation and the action of enzymes as it takes place —**zymologic** /zímə lójjik/ *adj* —**zymologist** *n*

zymolysis /zī mólləssiss/ *n* the action of enzymes in the process of fermentation (*technical*) —**zymolytic** /zímə líttik/ *adj*

zymometer /zī mómmitər/ *n* an instrument that measures degrees of fermentation

zymosis /zī mōssiss/ *n* BIOCHEM same as **zymolysis** [Early 18C. < Greek *zumōsis* 'fermentation' < *zumoun* 'to leaven' < *zumē* (see ZYMO-)]

zymotic /zī móttik/ *adj* relating to, producing, or produced by fermentation [Mid-19C. < Greek *zumōtikos* 'causing fermentation' < *zumōsis* (see ZYMOSIS)] —**zymotically** *adv*

zymurgy /zímǝrji/ *n* the scientific study of fermentation processes involved in the production of alcoholic drinks [Mid-19C. < ZYMO-, after METALLURGY] —**zymurgic** /zī múrjik/ *adj*

Zyrian /zírri ən/ *n* the Komi language, particularly its northern dialect [Late 19C. < Russian *Zyryanin*] —**Zyrian** *adj*

zzz /zz/ *n* a representation of the sound made by somebody sleeping or snoring, often used in cartoons (*humorous*)

TABLES, CHARTS, AND COMPOSITE PICTURES

The following tables, charts, and composite pictures can be found at their alphabetical entry:

Aircraft
Alphabets
Angles
Beaufort scale
Bible, Books of the
Boats
Braille
Brass instruments
Bridges
Calendars and festivals
Cloud formations
Constellations
Crosses
Currencies
Deserts
Diacritics, Common
Domains, Internet
Elements, Chemical
Emoticons
Fungi
Geological time
Geometry
Hats
Herbs
Keyboard instruments
Lakes
Leaf shapes
Map projections
Measurements
Military ranks
Moon, Phases of the
Mountains
Notation, Musical
Oceans and seas
Percussion instruments
Periodic table
Presidents of the United States
Prime Ministers of Canada, Britain, Australia, and New Zealand
Richter scale
Rivers
Roofs
Runes
San Andreas Fault
Semaphore
Shoes
Stringed instruments
Time zones
Triangles
Trigrams
Volcanoes
Waterfalls
Weather symbols
Woodwind instruments